2024
Harris
Ohio
Services Directory

Exclusive Provider of Dun & Bradstreet Library Solutions

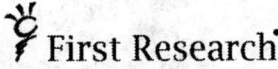

Published July 2024 next update July 2025

WARNING: Purchasers and users of this directory may not use this directory to compile mailing lists, other marketing aids and other types of data, which are sold or otherwise provided to third parties. Such use is wrongful, illegal and a violation of the federal copyright laws.

CAUTION: Because of the many thousands of establishment listings contained in this directory and the possibilities of both human and mechanical error in processing this information, Mergent Inc. cannot assume liability for the correctness of the listings or information on which they are based. Hence, no information contained in this work should be relied upon in any instance where there is a possibility of any loss or damage as a consequence of any error or omission in this volume.

Publisher

Mergent Inc.
444 Madison Ave
New York, NY 10022

©Mergent Inc All Rights Reserved
2024 Mergent Business Press
ISSN 1080-2614
ISBN 979-8-89251-120-9

TABLE OF CONTENTS

Summary of Contents & Explanatory Notes 4
User's Guide to Listings 6

Geographic Section
County/City Cross-Reference Index 9
Firms Listed by Location City 13

Standard Industrial Classification (SIC) Section
SIC Alphabetical Index 737
SIC Numerical Index 741
Firms Listed by SIC 747

Alphabetic Section
Firms Listed by Firm Name 983

Services Section
Services Index 1265
Firms Listed by Service Category 1275

SUMMARY OF CONTENTS

Number of Companies 15,844
Number of Decision Makers 24,500
Minimum Number of Employees 27

EXPLANATORY NOTES

How to Cross-Reference in This Directory

Sequential Entry Numbers. Each establishment in the Geographic Section is numbered sequentially (G-0000). The number assigned to each establishment is referred to as its "entry number." To make cross-referencing easier, each listing in the Geographic, SIC, Alphabetic and Product Sections includes the establishment's entry number. To facilitate locating an entry in the Geographic Section, the entry numbers for the first listing on the left page and the last listing on the right page are printed at the top of the page next to the city name.

Source Suggestions Welcome

Although all known sources were used to compile this directory, it is possible that companies were inadvertently omitted. Your assistance in calling attention to such omissions would be greatly appreciated. A special form on the facing page will help you in the reporting process.

Analysis

Every effort has been made to contact all firms to verify their information. The one exception to this rule is the annual sales figure, which is considered by many companies to be confidential information. Therefore, estimated sales have been calculated by multiplying the nationwide average sales per employee for the firm's major SIC/NAICS code by the firm's number of employees. Nationwide averages for sales per employee by SIC/NAICS codes are provided by the U.S. Department of Commerce and are updated annually. All sales—sales (est)—have been estimated by this method. The exceptions are parent companies (PA), division headquarters (DH) and headquarter locations (HQ) which may include an actual corporate sales figure—sales (corporate-wide) if available.

Types of Companies

Descriptive and statistical data are included for companies in the entire state. These comprise manufacturers, machine shops, fabricators, assemblers and printers. Also identified are corporate offices in the state.

Employment Data

This directory contains companies with 27 or more employees. The employment figure shown in the Geographic Section includes male and female employees and embraces all levels of the company: administrative, clerical, sales and maintenance. This figure is for the facility listed and does not include other plants or offices. It should be recognized that these figures represent an approximate year-round average. These employment figures are broken into codes A through G and used in the Product and SIC Sections to further help you in qualifying a company. Be sure to check the footnotes on the bottom of pages for the code breakdowns.

Standard Industrial Classification (SIC)

The Standard Industrial Classification (SIC) system used in this directory was developed by the federal government for use in classifying establishments by the type of activity they are engaged in. The SIC classifications used in this directory are from the 1987 edition published by the U.S. Government's Office of Management and Budget. The SIC system separates all activities into broad industrial divisions (e.g., manufacturing, mining, retail trade). It further subdivides each division. The range of manufacturing industry classes extends from two-digit codes (major industry group) to four-digit codes (product).

For example:

Industry Breakdown	Code	Industry, Product, etc.
*Major industry group	20	Food and kindred products
Industry group	203	Canned and frozen foods
*Industry	2033	Fruits and vegetables, etc.

*Classifications used in this directory

Only two-digit and four-digit codes are used in this directory.

Arrangement

1. The **Geographic Section** contains complete in-depth corporate data. This section is sorted by cities listed in alphabetical order and companies listed alphabetically within each city. A County/City Index for referencing cities within counties precedes this section.

> IMPORTANT NOTICE: It is a violation of both federal and state law to transmit an unsolicited advertisement to a facsimile machine. Any user of this product that violates such laws may be subject to civil and criminal penalties, which may exceed $500 for each transmission of an unsolicited facsimile. Mergent Inc. provides fax numbers for lawful purposes only and expressly forbids the use of these numbers in any unlawful manner.

2. The **Standard Industrial Classification (SIC) Section** lists companies under approximately 500 four-digit SIC codes. An alphabetical and a numerical index precedes this section. A company can be listed under several codes. The codes are in numerical order with companies listed alphabetically under each code.

3. The **Alphabetic Section** lists all companies with their full physical or mailing addresses and telephone number.

4. The **Services Section** lists companies under unique Harris categories. An index precedes this section. Companies can be listed under several categories.

USER'S GUIDE TO LISTINGS

GEOGRAPHIC SECTION

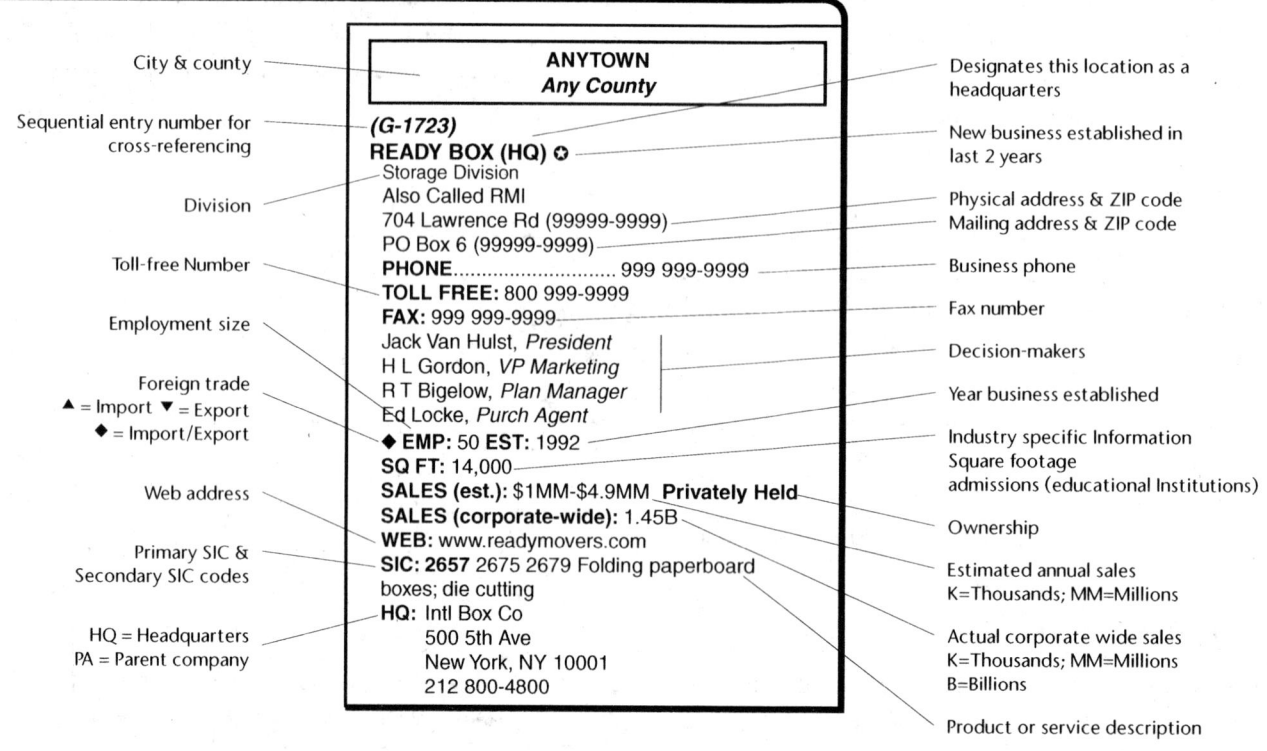

SIC SECTION

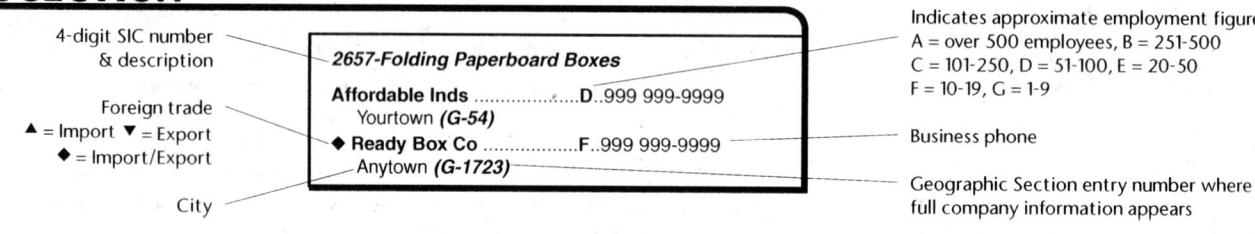

ALPHABETIC SECTION

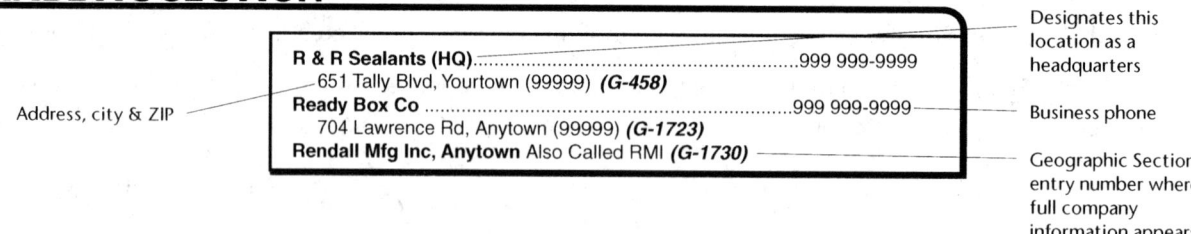

SERVICES SECTION

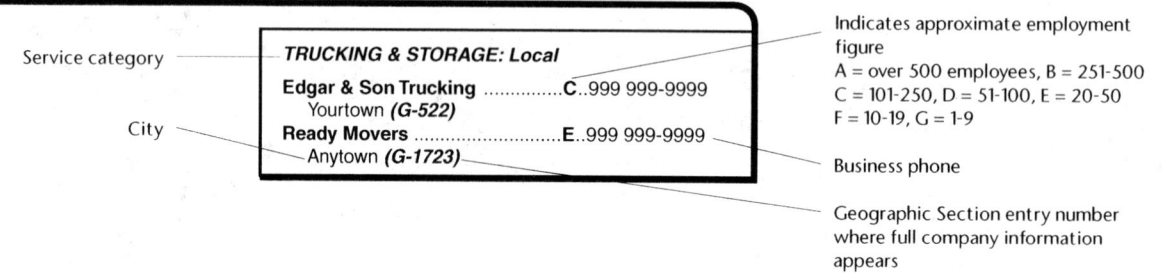

GEOGRAPHIC SECTION

Companies sorted by city in alphabetical order
In-depth company data listed

STANDARD INDUSTRIAL CLASSIFICATIONS

Alphabetical index of classification descriptions
Numerical index of classification descriptions
Companies sorted by SIC product groupings

ALPHABETIC SECTION

Company listings in alphabetical order

SERVICES INDEX

Service categories listed in alphabetical order

SERVICES SECTION

Companies sorted by service classifications

COUNTY/CITY CROSS-REFERENCE INDEX

Adams
Manchester .... (G-10238)
Peebles .... (G-12288)
Seaman .... (G-12944)
West Union .... (G-14864)
Winchester .... (G-15283)

Allen
Beaverdam .... (G-952)
Bluffton .... (G-1276)
Delphos .... (G-7836)
Harrod .... (G-9122)
Lima .... (G-9860)
Spencerville .... (G-13187)

Ashland
Ashland .... (G-471)
Loudonville .... (G-10108)
Perrysville .... (G-12391)
Polk .... (G-12512)

Ashtabula
Andover .... (G-437)
Ashtabula .... (G-517)
Austinburg .... (G-632)
Conneaut .... (G-6937)
Geneva .... (G-8783)
Jefferson .... (G-9537)
Orwell .... (G-12177)
Rock Creek .... (G-12733)

Athens
Albany .... (G-373)
Athens .... (G-554)
Glouster .... (G-8835)
Nelsonville .... (G-11541)
The Plains .... (G-13615)

Auglaize
Cridersville .... (G-7028)
Lima .... (G-9989)
Minster .... (G-11315)
New Bremen .... (G-11596)
New Knoxville .... (G-11617)
Saint Marys .... (G-12827)
Wapakoneta .... (G-14481)

Belmont
Barnesville .... (G-716)
Bellaire .... (G-1006)
Belmont .... (G-1053)
Bethesda .... (G-1097)
Bridgeport .... (G-1375)
Flushing .... (G-8601)
Martins Ferry .... (G-10465)
Powhatan Point .... (G-12610)
Saint Clairsville .... (G-12772)
Shadyside .... (G-12969)

Brown
Georgetown .... (G-8796)
Lake Waynoka .... (G-9653)
Mount Orab .... (G-11469)
Ripley .... (G-12727)
Sardinia .... (G-12941)

Butler
College Corner .... (G-5222)
Fairfield .... (G-8388)
Fairfield Township ...... (G-8456)
Hamilton .... (G-9015)
Liberty Township .... (G-9847)
Middletown .... (G-11149)
Monroe .... (G-11333)
Okeana .... (G-12086)
Oxford .... (G-12200)
Seven Mile .... (G-12962)
Somerville .... (G-13167)
Trenton .... (G-14123)
West Chester .... (G-14646)

Carroll
Carrollton .... (G-1902)
Malvern .... (G-10233)
Sherrodsville .... (G-13012)

Champaign
Saint Paris .... (G-12837)
Urbana .... (G-14297)
Woodstock .... (G-15305)

Clark
Donnelsville .... (G-7870)
Medway .... (G-10907)
New Carlisle .... (G-11600)
Springfield .... (G-13212)

Clermont
Amelia .... (G-409)
Batavia .... (G-726)
Bethel .... (G-1091)
Cincinnati .... (G-2095)
Goshen .... (G-8837)
Loveland .... (G-10125)
Miamiville .... (G-11108)
Milford .... (G-11214)
Moscow .... (G-11457)
New Richmond .... (G-11676)
Owensville .... (G-12199)
Williamsburg .... (G-15176)

Clinton
Blanchester .... (G-1116)
Clarksville .... (G-3730)
New Vienna .... (G-11680)
Sabina .... (G-12771)
Wilmington .... (G-15237)

Columbiana
Columbiana .... (G-5231)
East Liverpool .... (G-8178)
East Palestine .... (G-8195)
Hanoverton .... (G-9095)
Kensington .... (G-9554)
Lisbon .... (G-9996)
Negley .... (G-11540)
New Waterford .... (G-11684)
Salem .... (G-12839)
Salineville .... (G-12859)
Wellsville .... (G-14642)

Coshocton
Coshocton .... (G-6977)
Warsaw .... (G-14591)
West Lafayette .... (G-14855)

Crawford
Bucyrus .... (G-1495)
Crestline .... (G-7020)
Galion .... (G-8740)
New Washington .... (G-11681)

Cuyahoga
Bay Village .... (G-757)
Beachwood .... (G-762)
Bedford .... (G-953)
Bedford Heights .... (G-994)
Berea .... (G-1061)
Brecksville .... (G-1342)
Broadview Heights .... (G-1383)
Brook Park .... (G-1405)
Brooklyn .... (G-1409)
Brooklyn Heights .... (G-1413)
Brookpark .... (G-1429)
Chagrin Falls .... (G-1953)
Cleveland .... (G-3738)
Cleveland Heights .... (G-5177)
Euclid .... (G-8335)
Garfield Heights .... (G-8775)
Gates Mills .... (G-8781)
Glenwillow .... (G-8834)
Highland Heights .... (G-9163)
Independence .... (G-9394)
Lakewood .... (G-9657)
Maple Heights .... (G-10333)
Mayfield Heights .... (G-10784)
Mayfield Village .... (G-10794)
Middleburg Heights ...... (G-11113)
Moreland Hills .... (G-11452)
Newburgh Heights .... (G-11757)
North Olmsted .... (G-11893)
North Royalton .... (G-11937)
Oakwood Village .... (G-12055)
Olmsted Falls .... (G-12088)
Olmsted Twp .... (G-12089)
Parma .... (G-12248)
Pepper Pike .... (G-12297)
Richmond Heights .... (G-12715)
Rocky River .... (G-12738)
Seven Hills .... (G-12951)
Shaker Heights .... (G-12972)
Solon .... (G-13061)
South Euclid .... (G-13170)
Strongsville .... (G-13437)
University Heights ...... (G-14274)
Walton Hills .... (G-14476)
Warrensville Heights (G-14579)
Westlake .... (G-15029)
Woodmere .... (G-15298)

Darke
Ansonia .... (G-446)
Arcanum .... (G-453)
Greenville .... (G-8867)
New Madison .... (G-11634)
New Weston .... (G-11685)
Osgood .... (G-12180)
Rossburg .... (G-12764)
Union City .... (G-14239)
Versailles .... (G-14412)
Yorkshire .... (G-15538)

Defiance
Defiance .... (G-7742)
Hicksville .... (G-9158)
Sherwood .... (G-13013)

Delaware
Columbus .... (G-5243)
Delaware .... (G-7776)
Galena .... (G-8735)
Lewis Center .... (G-9803)
Ostrander .... (G-12182)
Powell .... (G-12582)
Sunbury .... (G-13514)
Westerville .... (G-14876)

Erie
Birmingham .... (G-1107)
Castalia .... (G-1914)
Huron .... (G-9384)
Kelleys Island .... (G-9552)
Milan .... (G-11205)
Sandusky .... (G-12861)
Vermilion .... (G-14404)

Fairfield
Bremen .... (G-1372)
Carroll .... (G-1899)
Lancaster .... (G-9690)
Millersport .... (G-11297)
Pickerington .... (G-12396)
Sugar Grove .... (G-13507)

Fayette
Jeffersonville .... (G-9540)
Wshngtn Ct Hs .... (G-15476)

Franklin
Blacklick .... (G-1108)
Canal Winchester .... (G-1597)
Columbus .... (G-5286)
Dublin .... (G-7918)
Etna .... (G-8328)
Gahanna .... (G-8710)
Galloway .... (G-8771)
Grove City .... (G-8893)
Groveport .... (G-8967)
Hilliard .... (G-9174)
Lockbourne .... (G-10009)
New Albany .... (G-11551)
Obetz .... (G-12078)
Reynoldsburg .... (G-12649)
Upper Arlington .... (G-14275)
Urbancrest .... (G-14318)
Westerville .... (G-14955)
Whitehall .... (G-15135)
Worthington .... (G-15403)

Fulton
Archbold .... (G-454)
Delta .... (G-7849)
Lyons .... (G-10187)
Metamora .... (G-11016)
Swanton .... (G-13525)
Wauseon .... (G-14597)

Gallia
Bidwell .... (G-1103)
Cheshire .... (G-2029)
Gallipolis .... (G-8752)
Patriot .... (G-12280)
Rio Grande .... (G-12726)
Vinton .... (G-14425)

Geauga
Burton .... (G-1525)
Chagrin Falls .... (G-1972)
Chardon .... (G-1993)
Chesterland .... (G-2032)
Huntsburg .... (G-9380)
Middlefield .... (G-11138)
Newbury .... (G-11759)
Novelty .... (G-12036)
Thompson .... (G-13617)

Greene
Beavercreek .... (G-854)
Beavercreek Township .. (G-933)
Bellbrook .... (G-1016)
Dayton .... (G-7123)
Fairborn .... (G-8365)
Jamestown .... (G-9534)
Wright Patterson Afb (G-15473)
Xenia .... (G-15497)
Yellow Springs .... (G-15534)

Guernsey
Buffalo .... (G-1521)
Byesville .... (G-1534)
Cambridge .... (G-1552)
Derwent .... (G-7863)
Kimbolton .... (G-9640)
Old Washington .... (G-12087)
Senecaville .... (G-12950)

Hamilton
Addyston .... (G-4)
Arlington Heights .... (G-470)
Blue Ash .... (G-1119)
Camp Dennison .... (G-1590)
Cincinnati .... (G-2117)
Cleves .... (G-5186)
Harrison .... (G-9096)
Hooven .... (G-9317)
Miamitown .... (G-11106)
Montgomery .... (G-11361)
North Bend .... (G-11803)
Norwood .... (G-12032)
Sharonville .... (G-12992)
Symmes Township .... (G-13580)
Symmes Twp .... (G-13582)
Terrace Park .... (G-13613)
Walnut Hills .... (G-14474)
West Chester .... (G-14797)
Wyoming .... (G-15496)

Hancock
Arlington .... (G-469)
Findlay .... (G-8504)
Van Buren .... (G-14338)

Hardin

2024 Harris Ohio Services Directory

COUNTY/CITY CROSS-REFERENCE

	ENTRY #
Ada	(G-1)
Forest	(G-8602)
Kenton	(G-9609)
Mc Guffey	(G-10802)
Mount Victory	(G-11512)

Harrison
Bowerston	(G-1301)
Cadiz	(G-1538)
Freeport	(G-8663)
Hopedale	(G-9318)
Jewett	(G-9543)
Scio	(G-12942)

Henry
Deshler	(G-7865)
Liberty Center	(G-9846)
Napoleon	(G-11515)
Ridgeville Corners	(G-12725)

Highland
Greenfield	(G-8863)
Hillsboro	(G-9248)
Lynchburg	(G-10183)

Hocking
Logan	(G-10021)
Rockbridge	(G-12735)

Holmes
Berlin	(G-1089)
Holmesville	(G-9316)
Killbuck	(G-9638)
Lakeville	(G-9656)
Millersburg	(G-11272)
Mount Hope	(G-11466)
Walnut Creek	(G-14471)
Winesburg	(G-15290)

Huron
Bellevue	(G-1040)
Greenwich	(G-8892)
Monroeville	(G-11356)
New London	(G-11632)
Norwalk	(G-11998)
Plymouth	(G-12501)
Wakeman	(G-14458)
Willard	(G-15166)

Jackson
Jackson	(G-9515)
Wellston	(G-14636)

Jefferson
Amsterdam	(G-435)
Bergholz	(G-1088)
Brilliant	(G-1378)
Dillonvale	(G-7869)
Mingo Junction	(G-11313)
Rayland	(G-12647)
Steubenville	(G-13315)
Stratton	(G-13407)
Toronto	(G-14121)
Wintersville	(G-15291)

Knox
Centerburg	(G-1932)
Fredericktown	(G-8659)
Gambier	(G-8774)
Mount Vernon	(G-11476)

Lake
	ENTRY #
Concord Township	(G-6922)
Eastlake	(G-8200)
Grand River	(G-8848)
Kirtland	(G-9645)
Madison	(G-10211)
Mentor	(G-10908)
Mentor On The Lake	(G-11014)
Painesville	(G-12219)
Perry	(G-12303)
Wickliffe	(G-15145)
Willoughby	(G-15182)
Willoughby Hills	(G-15230)
Willowick	(G-15235)

Lawrence
Chesapeake	(G-2028)
Coal Grove	(G-5211)
Ironton	(G-9501)
Kitts Hill	(G-9647)
Proctorville	(G-12612)
South Point	(G-13173)

Licking
Croton	(G-7030)
Etna	(G-8332)
Granville	(G-8849)
Heath	(G-9133)
Hebron	(G-9141)
Johnstown	(G-9544)
Newark	(G-11686)
Pataskala	(G-12269)
Saint Louisville	(G-12826)
Utica	(G-14328)

Logan
Bellefontaine	(G-1019)
De Graff	(G-7739)
East Liberty	(G-8171)
Huntsville	(G-9383)
Lakeview	(G-9655)
Lewistown	(G-9843)
West Liberty	(G-14859)
West Mansfield	(G-14862)
Zanesfield	(G-15764)

Lorain
Amherst	(G-421)
Avon	(G-638)
Avon Lake	(G-670)
Columbia Station	(G-5223)
Elyria	(G-8231)
Grafton	(G-8838)
Lagrange	(G-9650)
Lorain	(G-10052)
North Ridgeville	(G-11921)
Oberlin	(G-12062)
Sheffield Lake	(G-12996)
Sheffield Village	(G-12997)
South Amherst	(G-13168)
Wellington	(G-14629)

Lucas
Holland	(G-9276)
Maumee	(G-10682)
Oregon	(G-12128)
Ottawa Hills	(G-12197)
Sylvania	(G-13535)
Toledo	(G-13670)
Waterville	(G-14593)
Whitehouse	(G-15137)

Madison
	ENTRY #
London	(G-10037)
Mount Sterling	(G-11474)
Plain City	(G-12463)
West Jefferson	(G-14847)

Mahoning
Austintown	(G-635)
Boardman	(G-1284)
Campbell	(G-1591)
Canfield	(G-1621)
Lowellville	(G-10167)
New Middletown	(G-11635)
New Springfield	(G-11679)
North Jackson	(G-11871)
North Lima	(G-11881)
Petersburg	(G-12394)
Poland	(G-12502)
Sebring	(G-12945)
Struthers	(G-13499)
Youngstown	(G-15539)

Marion
La Rue	(G-9648)
Marion	(G-10416)
Morral	(G-11453)
Prospect	(G-12616)
Waldo	(G-14470)

Medina
Brunswick	(G-1449)
Chippewa Lake	(G-2094)
Hinckley	(G-9269)
Lodi	(G-10018)
Medina	(G-10805)
Seville	(G-12963)
Sharon Center	(G-12989)
Valley City	(G-14331)
Wadsworth	(G-14426)
Westfield Center	(G-15023)

Meigs
Middleport	(G-11147)
Pomeroy	(G-12513)
Portland	(G-12542)

Mercer
Burkettsville	(G-1524)
Celina	(G-1916)
Coldwater	(G-5212)
Fort Recovery	(G-8606)
Maria Stein	(G-10353)
Rockford	(G-12737)
Saint Henry	(G-12824)

Miami
Bradford	(G-1340)
Covington	(G-7017)
Piqua	(G-12434)
Tipp City	(G-13650)
Troy	(G-14129)

Monroe
Clarington	(G-3729)
Woodsfield	(G-15300)

Montgomery
Beavercreek	(G-919)
Brookville	(G-1444)
Centerville	(G-1938)
Clayton	(G-3731)
Dayton	(G-7145)
Englewood	(G-8302)
Germantown	(G-8803)
Huber Heights	(G-9323)
Kettering	(G-9625)
Miamisburg	(G-11017)
Moraine	(G-11388)
New Lebanon	(G-11619)
Oakwood	(G-12048)
Trotwood	(G-14127)
Vandalia	(G-14363)
West Carrollton	(G-14644)

Morgan
Malta	(G-10231)
Mcconnelsville	(G-10803)

Morrow
Marengo	(G-10352)
Mount Gilead	(G-11459)

Muskingum
Dresden	(G-7917)
Frazeysburg	(G-8656)
Nashport	(G-11535)
New Concord	(G-11609)
Roseville	(G-12763)
South Zanesville	(G-13186)
Zanesville	(G-15765)

Noble
Caldwell	(G-1545)
Dexter City	(G-7867)

Ottawa
Curtice	(G-7031)
Elmore	(G-8230)
Genoa	(G-8793)
Lakeside	(G-9654)
Marblehead	(G-10351)
Oak Harbor	(G-12044)
Port Clinton	(G-12516)
Put In Bay	(G-12617)

Paulding
Antwerp	(G-447)
Haviland	(G-9132)
Oakwood	(G-12053)
Paulding	(G-12281)

Perry
Glenford	(G-8832)
New Lexington	(G-11621)
Thornville	(G-13619)

Pickaway
Ashville	(G-551)
Circleville	(G-3701)
Orient	(G-12151)

Pike
Piketon	(G-12414)
Waverly	(G-14610)

Portage
Atwater	(G-602)
Aurora	(G-603)
Deerfield	(G-7740)
Garrettsville	(G-8779)
Hiram	(G-9274)
Kent	(G-9555)

(Portage cont.)
	ENTRY #
Mantua	(G-10328)
Mogadore	(G-11322)
North Benton	(G-11805)
Randolph	(G-12618)
Ravenna	(G-12619)
Rootstown	(G-12759)
Streetsboro	(G-13408)
Windham	(G-15288)

Preble
Camden	(G-1589)
Eaton	(G-8210)
Lewisburg	(G-9841)
New Paris	(G-11637)
West Alexandria	(G-14643)

Putnam
Columbus Grove	(G-6921)
Kalida	(G-9551)
Leipsic	(G-9801)
Ottawa	(G-12185)
Ottoville	(G-12198)
Pandora	(G-12245)

Richland
Bellville	(G-1047)
Lexington	(G-9844)
Lucas	(G-10172)
Mansfield	(G-10241)
Ontario	(G-12095)
Shelby	(G-13004)
Shiloh	(G-13014)

Ross
Bainbridge	(G-685)
Chillicothe	(G-2044)
Frankfort	(G-8629)

Sandusky
Burgoon	(G-1523)
Clyde	(G-5198)
Fremont	(G-8664)
Gibsonburg	(G-8806)
Helena	(G-9157)
Lindsey	(G-9995)
Vickery	(G-14418)
Woodville	(G-15306)

Scioto
Franklin Furnace	(G-8653)
Lucasville	(G-10173)
Mc Dermott	(G-10800)
Minford	(G-11312)
New Boston	(G-11593)
Portsmouth	(G-12543)
South Webster	(G-13185)
Wheelersburg	(G-15127)

Seneca
Attica	(G-598)
Bascom	(G-725)
Bettsville	(G-1098)
Bloomville	(G-1118)
Flat Rock	(G-8600)
Fostoria	(G-8613)
Green Springs	(G-8858)
New Riegel	(G-11677)
Tiffin	(G-13624)

Shelby
Anna	(G-442)

COUNTY/CITY CROSS-REFERENCE

| ENTRY # | ENTRY # | ENTRY # | ENTRY # | ENTRY # |

Botkins .... (G-1298)
Fort Loramie .... (G-8603)
Jackson Center .... (G-9531)
Russia .... (G-12770)
Sidney .... (G-13017)

Stark

Alliance .... (G-374)
Beach City .... (G-761)
Brewster .... (G-1373)
Canal Fulton .... (G-1592)
Canton .... (G-1647)
East Canton .... (G-8169)
East Sparta .... (G-8199)
Hartville .... (G-9124)
Louisville .... (G-10111)
Magnolia .... (G-10223)
Massillon .... (G-10626)
Middlebranch .... (G-11112)
Minerva .... (G-11305)
Navarre .... (G-11536)
North Canton .... (G-11806)
North Lawrence .... (G-11880)
Paris .... (G-12247)
Uniontown .... (G-14240)
Waynesburg .... (G-14621)
Wilmot .... (G-15281)

Summit

Akron .... (G-5)
Barberton .... (G-692)
Bath .... (G-754)

Clinton .... (G-5197)
Copley .... (G-6946)
Coventry Township ... (G-7006)
Cuyahoga Falls .... (G-7032)
Fairlawn .... (G-8467)
Green .... (G-8857)
Hudson .... (G-9327)
Macedonia .... (G-10188)
Munroe Falls .... (G-11513)
New Franklin .... (G-11614)
Northfield .... (G-11951)
Norton .... (G-11989)
Peninsula .... (G-12293)
Richfield .... (G-12684)
Silver Lake .... (G-13060)
Stow .... (G-13352)
Tallmadge .... (G-13586)
Twinsburg .... (G-14171)

Trumbull

Brookfield .... (G-1406)
Cortland .... (G-6968)
Fowler .... (G-8628)
Girard .... (G-8808)
Hartford .... (G-9123)
Hubbard .... (G-9319)
Kinsman .... (G-9644)
Leavittsburg .... (G-9751)
Masury .... (G-10677)
Mc Donald .... (G-10801)
Mineral Ridge .... (G-11302)
Newton Falls .... (G-11774)

Niles .... (G-11779)
Vienna .... (G-14419)
Warren .... (G-14494)

Tuscarawas

Baltic .... (G-688)
Bolivar .... (G-1293)
Dennison .... (G-7855)
Dover .... (G-7871)
Dundee .... (G-8168)
Midvale .... (G-11203)
Mineral City .... (G-11301)
New Philadelphia ..... (G-11638)
Newcomerstown .... (G-11766)
Port Washington .... (G-12541)
Strasburg .... (G-13403)
Sugarcreek .... (G-13508)
Uhrichsville .... (G-14233)

Union

Marysville .... (G-10473)
Milford Center .... (G-11265)
Richwood .... (G-12724)

Van Wert

Middle Point .... (G-11110)
Van Wert .... (G-14339)

Vinton

Mc Arthur .... (G-10798)
New Plymouth .... (G-11675)

Warren

Carlisle .... (G-1898)
Franklin .... (G-8631)
Kings Mills .... (G-9642)
Lebanon .... (G-9752)
Maineville .... (G-10224)
Mason .... (G-10517)
Middletown .... (G-11193)
Morrow .... (G-11455)
Oregonia .... (G-12149)
Pleasant Plain .... (G-12499)
South Lebanon .... (G-13172)
Springboro .... (G-13191)
Waynesville .... (G-14622)

Washington

Belpre .... (G-1056)
Beverly .... (G-1099)
Little Hocking .... (G-10008)
Marietta .... (G-10355)
Waterford .... (G-14592)

Wayne

Apple Creek .... (G-449)
Burbank .... (G-1522)
Dalton .... (G-7120)
Doylestown .... (G-7912)
Fredericksburg .... (G-8658)
Kidron .... (G-9635)
Mount Eaton .... (G-11458)
Orrville .... (G-12155)
Rittman .... (G-12729)

Shreve .... (G-13015)
West Salem .... (G-14863)
Wooster .... (G-15307)

Williams

Bryan .... (G-1477)
Edgerton .... (G-8226)
Edon .... (G-8229)
Montpelier .... (G-11381)
Pioneer .... (G-12433)
Stryker .... (G-13504)
West Unity .... (G-14874)

Wood

Bowling Green .... (G-1302)
Bradner .... (G-1341)
Grand Rapids .... (G-8845)
Luckey .... (G-10182)
Millbury .... (G-11266)
North Baltimore .... (G-11800)
Northwood .... (G-11968)
Pemberville .... (G-12289)
Perrysburg .... (G-12313)
Rossford .... (G-12765)
Walbridge .... (G-14460)
Wayne .... (G-14620)

Wyandot

Carey .... (G-1894)
Sycamore .... (G-13532)
Upper Sandusky ...... (G-14284)

GEOGRAPHIC SECTION

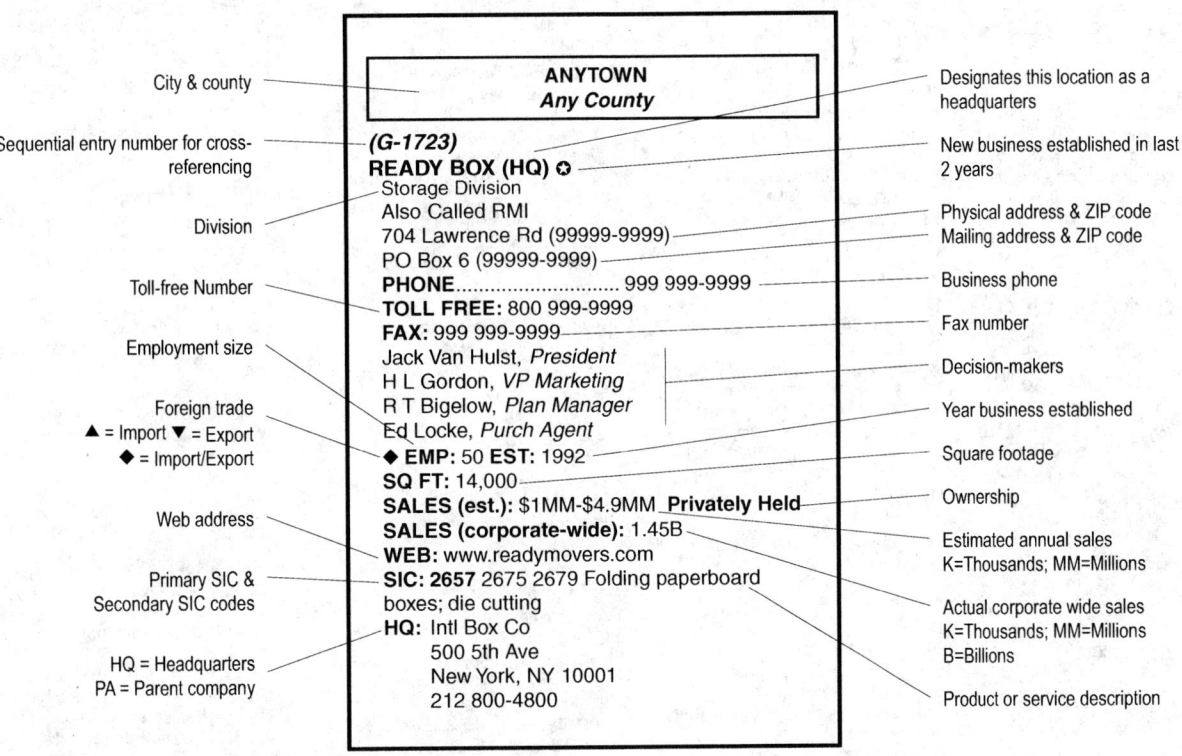

See footnotes for symbols and codes identification.
- This section is in alphabetical order by city.
- Companies are sorted alphabetically under their respective cities.
- To locate cities within a county refer to the County/City Cross Reference Index.

IMPORTANT NOTICE: It is a violation of both federal and state law to transmit an unsolicited advertisement to a facsimile machine. Any user of this product that violates such laws may be subject to civil and criminal penalties which may exceed $500 for each transmission of an unsolicited facsimile. Harris InfoSource provides fax numbers for lawful purposes only and expressly forbids the use of these numbers in any unlawful manner.

Ada
Hardin County

(G-1)
COMMUNITY HLTH PRFSSIONALS INC
Also Called: Ada Visiting Nurses
1200 S Main St (45810-2616)
PHONE.............................419 634-7443
Claudia Crawford, *Mgr*
EMP: 47
SALES (corp-wide): 12.27MM **Privately Held**
Web: www.comhealthpro.org
SIC: 8082 8051 Visiting nurse service; Skilled nursing care facilities
PA: Community Health Professionals, Inc.
1159 Westwood Dr
Van Wert OH 45891
419 238-9203

(G-2)
MIDDLEFIELD BANKING COMPANY
118 S Main St (45810-1255)
PHONE.............................419 634-5015
Tom Caldwell, *Brnch Mgr*

EMP: 55
Web: www.middlefieldbank.bank
SIC: 6022 State commercial banks
HQ: The Middlefield Banking Company
15985 E High St
Middlefield OH 44062
440 632-1666

(G-3)
MIDWEST REHAB INC (PA)
118 E Highland Ave (45810-1120)
PHONE.............................419 692-3405
Steve Zuber, *Pr*
EMP: 54 **EST:** 1992
SALES (est): 2.03MM **Privately Held**
Web: www.midwestrehab.net
SIC: 8049 Physical therapist

Addyston
Hamilton County

(G-4)
INEOS ABS (USA) LLC
Also Called: Ineos
356 Three Rivers Pkwy (45001)
P.O. Box 39 (45001)
PHONE.............................513 467-2400

Clint Herring, *VP*
Rebecca Libourel, *
◆ **EMP:** 185 **EST:** 2007
SQ FT: 372,600
SALES (est): 48.67MM
SALES (corp-wide): 917.38K **Privately Held**
Web: www.ineos-abs.com
SIC: 2821 7389 Plastics materials and resins ; Business Activities at Non-Commercial Site
HQ: Ineos Industries Limited
Hawkslease
Lyndhurst HANTS SO43
238 028-7000

Akron
Summit County

(G-5)
21ST CENTURY FINANCIAL INC
130 Springside Dr Ste 100 (44333-4543)
PHONE.............................330 668-9065
Charlie Parks, *Pr*
Mike Sarver, *
EMP: 62 **EST:** 1996
SALES (est): 6.99MM **Privately Held**

Web: www.xxiadvisors.com
SIC: 6311 Life insurance

(G-6)
365 HOLDINGS LLC
115 W Bartges St (44311-1008)
PHONE.............................800 403-8182
EMP: 63 **EST:** 2017
SALES (est): 6.16MM **Privately Held**
Web: www.365-holdings.com
SIC: 7389 Packaging and labeling services

(G-7)
50 X 20 HOLDING COMPANY INC
779 White Pond Dr (44320-1136)
PHONE.............................330 865-4663
Guy Robinson, *Brnch Mgr*
EMP: 34
SALES (corp-wide): 114.18MM **Privately Held**
Web: www.schumacherhomes.com
SIC: 1521 Single-family housing construction
PA: 50 X 20 Holding Company, Inc.
2715 Wise Ave Nw
Canton OH 44708
330 478-4500

Akron - Summit County (G-8)

GEOGRAPHIC SECTION

(G-8)
A CRANO EXCAVATING INC
1505 Industrial Pkwy (44310-2603)
PHONE..................................330 630-1061
James V Riter, *Pr*
Anthony Riter, *
Raymond Riter, *
EMP: 40 **EST:** 1945
SALES (est): 8.6MM **Privately Held**
Web: www.acrano.com
SIC: 1623 1794 Oil and gas line and compressor station construction; Excavation and grading, building construction

(G-9)
A J AMER AGENCY INC (HQ)
Also Called: Amer Insurance
3737 Embassy Pkwy Ste 260 (44333-8381)
PHONE..................................330 665-9966
Charles Tennent, *Pr*
Hamilton Amer, *
EMP: 43 **EST:** 1923
SALES (est): 4.79MM
SALES (corp-wide): 10.07B **Publicly Held**
SIC: 6411 Insurance brokers, nec
PA: Arthur J. Gallagher & Co.
2850 Golf Rd
Rolling Meadows IL 60008
630 773-3800

(G-10)
A J AMER AGENCY INC
231 Springside Dr Ste 205 (44333-4516)
PHONE..................................330 665-9966
Kevin Copeland, *Brnch Mgr*
EMP: 33
SALES (corp-wide): 10.07B **Publicly Held**
SIC: 6411 Insurance brokers, nec
HQ: A. J. Amer Agency, Inc.
3737 Embassy Pkwy Ste 260
Akron OH 44333
330 665-9966

(G-11)
A-A BLUEPRINT CO INC
2757 Gilchrist Rd (44305-4400)
PHONE..................................330 794-8803
Daisy Scalia, *Prin*
John Scalia, *
EMP: 32 **EST:** 1968
SQ FT: 30,000
SALES (est): 4.85MM **Privately Held**
Web: www.aablueprint.com
SIC: 2791 2759 7334 2789 Typesetting; Letterpress printing; Photocopying and duplicating services; Bookbinding and related work

(G-12)
ACCEL SCHOOLS OHIO LLC
Also Called: Hope Acadamies
107 S Arlington St (44306-1328)
PHONE..................................330 535-7728
Sally Porter, *Prin*
EMP: 116
SQ FT: 28,437
SALES (corp-wide): 13.26MM **Privately Held**
Web: www.accelschools.com
SIC: 4141 Local bus charter service
PA: Accel Schools Ohio Llc
5730 Broadview Rd
Cleveland OH 44134
216 583-5230

(G-13)
ACCESS INC
Also Called: AKRON CITIZEN'S COALITION FOR
230 W Market St (44303-2197)
P.O. Box 1007 (44309-1007)
PHONE..................................330 535-2999
Silvia Hines, *Ex Dir*
EMP: 43 **EST:** 1983
SQ FT: 9,050
SALES (est): 1.82MM **Privately Held**
Web: www.access-shelter.org
SIC: 8322 Social service center

(G-14)
ACRO TOOL & DIE COMPANY
Also Called: Metalcraft Solutions
325 Morgan Ave (44311-2494)
PHONE..................................330 773-5173
Pamela Thielo, *Pr*
T T Thompson, *
Pamela Perrin, *
▲ **EMP:** 37 **EST:** 1951
SQ FT: 27,000
SALES (est): 4.69MM **Privately Held**
Web: www.acrotool.com
SIC: 0781 0811 3541 3444 Landscape services; Christmas tree farm; Machine tools, metal cutting type; Sheet metalwork

(G-15)
ACTIONLINK LLC
286 N Cleveland Massillon Rd # 200 (44333-2492)
PHONE..................................888 737-8757
Bruce Finn, *Pr*
Delbert Tanner, *COO*
EMP: 2000 **EST:** 2002
SQ FT: 12,000
SALES (est): 94.76MM
SALES (corp-wide): 1.88B **Privately Held**
Web: www.actionlink.com
SIC: 8748 Business consulting, nec
HQ: Acosta Inc.
6600 Corporate Ctr Pkwy
Jacksonville FL 32216
904 281-9800

(G-16)
ACU-SERVE CORP (PA)
121 S Main St Ste 102 (44308-1436)
PHONE..................................330 923-5258
Angie Barone, *Pr*
Timothy Barone, *VP*
EMP: 140 **EST:** 1993
SALES (est): 13.52MM **Privately Held**
Web: www.acuservecorp.com
SIC: 7372 6411 Prepackaged software; Medical insurance claim processing, contract or fee basis

(G-17)
ADVANCED AUTO GLASS INC (PA)
44 N Union St (44304-1347)
PHONE..................................412 373-6675
TOLL FREE: 800
Greg Pattakos, *Pr*
Christina Pattakos, *
▲ **EMP:** 29 **EST:** 1984
SQ FT: 4,400
SALES (est): 4.06MM
SALES (corp-wide): 4.06MM **Privately Held**
Web: www.unibancanada.ca
SIC: 7536 1793 Automotive glass replacement shops; Glass and glazing work

(G-18)
ADVANCED POLY-PACKAGING INC (PA)
1331 Emmitt Rd (44306-3807)
P.O. Box 7040 (44306-0040)
PHONE..................................330 785-4000
▲ **EMP:** 116 **EST:** 1978
SALES (est): 20.59MM
SALES (corp-wide): 20.59MM **Privately Held**
Web: ecom.advancedpoly.com
SIC: 3565 5199 Packaging machinery; Packaging materials

(G-19)
AKROCHEM CORPORATION (PA)
3770 Embassy Pkwy (44333-8367)
PHONE..................................330 535-2100
◆ **EMP:** 60 **EST:** 1929
SALES (est): 139.59MM
SALES (corp-wide): 139.59MM **Privately Held**
Web: www.akrochem.com
SIC: 5169 2851 Synthetic resins, rubber, and plastic materials; Paints and paint additives

(G-20)
AKRON ART MUSEUM
1 S High St (44308-1801)
PHONE..................................330 376-9185
Jon Fiume, *CEO*
Mitchell Kahan, *
Susan Schweitzer, *
EMP: 75 **EST:** 1922
SQ FT: 3,312
SALES (est): 6.9MM **Privately Held**
Web: www.akronartmuseum.org
SIC: 8412 Museum

(G-21)
AKRON BLIND CENTER & WORKSHOP (PA)
Also Called: VISON SUPPORT SERVICES
325 E Market St (44304-1340)
P.O. Box 1864 (44309-1864)
PHONE..................................330 253-2555
Kristen Baysinger, *Ex Dir*
EMP: 41 **EST:** 1948
SQ FT: 15,000
SALES (est): 141.01K
SALES (corp-wide): 141.01K **Privately Held**
Web: www.akronblindcenter.org
SIC: 8331 Job training services

(G-22)
AKRON BOARD OF EDUCATION
10 N Main St (44308-1958)
PHONE..................................330 761-1660
David James, *Ex Dir*
EMP: 42
SALES (corp-wide): 454.11MM **Privately Held**
Web: www.akronschools.com
SIC: 1541 Industrial buildings and warehouses
PA: Akron Board Of Education
10 N Main St Unit 1
Akron OH 44308
330 761-1661

(G-23)
AKRON CITY HOSPITAL INC
525 E Market St (44304-1698)
PHONE..................................330 253-5046
Albert F Gilbert, *Pr*
Albert F Gilbert, *Pr*
Barbara Hiney, *
Beth O'brien, *Ex VP*
James B Pickering, *
EMP: 2900 **EST:** 1890
SQ FT: 850,000
SALES (est): 70.01MM **Privately Held**
Web: www.summahealth.org
SIC: 8062 General medical and surgical hospitals

(G-24)
AKRON CMNTY SVC CTR URBAN LEAG
Also Called: AKRON COMMUNITY SERV CENTER
440 Vernon Odom Blvd (44307-2108)
PHONE..................................234 542-4141
Fred Wright, *Pr*
EMP: 28 **EST:** 1945
SALES (est): 4.76MM **Privately Held**
Web: www.akronurbanleague.org
SIC: 8322 Social service center

(G-25)
AKRON ELECTRIC INC
1025 Eaton Ave (44303-1313)
PHONE..................................330 745-8891
George Ostich, *Pr*
EMP: 40 **EST:** 1981
SQ FT: 13,000
SALES (est): 1.97MM
SALES (corp-wide): 49.84MM **Privately Held**
Web: www.akronelectric.com
SIC: 5063 Boxes and fittings, electrical
PA: Akron Foundry Co.
2728 Wingate Ave
Akron OH 44314
330 745-3101

(G-26)
AKRON ENERGY SYSTEMS LLC
222 Opportunity Pkwy (44307-2232)
PHONE..................................330 374-0600
Donald J Hoffman, *Managing Member*
Marc Divis, *
EMP: 37 **EST:** 1970
SALES (est): 42.32MM **Privately Held**
Web: www.akronenergysystems.com
SIC: 4961 Steam heating systems (suppliers of heat)

(G-27)
AKRON FAMILY INSTITUTE INC
3469 Fortuna Dr (44312-5281)
PHONE..................................330 644-3469
Steven Perkins, *Pr*
John Leedy, *Sec*
EMP: 32 **EST:** 1984
SALES (est): 803.93K **Privately Held**
Web: www.akronfamilyinstitute.com
SIC: 8322 General counseling services

(G-28)
AKRON FOUNDRY CO (PA)
2728 Wingate Ave (44314-1300)
P.O. Box 27028 (44319-7028)
PHONE..................................330 745-3101
George Ostich, *Pr*
Geraldine Ostich, *
Michael Ostich, *
Ronald C Allan, *
EMP: 175 **EST:** 1969
SQ FT: 100,000
SALES (est): 49.84MM
SALES (corp-wide): 49.84MM **Privately Held**
Web: www.akronfoundry.com
SIC: 3369 5063 3365 3363 Castings, except die-castings, precision; Boxes and fittings, electrical; Aluminum foundries; Aluminum die-castings

(G-29)
AKRON GENERAL FOUNDATION
400 Wabash Ave (44307)
PHONE..................................330 344-6888
Karen Bozzelli, *Pr*
Steven P Bossart Dtr, *Prin*
Evelyn Burkhart Dtr, *Prin*
EMP: 122 **EST:** 1973
SALES (est): 2.29MM
SALES (corp-wide): 14.48B **Privately Held**
Web: www.akrongeneral.org

GEOGRAPHIC SECTION

Akron - Summit County (G-50)

SIC: 8322 Individual and family services
HQ: Akron General Medical Center Inc
1 Akron General Ave
Akron OH 44307
330 344-6000

(G-30)
AKRON GENERAL HEALTH SYSTEM
Also Called: Akron Gen Spt & Physcl Therapy
4125 Medina Rd Ofc (44333-4566)
PHONE..................330 665-8200
Todd Dawfon, Dir
EMP: 529
SALES (corp-wide): 14.48B Privately Held
Web: www.akrongeneral.org
SIC: 8049 Physical therapist
HQ: Akron General Health System
1 Akron General Ave
Akron OH 44307
330 344-6000

(G-31)
AKRON GENERAL HEALTH SYSTEM (HQ)
1 Akron General Ave (44307-2432)
PHONE..................330 344-6000
Thomas L Stover, Pr
Pat Mcmahon, CFO
Daniel P Cunningham, Sr VP
EMP: 440 EST: 1986
SQ FT: 1,027,000
SALES (est): 544.48MM
SALES (corp-wide): 14.48B Privately Held
Web: www.akrongeneral.org
SIC: 8741 Hospital management
PA: The Cleveland Clinic Foundation
9500 Euclid Ave
Cleveland OH 44195
216 636-8335

(G-32)
AKRON GENERAL MEDICAL CENTER (DH)
Also Called: Edwin Shaw Rehabilitation Hosp
1 Akron General Ave (44307-2432)
PHONE..................330 344-6000
TOLL FREE: 800
F William Steere, Ch Bd
EMP: 571 EST: 1914
SQ FT: 1,027,000
SALES (est): 544.48MM
SALES (corp-wide): 14.48B Privately Held
Web: www.akrongeneral.org
SIC: 8062 General medical and surgical hospitals
HQ: Akron General Health System
1 Akron General Ave
Akron OH 44307
330 344-6000

(G-33)
AKRON HARDWARE CONSULTANTS INC (PA)
1100 Killian Rd (44312-4730)
PHONE..................330 644-7167
Roy Crute, Pr
Thomas Orihel, *
EMP: 37 EST: 1960
SQ FT: 28,000
SALES (est): 10.64MM
SALES (corp-wide): 10.64MM Privately Held
Web: www.bannersolutions.com
SIC: 5072 Builders' hardware, nec

(G-34)
AKRON MANAGEMENT CORP
Also Called: Firestone Country Club
452 E Warner Rd (44319-1925)
PHONE..................330 644-8441
Mark Gore, Genl Mgr
EMP: 260 EST: 1950
SQ FT: 3,700
SALES (est): 7.54MM
SALES (corp-wide): 2.44B Privately Held
Web: www.invitedclubs.com
SIC: 7997 5941 5812 5813 Golf club, membership; Golf goods and equipment; Eating places; Cocktail lounge
HQ: Clubcorp Usa, Inc.
5215 N O Connor Blvd # 2
Irving TX 75039
972 243-6191

(G-35)
AKRON RADIOLOGY INC
525 E Market St (44304-1619)
PHONE..................330 375-3043
Malay Mody, Pr
Edward Bury, Pr
EMP: 47 EST: 1991
SALES (est): 23.74MM Privately Held
Web: www.akronradiology.com
SIC: 8062 General medical and surgical hospitals

(G-36)
AKRON RUBBER DEV LAB INC (PA)
2887 Gilchrist Rd (44305-4415)
PHONE..................330 794-6600
Timothy Samples, CEO
Jerry Leyden, *
Deborah Samples, *
Alice J Samples Incorp, Prin
Leo H Samples Incorp, Prin
EMP: 65 EST: 1962
SALES (est): 15.1MM
SALES (corp-wide): 15.1MM Privately Held
Web: www.ardl.com
SIC: 8734 Testing laboratories

(G-37)
AKRON RUBBERDUCKS
300 S Main St (44308-1204)
PHONE..................330 253-5151
Ken Babby, CEO
EMP: 57 EST: 2018
SALES (est): 815.42K Privately Held
Web: www.akronrubberducks.com
SIC: 7941 Football club

(G-38)
AKRON SUMMIT CMNTY ACTION AGCY (PA)
Also Called: COMMUNITY ACTION AKRON SUMMIT
55 E Mill St (44308-1405)
P.O. Box 2000 (44309-2000)
PHONE..................330 376-7730
Malcolm J Costa, Pr
EMP: 330 EST: 1965
SQ FT: 8,908
SALES (est): 43.52MM
SALES (corp-wide): 43.52MM Privately Held
Web: www.ca-akron.org
SIC: 8351 Head Start center, except in conjunction with school

(G-39)
AKRON ZOOLOGICAL PARK
Also Called: AKRON ZOO
500 Edgewood Ave (44307-2199)
PHONE..................330 375-2550
L Patricia Simmons, CEO
Robert Littman, *
David Drechler, *
EMP: 50 EST: 1950
SQ FT: 35,000
SALES (est): 21.45MM Privately Held
Web: www.akronzoo.org
SIC: 8422 Zoological garden, noncommercial

(G-40)
AKRON-CANTON REGIONAL FOODBANK (PA)
350 Opportunity Pkwy (44307-2234)
PHONE..................330 535-6900
Daniel R Flowers, CEO
Peggy Susniskas, *
Bernett Williams, *
Patricia Gibbs, *
Laura Bennett, *
EMP: 49 EST: 1982
SQ FT: 87,000
SALES (est): 55.59MM Privately Held
Web: www.akroncantonfoodbank.org
SIC: 8322 Social service center

(G-41)
AKRON-RBAN MNRITY ALCHLISM DRG
Also Called: Urban Minority Alcoholism
665 W Market St Ste 2d (44303-1438)
PHONE..................330 379-3467
EMP: 34 EST: 1985
SALES (est): 1.2MM Privately Held
Web: www.akronumadaop.com
SIC: 8322 8069 Alcoholism counseling, nontreatment; Alcoholism rehabilitation hospital

(G-42)
AKRON-SMMIT CNVNTION VSTORS BU
Also Called: JOHN S KNIGHT CENTER
77 E Mill St (44308-1459)
PHONE..................330 374-7560
Gregg Mervis, Pr
▲ EMP: 35 EST: 1973
SALES (est): 7.68MM Privately Held
Web: www.visitakron-summit.org
SIC: 7389 Convention and show services

(G-43)
ALCO-CHEM INC (PA)
Also Called: Alco
45 N Summit St (44308-1933)
PHONE..................330 253-3535
Anthony Mandala Junior, Pr
Bart Mandala, *
Robert Mandala, *
▲ EMP: 34 EST: 1966
SQ FT: 22,000
SALES (est): 21.28MM
SALES (corp-wide): 21.28MM Privately Held
Web: www.alco-chem.com
SIC: 5087 2869 2842 Janitors' supplies; Industrial organic chemicals, nec; Polishes and sanitation goods

(G-44)
ALPHA PHI ALPHA HOMES INC
Also Called: Cwv Family Housing
695 Dunbar Dr (44311-1315)
PHONE..................330 376-9956
Beverly Lomax, Mgr
EMP: 35
SQ FT: 2,400
SALES (corp-wide): 2.39MM Privately Held
Web: www.alphahomes.org
SIC: 6531 Real estate managers
PA: Alpha Phi Alpha Homes Incorporated
662 Wolf Ledges Pkwy
Akron OH
330 376-8787

(G-45)
ALPHA PHI ALPHA HOMES INC
730 Callis Dr (44311-1313)
PHONE..................330 376-2115
Beverly Lomax, Genl Mgr
EMP: 34
SALES (corp-wide): 2.39MM Privately Held
Web: www.alphahomes.org
SIC: 7299 6513 Apartment locating service; Apartment building operators
PA: Alpha Phi Alpha Homes Incorporated
662 Wolf Ledges Pkwy
Akron OH
330 376-8787

(G-46)
AMERICAN NATIONAL RED CROSS
Also Called: American Nat Red Cross - Blood
501 W Market St (44303-1842)
PHONE..................330 535-6131
EMP: 52
SALES (corp-wide): 3.18B Privately Held
Web: www.redcross.org
SIC: 8322 Social service center
PA: The American National Red Cross
431 18th St Nw
Washington DC 20006
202 737-8300

(G-47)
AMERICAN NATIONAL RED CROSS
Also Called: American Red Cross
501 W Market St (44303-1842)
PHONE..................330 535-6131
EMP: 31
SALES (corp-wide): 3.18B Privately Held
Web: www.redcross.org
SIC: 8322 Social service center
PA: The American National Red Cross
431 18th St Nw
Washington DC 20006
202 737-8300

(G-48)
AMERICAN PLASTICS INC
Also Called: Ego of Indiana
1914 Akron Peninsula Rd (44313-4810)
PHONE..................330 945-4100
Dale Schiff, Pr
Michael Temple, *
▲ EMP: 60 EST: 1993
SQ FT: 6,000
SALES (est): 6.13MM Privately Held
Web: www.americanplastics.com
SIC: 5162 Plastics materials, nec

(G-49)
AMPERSAND GROUP LLC
1946 S Arlington St (44306-4285)
PHONE..................330 379-0044
EMP: 30 EST: 2004
SALES (est): 2.21MM Privately Held
Web: www.theampersandgroup.com
SIC: 5961 7389 Electronic shopping; Financial services

(G-50)
ANESTHESIOLOGY ASSOC OF AKRON
1 Akron General Ave (44307-2432)
PHONE..................330 344-6401
Paul Korytkowski, Pr
EMP: 39 EST: 1969
SALES (est): 809.75K Privately Held
Web: www.akrongeneral.org
SIC: 8011 Anesthesiologist

Akron - Summit County (G-51) GEOGRAPHIC SECTION

(G-51)
ANSWERNET INC
411 Wolf Ledges Pkwy Ste 201
(44311-1052)
PHONE.................978 710-5856
EMP: 37
SALES (corp-wide): 47.9MM **Privately Held**
Web: www.answernet.com
SIC: 7389 Telephone answering service
PA: Answernet, Inc.
  3930 Commerce Ave
  Willow Grove PA 19090
  800 411-5777

(G-52)
ANSWERNET INC
120 E Mill St (44308-1731)
PHONE.................877 864-2251
Cindy Smith, *Mgr*
EMP: 38
SALES (corp-wide): 47.9MM **Privately Held**
Web: www.answernet.com
SIC: 7389 Telephone answering service
PA: Answernet, Inc.
  3930 Commerce Ave
  Willow Grove PA 19090
  800 411-5777

(G-53)
APPLE GROWTH PARTNERS INC (PA)
1540 W Market St (44313-7114)
PHONE.................330 867-7350
Harold Gaar, *CEO*
David Gaino, *
Erica Ishida, *
Ivan Mahovlic, *
Karl Driggs, *
▲ **EMP**: 70 **EST**: 1948
SQ FT: 2,500
SALES (est): 25.02MM
SALES (corp-wide): 25.02MM **Privately Held**
Web: www.applegrowth.com
SIC: 8748 8721 Business consulting, nec; Certified public accountant

(G-54)
ARCADIA SERVICES INC
Also Called: Arcadia Health Care
1650 W Market St Ste 27 (44313-7007)
PHONE.................330 869-9520
Kathy Kozachenko, *Mgr*
EMP: 32
SALES (corp-wide): 25.38MM **Privately Held**
Web: www.arcadiahomecare.com
SIC: 7363 8082 Medical help service; Home health care services
PA: Arcadia Services, Inc.
  20750 Civic Center Dr # 100
  Southfield MI 48076
  248 352-7530

(G-55)
ARDMORE INC
981 E Market St (44305-2443)
PHONE.................330 535-2601
Yvette Diaz, *Ex Dir*
EMP: 90 **EST**: 1975
SQ FT: 12,000
SALES (est): 6.38MM **Privately Held**
Web: www.ardmoreinc.org
SIC: 8361 8699 Retarded home; Charitable organization

(G-56)
ARTEMIS FINE ARTS INC
Also Called: Artemis Fine Art Services
320 Ely Rd (44313-4514)
PHONE.................214 357-2577
Eric Smith, *Pr*
▲ **EMP**: 30 **EST**: 2000
SALES (est): 4.88MM **Privately Held**
Web: www.goafa.com
SIC: 4213 Trucking, except local

(G-57)
B F G FEDERAL CREDIT UNION (PA)
445 S Main St Ste B (44311-1056)
PHONE.................330 374-2990
Owen Dibert, *Ch Bd*
Betty Phillips, *
EMP: 44 **EST**: 1935
SQ FT: 29,000
SALES (est): 5.06MM
SALES (corp-wide): 5.06MM **Privately Held**
Web: www.bfgfcu.org
SIC: 6061 Federal credit unions

(G-58)
BABCOCK & WILCOX CNSTR CO LLC (HQ)
1200 E Market St Ste 651 (44305-4067)
PHONE.................330 753-9750
E James Ferland, *CEO*
Jenny L Apker, *
Mark S Low, *
D Paul Scavuzzo, *
EMP: 94 **EST**: 1867
SALES (est): 42.57MM
SALES (corp-wide): 999.35MM **Publicly Held**
Web: www.babcock.com
SIC: 1629 Power plant construction
PA: Babcock & Wilcox Enterprises, Inc.
  1200 E Market St Ste 650
  Akron OH 44305
  330 753-4511

(G-59)
BABCOCK & WILCOX COMPANY (HQ)
1200 E Market St Ste 650 (44305)
P.O. Box 351 (44203)
PHONE.................330 753-4511
Mark Low, *Sr VP*
Jimmy Morgan, *
Louis Salamone, *
◆ **EMP**: 1000 **EST**: 1867
SQ FT: 16,000
SALES (est): 896.25MM
SALES (corp-wide): 999.35MM **Publicly Held**
Web: www.babcock.com
SIC: 1629 1711 3443 7699 Industrial plant construction; Plumbing, heating, air-conditioning; Fabricated plate work (boiler shop); Boiler and heating repair services
PA: Babcock & Wilcox Enterprises, Inc.
  1200 E Market St Ste 650
  Akron OH 44305
  330 753-4511

(G-60)
BABCOCK & WILCOX HOLDINGS INC
1200 E Market St Ste 650 (44305-4067)
PHONE.................704 625-4900
EMP: 2400 **EST**: 2017
SALES (est): 48.92MM **Privately Held**
Web: www.babcock.com
SIC: 3511 8711 Turbines and turbine generator sets; Engineering services

(G-61)
BARBICAS CONSTRUCTION CO
124 Darrow Rd Ste 1 (44305-3835)
PHONE.................330 733-9101
Carla Barbicas, *Pr*
Elia Barbicas, *
EMP: 36 **EST**: 1947
SQ FT: 9,600
SALES (est): 5.23MM **Privately Held**
Web: www.barbicas.com
SIC: 1771 1611 Blacktop (asphalt) work; Surfacing and paving

(G-62)
BATH MANOR LIMITED PARTNERSHIP
Also Called: Bath Manor Special Care Centre
2330 Smith Rd (44333-2927)
PHONE.................330 836-1006
Morton J Weisburg, *Pr*
EMP: 485 **EST**: 1991
SALES (est): 12.82MM
SALES (corp-wide): 655.44MM **Privately Held**
Web: www.saberhealth.com
SIC: 8051 Convalescent home with continuous nursing care
PA: Saber Healthcare Group, L.L.C.
  23700 Commerce Park
  Beachwood OH 44122
  216 292-5706

(G-63)
BBS & ASSOCIATES INC
130 Springside Dr Ste 200 (44333-4553)
PHONE.................330 665-5227
Dale Berkey, *Pr*
Phyllis Laskowski, *
Doug Brendel, *
Jim Alexander, *
EMP: 32 **EST**: 1985
SALES (est): 3.96MM **Privately Held**
Web: www.servantheart.com
SIC: 7389 7311 8748 Fund raising organizations; Advertising agencies; Business consulting, nec

(G-64)
BEAVER DAM HEALTH CARE CENTER
Also Called: Beverly
721 Hickory St (44303-2213)
PHONE.................330 762-6486
Michael Jordan, *Mgr*
EMP: 27
SALES (corp-wide): 825.65MM **Privately Held**
Web: www.beaverdamhcc.com
SIC: 8059 8051 Convalescent home; Skilled nursing care facilities
PA: Golden Living Llc
  5220 Tennyson Pkwy # 400
  Plano TX 75024
  972 372-6300

(G-65)
BENEFICIAL BUILDING SVCS INC (PA)
1830 13th St Sw (44314-2907)
PHONE.................330 848-2556
James Lawson, *Pr*
Paul Carnifac, *
EMP: 54 **EST**: 1983
SQ FT: 500
SALES (est): 1.91MM
SALES (corp-wide): 1.91MM **Privately Held**
Web: www.beneficialbuildingservices.com
SIC: 7349 Janitorial service, contract basis

(G-66)
BERNS ONEILL SEC & SAFETY LLC
Also Called: Boss Investigations
1000 N Main St (44310-1452)
PHONE.................330 374-9133
Dan O'neill, *Managing Member*
EMP: 30 **EST**: 2003
SQ FT: 2,000
SALES (est): 2.89MM
SALES (corp-wide): 9.54MM **Privately Held**
SIC: 7361 Placement agencies
PA: Professional Placement Services Llc
  34200 Solon Rd
  Solon OH 44139
  440 914-0090

(G-67)
BEST WESTERN EXECUTIVE INN
Also Called: Best Western
2677 Gilchrist Rd Unit 1 (44305-4439)
PHONE.................330 794-1050
Dilu Dinani, *Pt*
Haider Ladha, *Pt*
EMP: 27 **EST**: 1986
SQ FT: 73,823
SALES (est): 489.01K **Privately Held**
Web: best-western-executive-inn-of-akron-oh-us.booked.net
SIC: 7011 Hotels and motels

(G-68)
BIO-MDCAL APPLCATIONS OHIO INC
Also Called: Greater Akron Dialysis Center
345 Bishop St (44307-2401)
PHONE.................330 376-4905
Dottie Sample, *Ex Dir*
EMP: 28
SQ FT: 2,000
SALES (corp-wide): 21.15B **Privately Held**
Web: www.fmcna.com
SIC: 8092 Kidney dialysis centers
HQ: Bio-Medical Applications Of Ohio, Inc.
  920 Winter St
  Waltham MA 02451

(G-69)
BIT MINING LIMITED ✪
428 Seiberling St (44306-3205)
PHONE.................346 204-8537
Xianfeng Yang, *CEO*
Bo Yu, *Ch Bd*
Qiang Yuan, *CFO*
EMP: 74 **EST**: 2023
SALES (est): 1.55MM **Privately Held**
SIC: 6799 Investors, nec

(G-70)
BLICK CLINIC INC (PA)
640 W Market St (44303-1465)
PHONE.................330 762-5425
Karin Loper-orr, *Pr*
EMP: 80 **EST**: 1969
SQ FT: 15,600
SALES (est): 13.67MM
SALES (corp-wide): 13.67MM **Privately Held**
Web: www.blickclinic.org
SIC: 8093 8322 Mental health clinic, outpatient; Individual and family services

(G-71)
BLICK CLINIC INC
682 W Market St (44303-1414)
PHONE.................330 762-5425
EMP: 135
SQ FT: 11,400
SALES (corp-wide): 13.67MM **Privately Held**
Web: www.blickcenter.org

GEOGRAPHIC SECTION

Akron - Summit County (G-93)

SIC: 8093 Mental health clinic, outpatient
PA: Blick Clinic, Inc.
640 W Market St
Akron OH 44303
330 762-5425

(G-72)
BOGIE INDUSTRIES INC LTD
Also Called: Weaver Fab & Finishing
1100 Home Ave (44310-3504)
PHONE.................330 745-3105
Jim Lauer, Pr
Fuzzy Helton, *
Marian Lauer, *
EMP: 38 EST: 1998
SQ FT: 40,000
SALES (est): 8.99MM Privately Held
Web: www.weaverfab.com
SIC: 3444 1799 3399 Sheet metalwork; Coating of metal structures at construction site; Powder, metal

(G-73)
BRAKEFIRE INCORPORATED
Also Called: Akron Welding & Spring Co
451 Kennedy Rd (44305-4423)
PHONE.................330 535-4343
Kenneth G May, Mgr
EMP: 36
SALES (corp-wide): 50.11MM Privately Held
Web: www.silcofs.com
SIC: 5087 Firefighting equipment
PA: Brakefire, Incorporated
10200 Reading Rd
Cincinnati OH 45241
513 733-5655

(G-74)
BREEZE 33 PRODUCTS LLC
Also Called: Breeze33
2620 Ridgewood Rd (44313-3527)
PHONE.................833 273-3950
Marc D Blaushild, Managing Member
EMP: 62 EST: 2017
SALES (est): 8.46MM Privately Held
Web: www.breeze33.com
SIC: 5075 Warm air heating and air conditioning
PA: Famous Enterprises, Inc.
2620 Ridgewood Rd Ste 200
Akron OH 44313

(G-75)
BRENNAN MANNA & DIAMOND LLC (PA)
75 E Market St (44308-2010)
PHONE.................330 253-5060
Joy Westfall, Off Mgr
EMP: 27 EST: 2000
SQ FT: 6,800
SALES (est): 19.29MM
SALES (corp-wide): 19.29MM Privately Held
Web: www.bmdllc.com
SIC: 8111 General practice law office

(G-76)
BROOKDALE LVING CMMUNITIES INC
100 Brookmont Rd Ofc (44333-9268)
PHONE.................330 666-4545
EMP: 50
SALES (corp-wide): 4.53B Publicly Held
SIC: 8051 Skilled nursing care facilities
HQ: Brookdale Living Communities, Inc.
515 N State St Ste 1750
Chicago IL 60654

(G-77)
BUCKINGHAM DLTTLE BRROUGHS LLC (PA)
3800 Embassy Pkwy Ste 300 (44333)
PHONE.................330 376-5300
Nicholas T George, Pr
Patrick J Keating, Vice Chairman*
Donald B Leach Junior, Asst VP
Jeffrey A Halm, *
Steven A Dimengo, *
EMP: 165 EST: 1913
SQ FT: 70,000
SALES (est): 42.23K
SALES (corp-wide): 42.23K Privately Held
Web: www.bdblaw.com
SIC: 8111 General practice attorney, lawyer

(G-78)
BUREAU VERITAS NORTH AMER INC
520 S Main St Ste 2444 (44311-1087)
PHONE.................330 252-5100
Barb Hana, Pr
EMP: 29
SALES (corp-wide): 286.3MM Privately Held
Web: www.bvna.com
SIC: 8748 Environmental consultant
HQ: Bureau Veritas North America, Inc.
16800 Grnspint Pk Dr Ste
Houston TX 77060
954 236-8100

(G-79)
CANAL PHYSICIAN GROUP
1 Akron General Ave (44307-2432)
PHONE.................330 344-4000
Kim Roberts, Mgr
EMP: 49 EST: 2002
SALES (est): 675.49K Privately Held
Web: www.akrongeneral.org
SIC: 8011 General and family practice, physician/surgeon

(G-80)
CARDINAL GROUP INC
180 E Miller Ave (44301-1349)
PHONE.................330 252-1047
Bethann Skidmore, CEO
EMP: 168 EST: 2002
SALES (est): 24.76MM Privately Held
Web: www.cardinal-group.com
SIC: 1541 1761 7349 Industrial buildings and warehouses; Roofing, siding, and sheetmetal work; Cleaning service, industrial or commercial

(G-81)
CARROLLS LLC
Also Called: National Tire Wholesale
2880 Gilchrist Rd (44305-4416)
PHONE.................330 733-8100
Jeff Schaber, Mgr
EMP: 30
Web: www.carrollorg.com
SIC: 5014 Automobile tires and tubes
HQ: Carroll's, Llc
4281 Old Dixie Hwy
Atlanta GA 30354
404 366-5476

(G-82)
CARTER-JONES LUMBER COMPANY
Also Called: Carter Lumber
172 N Case Ave (44305-2599)
PHONE.................330 784-5441
Mike Smead, Mgr
EMP: 30
SALES (corp-wide): 2.57B Privately Held
Web: www.carterlumber.com
SIC: 5211 5031 5251 Lumber products; Lumber, plywood, and millwork; Hardware stores
HQ: The Carter-Jones Lumber Company
601 Tallmadge Rd
Kent OH 44240
330 673-6100

(G-83)
CAVANAUGH BUILDING CORPORATION
1744 Collier Rd (44320-3908)
PHONE.................330 753-6658
EMP: 60 EST: 1983
SALES (est): 15.44MM Privately Held
Web: www.cavanaughbuilding.com
SIC: 1542 1541 Commercial and office building, new construction; Industrial buildings, new construction, nec

(G-84)
CBIZ ACCNTING TAX ADVSORY OHIO
4040 Embassy Pkwy Ste 100 (44333-8354)
PHONE.................330 668-6500
Jeffery Walters, Dir
EMP: 216 EST: 1986
SALES (est): 1.55MM Publicly Held
Web: www.cbiz.com
SIC: 8721 Certified public accountant
PA: Cbiz, Inc.
5959 Rckside Wods Blvd N
Cleveland OH 44131

(G-85)
CENTER FOR UROLOGIC HEALTH LLC (PA)
Also Called: Physicians Urology Centre
95 Arch St Ste 165 (44304-1488)
PHONE.................330 375-0924
EMP: 36 EST: 1995
SALES (est): 5.26MM Privately Held
Web: www.summahealth.org
SIC: 8011 Urologist

(G-86)
CENTRAL COCA-COLA BTLG CO INC
Also Called: Coca-Cola
1560 Triplett Blvd (44306-3306)
PHONE.................330 875-1487
EMP: 34
SALES (corp-wide): 45.75B Publicly Held
Web: www.coca-cola.com
SIC: 2086 8741 Bottled and canned soft drinks; Management services
HQ: Central Coca-Cola Bottling Company, Inc.
555 Taxter Rd Ste 550
Elmsford NY 10523
914 789-1100

(G-87)
CHEMSTRESS CONSULTANT COMPANY (PA)
39 S Main St Ste 315 (44308-1856)
PHONE.................330 535-5591
Robert Handelman, Ch
James Kehres, *
Jean E Hagen, *
Paul K Christoff, *
Wiliam R Ferguson, *
EMP: 150 EST: 1965
SQ FT: 70,000
SALES (est): 24.71MM
SALES (corp-wide): 24.71MM Privately Held
Web: www.chemstress.com
SIC: 8711 8712 8741 Consulting engineer; Architectural services; Construction management

(G-88)
CHILDRENS HOME CARE GROUP
185 W Cedar St Ste 203 (44307-2447)
PHONE.................330 543-5000
EMP: 280 EST: 1988
SALES (est): 7.07MM Privately Held
SIC: 8082 Home health care services

(G-89)
CHILDRENS HOSP MED CTR AKRON
1463 Canton Rd # A (44312-4022)
PHONE.................330 253-4931
EMP: 54
SALES (corp-wide): 1.4B Privately Held
Web: www.akronchildrens.org
SIC: 8069 8031 8011 Childrens' hospital; Offices and clinics of osteopathic physicians; Pediatrician
PA: Childrens Hospital Medical Center Of Akron
1 Perkins Sq
Akron OH 44308
330 543-1000

(G-90)
CHILDRENS HOSP MED CTR AKRON
Also Called: Ask Childrens
1 Perkins Sq (44308-1063)
PHONE.................330 543-8004
Cheryl Ballentine, Prin
EMP: 54
SALES (corp-wide): 1.4B Privately Held
Web: www.akronchildrens.org
SIC: 8069 8011 Childrens' hospital; Offices and clinics of medical doctors
PA: Childrens Hospital Medical Center Of Akron
1 Perkins Sq
Akron OH 44308
330 543-1000

(G-91)
CHILDRENS HOSP MED CTR AKRON
Also Called: Critical Care
1 Perkins Sq (44308-1063)
PHONE.................330 543-8639
James Besunder, Prin
EMP: 54
SALES (corp-wide): 1.4B Privately Held
Web: www.akronchildrens.org
SIC: 8011 8031 Pediatrician; Offices and clinics of osteopathic physicians
PA: Childrens Hospital Medical Center Of Akron
1 Perkins Sq
Akron OH 44308
330 543-1000

(G-92)
CHILDRENS HOSP MED CTR AKRON
Also Called: Akron Childrens Hospital
214 W Bowery St (44308-1046)
PHONE.................330 543-8503
Bradley Riemenschneide, Prin
EMP: 55
SALES (corp-wide): 1.4B Privately Held
Web: www.akronchildrens.org
SIC: 8011 8351 Medical centers; Child day care services
PA: Childrens Hospital Medical Center Of Akron
1 Perkins Sq
Akron OH 44308
330 543-1000

(G-93)
CHILDRENS HOSP MED CTR AKRON
6100 Whipple Ave. Nw Ste 5200 (44308)
PHONE.................330 543-8521
EMP: 54
SALES (corp-wide): 1.4B Privately Held

Akron - Summit County (G-94)   GEOGRAPHIC SECTION

Web: www.akronchildrens.org
SIC: 8062 General medical and surgical hospitals
PA: Childrens Hospital Medical Center Of Akron
1 Perkins Sq
Akron OH 44308
330 543-1000

(G-94)
CHILDRENS HOSP MED CTR AKRON
525 E Market St (44304-1619)
PHONE..................................330 375-3528
EMP: 54
SALES (corp-wide): 1.4B Privately Held
Web: www.akronchildrens.org
SIC: 8062 General medical and surgical hospitals
PA: Childrens Hospital Medical Center Of Akron
1 Perkins Sq
Akron OH 44308
330 543-1000

(G-95)
CHILDRENS HOSP MED CTR AKRON
701 White Pond Dr Ste 100 (44320-1193)
PHONE..................................330 865-1252
EMP: 55
SALES (corp-wide): 1.4B Privately Held
Web: www.akronchildrens.org
SIC: 8062 General medical and surgical hospitals
PA: Childrens Hospital Medical Center Of Akron
1 Perkins Sq
Akron OH 44308
330 543-1000

(G-96)
CHILDRENS HOSP MED CTR AKRON
1 Perkins Sq Ste 214 (44308-1063)
PHONE..................................330 543-1000
EMP: 54
SALES (corp-wide): 1.4B Privately Held
Web: www.akronchildrens.org
SIC: 8062 General medical and surgical hospitals
PA: Childrens Hospital Medical Center Of Akron
1 Perkins Sq
Akron OH 44308
330 543-1000

(G-97)
CHILDRENS HOSP MED CTR AKRON
215 W Bowery St Ste 2200 (44308-1069)
PHONE..................................330 543-8260
Cyndee Winter, *Mgr*
EMP: 54
SALES (corp-wide): 1.4B Privately Held
Web: www.akronchildrens.org
SIC: 8062 General medical and surgical hospitals
PA: Childrens Hospital Medical Center Of Akron
1 Perkins Sq
Akron OH 44308
330 543-1000

(G-98)
CHILDRENS HOSP MED CTR AKRON (PA)
Also Called: AKRON CHILDREN'S HOSPITAL
1 Perkins Sq (44308-1063)
PHONE..................................330 543-1000
TOLL FREE: 800
William Considine, *CEO*
Walt Schwoeble, *
Spencer A Kowal, *
Craig Mcghee, *CAO*
Kim Moses, *CLO**
EMP: 3462 EST: 1891
SQ FT: 356,000
SALES (est): 1.4B
SALES (corp-wide): 1.4B Privately Held
Web: www.akronchildrens.org
SIC: 8062 General medical and surgical hospitals

(G-99)
CHILDRENS HOSP MED CTR AKRON
300 Locust St (44302-1821)
PHONE..................................330 543-8530
EMP: 54
SALES (corp-wide): 1.4B Privately Held
Web: www.akronchildrens.org
SIC: 8062 General medical and surgical hospitals
PA: Childrens Hospital Medical Center Of Akron
1 Perkins Sq
Akron OH 44308
330 543-1000

(G-100)
CITY OF AKRON
Sewer Department
2460 Akron Peninsula Rd (44313-4710)
PHONE..................................330 375-2666
EMP: 27
SQ FT: 240
SALES (corp-wide): 395.24MM Privately Held
Web: www.akronohio.gov
SIC: 4952 Sewerage systems
PA: City Of Akron
166 S High St Rm 502
Akron OH 44308
330 375-2720

(G-101)
CITY OF AKRON
Also Called: Utilities Business Office, The
1180 S Main St Ste 110 (44301-1253)
PHONE..................................330 375-2650
EMP: 27
SALES (corp-wide): 395.24MM Privately Held
Web: www.akronohio.gov
SIC: 4953 4212 Recycling, waste materials; Garbage collection and transport, no disposal
PA: City Of Akron
166 S High St Rm 502
Akron OH 44308
330 375-2720

(G-102)
CITY OF AKRON
Also Called: Alcohol, Drug Addiction
100 W Cedar St Ste 300 (44307-2572)
PHONE..................................330 564-4075
EMP: 27
SALES (corp-wide): 395.24MM Privately Held
Web: www.akronohio.gov
SIC: 9431 6513 Administration of public health programs; Apartment building operators
PA: City Of Akron
166 S High St Rm 502
Akron OH 44308
330 375-2720

(G-103)
CITY OF AKRON
Bureau of Engineering
166 S High St Rm 701 (44308-1627)
PHONE..................................330 375-2355
EMP: 117
SALES (corp-wide): 395.24MM Privately Held
Web: www.akronohio.gov
SIC: 8711 9111 Engineering services; Mayors' office
PA: City Of Akron
166 S High St Rm 502
Akron OH 44308
330 375-2720

(G-104)
CIVIL SERVICE PERSONNEL ASSN
Also Called: Cspa
720 Wolf Ledges Pkwy Ste 203 (44311-1521)
PHONE..................................330 434-2772
Charles Victor, *Pr*
Andy Doyle, *Treas*
Joey Anderson, *Sec*
William Blankenship, *VP*
EMP: 34 EST: 1993
SALES (est): 333.85K Privately Held
Web: www.cspaunion.com
SIC: 8631 Labor union

(G-105)
CLEARPATH HM HLTH HOSPICE LLC
Also Called: Clearpath Home Health
577 Grant St Ste C (44311-1535)
PHONE..................................330 784-2162
Ruth Self, *Managing Member*
EMP: 43 EST: 2004
SALES (est): 8.42MM Privately Held
Web: www.clearpathhomehealth.com
SIC: 8082 Visiting nurse service

(G-106)
CLEARWATER SERVICES INC (PA)
Also Called: Clearwater Systems
1411 Vernon Odom Blvd (44320-4086)
P.O. Box 8440 (44320-0100)
PHONE..................................330 836-4946
Jerome P Kovach Junior, *CEO*
EMP: 35 EST: 2014
SQ FT: 13,000
SALES (est): 23.2MM
SALES (corp-wide): 23.2MM Privately Held
Web: www.clearwatersystems.com
SIC: 4941 7389 Water supply; Water softener service

(G-107)
CLEVELAND CLINIC FOUNDATION
1 Park West Blvd Ste 150 (44320-4230)
PHONE..................................330 864-8060
Michael P Harrington, *Brnch Mgr*
EMP: 33
SALES (corp-wide): 14.48B Privately Held
Web: www.clevelandclinic.org
SIC: 8062 General medical and surgical hospitals
PA: The Cleveland Clinic Foundation
9500 Euclid Ave
Cleveland OH 44195
216 636-8335

(G-108)
CLEVELAND CLNIC AKRON GEN VSTI (PA)
1 Home Care Pl (44320-3901)
PHONE..................................330 745-1601
Karen Talbott, *Pr*
Jerry Bauman, *
Tom Lyzen, *
EMP: 325 EST: 1947
SQ FT: 20,000
SALES (est): 16.73MM
SALES (corp-wide): 16.73MM Privately Held
Web: www.vnsi.org
SIC: 8082 Visiting nurse service

(G-109)
CLEVELAND ELC ILLUMINATING CO (HQ)
76 S Main St (44308)
PHONE..................................800 589-3101
John E Skory, *Pr*
Mark T Clark, *Ex VP*
Harvey L Wagner, *VP*
L L Vespoli, *Ex VP*
J F Pearson, *VP*
EMP: 100 EST: 1892
SALES (est): 1.16B Publicly Held
Web: www.firstenergycorp.com
SIC: 4911 Generation, electric power
PA: Firstenergy Corp.
76 S Main St
Akron OH 44308

(G-110)
CLUNK HOOSE CO LPA
495 Wolf Ledges Pkwy Ste 1 (44311-1084)
PHONE..................................330 922-5492
John Clunk, *Pr*
EMP: 35 EST: 2009
SALES (est): 6.87MM Privately Held
Web: www.clunkhoose.com
SIC: 8111 General practice attorney, lawyer

(G-111)
COHEN & COMPANY LTD
3500 Embassy Pkwy Ste 100 (44333-8373)
PHONE..................................330 374-1040
J Michael Kolk, *Pt*
EMP: 104
SALES (corp-wide): 36MM Privately Held
Web: www.cohencpa.com
SIC: 8721 Certified public accountant
PA: Cohen & Company, Ltd.
1350 Euclid Ave Ste 800
Cleveland OH 44115
216 579-1040

(G-112)
COLEMAN PROFESSIONAL SERVICES
3043 Sanitarium Rd Ste 2 (44312-4600)
PHONE..................................330 394-8831
EMP: 31
SALES (est): 1.06MM Privately Held
Web: www.colemanservices.org
SIC: 8093 Mental health clinic, outpatient

(G-113)
COLEMAN PROFESSIONAL SVCS INC
3043 Sanitarium Rd Ste 2 (44312-4600)
PHONE..................................330 744-2991
EMP: 53
SALES (corp-wide): 67.31MM Privately Held
Web: www.colemanservices.org
SIC: 8093 Mental health clinic, outpatient
PA: Coleman Professional Services, Inc.
5982 Rhodes Rd
Kent OH 44240
330 673-1347

(G-114)
COMBS MANUFACTURING INC
380 Kennedy Rd (44305-4422)
PHONE..................................330 784-3151
▲ EMP: 70
SIC: 3599 7692 2421 Machine shop, jobbing and repair; Welding repair; Sawmills and planing mills, general

GEOGRAPHIC SECTION   Akron - Summit County (G-137)

(G-115)
COMMERCIAL TIME SHARING INC
Also Called: C T I
2740 Cory Ave (44314-1339)
PHONE..................................330 644-3059
David L Poling, *Ch Bd*
Ronald Symens, *
Kathleen Symens, *
EMP: 29 **EST:** 1978
SQ FT: 8,000
SALES (est): 6.01MM **Privately Held**
Web: www.comtime.com
SIC: 7373 7371 5045 Systems integration services; Computer software development; Computer software

(G-116)
COMMUNITY DRUG BOARD INC (PA)
725 E Market St (44305-2421)
PHONE..................................330 315-5590
Theodore P Ziegler, *CEO*
Pamela J Crislip, *
Janet Wagner, *
EMP: 90 **EST:** 1974
SQ FT: 17,000
SALES (est): 11.53MM
SALES (corp-wide): 11.53MM **Privately Held**
Web: www.chcaddiction.org
SIC: 8093 8322 Substance abuse clinics (outpatient); Substance abuse counseling

(G-117)
COMMUNITY DRUG BOARD INC
Also Called: Ramar-Genesis
380 S Portage Path (44320-2326)
PHONE..................................330 996-5114
EMP: 90
SALES (corp-wide): 11.53MM **Privately Held**
Web: www.chcaddiction.org
SIC: 8093 Substance abuse clinics (outpatient)
PA: Community Drug Board, Inc.
725 E Market St
Akron OH 44305
330 315-5590

(G-118)
COMMUNITY SUPPORT SERVICES INC (PA)
47 N Arlington St (44305)
PHONE..................................330 253-9388
Terry Dalton, *CEO*
James Bonnervall, *
Terrence B Dalton, *
James E Bournival, *
Robert W Hermanowski, *
EMP: 201 **EST:** 1988
SALES (est): 26.46MM
SALES (corp-wide): 26.46MM **Privately Held**
Web: www.cssbh.org
SIC: 8093 8331 8361 Mental health clinic, outpatient; Vocational rehabilitation agency; Emotionally disturbed home

(G-119)
CONCORD TESTA HOTEL ASSOC LLC
Also Called: Courtyard By Marriott
41 Furnace St (44308-1914)
PHONE..................................330 252-9228
EMP: 99 **EST:** 2014
SALES (est): 2.78MM **Privately Held**
Web: courtyard.marriott.com
SIC: 7011 Hotels and motels

(G-120)
CONDUENT CARE SOLUTIONS LLC
2717 S Arlington Rd Ste B (44312-4725)
PHONE..................................330 644-0927
Cheryl Mcardle, *Brnch Mgr*
EMP: 50
SIC: 6411 Medical insurance claim processing, contract or fee basis
PA: Conduent Care Solutions, Llc
100 Campus Dr Ste 200
Florham Park NJ 07932

(G-121)
CONSOLIDUS LLC
526 S Main St Ste 804 (44311)
PHONE..................................330 319-7200
Jeffrey Jones, *Mgr*
EMP: 39 **EST:** 2006
SQ FT: 2,000
SALES (est): 6.13MM **Privately Held**
Web: www.consolidus.com
SIC: 8743 Sales promotion

(G-122)
CONSTRUCTION MECHANICS INC
1025 S Broadway St (44311-2340)
P.O. Box 3564 (44223-7564)
PHONE..................................330 630-9239
Stephen Milkovich, *Pr*
EMP: 172 **EST:** 2009
SALES (est): 7.2MM **Privately Held**
Web: www.constructionmechanics.com
SIC: 1521 Single-family housing construction

(G-123)
CORNERSTONE MED SVCS - MDWEST
453 S High St Ste 201 (44311-4417)
PHONE..................................330 374-0229
EMP: 35 **EST:** 2004
SQ FT: 11,000
SALES (est): 2.06MM **Privately Held**
SIC: 7352 5047 Medical equipment rental; Medical equipment and supplies

(G-124)
COTTER MDSE STOR OF OHIO
1564 Firestone Pkwy (44301-1626)
P.O. Box 808 (44309-0808)
PHONE..................................330 773-9177
Chris Geib, *Pr*
Howard D Heater, *
EMP: 44 **EST:** 1987
SQ FT: 500,000
SALES (est): 891.89K
SALES (corp-wide): 9.95MM **Privately Held**
Web: www.cotterwhse.com
SIC: 4225 General warehousing
PA: The Cotter Merchandise Storage Company
1564 Firestone Pkwy
Akron OH 44301
330 315-2755

(G-125)
COTTER MOVING & STORAGE CO
Also Called: A-Advnced Mvg Stor Systms-Self
265 W Bowery St (44308-1034)
P.O. Box 529 (44309-0529)
PHONE..................................330 535-5115
Harry L Bord, *Pr*
Fred Bord, *
William C Bord, *
EMP: 32 **EST:** 1882
SQ FT: 250,000
SALES (est): 2.43MM **Privately Held**
Web: www.cottermoving.com

SIC: 4213 4225 4212 Trucking, except local; General warehousing and storage; Local trucking, without storage

(G-126)
CRYSTAL CLINIC INC
1622 E Turkeyfoot Lake Rd Ste 200 (44312-5277)
PHONE..................................330 644-7436
EMP: 41
SALES (corp-wide): 54.91MM **Privately Held**
Web: www.crystalclinic.com
SIC: 8011 Orthopedic physician
PA: Crystal Clinic, Inc.
3975 Embassy Pkwy Ste A
Akron OH 44333
330 668-4040

(G-127)
CRYSTAL CLINIC SURGERY CTR LLC
3975 Embassy Pkwy Ste 202 (44333-8395)
PHONE..................................330 668-4040
Ronald R Suntken, *Pr*
Thomas J Reilly Md, *Prin*
Robert Bell, *
J W Ewing, *
Jim Miltner, *
EMP: 48 **EST:** 1989
SQ FT: 6,800
SALES (est): 19.55MM **Privately Held**
Web: www.crystalclinic.com
SIC: 8011 Orthopedic physician

(G-128)
CRYSTAL CLNIC ORTHPDIC CTR LLC
20 Olive St Ste 200 (44310-3169)
PHONE..................................330 535-3396
EMP: 88
SALES (corp-wide): 54.91MM **Privately Held**
Web: www.crystalclinic.com
SIC: 8011 Orthopedic physician
HQ: Crystal Clinic Orthopaedic Center, Llc
3925 Embassy Pkwy Ste 250
Akron OH 44333
330 668-4040

(G-129)
CTI ENGINEERS INC
17 S Main St (44308-1803)
PHONE..................................330 294-5996
Richard W Reed, *Prin*
EMP: 54 **EST:** 1995
SALES (est): 1.22MM **Privately Held**
Web: www.ctiengr.com
SIC: 8711 Consulting engineer

(G-130)
CYO & COMMUNITY SERVICES INC (PA)
Also Called: Cyo
795 Russell Ave (44307-1115)
PHONE..................................330 762-2961
Donald P Finn, *Ex Dir*
EMP: 40 **EST:** 1936
SALES (est): 1.02MM
SALES (corp-wide): 1.02MM **Privately Held**
Web: www.ccdocle.org
SIC: 8661 8322 Religious organizations; Individual and family services

(G-131)
DAN MARCHETTA CNSTR CO INC
525 N Cleveland Massillon Rd Ste 109 (44333)
PHONE..................................330 668-4800
Daniel T Marchetta Junior, *Pr*
Joseph Marchetta, *
Michael Marchetta, *

EMP: 30 **EST:** 1957
SQ FT: 3,000
SALES (est): 5MM **Privately Held**
Web: www.marchetta.com
SIC: 1542 1521 Commercial and office building, new construction; New construction, single-family houses

(G-132)
DAVID A LEVY INC
Also Called: Levy & Associates
345 Springside Dr (44333-2434)
PHONE..................................330 352-1289
David A Levy, *Pr*
EMP: 28 **EST:** 1990
SQ FT: 7,494
SALES (est): 2.04MM **Privately Held**
Web: www.dalevy.com
SIC: 8712 Architectural engineering

(G-133)
DETROIT WESTFIELD LLC
Also Called: Holiday Inn
4073 Medina Rd (44333-2476)
PHONE..................................330 666-4131
Fred Lami, *Pt*
Louie Lemaster, *Genl Mgr*
EMP: 84 **EST:** 1976
SQ FT: 106,335
SALES (est): 919.7K **Privately Held**
Web: www.holidayinn.com
SIC: 7011 5812 Hotels and motels; Restaurant, family: independent

(G-134)
DIGEST HEALTH CENTER LTD
Also Called: Amsurg
570 White Pond Dr Ste 150 (44320-4207)
PHONE..................................330 869-0178
Duane Roe, *Prin*
EMP: 39 **EST:** 2003
SQ FT: 19,200
SALES (est): 6.06MM **Privately Held**
Web: www.dhcakron.com
SIC: 8011 Gastronomist

(G-135)
DLZ OHIO INC
Also Called: Dlz
1 Canal Square Plz Ste 1300 (44308-1037)
PHONE..................................330 923-0401
EMP: 45
SQ FT: 11,667
Web: www.dlz.com
SIC: 8711 Consulting engineer
HQ: Dlz Ohio, Inc.
6121 Huntley Rd
Columbus OH 43229
614 888-0040

(G-136)
DOUG BIGELOW CHEVROLET INC
Also Called: Doug Chevrolet
894 Robinwood Hills Dr (44333-1550)
PHONE..................................330 644-7500
EMP: 75
SIC: 5511 5521 7538 7532 Automobiles, new and used; Used car dealers; General automotive repair shops; Top and body repair and paint shops

(G-137)
DOWNTOWN AKRON PARTNERSHIP INC
Also Called: DAT
103 S High St Fl 4 (44308-1461)
PHONE..................................330 374-7676
Suzie Graham, *Ex Dir*
Clair Dickinson Board, *Ch*
EMP: 50 **EST:** 1995
SALES (est): 1.5MM **Privately Held**

Akron - Summit County (G-138)　　　GEOGRAPHIC SECTION

Web: www.downtownakron.com
SIC: 8699 Charitable organization

(G-138)
DRB HOLDINGS LLC
3245 Pickle Rd (44312-5333)
PHONE..................................330 645-3299
Bill Morgenstern, *CEO*
EMP: 285 **EST:** 2003
SALES (est): 10.71MM **Privately Held**
Web: www.drb.com
SIC: 7373 7371 7372 Systems software development services; Custom computer programming services; Prepackaged software

(G-139)
DRB SYSTEMS LLC (HQ)
Also Called: Drb Tunnel Solutions
3245 Pickle Rd (44312-5333)
P.O. Box 550 (44685-0550)
PHONE..................................330 645-3299
Dale Brott, *Pr*
Donald A Brott, *
Kenneth Brott, *
EMP: 259 **EST:** 1984
SALES (est): 86.19MM
SALES (corp-wide): 3.1B **Publicly Held**
Web: www.drb.com
SIC: 7373 7371 7372 Systems software development services; Custom computer programming services; Prepackaged software
PA: Vontier Corporation
　5438 Wade Park Blvd # 601
　Raleigh NC 27607
　984 275-6000

(G-140)
DRIPS HOLDINGS LLC
1700 W Market St Ste 173 (44313-7002)
PHONE..................................512 643-7477
Aaron Christopher Evans, *CEO*
EMP: 99 **EST:** 2017
SALES (est): 4.74MM **Privately Held**
Web: www.drips.com
SIC: 8999 Communication services

(G-141)
DRIVERGE VHCL INNOVATIONS LLC (HQ)
2000 Brittain Rd Ste 200 (44310-1804)
PHONE..................................330 861-1118
William Koeblitz, *
Taylor Clark, *
Gerhard Schmidt, *
▲ **EMP:** 36 **EST:** 2012
SALES (est): 58.46MM
SALES (corp-wide): 218.57MM **Privately Held**
Web: www.driverge.com
SIC: 7532 5511 Customizing services, nonfactory basis; Automobiles, new and used
PA: Wmk, Llc
　4199 Knross Lkes Pkwy Ste
　Richfield OH 44286
　234 312-2000

(G-142)
DUNBAR ARMORED INC
830 Moe Dr Ste C (44310-2569)
PHONE..................................330 630-0603
Jim Dunbar, *Pr*
EMP: 32
SALES (corp-wide): 4.87B **Publicly Held**
Web: www.dunbarsecurity.com
SIC: 7381 Armored car services
HQ: Dunbar Armored, Inc.
　50 Schilling Rd
　Hunt Valley MD 21031
　410 584-9800

(G-143)
E & V VENTURES INC (PA)
Also Called: Two Men and A Truck
1511 E Market St (44305-4208)
PHONE..................................330 794-6683
EMP: 30 **EST:** 1995
SALES (est): 2.68MM **Privately Held**
Web: www.twomenandatruck.com
SIC: 4212 Moving services

(G-144)
EAST COMMUNITY LEARNING CENTER
80 Brittain Rd (44305-4222)
PHONE..................................330 814-7412
EMP: 58 **EST:** 2018
SALES (est): 190.27K **Privately Held**
Web: eastclchigh.akronschools.com
SIC: 8322 Community center

(G-145)
EAST OHIO GAS COMPANY
Also Called: Dominion Energy Ohio
2100 Eastwood Ave (44305-1998)
P.O. Box 94633 (44101-4633)
PHONE..................................800 362-7557
EMP: 65
SALES (corp-wide): 39.69B **Privately Held**
Web: www.dominiongaschoice.com
SIC: 4924 Natural gas distribution
HQ: The East Ohio Gas Company
　1201 E 55th St
　Cleveland OH 44103
　800 362-7557

(G-146)
EMERGE MINISTRIES INC
900 Mull Ave (44313-7597)
PHONE..................................330 865-8351
Clayton Glickert, *Pr*
Richard D Dobbins, *
Reverend Carl L Miller, *Sec*
Doctor Donald A Lichi, *Education Vice President*
Norma Rowe, *
EMP: 44 **EST:** 1973
SQ FT: 25,000
SALES (est): 3.93MM **Privately Held**
Web: www.emerge.org
SIC: 8322 7841 5942 General counseling services; Video disk/tape rental to the general public; Books, religious

(G-147)
EMPIRE ENTERPRISES INC
Also Called: Empire Wholesale Lumber Co
3677 Embassy Pkwy (44333-8382)
P.O. Box 1248 (44210-1248)
PHONE..................................330 665-7800
EMP: 47
SIC: 5031 5032 Lumber: rough, dressed, and finished; Brick, stone, and related material

(G-148)
EMPIRE WHOLESALE LUMBER COMPANY
3677 Embassy Pkwy (44333-8382)
P.O. Box 1248 (44210-1248)
PHONE..................................330 665-7800
▲ **EMP:** 47
Web: www.empirewholesale.com
SIC: 5031 Lumber: rough, dressed, and finished

(G-149)
ENERGY HARBOR CORP (HQ)
168 E Market St (44308-2014)
PHONE..................................888 254-6359
John Judge, *Pr*

Stephen Burnazian, *COMMERCIAL*
Jason Petrik, *Ex VP*
John Kiani, *Ofcr*
David Hamilton, *NUCLEAR*
EMP: 31 **EST:** 2019
SALES (est): 8.6B
SALES (corp-wide): 14.78B **Publicly Held**
Web: www.energyharbor.com
SIC: 4911 Electric services
PA: Vistra Corp.
　6555 Sierra Dr
　Irving TX 75039
　214 812-4600

(G-150)
ENERGY HARBOR LLC
168 E Market St (44308-2014)
PHONE..................................888 254-6356
John W Judge, *Pr*
Stephen Burnazian, *Ex VP*
John Kiani, *Ofcr*
David Hamilton, *NUCLEAR*
EMP: 2600 **EST:** 1997
SALES (est): 413.67MM
SALES (corp-wide): 14.78B **Publicly Held**
Web: www.energyharbor.com
SIC: 4911 Distribution, electric power
HQ: Energy Harbor Corp.
　168 E Market St
　Akron OH 44308
　888 254-6359

(G-151)
FAIRLAWN PARTNERS LLC
3600 Embassy Pkwy Ste 100 (44333-8337)
PHONE..................................330 576-1100
EMP: 35 **EST:** 1980
SALES (est): 5.5MM **Privately Held**
Web: www.buaweb.com
SIC: 6411 Insurance brokers, nec
HQ: Specialty Program Group Llc
　180 River Rd
　Summit NJ 07901
　908 790-6884

(G-152)
FALLSWAY EQUIPMENT CO INC (PA)
Also Called: Fallsway Equipment Company
1277 Devalera St (44310-2454)
P.O. Box 4537 (44310-0537)
PHONE..................................330 633-6000
TOLL FREE: 800
Harry Fairhurst, *CEO*
Gregory Fairhurst, *
▲ **EMP:** 114 **EST:** 1959
SQ FT: 92,140
SALES (est): 48.2MM
SALES (corp-wide): 48.2MM **Privately Held**
Web: www.fallsway.com
SIC: 5084 5511 7699 7359 Trucks, industrial ; Trucks, tractors, and trailers: new and used; Industrial truck repair; Industrial truck rental

(G-153)
FAMILY DENTAL TEAM INC (PA)
620 Ridgewood Xing Ste K (44333)
PHONE..................................330 733-7911
Mark Grucella, *Prin*
EMP: 30 **EST:** 1979
SQ FT: 4,000
SALES (est): 4.74MM
SALES (corp-wide): 4.74MM **Privately Held**
Web: www.akronbestdentist.com
SIC: 8021 Dentists' office

(G-154)
FAMOUS DISTRIBUTION INC (HQ)
Also Called: Famous Supply Companies

2620 Ridgewood Rd (44313-3527)
P.O. Box 951344 (44193-0011)
PHONE..................................330 762-9621
Jay Blaushild, *Ch*
Marc Blaushild, *
Dale Newman, *
EMP: 60 **EST:** 1933
SQ FT: 200,000
SALES (est): 201.89MM **Privately Held**
SIC: 5074 5075 5085 5023 Plumbing fittings and supplies; Furnaces, warm air; Valves and fittings; Kitchenware
PA: Famous Enterprises, Inc.
　2620 Ridgewood Rd Ste 200
　Akron OH 44313

(G-155)
FAMOUS DISTRIBUTION INC
Also Called: Johnson Contrls Authorized Dlr
166 N Union St (44304-1355)
PHONE..................................330 434-5194
EMP: 41
Web: www.johnsoncontrols.com
SIC: 5075 5074 Furnaces, warm air; Plumbing and hydronic heating supplies
HQ: Famous Distribution Inc
　2620 Ridgewood Rd
　Akron OH 44313
　330 762-9621

(G-156)
FAMOUS ENTERPRISES INC (PA)
Also Called: Famous Supply
2620 Ridgewood Rd Ste 200 (44313-3507)
PHONE..................................330 762-9621
EMP: 45 **EST:** 1933
SQ FT: 20,000
SALES (est): 462.89MM **Privately Held**
Web: www.famous-supply.com
SIC: 5075 5031 5074 7699 Warm air heating equipment and supplies; Lumber, plywood, and millwork; Plumbing and hydronic heating supplies; Industrial equipment services

(G-157)
FAMOUS INDUSTRIES INC (DH)
Also Called: Johnson Contrls Authorized Dlr
2620 Ridgewood Rd Ste 200 (44313-3507)
PHONE..................................330 535-1811
Pat Mccaffrey, *Pr*
EMP: 50 **EST:** 1948
SALES (est): 51.14MM
SALES (corp-wide): 3.83B **Privately Held**
Web: www.johnsoncontrols.com
SIC: 3444 5065 5074 Metal ventilating equipment; Telephone equipment; Plumbing and heating valves
HQ: Flex-Tek Group Llc
　1473 Gould Dr
　Cookeville TN 38506
　931 432-7212

(G-158)
FINDAWAY WORLD LLC
354 Ely Rd (44313-4564)
PHONE..................................330 794-7758
Blake Squires, *Brnch Mgr*
EMP: 50
Web: www.playaway.com
SIC: 7389 Business Activities at Non-Commercial Site
PA: Findaway World Llc
　31999 Aurora Rd
　Solon OH 44139

(G-159)
FIRST AMERICAN
50 S Main St Ste 1210 (44308-1831)
PHONE..................................330 379-2320
EMP: 73

GEOGRAPHIC SECTION

Akron - Summit County (G-182)

Web: www.firstam.com
SIC: 6141 Personal credit institutions
HQ: First American
215 S State St Ste 280
Salt Lake City UT 84111
801 578-8888

(G-160)
FIRST ASSEMBLY OF GOD
Also Called: Akron First Academy Preschool
1175 W Market St (44313-7122)
PHONE.................330 836-1436
Lauri Jarvis, *Dir*
EMP: 49 EST: 1980
SQ FT: 33,232
SALES (est): 3.03MM **Privately Held**
SIC: 8351 8211 Preschool center; Kindergarten

(G-161)
FIRSTENERGY CORP (PA)
Also Called: Firstenergy
76 S Main St (44308)
PHONE.................800 736-3402
Brian X Tierney, *Pr*
John W Somerhalder Ii, *Non-Executive Chairman of the Board*
Toby L Thomas, *COO*
K Jon Taylor, *Sr VP*
Hyun Park, *CLO*
EMP: 1618 EST: 1996
SALES (est): 12.87MM **Publicly Held**
Web: www.firstenergycorp.com
SIC: 4911 Distribution, electric power

(G-162)
FIRSTMERIT BANK NATIONAL ASSOCIATION
Also Called: Firstmerit Bank
106 S Main St Fl 5 (44308-1412)
PHONE.................330 384-7201
EMP: 2836
SIC: 6021 National commercial banks

(G-163)
FIRSTMERIT CORPORATION
Iii Cascade Plz Fl 7 (44308)
PHONE.................330 996-6300
EMP: 4112
Web: www.huntington.com
SIC: 6021 National commercial banks

(G-164)
FLEXSYS AMERICA LP (HQ)
Also Called: Flexsys America
260 Springside Dr (44333-4554)
PHONE.................330 666-4111
◆ EMP: 65 EST: 1995
SQ FT: 85,000
SALES (est): 52.96MM
SALES (corp-wide): 105.28MM **Privately Held**
SIC: 3069 8731 2899 2823 Reclaimed rubber and specialty rubber compounds; Commercial physical research; Chemical preparations, nec; Cellulosic manmade fibers
PA: Flexsys Holdings, Inc.
260 Springside Dr
Akron OH 44333
330 666-4111

(G-165)
FLEXSYS INC (PA)
260 Springside Dr (44333-4554)
PHONE.................212 605-6000
Sandip Tyagi, *CEO*
Tony Lee, *Treas*
EMP: 500 EST: 2021
SALES (est): 360MM
SALES (corp-wide): 360MM **Privately Held**

Web: www.flexsys.com
SIC: 2819 7389 Industrial inorganic chemicals, nec; Business Activities at Non-Commercial Site

(G-166)
FORMU3 INTERNATIONAL INC (PA)
395 Springside Dr (44333-2434)
PHONE.................330 668-1461
Charles Sekeres, *Pr*
EMP: 35 EST: 1971
SALES (est): 4.8MM
SALES (corp-wide): 4.8MM **Privately Held**
SIC: 8093 7299 Weight loss clinic, with medical staff; Diet center, without medical staff

(G-167)
FOTOSAV INC
1479 Exeter Rd (44306-3856)
PHONE.................330 436-6500
Adam Fried, *CEO*
EMP: 50 EST: 2012
SQ FT: 42,000
SALES (est): 725.35K **Privately Held**
SIC: 7221 Photographic studios, portrait

(G-168)
FRED MARTIN NISSAN LLC
3388 S Arlington Rd (44312-5257)
PHONE.................330 644-8888
EMP: 45 EST: 2003
SALES (est): 9.52MM **Privately Held**
Web: www.fredmartinnissan.com
SIC: 5511 7539 Automobiles, new and used; Automotive repair shops, nec

(G-169)
FRED W ALBRECHT GROCERY CO
Also Called: Acme
3979 Medina Rd (44333-2444)
PHONE.................330 666-6781
Bill Haliko, *Mgr*
EMP: 149
SALES (corp-wide): 455.09K **Privately Held**
Web: www.acmestores.com
SIC: 5411 5912 7384 Grocery stores, chain; Drug stores and proprietary stores; Photofinish laboratories
PA: The Fred W Albrecht Grocery Company
2700 Gilchrist Rd Ste A
Akron OH 44305
330 733-2263

(G-170)
FULL SPECTRUM MARKETING LLC
50 S Main St (44308-1830)
PHONE.................330 541-9456
Josh Gordon, *Pr*
EMP: 31 EST: 2015
SALES (est): 1.88MM **Privately Held**
Web: www.fsm.agency
SIC: 8742 Marketing consulting services

(G-171)
GBC DESIGN INC
565 White Pond Dr (44320-1123)
PHONE.................330 836-0228
Gary Rouse, *Pr*
Sy Cymerman, *Pr*
EMP: 35 EST: 1945
SQ FT: 10,000
SALES (est): 4.63MM **Privately Held**
Web: www.gbcdesign.com
SIC: 8712 8711 8713 Architectural services; Consulting engineer; Surveying services

(G-172)
GBD LEGACY LLC
1050 Ghent Rd (44333-2638)
PHONE.................330 441-0785
EMP: 47
SALES (corp-wide): 5.66MM **Privately Held**
Web: www.nscstaffing.com
SIC: 8111 Legal services
PA: Gbd Legacy, Llc
635 Burlington Ave
Logansport IN 46947
866 456-1456

(G-173)
GENERAL TRANSPORT & CONS INC
1100 Jenkins Blvd (44306-3754)
P.O. Box 7727 (44306-0727)
PHONE.................330 645-6055
Joe M Ostrowske, *Pr*
John Troy, *VP*
Michelle Troy, *Sec*
EMP: 41 EST: 1984
SQ FT: 5,000
SALES (est): 3.26MM **Privately Held**
Web: www.generaltransport.com
SIC: 4213 Trucking, except local

(G-174)
GENERAL TRANSPORT INCORPORATED
1100 Jenkins Blvd (44306)
P.O. Box 7727 (44306)
PHONE.................330 786-3400
Harold Joseph Ostrowske, *Pr*
Joe M Ostrowske, *Prin*
John Troy, *
Michelle Troy, *
EMP: 42 EST: 1985
SQ FT: 5,000
SALES (est): 9.99MM **Privately Held**
Web: www.generaltransport.com
SIC: 4213 Trucking, except local

(G-175)
GENESIS CORP
Also Called: Genesis 10
1 Cascade Plz Ste 1230 (44308-1144)
PHONE.................330 597-4100
Nate Gram, *Brnch Mgr*
EMP: 85
SALES (corp-wide): 197.65MM **Privately Held**
Web: www.genesis10.com
SIC: 7379 Online services technology consultants
PA: Genesis Corp.
950 3rd Ave Fl 26
New York NY 10022
212 688-5522

(G-176)
GLAUS PYLE SCHMER BRNS DHVEN I (PA)
Also Called: Gpd Group
520 S Main St Ste 2531 (44311-1073)
PHONE.................330 572-2100
Darrin Kotecki, *Pr*
James Shives, *
Jeff Evans, *
Mark Salopek, *
EMP: 270 EST: 1961
SQ FT: 20,000
SALES (est): 122.1MM
SALES (corp-wide): 122.1MM **Privately Held**
Web: www.gpdgroup.com
SIC: 8711 8712 Consulting engineer; Architectural services

(G-177)
GLENCOE RESTORATION GROUP LLC
Also Called: Grgstormpro
513 James Ave (44312-3667)
PHONE.................330 752-1244
Whitney Philips, *Managing Member*
EMP: 32 EST: 2011
SQ FT: 1,600
SALES (est): 2.47MM **Privately Held**
Web: www.glencoerestoration.com
SIC: 1531 Operative builders

(G-178)
GLOBAL EXEC SLUTIONS GROUP LLC
Also Called: Mri Network
3505 Embassy Pkwy Ste 200 (44333-8404)
PHONE.................330 666-3354
James Chadbourne Mg, *Dir*
EMP: 27 EST: 2001
SQ FT: 14,000
SALES (est): 4.35MM **Privately Held**
Web: www.globalesg.com
SIC: 7361 Executive placement

(G-179)
GOODYEAR TIRE & RUBBER COMPANY (PA)
Also Called: Goodyear
200 E Innovation Way (44316)
PHONE.................330 796-2121
Mark Stewart, *Pr*
Laurette T Koellner, *
Christina L Zamarro, *Chief Financial Officer USA*
Darren R Wells, *CAO*
David E Phillips, *CLO*
◆ EMP: 2602 EST: 1898
SALES (est): 20.07B
SALES (corp-wide): 20.07B **Publicly Held**
Web: www.goodyear.com
SIC: 3011 5531 7534 7538 Inner tubes, all types; Automotive tires; Tire retreading and repair shops; General automotive repair shops

(G-180)
GPD SERVICES COMPANY INC (PA)
Also Called: Gpd Associates
520 S Main St Ste 2531 (44311-1073)
PHONE.................330 572-2100
David B Granger, *Pr*
Darrin Kotecki, *
David B Granger, *Dir*
EMP: 173 EST: 1981
SALES (est): 10.01MM
SALES (corp-wide): 10.01MM **Privately Held**
Web: www.gpdservicesinc.com
SIC: 8712 Architectural services

(G-181)
GREENLEAF FAMILY CENTER (PA)
580 Grant St (44311-9910)
PHONE.................330 376-9494
Judy Joyce, *Pr*
EMP: 28 EST: 1912
SQ FT: 8,000
SALES (est): 2.92MM
SALES (corp-wide): 2.92MM **Privately Held**
Web: www.greenleafctr.org
SIC: 8322 General counseling services

(G-182)
HANNA CAMBELL & POWELL
3737 Embassy Pkwy Ste 100 (44333-8380)
PHONE.................330 670-7300
Timothy Campbell, *Pt*

David Hanna, *Pt*
Donald Powell, *Pt*
Timothy Cambell, *Pt*
EMP: 50 **EST:** 1999
SALES (est): 3.22MM **Privately Held**
Web: www.hcplaw.net
SIC: 8111 Corporate, partnership and business law

(G-183)
HARDWARE SUPPLIERS OF AMERICA INC
Also Called: Hsi
1100 Killian Rd (44312-4730)
PHONE..............................330 644-7167
▲ **EMP:** 85
SIC: 5072 Builders' hardware, nec

(G-184)
HARRY C LOBALZO & SONS INC
Also Called: Hobart Sales & Service
61 N Cleveland Massillon Rd Unit A (44333)
PHONE..............................330 666-6758
Mike Lobalzo, *Ch*
Joe Saporito, *
Rick Lobalzo, *Vice Chairman*
▲ **EMP:** 45 **EST:** 1956
SQ FT: 20,000
SALES (est): 10.79MM **Privately Held**
Web: www.retailfoodequip.com
SIC: 5046 7699 3556 Restaurant equipment and supplies, nec; Restaurant equipment repair; Food products machinery

(G-185)
HARTVILLE GROUP INC (PA)
1210 Massillon Rd (44306-3327)
PHONE..............................330 484-8166
Dennis C Rushovich, *Pr*
Nicholas J Leighton, *Ch Bd*
Christopher R Sachs, *CFO*
Christopher Edgar, *CMO*
Hirsch C Ribakow, *Insurance Compliance*
EMP: 64 **EST:** 2000
SQ FT: 12,395
SALES (est): 32.19MM
SALES (corp-wide): 32.19MM **Privately Held**
Web: www.aspcapetinsurance.com
SIC: 6399 Health insurance for pets

(G-186)
HARWICK STANDARD DIST CORP (PA)
60 S Seiberling St (44305-4217)
PHONE..............................330 798-9300
Ernie Pouttu, *Pr*
Jeffrey J Buda, *
David Sultz, *
Dan Davis, *
William Caplan, *
◆ **EMP:** 60 **EST:** 1932
SQ FT: 160,000
SALES (est): 48.82MM
SALES (corp-wide): 48.82MM **Privately Held**
Web: www.harwick.com
SIC: 5169 Chemicals, industrial and heavy

(G-187)
HASENSTAB ARCHITECTS INC
190 N Union St Ste 400 (44304-1362)
PHONE..............................330 434-4464
Dennis Check, *Pr*
Robert Medziuch, *
EMP: 37 **EST:** 1982
SALES (est): 6.04MM **Privately Held**
Web: www.hasenstabinc.com
SIC: 8712 Architectural engineering

(G-188)
HAT WHITE MANAGEMENT LLC
Also Called: Life Skills Center
121 S Main St Ste 500 (44308-1426)
PHONE..............................800 525-7967
EMP: 116
Web: www.whitehatmgmt.com
SIC: 4142 8741 Bus charter service, except local; Business management

(G-189)
HATTIE LRLHAM CTR FOR CHLDREN
540 S Main St Ste 412 (44311-1079)
PHONE..............................330 274-2272
EMP: 41
SALES (corp-wide): 61.41MM **Privately Held**
Web: www.hattielarlham.org
SIC: 8361 Mentally handicapped home
PA: Hattie Larlham Center For Children With Disabilities
9772 Diagonal Rd
Mantua OH 44255
330 274-2272

(G-190)
HAVEN REST MINISTRIES INC (PA)
175 E Market St (44308-2011)
P.O. Box 547 (44309-0547)
PHONE..............................330 535-1563
James Cummins, *Pr*
Doctor Forest Crocker, *VP*
EMP: 90 **EST:** 1942
SQ FT: 45,851
SALES (est): 1.04MM
SALES (corp-wide): 1.04MM **Privately Held**
Web: www.havenofrest.org
SIC: 8661 8322 Non-denominational church; Individual and family services

(G-191)
HERITAGE CROSSING
251 N Cleveland Massillon Rd (44333-2423)
PHONE..............................330 510-3110
EMP: 27 **EST:** 2019
SALES (est): 5.64MM **Privately Held**
Web: www.experiencesrliving.com
SIC: 8361 Aged home

(G-192)
HIGH LINE CORPORATION
Also Called: Casnet
2420 Wedgewood Dr Ste 20 (44312-2414)
PHONE..............................330 848-8800
Bradley D Bowers, *Pr*
EMP: 50 **EST:** 1992
SALES (est): 5.12MM **Privately Held**
Web: www.vitalrecordscontrol.com
SIC: 7389 5999 7629 4226 Microfilm recording and developing service; Telephone and communication equipment; Electrical repair shops; Document and office records storage

(G-193)
HITCHCOCK FLEMING & ASSOC INC
Also Called: H F A
388 S Main St Ste 350 (44311-1080)
PHONE..............................330 376-2111
Charles Abraham, *Mng Pt*
Jack Deleo, *
Nick Betro, *
Charles Abraham, *Mng Pt*
EMP: 90 **EST:** 1940
SALES (est): 13.87MM **Privately Held**
Web: www.teamhfa.com
SIC: 7311 Advertising consultant

(G-194)
HOLLAND OIL COMPANY (PA)
1485 Marion Ave (44313-7625)
PHONE..............................330 835-1815
Lisa M Holland-toth, *Pr*
Michael J Toth, *
John Ballard, *
Lynn Gorman, *
Carl Hummel, *
EMP: 70 **EST:** 1954
SQ FT: 20,000
SALES (est): 54.96MM
SALES (corp-wide): 54.96MM **Privately Held**
Web: www.circlek.com
SIC: 5541 5172 5411 Filling stations, gasoline; Gasoline; Convenience stores

(G-195)
HOME DEPOT USA INC
Also Called: Home Depot, The
2811 S Arlington Rd (44312)
PHONE..............................330 245-0280
Eric Hilgert, *Brnch Mgr*
EMP: 179
SQ FT: 119,856
SALES (corp-wide): 152.67B **Publicly Held**
Web: www.homedepot.com
SIC: 5211 7359 Home centers; Tool rental
HQ: Home Depot U.S.A., Inc.
2445 Springfield Ave
Vauxhall NJ 07088

(G-196)
HUDSON L SURGCENTER L C
2215 E Waterloo Rd Ste 313 (44312-3856)
PHONE..............................330 655-5460
Anne Breuker, *Prin*
EMP: 31 **EST:** 2005
SALES (est): 2.06MM **Privately Held**
Web: www.surgcenterhudson.com
SIC: 8011 Offices and clinics of medical doctors

(G-197)
HUNTINGTON NATIONAL BANK
1411 S Arlington St (44306-3711)
PHONE..............................330 786-9950
Lisa Mcelwain, *Mgr*
EMP: 31
SALES (corp-wide): 10.84B **Publicly Held**
Web: www.huntington.com
SIC: 6029 Commercial banks, nec
HQ: The Huntington National Bank
41 S High St
Columbus OH 43215
614 480-4293

(G-198)
HUNTINGTON NATIONAL BANK
Also Called: Firstmerit Bank
855 W Market St (44303-1019)
PHONE..............................330 762-4210
Lucy Statin, *Supervisor*
EMP: 36
SALES (corp-wide): 10.84B **Publicly Held**
Web: www.huntington.com
SIC: 6029 Commercial banks, nec
HQ: The Huntington National Bank
41 S High St
Columbus OH 43215
614 480-4293

(G-199)
HUNTINGTON NATIONAL BANK
1525 S Hawkins Ave (44320-4054)
PHONE..............................330 869-5950
Barb Patrino, *Brnch Mgr*
EMP: 31
SALES (corp-wide): 10.84B **Publicly Held**
Web: www.huntington.com
SIC: 6029 Commercial banks, nec
HQ: The Huntington National Bank
41 S High St
Columbus OH 43215
614 480-4293

(G-200)
IMCD US LLC
1779 Marvo Dr (44306-4331)
PHONE..............................216 228-8900
John Mastrantoni, *Brnch Mgr*
EMP: 111
Web: www.imcdus.com
SIC: 4225 Warehousing, self storage
HQ: Imcd Us, Llc
2 Equity Way Ste 210
Westlake OH 44145
216 228-8900

(G-201)
INFOCISION MANAGEMENT CORP (PA)
Also Called: Infocision
325 Springside Dr (44333-4504)
PHONE..............................330 668-1411
Craig Taylor, *CEO*
Steve Boyazis, *Pr*
Gary Taylor, *Ch Bd*
Ken Dawson, *Sr VP*
Mike Langenfeld, *Sr VP*
EMP: 356 **EST:** 1982
SQ FT: 38,000
SALES (est): 115.4MM
SALES (corp-wide): 115.4MM **Privately Held**
Web: www.infocision.com
SIC: 7389 Telemarketing services

(G-202)
INSTALLED BUILDING PDTS LLC
Also Called: Nooney & Moses
2783 Gilchrist Rd Unit B (44305-4406)
PHONE..............................330 798-9640
James Pope, *Prin*
EMP: 59
SALES (corp-wide): 2.78B **Publicly Held**
Web: www.installedbuildingproducts.com
SIC: 1742 Insulation, buildings
HQ: Installed Building Products Llc
495 S High St Ste 150
Columbus OH 43215
614 221-3399

(G-203)
INTEGRTED WLLNESS PARTNERS LLC
19 N High St (44308-1912)
PHONE..............................330 762-9102
Sabreena Riley, *Prin*
EMP: 40 **EST:** 2018
SALES (est): 2.34MM **Privately Held**
Web: www.integrated-wellness-partners.com
SIC: 7299 Miscellaneous personal service

(G-204)
IRACE INC
Also Called: Irace Automotive
2265 W Market St (44313-6907)
PHONE..............................330 836-7247
Jim Irace, *Prin*
EMP: 28 **EST:** 2001
SQ FT: 2,448
SALES (est): 4.48MM **Privately Held**
Web: www.iraceautomotive.com
SIC: 5541 7538 7539 Gasoline service stations; General automotive repair shops; Automotive repair shops, nec

GEOGRAPHIC SECTION

Akron - Summit County (G-226)

(G-205)
J & P ASSET MANAGEMENT INC
4737 Arbour Green Dr (44333-1664)
PHONE.................216 408-7693
Jim Overman, *Prin*
EMP: 73 **EST:** 2017
SALES (est): 9.2MM **Privately Held**
Web: www.jpassetmanagement.com
SIC: 8741 Financial management for business

(G-206)
J RAYL TRANSPORT INC (PA)
1016 Triplett Blvd # 1 (44306-3007)
PHONE.................330 784-1134
Jeremy Rayl, *CEO*
Tim Rayl, *Pr*
Ryan Richards, *VP*
Jim St John, *VP*
Dan Rafferty, *VP*
EMP: 86 **EST:** 1977
SQ FT: 10,000
SALES (est): 49.06MM
SALES (corp-wide): 49.06MM **Privately Held**
Web: www.jrayl.com
SIC: 4213 4731 4231 Trucking, except local; Truck transportation brokers; Trucking terminal facilities

(G-207)
J W DIDADO ELECTRIC INC
1033 Kelly Ave (44306-3143)
PHONE.................330 374-0070
EMP: 150 **EST:** 1958
SQ FT: 6,500
SALES (est): 46.55MM
SALES (corp-wide): 20.88B **Publicly Held**
Web: www.jwdidado.com
SIC: 1731 General electrical contractor
PA: Quanta Services, Inc.
   2727 North Loop W
   Houston TX 77008
   713 629-7600

(G-208)
J W GEOPFERT CO INC
Also Called: Geopfert Company, The
1024 Home Ave (44310-3579)
PHONE.................330 762-2293
Thomas Geopfert Junior, *Pr*
Thomas Geopfert Senior, *Ch*
Joseph Geopfert, *
Jean Geopfert, *
EMP: 32 **EST:** 1953
SQ FT: 6,100
SALES (est): 6.8MM **Privately Held**
Web: www.geopfert.com
SIC: 1711 Warm air heating and air conditioning contractor

(G-209)
JB DOLLAR STRETCHER
1653 Merriman Rd Ste 203 (44313-5287)
PHONE.................614 436-2800
John Cook, *Ex VP*
EMP: 44 **EST:** 2007
SALES (est): 635.35K **Privately Held**
SIC: 7319 Advertising, nec

(G-210)
JENNINGS HEATING COMPANY INC
Also Called: Jennings Heating & Cooling
2279 Romig Rd (44320-3823)
PHONE.................330 784-1286
Mike Foraker, *Pr*
Marshall Jennings, *
Fred S Jennings, *
EMP: 47 **EST:** 1933
SALES (est): 9.94MM **Privately Held**
Web: www.jenningsheating.com

SIC: 1711 Warm air heating and air conditioning contractor

(G-211)
JERSEY CENTRAL PWR & LIGHT CO (HQ)
Also Called: FIRSTENERGY
76 S Main St (44308-1812)
PHONE.................800 736-3402
TOLL FREE: 800
Donald M Lynch, *Pr*
Marlene A Barwood, *CAO**
▲ **EMP:** 272 **EST:** 1925
SALES (est): 1.81B **Publicly Held**
Web: www.firstenergycorp.com
SIC: 4911 Generation, electric power
PA: Firstenergy Corp.
   76 S Main St
   Akron OH 44308

(G-212)
JSC EMPLOYEE LEASING CORP (PA)
1560 Firestone Pkwy (44301-1626)
PHONE.................330 773-8971
Jack Jeter, *Pr*
Nicholas George, *Sec*
Pam Love, *Ex VP*
EMP: 92 **EST:** 1971
SQ FT: 150,000
SALES (est): 19.37MM
SALES (corp-wide): 19.37MM **Privately Held**
SIC: 2522 5021 Office cabinets and filing drawers, except wood; Filing units

(G-213)
JW DIDADO ELECTRIC LLC
Also Called: J.W. Didado Electric
1033 Kelly Ave (44306-3143)
PHONE.................330 374-0070
Gary Didado, *Pr*
EMP: 59 **EST:** 2015
SQ FT: 15,000
SALES (est): 13.86MM
SALES (corp-wide): 20.88B **Publicly Held**
Web: www.jwdidado.com
SIC: 1731 General electrical contractor
PA: Quanta Services, Inc.
   2727 North Loop W
   Houston TX 77008
   713 629-7600

(G-214)
JWT ACTION (DH)
Also Called: JWT Action
388 S Main St Ste 410 (44311-4407)
PHONE.................330 376-6148
EMP: 60 **EST:** 1943
SALES (est): 10.99MM
SALES (corp-wide): 18.5B **Privately Held**
SIC: 7311 Advertising agencies
HQ: Wunderman Thompson Llc
   175 Greenwich St Fl 16
   New York NY 10007
   212 210-7000

(G-215)
KENMORE CONSTRUCTION CO INC (PA)
700 Home Ave (44310-4190)
PHONE.................330 762-8936
William A Scala, *Pr*
Paul Scala, *
Janet Smith, *
▲ **EMP:** 101 **EST:** 1956
SQ FT: 3,000
SALES (est): 44.06MM
SALES (corp-wide): 44.06MM **Privately Held**
Web: www.kenmorecompanies.com

SIC: 1611 5032 General contractor, highway and street construction; Sand, construction

(G-216)
KEYSTONE TECHNOLOGY CONS
Also Called: Keystone Business Solutions
787 Wye Rd (44333-2268)
PHONE.................330 666-6200
Greg Cordray, *Prin*
Greg Cordray, *Pr*
Brian Fontanella, *
David Howard, *
EMP: 36 **EST:** 1997
SALES (est): 5.59MM **Privately Held**
Web: www.keystonecorp.com
SIC: 7379 Computer related consulting services

(G-217)
KRUMROY-COZAD CNSTR CORP
376 W Exchange St (44302-1703)
PHONE.................330 376-4136
Daniel J Cozad, *Pr*
EMP: 50 **EST:** 1913
SQ FT: 3,226
SALES (est): 6.77K **Privately Held**
Web: www.krumroy-cozadconstruction.com
SIC: 1542 Commercial and office building, new construction

(G-218)
LAKE ERIE ELECTRIC INC
1888 Brown St (44301-3143)
PHONE.................330 724-1241
John Kellamis, *Brnch Mgr*
EMP: 101
SALES (corp-wide): 111.7MM **Privately Held**
Web: www.lakeerieelectric.com
SIC: 1731 General electrical contractor
PA: Lake Erie Electric, Inc.
   25730 1st St
   Westlake OH 44145
   440 835-5565

(G-219)
LAW OFFCES OF JOHN D CLUNK A L
495 Wolf Ledges Pkwy Ste 1 (44311-1084)
PHONE.................330 436-0300
John D Clunk, *Owner*
EMP: 55 **EST:** 1999
SALES (est): 1.75MM **Privately Held**
Web: www.clunkhoose.com
SIC: 8111 Bankruptcy law

(G-220)
LEGAL DFNDERS OFF SMMIT CNTY O
1 Cascade Plz Ste 1940 (44308-1121)
PHONE.................330 434-3461
EMP: 62 **EST:** 1999
SALES (est): 2.96MM **Privately Held**
Web: blogs.uakron.edu
SIC: 8111 Legal services

(G-221)
LINCARE INC
Also Called: America's Best Medical
1566 Akron Peninsula Rd Ste 2 (44313-7980)
PHONE.................330 928-0884
Rob Dellaposta, *Mgr*
EMP: 29
Web: www.lincare.com
SIC: 7352 Medical equipment rental
HQ: Lincare Inc.
   19387 Us Highway 19 N
   Clearwater FL 33764
   727 530-7700

(G-222)
LINDE GAS & EQUIPMENT INC
Also Called: Praxair
1760 E Market St (44305-4245)
PHONE.................330 376-2242
Brian Mccormick, *Brnch Mgr*
EMP: 30
Web: www.lindeus.com
SIC: 5084 Welding machinery and equipment
HQ: Linde Gas & Equipment Inc.
   10 Riverview Dr
   Danbury CT 06810
   844 445-4633

(G-223)
LKQ TRIPLETTASAP INC (HQ)
Also Called: Triplett ASAP
1435 Triplett Blvd (44306-3303)
PHONE.................330 733-6333
Stuart Willen, *Pr*
EMP: 120 **EST:** 1953
SQ FT: 25,000
SALES (est): 23.47MM
SALES (corp-wide): 13.87B **Publicly Held**
Web: www.lkqcorp.com
SIC: 5015 5521 Automotive supplies, used: wholesale and retail; Used car dealers
PA: Lkq Corporation
   500 W Madison St Ste 2800
   Chicago IL 60661
   312 621-1950

(G-224)
LORAIN CNTY BYS GIRLS CLB INC
Also Called: Lorain County Boys and Girls Club, Inc.
889 Jonathan Ave (44306-3606)
PHONE.................330 773-3375
Alex Andrew, *Brnch Mgr*
EMP: 27
SALES (corp-wide): 6.24MM **Privately Held**
Web: www.loraincountybgc.com
SIC: 8641 Youth organizations
PA: Boys & Girls Clubs Of Northeast Ohio
   4111 Pearl Ave
   Lorain OH 44055
   440 775-2582

(G-225)
LOWES HOME CENTERS LLC
Also Called: Lowe's
186 N Cleveland Massillon Rd (44333-2467)
PHONE.................330 665-9356
Mike Hoffmeier, *Mgr*
EMP: 153
SALES (corp-wide): 86.38B **Publicly Held**
Web: www.lowes.com
SIC: 5211 5031 5722 5064 Home centers; Building materials, exterior; Household appliance stores; Electrical appliances, television and radio
HQ: Lowe's Home Centers, Llc
   1000 Lowes Blvd
   Mooresville NC 28117
   336 658-4000

(G-226)
LUNAR COW DESIGN INC
120 E Mill St Ste 415 (44308-1710)
PHONE.................330 836-0911
Ben Harris, *Pr*
EMP: 60
SQ FT: 4,800
SALES (est): 1.23MM **Privately Held**
SIC: 7374 Computer graphics service

Akron - Summit County (G-227) — GEOGRAPHIC SECTION

(G-227)
MAXIM HEALTHCARE SERVICES INC
Also Called: Akron Homecare Adult
3737 Embassy Pkwy Ste 300 (44333-8379)
PHONE.................................330 670-1054
Mike Schweninger, *Brnch Mgr*
EMP: 92
Web: www.maximhealthcare.com
SIC: 7363 Medical help service
PA: Maxim Healthcare Services, Inc.
7227 Lee Deforest Dr
Columbia MD 21046

(G-228)
MEDLINK OF OHIO INC
Also Called: Nursefinders
1225 E Waterloo Rd (44306-3805)
PHONE.................................330 773-9434
Doti Johnson, *Mgr*
EMP: 300
SALES (corp-wide): 371.62B **Publicly Held**
Web: www.nursefinders.com
SIC: 7361 7363 Nurses' registry; Temporary help service
HQ: Medlink Of Ohio, Inc
20600 Chagrin Blvd # 290
Cleveland OH 44122
216 751-5900

(G-229)
METRO REGIONAL TRANSIT AUTH (PA)
416 Kenmore Blvd (44301-1099)
PHONE.................................330 762-0341
Richard Enty, *Ex Dir*
Saundra Foster, *
Bernard Bear, *
Dean J Harris, *
Scott C Meyer, *
EMP: 237 **EST:** 1969
SQ FT: 300,000
SALES (est): 49.74MM
SALES (corp-wide): 49.74MM **Privately Held**
Web: www.yourmetrobus.org
SIC: 4111 Bus transportation

(G-230)
METRO REGIONAL TRANSIT AUTH
631 S Broadway St (44311-1000)
PHONE.................................330 762-0341
EMP: 125
SALES (corp-wide): 49.74MM **Privately Held**
Web: www.yourmetrobus.org
SIC: 4111 Bus line operations
PA: Metro Regional Transit Authority
416 Kenmore Blvd
Akron OH 44301
330 762-0341

(G-231)
METROPOLITAN EDISON COMPANY (HQ)
Also Called: Met-Ed
76 S Main St (44308)
PHONE.................................800 736-3402
Mark T Clark, *Ex VP*
Harvey L Wagner, *CAO*
Leila L Vespoli, *Ex VP*
James F Pearson, *VP*
EMP: 102 **EST:** 1922
SALES (est): 864.03MM **Publicly Held**
Web: www.firstenergycorp.com
SIC: 4911 Distribution, electric power
PA: Firstenergy Corp.
76 S Main St
Akron OH 44308

(G-232)
METROPOLITAN SECURITY SVCS INC
Also Called: Walden Security
2 S Main St (44308-1813)
PHONE.................................330 253-6459
EMP: 145
Web: www.waldensecurity.com
SIC: 7381 Security guard service
PA: Metropolitan Security Services, Inc.
100 E 10th St Ste 400
Chattanooga TN 37402

(G-233)
MILLENNIUM CPITL RECOVERY CORP
388 S Main St Ste 320 (44311-1044)
PHONE.................................330 805-9063
Robert Bronchetti, *Pr*
Jayne Bronchetti, *
EMP: 40 **EST:** 1999
SALES (est): 5.58MM **Privately Held**
Web: www.nationwiderecoverymanagers.com
SIC: 7322 Collection agency, except real estate

(G-234)
MILLERS RENTAL AND SLS CO INC (PA)
2023 Romig Rd (44320-3819)
PHONE.................................330 753-8600
John J Miller, *CEO*
John P Miller, *
Daniel E Craig, *
Frank P Pamer, *
EMP: 60 **EST:** 1949
SQ FT: 14,000
SALES (est): 10.57MM
SALES (corp-wide): 10.57MM **Privately Held**
Web: www.millers.com
SIC: 7352 5999 Medical equipment rental; Hospital equipment and supplies

(G-235)
MOBILE MEALS (PA)
1357 Home Ave Ste 1 (44310-2549)
PHONE.................................330 376-7717
Dana Downing, *Pr*
Kathleen Downing, *
EMP: 88 **EST:** 1971
SQ FT: 6,500
SALES (est): 4.96MM
SALES (corp-wide): 4.96MM **Privately Held**
Web: www.fcsserves.org
SIC: 8322 Meal delivery program

(G-236)
MODERN BUILDERS SUPPLY INC
Also Called: Modern Builders Supply
809 E Exchange St (44306-1127)
P.O. Box 7099 (44306-0099)
PHONE.................................330 376-1031
Joe Reitenbach, *Mgr*
EMP: 35
SQ FT: 6,013
SALES (corp-wide): 346.23MM **Privately Held**
Web: www.modernbuilderssupply.com
SIC: 5039 5211 Prefabricated structures; Lumber and other building materials
PA: Modern Builders Supply, Inc.
3500 Phillips Ave
Toledo OH 43608
419 241-3961

(G-237)
MORE THAN GOURMET HOLDINGS INC
929 Home Ave (44310-4107)
PHONE.................................330 762-6652
Brad Sacks, *CEO*
▲ **EMP:** 50 **EST:** 1993
SALES (est): 21.29MM **Privately Held**
Web: www.morethangourmet.com
SIC: 5149 2032 Seasonings, sauces, and extracts; Soups and broths, canned, jarred, etc.
HQ: Ajinomoto Health & Nutrition North America, Inc.
250 E Devon Ave
Itasca IL 60143
630 931-6800

(G-238)
MYERS INDUSTRIES INC (PA)
Also Called: Myers Industries
1293 S Main St (44301-1339)
PHONE.................................330 253-5592
Michael Mcgaugh, *Pr*
F Jack Liebau Junior, *Ch Bd*
Sonal P Robinson, *Ex VP*
Daniel W Hoehn, *Corporate Controller*
Lorelei Evans, *Pers/VP*
EMP: 50 **EST:** 1933
SQ FT: 129,000
SALES (est): 813.07MM
SALES (corp-wide): 813.07MM **Publicly Held**
Web: www.myersindustries.com
SIC: 3089 3086 3069 3052 Pallets, plastics; Plastics foam products; Rubber automotive products; Automobile hose, rubber

(G-239)
NATIONWIDE CHILDRENS HOSPITAL
Also Called: Central Billing Office
1 Canal Square Plz Ste 110 (44308-1037)
PHONE.................................330 253-5200
Melanie Polack, *Mgr*
EMP: 152
SALES (corp-wide): 3.6B **Privately Held**
Web: www.nationwidechildrens.org
SIC: 8069 8721 Childrens' hospital; Billing and bookkeeping service
PA: Nationwide Children's Hospital
700 Childrens Dr
Columbus OH 43205
614 722-2000

(G-240)
NEO ADMINISTRATION COMPANY
525 N Cleveland Massillon Rd Ste 204 (44333-3361)
PHONE.................................330 864-0690
Janet Palcko, *Mng Pt*
EMP: 98 **EST:** 1990
SALES (est): 6.13MM **Privately Held**
Web: www.flexneo.com
SIC: 6324 Health Maintenance Organization (HMO), insurance only
PA: Benefit Administration Services International Corporation
9246 Portage Indus Dr
Portage MI 49024

(G-241)
NETWORK POLYMERS INC
1353 Exeter Rd (44306-3853)
PHONE.................................330 773-2700
◆ **EMP:** 29
Web: www.networkpolymers.com
SIC: 2821 5162 Plastics materials and resins; Plastics resins

(G-242)
NEXTCABLE CORPORATION
302 N Cleveland Massillon Rd (44333-9303)
PHONE.................................330 576-3154
Eric Frank, *Brnch Mgr*
EMP: 40
Web: www.nextecgroup.com
SIC: 7379 Computer related consulting services
PA: Nextcable Corporation
1111 Loper St Ste 810
Houston TX 77017

(G-243)
NIGHTINGALE HOLDINGS LLC
Also Called: Pebble Creek
670 Jarvis Rd (44319-2538)
PHONE.................................330 645-0200
EMP: 441 **EST:** 1998
SALES (est): 13.81MM **Privately Held**
Web: www.communicarehealth.com
SIC: 8051 Convalescent home with continuous nursing care

(G-244)
NORTHAST OHIO NEPHROLOGY ASSOC
Also Called: Northeast Ohio Nephrology
411 E Market St (44304-1542)
PHONE.................................330 252-0600
Susan Ray, *Pr*
EMP: 27 **EST:** 1975
SQ FT: 5,305
SALES (est): 2.32MM **Privately Held**
Web: www.neonephrology.com
SIC: 8011 Nephrologist

(G-245)
OAK ASSOCIATES LTD
3800 Embassy Pkwy (44333-8387)
PHONE.................................330 666-5263
James D Oelschlager, *Managing Member*
Vanita B Oelschlager, *
Edward Yardeni, *
EMP: 45 **EST:** 1985
SALES (est): 10.48MM **Privately Held**
Web: www.oakltd.com
SIC: 6282 Investment advisory service

(G-246)
OECONNECTION LLC (PA)
Also Called: Assured Performance Coop
3600 Embassy Pkwy Ste 300 (44333-8337)
PHONE.................................888 776-5792
Patrick C Brown, *Pr*
Chris Chapman, *CFO*
EMP: 83 **EST:** 2000
SALES (est): 25.36MM
SALES (corp-wide): 25.36MM **Privately Held**
Web: www.oeconnection.com
SIC: 7371 Computer software development

(G-247)
OHIO AUTOMOBILE CLUB
Also Called: Akron Automobile Club
100 Rosa Parks Dr (44311-2015)
PHONE.................................330 762-0631
Kevin Thomas, *Reg Pr*
EMP: 83
SALES (corp-wide): 74.32MM **Privately Held**
Web: cluballiance.aaa.com
SIC: 8699 Automobile owners' association
PA: The Ohio Automobile Club
90 E Wilson Bridge Rd # 1
Worthington OH 43085
614 431-7901

GEOGRAPHIC SECTION Akron - Summit County (G-270)

(G-248)
OHIO DEPT JOB & FMLY SVCS
Also Called: Job Service of Ohio
161 S High St Ste 300 (44308-1714)
PHONE.................................330 484-5402
Barbara Frank, *Dir*
EMP: 34
Web: jfs.ohio.gov
SIC: 7361 9441 Employment agencies; Administration of social and manpower programs, State government
HQ: Ohio Department Of Job And Family Services
30 E Broad St Fl 32
Columbus OH 43215

(G-249)
OHIO EDISON COMPANY (HQ)
76 S Main St Bsmt (44308-1817)
PHONE.................................800 736-3402
James F Pearson, *Sr VP*
Harvey L Wagner, *
EMP: 126 **EST:** 1930
SALES (est): 1.4B **Publicly Held**
Web: www.firstenergycorp.com
SIC: 4911 Generation, electric power
PA: Firstenergy Corp.
76 S Main St
Akron OH 44308

(G-250)
OHIO FABRICATORS INC
Also Called: Fab3 Group, The
1452 Kenmore Blvd (44314-1659)
PHONE.................................330 745-4406
John Sickle Junior, *Pr*
EMP: 65 **EST:** 1970
SQ FT: 25,000
SALES (est): 4.94MM **Privately Held**
Web: www.tinshops.com
SIC: 1761 1711 7389 Sheet metal work, nec; Heating and air conditioning contractors; Industrial and commercial equipment inspection service

(G-251)
OHIO GASKET AND SHIM CO INC (PA)
Also Called: Ogs Industries
976 Evans Ave (44305-1019)
PHONE.................................330 630-0626
John S Bader, *Pr*
Thomas Bader, *
◆ **EMP:** 45 **EST:** 1959
SQ FT: 84,000
SALES (est): 21.3MM
SALES (corp-wide): 21.3MM **Privately Held**
Web: www.ogsindustries.com
SIC: 3469 3053 3599 3499 Stamping metal for the trade; Gaskets, all materials; Machine shop, jobbing and repair; Shims, metal

(G-252)
OHIO HEALTH CHOICE INC (DH)
400 E Market St Ste 400 (44304-1541)
P.O. Box 2090 (44309-2090)
PHONE.................................800 554-0027
Bryan Kennedy, *Pr*
Michael Rutherford, *
EMP: 58 **EST:** 1999
SQ FT: 8,100
SALES (est): 24.54MM
SALES (corp-wide): 1.78B **Privately Held**
Web: www.ohiohealthchoice.com
SIC: 6324 Group hospitalization plans
HQ: Summa Health System Corp.
95 Arch St Ste G50
Akron OH 44304

(G-253)
OHIO LIVING
Also Called: Rockynol Retirement Community
1150 W Market St (44313-7129)
PHONE.................................330 867-2150
Thomas R Miller, *Brnch Mgr*
EMP: 305
Web: www.ohioliving.org
SIC: 8051 Skilled nursing care facilities
PA: Ohio Living
9200 Worthington Rd # 300
Westerville OH 43082

(G-254)
OHIO MAINT & RENOVATION INC (PA)
Also Called: Commercial Maintenance & Repr
124 Darrow Rd (44305-3835)
PHONE.................................330 315-3101
Steven Harvey, *CEO*
Steven E Harvey, *
Mike Abel, *
EMP: 40 **EST:** 2000
SALES (est): 6.4MM
SALES (corp-wide): 6.4MM **Privately Held**
SIC: 1542 Commercial and office building contractors

(G-255)
OMEGA TITLE AGENCY LLC
495 Wolf Ledges Pkwy Ste 1 (44311-1084)
PHONE.................................330 436-0600
EMP: 53 **EST:** 2010
SALES (est): 9.93MM **Privately Held**
Web: www.omegatitlellc.com
SIC: 6361 Title insurance

(G-256)
ORIANA HOUSE INC
941 Sherman St (44311-2467)
P.O. Box 1501 (44309-1501)
PHONE.................................330 374-9610
James Lawrence, *Pr*
EMP: 264
SALES (corp-wide): 68.05MM **Privately Held**
Web: www.orianahouse.org
SIC: 8322 Substance abuse counseling
PA: Oriana House, Inc.
885 E Buchtel Ave
Akron OH 44305
330 535-8116

(G-257)
ORIANA HOUSE INC (PA)
885 E Buchtel Ave (44305-2338)
P.O. Box 1501 (44309-1501)
PHONE.................................330 535-8116
James Lawrence, *Pr*
Bernard Rochford, *
Anne Connell-freund, *Ex VP*
Joyce Allen, *
George Debord, *
EMP: 65 **EST:** 1981
SALES (est): 68.05MM
SALES (corp-wide): 68.05MM **Privately Held**
Web: www.orianahouse.org
SIC: 8322 9111 Alcoholism counseling, nontreatment; County supervisors' and executives' office

(G-258)
ORIANA HOUSE INC
Also Called: A D M Crisis Center
15 Frederick Ave (44310-2904)
PHONE.................................330 996-7730
Tammy Johnson, *Mgr*
EMP: 60
SALES (corp-wide): 68.05MM **Privately Held**

Web: www.orianahouse.org
SIC: 8322 8069 Emergency social services; Drug addiction rehabilitation hospital
PA: Oriana House, Inc.
885 E Buchtel Ave
Akron OH 44305
330 535-8116

(G-259)
OXCYON INC
127 N Cleveland Massillon Rd (44333-2422)
PHONE.................................440 239-3345
Samuel Keller, *CEO*
EMP: 42 **EST:** 2000
SALES (est): 7.74MM **Privately Held**
Web: www.oxcyon.com
SIC: 4813 Internet host services

(G-260)
PARAGON OBSTETRICS & GYNE ASSO
Also Called: Fairlawn Obgyn Assocs
1 Park West Blvd Ste 200 (44320-4219)
PHONE.................................330 665-8270
John Black, *Pr*
EMP: 100 **EST:** 1989
SALES (est): 4.21MM **Privately Held**
SIC: 8011 Obstetrician

(G-261)
PARK LANE MANOR AKRON INC
Also Called: Rti
744 Colette Dr (44306-2208)
PHONE.................................330 724-3315
Robert Abassi, *Pr*
EMP: 50 **EST:** 1952
SALES (est): 1.35MM **Privately Held**
SIC: 6513 Apartment building operators

(G-262)
PASTORAL CNSLING SVC SMMIT CNT
Also Called: Red Oak Behavioral Health
611 W Market St (44303-1411)
PHONE.................................330 996-4600
Megan Kleidon, *CEO*
Byron Arledge, *
EMP: 145 **EST:** 1963
SALES (est): 343.44K **Privately Held**
Web: www.redoakbh.org
SIC: 8322 8049 General counseling services; Psychiatric social worker

(G-263)
PENNSYLVANIA ELECTRIC COMPANY (HQ)
Also Called: Penelec
2800 Pottsville Pike (44308)
PHONE.................................800 545-7741
Mark T Clark, *Ex VP*
Leila L Vespoli, *Ex VP*
Harvey L Wagner, *CAO*
James F Pearson, *VP*
EMP: 89 **EST:** 1919
SALES (est): 823.84MM **Publicly Held**
Web: www.firstenergycorp.com
SIC: 4911 Electric services
PA: Firstenergy Corp.
76 S Main St
Akron OH 44308

(G-264)
PENNSYLVANIA POWER COMPANY (DH)
Also Called: Penn Power
76 S Main St Bsmt (44308)
PHONE.................................800 720-3600
TOLL FREE: 800
Anthony J Alexander, *Pr*

T M Welsh, *
Robert Wuschinske, *
EMP: 140 **EST:** 1930
SQ FT: 40,000
SALES (est): 257.41MM **Publicly Held**
SIC: 4911 Distribution, electric power
HQ: Ohio Edison Company
76 S Main St Bsmt
Akron OH 44308
800 736-3402

(G-265)
PERRIN ASPHALT CO INC
525 Dan St (44310-3987)
PHONE.................................330 253-1020
Charles W Perrin, *Pr*
Michael A Perrin, *
Pamela J Perrin, *
Kimberly A Perrin, *
Timothy P Perrin, *
EMP: 100 **EST:** 1963
SALES (est): 15.7MM **Privately Held**
Web: www.perrinasphalt.com
SIC: 1771 Blacktop (asphalt) work

(G-266)
PETERMANN LTD
860 S Arlington St (44306-2455)
PHONE.................................330 773-4222
Mathew Gaugler, *Brnch Mgr*
EMP: 173
Web: www.petermannbus.com
SIC: 4151 School buses
HQ: Petermann Ltd
1861 Section Rd
Cincinnati OH 45237

(G-267)
PLUS ONE COMMUNICATIONS LLC
1115 S Main St (44301-1205)
PHONE.................................330 255-4500
Jill Madden, *
EMP: 500 **EST:** 2008
SQ FT: 50,000
SALES (est): 28.22MM **Privately Held**
SIC: 7379 Computer related maintenance services

(G-268)
PORTAGE COUNTRY CLUB COMPANY
240 N Portage Path (44303-1299)
PHONE.................................330 836-8565
Robert J Le Fever, *Genl Mgr*
EMP: 80 **EST:** 1905
SQ FT: 52,275
SALES (est): 6.92MM **Privately Held**
Web: www.portagecc.org
SIC: 7997 Country club, membership

(G-269)
PORTAGE PATH BEHAVIORAL HEALTH (PA)
340 S Broadway St (44308-1529)
PHONE.................................330 253-3100
Jerome Kraker, *Pr*
Tim Morgan, *
Phil Heislman, *
EMP: 68 **EST:** 1968
SQ FT: 12,000
SALES (est): 12.13MM
SALES (corp-wide): 12.13MM **Privately Held**
Web: www.portagepath.org
SIC: 8093 Mental health clinic, outpatient

(G-270)
PORTAGE PATH BEHAVORIAL HEALTH
Also Called: Emergency Psychiatric Svc

Akron - Summit County (G-271)   GEOGRAPHIC SECTION

10 Penfield Ave (44310-2912)
PHONE.................................330 762-6110
EMP: 41
SALES (corp-wide): 12.13MM Privately Held
Web: www.portagepath.org
SIC: 8093 4119 Mental health clinic, outpatient; Ambulance service
PA: Portage Path Behavioral Health
340 S Broadway St
Akron OH 44308
330 253-3100

(G-271)
POWER ENGINEERS INCORPORATED
Also Called: P E I
1 S Main St Ste 501 (44308-1857)
PHONE.................................234 678-9875
EMP: 34
SALES (corp-wide): 509.69MM Privately Held
Web: www.powereng.com
SIC: 8711 Consulting engineer
PA: Power Engineers, Incorporated
3940 Glenbrook Dr
Hailey ID 83333
208 788-3456

(G-272)
PROFESSIONAL ELECTRIC PDTS CO
Also Called: Pepco
1140 E Waterloo Rd (44306-3804)
PHONE.................................330 896-3790
John Borkey, Brnch Mgr
EMP: 27
SALES (corp-wide): 12.53MM Privately Held
Web: www.pepconet.com
SIC: 5063 Electrical supplies, nec
HQ: Professional Electric Products Co Inc
33210 Lakeland Blvd
Eastlake OH 44095
800 872-7000

(G-273)
PROFESSIONALS GROUP LLC
Also Called: Professionals Group
2022 Adelaide Blvd (44305-4333)
PHONE.................................330 957-5114
Keith Burnette, CEO
EMP: 30 EST: 2016
SALES (est): 2.47MM Privately Held
SIC: 7361 Registries

(G-274)
PTA ENGINEERING INC
275 Springside Dr Ste 300 (44333-4550)
PHONE.................................330 666-3702
James Peters, Pr
Tom Bandwin, VP
Dave Tzchantz, Sec
EMP: 42 EST: 1954
SQ FT: 120,000
SALES (est): 4.67MM Privately Held
Web: www.ptaengineering.com
SIC: 8711 Consulting engineer

(G-275)
QT EQUIPMENT COMPANY (PA)
151 W Dartmore Ave (44301-2462)
PHONE.................................330 724-3055
Daniel Root, Pr
Dave Root, *
▼ EMP: 35 EST: 1992
SQ FT: 20,000
SALES (est): 10.3MM Privately Held
Web: www.qtequipment.com
SIC: 7532 5531 3713 Body shop, trucks; Automotive tires; Utility truck bodies

(G-276)
R & R TRUCK SALES INC
1650 E Waterloo Rd (44306-4103)
P.O. Box 7309 (44306-0309)
PHONE.................................330 784-5881
George Ralich, Pr
Daniel Ralich, *
Steven Ralich, *
EMP: 30 EST: 1983
SQ FT: 30,000
SALES (est): 13.17MM Privately Held
Web: www.rrtrucksales.net
SIC: 5511 5012 Trucks, tractors, and trailers: new and used; Trucks, commercial

(G-277)
RED ROOF INNS INC
Also Called: Red Roof Inn
2939 S Arlington Rd (44312-4717)
PHONE.................................330 644-7748
Michael Crook, Brnch Mgr
EMP: 45
Web: www.redroof.com
SIC: 7011 Hotels and motels
HQ: Red Roof Inns, Inc.
7815 Walton Pkwy
New Albany OH 43054
614 744-2600

(G-278)
REHABILITATION SUPPORT SVCS
594 W Market St (44303-1839)
P.O. Box 1492 (44309-1492)
PHONE.................................330 252-9012
Nancy Young, Prin
EMP: 49 EST: 2008
SALES (est): 407.12K Privately Held
SIC: 8093 Rehabilitation center, outpatient treatment

(G-279)
RENNER KNNER GREVE BBAK TYLOR (PA)
Also Called: Renner Kenner
106 S Main St (44308-1417)
PHONE.................................330 376-1242
Edward Grieve, Pt
Phillip Kenner, *
Reese Taylor, *
Donald J Bobak, *
EMP: 37 EST: 1917
SQ FT: 4,500
SALES (est): 4.39MM
SALES (corp-wide): 4.39MM Privately Held
Web: www.rennerkenner.com
SIC: 8111 General practice attorney, lawyer

(G-280)
REPROS INC (PA)
1518 Copley Rd (44320)
P.O. Box 727 (44309)
PHONE.................................330 247-3747
Lou Laguardia, Ch Bd
Daniel Laguardia, *
Mike Laguardia, *
Lou Laguardia Junior, VP Opers
EMP: 27 EST: 1989
SQ FT: 10,000
SALES (est): 17.52MM Privately Held
Web: www.reprosinc.com
SIC: 5044 7334 5049 Blueprinting equipment; Blueprinting service; Scientific and engineering equipment and supplies

(G-281)
REVVITY HEALTH SCIENCES INC
520 S Main St Ste 2423 (44311-1086)
PHONE.................................330 825-4525
Chritine Gradisher, Mgr
EMP: 44
SALES (corp-wide): 2.75B Publicly Held
Web: www.perkinelmer.com
SIC: 2835 2836 5049 Diagnostic substances; Biological products, except diagnostic; Laboratory equipment, except medical or dental
HQ: Revvity Health Sciences, Inc.
940 Winter St
Waltham MA 02451
781 663-6900

(G-282)
RICHARDS WHL FENCE CO INC
Also Called: Richard's Fence Company
1600 Firestone Pkwy (44301-1659)
PHONE.................................330 773-0423
Richard Peterson, Pr
Bill Peterson, *
▲ EMP: 30 EST: 1968
SQ FT: 235,000
SALES (est): 12.28MM Privately Held
Web: www.richardsfence.com
SIC: 3315 5039 Chain link fencing; Wire fence, gates, and accessories

(G-283)
RISQUE SOLES LLC
854 Storer Ave (44320-3744)
P.O. Box 181365 (44118-7365)
PHONE.................................216 965-5261
EMP: 34 EST: 2021
SALES (est): 1.07MM Privately Held
SIC: 8742 Retail trade consultant

(G-284)
ROB LYNN INC
Also Called: Thomasville Limosine Service
330 Kennedy Rd (44305-4422)
PHONE.................................330 773-6470
Jim Thomas, Pr
Darlene Thomas, *
EMP: 30 EST: 1972
SALES (est): 796.67K Privately Held
SIC: 4119 Limousine rental, with driver

(G-285)
RODERICK LINTON BELFANCE LLP
50 S Main St Fl 10 (44308-1849)
PHONE.................................330 434-3000
Katherine Belfance, Pt
EMP: 43 EST: 2014
SALES (est): 5.07MM Privately Held
Web: www.rlbllp.com
SIC: 8111 General practice law office

(G-286)
ROETZEL ANDRESS A LGAL PROF AS (PA)
222 S Main St Ste 400 (44308-1500)
PHONE.................................330 376-2700
Robert E Blackham, CEO
Joseph Maslowski, *
Paul L Jackson, *
EMP: 130 EST: 1872
SQ FT: 115,000
SALES (est): 43.22MM
SALES (corp-wide): 43.22MM Privately Held
Web: www.ralaw.com
SIC: 8111 General practice attorney, lawyer

(G-287)
ROOFSMITH RESTORATION INC
122 Western Ave (44313-6332)
PHONE.................................330 812-4245
Michael Farish, Pr
Michael Farist, Pr
EMP: 55 EST: 2010
SALES (est): 5.36MM Privately Held
Web: www.roof-smith.com
SIC: 1761 Roofing contractor

(G-288)
RUBBER CITY MACHINERY CORP
Also Called: R C M
One Thousand Sweitzer Avenue (44311)
P.O. Box 2043 (44309-2043)
PHONE.................................330 434-3500
George B Sobieraj, Pr
Robert J Westfall, *
Bernie Sobieraj, *
Robert F Longano, Prin
▲ EMP: 32 EST: 1980
SQ FT: 100,000
SALES (est): 5.7MM Privately Held
Web: www.rcmc.com
SIC: 3559 5084 7629 Rubber working machinery, including tires; Industrial machinery and equipment; Electrical repair shops

(G-289)
RUBBER CITY RADIO GROUP INC (PA)
Also Called: Wqmx 94.9 FM
1795 W Market St (44313-7001)
PHONE.................................330 869-9800
Thomas Mandel, Pr
EMP: 79 EST: 1988
SALES (est): 10.28MM Privately Held
Web: www.wqmx.com
SIC: 4832 Radio broadcasting stations

(G-290)
RUBBERMAID INCORPORATED
Also Called: Rubbermaid
3009 Gilchrist Rd (44305-4419)
PHONE.................................330 733-7771
EMP: 79
SALES (corp-wide): 8.13B Publicly Held
Web: www.newellbrands.com
SIC: 5023 Homefurnishings
HQ: Rubbermaid Incorporated
6655 Pachtree Dunwoody Rd
Atlanta GA 30328
888 895-2110

(G-291)
RVC INC
Also Called: Mill Paper Packaging
131 N Summit St (44304-1277)
P.O. Box 1911 (44309-1911)
PHONE.................................330 535-2211
Jeff Robertson, Mgr
EMP: 35
SALES (corp-wide): 573.33MM Privately Held
Web: www.intfiber.com
SIC: 5113 Industrial and personal service paper
HQ: Rvc Inc.
1560 Firestone Pkwy
Akron OH 44301
330 535-1001

(G-292)
S GARY SHMKER RGGING TRNSPT L
Also Called: Shoemaker Rigging
3385 Miller Park Rd (44312-5341)
PHONE.................................330 899-9090
EMP: 30 EST: 2013
SQ FT: 3,000
SALES (est): 2.82MM Privately Held
Web: www.shoemakerrigging.com
SIC: 1796 Machine moving and rigging

(G-293)
SACS CNSLTING TRAINING CTR INC
Also Called: Sacs Cnslting Invstigative Svc
520 S Main St Ste 2516 (44311-1073)
PHONE.................................330 255-1101

GEOGRAPHIC SECTION

Akron - Summit County (G-315)

Timothy Dimoff, *Pr*
Michelle Dimoff, *CFO*
Anthony Wellendorf, *COO*
Helen Farmer Domestic, *Prin*
EMP: 31 **EST:** 1990
SALES (est): 1.52MM **Privately Held**
Web: www.sacsconsulting.com
SIC: 8742 Training and development consultant

(G-294)
SAMUEL JOSEPH CORP
675 Cuyahoga St (44310-1954)
PHONE.................330 983-6557
Billy Glass, *CEO*
EMP: 50 **EST:** 2012
SALES (est): 850.39K **Privately Held**
SIC: 7389 1531 Design services; Cooperative apartment developers

(G-295)
SCANDINAVIAN TOB GROUP LN LTD
Also Called: Stg Lane
1424 Diagonal Rd (44320-4016)
PHONE.................770 934-4594
J Kelly Michols, *CEO*
W David Parrish, *Finance Treasurer*
Phil Gee, *Managing Director US Operations*
Daniel Mcgee, *Sec*
Elliot Fledz, *Asst Tr*
◆ **EMP:** 130 **EST:** 1975
SALES (est): 22.36MM **Privately Held**
Web: www.st-group.com
SIC: 2131 5194 Smoking tobacco; Tobacco and tobacco products

(G-296)
SELECT SPCLTY HSPTAL-AKRON LLC
200 E Market St (44308-2015)
P.O. Box 2090 (44309-2090)
PHONE.................330 761-7500
Jeffrey Houck, *Prin*
EMP: 85 **EST:** 2000
SALES (est): 23.96MM
SALES (corp-wide): 6.2B **Publicly Held**
Web: www.selectspecialtyhospitals.com
SIC: 8069 8361 8051 Alcoholism rehabilitation hospital; Residential care; Skilled nursing care facilities
HQ: Sempercare, Inc.
    4716 Old Gettysburg Rd
    Mechanicsburg PA 17055
    717 972-1100

(G-297)
SEQUOIA FINANCIAL GROUP LLC (PA)
3500 Embassy Pkwy Ste 100 (44333-8327)
PHONE.................330 375-9480
Tom Haught, *Pr*
Chris Redhead, *Ex VP*
Chad Roope, *CIO*
Kevin Tichnell, *STRATEGY ACQUISITIONS*
Joseph Glick, *Ex VP*
EMP: 32 **EST:** 1991
SALES (est): 11.7MM **Privately Held**
Web: www.sequoia-financial.com
SIC: 8742 6282 7389 Financial consultant; Investment advice; Financial services

(G-298)
SHAW JEWISH COMMUNITY CENTER
Also Called: EARLY CHILDHOOD EDUCATION
750 White Pond Dr (44320-1128)
PHONE.................330 867-7850
Michael Wise, *CEO*
Irving Sugerman, *
EMP: 62 **EST:** 1924
SQ FT: 100,000
SALES (est): 6.18MM **Privately Held**
Web: www.shawjcc.org
SIC: 8322 Community center

(G-299)
SHIN-ETSU SILICONES OF AMERICA INC (HQ)
1150 Damar Dr (44305-1066)
PHONE.................330 630-9460
◆ **EMP:** 150 **EST:** 1985
SALES (est): 102.95MM **Privately Held**
Web: www.shinetsusilicones.com
SIC: 5169 2822 2869 Silicon lubricants; Silicone rubbers; Industrial organic chemicals, nec
PA: Shin-Etsu Chemical Co., Ltd.
    1-4-1, Marunouchi
    Chiyoda-Ku TKY 100-0

(G-300)
SIGNET MANAGEMENT CO LTD
19 N High St (44308-1912)
PHONE.................330 762-9102
Anthony S Manna, *Ch*
EMP: 200 **EST:** 1995
SALES (est): 4.1MM **Privately Held**
Web: www.signetllc.com
SIC: 8742 Business management consultant

(G-301)
SILCO FIRE PROTECTION COMPANY
451 Kennedy Rd (44305-4423)
PHONE.................330 535-4343
James Fraser, *Pr*
Marc Ollier, *
EMP: 152 **EST:** 1912
SQ FT: 7,500
SALES (est): 4.78MM
SALES (corp-wide): 50.11MM **Privately Held**
Web: www.silcofs.com
SIC: 7389 Fire extinguisher servicing
PA: Brakefire, Incorporated
    10200 Reading Rd
    Cincinnati OH 45241
    513 733-5655

(G-302)
SIMPLY EZ HM DLVRED MALS NRTHA
1130 Damar Dr (44305-1066)
PHONE.................330 633-7490
EMP: 52
SALES (est): 617.79K **Privately Held**
SIC: 8322 Individual and family services
PA: Simply Ez Home Delivered Meals Of Northeast Ohio, Llc
    6412 Fairfield Dr Ste F
    Northwood OH 43619

(G-303)
SIRPILLA RECRTL VHCL CTR INC
Also Called: Freedom Rv
1005 Interstate Pkwy (44312-5289)
PHONE.................330 494-2525
TOLL FREE: 800
John A Sirpilla Junior, *Pr*
EMP: 50 **EST:** 1959
SQ FT: 23,000
SALES (est): 877.12K **Privately Held**
SIC: 5561 7699 Travel trailers: automobile, new and used; Mobile home repair

(G-304)
SMITHERS GROUP INC (PA)
121 S Main St Ste 300 (44308-1426)
PHONE.................330 762-7441
Michael J Hochschwender, *CEO*
Steve Mihnovets, *VP Fin*
Gregory J Dziak, *Prin*
EMP: 55 **EST:** 2002
SALES (est): 115.78MM
SALES (corp-wide): 115.78MM **Privately Held**
Web: www.smithers.com
SIC: 8742 Business management consultant

(G-305)
SMITHERS MSE INC (HQ)
Also Called: Smithers Rapra
425 W Market St (44303-2044)
PHONE.................330 762-7441
J Michael Hochschwender, *CEO*
J Michael Hochschwender, *Pr*
Douglas Domeck, *VP Opers*
Steve Mihnovets, *VP Fin*
EMP: 51 **EST:** 1925
SQ FT: 20,000
SALES (est): 36.78MM
SALES (corp-wide): 115.78MM **Privately Held**
Web: www.smithers.com
SIC: 8742 8734 8731 Business management consultant; Product testing laboratories; Environmental research
PA: The Smithers Group Inc
    121 S Main St Ste 300
    Akron OH 44308
    330 762-7441

(G-306)
SMITHERS TIRE AUTO TSTG OF TXA
Also Called: Smithers Trnsp Test Ctrs
425 W Market St (44303-2044)
PHONE.................330 762-7441
J Hoschschwender, *Pr*
EMP: 179 **EST:** 1984
SALES (est): 6.6MM
SALES (corp-wide): 115.78MM **Privately Held**
Web: www.smithers.com
SIC: 8734 Product testing laboratories
HQ: Smithers Mse Inc
    425 W Market St
    Akron OH 44303
    330 762-7441

(G-307)
SOFTWARE CRAFTSMANSHIP GUILD
526 S Main St (44311-4401)
PHONE.................330 888-8519
Eric Wise, *Pr*
EMP: 49 **EST:** 2013
SALES (est): 814.47K **Privately Held**
Web: www.thesoftwareguild.com
SIC: 8331 Vocational training agency

(G-308)
ST PAULS CATHOLIC CHURCH (PA)
433 Mission Dr (44301-2710)
PHONE.................330 724-1263
Pastor Ralph Thomas, *Prin*
EMP: 50 **EST:** 1919
SQ FT: 2,000
SALES (est): 856.16K
SALES (corp-wide): 856.16K **Privately Held**
Web: www.stpaulparishakron.org
SIC: 8661 8351 8211 Catholic Church; Preschool center; Catholic elementary school

(G-309)
STAN HYWET HALL AND GRDNS INC
714 N Portage Path (44303-1399)
PHONE.................330 836-5533
Harry Lynch, *CEO*
Joyce Johnson, *
William Binnie, *
EMP: 62 **EST:** 1955
SQ FT: 5,000
SALES (est): 6.67MM **Privately Held**
Web: www.stanhywet.org
SIC: 8412 8422 Museum; Botanical and zoological gardens

(G-310)
STEADY CARE BEHAVIORAL LLC
723 E Tallmadge Ave Rear (44310-2419)
PHONE.................330 956-1190
Jerome Armstead, *CEO*
EMP: 40 **EST:** 2019
SALES (est): 972.8K **Privately Held**
SIC: 8322 Individual and family services

(G-311)
STEWART & CALHOUN FNRL HM INC
529 W Thornton St (44307-1799)
PHONE.................330 535-1543
William E Calhoun, *Pr*
James V Stewart, *VP*
EMP: 27 **EST:** 1963
SALES (est): 992.22K **Privately Held**
Web: www.calhounfuneral.com
SIC: 7261 5087 Funeral home; Concrete burial vaults and boxes

(G-312)
STRATOS WEALTH PARTNERS
291 N Cleveland Massillon Rd Ste 100 (44333-4513)
PHONE.................330 666-8131
James Lupica, *Mgr*
EMP: 30 **EST:** 2015
SALES (est): 148.23K **Privately Held**
Web: www.stratoswealthpartners.com
SIC: 8742 Financial consultant

(G-313)
SUMMA AKRON CY ST THMAS HSPTAL
525 E Market St (44304-1619)
PHONE.................330 375-3159
Thomas A Clark, *Ch*
EMP: 2572 **EST:** 2002
SALES (est): 5.83MM
SALES (corp-wide): 1.78B **Privately Held**
Web: www.summahealth.org
SIC: 8062 General medical and surgical hospitals
PA: Summa Health System
    1077 Gorge Blvd
    Akron OH 44310
    330 375-3000

(G-314)
SUMMA HEALTH
Also Called: Akron City Hospital
55 Arch St Ste 1b (44304-1436)
PHONE.................330 375-3315
Steven Radwany, *Dir*
EMP: 209
SALES (corp-wide): 1.78B **Privately Held**
Web: www.summahealth.org
SIC: 8062 General medical and surgical hospitals
PA: Summa Health System
    1077 Gorge Blvd
    Akron OH 44310
    330 375-3000

(G-315)
SUMMA HEALTH
Also Called: Summa Park West
1 Park West Blvd Ste 130 (44320-4230)
PHONE.................330 864-8060
EMP: 60
SALES (corp-wide): 1.78B **Privately Held**
Web: www.summahealth.org
SIC: 8062 General medical and surgical hospitals
PA: Summa Health System

Akron - Summit County (G-316)

1077 Gorge Blvd
Akron OH 44310
330 375-3000

(G-316)
SUMMA HEALTH SYSTEM (PA)
141 N Forge St (44304-1407)
PHONE.................................330 375-3000
EMP: 81 **EST:** 2019
SALES (est): 176.16MM
SALES (corp-wide): 176.16MM **Privately Held**
Web: www.summahealth.org
SIC: 8062 General medical and surgical hospitals

(G-317)
SUMMA HEALTH SYSTEM
141 N Forge St (44304-1407)
PHONE.................................330 375-3000
EMP: 105
SALES (corp-wide): 1.78B **Privately Held**
Web: www.summahealth.org
SIC: 8062 General medical and surgical hospitals
PA: Summa Health System
1077 Gorge Blvd
Akron OH 44310
330 375-3000

(G-318)
SUMMA HEALTH SYSTEM
Also Called: Summa Care
1200 E Market St Ste 400 (44305-4066)
PHONE.................................330 535-7319
Charles Vignos, *Brnch Mgr*
EMP: 404
SALES (corp-wide): 1.78B **Privately Held**
Web: www.summahealth.org
SIC: 8062 General medical and surgical hospitals
PA: Summa Health System
1077 Gorge Blvd
Akron OH 44310
330 375-3000

(G-319)
SUMMA HEALTH SYSTEM
Also Called: Summa Purchasing Department
820 W Wilbeth Rd (44314-1720)
PHONE.................................330 798-5026
Cliff Deveny Md, *Pr*
EMP: 164
SALES (corp-wide): 1.78B **Privately Held**
Web: www.summahealth.org
SIC: 8062 General medical and surgical hospitals
PA: Summa Health System
1077 Gorge Blvd
Akron OH 44310
330 375-3000

(G-320)
SUMMA HEALTH SYSTEM
1260 Independence Ave (44310-1812)
PHONE.................................330 928-8700
EMP: 60
SALES (corp-wide): 1.78B **Privately Held**
Web: www.summahealth.org
SIC: 8062 General medical and surgical hospitals
PA: Summa Health System
1077 Gorge Blvd
Akron OH 44310
330 375-3000

(G-321)
SUMMA HEALTH SYSTEM CORP (HQ)
Also Called: Summa Hlth Sys Breast Imaging
95 Arch St Ste G50 (44304-1477)
PHONE.................................330 375-4848
EMP: 50 **EST:** 1986
SALES (est): 375.82MM
SALES (corp-wide): 1.78B **Privately Held**
Web: www.summahealth.org
SIC: 8741 6324 Hospital management; Group hospitalization plans
PA: Summa Health System
1077 Gorge Blvd
Akron OH 44310
330 375-3000

(G-322)
SUMMA INSURANCE COMPANY INC (DH)
Also Called: Summacare
10 N Main St (44308-1958)
P.O. Box 3620 (44309-3620)
PHONE.................................800 996-8411
Martin P Hauser, *Pr*
Claude Vincenti, *
Annette M Ruby, *
EMP: 290 **EST:** 1995
SALES (est): 346.88MM
SALES (corp-wide): 1.78B **Privately Held**
Web: www.summacare.com
SIC: 6321 6311 Health insurance carriers; Life insurance
HQ: Summa Health System Corp.
95 Arch St Ste G50
Akron OH 44304

(G-323)
SUMMA REHAB HOSPITAL LLC
Also Called: SUMMA REHAB HOSPITAL
29 N Adams St (44304-1641)
PHONE.................................330 572-7300
EMP: 87 **EST:** 2010
SALES (est): 31.54MM **Privately Held**
Web: www.summarehabhospital.com
SIC: 8093 Rehabilitation center, outpatient treatment

(G-324)
SUMMIT COUNTY
1867 W Market St Ste B2 (44313-6906)
PHONE.................................330 762-3500
William Zumbar, *Ex Dir*
EMP: 39
SALES (corp-wide): 494.44MM **Privately Held**
Web: www.admboard.org
SIC: 8069 9111 Drug addiction rehabilitation hospital; Executive offices
PA: Summit County
650 Dan St
Akron OH 44310
330 643-2500

(G-325)
SUMMIT COUNTY
Also Called: Coroner's Office
85 N Summit St (44308-1950)
PHONE.................................330 643-2101
EMP: 54
SALES (corp-wide): 494.44MM **Privately Held**
Web: www.summitcasagal.org
SIC: 8071 Medical laboratories
PA: Summit County
650 Dan St
Akron OH 44310
330 643-2500

(G-326)
SUMMIT COUNTY
538 E South St (44311-1848)
PHONE.................................330 643-2850
Allan Brubaker, *Brnch Mgr*
EMP: 165
SQ FT: 1,368
SALES (corp-wide): 494.44MM **Privately Held**
Web: www.summitcasagal.org
SIC: 8711 9111 Engineering services; County supervisors' and executives' office
PA: Summit County
650 Dan St
Akron OH 44310
330 643-2500

(G-327)
SUPREME XPRESS TRNSP INC
810 S Main St Ste 159 (44311-1518)
PHONE.................................234 738-4047
Clarence Hunt, *Prin*
Pamela Johnson, *Prin*
EMP: 55 **EST:** 2021
SALES (est): 1.48MM **Privately Held**
SIC: 4731 Freight transportation arrangement

(G-328)
SYNTHOMER INC
2990 Gilchrist Rd (44305-4418)
PHONE.................................330 794-6300
Bill Beers, *Mgr*
EMP: 83
SQ FT: 117,299
SALES (corp-wide): 2.46B **Privately Held**
Web: www.omnova.com
SIC: 8731 Commercial physical research
HQ: Synthomer Inc.
25435 Harvard Rd
Beachwood OH 44122
216 682-7000

(G-329)
TASTY PURE FOOD COMPANY (PA)
1557 Industrial Pkwy (44310-2603)
PHONE.................................330 434-8141
Jim K Heilmeier, *Pr*
William Heilmeier, *
EMP: 33 **EST:** 1923
SQ FT: 20,000
SALES (est): 9.63MM
SALES (corp-wide): 9.63MM **Privately Held**
Web: www.tastypure.com
SIC: 5147 5142 5141 Meats, fresh; Packaged frozen goods; Groceries, general line

(G-330)
TC ARCHITECTS INC
430 Grant St (44311-1190)
PHONE.................................330 867-1093
Susan Allen, *VP*
Robert Chordar, *Pr*
EMP: 35 **EST:** 1951
SQ FT: 3,000
SALES (est): 5.13MM **Privately Held**
Web: www.tcarchitects.com
SIC: 8712 7389 Architectural engineering; Interior designer

(G-331)
TENNIS UNLIMITED INC
Also Called: Towpath Racquet Club
2108 Akron Peninsula Rd (44313-4804)
P.O. Box 341 (44222-0341)
PHONE.................................330 928-8763
Dallas Aleman, *Pr*
Nancy Aleman, *
EMP: 31 **EST:** 1967
SQ FT: 50,000
SALES (est): 987.47K **Privately Held**
Web: www.towpathtennis.com
SIC: 7997 5941 Tennis club, membership; Tennis goods and equipment

(G-332)
THE FAMOUS MANUFACTURING CO
2620 Ridgewood Rd Ste 200 (44313-3507)
PHONE.................................330 762-9621
Jay Blaushild, *Pr*
EMP: 317 **EST:** 2001
SALES (est): 5.25MM **Privately Held**
SIC: 5075 5074 Furnaces, heating: electric; Plumbing and hydronic heating supplies
PA: Famous Enterprises, Inc.
2620 Ridgewood Rd Ste 200
Akron OH 44313

(G-333)
THEKEN SPINE LLC
1800 Triplett Blvd (44306-3311)
PHONE.................................330 733-7600
Jolene Maurer, *CFO*
EMP: 189 **EST:** 2013
SALES (est): 2.48MM
SALES (corp-wide): 746.64MM **Privately Held**
Web: www.nextsteparthropedix.com
SIC: 8011 Physicians' office, including specialists
HQ: Seaspine Holdings Corporation
5770 Armada Dr
Carlsbad CA 92008
760 727-8399

(G-334)
TIMELINE CONSTRUCTION LLC
80 Cole Ave (44301-1605)
PHONE.................................330 595-4462
EMP: 28
SALES (corp-wide): 974.67K **Privately Held**
SIC: 1521 General remodeling, single-family houses
PA: Timeline Construction Llc
80 Cole Ave
Akron OH 44301
330 618-2108

(G-335)
TOLEDO EDISON COMPANY (HQ)
Also Called: FIRSTENERGY
76 S Main St Bsmt (44308-1817)
PHONE.................................800 447-3333
TOLL FREE: 800
Anthony J Alexander, *CEO*
C E Jones, *Pr*
Mark T Clark, *
Harvey L Wagner, *CAO*
L L Vespoli, *Ex VP*
EMP: 103 **EST:** 1901
SALES (est): 458.82MM **Publicly Held**
Web: www.firstenergycorp.com
SIC: 4911 Distribution, electric power
PA: Firstenergy Corp.
76 S Main St
Akron OH 44308

(G-336)
TOTAL QUALITY LOGISTICS LLC
50 S Main St Ste 900 (44308-1866)
PHONE.................................513 831-2600
EMP: 71
SALES (corp-wide): 8.85B **Privately Held**
Web: www.tql.com
SIC: 4731 Truck transportation brokers
HQ: Total Quality Logistics, Llc
4289 Ivy Pointe Blvd
Cincinnati OH 45245

(G-337)
TRI-C CONSTRUCTION COMPANY INC
1765 Merriman Rd (44313-5251)
PHONE.................................330 836-2722
EMP: 50 **EST:** 1990
SALES (est): 4.15MM **Privately Held**
Web: www.cedarwoodcompanies.com

GEOGRAPHIC SECTION

Akron - Summit County (G-359)

SIC: 8741 1542 Construction management; Commercial and office building contractors

(G-338)
TURNSERV LLC
231 Springside Dr Ste 150 (44333-4534)
P.O. Box 741 (44240-0014)
PHONE..................................216 600-8876
Tyler Dunagin, *Pr*
EMP: 44 **EST:** 2018
SALES (est): 1.15MM **Privately Held**
Web: www.turnserv.com
SIC: 8741 6531 Construction management; Real estate managers

(G-339)
UNION PROCESS INC
1925 Akron Peninsula Rd (44313-4896)
PHONE..................................330 929-3333
Arno Szegvari, *Pr*
Emery Li, *VP*
Margaret Szegvari, *
Anita Szegvari, *
▲ **EMP:** 35 **EST:** 1944
SQ FT: 30,000
SALES (est): 10.75MM **Privately Held**
Web: www.unionprocess.com
SIC: 5084 Industrial machinery and equipment

(G-340)
UNITED DISABILITY SERVICES INC
1275 Sweitzer Ave (44301-1346)
PHONE..................................330 379-3337
Kay Shellenberger, *Mgr*
EMP: 54
SALES (corp-wide): 9.35MM **Privately Held**
Web: www.udsakron.org
SIC: 8093 8322 Mental health clinic, outpatient; Adult day care center
PA: United Disability Services, Inc.
    701 S Main St
    Akron OH 44311
    330 374-1169

(G-341)
UNITED DISABILITY SERVICES INC (PA)
701 S Main St (44311-1019)
PHONE..................................330 374-1169
Gary Knuth, *Ex Dir*
EMP: 85 **EST:** 1949
SQ FT: 78,000
SALES (est): 9.35MM
SALES (corp-wide): 9.35MM **Privately Held**
Web: www.udsakron.org
SIC: 8331 8322 8093 Job training and related services; Social services for the handicapped; Rehabilitation center, outpatient treatment

(G-342)
UNITED WAY SUMMIT AND MEDINA (PA)
Also Called: United Way
37 N High St Ste A (44308-1973)
PHONE..................................330 762-7601
James Mullen, *Pr*
EMP: 51 **EST:** 1951
SQ FT: 13,000
SALES (est): 14.45MM
SALES (corp-wide): 14.45MM **Privately Held**
Web: www.uwsummitmedina.org
SIC: 8322 Social service center

(G-343)
UNIVERSAL NURSING SERVICES (PA)
483 Augusta Dr (44333-9214)
PHONE..................................330 434-7318
Gloria Rookard, *Pr*
David Rookard, *
Derrick Rookard, *
EMP: 50 **EST:** 1982
SQ FT: 4,800
SALES (est): 4.21MM
SALES (corp-wide): 4.21MM **Privately Held**
Web: www.universalnursinginc.com
SIC: 8082 Home health care services

(G-344)
URS GROUP INC
Also Called: URS
564 White Pond Dr (44320-1100)
PHONE..................................330 836-9111
Michael Burgess, *Mgr*
EMP: 281
SALES (corp-wide): 14.38B **Publicly Held**
Web: www.aecom.com
SIC: 8712 8711 Architectural engineering; Professional engineer
HQ: Urs Group, Inc.
    300 S Grand Ave Ste 900
    Los Angeles CA 90071
    213 593-8000

(G-345)
US CAPITAL INC
423 S Rose Blvd (44320-1307)
PHONE..................................330 867-4525
Peter Hamo, *CEO*
Susan Hamo, *Pr*
EMP: 30 **EST:** 2002
SALES (est): 873.65K **Privately Held**
Web: www.uscapitalcorp.com
SIC: 6726 Investment offices, nec

(G-346)
USIC LOCATING SERVICES LLC
441 Munroe Falls Rd (44312)
PHONE..................................330 733-9393
Shaun Corrin, *Mgr*
EMP: 55
Web: www.usicllc.com
SIC: 8713 Surveying services
HQ: Usic Locating Services, Llc
    9045 River Rd Ste 200
    Indianapolis IN 46240
    317 575-7800

(G-347)
VALMARK FINANCIAL GROUP LLC
130 Springside Dr Ste 300 (44333-2489)
PHONE..................................330 576-1234
Lawrence J Rybka, *Pr*
Caleb Callahan, *COO*
EMP: 198 **EST:** 2000
SQ FT: 15,000
SALES (est): 13.6MM **Privately Held**
Web: www.valmarkfg.com
SIC: 6411 6211 Insurance agents, brokers, and service; Security brokers and dealers

(G-348)
VAN DEVERE INC (PA)
Also Called: Van Devere Buick
300 W Market St (44303-2185)
PHONE..................................330 253-6137
Michael Van Devere, *Pr*
Shirley A Van Devere, *
EMP: 84 **EST:** 1947
SALES (est): 81.46MM
SALES (corp-wide): 81.46MM **Privately Held**
Web: www.buickvandevere.com
SIC: 5511 7515 Automobiles, new and used; Passenger car leasing

(G-349)
VANTAGE AGING (PA)
388 S Main St Ste 325 (44311-1045)
PHONE..................................330 253-4597
Karen Hrdlicka, *Pr*
Melinda Smith Yeargin, *
Leann Schaeffer, *Vice Chairman*
Amy Marsteller, *
EMP: 67 **EST:** 1975
SALES (est): 11.1MM
SALES (corp-wide): 11.1MM **Privately Held**
Web: www.vantageaging.org
SIC: 8322 Senior citizens' center or association

(G-350)
VANTAGE AGING
1155 E Tallmadge Ave (44310-3529)
PHONE..................................330 785-9770
Catherine Lewis, *Pr*
EMP: 417
SALES (corp-wide): 11.1MM **Privately Held**
Web: www.vantageaging.org
SIC: 8322 Senior citizens' center or association
PA: Vantage Aging
    388 S Main St Ste 325
    Akron OH 44311
    330 253-4597

(G-351)
VICTIM ASSISTANCE PROGRAM INC
137 S Main St Ste 300 (44308-1416)
PHONE..................................330 376-7022
Leanne Graham, *CEO*
Leanne Graham, *Ex Dir*
EMP: 36 **EST:** 1972
SALES (est): 2.21MM **Privately Held**
Web: www.victimassistanceprogram.org
SIC: 8322 Social service center

(G-352)
VINSON GROUP LLC
283 E Waterloo Rd (44319-1238)
PHONE..................................440 283-8832
EMP: 47 **EST:** 2016
SALES (est): 1.19MM **Privately Held**
Web: www.vinsonedu.com
SIC: 7379 Online services technology consultants

(G-353)
VIRTUAL HOLD TECH SLUTIONS LLC (DH)
Also Called: Mindful
3875 Embassy Pkwy Ste 350 (44333)
PHONE..................................330 670-2200
EMP: 29 **EST:** 1995
SQ FT: 18,000
SALES (est): 23.35MM
SALES (corp-wide): 534MM **Privately Held**
Web: www.getmindful.com
SIC: 7371 7372 Computer software development; Prepackaged software
HQ: Medallia, Inc.
    6220 Stnrdge Mall Rd Fl 2
    Pleasanton CA 94588
    650 321-3000

(G-354)
WALTS CLEANING CONTRS INC
515 E Turkeyfoot Lake Rd Ste E (44319-4102)
PHONE..................................330 899-0040
Charles Lancaster, *Pr*
EMP: 43 **EST:** 1979
SQ FT: 3,000
SALES (est): 2.02MM **Privately Held**
Web: www.waltscleaning.com
SIC: 7699 Cleaning services

(G-355)
WEAVER INDUSTRIES INC
636 W Exchange St (44302-1306)
PHONE..................................330 379-3606
Jean Fish, *Mgr*
EMP: 74
SALES (corp-wide): 7.88MM **Privately Held**
Web: www.weaverindustries.org
SIC: 7389 Packaging and labeling services
PA: Weaver Industries, Inc.
    520 S Main St Ste 2441
    Akron OH 44311
    330 379-3660

(G-356)
WEAVER INDUSTRIES INC (PA)
520 S Main St Ste 2441 (44311-1071)
PHONE..................................330 379-3660
Jeff Johnson, *Ex Dir*
EMP: 30 **EST:** 1971
SQ FT: 20,000
SALES (est): 7.88MM
SALES (corp-wide): 7.88MM **Privately Held**
Web: www.weaverindustries.org
SIC: 7389 8331 Packaging and labeling services; Job training and related services

(G-357)
WEAVER INDUSTRIES INC
340 N Cleveland Massillon Rd (44333-9302)
PHONE..................................330 666-5114
Claire Poirer-keys, *Mgr*
EMP: 249
SALES (corp-wide): 7.88MM **Privately Held**
Web: www.weaverindustries.org
SIC: 7389 8331 Packaging and labeling services; Job training and related services
PA: Weaver Industries, Inc.
    520 S Main St Ste 2441
    Akron OH 44311
    330 379-3660

(G-358)
WEAVER INDUSTRIES INC
Also Called: Weaver Secure Shred
2337 Romig Rd Ste 2 (44320-3824)
PHONE..................................330 745-2400
EMP: 141
SALES (corp-wide): 7.88MM **Privately Held**
Web: www.weaverindustries.org
SIC: 7389 Document and office record destruction
PA: Weaver Industries, Inc.
    520 S Main St Ste 2441
    Akron OH 44311
    330 379-3660

(G-359)
WEST CHSTER DNTSTRY DR JFFREY
1575 Vernon Odom Blvd (44320-4091)
PHONE..................................330 753-7734
EMP: 30 **EST:** 2013
SALES (est): 745.03K **Privately Held**
SIC: 8011 8021 Offices and clinics of medical doctors; Dentists' office

Akron - Summit County (G-360)

(G-360)
WHITESPACE DESIGN GROUP INC
Also Called: Whitespace Creative
243 Furnace St (44304-1284)
PHONE..................................330 762-9320
EMP: 30 **EST:** 1995
SQ FT: 17,000
SALES (est): 3.8MM **Privately Held**
Web: www.whitespace-creative.com
SIC: 8743 7336 7311 Public relations services; Commercial art and graphic design; Advertising agencies

(G-361)
WILLIAMS CONCRETE CNSTR CO INC
753 W Waterloo Rd (44314-1500)
PHONE..................................330 745-6388
Christopher Williams, *Pr*
Nancy C Williams, *
EMP: 32 **EST:** 1975
SQ FT: 4,000
SALES (est): 2.54MM **Privately Held**
Web: www.williamsconcreteohio.com
SIC: 1771 Concrete pumping

(G-362)
WINDSONG HEALTHCARE GROUP LLC
Also Called: Windsong Care Center
120 Brookmont Rd (44333-3089)
PHONE..................................216 292-5706
Teresa Lane, *Admn*
EMP: 80
SALES (corp-wide): 2.54MM **Privately Held**
Web: www.phxhealthohio.com
SIC: 8051 Skilled nursing care facilities
PA: Windsong Healthcare Group, Llc
120 Brookmont Rd
Akron OH 44333
330 666-7373

(G-363)
WOLCOTT SYSTEMS GROUP LLC
Also Called: Wolcott Group
3700 Embassy Pkwy Ste 430 (44333-8388)
PHONE..................................330 666-5900
EMP: 50 **EST:** 1994
SQ FT: 6,000
SALES (est): 4.74MM **Privately Held**
SIC: 8748 Systems engineering consultant, ex. computer or professional

(G-364)
WYANT LEASING CO LLC
Also Called: Wyant Woods Care Center
200 Wyant Rd (44313-4228)
PHONE..................................330 836-7953
EMP: 37 **EST:** 2005
SALES (est): 8.26MM **Privately Held**
Web: www.communicarehealth.com
SIC: 8051 Skilled nursing care facilities

(G-365)
WZ MANAGEMENT INC
3417 E Waterloo Rd (44312-4036)
P.O. Box 6258 (44312-0258)
PHONE..................................330 628-4881
Sidney Zetzer, *Pr*
Shirley Zetzer, *Sec*
◆ **EMP:** 32 **EST:** 1946
SALES (est): 6.36MM **Privately Held**
Web: www.samwinermotors.com
SIC: 5013 5531 Truck parts and accessories ; Truck equipment and parts

(G-366)
XPERT STAFFING LLC
692 Virginia Ave (44306-2033)
P.O. Box 13404 (44334-8804)
PHONE..................................330 969-9949
EMP: 63 **EST:** 2005
SQ FT: 1,200
SALES (est): 1.94MM **Privately Held**
SIC: 7361 Employment agencies

(G-367)
XTREME ELEMENTS LLC
1016 Morse St (44320-3926)
PHONE..................................330 612-0075
Hugh B Lookhart, *Managing Member*
EMP: 150 **EST:** 2003
SALES (est): 23.31MM **Privately Held**
Web: www.xeconstruction.com
SIC: 1611 Concrete construction: roads, highways, sidewalks, etc.

(G-368)
YOUNG MNS CHRSTN ASSN OF AKRON
Also Called: Canal Square Branch
1 Canal Square Plz (44308-1037)
PHONE..................................330 376-1335
Douglas R Kohl, *Pr*
EMP: 38
SALES (corp-wide): 21.21MM **Privately Held**
Web: www.akronymca.org
SIC: 8641 8351 Recreation association; Child day care services
PA: The Young Men's Christian Association Of Akron Ohio
50 S Mn St Ste Ll100
Akron OH 44308
330 376-1335

(G-369)
YOUNG MNS CHRSTN ASSN OF AKRON
Also Called: Hope Early Care & Educatn Ctr
475 Ohio St (44304-1421)
PHONE..................................330 434-5900
Nicole Sims, *Brnch Mgr*
EMP: 37
SALES (corp-wide): 21.21MM **Privately Held**
Web: www.akronymca.org
SIC: 8641 Youth organizations
PA: The Young Men's Christian Association Of Akron Ohio
50 S Mn St Ste Ll100
Akron OH 44308
330 376-1335

(G-370)
YOUNG MNS CHRSTN ASSN OF AKRON
Also Called: Khol Family YMCA
50 S Main St Ste Ll100 (44308-1859)
PHONE..................................330 376-1335
EMP: 38
SALES (corp-wide): 21.21MM **Privately Held**
Web: www.akronymca.org
SIC: 8641 Youth organizations
PA: The Young Men's Christian Association Of Akron Ohio
50 S Mn St Ste Ll100
Akron OH 44308
330 376-1335

(G-371)
YOUNG MNS CHRSTN ASSN OF AKRON
Also Called: YMCA
350 E Wilbeth Rd (44301-2624)
PHONE..................................330 724-1255
Melissa Roddy, *Ofcr*
EMP: 38

SALES (corp-wide): 21.21MM **Privately Held**
Web: www.akronymca.org
SIC: 8641 8351 Youth organizations; Child day care services
PA: The Young Men's Christian Association Of Akron Ohio
50 S Mn St Ste Ll100
Akron OH 44308
330 376-1335

(G-372)
YOUNG MNS CHRSTN ASSN OF AKRON
Also Called: North Hill YMCA
210 E North St (44304-1246)
PHONE..................................330 983-5573
Frances Varner, *Dir*
EMP: 38
SALES (corp-wide): 21.21MM **Privately Held**
Web: www.akronymca.org
SIC: 8641 7991 8351 7032 Youth organizations; Physical fitness facilities; Child day care services; Youth camps
PA: The Young Men's Christian Association Of Akron Ohio
50 S Mn St Ste Ll100
Akron OH 44308
330 376-1335

Albany
Athens County

(G-373)
VETERANS OF FOREIGN WARS OF US
3025 Dickson Rd (45710-9140)
PHONE..................................740 698-8841
EMP: 65
SALES (corp-wide): 105.25MM **Privately Held**
SIC: 8641 Veterans' organization
PA: Veterans Of Foreign Wars Of The United States
406 W 34th St Fl 11
Kansas City MO 64111
816 756-3390

Alliance
Stark County

(G-374)
ALLIANCE CITIZENS HEALTH ASSN
200 E State St (44601-4936)
PHONE..................................330 596-6000
Stan Jonas, *CEO*
EMP: 87 **EST:** 1921
SQ FT: 30,000
SALES (est): 9.6MM **Privately Held**
Web: www.aultmanalliance.org
SIC: 8062 General medical and surgical hospitals

(G-375)
ALLIANCE COMMUNITY HOSPITAL (PA)
Also Called: Community Care Center
200 E State St (44601-4936)
PHONE..................................330 596-6000
EMP: 85 **EST:** 1900
SALES (est): 246.87MM
SALES (corp-wide): 246.87MM **Privately Held**
Web: www.aultmanalliance.org
SIC: 8062 General medical and surgical hospitals

(G-376)
BUCKEYE STATE CREDIT UNION INC
1010 W State St (44601-4622)
PHONE..................................330 823-7930
Renee Kuhn, *Brnch Mgr*
EMP: 38
SALES (corp-wide): 3.92MM **Privately Held**
Web: www.buckeyecu.org
SIC: 6062 State credit unions, not federally chartered
PA: Buckeye State Credit Union, Inc.
197 E Thornton St
Akron OH 44311
330 253-9197

(G-377)
CANTERBURY VLLA OPRATIONS CORP
Also Called: Canterbury Villa of Alliance Center
1785 N Freshley Ave (44601-8772)
PHONE..................................330 821-4000
Brian Colleran, *Pr*
EMP: 29 **EST:** 2002
SALES (est): 7.29MM
SALES (corp-wide): 24.56MM **Privately Held**
Web: www.canterbury-villa.net
SIC: 8051 Skilled nursing care facilities
PA: Ballantrae Healthcare, Llc
1128 Pennsylvania St Ne
Albuquerque NM 87110
505 366-5200

(G-378)
CHILDRENS HOSP MED CTR AKRON
1826 S Arch Ave (44601-4332)
PHONE..................................330 823-7311
Georgene Gross, *Pr*
EMP: 54
SALES (corp-wide): 1.4B **Privately Held**
Web: www.akronchildrens.org
SIC: 8062 General medical and surgical hospitals
PA: Childrens Hospital Medical Center Of Akron
1 Perkins Sq
Akron OH 44308
330 543-1000

(G-379)
CITY OF ALLIANCE
Also Called: Wastewater Treatment Plant
12251 Rockhill Ave Ne (44601-1063)
PHONE..................................330 829-2220
Joseph Amabeli, *Mgr*
EMP: 39
SALES (corp-wide): 19.44MM **Privately Held**
Web: www.cityofalliance.com
SIC: 4952 Sewerage systems
PA: City Of Alliance
504 E Main St Ste 1
Alliance OH 44601
330 823-5900

(G-380)
CLEVELAND CLINIC MERCY HOSP
Also Called: Mercy Health Center Alliance
149 E Simpson St (44601-4219)
PHONE..................................330 823-3856
Dave Kelly, *Prin*
EMP: 421
SALES (corp-wide): 14.48B **Privately Held**
Web: www.cantonmercy.org
SIC: 8062 General medical and surgical hospitals
HQ: Cleveland Clinic Mercy Hospital
1320 Mercy Dr Nw
Canton OH 44708
330 489-1000

GEOGRAPHIC SECTION

Alliance - Stark County (G-400)

(G-381)
DINO PERSICHETTI
Also Called: Perkins Family Restaurant
20040 Harrisburg Westville Rd (44601)
PHONE.................................330 821-9600
Richard Fielgar, *Genl Mgr*
Dino Persichetti, *
Phillip Constantine, *
Richard Felgar, *
EMP: 64 **EST:** 1969
SQ FT: 2,788
SALES (est): 419.89K **Privately Held**
Web: www.perkinsrestaurants.com
SIC: 5812 7011 Restaurant, family: chain; Motor inn

(G-382)
FAMILY MEDICAL CTR OF ALIANCE
149 E Simpson St (44601)
PHONE.................................330 823-3856
Donald E Carter, *CEO*
Michael L Mcgrady, *Pr*
Duane K Kuentz, *
EMP: 40 **EST:** 1977
SQ FT: 5,800
SALES (est): 2.27MM **Privately Held**
SIC: 8011 General and family practice, physician/surgeon

(G-383)
HOLIDAY INN EX HT & SUITES
Also Called: Holiday Inn
2341 W State St (44601-3530)
PHONE.................................330 821-6700
Mildred Gurley, *Genl Mgr*
EMP: 37 **EST:** 2000
SQ FT: 12,552
SALES (est): 620.39K **Privately Held**
Web: www.hiexpress.com
SIC: 7011 Hotels and motels

(G-384)
ICC LOWE PACE LLC
1641 S Arch Ave (44601-4316)
P.O. Box 3622 (44601-7622)
PHONE.................................330 823-7223
Barbara Abraham, *Dir*
EMP: 36
SQ FT: 3,394
SALES (corp-wide): 10.89B **Publicly Held**
SIC: 7311 Advertising agencies
HQ: Icc Lowe Pace, Llc
5 Sylvan Way Ste 110
Parsippany NJ 07054

(G-385)
KEYBANK NATIONAL ASSOCIATION
960 W State St Ste 210 (44601-4685)
PHONE.................................330 823-9615
Mary Ann Casper, *Mgr*
EMP: 44
SALES (corp-wide): 10.4B **Publicly Held**
Web: www.key.com
SIC: 6021 National commercial banks
HQ: Keybank National Association
127 Public Sq Ste 5600
Cleveland OH 44114
800 539-2968

(G-386)
KISHAN INC
Also Called: Alliance Super 8
2330 W State St (44601)
PHONE.................................330 821-5688
Roy Patel, *Pr*
Sue Sanor, *Mgr*
EMP: 60 **EST:** 1994
SQ FT: 16,376
SALES (est): 399.77K **Privately Held**
Web: www.wyndhamhotels.com
SIC: 7011 Hotels and motels

(G-387)
KUNTZMAN TRUCKING INC (PA)
13515 Oyster Rd (44601-2064)
PHONE.................................330 821-9160
Virgil Waters, *Ch Bd*
Kenneth Boatright, *
EMP: 43 **EST:** 1997
SQ FT: 32,000
SALES (est): 2.88MM
SALES (corp-wide): 2.88MM **Privately Held**
Web: www.kmantrucking.com
SIC: 4213 4212 Contract haulers; Local trucking, without storage

(G-388)
LAVERY CHEVROLET-BUICK INC (PA)
Also Called: Lavery Buick
1096 W State St (44601-4694)
P.O. Box 3545 (44601-7545)
PHONE.................................330 823-1100
Thomas C Lavery, *Ch Bd*
William Lavery, *
Pat Bland, *
EMP: 36 **EST:** 1965
SQ FT: 31,000
SALES (est): 8.7MM
SALES (corp-wide): 8.7MM **Privately Held**
Web: www.laveryauto.com
SIC: 5511 7538 7532 7515 Automobiles, new and used; General automotive repair shops; Top and body repair and paint shops; Passenger car leasing

(G-389)
LOWES HOME CENTERS LLC
Also Called: Lowe's
2595 W State St (44601-5604)
PHONE.................................330 829-2700
Keith Fosse, *Mgr*
EMP: 143
SALES (corp-wide): 86.38B **Publicly Held**
Web: www.lowes.com
SIC: 5211 5031 5722 5064 Home centers; Building materials, exterior; Household appliance stores; Electrical appliances, television and radio
HQ: Lowe's Home Centers, Llc
1000 Lowes Blvd
Mooresville NC 28117
336 658-4000

(G-390)
MAC MANUFACTURING INC (HQ)
Also Called: Mac
14599 Commerce St Ne (44601)
PHONE.................................330 823-9900
Michael Conny, *Prin*
Dan Tubbs, *
Jenny Conny, *
Steve Hallas, *Prin*
Bill Ogden, *Prin*
▲ **EMP:** 700 **EST:** 1995
SALES (est): 108.7MM **Privately Held**
Web: www.mactrailer.com
SIC: 3715 5012 Truck trailers; Trailers for trucks, new and used
PA: Mac Trailer Manufacturing, Inc.
14599 Commerce St Ne
Alliance OH 44601

(G-391)
MAC TRAILER MANUFACTURING INC (PA)
14599 Commerce St Ne (44601-1003)
PHONE.................................800 795-8454
Michael A Conny, *Pr*
Bill Ogden, *CFO*
◆ **EMP:** 1300 **EST:** 1992
SQ FT: 220,000
SALES (est): 182.08MM **Privately Held**
Web: www.mactrailer.com
SIC: 3715 5012 5013 5015 Truck trailers; Trailers for trucks, new and used; Motor vehicle supplies and new parts; Motor vehicle parts, used

(G-392)
MCCREA OPERATING COMPANY LLC
Also Called: MCCREA MANOR NURSING & REHABIL
2040 Mccrea St (44601-2703)
PHONE.................................330 823-9055
Joseph Hazelbaker, *Prin*
Brian Hazelbaker, *Prin*
Ralph Hazelbaker, *Prin*
EMP: 66 **EST:** 2020
SALES (est): 3.04MM **Privately Held**
Web: www.mccreamanor.com
SIC: 8059 Nursing and personal care, nec

(G-393)
NIHON KOHDEN AMERICA INC
Also Called: NIHON KOHDEN AMERICA, INC.
10700 Lair Rd Ne (44601-7933)
PHONE.................................330 935-0184
M Kesterke, *Brnch Mgr*
EMP: 44
Web: us.nihonkohden.com
SIC: 5047 Medical equipment and supplies
HQ: Nihon Kohden America, Llc
15353 Barranca Pkwy
Irvine CA 92618
949 580-1555

(G-394)
OHIO EYE ALLIANCE INC (PA)
985 S Sawburg Ave (44601-3515)
PHONE.................................330 823-1680
TOLL FREE: 800
Sanjeev Dewan Md, *Pr*
Richard Lehrer Md, *Pr*
Doctor Dewan Md, *VP*
EMP: 32 **EST:** 1892
SQ FT: 8,000
SALES (est): 4.46MM
SALES (corp-wide): 4.46MM **Privately Held**
Web: www.ohioeye.com
SIC: 8011 Opthalmologist

(G-395)
PENNSYLVANIA STEEL COMPANY INC
432 Keystone St (44601-1722)
PHONE.................................330 823-7383
Joseph M Dombrowski, *CEO*
EMP: 35
SALES (corp-wide): 108.8MM **Privately Held**
SIC: 5051 Steel
PA: Pennsylvania Steel Company, Inc.
1717 Woodhaven Dr
Bensalem PA 19020
215 633-9600

(G-396)
PEREGRINE HEALTH SERVICES INC
Also Called: McCrea Manor Nursing
2040 Mccrea St (44601-2703)
PHONE.................................330 823-9005
Nicole Dandee, *Brnch Mgr*
EMP: 92
SALES (corp-wide): 9.05MM **Privately Held**
Web: www.ltcoh.com
SIC: 8051 8093 Skilled nursing care facilities; Rehabilitation center, outpatient treatment
PA: Peregrine Health Services, Inc.
1661 Old Henderson Rd
Columbus OH 43220
614 459-2656

(G-397)
ROBERTSON HEATING SUP CO OHIO (PA)
Also Called: Robertson
2155 W Main St (44601-2190)
P.O. Box 2448 (44601-0448)
PHONE.................................800 433-9532
Scott Robertson, *Pr*
Ed Robertson, *
Susan Neil, *
EMP: 107 **EST:** 1946
SQ FT: 137,000
SALES (est): 9.81MM
SALES (corp-wide): 9.81MM **Privately Held**
Web: www.robertsonheatingsupply.com
SIC: 5075 5074 Warm air heating and air conditioning; Plumbing and hydronic heating supplies

(G-398)
ROBERTSON HTG SUP ALIANCE OHIO (HQ)
2155 W Main St (44601-2190)
P.O. Box 2448 (44601-0448)
PHONE.................................330 821-9180
Scott Robertson, *Pr*
Larry Smith, *
Edward Robertson, *
Susan Neil, *
▲ **EMP:** 100 **EST:** 1946
SALES (est): 32.11MM
SALES (corp-wide): 85.52MM **Privately Held**
Web: www.rhs1.com
SIC: 5074 5999 5722 Plumbing fittings and supplies; Plumbing and heating supplies; Air conditioning room units, self-contained
PA: Robertson Heating Supply Co Of Columbus, Ohio
2155 W Main St
Alliance OH 44601
330 821-9180

(G-399)
ROBERTSON HTG SUP CLUMBUS OHIO (PA)
Also Called: Robertson Heating Supply
2155 W Main St (44601-2190)
P.O. Box 2448 (44601-0448)
PHONE.................................330 821-9180
Scott Robertson, *Pr*
Ed Robertson, *
Geoff Alpert, *
Scott Middleton, *
Kevin Duro, *
EMP: 105 **EST:** 1961
SQ FT: 60,000
SALES (est): 85.52MM
SALES (corp-wide): 85.52MM **Privately Held**
Web: www.rhs1.com
SIC: 5075 Warm air heating and air conditioning

(G-400)
ROWND METAL SALES INC
Also Called: SMS
432 Keystone St (44601-1722)
EMP: 35 **EST:** 1989
SQ FT: 70,000
SALES (est): 16.24MM **Privately Held**
Web: www.pasteel.com
SIC: 5051 Steel

Alliance - Stark County

(G-401)
STEEL EQP SPECIALISTS INC (PA)
Also Called: S.E.S. Engineering
1507 Beeson St Ne (44601-2142)
PHONE..................330 823-8260
James R Boughton, *CEO*
T Virgil Huggett, *Ch Bd*
Donald Watkins, *Ex VP*
Wayne W Weisenburger, *VP*
Allan Wolfgang, *VP*
▲ **EMP:** 72 **EST:** 1976
SQ FT: 32,000
SALES (est): 27.78MM
SALES (corp-wide): 27.78MM **Privately Held**
Web: www.seseng.com
SIC: 7699 3599 7629 3593 Industrial machinery and equipment repair; Custom machinery; Electrical repair shops; Fluid power cylinders and actuators

(G-402)
STONE CREEK ALLIANCE INC
1280 S Sawburg Ave (44601-3518)
PHONE..................330 856-4232
Michael Slyk, *Prin*
Dan D'amico, *Prin*
EMP: 35 **EST:** 2019
SALES (est): 1.47MM **Privately Held**
Web: www.stonecreekalf.com
SIC: 8361 Aged home

(G-403)
SURGERY ALLIANCE LTD
975 S Sawburg Ave (44601-3515)
PHONE..................330 821-7997
Philip C Roholt, *Pr*
EMP: 43 **EST:** 1995
SQ FT: 8,200
SALES (est): 5.52MM **Privately Held**
SIC: 8062 General medical and surgical hospitals

(G-404)
WEST BRANCH LOCAL SCHOOL DST
Also Called: West Branch Preschool
2900 Knox School Rd (44601-9021)
PHONE..................330 938-1122
EMP: 40
SALES (corp-wide): 19.86MM **Privately Held**
SIC: 8351 Preschool center
PA: West Branch Local School District
14277 S Main St
Beloit OH 44609
330 938-9324

(G-405)
WIELAND METAL SVCS FOILS LLC
2081 Mccrea St (44601-2704)
PHONE..................330 823-1700
Kevin Bense, *Pr*
Robert M James, *VP*
Marc R Bacon, *CFO*
Greg Keown, *Genl Mgr*
▲ **EMP:** 53 **EST:** 1986
SQ FT: 80,000
SALES (est): 28.04MM **Privately Held**
SIC: 3341 3353 3471 3497 Secondary nonferrous metals; Aluminum sheet, plate, and foil; Plating and polishing; Metal foil and leaf
HQ: Wieland Metal Services, Llc
301 Metro Center Blvd # 204
Warwick RI 02886
401 736-2600

(G-406)
WIELAND ROLLED PDTS N AMER LLC
Also Called: Olin Brass
2081 Mccrea St (44601-2704)
PHONE..................330 823-1700
Beth Tirey, *Genl Mgr*
EMP: 314
Web: www.wieland.com
SIC: 5051 Metals service centers and offices
HQ: Wieland Rolled Products North America, Llc
4801 Olympia Park Plz # 3
Louisville KY 40241

(G-407)
WINKLE INDUSTRIES INC
2080 W Main St (44601-2187)
PHONE..................330 823-9730
Joe Schatz, *CEO*
Beth A Felger, *
Christina M Schatz, *
▲ **EMP:** 55 **EST:** 1949
SQ FT: 85,000
SALES (est): 11.57MM **Privately Held**
Web: www.winkleindustries.com
SIC: 7699 3499 5063 Industrial machinery and equipment repair; Magnets, permanent: metallic; Control and signal wire and cable, including coaxial

(G-408)
YMCA
205 S Union Ave (44601-2593)
PHONE..................330 823-1930
Dale Nissley, *Dir*
EMP: 35 **EST:** 1921
SQ FT: 12,000
SALES (est): 243.11K **Privately Held**
Web: www.ymcastark.org
SIC: 8641 7991 8351 7032 Youth organizations; Physical fitness facilities; Child day care services; Youth camps

Amelia
Clermont County

(G-409)
A & A SAFETY INC (PA)
1126 Ferris Rd (45102-1892)
PHONE..................513 943-6100
William N Luttmer, *Pr*
Francis Luttmer, *
EMP: 50 **EST:** 1979
SQ FT: 12,300
SALES (est): 22.88MM
SALES (corp-wide): 22.88MM **Privately Held**
Web: www.aasafetyinc.com
SIC: 7359 3993 5084 1721 Work zone traffic equipment (flags, cones, barrels, etc.); Signs and advertising specialties; Safety equipment; Painting and paper hanging

(G-410)
AMERICAN DREAM SOLAR & WIN INC
Also Called: Solar Is Freedom
4007 Bach Buxton Rd (45102)
PHONE..................513 543-5645
Antonio Ranieri, *Pr*
EMP: 100 **EST:** 2016
SALES (est): 10.41MM **Privately Held**
Web: www.solarisfreedom.com
SIC: 1711 Solar energy contractor

(G-411)
AMERICAN FAMILY HOME INSUR CO
7000 Midland Blvd (45102)
P.O. Box 5323 (45201)
PHONE..................513 943-7100
EMP: 41 **EST:** 1965
SALES (est): 9.78MM
SALES (corp-wide): 3.29B **Privately Held**
Web: policyholders.amig.com
SIC: 6411 Insurance agents, nec
HQ: American Modern Insurance Group, Inc.
7000 Midland Blvd
Amelia OH 45102

(G-412)
AMERICAN MODERN HOME SVC CO
7000 Midland Blvd (45102-2608)
PHONE..................513 943-7100
W Todd Gray, *Pr*
EMP: 32 **EST:** 2009
SALES (est): 50.78MM
SALES (corp-wide): 3.29B **Privately Held**
Web: policyholders.amig.com
SIC: 6321 Reinsurance carriers, accident and health
HQ: American Modern Insurance Group, Inc.
7000 Midland Blvd
Amelia OH 45102

(G-413)
AMERICAN MODRN INSUR GROUP INC (DH)
Also Called: American Modern Home Insur Co
7000 Midland Blvd (45102)
P.O. Box P.O. Box 5323 (45201)
PHONE..................800 543-2644
John W Hayden, *Pr*
Michael Flowers, *
James P Tierney, *
John Campbell, *BICA Vice President**
Tammy Nelson, *CMO**
EMP: 108 **EST:** 1994
SALES (est): 295.96MM
SALES (corp-wide): 3.29B **Privately Held**
Web: policyholders.amig.com
SIC: 6411 Insurance agents and brokers
HQ: Midland-Guardian Co.
7000 Midland Blvd
Amelia OH 45102
513 943-7100

(G-414)
AMERICAN MODRN SELECT INSUR CO
7000 Midland Blvd (45102)
PHONE..................513 943-7100
EMP: 154 **EST:** 2008
SALES (est): 3.51MM
SALES (corp-wide): 3.29B **Privately Held**
Web: policyholders.amig.com
SIC: 6411 Insurance agents, nec
HQ: American Modern Home Insurance Company
7000 Midland Blvd
Amelia OH 45102
513 943-7100

(G-415)
AMERICAN WESTERN HOME INSUR CO
7000 Midland Blvd (45102)
PHONE..................513 943-7100
Thomas Rohs, *Pr*
Joseph P Hayden Junior, *Ch Bd*
Robert W Hayden, *
John Von Lehman, *
John R Labar, *
EMP: 530 **EST:** 1977
SALES (est): 11.88MM
SALES (corp-wide): 3.29B **Privately Held**
Web: policyholders.amig.com
SIC: 6331 Fire, marine, and casualty insurance
HQ: American Modern Home Insurance Company
7000 Midland Blvd
Amelia OH 45102
513 943-7100

(G-416)
CLERMONT COUNSELING CENTER (PA)
Also Called: Lifepoint Solutions
43 E Main St (45102-1993)
PHONE..................513 947-7000
Arlene Herman, *CEO*
EMP: 30 **EST:** 1970
SALES (est): 676.3K
SALES (corp-wide): 676.3K **Privately Held**
Web: www.clermontcounseling.org
SIC: 8322 General counseling services

(G-417)
KOEBBE PRODUCTS INC (PA)
1132 Ferris Rd (45102-1020)
PHONE..................513 753-4200
Dick Koebbe, *Pr*
EMP: 60 **EST:** 1969
SQ FT: 38,400
SALES (est): 19.74MM
SALES (corp-wide): 19.74MM **Privately Held**
Web: www.egerproducts.com
SIC: 3644 3544 5039 Insulators and insulation materials, electrical; Forms (molds), for foundry and plastics working machinery; Ceiling systems and products

(G-418)
MIDLAND COMPANY
Also Called: American Western Home Insur
7000 Midland Blvd (45102-2608)
PHONE..................513 947-5503
John W Hayden, *Pr*
Joseph P Hayden Iii, *Ch Bd*
W Todd Gray, *CAO**
John I Von Lehman, *
Paul T Brizzolara, *
EMP: 1200 **EST:** 1938
SQ FT: 275,000
SALES (est): 229.08MM
SALES (corp-wide): 3.29B **Privately Held**
Web: policyholders.amig.com
SIC: 6331 4449 Property damage insurance; Intracoastal (freight) transportation
HQ: Munich-American Holding Corporation
555 College Rd E
Princeton NJ 08540
609 243-4876

(G-419)
MIDLAND-GUARDIAN CO (HQ)
7000 Midland Blvd (45102-2608)
P.O. Box 5323 (45201-5323)
PHONE..................513 943-7100
Andreas Kleiner, *Pr*
Matt Mcconnell, *Treas*
Todd Gray, *
EMP: 650 **EST:** 1952
SALES (est): 496.9MM
SALES (corp-wide): 3.29B **Privately Held**
Web: policyholders.amig.com
SIC: 6311 6331 Life insurance carriers; Fire, marine, and casualty insurance: stock
PA: Munchener Ruckversicherungs-Gesellschaft Ag In Munchen
Koniginstr. 107
Munchen BY 80802
8938910

GEOGRAPHIC SECTION   Andover - Ashtabula County (G-440)

(G-420)
SUNRISE NURSING HEALTHCARE LLC
3434 State Route 132 (45102-2012)
PHONE..........................513 797-5144
Gil Salinas, *Admn*
EMP: 66 **EST:** 2020
SALES (est): 4.22MM **Privately Held**
Web:
www.sunrisenursinghealthcare.com
SIC: 8082 Home health care services

Amherst
Lorain County

(G-421)
AMHERST HOSPITAL ASSOCIATION
Also Called: E M H Regional Medical Center
254 Cleveland Ave (44001-1699)
PHONE..........................440 988-6000
Kristi Sink, *Pr*
David Cook, *
EMP: 57 **EST:** 1917
SQ FT: 90,000
SALES (est): 7.5MM **Privately Held**
Web: www.specialtyhospitaloflorain.org
SIC: 8062 General medical and surgical hospitals

(G-422)
AMHERST MANOR INC
Also Called: Amherst Manor Nursing Home
175 N Lake St (44001-1332)
P.O. Box 88126 (60188-0126)
PHONE..........................440 988-4415
Donel Sprenger, *Pr*
Anthony Sprenger, *
EMP: 450 **EST:** 1973
SQ FT: 30,000
SALES (est): 8.82MM **Privately Held**
Web: www.sprengerhealthcare.com
SIC: 8051 Skilled nursing care facilities
PA: Sprenger Enterprises, Inc.
   3905 Oberlin Ave Ste 1
   Lorain OH 44053

(G-423)
BAYMARK HEALTH SERVICES LA INC
530 N Leavitt Rd (44001-1131)
PHONE..........................440 328-4213
EMP: 115
SALES (corp-wide): 106.29MM **Privately Held**
Web: www.medmark.com
SIC: 8093 Substance abuse clinics (outpatient)
PA: Baymark Health Services Of Louisiana, Inc.
   1720 Lakepointe Dr # 117
   Lewisville TX 75057
   214 379-3300

(G-424)
BINDU ASSOCIATES LLC ELYRIA
Also Called: Country Suites By Carlson
99 Cortland Cir (44001)
PHONE..........................440 324-0099
EMP: 28 **EST:** 2000
SALES (est): 975.26K **Privately Held**
Web: www.radissonhotels.com
SIC: 7011 Hotels and motels

(G-425)
BON SECOURS MERCY HEALTH INC
Also Called: Poison & Toxic Control Center
360 Cleveland Ave (44001-1622)
PHONE..........................440 233-1000
Ed Oley, *Brnch Mgr*

EMP: 4000
SALES (corp-wide): 6.92B **Privately Held**
Web: www.bonsecours.com
SIC: 8063 8062 Psychiatric hospitals; General medical and surgical hospitals
PA: Bon Secours Mercy Health, Inc.
   1701 Mercy Health Pl
   Cincinnati OH 45237
   513 956-3729

(G-426)
CLOVERVALE FARMS LLC (DH)
Also Called: Clovervale Foods
8133 Cooper Foster Park Rd (44001)
PHONE..........................440 960-0146
Richard Cawrse Junior, *Pr*
Suzanne Graham, *
Richard Cecil, *
EMP: 100 **EST:** 1920
SQ FT: 38,000
SALES (est): 28.27MM
SALES (corp-wide): 52.88B **Publicly Held**
Web: clovervalefarms.openfos.com
SIC: 2032 2033 2038 0191 Puddings, except meat; packaged in cans, jars, etc.; Fruits; packaged in cans, jars, etc.; Frozen specialties, nec; General farms, primarily crop
HQ: Advancepierre Foods, Inc.
   9990 Prnceton Glendale Rd
   West Chester OH 45246
   513 874-8741

(G-427)
ED MULLINAX FORD LLC
Also Called: Autonation Ford Amherst
8000 Leavitt Rd (44001-2712)
P.O. Box 280 (44001-0280)
PHONE..........................440 984-2431
Dennis Pritt, *Mgr*
Michael J Jackson, *
EMP: 250 **EST:** 1970
SALES (est): 45.62MM
SALES (corp-wide): 26.95B **Publicly Held**
Web: www.autonationfordamherst.com
SIC: 5511 7538 7532 5521 Automobiles, new and used; General automotive repair shops; Top and body repair and paint shops ; Used car dealers
HQ: An Dealership Holding Corp.
   200 Sw 1st Ave
   Fort Lauderdale FL 33301
   954 769-7000

(G-428)
EDWARDS LAND CLEARING INC
Also Called: Edwards Tree Service
49090 Cooper Foster Park Rd (44001-9649)
PHONE..........................440 988-4477
EMP: 40 **EST:** 1972
SALES (est): 2.2MM **Privately Held**
Web: www.edwardslandclearingandtreeservice.com
SIC: 0783 1629 Planting, pruning, and trimming services; Land clearing contractor

(G-429)
GRACE HOSPITAL
254 Cleveland Ave (44001-1620)
PHONE..........................216 687-4013
Vickie Kayatin, *Prin*
EMP: 59
SALES (corp-wide): 9.47MM **Privately Held**
Web: www.gracehospital.org
SIC: 8062 General medical and surgical hospitals
PA: Grace Hospital
   2307 W 14th St
   Cleveland OH 44113

216 687-1500

(G-430)
KTM NORTH AMERICA INC (PA)
Also Called: Gasgas North America
1119 Milan Ave (44001-1319)
PHONE..........................855 215-6360
Di Stefan Pierer, *CEO*
Rod Bush, *
Selvaraj Narayana, *
John S Harden, *
Jon-erik Burleson, *Treas*
▲ **EMP:** 87 **EST:** 1992
SQ FT: 5,000
SALES (est): 53.86MM **Privately Held**
Web: www.ktm.com
SIC: 5012 3751 Motorcycles; Motorcycles, bicycles and parts

(G-431)
LORMET COMMUNITY FEDERAL CR UN (PA)
2051 Cooper Foster Park Rd (44001-1208)
PHONE..........................440 960-6600
Daniel Cwalina, *CEO*
Wendy Meincke, *CFO*
EMP: 36 **EST:** 1936
SQ FT: 2,718
SALES (est): 6.92MM
SALES (corp-wide): 6.92MM **Privately Held**
Web: www.lormet.com
SIC: 6061 Federal credit unions

(G-432)
SLIMANS SALES & SERVICE INC
Also Called: Slimans Chrysler Plymouth Dodge
7498 Leavitt Rd (44001-2457)
PHONE..........................440 988-4484
Paul Sliman, *Pr*
Wendy Sliman, *
Barbara Sliman, *
Ben Gray, *
EMP: 32 **EST:** 1951
SQ FT: 20,000
SALES (est): 17.15MM **Privately Held**
Web: www.slimans.net
SIC: 5511 5012 Automobiles, new and used; Automobiles and other motor vehicles

(G-433)
SPECIALTY HOSPITAL OF LORAIN
254 Cleveland Ave (44001-1620)
PHONE..........................440 988-6088
Jeffrey R Popp, *Prin*
EMP: 27 **EST:** 2012
SALES (est): 6.88MM **Privately Held**
Web: www.specialtyhospitaloflorain.org
SIC: 8062 General medical and surgical hospitals

(G-434)
STAR BUILDERS INC
46405 Telegraph Rd (44001-2855)
P.O. Box 109 (44001-0109)
PHONE..........................440 986-5951
TOLL FREE: 800
Richard Mulder, *CEO*
Kalyn Wise, *
Todd Mealwitz, *
EMP: 30 **EST:** 1957
SQ FT: 30,000
SALES (est): 4.72MM **Privately Held**
Web: www.starinc.cc
SIC: 1542 1541 Commercial and office building, new construction; Industrial buildings and warehouses

Amsterdam
Jefferson County

(G-435)
APEX ENVIRONMENTAL LLC (PA)
11 County Road 78 (43903-7942)
P.O. Box 157 (43903-0157)
PHONE..........................740 543-4389
Antony Rosso, *CEO*
EMP: 37 **EST:** 2015
SQ FT: 2,500
SALES (est): 18.39MM **Privately Held**
SIC: 1629 Waste disposal plant construction

(G-436)
EDISON LOCAL SCHOOL DISTRICT
Also Called: Edison Bus Garage
8235 Amsterdam Rd Se (43903-9727)
PHONE..........................740 543-4011
Florence Mader, *Mgr*
EMP: 41
SALES (corp-wide): 28.16MM **Privately Held**
Web: www.edisonwildcats.org
SIC: 8211 7514 Public senior high school; Passenger car rental
PA: Edison Local School District
   14890 State Route 213
   Hammondsville OH 43930
   740 282-0065

Andover
Ashtabula County

(G-437)
ANDOVER BANCORP INC (PA)
19 Public Sq (44003)
P.O. Box 1300 (44003)
PHONE..........................440 293-7605
Larry W Park, *Pr*
James Greenfield, *VP*
EMP: 50 **EST:** 1984
SALES (est): 16.86MM **Privately Held**
Web: www.andover.bank
SIC: 6022 State commercial banks

(G-438)
ANDOVER VLG RTREMENT CMNTY LTD
486 S Main St (44003-9602)
PHONE..........................440 293-5416
EMP: 81 **EST:** 1981
SALES (est): 8.22MM **Privately Held**
Web: www.andovervillagesnr.com
SIC: 8051 Convalescent home with continuous nursing care

(G-439)
JEFFERSON REHAB & WELLNESS LLC
6752 Twitchell Rd (44003-9536)
PHONE..........................440 576-0043
EMP: 30
SALES (corp-wide): 217.6K **Privately Held**
Web: www.jeffersonrehabwellness.com
SIC: 8361 Rehabilitation center, residential; health care incidental
PA: Jefferson Rehabilitation And Wellness, Llc
   42 S Chestnut St
   Jefferson OH 44047
   440 576-0043

(G-440)
SEELEY ENTERPRISES COMPANY (PA)
Also Called: Seeley Medical

Andover - Ashtabula County (G-441)

104 Parker Dr (44003-9481)
PHONE..................................440 293-6600
Mario Lacute, *CEO*
Donald Bellante, *
Ann Lacute, *
Glenna Gallagher, *
Joe Petrolla, *
EMP: 35 **EST:** 1978
SQ FT: 12,000
SALES (est): 16.94MM
SALES (corp-wide): 16.94MM **Privately Held**
Web: www.seeleymedical.com
SIC: 5999 7352 Medical apparatus and supplies; Medical equipment rental

(G-441)
SEELEY MEDICAL OXYGEN CO (HQ)
104 Parker Dr (44003-9481)
PHONE..................................440 255-7163
Mario Lacute, *Pr*
Donald Bellante, *
Ann Lacute, *
EMP: 45 **EST:** 1955
SQ FT: 15,000
SALES (est): 10.46MM
SALES (corp-wide): 16.94MM **Privately Held**
Web: www.seeleymedical.com
SIC: 5047 7352 Medical equipment and supplies; Medical equipment rental
PA: Seeley Enterprises Company
104 Parker Dr
Andover OH 44003
440 293-6600

Anna
Shelby County

(G-442)
AGRANA FRUIT US INC
16197 County Road 25a (45302-9498)
PHONE..................................937 693-3821
Jeff Elliot, *Mgr*
EMP: 150
SALES (corp-wide): 68.66MM **Privately Held**
Web: us.agrana.com
SIC: 8734 2099 2087 Food testing service; Food preparations, nec; Flavoring extracts and syrups, nec
HQ: Agrana Fruit Us, Inc.
6850 Southpointe Pkwy
Brecksville OH 44141
440 546-1199

(G-443)
NOLL FISHER INCORPORATED
Also Called: Noll - Fisher
214 W Main St (45302)
P.O. Box 199 (45302-0199)
PHONE..................................937 394-4181
Michael Noll, *Pr*
Mark Noll, *
EMP: 30 **EST:** 1948
SQ FT: 7,100
SALES (est): 2.41MM **Privately Held**
Web: www.honeywell.com
SIC: 1731 1711 General electrical contractor; Mechanical contractor

(G-444)
TRI COUNTY VETERINARY SERVICE
16200 County Road 25a (45302-9723)
PHONE..................................937 693-2131
Ken Gloyeske, *CEO*
Timothy Woodward, *VP*
EMP: 29 **EST:** 1958
SQ FT: 4,500
SALES (est): 4.71MM **Privately Held**
Web: www.tricountyvetservice.com
SIC: 0741 0742 Veterinarian, livestock; Veterinarian, animal specialties

(G-445)
WELLS BROTHERS INC
Also Called: Honeywell Authorized Dealer
105 Shue Dr (45302-8402)
PHONE..................................937 394-7559
Curt Wells, *Pr*
Ken Steinke, *
Sandy Wells, *
Jerry Wells, *
EMP: 82 **EST:** 1989
SALES (est): 26.99MM **Privately Held**
Web: www.wellsbrothers.com
SIC: 1731 1711 General electrical contractor; Plumbing contractors

Ansonia
Darke County

(G-446)
SHUR-GREEN FARMS LLC
9159 State Route 118 (45303-9778)
PHONE..................................937 547-9633
EMP: 64 **EST:** 2013
SALES (est): 3.03MM **Privately Held**
Web: www.shurgreen.net
SIC: 0213 4953 Hogs; Recycling, waste materials

Antwerp
Paulding County

(G-447)
ANTWERP MNOR ASSSTED LVING LLC
204 Archer Dr (45813-8499)
P.O. Box 759 (45813-0759)
PHONE..................................419 258-1500
Kenneth Wilson, *Pr*
EMP: 40 **EST:** 2018
SALES (est): 2.32MM **Privately Held**
Web: www.antwerpmanor.com
SIC: 8361 Aged home

(G-448)
SCHROEDER ASSOCIATES INC (PA)
5554 County Road 424 (45813-9420)
P.O. Box 1084 (45813-1084)
PHONE..................................419 258-5075
Easther H Schroeder, *Prin*
Charles Schroeder, *Prin*
EMP: 30 **EST:** 1956
SQ FT: 10,000
SALES (est): 2.23MM
SALES (corp-wide): 2.23MM **Privately Held**
Web: www.reyesschroederlaw.com
SIC: 4213 4789 6411 Trucking, except local; Pipeline terminal facilities, independently operated; Insurance agents and brokers

Apple Creek
Wayne County

(G-449)
ELDORADO STONE LLC
Stone Craft
167 Maple St (44606-9599)
PHONE..................................330 698-3931
Melanie Garcia, *Mgr*
EMP: 30
Web: www.eldoradostone.com
SIC: 3272 1771 Concrete products, precast, nec; Concrete work
HQ: Eldorado Stone Llc
3817 Ocean Ranch Blvd # 114
Oceanside CA 92056
800 925-1491

(G-450)
ESPT LIQUIDATION INC
339 Mill St (44606-9541)
P.O. Box 458 (44606-0458)
PHONE..................................330 698-4711
Leonard Buckner, *Pr*
EMP: 75 **EST:** 1960
SQ FT: 88,000
SALES (est): 8.87MM **Privately Held**
Web: www.euclidmedicalproducts.com
SIC: 5047 5113 Medical and hospital equipment; Paper tubes and cores

(G-451)
NORTH CENTRAL INSULATION INC
7538 E Lincoln Way (44606-9584)
PHONE..................................330 262-1998
Lyle Dudgeon, *Mgr*
EMP: 65
SALES (corp-wide): 24.79MM **Privately Held**
Web: www.nci-ins.com
SIC: 1741 1742 Foundation building; Insulation, buildings
PA: North Central Insulation, Inc.
7539 State Route 13
Bellville OH 44813
419 886-2030

(G-452)
PRECISION PRODUCTS GROUP INC
Also Called: Euclid Medical Products
339 Mill St (44606-9541)
PHONE..................................330 698-4711
Ray Schroeder, *Mgr*
EMP: 75
Web: www.euclidmedicalproducts.com
SIC: 5047 5113 Medical and hospital equipment; Paper tubes and cores
PA: Precision Products Group, Inc.
8770 Guion Rd Ste A
Indianapolis IN 46268

Arcanum
Darke County

(G-453)
BRUMBAUGH CONSTRUCTION INC
3520 State Route 49 (45304-9731)
P.O. Box 309 (45304-0309)
PHONE..................................937 692-5107
Joe Raterman, *CEO*
Herbert W Cox, *Prin*
Scott Myers, *
Ralph E Brumbaugh, *Prin*
Diane Wills, *
▲ **EMP:** 43 **EST:** 1961
SQ FT: 3,000
SALES (est): 21.71MM **Privately Held**
Web: www.brumbaughconstruction.com
SIC: 1542 1622 Commercial and office building, new construction; Bridge construction

Archbold
Fulton County

(G-454)
2023 VENTURES INC
595 E Lugbill Rd (43502-1560)
◆ **EMP:** 80 **EST:** 1997
Web: www.graniteind.com
SIC: 6719 Investment holding companies, except banks

(G-455)
COMMUNITY HLTH PRFSSIONALS INC
Also Called: Community Health Professionals
230 Westfield Dr (43502-1047)
PHONE..................................419 445-5128
Brent Tow, *Brnch Mgr*
EMP: 31
SALES (corp-wide): 12.27MM **Privately Held**
Web: www.comhealthpro.org
SIC: 8082 Visiting nurse service
PA: Community Health Professionals, Inc.
1159 Westwood Dr
Van Wert OH 45891
419 238-9223

(G-456)
COMMUNITY HSPTALS WLLNESS CTRS
Also Called: Archbold Hospital
121 Westfield Dr Ste 1 (43502-1005)
PHONE..................................419 445-2015
Rusty O Brunicardi, *COO*
EMP: 34
SALES (corp-wide): 77.07MM **Privately Held**
Web: www.chwchospital.org
SIC: 8062 General medical and surgical hospitals
PA: Community Hospitals And Wellness Centers
433 W High St
Bryan OH 43506
419 636-1131

(G-457)
FARMERS & MERCHANTS STATE BANK (HQ)
Also Called: F&M Bank
307-11 N Defiance St (43502)
P.O. Box 216 (43502)
PHONE..................................419 446-2501
Lars B Eller, *Pr*
Eric Faust, *CRO*
Benet Rupp, *
David Gerken, *Chief Lending Officer*
Tim Carsey, *
EMP: 115 **EST:** 1897
SALES (est): 116.33MM
SALES (corp-wide): 155.85MM **Publicly Held**
Web: www.fm.bank
SIC: 6022 State trust companies accepting deposits, commercial
PA: Farmers & Merchants Bancorp, Inc.
307 N Defiance St
Archbold OH 43502
419 446-2501

(G-458)
FARMERS MERCHANTS BANCORP INC (PA)
307 N Defiance St (43502-1162)
P.O. Box 216 (43502-0216)
PHONE..................................419 446-2501
Lars B Eller, *Pr*
Jack C Johnson, *Ch Bd*
Kevin J Sauder, *V Ch Bd*
Barbara J Britenriker, *Ex VP*
Rex D Rice, *Chief Lending Officer*
EMP: 56 **EST:** 1985
SALES (est): 155.85MM
SALES (corp-wide): 155.85MM **Publicly Held**
Web: www.fm.bank

GEOGRAPHIC SECTION   Ashland - Ashland County (G-479)

SIC: 6022 State trust companies accepting deposits, commercial

(G-459)
GERALD GRAIN CENTER INC
3265 County Road 24 (43502-9415)
PHONE....................419 445-2451
Chet Phillips, *Brnch Mgr*
EMP: 30
SALES (corp-wide): 20.13MM **Privately Held**
Web: www.geraldgrain.com
SIC: 3523 5191 Elevators, farm; Animal feeds
PA: Gerald Grain Center, Inc.
14540 County Road U
Napoleon OH 43545
419 598-8015

(G-460)
HAULOTTE GROUP BILJAX INC
125 Taylor Pkwy (43502-9122)
PHONE....................567 444-4159
EMP: 35 EST: 2015
SALES (est): 8.35MM **Privately Held**
Web: www.biljax.com
SIC: 5032 Plastering materials

(G-461)
LIECHTY INC (DH)
1701 S Defiance St (43502-9798)
P.O. Box 67 (43502-0067)
PHONE....................419 445-1565
Orval Jay Beck, *Pr*
EMP: 30 EST: 1934
SALES (est): 10.27MM
SALES (corp-wide): 33.49MM **Privately Held**
Web: www.liechtyfarmequip.com
SIC: 5083 Agricultural machinery and equipment
HQ: Kenn-Feld Group, Llc
5068 E 100 N
Bluffton IN 46714

(G-462)
MBC HOLDINGS INC (PA)
1613 S Defiance St (43502)
P.O. Box 30 (43502)
PHONE....................419 445-1015
EMP: 39 EST: 1994
SALES (est): 196.71MM **Privately Held**
Web: www.mbcholdings.net
SIC: 1622 1611 Bridge construction; Highway and street paving contractor

(G-463)
MILLER BROS CONST INC
1613 S Defiance St (43502-9488)
P.O. Box 30 (43502-0030)
PHONE....................419 445-1015
Bradley D Miller, *Pr*
Sean Miley, *
Scott Jaskela, *
Larry Winkleman, *
Mark F Murray, *
EMP: 600 EST: 1945
SQ FT: 48,000
SALES (est): 181.29MM **Privately Held**
Web: www.mbcholdings.com
SIC: 1611 Highway and street paving contractor
PA: Mbc Holdings, Inc.
1613 S Defiance St
Archbold OH 43502

(G-464)
NORTHWEST OHIO COMPUTER ASSN (PA)
Also Called: Northern Bckeye Edcatn Council
209 Nolan Pkwy (43502-8404)
PHONE....................419 267-5565
John Mohler, *Ex Dir*
EMP: 35 EST: 1981
SQ FT: 6,000
SALES (est): 7.49MM
SALES (corp-wide): 7.49MM **Privately Held**
Web: www.nwoca.org
SIC: 7374 8211 Data processing service; Elementary and secondary schools

(G-465)
NWOCA WEST
209 Nolan Pkwy (43502-8404)
PHONE....................419 267-2544
EMP: 36 EST: 1985
SALES (est): 171.78K **Privately Held**
Web: www.nwoca.org
SIC: 8699 Membership organizations, nec

(G-466)
QUADCO REHABILITATION CTR INC
Also Called: Northwest Products Div
600 Oak St (43502-1579)
P.O. Box 336 (43502-0336)
PHONE....................419 445-1950
Phillip Zuver, *Brnch Mgr*
EMP: 35
SALES (corp-wide): 1.38MM **Privately Held**
Web: www.quadcorehab.org
SIC: 8331 2448 Vocational rehabilitation agency; Wood pallets and skids
PA: Quadco Rehabilitation Center, Inc.
427 N Defiance St
Stryker OH 43557
419 682-1011

(G-467)
SAUDER WOODWORKING CO (PA)
Also Called: Sauder
502 Middle St (43502-1500)
P.O. Box 156 (43502-0156)
PHONE....................419 446-2711
Kevin Sauder, *CEO*
Patrick Sauder, *Ex VP*
◆ EMP: 2100 EST: 1934
SQ FT: 5,000,000
SALES (est): 543.69MM
SALES (corp-wide): 543.69MM **Privately Held**
Web: www.sauder.com
SIC: 5021 2512 Household furniture; Upholstered household furniture

(G-468)
T J AUTOMATION INC
U075 State Route 66 (43502-9505)
PHONE....................419 267-5687
Tracy Hammersmith, *Pr*
EMP: 30 EST: 1997
SQ FT: 12,000
SALES (est): 10.78MM **Privately Held**
Web: www.tjautomationinc.com
SIC: 5084 Industrial machinery and equipment

Arlington
Hancock County

(G-469)
EVANGLCAL LTHRAN GOOD SMRTAN S
Also Called: Good Samaritan Soc - Arlington
100 Powell Dr (45814-9500)
P.O. Box 5038 (57117-5038)
PHONE....................419 365-5115
Austin Gerber, *Brnch Mgr*
EMP: 240
Web: www.good-sam.com
SIC: 8059 8051 Nursing home, except skilled and intermediate care facility; Skilled nursing care facilities
HQ: The Evangelical Lutheran Good Samaritan Society
4800 W 57th St
Sioux Falls SD 57108
866 928-1635

Arlington Heights
Hamilton County

(G-470)
MITER MASONRY CONTRACTORS
421 Maple Ave (45215-5425)
PHONE....................513 821-3334
Thomas Krallman, *Pr*
Anne M Krallman, *
EMP: 40 EST: 1982
SQ FT: 8,000
SALES (est): 3.58MM **Privately Held**
SIC: 1741 Masonry and other stonework

Ashland
Ashland County

(G-471)
ABERS GARAGE INC (PA)
Also Called: Aber's Truck Center
1729 Claremont Ave (44805-3594)
PHONE....................419 281-5500
Danny Aber, *Pr*
Jerry Aber, *
Allen Aber, *
Frances Aber, *
EMP: 45 EST: 1950
SQ FT: 26,000
SALES (est): 14.86MM
SALES (corp-wide): 14.86MM **Privately Held**
Web: www.aberstruckcenter.com
SIC: 5511 7538 7549 5012 Trucks, tractors, and trailers: new and used; General truck repair; Towing service, automotive; Automobiles and other motor vehicles

(G-472)
APPLESEED CMNTY MNTAL HLTH CTR
Also Called: APPLESEED COUNSELING
2233 Rocky Ln (44805-4701)
PHONE....................419 281-3716
Jerry Strausaugh, *Dir*
EMP: 77 EST: 1992
SALES (est): 6.66MM **Privately Held**
Web: www.appleseedmentalhealth.com
SIC: 8049 8093 Clinical psychologist; Specialty outpatient clinics, nec

(G-473)
ASHLAND CITY SCHOOL DISTRICT
Also Called: Reagan Elementary School
850 Jackson Dr (44805-4254)
PHONE....................419 289-7967
Stephen Mcdonnell, *Prin*
EMP: 75
SALES (corp-wide): 44.49MM **Privately Held**
Web: www.ashlandcityschools.org
SIC: 8211 8351 Public junior high school; Preschool center
PA: Ashland City Schools Pto
1407 Claremont Ave
Ashland OH 44805
419 289-1117

(G-474)
ASHLAND CLEANING LLC
1965 S Baney Rd (44805-4502)
PHONE....................419 281-1747
Melinda Turk, *Prin*
EMP: 50 EST: 2005
SALES (est): 2.25MM **Privately Held**
Web: www.ashlandcleaning.com
SIC: 7349 Janitorial service, contract basis

(G-475)
ASHLAND HOME TOWNE PHRM INC
849 Smith Rd (44805-3644)
P.O. Box 328 (44805-0328)
PHONE....................419 281-4040
Matthew Maiyer, *Pr*
EMP: 47 EST: 1966
SALES (est): 905.51K **Privately Held**
Web: www.ashland.edu
SIC: 8741 Business management

(G-476)
ASHLAND TRAINING CENTER
Also Called: Loudonville Training Center
228 Maple St (44805-3212)
PHONE....................419 281-2767
Shannon Richter, *Dir*
Kathy Wigal, *Dir*
Kanon Rector, *Admn*
EMP: 37 EST: 1975
SALES (est): 244.42K **Privately Held**
Web: www.ashland.edu
SIC: 8351 7032 Preschool center; Summer camp, except day and sports instructional

(G-477)
ASPEN MANAGEMENT USA LLC (PA)
1566 County Road 1095 (44805-9592)
PHONE....................419 281-3367
David Wurster, *Pr*
Thomas Wurster, *VP*
Ann Wurster, *Treas*
EMP: 36 EST: 2004
SALES (est): 2.31MM
SALES (corp-wide): 2.31MM **Privately Held**
Web: www.aspenmanagementusa.com
SIC: 6513 Apartment building operators

(G-478)
ATLAS BOLT & SCREW COMPANY LLC (DH)
Also Called: Atlas Fasteners For Cnstr
1628 Troy Rd (44805-1398)
PHONE....................419 289-6171
Robert W Moore, *Pr*
Robert C Gluth, *Ex VP*
Robert Webb, *Sec*
▲ EMP: 175 EST: 1986
SQ FT: 75,000
SALES (est): 47.18MM
SALES (corp-wide): 364.48B **Publicly Held**
Web: www.atlasfasteners.com
SIC: 3452 5085 5051 5072 Washers, metal; Fasteners, industrial: nuts, bolts, screws, etc.; Metals service centers and offices; Hardware
HQ: Marmon Group Llc
181 W Madison St Ste 3900
Chicago IL 60602
312 372-9500

(G-479)
BALL BOUNCE AND SPORT INC (PA)
Also Called: Hedstrom Entertainment
1 Hedstrom Dr (44805-3586)

Ashland - Ashland County (G-480)

GEOGRAPHIC SECTION

PHONE.................................419 289-9310
James Purtell, *Pr*
Scott Fickes, *
◆ **EMP:** 35 **EST:** 2004
SQ FT: 187,000
SALES (est): 46.04MM
SALES (corp-wide): 46.04MM **Privately Held**
Web: www.hedstrom.com
SIC: 5092 Toys and hobby goods and supplies

(G-480)
BCU ELECTRIC INC
1019 Us Highway 250 N (44805-9474)
PHONE.................................419 281-8944
Bennie Uselton, *Pr*
Brenda Uselton, *
EMP: 75 **EST:** 1990
SQ FT: 6,000
SALES (est): 12.33MM **Privately Held**
Web: www.bcuelectric.com
SIC: 1731 General electrical contractor

(G-481)
BENDON INC
Also Called: Primary Colors Design Corp.
1191 Commerce Pkwy (44805-8955)
PHONE.................................419 903-0403
Ben Ferguson, *CEO*
EMP: 94
SALES (corp-wide): 28.5MM **Privately Held**
Web: www.bendonpub.com
SIC: 4225 General warehousing and storage
PA: Bendon, Inc.
  1840 S Baney Rd
  Ashland OH 44805
  419 207-3600

(G-482)
BENDON INC (PA)
Also Called: Bendon Publishing Intl
1840 S Baney Rd (44805-3524)
PHONE.................................419 207-3600
Benjamin Ferguson, *CEO*
Benjamin Ferguson, *Pr*
Terry Gerwig, *
Jenny Hastings, *
David Swank, *
▲ **EMP:** 54 **EST:** 2001
SQ FT: 220,000
SALES (est): 28.5MM
SALES (corp-wide): 28.5MM **Privately Held**
Web: www.bendonpub.com
SIC: 5999 5961 5092 2731 Educational aids and electronic training materials; Educational supplies and equipment, mail order; Educational toys; Books, publishing only

(G-483)
BOOKMASTERS INC (HQ)
Also Called: Baker & Taylor Publisher Svcs
30 Amberwood Pkwy (44805-9765)
PHONE.................................419 281-1802
Raymond Sevin, *Pr*
Thomas Wurster, *
◆ **EMP:** 157 **EST:** 1972
SQ FT: 180,000
SALES (est): 49.92MM **Privately Held**
Web: www.btpubservices.com
SIC: 7389 2752 2731 2791 Printers' services: folding, collating, etc.; Commercial printing, lithographic; Book publishing; Typesetting
PA: Baker & Taylor, Llc
  2810 Clseum Cntre Dr Ste
  Charlotte NC 28217

(G-484)
BRETHREN CARE INC
Also Called: BLOOMFIELD COTTAGES
2140 Center St Ofc (44805-4380)
PHONE.................................419 289-0803
Jay Brooks, *CEO*
EMP: 200 **EST:** 1970
SQ FT: 38,000
SALES (est): 19.13MM **Privately Held**
Web: www.brethrencarevillage.org
SIC: 8052 6513 8051 Intermediate care facilities; Apartment building operators; Skilled nursing care facilities

(G-485)
BRETHREN CARE VILLAGE LLC
2140 Center St (44805-4376)
PHONE.................................419 289-1585
Troy Snyder, *CEO*
Matthew Mcfarland, *CFO*
EMP: 99 **EST:** 2016
SQ FT: 49,810
SALES (est): 9.29MM **Privately Held**
Web: www.brethrencarevillage.org
SIC: 8051 Skilled nursing care facilities

(G-486)
CABINET RESTYLERS INC
Also Called: Cabinet Restylers
419 E 8th St (44805-1953)
PHONE.................................419 281-8449
Eric Thiel, *Pr*
Denise Appleby, *VP*
EMP: 56 **EST:** 1968
SQ FT: 50,000
SALES (est): 9.23MM **Privately Held**
Web: www.thiels.com
SIC: 1751 2541 5211 1799 Window and door (prefabricated) installation; Cabinets, lockers, and shelving; Cabinets, kitchen; Bathtub refinishing

(G-487)
CATHOLIC CHARITIES CORPORATION
Also Called: St Edward Elementary School
433 Cottage St (44805-2125)
PHONE.................................419 289-7456
Sue Ellen Valentine, *Prin*
EMP: 78
Web: www.stedwardashland.org
SIC: 8399 8211 8661 Fund raising organization, non-fee basis; Catholic elementary and secondary schools; Catholic Church
PA: Catholic Charities Corporation
  7911 Detroit Ave
  Cleveland OH 44102

(G-488)
CATHOLIC CHARITIES CORPORATION
Also Called: Catholic Chrties Svcs Ashland
34 W 2nd St Ste 18 (44805-2201)
PHONE.................................419 289-1903
EMP: 78
Web: www.catholiccharitiesusa.org
SIC: 8399 8322 Fund raising organization, non-fee basis; Child related social services
PA: Catholic Charities Corporation
  7911 Detroit Ave
  Cleveland OH 44102

(G-489)
CELLCO PARTNERSHIP
Also Called: Verizon Wireless
1441 Claremont Ave (44805-3532)
PHONE.................................419 281-1714
EMP: 71
SALES (corp-wide): 133.97B **Publicly Held**
Web: www.verizonwireless.com
SIC: 4812 Cellular telephone services
HQ: Cellco Partnership
  1 Verizon Way
  Basking Ridge NJ 07920

(G-490)
CENTERRA CO-OP (PA)
813 Clark Ave (44805-1967)
PHONE.................................419 281-2153
Jean Bratton, *CEO*
William Bullock, *
EMP: 30 **EST:** 2003
SALES (est): 174.64MM
SALES (corp-wide): 174.64MM **Privately Held**
Web: www.centerracoop.com
SIC: 5983 5261 5999 2048 Fuel oil dealers; Fertilizer; Feed and farm supply; Bird food, prepared

(G-491)
CHANDLER SYSTEMS INCORPORATED
Also Called: Best Controls Company
710 Orange St (44805-1725)
PHONE.................................888 363-9434
William Chandler III, *Pr*
Polly Chandler, *
Bill Chandler, *
▲ **EMP:** 65 **EST:** 1993
SQ FT: 52,000
SALES (est): 20.61MM **Privately Held**
Web: www.chandlersystemsinc.com
SIC: 5074 3625 Water purification equipment ; Relays and industrial controls

(G-492)
CHARLES RIVER LABS ASHLAND LLC
1407 George Rd (44805)
PHONE.................................419 282-8700
David Spaight, *CEO*
John Maxwell, *
Howard Moody, *CIO*
EMP: 670 **EST:** 2004
SALES (est): 52.82MM
SALES (corp-wide): 4.13B **Publicly Held**
Web: www.criver.com
SIC: 8731 Biotechnical research, commercial
HQ: Charles River Laboratories Sa Usa, Inc.
  251 Ballardvale St
  Wilmington MA 01887
  919 245-3114

(G-493)
CHILDRENS HOSP MED CTR AKRON
2212 Mifflin Ave (44805-8848)
PHONE.................................419 281-3077
EMP: 55
SALES (corp-wide): 1.4B **Privately Held**
Web: www.akronchildrens.org
SIC: 8062 General medical and surgical hospitals
PA: Childrens Hospital Medical Center Of Akron
  1 Perkins Sq
  Akron OH 44308
  330 543-1000

(G-494)
COMPANIONS OF ASHLAND LLC (PA)
1241 E Main St (44805-2810)
PHONE.................................419 281-2273
EMP: 42 **EST:** 2004
SALES (est): 2.64MM
SALES (corp-wide): 2.64MM **Privately Held**
Web: www.companionshealthtechcenter.com
SIC: 8082 Home health care services

(G-495)
D-R TRAINING CENTER & WORKSHOP
Also Called: DALE-ROY SCHOOL & TRAINING CEN
1256 Center St (44805-4101)
PHONE.................................419 289-0470
Ron Pagano, *Superintnt*
Jerry Simon, *
EMP: 70 **EST:** 1963
SQ FT: 5,000
SALES (est): 1.07MM **Privately Held**
Web: www.ashlandcbdd.org
SIC: 8211 8331 8361 School for retarded, nec; Sheltered workshop; Residential care

(G-496)
DELL WILLO NURSERY INC (PA)
Also Called: Willodell Nurs Grdn & Lawn Ctr
1398 Us Highway 42 (44805-9730)
PHONE.................................419 289-0606
Daniel Quinn Junior, *Pr*
Maxine Quinn, *
Susan Sale, *
EMP: 36 **EST:** 1936
SQ FT: 8,000
SALES (est): 2.08MM
SALES (corp-wide): 2.08MM **Privately Held**
Web: www.willodellnursery.com
SIC: 0782 5261 Landscape contractors; Retail nurseries

(G-497)
DONLEY FORD-LINCOLN INC (PA)
1641 Claremont Ave (44805-3536)
P.O. Box 405 (44805-0405)
PHONE.................................419 281-3673
Scott Donley, *Pr*
EMP: 45 **EST:** 1977
SQ FT: 25,000
SALES (est): 24.99MM
SALES (corp-wide): 24.99MM **Privately Held**
Web: www.donleyfordashland.net
SIC: 5511 5012 Automobiles, new and used; Automobiles and other motor vehicles

(G-498)
FIRST-KNOX NATIONAL BANK
Also Called: Farmer's and Savings Bank
1000 Sugarbush Dr (44805-9489)
PHONE.................................419 289-6137
Hal Sheaffer, *Mgr*
EMP: 30
SALES (corp-wide): 564.3MM **Publicly Held**
Web: www.parknationalbank.com
SIC: 6021 National commercial banks
HQ: The First-Knox National Bank
  1 S Main St
  Mount Vernon OH 43050
  740 399-5500

(G-499)
GOOD SHEPHERD HOME FOR AGED
Also Called: The Good Shepherd
622 Center St (44805-3343)
PHONE.................................614 228-5200
Marshall G Moore, *CEO*
Larry Crowell, *
Phil Helser, *
Henry Kassab, *
EMP: 170 **EST:** 1956
SQ FT: 82,651
SALES (est): 13.54MM **Privately Held**
Web: www.seniorlivinglss.com

GEOGRAPHIC SECTION

Ashtabula - Ashtabula County (G-521)

SIC: 8051 Convalescent home with continuous nursing care

(G-500)
GUENTHER MECHANICAL INC
1248 Middle Rowsburg Rd (44805-2813)
P.O. Box 97 (44805-0097)
PHONE.............................419 289-6900
Herbert E Guenther, *Pr*
James B Andrews, *
Jim Cutright, *
EMP: 120 **EST:** 1961
SQ FT: 35,000
SALES (est): 24.57MM **Privately Held**
Web: www.guenthermechanical.com
SIC: 1711 Mechanical contractor

(G-501)
HOSPICE NORTH CENTRAL OHIO INC (PA)
1021 Dauch Dr (44805-8845)
PHONE.............................419 281-7107
EMP: 32 **EST:** 1985
SQ FT: 6,500
SALES (est): 5.72MM **Privately Held**
Web: www.hospiceofnorthcentralohio.org
SIC: 8082 8051 8059 Home health care services; Skilled nursing care facilities; Rest home, with health care

(G-502)
HUNTINGTON NATIONAL BANK
308 Eastern Ave (44805-3262)
PHONE.............................419 281-6020
Carolyn Stoler, *Brnch Mgr*
EMP: 36
SALES (corp-wide): 10.84B **Publicly Held**
Web: www.huntington.com
SIC: 6029 6021 Commercial banks, nec; National commercial banks
HQ: The Huntington National Bank
41 S High St
Columbus OH 43215
614 480-4293

(G-503)
HUNTINGTON NATIONAL BANK
132 W Main St (44805-2103)
PHONE.............................419 281-2541
Mark Lempe, *VP*
EMP: 31
SALES (corp-wide): 10.84B **Publicly Held**
Web: www.huntington.com
SIC: 6029 Commercial banks, nec
HQ: The Huntington National Bank
41 S High St
Columbus OH 43215
614 480-4293

(G-504)
KINGSTON HEALTHCARE COMPANY
Also Called: Kingston of Ashland
20 Amberwood Pkwy (44805-9439)
PHONE.............................419 281-3859
Timothy Callahan, *Brnch Mgr*
EMP: 44
Web: www.kingstonhealthcare.com
SIC: 8051 Convalescent home with continuous nursing care
PA: Kingston Healthcare Company
1 Seagate Ste 1960
Toledo OH 43604

(G-505)
LIPPERT ENTERPRISES INC (PA)
1327 Faultless Dr (44805-1292)
PHONE.............................419 281-8084
◆ **EMP:** 35 **EST:** 1954
SALES (est): 10.36MM
SALES (corp-wide): 10.36MM **Privately Held**

Web: www.lippertent.com
SIC: 5013 5088 Truck parts and accessories; Transportation equipment and supplies

(G-506)
LUTHERAN SCIAL SVCS CENTL OHIO
Also Called: Good Shepard, The
622 Center St (44805-3343)
P.O. Box 112 (44805-0112)
PHONE.............................419 289-3523
Joe Abraham, *Mgr*
EMP: 30
SALES (corp-wide): 24.05MM **Privately Held**
Web: www.lssnetworkofhope.org
SIC: 8051 Skilled nursing care facilities
PA: Lutheran Social Services Of Central Ohio
500 W Wilson Bridge Rd
Worthington OH 43085
419 289-3523

(G-507)
MCGRAW-HILL SCHL EDCATN HLDNGS
Also Called: Mc Graw-Hill Educational Pubg
1250 George Rd (44805-8916)
PHONE.............................419 207-7400
Maryellen Valaitis, *Prin*
EMP: 750
Web: www.mheducation.com
SIC: 2731 5192 Books, publishing and printing; Books, periodicals, and newspapers
HQ: Mcgraw-Hill School Education Holdings, Llc
2 Penn Plz Fl 20
New York NY 10121
646 766-2000

(G-508)
RANDALL R LEAB
Also Called: Accessibility
1895 Township Road 1215 (44805-9414)
PHONE.............................330 689-6263
Randall R Leab, *CFO*
EMP: 45 **EST:** 2013
SALES (est): 214.78K **Privately Held**
SIC: 8399 Community development groups

(G-509)
SAMARITAN PROFESSIONAL CORP
1025 Center St (44805-4011)
PHONE.............................419 289-0491
Danny Boggs, *Pr*
EMP: 50 **EST:** 1996
SALES (est): 8.77MM **Privately Held**
Web: www.uhhospitals.org
SIC: 8062 General medical and surgical hospitals

(G-510)
SAMARITAN REGIONAL HEALTH SYS (PA)
Also Called: Peoples Hospital
1025 Center St (44805-4097)
PHONE.............................419 289-0491
Danny L Boggs, *CEO*
Mary Macdonald, *
Anne Beer, *
Matthew Bernhard, *
Mary Griest, *
EMP: 349 **EST:** 1910
SQ FT: 128,700
SALES (est): 73.97MM
SALES (corp-wide): 73.97MM **Privately Held**
Web: www.uhhospitals.org

SIC: 8062 General medical and surgical hospitals

(G-511)
SAMARITAN REGIONAL HEALTH SYS
Also Called: Samaritan Health & Rehab Ctr
2163 Claremont Ave (44805-3547)
PHONE.............................419 281-1330
Don Harris, *Dir*
EMP: 69
SALES (corp-wide): 73.97MM **Privately Held**
Web: www.uhhospitals.org
SIC: 8062 8049 General medical and surgical hospitals; Occupational therapist
PA: Samaritan Regional Health System
1025 Center St
Ashland OH 44805
419 289-0491

(G-512)
SAMARITAN REGIONAL HEALTH SYS
Also Called: Baney Rd Medical Office Bldg
1941 S Baney Rd (44805-4507)
PHONE.............................419 289-0491
Patty Krispinsky, *Brnch Mgr*
EMP: 54
SALES (corp-wide): 73.97MM **Privately Held**
Web: www.uhhospitals.org
SIC: 8062 General medical and surgical hospitals
PA: Samaritan Regional Health System
1025 Center St
Ashland OH 44805
419 289-0491

(G-513)
SUPER 8
Also Called: Super 8 Motel
736 Us Highway 250 E (44805-8930)
PHONE.............................419 529-0444
Bob Patel, *Owner*
EMP: 29 **EST:** 1998
SALES (est): 243.34K **Privately Held**
Web: www.wyndhamhotels.com
SIC: 7011 Hotels and motels

(G-514)
VALLEY TRANSPORTATION INC
Also Called: Valley Fleet
1 Valley Dr (44805)
P.O. Box 305 (44805-0305)
PHONE.............................419 289-6200
Steven Aber, *Pr*
Shawn Aber, *
Karen Aber, *
EMP: 28 **EST:** 1973
SQ FT: 20,000
SALES (est): 7.51MM **Privately Held**
Web: www.valleytransportation.net
SIC: 4212 Local trucking, without storage

(G-515)
VISITING NRSE ASSN OF CLVELAND
Also Called: Visiting Nurse Assn Ashland
1165 E Main St (44805-2831)
PHONE.............................419 281-2480
EMP: 249
SALES (corp-wide): 13.3MM **Privately Held**
Web: www.vnaohio.org
SIC: 8082 Visiting nurse service
PA: The Visiting Nurse Association Of Cleveland
925 Keynote Cir Ste 300
Brooklyn Heights OH 44131
216 931-1400

(G-516)
Y M C A OF ASHLAND OHIO INC
Also Called: YMCA
207 Miller St (44805-2484)
PHONE.............................419 289-0626
Jerry Seiter, *Ex Dir*
EMP: 55 **EST:** 1906
SQ FT: 443,000
SALES (est): 1.43MM **Privately Held**
Web: www.ashlandy.org
SIC: 8641 7991 8351 7032 Youth organizations; Physical fitness facilities; Child day care services; Youth camps

Ashtabula
Ashtabula County

(G-517)
ASHTABULA AREA CITY SCHOOL DST
Also Called: Transportation Department
5921 Gerald Rd (44004-9450)
PHONE.............................440 992-1221
Al Peck, *Prin*
EMP: 30
SALES (corp-wide): 52.74MM **Privately Held**
Web: www.aacs.net
SIC: 8211 7538 Public senior high school; General automotive repair shops
PA: Ashtabula Area City School District
6610 Sanborn Rd
Ashtabula OH 44004
440 992-1200

(G-518)
ASHTABULA CLINIC INC (PA)
2422 Lake Ave (44004-4982)
PHONE.............................440 997-6980
Morris Wasylenki Md, *Pr*
Glenn E Eippert Md, *VP*
James M Cho Md, *Sec*
Suk K Choi, *
EMP: 81 **EST:** 1969
SQ FT: 13,000
SALES (est): 9.73MM
SALES (corp-wide): 9.73MM **Privately Held**
Web: www.acmchealth.org
SIC: 8011 Clinic, operated by physicians

(G-519)
ASHTABULA CNTY CMNTY ACTION AG
6920 Austinburg Rd (44004-9393)
PHONE.............................440 997-1721
EMP: 41 **EST:** 1978
SALES (est): 11.49MM **Privately Held**
Web: www.211ashtabula.org
SIC: 8322 Social service center

(G-520)
ASHTABULA CNTY EDUCTL SVC CTR
2630 W 13th St Ste A (44004-2405)
P.O. Box 186 (44047-0186)
PHONE.............................440 576-4085
John Rubesich, *Superintnt*
EMP: 40 **EST:** 1917
SALES (est): 134.53K **Privately Held**
Web: www.ashtabulaesc.org
SIC: 8211 8748 Specialty education; Business consulting, nec

(G-521)
ASHTABULA COUNTY COMMNTY ACTN (PA)
Also Called: ACCAA
6920 Austinburg Rd (44004-9393)

Ashtabula - Ashtabula County (G-522)   GEOGRAPHIC SECTION

P.O. Box 2610 (44005-2610)
PHONE..............................440 997-1721
Richard J Pepperney, *Ex Dir*
Steve Cervas, *
Judith Barris, *
EMP: 168 **EST:** 1965
SQ FT: 17,380
SALES (est): 9.78MM
SALES (corp-wide): 9.78MM **Privately Held**
Web: www.accaa.org
SIC: 8399 Antipoverty board

(G-522)
ASHTABULA COUNTY MEDICAL CTR (PA)
2420 Lake Ave (44004-4970)
PHONE..............................440 997-2262
Michael Habowski, *CEO*
Joe Giangola, *Ch*
Bill Dingledine, *Sec*
Donal Kepner, *CFO*
EMP: 750 **EST:** 1902
SQ FT: 270,000
SALES (est): 179MM
SALES (corp-wide): 179MM **Privately Held**
Web: www.acmchealth.org
SIC: 8062 General medical and surgical hospitals

(G-523)
ASHTABULA COUNTY MEDICAL CTR
2422 Lake Ave (44004-4985)
PHONE..............................440 997-6960
EMP: 372
SALES (corp-wide): 179MM **Privately Held**
Web: www.acmchealth.org
SIC: 8062 8011 General medical and surgical hospitals; Offices and clinics of medical doctors
PA: Ashtabula County Medical Center
2420 Lake Ave
Ashtabula OH 44004
440 997-2262

(G-524)
ASHTABULA COUNTY MEDICAL CTR
2515 Lake Ave (44004-4955)
PHONE..............................440 997-6680
EMP: 373
SALES (corp-wide): 179MM **Privately Held**
Web: www.acmchealth.org
SIC: 8062 General medical and surgical hospitals
PA: Ashtabula County Medical Center
2420 Lake Ave
Ashtabula OH 44004
440 997-2262

(G-525)
ASHTABULA DENTAL ASSOC INC
Also Called: Laukhuf, Gary DDS
5005 State Rd (44004-6265)
PHONE..............................440 992-3146
William Sockman, *Pr*
Gregory Seymour D.d.s., *VP*
▲ **EMP:** 38 **EST:** 1955
SQ FT: 7,700
SALES (est): 2.07MM **Privately Held**
Web: www.ashtabuladentalonline.com
SIC: 8021 Dentists' office

(G-526)
ASHTABULA RGIONAL HM HLTH SVCS
2131 Lake Ave Ste 2 (44004-3466)
P.O. Box 1428 (44005-1428)
PHONE..............................440 992-4663

Kerry Gerken, *Pr*
EMP: 38 **EST:** 1974
SQ FT: 1,200
SALES (est): 4.02MM **Privately Held**
Web: www.acmchealth.org
SIC: 8082 Visiting nurse service

(G-527)
COMMUNITY CARE AMBLANCE NETWRK (PA)
115 E 24th St (44004)
P.O. Box 1340 (44005)
PHONE..............................440 992-1401
Julie Rose, *Ex Dir*
EMP: 75 **EST:** 1984
SQ FT: 36,000
SALES (est): 17MM
SALES (corp-wide): 17MM **Privately Held**
Web: www.ccan.org
SIC: 4119 Ambulance service

(G-528)
COMMUNITY CNSLING CTR ASHTBULA (PA)
2801 C Ct Unit 2 (44004)
PHONE..............................440 998-4210
Kathy L Regal, *CEO*
EMP: 50 **EST:** 1961
SALES (est): 7.98MM
SALES (corp-wide): 7.98MM **Privately Held**
Web: www.cccohio.com
SIC: 8093 Mental health clinic, outpatient

(G-529)
COUNTING BLESSINGS HM CARE LLC
4310 Main Ave (44004-6853)
PHONE..............................440 850-1050
Jessica Tringali, *Managing Member*
EMP: 30 **EST:** 2020
SALES (est): 591.82K **Privately Held**
Web: www.cbhomecare.info
SIC: 8082 Home health care services

(G-530)
COUNTRY CLB RETIREMENT CTR LLC
Also Called: Country Club Center III
925 E 26th St (44004-5061)
PHONE..............................440 992-0022
Gabriella Vendetti, *Mgr*
EMP: 60
SALES (corp-wide): 12.27MM **Privately Held**
Web: www.countryclubretirementcampus.com
SIC: 8051 Skilled nursing care facilities
PA: Country Club Retirement Center, Llc
55801 Conno Mara Dr
Bellaire OH 43906
740 671-9330

(G-531)
COUNTY OF ASHTABULA
Also Called: Ashtabula Cnty Chldren Svcs Bd
3914 C Ct (44004-4572)
P.O. Box 1175 (44005-1175)
PHONE..............................440 998-1811
Diane Solembrino, *Dir*
EMP: 165
SALES (corp-wide): 102.04MM **Privately Held**
Web: www.ashtabuladd.org
SIC: 8322 Child related social services
PA: County Of Ashtabula
2505 S Ridge Rd E
Ashtabula OH 44004
440 224-2155

(G-532)
DELTA RAILROAD CNSTR INC (DH)
2648 W Prospect Rd Frnt (44004-6372)
P.O. Box 1398 (44005-1398)
PHONE..............................440 992-2997
Larry F Laurello, *Pr*
Linda Laurello, *
Rick R Ryel, *
▲ **EMP:** 100 **EST:** 1957
SQ FT: 82,000
SALES (est): 41.55MM
SALES (corp-wide): 576.11MM **Privately Held**
Web: www.deltarr.com
SIC: 1629 Railroad and railway roadbed construction
HQ: Salcef Usa, Inc.
1209 N Orange St
Wilmington DE

(G-533)
DETREX CORPORATION
1100 State Rd (44004-3943)
PHONE..............................440 997-6131
Tom Steiv, *Mgr*
EMP: 29
Web: www.detrexchemicals.com
SIC: 5169 Chemicals and allied products, nec
HQ: Detrex Corporation
1000 Belt Line Ave
Cleveland OH 44109
216 749-2605

(G-534)
EAST OHIO GAS COMPANY
Also Called: Dominion Energy Ohio
7001 Center Rd (44004-8948)
PHONE..............................216 736-6120
Dave Findley, *Brnch Mgr*
EMP: 83
SALES (corp-wide): 39.69B **Privately Held**
Web: www.dominiongaschoice.com
SIC: 4924 Natural gas distribution
HQ: The East Ohio Gas Company
1201 E 55th St
Cleveland OH 44103
800 362-7557

(G-535)
FHS CARINGTON INC
Also Called: Carington Park
2217 West Ave (44004-3107)
PHONE..............................440 964-8446
Daniel Parker, *Pr*
John Krystowski, *Treas*
Ryan Kray, *Sec*
EMP: 35 **EST:** 2019
SALES (est): 13.76MM **Privately Held**
Web: www.carington-park.net
SIC: 8051 Convalescent home with continuous nursing care

(G-536)
GOODWILL INDS ASHTABULA INC (PA)
Also Called: Goodwill Industry
621 Goodwill Dr (44004-3232)
P.O. Box 2926 (44005-2926)
PHONE..............................440 964-3565
Phillip Johnston, *CEO*
Doreen Nowakowski, *
EMP: 100 **EST:** 1935
SQ FT: 35,000
SALES (est): 4.73MM
SALES (corp-wide): 4.73MM **Privately Held**
Web: www.goodwillready.org
SIC: 8331 5932 Vocational rehabilitation agency; Used merchandise stores

(G-537)
HUNTINGTON NATIONAL BANK
4366 Main Ave (44004-6801)
PHONE..............................440 992-7342
Patricia Shells, *Brnch Mgr*
EMP: 46
SALES (corp-wide): 10.84B **Publicly Held**
Web: www.huntington.com
SIC: 6029 6022 Commercial banks, nec; State commercial banks
HQ: The Huntington National Bank
41 S High St
Columbus OH 43215
614 480-4293

(G-538)
ID NETWORKS INC
7720 Jefferson Rd (44004-9025)
P.O. Box 2986 (44005-2986)
PHONE..............................440 992-0062
Douglas G Blenman, *Pr*
Bonnie Blenman, *
EMP: 31 **EST:** 1982
SALES (est): 5.95MM **Privately Held**
Web: www.idnetworks.com
SIC: 7373 Systems software development services

(G-539)
ITEN DEFENSE LLC
3500 N Ridge Rd W (44004-6370)
PHONE..............................440 990-2440
Damon Walsh, *CEO*
Grey Chapman, *
Keith Harrison, *
EMP: 57 **EST:** 2019
SALES (est): 9.12MM
SALES (corp-wide): 9.12MM **Privately Held**
Web: www.itendefense.com
SIC: 7389 Personal service agents, brokers, and bureaus
PA: Ohio Armor Holdings, Llc
3500 N Ridge Rd W
Ashtabula OH 44004
440 990-2440

(G-540)
LOWES HOME CENTERS LLC
Also Called: Lowe's
2416 Dillon Dr (44004-4102)
PHONE..............................440 998-6555
John Matras, *Mgr*
EMP: 143
SALES (corp-wide): 86.38B **Publicly Held**
Web: www.lowes.com
SIC: 5211 5031 5722 5064 Home centers; Building materials, exterior; Household appliance stores; Electrical appliances, television and radio
HQ: Lowe's Home Centers, Llc
1000 Lowes Blvd
Mooresville NC 28117
336 658-4000

(G-541)
LT HARNETT TRUCKING INC
2440 State Rd (44004-4163)
PHONE..............................440 997-5528
Chuck Hughes, *Brnch Mgr*
EMP: 48
SALES (corp-wide): 552.56MM **Privately Held**
Web: www.quantixscs.com
SIC: 4212 4213 Local trucking, without storage; Trucking, except local
HQ: L.T. Harnett Trucking, Inc.
7431 State Route 7
Kinsman OH 44428
330 876-2701

GEOGRAPHIC SECTION
Athens - Athens County (G-563)

(G-542)
NORFOLK SOUTHERN CORPORATION
Also Called: Norfolk Southern Ashtabula
Bridge Street (44004)
Rural Route 2886 (44004)
PHONE..............................440 992-2238
Pete Candela, *Mgr*
EMP: 57
SALES (corp-wide): 12.16B **Publicly Held**
Web: www.norfolksouthern.com
SIC: 4011 Railroads, line-haul operating
PA: Norfolk Southern Corporation
   650 W Peachtree St Nw
   Atlanta GA 30308
   855 667-3655

(G-543)
NORTHCOAST CONSULT LLC
5715 Nathan Ave Ste B (44004-7330)
PHONE..............................440 291-8987
Daryl Jackson, *Managing Member*
Daryl Colbert, *Managing Member**
Sal Jackson, *
EMP: 32 **EST:** 2018
SALES (est): 1.37MM **Privately Held**
SIC: 8748 Business consulting, nec

(G-544)
OUICARE RCRTMENT STFFING SVCS
1110 Lake Ave (44004-2930)
PHONE..............................440 536-4829
Ouida King, *CEO*
EMP: 32 **EST:** 2018
SALES (est): 2.12MM **Privately Held**
SIC: 7361 8059 Employment agencies; Personal care home, with health care

(G-545)
PAYNE TRUCKING CO
1635 E 6th St (44004-3721)
PHONE..............................440 998-5538
EMP: 35 **EST:** 2019
SALES (est): 954.79K **Privately Held**
Web: www.paynetrucking.com
SIC: 4212 Local trucking, without storage

(G-546)
PINNEY DOCK & TRANSPORT LLC
1149 E 5th St (44004-3513)
P.O. Box 41 (44005-0041)
PHONE..............................440 964-7186
◆ **EMP:** 57 **EST:** 1953
SQ FT: 20,000
SALES (est): 1.65MM **Publicly Held**
SIC: 3731 4491 5032 Drydocks, floating; Docks, piers and terminals; Limestone
PA: Kinder Morgan Inc
   1001 La St Ste 1000
   Houston TX 77002

(G-547)
RENTOKIL NORTH AMERICA INC
1618 W 7th St (44004-2877)
PHONE..............................440 964-5641
EMP: 33
SALES (corp-wide): 6.7B **Privately Held**
Web: www.jcehrlich.com
SIC: 0721 5999 7342 Weed control services, after planting; Pets and pet supplies; Pest control services
HQ: Rentokil North America, Inc.
   1125 Berkshire Blvd # 15
   Wyomissing PA 19610
   470 643-3300

(G-548)
SALUTARY PROVIDERS INC
Also Called: Carington Park
2217 West Ave (44004-3107)
PHONE..............................440 964-8446
EMP: 200
SALES (corp-wide): 8.32MM **Privately Held**
Web: www.carington-park.net
SIC: 8059 8052 8051 Convalescent home; Intermediate care facilities; Skilled nursing care facilities
PA: Salutary Providers Inc
   8230 Beckett Park Dr
   Hamilton OH

(G-549)
SHAWNEE OPTICAL INC
3705 State Rd (44004-5904)
PHONE..............................440 997-2020
Bob Leonardi, *Brnch Mgr*
EMP: 33
SALES (corp-wide): 1.06MM **Privately Held**
Web: www.shawneeoptical.com
SIC: 8042 5995 5049 Contact lens specialist optometrist; Optical goods stores; Optical goods
PA: Shawnee Optical Inc
   2240 E 38th St Ste 2
   Erie PA 16510
   814 824-3937

(G-550)
STAN-KELL LLC
2621 West Ave (44004-3115)
P.O. Box 429 (44005-0429)
PHONE..............................440 998-1116
Brian Lewis, *Pr*
Steve Berndt, *VP*
EMP: 30 **EST:** 1963
SQ FT: 18,450
SALES (est): 1.96MM **Privately Held**
Web: www.pencotool.com
SIC: 3544 3599 7692 Industrial molds; Machine shop, jobbing and repair; Welding repair

Ashville
Pickaway County

(G-551)
CITIZENS BANK OF ASHVILLE OHIO
Also Called: Citizens Bank
26 Main St E (43103-1512)
P.O. Box 227 (43103-0227)
PHONE..............................740 983-2511
EMP: 27 **EST:** 1894
SALES (est): 4.82MM **Privately Held**
Web: www.ashvilleohio.net
SIC: 6022 State trust companies accepting deposits, commercial

(G-552)
COUNTY OF PICKAWAY
Also Called: Dept of Human Service
16405 Us Highway 23 (43103-9610)
P.O. Box 610 (43113-0610)
PHONE..............................740 474-7588
Rojanne Woodward, *Brnch Mgr*
EMP: 32
SALES (corp-wide): 53.99MM **Privately Held**
Web: www.pickaway.org
SIC: 8322 9111 Individual and family services ; County supervisors' and executives' office
PA: County Of Pickaway
   139 W Franklin St
   Circleville OH 43113
   740 474-6093

(G-553)
NOXIOUS VEGETATION CONTROL INC
Also Called: Novco
14923 State Route 104 (43103-9411)
PHONE..............................614 486-8994
Charles W Thomas, *Pr*
Todd Thomas, *
Clarence Wissiner, *
EMP: 100 **EST:** 1960
SQ FT: 8,000
SALES (est): 8.91MM **Privately Held**
Web: www.novcoinc.com
SIC: 5191 Herbicides

Athens
Athens County

(G-554)
AFA BEAUTY INC
385 Richland Ave (45701-3206)
PHONE..............................740 331-1655
Abdaiiah Alhamayel, *Pr*
EMP: 41 **EST:** 2010
SALES (est): 199.24K **Privately Held**
SIC: 7231 Cosmetology school

(G-555)
APPALCHIAN CMNTY VSTING NRSE A
444 W Union St Ste C (45701-2340)
PHONE..............................740 594-8226
Margaret Frey, *Dir*
Deborah Sechkar, *
EMP: 35 **EST:** 1982
SQ FT: 8,000
SALES (est): 2.81MM **Privately Held**
Web: www.ohiohealth.com
SIC: 8062 General medical and surgical hospitals

(G-556)
ATHENS OH STATE 405 LLC
Also Called: Hampton Inn
986 E State St (45701-2116)
PHONE..............................740 593-5600
Sandra Bostle, *Managing Member*
EMP: 38 **EST:** 2005
SALES (est): 707.47K **Privately Held**
Web: www.hilton.com
SIC: 7011 Hotels and motels

(G-557)
ATHENS COUNTY BOARD OF DEV (PA)
801 W Union St (45701-9411)
PHONE..............................740 594-3539
Kevin Davis, *Superintnt*
EMP: 41 **EST:** 1968
SQ FT: 1,200
SALES (est): 1.01MM
SALES (corp-wide): 1.01MM **Privately Held**
Web: www.athenscbdd.org
SIC: 8322 Social services for the handicapped

(G-558)
ATHENS GOLF & COUNTRY CLUB (PA)
Also Called: ATHENS COUNTRY CLUB
7606 Country Club Rd (45701-8844)
PHONE..............................740 592-1655
Rick Oremus, *Pr*
Rick Frame, *
Mark Felcman, *
EMP: 45 **EST:** 1921
SQ FT: 5,000
SALES (est): 1.31MM
SALES (corp-wide): 1.31MM **Privately Held**
Web: www.athenscc.com
SIC: 7997 Country club, membership

(G-559)
ATHENS MOLD AND MACHINE INC
180 Mill St (45701-2627)
P.O. Box 847 (45701-0847)
PHONE..............................740 593-6613
Jack D Thornton, *Pr*
Mark Thornton, *
EMP: 81 **EST:** 1985
SQ FT: 70,000
SALES (est): 7.81MM **Privately Held**
Web: www.tiremolds.com
SIC: 3544 3599 7692 Special dies and tools; Machine shop, jobbing and repair; Welding repair

(G-560)
ATHENS SURGERY CENTER LTD
75 Hospital Dr Ste 100 (45701-2858)
PHONE..............................740 566-4504
Susan Hunter, *Admn*
EMP: 47 **EST:** 2003
SALES (est): 7.69MM **Privately Held**
Web: www.ohiohealth.com
SIC: 8011 Surgeon

(G-561)
CITY OF ATHENS
Also Called: City Garage
387 W State St (45701-1527)
PHONE..............................740 592-3343
Andy Stone, *Dir*
EMP: 29
SALES (corp-wide): 25.51MM **Privately Held**
Web: ci.athens.oh.us
SIC: 7538 7549 General automotive repair shops; Automotive maintenance services
PA: City Of Athens
   8 E Washington St Ste 101
   Athens OH 45701
   740 592-3338

(G-562)
CORPORTION FOR OHIO APPLCHIAN (PA)
Also Called: COAD
1 Pinchot Pl (45701-2135)
P.O. Box 787 (45701-0787)
PHONE..............................740 594-8499
Megan Riddlebarger, *Ex Dir*
Ronald Rees, *
Owen Yoder, *
EMP: 32 **EST:** 1971
SQ FT: 168
SALES (est): 25.67MM
SALES (corp-wide): 25.67MM **Privately Held**
Web: www.coadinc.org
SIC: 8322 Social service center

(G-563)
CVS REVCO DS INC
Also Called: CVS
555 E State St (45701-2104)
PHONE..............................740 593-8501
Al North, *Genl Mgr*
EMP: 75
SALES (corp-wide): 357.78B **Publicly Held**
Web: www.cvs.com
SIC: 5912 7384 Drug stores; Photofinishing laboratory
HQ: Cvs Revco D.S., Inc.
   1 Cvs Dr
   Woonsocket RI 02895
   401 765-1500

Athens - Athens County (G-564)   GEOGRAPHIC SECTION

(G-564)
DAVID R WHITE SERVICES INC (PA)
Also Called: Fire Place For Embers Only
5315 Hebbardsville Rd (45701-8973)
P.O. Box 250 (45701-0250)
PHONE..................................740 594-8381
Gayman Chambers, *Pr*
EMP: 38 **EST:** 1977
SQ FT: 16,000
SALES (est): 4.37MM
SALES (corp-wide): 4.37MM **Privately Held**
Web: www.davidwhiteservices.com
SIC: 1711 Warm air heating and air conditioning contractor

(G-565)
DAYS INN HTELS ATHENS CLMBUS R
Also Called: Days Inn
330 Columbus Rd (45701-1336)
PHONE..................................740 593-6655
Bob Esai, *Pr*
EMP: 39 **EST:** 1988
SALES (est): 284.34K **Privately Held**
Web: www.wyndhamhotels.com
SIC: 7011 Hotels and motels

(G-566)
DON WOOD INC
Also Called: Don Wood Bick Oldsmbile Pntiac
900 E State St (45701)
PHONE..................................740 593-6641
Don Wood, *CEO*
EMP: 45 **EST:** 1955
SQ FT: 10,000
SALES (est): 18.51MM **Privately Held**
Web: www.donwood.com
SIC: 5511 7538 Automobiles, new and used; General automotive repair shops

(G-567)
ECHOING HILLS VILLAGE INC
Also Called: Echoing Meadows
507 Richland Ave (45701-3700)
PHONE..................................740 594-3541
Mark Hutchinson, *Dir*
EMP: 65
SALES (corp-wide): 39.8MM **Privately Held**
Web: www.ehvi.org
SIC: 7032 8361 Sporting and recreational camps; Residential care
PA: Echoing Hills Village, Inc.
36272 County Road 79
Warsaw OH 43844
740 327-2311

(G-568)
G & J PEPSI-COLA BOTTLERS INC
Also Called: Pepsi-Cola
2001 E State St (45701-2125)
PHONE..................................740 593-3366
Curt Allison, *Brnch Mgr*
EMP: 44
SALES (corp-wide): 404.54MM **Privately Held**
Web: www.gjpepsi.com
SIC: 2086 5149 Carbonated soft drinks, bottled and canned; Beverages, except coffee and tea
PA: G & J Pepsi-Cola Bottlers Inc
9435 Waterstone Blvd # 300
Cincinnati OH 45249
513 785-6060

(G-569)
GOOD INC
Also Called: Good Cleaners Laundry
21 W State St (45701-2559)
P.O. Box 150 (45701-0150)
PHONE..................................740 592-9667
Peter L Good, *Pr*
Barbara Good, *
Kimberly Good-kelly, *Sec*
EMP: 64 **EST:** 1956
SQ FT: 1,500
SALES (est): 2.49MM **Privately Held**
Web: www.goodrentals.biz
SIC: 7216 7215 6514 6512 Drycleaning plants, except rugs; Laundry, coin-operated ; Residential building, four or fewer units: operation; Commercial and industrial building operation

(G-570)
HAVAR INC (PA)
396 Richland Ave (45701-3204)
P.O. Box 460 (45701-0460)
PHONE..................................740 594-3533
Debby Schmieding, *Dir*
EMP: 75 **EST:** 1972
SQ FT: 3,300
SALES (est): 4.93MM
SALES (corp-wide): 4.93MM **Privately Held**
Web: www.havar.org
SIC: 8361 8322 Residential care; Individual and family services

(G-571)
HEALTH RECOVERY SERVICES INC (PA)
224 Columbus Rd Ste 102 (45701-1350)
P.O. Box 724 (45701-0724)
PHONE..................................740 592-6720
Doctor Joe Gay, *Ex Dir*
Virgina Smith, *
EMP: 185 **EST:** 1975
SALES (est): 10.99MM
SALES (corp-wide): 10.99MM **Privately Held**
Web: www.hrs.org
SIC: 8069 8361 Alcoholism rehabilitation hospital; Rehabilitation center, residential: health care incidental

(G-572)
HOCKING VLY BNK OF ATHENS CO (HQ)
7 W Stimson Ave (45701-2649)
PHONE..................................740 592-4441
Benedict Weissenrieder, *CEO*
Tammy Bobo, *
EMP: 45 **EST:** 1963
SALES (est): 11.25MM **Privately Held**
Web: www.hvbonline.com
SIC: 6022 State trust companies accepting deposits, commercial
PA: Hocking Valley Bancshares, Inc.
7 W Stimson Ave
Athens OH 45701

(G-573)
HOCKINS ATHENS PRRY CMNTY ACTI (PA)
11100 State Route 550 (45701-8839)
PHONE..................................740 385-3644
Robert W Garbo, *Ex Dir*
EMP: 30 **EST:** 1965
SQ FT: 7,600
SALES (est): 35.22MM
SALES (corp-wide): 35.22MM **Privately Held**
Web: www.thiestalle.com
SIC: 8322 8331 Social service center; Job training and related services

(G-574)
HOLZER CLINIC LLC
2131 E State St (45701-2138)
PHONE..................................740 589-3100
EMP: 40
SALES (corp-wide): 337.52MM **Privately Held**
Web: www.holzerclinic.com
SIC: 8062 General medical and surgical hospitals
HQ: Holzer Clinic Llc
90 Jackson Pike
Gallipolis OH 45631
740 446-5411

(G-575)
HOPEWELL HEALTH CENTERS INC
Also Called: Hopewell Health Centers
90 Hospital Dr (45701-2301)
PHONE..................................740 594-5045
George Wigley, *Prin*
EMP: 90
SALES (corp-wide): 66.73MM **Privately Held**
Web: www.hopewellhealth.org
SIC: 8093 Mental health clinic, outpatient
PA: Hopewell Health Centers, Inc.
1049 Western Ave
Chillicothe OH 45601
740 773-1006

(G-576)
HOPEWELL HEALTH CENTERS INC
Also Called: Hopewell Health Centers
25 Hocking St (45701-6304)
PHONE..................................740 592-3504
J Hinton, *Pr*
EMP: 47
SALES (corp-wide): 66.73MM **Privately Held**
Web: www.hopewellhealth.org
SIC: 8093 Mental health clinic, outpatient
PA: Hopewell Health Centers, Inc.
1049 Western Ave
Chillicothe OH 45601
740 773-1006

(G-577)
HOPEWELL HEALTH CENTERS INC
Also Called: Wic Program
315 W Union St (45701-2335)
P.O. Box 702 (45701-0702)
PHONE..................................740 757-2352
Heidi Anderson, *Dir*
EMP: 35
SALES (corp-wide): 66.73MM **Privately Held**
Web: www.hopewellhealth.org
SIC: 8093 Mental health clinic, outpatient
PA: Hopewell Health Centers, Inc.
1049 Western Ave
Chillicothe OH 45601
740 773-1006

(G-578)
JOINT IMPLANT SURGEONS INC A
20 University Estates Blvd Unit 100 (45701-2967)
PHONE..................................740 566-4640
EMP: 35
SALES (corp-wide): 4.48MM **Privately Held**
Web: www.jisortho.com
SIC: 8011 Orthopedic physician
PA: Joint Implant Surgeons, Inc. A
7277 Smiths Mill Rd # 200
New Albany OH 43054
614 221-6331

(G-579)
KIMES CONVALESCENT CENTER LTD
75 Kimes Ln (45701-3899)
PHONE..................................740 593-3391
Richard Buckley, *Owner*
EMP: 67 **EST:** 1965
SALES (est): 478.77K **Privately Held**
Web: www.kimesnursingandrehab.com
SIC: 8051 Convalescent home with continuous nursing care

(G-580)
LAUGHLIN MUSIC & VENDING SVC (PA)
Also Called: Laughlin Music and Vending Svc
148 W Union St (45701-2728)
P.O. Box 547 (45701-0547)
PHONE..................................740 593-7778
Harold D Laughlin, *Pr*
Naomi Laughlin, *
Dewey Laughlin, *
EMP: 29 **EST:** 1949
SQ FT: 100,000
SALES (est): 875K
SALES (corp-wide): 875K **Privately Held**
Web: www.laughlinvending.com
SIC: 5962 5063 5087 Sandwich and hot food vending machines; Electrical apparatus and equipment; Laundry equipment and supplies

(G-581)
LAURELS OF ATHENS
70 Columbus Circle (45701-1370)
PHONE..................................740 592-1000
Shaun Genter, *Admn*
EMP: 46 **EST:** 2011
SALES (est): 11.41MM **Privately Held**
Web: www.cienahealthcare.com
SIC: 8051 Convalescent home with continuous nursing care

(G-582)
LOWES HOME CENTERS LLC
Also Called: Lowe's
983 E State St (45701-2117)
PHONE..................................740 589-3750
Dave Matter, *Prin*
EMP: 143
SALES (corp-wide): 86.38B **Publicly Held**
Web: www.lowes.com
SIC: 5211 5031 5722 5064 Home centers; Building materials, exterior; Household appliance stores; Electrical appliances, television and radio
HQ: Lowe's Home Centers, Llc
1000 Lowes Blvd
Mooresville NC 28117
336 658-4000

(G-583)
OHIO DEPT MNTAL HLTH ADDCTION
Also Called: Appalachian Bhvioral Healthcare
100 Hospital Dr (45701-2301)
PHONE..................................740 594-5000
EMP: 106
Web: www.hopewellhealth.org
SIC: 8093 9431 Mental health clinic, outpatient; Administration of public health programs, State government
HQ: Ohio Department Of Mental Health And Addiction Services
30 E Broad St Fl 36
Columbus OH 43215

(G-584)
OHIO HLTH PHYSCN GROUP HRITG C
Also Called: River Rose Obstetrics & Gyneco
75 Hospital Dr Ste 216 (45701-2859)
PHONE..................................740 594-8819
Richard F Castrop, *Managing Member*
EMP: 48 **EST:** 2004
SALES (est): 10.37MM **Privately Held**
Web: www.ohiohealth.com
SIC: 8062 General medical and surgical hospitals

(G-585)
OHIO VALLEY HOME HEALTH INC
2097 E State St Ste B1 (45701-2156)
PHONE................................740 249-4219
Summer Atkinson, *Brnch Mgr*
EMP: 46
SALES (corp-wide): 4.05MM **Privately Held**
Web: www.ohioishome.com
SIC: 8082 Home health care services
PA: Ohio Valley Home Health Inc
1480 Jackson Pike
Gallipolis OH 45631
740 441-1393

(G-586)
RADIOLOGY ASSOCIATES ATHENS
Also Called: Radiology Associates
55 Hospital Dr (45701-2302)
P.O. Box 2608 (45701-5408)
PHONE................................740 593-5551
John Murrey D.o.s., *Owner*
EMP: 29 **EST:** 1986
SALES (est): 295.87K **Privately Held**
Web: www.athensradiology.com
SIC: 8011 Radiologist

(G-587)
RVC ARCHITECTS INC
131 W State St (45701-2221)
PHONE................................740 592-5615
David C Reiser, *Pr*
John Valentour, *Treas*
David Callahan, *Sec*
EMP: 37 **EST:** 1973
SQ FT: 3,000
SALES (est): 3.11MM **Privately Held**
Web: www.rvcarchitects.com
SIC: 8712 Architectural engineering

(G-588)
SAHAJ HOSPITALITY LTD
997 E State St (45701-2117)
PHONE................................740 593-5565
EMP: 77
SALES (corp-wide): 32.59K **Privately Held**
SIC: 7011 Hotels and motels
PA: Sahaj Hospitality, Ltd.
2929 Kenny Rd
Columbus OH

(G-589)
SHELTRING ARMS HOSP FNDTION IN
Also Called: Ohiohealth O'Bleness Hospital
55 Hospital Dr (45701-2302)
PHONE................................740 592-9300
Mark Seckinger, *Pr*
Greg Long, *
Sandy Leasure, *
Larry Thornhill, *
Lynn Anastas, *
EMP: 368 **EST:** 1948
SQ FT: 127,500
SALES (est): 81.94MM
SALES (corp-wide): 4.29B **Privately Held**
Web: www.ohiohealth.com
SIC: 8062 General medical and surgical hospitals
PA: Ohiohealth Corporation
3430 Ohhalth Pkwy 5th Flr
Columbus OH 43202
614 788-8860

(G-590)
SOUTHAST OHIO SRGCAL SITES LLC
20 University Estates Blvd Ste 110 (45701-2838)
PHONE................................740 856-9044
Keith Berend, *CEO*
Keith Beren, *CEO*
EMP: 27 **EST:** 2014
SALES (est): 4.62MM
SALES (corp-wide): 20.55B **Publicly Held**
Web: www.seosurgical.com
SIC: 8062 General medical and surgical hospitals
PA: Tenet Healthcare Corporation
14201 Dallas Pkwy
Dallas TX 75254
469 893-2200

(G-591)
SOUTHSTERN OHIO VLNTARY EDCATN
Also Called: Seovec
221 Columbus Rd (45701-1335)
P.O. Box 1250 (45701-1250)
PHONE................................740 594-7663
Ronald L Smith, *CEO*
Robert L Lindsey, *OF COMPUTER SERVICES*
EMP: 50 **EST:** 1969
SQ FT: 5,500
SALES (est): 133.52K **Privately Held**
SIC: 7374 4813 Data processing and preparation; Internet connectivity services

(G-592)
SUNPOWER INC
2005 E State St Ste 104 (45701-2125)
PHONE................................740 594-2221
Jeffrey Hatfield, *VP*
EMP: 95 **EST:** 1974
SQ FT: 16,000
SALES (est): 20.87MM
SALES (corp-wide): 6.6B **Publicly Held**
Web: www.sunpowerinc.com
SIC: 8731 8711 8733 3769 Commercial physical research; Engineering services; Physical research, noncommercial; Space vehicle equipment, nec
HQ: Advanced Measurement Technology, Inc.
801 S Illinois Ave
Oak Ridge TN 37830
865 482-4411

(G-593)
TRI COUNTY MENTAL HEALTH SVCS (PA)
Also Called: TRAC
90 Hospital Dr (45701-2301)
PHONE................................740 592-3091
TOLL FREE: 888
George P Weigly Ph.d., *CEO*
George Weigly, *Ex Dir*
EMP: 95 **EST:** 1971
SALES (est): 170.87K
SALES (corp-wide): 170.87K **Privately Held**
Web: www.hopewellhealth.org
SIC: 8093 8361 8011 Mental health clinic, outpatient; Mentally handicapped home; Offices and clinics of medical doctors

(G-594)
TRI COUNTY MENTAL HEALTH SVCS
90 Hospital Dr (45701-2301)
PHONE................................740 594-5045
EMP: 109
SALES (corp-wide): 170.87K **Privately Held**
Web: www.hopewellhealth.org
SIC: 8093 Mental health clinic, outpatient
PA: Tri County Mental Health Services Inc
90 Hospital Dr
Athens OH 45701
740 592-3091

(G-595)
TS TECH AMERICAS INC
TS Tech North America
10 Kenny Dr (45701-9406)
PHONE................................740 593-5958
Bill Hass, *Mgr*
EMP: 134
Web: www.tstech.com
SIC: 5099 Child restraint seats, automotive
HQ: Ts Tech Americas, Inc.
8458 E Broad St
Reynoldsburg OH 43068
614 575-4100

(G-596)
UNITED PARCEL SERVICE INC
Also Called: UPS
1 Kenny Dr (45701-9406)
PHONE................................740 592-4570
Matthew Kazmirski, *Mgr*
EMP: 52
SALES (corp-wide): 90.96B **Publicly Held**
Web: www.ups.com
SIC: 4215 Parcel delivery, vehicular
HQ: United Parcel Service, Inc.
55 Glenlake Pkwy
Atlanta GA 30328
404 828-6000

(G-597)
UNIVERSITY MEDICAL ASSOC INC
350 Parks Hall (45701-1359)
PHONE................................740 593-0753
Scott Jenkinson, *Prin*
EMP: 85 **EST:** 2003
SALES (est): 811.52K **Privately Held**
SIC: 8062 General medical and surgical hospitals

Attica
Seneca County

(G-598)
BECK SUPPLIERS INC
15025 E. Us 224 (44807)
PHONE................................419 426-3051
Ed Willman, *Brnch Mgr*
EMP: 27
SALES (corp-wide): 89.45MM **Privately Held**
Web: www.becksuppliers.com
SIC: 5171 5541 5411 5984 Petroleum bulk stations; Filling stations, gasoline; Convenience stores; Liquefied petroleum gas dealers
PA: Beck Suppliers, Inc.
1000 N Front St
Fremont OH 43420
800 232-5645

(G-599)
CLAY DISTRIBUTING CO
15025 E Us 224 (44807)
P.O. Box 581 (44807-0581)
PHONE................................419 426-3051
Doug Beck, *Pr*
Dean Beck, *
Brian Beck, *
EMP: 133 **EST:** 1949
SALES (est): 1.63MM
SALES (corp-wide): 89.45MM **Privately Held**
SIC: 5172 Petroleum products, nec
PA: Beck Suppliers, Inc.
1000 N Front St
Fremont OH 43420
800 232-5645

(G-600)
NORTH CENTRAL ELC COOP INC
350 Stump Pike Rd (44807-9571)
P.O. Box 475 (44807-0475)
PHONE................................800 426-3072
Richard Reichert, *Pr*
Denny Schendler, *VP*
Duane E Frankard, *Treas*
Eileen Dabell, *Sec*
Markus I Bryant, *Genl Mgr*
EMP: 44 **EST:** 1936
SQ FT: 27,000
SALES (est): 30.23MM **Privately Held**
Web: www.ncelec.org
SIC: 4911 Distribution, electric power

(G-601)
R & R CHIROPRACTIC
26 N Main St (44807-9001)
PHONE................................419 425-2225
Renee Suzanne Perry, *Brnch Mgr*
EMP: 29
SIC: 8041 7299 Offices and clinics of chiropractors; Massage parlor and steam bath services
PA: R & R Chiropractic
402 Tiffin Ave
Findlay OH 45840

Atwater
Portage County

(G-602)
ZENITH SYSTEMS LLC
9627 Price St Ne (44201-9602)
PHONE................................216 406-7916
Paul Francisco, *Pr*
EMP: 340
Web: www.zenithsystems.com
SIC: 1731 Communications specialization
PA: Zenith Systems, Llc
5055 Corbin Dr
Cleveland OH 44128

Aurora
Portage County

(G-603)
ANNA MARIA OF AURORA INC (PA)
Also Called: Kensington Care Center
889 N Aurora Rd (44202-9537)
PHONE................................330 562-6171
Robert J Norton Junior, *Pr*
George Norton, *
EMP: 200 **EST:** 1964
SQ FT: 100,000
SALES (est): 24.52MM
SALES (corp-wide): 24.52MM **Privately Held**
Web: www.annamariaofaurora.com
SIC: 8051 Skilled nursing care facilities

(G-604)
ANNA MARIA OF AURORA INC
849 Rural Rd (44202)
PHONE................................330 562-3120
Robert J Norton Junior, *Pr*
EMP: 100
SALES (corp-wide): 24.52MM **Privately Held**
Web: www.annamariaofaurora.com
SIC: 8051 Skilled nursing care facilities
PA: Anna Maria Of Aurora, Inc.
889 N Aurora Rd
Aurora OH 44202
330 562-6171

Aurora - Portage County (G-605)

GEOGRAPHIC SECTION

(G-605)
AURORA HOTEL PARTNERS LLC
Also Called: Aurora Inn Hotel & Event Ctr
30 Shawnee Trl (44202-9385)
PHONE......................330 562-0767
EMP: 50
SQ FT: 42,682
SALES (est): 1.54MM **Privately Held**
Web: www.aurorainnohio.com
SIC: 7011 6513 5812 Resort hotel, franchised; Residential hotel operation; American restaurant

(G-606)
AURORA MANOR LTD PARTNERSHIP
Also Called: Aurora Mnor Spcial Care Centre
101 S Bissell Rd (44202-9170)
PHONE......................330 562-5000
Christa Mayes, *Admn*
EMP: 481 **EST:** 1990
SALES (est): 25.61MM
SALES (corp-wide): 655.44MM **Privately Held**
Web: www.saberhealth.com
SIC: 8051 8093 Convalescent home with continuous nursing care; Rehabilitation center, outpatient treatment
PA: Saber Healthcare Group, L.L.C.
23700 Commerce Park
Beachwood OH 44122
216 292-5706

(G-607)
B & I HOTEL MANAGEMENT LLC
Also Called: Bertram Inn
600 N Aurora Rd (44202-7107)
PHONE......................330 995-0200
Dale A Bradford, *Managing Member*
EMP: 150 **EST:** 2000
SALES (est): 10.47MM **Privately Held**
Web: www.thebertraminn.com
SIC: 7011 7991 5813 5812 Inns; Physical fitness facilities; Drinking places; Eating places

(G-608)
BARRINGTON GOLF CLUB INC (PA)
350 N Aurora Rd (44202-7104)
PHONE......................330 995-0600
Jack Nicklaus, *Prin*
Richard A Rosner, *
EMP: 52 **EST:** 1990
SALES (est): 4.58MM
SALES (corp-wide): 4.58MM **Privately Held**
Web: www.barringtongolfclub.com
SIC: 7997 Country club, membership

(G-609)
BARRINGTON GOLF CLUB INC
680 N Aurora Rd (44202-7107)
PHONE......................330 995-0821
EMP: 68
SALES (corp-wide): 4.58MM **Privately Held**
Web: www.barringtongolfclub.com
SIC: 7997 Country club, membership
PA: Barrington Golf Club, Inc.
350 N Aurora Rd
Aurora OH 44202
330 995-0600

(G-610)
CABI C AYDIN DDS INC
Also Called: Cabi C Aydin DDS
485 N Aurora Rd (44202-8721)
P.O. Box 624 (44202-0624)
PHONE......................330 562-1644
C Aydin Cabi D.d.s., *Pr*
EMP: 41 **EST:** 1992
SALES (est): 373.88K **Privately Held**
Web: www.cabidentist.com
SIC: 8021 Dentists' office

(G-611)
CITY OF AURORA
158 W Pioneer Trl (44202-9420)
PHONE......................330 562-8662
Ann Womer Benjamin, *Mayor*
EMP: 34
SALES (corp-wide): 28.62MM **Privately Held**
Web: www.auroraoh.com
SIC: 1611 9111 Highway and street maintenance; Executive offices, Local government
PA: City Of Aurora
130 S Chillicothe Rd
Aurora OH 44202
330 562-6131

(G-612)
EYEMED VISION
295 Westview Dr (44202-9222)
PHONE......................330 995-0597
EMP: 56 **EST:** 2014
SALES (est): 190.26K **Privately Held**
Web: www.eyemed.com
SIC: 8042 Offices and clinics of optometrists

(G-613)
GEO GLOBAL PARTNERS LLC
125 Lena Dr (44202-9202)
PHONE......................561 598-6000
EMP: 28 **EST:** 2018
SALES (est): 778.54K **Privately Held**
Web: store.ggp-us.com
SIC: 8748 Business consulting, nec

(G-614)
GEOGLOBAL PARTNERS LLC
125 Lena Dr (44202-9202)
PHONE......................561 598-6000
Daniel Owen, *
Michael Selk, *
◆ **EMP:** 53 **EST:** 2003
SALES (est): 42.75MM
SALES (corp-wide): 189.01MM **Privately Held**
Web: store.ggp-us.com
SIC: 5023 5191 Decorative home furnishings and supplies; Garden supplies
HQ: Oase Gmbh
Tecklenburger Str. 161
Horstel NW 48477

(G-615)
GODFREY & WING INC (PA)
220 Campus Dr (44202-6663)
PHONE......................330 562-1440
Alexander Alford, *CEO*
Christopher Gilmore, *
Karen Gilmore, *
Brad Welch, *
▲ **EMP:** 41 **EST:** 1947
SQ FT: 68,000
SALES (est): 19.38MM
SALES (corp-wide): 19.38MM **Privately Held**
Web: www.godfreywing.com
SIC: 3479 8734 Coating of metals with plastic or resins; Testing laboratories

(G-616)
MARC GLASSMAN INC
Also Called: Marc's 45
300 Aurora Commons Cir (44202-8828)
PHONE......................330 995-9246
EMP: 109
SALES (corp-wide): 1.03B **Privately Held**
Web: www.marcs.com
SIC: 5331 7384 5912 Variety stores; Photofinish laboratories; Drug stores and proprietary stores
PA: Marc Glassman, Inc.
5841 W 130th St
Cleveland OH 44130
216 265-7700

(G-617)
MCMASTER-CARR SUPPLY COMPANY
200 Aurora Industrial Pkwy (44202-8090)
P.O. Box 94930 (44101-4930)
PHONE......................330 995-5500
Steve Lloyd, *Mgr*
EMP: 675
SALES (corp-wide): 621.02MM **Privately Held**
Web: www.mcmaster.com
SIC: 5085 Industrial supplies
PA: Mcmaster-Carr Supply Company
600 N County Line Rd
Elmhurst IL 60126
630 834-9600

(G-618)
MILL DISTRIBUTORS INC
45 Aurora Industrial Pkwy (44202-8088)
PHONE......................330 995-9200
Thomas H Wieder, *Pr*
Douglas M Wieder, *
◆ **EMP:** 53 **EST:** 1926
SQ FT: 40,000
SALES (est): 24.27MM **Privately Held**
Web: www.milldist.com
SIC: 5023 5021 Blankets; Furniture

(G-619)
NATIONAL BIOCHEMICALS LLC
220 Lena Dr (44202-9244)
PHONE......................330 425-2522
▲ **EMP:** 36
SIC: 5169 Chemicals and allied products, nec

(G-620)
PARTSSOURCE INC
777 Lena Dr (44202-8025)
PHONE......................330 562-9900
Philip Settimi, *Pr*
Mark Tomasetti, *
Patrick Blake, *
Mike Maguire, *Senior Vice President Cash*
Guy Mansueto, *CMO*
EMP: 210 **EST:** 2001
SQ FT: 75,000
SALES (est): 162.75MM
SALES (corp-wide): 1.8MM **Privately Held**
Web: www.partssource.com
SIC: 5047 Medical equipment and supplies
HQ: Bain Capital Private Equity, Lp
200 Clarendon St
Boston MA 02116

(G-621)
PREMIUM OUTLET PARTNERS LP
Aurora Farms Market
549 S Chillicothe Rd Ste 185 (44202-8800)
PHONE......................330 562-2000
Claude Hopkins, *Mgr*
EMP: 96
Web: www.simon.com
SIC: 6512 Shopping center, property operation only
HQ: Premium Outlet Partners, L.P.
225 W Washington St
Indianapolis IN 46204

(G-622)
PROGRESSIVE AURORA LLC
Also Called: Avenue At Aurora
425 S Chillicothe Rd (44202-6548)
PHONE......................330 995-0094
Eitan Flank, *Managing Member*
EMP: 27 **EST:** 2011
SALES (est): 8.63MM **Privately Held**
Web: www.avenueataurora.com
SIC: 8051 Skilled nursing care facilities

(G-623)
R & G NURSING CARE INC
Also Called: Kensington At Anna Maria
849 N Aurora Rd (44202-9537)
PHONE......................330 562-3120
Robert Norton, *Pr*
Aaron Baker, *
Christopher Norton, *
EMP: 150 **EST:** 1992
SALES (est): 3.64MM **Privately Held**
SIC: 8052 Intermediate care facilities

(G-624)
ROBECK FLUID POWER CO
Also Called: Robeck
350 Lena Dr (44202-8098)
PHONE......................330 562-1140
Peter Becker, *Pr*
Ken Traeger, *
Ida Becker, *
▲ **EMP:** 65 **EST:** 1983
SQ FT: 6,000
SALES (est): 26.14MM **Privately Held**
Web: www.robeckfluidpower.com
SIC: 5084 3593 3594 3494 Hydraulic systems equipment and supplies; Fluid power cylinders and actuators; Fluid power pumps and motors; Valves and pipe fittings, nec

(G-625)
ROBINSON HEALTH SYSTEM INC
Also Called: Robinson Health Affiliates
700 Walden Pl (44202-7548)
PHONE......................330 562-3169
Jane Davis, *Mgr*
EMP: 3542
SALES (corp-wide): 878.24MM **Privately Held**
Web: www.robinsonmemorial.org
SIC: 8062 8011 8031 General medical and surgical hospitals; General and family practice, physician/surgeon; Offices and clinics of osteopathic physicians
HQ: Robinson Health System, Inc.
6847 N Chestnut St
Ravenna OH 44266
330 297-0811

(G-626)
ROVISYS COMPANY (PA)
1455 Danner Dr (44202-9273)
PHONE......................330 562-8600
John W Robertson, *
Pete Madonia, *CFO*
Joel Spafford, *
EMP: 67 **EST:** 1989
SQ FT: 35,000
SALES (est): 115.17MM **Privately Held**
Web: www.rovisys.com
SIC: 7373 Computer integrated systems design

(G-627)
RP GATTA INC
435 Gentry Dr (44202-7538)
PHONE......................330 562-2288
Raymond Gatta, *Pr*
Raymond P Gatta, *
Katherine E Gatta, *

▲ = Import ▼ = Export
◆ = Import/Export

GEOGRAPHIC SECTION

◆ **EMP:** 71 **EST:** 1985
SQ FT: 28,000
SALES (est): 9.51MM **Privately Held**
Web: www.rpgatta.com
SIC: 5084 Industrial machinery and equipment

(G-628)
TECHNICAL CONSUMER PDTS INC
Also Called: T C P
325 Campus Dr (44202)
PHONE.................................330 995-6111
Ellis Yan, *CEO*
Naiqi Zhao, *Senior Vice President Information Technology**
Jim Connolly, *Senior Vice President Global Retail**
Bill Tortora Senior, *Coll Vice President*
◆ **EMP:** 385 **EST:** 1993
SQ FT: 159,000
SALES (est): 216.38MM **Privately Held**
Web: www.tcpi.com
SIC: 5063 Lighting fittings and accessories
HQ: Quality Light Source Gmbh
C/O Sibla Services Ag
Zug ZG 6300

(G-629)
WALDEN CLUB
1119 Aurora Hudson Rd (44202-7512)
PHONE.................................330 995-7162
Manuel Barenholtz, *Pr*
EMP: 40 **EST:** 1969
SQ FT: 10,000
SALES (est): 661.55K **Privately Held**
Web: www.yourwalden.com
SIC: 7997 5941 5812 Golf club, membership; Golf goods and equipment; Eating places

(G-630)
WATERWAY GAS & WASH COMPANY
Also Called: BP
7010 N Aurora Rd (44202-9626)
PHONE.................................330 995-2900
Shayne Roche, *Genl Mgr*
EMP: 37
SALES (corp-wide): 381.21MM **Privately Held**
Web: www.waterway.com
SIC: 7542 Washing and polishing, automotive
PA: Waterway Gas & Wash Company
727 Goddard Ave
Chesterfield MO 63005
636 537-1111

(G-631)
WS ONE INVESTMENT USA LLC (PA)
Also Called: Ws1
1263 S Chillicothe Rd (44202-8002)
PHONE.................................855 895-3728
Shiraz Khan, *Pr*
EMP: 100 **EST:** 2015
SALES (est): 9.75MM
SALES (corp-wide): 9.75MM **Privately Held**
Web: www.ws1.com
SIC: 6799 Investors, nec

Austinburg
Ashtabula County

(G-632)
NASSIEF AUTOMOTIVE INC
Also Called: Nassief Honda
2920 Gh Dr (44010-9793)
PHONE.................................440 997-5151
George Nassief, *CEO*
Todd Nassief, *
Helen Nassief, *
Ann Nassief, *
EMP: 31 **EST:** 1938
SQ FT: 10,000
SALES (est): 2.44MM **Privately Held**
Web: www.victory440.com
SIC: 5511 7538 Automobiles, new and used; General automotive repair shops

(G-633)
PIKES INC
Also Called: Hampton Inn
2900 Gh Dr # H (44010-9793)
PHONE.................................440 275-2000
EMP: 37 **EST:** 1996
SALES (est): 398.1K **Privately Held**
Web: www.hilton.com
SIC: 7011 Hotels and motels

(G-634)
UNITED PARCEL SERVICE INC
Also Called: UPS
1553 State Route 45 (44010-9749)
PHONE.................................440 275-3301
Carol Bianchi, *Mgr*
EMP: 31
SALES (corp-wide): 90.96B **Publicly Held**
Web: www.ups.com
SIC: 4215 Parcel delivery, vehicular
HQ: United Parcel Service, Inc.
55 Glenlake Pkwy
Atlanta GA 30328
404 828-6000

Austintown
Mahoning County

(G-635)
ALL STAR MGMT INC
Also Called: Comfort Inn
5425 Clarkins Dr (44515-1120)
PHONE.................................330 792-9740
Mitesh Kalthia, *Prin*
EMP: 29 **EST:** 2006
SALES (est): 203.27K **Privately Held**
Web: www.choicehotels.com
SIC: 7011 Hotels and motels

(G-636)
RHIEL SUPPLY CO (PA)
Also Called: Rhiel Supply Co, The
3735 Oakwood Ave (44515-3050)
PHONE.................................330 799-7777
Toby Mirto, *VP*
Daniel F Mirto, *
J D Mirto, *
EMP: 27 **EST:** 1950
SQ FT: 30,000
SALES (est): 7.53MM
SALES (corp-wide): 7.53MM **Privately Held**
Web: www.rhiel.com
SIC: 5087 5169 Janitors' supplies; Swimming pool and spa chemicals

(G-637)
XALOY LLC (PA)
375 Victoria Rd Ste 1 (44515-2053)
PHONE.................................330 726-4000
Kamal K Tiwari, *CEO*
Keith Young, *
◆ **EMP:** 190 **EST:** 2021
SALES (est): 106.67MM
SALES (corp-wide): 106.67MM **Privately Held**
Web: www.xaloy.com
SIC: 3089 8711 Automotive parts, plastic; Engineering services

Avon
Lorain County

(G-638)
AVON HERITAGE BOOSTERS
37545 Detroit Rd (44011-2133)
PHONE.................................440 934-5111
EMP: 41 **EST:** 2011
SALES (est): 130.63K **Privately Held**
SIC: 8641 Booster club

(G-639)
AVON-OAKS COUNTRY CLUB
32300 Detroit Rd (44011-2097)
PHONE.................................440 892-0660
Judd Stevenson, *Dir*
EMP: 65 **EST:** 1959
SQ FT: 30,000
SALES (est): 4.98MM **Privately Held**
Web: www.avonoakscc.com
SIC: 7997 Country club, membership

(G-640)
BENDIX COML VHCL SYSTEMS LLC (DH)
Also Called: Bendix
35500 Chester Rd (44011)
P.O. Box 4016 (44035)
PHONE.................................440 329-9000
Piotr Sroka, *Pr*
Piotr Sroka, *Pr*
Carlos Hungria, *
Dave Kralic, *
◆ **EMP:** 350 **EST:** 2001
SALES (est): 997.21MM
SALES (corp-wide): 2.67MM **Privately Held**
Web: www.bendix.com
SIC: 3714 5013 5088 Motor vehicle brake systems and parts; Automotive supplies and parts; Combat vehicles
HQ: Knorr-Bremse Ag
Moosacher Str. 80
Munchen BY 80809
8935470

(G-641)
BRIMAR PACKAGING INC
37520 Colorado Ave (44011-1534)
PHONE.................................440 934-3080
EMP: 40 **EST:** 1992
SALES (est): 2.57MM **Privately Held**
Web: www.brimarpackaging.com
SIC: 2449 2653 5085 2657 Wood containers, nec; Boxes, corrugated: made from purchased materials; Commercial containers; Folding paperboard boxes

(G-642)
CENTER CLEANING SERVICES INC
34100 Mills Rd (44011-2472)
P.O. Box 39035 (44039-0035)
PHONE.................................440 327-5099
Shawn Mueller, *Pr*
EMP: 100 **EST:** 1982
SALES (est): 1.18MM **Privately Held**
Web: www.perfectdomain.com
SIC: 7349 Cleaning service, industrial or commercial

(G-643)
CHAMBRLAIN HRDLCKA WHITE WLLAM
36368 Detroit Rd Ste A (44011-2843)
PHONE.................................216 589-9280
Henry Chamberlain, *Brnch Mgr*
EMP: 61
SALES (corp-wide): 46.57MM **Privately Held**
Web: www.chamberlainlaw.com
SIC: 8111 General practice attorney, lawyer
PA: Chamberlain, Hrdlicka, White, Williams & Aughtry, P.C.
1200 Smith St
Houston TX 77002
713 658-1818

(G-644)
CHEMTRON CORPORATION (PA)
Also Called: Chemtron
35850 Schneider Ct (44011-1298)
PHONE.................................440 937-6348
TOLL FREE: 800
Andrew Kuhar, *Pr*
Michael Guenther, *
EMP: 43 **EST:** 1964
SQ FT: 16,500
SALES (est): 21.28MM
SALES (corp-wide): 21.28MM **Privately Held**
Web: www.chemtron-corp.com
SIC: 4953 4959 Recycling, waste materials; Environmental cleanup services

(G-645)
CLEVELAND CLINIC AVON HOSPITAL
33300 Cleveland Clinic Blvd (44011-1172)
PHONE.................................440 695-5000
EMP: 99 **EST:** 2016
SQ FT: 212,000
SALES (est): 166.22MM
SALES (corp-wide): 14.48B **Privately Held**
Web: www.ccf.org
SIC: 8062 General medical and surgical hospitals
PA: The Cleveland Clinic Foundation
9500 Euclid Ave
Cleveland OH 44195
216 636-8335

(G-646)
CLEVELAND CLINIC FNDTN-CARDIO
33100 Cleveland Clinic Blvd (44011-1390)
PHONE.................................440 695-4000
Brian Thomas, *Admn*
EMP: 36 **EST:** 2014
SALES (est): 48.54MM **Privately Held**
Web: www.clevelandclinic.org
SIC: 8099 Health and allied services, nec

(G-647)
CLEVELAND CLINIC FOUNDATION
33355 Health Campus Blvd (44011-1399)
PHONE.................................440 937-9099
EMP: 41
SALES (corp-wide): 14.48B **Privately Held**
Web: my.clevelandclinic.org
SIC: 8062 General medical and surgical hospitals
PA: The Cleveland Clinic Foundation
9500 Euclid Ave
Cleveland OH 44195
216 636-8335

(G-648)
COCHIN TECHNOLOGIES LLC
Also Called: Delight Connection
37854 Briar Lakes Dr (44011-3105)
PHONE.................................440 941-4856
Robin Roy, *Prin*
EMP: 50 **EST:** 2010
SALES (est): 1.38MM **Privately Held**
Web: www.cochintechnologies.com
SIC: 7371 Computer software development

(G-649)
DENTALONE PARTNERS INC
Also Called: Dentalworks
36050 Detroit Rd (44011-1683)

Avon - Lorain County (G-650)

PHONE..............................440 934-0147
EMP: 107
SALES (corp-wide): 85.13MM **Privately Held**
Web: www.dentalworks.com
SIC: 8021 Dental clinic
PA: Dentalone Partners, Inc.
  6700 Pinecrest Dr Ste 150
  Plano TX 75024
  972 755-0800

(G-650)
EMH REGIONAL MEDICAL CENTER
Also Called: Fitness Center
1997 Healthway Dr (44011-2834)
PHONE..............................440 988-6800
Sabarras George, *Mgr*
EMP: 95
SALES (corp-wide): 878.24MM **Privately Held**
Web: www.uhhospitals.org
SIC: 8062 7991 Hospital, affiliated with AMA residency; Physical fitness facilities
HQ: Emh Regional Medical Center
  630 E River St
  Elyria OH 44035
  440 329-7500

(G-651)
FREEMAN MANUFACTURING & SUP CO (PA)
1101 Moore Rd (44011-4043)
PHONE..............................440 934-1902
Lou Turco, *Pr*
Gerald W Rusk, *Ch Bd*
EMP: 50 **EST:** 1942
SQ FT: 110,000
SALES (est): 50.71MM
SALES (corp-wide): 50.71MM **Privately Held**
Web: www.freemansupply.com
SIC: 5084 3087 3543 2821 Industrial machinery and equipment; Custom compound purchased resins; Industrial patterns; Plastics materials and resins

(G-652)
GREAT LAKES COMPUTER CORP
33675 Lear Industrial Pkwy (44011-1370)
PHONE..............................440 937-1100
Jim Manco, *CEO*
Robert Martin, *
EMP: 60 **EST:** 1980
SQ FT: 20,000
SALES (est): 5.35MM **Privately Held**
Web: www.greatlakescomputer.com
SIC: 7378 5734 Computer peripheral equipment repair and maintenance; Computer and software stores

(G-653)
HEALTHSOURCE CHIROPRACTIC INC
36901 American Way Ste 7 (44011-4058)
PHONE..............................440 934-5858
Chris Tomshack, *CEO*
EMP: 47 **EST:** 2005
SALES (est): 4.06MM **Privately Held**
Web: www.healthsourcechiro.com
SIC: 8041 Offices and clinics of chiropractors

(G-654)
HOME DEPOT USA INC
Also Called: Home Depot, The
35930 Detroit Rd (44011)
PHONE..............................440 937-2240
Ronald W Salazar, *Mgr*
EMP: 110
SALES (corp-wide): 152.67B **Publicly Held**
Web: www.homedepot.com
SIC: 5211 7359 Home centers; Tool rental
HQ: Home Depot U.S.A., Inc.
  2445 Springfield Ave
  Vauxhall NJ 07088

(G-655)
HUNTINGTON NATIONAL BANK
Also Called: Avon Branch
2085 Center Rd (44011-1824)
PHONE..............................440 937-5545
Dennis Nakoneczny, *Pr*
EMP: 31
SALES (corp-wide): 10.84B **Publicly Held**
Web: www.huntington.com
SIC: 6029 Commercial banks, nec
HQ: The Huntington National Bank
  41 S High St
  Columbus OH 43215
  614 480-4293

(G-656)
JENNE INC
Also Called: Jenne
33665 Chester Rd (44011-1307)
PHONE..............................440 835-0040
Rose Jenne, *Ch*
Dave Johnson, *Vice Chairman**
Ray Jenne Junior, *Prin*
Dean Jenne, *
▲ **EMP:** 207 **EST:** 1986
SQ FT: 126,000
SALES (est): 51.45MM **Privately Held**
Web: www.jenne.com
SIC: 7371 7382 Software programming applications; Security systems services

(G-657)
JLW - TW CORP
Also Called: Suntan Supply
35350 Chester Rd (44011-1255)
PHONE..............................440 937-7775
William Gallagherr, *Pr*
William Gallagher, *
Martin F Gallagher, *
EMP: 50 **EST:** 2007
SALES (est): 8.86MM **Privately Held**
Web: www.suntansupply.org
SIC: 5047 Medical and hospital equipment

(G-658)
KAISER FOUNDATION HOSPITALS
Also Called: Avon Medical Offices
36711 American Way (44011-4062)
PHONE..............................216 524-7377
EMP: 29
SALES (corp-wide): 70.8B **Privately Held**
Web: www.kaisercenter.com
SIC: 8011 Medical centers
HQ: Kaiser Foundation Hospitals Inc
  1 Kaiser Plz
  Oakland CA 94612
  510 271-6611

(G-659)
KMU TRUCKING & EXCVTG LLC
4436 Center Rd (44011-2369)
PHONE..............................440 934-1008
Kevin Urig, *Pr*
Lorie Urig, *
Keith Urig, *
EMP: 30 **EST:** 1992
SALES (est): 9.63MM **Privately Held**
Web: www.kmuexcavating.com
SIC: 1794 4212 Excavation and grading, building construction; Local trucking, without storage

(G-660)
LOWES HOME CENTERS LLC
Also Called: Lowe's
1445 Center Rd (44011-1238)
PHONE..............................440 937-3500
Greg Fillar, *Mgr*
EMP: 138
SALES (corp-wide): 86.38B **Publicly Held**
Web: www.lowes.com
SIC: 5211 5031 5722 5064 Home centers; Building materials, exterior; Household appliance stores; Electrical appliances, television and radio
HQ: Lowe's Home Centers, Llc
  1000 Lowes Blvd
  Mooresville NC 28117
  336 658-4000

(G-661)
MEDICAL DIAGNOSTIC LAB INC (PA)
Also Called: Premier Physican Centers
36711 American Way Ste 2a (44011-4061)
P.O. Box 74692 (44194-0775)
PHONE..............................440 333-1375
M Sowden, *Mgr*
EMP: 30 **EST:** 1995
SALES (est): 16.85MM
SALES (corp-wide): 16.85MM **Privately Held**
Web: www.premierphysicians.net
SIC: 8011 8071 General and family practice, physician/surgeon; Testing laboratories

(G-662)
NORTH COAST BEARINGS LLC
Also Called: After Market Products
1141 Jaycox Rd (44011)
PHONE..............................440 930-7600
William Hagy, *Pr*
▲ **EMP:** 50 **EST:** 1983
SALES (est): 22.84MM **Privately Held**
Web: www.dtcomponents.com
SIC: 5085 Bearings

(G-663)
R & J INVESTMENT CO INC
Also Called: Avon Oaks Nursing Home
37800 French Creek Rd (44011-1763)
PHONE..............................440 934-5204
Joan E Reidy, *Pr*
Richard J Reidy, *
Juliette Reidy, *
EMP: 130 **EST:** 1965
SQ FT: 75,000
SALES (est): 9.27MM **Privately Held**
Web: www.avonoaks.net
SIC: 8051 8351 Convalescent home with continuous nursing care; Child day care services

(G-664)
ROCK PILE INC
900 Nagel Rd (44011-1325)
PHONE..............................440 937-5100
TOLL FREE: 800
Brian Mc Keown, *Pr*
Jennifer Mc Keown, *Sec*
Erin Mc Keown, *Treas*
Mary Mc Keown, *VP*
EMP: 30 **EST:** 1986
SQ FT: 44,000
SALES (est): 2.44MM **Privately Held**
Web: www.therockpile.com
SIC: 5261 5083 Lawn and garden supplies; Landscaping equipment

(G-665)
STACK HEATING AND COOLING LLC
Also Called: Stack Heating Cooling & Elc
37520 Colorado Ave (44011-1587)
PHONE..............................440 937-9134
Andy Stack, *CEO*
Andy Stack, *Prin*
Brian Stack, *
EMP: 60 **EST:** 1989
SALES (est): 9.82MM **Privately Held**
Web: www.stackheating.com
SIC: 1711 Warm air heating and air conditioning contractor

(G-666)
TRI-TECH MEDICAL INC
Also Called: Tri-Tech Pipeline
35401 Avon Commerce Pkwy (44011-1374)
PHONE..............................800 253-8692
Don L Daviess, *CEO*
Donald M Simo, *
James L Lucas, *
Russell J Godfrey, *
◆ **EMP:** 40 **EST:** 1989
SQ FT: 26,500
SALES (est): 9.44MM **Privately Held**
Web: www.tri-techmedical.com
SIC: 5047 Medical equipment and supplies

(G-667)
WHITTGUARD SECURITY SVCS INC
37435 Colorado Ave (44011-1531)
PHONE..............................440 288-7233
James Whitt, *Owner*
EMP: 130 **EST:** 2004
SQ FT: 3,000
SALES (est): 4.79MM **Privately Held**
Web: www.whittguard.com
SIC: 7381 Security guard service

(G-668)
WICKENS HERZER PANZA CO
35765 Chester Rd (44011-1262)
PHONE..............................440 695-8000
David L Herzer, *Pr*
EMP: 98 **EST:** 1976
SQ FT: 30,000
SALES (est): 15.65MM **Privately Held**
Web: www.wickenslaw.com
SIC: 8111 General practice law office

(G-669)
WILLOWAY NURSERIES INC (PA)
4534 Center Rd (44011-2368)
P.O. Box 299 (44011-0299)
PHONE..............................440 934-4435
Tom Demaline, *Pr*
Cathy Kowalczyk, *
▲ **EMP:** 148 **EST:** 1953
SQ FT: 5,000
SALES (est): 28.86MM
SALES (corp-wide): 28.86MM **Privately Held**
Web: www.willowaynurseries.com
SIC: 0181 Shrubberies, grown in field nurseries

Avon Lake
Lorain County

(G-670)
ALUMALLOY METALCASTING COMPANY
33665 Walker Rd (44012-1044)
PHONE..............................440 930-2222
Dennis Daniels, *Pr*
Chris Daniels, *
EMP: 65 **EST:** 1981
SQ FT: 11,000
SALES (est): 23.8MM **Privately Held**
Web: www.alumalloymetalcasting.com
SIC: 5051 Steel

(G-671)
APPLIED SPECIALTIES INC
Also Called: Asi Chemical Company
33555 Pin Oak Pkwy (44012-2319)
P.O. Box 307 (44012-0307)

GEOGRAPHIC SECTION

PHONE...............................440 933-9442
◆ **EMP:** 30 **EST:** 1981
SALES (est): 8.46M **Privately Held**
Web: www.appliedspecialties.com
SIC: 2899 8742 Water treating compounds; Industry specialist consultants

(G-672)
AVIENT CORPORATION (PA)
Also Called: Avient
33587 Walker Rd (44012)
PHONE...............................440 930-1000
Robert M Patterson, *Ch Bd*
Jamie A Beggs, *Sr VP*
Lisa K Kunkle, *Sr VP*
Joao Jose San Martin Neto, *Chief Human Resource Officer*
Joel R Rathbun, *Sr VP*
◆ **EMP:** 73 **EST:** 1885
SALES (est): 3.14B **Publicly Held**
Web: www.avient.com
SIC: 2821 3087 5162 3081 Thermoplastic materials; Custom compound purchased resins; Resins; Unsupported plastics film and sheet

(G-673)
AVON LAKE SHEET METAL CO
33574 Pin Oak Pkwy (44012-2320)
P.O. Box 64 (44012-0064)
PHONE...............................440 933-3505
Carl Wetzig Junior, *Pr*
Gary Wightman, *
EMP: 38 **EST:** 1953
SQ FT: 32,000
SALES (est): 8.06MM **Privately Held**
Web: www.avonlakesheetmetal.com
SIC: 3444 1761 Sheet metalwork; Sheet metal work, nec

(G-674)
AVON LAKE VET HOLDINGS INC
Also Called: Avon Lake Animal Care Center
124 Miller Rd (44012-1015)
PHONE...............................440 933-5297
James Haddad, *Pr*
John H Simpson D.v.m., *Prin*
EMP: 45 **EST:** 1956
SQ FT: 2,000
SALES (est): 2.56MM **Privately Held**
Web: www.avonlakeanimalclinic.com
SIC: 0742 0752 Animal hospital services, pets and other animal specialties; Grooming services, pet and animal specialties

(G-675)
BEARING TECHNOLOGIES LTD (PA)
Also Called: Coast To Coast
33554 Pin Oak Pkwy (44012-2320)
PHONE...............................800 597-3486
Laz Tromler, *CEO*
Jeff Hrehocik, *
▲ **EMP:** 60 **EST:** 1997
SQ FT: 230,000
SALES (est): 23.91MM
SALES (corp-wide): 23.91MM **Privately Held**
Web: www.brgtec.com
SIC: 5085 Bearings

(G-676)
CITY OF AVON LAKE
Also Called: Water & Sewer Department
201 Miller Rd (44012-1004)
PHONE...............................440 933-6226
EMP: 36
SALES (corp-wide): 27.67MM **Privately Held**
Web: www.avonlakewater.org

SIC: 4941 4952 Water supply; Sewerage systems
PA: City Of Avon Lake
150 Avon Belden Rd
Avon Lake OH 44012
440 933-6141

(G-677)
ED TOMKO CHRYSLER JEEP DDGE IN
Also Called: Ed Tomko
33725 Walker Rd (44012-1010)
PHONE...............................440 835-5900
Edward P Tomko, *Pr*
Dolores Tomko, *
Paul E Tomko, *
EMP: 29 **EST:** 1977
SQ FT: 8,000
SALES (est): 6.87MM **Privately Held**
Web: www.edtomkochryslerjeepdodge.com
SIC: 5511 7538 7515 5012 Automobiles, new and used; General automotive repair shops; Passenger car leasing; Automobiles and other motor vehicles

(G-678)
ELECTRA SOUND INC (PA)
Also Called: Electrasound TV & Appl Svc
32483 English Turn (44012-3321)
PHONE...............................216 433-9600
TOLL FREE: 800
Robert C Masa Junior, *CEO*
Patricia Masa, *
Charles C Masa, *
EMP: 70 **EST:** 1968
SALES (est): 12.2MM
SALES (corp-wide): 12.2MM **Privately Held**
Web: www.techni-car.com
SIC: 3694 7622 5065 5731 Automotive electrical equipment, nec; Television repair shop; Sound equipment, electronic; Automotive sound equipment

(G-679)
GENTRY HEALTH SERVICES INC (PA)
33381 Walker Rd Ste A (44012-1456)
PHONE...............................330 721-1077
Timothy Johnson, *Pr*
EMP: 58 **EST:** 2014
SALES (est): 497.8MM
SALES (corp-wide): 497.8MM **Privately Held**
Web: www.gentryhealthservices.com
SIC: 8052 Home for the mentally retarded, with health care

(G-680)
KOPF CONSTRUCTION CORPORATION (PA)
420 Avon Belden Rd Ste A (44012-2294)
PHONE...............................440 933-6908
Herman R Kopf Junior, *Pr*
EMP: 99 **EST:** 1965
SQ FT: 1,609
SALES (est): 9.95MM
SALES (corp-wide): 9.95MM **Privately Held**
SIC: 1521 1522 New construction, single-family houses; Multi-family dwelling construction, nec

(G-681)
MT BUSINESS TECHNOLOGIES INC
Also Called: Mt Business Technologies
33588 Pin Oak Pkwy (44012-2320)
PHONE...............................440 933-7682
Donald Cole, *Mgr*
EMP: 165

SALES (corp-wide): 6.89B **Publicly Held**
Web: www.mtbt.com
SIC: 5044 Office equipment
HQ: Mt Business Technologies, Inc.
1150 National Pkwy
Mansfield OH 44906
419 529-6100

(G-682)
OPTUMRX HOME DELIVERY OHIO LLC
Also Called: Ips
33381 Walker Rd (44012-1456)
PHONE...............................440 930-5520
Douglas Boodjeh, *Ch*
Thomas Mc Connell, *
EMP: 61 **EST:** 1985
SALES (est): 3.48MM
SALES (corp-wide): 371.62B **Publicly Held**
Web: www.catamaranhomedelivery.com
SIC: 5961 5122 Pharmaceuticals, mail order; Drugs, proprietaries, and sundries
HQ: Optumrx Health Solutions, Llc
800 King Farm Blvd # 400
Rockville MD 20850

(G-683)
PHOENIX ADMINISTRATORS LLC
Also Called: Performance Health
33479 Lake Rd (44012)
PHONE...............................440 628-4235
Todd Houston, *Pr*
Jeannette Hobson, *
EMP: 48 **EST:** 2015
SALES (est): 2.41MM **Privately Held**
SIC: 8741 Administrative management

(G-684)
WATTEREDGE LLC (DH)
Also Called: Watteredge
567 Miller Rd (44012-2304)
PHONE...............................440 933-6110
Joseph P Langhenry, *Pr*
◆ **EMP:** 64 **EST:** 1970
SQ FT: 65,000
SALES (est): 25.11MM
SALES (corp-wide): 1.7B **Privately Held**
Web: www.watteredge.com
SIC: 5085 3643 5051 3052 Industrial supplies; Current-carrying wiring services; Metals service centers and offices; Rubber and plastics hose and beltings
HQ: Coleman Cable, Llc
1 Overlook Pt
Lincolnshire IL 60069
847 672-2300

Bainbridge
Ross County

(G-685)
LIGHTHOUSE YOUTH SERVICES INC
Also Called: Paint Creek Youth Center
1071 Tong Hollow Rd (45612-1500)
P.O. Box 586 (45612-0586)
PHONE...............................740 634-3094
Renee Hagan, *Dir*
EMP: 41
SALES (corp-wide): 30.45MM **Privately Held**
Web: www.lys.org
SIC: 8322 8361 Youth center; Juvenile correctional facilities
PA: Lighthouse Youth Services, Inc.
401 E Mcmillan St
Cincinnati OH 45206
513 221-3350

(G-686)
ROCKHOLD BANK
101 E Main St (45612-1102)
P.O. Box 506 (45612-0506)
PHONE...............................740 634-2331
Jonathan Wisecup, *CEO*
Rick Givens, *VP*
William Hubbard, *Dir*
John Scott Iii, *Ch*
Megan Brumfield, *Dir*
EMP: 30 **EST:** 1867
SALES (est): 2.47MM **Privately Held**
Web: www.joinbsb.com
SIC: 6022 State trust companies accepting deposits, commercial
PA: Rockhold-Brown Bancshares, Inc.
101 E Main St
Bainbridge OH

(G-687)
WKHR RADIO INC
Also Called: FM 91 Point 5
17425 Snyder Rd (45612)
PHONE...............................440 708-0915
Rowland Shepard, *VP*
EMP: 30 **EST:** 1999
SALES (est): 92.28K **Privately Held**
Web: www.wkhr.org
SIC: 4832 Radio broadcasting stations

Baltic
Tuscarawas County

(G-688)
FLEX TECHNOLOGIES INC
Also Called: Poly Flex
3430 State Route 93 (43804-9705)
P.O. Box 300 (43804-0300)
PHONE...............................330 897-6311
Brian Harrison, *Mgr*
EMP: 53
SQ FT: 20,000
SALES (corp-wide): 6MM **Privately Held**
Web: www.flextechnologies.com
SIC: 2821 5169 3087 Molding compounds, plastics; Synthetic resins, rubber, and plastic materials; Custom compound purchased resins
PA: Flex Technologies, Inc.
5479 Gundy Dr
Midvale OH 44653
740 922-5992

(G-689)
GMI HOLDINGS INC
Also Called: Genie Company, The
606 N Ray St (43804-9093)
P.O. Box 284 (43804-0284)
PHONE...............................330 897-4424
Rick Johnson, *Dir*
EMP: 167
Web: www.geniecompany.com
SIC: 1751 Garage door, installation or erection
HQ: Gmi Holdings, Inc.
1 Door Dr
Mount Hope OH 44660
800 354-3643

(G-690)
KEIM LUMBER COMPANY
State Rte 557 (43804)
PHONE...............................330 893-2251
Bill Keim, *Brnch Mgr*
EMP: 60
SALES (corp-wide): 49.38MM **Privately Held**
Web: www.keimlumber.cc

Baltic - Tuscarawas County (G-691)   **GEOGRAPHIC SECTION**

SIC: 5211 5031 Planing mill products and lumber; Lumber: rough, dressed, and finished
PA: Keim Lumber Company
4465 State Route 557
Millersburg OH 44654
330 893-2251

(G-691)
SCHLABACH WOOD DESIGN INC
52567 State Route 651 (43804-9520)
PHONE.................................330 897-2600
Willis Schlabach, Pr
EMP: 32 **EST:** 1994
SQ FT: 9,000
SALES (est): 2.74MM **Privately Held**
Web: www.schlabachwooddesign.com
SIC: 1751 5211 Cabinet and finish carpentry; Cabinets, kitchen

Barberton
Summit County

(G-692)
AKRON RUBBER DEV LAB INC
75 Robinson Ave (44203-3500)
PHONE.................................330 794-6600
EMP: 35
SALES (corp-wide): 15.1MM **Privately Held**
Web: www.ardl.com
SIC: 8734 Testing laboratories
PA: Akron Rubber Development Laboratory, Incorporated
2887 Gilchrist Rd
Akron OH 44305
330 794-6600

(G-693)
ARIS HORTICULTURE INC (PA)
Also Called: Yoder Trading Company
115 3rd St Se (44203-4208)
PHONE.................................330 745-2143
G Ramsey Yoder, Ch
William Rasbach, *
Scott Schaefer, *
Thomas D Doak, Vice Chairman*
William Riffey, *
▲ **EMP:** 85 **EST:** 1919
SQ FT: 28,000
SALES (est): 92.07MM
SALES (corp-wide): 92.07MM **Privately Held**
Web: www.arishort.com
SIC: 0181 Nursery stock, growing of

(G-694)
BARBERTON LAUNDRY AND CLG INC
Also Called: Liniform Service
1050 Northview Ave (44203-7197)
PHONE.................................330 825-6911
TOLL FREE: 800
A Edward Good, Ch
Bertha Jenkins, *
Patricia Shultz, *
EMP: 58 **EST:** 1924
SQ FT: 35,000
SALES (est): 4.8MM **Privately Held**
Web: www.liniform.com
SIC: 7299 7213 4215 Clothing rental services ; Uniform supply; Package delivery, vehicular

(G-695)
BLIND & SON LLC
Also Called: Tri-County Heating & Cooling
344 4th St Nw (44203-2212)
PHONE.................................330 753-7711
William Blind, Managing Member
John Hartman, *
David Zahn, *
Joe Bilota, *
EMP: 80 **EST:** 1937
SQ FT: 15,000
SALES (est): 16.46MM **Privately Held**
Web: www.blindandsons.com
SIC: 1711 Warm air heating and air conditioning contractor

(G-696)
CHRISTIAN HLTHCARE MNSTRIES IN
127 Hazelwood Ave (44203-1316)
P.O. Box 29 (44203-0029)
PHONE.................................330 848-1511
Howard Russell, Ex Dir
Roger Kittelson, *
EMP: 40 **EST:** 1961
SALES (est): 752.91MM **Privately Held**
Web: www.chministries.org
SIC: 8011 Offices and clinics of medical doctors

(G-697)
FRED CRDNAL ATHC SCHLRSHIP FUN
39 20th St Sw (44203-7105)
PHONE.................................812 801-7641
EMP: 45 **EST:** 2018
SALES (est): 51.74K **Privately Held**
Web: www.americoldrealty.com
SIC: 8641 Civic and social associations

(G-698)
ICON WORLD ENTERTAINMENT LLC
467 W Paige Ave Ste A (44203-2563)
PHONE.................................330 615-7008
EMP: 56 **EST:** 2015
SQ FT: 13,800
SALES (est): 1.18MM **Privately Held**
SIC: 7812 Motion picture production

(G-699)
INTEGRITY PROCESSING LLC (PA)
1055 Wooster Rd N (44203-1352)
P.O. Box 342 (44022-0342)
PHONE.................................330 285-6937
Gerald F Robinson, Managing Member
EMP: 30 **EST:** 2012
SALES (est): 1.01MM **Privately Held**
Web: www.integrityprocessingllc.com
SIC: 7699 Plastics products repair

(G-700)
MALCO PRODUCTS INC (PA)
Also Called: Malco Products
361 Fairview Ave (44203-2700)
P.O. Box 892 (44203-0892)
PHONE.................................330 753-0361
◆ **EMP:** 175 **EST:** 1953
SALES (est): 63.82MM
SALES (corp-wide): 63.82MM **Privately Held**
Web: www.malcopro.com
SIC: 2842 8742 2899 2841 Polishes and sanitation goods; Marketing consulting services; Chemical preparations, nec; Soap and other detergents

(G-701)
MANOR CARE BARBERTON OH LLC ✪
Also Called: Promedica Sklled Nrsing Rhbltt
85 3rd St Se (44203-4299)
PHONE.................................330 753-5005
EMP: 48 **EST:** 2022
SALES (est): 14.92MM **Privately Held**
SIC: 8051 Skilled nursing care facilities

(G-702)
PLEASANT VIEW NURSING HOME INC
220 3rd St Se (44203-4235)
PHONE.................................330 848-5028
Richard Morris, Brnch Mgr
EMP: 90
SALES (corp-wide): 9.66MM **Privately Held**
Web: www.pleasantviewhealthcare.com
SIC: 8052 Personal care facility
PA: Pleasant View Nursing Home, Inc.
401 Snyder Ave
Barberton OH 44203
330 745-6028

(G-703)
PLEASANT VIEW NURSING HOME INC (PA)
Also Called: Pleasant View Health Care Ctr
401 Snyder Ave (44203-4131)
PHONE.................................330 745-6028
Richard Morris, Pr
Eileen Morris, *
EMP: 59 **EST:** 1950
SALES (est): 9.66MM
SALES (corp-wide): 9.66MM **Privately Held**
Web: www.pleasantviewhealthcare.com
SIC: 8051 Convalescent home with continuous nursing care

(G-704)
PROFIT TRACK LTD
588 W Tuscarawas Ave (44203-2522)
PHONE.................................330 848-2730
Mike Markwood, Brnch Mgr
EMP: 29
SALES (corp-wide): 2.33MM **Privately Held**
SIC: 8748 7832 Business consulting, nec; Motion picture theaters, except drive-in
PA: Profit Track, Ltd.
524 W Park Ave
Barberton OH 44203
330 352-0542

(G-705)
RITE AID OF OHIO INC
Also Called: Rite Aid
1403 Wooster Rd W (44203-7374)
PHONE.................................330 706-1004
Mindy Durst, Mgr
EMP: 47
SALES (corp-wide): 24.09B **Publicly Held**
Web: www.riteaid.com
SIC: 5912 7384 Drug stores; Photofinishing laboratory
HQ: Rite Aid Of Ohio, Inc.
1200 Intrepid Ave Ste 2
Philadelphia PA 19112

(G-706)
RONDY FLEET SERVICES INC
255 Wooster Rd N (44203-8206)
PHONE.................................330 745-9016
Donald Rondy, Pr
Frank Moore, VP
Ronna Rondy, Sec
EMP: 48 **EST:** 1986
SALES (est): 1.92MM
SALES (corp-wide): 26.25MM **Privately Held**
SIC: 4731 7538 Freight transportation arrangement; General automotive repair shops
HQ: Tahoma Rubber & Plastics, Inc.
255 Wooster Rd N
Barberton OH 44203
330 745-9016

(G-707)
RT80 EXPRESS INC
4409 S Cleveland Massillon Rd (44203-5703)
P.O. Box 269 (44203-0269)
PHONE.................................330 706-0900
David Bilinovich, Pr
Pam Bilinovich, VP
EMP: 40 **EST:** 1993
SQ FT: 140,000
SALES (est): 849.48K **Privately Held**
Web: www.route80express.com
SIC: 4212 4213 Local trucking, without storage; Trucking, except local

(G-708)
S A COMUNALE CO INC (DH)
Also Called: Sprinkfab
2900 Newpark Dr (44203-1050)
P.O. Box 150 (44203-0150)
PHONE.................................330 706-3040
EMP: 160 **EST:** 1973
SALES (est): 101.31MM
SALES (corp-wide): 12.58B **Publicly Held**
Web: www.sacomunale.com
SIC: 1711 Mechanical contractor
HQ: Emcor Construction Services, Inc.
301 Merritt Seven 6th Fl
Norwalk CT 06851

(G-709)
SMITH AMBULANCE SERVICE INC
594 Hudson Run Rd (44203-3934)
PHONE.................................330 825-0205
Robert L Smith, Brnch Mgr
EMP: 45
Web: www.smithambulance.com
SIC: 4119 Ambulance service
PA: Smith Ambulance Service, Inc.
214 W 3rd St
Dover OH 44622

(G-710)
SUMMA BARBERTON CITIZENS HOSPITAL
Also Called: Summa Barberton Hospital
155 5th St Ne (44203-3332)
P.O. Box 2090 (44309-2090)
PHONE.................................330 615-3000
EMP: 1100
Web: www.summahealth.org
SIC: 8062 General medical and surgical hospitals

(G-711)
SUMMA HEALTH
Labcare Plus
155 5th St Ne (44203-3332)
PHONE.................................330 615-5200
Richard Adams, Brnch Mgr
EMP: 822
SALES (corp-wide): 1.78B **Privately Held**
Web: www.summahealth.org
SIC: 8062 General medical and surgical hospitals
PA: Summa Health System
1077 Gorge Blvd
Akron OH 44310
330 375-3000

(G-712)
SUMMA HEALTH
Also Called: Lab Care
165 5th St Se Ste A (44203-9001)
PHONE.................................330 753-3649
Fran Royer, Mgr
EMP: 60
SALES (corp-wide): 1.78B **Privately Held**
Web: www.summahealth.org

▲ = Import ▼ = Export
◆ = Import/Export

GEOGRAPHIC SECTION

SIC: 8062 8071 General medical and surgical hospitals; Medical laboratories
PA: Summa Health System
1077 Gorge Blvd
Akron OH 44310
330 375-3000

(G-713)
SUMMA HEALTH SYSTEM
Also Called: Summa Barberton Hospital
155 5th St Ne (44203-3332)
PHONE..................330 615-3000
EMP: 718
SALES (corp-wide): 1.78B Privately Held
Web: www.summahealth.org
SIC: 8062 General medical and surgical hospitals
PA: Summa Health System
1077 Gorge Blvd
Akron OH 44310
330 375-3000

(G-714)
TAHOMA ENTERPRISES INC (PA)
255 Wooster Rd N (44203-2560)
PHONE..................330 745-9016
William P Herrington, CEO
EMP: 100 EST: 2007
SALES (est): 26.25MM
SALES (corp-wide): 26.25MM Privately Held
SIC: 3069 3089 5199 5162 Reclaimed rubber (reworked by manufacturing processes); Plastics processing; Foams and rubber; Plastics products, nec

(G-715)
TAHOMA RUBBER & PLASTICS INC (HQ)
Also Called: Rondy & Co.
255 Wooster Rd N (44203-2560)
PHONE..................330 745-9016
William P Herrington, CEO
▼ EMP: 100 EST: 1965
SQ FT: 750,000
SALES (est): 17.69MM
SALES (corp-wide): 26.25MM Privately Held
Web: www.tahomarubberplastics.com
SIC: 3069 3089 5199 5162 Reclaimed rubber (reworked by manufacturing processes); Plastics processing; Foams and rubber; Plastics products, nec
PA: Tahoma Enterprises, Inc.
255 Wooster Rd N
Barberton OH 44203
330 745-9016

Barnesville
Belmont County

(G-716)
ALTERNATIVE RESIDENCES TWO INC
Also Called: Mainstreet Group Home
320 E Main St (43713-1410)
PHONE..................740 425-1565
Tonya Mangerie, Dir
EMP: 70
SALES (corp-wide): 2.27MM Privately Held
SIC: 8361 Mentally handicapped home
PA: Alternative Residences Two, Inc.
100 W Main St Lowr
Saint Clairsville OH 43950
740 526-0514

(G-717)
BARNESVILLE HOSPITAL ASSN INC (PA)
639 W Main St (43713-1039)
P.O. Box 309 (43713-0309)
PHONE..................740 425-3941
Richard Doan, CEO
Willie Cooper-lohr, CFO
David Phillips, *
EMP: 277 EST: 1940
SQ FT: 60,000
SALES (est): 23.46MM
SALES (corp-wide): 23.46MM Privately Held
Web: www.barnesvillehospital.com
SIC: 8062 Hospital, affiliated with AMA residency

(G-718)
HEALTH CARE SOLUTIONS INC
Also Called: HEALTH CARE SOLUTIONS, INC
114 Mill St (43713-1352)
PHONE..................304 243-9605
Jay Grob, Mgr
EMP: 212
Web: www.nyuhealthcaresolutions.com
SIC: 5047 Medical equipment and supplies
PA: Healthcare Solutions, Inc.
3741 Plaza Dr Ste 1a
Ann Arbor MI 48108

(G-719)
LINCARE INC
Also Called: Health Care Solutions
114 Mill St (43713-1352)
PHONE..................304 243-9605
Jay Grob, Mgr
EMP: 29
Web: www.lincare.com
SIC: 7352 Medical equipment rental
HQ: Lincare Inc.
19387 Us Highway 19 N
Clearwater FL 33764
727 530-7700

(G-720)
OHIO HILLS HEALTH SERVICES (PA)
101 E Main St (43713-1005)
P.O. Box 43 (43713-0043)
PHONE..................740 425-5165
William E Chaney, Pr
Charles Bardell, *
Linda Tacosik, *
Candy Lendon, *
EMP: 55 EST: 1976
SALES (est): 9.81MM
SALES (corp-wide): 9.81MM Privately Held
Web: www.ohiohillshealthcenters.com
SIC: 8011 Clinic, operated by physicians

(G-721)
SOUTH CENTRAL POWER COMPANY
Also Called: Belmont Division
37801 Barnesville Bethesda Rd (43713)
PHONE..................740 425-4018
Jim Meyers, Brnch Mgr
EMP: 63
SALES (corp-wide): 369.45MM Privately Held
Web: www.southcentralpower.com
SIC: 4911 Distribution, electric power
PA: South Central Power Company Inc
720 Mill Park Dr
Lancaster OH 43130
740 653-4422

(G-722)
SOUTHEASTERN HEALTH CARE CTR
Also Called: Barnesville Health Care Center
400 Carrie Ave (43713-1317)
PHONE..................740 425-3648
Dale Shonk, Pr
EMP: 65 EST: 1976
SQ FT: 40,000
SALES (est): 7.34MM
SALES (corp-wide): 12.43MM Privately Held
SIC: 8052 8051 Intermediate care facilities; Skilled nursing care facilities
PA: S.F.T. Health Care Inc
5890 Mayfair Rd
Canton OH 44720
330 499-6358

(G-723)
TRI-VALLEY EQUIPMENT SALES INC
Main St W (43713)
PHONE..................740 695-5895
Terry Lee Wright, Brnch Mgr
EMP: 39
SALES (corp-wide): 4.65MM Privately Held
Web: www.trivalleyequip.com
SIC: 7542 Carwash, self-service
PA: Tri-Valley Equipment Sales, Inc.
117 N Sugar St
Saint Clairsville OH 43950
740 695-5895

(G-724)
WALTON RETIREMENT HOME
1254 E Main St (43713-9108)
PHONE..................740 425-2344
Nirmal Kaul, Dir
EMP: 28 EST: 1944
SALES (est): 1.25MM Privately Held
Web: www.waltonhome.org
SIC: 8361 Aged home

Bascom
Seneca County

(G-725)
MID-WOOD INC
6100 W Poplar St (44809)
PHONE..................419 937-2233
Bruce Mathias, Brnch Mgr
EMP: 30
SALES (corp-wide): 16.88MM Privately Held
Web: www.mid-wood.com
SIC: 5153 Grains
PA: Mid-Wood, Inc.
12965 Defiance Pike
Cygnet OH
419 352-5231

Batavia
Clermont County

(G-726)
BACHMANS INC
Also Called: Honeywell Authorized Dealer
4058 Clough Woods Dr (45103-2586)
PHONE..................513 943-5300
Marc E Bachman, Pr
Rod E Bachman, *
EMP: 30 EST: 1955
SQ FT: 16,500
SALES (est): 9.57MM Privately Held
Web: www.bachmansinc.com
SIC: 1711 Warm air heating and air conditioning contractor

(G-727)
BANSI & PRATIMA INC
Also Called: Microtel
1839 Clough Pike (45103-2621)
PHONE..................513 735-0453
Pratima Patel, CEO
Bhavesh Patel, Pr
EMP: 55 EST: 1997
SALES (est): 239.22K Privately Held
Web: www.hiexpress.com
SIC: 7011 Hotels and motels

(G-728)
BENCHMARK BUILDING SUPPLY INC
4701 State Route 276 (45103-2002)
PHONE..................513 732-2522
Derek C Smith, CEO
EMP: 40 EST: 2020
SALES (est): 2.91MM Privately Held
SIC: 5099 Durable goods, nec

(G-729)
BURD BROTHERS INC (PA)
4294 Armstrong Blvd (45103-1600)
P.O. Box 324 (45103-0324)
PHONE..................800 538-2873
Gayle Burdick, Ch
Dick Burdick, *
Tyler Burdick, *
Erin Burdick, *
EMP: 45 EST: 1993
SALES (est): 11.19MM Privately Held
Web: www.burdbrothers.com
SIC: 4213 4225 Contract haulers; General warehousing

(G-730)
CARINGTON HEALTH SYSTEMS
Also Called: Batavia Nrsing Cnvalescent Inn
4000 Golden Age Dr (45103-1913)
PHONE..................513 732-6500
Steve Chaney, Admn
EMP: 591
SALES (corp-wide): 58.43MM Privately Held
Web: www.batavia-care.net
SIC: 8051 Convalescent home with continuous nursing care
PA: Carington Health Systems
8200 Beckett Park Dr
Hamilton OH 45011
513 682-2700

(G-731)
CHILD FOCUS INC
2337 Clermont Center Dr (45103-1959)
PHONE..................513 732-8800
Jim Carter, Brnch Mgr
EMP: 43
SALES (corp-wide): 20.97MM Privately Held
Web: www.child-focus.org
SIC: 8322 Child related social services
PA: Child Focus, Inc.
4629 Aicholtz Rd
Cincinnati OH 45244
513 752-1555

(G-732)
CLERMONT CNTY WTR RSURCES DEPT
4400 Haskell Ln (45103-2990)
PHONE..................513 732-7970
Lyle Bloom, Dir
EMP: 97 EST: 1957
SQ FT: 11,000
SALES (est): 23.42MM Privately Held
Web: www.clermontcountyohio.gov
SIC: 4952 Sewerage systems

Batavia - Clermont County (G-733)

(G-733)
CLERMONT COUNTY CMNTY SVCS INC (PA)
3003 Hospital Dr (45103-2689)
PHONE.................513 732-2277
Billie Kuntz, *Dir*
Joyce A Richardson, *
EMP: 35 **EST:** 1984
SQ FT: 10,000
SALES (est): 2.46MM **Privately Held**
Web: www.cccsi.org
SIC: 8322 9111 Individual and family services; County supervisors' and executives' office

(G-734)
CLERMONT RECOVERY CENTER INC
1088 Wasserman Way Ste C (45103-1974)
PHONE.................513 735-8100
EMP: 46 **EST:** 1975
SALES (est): 10.08MM **Privately Held**
Web: www.recoveryctr.org
SIC: 8093 Mental health clinic, outpatient

(G-735)
CLERMONT SENIOR SERVICES INC (PA)
Also Called: CLERMONT SENIOR SERVICES
2085 James E Sauls Sr Dr (45103-3255)
PHONE.................513 724-1255
Cynthia Jenkins-gramke, *CEO*
Gregory Carson, *
EMP: 72 **EST:** 1973
SQ FT: 33,000
SALES (est): 7.07MM
SALES (corp-wide): 7.07MM **Privately Held**
Web: www.clermontseniors.com
SIC: 8322 Senior citizens' center or association

(G-736)
COUNTY OF CLERMONT
Also Called: Clermont Cnty Cmmon Pleas Crt
270 E Main St Ste 8 (45103-3031)
PHONE.................513 732-7265
Bruce Gibson, *Dir*
EMP: 38
SQ FT: 2,243
SALES (corp-wide): 183.15MM **Privately Held**
Web: www.clermontcountyohio.gov
SIC: 8322 9111 Probation office; County supervisors' and executives' office
PA: County Of Clermont
    177 E Main St
    Batavia OH 45103
    513 732-7980

(G-737)
COUNTY OF CLERMONT
Also Called: Clermont Cnty Hlth Recovery Bd
2337 Clermont Center Dr (45103-1959)
PHONE.................513 732-5400
EMP: 63
SALES (corp-wide): 183.15MM **Privately Held**
Web: www.clermontcountyohio.gov
SIC: 8069 Drug addiction rehabilitation hospital
PA: County Of Clermont
    177 E Main St
    Batavia OH 45103
    513 732-7980

(G-738)
COUNTY OF CLERMONT
Also Called: Division of Water Resources
4400 Haskell Ln (45103-2990)
PHONE.................513 732-7970
Lyle Bloom, *Dir*
EMP: 44
SALES (corp-wide): 183.15MM **Privately Held**
Web: www.clermontcountyohio.gov
SIC: 1623 Water, sewer, and utility lines
PA: County Of Clermont
    177 E Main St
    Batavia OH 45103
    513 732-7980

(G-739)
COUNTY OF CLERMONT
Also Called: Information Systems Dept
2279 Clermont Center Dr (45103-1956)
PHONE.................513 732-7661
Steve Rybolt, *Mgr*
EMP: 49
SQ FT: 1,320
SALES (corp-wide): 183.15MM **Privately Held**
Web: www.clermontcountyohio.gov
SIC: 8999 9121 Information bureau; County commissioner
PA: County Of Clermont
    177 E Main St
    Batavia OH 45103
    513 732-7980

(G-740)
FREEMAN SCHWABE MACHINERY LLC
Also Called: F S
4064 Clough Woods Dr (45103-2586)
PHONE.................513 947-2888
▲ **EMP:** 30 **EST:** 2006
SALES (est): 10.1MM **Privately Held**
Web: www.freemanschwabe.com
SIC: 5084 Industrial machinery and equipment

(G-741)
GLOBAL SCRAP MANAGEMENT INC
Also Called: G S M
4340 Batavia Rd (45103-3342)
PHONE.................513 576-6600
EMP: 40
Web: www.globalscrap.net
SIC: 4953 Recycling, waste materials

(G-742)
KAESER AND BLAIR INCORPORATED (PA)
4236 Grissom Dr (45103-1696)
PHONE.................513 732-6400
▲ **EMP:** 82 **EST:** 1894
SALES (est): 23.71MM
SALES (corp-wide): 23.71MM **Privately Held**
Web: www.kaeser-blair.com
SIC: 5199 Advertising specialties

(G-743)
MERCY HLTH - CLERMONT HOSP LLC
Also Called: Mercy Health - Clermont Hosp
3000 Hospital Dr (45103-1921)
PHONE.................513 732-8200
Mark Shuagerman, *Pr*
Arlene Cooper, *
EMP: 720 **EST:** 1973
SQ FT: 230,000
SALES: 121.16MM
SALES (corp-wide): 6.92B **Privately Held**
Web: www.clermontcountyohio.gov
SIC: 8062 8011 General medical and surgical hospitals; Clinic, operated by physicians
HQ: Mercy Health Cincinnati Llc
    1701 Mercy Health Pl
    Cincinnati OH 45237
    513 952-5000

(G-744)
OHIO DEPT DVLPMNTAL DSBILITIES
Also Called: Southwest Ohio Dvlopmental Ctr
4399 E Bauman Ln (45103-1685)
PHONE.................513 732-9200
Nancy Mcavoy, *Prin*
EMP: 247
SIC: 8322 9431 Family counseling services; Administration of public health programs, State government
HQ: Ohio Department Of Developmental Disabilities
    30 E Broad St Fl 13
    Columbus OH 43215

(G-745)
PERRY INTERIORS INC
4054 Clough Woods Dr (45103-2586)
PHONE.................513 761-9333
Karen Perry, *Pr*
Rick Perry, *
EMP: 30 **EST:** 1999
SQ FT: 3,500
SALES (est): 2.45MM **Privately Held**
Web: www.perryinteriors.com
SIC: 1721 Residential painting

(G-746)
PROVISION LIVING LLC
4299 Bach Buxton Rd (45103)
PHONE.................513 970-9201
EMP: 61
Web: www.provisionliving.com
SIC: 8361 Aged home
PA: Provision Living, Llc
    9450 Manchester Rd # 207
    Saint Louis MO 63119

(G-747)
SPORTSMANS MARKET INC
Also Called: Sportys Pilot Shop
2001 Sportys Dr (45103-9719)
PHONE.................513 735-9100
Michael Wolf, *CEO*
Harold Shevers Junior, *Ch Bd*
Michael J Wolf, *
John P Lynch, *
Marc A Liggett, *
▲ **EMP:** 172 **EST:** 1961
SQ FT: 120,000
SALES (est): 47.94MM **Privately Held**
Web: www.sportys.com
SIC: 5599 5088 Aircraft instruments, equipment or parts; Aircraft equipment and supplies, nec

(G-748)
STRICKER BROS INC
Also Called: Stricker Auto Sales
4955 Benton Rd (45103-1203)
PHONE.................513 732-1152
TOLL FREE: 800
John M Stricker, *Pr*
Arthur J Stricker, *
▼ **EMP:** 50 **EST:** 1956
SQ FT: 2,500
SALES (est): 8.93MM **Privately Held**
Web: www.strickerbros.com
SIC: 5521 5015 5531 Automobiles, used cars only; Automotive supplies, used: wholesale and retail; Auto and truck equipment and parts

(G-749)
TOWNE CONSTRUCTION SVCS LLC
Also Called: Towne Properties Machine Group
500 Kent Rd Ste A (45103-1703)
PHONE.................513 561-3700
EMP: 150 **EST:** 2005
SALES (est): 32.54MM
SALES (corp-wide): 59.97MM **Privately Held**
Web: www.townescapes.com
SIC: 1771 Concrete work
PA: Original Partners Limited Partnership
    1055 Saint Paul Pl
    Cincinnati OH 45202
    513 381-8696

(G-750)
TRENDCO SUPPLY INC (PA)
Also Called: Pace America
1236 Clough Pike Ste B (45103-2597)
PHONE.................513 752-1871
▲ **EMP:** 31 **EST:** 1978
SALES (est): 16.2MM
SALES (corp-wide): 16.2MM **Privately Held**
Web: www.trendcosupply.com
SIC: 5046 5113 5087 Restaurant equipment and supplies, nec; Industrial and personal service paper; Janitors' supplies

(G-751)
UNIVERSAL PACKG SYSTEMS INC
Also Called: Paklab
5055 State Route 276 (45103-1211)
PHONE.................513 732-2000
Richard Burton, *Brnch Mgr*
EMP: 158
SALES (corp-wide): 379.38MM **Privately Held**
Web: www.paklab.com
SIC: 2844 7389 3565 2671 Cosmetic preparations; Packaging and labeling services; Bottling machinery: filling, capping, labeling; Plastic film, coated or laminated for packaging
PA: Universal Packaging Systems, Inc.
    14570 Monte Vista Ave
    Chino CA 91710
    909 517-2442

(G-752)
UNIVERSAL PACKG SYSTEMS INC
5069 State Route 276 (45103-1211)
PHONE.................513 735-4777
EMP: 158
SALES (corp-wide): 379.38MM **Privately Held**
Web: www.paklab.com
SIC: 2844 7389 3565 2671 Cosmetic preparations; Packaging and labeling services; Bottling machinery: filling, capping, labeling; Plastic film, coated or laminated for packaging
PA: Universal Packaging Systems, Inc.
    14570 Monte Vista Ave
    Chino CA 91710
    909 517-2442

(G-753)
UTILITY TRAILER MFG CO
Also Called: UTILITY TRAILER MANUFACTURING COMPANY
4225 Curliss Ln (45103-3217)
PHONE.................513 436-2600
Del Eastman, *Mgr*
EMP: 304
SALES (corp-wide): 897.7MM **Privately Held**
Web: www.utilitytrailer.com
SIC: 4225 General warehousing and storage
PA: Utility Trailer Manufacturing Company, Llc
    17295 E Railroad St
    City Of Industry CA 91748
    626 965-1514

Bath
Summit County

(G-754)
OLD TRAIL SCHOOL
2315 Ira Rd (44210)
P.O. Box 827 (44210)
PHONE..................330 666-1118
Sarah L Johnston, *Headmaster*
EMP: 85 **EST:** 1920
SQ FT: 100,000
SALES (est): 12.15MM **Privately Held**
Web: www.oldtrail.org
SIC: 8211 8351 Private elementary school; Preschool center

(G-755)
WESTERN RESERVE HISTORICAL SOC
Also Called: Hale Farm & Village
2686 Oak Hill Dr (44210)
P.O. Box 296 (44210-0296)
PHONE..................330 666-3711
Margaret Tramontine, *Dir*
EMP: 33
SALES (corp-wide): 4.63MM **Privately Held**
Web: www.wrhs.org
SIC: 8412 Museum
PA: Western Reserve Historical Society
10825 East Blvd
Cleveland OH 44106
216 721-5722

(G-756)
WILLORY LLC
1970 N Cleveland Massillon Rd Unit 50 (44210-5367)
P.O. Box 50 (44210-0050)
PHONE..................330 576-5486
EMP: 37 **EST:** 2010
SALES (est): 3.48MM **Privately Held**
Web: www.willory.com
SIC: 7361 Executive placement

Bay Village
Cuyahoga County

(G-757)
AMERICAN PLUMBING
31400 Fairwin Dr (44140-1443)
PHONE..................440 871-8293
Don Cowles, *Brnch Mgr*
EMP: 37
Web: www.americanplumbing1.com
SIC: 1711 Plumbing contractors
PA: American Plumbing
1063 Bradley Rd
Westlake OH 44145

(G-758)
BRADLEY BAY ASSISTED LIVING
605 Bradley Rd (44140-1670)
PHONE..................440 871-4509
John O'neal, *Owner*
John O' Neal, *Owner*
EMP: 31 **EST:** 2001
SALES (est): 413.89K **Privately Held**
Web: www.oneillhc.com
SIC: 8361 8082 Rest home, with health care incidental; Home health care services

(G-759)
GASTRNTRLOGY ASSOC CLVLAND INC (PA)
428 Bassett Rd (44140-1800)
PHONE..................216 593-7700
James Andrassy, *CEO*
Mario D Kamionkowski, *
Michael H Frankel, *
Brian Kirsh, *
Jack S Lissauer, *
EMP: 29 **EST:** 1965
SALES (est): 4.96MM
SALES (corp-wide): 4.96MM **Privately Held**
Web: www.gastro-associates.com
SIC: 8011 Gastronomist

(G-760)
HUNTINGTON NATIONAL BANK
355 Dover Center Rd (44140-2298)
PHONE..................216 515-0029
Cheryl Mullen, *Prin*
EMP: 36
SALES (corp-wide): 10.84B **Publicly Held**
Web: www.huntington.com
SIC: 6029 6021 Commercial banks, nec; National commercial banks
HQ: The Huntington National Bank
41 S High St
Columbus OH 43215
614 480-4293

Beach City
Stark County

(G-761)
GRABILL PLUMBING & HEATING
Also Called: Graybill Gallery Kitchens Bath
10235 Manchester Ave Sw (44608-9756)
PHONE..................330 756-2075
Luke Grabill, *Pr*
Grant Grabill, *
Karla Ferguson, *
EMP: 28 **EST:** 1965
SALES (est): 5.13MM **Privately Held**
Web: www.grabill.com
SIC: 1711 Plumbing contractors

Beachwood
Cuyahoga County

(G-762)
16644 SNOW RD LLC
Also Called: Howard Johnson
26949 Chagrin Blvd (44122-4230)
PHONE..................216 676-5200
EMP: 28 **EST:** 2011
SALES (est): 214.26K **Privately Held**
Web: www.wyndhamhotels.com
SIC: 7011 Hotels and motels

(G-763)
AERO COMMUNICATIONS INC
25101 Chagrin Blvd # 350 (44122-5687)
PHONE..................734 467-8121
EMP: 1600
SIC: 1623 Telephone and communication line construction

(G-764)
AERODYNMICS INC ARDYNAMICS INC
25700 Science Park Dr Ste 210 (44122-7319)
PHONE..................404 596-8751
Scott Beale, *CEO*
EMP: 30 **EST:** 2013
SALES (est): 743.16K **Privately Held**
SIC: 4522 Flying charter service

(G-765)
ALTRUISM SOCIETY INC
3695 Green Rd Unit 22896 (44122-7945)
P.O. Box 22896 (44122-0896)
PHONE..................877 283-4001
James Abrams, *CEO*
Jaicynthia Farmer, *
EMP: 99 **EST:** 2015
SALES (est): 1.91MM **Privately Held**
Web: www.altruismsociety.org
SIC: 6732 8611 8322 1611 Trusts: educational, religious, etc.; Community affairs and services; Emergency social services; General contractor, highway and street construction

(G-766)
AMIN TUROCY & WATSON LLP (PA)
200 Park Ave Ste 300 (44122-4296)
PHONE..................216 696-8730
Himanshu S Amin, *Genl Pt*
Gregory Turocy, *
EMP: 49 **EST:** 1999
SALES (est): 5.06MM **Privately Held**
Web: www.thepatentattorneys.com
SIC: 8111 Corporate, partnership and business law

(G-767)
BEACHWOOD CINEMA LLC
Also Called: Silverspot Cinema
10 Park Ave Ste 218 (44122-4237)
PHONE..................954 840-8150
Richard Corredera, *
EMP: 30 **EST:** 2019
SALES (est): 506.54K **Privately Held**
SIC: 7832 Motion picture theaters, except drive-in

(G-768)
BEACHWOOD LODGING LLC
Also Called: Hampton Inn & Suites Beachwood
3840 Orange Pl (44122-4488)
PHONE..................216 831-3735
David H Baldauf, *Prin*
Nick Lamparelli, *
EMP: 28 **EST:** 2004
SALES (est): 1.19MM **Privately Held**
Web: www.hilton.com
SIC: 7011 Hotels and motels

(G-769)
BNY MELLON NATIONAL ASSN
3333 Richmond Rd Ste 110 (44122-4194)
PHONE..................216 595-8769
EMP: 274
SALES (corp-wide): 17.5B **Publicly Held**
Web: www.bnymellon.com
SIC: 6021 National commercial banks
HQ: Bny Mellon, National Association
500 Grant St
Pittsburgh PA 15219
412 234-5000

(G-770)
BRAND PROTECT PLUS LLC
23945 Mercantile Rd (44122-5939)
PHONE..................216 539-1880
Chuck H Strobel, *Prin*
EMP: 39 **EST:** 2012
SALES (est): 4.53MM **Privately Held**
Web: www.brandprotectplus.com
SIC: 7389 Teleconferencing services

(G-771)
BUCKEYE RUBBER & PACKING CO
23940 Mercantile Rd (44122-5989)
PHONE..................216 464-8900
William Bauer Junior, *Pr*
▲ **EMP:** 45 **EST:** 1937
SQ FT: 30,000
SALES (est): 21.7MM **Privately Held**
Web: www.buckeyerubber.com
SIC: 5085 Gaskets and seals

(G-772)
CARLISLE MCNLLIE RINI KRMER UL
24755 Chagrin Blvd (44122-5682)
PHONE..................216 360-7200
Richard Mcnellie, *Pr*
William Rini, *
Herbert Kramer, *
Phyllis Ulrich, *
James Sassano, *
EMP: 40 **EST:** 1979
SQ FT: 5,000
SALES (est): 3.82MM **Privately Held**
Web: www.carlisle-law.com
SIC: 8111 General practice attorney, lawyer

(G-773)
CARP COSMETIC SURGERY CTR INC
24300 Chagrin Blvd (44122-5639)
PHONE..................216 416-1221
EMP: 90
SALES (corp-wide): 2.19MM **Privately Held**
Web: www.carpcosmetic.com
SIC: 8011 Plastic surgeon
PA: Carp Cosmetic Surgery Center, Inc.
4031 Massillon Rd Ste A
Uniontown OH 44685
216 416-1221

(G-774)
CENTER AL HEALTH
3690 Orange Pl Ste 320 (44122-4432)
PHONE..................216 831-8118
EMP: 50 **EST:** 2017
SALES (est): 110.42K **Privately Held**
SIC: 8099 Health and allied services, nec

(G-775)
CHAGRIN SURGERY CENTER LLC
3755 Orange Pl Ste 102 (44122-4455)
PHONE..................216 839-1800
Seth J Silberman, *Prin*
EMP: 31 **EST:** 2007
SALES (est): 4.67MM **Privately Held**
SIC: 8011 Surgeon

(G-776)
CHARLES SCHWAB CORPORATION
Also Called: Charles Schwab
511 Park Ave Ste 145 (44122-4255)
PHONE..................800 435-4000
Jeffrey L Hurst, *Prin*
EMP: 48
SALES (corp-wide): 18.84B **Publicly Held**
Web: www.schwab.com
SIC: 6211 Brokers, security
PA: The Charles Schwab Corporation
3000 Schwab Way
Westlake TX 76262
817 859-5000

(G-777)
CLEVELAND BCHWOOD HSPTLITY LLC
Also Called: Hilton Cleveland/Beachwood
3663 Park East Dr (44122-4315)
PHONE..................216 464-5950
EMP: 99 **EST:** 2006
SALES (est): 2.51MM **Privately Held**
SIC: 7011 Hotels and motels

(G-778)
CLEVELAND CLINIC FOUNDATION
Also Called: Beachwood Family Health Center

Beachwood - Cuyahoga County (G-779)

26900 Cedar Rd (44122-1191)
PHONE..................216 839-3000
Molly Cissell, *Admn*
EMP: 66
SALES (corp-wide): 14.48B **Privately Held**
Web: www.clevelandclinic.org
SIC: 8099 Childbirth preparation clinic
PA: The Cleveland Clinic Foundation
  9500 Euclid Ave
  Cleveland OH 44195
  216 636-8335

(G-779)
CLEVELAND CLINIC FOUNDATION
Also Called: Cleveland Clnic Ctr For Cntnue
3050 Science Park Dr Bldg 3 (44122-7316)
PHONE..................216 448-0770
William D Carey, *Dir*
EMP: 82
SALES (corp-wide): 14.48B **Privately Held**
Web: www.clevelandclinic.org
SIC: 8099 Medical services organization
PA: The Cleveland Clinic Foundation
  9500 Euclid Ave
  Cleveland OH 44195
  216 636-8335

(G-780)
CLEVELAND CLINIC FOUNDATION
Also Called: Cole Eye Institute
2000 Auburn Dr Ste 300 (44122-4328)
PHONE..................216 831-0120
Peter Nintcheff, *Brnch Mgr*
EMP: 90
SALES (corp-wide): 14.48B **Privately Held**
Web: www.clevelandclinic.org
SIC: 8062 General medical and surgical hospitals
PA: The Cleveland Clinic Foundation
  9500 Euclid Ave
  Cleveland OH 44195
  216 636-8335

(G-781)
CLEVELAND CLINIC FOUNDATION
Also Called: Cleveland Clinic
3025 Science Park Dr (44122-7333)
PHONE..................216 448-0116
EMP: 49
SALES (corp-wide): 14.48B **Privately Held**
Web: www.clevelandclinic.org
SIC: 8062 General medical and surgical hospitals
PA: The Cleveland Clinic Foundation
  9500 Euclid Ave
  Cleveland OH 44195
  216 636-8335

(G-782)
CLEVELAND CLINIC FOUNDATION
Also Called: Cleveland Clinic ADM Campus
25900 Science Park Dr Bldg 2 (44122-7318)
PHONE..................800 223-2273
EMP: 90
SALES (corp-wide): 14.48B **Privately Held**
Web: www.clevelandclinic.org
SIC: 8062 General medical and surgical hospitals
PA: The Cleveland Clinic Foundation
  9500 Euclid Ave
  Cleveland OH 44195
  216 636-8335

(G-783)
CLEVELAND CLINIC FOUNDATION
Also Called: Cleveland Clinic
3025 Science Park Dr (44122-7333)
PHONE..................216 455-6400
EMP: 33
SALES (corp-wide): 14.48B **Privately Held**

Web: www.clevelandclinic.org
SIC: 8062 General medical and surgical hospitals
PA: The Cleveland Clinic Foundation
  9500 Euclid Ave
  Cleveland OH 44195
  216 636-8335

(G-784)
CORNELIA C HODGSON - ARCHITEC (PA)
23240 Chagrin Blvd Ste 350 (44122-5404)
PHONE..................216 593-0057
Cornelia Hodgson, *Pr*
EMP: 47 **EST**: 2009
SQ FT: 5,000
SALES (est): 2.36MM **Privately Held**
SIC: 8712 Architectural engineering

(G-785)
CROSSCOUNTRY MORTGAGE LLC
29225 Chagrin Blvd Ste 350 (44122-4645)
PHONE..................216 314-0107
EMP: 56
SALES (corp-wide): 803.24MM **Privately Held**
Web: www.crosscountrymortgage.com
SIC: 6162 Mortgage bankers and loan correspondents
PA: Crosscountry Mortgage, Llc
  6850 Miller Rd
  Brecksville OH 44141
  440 845-3700

(G-786)
DATATRAK INTERNATIONAL INC
3690 Orange Pl Ste 375 (44122-4466)
PHONE..................440 443-0082
James R Ward, *Pr*
Julia Henderson, *
Alex Tabatabai, *
EMP: 47 **EST**: 1991
SQ FT: 4,300
SALES (est): 7.16MM **Privately Held**
Web: www.fountayn.com
SIC: 7374 7372 Data processing and preparation; Prepackaged software

(G-787)
DIAMONDS PEARLS HLTH SVCS LLC
Also Called: DIAMONDS & PEARLS RCH
23611 Chagrin Blvd Ste 226 (44122-5540)
PHONE..................216 752-8500
EMP: 90 **EST**: 2003
SQ FT: 2,680
SALES (est): 580.87K **Privately Held**
Web: www.dphealthservices.com
SIC: 8082 Home health care services

(G-788)
EATON LEASING CORPORATION
1000 Eaton Blvd (44122)
PHONE..................216 382-2292
Richard Fearon, *Pr*
Billie Rawot, *VP*
EMP: 500 **EST**: 1981
SQ FT: 1,200
SALES (est): 60.88MM **Privately Held**
SIC: 7359 3612 3594 3593 Equipment rental and leasing, nec; Transformers, except electric; Fluid power pumps and motors; Fluid power cylinders and actuators
HQ: Eaton Corporation
  1000 Eaton Blvd
  Cleveland OH 44122
  440 523-5000

(G-789)
EMBASSY HEALTHCARE MGT INC (PA)

Also Called: Embassy Healthcare
25201 Chagrin Blvd Ste 190 (44122-5600)
PHONE..................216 378-2050
Aaron Handler, *Pr*
Darla Handler, *Prin*
EMP: 30 **EST**: 1998
SALES (est): 192.83MM
SALES (corp-wide): 192.83MM **Privately Held**
Web: www.embassyhealthcare.net
SIC: 8051 Skilled nursing care facilities

(G-790)
EVERSIDE HEALTH LLC
25700 Science Park Dr Ste 120 (44122-7319)
PHONE..................216 672-0211
EMP: 30
SALES (corp-wide): 478.59MM **Privately Held**
Web: www.eversidehealth.com
SIC: 8099 Childbirth preparation clinic
HQ: Everside Health, Llc
  1400 Wewatta St Ste 350
  Denver CO 80202
  866 808-6005

(G-791)
FIRST FEDERAL CREDIT CONTROL
Also Called: Interntnal Spcial Adit Systems
25700 Science Park Dr (44122-7312)
PHONE..................216 360-2000
TOLL FREE: 800
Norm Shafran, *Pr*
Brian Himmel, *
EMP: 43 **EST**: 1970
SALES (est): 3.29MM **Privately Held**
Web: www.ffcc.com
SIC: 7322 Collection agency, except real estate

(G-792)
FLASHHOUSE INC
29225 Chagrin Blvd Ste 300 (44122-4645)
PHONE..................216 600-0504
Stephen London, *CEO*
EMP: 35 **EST**: 2021
SALES (est): 1.09MM **Privately Held**
Web: www.hifello.com
SIC: 6531 Real estate agents and managers

(G-793)
FOX INTERNATIONAL LIMITED INC
23645 Mercantile Rd Ste B (44122)
PHONE..................216 454-1001
▼ **EMP**: 150
SIC: 5065 7389 5087 Electronic parts and equipment, nec; Telemarketing services; Firefighting equipment

(G-794)
GCI CONSTRUCTION LLC (HQ)
25101 Chagrin Blvd (44122-5643)
PHONE..................216 831-6100
Larry Goldberg, *Pr*
EMP: 33 **EST**: 2000
SALES (est): 47.89MM
SALES (corp-wide): 92.53MM **Privately Held**
Web: www.goldbergcompanies.com
SIC: 1522 1521 Multi-family dwelling construction, nec; Single-family housing construction
PA: Goldberg Companies, Inc.
  25101 Chagrin Blvd # 300
  Beachwood OH 44122
  216 831-6100

(G-795)
GOTTLIEB & SONS INC (PA)
25201 Chagrin Blvd (44122-5635)
PHONE..................216 771-4785
Saul Gottlieb, *Pr*
Jeff Gottlieb, *VP*
Alan Gottlieb, *VP*
Jerry Gottlieb, *VP*
Bernice Gottlieb, *Sec*
◆ **EMP**: 40 **EST**: 1949
SQ FT: 3,200
SALES (est): 3.05MM
SALES (corp-wide): 3.05MM **Privately Held**
Web: www.gottlieb-sons.com
SIC: 5094 5944 Diamonds (gems); Jewelry stores

(G-796)
GREATER CLVLAND HM HLTH CARE I
23811 Chagrin Blvd Ste 280 (44122-5525)
PHONE..................440 232-4995
Mohamed Ahmed, *Prin*
April Yaros, *
Omar Igeh, *
Kathy Bryne, *
EMP: 85 **EST**: 2010
SALES (est): 2.24MM **Privately Held**
Web: www.greaterclevelandhhc.com
SIC: 8082 Home health care services

(G-797)
HEALTH DATA MGT SOLUTIONS INC
3201 Enterprise Pkwy (44122-7330)
PHONE..................216 595-1232
Denise Zeman, *Brnch Mgr*
EMP: 100
Web: www.hdms.com
SIC: 8099 Blood related health services
PA: Health Data & Management Solutions, Inc.
  233 Spring St Rm 12e
  New York NY 10013

(G-798)
HELPING U HOME HEALTH CARE LLC
23533 Mercantile Rd Ste 106 (44122)
PHONE..................440 724-3754
Tanya Zelenkov, *Prin*
Alina Lakhter, *Prin*
EMP: 30 **EST**: 2021
SALES (est): 625.96K **Privately Held**
SIC: 8082 Home health care services

(G-799)
HIGHLAND SPRINGS LLC
4199 Millpond Dr (44122-5731)
PHONE..................216 591-9433
EMP: 75 **EST**: 2015
SALES (est): 19.56MM **Privately Held**
Web: www.highlandspringshealth.com
SIC: 8093 Mental health clinic, outpatient

(G-800)
HOME CARE NETWORK INC
3601 Green Rd Ste 202 (44122-5719)
PHONE..................216 378-9011
Connie Cahoon, *Brnch Mgr*
EMP: 144
Web: www.hcnmidwest.net
SIC: 7361 8082 Nurses' registry; Visiting nurse service
PA: Home Care Network, Inc.
  1191 Lyons Rd
  Dayton OH 45458

GEOGRAPHIC SECTION
Beachwood - Cuyahoga County (G-821)

(G-801)
IA URBAN HTELS BCHWOOD TRS LLC
Also Called: Embassy Suites
3775 Park East Dr (44122-4307)
PHONE.................216 765-8066
EMP: 99 EST: 2008
SQ FT: 66,940
SALES (est): 4.19MM **Privately Held**
Web: www.hilton.com
SIC: 7011 Hotels and motels

(G-802)
INSIGHT2PROFIT LLC (PA)
Also Called: Insight2profit
3333 Richmond Rd Ste 200 (44122-4196)
PHONE.................440 646-9490
Carl Will, *CEO*
Chris Donnelly, *Dir*
Chaz Napoli, *COO*
Jay Yellen, *Dir*
Yolanda Moore, *VP*
EMP: 38 EST: 2009
SALES (est): 13.75MM
SALES (corp-wide): 13.75MM **Privately Held**
Web: www.insight2profit.com
SIC: 8748 Agricultural consultant

(G-803)
INTEREX INC
3700 Park East Dr Ste 250 (44122-4318)
PHONE.................646 905-0091
Jamie Fraser, *CEO*
EMP: 50 EST: 1997
SALES (est): 2.05MM **Privately Held**
SIC: 8748 7361 Business consulting, nec; Employment agencies

(G-804)
JEWISH FMLY SVC ASSN CLVLAND O (PA)
Also Called: JEWISH COMMUNITY CARE AT HOME
29125 Chagrin Blvd (44122-4609)
PHONE.................216 292-3999
Robert Shakno, *CEO*
David Hlavac, *
EMP: 50 EST: 1907
SQ FT: 16,000
SALES (est): 5.02MM
SALES (corp-wide): 5.02MM **Privately Held**
Web: www.jfsa-cleveland.org
SIC: 8322 Social service center

(G-805)
JEWISH FMLY SVC ASSN CLVLAND O
Also Called: Professional Services
29125 Chagrin Blvd (44122-4609)
PHONE.................216 292-3999
Kathy Levine, *Dir*
EMP: 450
SALES (corp-wide): 5.02MM **Privately Held**
Web: www.jfsa-cleveland.org
SIC: 8322 Social service center
PA: Jewish Family Service Association Of Cleveland, Ohio
29125 Chagrin Blvd
Beachwood OH 44122
216 292-3999

(G-806)
KIRTLAND CAPITAL PARTNERS LP (PA)
Also Called: K C P
3201 Enterprise Pkwy Ste 200 (44122)
PHONE.................216 593-0100
◆ EMP: 46 EST: 1992
SQ FT: 4,031
SALES (est): 44.69MM **Privately Held**
Web: www.kirtlandcapital.com
SIC: 5051 3312 3498 3494 Metals service centers and offices; Tubes, steel and iron; Fabricated pipe and fittings; Valves and pipe fittings, nec

(G-807)
LAKE HOSPITAL SYSTEM INC
Also Called: Beachwood Medical Center
25501 Chagrin Blvd (44122-5603)
PHONE.................216 545-4800
EMP: 107
SALES (corp-wide): 878.24MM **Privately Held**
Web: www.uhhospitals.org
SIC: 8062 General medical and surgical hospitals
HQ: Lake Hospital System, Inc.
7590 Auburn Rd
Concord Township OH 44077
440 375-8100

(G-808)
MANDEL JCC
26001 S Woodland Rd (44122-3367)
PHONE.................781 934-5774
EMP: 29 EST: 2019
SALES (est): 13.71MM **Privately Held**
Web: www.mandeljcc.org
SIC: 8322 Community center

(G-809)
MANDEL JWISH CMNTY CTR OF CLVL
Also Called: Mandel Jcc
26001 S Woodland Rd (44122-3367)
PHONE.................216 831-0700
Michael Hyman, *CEO*
Elizabeth Nudelman, *
Gilon Rubanenko, *
EMP: 150 EST: 1948
SQ FT: 93,000
SALES (est): 13.14MM **Privately Held**
Web: www.mandeljcc.org
SIC: 8322 Community center

(G-810)
MARSH BERRY & COMPANY LLC (PA)
28601 Chagrin Blvd Ste 400 (44122-4556)
PHONE.................440 637-8122
John Wepler, *CEO*
Douglas A Yoh, *
Valerie Weber, *
John Wepler, *Ex VP*
Lawrence J Marsh, *
EMP: 27 EST: 1975
SALES (est): 12.18MM
SALES (corp-wide): 12.18MM **Privately Held**
Web: www.marshberry.com
SIC: 8742 8741 6211 Business management consultant; Management services; Investment bankers

(G-811)
MASTER BUILDERS LLC (HQ)
Also Called: Degussa Construction
23700 Chagrin Blvd (44122-5506)
PHONE.................800 228-3318
Anthony Price, *CEO*
◆ EMP: 50 EST: 1911
SALES (est): 467.64MM **Privately Held**
Web: master-builders-solutions.basf.us
SIC: 2899 2851 1799 Concrete curing and hardening compounds; Epoxy coatings; Caulking (construction)
PA: Sika Ag
Zugerstrasse 50
Baar ZG 6341

(G-812)
MASTERBRAND CABINETS LLC (HQ)
Also Called: Decora
3300 Enterprise Pkwy Ste 300 (44122)
P.O. Box 420 (47547-0420)
PHONE.................812 482-2527
Dave Banyard, *Pr*
Angela M Pla, *
Matthew C Lenz, *
Andi Simon, *
▲ EMP: 300 EST: 1986
SALES (est): 1.3B
SALES (corp-wide): 2.73B **Publicly Held**
Web: www.masterbrand.com
SIC: 2434 7371 Wood kitchen cabinets; Computer software development
PA: Masterbrand, Inc.
1 Masterbrand Cabinets Dr
Jasper IN 47546
812 482-2527

(G-813)
MCM CAPITAL PARTNERS II LP (PA)
25201 Chagrin Blvd Ste 360 (44122-5633)
PHONE.................216 514-1840
Mark Mansour, *Mng Pt*
Steve Ross, *Ex Dir*
James Poffenberger, *Ex Dir*
Gerry Weimann, *Ex Dir*
EMP: 343 EST: 1992
SQ FT: 5,000
SALES (est): 25.5MM **Privately Held**
Web: www.mcmcapital.com
SIC: 6799 Investors, nec

(G-814)
MEDIC MANAGEMENT GROUP LLC (PA)
3201 Enterprise Pkwy Ste 370 (44122)
PHONE.................330 670-5316
Thomas Ferkovic, *Pr*
EMP: 87 EST: 1999
SALES (est): 10.97MM
SALES (corp-wide): 10.97MM **Privately Held**
Web: www.medicmgmt.com
SIC: 8721 Billing and bookkeeping service

(G-815)
METROHEALTH SYSTEM
Also Called: Metrohealth Beachwood Hlth Ctr
3609 Park East Dr Ste 300 (44122-4309)
PHONE.................216 765-0733
EMP: 355
SALES (corp-wide): 620.72MM **Privately Held**
Web: www.metrohealth.org
SIC: 8062 General medical and surgical hospitals
PA: The Metrohealth System
2500 Metrohealth Dr
Cleveland OH 44109
216 778-7800

(G-816)
METROHEALTH SYSTEM
Also Called: Metrohlth Pepper Pike Hlth Ctr
3609 Park East Dr Ste 206 (44122-4309)
PHONE.................216 591-0523
EMP: 177
SALES (corp-wide): 620.72MM **Privately Held**
Web: www.metrohealth.org
SIC: 8062 General medical and surgical hospitals
PA: The Metrohealth System
2500 Metrohealth Dr
Cleveland OH 44109
216 778-7800

(G-817)
MIM SOFTWARE INC (PA)
25800 Science Park Dr Ste 180 (44122-7311)
PHONE.................216 455-0600
Andrew Nelson, *CEO*
Jonathan Piper, *
Peter Simmelink, *
Jerimy Brockway, *
Mark Cain, *
EMP: 160 EST: 2003
SALES (est): 35.87MM
SALES (corp-wide): 35.87MM **Privately Held**
Web: www.mimsoftware.com
SIC: 7372 Application computer software

(G-818)
MOLE CONSTRUCTORS INC
3201 Enterprise Pkwy Ste 220 (44122)
PHONE.................440 248-0616
Victor J Scaravilli, *CEO*
Lawrence William, *Prin*
EMP: 809 EST: 1995
SALES (est): 3.12MM
SALES (corp-wide): 1.6B **Publicly Held**
Web: www.southlandholdings.com
SIC: 8711 Construction and civil engineering
HQ: Southland Holdings, Inc.
1100 Kubota Dr
Grapevine TX 76051
817 293-4263

(G-819)
MONTEFIORE HOME
1 David Myers Pkwy (44122)
PHONE.................216 360-9080
Lauren B Rock, *CEO*
Mark Weiss, *
EMP: 450 EST: 1881
SQ FT: 180,000
SALES (est): 24.53MM
SALES (corp-wide): 39.28MM **Privately Held**
Web: www.menorahpark.org
SIC: 8051 Skilled nursing care facilities
PA: Menorah Park Center For Senior Living Bet Moshav Zekenim Hadati
27100 Cedar Rd
Cleveland OH 44122
216 831-6500

(G-820)
MURWOOD REAL ESTATE GROUP LLC
Also Called: Keller Williams Realtors
29225 Chagrin Blvd (44122-4629)
PHONE.................216 839-5500
EMP: 28 EST: 2002
SALES (est): 1.65MM **Privately Held**
Web: www.kw.com
SIC: 6531 Real estate agent, residential

(G-821)
NORTH EAST OHIO HEALTH SVCS (PA)
Also Called: Connectons Hlth Wllness Advcac
24200 Chagrin Blvd (44122-5529)
PHONE.................216 831-6466
Esther Pla, *CEO*
James Nagle, *
EMP: 52 EST: 1969
SQ FT: 12,000
SALES (est): 5.06MM
SALES (corp-wide): 5.06MM **Privately Held**
Web: www.connectionscleveland.org
SIC: 8322 8093 General counseling services; Specialty outpatient clinics, nec

Beachwood - Cuyahoga County (G-822)

GEOGRAPHIC SECTION

(G-822)
NORTHCOAST HEALTH CARE GROUP
3733 Park East Dr Ste 250 (44122-4334)
PHONE..................................330 856-2656
Melissa Miller, *Mgr*
EMP: 34
SALES (corp-wide): 1.17K **Privately Held**
SIC: 8082 Home health care services
HQ: Northcoast Health Care Group, Inc
  6600 France Ave S Ste 510
  Minneapolis MN 55435

(G-823)
ONE80 INTERMEDIARIES INC
Also Called: Interntnal Excess Prgram Mnger
3700 Park East Dr Ste 250 (44122-4318)
PHONE..................................617 330-5700
Matthew Power, *Mgr*
EMP: 50
SALES (corp-wide): 1.03B **Privately Held**
Web: www.one80.com
SIC: 6411 Insurance brokers, nec
HQ: One80 Intermediaries Inc.
  160 Federal St Fl 4
  Boston MA 02110
  216 797-9700

(G-824)
OXFORD HARRIMAN & CO AM LLC ✿
3201 Enterprise Pkwy Ste 400 (44122)
PHONE..................................216 755-7150
Dennis Barba, *CEO*
EMP: 33 **EST:** 2022
SALES (est): 994.39K **Privately Held**
SIC: 8748 Business consulting, nec

(G-825)
PENSKE LOGISTICS LLC
Also Called: Penske Logistics
3000 Auburn Dr Ste 100 (44122-4333)
PHONE..................................216 765-5475
Peter Smith, *Ch Bd*
EMP: 75
SALES (corp-wide): 2.11B **Privately Held**
Web: www.penskelogistics.com
SIC: 7513 Truck rental and leasing, no drivers
HQ: Penske Logistics Llc
  Rte 10 Green Hills
  Reading PA 19603
  610 775-6000

(G-826)
PRECISION DIAGNOSTIC IMAGING
3609 Park East Dr Ste 101 (44122-4331)
PHONE..................................216 360-8300
Kim Paul, *Brnch Mgr*
EMP: 100
Web: www.imagelinkmri.com
SIC: 8071 X-ray laboratory, including dental
HQ: Precision Diagnostic Imaging
  4400 Rockside Rd
  Cleveland OH

(G-827)
PREFERRED MEDICAL GROUP INC
23600 Commerce Park (44122-5817)
PHONE..................................404 403-8310
EMP: 140
SALES (corp-wide): 21.42MM **Privately Held**
Web: www.preferredvasculargroup.com
SIC: 8082 Home health care services
PA: Preferred Medical Group, Inc.
  9140 Crsea Del Fntana Way
  Naples FL 34109
  239 597-2010

(G-828)
QUADAX INC
25201 Chagrin Blvd Ste 290 (44122-5633)
PHONE..................................216 765-1144
Catherine Sicker, *Pr*
EMP: 246
SALES (corp-wide): 40.39MM **Privately Held**
Web: www.quadax.com
SIC: 8721 Billing and bookkeeping service
PA: Quadax, Inc.
  7500 Old Oak Blvd
  Middleburg Heights OH 44130
  440 777-6300

(G-829)
RCT ENGINEERING INC (PA)
24880 Shaker Blvd (44122-2356)
PHONE..................................561 684-7534
EMP: 28 **EST:** 1996
SQ FT: 3,800
SALES (est): 1.22MM **Privately Held**
SIC: 8711 Structural engineering

(G-830)
RETINA ASSOCIATE OF CLEVELAND (PA)
3401 Enterprise Pkwy Ste 300 (44122)
PHONE..................................216 831-5700
Lawrence J Singerman, *Pr*
Doctor Lawrence J Singerman, *Pr*
Doctor Michael Novak, *VP*
David Miller, *
EMP: 35 **EST:** 1984
SQ FT: 5,000
SALES (est): 10.97MM
SALES (corp-wide): 10.97MM **Privately Held**
Web: www.retina-doctors.com
SIC: 8011 Opthalmologist

(G-831)
RODDY GROUP INC
24500 Chagrin Blvd Ste 200 (44122-5646)
PHONE..................................216 763-0088
Matthew Roddy, *Pr*
EMP: 30 **EST:** 1998
SALES (est): 1.1MM **Privately Held**
SIC: 7322 Adjustment bureau, except insurance

(G-832)
SABER HEALTHCARE GROUP LLC
25825 Science Park Dr (44122-7323)
PHONE..................................216 464-4300
EMP: 34
SALES (corp-wide): 655.44MM **Privately Held**
Web: www.saberhealth.com
SIC: 8051 Convalescent home with continuous nursing care
PA: Saber Healthcare Group, L.L.C.
  23700 Commerce Park
  Beachwood OH 44122
  216 292-5706

(G-833)
SABER HEALTHCARE GROUP LLC (PA)
23700 Commerce Park (44122-5827)
PHONE..................................216 292-5706
William Weisberg, *Managing Member*
Michael E Defrank, *
EMP: 50 **EST:** 2001
SALES (est): 655.44MM
SALES (corp-wide): 655.44MM **Privately Held**
Web: www.saberhealth.com

SIC: 8051 8741 Convalescent home with continuous nursing care; Nursing and personal care facility management

(G-834)
SAFEGARD BCKGRUND SCRENING LLC
2000 Auburn Dr Ste 200 (44122-4328)
PHONE..................................877 700-7345
EMP: 50 **EST:** 2009
SALES (est): 3.64MM **Privately Held**
Web: www.safeguardcertify.com
SIC: 8742 7323 7363 Human resource consulting services; Credit reporting services; Labor resource services

(G-835)
SERVUS LLC
2000 Auburn Dr Ste 200 (44122-4328)
PHONE..................................844 737-8871
Scott Marincek, *Managing Member*
EMP: 2600 **EST:** 2006
SALES (est): 25.22MM **Privately Held**
Web: www.servus.vet
SIC: 8744 Facilities support services

(G-836)
SHAQ INC
Also Called: Shaw Stainless
22901 Millcreek Blvd Ste 650 (44122)
PHONE..................................770 427-0402
EMP: 70 **EST:** 2021
SALES (est): 12.11MM
SALES (corp-wide): 2.16B **Publicly Held**
SIC: 5085 5051 3312 Valves and fittings; Pipe and tubing, steel; Stainless steel
PA: Olympic Steel, Inc.
  22901 Mllcreek Blvd Ste 6
  Cleveland OH 44122
  216 292-3800

(G-837)
SHIELDS CAPITAL CORPORATION
20600 Chagrin Blvd Ste 800 (44122-5327)
PHONE..................................216 767-1340
Robert Snapper, *Prin*
EMP: 55
SALES (corp-wide): 22.88MM **Privately Held**
Web: www.wellingtonshields.com
SIC: 6799 Investors, nec
PA: Shields Capital Corporation
  140 Broadway Ste 4400
  New York NY 10005
  212 320-3000

(G-838)
SIKA MBCC US LLC
Also Called: Master Bldrs Sltons Cnstr Syst
23700 Chagrin Blvd (44122-5506)
PHONE..................................216 839-7500
Boris Gorella, *CEO*
Christian Hammel, *CFO*
Karsten Eller, *COO*
Bruce Christensen, *Pr*
EMP: 512 **EST:** 2020
SALES (est): 134.1MM **Privately Held**
Web: www.master-builders-solutions.com
SIC: 1771 2891 1799 Flooring contractor; Sealants; Coating, caulking, and weather, water, and fireproofing
HQ: Master Builders Solutions Admixtures Us, Llc
  23700 Chagrin Blvd
  Beachwood OH 44122
  216 839-7500

(G-839)
SITE CENTERS CORP (PA)
3300 Enterprise Pkwy (44122-7200)
PHONE..................................216 755-5500
David R Lukes, *Pr*
Terrance R Ahern, *
Michael A Makinen, *Ex VP*
Matthew L Ostrower, *Ex VP*
Christa A Vesy, *CAO*
EMP: 150 **EST:** 1965
SALES (est): 546.27MM
SALES (corp-wide): 546.27MM **Privately Held**
Web: www.sitecenters.com
SIC: 6798 Real estate investment trusts

(G-840)
SPITZ LAW FIRM LLC
25825 Science Park Dr Ste 200 (44122-7315)
PHONE..................................216 291-4744
Brian D Spitz, *Prin*
EMP: 78 **EST:** 2007
SALES (est): 4.86MM **Privately Held**
Web: www.calltherightattorney.com
SIC: 8111 General practice law office

(G-841)
STRATOS WEALTH PARTNERS LTD
3750 Park East Dr (44122-4348)
PHONE..................................440 519-2500
Jeffrey Concepcion, *CEO*
EMP: 108 **EST:** 2012
SALES (est): 22.67MM
SALES (corp-wide): 22.67MM **Privately Held**
Web: www.stratoswealthpartners.com
SIC: 8742 Financial consultant
PA: Man On The Moon, Llc
  6241 Riverside Dr Ste 1n
  Dublin OH 43017
  614 886-9395

(G-842)
SYNTHOMER LLC
25435 Harvard Rd (44122-6201)
PHONE..................................678 400-6655
Calum G Maclean, *CEO*
◆ **EMP:** 56 **EST:** 2012
SALES (est): 23.25MM
SALES (corp-wide): 2.46B **Privately Held**
Web: www.synthomer.com
SIC: 5169 5198 Adhesives and sealants; Paints
PA: Synthomer Plc
  Temple Mead
  Harlow CM20
  127 943-6211

(G-843)
TELARC INTERNATIONAL CORP
23412 Commerce Park (44122-5813)
PHONE..................................216 464-2313
Robert Woods, *Pr*
Jack Renner, *
Scott Peplin, *
EMP: 50 **EST:** 1985
SQ FT: 14,000
SALES (est): 3.31MM **Privately Held**
Web: www.telarc.com
SIC: 5099 7389 Compact discs; Music recording producer

(G-844)
TOA TECHNOLOGIES INC (PA)
3333 Richmond Rd Ste 420 (44122-4194)
PHONE..................................216 925-5950
Yuval Brisker, *Pr*
Irad Carmi, *
Brian Cook, *
Bruce Grainger, *

GEOGRAPHIC SECTION

Beavercreek - Greene County (G-864)

Michael Mcdonnell, *VP*
EMP: 216 **EST:** 2003
SALES (est): 25.39MM
SALES (corp-wide): 25.39MM **Privately Held**
Web: www.oracle.com
SIC: 7372 Prepackaged software

(G-845)
TOWER REAL ESTATE GROUP LLC
Also Called: Millennia Commercial Group Ltd
1000 Eaton Blvd (44122)
PHONE..................216 520-1250
Douglas L Miller, *Pr*
EMP: 610 **EST:** 2019
SALES (est): 243.94M
SALES (corp-wide): 198.28MM **Privately Held**
SIC: 8742 Management consulting services
PA: Millennia Housing Management, Ltd.
  4000 Key Tower 127 Pub Sq
  Cleveland OH 44114
  216 520-1250

(G-846)
TREMCO CPG INC (HQ)
3735 Green Rd (44122-5730)
PHONE..................216 292-5000
Paul Hoogenboom, *Pr*
EMP: 67 **EST:** 2021
SALES (est): 526.27MM
SALES (corp-wide): 7.26B **Publicly Held**
Web: www.tremcosealants.com
SIC: 5032 Brick, stone, and related material
PA: Rpm International Inc.
  2628 Pearl Rd
  Medina OH 44256
  330 273-5090

(G-847)
TREMCO INCORPORATED (HQ)
3735 Green Rd (44122-5730)
◆ **EMP:** 265 **EST:** 1980
SALES (est): 740.14MM
SALES (corp-wide): 7.26B **Publicly Held**
Web: www.tremcocpg.com
SIC: 2891 2952 1761 1752 Sealants; Roofing materials; Roofing contractor; Floor laying and floor work, nec
PA: Rpm International Inc.
  2628 Pearl Rd
  Medina OH 44256
  330 273-5090

(G-848)
UNIVERSITY HOSPITALS CLEVELAND
Also Called: Uh Landerbrook Health Center
26001 S Woodland Rd (44122-3367)
PHONE..................440 646-2626
EMP: 1697
SALES (corp-wide): 878.24MM **Privately Held**
Web: www.uhhospitals.org
SIC: 8062 General medical and surgical hospitals
HQ: University Hospitals Cleveland Medical Center
  11100 Euclid Ave
  Cleveland OH 44106

(G-849)
UNIVERSITY HSPTALS CLVLAND MED
Also Called: University Ophthalmologist
26001 S Woodland Rd (44122-3367)
PHONE..................216 378-6240
Doctor Suber Suang, *Prin*
EMP: 1234
SQ FT: 18,498
SALES (corp-wide): 878.24MM **Privately Held**
Web: www.uhhospitals.org
SIC: 8062 8011 General medical and surgical hospitals; Offices and clinics of medical doctors
HQ: University Hospitals Cleveland Medical Center
  11100 Euclid Ave
  Cleveland OH 44106

(G-850)
UNIVERSITY HSPTALS CLVLAND MED
Also Called: Alzheimer Center
23215 Commerce Park Ste 300 (44122-5803)
PHONE..................216 342-5556
EMP: 1851
SALES (corp-wide): 878.24MM **Privately Held**
Web: www.uhhospitals.org
SIC: 8062 8011 General medical and surgical hospitals; Offices and clinics of medical doctors
HQ: University Hospitals Cleveland Medical Center
  11100 Euclid Ave
  Cleveland OH 44106

(G-851)
WALNUT RIDGE STRGC MGT CO LLC
100 Park Ave Ste 400 (44122-8204)
PHONE..................234 678-3900
Jeanette M Thomas, *Managing Member*
EMP: 70 **EST:** 2009
SALES (est): 4.99MM **Privately Held**
Web: www.lkflt.org
SIC: 8741 Financial management for business

(G-852)
WORLD SYNERGY ENTERPRISES INC
Also Called: Formation V Consulting
3700 Park East Dr Ste 350 (44122-4339)
PHONE..................440 349-4940
Glenn Smith, *Pr*
EMP: 27 **EST:** 1998
SQ FT: 3,000
SALES (est): 3.51MM **Privately Held**
Web: www.worldsynergy.com
SIC: 7379 Computer related consulting services

(G-853)
ZINNER & CO
3201 Enterprise Pkwy Ste 410 (44122)
PHONE..................216 831-0733
Donald J Zinner, *Pt*
David Antine, *Pt*
Sidney Brode, *Pt*
Jill Giesy, *Pt*
EMP: 41 **EST:** 1939
SQ FT: 5,000
SALES (est): 3.1MM **Privately Held**
Web: www.zinnerco.com
SIC: 8721 Certified public accountant

Beavercreek
Greene County

(G-854)
22ND CENTURY TECHNOLOGIES INC
2601 Commons Blvd Ste 130 (45431-3830)
PHONE..................866 537-9191
Satvinder Singh, *Pr*
EMP: 420
SALES (corp-wide): 100.85MM **Privately Held**
Web: www.tscti.com
SIC: 7371 Computer software systems analysis and design, custom
PA: 22nd Century Technologies Inc.
  8251 Greensboro Dr # 900
  Mc Lean VA 22102
  732 537-9191

(G-855)
A M MANAGEMENT INC
2000 Zink Rd (45324-2018)
PHONE..................937 426-6500
Diana Spiegel, *Brnch Mgr*
EMP: 44
SALES (corp-wide): 4.4MM **Privately Held**
Web: www.ammanagement.net
SIC: 7021 Dormitory, commercially operated
PA: A M Management Inc
  2871 Heinz Rd Ste B
  Iowa City IA 52240
  319 354-1961

(G-856)
ALTAMIRA TECHNOLOGIES CORP
2850 Presidential Dr Ste 200 (45324-6298)
PHONE..................937 490-4804
Amber Scott, *Contracts Vice President*
EMP: 170
SALES (corp-wide): 47.57MM **Privately Held**
Web: www.altamiracorp.com
SIC: 7373 Systems integration services
HQ: Altamira Technologies Corporation
  8201 Greensboro Dr # 800
  Mc Lean VA 22102
  703 813-2100

(G-857)
ARCADIA SERVICES INC
Arcadia Health Care
2440 Dayton Xenia Rd Ste C (45434-7123)
PHONE..................937 912-5800
Cathy Sparling, *COO*
EMP: 36
SALES (corp-wide): 25.38MM **Privately Held**
Web: www.arcadiahomecare.com
SIC: 7363 8082 Medical help service; Home health care services
PA: Arcadia Services, Inc.
  20750 Civic Center Dr # 100
  Southfield MI 48076
  248 352-7530

(G-858)
ARCTOS MISSION SOLUTIONS LLC
2601 Mission Point Blvd (45431-6600)
PHONE..................813 609-5591
James Fugit, *CEO*
Steven Shugart, *
Todd J Schweitzer, *
Brian Overstreet, *
David Joseph, *
EMP: 40 **EST:** 2008
SALES (est): 4.65MM
SALES (corp-wide): 67.58MM **Privately Held**
Web: www.arctos-us.com
SIC: 7379 5045 3728 Computer related consulting services; Computers, peripherals, and software; Aircraft parts and equipment, nec
HQ: Arctos, Llc
  2601 Mssion Pt Blvd Ste 3
  Beavercreek OH 45431
  478 923-9995

(G-859)
ARCTOS TECH SOLUTIONS LLC (DH)
2601 Mission Point Blvd Ste 300 (45431-6600)
PHONE..................937 426-2808
EMP: 72 **EST:** 1961
SALES (est): 53.67MM
SALES (corp-wide): 67.58MM **Privately Held**
Web: www.arctos-us.com
SIC: 8711 7812 7221 Engineering services; Audio-visual program production; Photographic studios, portrait
HQ: Arctos, Llc
  2601 Mssion Pt Blvd Ste 3
  Beavercreek OH 45431
  478 923-9995

(G-860)
ARRAY INFORMATION TECH INC
2689 Commons Blvd Ste 105 (45431-3832)
PHONE..................937 203-3209
EMP: 43
SALES (corp-wide): 9.87B **Privately Held**
Web: www.arrayinfotech.com
SIC: 7379 Computer related consulting services
HQ: Array Information Technology, Inc.
  7474 Greenway Center Dr # 60
  Greenbelt MD 20770
  301 345-8188

(G-861)
AZIMUTH CORPORATION
2970 Presidential Dr Ste 200 (45324-6712)
PHONE..................937 256-8571
Valerie Rossi, *Pr*
Charles Rossi, *VP*
EMP: 110 **EST:** 2001
SQ FT: 3,286
SALES (est): 24.67MM **Privately Held**
Web: www.azimuth-corp.com
SIC: 8711 8731 8742 Consulting engineer; Commercial physical research; Management consulting services

(G-862)
BAE SYSTEMS SCIENCE & TECHNOLOGY INC
3725 Pentagon Blvd Ste 110 (45431-2775)
EMP: 2900
SIC: 8711 Engineering services

(G-863)
BEAVERCREEK MEDICAL CENTER
Also Called: GRANDVIEW HOSPITAL & MEDICAL C
3535 Pentagon Blvd (45431-1705)
PHONE..................937 702-4000
Ann Hopkins, *Mgr*
EMP: 160 **EST:** 2017
SALES (est): 264.75MM
SALES (corp-wide): 2.46B **Privately Held**
Web: www.ketteringhealth.org
SIC: 8062 General medical and surgical hospitals
HQ: Dayton Osteopathic Hospital
  405 W Grand Ave
  Dayton OH 45405
  937 762-1629

(G-864)
BOOZ ALLEN HAMILTON INC
3800 Pentagon Blvd Ste 110 (45431-2199)
PHONE..................937 912-6400
Michael Mushala, *Mgr*
EMP: 31
SALES (corp-wide): 9.26B **Publicly Held**
Web: www.boozallen.com
SIC: 8742 Human resource consulting services
HQ: Booz Allen Hamilton Inc.
  8283 Greensboro Dr # 700
  Mc Lean VA 22102
  703 902-5000

Beavercreek - Greene County (G-865)   **GEOGRAPHIC SECTION**

(G-865)
BOOZ ALLEN HAMILTON INC
3800 Pentagon Blvd Ste 110 (45431-2199)
PHONE..................................937 429-5580
Charles Flowers, *Brnch Mgr*
EMP: 57
SALES (corp-wide): 9.26B **Publicly Held**
Web: www.boozallen.com
SIC: 8742 Business management consultant
HQ: Booz Allen Hamilton Inc.
   8283 Greensboro Dr # 700
   Mc Lean VA 22102
   703 902-5000

(G-866)
BTAS INC (PA)
Also Called: Business Tech & Solutions
4391 Dayton Xenia Rd (45432-1803)
PHONE..................................937 431-9431
EMP: 80 **EST:** 1995
SQ FT: 7,500
SALES (est): 24.8MM **Privately Held**
Web: www.btas.com
SIC: 8742 7374 7371 Business management consultant; Data processing and preparation; Custom computer programming services

(G-867)
C H DEAN LLC (PA)
Also Called: Dean Financial Management
3500 Pentagon Blvd Ste 200 (45431-2376)
PHONE..................................937 222-9531
Pamala Miller, *Managing Member*
Dennis D Dean, *
Stephen M Miller, *
Mark E Schutter, *
Ronald A Best Phr, *
EMP: 60 **EST:** 1975
SQ FT: 26,000
SALES (est): 8.37MM
SALES (corp-wide): 8.37MM **Privately Held**
Web: www.chdean.com
SIC: 6282 8721 8742 Investment counselors; Accounting services, except auditing; Management consulting services

(G-868)
CACI MTL SYSTEMS INC
2685 Hibiscus Way Ste 200 (45431-1296)
PHONE..................................937 429-2771
J P London, *Ch Bd*
EMP: 88
SALES (corp-wide): 6.7B **Publicly Held**
Web: www.caci.com
SIC: 7373 Computer systems analysis and design
HQ: Caci Mtl Systems, Inc.
   1100 N Glebe Rd Ste 200
   Arlington VA 22201
   703 841-7800

(G-869)
CACI MTL SYSTEMS INC
3481 Dayton Xenia Rd Ste A (45432-2730)
PHONE..................................937 426-3111
J P London, *Ch Bd*
EMP: 88
SALES (corp-wide): 6.7B **Publicly Held**
Web: www.caci.com
SIC: 7373 Computer integrated systems design
HQ: Caci Mtl Systems, Inc.
   1100 N Glebe Rd Ste 200
   Arlington VA 22201
   703 841-7800

(G-870)
CADX SYSTEMS INC
2689 Commons Blvd Ste 100 (45431-3832)
PHONE..................................937 431-1464
James Corbett, *Pr*
EMP: 71 **EST:** 2002
SALES (est): 1.58MM
SALES (corp-wide): 17.32MM **Publicly Held**
SIC: 8071 Testing laboratories
PA: Icad, Inc.
   98 Spit Brook Rd Ste 100
   Nashua NH 03062
   603 882-5200

(G-871)
CHOICE HEALTHCARE LIMITED
1257 N Fairfield Rd (45432-2633)
PHONE..................................937 254-6220
Megan Upchurch, *Admn*
Cammy Burns, *Prin*
EMP: 80 **EST:** 2000
SALES (est): 2.68MM **Privately Held**
SIC: 8082 Visiting nurse service

(G-872)
CLEAR CREEK APPLIED TECH (PA)
3855 Colonel Glenn Hwy Ste 100 (45324-2298)
PHONE..................................937 912-5438
Martin March, *CEO*
Arnold Talcott, *Pur Mgr*
Brad Dunaway, *COO*
EMP: 35 **EST:** 2006
SQ FT: 2,000
SALES (est): 5.13MM **Privately Held**
Web: www.jfti.com
SIC: 8711 Consulting engineer

(G-873)
COMPUNET CLINICAL LABS LLC
3535 Pentagon Blvd (45431-1705)
PHONE..................................937 912-9017
John Manier, *Brnch Mgr*
EMP: 48
SALES (corp-wide): 2.41MM **Privately Held**
Web: www.compunetlab.com
SIC: 8071 Medical laboratories
HQ: Compunet Clinical Laboratories, Llc
   2308 Sandridge Dr
   Moraine OH 45439
   937 296-0844

(G-874)
COURTYARD BY MARRIOTT
Also Called: Courtyard By Marriott
2777 Fairfield Commons Blvd (45431)
PHONE..................................937 429-5203
Dan Petterson, *Prin*
EMP: 40 **EST:** 2007
SALES (est): 846.3K **Privately Held**
Web: www.marriott.com
SIC: 7011 Hotels and motels

(G-875)
CREDENCE MGT SLTIONS LTD LBLTY
2940 Presidential Dr Ste 230 (45324-6762)
PHONE..................................571 620-7586
Siddhartha Chowdhary, *CEO*
EMP: 198
Web: www.credence-llc.com
SIC: 7379 Computer related consulting services
PA: Credence Management Solutions Limited Liability Company
   8609 Wstwd Ctr Dr Ste 3
   Vienna VA 22182

(G-876)
CREEK TECHNOLOGIES COMPANY
Also Called: Creek Tech
2372 Lakeview Dr Ste H (45431-2566)
PHONE..................................937 272-4581
Lee Allen Culver, *Pr*
EMP: 120 **EST:** 2007
SQ FT: 16,000
SALES (est): 9.85MM **Privately Held**
Web: www.creek-technologies.com
SIC: 7379 Computer related maintenance services

(G-877)
DEATON ENTERPRISES INC
Also Called: Finer Services
1619 Mardon Dr (45432-1921)
PHONE..................................937 320-6200
Chris Hill, *Genl Mgr*
EMP: 215
SALES (corp-wide): 2.1MM **Privately Held**
SIC: 7349 Maid services, contract or fee basis
PA: Deaton Enterprises, Inc.
   4108 Dayton Xenia Rd
   Beavercreek OH 45432
   937 429-9844

(G-878)
DRS SIGNAL TECHNOLOGIES INC
4393 Dayton Xenia Rd (45432-1803)
PHONE..................................937 429-7470
Leo Torresani, *Pr*
EMP: 47 **EST:** 1990
SALES (est): 2.73MM
SALES (corp-wide): 15.28B **Publicly Held**
Web: www.leonardodrs.com
SIC: 3825 7371 Electrical energy measuring equipment; Custom computer programming services
HQ: Leonardo Drs, Inc.
   2345 Crystal Dr Ste 1000
   Arlington VA 22202
   703 416-8000

(G-879)
EDICT SYSTEMS INC
2434 Esquire Dr (45431-2573)
PHONE..................................937 429-4288
Ason K Wadzinski, *Ch Bd*
EMP: 45 **EST:** 1989
SQ FT: 12,000
SALES (est): 11.71MM
SALES (corp-wide): 12.55MM **Privately Held**
Web: www.edictsystems.com
SIC: 7372 Prepackaged software
PA: Advant-E Corporation
   2434 Esquire Dr
   Beavercreek OH 45431
   937 429-4288

(G-880)
GERMAIN OF BEAVERCREEK II LLC
Also Called: Germain Honda of Beavercreek
2300 Heller Dr (45434-7225)
P.O. Box 340400 (45434-0400)
PHONE..................................937 429-2400
Stephen Germain, *Managing Member*
Jerry Poland, *
John Malishenko, *
EMP: 100 **EST:** 2014
SALES (est): 24.99MM **Privately Held**
Web: www.germainhondaofbeavercreek.com
SIC: 5511 7538 Automobiles, new and used; General automotive repair shops

(G-881)
GORDON W WOMACK DDS
3300 Kemp Rd (45431-4200)
PHONE..................................937 426-2653
Gordon W Womack D.d.s., *Owner*
EMP: 31 **EST:** 1986
SALES (est): 922.87K **Privately Held**
Web: www.beavercreekpediatricdentistry.com
SIC: 8021 Dentists' office

(G-882)
HOME EXPERTS REALTY
4230 Dayton Xenia Rd (45432-1801)
PHONE..................................937 705-6336
EMP: 79 **EST:** 2017
SALES (est): 1.11MM **Privately Held**
Web: www.homeexpertsrealty.net
SIC: 6531 Real estate agent, residential

(G-883)
HOSPICE OF MIAMI VALLEY LLC
2601 Mission Point Blvd Ste 300 (45431)
PHONE..................................937 458-6028
Carol L Brad, *CEO*
EMP: 28 **EST:** 2008
SALES (est): 7.84MM **Privately Held**
Web: www.hospiceofthemiamivalley.org
SIC: 8052 Personal care facility

(G-884)
ILLUMINATION WORKS LLC
2689 Commons Blvd Ste 120 (45431-3832)
PHONE..................................937 938-1321
Jonathon J Mitchell, *Managing Member*
EMP: 85 **EST:** 2006
SQ FT: 6,200
SALES (est): 12.98MM **Privately Held**
Web: www.ilwllc.com
SIC: 7379 7374 8711 8748 Data processing consultant; Data processing and preparation; Consulting engineer; Business consulting, nec

(G-885)
KBR WYLE SERVICES LLC
2601 Mission Point Blvd Ste 300 (45431)
PHONE..................................937 912-3470
Douglas Van Kirk, *Sec*
EMP: 49
Web: www.kbr.com
SIC: 8734 Testing laboratories
HQ: Kbr Wyle Services, Llc
   601 Jefferson St Ste 7911
   Houston TX 77002

(G-886)
LEIDOS INC
3745 Pentagon Blvd (45431-2369)
PHONE..................................937 656-8433
Dennis Anders, *Brnch Mgr*
EMP: 77
Web: www.leidos.com
SIC: 8731 7371 7373 8742 Commercial physical research; Computer software development; Systems engineering, computer related; Training and development consultant
HQ: Leidos, Inc.
   1750 Presidents St
   Reston VA 20190
   571 526-6000

(G-887)
LIFECYCLE SOLUTIONS JV LLC
2689 Commons Blvd Ste 120 (45431)
PHONE..................................937 938-1321
Jonathon Mitchell, *Pt*
EMP: 99 **EST:** 2017
SALES (est): 1.32MM **Privately Held**
Web: www.ilwllc.com
SIC: 7371 Custom computer programming services

(G-888)
LINQUEST CORPORATION
2647 Commons Blvd (45431-3704)

PHONE..............................937 306-6040
Greg Dawson, VP
EMP: 99
SALES (corp-wide): 116.91MM Privately Held
Web: www.linquest.com
SIC: 8711 Engineering services
PA: Linquest Corporation
 2551 Dulles View Dr # 200
 Herndon VA 20171
 323 924-1600

(G-889)
LOWES HOME CENTERS LLC
Also Called: Lowe's
2850 Centre Dr Ste I (45324-2675)
PHONE..............................937 427-1110
EMP: 148
SALES (corp-wide): 86.38B Publicly Held
Web: www.lowes.com
SIC: 5211 5031 5722 5064 Home centers; Building materials, exterior; Household appliance stores; Electrical appliances, television and radio
HQ: Lowe's Home Centers, Llc
 1000 Lowes Blvd
 Mooresville NC 28117
 336 658-4000

(G-890)
MCKEEVER & NIEKAMP ELECTRIC
1834 Woods Dr (45432-2261)
PHONE..............................937 431-9363
Larry A Mckeever, Pr
Doug Niekamp, *
EMP: 49 EST: 1993
SQ FT: 3,000
SALES (est): 5.16MM Privately Held
Web: www.mnelectric.biz
SIC: 1731 General electrical contractor

(G-891)
MCR LLC
2601 Mission Point Blvd Ste 320 (45431)
PHONE..............................937 879-5055
Kurt Gwaltney, Mgr
EMP: 49
SALES (corp-wide): 30.84MM Privately Held
Web: www.spa.com
SIC: 8741 Administrative management
PA: Mcr, Llc
 2010 Corp Rdg Ste 850
 Mclean VA 22102
 703 506-4600

(G-892)
PAYAL DEVELOPMENT LLC
Also Called: Country Suites By Carlson
3971 Colonel Glenn Hwy (45324-2032)
PHONE..............................937 429-2222
EMP: 32 EST: 2000
SALES (est): 905.46K Privately Held
Web: www.radissonhotels.com
SIC: 7011 Hotels and motels

(G-893)
PERDUCO GROUP INC
2647 Commons Blvd (45431-3704)
PHONE..............................937 401-0268
EMP: 44 EST: 2011
SQ FT: 4,580
SALES (est): 2.76MM
SALES (corp-wide): 116.91MM Privately Held
Web: www.linquest.com
SIC: 8741 8742 Management services; Management consulting services
PA: Linquest Corporation
 2551 Dulles View Dr # 200
 Herndon VA 20171
 323 924-1600

(G-894)
PH FAIRBORN HT OWNER 2800 LLC
Also Called: Holiday Inn
2800 Presidential Dr (45324-6264)
PHONE..............................937 426-7800
Nathaniel Hamilton, Genl Mgr
EMP: 85 EST: 2017
SALES (est): 2.82MM Privately Held
Web: www.holidayinn.com
SIC: 7011 Hotels and motels

(G-895)
PRIMARY CR NTWRK PRMR HLTH PRT
722 N Fairfield Rd (45434-5918)
PHONE..............................937 208-7000
EMP: 43
SALES (corp-wide): 25.36MM Privately Held
Web: www.premierhealth.com
SIC: 8011 General and family practice, physician/surgeon
PA: Primary Care Network Of Premier Health Partners
 110 N Main St Ste 350
 Dayton OH 45402
 937 226-7085

(G-896)
QUEST GYMNSTICS EXTREME SPT CT
3820 Kemp Rd (45431-2351)
PHONE..............................937 426-3547
Harold Debolt, *
EMP: 28 EST: 2017
SALES (est): 600K Privately Held
Web: www.questextreme.com
SIC: 7999 Gymnastic instruction, non-membership

(G-897)
R ROBNSONS TWING RECOVERY LLC
1859 N Central Dr (45432-2011)
PHONE..............................937 458-3666
Robert Robinson, Brnch Mgr
EMP: 27
Web: www.rrobinsons.com
SIC: 7549 Towing service, automotive
PA: R. Robinson's Towing & Recovery L.L.C.
 3800 State Route 444
 Fairborn OH 45324

(G-898)
RADIANCE TECHNOLOGIES INC
3715 Pentagon Blvd (45431-2369)
PHONE..............................937 425-0747
William C Bailey, CEO
EMP: 117
SALES (corp-wide): 376.73MM Privately Held
Web: www.radiancetech.com
SIC: 8731 Commercial physical research
PA: Radiance Technologies, Inc.
 310 Bob Heath Dr Nw
 Huntsville AL 35806
 256 704-3400

(G-899)
RAINBOW DATA SYSTEMS INC
2358 Lakeview Dr Ste A (45431)
PHONE..............................937 431-8000
John H Kim, Pr
Doug Mummert, *
Sam Morgan, *
Deanna Collier, *
EMP: 34 EST: 1996

SQ FT: 7,100
SALES (est): 14.51MM Privately Held
Web: www.rainbowdata.com
SIC: 7379 7371 7373 Computer related consulting services; Custom computer programming services; Computer integrated systems design

(G-900)
RGBSI AEROSPACE & DEFENSE LLC
Also Called: Rgbsi A&D
2850 Presidential Dr Ste 120 (45324-6298)
PHONE..............................248 761-0412
Shweta Kumar, Pr
EMP: 90 EST: 2020
SALES (est): 9.53MM
SALES (corp-wide): 84.19MM Privately Held
Web: www.rgbsiaero.com
SIC: 8731 Commercial physical research
PA: Rapid Global Business Solutions, Inc.
 1200 Stephenson Hwy
 Troy MI 48083
 248 589-1135

(G-901)
RIVERSIDE RESEARCH INSTITUTE
2640 Hibiscus Way (45431-1798)
PHONE..............................937 431-3810
Brian O'connor, Mgr
EMP: 118
SALES (corp-wide): 139.33MM Privately Held
Web: www.riversideresearch.org
SIC: 8733 Research institute
PA: Riverside Research Institute
 100 William St
 New York NY 10038
 212 563-4545

(G-902)
ROUND ROOM LLC
3301 Dayton Xenia Rd (45432-2758)
PHONE..............................937 429-2230
EMP: 29
Web: www.tccrocks.com
SIC: 4813 Local and long distance telephone communications
PA: Round Room, Llc
 525 Congressional Blvd
 Carmel IN 46032

(G-903)
RYAN G HARRIS DMD
1205 Meadow Bridge Dr (45434-6380)
PHONE..............................937 426-5411
Ryan Harris, Pr
EMP: 29
Web: www.harrisperio.com
SIC: 8021 Periodontist
PA: Ryan G Harris Dmd
 5138 Cedar Village Dr
 Mason OH 45040

(G-904)
SERCO INC
2661 Commons Blvd (45431-3704)
PHONE..............................502 364-8157
Dan Coots, Mgr
EMP: 56
SALES (corp-wide): 6.07B Privately Held
Web: www.serco.com
SIC: 8744 Facilities support services
HQ: Serco Inc.
 12930 Worldgate Dr # 600
 Herndon VA 20170

(G-905)
SIEBENTHALER COMPANY (PA)
Also Called: Siebenthaler's Garden Center
2074 Beaver Valley Rd (45434-6976)
PHONE..............................937 274-1154
Robert Siebenthaler, Pr
R Jeffrey Siebenthaler, *
Michael Fanning, *
David C Ruppert, *
EMP: 90 EST: 1870
SQ FT: 3,000
SALES (est): 9.75MM
SALES (corp-wide): 9.75MM Privately Held
Web: www.siebenthaler.com
SIC: 0782 5193 5261 Landscape contractors ; Nursery stock; Retail nurseries and garden stores

(G-906)
SIERRA NEVADA CORPORATION
2611 Commons Blvd (45431-3704)
PHONE..............................937 431-2800
William Sullivan, Prin
EMP: 111
SALES (corp-wide): 2.38B Privately Held
Web: www.sncorp.com
SIC: 8731 3577 Electronic research; Computer peripheral equipment, nec
PA: Sierra Nevada Corporation
 444 Salomon Cir
 Sparks NV 89434
 775 331-0222

(G-907)
SOLUTONS THRUGH INNVTIVE TECH (PA)
Also Called: STI-TEC
3152 Presidential Dr (45324-2039)
PHONE..............................937 320-9994
Alvin Hall Senior, Ch Bd
Charles Colon Iii, CEO
EMP: 56 EST: 2000
SQ FT: 2,000
SALES (est): 27.31MM
SALES (corp-wide): 27.31MM Privately Held
Web: www.sti-tec.com
SIC: 7371 8711 8999 8731 Computer software development and applications; Engineering services; Scientific consulting; Biotechnical research, commercial

(G-908)
SRC INC
2900 Presidential Dr Ste 240 (45324-6259)
PHONE..............................937 431-0717
EMP: 27
SALES (corp-wide): 287.79MM Privately Held
Web: www.srcinc.com
SIC: 8733 Noncommercial biological research organization
PA: Src, Inc.
 7502 Round Pond Rd
 North Syracuse NY 13212
 315 452-8000

(G-909)
SUMARIA SYSTEMS LLC
3164 Presidential Dr (45324-2039)
PHONE..............................937 429-6070
EMP: 131
SALES (corp-wide): 100.85MM Privately Held
Web: www.sumaria.com
SIC: 7373 8711 7374 7371 Computer integrated systems design; Consulting engineer; Data processing and preparation; Custom computer programming services
PA: Sumaria Systems, Llc
 8 Essex Center Dr Ste 210
 Peabody MA 01960
 978 739-4200

Beavercreek - Greene County (G-910)
GEOGRAPHIC SECTION

(G-910)
SYTRONICS INC
4433 Dayton Xenia Rd Bldg 1 (45432-1805)
PHONE..............................937 431-6100
Barrett Myers, *Pr*
Sonja Johannes, *Sec*
EMP: 35 **EST:** 1983
SQ FT: 22,000
SALES (est): 5.58MM **Privately Held**
Web: www.sytronics.com
SIC: 8732 8731 7373 Commercial nonphysical research; Commercial physical research; Computer systems analysis and design

(G-911)
TYTO GOVERNMENT SOLUTIONS INC
Also Called: AT&T
2940 Presidential Dr Ste 390 (45324-6762)
PHONE..............................937 306-3030
Kirk Dunker, *Genl Mgr*
EMP: 31
SQ FT: 1,500
Web: www.gotyto.com
SIC: 8742 Management consulting services
HQ: Tyto Government Solutions, Inc.
12901 Worldgate Dr
Herndon VA 20170
703 885-7900

(G-912)
UNIVERSAL ONE INC
Also Called: Univerrsal 1 Credit Union
2450 Esquire Dr (45431-2573)
P.O. Box 341090 (45434-1090)
PHONE..............................937 431-3100
Loren Rush, *Brnch Mgr*
EMP: 69
Web: www.u1cu.org
SIC: 6061 Federal credit unions
PA: Universal One Inc
1080 N Bridge St Ste 47a
Chillicothe OH 45601

(G-913)
VANA SOLUTIONS LLC
3610 Pentagon Blvd Ste 110 (45431)
PHONE..............................937 242-6399
EMP: 50 **EST:** 2004
SALES (est): 6.32MM **Privately Held**
Web: www.vanasolutions.com
SIC: 7379 Computer related maintenance services

(G-914)
WINGATE BY WYNDHAM DYTON FRBOR
Also Called: Wingate By Wyndham
3055 Presidential Dr (45324-6221)
PHONE..............................937 912-9350
Sara Sohi, *Owner*
EMP: 27 **EST:** 2010
SALES (est): 195.64K **Privately Held**
Web: www.wyndhamhotels.com
SIC: 7011 Hotels

(G-915)
WRIGHT EXECUTIVE HT LTD PARTNR (PA)
Also Called: Homewood Suites
2800 Presidential Dr (45324-6296)
PHONE..............................937 426-7800
Karl Williard, *Dir*
Miller-valentine Realty, *General PAR*
Steve Groppe, *Genl Mgr*
EMP: 70 **EST:** 1987
SALES (est): 6.28MM **Privately Held**
Web: www.holidayinn.com

SIC: 7011 Hotels and motels

(G-916)
WRIGHT STATE UNIVERSITY
Also Called: Quest Diagnostics
3640 Colonel Glenn Hwy (45324-2096)
PHONE..............................937 775-3333
Simone Polk, *Mgr*
EMP: 47
SALES (corp-wide): 159.41MM **Privately Held**
Web: www.wright.edu
SIC: 5063 8221 Electrical apparatus and equipment; University
PA: Wright State University
3640 Colonel Glenn Hwy
Dayton OH 45435
937 775-3333

(G-917)
WRIGHT-PATT CREDIT UNION INC (PA)
3560 Pentagon Blvd (45431-2779)
P.O. Box 340134 (45434-0134)
PHONE..............................937 912-7000
Doug Fecher, *Pr*
Kim Test, *
EMP: 254 **EST:** 1932
SQ FT: 46,000
SALES (est): 382.11MM
SALES (corp-wide): 382.11MM **Privately Held**
Web: www.wpcu.coop
SIC: 6062 State credit unions, not federally chartered

(G-918)
YOUNGLEARNERSWORLD
2308 Lakeview Dr (45431-2563)
PHONE..............................937 426-5437
Thomas Baker, *Dir*
EMP: 33
Web: www.younglearnersworld.com
SIC: 8351 Preschool center
PA: Younglearnersworld
2021 Wyoming St
Dayton OH 45410

Beavercreek
Montgomery County

(G-919)
BRAKEFIRE INCORPORATED
Also Called: Silco Fire Protection Company
4099 Industrial Ln (45430-1016)
PHONE..............................937 426-9717
Jim Wrobleski, *Brnch Mgr*
EMP: 44
SALES (corp-wide): 50.11MM **Privately Held**
Web: www.silcofs.com
SIC: 5087 Floor machinery, maintenance
PA: Brakefire, Incorporated
10200 Reading Rd
Cincinnati OH 45241
513 733-5655

(G-920)
COLDWELL BNKR HRITG RLTORS DYT
4060 Executive Dr (45430-1061)
PHONE..............................937 482-0082
Howard Back, *Prin*
EMP: 132 **EST:** 2008
SALES (est): 5.64MM **Privately Held**
Web: www.coldwellbankerishome.com
SIC: 6531 Real estate agent, residential

(G-921)
COMPUNET CLINICAL LABS LLC
75 Sylvania Dr (45440-3237)
PHONE..............................937 427-2655
Linda Blumme, *Mgr*
EMP: 48
SALES (corp-wide): 2.41MM **Privately Held**
Web: www.compunetlab.com
SIC: 8071 Medical laboratories
HQ: Compunet Clinical Laboratories, Llc
2308 Sandridge Dr
Moraine OH 45439
937 296-0844

(G-922)
DEDICATED NURSING ASSOC INC
70 Birch Aly Ste 240 (45440-1477)
PHONE..............................888 465-6929
EMP: 124
Web: www.dedicatednurses.com
SIC: 8051 7361 7363 Skilled nursing care facilities; Nurses' registry; Medical help service
PA: Dedicated Nursing Associates, Inc.
6536 State Route 22
Delmont PA 15626

(G-923)
GREATER DAYTON CNSTR LTD
Also Called: Oberer Thompson Co
4197 Research Blvd (45430)
PHONE..............................937 426-3577
Greg Thompson, *Pt*
Robin Collier, *
EMP: 74 **EST:** 1988
SQ FT: 13,500
SALES (est): 39.66MM **Privately Held**
Web: www.greaterdaytonconstruction.com
SIC: 1542 1521 1522 Commercial and office building, new construction; New construction, single-family houses; Residential construction, nec

(G-924)
HCF OF CRESTVIEW INC
Also Called: Village At The Greene
4381 Tonawanda Trl (45430-1961)
PHONE..............................937 426-5033
Patrice Gerber, *Prin*
EMP: 50 **EST:** 1991
SQ FT: 26,580
SALES (est): 10.6MM **Privately Held**
Web: www.villageatgreene.com
SIC: 8051 Convalescent home with continuous nursing care

(G-925)
MANATRON INC (DH)
4105 Executive Dr (45430-1071)
PHONE..............................937 431-4000
Allen Peat, *Pr*
Nan W Warner, *
EMP: 34 **EST:** 1967
SQ FT: 12,000
SALES (est): 6.62MM
SALES (corp-wide): 10.66B **Publicly Held**
Web: www.aumentumtech.com
SIC: 7373 5045 Turnkey vendors, computer systems; Computer peripheral equipment
HQ: Manatron, Inc.
2429 Military Rd Ste 300
Niagara Falls NY 14304
269 567-2900

(G-926)
MANATRON SABRE SYSTEMS AND SVC (DH)
4105 Executive Dr (45430-1071)
PHONE..............................937 431-4000

Dan Muthard, *Pr*
EMP: 68 **EST:** 1994
SALES (est): 20.62MM
SALES (corp-wide): 10.66B **Publicly Held**
SIC: 5045 6531 Computer software; Appraiser, real estate
HQ: Manatron, Inc.
2429 Military Rd Ste 300
Niagara Falls NY 14304
269 567-2900

(G-927)
MATRIX RESEARCH INC
3844 Research Blvd (45430-2104)
PHONE..............................937 427-8433
Robert Hawley, *Pr*
Robert W Hawley, *
James Lutz, *
William Pierson, *
EMP: 80 **EST:** 2005
SQ FT: 4,000
SALES (est): 16.31MM **Privately Held**
Web: www.matrixresearch.com
SIC: 3829 8711 Measuring and controlling devices, nec; Engineering services

(G-928)
NAKED LIME
2405 County Line Rd (45430-1573)
PHONE..............................855 653-5463
EMP: 33
SALES (est): 1.17MM **Privately Held**
Web: www.nakedlime.com
SIC: 8742 Marketing consulting services

(G-929)
RESONANT SCIENCES LLC
3975 Research Blvd (45430-2107)
PHONE..............................937 431-8180
Jeremy North, *Pr*
EMP: 49 **EST:** 2014
SALES (est): 10.47MM **Privately Held**
Web: www.resonantsciences.com
SIC: 8711 3825 Aviation and/or aeronautical engineering; Radio frequency measuring equipment

(G-930)
SAWDEY SOLUTION SERVICES INC (PA)
1430 Oak Ct Ste 304 (45430-1065)
PHONE..............................937 490-4060
Constance Sawdey, *Pr*
Jeffrey Sawdey, *VP*
EMP: 27 **EST:** 2001
SALES (est): 35.7MM
SALES (corp-wide): 35.7MM **Privately Held**
Web: www.sawdeysolutionservices.com
SIC: 7371 8748 8711 Custom computer programming services; Systems engineering consultant, ex. computer or professional; Consulting engineer

(G-931)
TACG LLC (PA)
Also Called: Tacg
1430 Oak Ct Ste 100 (45430-1064)
PHONE..............................937 203-8201
Todd Vikan, *COO*
Brian Chaney, *
EMP: 35 **EST:** 2006
SALES (est): 11.75MM **Privately Held**
Web: www.copperrivermc.com
SIC: 7382 8742 Security systems services; Business management consultant

(G-932)
THE SCHAEFER GROUP INC (PA)
1300 Grange Hall Rd (45430-1013)
PHONE..............................937 253-3342

GEOGRAPHIC SECTION

Beaverdam - Allen County (G-952)

▲ **EMP:** 50 **EST:** 1956
SALES (est): 20.24MM
SALES (corp-wide): 20.24MM **Privately Held**
Web: www.theschaefergroup.com
SIC: 3567 1741 Metal melting furnaces, industrial: electric; Refractory or acid brick masonry

Beavercreek Township
Greene County

(G-933)
CAPABLITY ANLIS MSRMENT ORGNZT
Also Called: Camo
4027 Colonel Glenn Hwy Ste 100 (45431-1673)
PHONE.................937 260-9373
Kurt Rinke, *CEO*
Kurt J Rinke, *CEO*
Edward Rinke, *COO*
EMP: 30 **EST:** 2011
SALES (est): 3.8MM
SALES (corp-wide): 116.91MM **Privately Held**
Web: www.camollc.org
SIC: 8711 Engineering services
PA: Linquest Corporation
2551 Dulles View Dr # 200
Herndon VA 20171
323 924-1600

(G-934)
COLDWELL BNKR HRITG RLTORS LLC
Also Called: Coldwell Banker
4139 Colonel Glenn Hwy (45431-1652)
PHONE.................937 426-6060
Bruce Dolbeer, *Mgr*
EMP: 29
SALES (corp-wide): 8.98MM **Privately Held**
Web: www.coldwellbankerishome.com
SIC: 6531 Real estate agent, residential
PA: Coldwell Banker Heritage Realtors Llc
4486 Indian Ripple Rd
Dayton OH 45440
937 434-7600

(G-935)
DAVE DENNIS INC
Also Called: Dave Dennis Auto Group
4232 Colonel Glenn Hwy (45431-1604)
PHONE.................937 429-5566
Andre Matre, *CEO*
Ulysses Ponder, *
Julie Parrott, *
Dwayne Owens, *
EMP: 92 **EST:** 1969
SQ FT: 31,000
SALES (est): 23.36MM **Privately Held**
Web: www.davedennis.com
SIC: 5511 7532 7538 5531 Automobiles, new and used; Body shop, automotive; General automotive repair shops; Automotive parts

(G-936)
DAYTON AEROSPACE INC
4141 Colonel Glenn Hwy Ste 252 (45431-5102)
PHONE.................937 426-4300
Robert Matthews, *Pr*
David Waite, *
Gary Poleskey, *
Robert Raggio, *
Charles Craw Junior, *VP*
EMP: 30 **EST:** 1984
SQ FT: 6,337
SALES (est): 5.17MM **Privately Held**
Web: www.daytonaero.com
SIC: 8742 Business management consultant

(G-937)
DCS CORPORATION
4027 Colonel Glenn Hwy Ste 210 (45431-1673)
PHONE.................937 306-7180
EMP: 89
SALES (corp-wide): 196.63MM **Privately Held**
Web: www.dcscorp.com
SIC: 8711 Consulting engineer
PA: Dcs Corporation
6909 Metro Pk Dr Ste 500
Alexandria VA 22310
571 227-6000

(G-938)
DCS CORPORATION
4027 Colonel Glenn Hwy Ste 210 (45431-1673)
PHONE.................781 419-6370
Jim Benbow, *Mgr*
EMP: 150
SALES (corp-wide): 196.63MM **Privately Held**
Web: www.dcscorp.com
SIC: 8711 Consulting engineer
PA: Dcs Corporation
6909 Metro Pk Dr Ste 500
Alexandria VA 22310
571 227-6000

(G-939)
FRONTIER TECHNOLOGY INC (PA)
Also Called: Fti
4141 Colonel Glenn Hwy Ste 140 (45431-1662)
PHONE.................937 429-3302
Ron Shroder, *CEO*
Lincoln Hudson, *
Jose L Hidalgo, *
Connie R Edwards, *
Tim Hinds, *
EMP: 30 **EST:** 1985
SQ FT: 3,834
SALES (est): 24.73MM
SALES (corp-wide): 24.73MM **Privately Held**
Web: www.ftidefense.com
SIC: 7371 8711 Computer software development and applications; Consulting engineer

(G-940)
HII MISSION TECHNOLOGIES CORP
2310 National Rd (45324-2687)
PHONE.................937 426-3421
EMP: 200
Web: www.hii.com
SIC: 8731 Commercial physical research
HQ: Hii Mission Technologies Corp.
8350 Broad St Ste 1400
Mc Lean VA 22102
703 918-4480

(G-941)
HUMANIT SOLUTIONS LLC
4058 Colonel Glenn Hwy (45431-1602)
PHONE.................937 901-7576
EMP: 86 **EST:** 2016
SQ FT: 1,500
SALES (est): 5.56MM **Privately Held**
Web: www.humanit.us
SIC: 7379 7371 7373 8748 Computer related consulting services; Custom computer programming services; Systems software development services; Systems analysis and engineering consulting services

(G-942)
JOES LDSCPG BEAVERCREEK INC
Also Called: Joe's Landscaping
2500 National Rd (45324-2011)
PHONE.................937 427-1133
Joe Leopard, *Pr*
EMP: 30 **EST:** 1985
SQ FT: 5,000
SALES (est): 2.33MM **Privately Held**
Web: www.joeslandscaping.com
SIC: 0781 Landscape services

(G-943)
MACAULAY-BROWN INC
Also Called: Macb
2310 National Rd (45324-2687)
PHONE.................937 426-3421
EMP: 639
Web: www.macb.com
SIC: 8711 8733 Consulting engineer; Research institute

(G-944)
NEXTGEN FEDERAL SYSTEMS LLC
4031 Colonel Glenn Hwy Ste T-101 (45431-2700)
PHONE.................304 413-0208
Jayachandra Reddy, *Prin*
EMP: 206 **EST:** 2010
SALES (est): 5.11MM **Privately Held**
Web: www.nextgenfed.com
SIC: 7371 Computer software systems analysis and design, custom

(G-945)
NORTHROP GRMMAN TCHNCAL SVCS I
Also Called: Ngts
4065 Colonel Glenn Hwy (45431-1601)
PHONE.................937 320-3100
Saju Kuruvilla, *Brnch Mgr*
EMP: 66
SIC: 3812 8711 7373 Search and navigation equipment; Engineering services; Computer integrated systems design
HQ: Northrop Grumman Technical Services, Inc.
7575 Colshire Dr
Mc Lean VA 22102
703 556-1144

(G-946)
PEERLESS TECHNOLOGIES CORP
Also Called: Ptech
2300 National Rd (45324-2009)
PHONE.................937 490-5000
Michael C Bridges, *Pr*
Andrea M Kunk, *
EMP: 60 **EST:** 2000
SQ FT: 17,000
SALES (est): 17.94MM **Privately Held**
Web: www.epeerless.com
SIC: 8731 Computer (hardware) development

(G-947)
QUANTECH SERVICES INC
4141 Colonel Glenn Hwy Ste 273 (45431-1676)
PHONE.................937 490-8461
Maryanne E Cromwell, *Prin*
EMP: 144
SALES (corp-wide): 41.25MM **Privately Held**
Web: www.quantechserv.com
SIC: 8999 Artists and artists' studios
PA: Quantech Services Inc.
1 Hartwell Pl Ste 2
Lexington MA 02421
781 271-9757

(G-948)
SIERTEK LTD (PA)
4141 Colonel Glenn Hwy Ste 250 (45431-1600)
PHONE.................937 623-2466
Raul Sierra, *CEO*
EMP: 30 **EST:** 2007
SALES (est): 10.5MM **Privately Held**
Web: www.siertek.com
SIC: 8711 7371 7373 7376 Engineering services; Custom computer programming services; Computer integrated systems design; Computer facilities management

(G-949)
SONOCO PRODUCTS COMPANY
Sonoco Consumer Products
761 Space Dr (45434-7171)
PHONE.................937 429-0040
Norwood Bizzell, *Mgr*
EMP: 62
SALES (corp-wide): 6.78B **Publicly Held**
Web: www.sonoco.com
SIC: 2655 5113 2891 Cans, fiber: made from purchased material; Paper tubes and cores; Adhesives and sealants
PA: Sonoco Products Company
1 N 2nd St
Hartsville SC 29550
843 383-7000

(G-950)
STANLEY STEEMER INTL INC
Also Called: Dayton 009
824 Space Dr (45434-7163)
PHONE.................614 764-2007
Gary Lettice, *Brnch Mgr*
EMP: 34
SALES (corp-wide): 263.72MM **Privately Held**
Web: www.stanleysteemer.com
SIC: 7217 Carpet and furniture cleaning on location
PA: Stanley Steemer International, Inc.
5800 Innovation Dr
Dublin OH 43016
614 764-2007

(G-951)
TRACTOR SUPPLY COMPANY
Also Called: Tractor Supply 492
610 Orchard Ln (45434-6167)
PHONE.................937 320-1855
Gary Hedrickson, *Mgr*
EMP: 31
SALES (corp-wide): 14.56B **Publicly Held**
Web: www.tractorsupply.com
SIC: 5191 Farm supplies
PA: Tractor Supply Company
5401 Virginia Way
Brentwood TN 37027
615 440-4000

Beaverdam
Allen County

(G-952)
BLUE BEACON USA LP II
Also Called: Blue Beacon of Beaverdam
413 E Main St (45808-9728)
PHONE.................419 643-8146
Mike Kreager, *Brnch Mgr*
EMP: 39
SALES (corp-wide): 88.72MM **Privately Held**
Web: www.bluebeacon.com
SIC: 7542 Washing and polishing, automotive
PA: Blue Beacon U.S.A., L.P. Ii

Bedford - Cuyahoga County (G-953) GEOGRAPHIC SECTION

500 Graves Blvd
Salina KS 67401
785 825-2221

Bedford
Cuyahoga County

(G-953)
APEX PEST CONTROL SERVICE INC
26118 Broadway Ave Ste E (44146-6530)
 PHONE.................................440 461-6530
James W Stocker, *Pr*
EMP: 33 **EST:** 1969
SQ FT: 900
SALES (est): 1.11MM **Privately Held**
Web: www.apexpestcontrol.net
SIC: 7342 Pest control in structures

(G-954)
AXIOM AUTOMOTIVE TECH INC
7350 Young Dr (44146-5357)
 PHONE.................................800 321-8830
Ted Kachel, *Pr*
David Pecore, *
Robert Fitzsimmons, *
◆ **EMP:** 800 **EST:** 1997
SALES (est): 42.06MM **Privately Held**
SIC: 5013 Motor vehicle supplies and new parts

(G-955)
BAF HOLDING COMPANY
26050 Richmond Rd (44146-1436)
 PHONE.................................440 287-2200
Brian Fox, *Pr*
Keith Karakul, *
A Richard Valore, *
EMP: 35 **EST:** 1992
SALES (est): 8.36MM **Privately Held**
Web: www.envirochemical.com
SIC: 5087 Janitors' supplies

(G-956)
CIULLA SMITH & DALE LLP
25 Tarbell Ave (44146-3682)
 PHONE.................................440 439-4700
Joseph Ciulla, *Brnch Mgr*
EMP: 28
SALES (corp-wide): 2.25MM **Privately Held**
Web: www.theciullagroup.com
SIC: 8721 Certified public accountant
PA: Ciulla Smith & Dale Llp
  6364 Pearl Rd Ste 4
  Cleveland OH 44130
  440 884-2036

(G-957)
COMFORT SYSTEMS USA OHIO INC (HQ)
Also Called: Comfort Systems USA
7401 First Pl Ste A (44146-6723)
 PHONE.................................440 703-1600
Daniel Lemons, *Pr*
EMP: 50 **EST:** 1979
SQ FT: 21,000
SALES (est): 26.32MM
SALES (corp-wide): 5.21B **Publicly Held**
Web: www.comfortsystemsusaohio.com
SIC: 1711 Mechanical contractor
PA: Comfort Systems Usa, Inc.
  675 Bering Dr Ste 400
  Houston TX 77057
  713 830-9600

(G-958)
DARKO INC
26401 Richmond Rd (44146-1443)
 PHONE.................................330 425-9805
Dean Rinicella, *Pr*
Dan Rinicella Junior, *VP*
Derek Rinicella, *
▲ **EMP:** 50 **EST:** 1974
SQ FT: 72,000
SALES (est): 10.56MM **Privately Held**
Web: www.darkoinc.com
SIC: 8742 Marketing consulting services

(G-959)
DBS FINANCIAL
424 Broadway Ave (44146-2603)
 PHONE.................................440 232-0001
EMP: 39
SALES (corp-wide): 293.27K **Privately Held**
Web: www.abcmotorcredit.com
SIC: 6282 Investment advice
PA: Dbs Financial
  3081 Gilchrist Rd Ste 100
  Akron OH 44305
  330 848-8300

(G-960)
FOWLER ELECTRIC CO
26185 Broadway Ave (44146-6512)
 PHONE.................................440 735-2385
Richard Trela, *Managing Member*
Scott Jordan, *Managing Member*
EMP: 48 **EST:** 1963
SALES (est): 9.01MM **Privately Held**
Web: www.oneezcall.com
SIC: 1711 1731 Mechanical contractor; General electrical contractor

(G-961)
GRACE HOSPITAL
44 Blaine Ave (44146-2709)
 PHONE.................................216 687-1500
EMP: 67
SALES (corp-wide): 9.47MM **Privately Held**
Web: www.gracehospital.org
SIC: 8062 General medical and surgical hospitals
PA: Grace Hospital
  2307 W 14th St
  Cleveland OH 44113
  216 687-1500

(G-962)
GUARDIAN PROTECTION SVCS INC
Also Called: Guardian Home Technology
7710 First Pl Ste H (44146-6718)
 PHONE.................................330 797-1570
EMP: 40
Web: www.guardianprotection.com
SIC: 1731 5999 7382 Fire detection and burglar alarm systems specialization; Alarm signal systems; Security systems services
HQ: Guardian Protection Services, Inc.
  174 Thorn Hill Rd
  Warrendale PA 15086
  412 788-2580

(G-963)
GUIDING FNDTONS SPPORT SVCS LL
466 Northfield Rd Ste 100 (44146-2287)
 PHONE.................................440 485-3772
Latierra Longmire, *Pt*
EMP: 56 **EST:** 2018
SALES (est): 1.19MM **Privately Held**
Web: www.guidingfoundationsupportservices.org
SIC: 8641 8059 Civic and social associations ; Personal care home, with health care

(G-964)
HANDL-IT INC
7120 Krick Rd Ste 1a (44146-4444)
 PHONE.................................440 439-9400
Jerry Peters, *Brnch Mgr*
EMP: 44
Web: www.handlit.com
SIC: 5063 Light bulbs and related supplies
PA: Handl-It, Inc
  360 Highland Rd E Ste 2
  Macedonia OH 44056

(G-965)
HOME INSTEAD SENIOR CARE
7650 First Pl Ste H (44146-6732)
 PHONE.................................440 914-1400
Scott Radcliss, *Pr*
EMP: 27 **EST:** 2001
SALES (est): 2.01MM **Privately Held**
Web: www.homeinstead.com
SIC: 8082 Home health care services

(G-966)
INDUSTRIAL FIRST INC (PA)
25840 Miles Rd Ste 2 (44146-1426)
 PHONE.................................216 991-8605
Steven F Lau, *Pr*
Steven F Lau, *Pr*
Frank Burkosky, *
EMP: 125 **EST:** 1936
SQ FT: 6,400
SALES (est): 32.95MM
SALES (corp-wide): 32.95MM **Privately Held**
Web: www.industrialfirst.com
SIC: 1741 1761 1791 Masonry and other stonework; Siding contractor; Structural steel erection

(G-967)
INTERSTATE-MCBEE LLC (PA)
7440 Oak Leaf Rd (44146)
 PHONE.................................216 881-0015
Alfred J Buescher, *Managing Member*
Anne Buescher, *
◆ **EMP:** 150 **EST:** 2000
SALES (est): 98.25MM **Privately Held**
Web: www.interstate-mcbee.com
SIC: 5084 5013 Engines and parts, diesel; Automotive supplies and parts

(G-968)
JADE-STERLING STEEL CO INC (PA)
26400 Richmond Rd (44146)
P.O. Box 1090 (44087)
 PHONE.................................330 425-3141
Scott Herman, *Pr*
Howard Fertel, *
Dean Musarra, *
Matthew Griswold, *
▲ **EMP:** 45 **EST:** 1965
SQ FT: 375,000
SALES (est): 50.5MM
SALES (corp-wide): 50.5MM **Privately Held**
Web: www.jadesterling.com
SIC: 5051 Steel

(G-969)
LOVEMAN STEEL CORPORATION
5455 Perkins Rd (44146-1856)
 PHONE.................................440 232-6200
Anthony Murru, *CEO*
Robin Davis Ray, *Prin*
David Loveman, *
Rob Loveman, *
James Loveman, *
◆ **EMP:** 75 **EST:** 1928
SQ FT: 80,000
SALES (est): 14.18MM **Privately Held**
Web: www.lovemansteel.com

SIC: 5051 3443 Plates, metal; Weldments

(G-970)
LOWES HOME CENTERS LLC
Also Called: Lowe's
24500 Miles Rd (44146-1314)
 PHONE.................................216 831-2860
John Lerch, *Mgr*
EMP: 143
SALES (corp-wide): 86.38B **Publicly Held**
Web: www.lowes.com
SIC: 5211 5031 5722 5064 Home centers; Building materials, exterior; Household appliance stores; Electrical appliances, television and radio
HQ: Lowe's Home Centers, Llc
  1000 Lowes Blvd
  Mooresville NC 28117
  336 658-4000

(G-971)
MCBEE SUPPLY CORPORATION
Also Called: Interstate-Mcbee
7440 Oak Leaf Rd (44146-5400)
 PHONE.................................216 881-0015
Ann Buescher, *Pr*
Brad Buescher, *
▲ **EMP:** 100 **EST:** 1958
SQ FT: 65,000
SALES (est): 23.71MM **Privately Held**
Web: www.interstate-mcbee.com
SIC: 5013 Automotive supplies and parts

(G-972)
MCCARTHY BURGESS & WOLFF INC (PA)
Also Called: McCarthy, Burgess & Wolff
26000 Cannon Rd (44146-1807)
 PHONE.................................440 735-5100
Freida M Wolff, *Pr*
Stephen Wolff, *
EMP: 140 **EST:** 1980
SQ FT: 21,000
SALES (est): 26.5MM
SALES (corp-wide): 26.5MM **Privately Held**
Web: www.mbandw.com
SIC: 7322 Collection agency, except real estate

(G-973)
MEDICAL SERVICE COMPANY (PA)
24000 Broadway Ave (44146-6329)
 PHONE.................................440 232-3000
Joel D Marx, *Pr*
John Geller, *VP*
Darrel Lowery, *Pr*
Dana Mclaughlin, *VP Fin*
EMP: 99 **EST:** 1949
SQ FT: 4,000
SALES (est): 42.38MM
SALES (corp-wide): 42.38MM **Privately Held**
Web: www.medicalserviceco.com
SIC: 5912 7352 Drug stores; Medical equipment rental

(G-974)
NOBLEINVESTMENTS LLC
195 Columbus St (44146-2837)
 PHONE.................................216 856-6555
EMP: 40 **EST:** 2020
SALES (est): 178.47K **Privately Held**
SIC: 8999 Personal services

(G-975)
NORFOLK SOUTHERN RAILWAY CO
Also Called: Norfolk Southern
7847 Northfield Rd (44146-5522)
 PHONE.................................440 439-1827
Allan Carter, *Superintnt*

EMP: 61
SALES (corp-wide): 12.16B **Publicly Held**
Web: www.norfolksouthern.com
SIC: 4011 Railroads, line-haul operating
HQ: Norfolk Southern Railway Company
    650 W Peachtree St Nw
    Atlanta GA 30308
    855 667-3655

(G-976)
NPK CONSTRUCTION EQUIPMENT INC (HQ)
7550 Independence Dr (44146-5541)
PHONE..............................440 232-7900
Dan Tyrell, *Pr*
Nick Shah, *
◆ EMP: 60 EST: 1985
SQ FT: 150,000
SALES (est): 57.56MM **Privately Held**
Web: www.npkce.com
SIC: 5082 3599 3546 3532 General construction machinery and equipment; Machine shop, jobbing and repair; Power-driven handtools; Mining machinery
PA: Nippon Pneumatic Manufacturing Co.,Ltd.
    4-11-5, Kamiji, Higashinari-Ku
    Osaka OSK 537-0

(G-977)
NVR INC
Also Called: Ryan Homes
6245 Sparrowhawk Way (44146-3165)
PHONE..............................440 232-5534
EMP: 33
Web: www.nvrinc.com
SIC: 1521 New construction, single-family houses
PA: Nvr, Inc.
    11700 Plz Amer Dr Ste 500
    Reston VA 20190

(G-978)
OAKWOOD HOSPITALITY CORP
Also Called: Holiday Inn
23303 Oakwood Commons Dr (44146-5700)
PHONE..............................440 786-1998
EMP: 28 EST: 1994
SALES (est): 473.56K **Privately Held**
Web: www.hiexpress.com
SIC: 7011 Hotels and motels

(G-979)
OLYMPIC STEEL INC
5080 Richmond Rd (44146-1329)
PHONE..............................216 292-3800
EMP: 156
SALES (corp-wide): 2.16B **Publicly Held**
Web: www.olysteel.com
SIC: 5051 Steel
PA: Olympic Steel, Inc.
    22901 Mllcreek Blvd Ste 6
    Cleveland OH 44122
    216 292-3800

(G-980)
PARTNERS AUTO GROUP BDFORD INC
Also Called: Mazda Saab of Bedford
22501 Rockside Rd (44146-1548)
PHONE..............................440 439-2323
Chris Hudak, *Pr*
Jerald Loretitsch, *
EMP: 52 EST: 1972
SALES (est): 11.54MM **Privately Held**
Web: www.mazdausa.com
SIC: 5511 7515 Automobiles, new and used; Passenger car leasing

(G-981)
RENAISSANCE HOME HEALTH CARE
5311 Northfield Rd (44146-1188)
PHONE..............................216 662-8702
Patricia Eady, *Pr*
EMP: 27 EST: 1947
SALES (est): 838.12K **Privately Held**
Web: www.clevelandhomehealthcareservice.com
SIC: 8099 Health screening service

(G-982)
RIDGECREST HEALTHCARE GROUP IN
26691 Richmond Rd (44146-1421)
PHONE..............................216 292-5706
William Weisberg, *Prin*
EMP: 29 EST: 2010
SALES (est): 559.68K **Privately Held**
Web: www.saberhealth.com
SIC: 8051 Convalescent home with continuous nursing care

(G-983)
ROSELAND LANES INC
Also Called: Roseland Lanes I
26383 Broadway Ave (44146-6516)
PHONE..............................440 439-0097
Peter Scimone, *Pr*
Anna Marie Slaby, *
Rosalie Scimone, *
EMP: 60 EST: 1961
SQ FT: 20,000
SALES (est): 2.34MM **Privately Held**
Web: www.roselandlanes.com
SIC: 7933 5812 Ten pin center; Snack bar

(G-984)
S B MORABITO TRUCKING INC
7353 Dunham Rd (44146-4149)
PHONE..............................216 441-3070
Sebastian Morabito Junior, *Pr*
Tony Morabito, *
EMP: 100 EST: 1956
SALES (est): 5.72MM **Privately Held**
SIC: 4212 Local trucking, without storage

(G-985)
SMITH & OBY SERVICE CO
7676 Northfield Rd (44146-5519)
PHONE..............................440 735-5322
Gary Y Klie, *Pr*
Ted Macfarlane, *Prin*
EMP: 27 EST: 1986
SALES (est): 2.37MM **Privately Held**
Web: www.smithandoby.com
SIC: 1711 7699 7623 Warm air heating and air conditioning contractor; Boiler and heating repair services; Air conditioning repair

(G-986)
SMYLIE ONE HEATING & COOLING
Also Called: Honeywell Authorized Dealer
5108 Richmond Rd (44146-1331)
PHONE..............................440 449-4328
Shari Rosen, *Pr*
Steven Smiley, *
EMP: 45 EST: 2003
SALES (est): 10.19MM **Privately Held**
Web: www.smylieone.com
SIC: 1711 Warm air heating and air conditioning contractor

(G-987)
STATE CREST CARPET & FLOORING (PA)
5400 Perkins Rd (44146-1857)
PHONE..............................440 232-3980
Dennis Chiancone, *Pr*
Janice Redina, *
◆ EMP: 27 EST: 1956
SQ FT: 36,000
SALES (est): 24.56MM
SALES (corp-wide): 24.56MM **Privately Held**
Web: www.statecrest.com
SIC: 5023 Carpets

(G-988)
TIM LALLY CHEVROLET INC
19000 Rockside Rd (44146-2033)
P.O. Box 46400 (44146-0400)
PHONE..............................440 232-2000
EMP: 97 EST: 1928
SALES (est): 14.12MM **Privately Held**
Web: www.neovc.org
SIC: 5511 7538 Automobiles, new and used; General automotive repair shops

(G-989)
TORQ CORPORATION
Also Called: Torq
32 W Monroe Ave (44146-3693)
PHONE..............................440 232-4100
James E Taylor, *CEO*
John P Taylor, *
Marian Knapik, *
▲ EMP: 29 EST: 1951
SQ FT: 22,000
SALES (est): 5.08MM **Privately Held**
Web: www.torq.com
SIC: 5063 Electrical apparatus and equipment

(G-990)
TUCKER LANDSCAPING INC
Also Called: Tucker Landscaping Company
1000 Broadway Ave (44146-4521)
PHONE..............................440 786-9840
Austin W Tucker, *Pt*
EMP: 90 EST: 2004
SQ FT: 4,160
SALES (est): 4.77MM **Privately Held**
Web: www.tuckerlandscaping.com
SIC: 0781 Landscape services

(G-991)
UH REGIONAL HOSPITALS
Also Called: University Hsptals Bdford Med
44 Blaine Ave (44146-2709)
PHONE..............................440 735-3900
Cliff Megerian, *CEO*
EMP: 74 EST: 2000
SALES (est): 23.11MM **Privately Held**
Web: www.uhhospitals.org
SIC: 8062 General medical and surgical hospitals

(G-992)
UNIVERSITY MEDNET
22750 Rockside Rd Ste 210 (44146-1576)
PHONE..............................440 285-9079
EMP: 150
SALES (corp-wide): 10.47MM **Privately Held**
SIC: 8011 Clinic, operated by physicians
PA: University Mednet
    18599 Lake Shore Blvd
    Euclid OH 44119
    216 383-0100

(G-993)
WMK LLC
Also Called: Mobilityworks
5040 Richmond Rd (44146-1329)
PHONE..............................440 951-4335
EMP: 35
SALES (corp-wide): 218.57MM **Privately Held**
Web: www.mobilityworks.com
SIC: 7532 5999 1799 Van conversion; Technical aids for the handicapped; Home/office interiors finishing, furnishing and remodeling
PA: Wmk, Llc
    4199 Knross Lkes Pkwy Ste
    Richfield OH 44286
    234 312-2000

Bedford Heights
Cuyahoga County

(G-994)
B&L ACQUISITION GROUP LLC
Also Called: Coit Clg & Restoration Svcs
23580 Miles Rd (44128-5433)
PHONE..............................216 626-0040
Brad Hunsucker, *Pr*
EMP: 50 EST: 2021
SALES (est): 711.3K **Privately Held**
Web: www.coit.com
SIC: 7217 Carpet and upholstery cleaning

(G-995)
BASS FAMILY LLC
26701 Richmond Rd (44146)
EMP: 159 EST: 1975
SALES (est): 26.32MM **Privately Held**
Web: www.bass-security.com
SIC: 5251 7382 Door locks and lock sets; Security systems services

(G-996)
BUCKEYE HEATING AND AC SUP INC (PA)
5075 Richmond Rd (44146-1384)
PHONE..............................216 831-0066
John Wortendyke, *Pr*
Louis Tisch, *
EMP: 35 EST: 1975
SQ FT: 30,000
SALES (est): 9.5MM
SALES (corp-wide): 9.5MM **Privately Held**
Web: www.buckeyesupply.com
SIC: 5078 5075 Refrigeration equipment and supplies; Warm air heating and air conditioning

(G-997)
CLEVELAND BALLET
23020 Miles Rd (44128)
PHONE..............................216 320-9000
Larry Goodman, *Pr*
EMP: 40 EST: 2014
SALES (est): 1.22MM **Privately Held**
Web: www.clevelandballet.org
SIC: 7922 Theatrical producers and services

(G-998)
HATTIE LRLHAM CTR FOR CHLDREN
26901 Cannon Rd (44146-1809)
PHONE..............................440 232-9320
Hattie Larlham, *Prin*
EMP: 40
SALES (corp-wide): 61.41MM **Privately Held**
Web: www.hattielarlham.org
SIC: 8361 Mentally handicapped home
PA: Hattie Larlham Center For Children With Disabilities
    9772 Diagonal Rd
    Mantua OH 44255
    330 274-2272

(G-999)
MUNICIPAL BUILDING INSPECTION
24850 Aurora Rd Ste A (44146-1747)
PHONE..............................440 399-0850
Bradley Resnick, *VP*

Bedford Heights - Cuyahoga County (G-1000)   GEOGRAPHIC SECTION

Jeff Filarski, *Chief Building Official*
Rick Loconti, *Chief Building Official*
Robert Apanasewicz, *Chief Building*
David Strichko, *Chief Building Official*
EMP: 239 **EST:** 2012
SALES (est): 285.06K
SALES (corp-wide): 45.42MM **Privately Held**
Web: www.mbislimited.com
SIC: 8748 4785 Business consulting, nec; Inspection and fixed facilities
HQ: Safebuilt Ohio, Llc
    444 N Cleveland Ave
    Loveland CO 80537
    877 230-5019

(G-1000)
OWNERS MANAGEMENT COMPANY
Also Called: Rockside Park Towers
25400 Rockside Rd (44146-1932)
PHONE.................................440 232-6093
Kathleen Grumbach, *Mgr*
EMP: 54
SALES (corp-wide): 26.01MM **Privately Held**
Web: www.rocksideparktowers.com
SIC: 6513 Apartment building operators
HQ: Owner's Management Company Inc
    25250 Rockside Rd Ste 1
    Cleveland OH 44146
    440 439-3800

(G-1001)
RISER FOODS COMPANY (HQ)
Also Called: American Seaway
5300 Richmond Rd (44146-1389)
PHONE.................................216 292-7000
David S Shapiro, *Ch*
Laura Shapira Karet, *
John Lucot, *
Mark Minnaugh, *
EMP: 100 **EST:** 1987
SQ FT: 1,000,000
SALES (est): 52.49MM
SALES (corp-wide): 1.43B **Privately Held**
SIC: 5411 5141 5146 5199 Supermarkets, chain; Groceries, general line; Seafoods; General merchandise, non-durable
PA: Giant Eagle, Inc.
    101 Kappa Dr
    Pittsburgh PA 15238
    866 620-0216

(G-1002)
SABER HEALTHCARE HOLDINGS LLC
26691 Richmond Rd Frnt (44146-1422)
PHONE.................................216 292-5706
George S Repchick, *Pr*
EMP: 27 **EST:** 2011
SALES (est): 723.23K **Privately Held**
Web: www.saberhealth.com
SIC: 8051 Skilled nursing care facilities

(G-1003)
UNIVERSAL WINDOWS DIRECT
24801 Rockside Rd (44146-1962)
PHONE.................................440 232-9060
EMP: 57 **EST:** 2019
SALES (est): 9.16MM **Privately Held**
Web: www.universalwindowsdirect.com
SIC: 5031 Windows

(G-1004)
WAXMAN CONSUMER PDTS GROUP INC (HQ)
Also Called: Waxman Consumer Products Group
24460 Aurora Rd (44146-1728)
PHONE.................................440 439-1830
▲ **EMP:** 75 **EST:** 1994

SQ FT: 9,000
SALES (est): 46.38MM
SALES (corp-wide): 99.88MM **Privately Held**
Web: www.spraysensations.com
SIC: 5072 5074 Casters and glides; Plumbing and hydronic heating supplies
PA: Waxman Industries, Inc.
    24460 Aurora Rd
    Bedford Heights OH 44146
    440 439-1830

(G-1005)
WAXMAN INDUSTRIES INC (PA)
24460 Aurora Rd (44146-1794)
PHONE.................................440 439-1830
Larry Waxman, *Pr*
Melvin Waxman, *Ch Bd*
Laurence Waxman, *Pr*
Mark Wester, *Sr VP*
◆ **EMP:** 110 **EST:** 1962
SQ FT: 21,000
SALES (est): 99.88MM
SALES (corp-wide): 99.88MM **Privately Held**
Web: www.waxmanind.com
SIC: 5072 5074 3494 3491 Hardware; Plumbing and hydronic heating supplies; Valves and pipe fittings, nec; Industrial valves

Bellaire
Belmont County

(G-1006)
BELLAIRE HARBOR SERVICE LLC
Also Called: Harbor Services
4102 Jefferson St (43906-1282)
P.O. Box 29 (43906-0029)
PHONE.................................740 676-4305
EMP: 43 **EST:** 2006
SALES (est): 4.6MM **Privately Held**
Web: www.bellaireharbor.com
SIC: 4492 Marine towing services

(G-1007)
BELMONT COMMUNITY HOSPITAL (DH)
4697 Harrison St (43906-1303)
P.O. Box 653 (43906-0653)
PHONE.................................740 671-1200
John De Blasis, *Admn*
EMP: 259 **EST:** 1912
SQ FT: 98,000
SALES (est): 9.87MM
SALES (corp-wide): 4.66B **Privately Held**
SIC: 8062 General medical and surgical hospitals
HQ: Wheeling Hospital, Inc.
    1 Medical Park
    Wheeling WV 26003
    304 243-3000

(G-1008)
BELMONT FEDERAL SAV & LN ASSN (PA)
3301 Guernsey St (43906)
P.O. Box 654 (43906)
PHONE.................................740 676-1165
Thomas Poe, *Pr*
Ray Wise, *VP*
Nancy Veres, *VP*
James Trouten, *Sec*
EMP: 48 **EST:** 1885
SQ FT: 5,000
SALES (est): 5.04MM
SALES (corp-wide): 5.04MM **Privately Held**
Web: www.belmont-savings.com

SIC: 6035 Federal savings and loan associations

(G-1009)
COMMUNITY ACTION COMM BLMONT C
Also Called: Indian Learning Head Start
4129 Noble St (43906-1246)
PHONE.................................740 676-0800
EMP: 93
SALES (corp-wide): 5.58MM **Privately Held**
Web: www.cacbelmont.org
SIC: 8322 Social service center
PA: Community Action Commission Of Belmont County
    153 1/2 W Main St
    Saint Clairsville OH 43950
    740 695-0293

(G-1010)
COUNTRY CLB RETIREMENT CTR LLC (PA)
55801 Conno Mara Dr (43906-9698)
PHONE.................................740 671-9330
David Taylor, *Prin*
Mark Bradley, *
John E Holland, *
EMP: 100 **EST:** 1986
SALES (est): 12.27MM
SALES (corp-wide): 12.27MM **Privately Held**
Web: www.countryclubretirementcampus.com
SIC: 8059 8052 8051 Nursing home, except skilled and intermediate care facility; Intermediate care facilities; Skilled nursing care facilities

(G-1011)
ENERSTAR RENTALS AND SVCS LTD
55643 High Ridge Rd (43906-9723)
PHONE.................................570 360-3271
EMP: 32
SALES (corp-wide): 13.36MM **Privately Held**
Web: www.enerstarsolutions.com
SIC: 7359 Equipment rental and leasing, nec
HQ: Enerstar Rentals And Services Ltd.
    210 S Washington St
    Pottstown PA 19464
    570 494-6277

(G-1012)
EXTRAS SUPPORT STAFFING
3494 Noble St (43906-1214)
PHONE.................................740 671-3996
Mario Iacojelli, *Brnch Mgr*
EMP: 105
SALES (corp-wide): 18.58MM **Privately Held**
Web: www.extrasstaffing.com
SIC: 7363 Temporary help service
HQ: Extras Support Staffing
    430 29th St
    Parkersburg WV 26101
    304 485-4000

(G-1013)
IRISH YOUTH SPORTS INC
5120 Guernsey St (43906-9547)
PHONE.................................859 257-7910
Nikki Liberatore, *Prin*
EMP: 34 **EST:** 2008
SALES (est): 9.63K **Privately Held**
Web: www.irishyouthsports.com
SIC: 8699 Membership organizations, nec

(G-1014)
OHIO VLY ATHC CONFERENCE INC
64962 Breezy Point Ln (43906-9721)
PHONE.................................740 671-3269
Dan Doyle, *Pr*
Tom Rataiczak, *
EMP: 29 **EST:** 2008
SALES (est): 523.63K **Privately Held**
Web: www.ovac.org
SIC: 8699 Athletic organizations

(G-1015)
PHOENIX TECHNOLOGY SERVICES
4 Commerce Pkwy (43906-1704)
PHONE.................................740 325-1138
EMP: 30 **EST:** 2016
SALES (est): 135.8K **Privately Held**
Web: www.phxtech.com
SIC: 8731 Commercial physical research

Bellbrook
Greene County

(G-1016)
FORGE LLC
Also Called: Sparkbox
15 N Main St (45305-2010)
PHONE.................................937 461-6560
Benjamin Callahan, *Managing Member*
Robert Harr, *Prin*
EMP: 45 **EST:** 2010
SALES (est): 6.03MM **Privately Held**
Web: www.sparkbox.com
SIC: 7371 Custom computer programming services

(G-1017)
HUNTINGTON NATIONAL BANK
2010 S Lakeman Dr (45305-1431)
PHONE.................................937 848-6861
William Dougherty, *Brnch Mgr*
EMP: 31
SALES (corp-wide): 10.84B **Publicly Held**
Web: www.huntington.com
SIC: 6029 6021 Commercial banks, nec; National commercial banks
HQ: The Huntington National Bank
    41 S High St
    Columbus OH 43215
    614 480-4293

(G-1018)
LBK HEALTH CARE INC (PA)
4336 W Franklin St Ste A (45305-1551)
PHONE.................................937 296-1550
Linda Black-kurek, *Prin*
EMP: 42 **EST:** 1992
SALES (est): 3.43MM **Privately Held**
SIC: 8721 Billing and bookkeeping service

Bellefontaine
Logan County

(G-1019)
ASPC CORP
1 Hunter Pl (43311-3002)
PHONE.................................937 593-7010
EMP: 234
Web: www.acusport.com
SIC: 5091 Firearms, sporting

(G-1020)
BELLEFONTAINE LODGING INC
Also Called: Comfort Inn
260 Northview Dr (43311-9316)
PHONE.................................937 599-6666
Roy Smith, *Pr*

GEOGRAPHIC SECTION   Bellevue - Huron County (G-1040)

EMP: 52 EST: 1988
SALES (est): 871.92K Privately Held
Web: www.choicehotels.com
SIC: 7011 Hotels and motels

(G-1021)
BELLETECH CORP
20 Hunter Pl (43311-3000)
PHONE..................................937 599-3774
Mark Mcintyre, VP
EMP: 131
Web: www.belletechcorp.com
SIC: 7536 Automotive glass replacement shops
HQ: Belletech Corp.
    700 W Lake Ave
    Bellefontaine OH 43311
    937 599-3774

(G-1022)
BIG GRENS LAWN SVC SNOW PLWING
914 Township Road 219 W (43311-9376)
PHONE..................................937 539-8163
Jeremy Gildow, Pr
Jeremy R Gildow, *
EMP: 35 EST: 2006
SALES (est): 2.08MM Privately Held
Web: www.biggreens.com
SIC: 0782 Lawn care services

(G-1023)
CHOICE PROPERTIES REAL ESTATE
245 S Main St (43311-1701)
PHONE..................................937 593-7216
Karen Frymyer, Brnch Mgr
EMP: 91
Web: www.cprealestate.com
SIC: 6531 Real estate agent, residential
PA: Choice Properties Real Estate
    408 E Main St
    Russells Point OH 43348

(G-1024)
COUNTY OF LOGAN
1991 County Road 13 (43311-9322)
PHONE..................................937 592-2791
Scott Coleman, Brnch Mgr
EMP: 31
SALES (corp-wide): 54.61MM Privately Held
Web: www.lceo.us
SIC: 8711 Engineering services
PA: County Of Logan
    100 S Madriver St
    Bellefontaine OH 43311
    937 599-7209

(G-1025)
COUNTY OF LOGAN
Also Called: Logan Cnty Bd Mntal Rtardation
1851 State Route 47 W (43311-9328)
P.O. Box 710 (43311-0710)
PHONE..................................937 292-3031
Joseph F Mancuso, Superintnt
EMP: 31
SALES (corp-wide): 54.61MM Privately Held
Web: www.logancountyohio.com
SIC: 8611 Chamber of Commerce
PA: County Of Logan
    100 S Madriver St
    Bellefontaine OH 43311
    937 599-7209

(G-1026)
COUNTY OF LOGAN
Also Called: Logan Cnty Prbate Juvenile Crt
101 S Main St Rm 1 (43311-2055)
PHONE..................................937 599-7252
Linda Brunke, Prin

EMP: 31
SALES (corp-wide): 54.61MM Privately Held
Web: www.logancountyohio.com
SIC: 8743 9211 Public relations services; Courts
PA: County Of Logan
    100 S Madriver St
    Bellefontaine OH 43311
    937 599-7209

(G-1027)
COUNTY OF LOGAN
Also Called: Logan Acres
2739 County Road 91 (43311-9007)
PHONE..................................937 592-2901
Andrew Hershderger, Mgr
EMP: 173
SALES (corp-wide): 54.61MM Privately Held
Web: www.loganacres.com
SIC: 8361 8051 Aged home; Skilled nursing care facilities
PA: County Of Logan
    100 S Madriver St
    Bellefontaine OH 43311
    937 599-7209

(G-1028)
COUNTY OF LOGAN
Also Called: Logan County Childrens Svcs
1100 S Detroit St (43311-9702)
PHONE..................................937 599-7290
John Holtkamp, Dir
EMP: 31
SALES (corp-wide): 54.61MM Privately Held
Web: www.logancountyohio.com
SIC: 8322 Child related social services
PA: County Of Logan
    100 S Madriver St
    Bellefontaine OH 43311
    937 599-7209

(G-1029)
HUNTINGTON NATIONAL BANK
201 E Columbus Ave (43311-2051)
PHONE..................................937 593-2010
Barbara Klinger, Brnch Mgr
EMP: 31
SALES (corp-wide): 10.84B Publicly Held
Web: www.huntington.com
SIC: 6029 6022 Commercial banks, nec; State commercial banks
HQ: The Huntington National Bank
    41 S High St
    Columbus OH 43215
    614 480-4293

(G-1030)
LINK CONSTRUCTION GROUP INC
895 County Road 32 N (43311-9210)
PHONE..................................937 292-7774
David Link, Pr
Reno Stapleton, *
Richard Dyer, *
EMP: 40 EST: 1997
SQ FT: 1,500
SALES (est): 15.47MM Privately Held
Web: www.linkconstructiongroup.com
SIC: 1542 1541 Commercial and office building contractors; Industrial buildings and warehouses

(G-1031)
LOGAN VIEW LLC
Also Called: Credit Care
112 Dowell Ave (43311-2305)
P.O. Box 117 (43311-0117)
PHONE..................................937 592-3902
EMP: 34

SALES (corp-wide): 329.98K Privately Held
Web: www.loganviewhomemedical.com
SIC: 7322 Collection agency, except real estate
HQ: Logan View Llc
    110 Dowell Ave
    Bellefontaine OH 43311
    937 593-2100

(G-1032)
LOWES HOME CENTERS LLC
Also Called: Lowe's
2168 Us Highway 68 S (43311-8904)
PHONE..................................937 599-4000
Jeremy Givens, Mgr
EMP: 91
SALES (corp-wide): 86.38B Publicly Held
Web: www.lowes.com
SIC: 5211 5031 5722 5064 Home centers; Building materials, exterior; Household appliance stores; Electrical appliances, television and radio
HQ: Lowe's Home Centers, Llc
    1000 Lowes Blvd
    Mooresville NC 28117
    336 658-4000

(G-1033)
MARY RTAN HLTH ASSN LOGAN CNTY (PA)
Also Called: Mary Rutan Hospital
205 E Palmer Rd (43311-2281)
PHONE..................................937 592-4015
Mandy Goble, Pr
Ron Carmin, *
Kelli Zimmerly, *
EMP: 44 EST: 1974
SQ FT: 145,000
SALES (est): 329.98K
SALES (corp-wide): 329.98K Privately Held
Web: www.maryrutan.org
SIC: 8741 Hospital management

(G-1034)
MARY RUTAN HOSPITAL (HQ)
Also Called: MARY RUTAN HOSPITAL
205 E Palmer Rd (43311-2298)
PHONE..................................937 592-4015
Thomas Simon, Ch Bd
Mandy Goble, Prin
Ron Carmen, *
Kelli Zimmerly, *
EMP: 650 EST: 1919
SQ FT: 90,000
SALES (est): 123.99MM
SALES (corp-wide): 329.98K Privately Held
Web: www.maryrutan.org
SIC: 8062 General medical and surgical hospitals
PA: Mary Rutan Health Association Of Logan County
    205 E Palmer Rd
    Bellefontaine OH 43311
    937 592-4015

(G-1035)
PANNU PETROLEUM INC
1504 S Main St (43311-1506)
PHONE..................................937 599-5454
EMP: 31
SIC: 5172 Petroleum products, nec
PA: Pannu Petroleum, Inc.
    2183 Oakbrook Blvd
    Beavercreek OH 45434

(G-1036)
POWERBILT MTL HDLG SLTIONS LLC
230 Reynolds Ave (43311-3003)
PHONE..................................937 592-5660
Richard Hauck, Managing Member
Nathaniel Hauck, *
EMP: 65 EST: 2000
SQ FT: 3,200
SALES (est): 25MM Privately Held
Web: www.powerbuilt.net
SIC: 5084 5063 Materials handling machinery; Lighting fixtures, commercial and industrial

(G-1037)
ROBINSON INVESTMENTS LTD
811 N Main St (43311-2376)
P.O. Box 508 (43311-0508)
PHONE..................................937 593-1849
Mark Robinson, Pr
Matt Robinson, *
Penny Robinson, *
Scott Robinson, *
Jerry Robinson, *
EMP: 37 EST: 1998
SQ FT: 70,000
SALES (est): 8.24MM Privately Held
Web: www.robinsoninvestmentsltd.com
SIC: 6512 Commercial and industrial building operation

(G-1038)
SUPERIOR ENVMTL SOLUTIONS LLC
Also Called: Resource-One, An SES Company
471 County Road 32 N (43311-9326)
PHONE..................................937 593-0425
EMP: 55
SALES (corp-wide): 108.19MM Privately Held
Web: www.sesinc.com
SIC: 8748 Environmental consultant
PA: Superior Environmental Solutions Llc
    9996 Joseph James Dr
    West Chester OH 45246
    513 874-8355

(G-1039)
THOMPSON DUNLAP HEYDINGER LTD
1111 Rush Ave (43311-9488)
P.O. Box 68 (43311-0068)
PHONE..................................937 593-6065
Robert Macdonald, Pt
Thomas Heydinger, Pt
Dave Watkins, Pt
Howard Traul, Pt
EMP: 27 EST: 1996
SALES (est): 4.16MM Privately Held
Web: www.tdhlaw.com
SIC: 8111 General practice law office

Bellevue
Huron County

(G-1040)
ADVANCED NEUROLOGIC ASSOC INC
5433 State Route 113 (44811-9708)
PHONE..................................419 483-2403
Stanley L Ruby, Pr
Steven Benedict, Prin
EMP: 38 EST: 2003
SALES (est): 1.69MM Privately Held
Web: www.advneuroassoc.com
SIC: 8011 Neurologist

Bellevue - Huron County (G-1041)

(G-1041)
BELLEVUE HEALTHCARE GROUP LLC
Also Called: Bellevue Care Center
1 Audrich Sq (44811-9700)
PHONE..................................419 483-6225
Cindy Starkey, *Admn*
EMP: 117
SALES (corp-wide): 4.19MM **Privately Held**
Web: www.saberhealth.com
SIC: 8051 Convalescent home with continuous nursing care
PA: Bellevue Healthcare Group, Llc
26691 Richmond Rd
Bedford OH 44146
216 292-5706

(G-1042)
BELLEVUE HOSPITAL (PA)
1400 W Main St Frnt (44811-8952)
PHONE..................................419 483-4040
Sara K Brokaw, *Pr*
Doctor Valerie Hepburn, *Pr*
Alan Ganci, *
EMP: 385 **EST:** 1915
SQ FT: 70,000
SALES (est): 58.89MM
SALES (corp-wide): 58.89MM **Privately Held**
Web: www.bellevuehospital.com
SIC: 8062 General medical and surgical hospitals

(G-1043)
BENCHMARK NATIONAL CORPORATION
400 N Buckeye St (44811-1210)
PHONE..................................419 843-6691
Gary A Cooper, *Brnch Mgr*
EMP: 36
SALES (corp-wide): 5.73MM **Privately Held**
Web: www.benchmarknational.com
SIC: 8748 8742 7389 Business consulting, nec; Quality assurance consultant; Inspection and testing services
PA: Benchmark National Corporation
3161 N Republic Blvd
Toledo OH 43615
419 843-6691

(G-1044)
FIRELANDS FEDERAL CREDIT UNION (PA)
300 North St (44811-1462)
P.O. Box 8005 (44811-8005)
PHONE..................................419 483-4180
Kevin L Wadsworth, *Pr*
Jacquelyn Wells, *VP*
Deborah Houle, *Lending Vice President*
EMP: 41 **EST:** 1957
SQ FT: 10,000
SALES (est): 22.32MM
SALES (corp-wide): 22.32MM **Privately Held**
Web: www.firelandsfcu.org
SIC: 6061 6163 Federal credit unions; Loan brokers

(G-1045)
GREAT LAKES PACKERS INC (PA)
400 Great Lakes Pkwy (44811-1165)
P.O. Box 366 (44811-0366)
PHONE..................................419 483-2956
Jerome Fritz, *Pr*
EMP: 50 **EST:** 1976
SQ FT: 31,500
SALES (est): 43.25MM
SALES (corp-wide): 43.25MM **Privately Held**
Web: www.greatlakespackers.com
SIC: 0723 Vegetable packing services

(G-1046)
WP7PRO INC (DH)
Also Called: Woodard Photographic, Inc.
550 Goodrich Rd (44811-1139)
P.O. Box 8001 (44811-8001)
PHONE..................................419 483-3364
George Woodard, *Pr*
Marc Woodard, *
Roger Wilburn, *
EMP: 40 **EST:** 1965
SQ FT: 18,763
SALES (est): 4.94MM
SALES (corp-wide): 2.47B **Privately Held**
Web: www.woodardphotographic.com
SIC: 7335 7221 Commercial photography; School photographer
HQ: Lifetouch Inc.
11000 Viking Dr
Eden Prairie MN 55344
952 826-4000

Bellville
Richland County

(G-1047)
CONSULATE MANAGEMENT CO LLC
Also Called: Country Meadow Care Center
4910 Algire Rd (44813-9263)
PHONE..................................419 886-3922
Phil Critcher, *Dir*
EMP: 229
SALES (corp-wide): 491MM **Privately Held**
Web: www.consulatehc.com
SIC: 8051 Skilled nursing care facilities
HQ: Consulate Management Company, Llc
800 Concourse Pkwy S # 200
Maitland FL 32751
407 571-1550

(G-1048)
COUNTRY MEADOW CARE CENTER LLC
Also Called: Country Mdow Rhbltion Nrsing
4910 Algire Rd (44813-9263)
PHONE..................................419 886-3922
Phil Kritcher, *Ex Dir*
EMP: 47 **EST:** 2017
SALES (est): 4MM **Privately Held**
Web: www.consulatehc.com
SIC: 8093 8059 Rehabilitation center, outpatient treatment; Nursing home, except skilled and intermediate care facility

(G-1049)
GORMAN-RUPP COMPANY
Also Called: Division Gorman-Rupp Company
180 Hines Ave (44813-1234)
PHONE..................................419 886-3001
Michael Hill, *Genl Mgr*
EMP: 46
SQ FT: 12,000
SALES (corp-wide): 659.51MM **Publicly Held**
Web: www.gripumps.com
SIC: 5084 Pumps and pumping equipment, nec
PA: Gorman-Rupp Company
600 S Airport Rd
Mansfield OH 44903
419 755-1011

(G-1050)
HEARTLAND VALLEY METALS LLC
500 Main St (44813-1302)
PHONE..................................419 886-0220
EMP: 78
SALES (corp-wide): 4.05MM **Privately Held**
Web: www.midohiotubing.com
SIC: 5051 Steel
PA: Heartland Valley Metals, Llc
3 Township Road 200
Centerburg OH 43011
419 883-2066

(G-1051)
INTEGRITY PIPELINE SERVICES LLC
500 S Mn St (44813)
P.O. Box 225 (43019-0225)
PHONE..................................419 886-9907
EMP: 62
SIC: 1623 Water, sewer, and utility lines

(G-1052)
VALLEY VIEW MANAGEMENT CO INC
Also Called: Comfort Inn
855 Comfort Plaza Dr (44813-1267)
PHONE..................................419 886-4000
James W Haring, *Pr*
Daniel Galat, *
EMP: 29 **EST:** 1989
SALES (est): 1.72MM **Privately Held**
Web: www.choicehotels.com
SIC: 7011 Hotels and motels

Belmont
Belmont County

(G-1053)
50 X 20 HOLDING COMPANY INC
Also Called: Schumacher Homes
41201 Bond Dr (43718-7502)
PHONE..................................740 238-4262
Greg Mcquaid, *Brnch Mgr*
EMP: 34
SALES (corp-wide): 114.18MM **Privately Held**
Web: www.schumacherhomes.com
SIC: 1521 New construction, single-family houses
PA: 50 X 20 Holding Company, Inc.
2715 Wise Ave Nw
Canton OH 44708
330 478-4500

(G-1054)
CONTRLLED CHAOS ENRGY SVCS LLC
43510 National Rd (43718-9672)
PHONE..................................740 257-0724
Frederick Lang, *Managing Member*
Jesseca Lang, *
EMP: 40 **EST:** 2021
SALES (est): 6MM **Privately Held**
SIC: 4789 Freight car loading and unloading

(G-1055)
STINGRAY PRESSURE PUMPING LLC (PA)
42739 National Rd (43718-9669)
PHONE..................................405 648-4177
Bob Maughmer, *Managing Member*
▲ **EMP:** 69 **EST:** 2012
SALES (est): 125.79MM
SALES (corp-wide): 125.79MM **Privately Held**
Web: www.mammothenergy.com
SIC: 1389 Gas field services, nec

Belpre
Washington County

(G-1056)
KRATON POLYMERS US LLC
Also Called: Kraton Polymers
2419 State Route 618 (45714)
P.O. Box 235 (45714-0235)
PHONE..................................740 423-7571
Bob Rose, *Brnch Mgr*
EMP: 400
Web: www.kraton.com
SIC: 2822 5169 2821 Synthetic rubber; Synthetic resins, rubber, and plastic materials; Plastics materials and resins
HQ: Kraton Polymers U.S. Llc
9950 Woodloch Forest Dr
Spring TX 77380
281 504-4700

(G-1057)
MARIETTA MEMORIAL HOSPITAL
809 Farson St (45714-1009)
PHONE..................................740 401-0362
EMP: 57
SALES (corp-wide): 454.22MM **Privately Held**
Web: www.mhsystem.org
SIC: 8062 General medical and surgical hospitals
PA: Marietta Memorial Hospital Inc
401 Matthew St
Marietta OH 45750
740 374-1400

(G-1058)
OHIO VLY AMBLTORY SRGERY CTR L
608 Washington Blvd (45714-2465)
P.O. Box 369 (45714-0369)
PHONE..................................740 423-4684
David Catalino Mendoza, *Prin*
EMP: 31 **EST:** 2007
SALES (est): 6.08MM **Privately Held**
Web: www.ohiovalleyasc.com
SIC: 8011 Ambulatory surgical center

(G-1059)
STATIONERS INC
Also Called: Garrison Brewer
214 Stone Rd (45714-2348)
PHONE..................................740 423-1400
FAX: 740 423-1612
EMP: 30
SALES (corp-wide): 61.29MM **Publicly Held**
SIC: 4225 5943 5712 General warehousing and storage; Office forms and supplies; Office furniture
HQ: Stationers, Inc.
100 Industrial Ln
Huntington WV 25702
304 528-2780

(G-1060)
STONEGATE CONSTRUCTION INC
1378 Way Rd (45714-9633)
PHONE..................................740 423-9170
EMP: 46 **EST:** 1995
SQ FT: 1,800
SALES (est): 23.9MM **Privately Held**
Web: www.stonegateweb.com
SIC: 1611 1794 General contractor, highway and street construction; Excavation work

Berea
Cuyahoga County

(G-1061)
ASANA HOSPICE CLEVELAND LLC
Also Called: Asana Hospice Palliative Care
885 W Bagley Rd (44017-2903)
PHONE.................................419 903-0300
Tina Krajnikovich, *Prin*
EMP: 35 **EST:** 2018
SALES (est): 2.43MM **Publicly Held**
SIC: 8052 Personal care facility
PA: Amedisys, Inc.
 3854 American Way Ste A
 Baton Rouge LA 70816

(G-1062)
B-W BASEBALL
275 Eastland Rd (44017-2005)
PHONE.................................440 826-2182
Joe Kilburg, *Prin*
EMP: 50 **EST:** 2010
SALES (est): 176.58K **Privately Held**
Web: www.bw.edu
SIC: 7997 Baseball club, except professional and semi-professional

(G-1063)
BW ALUMNI ASSOCIATION
279 Front St (44017-1757)
PHONE.................................440 826-2104
EMP: 64 **EST:** 2018
SALES (est): 239.65K **Privately Held**
Web: www.bw.edu
SIC: 6512 Commercial and industrial building operation

(G-1064)
CHARLIE TOWING SERVICE INC
Also Called: Charlie's Towing Svc
55 Lou Groza Blvd (44017-1237)
PHONE.................................440 234-5300
Charles Valentine, *CEO*
EMP: 30 **EST:** 1981
SQ FT: 8,000
SALES (est): 1MM **Privately Held**
Web: www.charliestowing.com
SIC: 7549 Towing service, automotive

(G-1065)
CLEVELAND BROWNS FOOTBALL LLC
Also Called: Cleveland Browns
76 Lou Groza Blvd (44017-1269)
PHONE.................................440 891-5000
EMP: 150 **EST:** 1998
SQ FT: 10,000
SALES (est): 48.14MM **Privately Held**
Web: www.clevelandbrowns.com
SIC: 7941 Football club

(G-1066)
COMMUNICARE HEALTH SVCS INC
Also Called: Berea Alzheimer's Care Center
49 Sheldon Rd (44017-1136)
PHONE.................................440 234-0454
Haleigh Niece, *Ex Dir*
EMP: 100
SALES (corp-wide): 392.92MM **Privately Held**
Web: www.communicarehealth.com
SIC: 8051 Convalescent home with continuous nursing care
PA: Communicare Health Services, Inc.
 10123 Alliance Rd
 Blue Ash OH 45242
 513 530-1654

(G-1067)
CUYAHOGA COUNTY AG SOC
Also Called: Cuyahoga County Fair
164 Eastland Rd (44017-2066)
P.O. Box 135 (44017-0135)
PHONE.................................440 243-0090
Timothy Fowler, *Pr*
EMP: 30 **EST:** 1898
SALES (est): 861.88K **Privately Held**
Web: www.cuyfair.com
SIC: 8641 7999 Civic associations; Agricultural fair

(G-1068)
ESTABROOK CORPORATION (PA)
700 W Bagley Rd (44017-2900)
P.O. Box 804 (44017-0804)
PHONE.................................440 234-8566
Jeffrey W Tarr, *Pr*
Kelly Sutula, *
EMP: 30 **EST:** 1965
SQ FT: 25,000
SALES (est): 26.22MM
SALES (corp-wide): 26.22MM **Privately Held**
Web: www.estabrookcorp.com
SIC: 5084 7699 Pumps and pumping equipment, nec; Industrial machinery and equipment repair

(G-1069)
FASTENER INDUSTRIES INC
Also Called: Ohio Nut & Bolt Company Div
33 Lou Groza Blvd (44017-1237)
PHONE.................................440 891-2031
Tim Morgan, *Mgr*
EMP: 50
SALES (corp-wide): 46.16MM **Privately Held**
Web: www.fastenerind.com
SIC: 3452 5084 Bolts, nuts, rivets, and washers; Lift trucks and parts
PA: Fastener Industries, Inc.
 1 Berea Cmns Ste 209
 Berea OH 44017
 440 243-0034

(G-1070)
FRONT LEASING CO LLC
Also Called: Aristcrat Brea Sklled Nrsing R
255 Front St (44017-1943)
PHONE.................................440 243-4000
EMP: 35 **EST:** 2004
SALES (est): 1.91MM **Privately Held**
SIC: 8051 Convalescent home with continuous nursing care

(G-1071)
HUNTINGTON NATIONAL BANK
31 E Bridge St Ste 203 (44017-1941)
PHONE.................................440 202-3050
EMP: 31
SALES (corp-wide): 10.84B **Publicly Held**
Web: www.huntington.com
SIC: 6029 Commercial banks, nec
HQ: The Huntington National Bank
 41 S High St
 Columbus OH 43215
 614 480-4293

(G-1072)
KUEHNE + NAGEL INC
1 Berea Cmns Ste 3 (44017-2534)
P.O. Box 81187 (44181-0187)
PHONE.................................440 243-6070
Juergen Habner, *Mgr*
EMP: 106
Web: us.kuehne-nagel.com
SIC: 4731 Freight forwarding
HQ: Kuehne + Nagel Inc.
 10 Exchange Pl Fl 19-20
 Jersey City NJ 07302
 201 413-5500

(G-1073)
MAKOVICH PUSTI ARCHITECTS INC
111 Front St (44017-1912)
PHONE.................................440 891-8910
Ronald Makovich, *Pr*
David Pusti, *VP*
EMP: 28 **EST:** 1986
SQ FT: 4,000
SALES (est): 4.19MM **Privately Held**
Web: www.mparc.com
SIC: 8712 Architectural engineering

(G-1074)
MIDWEST TRANSATLANTIC LINES INC (PA)
1230 W Bagley Rd (44017-2910)
P.O. Box 81337 (44181-0337)
PHONE.................................440 243-1993
◆ **EMP:** 41 **EST:** 1980
SALES (est): 17.99MM
SALES (corp-wide): 17.99MM **Privately Held**
Web: www.mtalines.com
SIC: 4731 4412 Customhouse brokers; Deep sea foreign transportation of freight

(G-1075)
NORTHEAST CARE CENTER INC
Also Called: Maple House
250 Maplelawn Dr (44017-2815)
PHONE.................................440 234-9407
EMP: 74
SQ FT: 4,558
SALES (corp-wide): 79.39K **Privately Held**
Web: www.necare.org
SIC: 8361 8052 8059 Mentally handicapped home; Intermediate care facilities; Home for the mentally retarded, ex. skilled or intermediate
PA: Northeast Care Center, Inc.
 13405 York Rd
 Cleveland OH
 440 582-3300

(G-1076)
OHIO TPK & INFRASTRUCTURE COMM (DH)
Also Called: EXECUTIVE OFFICE
682 Prospect St (44017-2711)
P.O. Box 460 (44017-0460)
PHONE.................................440 234-2081
Randy Cole, *CEO*
Sandy Barber, *
Jerry N Hruby, *
Joseph Balog, *Vice Chairman**
George Dixon, *Board Manager**
EMP: 125 **EST:** 1949
SQ FT: 55,000
SALES (est): 378.58MM **Privately Held**
Web: www.ohioturnpike.org
SIC: 4785 Toll road operation
HQ: Executive Office State Of Ohio
 77 S High St Fl 30
 Columbus OH 43215

(G-1077)
OHIO TPK & INFRASTRUCTURE COMM
Also Called: Amherst Maintenance Bldg
682 Prospect St (44017-2711)
PHONE.................................440 234-2081
Dan Castrigano, *Chief*
EMP: 82
Web: www.ohioturnpike.org
SIC: 1611 0782 9621 Highway and street maintenance; Highway lawn and garden maintenance services; Regulation, administration of transportation
HQ: Ohio Turnpike And Infrastructure Commission
 682 Prospect St
 Berea OH 44017
 440 234-2081

(G-1078)
OHIOGUIDESTONE
343 W Bagley Rd (44017-1370)
PHONE.................................440 234-2006
EMP: 258
SALES (corp-wide): 86.77MM **Privately Held**
Web: www.ohioguidestone.org
SIC: 8051 Skilled nursing care facilities
PA: Ohioguidestone
 434 Eastland Rd
 Berea OH 44017
 440 234-2006

(G-1079)
OHIOGUIDESTONE (PA)
434 Eastland Rd (44017-1217)
PHONE.................................440 234-2006
Richard Frank, *CEO*
Donna Keegan, *
EMP: 50 **EST:** 1864
SQ FT: 53,000
SALES (est): 86.77MM
SALES (corp-wide): 86.77MM **Privately Held**
Web: www.ohioguidestone.org
SIC: 8322 8361 8351 8051 Child related social services; Emotionally disturbed home ; Child day care services; Skilled nursing care facilities

(G-1080)
ROCKY RIVER LEASING CO LLC
Also Called: NORTHWESTERN HEALTHCARE CENTER
570 N Rocky River Dr (44017-1613)
PHONE.................................440 243-5688
EMP: 44 **EST:** 2008
SALES (est): 9.02MM **Privately Held**
Web: www.communicarehealth.com
SIC: 8051 Convalescent home with continuous nursing care

(G-1081)
SOUND COM CORPORATION
Also Called: Sound Com System
227 Depot St (44017-1860)
PHONE.................................440 234-2604
Paul Winkler, *Pr*
Paul Fussner, *
Carl Mclaughlin, *COO*
EMP: 70 **EST:** 1974
SQ FT: 10,500
SALES (est): 26.58MM
SALES (corp-wide): 6.6B **Publicly Held**
Web: www.soundcom.net
SIC: 5065 Communication equipment
PA: Ametek, Inc.
 1100 Cassatt Rd
 Berwyn PA 19312
 610 647-2121

(G-1082)
SOUTHWEST SPORTS CENTER INC
Also Called: Dairy Queen
1005 W Bagley Rd (44017-2907)
PHONE.................................440 234-6448
Richard C Straub Senior, *Pr*
Richard Straub, *Owner*
EMP: 49 **EST:** 1978
SQ FT: 2,000

SALES (est): 451.32K **Privately Held**
Web: www.dairyqueen.com
SIC: **5812** 7999 Ice cream stands or dairy bars; Golf driving range

(G-1083)
T & L ENTERPRISES INC
Also Called: ServiceMaster
1060 W Bagley Rd Ste 101 (44017-2938)
PHONE....................440 234-5900
Terry D Litt, *Pr*
Elizabeth Litt, *
EMP: 30 EST: 1979
SQ FT: 3,000
SALES (est): 953.62K **Privately Held**
Web: www.servicemaster.com
SIC: **7349** Building maintenance services, nec

(G-1084)
T ALLEN INC
200 Depot St (44017-1810)
P.O. Box 625 (44017-0625)
PHONE....................440 234-2366
Gareth Vaughan, *Pr*
EMP: 106 EST: 1987
SQ FT: 4,500
SALES (est): 1.2MM
SALES (corp-wide): 265.68MM **Privately Held**
Web: www.tallencarpentry.com
SIC: **1751** Carpentry work
PA: The Albert M Higley Company
3636 Euclid Ave
Cleveland OH 44115
216 861-2050

(G-1085)
TJM EXPRESS INC
212 Sandstone Ridge Way (44017-1085)
PHONE....................216 385-4164
James R Mccarthy, *Pr*
EMP: 27 EST: 2015
SALES (est): 2.2MM **Privately Held**
SIC: **4731** Freight forwarding

(G-1086)
WEEKLEYS MAILING SERVICE INC
1420 W Bagley Rd (44017-2935)
PHONE....................440 234-4325
Thomas Weekley, *Pr*
Gerald Milton, *
Vera Rutz, *
EMP: 100 EST: 1945
SQ FT: 63,000
SALES (est): 9.42MM **Privately Held**
Web: www.weekleysmailing.com
SIC: **7331** Mailing service

(G-1087)
WEST SIDE DTSCHER FRUEN VEREIN
Also Called: ALTENHEIM
520 Abbyshire Dr (44017-1404)
PHONE....................440 238-3361
EMP: 300 EST: 1887
SALES (est): 21.91MM **Privately Held**
SIC: **8051** Skilled nursing care facilities

Bergholz
Jefferson County

(G-1088)
ROSEBUD MINING COMPANY
Also Called: Bergholz 7
9076 County Road 53 (43908-7948)
PHONE....................740 768-2275
William Denoon, *Brnch Mgr*
EMP: 90

SALES (corp-wide): 221.86MM **Privately Held**
Web: www.rosebudmining.com
SIC: **1222** 1221 Bituminous coal-underground mining; Bituminous coal and lignite-surface mining
PA: Rosebud Mining Company
301 Market St
Kittanning PA 16201
724 545-6222

Berlin
Holmes County

(G-1089)
BERLIN GRANDE HOTEL LTD
4787 Township Rd 366 (44610)
P.O. Box 449 (44610-0449)
PHONE....................330 403-3050
EMP: 43 EST: 2009
SALES (est): 825.62K **Privately Held**
Web: www.berlingrandehotel.com
SIC: **7011** Hotels

(G-1090)
CHOICE HOTELS INTL INC
Also Called: Comfort Suites Berlin
4810 Tr 366 N St (44610)
P.O. Box 331 (44610-0331)
PHONE....................330 729-5645
Kent Miller, *Brnch Mgr*
EMP: 30
SALES (corp-wide): 1.54B **Publicly Held**
Web: www.choicehotels.com
SIC: **7011** Hotels
PA: Choice Hotels International, Inc.
1 Choice Hotels Cir # 400
Rockville MD 20850
301 592-5000

Bethel
Clermont County

(G-1091)
H & G NURSERY HOME INC
Also Called: MORRIS NURSING HOME
322 S Charity St (45106-1324)
P.O. Box 29 (45106-0029)
PHONE....................513 734-7401
Mary Leget, *Dir*
Patrick L Gregory, *VP*
EMP: 47 EST: 1982
SQ FT: 2,840
SALES (est): 1.86MM **Privately Held**
Web: www.hg-nh.com
SIC: **8052** 8051 Intermediate care facilities; Skilled nursing care facilities

(G-1092)
HOUCK ASPHALT MAINTENANCE LLC
2656 State Route 222 (45106-8222)
PHONE....................513 734-4500
Bryan Shively, *Pr*
John Houck, *
Brian Shively, *
EMP: 30 EST: 1992
SQ FT: 2,732
SALES (est): 2.42MM **Privately Held**
Web: www.houckasphalt.com
SIC: **1611** 7521 1721 1771 Surfacing and paving; Parking lots; Pavement marking contractor; Concrete work

(G-1093)
M M CONSTRUCTION
1924 State Route 222 (45106)
PHONE....................513 553-0106

Mark Sturgill, *Pr*
EMP: 50 EST: 2015
SALES (est): 2.31MM **Privately Held**
SIC: **1521** Single-family housing construction

(G-1094)
SMITH & SCHAEFER INC
Also Called: Smith & Schaefer
202 E Plane St # 400 (45106-1402)
PHONE....................216 226-6700
Thomas J Stollenwerk, *Pr*
John J Abell, *
Gary Wagner, *
EMP: 47 EST: 1952
SQ FT: 16,000
SALES (est): 4.81MM **Privately Held**
Web: www.smithandschaefer.com
SIC: **5047** 5049 5021 Hospital equipment and furniture; Laboratory equipment, except medical or dental; Office and public building furniture

(G-1095)
TRIHEALTH INC
Also Called: Bethel Rgional Fmly Healthcare
210 N Union St (45106-1124)
PHONE....................513 734-9050
EMP: 163
Web: www.trihealth.com
SIC: **8099** Childbirth preparation clinic
HQ: Trihealth, Inc.
625 Eden Park Dr
Cincinnati OH 45202
513 569-5400

(G-1096)
UTTER CONSTRUCTION INC
1302 State Route 133 (45106-8449)
PHONE....................513 876-2246
Doug Utter, *Pr*
Dwayne K Utter, *
Shiela G Defau, *
EMP: 150 EST: 1996
SALES (est): 17.53MM **Privately Held**
Web: www.utterinc.com
SIC: **1794** Excavation work

Bethesda
Belmont County

(G-1097)
RES-CARE INC
39555 National Rd (43719-9762)
PHONE....................740 782-1476
Gloria Llewellyn, *Ex Dir*
EMP: 55
SALES (corp-wide): 8.83B **Publicly Held**
Web: www.rescare.com
SIC: **8082** Home health care services
HQ: Res-Care, Inc.
805 N Whittington Pkwy
Louisville KY 40222
502 394-2100

Bettsville
Seneca County

(G-1098)
CARMEUSE LIME INC
Also Called: Carmeuse Natural Chemicals
1967 W County Rd 42 (44815)
P.O. Box 708 (44815-0708)
PHONE....................419 986-5200
Thomas A Buck, *CEO*
EMP: 47
SALES (corp-wide): 2.67MM **Privately Held**
Web: www.carmeuse.com

SIC: **1422** Crushed and broken limestone
HQ: Carmeuse Lime, Inc.
11 Stanwix St Fl 21
Pittsburgh PA 15222
412 995-5500

Beverly
Washington County

(G-1099)
ADKINS TIMBER PRODUCTS INC
Also Called: Nmoble Hardwoods
22180 State Rte 60 (45715)
P.O. Box 387 (45715-0387)
PHONE....................740 984-2768
Alan Adkins, *Pr*
Allen Adkins, *
Randy Adkins, *
Kevin Adkins, *
EMP: 28 EST: 1976
SALES (est): 2.29MM **Privately Held**
SIC: **5031** Lumber: rough, dressed, and finished

(G-1100)
CITIZENS BANK COMPANY (HQ)
Also Called: CITIZENS BANK
501 5th St (45715-8916)
P.O. Box 128 (45715-0128)
PHONE....................740 984-2381
Todd A Hilverding, *CEO*
Loretta Linn, *
EMP: 28 EST: 1904
SALES (est): 13.01MM **Privately Held**
Web: www.thecitizens.com
SIC: **6022** State trust companies accepting deposits, commercial
PA: Muskingum Valley Bancshares, Inc.
Ullman & Fifth Sts # 5
Beverly OH 45715

(G-1101)
LARRY LANG EXCAVATING INC
19371 State Route 60 (45715-5055)
PHONE....................740 984-4750
Larry D Lang, *Pr*
EMP: 30 EST: 1982
SALES (est): 5.55MM **Privately Held**
Web: www.langspouredwalls.com
SIC: **1794** Excavation and grading, building construction

(G-1102)
STEPHENS-MATTHEWS MKTG LLC
605 Center St (45715-2504)
P.O. Box 1208 (45715-1208)
PHONE....................740 984-8011
David Stephens, *Pr*
Larry L Mathews, *
EMP: 32 EST: 1984
SQ FT: 3,500
SALES (est): 4.41MM
SALES (corp-wide): 124.33MM **Privately Held**
Web: www.stephens-matthews.com
SIC: **6411** Insurance agents, nec
PA: Amerilife Group, Llc
2650 Mccormick Dr
Clearwater FL 33759
727 726-0726

Bidwell
Gallia County

(G-1103)
CARMICHAEL EQUIPMENT INC (PA)
668 Pinecrest Dr (45614-9275)
PHONE....................740 446-2412

TOLL FREE: 800
John Carmichael, Pr
Loralee Carmichael, *
EMP: 35 EST: 1995
SQ FT: 39,000
SALES (est): 4.22MM Privately Held
Web: www.careq.com
SIC: 5999 5261 5082 Farm equipment and supplies; Lawn and garden equipment; Contractor's materials

(G-1104)
HOLZER SENIOR CARE CENTER
380 Colonial Dr (45614-9215)
PHONE...............................740 446-5001
Charles I Adkins Junior, Prin
EMP: 47 EST: 1996
SALES (est): 5.06MM Privately Held
SIC: 8051 8741 Skilled nursing care facilities; Nursing and personal care facility management

(G-1105)
MPW INDUSTRIAL SVCS GROUP INC
2860 State Route 850 (45614-9287)
PHONE...............................740 245-5393
EMP: 37
SALES (corp-wide): 213.53MM Privately Held
Web: www.mpwservices.com
SIC: 7349 Cleaning service, industrial or commercial
PA: Mpw Industrial Services Group, Inc.
9711 Lancaster Rd
Hebron OH 43025
740 927-8790

(G-1106)
TRIMAT CONSTRUCTION INC
13621 State Route 554 (45614-9425)
P.O. Box 10 (45614-0010)
PHONE...............................740 388-9515
Matthew Toler, Pr
Patrica Toler, *
EMP: 45 EST: 1991
SQ FT: 3,000
SALES (est): 1.12MM Privately Held
Web: www.trimatconstruction.com
SIC: 1521 1794 New construction, single-family houses; Excavation work

Birmingham
Erie County

(G-1107)
BETTCHER INDUSTRIES INC (PA)
Also Called: Bettcher Industries
6801 State Rte 60 (44816)
P.O. Box 336 (44089)
PHONE...............................440 965-4422
Tim Swanson, CEO
Kevin Harry, *
▲ EMP: 165 EST: 1944
SQ FT: 65,000
SALES (est): 131.48MM
SALES (corp-wide): 131.48MM Privately Held
Web: www.bettcher.com
SIC: 5084 Food product manufacturing machinery

Blacklick
Franklin County

(G-1108)
AMERICAN FINANCIAL NETWORK INC
6833 Clark State Rd (43004-7500)

PHONE...............................714 831-4000
EMP: 37
SALES (corp-wide): 201.91MM Privately Held
Web: www.afncorp.com
SIC: 6282 Investment advice
PA: American Financial Network, Inc.
10 Pointe Dr Ste 330
Brea CA 92821
714 831-4000

(G-1109)
AMERISCAPE INC
6751 Taylor Rd Unit D1 (43004-8313)
P.O. Box 663 (43054-0663)
PHONE...............................614 863-5400
Bill Duraney, Pr
EMP: 45 EST: 1991
SALES (est): 1.01MM Privately Held
Web: www.ameriscape.com
SIC: 0782 Landscape contractors

(G-1110)
ATRIUM BUYING CORPORATION
1010 Jackson Hole Dr Ste 100 (43004-6050)
PHONE...............................740 966-8200
David Hirsh, CEO
Jason Tu, *
Jackie Hutson, *
Joe Reiber, *
◆ EMP: 100 EST: 1995
SQ FT: 25,000
SALES (est): 10.49MM Privately Held
SIC: 5137 Handbags

(G-1111)
INDUSTRIAL CONT SVCS - CA LLC
1385 Blatt Blvd (43004)
PHONE...............................614 864-1900
EMP: 271
SIC: 5085 Industrial supplies
HQ: Industrial Container Services - Ca, Llc
1540 S Greenwood Ave
Montebello CA 90640

(G-1112)
JEFFERSON GOLF & COUNTRY CLUB
7271 Jefferson Meadows Dr (43004-9811)
PHONE...............................614 759-7500
Earl Berry, Pr
EMP: 75 EST: 1989
SQ FT: 7,980
SALES (est): 6.19MM Privately Held
Web: www.jeffersoncountryclub.com
SIC: 7997 Golf club, membership

(G-1113)
JESS HOWARD ELECTRIC COMPANY
6630 Taylor Rd (43004-8661)
P.O. Box 400 (43004-0400)
PHONE...............................614 864-2167
Jess E Howard, CEO
John Howard, *
Francis Bolton, *
Bill Walt, *
Mel Haywood, *
EMP: 140 EST: 1945
SQ FT: 70,000
SALES (est): 38.17MM Privately Held
Web: www.jesshoward.com
SIC: 1731 General electrical contractor

(G-1114)
UNIFIRST CORPORATION
Also Called: Unifirst
211 Reynoldsburg New Albany Rd (43004-8700)
PHONE...............................614 575-9999
Douglas Parfker, Brnch Mgr

EMP: 50
SALES (corp-wide): 2.23B Publicly Held
Web: www.unifirst.com
SIC: 7218 7213 Work clothing supply; Uniform supply
PA: Unifirst Corporation
68 Jonspin Rd
Wilmington MA 01887
978 658-8888

(G-1115)
YARDMASTER OF COLUMBUS INC
570 Reynoldsburg New Albany Rd (43004-9688)
P.O. Box 650 (43004-0650)
PHONE...............................614 863-4510
Robert Slingluff, Pr
Kurt Kluznik, VP
Rick Colwell, Sec
EMP: 27 EST: 1991
SALES (est): 980.61K Privately Held
Web: www.yardmaster.com
SIC: 0781 4959 Landscape architects; Snowplowing

Blanchester
Clinton County

(G-1116)
DUVALL AUTOMOTIVE LLC
805 E Center St (45107-1309)
PHONE...............................513 836-6447
EMP: 27
Web: www.duvallautomotive.com
SIC: 7538 General automotive repair shops
PA: Duvall Automotive, Llc
3780 Nicholson Rd
Clarksville OH 45113

(G-1117)
FULFLO SPECIALTIES COMPANY
Also Called: True Torq
459 E Fancy St (45107-1462)
PHONE...............................937 783-2411
Thomas Ruthman, Pr
David Locaputo, Genl Mgr
EMP: 33 EST: 1939
SQ FT: 30,000
SALES (est): 14.01MM
SALES (corp-wide): 29.79MM Privately Held
Web: www.fulflo.com
SIC: 5085 Valves and fittings
PA: Ruthman Pump And Engineering, Inc
7236 Tylers Corner Dr
West Chester OH 45069
513 559-1901

Bloomville
Seneca County

(G-1118)
HANNAH FARM LLC
8240 S Township Road 171 (44818-9449)
PHONE...............................419 295-3929
Chris Ziegler, Brnch Mgr
EMP: 39
SALES (corp-wide): 244.32K Privately Held
SIC: 0191 General farms, primarily crop
PA: Hannah Farm, Llc
1167 W Ohio Pike
Amelia OH

Blue Ash
Hamilton County

(G-1119)
4MYBENEFITS INC
4665 Cornell Rd Ste 331 (45241-2455)
PHONE...............................513 891-6726
Gerald A Peter, Pr
Justin Peter, *
Jason Peter, *
Linda Peter, *
▲ EMP: 30 EST: 1999
SALES (est): 5.46MM Privately Held
Web: www.4mybenefits.com
SIC: 8742 6411 Human resource consulting services; Insurance information and consulting services

(G-1120)
5901 PFFFER RD HTELS SITES LLC
Also Called: Clarion Hotel Suites
5901 Pfeiffer Rd (45242-4821)
PHONE...............................513 793-4500
Jose Machuca, Genl Mgr
EMP: 31 EST: 1993
SALES (est): 477.92K Privately Held
Web: www.clarioncincinnati.com
SIC: 7011 5812 Hotels; Eating places

(G-1121)
ACKERMAN CHACCO COMPANY INC
10770 Kenwood Rd (45242-2823)
PHONE...............................513 791-4252
EMP: 32
SIC: 5072 5082 5085 7359 Hardware; General construction machinery and equipment; Fasteners and fastening equipment; Tool rental

(G-1122)
ADVANCED TESTING LAB INC
Also Called: Advanced Testing Laboratories
6954 Cornell Rd Ste 200 (45242-3001)
PHONE...............................513 489-8447
Greg Neal, Pr
EMP: 250 EST: 1987
SALES (est): 28.67MM
SALES (corp-wide): 286.3MM Privately Held
Web: www.atlscience.com
SIC: 8734 Testing laboratories
PA: Bureau Veritas
40 52 Immeuble Newtime
Neuilly Sur Seine 92200
969391009

(G-1123)
ADVANCED TESTING MGT GROUP INC
6954 Cornell Rd Ste 200 (45242-3001)
PHONE...............................513 489-8447
Greg Neal, Pr
Elizabeth Horton, *
Dorothy S Stammer, *
Dieter Stammer, *
EMP: 55 EST: 1987
SQ FT: 6,000
SALES (est): 3.58MM Privately Held
Web: www.advancedtesting.net
SIC: 8734 Testing laboratories

(G-1124)
ADVANTECH CORPORATION
Also Called: Advantech Indus Automtn Group
4445 Lake Forest Dr Ste 200 (45242-3743)
PHONE...............................513 742-8895
Roy Wang, Brnch Mgr
EMP: 70
Web: www.advantech.com

Blue Ash - Hamilton County (G-1125)

GEOGRAPHIC SECTION

SIC: **5045** Computer peripheral equipment
HQ: Advantech Corporation
380 Fairview Way
Milpitas CA 95035
408 519-3800

(G-1125)
ADVIZEX TECHNOLOGIES LLC
10260 Alliance Rd Ste 205 (45242-4743)
PHONE..................513 229-8400
Gary Hoying, *Brnch Mgr*
EMP: 34
Web: www.advizex.com
SIC: **7373** Value-added resellers, computer systems
PA: Advizex Technologies, Llc
6480 Rckside Wods Blvd St
Independence OH 44131

(G-1126)
AKKODIS INC
4665 Cornell Rd Ste 155 (45241-2471)
PHONE..................513 769-9797
EMP: 183
Web: www.modis.com
SIC: **7371** Computer software systems analysis and design, custom
HQ: Akkodis, Inc.
4800 Deerwood Campus Pkwy
Jacksonville FL 32246
904 360-2300

(G-1127)
ALLEGION S&S HOLDING CO INC
Steelcraft Manufacturing
9017 Blue Ash Rd (45242-6816)
PHONE..................513 766-4300
William Moore, *Brnch Mgr*
EMP: 110
Web: www.allegion.com
SIC: **4225** General warehousing
HQ: Allegion S&S Holding Company Inc.
11819 N Penn St
Carmel IN 46032
317 810-3700

(G-1128)
ALLWORTH FINANCIAL LP
Also Called: Hanson McClain Advisors
9987 Carver Rd (45242-5554)
PHONE..................513 469-7500
Patrick C Mcclain, *Brnch Mgr*
EMP: 30
Web: www.allworthfinancial.com
SIC: **8742** **6282** Financial consultant; Investment advisory service
PA: Allworth Financial, L.P.
8775 Folsom Blvd Ste 100
Sacramento CA 95826

(G-1129)
ALPHA & OMEGA BLDG SVCS INC
11319 Grooms Rd (45242-1405)
PHONE..................513 429-5082
Jim Baker, *CEO*
EMP: 334
SALES (corp-wide): 16.61MM **Privately Held**
Web: www.aobuildingservices.com
SIC: **7349** Janitorial service, contract basis
PA: Alpha & Omega Building Services, Inc.
2843 Culver Ave Ste A
Dayton OH 45429
937 298-2125

(G-1130)
AMERIGROUP OHIO INC
10123 Alliance Rd Ste 140 (45242-4707)
P.O. Box 62509 (23466-2509)
PHONE..................513 733-2300
Gary Radke, *Prin*

EMP: 143 EST: 2007
SALES (est): 3.6MM
SALES (corp-wide): 171.34B **Publicly Held**
SIC: **6324** Health Maintenance Organization (HMO), insurance only
HQ: Amerigroup Corporation
4425 Corp Ln Ste 160
Virginia Beach VA 23462

(G-1131)
ASCENDUM SOLUTIONS LLC (HQ)
Also Called: Ascendum Solutions
10290 Alliance Rd (45242-4710)
PHONE..................513 792-5100
Kris Nair, *Pt*
Diane Holle, *Managing Member*
EMP: 31 EST: 2008
SALES (est): 43.76MM **Privately Held**
Web: www.voraventures.com
SIC: **7379** Computer related consulting services
PA: Vora Ventures Llc
10290 Alliance Rd
Blue Ash OH 45242

(G-1132)
BELCAN LLC (PA)
Also Called: Belcan
10151 Carver Rd Ste 105 (45242-4760)
PHONE..................513 891-0972
Lance H Kwasniewski, *CEO*
Beth Ferris, *CFO*
EMP: 3000 EST: 1958
SALES (est): 751.87MM
SALES (corp-wide): 751.87MM **Privately Held**
Web: www.belcan.com
SIC: **7363** **8711** Engineering help service; Engineering services

(G-1133)
BELCAN LLC
Multimedia Services Division
10151 Carver Rd Ste 105 (45242-4760)
PHONE..................513 985-7777
Patrick Wagonfield, *Prin*
EMP: 42
SALES (corp-wide): 751.87MM **Privately Held**
Web: www.belcan.com
SIC: **8711** Engineering services
PA: Belcan, Llc
10151 Carver Rd Ste 105
Blue Ash OH 45242
513 891-0972

(G-1134)
BELCAN CORPORATION
10151 Carver Rd Ste 105 (45242-4760)
PHONE..................513 891-0972
Lance Kwasniewski, *CEO*
Beth Ferris, *CFO*
Neal Montour, *Pr*
Terry Williams, *CIO*
EMP: 48 EST: 2002
SALES (est): 4.75MM **Privately Held**
SIC: **7373** Systems engineering, computer related

(G-1135)
BELCAN ENGINEERING GROUP LLC (HQ)
10151 Carver Rd (45242-4758)
PHONE..................513 891-0972
Lance Kwasniewski, *CEO*
Lance Kwasniewski, *Pr*
Elizabeth Ferris, *
Michael Wirth, *CAO*
EMP: 1100 EST: 1991
SQ FT: 104,000

SALES (est): 363.47MM
SALES (corp-wide): 751.87MM **Privately Held**
Web: www.belcan.com
SIC: **8711** Engineering services
PA: Belcan, Llc
10151 Carver Rd Ste 105
Blue Ash OH 45242
513 891-0972

(G-1136)
BELCAN SVCS GROUP LTD PARTNR (HQ)
Also Called: Belflex Staffing Network
10151 Carver Rd (45242-4758)
PHONE..................513 891-0972
Lance Kwasniewski, *Genl Pt*
Mike Wirth, *Pt*
Elizabeth Ferris, *Pt*
EMP: 200 EST: 1958
SALES (est): 205.23MM
SALES (corp-wide): 751.87MM **Privately Held**
Web: www.belcan.com
SIC: **7363** Engineering help service
PA: Belcan, Llc
10151 Carver Rd Ste 105
Blue Ash OH 45242
513 891-0972

(G-1137)
BLUE-KENWOOD LLC
Also Called: Hilton
5300 Cornell Rd (45242-2002)
PHONE..................513 469-6900
EMP: 40 EST: 2008
SALES (est): 2.36MM **Privately Held**
Web: www.hilton.com
SIC: **7011** Resort hotel

(G-1138)
BLUESPRING SOFTWARE INC (HQ)
10290 Alliance Rd (45242-4710)
PHONE..................513 794-1764
Blaine Clark, *Pr*
Mahendra Vora, *Ch*
Micah Zimmerman, *CFO*
EMP: 27 EST: 1996
SQ FT: 9,000
SALES (est): 17.25MM **Privately Held**
Web: www.bluespringsoftware.com
SIC: **7371** **4813** **7375** Computer software development; Internet connectivity services; Information retrieval services
PA: Vora Ventures Llc
10290 Alliance Rd
Blue Ash OH 45242

(G-1139)
BUCKEYE HOME HEALTH CARE
10921 Reed Hartman Hwy Ste 310 (45242-2830)
PHONE..................513 791-6446
EMP: 152
Web: www.buckeyehomehealthcare.com
SIC: **8082** Home health care services
PA: Buckeye Home Health Care
7750 Paragon Rd
Dayton OH 45459

(G-1140)
CANGEN HOLDINGS INC
10200 Alliance Rd Ste 200 (45242-4716)
PHONE..................770 458-4882
Paul Cusolito, *Brnch Mgr*
EMP: 368
SIC: **5084** Industrial machinery and equipment
HQ: Cangen Holdings, Inc.
1057 Vijay Dr
Atlanta GA 30341

(G-1141)
CARDIOSOLUTION LLC
Also Called: Vitalsolution
4675 Cornell Rd Ste 100 (45241-2498)
PHONE..................513 618-2394
Perrin Peacock, *Pr*
EMP: 50 EST: 2011
SALES (est): 6.37MM
SALES (corp-wide): 461.91MM **Privately Held**
Web: www.vitalsolution.com
SIC: **8748** Business consulting, nec
PA: Ingenovis Health, Inc.
5700 S Quebec St Ste 300
Greenwood Village CO 80111
855 271-1767

(G-1142)
CASSADY SCHILLER & ASSOC INC
4555 Lake Forest Dr Ste 400 (45242-3785)
PHONE..................513 483-6699
David Cassady, *Pr*
EMP: 190 EST: 1990
SALES (est): 9.96MM **Privately Held**
Web: www.cassadyschiller.com
SIC: **8721** Certified public accountant

(G-1143)
CAVALIER DISTRIBUTING COMPANY (PA)
4650 Lake Forest Dr Ste 580 (45242-3756)
PHONE..................513 247-9222
George T Fisher, *Pr*
▲ EMP: 70 EST: 1992
SQ FT: 12,000
SALES (est): 30.31MM **Privately Held**
Web: www.cavbeer.com
SIC: **5181** Beer and other fermented malt liquors

(G-1144)
CEI PHYSICIANS PSC LLC (PA)
Also Called: Cincinnati Eye Institute
1945 Cei Dr (45242-5664)
PHONE..................513 984-5133
Clyde Bell, *Pr*
Robert E Brant, *
Carry Mcgehee, *VP*
Bobby Shaw, *
EMP: 160 EST: 1968
SQ FT: 44,000
SALES (est): 54.85MM
SALES (corp-wide): 54.85MM **Privately Held**
Web: www.cincinnatieye.com
SIC: **8011** Opthalmologist

(G-1145)
CEI VISION PARTNERS LLC
Also Called: Cvp Health
1945 Cei Dr (45242-5664)
PHONE..................513 569-3114
Clyde Bell, *CEO*
EMP: 100 EST: 2018
SALES (est): 11.09MM **Privately Held**
SIC: **8011** Offices and clinics of medical doctors

(G-1146)
CEQUENCE SECURITY INC
10805 Indeco Dr Ste B (45241-2965)
PHONE..................650 437-6338
EMP: 110
SALES (corp-wide): 1.17MM **Privately Held**
SIC: **7372** Prepackaged software
PA: Cequence Security, Inc.
100 S Murphy Ave Ste 300
Sunnyvale CA
844 978-3258

GEOGRAPHIC SECTION
Blue Ash - Hamilton County (G-1169)

(G-1147)
CERKL INCORPORATED
Also Called: Cerkl
11126 Kenwood Rd (45242-1897)
P.O. Box 42458 (45242-0458)
PHONE.................513 813-8425
Tarek Kamil, *CEO*
EMP: 100 **EST:** 2014
SALES (est): 11.33MM **Privately Held**
Web: www.cerkl.com
SIC: 2741 7371 7372 Internet publishing and broadcasting; Software programming applications; Prepackaged software

(G-1148)
CH2M HILL ENGINEERS INC
10123 Alliance Rd Ste 300 (45242-4714)
PHONE.................513 530-5520
Tom Murphy, *Brnch Mgr*
EMP: 120
SQ FT: 3,000
SALES (corp-wide): 14.92B **Publicly Held**
SIC: 8711 Consulting engineer
HQ: Ch2m Hill Engineers, Inc.
   6312 S Fiddlers Green Cir 300n
   Greenwood Village CO 80111
   720 286-2000

(G-1149)
CHAPTER TWO INC (PA)
4555 Lake Forest Dr Ste 220 (45242-3785)
PHONE.................513 792-5100
Phyllis Adams, *Pr*
EMP: 80 **EST:** 1982
SQ FT: 5,000
SALES (est): 4.72MM
SALES (corp-wide): 4.72MM **Privately Held**
SIC: 7379 7361 Data processing consultant; Employment agencies

(G-1150)
CIVIL & ENVIRONMENTAL CONS INC
10300 Alliance Rd (45242-4734)
PHONE.................513 985-0226
EMP: 34
SALES (corp-wide): 179.1MM **Privately Held**
Web: www.cecinc.com
SIC: 0781 8711 Landscape architects; Civil engineering
PA: Civil & Environmental Consultants, Inc.
   700 Cherrington Pkwy
   Moon Twp PA 15108
   412 429-2324

(G-1151)
CLIPPER MAGAZINE LLC
4601 Malsbary Rd # 1 (45242-5632)
PHONE.................513 794-4100
EMP: 60
SALES (corp-wide): 74.79MM **Privately Held**
Web: www.clippermagazine.com
SIC: 7331 Direct mail advertising services
PA: Clipper Magazine, Llc
   3708 Hempland Rd
   Mountville PA 17554
   717 569-5100

(G-1152)
CLOSETS BY DESIGN
11275 Deerfield Rd (45242-2023)
PHONE.................513 469-6130
Glen Grosser, *Pr*
EMP: 28 **EST:** 2001
SALES (est): 5.91MM **Privately Held**
Web: www.closetsbydesign.com
SIC: 1799 Closet organizers, installation and design

(G-1153)
CLUBESSENTIAL LLC (PA)
Also Called: Clubessential Holdings
9987 Carver Rd (45242-5553)
PHONE.................800 448-1475
Randy Eckels, *CEO*
Rob Decarlo, *
EMP: 41 **EST:** 2002
SALES (est): 30.36MM **Privately Held**
Web: www.clubessential.com
SIC: 7371 7374 Computer software development; Computer graphics service

(G-1154)
CMP I BLUE ASH OWNER LLC
Also Called: Courtyard Cincinnati Blue Ash
4625 Lake Forest Dr (45242-3729)
PHONE.................513 733-4334
Rick Kimmel, *Mgr*
EMP: 63 **EST:** 2008
SALES (est): 3.36MM
SALES (corp-wide): 196.32MM **Privately Held**
Web: www.blueash.com
SIC: 7011 Hotels and motels
PA: Cmp I Owner-T, Llc
   399 Park Ave Fl 18
   New York NY

(G-1155)
COHESION CONSULTING LLC
5151 Pfeiffer Rd Ste 105 (45242-4871)
PHONE.................513 587-7700
EMP: 63
SALES (corp-wide): 4.79MM **Privately Held**
Web: www.suncoastmarinesurveyor.com
SIC: 8748 Systems engineering consultant, ex. consultant or professional
PA: Cohesion Consulting Llc
   701 S Howard Ave
   Tampa FL 33606
   813 999-3100

(G-1156)
COMDOC INC
Also Called: Com Doc
9999 Carver Rd Ste 100 (45242-5584)
PHONE.................513 766-8124
EMP: 45
SALES (corp-wide): 6.89B **Publicly Held**
Web: www.comdoc.com
SIC: 5044 5021 Copying equipment; Office and public building furniture
HQ: Comdoc, Inc.
   8247 Pittsburg Ave Nw
   North Canton OH 44720
   330 896-2346

(G-1157)
COMMUNICARE HEALTH SVCS INC (PA)
Also Called: Communicare Health Services
10123 Alliance Rd (45242-4707)
PHONE.................513 530-1654
Stephen L Rosedale, *Pr*
Beatrice Rosedale, *
Michele Hoft, *
EMP: 40 **EST:** 1984
SALES (est): 392.92MM
SALES (corp-wide): 392.92MM **Privately Held**
Web: www.communicarehealth.com
SIC: 8741 Hospital management

(G-1158)
COMPLETE MECHANICAL SVCS LLC
Also Called: Cincinnati Mechanical Svcs LLC
11399 Grooms Rd (45242-1405)
PHONE.................513 489-3080
Bruce Ducker, *

Daniel G Dulle, *
Robert Sambrookes, *
Wyane Miller, *
EMP: 97 **EST:** 2000
SQ FT: 20,000
SALES (est): 24.79MM **Privately Held**
Web: www.completemech.com
SIC: 1711 3443 Mechanical contractor; Tank towers, metal plate

(G-1159)
COUNCIL ON AGING STHWSTERN OHI
4601 Malsbary Rd (45242-5632)
PHONE.................513 721-1025
TOLL FREE: 800
Suzanne Burke, *Ex Dir*
EMP: 200 **EST:** 1971
SQ FT: 31,000
SALES (est): 95.81MM **Privately Held**
Web: www.help4seniors.org
SIC: 8399 8322 Council for social agency; Individual and family services

(G-1160)
COUNSELING SOURCE INC
Also Called: Rehab Continuum, The
10921 Reed Hartman Hwy Ste 133 (45242-2851)
PHONE.................513 984-9838
David Turner, *Pr*
EMP: 33 **EST:** 1993
SALES (est): 4.58MM **Privately Held**
Web: www.thecounselingsource.com
SIC: 8093 Mental health clinic, outpatient

(G-1161)
COUNTY OF HAMILTON
Also Called: Hamilton County Coroner
4477 Carver Woods Dr (45242-5545)
PHONE.................513 946-8757
Lakshmi K Sammarco, *Coroner*
EMP: 42
SALES (corp-wide): 1.06MM **Privately Held**
Web: www.hamilton-co.org
SIC: 8049 Coroner
PA: County Of Hamilton
   138 E Court St Rm 607
   Cincinnati OH 45202
   513 946-4400

(G-1162)
CROSSCOUNTRY MORTGAGE LLC
4700 Ashwood Dr (45241-2465)
PHONE.................513 373-4240
EMP: 56
SALES (corp-wide): 803.24MM **Privately Held**
Web: www.crosscountrymortgage.com
SIC: 6162 Mortgage bankers and loan correspondents
PA: Crosscountry Mortgage, Llc
   6850 Miller Rd
   Brecksville OH 44141
   440 845-3700

(G-1163)
DORAN MFG LLC
4362 Glendale Milford Rd (45242-3706)
PHONE.................866 816-7233
Dave Robinson, *CFO*
EMP: 75 **EST:** 2003
SQ FT: 10,000
SALES (est): 3.61MM **Privately Held**
Web: www.doranmfg.com
SIC: 5013 3714 Motor vehicle supplies and new parts; Sanders, motor vehicle safety
PA: Evolving Enterprises, Inc.
   8748 Old Indian Hill Rd
   Cincinnati OH 45243

(G-1164)
DUGAN & MEYERS LLC (PA)
11110 Kenwood Rd (45242-1818)
PHONE.................513 891-4300
Jeff Kelly, *CFO*
EMP: 69 **EST:** 2016
SALES (est): 53.77MM
SALES (corp-wide): 53.77MM **Privately Held**
Web: www.dugan-meyers.com
SIC: 1541 Industrial buildings, new construction, nec

(G-1165)
DVA HLTHCARE - STHWEST OHIO LL
Also Called: Blue Ash Dialysis
10600 Mckinley Rd (45242-3716)
PHONE.................513 733-8215
John Winstel, *Brnch Mgr*
EMP: 39
SIC: 8092 Kidney dialysis centers
HQ: Dva Healthcare - Southwest Ohio, Llc
   2000 16th St
   Denver CO 80202
   253 733-4501

(G-1166)
E-VOLVE SYSTEMS LLC (DH)
Also Called: E-Volve Systems An E Tech Grou
4600 Mcauley Pl Ste 120 (45242-4765)
PHONE.................765 543-8123
Kevin Stout, *Pr*
EMP: 28 **EST:** 2010
SALES (est): 5.22MM
SALES (corp-wide): 106.23MM **Privately Held**
Web: www.e-volvesystems.com
SIC: 8711 8742 Consulting engineer; Industrial consultant
HQ: E-Technologies Group, Llc
   8614 Jacquemin Dr
   West Chester OH 45069

(G-1167)
ENERVISE INCORPORATED (PA)
10226 Alliance Rd (45242-4710)
PHONE.................513 761-6000
Thomas Winstel, *CEO*
Mary Seaman, *
Dave Plouffe, *
EMP: 74 **EST:** 1985
SQ FT: 22,000
SALES (est): 16MM
SALES (corp-wide): 16MM **Privately Held**
Web: www.enervise.com
SIC: 1711 Mechanical contractor

(G-1168)
ENGINRING EXCLLNCE NAT ACCNTS
4360 Glendale Milford Rd (45242-3706)
PHONE.................844 969-3923
Jenine Kraus, *Pr*
EMP: 99 **EST:** 2008
SALES (est): 9.33MM
SALES (corp-wide): 17.93B **Privately Held**
SIC: 1711 Heating and air conditioning contractors
HQ: Sehac Holdings Llc
   3820 American Dr Ste 200
   Plano TX

(G-1169)
ENTERPRISE HOLDINGS INC
Also Called: Enterprise Rent-A-Car
4600 Mcauley Pl Ste 150 (45242-4765)
PHONE.................513 538-6200
Leandra Carlfeldt, *Mgr*
EMP: 49
SALES (corp-wide): 7.04B **Privately Held**
Web: www.enterprise.com

Blue Ash - Hamilton County (G-1170) GEOGRAPHIC SECTION

SIC: 7514 7515 Rent-a-car service; Passenger car leasing
HQ: Enterprise Mobility
600 Corporate Park Dr
Saint Louis MO 63105
314 512-5000

(G-1170)
ETHICON ENDO-SURGERY INC (HQ)
4545 Creek Rd (45242-2839)
PHONE.................513 337-7000
Andrew K Ekdahl, Pr
▲ EMP: 1440 EST: 1992
SQ FT: 31,330
SALES (est): 783.51MM
SALES (corp-wide): 85.16B Publicly Held
SIC: 3841 5047 Surgical instruments and apparatus; Medical equipment and supplies
PA: Johnson & Johnson
1 Johnson & Johnson Plz
New Brunswick NJ 08933
732 524-0400

(G-1171)
F+W MEDIA INC
Also Called: Novel Writing Workshop
9912 Carver Rd Ste 100 (45242-5541)
P.O. Box 78000 (48278-0001)
PHONE.................513 531-2690
▲ EMP: 650
Web: www.goldenpeakmedia.com
SIC: 2721 2731 4813 Magazines: publishing only, not printed on site; Books, publishing only; Online service providers

(G-1172)
FEINTOOL EQUIPMENT CORPORATION
6833 Creek Rd (45242-4121)
PHONE.................513 791-1118
Lars Reich, Genl Mgr
▲ EMP: 35 EST: 1976
SQ FT: 29,000
SALES (est): 8.8MM Privately Held
Web: www.feintool.com
SIC: 5084 Industrial machinery and equipment
HQ: Feintool U.S. Operations, Inc.
11280 Cornell Park Dr
Cincinnati OH 45242
513 247-0110

(G-1173)
FINANCIAL MANAGEMENT GROUP
4665 Cornell Rd Ste 160 (45241-2455)
PHONE.................513 984-6696
EMP: 54 EST: 1989
SALES (est): 192.88K Privately Held
Web: www.twpteam.com
SIC: 8742 6282 Financial consultant; Investment advice

(G-1174)
FIRST DATA GVRNMNT SOLUTNS INC (DH)
11311 Cornell Park Dr Ste 300 (45242-1889)
PHONE.................513 489-9599
Michael D Capellas, CEO
EMP: 125 EST: 1998
SALES (est): 13.31MM
SALES (corp-wide): 19.09B Publicly Held
SIC: 7371 Custom computer programming services
HQ: First Data Corporation
600 N Vel R Phillips Ave
Milwaukee WI 53203

(G-1175)
FISHBECK THMPSON CARR HBER INC
11353 Reed Hartman Hwy Ste 500 (45241-2443)
PHONE.................513 469-2370
Peter Soltys, Mgr
EMP: 50
SALES (corp-wide): 90.3MM Privately Held
Web: www.fishbeck.com
SIC: 8711 Consulting engineer
PA: Fishbeck, Thompson, Carr & Huber, Inc.
1515 Arboretum Dr Se
Grand Rapids MI 49546
616 575-3824

(G-1176)
FOUR O CORPORATION (DH)
Also Called: Oil Distributing Co
9395 Kenwood Rd (45242-6819)
PHONE.................513 941-2800
EMP: 50 EST: 1961
SALES (est): 91.02MM Privately Held
SIC: 5171 Petroleum bulk stations and terminals
HQ: Reladyne Llc
8280 Montgomery Rd # 101
Cincinnati OH 45236
513 489-6000

(G-1177)
FUSION ALLIANCE LLC
4555 Lake Forest Dr Ste 325 (45242-3785)
PHONE.................513 563-8444
EMP: 103
SALES (corp-wide): 49.95MM Privately Held
Web: digital.neweratech.com
SIC: 7371 Computer software development
HQ: Fusion Alliance, Llc
301 Pnnsylvnia Pkwy Ste 2
Carmel IN 46032
317 955-1300

(G-1178)
GIRL SCOUTS OF WESTERN OHIO (PA)
4930 Cornell Rd (45242-1804)
PHONE.................513 489-1025
Barbara J Bonifas, CEO
EMP: 45 EST: 1963
SQ FT: 6,000
SALES (est): 13.28MM
SALES (corp-wide): 13.28MM Privately Held
Web: www.gswo.org
SIC: 8641 Girl Scout organization

(G-1179)
GLOBAL MEDICAL PRODUCTS LLC
11253 Williamson Rd (45241)
PHONE.................630 521-9545
Emmett Bailey, Managing Member
EMP: 48 EST: 2008
SALES (est): 8.32MM Privately Held
Web: www.globalmedicalproducts.net
SIC: 5047 Medical equipment and supplies

(G-1180)
GROUNDSYSTEMS LLC (PA)
11315 Williamson Rd (45242-2232)
PHONE.................800 570-0213
Rachel Rorie, Pr
Michael Rorie, *
EMP: 35 EST: 2013
SALES (est): 17.09MM
SALES (corp-wide): 17.09MM Privately Held

Web: www.groundsystems.net
SIC: 0782 Lawn care services

(G-1181)
HH FRANCHISING SYSTEMS INC
Also Called: Home Helpers Home Care
10101 Alliance Rd Ste 300 (45242-4736)
PHONE.................513 563-8339
Emma Dickison, Pr
Keith Tilley, CFO
EMP: 93 EST: 1997
SALES (est): 16.4MM Privately Held
Web: www.homehelpershomecare.com
SIC: 8082 Home health care services

(G-1182)
HILLS DEVELOPERS INC
4901 Hunt Rd Ste 300 (45242-6990)
PHONE.................513 984-0300
Murray Guttman, Ch Bd
Stephen Guttman, *
Harold Guttman, *
Louis Guttman, *
EMP: 175 EST: 1981
SQ FT: 16,000
SALES (est): 11.22MM Privately Held
Web: www.hillsproperties.com
SIC: 8741 Construction management

(G-1183)
HILLS PROPERTY MANAGEMENT INC (PA)
Also Called: Hills Real Estate Group
4901 Hunt Rd Ste 300 (45242-6990)
PHONE.................513 984-0300
Steve Guttman, Pr
Louis Guttman, VP
EMP: 70 EST: 1986
SQ FT: 2,000
SALES (est): 22.29MM
SALES (corp-wide): 22.29MM Privately Held
Web: www.hillsproperties.com
SIC: 6513 6512 Apartment building operators ; Nonresidential building operators

(G-1184)
INFOTRUST LLC
4340 Glendale Milford Rd Ste 200 (45242)
PHONE.................513 403-2107
EMP: 99 EST: 2018
SALES (est): 126.19K Privately Held
Web: www.infotrust.com
SIC: 6512 Commercial and industrial building operation

(G-1185)
INTERACT ONE INC
4665 Cornell Rd Ste 255 (45241-2455)
PHONE.................513 469-7042
Brian Dwyer, Pr
Brian Dwyer, Pr
Maryellen Dwyer, *
EMP: 32 EST: 1998
SALES (est): 2.09MM Privately Held
Web: www.interactone.com
SIC: 7374 Computer graphics service

(G-1186)
ITCUBE LLC
10999 Reed Hartman Hwy Ste 237 (45242-8331)
PHONE.................513 891-7300
EMP: 27 EST: 2006
SALES (est): 4.71MM Privately Held
Web: www.itcubebpo.com
SIC: 7371 Computer software development

(G-1187)
ITW AIR MANAGEMENT
10125 Carver Rd (45242-4798)
PHONE.................513 891-7474
Tom Long, Contrlr
EMP: 34 EST: 2015
SALES (est): 4.05MM Privately Held
Web: www.itw-air.com
SIC: 8741 Management services

(G-1188)
J M SEALTS COMPANY
4755 Lake Forest Dr Ste 100 (45242-3858)
PHONE.................419 224-8075
Larry Easterday, Pr
EMP: 46 EST: 1883
SQ FT: 60,000
SALES (est): 5.24MM Privately Held
SIC: 5141 5142 Food brokers; Packaged frozen goods

(G-1189)
J PETERMAN COMPANY LLC
Also Called: J. Peterman
5345 Creek Rd (45242-3935)
PHONE.................888 647-2555
▲ EMP: 35 EST: 1999
SQ FT: 15,000
SALES (est): 8.07MM Privately Held
Web: www.jpeterman.com
SIC: 5136 5611 5621 5137 Apparel belts, men's and boys'; Men's and boys' clothing stores; Women's clothing stores; Women's and children's clothing

(G-1190)
JAI BAPA SWAMI LLC
Also Called: Hampton Inn Cncinnati Blue Ash
4761 Creek Rd (45242-0247)
PHONE.................513 791-2822
Laura Wigle, Prin
EMP: 33 EST: 2009
SALES (est): 1.7MM Privately Held
Web: www.hilton.com
SIC: 7011 Hotels and motels

(G-1191)
JATIGA INC (PA)
Also Called: Hanser Music Group
9933 Alliance Rd Ste 1 (45242-5662)
PHONE.................859 817-7100
John Hanser Iii, Pr
Gary Hanser, *
Timothy Hanser, *
David Rasfeld, *
▲ EMP: 80 EST: 1924
SALES (est): 4.06MM
SALES (corp-wide): 4.06MM Privately Held
SIC: 3931 5099 Musical instruments; Musical instruments

(G-1192)
JP OUTFITTERS LLC
5345 Creek Rd (45242-3935)
PHONE.................513 745-1137
EMP: 45 EST: 2019
SALES (est): 4.56MM Privately Held
Web: www.jpeterman.com
SIC: 5136 Apparel belts, men's and boys'

(G-1193)
KALEIDOSCOPE INNOVATION
4362 Creek Rd (45241-2924)
PHONE.................513 791-3009
EMP: 107 EST: 2020
SALES (est): 5.13MM Privately Held
Web: www.kascope.com
SIC: 8741 Management services

GEOGRAPHIC SECTION
Blue Ash - Hamilton County (G-1215)

(G-1194)
KALEIDOSCOPE PROTOTYPING LLC
4362 Creek Rd (45241-2924)
PHONE..............................513 206-9137
Matthew P Komau, *Prin*
EMP: 50 **EST:** 2019
SALES (est): 978.14K Privately Held
Web: www.kascope.com
SIC: 8742 Management consulting services
PA: Infosys Limited
 Plot No. 44 & 97a, Electronics City
 Bengaluru KA 56010

(G-1195)
KINDER GARDEN SCHOOL
10969 Reed Hartman Hwy (45242-2821)
PHONE..............................513 791-4300
Tami Lanham, *Owner*
EMP: 29 **EST:** 2004
SALES (est): 446.25K Privately Held
Web: www.kindergardenschool.com
SIC: 8351 Preschool center

(G-1196)
KOORSEN FIRE & SECURITY INC
10608 Millington Ct (45242-4015)
PHONE..............................513 398-4300
EMP: 44
SALES (corp-wide): 150.64MM Privately Held
Web: www.koorsen.com
SIC: 7382 Security systems services
PA: Koorsen Fire & Security, Inc.
 2719 N Arlington Ave
 Indianapolis IN 46218
 317 542-1800

(G-1197)
LAN SOLUTIONS INC
Also Called: Intrust It
9850 Redhill Dr (45242)
PHONE..............................513 469-6500
Timothy J Rettig, *Pr*
EMP: 60 **EST:** 1992
SQ FT: 4,300
SALES (est): 9.96MM Privately Held
Web: www.intrust-it.com
SIC: 7379 Online services technology consultants

(G-1198)
LANDRUM & BROWN INCORPORATED (PA)
4445 Lake Forest Dr Ste 700 (45242-3733)
PHONE..............................513 530-5333
Beth Hess, *Admn*
Mark Perryman, *
Berta Fernandez, *
James Adams, *
Brian Reed, *
EMP: 50 **EST:** 1984
SALES (est): 25.11MM
SALES (corp-wide): 25.11MM Privately Held
Web: www.landrumbrown.com
SIC: 8748 8742 Business consulting, nec; Transportation consultant

(G-1199)
LANG FINANCIAL GROUP INC
4225 Malsbary Rd Ste 100 (45242-5561)
PHONE..............................513 699-2966
Stanford L Lang, *Ch Bd*
EMP: 40 **EST:** 1958
SQ FT: 8,700
SALES (est): 7.04MM Privately Held
Web: www.langgroup.com

SIC: 6411 8742 6282 Insurance agents, nec; Financial consultant; Investment advice

(G-1200)
LEADEC CORP (DH)
Also Called: Leadec Services
9395 Kenwood Rd Ste 200 (45242-6819)
PHONE..............................513 731-3590
William Bell, *CEO*
Donald G Morsch, *
▲ **EMP:** 34 **EST:** 1984
SQ FT: 18,000
SALES (est): 341.34MM
SALES (corp-wide): 2.67MM Privately Held
Web: www.leadec-services.com
SIC: 7349 8741 3714 Building cleaning service; Management services; Motor vehicle parts and accessories
HQ: Leadec Holding Bv & Co. Kg
 Meitnerstr. 11
 Stuttgart BW 70563
 71178410

(G-1201)
LENDKEY TECHNOLOGIES INC
9999 Carver Rd Ste 400 (45242-5584)
PHONE..............................646 626-7396
Vincent Passione, *Ch Bd*
Raymond Dury, *CIO*
Lewis Goldman, *CMO*
Christian Widhalm, *CRO*
EMP: 133 **EST:** 2010
SALES (est): 12.91MM Privately Held
Web: www.lendkey.com
SIC: 8741 Management services

(G-1202)
LSI INDUSTRIES INC
LSI Midwest Lighting
10000 Alliance Rd (45242-4706)
PHONE..............................913 281-1100
Dennis Oberling, *Mgr*
EMP: 200
SALES (corp-wide): 496.98MM Publicly Held
Web: www.lsicorp.com
SIC: 3646 5063 Commercial lighting fixtures; Lighting fixtures
PA: Lsi Industries Inc.
 10000 Alliance Rd
 Cincinnati OH 45242
 513 793-3200

(G-1203)
LSI LIGHTRON INC
10000 Alliance Rd (45242-4706)
PHONE..............................845 562-5500
Gene Littman, *CEO*
Barry White, *
▲ **EMP:** 1000 **EST:** 1946
SALES (est): 322.71MM
SALES (corp-wide): 496.98MM Publicly Held
Web: www.lsicorp.com
SIC: 3646 5063 Commercial lighting fixtures; Electrical apparatus and equipment
PA: Lsi Industries Inc.
 10000 Alliance Rd
 Cincinnati OH 45242
 513 793-3200

(G-1204)
LUMINEX HM DCOR FRGRNCE HLDG C (PA)
Also Called: Luminex HD&f Company
10521 Millington Ct (45242-4022)
PHONE..............................513 563-1113
Calvin Johnston, *CEO*
EMP: 498 **EST:** 2016
SALES (est): 260.78MM

SALES (corp-wide): 260.78MM Privately Held
Web: www.candle-lite.com
SIC: 5023 2844 Decorative home furnishings and supplies; Perfumes, cosmetics and other toilet preparations

(G-1205)
LYNX EMS LLC
10123 Alliance Rd (45242-4707)
PHONE..............................513 530-1600
Yitzhak Rosedale, *Prin*
Sandra Smiddy, *
EMP: 29 **EST:** 2017
SALES (est): 5.24MM
SALES (corp-wide): 392.92MM Privately Held
Web: www.lynx911.com
SIC: 4119 Local passenger transportation, nec
PA: Communicare Health Services, Inc.
 10123 Alliance Rd
 Blue Ash OH 45242
 513 530-1654

(G-1206)
MARKETVISION RESEARCH INC (PA)
5151 Pfeiffer Rd Ste 300 (45242-4854)
PHONE..............................513 791-3100
Tyler Mcmullen, *CEO*
EMP: 70 **EST:** 1983
SQ FT: 20,500
SALES (est): 21.24MM
SALES (corp-wide): 21.24MM Privately Held
Web: www.mv-research.com
SIC: 8732 Market analysis or research

(G-1207)
MD OMG EMP LLC (HQ)
Also Called: Communicare Family of Company
10123 Alliance Rd (45242-4707)
PHONE..............................513 489-7100
EMP: 68 **EST:** 1994
SALES (est): 45.66MM
SALES (corp-wide): 392.92MM Privately Held
Web: www.communicarehealth.com
SIC: 8051 Skilled nursing care facilities
PA: Communicare Health Services, Inc.
 10123 Alliance Rd
 Blue Ash OH 45242
 513 530-1654

(G-1208)
MEDUS TRAVELERS
4555 Lake Forest Dr Ste 540 (45242-3732)
PHONE..............................513 678-2179
Michael Riley, *Prin*
EMP: 75 **EST:** 2018
SALES (est): 4.16MM Privately Held
Web: www.medusinc.com
SIC: 4724 Travel agencies

(G-1209)
MERCHANDISING SERVICES CO
10999 Reed Hartman Hwy Ste 200 (45242-8331)
PHONE..............................866 479-8246
Mike Buschelmann, *Pr*
EMP: 62
SALES (corp-wide): 5.07MM Privately Held
Web: www.merchandisingservicesco.com
SIC: 8742 Merchandising consultant
PA: Merchandising Services, Co.
 9891 Montgomery Rd # 320
 Montgomery OH 45242

866 479-8246

(G-1210)
META MANUFACTURING CORPORATION
8901 Blue Ash Rd Ste 1 (45242-7809)
PHONE..............................513 793-6382
David Mc Swain, *Pr*
EMP: 50 **EST:** 1988
SQ FT: 54,000
SALES (est): 6.02MM Privately Held
Web: www.metamfg.com
SIC: 3599 7692 Machine shop, jobbing and repair; Welding repair

(G-1211)
MODERN OFFICE METHODS INC
Also Called: M.O.M.
11235 Williamson Rd (45241-2230)
PHONE..............................513 791-0909
Derrick Holmes, *Mgr*
EMP: 34
SALES (corp-wide): 45.16MM Privately Held
Web: www.momnet.com
SIC: 7359 7629 5044 Office machine rental, except computers; Business machine repair, electric; Office equipment
PA: Modern Office Methods, Inc.
 4747 Lake Forest Dr
 Cincinnati OH 45242
 513 791-0909

(G-1212)
MOLLOY ROOFING COMPANY
Also Called: Blue Ash Roofing Co
11099 Deerfield Rd (45242-4111)
PHONE..............................513 791-7400
David Molloy, *Prin*
EMP: 31 **EST:** 1958
SQ FT: 10,000
SALES (est): 3.2MM Privately Held
Web: www.molloyroofing.com
SIC: 1761 Roofing contractor

(G-1213)
MPF SALES AND MKTG GROUP LLC
11243 Cornell Park Dr (45242-1811)
PHONE..............................513 793-6241
Mike Marek, *Managing Member*
EMP: 200 **EST:** 2010
SALES (est): 24.36MM Privately Held
Web: www.epicsales.com
SIC: 5141 Food brokers

(G-1214)
NATIONAL HEATING AND AC CO
4300 Creek Rd (45241-2924)
PHONE..............................513 621-4620
Scott Braun, *Pr*
EMP: 33 **EST:** 1963
SALES (est): 5.04MM Privately Held
Web: www.nationalheatingandac.com
SIC: 1711 Warm air heating and air conditioning contractor

(G-1215)
NIGHTINGALE HOLDINGS LLC (PA)
4700 Ashwood Dr Ste 200 (45241-2424)
PHONE..............................513 489-7100
Steve Rosedale, *Pr*
Ms. Hawkins, *Contrlr*
EMP: 800 **EST:** 2000
SALES (est): 12.74MM
SALES (corp-wide): 12.74MM Privately Held
SIC: 8051 Skilled nursing care facilities

(PA)=Parent Co (HQ)=Headquarters
✿ = New Business established in last 2 years

Blue Ash - Hamilton County (G-1216) **GEOGRAPHIC SECTION**

(G-1216)
OCTAVIA WEALTH ADVISORS LLC
9999 Carver Rd Ste 130 (45242-5585)
PHONE.................................513 762-7775
EMP: 41 **EST:** 2020
SALES (est): 9.22MM **Privately Held**
Web: www.octaviawa.com
SIC: 6282 Investment advisory service

(G-1217)
OHIO VALLEY ELEC SVCS LLC
4585 Cornell Rd (45241-2439)
PHONE.................................513 771-2410
Steve Ortner, *Pr*
Mike Nienhaus, *
EMP: 85 **EST:** 2002
SQ FT: 8,000
SALES (est): 24.67MM **Privately Held**
Web: www.ohiovalleyelectric.com
SIC: 1731 General electrical contractor

(G-1218)
OXFORD PHYSICAL THERAPY INC
Also Called: OXFORD PHYSICAL THERAPY INC
9395 Kenwood Rd Ste 101 (45242-6819)
PHONE.................................513 745-9877
Peter Zulia, *Brnch Mgr*
EMP: 46
Web: www.oxfordphysicaltherapy.com
SIC: 8049 Physical therapist
PA: Oxford Physical Therapy And
   Rehabilitation, Inc.
   345 S College Ave
   Oxford OH 45056

(G-1219)
PCMS DATAFIT INC
Also Called: Pcms
4270 Glendale Milford Rd (45242-3704)
PHONE.................................513 587-3100
Richard Smith, *Pr*
Jon Stretton, *CCO**
EMP: 68 **EST:** 2000
SALES (est): 22.3MM **Privately Held**
Web: www.flooid.com
SIC: 7371 7373 Computer software writing services; Computer integrated systems design
HQ: Flooid Limited
   P C M S House
   Coventry W MIDLANDS CV4 8
   247 669-4455

(G-1220)
PEDCO E & A SERVICES INC
10300 Alliance Rd (45242-4734)
PHONE.................................513 782-4920
Michael Walsh, *CEO*
Kenneth Hover, *
William Giesler, *
Steve Weidner, *
EMP: 75 **EST:** 1981
SALES (est): 10.34MM **Privately Held**
Web: www.pedcoea.com
SIC: 8711 8712 7389 Consulting engineer; Architectural engineering; Interior designer

(G-1221)
PEPPER CNSTR CO OHIO LLC
4350 Glendale Milford Rd Ste 160 (45242-3700)
PHONE.................................513 563-7700
EMP: 38
SALES (corp-wide): 1.32B **Privately Held**
Web: www.pepperconstruction.com
SIC: 1542 Commercial and office building, new construction
HQ: Pepper Construction Company Of Ohio, Llc
   5185 Blazer Pkwy
   Dublin OH 43017
   614 793-4477

(G-1222)
PRIORITY DISPATCH INC (PA)
4665 Malsbary Rd (45242-5645)
PHONE.................................513 791-3900
R Jeffrey Thomas, *Pr*
Beth Dusha, *
EMP: 40 **EST:** 1973
SQ FT: 20,000
SALES (est): 24.29MM
SALES (corp-wide): 24.29MM **Privately Held**
Web: www.prioritydispatch.com
SIC: 4212 Delivery service, vehicular

(G-1223)
PROCAMPS INC
10001 Alliance Rd (45242-4751)
PHONE.................................513 745-5855
Gregg Darbyshire, *Pr*
EMP: 30 **EST:** 2011
SALES (est): 4.27MM **Privately Held**
Web: www.procamps.com
SIC: 7032 Sporting and recreational camps

(G-1224)
PROCTER & GAMBLE DISTRG LLC
Also Called: Procter & Gamble
11510 Reed Hartman Hwy (45241-2422)
PHONE.................................513 626-2500
Tony Burns, *Brnch Mgr*
EMP: 273
SALES (corp-wide): 82.01B **Publicly Held**
SIC: 5169 5122 5149 5113 Detergents; Drugs, proprietaries, and sundries; Groceries and related products, nec; Napkins, paper
HQ: Procter & Gamble Distributing Llc
   1 Procter And Gamble Plz
   Cincinnati OH 45202
   513 983-1100

(G-1225)
PROFESSIONAL RADIOLOGY INC
Also Called: PRI
9825 Kenwood Rd Ste 105 (45242-6252)
PHONE.................................513 872-4500
W Wallace White Md, *Pr*
Raymond C Rost Md, *VP*
Steve J Polmeranz Md, *Pr*
James J Masters Md, *Sec*
EMP: 44 **EST:** 1962
SALES (est): 6.32MM **Privately Held**
Web: www.professionalradiology.com
SIC: 8011 Radiologist

(G-1226)
PULMONARY SOLUTIONS INC
4701 Creek Rd Ste 100 (45242-8330)
PHONE.................................937 393-0991
Jean Dennig, *Pr*
William M Copeland, *
EMP: 35 **EST:** 1998
SALES (est): 814.45K **Privately Held**
SIC: 8093 8082 Respiratory therapy clinic; Home health care services

(G-1227)
QUEST DEF SYSTEMS SLUTIONS INC
10300 Alliance Rd Ste 500 (45242-4767)
PHONE.................................513 628-4521
Robert Harvey, *Pr*
EMP: 100 **EST:** 2019
SALES (est): 15.04MM **Privately Held**
Web: www.quest-global.com
SIC: 7379 Computer related consulting services
HQ: Quest Global Services-Na, Inc.
   175 Addison Rd
   Windsor CT 06095

(G-1228)
R A MUELLER INC
11270 Cornell Park Dr (45242-1887)
PHONE.................................513 489-5200
EMP: 46 **EST:** 1952
SALES (est): 10.06MM **Publicly Held**
Web: www.ramueller.com
SIC: 5084 Chemical process equipment
PA: Dxp Enterprises, Inc.
   5301 Hollister St
   Houston TX 77040

(G-1229)
RA CONSULTANTS LLC
10856 Kenwood Rd (45242-2812)
PHONE.................................513 469-6600
Marijo Flamm, *
EMP: 46 **EST:** 2004
SALES (est): 5.26MM **Privately Held**
Web: www.raconsultantsllc.com
SIC: 8711 3679 Civil engineering; Commutators, electronic

(G-1230)
RAINBOW RASCALS LRNG CTR INC
Also Called: Rainbow Child Development Ctr
10631 Techwoods Cir (45242-2846)
PHONE.................................513 769-7529
EMP: 72
SQ FT: 5,840
SALES (corp-wide): 77.32K **Privately Held**
Web: www.boulderrainbow.com
SIC: 8351 8322 Group day care center; Individual and family services
PA: Rainbow Rascals Learning Center, Inc.
   5660 Sioux Dr
   Boulder CO 80303
   303 499-3038

(G-1231)
RANDSTAD PROFESSIONALS US LLC
4600 Mcauley Pl Ste 140 (45242-4765)
PHONE.................................513 791-8600
EMP: 90
SALES (corp-wide): 28.63B **Privately Held**
Web: www.randstadusa.com
SIC: 7361 Executive placement
HQ: Randstad Professionals Us, Llc
   150 Presidential Way
   Woburn MA 01801

(G-1232)
RAYMOND STORAGE CONCEPTS INC (PA)
5480 Creek Rd Unit 1 (45242-4002)
PHONE.................................513 891-7290
Scott Wolcott, *Pr*
Tim Fahey, *
Joe Nartker, *
Tim Crowe, *
▲ **EMP:** 90 **EST:** 1980
SQ FT: 15,000
SALES (est): 75.94MM
SALES (corp-wide): 75.94MM **Privately Held**
Web: www.raymondsci.com
SIC: 5084 7699 Materials handling machinery; Industrial equipment services

(G-1233)
RBG INC
Also Called: Resource One
6043 Interstate Cir (45242-1414)
PHONE.................................513 247-0175
EMP: 33
SIC: 4953 Recycling, waste materials

(G-1234)
RECO LLC
Also Called: Richard Equipment Co
6860 Ashfield Dr (45242-4108)
▲ **EMP:** 40 **EST:** 1961
SQ FT: 6,400
SALES (est): 20.73MM **Publicly Held**
SIC: 5082 General construction machinery and equipment
PA: Wesco International, Inc.
   225 W Stn Sq Dr Ste 700
   Pittsburgh PA 15219

(G-1235)
REQ/JQH HOLDINGS INC
Also Called: International Merchants
4243 Hunt Rd Ste 2 (45242-6645)
PHONE.................................513 891-1066
EMP: 334
Web: www.birminghammarriott.com
SIC: 7011 6552 Hotels and motels; Land subdividers and developers, commercial

(G-1236)
RESIDENCE INN BY MARRIOTT LLC
Also Called: Residence Inn By Marriott
11401 Reed Hartman Hwy (45241-2470)
PHONE.................................513 530-5060
John Secola, *Brnch Mgr*
EMP: 42
SALES (corp-wide): 23.71B **Publicly Held**
Web: www.marriott.com
SIC: 7011 Hotels and motels
HQ: Residence Inn By Marriott, Llc
   10400 Fernwood Rd
   Bethesda MD 20817

(G-1237)
RETIREMENT CORP OF AMERICA
10300 Alliance Rd Ste 100 (45242-4770)
PHONE.................................513 769-4040
EMP: 64 **EST:** 1988
SALES (est): 4.38MM
SALES (corp-wide): 12.64B **Publicly Held**
SIC: 6022 State trust companies accepting deposits, commercial
PA: Fifth Third Bancorp
   38 Fountain Square Plz
   Cincinnati OH 45263
   800 972-3030

(G-1238)
RIVER CITY MORTGAGE LLC
4555 Lake Forest Dr Ste 450 (45242-3760)
PHONE.................................513 631-6400
EMP: 157 **EST:** 2010
SALES (est): 29.34MM **Privately Held**
Web: www.rchomeloans.com
SIC: 6162 Mortgage bankers

(G-1239)
SAMUELS PRODUCTS INC
9851 Redhill Dr (45242-5694)
PHONE.................................513 891-4456
Millard Samuels, *Pr*
Thomas J Samuels, *
William Fitzpatric, *
EMP: 30 **EST:** 1903
SQ FT: 61,000
SALES (est): 5.66MM **Privately Held**
Web: www.samuelsproducts.com
SIC: 2759 5122 Flexographic printing; Druggists' sundries, nec

(G-1240)
SANDY SHORES PARTNERS INC
11275 Deerfield Rd (45242-2023)
PHONE.................................513 469-6130

GEOGRAPHIC SECTION

Blue Ash - Hamilton County (G-1264)

EMP: 73 **EST:** 2020
SALES (est): 1.52MM **Privately Held**
SIC: 7011 Resort hotel

(G-1241)
SCHAEFER GROUP INC
Also Called: Schaefer Group
11310 Tamarco Dr (45242-2108)
PHONE.................513 489-2420
Kathy Miller, *Mgr*
EMP: 37
SALES (corp-wide): 20.24MM **Privately Held**
Web: www.theschaefergroup.com
SIC: 7699 Boiler repair shop
PA: The Schaefer Group Inc
1300 Grange Hall Rd
Beavercreek OH 45430
937 253-3342

(G-1242)
SCHAEFFERS INVESTMENT RESEARCH INC
Also Called: Option Advisor, The
5151 Pfeiffer Rd Ste 450 (45242-4865)
PHONE.................513 589-3800
EMP: 65 **EST:** 1981
SALES (est): 7.01MM **Privately Held**
Web: www.schaeffersresearch.com
SIC: 2741 6282 2721 Newsletter publishing; Investment advice; Periodicals

(G-1243)
SCHILL LDSCPG LAWN CARE SVCS L
Also Called: Grasscor Lawn & Landscapes
8915 Blue Ash Rd Ste 1 (45242-7809)
PHONE.................513 271-5296
Alex Sulfsted, *Mgr*
EMP: 71
Web: www.schilllandscaping.com
SIC: 0781 Landscape services
PA: Schill Landscaping And Lawn Care Services, Llc
5000 Mills Indus Pkwy
North Ridgeville OH 44039

(G-1244)
SKILLED IN MANAGEMENT CO LLC
Also Called: Communicare
10123 Alliance Rd (45242-4707)
PHONE.................513 489-7100
EMP: 99 **EST:** 2017
SALES (est): 6.18MM **Privately Held**
SIC: 8051 Extended care facility

(G-1245)
SOGETI USA LLC
4445 Lake Forest Dr Ste 550 (45242-3734)
PHONE.................513 824-3000
John Rogan, *Mgr*
EMP: 115
SALES (corp-wide): 415.14MM **Privately Held**
Web: us.sogeti.com
SIC: 7379 Online services technology consultants
HQ: Sogeti Usa Llc
10100 Innovation Dr # 200
Miamisburg OH 45342
937 291-8100

(G-1246)
SUMMIT ORTHO HOME CARE
4600 Mcauley Pl Ste 150 (45242-4765)
PHONE.................513 898-3750
EMP: 75 **EST:** 2018
SALES (est): 11.7MM **Privately Held**
Web: www.summit-ortho.com

SIC: 8082 Home health care services

(G-1247)
SUNDANCE PROPERTY MGT LLC (PA)
Also Called: Sundance Real Estate Holdings
9918 Carver Rd Ste 110 (45242-5530)
PHONE.................513 489-3363
Russell D Kornman, *Pr*
Deborah L Kitching, *
Mark Hill, *
Doug Murphy, *
EMP: 33 **EST:** 1993
SQ FT: 5,000
SALES (est): 9.84MM **Privately Held**
Web: www.sundancemanagement.com
SIC: 6531 Real estate managers

(G-1248)
SW GRIFFIN CO LLC
4910 Hunt Rd Unit 2328 (45242-7150)
PHONE.................513 601-3894
Sophia Stevenson, *CEO*
John Stevenson, *
Sophia Stevenson, *Pr*
EMP: 34 **EST:** 2010
SALES (est): 1.59MM **Privately Held**
SIC: 1795 Wrecking and demolition work

(G-1249)
SW GRIFFIN CO LLC
4910 Hunt Rd (45242-7092)
PHONE.................513 678-4741
EMP: 32
SALES (est): 1.38MM **Privately Held**
SIC: 1795 Wrecking and demolition work

(G-1250)
SWAPALEASE INC
Also Called: Swapalease.com
11224 Cornell Park Dr (45242-1812)
PHONE.................513 381-0100
Richard Joseph, *Pr*
Ronald Joseph Junior, *VP*
EMP: 52 **EST:** 1999
SALES (est): 1.8MM **Privately Held**
Web: www.swapalease.com
SIC: 7515 Passenger car leasing

(G-1251)
SYCAMORE SENIOR CENTER (PA)
Also Called: Mt View Terrace
4455 Carver Woods Dr (45242-5560)
PHONE.................513 984-1234
Ray Kingsbury, *VP*
Jim Formal, *
EMP: 90 **EST:** 1971
SALES (est): 2.15MM
SALES (corp-wide): 2.15MM **Privately Held**
Web: www.sycamoreseniorcenter.org
SIC: 8322 Senior citizens' center or association

(G-1252)
TEMENOS
4156 Crossgate Ln (45236)
PHONE.................513 791-7022
EMP: 51 **EST:** 1995
SALES (est): 78.76K **Privately Held**
Web: www.temenos.com
SIC: 8049 8299 Dietician; Meditation therapy

(G-1253)
THE PAYNE FIRM INC
11231 Cornell Park Dr (45242-1811)
PHONE.................513 489-2255
EMP: 35
Web: www.paynefirm.com

SIC: 8748 Environmental consultant

(G-1254)
THOMAS RITTER OD INC
Also Called: Ritter & Hagee Optemetrists
9912 Carver Rd Ste 101 (45242-5541)
PHONE.................513 984-0202
Thomas G Ritter O.d., *Pr*
Mark Hagee O.d., *VP*
EMP: 28 **EST:** 1978
SQ FT: 1,000
SALES (est): 3.18MM **Privately Held**
Web: www.ritterhagee.com
SIC: 8042 Specialized optometrists

(G-1255)
TIME WARNER CABLE ENTPS LLC
Also Called: Time Warner
11325 Reed Hartman Hwy Ste 100 (45241-2493)
PHONE.................513 489-5000
Mary Egloff, *Mgr*
EMP: 41
SALES (corp-wide): 54.61B **Publicly Held**
SIC: 4841 Cable television services
HQ: Time Warner Cable Enterprises Llc
400 Atlantic St Ste 6
Stamford CT 06901

(G-1256)
TRAINCROFT INC
Also Called: Traincroft Staffing Associates
10901 Reed Hartman Hwy Ste 305 (45242-2835)
PHONE.................513 792-0291
Michael Ballard, *Brnch Mgr*
EMP: 35
SALES (corp-wide): 9.63MM **Privately Held**
Web: www.traincroft.com
SIC: 7361 Executive placement
PA: Traincroft Inc.
0 Governors Ave Ste 38
Medford MA 02155
781 393-6943

(G-1257)
TRIHEALTH INC
4665 Cornell Rd Ste 350 (45241-2460)
PHONE.................513 891-1627
Rick Hassler, *Dir*
EMP: 244
Web: www.trihealth.com
SIC: 8741 8011 Hospital management; Offices and clinics of medical doctors
HQ: Trihealth, Inc.
625 Eden Park Dr
Cincinnati OH 45202
513 569-5400

(G-1258)
TRUEPOINT INC
4901 Hunt Rd Ste 200 (45242-6990)
PHONE.................513 792-6648
Michael J Chasnoff, *Pr*
Janel Carroll, *
John Azens, *
EMP: 32 **EST:** 1990
SALES (est): 1.64MM **Privately Held**
Web: www.truepointwealth.com
SIC: 8742 Financial consultant

(G-1259)
TRUEPOINT WEALTH COUNSEL LLC (PA)
9999 Carver Rd Ste 200 (45242-5587)
PHONE.................513 792-6648
Michael J Chasnoff, *CEO*
EMP: 50 **EST:** 2014
SALES (est): 9.13MM
SALES (corp-wide): 9.13MM **Privately Held**

Web: www.truepointwealth.com
SIC: 6282 Investment advisory service

(G-1260)
TRUSTAFF MANAGEMENT LLC
Also Called: Trustaff Travel Nurses
4675 Cornell Rd Ste 100 (45241-2498)
PHONE.................513 272-3999
Brent Loring, *CEO*
Doug Dean, *Pr*
Sean Loring, *Pr*
Pam Oliver, *COO*
Gregg Harris, *CAO*
EMP: 2000 **EST:** 2002
SQ FT: 40,000
SALES (est): 116.32MM
SALES (corp-wide): 461.91MM **Privately Held**
Web: www.trustaff.com
SIC: 7361 Executive placement
PA: Ingenovis Health, Inc.
5700 S Quebec St Ste 300
Greenwood Village CO 80111
855 271-1767

(G-1261)
ULTIMATE REHAB LTD
9403 Kenwood Rd (45242-6820)
PHONE.................513 563-8777
Lorie Macdonald, *CEO*
Thomas Macdonald, *
Kelley Robinson, *
EMP: 85 **EST:** 2002
SALES (est): 5.05MM **Privately Held**
Web: www.ultimaterehabltd.com
SIC: 8093 Rehabilitation center, outpatient treatment

(G-1262)
UNIFUND CCR LLC
10625 Techwoods Cir (45242-2846)
PHONE.................513 489-8877
David G Rosenberg, *CEO*
EMP: 100 **EST:** 2011
SALES (est): 17.06MM **Privately Held**
Web: www.unifund.com
SIC: 6153 Buying of installment notes

(G-1263)
UNIFUND CORPORATION
Also Called: Rushcard
10625 Techwoods Cir (45242-2846)
PHONE.................513 489-8877
David G Rosenberg, *CEO*
EMP: 50 **EST:** 1986
SQ FT: 12,000
SALES (est): 24.23MM **Privately Held**
Web: www.unifund.com
SIC: 6153 Buying of installment notes

(G-1264)
UNIVERSITY OF CINCINNATI
Also Called: Center For Executive Education
4450 Carver Woods Dr Ste 3 (45242-5527)
P.O. Box 210177 (45221-0177)
PHONE.................513 556-6932
Rajan Kamath, *Mgr*
EMP: 30
SALES (corp-wide): 914.68MM **Privately Held**
Web: www.uc.edu
SIC: 8741 8221 Management services; University
PA: University Of Cincinnati
2600 Clifton Ave
Cincinnati OH 45220
513 556-6000

Blue Ash - Hamilton County (G-1265) GEOGRAPHIC SECTION

(G-1265)
VACO CINCINNATI LLC
9987 Carver Rd Ste 440 (45242-5563)
PHONE.................................513 239-5674
Steve Shoemake, *Managing Member*
EMP: 327 **EST:** 2015
SALES (est): 481.03K
SALES (corp-wide): 472MM **Privately Held**
SIC: 7361 Executive placement
PA: Vaco Llc
  5501 Virginia Way Ste 120
  Brentwood TN 37027
  615 301-4099

(G-1266)
VACO LLC
4500 Cooper Rd Ste 101 (45242-5600)
PHONE.................................513 239-5674
Jay Hollomon, *Managing Member*
EMP: 73
SALES (corp-wide): 472MM **Privately Held**
Web: www.vaco.com
SIC: 7361 Executive placement
PA: Vaco Llc
  5501 Virginia Way Ste 120
  Brentwood TN 37027
  615 301-4099

(G-1267)
VALICOR FEDERAL SERVICES LLC
11140 Deerfield Rd (45242-2022)
PHONE.................................313 724-8600
Vanessa Willett, *Pr*
EMP: 35
SALES (corp-wide): 2.27MM **Privately Held**
Web: www.valicor.com
SIC: 1542 Commercial and office buildings, renovation and repair
PA: Valicor Federal Services, Llc
  27140 Princeton St
  Inkster MI 48141
  313 236-5660

(G-1268)
VARIOUS VIEWS RESEARCH INC
11353 Reed Hartman Hwy Ste 200 (45241-2443)
PHONE.................................513 489-9000
Mirjana Popovich, *CEO*
Sharon Lally, *
EMP: 55 **EST:** 2007
SQ FT: 13,788
SALES (est): 2.24MM **Privately Held**
Web: www.variousviews.com
SIC: 8732 Market analysis or research

(G-1269)
VENDORINSIGHT
9987 Carver Rd Ste 130 (45242-5554)
PHONE.................................800 997-2674
EMP: 50 **EST:** 2019
SALES (est): 124.25K **Privately Held**
Web: www.mitratech.com
SIC: 7371 Computer software development

(G-1270)
VERDANT COMMERCIAL CAPITAL LLC
9987 Carver Rd Ste 110 (45242)
PHONE.................................513 769-2033
Mike Rooney, *CEO*
Amanda Lindsey, *
Chris Kelley, *
Margaret Irvin, *
EMP: 46 **EST:** 2017
SALES (est): 12MM **Privately Held**
Web: www.verdantcc.com

SIC: 6799 Venture capital companies

(G-1271)
VONLEHMAN & COMPANY INC
9987 Carver Rd Ste 120 (45242-5554)
PHONE.................................513 891-5911
EMP: 40
SALES (corp-wide): 9.85MM **Privately Held**
Web: www.vlcpa.com
SIC: 8721 Certified public accountant
PA: Vonlehman & Company, Inc.
  810 Wrightsummit Pkwy # 200
  Ft Wright KY 41011
  513 891-5911

(G-1272)
VORA VENTURES LLC (PA)
10290 Alliance Rd (45242-4710)
PHONE.................................513 792-5100
Mahendra B Vora, *Managing Member*
Kevin Dooley, *CSO*
EMP: 385 **EST:** 2006
SALES (est): 94.49MM **Privately Held**
Web: www.voraventures.com
SIC: 8741 Business management

(G-1273)
WASHINGTON MD LEASING CO LLC (HQ)
Also Called: South River Healthcare Center
10123 Alliance Rd (45242-4707)
PHONE.................................513 489-7100
EMP: 49 **EST:** 2021
SALES (est): 54.29MM
SALES (corp-wide): 392.92MM **Privately Held**
Web: www.communicarehealth.com
SIC: 8051 Convalescent home with continuous nursing care
PA: Communicare Health Services, Inc.
  10123 Alliance Rd
  Blue Ash OH 45242
  513 530-1654

(G-1274)
WOLF MACHINE COMPANY (PA)
5570 Creek Rd (45242-4004)
PHONE.................................513 791-5194
Scott E Andre, *Pr*
EMP: 35 **EST:** 1888
SQ FT: 50,000
SALES (est): 17.69MM
SALES (corp-wide): 17.69MM **Privately Held**
Web: www.wolfmachine.com
SIC: 5084 3552 3556 3546 Machine tools and accessories; Textile machinery; Food products machinery; Power-driven handtools

(G-1275)
YOUNG MNS CHRSTN ASSN GRTER CN
Also Called: Blue Ash YMCA
5000 Ymca Dr (45242-7444)
PHONE.................................513 791-5000
Paul Waldsmith, *Ex Dir*
EMP: 349
SQ FT: 16,506
SALES (corp-wide): 44.55MM **Privately Held**
Web: www.myy.org
SIC: 8641 7336 8351 7997 Youth organizations; Commercial art and graphic design; Child day care services; Membership sports and recreation clubs
PA: Young Mens Christian Association Of Greater Cincinnati
  1105 Elm St
  Cincinnati OH 45202

513 651-2100

Bluffton
Allen County

(G-1276)
A TO Z PORTION CTRL MEATS INC
201 N Main St (45817-1283)
PHONE.................................419 358-2926
Lee Ann Kagy, *Pr*
Sean Kagy, *
Leslie Barnes, *
EMP: 34 **EST:** 1945
SQ FT: 20,000
SALES (est): 9.64MM **Privately Held**
Web: www.atozmeats.com
SIC: 5142 2013 Meat, frozen: packaged; Sausages and other prepared meats

(G-1277)
BLANCHARD VLY RGIONAL HLTH CTR
Also Called: Bluffton Campus
139 Garau St (45817-1027)
P.O. Box 48 (45817-0048)
PHONE.................................419 358-9010
William Watkins, *Dir*
EMP: 185
SALES (corp-wide): 32.58MM **Privately Held**
Web: www.bvhealthsystem.org
SIC: 8062 General medical and surgical hospitals
HQ: Blanchard Valley Regional Health Center
  1900 S Main St
  Findlay OH 45840
  419 423-4500

(G-1278)
BLUFFTON COMMUNITY HOSPITAL
139 Garau St (45817-1027)
P.O. Box 48 (45817-0048)
PHONE.................................419 358-9010
Clifford K Harmon, *Admn*
William D Watkins, *
EMP: 105 **EST:** 1936
SQ FT: 39,062
SALES (est): 26.19MM **Privately Held**
Web: www.bvhealthsystem.org
SIC: 8062 General medical and surgical hospitals

(G-1279)
BLUFFTON STONE CO
310 Quarry Dr (45817)
P.O. Box 26 (45817-0026)
PHONE.................................419 358-6941
Brent Gerken, *Pr*
Mike Gerken, *Sec*
EMP: 39 **EST:** 1930
SQ FT: 1,800
SALES (est): 1.87MM **Privately Held**
Web: www.bluffton.edu
SIC: 1422 3274 2951 Crushed and broken limestone; Lime; Asphalt paving mixtures and blocks

(G-1280)
CARPE DIEM INDUSTRIES LLC
Also Called: Diamond Machine and Mfg
505 E Jefferson St (45817-1349)
PHONE.................................419 358-0129
Ryan Smith, *Mgr*
EMP: 55
SQ FT: 271,000
SALES (corp-wide): 9.25MM **Privately Held**
Web: www.colonialsurfacesolutions.com

SIC: 3471 3398 3479 1799 Cleaning and descaling metal products; Metal heat treating; Painting of metal products; Coating of metal structures at construction site
PA: Carpe Diem Industries, Llc
  4599 Campbell Rd
  Columbus Grove OH 45830
  419 659-5639

(G-1281)
GROB SYSTEMS INC
Also Called: Machine Tool Division
1070 Navajo Dr (45817-9666)
PHONE.................................419 358-9015
Michael Hutecker, *CEO*
David Kuenzli, *Sec*
◆ **EMP:** 590 **EST:** 1981
SQ FT: 262,000
SALES (est): 151.63MM
SALES (corp-wide): 355.83K **Privately Held**
Web: www.grobgroup.com
SIC: 3535 7699 Robotic conveyors; Industrial equipment services
PA: Grob-Werke Burkhart Grob E.K.
  Industriestr. 4
  Mindelheim BY 87719
  82619960

(G-1282)
MENNONITE MEMORIAL HOME
Also Called: Maple Crest
700 Maple Crest Ct (45817-8552)
PHONE.................................419 358-7654
Daren Lee, *Mgr*
EMP: 75
SALES (corp-wide): 13.01MM **Privately Held**
Web: www.mhcoliving.org
SIC: 8051 Skilled nursing care facilities
PA: Mennonite Memorial Home
  410 W Elm St
  Bluffton OH 45817
  419 358-1015

(G-1283)
MENNONITE MEMORIAL HOME (PA)
Also Called: Maple Crest Senior Living Vlg
410 W Elm St (45817-1122)
PHONE.................................419 358-1015
Laura Voth, *CEO*
David Lynn Thompson, *
EMP: 200 **EST:** 1947
SQ FT: 65,000
SALES (est): 13.01MM
SALES (corp-wide): 13.01MM **Privately Held**
Web: www.mhcoliving.org
SIC: 8052 8059 8051 Intermediate care facilities; Personal care home, with health care; Skilled nursing care facilities

Boardman
Mahoning County

(G-1284)
ASHLEY ENTERPRISES LLC (PA)
Also Called: Briarfield At Ashley Circle
1419 Boardman Canfield Rd Ste 500 (44512-8062)
PHONE.................................330 726-5790
Edward Reese, *Managing Member*
Rob Rupeka, *CFO*
EMP: 93 **EST:** 2003
SQ FT: 33,991
SALES (est): 5.54MM
SALES (corp-wide): 5.54MM **Privately Held**
Web: www.briarfield.net

SIC: 8051 Skilled nursing care facilities

(G-1285)
BEEGHLY NURSING LLC
Also Called: Beeghly Oaks Ctr For Rhbltttion
6505 Market St Bldg D (44512-3459)
PHONE.................................330 884-2300
EMP: 99 EST: 2018
SALES (est): 4.97MM Privately Held
SIC: 8051 Skilled nursing care facilities

(G-1286)
CHILDRENS HOSP MED CTR AKRON
6505 Market St Ste 2100 (44512-3457)
PHONE.................................330 746-8040
EMP: 55
SALES (corp-wide): 1.4B Privately Held
Web: www.akronchildrens.org
SIC: 8069 8062 8031 8011 Childrens' hospital; General medical and surgical hospitals; Offices and clinics of osteopathic physicians; Offices and clinics of medical doctors
PA: Childrens Hospital Medical Center Of Akron
1 Perkins Sq
Akron OH 44308
330 543-1000

(G-1287)
DRUND LTD
945 Boardman Canfield Rd Ste 8 (44512-4239)
PHONE.................................330 402-5944
Edward Smith, Prin
EMP: 54 EST: 2013
SQ FT: 2,800
SALES (est): 905.63K Privately Held
Web: team.drund.com
SIC: 7371 Computer software development and applications

(G-1288)
GORANT CHOCOLATIER LLC (PA)
Also Called: Gorant's Yum Yum Tree
8301 Market St (44512-6257)
P.O. Box 1014 (44406-5014)
PHONE.................................330 726-8821
Joseph M Miller, Managing Member
Gary Weiss, Pr
EMP: 120 EST: 1946
SQ FT: 60,000
SALES (est): 27.29MM
SALES (corp-wide): 27.29MM Privately Held
Web: www.gorant.com
SIC: 5441 5947 5145 3999 Candy; Greeting cards; Candy; Candles

(G-1289)
HERCULES LED LLC
5411 Market St (44512-2615)
PHONE.................................844 437-2533
James Rosan, Managing Member
EMP: 35 EST: 2014
SALES (est): 3.42MM Privately Held
Web: www.herculesled.com
SIC: 5211 8748 Energy conservation products; Energy conservation consultant

(G-1290)
RL BEST COMPANY
723 Bev Rd (44512-6243)
PHONE.................................330 758-8601
Richard L Best, CEO
Ted Best, Pr
Mark Best, VP
William Kavanaugh, VP
◆ EMP: 32 EST: 1972
SQ FT: 35,000
SALES (est): 4.7MM Privately Held

Web: www.sms-group.com
SIC: 7539 3599 Machine shop, automotive; Machine shop, jobbing and repair

(G-1291)
SOUTH I LEASING CO LLC
Also Called: Greenbriar Boardman
8064 South Ave (44512-6153)
PHONE.................................513 530-1600
Richard Odenthal, Prin
Sandra Smiddy, *
EMP: 50 EST: 2008
SALES (est): 1.62MM Privately Held
SIC: 7359 Equipment rental and leasing, nec

(G-1292)
ST ELZABETH BOARDMAN HLTH CTR
8401 Market St (44512-6725)
PHONE.................................330 729-4580
Gary Kabetso, Genl Mgr
EMP: 41 EST: 2014
SALES (est): 271.15MM Privately Held
Web: www.boardmantraining.com
SIC: 8099 8062 Childbirth preparation clinic; General medical and surgical hospitals

Bolivar
Tuscarawas County

(G-1293)
DCHM INC
11155 State Route 212 Ne (44612-8746)
PHONE.................................330 874-3435
EMP: 54
Web: www.choicehotels.com
SIC: 7011 Hotels and motels
PA: Dchm, Inc.
2024 State Route 39 Nw
Dover OH 44622

(G-1294)
ELEET CRYOGENICS INC (PA)
11132 Industrial Pkwy Nw (44612-8993)
PHONE.................................330 874-4009
▲ EMP: 33 EST: 1997
SQ FT: 47,000
SALES (est): 11.58MM Privately Held
Web: www.eleetcryogenics.com
SIC: 3443 7353 2761 5088 Cryogenic tanks, for liquids and gases; Oil field equipment, rental or leasing; Manifold business forms; Tanks and tank components

(G-1295)
MEGCO MANAGEMENT INC
Also Called: Hennis Care Center of Bolivar
300 Yant St (44612-9712)
PHONE.................................330 874-9999
David Hennis, Admn
EMP: 120 EST: 1999
SALES (est): 10.3MM Privately Held
Web: www.henniscarecentre.com
SIC: 8051 Convalescent home with continuous nursing care

(G-1296)
OHIO MACHINERY CO
Also Called: Caterpillar Authorized Dealer
10955 Industrial Pkwy Nw (44612-8991)
PHONE.................................330 874-1003
Janie Rogers, Brnch Mgr
EMP: 37
SALES (corp-wide): 185.86MM Privately Held
Web: www.ohiocat.com
SIC: 7699 5082 Hydraulic equipment repair; Construction and mining machinery
PA: Ohio Machinery Co.

3993 E Royalton Rd
Broadview Heights OH 44147
440 526-6200

(G-1297)
PRIMARY PACKAGING INCORPORATED
10810 Industrial Pkwy Nw (44612-8990)
PHONE.................................330 874-3131
Jeffrey Thrams, Pr
Joseph Kaplan, *
John Hiltner, *
Jim O'brien, Sec
EMP: 85 EST: 1990
SQ FT: 50,000
SALES (est): 23.6MM Privately Held
Web: www.primarypackaging.com
SIC: 5199 Packaging materials

Botkins
Shelby County

(G-1298)
BEEM CONSTRUCTION INC
225 S Mill St (45306-8023)
P.O. Box 208 (45306-0208)
PHONE.................................937 693-3176
Roger Barlage, Pr
Donald Eilerman, *
Steven Eilerman, *
EMP: 45 EST: 1977
SQ FT: 8,000
SALES (est): 3.75MM Privately Held
Web: www.beemconstruction.com
SIC: 1541 Industrial buildings, new construction, nec

(G-1299)
BROWN INDUSTRIAL INC
311 W South St (45306-8019)
P.O. Box 74 (45306-0074)
PHONE.................................937 693-3838
Christopher D Brown, Pr
Ruth C Brown, *
Craig D Brown, *
EMP: 45 EST: 1937
SQ FT: 32,000
SALES (est): 9.14MM Privately Held
Web: www.brownindustrial.com
SIC: 3713 5012 5084 7692 Truck bodies (motor vehicles); Truck bodies; Industrial machinery and equipment; Automotive welding

(G-1300)
SCHNIPPEL CONSTRUCTION INC
302 N Main St (45306-8039)
P.O. Box 477 (45306-0477)
PHONE.................................937 693-3831
Thomas J Schnippel, Pr
Tracy Cooper, *
EMP: 30 EST: 1952
SQ FT: 9,000
SALES (est): 8.84MM Privately Held
Web: www.schnippelconstruction.com
SIC: 1522 1541 1542 Multi-family dwelling construction, nec; Industrial buildings, new construction, nec; Commercial and office building, new construction

Bowerston
Harrison County

(G-1301)
CARRIAGE INN BOWERSTON INC
Also Called: Sunny Slope Nursing Home
102 Boyce Dr (44695-9701)
PHONE.................................740 269-8001

Bob Huff, Pr
EMP: 46 EST: 1964
SQ FT: 9,700
SALES (est): 3.07MM Privately Held
SIC: 8051 Convalescent home with continuous nursing care

Bowling Green
Wood County

(G-1302)
ACTION BAR LLC
238 N Main St (43402-2420)
PHONE.................................419 250-1938
Nathan Cordes, Managing Member
EMP: 41 EST: 2015
SALES (est): 301.13K Privately Held
SIC: 8621 Bar association

(G-1303)
ARGO-HYTOS INC
1835 N Research Dr (43402-8548)
P.O. Box 28 (43402-0028)
PHONE.................................419 353-6070
Christian H Kienzle, Pr
Larry Gerken, *
Walter Bader, *
▲ EMP: 1200 EST: 1998
SQ FT: 6,200
SALES (est): 91.42MM
SALES (corp-wide): 4.87B Privately Held
Web: www.argo-hytos-us.com
SIC: 5084 Hydraulic systems equipment and supplies
HQ: Argo-Hytos Group Ag
Neuhofstrasse 1
Baar ZG 6340

(G-1304)
BEHAVRAL CNNCTIONS WD CNTY INC
1010 N Prospect St (43402-1335)
P.O. Box 8970 (43623-0970)
PHONE.................................419 352-5387
EMP: 44
SALES (corp-wide): 867 Privately Held
Web: www.harbor.org
SIC: 8093 Mental health clinic, outpatient
PA: Behavioral Connections Of Wood County, Inc.
280 S Main St
Bowling Green OH 43402
419 352-5387

(G-1305)
BEHAVRAL CNNCTIONS WD CNTY INC
Also Called: Women's Residential
1033 Devlac Grv (43402-4501)
P.O. Box 29 (43402-0029)
PHONE.................................419 352-5561
Mark Haskins, Dir
EMP: 33
SALES (corp-wide): 867 Privately Held
Web: www.harbor.org
SIC: 8093 8069 Alcohol clinic, outpatient; Alcoholism rehabilitation hospital
PA: Behavioral Connections Of Wood County, Inc.
280 S Main St
Bowling Green OH 43402
419 352-5387

(G-1306)
BEHAVRAL CNNCTIONS WD CNTY INC
320 W Gypsy Lane Rd Ste A (43402-4571)
PHONE.................................419 352-5387
Richard Goldberg, Dir

Bowling Green - Wood County (G-1307)

GEOGRAPHIC SECTION

EMP: 29
SALES (corp-wide): 867 **Privately Held**
Web: www.harbor.org
SIC: 8093 8069 Alcohol clinic, outpatient; Drug addiction rehabilitation hospital
PA: Behavioral Connections Of Wood County, Inc.
280 S Main St
Bowling Green OH 43402
419 352-5387

(G-1307)
BETCO CORPORATION (PA)
400 Van Camp Rd (43402-9062)
PHONE.................................419 241-2156
Paul C Betz, *CEO*
James Betz, *
Tony Lyons, *
▲ **EMP:** 200 **EST:** 1950
SQ FT: 90,000
SALES (est): 140.16MM
SALES (corp-wide): 140.16MM **Privately Held**
Web: www.betco.com
SIC: 5087 Janitors' supplies

(G-1308)
BINKELMAN CORPORATION (PA)
828 Van Camp Rd (43402-9379)
PHONE.................................419 537-9333
Dan Kazmierczak, *Pr*
Brad Fitzgerald, *
Dave Grana, *
Clay Grieffendorf, *
EMP: 33 **EST:** 1946
SQ FT: 30,000
SALES (est): 11.08MM
SALES (corp-wide): 11.08MM **Privately Held**
Web: www.binkelman.com
SIC: 5085 Power transmission equipment and apparatus

(G-1309)
BIOTEST PHARMACEUTICALS CORP
Also Called: Biotest Plasma Center
1616 E Wooster St Unit 39 (43402-3478)
PHONE.................................419 819-3068
Ileana Carlisle, *Prin*
EMP: 50 **EST:** 2018
SALES (est): 629.01K **Privately Held**
SIC: 8099 Blood bank

(G-1310)
BOWLING GREEN CLINIC INC
1039 Haskins Rd Unit A (43402-9066)
PHONE.................................419 352-1121
Mohammad Sidiq, *Pr*
EMP: 49 **EST:** 1972
SALES (est): 2.7MM **Privately Held**
Web: www.woodcountyhospital.org
SIC: 8062 General medical and surgical hospitals

(G-1311)
BOWLING GREEN COUNTRY CLUB INC
923 Fairview Ave (43402-1722)
PHONE.................................419 352-5546
Stu Sterns, *Pr*
EMP: 27 **EST:** 1937
SQ FT: 5,000
SALES (est): 663.46K **Privately Held**
Web: www.bgcountryclub.com
SIC: 7997 7992 Country club, membership; Public golf courses

(G-1312)
BOWLING GREEN LINCOLN INC
Also Called: Bowling Green Lincoln Auto SL
1079 N Main St (43402-1302)
PHONE.................................419 352-2553
John Heffernan, *Pr*
Carl Heffernan Junior, *Pr*
Kay C Heffernan, *
EMP: 28
SQ FT: 37,000
SALES (est): 21.14MM **Privately Held**
Web: www.bowlinggreenlincolnauto.com
SIC: 5511 7538 Automobiles, new and used; General automotive repair shops

(G-1313)
CMC GROUP INC (PA)
12836 S Dixie Hwy (43402-9697)
PHONE.................................419 354-2591
Albert J Caperna, *Ch*
Craig Dixon, *
Jeff Palmer, *
Bob Copple, *
Tammy Corral, *
▲ **EMP:** 66 **EST:** 1999
SQ FT: 2,268
SALES (est): 52.62MM
SALES (corp-wide): 52.62MM **Privately Held**
Web: www.cmcgp.com
SIC: 2759 7389 Labels and seals: printing, nsk; Telemarketing services

(G-1314)
COUNTY OF WOOD
Also Called: Wood Haven Health Care
1965 E Gypsy Lane Rd (43402-9396)
PHONE.................................419 353-8411
David Cecil, *Admn*
EMP: 62
SQ FT: 400,000
SALES (corp-wide): 130MM **Privately Held**
Web: www.woodhavenhealthcare.com
SIC: 8051 9111 Convalescent home with continuous nursing care; County supervisors' and executives' office
PA: County Of Wood
1 Courthouse Sq
Bowling Green OH 43402
419 354-9100

(G-1315)
COUNTY OF WOOD
Also Called: Wood County Health Department
1840 E Gypsy Lane Rd (43402-9173)
PHONE.................................419 352-8402
Ben Batey, *Ex Dir*
EMP: 78
SALES (corp-wide): 130MM **Privately Held**
Web: www.woodcountyhealth.org
SIC: 9431 8399 Administration of public health programs, County government; Health systems agency
PA: County Of Wood
1 Courthouse Sq
Bowling Green OH 43402
419 354-9100

(G-1316)
DAYMARK SAFETY SYSTEMS
12830 S Dixie Hwy (43402-9697)
PHONE.................................419 353-2458
◆ **EMP:** 56 **EST:** 2005
SALES (est): 7.47MM
SALES (corp-wide): 52.62MM **Privately Held**
Web: www.daymarksafety.com
SIC: 1731 Safety and security specialization
PA: Cmc Group, Inc.
12836 S Dixie Hwy
Bowling Green OH 43402
419 354-2591

(G-1317)
DEBMAR INC
Also Called: Herritage Inn
1069 Klotz Rd (43402-4820)
PHONE.................................419 728-7010
Mark Manley, *Pr*
Deborah Manley, *VP*
Larry Manley, *Sec*
EMP: 55 **EST:** 1982
SQ FT: 20,000
SALES (est): 2.56MM **Privately Held**
Web: www.heritagecorner.com
SIC: 8059 8052 8051 Personal care home, with health care; Intermediate care facilities ; Skilled nursing care facilities

(G-1318)
EASTWOOD LOCAL SCHOOLS
10142 Dowling Rd (43402-9684)
PHONE.................................419 833-1196
Marcia Mohre, *Prin*
EMP: 38 **EST:** 2018
SALES (est): 194.48K **Privately Held**
Web: www.eastwoodschools.org
SIC: 8748 Educational consultant

(G-1319)
FALCON PLAZA LLC
Also Called: Best Western Falcon Plaza Mtl
1450 E Wooster St Ste 401 (43402-3260)
PHONE.................................419 352-4671
Jacob C Bishop, *Pr*
EMP: 28 **EST:** 1963
SALES (est): 502.16K **Privately Held**
Web: www.bestwestern.com
SIC: 7011 Motels

(G-1320)
FOX
1010 N Main St (43402-1301)
PHONE.................................419 352-1673
Bill Wammes, *Prin*
EMP: 36 **EST:** 2010
SALES (est): 251.74K **Privately Held**
SIC: 4226 Household goods and furniture storage

(G-1321)
HCF OF BOWL GREEN CARE CTR INC
Also Called: HEALTH CARE FACILITIES
850 W Poe Rd (43402-1219)
PHONE.................................419 352-7558
Tom Blakely, *CEO*
EMP: 183 **EST:** 2003
SALES (est): 8.7MM
SALES (corp-wide): 305.93MM **Privately Held**
Web: www.bgcarecenter.com
SIC: 8051 Convalescent home with continuous nursing care
PA: Hcf Management, Inc.
1100 Shawnee Rd
Lima OH 45805
419 999-2010

(G-1322)
HCF OF BOWLING GREEN INC
1021 W Poe Rd (43402-9362)
PHONE.................................419 352-4694
EMP: 163 **EST:** 2002
SALES (est): 16.74MM
SALES (corp-wide): 305.93MM **Privately Held**
Web: www.bowlinggreenmanor.com
SIC: 8051 Convalescent home with continuous nursing care
PA: Hcf Management, Inc.
1100 Shawnee Rd
Lima OH 45805
419 999-2010

(G-1323)
HERITAGE CORNER HEALTH CARE CA
1069 Klotz Rd (43402-4820)
PHONE.................................419 353-3759
Mathew Manley, *Pr*
EMP: 27 **EST:** 2015
SALES (est): 2.66MM **Privately Held**
Web: www.heritagecorner.com
SIC: 8099 Health and allied services, nec

(G-1324)
HERITAGE CORNER NURSING HM LLC
1069 Klotz Rd Ste B (43402-4832)
PHONE.................................419 728-7010
EMP: 30 **EST:** 2010
SALES (est): 308.06K **Privately Held**
Web: www.heritagecorner.com
SIC: 8051 Skilled nursing care facilities

(G-1325)
HPJ INDUSTRIES INC (PA)
118 N Main St (43402-2418)
P.O. Box 860 (43402-0860)
PHONE.................................419 278-1000
Scott M Rothweiler, *Pr*
Chris Beck, *
EMP: 49 **EST:** 2004
SALES (est): 28.78MM
SALES (corp-wide): 28.78MM **Privately Held**
Web: www.hpjind.com
SIC: 4953 Recycling, waste materials

(G-1326)
KELLERMEYER COMPANY
475 W Woodland Cir (43402-8834)
P.O. Box 66 (43402-0066)
PHONE.................................419 255-3022
EMP: 74
SIC: 5169 5085 5087 5113 Chemicals and allied products, nec; Industrial supplies; Janitors' supplies; Industrial and personal service paper

(G-1327)
MONTESSORI SCHOOL BOWL GREEN
515 Sand Ridge Rd (43402-4423)
PHONE.................................419 352-4203
Sandra Earle, *Pr*
Randy Huber, *VP*
EMP: 35 **EST:** 1980
SQ FT: 70,000
SALES (est): 1.38MM **Privately Held**
Web: www.montessorischoolbg.org
SIC: 8351 Montessori child development center

(G-1328)
NICHOLS PAPER & SUPPLY CO
Also Called: Nichols
475 W Woodland Cir (43402-8834)
PHONE.................................419 255-3022
EMP: 53
SQ FT: 1,629
SALES (corp-wide): 1.65B **Privately Held**
Web: www.enichols.com
SIC: 5087 Janitors' supplies
HQ: Nichols Paper & Supply Co.
1391 Judson Rd
Norton Shores MI 49456
231 799-2120

(G-1329)
NORTHWESTERN WATER & SEWER DST
12560 Middleton Pike (43402-8289)
P.O. Box 348 (43402-0348)

GEOGRAPHIC SECTION

Brecksville - Cuyahoga County (G-1349)

PHONE..............419 354-9090
Jerry Greiner, *Ex Dir*
EMP: 49 **EST:** 1994
SQ FT: 30,000
SALES (est): 32.43MM **Privately Held**
Web: www.nwwsd.org
SIC: 4952 4941 Sewerage systems; Water supply

(G-1330)
PHOENIX TECHNOLOGIES INTL LLC (HQ)
Also Called: Pti
1098 Fairview Ave (43402-1233)
PHONE..............419 353-7738
Thomas E Brady, *Managing Member*
▲ **EMP:** 50 **EST:** 1992
SQ FT: 100,000
SALES (est): 32.1MM **Privately Held**
Web: www.phoenixtechnologies.net
SIC: 3085 5169 Plastics bottles; Synthetic resins, rubber, and plastic materials
PA: Far Eastern New Century Corporation
36f, No. 207, Dunhua S. Rd., Sec. 2
Taipei City TAP 10605

(G-1331)
POGGEMEYER DESIGN GROUP INC (HQ)
Also Called: PDG
1168 N Main St (43402-1352)
PHONE..............419 244-8074
Jack A Jones, *Ch*
Charlene Kerr, *
Larry Carroll, *
Michael Atherine, *
EMP: 110 **EST:** 1968
SQ FT: 50,000
SALES (est): 43.78MM
SALES (corp-wide): 458.93MM **Privately Held**
Web: www.kleinfelder.com
SIC: 8711 8712 8713 8748 Professional engineer; Architectural services; Surveying services; City planning
PA: The Kleinfelder Group Inc
770 1st Ave Ste 400
San Diego CA 92101
619 831-4600

(G-1332)
SALO INC
Also Called: Interim Healthcare
1216 W Wooster St (43402-2637)
PHONE..............419 419-0038
EMP: 187
SALES (corp-wide): 52.16MM **Privately Held**
Web: www.interimhealthcare.com
SIC: 8082 7363 Home health care services; Help supply services
PA: Salo, Inc.
300 W Wlson Brdge Rd Ste
Columbus OH 43085
614 436-9404

(G-1333)
STARSHIP TECHNOLOGIES INC
707 N College Dr (43403-0001)
PHONE..............440 251-7096
EMP: 175
SALES (corp-wide): 2.72MM **Privately Held**
SIC: 7371 Computer software development and applications
PA: Starship Technologies, Inc.
535 Mission St Fl 19
San Francisco CA 94105
844 445-5333

(G-1334)
WOOD CNTY CMMTTEE ON AGING INC (PA)
140 S Grove St (43402-2819)
PHONE..............419 353-5661
James Stainbrook, *Dir*
Denise Niese, *
EMP: 32 **EST:** 1975
SALES (est): 4.26MM
SALES (corp-wide): 4.26MM **Privately Held**
Web: www.wccoa.net
SIC: 8322 Senior citizens' center or association

(G-1335)
WOOD COUNTY CHLD SVCS ASSN
Also Called: CHILDREN'S RESOURCE CENTER
1045 Klotz Rd (43402)
P.O. Box 738 (43402)
PHONE..............419 352-7588
TOLL FREE: 888
J Lafond, *Ex Dir*
Timothy Scherer, *
Janelle Lafond, *
EMP: 37 **EST:** 1974
SQ FT: 29,900
SALES (est): 6.48MM **Privately Held**
Web: www.crcwoodcounty.org
SIC: 8322 8361 8093 Child related social services; Residential care; Specialty outpatient clinics, nec

(G-1336)
WOOD COUNTY HOSPITAL (PA)
Also Called: Wch
950 W Wooster St (43402)
PHONE..............419 354-8900
Stanley Korducki, *Pr*
EMP: 530 **EST:** 1951
SQ FT: 130,000
SALES (est): 120.06MM
SALES (corp-wide): 120.06MM **Privately Held**
Web: www.woodcountyhospital.org
SIC: 8062 General medical and surgical hospitals

(G-1337)
WOOD HEALTH COMPANY LLC
745 Haskins Rd Ste B (43402-1600)
PHONE..............419 353-7069
EMP: 100 **EST:** 2003
SALES (est): 7.55MM **Privately Held**
SIC: 8011 Medical centers

(G-1338)
WOOD LANE RESIDENTIAL SVCS INC
545 Pearl St Ste A (43402-2784)
PHONE..............419 353-9577
Jessica Blakely, *CEO*
Tonia Peters, *
EMP: 99 **EST:** 1980
SALES (est): 12.2MM **Privately Held**
Web: www.wlrs.org
SIC: 8052 Intermediate care facilities

(G-1339)
WRYNECK DEVELOPMENT LLC
Also Called: Stone Ridge Golf Club
1553 Muirfield Dr (43402-5230)
PHONE..............419 354-2535
EMP: 48 **EST:** 1998
SQ FT: 20,000
SALES (est): 1.57MM **Privately Held**
Web: www.stoneridgegolfclub.org
SIC: 7992 Public golf courses

Bradford
Miami County

(G-1340)
BRADFORD FIRE RESCUE SVCS INC
200 S Miami Ave (45308-1322)
PHONE..............937 448-2686
Ron Hoelscher, *CEO*
Dave Richard, *
Terry Applegate, *
Randy Patty, *
EMP: 40 **EST:** 1946
SALES (est): 1MM **Privately Held**
Web: www.bradfordoh.com
SIC: 4119 Local passenger transportation, nec

Bradner
Wood County

(G-1341)
AMERICAN WARMING AND VENT
Also Called: Reed Air Products
120 Plin St (43406-7735)
P.O. Box 677 (43406-0677)
PHONE..............419 288-2703
Stewart E Reed, *Pr*
John Reed, *
EMP: 75 **EST:** 1960
SALES (est): 4.12MM **Privately Held**
Web: www.awv.com
SIC: 5031 5039 Doors and windows; Air ducts, sheet metal

Brecksville
Cuyahoga County

(G-1342)
AHOLA CORPORATION
6820 W Snowville Rd (44141-3214)
PHONE..............440 717-7620
Mark Ahola, *Pr*
EMP: 88 **EST:** 1967
SQ FT: 21,000
SALES (est): 10.59MM **Privately Held**
Web: www.ahola.com
SIC: 8721 Payroll accounting service

(G-1343)
APPLIED MEDICAL TECHNOLOGY INC
Also Called: Amt
8006 Katherine Blvd (44141-4202)
PHONE..............440 717-4000
George J Picha, *Pr*
Robert J Crump, *
EMP: 30 **EST:** 1979
SQ FT: 14,000
SALES (est): 8.21MM **Privately Held**
Web: www.appliedmedical.net
SIC: 3841 3083 8731 Surgical and medical instruments; Laminated plastics plate and sheet; Medical research, commercial

(G-1344)
ARISE INCORPORATED
7000 S Edgerton Rd Ste 100 (44141-3199)
PHONE..............440 746-8860
William Ramonas, *Pr*
EMP: 30 **EST:** 1993
SALES (est): 10.09MM
SALES (corp-wide): 505.19K **Privately Held**
Web: www.ariseco.com
SIC: 1711 Boiler maintenance contractor
HQ: Tuv Sud America Inc.
401 Edgewater Pl Ste 500
Wakefield MA 01880
978 573-2500

(G-1345)
BPI INFRMTION SYSTEMS OHIO INC
6055 W Snowville Rd (44141-3245)
PHONE..............440 717-4112
Gary Ellis, *Pr*
George Stoll, *
Joyce Ellis, *
EMP: 50 **EST:** 1983
SQ FT: 12,000
SALES (est): 7.25MM **Privately Held**
Web: www.bpiohio.com
SIC: 7378 7373 Computer maintenance and repair; Computer integrated systems design

(G-1346)
BRECKSVLLE HALTHCARE GROUP INC
Also Called: OAKS OF BRECKSVILLE, THE
8757 Brecksville Rd (44141-1919)
PHONE..............440 546-0643
Repchick S George, *Pr*
EMP: 33 **EST:** 2011
SALES (est): 6.65MM **Privately Held**
Web: www.saberhealth.com
SIC: 8093 8099 Rehabilitation center, outpatient treatment; Physical examination and testing services

(G-1347)
CHANDLER PRODUCTS LLC
10147 Brecksville Rd (44141-3205)
PHONE..............216 481-4400
Ron Kiter, *Managing Member*
EMP: 31 **EST:** 2010
SALES (est): 6.65MM
SALES (corp-wide): 504.83MM **Privately Held**
Web: www.chandlerproducts.com
SIC: 5085 Fasteners, industrial: nuts, bolts, screws, etc.
HQ: Elgin Fastener Group, Llc
288 Holbrook Dr
Wheeling IL 60090

(G-1348)
CHILDRENS HOSP MED CTR AKRON
7001 S Edgerton Rd Ste 1 (44141-4207)
PHONE..............440 526-4543
EMP: 54
SALES (corp-wide): 1.4B **Privately Held**
Web: www.akronchildrens.org
SIC: 8062 General medical and surgical hospitals
PA: Childrens Hospital Medical Center Of Akron
1 Perkins Sq
Akron OH 44308
330 543-1000

(G-1349)
CITY OF BRECKSVILLE
Also Called: Brecksville Community Center
1 Community Dr (44141-2326)
PHONE..............440 526-4109
Tom Tupa, *Dir*
EMP: 45
SALES (corp-wide): 37.55MM **Privately Held**
Web: www.brecksville.oh.us
SIC: 8322 7991 Community center; Physical fitness facilities
PA: City Of Brecksville
9069 Brecksville Rd
Cleveland OH 44141
440 526-4351

Brecksville - Cuyahoga County (G-1350)

(G-1350)
CITY OF BRECKSVILLE
Also Called: Brecksville City Service Dept
9069 Brecksville Rd (44141-2367)
PHONE.................................440 526-1384
Robert Pech, *Dir*
EMP: 134
SALES (corp-wide): 37.55MM **Privately Held**
Web: www.brecksville.oh.us
SIC: 1611 Highway and street maintenance
PA: City Of Brecksville
9069 Brecksville Rd
Cleveland OH 44141
440 526-4351

(G-1351)
CLINICAL TECHNOLOGY INC
7005 S Edgerton Rd (44141-4203)
PHONE.................................440 526-0160
Dennis Forchione, *Pr*
Dennis A Forchione, *
Dominic Verrilli, *
Michael Forchione, *
EMP: 40 **EST:** 1978
SQ FT: 11,000
SALES (est): 9.42MM **Privately Held**
Web: www.clinical-tech.com
SIC: 5047 Patient monitoring equipment

(G-1352)
CROSSCOUNTRY MORTGAGE LLC (PA)
Also Called: Bestrateusa
6850 Miller Rd (44141-3287)
PHONE.................................440 845-3700
Ronald Leonhardt Junior, *Pr*
Barbara Voytek, *
EMP: 414 **EST:** 2003
SQ FT: 1,695
SALES (est): 803.24MM
SALES (corp-wide): 803.24MM **Privately Held**
Web: www.crosscountrymortgage.com
SIC: 6163 6162 6211 Mortgage brokers arranging for loans, using money of others; Mortgage bankers and loan correspondents; Mortgages, buying and selling

(G-1353)
HASTINGS WATER WORKS INC
10331 Brecksville Rd (44141-3335)
PHONE.................................440 832-7700
David J Hastings, *Pr*
EMP: 35 **EST:** 1992
SQ FT: 17,000
SALES (est): 5.34MM **Privately Held**
Web: www.hastingswaterworks.com
SIC: 7389 Swimming pool and hot tub service and maintenance

(G-1354)
HOUSE OF LA ROSE CLEVELAND
Also Called: House of La Rose
6745 Southpointe Pkwy (44141-3267)
PHONE.................................440 746-7500
Thomas A La Rose, *Ch Bd*
Joseph F La Rose, *
Peter C La Rose, *
James P La Rose, *
Thomas G Knoll, *
EMP: 210 **EST:** 1979
SQ FT: 153,000
SALES (est): 45.67MM **Privately Held**
Web: www.houseoflarose.com
SIC: 5181 Beer and other fermented malt liquors

(G-1355)
IC HOLDING COMPANY
10060 Brecksville Rd (44141-3293)
P.O. Box 470665 (44147-0665)
PHONE.................................440 746-9200
Walter P Kerr, *Pr*
Marc A Lockemer, *VP*
Richard Kreal, *VP*
Brian Emsley, *Treas*
EMP: 111 **EST:** 1997
SQ FT: 19,400
SALES (est): 15.86MM **Privately Held**
SIC: 1541 Renovation, remodeling and repairs: industrial buildings

(G-1356)
KRISH SERVICES GROUP INC
10091 Brecksville Rd (44141-3376)
PHONE.................................813 784-0039
Peruri Srinivasulu, *CEO*
EMP: 35 **EST:** 2011
SALES (est): 1.29MM **Privately Held**
Web: www.krishservicesgroup.com
SIC: 7371 Computer software development

(G-1357)
LEVEL SEVEN
Also Called: S. B. Stone & Company
8803 Brecksville Rd Unit 7 (44141-1932)
PHONE.................................216 524-9055
Stuart Taylor, *Managing Member*
Lisa Locklear, *Mktg Dir*
EMP: 75 **EST:** 2010
SALES (est): 8.73MM **Privately Held**
Web: www.lvlsvn.com
SIC: 8742 Management consulting services

(G-1358)
LLC MOON DYE
6580 Glen Coe Dr (44141-2883)
PHONE.................................440 623-9016
Dipak Shah, *Prin*
EMP: 29 **EST:** 2007
SALES (est): 480.39K **Privately Held**
SIC: 7011 Hotels and motels

(G-1359)
METROHEALTH SYSTEM
Also Called: Metrohlth Brcksvlle Hlth Srger
9200 Treeworth Blvd (44141-2591)
PHONE.................................216 957-9000
Mario Pisano, *Admn*
EMP: 106
SALES (corp-wide): 620.72MM **Privately Held**
Web: www.metrohealth.org
SIC: 8011 Offices and clinics of medical doctors
PA: The Metrohealth System
2500 Metrohealth Dr
Cleveland OH 44109
216 778-7800

(G-1360)
OHIO BELL TELEPHONE COMPANY (DH)
Also Called: AT&T Ohio
6889 W Snowville Rd (44141-3213)
PHONE.................................216 822-9700
EMP: 869 **EST:** 1921
SQ FT: 100,000
SALES (est): 569.85MM
SALES (corp-wide): 122.43B **Publicly Held**
SIC: 4813 8721 Local and long distance telephone communications; Billing and bookkeeping service
HQ: At&T Teleholdings, Inc.
30 S Wacker Dr Fl 34
Chicago IL 60606
800 288-2020

(G-1361)
OPTION CARE BRECKSVILLE O
Also Called: Option Care
6955 Treeline Dr (44141-3372)
PHONE.................................440 627-2031
EMP: 44 **EST:** 2017
SALES (est): 492.44K **Privately Held**
Web: www.optioncarehealth.com
SIC: 8082 Home health care services

(G-1362)
PHYSICIANS AMBULANCE SVC INC (PA)
Also Called: Physicians Medical Trnspt Team
6670 W Snowville Rd Ste 2 (44141-4300)
PHONE.................................216 454-4911
Ron Hess, *Pr*
Terry Finnerty, *
EMP: 40 **EST:** 2000
SALES (est): 11.7MM
SALES (corp-wide): 11.7MM **Privately Held**
Web: www.physiciansambulance.com
SIC: 4119 Ambulance service

(G-1363)
POMEROY IT SOLUTIONS SLS INC
6670 W Snowville Rd Ste 3 (44141-4300)
PHONE.................................440 717-1364
Hal Loughry, *Genl Mgr*
EMP: 49
Web: www.pomeroy.com
SIC: 1731 7373 8243 7378 Computer installation; Computer integrated systems design; Data processing schools; Computer maintenance and repair
HQ: Pomeroy It Solutions Sales Company, Inc.
1020 Petersburg Rd
Hebron KY 41048

(G-1364)
REGIONAL INCOME TAX AGENCY (PA)
10107 Brecksville Rd (44141-3205)
PHONE.................................800 860-7482
Rick Carbone, *Ex Dir*
EMP: 125 **EST:** 1971
SQ FT: 33,000
SALES (est): 14.1MM
SALES (corp-wide): 14.1MM **Privately Held**
Web: www.ritaohio.com
SIC: 7291 Tax return preparation services

(G-1365)
RENASCENT SALVAGE HOLDINGS LLC
6910 Carriage Hill Dr (44141-1259)
P.O. Box 786 (44236-0786)
PHONE.................................216 539-1033
EMP: 35 **EST:** 2017
SALES (est): 2.05MM **Privately Held**
SIC: 5015 Automotive parts and supplies, used

(G-1366)
SCG FIELDS LLC
10303 Brecksville Rd (44141-3335)
PHONE.................................440 546-1200
Christopher Franks, *
Joseph Smith, *
EMP: 50 **EST:** 2012
SALES (est): 11.26MM **Privately Held**
Web: www.scgfields.com
SIC: 1629 Athletic field construction

(G-1367)
SOUTH SUBURBAN MONTESSORI ASSN
4450 Oakes Rd Bldg 7 (44141)
P.O. Box 470216 (44147)
PHONE.................................440 526-1966
Amy Mackie-barr, *Prin*
EMP: 35 **EST:** 1970
SALES (est): 1.89MM **Privately Held**
Web: www.ssmsmontessori.net
SIC: 8351 Montessori child development center

(G-1368)
SPORTS SURFACES CNSTR LLC
Also Called: Sports Construction Group
10303 Brecksville Rd (44141-3335)
PHONE.................................440 546-1200
Christopher Franks, *Managing Member*
EMP: 32 **EST:** 2004
SALES (est): 16.79MM **Privately Held**
Web: www.scgfields.com
SIC: 1629 Athletic field construction

(G-1369)
SYSTEM SEALS INC
6600 W Snowville Rd (44141-3257)
PHONE.................................216 220-1800
EMP: 28
SALES (corp-wide): 1.01MM **Privately Held**
Web: www.systemseals.com
SIC: 3953 5084 Embossing seals and hand stamps; Hydraulic systems equipment and supplies
HQ: System Seals, Inc.
9505 Midwest Ave
Cleveland OH 44125

(G-1370)
TRUE NORTH ENERGY LLC (PA)
10346 Brecksville Rd (44141-3338)
PHONE.................................877 245-9336
W Geoffrey Lyden Iii, *Managing Member*
EMP: 35 **EST:** 1999
SQ FT: 18,000
SALES (est): 265.72MM
SALES (corp-wide): 265.72MM **Privately Held**
Web: www.truenorthstores.com
SIC: 5541 5172 Filling stations, gasoline; Gasoline

(G-1371)
WD BPI LLC
Also Called: Bpi Information Systems
6055 W Snowville Rd (44141-3245)
PHONE.................................440 717-4112
Ross Butler, *Prin*
Joyce Ellis, *Prin*
George Stoll, *Prin*
EMP: 34 **EST:** 2021
SALES (est): 5.7MM **Privately Held**
Web: www.bpiohio.com
SIC: 7378 Computer maintenance and repair

Bremen
Fairfield County

(G-1372)
WESTERMAN INC (PA)
245 N Broad St (43107-1003)
P.O. Box 125 (43107-0125)
PHONE.................................800 338-8265
John Moorefield, *Ch*
Jacob Garrett, *
Nick Chrzanowski, *
Dave Cline, *
Brian Kariker, *
◆ **EMP:** 185 **EST:** 1957
SQ FT: 150,000
SALES (est): 126.49MM

GEOGRAPHIC SECTION

Broadview Heights - Cuyahoga County (G-1394)

SALES (corp-wide): 126.49MM **Privately Held**
Web: www.westermaninc.com
SIC: 3825 1389 Electrical energy measuring equipment; Oil field services, nec

Brewster
Stark County

(G-1373)
BREWSTER PARKE INC
Also Called: Brewster Convalescent Center
264 Mohican St Ne (44613-1126)
PHONE...............................330 767-4179
David E Childs, *Pr*
Cheryl Childs, *
EMP: 84 **EST:** 1973
SQ FT: 9,000
SALES (est): 4.19MM **Privately Held**
Web: www.brewsterparke.com
SIC: 8059 8052 8051 Convalescent home; Intermediate care facilities; Skilled nursing care facilities

(G-1374)
WHEELING & LAKE ERIE RLWY CO
100 East First St (44613-1202)
P.O. Box 96 (44613-0096)
PHONE...............................330 767-3401
Larry R Parsons, *Ch*
Jonathan Chastek, *
Donna L Phillips, *
Alec Jarvis, *CLO*
EMP: 416 **EST:** 1990
SQ FT: 33,000
SALES (est): 20.72MM **Privately Held**
Web: www.wlerwy.com
SIC: 4011 Railroads, line-haul operating
PA: Wheeling Corporation
    100 1st St Se
    Brewster OH 44613

Bridgeport
Belmont County

(G-1375)
BRIDGEPORT AUTO PARTS INC (PA)
56104 National Rd Ste 110 (43912-2506)
PHONE...............................740 635-0441
Tim Conway, *Pr*
Timothy A Conway, *
EMP: 35 **EST:** 1946
SALES (est): 5.05MM
SALES (corp-wide): 5.05MM **Privately Held**
SIC: 5013 5531 Automotive supplies and parts; Automotive parts

(G-1376)
ERB ELECTRIC CO
500 Hall St Ste 1 (43912-1324)
PHONE...............................740 633-5055
Tom Knight, *Pr*
Marianne Knight, *
Kathy Heil, *
Ray Heil, *
EMP: 200 **EST:** 1958
SALES (est): 24.16MM **Privately Held**
Web: www.erbelectric.com
SIC: 1731 General electrical contractor

(G-1377)
RECON
54382 National Rd (43912-9804)
PHONE...............................740 609-3050
Ray Hieronymus, *Pr*
EMP: 99 **EST:** 2017
SALES (est): 8.69MM **Privately Held**
Web: www.reconoilfieldservices.com
SIC: 1389 Oil field services, nec

Brilliant
Jefferson County

(G-1378)
BUCKEYE POWER INC
Also Called: Cardinal Plant
306 County Road 7e (43913-1002)
PHONE...............................740 598-6534
Doug Shearn, *Mgr*
EMP: 136
SALES (corp-wide): 832.7MM **Privately Held**
Web: www.ohioec.org
SIC: 4911 Generation, electric power
PA: Buckeye Power, Inc.
    6677 Busch Blvd
    Columbus OH 43229
    614 781-0573

(G-1379)
CARDINAL OPERATING COMPANY
306 County Road 7e (43913-1002)
PHONE...............................740 598-4164
E Linn Draper Junior, *Pr*
Richard K Byrne, *
William J Lhota, *
John F Dilorenzo Junior, *Sec*
Myron Kempfer, *
EMP: 397 **EST:** 1967
SQ FT: 200,000
SALES (est): 58.7MM **Privately Held**
Web: www.cardinalopco.com
SIC: 4911 Generation, electric power

(G-1380)
FRALEY & SCHILLING INC
708 Dandy Ln (43913)
PHONE...............................740 598-4118
Jon Patton, *Mgr*
EMP: 31
SALES (corp-wide): 50.35MM **Privately Held**
Web: www.drivefs.com
SIC: 4213 4212 Contract haulers; Local trucking, without storage
PA: Fraley & Schilling Inc
    1920 S State Road 3
    Rushville IN 46173
    765 932-5977

(G-1381)
UNITED PARCEL SERVICE INC
Also Called: UPS
500 Labelle St (43913-1165)
PHONE...............................740 598-4293
EMP: 31
SALES (corp-wide): 90.96B **Publicly Held**
Web: www.ups.com
SIC: 4215 Parcel delivery, vehicular
HQ: United Parcel Service, Inc.
    55 Glenlake Pkwy
    Atlanta GA 30328
    404 828-6000

(G-1382)
WELLS TOWNSHIP
409 Prospect St (43913-1218)
PHONE...............................740 598-9602
Cheryl Roe, *Sec*
EMP: 46
Web: www.wellstownship.net
SIC: 4959 9221 Road, airport, and parking lot maintenance services; Police protection
PA: Wells Township
    107 Steuben St
    Brilliant OH 43913
    740 598-4152

Broadview Heights
Cuyahoga County

(G-1383)
BABIN BUILDING SOLUTIONS LLC
4101 E Royalton Rd (44147-3122)
PHONE...............................216 292-2500
EMP: 35
Web: www.babinbuildingsolutions.com
SIC: 5031 5211 5072 Kitchen cabinets; Home centers; Hardware

(G-1384)
CLEVELAND CLINIC FOUNDATION
2001 E Royalton Rd (44147-2811)
PHONE...............................440 986-4000
Mark Lang, *Mgr*
EMP: 41
SALES (corp-wide): 14.48B **Privately Held**
Web: www.clevelandclinic.org
SIC: 8062 General medical and surgical hospitals
PA: The Cleveland Clinic Foundation
    9500 Euclid Ave
    Cleveland OH 44195
    216 636-8335

(G-1385)
CLEVELAND CLINIC FOUNDATION
2525 E Royalton Rd Ste 1 (44147-2842)
PHONE...............................440 717-1370
EMP: 33
SALES (corp-wide): 14.48B **Privately Held**
Web: www.clevelandclinic.org
SIC: 8062 General medical and surgical hospitals
PA: The Cleveland Clinic Foundation
    9500 Euclid Ave
    Cleveland OH 44195
    216 636-8335

(G-1386)
CLINICL OTCMS MNGMNT SYST LLC
Also Called: Coms Interactive
9200 S Hills Blvd Ste 200 (44147-3520)
PHONE...............................330 650-9900
EMP: 59 **EST:** 2009
SQ FT: 1,400
SALES (est): 8.14MM
SALES (corp-wide): 77.37MM **Privately Held**
SIC: 7372 Business oriented computer software
HQ: Pointclickcare Technologies Inc
    5570 Explorer Dr
    Mississauga ON L4W 0
    905 858-8885

(G-1387)
EMERALD RESOURCE GROUP INC
1 Eagle Valley Ct (44147-2982)
PHONE...............................440 922-9000
Mark Krusinski, *Pr*
EMP: 35 **EST:** 1997
SALES (est): 2.34MM **Privately Held**
Web: www.emeraldresourcegroup.com
SIC: 7361 Executive placement

(G-1388)
EXTREME MKTG & PROMOTIONS INC
9403 Scottsdale Dr (44147-2361)
PHONE...............................440 237-8400
Dominick Palazzo, *Owner*
EMP: 63 **EST:** 2013
SALES (est): 1.6MM **Privately Held**
Web: www.extrememp.com
SIC: 8742 Marketing consulting services

(G-1389)
FAMILY HERITG LF INSUR CO AMER (HQ)
6001 E Royalton Rd Ste 200 (44147-3527)
P.O. Box 470608 (44147-0608)
PHONE...............................440 922-5222
Howard Lewis, *CEO*
Ken Matson, *Pr*
EMP: 89 **EST:** 1989
SQ FT: 16,000
SALES (est): 80.02MM
SALES (corp-wide): 5.45B **Publicly Held**
Web: home.globelifeinsurance.com
SIC: 6311 Life insurance
PA: Globe Life Inc.
    3700 S Stonebridge Dr
    Mckinney TX 75070
    972 569-4000

(G-1390)
FIRST CHOICE HOMECARE INC
601 Towpath Trl Ste C (44147-4704)
PHONE...............................440 717-1984
EMP: 35
SIC: 7352 Medical equipment rental

(G-1391)
HMT ASSOCIATES INC
335 Treeworth Blvd (44147-2985)
PHONE...............................216 369-0109
Patti Conti, *Prin*
EMP: 41 **EST:** 1997
SALES (est): 8.15MM **Privately Held**
Web: www.hmtassociates.com
SIC: 8742 Marketing consulting services

(G-1392)
MERRILL LYNCH PRCE FNNER SMITH
Also Called: Merrill Lynch
6001 E Royalton Rd (44147-3527)
PHONE...............................440 526-8880
EMP: 53
SALES (corp-wide): 93.85B **Publicly Held**
Web: www.ml.com
SIC: 6211 Security brokers and dealers
HQ: Merrill Lynch, Pierce, Fenner & Smith Incorporated
    111 8th Ave
    New York NY 10011
    800 637-7455

(G-1393)
NELSON LABS FAIRFIELD INC
9100 S Hills Blvd (44147-3518)
PHONE...............................973 227-6882
Daniel L Prince, *Pr*
EMP: 50 **EST:** 1970
SALES (est): 10.56MM
SALES (corp-wide): 1.05B **Publicly Held**
Web: www.nelsonlabs.com
SIC: 3841 8734 Diagnostic apparatus, medical; Testing laboratories
PA: Sotera Health Company
    9100 S Hills Blvd Ste 300
    Broadview Heights OH 44147
    440 262-1410

(G-1394)
OHIO MACHINERY CO (PA)
Also Called: Caterpillar Authorized Dealer
3993 E Royalton Rd (44147-2898)
PHONE...............................440 526-6200
Ken Taylor, *Pr*
Paul Liesem, *
Kelly Love, *
Eric W Emch, *
David J Blocksom, *

(PA)=Parent Co (HQ)=Headquarters
✿ = New Business established in last 2 years

2024 Harris Ohio Services Directory

◆ **EMP:** 160 **EST:** 1946
SQ FT: 92,000
SALES (est): 185.86MM
SALES (corp-wide): 185.86MM **Privately Held**
Web: www.ohiocat.com
SIC: 7513 6159 7699 5082 Truck rental, without drivers; Machinery and equipment finance leasing; Aircraft and heavy equipment repair services; General construction machinery and equipment

(G-1395)
OHIO MACHINERY CO
Also Called: Caterpillar
900 Ken Mar Industrial Pkwy (44147-2992)
PHONE..................................440 526-0520
Greg Deanna, *Brnch Mgr*
EMP: 80
SALES (corp-wide): 185.86MM **Privately Held**
Web: www.ohiocat.com
SIC: 5082 General construction machinery and equipment
PA: Ohio Machinery Co.
3993 E Royalton Rd
Broadview Heights OH 44147
440 526-6200

(G-1396)
SOTERA HEALTH COMPANY (PA)
9100 S Hills Blvd Ste 300 (44147)
PHONE..................................440 262-1410
Michael B Petras Junior, *Ch Bd*
Michael F Biehl, *CAO*
Matthew Klaben, *INTERIM SENIOR VICE PRESIDENT*
Jon Lyons, *Sr VP*
EMP: 28 **EST:** 2015
SALES (est): 1.05B
SALES (corp-wide): 1.05B **Publicly Held**
Web: www.soterahealth.com
SIC: 8734 Testing laboratories

(G-1397)
SOTERA HEALTH HOLDINGS LLC
Also Called: Nelson Laboratories
9100 S Hills Blvd Ste 300 (44147)
PHONE..................................440 262-1410
Michael B Petras Junior, *CEO*
Scott J Leffler, *
EMP: 368 **EST:** 2015
SALES (est): 10.36MM
SALES (corp-wide): 1.05B **Publicly Held**
Web: www.sterigenics.com
SIC: 8734 6799 Testing laboratories; Investors, nec
PA: Sotera Health Company
9100 S Hills Blvd Ste 300
Broadview Heights OH 44147
440 262-1410

(G-1398)
SOTERA HEALTH LLC (HQ)
9100 S Hills Blvd Ste 300 (44147-3525)
PHONE..................................440 262-1410
Michael B Petras Junior, *CEO*
EMP: 100 **EST:** 2004
SALES (est): 513.94MM
SALES (corp-wide): 1.05B **Publicly Held**
Web: www.soterahealth.com
SIC: 7389 Product sterilization service
PA: Sotera Health Company
9100 S Hills Blvd Ste 300
Broadview Heights OH 44147
440 262-1410

(G-1399)
SOTERA HEALTH SERVICES LLC
9100 S Hills Blvd Ste 300 (44147-3525)
PHONE..................................440 262-1410
Michael B Petras Junior, *CEO*
EMP: 92 **EST:** 2020
SALES (est): 2.04MM
SALES (corp-wide): 1.05B **Publicly Held**
Web: www.soterahealth.com
SIC: 8734 Testing laboratories
PA: Sotera Health Company
9100 S Hills Blvd Ste 300
Broadview Heights OH 44147
440 262-1410

(G-1400)
SOTERA HEALTH TOPCO PARENT LP
9100 S Hills Blvd Ste 300 (44147-3525)
PHONE..................................440 262-1410
Michael B Petras Junior, *Ch Bd*
EMP: 2900 **EST:** 2015
SALES (est): 5.46MM **Privately Held**
Web: www.soterahealth.com
SIC: 8071 Medical laboratories

(G-1401)
TK ELEVATOR CORPORATION
9200 Market Pl (44147-2863)
PHONE..................................440 717-0080
Lou Cozza, *Mgr*
EMP: 154
SALES (corp-wide): 2.67MM **Privately Held**
Web: www.tkelevator.com
SIC: 5084 7699 Elevators; Elevators: inspection, service, and repair
HQ: Tk Elevator Corporation
788 Cir 75 Pkwy Se # 500
Atlanta GA 30339
678 319-3240

(G-1402)
UNITED FD COML WKRS UN LCAL 88 (PA)
Also Called: UFCW LOCAL 880
9199 Market Pl Ste 2 (44147-2870)
PHONE..................................216 241-5930
Thomas H Robertson, *Pr*
Robert W Grauvogl, *
EMP: 43 **EST:** 1937
SQ FT: 30,000
SALES (est): 64.72K
SALES (corp-wide): 64.72K **Privately Held**
Web: www.ufcwlocal880.org
SIC: 8631 6512 Labor union; Commercial and industrial building operation

(G-1403)
UNIVERSITY HSPTALS CLVLAND MED
Also Called: Uh Urgent Care Broadview Hts
5901 E Royalton Rd (44147-3532)
PHONE..................................440 499-5900
EMP: 1080
SALES (corp-wide): 878.24MM **Privately Held**
Web: www.uhhospitals.org
SIC: 8011 Medical centers
HQ: University Hospitals Cleveland Medical Center
11100 Euclid Ave
Cleveland OH 44106

(G-1404)
WARWICK COMMUNICATIONS INC (PA)
Also Called: C C I
405 Ken Mar Industrial Pkwy (44147-4614)
PHONE..................................216 787-0300
Steve Leopold, *CEO*
Heidi Murphy, *
Laura Green, *
EMP: 30 **EST:** 1942
SQ FT: 25,000
SALES (est): 5.02MM
SALES (corp-wide): 5.02MM **Privately Held**
Web: www.warwickinc.com
SIC: 7359 5065 Electronic equipment rental, except computers; Telephone equipment

Brook Park
Cuyahoga County

(G-1405)
ANALEX CORPORATION
Also Called: Arcfield
1000 Apollo Dr (44142)
PHONE..................................703 721-6001
Kevin Kelly, *Mgr*
EMP: 40
SALES (corp-wide): 8.69B **Privately Held**
Web: www.arcfield.com
SIC: 7371 Computer software development
HQ: Analex Corporation
14295 Pk Madow Dr Ste 500
Chantilly VA 20151
703 721-6001

Brookfield
Trumbull County

(G-1406)
KIRILA CONTRACTORS INC
505 Bedford Rd Se (44403-9750)
P.O. Box 179 (44403-0179)
PHONE..................................330 448-4055
Ronald Kirila, *Pr*
Robert Kirila, *
Paul Kirila, *
Ronald Kirila Junior, *VP*
William Kirila Junior, *VP*
EMP: 70 **EST:** 1956
SQ FT: 50,000
SALES (est): 11.62MM **Privately Held**
Web: www.kirila.com
SIC: 1794 Excavation and grading, building construction

(G-1407)
UNITED STEEL SERVICE LLC (HQ)
Also Called: Uniserv
4500 Parkway Dr (44403-8720)
P.O. Box 149 (44403-0149)
PHONE..................................330 448-4057
▲ **EMP:** 120 **EST:** 1951
SQ FT: 50,000
SALES (est): 28.35MM
SALES (corp-wide): 44.18MM **Privately Held**
Web: www.unitedsteelservice.com
SIC: 5051 Steel
PA: P. I. & I. Motor Express, Inc.
908 Broadway St
Masury OH 44438
330 448-4035

(G-1408)
YANKEE LAKE INC
Also Called: Village Party Center
1800 State Route 7 Ne (44403-9732)
PHONE..................................330 448-8866
John A Jurko, *Pr*
Geralyn H Jurko, *VP*
Jane E Gentile, *Treas*
EMP: 28 **EST:** 1928
SALES (est): 548.73K **Privately Held**
Web: www.yankee-lake.org
SIC: 5813 7911 5812 5921 Tavern (drinking places); Dance hall or ballroom operation; Caterers; Beer (packaged)

Brooklyn
Cuyahoga County

(G-1409)
FERROUS METAL TRANSFER CO
11103 Memphis Ave (44144-2055)
PHONE..................................216 671-8500
Eduardo Gonzalez, *Pr*
Reed Mcgivney, *Ex VP*
Jim Stratton, *
Anthony Potelicki, *
David Hill, *
EMP: 36 **EST:** 1989
SQ FT: 1,000
SALES (est): 2.67MM **Privately Held**
Web: www.ferrousmetaltransfer.com
SIC: 4212 4213 1541 1611 Lumber and timber trucking; Heavy hauling, nec; Steel building construction; General contractor, highway and street construction

(G-1410)
KEYBANK NATIONAL ASSOCIATION
Also Called: Keybank
4900 Tiedeman Rd (44144-2338)
PHONE..................................800 539-8336
EMP: 38
SALES (corp-wide): 10.4B **Publicly Held**
Web: www.key.com
SIC: 6021 National commercial banks
HQ: Keybank National Association
127 Public Sq Ste 5600
Cleveland OH 44114
800 539-2968

(G-1411)
TRG STUDIOS INC
Also Called: Reuben Group, The
1 American Rd (44144-2354)
PHONE..................................216 781-8644
Martin Reuben, *CEO*
EMP: 35 **EST:** 1982
SQ FT: 7,600
SALES (est): 4.93MM **Privately Held**
Web: www.trgreality.com
SIC: 7335 Photographic studio, commercial

(G-1412)
VICTORY CAPITAL HOLDINGS INC (PA)
Also Called: VICTORY
4900 Tiedeman Rd Fl 4 (44144)
PHONE..................................216 898-2400
David C Brown, *Ch Bd*
Michael D Policarpo, *Pr*
Nina Gupta, *CLO*
EMP: 29 **EST:** 2013
SALES (est): 821.03MM
SALES (corp-wide): 821.03MM **Publicly Held**
Web: investor.vcm.com
SIC: 6282 6722 Investment advisory service; Management investment, open-end

Brooklyn Heights
Cuyahoga County

(G-1413)
BRILLIANT ELECTRIC SIGN CO LTD
4811 Van Epps Rd (44131-1082)
PHONE..................................216 741-3800
James R Groh, *Managing Member*
EMP: 55 **EST:** 1929
SQ FT: 55,000
SALES (est): 5.05MM **Privately Held**
Web: www.brilliantsign.com
SIC: 3993 1799 Electric signs; Sign installation and maintenance

GEOGRAPHIC SECTION
Brookpark - Cuyahoga County (G-1434)

(G-1414)
CI DISPOSITION CO
1000 Valley Belt Rd (44131-1433)
PHONE..............................216 587-5200
Gary Tarnowski, *VP*
EMP: 89 EST: 1952
SQ FT: 56,000
SALES (est): 2.07MM **Privately Held**
SIC: 3699 5085 Linear accelerators; Industrial supplies

(G-1415)
CLEVELAND CONCRETE CNSTR INC (PA)
Also Called: Cleveland Cement Contractors
4823 Van Epps Rd (44131-1015)
PHONE..............................216 741-3954
Ronald Simonetti, *CEO*
Michael H Simonetti, *
Steven Murphy, *
Jim Simonetti, *
EMP: 98 EST: 1944
SQ FT: 10,000
SALES (est): 27.17MM
SALES (corp-wide): 27.17MM **Privately Held**
Web: www.clevelandcement.com
SIC: 1771 Foundation and footing contractor

(G-1416)
DEDICATED TRANSPORT LLC (HQ)
700 W Resource Dr (44131-1836)
PHONE..............................216 641-2500
Tom Mcdermott, *Pr*
Tom Mcdermott, *SED Vice President*
Franklin Price, *
EMP: 120 EST: 2004
SQ FT: 6,000
SALES (est): 20.39MM **Privately Held**
SIC: 4212 4213 Local trucking, without storage; Contract haulers
PA: Dedicated Transport Holdings, Llc
    700 W Resource Dr
    Brooklyn Heights OH 44131

(G-1417)
ELECTRICAL APPL REPR SVC INC
5805 Valley Belt Rd (44131-1423)
PHONE..............................216 459-8700
Tom Roberts, *Pr*
Kenneth Roberts, *
Gloria Crist, *
Walter Novak, *Adviser**
EMP: 30 EST: 1953
SQ FT: 12,500
SALES (est): 3.5MM **Privately Held**
Web: www.electapplrep.com
SIC: 7629 7623 Electrical equipment repair services; Refrigeration service and repair

(G-1418)
FLEET TEAM
1425 Valley Belt Rd (44131-1440)
PHONE..............................614 699-2500
David Bongorno, *Prin*
Paul Libassi, *Prin*
EMP: 50 EST: 2011
SALES (est): 10.1MM **Privately Held**
Web: www.fleetteam.com
SIC: 7699 Industrial machinery and equipment repair

(G-1419)
GNCO INC (PA)
1395 Valley Belt Rd (44131-1438)
PHONE..............................216 706-2349
John Champ, *Prin*
EMP: 28 EST: 2019
SALES (est): 246.16MM
SALES (corp-wide): 246.16MM **Privately Held**

Web: www.kubota.com
SIC: 5084 Industrial machinery and equipment

(G-1420)
J V JANITORIAL SERVICES INC
1000 Resource Dr (44131-1399)
PHONE..............................216 749-1150
Joseph N Vocaire Senior, *Pr*
EMP: 200 EST: 1975
SQ FT: 6,600
SALES (est): 4.58MM **Privately Held**
Web: www.jvjanitorial.com
SIC: 7349 Janitorial service, contract basis

(G-1421)
JACKPOT PALLETS LLC
Also Called: Jackpot Pallets Wholesale
4770 Van Epps Rd Ste 107 (44131-1058)
PHONE..............................877 770-0005
Sanad Nassar, *CEO*
EMP: 35 EST: 2020
SALES (est): 3.92MM **Privately Held**
Web: www.jackpotpalletswholesale.com
SIC: 5031 Pallets, wood

(G-1422)
JANTECH BUILDING SERVICES INC
4963 Schaaf Ln (44131-1034)
PHONE..............................216 661-6102
William Rosby, *Pr*
Jeff Thayer, *
EMP: 50 EST: 1997
SQ FT: 3,000
SALES (est): 1.41MM **Privately Held**
Web: www.jantechinc.com
SIC: 7349 Janitorial service, contract basis

(G-1423)
KAISER FOUNDATION HOSPITALS
Also Called: Bedford Medical Offices
5400 Lancaster Dr (44131-1832)
PHONE..............................216 524-7377
EMP: 33
SALES (corp-wide): 70.8B **Privately Held**
Web: www.kaisercenter.com
SIC: 8011 Offices and clinics of medical doctors
HQ: Kaiser Foundation Hospitals Inc
    1 Kaiser Plz
    Oakland CA 94612
    510 271-6611

(G-1424)
KAISER FOUNDATION HOSPITALS
Also Called: Parma Medical Center
5400 Lancaster Dr (44131-1832)
PHONE..............................800 524-7377
EMP: 33
SALES (corp-wide): 70.8B **Privately Held**
Web: www.kaisercenter.com
SIC: 8011 Medical centers
HQ: Kaiser Foundation Hospitals Inc
    1 Kaiser Plz
    Oakland CA 94612
    510 271-6611

(G-1425)
MULTI-FLOW DISPENSERS OHIO INC (PA)
4705 Van Epps Rd (44131-1013)
PHONE..............................216 641-0200
Stanley Klein, *Pr*
EMP: 60 EST: 1963
SQ FT: 17,000
SALES (est): 19.1MM
SALES (corp-wide): 19.1MM **Privately Held**
Web: www.multiflowdispensers.com

SIC: 5145 7359 Syrups, fountain; Vending machine rental

(G-1426)
OHIO DESK COMPANY
4851 Van Epps Rd Ste A (44131-1052)
PHONE..............................216 623-0600
EMP: 50
SALES (corp-wide): 27.8MM **Privately Held**
Web: www.ohiodesk.com
SIC: 4225 General warehousing and storage
PA: The Ohio Desk Company
    1122 Prospect Ave E
    Cleveland OH 44115
    216 623-0600

(G-1427)
SOLAR TESTING LABORATORIES INC (PA)
1125 Valley Belt Rd (44131-1434)
PHONE..............................216 741-7007
George J Ata, *Pr*
Edward A Zielinski, *
Michael Kichurchak, *
EMP: 75 EST: 1969
SQ FT: 20,000
SALES (est): 4.64MM
SALES (corp-wide): 4.64MM **Privately Held**
Web: www.stlohio.com
SIC: 8748 Testing services

(G-1428)
TOWLIFT INC (HQ)
1395 Valley Belt Rd (44131-1474)
PHONE..............................216 749-6800
TOLL FREE: 800
David H Cannon, *Pr*
David Bongorno, *VP Fin*
▲ EMP: 121 EST: 1965
SQ FT: 28,000
SALES (est): 117.29MM
SALES (corp-wide): 246.16MM **Privately Held**
Web: www.towlift.com
SIC: 5084 7699 7359 Materials handling machinery; Industrial machinery and equipment repair; Equipment rental and leasing, nec
PA: Gnco, Inc.
    1395 Valley Belt Rd
    Brooklyn Heights OH 44131
    216 706-2349

Brookpark
Cuyahoga County

(G-1429)
CAR PARTS WAREHOUSE INC (PA)
Also Called: C P W
5200 W 130th St (44142-1804)
PHONE..............................216 281-4500
Tony Difiore, *Pr*
Carmelina Di Fiore, *
▲ EMP: 30 EST: 1985
SQ FT: 70,000
SALES (est): 48.99MM
SALES (corp-wide): 48.99MM **Privately Held**
Web: www.carpartswarehouse.net
SIC: 5013 5531 Automotive supplies; Automotive parts

(G-1430)
CEC COMBUSTION SAFETY LLC (DH)
2100 Apollo Dr (44142-4103)
PHONE..............................216 749-2992

EMP: 42 EST: 1984
SQ FT: 25,000
SALES (est): 10.42MM
SALES (corp-wide): 36.66B **Publicly Held**
Web: process.honeywell.com
SIC: 8711 7389 Consulting engineer; Industrial and commercial equipment inspection service
HQ: Eclipse, Inc.
    201 E 18th St
    Muncie IN 47302

(G-1431)
CERAMIC HOLDINGS INC (DH)
Also Called: Cetek
20600 Sheldon Rd (44142-1312)
PHONE..............................216 362-3900
Derek Scott, *Pr*
Kathlene Stevens, *
◆ EMP: 120 EST: 1981
SALES (est): 27.04MM **Privately Held**
Web: www.integratedglobal.com
SIC: 7629 7692 Electrical repair shops; Welding repair
HQ: Fosbel Holding, Inc.
    20600 Sheldon Rd
    Cleveland OH 44142

(G-1432)
CREDIT FIRST NA
6275 Eastland Rd (44142-1399)
PHONE..............................216 362-5000
Alfred Policy, *CEO*
Alan Meier, *CFO*
EMP: 52 EST: 1993
SQ FT: 25,000
SALES (est): 51.17MM **Privately Held**
Web: www.cfna.com
SIC: 6021 National commercial banks
HQ: Bridgestone Retail Operations, Llc
    333 E Lake St Ste 300
    Bloomingdale IL 60108
    630 259-9000

(G-1433)
DISTRIBUTION DATA INCORPORATED (PA)
Also Called: Ddi
16101 Snow Rd Ste 200 (44142-2817)
P.O. Box 818019 (44181-8019)
PHONE..............................216 362-3009
Robert W Hartig, *Pr*
Charles C Deems, *
Lynn M Hartig, *
Debbie Zillich, *
EMP: 90 EST: 1985
SQ FT: 34,000
SALES (est): 24.72MM
SALES (corp-wide): 24.72MM **Privately Held**
Web: www.ddiservices.com
SIC: 5199 7371 8742 4731 Art goods and supplies; Custom computer programming services; Transportation consultant; Freight forwarding

(G-1434)
EDUCATION ALTERNATIVES (PA)
5445 Smith Rd (44142-2026)
PHONE..............................216 332-9360
Jerry Swartz, *Ex Dir*
Gerald Swartz, *
EMP: 57 EST: 1999
SALES (est): 18.23MM
SALES (corp-wide): 18.23MM **Privately Held**
Web: www.easchools.org
SIC: 8211 8093 Private special education school; Rehabilitation center, outpatient treatment

(PA)=Parent Co (HQ)=Headquarters
✪ = New Business established in last 2 years

Brookpark - Cuyahoga County (G-1435)

(G-1435)
HUNTINGTON NATIONAL BANK
5881 Smith Rd (44142-2005)
PHONE..................................216 515-0013
Linda Chovan, *Mgr*
EMP: 31
SALES (corp-wide): 10.84B **Publicly Held**
Web: www.huntington.com
SIC: 6029 6021 Commercial banks, nec; National commercial banks
HQ: The Huntington National Bank
41 S High St
Columbus OH 43215
614 480-4293

(G-1436)
LAKEFRONT LINES INC (DH)
13315 Brookpark Rd (44142-1822)
P.O. Box 81172 (44181-0172)
PHONE..................................216 267-8810
Chris Goebel, *CEO*
Tom Goebel, *Genl Mgr*
Christopher Goebel, *Asst Mgr*
EMP: 175 **EST:** 1965
SQ FT: 48,000
SALES (est): 23.97MM **Privately Held**
Web: www.lakefrontlines.com
SIC: 4119 4142 4141 Local passenger transportation, nec; Bus charter service, except local; Local bus charter service
HQ: Coach Usa, Inc.
160 S Route 17 N
Paramus NJ 07652

(G-1437)
LAKEWOOD CHRYSLER-PLYMOUTH
Also Called: Spitzer Lakewood
13001 Brookpark Rd (44142-1819)
PHONE..................................216 521-1000
William Burke, *VP*
Allan Spitzer, *
EMP: 47 **EST:** 1949
SQ FT: 30,000
SALES (est): 7.2MM **Privately Held**
Web: www.chrysler.com
SIC: 5511 7538 7515 Automobiles, new and used; General automotive repair shops; Passenger car leasing

(G-1438)
NORTH COAST LOGISTICS INC (PA)
18901 Snow Rd Frnt (44142-1471)
PHONE..................................216 362-7159
Patricia A Gazey, *Pr*
William Harrison, *
▲ **EMP:** 40 **EST:** 1992
SQ FT: 575,000
SALES (est): 18.53MM **Privately Held**
Web: www.northcoastlogistics.com
SIC: 4225 General warehousing

(G-1439)
SMITHFIELD DIRECT LLC
Also Called: Armour
15751 Commerce Park Dr (44142-2018)
PHONE..................................216 267-6196
Ray Owsiak, *Prin*
EMP: 107
Web: carando.sfdbrands.com
SIC: 5147 Meats, fresh
HQ: Smithfield Direct, Llc
4225 Naperville Rd # 600
Lisle IL 60532

(G-1440)
STANDARD CONTG & ENGRG INC
Also Called: S C E
6356 Eastland Rd (44142-1302)
PHONE..................................440 243-1001
Russell Metzger, *Pr*
Gary Barnhill, *
George Wonkovich, *
EMP: 75 **EST:** 1991
SQ FT: 6,000
SALES (est): 16.91MM **Privately Held**
Web: www.standardcontracting.com
SIC: 1541 1771 1794 1796 Industrial buildings, new construction, nec; Concrete work; Excavation work; Machine moving and rigging

(G-1441)
SWX ENTERPRISES INC
5231 Engle Rd (44142-1531)
PHONE..................................216 676-4600
Dean Armanini, *Pr*
EMP: 50 **EST:** 1990
SQ FT: 25,000
SALES (est): 2.35MM **Privately Held**
SIC: 4213 Trucking, except local

(G-1442)
VICTORY PACKAGING LP
18300 Snow Rd (44142-1415)
PHONE..................................216 898-9130
Ray Stachura, *Brnch Mgr*
EMP: 84
SALES (corp-wide): 20.31B **Publicly Held**
Web: www.victorypackaging.com
SIC: 5199 Packaging materials
HQ: Victory Packaging, L.P.
3555 Timmons Ln Ste 1440
Houston TX 77027
713 961-3299

(G-1443)
WELDERS SUPPLY INC
5575 Engle Rd (44142-1533)
PHONE..................................216 267-4470
EMP: 45
SALES (corp-wide): 12.38MM **Privately Held**
SIC: 7692 5999 5984 Welding repair; Welding supplies; Propane gas, bottled
HQ: Welders Supply Inc
2020 Train Ave
Cleveland OH 44113
216 241-1696

Brookville
Montgomery County

(G-1444)
A BROWN AND SONS NURSERY INC
11506 Dayton Greenville Pike (45309-8652)
P.O. Box 427 (45354-0427)
PHONE..................................937 836-5826
Kenneth Brown, *Pr*
John Brown, *
Michael Brown, *
Harry Brown, *
EMP: 60 **EST:** 1959
SALES (est): 4.63MM **Privately Held**
Web: www.brownsnursery.com
SIC: 0181 5431 Nursery stock, growing of; Vegetable stands or markets

(G-1445)
BROOKVILLE ENTERPRISES INC
Also Called: BROOKHAVEN NURSING & CARE CENT
1 Country Ln (45309-9268)
PHONE..................................937 833-2133
Mike Mckinniss, *Ex Dir*
Dale Baughman, *
Terry Miller, *
EMP: 125 **EST:** 1972
SQ FT: 32,500
SALES (est): 9.46MM **Privately Held**
Web: www.brookhavenoh.org
SIC: 8052 8051 Intermediate care facilities; Skilled nursing care facilities

(G-1446)
MIAMI VLY CHILD DEV CTRS INC
75 June Pl (45309-1621)
PHONE..................................937 833-6600
Cheryl Warren, *Brnch Mgr*
EMP: 50
SALES (corp-wide): 43.26MM **Privately Held**
Web: www.mvcdc.org
SIC: 8351 Head Start center, except in conjunction with school
PA: Miami Valley Child Development Centers, Inc.
215 Horace St
Dayton OH 45402
937 226-5664

(G-1447)
ODW LOGISTICS INC
1 Collective Way Ste B (45309-8878)
PHONE..................................937 770-5602
EMP: 28
SALES (corp-wide): 529.12MM **Privately Held**
Web: www.odwlogistics.com
SIC: 4789 Cargo loading and unloading services
PA: Odw Logistics, Inc.
400 W Nationwide Blvd # 200
Columbus OH 43215
614 549-5000

(G-1448)
RITE AID OF OHIO INC
Also Called: Rite Aid
437 N Wolf Creek St (45309-1214)
PHONE..................................937 833-2174
Linda Ewlens, *Mgr*
EMP: 47
SALES (corp-wide): 24.09B **Publicly Held**
Web: www.riteaid.com
SIC: 5912 7384 Drug stores; Photofinishing laboratory
HQ: Rite Aid Of Ohio, Inc.
1200 Intrepid Ave Ste 2
Philadelphia PA 19112

Brunswick
Medina County

(G-1449)
ADVANCED ELEC SPECIALISTS INC
Also Called: AES
1258 Industrial Pkwy N # 2 (44212-2369)
PHONE..................................330 237-9930
Jason Galata, *Pr*
EMP: 77 **EST:** 2003
SALES (est): 3.96MM **Privately Held**
SIC: 1731 Electrical work

(G-1450)
ALL CONSTRUCTION SERVICES INC
Also Called: All Construction/Mooney Moses
945 Industrial Pkwy N (44212-4321)
PHONE..................................330 225-1653
David J Le Hotan, *Pr*
Michael J Fox, *
EMP: 275 **EST:** 1994
SQ FT: 12,000
SALES (est): 1.81MM
SALES (corp-wide): 2.78B **Publicly Held**
Web: www.allconstructionohio.com
SIC: 1742 Insulation, buildings
HQ: Installed Building Products Llc
495 S High St Ste 150
Columbus OH 43215
614 221-3399

(G-1451)
BLACKHAWK INDUSTRIAL DIST INC
2845 Interstate Pkwy (44212-4326)
PHONE..................................918 610-4719
Bill Scheller, *Brnch Mgr*
EMP: 32
Web: www.bhid.com
SIC: 5085 Industrial supplies
PA: Blackhawk Industrial Distribution, Inc.
10810 E 45th St Ste 100
Tulsa OK 74146

(G-1452)
BRUNSWICK SENIOR LIVING LLC
Also Called: Danbury Brunswick
3430 Brunswick Lake Pkwy (44212-3673)
PHONE..................................330 460-4244
William J Lemmon, *Managing Member*
EMP: 47 **EST:** 2015
SALES (est): 1.37MM **Privately Held**
SIC: 6531 Real estate agents and managers

(G-1453)
CHS THERAPY REHAB HOLDINGS LLC
2875 Center Rd (44212-2319)
PHONE..................................888 995-1305
EMP: 37
SALES (est): 341.55K **Privately Held**
SIC: 8099 Health and allied services, nec

(G-1454)
CONTINING HLTHCARE SLTIONS INC
2875 Center Rd Ste 6 (44212-2319)
PHONE..................................419 529-7272
▼ **EMP:** 52
SALES (est): 3.51MM **Privately Held**
Web: www.continuinghc.com
SIC: 8099 Blood bank

(G-1455)
DIGESTIVE DISEASE CONSULTANTS
1299 Industrial Pkwy N Ste 110 (44212-6366)
PHONE..................................330 225-6468
David Myers, *Owner*
EMP: 27 **EST:** 2004
SALES (est): 3.37MM **Privately Held**
Web: www.mygidocs.com
SIC: 8011 Gastronomist

(G-1456)
FOOD SAMPLE EXPRESS LLC
2945 Carquest Dr (44212-4447)
PHONE..................................330 225-3550
Jeffrey M Wood, *Managing Member*
EMP: 90 **EST:** 2000
SALES (est): 4.88MM **Privately Held**
SIC: 5141 Groceries, general line

(G-1457)
HUNTINGTON NATIONAL BANK
1344 Pearl Rd (44212-2808)
PHONE..................................330 225-3946
EMP: 31
SALES (corp-wide): 10.84B **Publicly Held**
Web: www.huntington.com
SIC: 6029 Commercial banks, nec
HQ: The Huntington National Bank
41 S High St
Columbus OH 43215
614 480-4293

(G-1458)
ICS LABORATORIES INC
1072 Industrial Pkwy N (44212-4318)
PHONE..................................330 220-0515

GEOGRAPHIC SECTION

Dale Pfriem, *Pr*
EMP: 36 **EST:** 1995
SQ FT: 7,000
SALES (est): 7.81MM **Privately Held**
Web: www.icslabs.com
SIC: 8734 Product testing laboratories

(G-1459)
INDEPENDENT RESEARCH GROUP INC
1575 Pearl Rd (44212-3468)
P.O. Box 398 (44212-0398)
PHONE..................................330 273-3380
David Mclaughlin, *Pr*
EMP: 74 **EST:** 1983
SALES (est): 1.08MM **Privately Held**
SIC: 7381 8732 Private investigator; Market analysis or research

(G-1460)
INTEGRATED MARKETING TECH INC
Also Called: IMT
2945 Carquest Dr (44212-4447)
PHONE..................................330 225-3550
▲ **EMP:** 100 **EST:** 1995
SQ FT: 120,000
SALES (est): 20.13MM **Privately Held**
Web: www.imtco.com
SIC: 7363 7374 Labor resource services; Data processing service

(G-1461)
KHM CONSULTING INC
Also Called: Khm Travel Group
50 Pearl Rd Ste 300 (44212-5703)
PHONE..................................330 460-5635
Richard Zimmerman, *Pr*
EMP: 45 **EST:** 2005
SALES (est): 21.28MM **Privately Held**
Web: www.khmtravel.com
SIC: 4724 Tourist agency arranging transport, lodging and car rental

(G-1462)
MAPLESIDE VALLEY LLC (PA)
Also Called: Mapleside Bakery
294 Pearl Rd (44212-1118)
PHONE..................................330 225-5576
William Eyssen Junior, *Prin*
David Eyssen, *Prin*
EMP: 75 **EST:** 1927
SQ FT: 9,900
SALES (est): 4.7MM
SALES (corp-wide): 4.7MM **Privately Held**
Web: www.mapleside.com
SIC: 0175 0172 5947 5812 Apple orchard; Grapes; Gift shop; Eating places

(G-1463)
MBD TRANSPORT LLC
3906 Turnbridge Ct Unit 311 (44212)
P.O. Box 1199 (44212-8699)
PHONE..................................513 449-0777
Trevor Wright, *Pr*
Idrissa Deera, *
EMP: 51 **EST:** 2009
SALES (est): 1.65MM **Privately Held**
Web: www.mbdtransportllc.com
SIC: 7389 7549 Courier or messenger service; Towing services

(G-1464)
NATIONAL DENTEX LLC
Also Called: Ndx Salem
2868 Westway Dr Ste G (44212-5661)
PHONE..................................216 671-0577
Vicky Rice, *Brnch Mgr*
EMP: 68
SALES (corp-wide): 339.71MM **Privately Held**
Web: www.nationaldentex.com

SIC: 8072 Crown and bridge production
HQ: National Dentex, Llc
  1701 Military Trl Ste 150
  Jupiter FL 33458
  800 678-4140

(G-1465)
NATIONS EXPRESS INC
3931 Center Rd (44212-3087)
PHONE..................................440 234-4330
Joe Werner, *Brnch Mgr*
EMP: 32
SALES (corp-wide): 231.81MM **Privately Held**
Web: www.neirecruiting.com
SIC: 4731 Freight forwarding
HQ: Nations Express, Inc.
  17015 Kenton Dr Ste 205
  Cornelius NC 28031
  888 997-9911

(G-1466)
PATRICIAN INC
Also Called: Patrician Skilled Nursing Ctr
1026 Pearl Rd Ste 5 (44212-2519)
PHONE..................................440 237-3104
Doula Gaitanaros, *Pr*
Basil Gaitanaros, *
EMP: 210 **EST:** 1979
SQ FT: 68,000
SALES (est): 8.6MM **Privately Held**
SIC: 8051 Skilled nursing care facilities

(G-1467)
POINT RECOGNITION LTD
1015 Industrial Pkwy N (44212-4319)
PHONE..................................330 220-6777
EMP: 30 **EST:** 1985
SQ FT: 4,200
SALES (est): 4.99MM **Privately Held**
Web: www.pointrecognition.com
SIC: 5094 7389 Coins, medals, and trophies; Engraving service

(G-1468)
PRECISION SUPPLY COMPANY INC
2845 Interstate Pkwy (44212-4326)
PHONE..................................330 225-5530
Alfred J Koch, *CEO*
Bob Koch, *
Tracy Lehnecker, *
EMP: 75 **EST:** 1973
SQ FT: 18,630
SALES (est): 10MM **Privately Held**
Web: www.bhid.com
SIC: 5084 5085 Machine tools and accessories; Industrial supplies
PA: Blackhawk Industrial Distribution, Inc.
  10810 E 45th St Ste 100
  Tulsa OK 74146

(G-1469)
ROLLING HLLS RHAB WELLNESS CTR
4426 Homestead Dr (44212-2506)
PHONE..................................330 225-9121
Dan Shiller, *Pr*
Basil Gaitanaros, *
Mary Traczyk, *
Michael Traczyk, *
EMP: 50 **EST:** 1967
SQ FT: 15,000
SALES (est): 1.89MM **Privately Held**
Web: www.pearlviewcarecenter.com
SIC: 8051 Convalescent home with continuous nursing care

(G-1470)
SPECIAL SERVICE TRANSPORTATION INC

1529 Substation Rd (44212-3227)
PHONE..................................330 273-0755
EMP: 45 **EST:** 1946
SALES (est): 5.4MM **Privately Held**
Web: www.specialservicetrans.com
SIC: 4213 4212 Contract haulers; Local trucking, without storage

(G-1471)
TMR INC
2945 Carquest Dr (44212-4447)
PHONE..................................330 220-8564
Peter Howe, *Ch Bd*
Jason Atkins, *Pr*
▲ **EMP:** 46 **EST:** 1976
SQ FT: 210,000
SALES (est): 1.29MM **Privately Held**
SIC: 7334 7331 Photocopying and duplicating services; Direct mail advertising services

(G-1472)
VOESTLPINE PRECISION STRIP LLC (HQ)
3052 Interstate Pkwy (44212-4324)
PHONE..................................330 220-7800
◆ **EMP:** 45 **EST:** 2006
SALES (est): 44.65MM
SALES (corp-wide): 19.29B **Privately Held**
Web: www.voestalpine.com
SIC: 5051 Iron or steel semifinished products
PA: Voestalpine Ag
  Voest-Alpine-StraBe 1
  Linz 4020
  5030415

(G-1473)
W W WILLIAMS COMPANY LLC
Also Called: Midwest Division - Brunswick
1176 Industrial Pkwy N (44212-2342)
PHONE..................................330 225-7751
Alan Gatlin, *CEO*
EMP: 50
SALES (corp-wide): 1.47B **Privately Held**
Web: www.wwwilliams.com
SIC: 7538 7537 5084 Diesel engine repair: automotive; Automotiv e transmission repair shops; Engines and parts, diesel
HQ: The W W Williams Company Llc
  400 Metro Pl N Ste 201
  Dublin OH 43017
  614 228-5000

(G-1474)
W W WILLIAMS MIDWEST INC
1176 Industrial Pkwy N (44212-2342)
PHONE..................................330 225-7751
EMP: 50
SIC: 5084 7538 7537 Industrial machinery and equipment; Diesel engine repair: automotive; Automotiv e transmission repair shops

(G-1475)
WILLOWOOD CARE CENTER
Also Called: WILLOWOOD NURSING
1186 Hadcock Rd (44212-3061)
PHONE..................................330 225-3156
EMP: 121 **EST:** 1965
SQ FT: 27,150
SALES (est): 9.21MM **Privately Held**
Web: www.carecorehealth.com
SIC: 8051 8742 Convalescent home with continuous nursing care; Management consulting services

(G-1476)
WINKING LIZARD INC
3634 Center Rd (44212-4446)
PHONE..................................330 220-9944
Jim Callam, *Brnch Mgr*

EMP: 39
SALES (corp-wide): 28.01MM **Privately Held**
Web: www.winkinglizard.com
SIC: 5812 7299 Fast food restaurants and stands; Banquet hall facilities
PA: Winking Lizard, Inc.
  25380 Miles Rd
  Bedford OH 44146
  216 831-0022

Bryan
Williams County

(G-1477)
ADVANCED RHBILITATION TECH LTD
Also Called: Art
525 Winzeler Dr # 1 (43506-8303)
PHONE..................................419 636-2684
Dustin L Schlachter, *Managing Member*
Lynn Schlachter, *
EMP: 33 **EST:** 2007
SALES (est): 5.5MM **Privately Held**
Web: www.artcoatingtech.com
SIC: 7389 7699 1623 Sewer inspection service; Sewer cleaning and rodding; Water, sewer, and utility lines

(G-1478)
AIRMATE CO INC
16280 County Road D (43506-9552)
PHONE..................................419 636-3184
Carol Schreder Czech, *Pr*
Carol Schreder, *
Neil Oberlin, *
▲ **EMP:** 57 **EST:** 1946
SQ FT: 24,000
SALES (est): 7.55MM **Privately Held**
Web: www.airmateplasticfabrication.com
SIC: 3823 7311 Process control instruments; Advertising consultant

(G-1479)
ANDERSON & VREELAND INC
Also Called: Anderson Vreeland Midwest
15348 Us Highway 127 Ew (43506)
P.O. Box 527 (43506-0527)
PHONE..................................419 636-5002
EMP: 80
SQ FT: 3,000
SALES (corp-wide): 49.53MM **Privately Held**
Web: www.andersonvreeland.com
SIC: 5084 3555 3542 2796 Printing trades machinery, equipment, and supplies; Printing trades machinery; Machine tools, metal forming type; Platemaking services
PA: Anderson & Vreeland, Inc.
  8 Evans St
  Fairfield NJ 07004
  973 227-2270

(G-1480)
COMMUNITY HOSPITALS
433 W High St (43506-1690)
PHONE..................................419 636-1131
Phillip Ennen, *CEO*
EMP: 484 **EST:** 2012
SALES (est): 5.13MM
SALES (corp-wide): 77.07MM **Privately Held**
Web: www.chwhospital.org
SIC: 8062 General medical and surgical hospitals
PA: Community Hospitals And Wellness Centers
  433 W High St
  Bryan OH 43506
  419 636-1131

Bryan - Williams County (G-1481)

(G-1481)
COMMUNITY HOSPITALS WELLNESS
442 W High St (43506-1681)
PHONE..............................419 636-1131
Mahmoud H Afifi Md, *Prin*
EMP: 51 **EST:** 2015
SALES (est): 18.64MM **Privately Held**
SIC: 8062 General medical and surgical hospitals

(G-1482)
COMMUNITY HSPTALS WLLNESS CTRS (PA)
Also Called: Chwc
433 W High St (43506-1690)
PHONE..............................419 636-1131
Phil Ennen, *CEO*
Chad Tinkel, *
EMP: 101 **EST:** 1969
SQ FT: 50,000
SALES (est): 77.07MM
SALES (corp-wide): 77.07MM **Privately Held**
Web: www.chwchospital.org
SIC: 8062 General medical and surgical hospitals

(G-1483)
CROSSCOUNTRY MORTGAGE LLC
1607 W High St (43506-1598)
PHONE..............................419 636-4663
EMP: 46
SALES (corp-wide): 803.24MM **Privately Held**
Web: www.crosscountrymortgage.com
SIC: 6162 Mortgage bankers and loan correspondents
PA: Crosscountry Mortgage, Llc
6850 Miller Rd
Brecksville OH 44141
440 845-3700

(G-1484)
F F & W INC
Also Called: Colonial Manor Motel
924 E High St (43506-1827)
P.O. Box 846 (43506-0846)
PHONE..............................419 636-3123
Gary Welling, *Pr*
Warren Fisher, *Prin*
EMP: 27 **EST:** 1977
SALES (est): 475.76K **Privately Held**
Web: colonial-manor-motel.business.site
SIC: 7011 Motels

(G-1485)
HUNTINGTON NATIONAL BANK
310 S Main St (43506-1756)
PHONE..............................419 636-1164
Steve Collins, *Prin*
EMP: 31
SALES (corp-wide): 10.84B **Publicly Held**
Web: www.huntington.com
SIC: 6029 6022 Commercial banks, nec; State commercial banks
HQ: The Huntington National Bank
41 S High St
Columbus OH 43215
614 480-4293

(G-1486)
L E SMITH COMPANY (PA)
1030 E Wilson St (43506)
P.O. Box 766 (43506)
PHONE..............................419 636-4555
Laura Juarez, *Pr*
Craig Francisco, *
Mindy Hess, *
Steve Smith, *
Mari Ivan, *
▲ **EMP:** 100 **EST:** 1950

SQ FT: 90,000
SALES (est): 12.22MM
SALES (corp-wide): 12.22MM **Privately Held**
Web: www.lesmith.com
SIC: 2431 5072 2541 Interior and ornamental woodwork and trim; Builders' hardware, nec; Wood partitions and fixtures

(G-1487)
MANSFELD OHIO ARIE NO 336 FRTN (PA)
Also Called: Foe 2233
221 S Walnut St (43506-1720)
PHONE..............................419 636-7812
Denny Baer, *Pr*
Chuck Cunnigham, *
Tim Lewis, *
EMP: 33 **EST:** 1898
SQ FT: 21,000
SALES (est): 4.44MM
SALES (corp-wide): 4.44MM **Privately Held**
Web: www.foe.com
SIC: 8641 7371 Fraternal associations; Computer software development and applications

(G-1488)
MIDWEST CMNTY HLTH ASSOC INC (HQ)
Also Called: Parkview Physicians Group
442 W High St Ste 3 (43506-1685)
PHONE..............................419 633-4034
TOLL FREE: 800
Randall Bauman, *Pr*
Stacey Beck, *
James Hamilton, *
EMP: 175 **EST:** 1965
SALES (est): 26.02MM **Privately Held**
SIC: 8062 General medical and surgical hospitals
PA: Parkview Health System, Inc.
10501 Corporate Dr
Fort Wayne IN 46845

(G-1489)
OBERLIN INVESTMENTS LLC
209 N Main St (43506-1319)
P.O. Box 998 (43506-0998)
PHONE..............................419 636-4001
EMP: 30 **EST:** 1999
SALES (est): 3.55MM **Privately Held**
SIC: 6211 Brokers, security

(G-1490)
OHIO GAS COMPANY
715 E Wilson St (43506-1848)
P.O. Box 528 (43506-0528)
PHONE..............................419 636-3642
Doug Saul, *Dir*
EMP: 31
SALES (corp-wide): 46.55MM **Privately Held**
Web: www.ohiogas.com
SIC: 4922 Natural gas transmission
HQ: Ohio Gas Company
206 W High St
Bryan OH 43506
419 636-1117

(G-1491)
OHIO GAS COMPANY (HQ)
200 W High St (43506-1612)
P.O. Box 528 (43506-0528)
PHONE..............................419 636-1117
Richard Hallett, *Pr*
Kim Watkins, *
Bob Eyre, *GAS SYS**
Douglas Saul, *
Dee Swanson, *

EMP: 30 **EST:** 1914
SQ FT: 15,000
SALES (est): 22.84MM
SALES (corp-wide): 41.99MM **Privately Held**
Web: www.ohiogas.com
SIC: 4924 Natural gas distribution
PA: Nwo Resources, Inc.
206 W High St
Bryan OH 43506
419 636-1117

(G-1492)
POTTER INC (PA)
Also Called: Potter
630 Commerce Dr (43506-8864)
PHONE..............................419 636-5624
Steve Voigt, *Pr*
Dave Gorzelanczyk, *
Marie Campbell Watkins, *
▲ **EMP:** 30 **EST:** 1977
SQ FT: 37,000
SALES (est): 8MM
SALES (corp-wide): 8MM **Privately Held**
Web: www.potter-inc.com
SIC: 5199 Baskets

(G-1493)
POWER TRAIN COMPONENTS INC
509 E Edgerton St (43506-1315)
P.O. Box 805 (43506-0805)
PHONE..............................419 636-4430
Delton R Nihart, *Ch Bd*
Jack Nihart, *
◆ **EMP:** 55 **EST:** 1978
SQ FT: 60,000
SALES (est): 9.23MM **Privately Held**
Web: www.ptcauto.com
SIC: 5013 Truck parts and accessories

(G-1494)
TRANE TECHNOLOGIES COMPANY LLC
Also Called: Ingersoll-Rand
209 N Main St (43506-1319)
P.O. Box 151 (43506-0151)
PHONE..............................419 633-6800
EMP: 49
Web: www.tranetechnologies.com
SIC: 3546 4225 3823 3594 Power-driven handtools; General warehousing and storage; Process control instruments; Fluid power pumps and motors
HQ: Ingersoll-Rand Industrial U.S., Inc.
800 Beaty St Ste E
Davidson NC 28036
704 655-4000

Bucyrus
Crawford County

(G-1495)
ALTERCARE OF BUCYRUS INC
1929 Whetstone St (44820-3564)
PHONE..............................419 562-7644
Cathy Rox, *Admn*
EMP: 40 **EST:** 1992
SALES (est): 6.13MM **Privately Held**
Web: www.altercareonline.com
SIC: 8051 Convalescent home with continuous nursing care

(G-1496)
BROKEN ARROW INC
1649 Marion Rd (44820-3116)
PHONE..............................419 562-3480
Jayne Hanning, *Ex Dir*
EMP: 32 **EST:** 1991
SALES (est): 1.22MM **Privately Held**

SIC: 8322 8699 8059 Social services for the handicapped; Charitable organization; Personal care home, with health care

(G-1497)
BUCYRUS COMMUNITY HOSPITAL INC
629 N Sandusky Ave (44820-1821)
PHONE..............................419 562-4677
Jerry Morasko, *Prin*
Andrew Daniels, *
Doctor Samantha Bark, *Prin*
Doctor Christopher Cannell, *Prin*
Doctor Robert Dawson, *Prin*
EMP: 165 **EST:** 1956
SQ FT: 75,000
SALES (est): 91.71K
SALES (corp-wide): 444.64K **Privately Held**
Web: www.bchonline.org
SIC: 8062 Hospital, affiliated with AMA residency
PA: Avita Health System
269 Portland Way S
Galion OH 44833
419 468-4841

(G-1498)
BUCYRUS COMMUNITY HOSPITAL LLC
629 N Sandusky Ave (44820-1821)
PHONE..............................419 562-4677
EMP: 95 **EST:** 2010
SALES (est): 52.8K
SALES (corp-wide): 444.64K **Privately Held**
Web: www.bchonline.org
SIC: 8062 General medical and surgical hospitals
PA: Avita Health System
269 Portland Way S
Galion OH 44833
419 468-4841

(G-1499)
BUCYRUS COMMUNITY PHYSICIANS
140 Hill St Ste A (44820-1566)
PHONE..............................419 563-9801
Michael Landes, *Brnch Mgr*
EMP: 68
SIC: 8099 Medical services organization
PA: Bucyrus Community Physicians Inc
139 Gaius St
Bucyrus OH 44820

(G-1500)
COLUMBIA GAS OF OHIO INC
Also Called: Columbia
231 S Poplar St (44820-2211)
P.O. Box 270 (44820-0270)
PHONE..............................419 562-4003
Brian Black, *Brnch Mgr*
EMP: 75
SALES (corp-wide): 5.51B **Publicly Held**
Web: www.columbiagasohio.com
SIC: 4924 Natural gas distribution
HQ: Columbia Gas Of Ohio, Inc.
290 W Nationwide Blvd # 1
Columbus OH 43215
614 460-6000

(G-1501)
COMMUNITY COUNSELING SVCS INC
2458 Stetzer Rd (44820-2066)
P.O. Box 765 (44820-0765)
PHONE..............................419 562-2000
Tom Saccenti, *Dir*
EMP: 35 **EST:** 1972
SQ FT: 4,600
SALES (est): 3.03MM **Privately Held**

GEOGRAPHIC SECTION

Bucyrus - Crawford County (G-1520)

Web: www.communitycounseling.info
SIC: **8093** 8322 8069 Mental health clinic, outpatient; Crisis intervention center; Alcoholism rehabilitation hospital

(G-1502)
COUNTY OF CRAWFORD
Also Called: Crawford Cnty Job & Fmly Svcs
224 Norton Way (44820-1831)
PHONE..............................419 562-0015
Thomas M O'leary, *Dir*
EMP: 43
SALES (corp-wide): 54.43MM **Privately Held**
Web: www.crawfordcountymuni.org
SIC: **8331** Job training services
PA: County Of Crawford
  112 E Mansfield St # 304
  Bucyrus OH 44820
  419 562-5871

(G-1503)
COUNTY OF CRAWFORD
Also Called: Crawford Cnty Council On Aging
200 S Spring St (44820-2227)
P.O. Box 166 (44820-0166)
PHONE..............................419 562-3050
EMP: 38
SALES (corp-wide): 54.43MM **Privately Held**
Web: www.crawfordcountyaging.com
SIC: **8322** Senior citizens' center or association
PA: County Of Crawford
  112 E Mansfield St # 304
  Bucyrus OH 44820
  419 562-5871

(G-1504)
COUNTY OF CRAWFORD
Also Called: Health Department
1520 Isaac Beal Rd (44820-9604)
PHONE..............................419 562-5871
EMP: 29
SALES (corp-wide): 54.43MM **Privately Held**
Web: www.crawfordcountymuni.org
SIC: **8621** Health association
PA: County Of Crawford
  112 E Mansfield St # 304
  Bucyrus OH 44820
  419 562-5871

(G-1505)
COUNTY OF CRAWFORD
815 Whetstone St (44820-3359)
PHONE..............................419 562-7731
Tim Marcom, *Prin*
EMP: 52
SALES (corp-wide): 54.43MM **Privately Held**
Web: www.crawfordcountyengineer.com
SIC: **8711** Civil engineering
PA: County Of Crawford
  112 E Mansfield St # 304
  Bucyrus OH 44820
  419 562-5871

(G-1506)
CRAWFORD COUNTY CHILDREN SVCS (PA)
Also Called: Children's Service Board
224 Norton Way (44820-1831)
PHONE..............................419 562-1200
Kathy Scott, *Dir*
EMP: 28 EST: 1911
SALES (est): 815.09K
SALES (corp-wide): 815.09K **Privately Held**
Web: www.crawfordcountyjfs.org

SIC: **8322** Child related social services

(G-1507)
DESIGN BUILT CONSTRUCTION INC
825 E Mansfield St (44820-1964)
PHONE..............................419 563-0185
Jim Teynor, *Pr*
Kenneth Heil, *
Jeff Teynor, *
Joe Teynor, *
Jerome Teynor, *
EMP: 29 EST: 1993
SALES (est): 1.45MM **Privately Held**
SIC: **1741** Masonry and other stonework

(G-1508)
FARMERS CITIZENS BANK (DH)
105 Washington Sq (44820-2252)
P.O. Box 567 (44820-0567)
PHONE..............................419 562-7040
Coleman Clougherty, *CEO*
Robert D Hord, *
EMP: 43 EST: 1907
SQ FT: 24,000
SALES (est): 16.75MM
SALES (corp-wide): 327.03MM **Publicly Held**
Web: www.fcbank.bank
SIC: **6022** State trust companies accepting deposits, commercial
HQ: Cnb Bank
  1 S 2nd St
  Clearfield PA 16830
  814 765-9621

(G-1509)
HORD LIVESTOCK COMPANY INC
887 State Route 98 (44820-8646)
PHONE..............................419 562-0277
Robert Hord, *Prin*
EMP: 46
SALES (corp-wide): 11.3MM **Privately Held**
Web: www.hordlivestock.com
SIC: **5154** Livestock
PA: Hord Livestock Company Inc.
  911 State Route 98
  Bucyrus OH 44820
  419 562-9885

(G-1510)
J & F CONSTRUCTION AND DEV INC
Also Called: J & F Construction
2141 State Route 19 (44820-9569)
PHONE..............................419 562-6662
James Mayes, *Pr*
Steve Bridgford, *
Brock Mayes, *
EMP: 28 EST: 1978
SQ FT: 5,000
SALES (est): 14.87MM **Privately Held**
Web: www.jfconstruction.com
SIC: **1542** 1541 Commercial and office building, new construction; Industrial buildings and warehouses

(G-1511)
KINN BROS PLBG HTG & AC INC
527 Whetstone St (44820-2940)
PHONE..............................419 562-1484
Lon Kinn, *Pr*
Kip Kinn, *VP*
EMP: 28 EST: 1980
SQ FT: 2,500
SALES (est): 897.39K **Privately Held**
Web: www.kinnbrothers.com
SIC: **1711** 5722 Plumbing contractors; Electric household appliances, major

(G-1512)
MARYHAVEN INC
137 Stetzer Rd (44820-2076)
PHONE..............................419 562-1740
Paul Coleman, *Brnch Mgr*
EMP: 28
SALES (corp-wide): 32.39MM **Privately Held**
Web: www.maryhaven.com
SIC: **8069** Alcoholism rehabilitation hospital
PA: Maryhaven, Inc.
  1791 Alum Creek Dr
  Columbus OH 43207
  614 449-1530

(G-1513)
NATIONAL LIME AND STONE CO
4580 Bethel Rd (44820-9754)
P.O. Box 69 (44820-0069)
PHONE..............................419 562-0771
Eric Johnson, *Prin*
EMP: 28
SALES (corp-wide): 167.89MM **Privately Held**
Web: www.natlime.com
SIC: **1411** 3281 1422 Limestone, dimension-quarrying; Cut stone and stone products; Crushed and broken limestone
PA: The National Lime And Stone Company
  551 Lake Cascade Pkwy
  Findlay OH 45840
  419 422-4341

(G-1514)
OHIO MUTUAL INSURANCE COMPANY (PA)
Also Called: Ohio Mutual Insurance Group
1725 Hopley Ave (44820-3596)
P.O. Box 111 (44820-0111)
PHONE..............................419 562-3011
Jim Kennedy, *Pr*
Michael Brogan, *Claims Vice President*
Thomas Holtshouse, *Product Vice President*
David Hendrix, *
Randy O'conner, *Underwriting Vice President*
EMP: 120 EST: 1901
SQ FT: 26,000
SALES (est): 100.54MM
SALES (corp-wide): 100.54MM **Privately Held**
Web: public.omig.com
SIC: **6411** 6331 Insurance brokers, nec; Fire, marine, and casualty insurance: mutual

(G-1515)
OHIO UNITED AGENCY INC
1725 Hopley Ave (44820-3569)
P.O. Box 111 (44820-0111)
PHONE..............................419 562-3011
James J Kennedy, *Pr*
David Hendrix, *CFO*
EMP: 44 EST: 1968
SQ FT: 1,500
SALES (est): 1.53MM
SALES (corp-wide): 100.54MM **Privately Held**
Web: public.omig.com
SIC: **6411** 7374 7514 Insurance agents, nec; Data processing service; Passenger car rental
HQ: Centurion Financial, Inc.
  1725 Hopley Ave
  Bucyrus OH 44820
  419 562-3011

(G-1516)
PEOPLES SAVINGS AND LOAN CO (PA)
300 S Walnut St (44820-2330)
PHONE..............................419 562-6896
David Coffman, *CEO*
Steven Shields, *
Renae Cox, *
EMP: 30 EST: 1888
SALES (est): 4.92MM **Privately Held**
Web: www.psalc.com
SIC: **6035** Federal savings and loan associations

(G-1517)
QUALITOR SUBSIDIARY H INC
1232 Whetstone St (44820-3539)
PHONE..............................419 562-7987
Andrew Ason, *Pr*
Ralph Reins, *
EMP: 127 EST: 1984
SALES (est): 5.08MM
SALES (corp-wide): 8.03B **Privately Held**
SIC: **3714** 3451 3429 5013 Motor vehicle brake systems and parts; Screw machine products; Hardware, nec; Automotive supplies and parts
HQ: Transportation Aftermarket Enterprise Inc
  1840 Mccullough St
  Lima OH

(G-1518)
TIMKEN COMPANY
2325 E Mansfield St (44820-2094)
P.O. Box 391 (44820-0391)
PHONE..............................419 563-2200
Jack Yohe, *Brnch Mgr*
EMP: 74
SQ FT: 400,000
SALES (corp-wide): 4.77B **Publicly Held**
Web: www.timken.com
SIC: **5085** Bearings
PA: The Timken Company
  4500 Mount Pleasant St Nw
  North Canton OH 44720
  234 262-3000

(G-1519)
VELVET ICE CREAM COMPANY
Also Called: Bucyrus Ice Company
1233 Whetstone St (44820-3540)
PHONE..............................419 562-2009
TOLL FREE: 800
Jack Rogers, *Mgr*
EMP: 30
SALES (corp-wide): 21.87MM **Privately Held**
Web: www.velveticecream.com
SIC: **5143** 2097 Ice cream and ices; Manufactured ice
PA: Velvet Ice Cream Company
  11324 Mount Vernon Rd
  Utica OH 43080
  740 892-3921

(G-1520)
WAYCRAFT INC
118 River St (44820-1536)
PHONE..............................419 563-0550
Mark Barron, *Pr*
W Michael Miller, *
EMP: 125 EST: 1968
SQ FT: 44,000
SALES (est): 944.6K **Privately Held**
Web: www.waycraftinc.com
SIC: **8331** Vocational rehabilitation agency

Buffalo
Guernsey County

(G-1521)
UNITED HSPTALITY SOLUTIONS LLC
11998 Clay Pike Rd (43722-9900)
P.O. Box 98 (43722-0098)
PHONE.................................800 238-0487
Jennifer Yontz-orlando, *Managing Member*
EMP: 29 **EST:** 2003
SQ FT: 1,200
SALES (est): 451.21K **Privately Held**
SIC: 7011 Hotels and motels

Burbank
Wayne County

(G-1522)
RON BURGE TRUCKING INC
Also Called: Burge, Ron
1876 W Britton Rd (44214-9729)
PHONE.................................330 624-5373
Mike Burge, *Pr*
Scott Burge, *
Annette Burge, *
Sandra Burge, *Stockholder**
EMP: 30 **EST:** 1957
SQ FT: 2,000
SALES (est): 2.49MM **Privately Held**
Web: www.ronburgetrucking.com
SIC: 4213 Contract haulers

Burgoon
Sandusky County

(G-1523)
C I E INC
2704 County Road 13 (43407-9750)
PHONE.................................419 986-5566
Marylin Broski, *Brnch Mgr*
EMP: 273
SALES (corp-wide): 10.14MM **Privately Held**
Web: www.eciinc.net
SIC: 6513 8361 Retirement hotel operation; Geriatric residential care
PA: C I E Inc
 2036 E Township Road 122
 Tiffin OH 44883
 419 443-0767

Burkettsville
Mercer County

(G-1524)
KLINGSHIRN & SONS TRUCKING
Also Called: Klingshirn, Tom & Sons Trckng
14884 St Rt 118 S (45310)
P.O. Box 98 (45310)
PHONE.................................937 338-5000
Thomas P Klingshirn, *Pr*
Robert Klingshirn, *
Paul Klingshirn, *
Mary Ann Klingshirn, *
Joe Klingshirn, *
EMP: 40 **EST:** 1960
SALES (est): 2.7MM **Privately Held**
Web: www.klingshirnandsons.com
SIC: 4213 4212 Contract haulers; Local trucking, without storage

Burton
Geauga County

(G-1525)
BERKSHIRE LOCAL SCHOOL DST
14259 Claridon Troy Rd (44021-9521)
P.O. Box 406 (44021-0406)
PHONE.................................440 834-4123
Doug Delong, *Brnch Mgr*
EMP: 35
SALES (corp-wide): 29.39MM **Privately Held**
Web: www.berkshireschools.org
SIC: 4731 Transportation agents and brokers
PA: Berkshire Local School District
 14259 Claridon Troy Rd
 Burton OH 44021
 440 834-4123

(G-1526)
BFG SUPPLY CO LLC (PA)
Also Called: Bfg Supply Co.
14500 Kinsman Rd (44021-9423)
P.O. Box 479 (44021-0479)
PHONE.................................800 883-0234
David C Daily, *Pr*
Nicole Krizner, *VP*
Jim Smeltzer, *Treas*
◆ **EMP:** 30 **EST:** 1972
SQ FT: 32,000
SALES (est): 183.31MM
SALES (corp-wide): 183.31MM **Privately Held**
SIC: 5191 5261 Garden supplies; Garden supplies and tools, nec

(G-1527)
FIRST TRANSIT INC
13571 W Spring St (44021-9100)
PHONE.................................440 834-1020
Bud Jordan, *Brnch Mgr*
EMP: 61
SALES (corp-wide): 4.23MM **Privately Held**
Web: www.transdevna.com
SIC: 4111 Local and suburban transit
HQ: First Transit, Inc.
 600 Vine St Ste 1400
 Cincinnati OH 45202
 513 241-2200

(G-1528)
HEXPOL COMPOUNDING LLC
Also Called: Burton Rubber Processing
14330 Kinsman Rd (44021-9648)
PHONE.................................440 834-4644
John Gorrell, *Mgr*
EMP: 200
SALES (corp-wide): 2.12B **Privately Held**
Web: www.hexpol.com
SIC: 3087 2865 5162 2899 Custom compound purchased resins; Dyes and pigments; Resins; Chemical preparations, nec
HQ: Hexpol Compounding Llc
 14330 Kinsman Rd
 Burton OH 44021
 440 834-4644

(G-1529)
HUNTINGTON NATIONAL BANK
14522 Main St (44021-9029)
P.O. Box 407 (44021-0407)
PHONE.................................440 834-4481
Charels Bixler, *Mgr*
EMP: 31
SALES (corp-wide): 10.84B **Publicly Held**
Web: www.huntington.com
SIC: 6029 6021 Commercial banks, nec; National commercial banks
HQ: The Huntington National Bank
 41 S High St
 Columbus OH 43215
 614 480-4293

(G-1530)
IMPULLITTI LANDSCAPING LLC
14659 Ravenna Rd (44021-9713)
PHONE.................................440 834-1866
Wayne Impullitti, *Pr*
EMP: 95 **EST:** 1964
SALES (est): 9.5MM **Privately Held**
Web: www.enjoytheview.com
SIC: 0781 Landscape services

(G-1531)
MONROE PLUMBING INC
13745 Hale Rd (44021-9595)
P.O. Box 577 (44021-0577)
PHONE.................................440 708-0006
Brian Monroe, *Pr*
Keith Monroe, *
EMP: 35 **EST:** 1987
SQ FT: 16,000
SALES (est): 2.56MM **Privately Held**
Web: www.monroeplumbing.net
SIC: 1711 Plumbing contractors

(G-1532)
ORIANA HOUSE INC
13820 Hale Rd (44021-9105)
PHONE.................................216 881-7882
EMP: 40 **EST:** 2019
SALES (est): 224.05K **Privately Held**
Web: www.orianahouse.org
SIC: 8322 Substance abuse counseling

(G-1533)
STEPHEN M TRUDICK
Also Called: Hardwood Lumber Co
13813 Station Road (44021)
P.O. Box 15 (44021)
PHONE.................................440 834-1891
Stephen M Trudick, *Owner*
▲ **EMP:** 41 **EST:** 1958
SQ FT: 80,000
SALES (est): 2.29MM **Privately Held**
Web: www.hardwood-lumber.com
SIC: 3991 2426 5031 3442 Brooms and brushes; Dimension, hardwood; Lumber: rough, dressed, and finished; Metal doors, sash, and trim

Byesville
Guernsey County

(G-1534)
EAST OHIO GAS COMPANY
Also Called: Dominion Energy Ohio
60755 Country Club Rd (43723-9730)
PHONE.................................740 439-2721
Larry Blake, *Brnch Mgr*
EMP: 55
SALES (corp-wide): 39.69B **Privately Held**
Web: www.dominiongaschoice.com
SIC: 4924 Natural gas distribution
HQ: The East Ohio Gas Company
 1201 E 55th St
 Cleveland OH 44103
 800 362-7557

(G-1535)
KERRY INC
Also Called: Kerry Ingredients
100 Hope Ave (43723-9460)
PHONE.................................760 685-2548
EMP: 45
Web: www.kerry.com
SIC: 2656 5149 Food containers (liquid tight), including milk cartons; Condiments
HQ: Kerry Inc.
 3400 Millington Rd
 Beloit WI 53511
 608 363-1200

(G-1536)
STEVE CRAWFORD TRUCKING INC
Also Called: Steve Crwford Trucking-Se Ohio
59965 Olive St (43723-9673)
P.O. Box 32 (43723-0032)
PHONE.................................866 748-9505
EMP: 43
SALES (corp-wide): 1.25MM **Privately Held**
Web: www.stevecrawfordbusiness.com
SIC: 4212 Local trucking, without storage
PA: Steve Crawford Trucking, Inc.
 5988 Mid Rivrs Mall Dr # 216
 Saint Peters MO 63304
 314 475-5888

(G-1537)
UNITED AMBLNCE SVC OF CMBRIDGE
217 Watson Ave (43723-1210)
P.O. Box 1118 (43725-6118)
PHONE.................................740 685-2277
EMP: 27
SALES (corp-wide): 107.1MM **Privately Held**
SIC: 4119 Ambulance service
HQ: United Ambulance Service Of Cambridge, Inc
 1331 Campbell Ave
 Cambridge OH 43725
 740 439-7787

Cadiz
Harrison County

(G-1538)
CARRIAGE INN OF CADIZ INC
308 W Warren St (43907-1077)
PHONE.................................740 942-8084
Ken Bernsen, *Pr*
Lynne Huff, *
EMP: 54 **EST:** 1982
SALES (est): 13.81MM **Privately Held**
Web: www.carriageinnofcadiz.com
SIC: 8051 8322 Convalescent home with continuous nursing care; Rehabilitation services

(G-1539)
HARRISON COMMUNITY HOSPITAL INC
951 E Market St (43907-9799)
PHONE.................................740 942-4631
EMP: 200
SIC: 8062 Hospital, affiliated with AMA residency

(G-1540)
HARRISON TOWNSHIP
Also Called: Department Job and Family Svcs
520 N Main St (43907-1276)
P.O. Box 239 (43907-0239)
PHONE.................................740 942-2171
Sott Blackburn, *Dir*
EMP: 40
Web: www.harrisoncountyohio.org
SIC: 8322 9111 Public welfare center; County supervisors' and executives' office
PA: Harrison Township
 100 W Market St
 Cadiz OH 43907

GEOGRAPHIC SECTION

Cambridge - Guernsey County (G-1563)

740 942-4623

(G-1541)
ISI SYSTEMS INC (PA)
43029 Industrial Park Rd (43907-9639)
P.O. Box 156 (43906-0156)
PHONE................................740 942-0050
Christine Wallace, *Pr*
William Wallace, *
EMP: 30 **EST:** 1971
SQ FT: 10,000
SALES (est): 5.17MM
SALES (corp-wide): 5.17MM **Privately Held**
Web: www.isisystems.net
SIC: 1629 Industrial plant construction

(G-1542)
OHIO MACHINERY CO
Also Called: Ohio Cat
1016 E Market St (43907-9728)
PHONE................................740 942-4626
Frank Keller, *Mgr*
EMP: 62
SALES (corp-wide): 185.86MM **Privately Held**
Web: www.ohiocat.com
SIC: 5082 General construction machinery and equipment
PA: Ohio Machinery Co.
  3993 E Royalton Rd
  Broadview Heights OH 44147
  440 526-6200

(G-1543)
RITE AID OF OHIO INC
Also Called: Rite Aid
651 Lincoln Ave (43907-9498)
PHONE................................740 942-3101
Jim Seele, *Mgr*
EMP: 47
SALES (corp-wide): 24.09B **Publicly Held**
Web: www.riteaid.com
SIC: 5912 7384 Drug stores; Photofinishing laboratory
HQ: Rite Aid Of Ohio, Inc.
  1200 Intrepid Ave Ste 2
  Philadelphia PA 19112

(G-1544)
WHEELING HOSPITAL INC
Also Called: Harrison Community Hospital
951 E Market St (43907-9799)
PHONE................................740 942-4631
Anthony Martinelli, *Brnch Mgr*
EMP: 150
SALES (corp-wide): 4.66B **Privately Held**
Web: www.wvumedicine.org
SIC: 8062 Hospital, affiliated with AMA residency
HQ: Wheeling Hospital, Inc.
  1 Medical Park
  Wheeling WV 26003
  304 243-3000

Caldwell
Noble County

(G-1545)
ANTERO RESOURCES CORPORATION
44510 Marietta Rd (43724-9209)
PHONE................................303 357-7310
Austin Beeler, *Mgr*
EMP: 33
Web: www.anteroresources.com
SIC: 1382 Oil and gas exploration services
PA: Antero Resources Corporation
  1615 Wynkoop St
  Denver CO 80202

(G-1546)
BEST WESTERN CALDWELL INN INC
Also Called: Best Western
44128 Fairground Rd (43724-9680)
PHONE................................740 732-7599
Roman B Lori, *Pr*
Karen Mcgilton, *Mgr*
EMP: 27 **EST:** 1997
SALES (est): 470K **Privately Held**
Web: www.bestwestern.com
SIC: 7011 Hotels and motels

(G-1547)
BRADEN MED SERVICES INC
Also Called: Gillespie Drug
44519 Marietta Rd (43724-9209)
PHONE................................740 732-2356
James Scott Braden, *Pr*
Diane R Braden, *
Melissa Zwick, *
EMP: 34 **EST:** 1991
SQ FT: 5,000
SALES (est): 2.69MM **Privately Held**
Web: www.gillespiesdrugs.com
SIC: 8082 7352 5122 5169 Home health care services; Medical equipment rental; Pharmaceuticals; Oxygen

(G-1548)
COMMUNITY SAVINGS
425 Main St (43724)
P.O. Box 320 (43724)
PHONE................................740 732-5678
Barry Parmiter, *Pr*
Brady Miller, *VP*
Kristina Tipton, *Treas*
EMP: 39 **EST:** 1885
SALES (est): 3.9MM **Privately Held**
Web: www.mycommunitysavings.com
SIC: 6022 State commercial banks

(G-1549)
G M N TRI CNTY CMNTY ACTION CM (PA)
615 North St (43724-1123)
PHONE................................740 732-2388
Gary Ricer, *Ex Dir*
EMP: 40 **EST:** 1965
SQ FT: 4,000
SALES (est): 8.64MM
SALES (corp-wide): 8.64MM **Privately Held**
Web: www.gmntrico.org
SIC: 8322 Social service center

(G-1550)
IEH AUTO PARTS LLC
218 West St (43724-1337)
PHONE................................740 732-2395
Wally Olson, *Brnch Mgr*
EMP: 37
Web: autoplus1.cypresstg.com
SIC: 5013 Automotive supplies and parts
HQ: Ieh Auto Parts Llc
  112 Townpark Dr Nw # 300
  Kennesaw GA 30144
  770 701-5000

(G-1551)
SUMMIT ACRES INC (PA)
Also Called: Summit Acres Nursing Home
44565 Sunset Rd (43724-9731)
PHONE................................740 732-2364
Leander Crock, *Pr*
Edward Hupp, *
Malcolm Parks, *
Donald Crock, *
EMP: 200 **EST:** 1965
SQ FT: 54,000
SALES (est): 8.45MM
SALES (corp-wide): 8.45MM **Privately Held**
Web: summitacres.altercareonline.com
SIC: 8093 8052 8082 Rehabilitation center, outpatient treatment; Intermediate care facilities; Home health care services

Cambridge
Guernsey County

(G-1552)
AFC CABLE SYSTEMS INC
829 Georgetown Rd (43725)
PHONE................................740 435-3340
Bob Koscoe, *Brnch Mgr*
EMP: 37
Web: www.atkore.com
SIC: 5063 Wire and cable
HQ: Afc Cable Systems, Inc.
  16100 Lathrop Ave
  Harvey IL 60426
  508 998-1131

(G-1553)
ALLWELL BEHAVIORAL HEALTH SVCS
Also Called: In Place, The
917 Batte Ave (43725-1853)
PHONE................................740 432-7155
Karen Wheatley, *Mgr*
EMP: 30
SALES (corp-wide): 15.97MM **Privately Held**
Web: www.allwell.org
SIC: 8093 7999 Mental health clinic, outpatient; Recreation center
PA: Allwell Behavioral Health Services
  2845 Bell St
  Zanesville OH 43701
  740 454-9766

(G-1554)
AREA AGENCY ON AGING REG 9 INC
Also Called: Area Agency On Aging
710 Wheeling Ave (43725-2332)
PHONE................................740 439-4478
James Endly, *CEO*
EMP: 54 **EST:** 1975
SQ FT: 15,000
SALES (est): 49.06MM **Privately Held**
Web: www.aaa9.org
SIC: 8322 Senior citizens' center or association

(G-1555)
BASIC SYSTEMS INC
9255 Cadiz Rd (43725-9564)
PHONE................................740 432-3001
EMP: 100 **EST:** 1982
SALES (est): 17.48MM **Privately Held**
Web: www.basic-systems.com
SIC: 8711 Designing: ship, boat, machine, and product

(G-1556)
BLUE RACER MIDSTREAM LLC
11388 E Pike Rd Unit B (43725-9669)
PHONE................................740 630-7556
EMP: 66 **EST:** 2013
SALES (est): 3.31MM **Privately Held**
Web: www.blueracermidstream.com
SIC: 1382 Oil and gas exploration services

(G-1557)
CAMBRDGE PRPERTY INVESTORS LTD
Also Called: Holiday Inn
2248 Southgate Pkwy (43725-3038)
P.O. Box 96 (43723-0096)
PHONE................................740 432-7313
Richard Lenhart, *Pt*
Kelly Lenhart, *
EMP: 28 **EST:** 1998
SALES (est): 616.66K **Privately Held**
Web: www.holidayinn.com
SIC: 7011 Hotels and motels

(G-1558)
CAMBRIDGE ASSOCIATES LTD
Also Called: Holiday Inn
2248 Southgate Pkwy (43725-3038)
P.O. Box 15395 (43215-0395)
PHONE................................740 432-7313
Ralph Ray, *Genl Mgr*
EMP: 49
SALES (corp-wide): 1.44MM **Privately Held**
Web: www.cambridgeassociates.com
SIC: 7011 Hotels and motels
PA: Cambridge Associates Ltd
  2002 Richard Jones Rd 105c
  Nashville TN 37215
  615 385-4946

(G-1559)
CAMBRIDGE BEHAVIORAL HOSPITAL
66755 State St (43725-8757)
PHONE................................740 432-4906
EMP: 130 **EST:** 2010
SALES (est): 5MM **Privately Held**
Web: www.cbhohio.com
SIC: 8063 8069 Mental hospital, except for the mentally retarded; Substance abuse hospitals

(G-1560)
CAMBRIDGE PACKAGING INC
Also Called: Cambridge Box & Gift Shop
60794 Southgate Rd (43725-9414)
PHONE................................740 432-3351
Larry Knellinger, *Pr*
Margaret F Knellinger, *
Bill Knellinger, *
Rick Knellinger, *
EMP: 31 **EST:** 1982
SQ FT: 26,000
SALES (est): 5.48MM **Privately Held**
Web: www.cambridgepackaging.com
SIC: 2653 5199 Boxes, corrugated: made from purchased materials; Packaging materials

(G-1561)
CAMBRIDGE SURGICAL SUITES LLC
61605 Southgate Rd (43725-9114)
PHONE................................740 421-4455
EMP: 28 **EST:** 2021
SALES (est): 934.22K **Privately Held**
Web: www.cambridgess.com
SIC: 7011 Hotels

(G-1562)
CAMCO FINANCIAL CORPORATION
814 Wheeling Ave (43725-2317)
PHONE................................740 435-2020
EMP: 220
SIC: 6036 Savings and loan associations, not federally chartered

(G-1563)
CATHOLIC CHRTIES STHSTERN OHIO
Also Called: St Benedict School
220 N 7th St (43725-1838)
PHONE................................740 432-6751
Jane Rush, *Prin*

Cambridge - Guernsey County (G-1564) — GEOGRAPHIC SECTION

EMP: 97
SALES (corp-wide): 25.04MM **Privately Held**
Web: www.catholiccharitiesusa.org
SIC: 8322 8211 Individual and family services; Catholic elementary school
PA: Catholic Charities Of Southeastern Ohio
422 Washington St Ste 1
Steubenville OH 43952
740 282-3631

(G-1564)
COLUMBIA GAS OF OHIO INC
Also Called: Columbia
98 Steubenville Ave (43725-2211)
PHONE................................559 683-1567
Mark Hill, *Mgr*
EMP: 77
SALES (corp-wide): 5.51B **Publicly Held**
Web: www.columbiagasohio.com
SIC: 4924 Natural gas distribution
HQ: Columbia Gas Of Ohio, Inc.
290 W Nationwide Blvd # 1
Columbus OH 43215
614 460-6000

(G-1565)
COUNTY OF GUERNSEY
Also Called: Guernsey Cnty Wtr & Sewer Dept
11272 E Pike Rd (43725-9669)
PHONE................................740 439-1269
Clarence Ridgley, *Superintnt*
EMP: 27
Web: www.guernseycounty.org
SIC: 4941 9111 Water supply; County supervisors' and executives' office
PA: County Of Guernsey
627 Wheeling Ave Rm 301
Cambridge OH 43725
740 432-9243

(G-1566)
COUNTY OF GUERNSEY
Also Called: Guernsey County Senior Center
1022 Carlisle Ave (43725-2420)
PHONE................................740 439-6681
Shon Gress, *Dir*
EMP: 27
Web: www.guernseycounty.org
SIC: 8322 Senior citizens' center or association
PA: County Of Guernsey
627 Wheeling Ave Rm 301
Cambridge OH 43725
740 432-9243

(G-1567)
COUNTY OF GUERNSEY
Also Called: Guernsey Cnty Children Svcs Bd
274 Highland Ave (43725-2571)
PHONE................................740 439-5555
Kelly Lynch, *Ex Dir*
EMP: 27
Web: www.guernseycounty.org
SIC: 8351 9111 Child day care services; County supervisors' and executives' office
PA: County Of Guernsey
627 Wheeling Ave Rm 301
Cambridge OH 43725
740 432-9243

(G-1568)
DUNNING MOTOR SALES INC
9108 Southgate Rd (43725-8005)
PHONE................................740 439-4465
John Dunning Junior, *Genl Mgr*
John Dunning Junior, *Pr*
Nancy S Dunning, *
EMP: 45 **EST:** 1975

SALES (est): 19.03MM **Privately Held**
Web: www.dunningmotorsales.com
SIC: 5511 7538 7515 Automobiles, new and used; General automotive repair shops; Passenger car leasing

(G-1569)
DYNO NOBEL TRANSPORTATION
Also Called: Dyno Transportation
850 Woodlawn Ave (43725-2959)
PHONE................................740 439-5050
Bobby Bickford, *Brnch Mgr*
EMP: 52
SIC: 4212 Delivery service, vehicular
HQ: Dyno Nobel Transportation, Inc
6440 S Millrock Dr # 150
Salt Lake City UT 84121
801 364-4800

(G-1570)
EQUITY LODGING LLC
Also Called: Comfort Inn
2327 Southgate Pkwy (43725-3035)
PHONE................................740 435-0427
Tim R Longstreth, *Pr*
Tori Neptune, *Acctnt*
Tim R Longstreth, *Prin*
EMP: 31 **EST:** 1998
SALES (est): 522.56K **Privately Held**
Web: www.choicehotels.com
SIC: 7011 Hotels and motels

(G-1571)
G M N TRI CNTY CMNTY ACTION CM
Also Called: G M N
60901 Beech Grove Ln (43725-8909)
PHONE................................740 732-2388
Kay Davis, *Dir*
EMP: 32
SALES (corp-wide): 8.64MM **Privately Held**
Web: www.gmntrico.org
SIC: 8351 Head Start center, except in conjunction with school
PA: G M N Tri County Community Action Committee
615 North St
Caldwell OH 43724
740 732-2388

(G-1572)
GOODWILL INDS CENTL OHIO INC
Also Called: Goodwill Industries
1712 Southgate Pkwy (43725-3024)
PHONE................................740 439-7000
Vickie Frick, *Mgr*
EMP: 36
SALES (corp-wide): 59.87MM **Privately Held**
Web: www.goodwillcolumbus.org
SIC: 8699 8331 5932 Charitable organization; Vocational rehabilitation agency; Used merchandise stores
PA: Goodwill Industries Of Central Ohio, Inc.
605 S Front St
Columbus OH 43215
614 294-5181

(G-1573)
GUERNSEY HEALTH SYSTEMS (HQ)
1341 Clark St (43725-9614)
P.O. Box 610 (43725-0610)
PHONE................................740 439-3561
Philip Hearing, *CEO*
Philip Hearing, *Pr*
Donald P Huelskamp, *
EMP: 550 **EST:** 1985
SQ FT: 211,000
SALES (est): 442.45K
SALES (corp-wide): 107.1MM **Privately Held**

Web: www.ohiohealth.com
SIC: 4119 8062 8052 Local passenger transportation, nec; General medical and surgical hospitals; Intermediate care facilities
PA: Southeastern Ohio Regional Medical Center
1341 N Clark St
Cambridge OH 43725
740 439-3561

(G-1574)
HUNTINGTON NATIONAL BANK
Also Called: Cambridge Savings Bank
175 N 11th St (43725-2459)
PHONE................................740 439-5533
Monica Rocker, *Mgr*
EMP: 41
SALES (corp-wide): 10.84B **Publicly Held**
Web: www.huntington.com
SIC: 6029 Commercial banks, nec
HQ: The Huntington National Bank
41 S High St
Columbus OH 43215
614 480-4293

(G-1575)
MEDICAL ASSOC CAMBRIDGE INC
1515 Maple Dr (43725-1162)
PHONE................................740 439-3515
Mark T Goggin, *Prin*
Douglas A Rush, *
Patrick D Goggin, *
Kayode Ojedele, *
EMP: 55 **EST:** 1974
SALES (est): 5.25MM **Privately Held**
Web: www.medicalassociatescare.com
SIC: 8011 General and family practice, physician/surgeon

(G-1576)
MOSSER GLASS INC
9279 Cadiz Rd (43725-9564)
PHONE................................740 439-1827
Timmy J Mosser, *Pr*
Thomas R Mosser, *
Timmy J Mosser, *VP*
Mindy Hartly, *
▲ **EMP:** 30 **EST:** 1961
SALES (est): 2.36MM **Privately Held**
Web: www.mosserglass.com
SIC: 3229 5199 5719 Novelty glassware; Glassware, novelty; Glassware

(G-1577)
NICOLOZAKES TRCKG & CNSTR INC
8555 Georgetown Rd (43725-8866)
P.O. Box 670 (43725-0670)
PHONE................................740 432-5648
William Nicolozakes, *Pr*
William A Nicolozakes, *
Dean S Nicolozakes, *
James A Nicolozakes, *
Basil J Nicolozakes, *
EMP: 30 **EST:** 1953
SQ FT: 32,600
SALES (est): 4.71MM **Privately Held**
Web: www.nicolozakes.com
SIC: 1541 4212 4213 1794 Industrial buildings, new construction, nec; Light haulage and cartage, local; Heavy machinery transport; Excavation and grading, building construction

(G-1578)
OHIO BRIDGE CORPORATION
Also Called: U.S. Bridge
201 Wheeling Ave (43725-2256)
P.O. Box 757 (43725-0757)
PHONE................................740 432-6334
Daniel Rogovin, *CEO*

Richard Rogovin, *
▼ **EMP:** 140 **EST:** 1952
SQ FT: 250,000
SALES (est): 22.38MM **Privately Held**
Web: www.usbridge.com
SIC: 1622 3449 Bridge construction; Bars, concrete reinforcing; fabricated steel

(G-1579)
PICOMA INDUSTRIES INC
9208 Jeffrey Dr (43725-9417)
PHONE................................740 432-2146
Jim Hays, *Pr*
Tony Frabotta, *VP*
Tim Feeney, *Dir*
EMP: 29 **EST:** 1988
SALES (est): 1.07MM **Privately Held**
Web: www.picoma.com
SIC: 5074 Plumbing and heating valves
PA: Zekelman Industries, Inc.
227 W Monroe St Ste 2600
Chicago IL 60606

(G-1580)
RED CARPET HEALTH CARE CENTER
8420 Georgetown Rd (43725-9770)
PHONE................................740 439-4401
Vern Beynon, *Admn*
Dale Shonk, *VP*
Arnold Tuber, *Sec*
EMP: 27 **EST:** 1976
SQ FT: 35,000
SALES (est): 5.09MM
SALES (corp-wide): 12.43MM **Privately Held**
Web: www.redcarpethealthcarecenter.com
SIC: 8059 8051 Rest home, with health care; Skilled nursing care facilities
PA: S.F.T. Health Care Inc
5890 Mayfair Rd
Canton OH 44720
330 499-6358

(G-1581)
SALO INC
Also Called: Interim Services
2146 Southgate Pkwy Ste 7 (43725-3096)
PHONE................................740 432-2966
Lisa Moore, *Mgr*
EMP: 281
SALES (corp-wide): 52.16MM **Privately Held**
Web: www.interimhealthcare.com
SIC: 8082 Home health care services
PA: Salo, Inc.
300 W Wilson Brdge Rd Ste
Columbus OH 43085
614 436-9404

(G-1582)
SOUTHEASTERN EQUIPMENT CO INC (PA)
10874 E Pike Rd (43725-9615)
P.O. Box 536 (43725-0536)
PHONE................................740 432-6303
▲ **EMP:** 45 **EST:** 1957
SALES (est): 83.65MM **Privately Held**
Web: www.southeasternequip.com
SIC: 5082 General construction machinery and equipment

(G-1583)
SOUTHSTERN OHIO PHYSICIANS INC
Also Called: Sarap, Michael D MD
1230 Clark St Apt B (43725-9807)
PHONE................................740 432-5685
Michael D Sarap, *Pr*
EMP: 27 **EST:** 1966

SALES (est): 651.18K Privately Held
Web: www.seophysicians.com
SIC: 8011 Surgeon

(G-1584)
SOUTHSTERN OHIO RGONAL MED CTR (PA)
Also Called: Southeastern Med
1341 Clark St (43725)
P.O. Box 610 (43725)
PHONE.................................740 439-3561
Wendy Elliott, Pr
Raymond Chorey, *
Donald Huelskamp, *
EMP: 40 EST: 1954
SQ FT: 211,000
SALES (est): 107.1MM
SALES (corp-wide): 107.1MM Privately Held
Web: www.ohiohealth.com
SIC: 8062 General medical and surgical hospitals

(G-1585)
SUPERIOR MED LLC (PA)
1251 Clark St (43725-9612)
P.O. Box 501 (43725-0501)
PHONE.................................740 439-8839
EMP: 33 EST: 1990
SALES (est): 2.93MM Privately Held
Web: www.ohiohealth.com
SIC: 8062 General medical and surgical hospitals

(G-1586)
US HOTEL OSP VENTURES LLC
Also Called: Salt Fork Lodge Conference Ctr
Us Route 22 E (43725)
PHONE.................................740 435-9000
EMP: 29
SALES (corp-wide): 5.81MM Privately Held
Web: www.saltforkparklodge.com
SIC: 7011 Resort hotel
PA: U.S. Hotel Osp Ventures, Llc
3200 W Maple St Ste 2001
Sioux Falls SD 57107
605 334-2371

(G-1587)
VAN DYNE-CROTTY CO
Also Called: Spirit
1305 Marquand Ave (43725-2934)
PHONE.................................740 432-7503
Don Holt, Mgr
EMP: 55
SALES (corp-wide): 16MM Privately Held
Web: www.getspirit.com
SIC: 7218 Industrial uniform supply
PA: Van Dyne-Crotty Co.
2150 Fairwood Ave
Columbus OH 43207
614 684-0048

(G-1588)
ZEKELMAN INDUSTRIES INC
Also Called: Wheatland Tube Company
9208 Jeffrey Dr (43725-9417)
PHONE.................................740 432-2146
Ned Feeney, Pr
EMP: 186
SQ FT: 58,000
Web: www.zekelman.com
SIC: 3317 3498 5074 3644 Pipes, seamless steel; Fabricated pipe and fittings; Plumbing fittings and supplies; Noncurrent-carrying wiring devices
PA: Zekelman Industries, Inc.
227 W Monroe St Ste 2600
Chicago IL 60606

Camden
Preble County

(G-1589)
COUNCIL ON RUR SVC PRGRAMS INC
8263 Us Route 127 (45311-8798)
PHONE.................................937 452-1090
EMP: 56
SALES (corp-wide): 19.72MM Privately Held
Web: www.councilonruralservices.org
SIC: 8351 Head Start center, except in conjunction with school
PA: Council On Rural Service Programs, Inc.
201 Robert M Davis Pkwy B
Piqua OH 45356
937 778-5220

Camp Dennison
Hamilton County

(G-1590)
AIM MRO LLC
8500 Glendale Milford Rd (45111-9714)
PHONE.................................513 831-2938
Barry F Bucher, Managing Member
▲ EMP: 40 EST: 2001
SALES (est): 9.4MM Privately Held
Web: www.aimmro.com
SIC: 5088 Aircraft and space vehicle supplies and parts
PA: Aim Mro Holdings, Llc
375 Center St 175
Miamiville OH 45147

Campbell
Mahoning County

(G-1591)
APBN INC
670 Robinson Rd (44405-2031)
P.O. Box 637 (44405-0637)
PHONE.................................724 964-8252
Diane Katsourakis, Pr
Vasalis Katsourakis, *
Nikita Katsourakis, *
EMP: 37 EST: 2005
SALES (est): 2.14MM Privately Held
Web: www.apbninc.com
SIC: 1721 Bridge painting

Canal Fulton
Stark County

(G-1592)
AVALON FOODSERVICE INC
1 Avalon Dr (44614-8893)
P.O. Box 536 (44614-0536)
PHONE.................................330 854-4551
Andrew Schroer, Pr
EMP: 120 EST: 1957
SQ FT: 100,000
SALES (est): 56.89MM Privately Held
Web: www.avalonfoods.com
SIC: 5142 5149 5169 5113 Packaged frozen goods; Canned goods: fruit, vegetables, seafood, meats, etc.; Chemicals and allied products, nec; Industrial and personal service paper

(G-1593)
BJAAM ENVIRONMENTAL INC
Also Called: Bjaam Environmental
472 Elm Ridge Ave (44614-9369)
P.O. Box 523 (44614-0523)
PHONE.................................330 854-5300
Brett Urian, Pr
Troy Schultz, *
Williams Pidcock, *
Sean Hetrick, *
EMP: 50 EST: 1989
SQ FT: 26,000
SALES (est): 8.84MM Privately Held
Web: www.bjaam.com
SIC: 8748 Environmental consultant

(G-1594)
SKIPCO FINANCIAL ADJUSTERS INC (PA)
Also Called: Skipco
700 Elm Ridge Ave (44614-9380)
P.O. Box 606 (44614-0606)
PHONE.................................330 854-4800
Robert Blowers, Pr
Cynthia Blowers, *
Keith Blowers, *
EMP: 60 EST: 1978
SQ FT: 17,000
SALES (est): 9.59MM
SALES (corp-wide): 9.59MM Privately Held
Web: www.skipco.com
SIC: 7389 5521 Auctioneers, fee basis; Used car dealers

(G-1595)
USA PRECAST CONCRETE LIMITED
801 Elm Ridge Ave (44614-9396)
P.O. Box 613 (44614-0613)
PHONE.................................330 854-9600
Jeffrey Augustine, VP
Timothy Gesaman, *
Krista Gesaman, *
Jeff Augustine, *
Wendy Potashnik, *
EMP: 60 EST: 2016
SALES (est): 3.18MM Privately Held
Web: www.usaprecast.com
SIC: 1771 Concrete work

(G-1596)
ZVN PROPERTIES INC
Also Called: Zvn Properties
957 Cherry St E (44614-9609)
P.O. Box 583 (44614-0583)
PHONE.................................330 854-5890
Rick Hoback, Pr
Richard Hoback, *
Bryan Lysikowski, *
David Dolan, *
EMP: 65 EST: 2007
SQ FT: 44,000
SALES (est): 10.03MM Privately Held
Web: www.zvnproperties.com
SIC: 6512 Nonresidential building operators

Canal Winchester
Franklin County

(G-1597)
A K ATHLETIC EQUIPMENT INC
8015 Howe Industrial Pkwy (43110-7890)
PHONE.................................614 920-3069
Angela Katz, Pr
EMP: 34 EST: 1993
SQ FT: 32,000
SALES (est): 7.5MM Privately Held
Web: www.akathletics.com

SIC: 3496 5091 Mats and matting; Gymnasium equipment

(G-1598)
ATWOOD ROPE MANUFACTURING INC
121 N Trine St (43110-1154)
PHONE.................................614 920-0534
Curtis Atwood, Pr
Curtis Atwood, Owner
▲ EMP: 40 EST: 2000
SALES (est): 3.87MM Privately Held
Web: www.atwoodrope.com
SIC: 5091 5085 2298 Boat accessories and parts; Rope, cord, and thread; Ropes and fiber cables

(G-1599)
BREWDOG FRANCHISING LLC
Also Called: Brewdog
96 Gender Rd (43110-7539)
PHONE.................................614 908-3051
EMP: 50 EST: 2020
SALES (est): 4.44MM Privately Held
Web: www.brewdog.com
SIC: 5813 6794 Bars and lounges; Franchises, selling or licensing

(G-1600)
CAPSA SOLUTIONS LLC (PA)
Also Called: Capsa Healthcare
8170 Dove Pkwy (43110-9674)
PHONE.................................800 437-6633
Eric Webb, Pr
Jeff Strickler, *
◆ EMP: 150 EST: 1967
SQ FT: 110,000
SALES (est): 111.12MM
SALES (corp-wide): 111.12MM Privately Held
Web: www.capsahealthcare.com
SIC: 5047 Medical equipment and supplies

(G-1601)
CENTRAL OHIO PRIMARY CARE
6201 Gender Rd (43110-2007)
PHONE.................................614 834-8042
EMP: 36
Web: www.copcp.com
SIC: 8011 General and family practice, physician/surgeon
PA: Central Ohio Primary Care Physicians, Inc.
655 Africa Rd
Westerville OH 43082

(G-1602)
CITY OF CANAL WINCHESTER
22 S Trine St (43110-1230)
PHONE.................................614 837-8276
Jennifer Paswell, Dir
EMP: 77
Web: www.canalwinchesterohio.gov
SIC: 8322 9111 Senior citizens' center or association; Mayors' office
PA: City Of Canal Winchester
45 E Waterloo St
Canal Winchester OH 43110
614 837-6937

(G-1603)
DAVID EVANGELICAL LUTHERAN CH
Also Called: David Lutheran Chrn Pre-School
300 Groveport Pike (43110-9747)
PHONE.................................614 920-3517
Charlotte Nau, Pr
EMP: 30 EST: 1955
SALES (est): 455.21K Privately Held
Web: www.davidlutheran.org

Canal Winchester - Franklin County (G-1604)   GEOGRAPHIC SECTION

SIC: **8351** 8211 Child day care services; Private elementary and secondary schools

(G-1604)
DYSART CORPORATION
48 Elm St (43110-1167)
PHONE................614 837-1201
▲ EMP: 50
Web: www.dysartinc.com
SIC: **4783** Packing goods for shipping

(G-1605)
EMBASSY WINCHESTER LLC
Also Called: Winchester Care Rehabilitation
36 Lehman Dr (43110-1006)
PHONE................614 834-2273
EMP: 99 EST: 2020
SALES (est): 1.61MM **Privately Held**
SIC: **8051** Skilled nursing care facilities

(G-1606)
FEECORP CORPORATION (PA)
Also Called: F E E
7995 Allen Rd Nw (43110-9206)
P.O. Box 447 (43147-0447)
PHONE................614 837-3010
Karen Fee, *Pr*
Dawn Fee, *
Casandra Fee, *
EMP: 50 EST: 1992
SQ FT: 2,400
SALES (est): 10.17MM **Privately Held**
SIC: **1799** Exterior cleaning, including sandblasting

(G-1607)
GENERAL TEMPERATURE CTRL INC
970 W Walnut St (43110-9757)
PHONE................614 837-3888
Bob Billings, *CEO*
Brenda Billings, *
L R Billings Junior, *Prin*
Patricia Ann Woodard, *
Brian Ray Woodard, *
EMP: 30 EST: 1987
SQ FT: 10,000
SALES (est): 9.19MM **Privately Held**
Web: www.gtc.cc
SIC: **1711** Mechanical contractor

(G-1608)
HOME INSTEAD SENIOR CARE
9263 Lithopolis Rd Nw (43110-8996)
PHONE................614 432-8524
EMP: 40 EST: 1996
SALES (est): 907.72K **Privately Held**
Web: www.homeinstead.com
SIC: **8082** Home health care services

(G-1609)
HUNTINGTON NATIONAL BANK
37 S High St (43110-1212)
PHONE................614 480-0008
Fred C Ballard, *Asst VP*
EMP: 36
SQ FT: 37,460
SALES (corp-wide): 10.84B **Publicly Held**
Web: www.huntington.com
SIC: **6029** 6021 Commercial banks, nec; National commercial banks
HQ: The Huntington National Bank
41 S High St
Columbus OH 43215
614 480-4293

(G-1610)
KINDRED NURSING CENTERS E LLC
Also Called: MGM Hlth Care Wnchster Pl Nrsi
36 Lehman Dr (43110-1006)
PHONE................614 837-9666

Seth White, *Admn*
EMP: 98
SALES (corp-wide): 13.68B **Privately Held**
Web: www.kindredhospitals.com
SIC: **8051** Convalescent home with continuous nursing care
HQ: Kindred Nursing Centers East, L.L.C.
680 S 4th St
Louisville KY 40202
502 596-7300

(G-1611)
KLAMFOTH INC
6630 Hill Rd (43110-1306)
PHONE................614 833-5007
Pam Klamfoth, *Pr*
Scott Klamfoth, *
EMP: 30 EST: 1984
SALES (est): 936.01K **Privately Held**
Web: www.klamfothinc.com
SIC: **0781** 0782 4959 Landscape planning services; Lawn care services; Snowplowing

(G-1612)
MEDVET ASSOCIATES LLC
Also Called: Medvet Diley Hill
9696 Basil Western Rd (43110-9202)
PHONE................614 829-5070
Jo Colliton, *Brnch Mgr*
EMP: 97
Web: www.medvet.com
SIC: **0742** Animal hospital services, pets and other animal specialties
PA: Medvet Associates, Llc
350 E Wilson Bridge Rd
Worthington OH 43085

(G-1613)
MILL TECH LLC
6355 Rutherford Dr (43110-3206)
PHONE................614 496-9778
Kevin Henderson, *Pt*
Kevin L Henderson, *Managing Member*
EMP: 30 EST: 2000
SQ FT: 20,000
SALES (est): 4.47MM **Privately Held**
Web: www.milltechllc.com
SIC: **1751** 5712 Cabinet building and installation; Cabinet work, custom

(G-1614)
ONEIL TENT CO INC
895 W Walnut St (43110-9436)
PHONE................614 837-6352
Dennis Ritchey, *Pr*
Brian Ritchey, *
Fred Waller, *
Tim Ritchey, *
EMP: 47 EST: 1960
SQ FT: 40,000
SALES (est): 1.37MM **Privately Held**
Web: www.oneiltents.com
SIC: **7359** Party supplies rental services

(G-1615)
PROMPT PRVATE NURSING CARE INC
26 W Waterloo St (43110-1140)
PHONE................614 834-1105
Betsy Feeney, *Pr*
Dan Feeney, *
EMP: 66 EST: 1989
SALES (est): 1.33MM **Privately Held**
SIC: **8082** Home health care services

(G-1616)
SEALS CONSTRUCTION INC
10283 Busey Rd Nw (43110-9629)
PHONE................614 836-7200
Andy Seals, *Pr*
EMP: 47 EST: 1999

SQ FT: 12,000
SALES (est): 3.59MM **Privately Held**
Web: www.sealscoinc.com
SIC: **1794** Excavation and grading, building construction

(G-1617)
TRI COUNTY FAMILY PHYSICIANS
11925 Lithopolis Rd Nw (43110-9535)
PHONE................614 837-6363
Fred Hennis, *Prin*
EMP: 31 EST: 1977
SALES (est): 559.09K **Privately Held**
Web: www.copcp.com
SIC: **8011** General and family practice, physician/surgeon

(G-1618)
TS TRIM INDUSTRIES INC (DH)
6380 Canal St (43110-9640)
PHONE................614 837-4114
▲ EMP: 400 EST: 1986
SALES (est): 84.46MM **Privately Held**
Web: www.tstech.com
SIC: **5013** 3465 3714 3083 Automotive supplies and parts; Moldings or trim, automobile; stamped metal; Motor vehicle parts and accessories; Laminated plastics plate and sheet
HQ: Ts Tech Americas, Inc.
8458 E Broad St
Reynoldsburg OH 43068
614 575-4100

(G-1619)
WINCHESTER PLACE LEASING LLC
Also Called: Winchester Care Rehabilitation
36 Lehman Dr (43110-1099)
PHONE................614 834-2273
Eli Gunzburg, *Mgr*
EMP: 99 EST: 2017
SQ FT: 52,214
SALES (est): 7.3MM
SALES (corp-wide): 7.3MM **Privately Held**
Web: www.embassyhealthcare.net
SIC: **8051** Mental retardation hospital
PA: Aspenwood Holdings, Llc
25550 Chagrin Blvd # 103
Beachwood OH 44122
216 367-1214

(G-1620)
WORLD HARVEST CHURCH INC (PA)
Also Called: Breakthrough Media Ministries
4595 Gender Rd (43110-9149)
P.O. Box 428 (43110-0428)
PHONE................614 837-1990
Pastor Rodney Parsley, *Prin*
EMP: 200 EST: 1976
SQ FT: 200,000
SALES (est): 23.49MM
SALES (corp-wide): 23.49MM **Privately Held**
Web: www.whc.life
SIC: **7812** 2731 Video tape production; Books, publishing and printing

---

Canfield
Mahoning County

(G-1621)
BLOOD & CANCER CENTER INC
3695 Boardman Canfield Rd (44406-9009)
PHONE................330 533-3040
Sudershan Garg, *Pr*
Eledath Krishnan, *VP*
EMP: 31 EST: 1988
SALES (est): 2.42MM **Privately Held**
Web: www.regionalbccenter.com

SIC: **8011** Oncologist

(G-1622)
BODINE PERRY LLC (PA)
Also Called: Dgperry, Pllc
3711 Starrs Centre Dr Ste 2 (44406)
PHONE................330 702-8100
EMP: 50
SALES (est): 7.19MM **Privately Held**
Web: www.dgperry.com
SIC: **8721** 8742 Certified public accountant; Financial consultant

(G-1623)
CANFIELD METAL COATING CORP
460 W Main St (44406-1434)
PHONE................330 702-3876
Ronald W Jandrokovic, *Pr*
George S Bokros, *
Paul Pirko, *
EMP: 52 EST: 2001
SALES (est): 12.41MM
SALES (corp-wide): 1.91B **Publicly Held**
Web: www.materialsciencescorp.com
SIC: **3479** 5051 Galvanizing of iron, steel, or end-formed products; Metals service centers and offices
HQ: Handy & Harman Ltd.
590 Madison Ave Fl 32
New York NY 10022

(G-1624)
CASALS HAIR SALON INC (PA)
Also Called: Casal Day Spa and Salon
4030 Boardman Canfield Rd (44406-9505)
PHONE................330 533-6766
EMP: 33 EST: 1993
SALES (est): 1.13MM **Privately Held**
Web: www.casalsspa.com
SIC: **7231** Manicurist, pedicurist

(G-1625)
CENTERFIELD INSUR FINCL CO LLC (PA) ✪
900 Blueberry Hill Dr (44406-1040)
PHONE................330 501-9719
Jason Cohen, *Managing Member*
EMP: 45 EST: 2022
SALES (est): 62.79MM
SALES (corp-wide): 62.79MM **Privately Held**
SIC: **6282** Investment advice

(G-1626)
CLEVELAND CLINIC FOUNDATION
3736 Boardman Canfield Rd Ste 1 (44406-7020)
PHONE................330 533-8350
Can Fagan, *Brnch Mgr*
EMP: 33
SALES (corp-wide): 14.48B **Privately Held**
Web: www.clevelandclinic.org
SIC: **8062** General medical and surgical hospitals
PA: The Cleveland Clinic Foundation
9500 Euclid Ave
Cleveland OH 44195
216 636-8335

(G-1627)
COY BROS INC
433 Fairground Blvd (44406-1551)
P.O. Box 416 (44406-0416)
PHONE................330 533-6864
Arlan Coy, *Pr*
Patricia Coy, *
EMP: 32 EST: 1920
SALES (est): 3.92MM **Privately Held**
Web: www.wrighthealthclinic.com

GEOGRAPHIC SECTION

Canton - Stark County (G-1649)

SIC: 4213 Trucking, except local

(G-1628)
FARMERS NAT BNK OF CANFIELD (HQ)
Also Called: Farmers National Bank
20 S Broad St (44406)
P.O. Box 555 (44406)
PHONE.................330 533-3341
Kevin Helmick, *Pr*
Carl D Culp, *
Mark R Witmer Sevp, *Chief Business Officer*
James R Vansickle, *CRO*
Troy Adair, *
EMP: 61 **EST:** 1887
SQ FT: 25,000
SALES (est): 142.61MM
SALES (corp-wide): 255.2MM **Publicly Held**
Web: www.farmersbankgroup.com
SIC: 6022 State commercial banks
PA: Farmers National Banc Corp.
20 S Broad St
Canfield OH 44406
330 533-3341

(G-1629)
FARMERS NATIONAL BANC CORP (PA)
20 S Broad St (44406)
P.O. Box 555 (44406)
PHONE.................330 533-3341
Kevin J Helmick, *Pr*
Terry A Moore, *Ch Bd*
Lance J Ciroli, *Non-Executive Chairman of the Board*
James R Smail, *Non-Executive Vice Chairman of the Board*
EMP: 59 **EST:** 1983
SALES (est): 255.2MM
SALES (corp-wide): 255.2MM **Publicly Held**
Web: www.farmersbankgroup.com
SIC: 6022 State commercial banks

(G-1630)
HERITAGE COOPERATIVE INC
364 Lisbon St (44406-1422)
P.O. Box 369 (44406-0369)
PHONE.................330 533-5551
George F Rellinger, *Ch*
EMP: 44 **EST:** 2009
SALES (est): 11.41MM **Privately Held**
Web: www.heritagecooperative.com
SIC: 5153 Grains

(G-1631)
HILL BARTH & KING LLC (PA)
Also Called: Hbk
6603 Summit Dr (44406-9509)
P.O. Box 3406 (44513-3406)
PHONE.................330 758-8613
Christopher M Allegretti, *CEO*
EMP: 50 **EST:** 1949
SQ FT: 15,000
SALES (est): 46.2MM
SALES (corp-wide): 46.2MM **Privately Held**
Web: www.hbkcpa.com
SIC: 8721 8741 Certified public accountant; Financial management for business

(G-1632)
IES SYSTEMS INC
464 Lisbon St (44406-1423)
P.O. Box 89 (44406-0089)
PHONE.................330 533-6683
Mark Brucoli, *Pr*
Rob Mcandrew, *Ex VP*
David Wigal, *
Bill Yobi, *
Kelly Weiss, *
EMP: 45 **EST:** 2000
SQ FT: 27,000
SALES (est): 8.67MM **Privately Held**
Web: www.ies-us.com
SIC: 7389 3821 Design, commercial and industrial; Laboratory apparatus and furniture

(G-1633)
KALEIDOSCOPE PROJECT INC
6610 Pheasant Run Dr (44406-8742)
PHONE.................330 702-1822
Richard A Simmons, *Pr*
EMP: 100 **EST:** 2006
SALES (est): 2.25MM **Privately Held**
SIC: 8742 General management consultant

(G-1634)
L CALVIN JONES & COMPANY
3744 Starrs Centre Dr (44406-8001)
P.O. Box 159 (44406-0159)
PHONE.................330 533-1195
Alvin Miller Junior, *Pr*
EMP: 34 **EST:** 1911
SALES (est): 2.91MM **Privately Held**
Web: www.lcalvinjones.com
SIC: 6331 Fire, marine and casualty insurance and carriers

(G-1635)
MYERS EQUIPMENT CORPORATION
8860 Akron Canfield Rd (44406-8770)
PHONE.................330 533-5556
David Myers, *Pr*
▼ **EMP:** 40 **EST:** 1949
SQ FT: 40,000
SALES (est): 5.72MM **Privately Held**
Web: www.myersequip.com
SIC: 5013 Automotive supplies and parts

(G-1636)
OHIO LIVING HOLDINGS
Also Called: Ohio Lving HM Hlth Grter Yngst
6715 Tippecanoe Rd Ste E201 (44406-7120)
PHONE.................330 533-4350
Laurence C Gumina, *Prin*
Kevin Futryk, *
Paul Flannery, *
Barbara Sears, *
Zaafat Raki, *
EMP: 35 **EST:** 2010
SALES (est): 889.29K **Privately Held**
Web: www.ohioliving.org
SIC: 8051 Skilled nursing care facilities

(G-1637)
PANTHERX SPECIALTY LLC
6715 Tippecanoe Rd Ste C1 (44406-8180)
PHONE.................855 726-8479
Timothy Davis, *Brnch Mgr*
EMP: 45
SALES (corp-wide): 46.13MM **Privately Held**
Web: www.pantherxrare.com
SIC: 5122 Drugs, proprietaries, and sundries
PA: Pantherx Specialty Llc
24 Summit Park Dr Ste 101
Pittsburgh PA 15275
412 246-9858

(G-1638)
PAUL HRNCHAR FORD-MERCURY INC
Also Called: Hrnchar's Fairway Ford
366 W Main St (44406-1477)
PHONE.................330 533-3673
Paul J Hrnchar, *Pr*
EMP: 40 **EST:** 1998
SQ FT: 30,000
SALES (est): 9.82MM **Privately Held**
Web: www.fairwayfordohio.com
SIC: 5511 7539 7532 Automobiles, new and used; Automotive repair shops, nec; Body shop, automotive

(G-1639)
ROHOLT VISION INSTITUTE INC
25 Manor Hill Dr Ste 300 (44406-1537)
PHONE.................330 702-8755
Philip Roholt, *Pr*
EMP: 30
SALES (corp-wide): 3.97MM **Privately Held**
Web: www.roholtvision.com
SIC: 8011 Opthalmologist
PA: Roholt Vision Institute, Inc
5890 Mayfair Rd
Canton OH 44720
330 305-2200

(G-1640)
SCHROEDEL SCULLIN & BESTIC LLC
Also Called: Ssb Cpas
196 N Broad St Ste A (44406-1291)
PHONE.................330 533-1131
Richard Scullin, *
Gregory Bestic, *
EMP: 40 **EST:** 1980
SALES (est): 2.64MM **Privately Held**
Web: www.ssb-cpa.com
SIC: 8721 Certified public accountant

(G-1641)
SEBASTIANI TRUCKING INC
61 Railroad St (44406-1440)
PHONE.................330 286-0059
EMP: 56 **EST:** 1965
SQ FT: 2,500
SALES (est): 2.43MM **Privately Held**
SIC: 4212 Dump truck haulage

(G-1642)
SURGERY CENTER CANFIELD LLC
4147 Westford Pl (44406-8086)
PHONE.................330 449-0030
EMP: 47 **EST:** 2002
SALES (est): 8.03MM
SALES (corp-wide): 20.55B **Publicly Held**
Web: www.canfieldsc.com
SIC: 8011 Surgeon
PA: Tenet Healthcare Corporation
14201 Dallas Pkwy
Dallas TX 75254
469 893-2200

(G-1643)
THOMAS PACKER & CO (PA)
6601 Westford Pl Ste 101 (44406-7005)
PHONE.................330 533-9777
Phillip Dennison, *Pr*
Gregory L Gett, *
John Donchess, *
John Cournan, *
Patricia Czechowski, *OF AMDIN Operations*
EMP: 47 **EST:** 1923
SALES (est): 6.65MM
SALES (corp-wide): 6.65MM **Privately Held**
Web: www.packerthomas.com
SIC: 8721 Certified public accountant

(G-1644)
TIPPECANOE COUNTRY CLUB INC
Also Called: Tippecanoe Pro Shop
5870 Tippecanoe Rd (44406-9538)
P.O. Box 86 (44406-0086)
PHONE.................330 758-7518
Adnan Folloum, *Mgr*
EMP: 35 **EST:** 1941
SQ FT: 34,000
SALES (est): 2.44MM **Privately Held**
Web: www.tippecanoeccohio.com
SIC: 7997 5941 7991 5812 Country club, membership; Golf goods and equipment; Physical fitness facilities; Eating places

(G-1645)
WSB REHABILITATION SVCS INC (PA)
Also Called: Blue Sky Therapy
510 W Main St (44406-1454)
PHONE.................330 533-1338
Renee Bucci Halfhill, *Pr*
EMP: 76 **EST:** 1992
SALES (est): 23MM
SALES (corp-wide): 23MM **Privately Held**
Web: www.blueskytherapy.net
SIC: 8093 Rehabilitation center, outpatient treatment

(G-1646)
YOUNGSTOWN ORTHPEDIC ASSOC LTD
6470 Tippecanoe Rd Ste A (44406-7036)
PHONE.................330 726-1466
Robert Cutticakuo, *Dir*
James Kerrigan, *
Joseph Stephko, *
James Jamison, *
Leslie Schwendeman, *
EMP: 30 **EST:** 1969
SQ FT: 2,000
SALES (est): 6.76MM **Privately Held**
Web: www.youngstownortho.com
SIC: 8011 Orthopedic physician

Canton
Stark County

(G-1647)
3E COMPANY ENVIRONMENTAL ECOLO
Also Called: 3E COMPANY ENVIRONMENTAL, ECOLOGICAL AND ENGINEERING
4450 Belden Village St Nw Ste 407 (44718-2552)
PHONE.................330 451-4900
Janet Iglesias, *Brnch Mgr*
EMP: 112
Web: www.3eco.com
SIC: 8748 Environmental consultant
PA: 3e Company Environmental, Ecological And Engineering
3207 Grey Hawk Ct
Carlsbad CA 92010

(G-1648)
415 GROUP INC (PA)
4300 Munson St Nw Ste 100 (44718-3669)
P.O. Box 35334 (44735-5334)
PHONE.................330 492-0094
Frank Monaco, *Pr*
Scott Whetstone, *
EMP: 38 **EST:** 1981
SALES (est): 7.06MM
SALES (corp-wide): 7.06MM **Privately Held**
Web: www.415group.com
SIC: 8721 Certified public accountant

(G-1649)
4859 HILLS & DALES INC
Also Called: Canterbury Enterprises
4150 Belden Village St Nw Ste 108 (44718)
PHONE.................330 479-9175
Ron Canterbury Junior, *Pr*

(PA)=Parent Co (HQ)=Headquarters
✛ = New Business established in last 2 years

2024 Harris Ohio Services Directory

Canton - Stark County (G-1650) GEOGRAPHIC SECTION

Anna Musleve, *
EMP: 75 **EST:** 1996
SALES (est): 2.1MM **Privately Held**
SIC: 0782 Landscape contractors

(G-1650)
50 X 20 HOLDING COMPANY INC (PA)
Also Called: Schumacher Homes
2715 Wise Ave Nw (44708-1641)
PHONE.................................330 478-4500
Paul T Schumacher, *Pr*
William Schumacher, *
EMP: 57 **EST:** 1991
SQ FT: 250,000
SALES (est): 104.35MM
SALES (corp-wide): 104.35MM **Privately Held**
Web: www.schumacherhomes.com
SIC: 1521 New construction, single-family houses

(G-1651)
A BLESSED PATH INC
Also Called: Scenic View Transportation
2380 Nimishillen Church Rd Ne (44721-1026)
P.O. Box 417 (44632-0417)
PHONE.................................330 244-0657
Connor Orban, *Pr*
Aleena Orban, *
EMP: 65 **EST:** 2007
SALES (est): 836.73K **Privately Held**
Web: www.scenicviewtransportation.com
SIC: 8699 4119 Charitable organization; Limousine rental, with driver

(G-1652)
ABBOTT ELECTRIC INC (PA)
1935 Allen Ave Se (44707-3605)
PHONE.................................330 452-6601
James D Abbott, *Pr*
Michael C Abbott, *
Nancy Abbott, *
Brent R Fatzinger, *
Steve Abbott, *
EMP: 63 **EST:** 1978
SQ FT: 5,000
SALES (est): 25.29MM
SALES (corp-wide): 25.29MM **Privately Held**
Web: www.abbottelectric.com
SIC: 1731 General electrical contractor

(G-1653)
ABSOLUTE PHARMACY INC
7167 Keck Park Cir Nw (44720-6301)
PHONE.................................330 498-8200
EMP: 30 **EST:** 1995
SALES (est): 3.65MM **Privately Held**
SIC: 5122 Pharmaceuticals

(G-1654)
ACUTE CARE SPECIALTY HOSPITAL
2600 6th St Sw (44710-1702)
PHONE.................................330 363-4860
Ileen Good, *Prin*
EMP: 46 **EST:** 2009
SALES (est): 1.62MM **Privately Held**
Web: www.aultman.org
SIC: 8062 General medical and surgical hospitals

(G-1655)
ADELMANS TRUCK PARTS CORP (PA)
Also Called: Adelman's Truck Sales
2000 Waynesburg Dr Se (44707-2194)
PHONE.................................330 456-0206
Carl Adelman, *Pr*
Larry Adelman, *
♦ **EMP:** 30 **EST:** 1921
SQ FT: 120,000
SALES (est): 10.01MM
SALES (corp-wide): 10.01MM **Privately Held**
Web: www.adelmans.com
SIC: 5013 3714 Truck parts and accessories; Power transmission equipment, motor vehicle

(G-1656)
ADVANTAGE APPLIANCE SERVICES
Also Called: Absolute Health Services
7235 Whipple Ave Nw (44720-7101)
P.O. Box 497 (44232-0497)
PHONE.................................330 498-8101
Gereld Schroer Senior, *Pr*
Jerry Schroer Junior, *VP*
EMP: 34 **EST:** 1994
SQ FT: 27,000
SALES (est): 1.02MM **Privately Held**
SIC: 5047 Medical equipment and supplies

(G-1657)
ALBERT T DOMINGO MS MD INC
3120 Parkway St Nw Ste A (44708-3982)
PHONE.................................330 452-9460
Marc Fiorentino, *Prin*
EMP: 49 **EST:** 2005
SALES (est): 4MM **Privately Held**
Web: www.drdomingo.com
SIC: 8011 Gynecologist

(G-1658)
ALCO-CHEM INC
1303 Park Ave Sw (44706-5403)
PHONE.................................330 833-8551
Alco Chem, *Pr*
EMP: 34
SALES (corp-wide): 21.28MM **Privately Held**
Web: www.alco-chem.com
SIC: 7629 5113 5087 Electrical household appliance repair; Paper, wrapping or coarse, and products; Janitors' supplies
PA: Alco-Chem, Inc.
  45 N Summit St
  Akron OH 44308
  330 253-3535

(G-1659)
ALLEN-KEITH CONSTRUCTION CO (PA)
Also Called: Service Master By Allen Keith
2735 Greensburg Rd (44720-1423)
PHONE.................................330 266-2220
Daniel Hanlon, *CEO*
Thomas Hocking, *
EMP: 93 **EST:** 1975
SQ FT: 38,000
SALES (est): 10MM
SALES (corp-wide): 10MM **Privately Held**
Web: www.allenkeith.com
SIC: 7349 1541 7217 Building maintenance services, nec; Industrial buildings and warehouses; Carpet and upholstery cleaning

(G-1660)
ALLIANCE IMAGING INC
4825 Higbee Ave Nw Ste 201 (44718-2567)
PHONE.................................330 493-5100
Shawn Smith, *VP*
Randy Skiles, *
EMP: 77 **EST:** 1987
SQ FT: 5,000
SALES (est): 3.95MM
SALES (corp-wide): 825.15MM **Privately Held**
Web: www.allianceimagingbeldenvillage.com
SIC: 8071 8731 X-ray laboratory, including dental; Commercial physical research
HQ: Alliance Healthcare Services, Inc.
  18201 Von Karman Ave # 6
  Irvine CA 92612
  800 544-3215

(G-1661)
ALLURE SCENTS LLC
1405 22nd St Ne (44714-2003)
PHONE.................................330 312-2019
EMP: 31 **EST:** 2020
SALES (est): 72.94K **Privately Held**
SIC: 4119 Limousine rental, with driver

(G-1662)
ALPHA MEDIA LLC
Also Called: Whbc-FM
550 Market Ave S (44702-2112)
PHONE.................................330 456-7166
Adam Miller, *General*
EMP: 49
SALES (corp-wide): 441.62MM **Privately Held**
Web: www.alphamediausa.com
SIC: 4832 Radio broadcasting stations
HQ: Alpha Media Llc
  1211 Sw 5th Ave Ste 600
  Portland OR 97204

(G-1663)
ALTERCARE NOBLES POND INC
Also Called: Altercare of Ohio
7006 Fulton Dr Nw (44718-1521)
PHONE.................................330 834-4800
Brenda Pedro, *Admn*
EMP: 27 **EST:** 2006
SQ FT: 38,892
SALES (est): 6.38MM **Privately Held**
Web: noblespond.altercareonline.com
SIC: 8052 8051 Intermediate care facilities; Skilled nursing care facilities

(G-1664)
ALTERCARE OF OHIO INC
7235 Whipple Ave Nw (44720-7101)
P.O. Box 497 (44232-0497)
PHONE.................................330 498-8110
Gerald F Schroer, *Pr*
EMP: 48 **EST:** 1983
SALES (est): 1.06MM **Privately Held**
SIC: 8322 Rehabilitation services

(G-1665)
AMERICAN NATIONAL RED CROSS
Also Called: Red Cross
408 9th St Sw (44707-4714)
PHONE.................................330 452-1111
Sia Pope, *Ex Dir*
EMP: 41
SALES (corp-wide): 3.18B **Privately Held**
Web: www.redcross.org
SIC: 8322 Social service center
PA: The American National Red Cross
  431 18th St Nw
  Washington DC 20006
  202 737-8300

(G-1666)
AMERIDIAL INC (HQ)
4877 Higbee Ave Nw Fl 2 (44718-2566)
PHONE.................................234 542-5036
Partho Choudhury, *Pr*
James Mcgeorge, *Ch*
Matt Mcgeorge, *Ex VP*
Richard Smalley, *
EMP: 429 **EST:** 1987
SQ FT: 3,000
SALES (est): 48.77MM
SALES (corp-wide): 224.77MM **Privately Held**
Web: www.fusioncx.com
SIC: 7389 Telemarketing services
PA: Fusion Bpo Services, Inc.
  1147 E Lone Peak Ln
  Draper UT 84020
  866 581-0038

(G-1667)
ANSWERCARE LLC
4150 Belden Village St Nw Ste 307 (44718-2595)
PHONE.................................855 213-1511
Jordan P Bucar, *Managing Member*
EMP: 55 **EST:** 2012
SQ FT: 1,500
SALES (est): 1.9MM **Privately Held**
Web: www.helpathome.com
SIC: 8082 Home health care services

(G-1668)
ANTHEM INSURANCE COMPANIES INC
Also Called: Blue Cross
4150 Belden Village St Nw Ste 506 (44718-2595)
PHONE.................................330 492-2151
Eloise Walls, *Brnch Mgr*
EMP: 168
SALES (corp-wide): 171.34B **Publicly Held**
Web: www.anthem.com
SIC: 6324 Group hospitalization plans
HQ: Anthem Insurance Companies, Inc.
  220 Virginia Ave
  Indianapolis IN 46204
  317 488-6000

(G-1669)
APPALACHIAN POWER COMPANY
301 Cleveland Ave Sw (44702-1623)
P.O. Box 24400 (44701-4400)
PHONE.................................330 438-7102
EMP: 145
SALES (corp-wide): 18.9B **Privately Held**
Web: www.appalachianpower.com
SIC: 4911 Distribution, electric power
HQ: Appalachian Power Company
  1 Riverside Plz
  Columbus OH 43215
  614 716-1000

(G-1670)
ARCHER CORPORATION
Also Called: Archer Sign
1917 Henry Ave Sw (44706-2941)
PHONE.................................330 455-9995
Jerry Archer, *CEO*
Michael Minor, *
EMP: 40 **EST:** 1965
SQ FT: 70,000
SALES (est): 7.44MM **Privately Held**
Web: www.archersign.com
SIC: 1799 3993 Sign installation and maintenance; Signs and advertising specialties

(G-1671)
ASTORIA SNF INC
3537 12th St Nw (44708-3818)
PHONE.................................330 455-5500
Timothy A Chesney, *Pr*
EMP: 27 **EST:** 2010
SALES (est): 7.89MM **Privately Held**
Web: www.astoriaskilled.com
SIC: 8051 Convalescent home with continuous nursing care

GEOGRAPHIC SECTION
Canton - Stark County (G-1691)

(G-1672)
ASW GLOBAL LLC
Also Called: Asw Akron Logistic
2150 International Pkwy (44720-1373)
PHONE...................................330 899-1003
Bruce Paisley, *Brnch Mgr*
EMP: 37
SALES (corp-wide): 50.24MM **Privately Held**
Web: www.aswglobal.com
SIC: 4225 General warehousing
PA: Asw Global, Llc
3375 Gilchrist Rd
Mogadore OH 44260
330 733-6291

(G-1673)
ATLANTIC FISH & DISTRG CO
Also Called: Atlantic Food Distributors
430 6th St Se (44702-1158)
PHONE...................................330 454-1307
Stan S Manolakis, *Prin*
Debbi Vinton, *
Tiffany Manolakis, *
Barbara Wyatt, *
EMP: 41 EST: 1960
SQ FT: 3,000
SALES (est): 23.86MM **Privately Held**
Web: www.atlanticfoods.biz
SIC: 5141 Food brokers

(G-1674)
AULTCARE CORP
2600 6th St Sw (44710-1702)
PHONE...................................330 363-6360
Rick Haines, *Pr*
Allen Rovner Md, *Pr*
Paul Welch Md, *Sec*
Robert Mann, *
EMP: 300 EST: 1986
SALES (est): 59.47MM
SALES (corp-wide): 77.49MM **Privately Held**
Web: www.aultcare.com
SIC: 6324 Group hospitalization plans
PA: Aultman Health Foundation
2600 6th St Sw
Canton OH 44710
330 452-9911

(G-1675)
AULTCARE HOLDING COMPANY
2600 6th St Sw (44710)
P.O. Box 6910 (44706)
PHONE...................................330 452-9911
Rick Hang, *Pr*
EMP: 300 EST: 1986
SALES (est): 115.56MM
SALES (corp-wide): 77.49MM **Privately Held**
Web: www.aultcare.com
SIC: 6324 Group hospitalization plans
PA: Aultman Health Foundation
2600 6th St Sw
Canton OH 44710
330 452-9911

(G-1676)
AULTCARE INSURANCE COMPANY
Also Called: Aultcare
2600 6th St Sw (44710-1702)
P.O. Box 6910 (44706-0910)
PHONE...................................330 363-6360
EMP: 400 EST: 1989
SALES (est): 99.96MM
SALES (corp-wide): 77.49MM **Privately Held**
Web: www.aultcare.com
SIC: 6321 Health insurance carriers
PA: Aultman Health Foundation
2600 6th St Sw
Canton OH 44710
330 452-9911

(G-1677)
AULTMAN HEALTH FOUNDATION
6100 Whipple Ave Nw (44720-7618)
PHONE...................................330 305-6999
Cindy Spondsellar, *Mgr*
EMP: 301
SALES (corp-wide): 77.49MM **Privately Held**
Web: www.aultman.org
SIC: 8062 General medical and surgical hospitals
PA: Aultman Health Foundation
2600 6th St Sw
Canton OH 44710
330 452-9911

(G-1678)
AULTMAN HEALTH FOUNDATION (PA)
2600 6th St Sw (44710-1702)
PHONE...................................330 452-9911
Christopher Remark, *CEO*
EMP: 37 EST: 1891
SQ FT: 1,000,000
SALES (est): 77.49MM
SALES (corp-wide): 77.49MM **Privately Held**
Web: www.aultman.org
SIC: 8062 General medical and surgical hospitals

(G-1679)
AULTMAN HOSPITAL (HQ)
2600 6th St Sw (44710-1702)
PHONE...................................330 452-9911
Christopher E Remark, *CEO*
Edward J Roth Iii, *Pr*
Mark Wright, *CFO*
George Film, *Contrlr*
EMP: 2900 EST: 1891
SQ FT: 700,000
SALES (est): 586.28MM
SALES (corp-wide): 77.49MM **Privately Held**
Web: www.aultman.org
SIC: 8062 8069 8221 General medical and surgical hospitals; Specialty hospitals, except psychiatric; Colleges and universities
PA: Aultman Health Foundation
2600 6th St Sw
Canton OH 44710
330 452-9911

(G-1680)
AULTMAN MSO INC
Also Called: Aultman Mso
4455 Dressler Rd Nw Ste 201 (44718-2785)
PHONE...................................330 479-8705
EMP: 44 EST: 1997
SALES (est): 3.14MM **Privately Held**
Web: www.aultmanmso.com
SIC: 8062 General medical and surgical hospitals

(G-1681)
AULTMAN NORTH CANTON MED GROUP (PA)
Also Called: NCMF
6046 Whipple Ave Nw (44720-7616)
PHONE...................................330 433-1200
Nicholas Cleary, *CEO*
Tmothy Murphy, *
Carol Pontius, *
John Humphrey Md, *Ex Dir*
EMP: 213 EST: 1971
SQ FT: 93,398
SALES (est): 462.92K
SALES (corp-wide): 462.92K **Privately Held**
Web: www.aultmandocs.com
SIC: 8062 General medical and surgical hospitals

(G-1682)
AULTMAN NORTH CANTON MED GROUP
Also Called: Cancer Center
2600 6th St Sw (44710-1702)
PHONE...................................330 363-6333
Traci Hocking, *Brnch Mgr*
EMP: 32
SALES (corp-wide): 462.92K **Privately Held**
Web: www.aultmandocs.com
SIC: 8011 8093 Clinic, operated by physicians; Specialty outpatient clinics, nec
PA: Aultman North Canton Medical Group
6046 Whipple Ave Nw
Canton OH 44720
330 433-1200

(G-1683)
AULTMAN NORTH INC
6100 Whipple Ave Nw (44720-7618)
PHONE...................................330 305-6999
David Thiel, *VP*
Mark Wright, *CFO*
EMP: 52 EST: 1984
SALES (est): 56.3MM
SALES (corp-wide): 77.49MM **Privately Held**
Web: www.aultman.org
SIC: 8062 8011 General medical and surgical hospitals; Opthalmologist
HQ: The Aultman Hospital
2600 6th St Sw
Canton OH 44710
330 452-9911

(G-1684)
B-TEK SCALES LLC
1510 Metric Ave Sw (44706-3088)
PHONE...................................330 471-8900
Kraig F Brechbuhler, *Pr*
Andrew Brechbuhler, *
Rei Tritt, *
▲ EMP: 50 EST: 2003
SQ FT: 65,000
SALES (est): 9.13MM
SALES (corp-wide): 21.72MM **Privately Held**
Web: www.b-tek.com
SIC: 7371 5046 Software programming applications; Scales, except laboratory
PA: Brechbuhler Scales, Inc.
1424 Scales St Sw
Canton OH 44706
330 458-3060

(G-1685)
BELCAP INC
700 Tuscarawas St W (44702-2048)
P.O. Box 20910 (44701-0910)
PHONE...................................330 456-0031
Robert Belden, *Pr*
William H Belden Junior, *CEO*
James Leahy, *
EMP: 42 EST: 1991
SQ FT: 10,500
SALES (est): 862.9K
SALES (corp-wide): 140.04MM **Privately Held**
SIC: 8742 Management consulting services
HQ: The Belden Brick Company Llc
700 Tuscarawas St W Uppr
Canton OH 44702
330 456-0031

(G-1686)
BETHANY NURSING HOME INC
626 34th St Nw (44709-2977)
PHONE...................................330 492-7171
John Baum, *Pr*
Elizabeth Baum, *
Mary Meyer, *
EMP: 50 EST: 1968
SQ FT: 16,000
SALES (est): 8.42MM **Privately Held**
Web: www.bethanynh.com
SIC: 8051 Convalescent home with continuous nursing care

(G-1687)
BETTER BUS BUR SRVING CNTON RE
Also Called: BETTER BUSINESS BUREAU
1434 Cleveland Ave Nw (44703-3103)
P.O. Box 8017 (44711-8017)
PHONE...................................330 454-9401
TOLL FREE: 800
Frank Salone, *Pr*
EMP: 27 EST: 1961
SALES (est): 836.24K **Privately Held**
Web: www.bbb.org
SIC: 8611 Better Business Bureau

(G-1688)
BOCK & CLARK CORPORATION (HQ)
Also Called: Alta
4580 Stephens Cir Nw Ste 300 (44718-3644)
PHONE...................................330 665-4821
TOLL FREE: 800
EMP: 40 EST: 1973
SALES (est): 6.38MM
SALES (corp-wide): 861.74MM **Publicly Held**
Web: www.nv5.com
SIC: 6531 Real estate managers
PA: Nv5 Global, Inc.
200 S Park Rd Ste 350
Hollywood FL 33021
954 495-2112

(G-1689)
BRECHBUHLER SCALES INC (PA)
1424 Scales St Sw (44706-3096)
PHONE...................................330 458-3060
TOLL FREE: 800
Dennis Thomas, *Pr*
EMP: 50 EST: 1929
SQ FT: 90,000
SALES (est): 21.72MM
SALES (corp-wide): 21.72MM **Privately Held**
Web: www.brechbuhler.com
SIC: 7699 5046 Scale repair service; Scales, except laboratory

(G-1690)
BROOKWOOD MANAGEMENT CO LLC
Also Called: Sanctuary, The
2017 Applegrove St Nw (44720-6280)
PHONE...................................330 499-7721
Dixie Lee, *Genl Mgr*
EMP: 42
Web: www.brookwoodmgt.com
SIC: 7992 Public golf courses
PA: Brookwood Management Company, Llc
8230 Pittsburg Ave Nw
North Canton OH 44720

(G-1691)
BROOKWOOD MANAGEMENT COMPANY
Also Called: Danbury Senior Living
181 Applegrove St Ne (44720-1696)

Canton - Stark County (G-1692)

PHONE..................330 497-8718
Barbara Hebb, *Genl Mgr*
EMP: 41
Web: www.brookwoodmgt.com
SIC: 8322 Adult day care center
PA: Brookwood Management Company, Llc
8230 Pittsburg Ave Nw
North Canton OH 44720

(G-1692)
BUCKEYE PAPER CO INC
5233 Southway St Sw Ste 523
(44706-1943)
P.O. Box 711 (44648-0711)
PHONE..................330 477-5925
Edward N Bast Senior, *Pr*
Edward Bast Junior, *VP*
▼ **EMP:** 32 **EST:** 1981
SQ FT: 54,000
SALES (est): 7.06MM **Privately Held**
Web: www.buckeyepaper.com
SIC: 2679 5113 Paper products, converted, nec; Industrial and personal service paper

(G-1693)
BUCKINGHAM DLTTLE BRROUGHS LLC
4277 Munson St Nw (44718-2982)
PHONE..................330 492-8717
Joseph J Feltes, *In Charge*
EMP: 36
SALES (corp-wide): 42.23K **Privately Held**
Web: www.bdblaw.com
SIC: 8111 General practice attorney, lawyer
PA: Buckingham, Doolittle & Burroughs, Llc
3800 Embassy Pkwy
Akron OH 44333
330 376-5300

(G-1694)
CA-MJ HOTEL ASSOCIATES LTD
Also Called: Courtyard By Marriott Canton
4375 Metro Cir Nw (44720-7715)
PHONE..................330 494-6494
EMP: 61 **EST:** 1994
SALES (est): 3.47MM **Privately Held**
Web: courtyard.marriott.com
SIC: 7011 Hotels and motels
PA: Meyer Jabara Hotels, Llc
7 Kenosia Ave, Ste 2a
Danbury CT 06810

(G-1695)
CAIN MOTORS INC
Also Called: Cain B M W
6527 Whipple Ave Nw (44720-7339)
PHONE..................330 494-5588
David Cain, *Pr*
Brian Cain, *
EMP: 49 **EST:** 1952
SQ FT: 17,000
SALES (est): 8.64MM
SALES (corp-wide): 10.82MM **Privately Held**
Web: www.cainmotors.com
SIC: 5511 7538 5521 Automobiles, new and used; General automotive repair shops; Used car dealers
PA: Five Star Automotive Group, Llc
495 Watson Blvd
Warner Robins GA

(G-1696)
CANTON ALTMAN EMRGNCY PHYSCANS
2600 6th St Sw (44710-1702)
PHONE..................330 456-2695
Paul Ricks, *Pr*
EMP: 38 **EST:** 1984
SALES (est): 2.63MM **Privately Held**
Web: www.aultman.org
SIC: 8062 General medical and surgical hospitals

(G-1697)
CANTON ASSSTED LVING RHBLTTION
836 34th St Nw (44709-2947)
PHONE..................330 492-7131
EMP: 34 **EST:** 1995
SALES (est): 2.57MM **Privately Held**
Web: www.cantonchristianhome.org
SIC: 8051 8052 Convalescent home with continuous nursing care; Intermediate care facilities

(G-1698)
CANTON CHRISTIAN HOME INC
Also Called: C C H
2550 Cleveland Ave Nw (44709-3306)
PHONE..................330 456-0004
Tom K Strobl, *Ex Dir*
EMP: 88 **EST:** 1976
SQ FT: 154,000
SALES (est): 8.63MM **Privately Held**
Web: www.cantonchristianhome.org
SIC: 8051 Skilled nursing care facilities

(G-1699)
CANTON CITY SCHOOL DISTRICT
Also Called: Canton School Trnsp Dept
2030 Cleveland Ave Sw (44707-3657)
PHONE..................330 456-6710
Sheena Miller, *Dir*
EMP: 100
SALES (corp-wide): 185.95MM **Privately Held**
Web: www.ccsdistrict.org
SIC: 4151 School buses
PA: Canton City School District
305 Mckinley Ave Nw
Canton OH 44702
330 438-2500

(G-1700)
CANTON COUNTRY DAY SCHOOL
3000 Demington Ave Nw (44718-3399)
PHONE..................330 453-8279
David Costello, *Headmaster*
EMP: 48 **EST:** 1964
SQ FT: 30,000
SALES (est): 2.95MM **Privately Held**
Web: www.cantoncountryday.org
SIC: 8211 8351 Private elementary school; Child day care services

(G-1701)
CANTON FLOORS INC
Also Called: CFI Interiors
3944 Fulton Dr Nw (44718-3094)
PHONE..................330 492-1121
Rollie L Layfield, *Pr*
Wayne Kroll, *
Gary W Frank, *
I K Sapienza, *
EMP: 40 **EST:** 1951
SQ FT: 15,200
SALES (est): 12.39MM **Privately Held**
SIC: 1542 Commercial and office buildings, renovation and repair

(G-1702)
CANTON MONTESSORI ASSOCIATION
Also Called: Canton Montessori School
125 15th St Nw (44703-3207)
PHONE..................330 452-0148
Pam Butler, *Dir*
EMP: 44 **EST:** 1968
SALES (est): 903.51K **Privately Held**
Web: www.cantonmontessori.org

SIC: 8351 Preschool center

(G-1703)
CANTON OPHTHALMOLOGY ASSOC INC
2600 Tuscarawas St W Ste 200 (44708-4693)
PHONE..................330 456-0047
Frank J Weinstock Md, *Pr*
Doctor Jamie Zucker, *Sec*
EMP: 40 **EST:** 1971
SALES (est): 4.98MM **Privately Held**
Web: www.coaeye.com
SIC: 8011 Opthalmologist

(G-1704)
CANTON RHBLTTION NRSING CTR LL
Also Called: Hall Fame Rhbltion Nrsing Ctr
2714 13th St Nw (44708-3121)
PHONE..................330 456-2842
Isaak Markovits, *Mgr*
EMP: 27 **EST:** 2020
SALES (est): 1.48MM **Privately Held**
SIC: 8741 Nursing and personal care facility management

(G-1705)
CANTON SCHL EMPLYEES FDRAL CR (PA)
1380 Market Ave N (44714-2606)
PHONE..................330 452-9801
Robert Hallier, *Pr*
EMP: 36 **EST:** 1938
SALES (est): 27.64MM
SALES (corp-wide): 27.64MM **Privately Held**
Web: www.csefcu.com
SIC: 6061 Federal credit unions

(G-1706)
CENTRAL ALLIED ENTERPRISES INC (PA)
1243 Raff Rd Sw (44710-1498)
P.O. Box 80449 (44708-0449)
PHONE..................330 477-6751
EMP: 47 **EST:** 1929
SALES (est): 21.96MM
SALES (corp-wide): 21.96MM **Privately Held**
Web: www.shellyco.com
SIC: 1611 2951 1442 Highway and street construction; Asphalt and asphaltic paving mixtures (not from refineries); Construction sand and gravel

(G-1707)
CENTRAL WHSE OPERATIONS INC
2207 Kimball Rd Se (44707-3631)
PHONE..................330 453-3709
Ronald R Sibila, *Ch Bd*
Douglas J Sibila, *
Dan Stemple, *
Larry P Kelley, *
EMP: 53 **EST:** 2007
SALES (est): 12.68MM **Privately Held**
Web: www.peoplesservices.com
SIC: 4225 General warehousing
PA: Peoples Services, Inc.
2207 Kimball Rd Se
Canton OH 44707

(G-1708)
CHILD ADLSCENT BEHAVIORAL HLTH (PA)
919 2nd St Ne (44704-1132)
PHONE..................330 454-7917
Michael Johnson, *Ex Dir*
Lillian Blosfield, *
EMP: 50 **EST:** 1976

SALES (est): 8.59MM
SALES (corp-wide): 8.59MM **Privately Held**
Web: www.childandadolescent.org
SIC: 8093 Mental health clinic, outpatient

(G-1709)
CINTAS CORPORATION NO 2
Also Called: Cintas
3865 Highland Park Nw (44720-4537)
P.O. Box 3010 (44720-8010)
PHONE..................330 966-7800
TOLL FREE: 800
EMP: 81
SQ FT: 17,084
SALES (corp-wide): 8.82B **Publicly Held**
Web: www.cintas.com
SIC: 5084 2326 2337 Safety equipment; Work uniforms; Uniforms, except athletic: women's, misses', and juniors'
HQ: Cintas Corporation No. 2
6800 Cintas Blvd
Mason OH 45040

(G-1710)
CJU ENTERPRISES INC
2830 Cleveland Ave Nw (44709-3204)
PHONE..................330 493-1800
EMP: 65 **EST:** 1928
SALES (est): 7.98MM **Privately Held**
Web: www.amsterkirtz.com
SIC: 5194 5145 5149 Cigarettes; Confectionery; Groceries and related products, nec

(G-1711)
CLAYS HERITAGE CARPET INC (PA)
Also Called: Heritage Carpet & HM Dctg Ctrs
1440 N Main St (44720-1640)
PHONE..................330 497-1280
Dennis Clay, *Pr*
Paula Clay, *Sec*
EMP: 37 **EST:** 1979
SQ FT: 3,850
SALES (est): 2.42MM
SALES (corp-wide): 2.42MM **Privately Held**
Web: www.heritage-carpet.com
SIC: 5713 5211 1752 Carpets; Lumber and other building materials; Floor laying and floor work, nec

(G-1712)
CLEVELAND CLINIC MERCY HOSP
6200 Whipple Ave Nw (44720-7624)
PHONE..................330 966-8884
Eldon Jones, *Prin*
EMP: 420
SALES (corp-wide): 14.48B **Privately Held**
Web: www.cantonmercy.org
SIC: 8062 General medical and surgical hospitals
HQ: Cleveland Clinic Mercy Hospital
1320 Mercy Dr Nw
Canton OH 44708
330 489-1000

(G-1713)
CLEVELAND CLINIC MERCY HOSP
1459 Superior Ave Ne (44705-1964)
PHONE..................330 588-4892
Pam Barner, *Dir*
EMP: 421
SALES (corp-wide): 14.48B **Privately Held**
Web: www.cantonmercy.org
SIC: 8062 General medical and surgical hospitals
HQ: Cleveland Clinic Mercy Hospital
1320 Mercy Dr Nw
Canton OH 44708
330 489-1000

GEOGRAPHIC SECTION
Canton - Stark County (G-1735)

(G-1714)
CLEVELAND CLINIC MERCY HOSP
Also Called: Mercy Medical Center Hospice
4369 Whipple Ave Nw (44718-2643)
PHONE.................................330 649-4380
Maria Thompson, *Dir*
EMP: 481
SALES (corp-wide): 14.48B **Privately Held**
Web: www.cantonmercy.org
SIC: 8062 General medical and surgical hospitals
HQ: Cleveland Clinic Mercy Hospital
 1320 Mercy Dr Nw
 Canton OH 44708
 330 489-1000

(G-1715)
CLEVELAND CLINIC MERCY HOSP
Also Called: Mercy Medical Center
1320 Mercy Dr Nw (44708-2614)
PHONE.................................330 489-1329
EMP: 301
SALES (corp-wide): 14.48B **Privately Held**
Web: www.cantonmercy.org
SIC: 8062 General medical and surgical hospitals
HQ: Cleveland Clinic Mercy Hospital
 1320 Mercy Dr Nw
 Canton OH 44708
 330 489-1000

(G-1716)
CLEVELAND CLINIC MERCY HOSP
Also Called: Mercy Medical Center Hospice
1320 Mercy Dr Nw (44708-2614)
PHONE.................................330 492-8803
EMP: 421
SALES (corp-wide): 14.48B **Privately Held**
Web: www.cantonmercy.org
SIC: 8062 General medical and surgical hospitals
HQ: Cleveland Clinic Mercy Hospital
 1320 Mercy Dr Nw
 Canton OH 44708
 330 489-1000

(G-1717)
CLEVELAND CLINIC MERCY HOSP (HQ)
1320 Mercy Dr Nw (44708-2614)
PHONE.................................330 489-1000
Timothy Crone, *Pr*
Carolyn Capuano, *
David Gormsen, *
Barbara Yingling, *
David Stewart, *
EMP: 40 **EST:** 2019
SQ FT: 1,000,000
SALES (est): 320.54MM
SALES (corp-wide): 14.48B **Privately Held**
Web: www.cantonmercy.org
SIC: 8062 General medical and surgical hospitals
PA: The Cleveland Clinic Foundation
 9500 Euclid Ave
 Cleveland OH 44195
 216 636-8335

(G-1718)
COMMQUEST SERVICES INC
Also Called: COMMUNITY SERVICES OF STARK CO
625 Cleveland Ave Nw (44702-1805)
PHONE.................................330 455-0374
John Kaminiski, *Pr*
Jeffrey Bigler, *
Keith Hochadel, *
Richard Craig, *
Shannon English-hexamer, *VP*
EMP: 103 **EST:** 1919
SQ FT: 8,500
SALES (est): 22.88MM **Privately Held**
Web: www.commquest.org
SIC: 8322 8742 Family service agency; Management consulting services

(G-1719)
COMMUNICARE HEALTH SVCS INC
Also Called: Pines Healthcare Center, The
3015 17th St Nw (44708-6004)
PHONE.................................330 454-6508
Kim Frankberger, *Admn*
EMP: 42
SALES (corp-wide): 392.92MM **Privately Held**
Web: www.communicarehealth.com
SIC: 8051 Convalescent home with continuous nursing care
PA: Communicare Health Services, Inc.
 10123 Alliance Rd
 Blue Ash OH 45242
 513 530-1654

(G-1720)
COMMUNITY RSTRTION CTRS INC ST
1432 Tuscarawas St E (44707-3166)
PHONE.................................330 456-3565
Deion Cash, *Ex Dir*
EMP: 55 **EST:** 1972
SQ FT: 9,658
SALES (est): 1.86MM **Privately Held**
SIC: 8361 Halfway group home, persons with social or personal problems

(G-1721)
CONCORDE THERAPY GROUP INC (PA)
4645 Belpar St Nw (44718-3602)
PHONE.................................330 493-4210
Timothy C Murphy, *Pr*
Mark Mottice, *
EMP: 149 **EST:** 1988
SQ FT: 21,000
SALES (est): 5.04MM **Privately Held**
Web: www.concordetherapygroup.com
SIC: 8049 8021 Physiotherapist; Offices and clinics of dentists

(G-1722)
CORRECTNAL HLTH CARE GROUP INC
4500 Atlantic Blvd Ne (44705-4374)
PHONE.................................330 454-6766
Johnathon Stump, *Pr*
EMP: 27 **EST:** 1985
SQ FT: 1,200
SALES (est): 760.24K **Privately Held**
SIC: 8049 Nurses, registered and practical

(G-1723)
COST SHARING SOLUTIONS LLC
2824 Woodlawn Ave Nw (44708-1467)
PHONE.................................330 915-6800
EMP: 38 **EST:** 2014
SALES (est): 5.67MM **Privately Held**
Web: www.costsharingsolutions.com
SIC: 8742 Marketing consulting services

(G-1724)
COUNTY OF STARK
Also Called: Stark County Engineer
5165 Southway St Sw (44706-1962)
PHONE.................................330 477-6781
Keith Bennett, *Prin*
EMP: 210
SQ FT: 20,626
SALES (corp-wide): 294.05MM **Privately Held**
Web: www.starkcountyohio.gov
SIC: 8711 Engineering services
PA: County Of Stark
 110 Central Plz S Ste 240
 Canton OH 44702
 330 451-7371

(G-1725)
COUNTY OF STARK
Also Called: Stark County Sewer Dept
1701 Mahoning Rd Ne (44705-1471)
P.O. Box 9972 (44711-0972)
PHONE.................................330 451-2303
Mike Armogida, *Mgr*
EMP: 189
SQ FT: 17,924
SALES (corp-wide): 294.05MM **Privately Held**
Web: www.starkcountyohio.gov
SIC: 4952 Sewerage systems
PA: County Of Stark
 110 Central Plz S Ste 240
 Canton OH 44702
 330 451-7371

(G-1726)
COUNTY OF STARK
Also Called: Data Processing
225 4th St Ne (44702-1256)
PHONE.................................330 451-7232
Rebecca Spilios, *Mgr*
EMP: 29
SQ FT: 7,800
SALES (corp-wide): 294.05MM **Privately Held**
Web: www.starkcountyohio.gov
SIC: 7374 9111 Data processing service; County supervisors' and executives' office
PA: County Of Stark
 110 Central Plz S Ste 240
 Canton OH 44702
 330 451-7371

(G-1727)
COUNTY OF STARK
Also Called: Mhrs Board of Stark County
121 Cleveland Ave Sw (44702-1903)
PHONE.................................330 455-6644
EMP: 119
SALES (corp-wide): 294.05MM **Privately Held**
Web: www.starkmhar.org
SIC: 8069 Drug addiction rehabilitation hospital
PA: County Of Stark
 110 Central Plz S Ste 240
 Canton OH 44702
 330 451-7371

(G-1728)
CROSS TRUCK EQUIPMENT CO INC
1801 Perry Dr Sw (44706-1923)
P.O. Box 80509 (44708-0509)
PHONE.................................330 477-8151
M Lucille Cross, *Pr*
John Cross, *
Glenn G Cross, *
Ivan Bruce Hart, *
EMP: 30 **EST:** 1950
SQ FT: 45,000
SALES (est): 9.25MM **Privately Held**
Web: www.crosstruck.com
SIC: 5084 5013 Trucks, industrial; Truck parts and accessories

(G-1729)
CUSTOM CABLE CONSTRUCTION INC
Also Called: Custom Utilicom
3670 Progress St Ne (44705-4438)
P.O. Box 7495 (44705-0495)
PHONE.................................330 351-1207
Anthony Chirumbolo, *CEO*
George Chirumbolo, *
Leeann Chirumbolo, *
EMP: 60 **EST:** 2004
SQ FT: 16,000
SALES (est): 11.66MM **Privately Held**
SIC: 1623 Transmitting tower (telecommunication) construction

(G-1730)
D & L ENERGY INC
3930 Fulton Dr Nw Ste 200 (44718-3040)
PHONE.................................330 270-1201
Ben W Lupo, *CEO*
Susan A Faith, *Pr*
EMP: 35 **EST:** 1986
SQ FT: 13,637
SALES (est): 2.33MM **Privately Held**
SIC: 1311 Natural gas production

(G-1731)
DAMARC INC
Also Called: Harding Park Cycle
4330 Kirby Ave Ne (44705-4348)
PHONE.................................330 454-6171
Daniel Harding, *Pr*
EMP: 28 **EST:** 1984
SQ FT: 40,000
SALES (est): 4.22MM **Privately Held**
Web: www.parkcycle.com
SIC: 5571 7699 Motorcycles; Motorcycle repair service

(G-1732)
DAY KETTERER LTD (PA)
200 Market Ave N Ste 300 (44702-1436)
P.O. Box 24213 (44701-4213)
PHONE.................................330 455-0173
James R Blake, *Pt*
EMP: 52 **EST:** 1872
SQ FT: 35,000
SALES (est): 9.96MM
SALES (corp-wide): 9.96MM **Privately Held**
Web: www.dayketterer.com
SIC: 8111 General practice law office

(G-1733)
DEHOFF AGENCY INC
Also Called: Prudential Dehoff Realtors
821 S Main St (44720-3197)
PHONE.................................330 499-8153
Robert J Dehoff, *Pr*
Linda Dehoff, *Sec*
EMP: 44 **EST:** 1962
SQ FT: 3,000
SALES (est): 7.89MM **Privately Held**
Web: www.dehoff.com
SIC: 6531 6552 Real estate agent, commercial; Land subdividers and developers, commercial

(G-1734)
DENTAL SUPPORT SPECIALTIES LLC
Also Called: Dss
4774 Munson St Nw (44718-3634)
PHONE.................................330 639-1333
Mary Beth Bajornas, *Managing Member*
EMP: 35 **EST:** 2012
SALES (est): 3.45MM **Privately Held**
Web: www.dentalsupportspecialties.com
SIC: 8021 Offices and clinics of dentists

(G-1735)
DETROIT DIESEL CORPORATION
515 11th St Se (44707-3811)
PHONE.................................330 430-4300
Jerry Reaves, *Mgr*
EMP: 285
SALES (corp-wide): 60.75B **Privately Held**

Canton - Stark County (G-1736) — GEOGRAPHIC SECTION

Web: www.demanddetroit.com
SIC: 5084   Engines and parts, diesel
HQ: Detroit Diesel Corporation
    13400 W Outer Dr
    Detroit MI 48239
    313 592-5000

(G-1736)
DIEBOLD SELF SERVICE SYSTEMS (PA)
5995 Mayfair Rd (44720-1511)
P.O. Box 3077 (44720-8077)
PHONE..................330 490-5099
Thomas Swidarski, CEO
▲ EMP: 600 EST: 1988
SQ FT: 1,000
SALES (est): 36.36MM Privately Held
SIC: 5049   Bank equipment and supplies

(G-1737)
DIVINE STRINGS INVESTMENT LLC
6545 Market Ave N Ste 100 (44721-2430)
PHONE..................937 241-0782
EMP: 51 EST: 2021
SALES (est): 2.2MM Privately Held
SIC: 6798   Real estate investment trusts

(G-1738)
DOWNTOWN FORD LINCOLN INC
1423 Tuscarawas St W (44702-2037)
PHONE..................330 456-2781
Donald Schneider, Pr
Brad A Black, General Vice President*
Jayne A Montgomery, *
EMP: 98 EST: 1985
SQ FT: 35,000
SALES (est): 9.37MM Privately Held
Web: www.libertyfordcanton.com
SIC: 5511 5012 7538 7532   Automobiles, new and used; Automobiles and other motor vehicles; General automotive repair shops; Collision shops, automotive

(G-1739)
EAGLE INDUSTRIAL PAINTING LLC
1311 Chantilly Cir Ne (44721-3912)
PHONE..................330 866-5965
Steve Zoumberakis, Managing Member
EMP: 30 EST: 2013
SALES (est): 2.08MM Privately Held
Web: www.eagleindustrialpainting.com
SIC: 1721   Industrial painting

(G-1740)
EARLY CHILDHOOD RESOURCE CTR
1718 Cleveland Ave Nw (44703-1214)
PHONE..................330 491-3272
Geri Ash Grove, Dir
EMP: 60 EST: 1926
SALES (est): 2.41MM Privately Held
Web: www.ecresourcecenter.org
SIC: 8361   Residential care for children

(G-1741)
EAST OHIO GAS COMPANY
Also Called: Dominion Energy Ohio
5433 West Blvd Nw (44718-1423)
PHONE..................330 266-2161
Thomas Newland, Brnch Mgr
EMP: 74
SALES (corp-wide): 39.69B Privately Held
Web: www.dominiongaschoice.com
SIC: 4924   Natural gas distribution
HQ: The East Ohio Gas Company
    1201 E 55th St
    Cleveland OH 44103
    800 362-7557

(G-1742)
EAST OHIO GAS COMPANY
Dominion Energy Ohio
4725 Southway St Sw (44706-1936)
PHONE..................330 477-9411
Nancy Mcclenaghan, Brnch Mgr
EMP: 65
SALES (corp-wide): 39.69B Privately Held
Web: www.dominiongaschoice.com
SIC: 4924   Natural gas distribution
HQ: The East Ohio Gas Company
    1201 E 55th St
    Cleveland OH 44103
    800 362-7557

(G-1743)
EAST OHIO GAS COMPANY
Dominion Energy Ohio
7015 Freedom Ave Nw (44720-7381)
PHONE..................330 499-2501
Greg Theirl, Brnch Mgr
EMP: 74
SALES (corp-wide): 39.69B Privately Held
Web: www.dominiongaschoice.com
SIC: 4924   Natural gas distribution
HQ: The East Ohio Gas Company
    1201 E 55th St
    Cleveland OH 44103
    800 362-7557

(G-1744)
ECKINGER CONSTRUCTION COMPANY
2340 Shepler Church Ave Sw (44706-3093)
PHONE..................330 453-2566
Tom Eckinger, CEO
Philip Eckinger, *
Jeremy Eckinger, *
Janice Holdsworth, *
EMP: 47 EST: 1923
SQ FT: 18,740
SALES (est): 25.26MM Privately Held
Web: www.eckinger.com
SIC: 1542   Commercial and office building, new construction

(G-1745)
EMERITUS CORPORATION
Also Called: Emeritus Assisted Living
4507 22nd St Nw Apt 33 (44708-6211)
PHONE..................330 477-5727
Sue Rohr, Brnch Mgr
EMP: 154
SALES (corp-wide): 2.83B Publicly Held
Web: www.brookdale.com
SIC: 8051   Skilled nursing care facilities
HQ: Emeritus Corporation
    6737 W Wa St Ste 2300
    Milwaukee WI 53214

(G-1746)
EMP HOLDINGS LTD
4535 Dressler Rd Nw (44718-2545)
PHONE..................330 493-4443
EMP: 48 EST: 2000
SALES (est): 6.35MM Privately Held
Web: www.usacs.com
SIC: 7363   Medical help service

(G-1747)
ENVIRITE OF OHIO INC
Also Called: Eq Ohio
2050 Central Ave Se (44707)
PHONE..................330 456-6238
Jeffrey R Feeler, Pr
Eric Gerratt, *
Simon Bell, *
Wayne Ipsen, *
EMP: 50 EST: 2001
SALES (est): 26.47MM
SALES (corp-wide): 14.96B Publicly Held
Web: www.waste.com
SIC: 4953 8734   Recycling, waste materials; Hazardous waste testing
HQ: Us Ecology Holdings, Inc.
    101 S Cptol Blvd Ste 1000
    Boise ID 83702
    208 331-8400

(G-1748)
ERIE INDEMNITY COMPANY
4690 Munson St Nw (44718-3636)
PHONE..................330 433-6300
EMP: 183
SALES (corp-wide): 3.27B Publicly Held
Web: www.erieinsurance.com
SIC: 6411 8741   Insurance agents, nec; Management services
PA: Erie Indemnity Company
    100 Erie Insurance Pl
    Erie PA 16530
    814 870-2000

(G-1749)
ERIE INSUR EXCH ACTVTIES ASSN
4690 Munson St Nw Ste A (44718-3636)
P.O. Box 9031 (44711-9031)
PHONE..................330 433-1925
Mark Hammerstein, Mgr
EMP: 32
SALES (corp-wide): 1.24B Privately Held
Web: www.erieinsurance.com
SIC: 6411   Insurance agents, nec
PA: The Erie Insurance Exchange
    Activities Association Inc
    100 Erie Insurance Pl
    Erie PA 16530
    800 458-0811

(G-1750)
ESBER BEVERAGE COMPANY
2217 Bolivar Rd Sw (44706-3099)
PHONE..................330 456-4361
TOLL FREE: 800
Gary Esber, Pr
▲ EMP: 50 EST: 1937
SQ FT: 40,000
SALES (est): 14.98MM Privately Held
Web: www.esberbeverage.com
SIC: 5181 5182 5149   Ale; Wine and distilled beverages; Beverages, except coffee and tea

(G-1751)
FAMILY MEDICINE STARK COUNTY
6512 Whipple Ave Nw (44720-7340)
PHONE..................330 499-5600
Gust Pantelas Md, Pr
Matthew Li Cause Md, VP
EMP: 32 EST: 1989
SALES (est): 3.69MM Privately Held
Web: www.familymedicinestark.com
SIC: 8011   General and family practice, physician/surgeon

(G-1752)
FAMILY PHYSICIANS INC
4860 Frank Ave Nw (44720-7498)
PHONE..................330 494-7099
Thomas Shemory, Pr
Doctor Gregory A Haban, VP
Doctor Paul Bortos, Sec
Doctor Howard Marshall, Treas
Melanie Mirande, *
EMP: 46 EST: 1981
SQ FT: 20,000
SALES (est): 8.62MM Privately Held
Web: www.familyphysicansinc.org
SIC: 8011   Physicians' office, including specialists

(G-1753)
FIRST CHRISTIAN CHURCH
6900 Market Ave N (44721-2437)
PHONE..................330 445-2700
Pastor John Hampton, Prin
EMP: 34 EST: 1892
SQ FT: 107,000
SALES (est): 3.15MM Privately Held
Web: www.firstchristian.com
SIC: 8661 8351   Miscellaneous denomination church; Preschool center

(G-1754)
FIRSTMERIT MORTGAGE CORP
4455 Hills And Dales Rd Nw (44708-1505)
PHONE..................330 478-3400
EMP: 85 EST: 1995
SALES (est): 16.04MM
SALES (corp-wide): 10.84B Publicly Held
SIC: 6162   Mortgage bankers
HQ: The Huntington National Bank
    41 S High St
    Columbus OH 43215
    614 480-4293

(G-1755)
FLAMOS ENTERPRISES INC
Also Called: Stark Sandblasting & Pntg Co
1501 Raff Rd Sw Ste 1 (44710-2356)
PHONE..................330 478-0009
EMP: 50
Web: www.apacheip.com
SIC: 1799 7389 1721   Sandblasting of building exteriors; Interior decorating; Industrial painting

(G-1756)
FOXHIRE LLC
4883 Dressler Rd Nw Ste 103 (44718-3635)
PHONE..................330 454-3508
EMP: 49 EST: 2020
SALES (est): 6.22MM Privately Held
Web: www.foxhire.com
SIC: 7379   Computer related services, nec

(G-1757)
FOXTROT AVIATION SERVICES LLC
5440 Fulton Dr Nw Ste 201 (44718-1762)
PHONE..................330 806-7477
EMP: 40 EST: 2010
SALES (est): 5.53MM Privately Held
Web: www.foxtrotaviation.com
SIC: 4581 7361   Aircraft cleaning and janitorial service; Employment agencies

(G-1758)
FURBAY ELECTRIC SUPPLY CO (PA)
208 Schroyer Ave Sw (44702-2039)
P.O. Box 6268 (44706-0268)
PHONE..................330 454-3033
Timothy Furbay, Pr
Jean Furbay, *
EMP: 37 EST: 1934
SQ FT: 35,000
SALES (est): 41.4MM
SALES (corp-wide): 41.4MM Privately Held
Web: www.furbay.com
SIC: 5063   Electrical supplies, nec

(G-1759)
GASPAR INC
Also Called: Gaspar
1545 Whipple Ave Sw (44710-1373)
PHONE..................330 477-2222
Gary W Gaspar, Pr
Judy Gaspar, *
EMP: 55 EST: 1967
SQ FT: 36,000

SALES (est): 8.71MM **Privately Held**
Web: www.gasparinc.com
SIC: 3443 7692 3444 Tanks, standard or custom fabricated: metal plate; Welding repair; Sheet metalwork

(G-1760)
GASTRNTEROLOGY SPECIALISTS INC
2726 Fulton Dr Nw (44718-3506)
PHONE.................................330 455-5011
Michael Van Ness, *Pr*
EMP: 49 **EST:** 1989
SALES (est): 6.15MM **Privately Held**
Web: www.gsiohio.com
SIC: 8011 Gastronomist

(G-1761)
GERDAU MCSTEEL ATMSPHERE ANNLI
Also Called: Advanced Bar Technology
1501 Raff Rd Sw (44710-2356)
PHONE.................................330 478-0314
Saminathan Ramaswamy, *Prin*
EMP: 28
SQ FT: 31,316
SALES (corp-wide): 1.56B **Privately Held**
SIC: 7389 3398 Metal cutting services; Metal heat treating
HQ: Gerdau Macsteel Atmosphere Annealing
209 W Mount Hope Ave # 1
Lansing MI 48910
517 782-0415

(G-1762)
GERVASI VINYRD ITLN BISTRO LLC
Also Called: Gervasi Vineyard
1700 55th St Ne (44721-3401)
PHONE.................................330 497-1000
Ted Swaldo, *Managing Member*
EMP: 88 **EST:** 2009
SALES (est): 11.38MM **Privately Held**
Web: www.gervasivineyard.com
SIC: 5182 Wine

(G-1763)
GLOBAL INSULATION INC (PA)
Also Called: Chempower Sheetmetal
4450 Belden Village St Nw Ste 406 (44718-2552)
PHONE.................................330 479-3100
Patrick F Byrne, *Pr*
Dale Crumley, *
EMP: 38 **EST:** 2000
SQ FT: 1,200
SALES (est): 4.34MM **Privately Held**
Web: www.cisystems.us
SIC: 1742 1761 Insulation, buildings; Sheet metal work, nec

(G-1764)
GOODWILL INDS RHBILITATION CTR (PA)
408 9th St Sw (44707-4799)
PHONE.................................330 454-9461
Ken Weber, *CEO*
Harold G Oswald, *
Gene Dechellis, *
Sharon Gonzales, *
EMP: 225 **EST:** 1920
SQ FT: 76,000
SALES (est): 8.16MM
SALES (corp-wide): 8.16MM **Privately Held**
Web: www.goodwillgoodskills.org
SIC: 8322 8331 Rehabilitation services; Community service employment training program

(G-1765)
GOVPLUS LLC
Also Called: GOVPLUS LLC
400 Tuscarawas St W Ste 1 (44702-2044)
PHONE.................................330 580-1913
Kevin Kamper, *Brnch Mgr*
EMP: 35
SALES (corp-wide): 12.19B **Publicly Held**
Web: www.citizensbank.com
SIC: 6022 State commercial banks
HQ: Citizens Bank, National Association
1 Citizens Plz
Providence RI 02903
401 456-7096

(G-1766)
GRACO OHIO INC
Also Called: Profiol
8400 Port Jackson Ave Nw (44720-5464)
PHONE.................................330 494-1313
EMP: 49
SQ FT: 832
SALES (corp-wide): 2.2B **Publicly Held**
Web: www.graco.com
SIC: 5084 Pumps and pumping equipment, nec
HQ: Graco Ohio Inc.
8400 Port Jackson Ave Nw
North Canton OH 44720
330 494-1313

(G-1767)
HABITAT FOR HMNITY E CNTL OHIO
1400 Raff Rd Sw (44710-2320)
PHONE.................................330 915-5888
Beth Lechner, *Prin*
EMP: 35 **EST:** 1998
SALES (est): 7.34MM **Privately Held**
Web: www.habitateco.org
SIC: 8399 Community development groups

(G-1768)
HALL OF FAME VILLAGE
2626 Fulton Dr Nw (44718-3504)
PHONE.................................714 337-0333
Brian Parisi, *Prin*
EMP: 38 **EST:** 2019
SALES (est): 1.62MM **Privately Held**
Web: www.profootballhof.com
SIC: 8412 Museum

(G-1769)
HAMMONTREE & ASSOCIATES LTD (PA)
5233 Stoneham Rd (44720-1594)
PHONE.................................330 499-8817
TOLL FREE: 800
Bruce Bair, *Pt*
Charles F Hammontree, *Pt*
Barbara H Bennett, *Pt*
Keith A Bennett, *Pt*
EMP: 46 **EST:** 1966
SQ FT: 10,800
SALES (est): 9.4MM
SALES (corp-wide): 9.4MM **Privately Held**
Web: www.hammontree-engineers.com
SIC: 8711 8713 Consulting engineer; Surveying services

(G-1770)
HANNON COMPANY (PA)
Also Called: Charles Rewinding Div
1605 Waynesburg Dr Se (44707-2137)
PHONE.................................330 456-4728
Christopher Meister, *Pr*
Mike Mcallister, *Superintnt*
Gary Gonzalez, *
Gary Griswold, *
Ann Paris, *
EMP: 75 **EST:** 1926
SQ FT: 65,000

SALES (est): 35.51MM
SALES (corp-wide): 35.51MM **Privately Held**
Web: www.hannonelectric.com
SIC: 3621 3825 5084 3699 Motors, electric; Test equipment for electronic and electrical circuits; Industrial machinery and equipment ; Electrical equipment and supplies, nec

(G-1771)
HILL TECHNICAL SERVICES INC
Also Called: Hill & Associates
4791 Munson St Nw (44718-3612)
PHONE.................................330 494-3656
Charles F Hill, *Pr*
EMP: 30 **EST:** 1987
SQ FT: 750
SALES (est): 1.44MM **Privately Held**
SIC: 8711 Engineering services

(G-1772)
HILSCHER-CLARKE ELECTRIC CO (PA)
Also Called: Hilscher-Clarke
519 4th St Nw (44703-2699)
PHONE.................................330 452-9806
Ronald Becker, *CEO*
John Fether, *
Ronald D Becker, *
Scott A Goodspeed, *
Barb Zwick, *
EMP: 30 **EST:** 1946
SQ FT: 26,000
SALES (est): 65.49MM
SALES (corp-wide): 65.49MM **Privately Held**
Web: www.hilscher-clarke.com
SIC: 1731 General electrical contractor

(G-1773)
HOF FITNESS CENTER INC
Also Called: Hall of Fame Fitness Center
2700 Roberts Ave Nw (44709-3442)
PHONE.................................330 455-0555
David Thomas, *Pr*
Robert Thomas, *
EMP: 60 **EST:** 1975
SQ FT: 200,000
SALES (est): 2.15MM **Privately Held**
Web: www.hoffitnesscenter.com
SIC: 7997 5941 Membership sports and recreation clubs; Specialty sport supplies, nec

(G-1774)
HOF VILLAGE NEWCO LLC
Also Called: Hof Vllage Cnstlltion Ctr For 2014 Champions Gateway (44708-2605)
PHONE.................................330 458-9176
Brian Parisi, *Prin*
Jason Krom, *
EMP: 125 **EST:** 2015
SALES (est): 7.49MM
SALES (corp-wide): 24.13MM **Publicly Held**
Web: www.hofvillage.com
SIC: 7999 Indoor court clubs
PA: Hall Of Fame Resort & Entertainment Company
2626 Fulton Dr Nw
Canton OH 44718
330 458-9176

(G-1775)
HOLMES LUMBER & BLDG CTR INC
1532 Perry Dr Sw (44710-1039)
PHONE.................................330 479-8314
EMP: 46
SALES (corp-wide): 32.18MM **Privately Held**
Web: www.holmeslumber.com

SIC: 5031 5211 2439 2434 Lumber, plywood, and millwork; Lumber and other building materials; Structural wood members, nec; Wood kitchen cabinets
PA: Holmes Lumber & Building Center, Inc.
6139 Hc 39
Millersburg OH 44654
330 674-9060

(G-1776)
HOME DEPOT USA INC
Also Called: Home Depot, The
4873 Portage St Nw (44720)
PHONE.................................330 497-1810
Jay Hissom, *Brnch Mgr*
EMP: 167
SQ FT: 111,806
SALES (corp-wide): 152.67B **Publicly Held**
Web: www.homedepot.com
SIC: 5211 7359 Home centers; Tool rental
HQ: Home Depot U.S.A., Inc.
2445 Springfield Ave
Vauxhall NJ 07088

(G-1777)
HUGHES KITCHENS AND BATH LLC
1258 Cleveland Ave Nw (44703-3147)
PHONE.................................330 455-5269
EMP: 30 **EST:** 1948
SQ FT: 80,000
SALES (est): 4.96MM **Privately Held**
Web: www.hugheskitchens.com
SIC: 1521 General remodeling, single-family houses

(G-1778)
HUNTINGTON NATIONAL BANK
3315 Cleveland Ave Nw (44709-2816)
PHONE.................................330 966-5232
Tom Lascosela, *Brnch Mgr*
EMP: 31
SALES (corp-wide): 10.84B **Publicly Held**
Web: www.huntington.com
SIC: 6029 6021 Commercial banks, nec; National commercial banks
HQ: The Huntington National Bank
41 S High St
Columbus OH 43215
614 480-4293

(G-1779)
INCEPT CORPORATION
4150 Belden Village St Nw Ste 205 (44718-2595)
PHONE.................................330 649-8000
EMP: 200 **EST:** 1992
SQ FT: 10,000
SALES (est): 18.25MM **Privately Held**
Web: www.inceptresults.com
SIC: 7389 Telemarketing services

(G-1780)
INSTITUTE OF JAW FCIAL SRGERY
4181 Holiday St Nw (44718-2531)
PHONE.................................330 493-1605
Michael Zetz, *Pr*
David Ash, *VP*
Richard Sundheimer, *Sec*
EMP: 64 **EST:** 1983
SALES (est): 2.31MM **Privately Held**
Web: www.jawandfacialsurgery.com
SIC: 8021 Dental surgeon

(G-1781)
INSURANCE PARTNERS AGENCY LLC
Also Called: Sirak Insurance Partners
4700 Dressler Rd Nw (44718-2570)
PHONE.................................330 493-3211
EMP: 48

Canton - Stark County (G-1782) — GEOGRAPHIC SECTION

SALES (corp-wide): 11.88MM **Privately Held**
Web: www.inspartners.com
SIC: **6411** Insurance agents, nec
PA: Insurance Partners Agency, Llc
26865 Center Ridge Rd
Westlake OH 44145
440 926-2561

(G-1782)
IRONROCK CAPITAL INCORPORATED
Also Called: Metropolitan Ceramics Div
1201 Millerton St Se (44707-2209)
P.O. Box 9240 (44711-9240)
PHONE..................................330 484-4887
Guy F Renkert, *Pr*
C W Keplinger, *
H S Renkert, *
▲ EMP: 100 EST: 1866
SQ FT: 100,000
SALES (est): 24.31MM **Privately Held**
Web: www.ironrock.com
SIC: **1743** Tile installation, ceramic

(G-1783)
JANSON INDUSTRIES
1200 Garfield Ave Sw (44706-1639)
P.O. Box 6090 (44706-0090)
PHONE..................................330 455-7029
Richard Janson, *Pt*
Eric H Janson, *Mng Pt*
EMP: 100 EST: 1927
SQ FT: 120,000
SALES (est): 14.9MM **Privately Held**
Web: www.jansonindustries.com
SIC: **1799** 2391 3999 Rigging and scaffolding; Curtains and draperies; Stage hardware and equipment, except lighting

(G-1784)
JMT CARTAGE INC
1712 N Park Ave Nw (44708-3043)
PHONE..................................330 478-2430
Jeffrey M Tomich, *Pr*
EMP: 35 EST: 1992
SALES (est): 2.39MM **Privately Held**
Web: www.jmtcartage.com
SIC: **4212** 4213 Light haulage and cartage, local; Contract haulers

(G-1785)
JMW WELDING AND MFG INC
512 45th St Sw (44706-4432)
PHONE..................................330 484-2428
John Slutz, *Pr*
Michael Slutz, *
Neal Slutz, *
EMP: 30 EST: 1983
SQ FT: 12,000
SALES (est): 2.71MM **Privately Held**
Web: www.jmwcompanies.net
SIC: **3443** 7692 Industrial vessels, tanks, and containers; Welding repair

(G-1786)
JOHNSON CNTRLS SEC SLTIONS LLC
5590 Lauby Rd Ste 6 (44720-1500)
PHONE..................................330 497-0850
Brad Wilamson, *Genl Mgr*
EMP: 50
Web: datasource.johnsoncontrols.com
SIC: **7382** Burglar alarm maintenance and monitoring
HQ: Johnson Controls Security Solutions Llc
6600 Congress Ave
Boca Raton FL 33487
561 264-2071

(G-1787)
JUNCTION TAVERN INC
2925 Westdale Rd Nw (44708-1250)
PHONE..................................330 477-4694
EMP: 98
SALES (corp-wide): 222.87K **Privately Held**
SIC: **1794** Excavation work
PA: Junction Tavern, Inc.
3011 Tuscarawas St W
Canton OH 44708
330 453-3780

(G-1788)
K HOVNANIAN SUMMIT HOMES LLC (HQ)
Also Called: Summit Homes
2000 10th St Ne (44705-1414)
PHONE..................................330 454-4048
Ricky Haney, *
EMP: 50 EST: 1985
SALES (est): 257.12MM
SALES (corp-wide): 2.76B **Publicly Held**
Web: www.khov.com
SIC: **1521** New construction, single-family houses
PA: Hovnanian Enterprises, Inc.
90 Matawan Rd Fl 5
Matawan NJ 07747
732 747-7800

(G-1789)
KAMES INC
Also Called: Kame's Sports Center
8516 Cleveland Ave Nw (44720-7908)
PHONE..................................330 499-4558
EMP: 35 EST: 1968
SALES (est): 1.78MM **Privately Held**
Web: www.kamessports.com
SIC: **5941** 5091 Hunting equipment; Hunting equipment and supplies

(G-1790)
KEMPTHORN MOTORS INC (PA)
Also Called: Jaguar Volvo
1449 Cleveland Ave Nw (44703)
PHONE..................................800 451-3877
TOLL FREE: 800
Eric Kempthorn, *Pr*
EMP: 100 EST: 1930
SQ FT: 25,000
SALES (est): 26.01MM
SALES (corp-wide): 26.01MM **Privately Held**
Web: www.kempthorn.com
SIC: **5511** 5521 7538 7515 Automobiles, new and used; Used car dealers; General automotive repair shops; Passenger car leasing

(G-1791)
KEYBANK NATIONAL ASSOCIATION
Also Called: Keybank
4428 Tuscarawas St W (44708-5361)
P.O. Box 9950 (44711-0950)
PHONE..................................330 477-6787
Joyce Swallow, *Mgr*
EMP: 57
SALES (corp-wide): 10.4B **Publicly Held**
Web: www.key.com
SIC: **6021** National commercial banks
HQ: Keybank National Association
127 Public Sq Ste 5600
Cleveland OH 44114
800 539-2968

(G-1792)
KRUGLIAK WLKINS GRFFTHS DGHRTY (PA)
4775 Munson St Nw (44718-3612)
P.O. Box 36963 (44735-6963)
PHONE..................................330 497-0700
Terry Moore, *Dir*
EMP: 68 EST: 1965
SQ FT: 23,000
SALES (est): 11.43MM
SALES (corp-wide): 11.43MM **Privately Held**
Web: www.kwgd.com
SIC: **8111** General practice attorney, lawyer

(G-1793)
LAJD WAREHOUSING & LEASING INC
935 Mckinley Ave Nw (44703-2072)
PHONE..................................330 452-5010
Leo A Dick, *Pr*
Lawrence J Dick, *
▲ EMP: 65 EST: 1922
SQ FT: 50,000
SALES (est): 9.44MM **Privately Held**
Web: www.liparifoods.com
SIC: **5149** Specialty food items

(G-1794)
LIFECARE FMLY HLTH DNTL CTR IN
Also Called: Lifecare Family Health
2725 Lincoln St E (44707-2769)
PHONE..................................330 454-2000
Eric D Riley, *Dir*
Kay Seeberger, *
Janet Mcpeek, *CFO*
EMP: 35 EST: 1993
SQ FT: 16,552
SALES (est): 7.63MM **Privately Held**
Web: www.lifecarefhdc.org
SIC: **8011** Clinic, operated by physicians

(G-1795)
LIFETOUCH NAT SCHL STUDIOS INC
Also Called: Lifetouch
1300 S Main St Ste 300 (44720-4252)
P.O. Box 8001 (44811-8001)
PHONE..................................330 497-1291
Barry Weber, *Mgr*
EMP: 29
SALES (corp-wide): 2.47B **Privately Held**
Web: www.lifetouch.com
SIC: **7221** Photographer, still or video
HQ: Lifetouch National School Studios Inc.
11000 Viking Dr Ste 300
Eden Prairie MN 55344
952 826-4000

(G-1796)
LIGHT SPEED LGISTICS LTD LBLTY
2516 3rd St Ne (44704-2302)
PHONE..................................330 412-0567
EMP: 129 EST: 2019
SALES (est): 4.49MM **Privately Held**
SIC: **4215** Package delivery, vehicular

(G-1797)
LOWES HOME CENTERS LLC
Also Called: Lowe's
6375 Strip Ave Nw (44720-7097)
PHONE..................................330 497-2720
EMP: 162
SALES (corp-wide): 86.38B **Publicly Held**
Web: www.lowes.com
SIC: **5211** 5031 5722 5064 Home centers; Building materials, exterior; Household appliance stores; Electrical appliances, television and radio
HQ: Lowe's Home Centers, Llc
1000 Lowes Blvd
Mooresville NC 28117
336 658-4000

(G-1798)
M CONLEY COMPANY (PA)
Also Called: Network
1312 4th St Se (44707-3243)
P.O. Box 21270 (44701-1270)
PHONE..................................330 456-8243
Robert Stuart Iii, *CEO*
Eric Conley, *
James Winafeld, *
EMP: 100 EST: 1918
SQ FT: 75,000
SALES (est): 42.77MM
SALES (corp-wide): 42.77MM **Privately Held**
Web: www.mconley.com
SIC: **5087** 5084 5113 Janitors' supplies; Safety equipment; Paper, wrapping or coarse, and products

(G-1799)
MALONEY & ASSOCIATES INC
Also Called: Canton Chair Rental
4850 Southway St Sw (44706-1947)
PHONE..................................330 477-7719
TOLL FREE: 800
Tim Moloney Senior, *Pr*
R C Maloney, *
Helen L Maloney, *
EMP: 46 EST: 1972
SQ FT: 20,000
SALES (est): 4.35MM **Privately Held**
Web: www.cantonchairrental.com
SIC: **7359** Party supplies rental services

(G-1800)
MARTIN LOGISTICS INCORPORATED
4526 Louisville St Ne (44705)
P.O. Box 9605 (44711)
PHONE..................................330 456-8000
Alice F Martin, *Pr*
EMP: 51 EST: 1997
SQ FT: 30,000
SALES (est): 4.9MM **Privately Held**
Web: www.martinlogistics.com
SIC: **4731** Freight forwarding

(G-1801)
MAYFLOWER NURSING HOME INC
Also Called: Sumser Health Care Center
836 34th St Nw (44709-2947)
PHONE..................................330 492-7131
Shirley Armstrong, *Pr*
EMP: 42 EST: 1958
SQ FT: 55,000
SALES (est): 516.65K **Privately Held**
SIC: **8051** 8059 Convalescent home with continuous nursing care; Personal care home, with health care

(G-1802)
MCKINLEY AIR TRANSPORT INC
5430 Lauby Rd Bldg 4 (44720-1576)
P.O. Box 2406 (44720-0406)
PHONE..................................330 497-6956
Don J Armen, *Pr*
EMP: 40 EST: 1934
SQ FT: 38,000
SALES (est): 4.8MM **Privately Held**
Web: www.mckinleyair.com
SIC: **5599** 4581 5172 4522 Aircraft, self-propelled; Aircraft cleaning and janitorial service; Aircraft fueling services; Flying charter service

(G-1803)
MCKINLEY HEALTH CARE CTR LLC
800 Market Ave N (44702-1083)
PHONE..................................330 456-1014
Robert Knapp, *Prin*
EMP: 99 EST: 1999

GEOGRAPHIC SECTION
Canton - Stark County (G-1826)

SALES (est): 7.91MM **Privately Held**
Web: www.mckinleyhc.com
SIC: 8052 Intermediate care facilities

(G-1804)
MEP HEALTH LLC
4535 Dressler Rd Nw (44718-2545)
P.O. Box 17723 (04915-4072)
PHONE..................................330 492-4559
Tina Frick, *Admn*
Paul Miltiades, *Admn*
EMP: 34 **EST:** 1997
SALES (est): 4.28MM **Privately Held**
Web: www.usacs.com
SIC: 8062 General medical and surgical hospitals

(G-1805)
MEYERS LAKE SPORTSMANS CLB INC
1672 N Park Ave Nw (44708-3041)
PHONE..................................330 456-1025
James Scott, *Pr*
EMP: 70 **EST:** 2020
SALES (est): 232.63K **Privately Held**
SIC: 7997 Gun and hunting clubs

(G-1806)
MICHAEL BAKER INTL INC
101 Cleveland Ave Nw Ste 106 (44702-1707)
PHONE..................................330 453-3110
Michael Baker, *Brnch Mgr*
EMP: 40
SALES (corp-wide): 1.04B **Privately Held**
SIC: 8711 8741 Civil engineering; Management services
HQ: Michael Baker International, Inc.
500 Grant St Ste 5400
Pittsburgh PA 15219
412 269-6300

(G-1807)
MIDWEST INDUSTRIAL SUPPLY INC (PA)
Also Called: Midwest
1101 3rd St Se (44707-3230)
P.O. Box 8431 (44711-8431)
PHONE..................................330 456-3121
Robert Vitale, *Pr*
Steven Vitale, *
▲ **EMP:** 30 **EST:** 1975
SQ FT: 40,000
SALES (est): 37.63MM
SALES (corp-wide): 37.63MM **Privately Held**
Web: www.midwestind.com
SIC: 5084 Industrial machinery and equipment

(G-1808)
MILLER & CO PORTABLE TOIL SVCS
2400 Shepler Church Ave Sw (44706-4112)
PHONE..................................330 453-9472
Ronald Miller Junior, *Pr*
EMP: 50 **EST:** 1999
SQ FT: 40,000
SALES (est): 9.05MM **Privately Held**
Web: www.unitedsiteservices.com
SIC: 7359 Portable toilet rental

(G-1809)
MIRACLE PLUMBING & HEATING CO
Also Called: Honeywell Authorized Dealer
2121 Whipple Ave Nw (44708-2361)
PHONE..................................330 477-2402
Steven J Brown, *Pr*
EMP: 35 **EST:** 1927
SALES (est): 4.97MM **Privately Held**
Web: www.miracle1927.com

SIC: 1711 1623 Warm air heating and air conditioning contractor; Water main construction

(G-1810)
MORROW CONTROL AND SUPPLY INC (PA)
Also Called: Johnson Contrls Authorized Dlr
810 Marion Motley Ave Ne (44705-1430)
PHONE..................................330 452-9791
Richard Schwane, *Pr*
EMP: 35 **EST:** 1952
SQ FT: 100,000
SALES (est): 16.76MM
SALES (corp-wide): 16.76MM **Privately Held**
Web: www.winstelcontrols.com
SIC: 5074 Heating equipment (hydronic)

(G-1811)
MPLX TERMINALS LLC
Also Called: Marathon Canton Refinery
2408 Gambrinus Ave Sw (44706-2365)
PHONE..................................330 479-5539
Mike Armbrester, *Brnch Mgr*
EMP: 78
SIC: 5172 2951 Gasoline; Asphalt paving mixtures and blocks
HQ: Mplx Terminals Llc
200 E Hardin St
Findlay OH 45840
419 421-2414

(G-1812)
MULLINAX FORD NORTH CANTON INC
Also Called: Autonation Ford North Canton
5900 Whipple Ave Nw (44720-7614)
PHONE..................................330 238-3206
Brian Gilmore, *Mgr*
Charles E Mullinax, *
Janet Mullinax, *
Larry Mullinax, *
EMP: 125 **EST:** 1992
SQ FT: 40,000
SALES (est): 12.41MM
SALES (corp-wide): 26.95B **Publicly Held**
Web: www.autonationfordnorthcanton.com
SIC: 5511 5521 7515 Automobiles, new and used; Used car dealers; Passenger car leasing
HQ: An Dealership Holding Corp.
200 Sw 1st Ave
Fort Lauderdale FL 33301
954 769-7000

(G-1813)
MULTI-CNTY JVNILE ATTNTION SYS (PA)
815 Faircrest St Sw (44706-4844)
PHONE..................................330 484-6471
Donald Thernes, *Superintnt*
Ruth Martin, *
EMP: 100 **EST:** 1974
SALES (est): 8.57MM
SALES (corp-wide): 8.57MM **Privately Held**
Web: www.mcjas.org
SIC: 8322 Individual and family services

(G-1814)
MY COMMUNITY HEALTH CENTER
2600 7th St Sw (44710-1709)
PHONE..................................330 363-6242
Terry L Regula, *CEO*
Terry Regula, *
EMP: 40 **EST:** 2016
SALES (est): 7.39MM **Privately Held**
Web: www.mycomhc.org

SIC: 8011 Physicians' office, including specialists

(G-1815)
N MARKET BEHAVIORAL HOSP LLC
Also Called: Sunrise Vista Hlth & Wellnesss
1223 Market Ave N (44714-2603)
PHONE..................................513 530-1600
Richard Odenthal, *Prin*
Sandra Smiddy, *
EMP: 50 **EST:** 2019
SALES (est): 2.45MM **Privately Held**
Web: www.sunrisevistahealth.com
SIC: 8093 Mental health clinic, outpatient

(G-1816)
N P MOTEL SYSTEM INC
Also Called: 8motel
3950 Convenience Cir Nw (44718-2661)
PHONE..................................330 492-5030
Norman Patel, *Pr*
EMP: 41 **EST:** 1981
SQ FT: 3,000
SALES (est): 181.47K **Privately Held**
SIC: 7011 Motels

(G-1817)
NATIONAL FOOTBALL MUSEUM INC
Also Called: Professional Football Hall Fame
2121 George Halas Dr Nw (44708-2630)
PHONE..................................330 456-8207
David Baker, *Pr*
George Veras, *Executive Producer**
Joe Horrigan, *Executive Producer**
Steve Strawbridge, *CAO**
Pete Fierle, *CSO**
EMP: 31 **EST:** 1963
SQ FT: 83,000
SALES (est): 44.34K **Privately Held**
Web: www.nationalfootballmuseum.com
SIC: 7941 Football club

(G-1818)
NATIONWIDE
Also Called: Nationwide
3101 Cleveland Ave Nw (44709-2812)
PHONE..................................800 421-3535
EMP: 31 **EST:** 2012
SALES (est): 171.95K **Privately Held**
Web: www.nationwide.com
SIC: 6411 Insurance agents, nec

(G-1819)
NATIONWIDE MUTUAL INSURANCE CO
Also Called: Nationwide
1000 Market Ave N (44702-1025)
P.O. Box 182144 (43218-2144)
PHONE..................................330 489-5000
Barbara Moses, *Mgr*
EMP: 44
SALES (corp-wide): 11.75B **Privately Held**
Web: www.nationwide.com
SIC: 6411 Insurance agents, nec
PA: Nationwide Mutual Insurance Company
1 Nationwide Plz
Columbus OH 43215
614 249-7111

(G-1820)
NIMISHILLEN & TUSCARAWAS LLC
2633 8th St Ne (44704-2311)
PHONE..................................330 438-5821
Steve Sinnott, *Genl Mgr*
EMP: 67 **EST:** 1999
SALES (est): 3.95MM **Privately Held**
SIC: 4011 Railroads, line-haul operating
HQ: Republic Steel
2633 8th St Ne
Canton OH 44704
330 438-5435

(G-1821)
NORTHEAST PROFESSIONAL HM CARE (PA)
4580 Stephens Cir Nw Ste 301 (44718-3646)
PHONE..................................330 966-2311
Anthony John Vallone, *Pr*
Eusnook Vallone, *
EMP: 95 **EST:** 1995
SALES (est): 4.3MM
SALES (corp-wide): 4.3MM **Privately Held**
Web: www.neprohomecare.com
SIC: 8082 Visiting nurse service

(G-1822)
OHIO HEAD & NECK SURGEONS INC (PA)
Also Called: Canton Allergy Lab
4912 Higbee Ave Nw Ste 200 (44718-2599)
PHONE..................................330 492-2844
Steven J Ossakow, *Pr*
EMP: 35 **EST:** 1964
SALES (est): 4.83MM
SALES (corp-wide): 4.83MM **Privately Held**
Web: www.ohioheadandneck.com
SIC: 8011 Ears, nose, and throat specialist: physician/surgeon

(G-1823)
OHIO POOLS & SPAS INC (PA)
6815 Whipple Ave Nw (44720-7335)
PHONE..................................330 494-7755
Richard A Annis, *Pr*
▲ **EMP:** 34 **EST:** 1957
SQ FT: 8,000
SALES (est): 4.58MM
SALES (corp-wide): 4.58MM **Privately Held**
Web: www.ohiopools.com
SIC: 1799 Swimming pool construction

(G-1824)
OHIOGUIDESTONE
4579 Everhard Rd Nw (44718-2425)
PHONE..................................440 234-2006
EMP: 112
SALES (corp-wide): 86.77MM **Privately Held**
Web: www.ohioguidestone.org
SIC: 8322 Child related social services
PA: Ohioguidestone
434 Eastland Rd
Berea OH 44017
440 234-2006

(G-1825)
OMNI MEDICAL CENTER
4760 Belpar St Nw (44718-3603)
P.O. Box 36959 (44735-6959)
PHONE..................................330 492-5565
EMP: 31 **EST:** 1995
SALES (est): 541.13K **Privately Held**
Web: www.orthounitedohio.com
SIC: 8011 Orthopedic physician

(G-1826)
ORTHORPDICS MLTSPCIALTY NETWRK (PA)
4760 Belpar St Nw (44718-3603)
PHONE..................................330 493-1630
Stephen A Lohr, *CEO*
Michael D London, *Sec*
EMP: 30 **EST:** 1972
SALES (est): 4.7MM
SALES (corp-wide): 4.7MM **Privately Held**
Web: www.orthounitedohio.com
SIC: 8011 Orthopedic physician

Canton - Stark County (G-1827)

(G-1827)
PATHWAY CARING FOR CHILDREN (PA)
4895 Dressler Rd Nw Ste A (44718-2571)
PHONE..................................330 493-0083
Eric Belden, *CEO*
Gregg Umberger, *
EMP: 60 **EST**: 1972
SQ FT: 21,000
SALES (est): 6.02MM
SALES (corp-wide): 6.02MM **Privately Held**
Web: www.pathwaycfc.org
SIC: 8361 Children's home

(G-1828)
PATRIOT SOFTWARE LLC
4883 Dressler Rd Nw Ste 301 (44718-3665)
PHONE..................................877 968-7147
Michael J Kappel, *Pr*
Todd Schmitt, *
EMP: 100 **EST**: 2002
SQ FT: 1,120
SALES (est): 13.67MM **Privately Held**
Web: www.patriotsoftware.com
SIC: 7372 Business oriented computer software

(G-1829)
PEOPLE DEVELOPED SYSTEMS INC
4914 Hills And Dales Rd Nw (44708-1406)
PHONE..................................330 479-7823
Donna Learned, *Pr*
Robert Learned, *
EMP: 60 **EST**: 1993
SQ FT: 1,600
SALES (est): 258.59K **Privately Held**
SIC: 8699 Personal interest organization

(G-1830)
PREFERRED TEMPORARY SVCS INC
4791 Munson St Nw (44718-3612)
PHONE..................................330 494-5502
Charles Hill, *CEO*
EMP: 30 **EST**: 1994
SALES (est): 1.92MM **Privately Held**
SIC: 7363 Temporary help service

(G-1831)
PRO AUDIO VIDEO INC
1620 30th St Ne (44714-1628)
P.O. Box 155 (44685-0155)
PHONE..................................330 494-2100
Michael E White, *Pr*
EMP: 54 **EST**: 1985
SQ FT: 40,000
SALES (est): 437.86K **Privately Held**
Web: www.pro-av.com
SIC: 7929 Disc jockey service

(G-1832)
PROFESSIONAL SECURITY BUR INC
318 Cleveland Ave Nw (44702-1501)
PHONE..................................330 438-6800
Margaret Gursky, *Pr*
▲ **EMP**: 60 **EST**: 1977
SQ FT: 500
SALES (est): 1.59MM **Privately Held**
SIC: 7381 Security guard service

(G-1833)
PSC METALS LLC
3101 Varley Ave Sw (44706-3544)
PHONE..................................330 484-7610
Andrew Luntz, *Brnch Mgr*
EMP: 78
Web: www.pscmetals.com
SIC: 4953 Recycling, waste materials
HQ: Psc Metals, Llc
 2411 N Glassell St
 Orange CA 92865
 440 753-5400

(G-1834)
PUBLIC SERVICE COMPANY OKLA
301 Cleveland Ave (44702)
P.O. Box 24404 (44701-4404)
PHONE..................................888 216-3523
EMP: 79
SALES (corp-wide): 18.98B **Privately Held**
Web: www.psoklahoma.com
SIC: 4911 Distribution, electric power
HQ: Public Service Company Of Oklahoma
 212 E 6th St
 Tulsa OK 74119
 888 216-3523

(G-1835)
PULL-A-PART LLC
1551 Belden Ave Se (44707-2657)
PHONE..................................330 456-8349
EMP: 32
SALES (corp-wide): 119.55MM **Privately Held**
Web: www.pullapart.com
SIC: 5015 Automotive parts and supplies, used
PA: Pull-A-Part, Llc
 4473 Tilly Mill Rd
 Atlanta GA 30360
 404 607-7000

(G-1836)
QUALITY CMFORT LIVING SVCS LLC
4117 Whipple Ave Nw (44718-4808)
P.O. Box 36302 (44735-6302)
PHONE..................................330 280-7659
EMP: 70 **EST**: 2014
SALES (est): 2.21MM **Privately Held**
Web: www.qclsinspired.com
SIC: 8082 Home health care services

(G-1837)
QUEST RECOVERY PREVENTION SVCS (PA)
1341 Market Ave N (44714-2624)
PHONE..................................330 453-8252
Keith Hochadel, *CEO*
Beth Devitt, *
Ivan Rosa, *
EMP: 111 **EST**: 1969
SQ FT: 12,000
SALES (est): 7.13MM **Privately Held**
Web: www.commquest.org
SIC: 8322 Substance abuse counseling

(G-1838)
QUICK DELIVERY SERVICE INC (HQ)
2207 Kimball Rd Se (44707-3631)
P.O. Box 20109 (44701-0109)
PHONE..................................330 453-3709
Douglas J Sibila, *Pr*
Larry Kelley, *
EMP: 30 **EST**: 2009
SALES (est): 5.3MM **Privately Held**
Web: www.peoplesservices.com
SIC: 4212 Delivery service, vehicular
PA: Peoples Services, Inc.
 2207 Kimball Rd Se
 Canton OH 44707

(G-1839)
R G SMITH COMPANY (PA)
Also Called: Rgs
1249 Dueber Ave Sw (44706-1635)
P.O. Box 9067 (44711-9067)
PHONE..................................330 456-3415
EMP: 95 **EST**: 1909
SALES (est): 21.47MM
SALES (corp-wide): 21.47MM **Privately Held**
Web: www.rgscontractors.com
SIC: 3444 1761 1541 3496 Ducts, sheet metal; Roofing contractor; Industrial buildings and warehouses; Miscellaneous fabricated wire products

(G-1840)
RADIOLOGY ASSOC CANTON INC
2600 6th St Sw (44710-1702)
PHONE..................................330 363-2842
John Vizzuso, *CEO*
EMP: 27 **EST**: 1971
SALES (est): 1.56MM **Privately Held**
Web: www.radcanton.com
SIC: 8721 Billing and bookkeeping service

(G-1841)
RED ROBIN GOURMET BURGERS INC
Also Called: Red Robin
6522 Strip Ave Nw (44720-9203)
PHONE..................................330 305-1080
EMP: 138
SALES (corp-wide): 1.3B **Publicly Held**
Web: www.redrobin.com
SIC: 5812 6794 Restaurant, family: chain; Franchises, selling or licensing
PA: Red Robin Gourmet Burgers Inc
 10000 E Gddes Ave Ste 500
 Englewood CO 80112
 303 846-6000

(G-1842)
RED ROOF INNS INC
Also Called: Red Roof Inn
5353 Inn Cir Nw (44720-7555)
PHONE..................................330 499-1970
Vicki Hinkle, *Brnch Mgr*
EMP: 45
SQ FT: 16,128
Web: www.redroof.com
SIC: 7011 Hotels and motels
HQ: Red Roof Inns, Inc.
 7815 Walton Pkwy
 New Albany OH 43054
 614 744-2600

(G-1843)
REED FUNERAL HOME INC
705 Raff Rd Sw (44710-1597)
P.O. Box 80367 (44708-0367)
PHONE..................................330 477-6721
Elizabeth Reed, *Pr*
Carol Reed, *VP*
Dennis Reed, *Pr*
EMP: 31 **EST**: 1946
SALES (est): 496.11K **Privately Held**
Web: www.reedfuneralhome.com
SIC: 7261 Funeral home

(G-1844)
REPUBLIC N&T RAILROAD INC
2633 8th St Ne (44704-2311)
PHONE..................................330 438-5826
Jim Murphy, *Mgr*
EMP: 48 **EST**: 2003
SALES (est): 2.19MM **Privately Held**
SIC: 4011 Railroads, line-haul operating
HQ: Republic Steel
 2633 8th St Ne
 Canton OH 44704
 330 438-5435

(G-1845)
REPUBLIC TELCOM WORLDWIDE LLC (HQ)
3939 Everhard Rd Nw (44709-4004)
PHONE..................................330 966-4586
Aaron Stryker, *Genl Mgr*
EMP: 150 **EST**: 2007
SALES (est): 11.82MM **Privately Held**
SIC: 7389 Telephone services
PA: Arthur Middleton Capital Holdings, Inc.
 8000 Freedom Ave Nw
 North Canton OH 44720

(G-1846)
RES-CARE INC
2424 Market Ave N (44714-1942)
PHONE..................................330 452-2913
Cindy Brown, *Dir*
EMP: 55
SALES (corp-wide): 8.83B **Publicly Held**
Web: www.rescare.com
SIC: 8082 Home health care services
HQ: Res-Care, Inc.
 805 N Whittington Pkwy
 Louisville KY 40222
 502 394-2100

(G-1847)
RUAN TRANSPORT CORPORATION
3800 Commerce St Sw (44706-3367)
PHONE..................................330 484-1450
EMP: 37
SALES (corp-wide): 7.23MM **Privately Held**
Web: www.ruan.com
SIC: 4213 Contract haulers
HQ: Ruan Transport Corporation
 666 Grand Ave Ste 3100
 Des Moines IA 50309
 515 245-2500

(G-1848)
RUKH-JAGI HOLDINGS LLC
Also Called: Holiday Inn Canton
4520 Everhard Rd Nw (44718-2407)
PHONE..................................330 494-2770
EMP: 100 **EST**: 2004
SALES (est): 5.16MM **Privately Held**
Web: www.holidayinn.com
SIC: 7011 Hotels and motels

(G-1849)
SCHAUER GROUP INCORPORATED (PA)
Also Called: Nationwide
200 Market Ave N Ste 100 (44702-1435)
PHONE..................................330 453-7721
David T Schauer, *Pr*
Ronald Repp, *Sr VP*
Tim Pentivegna, *VP*
William T Schauer, *Treas*
EMP: 35 **EST**: 1904
SQ FT: 11,000
SALES (est): 8.64MM
SALES (corp-wide): 8.64MM **Privately Held**
Web: www.schauergroup.com
SIC: 6411 Insurance agents, nec

(G-1850)
SELINSKY FORCE LLC
4015 23rd St Sw (44706-2313)
PHONE..................................330 477-4527
Steve Miller, *Brnch Mgr*
EMP: 200
Web: www.selinskyforce.com
SIC: 7353 Heavy construction equipment rental
PA: The Selinsky Force Llc
 5365 E Center Dr Ne Ste C
 Canton OH 44721

(G-1851)
SHARE AND KARE INC
110 15th St Ne (44714-2507)
PHONE..................................330 493-6600
Karen Gobel, *Brnch Mgr*
EMP: 69

GEOGRAPHIC SECTION
Canton - Stark County (G-1875)

Web: www.shareandkare.com
SIC: 8351 Group day care center
PA: Share And Kare Inc
4389 Whipple Ave Nw
Canton OH 44718

(G-1852)
SIRAK FINANCIAL SERVICES INC (PA)
Also Called: Sirak Financial Companies
4700 Dressler Rd Nw (44718-2570)
PHONE..................................330 493-0642
Gary D Sirak, Pr
Wayne E S Arnold, *
EMP: 60 EST: 1956
SQ FT: 22,000
SALES (est): 9.73MM
SALES (corp-wide): 9.73MM Privately Held
Web: www.sirakfinancial.com
SIC: 6211 6411 Stock brokers and dealers; Pension and retirement plan consultants

(G-1853)
SKGAI HOLDINGS INC
4665 Belpar St Nw (44718-3602)
P.O. Box 36329 (44735-6329)
PHONE..................................330 493-1480
Sanjiv Khetarpal, Pr
Kathy Farley-white, Mgr
EMP: 53 EST: 1971
SQ FT: 4,500
SALES (est): 7.41MM Privately Held
Web: www.gastro-ohio.com
SIC: 8011 Gastronomist

(G-1854)
SLESNICK IRON & METAL CO
Also Called: Auto Crushers
927 Warner Rd Se (44707-3337)
PHONE..................................330 453-8475
TOLL FREE: 800
W Stanley Slesnick, Pr
Edward Slesnick, *
Jeffrey Slesnick, *
EMP: 42 EST: 1920
SQ FT: 3,000
SALES (est): 5.2MM Privately Held
Web: www.slesnicksteel.com
SIC: 5093 Ferrous metal scrap and waste

(G-1855)
SOLMAN INC
2716 Shepler Church Ave Sw (44706-4114)
PHONE..................................330 580-5188
Joe Halter, Pr
EMP: 50
SALES (est): 5.47MM Privately Held
SIC: 5051 Steel

(G-1856)
STANDARD PLUMBING & HEATING CO (HQ)
435 Walnut Ave Se (44702-1348)
P.O. Box 20650 (44701-0650)
PHONE..................................330 453-5150
David Grabowsky, Pr
Herman C Grabowsky, *
May C Grabowsky, *
Robert W Grabowsky, *
EMP: 60 EST: 1912
SQ FT: 20,000
SALES (est): 31.02MM
SALES (corp-wide): 274.77MM Privately Held
Web: www.standardpandh.com
SIC: 1711 Plumbing contractors
PA: Premistar, Llc
10 Parkway North Blvd # 100
Deerfield IL 60015
847 729-9450

(G-1857)
STARK AREA REGIONAL TRNST AUTH (PA)
Also Called: Sarta
1600 Gateway Blvd Se (44707-3544)
PHONE..................................330 477-2782
Kirt Conrad, Ex Dir
EMP: 207 EST: 1971
SQ FT: 100,000
SALES (est): 21.34MM
SALES (corp-wide): 21.34MM Privately Held
Web: www.sartaonline.com
SIC: 4111 Bus transportation

(G-1858)
STARK COUNTY BOARD OF DEVELOPM
Also Called: Workshops, The
4065 Bradley Cir Nw (44718-2565)
PHONE..................................330 477-5200
H Michael Miller, CEO
Gary Braun, *
EMP: 600 EST: 1968
SALES (est): 18.47MM Privately Held
Web: www.starkdd.org
SIC: 8331 8093 Sheltered workshop; Mental health clinic, outpatient

(G-1859)
STARK COUNTY NEUROLOGISTS INC
4105 Holiday St Nw (44718-2531)
P.O. Box 35006 (44735-5006)
PHONE..................................330 494-2097
Alok Bhagap, Pr
Doctor Morris Kinast, VP
Doctor Jay P Berke, Sec
Doctor Leon Rosenberg, Treas
EMP: 39 EST: 1964
SQ FT: 3,100
SALES (est): 981.18K Privately Held
Web: www.neurocarecenter.com
SIC: 8011 Neurologist

(G-1860)
STARK COUNTY PARK DISTRICT
5300 Tyner Ave Nw (44708-5041)
PHONE..................................330 477-3552
Bob Fonte, Dir
EMP: 108 EST: 1994
SQ FT: 2,912
SALES (est): 224.32K Privately Held
Web: www.starkparks.com
SIC: 7999 Recreation services

(G-1861)
STOLLE MACHINERY COMPANY LLC
4150 Belden Village St Nw Ste 504 (44718-2595)
PHONE..................................330 493-0444
Jim Mcclung, Brnch Mgr
EMP: 53
SALES (corp-wide): 492.99MM Privately Held
Web: www.stollemachinery.com
SIC: 5084 Industrial machinery and equipment
PA: Stolle Machinery Company, Llc
6949 S Potomac St
Centennial CO 80112
303 708-9044

(G-1862)
STONE CRSSING ASSSTED LVING LL
Also Called: Glenwood Assisted Living
820 34th St Nw (44709-2966)
PHONE..................................330 492-7131

EMP: 250 EST: 2017
SALES (est): 2.47MM Privately Held
SIC: 8051 Skilled nursing care facilities

(G-1863)
SUGAR CREEK VLY FRM & GAME CLB
2505 Grove St Ne (44721-3315)
P.O. Box 26 (44652-0026)
PHONE..................................330 492-3071
EMP: 30 EST: 2011
SALES (est): 282.61K Privately Held
SIC: 0191 General farms, primarily crop

(G-1864)
SUNOHIO INC
1515 Bank Pl Sw (44706-1602)
PHONE..................................330 477-6769
Dale A Bissonette, Pr
Charles A Baker Junior, VP
EMP: 60 EST: 1997
SQ FT: 29,409
SALES (est): 2.96MM Privately Held
SIC: 8744 Facilities support services

(G-1865)
SUNSET HILLS CEMETERY CORP
5001 Everhard Rd Nw (44718-2473)
PHONE..................................330 494-2051
Victor M Evans, Pr
E Keith Payne, *
Floyd E Bennett, *
EMP: 35 EST: 1984
SQ FT: 12,600
SALES (est): 8.04K
SALES (corp-wide): 4.1B Publicly Held
Web: www.sunsethillsbp.com
SIC: 7261 Funeral home
PA: Service Corporation International
1929 Allen Pkwy
Houston TX 77019
713 522-5141

(G-1866)
SUPERIOR PAVING & MATERIALS
5947 Whipple Ave Nw (44720-7613)
PHONE..................................330 499-5849
Marlene Oster, Pr
EMP: 35 EST: 1984
SQ FT: 3,000
SALES (est): 4.41MM Privately Held
Web: www.ostersandandgravelnorthcantonoh.com
SIC: 1611 Highway and street paving contractor

(G-1867)
SUPREME ACQUISITION HOLDG LLC
6545 Market Ave N Ste 100 (44721-2430)
PHONE..................................330 906-2509
Clarence L Hunt, Prin
Pamela Rae, Prin
EMP: 55 EST: 2014
SIC: 6719 Holding companies, nec

(G-1868)
TAB CONSTRUCTION COMPANY INC
530 Walnut Ave Ne (44702-1273)
PHONE..................................330 454-5228
EMP: 50 EST: 1993
SALES (est): 9.8MM Privately Held
SIC: 1611 1542 Highway and street construction; Nonresidential construction, nec

(G-1869)
TEBO FINANCIAL SERVICES INC
4740 Belpar St Nw Ste A (44718-3685)
PHONE..................................234 207-2500
Robert L Bowman, Pr

Robert M James, *
Roy A Baker Junior, VP
EMP: 48 EST: 1993
SALES (est): 5.8MM Privately Held
Web: www.tebofinancialservices.com
SIC: 7389 Financial services

(G-1870)
TERMINAL WAREHOUSE INC
2207 Kimball Rd Se (44707-3631)
P.O. Box 20109 (44701-0109)
PHONE..................................330 773-2056
▲ EMP: 130
SALES (est): 19.79MM Privately Held
Web: www.terminalwhse.com
SIC: 4225 General warehousing

(G-1871)
THE BEAVER EXCAVATING CO (PA)
2000 Beaver Place Ave Sw (44706-1963)
P.O. Box 6059 (44706-0059)
PHONE..................................330 478-2151
TOLL FREE: 800
EMP: 975 EST: 1953
SALES (est): 199.83MM
SALES (corp-wide): 199.83MM Privately Held
Web: www.beaverexcavating.com
SIC: 1794 1611 1771 1623 Excavation and grading, building construction; Highway and street construction; Foundation and footing contractor; Sewer line construction

(G-1872)
THE SELINSKY FORCE LLC (PA)
5365 E Center Dr Ne Ste C (44721-3734)
PHONE..................................330 477-4527
EMP: 51 EST: 2007
SALES (est): 41.15MM Privately Held
Web: www.selinskyforce.com
SIC: 7353 Heavy construction equipment rental

(G-1873)
THRASHER GROUP INC
400 3rd St Se Ste 309 (44702-1100)
PHONE..................................330 620-4790
EMP: 52
SALES (corp-wide): 59.55MM Privately Held
Web: www.thethrashergroup.com
SIC: 8711 Civil engineering
PA: The Thrasher Group Inc
600 White Oaks Blvd
Bridgeport WV 26330
304 624-4108

(G-1874)
TZANGAS PLAKAS MANNOS RECUPERO (PA)
200 Market Ave N Ste 300 (44702-1436)
PHONE..................................330 453-5466
TOLL FREE: 877
George J Tzangas, Pt
Leonide E Plakos, Pt
James J Mannos, Pt
EMP: 30 EST: 1980
SALES (est): 4.86MM
SALES (corp-wide): 4.86MM Privately Held
Web: www.lawlion.com
SIC: 8111 General practice attorney, lawyer

(G-1875)
UNITED WAY GRTER STARK CNTY IN
Also Called: UNITED WAY
401 Market Ave N Ste 300 (44702-1502)
PHONE..................................330 491-0445
Maria Heege, *
EMP: 35 EST: 2005
SALES (est): 6.56MM Privately Held

Web: www.uwstark.org
SIC: 8322 Social service center

(G-1876)
US ACUTE CARE SOLUTIONS LLC
4535 Dressler Rd Nw (44718-2545)
PHONE.................................800 828-0898
James Frary, CEO
Dominic J Bagnoli, *
Matt Patlovany, *
Amer Z Aldeen, CMO*
Tina Latimer, CCO*
EMP: 210 EST: 2015
SALES (est): 59.59MM Privately Held
Web: www.usacs.com
SIC: 8011 Physicians' office, including specialists

(G-1877)
USACS MANAGEMENT GROUP LTD
Also Called: Emergency Medicine Physicians
4535 Dressler Rd Nw (44718-2545)
PHONE.................................330 493-4443
EMP: 60 EST: 1995
SQ FT: 24,000
SALES (est): 16.13MM Privately Held
Web: www.usacs.com
SIC: 8741 8011 Hospital management; Offices and clinics of medical doctors

(G-1878)
USACS MEDICAL GROUP LTD
4535 Dressler Rd Nw (44718-2545)
PHONE.................................330 493-4443
EMP: 51 EST: 2007
SALES (est): 962.85K Privately Held
Web: www.usacsbill.com
SIC: 8011 Offices and clinics of medical doctors

(G-1879)
VALVOLINE INSTANT OIL CHNGE FR
Also Called: Valvoline Instant Oil Change
2203 Columbus Rd Ne (44705-2531)
PHONE.................................330 453-4549
EMP: 44
Web: www.valvoline.com
SIC: 7549 Automotive maintenance services
HQ: Valvoline Instant Oil Change Franchising, Inc.
    100 Valvoline Way
    Lexington KY 40509

(G-1880)
VELVET BLUE TRANSPORT CO INC
4821 Corporate St Sw (44706-1906)
PHONE.................................330 478-1426
EMP: 40 EST: 1981
SALES (est): 2.01MM Privately Held
SIC: 4213 Refrigerated products transport

(G-1881)
VISUAL EDGE TECHNOLOGY INC (PA)
3874 Highland Park Nw (44720-4538)
PHONE.................................330 494-9694
Austin Vanchieri, Ch Bd
Yvonne Brown, *
EMP: 130 EST: 1986
SQ FT: 52,000
SALES (est): 270MM
SALES (corp-wide): 270MM Privately Held
Web: www.visualedgeit.com
SIC: 5044 5065 Copying equipment; Facsimile equipment

(G-1882)
W L LOGAN TRUCKING COMPANY
Also Called: Logan Logistics

3224 Navarre Rd Sw (44706-1897)
PHONE.................................330 478-1404
William Logan Junior, Prin
William L Logan Senior, Ch Bd
Betty Jane Logan, *
William L Logan Junior, VP
Robert Logan, *
EMP: 125 EST: 1952
SQ FT: 30,000
SALES (est): 20.37MM Privately Held
Web: www.logantrucking.com
SIC: 4212 4213 Local trucking, without storage; Contract haulers

(G-1883)
WARSTLER BROS LANDSCAPING INC
4125 Salway Ave Nw (44718-2953)
PHONE.................................330 492-9500
Shawn Warstlet, Pr
Shawn Warstler, *
EMP: 33 EST: 1984
SQ FT: 3,360
SALES (est): 1.11MM Privately Held
Web: www.warstlerbros.com
SIC: 0782 4959 8748 4971 Landscape contractors; Snowplowing; Lighting consultant; Irrigation systems

(G-1884)
WAYMAKER MEDSTAFF LLC
5458 Fulton Dr Nw Ste B (44718-4309)
PHONE.................................330 526-8594
Leberliza Stalcup, CEO
EMP: 40 EST: 2019
SALES (est): 656.71K Privately Held
Web: www.waymakermedstaff.com
SIC: 8399 Health systems agency

(G-1885)
WELLNESS GROVE LLC
4200 Munson St Nw (44718-2981)
PHONE.................................330 244-1566
Shaun Swiger, Prin
EMP: 31 EST: 2020
SALES (est): 523.87K Privately Held
Web: www.wellnessgrove.com
SIC: 8322 General counseling services

(G-1886)
WINDSOR MEDICAL CENTER INC
1454 E Maple St (44720-2634)
PHONE.................................330 499-8300
Thomas Sawllen, Pr
EMP: 100 EST: 1961
SQ FT: 10,000
SALES (est): 3.38MM Privately Held
Web: www.windsormedicalcenter.com
SIC: 8059 8661 8052 8051 Personal care home, with health care; Religious organizations; Intermediate care facilities; Skilled nursing care facilities

(G-1887)
WORKSHOPS INC
4065 Bradley Cir Nw (44718-2565)
PHONE.................................330 479-3958
Ryan Heckert, CEO
Michael Testa, *
Lorie Travaglino, *
EMP: 100 EST: 1968
SALES (est): 7.04MM Privately Held
Web: www.choosetwi.com
SIC: 8331 Community service employment training program

(G-1888)
WYOMING CASING SERVICE INC
1414 Raff Rd Sw (44710-2320)
PHONE.................................330 479-8785
EMP: 70

SALES (corp-wide): 49.6MM Privately Held
Web: www.wyomingcasing.com
SIC: 1389 Oil field services, nec
PA: Wyoming Casing Service, Inc.
    198 40th St E
    Dickinson ND 58601
    701 225-8521

(G-1889)
YOUNG MNS CHRSTN ASSN CNTL STA
Also Called: YMCA Child Care
200 Charlotte St Nw (44720-2404)
PHONE.................................330 305-5437
Sherry Sampson, Brnch Mgr
EMP: 54
SALES (corp-wide): 20.07MM Privately Held
Web: www.ymcastark.org
SIC: 8641 7991 8351 7032 Youth organizations; Physical fitness facilities; Child day care services; Youth camps
PA: Young Mens Christian Association Of Central Stark County, Inc.
    4700 Dressler Rd Nw
    Canton OH 44718
    330 491-9622

(G-1890)
YOUNG MNS CHRSTN ASSN CNTL STA
Also Called: Gymnastics Center
7241 Whipple Ave Nw (44720-7137)
PHONE.................................330 498-4082
Colleen Ekle, Brnch Mgr
EMP: 84
SALES (corp-wide): 20.07MM Privately Held
Web: www.ymcastark.org
SIC: 8641 7991 8351 7032 Youth organizations; Physical fitness facilities; Child day care services; Youth camps
PA: Young Mens Christian Association Of Central Stark County, Inc.
    4700 Dressler Rd Nw
    Canton OH 44718
    330 491-9622

(G-1891)
YOUNG TRUCK SALES INC (PA)
Also Called: Jay-Mac
4970 Southway St Sw (44706-1940)
P.O. Box 6118 (44706-0118)
PHONE.................................330 477-6271
TOLL FREE: 800
Richard A Young, Ch Bd
Craig Young, *
Robert P Young, *
Nellie M Young, *
EMP: 50 EST: 1954
SQ FT: 31,000
SALES (est): 33.96MM
SALES (corp-wide): 33.96MM Privately Held
Web: www.youngtrucks.com
SIC: 5511 5013 7538 Automobiles, new and used; Truck parts and accessories; General automotive repair shops

(G-1892)
YOUNG WNS CHRSTN ASSN OF CNTON
Also Called: YWCA
1700 Gateway Blvd Se (44707-3518)
PHONE.................................330 453-0789
Sandy Markert, Brnch Mgr
EMP: 51
SALES (corp-wide): 5.69MM Privately Held
Web: www.ywcacanton.org

SIC: 8641 7991 8351 7032 Youth organizations; Physical fitness facilities; Child day care services; Youth camps
PA: The Young Womens Christian Association Of Canton Ohio
    231 6th St Ne
    Canton OH 44702
    330 453-7644

(G-1893)
ZIEGLER BOLT & PARTS CO (PA)
Also Called: Ziegler Bolt & Nut House
4848 Corporate St Sw (44706-1907)
P.O. Box 80369 (44708-0369)
PHONE.................................330 478-2542
William A Ziegler Junior, Pr
Janet Hanacek, *
EMP: 86 EST: 1964
SQ FT: 80,000
SALES (est): 24.36MM
SALES (corp-wide): 24.36MM Privately Held
Web: www.zieglerbolt.com
SIC: 5085 5072 Fasteners, industrial: nuts, bolts, screws, etc.; Hardware

Carey
Wyandot County

(G-1894)
NATIONAL LIME AND STONE CO
370 N Patterson St (43316-1057)
P.O. Box 8 (43316-0008)
PHONE.................................419 396-7671
Ryan Phillips, Brnch Mgr
EMP: 40
SALES (corp-wide): 167.89MM Privately Held
Web: www.natlime.com
SIC: 1422 3291 3281 3274 Lime rock, ground; Abrasive products; Cut stone and stone products; Lime
PA: The National Lime And Stone Company
    551 Lake Cascade Pkwy
    Findlay OH 45840
    419 422-4341

(G-1895)
VAUGHN INDUSTRIES LLC (PA)
Also Called: Vaughn
1201 E Findlay St (43316-9686)
P.O. Box 96 (43316-0096)
PHONE.................................419 396-3900
Timothy Vaughn, Managing Member
Timothy L Vaughn, Managing Member*
Roger Woods, *
Gregg Vaughn, *
Matthew Plotts, *
▲ EMP: 300 EST: 1963
SQ FT: 12,800
SALES (est): 88.39MM
SALES (corp-wide): 88.39MM Privately Held
Web: www.vaughnindustries.com
SIC: 1731 1711 General electrical contractor ; Mechanical contractor

(G-1896)
VULCAN ENTERPRISES INC
Also Called: Vulcan Fire Protection
2600 State Highway 568 Ste A (43316-1142)
PHONE.................................419 396-3535
Joyce Hunter, CEO
Larry Walters, *
Michael Kenn, *
Armando A Madrigal, *
EMP: 37 EST: 1990
SQ FT: 10,000

SALES (est): 5.72MM **Privately Held**
Web: www.vulcanfireprotection-oh.com
SIC: **1711** Fire sprinkler system installation

(G-1897)
WOODSIDE PROPERTIES I LTD
Also Called: Eaglewood Care Center
821 E Findlay St (43316-9685)
PHONE..............................419 396-7287
Cynthia Athens, *Mgr*
EMP: 50 EST: 1995
SALES (est): 1.2MM **Privately Held**
SIC: **8051** Skilled nursing care facilities

Carlisle
Warren County

(G-1898)
NARROW WAY CUSTOM TECH INC
100 Industry Dr (45005-6304)
PHONE..............................937 743-1611
Timothy Williams, *Pr*
EMP: 29 EST: 1998
SQ FT: 5,600
SALES (est): 4.18MM **Privately Held**
Web: www.narrowway100.com
SIC: **3599 7629** Custom machinery; Electrical repair shops

Carroll
Fairfield County

(G-1899)
BOBBY LAYMAN CADILLAC GMC INC
Also Called: Bobby Layman Cadillac
3733 Claypool Dr (43112-9795)
PHONE..............................740 654-9590
Mick Layman, *Pr*
Robert A Layman, *
Linda Layman, *
EMP: 32 EST: 1989
SALES (est): 4.95MM **Privately Held**
Web: www.bobbylaymancars.net
SIC: **5511 7539** Automobiles, new and used; Automotive repair shops, nec

(G-1900)
COMPANY WRENCH LTD (PA)
4805 Scooby Ln (43112-9446)
PHONE..............................740 654-5304
Cameron Gabbard, *Pr*
Jason Templeton, *VP*
Scott Carpenter, *CFO*
Brad Hutchinson, *Ch*
Justin Owen, *Sec*
▲ EMP: 65 EST: 1999
SQ FT: 40,000
SALES (est): 90MM
SALES (corp-wide): 90MM **Privately Held**
Web: www.companywrench.com
SIC: **5082** General construction machinery and equipment

(G-1901)
FAIRFIELD INDUSTRIES INC
4465 Coonpath Rd (43112-9705)
P.O. Box 160 (43112-0160)
PHONE..............................740 409-1539
Terry Morris, *Prin*
EMP: 37 EST: 1975
SALES (est): 466.46K **Privately Held**
Web: www.fairfielddd.com
SIC: **5812 8699 8412** Coffee shop; Charitable organization; Art gallery

Carrollton
Carroll County

(G-1902)
ALTERNATIVE RESIDENCES TWO INC
Also Called: Carrollton Habilitation Center
520 S Lisbon St (44615-9582)
PHONE..............................330 627-7552
Jenny Brendel, *Brnch Mgr*
EMP: 70
SALES (corp-wide): 2.27MM **Privately Held**
SIC: **8361** Mentally handicapped home
PA: Alternative Residences Two, Inc.
    100 W Main St Lowr
    Saint Clairsville OH 43950
    740 526-0514

(G-1903)
CARROLL ELECTRIC COOP INC
250 Canton Rd Nw (44615-8403)
P.O. Box 67 (44615-0067)
PHONE..............................330 627-2116
Lary Sanders, *Pr*
EMP: 27 EST: 1937
SQ FT: 11,000
SALES (est): 25.55MM **Privately Held**
Web: www.cecpower.coop
SIC: **4911** Distribution, electric power

(G-1904)
CLEVELAND CLINIC MERCY HOSP
Also Called: Timken Mercy Health Center
125 Canton Rd Nw (44615-1009)
PHONE..............................330 627-7641
Jack Topeleski, *Owner*
EMP: 421
SALES (corp-wide): 14.48B **Privately Held**
Web: www.cantonmercy.org
SIC: **8011 8093** Clinic, operated by physicians; Specialty outpatient clinics, nec
HQ: Cleveland Clinic Mercy Hospital
    1320 Mercy Dr Nw
    Canton OH 44708
    330 489-1000

(G-1905)
COUNTY OF CARROLL
Carroll County Transit/Caravan
2205 Commerce Dr (44615)
P.O. Box 185 (44615-0185)
PHONE..............................330 627-1900
Patti Manfull, *Dir*
EMP: 33
SQ FT: 2,000
Web: www.carrollcountyohio.us
SIC: **4119** Local passenger transportation, nec
PA: County Of Carroll
    119 S Lisbon St Ste 203
    Carrollton OH 44615
    330 627-2250

(G-1906)
COUNTY OF CARROLL
Also Called: Board of Mental Retardation
2167 Kensington Rd Ne (44615-8626)
P.O. Box 429 (44615-0429)
PHONE..............................330 627-7651
Alicia Hall, *Prin*
EMP: 60
Web: www.carrollcountyohio.us
SIC: **9431 8093** Mental health agency administration, government; Rehabilitation center, outpatient treatment
PA: County Of Carroll
    119 S Lisbon St Ste 203
    Carrollton OH 44615

330 627-2250

(G-1907)
EFFICIENT SERVICES OHIO INC
Also Called: Eso
277 Steubenville Rd Se (44615-9601)
PHONE..............................330 627-4440
Bryan T Shaw, *CEO*
EMP: 30 EST: 2012
SALES (est): 4.91MM **Privately Held**
Web: www.esohio.com
SIC: **5039** Soil erosion control fabrics

(G-1908)
GUESS MOTORS INC (PA)
457 Steubenville Rd Se (44615-9608)
PHONE..............................866 890-0522
TOLL FREE: 888
EMP: 30 EST: 1965
SQ FT: 12,000
SALES (est): 8.07MM **Privately Held**
Web: www.buyguess.com
SIC: **5511 7538** Automobiles, new and used; General automotive repair shops

(G-1909)
HOSPICE TUSCARAWAS COUNTY INC
Also Called: Community Hospice Carroll Cnty
789 N Lisbon St (44615-9401)
PHONE..............................330 627-4796
Roselle Furbee, *Brnch Mgr*
EMP: 37
Web: www.ohioshospice.org
SIC: **8052** Personal care facility
PA: Hospice Of Tuscarawas County, Inc.
    716 Commercial Ave Sw
    New Philadelphia OH 44663

(G-1910)
NOMAC DRILLING LLC
1258 Panda Rd Se (44615-9657)
PHONE..............................330 476-7040
EMP: 139
SALES (corp-wide): 4.15B **Publicly Held**
Web: www.patenergy.com
SIC: **1381** Drilling oil and gas wells
HQ: Nomac Drilling, L.L.C.
    3400 S Radio Rd
    El Reno OK 73036
    405 422-2754

(G-1911)
OHIO FFA CAMPS INC
Also Called: F F A CAMP MUSKINGUM
3266 Dyewood Rd Sw (44615-9246)
PHONE..............................330 627-2208
Todd Davis, *Dir*
EMP: 35 EST: 1942
SQ FT: 1,000
SALES (est): 2.37MM **Privately Held**
Web: www.ffacamp.com
SIC: **7032** Recreational camps

(G-1912)
RES-CARE INC
Also Called: RES Care OH
520 S Lisbon St (44615-9582)
PHONE..............................330 627-7552
Jenny Brendel, *Mgr*
EMP: 75
SALES (corp-wide): 8.83B **Publicly Held**
Web: www.rescare.com
SIC: **8052** Home for the mentally retarded, with health care
HQ: Res-Care, Inc.
    805 N Whittington Pkwy
    Louisville KY 40222
    502 394-2100

(G-1913)
ST JOHNS VILLA
Also Called: Villa Restaurant
701 Crest St Nw (44615)
P.O. Box 457 (44615)
PHONE..............................330 627-4662
Sister Elaine Weber, *Pr*
EMP: 145 EST: 1991
SQ FT: 60,000
SALES (est): 6MM **Privately Held**
Web: www.stjohnsvilla.net
SIC: **5812 8351 8052 8361** Eating places; Child day care services; Intermediate care facilities; Mentally handicapped home

Castalia
Erie County

(G-1914)
AUTOMATION ZONE INC
508 Lucas St E (44824-9600)
PHONE..............................419 684-8050
Ken Bragg, *Pr*
Kelly Garbe, *
EMP: 47 EST: 2001
SQ FT: 5,000
SALES (est): 9.82MM **Privately Held**
Web: www.theazone.net
SIC: **1731 8711** Access control systems specialization; Industrial engineers

(G-1915)
PLAYLAND DAY CARE LTD
314 Lucas St E (44824)
PHONE..............................419 625-8200
Jeffrey S Berquist, *Prin*
EMP: 30 EST: 1971
SALES (est): 351.97K **Privately Held**
SIC: **8351** Group day care center

Celina
Mercer County

(G-1916)
ARMCORP CONSTRUCTION INC
8511 State Route 703 (45822-2940)
PHONE..............................419 778-7024
Timothy J Rosengarten, *Pr*
Mary Rosengarten, *
EMP: 59 EST: 2009
SQ FT: 2,200
SALES (est): 17.5MM **Privately Held**
Web: www.armcorpinc.com
SIC: **1542** Commercial and office building, new construction

(G-1917)
BRUNS CONSTRUCTION ENTPS LLC
6781 Hellwarth Rd (45822-9273)
PHONE..............................419 586-9367
EMP: 35 EST: 2019
SALES (est): 8.53MM **Privately Held**
Web: www.rcs1951.com
SIC: **1521** New construction, single-family houses

(G-1918)
CELINA ENTERPRISES LLC (PA)
5481 State Route 29 (45822-9210)
PHONE..............................419 586-3610
Jeff Grieshop, *Prin*
Jill Roy, *
EMP: 64 EST: 2021
SALES (est): 2.52MM
SALES (corp-wide): 2.52MM **Privately Held**
Web: www.celinatent.com

Celina - Mercer County (G-1919)

SIC: 7359 Party supplies rental services

(G-1919)
CELINA MUTUAL INSURANCE CO (PA)
Also Called: Celina Insurance Group
1 Insurance Sq (45822-1659)
PHONE.................................800 552-5181
William W Montgomery, *Pr*
Donald W Montgomery, *
Phillip Fullenkamp, *
Michael S Kleinhenz, *
EMP: 130 EST: 1919
SQ FT: 75,000
SALES (est): 96.07MM
SALES (corp-wide): 96.07MM **Privately Held**
Web: www.celinainsurance.com
SIC: 6331 Fire, marine, and casualty insurance: mutual

(G-1920)
COMMUNITY HLTH PRFSSIONALS INC
Also Called: Celina Visting Nurses
816 Pro Dr (45822-1360)
PHONE.................................419 586-1999
Deb Garwood, *Mgr*
EMP: 32
SALES (corp-wide): 12.27MM **Privately Held**
Web: www.comhealthpro.org
SIC: 8082 Visiting nurse service
PA: Community Health Professionals, Inc.
1159 Westwood Dr
Van Wert OH 45891
419 238-9223

(G-1921)
COMMUNITY HLTH PRFSSIONALS INC
Also Called: Private Duty & Visiting Nurses
816 Pro Dr (45822-1360)
PHONE.................................419 586-6266
Caprice Smith, *Mgr*
EMP: 48
SALES (corp-wide): 12.27MM **Privately Held**
Web: www.comhealthpro.org
SIC: 8082 7361 Visiting nurse service; Nurses' registry
PA: Community Health Professionals, Inc.
1159 Westwood Dr
Van Wert OH 45891
419 238-9223

(G-1922)
FANNING/HOWEY ASSOCIATES INC (PA)
Also Called: Fanning Howey
1200 Irmscher Blvd (45822-8305)
PHONE.................................419 586-2292
EMP: 30 EST: 1952
SALES (est): 23.29MM
SALES (corp-wide): 23.29MM **Privately Held**
Web: www.fhai.com
SIC: 8712 8748 Architectural engineering; Business consulting, nec

(G-1923)
FOUNDTONS BHVRAL HLTH SVCS INC
4761 State Route 29 (45822)
PHONE.................................419 584-1000
Brian Angle, *Dir*
EMP: 52 EST: 1975
SALES (est): 3.88MM **Privately Held**
Web: www.foundationsbhs.org

SIC: 8093 Mental health clinic, outpatient

(G-1924)
GARDENS AT CELINA OPER CO LLC
Also Called: GARDENS AT CELINA
1301 Myers Rd (45822-4114)
PHONE.................................419 584-0100
Joseph Hazelbaker, *Prin*
Brian Hazelbaker, *Prin*
Ralph Hazelbaker, *Prin*
EMP: 47 EST: 2020
SALES (est): 2.59MM **Privately Held**
SIC: 8059 Nursing and personal care, nec

(G-1925)
HCF OF CELINA INC (HQ)
Also Called: HEALTH CARE FACILITIES
1001 Myers Rd (45822-1137)
PHONE.................................419 586-6645
Barbara Masella, *VP*
Carrie Vanass, *Prin*
Jim Unverferph, *Pr*
EMP: 86 EST: 1978
SALES (est): 7.94MM
SALES (corp-wide): 305.93MM **Privately Held**
Web: www.celinamanor.com
SIC: 8051 Convalescent home with continuous nursing care
PA: Hcf Management, Inc.
1100 Shawnee Rd
Lima OH 45805
419 999-2010

(G-1926)
MERCER CNTY JINT TWNSHIP CMNTY
Also Called: Community Medical Center
950 S Main St (45822-2413)
PHONE.................................419 586-1611
Vivian Hillwaret, *Mgr*
EMP: 66
SALES (corp-wide): 49.12MM **Privately Held**
Web: www.mercer-health.com
SIC: 8062 8011 General medical and surgical hospitals; Offices and clinics of medical doctors
PA: Mercer County Joint Township Community Hospital
800 W Main St
Coldwater OH 45828
419 678-2341

(G-1927)
MERCER CNTY JOINT TOWNSHP HOSP
Mercer Health Home Care
909 E Wayne St Ste 126oh (45822-3304)
PHONE.................................419 584-0143
Lisa Muhlenkamp, *Brnch Mgr*
EMP: 66
SALES (corp-wide): 49.12MM **Privately Held**
Web: www.mercer-health.com
SIC: 8082 Home health care services
PA: Mercer County Joint Township Community Hospital
800 W Main St
Coldwater OH 45828
419 678-2341

(G-1928)
MIDWEST LOGISTICS SYSTEMS LTD (HQ)
8779 State Route 703 (45822-2936)
PHONE.................................419 584-1414
F Edward Voelker, *Pr*
Ellen Welker, *VP*
David L Demoss, *Sec*
EMP: 74 EST: 1998

SALES (est): 102.84MM
SALES (corp-wide): 5.5B **Publicly Held**
Web: www.midwestlogisticssystems.com
SIC: 4212 Local trucking, without storage
PA: Schneider National, Inc.
3101 S Packerland Dr
Green Bay WI 54313
920 592-2000

(G-1929)
ORTHODONTIC ASSOCIATES LLC
Also Called: Fowler, Gary J DDS Ms
724 E Wayne St (45822-1356)
PHONE.................................419 229-8771
Thomas Ahman, *Pr*
EMP: 50 EST: 1952
SALES (est): 4.95MM **Privately Held**
Web: www.smilecreators.net
SIC: 8021 Orthodontist

(G-1930)
UNITED PARCEL SERVICE INC
Also Called: UPS
1851 Industrial Dr (45822-1377)
PHONE.................................419 586-8556
Steve Hoyne, *Brnch Mgr*
EMP: 31
SALES (corp-wide): 90.96B **Publicly Held**
Web: www.ups.com
SIC: 4215 Parcel delivery, vehicular
HQ: United Parcel Service, Inc.
55 Glenlake Pkwy
Atlanta GA 30328
404 828-6000

(G-1931)
VERSA-PAK LTD
500 Staeger Rd (45822)
P.O. Box 69 (45822)
PHONE.................................419 586-5466
Jeffrey C Bruns, *Rep*
Kenneth Gerlach, *
Mark A Bruns, *
EMP: 45 EST: 2000
SQ FT: 23,000
SALES (est): 21.72MM **Privately Held**
Web: www.versa-pak.com
SIC: 5199 2671 Packaging materials; Plastic film, coated or laminated for packaging

Centerburg
Knox County

(G-1932)
CENTERBURG PNTE HLTHCARE GROUP
Also Called: Centerburg Pointe
4531 Columbus Rd (43011-9401)
PHONE.................................740 625-5401
George S Repchick, *Pr*
William I Weisberg, *
EMP: 230 EST: 2010
SALES (est): 3.34MM
SALES (corp-wide): 655.44MM **Privately Held**
Web: www.saberhealth.com
SIC: 8051 Convalescent home with continuous nursing care
PA: Saber Healthcare Group, L.L.C.
23700 Commerce Park
Beachwood OH 44122
216 292-5706

(G-1933)
CENTERBURG TWO LLC
Also Called: Centerburg Respiratory and Specialty Rehab Center
212 Fairview St (43011-8314)
PHONE.................................740 625-5774

George Repchick, *Pr*
William Weisberg, *
EMP: 73 EST: 2007
SALES (est): 6.73MM
SALES (corp-wide): 655.44MM **Privately Held**
Web: www.saberhealth.com
SIC: 8051 Convalescent home with continuous nursing care
PA: Saber Healthcare Group, L.L.C.
23700 Commerce Park
Beachwood OH 44122
216 292-5706

(G-1934)
COOPER ADEL VU & ASSOC LPA
36 W Main St (43011-7048)
PHONE.................................740 625-4220
Mitchell J Adel, *Pr*
EMP: 52 EST: 2012
SALES (est): 4.49MM **Privately Held**
Web: www.cooperadelvu.com
SIC: 8742 Management consulting services

(G-1935)
DAMASCUS CTHLIC MISSION CAMPUS
3 Township Road 200 (43011-9674)
PHONE.................................740 480-1288
EMP: 41 EST: 2016
SALES (est): 668.3K **Privately Held**
Web: www.damascus.net
SIC: 8699 Charitable organization

(G-1936)
SHREDDED BEDDING CORPORATION (PA)
Also Called: SBC Recycling
6328 Bennington Chapel Rd (43011-9312)
PHONE.................................740 893-3567
EMP: 58 EST: 1993
SALES (est): 9.71MM **Privately Held**
SIC: 7389 4953 5093 Brokers' services; Recycling, waste materials; Scrap and waste materials

(G-1937)
TABLE ROCK GOLF CLUB INC
3005 Wilson Rd (43011-9467)
PHONE.................................740 625-6859
TOLL FREE: 800
Kathy Butler, *Pr*
Jim Butler, *
EMP: 35 EST: 1973
SQ FT: 4,500
SALES (est): 1.12MM **Privately Held**
Web: www.tablerockgc.com
SIC: 7992 Public golf courses

Centerville
Montgomery County

(G-1938)
ABC SCRIBES LTD
6784 Loop Rd Ste 210 (45459-2161)
PHONE.................................937 705-5471
Kim Kwiatek, *Prin*
EMP: 37 EST: 2010
SALES (est): 122.23K **Privately Held**
SIC: 7338 Secretarial and typing service

(G-1939)
AYDELOTT EQUIPMENT INC
Also Called: A E I
119 Compark Rd (45459-4803)
PHONE.................................888 293-3568
◆ EMP: 32 EST: 1990
SALES (est): 22.91MM **Privately Held**
Web: www.aydelott.com

GEOGRAPHIC SECTION
Chagrin Falls - Cuyahoga County (G-1961)

SIC: 5046 Commercial cooking and food service equipment

(G-1940)
CENTERVILLE FITNESS INC
Also Called: Club 51 Fitness
51 E Spring Valley Pike (45458-3801)
PHONE...................................937 291-7990
Michael Brunett, *Pr*
EMP: 35 **EST:** 2010
SQ FT: 40,000
SALES (est): 1.41MM **Privately Held**
Web: www.club51fitness.com
SIC: 7991 Health club

(G-1941)
CLYO INTERNAL MEDICINE INC
7073 Clyo Rd (45459-4816)
PHONE...................................937 435-5857
R Jeffrey Taylor, *Pr*
EMP: 31 **EST:** 2003
SALES (est): 650.59K
SALES (corp-wide): 3.6B **Privately Held**
SIC: 8011 Physicians' office, including specialists
HQ: Ipc Healthcare, Inc.
  4605 Lnkrshim Blvd Ste 61
  North Hollywood CA 91602
  888 447-2362

(G-1942)
CMT II ADVISORS LLC
6485 Centerville Business Pkwy (45459-2673)
PHONE...................................937 434-3095
Bev Yates, *Managing Member*
EMP: 45 **EST:** 2001
SALES (est): 3.13MM **Privately Held**
SIC: 6282 Investment advisory service

(G-1943)
DAYTON OB GYN
330 N Main St Ste 200 (45459-4459)
PHONE...................................937 439-7550
Ahmed Moezzi, *Pr*
Michael Thesing, *VP*
Brent Imbody, *VP*
EMP: 47 **EST:** 1986
SQ FT: 46,000
SALES (est): 1.91MM **Privately Held**
Web: www.premierhealth.com
SIC: 8011 Gynecologist

(G-1944)
DAYTON OSTEOPATHIC HOSPITAL
Also Called: Dayton Spt Mdicine Centerville
7677 Yankee St Ste 110 (45459-3475)
PHONE...................................937 401-6400
EMP: 27
SALES (corp-wide): 2.46B **Privately Held**
Web: www.ketteringhealth.com
SIC: 8062 General medical and surgical hospitals
HQ: Dayton Osteopathic Hospital
  405 W Grand Ave
  Dayton OH 45405
  937 762-1629

(G-1945)
GRISMER TIRE COMPANY (PA)
1099 S Main St (45458-3840)
P.O. Box 337 (45401-0337)
PHONE...................................937 643-2526
Charles L Marshall Ii, *Pr*
John L Marshall, *
Robert Hupp, *
▲ **EMP:** 28 **EST:** 1932
SQ FT: 40,000
SALES (est): 18.33MM
SALES (corp-wide): 18.33MM **Privately Held**
Web: www.grismertire.com
SIC: 5531 7538 5014 7534 Automotive tires; General automotive repair shops; Automobile tires and tubes; Rebuilding and retreading tires

(G-1946)
IRONGATE INC (PA)
Also Called: Irongate Realtors
122 N Main St (45459-4621)
PHONE...................................937 433-3300
Steven Brown, *Pr*
Steven Brown, *Sec*
Greg Gillen, *
EMP: 80 **EST:** 1960
SALES (est): 24.13MM
SALES (corp-wide): 24.13MM **Privately Held**
Web: www.irongaterealtors.com
SIC: 6531 6311 Real estate agent, residential ; Mutual association life insurance

(G-1947)
MCM ELECTRONICS INC
650 Congress Park Dr (45459-4000)
P.O. Box 750275 (45475-0275)
PHONE...................................888 235-4692
◆ **EMP:** 109
Web: electronics.mcmelectronics.com
SIC: 5065 Electronic parts and equipment, nec

(G-1948)
OHIO ALLERGY ASSOCIATES INC (PA)
Also Called: Allergy & Asthma Centre Dayton
8039 Washington Village Dr Ste 100 (45458-1877)
PHONE...................................937 435-8999
Arturo J Bonnin, *Prin*
EMP: 28 **EST:** 1996
SALES (est): 2.97MM **Privately Held**
Web: www.allergyasthmadayton.com
SIC: 8011 Allergist

(G-1949)
ORTHOPEDIC ASSOC SW OHIO INC (PA)
7677 Yankee St Ste 110 (45459-3475)
PHONE...................................937 415-9100
Jan E Faunders, *
Jan E Faunders, *
H Brent Bamberger, *
Sally Chaytor, *
EMP: 30 **EST:** 1985
SALES (est): 29.65MM **Privately Held**
Web: www.oadoctors.com
SIC: 8011 Orthopedic physician

(G-1950)
PREMIER SPORTS MEDICINE
2350 Miami Valley Dr Ste 320 (45459-4778)
PHONE...................................937 312-1661
EMP: 32 **EST:** 2016
SALES (est): 59.55K **Privately Held**
Web: www.premierhealth.com
SIC: 8011 Orthopedic physician

(G-1951)
PURE HEALTH CARE LLC
2200 Miami Valley Dr (45459-4783)
PHONE...................................937 668-7873
EMP: 30 **EST:** 2018
SALES (est): 572.68K **Privately Held**
Web: www.purehealthcare.org
SIC: 8082 8059 Home health care services; Personal care home, with health care

(G-1952)
TOTAL QUALITY LOGISTICS LLC
6525 Centerville Business Pkwy (45459-2686)
PHONE...................................800 580-3101
Matt Howard, *Prin*
EMP: 108
SALES (corp-wide): 8.85B **Privately Held**
Web: www.tql.com
SIC: 4731 Truck transportation brokers
HQ: Total Quality Logistics, Llc
  4289 Ivy Pointe Blvd
  Cincinnati OH 45245

Chagrin Falls
Cuyahoga County

(G-1953)
BEAVER DAM HEALTH CARE CENTER
Also Called: Hamlet Manor
150 Cleveland St (44022-2985)
PHONE...................................440 247-4200
Bartlett T Bell, *Brnch Mgr*
EMP: 37
SQ FT: 41,000
SALES (corp-wide): 825.65MM **Privately Held**
Web: www.beaverdamhcc.com
SIC: 8051 Skilled nursing care facilities
PA: Golden Living Llc
  5220 Tennyson Pkwy # 400
  Plano TX 75024
  972 372-6300

(G-1954)
CELLCO PARTNERSHIP
Also Called: Verizon Wireless
16 S Main St (44022-3218)
PHONE...................................440 893-6100
EMP: 71
SALES (corp-wide): 133.97B **Publicly Held**
Web: www.verizonwireless.com
SIC: 4812 Cellular telephone services
HQ: Cellco Partnership
  1 Verizon Way
  Basking Ridge NJ 07920

(G-1955)
CHAGRIN VALLEY COUNTRY CLUB CO
4700 Som Center Rd (44022-2399)
PHONE...................................440 248-4310
Jack Goldberg, *Ex Dir*
Alan Matta, *
EMP: 100 **EST:** 1925
SQ FT: 30,000
SALES (est): 9.34MM **Privately Held**
Web: www.cvcclub.com
SIC: 7997 Country club, membership

(G-1956)
CLEVELAND CLNIC CHGRIN FLS FML
551 Washington St (44022-4403)
PHONE...................................440 893-9393
Lisa Ramage, *Mgr*
Kim Reidel, *Prin*
EMP: 492 **EST:** 2004
SALES (est): 7.01MM
SALES (corp-wide): 14.48B **Privately Held**
Web: my.clevelandclinic.org
SIC: 8011 Clinic, operated by physicians
PA: The Cleveland Clinic Foundation
  9500 Euclid Ave
  Cleveland OH 44195
  216 636-8335

(G-1957)
D E WILLIAMS ELECTRIC INC
168 Solon Rd Ste B (44022-3100)
P.O. Box 180 (44022-0180)
PHONE...................................440 543-1222
Briana Harper, *Pr*
Ted Williams, *
Dan E Williams, *
Douglas Williams, *
EMP: 50 **EST:** 1952
SQ FT: 12,000
SALES (est): 3.87MM **Privately Held**
Web: www.dewilliamselectric.com
SIC: 1731 General electrical contractor

(G-1958)
FOR WOMEN LIKE ME INC (PA)
Also Called: Fwlm
46 Shopping Plz Ste 155 (44022-3022)
PHONE...................................407 848-7339
Arline Burks, *CEO*
Dakkota Gant, *
Marsha Robles, *
Julie Turner, *
Kathy Chislom, *
◆ **EMP:** 42 **EST:** 1988
SQ FT: 5,000
SALES (est): 866.99K
SALES (corp-wide): 866.99K **Privately Held**
SIC: 7812 5137 5621 5136 Television film production; Women's and children's clothing ; Women's clothing stores; Men's and boy's clothing

(G-1959)
HAMLET VILLAGE IN CHAGRIN FLS (PA)
200 Hamlet Hills Dr Ofc (44022-2838)
PHONE...................................216 263-6033
John Eigen, *Ex Dir*
EMP: 45 **EST:** 2004
SALES (est): 8.48MM
SALES (corp-wide): 8.48MM **Privately Held**
Web: www.hamletretirement.com
SIC: 6513 Retirement hotel operation

(G-1960)
HAMLET VILLAGE IN CHAGRIN FLS
Also Called: Hamlet Nursing Home
150 Cleveland St (44022-2985)
PHONE...................................440 247-4200
John Eigen, *Brnch Mgr*
EMP: 105
SALES (corp-wide): 8.48MM **Privately Held**
Web: www.hamletretirement.com
SIC: 8059 Rest home, with health care
PA: Hamlet Village In Chagrin Falls
  200 Hamlet Hills Dr Ofc
  Chagrin Falls OH 44022
  216 263-6033

(G-1961)
LAKE HORRY ELECTRIC (PA)
Also Called: Hirsch Division
255 Bramley Ct (44022-3613)
PHONE...................................440 808-8791
Ronald Hirsch, *Pr*
Michael Simon, *
Birdie Hirsch, *
EMP: 100 **EST:** 1967
SQ FT: 12,000
SALES (est): 4.39MM
SALES (corp-wide): 4.39MM **Privately Held**
SIC: 1731 General electrical contractor

Chagrin Falls - Cuyahoga County (G-1962)

GEOGRAPHIC SECTION

(G-1962)
LANTERN OF CHAGRIN VALLEY
5277 Chillicothe Rd (44022-4334)
PHONE.................................440 996-5084
Heather Grice, *Prin*
EMP: 36 **EST:** 2015
SALES (est): 2.49MM **Privately Held**
Web: www.lanternlifestyle.com
SIC: 8361 Residential care

(G-1963)
MUSICAL UPCMING STARS IN CLSSI
3939 Lander Rd (44022-1328)
PHONE.................................216 702-7047
Manny Nast, *Pr*
Jodi Kanter, *Dir*
EMP: 29 **EST:** 2010
SALES (est): 195.27K **Privately Held**
Web: www.starsintheclassics.org
SIC: 7929 Musician

(G-1964)
REAL ESTATE MORTGAGE CORP
200 Jackson Dr (44022-1556)
PHONE.................................440 356-5373
Mark Johnston, *Pr*
EMP: 53 **EST:** 1988
SQ FT: 4,000
SALES (est): 2.28MM
SALES (corp-wide): 28.65MM **Privately Held**
SIC: 6162 Mortgage bankers and loan correspondents
PA: The American Eagle Mortgage Co Llc
6145 Park Sq Dr Ste 4
Lorain OH 44053
440 988-2900

(G-1965)
ROBOTS AND PENCILS LP
7 1/2 N Franklin St (44022-3009)
PHONE.................................866 515-9897
Tracey Zimmerman, *Pt*
EMP: 117 **EST:** 2017
SALES (est): 24.8MM **Privately Held**
Web: www.robotsandpencils.com
SIC: 7371 Computer software development

(G-1966)
SNAVELY BUILDING COMPANY (PA)
7139 Pine St Ste 110 (44022-3401)
PHONE.................................440 585-9091
John P Snavely, *Ch*
John P Snavely, *Ch Bd*
Peter Snavely, *
Paul Snavely, *
John E Withrow, *
EMP: 30 **EST:** 1988
SQ FT: 6,000
SALES (est): 24.67MM
SALES (corp-wide): 24.67MM **Privately Held**
Web: www.snavely.com
SIC: 1542 1521 1522 Commercial and office building, new construction; New construction, single-family houses; Apartment building construction

(G-1967)
SNAVELY DEVELOPMENT COMPANY (PA)
7139 Pine St (44022-3401)
PHONE.................................440 585-9091
Peter Snavely Senior, *Pr*
Brad Lohan, *Finance*
EMP: 40 **EST:** 1980
SQ FT: 6,000
SALES (est): 8.91MM
SALES (corp-wide): 8.91MM **Privately Held**
Web: www.snavely.com

SIC: 1521 1522 New construction, single-family houses; Multi-family dwellings, new construction

(G-1968)
STATESIDE UNDWRT AGCY INC
13 1/2 N Franklin St Ste 1 (44022-3009)
PHONE.................................440 893-9917
EMP: 41
SALES (corp-wide): 96.23MM **Privately Held**
Web: www.statesideunderwriting.com
SIC: 6411 Insurance brokers, nec
HQ: Stateside Underwriting Agency, Inc.
265 Exchange Dr Ste 101
Crystal Lake IL 60014

(G-1969)
STOUFFER REALTY LLC
68 Olive St (44022-3117)
PHONE.................................440 247-4210
EMP: 42
SALES (corp-wide): 224.25K **Privately Held**
Web: www.stoufferrealty.com
SIC: 6531 Real estate brokers and agents
PA: Stouffer Realty Llc
8748 Brecksville Rd
Brecksville OH 44141
440 526-6700

(G-1970)
VERTICAL KNOWLEDGE LLC (HQ)
8 E Washington St Ste 200 (44022)
PHONE.................................216 920-7790
Matt Carpenter, *CEO*
EMP: 45 **EST:** 2006
SALES (est): 10.46MM **Privately Held**
Web: www.vk.ai
SIC: 7379 Online services technology consultants
PA: Babel Street, Inc.
1818 Library St Ste 500
Reston VA 20190

(G-1971)
W HOME COLLECTION LLC
Also Called: W Design Interiors
86 West St (44022-2759)
PHONE.................................440 247-4474
Wendy Berry, *Managing Member*
Catherine Stenta, *Prin*
EMP: 36 **EST:** 2014
SALES (est): 844.4K **Privately Held**
Web: www.wdesign.com
SIC: 7389 5712 Interior designer; Furniture stores

Chagrin Falls
Geauga County

(G-1972)
ALLIED POWER TRANSMISSION CO
10160 Queens Way Unit 3 (44023-5434)
PHONE.................................440 708-1006
Jim J Steiner, *Pr*
James Mcdevitt, *Mgr*
EMP: 40 **EST:** 1946
SQ FT: 8,000
SALES (est): 3.36MM **Privately Held**
Web: www.allied.com
SIC: 5063 5085 Motors, electric; Power transmission equipment and apparatus

(G-1973)
APEC ENGINEERING INC
7416 Pettibone Rd (44023-4941)
PHONE.................................440 708-2303
David M Berry, *Prin*

EMP: 44 **EST:** 2009
SALES (est): 4.5MM **Privately Held**
Web: www.apecengineering.com
SIC: 8711 Electrical or electronic engineering

(G-1974)
CHAGRIN VALLEY ATHC CLB INC
17260 Snyder Rd (44023-2724)
PHONE.................................440 543-5141
James M Rosenberger, *Pr*
Hollis H Rosenberger, *
EMP: 100 **EST:** 1968
SALES (est): 4.75MM **Privately Held**
Web: www.cvaclub.com
SIC: 7997 Membership sports and recreation clubs

(G-1975)
CHERISHED COMPANIONS HOME CARE
7181 Chagrin Rd Ste 200 (44023-1128)
PHONE.................................440 273-7230
Douglas A Wilber, *Pr*
EMP: 59 **EST:** 2016
SALES (est): 1.21MM **Privately Held**
Web: www.cherishedagency.com
SIC: 8082 Home health care services

(G-1976)
CUSTOM MATERIALS INC
Also Called: C M I Group
16865 Park Circle Dr (44023-4591)
PHONE.................................440 543-8284
Anthony D Borrelli, *Prin*
Robert G Boes, *Prin*
Yaro Mraz, *Prin*
Hillary T Robinson, *
Taylor D Robinson, *
▲ **EMP:** 70 **EST:** 1964
SQ FT: 50,000
SALES (est): 12.97MM **Privately Held**
Web: www.custommaterials.com
SIC: 8711 Engineering services

(G-1977)
EXCALIBUR COLLISION INC
9935 Washington St (44023-5483)
PHONE.................................440 708-9898
William E Collins, *Pr*
Mitch Rudolph, *VP*
EMP: 38 **EST:** 2005
SQ FT: 13,000
SALES (est): 640.89K **Privately Held**
SIC: 7532 Collision shops, automotive

(G-1978)
HEMLOCK LANDSCAPES INC
7209 Chagrin Rd Ste A (44023-1129)
PHONE.................................440 247-3631
Dennis Barriball, *Pr*
Lauren Barriball, *Treas*
EMP: 41 **EST:** 1981
SQ FT: 4,500
SALES (est): 4.8MM **Privately Held**
Web: www.hemlocklandscapes.com
SIC: 0781 0782 Landscape services; Landscape contractors

(G-1979)
HIGHWAY AUTO CENTER LLC
Also Called: Highway Auto Body
8410 Washington St (44023-4581)
PHONE.................................440 543-9569
EMP: 28 **EST:** 1977
SALES (est): 5.55MM **Privately Held**
Web: www.highwayautocenter.com
SIC: 7538 7532 General automotive repair shops; Body shop, automotive

(G-1980)
IMS COMPANY
Also Called: Injection Molders Supply
10373 Stafford Rd (44023-5296)
PHONE.................................440 543-1615
Brad G Morse, *CEO*
Mary Ann Morris, *
Jeffrey Sawicki, *
◆ **EMP:** 60 **EST:** 1960
SQ FT: 62,000
SALES (est): 24.15MM **Privately Held**
Web: www.imscompany.com
SIC: 5084 Plastic products machinery

(G-1981)
IRISH ENVY LLC
Also Called: Massage Envy
48 Windward Way (44023-6706)
PHONE.................................440 808-8000
Kevin Flynn, *Managing Member*
EMP: 30 **EST:** 2009
SALES (est): 610.89K **Privately Held**
Web: www.irishenvy.com
SIC: 7299 Massage parlor

(G-1982)
JDD INC (PA)
17800 Chillicothe Rd Ste 250a
(44023-4885)
PHONE.................................216 464-8855
James Vaughan Junior, *Pr*
EMP: 92 **EST:** 1994
SALES (est): 2.32MM
SALES (corp-wide): 2.32MM **Privately Held**
Web: www.jdd-inc.com
SIC: 7349 Janitorial service, contract basis

(G-1983)
JUDSON SERVICES INC
16600 Warren Ct (44023-1173)
PHONE.................................216 791-2004
EMP: 48
SALES (corp-wide): 1.74MM **Privately Held**
Web: www.judsonsmartliving.org
SIC: 8361 Aged home
PA: Judson Services, Inc.
2181 Ambleside Dr
Cleveland OH 44106
216 791-2004

(G-1984)
LOWES INVESTMENTS INC
Also Called: Lowe's Greenhouses & Gift Shop
16540 Chillicothe Rd (44023-4328)
PHONE.................................440 543-5123
Jeffrey B Griff, *Pr*
Mary Lynn Griff, *
EMP: 35 **EST:** 1953
SQ FT: 40,000
SALES (est): 2.2MM **Privately Held**
Web: www.lowesgreenhouse.com
SIC: 5992 0181 5947 Flowers, fresh; Foliage, growing of; Gift shop

(G-1985)
M&C HOTEL INTERESTS INC
Also Called: Pine Lake Trout Club
17021 Chillicothe Rd (44023-4617)
P.O. Box 23282 (44023-0282)
PHONE.................................440 543-1331
Sandra Hughes, *Brnch Mgr*
EMP: 128
Web: www.richfield.com
SIC: 8741 7997 Hotel or motel management; Membership sports and recreation clubs
HQ: M&C Hotel Interests, Inc.
6560 Greenwood Plaza Blvd
Greenwood Village CO 80111

▲ = Import ▼ = Export
◆ = Import/Export

(G-1986)
MEDHURST MASON CONTRACTORS INC
17111 Munn Rd Ste 1 (44023-5427)
PHONE..................................440 543-8885
Robert Medhurst, *Pr*
Carol Medhurst, *
EMP: 115 **EST:** 1976
SQ FT: 7,900
SALES (est): 4.27MM **Privately Held**
SIC: 1741 Bricklaying

(G-1987)
PROS FREIGHT CORPORATION
16687 Hilltop Park Pl (44023-4500)
PHONE..................................440 543-7555
Elaine R Moore, *Pr*
EMP: 30 **EST:** 1975
SQ FT: 2,000
SALES (est): 2.13MM **Privately Held**
Web: www.proscorp.com
SIC: 4213 Contract haulers

(G-1988)
ROUNDTABLE LEARNING LLC
8401 Chagrin Rd Ste 6 (44023-4702)
PHONE..................................440 220-5252
Dan Grajzl, *Pr*
Tanya Loncar, *Client Services Vice President*
James Lorentz, *Strategic Partner*
Jim Wenger, *Development*
EMP: 49 **EST:** 1998
SQ FT: 3,500
SALES (est): 4.21MM **Privately Held**
Web: www.roundtablelearning.com
SIC: 8299 4813 Educational services; Internet host services

(G-1989)
SCHNEIDER SADDLERY LLC
Also Called: Billy Royal
8255 Washington St (44023)
PHONE..................................440 543-2700
Donald Schneider, *Pr*
Stanley Schneider, *
◆ **EMP:** 35 **EST:** 1966
SQ FT: 40,000
SALES (est): 7.12MM **Privately Held**
Web: www.sstack.com
SIC: 5941 5699 5091 5961 Saddlery and equestrian equipment; Riding apparel; Sporting and recreation goods; Mail order house, nec

(G-1990)
SMALL HNDS BIG DRAMS LRNG CTRS
8505 Tanglewood Sq Ste T26 (44023-6434)
PHONE..................................440 708-0559
EMP: 35 **EST:** 2002
SQ FT: 4,757
SALES (est): 696.39K **Privately Held**
Web: www.smallhandsbigdreams.com
SIC: 8351 Group day care center

(G-1991)
SOUTH FRANKLIN CIRCLE
16575 S Franklin St (44023-1002)
PHONE..................................440 247-1300
Rob Lucarelli, *Dir*
EMP: 54
Web: www.judsonsmartliving.org
SIC: 6513 Retirement hotel operation
PA: South Franklin Circle
16600 Warren Ct
Chagrin Falls OH 44023

(G-1992)
ULL INC
9812 Washington St (44023-5486)
P.O. Box 23399 (44023-0399)
PHONE..................................440 543-5195
Marilyn Ullman, *Pr*
Joshua R Cilley, *
Lee Sparbeck, *Prin*
Kim Ullman, *
Bernd O Bryant, *
EMP: 42 **EST:** 1966
SQ FT: 20,000
SALES (est): 17.52MM **Privately Held**
SIC: 5172 5983 Petroleum products, nec; Fuel oil dealers

Chardon
Geauga County

(G-1993)
ABB INC
Also Called: ABB, INC.
9145 Cambridge Rd (44024-9621)
PHONE..................................440 725-2968
EMP: 41
Web: www.abb.com
SIC: 5063 Electrical apparatus and equipment
HQ: Abb Inc.
305 Gregson Dr
Cary NC 27511

(G-1994)
AYRSHIRE INC (PA)
191 5th Ave (44024-1005)
P.O. Box 172 (44024-0172)
PHONE..................................440 286-9507
Randall Darling, *Pr*
Ken Jamison, *
D M Dworken, *
H W Bernstein, *
M E Resnick, *
EMP: 40 **EST:** 1975
SQ FT: 5,000
SALES (est): 20.15MM
SALES (corp-wide): 20.15MM **Privately Held**
Web: www.ayrshireinc.com
SIC: 1541 Industrial buildings, new construction, nec

(G-1995)
CENTER FOR DIALYSIS CARE
12340 Bass Lake Rd (44024-8327)
PHONE..................................440 286-4103
Jennifer Hoppert, *Mgr*
EMP: 28 **EST:** 1998
SALES (est): 710.66K **Privately Held**
Web: www.cdcare.org
SIC: 8071 8011 Medical laboratories; Clinic, operated by physicians

(G-1996)
CHARDON LAKES GOLF COURSE INC (PA)
470 South St (44024-2804)
PHONE..................................440 285-4653
Tom Bond, *Genl Mgr*
Rick Heterstrom, *
Jerry Peterson, *
Tom Bond M, *Prin*
EMP: 40 **EST:** 1988
SQ FT: 300
SALES (est): 916.25K **Privately Held**
Web: www.chardonlakes.com
SIC: 7992 Public golf courses

(G-1997)
CHARDON TOOL & SUPPLY CO INC
115 Parker Ct (44024-1112)
P.O. Box 291 (44024-0291)
PHONE..................................440 286-6440
Weldon Bennett, *Pr*
EMP: 40 **EST:** 1986
SQ FT: 4,800
SALES (est): 4.41MM **Privately Held**
Web: www.chardontool.com
SIC: 3545 5085 Diamond cutting tools for turning, boring, burnishing, etc.; Diamonds, industrial: natural, crude

(G-1998)
COUNTY OF GEAUGA
Also Called: Geauga County Jobs & Fmly Svcs
12611 Ravenwood Dr Ste 150 (44024-9340)
P.O. Box 309 (44024-0309)
PHONE..................................440 285-9141
Tim Taylor, *Dir*
EMP: 64
SALES (corp-wide): 103.12MM **Privately Held**
Web: www.geauga.org
SIC: 8322 Public welfare center
PA: County Of Geauga
470 Center St Bldg 4
Chardon OH 44024
440 285-2222

(G-1999)
GARDENLIFE INC
Also Called: Grimes Seeds
10010 Mitchells Mill Rd (44024)
PHONE..................................800 241-7333
Gary S Grimes, *Ch Bd*
Rodney Ledrew, *
EMP: 35 **EST:** 1925
SALES (est): 4.88MM **Privately Held**
SIC: 5191 Seeds: field, garden, and flower

(G-2000)
GEAUGA MECHANICAL COMPANY
12585 Chardon Windsor Rd (44024-8968)
PHONE..................................440 285-2000
Bruce Berman, *Pr*
Ted R Berman, *
Tom Wadsworth, *
Tim Berman, *
EMP: 72 **EST:** 1950
SQ FT: 15,000
SALES (est): 20.77MM **Privately Held**
Web: www.geaugamechanical.com
SIC: 1711 1761 Warm air heating and air conditioning contractor; Sheet metal work, nec

(G-2001)
GEAUGA PARK DISTRICT
9160 Robinson Rd (44024-9148)
PHONE..................................440 415-5661
John Oros, *Prin*
EMP: 75 **EST:** 2021
SALES (est): 1.55MM **Privately Held**
Web: www.geaugaparkdistrict.org
SIC: 8641 Civic associations

(G-2002)
GEAUGA REGIONAL HOSP HM CARE
13207 Ravenna Rd (44024-7032)
PHONE..................................440 285-6834
Andrew R Nara Md, *Prin*
EMP: 35 **EST:** 2003
SALES (est): 1.12MM **Privately Held**
SIC: 8062 General medical and surgical hospitals

(G-2003)
GEM ELECTRIC
12577 Gar Hwy (44024-9201)
PHONE..................................440 286-6200
Patrick Nusrala, *Owner*
EMP: 27 **EST:** 1985
SQ FT: 3,000
SALES (est): 2.97MM **Privately Held**
Web: www.gem-electric.com
SIC: 1731 General electrical contractor

(G-2004)
HEATHERHILL CARE COMMUNITIES
12340 Bass Lake Rd (44024-8327)
PHONE..................................440 285-4040
Jim Homa, *Pr*
Andy Bragalone, *
EMP: 28 **EST:** 2006
SALES (est): 1.31MM **Privately Held**
Web: www.heatherhill-care.net
SIC: 8051 Convalescent home with continuous nursing care

(G-2005)
HUNTINGTON NATIONAL BANK
Also Called: Firstmerit Bank
376 Center St (44024-1104)
PHONE..................................440 285-2111
Beverly Book, *Mgr*
EMP: 36
SALES (corp-wide): 10.84B **Publicly Held**
Web: www.huntington.com
SIC: 6029 Commercial banks, nec
HQ: The Huntington National Bank
41 S High St
Columbus OH 43215
614 480-4293

(G-2006)
IBOLD & OBRIEN INC
Also Called: Evans, Jonathon P
401 South St Ste 1a (44024-2820)
PHONE..................................440 279-0688
Jerry Peterson, *Pr*
Dennis J Ibold, *Pr*
Jerry Petersen, *VP*
Michael J Ibold, *Treas*
EMP: 39 **EST:** 1977
SALES (est): 4.26MM **Privately Held**
Web: www.iboldobrien.com
SIC: 8111 General practice law office

(G-2007)
INSURNCE SPECIALISTS GROUP INC
Also Called: Love Insurance Agency
373 Center St Ste A (44024-8952)
PHONE..................................440 975-0309
Robert J Love, *Pr*
James P Love, *VP*
John C Love, *Sec*
EMP: 36 **EST:** 2001
SALES (est): 1.99MM **Privately Held**
Web: www.loveinsurance.com
SIC: 6411 Insurance agents, nec

(G-2008)
INTELLINET CORPORATION (PA)
150 Center St (44024-1179)
PHONE..................................216 289-4100
Richard E Taton, *CEO*
Ronald J Taton, *Pr*
John Odonnell, *VP*
EMP: 61 **EST:** 1997
SALES (est): 8.25MM
SALES (corp-wide): 8.25MM **Privately Held**
Web: www.intellinetcorp.com
SIC: 4813 Internet connectivity services

Chardon - Geauga County (G-2009)

(G-2009)
LAKE HEALTH INC
510 5th Ave Ste C130 (44024-2910)
PHONE..............................440 279-1500
Robert B Tracz, *Prin*
EMP: 57 **EST:** 2003
SALES (est): 2.15MM **Privately Held**
Web: www.uhhospitals.org
SIC: 8062 General medical and surgical hospitals

(G-2010)
MAPLE GROVE ENTERPRISES INC
Also Called: First Light Home Care
526 Water St (44024-1147)
PHONE..............................440 286-1342
Annette Smith, *Pr*
EMP: 54 **EST:** 2011
SALES (est): 2.53MM **Privately Held**
Web: www.maplegroveenterprises.com
SIC: 8082 Home health care services

(G-2011)
MAPLEVIEW COUNTRY VILLA
775 South St (44024-2800)
PHONE..............................440 286-8176
Mckenzie Kretch, *Admn*
Admiral Mckenzie Kretch, *Prin*
EMP: 62 **EST:** 2015
SALES (est): 15.59MM **Privately Held**
Web: www.lhshealth.com
SIC: 8051 Skilled nursing care facilities

(G-2012)
MCI COMMUNICATIONS SVCS LLC
Also Called: Verizon Business
12956 Taylor Wells Rd (44024-7910)
PHONE..............................440 635-0418
Dane Oneill, *Brnch Mgr*
EMP: 67
SALES (corp-wide): 136.84B **Publicly Held**
SIC: 4813 Long distance telephone communications
HQ: Mci Communications Services Llc
22001 Loudoun County Pkwy
Ashburn VA 20147
703 886-5600

(G-2013)
NMS WEALTH MANAGEMENT LLC
121 South St (44024-1306)
PHONE..............................440 286-5222
Shawn Neece, *Prin*
EMP: 27 **EST:** 2013
SALES (est): 720.16K **Privately Held**
Web: www.nmswealthmanagement.com
SIC: 8741 Financial management for business

(G-2014)
PARKSIDE CARE CORPORATION
Also Called: Hospice of Care
11250 Thwing Rd (44024-8407)
PHONE..............................440 286-2273
Jason Baker, *CEO*
EMP: 80 **EST:** 1984
SALES (est): 2.71MM **Privately Held**
Web: www.carecorponline.com
SIC: 8082 Home health care services

(G-2015)
RAVENWOOD MENTAL HLTH CTR INC (PA)
Also Called: Ravenwood Health
12557 Ravenwood Dr (44024-9009)
PHONE..............................440 285-3568
Vicki Clark, *CEO*
EMP: 35 **EST:** 1966
SALES (est): 11.31MM
SALES (corp-wide): 11.31MM **Privately Held**
Web: www.ravenwoodhealth.org
SIC: 8093 Mental health clinic, outpatient

(G-2016)
RESIDENCE OF CHARDON
Also Called: Residents of Chardon
501 Chardon Windsor Rd (44024-8944)
PHONE..............................440 286-2277
Admiral Christin Johnson, *Prin*
EMP: 46 **EST:** 2000
SALES (est): 2.2MM **Privately Held**
Web: www.chardon.k12.oh.us
SIC: 8052 Intermediate care facilities

(G-2017)
RHEIN CHEMIE CORPORATION
145 Parker Ct (44024-1112)
PHONE..............................440 279-2367
◆ **EMP:** 250
Web: www.lanxess.com
SIC: 3069 5169 Reclaimed rubber and specialty rubber compounds; Industrial chemicals

(G-2018)
RONYAK PAVING INC
12063 Fowlers Mill Rd (44024-9399)
PHONE..............................440 279-0616
David W Ronyak, *Prin*
EMP: 28 **EST:** 2010
SALES (est): 2.02MM **Privately Held**
Web: www.ronyakbros.com
SIC: 1611 Highway and street paving contractor

(G-2019)
SAND RIDGE GOLF CLUB
12150 Mayfield Rd (44024-8448)
PHONE..............................440 285-8088
EMP: 50 **EST:** 1995
SALES (est): 1.31MM **Privately Held**
Web: www.mayfieldsandridge.com
SIC: 7997 5941 5812 Golf club, membership; Sporting goods and bicycle shops; Box lunch stand

(G-2020)
SISTERS OF NTRE DAME OF CHRDON
Also Called: Notre Dame Pre-School
13000 Auburn Rd (44024-9337)
PHONE..............................440 279-0575
Jennifer Hanna, *Dir*
EMP: 33
SALES (corp-wide): 22.32MM **Privately Held**
Web: www.sndusa.org
SIC: 8351 Preschool center
PA: The Sisters Of Notre Dame Of The United States
13000 Auburn Rd
Chardon OH 44024
440 286-7101

(G-2021)
STAT INTEGRATED TECH INC (PA)
Also Called: Aqua Doc Lake & Pond MGT
10779 Mayfield Rd (44024-9323)
P.O. Box 625 (44026-0625)
PHONE..............................440 286-7663
Jeanine Wilson, *Pr*
EMP: 34 **EST:** 1983
SALES (est): 9.89MM
SALES (corp-wide): 9.89MM **Privately Held**
Web: www.aquadocinc.com
SIC: 8741 Management services

(G-2022)
UH REGIONAL HOSPITALS
13207 Ravenna Rd (44024-7032)
PHONE..............................440 285-6000
EMP: 613
SALES (corp-wide): 878.24MM **Privately Held**
Web: www.uhhospitals.org
SIC: 8062 General medical and surgical hospitals
HQ: Uh Regional Hospitals
27100 Chardon Rd
Richmond Heights OH 44143
440 585-6439

(G-2023)
UNIVERSAL DISPOSAL INC
9954 Old State Rd (44024-9521)
P.O. Box 1065 (44024-5065)
PHONE..............................440 286-3153
Murl Clemson, *Pr*
Bill Clemson, *
Shirley Clemson, *
EMP: 50 **EST:** 1962
SQ FT: 1,500
SALES (est): 3.12MM **Privately Held**
Web: www.universaldisposalinc.com
SIC: 4212 Garbage collection and transport, no disposal

(G-2024)
UNIVERSITY HSPTALS HLTH SYSTM- (PA)
Also Called: Heather Hl Rehabilitation Hosp
12340 Bass Lake Rd (44024-8327)
PHONE..............................440 285-4040
Louise Alexander, *Ch Bd*
Susan Juris, *
David Pasco, *
EMP: 500 **EST:** 1935
SQ FT: 39,000
SALES (est): 22.59MM
SALES (corp-wide): 22.59MM **Privately Held**
Web: www.heatherhill-care.net
SIC: 8069 8059 8052 8051 Specialty hospitals, except psychiatric; Convalescent home; Intermediate care facilities; Skilled nursing care facilities

(G-2025)
VAN BOXEL STOR SOLUTIONS LLC
13770 Gar Hwy (44024-9288)
PHONE..............................440 721-1504
Kyle Van Boxel, *Managing Member*
EMP: 50 **EST:** 2015
SALES (est): 2.44MM **Privately Held**
SIC: 4225 5032 5023 General warehousing and storage; Brick, stone, and related material; Wood flooring

(G-2026)
WATER LEASING CO LLC
Also Called: CHARDON HEALTHCARE CENTER
620 Water St (44024-1149)
PHONE..............................440 285-9400
Stephen L Rosedale, *Managing Member*
Ronald S Wilheim, *Managing Member*
EMP: 39 **EST:** 2008
SALES (est): 7.9MM **Privately Held**
Web: www.communicarehealth.com
SIC: 8051 Convalescent home with continuous nursing care

(G-2027)
YOUNG MNS CHRSTN ASSN GRTER CL
Also Called: YMCA
12460 Bass Lake Rd (44024-8315)
PHONE..............................440 285-7543
Alexandria Nichols, *Brnch Mgr*
EMP: 42
SALES (corp-wide): 25.51MM **Privately Held**
Web: www.clevelandymca.org
SIC: 8641 7991 8351 7032 Youth organizations; Physical fitness facilities; Child day care services; Youth camps
PA: Young Men's Christian Association Of Greater Cleveland
1301 E 9th St Fl 9
Cleveland OH 44114
216 781-1337

Chesapeake
Lawrence County

(G-2028)
BIG SANDY FURNITURE INC
Also Called: Big Sandy Superstore
45 County Rd 407 (45619)
PHONE..............................740 894-4242
EMP: 68
Web: www.bigsandysuperstore.com
SIC: 4225 5712 General warehousing and storage; Furniture stores
HQ: Big Sandy Furniture, Inc.
8375 Gallia Pike
Franklin Furnace OH 45629
740 574-2113

Cheshire
Gallia County

(G-2029)
GALLI-MIGS CMNTY ACTION AGCY I (PA)
8317 State Route 7 N (45620-9001)
P.O. Box 272 (45620-0272)
PHONE..............................740 367-7341
Tom Reed, *Ex Dir*
Michael Davenport, *
Tony Gallagher, *
Linda Lester, *
EMP: 28 **EST:** 1965
SQ FT: 3,600
SALES (est): 5.3MM
SALES (corp-wide): 5.3MM **Privately Held**
Web: galliameigscaa.webs.com
SIC: 8322 Individual and family services

(G-2030)
GAVIN AEP PLANT
7397 State Route 7 N (45620-7500)
P.O. Box 271 (45620-0271)
PHONE..............................740 925-3166
EMP: 28 **EST:** 2010
SALES (est): 9.36MM **Privately Held**
Web: www.aep.com
SIC: 4911 Generation, electric power

(G-2031)
GAVIN POWER LLC
Also Called: Gavin Generating Station
7397 State Route 7 N (45620-7500)
P.O. Box 271 (45620-0271)
PHONE..............................740 925-3140
EMP: 96 **EST:** 2016
SALES (est): 53.22MM
SALES (corp-wide): 53.22MM **Privately Held**
Web: www.gavinpowerccr.com
SIC: 4911 Generation, electric power
PA: Lightstone Generation Llc
460 Park Ave
New York NY 10022

GEOGRAPHIC SECTION

Chillicothe - Ross County (G-2052)

212 616-9969

Chesterland
Geauga County

(G-2032)
BREMEC GROUP INC
Also Called: Bremec Group
12265 Chillicothe Rd (44026-2109)
PHONE.................................440 951-0770
Robert Bremec, *Pr*
EMP: 37 **EST:** 1980
SQ FT: 3,000
SALES (est): 1.88MM **Privately Held**
Web: www.bremec.com
SIC: 0782 4959 0781 Landscape contractors; Snowplowing; Landscape counseling and planning

(G-2033)
CLEVELAND CLINIC FOUNDATION
Also Called: Cleveland Clinic, The
8254 Mayfield Rd Ste 4 (44026-2562)
PHONE.................................440 729-9000
EMP: 33
SALES (corp-wide): 14.48B **Privately Held**
Web: my.clevelandclinic.org
SIC: 8062 General medical and surgical hospitals
PA: The Cleveland Clinic Foundation
9500 Euclid Ave
Cleveland OH 44195
216 636-8335

(G-2034)
CVS REVCO DS INC
Also Called: CVS
8519 Mayfield Rd (44026)
PHONE.................................440 729-9070
Ron Maurer, *Mgr*
EMP: 100
SALES (corp-wide): 357.78B **Publicly Held**
Web: www.cvs.com
SIC: 5912 7384 Drug stores; Photofinishing laboratory
HQ: Cvs Revco D.S., Inc.
1 Cvs Dr
Woonsocket RI 02895
401 765-1500

(G-2035)
FARMERS NAT BNK OF CANFIELD
Also Called: Farmers National Bank
8389 Mayfield Rd Ste B-1 (44026-2579)
PHONE.................................440 564-1520
Kevin Helmick, *Brnch Mgr*
EMP: 36
SALES (corp-wide): 255.2MM **Publicly Held**
Web: www.farmersbankgroup.com
SIC: 6021 National commercial banks
HQ: The Farmers National Bank Of Canfield
20 S Broad St
Canfield OH 44406
330 533-3341

(G-2036)
INNOVEST GLOBAL INC (PA)
8834 Mayfield Rd (44026-2690)
P.O. Box 179 (44045-0179)
PHONE.................................216 815-1122
Damon Mintz, *CEO*
Daniel G Martin, *Ch*
Indrani Egleston, *Ex VP*
EMP: 54 **EST:** 1997
SALES (est): 21.34MM
SALES (corp-wide): 21.34MM **Privately Held**
Web: www.innovestglobal.com
SIC: 8731 Biological research

(G-2037)
JP COMPASS CNSULTING CNSTR INC
Also Called: JP Compass
7948 Mayfield Rd (44026-2437)
PHONE.................................440 635-0500
John P Park, *Pr*
EMP: 32 **EST:** 2005
SALES (est): 2.15MM **Privately Held**
Web: www.compassstudio.com
SIC: 8741 Construction management

(G-2038)
LITIGATION MANAGEMENT INC
7976 Mayfield Rd (44026-2483)
PHONE.................................440 484-2000
Elizabeth Juliano, *CEO*
EMP: 141 **EST:** 1984
SALES (est): 22.75MM **Privately Held**
Web: www.lmiweb.com
SIC: 8111 Legal aid service

(G-2039)
MAIN SAIL LLC
8279 Mayfield Rd Unit 12 (44026-2540)
PHONE.................................216 472-5100
D Brian Conley, *Managing Member*
D Brian Conley, *Mng Pt*
Scott Harris, *
Robert Mackinley, *
Ken Conley, *
EMP: 50 **EST:** 2001
SQ FT: 5,000
SALES (est): 8.7MM **Privately Held**
Web: www.mainsailgroup.com
SIC: 7379 Online services technology consultants

(G-2040)
MATO INC
Also Called: Avanti Salon
8027 Mayfield Rd (44026-2438)
PHONE.................................440 729-9008
Marisa Paterniti, *Pr*
Tony Paterniti, *VP*
EMP: 47 **EST:** 1992
SQ FT: 1,450
SALES (est): 1.61MM **Privately Held**
Web: www.avantisalon.com
SIC: 7231 Hairdressers

(G-2041)
METZENBAUM SHELTERED INDS INC
Also Called: MSI
8090 Cedar Rd (44026-3465)
P.O. Box 538 (44065-0538)
PHONE.................................440 729-1919
Robert Voss, *Prgrm Mgr*
Robert Preston, *
Diane Buehner, *Head Secretary**
EMP: 73 **EST:** 1969
SQ FT: 12,000
SALES (est): 1.51MM **Privately Held**
Web: www.geaugadd.org
SIC: 8331 7389 3672 Sheltered workshop; Packaging and labeling services; Printed circuit boards

(G-2042)
PULSE LTD LLC
12628 Chillicothe Rd (44026-2558)
PHONE.................................216 570-7732
Jeffrey Maguire, *CEO*
EMP: 30 **EST:** 2009
SALES (est): 3.21MM **Privately Held**
Web: www.pulsellc.com

(G-2043)
SYCAMORE LAKE INC
Also Called: Alpine Valley Ski Area
10620 Mayfield Rd (44026-2738)
PHONE.................................440 729-9775
Thomas Apthorp, *Pr*
S Sandy Sutlo, *
EMP: 37 **EST:** 1963
SQ FT: 22,000
SALES (est): 2.59MM
SALES (corp-wide): 88.9B **Publicly Held**
Web: www.alpinevalleyohio.com
SIC: 7011 5812 Ski lodge; Caterers
HQ: Vail Resorts, Inc.
390 Intrlcken Cres Ste 10
Broomfield CO 80021

Chillicothe
Ross County

(G-2044)
ADENA HEALTH SYSTEM
Also Called: Adena Plmnlogy Crtcal Care Sle
4437 State Route 159 Ste 240
(45601-7065)
PHONE.................................740 779-8700
Michael Dennis, *Prin*
EMP: 27
SALES (corp-wide): 678.56MM **Privately Held**
Web: www.adena.org
SIC: 8062 Hospital, med school affiliated with nursing and residency
PA: Adena Health System
272 Hospital Rd
Chillicothe OH 45601
740 779-7500

(G-2045)
ADENA HEALTH SYSTEM
Also Called: Southern Ohio Cardiology Assoc
4439 State Route 159 Ste 204
(45601-8207)
PHONE.................................740 779-4300
Shashikant B Patel, *Pr*
EMP: 33
SALES (corp-wide): 678.56MM **Privately Held**
Web: www.adena.org
SIC: 8062 8011 Hospital, med school affiliated with nursing and residency; Cardiologist and cardio-vascular specialist
PA: Adena Health System
272 Hospital Rd
Chillicothe OH 45601
740 779-7500

(G-2046)
ADENA HEALTH SYSTEM
Also Called: Parks Ob Gyn Assoc
4439 State Route 159 Ste 120
(45601-8207)
PHONE.................................740 779-7201
Heidi Streitenberger, *Mgr*
EMP: 29
SALES (corp-wide): 678.56MM **Privately Held**
Web: www.adena.org
SIC: 8062 8031 Hospital, med school affiliated with nursing and residency; Offices and clinics of osteopathic physicians
PA: Adena Health System
272 Hospital Rd
Chillicothe OH 45601
740 779-7500

(G-2047)
ADENA HEALTH SYSTEM (PA)
Also Called: ADENA REGIONAL MEDICAL CENTER
272 Hospital Rd (45601-9031)
PHONE.................................740 779-7500
TOLL FREE: 800
Jeffrey J Graham, *Pr*
Lisa Carlson, *CFO*
Kathi Edrington, *COO*
Sharon Wisecup, *Dir*
EMP: 2000 **EST:** 1895
SQ FT: 690,000
SALES (est): 678.56MM
SALES (corp-wide): 678.56MM **Privately Held**
Web: www.adena.org
SIC: 8062 Hospital, med school affiliated with nursing and residency

(G-2048)
ADENA HEALTH SYSTEM
Also Called: Adena Rhblitation Wellness Ctr
445 Shawnee Ln (45601-4145)
PHONE.................................740 779-4801
R Sorrell, *Mgr*
EMP: 30
SALES (corp-wide): 678.56MM **Privately Held**
Web: www.adena.org
SIC: 8062 Hospital, med school affiliated with nursing and residency
PA: Adena Health System
272 Hospital Rd
Chillicothe OH 45601
740 779-7500

(G-2049)
ADENA REGIONAL MEDICAL CENTER
Western Ave. (45601)
PHONE.................................740 779-4050
Allen Rupiper, *CEO*
EMP: 35 **EST:** 1991
SALES (est): 1.76MM **Privately Held**
Web: www.adena.org
SIC: 8062 General medical and surgical hospitals

(G-2050)
AMERICAN HEALTH FOUNDATION INC
Also Called: Liberty Village Senior Cmnty
1839 Western Ave (45601-1038)
PHONE.................................614 798-5110
Barbara Wright, *Mgr*
EMP: 792
Web: www.abbingtononline.com
SIC: 8361 Aged home
PA: American Health Foundation, Inc.
5920 Venture Dr Ste 100
Dublin OH 43017

(G-2051)
BEST WESTERN ADENA INN
Also Called: Best Western
1250 N Bridge St (45601-1852)
PHONE.................................877 722-3422
Dinesh Patel, *Prin*
EMP: 27 **EST:** 2008
SALES (est): 278.09K **Privately Held**
Web: www.bestwestern.com
SIC: 7011 Hotels and motels

(G-2052)
BIG SANDY FURNITURE INC
1404 N Bridge St (45601-4101)
PHONE.................................740 775-4244
Mike Farmer, *Brnch Mgr*
EMP: 68

Chillicothe - Ross County (G-2053)

Web: www.bigsandysuperstore.com
SIC: **4225** 5722 5712 General warehousing and storage; Electric household appliances, major; Furniture stores
HQ: Big Sandy Furniture, Inc.
 8375 Gallia Pike
 Franklin Furnace OH 45629
 740 574-2113

(G-2053)
BUCKEYE CHECK CASHING INC
860 N Bridge St (45601-1702)
PHONE..................................740 851-4073
EMP: 35
Web: www.ccfi.com
SIC: **6099** Check cashing agencies
HQ: Buckeye Check Cashing, Inc.
 5165 Emerald Pkwy Ste 100
 Dublin OH 43017
 614 798-5900

(G-2054)
CHILLCTH-ROSS CHILD CARE CTR I
Also Called: Play & Learn Express
369 N High St (45601-1632)
PHONE..................................740 775-7772
Bonnie Maughmer, *Pr*
David Maughmer, *VP*
EMP: 30 **EST:** 1991
SQ FT: 7,000
SALES (est): 628.43K **Privately Held**
Web: www.playandlearnexpress.com
SIC: **8351** Preschool center

(G-2055)
CHILLICOTHE BOWLING LANES INC
Also Called: Shawnee Trophies & Sptg Gds
1680 N Bridge St (45601-4105)
PHONE..................................740 773-3300
John Corcoran, *Pr*
Walter Highland, *
Kenneth De Long, *
EMP: 29 **EST:** 1959
SQ FT: 39,600
SALES (est): 462.92K **Privately Held**
Web: www.shawneelanes.com
SIC: **7933** 5812 5813 5941 Ten pin center; Snack bar; Cocktail lounge; Bowling equipment and supplies

(G-2056)
CHILLICOTHE INN
24 N Bridge St (45601-2614)
PHONE..................................740 774-2512
John R Molnar, *Pr*
Rose Marie Molnar, *Sec*
EMP: 27 **EST:** 1987
SALES (est): 245.97K **Privately Held**
Web: www.chillicotheinn.com
SIC: **7011** Motels

(G-2057)
CHILLICOTHE LONG-TERM CARE INC
Also Called: Westmoreland Place
230 Cherry St (45601-2301)
PHONE..................................740 773-6161
David Dixon, *Admn*
EMP: 140
SALES (corp-wide): 10.08MM **Privately Held**
Web: www.westmorelandplace.com
SIC: **8051** Convalescent home with continuous nursing care
PA: Chillicothe Long-Term Care, Inc.
 7265 Kenwood Rd Ste 300
 Cincinnati OH 45236
 740 773-6470

(G-2058)
CHILLICOTHE MOTEL LLC
Also Called: Comfort Inn
20 N Plaza Blvd (45601-1757)
PHONE..................................740 773-3903
EMP: 51 **EST:** 1986
SQ FT: 40,000
SALES (est): 538.5K **Privately Held**
Web: www.choicehotels.com
SIC: **7011** 7991 Hotels and motels; Physical fitness facilities

(G-2059)
CHILLICOTHE STEEL COMPANY
1393 Industrial Dr (45601-3978)
P.O. Box 246 (45601-0246)
PHONE..................................740 772-2481
Jeff Crace, *Pr*
Peggy Sickels, *Sec*
EMP: 40 **EST:** 1992
SALES (est): 33.54MM **Privately Held**
Web: www.chillicothesteel.com
SIC: **5051** Steel

(G-2060)
CHILLICOTHE TELEPHONE COMPANY (HQ)
68 E Main St (45601-2503)
P.O. Box 480 (45601-0480)
PHONE..................................740 772-8200
William Mc Kell, *CEO*
Jack E Thomson, *Sec*
EMP: 130 **EST:** 1927
SQ FT: 80,000
SALES (est): 54.97MM **Privately Held**
SIC: **4813** 4841 Local telephone communications; Cable television services
PA: Horizon Telcom, Inc.
 68 E Main St
 Chillicothe OH 45601

(G-2061)
CONNECT TRNSP SVCS LLC
1338 Delano Rd (45601-8440)
PHONE..................................740 656-5042
Arthur Dunkle, *Mgr*
EMP: 47 **EST:** 2018
SQ FT: 7,000
SALES (est): 1.96MM **Privately Held**
SIC: **4119** Local passenger transportation, nec

(G-2062)
COUNTY OF ROSS
Also Called: South Cntl Ohio Rgnal Jvnile D
184 Cattail Rd (45601-9404)
PHONE..................................740 773-4169
Cathy Fenner, *Superintnt*
EMP: 41
SALES (corp-wide): 64.95MM **Privately Held**
Web: co.ross.oh.us
SIC: **8361** 9223 Juvenile correctional facilities ; Detention center, government
PA: County Of Ross
 2 N Paint St Ste H
 Chillicothe OH 45601
 740 702-3085

(G-2063)
COURT DIALYSIS LLC
Also Called: DAVITA
1180 N Bridge St (45601-1793)
P.O. Box 2037 (98401-2037)
PHONE..................................740 773-3733
Jim Hilger, *Prin*
EMP: 29 **EST:** 2011
SALES (est): 4.29MM **Publicly Held**
SIC: **8092** Kidney dialysis centers
PA: Davita Inc.
 2000 16th St
 Denver CO 80202

(G-2064)
FIRST CAPITAL ENTERPRISES INC
505 E 7th St (45601-3632)
P.O. Box 1747 (45601-5747)
PHONE..................................740 773-2166
Ron Sarrar, *Dir*
EMP: 60 **EST:** 1972
SQ FT: 18,000
SALES (est): 1.63MM **Privately Held**
Web: www.firstcapitalenterprises.com
SIC: **8331** 8699 Sheltered workshop; Charitable organization

(G-2065)
FNS INC
Also Called: Family Nursing Services
24 Star Dr (45601-9845)
PHONE..................................740 775-5463
Ken Kevorkian, *Dir Fin*
EMP: 50 **EST:** 2017
SALES (est): 1.03MM
SALES (corp-wide): 8.81MM **Privately Held**
SIC: **8082** Visiting nurse service
PA: Hcf Home Care, Inc.
 1100 Shawnee Rd
 Lima OH 45805
 419 999-2010

(G-2066)
GOODS HANDS SUPPORTED LIVING
Also Called: GOODS HANDS SUPPORTED LIVING
263 Delano Ave (45601-2251)
PHONE..................................740 773-4170
EMP: 28
SALES (corp-wide): 4.44MM **Privately Held**
Web: www.ghslohio.org
SIC: **8082** Home health care services
PA: Goods Hands Supported Living, Ltd.
 2491 E Dblin Granville Rd
 Columbus OH 43229
 614 899-7320

(G-2067)
GOODWILL INDS S CENTL OHIO (PA)
Also Called: Goodwill Industries
1285 Industrial Dr (45601)
P.O. Box 93 (45601)
PHONE..................................740 702-4000
Marvin Jones, *CEO*
Mark Hughes, *COO*
Wanda Lanzer, *CFO*
EMP: 80 **EST:** 1959
SALES (est): 4.39MM
SALES (corp-wide): 4.39MM **Privately Held**
Web: www.gwisco.org
SIC: **5932** 8331 Clothing, secondhand; Community service employment training program

(G-2068)
HERRNSTEIN CHRYSLER INC
Also Called: Herrnstein Auto Group
133 Marietta Rd (45601)
P.O. Box 266 (45601)
PHONE..................................740 773-2203
TOLL FREE: 800
Bart Herrnstein, *Pr*
Bart Herrnstein, *VP*
William B Herrnstein, *
Linda Herrnstein, *
EMP: 125 **EST:** 1944
SQ FT: 11,500
SALES (est): 24.64MM **Privately Held**
Web: www.herrnsteinchrysler.net
SIC: **5511** 7549 Automobiles, new and used; Automotive maintenance services

(G-2069)
HOMELAND CREDIT UNION INC (PA)
310 Caldwell St (45601-3331)
P.O. Box 1974 (45601-5974)
PHONE..................................740 775-3024
Michael Spindler, *CEO*
EMP: 30 **EST:** 1932
SQ FT: 3,500
SALES (est): 16.43MM
SALES (corp-wide): 16.43MM **Privately Held**
Web: www.homelandcu.com
SIC: **6062** State credit unions, not federally chartered

(G-2070)
HOPEWELL HEALTH CENTERS INC (PA)
1049 Western Ave (45601-1104)
P.O. Box 188 (45601-0188)
PHONE..................................740 773-1006
Mark Bridenbaugh, *CEO*
Kathy Cecil, *
EMP: 50 **EST:** 1986
SALES (est): 66.73MM
SALES (corp-wide): 66.73MM **Privately Held**
Web: www.hopewellhealth.org
SIC: **8011** Clinic, operated by physicians

(G-2071)
HORIZON PCS INC (HQ)
68 E Main St (45601)
PHONE..................................740 772-8200
William A Mckell, *Pr*
Peter M Holland, *
Steven Burkhardt, *
Alan G Morse, *
EMP: 200 **EST:** 2000
SALES (est): 41.35MM **Privately Held**
Web: www.horizonconnects.com
SIC: **4812** Radiotelephone communication
PA: Horizon Telcom, Inc.
 68 E Main St
 Chillicothe OH 45601

(G-2072)
INGLE-BARR INC (PA)
Also Called: Ibi
20 Plyleys Ln (45601)
P.O. Box 874 (45601)
PHONE..................................740 702-6117
Jeffrey Poole, *Pr*
Rod Poole, *
EMP: 100 **EST:** 1967
SQ FT: 6,500
SALES (est): 19.09MM
SALES (corp-wide): 19.09MM **Privately Held**
Web: www.4ibi.com
SIC: **1521** 1541 1542 2541 General remodeling, single-family houses; Renovation, remodeling and repairs: industrial buildings; Commercial and office building, new construction; Bar fixtures, wood

(G-2073)
INTERGNCY EMPLYEES CHILD CARE
17273 State Route 104 (45601-9718)
PHONE..................................740 772-7086
Jodi Riber, *Ex Dir*
Anita Sparkes, *
EMP: 45 **EST:** 1987
SALES (est): 506.72K **Privately Held**
SIC: **8351** Group day care center

GEOGRAPHIC SECTION
Cincinnati - Clermont County (G-2095)

(G-2074)
J & W ENTERPRISES INC (PA)
Also Called: ERA
159 E Main St (45601-2507)
P.O. Box 2066 (45601-8066)
PHONE.................................740 774-4500
EMP: 30 **EST:** 1989
SQ FT: 6,000
SALES (est): 2.34MM **Privately Held**
Web: www.era.com
SIC: 6531 1521 Real estate agent, residential ; New construction, single-family houses

(G-2075)
J B EXPRESS INC
27311 Old Route 35 (45601-8110)
P.O. Box 91 (45601-0091)
PHONE.................................740 702-9830
EMP: 60 **EST:** 1996
SQ FT: 24,440
SALES (est): 18.47MM **Privately Held**
Web: www.jbexpress.com
SIC: 4731 1623 4225 Transportation agents and brokers; Oil and gas pipeline construction; General warehousing and storage

(G-2076)
KHC INC
Also Called: Kendal Home Care
24 Star Dr (45601-9845)
PHONE.................................740 775-5463
Marilyn Haines, *Branch Administrator*
EMP: 100 **EST:** 2017
SALES (est): 4.85MM
SALES (corp-wide): 8.81MM **Privately Held**
Web: www.kendallhomecare.com
SIC: 8082 Home health care services
PA: Hcf Home Care, Inc.
1100 Shawnee Rd
Lima OH 45805
419 999-2010

(G-2077)
KINDRED NURSING CENTERS E LLC
Also Called: Kindred Trnstnal Care Rhbltton
60 Marietta Rd (45601-9433)
PHONE.................................740 772-5900
Christina Schramm, *Dir*
EMP: 105
SALES (corp-wide): 13.68B **Privately Held**
Web: www.shcofchillicothe.com
SIC: 8051 Convalescent home with continuous nursing care
HQ: Kindred Nursing Centers East, L.L.C.
680 S 4th St
Louisville KY 40202
502 596-7300

(G-2078)
LITTER DISTRIBUTING CO INC
Also Called: Classic Brands
656 Hospital Rd (45601-9030)
PHONE.................................740 774-2831
EMP: 53
Web: www.classicbrandsoh.com
SIC: 5181 Beer and other fermented malt liquors
HQ: Litter Distributing Company, Inc.
656 Hospital Rd
Chillicothe OH 45601
740 775-2063

(G-2079)
LOWES HOME CENTERS LLC
Also Called: Lowe's
867 N Bridge St (45601-1775)
PHONE.................................740 773-7777
Denny Gray, *Mgr*
EMP: 148
SALES (corp-wide): 86.38B **Publicly Held**
Web: www.lowes.com
SIC: 5211 5031 5722 5064 Home centers; Building materials, exterior; Household appliance stores; Electrical appliances, television and radio
HQ: Lowe's Home Centers, Llc
1000 Lowes Blvd
Mooresville NC 28117
336 658-4000

(G-2080)
OHIO DEPT MNTAL HLTH ADDCTION
Also Called: Paint Vly Alchol DRG Addction
394 Chestnut St (45601-2305)
PHONE.................................740 773-2283
Junie Johnson, *Ex Dir*
EMP: 93
Web: www.pvadamh.org
SIC: 8322 Rehabilitation services
HQ: Ohio Department Of Mental Health And Addiction Services
30 E Broad St Fl 36
Columbus OH 43215

(G-2081)
OPTIMAS OE SOLUTIONS LLC
Also Called: Fastenal
101 S Mcarthur St (45601-3630)
PHONE.................................740 774-4553
Robert Hitchens, *Brnch Mgr*
EMP: 42
SALES (corp-wide): 673.07MM **Privately Held**
Web: www.optimas.com
SIC: 5085 Industrial supplies
HQ: Optimas Oe Solutions, Llc
1441 N Wood Dale Rd
Wood Dale IL 60191
224 999-1000

(G-2082)
PETLAND INC (PA)
250 Riverside St (45601-2611)
PHONE.................................740 775-2464
Edward Kunzelman, *Ch*
Joe Watson, *
Mike Voinovich, *
Steve Huggins, *
EMP: 50 **EST:** 1967
SQ FT: 40,000
SALES (est): 48.49MM
SALES (corp-wide): 48.49MM **Privately Held**
Web: www.petland.com
SIC: 5999 6794 Pets; Franchises, selling or licensing

(G-2083)
RON NEFF REAL ESTATE (PA)
Also Called: Ron Neff Her Realtors
75 W 2nd St (45601-3111)
PHONE.................................740 773-4670
Ron Neff, *Owner*
EMP: 27 **EST:** 1980
SALES (est): 1.05MM
SALES (corp-wide): 1.05MM **Privately Held**
SIC: 6531 Real estate brokers and agents

(G-2084)
ROSS CNTY CMNTY ACTION COMM IN (PA)
250 N Woodbridge Ave (45601-2245)
PHONE.................................740 702-7222
Ed Alexinas, *Prin*
EMP: 51 **EST:** 1966
SALES (est): 10.56MM **Privately Held**
Web: www.rossccac.org
SIC: 8399 Community action agency

(G-2085)
ROSS COUNTY CHILDREN SVCS CTR (PA)
Also Called: Ross Cnty Job Fmly Svcs Chldre
150 E 2nd St (45601-2525)
P.O. Box 469 (45601-0469)
PHONE.................................740 773-2651
Robert Gallagher, *CEO*
Thomas E Williamson, *
EMP: 35 **EST:** 1987
SALES (est): 2.45MM
SALES (corp-wide): 2.45MM **Privately Held**
Web: www.thechildprotectioncenter.org
SIC: 8322 Child related social services

(G-2086)
ROSS COUNTY HEALTH DISTRICT
150 E 2nd St (45601-2295)
PHONE.................................740 775-1114
Wanda Medcalf, *Dir*
EMP: 43 **EST:** 1974
SALES (est): 7.87MM **Privately Held**
Web: www.rosscountyhealth.org
SIC: 8082 Home health care services

(G-2087)
ROSS COUNTY HOME HEALTH LLC
1550 Western Ave # A (45601-1056)
PHONE.................................740 775-1114
Gerald Vallee, *Prin*
Wanda Whetsel, *
Joseph Vallee, *
EMP: 57 **EST:** 2017
SALES (est): 1.09MM **Privately Held**
SIC: 8082 Home health care services

(G-2088)
ROSS COUNTY WATER COMPANY INC
Also Called: Rural Water Utility
663 Fairgrounds Rd (45601-9715)
P.O. Box 1690 (45601-5690)
PHONE.................................740 774-4117
Michael Riffle, *Pr*
Clyde Hawkins, *
William Neal, *
EMP: 33 **EST:** 1970
SQ FT: 3,000
SALES (est): 9.46MM **Privately Held**
Web: www.rosscowater.org
SIC: 4941 Water supply

(G-2089)
RUMPKE/KENWORTH CONTRACT
Also Called: Kenworth Truck Co
65 Kenworth Dr (45601-8829)
PHONE.................................740 774-5111
Judy Nctigue, *Brnch Mgr*
▲ **EMP:** 53 **EST:** 2010
SALES (est): 47.38MM **Privately Held**
Web: kenworthofcincinnatiinc.kenworth.com
SIC: 5084 5511 Trucks, industrial; Trucks, tractors, and trailers: new and used

(G-2090)
SCIOT-PINT VLY MENTAL HLTH CTR (PA)
4449 State Route 159 (45601-8620)
P.O. Box 6179 (45601-6179)
PHONE.................................740 775-1260
Gary Kreuchauf, *Ex Dir*
EMP: 101 **EST:** 1966
SQ FT: 25,000
SALES (est): 14.09MM
SALES (corp-wide): 14.09MM **Privately Held**
Web: www.spvmhc.org
SIC: 8322 8093 General counseling services ; Mental health clinic, outpatient

(G-2091)
SCIOTO LODGING INC
Also Called: Holiday Inn
547 Plyleys Ln Apt 18 (45601-2017)
PHONE.................................740 851-6140
Llyod Abdol, *Pr*
EMP: 59 **EST:** 1998
SALES (est): 757.3K **Privately Held**
Web: www.holidayinn.com
SIC: 7011 Hotels and motels

(G-2092)
TENNESSEE CENTERSTONE INC
455 Shawnee Ln (45601-4145)
PHONE.................................740 779-4888
Stephanie Sharpnack, *Brnch Mgr*
EMP: 33
SALES (corp-wide): 102.95MM **Privately Held**
Web: www.centerstone.org
SIC: 8322 General counseling services
PA: Centerstone Of Tennessee, Inc.
44 Vantage Way
Nashville TN 37228
615 463-6610

(G-2093)
VETERANS HEALTH ADMINISTRATION
Also Called: Chillicothe VA Medical Center
17273 State Route 104 (45601-9718)
PHONE.................................740 773-1141
EMP: 1100
Web: benefits.va.gov
SIC: 8011 9451 Medical centers; Administration of veterans' affairs, Federal government
HQ: Veterans Health Administration
810 Vermont Ave Nw
Washington DC 20420

Chippewa Lake
Medina County

(G-2094)
THE OAKS LODGE
5878 Longacre Ln (44215-9778)
P.O. Box 32 (44215-0032)
PHONE.................................330 769-2601
TOLL FREE: 800
Bonnie Druschel, *Pr*
Donald R Casper, *
EMP: 61 **EST:** 1949
SQ FT: 10,393
SALES (est): 475.98K **Privately Held**
Web: www.theoakslakeside.com
SIC: 5812 5813 7299 Restaurant, family: independent; Cocktail lounge; Banquet hall facilities

Cincinnati
Clermont County

(G-2095)
5ME LLC
4270 Ivy Pointe Blvd Ste 100 (45245-0004)
P.O. Box 541085 (45254-1085)
PHONE.................................513 719-1600
William A Horwarth, *Pr*
Jeffery Price, *
Chris Chapman, *
EMP: 45 **EST:** 2013
SALES (est): 9.68MM
SALES (corp-wide): 9.68MM **Privately Held**

Cincinnati - Clermont County (G-2096)

Web: www.5me.com
SIC: 3544 8742 Special dies, tools, jigs, and fixtures; Business management consultant
PA: 5me Holdings Llc
4270 Ivy Pointe Blvd # 240
Cincinnati OH 45245
859 534-4872

(G-2096)
AMERATHON LLC (HQ)
671 Ohio Pike Ste K (45245-2136)
PHONE..............................513 752-7300
Debbie Martin, *Pr*
Christopher Martin, *
Tom Kaylor, *
Jim Jackson, *
EMP: 450 EST: 2014
SQ FT: 25,000
SALES (est): 82.57MM **Privately Held**
SIC: 8071 Ultrasound laboratory
PA: American Health S, Llc
15712 Sw 41st St Ste 11
Davie FL 33331

(G-2097)
AMERICAN HEALTH IMAGING S LLC
Also Called: American Health Associates
665 Ohio Pike (45245-2117)
PHONE..............................513 752-7300
EMP: 877
SALES (corp-wide): 27.99MM **Privately Held**
Web: www.themedlab.com
SIC: 8071 Medical laboratories
PA: American Health Imaging S, Llc
15712 Sw 41st St Ste 16
Davie FL 33331
513 752-7300

(G-2098)
BEECHMONT FORD INC (PA)
600 Ohio Pike (45245-2118)
PHONE..............................513 752-6611
Mark Williams, *Pr*
Lorine Williams, *
Dan Rapier, *
EMP: 120 EST: 1970
SQ FT: 25,000
SALES (est): 23.24MM
SALES (corp-wide): 23.24MM **Privately Held**
Web: www.beechmontford.com
SIC: 5511 7538 7515 5531 Automobiles, new and used; General automotive repair shops; Passenger car leasing; Auto and home supply stores

(G-2099)
CHILDRENS HOSPITAL MEDICAL CTR
796 Cincinnati Batavia Pike (45245-1262)
PHONE..............................513 636-6036
Jean Kinman, *Brnch Mgr*
EMP: 442
SALES (corp-wide): 2.94B **Privately Held**
Web: www.cincinnatichildrens.org
SIC: 8062 General medical and surgical hospitals
PA: Children's Hospital Medical Center
3333 Burnet Ave
Cincinnati OH 45229
513 636-4200

(G-2100)
CLERMONT HILLS CO LLC
Also Called: Holiday Inn
4501 Eastgate Blvd (45245-1201)
PHONE..............................513 752-4400
Jacquie A Dowdy, *Managing Member*
EMP: 96 EST: 1983
SALES (est): 1.74MM **Privately Held**

Web: www.holidayinn.com
SIC: 7011 Hotels and motels

(G-2101)
CURTISS-WRIGHT FLOW CTRL CORP
Also Called: Qualtech NP
4600 E Tech Dr (45245-1000)
PHONE..............................513 528-7900
EMP: 82
SALES (corp-wide): 2.85B **Publicly Held**
Web: www.curtisswright.com
SIC: 3443 8734 Fabricated plate work (boiler shop); Testing laboratories
HQ: Curtiss-Wright Flow Control Corporation
1966 Broadhollow Rd Ste E
Farmingdale NY 11735
631 293-3800

(G-2102)
DNV HEALTHCARE USA INC
4435 Aicholtz Rd Ste 900 (45245-2038)
PHONE..............................281 396-1610
Yehuda Dror, *Brnch Mgr*
EMP: 44
Web: www.dnvhealthcareportal.com
SIC: 8621 Medical field-related associations
HQ: Dnv Healthcare Usa Inc.
1400 Ravello Rd
Katy TX 77449
281 396-1000

(G-2103)
EASTGATE HEALTH CARE CENTER
Also Called: CARESPRING
4400 Glen Este Withamsville Rd (45245)
PHONE..............................513 752-3710
Henry Schneider, *Pr*
Barry Bortz, *
EMP: 64 EST: 1985
SQ FT: 87,000
SALES (est): 17.28MM
SALES (corp-wide): 84.56MM **Privately Held**
Web: www.carespring.com
SIC: 8051 Skilled nursing care facilities
PA: Carespring Health Care Management, Llc
390 Wards Corner Rd
Loveland OH 45140
513 943-4000

(G-2104)
FINNEY LAW FIRM LLC
4270 Ivy Pointe Blvd Ste 225 (45245-0004)
PHONE..............................513 943-6650
Christopher P Finney, *Prin*
EMP: 46 EST: 2013
SALES (est): 4.92MM **Privately Held**
Web: www.finneylawfirm.com
SIC: 8111 General practice attorney, lawyer

(G-2105)
GENERAL DATA COMPANY INC (PA)
4354 Ferguson Dr (45245-1667)
P.O. Box 541165 (45254-1165)
PHONE..............................513 752-7978
Peter Wenzel, *Pr*
Jim Burns, *
Erin Johnson, *
Michele Marsh, *
◆ EMP: 280 EST: 1980
SQ FT: 175,000
SALES (est): 91.21MM
SALES (corp-wide): 91.21MM **Privately Held**
Web: www.general-data.com

SIC: 2679 5046 5084 2759 Labels, paper: made from purchased material; Commercial equipment, nec; Printing trades machinery, equipment, and supplies; Commercial printing, nec

(G-2106)
HAMPTON INN
858 Eastgate North Dr (45245-1588)
PHONE..............................513 752-8584
Andrew Crum, *Genl Mgr*
EMP: 49 EST: 1999
SALES (est): 369.02K **Privately Held**
Web: www.hilton.com
SIC: 7011 Hotels and motels

(G-2107)
KGBO HOLDINGS INC (PA)
4289 Ivy Pointe Blvd (45245-0002)
P.O. Box 799 (45150-0799)
PHONE..............................513 831-2600
Kenneth Oaks, *Pr*
EMP: 94 EST: 2006
SQ FT: 100,000
SALES (est): 8.85B
SALES (corp-wide): 8.85B **Privately Held**
SIC: 4731 Truck transportation brokers

(G-2108)
KIDS FIRST ACADEMY LLC
756 Ohio Pike (45245-2156)
PHONE..............................513 752-2811
EMP: 32 EST: 1996
SALES (est): 336.67K **Privately Held**
Web: www.kids1stacademy.com
SIC: 8351 Preschool center

(G-2109)
KILBOURNE MEDICAL LABORATORIES INC
Also Called: Kilbourne Medical Labs
665 Ohio Pike (45245-2117)
PHONE..............................513 385-5457
EMP: 136
SIC: 8071 Blood analysis laboratory

(G-2110)
LNS AMERICA INC (DH)
4621 E Tech Dr (45245-1044)
PHONE..............................513 528-5674
Jeff Mcmullen, *CEO*
▲ EMP: 46 EST: 1980
SQ FT: 52,000
SALES (est): 97.05MM
SALES (corp-wide): 3.26B **Privately Held**
Web: www.lns-northamerica.com
SIC: 5084 Machine tools and accessories
HQ: Lns Sarl
Route De Frinvillier
Orvin BE 2534

(G-2111)
NATIONWIDE CHILDRENS HOSPITAL
796 Cincinnati Batavia Pike Ste 200 (45245-1262)
PHONE..............................513 636-6000
Donna Kinnemeyer, *Mgr*
EMP: 152
SALES (corp-wide): 3.6B **Privately Held**
Web: www.nationwidechildrens.org
SIC: 8062 General medical and surgical hospitals
PA: Nationwide Children's Hospital
700 Childrens Dr
Columbus OH 43205
614 722-2000

(G-2112)
PRESSLEY RIDGE FOUNDATION
4355 Ferguson Dr Ste 125 (45245-5149)

PHONE..............................513 752-4548
Matthew Mitchell, *Brnch Mgr*
EMP: 141
Web: www.pressleyridge.org
SIC: 8322 Individual and family services
PA: Pressley Ridge Foundation
5500 Corporate Dr Ste 400
Pittsburgh PA 15237

(G-2113)
STEWART ADVNCED LAND TITLE LTD (PA)
792 Eastgate South Dr (45245-1592)
PHONE..............................513 753-2800
Gregory Traynor, *Pr*
EMP: 36 EST: 2001
SALES (est): 7.49MM
SALES (corp-wide): 7.49MM **Privately Held**
SIC: 6361 Title insurance

(G-2114)
TATA CONSULTANCY SERVICES LTD
4270 Ivy Pointe Blvd Ste 400 (45245-0003)
PHONE..............................515 553-8300
EMP: 76
Web: www.tcs.com
SIC: 8748 Business consulting, nec
HQ: Tata Consultancy Services Limited
9th Floor, Nirmal Building,
Mumbai MH 40002

(G-2115)
THARALDSON HOSPITALITY MGT
Also Called: Fairfield Inn
4521 Eastgate Blvd (45245-1201)
PHONE..............................513 947-9402
Joyce Jabornick, *Mgr*
EMP: 103
Web: www.tharaldson.com
SIC: 7011 Motels
PA: Tharaldson Hospitality Management
4520 36th Ave S
Fargo ND 58104

(G-2116)
TOTAL QUALITY LOGISTICS LLC
4270 Ivy Pointe Blvd (45245-0003)
PHONE..............................513 831-2600
EMP: 76
SALES (corp-wide): 8.85B **Privately Held**
Web: www.tql.com
SIC: 4731 Transportation agents and brokers
HQ: Total Quality Logistics, Llc
4289 Ivy Pointe Blvd
Cincinnati OH 45245

Cincinnati
Hamilton County

(G-2117)
022808 KENWOOD LLC
Also Called: Liberty Dialysis - Kenwood
8251 Pine Rd Ste 110 (45236-2193)
PHONE..............................513 745-0800
Ron Kuerbitz, *CEO*
EMP: 29
SALES (corp-wide): 1.87MM **Privately Held**
SIC: 8092 Kidney dialysis centers
PA: 022808 Kenwood Llc
920 Winter St
Waltham MA 02451
781 699-9000

(G-2118)
11689 SHARON WEST INC
Also Called: Sonesta Es Cncnnati Shrnvlle W
11689 Chester Rd (45246-2803)

GEOGRAPHIC SECTION

Cincinnati - Hamilton County (G-2143)

PHONE..................513 771-2525
EMP: 28 EST: 2018
SALES (est): 300.07K **Privately Held**
Web: www.sonesta.com
SIC: 7011 Hotels

(G-2119)
151 W 4TH CINCINNATI LLC
151 W 4th St (45202-2744)
PHONE..................312 283-3683
William Bennett, *Prin*
Kayley Dicicco, *
EMP: 75 EST: 2019
SALES (est): 4.53MM **Privately Held**
Web: www.4thandelmselfstorage.com
SIC: 4225 Warehousing, self storage

(G-2120)
1ST CHOICE SECURITY INC
2245 Gilbert Ave Ste 400 (45206-3000)
PHONE..................513 381-6789
Alan Grissinger, *Pr*
EMP: 175 EST: 1996
SQ FT: 1,200
SALES (est): 4.85MM **Privately Held**
Web: www.1stchoicesecurityservices.com
SIC: 7381 Security guard service

(G-2121)
2060 DIGITAL LLC
4800 Kennedy Ave (45209-7544)
PHONE..................513 699-5012
EMP: 39
SALES (corp-wide): 8.74MM **Privately Held**
Web: www.2060digital.com
SIC: 7371 Custom computer programming services
PA: 2060 Digital, Llc
    3415 University Ave W
    Saint Paul MN 55114
    425 653-9462

(G-2122)
2MC MANAGEMENT LLC
Also Called: Fast Track It
7660 School Rd (45249-1528)
PHONE..................513 771-1700
David J Hrina, *Prin*
EMP: 34 EST: 2014
SALES (est): 9.65MM **Privately Held**
Web: www.bidfta.com
SIC: 7389 Auctioneers, fee basis

(G-2123)
3CRE ADVISORS LLC
7815 Cooper Rd Ste C (45242-7649)
PHONE..................513 745-9333
Tryfon Christoforou, *Prin*
EMP: 54 EST: 2016
SALES (est): 938.5K **Privately Held**
Web: www.3cre.com
SIC: 6531 Real estate agent, commercial

(G-2124)
506 PHELPS HOLDINGS LLC
Also Called: Residence Inn By Marriott
506 E 4th St (45202-3303)
PHONE..................513 651-1234
EMP: 39 EST: 2010
SALES (est): 3.48MM **Privately Held**
Web: www.topoftheparkcincinnati.com
SIC: 7011 Hotels

(G-2125)
609 WALNUT HOTEL LLC
Also Called: 21c Museum Hotel Cincinnati
609 Walnut St Ste 2 (45202-1191)
PHONE..................513 578-6600
Steve Wilson, *
EMP: 37 EST: 2009
SALES (est): 13.56MM **Privately Held**
Web: www.21cmuseumhotels.com
SIC: 7011 Hotel, franchised

(G-2126)
6300 SHARONVILLE ASSOC LLC
Also Called: Doubletree Hotel
6300 E Kemper Rd (45241-2360)
PHONE..................513 489-3636
David Sundermann, *Prin*
EMP: 39 EST: 2012
SALES (est): 1.45MM **Privately Held**
Web: www.hilton.com
SIC: 7011 Hotels and motels

(G-2127)
8451 LLC (HQ)
100 W 5th St (45202-2704)
PHONE..................513 632-1020
Simon Hay, *CEO*
EMP: 84 EST: 2003
SQ FT: 40,000
SALES (est): 51.66MM
SALES (corp-wide): 150.04B **Publicly Held**
Web: www.8451.com
SIC: 8732 Market analysis or research
PA: The Kroger Co
    1014 Vine St
    Cincinnati OH 45202
    513 762-4000

(G-2128)
A & A WALL SYSTEMS INC
11589 Deerfield Rd (45242-1419)
PHONE..................513 489-0086
Michele Mcintyre, *Pr*
Dale Adkins, *
EMP: 30 EST: 1959
SQ FT: 6,000
SALES (est): 754.68K **Privately Held**
Web: www.aawallsystems.com
SIC: 1742 Drywall

(G-2129)
A CHILDS HOPE INTL INC
2430 E Kemper Rd Unit A (45241-5806)
PHONE..................513 771-2244
Lawrence Bergeron, *Ex Dir*
Paul Linsley, *Ch*
Deanna Linsley, *Sec*
Mark Morris, *Treas*
EMP: 34 EST: 2011
SALES (est): 2.14MM **Privately Held**
Web: www.thechildrenarewaiting.org
SIC: 8351 Child day care services

(G-2130)
A ONE FINE DRY CLEANERS INC
6211 Montgomery Rd (45213-1403)
PHONE..................513 731-7950
Mark Folzenlogen, *Brnch Mgr*
EMP: 41
SQ FT: 2,856
Web: www.a-onecleaners.com
SIC: 7216 Cleaning and dyeing, except rugs
PA: A One Fine Dry Cleaners Inc
    6223 Montgomery Rd
    Cincinnati OH 45213

(G-2131)
A-1 QLITY LGSTCAL SLUTIONS LLC (PA)
3055 Blue Rock Rd (45239-6320)
PHONE..................513 353-0173
William Foster, *Pr*
EMP: 45 EST: 2010
SALES (est): 4.78MM
SALES (corp-wide): 4.78MM **Privately Held**
Web: www.a1qls.com
SIC: 4789 Transportation services, nec

(G-2132)
A-E DOOR SALES AND SERVICE INC (PA)
Also Called: A-E Door and Window Sales
1260 W Sharon Rd (45240-2917)
PHONE..................513 742-1984
EMP: 40 EST: 1980
SALES (est): 8.4MM
SALES (corp-wide): 8.4MM **Privately Held**
Web: www.aedoorsales.com
SIC: 1751 5031 Garage door, installation or erection; Doors, garage

(G-2133)
AAA CLUB ALLIANCE INC
Also Called: AAA Worldwide Travel Service
8176 Montgomery Rd (45236-2904)
PHONE..................513 984-3553
Debbie Doll, *Brnch Mgr*
EMP: 36
SQ FT: 54,618
SALES (corp-wide): 502.74MM **Privately Held**
Web: cluballiance.aaa.com
SIC: 4724 8699 Travel agencies; Automobile owners' association
PA: Aaa Club Alliance Inc.
    1 River Pl
    Wilmington DE 19801
    302 299-4700

(G-2134)
AAA CLUB ALLIANCE INC
15 W Central Pkwy (45202-1005)
PHONE..................513 762-3301
Thomas C Wiedemann, *CEO*
EMP: 1000
SALES (corp-wide): 502.74MM **Privately Held**
SIC: 4724 8699 Travel agencies; Automobile owners' association
PA: Aaa Club Alliance Inc.
    1 River Pl
    Wilmington DE 19801
    302 299-4700

(G-2135)
ABM JANITORIAL SERVICES INC
354 Gest St (45203-1822)
PHONE..................513 731-1418
Brian Planicka, *Mgr*
EMP: 54
SALES (corp-wide): 8.1B **Publicly Held**
Web: www.abm.com
SIC: 7349 Janitorial service, contract basis
HQ: Abm Janitorial Services, Inc.
    1111 Fannin St Ste 1500
    Houston TX 77002
    866 624-1520

(G-2136)
ABS TRANSITIONS LLC
4861 Duck Creek Rd (45227-1421)
PHONE..................513 832-2884
Amy Bailey, *Ex Dir*
EMP: 45 EST: 2016
SALES (est): 2.72MM **Privately Held**
Web: www.transitions-bh.com
SIC: 8748 Business consulting, nec

(G-2137)
ACCENTURE LLP
201 E 4th St Ste 1600 (45202-4249)
PHONE..................513 455-1000
Nathan Beadle, *Mgr*
EMP: 111
Web: www.accenture.com
SIC: 8742 Business management consultant
HQ: Accenture Llp
    500 W Madison St
    Chicago IL 60661
    312 693-5009

(G-2138)
ACCENTURE LLP
425 Walnut St Ste 1200 (45202-3928)
PHONE..................513 651-2444
Edward Harbach, *Brnch Mgr*
EMP: 29
Web: www.accenture.com
SIC: 8742 Business management consultant
HQ: Accenture Llp
    500 W Madison St
    Chicago IL 60661
    312 693-5009

(G-2139)
ACCS DAY CARE CENTERS INC
1705 Section Rd (45237-3313)
PHONE..................513 841-2227
Jamica Thomas, *Pr*
Derek Edwards, *
EMP: 28 EST: 2013
SALES (est): 492.18K **Privately Held**
SIC: 8351 Group day care center

(G-2140)
ACE DORAN HAULING & RIGGING CO
10765 Medallion Dr (45241-4828)
PHONE..................513 681-7900
Daniel J Doran, *Pr*
EMP: 60 EST: 1913
SALES (est): 13.14MM **Privately Held**
Web: www.acedoran.com
SIC: 4213 Trucking, except local
HQ: Bennett Motor Express, Llc
    1001 Industrial Pkwy
    Mcdonough GA 30253
    770 957-1866

(G-2141)
ACKERMANN ENTERPRISES INC
5801 Madison Rd (45227-1707)
PHONE..................513 842-3100
Thomas B Ackermann, *Pr*
Dobbs Ackerman, *Sec*
EMP: 67 EST: 1966
SALES (est): 4.23MM **Privately Held**
Web: www.ackermanngroup.com
SIC: 1522 1521 Apartment building construction; New construction, single-family houses

(G-2142)
ACKERMANN GROUP
5801 Madison Rd (45227-1707)
PHONE..................513 480-5204
Chris Kohnen, *Prin*
EMP: 82 EST: 2017
SALES (est): 3.23MM **Privately Held**
Web: www.ackermanngroup.com
SIC: 6531 Real estate agents and managers

(G-2143)
ACTIVE DAY INC
Also Called: Almost Family
2600 Civic Center Dr (45231-1312)
PHONE..................513 984-8000
Kim Chalfont, *Dir*
EMP: 29
Web: www.activeday.com
SIC: 8322 Adult day care center
PA: Active Day, Inc.
    6 Neshaminy Interplex Dr # 401
    Trevose PA 19053

Cincinnati - Hamilton County (G-2144)

(G-2144)
ADDICTION SERVICES COUNCIL
Also Called: CASA
2828 Vernon Pl (45219-2414)
PHONE.................513 281-7880
Nan Franks, *CEO*
Daina Dennis, *COO*
EMP: 31 **EST**: 1955
SQ FT: 4,000
SALES (est): 2.35MM **Privately Held**
Web: www.addictionservicescouncil.org
SIC: 8322 Alcoholism counseling, nontreatment

(G-2145)
ADLETA INC
Also Called: Adleta Construction
389 S Wayne Ave (45215-4522)
PHONE.................513 554-1469
Robert Adleta Senior, *Pr*
Robert Adleta Ii, *VP*
Mary Lee Holthous, *
Bob Dunn, *
Tim Adleta, *
EMP: 35 **EST**: 1978
SQ FT: 2,000
SALES (est): 6.22MM **Privately Held**
Web: www.adletagroup.com
SIC: 1771 1623 Concrete work; Sewer line construction

(G-2146)
ADVANCE IMPLANT DENTISTRY INC
5823 Wooster Pike (45227-4505)
PHONE.................513 271-0821
Scott E Sayre, *Pr*
Janet Sayre, *
Robert Buechner, *
EMP: 57 **EST**: 1978
SQ FT: 1,600
SALES (est): 7.98MM **Privately Held**
Web: www.nofeardentist.com
SIC: 8021 Dentists' office

(G-2147)
ADVANCE TRNSP SYSTEMS INC
Also Called: Ats Transportation Services
2 Crowne Point Ct Ste 300 (45241-5424)
PHONE.................513 818-4311
Robert Wyenandt, *Pr*
Robert L Wyenandt, *
EMP: 55 **EST**: 1980
SALES (est): 24.35MM **Privately Held**
Web: www.atslogistics.com
SIC: 4213 Trucking, except local

(G-2148)
ADVANCED CSMTC SRGERY LSER CTR
Also Called: Hj Services
3805 Edwards Rd Ste 100 (45209-1939)
PHONE.................513 351-3223
Jon Mendelsohn, *Pr*
EMP: 43 **EST**: 2001
SALES (est): 7.22MM **Privately Held**
Web: www.351face.com
SIC: 8011 Plastic surgeon

(G-2149)
ADVANTAGE RESOURCING AMER INC (HQ)
Also Called: Advantage Staffing
201 E 4th St Ste 800 (45202-4248)
PHONE.................781 472-8900
EMP: 30 **EST**: 1995
SALES (est): 454.44MM **Privately Held**
Web: www.advantageresourcing.com
SIC: 7361 Labor contractors (employment agency)
PA: Recruit Holdings Co., Ltd.
1-9-2, Marunouchi
Chiyoda-Ku TKY 100-0

(G-2150)
ADVANTAGE TCHNCAL RSURCING INC
201 E 4th St Ste 800 (45202-4248)
PHONE.................513 651-1111
Hitoshi Motohara, *Pr*
Geno Cutolo, *
Jennifer Prospero, *
EMP: 500 **EST**: 1997
SALES (est): 47.75MM **Privately Held**
Web: www.advantageresourcing.com
SIC: 7361 Employment agencies
HQ: Advantage Resourcing America, Inc.
201 E 4th St Ste 800
Cincinnati OH 45202

(G-2151)
ADVANTAGE TECHNICAL SVCS INC
191 Rosa Parks St (45202-2573)
PHONE.................513 852-4891
EMP: 55 **EST**: 2018
SALES (est): 575.43K **Privately Held**
Web: www.advantagetsi.com
SIC: 7361 Employment agencies

(G-2152)
ADVENT MEDIA GROUP LLC
537 E Pete Rose Way (45202-3578)
PHONE.................513 421-2267
Rob Lutz, *CEO*
EMP: 47 **EST**: 2003
SALES (est): 4.52MM **Privately Held**
Web: www.adventmediagroup.com
SIC: 7311 Advertising agencies

(G-2153)
AECOM
525 Vine St Ste 1800 (45202-3142)
PHONE.................513 651-3440
Perry Sole, *Brnch Mgr*
EMP: 60
SALES (corp-wide): 14.38B **Publicly Held**
Web: www.aecom.com
SIC: 8748 Environmental consultant
PA: Aecom
13355 Noel Rd Ste 400
Dallas TX 75240
972 788-1000

(G-2154)
AFC HOLDING COMPANY INC (HQ)
1 E 4th St (45202)
PHONE.................513 579-2121
EMP: 55 **EST**: 1994
SQ FT: 600,000
SALES (est): 59.54MM **Publicly Held**
SIC: 6331 6311 Property damage insurance; Life insurance
PA: American Financial Group, Inc.
301 E 4th St
Cincinnati OH 45202

(G-2155)
AGAR LLC
1205 Walnut St (45202-7153)
PHONE.................513 549-4576
Linda Agar, *Prin*
EMP: 39 **EST**: 2013
SALES (est): 4.9MM **Privately Held**
Web: www.theagar.com
SIC: 8742 Transportation consultant

(G-2156)
AGILE PURSUITS INC
One Procter & Gamble Plaza (45202-3315)
PHONE.................513 945-9908
Joseph A Stegbauer, *Pr*
EMP: 70 **EST**: 2006
SALES (est): 4.55MM
SALES (corp-wide): 82.01B **Publicly Held**
SIC: 8741 Management services
PA: The Procter & Gamble Company
1 Procter & Gamble Plz
Cincinnati OH 45202
513 983-1100

(G-2157)
AL NEYER LLC (PA)
302 W 3rd St (45202-3436)
PHONE.................513 271-6400
Molly North, *Pr*
David Neyer, *
EMP: 56 **EST**: 2006
SALES (est): 22.92MM **Privately Held**
Web: www.neyer.com
SIC: 6531 Real estate managers

(G-2158)
ALBERT MIKE LEASING (PA)
10340 Evendale Dr (45241-2512)
PHONE.................513 563-1400
Robert Betagole, *CEO*
Marty Betagole, *
Richard Betagole, *
Donald Miller, *
John Betagole, *
▼ **EMP**: 169 **EST**: 1928
SQ FT: 56,000
SALES (est): 48.67MM
SALES (corp-wide): 48.67MM **Privately Held**
Web: www.mikealbert.com
SIC: 7515 7513 5521 5012 Passenger car leasing; Truck leasing, without drivers; Automobiles, used cars only; Automobiles

(G-2159)
ALEXANDER & ASSOCIATES CO (PA)
4625 Este Ave (45232-1760)
PHONE.................513 731-7800
Thomas Luebbe, *Pr*
Thomas Rowe, *
▲ **EMP**: 130 **EST**: 1943
SALES (est): 48.76MM
SALES (corp-wide): 48.76MM **Privately Held**
Web: www.alexanderandassoc.com
SIC: 8711 Consulting engineer

(G-2160)
ALEXZANDER ANGELS LLC
478 Maple Circle Dr (45246-1510)
PHONE.................678 984-3093
EMP: 30 **EST**: 2021
SALES (est): 638.88K **Privately Held**
SIC: 8082 7389 Home health care services; Business Activities at Non-Commercial Site

(G-2161)
ALL MY SONS MVG STOR CNCNNATI
Also Called: All My Sons Moving & Storage
3010 Harris Ave (45212-2404)
PHONE.................513 440-5924
Patrick J O'neill, *Pr*
EMP: 70 **EST**: 2000
SALES (est): 2.59MM **Privately Held**
Web: www.allmysons.com
SIC: 4212 Moving services
PA: All My Sons Business Development Corporation
2400 Old Mill Rd
Carrollton TX 75007

(G-2162)
ALLIANCE CUSTOMS CLEARANCE
4010 Executive Park Dr Ste 300 (45241-4013)
PHONE.................513 794-9400
Scott Teets, *Genl Mgr*
EMP: 46
SALES (corp-wide): 524.08MM **Privately Held**
Web: www.alliance.com
SIC: 4731 Freight forwarding
HQ: Alliance Customs Clearance Inc
516 Sylvan Ave
Englewood Cliffs NJ 07632

(G-2163)
ALLIED CAR WASH INC
Also Called: AAA Auto Wash
3330 Central Pkwy (45225-2307)
PHONE.................513 559-1733
Emina Short, *Finance*
EMP: 45 **EST**: 2017
SALES (est): 659.31K **Privately Held**
Web: cluballiance.aaa.com
SIC: 7542 Carwash, automatic

(G-2164)
ALLIED CASH ADVANCE CAL LLC
7755 Montgomery Rd Ste 400 (45236-4291)
PHONE.................800 528-1974
EMP: 82 **EST**: 2013
SALES (est): 3.63MM
SALES (corp-wide): 696.24MM **Privately Held**
Web: www.alliedcash.com
SIC: 6099 Check cashing agencies
HQ: Allied Cash Holdings Llc
7755 Montgomery Rd # 400
Cincinnati OH 45236

(G-2165)
ALLIED CASH ADVANCE OHIO LLC
Also Called: Allied Cash Advance
7755 Montgomery Rd Ste 400 (45236-4197)
PHONE.................800 528-1974
Douglass D Clark, *
Roger W Dean, *
Roger A Craig, *
EMP: 176 **EST**: 2014
SALES (est): 26.76MM
SALES (corp-wide): 696.24MM **Privately Held**
Web: www.alliedcash.com
SIC: 6099 Check cashing agencies
HQ: Allied Cash Holdings Llc
7755 Montgomery Rd # 400
Cincinnati OH 45236

(G-2166)
ALLIED CASH HOLDINGS LLC (HQ)
Also Called: Allied Cash Advance
7755 Montgomery Rd Ste 400 (45236-4197)
EMP: 58 **EST**: 2004
SQ FT: 5,400
SALES (est): 107.06MM
SALES (corp-wide): 696.24MM **Privately Held**
Web: www.alliedcash.com
SIC: 6099 Check cashing agencies
PA: Cng Financial Corporation
7755 Montgomery Rd # 400
Cincinnati OH 45236
513 336-7735

(G-2167)
ALLIED CONSTRUCTION INDUSTRIES
3 Kovach Dr (45215-1000)
PHONE.................513 221-8020
Terry Phillips, *Ex Dir*
EMP: 56 **EST**: 1929
SQ FT: 3,200
SALES (est): 1.44MM **Privately Held**

Cincinnati - Hamilton County (G-2190)

Web: www.aci-construction.org
SIC: 8611 Trade associations

(G-2168)
ALLIED SECURITY LLC
110 Boggs Ln Ste 140 (45246-3143)
PHONE.................513 771-3776
Tim Cember, *Mgr*
EMP: 86
SALES (corp-wide): 946.48MM **Privately Held**
Web: www.aus.com
SIC: 7381 Security guard service
HQ: Allied Security Llc
    161 Washington St Ste 600
    Conshohocken PA 19428
    484 351-1300

(G-2169)
ALLIED WINDOW INC
11111 Canal Rd (45241-1861)
PHONE.................513 559-1212
David Martin, *Pr*
Sonya Martin, *
Richard Young, *
EMP: 40 EST: 1950
SQ FT: 15,000
SALES (est): 8.35MM **Privately Held**
Web: www.alliedwindow.com
SIC: 5031 Windows

(G-2170)
ALPHA INVESTMENT PARTNERSHIP (PA)
Also Called: Cincinnati Equitable Insurance
525 Vine St Ste 1925 (45202)
P.O. Box 2405 (45201)
PHONE.................513 621-1826
EMP: 58 EST: 1995
SALES (est): 26.62MM **Privately Held**
Web: www.axa.com
SIC: 6311 Life insurance

(G-2171)
ALPS SERVICES INC
12073 Sheraton Ln (45246-1611)
PHONE.................513 772-4746
EMP: 28
Web: www.alpsservices.com
SIC: 6411 Insurance claim adjusters, not employed by insurance company
PA: Alps Services, Inc.
    10653 Chester Rd
    Cincinnati OH 45215

(G-2172)
ALRO STEEL CORPORATION
10310 S Medallion Dr (45241-4836)
PHONE.................513 769-9999
Rick Tennenholtz, *Brnch Mgr*
EMP: 85
SALES (corp-wide): 3.43B **Privately Held**
Web: www.alro.com
SIC: 5051 Steel
PA: Alro Steel Corporation
    3100 E High St
    Jackson MI 49203
    517 787-5500

(G-2173)
ALTA IT SERVICES LLC
511 W Bay St Ste 480 (45242)
PHONE.................813 999-3101
John Owens, *Mgr*
EMP: 170
Web: www.altaits.com
SIC: 8742 7373 7363 Management information systems consultant; Systems integration services; Office help supply service
HQ: Alta It Services, Llc
    9210 Corp Blvd Ste 200
    Rockville MD 20850
    301 948-8700

(G-2174)
ALTORIA SOLUTIONS LLC
600 Vine St Ste 1904 (45202-2429)
PHONE.................513 612-2007
EMP: 45 EST: 2001
SQ FT: 3,000
SALES (est): 2.18MM **Privately Held**
Web: www.altoria.com
SIC: 4813 Online service providers

(G-2175)
AMBULATORY MEDICAL CARE INC (PA)
Also Called: Doctor's Urgent Care Offices
7312 Beechmont Ave (45230-4119)
PHONE.................513 831-8555
Paul J Amrhein, *Pr*
Dean Judkins, *
Paul Amrhein, *
EMP: 35 EST: 1982
SALES (est): 21.61MM
SALES (corp-wide): 21.61MM **Privately Held**
Web: www.culturestrike.org
SIC: 8011 Clinic, operated by physicians

(G-2176)
AMEND CONSULTING LLC
538 Reading Rd Ste 300 (45202-1493)
PHONE.................513 399-6300
David Velie, *Prin*
EMP: 100 EST: 2005
SALES (est): 5.02MM **Privately Held**
Web: www.amendllc.com
SIC: 8741 Business management

(G-2177)
AMERICAN CMPASSIONATE CARE LLC
5960 Glenway Ave (45238-2009)
PHONE.................513 443-8156
Alysa Croxton, *Prin*
James Mayweather, *Prin*
EMP: 47 EST: 2014
SALES (est): 2.04MM **Privately Held**
Web: www.americancompassionatecare.com
SIC: 8082 Home health care services

(G-2178)
AMERICAN EMPIRE SRPLS LNES INS
Also Called: American Empire Insurance
515 Main St (45202-3223)
P.O. Box 5423 (45201-5423)
PHONE.................513 369-3000
Bob Nelson, *Pr*
Chet Nalepa, *
Matt Held, *
EMP: 47 EST: 1986
SQ FT: 20,000
SALES (est): 9.59MM **Publicly Held**
SIC: 6331 Fire, marine, and casualty insurance
HQ: Great American Risk Solutions Surplus Lines Insurance Company
    580 Walnut St
    Cincinnati OH 45202
    513 369-3000

(G-2179)
AMERICAN FINANCIAL CORPORATION
580 Walnut St Fl 9 (45202-3193)
PHONE.................513 579-2121
James Evans, *Prin*
EMP: 195 EST: 2007
SALES (est): 59.54MM **Publicly Held**
Web: www.greatamericaninsurancegroup.com
SIC: 6331 Fire, marine, and casualty insurance
HQ: Afc Holding Company Inc
    One East Fourth St
    Cincinnati OH 45202

(G-2180)
AMERICAN FINANCIAL GROUP INC (PA)
301 E 4th St (45202)
PHONE.................513 579-2121
John B Berding, *Pr*
Brian S Hertzman, *Sr VP*
Michelle A Gillis, *CAO*
EMP: 549 EST: 1872
SALES (est): 7.83B **Publicly Held**
Web: www.afginc.com
SIC: 6411 Property and casualty insurance agent

(G-2181)
AMERICAN HERITAGE GIRLS INC
Also Called: AHG
35 Tri County Pkwy (45246-3207)
PHONE.................513 771-2025
Patty Garibay, *Ex Dir*
EMP: 70 EST: 1995
SALES (est): 4.77MM **Privately Held**
Web: www.americanheritagegirls.org
SIC: 8641 Youth organizations

(G-2182)
AMERICAN HOMES 4 RENT
11802 Conrey Rd Ste 100 (45249-1077)
PHONE.................513 429-7174
EMP: 34 EST: 2013
SALES (est): 242.87K **Privately Held**
Web: www.amh.com
SIC: 6531 Real estate agents and managers

(G-2183)
AMERICAN MONEY MANAGEMENT CORP
301 E 4th St 27th Fl (45202-4245)
PHONE.................513 579-2592
S Craig Lindner, *Ch Bd*
John B Berding, *
Sandra W Heimann, *
Jason J Maney, *
EMP: 38 EST: 1973
SQ FT: 2,000
SALES (est): 10.49MM **Publicly Held**
SIC: 6331 Fire, marine, and casualty insurance
PA: American Financial Group, Inc.
    301 E 4th St
    Cincinnati OH 45202

(G-2184)
AMERICAN NURSING CARE INC
4750 Wesley Ave Ste Q (45212-2273)
PHONE.................513 731-4600
Amy Owens, *Mgr*
EMP: 314
Web: www.americannursingcare.com
SIC: 8051 8082 Skilled nursing care facilities; Home health care services
HQ: American Nursing Care, Inc.
    6281 Tri Ridge Blvd # 300
    Loveland OH 45140
    513 576-0262

(G-2185)
AMERICAN NURSING CARE INC
4460 Red Bank Rd Ste 100 (45227-2173)
PHONE.................513 245-1500
Victoria Dixon, *Prin*
EMP: 217
Web: www.americannursingcare.com
SIC: 8051 Skilled nursing care facilities
HQ: American Nursing Care, Inc.
    6281 Tri Ridge Blvd # 300
    Loveland OH 45140
    513 576-0262

(G-2186)
AMERICAN RED CROSS
Also Called: Cincinnati Area Chapter
2111 Dana Ave (45207-1303)
PHONE.................513 579-3000
Trish Smitson, *CEO*
EMP: 1382 EST: 1905
SQ FT: 26,147
SALES (est): 6.12MM
SALES (corp-wide): 3.18B **Privately Held**
Web: www.redcross.org
SIC: 8322 Social service center
PA: The American National Red Cross
    431 18th St Nw
    Washington DC 20006
    202 737-8300

(G-2187)
AMERICAN RISK SERVICES LLC
Also Called: ARS
1130 Congress Ave Ste A (45246-4485)
PHONE.................513 772-3712
Scott Satterthwaite, *Managing Member*
EMP: 31 EST: 2007
SALES (est): 5.49MM **Privately Held**
Web: www.assuredpartners.com
SIC: 6411 Insurance brokers, nec
PA: Assuredpartners, Inc.
    450 S Orange Ave Fl 4
    Orlando FL 32801

(G-2188)
AMERICAN WELDING & GAS INC
1210 Glendale Milford Rd (45215-1209)
PHONE.................859 519-8772
Jason Krieger, *Brnch Mgr*
EMP: 35
SALES (corp-wide): 166.62MM **Privately Held**
Web: www.awggases.com
SIC: 5084 Welding machinery and equipment
PA: American Welding & Gas, Inc.
    4900 Falls Of Neuse Rd # 150
    Raleigh NC 27609
    984 222-2600

(G-2189)
AMERIPRIDE SERVICES INC
Also Called: AMERIPRIDE SERVICES, INC.
4936 Montgomery Rd (45212-2127)
PHONE.................859 371-4037
Sam Hooks, *Mgr*
EMP: 76
SALES (corp-wide): 2.83B **Publicly Held**
Web: www.ameripride.com
SIC: 7213 Uniform supply
HQ: Ameripride Services, Llc
    10801 Wayzata Blvd # 100
    Minnetonka MN 55305
    800 750-4628

(G-2190)
AMERITAS LIFE INSURANCE CORP
1876 Waycross Rd (45240-2825)
PHONE.................866 696-7478
EMP: 1200
SALES (corp-wide): 2.36B **Privately Held**
Web: www.ameritas.com
SIC: 6311 6321 Mutual association life insurance; Mutual accident and health associations
HQ: Ameritas Life Insurance Corp.
    5900 O St

Cincinnati - Hamilton County (G-2191) GEOGRAPHIC SECTION

Lincoln NE 68510
402 467-1122

(G-2191)
AMERITAS LIFE INSURANCE CORP
1876 Waycross Rd (45240-2825)
P.O. Box 40888 (45240-0888)
PHONE..................................513 595-2334
Joann M Martin, *CEO*
Steven J Valerius, *
Tim L Stonehocker, *
J Thomas Burkhard, *
Cheryl L Heilman, *
EMP: 240 **EST:** 2011
SALES (est): 855.35K **Privately Held**
Web: www.ameritas.com
SIC: 6311 Life insurance

(G-2192)
AMG CONSULTANTS INC
700 W Pete Rose Way (45203-1892)
PHONE..................................917 600-3773
Enoch Frank, *Pr*
EMP: 50
SALES (est): 1.21MM **Privately Held**
SIC: 8742 Marketing consulting services

(G-2193)
AMORSO AT HM SNIOR DSBLITY CAR
1821 Summit Rd Ste 113 (45237-2818)
PHONE..................................513 761-6500
EMP: 30 **EST:** 2015
SALES (est): 1MM **Privately Held**
Web: www.amorsohomecare.com
SIC: 8082 Home health care services

(G-2194)
AMPAC HOLDINGS LLC (HQ)
Also Called: Proampac
12025 Tricon Rd (45246-1719)
PHONE..................................513 671-1777
Greg Tucker, *Managing Member*
◆ **EMP:** 700 **EST:** 2001
SQ FT: 220,000
SALES (est): 420.05MM
SALES (corp-wide): 1.58B **Privately Held**
Web: www.proampac.com
SIC: 2673 2677 3081 2674 Plastic bags: made from purchased materials; Envelopes ; Unsupported plastics film and sheet; Shopping bags: made from purchased materials
PA: Proampac Holdings Inc.
12025 Tricon Rd
Cincinnati OH 45246
513 671-1777

(G-2195)
AMPAC PACKAGING LLC (HQ)
Also Called: Ampac
12025 Tricon Rd (45246-1719)
PHONE..................................513 671-1777
John Baumann, *CEO*
◆ **EMP:** 106 **EST:** 2006
SALES (est): 412.5MM
SALES (corp-wide): 1.58B **Privately Held**
Web: www.proampac.com
SIC: 3086 5084 Packaging and shipping materials, foamed plastics; Processing and packaging equipment
PA: Proampac Holdings Inc.
12025 Tricon Rd
Cincinnati OH 45246
513 671-1777

(G-2196)
ANCHOR FLANGE COMPANY (PA)
Also Called: Anchor Fluid Power
5553 Murray Ave (45227-2707)
PHONE..................................513 527-3512
▲ **EMP:** 79 **EST:** 1983
SALES (est): 17.98MM
SALES (corp-wide): 17.98MM **Privately Held**
Web: www.anchorfluidpower.com
SIC: 3462 5085 3594 3494 Flange, valve, and pipe fitting forgings, ferrous; Industrial supplies; Fluid power pumps and motors; Valves and pipe fittings, nec

(G-2197)
ANDERSON HEALTHCARE LTD
Also Called: Anderson Nrsing Rhbltation Ctr
8139 Beechmont Ave (45255-3152)
P.O. Box 541084 (45254-1084)
PHONE..................................513 474-6200
Linda Wagschal, *
EMP: 50 **EST:** 1996
SQ FT: 44,000
SALES (est): 16.28MM **Privately Held**
Web: www.theanderson.com
SIC: 8051 8069 Convalescent home with continuous nursing care; Specialty hospitals, except psychiatric

(G-2198)
ANDERSON HILLS PEDIATRICS INC
7400 Jager Ct (45230-4344)
PHONE..................................513 232-8100
Lori B Gordley D.o.s. Md, *Prin*
William Broderick Md, *Prin*
Jon Venneymer Md, *Prin*
James Depiore Md, *Prin*
Meri Scrader Md, *Prin*
EMP: 60 **EST:** 1975
SQ FT: 4,750
SALES (est): 8.73MM **Privately Held**
Web: www.ahpediatrics.com
SIC: 8011 Pediatrician

(G-2199)
ANDERSON JEFFERY R RE INC
3805 Edwards Rd Ste 700 (45209-1955)
PHONE..................................513 241-5800
Jeffrey R Anderson, *Pr*
EMP: 50 **EST:** 1979
SQ FT: 30,000
SALES (est): 7.49MM **Privately Held**
Web: www.anderson-realestate.com
SIC: 6512 Commercial and industrial building operation

(G-2200)
ANDERSON LITTLE
8516 Beechmont Ave (45255-4708)
PHONE..................................513 474-7800
Robin Beier, *Dir*
Robin L Beier, *Dir*
EMP: 38 **EST:** 1999
SALES (est): 823.37K **Privately Held**
Web: www.thelittleanderson.com
SIC: 8351 Group day care center

(G-2201)
ANDERSON TOWNSHIP PARK DST
Also Called: Beech Acres Park
6910 Salem Rd (45230-2959)
PHONE..................................513 474-0003
Brian Jordan, *Finance*
EMP: 40
SALES (corp-wide): 2.41MM **Privately Held**
Web: www.andersonparks.com
SIC: 7999 Recreation services
PA: Anderson Township Park District
8249 Clough Pike
Cincinnati OH 45244
513 474-0003

(G-2202)
ANDERSON TWNSHIP HSTRCAL SOC I
6550 Clough Pike (45244-4029)
P.O. Box 30174 (45230-0174)
PHONE..................................513 231-2114
Sue A Wettstein, *Pr*
Robert Radcliffe, *
Carol Voorhees, *
Albert Wettstein, *
EMP: 45 **EST:** 1975
SALES (est): 108.02K **Privately Held**
Web: www.andersontownshiphistoricalsociety.org
SIC: 8412 Historical society

(G-2203)
ANDYDANDY CENTER LLC
3804 Church St (45244-2437)
PHONE..................................513 272-6141
EMP: 28
SALES (corp-wide): 162.27K **Privately Held**
SIC: 7389 Business Activities at Non-Commercial Site
PA: Andydandy Center, Llc
4601 Malsbary Rd
Blue Ash OH 45242
513 272-6141

(G-2204)
ANESTHSIA ASSOC CINCINNATI INC
2139 Auburn Ave (45219-2906)
P.O. Box 40574 (45240-0574)
PHONE..................................513 585-0577
Donald Adkins, *Dir*
EMP: 1155 **EST:** 1961
SALES (est): 11.3MM
SALES (corp-wide): 3.6B **Privately Held**
SIC: 8011 Anesthesiologist
HQ: Team Health Holdings, Inc.
265 Brkview Cntre Way Ste
Knoxville TN 37919
865 693-1000

(G-2205)
ANHEUSER-BUSCH LLC
Also Called: Anheuser-Busch
600 Vine St Ste 1002 (45202-2400)
PHONE..................................513 381-3927
Dirk Disper, *Brnch Mgr*
EMP: 29
SALES (corp-wide): 1.31B **Privately Held**
Web: www.budweisertours.com
SIC: 5181 Beer and other fermented malt liquors
HQ: Anheuser-Busch, Llc
1 Busch Pl
Saint Louis MO 63118
800 342-5283

(G-2206)
AP CCHMC
3333 Burnet Ave (45229-3026)
PHONE..................................513 636-4200
EMP: 53 **EST:** 2013
SALES (est): 11.77MM **Privately Held**
Web: www.cincinnatichildrens.org
SIC: 8011 Pediatrician

(G-2207)
APC2 INC (PA)
Also Called: Appearance Plus
6812 Clough Pike (45244-4037)
PHONE..................................513 231-5540
Jonathon Lindy, *Pr*
EMP: 50 **EST:** 1984
SALES (est): 2.22MM
SALES (corp-wide): 2.22MM **Privately Held**
Web: www.appearanceplus.com

SIC: 7216 7212 Cleaning and dyeing, except rugs; Laundry and drycleaner agents

(G-2208)
APEX ENVIRONMENTAL SERVICES L
19 E 72nd St (45216-2053)
PHONE..................................513 772-2739
John Thomas, *CEO*
Bill Evans, *
EMP: 101 **EST:** 1998
SALES (est): 2.38MM **Privately Held**
Web: www.apexservicesllc.com
SIC: 7349 5113 Janitorial service, contract basis; Industrial and personal service paper

(G-2209)
APEX RESTORATION CONTRS LTD (PA)
6315 Warrick St (45227-2540)
P.O. Box 80850 (48308-0850)
PHONE..................................513 489-1795
Daniel P Mc Neil, *Managing Member*
EMP: 30 **EST:** 1997
SQ FT: 10,200
SALES (est): 6.52MM
SALES (corp-wide): 6.52MM **Privately Held**
Web: www.apexrest.com
SIC: 1521 1542 General remodeling, single-family houses; Commercial and office buildings, renovation and repair

(G-2210)
APOLLO HEATING & AC INC
4538 Camberwell Rd (45209-1155)
PHONE..................................513 271-3600
Chad Lyons, *Pr*
EMP: 35 **EST:** 1969
SALES (est): 7.04MM
SALES (corp-wide): 587.54MM **Privately Held**
Web: www.apollohome.com
SIC: 1711 1731 Warm air heating and air conditioning contractor; Electrical work
PA: Essential Services Intermediate Holding Corporation
3416 Robards Ct
Louisville KY 40218
502 657-1903

(G-2211)
APS ACQUISITION LLC (DH)
201 E 4th St Ste 900 (45202-4160)
PHONE..................................513 719-2600
EMP: 33 **EST:** 2014
SALES (est): 32.82MM
SALES (corp-wide): 357.78B **Publicly Held**
SIC: 5122 Drugs, proprietaries, and sundries
HQ: Neighborcare Pharmacy Services, Inc.
201 E 4th St Ste 900
Cincinnati OH 45202

(G-2212)
ARCHDIOCESE OF CINCINNATI
Also Called: St Bartholomew Cons School
9375 Winton Rd (45231-3967)
PHONE..................................513 729-1725
Leanora Roach, *Prin*
EMP: 40
SALES (corp-wide): 222.98MM **Privately Held**
Web: www.catholicaoc.org
SIC: 7032 Girls' camp
PA: Archdiocese Of Cincinnati
100 E 8th St Fl 8
Cincinnati OH 45202
513 421-3131

GEOGRAPHIC SECTION

Cincinnati - Hamilton County (G-2237)

(G-2213)
ARCHDIOCESE OF CINCINNATI
Gate of Heaven Cemetery
11000 Montgomery Rd (45249-2307)
PHONE................................513 489-0300
Gary Raffel, *Dir*
EMP: 112
SALES (corp-wide): 222.98MM **Privately Held**
Web: www.gateofheaven.org
SIC: 6553 0782 Cemeteries, real estate operation; Lawn and garden services
PA: Archdiocese Of Cincinnati
100 E 8th St Fl 8
Cincinnati OH 45202
513 421-3131

(G-2214)
ARCHIABLE ELECTRIC COMPANY
3803 Ford Cir (45227-3403)
PHONE................................513 621-1307
James Schroth, *Pr*
Barbara Ruehlmann, *
EMP: 65 **EST:** 1919
SQ FT: 10,000
SALES (est): 9.2MM **Privately Held**
Web: www.archiableelectric.com
SIC: 1731 General electrical contractor

(G-2215)
ARENA MANAGEMENT HOLDINGS LLC
Also Called: Heritage Bank Center
100 Broadway St Ste 300 (45202-3514)
PHONE................................513 421-4111
EMP: 600 **EST:** 2001
SQ FT: 123,208
SALES (est): 25.29MM **Privately Held**
Web: www.heritagebankcenter.com
SIC: 7941 6531 Sports field or stadium operator, promoting sports events; Real estate agents and managers

(G-2216)
ARLING LUMBER INCORPORATED
771 Neeb Rd (45233-4698)
PHONE................................513 451-5700
EMP: 30
Web: www.arlinglumber.com
SIC: 5031 Lumber, plywood, and millwork

(G-2217)
ARLINGTON MEMORIAL GRDNS ASSN
Also Called: ARLINGTON MEMORIAL GARDENS, TH
2145 Compton Rd (45231-3009)
PHONE................................513 521-7003
Leroy Meier, *Ch Bd*
Edwin Friedhoff, *
Daniel Applegate, *
Julie Hoffman, *
EMP: 27 **EST:** 1936
SQ FT: 10,000
SALES (est): 3.88MM **Privately Held**
Web: www.amgardens.org
SIC: 6553 Cemeteries, real estate operation

(G-2218)
ASSOCIATED BANK
312 Walnut St Ste 3450 (45202-4026)
PHONE................................513 246-2200
EMP: 28 **EST:** 2019
SALES (est): 248.2K **Privately Held**
Web: newsroom.associatedbank.com
SIC: 5044 Bank automatic teller machines

(G-2219)
ASSOCIATED PREMIUM CORPORATION
1870 Summit Rd (45237-2804)
PHONE................................513 679-4444
◆ **EMP:** 40 **EST:** 1975
SALES (est): 9.29MM **Privately Held**
Web: www.apcpromos.com
SIC: 5199 5064 3993 3911 Advertising specialties; Electrical appliances, television and radio; Signs and advertising specialties; Jewelry, precious metal

(G-2220)
ASSURECARE LLC
250 W Court St Ste 450e (45202-1088)
PHONE................................513 618-2150
Mahendra Vora, *Ofcr*
Greg Silence, *VP*
Thomas M Mack, *VP*
Dan Falke, *VP*
EMP: 35 **EST:** 2014
SQ FT: 50,000
SALES (est): 6.77MM **Privately Held**
Web: www.assurecare.com
SIC: 7371 8082 Computer software development; Home health care services
PA: Vora Ventures Llc
10290 Alliance Rd
Blue Ash OH 45242

(G-2221)
ASTORIA PLACE CINCINNATI LLC
3627 Harvey Ave (45229-2005)
PHONE................................513 961-8881
Michael Nudell, *Prin*
EMP: 250 **EST:** 2018
SALES (est): 6.05MM **Privately Held**
SIC: 8742 General management consultant

(G-2222)
ASTORIA PLACE SILVERTON LLC
6922 Ohio Ave (45236-3506)
PHONE................................513 793-2090
Laura Ritterbach, *
EMP: 85 **EST:** 2018
SALES (est): 5.92MM **Privately Held**
SIC: 8059 Nursing home, except skilled and intermediate care facility

(G-2223)
AT HOSPITALITY LLC
5375 Medpace Way (45227-1543)
PHONE................................513 527-9962
EMP: 100 **EST:** 2014
SALES (est): 4.51MM **Privately Held**
SIC: 7011 Hotels

(G-2224)
AT&T CORP
Also Called: AT&T Corp.
11711 Princeton Pike (45246)
PHONE................................513 407-4446
EMP: 69
SALES (corp-wide): 122.43B **Publicly Held**
Web: www.att.com
SIC: 4813 Telephone communication, except radio
HQ: At&T Enterprises, Llc
208 S Akard St
Dallas TX 75202
800 403-3302

(G-2225)
ATHLETIC TRINING SOLUTIONS LLC
7430 Bridge Point Pass (45248-1916)
PHONE................................513 295-1756
Matthew Smith, *Prin*
EMP: 35 **EST:** 2015
SALES (est): 3.25MM **Privately Held**
Web: www.atsbwc.com
SIC: 8699 Athletic organizations

(G-2226)
ATKINS & STANG INC
1031 Meta Dr (45237-5007)
PHONE................................513 242-8300
Fred Stang, *Pr*
Randall Stortz, *
Susan Ochs, *
EMP: 69 **EST:** 1984
SQ FT: 28,000
SALES (est): 10.55MM **Privately Held**
Web: www.atkinsandstang.com
SIC: 1731 General electrical contractor

(G-2227)
ATLANTIC FOODS CORP
1999 Section Rd (45237-3343)
PHONE................................513 772-3535
Gary Grefer, *Pr*
Stuart Goret, *
Jeff Busch, *
Stuart Berning, *
Rick Breeden Transportation, *Supervisor*
▲ **EMP:** 65 **EST:** 2001
SALES (est): 22.69MM **Privately Held**
Web: www.atlanticfoods.com
SIC: 5149 Specialty food items

(G-2228)
ATM SOLUTIONS INC (PA)
Also Called: Asi Technical Services
551 Northland Blvd (45240-3212)
PHONE................................513 742-4900
Paul Scott, *Pr*
Neil Scott, *
EMP: 100 **EST:** 1996
SALES (est): 19.23MM
SALES (corp-wide): 19.23MM **Privately Held**
Web: www.atm-solutions.com
SIC: 7699 Automated teller machine (ATM) repair

(G-2229)
AUGUST GROH & SONS INC
8832 Reading Rd (45215-4815)
PHONE................................513 821-0090
Jo Groh, *Pr*
Richard T Groh, *
Tom Mooran, *
EMP: 50 **EST:** 1926
SQ FT: 10,000
SALES (est): 4.35MM **Privately Held**
Web: www.groh.com
SIC: 1721 7349 Commercial painting; Building and office cleaning services

(G-2230)
AWH HOLDINGS INC
Also Called: Woods Hardware
125 E 9th St (45202-2127)
PHONE................................513 241-2614
Matthew Woods, *COO*
Laura Woods, *
Steven Woods, *
EMP: 80 **EST:** 2017
Web: stores.truevalue.com
SIC: 6719 5231 Holding companies, nec; Paint, glass, and wallpaper stores

(G-2231)
AWS
2718 E Camp Rd (45241)
PHONE................................513 648-9360
Angie Honshell, *Prin*
EMP: 30
SALES (corp-wide): 2.74MM **Privately Held**
Web: www.awscpas.com
SIC: 8052 Home for the mentally retarded, with health care
PA: Aws
5440 25th St
Columbus IN 47203
812 376-3906

(G-2232)
AXCESS RCVERY CR SOLUTIONS INC
4540 Cooper Rd Ste 305 (45242-5649)
PHONE................................513 229-6700
Jerry R Williams, *Pr*
Stephen J Schaller, *
Robert W Neu, *
EMP: 50 **EST:** 2007
SALES (est): 1.22MM **Privately Held**
SIC: 7322 Collection agency, except real estate

(G-2233)
AZTEC SERVICES GROUP INC
Also Called: Aztec Demolition & Envmtl Co
3814 William P Dooley Byp (45223-2664)
PHONE................................513 541-2002
Albert C Meininger, *Pr*
Tom Coon, *
EMP: 100 **EST:** 2013
SQ FT: 2,000
SALES (est): 12.31MM **Privately Held**
Web: www.aztecservices.com
SIC: 1795 8744 Wrecking and demolition work; Environmental remediation

(G-2234)
B & J ELECTRICAL COMPANY INC
6265 Wiehe Rd (45237-4211)
PHONE................................513 351-7100
Gary Lee Janzen, *Ch*
Shannon Ernst, *
Debbie Janzen, *
Kirsten Janzen, *
Peggy Deorger, *
EMP: 45 **EST:** 1974
SALES (est): 10MM **Privately Held**
Web: www.bjelectrical.com
SIC: 1731 General electrical contractor

(G-2235)
B D S INC (PA)
3500 Southside Ave (45204-1138)
PHONE................................513 921-8441
William Lindsey, *Pr*
EMP: 35 **EST:** 1985
SALES (est): 2.51MM **Privately Held**
SIC: 4226 4225 Liquid storage; General warehousing and storage

(G-2236)
BAKER & HOSTETLER LLP
312 Walnut St Ste 3200 (45202-4074)
PHONE................................513 929-3400
David G Holcombe, *Mng Pt*
EMP: 93
SALES (corp-wide): 309.55K **Privately Held**
Web: www.bakerlaw.com
SIC: 8111 General practice attorney, lawyer
PA: Baker & Hostetler Llp
127 Public Sq Ste 2000
Cleveland OH 44114
216 621-0200

(G-2237)
BARNES DENNIG & CO LTD (PA)
150 E 4th St Ste 300 (45202-4186)
PHONE................................513 241-8313
William J Cloppert, *Prin*
Bradley S Chaffin, *Pt*
James A Donnellon, *Pt*
Steven T Hube, *Pt*
Alan E Bieber, *Pt*
EMP: 44 **EST:** 1965
SQ FT: 19,549

Cincinnati - Hamilton County (G-2238)   GEOGRAPHIC SECTION

SALES (est): 10.22MM
SALES (corp-wide): 10.22MM **Privately Held**
Web: www.barnesdennig.com
SIC: 8721 Certified public accountant

(G-2238)
BARTLETT & CO LLC
600 Vine St Ste 2100 (45202-3896)
PHONE..................513 621-4612
Kelley J Downing, *Pr*
EMP: 56 EST: 1898
SQ FT: 28,000
SALES (est): 9.09MM **Privately Held**
Web: www.bartlett1898.com
SIC: 6282 Investment advisory service

(G-2239)
BATTERII LLC
1008 Race St Ste 4 (45202-1091)
PHONE..................513 379-3595
EMP: 29 EST: 2012
SALES (est): 3.03MM **Privately Held**
Web: www.batterii.com
SIC: 7371 Computer software development and applications

(G-2240)
BAXTER HDELL DNNLLY PRSTON INC (PA)
Also Called: Bhdp Architecture
302 W 3rd St Ste 500 (45202-3434)
PHONE..................513 271-1634
Michael Habel, *CEO*
Richard Krzyminski, *
Anthony Berger, *
Patrick Donnelly, *
Barry Bayer, *
EMP: 101 EST: 1937
SQ FT: 24,000
SALES (est): 24.6MM
SALES (corp-wide): 24.6MM **Privately Held**
Web: www.bhdp.com
SIC: 8741 8712 8742 7373 Construction management; Architectural engineering; Management consulting services; Computer integrated systems design

(G-2241)
BBDO WORLDWIDE INC
Also Called: BBDO
700 W Pete Rose Way (45203-1892)
PHONE..................513 861-3668
Susan Davidson, *Pdt Mgr*
EMP: 47
SALES (corp-wide): 14.69B **Publicly Held**
Web: www.bbdo.com
SIC: 7311 Advertising consultant
HQ: Bbdo Worldwide Inc.
1285 Ave Of The Amrcas Fl
New York NY 10019
212 459-5000

(G-2242)
BEACON ELECTRIC COMPANY
Also Called: Beacon Electrical Contractors
7815 Redsky Dr (45249-1636)
PHONE..................513 851-0731
William K Schubert, *CEO*
Joe Mellencamp, *
Bonnie Klein, *
David Earlywine, *
Kenneth K Butler, *
EMP: 100 EST: 1983
SQ FT: 10,000
SALES (est): 29.27MM **Privately Held**
Web: www.beacon-electric.com
SIC: 1731 General electrical contractor

(G-2243)
BEACON ORTHPAEDCS & SPRTS MED
6480 Harrison Ave Ste 100 (45247-7961)
PHONE..................513 354-3700
John W Wolf Junior, *Brnch Mgr*
EMP: 393
SALES (corp-wide): 178.48MM **Privately Held**
Web: www.beaconortho.com
SIC: 8011 Orthopedic physician
PA: Beacon Orthopaedics & Sports Medicine, Ltd.
500 E Business Way
Cincinnati OH 45241
513 354-3700

(G-2244)
BEACON ORTHPDICS SPT MDCINE LT
8099 Cornell Rd (45249-2231)
PHONE..................513 985-2252
EMP: 855
SALES (corp-wide): 178.48MM **Privately Held**
Web: www.orthocincy.com
SIC: 8011 Orthopedic physician
PA: Beacon Orthopaedics & Sports Medicine, Ltd.
500 E Business Way
Cincinnati OH 45241
513 354-3700

(G-2245)
BEACON ORTHPDICS SPT MDCINE LT (PA)
Also Called: Beacon Orthopedics
500 E Business Way (45241-2374)
PHONE..................513 354-3700
John W Wolf Junior, *Pr*
John Gallagher Md, *VP*
Roger Meyer Md, *Sec*
EMP: 100 EST: 1972
SALES (est): 178.48MM
SALES (corp-wide): 178.48MM **Privately Held**
Web: www.beaconortho.com
SIC: 8011 Orthopedic physician

(G-2246)
BEECH ACRES PARENTING CENTER (PA)
Also Called: BEECH ACRES THERAPUTIC FOSTER
615 Elsinore Pl (45202-1455)
PHONE..................513 231-6630
James Mason, *Pr*
Richard Sorg, *TX Vice President*
Karen Sandker, *
David T Wallace, *
EMP: 85 EST: 1849
SALES (est): 16.63MM
SALES (corp-wide): 16.63MM **Privately Held**
Web: www.beechacres.org
SIC: 8322 Adoption services

(G-2247)
BEECHMONT CHEVROLET INC
Also Called: Beechmont Chevrolet
7600 Beechmont Ave (45255-4202)
PHONE..................513 624-1100
William F Woeste Junior, *Pr*
Margot Woeste, *
Cynthia Mac Connell, *
EMP: 55 EST: 1946
SQ FT: 29,000
SALES (est): 2.64MM **Privately Held**
Web: www.chevrolet.com
SIC: 5511 7539 5013 5012 Automobiles, new and used; Automotive repair shops, nec; Motor vehicle supplies and new parts; Automobiles

(G-2248)
BEECHMONT MOTORS INC (PA)
Also Called: Beechmont Porsche
8639 Beechmont Ave (45255-4709)
PHONE..................513 388-3883
William Woeste Junior, *Pr*
Margo Woeste, *
Cynthia S Connell Mac, *Sec*
EMP: 30 EST: 1971
SQ FT: 60,000
SALES (est): 10.27MM
SALES (corp-wide): 10.27MM **Privately Held**
Web: www.audicincinnatieast.com
SIC: 5511 7539 5012 5013 Automobiles, new and used; Automotive repair shops, nec; Automobiles; Motor vehicle supplies and new parts

(G-2249)
BEECHMONT MOTORS T INC
8667 Beechmont Ave (45255-4709)
PHONE..................513 388-3800
William F Woeste Junior, *Pr*
Margot Woeste, *
Cynthia Mac Connell, *
EMP: 70 EST: 1948
SQ FT: 20,000
SALES (est): 9.33MM **Privately Held**
Web: www.beechmonttoyota.com
SIC: 5511 7539 5012 5013 Automobiles, new and used; Automotive repair shops, nec; Automobiles; Motor vehicle supplies and new parts

(G-2250)
BEECHMONT RACQUET CLUB INC
Also Called: Beechmont Racquet and Fitness
435 Ohio Pike (45255-3712)
PHONE..................513 528-5700
William Atkins, *Pr*
Helen Atkins, *
Bradon Atkins, *
EMP: 40 EST: 1966
SQ FT: 160,000
SALES (est): 873.53K **Privately Held**
Web: www.beechmontfitness.com
SIC: 7991 7997 Health club; Racquetball club, membership

(G-2251)
BEECHWOOD HOME
2140 Pogue Ave (45208-3299)
PHONE..................513 321-9294
Patricia Clark, *CEO*
Tim Owens, *
EMP: 150 EST: 1892
SQ FT: 53,000
SALES (est): 11.11MM **Privately Held**
Web: www.beechwoodhome.com
SIC: 8051 Convalescent home with continuous nursing care

(G-2252)
BEECHWOOD TERRACE CARE CTR INC
Also Called: Forest Hills Care Center
8700 Moran Rd (45244-1986)
PHONE..................513 578-6200
Harold Sosna, *Pr*
EMP: 40 EST: 2007
SALES (est): 8.96MM **Privately Held**
Web: www.foresthillscarecenter.com
SIC: 8051 Convalescent home with continuous nursing care

(G-2253)
BELCAN LLC
Also Called: Belcan Engineering Services
7785 E Kemper Rd (45249-1611)
PHONE..................513 277-3100
EMP: 250
SALES (corp-wide): 751.87MM **Privately Held**
Web: www.belcan.com
SIC: 8711 Engineering services
PA: Belcan, Llc
10151 Carver Rd Ste 105
Blue Ash OH 45242
513 891-0972

(G-2254)
BELCAN STAFFING SOLUTION
127 W 4th St (45202-2705)
PHONE..................513 241-8367
Ralph Anderson, *CEO*
EMP: 39 EST: 2017
SALES (est): 243.59K **Privately Held**
Web: www.belcan.com
SIC: 7371 Custom computer programming services

(G-2255)
BELFLEX STAFFING NETWORK LLC (HQ)
11591 Goldcoast Dr (45249)
PHONE..................513 488-8588
Jason Mccaw, *CEO*
Timothy Mueller, *
Robert Baer, *
EMP: 125 EST: 1998
SALES (est): 51.22MM
SALES (corp-wide): 112.31MM **Privately Held**
Web: www.belflex.com
SIC: 7361 7363 Labor contractors (employment agency); Help supply services
PA: Elwood Staffing Services, Inc.
4111 Central Ave
Columbus IN 47203
812 372-6200

(G-2256)
BELTING COMPANY OF CINCINNATI (PA)
Also Called: Cbt Company
5500 Ridge Ave (45213-2516)
PHONE..................513 621-9050
James E Stahl Junior, *Pr*
Patricia M Stahl, *
▲ EMP: 110 EST: 1955
SQ FT: 95,000
SALES (est): 264.36MM
SALES (corp-wide): 264.36MM **Privately Held**
Web: www.cbtcompany.com
SIC: 5085 5063 Bearings; Power transmission equipment, electric

(G-2257)
BELVEDERE CORPORATION
35 W 5th St (45202-2801)
PHONE..................513 241-3888
Greg Power, *Pr*
EMP: 305 EST: 1984
SALES (est): 14.83MM **Privately Held**
Web: www.ohtels.es
SIC: 6512 Commercial and industrial building operation

(G-2258)
BETHESDA HOSPITAL INC (DH)
Also Called: Bethesda North Hospital
4750 Wesley Ave (45212-2244)
PHONE..................513 569-6100
John Prout, *Pr*

Craig Rucker, *
EMP: 1390 EST: 1894
SALES (est): 850MM Privately Held
Web: www.trihealth.com
SIC: 8062 General medical and surgical hospitals
HQ: Bethesda, Inc.
619 Oak St 7 N
Cincinnati OH 45206
513 569-6400

(G-2259)
BETHESDA HOSPITAL INC
Bethesda Care-Sharonville
3801 Hauck Rd Frnt (45241-4607)
PHONE..................513 563-1505
Jay Fultz, Prin
EMP: 54
Web: www.trihealth.com
SIC: 8011 8062 Primary care medical clinic; General medical and surgical hospitals
HQ: Bethesda Hospital, Inc.
4750 Wesley Ave
Cincinnati OH 45212
513 569-6100

(G-2260)
BHE ENVIRONMENTAL INC
11733 Chesterdale Rd (45246-3405)
EMP: 130
SIC: 8748 Environmental consultant

(G-2261)
BIG VILLAGE INSIGHTS INC
110 Boggs Ln Ste 380 (45246-3150)
PHONE..................513 772-7580
Randy Thamen, Brnch Mgr
EMP: 82
SALES (corp-wide): 44.55MM Publicly Held
Web: www.big-village.com
SIC: 8732 Market analysis or research
HQ: Big Village Insights, Inc.
301 Carnegie Ctr Ste 301 # 301
Princeton NJ 08540

(G-2262)
BILLS BATTERY COMPANY INC
5221 Crookshank Rd (45238-3392)
P.O. Box 58305 (45258-0305)
PHONE..................513 922-0100
Michael F Hartoin, Pr
Michael Hartoin, *
Ronald Hartoin, *
Helen Hartoin, *
EMP: 28 EST: 1946
SQ FT: 40,000
SALES (est): 4.84MM Privately Held
Web: www.kahny.com
SIC: 5013 Automotive batteries

(G-2263)
BIZ COM ELECTRIC LLC
682 Tuxedo Pl (45206-1155)
PHONE..................513 961-7200
Bruce M Cummins, Pr
Larry Ayer, *
EMP: 35 EST: 1984
SALES (est): 8.61MM Privately Held
Web: www.bizcomelec.com
SIC: 1731 General electrical contractor

(G-2264)
BLACK STONE CINCINNATI LLC (DH)
Also Called: Assisted Care By Black Stone
4700 E Galbraith Rd Fl 3 (45236)
PHONE..................513 924-1370
David Tramontana, CEO
Christine Doggett, VP
Jenny Sand, Prin

Billie Agnone, Prin
Steve Black, Prin
EMP: 82 EST: 1996
SALES (est): 2.25MM
SALES (corp-wide): 371.62B Publicly Held
Web: www.blackstonehc.com
SIC: 8082 Home health care services
HQ: Lhc Group, Inc.
901 Hugh Wallis Rd S
Lafayette LA 70508
337 233-1307

(G-2265)
BLUE & CO LLC
720 E Pete Rose Way Ste 100 (45202-3583)
PHONE..................513 241-4507
Stephen Mann, Brnch Mgr
EMP: 51
SALES (corp-wide): 37.69MM Privately Held
Web: www.blueandco.com
SIC: 8721 Certified public accountant
PA: Blue & Co., Llc
12800 N Meridian St # 400
Carmel IN 46032
317 939-3576

(G-2266)
BLUE ASH HEALTHCARE GROUP INC
Also Called: BLUE ASH CARE CENTER
4900 Cooper Rd (45242-6915)
PHONE..................513 793-3362
George Repchick, Pr
EMP: 44 EST: 1998
SALES (est): 3.48MM Privately Held
Web: www.saberhealth.com
SIC: 8051 8059 Skilled nursing care facilities ; Nursing home, except skilled and intermediate care facility

(G-2267)
BLUE CHIP 2000 COML CLG INC
Also Called: Blue Chip Pros
7250 Edington Dr (45249-1063)
PHONE..................513 561-2999
Daniel F Hopkins, Pr
Gary J Hopkins, *
EMP: 2500 EST: 2007
SALES (est): 86.48MM Privately Held
Web: www.bluechip2000.com
SIC: 7349 Cleaning service, industrial or commercial

(G-2268)
BLUE CHIP PAVEMENT MAINTENANCE INC
4320 Mount Carmel Rd (45244-1642)
PHONE..................513 321-9595
EMP: 83
Web: www.bluechipp.com
SIC: 1799 8611 Parking lot maintenance; Business associations

(G-2269)
BODY ALIVE CORPORATE LLC
Also Called: Body Alive Fitness
8110 Montgomery Rd Ste 3 (45236-2931)
PHONE..................513 834-8043
Tara Ballinger, Prin
EMP: 56 EST: 2016
SALES (est): 563.99K Privately Held
Web: www.bodyalivefitness.com
SIC: 7991 Physical fitness facilities

(G-2270)
BON SCURS MRCY HLTH FOUNDATION

1701 Mercy Health Pl (45237-6147)
PHONE..................513 952-4019
EMP: 55 EST: 2011
SALES (est): 63.08MM Privately Held
Web: www.givebsmh.org
SIC: 8062 General medical and surgical hospitals

(G-2271)
BON SECOURS MERCY HEALTH INC
Also Called: Accounts Pyble Sso Mrcy AP Shr
1701 Mercy Health Pl (45237-6147)
P.O. Box 5203 (45201-5203)
PHONE..................513 639-2800
EMP: 43
SALES (corp-wide): 6.92B Privately Held
Web: www.bonsecours.com
SIC: 8062 General medical and surgical hospitals
PA: Bon Secours Mercy Health, Inc.
1701 Mercy Health Pl
Cincinnati OH 45237
513 956-3729

(G-2272)
BON SECOURS MERCY HEALTH INC
Also Called: Mercy Anderson Ambulatory Ctr
7520 State Rd (45255-2439)
PHONE..................513 624-1950
Julie Hanser, Prin
EMP: 43
SALES (corp-wide): 6.92B Privately Held
Web: www.bonsecours.com
SIC: 8062 General medical and surgical hospitals
PA: Bon Secours Mercy Health, Inc.
1701 Mercy Health Pl
Cincinnati OH 45237
513 956-3729

(G-2273)
BON SECOURS MERCY HEALTH INC
1701 Mercy Health Pl (45237-6147)
PHONE..................513 639-2800
John M Starcher Junior, Pr
EMP: 1000
SALES (corp-wide): 6.92B Privately Held
Web: www.bonsecours.com
SIC: 8062 General medical and surgical hospitals
PA: Bon Secours Mercy Health, Inc.
1701 Mercy Health Pl
Cincinnati OH 45237
513 956-3729

(G-2274)
BON SECOURS MERCY HEALTH INC (PA)
Also Called: Mercy Health
1701 Mercy Health Pl (45237-6147)
PHONE..................513 956-3729
John M Starcher Junior, Pr
Don Kline, COO
Wael Haidar, CCO
David Cannady, CSO
Jean Haynes Cpho, Prin
EMP: 70 EST: 1983
SQ FT: 31,000
SALES (est): 6.92B
SALES (corp-wide): 6.92B Privately Held
Web: www.bonsecours.com
SIC: 8062 8099 General medical and surgical hospitals; Medical services organization

(G-2275)
BP FINANCIAL GROUP INC
415 Glensprings Dr Ste 201 (45246-2317)
PHONE..................513 851-8525
Brian Popp, Pr
Todd Bitter, *

EMP: 35 EST: 1999
SQ FT: 3,500
SALES (est): 2.22MM Privately Held
SIC: 6163 Mortgage brokers arranging for loans, using money of others

(G-2276)
BRAKEFIRE INCORPORATED (PA)
Also Called: Silco Fire Protection Company
10200 Reading Rd (45241-3112)
PHONE..................513 733-5655
EMP: 65 EST: 1959
SALES (est): 42.08MM
SALES (corp-wide): 42.08MM Privately Held
Web: www.silcofs.com
SIC: 5087 7699 Firefighting equipment; Fire control (military) equipment repair

(G-2277)
BRANDIENCE LLC
3251 Riverside Dr (45226-1011)
PHONE..................513 333-4100
EMP: 32 EST: 2018
SALES (est): 6.72MM Privately Held
Web: www.brandience.com
SIC: 7311 Advertising agencies

(G-2278)
BRCOM INC (DH)
201 E 4th St (45202)
PHONE..................513 397-9900
Cassidy F John, CEO
EMP: 51 EST: 1992
SALES (est): 266.3MM
SALES (corp-wide): 3.15B Privately Held
SIC: 4813 Voice telephone communications
HQ: Cincinnati Bell Inc.
221 E 4th St Ste 700
Cincinnati OH 45202
513 397-9900

(G-2279)
BRENDAMOUR MOVING & STOR INC
2630 Glendale Milford Rd Ste D (45241-4835)
PHONE..................800 354-9715
TOLL FREE: 800
EMP: 65 EST: 1994
SALES (est): 10.54MM Privately Held
Web: www.brendamourlogistics.com
SIC: 4214 4213 Household goods moving and storage, local; Trucking, except local

(G-2280)
BRG REALTY GROUP LLC (PA)
Also Called: Berkshire Realty Group
7265 Kenwood Rd Ste 111 (45236-4411)
PHONE..................513 936-5960
EMP: 154 EST: 2005
SALES (est): 22.39MM Privately Held
SIC: 6513 Apartment building operators

(G-2281)
BRIDGE
1515 Carll St (45225-2012)
PHONE..................513 244-3985
Dominic Turner, Prin
EMP: 32 EST: 2011
SALES (est): 417.28K Privately Held
SIC: 8093 Substance abuse clinics (outpatient)

(G-2282)
BROADBAND EXPRESS LLC
11359 Mosteller Rd (45241-1827)
PHONE..................513 834-8085
Dusty Banks, Brnch Mgr
EMP: 55
SALES (corp-wide): 4.18B Publicly Held

Cincinnati - Hamilton County (G-2283) GEOGRAPHIC SECTION

Web: recruiting.ultipro.com
SIC: 1731 Cable television installation
HQ: Broadband Express, Llc
374 Westdale Ave Ste B
Westerville OH 43082
614 823-6464

(G-2283)
BROOKWOOD REALTY COMPANY
Also Called: Brookwood Retirement Community
12100 Reed Hartman Hwy Apt 118 (45241-6071)
PHONE..................................513 530-9555
Steven Boymel, *Pr*
EMP: 100 EST: 1985
SALES (est): 9.82MM **Privately Held**
SIC: 6512 8052 8051 Commercial and industrial building operation; Intermediate care facilities; Skilled nursing care facilities

(G-2284)
BSI ENGINEERING LLC (PA)
300 E Business Way Ste 300 (45241)
PHONE..................................513 201-3100
Phil Beirne, *Pr*
Dan Prickel, *
John Garmany, *
EMP: 130 EST: 2007
SQ FT: 17,000
SALES (est): 33.11MM **Privately Held**
Web: www.bsiengr.com
SIC: 8711 Consulting engineer

(G-2285)
BUCKEYE CHECK CASHING INC
7680 Montgomery Rd (45236-4204)
PHONE..................................513 936-9995
EMP: 35
Web: www.ccfi.com
SIC: 6099 Check cashing agencies
HQ: Buckeye Check Cashing, Inc.
5165 Emerald Pkwy Ste 100
Dublin OH 43017
614 798-5900

(G-2286)
BUCKEYE CHECK CASHING INC
10990 Hamilton Ave (45231-1452)
PHONE..................................513 851-3100
EMP: 35
Web: www.ccfi.com
SIC: 6099 Check cashing agencies
HQ: Buckeye Check Cashing, Inc.
5165 Emerald Pkwy Ste 100
Dublin OH 43017
614 798-5900

(G-2287)
BUCKEYE CHECK CASHING INC
2003 W Galbraith Rd (45239-4326)
PHONE..................................513 931-7300
EMP: 35
Web: www.ccfi.com
SIC: 6099 Check cashing agencies
HQ: Buckeye Check Cashing, Inc.
5165 Emerald Pkwy Ste 100
Dublin OH 43017
614 798-5900

(G-2288)
BUCKEYE CHECK CASHING INC
9385 Colerain Ave (45251-2013)
PHONE..................................513 741-3777
EMP: 35
Web: www.ccfi.com
SIC: 6099 Check cashing agencies
HQ: Buckeye Check Cashing, Inc.
5165 Emerald Pkwy Ste 100
Dublin OH 43017
614 798-5900

(G-2289)
BUILDING 8 INC
Also Called: J & N
10995 Canal Rd (45241-1886)
PHONE..................................513 771-8000
Thomas J Kuechly, *Pr*
Mary L Kuechly, *
David W Blocker, *
Nick Kuechly, *
▲ EMP: 27 EST: 1954
SQ FT: 68,000
SALES (est): 16.12MM
SALES (corp-wide): 276.08MM **Privately Held**
SIC: 5013 Automotive supplies and parts
PA: Arrowhead Engineered Products, Inc.
3705 95th Ave Ne
Circle Pines MN 55014
763 255-2555

(G-2290)
BURKE INC (PA)
Also Called: Burke Institute
500 W 7th St (45203-1543)
PHONE..................................513 241-5663
Jeff Miller, *CEO*
Micheal H Baumgardner, *
Mike Webster, *
Stacy Mcwhorter, *Sr VP*
Andrew Ma, *VP*
EMP: 202 EST: 1931
SQ FT: 51,000
SALES (est): 48.55MM **Privately Held**
Web: www.burke.com
SIC: 8732 8742 Market analysis or research; Management consulting services

(G-2291)
BURKE MANLEY LPA
225 W Court St (45202-1012)
PHONE..................................513 721-5525
Robert Manley, *Pr*
Bonnie Bockelman, *
EMP: 42 EST: 1979
SALES (est): 5.4MM **Privately Held**
Web: www.manleyburke.com
SIC: 8111 General practice attorney, lawyer

(G-2292)
BURLINGTON HOUSE INC
2222 Springdale Rd (45231-1805)
PHONE..................................513 851-7888
Stephen L Rosedale, *Pr*
Beatrice W Rosedale, *VP*
EMP: 50 EST: 1990
SQ FT: 2,682
SALES (est): 10.91MM **Privately Held**
Web: www.communicarehealth.com
SIC: 8051 Convalescent home with continuous nursing care

(G-2293)
BUSINESS EQUIPMENT CO INC
Also Called: Beco Legal Systems
11590 Century Blvd (45246-3326)
PHONE..................................513 948-1500
Michael Brookbank, *Pr*
John Brookbank, *VP*
EMP: 45 EST: 1941
SALES (est): 5.71MM **Privately Held**
SIC: 7371 Computer software development

(G-2294)
BUSKEN BAKERY INC (PA)
2675 Madison Rd (45208-1389)
PHONE..................................513 871-2114
D Page Busken, *Pr*
Brian Busken, *
EMP: 90 EST: 1928
SQ FT: 21,000
SALES (est): 18.43MM
SALES (corp-wide): 18.43MM **Privately Held**
Web: www.busken.com
SIC: 2045 5461 5149 Blended flour: from purchased flour; Bread; Bakery products

(G-2295)
BYER STEEL INC
200 W North Bend Rd (45216-1728)
PHONE..................................513 821-6400
Burke Byer, *Pr*
Shawn Eddy, *
Jay Binder, *
Jonas Allen, *
Jeff Ginter, *
EMP: 49 EST: 2010
SQ FT: 100,000
SALES (est): 23.13MM **Privately Held**
Web: www.byersteelminded.com
SIC: 5051 Steel

(G-2296)
BYER STEEL SERVICE CENTER INC
Also Called: Byer Steel
200 Wn Bend Rd (45216)
PHONE..................................513 821-6400
TOLL FREE: 800
EMP: 38 EST: 1933
SALES (est): 12.53MM
SALES (corp-wide): 22.05MM **Privately Held**
Web: www.byersteel.com
SIC: 5051 Steel
PA: Byer Steel Recycling, Inc.
200 W North Bend Rd
Cincinnati OH 45216
513 948-0300

(G-2297)
BYRIDER FINANCE INC
8581 Beechmont Ave (45255-4784)
PHONE..................................513 407-4140
EMP: 52
Web: www.jdbyrider.com
SIC: 7389 Financial services
HQ: Byrider Finance, Inc.
12802 Hmlton Crssing Blvd
Carmel IN 46032

(G-2298)
C MICAH RAND INC
Also Called: Brookwood Retirement Community
12100 Reed Hartman Hwy (45241-6071)
PHONE..................................513 605-2000
Steve Boymel, *Pr*
EMP: 150 EST: 1984
SQ FT: 180,000
SALES (est): 14.53MM **Privately Held**
SIC: 8051 Convalescent home with continuous nursing care

(G-2299)
C&C CLEAN TEAM ENTERPRISES LLC
Also Called: Widmer's
2016 Madison Rd (45208-3238)
PHONE..................................513 321-5100
Steve Carico, *Managing Member*
EMP: 250 EST: 2007
SALES (est): 3.23MM **Privately Held**
Web: www.widmersisclean.com
SIC: 7212 7217 Garment pressing and cleaners' agents; Carpet and upholstery cleaning

(G-2300)
CADRE COMPUTER RESOURCES CO (PA)
Also Called: Cadre Information Security
625 Eden Park Dr (45202-6069)
PHONE..................................513 762-7350
Sandra E Laney, *CEO*
Steven W Snider, *
Stephen M Krumpelman, *
EMP: 41 EST: 2001
SALES (est): 30.83MM
SALES (corp-wide): 30.83MM **Privately Held**
Web: www.cadre.net
SIC: 7379 Online services technology consultants

(G-2301)
CALFEE HALTER & GRISWOLD LLP
255 E 5th St (45202-4700)
PHONE..................................513 693-4880
Shelli Spine, *Off Mgr*
EMP: 44
SALES (corp-wide): 46.79MM **Privately Held**
Web: www.calfee.com
SIC: 8111 General practice attorney, lawyer
PA: Calfee, Halter & Griswold Llp
The Clfee Bldg 1405 E 6th
Cleveland OH 44114
216 622-8200

(G-2302)
CAMARGO CLUB
8605 Shawnee Run Rd (45243-2811)
PHONE..................................513 561-9292
Joseph Beech Iii, *VP*
Doug Postler, *
EMP: 105 EST: 1925
SQ FT: 7,000
SALES (est): 5.31MM **Privately Held**
Web: www.camargoclub.org
SIC: 7997 Country club, membership

(G-2303)
CAMELOT COMMUNITY CARE INC
7162 Reading Rd Ste 300 (45237-3899)
PHONE..................................513 961-5900
Steve Tutt, *Ex Dir*
EMP: 101
Web: www.camelotcommunitycare.org
SIC: 8322 Child related social services
PA: Camelot Community Care, Inc.
15500 Roosevelt Blvd # 304
Clearwater FL 33760

(G-2304)
CAMPBELL SALES COMPANY
8805 Governors Hill Dr Ste 300 (45249-3318)
PHONE..................................513 697-2900
Keith Olscamp, *Mgr*
EMP: 398
SALES (corp-wide): 9.36B **Publicly Held**
Web: www.campbellsoupcompany.com
SIC: 8743 Sales promotion
HQ: Campbell Sales Company
1 Campbell Pl
Camden NJ 08103
856 342-4800

(G-2305)
CANCER FAMILY CARE INC
4790 Red Bank Rd Ste 128 (45227-1509)
PHONE..................................513 731-3346
Brent Seelmeyer, *Ex Dir*
EMP: 34 EST: 1971
SALES (est): 1.13MM **Privately Held**
Web: www.cancerfamilycare.org
SIC: 8322 Social service center

(G-2306)
CAPITAL INVESTMENT GROUP LLC
525 Vine St Ste 1605 (45202-3132)
PHONE..................................513 241-5090

GEOGRAPHIC SECTION — Cincinnati - Hamilton County

David Bastos, Pr
EMP: 44 **EST:** 2008
SALES (est): 8.74MM **Privately Held**
Web: www.cigcommunities.com
SIC: 6799 Investors, nec

(G-2307)
CARDIAC VSCLAR THRCIC SURGEONS
4030 Smith Rd Ste 300 (45209-1974)
PHONE................513 421-3494
Steven Park, Pr
Creighton Wright, VP
EMP: 75 **EST:** 1968
SALES (est): 3.9MM
SALES (corp-wide): 6.92B **Privately Held**
SIC: 8011 Cardiologist and cardio-vascular specialist
PA: Bon Secours Mercy Health, Inc.
   1701 Mercy Health Pl
   Cincinnati OH 45237
   513 956-3729

(G-2308)
CARDINAL SOLUTIONS GROUP INC (HQ)
7755 Montgomery Rd Ste 510 (45236-4291)
PHONE................513 984-6700
Kelly P Conway, Pr
EMP: 52 **EST:** 1996
SALES (est): 24.27MM **Publicly Held**
Web: www.cardinalgroup.com
SIC: 7379 Online services technology consultants
PA: Insight Enterprises, Inc.
   2701 E Insight Way
   Chandler AZ 85286

(G-2309)
CARE MEDICAL INC
8340 Reading Rd (45237-1407)
PHONE................513 821-7272
Todd Wirtz, Pr
EMP: 42 **EST:** 1983
SQ FT: 10,000
SALES (est): 6.19MM **Privately Held**
Web: www.caremedicalonline.com
SIC: 5999 7352 Medical apparatus and supplies; Medical equipment rental

(G-2310)
CAREERBUILDER LLC
8044 Montgomery Rd Ste 505 (45236-2919)
PHONE................513 297-3707
EMP: 42
SALES (corp-wide): 32.64B **Publicly Held**
Web: www.careerbuildercareers.com
SIC: 8331 Job counseling
HQ: Careerbuilder, Llc
   200 N La Salle St # 1100
   Chicago IL 60601
   773 527-3600

(G-2311)
CAREFIRST URGENT CARE LLC
Also Called: Beechmont Urgent Care
7300 Beechmont Ave (45230-4119)
PHONE................513 868-2345
Jessi Davis, Mgr
EMP: 81 **EST:** 2014
SALES (est): 3.81MM **Privately Held**
Web: www.carefirsturgentcares.com
SIC: 8011 Freestanding emergency medical center

(G-2312)
CAREFOR PLACE NURSING HOME INC
Also Called: Terrace View Gardens
3904 N Bend Rd (45211-4855)
PHONE................513 481-2201
Arleene Keller, Pr
EMP: 31 **EST:** 1997
SALES (est): 4.83MM **Privately Held**
Web: www.terrace-view.net
SIC: 8051 Convalescent home with continuous nursing care

(G-2313)
CARESTAR INC (PA)
Also Called: Carestar
5566 Cheviot Rd (45247-7094)
PHONE................513 618-8300
Thomas J Gruber, Pr
Jack Kersjes, *
EMP: 181 **EST:** 1988
SQ FT: 15,000
SALES (est): 27.26MM
SALES (corp-wide): 27.26MM **Privately Held**
Web: www.carestar.com
SIC: 7361 8082 Nurses' registry; Home health care services

(G-2314)
CARING PLACE HEALTHCARE GROUP
779 Glendale Milford Rd (45215-1161)
PHONE................513 771-1779
Barry Kohn, Managing Member
EMP: 58 **EST:** 2004
SALES (est): 42.8MM **Privately Held**
Web: www.caringplacehcg.com
SIC: 8051 Convalescent home with continuous nursing care

(G-2315)
CARINGTON HEALTH SYSTEMS
Also Called: Glencare Center
3627 Harvey Ave (45229-2005)
PHONE................513 961-8881
Bob Bishop, Admn
EMP: 496
SALES (corp-wide): 58.43MM **Privately Held**
Web: www.carington.com
SIC: 8051 8049 Convalescent home with continuous nursing care; Physical therapist
PA: Carington Health Systems
   8200 Beckett Park Dr
   Hamilton OH 45011
   513 682-2700

(G-2316)
CARUSO INC (PA)
3465 Hauck Rd (45241-1601)
PHONE................513 860-9200
Jim Caruso, CEO
Mike Caruso, *
Steve Caruso, *
James S Caruso, *
Wayne Kramer, *
▲ **EMP:** 42 **EST:** 1926
SQ FT: 155,000
SALES (est): 41.72MM
SALES (corp-wide): 41.72MM **Privately Held**
Web: www.carusousa.com
SIC: 4225 General warehousing and storage

(G-2317)
CAS-KER COMPANY INC
2550 Civic Center Dr (45231-1310)
PHONE................513 674-7700
Patrick J Cassedy, Pr
Thomas J Cassedy, *
Daniel B Cassedy, *
Richard Foster, *
▲ **EMP:** 38 **EST:** 1926
SQ FT: 21,750
SALES (est): 2.38MM **Privately Held**
Web: www.jewelerssupplies.com
SIC: 5094 Jewelry

(G-2318)
CASCO MFG SOLUTIONS INC
3107 Spring Grove Ave (45225-1821)
PHONE................513 681-0003
Thomas Mangold, Ch
Melissa Mangold, *
Terri Mangold, *
▲ **EMP:** 60 **EST:** 1959
SQ FT: 72,000
SALES (est): 9.93MM **Privately Held**
Web: www.cascomfg.com
SIC: 2515 7641 3841 2522 Mattresses, containing felt, foam rubber, urethane, etc.; Upholstery work; Surgical and medical instruments; Office furniture, except wood

(G-2319)
CASSIDY TRLEY COML RE SVCS INC
Also Called: Colliers Turley Martin Tucker
300 E Business Way Ste 190 (45241)
PHONE................513 771-2580
Mamie Castleberry, Brnch Mgr
EMP: 76
SALES (corp-wide): 9.49B **Privately Held**
Web: www.ctmt.com
SIC: 6531 Real estate agent, commercial
HQ: Cassidy Turley Commercial Real Estate Services Inc.
   7700 Forsyth Blvd Ste 900
   Saint Louis MO 63105
   314 862-7100

(G-2320)
CATALYST RECOVERY LA LLC (PA)
1 Landy Ln (45215-3405)
PHONE................513 354-3640
EMP: 84 **EST:** 2004
SALES (est): 19.13MM
SALES (corp-wide): 19.13MM **Privately Held**
Web: catalysts.evonik.com
SIC: 7389 Business Activities at Non-Commercial Site

(G-2321)
CATANZARO FRANK J SONS DGHTERS
535 Shepherd Ave (45215-3115)
PHONE................800 827-4020
Frank C Catanzaro, Ch
EMP: 99 **EST:** 1972
SALES (est): 9.15MM **Privately Held**
SIC: 5142 5147 5148 5149 Packaged frozen goods; Meats and meat products; Fruits, fresh; Canned goods: fruit, vegetables, seafood, meats, etc.

(G-2322)
CATHEDRAL HOLDINGS INC
302 W 3rd St Ste 800 (45202-3426)
PHONE................513 271-6400
Molly North, Managing Member
David F Neyer, *
William L Neyer, *
Cassie J Belmonte, Finance Accounting Vice President*
James T Neyer, Asset Management Vice President*
EMP: 80 **EST:** 1920
SQ FT: 17,837
SALES (est): 364.06K **Privately Held**
SIC: 6552 1522 1541 1542 Land subdividers and developers, commercial; Multi-family dwelling construction, nec; Industrial buildings and warehouses; Commercial and office building contractors

(G-2323)
CATHOLIC CHRTIES OF STHWSTERN (PA)
Also Called: CATHOLIC CHARITIES
7162 Reading Rd Ste 604 (45237-3819)
PHONE................513 241-7745
M Kathleen Donnellan, Ex Dir
Gene Johnson, *
EMP: 90 **EST:** 1914
SALES (est): 7.78MM
SALES (corp-wide): 7.78MM **Privately Held**
Web: www.ccswoh.org
SIC: 8322 4119 Social service center; Local passenger transportation, nec

(G-2324)
CATHOLIC HLTHCARE PRTNERS FNDT
1701 Mercy Health Pl (45237-6147)
PHONE................513 639-2800
EMP: 65 **EST:** 2011
SALES (est): 8.1MM **Privately Held**
Web: www.mercy.com
SIC: 8062 General medical and surgical hospitals

(G-2325)
CBS PERSONNEL SERVICES LLC
Also Called: Staffmark
201 E 4th St (45202-4248)
PHONE................513 651-3600
EMP: 700
SIC: 7361 7363 Labor contractors (employment agency); Labor resource services

(G-2326)
CBST ACQUISITION LLC
Also Called: Dynus Technologies
6900 Steger Dr (45237-3096)
PHONE................513 361-9600
EMP: 90 **EST:** 1983
SQ FT: 80,000
SALES (est): 9.95MM **Privately Held**
SIC: 5065 7629 3357 7622 Telephone equipment; Telecommunication equipment repair (except telephones); Fiber optic cable (insulated); Radio and television repair

(G-2327)
CBTS LLC
25 Merchant St (45246-3739)
PHONE................440 478-8447
Jeff Lackey, CEO
EMP: 40 **EST:** 2018
SALES (est): 54.11K **Privately Held**
Web: www.cbts.com
SIC: 7379 Computer related consulting services

(G-2328)
CBTS TECHNOLOGY SOLUTIONS LLC (DH)
Also Called: Cbts
25 Merchant St (45246-3700)
P.O. Box 2301 (45201-2301)
PHONE................513 841-2287
Theodore H Torbeck, CEO
Leigh R Fox, *
Christopher J Wilson, *
Don Verdon, *
John Burns, *
▼ **EMP:** 300 **EST:** 1987
SQ FT: 10,000
SALES (est): 175.44MM
SALES (corp-wide): 3.15B **Privately Held**
Web: www.cbts.com

Cincinnati - Hamilton County (G-2329) GEOGRAPHIC SECTION

SIC: 7379 5734 Computer related consulting services; Computer peripheral equipment
HQ: Cincinnati Bell Inc.
221 E 4th St Ste 700
Cincinnati OH 45202
513 397-9900

(G-2329)
CDC DISTRIBUTORS INC (PA)
10511 Medallion Dr (45241-3193)
PHONE.................................513 771-3100
▲ EMP: 75 EST: 1976
SALES (est): 35.25MM
SALES (corp-wide): 35.25MM Privately Held
Web: www.cdcdist.com
SIC: 5023 5251 Floor coverings; Tools, hand

(G-2330)
CDW TECHNOLOGIES LLC
9349 Waterstone Blvd Ste 150 (45249-8320)
PHONE.................................513 677-4100
Chris Ashcraft, Brnch Mgr
EMP: 388
SIC: 5045 Computers, peripherals, and software
HQ: Cdw Technologies Llc
5525 Nobel Dr Ste 200
Fitchburg WI 53711

(G-2331)
CEDAR MEDICAL GROUP
Also Called: Lake Rdge Vlla Hlth Care Rehab
7220 Pippin Rd (45239-4607)
PHONE.................................513 729-2300
Herman Moskowitz, Pr
Bernard Moskowitz, *
EMP: 85 EST: 1987
SALES (est): 7.22MM Privately Held
Web: www.carecorehealth.com
SIC: 8051 Extended care facility

(G-2332)
CENTER FOR ADDICTION TREATMENT
830 Ezzard Charles Dr (45214-2525)
PHONE.................................513 381-6672
Patti Webb, CEO
Sharlene Brown, *
EMP: 95 EST: 1970
SQ FT: 31,000
SALES (est): 8.1MM Privately Held
Web: www.catsober.org
SIC: 8069 8093 8063 Alcoholism rehabilitation hospital; Specialty outpatient clinics, nec; Psychiatric hospitals

(G-2333)
CENTRAL BUSINESS EQUIPMENT CO
Also Called: Patterson Pope
10321 S Medallion Dr (45241-4825)
PHONE.................................513 891-4430
Dennis Hammack, Pr
EMP: 27 EST: 2011
SALES (est): 10.99MM
SALES (corp-wide): 87.69MM Privately Held
Web: www.pattersonpope.com
SIC: 5021 Filing units
PA: Patterson Pope, Inc.
3001 N Graham St
Charlotte NC 28206
704 523-4400

(G-2334)
CENTRAL CLINIC OUTPATIENT SVCS
311 Albert Sabin Way (45229-2838)
PHONE.................................513 558-9005
Kathleen Fields, CFO
Walter Smitson, *
EMP: 99 EST: 2017
SALES (est): 5.59MM Privately Held
Web: www.centralclinic.org
SIC: 8099 Health and allied services, nec

(G-2335)
CENTRAL CMNTY HLTH BD HMLTON C (PA)
532 Maxwell Ave (45219-2408)
PHONE.................................513 559-2000
Emmett Cooper, Admn
Bennett Cooper Junior, Ex Dir
EMP: 100 EST: 1970
SQ FT: 2,500
SALES (est): 7.49MM
SALES (corp-wide): 7.49MM Privately Held
Web: www.cchbinc.com
SIC: 8063 8093 Mental hospital, except for the mentally retarded; Specialty outpatient clinics, nec

(G-2336)
CENTRAL INSULATION SYSTEMS INC
Also Called: Central Environmental Systems
300 Murray Rd (45217-1011)
PHONE.................................513 242-0600
Steve Kirby, Pr
Kathy Kirby, *
EMP: 50 EST: 1988
SQ FT: 30,000
SALES (est): 8.93MM Privately Held
Web: www.centralinsulation.com
SIC: 1799 1742 Asbestos removal and encapsulation; Insulation, buildings

(G-2337)
CENTRAL READY MIX LLC (PA)
6310 E Kemper Rd Ste 125 (45241-2370)
P.O. Box 70 (45050-0070)
PHONE.................................513 402-5001
TOLL FREE: 888
EMP: 30 EST: 1934
SQ FT: 8,000
SALES (est): 11.19MM
SALES (corp-wide): 11.19MM Privately Held
Web: www.centralrm.com
SIC: 3273 1442 Ready-mixed concrete; Sand mining

(G-2338)
CENTRAL STEEL AND WIRE CO LLC
525 Township Ave (45216)
P.O. Box 14148 (45250)
PHONE.................................513 242-2233
Tom Rogina, Brnch Mgr
EMP: 50
Web: www.centralsteel.com
SIC: 5051 Steel
HQ: Central Steel And Wire Company, Llc
23301 S Central Ave
University Park IL 60484
773 471-3800

(G-2339)
CFM RELIGION PUBG GROUP LLC (PA)
8805 Governors Hill Dr Ste 400 (45249-3314)
PHONE.................................513 931-4050
Matthew Thibeau, Pr
EMP: 52 EST: 2007
SALES (est): 43.18MM Privately Held
Web: www.cfmpublishing.com

SIC: 2721 8741 Magazines: publishing only, not printed on site; Management services

(G-2340)
CGH-GLOBAL SECURITY LLC
4957 Cinnamon Cir (45244-1210)
PHONE.................................800 376-0655
Andrew Glassmeyer, CEO
EMP: 32 EST: 2016
SALES (est): 1.8MM
SALES (corp-wide): 8.7MM Privately Held
SIC: 7389
PA: Cgh-Global, Llc
47 Harness Creek View Ct
Annapolis MD 21403
800 376-0655

(G-2341)
CGH-GLOBAL TECHNOLOGIES LLC
4957 Cinnamon Cir (45244-1210)
PHONE.................................800 376-0655
Andrew Glassmeyer, CEO
EMP: 32 EST: 2016
SALES (est): 2.25MM
SALES (corp-wide): 8.7MM Privately Held
SIC: 8748 Business consulting, nec
PA: Cgh-Global, Llc
47 Harness Creek View Ct
Annapolis MD 21403
800 376-0655

(G-2342)
CH2M HILL INC
1880 Waycross Rd (45240-2825)
PHONE.................................513 243-5070
Mike Bartlett, Prin
EMP: 83 EST: 2013
SALES (est): 4MM Privately Held
Web: www.jacobs.com
SIC: 8711 Consulting engineer

(G-2343)
CH2M HILL ENGINEERS INC
1880 Waycross Rd (45240-2825)
PHONE.................................720 286-2000
Fred M Brune, Pr
EMP: 51
SALES (corp-wide): 14.92B Publicly Held
SIC: 8711 Consulting engineer
HQ: Ch2m Hill Engineers, Inc.
6312 S Fiddlers Green Cir 300n
Greenwood Village CO 80111
720 286-2000

(G-2344)
CHAMPION CLG SPECIALISTS INC
8391 Blue Ash Rd (45236-1986)
PHONE.................................513 871-2333
TOLL FREE: 888
Chris Kurtz, Pr
Pat Kurtz, *
EMP: 30 EST: 1982
SQ FT: 12,000
SALES (est): 5.6MM Privately Held
Web: www.championcleaning.net
SIC: 7349 Cleaning service, industrial or commercial

(G-2345)
CHAMPION OPCO LLC (DH)
Also Called: Champion Windows
12121 Champion Way (45241-6419)
PHONE.................................513 327-7338
Jim Mishler, CEO
Donald R Jones, *
Joe Faisant, *
▲ EMP: 300 EST: 2007
SQ FT: 500,000
SALES (est): 496.44MM Privately Held
Web: www.championwindow.com

SIC: 3089 1761 3442 Window frames and sash, plastics; Siding contractor; Storm doors or windows, metal
HQ: Great Day Improvements, Llc
700 Highland Rd E
Macedonia OH 44056

(G-2346)
CHAMPLIN HAUPT ARCHITECTS INC (PA)
Also Called: Champlin Architecture
720 E Pete Rose Way Ste 140 (45202-3579)
PHONE.................................513 241-4474
Robert A Schilling Junior, Pr
Michael J Battoclette, *
Joan Tepe Wurtenberger, *
John Wyler, Stockholder*
EMP: 50 EST: 1978
SQ FT: 6,900
SALES (est): 10.91MM
SALES (corp-wide): 10.91MM Privately Held
Web: www.thinkchamplin.com
SIC: 8712 Architectural engineering

(G-2347)
CHARLES W POWERS & ASSOC INC
Also Called: Powers Agency
151 W 4th St Unit 36 (45202-2724)
PHONE.................................513 721-5353
Lori Powers, CEO
Charles W Powers, *
Mark Wesling, *
Melissa Mccann, CFO
Jennifer King, *
EMP: 31 EST: 1986
SALES (est): 2.38MM Privately Held
Web: www.powersagency.com
SIC: 7311 Advertising consultant

(G-2348)
CHC FABRICATING CORP (PA)
10270 Wayne Ave (45215-1127)
PHONE.................................513 821-7757
EMP: 58 EST: 1961
SALES (est): 4.25MM
SALES (corp-wide): 4.25MM Privately Held
Web: www.chcfab.com
SIC: 1791 3446 3441 Structural steel erection; Stairs, staircases, stair treads: prefabricated metal; Fabricated structural metal

(G-2349)
CHECK N GO OF FLORIDA INC
7755 Montgomery Rd Ste 400 (45236-4197)
PHONE.................................513 336-7735
Douglas D Clark, Prin
EMP: 90 EST: 1995
SALES (est): 18.74MM
SALES (corp-wide): 696.24MM Privately Held
Web: www.checkngo.com
SIC: 6099 Check cashing agencies
PA: Cng Financial Corporation
7755 Montgomery Rd # 400
Cincinnati OH 45236
513 336-7735

(G-2350)
CHECK N GO OF MISSOURI INC
Also Called: Check N Go
7755 Montgomery Rd Ste 400 (45236-4197)
PHONE.................................513 531-2288
Charlene Lambert, Prin
EMP: 30 EST: 1998
SALES (est): 8.02MM

GEOGRAPHIC SECTION
Cincinnati - Hamilton County (G-2371)

SALES (corp-wide): 696.24MM **Privately Held**
Web: www.checkngo.com
SIC: 6099 Check cashing agencies
PA: Cng Financial Corporation
   7755 Montgomery Rd # 400
   Cincinnati OH 45236
   513 336-7735

(G-2351)
CHECK N GO OF WASHINGTON INC
Also Called: Check N Go
7755 Montgomery Rd Ste 400
(45236-4197)
PHONE..................................800 561-2274
Douglas D Clark, *Prin*
EMP: 30 EST: 2003
SALES (est): 10.13MM
SALES (corp-wide): 696.24MM **Privately Held**
Web: www.checkngo.com
SIC: 6141 Licensed loan companies, small
PA: Cng Financial Corporation
   7755 Montgomery Rd # 400
   Cincinnati OH 45236
   513 336-7735

(G-2352)
CHEMED CORPORATION (PA)
Also Called: Chemed
255 E 5th St Ste 2600 (45202)
PHONE..................................513 762-6690
Kevin J Mcnamara, *Pr*
George J Walsh Iii, *Ch Bd*
Michael D Witzeman, *CFO*
Brian C Judkins, *CLO*
Michael D Witzeman, *CAO*
EMP: 222 EST: 1970
SALES (est): 2.26B
SALES (corp-wide): 2.26B **Publicly Held**
Web: www.chemed.com
SIC: 8082 1711 7699 Visiting nurse service; Plumbing, heating, air-conditioning; Sewer cleaning and rodding

(G-2353)
CHEVIOT FINANCIAL CORP
3723 Glenmore Ave (45211-4720)
PHONE..................................513 661-0457
EMP: 111
Web: www.cheviotsavings.com
SIC: 6021 National commercial banks

(G-2354)
CHICAGO MSO INC (PA)
Also Called: Cmso
6136 Campus Ln (45230-1682)
PHONE..................................513 624-8300
Danielle D Lydon, *Pr*
Daniell Lydon, *
David Wirsing, *
Michelle R Ruscher, *
Dan Clark, *
EMP: 40 EST: 1997
SQ FT: 4,000
SALES (est): 1.14MM
SALES (corp-wide): 1.14MM **Privately Held**
SIC: 8721 Billing and bookkeeping service

(G-2355)
CHILD FOCUS INC (PA)
4629 Aicholtz Rd (45244)
PHONE..................................513 752-1555
James Carter, *CEO*
Sandy Lock, *
EMP: 75 EST: 1977
SQ FT: 27,000
SALES (est): 20.97MM
SALES (corp-wide): 20.97MM **Privately Held**
Web: www.child-focus.org
SIC: 8322 8093 8351 Child related social services; Mental health clinic, outpatient; Head Start center, except in conjunction with school

(G-2356)
CHILDRENS H CINCINNATI
3244 Burnet Ave (45229-3019)
PHONE..................................513 803-2707
Sam Kiger, *Proj Mgr*
EMP: 170 EST: 2018
SALES (est): 28.42MM **Privately Held**
Web: www.cincinnatichildrens.org
SIC: 8062 General medical and surgical hospitals

(G-2357)
CHILDRENS HM OF CNCINNATI OHIO
Also Called: CHILDREN'S HOME SCHOOL
5050 Madison Rd (45227-1491)
PHONE..................................513 272-2800
Ellen Johnson, *Ex Dir*
EMP: 200 EST: 1864
SQ FT: 84,000
SALES (est): 40.09MM **Privately Held**
Web: www.bestpoint.org
SIC: 8322 Child related social services

(G-2358)
CHILDRENS HOSPITAL
5642 Hamilton Ave 1flr (45224-3114)
PHONE..................................513 636-9900
Randall Nagal, *Prin*
EMP: 135 EST: 1977
SALES (est): 4.08MM **Privately Held**
Web: cincinnatichildrens.giftlegacy.com
SIC: 8062 8011 General medical and surgical hospitals; Offices and clinics of medical doctors

(G-2359)
CHILDRENS HOSPITAL
3373 Burnet Ave (45229-3026)
PHONE..................................513 636-4051
Diane Holbrook, *Prin*
EMP: 100 EST: 2001
SALES (est): 46.05MM **Privately Held**
Web: www.cincinnatichildrens.org
SIC: 8062 General medical and surgical hospitals

(G-2360)
CHILDRENS HOSPITAL MEDICAL CTR
2750 Beekman St (45225-2049)
PHONE..................................513 541-4500
EMP: 600
SALES (corp-wide): 2.94B **Privately Held**
Web: www.cincinnatichildrens.org
SIC: 8062 General medical and surgical hospitals
PA: Children's Hospital Medical Center
   3333 Burnet Ave
   Cincinnati OH 45229
   513 636-4200

(G-2361)
CHILDRENS HOSPITAL MEDICAL CTR
Also Called: Cincinnati Chld Hosp Med Ctr
6941 Moorfield Dr (45230-2223)
PHONE..................................513 636-4200
Jill Guilfoile, *Prin*
EMP: 979
SALES (corp-wide): 2.94B **Privately Held**
Web: www.cincinnatichildrens.org
SIC: 8062 General medical and surgical hospitals
PA: Children's Hospital Medical Center
   3333 Burnet Ave
   Cincinnati OH 45229
   513 636-4200

(G-2362)
CHILDRENS HOSPITAL MEDICAL CTR
Heart Institute Diagnostic Lab
240 Albert Sabin Way Rm S4.381
(45229-2842)
PHONE..................................513 803-1751
Wenying Zhang, *Dir*
EMP: 505
SALES (corp-wide): 2.94B **Privately Held**
Web: www.cincinnatichildrens.org
SIC: 8062 General medical and surgical hospitals
PA: Children's Hospital Medical Center
   3333 Burnet Ave
   Cincinnati OH 45229
   513 636-4200

(G-2363)
CHILDRENS HOSPITAL MEDICAL CTR
2900 Vernon Pl (45219-2436)
PHONE..................................513 636-4200
EMP: 916
SALES (corp-wide): 2.94B **Privately Held**
Web: www.cincinnatichildrens.org
SIC: 8062 General medical and surgical hospitals
PA: Children's Hospital Medical Center
   3333 Burnet Ave
   Cincinnati OH 45229
   513 636-4200

(G-2364)
CHILDRENS HOSPITAL MEDICAL CTR
Cincinnati Chld Hosp Med Ctr
2800 Winslow Ave Fl 3 (45206-1144)
PHONE..................................513 636-4366
Cynthia Kuelbs, *Dir*
EMP: 916
SALES (corp-wide): 2.94B **Privately Held**
Web: www.cincinnatichildrens.org
SIC: 8062 General medical and surgical hospitals
PA: Children's Hospital Medical Center
   3333 Burnet Ave
   Cincinnati OH 45229
   513 636-4200

(G-2365)
CHILDRENS HOSPITAL MEDICAL CTR
Chmc Research Foundation
3333 Burnet Ave Fl 6 (45229-3039)
PHONE..................................513 636-4288
EMP: 916
SQ FT: 3,598
SALES (corp-wide): 2.94B **Privately Held**
Web: www.cincinnatichildrens.org
SIC: 8062 General medical and surgical hospitals
PA: Children's Hospital Medical Center
   3333 Burnet Ave
   Cincinnati OH 45229
   513 636-4200

(G-2366)
CHILDRENS HOSPITAL MEDICAL CTR
3333 Burnet Ave (45229-3039)
PHONE..................................513 636-8778
EMP: 347
SALES (corp-wide): 2.94B **Privately Held**
Web: www.cincinnatichildrens.org
SIC: 8062 General medical and surgical hospitals
PA: Children's Hospital Medical Center
   3333 Burnet Ave
   Cincinnati OH 45229
   513 636-4200

(G-2367)
CHILDRENS HOSPITAL MEDICAL CTR
Also Called: Outpatient Anderson
7495 State Rd Ste 355 (45255-6402)
PHONE..................................513 636-6100
Vince Paradisco, *Mgr*
EMP: 253
SALES (corp-wide): 2.94B **Privately Held**
Web: www.cincinnatichildrens.org
SIC: 8733 8093 Medical research; Specialty outpatient clinics, nec
PA: Children's Hospital Medical Center
   3333 Burnet Ave
   Cincinnati OH 45229
   513 636-4200

(G-2368)
CHILDRENS HOSPITAL MEDICAL CTR (PA)
Also Called: Children's Home Healthcare
3333 Burnet Ave (45229)
PHONE..................................513 636-4200
Steve Davis, *CEO*
Michael Fisher, *
Dorine Seaquist, *
Thomas Boat, *
Teresa Bowling, *
EMP: 1181 EST: 1883
SQ FT: 1,803,000
SALES (est): 2.94B
SALES (corp-wide): 2.94B **Privately Held**
Web: www.cincinnatichildrens.org
SIC: 8733 8069 8731 Medical research; Childrens' hospital; Biotechnical research, commercial

(G-2369)
CHILDRENS HOSPITAL MEDICAL CTR
Also Called: Cincinnati Childrens Hospital
3401 Burnet Ave (45229-2807)
PHONE..................................513 636-4200
EMP: 537
SALES (corp-wide): 2.94B **Privately Held**
Web: www.cincinnatichildrens.org
SIC: 8733 8069 8731 Medical research; Childrens' hospital; Biotechnical research, commercial
PA: Children's Hospital Medical Center
   3333 Burnet Ave
   Cincinnati OH 45229
   513 636-4200

(G-2370)
CHILDRENS HOSPITAL MEDICAL CTR
Also Called: Cincinnati Children's Hospital
3350 Elland Ave (45229-3039)
PHONE..................................513 636-4200
EMP: 3853
SALES (corp-wide): 2.94B **Privately Held**
Web: www.cincinnatichildrens.org
SIC: 4225 General warehousing
PA: Children's Hospital Medical Center
   3333 Burnet Ave
   Cincinnati OH 45229
   513 636-4200

(G-2371)
CHILDRENS HOUSE LLC
11161 Montgomery Rd (45249-2308)
PHONE..................................513 451-4551

Amanda Ballman, *Dir*
EMP: 27
SALES (corp-wide): 5.7MM **Privately Held**
Web: www.thechildrenshousecincinnati.com
SIC: 8351 Group day care center
PA: The Children's House Llc
6155 Bridgetown Rd
Cincinnati OH 45248
513 574-9335

(G-2372)
CHILLICOTHE LONG-TERM CARE INC (PA)
Also Called: Westmoreland Place
7265 Kenwood Rd Ste 300 (45236-4414)
PHONE.................................740 773-6470
James Farley, *Pr*
Michael Scharfenberger, *Ex VP*
EMP: 80 **EST:** 1986
SQ FT: 50,000
SALES (est): 10.08MM
SALES (corp-wide): 10.08MM **Privately Held**
Web: www.westmorelandplace.com
SIC: 8051 Convalescent home with continuous nursing care

(G-2373)
CHIQUITA BRNDS INTL FOUNDATION
250 E 5th St (45202-4119)
PHONE.................................980 636-5000
FAX: 513 784-6648
EMP: 76
SALES (est): 6.3MM **Privately Held**
SIC: 8699 Charitable organization

(G-2374)
CHIRST HOSPITAL SURGERY CENTER
4850 Red Bank Rd Fl 1 (45227-1546)
PHONE.................................513 272-3448
EMP: 47 **EST:** 2000
SALES (est): 7.95MM **Privately Held**
Web: www.thechristhospital.com
SIC: 8062 General medical and surgical hospitals

(G-2375)
CHMC CMNTY HLTH SVCS NETWRK
Also Called: CHILDREN'S HOME HEALTHCARE
3333 Burnet Ave (45229-3026)
PHONE.................................513 636-8778
EMP: 3222 **EST:** 1995
SALES (est): 4.02MM
SALES (corp-wide): 2.94B **Privately Held**
Web: www.cincinnatichildrens.org
SIC: 8062 General medical and surgical hospitals
PA: Children's Hospital Medical Center
3333 Burnet Ave
Cincinnati OH 45229
513 636-4200

(G-2376)
CHRIST HOSPITAL
4803 Montgomery Rd Ste 114 (45212-1152)
PHONE.................................513 631-3300
Mona Fry, *Brnch Mgr*
EMP: 66
SALES (corp-wide): 1.3B **Privately Held**
Web: www.thechristhospital.com
SIC: 8062 General medical and surgical hospitals
PA: The Christ Hospital
2139 Auburn Ave
Cincinnati OH 45219
513 585-2000

(G-2377)
CHRIST HOSPITAL
Also Called: Christ Hospital, The
2355 Norwood Ave Ste 1 (45212-2750)
PHONE.................................513 351-0800
EMP: 57
SALES (corp-wide): 1.3B **Privately Held**
Web: www.thechristhospital.com
SIC: 8062 General medical and surgical hospitals
PA: The Christ Hospital
2139 Auburn Ave
Cincinnati OH 45219
513 585-2000

(G-2378)
CHRIST HOSPITAL
2139 Auburn Ave (45219-2989)
PHONE.................................513 585-2000
EMP: 27 **EST:** 2011
SALES (est): 3.05MM **Privately Held**
Web: www.thechristhospital.com
SIC: 8062 General medical and surgical hospitals

(G-2379)
CHRIST HOSPITAL
Also Called: Spectrum Rehabilitation
7545 Beechmont Ave Ste E (45255-4238)
PHONE.................................513 688-1111
Raymond C Rost, *Prin*
EMP: 57
SALES (corp-wide): 1.3B **Privately Held**
Web: www.thechristhospital.com
SIC: 8062 8049 Hospital, med school affiliated with nursing and residency; Physical therapist
PA: The Christ Hospital
2139 Auburn Ave
Cincinnati OH 45219
513 585-2000

(G-2380)
CHRIST HOSPITAL (PA)
Also Called: Christ Hospital Health Network
2139 Auburn Ave (45219-2989)
PHONE.................................513 585-2000
Deborah Hayes, *Pr*
Admiral Jack Cook, *Prin*
Mike Keating, *
Heather Adkins, *
Chris Bergman, *
EMP: 1500 **EST:** 1891
SALES (est): 1.73MM
SALES (corp-wide): 1.73MM **Privately Held**
Web: www.thechristhospital.com
SIC: 8062 Hospital, med school affiliated with nursing and residency

(G-2381)
CHRIST HOSPITAL
2123 Auburn Ave Ste 722 (45219-2906)
PHONE.................................513 651-0094
EMP: 57
SALES (corp-wide): 1.3B **Privately Held**
Web: www.thechristhospital.com
SIC: 8062 General medical and surgical hospitals
PA: The Christ Hospital
2139 Auburn Ave
Cincinnati OH 45219
513 585-2000

(G-2382)
CHRIST HOSPITAL
Also Called: Surgery Center
4850 Red Bank Rd Fl 1 (45227-1546)
PHONE.................................513 272-3448
EMP: 57
SALES (corp-wide): 1.3B **Privately Held**

(G-2383)
CHRIST HOSPITAL
Also Called: Glenway Family Medicine
5649 Harrison Rd Ste C (45248-1744)
PHONE.................................513 347-2300
EMP: 65
SALES (corp-wide): 1.3B **Privately Held**
Web: www.thechristhospital.com
SIC: 8062 General medical and surgical hospitals
PA: The Christ Hospital
2139 Auburn Ave
Cincinnati OH 45219
513 585-2000

(G-2384)
CHRIST HOSPITAL
11140 Montgomery Rd (45249-2309)
PHONE.................................513 561-7809
EMP: 56
SALES (corp-wide): 1.3B **Privately Held**
Web: www.thechristhospital.com
SIC: 8062 8031 8011 General medical and surgical hospitals; Offices and clinics of osteopathic physicians; Offices and clinics of medical doctors
PA: The Christ Hospital
2139 Auburn Ave
Cincinnati OH 45219
513 585-2000

(G-2385)
CHRISTIAN BENEVOLENT ASSN (PA)
8097 Hamilton Ave (45231-2321)
PHONE.................................513 931-5000
J Donald Sams, *CEO*
Roger Schwartz, *Business Administrator*
EMP: 200 **EST:** 1960
SALES (est): 2.09MM
SALES (corp-wide): 2.09MM **Privately Held**
Web: www.christianvillages.org
SIC: 8741 Nursing and personal care facility management

(G-2386)
CHRISTIAN COMMUNITY HLTH SVCS
Also Called: CROSSROAD HEALTH CENTER
5 E Liberty St Ste 4 (45202-8202)
PHONE.................................513 381-2247
▲ **EMP:** 37 **EST:** 1992
SALES (est): 10.1MM **Privately Held**
Web: www.crossroadhc.org
SIC: 8011 Clinic, operated by physicians

(G-2387)
CHS NORWOOD INC
Also Called: Woods Edge Point
1171 Towne St (45216-2227)
PHONE.................................513 242-1360
Carol Bottonari, *Dir*
EMP: 45 **EST:** 1997
SALES (est): 2.23MM **Privately Held**
Web: www.woods-edge.net
SIC: 8051 Convalescent home with continuous nursing care

(G-2388)
CHS-NORWOOD INC
Also Called: Harmony Court
6969 Glenmeadow Ln (45237-3001)
PHONE.................................513 351-7007
Laurie Westermeyer, *Admn*
Glyndon Powell, *
EMP: 160 **EST:** 2001
SALES (est): 25.88MM
SALES (corp-wide): 58.43MM **Privately Held**
Web: www.harmony-court.net
SIC: 8051 Convalescent home with continuous nursing care
PA: Carington Health Systems
8200 Beckett Park Dr
Hamilton OH 45011
513 682-2700

(G-2389)
CIMCOOL INDUSTRIAL PDTS LLC (DH)
Also Called: Cimcool
3000 Disney St (45209-5028)
PHONE.................................513 458-8100
▲ **EMP:** 42 **EST:** 2009
SALES (est): 94.4MM
SALES (corp-wide): 5.31MM **Privately Held**
Web: www.cimcool.com
SIC: 5169 Chemicals and allied products, nec
HQ: Dubois Chemicals, Inc.
3630 E Kemper Rd
Sharonville OH 45241

(G-2390)
CIMX LLC
Also Called: Cimx Software
2368 Victory Pkwy Ste 120 (45206-2810)
PHONE.................................513 248-7700
EMP: 30 **EST:** 1996
SALES (est): 4.22MM **Privately Held**
Web: www.cimx.com
SIC: 7372 7371 Prepackaged software; Custom computer programming services

(G-2391)
CINCINNATI - VULCAN COMPANY
5353 Spring Grove Ave (45217-1026)
PHONE.................................513 242-5300
Garry C Ferraris, *Pr*
EMP: 87 **EST:** 1912
SQ FT: 6,000
SALES (est): 2.24MM
SALES (corp-wide): 11.67MM **Privately Held**
SIC: 5983 2992 5171 2899 Fuel oil dealers; Oils and greases, blending and compounding; Petroleum bulk stations; Chemical preparations, nec
HQ: Coolant Control, Inc.
5353 Spring Grove Ave
Cincinnati OH 45217
513 471-8770

(G-2392)
CINCINNATI AIR CONDITIONING CO
Also Called: Honeywell Authorized Dealer
2080 Northwest Dr (45231-1700)
PHONE.................................513 721-5622
Mark Radtke, *Pr*
Michael Geiger, *
EMP: 55 **EST:** 1939
SQ FT: 30,000
SALES (est): 15.51MM **Privately Held**
Web: www.cincinnatiair.com
SIC: 1711 3822 Warm air heating and air conditioning contractor; Environmental controls

(G-2393)
CINCINNATI ANMAL RFRRAL EMRGNC
Also Called: Care Center
6995 East Kimper Rd (45249-1024)

GEOGRAPHIC SECTION

Cincinnati - Hamilton County (G-2415)

PHONE..................513 530-0911
EMP: 68 EST: 2000
SALES (est): 5.81MM Privately Held
Web: www.carecentervets.com
SIC: 0742 Animal hospital services, pets and other animal specialties

(G-2394)
CINCINNATI AREA SNIOR SVCS INC (PA)
644 Linn St Ste 304 (45203-1733)
PHONE..................513 721-4330
Elizabeth Patterson, *Ex Dir*
Tracy Collins, *
Jim Boesch, *
EMP: 55 EST: 1966
SQ FT: 9,000
SALES (est): 4.42MM
SALES (corp-wide): 4.42MM Privately Held
Web: www.muchmorethanameal.org
SIC: 8322 Senior citizens' center or association

(G-2395)
CINCINNATI ASSN FOR THE BLIND
2045 Gilbert Ave (45202-1403)
PHONE..................513 221-8558
TOLL FREE: 888
John Mitchell, *CEO*
Ginny Backscheider, *SERVICES**
Jennifer Dubois, *
Amy Scrivner, *OF Development COMMUNITY Relations**
Bill Neyer, *OF Business Development**
▲ EMP: 125 EST: 1910
SQ FT: 88,000
SALES (est): 12.08MM Privately Held
Web: www.cincyblind.org
SIC: 8331 8322 2891 Sheltered workshop; Association for the handicapped; Adhesives and sealants

(G-2396)
CINCINNATI ASSN FOR THE PRFRMG (PA)
650 Walnut St (45202-2517)
PHONE..................513 744-3344
Dudly S Taft, *Ch*
Steve Loftin, *
EMP: 75 EST: 1878
SQ FT: 200,000
SALES (est): 26.72MM
SALES (corp-wide): 26.72MM Privately Held
Web: www.cincinnatiarts.org
SIC: 8641 Dwelling-related associations

(G-2397)
CINCINNATI BALLET COMPANY INC
Also Called: Cincinnati Ballet
1801 Gilbert Ave (45202-1402)
PHONE..................513 621-5219
Deborah Brant, *Pr*
Melissa Santomo, *
EMP: 30 EST: 1958
SQ FT: 27,595
SALES (est): 12.64MM Privately Held
Web: www.cballet.org
SIC: 7911 Dance studio and school

(G-2398)
CINCINNATI BELL INC (DH)
Also Called: Altafiber
221 E 4th St (45202-4118)
P.O. Box 2301 (45201-2301)
PHONE..................513 397-9900
Leigh R Fox, *Pr*
Joshua T Duckworth, *CFO*
Thomas E Simpson, *COO*
Christi H Cornette, *CCO*
Kevin J Murray, *CIO*
◆ EMP: 271 EST: 1873
SQ FT: 200,000
SALES (est): 1.82B
SALES (corp-wide): 3.15B Privately Held
Web: www.altafiber.com
SIC: 7373 7374 7379 4813 Systems software development services; Data processing service; Computer related consulting services; Local and long distance telephone communications
HQ: Red Fiber Parent Llc
125 W 55th St
New York NY 10019
212 231-1000

(G-2399)
CINCINNATI BELL TELE CO LLC (DH)
Also Called: Cincinnati Bell Telephone Co
221 E 4th St 103-710 (45202-4124)
P.O. Box 2301 (45201-2301)
PHONE..................513 397-9900
Brian A Ross, *CFO*
Rodney D Dir, *
Mark Peterson, *
EMP: 275 EST: 1873
SQ FT: 100,000
SALES (est): 751.38MM
SALES (corp-wide): 3.15B Privately Held
Web: www.cincinnatibell.com
SIC: 4813 Local telephone communications
HQ: Cincinnati Bell Inc.
221 E 4th St Ste 700
Cincinnati OH 45202
513 397-9900

(G-2400)
CINCINNATI BELL WIRELESS COMPANY
221 E 4th St Ste 113 (45202-4137)
P.O. Box 2301 (45201-2301)
PHONE..................513 397-9548
EMP: 250
Web: www.altafiber.com
SIC: 4812 4813 5731 Cellular telephone services; Telephone communication, except radio; Radio, television, and electronic stores

(G-2401)
CINCINNATI BENGALS INC (PA)
Also Called: Ohio Valley Sports, Inc.
1 Paycor Stadium (45202-3492)
PHONE..................513 621-3550
Michael Brown, *CEO*
Andrew R Berger, *
William Scanlom, *
EMP: 645 EST: 1966
SALES (est): 53.82MM
SALES (corp-wide): 53.82MM Privately Held
Web: www.bengals.com
SIC: 7941 Football club

(G-2402)
CINCINNATI BULK TERMINALS LLC
Also Called: Cincinnati Bulk Terminals
895 Mehring Way (45203-1906)
PHONE..................513 621-4800
Jack Weiss, *Managing Member*
EMP: 50 EST: 1887
SALES (est): 2.67MM Privately Held
Web: www.cinbulk.com
SIC: 4491 Marine terminals

(G-2403)
CINCINNATI CIRCUS COMPANY LLC
6433 Wiehe Rd (45237-4215)
PHONE..................513 921-5454
Dave Willacker, *Managing Member*
EMP: 85 EST: 2010
SALES (est): 4.73MM Privately Held
Web: www.cincinnaticircus.com
SIC: 7929 Entertainment service

(G-2404)
CINCINNATI CNSLTING CONSORTIUM
220 Wyoming Ave (45215-4308)
PHONE..................513 233-0011
Richard Bruder, *Pr*
EMP: 29 EST: 1999
SALES (est): 824.26K Privately Held
Web: www.cincconsult.com
SIC: 8742 Business management consultant

(G-2405)
CINCINNATI COUNTRY CLUB
2348 Grandin Rd (45208-3399)
PHONE..................513 533-5200
Pat O'callaghan, *Genl Mgr*
EMP: 125 EST: 1902
SQ FT: 75,000
SALES (est): 13.37MM Privately Held
Web: www.cincinnaticountryclub.com
SIC: 7997 Country club, membership

(G-2406)
CINCINNATI CTR FOR PSYCHTHRAPY
3001 Highland Ave (45219-2315)
PHONE..................513 961-8484
EMP: 36 EST: 1974
SALES (est): 1.63MM Privately Held
Web: www.cincinnatipsychcenter.com
SIC: 8011 Psychiatrist

(G-2407)
CINCINNATI CYCLONES LLC
100 Broadway St Fl 3 (45202-3514)
PHONE..................513 421-7825
EMP: 41 EST: 2015
SALES (est): 119.58K Privately Held
Web: www.cycloneshockey.com
SIC: 7941 Sports clubs, managers, and promoters

(G-2408)
CINCINNATI DENTAL SERVICES (PA)
121 E Mcmillan St (45219-2606)
P.O. Box 36444 (45236-0444)
PHONE..................513 721-8888
Larry Faust, *Pr*
Missy Garvin, *VP*
Fred White Junior, *Mgr*
Steve Jones, *VP*
EMP: 75 EST: 1969
SQ FT: 18,500
SALES (est): 5.17MM
SALES (corp-wide): 5.17MM Privately Held
Web: www.cincinnatidentalservices.com
SIC: 8021 Dentists' office

(G-2409)
CINCINNATI DERMATOLOGY CTR LLC
Also Called: Mona Dermatology
7730 Montgomery Rd Ste 200 (45236-4284)
PHONE..................513 984-4800
Mona Salem Foad, *Prin*
EMP: 33 EST: 2008
SALES (est): 8.57MM Privately Held
Web: www.monadermatology.com
SIC: 8011 Dermatologist

(G-2410)
CINCINNATI EARLY LEARNING CTR (PA)
1301 E Mcmillan St (45206-2222)
PHONE..................513 961-2690
Patricia Gleason, *Ex Dir*
EMP: 30 EST: 1980
SALES (est): 5.06MM
SALES (corp-wide): 5.06MM Privately Held
Web: www.celcinc.org
SIC: 8351 Preschool center

(G-2411)
CINCINNATI FIFTH STREET HT LLC
Also Called: Cincinnati Hyatt Regency
151 W 5th St (45202-2703)
PHONE..................513 579-1234
Manuel Artime, *Admn*
Joe Pinto, *
EMP: 99 EST: 2015
SQ FT: 100,000
SALES (est): 4.9MM Privately Held
Web: cincinnati.hyatt.com
SIC: 7011 Hotels

(G-2412)
CINCINNATI HOME CARE INC
742 Waycross Rd (45240-3141)
PHONE..................513 771-2760
Vinna Ugwu, *Prin*
Obinna Ugwu, *
Lisa Spicer, *
EMP: 65 EST: 2007
SALES (est): 4.97MM Privately Held
Web: www.cincinnatihomecareinc.com
SIC: 8082 Home health care services

(G-2413)
CINCINNATI INSTITUTE FINE ARTS (PA)
Also Called: ARTSWAVE
20 East Central Pkwy Ste 2 (45202-7239)
PHONE..................513 871-2787
Mary Mccullough-hudson, *CEO*
Theresa Haught, *
Sue Reichelderfer, *
EMP: 27 EST: 1927
SQ FT: 4,000
SALES (est): 18.17MM
SALES (corp-wide): 18.17MM Privately Held
Web: www.artswave.org
SIC: 8699 Charitable organization

(G-2414)
CINCINNATI LNDMARK PRODUCTIONS (PA)
Also Called: CINCINNATI YOUNG PEOPLE'S THEA
4990 Glenway Ave (45238-3902)
P.O. Box 5255 (45205-0255)
PHONE..................513 241-6550
Timothy Perrino, *Ex Dir*
EMP: 27 EST: 2006
SQ FT: 11,650
SALES (est): 2.89MM Privately Held
Web: www.cincinnatilandmarkproductions.com
SIC: 7922 Performing arts center production

(G-2415)
CINCINNATI MUSEUM ASSOCIATION (PA)
Also Called: CINCINNATI ART MUSEUM
953 Eden Park Dr (45202-1557)
PHONE..................513 721-5204
Andrew Dewitt, *Pr*
Valerie Newell, *
▲ EMP: 170 EST: 1881
SQ FT: 300,000
SALES (est): 25.97MM
SALES (corp-wide): 25.97MM Privately Held
Web: www.cincinnatiartmuseum.org

Cincinnati - Hamilton County (G-2416)

SIC: 8412 8299 Museum; Art school, except commercial

(G-2416)
CINCINNATI MUSEUM CENTER (PA)
1301 Western Ave Ste 2253 (45203-1120)
PHONE..................513 287-7000
Douglass Mcdonald, *Pr*
EMP: 283 EST: 1987
SALES (est): 34.02MM **Privately Held**
Web: www.cincymuseum.org
SIC: 7832 8412 8231 Motion picture theaters, except drive-in; Museums and art galleries; Libraries

(G-2417)
CINCINNATI NETHERLAND HT LLC
Also Called: Hilton
35 W 5th St (45202-2801)
PHONE..................513 421-9100
EMP: 350 EST: 1983
SALES (est): 24.77MM **Privately Held**
Web: www.hilton.com
SIC: 7011 Resort hotel

(G-2418)
CINCINNATI OPERA ASSOCIATION
1243 Elm St (45202-7531)
PHONE..................513 768-5500
Patricia K Beggs, *CEO*
Robert W Olson, *
Darlene Zoz, *
Cathy Crain, *
EMP: 27 EST: 1920
SALES (est): 9.06MM **Privately Held**
Web: www.cincinnatiopera.org
SIC: 7922 Theatrical companies

(G-2419)
CINCINNATI PUBLIC RADIO INC
Also Called: W G U C-FM RADIO
1223 Central Pkwy (45214-2834)
PHONE..................513 352-9185
EMP: 36 EST: 1994
SQ FT: 20,000
SALES (est): 14.36MM **Privately Held**
Web: www.cinradio.org
SIC: 4832 Radio broadcasting stations, music format

(G-2420)
CINCINNATI REDS LLC (PA)
100 Joe Nuxhall Way (45202)
PHONE..................513 765-7000
Robert Castellini, *CEO*
Carl Lindnert, *
◆ EMP: 125 EST: 1869
SQ FT: 5,000
SALES (est): 50.52MM
SALES (corp-wide): 50.52MM **Privately Held**
Web: www.mlb.com
SIC: 7941 Baseball club, professional and semi-professional

(G-2421)
CINCINNATI REDS LLC
100 Main Street (45202)
PHONE..................513 765-7923
EMP: 125
SALES (corp-wide): 50.52MM **Privately Held**
Web: www.mlb.com
SIC: 7941 Baseball club, professional and semi-professional
PA: The Cincinnati Reds Llc
100 Joe Nuxhall Way
Cincinnati OH 45202
513 765-7000

(G-2422)
CINCINNATI SPEECH HEARING CTR (PA)
2825 Burnet Ave Ste 401 (45219-2426)
PHONE..................513 221-0527
Carol P Leslie, *Ex Dir*
EMP: 34 EST: 1925
SQ FT: 9,000
SALES (est): 40.21K
SALES (corp-wide): 40.21K **Privately Held**
Web: www.hearingspeechdeaf.org
SIC: 8099 8093 Hearing testing service; Speech defect clinic

(G-2423)
CINCINNATI SPORTS MALL INC
Also Called: Cincinnati Sports Club
3950 Red Bank Rd Ste A (45227-3430)
PHONE..................513 527-4000
Christopher L Fister, *Pr*
Charles Reynolds, *
Daniel A Funk Md, *Owner*
EMP: 154 EST: 1989
SQ FT: 100,000
SALES (est): 6.6MM **Privately Held**
Web: www.cincinnatisportsclub.com
SIC: 6512 7991 7997 Nonresidential building operators; Athletic club and gymnasiums, membership; Membership sports and recreation clubs

(G-2424)
CINCINNATI STEEL PRODUCTS CO
4540 Steel Pl (45209-1161)
PHONE..................513 871-4444
TOLL FREE: 800
James S Todd, *CEO*
Tom Brown, *
Thomas Rutter, *
EMP: 50 EST: 1933
SQ FT: 75,000
SALES (est): 5.65MM **Privately Held**
Web: www.cincinnatisteel.com
SIC: 5051 Steel

(G-2425)
CINCINNATI SYMPHONY ORCHESTRA (PA)
Also Called: RIVERBEND MUSIC CENTER
1241 Elm St (45202-7531)
PHONE..................513 621-1919
Melody Sawyer Richardson, *Ch*
Leonard M Randolph Junior, *Sec*
L Timothy Giglio, *
EMP: 150 EST: 1894
SQ FT: 10,000
SALES (est): 55.15MM
SALES (corp-wide): 55.15MM **Privately Held**
Web: www.cincinnatisymphony.org
SIC: 7929 Symphony orchestra

(G-2426)
CINCINNATI SYMPHONY ORCHESTRA
Also Called: Riverbend Music Center
1229 Elm St (45202-7531)
PHONE..................513 381-3300
EMP: 52
SALES (corp-wide): 55.15MM **Privately Held**
Web: www.cincinnatisymphony.org
SIC: 7929 Symphony orchestra
PA: Cincinnati Symphony Orchestra
1241 Elm St
Cincinnati OH 45202
513 621-1919

(G-2427)
CINCINNATI TESTING LABORATORIES INC (HQ)
Also Called: Cincinnati Testing Labs
1775 Carillion Blvd (45240-2805)
PHONE..................513 851-3313
EMP: 32 EST: 1946
SALES (est): 10.03MM
SALES (corp-wide): 24.93MM **Privately Held**
Web: www.metcutctl.com
SIC: 8734 Product testing laboratory, safety or performance
PA: Metcut Research Associates Inc.
3980 Rosslyn Dr
Cincinnati OH 45209
513 271-5100

(G-2428)
CINCINNATI TESTING LABS INC
417 Northland Blvd (45240-3210)
PHONE..................513 851-3313
Laurie Hash, *Brnch Mgr*
EMP: 33
SALES (corp-wide): 24.93MM **Privately Held**
Web: www.metcutctl.com
SIC: 8734 Testing laboratories
HQ: Cincinnati Testing Laboratories, Inc.
1775 Carillion Blvd
Cincinnati OH 45240
513 851-3313

(G-2429)
CINCINNATI TRNING TRML SVCS IN (PA)
Also Called: Ctts
4000 Executive Park Dr Ste 402 (45241-4009)
PHONE..................513 563-4474
Patricia E Fraley, *Pr*
Kathleen A Mc Connell, *VP*
EMP: 67 EST: 1985
SQ FT: 2,600
SALES (est): 4.84MM
SALES (corp-wide): 4.84MM **Privately Held**
Web: www.ctts.com
SIC: 7379 7373 Data processing consultant; Computer integrated systems design

(G-2430)
CINCINNATI USA RGIONAL CHAMBER
3 E 4th St Ste 200 (45202-3746)
PHONE..................513 579-3100
Jill P Meyer, *Pr*
Karen Michelsen, *
Tom Farrell, *Vice President Business**
Shasta Haddad, *Strategy Vice President**
Brendon J Cull, *
EMP: 75 EST: 1839
SQ FT: 24,900
SALES (est): 9.15MM **Privately Held**
Web: www.cincinnatichamber.com
SIC: 8611 Chamber of Commerce

(G-2431)
CINCINNATI WORKS CORP
708 Walnut St Ste 200 (45202-2030)
PHONE..................513 744-9675
EMP: 136 EST: 1996
SALES (est): 4.4MM **Privately Held**
Web: www.cincinnatiworks.org
SIC: 8331 Job training services

(G-2432)
CINCINNATI YOUTH COLLABORATIVE
301 Oak St (45219)
P.O. Box 18264 (45218)
PHONE..................513 475-4165
Myrtis Powell, *Ex Dir*
Jenny Keller, *VP*
Bill Russel, *VP*
EMP: 47 EST: 1987
SQ FT: 800
SALES (est): 3.3MM **Privately Held**
Web: www.cycyouth.org
SIC: 8322 Youth center

(G-2433)
CINCINNATIAN HOTEL
Also Called: Cincinnatian Hotel, The
601 Vine St (45202-2408)
PHONE..................513 381-3000
Rick Foreman, *Contrlr*
EMP: 47 EST: 1985
SQ FT: 105,160
SALES (est): 1.87MM **Privately Held**
Web: www.cincinnatianhotel.com
SIC: 7011 Hotels

(G-2434)
CINCINNT-HMLTON CNTY CMNTY ACT (PA)
1740 Langdon Farm Rd Ste 300 (45237-1157)
PHONE..................513 569-1840
Gwen L Robinson, *Pr*
Diana Paternoster, *
Stephanie Moes, *
Mark B Lawson, *
Chandra Mathews-smith, *Prin*
EMP: 145 EST: 1964
SQ FT: 28,000
SALES (est): 27.19MM
SALES (corp-wide): 27.19MM **Privately Held**
Web: www.cincy-caa.org
SIC: 8322 Social service center

(G-2435)
CINCINNT-HMLTON CNTY CMNTY ACT
880 W Court St (45203-1309)
PHONE..................513 354-3900
Gwen Robinson, *Mgr*
EMP: 49
SALES (corp-wide): 27.19MM **Privately Held**
Web: www.cincy-caa.org
SIC: 8322 Social service center
PA: Cincinnati-Hamilton County Community Action Agency
1740 Langdon Farm Rd
Cincinnati OH 45237
513 569-1840

(G-2436)
CINCINNTIS OPTMUM RSDNTIAL ENV
Also Called: Core
75 Tri County Pkwy (45246-3218)
PHONE..................513 771-2673
Martha A Adams, *Ex Dir*
EMP: 150 EST: 1986
SALES (est): 8.29MM **Privately Held**
Web: www.coreinc.org
SIC: 8361 Mentally handicapped home

(G-2437)
CINCO CREDIT UNION (PA)
Also Called: CINCO FAMILY FINANCIAL CENTER
49 William Howard Taft Rd (45219-1760)
PHONE..................513 281-9988
William C Page, *Pr*
Terry Tracey, *
Mark Schweinfurth, *
EMP: 50 EST: 1936

GEOGRAPHIC SECTION
Cincinnati - Hamilton County (G-2458)

SQ FT: 17,400
SALES (est): 5.12MM
SALES (corp-wide): 5.12MM **Privately Held**
Web: www.superiorcu.com
SIC: 6061 Federal credit unions

(G-2438)
CINCOM SYSTEMS INC (PA)
Also Called: Cincom
55 Merchant St (45246-3761)
PHONE.................513 612-2300
Thomas M Nies, *Ch Bd*
Donald Vick, *
Kenneth L Byrne, *
▲ EMP: 300 EST: 1968
SQ FT: 180,000
SALES (est): 37.04MM
SALES (corp-wide): 37.04MM **Privately Held**
Web: www.cincom.com
SIC: 7371 Computer software development

(G-2439)
CINCYSMILES FOUNDATION INC
Also Called: Greater Cncnnati Oral Hlth Cnc
5310 Rapid Run Rd Ste 101 (45238-4279)
PHONE.................513 621-0248
Lawrence F Hill, *Dir*
EMP: 35 EST: 1910
SALES (est): 2.22MM **Privately Held**
Web: www.cincysmiles.org
SIC: 8322 Individual and family services

(G-2440)
CINERGY CORP (DH)
139 E 4th St (45202-4003)
P.O. Box 960 (45201-0960)
PHONE.................513 421-9500
David L Hauser, *Pr*
Steven K Young, *
▲ EMP: 1700 EST: 1992
SQ FT: 300,000
SALES (est): 612.12MM
SALES (corp-wide): 29.06B **Publicly Held**
Web: www.cinergy.com
SIC: 4911 4924 Distribution, electric power; Natural gas distribution
HQ: Duke Energy Carolinas, Llc
526 S Church St
Charlotte NC 28202

(G-2441)
CINFED FEDERAL CREDIT UNION (PA)
Also Called: CINFED CREDIT UNION
4801 Kennedy Ave (45209-7543)
PHONE.................513 333-3800
Christine Kunnen, *Pr*
Jay Sigler, *CEO*
Eric Ketcham, *COO*
Wanda Handley, *VP*
EMP: 73 EST: 1934
SQ FT: 1,500
SALES (est): 31.35MM
SALES (corp-wide): 31.35MM **Privately Held**
Web: www.cinfed.com
SIC: 6061 Federal credit unions

(G-2442)
CINTAS CORPORATION (PA)
Also Called: Cintas
6800 Cintas Blvd (45262)
P.O. Box 625737 (45262-5737)
PHONE.................513 459-1200
Todd M Schneider, *Pr*
Scott D Farmer, *Ex Ch Bd*
James N Rozakis, *Ex VP*
J Michael Hansen, *Ex VP*
D Brock Denton, *Sr VP*

◆ EMP: 1500 EST: 1968
SALES (est): 8.82B
SALES (corp-wide): 8.82B **Publicly Held**
Web: www.cintas.com
SIC: 2326 2337 7218 5084 Work uniforms; Uniforms, except athletic: women's, misses', and juniors'; Industrial uniform supply; Safety equipment

(G-2443)
CINTAS CORPORATION
Also Called: Cintas Uniforms AP Fcilty Svcs
5570 Ridge Ave (45213-2516)
PHONE.................513 631-5750
Marie Seng, *Brnch Mgr*
EMP: 100
SALES (corp-wide): 8.82B **Publicly Held**
Web: www.cintas.com
SIC: 2326 2337 7218 5084 Work uniforms; Uniforms, except athletic: women's, misses', and juniors'; Industrial uniform supply; Safety equipment
PA: Cintas Corporation
6800 Cintas Blvd
Cincinnati OH 45262
513 459-1200

(G-2444)
CINTAS R US INC
6800 Cintas Blvd (45262)
PHONE.................513 459-1200
Scott Farmer, *CEO*
Richard T Farmer, *
EMP: 100 EST: 1956
SALES (est): 770.15K
SALES (corp-wide): 8.82B **Publicly Held**
Web: www.cintas.com
SIC: 7218 Industrial uniform supply
PA: Cintas Corporation
6800 Cintas Blvd
Cincinnati OH 45262
513 459-1200

(G-2445)
CINTAS SALES CORPORATION (HQ)
Also Called: Cintas
6800 Cintas Blvd (45262)
PHONE.................513 459-1200
Richard T Farmer, *Ch Bd*
Robert J Kohlhepp, *
Scott Farmer, *
Bill Gale, *
EMP: 450 EST: 1987
SALES (est): 22.08MM
SALES (corp-wide): 8.82B **Publicly Held**
SIC: 7218 2326 5136 5137 Industrial uniform supply; Work uniforms; Uniforms, men's and boys'; Uniforms, women's and children's
PA: Cintas Corporation
6800 Cintas Blvd
Cincinnati OH 45262
513 459-1200

(G-2446)
CINTECH LLC
Also Called: Cbts Technology Solutions
3280 Hageman Ave (45241-1907)
PHONE.................513 731-6000
Bryant Downey, *
EMP: 28 EST: 2009
SALES (est): 5.86MM
SALES (corp-wide): 3.15B **Privately Held**
Web: www.cintechconstruction.com
SIC: 7371 Computer software development
HQ: Cbts Technology Solutions Llc
25 Merchant St
Cincinnati OH 45246

(G-2447)
CINTECH CONSTRUCTION INC
4865 Duck Creek Rd (45227-1421)
PHONE.................513 563-1991
EMP: 30 EST: 1984
SALES (est): 23.6MM **Privately Held**
Web: www.cintechconstruction.com
SIC: 1542 Commercial and office building, new construction

(G-2448)
CIRCANA INC
Also Called: CIRCANA, INC.
250 E 5th St Ste 700 (45202-4183)
PHONE.................513 651-0500
Lynn Samford, *Mgr*
EMP: 130
SALES (corp-wide): 462.28MM **Privately Held**
Web: www.iriworldwide.com
SIC: 8732 Market analysis or research
PA: Circana, Llc
203 N Lasalle St Ste 1500
Chicago IL 60601
312 726-1221

(G-2449)
CITY BASE CINCINNATI LLC
5901 E Galbraith Rd Ste 200 (45236-2230)
P.O. Box 690388 (78269-0388)
PHONE.................210 907-7197
EMP: 50 EST: 2021
SALES (est): 380.68K **Privately Held**
Web: kenwood.citybasecinemas.com
SIC: 7832 Motion picture theaters, except drive-in

(G-2450)
CITY DASH LLC
Also Called: City Dash
949 Laidlaw Ave (45237-5003)
PHONE.................513 562-2000
Troy Burt, *Pr*
EMP: 170 EST: 1985
SQ FT: 10,000
SALES (est): 43.26MM **Privately Held**
Web: www.citydash.com
SIC: 4213 4215 4212 Less-than-truckload (LTL); Courier services, except by air; Local trucking, without storage

(G-2451)
CITY OF CINCINNATI
Also Called: Cincinnati Municipal Garage
1106 Bates Ave (45225-1302)
PHONE.................513 352-3680
EMP: 31
SALES (corp-wide): 901.5MM **Privately Held**
Web: www.cincinnati-oh.gov
SIC: 7521 Parking garage
PA: City Of Cincinnati
801 Plum St Rm 246
Cincinnati OH 45202
513 352-3221

(G-2452)
CITY OF CINCINNATI
Also Called: City of Cincinnati
4356 Dunham Ln (45238-3000)
PHONE.................513 471-9844
EMP: 30
SALES (corp-wide): 901.5MM **Privately Held**
Web: www.cincinnati-oh.gov
SIC: 8322 Senior citizens' center or association
PA: City Of Cincinnati
801 Plum St Rm 246
Cincinnati OH 45202
513 352-3221

(G-2453)
CITY OF CNCNNATI EMPLOYEES RTRM
801 Plum St (45202-1927)
PHONE.................513 591-6000
Jeff Mcelravy, *Prin*
EMP: 72 EST: 2009
SALES (est): 809.2K
SALES (corp-wide): 901.5MM **Privately Held**
Web: www.cincinnati-oh.gov
SIC: 6371 Pension, health, and welfare funds
PA: City Of Cincinnati
801 Plum St Rm 246
Cincinnati OH 45202
513 352-3221

(G-2454)
CIVIC GRDN CTR GRTER CNCINNATI
2715 Reading Rd (45206-1617)
PHONE.................513 221-0981
Vickie Ciotti, *Ex Dir*
EMP: 27 EST: 1942
SQ FT: 3,500
SALES (est): 570.94K **Privately Held**
Web: www.civicgardencenter.org
SIC: 8641 5947 Civic associations; Gift shop

(G-2455)
CLARKE FIRE PRTECTION PDTS INC
11407 Rockfield Ct (45241-1916)
PHONE.................513 771-2200
Terry Mcmahon, *Brnch Mgr*
EMP: 27
SQ FT: 8,000
SALES (corp-wide): 225.9MM **Privately Held**
Web: www.clarkepowerservices.com
SIC: 5084 Engines and parts, diesel
HQ: Clarke Fire Protection Products, Inc.
3133 E Kemper Rd
Cincinnati OH 45241

(G-2456)
CLARKE POWER SERVICES INC (PA)
Also Called: Clarke Detroit Diesel-Allison
3133 E Kemper Rd (45241-1516)
PHONE.................513 771-2200
Mark Andreae, *CEO*
Brad Abbot, *
Don Bixler, *
Dane Petrie, *
Kirk Andreae, *
◆ EMP: 100 EST: 1964
SQ FT: 62,000
SALES (est): 225.9MM
SALES (corp-wide): 225.9MM **Privately Held**
Web: www.clarkepowerservices.com
SIC: 5083 Farm and garden machinery

(G-2457)
CLERMONT COUNSELING CENTER
3730 Glenway Ave (45205-1354)
PHONE.................513 345-8555
Arlene Herman, *Brnch Mgr*
EMP: 60
SALES (corp-wide): 676.3K **Privately Held**
Web: www.clermontcounseling.com
SIC: 8322 General counseling services
PA: Clermont Counseling Center
43 E Main St
Amelia OH 45102
513 947-7000

(G-2458)
CLEVELAND EAST HTL LLC
8044 Montgomery Rd Ste 385 (45236-2919)

Cincinnati - Hamilton County (G-2459)

PHONE..................513 794-2566
William F O Brien, *Prin*
EMP: 28 **EST:** 2005
SALES (est): 234.87K **Privately Held**
SIC: 7011 Hotels

(G-2459)
CLIFTON CARE CENTER INC
Also Called: Communcare Clfton Pstcute Rhbl
625 Probasco St (45220-2710)
PHONE..................513 530-1600
Stephen L Rosedale, *Pr*
Ronald S Wilhelm, *Ex VP*
Charles R Stoltz, *Ex VP*
EMP: 113 **EST:** 1975
SQ FT: 26,000
SALES (est): 12.21MM
SALES (corp-wide): 392.92M **Privately Held**
Web: www.communicarehealth.com
SIC: 8051 Convalescent home with continuous nursing care
PA: Communicare Health Services, Inc.
10123 Alliance Rd
Blue Ash OH 45242
513 530-1654

(G-2460)
CLIPPARD INSTRUMENT LAB INC (PA)
Also Called: CLIPPARD MINIMATIC
7390 Colerain Ave (45239-5396)
PHONE..................513 521-4261
Harriet Clippard, *Prin*
Ralph Sparks, *
Wm Lippard Junior, *Prin*
▲ **EMP:** 200 **EST:** 1941
SQ FT: 84,000
SALES (est): 2.3MM
SALES (corp-wide): 2.3MM **Privately Held**
Web: www.clippard.com
SIC: 5084 Hydraulic systems equipment and supplies

(G-2461)
CLOVERNOOK INC (PA)
Also Called: Clovernook Hlth Care Pavilion
7025 Clovernook Ave (45231-5557)
P.O. Box 246 (45040-0246)
PHONE..................513 605-4000
Steve Boymel, *Pr*
EMP: 49 **EST:** 1981
SQ FT: 15,000
SALES (est): 7.65MM
SALES (corp-wide): 7.65MM **Privately Held**
Web: www.clovernookhc.com
SIC: 8051 Convalescent home with continuous nursing care

(G-2462)
CLOVERNOOK INC
Also Called: Clovernook Nursing Center
7025 Clovernook Ave (45231-5557)
PHONE..................513 605-4000
EMP: 71
SALES (corp-wide): 7.65MM **Privately Held**
Web: www.clovernookhc.com
SIC: 8051 8052 Skilled nursing care facilities; Intermediate care facilities
PA: Clovernook, Inc.
7025 Clovernook Ave
Cincinnati OH 45231
513 605-4000

(G-2463)
CLOVERNOOK COUNTRY CLUB
2035 W Galbraith Rd (45239-4364)
PHONE..................513 521-0333
Leslie Huesman, *Pr*
EMP: 84 **EST:** 1923
SQ FT: 12,000
SALES (est): 5.17MM **Privately Held**
Web: www.clovernookcc.com
SIC: 7997 Country club, membership

(G-2464)
CLOVERNOOK CTR FOR BLIND VSLLY (PA)
7000 Hamilton Ave (45231)
PHONE..................513 522-3860
Robin Usalis, *Pr*
Christopher Faust, *
Douglas Jacques, *
Betsy Baugh, *
Jacqueline L Conner, *
EMP: 125 **EST:** 1958
SQ FT: 40,000
SALES (est): 6.34MM
SALES (corp-wide): 6.34MM **Privately Held**
Web: www.clovernook.org
SIC: 2656 8322 7389 Paper cups, plates, dishes, and utensils; Rehabilitation services; Fund raising organizations

(G-2465)
CNG FINANCIAL CORPORATION (PA)
Also Called: Check N Go
7755 Montgomery Rd Ste 400 (45236-4197)
PHONE..................513 336-7735
Jared A Davis, *Pr*
David Davis, *
Stephen J Schaller, *
Robert M Beck Junior, *Prin*
EMP: 300 **EST:** 1994
SQ FT: 66,000
SALES (est): 696.24MM
SALES (corp-wide): 696.24MM **Privately Held**
Web: www.checkngo.com
SIC: 6099 Check cashing agencies

(G-2466)
CNG HOLDINGS INC
7755 Montgomery Rd Ste 400 (45236)
PHONE..................513 336-7735
A David Davis, *Pr*
Jared A Davis, *
Stephen J Schaller, *
Douglas D Clark, *
EMP: 3000 **EST:** 2006
Web: www.cng.com
SIC: 6719 Investment holding companies, except banks

(G-2467)
CNSLD HUMACARE- EMPLOYEE MGT (PA)
9435 Waterstone Blvd Ste 250 (45249)
PHONE..................513 605-3522
William B Southerland, *CEO*
EMP: 45 **EST:** 1995
SALES (est): 7.15MM
SALES (corp-wide): 7.15MM **Privately Held**
Web: www.humacare.net
SIC: 7361 Employment agencies

(G-2468)
COFFEE BREAK CORPORATION
Also Called: Restaurant Refreshment Service
1940 Losantiville Ave (45237-4106)
PHONE..................513 841-1100
Robert Walter, *Prin*
Robert Walter, *Pr*
Mary A Walter, *
Edward Walter, *
Robert C Porter Junior, *Prin*
EMP: 35 **EST:** 1973
SQ FT: 7,500
SALES (est): 9.36MM **Privately Held**
Web: www.coffeebreakroasting.com
SIC: 5149 5962 Coffee, green or roasted; Beverage vending machines

(G-2469)
COHESION CORPORATION
Also Called: Cohesion
511 W Bay St Ste 480 (45242)
PHONE..................813 999-3101
EMP: 170
SIC: 8742 7363 7373 Management information systems consultant; Office help supply service; Systems integration services

(G-2470)
COHO CREATIVE LLC
2331 Victory Pkwy (45206-2888)
PHONE..................513 751-7500
Daniel Brod, *Prin*
Julie Knight, *CFO*
EMP: 49 **EST:** 2002
SALES (est): 9.58MM **Privately Held**
Web: www.cohocreative.com
SIC: 8742 Marketing consulting services

(G-2471)
COLAS CONSTRUCTION USA INC
7374 Main St (45244-3015)
PHONE..................513 272-5648
John Harrington, *Pr*
Dustin Darby, *
Christian Ransinangue, *
Anthony Martino, *
EMP: 131 **EST:** 2020
SALES (est): 4.02MM
SALES (corp-wide): 90.36MM **Privately Held**
Web: www.colasusa.com
SIC: 1611 1622 8711 General contractor, highway and street construction; Tunnel construction; Engineering services
HQ: Colas Inc.
73 Hedqrters Plz N Towe 1
Morristown NJ 07960

(G-2472)
COLAS SOLUTIONS LLC
7374 Main St (45244-3015)
PHONE..................513 272-5648
Roger Hayner, *Pr*
EMP: 255 **EST:** 2010
SALES (est): 10.29MM
SALES (corp-wide): 90.36MM **Privately Held**
Web: www.colassolutions.com
SIC: 1611 1622 Highway and street construction; Bridge construction
HQ: Colas Inc.
73 Hedqrters Plz N Towe 1
Morristown NJ 07960

(G-2473)
COLDSTREAM COUNTRY CLUB
400 Asbury Rd (45255-4657)
PHONE..................513 231-3900
Mike Haehnle, *Genl Mgr*
EMP: 99 **EST:** 1959
SQ FT: 5,000
SALES (est): 6.79MM **Privately Held**
Web: www.coldstreamcc.com
SIC: 7997 Country club, membership

(G-2474)
COLDWELL BANKER WEST SHELL
7203 Wooster Pike (45227-3830)
PHONE..................513 271-7200
Beth Rouse, *Brnch Mgr*
EMP: 45
SALES (corp-wide): 25.71MM **Privately Held**
Web: www.coldwellbanker.com
SIC: 6531 Real estate agent, residential
PA: Coldwell Banker West Shell
9321 Montgomery Rd Ste C
Montgomery OH 45242
513 794-9494

(G-2475)
COLERAIN ANIMAL CLINIC INC (PA)
6340 Colerain Ave (45239-5534)
PHONE..................513 923-4400
John S Lies, *Pr*
EMP: 28 **EST:** 1966
SQ FT: 2,500
SALES (est): 4.86MM
SALES (corp-wide): 4.86MM **Privately Held**
SIC: 0742 Veterinarian, animal specialties

(G-2476)
COLERAIN DRY RDGE CHLDCARE LTD
Also Called: ABC Early Childhood Lrng Ctr
3998 Dry Ridge Rd (45252-1910)
PHONE..................513 923-4300
EMP: 33 **EST:** 2004
SQ FT: 8,700
SALES (est): 1.6MM **Privately Held**
Web: www.abceclc.com
SIC: 8351 Preschool center

(G-2477)
COLUMBUS LIFE INSURANCE CO
400 Broadway St (45202-3312)
P.O. Box 5737 (45201-5737)
PHONE..................513 361-6700
John H Bultema Iii, *Pr*
Donald Wuebbling, *Sec*
EMP: 140 **EST:** 1906
SALES (est): 2.19MM **Privately Held**
Web: www.westernsouthern.com
SIC: 6311 6411 Life insurance carriers; Insurance agents, brokers, and service
HQ: The Western & Southern Life Insurance Company
400 Broadway Mail Stop G
Cincinnati OH 45202
513 629-1800

(G-2478)
COMBINED TECHNOLOGIES INC (PA)
Also Called: Mobilcomm
1211 W Sharon Rd (45240-2916)
PHONE..................513 595-5900
Nancy Gleason, *Pr*
Gerrald Griffith, *Sec*
EMP: 28 **EST:** 1980
SQ FT: 42,000
SALES (est): 24.83MM
SALES (corp-wide): 24.83MM **Privately Held**
Web: www.mobilcomm.com
SIC: 7622 7359 5999 1731 Communication equipment repair; Mobile communication equipment rental; Communication equipment; Communications specialization

(G-2479)
COMCAGE LLC
Also Called: Oodle
2345 Ashland Ave (45206-2204)
PHONE..................513 549-4003
Jonathan Rhoads, *Managing Member*
EMP: 34 **EST:** 2009
SALES (est): 6.63MM **Privately Held**
Web: www.heyoodle.com
SIC: 7374 8742 7311 Computer graphics service; Marketing consulting services; Advertising agencies

GEOGRAPHIC SECTION
Cincinnati - Hamilton County (G-2500)

(G-2480)
COMEY & SHEPHERD LLC
7870 E Kemper Rd Ste 100 (45249-1675)
PHONE.....................513 489-2100
Jonathan Amster, *Brnch Mgr*
EMP: 59
SALES (corp-wide): 25.24MM **Privately Held**
Web: www.canningteam.com
SIC: 6531 Real estate agent, residential
PA: Comey & Shepherd, Llc
  6901 Wooster Pike
  Cincinnati OH 45227
  513 561-5800

(G-2481)
COMMONWEALTH TITLE DALLAS INC
Also Called: Commonwealth Land Title
30 Garfield Pl Ste 720 (45202-4363)
PHONE.....................513 985-0550
Beth Pietrandrea, *Brnch Mgr*
EMP: 1594
SIC: 6361 Real estate title insurance
HQ: Commonwealth Title Of Dallas, Inc.
  2651 N Harwood St Ste 260
  Dallas TX 75201

(G-2482)
COMMONWEALTH WAREHOUSE INC (PA)
400 Murray Rd (45217-1013)
PHONE.....................513 791-1966
Brent L Collins, *CEO*
Brian W Collins, *
Karen S Hamm, *
Vicki Collins, *
▲ **EMP:** 42 **EST:** 1986
SALES (est): 12.48MM
SALES (corp-wide): 12.48MM **Privately Held**
Web: www.commonwealthinc.com
SIC: 4225 General warehousing

(G-2483)
COMMUNITY INSURANCE COMPANY
Also Called: Anthem
1351 William Howard Taft Rd (45206-3085)
PHONE.....................859 282-7888
Dawn Caudill, *Mgr*
EMP: 48
SALES (corp-wide): 171.34B **Publicly Held**
Web: www.juliechafinhealthinsurance.com
SIC: 6324 Hospital and medical service plans
HQ: Community Insurance Company
  4361 Irwin Simpson Rd
  Mason OH 45040

(G-2484)
COMMUNITY MANAGEMENT CORP
375 W Galbraith Rd (45215-5037)
PHONE.....................513 761-6339
Mary Cieger, *Brnch Mgr*
EMP: 84
SALES (corp-wide): 4.85MM **Privately Held**
Web: www.cmcproperties.com
SIC: 6531 Real estate managers
PA: Community Management Corp
  10925 Reed Hartman Hwy # 200
  Blue Ash OH 45242
  513 984-3030

(G-2485)
COMPASS CLINICAL CONSULTING CO
2181 Victory Pkwy Ste 200 (45206-2907)
PHONE.....................513 241-0142
Cary D Gutbezahl, *Pr*
EMP: 29 **EST:** 1979
SALES (est): 1.75MM **Privately Held**
Web: www.tier1performance.com
SIC: 8748 Business consulting, nec

(G-2486)
COMPASS SCHOOL WATERSTONE LLC
9370 Waterstone Blvd (45249-8225)
PHONE.....................513 683-8833
Martin Brill, *Brnch Mgr*
EMP: 47
SALES (corp-wide): 259.13K **Privately Held**
Web: www.thegardnerschool.com
SIC: 8351 Preschool center
PA: Compass School Of Waterstone, Llc
  302 Innovation Dr Ste 130
  Franklin TN 37067
  804 762-4685

(G-2487)
COMPLETE CARE PROVIDERS INC
9888 Reading Rd (45241-3104)
PHONE.....................937 825-4698
James K Kitanga, *Pr*
EMP: 30 **EST:** 2010
SALES (est): 2.64MM **Privately Held**
Web: www.completecareprovider.com
SIC: 4731 Transportation agents and brokers

(G-2488)
COMPREHENSIVE HR SOLUTIONS LLC
Also Called: Sheakley
1 Sheakley Way (45246-3778)
PHONE.....................513 771-2277
Shari Herper, *VP*
EMP: 105 **EST:** 2013
SALES (est): 9.25MM **Privately Held**
Web: www.sheakley.com
SIC: 8742 Human resource consulting services

(G-2489)
COMPRHNSIVE CMNTY CHILD CARE O (PA)
Also Called: 4C FOR CHILDREN
2100 Sherman Ave Ste 300 (45212-2775)
PHONE.....................513 221-0033
Vanessa Freytag, *Pr*
EMP: 37 **EST:** 1972
SQ FT: 12,000
SALES (est): 10.89MM
SALES (corp-wide): 10.89MM **Privately Held**
Web: www.4cforchildren.org
SIC: 8322 Child guidance agency

(G-2490)
COMPRHNSIVE HALTHCARE SVCS INC
Also Called: Comprehensive Health Care Svcs
18 E 4th St Ste 100 (45202-3714)
PHONE.....................513 245-0100
EMP: 200 **EST:** 1993
SALES (est): 4.05MM **Privately Held**
SIC: 8082 7361 Home health care services; Employment agencies

(G-2491)
COMPUTER AIDED TECHNOLOGY LLC
Also Called: 3dvision Technologies
11500 Northlake Dr Ste 122 (45249-1650)
PHONE.....................513 745-2700
Richard Werneth, *Brnch Mgr*
EMP: 61

SALES (corp-wide): 220.47MM **Privately Held**
Web: www.cati.com
SIC: 7371 Computer software development
HQ: Computer Aided Technology, Llc
  739 E Fort Union Blvd
  Midvale UT 84047

(G-2492)
CONCENTRIX CVG CORPORATION (HQ)
Also Called: Concentrix
201 E 4th St (45202-4248)
PHONE.....................800 747-0583
Dennis J Polk, *CEO*
Christopher A Caldwell, *
Marshall W Witt, *
Steven L Richie, *
Mayank Bharat Vaishnav, *
EMP: 800 **EST:** 1996
SALES (est): 3.32B
SALES (corp-wide): 7.11B **Publicly Held**
Web: www.concentrix.com
SIC: 7374 7373 Data processing service; Computer integrated systems design
PA: Concentrix Corporation
  39899 Blentine Dr Ste 235
  Newark CA 94560
  800 747-0583

(G-2493)
CONCENTRIX CVG CSTMER MGT INTL (DH)
Also Called: Convergys Cstomer MGT Intl Inc
201 E 4th St Bsmt (45202-4248)
PHONE.....................513 268-7014
Andrea J Ayers, *CEO*
EMP: 51 **EST:** 2014
SALES (est): 775.92K
SALES (corp-wide): 7.11B **Publicly Held**
SIC: 7389 Telemarketing services
HQ: Convergys Customer Management Group Inc.
  201 E 4th St Bsmt
  Cincinnati OH 45202
  513 723-6104

(G-2494)
CONCENTRIX SOLUTIONS CORP
201 E 4th St (45202-4248)
PHONE.....................480 968-2496
EMP: 44
SALES (corp-wide): 7.11B **Publicly Held**
Web: www.concentrix.com
SIC: 7374 Data processing service
HQ: Concentrix Solutions Corporation
  3750 Monroe Ave
  Pittsford NY 14534

(G-2495)
CONSOLIDATED GRAIN & BARGE CO
CGB - Riverside
3164 Southside Ave (45204-1255)
PHONE.....................513 244-7400
Scott Thibault, *Brnch Mgr*
EMP: 32
SQ FT: 7,308
Web: www.cgbgrain.com
SIC: 5153 4221 Grains; Grain elevator, storage only
HQ: Consolidated Grain & Barge Company
  1127 Hwy 190 E Service Rd
  Covington LA 70433
  985 867-3500

(G-2496)
CONSTELLATION INSURANCE INC (HQ)
1 Financial Way Ste 100 (45242)

P.O. Box 237 (45201)
PHONE.....................513 794-6100
Gary T Huffman, *Pr*
Ronald Dolan, *Vice Chairman**
Arthur J Roberts, *
Larry J Adams, *CAO**
Christopher A Carlson, *
EMP: 700 **EST:** 1909
SALES (est): 488.7MM
SALES (corp-wide): 2.2MM **Privately Held**
Web: www.constellationinsurance.com
SIC: 6311 Mutual association life insurance
PA: Constellation Insurance Holdings, Inc.
  1 Financial Way Ste 100
  Cincinnati OH 45242
  513 794-6100

(G-2497)
CONSTLLTION INSUR HOLDINGS INC (PA)
1 Financial Way Ste 100 (45242)
PHONE.....................513 794-6100
Gary Huffman, *Ch Bd*
Michael S Haberkamp, *
Ronald Dolan, *
Roylene Broadwell, *
EMP: 750 **EST:** 1993
SALES (est): 2.2MM
SALES (corp-wide): 2.2MM **Privately Held**
Web: www.constellationinsurance.com
SIC: 6311 Mutual association life insurance

(G-2498)
CONSTRUCTCONNECT INC (HQ)
Also Called: Constructconnect
3825 Edwards Rd Ste 800 (45209-1289)
PHONE.....................800 364-2059
Dave Conway, *Pr*
Craig Tate, *
Scott Waterbury, *
Alex Hart, *
Joseph Madda, *CIO**
EMP: 249 **EST:** 1994
SQ FT: 63,000
SALES (est): 90.72MM
SALES (corp-wide): 5.37B **Publicly Held**
Web: www.constructconnect.com
SIC: 7371 5045 Computer software development; Computer software
PA: Roper Technologies, Inc.
  6901 Prof Pkwy E Ste 200
  Sarasota FL 34240
  941 556-2601

(G-2499)
CONSUMERS ENERGY COMPANY
P.O. Box 740309 (45274-0309)
PHONE.....................800 477-5050
EMP: 27
SALES (corp-wide): 7.46B **Publicly Held**
Web: www.consumersenergy.com
SIC: 4931 4911 4924 Electric and other services combined; Electric services; Natural gas distribution
HQ: Consumers Energy Company
  1 Energy Plaza Dr
  Jackson MI 49201
  517 788-0550

(G-2500)
CONTANDA TERMINALS LLC
3500 Southside Ave (45204-1138)
PHONE.....................513 921-8441
William Lindsey, *Managing Member*
▲ **EMP:** 42 **EST:** 1966
SQ FT: 12,000
SALES (est): 3.23MM
SALES (corp-wide): 219.16MM **Privately Held**
Web: www.bwcterminals.com

Cincinnati - Hamilton County (G-2501)

SIC: 4225 General warehousing and storage
PA: Contanda Llc
1111 Bagby St Ste 1800
Houston TX 77002
832 699-4001

(G-2501)
CONTEMPORARY ARTS CENTER
44 E 6th St (45202-3998)
PHONE.................513 721-0390
Raphaela Platow, *Dir*
Margaux Higgins, *
EMP: 40 **EST:** 1939
SQ FT: 80,000
SALES (est): 4.45MM **Privately Held**
Web: www.contemporaryartscenter.org
SIC: 8412 Arts or science center

(G-2502)
CONTRACTORS MATERIALS COMPANY
Also Called: Mmi of Kentucky
10320 S Medallion Dr (45241-4836)
P.O. Box 621227 (45262-1227)
PHONE.................513 733-3000
Martha C Luken, *Pr*
Daniel P King, *VP*
David L Friedman, *VP*
William H Luken, *Sec*
▲ **EMP:** 50 **EST:** 1923
SQ FT: 95,000
SALES (est): 15.13MM **Privately Held**
Web: www.cmcmmi.com
SIC: 5211 5051 Lumber and other building materials; Concrete reinforcing bars

(G-2503)
CONTRLLED ENVMT CRTFCTION SVCS
171 Container Pl (45246-1708)
PHONE.................513 870-0293
EMP: 29
Web: www.steris.com
SIC: 7389 Inspection and testing services
HQ: Controlled Environment Certification Services, Inc.
177 N Commerce Way
Bethlehem PA 18017
610 867-5302

(G-2504)
CONVALESCENT HOSPITAL FOR CHIL
3333 Burnet Ave (45229-3026)
PHONE.................513 636-4415
Robby Thompson, *Admn*
EMP: 47 **EST:** 2005
SALES (est): 18.65MM **Privately Held**
Web: www.cincinnatichildrens.org
SIC: 8062 General medical and surgical hospitals

(G-2505)
CONVERGINT TECHNOLOGIES LLC
Also Called: Post Browning
7812 Redsky Dr (45249-1632)
PHONE.................513 771-1717
EMP: 130
SALES (corp-wide): 3.37B **Privately Held**
Web: www.convergint.com
SIC: 5065 7699 Security control equipment and systems; Industrial machinery and equipment repair
HQ: Convergint Technologies Llc
1 Commerce Dr
Schaumburg IL 60173
847 620-5000

(G-2506)
CONVERGYS CSTMER MGT GROUP INC (DH)
201 E 4th St Bsmt (45202-4248)
P.O. Box 1638 (45201-1638)
PHONE.................513 723-6104
David F Dougherty, *Pr*
Andre S Valentine, *
Ronald E Schultz, *
▼ **EMP:** 300 **EST:** 1988
SQ FT: 100,000
SALES (est): 323.24MM
SALES (corp-wide): 7.11B **Publicly Held**
Web: www.concentrix.com
SIC: 7389 8732 Telemarketing services; Market analysis or research
HQ: Concentrix Cvg Corporation
201 E 4th St
Cincinnati OH 45202
800 747-0583

(G-2507)
CORE RESOURCES INC
7795 5 Mile Rd (45230-2355)
PHONE.................513 731-1771
Paul Kitzmiller, *CEO*
David Kitzmiller, *
EMP: 52 **EST:** 1990
SQ FT: 7,000
SALES (est): 9.61MM **Privately Held**
Web: www.core-1.com.
SIC: 8741 Construction management

(G-2508)
CORNERSTONE BRK INSUR SVCS AGC (PA)
Also Called: Cornerstone Brkg Insur Svc Agc
2101 Florence Ave (45206-2426)
PHONE.................513 241-7675
John Carroll, *CEO*
John Carroll, *Pr*
John Clark, *VP*
EMP: 39 **EST:** 1991
SALES (est): 10.33MM **Privately Held**
Web: www.crnstone.com
SIC: 6411 Insurance agents, nec

(G-2509)
CORNERSTONE CONTROLS INC (PA)
7131 E Kemper Rd (45249-1028)
PHONE.................513 489-2500
EMP: 35 **EST:** 1935
SALES (est): 22.24MM
SALES (corp-wide): 22.24MM **Privately Held**
Web: www.cornerstonecontrols.com
SIC: 5085 5065 Industrial supplies; Electronic parts and equipment, nec

(G-2510)
CORS & BASSETT LLC (PA)
537 E Pete Rose Way Ste 400 (45202-3578)
PHONE.................513 852-8200
David L Barth, *Managing Member*
▲ **EMP:** 75 **EST:** 1931
SALES (est): 9.87MM
SALES (corp-wide): 9.87MM **Privately Held**
Web: www.corsbassett.com
SIC: 8111 General practice attorney, lawyer

(G-2511)
COTTINGHAM RTIREMENT CMNTY INC
3995 Cottingham Dr (45241-1680)
PHONE.................513 563-3600
George Raymond Drew, *Pr*
EMP: 64 **EST:** 1984
SALES (est): 9.87MM **Privately Held**
Web: www.cottinghamretirementcommunity.com
SIC: 8051 Skilled nursing care facilities

(G-2512)
COUNTY OF HAMILTON
Also Called: Family & Children First
222 East Central Pkwy (45202-1225)
PHONE.................513 946-1800
Patti Eber, *Brnch Mgr*
EMP: 29
SALES (corp-wide): 1.06MM **Privately Held**
Web: www.hamilton-co.org
SIC: 8322 9441 Individual and family services; Administration of social and manpower programs
PA: County Of Hamilton
138 E Court St Rm 607
Cincinnati OH 45202
513 946-4400

(G-2513)
COWANS LLC
Also Called: Cowan's Auctions
5030 Oaklawn Dr Ste 1 (45227-1485)
PHONE.................513 871-1670
Jay Krehbiel, *Prin*
Nicole Joy, *
EMP: 99 **EST:** 2019
SALES (est): 2.77MM **Privately Held**
Web: cowans.hindmanauctions.com
SIC: 7389 Auctioneers, fee basis

(G-2514)
CRAFTSMAN ELECTRIC INC
3855 Alta Ave Ste 1 (45236-3932)
PHONE.................513 891-4426
Kathleen Fischer, *Pr*
Charles Fischer, *
▲ **EMP:** 90 **EST:** 1984
SQ FT: 16,000
SALES (est): 21MM **Privately Held**
Web: www.craftsmanelectric.com
SIC: 1731 General electrical contractor

(G-2515)
CRANLEY SURGICAL ASSOCIATES
Also Called: Mercy Health
3747 W Fork Rd (45247-7548)
PHONE.................513 961-4335
L R Roedersheimer, *Pr*
James J Arbough, *
Robert Cranley, *
EMP: 49 **EST:** 1971
SALES (est): 1.74MM **Privately Held**
SIC: 8011 Cardiologist and cardio-vascular specialist

(G-2516)
CREATIVE CONNECTIONS LLC
5558 Cheviot Rd (45247-7094)
PHONE.................513 389-0213
Tamela Peel, *Prin*
EMP: 75 **EST:** 2013
SALES (est): 2.8MM **Privately Held**
Web: www.creativeconnectionsllc.net
SIC: 8351 Child day care services

(G-2517)
CROSSROADS CENTER
311 Martin Luther King Dr E (45219-2581)
PHONE.................513 475-5300
Jacqueline P Butler, *Ex Dir*
EMP: 150 **EST:** 1954
SALES (est): 7.41MM **Privately Held**
Web: www.thecrossroadscenter.org
SIC: 8069 8361 8093 Alcoholism rehabilitation hospital; Residential care; Specialty outpatient clinics, nec

(G-2518)
CRST INTERNATIONAL INC
Also Called: C Rst Specialized Trnsp
11677 Chesterdale Rd (45246-3917)
PHONE.................513 552-1935
EMP: 37
SALES (corp-wide): 2.19B **Privately Held**
SIC: 4789 Cargo loading and unloading services
PA: Crst International, Inc.
3930 16th Ave Sw
Cedar Rapids IA 52401
319 396-4400

(G-2519)
CRYSTALWOOD INC
Also Called: Alois Alzheimer Center, The
70 Damon Rd (45218-1041)
PHONE.................513 605-1000
Stephen Boymel, *Pr*
EMP: 49 **EST:** 1983
SQ FT: 30,000
SALES (est): 10.27MM **Privately Held**
Web: www.alois.com
SIC: 8059 8361 8052 Rest home, with health care; Residential care; Intermediate care facilities

(G-2520)
CSA AMERICA INC
Also Called: Csa Group
635 W 7th St Ste 406 (45203-1549)
PHONE.................513 791-6918
EMP: 74
SALES (corp-wide): 367.35MM **Privately Held**
Web: www.csagroup.org
SIC: 8712 Architectural services
HQ: Csa America Standards, Inc.
8501 E Pleasant Valley Rd
Independence OH 44131
216 524-4990

(G-2521)
CTS CONSTRUCTION INC
Also Called: CTS Telecommunications
7275 Edington Dr (45249-1064)
PHONE.................513 489-8290
Rick Stezer, *Pr*
William Coate, *
Frederick Setzer Iii, *Treas*
Ronald D Wagner, *
Andrew Rotunno, *
EMP: 100 **EST:** 1993
SQ FT: 15,000
SALES (est): 18.92MM **Privately Held**
Web: www.ctstelecomm.com
SIC: 7378 8748 1796 1731 Computer maintenance and repair; Telecommunications consultant; Installing building equipment; Electrical work

(G-2522)
CUMBERLAND GAP LLC
Also Called: Ramada Inn Cumberland Hotel
2285 Banning Rd (45239-6611)
PHONE.................513 681-9300
EMP: 45 **EST:** 1994
SALES (est): 206.23K **Privately Held**
Web: www.wyndhamhotels.com
SIC: 7011 Hotels and motels

(G-2523)
CUMULUS MEDIA INC
Also Called: Warm 98
4805 Montgomery Rd Ste 300 (45212-2198)
PHONE.................513 241-9898
Karrie Subbrick, *Mgr*
EMP: 39
SALES (corp-wide): 844.55MM **Publicly Held**

GEOGRAPHIC SECTION
Cincinnati - Hamilton County (G-2548)

Web: www.foxcincinnati.com
SIC: 4832 Radio broadcasting stations
PA: Cumulus Media Inc.
780 Johnson Fy Rd Ne # 500
Atlanta GA 30342
404 949-0700

(G-2524)
CURBELL PLASTICS INC
Also Called: Curbell Plastics
11145 Ashburn Rd (45240-3814)
PHONE.................................513 742-9898
Tim Cassani, Brnch Mgr
EMP: 29
SALES (corp-wide): 294.07MM Privately Held
Web: www.curbellplastics.com
SIC: 5162 Plastics products, nec
HQ: Curbell Plastics, Inc.
7 Cobham Dr
Orchard Park NY 14127

(G-2525)
CURIOSITY LLC
Also Called: Curiosity Advertising
1140 Main St (45202-7236)
PHONE.................................513 744-6000
Matthew Fischer, Managing Member
EMP: 62 EST: 2009
SALES (est): 9.14MM Privately Held
Web: www.curiosity.fun
SIC: 7311 Advertising consultant

(G-2526)
CUSHMAN WAKEFIELD HOLDINGS INC
221 E 4th St Fl 26 (45202-4100)
PHONE.................................513 241-4880
EMP: 38
SALES (corp-wide): 9.49B Privately Held
Web: www.cushmanwakefield.com
SIC: 6531 8742 8732 Real estate agent, commercial; Real estate consultant; Market analysis, business, and economic research
HQ: Cushman & Wakefield Holdings, Inc.
1290 Ave Of The Americas
New York NY 10104
212 841-7500

(G-2527)
CUSTOM DESIGN BENEFITS INC
5589 Cheviot Rd (45247-7020)
PHONE.................................513 598-2929
M Steven Chapel, CEO
Julie Muller, *
EMP: 38 EST: 1991
SQ FT: 10,000
SALES (est): 22.33MM Privately Held
Web: www.customdesignbenefits.com
SIC: 6324 Hospital and medical service plans

(G-2528)
CWFF CHILD DEVELOPMENT CTR
434 Forest Ave (45229-2516)
PHONE.................................513 569-5660
Ennis F Tait, Ex Dir
EMP: 27 EST: 1972
SALES (est): 1.45MM Privately Held
SIC: 8351 Group day care center

(G-2529)
D & D ADVERTISING ENTPS INC
801 Evans St Ste 203 (45204-2075)
PHONE.................................513 921-6827
EMP: 30 EST: 1993
SALES (est): 856.25K Privately Held
Web: www.ddadvertising.com
SIC: 5199 Advertising specialties

(G-2530)
D JAMES INCORPORATED
Also Called: Hillebrand Nrsing Rhblttion Ct
4320 Bridgetown Rd (45211-4428)
PHONE.................................513 574-4550
James Glass, Pr
EMP: 200 EST: 1967
SQ FT: 2,953
SALES (est): 9.95MM Privately Held
Web: www.hillebrandhealth.com
SIC: 8051 Convalescent home with continuous nursing care

(G-2531)
D&A TRANSPORT LLC
1410 Springfield Pike Apt 33 (45215)
PHONE.................................513 570-7153
Deondrick Hardy, Prin
Abraham Yisrael, *
EMP: 30 EST: 2021
SALES (est): 1.5MM Privately Held
SIC: 4789 Transportation services, nec

(G-2532)
D&D FOUNDATION LLC
412 Dayton St (45214-2321)
P.O. Box 40239 (45240-0239)
PHONE.................................513 291-3191
EMP: 44 EST: 2019
SALES (est): 576.61K Privately Held
SIC: 7349 Janitorial service, contract basis

(G-2533)
D+H USA CORPORATION
Also Called: DH
312 Plum St Ste 500 (45202-4810)
PHONE.................................513 381-9400
EMP: 173
SALES (corp-wide): 1.24B Privately Held
SIC: 7372 Application computer software
HQ: D+H Usa Corporation
1320 Sw Broadway Ste 100
Portland OR 97204
407 804-6600

(G-2534)
DAG CONSTRUCTION CO INC
447 Ivy Trails Dr (45244-2129)
PHONE.................................513 542-8597
Dale S White Senior, CEO
Stephanie A Hall, *
Dale White Junior, VP
Jacqueline M White, *
Gregory J Webb, *
EMP: 40 EST: 1990
SALES (est): 10.11MM Privately Held
Web: www.dag-cons.com
SIC: 1542 1541 Commercial and office building, new construction; Renovation, remodeling and repairs: industrial buildings

(G-2535)
DAMASCUS STAFFING LLC
1832 Freeman Ave (45214-2117)
PHONE.................................513 954-8941
Todd Wurzburger, Managing Member
EMP: 60 EST: 2016
SALES (est): 2.12MM Privately Held
Web: www.teamdamascus.com
SIC: 7361 Employment agencies

(G-2536)
DANIEL DRAKE CTR FOR PST-CUTE
Also Called: Drake Center, LLC
151 W Galbraith Rd (45216-1015)
PHONE.................................513 418-2500
Rick Hinds, *
Charity Fannin, *
EMP: 800 EST: 1824
SQ FT: 400,000
SALES (est): 63.52MM Privately Held
Web: www.uchealth.com
SIC: 8051 Skilled nursing care facilities
PA: Uc Health, Llc.
3200 Burnet Ave
Cincinnati OH 45229

(G-2537)
DANIS BUILDING CONSTRUCTION CO
50 E-Business Way (45241-2397)
PHONE.................................513 984-9696
James Kee, Mgr
EMP: 27
Web: www.danis.com
SIC: 1542 1541 8741 Commercial and office building, new construction; Industrial buildings and warehouses; Construction management
PA: Danis Building Construction Company
3233 Newmark Dr
Miamisburg OH 45342

(G-2538)
DANSON INC
Also Called: Aegis Protective Services
3033 Robertson Ave (45209-1233)
PHONE.................................513 948-0066
Justin Dutro, Pr
Daniel G Dutro, *
EMP: 210 EST: 1993
SQ FT: 2,400
SALES (est): 18.87MM Privately Held
Web: www.aegis-ps.com
SIC: 7381 Security guard service

(G-2539)
DATA PROCESSING SCIENCES CORPORATION
Also Called: Dpsciences
2 Camargo Cyn (45243-2945)
PHONE.................................513 791-7100
▼ EMP: 65
SIC: 4813 5045 3669 3577 Telephone communication, except radio; Computers, peripherals, and software; Intercommunication systems, electric; Computer peripheral equipment, nec

(G-2540)
DATA RECOGNITION CORPORATION
3645 Park 42 Dr (45241-2075)
PHONE.................................513 588-7260
Sharon Woolf, Brnch Mgr
EMP: 34
SALES (corp-wide): 275.31MM Privately Held
Web: www.datarecognitioncorp.com
SIC: 8732 Economic research
PA: Data Recognition Corporation
13490 Bass Lake Rd
Maple Grove MN 55311
763 268-2000

(G-2541)
DAVEY RESOURCE GROUP INC
Also Called: New Age Communications Cnstr
1230 W 8th St (45203-1005)
PHONE.................................859 630-9879
Jay Martin, Mgr
EMP: 40
SALES (corp-wide): 1.51B Privately Held
Web: www.davey.com
SIC: 0783 Planting, pruning, and trimming services
HQ: Davey Resource Group, Inc.
295 S Water St Ste 300
Kent OH 44240
330 673-5685

(G-2542)
DAVID J JOSEPH COMPANY
Also Called: David J. Joseph Co-Metals, The
300 Pike St (45202-4222)
PHONE.................................513 419-6016
EMP: 42
SALES (corp-wide): 34.71B Publicly Held
Web: www.djj.com
SIC: 5093 Ferrous metal scrap and waste
HQ: The David J Joseph Company
300 Pike St
Cincinnati OH 45202
513 419-6200

(G-2543)
DAVID L BARTH LWYR
537 E Pete Rose Way (45202-3567)
PHONE.................................513 852-8228
EMP: 60
SALES (est): 1.59MM Privately Held
SIC: 8111 General practice attorney, lawyer

(G-2544)
DAYTON HEIDELBERG DISTRG CO
Also Called: Heidelberg Distributing Co
1518 Dalton Ave (45214-2018)
PHONE.................................513 421-5000
Toby Coston, VP
EMP: 294
SALES (corp-wide): 2.07B Privately Held
Web: www.heidelbergdistributing.com
SIC: 5181 Beer and other fermented malt liquors
HQ: Dayton Heidelberg Distributing Co., Llc
3601 Dryden Rd
Moraine OH 45439
937 222-8692

(G-2545)
DCS SANITATION MANAGEMENT INC
7864 Camargo Rd (45243-4300)
P.O. Box 43215 (45243-0215)
PHONE.................................513 891-4980
EMP: 1700
SIC: 7349 7342 Building cleaning service; Disinfecting services

(G-2546)
DE COACH TEAM LLC
Also Called: Decoach Rehabilitation Centre
100 Crowne Point Pl (45241-5427)
PHONE.................................513 942-4673
Mindy Brewer, Prin
Kim Barrows, *
EMP: 51 EST: 2017
SALES (est): 4.97MM Privately Held
Web: www.decoachrecovery.com
SIC: 8093 Rehabilitation center, outpatient treatment

(G-2547)
DE FOXX & ASSOCIATES INC (PA)
Also Called: Validex
324 W 9th St Fl 5 (45202-2043)
PHONE.................................513 621-5522
David E Foxx, Pr
Patricia Foxx, *
EMP: 350 EST: 1981
SQ FT: 25,000
SALES (est): 94.54MM
SALES (corp-wide): 94.54MM Privately Held
Web: www.defoxx.com
SIC: 8742 8741 Business management consultant; Construction management

(G-2548)
DEACONESS ASSOCIATIONS INC (PA)
615 Elsinore Pl Ste 900 (45202-1459)

Cincinnati - Hamilton County (G-2549)   GEOGRAPHIC SECTION

PHONE...................................513 559-2100
E Anthony Woods, *Pr*
EMP: 300 **EST:** 1986
SALES (est): 19.28MM
SALES (corp-wide): 19.28MM **Privately Held**
Web: www.deaconess-healthcare.com
SIC: 8059 Nursing home, except skilled and intermediate care facility

(G-2549)
DEACONESS HOSPITAL OF CINCINNA (PA)
Also Called: DEACONESS HOSPITAL
615 Elsinore Pl Ste 900 (45202-1459)
PHONE...................................513 559-2100
E Anthony Woods, *Ch*
James L Pahls, *
EMP: 176 **EST:** 1888
SQ FT: 649,000
SALES (est): 34.4MM
SALES (corp-wide): 34.4MM **Privately Held**
Web: www.deaconess-healthcare.com
SIC: 8062 General medical and surgical hospitals

(G-2550)
DEACONESS LONG TERM CARE INC (HQ)
330 Straight St Ste 310 (45219-1019)
P.O. Box 198027 (45219-8027)
PHONE...................................513 861-0400
EMP: 52 **EST:** 1993
SQ FT: 1,891
SALES (est): 19.24MM
SALES (corp-wide): 19.28MM **Privately Held**
Web: www.deaconess-healthcare.com
SIC: 8059 Nursing home, except skilled and intermediate care facility
PA: The Deaconess Associations Inc
615 Elsinore Pl Bldg B
Cincinnati OH 45202
513 559-2100

(G-2551)
DEACONESS LONG TERM CARE OF MI (PA)
Also Called: Camden Health Center
330 Straight St Ste 310 (45219-1019)
PHONE...................................513 487-3600
Ken Raupach, *COO*
EMP: 1500 **EST:** 1995
SALES (est): 42.27MM **Privately Held**
Web: www.deaconess-healthcare.com
SIC: 8059 8361 8052 8051 Nursing home, except skilled and intermediate care facility; Residential care; Intermediate care facilities; Skilled nursing care facilities

(G-2552)
DEBRA-KUEMPEL INC (HQ)
Also Called: De Bra - Kuempel
3976 Southern Ave (45227)
P.O. Box 701620 (45227)
PHONE...................................513 271-6500
Fred B De Bra, *Ch Bd*
Joe D Clark, *
Morris H Reed, *
Debbie Biggs, *
Bill Flaugher, *
EMP: 73 **EST:** 1944
SQ FT: 20,079
SALES (est): 59.73MM
SALES (corp-wide): 12.58B **Publicly Held**
Web: www.dkemcor.com
SIC: 3446 1711 3443 3441 Architectural metalwork; Mechanical contractor; Fabricated plate work (boiler shop); Fabricated structural metal

PA: Emcor Group, Inc.
301 Merritt 7
Norwalk CT 06851
203 849-7800

(G-2553)
DEER PARK ROOFING INC (PA)
7201 Blue Ash Rd (45236-3665)
PHONE...................................513 891-9151
Nicholas A Sabino, *Pr*
EMP: 36 **EST:** 1996
SQ FT: 23,000
SALES (est): 10.31MM **Privately Held**
Web: www.deerparkroofing.com
SIC: 1761 Roofing contractor

(G-2554)
DEI INCORPORATED
1550 Kemper Meadow Dr (45240-1638)
PHONE...................................513 825-5800
Richard D Grow, *Ch Bd*
Nedd Compton, *
Jeff Stupak, *
David Morton, *
EMP: 74 **EST:** 1985
SQ FT: 15,000
SALES (est): 20.35MM **Privately Held**
Web: www.dei-corp.com
SIC: 8712 Architectural engineering

(G-2555)
DELHI TOWNSHIP (PA)
934 Neeb Rd (45233-4101)
PHONE...................................513 922-0060
Gerard Schroeder, *Admn*
Ken Ryan, *
Jerome Luebbers, *
Michael Davis, *
Al Duebber, *
EMP: 70 **EST:** 1789
Web: www.delhi.oh.us
SIC: 9111 8322 City and town managers' office; Senior citizens' center or association

(G-2556)
DELOITTE & TOUCHE LLP
Also Called: Deloitte Consulting
250 E 5th St Fl 1600 (45202-4263)
P.O. Box 5340 (45201-5340)
PHONE...................................513 784-7100
Cathy Melching, *Admn*
EMP: 365
Web: www.deloitte.com
SIC: 8721 8748 8742 7291 Certified public accountant; Business consulting, nec; Management consulting services; Tax return preparation services
HQ: Deloitte & Touche Llp
30 Rockefeller Plz # 4350
New York NY 10112
212 492-4000

(G-2557)
DELTA ELECTRICAL CONTRS LTD
4890 Gray Rd (45232-1512)
PHONE...................................513 421-7744
Dale Scheidt, *Owner*
EMP: 31 **EST:** 1998
SQ FT: 18,000
SALES (est): 5.75MM **Privately Held**
Web: www.delta-electrical.com
SIC: 1731 General electrical contractor

(G-2558)
DERMATLOGISTS CENTL STATES LLC
Also Called: Docs
9349 Waterstone Blvd Fl 3 (45249-8320)
PHONE...................................888 414-3627
John Macke, *CEO*
EMP: 651 **EST:** 2017

SALES (est): 56.76MM **Privately Held**
Web: www.docsdermgroup.com
SIC: 8011 Dermatologist

(G-2559)
DESKEY ASSOCIATES INC
120 E 8th St (45202-2118)
PHONE...................................513 721-6800
Michael Busher, *Pr*
Douglas Studer, *
EMP: 90 **EST:** 1925
SALES (est): 9.86MM **Privately Held**
Web: www.deskey.com
SIC: 8711 8732 Designing: ship, boat, machine, and product; Market analysis or research

(G-2560)
DETOX HEALTH CARE CORP OHIO
11500 Northlake Dr Ste 400 (45249-1650)
PHONE...................................513 742-6310
Kim Toole, *Brnch Mgr*
EMP: 90
SALES (corp-wide): 33.71MM **Privately Held**
Web: www.detox.net
SIC: 8082 Home health care services
PA: Detox Health Care Corp Of Ohio
201 S Biscayne Blvd
Miami FL 33131
513 742-6310

(G-2561)
DHR INTERNATIONAL INC
312 Walnut St Ste 1600 (45202-4038)
PHONE...................................513 762-7690
Ted Plattenburg, *Ex VP*
EMP: 84
Web: www.dhrglobal.com
SIC: 7361 Executive placement
PA: Dhr International, Inc.
71 S Wacker Dr Ste 2700
Chicago IL 60606

(G-2562)
DIALYSIS CLINIC INC
499 E Mcmillan St (45206-1924)
PHONE...................................513 281-0091
Roy Danfro, *Mgr*
EMP: 65
SQ FT: 3,840
SALES (corp-wide): 1.99MM **Privately Held**
Web: www.dciinc.org
SIC: 8092 Kidney dialysis centers
PA: Dialysis Clinic, Inc.
1633 Church St Ste 500
Nashville TN 37203
615 327-3061

(G-2563)
DIERS2018CO INC
Also Called: Andy's Mirror and Glass
5618 Center Hill Ave (45216-2306)
PHONE...................................513 242-9250
Robert Diers, *CEO*
Rick Schiller, *
EMP: 30 **EST:** 1936
SQ FT: 22,000
SALES (est): 2.39MM **Privately Held**
Web: www.andysmirror.com
SIC: 1793 Glass and glazing work

(G-2564)
DIFFERENTIAL DEV SHOP LLC
815 Main St (45202-2112)
PHONE...................................513 205-8930
Timothy Metzner, *Pt*
Colin Flynn, *Pt*
Sean Mccosh, *Pt*
EMP: 37 **EST:** 2014

SALES (est): 2.04MM **Privately Held**
Web: www.differential.com
SIC: 7371 Computer software development

(G-2565)
DINSMORE & SHOHL LLP (PA)
255 E 5th St Ste 1900 (45202-1971)
PHONE...................................513 977-8200
George Vincent, *Pt*
EMP: 406 **EST:** 1909
SQ FT: 158,000
SALES (est): 169.43MM
SALES (corp-wide): 169.43MM **Privately Held**
Web: www.dinsmore.com
SIC: 8111 General practice attorney, lawyer

(G-2566)
DIRECT OPTIONS INC
Also Called: Direct Options
1325 Glendale Milford Rd (45215-1210)
PHONE...................................513 779-4416
Jan S Moore, *Pr*
Paul Wiehe, *
EMP: 28 **EST:** 1992
SALES (est): 4.44MM **Privately Held**
SIC: 8742 Marketing consulting services

(G-2567)
DIRECTIONS RESEARCH INC (PA)
401 E Court St Ste 200 (45202-1379)
PHONE...................................513 651-2990
Randolph Brooks, *Pr*
Steven Wilde, *
Greg Widmeyer, *
Tim Laake, *CMO*
EMP: 100 **EST:** 1988
SQ FT: 46,374
SALES (est): 36.13MM
SALES (corp-wide): 36.13MM **Privately Held**
Web: www.directionsresearch.com
SIC: 8732 Market analysis or research

(G-2568)
DITSCH USA LLC
311 Northland Blvd (45246-3690)
PHONE...................................513 782-8888
Gary Gottenbusch, *CEO*
Brian Tooley, *CFO*
EMP: 50 **EST:** 2014
SQ FT: 100,000
SALES (est): 11.26MM **Privately Held**
Web: www.ditsch.com
SIC: 2052 5149 Pretzels; Bakery products
HQ: Valora Holding Ag
Hofackerstrasse 40
Muttenz BL 4132

(G-2569)
DIVERSICARE ST THERESA LLC
Also Called: DIVERSICARE
7010 Rowan Hill Dr (45227-3380)
PHONE...................................513 271-7010
James R Mcknight Junior, *Prin*
Kerry Massey, *
Rebecca Bodie, *
Matthew Weishaar, *
EMP: 99 **EST:** 2013
SALES (est): 6.44MM
SALES (corp-wide): 1.03B **Privately Held**
Web: www.dvcr.com
SIC: 8051 Skilled nursing care facilities
HQ: Diversicare Healthcare Services, Inc.
1621 Galleria Blvd
Brentwood TN 37027

(G-2570)
DIVERSIFIED OPHTHALMICS INC
Also Called: Diversified SE Division
250 Mccullough St (45226-2145)

PHONE.................................803 783-3454
Sara Baldwin, *Mgr*
EMP: 42
SIC: 5048 3851 5049 Contact lenses;
  Contact lenses; Optical goods
HQ: Diversified Ophthalmics, Inc.
  250 Mccullough St
  Cincinnati OH
  800 852-8089

(G-2571)
DIVISIONS INC (PA)
Also Called: Divisions Maintenance Group
50 W 5th St (45202-3788)
  PHONE.................................859 448-9730
Gary Mitchell, *CEO*
Kyle Murray, *CSO*
Bill Volz, *Field Operations Vice President*
Brian Wint, *Finance*
Adam Wallace, *Senior Technical Director*
EMP: 246 EST: 1999
SQ FT: 18,000
SALES (est): 261MM
SALES (corp-wide): 261MM **Privately Held**
Web: www.divisionsmg.com
SIC: 7349 Building maintenance services, nec

(G-2572)
DJJ HOLDING CORPORATION (HQ)
Also Called: David J Joseph Company, The
300 Pike St (45202-4222)
  PHONE.................................513 419-6200
Craig A Feldman, *Pr*
David J Steigerwald, *RECYCLING*
Mark D Schaefer Evp Recycling, *Prin*
Christopher J Bedel, *Corporate Counsel*
Karen A Arnold, *Employee*
◆ EMP: 175 EST: 1972
SQ FT: 160,000
SALES (est): 275.12MM
SALES (corp-wide): 34.71B **Publicly Held**
Web: www.djj.com
SIC: 5093 5088 4741 Ferrous metal scrap and waste; Railroad equipment and supplies; Rental of railroad cars
PA: Nucor Corporation
  1915 Rexford Rd
  Charlotte NC 28211
  704 366-7000

(G-2573)
DONNELLON MCCARTHY ENTPS INC (PA)
Also Called: ABS Business Products
10855 Medallion Dr (45241-4829)
  PHONE.................................513 769-7800
James Donnellon, *Pr*
EMP: 31 EST: 1980
SQ FT: 17,000
SALES (est): 25.15MM
SALES (corp-wide): 25.15MM **Privately Held**
Web: dme.us.com
SIC: 5044 7699 Copying equipment; Office equipment and accessory customizing

(G-2574)
DONNELLON MCCARTHY INC (PA)
10855 Medallion Dr (45241-4829)
P.O. Box P.O Box Dept839 (45204)
  PHONE.................................513 769-7800
EMP: 50 EST: 1957
SALES (est): 24.97MM
SALES (corp-wide): 24.97MM **Privately Held**
Web: dme.us.com
SIC: 5044 Photocopy machines

(G-2575)
DOTLOOP LLC
700 W Pete Rose Way Ste 436 (45203-1919)
  PHONE.................................513 257-0550
EMP: 32 EST: 2012
SALES (est): 4.92MM
SALES (corp-wide): 1.95B **Publicly Held**
Web: www.dotloop.com
SIC: 7371 Computer software development
HQ: Zillow, Inc.
  1301 2nd Ave Fl 31
  Seattle WA 98101
  206 470-7000

(G-2576)
DRURY HOTELS COMPANY LLC
Also Called: Drury Inn Suites Cincinnati N
2265 E Sharon Rd (45241-1870)
  PHONE.................................513 771-5601
Kam Siu, *Brnch Mgr*
EMP: 29
SALES (corp-wide): 555.12MM **Privately Held**
Web: www.druryhotels.com
SIC: 7011 Hotels
PA: Drury Hotels Company, Llc
  13075 Manchester Rd # 100
  Saint Louis MO 63131
  314 429-2255

(G-2577)
DRY RUN LIMITED PARTNERSHIP
Also Called: Ivy Hills Country Club
7711 Ivy Hills Dr (45244-2575)
  PHONE.................................513 561-9119
William Hines, *Genl Pt*
E Michael Zicka, *Ltd Pt*
EMP: 46 EST: 1989
SALES (est): 3.13MM **Privately Held**
SIC: 7997 Country club, membership

(G-2578)
DUKE ENERGY BECKJORD LLC
139 E 4th St (45202-4034)
  PHONE.................................513 287-2561
Charles Whitlock, *Prin*
EMP: 632 EST: 2012
SALES (est): 8.98MM
SALES (corp-wide): 29.06B **Publicly Held**
SIC: 4911 Electric services
HQ: Duke Energy Ohio, Inc.
  139 E 4th St
  Cincinnati OH 45202
  704 382-3853

(G-2579)
DUKE ENERGY CENTER
525 Elm St (45202-2316)
  PHONE.................................513 419-7300
EMP: 50 EST: 2019
SALES (est): 2.45MM **Privately Held**
Web: www.duke-energycenter.com
SIC: 7389 Convention and show services

(G-2580)
DUKE ENERGY KENTUCKY INC
Also Called: CINergy-Ulh&p
139 E 4th St (45202-4034)
  PHONE.................................704 594-6200
James Rogers, *Vice Chairman*
Jim Henning, *
Jackson H Randolph, *
EMP: 200 EST: 1901
SQ FT: 300,000
SALES (est): 478.7MM
SALES (corp-wide): 29.06B **Publicly Held**
SIC: 4932 4931 Gas and other services combined; Electric and other services combined
HQ: Duke Energy Ohio, Inc.
  139 E 4th St
  Cincinnati OH 45202
  704 382-3853

(G-2581)
DUKE ENERGY OHIO INC
Also Called: Montford Heights
5445 Audro Dr (45247-7001)
  PHONE.................................800 544-6900
Eric Stolzenberger, *Brnch Mgr*
EMP: 5201
SALES (corp-wide): 29.06B **Publicly Held**
Web: datacache.duke-energy.com
SIC: 4911 Distribution, electric power
HQ: Duke Energy Ohio, Inc.
  139 E 4th St
  Cincinnati OH 45202
  704 382-3853

(G-2582)
DUKE ENERGY OHIO INC
Also Called: Brecon Distribution Center
7600 E Kemper Rd (45249-1610)
P.O. Box 5385 (45201-5385)
  PHONE.................................513 287-1120
Darrell Ingel, *Brnch Mgr*
EMP: 4312
SALES (corp-wide): 29.06B **Publicly Held**
Web: www.duke-energy.com
SIC: 4911 Distribution, electric power
HQ: Duke Energy Ohio, Inc.
  139 E 4th St
  Cincinnati OH 45202
  704 382-3853

(G-2583)
DUKE ENERGY OHIO INC (HQ)
Also Called: DUKE ENERGY
139 E 4th St (45202-4034)
  PHONE.................................704 382-3853
TOLL FREE: 800
Lynn J Good, *CEO*
Steven K Young, *Ex VP*
Brian D Savoy, *CAO*
▲ EMP: 100 EST: 1837
SALES (est): 2.51B
SALES (corp-wide): 29.06B **Publicly Held**
Web: www.duke-energy.com
SIC: 4922 4924 4931 4911 Natural gas transmission; Natural gas distribution; Electric and other services combined; Distribution, electric power
PA: Duke Energy Corporation
  526 S Church St
  Charlotte NC 28202
  704 382-3853

(G-2584)
DUKE ENERGY ONE INC
Also Called: Econic, A Duke Energy Company
139 E 4th St (45202-4034)
  PHONE.................................980 373-3931
Robert F Caldwell, *Pr*
Karl Newlin, *
David Maltz, *Corporate Secretary*
Nancy Wrigh, *Assistant Corporate Secretary*
EMP: 5134 EST: 2013
SALES (est): 9.8MM
SALES (corp-wide): 29.06B **Publicly Held**
SIC: 4911 Distribution, electric power
HQ: Duke Technologies, Inc.
  139 E 4th St
  Cincinnati OH 45202
  704 382-7904

(G-2585)
DUNBAR ARMORED INC
1257 W 7th St (45203-1001)
  PHONE.................................513 381-8000
Brian Baker, *Mgr*
EMP: 39
SALES (corp-wide): 4.87B **Publicly Held**
Web: www.dunbarsecurity.com
SIC: 7381 Security guard service
HQ: Dunbar Armored, Inc.
  50 Schilling Rd
  Hunt Valley MD 21031
  410 584-9800

(G-2586)
DUNNHUMBY INC
3825 Edwards Rd Ste 600 (45209-1293)
  PHONE.................................513 579-3400
Simon Hay, *CEO*
EMP: 204 EST: 2000
SALES (est): 31.38MM
SALES (corp-wide): 81.02B **Privately Held**
Web: www.dunnhumby.com
SIC: 8742 Marketing consulting services
PA: Tesco Plc
  Tesco House Ground Floor
  Welwyn Garden City HERTS AL7 1
  800505555

(G-2587)
DURGA LLC
11320 Chester Rd (45246-4003)
  PHONE.................................513 771-2080
EMP: 39 EST: 2011
SALES (est): 320.19K **Privately Held**
SIC: 7011 5812 5091 Hotels; American restaurant; Water slides (recreation park)

(G-2588)
DVA HLTHCARE - STHWEST OHIO LL
Also Called: Western Hills Dialysis
3267 Westbourne Dr (45248-5110)
  PHONE.................................513 347-0444
John Winstel, *Brnch Mgr*
EMP: 52
SIC: 8092 Kidney dialysis centers
HQ: Dva Healthcare - Southwest Ohio, Llc
  2000 16th St
  Denver CO 80202
  253 733-4501

(G-2589)
DVA HLTHCARE - STHWEST OHIO LL
Also Called: Winton Road Dialysis
6550 Winton Rd (45224-1327)
  PHONE.................................513 591-2900
John Winstel, *Brnch Mgr*
EMP: 52
SIC: 8092 Kidney dialysis centers
HQ: Dva Healthcare - Southwest Ohio, Llc
  2000 16th St
  Denver CO 80202
  253 733-4501

(G-2590)
DYNEGY COML ASSET MGT LLC
139 E 4th St (45202-4003)
  PHONE.................................513 287-5033
Charles Whitlock, *Pr*
EMP: 143 EST: 2000
SALES (est): 424.08MM
SALES (corp-wide): 14.78B **Publicly Held**
SIC: 4924 4911 Natural gas distribution; Generation, electric power
PA: Vistra Corp.
  6555 Sierra Dr
  Irving TX 75039
  214 812-4600

(G-2591)
E & J TRAILER SALES & SVC INC
610 Wayne Park Dr Ste 5 (45215-2847)
  PHONE.................................513 563-2550
Edward Focke, *Pr*
EMP: 35 EST: 1976
SQ FT: 40,000

Cincinnati - Hamilton County (G-2592)

SALES (est): 1.97MM **Privately Held**
Web: www.ejtrailer.com
SIC: **7519** Trailer rental

(G-2592)
E B MILLER CONTRACTING INC
1701 Mills Ave (45212-2825)
PHONE..................513 531-7030
EMP: 50
Web: www.ebmiller.com
SIC: **1721** Commercial painting

(G-2593)
EAGLE REALTY GROUP LLC
301 E 4th St (45202-4245)
PHONE..................513 361-4000
Mario San Marco, *Brnch Mgr*
EMP: 160
Web: www.westernsouthern.com
SIC: **6531** 6519 Real estate agent, commercial; Real property lessors, nec
HQ: Eagle Realty Group, Llc
   421 E 4th St
   Cincinnati OH 45202

(G-2594)
EAGLE REALTY GROUP LLC
2501 Erie Ave (45208-2032)
PHONE..................513 361-7750
Joann Riley, *Dir*
EMP: 137
Web: www.westernsouthern.com
SIC: **6531** Real estate agent, residential
HQ: Eagle Realty Group, Llc
   421 E 4th St
   Cincinnati OH 45202

(G-2595)
EAGLE REALTY GROUP LLC (DH)
421 E 4th St (45202-3317)
P.O. Box 1091 (45201-1091)
PHONE..................513 361-7700
Edward W Grout, *
Thomas M Stapleton, *
EMP: 28 EST: 1996
SQ FT: 49,200
SALES (est): 5.2MM **Privately Held**
Web: www.westernsouthern.com
SIC: **6531** 6552 Real estate managers; Land subdividers and developers, commercial
HQ: The Western & Southern Life
   Insurance Company
   400 Broadway Mail Stop G
   Cincinnati OH 45202
   513 629-1800

(G-2596)
EAGLEBURGMANN KE INC
Also Called: Eagle Burgmann EXT Joint Sol
3478 Hauck Rd (45241-4604)
PHONE..................859 746-0091
▲ EMP: 37
SIC: **7699** Industrial equipment services

(G-2597)
EARLE M JORGENSEN COMPANY
Also Called: EMJ Cincinnati
601 Redna Ter (45215-1108)
P.O. Box 15100 (45215-0100)
PHONE..................513 771-3223
Jeff Stethens, *General*
EMP: 30
SQ FT: 10,000
SALES (corp-wide): 14.81B **Publicly Held**
Web: www.emjmetals.com
SIC: **5051** Steel
HQ: Earle M. Jorgensen Company
   10650 Alameda St
   Lynwood CA 90262
   323 567-1122

(G-2598)
EAST GLBRITH HLTH CARE CTR INC (PA)
Also Called: Chamberlin Healthcare Center
3889 E Galbraith Rd (45236-1514)
PHONE..................513 984-5220
Joseph Schneider, *Pr*
EMP: 252 EST: 1977
SQ FT: 7,245
SALES (est): 10.55MM **Privately Held**
Web: www.glendalefloristglendale.com
SIC: **8059** Nursing home, except skilled and intermediate care facility

(G-2599)
EASTER SEALS TRISTATE (HQ)
Also Called: Easter Seals
8740 Montgomery Rd (45236-2152)
PHONE..................513 985-0515
Pamela Green, *Pr*
Peter Bloch, *
Rich Davis, *
Amy Balson, *
Dan Feigelson, *
EMP: 115 EST: 1940
SALES (est): 12.2MM
SALES (corp-wide): 16.26MM **Privately Held**
Web: www.easterseals.com
SIC: **8331** 8322 Vocational rehabilitation agency; Individual and family services
PA: Easter Seals Tristate, Llc
   2901 Gilbert Ave
   Cincinnati OH 45206
   513 281-2316

(G-2600)
EASTER SEALS TRISTATE LLC (PA)
2901 Gilbert Ave (45206-1211)
PHONE..................513 281-2316
EMP: 60 EST: 1972
SQ FT: 22,000
SALES (est): 16.26MM
SALES (corp-wide): 16.26MM **Privately Held**
Web: www.easterselsredwood.org
SIC: **8322** Social service center

(G-2601)
EBENEZER ROAD CORPORATION
Also Called: Western Hills Retirement Vlg
6210 Cleves Warsaw Pike (45233-4510)
PHONE..................513 941-0099
Barry A Kohn, *Pr*
Sam Boymel, *
Harold Sosna, *
EMP: 250 EST: 1983
SQ FT: 150,000
SALES (est): 13.28MM **Privately Held**
Web: www.caringplacehcg.com
SIC: **6513** 8052 8051 Retirement hotel operation; Intermediate care facilities; Skilled nursing care facilities

(G-2602)
EBTHCOM LLC
697 Wilmer Ave (45226)
PHONE..................513 242-3284
Mike Reynolds, *CFO*
EMP: 63 EST: 2013
SALES (est): 2.08MM **Privately Held**
Web: www.ebth.com
SIC: **6531** Selling agent, real estate

(G-2603)
ECKSTEIN ROOFING COMPANY
264 Stille Dr (45233-1647)
PHONE..................513 941-1511
James Eckstein Junior, *Pr*
EMP: 30 EST: 1945
SQ FT: 12,000
SALES (est): 2.49MM **Privately Held**
Web: www.ecksteinroofing.com
SIC: **1761** Sheet metal work, nec

(G-2604)
ECO ENGINEERING INC
Also Called: Invision Technologies Dist
11815 Highway Dr Ste 600 (45241-2065)
PHONE..................513 985-8300
Thomas Kirkpatrick, *Pr*
Susan Kirkpatrick, *
EMP: 58 EST: 1993
SQ FT: 11,000
SALES (est): 20.66MM **Privately Held**
Web: www.ecoengineering.com
SIC: **8748** 1731 8711 Energy conservation consultant; Electrical work; Engineering services

(G-2605)
ECOBRYT LLC
7747 Reinhold Dr (45237-2805)
PHONE..................877 326-2798
EMP: 30 EST: 2010
SQ FT: 1,700
SALES (est): 991.6K **Privately Held**
Web: www.cincinnatihoodcleaning.com
SIC: **7349** Exhaust hood or fan cleaning

(G-2606)
EGP 2022 VEHICLE INC (PA)
3874 Paxton Ave Unit 9299 (45209-7512)
P.O. Box 9299 (45209-0299)
PHONE..................866 538-1909
Michael Foster, *Pr*
Elizabeth Lundberg, *CFO*
EMP: 48 EST: 2003
SALES (est): 620.64K
SALES (corp-wide): 620.64K **Privately Held**
Web: www.hci.org
SIC: **8621** Professional organizations

(G-2607)
EIGHT ELEVEN GROUP LLC
Also Called: Technical Youth
455 Delta Ave Fl 4 (45226-1127)
PHONE..................513 533-7300
Kenny Holocher, *Brnch Mgr*
EMP: 150
SALES (corp-wide): 101.59MM **Privately Held**
Web: www.eightelevengroup.com
SIC: **7379** Online services technology consultants
PA: Eight Eleven Group, Llc
   6215 N College Ave
   Indianapolis IN 46220
   317 475-0079

(G-2608)
EKCO CLEANING INC
4055 Executive Park Dr Ste 240 (45241-4029)
PHONE..................513 733-8882
Peter Campanella, *Pr*
C Robert Kidder, *Ch Bd*
EMP: 220 EST: 1926
SALES (est): 33.9MM
SALES (corp-wide): 995.27MM **Privately Held**
SIC: **5199** 2392 3991 Broom, mop, and paint handles; Mops, floor and dust; Brushes, household or industrial
HQ: Instant Brands Llc
   3025 Highland Pkwy # 700
   Downers Grove IL 60515
   847 233-8600

(G-2609)
ELECTRIC MOTOR TECH LLC (PA)
Also Called: Emt
5217 Beech St (45217-1021)
PHONE..................513 821-9999
F Daniel Freshley, *Managing Member*
Dwaine York, *
Andy Butz, *
EMP: 42 EST: 1999
SQ FT: 30,000
SALES (est): 11.1MM
SALES (corp-wide): 11.1MM **Privately Held**
Web: www.electricmotortech.com
SIC: **7629** 5063 Electrical repair shops; Motors, electric

(G-2610)
ELECTRIC SERVICE CO INC
5331 Hetzell St (45227-1513)
PHONE..................513 271-6387
Helen Snyder, *Pr*
EMP: 34 EST: 1912
SQ FT: 35,000
SALES (est): 2.41MM **Privately Held**
Web: www.elscotransformers.com
SIC: **7629** 3677 3621 Electronic equipment repair; Transformers power supply, electronic type; Phase or rotary converters (electrical equipment)

(G-2611)
ELEVAR DESIGN GROUP INC
Also Called: Sfa Architects, Inc.
555 Carr St (45203-1815)
PHONE..................513 721-0600
Emilio Thomas Fernandez, *CEO*
EMP: 49 EST: 1967
SQ FT: 35,656
SALES (est): 11.55MM **Privately Held**
Web: www.elevar.com
SIC: **7389** 8712 8711 Design services; Architectural engineering; Engineering services

(G-2612)
EMCOR FACILITIES SERVICES INC
15 W Voorhees St (45215-4834)
PHONE..................513 948-8469
EMP: 69
SALES (corp-wide): 12.58B **Publicly Held**
Web: www.emcorfacilities.com
SIC: **1731** General electrical contractor
HQ: Emcor Facilities Services, Inc.
   9655 Reading Rd
   Cincinnati OH 45215
   888 846-9462

(G-2613)
EMCOR FACILITIES SERVICES INC (HQ)
Also Called: Viox Services
9655 Reading Rd (45215-3513)
PHONE..................888 846-9462
Michael Mcelrath, *Pr*
Tim Viox, *
Frank Riley, *
Brian Johnston, *
EMP: 100 EST: 1946
SQ FT: 38,000
SALES (est): 142.73MM
SALES (corp-wide): 12.58B **Publicly Held**
Web: www.emcorfacilities.com
SIC: **7349** Janitorial service, contract basis
PA: Emcor Group, Inc.
   301 Merritt 7
   Norwalk CT 06851
   203 849-7800

GEOGRAPHIC SECTION
Cincinnati - Hamilton County (G-2635)

(G-2614)
EMERALD HILTON DAVIS LLC
Also Called: Emerald Specialties Group
2235 Langdon Farm Rd (45237-4712)
PHONE.................................513 841-0057
James Donnelly, *Managing Member*
▲ **EMP:** 70 **EST:** 2006
SALES (est): 38.67MM **Privately Held**
SIC: 5169 Chemicals and allied products, nec
HQ: Dystar L.P.
  9844 Southern Pine Blvd A
  Charlotte NC 28273

(G-2615)
EMERITUS CORPORATION
Also Called: The Lodge of Montgomery
12050 Montgomery Rd Ofc (45249-2100)
PHONE.................................513 683-9966
Betty Hudson, *Brnch Mgr*
EMP: 51
SALES (corp-wide): 2.83B **Publicly Held**
Web: www.brookdale.com
SIC: 6513 8052 Retirement hotel operation; Intermediate care facilities
HQ: Emeritus Corporation
  6737 W Wa St Ste 2300
  Milwaukee WI 53214

(G-2616)
EMERSION DESIGN LLC
Also Called: Emersion Design
310 Culvert St Ste 100 (45202-2229)
PHONE.................................513 841-9100
EMP: 28 **EST:** 2007
SQ FT: 5,000
SALES (est): 4.9MM **Privately Held**
Web: www.emersiondesign.com
SIC: 8711 7389 8748 8712 Structural engineering; Design services; Urban planning and consulting services; Architectural services

(G-2617)
EMPOWER LEARN CREATE INC
3310 Ruther Ave (45220-2111)
PHONE.................................513 961-2825
Kelly Hibham, *Pr*
EMP: 27 **EST:** 1985
SALES (est): 2.44MM **Privately Held**
Web: www.empowerlearncreate.org
SIC: 8351 Preschool center

(G-2618)
EMPOWER MEDIA PARTNERS LLC (PA)
15 E 14th St (45202-7001)
PHONE.................................513 871-7779
Jim Price, *Pr*
Joseph Lowry, *
EMP: 150 **EST:** 1986
SQ FT: 40,000
SALES (est): 64.28MM
SALES (corp-wide): 64.28MM **Privately Held**
Web: www.empowermm.com
SIC: 7319 Media buying service

(G-2619)
ENCLOSURE SUPPLIERS LLC
Also Called: Champion
12119 Champion Way (45241-6419)
PHONE.................................513 782-3900
▲ **EMP:** 30 **EST:** 1990
SQ FT: 160,000
SALES (est): 12.14MM **Privately Held**
Web: www.esi-blinds.com
SIC: 3448 5031 3231 Prefabricated metal buildings; Lumber, plywood, and millwork; Products of purchased glass
HQ: Champion Opco, Llc
  12121 Champion Way
  Cincinnati OH 45241
  513 327-7338

(G-2620)
ENERFAB LLC (PA)
4430 Chickering Ave (45232-1931)
PHONE.................................513 641-0500
Wendell R Bell, *CEO*
Dave Herche, *
Jeffrey P Hock, *
Daniel J Sillies, *
Mark Schoettmer, *
◆ **EMP:** 330 **EST:** 1912
SQ FT: 180,000
SALES (est): 550.89MM
SALES (corp-wide): 550.89MM **Privately Held**
Web: www.enerfab.com
SIC: 3443 1629 1541 1711 Tanks, standard or custom fabricated: metal plate; Power plant construction; Industrial buildings and warehouses; Mechanical contractor

(G-2621)
ENERFAB POWER & INDUSTRIAL INC
4955 Spring Grove Ave (45232-1925)
PHONE.................................513 470-5526
EMP: 1044
SALES (corp-wide): 550.89MM **Privately Held**
SIC: 1711 Solar energy contractor
HQ: Enerfab Power & Industrial, Inc.
  4430 Chickering Ave
  Cincinnati OH 45232
  513 641-0500

(G-2622)
ENERFAB PROCESS SOLUTIONS LLC
4430 Chickering Ave (45232)
PHONE.................................513 641-0500
EMP: 60
SALES (corp-wide): 564.11K **Privately Held**
SIC: 1542 Nonresidential construction, nec
PA: Enerfab Process Solutions, Llc
  4955 Spring Grove Avenue
  Cincinnati OH

(G-2623)
ENSEMBLE HEALTH PARTNERS INC
11511 Reed Hartman Hwy (45241-2421)
PHONE.................................704 765-3715
Judson Ivy, *Pr*
Allyson Evenson, *CAO*
Shannon White, *COO*
Robert Snead, *CFO*
EMP: 6600 **EST:** 2021
SQ FT: 400,296
SALES (est): 141.01MM **Privately Held**
Web: www.ensemblehp.com
SIC: 8741 Management services

(G-2624)
ENSEMBLE RCM LLC
Also Called: Ensemble Health Partners
11511 Reed Hartman Hwy (45241-2421)
PHONE.................................704 765-3715
Judson Ivy, *Managing Member*
Shannon White, *
John Erickson, *
Lisa Carter, *
Pieter Schouten, *Chief Analytics Officer*
EMP: 7000 **EST:** 2014
SALES (est): 222.31MM
SALES (corp-wide): 6.92B **Privately Held**
Web: www.ensemblehp.com
SIC: 8741 Financial management for business
PA: Bon Secours Mercy Health, Inc.
  1701 Mercy Health Pl
  Cincinnati OH 45237
  513 956-3729

(G-2625)
ENSEMBLE THEATRE CINCINNATI
Also Called: ETC
1127 Vine St (45202-7226)
PHONE.................................513 421-3555
D Lynn Meyers, *Dir*
EMP: 32 **EST:** 1986
SQ FT: 8,400
SALES (est): 2.57MM **Privately Held**
Web: www.ensemblecincinnati.org
SIC: 7922 Theatrical companies

(G-2626)
ENVIRNMNTAL SLTONS INNVTONS IN (PA)
4525 Este Ave (45232-1762)
PHONE.................................513 451-1777
Virgil Brack Junior, *CEO*
Taina Pankiewicz, *
EMP: 34 **EST:** 2003
SQ FT: 8,000
SALES (est): 7.76MM
SALES (corp-wide): 7.76MM **Privately Held**
Web: www.environmentalsi.com
SIC: 8748 Environmental consultant

(G-2627)
ENVIRONMENTAL ENTERPRISES INC (PA)
Also Called: E E I
10163 Cincinnati Dayton Rd (45241-1005)
PHONE.................................513 772-2818
EMP: 140 **EST:** 1976
SALES (est): 17.04MM
SALES (corp-wide): 17.04MM **Privately Held**
Web: www.eeienv.com
SIC: 8734 4212 4953 4959 Hazardous waste testing; Hazardous waste transport; Chemical detoxification; Toxic or hazardous waste cleanup

(G-2628)
ENVIRONMENTAL QUALITY MGT (DH)
Also Called: E Q M
1800 Carillion Blvd (45240-2788)
PHONE.................................513 825-7500
Scott Harris, *Pr*
EMP: 88 **EST:** 1990
SQ FT: 30,000
SALES (est): 50.14MM
SALES (corp-wide): 2.72B **Privately Held**
Web: www.eqm.com
SIC: 8748 1799 Environmental consultant; Asbestos removal and encapsulation
HQ: Asrc Industrial Services, Llc
  1501 W Ftnhead Pkwy # 550
  Tempe AZ 85282
  707 644-7455

(G-2629)
ENVISION
3030 W Fork Rd (45211-1944)
PHONE.................................513 389-7500
EMP: 35 **EST:** 2018
SALES (est): 453.64K **Privately Held**
Web: www.envisionohio.org
SIC: 8699 Charitable organization

(G-2630)
ENVISION CORPORATION
Also Called: Envision Children
8 Enfield St (45218-1435)
PHONE.................................513 772-5437
Matthew Hughes, *Ex Dir*
EMP: 53 **EST:** 2003
SQ FT: 2,000
SALES (est): 1.37MM **Privately Held**
Web: www.envisionchildren.org
SIC: 8748 Testing service, educational or personnel

(G-2631)
EPIPHEO INC
Also Called: Epipheo
2681 Cyclorama Dr (45211-8314)
PHONE.................................888 687-7620
Lucas Cole, *Prin*
John Herman, *
Jeremy Pryor, *
Stephen Mowry, *
Benjamin Crawford, *
EMP: 30 **EST:** 2009
SALES (est): 5.16MM **Privately Held**
Web: www.epipheo.com
SIC: 7311 8742 Advertising agencies; Marketing consulting services

(G-2632)
EPISCOPAL RETIREMENT HOMES INC
Also Called: Marjorie P Lee Rtirement Cmnty
3550 Shaw Ave Ofc (45208-1416)
PHONE.................................513 871-2090
Ginny Uehlin, *Admn*
EMP: 140
SQ FT: 2,850
SALES (est): 37.2MM **Privately Held**
Web: www.episcopalretirement.com
SIC: 6513 Retirement hotel operation
PA: Episcopal Retirement Homes, Inc.
  3870 Virginia Ave Ste 2
  Cincinnati OH 45227
  513 271-9610

(G-2633)
EPISCOPAL RETIREMENT HOMES INC
Also Called: Dupree House
3939 Erie Ave (45208-1954)
PHONE.................................513 561-6363
Laura Lamb, *Brnch Mgr*
EMP: 126
SALES (corp-wide): 37.2MM **Privately Held**
Web: www.episcopalretirement.com
SIC: 6513 Retirement hotel operation
PA: Episcopal Retirement Homes, Inc.
  3870 Virginia Ave Ste 2
  Cincinnati OH 45227
  513 271-9610

(G-2634)
EPISCPAL RTRMENT SVCS AFFRDBL
3870 Virginia Ave (45227-3431)
PHONE.................................513 271-9610
EMP: 68 **EST:** 2012
SALES (est): 8.17MM **Privately Held**
Web: www.episcopalretirement.com
SIC: 6513 Retirement hotel operation

(G-2635)
ERNEST V THOMAS JR (PA)
Also Called: Thomas & Thomas
2323 Park Ave (45206-2711)
PHONE.................................513 961-5311
Ernest V Thomas Iii, *Owner*
EMP: 50 **EST:** 1947
SQ FT: 4,500
SALES (est): 2.14MM
SALES (corp-wide): 2.14MM **Privately Held**

Cincinnati - Hamilton County (G-2636)

Web: www.tt-law.com
SIC: 8111 General practice attorney, lawyer

(G-2636)
ERNST & YOUNG LLP
1900 Scripps Ctr (45202-4065)
PHONE..................513 612-1594
EMP: 42
Web: www.ey.com
SIC: 8721 Certified public accountant
HQ: Ernst & Young Llp
1 Manhattan W Fl 6
New York NY 10001
703 747-0049

(G-2637)
ERNST & YOUNG LLP
Also Called: Ey
221 E 4th St Ste 2900 (45202-4095)
PHONE..................513 612-1400
Stanley Brown, Brnch Mgr
EMP: 157
Web: www.ey.com
SIC: 8721 8742 Certified public accountant;
Business management consultant
HQ: Ernst & Young Llp
1 Manhattan W Fl 6
New York NY 10001
703 747-0049

(G-2638)
EUCLID HEALTH CARE INC (PA)
Also Called: Madeira Health Care Center
7885 Camargo Rd (45243-2651)
PHONE..................513 561-6400
Harold Sosna, Pr
EMP: 128 EST: 1970
SALES (est): 9.34MM
SALES (corp-wide): 9.34MM **Privately Held**
SIC: 8051 Skilled nursing care facilities

(G-2639)
EVANS LANDSCAPING INC
3700 Round Bottom Rd (45244-2413)
PHONE..................513 271-1119
EMP: 50 EST: 1980
SALES (est): 20.65MM **Privately Held**
Web: www.evanslandscaping.com
SIC: 5191 5261 0781 1794 Farm supplies;
Lawn and garden supplies; Landscape
services; Excavation work

(G-2640)
EVANSTON BLLDOGS YUTH FTBALL A
3060 Durrell Ave (45207-1716)
PHONE..................513 254-9500
Peterson Mingo, Prin
Milan Lanier, *
EMP: 30 EST: 2017
SALES (est): 217.61K **Privately Held**
Web: www.evanstoncinci.org
SIC: 8699 Charitable organization

(G-2641)
EVERGREEN PHARMACEUTICAL LLC (DH)
201 E 4th St Ste 900 (45202-4160)
PHONE..................513 719-2600
Carl Wood, Pr
EMP: 300 EST: 1962
SQ FT: 40,000
SALES (est): 95.51MM
SALES (corp-wide): 357.78B **Publicly Held**
SIC: 5122 Pharmaceuticals
HQ: Omnicare Holding Company
1105 N Market St Ste 1300
Cincinnati OH 45202

(G-2642)
EVERGREEN PHRM CAL LLC (DH)
201 E 4th St Ste 900 (45202-4160)
PHONE..................513 719-2600
Elizabeth A Haley, Pr
EMP: 30 EST: 2004
SALES (est): 4.61MM
SALES (corp-wide): 357.78B **Publicly Held**
SIC: 5122 Pharmaceuticals
HQ: Omnicare Holding Company
1105 N Market St Ste 1300
Cincinnati OH 45202

(G-2643)
EVERY CHILD SUCCEEDS INC
3333 Burnet Ave (45229-3026)
PHONE..................513 636-2830
Judith Van Ginkle, Pr
EMP: 32 EST: 1999
SALES (est): 7.96MM **Privately Held**
Web: www.everychildsucceeds.org
SIC: 8082 Home health care services

(G-2644)
EXECUTIVE JET MANAGEMENT INC (DH)
4556 Airport Rd (45226-1601)
PHONE..................513 979-6600
Robert Molsbergen, Pr
Christine Leber, *
Colleen Nissl, *
EMP: 280 EST: 1988
SQ FT: 78,000
SALES (est): 127.04MM
SALES (corp-wide): 364.48B **Publicly Held**
Web: www.executivejetmanagement.com
SIC: 4522 8741 4581 4512 Flying charter
service; Management services; Airports,
flying fields, and services; Air
transportation, scheduled
HQ: Netjets Inc.
4111 Bridgeway Ave
Columbus OH 43219

(G-2645)
F L EMMERT COMPANY
2007 Dunlap St (45214-2309)
PHONE..................513 721-5808
Ken Rod, VP Opers
EMP: 27 EST: 2011
SALES (est): 3.48MM **Privately Held**
Web: www.emmert.com
SIC: 0723 Crop preparation services for market

(G-2646)
FALU CORPORATION
Also Called: Falu Security
9435 Waterstone Blvd Ste 140 (45249-8229)
PHONE..................502 641-8106
Hector Falu, CEO
EMP: 33 EST: 2005
SALES (est): 1.51MM **Privately Held**
Web: www.falucorporation.com
SIC: 7381 Security guard service

(G-2647)
FAMILY MOTOR COACH ASSN INC (PA)
8291 Clough Pike (45244-2756)
PHONE..................513 474-3622
Lana Makin, CEO
EMP: 46 EST: 1963
SQ FT: 22,000
SALES (est): 14.9MM
SALES (corp-wide): 14.9MM **Privately Held**

Web: www.fmca.com
SIC: 8641 2721 Social associations;
Magazines: publishing and printing

(G-2648)
FAMILY SERVICE (PA)
Also Called: United Way
3730 Glenway Ave (45205-1354)
PHONE..................513 381-6300
Arlene Herman, Pr
John Sarra, *
Mark Schneider, *
EMP: 50 EST: 1879
SQ FT: 10,500
SALES (est): 416.56K
SALES (corp-wide): 416.56K **Privately Held**
Web: www.familyservicecincy.org
SIC: 8322 Family counseling services

(G-2649)
FATH MANAGEMENT COMPANY
Also Called: Aspen Village Apartments
2703 Erlene Dr Ofc (45238-2800)
PHONE..................513 662-3724
Anita Qually, Mgr
EMP: 33
SALES (corp-wide): 23.7MM **Privately Held**
Web: www.fathproperties.com
SIC: 6513 Apartment hotel operation
PA: Fath Management Company
255 E 5th St Ste 2300
Cincinnati OH 45202
513 562-8490

(G-2650)
FAY LIMITED PARTNERSHIP
Also Called: Fay Apartments
3710 President Dr (45225-1016)
PHONE..................513 542-8333
Jerry Bowen, Mgr
EMP: 30
SQ FT: 2,501
SALES (corp-wide): 1.86MM **Privately Held**
SIC: 6513 Apartment building operators
PA: Fay Limited Partnership
36 E 4th St 1320
Cincinnati OH 45202
513 241-1911

(G-2651)
FAY LIMITED PARTNERSHIP (PA)
36 E 4th St # 1320 (45202-3725)
PHONE..................513 241-1911
David Hendy, Pt
Ken Kerr, Pt
EMP: 35 EST: 1986
SQ FT: 1,000,000
SALES (est): 1.86MM
SALES (corp-wide): 1.86MM **Privately Held**
SIC: 6513 6531 Apartment building operators
; Real estate agents and managers

(G-2652)
FC CINCINNATI LTD
14 E 4th St 3rd Fl (45202-3702)
PHONE..................513 977-5425
EMP: 243 EST: 1995
SALES (est): 1.51MM **Privately Held**
Web: www.fccincinnati.com
SIC: 7941 Soccer club

(G-2653)
FEDERAL CARD SERVICES LLC
263 Stille Dr (45233-1646)
PHONE..................513 429-4459
Matias Gainza Eurnekian, CEO
Phil Emery, COO

EMP: 50 EST: 2014
SALES (est): 4.8MM **Privately Held**
Web: www.fcsmetalcard.com
SIC: 7389 Credit card service

(G-2654)
FEDERAL HOME LN BNK CINCINNATI (PA)
221 E 4th St (45201)
P.O. Box 598 (45201)
PHONE..................513 852-7500
Andrew S Howell, Pr
Donald J Mullineaux, *
James A England, *
Donald R Able, Ex VP
Stephen J Sponaugle, Ex VP
EMP: 200 EST: 1932
SQ FT: 79,000
SALES (est): 6.96B
SALES (corp-wide): 6.96B **Privately Held**
Web: www.fhlbcin.com
SIC: 6111 Federal and federally sponsored credit agencies

(G-2655)
FEDERAL HOME LN BNK CINCINNATI
1000 Atrium 2 (45202)
P.O. Box 598 (45201-0598)
PHONE..................513 852-5719
Charles Thiemann, Mgr
EMP: 230
SALES (corp-wide): 6.96B **Privately Held**
Web: www.fhlbcin.com
SIC: 6022 State commercial banks
PA: Federal Home Loan Bank Of Cincinnati
221 E 4th St 600 Atrium T
Cincinnati OH 45201
513 852-7500

(G-2656)
FEDERAL RESERVE BANK CLEVELAND
150 E 4th St Fl 1 (45202-4080)
P.O. Box 999 (45201-0999)
PHONE..................513 721-4787
Barbara Henshaw, Genl Mgr
EMP: 225
Web: www.clevelandfed.org
SIC: 6035 Federal savings banks
HQ: Federal Reserve Bank Of Cleveland
1455 E 6th St
Cleveland OH 44114
216 579-2000

(G-2657)
FENTON RIGGING & CONTG INC
Also Called: Fenton
2150 Langdon Farm Rd (45237-4791)
PHONE..................513 631-5500
Michael Besl, Pr
William C Besl, *
Timothy W Besl, *
▲ EMP: 150 EST: 1893
SQ FT: 6,800
SALES (est): 36.72MM **Privately Held**
Web: www.fenton1898.com
SIC: 1622 1796 Bridge, tunnel, and elevated
highway construction; Machine moving and rigging

(G-2658)
FERGUSON ENTERPRISES LLC
Also Called: Ferguson Supply
11860 Mosteller Rd Ste B (45241-1525)
PHONE..................513 771-6000
Billy Brinck, Brnch Mgr
EMP: 44
SALES (corp-wide): 29.73B **Privately Held**
Web: www.ferguson.com

SIC: 5074 5085 Plumbing fittings and supplies; Valves and fittings
HQ: Ferguson Enterprises, Llc
751 Lakefront Cmns
Newport News VA 23606
757 969-4011

(G-2659)
FERN EXPOSITION SERVICES LLC (HQ)
Also Called: George Fern Company
645 Linn St (45203-1722)
PHONE..................................888 621-3376
Aaron Bludworth, Pr
Mark Epstein, *
Sheila Pannell, *
Michael Cox, *
John Barclay, *
▲ EMP: 30 EST: 2005
SQ FT: 500,000
SALES (est): 44.05MM
SALES (corp-wide): 148.27MM Privately Held
Web: www.fernexpo.com
SIC: 7359 Electronic equipment rental, except computers
PA: Nth Degree, Inc.
3237 Stllite Blvd Ste 600
Duluth GA 30096
404 296-5282

(G-2660)
FIDUCIUS
151 W 4th St Ste 300 (45202-2734)
PHONE..................................513 645-5400
EMP: 28 EST: 2019
SALES (est): 252.36K Privately Held
Web: www.getfiducius.com
SIC: 7389 Financial services

(G-2661)
FIELDS DIALYSIS LLC
Also Called: Norwood Dialysis
2300 Wall St Ste 0 (45212-2781)
PHONE..................................513 531-2111
Jim Hilger, Brnch Mgr
EMP: 37
SIC: 8092 Kidney dialysis centers
HQ: Fields Dialysis, Llc
5901 Montclair Blvd # 10
Milford OH 45150

(G-2662)
FIFTH THIRD BANCORP (PA)
38 Fountain Square Plz (45263)
PHONE..................................800 972-3030
Timothy N Spence, Ch Bd
Bryan Preston, Ex VP
Mark D Hazel, Ex VP
Nancy C Pinckney, Chief Human Resources Officer
Susan B Zaunbrecher, CLO
▲ EMP: 2047 EST: 1975
SALES (est): 12.64B
SALES (corp-wide): 12.64B Publicly Held
Web: www.53.com
SIC: 6022 State trust companies accepting deposits, commercial

(G-2663)
FIFTH THIRD BANK NATIONAL ASSN (DH)
Also Called: Fifth Third Bank
38 Fountain Square Plz (45202-3102)
PHONE..................................513 579-5203
Timothy N Spence, Pr
Don Coleman, *
Greg Carmichael, *
Brandon Ferrera, *
Kala Gibson, CORPORATE RESPONSIBILITY*

▲ EMP: 1800 EST: 1858
SALES (est): 9.37B
SALES (corp-wide): 12.64B Publicly Held
Web: locations.53.com
SIC: 6022 State trust companies accepting deposits, commercial
HQ: Fifth Third Financial Corporation
38 Fountain Sq Plz
Cincinnati OH 45202
513 579-5300

(G-2664)
FIFTH THIRD BANK NATIONAL ASSN
Also Called: Fifth Third Business Capital
38 Fountain Square Plz (45263-0001)
PHONE..................................513 579-5203
George Schaefer, Prin
EMP: 100
SALES (corp-wide): 12.64B Publicly Held
Web: locations.53.com
SIC: 6022 State trust companies accepting deposits, commercial
HQ: Fifth Third Bank, National Association
38 Fountain Square Plz
Cincinnati OH 45202
513 579-5203

(G-2665)
FIFTH THIRD EQUIPMENT FIN CO (DH)
38 Fountain Square Plz Ste 1090a4 (45202-3102)
P.O. Box 1com3a (45202)
PHONE..................................800 972-3030
George Schaefer Junior, Pr
David Jackson, Sr VP
Paul Reynolds, Sec
▲ EMP: 44 EST: 1972
SQ FT: 1,000
SALES (est): 17.95MM
SALES (corp-wide): 12.64B Publicly Held
SIC: 7359 Equipment rental and leasing, nec
HQ: Fifth Third Bank, National Association
38 Fountain Square Plz
Cincinnati OH 45202
513 579-5203

(G-2666)
FIFTH THIRD FINANCIAL CORP (HQ)
38 Fountain Square Plz (45202)
PHONE..................................513 579-5300
George A Schaefer Junior, Pr
▲ EMP: 500 EST: 2001
SQ FT: 30,000
SALES (est): 12.24K
SALES (corp-wide): 12.64B Publicly Held
SIC: 6022 State commercial banks
PA: Fifth Third Bancorp
38 Fountain Square Plz
Cincinnati OH 45263
800 972-3030

(G-2667)
FIFTH THIRD SECURITIES INC
2998 Cunningham Rd (45241-3384)
PHONE..................................513 346-2775
EMP: 56
SALES (corp-wide): 12.64B Publicly Held
Web: securitiesadvisors.53.com
SIC: 6211 Security brokers and dealers
HQ: Fifth Third Securities, Inc.
34 Fountain Square Plz
Cincinnati OH 45202
888 889-1025

(G-2668)
FIFTH THIRD SECURITIES INC
7101 Miami Ave (45243-2616)
PHONE..................................513 272-7755
EMP: 56
SALES (corp-wide): 12.64B Publicly Held

Web: securitiesadvisors.53.com
SIC: 6211 Bond dealers and brokers
HQ: Fifth Third Securities, Inc.
34 Fountain Square Plz
Cincinnati OH 45202
888 889-1025

(G-2669)
FINIT GROUP LLC
Also Called: Finit Solutions
8050 Hosbrook Rd Ste 326 (45236-2907)
PHONE..................................513 793-4648
EMP: 60 EST: 2002
SALES (est): 5.29MM Privately Held
Web: www.finit.com
SIC: 8742 Business management consultant

(G-2670)
FIRST CARE OHIO LLC
955 Redna Ter Ste 1 (45215-1112)
PHONE..................................513 563-8811
Dennis Lee Young, Prin
EMP: 72 EST: 2005
SALES (est): 10.5MM Privately Held
Web: www.firstcare.us
SIC: 4119 Ambulance service

(G-2671)
FIRST FINANCIAL BANK
255 E 5th St Ste 1100 (45202-4138)
PHONE..................................877 322-9530
Archie Brown Junior, Pr
EMP: 1366 EST: 2016
SALES (est): 205.2MM
SALES (corp-wide): 1.12B Publicly Held
Web: www.bankatfirst.com
SIC: 6022 State trust companies accepting deposits, commercial
PA: First Financial Bancorp.
255 E 5th St Ste 800
Cincinnati OH 45202
877 322-9530

(G-2672)
FIRST FINANCIAL BANK NAT ASSN (HQ)
255 E 5th St Ste 700 (45202)
PHONE..................................877 322-9530
Claude E Davis, Pr
EMP: 228 EST: 2002
SALES (est): 772.95MM
SALES (corp-wide): 1.12B Publicly Held
Web: www.bankatfirst.com
SIC: 6022 State commercial banks
PA: First Financial Bancorp.
255 E 5th St Ste 800
Cincinnati OH 45202
877 322-9530

(G-2673)
FIRST GROUP AMERICA
4105 Hoffman Ave (45236-2543)
P.O. Box 14009 (45250-0009)
PHONE..................................908 281-4589
EMP: 41 EST: 2018
SALES (est): 1.23MM Privately Held
SIC: 7011 Hotels and motels

(G-2674)
FIRST GROUP INVESTMENT PARTNR (DH)
600 Vine St Ste 1200 (45202-2474)
PHONE..................................513 241-2200
Alton Sloan, Pt
Phil Crookes, Pt
EMP: 100 EST: 1999
SALES (est): 31.05MM
SALES (corp-wide): 5.71B Privately Held
Web: www.firstgroupplc.com

SIC: 7513 4212 4213 4225 Truck leasing, without drivers; Local trucking, without storage; Trucking, except local; General warehousing
HQ: Firstbus Investments Limited
Oldmixon Crescent
Weston-Super-Mare BS24
122 465-0100

(G-2675)
FIRST SERVICES INC
600 Vine St Ste 1200 (45202-2474)
PHONE..................................513 241-2200
Brad Thomas, Pr
Wayne Johnson, *
EMP: 5036 EST: 2003
SALES (est): 1.05MM
SALES (corp-wide): 5.71B Privately Held
Web: www.transdevna.com
SIC: 8741 7539 Management services; Automotive repair shops, nec
HQ: Firstgroup Usa, Inc.
191 Rosa Parks St
Cincinnati OH 45202

(G-2676)
FIRST STAR LOGISTICS LLC (PA)
11461 Northlake Dr (45249-1641)
P.O. Box 498459 (45249-7459)
PHONE..................................812 637-3251
Kevin Bernhardt, CEO
Todd Hammerstrom, *
Alex Peralta, *
EMP: 45 EST: 2008
SALES (est): 28.21MM Privately Held
Web: www.firststarlogistics.com
SIC: 4731 Freight transportation arrangement

(G-2677)
FIRST STUDENT INC
1801 Transpark Dr (45229-1239)
PHONE..................................513 531-6888
John Nardini, Brnch Mgr
EMP: 96
Web: www.firststudentinc.com
SIC: 4151 School buses
PA: First Student, Inc.
191 Rosa Parks St Ste 800
Cincinnati OH 45202

(G-2678)
FIRST STUDENT INC
Also Called: Laidlaw Education Services
100 Hamilton Blvd (45215-5471)
PHONE..................................513 761-6100
Lisa Jajowka, Mgr
EMP: 33
Web: www.firststudentinc.com
SIC: 4151 School buses
PA: First Student, Inc.
191 Rosa Parks St Ste 800
Cincinnati OH 45202

(G-2679)
FIRST STUDENT INC
11786 Highway Dr (45241-2005)
PHONE..................................513 554-0105
EMP: 97
Web: www.firststudentinc.com
SIC: 4151 School buses
PA: First Student, Inc.
191 Rosa Parks St Ste 800
Cincinnati OH 45202

(G-2680)
FIRST STUDENT INC
Also Called: First Group America
100 Hamilton Blvd (45215-5471)
PHONE..................................513 761-5136
B Echelbarger, Brnch Mgr
EMP: 37

Cincinnati - Hamilton County (G-2681) GEOGRAPHIC SECTION

Web: www.firststudentinc.com
SIC: 4151 School buses
PA: First Student, Inc.
191 Rosa Parks St Ste 800
Cincinnati OH 45202

(G-2681)
FIRST STUDENT INC (PA)
191 Rosa Parks St Ste 800 (45202-2573)
PHONE..................513 241-2200
Paul Osland, Pr
Scot Spivey, Sr VP
Dean Suhre, *
Michael Petrucci, *
Leonardo Perez, VP
EMP: 50 EST: 1983
SQ FT: 61,461
SALES (est): 714.72MM Privately Held
Web: www.firststudentinc.com
SIC: 4151 4141 School buses; Local bus charter service

(G-2682)
FIRST TRANSIT INC (DH)
600 Vine St Ste 1400 (45202-2426)
P.O. Box 22192 Network Pl (60673-0001)
PHONE..................513 241-2200
Brad Thomas, Pr
Christian Gartner, Treas
Jim Tippen, CFO
◆ EMP: 75 EST: 1969
SQ FT: 15,000
SALES (est): 904.78MM
SALES (corp-wide): 4.23MM Privately Held
Web: www.transdevna.com
SIC: 8742 7539 8741 Transportation consultant; Automotive repair shops, nec; Management services
HQ: Transdev North America, Inc.
720 E Bttrfeld Rd Ste 300
Lombard IL 60148
630 571-7070

(G-2683)
FIRST VEHICLE SERVICES INC (DH)
600 Vine St Ste 1400 (45202-2426)
PHONE..................513 241-2200
Brad Thomas, Pr
Dale Domish, *
EMP: 200 EST: 1981
SALES (est): 53.85MM
SALES (corp-wide): 4.23MM Privately Held
Web: www.transdevna.com
SIC: 7549 Automotive maintenance services
HQ: First Transit, Inc.
600 Vine St Ste 1400
Cincinnati OH 45202
513 241-2200

(G-2684)
FIRSTGROUP AMERICA INC (DH)
Also Called: First Group of America
191 Rosa Parks St (45202-2573)
PHONE..................513 241-2200
Dennis Maple, Pr
Christian Gartner, *
Bruce Rasch, *
EMP: 58 EST: 1999
SALES (est): 119.39MM
SALES (corp-wide): 5.71B Privately Held
Web: www.firststudentinc.com
SIC: 4151 4111 4119 4131 School buses; Local and suburban transit; Local passenger transportation, nec; Intercity and rural bus transportation
HQ: Firstgroup Usa, Inc.
191 Rosa Parks St
Cincinnati OH 45202

(G-2685)
FIRSTGROUP AMERICA INC
Also Called: Laidlaw Transportation
191 Rosa Parks St (45202-2573)
PHONE..................513 419-8611
Martin Gilbert, Ch
EMP: 5063
SALES (corp-wide): 5.71B Privately Held
Web: www.firststudentinc.com
SIC: 4151 School buses
HQ: Firstgroup America, Inc.
191 Rosa Parks St
Cincinnati OH 45202
513 241-2200

(G-2686)
FIRSTGROUP AMERICA INC
705 Central Ave (45202-1967)
PHONE..................513 241-2200
Bruce Ballard, Mgr
EMP: 1767
SALES (corp-wide): 5.71B Privately Held
Web: www.firststudentinc.com
SIC: 4151 4111 4119 School buses; Local and suburban transit; Local passenger transportation, nec
HQ: Firstgroup America, Inc.
191 Rosa Parks St
Cincinnati OH 45202
513 241-2200

(G-2687)
FIRSTGROUP USA INC (HQ)
Also Called: First Transit
191 Rosa Parks St (45202-2573)
PHONE..................513 241-2200
Bruce Ballard, CEO
Tim O'toole, Ch
EMP: 425 EST: 1999
SALES (est): 1.23B
SALES (corp-wide): 5.71B Privately Held
Web: www.firstgroupplc.com
SIC: 7513 4212 4213 4225 Truck leasing, without drivers; Local trucking, without storage; Trucking, except local; General warehousing
PA: Firstgroup Plc
395 King Street
Aberdeen AB24
122 421-9225

(G-2688)
FITWORKS HOLDING LLC
5840 Cheviot Rd (45247-6225)
PHONE..................513 923-9931
Mike Korn, Brnch Mgr
EMP: 47
Web: www.fitworks.com
SIC: 7991 Health club
PA: Fitworks Holding, Llc
849 Brainard Rd
Cleveland OH 44143

(G-2689)
FITWORKS HOLDING LLC
Also Called: Fitworks Fitness & Spt Therapy
4600 Smith Rd Ste G (45212-2784)
PHONE..................513 531-1500
EMP: 47
Web: www.fitworks.com
SIC: 7991 Health club
PA: Fitworks Holding, Llc
849 Brainard Rd
Cleveland OH 44143

(G-2690)
FLYNN CRTIF PUB ACCNTNTS PSC I
7800 E Kemper Rd Ste 150 (45249-1666)
PHONE..................513 530-9200
Richard Flynn, Prin
EMP: 29 EST: 2007

SALES (est): 940.12K Privately Held
Web: www.flynncocpa.com
SIC: 8721 Certified public accountant

(G-2691)
FORCHT BANCORP INC
2110 Beechmont Ave (45230-1621)
PHONE..................513 231-7871
EMP: 921
Web: www.forchtbank.com
SIC: 6022 State commercial banks
HQ: Forcht Bancorp, Inc.
820 Master St
Corbin KY 40701

(G-2692)
FORCHT BANK NATIONAL ASSN
Also Called: Forcht Bank
3549 Columbia Pkwy (45226-2108)
PHONE..................513 231-7871
EMP: 62
Web: www.forchtbank.com
SIC: 6022 State commercial banks
HQ: Forcht Bank, National Association
2404 Sir Barton Way
Lexington KY 40509
859 264-2265

(G-2693)
FORD DEVELOPMENT CORP (PA)
Also Called: Trend Construction
11148 Woodward Ln (45241-1876)
PHONE..................513 772-1521
Robert J Henderson, CEO
Robert F Henderson, Pr
Andrew Kloenne, VP
EMP: 64 EST: 1971
SQ FT: 22,000
SALES (est): 46.24MM
SALES (corp-wide): 46.24MM Privately Held
Web: www.forddevelopment.com
SIC: 1542 1623 1794 Commercial and office building, new construction; Water, sewer, and utility lines; Excavation work

(G-2694)
FORD DEVELOPMENT CORP
Also Called: Ford Development Real Estate
11260 Chester Rd Ste 100 (45246-4079)
PHONE..................513 207-9118
EMP: 36
SALES (est): 46.24MM Privately Held
Web: www.forddevelopment.com
SIC: 6552 Subdividers and developers, nec
PA: Ford Development Corp.
11148 Woodward Ln
Cincinnati OH 45241
513 772-1521

(G-2695)
FORT WASH INV ADVISORS INC (DH)
303 Broadway St Ste 1100 (45202)
P.O. Box 2388 (45201)
PHONE..................513 361-7600
Maribeth S Rahe, Pr
EMP: 76 EST: 1990
SALES (est): 15.4MM Privately Held
Web: www.westernsouthern.com
SIC: 6282 Investment advisory service
HQ: The Western & Southern Life Insurance Company
400 Broadway Mail Stop G
Cincinnati OH 45202
513 629-1800

(G-2696)
FOSDICK & HILMER INC
525 Vine St Ste 1100 (45202-3141)
PHONE..................513 241-5640

Jim Pretz, Ch Bd
Joel Grubbs, *
Richard M Saunders, *
EMP: 56 EST: 1905
SQ FT: 16,000
SALES (est): 9.22MM Privately Held
Web: www.fosdickandhilmer.com
SIC: 8711 Consulting engineer

(G-2697)
FOSTER & MOTLEY INC
7755 Montgomery Rd Ste 100 (45236-4291)
PHONE..................513 561-6640
David A Foster, Pr
Mark Motley, VP
EMP: 55 EST: 1990
SALES (est): 4.78MM Privately Held
Web: www.fosterandmotley.com
SIC: 6282 Investment advisory service

(G-2698)
FOUNTAIN SQUARE MGT GROUP LLC
Also Called: Fsmg
1203 Walnut St 4th Fl (45202-3775)
PHONE..................513 621-4400
Bill Donabedian, Mgr
Timothy Szilasi, *
EMP: 50 EST: 2006
SQ FT: 12,000
SALES (est): 142.13K Privately Held
Web: www.myfountainsquare.com
SIC: 7929 Entertainment service

(G-2699)
FOUR ENTERTAINMENT GROUP
1502 Vine St (45202-7020)
PHONE..................513 721-0083
EMP: 41 EST: 2020
SALES (est): 686.87K Privately Held
Web: www.foureg.com
SIC: 7929 Entertainers and entertainment groups

(G-2700)
FRAMEWORK MI INC
9435 Waterstone Blvd Ste 140 (45249-8226)
PHONE..................513 444-2165
Danielle Lydon, CEO
EMP: 30 EST: 2011
SALES (est): 2.42MM Privately Held
Web: www.frameworkmi.org
SIC: 7371 Computer software development

(G-2701)
FRCH DESIGN WORLDWIDE - CINCIN
311 Elm St Ste 600 (45202-2774)
PHONE..................513 241-3000
James R Tippmann, CEO
James R Lazzari, *
Thomas E Horwitz, *
Sherry Walker, *
EMP: 275 EST: 1968
SQ FT: 22,000
SALES (est): 47.44MM
SALES (corp-wide): 58.51MM Privately Held
Web: www.nelsonworldwide.com
SIC: 8712 House designer
PA: Nelson Worldwide, Llc
100 S Indpdnc Mall W
Philadelphia PA 19106
215 925-6562

(G-2702)
FRED A NEMANN CO
6480 Bender Rd (45233-1552)
PHONE..................513 467-9400
Fred Nemann, Pr

GEOGRAPHIC SECTION

Cincinnati - Hamilton County (G-2724)

Sandra Timler, *
Tim Nemann, *
Fred Nemann Iii, VP
EMP: 48 **EST:** 1936
SQ FT: 3,000
SALES (est): 8.84MM **Privately Held**
SIC: 1611 1623 General contractor, highway and street construction; Water, sewer, and utility lines

(G-2703)
FREDERICK STEEL COMPANY LLC
Also Called: Bfs Supply
630 Glendale Milford Rd (45215-1105)
PHONE..................513 821-6400
Burke Byer, Prin
Timothy Nagy, Sec
Jay Binder, Prin
Jeff Ginter, Prin
Jonas Allen, Prin
EMP: 60 **EST:** 2013
SALES (est): 9.24MM
SALES (corp-wide): 99.72MM **Privately Held**
Web: www.fredericksteel.com
SIC: 1791 3441 Structural steel erection; Building components, structural steel
PA: Benjamin Steel Company, Inc.
  777 Benjamin Dr
  Springfield OH 45502
  937 322-8600

(G-2704)
FREE STORE/FOOD BANK INC (PA)
3401 Rosenthal Way (45204-3500)
PHONE..................513 482-4526
John Young, Pr
EMP: 45 **EST:** 1971
SALES (est): 74.25MM
SALES (corp-wide): 74.25MM **Privately Held**
Web: www.freestorefoodbank.org
SIC: 8322 Social service center

(G-2705)
FREE STORE/FOOD BANK INC
Meyerson Food Distribution
3401 Rosenthal Way (45204-3500)
PHONE..................513 241-1064
Steve Gibbs, Mgr
EMP: 42
SALES (corp-wide): 74.25MM **Privately Held**
Web: www.freestorefoodbank.org
SIC: 8322 Social services for the handicapped
PA: Free Store/Food Bank, Inc
  3401 Rosenthal Way
  Cincinnati OH 45204
  513 482-4526

(G-2706)
FREESTORE FOODBANK INC
3401 Rosenthal Way (45204-3500)
PHONE..................513 482-4500
EMP: 50 **EST:** 1971
SALES (est): 84.72MM **Privately Held**
Web: www.freestorefoodbank.org
SIC: 8322 Social service center

(G-2707)
FREKING MYERS & REUL LLC
600 Vine St Ste 900 (45202-4404)
PHONE..................513 721-1975
Randolph H Freking, Managing Member
Sheila Smith, *
Carrie Myers, *
EMP: 27 **EST:** 1991
SQ FT: 5,360
SALES (est): 2.46MM **Privately Held**
Web: www.fmr.law

SIC: 8111 General practice attorney, lawyer

(G-2708)
FREY ELECTRIC INC
5700 Cheviot Rd Ste A (45247-7101)
P.O. Box 53785 (45253-0785)
PHONE..................513 385-0700
David Frey, Pr
EMP: 60 **EST:** 1921
SQ FT: 16,000
SALES (est): 5.54MM **Privately Held**
Web: www.freyelectric.com
SIC: 1731 General electrical contractor

(G-2709)
FROST BROWN TODD LLC (PA)
3300 Great American Tower 301 E 4th St (45202)
PHONE..................513 651-6800
John Crockett, *
Bob Bolton, *
EMP: 294 **EST:** 1919
SALES (est): 96.01MM
SALES (corp-wide): 96.01MM **Privately Held**
Web: www.frostbrowntodd.com
SIC: 8111 General practice attorney, lawyer

(G-2710)
FROST ENGINEERING INC
3408 Beekman St (45223-2425)
PHONE..................513 541-6330
EMP: 42 **EST:** 1995
SQ FT: 15,000
SALES (est): 4.32MM **Privately Held**
Web: www.frosteng.net
SIC: 3556 8711 Smokers, food processing equipment; Engineering services

(G-2711)
FUND EVALUATION GROUP LLC (PA)
201 E 5th St Ste 1600 (45202-4156)
PHONE..................513 977-4400
Mary Bascom, *
Nolan M Bean, Co-CIO*
Keith M Berlin, *
EMP: 50 **EST:** 2002
SQ FT: 12,000
SALES (est): 45.16MM
SALES (corp-wide): 45.16MM **Privately Held**
Web: www.feg.com
SIC: 6282 7371 Investment advisory service; Computer software development and applications

(G-2712)
FUNDRIVER LLC
1114 Belvedere St (45202-1702)
P.O. Box 42370 (45242-0370)
PHONE..................513 618-8718
Steven Kapor, Pr
EMP: 33 **EST:** 2006
SALES (est): 4.62MM
SALES (corp-wide): 6.98MM **Privately Held**
Web: www.fundriver.com
SIC: 5045 Computer software
PA: Evertrue, Inc.
  33 Arch St Ste 1700
  Boston MA 02110
  954 829-4245

(G-2713)
FUTBOL CLUB CINCINNATI LLC
14 E 4th St Fl 3 (45202-3702)
PHONE..................513 977-5425
Jeffrey Berding, Prin
EMP: 135 **EST:** 2015
SALES (est): 2.24MM **Privately Held**

Web: www.fccincinnati.com
SIC: 7997 Membership sports and recreation clubs

(G-2714)
GALAXY ASSOCIATES INC
3630 E Kemper Rd (45241-2011)
PHONE..................513 731-6350
William D Oeters, Pr
Philip P Dober, *
Shawn Garver, *
EMP: 103 **EST:** 2002
SQ FT: 12,300
SALES (est): 25.05MM
SALES (corp-wide): 5.31MM **Privately Held**
Web: www.duboischemicals.com
SIC: 5169 Industrial chemicals
HQ: Dubois Chemicals, Inc.
  3630 E Kemper Rd
  Sharonville OH 45241

(G-2715)
GARDEN STREET IRON & METAL INC (PA)
2885 Spring Grove Ave (45225-2222)
PHONE..................513 721-4660
Earl J Weber Junior, Pr
Margaret Weber, *
▲ **EMP:** 39 **EST:** 1959
SQ FT: 43,000
SALES (est): 8.17MM
SALES (corp-wide): 8.17MM **Privately Held**
Web: www.gardenst.com
SIC: 4953 3341 3312 Recycling, waste materials; Secondary nonferrous metals; Blast furnaces and steel mills

(G-2716)
GASLIGHT HOLDINGS LLC
Also Called: Gaslight
5910 Hamilton Ave (45224)
PHONE..................513 470-3525
Peter Kananen, CEO
Doug Alcorn, *
EMP: 50 **EST:** 2017
SALES (est): 4.85MM **Privately Held**
Web: www.teamgaslight.com
SIC: 7372 Prepackaged software

(G-2717)
GATEWAY DISTRIBUTION LLC
Also Called: Gateway Distribution
11755 Lebanon Rd (45241-2038)
PHONE..................888 806-8206
Patrick Odell, Managing Member
EMP: 70 **EST:** 2020
SALES (est): 4.91MM **Privately Held**
Web: www.gatewaydistribution.net
SIC: 4212 Truck rental with drivers

(G-2718)
GATEWAY FREIGHT FORWARDING INC
11755 Lebanon Rd (45241-2038)
PHONE..................513 248-1514
EMP: 85
SIC: 4731 Freight forwarding

(G-2719)
GBQ PARTNERS LLC
5086 Wooster Rd (45226-2327)
PHONE..................513 871-3033
William Ernst, Brnch Mgr
EMP: 116
SALES (corp-wide): 14.27MM **Privately Held**
Web: www.gbq.com

SIC: 8721 Certified public accountant
PA: Gbq Partners Llc
  230 W St Ste 700
  Columbus OH 43215
  614 221-1000

(G-2720)
GE ENGINE SERVICES DIST LLC (DH)
1 Neumann Way (45215-1900)
PHONE..................513 243-2000
Dan Heintzelnan, Managing Member
▲ **EMP:** 149 **EST:** 1996
SALES (est): 91.27MM
SALES (corp-wide): 67.95B **Publicly Held**
SIC: 5088 Aircraft engines and engine parts
HQ: Ge Engine Services, Llc
  1 Aviation Way
  Cincinnati OH 45215
  513 243-2000

(G-2721)
GE ENGINE SERVICES LLC (HQ)
Also Called: GE
1 Neumann Way (45215-1900)
Drawer Mail Drop F 17 (45215)
PHONE..................513 243-2000
◆ **EMP:** 210 **EST:** 1996
SALES (est): 992.65MM
SALES (corp-wide): 67.95B **Publicly Held**
Web: www.geaerospace.com
SIC: 7699 Aircraft and heavy equipment repair services
PA: General Electric Company
  1 Aviation Way
  Cincinnati OH 45215
  617 443-3000

(G-2722)
GEICO GENERAL INSURANCE CO
Also Called: Geico
8044 Montgomery Rd (45236-2919)
PHONE..................513 794-3426
EMP: 320
SALES (corp-wide): 364.48B **Publicly Held**
Web: www.geico.com
SIC: 6411 Insurance agents, nec
HQ: Geico General Insurance Company
  1 Geico Plz
  Washington DC 20076

(G-2723)
GENERAL ELECTRIC COMPANY
Also Called: GE
201 W Crescentville Rd (45246-1733)
PHONE..................513 977-1500
Bill Fitzgerald, Mgr
EMP: 36
SALES (corp-wide): 67.95B **Publicly Held**
Web: www.ge.com
SIC: 7629 3769 3728 3537 Aircraft electrical equipment repair; Space vehicle equipment, nec; Aircraft parts and equipment, nec; Industrial trucks and tractors
PA: General Electric Company
  1 Aviation Way
  Cincinnati OH 45215
  617 443-3000

(G-2724)
GENERAL ELECTRIC COMPANY
Also Called: GE
8700 Governors Hill Dr (45249-1363)
PHONE..................513 583-3500
Steve Dublin, Brnch Mgr
EMP: 142
SQ FT: 7,273
SALES (corp-wide): 67.95B **Publicly Held**
Web: www.ge.com

Cincinnati - Hamilton County (G-2725)

SIC: 1731 7376 Electrical work; Computer facilities management
PA: General Electric Company
1 Aviation Way
Cincinnati OH 45215
617 443-3000

(G-2725)
GENERAL ELECTRIC COMPANY (PA)
Also Called: General Electric
1 Aviation Way (45215)
PHONE.................................617 443-3000
H Lawrence Culp Junior, *Ch Bd*
Rahul Ghai, *Sr VP*
L Kevin Cox, *Chief Human Resources Officer*
Michael J Holston, *Sr VP*
Robert Giglietti, *CAO*
EMP: 44087 **EST:** 1892
SALES (est): 67.95B
SALES (corp-wide): 67.95B **Publicly Held**
Web: www.ge.com
SIC: 3812 3519 4581 5088 Aircraft/aerospace flight instruments and guidance systems; Jet propulsion engines; Aircraft maintenance and repair services; Aircraft engines and engine parts

(G-2726)
GENERAL ELECTRIC CREDIT UNION (PA)
Also Called: Gecu
10485 Reading Rd (45241)
PHONE.................................513 243-4328
Timothy D Ballinger, *CEO*
Joan Moore, *
EMP: 90 **EST:** 1954
SQ FT: 23,000
SALES (est): 167.59MM
SALES (corp-wide): 167.59MM **Privately Held**
Web: www.gecreditunion.org
SIC: 6061 Federal credit unions

(G-2727)
GENERAL FACTORY SUPS CO INC
Also Called: Gfwd Supply
4811 Winton Rd (45232-1502)
PHONE.................................513 681-6300
Tim Stautberg, *Pr*
Robert Stautberg, *
Jeff Stautberg, *
EMP: 37 **EST:** 1946
SQ FT: 33,000
SALES (est): 11.89MM **Privately Held**
Web: www.genericerrormessage.com
SIC: 5085 Industrial supplies
PA: Waltz-Dettmer Supply Co.
4811 Winton Rd
Cincinnati OH 45232

(G-2728)
GENERAL TOOL COMPANY (PA)
101 Landy Ln (45215-3495)
PHONE.................................513 733-5500
William J Kramer Junior, *CEO*
William J Kramer Iii, *CFO*
John Cozad, *
Elliot Adams, *
Paul Kramer, *
▲ **EMP:** 235 **EST:** 1947
SQ FT: 150,000
SALES (est): 39.89MM
SALES (corp-wide): 39.89MM **Privately Held**
Web: www.gentool.com
SIC: 3599 3443 3444 3544 Machine shop, jobbing and repair; Fabricated plate work (boiler shop); Sheet metalwork; Special dies and tools

(G-2729)
GENPACT LLC
100 Tri County Pkwy Ste 200 (45246-3244)
PHONE.................................513 763-7660
EMP: 43
Web: www.genpact.com
SIC: 8711 3812 Mechanical engineering; Electronic field detection apparatus (aeronautical)
HQ: Genpact Llc
521 5th Ave Fl 14
New York NY 10175
212 896-6600

(G-2730)
GENTHERM MEDICAL LLC
Also Called: Cincinnati Sub-Zero Products
12011 Mosteller Rd (45241-1528)
PHONE.................................513 326-5252
Steve Berke, *Mgr*
EMP: 100
Web: www.gentherm.com
SIC: 8734 Testing laboratories
HQ: Gentherm Medical, Llc
12011 Mosteller Rd
Cincinnati OH 45241
513 772-8810

(G-2731)
GERBER LIFE AGENCY LLC
400 Broadway St (45202-3312)
PHONE.................................917 765-3572
Adam Erlebacher, *Managing Member*
Wen Lui, *Dir*
EMP: 35
SALES (est): 4.06MM **Privately Held**
SIC: 6311 Life insurance

(G-2732)
GILKEY WINDOW COMPANY INC (PA)
3625 Hauck Rd (45241-1605)
PHONE.................................513 769-4527
John M Gilkey, *Pr*
John M Gilkey, *Pr*
Sue Gilkey, *
▲ **EMP:** 98 **EST:** 1978
SQ FT: 56,000
SALES (est): 25.62MM
SALES (corp-wide): 25.62MM **Privately Held**
Web: www.gilkey.com
SIC: 5031 Doors and windows

(G-2733)
GILMAN PARTNERS
3960 Red Bank Rd Ste 200 (45227-3421)
PHONE.................................513 272-2400
Tom Gilman, *Mng Pt*
Barry Elkus, *Pt*
Marci Lauber, *Pt*
Rick Maier, *Pt*
Steve Wuest, *Pt*
EMP: 29 **EST:** 2014
SALES (est): 1.6MM **Privately Held**
Web: www.gilmanpartners.com
SIC: 7361 Executive placement

(G-2734)
GLOBE FURNITURE RENTALS INC (PA)
11745 Commons Dr (45246)
PHONE.................................513 771-8287
Paul Arnold, *Pr*
Maureen Thune, *
Victoria L Stiles, *
Anthony J Bellerdine, *
Michael G Connors, *
EMP: 85 **EST:** 1989
SQ FT: 12,500

SALES (est): 30.42MM
SALES (corp-wide): 30.42MM **Privately Held**
SIC: 6531 7359 5712 6513 Real estate agents and managers; Furniture rental; Furniture stores; Apartment building operators

(G-2735)
GODDARD SCHOOL
4430 Red Bank Rd (45227-2116)
PHONE.................................513 271-6311
EMP: 27 **EST:** 1997
SALES (est): 1.99MM **Privately Held**
Web: www.goddardschool.com
SIC: 8351 Preschool center

(G-2736)
GOERING CTR FOR FMLY/PRVATE BU
225 Calhoun St Ste 360 (45219-2192)
PHONE.................................513 556-7185
EMP: 64 **EST:** 1989
SALES (est): 1.92MM **Privately Held**
Web: business.uc.edu
SIC: 8742 Business planning and organizing services

(G-2737)
GOETTLE CO
12071 Hamilton Ave (45231-1032)
PHONE.................................513 825-8100
Dan Baker, *CFO*
EMP: 75 **EST:** 1975
SALES (est): 10.22MM **Privately Held**
Web: www.goettle.com
SIC: 1521 Single-family housing construction

(G-2738)
GOETTLE HOLDING COMPANY INC (PA)
Also Called: Goettle Construction
12071 Hamilton Ave (45231-1032)
PHONE.................................513 825-8100
Roger W Healey, *Prin*
Larry P Rayburn, *
Terrence Tucker, *
Douglas Keller, *
Dan Baker, *
▲ **EMP:** 129 **EST:** 1956
SQ FT: 15,000
SALES (est): 51.39MM
SALES (corp-wide): 51.39MM **Privately Held**
Web: www.goettle.com
SIC: 1799 1629 1771 1794 Shoring and underpinning work; Pile driving contractor; Foundation and footing contractor; Excavation work

(G-2739)
GOLD MEDAL PRODUCTS CO (PA)
Also Called: Gold Medal-Carolina
10700 Medallion Dr (45241-4807)
PHONE.................................513 769-7676
◆ **EMP:** 300 **EST:** 1931
SALES (est): 98.56MM
SALES (corp-wide): 98.56MM **Privately Held**
Web: www.gmpopcorn.com
SIC: 3556 3589 5145 3581 Food products machinery; Cooking equipment, commercial; Confectionery; Automatic vending machines

(G-2740)
GOLD STAR CHILI INC (PA)
Also Called: Gold Star Chili
650 Lunken Park Dr (45226-1800)
PHONE.................................513 231-4541

Roger David, *Pr*
Suhaila B David, *Stockholder**
Fahid S Daoud, *Stockholder**
Frank S Daoud, *Stockholder**
Basheer S David, *Stockholder**
EMP: 33 **EST:** 1965
SQ FT: 5,000
SALES (est): 22.38MM
SALES (corp-wide): 22.38MM **Privately Held**
Web: www.goldstarchili.com
SIC: 5812 2099 6794 5499 Chili stand; Food preparations, nec; Franchises, selling or licensing; Spices and herbs

(G-2741)
GOLDWAY TRANS LLC
Also Called: Goldway Trans
11811 Enterprise Dr (45241-1511)
PHONE.................................330 828-0008
Jamoliddin Tillaev, *Mgr*
EMP: 68 **EST:** 2017
SALES (est): 3.92MM **Privately Held**
SIC: 4789 Cargo loading and unloading services

(G-2742)
GOOD SAMARITAN HOSP CINCINNATI (HQ)
375 Dixmyth Ave (45220-2489)
PHONE.................................513 569-6251
Mark Clement, *CEO*
John S Prout, *
Robert L Walker, *
John R Robinson, *
Craig Rucker, *
EMP: 50 **EST:** 1852
SALES (est): 803.45MM **Privately Held**
Web: www.trihealth.com
SIC: 8062 8082 8011 General medical and surgical hospitals; Home health care services; Offices and clinics of medical doctors
PA: Commonspirit Health
444 W Lake St Ste 2500
Chicago IL 60606

(G-2743)
GORILLA GLUE COMPANY LLC (PA)
2101 E Kemper Rd (45241-1805)
PHONE.................................513 271-3300
Howard N Ragland Iii, *Pr*
Michael F Ragland, *VP*
◆ **EMP:** 419 **EST:** 1904
SQ FT: 44,000
SALES (est): 182.41MM
SALES (corp-wide): 182.41MM **Privately Held**
Web: www.gorillatough.com
SIC: 5085 5169 Adhesives, tape and plasters; Glue

(G-2744)
GOVERNMENT ACQUISITIONS INC
2060 Reading Rd Fl 4 (45202-1400)
PHONE.................................513 721-8700
Roger Brown, *CEO*
Roger Brown, *Owner*
Stan Jones, *
Bobby Brown, *
EMP: 35 **EST:** 1989
SQ FT: 20,000
SALES (est): 21.95MM **Privately Held**
Web: www.gov-acq.com
SIC: 7378 3577 5045 Computer maintenance and repair; Computer peripheral equipment, nec; Computer software

GEOGRAPHIC SECTION

Cincinnati - Hamilton County (G-2764)

(G-2745)
GP STRATEGIES CORPORATION
3794 E Galbraith Rd (45236-1506)
PHONE....................513 583-8810
EMP: 35
SALES (corp-wide): 515.16MM **Publicly Held**
SIC: 7379 8742 8331 Computer related consulting services; Management consulting services; Job training services
PA: Gp Strategies Corporation
11000 Broken Land Pkwy # 200
Columbia MD 21044
443 367-9600

(G-2746)
GRACE HOSPICE LLC
4850 Smith Rd Ste 100 (45212-2797)
PHONE....................513 458-5545
Mark Mitchell, Brnch Mgr
EMP: 109
Web: www.ghospice.com
SIC: 8052 Personal care facility
PA: Grace Hospice, Llc
500 Kirts Blvd Ste 250
Troy MI 48084

(G-2747)
GRACE MANAGEMENT INC
9191 Round Top Rd (45251-2446)
PHONE....................763 971-9271
EMP: 341
SALES (corp-wide): 49.15MM **Privately Held**
Web: www.northgateparkseniorliving.com
SIC: 8741 Management services
PA: Grace Management, Inc.
6900 Wedgwood Rd N # 300
Maple Grove MN 55311
763 544-9934

(G-2748)
GRACEWORKS ENHANCED LIVING
11430 Hamilton Ave (45231-6104)
PHONE....................513 825-3333
Kim Wurbalbacher, Brnch Mgr
EMP: 54
SALES (corp-wide): 8.97MM **Privately Held**
Web: www.graceworksenhancedliving.org
SIC: 8059 Nursing home, except skilled and intermediate care facility
PA: Graceworks Enhanced Living
11370 Springfield Pike
Cincinnati OH 45246
513 612-6500

(G-2749)
GRANT THORNTON LLP
4000 Smith Rd Ste 500 (45209-1967)
PHONE....................513 762-5000
Bob Taylor, Brnch Mgr
EMP: 34
SALES (corp-wide): 59.84MM **Privately Held**
Web: www.grantthornton.com
SIC: 8721 Accounting services, except auditing
HQ: Grant Thornton Llp
171 N Clark St Ste 200
Chicago IL 60601
312 856-0200

(G-2750)
GRAPHIC PACKAGING INTL LLC
Also Called: Altivity Packaging
4500 Beech St (45212-3402)
PHONE....................630 584-2900
Julie Robinson, Brnch Mgr
EMP: 83
Web: www.graphicpkg.com
SIC: 5199 Packaging materials
HQ: Graphic Packaging International, Llc
1500 Riveredge Pkwy # 100
Atlanta GA 30328

(G-2751)
GRAY & PAPE INC (PA)
1318 Main St Fl 1 (45202-6619)
PHONE....................513 287-7700
W Kevin Pape, Pr
EMP: 33 **EST:** 1986
SQ FT: 16,000
SALES (est): 9.6MM
SALES (corp-wide): 9.6MM **Privately Held**
Web: www.graypape.com
SIC: 8748 Environmental consultant

(G-2752)
GRAY MEDIA GROUP INC
Also Called: W X I X
635 W 7th St Ste 200 (45203-1549)
PHONE....................513 421-1919
Bill Lansey, Genl Mgr
EMP: 60
SALES (corp-wide): 3.28B **Publicly Held**
Web: www.wlbt.com
SIC: 4833 Television broadcasting stations
HQ: Gray Media Group, Inc.
201 Monroe St Fl 20
Montgomery AL 36104

(G-2753)
GRAYDON HEAD & RITCHEY LLP (PA)
312 Walnut St Ste 1800 (45202-3157)
P.O. Box 6464 (45201-6464)
PHONE....................513 621-6464
EMP: 137 **EST:** 1871
SALES (est): 10.86MM
SALES (corp-wide): 10.86MM **Privately Held**
Web: www.graydon.law
SIC: 8111 General practice law office

(G-2754)
GREAT AMERCN ALIANCE INSUR CO (DH)
301 E 4th St Fl 24 (45202)
P.O. Box 2575 (45201)
PHONE....................513 369-5000
Carl H Lindner Iii, Pr
Karen Holley Horrell, Sr VP
Gary J Gruber, Sr VP
EMP: 28 **EST:** 1973
SALES (est): 82.1MM **Publicly Held**
Web: www.greatamericaninsurancegroup.com
SIC: 6331 Fire, marine and casualty insurance and carriers
HQ: Great American Insurance Company
301 E 4th St
Cincinnati OH 45202
513 369-5000

(G-2755)
GREAT AMERICAN ASSURANCE
301 E 4th St Fl 8 (45202-4257)
PHONE....................513 369-5000
Carl H Lindner Iii, Pr
Karen Holley Horrell, Sr VP
EMP: 92 **EST:** 1905
SQ FT: 10,000
SALES (est): 30.44MM **Publicly Held**
Web: www.greatamericaninsurancegroup.com
SIC: 6331 Fire, marine and casualty insurance
HQ: Great American Insurance Company
301 E 4th St
Cincinnati OH 45202
513 369-5000

(G-2756)
GREAT AMERICAN HOLDING INC (HQ)
301 E 4th St (45202-4245)
PHONE....................513 369-3000
EMP: 73 **EST:** 2002
SALES (est): 911.12MM **Publicly Held**
Web: www.greatamericaninsurancegroup.com
SIC: 6331 Fire, marine, and casualty insurance
PA: American Financial Group, Inc.
301 E 4th St
Cincinnati OH 45202

(G-2757)
GREAT AMERICAN INSURANCE CO (HQ)
Also Called: Great American
301 E 4th St (45202)
P.O. Box 5420 (45201)
PHONE....................513 369-5000
Carl H Lindner Iii, CEO
Donald D Larson, COO
Karen H Horrell, Sr VP
Vito C Peraino, Sr VP
Michael E Sullivan Junior, Sr VP
◆ **EMP:** 3000 **EST:** 1942
SQ FT: 250,000
SALES (est): 1.47B **Publicly Held**
Web: www.gaig.com
SIC: 6331 6311 6321 Fire, marine, and casualty insurance; Life insurance; Accident and health insurance
PA: American Financial Group, Inc.
301 E 4th St
Cincinnati OH 45202

(G-2758)
GREAT AMERICAN SEC INSUR CO (DH)
580 Walnut St Ste S900 (45202-3193)
PHONE....................513 369-5000
Carl H Lindner Iii, Pr
Robert F Amory, Sr VP
Karen Holley Horrell Senior, General Vice President
David J Witzgall, VP
EMP: 33 **EST:** 1988
SQ FT: 100,000
SALES (est): 46.72MM **Publicly Held**
Web: www.greatamericaninsurancegroup.com
SIC: 6331 Fire, marine, and casualty insurance
HQ: Great American Insurance Company
301 E 4th St
Cincinnati OH 45202
513 369-5000

(G-2759)
GREAT AMRCN FNCL RESOURCES INC (HQ)
Also Called: Great American
250 E 5th St Ste 1000 (45202-4127)
PHONE....................513 333-5300
S Craig Lindner, Pr
Carl H Lindner, Ch Bd
Charles R Scheper, COO
Mark F Muething, Ex VP
Christopher P Miliano, CFO
EMP: 150 **EST:** 1987
SQ FT: 140,000
SALES (est): 508.44MM **Publicly Held**
Web: www.massmutualascend.com
SIC: 6331 Fire, marine, and casualty insurance
PA: American Financial Group, Inc.
301 E 4th St
Cincinnati OH 45202

(G-2760)
GREAT AMRCN PLAN ADMNSTRTORS I
525 Vine St Fl 7 (45202-3169)
PHONE....................513 412-2316
Mark Muething, Pr
EMP: 42 **EST:** 2008
SALES (est): 326.2K **Privately Held**
Web: www.greatamericaninsurancegroup.com
SIC: 6331 Fire, marine, and casualty insurance

(G-2761)
GREAT AMRCN RISK SLTONS SRPLS (DH)
Also Called: American Empire Srpls Lnes Ins
580 Walnut St (45202-3127)
PHONE....................513 369-3000
Robert A Nelson, CEO
Mark R Lonneman, Pr
EMP: 57 **EST:** 1977
SQ FT: 33,000
SALES (est): 103.56MM **Publicly Held**
Web: www.greatamericaninsurancegroup.com
SIC: 6331 Fire, marine, and casualty insurance: stock
HQ: Great American Insurance Company
301 E 4th St
Cincinnati OH 45202
513 369-5000

(G-2762)
GREAT LAKES COMPANIES INC
925 Laidlaw Ave (45237-5003)
PHONE....................513 554-0720
EMP: 66
SALES (corp-wide): 96.25MM **Privately Held**
Web: www.greatlakesway.com
SIC: 1521 Single-family housing construction
PA: Great Lakes Companies Inc
2608 Great Lakes Way
Hinckley OH
330 220-3900

(G-2763)
GREAT OAKS INST TECH CREER DEV
Also Called: Center For Employment Resource
3254 E Kemper Rd (45241-6421)
PHONE....................513 771-8840
Gary Gebhert, Dir
EMP: 44
SALES (corp-wide): 47.92MM **Privately Held**
Web: www.greatoaks.com
SIC: 8211 8299 8331 8249 Public adult education school; Educational service, nondegree granting: continuing educ.; Job training and related services; Vocational schools, nec
PA: Great Oaks Institute Of Technology & Career Development
110 Great Oaks Dr
Cincinnati OH 45241
513 613-3657

(G-2764)
GREAT OAKS INST TECH CREER DEV (PA)
110 Great Oaks Dr (45241-1573)
P.O. Box 62627 (45262-0627)
PHONE....................513 613-3657
Harry Snyder, Pr
Jon Quatman, *

Cincinnati - Hamilton County (G-2765)

Michelle Means Walker, *
Robert Giuffre, *
EMP: 98 **EST:** 1971
SQ FT: 10,000
SALES (est): 47.92MM
SALES (corp-wide): 47.92MM Privately Held
Web: www.greatoaks.com
SIC: 8211 8299 8331 8249 Public vocational/technical school; Educational service, nondegree granting: continuing educ.; Job training and related services; Vocational schools, nec

(G-2765)
GREAT PARKS FOREVER
10245 Winton Rd (45231-2626)
PHONE.................513 522-4357
Jack Sutton, *Prin*
EMP: 35 **EST:** 2006
SALES (est): 1.34MM Privately Held
Web: www.greatparks.org
SIC: 7033 Trailer parks and campsites

(G-2766)
GREAT PARKS HAMILTON COUNTY
Also Called: GLENWOOD GARDENS
377 Sheffield Rd (45240-4022)
PHONE.................513 521-7275
EMP: 221 **EST:** 2014
SALES (est): 843.94K Privately Held
Web: www.greatparks.org
SIC: 7999 Zoological garden, commercial

(G-2767)
GREATER CIN CARDI CONSULTS IN
Also Called: Greater Cnti Crdovascular Cons
2123 Auburn Ave (45219-2906)
PHONE.................513 751-4222
EMP: 50
SQ FT: 7,000
SALES (est): 3.49MM Privately Held
SIC: 8011 Cardiologist and cardio-vascular specialist

(G-2768)
GREATER CINCINNATI GASTRO ASSC (PA)
2925 Vernon Pl Ste 100 (45219-2425)
PHONE.................513 336-8636
Ronald Schneider, *Pr*
George Waissbluth, *
Michael Safdi, *
Alan Safdi, *
EMP: 60 **EST:** 1968
SQ FT: 6,000
SALES (est): 9.38MM
SALES (corp-wide): 9.38MM Privately Held
Web: www.ohiogi.com
SIC: 8011 Gastronomist

(G-2769)
GREATER CINCINNATI OB/GYN INC (PA)
2830 Victory Pkwy Ste 140 (45206-1786)
PHONE.................513 245-3103
EMP: 60 **EST:** 1985
SALES (est): 3.96MM Privately Held
SIC: 8011 Gynecologist

(G-2770)
GREATER CINCINNATI WATER WORKS ◊
4747 Spring Grove Ave (45232-1921)
PHONE.................513 591-7700
David Roger, *Prin*
EMP: 230 **EST:** 2022
SALES (est): 20.34MM
SALES (corp-wide): 901.5MM Privately Held
Web: portal.mygcww.org
SIC: 1623 Water, sewer, and utility lines
PA: City Of Cincinnati
801 Plum St Rm 246
Cincinnati OH 45202
513 352-3221

(G-2771)
GREATER CNCNNATI CNVNTION VSTO
525 Vine St Ste 1200 (45202-3174)
PHONE.................513 621-2142
Ben Lincoln, *Pr*
Cindi Flick, *VP*
Barrie Perks, *VP*
EMP: 53 **EST:** 1945
SQ FT: 10,000
SALES (est): 12.13MM Privately Held
Web: www.visitcincy.com
SIC: 7389 Convention and show services

(G-2772)
GREATER CNCNNATI DNTL LABS INC
3719 Struble Rd (45251-4951)
P.O. Box 53070 (45253-0070)
PHONE.................513 385-4222
Ken Blaylock, *Pr*
Robert Blaylock, *
Darlene Rogg, *
EMP: 49 **EST:** 1961
SALES (est): 4.49MM Privately Held
Web: www.greaterc.com
SIC: 8072 Denture production

(G-2773)
GREATER CNCNNATI TV EDCTL FNDT
Also Called: CHANNEL 48
1223 Central Pkwy (45214-2834)
PHONE.................513 381-4033
Susan Howarth, *CEO*
EMP: 70 **EST:** 1953
SQ FT: 84,210
SALES (est): 8.09MM Privately Held
Web: www.cetconnect.org
SIC: 4833 7812 Television broadcasting stations; Television film production

(G-2774)
GREEN TOWNSHIP HOSPITALITY LLC (PA)
Also Called: Holiday Inn
5505 Rybolt Rd (45248-1029)
PHONE.................513 574-6000
Katen Patel, *Managing Member*
EMP: 60 **EST:** 1965
SQ FT: 100,000
SALES (est): 5.14MM
SALES (corp-wide): 5.14MM Privately Held
Web: www.holidayinn.com
SIC: 7011 5812 Hotels and motels; Eating places

(G-2775)
GREIF INC
5500 Wooster Pike (45226-2227)
PHONE.................740 549-6000
EMP: 80
SALES (corp-wide): 5.22B Publicly Held
Web: www.greif.com
SIC: 5199 Packaging materials
PA: Greif, Inc.
425 Winter Rd
Delaware OH 43015
740 549-6000

(G-2776)
GREYHOUND LINES INC
600 Vine St Ste 1400 (45202-2426)
PHONE.................513 721-4450
Dave Leach, *CEO*
EMP: 48
SALES (corp-wide): 1.59B Privately Held
Web: www.greyhound.com
SIC: 4131 Intercity and rural bus transportation
HQ: Greyhound Lines, Inc.
350 N Saint Paul St # 300
Dallas TX 75201
214 849-8000

(G-2777)
GREYHOUND LINES INC
1005 Gilbert Ave (45202-1425)
PHONE.................513 421-7442
Virginia Purdy, *Mgr*
EMP: 36
SALES (corp-wide): 1.59B Privately Held
Web: www.greyhound.com
SIC: 4131 Intercity and rural bus transportation
HQ: Greyhound Lines, Inc.
350 N Saint Paul St # 300
Dallas TX 75201
214 849-8000

(G-2778)
GRIID INFRASTRUCTURE INC
2577 Duck Creek Rd (45212-4044)
PHONE.................513 268-6185
James D Kelly Iii, *Ch Bd*
Allan J Wallander, *CFO*
Gerard F King Ii, *COO*
EMP: 47 **EST:** 2018
SALES (est): 19.62MM Privately Held
Web: www.griid.com
SIC: 6231 Security exchanges

(G-2779)
GUARANTEED RATE INC
2654 Madison Rd (45208-1332)
PHONE.................513 609-4477
EMP: 120
Web: www.rate.com
SIC: 6162 Mortgage bankers and loan correspondents
PA: Guaranteed Rate, Inc.
3940 N Ravenswood Ave
Chicago IL 60613

(G-2780)
GUARDIAN LIFE INSUR CO AMER
419 Plum St (45202-2632)
PHONE.................513 579-1114
EMP: 44
SALES (corp-wide): 3.42B Privately Held
Web: www.guardianlife.com
SIC: 6311 Life insurance
PA: Guardian Life Insurance Company Of America
10 Hudson Yards Fl 22
New York NY 10001
212 598-8000

(G-2781)
GUARDIAN SAVINGS BANK
11333 Princeton Pike (45246-3201)
PHONE.................513 842-8900
EMP: 29
SALES (corp-wide): 43.29MM Privately Held
Web: www.guardiansavingsbank.com
SIC: 6163 6162 6029 6035 Loan brokers; Mortgage bankers and loan correspondents; Commercial banks, nec; Federal savings and loan associations
PA: Guardian Savings Bank
6100 W Chester Rd
West Chester OH 45069
513 942-3535

(G-2782)
GUARDIAN SAVINGS BANK
560 Ohio Pike (45255-3315)
PHONE.................513 528-8787
EMP: 46
SALES (corp-wide): 43.29MM Privately Held
Web: www.guardiansavingsbank.com
SIC: 6163 6035 Loan brokers; Federal savings institutions
PA: Guardian Savings Bank
6100 W Chester Rd
West Chester OH 45069
513 942-3535

(G-2783)
GUS HOLTHAUS SIGNS INC
Also Called: Holthaus Lackner Signs
817 Ridgeway Ave (45229-3222)
P.O. Box 29373 (45229-0373)
PHONE.................513 861-0060
Kevin Holthaus, *Pr*
Scott Holthaus, *
Kerry Holthaus, *
EMP: 40 **EST:** 1929
SQ FT: 38,600
SALES (est): 4.86MM Privately Held
Web: www.hlsigns.com
SIC: 3993 1799 Electric signs; Sign installation and maintenance

(G-2784)
GUS PERDIKAKIS ASSOCIATES
Also Called: GPA
9155 Governors Way Unit A (45249-4005)
P.O. Box 498612 (45249-8612)
PHONE.................513 583-0900
Gus G Perdikakis, *Pr*
Joann L Perdikakis, *
Lynn Perdikakis, *
EMP: 70 **EST:** 1979
SQ FT: 1,600
SALES (est): 9.65MM Privately Held
Web: www.trustingus.net
SIC: 8711 7361 Engineering services; Employment agencies

(G-2785)
GUSTAVE A LARSON COMPANY
Also Called: Progress Sup A Gstave A Larson
1201 Harrison Ave (45214-1719)
PHONE.................513 681-4089
Gary Sparks, *Brnch Mgr*
EMP: 48
SALES (corp-wide): 2.01B Privately Held
Web: www.galarson.com
SIC: 5078 Refrigeration equipment and supplies
HQ: Gustave A. Larson Company
W233n2869 Roundy Cir W
Pewaukee WI 53072
262 542-0200

(G-2786)
H HAFNER & SONS INC
5445 Wooster Pike (45226-2226)
PHONE.................513 321-1895
Justin Cooper, *Pr*
Linda Hafner, *
Andrew O Haefner, *
Maryellen Maltry, *
Paul J Hengge, *
EMP: 42 **EST:** 1923
SQ FT: 5,500
SALES (est): 9.18MM Privately Held
Web: www.hafners.com

GEOGRAPHIC SECTION

Cincinnati - Hamilton County (G-2810)

SIC: 5191 2499 4212 4953 Soil, potting and planting; Mulch, wood and bark; Dump truck haulage; Recycling, waste materials

(G-2787)
HABEGGER CORPORATION
Also Called: C A C Distributing
11413 Enterprise Park Dr (45241-1561)
PHONE..............................513 612-4700
John R Kinnamon, *Mgr*
EMP: 60
SQ FT: 29,320
SALES (corp-wide): 93.95MM **Privately Held**
Web: www.habeggercorp.com
SIC: 5074 5075 Heating equipment (hydronic); Air conditioning equipment, except room units, nec
PA: The Habegger Corporation
   4995 Winton Rd
   Cincinnati OH 45232
   513 853-6644

(G-2788)
HABEGGER CORPORATION (PA)
Also Called: Johnson Contrls Authorized Dlr
4995 Winton Rd (45232-1504)
PHONE..............................513 853-6644
Fred Habegger Iii, *Ch Bd*
John Dor, *
Mike Pope, *
▲ EMP: 49 EST: 1915
SQ FT: 20,000
SALES (est): 93.95MM
SALES (corp-wide): 93.95MM **Privately Held**
Web: www.habeggercorp.com
SIC: 5075 Warm air heating equipment and supplies

(G-2789)
HABITAT FOR HMNITY GRTER CNCNN
3970 N Bend Rd (45211-3569)
PHONE..............................513 389-1792
EMP: 39
Web: www.habitatcincinnati.org
SIC: 8399 Community development groups
PA: Habitat For Humanity Of Greater Cincinnati
   4910 Para Dr
   Cincinnati OH 45237

(G-2790)
HABITAT FOR HMNITY GRTER CNCNN (PA)
Also Called: CINCINNATI HABITAT FOR HUMANIT
4910 Para Dr (45237-5012)
PHONE..............................513 721-4483
EMP: 46 EST: 1986
SQ FT: 1,500
SALES (est): 9.76MM **Privately Held**
Web: www.habitatcincinnati.org
SIC: 8399 Community development groups

(G-2791)
HACKENSACK MERIDIAN HEALTH INC
Also Called: Carriage Court of Kenwood
4650 E Galbraith Rd (45236-2792)
PHONE..............................513 792-9697
K Pfeifer, *Dir Fin*
EMP: 80
Web: www.hackensackmeridianhealth.org
SIC: 8051 Skilled nursing care facilities
PA: Hackensack Meridian Health, Inc.
   343 Thornall St Ste 7
   Edison NJ 08837

(G-2792)
HAGGERTY LOGISTICS INC
95 W Crescentville Rd (45246-1730)
PHONE..............................734 713-9800
EMP: 93
SALES (corp-wide): 3.1B **Privately Held**
Web: www.haggertylogistics.com
SIC: 4789 Pipeline terminal facilities, independently operated
HQ: Haggerty Logistics, Inc.
   17900 Woodland Dr
   New Boston MI 48164
   734 397-6300

(G-2793)
HALO BRANDED SOLUTIONS INC
7800 E Kemper Rd Ste 100 (45249-1665)
PHONE..............................855 425-6266
Kent Wyant, *Brnch Mgr*
EMP: 29
SALES (corp-wide): 577.13MM **Privately Held**
Web: www.halo.com
SIC: 5199 Advertising specialties
PA: Halo Branded Solutions, Inc.
   1500 Halo Way
   Sterling IL 61081
   815 625-0980

(G-2794)
HAMILTON CNTY SOC FOR THE PRVN
Also Called: S P C A CINCINNATI
11900 Conrey Rd (45249-1014)
PHONE..............................513 541-6100
Harold Dates, *Dir*
EMP: 40 EST: 1907
SALES (est): 9.61MM **Privately Held**
Web: www.spcacincinnati.org
SIC: 8699 Animal humane society

(G-2795)
HAMILTON COUNTY EDUCTL SVC CTR
924 Waycross Rd (45240-3022)
PHONE..............................513 674-4200
Kathy Tirey, *Ex Dir*
EMP: 256
SALES (corp-wide): 44.79MM **Privately Held**
Web: www.hcesc.org
SIC: 8351 Head Start center, except in conjunction with school
PA: Hamilton County Educational Service Center
   11083 Hamilton Ave
   Cincinnati OH 45231
   513 674-4200

(G-2796)
HAMMOND NEAL MOORE LLC
441 Vine St Ste 3200 (45202-3005)
PHONE..............................513 381-2011
EMP: 60 EST: 1991
SALES (est): 8.37MM **Privately Held**
Web: www.hammondlawgroup.com
SIC: 8111 General practice law office

(G-2797)
HAMPTON INN DRY RIDGE
Also Called: Hampton By Hilton
310 Culvert St Ste 500 (45202-2200)
PHONE..............................859 823-7111
Phyllis Hunstein, *Mgr*
EMP: 28 EST: 2003
SALES (est): 353.64K **Privately Held**
Web: hampton-inn-dry-ridge.booked.net
SIC: 7011 Hotels and motels

(G-2798)
HAND AMBLATORY SURGERY CTR LLC
Also Called: Hand Surgery Center
2800 Winslow Ave # 201 (45206-1144)
PHONE..............................513 961-4263
EMP: 47 EST: 1998
SALES (est): 1.44MM **Privately Held**
Web: www.trihealth.com
SIC: 8011 Surgeon

(G-2799)
HANEY INC
Also Called: Haney PRC
5657 Wooster Pike (45227-4120)
PHONE..............................513 561-1441
Daniel E Haney, *Pr*
Matthew J Haney, *
EMP: 52 EST: 1989
SQ FT: 4,000
SALES (est): 11.6MM **Privately Held**
Web: www.haneypkg.com
SIC: 7336 Graphic arts and related design

(G-2800)
HARD ROCK CSINO CINCINNATI LLC
Also Called: Starbucks Licensed Store
1000 Broadway St (45202)
PHONE..............................513 250-3375
Dougy Phillips, *Managing Member*
EMP: 327 EST: 2010
SALES (est): 12.42MM **Privately Held**
Web: casino.hardrock.com
SIC: 7011 Casino hotel

(G-2801)
HARRIS DISTRIBUTING CO
4261 Crawford Ave (45223-1857)
PHONE..............................513 541-4222
Irma Harris, *Pr*
Carl Harris Junior, *VP*
Patricia Junker, *
Dennis A Harris, *
EMP: 30 EST: 1968
SALES (est): 2.12MM **Privately Held**
Web: www.harris3pl.com
SIC: 4213 Contract haulers

(G-2802)
HARRISON PAVILION
2171 Harrison Ave (45211-8159)
PHONE..............................513 662-5800
Skip Roos, *Prin*
EMP: 39 EST: 2008
SALES (est): 7.51MM **Privately Held**
Web: www.harrisonpavilionhc.com
SIC: 8322 8059 Rehabilitation services; Nursing home, except skilled and intermediate care facility

(G-2803)
HARTE-HANKS TRNSP SVCS
2950 Robinson Ave (45209)
PHONE..............................513 458-7600
Paul Lampone, *Mgr*
EMP: 55
SALES (corp-wide): 4.82MM **Privately Held**
SIC: 7331 Direct mail advertising services
PA: Harte-Hanks Transportation Services
   1400 E Nwport Ctr Dr 21
   Deerfield Beach FL 33442
   954 429-3771

(G-2804)
HARTWIG TRANSIT INC
11971 Reading Rd (45215-1543)
PHONE..............................513 563-1765
Caleb France, *Mgr*
EMP: 140
SQ FT: 3,648
SALES (corp-wide): 13.51MM **Privately Held**
SIC: 7538 Truck engine repair, except industrial
PA: Hartwig Transit, Inc.
   204 Christina Dr
   Dundee IL 60118
   847 749-1101

(G-2805)
HAUCK HOSPITALITY LLC
Also Called: Holiday Inn
3855 Hauck Rd (45241-1609)
PHONE..............................513 563-8330
EMP: 52 EST: 2006
SQ FT: 24,311
SALES (est): 1MM **Privately Held**
Web: www.kiwihospitality.com
SIC: 7011 5812 Hotels and motels; Eating places

(G-2806)
HAUSER INC
Also Called: Hauser Group, The
8260 Northcreek Dr Ste 200 (45236-2283)
PHONE..............................513 745-9200
Mark J Hauser, *Pr*
Mark J Hauser, *CEO*
Gary L Morgan, *
Paul M Swanson, *
Jim Hyer, *Employee*
EMP: 54 EST: 1971
SALES (est): 19.55MM **Privately Held**
Web: www.thehausergroup.com
SIC: 6411 Insurance agents, nec

(G-2807)
HC TRANSPORT INC
Also Called: For Hire Carrier
6045 Bridgetown Rd (45248-3049)
P.O. Box 111116 (45211-1116)
PHONE..............................513 574-1800
Edward Sedler, *Pr*
Clifford Riegler, *
EMP: 32 EST: 1997
SQ FT: 16,000
SALES (est): 7.98MM **Privately Held**
SIC: 4212 Delivery service, vehicular

(G-2808)
HEALTH CAROUSEL LLC (PA)
Also Called: Tailored Healthcare Staffing
4000 Smith Rd Ste 410 (45209-1967)
PHONE..............................855 665-4544
William Deville, *CEO*
Theodore Nelson, *
EMP: 150 EST: 2004
SALES (est): 119.22MM
SALES (corp-wide): 119.22MM **Privately Held**
Web: www.healthcarousel.com
SIC: 7363 Temporary help service

(G-2809)
HEALTH COLLABORATIVE
615 Elsinore Pl (45202-1459)
PHONE..............................513 618-3600
Craig Brammer, *CEO*
Robert Coogan, *
EMP: 97 EST: 1995
SALES (est): 22.26MM **Privately Held**
Web: www.healthcollab.org
SIC: 8621 8011 Professional organizations; Health maintenance organization

(G-2810)
HEALTH CROUSEL TRVL NETWRK LLC
3805 Edwards Rd Ste 700 (45209-1955)
PHONE..............................513 665-4544

Cincinnati - Hamilton County (G-2811)

Jonathan Kukulski, *Prin*
EMP: 50 **EST:** 2017
SALES (est): 8.63MM **Privately Held**
Web: www.healthcarousel.com
SIC: 8099 Health and allied services, nec

(G-2811)
HEALTHQUEST FIELDS ERTEL INC
Also Called: Healthquest
8390 E Kemper Rd Ste 310 (45249-1680)
PHONE..................513 774-9800
Kelly Greer, *Pr*
EMP: 100 **EST:** 2006
SALES (est): 809.02K **Privately Held**
Web: www.healthquestspine.com
SIC: 8041 8049 Offices and clinics of chiropractors; Physical therapist

(G-2812)
HEALTHSOURCE OF OHIO INC
Also Called: East Gate Pediatric Center
559 Old State Route 74 (45244-1518)
PHONE..................513 753-2820
EMP: 27
SALES (corp-wide): 67.96MM **Privately Held**
Web: www.healthsourceofohio.org
SIC: 8093 8011 Specialty outpatient clinics, nec; Pediatrician
PA: Healthsource Of Ohio, Inc.
424 Wards Corner Rd # 200
Loveland OH 45140
513 576-7700

(G-2813)
HEALTHSPAN INTEGRATED CARE
Also Called: Healthspan
1701 Mercy Health Pl (45237-6147)
PHONE..................216 621-5600
Kenneth Page, *CEO*
George Halverson, *
Patricia D Kennedy-scott, *Pr*
Denise Swanm, *
Thomas Revis, *
EMP: 1240 **EST:** 1964
SALES (est): 1.49MM
SALES (corp-wide): 6.92B **Privately Held**
Web: www.payhealthspan.com
SIC: 6324 Hospital and medical service plans
PA: Bon Secours Mercy Health, Inc.
1701 Mercy Health Pl
Cincinnati OH 45237
513 956-3729

(G-2814)
HEARING SPECH DEAF CTR GRTER C
2825 Burnet Ave Ste 330 (45219-2426)
PHONE..................513 221-0527
Janet Boothe, *CEO*
EMP: 35 **EST:** 1925
SALES (est): 2.77MM **Privately Held**
Web: www.hearingspeechdeaf.org
SIC: 8322 8699 Rehabilitation services; Charitable organization

(G-2815)
HEBREW UN CLLG-JWISH INST RLGI
American Jewish Achives
3101 Clifton Ave (45220-2488)
PHONE..................513 221-1875
Gary P Zola, *Mgr*
EMP: 50
SALES (corp-wide): 23.92MM **Privately Held**
Web: www.huc.edu
SIC: 8733 8221 Research institute; College, except junior
PA: Hebrew Union College-Jewish Institute Of Religion
3101 Clifton Ave
Cincinnati OH 45220
513 221-1875

(G-2816)
HEIDELBERG DISTRIBUTING C
10975 Medallion Dr (45241-4830)
PHONE..................513 771-9370
EMP: 52 **EST:** 2013
SALES (est): 1.28MM **Privately Held**
Web: www.heidelbergdistributing.com
SIC: 5181 Beer and other fermented malt liquors

(G-2817)
HENSLEY INDUSTRIES INC (PA)
Also Called: Hensley Industries
2150 Langdon Farm Rd (45237-4711)
PHONE..................513 769-6666
EMP: 49 **EST:** 1994
SQ FT: 182,000
SALES (est): 4.7MM **Privately Held**
Web: www.hensleyind.com
SIC: 1796 Machine moving and rigging

(G-2818)
HGC CONSTRUCTION CO (PA)
Also Called: H G C
2814 Stanton Ave (45206-1123)
PHONE..................513 861-8866
Mike Huseman, *Pr*
EMP: 100 **EST:** 1984
SQ FT: 22,000
SALES (est): 27.43MM
SALES (corp-wide): 27.43MM **Privately Held**
Web: www.hgcconstruction.com
SIC: 1751 1796 Carpentry work; Millwright

(G-2819)
HICON INC
93 Caldwell Dr # A (45216-1541)
PHONE..................513 242-3612
Wayne Moratschek, *Pr*
Steve Sprengard, *
EMP: 36 **EST:** 1977
SQ FT: 6,000
SALES (est): 5.56MM **Privately Held**
Web: www.hiconinc.com
SIC: 1741 1611 Masonry and other stonework; Highway and street paving contractor

(G-2820)
HIGH SCORE MENTOR LLC
1172 W Galbraith Rd Ste 211 (45231-5647)
PHONE..................513 485-2848
Christine Johnson, *Prin*
EMP: 45 **EST:** 2019
SALES (est): 1.49MM **Privately Held**
SIC: 8748 Business consulting, nec

(G-2821)
HILL-ROM INC
Also Called: Hill Rom
3478 Hauck Rd (45241-4604)
PHONE..................513 769-6343
EMP: 34
SALES (corp-wide): 14.81B **Publicly Held**
Web: www.hillrom.com
SIC: 7352 Medical equipment rental
HQ: Hill-Rom, Inc.
1069 State Rte 46 E
Batesville IN 47006
812 934-7777

(G-2822)
HILLMAN COMPANIES INC (DH)
Also Called: Hillman
10590 Hamilton Ave (45231)
PHONE..................513 851-4900
Douglas J Cahill, *Ch*
Robert O Kraft, *CFO*
George S Murphy, *VP Sls*
◆ **EMP:** 400 **EST:** 1964
SQ FT: 270,000
SALES (est): 1.37B
SALES (corp-wide): 1.48B **Publicly Held**
Web: www.hillmangroup.com
SIC: 5072 7699 Hardware; Key duplicating shop
HQ: Hman Intermediate Ii Holdings Corp.
10590 Hamilton Ave
Cincinnati OH 45231
513 851-4900

(G-2823)
HILLMAN GROUP INC (DH)
Also Called: Hardware Now
1280 Kemper Meadow Dr (45240-1632)
PHONE..................513 851-4900
Douglas Cahill, *Ch Bd*
Todd Spangler, *
Kim Corbitt, *
Robert Kraft, *
◆ **EMP:** 131 **EST:** 1998
SALES (est): 494.15MM
SALES (corp-wide): 1.48B **Publicly Held**
Web: www.hillmangroup.com
SIC: 5072 Hardware
HQ: The Hillman Companies Inc
10590 Hamilton Ave
Cincinnati OH 45231
513 851-4900

(G-2824)
HILLMAN SOLUTIONS CORP (PA)
10590 Hamilton Ave (45231)
PHONE..................513 851-4900
Doug Cahill, *Ch Bd*
Robert O Kraft, *CFO*
Gary L Seeds, *Ex VP*
George Murphy, *Ex VP*
Amanda Kitzberger, *VP*
EMP: 30 **EST:** 2014
SALES (est): 1.48B
SALES (corp-wide): 1.48B **Publicly Held**
Web: www.hillmangroup.com
SIC: 5072 Hardware

(G-2825)
HILLSBORO TRANSPORTATION CO
2889 E Crescentville Rd (45246)
P.O. Box 62595 (45262-0595)
PHONE..................513 772-9223
Jeff Duckwall, *VP*
EMP: 33
SQ FT: 4,800
SALES (corp-wide): 4.31MM **Privately Held**
Web: www.hillsborotransportation.com
SIC: 4213 Contract haulers
PA: Hillsboro Transportation Co.
6256 U S Rte 50 W
Hillsboro OH 45133
513 772-9223

(G-2826)
HILLTOP BASIC RESOURCES INC
Also Called: Hilltop Concrete
511 W Water St (45202-3400)
PHONE..................513 621-1500
Mike Marchioni, *Mgr*
EMP: 56
SQ FT: 1,758
SALES (corp-wide): 59.62MM **Privately Held**
Web: www.hilltopcompanies.com
SIC: 3273 3272 1442 Ready-mixed concrete; Concrete products, nec; Construction sand and gravel
PA: Hilltop Basic Resources, Inc.

50 E Rvrcnter Blvd Ste 10
Covington KY 41011
513 651-5000

(G-2827)
HINGE CONSULTING LLC
310 Culvert St Ste 301 (45202-4247)
PHONE..................513 404-1547
Fred Killingsworth, *CEO*
EMP: 31 **EST:** 2015
SALES (est): 1.69MM **Privately Held**
Web: www.hingecommerce.com
SIC: 8748 Business consulting, nec

(G-2828)
HIRSCH HOLDINGS INC
4 Kovach Dr Ste 470a (45215-1061)
PHONE..................513 733-4111
Leo Stenger, *Bmch Mgr*
EMP: 87
SIC: 5084 Printing trades machinery, equipment, and supplies
PA: Hirsch Holdings, Inc.
11515 Vanstory Dr Ste 145
Huntersville NC 28078

(G-2829)
HIXSON INCORPORATED
Also Called: Hixson Archtcts/Ngnrs/Nteriors
659 Van Meter St Ste 300 (45202-1568)
PHONE..................513 241-1230
J Wickliffe Ach, *Pr*
Bruce Mirrielees, *
William H Sander, *
Thomas J Benkert, *
William H Wiseman, *
EMP: 125 **EST:** 1948
SQ FT: 125,000
SALES (est): 28.79MM **Privately Held**
Web: www.hixson-inc.com
SIC: 8712 Architectural engineering

(G-2830)
HJ BENKEN FLOR & GREENHOUSES
6000 Plainfield Rd (45213-2335)
PHONE..................513 891-1040
Michael Benken, *Pr*
Kathleen A Benken, *
Timothy Clark, *
EMP: 46 **EST:** 1938
SQ FT: 6,500
SALES (est): 9.43MM **Privately Held**
Web: www.benkens.com
SIC: 5992 0181 5261 Flowers, fresh; Nursery stock, growing of; Retail nurseries and garden stores

(G-2831)
HOETING INC
Also Called: Hoeting Realtors
7601 Cheviot Rd (45247-4036)
PHONE..................513 385-5100
Carolyn Wedding, *Mgr*
EMP: 48
Web: www.hoeting.com
SIC: 6531 Real estate agent, residential
PA: Hoeting Inc
6048 Bridgetown Rd
Cincinnati OH 45248

(G-2832)
HOLTZ AGENCY LTD
4015 Executive Park Dr Ste 400 (45241-4017)
PHONE..................513 671-7220
Kevin Holtz, *Prin*
EMP: 36 **EST:** 2017
SALES (est): 1.41MM **Privately Held**
Web: www.holtzagency.com
SIC: 6411 Insurance agents, nec

GEOGRAPHIC SECTION
Cincinnati - Hamilton County (G-2856)

(G-2833)
HOME AT HEARTHSTONE
8028 Hamilton Ave (45231-2322)
PHONE.................................513 521-2700
Glenna Coffey, *Prin*
EMP: 44 **EST:** 2007
SALES (est): 7.68MM **Privately Held**
Web: www.hearthstone-care.net
SIC: 8051 8059 Convalescent home with continuous nursing care; Nursing home, except skilled and intermediate care facility

(G-2834)
HOME BLDRS ASSN GRTER CNCNNATI
11260 Chester Rd Ste 800 (45246-4007)
PHONE.................................513 851-6300
Dan Dressman, *Ex Dir*
EMP: 60 **EST:** 1939
SQ FT: 3,000
SALES (est): 637.72K **Privately Held**
Web: www.cincybuilders.com
SIC: 8611 Contractors' association

(G-2835)
HOME DEPOT USA INC
Also Called: Home Depot, The
520 Ohio Pike (45255)
PHONE.................................513 688-1654
Matt Hingle, *Mgr*
EMP: 185
SALES (corp-wide): 152.67B **Publicly Held**
Web: www.homedepot.com
SIC: 5211 7359 Home centers; Tool rental
HQ: Home Depot U.S.A., Inc.
2445 Springfield Ave
Vauxhall NJ 07088

(G-2836)
HOME DEPOT USA INC
Also Called: Home Depot, The
6300 Glenway Ave (45211)
PHONE.................................513 661-2413
Ken Hedges, *Prin*
EMP: 175
SALES (corp-wide): 152.67B **Publicly Held**
Web: www.homedepot.com
SIC: 5211 7359 Home centers; Tool rental
HQ: Home Depot U.S.A., Inc.
2445 Springfield Ave
Vauxhall NJ 07088

(G-2837)
HOME DEPOT USA INC
Also Called: Home Depot, The
3400 Highland Ave (45213)
PHONE.................................513 631-1705
Brenda Brown, *Mgr*
EMP: 158
SALES (corp-wide): 152.67B **Publicly Held**
Web: www.homedepot.com
SIC: 5211 7359 Home centers; Tool rental
HQ: Home Depot U.S.A., Inc.
2445 Springfield Ave
Vauxhall NJ 07088

(G-2838)
HOME GREEN HOME INC
1435 Vine St (45202-7094)
PHONE.................................513 900-1702
Heather Montanaro, *Pr*
EMP: 28 **EST:** 2007
SALES (est): 1.56MM **Privately Held**
SIC: 1521 Single-family housing construction

(G-2839)
HOME STATE PROTECTIVE SVCS LLC
Also Called: Hsps Special Operations
250 E 5th St 15th Fl (45202-4252)
P.O. Box 11593 (45211-0593)
PHONE.................................513 253-3095
Bobby Long, *Managing Member*
EMP: 50 **EST:** 2014
SALES (est): 2.29MM **Privately Held**
Web: www.hsprotectiveservices.com
SIC: 7381 Security guard service

(G-2840)
HOMEFRONT NURSING LLC
149 Northland Blvd (45246-3121)
PHONE.................................513 404-1189
Fred Ovie Okotie, *CEO*
EMP: 38 **EST:** 2009
SALES (est): 5.45MM **Privately Held**
Web: www.homefrontnursing.com
SIC: 8051 Skilled nursing care facilities

(G-2841)
HONORWORTH HOMECARE LLC
Also Called: Honorworth Homecare
4101 Spring Grove Ave (45223-2685)
PHONE.................................513 557-0093
Christine Johnson, *CEO*
Richard Hall, *
EMP: 32 **EST:** 2020
SALES (est): 1.34MM **Privately Held**
Web: www.honorworth.com
SIC: 8082 Home health care services

(G-2842)
HORAN CAPITAL ADVISORS LLC
4990 E Galbraith Rd (45236-6711)
PHONE.................................513 745-0707
Terence Horan Clu Chfc, *CEO*
Nicolas E Lance, *COO*
James R Hendricks, *CFO*
EMP: 51 **EST:** 2010
SALES (est): 2.19MM **Privately Held**
Web: www.horanassoc.com
SIC: 6799 Investors, nec

(G-2843)
HORIZON HEALTH MANAGEMENT LLC
3889 E Galbraith Rd (45236-1514)
PHONE.................................513 793-5220
Raymond Schneider, *Prin*
EMP: 45 **EST:** 2013
SALES (est): 629.54K **Privately Held**
SIC: 8051 Skilled nursing care facilities

(G-2844)
HORTER INVESTMENT MGT LLC
11726 7 Gables Rd (45249-1735)
PHONE.................................513 984-9933
Drew Horter, *Managing Member*
EMP: 40 **EST:** 2008
SALES (est): 10.8MM **Privately Held**
Web: www.horterinvestment.com
SIC: 6282 Investment advisory service

(G-2845)
HOSPICE CINCINNATI INC
5343 Hamilton Ave Apt 402 (45224-3132)
PHONE.................................513 389-5528
EMP: 100
Web: www.hospiceofcincinnati.org
SIC: 8052 Personal care facility
HQ: Hospice Of Cincinnati, Incorporated
4360 Cooper Rd Ste 200
Cincinnati OH 45242
513 891-7700

(G-2846)
HOSPICE CINCINNATI INC
Also Called: Tri Health Facility
5343 Hamilton Ave (45224-3130)
PHONE.................................513 598-5093
Steve West, *CEO*
EMP: 100
Web: www.hospiceofcincinnati.org
SIC: 8052 Personal care facility
HQ: Hospice Of Cincinnati, Incorporated
4360 Cooper Rd Ste 200
Cincinnati OH 45242
513 891-7700

(G-2847)
HOSPICE CINCINNATI INC
7691 5 Mile Rd Ste 100 (45230-4348)
PHONE.................................513 386-6000
Noel Hauser, *Prin*
EMP: 100
Web: www.hospiceofcincinnati.org
SIC: 8052 Personal care facility
HQ: Hospice Of Cincinnati, Incorporated
4360 Cooper Rd Ste 200
Cincinnati OH 45242
513 891-7700

(G-2848)
HOSPICE CINCINNATI INC (DH)
4360 Cooper Rd Ste 200 (45242-5636)
PHONE.................................513 891-7700
Gayle Mattson, *CEO*
Sandra Lobert, *
Leigh Gerdsen, *
Adhrain Griffith, *Finance*
Janet Montgomery, *
EMP: 100 **EST:** 1977
SALES (est): 63.5MM **Privately Held**
Web: www.hospiceofcincinnati.org
SIC: 8082 8051 Home health care services; Skilled nursing care facilities
HQ: Bethesda, Inc.
619 Oak St 7 N
Cincinnati OH 45206
513 569-6400

(G-2849)
HOSPICE SOUTHWEST OHIO INC
7625 Camargo Rd (45243-3107)
PHONE.................................513 770-0820
Joseph Killian, *CEO*
Steven Boymel, *
James Farley, *
Brent Dixon, *
Harold Sosna, *
EMP: 100 **EST:** 2005
SALES (est): 11.45MM **Privately Held**
Web: www.hswo.org
SIC: 8082 Home health care services

(G-2850)
HOST CINCINNATI HOTEL LLC
Also Called: Starwood Hotels & Resorts
21 E 5th St Ste A (45202-3120)
PHONE.................................513 621-7700
Wayne Bodington, *Genl Mgr*
EMP: 200 **EST:** 1999
SALES (est): 22.14MM
SALES (corp-wide): 5.31B **Publicly Held**
Web: westin.marriott.com
SIC: 7011 Hotels and motels
PA: Host Hotels & Resorts, Inc.
4747 Bethesda Ave # 1300
Bethesda MD 20814
240 744-1000

(G-2851)
HOWLAND LOGISTICS LLC
930 Tennessee Ave (45229-1006)
PHONE.................................513 469-5263
Jennifer Howland, *Managing Member*
Matthew Howland, *
EMP: 31 **EST:** 2018
SALES (est): 1.11MM **Privately Held**
Web: www.513howland.com
SIC: 4212 Petroleum haulage, local

(G-2852)
HP PRODUCTS CORPORATION
7135 E Kemper Rd (45249-1028)
PHONE.................................513 683-8553
Mike Brown, *Brnch Mgr*
EMP: 75
SALES (corp-wide): 29.73B **Privately Held**
Web: www.ferguson.com
SIC: 5087 Janitors' supplies
HQ: Hp Products Corporation
4220 Saguaro Trl
Indianapolis IN 46268
317 225-6779

(G-2853)
HST LESSEE CINCINNATI LLC
Also Called: Westin Cincinnati, The
21 E 5th St (45202-3114)
PHONE.................................513 852-2702
Monique Taylor, *Mgr*
EMP: 160 **EST:** 2006
SALES (est): 8.84MM
SALES (corp-wide): 5.31B **Publicly Held**
Web: www.westincincinnati.com
SIC: 7011 Hotels
HQ: Host Hotels & Resorts, L.P.
6903 Rockledge Dr # 1500
Bethesda MD 20817
240 744-1000

(G-2854)
HUBBARD RADIO CINCINNATI LLC
Also Called: Cincysavers
4800 Kennedy Ave (45209-7544)
PHONE.................................513 699-5100
Michael Fredrick, *Managing Member*
James Bryant, *Managing Member*
EMP: 99 **EST:** 2007
SALES (est): 8.98MM **Privately Held**
Web: www.wkrq.com
SIC: 4832 Radio broadcasting stations, music format

(G-2855)
HUMAN RESOURCE PROFILE INC
Also Called: Hr Profile
8506 Beechmont Ave (45255-4708)
PHONE.................................513 388-4300
Mark Owens, *Pr*
EMP: 34 **EST:** 1991
SQ FT: 4,500
SALES (est): 4.88MM **Privately Held**
Web: www.hrprofile.com
SIC: 7381 Private investigator

(G-2856)
HUMANA HEALTH PLAN OHIO INC
Also Called: Humana
111 Merchant St (45246-3730)
PHONE.................................513 784-5200
Wayne Thomas Smith, *Pr*
Walter Emerson Neely, *
EMP: 100 **EST:** 1986
SALES (est): 70.23MM
SALES (corp-wide): 106.37B **Publicly Held**
Web: www.humana.com
SIC: 6324 Health Maintenance Organization (HMO), insurance only
PA: Humana Inc.
500 W Main St
Louisville KY 40202
502 580-1000

Cincinnati - Hamilton County (G-2857)

(G-2857)
HUNTINGTON NATIONAL BANK
525 Vine St (45202-3121)
PHONE..................513 762-1860
Chad Todd, *Brnch Mgr*
EMP: 51
SALES (corp-wide): 10.84B **Publicly Held**
Web: www.huntington.com
SIC: 6029 6162 6021 Commercial banks, nec; Mortgage bankers; National commercial banks
HQ: The Huntington National Bank
41 S High St
Columbus OH 43215
614 480-4293

(G-2858)
HYDE PARK GOLF & COUNTRY CLUB
3740 Erie Ave (45208-1923)
PHONE..................513 871-3111
Jeff Mcgrath, *Pr*
Eric O'bryan, *Genl Mgr*
EMP: 75 EST: 1909
SALES (est): 6.92MM **Privately Held**
Web: www.hydeparkcc.com
SIC: 7997 Country club, membership

(G-2859)
HYDE PARK HEALTH CENTER
3763 Hopper Hill Rd (45255-5051)
PHONE..................513 272-0600
Aileen Jones, *Prin*
EMP: 35 EST: 2008
SALES (est): 8.22MM **Privately Held**
Web: www.trousdalelc.org
SIC: 8051 Skilled nursing care facilities

(G-2860)
HYDE PARK LDSCP & TREE SVC INC
Also Called: Hyde Park Landscaping
5055 Wooster Rd (45226-2353)
P.O. Box 8100 (45208-0100)
PHONE..................513 731-1334
Michael Shumrick, *Pr*
Vicki Seiter, *
EMP: 49 EST: 1972
SQ FT: 9,622
SALES (est): 4.84MM **Privately Held**
Web: www.hydeparklandscaping.com
SIC: 0782 0783 Landscape contractors; Planting, pruning, and trimming services

(G-2861)
HYDRO SYSTEMS COMPANY (DH)
3798 Round Bottom Rd (45244-2498)
PHONE..................513 271-8800
◆ EMP: 48 EST: 1963
SALES (est): 30.41MM
SALES (corp-wide): 8.44B **Publicly Held**
Web: www.hydrosystemsco.com
SIC: 5084 Pumps and pumping equipment, nec
HQ: Opw Fluid Transfer Group
4304 Nw Mattox Rd
Kansas City MO 64150

(G-2862)
HYPERQUAKE LLC
310 Culvert St, Ste-401 (45202-4247)
PHONE..................513 563-6555
Jeanne Bruce, *
Colin Crotty, *
EMP: 40 EST: 2000
SALES (est): 6.36MM **Privately Held**
Web: www.hyperquake.co
SIC: 7374 Computer graphics service

(G-2863)
IGEL TECHNOLOGY AMERICA LLC
2106 Florence Ave (45206-2427)
PHONE..................954 739-9990
Jim Volpenhein, *CEO*
EMP: 31 EST: 2009
SALES (est): 886.96K **Privately Held**
Web: www.igel.com
SIC: 7372 Prepackaged software

(G-2864)
IGNITE PHILANTHROPY
308 E 8th St Fl 6 (45202-2204)
PHONE..................513 381-1848
Annemarie Henkel, *Prin*
EMP: 28 EST: 2017
SALES (est): 3.26MM **Privately Held**
Web: www.ignitephilanthropy.com
SIC: 8742 Business management consultant

(G-2865)
IMFLUX INC
1 Procter And Gamble Plz (45202-3315)
PHONE..................513 488-1017
Mary Wagner, *CEO*
Kevin Wise, *
EMP: 80 EST: 2012
SALES (est): 24.03MM
SALES (corp-wide): 82.01B **Publicly Held**
Web: www.imflux.com
SIC: 7371 8741 Computer software development; Management services
PA: The Procter & Gamble Company
1 Procter & Gamble Plz
Cincinnati OH 45202
513 983-1100

(G-2866)
IMG COLLEGE LLC
Also Called: IMG Sports
2751 O Varsity Way Ste 870 (45221-0001)
PHONE..................513 556-4532
John Mason, *Prin*
EMP: 36
SALES (corp-wide): 461.62MM **Privately Held**
Web: www.learfield.com
SIC: 7319 Display advertising service
HQ: Img College, Llc
540 N Trade St
Winston Salem NC 27101

(G-2867)
INDIANA & OHIO RAIL CORP (DH)
Also Called: Central Railroad of Indiana
2856 Cypress Way (45212-2446)
PHONE..................513 860-1000
Bill Hudran, *CEO*
Gary Mareno, *
EMP: 30 EST: 1979
SQ FT: 5,700
SALES (est): 25.34MM
SALES (corp-wide): 17.93B **Privately Held**
SIC: 4011 Railroads, line-haul operating
HQ: Railtex, Inc.
1355 Central Pkwy S # 700
San Antonio TX 78232
210 301-7600

(G-2868)
INDUSTRIAL COMM & SOUND INC
Also Called: I C S
2105 Schappelle Ln (45240-2724)
PHONE..................614 276-8123
C K Satyapriya, *Pr*
Thomas A Volz, *
Allen Volz, *
EMP: 28 EST: 1948
SQ FT: 11,000
SALES (est): 9.92MM
SALES (corp-wide): 48.4MM **Privately Held**
Web: www.icands.com
SIC: 1731 Electronic controls installation
PA: Ctl Engineering, Inc.
2860 Fisher Rd
Columbus OH 43204
614 276-8123

(G-2869)
INFINITE TIERS INC
4055 Executive Park Dr Ste 140 (45241-2076)
PHONE..................513 769-1900
Husam Barkawi, *Prin*
EMP: 400 EST: 2004
SALES (est): 11MM **Privately Held**
Web: www.itgsoftware.com
SIC: 7371 Computer software development

(G-2870)
INFO-HOLD INC
Also Called: United Media Solutions
4120 Airport Rd (45226-1644)
PHONE..................513 248-5600
Joey Hazenfield, *CEO*
Joey C Hazenfield, *
Kevin Mccullough, *Ex VP*
EMP: 28 EST: 1988
SQ FT: 60,000
SALES (est): 2.47MM **Privately Held**
Web: www.infohold.com
SIC: 7371 5065 1731 Computer software systems analysis and design, custom; Sound equipment, electronic; Sound equipment specialization

(G-2871)
INFUSION PARTNERS INC (HQ)
Also Called: Texas Infusion Partners
4623 Wesley Ave Ste H (45212-2272)
PHONE..................513 396-6060
▲ EMP: 27 EST: 1994
SQ FT: 12,000
SALES (est): 12.72MM
SALES (corp-wide): 19.28MM **Privately Held**
Web: www.optioncarehealth.com
SIC: 8082 Home health care services
PA: The Deaconess Associations Inc
615 Elsinore Pl Bldg B
Cincinnati OH 45202
513 559-2100

(G-2872)
INNOVATIVE CLEANING SVCS & SUP
Also Called: Innovative Labor Clg Svcs Sup
4903 Vine St Ste 2 (45217-1252)
PHONE..................513 981-1287
Troy Parker, *Prin*
Darlene Parker, *
EMP: 60 EST: 2015
SALES (est): 1.95MM **Privately Held**
Web: www.innovativelaborandcleaningservice.com
SIC: 7342 Disinfecting and pest control services

(G-2873)
INSTRMNTATION CTRL SYSTEMS INC
Also Called: Ics Electrical Services
11355 Sebring Dr (45240-2796)
PHONE..................513 662-2600
John Guenther, *Pr*
▲ EMP: 43 EST: 1997
SQ FT: 15,500
SALES (est): 8.53MM **Privately Held**
Web: www.icselectricalservices.com
SIC: 1731 7629 3613 General electrical contractor; Electrical measuring instrument repair and calibration; Control panels, electric

(G-2874)
INTEGRA LIFESCIENCES CORP
Also Called: Integra Lifesciences
4900 Charlemar Dr Bldg A (45227-1595)
PHONE..................513 533-7923
EMP: 99
Web: www.integralife.com
SIC: 5047 Medical equipment and supplies
HQ: Integra Lifesciences Corporation
1100 Campus Rd
Princeton NJ 08540
609 275-0500

(G-2875)
INTEGRA RLTY RSRCES - CNCNNT/D
8241 Cornell Rd Ste 210 (45249-2285)
PHONE..................513 561-2305
Gary Wright, *Prin*
EMP: 250 EST: 2012
SALES (est): 504K
SALES (corp-wide): 18.75K **Privately Held**
SIC: 6531 Appraiser, real estate
PA: Integra Realty Resources, Inc.
7800 E Union Ave Ste 400
Denver CO 80237
212 255-7858

(G-2876)
INTEGRATED PROTECTION SVCS INC (PA)
Also Called: I P S
5303 Lester Rd (45213-2523)
PHONE..................513 631-5505
Garfield Hartman, *Pr*
Steve Ortner, *
Andy Boyd, *
Richard Keller, *
Peter Keller, *
EMP: 55 EST: 1999
SQ FT: 15,000
SALES (est): 13.65MM
SALES (corp-wide): 13.65MM **Privately Held**
Web: www.integratedprotection.com
SIC: 7382 Burglar alarm maintenance and monitoring

(G-2877)
INTEGRITY EX LOGISTICS LLC (DH)
4420 Cooper Rd Ste 400 (45242-5660)
P.O. Box 42275 (45242-0275)
PHONE..................888 374-5138
James Steger, *Managing Member*
Matt Ventura, *
Pete Ventura, *
Eric Arling, *
Greg Hamilton, *
EMP: 298 EST: 2007
SQ FT: 60,000
SALES (est): 132.24MM
SALES (corp-wide): 295.34MM **Privately Held**
Web: www.ielfreight.com
SIC: 4731 Domestic freight forwarding
HQ: Iel Holdco, Llc
4420 Cooper Rd Ste 400
Blue Ash OH 45242
937 684-8180

(G-2878)
INTERACT FOR HEALTH
Also Called: Health Fndtion of Grter Cncnna
8230 Montgomery Rd Ste 300 (45236-2292)
PHONE..................513 458-6600
Donald E Hoffman, *CEO*
Daniel Geeding, *CFO*
Patricia O'connor, *VP*
Christine Bennett, *Dir*
EMP: 30 EST: 1978
SALES (est): 8.93MM **Privately Held**

Web: www.interactforhealth.org
SIC: 8399 Fund raising organization, non-fee basis

(G-2879)
INTERACTIVE BUS SYSTEMS INC
130 Tri County Pkwy Ste 208 (45246-3289)
PHONE.................................513 984-2205
Jeff Jorgensen, Genl Mgr
EMP: 91
SALES (corp-wide): 45.9MM Privately Held
Web: www.ibs.com
SIC: 7379 Data processing consultant
PA: Interactive Business Systems, Inc.
2625 Bttrfeld Rd Ste 114w
Oak Brook IL 60523
630 571-9100

(G-2880)
INTERBRAND DESIGN FORUM LLC
700 W Pete Rose Way Ste 460 (45203-1892)
PHONE.................................513 421-2210
EMP: 225 EST: 1978
SALES (est): 20.32MM
SALES (corp-wide): 14.69B Publicly Held
Web: www.interbrand.com
SIC: 8742 7389 8711 Planning consultant; Interior design services; Engineering services
HQ: Interbrand Corporation
200 Varick St Fl 10
New York NY 10014
212 798-7500

(G-2881)
INTERBRAND HULEFELD INC
700 W Pete Rose Way Ste 460 (45203-1892)
PHONE.................................513 421-2210
Bruce Dyvbad, Pr
EMP: 49 EST: 1935
SQ FT: 23,000
SALES (est): 2.35MM
SALES (corp-wide): 14.69B Publicly Held
SIC: 7336 Graphic arts and related design
HQ: Interbrand Corporation
200 Varick St Fl 10
New York NY 10014
212 798-7500

(G-2882)
INTERNATIONAL HEALTHCARE CORP
Also Called: INTERNATIONAL HEALTHCARE CORPORATION
2837 Burnet Ave (45219-2401)
PHONE.................................513 731-3338
EMP: 51
SQ FT: 2,288
Web: www.iqhc.org
SIC: 8082 6411 Home health care services; Insurance agents, brokers, and service
PA: International Quality Healthcare Corporation.
6927 N Main St Ste 101
Dayton OH 45415

(G-2883)
INTERSTATE TRUCKWAY INC (PA)
Also Called: Truckway Leasing
1755 Dreman Ave (45223)
PHONE.................................513 542-5500
Ron Horstman, Pr
Jeff Barber, *
Robert Jones, *
Shawn Watson, *
EMP: 70 EST: 1952
SALES (est): 32.34MM Privately Held
Web: www.interstatetrailer.com

SIC: 7513 5012 Truck rental and leasing, no drivers; Commercial vehicles

(G-2884)
INTERSTOP CORPORATION
Also Called: Flow Control Technology
3956 Virginia Ave (45227-3412)
P.O. Box 1745 (60423-7674)
PHONE.................................513 272-1133
Walter Schaer, Pr
Irene Niggli, VP
▲ EMP: 48 EST: 1982
SQ FT: 32,000
SALES (est): 2.21MM Privately Held
SIC: 5084 Controlling instruments and accessories
PA: Rhi Magnesita Switzerland Ag
Bosch 83a
HUnenberg ZG 6331

(G-2885)
INTREN INC
Also Called: Midwest East Division
1267 Tennessee Ave (45229-1011)
PHONE.................................815 482-0651
Brian Carlin, Mgr
EMP: 29
SALES (corp-wide): 12B Publicly Held
Web: www.intren.com
SIC: 8711 Construction and civil engineering
HQ: Intren, Llc
18202 W Union Rd
Union IL 60180
815 923-2300

(G-2886)
ION MEDIA STATIONS INC
312 Walnut St Ste 2800 (45202)
PHONE.................................561 659-4122
R Brandon Burgess, Pr
EMP: 421 EST: 1994
SALES (est): 48.85MM
SALES (corp-wide): 2.29B Publicly Held
SIC: 4833 Television broadcasting stations
HQ: Ion Media Networks, Inc.
1100 Banyan Blvd
West Palm Beach FL 33401

(G-2887)
IOTCO LLC
250 E 5th St Ste 1500 (45202-4252)
PHONE.................................877 464-6826
Mohamed Abuali, Managing Member
Rizwan Pirani, *
EMP: 45 EST: 2017
SALES (est): 1.85MM Privately Held
Web: www.iotco.com
SIC: 8742 7371 Management consulting services; Software programming applications

(G-2888)
IPSOS-ASI LLC (DH)
Also Called: Ipsos Understanding Unlimited
3505 Columbia Pkwy Ste 300 (45226-2181)
PHONE.................................513 872-4300
EMP: 121 EST: 1996
SQ FT: 1,000
SALES (est): 4.96MM
SALES (corp-wide): 392.59K Privately Held
Web: www.ipsos-uu.com
SIC: 8732 Market analysis or research
PA: Ipsos America, Inc
180 Madison Ave Fl 22
New York NY 10016
212 265-3200

(G-2889)
ITA INC (PA)
Also Called: Ita Audio Visual Solutions
2162 Dana Ave (45207-1341)
PHONE.................................513 631-7000
EMP: 30 EST: 1982
SALES (est): 20.22MM
SALES (corp-wide): 20.22MM Privately Held
Web: www.ita.com
SIC: 5064 7359 Video cassette recorders and accessories; Audio-visual equipment and supply rental

(G-2890)
ITELLIGENCE OUTSOURCING INC (DH)
Also Called: Schmidt-Vogel Consulting
10856 Reed Hartman Hwy (45242-0209)
PHONE.................................513 956-2000
EMP: 80 EST: 2000
SQ FT: 4,000
SALES (est): 24.99MM Privately Held
Web: www.nttdata-solutions.com
SIC: 7379 Online services technology consultants
HQ: Ntt Data Business Solutions Inc.
10856 Reed Hartman Hwy
Cincinnati OH 45242

(G-2891)
J & E LLC
Also Called: Chavez Properties
250 W Court St Ste 200e (45202-1064)
PHONE.................................513 241-0429
Robert Chavez, Pt
Manuel Chavez Senior, Pt
EMP: 38 EST: 1979
SQ FT: 8,100
SALES (est): 3.4MM Privately Held
Web: www.chavezproperties.com
SIC: 6519 Real property lessors, nec

(G-2892)
JACK GRAY
Also Called: Jack, The
8044 Montgomery Rd (45236-2919)
PHONE.................................216 688-0466
Jack Gray, Owner
EMP: 51 EST: 1980
SALES (est): 4.5MM Privately Held
Web: www.jacksonwealth.com
SIC: 1521 6552 General remodeling, single-family houses; Subdividers and developers, nec

(G-2893)
JACKSON CONTROL CO INC
2710 E Kemper Rd (45241-1818)
PHONE.................................513 824-9850
EMP: 46
SALES (corp-wide): 113.02K Privately Held
SIC: 7373 Computer integrated systems design
PA: Jackson Control Co Inc
1640 W Carroll Ave
Chicago IL 60612
317 231-2200

(G-2894)
JACOBS ENGINEERING GROUP INC
2 Crowne Point Ct Ste 100 (45241-5428)
PHONE.................................513 595-7500
Tim Peter, Mgr
EMP: 40
SALES (corp-wide): 14.92B Publicly Held
Web: www.jacobs.com
SIC: 8711 Consulting engineer
HQ: Jacobs Engineering Group Inc.
1999 Bryan St Ste 3500

Dallas TX 75201
214 583-8500

(G-2895)
JACOBS MECHANICAL CO
Also Called: Jacobs
4500 W Mitchell Ave (45232-1912)
PHONE.................................513 681-6800
John E Mc Donald, Pr
EMP: 125 EST: 1922
SQ FT: 20,000
SALES (est): 23.6MM Privately Held
Web: www.jacobsmech.com
SIC: 1711 3444 Ventilation and duct work contractor; Sheet metalwork

(G-2896)
JAKE SWEENEY AUTOMOTIVE INC
33 W Kemper Rd (45246-2509)
PHONE.................................513 782-2800
EMP: 61 EST: 1970
SQ FT: 60,000
SALES (est): 11.79MM Privately Held
Web: www.jakesweeney.com
SIC: 8741 7538 7532 7515 Management services; General automotive repair shops; Top and body repair and paint shops; Passenger car leasing

(G-2897)
JAKE SWEENEY BODY SHOP
Also Called: Jake Sweeney Chevrolet Imports
169 Northland Blvd Ste 1 (45246-3154)
PHONE.................................513 782-1100
EMP: 88 EST: 1978
SQ FT: 21,892
SALES (est): 580.2K Privately Held
Web: www.jakesweeney.com
SIC: 7532 Body shop, automotive

(G-2898)
JAMES HUNT CONSTRUCTION CO INC
1865 Summit Rd (45237-2803)
PHONE.................................513 721-0559
Veronica Davis, Pr
Chris Davis, *
EMP: 30 EST: 1983
SQ FT: 5,000
SALES (est): 18.23MM Privately Held
Web: www.jameshuntconstruction.com
SIC: 1542 Commercial and office buildings, renovation and repair

(G-2899)
JANCOA JANITORIAL SERVICES INC
525 Vine St Ste 1600 (45202-3132)
PHONE.................................513 351-7200
Mary Miller, CEO
Anthony Miller, *
Mary Miller, VP
EMP: 275 EST: 1972
SALES (est): 9.85MM Privately Held
Web: www.jancoa.com
SIC: 7349 Janitorial service, contract basis

(G-2900)
JAO DISTRIBUTORS INC
Also Called: Gentile Bros
10310 Julian Dr (45215-1131)
PHONE.................................513 531-6000
EMP: 89
SIC: 5148 Fruits, fresh

(G-2901)
JAVITCH BLOCK LLC
Also Called: Mapother & Mapother Attorneys
700 Walnut St Ste 300 (45202-2011)
PHONE.................................513 381-3051
Robert K Hogan, Mgr

Cincinnati - Hamilton County (G-2902)
GEOGRAPHIC SECTION

EMP: 52
SALES (corp-wide): 41.42MM **Privately Held**
Web: www.jbllc.com
SIC: 8111 General practice law office
PA: Javitch Block Llc
1100 Superior Ave E
Cleveland OH 44114
216 623-0000

(G-2902)
JEDSON ENGINEERING INC (PA)
705 Central Ave (45202-1967)
PHONE..................513 965-5999
EMP: 90 **EST:** 1984
SQ FT: 20,000
SALES (est): 75.55MM **Privately Held**
Web: www.jedson.com
SIC: 8711 Industrial engineers

(G-2903)
JESS HAUER MASONRY INC
2400 W Kemper Rd (45231-1137)
PHONE..................513 521-2178
Michael Hauer, *Pr*
Denise Dunn, *
Jess Hauer, *
Jason Hauer, *
EMP: 39 **EST:** 1945
SQ FT: 2,450
SALES (est): 2.5MM **Privately Held**
Web: www.jesshauermasonry.com
SIC: 1741 Bricklaying

(G-2904)
JETSON ENGINEERING
705 Central Ave (45202-1967)
PHONE..................513 965-5999
EMP: 35
SALES (est): 7.03MM **Privately Held**
SIC: 8711 Consulting engineer

(G-2905)
JEWISH CMNTY CTR OF CINCINNATI
Also Called: MAYERSON JCC
8485 Ridge Rd (45236-1300)
PHONE..................513 761-7500
Roz Kaplan, *Ex Dir*
Miranda Brown, *
Tsipora Gopplieb, *
Christina Zaffiro, *
Marc Fisher, *
EMP: 97 **EST:** 1935
SQ FT: 150,000
SALES (est): 13.24MM **Privately Held**
Web: www.mayersonjcc.org
SIC: 8322 Community center

(G-2906)
JEWISH FMLY SVC OF CNCNNATI AR
8487 Ridge Rd (45236-1300)
PHONE..................513 469-1188
Beth Schwarthz, *Ex Dir*
Doug Sandor, *
Beth Schwartz, *Associate Executive Director*
John Youkilif, *
Jackie Orsi, *OF Development*
EMP: 46 **EST:** 1943
SALES (est): 7.95MM **Privately Held**
Web: www.jfscinti.org
SIC: 8322 Social service center

(G-2907)
JEWISH HOSPITAL
Also Called: Cholesterol Center, The
3200 Burnet Ave Fl 5 (45229-3028)
PHONE..................513 569-2434
Charles J Glueck, *Dir*
EMP: 49 **EST:** 1988
SALES (est): 1.84MM **Privately Held**
Web: www.mercy.com
SIC: 8011 8062 Internal medicine, physician/surgeon; General medical and surgical hospitals

(G-2908)
JEWISH HOSPITAL LLC
Also Called: Health Alliance Jewish Hosp
4777 E Galbraith Rd (45236-2814)
PHONE..................513 686-5970
Ken Hanover, *Dir*
EMP: 372
SALES (corp-wide): 88.72MM **Privately Held**
Web: www.mercy.com
SIC: 8062 General medical and surgical hospitals
PA: Jewish Hospital, Llc
4777 E Galbraith Rd
Cincinnati OH 45236
513 686-3000

(G-2909)
JEWISH HOSPITAL LLC
5310 Rapid Run Rd (45238-4279)
PHONE..................513 585-2668
Terri Campbell, *Brnch Mgr*
EMP: 372
SALES (corp-wide): 88.72MM **Privately Held**
Web: www.mercy.com
SIC: 8062 General medical and surgical hospitals
PA: Jewish Hospital, Llc
4777 E Galbraith Rd
Cincinnati OH 45236
513 686-3000

(G-2910)
JEWISH HOSPITAL LLC (PA)
4777 E Galbraith Rd (45236-2814)
P.O. Box 636641 (45263-6641)
PHONE..................513 686-3000
Steve Holman Senior, *Ex Dir*
▲ **EMP:** 584 **EST:** 1941
SALES (est): 88.72MM
SALES (corp-wide): 88.72MM **Privately Held**
Web: www.mercy.com
SIC: 8062 General medical and surgical hospitals

(G-2911)
JEWISH HOSPITAL CINCINNATI INC
4777 E Galbraith Rd (45236-2814)
PHONE..................513 686-3303
Patricia Davis-hagens, *Pr*
Craig Schmidt, *
▲ **EMP:** 2500 **EST:** 1850
SQ FT: 1,000,000
SALES (est): 339.51MM
SALES (corp-wide): 6.92B **Privately Held**
Web: www.mercy.com
SIC: 8062 General medical and surgical hospitals
HQ: Mercy Health Cincinnati Llc
1701 Mercy Health Pl
Cincinnati OH 45237
513 952-5000

(G-2912)
JFDB LTD
Also Called: Hvac Mech Cntrcto Plbg Ppfttin
10036 Springfield Pike (45215-1452)
PHONE..................513 870-0601
Jonathan Feldkamp, *Pr*
Joel Feldkamp, *
EMP: 150 **EST:** 2006
SQ FT: 18,000
SALES (est): 21.84MM **Privately Held**
Web: www.jfeldkampdesignbuild.com
SIC: 1711 3499 Mechanical contractor; Aerosol valves, metal

(G-2913)
JOHN R JURGENSEN CO (PA)
11641 Mosteller Rd (45241-1520)
PHONE..................513 771-0820
▲ **EMP:** 440 **EST:** 1930
SALES (est): 225.16MM
SALES (corp-wide): 225.16MM **Privately Held**
Web: www.jrjnet.com
SIC: 1611 1442 General contractor, highway and street construction; Sand mining

(G-2914)
JOHN STEWART COMPANY
6819 Montgomery Rd (45236-3818)
PHONE..................513 703-5412
John Stewart, *Brnch Mgr*
EMP: 27
SALES (corp-wide): 93.88MM **Privately Held**
Web: www.jsco.net
SIC: 6531 Real estate managers
PA: John Stewart Company
1388 Sutter St Ste 1100
San Francisco CA 94109
415 345-4400

(G-2915)
JOHNSON CNTRLS SEC SLTIONS LLC
4750 Wesley Ave Ste Q (45212-2273)
PHONE..................513 277-4966
Tereasa Schott, *Mgr*
EMP: 36
Web: datasource.johnsoncontrols.com
SIC: 7382 Burglar alarm maintenance and monitoring
HQ: Johnson Controls Security Solutions Llc
6600 Congress Ave
Boca Raton FL 33487
561 264-2071

(G-2916)
JOHNSON ELECTRIC SUPPLY CO (PA)
1841 Riverside Dr (45202-1738)
PHONE..................513 421-3700
Douglas Johnson, *Pr*
Robert White, *
Edward W Mohr, *
Robert D Johnson, *
A B Horton, *
EMP: 34 **EST:** 1907
SQ FT: 48,000
SALES (est): 25.91MM
SALES (corp-wide): 25.91MM **Privately Held**
Web: www.johnson-electric.com
SIC: 5063 Electrical construction materials

(G-2917)
JOHNSON INVESTMENT COUNSEL INC (PA)
3777 W Fork Rd (45247-7545)
PHONE..................800 541-0170
Timothy Johnson, *Pr*
EMP: 60 **EST:** 1965
SQ FT: 1,524
SALES (est): 236.54K
SALES (corp-wide): 236.54K **Privately Held**
Web: www.johnsoninv.com
SIC: 6282 Investment counselors

(G-2918)
JOHNSON TRUST COMPANY
Also Called: Johnson Institutional MGT
3777 W Fork Rd Fl 2 (45247-7575)
PHONE..................513 598-8859
Timothy E Johnson, *CEO*
EMP: 35 **EST:** 1998
SALES (est): 997.07K **Privately Held**
Web: www.johnsoninv.com
SIC: 6282 Investment counselors

(G-2919)
JOINT DEVELOPMENT & HSING CORP
1055 Saint Paul Pl (45202-6042)
PHONE..................513 381-8696
EMP: 70 **EST:** 1995
SALES (est): 8.15MM
SALES (corp-wide): 13.3MM **Privately Held**
SIC: 1522 Apartment building construction
PA: Towne Building Group Inc
1055 Saint Paul Pl
Cincinnati OH 45202
513 381-8696

(G-2920)
JONLE CO INC
Also Called: Jonle Heating & Cooling
4117 Bridgetown Rd (45211-4503)
PHONE..................513 662-2282
Gregory Leisgang, *Pr*
Julie Leisgang Gerhardt, *VP*
EMP: 35 **EST:** 1960
SQ FT: 9,000
SALES (est): 6.57MM **Privately Held**
Web: www.jonle.com
SIC: 1711 Warm air heating and air conditioning contractor

(G-2921)
JOSTIN CONSTRUCTION INC
Also Called: Jostin
2335 Florence Ave (45206-2430)
PHONE..................513 559-9390
Albert C Smitherman, *Pr*
EMP: 50 **EST:** 1998
SQ FT: 16,000
SALES (est): 16.39MM **Privately Held**
Web: www.jostinconstruction.com
SIC: 1771 Concrete work

(G-2922)
JUDSON CARE CENTER INC
2386 Kemper Ln (45206-2665)
PHONE..................513 662-5880
EMP: 548 **EST:** 1987
SALES (est): 7.61MM
SALES (corp-wide): 655.44MM **Privately Held**
Web: www.judsonvillage.com
SIC: 8051 8052 Skilled nursing care facilities ; Personal care facility
PA: Saber Healthcare Group, L.L.C.
23700 Commerce Park
Beachwood OH 44122
216 292-5706

(G-2923)
JUNIOR COOP SOC CHLDREN S HOSP
Also Called: Childern's Hospital Gift Shop
3333 Burnet Ave (45229-3026)
PHONE..................513 636-4310
Jean Pappas, *Prin*
EMP: 48 **EST:** 1945
SALES (est): 4.77MM **Privately Held**
Web: www.cincinnatichildrens.org
SIC: 8062 General medical and surgical hospitals

(G-2924)
JWT ACTION
35 E 7th St Ste 620 (45202-2446)
PHONE..................513 578-6721
EMP: 28
SALES (corp-wide): 18.5B **Privately Held**
SIC: 7311 Advertising agencies
HQ: Jwt Action
388 S Main St Ste 410
Akron OH 44311
330 376-6148

(G-2925)
K F T INC
726 Mehring Way (45203-1809)
PHONE..................513 241-5910
Ronald Eubanks, *Pr*
Richard Eubanks, *Stockholder**
EMP: 60 **EST:** 1941
SQ FT: 45,000
SALES (est): 4.88MM **Privately Held**
Web: www.tkf.com
SIC: 1796 3535 Millwright; Overhead conveyor systems

(G-2926)
K R DRENTH TRUCKING INC
119 E Court St (45202-1203)
PHONE..................708 983-6340
EMP: 81
Web: www.krdtrucking.com
SIC: 4212 Dump truck haulage
PA: K. R. Drenth Trucking, Inc.
10275 W Higgins Rd # 420
Rosemont IL 60018

(G-2927)
K&K TECHNICAL GROUP INC
3554 Blue Rock Rd (45239-5106)
PHONE..................513 202-1300
EMP: 200 **EST:** 1995
SALES (est): 15.3MM **Privately Held**
Web: www.kandktechnical.com
SIC: 7361 Executive placement

(G-2928)
K4 ARCHITECTURE LLC
555 Gest St (45203-1716)
PHONE..................513 455-5005
David Noell, *
John Schafer, *
Rick Posey, *
EMP: 60 **EST:** 1998
SQ FT: 25,000
SALES (est): 9.71MM **Privately Held**
Web: www.k4architecture.com
SIC: 8712 Architectural engineering

(G-2929)
KAO COLLINS INC (HQ)
1201 Edison Dr (45216-2277)
PHONE..................513 948-9000
Lawrence Gamblin, *Pr*
Lisa Gamblin, *Treas*
▲ **EMP:** 44 **EST:** 1995
SQ FT: 8,700
SALES (est): 36.91MM **Privately Held**
Web: www.kaocollins.com
SIC: 5043 5946 Photographic equipment and supplies; Camera and photographic supply stores
PA: Kao Corporation
1-14-10, Nihombashikayabacho
Chuo-Ku TKY 103-0

(G-2930)
KARING 4 KIDS LEARNING CENTER
9495 Coogan Dr (45231-2853)
PHONE..................513 931-5273
Salume Odubola, *Dir*
EMP: 29 **EST:** 2009
SALES (est): 738.88K **Privately Held**
Web: www.karing4kidslearningcenter.com
SIC: 8351 Preschool center

(G-2931)
KATZ TELLER BRANT HILD CO LPA
Also Called: Katz Teller
255 E 5th St Fl 24 (45202-4724)
PHONE..................513 721-4532
Katz Teller, *Pr*
Joseph Brant, *
Jerome S Teller, *
Guy Hild, *
Mark Jahnke, *
EMP: 65 **EST:** 1967
SALES (est): 8.99MM **Privately Held**
Web: www.katzteller.com
SIC: 8111 General practice attorney, lawyer

(G-2932)
KEATING MUETHING & KLEKAMP PLL (PA)
Also Called: Kmk
1 E 4th St Ste 1400 (45202-3752)
PHONE..................513 579-6400
Donald P Klekamp, *Sr Pt*
Paul V Muething, *
EMP: 350 **EST:** 1955
SQ FT: 60,000
SALES (est): 49.96MM
SALES (corp-wide): 49.96MM **Privately Held**
Web: www.kmklaw.com
SIC: 8111 General practice attorney, lawyer

(G-2933)
KEIDEL SUP LLC FKA KDEL SUP IN (HQ) ✪
Also Called: Keidel
1150 Tennessee Ave (45229-1010)
PHONE..................513 351-1600
Michael Barton, *Ch Bd*
Barry Keidel, *
EMP: 35 **EST:** 2023
SQ FT: 20,000
SALES (est): 22.12MM
SALES (corp-wide): 3.02B **Privately Held**
Web: www.keidel.com
SIC: 5074 5031 5099 Plumbing fittings and supplies; Kitchen cabinets; Firearms and ammunition, except sporting
PA: Winsupply Inc.
3110 Kettering Blvd
Moraine OH 45439
937 294-5331

(G-2934)
KEMBA CREDIT UNION INC
6230 Hamilton Ave (45224-2009)
PHONE..................513 541-3015
EMP: 104
SALES (corp-wide): 66.36MM **Privately Held**
Web: www.kemba.com
SIC: 6061 Federal credit unions
PA: Kemba Credit Union, Inc.
5600 Chppell Crssing Blvd
West Chester OH 45069
513 762-5070

(G-2935)
KENNEDY HEIGHTS MONTESSORI CTR
6620 Montgomery Rd (45213-1877)
PHONE..................513 631-8135
Marybeth Schneider, *Dir*
EMP: 33 **EST:** 1966
SALES (est): 1.23MM **Privately Held**
Web: www.kennedyheightsmontessori.org
SIC: 8351 Montessori child development center

(G-2936)
KENWOOD TER HLTH CARE CTR INC
Also Called: Kenwood Terrace Care Center
7450 Keller Rd (45243-1028)
PHONE..................513 793-2255
Harold Sosna, *Pr*
EMP: 145 **EST:** 1998
SALES (est): 10.79MM **Privately Held**
SIC: 8051 Convalescent home with continuous nursing care

(G-2937)
KENWORTH OF CINCINNATI INC
Also Called: PacLease
65 Partnership Way (45241-1570)
P.O. Box 62477 (45262-0477)
PHONE..................513 771-5831
Eldon Palmer, *Ch*
John Nichols, *
Jeffrey Curry, *
Jeffrey Gauger, *
EMP: 90 **EST:** 1961
SQ FT: 32,000
SALES (est): 9.22MM **Privately Held**
Web: www.palmertrucks.com
SIC: 5012 5013 7538 7513 Trucks, commercial; Truck parts and accessories; General automotive repair shops; Truck leasing, without drivers

(G-2938)
KERKAN ROOFING INC
Also Called: Kerkan
721 W Wyoming Ave (45215-4528)
PHONE..................513 821-0556
EMP: 72 **EST:** 1995
SQ FT: 20,000
SALES (est): 16.77MM **Privately Held**
Web: www.kerkan.com
SIC: 1761 Roofing contractor

(G-2939)
KERRY FORD INC (PA)
Also Called: Kerry Mitsubishi
155 W Kemper Rd (45246-2590)
PHONE..................513 671-6400
Patrick De Castro, *Pr*
Daniel J Brady, *
Paul W Krone, *
EMP: 100 **EST:** 1967
SQ FT: 50,000
SALES (est): 24.73MM
SALES (corp-wide): 24.73MM **Privately Held**
Web: www.quicklane.com
SIC: 5511 7538 7532 7515 Automobiles, new and used; General automotive repair shops; Top and body repair and paint shops ; Passenger car leasing

(G-2940)
KINETIC NUTRITION GROUP LLC
10270 Spartan Dr Ste S (45215)
PHONE..................513 279-8966
EMP: 35 **EST:** 2012
SALES (est): 3.49MM **Privately Held**
Web: www.kineticdogfood.com
SIC: 5149 Dog food

(G-2941)
KINGS TOYOTA INC
Also Called: Kings Toyota Scion
4700 Fields Ertel Rd (45249-8200)
PHONE..................513 583-4333
Gerald Carmichael, *Pr*
EMP: 95 **EST:** 1988
SALES (est): 21.56MM **Privately Held**
Web: www.kingstoyota.com
SIC: 5511 7515 7538 Automobiles, new and used; Passenger car leasing; General automotive repair shops

(G-2942)
KIRK & BLUM MANUFACTURING CO (DH)
4625 Red Bank Rd Ste 200 (45227-1552)
PHONE..................513 458-2600
◆ **EMP:** 200 **EST:** 1907
SQ FT: 250,000
SALES (est): 48.76MM **Publicly Held**
Web: www.cecoenviro.com
SIC: 1761 3444 3443 Sheet metal work, nec; Sheet metal specialties, not stamped; Fabricated plate work (boiler shop)
HQ: Ceco Group, Inc.
4625 Red Bank Rd Ste 200
Cincinnati OH 45227
513 458-2600

(G-2943)
KLOECKNER METALS CORPORATION
11501 Reading Rd (45241-2240)
PHONE..................513 769-4000
Darryl Grinstead, *Brnch Mgr*
EMP: 76
SALES (corp-wide): 7.56B **Privately Held**
Web: www.kloecknermetals.com
SIC: 5051 Steel
HQ: Kloeckner Metals Corporation
500 Colonial Center Pkwy # 500
Roswell GA 30076

(G-2944)
KLOSTERMAN BAKING CO LLC
1000 E Ross Ave (45217-1132)
PHONE..................513 242-5667
EMP: 62
SALES (corp-wide): 190.57MM **Privately Held**
Web: www.klostermanbakery.com
SIC: 5149 2051 Bakery products; Bread, cake, and related products
PA: Klosterman Baking Co., Llc
4760 Paddock Rd
Cincinnati OH 45229
513 242-1004

(G-2945)
KNOWLEDGEWORKS FOUNDATION (PA)
312 Plum St Ste 950 (45202)
PHONE..................513 929-4777
William Hite, *CEO*
Brian Ross, *
William E Mcneese, *Sr VP*
James L Scott, *CIO**
Andrew Benson, *
EMP: 43 **EST:** 1991
SQ FT: 8,000
SALES (est): 3.68MM
SALES (corp-wide): 3.68MM **Privately Held**
Web: www.knowledgeworks.org
SIC: 8299 8742 Educational services; Management consulting services

(G-2946)
KO TRANSMISSION COMPANY (DH)
139 E 4th St Rm 405-A (45202-4003)
PHONE..................513 287-3553
EMP: 30 **EST:** 1996
SQ FT: 300
SALES (est): 8.49MM
SALES (corp-wide): 29.06B **Publicly Held**
Web: www.kotransmission.com

Cincinnati - Hamilton County (G-2947)

SIC: 4922 Natural gas transmission
HQ: Duke Energy Ohio, Inc.
139 E 4th St
Cincinnati OH 45202
704 382-3853

(G-2947)
KOI ENTERPRISES INC
11849 Kemper Springs Dr Ste 1 (45240-6600)
PHONE..............................513 648-3020
EMP: 113
SALES (corp-wide): 525.52MM **Privately Held**
Web: www.koiautoparts.com
SIC: 5531 5013 Automotive parts; Automotive supplies and parts
HQ: K.O.I. Enterprises, Inc.
2701 Spring Grove Ave
Cincinnati OH 45225
513 357-2400

(G-2948)
KOI ENTERPRISES INC (HQ)
Also Called: K O I
2701 Spring Grove Ave (45225-2221)
P.O. Box 14240 (45250-0240)
PHONE..............................513 357-2400
David Wesselman, *Pr*
Greg Steppe, *
▲ **EMP:** 100 **EST:** 1946
SALES (est): 292.81MM
SALES (corp-wide): 525.52MM **Privately Held**
Web: www.koiautoparts.com
SIC: 5013 5531 Automotive supplies and parts; Auto and home supply stores
PA: Fisher Auto Parts, Inc.
512 Greenville Ave
Staunton VA 24401
540 885-8901

(G-2949)
KRAFT ELECTRICAL CONTG INC (PA)
Also Called: Kraft Electrical & Telecom Svs
5710 Hillside Ave (45233-1508)
PHONE..............................513 467-0500
Kelly Degregorio, *Pr*
John Kraft, *
Kimberly Kraft, *
Rich Voegeli, *Prin*
EMP: 49 **EST:** 1997
SALES (est): 22.8MM
SALES (corp-wide): 22.8MM **Privately Held**
Web: www.kecc.com
SIC: 1731 General electrical contractor

(G-2950)
KRAMER & FELDMAN INC
7636 Production Dr (45237-3209)
PHONE..............................513 821-7444
Daniel Kramer, *Pr*
Michael Feldman, *
Lori Feldman, *
EMP: 27 **EST:** 1992
SQ FT: 8,000
SALES (est): 4.73MM **Privately Held**
Web: www.kficontractors.com
SIC: 1542 1541 Commercial and office building contractors; Industrial buildings and warehouses

(G-2951)
KRELLER BUS INFO GROUP INC (PA)
Also Called: Kreller Group
817 Main St Ste 300 (45202-2153)
PHONE..............................513 723-8900
Joe Davidoski, *Pr*
Harvey Rosen, *

Scott Shaffer, *
EMP: 30 **EST:** 1991
SQ FT: 5,000
SALES (est): 7.09MM
SALES (corp-wide): 7.09MM **Privately Held**
Web: www.kreller.com
SIC: 7323 7381 Credit reporting services; Private investigator

(G-2952)
KRELLER CONSULTING GROUP INC
Also Called: Kreller Group
817 Main St Ste 700 (45202-2183)
PHONE..............................513 723-8900
Joseph M Davidoski, *Pr*
John Twomui, *Sec*
Bonnie Keller, *Treas*
EMP: 32 **EST:** 1989
SALES (est): 982.29K **Privately Held**
Web: www.krellerconsulting.com
SIC: 8742 Management information systems consultant

(G-2953)
KRLP INC
1014 Vine St (45202-1141)
PHONE..............................513 762-4000
David B Dillon, *CEO*
EMP: 25000 **EST:** 1997
SALES (est): 210.5MM
SALES (corp-wide): 150.04B **Publicly Held**
SIC: 5141 5411 Groceries, general line; Supermarkets, chain
PA: The Kroger Co
1014 Vine St
Cincinnati OH 45202
513 762-4000

(G-2954)
KROGER DEDICATED LOGISTICS CO (HQ)
1014 Vine St Ste 1000 (45202-1119)
PHONE..............................309 691-9670
David Dillon, *CEO*
James Arnold, *Pr*
EMP: 36 **EST:** 1997
SQ FT: 357,000
SALES (est): 4.43MM
SALES (corp-wide): 150.04B **Publicly Held**
Web: www.thekrogerco.com
SIC: 4213 Trucking, except local
PA: The Kroger Co
1014 Vine St
Cincinnati OH 45202
513 762-4000

(G-2955)
KS ENERGY SERVICES LLC
4320 Mount Carmel Rd (45244-1642)
PHONE..............................513 271-0276
EMP: 130
SALES (corp-wide): 2.13B **Privately Held**
Web: www.millerpipeline.com
SIC: 1623 Gas main construction
HQ: Ks Energy Services, Llc
19705 W Lincoln Ave
New Berlin WI 53146
262 574-5100

(G-2956)
KUEMPEL SERVICE INC
Also Called: Debra Kuempel
3976 Southern Ave (45227-3562)
PHONE..............................513 271-6500
Joseph Clark, *CEO*
John L Kuempel Junior, *VP*
EMP: 30 **EST:** 1981
SQ FT: 35,000

SALES (est): 9.41MM
SALES (corp-wide): 12.58B **Publicly Held**
Web: www.dkemcor.com
SIC: 1711 Mechanical contractor
PA: Emcor Group, Inc.
301 Merritt 7
Norwalk CT 06851
203 849-7800

(G-2957)
KW INTERNATIONAL INC
500 W Kemper Rd (45246-2202)
PHONE..............................513 942-8999
Harry Lee, *VP*
EMP: 87
Web: www.kwinternational.com
SIC: 4731 Freight forwarding
PA: Kw International, Inc.
18655 Bishop Ave
Carson CA 90746

(G-2958)
KYOCERA SENCO INDUS TLS INC (HQ)
8450 Broadwell Rd (45244-1612)
PHONE..............................513 388-2000
Cliff Mentrup, *CEO*
▲ **EMP:** 70 **EST:** 1948
SALES (est): 92.87MM **Privately Held**
Web: www.senco.com
SIC: 3546 7389 Power-driven handtools; Business services, nec
PA: Kyocera Corporation
6, Takedatobadonocho, Fushimi-Ku
Kyoto KYO 612-8

(G-2959)
KZF DESIGN INC
700 Broadway St (45202-6010)
PHONE..............................513 621-6211
Robert B Steele, *CEO*
William H Wilson Iii, *Pr*
Susan Williams, *
EMP: 74 **EST:** 1956
SQ FT: 36,000
SALES (est): 12.49MM **Privately Held**
Web: www.kzf.com
SIC: 8712 8711 Architectural engineering; Engineering services

(G-2960)
L & W SUPPLY CORPORATION
Also Called: Nexgen Building Supply
3274 Spring Grove Ave (45225-1338)
PHONE..............................513 723-1150
Jeff Worthington, *Mgr*
EMP: 35
SALES (corp-wide): 5.87MM **Privately Held**
Web: www.lwsupply.com
SIC: 5211 5032 Lumber products; Drywall materials
HQ: L & W Supply Corporation
300 S Rvrside Plz Ste 200
Chicago IL 60606
844 977-6785

(G-2961)
L2 SOURCE LLC
Also Called: L2 Source
4620 Wesley Ave Ste 200 (45212-2234)
PHONE..............................513 428-4530
EMP: 50 **EST:** 2018
SALES (est): 3.34MM **Privately Held**
Web: www.l2source.com
SIC: 7361 Employment agencies

(G-2962)
LADD INC
3603 Victory Pkwy (45229-2297)
PHONE..............................513 861-4089

David Robinson, *Prin*
EMP: 40 **EST:** 2002
SALES (est): 10.17MM **Privately Held**
Web: www.laddinc.org
SIC: 8361 Mentally handicapped home

(G-2963)
LAFAYETTE LIFE INSURANCE CO (DH)
400 Broadway St (45202-3312)
P.O. Box 5740 (45201-5740)
PHONE..............................800 443-8793
Larry Griypp, *Pr*
Jeffrey A Poxon, *
William Olds, *
Ronald Heibert, *
EMP: 185 **EST:** 1905
SQ FT: 102,000
SALES (est): 114.74MM **Privately Held**
Web: www.westernsouthern.com
SIC: 6311 Life insurance carriers
HQ: Western & Southern Financial Group, Inc.
400 Broadway
Cincinnati OH 45202
877 367-9734

(G-2964)
LAIDLAW TRANSIT SERVICES INC (DH)
600 Vine St Ste 1400 (45202-2426)
PHONE..............................513 241-2200
Mike Rushin, *Pr*
Jeff C Baker, *
EMP: 45 **EST:** 1995
SQ FT: 23,000
SALES (est): 102.23MM
SALES (corp-wide): 5.71B **Privately Held**
SIC: 4111 Local and suburban transit
HQ: Firstgroup America, Inc.
191 Rosa Parks St
Cincinnati OH 45202
513 241-2200

(G-2965)
LANGDON INC
9865 Wayne Ave (45215-1403)
P.O. Box 15308 (45215-0308)
PHONE..............................513 733-5955
David Sandman, *Pr*
Michael Sandman, *
▲ **EMP:** 40 **EST:** 1966
SQ FT: 42,000
SALES (est): 6.92MM **Privately Held**
Web: www.langdonsheetmetal.com
SIC: 3444 1711 3564 3446 Ducts, sheet metal; Warm air heating and air conditioning contractor; Blowers and fans; Architectural metalwork

(G-2966)
LAROSAS INC (PA)
2334 Boudinot Ave (45238-3492)
PHONE..............................513 347-5660
Donald S Buddy Larosa, *Prin*
Michael Larosa, *Prin*
Donald S Larosa, *
Mark Larosa, *
Joanne Larosa, *
EMP: 515 **EST:** 1954
SQ FT: 10,000
SALES (est): 46.7MM
SALES (corp-wide): 46.7MM **Privately Held**
Web: www.larosas.com
SIC: 5812 6794 5141 5921 Pizzeria, chain; Franchises, selling or licensing; Groceries, general line; Wine

GEOGRAPHIC SECTION
Cincinnati - Hamilton County (G-2988)

(G-2967)
LAWYERS TITLE CINCINNATI INC (HQ)
3500 Red Bank Rd (45227-4111)
PHONE...................513 421-1313
Timothy Griffin, *Pr*
Michael Fletcher, *
Ernie Overstreet, *
EMP: 60 **EST:** 1967
SQ FT: 10,000
SALES (est): 25.7MM **Publicly Held**
Web: www.ltcincy.com
SIC: 6361 Real estate title insurance
PA: Fidelity National Financial, Inc.
601 Riverside Ave
Jacksonville FL 32204

(G-2968)
LCA-VISION INC (HQ)
Also Called: Lasikplus
7840 Montgomery Rd (45236-4348)
PHONE...................513 792-9292
Craig Joffe, *CEO*
EMP: 28 **EST:** 1987
SQ FT: 30,000
SALES (est): 154.83MM
SALES (corp-wide): 154.83MM **Privately Held**
Web: www.lasikplus.com
SIC: 8011 Opthalmologist
PA: Vision Acquisition, Llc
7840 Montgomery Rd
Cincinnati OH 45236
513 792-9292

(G-2969)
LEGAL AID SOCIETY CINCINNATI (PA)
Also Called: LEGAL AID SOCIETY OF GREATER C
215 E 9th St Ste 200 (45202-1084)
PHONE...................513 241-9400
TOLL FREE: 800
Mary Asbury, *Ex Dir*
Gayle Bogardus, *
EMP: 70 **EST:** 1908
SQ FT: 21,000
SALES (est): 10.71MM
SALES (corp-wide): 10.71MM **Privately Held**
Web: www.lascinti.org
SIC: 8111 Legal aid service

(G-2970)
LEI HOME ENHANCEMENTS
11880 Kemper Springs Dr (45240-1640)
PHONE...................513 738-4663
EMP: 250 **EST:** 2011
SALES (est): 9.3MM **Privately Held**
Web: www.leihomeenhancements.com
SIC: 7299 6794 Home improvement and renovation contractor agency; Franchises, selling or licensing

(G-2971)
LEWIS BRSBOIS BSGARD SMITH LLP
250 E 5th St Ste 2000 (45202-4136)
PHONE...................859 663-9830
EMP: 35
SALES (corp-wide): 284.92MM **Privately Held**
Web: www.lewisbrisbois.com
SIC: 8111 General practice law office
PA: Lewis Brisbois Bisgaard & Smith Llp
633 W 5th St Ste 4000
Los Angeles CA 90071
213 250-1800

(G-2972)
LEYMAN MANUFACTURING CORP
Also Called: Leyman Liftgates
10335 Wayne Ave (45215-1128)
PHONE...................513 891-6210
John Mc Henry, *Pr*
Robert Drews Junior, *VP Sls*
Raymond B Leyman, *
William Margroum, *
▲ **EMP:** 90 **EST:** 1940
SQ FT: 50,000
SALES (est): 20.51MM **Privately Held**
Web: www.leymanlift.com
SIC: 5084 Materials handling machinery

(G-2973)
LIBBY PRSZYK KTHMAN HLDNGS INC
Also Called: L P K
19 Garfield Pl (45202-4310)
PHONE...................513 241-6401
Jerome Kathman, *Pr*
Dennis Geiger, *
John Recker, *INTL*
Phil Best, *
EMP: 90 **EST:** 1983
SQ FT: 125,000
SALES (est): 13.88MM **Privately Held**
Web: www.lpk.com
SIC: 7336 Graphic arts and related design

(G-2974)
LIBERTY NRSING CTR RVRSIDE LLC
315 Lilienthal St (45204-1170)
P.O. Box 11499 (45211-0499)
PHONE...................513 557-3621
EMP: 48 **EST:** 1982
SALES (est): 8.72MM **Privately Held**
Web: www.libertynursingcenters.com
SIC: 8051 8069 Convalescent home with continuous nursing care; Specialty hospitals, except psychiatric

(G-2975)
LIEBEL-FLARSHEIM COMPANY LLC
Also Called: Guerbet
2111 E Galbraith Rd (45237-1624)
P.O. Box 152760567 (45237)
PHONE...................513 761-2700
EMP: 186
SALES (corp-wide): 477.14MM **Privately Held**
Web: www.guerbet.com
SIC: 1541 Pharmaceutical manufacturing plant construction
HQ: Liebel-Flarsheim Company Llc
1034 S Brentwood Blvd
Saint Louis MO 63117
314 376-4768

(G-2976)
LIFECENTER ORGAN DONOR NETWORK (PA)
615 Elsinore Pl Ste 400 (45202-1455)
PHONE...................513 558-5555
David D Lewis, *Dir*
Jeff Matthews Md, *Ch*
EMP: 47 **EST:** 1981
SQ FT: 4,500
SALES (est): 21.37MM
SALES (corp-wide): 21.37MM **Privately Held**
Web: www.lifepassiton.org
SIC: 8099 Medical services organization

(G-2977)
LIGHTHOUSE YOUTH SERVICES INC (PA)
Also Called: LIGHTHOUSE YOUTH SERVICES
401 E Mcmillan St (45206-1922)
PHONE...................513 221-3350
Bob Mecum, *CEO*
Jean Sepate, *
Judy Oakman, *
EMP: 65 **EST:** 1969
SQ FT: 13,710
SALES (est): 30.45MM
SALES (corp-wide): 30.45MM **Privately Held**
Web: www.lys.org
SIC: 8322 Youth center

(G-2978)
LINCARE INC
10720 Makro Dr Ste A (45241-7514)
PHONE...................513 272-6050
Bob Davis, *Mgr*
EMP: 35
Web: www.lincare.com
SIC: 7352 Medical equipment rental
HQ: Lincare Inc.
19387 Us Highway 19 N
Clearwater FL 33764
727 530-7700

(G-2979)
LINCOLN MRCURY KINGS AUTO MALL (PA)
Also Called: Montgomery Jeep Eagle
9600 Kings Auto Mall Rd (45249-8240)
PHONE...................513 683-3800
Robert C Reichert, *Pr*
Gerald M Car Michael, *
Mark Pittman, *
Lou Galbraith, *
EMP: 50 **EST:** 1954
SQ FT: 23,000
SALES (est): 23.35MM
SALES (corp-wide): 23.35MM **Privately Held**
Web: www.lincolnofcincinnati.com
SIC: 5511 7514 7538 7515 Automobiles, new and used; Passenger car rental; General automotive repair shops; Passenger car leasing

(G-2980)
LINDHORST & DREIDAME CO LPA
Also Called: Lindhorst & Dreidame
312 Walnut St Ste 3100 (45202-4091)
PHONE...................513 421-6630
William Kirkham, *Pr*
EMP: 39 **EST:** 1942
SQ FT: 20,000
SALES (est): 6.05MM **Privately Held**
Web: www.lindhorstlaw.com
SIC: 8111 General practice attorney, lawyer

(G-2981)
LISNR INC (PA)
Also Called: Lisnr
1203 Main St 2nd Fl (45202-7611)
PHONE...................513 322-8400
Eric Allen, *CEO*
Rodney Williams, *CCO*
Anna Aguiar, *
Vicky Sagehorn, *
Eric Allen, *Pr*
EMP: 33 **EST:** 2014
SALES (est): 2.74MM
SALES (corp-wide): 2.74MM **Privately Held**
Web: www.lisnr.com
SIC: 7371 Computer software development

(G-2982)
LITTLE SSTERS OF POOR BLTMORE
Also Called: Archbishop Leibold Home
476 Riddle Rd (45220-2411)
PHONE...................513 281-8001
Motherjoseph Grenon, *Mgr*
EMP: 92
SQ FT: 13,932
SALES (corp-wide): 3.97MM **Privately Held**
Web: www.littlesistersofthepoor.org
SIC: 8361 8052 Aged home; Intermediate care facilities
PA: Little Sisters Of The Poor, Baltimore, Inc.
601 Maiden Choice Ln
Baltimore MD 21228
410 744-9367

(G-2983)
LIVING ARRNGMNTS FOR DVLPMNTLL
Also Called: L A D D
3603 Victory Pkwy (45229-2207)
PHONE...................513 861-5233
Susan Brownknight, *CEO*
Fred Valerius, *
EMP: 200 **EST:** 1975
SALES (est): 12.64MM **Privately Held**
Web: www.laddinc.org
SIC: 8361 Mentally handicapped home

(G-2984)
LMI TRANSPORTS INC
Also Called: Quality Carrier
10300 Evendale Dr Ste 4 (45241-7502)
PHONE...................513 921-4564
Jody Mangeot, *Pr*
Robert Moore, *
EMP: 38 **EST:** 2002
SALES (est): 2.35MM **Privately Held**
SIC: 4215 Courier services, except by air

(G-2985)
LOGISTICS LEGACY LLC
1085 Summer St (45204-2037)
PHONE...................513 244-3026
Ryan Canfield, *CEO*
Mike Lawry, *Pr*
Duke Heller, *Dir Opers*
EMP: 28 **EST:** 2006
SALES (est): 12.95MM **Privately Held**
Web: www.hglogisticsllc.com
SIC: 4731 Freight transportation arrangement

(G-2986)
LONDON COMPUTER SYSTEMS INC
Also Called: Lcs
9140 Waterstone Blvd (45249-7501)
PHONE...................513 583-0840
David Hegemann, *Pr*
EMP: 100 **EST:** 1987
SQ FT: 20,000
SALES (est): 13.28MM **Privately Held**
Web: www.lcs.com
SIC: 7379 7371 Online services technology consultants; Computer software development

(G-2987)
LOSANT IOT INC
1100 Sycamore St Fl 7 (45202-1361)
PHONE...................513 381-2947
Charles Key, *CEO*
EMP: 50 **EST:** 2015
SALES (est): 7.59MM **Privately Held**
Web: www.losant.com
SIC: 7371 Computer software development

(G-2988)
LOSANTIVILLE COUNTRY CLUB
3097 Losantiville Ave (45213-1398)
PHONE...................513 631-4133
Steve Vanburen, *Genl Mgr*
Marilyn Sferra, *
EMP: 85 **EST:** 1906

Cincinnati - Hamilton County (G-2989)

GEOGRAPHIC SECTION

SQ FT: 36,000
SALES (est): 4.09MM **Privately Held**
Web: www.losantivillecc.com
SIC: 7997 Country club, membership

(G-2989)
LOTH INC (PA)
Also Called: Asset Solutions
3574 E Kemper Rd (45241-2009)
PHONE.................513 554-4900
Jb Buse Junior, *CEO*
Rick Naber, *
Eric Roach, *
Walter Homan, *Stockholder*
EMP: 93 **EST:** 1994
SQ FT: 212,000
SALES (est): 56.34MM
SALES (corp-wide): 56.34MM **Privately Held**
Web: www.lothinc.com
SIC: 7389 8712 Design services; Architectural services

(G-2990)
LOWES HOME CENTERS LLC
Also Called: Lowe's
6150 Harrison Ave (45247-7848)
PHONE.................513 598-7050
Fausto Fuentes, *Brnch Mgr*
EMP: 148
SALES (corp-wide): 86.38B **Publicly Held**
Web: www.lowes.com
SIC: 5211 5031 5722 5064 Home centers; Building materials, exterior; Household appliance stores; Electrical appliances, television and radio
HQ: Lowe's Home Centers, Llc
1000 Lowes Blvd
Mooresville NC 28117
336 658-4000

(G-2991)
LOYAL AMERICAN LIFE INSUR CO
250 E 5th St 8th Fl (45202-4119)
PHONE.................800 633-6752
Charles Scheper, *Pr*
Robert A Adams, *
Edward C Dahmer Junior, *Sr VP*
Mark Muething, *
W Randolph Samples, *
EMP: 108 **EST:** 1955
SALES (est): 1.43MM
SALES (corp-wide): 195.26B **Publicly Held**
SIC: 6331 Fire, marine, and casualty insurance
HQ: Cigna Health And Life Insurance Company
900 Cottage Grove Rd
Bloomfield CT 06002

(G-2992)
LQ MANAGEMENT LLC
Also Called: La Quinta Inn
11029 Dowlin Dr (45241-1833)
PHONE.................513 771-0300
William Goetz, *Brnch Mgr*
EMP: 27
SALES (corp-wide): 1.4B **Publicly Held**
Web: www.lq.com
SIC: 7011 Hotels and motels
HQ: Lq Management L.L.C.
909 Hidden Rdg Ste 600
Irving TX 75038
214 492-6600

(G-2993)
LUCRUM INCORPORATED
7755 Montgomery Rd Ste 160 (45236-4197)
PHONE.................513 241-5949

EMP: 40
Web: www.lucruminc.com
SIC: 7379 7373 Computer related consulting services; Systems integration services

(G-2994)
LUMINAUT INC
1100 Sycamore St (45202-1361)
PHONE.................513 984-1070
Michael J Levally, *CEO*
Fredrick G Koehler Junior, *Pr*
Andrew Schaub, *Pr*
Nora Wiley, *VP*
Kirk Hodulik, *Prin*
EMP: 27 **EST:** 1979
SQ FT: 10,000
SALES (est): 866.83K **Privately Held**
Web: www.luminaut.com
SIC: 8712 Architectural engineering

(G-2995)
LUXFER MAGTECH INC (HQ)
Also Called: Heatermeals
2940 Highland Ave Ste 210 (45212-2402)
PHONE.................513 772-3066
Brian Purves, *CEO*
Marc Lamensdorf, *
Deborah Simsen, *
Deepak Madan, *
EMP: 37 **EST:** 2014
SALES (est): 7.78MM
SALES (corp-wide): 405MM **Privately Held**
Web: www.heatermeals.com
SIC: 2899 5149 Desalter kits, sea water; Groceries and related products, nec
PA: Luxfer Holdings Plc
Ancorage Gateway
Salford LANCS M50 3
161 300-0611

(G-2996)
LYONDELL CHEMICAL COMPANY
11530 Northlake Dr (45249-1642)
PHONE.................513 530-4000
Norma Maraschin, *Mgr*
EMP: 143
Web: www.lyondellbasell.com
SIC: 2869 2822 8731 Olefins; Polyethylene, chlorosulfonated, hypalon; Commercial physical research
HQ: Lyondell Chemical Company
1221 Mckinney St Ste 300
Houston TX 77010
713 309-7200

(G-2997)
LYTLE PARK INN LLC
311 Pike St (45202-4213)
PHONE.................513 621-4500
EMP: 32 **EST:** 2016
SALES (est): 3.74MM **Privately Held**
Web: www.thelytleparkhotel.com
SIC: 7011 Inns

(G-2998)
M T GOLF COURSE MANAGMENT INC (PA)
Also Called: Pebble Creek Golf Course
9799 Prechtel Rd (45252-2117)
PHONE.................513 923-1188
Michael R Macke, *CEO*
Mary J Padro, *
Mike Faillece, *
Carl F Tuke Junior, *Prin*
EMP: 50 **EST:** 1986
SQ FT: 15,000
SALES (est): 3.97MM
SALES (corp-wide): 3.97MM **Privately Held**
Web: www.pebblecreekgc.com

SIC: 1799 1629 Coating, caulking, and weather, water, and fireproofing; Golf course construction

(G-2999)
M-PACT CORPORATION
2323 Crowne Point Dr (45241-5405)
PHONE.................513 679-2023
Michael J Griffie, *Pr*
Steve Cooley, *Ofcr*
EMP: 31 **EST:** 2005
SALES (est): 2.16MM **Privately Held**
Web: www.m-pactcorp.com
SIC: 1731 General electrical contractor

(G-3000)
MACHINE DRIVE COMPANY
2513 Crescentville Rd (45241-1575)
PHONE.................513 793-7077
EMP: 52
SIC: 5063 3625 Electrical apparatus and equipment; Control equipment, electric

(G-3001)
MADEIRA VETERINARY HOSPITAL
7250 Miami Ave (45243-2129)
PHONE.................513 561-7467
Richard G Seaman, *Pr*
EMP: 28 **EST:** 1904
SQ FT: 3,000
SALES (est): 396.81K **Privately Held**
Web: www.vcahospitals.com
SIC: 0742 Animal hospital services, pets and other animal specialties

(G-3002)
MAE HOLDING COMPANY (PA)
7290 Deaconsbench Ct (45244-3708)
PHONE.................513 751-2424
George Thurner Iii, *Pr*
EMP: 32 **EST:** 1967
SQ FT: 80,000
SALES (est): 17.61MM
SALES (corp-wide): 17.61MM **Privately Held**
Web: www.aamco.com
SIC: 5031 5072 Door frames, all materials; Hardware

(G-3003)
MAIL CONTRACTORS AMERICA INC
3065 Cresecentville Rd (45262)
PHONE.................513 769-5967
EMP: 60
SALES (corp-wide): 497.12MM **Privately Held**
Web: www.mailcontractors.com
SIC: 4212 Local trucking, without storage
HQ: Mail Contractors Of America, Inc.
3809 Roundtop Dr
North Little Rock AR 72117

(G-3004)
MAIN HOSPITALITY HOLDINGS LLC
Also Called: AC Banks
135 Joe Nuxhall Way (45202-4143)
PHONE.................513 744-9900
EMP: 31 **EST:** 2017
SALES (est): 1.38MM **Privately Held**
Web: www.marriott.com
SIC: 7011 Hotels

(G-3005)
MAKETEWAH COUNTRY CLUB COMPANY
5401 Reading Rd (45237-5398)
PHONE.................513 242-9533
Charles Carpenter, *Pr*
EMP: 95 **EST:** 1910
SQ FT: 59,007

SALES (est): 5.72MM **Privately Held**
Web: www.maketewah.com
SIC: 7997 Country club, membership

(G-3006)
MAKING LIFE EASY LLC ✪
Also Called: Good Life
1731 Clayburn Cir (45240-1509)
PHONE.................513 280-0422
Erica Waldon, *Managing Member*
EMP: 64 **EST:** 2023
SALES (est): 1.13MM **Privately Held**
SIC: 7389 Business Activities at Non-Commercial Site

(G-3007)
MALLARD COVE SENIOR DEV LLC
Also Called: Mallard Cove Senior Living
1410 Mallard Cove Dr Ofc (45246-3930)
PHONE.................513 772-6655
Jonathan Levey, *Managing Member*
David A Smith, *Managing Member*
EMP: 105 **EST:** 2008
SALES (est): 9.55MM **Privately Held**
Web: www.mallardcoveseniorliving.com
SIC: 8051 Skilled nursing care facilities

(G-3008)
MAPLE KNOLL COMMUNITIES INC (PA)
Also Called: Maple Knoll Village
11100 Springfield Pike (45246)
PHONE.................513 782-2400
Rose Denman, *VP*
EMP: 400 **EST:** 1848
SQ FT: 323,000
SALES (est): 46.12MM
SALES (corp-wide): 46.12MM **Privately Held**
Web: www.mkcommunities.org
SIC: 8051 8052 8082 Convalescent home with continuous nursing care; Intermediate care facilities; Home health care services

(G-3009)
MARKETING RESEARCH SERVICES (DH)
Also Called: M R S I
310 Culvert St Fl 2 (45202-2229)
PHONE.................513 579-1555
Todd Earhart, *Pr*
Elise Delahanty, *
John Barth, *
Lori Kelley, *
Richard Brumfield, *
EMP: 95 **EST:** 1973
SQ FT: 30,000
SALES (est): 21.77MM
SALES (corp-wide): 44.55MM **Publicly Held**
Web: www.big-village.com
SIC: 8732 Market analysis or research
HQ: Big Village Insights, Inc.
301 Carnegie Ctr Ste 301 # 301
Princeton NJ 08540

(G-3010)
MARKETING RESEARCH SVCS INC
Also Called: MARKETING RESEARCH SERVICES, INC.
110 Boggs Ln Ste 380 (45246-3150)
PHONE.................513 772-7580
Valerie Enderle, *Mgr*
EMP: 102
SALES (corp-wide): 44.55MM **Publicly Held**
Web: www.big-village.com
SIC: 8732 Market analysis or research
HQ: Marketing Research Services, Inc
310 Culvert St Fl 2
Cincinnati OH 45202
513 579-1555

(G-3011)
MARKETING SUPPORT SERVICES INC (PA)
4921 Para Dr (45237-5011)
P.O. Box 37697 (45222-0697)
PHONE.................................513 752-1200
TOLL FREE: 800
Greg Fischer, *Pr*
Pam Fischer, *
▲ EMP: 45 EST: 1988
SQ FT: 100,000
SALES (est): 9.99MM **Privately Held**
Web: www.marketingsupportservices.com
SIC: 7311 Advertising agencies

(G-3012)
MARSH INC
Also Called: Marsh
333 E 8th St (45202-2205)
PHONE.................................513 421-1234
Edward E Betz, *Ch Bd*
Ken Neiheisel, *
Peter Costanzo, *
EMP: 90 EST: 1948
SQ FT: 12,000
SALES (est): 4.79MM **Privately Held**
Web: www.marshideas.com
SIC: 7335 8743 7336 Commercial photography; Promotion service; Package design

(G-3013)
MARTIN WILSON AND ASSOCIATES
Also Called: Martin & Associates
10385 Spartan Dr (45215-1220)
PHONE.................................513 772-7284
Kevin M Martin, *Pr*
Richard E Wilson, *VP*
EMP: 96 EST: 1988
SQ FT: 10,000
SALES (est): 4.93MM **Privately Held**
Web: www.martinandassoc.com
SIC: 8721 7379 Certified public accountant; Computer related consulting services

(G-3014)
MASSMUTUAL ASCEND LF INSUR CO (HQ)
Also Called: Great American
191 Rosa Parks St (45202-2573)
P.O. Box 5420 (45201-5420)
PHONE.................................800 854-3649
Mark Muething, *Pr*
▲ EMP: 33 EST: 1961
SALES (est): 208.38MM
SALES (corp-wide): 10.36B **Privately Held**
Web: www.massmutualascend.com
SIC: 6331 Fire, marine, and casualty insurance
PA: Massachusetts Mutual Life Insurance Company
1295 State St
Springfield MA 01111
413 744-8411

(G-3015)
MATLOCK ELECTRIC CO INC
2780 Highland Ave (45212)
PHONE.................................513 731-9600
TOLL FREE: 800
Thomas J Geoppinger, *Ch*
Joseph P Geoppinger, *Pr*
▼ EMP: 36 EST: 1920
SQ FT: 25,000
SALES (est): 8.3MM **Privately Held**
Web: www.matlockelectric.com
SIC: 7694 5063 3699 3612 Electric motor repair; Motors, electric; Electrical equipment and supplies, nec; Transformers, except electric

(G-3016)
MATRIX CLAIMS MANAGEMENT LLC
Also Called: Matrix Invstgations Consulting
644 Linn St Ste 900 (45203)
PHONE.................................513 351-1222
Brent Messmer, *Pr*
EMP: 80 EST: 2002
SQ FT: 6,400
SALES (est): 9.52MM **Privately Held**
Web: www.matrixtpa.com
SIC: 8742 Management consulting services

(G-3017)
MATTHEWS INTERNATIONAL CORP
Also Called: Pyramid Controls
5546 Fair Ln (45227-3402)
PHONE.................................513 679-7400
Mukesh Ram, *Pr*
Thomas E Martin, *
Stephen Kley, *
EMP: 31 EST: 1994
SALES (est): 8.59MM **Privately Held**
Web: www.pyramidcontrols.com
SIC: 8711 Electrical or electronic engineering

(G-3018)
MAXIM HEALTHCARE SERVICES INC
Also Called: Cincinnati Home Healthcare
34 Triangle Park Dr (45246-3411)
PHONE.................................513 793-6444
Mark Neumeyer, *Brnch Mgr*
EMP: 214
Web: www.maximhealthcare.com
SIC: 8082 Home health care services
PA: Maxim Healthcare Services, Inc.
7227 Lee Deforest Dr
Columbia MD 21046

(G-3019)
MAYERS ELECTRIC CO INC
4004 Erie Ct Ste B (45227-2167)
PHONE.................................513 272-2900
Howard Mayers, *Pr*
Jim Hopper, *
Steve Mayers, *
▲ EMP: 150 EST: 1948
SQ FT: 22,250
SALES (est): 22.12MM **Privately Held**
Web: www.mayerselectric.com
SIC: 1731 General electrical contractor

(G-3020)
MAYFIELD CLINIC INC (PA)
3825 Edwards Rd Ste 300 (45209-1288)
PHONE.................................513 221-1100
Michael J Gilligan, *Pr*
A Lee Greiner Md, *Ch*
William D Tobler Md, *Sec*
John M Tew Md, *Ch*
Ronald Warnick Md, *Treas*
EMP: 82 EST: 1937
SQ FT: 25,000
SALES (est): 26.7MM
SALES (corp-wide): 26.7MM **Privately Held**
Web: www.mayfieldclinic.com
SIC: 8011 Neurologist

(G-3021)
MAYFIELD SPINE SURGERY CTR LLC
4020 Smith Rd (45209-1936)
PHONE.................................513 619-5899
Mike Judge, *Genl Mgr*
EMP: 51 EST: 2009
SALES (est): 8.72MM
SALES (corp-wide): 20.55B **Publicly Held**
Web: www.mayfieldsurgerycenter.com

(G-3022)
MCCRACKEN GROUP INC
9145 Governors Way (45249-2037)
PHONE.................................513 697-2000
EMP: 32 EST: 2007
SALES (est): 1.71MM **Privately Held**
Web: www.mccrackengrp.com
SIC: 4813 5999 7389 Telephone communication, except radio; Telephone equipment and systems; Telephone services

(G-3023)
MCGILL SMITH PUNSHON INC
3700 Park 42 Dr Ste 190b (45241-2081)
PHONE.................................513 759-0004
Stephen C Roat, *Pr*
J Craig Rambo, *
Jim Watson, *
Stephanie Kirschner, *
EMP: 28 EST: 1984
SQ FT: 17,000
SALES (est): 7.33MM **Privately Held**
Web: www.mspdesign.com
SIC: 8711 8712 8713 0781 Consulting engineer; Architectural engineering; Surveying services; Landscape architects

(G-3024)
MECHANCAL OPTMZERS CNCNNATI HT
2145 Patterson St (45214-1843)
P.O. Box 14180 (45250-0180)
PHONE.................................513 467-1444
Jeffrey Wilmink, *Pr*
Ed Memory, *
EMP: 40 EST: 1997
SQ FT: 2,000
SALES (est): 5.48MM **Privately Held**
SIC: 1711 Warm air heating and air conditioning contractor

(G-3025)
MECHANCAL/INDUSTRIAL CONTG INC
Also Called: Honeywell Authorized Dealer
11863 Solzman Rd (45249-1236)
PHONE.................................513 489-8282
Clay Craig, *Pr*
Bill Sempsrott, *
EMP: 29 EST: 1983
SQ FT: 20,000
SALES (est): 2.4MM **Privately Held**
Web: www.mechanicalindustrial.com
SIC: 1711 Mechanical contractor

(G-3026)
MEDA-CARE TRANSPORTATION INC
10490 Taconic Ter (45215-1123)
PHONE.................................513 521-4799
Boris Galitsky, *Prin*
Rad Galitsky, *Pr*
EMP: 30 EST: 1994
SALES (est): 2.03MM **Privately Held**
Web: www.medacaretransportation.com
SIC: 4119 Ambulance service

(G-3027)
MEDICAL HOUSECALLS LLC
Also Called: Supportive Healthcare
4850 Smith Rd Ste 250 (45212-2733)
PHONE.................................513 699-9090
Scott Nix, *Pr*
EMP: 40 EST: 2021
SALES (est): 677.2K **Privately Held**
SIC: 8082 Home health care services

(G-3028)
MEDICAL RECOVERY SYSTEMS INC
Also Called: Mrsi
3372 Central Pkwy (45225)
PHONE.................................513 872-7000
Stephen I Caroll, *Pr*
EMP: 33 EST: 1988
SALES (est): 3.72MM **Privately Held**
Web: www.medicalrecovery.net
SIC: 8742 Hospital and health services consultant

(G-3029)
MEDICOUNT MANAGEMENT INC
10361 Spartan Dr (45215-1220)
P.O. Box 621005 (45262-1005)
PHONE.................................513 612-3144
Joseph Newcomb, *Pr*
Joseph D Newcomb, *
Joseph A Newcomb, *
Tim Newcomb, *Strategy Vice President*
EMP: 50 EST: 1995
SQ FT: 7,500
SALES (est): 4.82MM **Privately Held**
Web: www.medicount.com
SIC: 8721 Billing and bookkeeping service

(G-3030)
MEDPACE
4820 Red Bank Rd (45227-1539)
PHONE.................................513 254-1232
Gary L Heiman, *Prin*
EMP: 86 EST: 2010
SALES (est): 983.12K **Privately Held**
Web: www.medpace.com
SIC: 8742 Management consulting services

(G-3031)
MEDPACE INC (DH)
5375 Medpace Way (45227-1543)
PHONE.................................513 579-9911
August Troendle, *Pr*
August J Troendle, *
Kurt Brykman, *CRO*
EMP: 700 EST: 2002
SQ FT: 30,000
SALES (est): 590.93MM
SALES (corp-wide): 1.89B **Publicly Held**
Web: www.medpace.com
SIC: 8731 5122 5047 Biotechnical research, commercial; Pharmaceuticals; Medical equipment and supplies
HQ: Medpace Intermediateco, Inc.
5375 Medpace Way
Cincinnati OH 45227
513 579-9911

(G-3032)
MEDPACE BIOANALYTICAL LABS LLC
5365 Medpace Way (45227-1543)
PHONE.................................513 366-3260
August Troendle, *Pr*
Jesse Geiger, *
Stephen Ewald, *
EMP: 29 EST: 2008
SQ FT: 140,000
SALES (est): 9.06MM
SALES (corp-wide): 1.89B **Publicly Held**
Web: www.medpace.com
SIC: 8071 Testing laboratories
HQ: Medpace, Inc.
5375 Medpace Way
Cincinnati OH 45227

Cincinnati - Hamilton County (G-3033)

(G-3033)
MEDPACE HOLDINGS INC (PA)
Also Called: MEDPACE
5375 Medpace Way (45227)
PHONE.................................513 579-9911
August J Troendle, *Ch Bd*
Jesse J Geiger, *LABORATORY Operations*
Susan E Burwig, *Ofcr*
Stephen P Ewald, *Corporate Secretary*
EMP: 246 EST: 1992
SQ FT: 600,000
SALES (est): 1.89B
SALES (corp-wide): 1.89B **Publicly Held**
Web: www.medpace.com
SIC: **2834** 8731 Pharmaceutical preparations; Commercial physical research

(G-3034)
MEDVET ASSOCIATES LLC
Also Called: Medvet Cincinnati
3964 Red Bank Rd (45227-3408)
PHONE.................................513 561-0069
Cole Coffee, *Brnch Mgr*
EMP: 224
Web: www.medvet.com
SIC: **0742** Animal hospital services, pets and other animal specialties
PA: Medvet Associates, Llc
350 E Wilson Bridge Rd
Worthington OH 43085

(G-3035)
MEES DISTRIBUTORS INC (PA)
1541 W Fork Rd (45223-1203)
PHONE.................................513 541-2311
Howard Mees, *Pr*
▲ EMP: 50 EST: 1954
SQ FT: 58,000
SALES (est): 9.86MM
SALES (corp-wide): 9.86MM **Privately Held**
Web: www.meesdistributors.com
SIC: **5032** Ceramic construction materials, excluding refractory

(G-3036)
MEGEN CONSTRUCTION COMPANY INC (PA)
11130 Ashburn Rd (45240-3813)
PHONE.................................513 742-9191
EMP: 38 EST: 1993
SQ FT: 4,000
SALES (est): 24.29MM **Privately Held**
Web: www.megenconstruction.com
SIC: **1542** Commercial and office building, new construction

(G-3037)
MEINKINGS SERVICE LLC
Also Called: Meinking's Service
1756 Sherman Ave (45212-2545)
PHONE.................................513 631-5198
Mark Meinking, *Managing Member*
EMP: 27 EST: 1981
SQ FT: 8,500
SALES (est): 846.75K **Privately Held**
Web: www.meinkingservice.com
SIC: **7532** 7538 7549 Body shop, automotive; General automotive repair shops; Towing services

(G-3038)
MELLOTT & MELLOTT PLL
12 Walnut St Ste 2500 (45216-2453)
PHONE.................................513 241-2940
Donald Mellott Junior, *Pt*
Donald Mellot Senior, *Pt*
John Mellott, *Pt*
Rick Rumper, *Pt*
EMP: 41 EST: 1956
SALES (est): 2.82MM **Privately Held**
Web: www.mellottcpa.com
SIC: **8721** Certified public accountant

(G-3039)
MELS AUTO GLASS INC
11775 Reading Rd (45241-1548)
PHONE.................................513 563-7771
Lisa M Gabrielle, *Pr*
Melvin W Wolf, *
EMP: 30 EST: 1987
SQ FT: 8,000
SALES (est): 2.94MM **Privately Held**
Web: www.melsautoglass.com
SIC: **7536** Automotive glass replacement shops

(G-3040)
MERCY FRANCISCAN HOSP MT AIRY (PA)
2446 Kipling Ave (45239-6650)
PHONE.................................513 853-5101
Rodney Reider, *Pr*
Ruby Hemphil Crowford, *
Judy Daleiden, *
EMP: 1000 EST: 2004
SQ FT: 10,500
SALES (est): 47.11MM **Privately Held**
SIC: **8741** 8062 Hospital management; General medical and surgical hospitals

(G-3041)
MERCY HEALTH ANDERSON HOSPITAL
Also Called: Mercy Hospital Anderson
7500 State Rd (45255)
PHONE.................................513 624-4500
Patrica Shroer, *Pr*
Timothy L Prestridge, *
Nicole Barnett, *
EMP: 823 EST: 1942
SQ FT: 115,000
SALES (est): 236.02MM
SALES (corp-wide): 6.92B **Privately Held**
Web: www.mercy.com
SIC: **8062** General medical and surgical hospitals
HQ: Mercy Health Cincinnati Llc
1701 Mercy Health Pl
Cincinnati OH 45237
513 952-5000

(G-3042)
MERCY HEALTH CINCINNATI LLC (HQ)
Also Called: Mercy Health Cincinnati
1701 Mercy Health Pl (45237-6147)
PHONE.................................513 952-5000
Tom Urban, *CEO*
Kenneth C Page, *
Don Harmeyer, *
Michael W Garfield, *
Tonya Carter, *
EMP: 100 EST: 1982
SALES (est): 834.69MM
SALES (corp-wide): 6.92B **Privately Held**
Web: www.cincinnati.com
SIC: **8062** General medical and surgical hospitals
PA: Bon Secours Mercy Health, Inc.
1701 Mercy Health Pl
Cincinnati OH 45237
513 956-3729

(G-3043)
MERCY HEALTHPLEX ANDERSON LLC
201 E 5th St Ste 2500 (45202-4707)
PHONE.................................513 624-1871
EMP: 29 EST: 2016
SALES (est): 710.6K **Privately Held**
Web: www.mercyhealthplex.com
SIC: **7991** Health club

(G-3044)
MERCY HOSPITAL
11963 Lick Rd (45251-4117)
PHONE.................................513 870-7767
EMP: 177
SALES (corp-wide): 2.16B **Privately Held**
Web: www.northernlighthealth.org
SIC: **8062** General medical and surgical hospitals
HQ: Mercy Hospital
175 Fore River Pkwy
Portland ME 04102
207 879-3000

(G-3045)
MERCY HOSPITAL
7500 State Rd (45255-2439)
PHONE.................................513 624-4590
Patti Schrower, *Pr*
EMP: 76 EST: 2012
SALES (est): 36.57MM **Privately Held**
Web: www.hcafloridahealthcare.com
SIC: **8062** General medical and surgical hospitals

(G-3046)
MERCY MONTESSORI CENTER
2335 Grandview Ave (45206-2280)
PHONE.................................513 475-6700
Patty Normile, *Prin*
EMP: 41 EST: 1997
SALES (est): 1.59MM **Privately Held**
Web: www.mercymontessori.org
SIC: **8351** Montessori child development center

(G-3047)
MERCY ST THERESA CENTER INC
7010 Rowan Hill Dr Ste 200 (45227-3380)
PHONE.................................513 271-7010
EMP: 32 EST: 1990
SALES (est): 4.52MM **Privately Held**
Web: www.mercy.com
SIC: **8051** Skilled nursing care facilities

(G-3048)
MESA INDUSTRIES INC (PA)
Also Called: Airplaco Equipment Company
4027 Eastern Ave (45226-1747)
PHONE.................................513 321-2950
Terry S Segerberg, *CEO*
Kent Sexton, *
James R Sexton, *
◆ EMP: 32 EST: 1966
SQ FT: 100,000
SALES (est): 24.71MM
SALES (corp-wide): 24.71MM **Privately Held**
Web: www.mesa-intl.com
SIC: **3531** 5085 5082 Bituminous, cement and concrete related products and equip.; Hose, belting, and packing; Construction and mining machinery

(G-3049)
MESSER CONSTRUCTION CO
2495 Langdon Farm Rd (45237-4950)
PHONE.................................513 672-5000
Greg L Herrin, *VP*
EMP: 107
SALES (corp-wide): 1.35B **Privately Held**
Web: www.messer.com
SIC: **1542** Commercial and office building, new construction
PA: Messer Construction Co.
643 W Court St
Cincinnati OH 45203
513 242-1541

(G-3050)
MESSER CONSTRUCTION CO (PA)
Also Called: Frank Messer & Sons Cnstr Co
643 W Court St (45203-1511)
PHONE.................................513 242-1541
Tim Steigerwald, *Pr*
Tim Steigerwald, *Pr*
E Paul Hitter Junior, *CFO*
Kevin Cozart, *
Bernard Suer, *
EMP: 100 EST: 1968
SQ FT: 44,610
SALES (est): 1.35B
SALES (corp-wide): 1.35B **Privately Held**
Web: www.messer.com
SIC: **1542** 1541 1522 Hospital construction; Industrial buildings and warehouses; Hotel/motel, new construction

(G-3051)
MESSER CONSTRUCTION CO
1201 Glendale Milford Rd (45215-1247)
PHONE.................................513 482-7402
Greg L Herrin, *VP*
EMP: 106
SQ FT: 1,409
SALES (corp-wide): 1.35B **Privately Held**
Web: www.messer.com
SIC: **7353** Heavy construction equipment rental
PA: Messer Construction Co.
643 W Court St
Cincinnati OH 45203
513 242-1541

(G-3052)
METCUT RESEARCH ASSOCIATES INC (PA)
Also Called: Metcut Research, Inc.
3980 Rosslyn Dr (45209-1110)
PHONE.................................513 271-5100
John P Kahles, *Pr*
John H Clippinger, *
William P Koster, *
John H More, *
Robert T Keeler, *
EMP: 85 EST: 1948
SQ FT: 25,000
SALES (est): 24.93MM
SALES (corp-wide): 24.93MM **Privately Held**
Web: www.metcut.com
SIC: **8734** 3599 Metallurgical testing laboratory; Machine and other job shop work

(G-3053)
METROPLTAN SWER DST GRTER CNCN
Also Called: MSDGC
1600 Gest St (45204-2022)
PHONE.................................513 244-1300
Gerald Checco, *Dir*
James Parrott, *
EMP: 600 EST: 2002
SALES (est): 273.62MM **Privately Held**
Web: www.msdgc.org
SIC: **4952** Sewerage systems

(G-3054)
MIAMI CORPORATION (PA)
720 Anderson Ferry Rd (45238-4742)
PHONE.................................800 543-0448
Timothy J Niehaus, *Pr*
Kevin P Niehaus, *
Dan Niehaus, *
Edward Cappel, *
Robert Tomlinson, *
▲ EMP: 49 EST: 1923
SQ FT: 40,000
SALES (est): 25.76MM

GEOGRAPHIC SECTION
Cincinnati - Hamilton County (G-3076)

SALES (corp-wide): 25.76MM **Privately Held**
Web: www.miamicorp.com
SIC: 5131 5091 Upholstery fabrics, woven; Boat accessories and parts

(G-3055)
MIAMI VALLEY INTL TRCKS INC
Also Called: Idealease Miami Valley Intl
11775 Highway Dr Ste D (45241-2005)
PHONE.................................513 733-8500
EMP: 33
SALES (corp-wide): 23.45MM **Privately Held**
Web: www.mvigroup.net
SIC: 7513 Truck rental and leasing, no drivers
PA: Miami Valley International Trucks, Inc.
7655 Poe Ave
Dayton OH 45414
937 898-3660

(G-3056)
MICHAEL SCHUSTER ASSOC INC (PA)
Also Called: MSA Architects
316 W 4th St Ste 600 (45202-2677)
PHONE.................................513 241-5666
Michael Schuster, *Prin*
Richard Tripp, *Prin*
EMP: 39 **EST:** 1985
SQ FT: 10,000
SALES (est): 7.51MM
SALES (corp-wide): 7.51MM **Privately Held**
Web: www.msaarch.com
SIC: 8712 7389 Architectural engineering; Interior designer

(G-3057)
MICRO ELECTRONICS INC
Also Called: Micro Center
11755 Mosteller Rd Rear (45241-5505)
PHONE.................................513 782-8500
EMP: 125
SALES (corp-wide): 191.56MM **Privately Held**
SIC: 5734 5045 Personal computers; Computer peripheral equipment
PA: Micro Electronics, Inc.
4119 Leap Rd
Hilliard OH 43026
614 850-3000

(G-3058)
MIDWEST LAUNDRY INC
10110 Cincinnati Dayton Pike (45241-1006)
PHONE.................................513 563-5560
Tom Jaynes, *Genl Mgr*
EMP: 70 **EST:** 1991
SQ FT: 32,000
SALES (est): 2.45MM **Privately Held**
Web: www.midwestlaundryinc.com
SIC: 7211 7218 7216 7213 Power laundries, family and commercial; Industrial launderers; Drycleaning plants, except rugs; Linen supply

(G-3059)
MIDWEST MFG SOLUTIONS LLC
Also Called: Definity Partners
1 E 4th St (45202-3717)
P.O. Box 28 (45162-0028)
PHONE.................................513 381-7200
Ray Attiyah, *Admn*
EMP: 30 **EST:** 1997
SALES (est): 3.88MM **Privately Held**
SIC: 8742 Manufacturing management consultant

(G-3060)
MIDWESTERN PLUMBING SVC INC
3984 Bach Buxton Rd (45202)
PHONE.................................513 753-0050
Gene Hehemann, *Pr*
Eugene Heheman, *
Archie Wilson, *
EMP: 40 **EST:** 1978
SQ FT: 4,700
SALES (est): 8.09MM **Privately Held**
Web: www.midwestern-plumbing.com
SIC: 1711 6552 Plumbing contractors; Subdividers and developers, nec

(G-3061)
MIKE ALBERT FLEET SOLUTIONS
10340 Evendale Dr (45241-2512)
PHONE.................................800 985-3273
EMP: 247 **EST:** 2020
SALES (est): 10.24MM **Privately Held**
Web: www.mikealbert.com
SIC: 7515 Passenger car leasing

(G-3062)
MILESTONE FOOTBALL LEAGUE LLC
11537 Norbourne Dr (45240-2115)
PHONE.................................513 479-7602
EMP: 60 **EST:** 2020
SALES (est): 177.92K **Privately Held**
SIC: 7941 Football club

(G-3063)
MILLER BROS WALLPAPER COMPANY
Also Called: Miller Bros Paint & Decorating
8460 Beechmont Ave Ste A (45255-4782)
PHONE.................................513 231-4470
Eddy Mills, *Mgr*
EMP: 39
SALES (corp-wide): 4.99MM **Privately Held**
Web: miller-bros-paint.myshopify.com
SIC: 5198 5231 Paints; Paint
PA: Miller Bros. Wallpaper Company
4343 Montgomery Rd
Cincinnati OH 45212
513 531-1517

(G-3064)
MILLER-VALENTINE PARTNERS LTD (PA)
Also Called: Miller- Valentine Group
9349 Waterstone Blvd Ste 200
(45249-8320)
PHONE.................................937 293-0900
Bill Krul, *CEO*
Ed Blake, *Pr*
Sean Mcgory, *VP*
EMP: 80 **EST:** 1995
SALES (est): 23.33MM
SALES (corp-wide): 23.33MM **Privately Held**
Web: www.millervalentine.com
SIC: 6512 Commercial and industrial building operation

(G-3065)
MILLS CORPORATION
Also Called: Forest Fair Mall
600 Cincinnati Mills Dr (45240-1260)
PHONE.................................513 671-2882
Jim Childress, *Mgr*
EMP: 47
Web: www.themill.com
SIC: 6512 Shopping center, property operation only
HQ: The Mills Corporation
5425 Wisconsin Ave # 300
Chevy Chase MD 20815
301 968-6000

(G-3066)
MILLS FENCE CO LLC (PA)
6315 Wiehe Rd (45237-4213)
PHONE.................................513 631-0333
Kenneth Mills, *Pr*
John Lyttle, *
▲ **EMP:** 28 **EST:** 1970
SQ FT: 100,000
SALES (est): 10.75MM
SALES (corp-wide): 10.75MM **Privately Held**
Web: www.millsfence.com
SIC: 5039 1799 5211 Wire fence, gates, and accessories; Fence construction; Fencing

(G-3067)
MITCHELLS SALON & DAY SPA INC (PA)
5901 E Galbraith Rd Ste 230 (45236-2290)
PHONE.................................513 793-0900
Deborah M Schmidt, *Pr*
EMP: 90 **EST:** 1983
SQ FT: 11,000
SALES (est): 13.49MM
SALES (corp-wide): 13.49MM **Privately Held**
Web: www.mitchellssalon.com
SIC: 7231 7991 Hairdressers; Spas

(G-3068)
MITSUI SMITOMO MAR MGT USA INC
312 Elm St Ste 1250 (45202-2749)
PHONE.................................513 719-8480
Wendy Seidel, *Brnch Mgr*
EMP: 98
Web: www.msigusa.com
SIC: 6331 Fire, marine, and casualty insurance
HQ: Mitsui Sumitomo Marine Management (U.S.A.), Inc.
15 Independence Blvd # 1
Warren NJ 07059
800 711-1736

(G-3069)
MK CHILDCARE WARSAW AVE LLC
3711 Warsaw Ave (45205-1773)
PHONE.................................513 922-6279
EMP: 40 **EST:** 2016
SALES (est): 538.61K **Privately Held**
SIC: 8351 Child day care services

(G-3070)
MLM CHILDCARE LLC
16 Beaufort Hunt Ln (45242-4672)
PHONE.................................513 623-8243
EMP: 35 **EST:** 2016
SALES (est): 396.2K **Privately Held**
SIC: 8351 Child day care services

(G-3071)
MM ASCEND LIFE INV SVCS LLC (DH)
Also Called: Great American Advisors
301 E 4th St Fl 12 (45202-4245)
P.O. Box 5423 (45201-5423)
PHONE.................................513 333-6030
Peter Nerone, *Pr*
Athena Marie Purdon, *
Mark Muething, *
EMP: 30 **EST:** 1993
SQ FT: 9,000
SALES (est): 9.58MM
SALES (corp-wide): 10.36B **Privately Held**
Web: www.gaadvisors.com
SIC: 6411 6211 6282 Insurance agents, brokers, and service; Underwriters, security; Investment advice
HQ: Massmutual Ascend Life Insurance Company
191 Rosa Parks St
Cincinnati OH 45202
800 854-3649

(G-3072)
MOBILCOMM INC
1211 W Sharon Rd (45240-2916)
PHONE.................................513 742-5555
EMP: 84 **EST:** 1995
SALES (est): 5.66MM
SALES (corp-wide): 24.83MM **Privately Held**
Web: www.mobilcomm.com
SIC: 7622 7359 5999 5065 Communication equipment repair; Mobile communication equipment rental; Communication equipment; Electronic parts and equipment, nec
PA: Combined Technologies, Inc.
1211 W Sharon Rd
Cincinnati OH 45240
513 595-5900

(G-3073)
MODAL SHOP INC
Also Called: T M S
10310 Aerohub Blvd (45215)
PHONE.................................513 351-9919
Michael J Lally, *Pr*
Rick Bono, *
EMP: 70 **EST:** 1990
SALES (est): 22.05MM
SALES (corp-wide): 16.11B **Publicly Held**
Web: www.modalshop.com
SIC: 5084 7359 8711 Controlling instruments and accessories; Electronic equipment rental, except computers; Engineering services
HQ: Pcb Piezotronics, Inc.
3425 Walden Ave
Depew NY 14043
716 684-0001

(G-3074)
MODEL GROUP INC
1826 Race St (45202-7720)
PHONE.................................513 559-0048
Arthur Reckman, *Pr*
Stephen Smith, *
Shirley Poe, *
▲ **EMP:** 50 **EST:** 1978
SQ FT: 3,540
SALES (est): 12.27MM **Privately Held**
Web: www.modelgroup.net
SIC: 6531 Real estate managers

(G-3075)
MODERN BUILDERS SUPPLY INC
6225 Wiehe Rd (45237-4211)
PHONE.................................513 531-1000
David Phiem, *Mgr*
EMP: 28
SQ FT: 26,000
SALES (corp-wide): 346.23MM **Privately Held**
Web: www.modernbuilderssupply.com
SIC: 5033 5031 Roofing, siding, and insulation; Doors and windows
PA: Modern Builders Supply, Inc.
3500 Phillips Ave
Toledo OH 43608
419 241-3961

(G-3076)
MODERN OFFICE METHODS INC (PA)
Also Called: M.O.M.
4747 Lake Forest Dr Ste 200 (45242)
PHONE.................................513 791-0909

Cincinnati - Hamilton County (G-3077)

Robert J Mccarthy, *Ch Bd*
Kevin P Mccarthy, *Pr*
Steven Bandy, *
Ron Slageter, *
Silas P Rose, *
EMP: 85 **EST:** 1957
SQ FT: 10,000
SALES (est): 45.16MM
SALES (corp-wide): 45.16MM **Privately Held**
Web: www.momnet.com
SIC: **7359** 7629 5044 Office machine rental, except computers; Business machine repair, electric; Office equipment

(G-3077)
MONARCH CONSTRUCTION COMPANY
Also Called: Monarch
1654 Sherman Ave (45212-2598)
P.O. Box 12249 (45212-0249)
PHONE..................513 351-6900
Martin A Meisberger, *Pr*
Ronald A Koetters, *
Thomas P Butler, *
Jerome J Corbett Junior, *CFO*
EMP: 200 **EST:** 1963
SQ FT: 21,500
SALES (est): 42.45MM **Privately Held**
Web: www.monarchconstruction.cc
SIC: **1542** 1541 Commercial and office building, new construction; Industrial buildings and warehouses

(G-3078)
MONTGOMERY FAMILY MEDICINE
11029 Montgomery Rd (45249-2306)
PHONE..................513 891-2211
Thomas Grimm, *Pr*
EMP: 28 **EST:** 1954
SALES (est): 986.82K **Privately Held**
Web: www.trihealth.com
SIC: **8011** General and family practice, physician/surgeon

(G-3079)
MORELIA GROUP LLC
8600 Governors Hill Dr Ste 160 (45249-1360)
PHONE..................513 469-1500
EMP: 35 **EST:** 2010
SALES (est): 4.08MM **Privately Held**
Web: www.moreliagroup.com
SIC: **4813** Telephone communication, except radio

(G-3080)
MORRIS TECHNOLOGIES INC
11988 Tramway Dr (45241-1664)
PHONE..................513 733-1611
EMP: 45 **EST:** 1994
SQ FT: 25,000
SALES (est): 4.36MM **Privately Held**
SIC: **8711** 3999 3313 3841 Mechanical engineering; Models, except toy; Alloys, additive, except copper: not made in blast furnaces; Surgical and medical instruments

(G-3081)
MOTZ GROUP INC (PA)
1 Motz Way (45244-3600)
PHONE..................513 533-6452
Joseph Motz, *Pr*
Mark Heinlein, *
▲ **EMP:** 47 **EST:** 1994
SALES (est): 11.92MM
SALES (corp-wide): 11.92MM **Privately Held**
Web: www.themotzgroup.com

SIC: **1799** 0782 Artificial turf installation; Turf installation services, except artificial

(G-3082)
MOUNT NOTRE DAME HEALTH CENTER
699 E Columbia Ave (45215-3945)
PHONE..................513 821-7448
Elizabeth Bowyer, *Pr*
EMP: 33 **EST:** 2002
SALES (est): 1.82MM **Privately Held**
Web: www.mndhs.org
SIC: **8011** Offices and clinics of medical doctors

(G-3083)
MOUNT WASHINGTON BAPTIST CH
Also Called: Mt Washington Baptist Day Care
2005 Sutton Ave (45230-1670)
P.O. Box 30437 (45230-0437)
PHONE..................513 231-4334
Holly Mcintosh, *Dir*
EMP: 34
SQ FT: 15,882
Web: www.mwbcares.net
SIC: **8351** Child day care services
PA: Mt. Washington Baptist Church
2021 Sutton Ave
Cincinnati OH 45230

(G-3084)
MT AIRY DEVELOPMENT LLC
Also Called: Glenwood Behavioral Hlth Hosp
2446 Kipling Ave (45239-6650)
PHONE..................855 537-2301
Kim Peabody, *CEO*
EMP: 50 **EST:** 2018
SALES (est): 23.54MM **Publicly Held**
Web: www.glenwoodbehavioral.com
SIC: **8063** Mental hospital, except for the mentally retarded
PA: Acadia Healthcare Company, Inc.
6100 Tower Cir Ste 1000
Franklin TN 37067

(G-3085)
MT AIRY GRDNS RHBLTTION CARE
Also Called: MT. AIRY GARDENS REHABILITATIO
2250 Banning Rd (45239-6608)
PHONE..................513 591-0400
EMP: 27 **EST:** 2015
SALES (est): 8.22MM **Privately Held**
Web: www.mtairyrehab.com
SIC: **8051** Skilled nursing care facilities

(G-3086)
MT HEALTHY CHRISTIAN HOME INC
Also Called: CHRISTIAN BENEVOLENT ASSOCIATION OF GREATER CINCINNATI, THE
8097 Hamilton Ave (45231-2395)
PHONE..................513 931-5000
Rod Huron, *Ch Bd*
Kitty Garner, *
David Philips, *
EMP: 175 **EST:** 1964
SQ FT: 300,000
SALES (est): 6.31MM
SALES (corp-wide): 2.09MM **Privately Held**
Web: www.christianvillages.org
SIC: **8361** Aged home
PA: Christian Benevolent Association
8097 Hamilton Ave
Cincinnati OH 45231
513 931-5000

(G-3087)
MT WASHINGTON CARE CENTER INC
6900 Beechmont Ave (45230-2910)
PHONE..................513 231-4561
James Farley, *Pr*
Michael Scharfenberger, *
EMP: 50 **EST:** 1979
SALES (est): 16.54MM **Privately Held**
Web: www.mtwcc.com
SIC: **8051** 8322 6282 7389 Convalescent home with continuous nursing care; Individual and family services; Investment advice; Business Activities at Non-Commercial Site

(G-3088)
MUC HOLDINGS LLC
2368 Victory Pkwy Ste 320 (45206-2810)
P.O. Box 6368 (45206-0368)
PHONE..................513 417-8452
EMP: 39 **EST:** 2011
SALES (est): 1.67MM **Privately Held**
Web: www.mucltd.com
SIC: **7371** Computer software development

(G-3089)
MUNICH RE AMERICA SERVICES
1308 Race St Ste 300 (45202-7397)
PHONE..................609 480-6596
EMP: 50 **EST:** 1980
SALES (est): 2.29MM **Privately Held**
SIC: **8741** Management services

(G-3090)
MUSIC TEACHERS NAT ASSN INC
Also Called: MTNA
600 Vine St Ste 1710 (45202-2429)
PHONE..................513 421-1420
Gary Ingle, *CEO*
EMP: 44 **EST:** 1876
SALES (est): 2.59MM **Privately Held**
Web: www.mtna.org
SIC: **8621** Education and teacher association

(G-3091)
MUSILLO UNKENHOLT LLC
302 W 3rd St (45202-3497)
PHONE..................513 744-4080
EMP: 38 **EST:** 2017
SALES (est): 900.61K **Privately Held**
Web: www.muimmigration.com
SIC: **8111** General practice law office

(G-3092)
MV COMMERCIAL CONSTRUCTION LLC (PA)
Also Called: Miller Valentin Construction
9349 Waterstone Blvd Ste 200 (45249-8320)
PHONE..................513 774-8400
Elizabeth Mangan, *CEO*
Chris Knueven, *Pr*
Mike Dektas, *CFO*
EMP: 27 **EST:** 2000
SALES (est): 25.54MM
SALES (corp-wide): 25.54MM **Privately Held**
Web: www.millervalentine.com
SIC: **1541** Industrial buildings and warehouses

(G-3093)
MV RESIDENTIAL CNSTR LLC
Also Called: Sandoval 2 Gc Joint Venture
9349 Waterstone Blvd Ste 200 (45249-8320)
PHONE..................513 588-1000
Mike Green, *CEO*
Randy Humbert, *

Elizabeth A Mangan, *
EMP: 750 **EST:** 1963
SQ FT: 23,000
SALES (est): 29.12MM **Privately Held**
SIC: **1522** Residential construction, nec

(G-3094)
MV TRANSPORTATION INC
Also Called: Lancaster Transportation
1801 Transpark Dr (45229-1239)
P.O. Box 2583 (43130-5583)
PHONE..................740 681-5086
Chad Hockmay, *Mgr*
EMP: 292
SALES (corp-wide): 1.31B **Privately Held**
Web: www.mvtransit.com
SIC: **4111** Bus transportation
PA: Mv Transportation, Inc.
2711 N Hskell Ave Ste 150
Dallas TX 75204
972 391-4600

(G-3095)
NATIONAL MARKETSHARE GROUP (PA)
2155 W 8th St (45204-2051)
PHONE..................513 921-0800
William Burwinkel, *Pr*
Beth A Burwinkel, *Treas*
EMP: 36 **EST:** 1983
SQ FT: 18,000
SALES (est): 4.79MM
SALES (corp-wide): 4.79MM **Privately Held**
Web: www.nmsg.com
SIC: **5023** 5092 5013 5087 Homefurnishings; Toys, nec; Automotive supplies and parts; Janitors' supplies

(G-3096)
NATIONAL PSTAL MAIL HNDLERS UN
Also Called: Local 304
6509 Montgomery Rd (45213-1513)
PHONE..................513 625-7192
EMP: 66
SQ FT: 5,427
SALES (corp-wide): 33.5MM **Privately Held**
Web: www.npmhu.org
SIC: **8631** Labor union
PA: National Postal Mail Handlers Union
815 16th St Nw
Washington DC 20006
202 833-9095

(G-3097)
NATIONAL TAB LLC
1329 E Kemper Rd Ste 4210 (45246-5100)
PHONE..................513 860-2050
Joe Hertenstein, *Managing Member*
EMP: 34 **EST:** 2005
SALES (est): 2.61MM **Privately Held**
Web: www.nationaltab.com
SIC: **1711** Plumbing, heating, air-conditioning

(G-3098)
NATIONAL UNDGRD RR FRDOM CTR I
Also Called: FREEDOM CENTER
1301 Western Ave Ste 2253 (45203-1118)
PHONE..................513 333-7500
Kim Robinson, *CEO*
Daniel Hoffheimer, *
Edwin Rigaud, *
Spencer Crew, *
EMP: 48 **EST:** 1995
SALES (est): 4.23MM **Privately Held**
Web: www.freedomcenter.org
SIC: **8412** Museum

GEOGRAPHIC SECTION
Cincinnati - Hamilton County (G-3122)

(G-3099)
NAVISTONE INC
231 W 12th St Ste 200w (45202-8001)
PHONE..................................844 677-3667
Larry Kavanagh, *CEO*
Allen Abbott, *COO*
Efrain Torres, *CFO*
Lori Paikin, *CRO*
EMP: 38 **EST:** 2016
SALES (est): 3.91MM **Privately Held**
Web: www.navistone.com
SIC: 7371 7372 Computer software development; Application computer software

(G-3100)
NBDC II LLC
2127 W North Bend Rd (45224-2371)
PHONE..................................513 681-5439
Christopher Hildebrant, *Pr*
EMP: 40 **EST:** 2010
SQ FT: 11,500
SALES (est): 992.16K **Privately Held**
SIC: 8351 Child day care services

(G-3101)
NCS HEALTHCARE LLC (DH)
Also Called: Vangard Labs
201 E 4th St Ste 900 (45202-4160)
PHONE..................................513 719-2600
Cialdini James, *Prin*
EMP: 35 **EST:** 1995
SALES (est): 11.9MM
SALES (corp-wide): 357.78B **Publicly Held**
SIC: 5122 Pharmaceuticals
HQ: Omnicare Holding Company
1105 N Market St Ste 1300
Cincinnati OH 45202

(G-3102)
NEALS CONSTRUCTION COMPANY
Also Called: Neals Design Remodel
7770 E Kemper Rd (45249-1612)
PHONE..................................513 489-7700
Neal P Hendy, *CEO*
Steve Hendy, *
Allan Hendy, *
Neal Hendy Junior, *VP*
EMP: 29 **EST:** 1972
SQ FT: 3,000
SALES (est): 5.12MM **Privately Held**
Web: www.neals.com
SIC: 1521 General remodeling, single-family houses

(G-3103)
NEHEMIAH MANUFACTURING CO LLC
1907 South St (45204-2033)
PHONE..................................513 351-5700
Daniel Meyer, *CEO*
Richard T Palmer, *Pr*
Mike Pachko, *COO*
▲ **EMP:** 100 **EST:** 2009
SQ FT: 33,706
SALES (est): 27.6MM **Privately Held**
Web: www.nehemiahmfg.com
SIC: 2844 5122 Perfumes, cosmetics and other toilet preparations; Toiletries

(G-3104)
NEIGHBORCARE INC (DH)
201 E 4th St Ste 900 (45202-4160)
PHONE..................................513 719-2600
Elizabeth A Haley, *Pr*
Robert A Smith, *
John L Kordash, *
John F Gaither Junior, *Sr VP*
Richard W Hunt, *
EMP: 600 **EST:** 1985
SQ FT: 90,000
SALES (est): 522.95MM
SALES (corp-wide): 357.78B **Publicly Held**
SIC: 5122 5912 5047 7389 Pharmaceuticals; Drug stores and proprietary stores; Medical equipment and supplies; Purchasing service
HQ: Omnicare Holding Company
1105 N Market St Ste 1300
Cincinnati OH 45202

(G-3105)
NELSON STARK COMPANY
7685 Fields Ertel Rd Ste D2 (45241-6084)
PHONE..................................513 489-0866
Jeff Read, *Pr*
Mark Stark, *
Charles Nelson, *
Jeff Read, *VP*
H Joseph Iori, *
EMP: 170 **EST:** 1993
SQ FT: 45,000
SALES (est): 33.45MM **Privately Held**
Web: www.nelsonstark.com
SIC: 1711 1623 1794 Plumbing contractors; Water, sewer, and utility lines; Excavation work

(G-3106)
NESCO INC
11711 Princeton Pike Unit 301 (45246-2595)
PHONE..................................513 772-5870
EMP: 162
SALES (corp-wide): 514.23MM **Privately Held**
Web: www.nescoresource.com
SIC: 8742 Business planning and organizing services
PA: Nesco, Inc.
6140 Parkland Blvd # 110
Cleveland OH 44124
440 461-6000

(G-3107)
NETWORKING PARTNERS INC
Also Called: Product Fulfillment Solutions
185 Progress Pl (45246-1717)
PHONE..................................727 417-7447
William Coy, *Pr*
William M Coy, *
EMP: 125 **EST:** 2012
SALES (est): 5.41MM **Privately Held**
SIC: 4225 General warehousing

(G-3108)
NEW REPUBLIC ARCHITECTURE
433 E 13th St (45202-8808)
PHONE..................................513 800-8075
EMP: 42 **EST:** 2019
SALES (est): 1.18MM **Privately Held**
Web: www.newrepublicarchitecture.com
SIC: 8712 Architectural engineering

(G-3109)
NEW SCOTLAND HEALTH CARE LLC
Also Called: LINCOLN CRAWFORD CARE CENTER
1346 Lincoln Ave (45206-1341)
PHONE..................................513 861-2044
EMP: 28 **EST:** 2012
SALES (est): 8.63MM **Privately Held**
Web: www.lincolncrawford.com
SIC: 8051 Convalescent home with continuous nursing care

(G-3110)
NEW VIEW MANAGEMENT GROUP INC
10680 Mcswain Dr (45241-3167)
PHONE..................................513 733-4444
Joe Guerrera, *Pr*
EMP: 66 **EST:** 1995
SALES (est): 2.48MM **Privately Held**
Web: www.nvmodels.com
SIC: 7363 8249 7231 Modeling service; Vocational schools, nec; Beauty shops

(G-3111)
NEWS AMER MKTG IN-STORE SVCS L
221 E 4th St Ste 2410 (45202-4251)
PHONE..................................513 333-7373
J Cooke, *Prin*
EMP: 1911
SALES (corp-wide): 9.88B **Publicly Held**
Web: www.neptuneretailsolutions.com
SIC: 7319 Display advertising service
HQ: News America Marketing In-Store Services L.L.C.
20 Westport Rd Ste 320
Wilton CT 06897
203 563-6600

(G-3112)
NEXGEN ENTERPRISES INC
Also Called: Nexgen Building Supply
3274 Spring Grove Ave (45225-1338)
PHONE..................................513 618-0300
EMP: 320
Web: undercosnt.z14.web.core.windows.net
SIC: 5032 Brick, stone, and related material

(G-3113)
NEXTMED SYSTEMS INC (PA)
16 Triangle Park Dr (45246-3411)
PHONE..................................216 674-0511
David Shute, *CEO*
James Bennett, *
EMP: 44 **EST:** 1999
SQ FT: 3,000
SALES (est): 3.37MM
SALES (corp-wide): 3.37MM **Privately Held**
SIC: 7372 Business oriented computer software

(G-3114)
NEXXTSHOW LLC
645 Linn St (45203-1722)
EMP: 50
SIC: 7999 7389 Exposition operation; Advertising, promotional, and trade show services

(G-3115)
NEYER ARCHITECTS ENGINEERS INC
302 W 3rd St Ste 800 (45202-3426)
PHONE..................................513 271-6400
Dave Neyer, *Pr*
EMP: 39 **EST:** 1987
SALES (est): 374.68K **Privately Held**
Web: www.neyer.com
SIC: 8712 Architectural engineering

(G-3116)
NEYER REAL ESTATE MGT LLC
Also Called: Neyer Management
1111 Meta Dr (45237)
PHONE..................................513 618-6000
John Neyer, *Managing Member*
Robin Brankamp, *Managing Member**
Don Gruen, *Managing Member**
EMP: 107 **EST:** 2004
SALES (est): 13.69MM **Privately Held**
Web: www.neyermanagement.com
SIC: 6531 Real estate managers

(G-3117)
NIEMAN PLUMBING INC
2030 Stapleton Ct (45240-2778)
PHONE..................................513 851-5588
Drew Nieman, *Pr*
Jo Ellen Nieman, *
EMP: 95 **EST:** 1974
SQ FT: 20,000
SALES (est): 8.7MM **Privately Held**
Web: www.niemanplumbing.com
SIC: 1711 Septic system construction

(G-3118)
NOR-COM LLC
Also Called: Pixel Technologies
1441 Western Ave (45214-2041)
PHONE..................................859 689-7451
Scott Burkhart, *Pr*
EMP: 50 **EST:** 2021
SALES (est): 2.82MM **Privately Held**
Web: www.pixel.tech
SIC: 8748 Business consulting, nec

(G-3119)
NORTH SIDE BANK AND TRUST CO (PA)
4125 Hamilton Ave (45223-2246)
PHONE..................................513 542-7800
Clifford Coors, *Ch Bd*
John A Coors, *Pr*
Donald Beimesche, *VP*
EMP: 100 **EST:** 1891
SQ FT: 19,348
SALES (est): 37.13MM
SALES (corp-wide): 37.13MM **Privately Held**
Web: www.nsbt.net
SIC: 6022 State trust companies accepting deposits, commercial

(G-3120)
NORTH SIDE BANK AND TRUST CO
2739 Madison Rd (45209-2208)
PHONE..................................513 533-8000
Clifford Coors, *CEO*
EMP: 99
SALES (corp-wide): 37.13MM **Privately Held**
Web: www.nsbt.net
SIC: 6022 State trust companies accepting deposits, commercial
PA: The North Side Bank And Trust Company
4125 Hamilton Ave
Cincinnati OH 45223
513 542-7800

(G-3121)
NORTHBEND ARCHTCTURAL PDTS INC
2080 Waycross Rd (45240-2717)
PHONE..................................513 577-7988
Mark Smith, *Pr*
Richard Perkins, *
▲ **EMP:** 38 **EST:** 1996
SQ FT: 3,000
SALES (est): 4.67MM **Privately Held**
SIC: 1791 Structural steel erection

(G-3122)
NORTHERN KENTUCKY
2135 Dana Ave Ste 200 (45207-1327)
PHONE..................................513 563-7555
EMP: 55 **EST:** 2018
SALES (est): 1.03MM **Privately Held**
Web: www.potterestateplanning.com
SIC: 8111 General practice law office

Cincinnati - Hamilton County (G-3123) — GEOGRAPHIC SECTION

(G-3123)
NORTHGATE CHRYSLER DDGE JEEP I
8536 Colerain Ave (45251-2914)
PHONE..................513 385-3900
Peter Pannier, *Pr*
Kathy Hettesheimer, *
EMP: 60 **EST:** 1967
SQ FT: 40,000
SALES (est): 9.67MM **Privately Held**
Web: www.northgatechryslerdodgejeep.net
SIC: 5511 7538 7515 7532 Automobiles, new and used; General automotive repair shops; Passenger car leasing; Body shop, automotive

(G-3124)
NORTHGATE OPS LLC
Also Called: Xscape Theaters
9500 Colerain Ave (45251-2004)
PHONE..................812 945-4006
J Chance Ragains, *Prin*
EMP: 63 **EST:** 2014
SALES (est): 206.66K **Privately Held**
SIC: 7832 Motion picture theaters, except drive-in

(G-3125)
NORTHGATE PK RETIREMENT CMNTY
Also Called: Northgate Park
9191 Round Top Rd Ofc (45251-2465)
PHONE..................513 923-3711
Patricia Jett, *Dir*
EMP: 32 **EST:** 1987
SQ FT: 50,000
SALES (est): 5.1MM **Privately Held**
Web: www.northgateparkseniorliving.com
SIC: 8361 Aged home

(G-3126)
NORTHLICH LLC
Also Called: Northlich Public Relations
720 E Pete Rose Way (45202-3576)
PHONE..................513 421-8840
EMP: 103
Web: www.northlich.com
SIC: 7311 8743 7331 Advertising agencies; Public relations services; Direct mail advertising services

(G-3127)
NORTHWEST LOCAL SCHOOL DST
3308 Compton Rd (45251-2508)
PHONE..................513 923-1000
EMP: 47
SALES (corp-wide): 135.33MM **Privately Held**
Web: www.nwlsd.org
SIC: 8211 8351 Public elementary and secondary schools; Preschool center
PA: Northwest Local School District
3240 Banning Rd
Cincinnati OH 45239
513 923-1000

(G-3128)
NORWOOD ENDOSCOPY CENTER
4746 Montgomery Rd Ste 100 (45212-2626)
PHONE..................513 731-5600
EMP: 27 **EST:** 2009
SALES (est): 839.7K **Privately Held**
Web: www.ohiogi.com
SIC: 8011 Gastronomist

(G-3129)
NORWOOD HARDWARE AND SUPPLY CO
2906 Glendale Milford Rd (45241-3131)
PHONE..................513 733-1175
Matt Chabot, *CEO*
Matt Chabot, *Pr*
Matthew Chabot, *
Craig Chabot, *
Paul Sylvester, *
▲ **EMP:** 65 **EST:** 1946
SQ FT: 58,000
SALES (est): 20.17MM **Privately Held**
Web: www.norwoodhardware.com
SIC: 5072 5031 5023 Hardware; Metal doors, sash and trim; Homefurnishings

(G-3130)
NORWOOD HEALTH CARE CENTER LLC
1578 Sherman Ave (45212-2510)
PHONE..................513 351-0153
Herbert Seidner, *Managing Member*
EMP: 54 **EST:** 1965
SQ FT: 23,000
SALES (est): 1.4MM **Privately Held**
SIC: 8051 8052 8059 Convalescent home with continuous nursing care; Intermediate care facilities; Nursing home, except skilled and intermediate care facility

(G-3131)
NORWOOD HGHLNDS HEALTHCARE LLC
Also Called: Highlands Post Acute
1500 Sherman Ave (45212-2510)
PHONE..................513 351-0153
Mark Hancock, *
EMP: 66 **EST:** 2019
SALES (est): 3.99MM
SALES (corp-wide): 1.64B **Privately Held**
SIC: 8051 Skilled nursing care facilities
PA: Providence Group, Inc.
262 N University Ave
Farmington UT 84025
801 447-9829

(G-3132)
NOVELART MANUFACTURING COMPANY (PA)
Also Called: Topicz
2121 Section Rd (45237)
P.O. Box 37289 (45222)
PHONE..................513 351-7700
Adam Greenberg, *Pr*
EMP: 100 **EST:** 1903
SQ FT: 90,000
SALES (est): 49.66MM
SALES (corp-wide): 49.66MM **Privately Held**
Web: www.topicz.com
SIC: 5194 5145 5141 Tobacco and tobacco products; Confectionery; Food brokers

(G-3133)
NTT DATA BUS SOLUTIONS INC (DH)
10856 Reed Hartman Hwy (45242-0209)
PHONE..................513 956-2000
Herbert Vogel, *CEO*
Steven Niesman, *Pr*
Mark Mueller, *VP*
Steve Short, *VP*
Robert Fiorillo, *VP*
EMP: 45 **EST:** 1995
SALES (est): 45.52MM **Privately Held**
Web: www.nttdata-solutions.com
SIC: 7379 Online services technology consultants
HQ: Ntt Data Business Solutions Ag
Konigsbreede 1
Bielefeld NW 33605
521914480

(G-3134)
NUEROLOGICAL & SLEEP DISORDERS
Also Called: Fleet Management Institute
5240 E Galbraith Rd (45236-2879)
PHONE..................513 721-7533
EMP: 42 **EST:** 1995
SALES (est): 4.58MM **Privately Held**
Web: www.sleepmanagement.md
SIC: 8011 Specialized medical practitioners, except internal

(G-3135)
NUROTOCO MASSACHUSETTS INC
Also Called: Roto-Rooter
255 E 5th St 2500 Chemed Ctr (45202-4700)
PHONE..................513 762-6690
Spencer Lee, *CEO*
EMP: 28 **EST:** 1999
SALES (est): 4.37MM
SALES (corp-wide): 2.26B **Publicly Held**
Web: www.rotorooter.com
SIC: 7699 Sewer cleaning and rodding
HQ: Roto-Rooter Services Company
255 E 5th St Ste 2500
Cincinnati OH 45202
513 762-6690

(G-3136)
NURSE STAFFING CINCINNATI LLC (PA)
9157 Montgomery Rd Ste 206 (45242-7731)
PHONE..................513 984-8414
Don Day, *Managing Member*
EMP: 194 **EST:** 2002
SALES (est): 9.71MM
SALES (corp-wide): 9.71MM **Privately Held**
Web: www.cincinnatihealthcarestaffing.com
SIC: 7361 Executive placement

(G-3137)
NXSTAGE CINCINNATI LLC
Also Called: Nxstage Kidney Care Cincinnati
12065 Montgomery Rd (45249-1728)
PHONE..................513 712-1300
Jannie Heymaker, *Brnch Mgr*
EMP: 27
SALES (corp-wide): 187.85K **Privately Held**
Web: www.nxstage.com
SIC: 8092 Kidney dialysis centers
PA: Nxstage Cincinnati, Llc
920 Winter St
Waltham MA 02451
781 699-9000

(G-3138)
OAKTREE LLC
Also Called: Oak Hlls Nrsing Rehabilitation
4307 Bridgetown Rd (45211-4427)
P.O. Box 402399 (33140-0399)
PHONE..................513 598-8000
EMP: 70 **EST:** 2010
SQ FT: 72,000
SALES (est): 4.57MM **Privately Held**
SIC: 8051 Convalescent home with continuous nursing care

(G-3139)
OBSTETRIC ANESTHESIA ASSOC INC
Also Called: Good Samaritan Hospital
375 Dixmyth Ave (45220-2475)
PHONE..................513 862-1400
Martin Loon, *Prin*
Adelheid Kuchling, *Sec*
▲ **EMP:** 220 **EST:** 1981
SALES (est): 47.82MM **Privately Held**
Web: www.trihealth.com
SIC: 8011 Anesthesiologist

(G-3140)
OCI LLC ◯
8280 Montgomery Rd Ste 306 (45236-6101)
PHONE..................513 713-3751
Duncan Mclean, *Prin*
EMP: 76 **EST:** 2023
SALES (est): 6.9MM **Privately Held**
SIC: 5084 Industrial machinery and equipment

(G-3141)
OHAD INVESTMENT GROUP LLC
11005 Reading Rd Ste 1 (45241-1973)
PHONE..................513 426-5202
EMP: 40 **EST:** 2020
SALES (est): 2.5MM **Privately Held**
Web: www.ohad-group.com
SIC: 6798 Real estate investment trusts

(G-3142)
OHC OHIO CO-MANAGER LLC
4777 E Galbraith Rd (45236-2725)
PHONE..................513 751-2273
EMP: 28 **EST:** 2012
SALES (est): 69.04K **Privately Held**
SIC: 8741 Management services

(G-3143)
OHIO CASUALTY INSURANCE CO (DH)
Also Called: Liberty Mutual
1876 Waycross Rd (45240)
PHONE..................800 843-6446
Dan R Carmichael, *CEO*
Debra K Crane, *
Ralph G Goode, *
John S Kellington, *
Thomas E Schadler, *
EMP: 1200 **EST:** 1919
SALES (est): 379.63MM
SALES (corp-wide): 20.63B **Privately Held**
Web: www.ohioquotes.com
SIC: 6311 6331 Life insurance carriers; Workers' compensation insurance
HQ: Liberty Mutual Insurance Company
175 Berkeley St
Boston MA 02116
617 357-9500

(G-3144)
OHIO DEPT MNTAL HLTH ADDCTION
Also Called: Summit Bhvioral Healthcare Ctr
1101 Summit Rd (45237-2621)
PHONE..................513 948-3600
Dan Moles, *COO*
EMP: 146
Web: mha.ohio.gov
SIC: 8063 9431 Psychiatric hospitals; Mental health agency administration, government
HQ: Ohio Department Of Mental Health And Addiction Services
30 E Broad St Fl 36
Columbus OH 43215

(G-3145)
OHIO HEART AND VASCULAR
5885 Harrison Ave Ste 1900 (45248-1721)
PHONE..................513 206-1800
A Daniel Glassman, *Prin*
Andrew Daniel Glassman, *Prin*
EMP: 33 **EST:** 2007
SALES (est): 1.99MM **Privately Held**

Web: www.thechristhospital.com
SIC: 8062 General medical and surgical hospitals

(G-3146)
OHIO HEART HEALTH CENTER INC (PA)
237 William Howard Taft Rd (45219-2610)
PHONE.................513 351-9900
Pete L Caples, *Prin*
Dean Kereiakes, *
EMP: 30 EST: 1995
SALES (est): 7.77MM Privately Held
SIC: 8011 Cardiologist and cardio-vascular specialist

(G-3147)
OHIO LIVING
Also Called: Llanfair Retirement Community
1701 Llanfair Ave (45224-2972)
PHONE.................513 681-4230
Sheena Parton, *Brnch Mgr*
EMP: 406
Web: www.ohioliving.org
SIC: 8361 8052 8051 Aged home; Intermediate care facilities; Skilled nursing care facilities
PA: Ohio Living
9200 Worthington Rd # 300
Westerville OH 43082

(G-3148)
OHIO RIVER DIALYSIS LLC
Also Called: White Oak Home Training
5520 Cheviot Rd Ste B (45247-7069)
PHONE.................513 385-3580
Jim Hilger, *Brnch Mgr*
EMP: 27
Web: www.davita.com
SIC: 8092 Kidney dialysis centers
HQ: Ohio River Dialysis, Llc
601 Hawaii St
El Segundo CA 90245

(G-3149)
OHIO SHARED INFO SVCS INC
Also Called: OSIS
7870 E Kemper Rd (45249-1675)
PHONE.................513 677-5600
Jeff Lowrance, *CEO*
Bruce Gehring, *Pr*
Dave Chambers, *COO*
Scott Heaton, *VP*
Tom Shannon, *CFO*
EMP: 94 EST: 2000
SALES (est): 28.2MM Privately Held
Web: www.osisonline.net
SIC: 8741 Management services

(G-3150)
OHIO VALLEY FLOORING INC (PA)
Also Called: Ohio Valley Flooring
5555 Murray Ave (45227-2707)
PHONE.................513 271-3434
Alvin Hurt Iii, *CEO*
Jud Hurt, *
Mark Roflow, *
◆ EMP: 70 EST: 1978
SQ FT: 300,000
SALES (est): 49.02MM
SALES (corp-wide): 49.02MM Privately Held
Web: www.ovf.org
SIC: 5023 Carpets

(G-3151)
OHIO VALLEY WINE COMPANY LLC
Also Called: Ohio Valley Wine & Beer
1518 Dalton Ave (45214-2018)
PHONE.................513 771-9370
Steve Lowrey, *Pr*
Brian Cunningham Execvp Genmng r, *Prin*
Albert W Vontz Iii, *VP*
Tom Rouse, *
Greg Maurer, *
◆ EMP: 170 EST: 1974
SALES (est): 22.73MM Privately Held
Web: www.heidelbergdistributing.com
SIC: 5182 5181 Wine; Beer and other fermented malt liquors

(G-3152)
OHIO/OKLAHOMA HEARST TV INC (DH)
Also Called: Wlwt
1700 Young St (45202-6821)
PHONE.................513 412-5000
Richard Dyer, *Pr*
EMP: 51 EST: 1960
SALES (est): 21.98MM
SALES (corp-wide): 4.29B Privately Held
Web: www.wlwt.com
SIC: 4833 6794 Television broadcasting stations; Patent owners and lessors
HQ: Hearst Television, Inc.
214 N Tryon St Ste 3350
Charlotte NC 28202

(G-3153)
OK INTERIORS CORP
11100 Ashburn Rd (45240-3813)
PHONE.................513 742-3278
Todd Prewitt, *Pr*
Loren Schramm, *
Stephen Schramm, *
Gregory J Meurer, *
EMP: 150 EST: 1984
SQ FT: 18,500
SALES (est): 20.83MM Privately Held
Web: www.okinteriors.com
SIC: 1742 5031 1751 1752 Acoustical and ceiling work; Doors, nec; Window and door (prefabricated) installation; Access flooring system installation

(G-3154)
OKI AUCTION LLC
Also Called: Oki Auto Auction
120 Citycentre Dr (45216-1622)
PHONE.................513 679-7910
Anthony Schoenling, *
EMP: 75 EST: 2010
SALES (est): 2.47MM Privately Held
Web: www.okiautoauction.com
SIC: 7389 Auctioneers, fee basis

(G-3155)
OKL CAN LINE INC
11235 Sebring Dr (45240-2714)
Anthony Lacey, *CEO*
◆ EMP: 47 EST: 1983
SQ FT: 50,000
SALES (est): 11.04MM
SALES (corp-wide): 11.04MM Privately Held
Web: www.oklcan.com
SIC: 3565 7699 Bottling and canning machinery; Industrial machinery and equipment repair
PA: Allcan Global Services, Inc
11235 Sebring Dr
Cincinnati OH 45240
513 825-1655

(G-3156)
OLD TIME POTTERY LLC
1191 Smiley Ave (45240-1832)
PHONE.................513 825-5211
Ron Gribbins, *Brnch Mgr*
EMP: 54
SALES (corp-wide): 892.49MM Privately Held
Web: www.oldtimepottery.com
SIC: 5999 5023 Art, picture frames, and decorations; Homefurnishings
HQ: Old Time Pottery, Llc
480 River Rock Blvd
Murfreesboro TN 37128
615 890-6060

(G-3157)
OMNICARE LLC (DH)
900 Omnicare Ctr 201 E Fourth St (45202)
PHONE.................513 719-2600
Nitin Sahney, *CEO*
Ahmed Hassan, *
Robert O Kraft, *
Ashok Singh, *
Steve Skware, *
EMP: 250 EST: 1981
SALES (est): 1.83B
SALES (corp-wide): 357.78B Publicly Held
Web: www.omnicare.com
SIC: 5122 Pharmaceuticals
HQ: Cvs Pharmacy, Inc.
1 Cvs Dr
Woonsocket RI 02895
401 765-1500

(G-3158)
OMNICARE DISTRIBUTION CTR LLC
201 E 4th St Ste 1 (45202-4248)
PHONE.................419 720-8200
EMP: 100 EST: 2001
SALES (est): 43.03MM
SALES (corp-wide): 357.78B Publicly Held
Web: www.omnicare.com
SIC: 5122 Pharmaceuticals
HQ: Omnicare, Llc
900 Omncare Ctr 201 E 4th
Cincinnati OH 45202
513 719-2600

(G-3159)
OMNICARE PHARMACIES OF THE GP (DH)
201 E 4th St Ste 900 (45202-1513)
PHONE.................513 719-2600
EMP: 30 EST: 2014
SALES (est): 6.99MM
SALES (corp-wide): 357.78B Publicly Held
Web: www.omnicare.com
SIC: 5122 Drugs, proprietaries, and sundries
HQ: Omnicare Holding Company
1105 N Market St Ste 1300
Cincinnati OH 45202

(G-3160)
OMNICARE PHRM OF MIDWEST LLC (DH)
201 E 4th St Ste 900 (45202-1513)
PHONE.................513 719-2600
Joel Gemunder, *Prin*
EMP: 100 EST: 1964
SALES (est): 36.9MM
SALES (corp-wide): 357.78B Publicly Held
Web: www.omnicare.com
SIC: 5122 5912 2834 Drugs and drug proprietaries; Drug stores; Pharmaceutical preparations
HQ: Neighborcare Pharmacy Services, Inc.
201 E 4th St Ste 900
Cincinnati OH 45202

(G-3161)
OMNICARE PURCH LTD PARTNER INC
201 E 4th St Ste 900 (45202-1513)
PHONE.................800 990-6664
Janice Rice, *Prin*
EMP: 677 EST: 2014
SALES (est): 2.67MM
SALES (corp-wide): 357.78B Publicly Held
Web: www.omnicare.com
SIC: 8741 Business management
HQ: Omnicare, Llc
900 Omnicare Ctr 201 E 4th
Cincinnati OH 45202
513 719-2600

(G-3162)
ONCALL LLC
8044 Montgomery Rd Ste 700 (45236-2919)
PHONE.................513 381-4320
Walter R Dewees, *
Guy Bradley, *
Bob Hauser, *
EMP: 92 EST: 1996
SALES (est): 15.72MM
SALES (corp-wide): 18.5B Privately Held
Web: www.oncall-llc.com
SIC: 8742 General management consultant
HQ: Grey Healthcare Group Inc.
200 5th Ave Ste 500
New York NY 10010
212 886-3000

(G-3163)
ONCOLGY/HMATOLOGY CARE INC PSC (PA)
Also Called: O C I
5053 Wooster Rd (45226-2326)
PHONE.................513 751-2145
E Randolph Broun, *CEO*
EMP: 70 EST: 1984
SALES (est): 27.17MM Privately Held
Web: www.ohcare.com
SIC: 8011 Oncologist

(G-3164)
ONX HOLDINGS LLC (DH)
Also Called: Onx Enterprise Solutions
221 E 4th St (45202)
PHONE.................866 587-2287
EMP: 57 EST: 2006
SALES (est): 95.76MM
SALES (corp-wide): 3.15B Privately Held
Web: www.altafiber.com
SIC: 7379 7372 Computer related consulting services; Business oriented computer software
HQ: Cincinnati Bell Inc.
221 E 4th St Ste 700
Cincinnati OH 45202
513 397-9900

(G-3165)
OPTI LLC
5000 Willow Hills Ln (45243-4220)
PHONE.................212 651-7317
Chad Holsinger, *Managing Member*
EMP: 40 EST: 2017
SALES (est): 20MM Privately Held
SIC: 7311 8742 Advertising agencies; Marketing consulting services

(G-3166)
OPTUM INFUSION SVCS 550 LLC (DH)
Also Called: Diplomat Spclty Infusion Group
7167 E Kemper Rd (45249-1028)
PHONE.................866 442-4679
EMP: 63 EST: 2004
SALES (est): 50.08MM
SALES (corp-wide): 371.62B Publicly Held
Web: www.biorxhemophilia.com

Cincinnati - Hamilton County (G-3167) — **GEOGRAPHIC SECTION**

SIC: **5122** 8748 2834 5047 Pharmaceuticals; Business consulting, nec; Pharmaceutical preparations; Medical and hospital equipment
HQ: Optum, Inc.
  11000 Optum Cir
  Eden Prairie MN 55344
  952 936-1300

(G-3167)
ORGANIZED LIVING INC (PA)
Also Called: Organized Living
3100 E Kemper Rd (45241-1517)
  PHONE.....................513 489-9300
  John D Kokenge, *CEO*
  Patrick Taylor, *
  Steve Mccamley, *VP Mktg*
  Robert J Lamping, *
  Kevin Ball, *
  ◆ EMP: 40 EST: 1919
  SQ FT: 16,000
  SALES (est): 46.72MM
  SALES (corp-wide): 46.72MM **Privately Held**
  Web: www.organizedliving.com
  SIC: **3083** 3411 2542 1799 Laminated plastics plate and sheet; Metal cans; Partitions and fixtures, except wood; Home/office interiors finishing, furnishing and remodeling

(G-3168)
ORIGINAL PARTNERS LTD PARTNR (PA)
Also Called: Towne Properties
1055 Saint Paul Pl (45202-6042)
  PHONE.....................513 381-8696
  Neil K Bortz, *Ltd Pt*
  Marvin Rosenberg, *
  EMP: 150 EST: 1961
  SQ FT: 5,000
  SALES (est): 59.97MM
  SALES (corp-wide): 59.97MM **Privately Held**
  Web: www.towneproperties.com
  SIC: **6514** 6513 Dwelling operators, except apartments; Apartment building operators

(G-3169)
OROURKE WRECKING COMPANY
Also Called: O'Rourke Wrecking Company
660 Lunken Park Dr (45226-1800)
  PHONE.....................513 871-1400
  TOLL FREE: 800
  Michael Orourke, *Pr*
  EMP: 75 EST: 1996
  SQ FT: 20,000
  SALES (est): 14.08MM **Privately Held**
  Web: www.orourkewrecking.com
  SIC: **1795** Demolition, buildings and other structures

(G-3170)
ORTHOPEDIC CONS CINCINNATI
6620 Clough Pike (45244-4053)
  PHONE.....................513 753-7488
  Robert S Hiedt Senior, *Pr*
  EMP: 32
  SALES (corp-wide): 20.42MM **Privately Held**
  Web: www.orthocincy.com
  SIC: **8011** Orthopedic physician
  PA: Orthopedic Consultants Of Cincinnati
     7798 Discovery Dr Ste A
     West Chester OH 45069
     513 733-8894

(G-3171)
ORTHOPEDIC CONS CINCINNATI
Also Called: Wellington Orthopedics
6620 Clough Pike (45244-4053)
  PHONE.....................513 232-6677
  Julie Moore, *Mgr*
  EMP: 33
  SALES (corp-wide): 20.42MM **Privately Held**
  Web: www.orthocincy.com
  SIC: **8011** Orthopedic physician
  PA: Orthopedic Consultants Of Cincinnati
     7798 Discovery Dr Ste A
     West Chester OH 45069
     513 733-8894

(G-3172)
ORTHOPEDIC CONS CINCINNATI
Also Called: Wellington Orthpd Spt Medicine
7663 5 Mile Rd (45230-4340)
  PHONE.....................513 245-2500
  Sonya Hughes, *Genl Mgr*
  EMP: 33
  SALES (corp-wide): 20.42MM **Privately Held**
  Web: www.orthocincy.com
  SIC: **8011** Orthopedic physician
  PA: Orthopedic Consultants Of Cincinnati
     7798 Discovery Dr Ste A
     West Chester OH 45069
     513 733-8894

(G-3173)
ORTHOPEDIC CONS CINCINNATI
Also Called: Wellington Orthpd Spt Medicine
6909 Good Samaritan Dr (45247-5208)
  PHONE.....................513 347-9999
  EMP: 33
  SALES (corp-wide): 20.42MM **Privately Held**
  Web: www.orthocincy.com
  SIC: **8011** Orthopedic physician
  PA: Orthopedic Consultants Of Cincinnati
     7798 Discovery Dr Ste A
     West Chester OH 45069
     513 733-8894

(G-3174)
OSTERWISCH COMPANY INC
Also Called: Osterwisch
6755 Highland Ave (45236-3968)
  PHONE.....................513 791-3282
  James W Osterwisch, *Pr*
  Donald Osterwisch, *
  EMP: 80 EST: 1946
  SQ FT: 30,000
  SALES (est): 17.68MM **Privately Held**
  Web: www.osterwisch.com
  SIC: **1731** 1711 General electrical contractor; Warm air heating and air conditioning contractor

(G-3175)
OTIS ELEVATOR COMPANY
2463 Crowne Point Dr (45241-5407)
  PHONE.....................513 531-7888
  EMP: 116
  SALES (corp-wide): 14.21B **Publicly Held**
  Web: www.otis.com
  SIC: **5084** 7699 Elevators; Elevators: inspection, service, and repair
  HQ: Otis Elevator Company
     1 Carrier Pl
     Farmington CT 06032
     860 674-3000

(G-3176)
OUR LADY BELLEFONTE HOSP INC (HQ)
Also Called: Our Lady Bellefonte Hospital
1701 Mercy Health Pl (45237-6147)
  PHONE.....................606 833-3333
  Thom Morris, *Pr*
  Kevin Halter, *
  Pamela Hall, *
  John Wallenhorst, *
  Joe Buchheit, *
  EMP: 800 EST: 1953
  SALES (est): 166.53MM
  SALES (corp-wide): 6.92B **Privately Held**
  Web: www.bsmhealth.org
  SIC: **8062** 8082 8011 5999 Hospital, affiliated with AMA residency; Home health care services; Medical centers; Medical apparatus and supplies
  PA: Bon Secours Mercy Health, Inc.
     1701 Mercy Health Pl
     Cincinnati OH 45237
     513 956-3729

(G-3177)
OVERLAND XPRESS LLC (PA)
431 Ohio Pike Ste 311 (45255-3629)
  PHONE.....................513 528-1158
  Jason Brown, *Managing Member*
  Bledar Andoni, *
  EMP: 40 EST: 2005
  SQ FT: 1,600
  SALES (est): 15.94MM **Privately Held**
  Web: www.overlandxpress.com
  SIC: **4731** Freight forwarding

(G-3178)
OXFORD PHYSICAL THERAPY INC
Also Called: OXFORD PHYSICAL THERAPY INC
11003 Montgomery Rd (45249-2306)
  PHONE.....................513 469-1444
  EMP: 35
  Web: www.oxfordphysicaltherapy.com
  SIC: **8049** Physical therapist
  PA: Oxford Physical Therapy And Rehabilitation, Inc.
     345 S College Ave
     Oxford OH 45056

(G-3179)
P & M EXHAUST SYSTEMS WHSE INC
Also Called: Car-X Muffler & Brake
11843 Kemper Springs Dr (45240-1641)
  PHONE.....................513 825-2660
  Ranga Gorrepati, *Pr*
  Pallavi Gorrepati, *
  Madhavi Gorrepati, *
  Rayulu Gorrepati, *
  Ajay Gorrepati, *
  EMP: 27 EST: 1986
  SQ FT: 15,000
  SALES (est): 5.5MM **Privately Held**
  Web: www.carx.com
  SIC: **5013** Exhaust systems (mufflers, tail pipes, etc.)

(G-3180)
P C VPA
4623 Wesley Ave Ste P (45212-2272)
  PHONE.....................513 841-0777
  Meenakshi Sharma, *Bmch Mgr*
  EMP: 52
  Web: www.visitingphysicians.com
  SIC: **8082** Home health care services
  PA: P C Vpa
     500 Kirts Blvd
     Troy MI 48084

(G-3181)
PAIN SPCIALISTS CINCINNATI LLC
3328 Westbourne Dr (45248-5133)
  PHONE.....................513 922-2204
  EMP: 37 EST: 2015
  SALES (est): 5.31MM **Privately Held**
  Web: www.paincincinnati.com
  SIC: **8011** General and family practice, physician/surgeon

(G-3182)
PARAGON SALONS INC (PA)
6775 Harrison Ave (45247-3239)
  PHONE.....................513 574-7610
  Deborah Celek, *Pr*
  Steven Celek, *
  EMP: 40 EST: 1982
  SQ FT: 2,600
  SALES (est): 916.78K
  SALES (corp-wide): 916.78K **Privately Held**
  Web: www.paragonsalon.com
  SIC: **7991** Spas

(G-3183)
PARK HOTELS & RESORTS INC
Also Called: Hilton Cncnnati Netherland Plz
35 W 5th St (45202-2801)
  PHONE.....................513 421-9100
  EMP: 37
  SALES (corp-wide): 2.7B **Publicly Held**
  Web: www.pkhotelsandresorts.com
  SIC: **7011** Hotels
  PA: Park Hotels & Resorts Inc.
     1775 Tysons Blvd Fl 7
     Tysons VA 22102
     571 302-5757

(G-3184)
PARK PLACE OPERATIONS INC
Also Called: Hartsfield Atlanta Intl Arprt
250 W Court St Ste 200e (45202-1064)
  PHONE.....................513 241-0415
  William Miller, *Brnch Mgr*
  EMP: 29
  SALES (corp-wide): 51.29MM **Privately Held**
  Web: www.parkplaceparking.com
  SIC: **7521** Parking lots
  PA: Park Place Operations, Inc.
     250 W Court St Ste 200e
     Cincinnati OH 45202
     513 241-0415

(G-3185)
PARK PLACE OPERATIONS INC
Also Called: Downtown Fast Park
250 W Court St Ste 100e (45202-1046)
P.O. Box 6187 (45206-0187)
  PHONE.....................513 381-2179
  Ayo Owoeye, *Mgr*
  EMP: 43
  SALES (corp-wide): 51.29MM **Privately Held**
  Web: www.thefastpark.com
  SIC: **7521** Parking lots
  PA: Park Place Operations, Inc.
     250 W Court St Ste 200e
     Cincinnati OH 45202
     513 241-0415

(G-3186)
PARK PLACE OPERATIONS INC (PA)
Also Called: Airport Fast Park
250 W Court St Ste 200e (45202-1064)
  PHONE.....................513 241-0415
  EMP: 35 EST: 1974
  SALES (est): 51.29MM
  SALES (corp-wide): 51.29MM **Privately Held**
  Web: www.pca-star.com
  SIC: **7521** Parking garage

(G-3187)
PATIENTPINT HOSP SOLUTIONS LLC
8230 Montgomery Rd Ste 300 (45236-2200)
  PHONE.....................513 936-6800
  EMP: 114 EST: 2009
  SALES (est): 1.35MM
  SALES (corp-wide): 96.89MM **Privately Held**

GEOGRAPHIC SECTION
Cincinnati - Hamilton County (G-3208)

Web: www.patientpoint.com
SIC: 8742 Marketing consulting services
HQ: Patientpoint Holdings, Inc.
8230 Montgomery Rd # 300
Cincinnati OH 45236
513 936-6800

(G-3188)
PATIENTPOINT LLC (PA)
5901 E Galbraith Rd Ste R1000 (45236-2230)
PHONE..................513 936-6800
Mike Colette, *CEO*
Traver Hutchins, *CGO*
David Guthrie, *CPO*
Bill Jennings, *Chief Digital Officer*
EMP: 94 EST: 2014
SALES (est): 96.89MM
SALES (corp-wide): 96.89MM Privately Held
Web: www.patientpoint.com
SIC: 8062 General medical and surgical hospitals

(G-3189)
PATRICK J BURKE & CO
Also Called: Burke & Company
901 Adams Crossing Fl 1 (45202-1693)
PHONE..................513 455-8200
Patrick Burke, *Owner*
EMP: 41 EST: 1984
SALES (est): 5.72MM Privately Held
Web: www.burkecpa.com
SIC: 8721 7372 Certified public accountant; Prepackaged software

(G-3190)
PAYCOM SOFTWARE INC
255 E 5th St Ste 1420 (45202-4709)
PHONE..................888 678-0796
EMP: 170
SALES (corp-wide): 1.69B Publicly Held
Web: www.paycom.com
SIC: 8721 Payroll accounting service
PA: Paycom Software, Inc.
7501 W Memorial Rd
Oklahoma City OK 73142
405 722-6900

(G-3191)
PAYCOR INC (PA)
Also Called: Paycor
4811 Montgomery Rd (45212-2163)
PHONE..................513 381-0505
Robert J Coughlin, *Ch*
Steven G Haussler, *
Rick Chouteau, *
Tammy Jamison, *
Stacey Browning, *
EMP: 200 EST: 2001
SQ FT: 33,000
SALES (est): 421.78MM Privately Held
Web: www.paycor.com
SIC: 8721 Payroll accounting service

(G-3192)
PCMS INTERNATIONAL INC
25 Merchant St Ste 135 (45246-3740)
PHONE..................513 587-3100
Richard Smith, *Pr*
EMP: 90 EST: 2002
SALES (est): 4.14MM Privately Held
SIC: 7371 Computer software development

(G-3193)
PECK-HANNAFORD BRIGGS SVC CORP
Also Called: Peck Hannaford Briggs Service
4673 Spring Grove Ave (45232-1952)
PHONE..................513 681-1200
James G Briggs Junior, *Pr*

Jerry Govert, *
EMP: 57 EST: 1980
SQ FT: 4,000
SALES (est): 11.65MM
SALES (corp-wide): 57.91MM Privately Held
Web: www.peckhannafordbriggs.com
SIC: 1711 Warm air heating and air conditioning contractor
PA: Peck-Hannaford & Briggs Co, The (Inc)
4670 Chester Ave
Cincinnati OH 45232
513 681-4600

(G-3194)
PEGASUS TECHNICAL SERVICES INC
46 E Hollister St (45219-1704)
PHONE..................513 793-0094
EMP: 57 EST: 1996
SQ FT: 200
SALES (est): 5.34MM Privately Held
Web: www.ptsied.com
SIC: 8711 7371 7373 Consulting engineer; Custom computer programming services; Computer-aided design (CAD) systems service

(G-3195)
PENSION CORPORATION AMERICA
Also Called: ABG Advisors
2133 Luray Ave (45206-2604)
PHONE..................513 281-3366
Tom Seitz, *Pr*
Jim Eckeroe, *
EMP: 51 EST: 1977
SQ FT: 3,500
SALES (est): 2.63MM Privately Held
Web: www.pca401k.com
SIC: 8742 Financial consultant

(G-3196)
PERFECTION GROUP INC (PA)
Also Called: Honeywell Authorized Dealer
2649 Commerce Blvd (45241-1553)
PHONE..................513 772-7545
William J Albrecht, *CEO*
Anthony Apro, *
W John Albrecht Junior, *Sec*
Todd M Albrecht, *
EMP: 123 EST: 1983
SQ FT: 10,000
SALES (est): 51.92MM
SALES (corp-wide): 51.92MM Privately Held
Web: www.perfectiongroup.com
SIC: 1711 Mechanical contractor

(G-3197)
PERFECTION SERVICES INC
2649 Commerce Blvd (45241-1553)
PHONE..................513 772-7545
William Albrecht, *Pr*
William Albrecht, *CEO*
John E Shaw, *
EMP: 124 EST: 1972
SQ FT: 10,000
SALES (est): 8.8MM
SALES (corp-wide): 51.92MM Privately Held
Web: www.perfectiongroup.com
SIC: 1711 Mechanical contractor
PA: Perfection Group, Inc.
2649 Commerce Blvd
Cincinnati OH 45241
513 772-7545

(G-3198)
PERSONAL TOUCH HM CARE IPA INC
8260 Northcreek Dr Ste 140 (45236-2283)

PHONE..................513 984-9600
Barbie Wenman, *Mgr*
EMP: 230
SALES (corp-wide): 251.89MM Privately Held
Web: www.pthomecare.com
SIC: 8082 Home health care services
PA: Personal Touch Home Care Ipa, Inc.
1985 Marcus Ave Ste 202
New Hyde Park NY 11042
718 468-4747

(G-3199)
PETERBILT OF CINCINNATI
2550 Annuity Dr (45241-1502)
PHONE..................513 772-1740
Taylor Edwards, *Pr*
EMP: 278 EST: 1991
SQ FT: 50,000
SALES (est): 12.82MM
SALES (corp-wide): 147.46MM Privately Held
Web: www.peterbilt.com
SIC: 5012 5013 7538 Truck tractors; Truck parts and accessories; General truck repair
PA: W. D. Larson Companies Ltd., Inc.
500 Ford Rd
St Louis Park MN 55426
952 888-4934

(G-3200)
PETERMANN LTD (HQ)
Also Called: Petermann
1861 Section Rd (45237-3305)
PHONE..................513 351-7383
EMP: 31 EST: 1999
SALES (est): 67.74MM Privately Held
Web: www.petermannbus.com
SIC: 4119 4151 4141 Local passenger transportation, nec; School buses; Local bus charter service
PA: Mobico Group Plc
National Express House
Birmingham W MIDLANDS B5 6D

(G-3201)
PETERMANN NORTHEAST LLC
8041 Hosbrook Rd Ste 330 (45236-2909)
PHONE..................513 351-7383
Michael J Settle, *COO*
EMP: 237 EST: 2002
SALES (est): 2.35MM Privately Held
Web: www.petermannbus.com
SIC: 4151 School buses
HQ: National Express Llc
2601 Navistar Dr Bldg 4
Lisle IL 60532

(G-3202)
PETRO ENVIRONMENTAL TECH (PA)
Also Called: Petro Cells
8160 Corporate Park Dr Ste 300 (45242)
PHONE..................513 489-6789
Pete Mather, *Pr*
Mark Mather, *
Peter Mather, *
EMP: 40 EST: 1987
SQ FT: 7,500
SALES (est): 8.48MM
SALES (corp-wide): 8.48MM Privately Held
SIC: 1629 4959 Land preparation construction; Toxic or hazardous waste cleanup

(G-3203)
PFFA ACQUISITION LLC (PA)
1216 Central Pkwy (45202-7509)
PHONE..................859 835-6088
Neil Hornsby, *Managing Member*
Kurt Freyberger, *

Diane Tidwell, *
EMP: 99 EST: 2014
SALES (est): 2.77MM
SALES (corp-wide): 2.77MM Privately Held
SIC: 7941 Football club

(G-3204)
PFSC INC
2813 Gilbert Ave (45206-1210)
PHONE..................513 221-5080
Til Macconnel, *Prin*
EMP: 28 EST: 2005
SALES (est): 543.6K Privately Held
Web: www.pfscinc.com
SIC: 6159 General and industrial loan institutions

(G-3205)
PHARMACY CONSULTANTS LLC (DH)
Also Called: Omnicare of Spartanburg
201 E 4th St Ste 900 (45202-4160)
PHONE..................864 578-8788
Ed Bess, *Dir*
EMP: 44 EST: 1976
SALES (est): 5.58MM
SALES (corp-wide): 357.78B Publicly Held
SIC: 8742 Industry specialist consultants
HQ: Omnicare, Llc
900 Omncare Ctr 201 E 4th
Cincinnati OH 45202
513 719-2600

(G-3206)
PHILLIPS EDISON & COMPANY LLC (HQ)
Also Called: Phillips Edison & Company
11501 Northlake Dr Fl 1 (45249-1667)
PHONE..................513 554-1110
Jeffrey S Edison, *CEO*
Robert F Myers, *
Michael C Phillips, *
Bob Myers, *
John Caulfield, *
EMP: 27 EST: 2004
SQ FT: 5,000
SALES (est): 21.89MM Privately Held
Web: www.phillipsedison.com
SIC: 6531 6552 Real estate brokers and agents; Land subdividers and developers, commercial
PA: Edison Phillips Limited Partnership
11501 Northlake Dr Fl 1
Cincinnati OH 45249

(G-3207)
PHILLIPS EDISON INSTITUTIONAL
Also Called: Phillips Edison - ARC Shopping
11501 Northlake Dr (45249-1667)
PHONE..................513 554-1110
EMP: 33 EST: 2017
SALES (est): 484.47K Publicly Held
Web: www.phillipsedison.com
SIC: 8733 Research institute
PA: Phillips Edison & Company, Inc.
11501 Northlake Dr
Cincinnati OH 45249

(G-3208)
PHILLIPS SUPPLY COMPANY (PA)
1230 Findlay Street (1 Crosley Field Lane) (45214-2096)
PHONE..................513 579-1762
Pamela Rossmann, *Pr*
Claire B Phillips, *
Andrew Thompson, *
Eleanor Roth, *
▲ EMP: 55 EST: 1965
SQ FT: 40,000

Cincinnati - Hamilton County (G-3209)

SALES (est): 20.37MM
SALES (corp-wide): 20.37MM **Privately Held**
Web: www.phillipssupply.com
SIC: 5087 Janitors' supplies

(G-3209)
PHOTO-TYPE ENGRAVING COMPANY
Also Called: Photo Art
2150 Florence Ave (45206-2427)
PHONE.................................513 281-0999
Richard Olberding, *Owner*
EMP: 35
SALES (corp-wide): 43.97MM **Privately Held**
Web: www.phototype.com
SIC: 7335 Commercial photography
PA: The Photo-Type Engraving Company
2141 Gilbert Ave
Cincinnati OH 45206
513 281-0999

(G-3210)
PHOTO-TYPE ENGRAVING COMPANY
Gravity
2141 Gilbert Ave (45206-3021)
PHONE.................................513 475-5638
Richard Olberding, *Ch*
EMP: 35
SALES (corp-wide): 43.97MM **Privately Held**
Web: www.phototype.com
SIC: 7336 Package design
PA: The Photo-Type Engraving Company
2141 Gilbert Ave
Cincinnati OH 45206
513 281-0999

(G-3211)
PILLAR OF FIRE
Also Called: Star 93.3 FM
6275 Collegevue Pl (45224-1959)
PHONE.................................513 542-1212
Joseph W Gross, *Pr*
Christopher M Stanko, *
Robert B Dallenbach, *
Hunter T Barnes, *
Arturo Garza, *
EMP: 28 **EST:** 1921
SQ FT: 8,694
SALES (est): 2.43MM **Privately Held**
Web: www.invictus.church
SIC: 4832 8661 Radio broadcasting stations; Religious organizations

(G-3212)
PLANNED PRNTHOOD STHWEST OHIO (PA)
2314 Auburn Ave (45219-2802)
PHONE.................................513 721-7635
Jerry Lawson, *CEO*
Nina Schultz, *
Mike Moloney, *
Amy Kattman, *
Kelli Halter, *
EMP: 35 **EST:** 1929
SQ FT: 35,000
SALES (est): 11.15MM
SALES (corp-wide): 11.15MM **Privately Held**
Web: www.plannedparenthood.org
SIC: 8093 Family planning clinic

(G-3213)
PLEASANT RIDGE CARE CENTER INC (PA)
Also Called: Pleasant Ridge Care Center
5501 Verulam Ave (45213-2417)
PHONE.................................513 631-1310
EMP: 103 **EST:** 2008
SALES (est): 5.14MM **Privately Held**
SIC: 8051 Convalescent home with continuous nursing care

(G-3214)
PLK COMMUNITIES LLC (PA)
5905 E Galbraith Rd Ste 4100 (45236-0704)
PHONE.................................513 561-5080
EMP: 51 **EST:** 2010
SALES (est): 11.92MM **Privately Held**
Web: www.plkcommunities.com
SIC: 6531 Real estate managers

(G-3215)
PLS FINANCIAL SERVICES INC
702 Reading Rd (45202-1411)
PHONE.................................513 421-4200
EMP: 36
SALES (corp-wide): 501.55MM **Privately Held**
Web: www.pls247.com
SIC: 6099 Check cashing agencies
PA: Pls Financial Services, Inc.
1 S Wacker Dr Ste 3600
Chicago IL 60606
312 491-7300

(G-3216)
PNC BANC CORP OHIO (HQ)
Also Called: PNC Bank
201 E 5th St (45202-4152)
PHONE.................................513 651-8738
Barry Friedman, *VP*
Barry Friedman, *Sr VP*
EMP: 54 **EST:** 1968
SQ FT: 10,000
SALES (est): 10.95MM
SALES (corp-wide): 31.88B **Publicly Held**
Web: www.pnc.com
SIC: 6512 6021 Commercial and industrial building operation; National commercial banks
PA: The Pnc Financial Services Group Inc
300 5th Ave
Pittsburgh PA 15222
888 762-2265

(G-3217)
PNCEF LLC
995 Dalton Ave (45203-1100)
PHONE.................................513 421-9191
EMP: 58 **EST:** 1984
SALES (est): 16.07MM
SALES (corp-wide): 31.88B **Publicly Held**
SIC: 7359 Equipment rental and leasing, nec
PA: The Pnc Financial Services Group Inc
300 5th Ave
Pittsburgh PA 15222
888 762-2265

(G-3218)
PNG TELECOMMUNICATIONS INC (PA)
Also Called: Powernet Global Communications
8805 Governors Hill Dr Ste 250 (45249-3314)
PHONE.................................513 942-7900
EMP: 99 **EST:** 1992
SQ FT: 55,000
SALES (est): 26.09MM **Privately Held**
Web: www.powernetco.com
SIC: 4813 7375 Long distance telephone communications; Information retrieval services

(G-3219)
PNK (OHIO) LLC
Also Called: River Downs
6301 Kellogg Rd (45230-5237)
PHONE.................................513 232-8000
Anthony San Filippo, *CEO*
EMP: 700 **EST:** 2010
SALES (est): 50.39MM **Publicly Held**
Web: belterrapark.boydgaming.com
SIC: 7948 7993 Horse race track operation; Coin-operated amusement devices
HQ: Boyd Tciv, Llc
3883 Howard Hughes Pkwy
Las Vegas NV 89169
702 792-7200

(G-3220)
POISON INFORMATION CENTER
Also Called: Drug & Poison Information Ctr
3333 Burnet Ave 3rd Fl (45229-3026)
PHONE.................................513 636-5111
EMP: 43 **EST:** 1965
SALES (est): 2.91MM **Privately Held**
SIC: 8062 General medical and surgical hospitals

(G-3221)
PORTER WRGHT MORRIS ARTHUR LLP
250 E 5th St Ste 2200 (45202-5118)
PHONE.................................513 381-4700
David Croall, *Brnch Mgr*
EMP: 30
SALES (corp-wide): 47.71MM **Privately Held**
Web: www.porterwright.com
SIC: 8111 General practice attorney, lawyer
PA: Porter, Wright, Morris & Arthur Llp
41 S High St Ste 2900
Columbus OH 43215
614 227-2000

(G-3222)
POSITIVE BUS SOLUTIONS INC
Also Called: Pbsi
200 Northland Blvd # 100 (45246-3604)
PHONE.................................513 772-2555
Ray Cool, *Pr*
Tim Latham, *
Lloyd Mason, *
EMP: 56 **EST:** 1983
SQ FT: 15,000
SALES (est): 9.85MM **Privately Held**
Web: www.pbsinet.com
SIC: 7378 5045 7371 Computer and data processing equipment repair/maintenance; Computer software; Computer software development

(G-3223)
POSSIBLE WORLDWIDE LLC (HQ)
Also Called: Zaaz
302 W 3rd St Ste 900 (45202-3424)
P.O. Box 8500 4356 (19178-0001)
PHONE.................................513 381-1380
EMP: 50 **EST:** 2012
SALES (est): 22.19MM
SALES (corp-wide): 18.5B **Privately Held**
SIC: 7373 Computer integrated systems design
PA: Wpp Plc
22 Grenville Street
Jersey JE4 8
370 707-1411

(G-3224)
POST-BROWNING INC
7812 Redsky Dr (45249-1632)
PHONE.................................513 771-1717
EMP: 130
SIC: 5065 7699 Security control equipment and systems; Industrial machinery and equipment repair

(G-3225)
POSTAL FAMILY CREDIT UNION INC
1243 W 8th St (45203-1004)
P.O. Box 14403 (45250-0403)
PHONE.................................513 381-8600
Ann Martin, *Pr*
Richard Joesting, *Dir*
Dennis Marshner, *Sec*
EMP: 29 **EST:** 1932
SQ FT: 5,000
SALES (est): 2.44MM **Privately Held**
Web: www.urmycu.org
SIC: 6061 Federal credit unions

(G-3226)
POWER ENGINEERS INCORPORATED
Also Called: Environmental Division
11733 Chesterdale Rd (45246-3405)
PHONE.................................513 326-1500
Tim Gessner, *Brnch Mgr*
EMP: 35
SALES (corp-wide): 509.69MM **Privately Held**
Web: www.powereng.com
SIC: 8711 Consulting engineer
PA: Power Engineers, Incorporated
3940 Glenbrook Dr
Hailey ID 83333
208 788-3456

(G-3227)
PREMIER ESTATES 525 LLC
Also Called: Pristine Senior Living
1578 Sherman Ave (45212-2510)
PHONE.................................513 631-6800
Shari Bench, *Mgr*
EMP: 63 **EST:** 2017
SALES (est): 4.71MM
SALES (corp-wide): 24.45MM **Privately Held**
SIC: 8361 Aged home
PA: Trillium Healthcare Group, Llc
7349 Merchant Ct
Lakewood Ranch FL 34240
941 758-4745

(G-3228)
PREMIER ESTATES 526 LLC
Also Called: Premier Esttes Cncnnt-Rverview
5999 Bender Rd (45233-1601)
PHONE.................................513 922-1440
Brian Mccoy, *COO*
EMP: 80 **EST:** 2015
SALES (est): 2.29MM
SALES (corp-wide): 24.45MM **Privately Held**
SIC: 8361 Aged home
PA: Trillium Healthcare Group, Llc
7349 Merchant Ct
Lakewood Ranch FL 34240
941 758-4745

(G-3229)
PRESERVE OPERATING CO LLC
Also Called: Brookside Healthcare Center
315 Lilienthal St (45204-1170)
PHONE.................................513 471-8667
EMP: 50 **EST:** 2019
SALES (est): 1.19MM **Privately Held**
SIC: 8093 Rehabilitation center, outpatient treatment

(G-3230)
PRIORITY III CONTRACTING INC
5178 Crookshank Rd (45238-3304)
PHONE.................................513 922-0203

GEOGRAPHIC SECTION

Cincinnati - Hamilton County (G-3253)

EMP: 28 EST: 1995
SQ FT: 33,000
SALES (est): 1.16MM **Privately Held**
Web: www.priorityinsulation.com
SIC: **1799** Insulation of pipes and boilers

(G-3231)
PRISTINE SENIOR LIVING
Also Called: Premier Esttes Cncnnt-Rverside
315 Lilienthal St (45204-1170)
PHONE..................................513 471-8667
EMP: 60 EST: 2017
SALES (est): 1.83MM
SALES (corp-wide): 24.45MM **Privately Held**
Web: www.pristinesrriverside.com
SIC: **8361** Aged home
PA: Trillium Healthcare Group, Llc
7349 Merchant Ct
Lakewood Ranch FL 34240
941 758-4745

(G-3232)
PRN HEALTH SERVICES INC
8044 Montgomery Rd Ste 700 (45236-2919)
PHONE..................................513 792-2217
Anne Dejewski, *Brnch Mgr*
EMP: 334
Web: www.prnhealthservices.com
SIC: **7361** Employment agencies
PA: Prn Health Services, Inc.
1101 E South River St
Appleton WI 54915

(G-3233)
PRO FOOTBALL FCS
1216 Central Pkwy (45202-7509)
PHONE..................................513 381-3404
EMP: 47 EST: 2017
SALES (est): 894.39K **Privately Held**
SIC: **7941** Football club

(G-3234)
PRO ONCALL TECHNOLOGIES LLC (PA)
6902 E Kemper Rd (45249)
P.O. Box 498337 (45249)
PHONE..................................513 489-7660
John O Brian, *Pr*
Don Walter, *
▲ EMP: 30 EST: 1981
SQ FT: 10,000
SALES (est): 24.76MM
SALES (corp-wide): 24.76MM **Privately Held**
Web: www.prooncall.com
SIC: **5065** Telephone equipment

(G-3235)
PRO SENIORS INC
7162 Reading Rd Ste 1150 (45237-3849)
PHONE..................................513 345-4160
Rhonda Moore, *Ex Dir*
EMP: 30 EST: 1975
SALES (est): 2.98MM **Privately Held**
Web: www.proseniors.org
SIC: **8322** Senior citizens' center or association

(G-3236)
PROAMPAC HOLDINGS INC (PA)
Also Called: Proampac Intermediate
12025 Tricon Rd (45246)
PHONE..................................513 671-1777
Greg Tucker, *CEO*
Eric Bradford, *CFO*
EMP: 87 EST: 2015
SALES (est): 1.58B
SALES (corp-wide): 1.58B **Privately Held**
Web: www.proampac.com

SIC: **6722 7389 5199** Management investment, open-end; Packaging and labeling services; Packaging materials

(G-3237)
PROCESS CONSTRUCTION INC
2128 State Ave (45214-1614)
PHONE..................................513 251-2211
Klem Fennell, *Pr*
EMP: 37
SALES (corp-wide): 10.59MM **Privately Held**
Web: www.processconstruction.com
SIC: **1711** Mechanical contractor
PA: Process Construction, Inc.
1421 Queen City Ave
Cincinnati OH 45214
513 251-2211

(G-3238)
PROCESS CONSTRUCTION INC (PA)
Also Called: PCI Services
1421 Queen City Ave (45214)
P.O. Box 14186 (45250)
PHONE..................................513 251-2211
EMP: 53 EST: 1985
SALES (est): 10.59MM
SALES (corp-wide): 10.59MM **Privately Held**
Web: www.processconstruction.com
SIC: **1711** Mechanical contractor

(G-3239)
PROCESS PLUS LLC (HQ)
Also Called: Plus Group
135 Merchant St Ste 300 (45246-3759)
PHONE..................................513 742-7590
EMP: 51 EST: 1996
SQ FT: 32,000
SALES (est): 25.98MM
SALES (corp-wide): 110.61MM **Privately Held**
Web: www.plusgroups.com
SIC: **8711** Consulting engineer
PA: Salas O'brien Engineers, Inc.
305 S 11th St
San Jose CA 95112
408 282-1500

(G-3240)
PROCESS PLUS DESIGN BUILD LLC
Also Called: Design Build Plus
135 Merchant St Ste 300 (45246-3759)
PHONE..................................513 262-2261
Grant E Mitchell, *Managing Member*
EMP: 131 EST: 2001
SALES (est): 4.79MM **Privately Held**
Web: www.plusgroups.com
SIC: **7389** Design services

(G-3241)
PROCESS PLUS HOLDINGS INC
135 Merchant St Ste 300 (45246-3759)
PHONE..................................513 742-7590
Grant E Mitchell, *Dir*
EMP: 53 EST: 2000
SALES (est): 1.08MM
SALES (corp-wide): 110.61MM **Privately Held**
SIC: **7373** Office computer automation systems integration
HQ: Process Plus, Llc
135 Merchant St Ste 300
Cincinnati OH 45246

(G-3242)
PROCESS PUMP & SEAL INC
4317 Kugler Mill Rd (45236-1820)
PHONE..................................513 988-7000
Daniel Quenneville, *Pr*
EMP: 28 EST: 1984

SALES (est): 16.29MM **Privately Held**
Web: www.processpumpandseal.com
SIC: **5085 5084** Packing, industrial; Pumps and pumping equipment, nec

(G-3243)
PROCTER & GAMBLE DISTRG LLC
Also Called: Procter & Gamble
2 Procter And Gamble Plz (45202)
PHONE..................................513 945-7960
EMP: 107
SALES (corp-wide): 82.01B **Publicly Held**
SIC: **5169** Detergents
HQ: Procter & Gamble Distributing Llc
1 Procter And Gamble Plz
Cincinnati OH 45202
513 983-1100

(G-3244)
PROCTER GAMBLE US BUS SVCS CO
1 Procter And Gamble Plz (45202-3393)
PHONE..................................513 983-7777
Terry L Overbey, *Prin*
EMP: 103 EST: 2002
SALES (est): 10.89MM
SALES (corp-wide): 82.01B **Publicly Held**
SIC: **8732** Business economic service
PA: The Procter & Gamble Company
1 Procter & Gamble Plz
Cincinnati OH 45202
513 983-1100

(G-3245)
PROFESSIONAL MAINT OF COLUMBUS
Also Called: Professnal Mint Lttle Ohio Div
1 Crosley Field Ln (45214-2004)
PHONE..................................513 579-1762
Dale Barnett, *Pr*
Eldon Hall, *
EMP: 36 EST: 1960
SALES (est): 447.23K **Privately Held**
SIC: **8351 7349** Child day care services; Janitorial service, contract basis

(G-3246)
PROFESSNAL CBLING SLUTIONS LLC
11711 Chesterdale Rd (45246-3405)
PHONE..................................513 733-9473
EMP: 68 EST: 2003
SALES (est): 8.56MM **Privately Held**
Web: www.professionalcablingsolutions.com
SIC: **1731** Fiber optic cable installation

(G-3247)
PROFILL HOLDINGS LLC
255 W Crescentville Rd (45246-1713)
PHONE..................................513 742-4000
▲ EMP: 665
Web: www.profillholdings.com
SIC: **5199 5136 5137 6798** Advertising specialties; Men's and boy's clothing; Women's and children's clothing; Real estate investment trusts

(G-3248)
PROJETECH INC
Also Called: Projetech
3815 Harrison Ave (45211-4725)
PHONE..................................513 481-4900
Steven K Richmond, *CEO*
Debbie Herbers, *
EMP: 28 EST: 1992
SALES (est): 8.46MM
SALES (corp-wide): 1.38MM **Privately Held**
Web: www.projetech.com

SIC: **7371 7378** Computer software development and applications; Computer and data processing equipment repair/maintenance
HQ: Galanthus Partners Ltd
Flat 4
London

(G-3249)
PROKIDS
222 W 7th St (45202-2351)
PHONE..................................513 281-2000
Tracy Cook, *Ex Dir*
Carol Igoe, *Business Operations*
EMP: 49 EST: 1981
SALES (est): 4.36MM **Privately Held**
Web: www.prokids.org
SIC: **8322** Social service center

(G-3250)
PROLINK RESOURCES LLC
Also Called: Prolink
4600 Montgomery Rd Ste 300 (45212-2697)
PHONE..................................866 777-3704
EMP: 95
SALES (corp-wide): 681.54K **Privately Held**
Web: www.prolinkworks.com
SIC: **7361** Employment agencies
PA: Prolink Resources, Llc
10700 Montgomery Rd
Montgomery OH 45242
866 777-3704

(G-3251)
PROLINK STAFFING SERVICES LLC (PA)
4600 Montgomery Rd Ste 300 (45212-2600)
PHONE..................................513 489-5300
Anthony Munafor, *Managing Member*
EMP: 95 EST: 2013
SALES (est): 45.57MM
SALES (corp-wide): 45.57MM **Privately Held**
Web: www.prolinkworks.com
SIC: **7363** Temporary help service

(G-3252)
PROMEDICA HEALTH SYSTEM INC
Also Called: Heartland Hospice Services
3960 Red Bank Rd Ste 140 (45227-3421)
PHONE..................................513 831-5800
EMP: 283
SALES (corp-wide): 187.07MM **Privately Held**
Web: www.promedicaseniorcare.org
SIC: **8052** Personal care facility
PA: Promedica Health System, Inc.
100 Madison Ave
Toledo OH 43604
567 585-9600

(G-3253)
PROMOTION EXCTION PARTNERS LLC (DH)
Also Called: Pep
302 W 3rd St (45202-3437)
PHONE..................................513 826-0101
Dave Kroeger, *Managing Member*
Stephanie Bell, *Managing Member*
EMP: 36 EST: 2004
SALES (est): 52.37MM
SALES (corp-wide): 18.5B **Privately Held**
Web: www.peppromotions.com
SIC: **7331 7319 7389** Direct mail advertising services; Display advertising service; Advertising, promotional, and trade show services
HQ: Wpp Group Us Investments, Inc.

Cincinnati - Hamilton County (G-3254)
GEOGRAPHIC SECTION

100 Park Ave
New York NY 10017
212 632-2200

(G-3254)
PROSCAN IMAGING LLC (PA)
5400 Kennedy Ave (45213-2668)
PHONE.................513 281-3400
Steven Pomeranz, *Managing Member*
EMP: 100 **EST:** 1996
SALES (est): 96.84MM
SALES (corp-wide): 96.84MM **Privately Held**
Web: www.proscan.com
SIC: 8011 Radiologist

(G-3255)
PROTECTIVE PACKG SOLUTIONS LLC
10345 S Medallion Dr (45241-4825)
PHONE.................513 769-5777
EMP: 30 **EST:** 2011
SALES (est): 4.32MM **Privately Held**
Web: www.protectivepackagingsolutions.com
SIC: 2653 5199 Boxes, corrugated: made from purchased materials; Packaging materials

(G-3256)
PRUS CONSTRUCTION COMPANY
5325 Wooster Pike (45226-2224)
PHONE.................513 321-7774
Joseph M Prus, *Pr*
William J Prus, *
EMP: 130 **EST:** 1888
SALES (est): 33.35MM **Privately Held**
Web: www.prusconstruction.com
SIC: 1771 1622 Blacktop (asphalt) work; Bridge construction

(G-3257)
PSYCHPROS INC
2404 Auburn Ave (45219-2735)
PHONE.................513 651-9500
EMP: 32 **EST:** 1995
SQ FT: 3,240
SALES (est): 2.07MM **Privately Held**
Web: www.psychpros.com
SIC: 7361 Executive placement

(G-3258)
Q LABS LLC (PA)
Also Called: Q Laboratories
1911 Radcliff Dr (45204-1824)
PHONE.................513 471-1300
Jeffrey Rowe, *Pr*
EMP: 143 **EST:** 1966
SALES (est): 24.59MM
SALES (corp-wide): 24.59MM **Privately Held**
Web: www.qlaboratories.com
SIC: 8734 8731 Testing laboratories; Commercial physical research

(G-3259)
QC SOFTWARE LLC
50 E Business Way (45241-2397)
PHONE.................513 469-1424
Kevin Tedford, *CEO*
EMP: 50 **EST:** 1996
SQ FT: 2,900
SALES (est): 4.56MM
SALES (corp-wide): 40.69MM **Privately Held**
Web: www.kpisolutions.com
SIC: 7371 7372 Computer software development; Prepackaged software
PA: Kuecker Pulse Integration, L.P.
801 W Markey Rd
Belton MO 64012

844 574-1010

(G-3260)
QUALITY SUPPLY CO (PA)
Also Called: Quality Restaurant Supply
4020 Rev Dr (45232-1914)
PHONE.................937 890-6114
Leland D Manders, *Pr*
Bruce Feldman, *
Alan Moscowitz, *
Irvin Moscowitz, *
Mark Foster, *
EMP: 35 **EST:** 1985
SALES (est): 4.83MM
SALES (corp-wide): 4.83MM **Privately Held**
SIC: 5046 Commercial cooking and food service equipment

(G-3261)
QUALUS CORP (PA)
4040 Rev Dr (45232-1914)
PHONE.................800 434-0415
Paul Cody, *CEO*
Rodrigo Vogel, *
EMP: 80 **EST:** 2015
SQ FT: 15,600
SALES (est): 196.94MM
SALES (corp-wide): 196.94MM **Privately Held**
Web: www.qualuspowerservices.com
SIC: 7629 8711 6719 Electrical repair shops; Engineering services; Personal holding companies, except banks

(G-3262)
QUEEN CITY MECHANICALS INC
1950 Waycross Rd (45240-2827)
PHONE.................513 353-1430
Gary W Gilbert, *Pr*
Bryan Gilbert, *
Bradley Gilbert, *
Beverly Gilbert, *
EMP: 29 **EST:** 1983
SALES (est): 6.41MM **Privately Held**
Web: www.queencitymech.com
SIC: 1711 Plumbing contractors

(G-3263)
QUEEN CITY PHYSICIANS
Also Called: Queen City of Physicians
2475 W Galbraith Rd Ste 3 (45239-4369)
PHONE.................513 872-2061
Neil Deithsel, *Pr*
Victor R Smith, *
Charles Dietschel, *
Kathleen Lamping-arar, *Pt*
Ellen H Norby, *
EMP: 1546 **EST:** 1959
SQ FT: 1,800
SALES (est): 4.84MM **Privately Held**
Web: www.trihealth.com
SIC: 8011 Pediatrician
HQ: Trihealth, Inc.
625 Eden Park Dr
Cincinnati OH 45202
513 569-5400

(G-3264)
QUEEN CITY RACQUET CLUB LLC
11275 Chester Rd (45246-4014)
PHONE.................513 771-2835
Keven Shell, *Pr*
William P Martin, *
Carl Myers, *
EMP: 60 **EST:** 1971
SQ FT: 100,000
SALES (est): 806.92K **Privately Held**
Web: www.queencityfitness.com
SIC: 7991 Health club
PA: Central Investment Llc

7265 Kenwood Rd Ste 240
Cincinnati OH 45236

(G-3265)
QUEEN CITY REPROGRAPHICS
2863 E Sharon Rd (45241-1923)
PHONE.................513 326-2300
EMP: 105 **EST:** 1963
SALES (est): 11.43MM
SALES (corp-wide): 281.2MM **Publicly Held**
SIC: 5049 7334 7335 2752 Drafting supplies; Blueprinting service; Commercial photography; Lithographing on metal
PA: Arc Document Solutions, Inc.
12657 Alcosta Blvd # 200
San Ramon CA 94583
925 949-5100

(G-3266)
QUEEN CITY REPROGRAPHICS INC
Also Called: Resource Imaging Supply
2863 E Sharon Rd (45241-1923)
PHONE.................513 326-2300
EMP: 44
SIC: 7334 5112 Photocopying and duplicating services; Stationery and office supplies

(G-3267)
QUEEN CITY SKILLED CARE LLC
7265 Kenwood Rd Ste 370 (45236-4411)
PHONE.................513 802-5010
EMP: 51 **EST:** 2017
SALES (est): 12.67MM **Privately Held**
Web: www.queencityskilled.com
SIC: 8082 Home health care services

(G-3268)
QUEEN CITY TRANSPORTATION LLC
Also Called: Charter Bus Service
211 Township Ave # C (45216-2501)
PHONE.................513 941-8700
EMP: 300 **EST:** 1977
SALES (est): 9.96MM **Privately Held**
Web: www.queencitytransportation.com
SIC: 4141 4142 4151 Local bus charter service; Bus charter service, except local; School buses

(G-3269)
QUEENSGATE FOOD GROUP LLC
Also Called: Queensgate Foodservice
619 Linn St (45203-1794)
P.O. Box 14120 (45250-0120)
PHONE.................513 721-5503
EMP: 75 **EST:** 1999
SQ FT: 55,000
SALES (est): 24.02MM **Publicly Held**
Web: www.queensgatefoods.com
SIC: 5141 Food brokers
PA: The Chefs' Warehouse Inc
100 E Ridge Rd
Ridgefield CT 06877

(G-3270)
R E KRAMIG & CO INC
323 S Wayne Ave (45215-4522)
P.O. Box 9909 (45209-0909)
PHONE.................513 761-4010
George Kulesza, *Pr*
Howard H Horne, *
EMP: 200 **EST:** 1896
SQ FT: 65,000
SALES (est): 9.37MM **Privately Held**
SIC: 1799 5033 1742 Insulation of pipes and boilers; Insulation materials; Acoustical and insulation work

(G-3271)
R E WHITNEY INSUR AGCY LLC
Also Called: Whitney Insurance Group The
250 E 5th St Fl 15 (45202-4119)
PHONE.................877 652-7765
Russell Whitney, *Pr*
EMP: 75 **EST:** 2015
SALES (est): 100K **Privately Held**
SIC: 6411 Insurance agents, nec

(G-3272)
R L A UTILITIES
389 S Wayne Ave (45215-4522)
PHONE.................513 554-1453
Rob Adleta, *Pr*
Bob Adleta, *VP*
EMP: 28 **EST:** 2010
SALES (est): 5.53MM **Privately Held**
Web: www.adletagroup.com
SIC: 1623 Underground utilities contractor

(G-3273)
RAPID MORTGAGE COMPANY (PA)
Also Called: Rapid Aerial Imaging
7466 Beechmont Ave Unit 420 (45255-4109)
PHONE.................937 748-8888
Dennis M Fisher, *Pr*
David Rawson, *VP*
Chris Howard, *VP Opers*
EMP: 50 **EST:** 2002
SALES (est): 12.03MM
SALES (corp-wide): 12.03MM **Privately Held**
Web: www.rapidmortgage.com
SIC: 6162 7335 7389 7221 Bond and mortgage companies; Commercial photography; Mapmaking or drafting, including aerial; Photographer, still or video

(G-3274)
RAY HAMILTON COMPANIES
Also Called: Ray Hamilton Company
4817 Section Ave (45212-2118)
PHONE.................513 641-5400
Jay Wallis, *Pr*
EMP: 43 **EST:** 1986
SQ FT: 67,000
SALES (est): 2.23MM **Privately Held**
Web: www.rayhamilton.com
SIC: 4226 4212 4731 4214 Document and office records storage; Safe moving, local; Freight transportation arrangement; Furniture moving and storage, local

(G-3275)
READY SET GROW LLC
Also Called: Grey Matter
9863 Mistymorn Ln (45242-5451)
PHONE.................513 445-2939
Zachary Strauss, *Prin*
EMP: 30 **EST:** 2016
SALES (est): 661.73K **Privately Held**
Web: www.gogreymatter.com
SIC: 7371 Computer software development

(G-3276)
RED BANK HETZEL LP
Also Called: Holiday Inn
5311 Hetzell St (45227-1513)
PHONE.................513 834-9191
Lance Otis, *Genl Pt*
EMP: 50 **EST:** 2016
SALES (est): 2MM **Privately Held**
Web: www.holidayinn.com
SIC: 7011 Hotels and motels

(G-3277)
RED CARPET JANITORIAL SERVICE (PA)

GEOGRAPHIC SECTION
Cincinnati - Hamilton County (G-3300)

3478 Hauck Rd Ste D (45241-4604)
PHONE...................513 242-7575
Dale E Euller, *Pr*
EMP: 300 **EST:** 1971
SQ FT: 2,000
SALES (est): 4.14MM
SALES (corp-wide): 4.14MM **Privately Held**
Web: www.redcarpetjanitorial.com
SIC: 7699 Cleaning services

(G-3278)
REDI CINCINNATI LLC
3 E 4th St (45202-3744)
PHONE...................513 562-8474
EMP: 33 **EST:** 2016
SALES (est): 2.9MM **Privately Held**
Web: www.redicincinnati.com
SIC: 8611 Business associations

(G-3279)
REECE-CAMPBELL INC
10839 Chester Rd (45246-4707)
PHONE...................513 542-4600
EMP: 60 **EST:** 1982
SALES (est): 13.46MM **Privately Held**
SIC: 1542 Commercial and office building, new construction

(G-3280)
REGIONAL ACCEPTANCE CORP
Also Called: Regional Finance
8044 Montgomery Rd Ste 340 (45236-2938)
PHONE...................513 398-2106
EMP: 28
SALES (corp-wide): 33.25B **Publicly Held**
Web: www.truist.com
SIC: 6141 Personal credit institutions
HQ: Regional Acceptance Corporation
1424 E Fire Tower Rd
Greenville NC 27858
252 321-7700

(G-3281)
REHAB MEDICAL LLC
2860 Cooper Rd (45241-3368)
PHONE...................513 381-3740
Patrick Mcginley, *Brnch Mgr*
EMP: 97
Web: www.rehabmedical.com
SIC: 5047 8099 Medical equipment and supplies; Blood related health services
PA: Rehab Medical, Llc
6365 Castleplace Dr
Indianapolis IN 46250

(G-3282)
REHAB RESOURCES INC
8595 Beechmont Ave Ste 204 (45255-4740)
P.O. Box 541127 (45254-1127)
PHONE...................513 474-4123
Teresa Hollenkamp, *CEO*
EMP: 48 **EST:** 1999
SALES (est): 43.2K **Privately Held**
Web: www.rehabresources.net
SIC: 8322 Rehabilitation services

(G-3283)
REISENFELD & ASSOC LPA LLC (PA)
Also Called: Fojournerf Title Agency
3962 Red Bank Rd (45227-3408)
PHONE...................513 322-7000
Bradley A Reisenfeld, *Managing Member*
Sallie A Conyers, *
Matthew C Gladwell, *
Steven M Giordullo, *
Andy Schoenling, *
EMP: 165 **EST:** 1960
SQ FT: 38,000
SALES (est): 27.24MM
SALES (corp-wide): 27.24MM **Privately Held**
Web: www.reisenfeldlawfirm.com
SIC: 8111 General practice law office

(G-3284)
RELADYNE FLORIDA LLC
8280 Montgomery Rd Ste 101 (45236-6101)
P.O. Box 37589 (32236-7589)
PHONE...................904 354-8411
EMP: 100 **EST:** 2018
SALES (est): 25.46MM **Privately Held**
Web: www.reladyne.com
SIC: 5172 Petroleum products, nec

(G-3285)
RELADYNE INC (PA)
8280 Montgomery Rd Ste 101 (45236-6101)
PHONE...................513 941-2800
EMP: 152 **EST:** 2010
SALES (est): 2.39B **Privately Held**
Web: www.reladyne.com
SIC: 5172 Lubricating oils and greases

(G-3286)
RENDIGS FRY KIELY & DENNIS LLP (PA)
600 Vine St Ste 2602 (45202-2491)
PHONE...................513 381-9200
Thomas M Evans, *Prin*
J Kenneth Meagher, *Pt*
Ralph F Mitchell, *Pt*
W Roger Fry, *Pt*
William P Schroeder, *Pt*
EMP: 99 **EST:** 1940
SQ FT: 33,000
SALES (est): 56.37K
SALES (corp-wide): 56.37K **Privately Held**
Web: www.rendigs.com
SIC: 8111 General practice attorney, lawyer

(G-3287)
RENTOKIL NORTH AMERICA INC
Also Called: Ambius
3253 E Kemper Rd (45241-1518)
PHONE...................513 247-9300
Rosie Baker, *Mgr*
EMP: 50
SALES (corp-wide): 6.7B **Privately Held**
SIC: 7359 Live plant rental
HQ: Rentokil North America, Inc.
1125 Berkshire Blvd # 15
Wyomissing PA 19610
470 643-3300

(G-3288)
REPUBLIC BANK & TRUST COMPANY
8050 Hosbrook Rd Ste 220 (45236-2907)
PHONE...................513 651-3000
EMP: 30
Web: www.republicbank.com
SIC: 6022 State commercial banks
HQ: Republic Bank & Trust Company Inc
601 W Market St Ste 100
Louisville KY 40202
502 584-3600

(G-3289)
REPUBLIC SERVICES OHIO HLG LLC
11563 Mosteller Rd (45241-1831)
PHONE...................513 771-4200
David Barclay, *Prin*
EMP: 40 **EST:** 1998
SALES (est): 10.32MM
SALES (corp-wide): 14.96B **Publicly Held**
SIC: 4953 4212 Garbage: collecting, destroying, and processing; Local trucking, without storage
PA: Republic Services, Inc.
18500 N Allied Way
Phoenix AZ 85054
480 627-2700

(G-3290)
RES-CARE INC
Also Called: Rescare Workforce Services
5535 Fair Ln Ste A (45227-3440)
PHONE...................513 271-0708
EMP: 82
SALES (corp-wide): 8.83B **Publicly Held**
Web: www.rescare.com
SIC: 8052 Home for the mentally retarded, with health care
HQ: Res-Care, Inc.
805 N Whittington Pkwy
Louisville KY 40222
502 394-2100

(G-3291)
RESIDENCE INN BY MARRIOTT
Also Called: Residence Inn By Marriott
11689 Chester Rd (45246-2600)
PHONE...................513 771-2525
Dan Sirrine, *Prin*
EMP: 38 **EST:** 2007
SALES (est): 481.5K **Privately Held**
Web: residence-inn.marriott.com
SIC: 7011 Hotels and motels

(G-3292)
RESOLVIT RESOURCES LLC (HQ)
Also Called: Resolvit
1308 Race St Ste 200 (45202-7397)
PHONE...................513 619-5900
Mark Scofield, *Managing Member*
Lowell Lehmann, *
Craig Scates, *
Julie Sizelove, *
EMP: 45 **EST:** 2002
SALES (est): 22.25MM **Privately Held**
Web: www.aditiconsulting.com
SIC: 7379 Online services technology consultants
PA: Aditi Consulting Llc
11820 Northup Way Ste 305
Bellevue WA 98005

(G-3293)
REUPERT HEATING AND AC CO INC
5137 Crookshank Rd (45238-3386)
PHONE...................513 922-5050
Kenneth Reupert, *Pr*
Richard Reupert, *
Donald Reupert, *
EMP: 27 **EST:** 1947
SQ FT: 3,200
SALES (est): 2.11MM **Privately Held**
Web: www.reupert.com
SIC: 1711 Warm air heating and air conditioning contractor

(G-3294)
RHC INC (PA)
Also Called: RESIDENT HOME, THE
3030 W Fork Rd (45211-1944)
PHONE...................513 389-7501
Robert South, *Ch*
Peter Keiser, *
Russell Ferneding, *
EMP: 60 **EST:** 1963
SQ FT: 11,077
SALES (est): 9.97MM
SALES (corp-wide): 9.97MM **Privately Held**
Web: www.rhcorp.org
SIC: 8361 Mentally handicapped home

(G-3295)
RHINEGEIST LLC
Also Called: Rhinegeist Brewery
1910 Elm St (45202-7751)
PHONE...................513 381-1367
▲ **EMP:** 71 **EST:** 2013
SQ FT: 120,000
SALES (est): 40.02MM **Privately Held**
Web: www.rhinegeist.com
SIC: 5181 5813 Beer and other fermented malt liquors; Bars and lounges

(G-3296)
RICHARD GOETTLE INC
12071 Hamilton Ave (45231-1032)
PHONE...................513 825-8100
Douglas Keller, *CEO*
Daniel G Baker, *
◆ **EMP:** 99 **EST:** 1956
SALES (est): 51.39MM
SALES (corp-wide): 51.39MM **Privately Held**
Web: www.goettle.com
SIC: 5082 Contractor's materials
PA: Goettle Holding Company, Inc.
12071 Hamilton Ave
Cincinnati OH 45231
513 825-8100

(G-3297)
RICHARDS ELECTRIC SUP CO LLC (DH)
4620 Reading Rd (45229-1297)
PHONE...................513 242-8800
Mike Misrach, *Pr*
▲ **EMP:** 30 **EST:** 1939
SQ FT: 62,500
SALES (est): 120.14MM
SALES (corp-wide): 12.53MM **Privately Held**
Web: www.springfieldelectric.com
SIC: 5063 Electrical supplies, nec
HQ: Sonepar Management Us, Inc.
4400 Leeds Ave Ste 500
Charleston SC 29405
843 872-3500

(G-3298)
RIDE SHARE INFORMATION
Also Called: Oki Rgonal Council Governments
720 E Pete Rose Way Ste 420 (45202-3579)
PHONE...................513 621-6300
EMP: 33 **EST:** 1979
SALES (est): 4.49MM **Privately Held**
Web: www.oki.org
SIC: 8742 Administrative services consultant

(G-3299)
RIPPE & KINGSTON SYSTEMS INC (PA)
Also Called: Surepoint Technologies
4850 Smith Rd Ste 100 (45212)
PHONE...................513 977-4578
Tom Obermaier, *CEO*
Ron Sharp, *
Donald Schule, *
EMP: 59 **EST:** 1982
SALES (est): 10.51MM
SALES (corp-wide): 10.51MM **Privately Held**
Web: www.surepoint.com
SIC: 7379 7371 Computer related consulting services; Computer software development

(G-3300)
RIVER SERVICES INC
559 Liberty Hl Ste 1 (45202-6848)

Cincinnati - Hamilton County (G-3301)

PHONE.....................612 588-8141
Tim Privil, *Pr*
EMP: 108 **EST:** 1991
SALES (est): 1.06MM
SALES (corp-wide): 10.11MM **Privately Held**
Web: www.rtcltd.com
SIC: 4491 Marine terminals
PA: River Trading Company, Ltd.
559 Liberty Hl Ste 1
Cincinnati OH 45202
513 651-9444

(G-3301)
RIVER VALLEY DIALYSIS LLC
Also Called: Delhi Dialysis
5040 Delhi Rd (45238-5388)
PHONE.....................513 922-5900
EMP: 35
SIC: 8092 Kidney dialysis centers
HQ: River Valley Dialysis, Llc
601 Hawaii St
El Segundo CA 90245

(G-3302)
RIVER VALLEY DIALYSIS LLC
Also Called: Silverton Dialysis
6929 Silverton Ave (45236-3701)
PHONE.....................513 793-0555
James K Hilger, *CAO*
EMP: 35
SIC: 8092 Kidney dialysis centers
HQ: River Valley Dialysis, Llc
601 Hawaii St
El Segundo CA 90245

(G-3303)
RIVER VALLEY DIALYSIS LLC
Also Called: White Oak Dialysis
5520 Cheviot Rd Ste B (45247-7069)
PHONE.....................513 741-1062
EMP: 35
SIC: 8092 Kidney dialysis centers
HQ: River Valley Dialysis, Llc
601 Hawaii St
El Segundo CA 90245

(G-3304)
RIVERFRONT STEEL INC
10310 S Medallion Dr (45241-4836)
P.O. Box 62718 (45262-0718)
PHONE.....................513 769-9999
TOLL FREE: 800
▲ **EMP:** 95
Web: www.riverfrontsteel.com
SIC: 5051 Steel

(G-3305)
RIVERHILLS HEALTHCARE INC
8000 5 Mile Rd Ste 330 (45230-4367)
PHONE.....................513 624-6031
EMP: 46
SALES (corp-wide): 20.18MM **Privately Held**
Web: www.riverhillsneuro.com
SIC: 8099 Childbirth preparation clinic
PA: Riverhills Healthcare, Inc.
111 Wellington Pl Lowr
Cincinnati OH 45219
513 241-2370

(G-3306)
RIVERHILLS HEALTHCARE INC (PA)
111 Wellington Pl Lowr (45219-1709)
PHONE.....................513 241-2370
P Robert Schwetschenau, *Pr*
Colin Zadikoff Md, *Sec*
Peter Vicente, *
Linda Burnhardt, *
EMP: 38 **EST:** 1973
SQ FT: 22,224
SALES (est): 20.18MM
SALES (corp-wide): 20.18MM **Privately Held**
Web: www.riverhillsneuro.com
SIC: 8011 Neurologist

(G-3307)
RIVERSIDE CNSTR SVCS INC
218 W Mcmicken Ave (45214-2314)
PHONE.....................513 723-0900
Robert S Krejci, *Pr*
Timothy L Pierce, *
EMP: 32 **EST:** 1993
SQ FT: 21,000
SALES (est): 4.74MM **Privately Held**
Web: www.riversidearchitectural.com
SIC: 2431 1751 2434 Millwork; Carpentry work; Wood kitchen cabinets

(G-3308)
RLA UTILITIES LLC
389 Wade St (45214-2825)
PHONE.....................513 554-1470
Robert L Adleta Ii, *Pr*
EMP: 45 **EST:** 1996
SALES (est): 10.8MM **Privately Held**
Web: www.adletagroup.com
SIC: 1623 Sewer line construction

(G-3309)
RM ADVISORY GROUP INC
5300 Vine St (45217)
PHONE.....................513 242-2100
Robert Moskowitz, *Pr*
Ira Moskowitz, *
EMP: 35 **EST:** 1901
SQ FT: 70,000
SALES (est): 4.57MM **Privately Held**
SIC: 5093 3341 Ferrous metal scrap and waste; Secondary nonferrous metals

(G-3310)
RMS OF OHIO INC
Also Called: RMS
2824 E Kemper Rd (45241-1820)
PHONE.....................513 841-0990
Gwen Lee, *Dir*
EMP: 174
SALES (corp-wide): 9.41MM **Privately Held**
Web: www.teamrms.com
SIC: 8361 Residential care for the handicapped
PA: Rms Of Ohio, Inc.
733 E Dblin Grnvlle Rd St
Columbus OH 43229
614 844-6767

(G-3311)
RMT ACQUISITION INC
Also Called: Young & Bertke Air Systems Co.
3111 Spring Grove Ave (45225)
PHONE.....................513 241-5566
Roger Young, *Pr*
Tim Rohrer, *
Michael Munafo, *
Phillip C Young, *Stockholder*
EMP: 28 **EST:** 1920
SQ FT: 51,000
SALES (est): 4.47MM **Privately Held**
Web: www.youngbertke.com
SIC: 1761 3441 3564 3444 Sheet metal work, nec; Fabricated structural metal; Blowers and fans; Sheet metalwork

(G-3312)
ROBBINS KELLY PATTERSON TUCKER
312 Elm St Ste 2200 (45202-2748)
PHONE.....................513 721-3330
Fredric J Robbins, *Pr*
James M Kelly, *
Mark C Patterson, *
Jack Tucker, *
Thomas M Gaier, *
EMP: 45 **EST:** 1965
SALES (est): 6.19MM **Privately Held**
Web: www.rkpt.com
SIC: 8111 General practice attorney, lawyer

(G-3313)
ROBERT LUCKE HOMES INC
8825 Chapelsquare Ln Ste B (45249-4702)
PHONE.....................513 683-3300
Robert Lucke, *Pr*
EMP: 30 **EST:** 2006
SALES (est): 4.66MM **Privately Held**
Web: www.robertluckegroup.com
SIC: 1521 New construction, single-family houses

(G-3314)
ROBERT MCCABE COMPANY INC
Also Called: Mc Cabe Do-It-Center
10821 Montgomery Rd (45242-3212)
PHONE.....................513 469-2500
EMP: 40
SALES (corp-wide): 20.51MM **Privately Held**
Web: www.mccabedoitcenter.com
SIC: 5251 5072 5031 5211 Hardware stores; Hardware; Lumber, plywood, and millwork; Lumber products
PA: The Robert Mccabe Company Inc
118 Northeast Dr
Loveland OH 45140
513 683-2662

(G-3315)
ROCKFISH INTERACTIVE LLC
659 Van Meter St Ste 520 (45202-1585)
PHONE.....................513 381-1583
Kenny Tomlin, *CEO*
EMP: 34
SALES (corp-wide): 18.5B **Privately Held**
Web: www.rockfishdigital.com
SIC: 7311 Advertising agencies
HQ: Rockfish Interactive Llc
3100 S Market St Ste 100
Rogers AR 72758

(G-3316)
ROCKIN JUMP HOLDINGS LLC
Also Called: Rockin' Jump
8350 Colerain Ave (45239-3925)
PHONE.....................513 373-4260
EMP: 302
SALES (corp-wide): 51.07MM **Privately Held**
Web: www.rockinjump.com
SIC: 7999 Trampoline operation
HQ: Rockin' Jump Holdings, Llc
18 Crow Canyon Ct Ste 350
San Ramon CA 94583
925 401-7200

(G-3317)
ROGERS FAMILY DENTISTRY INC
Also Called: Rogers Family Dental Practice
8284 Beechmont Ave (45255-3153)
PHONE.....................513 231-1012
Douglas Rogers, *Pr*
EMP: 60 **EST:** 1973
SALES (est): 5.16MM
SALES (corp-wide): 10.99MM **Privately Held**
Web: www.rogersfamilydentist.com
SIC: 8021 Dentists' office
PA: Cordental Group Management, Llc
9825 Kenwood Rd Ste 200
Blue Ash OH 45242
855 876-4532

(G-3318)
ROLFES HENRY CO LPA (PA)
18 W 9th St (45202-2037)
PHONE.....................513 579-0080
Matthew J Smith, *Pr*
EMP: 38 **EST:** 1984
SALES (est): 8.28MM **Privately Held**
Web: www.rolfeshenry.com
SIC: 8111 General practice attorney, lawyer

(G-3319)
RONALD MCDNALD HSE CHRTIES GRT
341 Erkenbrecher Ave (45229-2813)
PHONE.....................513 636-7642
David Anderson, *Pr*
EMP: 27 **EST:** 1982
SQ FT: 56,000
SALES (est): 8.25MM **Privately Held**
Web: www.rmhcincinnati.org
SIC: 8322 Social service center

(G-3320)
ROSS SINCLAIRE & ASSOC LLC (PA)
700 Walnut St Ste 600 (45202)
PHONE.....................513 381-3939
Murray Sinclaire, *Managing Member*
EMP: 40 **EST:** 1981
SQ FT: 6,000
SALES (est): 20.79MM
SALES (corp-wide): 20.79MM **Privately Held**
Web: www.rsanet.com
SIC: 6211 Stock brokers and dealers

(G-3321)
ROTO RT INC (DH)
Also Called: Roto-Rooter
255 E 5th St Ste 2500 (45202-4725)
PHONE.....................513 762-6690
EMP: 35 **EST:** 1978
SALES (est): 23.84MM
SALES (corp-wide): 2.26B **Publicly Held**
Web: www.rotorooter.com
SIC: 7699 Sewer cleaning and rodding
HQ: Roto-Rooter Services Company
255 E 5th St Ste 2500
Cincinnati OH 45202
513 762-6690

(G-3322)
ROTO-ROOTER DEVELOPMENT CO (HQ)
Also Called: Roto-Rooter
255 E 5th St Ste 2500 (45202-4793)
PHONE.....................513 762-6690
Spencer S Lee, *Ch*
Edward L Hutton, *
Kevin J Mcnamara, *V Ch Bd*
Rick Arquilla, *
David Williams, *
EMP: 95 **EST:** 1983
SQ FT: 20,000
SALES (est): 504.82MM
SALES (corp-wide): 2.26B **Publicly Held**
Web: www.rotorooter.com
SIC: 7699 1711 Sewer cleaning and rodding; Plumbing contractors
PA: Chemed Corporation
255 E 5th St Ste 2600
Cincinnati OH 45202
513 762-6690

(G-3323)
ROTO-ROOTER GROUP INC (HQ)
Also Called: Roto-Rooter
255 E 5th St Ste 2500 (45202-4725)
PHONE.....................513 762-6690
Spencer Lee, *CEO*

Rick Arquilla, *Pr*
Frank Castillo, *Pr*
Gary H Sander, *Ex VP*
Robert Goldschmidt, *Ex VP*
EMP: 135 **EST:** 1984
SALES (est): 24.53MM
SALES (corp-wide): 2.26B **Publicly Held**
Web: www.rotorooter.com
SIC: 7699 Sewer cleaning and rodding
PA: Chemed Corporation
255 E 5th St Ste 2600
Cincinnati OH 45202
513 762-6690

(G-3324)
ROTO-ROOTER SERVICES COMPANY (DH)
Also Called: Roto-Rooter
255 E 5th St (45202-4793)
PHONE..............................513 762-6690
Spencer S Lee, *Ch*
Rick L Arquilla, *
David Williams, *
EMP: 100 **EST:** 1936
SALES (est): 213.8MM
SALES (corp-wide): 2.26B **Publicly Held**
Web: www.rotorooter.com
SIC: 7699 1711 Sewer cleaning and rodding; Plumbing contractors
HQ: Roto-Rooter Development Company
255 E 5th St Ste 2500
Cincinnati OH 45202
513 762-6690

(G-3325)
ROUGH BROTHERS MFG INC
5513 Vine St (45217-1022)
PHONE..............................513 242-0310
Richard Reilly, *Pr*
David Roberts, *
◆ **EMP:** 90 **EST:** 1992
SQ FT: 100,000
SALES (est): 86.1MM
SALES (corp-wide): 1.38B **Publicly Held**
Web: www.prospiant.com
SIC: 1542 3448 Greenhouse construction; Greenhouses, prefabricated metal
HQ: Rough Brothers Holding Co., Inc
3556 Lake Shore Rd # 100
Buffalo NY 14219
716 826-6500

(G-3326)
ROUNDTOWER TECHNOLOGIES LLC (DH)
5905 E Galbraith Rd Fl 3 (45236-2375)
PHONE..............................513 247-7900
EMP: 62 **EST:** 2007
SQ FT: 5,000
SALES (est): 36.75MM
SALES (corp-wide): 858.15MM **Privately Held**
Web: www.ahead.com
SIC: 7379 Computer related consulting services
HQ: Ahead, Inc.
401 N Michigan Ave # 3400
Chicago IL 60611

(G-3327)
RPC MECHANICAL SERVICES (HQ)
5301 Lester Rd (45213-2523)
PHONE..............................513 733-1641
John Lowe, *Pr*
EMP: 164 **EST:** 1937
SQ FT: 40,000
SALES (est): 22.73MM
SALES (corp-wide): 54.24MM **Privately Held**
Web: www.rpcmechanical.com

SIC: 1711 Mechanical contractor
PA: The Thomas J Dyer Company
5240 Lester Rd
Cincinnati OH 45213
513 321-8100

(G-3328)
RSW/US GP
Also Called: Reardon Smith Whittaker
6725 Miami Ave (45243-3109)
PHONE..............................513 898-0940
Mark Sneider, *Owner*
EMP: 45 **EST:** 2006
SALES (est): 5.92MM **Privately Held**
Web: www.rswus.com
SIC: 8748 Business consulting, nec

(G-3329)
RUDD EQUIPMENT COMPANY INC
11807 Enterprise Dr (45241-1511)
PHONE..............................513 321-7833
Mike Rudd, *Pr*
EMP: 62
Web: www.ruddequipment.com
SIC: 3462 7699 Construction or mining equipment forgings, ferrous; Industrial machinery and equipment repair
HQ: Rudd Equipment Company, Inc.
4344 Poplar Level Rd
Louisville KY 40213
502 456-4050

(G-3330)
RUMPKE CNSLD COMPANIES INC (PA)
Also Called: Rumpke Waste and Recycl Svcs
3990 Generation Dr (45251-4906)
PHONE..............................800 828-8171
William Rumpke Junior, *Pr*
Todd Rumpke, *
Jeff Rumpke, *
Phil Wehrman, *
EMP: 200 **EST:** 1988
SQ FT: 25,000
SALES (est): 1.28B **Privately Held**
Web: www.rumpke.com
SIC: 4953 Recycling, waste materials

(G-3331)
RUMPKE TRANSPORTATION CO LLC
Also Called: Rumpke Container Service
553 Vine St (45202-3105)
PHONE..............................513 242-4600
EMP: 263
Web: www.rumpke.com
SIC: 4953 3341 3231 2611 Recycling, waste materials; Secondary nonferrous metals; Products of purchased glass; Pulp mills
HQ: Rumpke Transportation Company, Llc
10795 Hughes Rd
Cincinnati OH 45251
513 851-0122

(G-3332)
RUMPKE WASTE INC (HQ)
Also Called: Rumpke
10795 Hughes Rd (45251-4598)
PHONE..............................513 851-0122
Bill Rumpke Senior, *Pr*
William J Rumpke, *
Bill Rumpke Junior, *COO*
EMP: 60 **EST:** 1978
SQ FT: 25,000
SALES (est): 443.04MM **Privately Held**
Web: www.rumpke.com
SIC: 4953 Recycling, waste materials
PA: Rumpke Consolidated Companies, Inc.
3990 Generation Dr
Cincinnati OH 45251

(G-3333)
RUMPKE WASTE INC
Also Called: Rumpke Recycling
5535 Vine St (45217-1003)
PHONE..............................513 242-4401
Larry Ochs, *Mgr*
EMP: 173
SQ FT: 51,870
Web: www.rumpke.com
SIC: 4953 4212 Recycling, waste materials; Local trucking, without storage
HQ: Rumpke Waste, Inc.
10795 Hughes Rd
Cincinnati OH 45251
513 851-0122

(G-3334)
RUSH TRUCK CENTERS OHIO INC (HQ)
Also Called: Rush Truck Center, Cincinnati
11775 Highway Dr (45241-2005)
PHONE..............................513 733-8500
EMP: 32 **EST:** 2012
SALES (est): 57.58MM
SALES (corp-wide): 7.93B **Publicly Held**
Web: www.rushfordtruckcincinnati.com
SIC: 5511 7538 5531 5014 Automobiles, new and used; General automotive repair shops; Auto and home supply stores; Tires and tubes
PA: Rush Enterprises, Inc.
555 S Ih 35 Ste 500
New Braunfels TX 78130
830 302-5200

(G-3335)
S & S HALTHCARE STRATEGIES LTD
1385 Kemper Meadow Dr (45240-1635)
PHONE..............................513 772-8866
EMP: 120 **EST:** 1994
SQ FT: 60,000
SALES (est): 66.92MM **Privately Held**
Web: www.ss-healthcare.com
SIC: 6411 Insurance adjusters

(G-3336)
SAATCHI & SAATCHI X INC
Also Called: Pg One Commerce
231 W 12th St Ste 600 (45202-8001)
PHONE..............................479 575-0200
Phillip Miller, *COO*
EMP: 30
SALES (corp-wide): 25.29MM **Privately Held**
Web: www.saatchix.net
SIC: 7311 Advertising agencies
HQ: Saatchi & Saatchi X, Inc.
605 W Lakeview Dr
Springdale AR 72764

(G-3337)
SADLER-NECAMP FINANCIAL SVCS
Also Called: Proware
7621 E Kemper Rd (45249-1609)
PHONE..............................513 489-5477
Randal R Sadler, *CEO*
Gregory Griffiths Special, *Project*
Melissa Sadler, *
Bret Sadler, *
Don Flischel, *
EMP: 40 **EST:** 1974
SQ FT: 7,400
SALES (est): 4.86MM **Privately Held**
Web: sadler-necamp-financial-services-inc-in-cincinnati-oh.cityfos.com
SIC: 7371 8748 5045 Computer software development; Systems engineering consultant, ex. computer or professional; Computers, peripherals, and software

(G-3338)
SAEC/KINETIC VISION INC
Also Called: Kinetic Vision
10651 Aerohub Blvd (45215-1271)
PHONE..............................513 793-4959
Richard Schweet, *Pr*
EMP: 130 **EST:** 1985
SQ FT: 28,000
SALES (est): 17.37MM **Privately Held**
Web: www.kinetic-vision.com
SIC: 8711 7371 Mechanical engineering; Computer software development and applications

(G-3339)
SAFRAN HUMN RSRCES SUPPORT INC (HQ)
111 Merchant St (45246-3730)
P.O. Box 15514 (45215-0514)
PHONE..............................513 552-3230
EMP: 72 **EST:** 1976
SQ FT: 5,000
SALES (est): 15.61MM
SALES (corp-wide): 650.78MM **Privately Held**
SIC: 8711 Consulting engineer
PA: Safran
2 Bd Du General Martial Valin
Paris 75015

(G-3340)
SAGE HOSPITALITY RESOURCES LLC
Also Called: Crowne Plz Cnncnnati Nrth-Coco
11320 Chester Rd (45246-4003)
PHONE..............................513 771-2080
Matthew Bryant, *Brnch Mgr*
EMP: 129
SALES (corp-wide): 286.23MM **Privately Held**
Web: www.ihg.com
SIC: 7011 Hotels
PA: Sage Hospitality Resources L.L.C.
1575 Welton St Ste 300
Denver CO 80202
303 595-7200

(G-3341)
SAINT JOSEPH ORPHANAGE (PA)
5400 Edalbert Dr (45239-7695)
PHONE..............................513 741-3100
Eric Cummins, *Pr*
Janet Nobel, *Assistant Executive Director**
EMP: 66 **EST:** 1979
SALES (est): 18.19MM
SALES (corp-wide): 18.19MM **Privately Held**
Web: www.newpath.org
SIC: 8361 Children's home

(G-3342)
SAINT JOSEPH ORPHANAGE
274 Sutton Rd (45230-3521)
PHONE..............................513 231-5010
Tom Uhl, *Brnch Mgr*
EMP: 75
SALES (corp-wide): 18.19MM **Privately Held**
Web: www.newpath.org
SIC: 8361 Orphanage
PA: Saint Joseph Orphanage
5400 Edalbert Dr
Cincinnati OH 45239
513 741-3100

(G-3343)
SAKRETE INC
5155 Fischer Ave (45217-1157)
PHONE..............................513 242-3644
John G Avril, *Ch Bd*

Cincinnati - Hamilton County (G-3344)

J Craig Avril, *
EMP: 35 **EST:** 1936
SQ FT: 35,000
SALES (est): 3.27MM **Privately Held**
SIC: 3273 6794 Ready-mixed concrete; Patent buying, licensing, leasing

(G-3344)
SALIX LTD
5712 Carthage Ave (45212-1030)
PHONE.................................513 381-2679
Robert Adams, *Brnch Mgr*
EMP: 54
Web: www.salixdata.com
SIC: 1721 Painting and paper hanging
PA: Salix, Ltd.
  600 Vine St Ste 2006
  Cincinnati OH 45202

(G-3345)
SALO INC
Also Called: Interim Services
8035 Hosbrook Rd (45236-2951)
PHONE.................................513 984-1110
EMP: 140
SALES (corp-wide): 52.16MM **Privately Held**
Web: www.interim-health.com
SIC: 8049 8082 Nurses and other medical assistants; Home health care services
PA: Salo, Inc.
  300 W Wlson Brdge Rd Ste
  Columbus OH 43085
  614 436-9404

(G-3346)
SALVATION ARMY
Also Called: Salvation Army
2250 Park Ave (45212-3200)
PHONE.................................937 461-2769
Michael Copland, *Prin*
EMP: 41
SALES (corp-wide): 2.41B **Privately Held**
Web: www.saconnects.org
SIC: 8661 7011 Nonchurch religious organizations; YMCA/YMHA hotel
HQ: The Salvation Army
  440 W Nyack Rd Ofc
  West Nyack NY 10994
  845 620-7200

(G-3347)
SCHERZINGER CORPORATION
Also Called: Scherzinger Trmt & Pest Ctrl
10557 Medallion Dr (45241-3193)
PHONE.................................513 531-7848
Steven Scherzinger, *Pr*
EMP: 85 **EST:** 1934
SQ FT: 13,500
SALES (est): 7.52MM **Privately Held**
Web: www.stopzbugs.com
SIC: 7342 0782 Termite control; Lawn care services

(G-3348)
SCHMIDT BUILDERS INC
9679 Cincinnati Columbus Rd (45241-1190)
PHONE.................................513 779-9300
Alan G Schmidt, *Pr*
Joseph Schwartz, *VP*
Judith Schmidt, *Sec*
Ken Kerr, *Treas*
EMP: 27 **EST:** 1985
SQ FT: 4,932
SALES (est): 2.52MM **Privately Held**
Web: www.schmidtbuilders.com
SIC: 1531 1542 1521 Speculative builder, single-family houses; Nonresidential construction, nec; Single-family housing construction

(G-3349)
SCHNEIDER HOME EQUIPMENT CO (PA)
7948 Pippin Rd (45239-4696)
PHONE.................................513 522-1200
Michael Schneider, *Pr*
Stanley C Schneider, *
Steven Scheider, *
Annette Littrell, *
EMP: 30 **EST:** 1936
SQ FT: 10,000
SALES (est): 2.02MM
SALES (corp-wide): 2.02MM **Privately Held**
Web: www.schneiderhomeequipment.com
SIC: 5031 5039 5211 Building materials, exterior; Awnings; Door and window products

(G-3350)
SCHOCH TILE & CARPET INC
Also Called: Schoch Tile
5282 Crookshank Rd (45238-3376)
PHONE.................................513 922-3466
Dennis Bley, *Pr*
Ruth Bley, *
EMP: 40 **EST:** 1927
SQ FT: 5,000
SALES (est): 4.44MM **Privately Held**
Web: www.schochtile.com
SIC: 1752 5713 Carpet laying; Floor covering stores

(G-3351)
SCRIPPS MEDIA INC (HQ)
Also Called: W P T V - T V
312 Walnut St Ste 2800 (45202-4019)
PHONE.................................513 977-3000
EMP: 53 **EST:** 1978
SALES (est): 497.82MM
SALES (corp-wide): 2.29B **Publicly Held**
Web: www.scripps.com
SIC: 4833 Television broadcasting stations
PA: The E W Scripps Company
  312 Walnut St
  Cincinnati OH 45202
  513 977-3000

(G-3352)
SCROGGINSGREAR INC
Also Called: William X Greene Bus Advisor
200 Northland Blvd (45246-3604)
PHONE.................................513 672-4281
Terry Grear, *Pr*
Mark D Scroggins, *
David C Scroggins, *
Paul R Trenz, *
Robert C Scroggins, *
EMP: 105 **EST:** 1946
SQ FT: 36,000
SALES (est): 16.83MM **Privately Held**
Web: www.scrogginsgrear.com
SIC: 8742 Business management consultant

(G-3353)
SECURITY FENCE GROUP INC (PA)
4260 Dane Ave (45223-1855)
PHONE.................................513 681-3700
Christine Frankenstein, *CEO*
Christine Frankenstein, *Pr*
George Frankenstein, *
Angela Case, *
EMP: 37 **EST:** 1960
SQ FT: 140,000
SALES (est): 18.5MM **Privately Held**
Web: www.sfence.com
SIC: 1611 1799 5039 1731 Guardrail construction, highways; Fence construction; Wire fence, gates, and accessories; General electrical contractor

(G-3354)
SEI - CINCINNATI LLC
7870 E Kemper Rd Ste 400 (45249-1675)
PHONE.................................513 459-1992
Maria Korengel, *VP*
EMP: 60 **EST:** 2003
SALES (est): 5.73MM **Privately Held**
Web: www.sei.com
SIC: 8742 Management consulting services

(G-3355)
SEILERS LANDSCAPING INC
7011 Plainfield Rd (45236-3735)
PHONE.................................513 791-2824
James F Seiler, *Pr*
Frank Seiler, *VP*
EMP: 33 **EST:** 1977
SQ FT: 2,160
SALES (est): 767.55K **Privately Held**
Web: www.seilerslandscaping.com
SIC: 0781 Landscape services

(G-3356)
SEILKOP INDUSTRIES INC (PA)
Also Called: Epcor Foundries
425 W North Bend Rd (45216-1731)
PHONE.................................513 761-1035
Dave Seilkop, *Pr*
Ken Seilkop, *
Robin Vogel, *
EMP: 50 **EST:** 1946
SQ FT: 35,000
SALES (est): 19.44MM
SALES (corp-wide): 19.44MM **Privately Held**
Web: www.seilkopindustries.com
SIC: 3363 3544 3553 3469 Aluminum die-castings; Special dies and tools; Pattern makers' machinery, woodworking; Patterns on metal

(G-3357)
SENIOR LIFESTYLE EVERGREEN LTD
230 W Galbraith Rd (45215-5223)
PHONE.................................513 948-2308
EMP: 43 **EST:** 1996
SALES (est): 617.8K **Privately Held**
Web: www.seniorlifestyle.com
SIC: 8051 Skilled nursing care facilities

(G-3358)
SENIOR STAR MANAGEMENT COMPANY
5435 Kenwood Rd (45227-1328)
PHONE.................................513 271-1747
Terry Bigger, *Brnch Mgr*
EMP: 75
SALES (corp-wide): 45.48MM **Privately Held**
Web: www.seniorstar.com
SIC: 8322 Senior citizens' center or association
PA: Senior Star Management Company
  1516 S Boston Ave Ste 301
  Tulsa OK 74119
  918 592-4400

(G-3359)
SENTRY LIFE INSURANCE COMPANY
4015 Executive Park Dr Ste 218 (45241-4017)
PHONE.................................513 733-0100
Paul Morton, *Brnch Mgr*
EMP: 245
SALES (corp-wide): 3.07B **Privately Held**
Web: www.sentry.com
SIC: 6411 6321 Insurance agents, brokers, and service; Health insurance carriers
HQ: Sentry Life Insurance Company
  1800 N Point Dr
  Stevens Point WI 54481
  715 346-6000

(G-3360)
SERV-A-LITE PRODUCTS INC (DH)
Also Called: A-1 Best Locksmith
10590 Hamilton Ave (45231-1764)
PHONE.................................309 762-7741
Thomas L Rowe, *Pr*
Mary J Rowe, *
▲ **EMP:** 216 **EST:** 1950
SQ FT: 115,000
SALES (est): 91.77MM
SALES (corp-wide): 1.48B **Publicly Held**
SIC: 5072 Hardware
HQ: The Hillman Companies Inc
  10590 Hamilton Ave
  Cincinnati OH 45231
  513 851-4900

(G-3361)
SERVALL ELECTRIC COMPANY INC
11697 Lebanon Rd (45241-2012)
P.O. Box 621078 (45262-1078)
PHONE.................................513 771-5584
Ryan Pogozalski, *CEO*
EMP: 45 **EST:** 1954
SQ FT: 4,000
SALES (est): 9.94MM **Privately Held**
Web: www.servallelectric.com
SIC: 1731 General electrical contractor

(G-3362)
SERVATII INC (PA)
Also Called: Servatii Pastry and Dealey
3888 Virginia Ave (45227-3410)
PHONE.................................513 271-5040
Gregory Gottenbusch, *Pr*
Gary Gottenbusch, *
EMP: 75 **EST:** 1963
SQ FT: 15,000
SALES (est): 14.87MM
SALES (corp-wide): 14.87MM **Privately Held**
Web: www.servatii.com
SIC: 5461 5149 Retail bakeries; Groceries and related products, nec

(G-3363)
SEVEN HILL ANESTHESIA LLC
10191 Evendale Commons Dr (45241-2689)
PHONE.................................513 865-5204
EMP: 49 **EST:** 2017
SALES (est): 1.03MM **Privately Held**
Web: www.sevenhillsanesthesia.com
SIC: 8011 Anesthesiologist

(G-3364)
SEVEN HLLS NEIGHBORHOOD HOUSES (PA)
Also Called: FINDLAY STREET NEIGHBORHOOD
901 Findlay St (45214-2135)
PHONE.................................513 407-5362
Melinda Butsch Kovacic, *Ch Bd*
Leonard Small, *
Melinda Butsch Kovacic Cnb, *Prin*
Alexis Kidd Zafer, *
EMP: 35 **EST:** 1961
SQ FT: 7,500
SALES (est): 950.75K
SALES (corp-wide): 950.75K **Privately Held**
Web: www.7hillsnh.com
SIC: 8322 Neighborhood center

GEOGRAPHIC SECTION

Cincinnati - Hamilton County (G-3385)

(G-3365)
SGK LLC
Also Called: Schawk
537 E Pete Rose Way Ste 100 (45202-3578)
PHONE.................513 569-9900
Rhett Warner, *Opers Mgr*
EMP: 145
SALES (corp-wide): 1.88B **Publicly Held**
Web: www.sgkinc.com
SIC: 7311 Advertising agencies
HQ: Sgk, Llc
  2 North Shore Center
  Pittsburgh PA 15212
  847 827-9494

(G-3366)
SGS NORTH AMERICA INC
Also Called: Automotive Div Of,
650 Northland Blvd Ste 600 (45240-3242)
PHONE.................513 674-7048
Mark Van Horck, *VP*
Mark Van Horck, *VP*
EMP: 38 **EST:** 2012
SALES (est): 495.76K **Privately Held**
SIC: 7549 Inspection and diagnostic service, automotive
HQ: Sgs North America Inc.
  201 Route 17 Fl 7
  Rutherford NJ 07070
  201 508-3000

(G-3367)
SHEAKLEY-UNISERVICE INC (PA)
1 Sheakley Way (45246-3774)
P.O. Box 42212 (45242-0212)
PHONE.................513 771-2277
Larry A Sheakley, *Ch*
EMP: 38 **EST:** 1965
SALES (est): 8.95MM
SALES (corp-wide): 8.95MM **Privately Held**
Web: www.sheakley.com
SIC: 8742 8721 Compensation and benefits planning consultant; Payroll accounting service

(G-3368)
SHELTERHOUSE VLNTR GROUP INC (PA)
Also Called: ALCOHOLIC DROP-IN CENTER
411 Gest St (45203-1730)
PHONE.................513 721-0643
Arlene Nolan, *CEO*
Don Gardner, *Pr*
Melissa Merritt, *Treas*
EMP: 49 **EST:** 1968
SQ FT: 2,000
SALES (est): 10.61MM
SALES (corp-wide): 10.61MM **Privately Held**
Web: www.shelterhousecincy.org
SIC: 8322 Aid to Families with Dependent Children (AFDC)

(G-3369)
SHERMAN FINANCIAL GROUP LLC
8600 Governors Hill Dr Ste 201 (45249-1388)
PHONE.................513 707-3000
Brian Gardner, *Brnch Mgr*
EMP: 447
SALES (corp-wide): 111.53MM **Privately Held**
Web: www.sfg.com
SIC: 6282 Investment advice
PA: Sherman Financial Group Llc
  200 Meeting St Ste 206
  Charleston SC 29401
  212 922-1616

(G-3370)
SHIHASI STARWIND NE LLP
Also Called: Comfort In Northeast
9011 Fields Ertel Rd (45249-8261)
PHONE.................513 683-9700
Admiral Miriam Haas, *Prin*
Subhas Patel, *Dir*
EMP: 32 **EST:** 1999
SALES (est): 126K **Privately Held**
SIC: 7011 Hotels

(G-3371)
SHOPTECH INDUSTRIAL SFTWR CORP
400 E Business Way Ste 300 (45241)
PHONE.................513 985-9900
Paul Ventura, *VP Mktg*
EMP: 35
Web: www.shoptech.com
SIC: 7371 Computer software development
HQ: Shoptech Industrial Software Corp.
  180 Glastonbury Blvd # 303
  Glastonbury CT 06033
  860 633-0740

(G-3372)
SHRINERS HSPITALS FOR CHILDREN
3229 Burnet Ave (45229-3018)
PHONE.................513 872-6000
Ronald Hitzler, *Admn*
EMP: 320
Web: www.shrinerschildrens.org
SIC: 8062 General medical and surgical hospitals
PA: Shriners Hospitals For Children
  2900 N Rocky Point Dr
  Tampa FL 33607

(G-3373)
SHRINERS INTERNATIONAL HDQTR
Also Called: SHRINER'S INTERNATIONAL HEADQUARTERS INC
3229 Burnet Ave (45229-3018)
PHONE.................800 875-8580
EMP: 61
Web: www.shrinersinternational.org
SIC: 8011 Medical centers
PA: Shriners Hospitals For Children
  2900 N Rocky Point Dr
  Tampa FL 33607

(G-3374)
SIBCY CLINE INC
Also Called: Kenwood Office
8040 Montgomery Rd (45236-2903)
PHONE.................513 793-2121
Stephanie Busam, *Mgr*
EMP: 121
SALES (corp-wide): 98.72MM **Privately Held**
Web: www.sibcycline.com
SIC: 6531 Real estate agent, residential
PA: Sibcy Cline, Inc.
  8044 Montgomery Rd # 300
  Cincinnati OH 45236
  513 984-4100

(G-3375)
SIBCY CLINE INC (PA)
Also Called: Sibcy Cline Realtors
8044 Montgomery Rd Ste 300 (45236-2922)
PHONE.................513 984-4100
Robert N Sibcy, *Pr*
James A Stofko, *
William D Borek, *
EMP: 82 **EST:** 1952
SQ FT: 30,000
SALES (est): 98.72MM
SALES (corp-wide): 98.72MM **Privately Held**
Web: www.sibcycline.com
SIC: 6531 Real estate agent, residential

(G-3376)
SIBCY CLINE INC
Also Called: Sibcy Cline Realtors
9250 Winton Rd (45231-3936)
PHONE.................513 931-7700
Beth Sehling, *Mgr*
EMP: 120
SALES (corp-wide): 98.72MM **Privately Held**
Web: www.sibcycline.com
SIC: 6531 Real estate agent, residential
PA: Sibcy Cline, Inc.
  8044 Montgomery Rd # 300
  Cincinnati OH 45236
  513 984-4100

(G-3377)
SIGMATEK SYSTEMS LLC (HQ)
Also Called: Sigma T E K
1445 Kemper Meadow Dr (45240-1637)
PHONE.................513 674-0005
Ben Terreblanche, *CEO*
EMP: 65 **EST:** 1993
SQ FT: 23,000
SALES (est): 26.66MM
SALES (corp-wide): 11.77B **Privately Held**
Web: www.sigmanest.com
SIC: 7372 Prepackaged software
PA: Sandvik Ab
  Hogbovagen 45
  Sandviken 811 3
  26260000

(G-3378)
SIKICH LLP
665 Balbriggan Ct (45255-5619)
PHONE.................513 482-1127
James A Sikich, *CEO*
EMP: 30
SALES (corp-wide): 105.04MM **Privately Held**
Web: www.sikich.com
SIC: 7379 Computer related consulting services
PA: Sikich Llp
  1415 W Diehl Rd Ste 400
  Naperville IL 60563
  877 279-1900

(G-3379)
SIMS-LOHMAN INC (PA)
Also Called: Sims-Lohman Fine Kitchens Gran
6325 Este Ave (45232)
PHONE.................513 651-3510
Steve Steinman, *CEO*
John Beiersdorfer, *
▲ **EMP:** 50 **EST:** 1974
SQ FT: 153,000
SALES (est): 96.65MM
SALES (corp-wide): 96.65MM **Privately Held**
Web: www.sims-lohman.com
SIC: 2435 5031 Hardwood veneer and plywood; Kitchen cabinets

(G-3380)
SISTERS OF CHRITY CNCNNATI OHI (HQ)
5900 Delhi Rd (45233-1680)
PHONE.................513 347-5200
Sister Bjoan Cook, *Pr*
Tim Moller, *
EMP: 178 **EST:** 1829
SQ FT: 60,000
SALES (est): 48.76MM **Privately Held**

Web: www.srcharitycinti.org
SIC: 8051 8661 Skilled nursing care facilities; Nonchurch religious organizations
PA: Commonspirit Health
  444 W Lake St Ste 2500
  Chicago IL 60606

(G-3381)
SJN DATA CENTER LLC (PA)
Also Called: Encore Technologies
4620 Wesley Ave (45212-2234)
PHONE.................513 386-7871
John Burns, *Pr*
Clay Stevens, *
EMP: 50 **EST:** 2011
SQ FT: 90,000
SALES (est): 41.14MM
SALES (corp-wide): 41.14MM **Privately Held**
Web: www.encore.tech
SIC: 8748 7378 7379 Systems engineering consultant, ex. computer or professional; Computer maintenance and repair; Online services technology consultants

(G-3382)
SKALLYS OLD WORLD BAKERY INC
Also Called: Skally's Restaurant
1933 W Galbraith Rd (45239-4767)
PHONE.................513 931-1411
Odette Skally, *Pr*
Drew Skally, *
EMP: 45 **EST:** 1977
SQ FT: 40,000
SALES (est): 12.53MM **Privately Held**
Web: www.oldworldbakery.com
SIC: 5149 5812 Bakery products; Eating places

(G-3383)
SKANSKA USA BUILDING INC
201 E 5th St Ste 2020 (45202-4164)
PHONE.................513 421-0082
Craig Eckert, *Brnch Mgr*
EMP: 96
SALES (corp-wide): 115.37MM **Privately Held**
Web: usa.skanska.com
SIC: 1541 1542 8741 Industrial buildings and warehouses; Nonresidential construction, nec; Management services
HQ: Skanska Usa Building Inc.
  389 Interpace Pkwy Ste 5
  Parsippany NJ 07054
  973 753-3500

(G-3384)
SKYLIGHT FINANCIAL GROUP LLC
3825 Edwards Rd Ste 210 (45209-1288)
PHONE.................513 579-8555
EMP: 99
SALES (corp-wide): 11.05MM **Privately Held**
Web: www.skylightfinancialgroup.com
SIC: 8742 Management consulting services
PA: Skylight Financial Group, Llc
  2012 W 25th St Ste 900
  Cleveland OH 44113
  216 621-5680

(G-3385)
SKYLIGHT PARTNERS INC
Also Called: Orchard
708 Walnut St (45202-2175)
PHONE.................513 381-5555
Richard Walker, *CEO*
EMP: 30 **EST:** 2016
SALES (est): 8.4MM **Privately Held**
Web: www.growatorchard.com
SIC: 7311 7374 Advertising agencies; Computer graphics service

Cincinnati - Hamilton County (G-3386)

(G-3386)
SL SEASONS LLC
7300 Dearwester Dr (45236-6119)
PHONE..................513 984-9400
Scharman O Sanders, *Prin*
EMP: 61 **EST:** 2003
SALES (est): 5.25MM
SALES (corp-wide): 244.88MM **Privately Held**
SIC: 8361 Aged home
PA: Senior Lifestyle Corporation
303 E Wacker Dr Ste 2400
Chicago IL 60601
312 673-4333

(G-3387)
SL WELLSPRING LLC
Also Called: Wellspring Health Care
8000 Evergreen Ridge Dr (45215-5750)
PHONE..................513 948-2339
EMP: 72 **EST:** 1989
SQ FT: 70,000
SALES (est): 3.9MM
SALES (corp-wide): 244.88MM **Privately Held**
Web: www.seniorlifestyle.com
SIC: 5051 Metals service centers and offices
PA: Senior Lifestyle Corporation
303 E Wacker Dr Ste 2400
Chicago IL 60601
312 673-4333

(G-3388)
SMARTPAY LEASING LLC
7755 Montgomery Rd Ste 400 (45236-4197)
PHONE..................800 374-5587
Ken Pedotto, *CEO*
EMP: 47 **EST:** 2015
SALES (est): 6.4MM **Privately Held**
Web: www.smartpaylease.com
SIC: 7359 Equipment rental and leasing, nec

(G-3389)
SMYTH AUTOMOTIVE INC (PA)
4275 Mount Carmel Tobasco Rd (45244-2319)
PHONE..................513 528-2800
Joseph M Smyth, *Pr*
Jim Smyth, *
Lynette Smithson, *
EMP: 87 **EST:** 1963
SQ FT: 23,000
SALES (est): 61.2MM
SALES (corp-wide): 61.2MM **Privately Held**
Web: www.smythautoparts.com
SIC: 5013 5531 Automotive supplies and parts; Automotive parts

(G-3390)
SNAPBLOX HOSTED SOLUTIONS LLC
131 Eight Mile Rd (45255-4612)
PHONE..................866 524-7707
Michael Earls, *Managing Member*
EMP: 30 **EST:** 2010
SALES (est): 737.32K **Privately Held**
Web: www.snapblox.com
SIC: 7379 7389 Computer related consulting services; Business services, nec

(G-3391)
SOCIETY OF THE TRANSFIGURATION (PA)
Also Called: Sisters of The Transfiguration
555 Albion Ave (45246-4649)
PHONE..................513 771-7462
Sister Ann, *Prin*
EMP: 66 **EST:** 1898

SALES (est): 6.29MM
SALES (corp-wide): 6.29MM **Privately Held**
Web: www.bethanyschool.org
SIC: 8661 8211 8059 7999 Catholic Church; Boarding school; Nursing home, except skilled and intermediate care facility; Recreation center

(G-3392)
SOFCO ERECTORS INC (PA)
10360 Wayne Ave (45215-1129)
PHONE..................513 771-1600
John Hesford, *Pr*
John C Hesford, *
Daniel Powell, *
John Hesford, *VP*
Roger Banner, *
EMP: 218 **EST:** 1992
SQ FT: 5,000
SALES (est): 23.73MM **Privately Held**
Web: www.sofcoerectors.com
SIC: 1791 Iron work, structural

(G-3393)
SOUTHWEST OHIO RGNAL TRNST AUT (PA)
Also Called: S O R T A
525 Vine St Ste 500 (45202-3133)
PHONE..................513 621-4455
Terry Garcia Cruz, *CEO*
Dave Etienne, *Dir*
EMP: 100 **EST:** 1880
SALES (est): 88.75MM
SALES (corp-wide): 88.75MM **Privately Held**
Web: www.go-metro.com
SIC: 4111 Bus line operations

(G-3394)
SOUTHWEST OHIO RGNAL TRNST AUT
Also Called: Mreto
1401 Bank St (45214-1737)
PHONE..................513 632-7511
Bill Speraul, *Mgr*
EMP: 765
SALES (corp-wide): 88.75MM **Privately Held**
Web: www.go-metro.com
SIC: 4111 Bus line operations
PA: Southwest Ohio Regional Transit Authority
525 Vine St Ste 500
Cincinnati OH 45202
513 621-4455

(G-3395)
SPECIALIZED ALTERNATIVES FOR F
Also Called: Safy of Cincinnati
11590 Century Blvd Ste 116 (45246-3326)
PHONE..................513 771-7239
Shawn Thornton, *Mgr*
EMP: 159
SALES (corp-wide): 22.34MM **Privately Held**
Web: www.safy.org
SIC: 8322 Child related social services
PA: Specialized Alternatives For Families And Youth Of Ohio, Inc.
10100 Elida Rd
Delphos OH 45833
419 695-8010

(G-3396)
SPECIALIZED PHARMACY SVCS LLC (DH)
Also Called: Specialized Pharmacy Svcs - N
201 E 4th St Ste 900 (45202-4160)
PHONE..................513 719-2600
John Workman, *CEO*

Cheryl D Hodges, *
Gary W Kadlec, *
Cecilia Temple, *
EMP: 50 **EST:** 1977
SQ FT: 28,000
SALES (est): 9.21MM
SALES (corp-wide): 357.78B **Publicly Held**
Web: www.specialtymailonline.com
SIC: 5122 Pharmaceuticals
HQ: Neighborcare Pharmacy Services, Inc.
201 E 4th St Ste 900
Cincinnati OH 45202

(G-3397)
SPRING GROVE CMTRY & ARBORETUM (PA)
4521 Spring Grove Ave (45232-1954)
PHONE..................513 681-7526
Gary M Freytag, *Pr*
David Kelly, *
Thomas L Smith, *
EMP: 75 **EST:** 1845
SALES (est): 13.21MM
SALES (corp-wide): 13.21MM **Privately Held**
Web: www.springgrove.org
SIC: 6553 Cemeteries, real estate operation

(G-3398)
SPRING GROVE RSRCE RCOVERY INC
4879 Spring Grove Ave (45232-1938)
PHONE..................513 681-6242
Alan Mckin, *CEO*
Roger Koenecke, *VP*
John P Lawton Senior, *Corporate Marketing Vice President*
Eugene Cookson, *Field Service Vice President*
Stephen E Dovell, *Disposal Service Vice President*
EMP: 49 **EST:** 1991
SQ FT: 50,000
SALES (est): 3.69MM
SALES (corp-wide): 5.41B **Publicly Held**
Web: www.cleanharbors.com
SIC: 4953 4212 Sanitary landfill operation; Local trucking, without storage
PA: Clean Harbors, Inc.
42 Longwater Dr
Norwell MA 02061
781 792-5000

(G-3399)
SPRING HILL SUITES
Also Called: Springhill Suites
610 Eden Park Dr (45202-6031)
PHONE..................513 381-8300
Volker Wellmann, *Genl Mgr*
EMP: 40 **EST:** 2009
SALES (est): 4.92MM
SALES (corp-wide): 23.71B **Publicly Held**
Web: springhillsuites.marriott.com
SIC: 7011 Hotels and motels
PA: Marriott International, Inc.
7750 Wisconsin Ave
Bethesda MD 20814
301 380-3000

(G-3400)
SPRINGDALE FAMILY MEDICINE PC
Also Called: Webb, Barry W
212 W Sharon Rd (45246-4137)
PHONE..................513 771-7213
Thomas Todd, *Pr*
Doctor Barry Webb, *VP*
Doctor Douglas L Hancher, *Sec*
EMP: 42 **EST:** 1937
SALES (est): 485.61K **Privately Held**
Web: www.springdale.org

SIC: 8011 General and family practice, physician/surgeon

(G-3401)
SPRINGDOT INC (PA)
Also Called: Springdot
2611 Colerain Ave (45214-1711)
PHONE..................513 542-4000
Josh Deutsch, *Pr*
Jeff Deutsch, *
John Brenner, *
Thomas Deutsch, *Stockholder**
EMP: 60 **EST:** 1904
SQ FT: 70,000
SALES (est): 11.11MM
SALES (corp-wide): 11.11MM **Privately Held**
Web: www.springdot.com
SIC: 2752 4899 2759 2675 Offset printing; Data communication services; Commercial printing, nec; Die-cut paper and board

(G-3402)
SQUIRE PATTON BOGGS (US) LLP
201 E 4th St Ste 324 (45202-4248)
PHONE..................513 361-1200
Scott Kane, *Mgr*
EMP: 30
SALES (corp-wide): 458.81MM **Privately Held**
Web: www.squirepattonboggs.com
SIC: 8111 Specialized law offices, attorneys
PA: Squire Patton Boggs (Us) Llp
1000 Key Tower 127 Pub Sq
Cleveland OH 44114
216 479-8500

(G-3403)
ST JOSEPH INFANT MATERNITY HM
Also Called: St Joseph S Home
10722 Wyscarver Rd (45241)
PHONE..................513 563-2520
Sister Marianne Van Vurst, *Dir*
Lynn Heper, *
EMP: 136 **EST:** 1873
SALES (est): 15.27MM **Privately Held**
Web: www.stjosephhome.org
SIC: 8052 8322 Home for the mentally retarded, with health care; Individual and family services

(G-3404)
STAFFMARK GROUP LLC (HQ)
191 Rosa Parks St Pmb 10 (45202-2573)
PHONE..................513 651-1111
Hitoshi Motohara, *Ch*
Geno A Cutolo, *
Kathryn S Bernard, *
William E Aglinsky, *
Yuichiro Miura, *
EMP: 75 **EST:** 1999
SALES (est): 478.52MM **Privately Held**
Web: www.staffmarkgroup.com
SIC: 7361 7363 Labor contractors (employment agency); Labor resource services
PA: Recruit Holdings Co., Ltd.
1-9-2, Marunouchi
Chiyoda-Ku TKY 100-0

(G-3405)
STAFFMARK INVESTMENT LLC (DH)
Also Called: Staffmark
201 E 4th St (45202-4248)
PHONE..................513 651-3600
David W Bartholomew, *CEO*
Clay Bullock, *
Kenny Berkemeyer, *
Sally Berrier, *
◆ **EMP:** 120 **EST:** 2000
SALES (est): 119.25MM **Privately Held**

GEOGRAPHIC SECTION

Cincinnati - Hamilton County (G-3425)

Web: www.staffmark.com
SIC: 7361 Labor contractors (employment agency)
HQ: Staffmark Group, Llc
191 Rosa Parks St Pmb 10
Cincinnati OH 45202
513 651-1111

(G-3406)
STAGNARO SABA PATTERSON CO LPA
7373 Beechmont Ave (45230-4100)
PHONE.................513 533-2700
William Patterson, *Brnch Mgr*
EMP: 30
Web: www.sspfirm.com
SIC: 8111   General practice law office
PA: Stagnaro, Saba & Patterson Co., L.P.A
2623 Erie Ave
Cincinnati OH 45208

(G-3407)
STAND ENERGY CORPORATION
1077 Celestial St Ste 110 (45202-1629)
PHONE.................513 621-1113
Matth Toebben, *Ch*
Judith Phillips, *
Lawrence Freeman, *
Jeffrey Crass, *
EMP: 34 EST: 1984
SQ FT: 4,580
SALES (est): 95.22MM **Privately Held**
Web: www.stand-energy.com
SIC: 4924   Natural gas distribution

(G-3408)
STANDARD INSURANCE COMPANY
Also Called: Employee Benefits Sls Svc Off
312 Elm St Ste 1400 (45202-2722)
PHONE.................513 241-7275
Jackie Voll, *Mgr*
EMP: 113
Web: www.standard.com
SIC: 6311   Life insurance carriers
HQ: Standard Insurance Company
900 Sw 5th Ave
Portland OR 97204
971 321-7000

(G-3409)
STANDARD TEXTILE CO INC (PA)
Also Called: Pridecraft Enterprises
1 Knollcrest Dr (45237-1608)
P.O. Box 371805 (45222-1805)
PHONE.................513 761-9255
Gary Heiman, *CEO*
Alex Heiman, *
Edward Frankel, *CAO**
Norman Frankel, *SALES**
Chris Bopp, *CIO**
◆ EMP: 300 EST: 1940
SQ FT: 150,000
SALES (est): 393.56MM
SALES (corp-wide): 393.56MM **Privately Held**
Web: www.standardtextile.com
SIC: 2299 7389 5023   Linen fabrics; Textile designers; Linens and towels

(G-3410)
STANDRDAERO COMPONENT SVCS INC (DH)
Also Called: Standardaero
11550 Mosteller Rd (45241-1832)
PHONE.................513 618-9588
Russell Ford, *CEO*
Michael Scott, *
Brent Fawkes, *
Kim Olson, *
EMP: 91 EST: 1953
SQ FT: 236,000
SALES (est): 51.24MM **Privately Held**
Web: www.standardaerocomponents.com
SIC: 7699   Aviation propeller and blade repair
HQ: Standard Aero (San Antonio) Inc.
3523 General Hudnell Dr
San Antonio TX 78226

(G-3411)
STANLEY STEEMER INTL INC
Also Called: Cincinnati 007
637 Redna Ter (45215-1108)
PHONE.................513 771-0213
Dustin Holmes, *Brnch Mgr*
EMP: 34
SALES (corp-wide): 263.72MM **Privately Held**
Web: www.stanleysteemer.com
SIC: 7217   Carpet and furniture cleaning on location
PA: Stanley Steemer International, Inc.
5800 Innovation Dr
Dublin OH 43016
614 764-2007

(G-3412)
STARFORCE NATIONAL CORPORATION
455 Delta Ave Ste 410 (45226-1178)
P.O. Box 21600 (45121-0600)
PHONE.................513 979-3600
Frank Mayfield Junior, *Ch Bd*
Judith Mc Cullough, *Sec*
Lauren Gibson, *VP*
EMP: 110 EST: 2001
SQ FT: 2,000
SALES (est): 9.2MM **Privately Held**
Web: www.starforcetransport.com
SIC: 4142   Bus charter service, except local

(G-3413)
STATE FARM GENERAL INSUR CO
Also Called: State Farm Insurance
6323 Glenway Ave (45211-6301)
PHONE.................513 662-7283
EMP: 63
SALES (corp-wide): 27.88B **Privately Held**
Web: www.statefarm.com
SIC: 6321 6036 6311   Health insurance carriers; State savings banks, not federally chartered; Life insurance carriers
HQ: State Farm General Insurance Co Inc
1 State Farm Plz
Bloomington IL 61701
309 766-2311

(G-3414)
STATE FARM GENERAL INSUR CO
Also Called: State Farm Insurance
2063 Beechmont Ave Ste 2 (45230-1699)
PHONE.................513 231-4975
Robert Donnelly, *Brnch Mgr*
EMP: 54
SALES (corp-wide): 27.88B **Privately Held**
Web: www.statefarm.com
SIC: 6411   Insurance agents and brokers
HQ: State Farm General Insurance Co Inc
1 State Farm Plz
Bloomington IL 61701
309 766-2311

(G-3415)
STEED HAMMOND PAUL INC (PA)
Also Called: Shp
312 Plum St Ste 700 (45202-2618)
PHONE.................513 381-2112
Lauren Della Bella, *Pr*
Susan Woollum, *
Thomas Fernandez, *
Ronald Hicks, *
Todd Thackery, *

EMP: 75 EST: 1981
SQ FT: 6,160
SALES (est): 12.51MM
SALES (corp-wide): 12.51MM **Privately Held**
Web: www.shpleadingdesign.com
SIC: 8712   Architectural engineering

(G-3416)
STERLING BUYING GROUP LLC
4540 Cooper Rd Ste 200 (45242-5649)
PHONE.................513 564-9000
Paul L Hunter, *Pr*
Jill Barnett, *
George Mahowald, *
Howard Cooper, *Managing Member**
Kevin Schifrin, *
EMP: 50 EST: 2006
SALES (est): 3.89MM
SALES (corp-wide): 9.65B **Publicly Held**
Web: www.sterlingb2bgroup.com
SIC: 7389 7373   Financial services; Systems integration services
HQ: Sterling Payment Technologies, Llc
5995 Windward Pkwy
Alpharetta GA 30005
813 637-9696

(G-3417)
STERLING MEDICAL ASSOCIATES
411 Oak St (45219-2504)
PHONE.................513 984-1800
Edwin Blatt, *Pr*
Richard Blatt, *
Doctor Ethel Blatt, *Sec*
Brandon Blatt, *
EMP: 70 EST: 1963
SQ FT: 15,000
SALES (est): 24.59MM
SALES (corp-wide): 45.39MM **Privately Held**
Web: www.sterlingoverseas.com
SIC: 8099   Medical services organization
PA: Sterling Medical Corporation
411 Oak St
Cincinnati OH 45219
513 984-1800

(G-3418)
STERLING MEDICAL CORPORATION (PA)
Also Called: Sterling Med Staffing Group
411 Oak St (45219)
PHONE.................513 984-1800
Richard Blatt, *CEO*
Edwin Blatt, *
Brandon Blatt, *
EMP: 120 EST: 1989
SQ FT: 15,000
SALES (est): 45.39MM
SALES (corp-wide): 45.39MM **Privately Held**
Web: www.sterlingmedcorp.com
SIC: 8741   Administrative management

(G-3419)
STERLING MEDICAL CORPORATION
411 Oak St (45219-2504)
PHONE.................513 984-1800
Kevin Korb, *Brnch Mgr*
EMP: 202
SALES (corp-wide): 45.39MM **Privately Held**
Web: www.sterlingmedcorp.com
SIC: 8741   Hospital management
PA: Sterling Medical Corporation
411 Oak St
Cincinnati OH 45219
513 984-1800

(G-3420)
STEVEN SCHAEFER ASSOCIATES INC (PA)
Also Called: Schaefer
537 E Pete Rose Way Ste 400
(45202-3578)
PHONE.................513 542-3300
Gregory J Riley, *Pr*
James Miller, *
Steven E Schaefer, *
Ed Schwieter, *
EMP: 52 EST: 1976
SQ FT: 13,000
SALES (est): 15.88MM
SALES (corp-wide): 15.88MM **Privately Held**
Web: www.schaefer-inc.com
SIC: 8711   Structural engineering

(G-3421)
STRATEGIC COMP
301 E 4th St Fl 24 (45202-4278)
PHONE.................770 225-3532
Pam Delaureal, *Pr*
EMP: 94 EST: 2015
SALES (est): 1.96MM **Privately Held**
Web: www.strategiccomp.com
SIC: 6021   National commercial banks

(G-3422)
STRATEGIC DATA SYSTEMS INC
11260 Chester Rd Ste 425 (45246-4052)
PHONE.................513 772-7374
Keith Stafford, *Mng Pt*
Keith Stafford, *Treas*
David Pledger, *Pr*
EMP: 198 EST: 1992
SQ FT: 1,500
SALES (est): 2.89MM **Privately Held**
Web: www.sds.io
SIC: 7371   Custom computer programming services

(G-3423)
STRIDAS LLC
8259 Beechmont Ave (45255-3151)
PHONE.................513 725-4626
Chris Painter, *Pr*
Paul Silk, *
EMP: 45 EST: 2012
SALES (est): 10.57MM **Privately Held**
Web: www.stridas.com
SIC: 4731   Freight transportation arrangement

(G-3424)
STRIVETOGETHER INC
125 E 9th St Fl 2 (45202-2127)
PHONE.................513 929-1150
EMP: 50 EST: 2018
SALES (est): 24.55MM **Privately Held**
Web: www.strivetogether.org
SIC: 8699   Charitable organization

(G-3425)
STUDENT LN FNDING RSOURCES LLC
Also Called: Student Loan Funding
1 W 4th St Ste 200 (45202-3634)
PHONE.................513 763-4300
James H Eickhoff Junior, *CEO*
EMP: 35 EST: 1981
SALES (est): 8.85MM
SALES (corp-wide): 4.83B **Publicly Held**
Web: www.studentloanxpress.com
SIC: 6111 6163 5932   Student Loan Marketing Association; Loan brokers; Used merchandise stores
HQ: Navient Solutions, Llc
123 S Justison St Ste 300
Wilmington DE 19801
703 810-3000

Cincinnati - Hamilton County (G-3426) — GEOGRAPHIC SECTION

(G-3426)
SUNRISE TREATMENT CENTER LLC (PA)
6460 Harrison Ave Ste 100 (45247-7958)
PHONE................................513 941-4999
Jeffrey Bill, *Managing Member*
EMP: 35 **EST:** 2007
SALES (est): 20.38MM
SALES (corp-wide): 20.38MM **Privately Held**
Web: www.sunrisetreatmentcenter.net
SIC: 8093 Substance abuse clinics (outpatient)

(G-3427)
SUNRISE TREATMENT CENTER LLC
680 Northland Blvd (45240-3248)
PHONE................................513 595-5340
Jeffrey P Bill Md, *CEO*
EMP: 27
SALES (corp-wide): 20.38MM **Privately Held**
Web: www.sunrisetreatmentcenter.net
SIC: 8093 Substance abuse clinics (outpatient)
PA: Sunrise Treatment Center, Llc
6460 Harrison Ave Ste 100
Cincinnati OH 45247
513 941-4999

(G-3428)
SUPER SYSTEMS INC (PA)
7205 Edington Dr (45249-1064)
PHONE................................513 772-0060
EMP: 32 **EST:** 1993
SQ FT: 5,000
SALES (est): 9.9MM **Privately Held**
Web: www.supersystems.com
SIC: 3829 5084 Measuring and controlling devices, nec; Industrial machinery and equipment

(G-3429)
SWS ENVIRONMENTAL SERVICE INC
5770 Park Rd (45243-3410)
PHONE................................513 793-7417
Donald E Savage, *Ch*
Sharon Savage Amato, *Pr*
EMP: 29 **EST:** 1977
SALES (est): 531.25K **Privately Held**
Web: www.sws-environmental.com
SIC: 1623 Water main construction

(G-3430)
SYSCO CINCINNATI LLC
Also Called: Sysco
10510 Evendale Dr (45241-2516)
PHONE................................513 563-6300
Michael Haunert, *Pr*
Daniel Pinsel, *
EMP: 483 **EST:** 2002
SALES (est): 105.69MM
SALES (corp-wide): 76.32B **Publicly Held**
Web: www.syscocincinnati.com
SIC: 5144 5149 5143 5113 Poultry and poultry products; Groceries and related products, nec; Dairy products, except dried or canned; Industrial and personal service paper
PA: Sysco Corporation
1390 Enclave Pkwy
Houston TX 77077
281 584-1390

(G-3431)
SYSTEMS EVOLUTION INC (PA)
11500 Northlake Dr Ste 450 (45249-1663)
PHONE................................513 459-1992
EMP: 38 **EST:** 1992
SALES (est): 10.7MM **Privately Held**
Web: www.sei.com
SIC: 7371 Computer software development

(G-3432)
TAFT MUSEUM OF ART
316 Pike St (45202-4293)
P.O. Box 631419 (45263-1419)
PHONE................................513 241-0343
Beth Siler, *Dir Fin*
EMP: 41 **EST:** 2008
SALES (est): 7.45MM **Privately Held**
Web: www.taftmuseum.org
SIC: 8412 Museum

(G-3433)
TAFT STETTINIUS HOLLISTER LLP (PA)
425 Walnut St Ste 1800 (45202-3920)
PHONE................................513 381-2838
Thomas T Terp, *Managing Member*
EMP: 278 **EST:** 1924
SQ FT: 114,000
SALES (est): 97.83MM
SALES (corp-wide): 97.83MM **Privately Held**
Web: www.taftlaw.com
SIC: 8111 General practice law office

(G-3434)
TALBERT HOUSE
3009 Burnet Ave (45219-2419)
PHONE................................513 872-8870
EMP: 66
SALES (corp-wide): 75.69MM **Privately Held**
Web: www.talberthouse.org
SIC: 8322 8361 Family counseling services; Residential care
PA: Talbert House
2600 Victory Pkwy
Cincinnati OH 45206
513 872-5863

(G-3435)
TALBERT HOUSE
1611 Emerson Ave (45239-4932)
PHONE................................513 541-1184
Neil F Tilow, *Brnch Mgr*
EMP: 28
SALES (corp-wide): 75.69MM **Privately Held**
Web: www.talberthouse.org
SIC: 8322 Substance abuse counseling
PA: Talbert House
2600 Victory Pkwy
Cincinnati OH 45206
513 872-5863

(G-3436)
TALBERT HOUSE
5837 Hamilton Ave (45224-2923)
PHONE................................513 751-7747
Suzanne Lukacs, *Brnch Mgr*
EMP: 58
SALES (corp-wide): 75.69MM **Privately Held**
Web: www.talberthouse.org
SIC: 8069 Drug addiction rehabilitation hospital
PA: Talbert House
2600 Victory Pkwy
Cincinnati OH 45206
513 872-5863

(G-3437)
TALBERT HOUSE
Also Called: Spring Grove Center
1817 Logan St Apt 508 (45202-8053)
PHONE................................513 541-0127
William Marshall, *Brnch Mgr*
EMP: 38
SALES (corp-wide): 75.69MM **Privately Held**
Web: www.talberthouse.org
SIC: 8322 Rehabilitation services
PA: Talbert House
2600 Victory Pkwy
Cincinnati OH 45206
513 872-5863

(G-3438)
TALBERT HOUSE
2880 Central Pkwy (45225-2302)
PHONE................................513 221-2398
EMP: 28
SALES (corp-wide): 75.69MM **Privately Held**
Web: www.talberthouse.org
SIC: 8322 Rehabilitation services
PA: Talbert House
2600 Victory Pkwy
Cincinnati OH 45206
513 872-5863

(G-3439)
TALBERT HOUSE (PA)
2600 Victory Pkwy (45206-1395)
PHONE................................513 872-5863
Neil F Tilow, *Pr*
Josh Arnold, *
William Hostler, *
Brad Mcmonigle, *VP*
Jay Treft, *
EMP: 70 **EST:** 1965
SQ FT: 40,000
SALES (est): 75.69MM
SALES (corp-wide): 75.69MM **Privately Held**
Web: www.talberthouse.org
SIC: 8322 Rehabilitation services

(G-3440)
TALBERT HOUSE
1617 Reading Rd (45202-1413)
PHONE................................513 629-2303
Weona Smithmyer, *Mgr*
EMP: 75
SALES (corp-wide): 75.69MM **Privately Held**
Web: www.talberthouse.org
SIC: 8051 Mental retardation hospital
PA: Talbert House
2600 Victory Pkwy
Cincinnati OH 45206
513 872-5863

(G-3441)
TALBERT HOUSE
Also Called: Talbert House
328 Mcgregor Ave Ste 106 (45219-3135)
PHONE................................513 684-7968
Victor Gray, *Mgr*
EMP: 66
SALES (corp-wide): 75.69MM **Privately Held**
Web: www.talberthouse.org
SIC: 8069 Alcoholism rehabilitation hospital
PA: Talbert House
2600 Victory Pkwy
Cincinnati OH 45206
513 872-5863

(G-3442)
TALBERT HOUSE HEALTH (HQ)
4868 Glenway Ave (45238-4402)
PHONE................................513 541-7577
Paul Guggenheim, *Dir*
Cordilia Schaber, *
John Francis, *
EMP: 35 **EST:** 1972
SQ FT: 13,000
SALES (est): 3.4MM
SALES (corp-wide): 75.69MM **Privately Held**

(G-3443)
TALBERT HOUSE
Web: www.talberthouse.org
SIC: 8322 General counseling services
PA: Talbert House
2600 Victory Pkwy
Cincinnati OH 45206
513 872-5863

(G-3443)
TANYAS IMAGE LLC (PA)
Also Called: Tanyas Image & Wellness Salon
2716 Erie Ave Ste 3 (45208-2135)
PHONE................................513 386-9981
EMP: 37 **EST:** 1999
SALES (est): 879.92K
SALES (corp-wide): 879.92K **Privately Held**
Web: www.tanyasimage.com
SIC: 7231 Hairdressers

(G-3444)
TCI
415 Greenwell Ave (45238-5302)
PHONE................................513 557-3200
Michael O'connor, *Prin*
EMP: 32 **EST:** 2010
SALES (est): 812.47K **Privately Held**
Web: www.tcibilling.com
SIC: 4832 Radio broadcasting stations

(G-3445)
TDG FACILITIES LLC
11400 Rockfield Ct (45241-1917)
PHONE................................513 834-6105
Paul Jostworth, *Managing Member*
EMP: 110 **EST:** 2016
SALES (est): 11.98MM **Privately Held**
Web: www.tdgfacilities.com
SIC: 7349 Janitorial service, contract basis

(G-3446)
TEASDALE FNTON CRPT CLG RSTRTI
12145 Centron Pl (45246-1704)
PHONE................................513 797-0900
EMP: 90 **EST:** 2006
SQ FT: 20,000
SALES (est): 33.61MM **Privately Held**
Web: www.teasdalefenton.com
SIC: 7217 7299 Carpet and upholstery cleaning; Home improvement and renovation contractor agency

(G-3447)
TEATING MUETING & KLEKAMP PLL
1 E 4th St Ste 1400 (45202-3752)
PHONE................................513 579-6462
EMP: 31
SALES (est): 2.67MM **Privately Held**
Web: www.kmklaw.com
SIC: 8111 General practice attorney, lawyer

(G-3448)
TECHNICAL AID CORPORATION (DH)
Also Called: TAC Worldwide Companies
201 E 4th St Ste 800 (45202-4248)
P.O. Box 9130 (02062-9130)
PHONE................................781 251-8000
EMP: 37 **EST:** 1969
SALES (est): 70.12MM **Privately Held**
SIC: 7363 Help supply services
HQ: Advantage Resourcing America, Inc.
201 E 4th St Ste 800
Cincinnati OH 45202

(G-3449)
TECHSOLVE INC
Also Called: TECHSOLVE
6705 Steger Dr (45237-3029)
PHONE................................513 948-2000
David R Linger, *Pr*

GEOGRAPHIC SECTION

Cincinnati - Hamilton County (G-3471)

Otto Henkel, *
Dana W Hullinger, *
Rick Henkel, *
Kara Valz, *
EMP: 51 **EST:** 1982
SQ FT: 22,000
SALES (est): 4.89MM **Privately Held**
Web: www.techsolve.org
SIC: 8742 8748 8711 Manufacturing management consultant; Business consulting, nec; Mechanical engineering

(G-3450)
TECTA AMERICA ZERO COMPANY LLC (HQ)
Also Called: Tecta America Kentucky
6225 Wiehe Rd (45237-4211)
PHONE.................................513 541-1848
Jonathan Wolf, *Pr*
Thomas M Miller, *
Edward Phillip, *
Jim Stark, *
EMP: 100 **EST:** 1969
SQ FT: 30,000
SALES (est): 27.56MM
SALES (corp-wide): 823.93MM **Privately Held**
Web: www.tectaamerica.com
SIC: 1761 Roofing contractor
PA: Tecta America Corp.
  9450 Bryn Mawr Ave
  Rosemont IL 60018
  847 581-3888

(G-3451)
TEMPOE LLC
Also Called: Smartpay
7755 Montgomery Rd Ste 400 (45236-4291)
PHONE.................................415 390-2620
Orlando Zayas, *Pr*
EMP: 42
SALES (corp-wide): 72.03MM **Privately Held**
Web: www.tempoe.com
SIC: 7359 Equipment rental and leasing, nec
PA: Tempoe, Llc
  7755 Montgomery Rd # 400
  Cincinnati OH 45236
  844 863-2948

(G-3452)
TENACK DIALYSIS LLC
Also Called: Montgomery Home Training
11135 Montgomery Rd (45249-2338)
PHONE.................................513 810-4369
John Winstel, *Brnch Mgr*
EMP: 45
SIC: 8092 Kidney dialysis centers
HQ: Tenack Dialysis, Llc
  2000 16th St
  Denver CO 80202
  253 733-4501

(G-3453)
TENDER HRTS AT HM SNIOR CARE I
9435 Waterstone Blvd Ste 140 (45249-8226)
PHONE.................................513 234-0805
Dan Lynch, *Prin*
EMP: 79 **EST:** 2010
SALES (est): 4.2MM **Privately Held**
Web: www.tenderheartsathomecare.com
SIC: 8361 8082 Geriatric residential care; Home health care services

(G-3454)
TENDER MERCIES INC
15 W 12th St (45202-7205)
P.O. Box 14465 (45250-0465)
PHONE.................................513 721-8666
EMP: 57
Web: www.tendermerciesinc.org
SIC: 8322 Individual and family services
PA: Tender Mercies, Inc.
  27 W 12th St
  Cincinnati OH 45202

(G-3455)
TENDER MERCIES INC (PA)
Also Called: TENDER MERCIES
27 W 12th St (45202-7205)
P.O. Box 14465 (45250-0465)
PHONE.................................513 721-8666
Marsha Spaeth, *CEO*
Kirsch Mary, *
EMP: 49 **EST:** 1985
SQ FT: 40,000
SALES (est): 3.58MM **Privately Held**
Web: www.tendermerciesinc.org
SIC: 8322 Emergency shelters

(G-3456)
TENNFREIGHT INC
4240 Airport Rd Ste 213 (45226-1622)
PHONE.................................615 977-2125
Sahib Niyazov, *Prin*
EMP: 28
SALES (est): 1.03MM **Privately Held**
SIC: 4213 Trucking, except local

(G-3457)
TERILLIUM INC
201 E 5th St Ste 2700 (45202)
PHONE.................................513 621-9500
Warren S Bach, *Pr*
Pamela H Bach, *
Chris Garrity, *
EMP: 206 **EST:** 1995
SALES (est): 31.31MM **Privately Held**
Web: www.terillium.com
SIC: 7379 7371 Computer related consulting services; Custom computer programming services

(G-3458)
TERRACON CONSULTANTS INC
Also Called: Terracon Consultants N1
611 Lunken Park Dr (45226-1813)
PHONE.................................513 321-5816
Jason Sander, *Brnch Mgr*
EMP: 130
Web: www.terracon.com
SIC: 8711 Consulting engineer
HQ: Terracon Consultants, Inc.
  10841 S Ridgeview Rd
  Olathe KS 66061

(G-3459)
TERRACON CONSULTANTS INC
611 Lunken Park Dr (45226-1813)
PHONE.................................513 321-5816
EMP: 300
Web: www.terracon.com
SIC: 8734 8711 8731 Testing laboratories; Engineering services; Commercial physical research

(G-3460)
TEVA WOMENS HEALTH LLC (DH)
5040 Duramed Rd (45213-2520)
PHONE.................................513 731-9900
Bruce L Downey, *Prin*
Lawrence A Glassman, *
Timothy J Holt, *
EMP: 250 **EST:** 1982
SQ FT: 28,200
SALES (est): 113.88MM **Privately Held**
Web: www.duramed.com
SIC: 5122 2834 7389 Patent medicines; Pharmaceutical preparations; Packaging and labeling services
HQ: Teva Pharmaceuticals Usa, Inc.
  400 Interpace Pkwy Bldg A
  Parsippany NJ 07054
  215 591-3000

(G-3461)
TFORCE FREIGHT INC
3250 E Kemper Rd (45241-1540)
PHONE.................................513 771-7555
Chris Timo, *Genl Mgr*
EMP: 35
SALES (corp-wide): 8.81B **Privately Held**
Web: www.tforcefreight.com
SIC: 4213 4231 Contract haulers; Trucking terminal facilities
HQ: Tforce Freight, Inc.
  1000 Semmes Ave
  Richmond VA 23224
  800 333-7400

(G-3462)
THE CHAS G BUCHY PACKING COMPANY
Also Called: Buchy Food Service
10510 Evendale Dr (45241-2516)
EMP: 38 **EST:** 1878
SALES (est): 4.55MM **Privately Held**
SIC: 5141 Food brokers

(G-3463)
THE CINCINNATI PLAYHOUSE IN THE PARK INC
Also Called: CINCINNATI PLAYHOUSE
962 Mount Adams Cir (45202)
P.O. Box 6537 (45206)
PHONE.................................513 345-2242
EMP: 172 **EST:** 1959
SALES (est): 14.06MM **Privately Held**
Web: www.cincyplay.com
SIC: 7922 Theatrical production services

(G-3464)
THE DAVID J JOSEPH COMPANY (HQ)
Also Called: D J J
300 Pike St Fl 3 (45202-4222)
P.O. Box 1078 (45201-1078)
PHONE.................................513 419-6200
◆ **EMP:** 170 **EST:** 1937
SALES (est): 1.24B
SALES (corp-wide): 34.71B **Publicly Held**
Web: www.djj.com
SIC: 5093 Ferrous metal scrap and waste
PA: Nucor Corporation
  1915 Rexford Rd
  Charlotte NC 28211
  704 366-7000

(G-3465)
THE F D LAWRENCE ELECTRIC COMPANY (PA)
3450 Beekman St (45223-2425)
PHONE.................................513 542-1100
EMP: 85 **EST:** 1904
SALES (est): 60.85MM
SALES (corp-wide): 60.85MM **Privately Held**
Web: www.fdlawrence.com
SIC: 5063 Electrical apparatus and equipment

(G-3466)
THE GEILER COMPANY
Also Called: LLC
6561 Glenway Ave (45211-4409)
P.O. Box 11324 (45211-0324)
PHONE.................................513 574-1200
EMP: 110 **EST:** 1900
SALES (est): 17.03MM **Privately Held**
Web: www.geiler.com
SIC: 1711 7623 Plumbing contractors; Refrigeration repair service

(G-3467)
THE OGARA GROUP INC (PA)
Also Called: Mobile Security Division
7870 E Kemper Rd Ste 460 (45249-1675)
P.O. Box 8576 (60093-8576)
PHONE.................................513 881-9800
Matt Burke, *CEO*
Thomas M O'gara, *Ch Bd*
Bill T O'gara, *CEO*
Michael J Lennon, *
Steven P Ratterman, *
EMP: 52 **EST:** 2002
SALES (est): 52.21MM
SALES (corp-wide): 52.21MM **Privately Held**
Web: www.ogaragroup.com
SIC: 7382 Security systems services

(G-3468)
THE PECK-HANNAFORD BRIGGS CO (PA)
Also Called: PH B
4670 Chester Ave (45232-1851)
PHONE.................................513 681-4600
James G Briggs Junior, *Pr*
Jerry A Govert, *
EMP: 193 **EST:** 1899
SQ FT: 40,000
SALES (est): 57.91MM
SALES (corp-wide): 57.91MM **Privately Held**
Web: www.peckhannafordbriggs.com
SIC: 1711 Mechanical contractor

(G-3469)
THE PHOTO-TYPE ENGRAVING COMPANY (PA)
Also Called: Olberding Brand Family
2141 Gilbert Ave (45206-3021)
PHONE.................................513 281-0999
EMP: 60 **EST:** 1919
SALES (est): 43.97MM
SALES (corp-wide): 43.97MM **Privately Held**
Web: www.phototype.com
SIC: 2754 7336 7335 2796 Commercial printing, gravure; Commercial art and graphic design; Commercial photography; Platemaking services

(G-3470)
THE RDI CORPORATION (PA)
4350 Glendale Milford Rd Ste 250 (45242)
PHONE.................................513 984-5927
EMP: 555 **EST:** 1979
SALES (est): 52.44MM
SALES (corp-wide): 52.44MM **Privately Held**
Web: www.rdi-connect.com
SIC: 8732 Market analysis or research

(G-3471)
THE SHEAKLEY GROUP INC (PA)
Also Called: S G I
1 Sheakley Way (45246-3774)
PHONE.................................513 771-2277
Larry Sheakley, *CEO*
Thomas E Pappas Junior, *VP*
EMP: 30 **EST:** 1986
SQ FT: 5,500
SALES (est): 23.72MM **Privately Held**
Web: www.sheakley.com
SIC: 8742 8721 8741 6411 Compensation and benefits planning consultant; Accounting, auditing, and bookkeeping; Management services; Insurance agents, brokers, and service

Cincinnati - Hamilton County (G-3472)

(G-3472)
THE UNION CENTRAL LIFE INSURANCE COMPANY
1876 Waycross Rd (45240-2899)
P.O. Box 40888 (45240-0888)
PHONE...................................866 696-7478
◆ **EMP:** 1200
Web: www.unioncentral.com
SIC: 6311 6321 Mutual association life insurance; Mutual accident and health associations

(G-3473)
THERMALTECH ENGINEERING INC (PA)
Also Called: Thermaltech Engineering
3960 Red Bank Rd Ste 250 (45227-3437)
PHONE...................................513 561-2271
Jeff Celuch, *Pr*
Charles T Young, *
EMP: 85 **EST:** 1980
SQ FT: 8,000
SALES (est): 29.21MM
SALES (corp-wide): 29.21MM **Privately Held**
Web: www.thermaltech.com
SIC: 8711 Consulting engineer

(G-3474)
THOMAS J DYER COMPANY (PA)
Also Called: Thomas J Dyer Company
5240 Lester Rd (45213-2522)
PHONE...................................513 321-8100
Thomas D Grote Senior, *CEO*
EMP: 164 **EST:** 1908
SQ FT: 29,600
SALES (est): 54.24MM
SALES (corp-wide): 54.24MM **Privately Held**
Web: www.tjdyer.com
SIC: 1711 Plumbing contractors

(G-3475)
THOMAS TRUCKING INC
2558 Apple Ridge Ln (45236-1331)
PHONE...................................513 731-8411
Callis A Thomas, *Pr*
Mark Thomas, *
Christine Thomas, *
Kathy Thomas-dawson, *Sec*
EMP: 40 **EST:** 1973
SQ FT: 2,000
SALES (est): 2.28MM **Privately Held**
Web: www.thomastruckinginc.com
SIC: 4213 Contract haulers

(G-3476)
THORSON BAKER & ASSOC INC
Also Called: THORSON BAKER & ASSOC, INC
2055 Reading Rd Ste 280 (45202-1467)
PHONE...................................513 579-8200
Nick Steinert, *Mgr*
EMP: 32
Web: www.thorsonbaker.com
SIC: 8711 Consulting engineer
PA: Baker Thorson & Associates Inc
 3030 W Streetsboro Rd
 Richfield OH 44286

(G-3477)
THP LIMITED INC
100 E 8th St Ste 3 (45202-2133)
PHONE...................................513 241-3222
James Millar, *Pr*
E James Millar, *
Mark H Hoffman, *
Shayne O Manning, *
Randy R Wilson, *
EMP: 55 **EST:** 1973

SQ FT: 20,000
SALES (est): 400K **Privately Held**
Web: www.thpltd.com
SIC: 8711 Consulting engineer

(G-3478)
TIAA-CREF INDVDUAL INSTNL SVCS
625 Eden Park Dr Ste 500 (45202-6016)
PHONE...................................614 659-1000
Paul Berg, *Mgr*
EMP: 96
SALES (corp-wide): 3.09B **Privately Held**
Web: www.tiaa.org
SIC: 8742 Financial consultant
HQ: Tiaa-Cref Individual & Institutional
 Services, Llc
 730 3rd Ave Ste 2a
 New York NY 10017

(G-3479)
TIGERSPIKE INC
201 E 4th St Ste 400 (45202-4243)
PHONE...................................646 330-4636
Luke W Janssen, *CEO*
Matthew Turnbull, *
◆ **EMP:** 30 **EST:** 2008
SALES (est): 4.88MM
SALES (corp-wide): 7.11B **Publicly Held**
Web: www.concentrix.com
SIC: 7311 Advertising agencies
HQ: Concentrix Solutions Corporation
 3750 Monroe Ave
 Pittsford NY 14534

(G-3480)
TILE SHOP LLC
Also Called: Rucker & Sill
11973 Lebanon Rd (45241-1701)
PHONE...................................513 554-4435
Chad Hoffman, *Brnch Mgr*
EMP: 30
SALES (corp-wide): 377.15MM **Publicly Held**
Web: www.tileshop.com
SIC: 1743 Tile installation, ceramic
HQ: The Tile Shop Llc
 14000 Carlson Pkwy
 Plymouth MN 55441
 763 541-1444

(G-3481)
TK ELEVATOR CORPORATION
934 Dalton Ave (45203-1102)
PHONE...................................513 241-6000
TOLL FREE: 888
Tom Zwick, *Brnch Mgr*
EMP: 154
SALES (corp-wide): 2.67MM **Privately Held**
Web: www.thyssenkruppelevator.com
SIC: 1796 7699 Elevator installation and conversion; Elevators: inspection, service, and repair
HQ: Tk Elevator Corporation
 788 Cir 75 Pkwy Se # 500
 Atlanta GA 30339
 678 319-3240

(G-3482)
TMI ELECTRICAL CONTRACTORS INC
Also Called: T M I
423 W Wyoming Ave (45215-3001)
PHONE...................................513 821-9900
EMP: 35 **EST:** 1983
SALES (est): 6.05MM **Privately Held**
Web: www.tmiss.net
SIC: 1731 General electrical contractor

(G-3483)
TOTAL HOMECARE SOLUTIONS LLC
4010 Executive Park Dr Ste 200 (45241-4042)
PHONE...................................513 277-0915
Adam Shoemaker, *
EMP: 50 **EST:** 2007
SALES (est): 5.62MM **Privately Held**
Web: www.thshomecare.com
SIC: 8082 Home health care services

(G-3484)
TOTAL MAINTENANCE SOLUTION INC
155 Tri County Pkwy Ste 105 (45246-3238)
PHONE...................................513 770-0925
Leroy Owens, *Pr*
EMP: 35 **EST:** 2010
SALES (est): 963.4K **Privately Held**
Web: www.tmswebinfo.com
SIC: 7349 Cleaning service, industrial or commercial

(G-3485)
TOTAL QUALITY LOGISTICS LLC
5130 Glencrossing Way Ste 3 (45238)
PHONE...................................513 831-2600
Joe Myers, *Brnch Mgr*
EMP: 76
SALES (corp-wide): 8.85B **Privately Held**
Web: www.tql.com
SIC: 4731 Truck transportation brokers
HQ: Total Quality Logistics, Llc
 4289 Ivy Pointe Blvd
 Cincinnati OH 45245

(G-3486)
TOUCHSTONE ADVISORS INC
221 E 4th St Ste 300 (45202-4124)
PHONE...................................800 638-8194
Jared Jenkins, *Prin*
EMP: 34 **EST:** 1993
SALES (est): 533.03K **Privately Held**
Web: www.westernsouthern.com
SIC: 6722 Money market mutual funds
HQ: The Western & Southern Life Insurance Company
 400 Broadway Mail Stop G
 Cincinnati OH 45202
 513 629-1800

(G-3487)
TOWARD INDEPENDENCE INC
Also Called: James Bower Home
5021 Oaklawn Dr (45227-1433)
PHONE...................................513 531-0804
EMP: 205
SALES (corp-wide): 15.46MM **Privately Held**
Web: www.ti-inc.org
SIC: 8361 Retarded home
PA: Toward Independence, Inc.
 81 E Main St
 Xenia OH 45385
 937 376-3996

(G-3488)
TOWNE BUILDING GROUP INC (PA)
1055 Saint Paul Pl (45202-6042)
PHONE...................................513 381-8696
Neil K Bortz, *Pr*
Max L Wiseman, *VP*
Philip T Montanus, *Prin*
Marvin Rosenberg, *Prin*
EMP: 65 **EST:** 1974
SQ FT: 2,000
SALES (est): 13.3MM
SALES (corp-wide): 13.3MM **Privately Held**
Web: www.towneprop.com

SIC: 1522 Apartment building construction

(G-3489)
TOWNE DEVELOPMENT GROUP LTD
1055 Saint Paul Pl Ste 300 (45202-6042)
PHONE...................................513 381-8696
Marvin Rosenberg, *
EMP: 32 **EST:** 1994
SQ FT: 1,200
SALES (est): 2.9MM **Privately Held**
SIC: 6552 1521 Land subdividers and developers, residential; New construction, single-family houses

(G-3490)
TOWNE PROPERTIES ASSET MGT (PA)
Also Called: Towne Properties Asset MGT
1055 Saint Paul Pl Ste 100 (45202-1687)
PHONE...................................513 381-8696
Bob Wahlke, *Pr*
Robert Wahlke, *
Phil Montanus, *
Neil Bortz, *
Robert E Wildermuth, *Prin*
EMP: 100 **EST:** 1989
SQ FT: 5,000
SALES (est): 23.73MM **Privately Held**
Web: www.towneproperties.com
SIC: 6513 Apartment building operators

(G-3491)
TOWNE PROPERTIES ASSOC INC
Also Called: Indian Creek Apartments
5701 Kugler Mill Rd (45236-2039)
PHONE...................................513 793-6976
Eric Grol, *Mgr*
EMP: 43
SALES (corp-wide): 33.35MM **Privately Held**
Web: www.towneprop.com
SIC: 6513 Apartment building operators
PA: Towne Properties Associates, Inc.
 1055 Saint Paul Pl # 100
 Cincinnati OH 45202
 513 381-8696

(G-3492)
TOWNE PROPERTIES ASSOC INC
Also Called: Towne Management Realty
11340 Montgomery Rd Ste 202 (45249-2377)
P.O. Box 691650 (45269-0001)
PHONE...................................513 489-4059
Char Ostholthoff, *Mgr*
EMP: 58
SALES (corp-wide): 33.35MM **Privately Held**
Web: www.towneprop.com
SIC: 6513 Apartment building operators
PA: Towne Properties Associates, Inc.
 1055 Saint Paul Pl # 100
 Cincinnati OH 45202
 513 381-8696

(G-3493)
TOWNE PROPERTIES ASSOC INC
11840 Kemper Springs Dr Ste C (45240-4130)
PHONE...................................513 874-3737
Wil Browning, *Mgr*
EMP: 57
SALES (corp-wide): 33.35MM **Privately Held**
Web: www.towneprop.com
SIC: 6513 6514 6531 Apartment building operators; Dwelling operators, except apartments; Real estate agents and managers
PA: Towne Properties Associates, Inc.
 1055 Saint Paul Pl # 100

Cincinnati OH 45202
513 381-8696

(G-3494)
TOWNE PROPERTIES ASSOC INC
Also Called: Racquet Club At Harper's Point
8675 E Kemper Rd (45249-2503)
PHONE..................................513 489-9700
Laura Wagner, Prin
EMP: 71
SALES (corp-wide): 33.35MM Privately Held
Web: www.clubatharperspoint.com
SIC: 7941 Sports field or stadium operator, promoting sports events
PA: Towne Properties Associates, Inc.
 1055 Saint Paul Pl # 100
 Cincinnati OH 45202
 513 381-8696

(G-3495)
TOWNE PROPERTIES ASSOCIATES INC (PA)
1055 Saint Paul Pl (45202-1687)
PHONE..................................513 381-8696
EMP: 100 EST: 1961
SALES (est): 33.35MM
SALES (corp-wide): 33.35MM Privately Held
Web: www.towneprop.com
SIC: 7941 Sports field or stadium operator, promoting sports events

(G-3496)
TOWNEPLACE SUITES BY MARRIOTT
Also Called: TownePlace Suites By Marriott
9369 Waterstone Blvd (45249-8218)
PHONE..................................513 774-0610
Pete Pordash, Prin
EMP: 39 EST: 2007
SALES (est): 400.88K Privately Held
Web: www.marriott.com
SIC: 7011 Hotel, franchised

(G-3497)
TOWNSHIP OF COLERAIN
Also Called: Fire Dept
3360 W Galbraith Rd (45239-3969)
PHONE..................................513 741-7551
Frank W Cook, Dir
EMP: 64
Web: www.colerain.org
SIC: 9224 8011 Fire department, not including volunteer; Freestanding emergency medical center
PA: Township Of Colerain
 4200 Springdale Rd
 Cincinnati OH 45251
 513 923-5000

(G-3498)
TP MECHANICAL CONTRACTORS LLC (HQ)
Also Called: Honeywell Authorized Dealer
1500 Kemper Meadow Dr (45240-1638)
PHONE..................................513 851-8881
Scott Teepe Senior, Pr
Bill Riddle, *
Jason Ralstin, *
EMP: 145 EST: 1987
SQ FT: 3,200
SALES (est): 116.96MM Privately Held
Web: www.tpmechanical.com
SIC: 1711 Mechanical contractor
PA: Temp-Con, Llc
 15670 S Keeler St
 Olathe KS 66062

(G-3499)
TPC PACKAGING SOLUTIONS INC (PA)
Also Called: TPC Packaging Solutions
11630 Deerfield Rd (45242-1422)
P.O. Box 42413 (45242-0413)
PHONE..................................513 489-8840
John Fette, CEO
Janet F Fette, *
Cynthia L Kagrise, *
Gail B Frazier, *
Tim L Thompson, *
◆ EMP: 80 EST: 1967
SQ FT: 62,500
SALES (est): 51.68MM
SALES (corp-wide): 51.68MM Privately Held
Web: www.tpcpack.com
SIC: 5113 5084 Pressure sensitive tape; Packaging machinery and equipment

(G-3500)
TRANS-CONTINENTAL SYSTEMS INC (PA)
Also Called: TCS
1718 Ralston Ave (45223-2415)
PHONE..................................513 769-4774
Gary W Stone, Prin
EMP: 30 EST: 1983
SALES (est): 8.33MM
SALES (corp-wide): 8.33MM Privately Held
Web: www.tcsohio.com
SIC: 4213 Trucking, except local

(G-3501)
TRANS-STATES EXPRESS INC
7750 Reinhold Dr (45237-2806)
PHONE..................................513 679-7100
William Edmund, Pr
Mary Edmund, *
EMP: 70 EST: 1982
SQ FT: 23,000
SALES (est): 4.93MM Privately Held
Web: www.transstatesexpress.com
SIC: 4213 4212 Contract haulers; Local trucking, without storage

(G-3502)
TRAVELERS PROPERTY CSLTY CORP
Also Called: Travelers Insurance
615 Elsinore Pl Bldg B (45202-1459)
PHONE..................................513 639-5300
Bruce Brizzi, Mgr
EMP: 178
SALES (corp-wide): 41.36B Publicly Held
Web: www.travelers.com
SIC: 6411 Insurance agents, nec
HQ: Travelers Property Casualty Insurance Company
 1 Tower Sq
 Hartford CT 06183

(G-3503)
TRI STATE URLOGIC SVCS PSC INC (PA)
Also Called: Urology Group
2000 Joseph E Sanker Blvd (45212)
PHONE..................................513 841-7400
Earl L Walz, CEO
EMP: 100 EST: 2010
SALES (est): 25.35MM
SALES (corp-wide): 25.35MM Privately Held
Web: www.urologygroup.com
SIC: 8011 Medical centers

(G-3504)
TRI STATE UROLOGIC SVCS PSC
Also Called: Urology Group
2450 Kipling Ave Ste G11 (45239-6650)
PHONE..................................513 681-2700
Debbie Livesay, Mgr
EMP: 126
Web: www.urologygroup.com
SIC: 8011 Urologist
PA: Tri State Urologic Services P.S.C., Inc
 350 Thomas More Pkwy
 Crestview Hills KY 41017

(G-3505)
TRI-STATE WHOLESALE BUILDING SUPPLIES INC
651 Evans St (45204)
PHONE..................................513 381-1231
EMP: 34 EST: 1970
SALES (est): 10.17MM Privately Held
Web: www.tri-statewholesale.com
SIC: 5023 Window covering parts and accessories

(G-3506)
TRIHEALTH INC
Also Called: Rudemiller Family Medicine
6350 Glenway Ave Ste 300 (45211-6380)
PHONE..................................513 481-9700
EMP: 407
Web: www.trihealth.com
SIC: 8011 Pediatrician
HQ: Trihealth, Inc.
 625 Eden Park Dr
 Cincinnati OH 45202
 513 569-5400

(G-3507)
TRIHEALTH INC
Also Called: Queen Cy Physcans Wstn Rdge In
6949 Good Samaritan Dr Ste 210 (45247-5205)
PHONE..................................513 931-2400
EMP: 122
Web: www.trihealth.com
SIC: 8011 General and family practice, physician/surgeon
HQ: Trihealth, Inc.
 625 Eden Park Dr
 Cincinnati OH 45202
 513 569-5400

(G-3508)
TRIHEALTH INC
Also Called: Dr Heuker
3260 Westbourne Dr (45248-5107)
PHONE..................................513 389-1400
EMP: 122
Web: www.trihealth.com
SIC: 8011 Offices and clinics of medical doctors
HQ: Trihealth, Inc.
 625 Eden Park Dr
 Cincinnati OH 45202
 513 569-5400

(G-3509)
TRIHEALTH INC
Also Called: Trihelth Orthpaedic Spine Inst
8311 Montgomery Rd (45236-2227)
PHONE..................................513 985-3700
Carol Ann Mackey, Prin
EMP: 163
Web: www.trihealth.com
SIC: 8733 Noncommercial research organizations
HQ: Trihealth, Inc.
 625 Eden Park Dr
 Cincinnati OH 45202
 513 569-5400

(G-3510)
TRIHEALTH INC
6909 Good Samaritan Dr Ste A (45247-5208)
PHONE..................................513 246-7000
EMP: 163
Web: www.trihealth.com
SIC: 8733 Noncommercial research organizations
HQ: Trihealth, Inc.
 625 Eden Park Dr
 Cincinnati OH 45202
 513 569-5400

(G-3511)
TRIHEALTH INC
1150 W 8th St Ste 120 (45203-1200)
PHONE..................................513 241-4135
Lisa Heine, Brnch Mgr
EMP: 81
Web: www.trihealth.com
SIC: 8741 Management services
HQ: Trihealth, Inc.
 625 Eden Park Dr
 Cincinnati OH 45202
 513 569-5400

(G-3512)
TRIHEALTH INC
Also Called: Senior Behaviroal Health
375 Dixmyth Ave (45220-2475)
PHONE..................................513 569-6777
Sue Harlow, Mgr
EMP: 1423
Web: www.trihealth.com
SIC: 8741 8093 Hospital management; Mental health clinic, outpatient
HQ: Trihealth, Inc.
 625 Eden Park Dr
 Cincinnati OH 45202
 513 569-5400

(G-3513)
TRIHEALTH INC
2753 Erie Ave (45208-2204)
PHONE..................................513 871-2340
EMP: 81
Web: www.trihealth.com
SIC: 8741 Hospital management
HQ: Trihealth, Inc.
 625 Eden Park Dr
 Cincinnati OH 45202
 513 569-5400

(G-3514)
TRIHEALTH INC
Also Called: Group Health Associates
7810 5 Mile Rd (45230-2356)
PHONE..................................513 624-5558
EMP: 488
Web: www.cgha.com
SIC: 8062 General medical and surgical hospitals
HQ: Trihealth, Inc.
 625 Eden Park Dr
 Cincinnati OH 45202
 513 569-5400

(G-3515)
TRIHEALTH INC
Also Called: Western Family Physicians
3425 North Bend Rd Ste A (45239-7660)
PHONE..................................513 853-4900
R Stephen Eby, Pr
Lisbeth Lazaron, VP
Jean Siebenaler, Ofcr
Richard Goldfarb, Ofcr
Lisa Cantor, Ofcr
EMP: 36 EST: 1989
SQ FT: 2,000
SALES (est): 1.07MM Privately Held

Cincinnati - Hamilton County (G-3516)

Web: www.trihealth.com
SIC: 8011 General and family practice, physician/surgeon

(G-3516)
TRIHEALTH INC
400 Martin Luther King Dr (45229-3314)
PHONE................................513 751-5900
Paulette Schalck, Brnch Mgr
EMP: 122
Web: www.trihealth.com
SIC: 8049 Midwife
HQ: Trihealth, Inc.
 625 Eden Park Dr
 Cincinnati OH 45202
 513 569-5400

(G-3517)
TRIHEALTH INC (HQ)
Also Called: Trihealth
625 Eden Park Dr (45202-6005)
PHONE................................513 569-5400
Mark Clement, CEO
John Prout, *
Joe Kessler, *
Claus Vonzychlin, *
William Groneman, *
EMP: 50 EST: 1994
SALES (est): 519.59MM Privately Held
Web: www.trihealth.com
SIC: 8062 8741 General medical and surgical hospitals; Hospital management
PA: Commonspirit Health
 444 W Lake St Ste 2500
 Chicago IL 60606

(G-3518)
TRIHEALTH INC
4030 Smith Rd (45209-1969)
PHONE................................513 221-4848
EMP: 203
Web: www.trihealth.com
SIC: 8099 Childbirth preparation clinic
HQ: Trihealth, Inc.
 625 Eden Park Dr
 Cincinnati OH 45202
 513 569-5400

(G-3519)
TRIHEALTH EVENDALE HOSPITAL (DH)
3155 Glendale Milford Rd (45241-3134)
PHONE................................513 454-2222
Ajay Mangal, Pr
EMP: 166 EST: 2003
SALES (est): 26.73MM Privately Held
Web: www.trihealth.com
SIC: 8062 General medical and surgical hospitals
HQ: Trihealth, Inc.
 625 Eden Park Dr
 Cincinnati OH 45202
 513 569-5400

(G-3520)
TRIHEALTH G LLC (DH)
Also Called: Group Health Associates
4600 Wesley Ave Ste N (45212-2274)
PHONE................................513 732-0700
Donna Nienaber, Corporate Counsel
EMP: 75 EST: 1974
SQ FT: 50,000
SALES (est): 92.39MM Privately Held
Web: www.cgha.com
SIC: 8011 Physicians' office, including specialists
HQ: Trihealth, Inc.
 625 Eden Park Dr
 Cincinnati OH 45202
 513 569-5400

(G-3521)
TRIHEALTH G LLC
Also Called: Trihelth Wns Svcs Advnced Gync
3219 Clifton Ave Ste 100 (45220-3035)
PHONE................................513 862-1888
Mark Clement, Managing Member
EMP: 130
Web: www.trihealth.com
SIC: 8011 Physicians' office, including specialists
HQ: Trihealth G, Llc
 4600 Wesley Ave Ste N
 Cincinnati OH 45212
 513 732-0700

(G-3522)
TRIHEALTH G LLC
Also Called: Group Health Associates
2001 Anderson Ferry Rd (45238-3325)
PHONE................................513 922-1200
EMP: 29
Web: www.cgha.com
SIC: 8049 8011 Physical therapist; Offices and clinics of medical doctors
HQ: Trihealth G, Llc
 4600 Wesley Ave Ste N
 Cincinnati OH 45212
 513 732-0700

(G-3523)
TRIHEALTH G LLC
Also Called: Northcreek Family Practice
8240 Northcreek Dr (45236-2377)
PHONE................................513 792-4700
Donna Nienaber, VP
EMP: 29
Web: www.trihealth.com
SIC: 8011 General and family practice, physician/surgeon
HQ: Trihealth G, Llc
 4600 Wesley Ave Ste N
 Cincinnati OH 45212
 513 732-0700

(G-3524)
TRIHEALTH ONCOLOGY INST LLC
Also Called: Oncology Partners Network
5520 Cheviot Rd (45247-7069)
PHONE................................513 451-4033
Richard Louis Meyer, Managing Member
J Bhaskaran, *
EMP: 55 EST: 1963
SQ FT: 1,900
SALES (est): 1.64MM Privately Held
Web: www.trihealth.com
SIC: 8011 Oncologist

(G-3525)
TRIHEALTH OS LLC (DH)
Also Called: Trihealth Orthpd & Spine Inst
8311 Montgomery Rd (45236-2227)
PHONE................................513 985-3700
Jay Koch, Ex Dir
EMP: 41 EST: 2012
SALES (est): 8.52MM Privately Held
Web: www.trihealth.com
SIC: 8099 8011 Medical services organization; Offices and clinics of medical doctors
HQ: Trihealth, Inc.
 625 Eden Park Dr
 Cincinnati OH 45202
 513 569-5400

(G-3526)
TRIHEALTH REHABILITATION HOSP
Also Called: SELECT PHYSICAL THEREPAHY AND
2155 Dana Ave (45207-1340)
P.O. Box 2034 (17055-0793)
PHONE................................513 601-0600
Mark Asmen, CEO
EMP: 113 EST: 2016
SALES (est): 29.3MM
SALES (corp-wide): 6.2B Publicly Held
Web: www.trihealthrehab.com
SIC: 8322 Rehabilitation services
HQ: Select Medical Corporation
 4714 Gettysburg Rd
 Mechanicsburg PA 17055
 717 972-1100

(G-3527)
TRIO TRUCKING INC
7750 Reinhold Dr (45237-2806)
PHONE................................513 679-7100
EMP: 73
SALES (corp-wide): 9.66MM Privately Held
Web: www.trioenterprises.com
SIC: 4213 4212 Trucking, except local; Local trucking, without storage
PA: Trio Trucking, Inc.
 7750 Reinhold Dr
 Cincinnati OH 45237
 513 679-7100

(G-3528)
TRIVERSITY CONSTRUCTION CO LLC
Also Called: Triversity Construction
921 Curtis St (45206-2618)
PHONE................................513 733-0046
Melvin Gravely, Managing Member
EMP: 95 EST: 2005
SALES (est): 17.54MM Privately Held
Web: www.trivc.com
SIC: 8741 Construction management

(G-3529)
TRK INVESTMENTS MONTGOMERY LLC
3045 Williams Creek Dr (45244-3257)
PHONE................................513 388-0186
EMP: 45 EST: 2017
SALES (est): 850.74K Privately Held
SIC: 7349 Building maintenance services, nec

(G-3530)
TROY STRAUSS CO LPA
150 E 4th St (45202-4186)
PHONE................................513 621-2120
EMP: 110 EST: 1953
SALES (est): 4.98MM Privately Held
Web: www.strausstroy.com
SIC: 8111 General practice law office

(G-3531)
TRUCARE PROVIDER SERVICES LLC
3600 Park 42 Dr Ste 3670 (45241)
P.O. Box 259 (45040)
PHONE................................513 201-5611
Kelly Lemuel, Pr
EMP: 133 EST: 2018
SALES (est): 3.79MM Privately Held
Web: www.trucareproviderservices.com
SIC: 8082 Home health care services

(G-3532)
TRUPARTNER CREDIT UNION INC (PA)
1717 Western Ave (45214-2007)
PHONE................................513 241-2050
William A Herring, Pr
EMP: 35 EST: 1937
SQ FT: 15,000
SALES (est): 7.84MM
SALES (corp-wide): 7.84MM Privately Held
Web: www.trupartnercu.org
SIC: 6061 Federal credit unions

(G-3533)
TRUST PROCESSING
11804 Conrey Rd (45249-1072)
PHONE................................513 774-8805
EMP: 27 EST: 2018
SALES (est): 216.38K Privately Held
Web: www.trustprocessing.com
SIC: 6733 Trusts, nec

(G-3534)
TSC APPAREL LLC (HQ)
Also Called: T-Shirt City
10856 Reed Hartman Hwy Ste 150 (45242-0229)
PHONE................................800 289-5400
Rick Mouty, CEO
Bob Winget, *
Denny Blazer, *
▲ EMP: 55 EST: 2000
SALES (est): 47.12MM
SALES (corp-wide): 522.19MM Privately Held
SIC: 5699 5137 T-shirts, custom printed; Sportswear, women's and children's
PA: S&S Activewear, Llc
 220 Remington Blvd Fl 3
 Bolingbrook IL 60440
 630 679-9940

(G-3535)
TURNBULL-WAHLERT CONSTRUCTION INC
5533 Fair Ln (45227-3414)
PHONE................................513 731-7300
EMP: 70 EST: 1995
SALES (est): 9.34MM Privately Held
Web: www.turnbull-wahlert.com
SIC: 8741 1542 1522 Construction management; Nonresidential construction, nec; Remodeling, multi-family dwellings

(G-3536)
TURNER CONSTRUCTION COMPANY
250 W Court St Ste 300w (45202-1095)
PHONE................................513 721-4224
Kenneth Butler, Brnch Mgr
EMP: 200
SQ FT: 7,000
Web: www.turnerconstruction.com
SIC: 1541 1542 1522 Industrial buildings, new construction, nec; Commercial and office building, new construction; Multi-family dwellings, new construction
HQ: Turner Construction Company Inc
 66 Hudson Blvd E
 New York NY 10001
 212 229-6000

(G-3537)
TURNKEY TECHNOLOGY LLC
6813 Harrison Ave (45247-3203)
PHONE................................513 725-2177
Chris Gherardini, Pr
EMP: 45 EST: 2021
SALES (est): 4.66MM
SALES (corp-wide): 686.58MM Privately Held
Web: www.turnkeyt.com
SIC: 7382 1731 Security systems services; Electrical work
PA: Pavion Corp.
 4151 Lafayette Center Dr # 70
 Chantilly VA 20151
 703 631-3377

GEOGRAPHIC SECTION
Cincinnati - Hamilton County (G-3560)

(G-3538)
TWG STAFFING LLC
Also Called: Vero Rn
8280 Montgomery Rd Ste 205 (45236-6101)
P.O. Box 49160 (45449-0160)
PHONE.................................877 293-3670
Brittany Rider, *CEO*
Charlene Adkins, *
EMP: 216 **EST:** 2016
SALES (est): 8.71MM **Privately Held**
Web: www.verorn.com
SIC: 7361 Nurses' registry

(G-3539)
TWISM ENTERPRISES LLC
Also Called: Valucadd Solutions
12110 Regency Run Ct Apt 9 (45240-1073)
PHONE.................................513 800-1098
EMP: 50 **EST:** 2016
SALES (est): 1.18MM **Privately Held**
SIC: 8712 8711 7373 8748 Architectural engineering; Mechanical engineering; Computer-aided engineering (CAE) systems service; Telecommunications consultant

(G-3540)
UBS FINANCIAL SERVICES INC
312 Walnut St Ste 3300 (45202-4045)
PHONE.................................513 576-5000
TOLL FREE: 800
Daniel Driscoll, *Mgr*
EMP: 39
SQ FT: 3,500
Web: www.ubs.com
SIC: 6211 Stock brokers and dealers
HQ: Ubs Financial Services Inc.
1200 Harbor Blvd
Weehawken NJ 07086
212 713-2000

(G-3541)
UC HEALTH LLC
3200 Burnet Ave (45229-3019)
PHONE.................................513 585-7600
Donald Kegg, *CEO*
EMP: 51
Web: www.uchealth.com
SIC: 6324 Health Maintenance Organization (HMO), insurance only
PA: Uc Health, Llc.
3200 Burnet Ave
Cincinnati OH 45229

(G-3542)
UC HEALTH LLC
222 Piedmont Ave Ste 6000 (45219-4223)
PHONE.................................513 475-7880
EMP: 85
Web: www.uchealth.com
SIC: 8011 Internal medicine, physician/ surgeon
PA: Uc Health, Llc.
3200 Burnet Ave
Cincinnati OH 45229

(G-3543)
UC HEALTH LLC
Also Called: Uc Helth Cncnnati Arthrtis Ass
3590 Lucille Dr Ste 1000 (45213-2675)
PHONE.................................513 271-5111
EMP: 51
Web: www.uchealth.com
SIC: 8011 Internal medicine, physician/ surgeon
PA: Uc Health, Llc.
3200 Burnet Ave
Cincinnati OH 45229

(G-3544)
UC HEALTH LLC
11590 Century Blvd Ste 102 (45246-3317)
PHONE.................................513 648-9077
EMP: 85
Web: www.uchealth.com
SIC: 8011 Internal medicine, physician/ surgeon
PA: Uc Health, Llc.
3200 Burnet Ave
Cincinnati OH 45229

(G-3545)
UC HEALTH LLC
Also Called: Alliance Health
3120 Burnet Ave Ste 203 (45229-3091)
PHONE.................................513 584-8600
James Peters, *Ex Dir*
EMP: 119
Web: www.uchealth.com
SIC: 8741 8062 Management services; General medical and surgical hospitals
PA: Uc Health, Llc.
3200 Burnet Ave
Cincinnati OH 45229

(G-3546)
UC HEALTH LLC (PA)
3200 Burnet Ave (45229-3019)
PHONE.................................513 585-6000
EMP: 800 **EST:** 1995
SALES (est): 1.7B **Privately Held**
Web: www.uchealth.com
SIC: 8741 8011 8733 Hospital management; Medical centers; Medical research

(G-3547)
UC HEALTH PARTNERS LLC
Also Called: Uc Health Varsity Vlg Imaging
222 Piedmont Ave (45219-4231)
PHONE.................................513 475-8524
EMP: 36 **EST:** 2009
SALES (est): 1.99MM **Privately Held**
Web: www.uchealth.com
SIC: 8011 Offices and clinics of medical doctors

(G-3548)
ULMER & BERNE LLP
600 Vine St Ste 2800 (45202-2409)
PHONE.................................513 698-5000
Scott Kadish, *Mgr*
EMP: 42
SALES (corp-wide): 50.31MM **Privately Held**
Web: www.ubglaw.com
SIC: 8111 General practice law office
PA: Ulmer & Berne Llp
1660 W 2nd St Ste 1100
Cleveland OH 44113
216 583-7000

(G-3549)
ULTIMUS FUND SOLUTIONS LLC (PA)
225 Pictoria Dr Ste 450 (45246-1617)
PHONE.................................513 587-3400
Gary Tenkman, *CEO*
Ian Martin, *
Michael K Neborak, *
EMP: 46 **EST:** 1999
SQ FT: 21,900
SALES (est): 24.16MM
SALES (corp-wide): 24.16MM **Privately Held**
Web: www.ultimusfundsolutions.com
SIC: 6799 Investors, nec

(G-3550)
UNION SAVINGS BANK (PA)
8534 E Kemper Rd Fl 1 (45249)
PHONE.................................513 247-0300
Chelen Reyes, *Pr*
Harry G Yeaggy, *Pr*
Robert Bogenschutz, *Sr VP*
Keith Wirtz, *CIO*
Richard Sweet, *Sr VP*
EMP: 46 **EST:** 1904
SQ FT: 30,000
SALES (est): 254.41MM
SALES (corp-wide): 254.41MM **Privately Held**
Web: www.usavingsbank.com
SIC: 6022 State commercial banks

(G-3551)
UNITED - MAIER SIGNS INC
1030 Straight St (45214-1734)
PHONE.................................513 681-6600
Antony E Maier, *Pr*
Elvera Maier, *
EMP: 54 **EST:** 1964
SQ FT: 18,000
SALES (est): 4.68MM **Privately Held**
Web: www.united-maier.com
SIC: 3993 1799 Electric signs; Sign installation and maintenance

(G-3552)
UNITED AUDIT SYSTEMS INC
Also Called: Uasi
1924 Dana Ave (45207-1212)
PHONE.................................513 723-1122
Ty C Hare, *Pr*
John De Fraites, *
Frank Kerley, *
Beverly J Bredenfoerder, *
Mary Stanfill, *
EMP: 206 **EST:** 1984
SQ FT: 16,000
SALES (est): 25.95MM **Privately Held**
Web: www.uasisolutions.com
SIC: 8742 Hospital and health services consultant

(G-3553)
UNITED DAIRY FARMERS INC (PA)
Also Called: U D F
3955 Montgomery Rd (45212-3798)
PHONE.................................513 396-8700
Brad Lindner, *Pr*
Marilyn Mitchell, *
EMP: 200 **EST:** 1940
SALES (est): 446.66MM
SALES (corp-wide): 446.66MM **Privately Held**
Web: www.udfinc.com
SIC: 5411 5143 2026 2024 Convenience stores, chain; Ice cream and ices; Milk processing (pasteurizing, homogenizing, bottling); Ice cream and ice milk

(G-3554)
UNITED HEALTHCARE OHIO INC
Also Called: United Healthcare
400 E Business Way Ste 100 (45241)
PHONE.................................513 603-6200
EMP: 67
SALES (corp-wide): 371.62B **Publicly Held**
Web: www.unitedhealthgroup.com
SIC: 6324 Health Maintenance Organization (HMO), insurance only
HQ: United Healthcare Of Ohio, Inc.
9200 Worthington Rd
Columbus OH 43085
614 410-7000

(G-3555)
UNITED PARCEL SERVICE INC
Also Called: UPS
500 Gest St (45203-1717)
PHONE.................................513 852-6135
EMP: 1207
SALES (corp-wide): 90.96B **Publicly Held**
Web: www.ups.com
SIC: 4215 Parcel delivery, vehicular
HQ: United Parcel Service, Inc.
55 Glenlake Pkwy
Atlanta GA 30328
404 828-6000

(G-3556)
UNITED PARCEL SERVICE INC
Also Called: UPS
640 W 3rd St (45202-3483)
PHONE.................................513 241-5289
EMP: 144
SALES (corp-wide): 90.96B **Publicly Held**
Web: www.ups.com
SIC: 4215 Parcel delivery, vehicular
HQ: United Parcel Service, Inc.
55 Glenlake Pkwy
Atlanta GA 30328
404 828-6000

(G-3557)
UNITED PARCEL SERVICE INC
Also Called: UPS
11141 Canal Rd (45241-1861)
PHONE.................................513 782-4000
EMP: 175
SALES (corp-wide): 90.96B **Publicly Held**
Web: www.ups.com
SIC: 4215 Parcel delivery, vehicular
HQ: United Parcel Service, Inc.
55 Glenlake Pkwy
Atlanta GA 30328
404 828-6000

(G-3558)
UNITED WAY GREATER CINCINNATI (PA)
Also Called: UNITED WAY
2400 Reading Rd (45202-1458)
PHONE.................................513 762-7100
Moira Weir, *Pr*
Yvonne L Gray, *
EMP: 100 **EST:** 1920
SQ FT: 70,000
SALES (est): 46.66MM
SALES (corp-wide): 46.66MM **Privately Held**
Web: www.uwgc.org
SIC: 8322 Social service center

(G-3559)
UNIV DERMATOLOGY
Also Called: Uc Health Dermatology
5575 Cheviot Rd Ste 1 (45247-7097)
PHONE.................................513 475-7630
Raymond Ringenbach Md, *Pr*
Br Brian Adams, *Pr*
EMP: 39 **EST:** 1978
SALES (est): 451.97K **Privately Held**
SIC: 8011 8093 Dermatologist; Specialty outpatient clinics, nec

(G-3560)
UNIVERSAL ADVG ASSOC INC
Also Called: Business Community Section
2530 Civic Center Dr (45231-1310)
P.O. Box 31132 (45231-0132)
PHONE.................................513 522-5000
Larry Vonderhaar, *Pr*
EMP: 49 **EST:** 1976
SQ FT: 7,500
SALES (est): 3.19MM **Privately Held**
Web: www.uaai.com

(PA)=Parent Co (HQ)=Headquarters
✪ = New Business established in last 2 years

Cincinnati - Hamilton County (G-3561)

SIC: **7311** 8611 Advertising consultant; Business associations

(G-3561)
UNIVERSAL CONTRACTING CORP
5151 Fishwick Dr (45216-2215)
PHONE.................................513 482-2700
Phillip J Neumann, *Pr*
EMP: 30 **EST:** 1957
SQ FT: 7,500
SALES (est): 10.02MM **Privately Held**
Web: www.unicon.cc
SIC: **1541** 1542 Industrial buildings, new construction, nec; Commercial and office building, new construction

(G-3562)
UNIVERSAL LAWNCARE LLC
1452 Waycross Rd (45240-2922)
PHONE.................................513 289-9391
EMP: 29
SALES (corp-wide): 28.84K **Privately Held**
SIC: **0782** Lawn care services
PA: Universal Lawncare Llc
  138 Hanover St
  Hamilton OH 45011
  513 805-5831

(G-3563)
UNIVERSAL PACKG SYSTEMS INC
Also Called: Paklab
470 Northland Blvd (45240-3211)
PHONE.................................513 674-9400
Jeff Topits, *Brnch Mgr*
EMP: 158
SALES (corp-wide): 379.38MM **Privately Held**
Web: www.paklab.com
SIC: **2844** 7389 3565 2671 Cosmetic preparations; Packaging and labeling services; Bottling machinery: filling, capping, labeling; Plastic film, coated or laminated for packaging
PA: Universal Packaging Systems, Inc.
  14570 Monte Vista Ave
  Chino CA 91710
  909 517-2442

(G-3564)
UNIVERSITY CNCNNATI MED CTR LL (HQ)
234 Goodman St (45219-2359)
PHONE.................................513 584-1000
Bryan Gibler, *CEO*
▲ **EMP:** 256 **EST:** 1996
SALES (est): 362.49K **Privately Held**
Web: www.uchealth.com
SIC: **8062** General medical and surgical hospitals
PA: Uc Health, Llc.
  3200 Burnet Ave
  Cincinnati OH 45229

(G-3565)
UNIVERSITY CNCNNATI PHYSCANS I (HQ)
Also Called: Uc Physicians
222 Piedmont Ave Ste 2200 (45219-4238)
PHONE.................................513 475-8521
Myles Pensak, *CEO*
Thomas Boat, *
Peter Iacobell, *
Dan Gahl, *
David J Fine, *
EMP: 40 **EST:** 1988
SQ FT: 2,800
SALES (est): 362.54MM **Privately Held**
Web: www.uchealth.com
SIC: **8011** Offices and clinics of medical doctors
PA: Uc Health, Llc.
  3200 Burnet Ave
  Cincinnati OH 45229

(G-3566)
UNIVERSITY EAR NOSE THROAT SPC
222 Piedmont Ave Ste 5200 (45219-4222)
PHONE.................................513 475-8403
Connie Foster, *Dir*
EMP: 210 **EST:** 1992
SALES (est): 900.55K
SALES (corp-wide): 914.68MM **Privately Held**
SIC: **8011** 8221 Ears, nose, and throat specialist: physician/surgeon; University
PA: University Of Cincinnati
  2600 Clifton Ave
  Cincinnati OH 45220
  513 556-6000

(G-3567)
UNIVERSITY EAR NOSE THROAT SPC
Also Called: Uc Health
231 Albert Sabin Way 6411 (45267-2827)
P.O. Box 670528 (45267-0001)
PHONE.................................513 558-4158
Myles Pensak, *Ch*
EMP: 44 **EST:** 1986
SALES (est): 1.85MM **Privately Held**
SIC: **8069** Eye, ear, nose, and throat hospital

(G-3568)
UNIVERSITY FAMILY PHYSICIANS
2123 Auburn Ave (45219-2906)
PHONE.................................513 929-0104
Laura J Ranz, *Brnch Mgr*
EMP: 45
SIC: **8011** General and family practice, physician/surgeon
PA: University Family Physicians Inc
  3235 Eden Ave
  Cincinnati OH 45267

(G-3569)
UNIVERSITY FAMILY PHYSICIANS
Also Called: Wyoming Family Practice Center
175 W Galbraith Rd (45216-1015)
PHONE.................................513 475-7505
Elouise Clark, *Mgr*
EMP: 45
Web: www.ucphysicians.com
SIC: **8011** Internal medicine, physician/surgeon
PA: University Family Physicians Inc
  3235 Eden Ave
  Cincinnati OH 45267

(G-3570)
UNIVERSITY HOSPITAL
2264 Westwood Northern Blvd (45225)
PHONE.................................513 584-1000
Rhonda Butler, *Prin*
EMP: 84
SALES (corp-wide): 25.52MM **Privately Held**
Web: www.uhhospitals.org
SIC: **8062** General medical and surgical hospitals
PA: University Hospital
  3315 N Ridge Rd E Ste 100
  Ashtabula OH 44004
  440 964-8387

(G-3571)
UNIVERSITY NEUROLOGY INC
222 Piedmont Ave Ste 3200 (45219-4217)
PHONE.................................513 475-8730
Joseph Broderick, *Pr*
Brett Kissela, *
Bratt Kissela, *
Neil Holsing, *
EMP: 43 **EST:** 1981
SALES (est): 772.37K **Privately Held**
SIC: **8011** Neurologist

(G-3572)
UNIVERSITY OF CINCINNATI
Also Called: Department of Anesthetia
231 Albert Sabin Way (45267-2827)
PHONE.................................513 558-4194
Doctor William Hurford, *Dir*
EMP: 35
SALES (corp-wide): 914.68MM **Privately Held**
Web: www.ucblueash.edu
SIC: **8011** 8221 Offices and clinics of medical doctors; University
PA: University Of Cincinnati
  2600 Clifton Ave
  Cincinnati OH 45220
  513 556-6000

(G-3573)
UNIVERSITY OF CINCINNATI
Also Called: Blood Center
3130 Highland Ave Fl 3 (45219-2399)
P.O. Box 670055 (45267-0001)
PHONE.................................513 558-1200
Ronald Sachner, *Dir*
EMP: 400
SALES (corp-wide): 914.68MM **Privately Held**
Web: www.hoxworth.org
SIC: **8011** 8221 Offices and clinics of medical doctors; University
PA: University Of Cincinnati
  2600 Clifton Ave
  Cincinnati OH 45220
  513 556-6000

(G-3574)
UNIVERSITY OF CINCINNATI
200 Albert Sabin Way (45267-2800)
PHONE.................................513 584-0618
EMP: 60
SALES (corp-wide): 914.68MM **Privately Held**
Web: www.uc.edu
SIC: **8011** Infectious disease specialist, physician/surgeon
PA: University Of Cincinnati
  2600 Clifton Ave
  Cincinnati OH 45220
  513 556-6000

(G-3575)
UNIVERSITY OF CINCINNATI
Also Called: University Hsptl-Uc Physicians
222 Piedmont Ave Ste 7000 (45219-4224)
PHONE.................................513 475-8771
Michael Nussbaum, *CEO*
EMP: 140
SALES (corp-wide): 914.68MM **Privately Held**
Web: www.uc.edu
SIC: **8011** 8221 General and family practice, physician/surgeon; University
PA: University Of Cincinnati
  2600 Clifton Ave
  Cincinnati OH 45220
  513 556-6000

(G-3576)
UNIVERSITY OF CINCINNATI
Also Called: University Cncnnati Purch Dept
51 Goodman St Ste 320 (45219-2736)
P.O. Box 210089 (45221-0089)
PHONE.................................513 556-2389
Thomas B Guerin, *Mgr*
EMP: 60
SALES (corp-wide): 914.68MM **Privately Held**
Web: www.ucphysicians.com
SIC: **7389** 8221 Purchasing service; University
PA: University Of Cincinnati
  2600 Clifton Ave
  Cincinnati OH 45220
  513 556-6000

(G-3577)
UNIVERSITY OF CINCINNATI
Also Called: College Conservatory of Music
290 Ccm Blvd (45221-0001)
P.O. Box 210003 (45221-0003)
PHONE.................................513 556-2700
Shellie Cash, *Prin*
EMP: 70
SALES (corp-wide): 914.68MM **Privately Held**
Web: ccm.uc.edu
SIC: **7911** 8221 Dance studios, schools, and halls; University
PA: University Of Cincinnati
  2600 Clifton Ave
  Cincinnati OH 45220
  513 556-6000

(G-3578)
UNIVERSITY OF CINCINNATI
Also Called: University Hospital
234 Goodman St (45219-2359)
PHONE.................................513 584-1000
EMP: 380
SALES (corp-wide): 914.68MM **Privately Held**
Web: www.uc.edu
SIC: **8062** 8221 General medical and surgical hospitals; University
PA: University Of Cincinnati
  2600 Clifton Ave
  Cincinnati OH 45220
  513 556-6000

(G-3579)
UNIVERSITY OF CINCINNATI
Also Called: University Hosp A & MBL Care
3200 Burnet Ave (45229-3019)
PHONE.................................513 584-7522
Dudley Smith, *Prin*
EMP: 1569
SALES (corp-wide): 914.68MM **Privately Held**
Web: www.uc.edu
SIC: **8062** 8221 Hospital, medical school affiliation; University
PA: University Of Cincinnati
  2600 Clifton Ave
  Cincinnati OH 45220
  513 556-6000

(G-3580)
UNIVERSITY OF CINCINNATI
Also Called: Univ Hospital, The
331 Albert Sabin Way (45229-2838)
PHONE.................................513 584-1000
EMP: 120
SALES (corp-wide): 914.68MM **Privately Held**
Web: www.uc.edu
SIC: **8062** 8221 Hospital, medical school affiliation; University
PA: University Of Cincinnati
  2600 Clifton Ave
  Cincinnati OH 45220
  513 556-6000

(G-3581)
UNIVERSITY OF CINCINNATI
Also Called: University Hosp Rdilology Dept
234 Goodman St (45219-2359)

PHONE..........................513 584-4396
Robert Lukin Md, *Ch*
EMP: 320
SALES (corp-wide): 914.68MM **Privately Held**
Web: www.starbucks.com
SIC: 8062 8221 General medical and surgical hospitals; University
PA: University Of Cincinnati
2600 Clifton Ave
Cincinnati OH 45220
513 556-6000

(G-3582)
UNIVERSITY OF CINCINNATI
Also Called: University Cincinnati Book Str
51 W Goodman Dr (45221-0001)
PHONE..........................513 556-4200
Mike Zimmerman, *Brnch Mgr*
EMP: 140
SALES (corp-wide): 914.68MM **Privately Held**
Web: www.uc.edu
SIC: 8741 5942 Administrative management; Book stores
PA: University Of Cincinnati
2600 Clifton Ave
Cincinnati OH 45220
513 556-6000

(G-3583)
UNIVERSITY OF CINCINNATI
Also Called: Uima
231 Albert Sabin Way Ste 6065 (45267-2827)
PHONE..........................513 558-4231
Bradley Britigan, *Brnch Mgr*
EMP: 110
SALES (corp-wide): 914.68MM **Privately Held**
Web: www.uc.edu
SIC: 8741 8221 Administrative management; University
PA: University Of Cincinnati
2600 Clifton Ave
Cincinnati OH 45220
513 556-6000

(G-3584)
UNIVERSITY OF CINCINNATI
Also Called: Band, The
147 Corry Blvd Ste 2100 (45221-0001)
PHONE..........................513 556-2263
Terren Frenz, *Admn*
EMP: 50
SALES (corp-wide): 914.68MM **Privately Held**
Web: www.uc.edu
SIC: 8641 8221 Civic and social associations ; Colleges and universities
PA: University Of Cincinnati
2600 Clifton Ave
Cincinnati OH 45220
513 556-6000

(G-3585)
UNIVERSITY OF CINCINNATI
170 Panzeca Way (45267-0001)
PHONE..........................513 558-4110
EMP: 40
SALES (corp-wide): 914.68MM **Privately Held**
Web: www.uc.edu
SIC: 8734 8221 Radiation laboratories; University
PA: University Of Cincinnati
2600 Clifton Ave
Cincinnati OH 45220
513 556-6000

(G-3586)
UNIVERSITY OF CINCINNATI
Also Called: Athletics Dept
2751 O'varsity Way Ste 880 (45221-0001)
P.O. Box 210021 (45221-0021)
PHONE..........................513 556-4603
Mike Bohn, *Dir*
EMP: 200
SALES (corp-wide): 914.68MM **Privately Held**
Web: www.uc.edu
SIC: 8699 8221 Athletic organizations; University
PA: University Of Cincinnati
2600 Clifton Ave
Cincinnati OH 45220
513 556-6000

(G-3587)
UNIVERSITY OF CINCINNATI
Also Called: Endocrine Lab
3125 Eden Ave (45219-2293)
P.O. Box 670547 (45267-0001)
PHONE..........................513 558-4444
David A'lessio, *Mgr*
EMP: 200
SQ FT: 1,203
SALES (corp-wide): 914.68MM **Privately Held**
Web: www.uc.edu
SIC: 8071 8221 Medical laboratories; University
PA: University Of Cincinnati
2600 Clifton Ave
Cincinnati OH 45220
513 556-6000

(G-3588)
UNIVERSITY OF CINCINNATI
Also Called: Breast Consultation Center
234 Goodman St (45219-2364)
PHONE..........................513 584-5331
Carolyn Thomas, *Dir*
EMP: 210
SALES (corp-wide): 914.68MM **Privately Held**
Web: www.uc.edu
SIC: 8071 8221 Testing laboratories; University
PA: University Of Cincinnati
2600 Clifton Ave
Cincinnati OH 45220
513 556-6000

(G-3589)
UNIVERSITY OF CINCINNATI
Also Called: Hoxworth Blood Center
3130 Highland Ave Fl 3 (45219-2399)
PHONE..........................513 558-1243
EMP: 220
SALES (corp-wide): 914.68MM **Privately Held**
Web: www.hoxworth.org
SIC: 8099 Blood related health services
PA: University Of Cincinnati
2600 Clifton Ave
Cincinnati OH 45220
513 556-6000

(G-3590)
UNIVERSITY OF CINCINNATI
Also Called: Administration Services Dept
51 Goodman Dr (45219-2720)
P.O. Box 210080 (45221-0080)
PHONE..........................513 556-6381
James Tucker, *Dir*
EMP: 70
SALES (corp-wide): 914.68MM **Privately Held**
Web: www.uc.edu

SIC: 8221 7349 5812 0782 University; Building maintenance services, nec; Eating places; Lawn and garden services
PA: University Of Cincinnati
2600 Clifton Ave
Cincinnati OH 45220
513 556-6000

(G-3591)
UNIVERSITY OF CINCINNATI
Also Called: Ucvp For Research
2614 Mecken Cir (45221-0001)
PHONE..........................513 556-4054
Nedille Pinto, *Prin*
EMP: 70
SALES (corp-wide): 914.68MM **Privately Held**
Web: grad.uc.edu
SIC: 8221 8732 University; Educational research
PA: University Of Cincinnati
2600 Clifton Ave
Cincinnati OH 45220
513 556-6000

(G-3592)
UNIVERSITY OF CINCINNATI
Also Called: Geological Department
500 Geo Physics Bldg 5th Fl (45221-0001)
P.O. Box 2210030 (45221-0001)
PHONE..........................513 556-3732
Arnold Miller, *Prin*
EMP: 70
SALES (corp-wide): 914.68MM **Privately Held**
Web: www.uc.edu
SIC: 8221 8711 University; Engineering services
PA: University Of Cincinnati
2600 Clifton Ave
Cincinnati OH 45220
513 556-6000

(G-3593)
UNIVERSITY OF CINCINNATI
Also Called: Arlette Child Family Rese
1 Bldg (45221-0001)
P.O. Box 210105 (45221-0105)
PHONE..........................513 556-3803
EMP: 40
SALES (corp-wide): 914.68MM **Privately Held**
Web: www.uc.edu
SIC: 8322 8221 Child related social services; University
PA: University Of Cincinnati
2600 Clifton Ave
Cincinnati OH 45220
513 556-6000

(G-3594)
UNIVERSITY OF CINCINNATI
Also Called: Cancer Center
234 Goodman St (45219-2359)
PHONE..........................513 584-3200
Barbara Stumps, *Mgr*
EMP: 40
SALES (corp-wide): 914.68MM **Privately Held**
Web: www.uc.edu
SIC: 8093 8221 Specialty outpatient clinics, nec; University
PA: University Of Cincinnati
2600 Clifton Ave
Cincinnati OH 45220
513 556-6000

(G-3595)
UNIVERSITY OF CINCINNATI PHYS
2830 Victory Pkwy Ste 320 (45206-3700)
PHONE..........................513 475-7934

EMP: 165
Web: www.uchealth.com
SIC: 8011 Offices and clinics of medical doctors
HQ: University Of Cincinnati Physicians, Inc.
222 Piedmont Ave Ste 2200
Cincinnati OH 45219

(G-3596)
UNIVERSITY RADIOLOGY ASSOC
Also Called: Uc Health
222 Piedmont Ave Ste 2100 (45219-4238)
PHONE..........................513 475-8760
Karen Krebs, *Prin*
EMP: 81 **EST:** 1989
SALES (est): 1.3MM **Privately Held**
SIC: 8011 8093 Radiologist; Specialty outpatient clinics, nec

(G-3597)
UNIVERSTY OF CINCINNTI MEDCL C
222 Piedmont Ave Ste 1200 (45219-4231)
PHONE..........................513 475-8000
EMP: 2372
Web: www.uchealth.com
SIC: 8011 Medical centers
HQ: University Of Cincinnati Medical Center, Llc
3199 Highland Ave
Cincinnati OH 45219
513 584-1000

(G-3598)
UPSHIFT WORK LLC
Also Called: Upshift
2300 Montana Ave Ste 301 (45211-3890)
PHONE..........................513 813-5695
Steve Anevski, *CEO*
EMP: 201 **EST:** 2016
SALES (est): 3.28MM **Privately Held**
Web: www.upshift.work
SIC: 7372 7363 Application computer software; Temporary help service

(G-3599)
UPTOWN RENTAL PROPERTIES LLC
2718 Short Vine St (45219-2019)
PHONE..........................513 861-9394
EMP: 45 **EST:** 1988
SQ FT: 2,289
SALES (est): 11.56MM **Privately Held**
Web: www.uptownrents.com
SIC: 6513 Apartment building operators

(G-3600)
URBAN LEAG GRTER STHWSTERN OHI
3458 Reading Rd (45229-3128)
PHONE..........................513 281-9955
Eddie Koen, *Pr*
Donna Jones Baker, *
Cato Mayberry, *
EMP: 54 **EST:** 1949
SQ FT: 27,000
SALES (est): 10.02MM **Privately Held**
Web: www.ulgso.org
SIC: 8322 Social service center

(G-3601)
UROLOGY CENTER LLC
2000 Joseph E Sanker Blvd (45212-1979)
PHONE..........................513 841-7500
EMP: 38 **EST:** 1997
SALES (est): 3.32MM **Privately Held**
Web: www.urologygroup.com
SIC: 8011 Urologist

Cincinnati - Hamilton County (G-3602)

(G-3602)
UROLOGY GROUP INC
Also Called: Wonnell, Dirk M
3301 Mercy Health Blvd Ste 525
(45211-1118)
PHONE..................513 662-0222
Alan Cordell Md, *Pr*
EMP: 27 **EST:** 1970
SQ FT: 1,000
SALES (est): 2.33MM **Privately Held**
Web: www.urologygroup.com
SIC: 8011 Urologist

(G-3603)
URS GROUP INC
Also Called: URS
525 Vine St Ste 1900 (45202-3124)
PHONE..................513 651-3440
Glenn Armstrong, *Brnch Mgr*
EMP: 314
SALES (corp-wide): 14.38B **Publicly Held**
Web: www.aecom.com
SIC: 8711 Consulting engineer
HQ: Urs Group, Inc.
300 S Grand Ave Ste 900
Los Angeles CA 90071
213 593-8000

(G-3604)
US BANK NATIONAL ASSOCIATION (HQ)
Also Called: US Bank
425 Walnut St Fl 14 (45202-3989)
PHONE..................513 632-4234
Andrew Cecere, *Ch Bd*
Jodi Richard, *Vice Chairman**
Mark Runkel, *TRANSFORMATION**
Terry Dolan, *Vice Chairman**
◆ **EMP:** 1150 **EST:** 1994
SQ FT: 244,000
SALES (est): 26.54B
SALES (corp-wide): 27.4B **Publicly Held**
Web: www.usbank.com
SIC: 6021 National commercial banks
PA: U.S. Bancorp
800 Nicollet Mall
Minneapolis MN 55402
651 466-3000

(G-3605)
US HEALTHCARE SYSTEM
3200 Burnet Ave (45229-3019)
PHONE..................513 585-1821
Ajitesh Kakade, *Prin*
EMP: 67 **EST:** 2010
SALES (est): 2.2B **Privately Held**
Web: www.uchealth.com
SIC: 8011 Offices and clinics of medical doctors

(G-3606)
US INSPECTION SERVICES INC
502 W Crescentville Rd (45246-1222)
PHONE..................513 671-7073
EMP: 73
SALES (corp-wide): 1.5B **Privately Held**
Web: www.acuren.com
SIC: 7389 Inspection and testing services
HQ: U.S. Inspection Services, Inc.
7333 Paragon Rd Ste 240
Dayton OH 45459

(G-3607)
US SECURITY ASSOCIATES INC
230 Northland Blvd Ste 307 (45246-0016)
PHONE..................937 454-9035
Lisa K Crawford, *Owner*
EMP: 264
SALES (corp-wide): 946.48MM **Privately Held**
Web: www.ussecurityassociates.com
SIC: 7381 Security guard service
HQ: U.S. Security Associates, Inc.
200 Mansell Ct E Fl 5
Roswell GA 30076

(G-3608)
USI INSURANCE SERVICES NAT INC
Also Called: Nationwide
720 E Pete Rose Way Ste 400
(45202-3579)
PHONE..................513 657-3116
Dixi Blackford, *Mgr*
EMP: 42
Web: www.usi.com
SIC: 6411 Insurance agents, nec
HQ: Usi Insurance Services National, Inc.
150 N Michigan Ave Fl 41
Chicago IL 60601
866 294-2571

(G-3609)
USI INSURANCE SERVICES NAT INC
312 Elm St Fl 24 (45202-2701)
PHONE..................513 852-6300
Donald E Friedrich, *Brnch Mgr*
EMP: 47
Web: www.usi.com
SIC: 6411 Insurance agents, nec
HQ: Usi Insurance Services National, Inc.
150 N Michigan Ave Fl 41
Chicago IL 60601
866 294-2571

(G-3610)
USI MIDWEST LLC (DH)
Also Called: USI
312 Elm St Ste 24 (45202-2992)
PHONE..................513 852-6300
Tom Cassady, *Pr*
Thomas Cassady, *
Ron Eslick, *
▲ **EMP:** 111 **EST:** 1895
SQ FT: 24,000
SALES (est): 22.3MM **Privately Held**
SIC: 6411 Insurance agents, nec
HQ: Usi Service Corporation
100 Summit Lake Dr # 400
Valhalla NY 10595

(G-3611)
USIC LOCATING SERVICES LLC
3478 Hauck Rd Ste D (45241-4604)
PHONE..................513 554-0456
EMP: 49
Web: www.usicllc.com
SIC: 1623 Underground utilities contractor
HQ: Usic Locating Services, Llc
9045 River Rd Ste 200
Indianapolis IN 46240
317 575-7800

(G-3612)
VALASSIS DIRECT MAIL INC
7722 Reinhold Dr (45237-2806)
P.O. Box 6450 (41022-6450)
PHONE..................859 283-2386
Scott Scaffer, *Mgr*
EMP: 66
Web: www.vericast.com
SIC: 7331 Mailing service
HQ: Valassis Direct Mail, Inc.
15955 La Cantera Pkwy
San Antonio TX 78256
800 437-0479

(G-3613)
VALLEY INTERIOR SYSTEMS INC (PA)
Also Called: Commercial Installers
2203 Fowler St (45206-2307)
P.O. Box 68109 (45206-8109)
PHONE..................513 961-0400
Mike Strawser, *CEO*
John W Strawser Senior, *Ch*
Jeff Hudepohl, *
Marcus Taulbee, *
Jim Melaragno, *
EMP: 350 **EST:** 1981
SQ FT: 9,000
SALES (est): 54.25MM
SALES (corp-wide): 54.25MM **Privately Held**
Web: www.buildwithvalley.com
SIC: 1742 Drywall

(G-3614)
VALVOLINE LLC
3901 River Rd (45204-1033)
PHONE..................513 557-3100
James Jones, *Brnch Mgr*
EMP: 160
Web: www.valvoline.com
SIC: 7549 Lubrication service, automotive
HQ: Valvoline Llc
100 Valvoline Way
Lexington KY 40509
859 357-7777

(G-3615)
VANTAGE AGING
Also Called: Senior Employment Center
644 Linn St Ste 1200 (45203-1742)
PHONE..................513 924-9100
Atala James, *Mgr*
EMP: 417
SALES (corp-wide): 11.1MM **Privately Held**
Web: www.vantageaging.org
SIC: 8322 Senior citizens' center or association
PA: Vantage Aging
388 S Main St Ste 325
Akron OH 44311
330 253-4597

(G-3616)
VARNEY DISPATCH INC
4 Triangle Park Dr Ste 404 (45246-3401)
PHONE..................513 682-4200
Gary Varney, *Pr*
Patty Varney, *
EMP: 40 **EST:** 1987
SQ FT: 22,000
SALES (est): 1.93MM **Privately Held**
SIC: 4212 Light haulage and cartage, local

(G-3617)
VEIN CLINICS OF AMERICA INC (HQ)
8044 Montgomery Rd Ste 525 (45236)
PHONE..................630 725-2700
Alton Shader, *Pr*
Daniel Doman, *
EMP: 40 **EST:** 1982
SALES (est): 90.9MM
SALES (corp-wide): 235.57MM **Privately Held**
Web: www.veinclinics.com
SIC: 8741 8011 Management services; Offices and clinics of medical doctors
PA: Integramed America, Inc.
2 Manhattanville Rd Fl 4
Purchase NY 10577
914 253-8000

(G-3618)
VELCO INC
Also Called: Coit
10280 Chester Rd (45215-1200)
PHONE..................513 772-4226
Dennis Desserich, *Pr*
Douglas Desserich, *
EMP: 27 **EST:** 1966
SQ FT: 27,000
SALES (est): 427.41K **Privately Held**
Web: www.servaid.com
SIC: 7217 7216 Carpet and furniture cleaning on location; Drapery, curtain drycleaning

(G-3619)
VENCO VENTURO INDUSTRIES LLC (PA)
Also Called: Venco/Venturo Div
12110 Best Pl (45241-1569)
PHONE..................513 772-8448
Brett Collins, *Pr*
Mike Strittholt, *
Dave Foster, *
▲ **EMP:** 41 **EST:** 1952
SQ FT: 100,000
SALES (est): 23.07MM
SALES (corp-wide): 23.07MM **Privately Held**
Web: www.venturo.com
SIC: 3713 5012 3714 5084 Truck bodies (motor vehicles); Truck bodies; Motor vehicle parts and accessories; Cranes, industrial

(G-3620)
VERSATEX LLC
324 W 9th St (45202-2043)
PHONE..................513 639-3119
Gerald Sparkman, *Pr*
Constance A Hill, *Legal Counsel*
EMP: 40 **EST:** 2010
SQ FT: 4,000
SALES (est): 5.15MM
SALES (corp-wide): 94.54MM **Privately Held**
Web: www.versatexmsp.com
SIC: 8742 Business management consultant
PA: D.E. Foxx & Associates, Inc.
324 W 9th St Fl 5
Cincinnati OH 45202
513 621-5522

(G-3621)
VERST GROUP LOGISTICS INC
11880 Enterprise Dr (45241-1512)
PHONE..................513 772-2494
Jeff Antrobus, *Brnch Mgr*
EMP: 45
SALES (corp-wide): 183.56MM **Privately Held**
Web: www.verstlogistics.com
SIC: 4225 4731 8741 General warehousing and storage; Freight transportation arrangement; Management services
PA: Verst Group Logistics, Inc.
300 Shorland Dr
Walton KY 41094
859 485-1212

(G-3622)
VERST GROUP LOGISTICS INC
Also Called: J C Buckles Transfer Co
11700 Enterprise Dr Ste 101 (45241)
PHONE..................859 379-1207
James Stadtmiller, *Brnch Mgr*
EMP: 200
SALES (corp-wide): 183.56MM **Privately Held**
Web: www.verstlogistics.com
SIC: 4225 General warehousing and storage
PA: Verst Group Logistics, Inc.
300 Shorland Dr
Walton KY 41094
859 485-1212

GEOGRAPHIC SECTION
Cincinnati - Hamilton County (G-3646)

(G-3623)
VERST GROUP LOGISTICS INC
Zenith Logistics
98 Glendale Milford Rd (45215-1101)
PHONE..................513 782-1725
Rich Grau, *VP*
EMP: 240
SALES (corp-wide): 183.56MM **Privately Held**
Web: www.verstlogistics.com
SIC: 4225 General warehousing
PA: Verst Group Logistics, Inc.
300 Shorland Dr
Walton KY 41094
859 485-1212

(G-3624)
VERTEX COMPUTER SYSTEMS INC
11260 Chester Rd Ste 300 (45246-4051)
PHONE..................513 662-6888
Murali Swamy, *Brnch Mgr*
EMP: 250
Web: www.vertexcs.com
SIC: 7371 Computer software development
PA: Vertex Computer Systems, Inc.
6090 Royalton Rd Pmb 343
North Royalton OH 44133

(G-3625)
VESTIS CORPORATION
Also Called: Aramark
P.O. Box 12131 (45212-0131)
PHONE..................513 533-1000
Rick Lachrop, *Genl Mgr*
EMP: 121
SALES (corp-wide): 2.83B **Publicly Held**
Web: www.vestis.com
SIC: 7213 Uniform supply
PA: Vestis Corporation
500 Colonial Center Pkwy # 1
Roswell GA 30076
470 226-3655

(G-3626)
VETERAN SECURITY PATROL CO
36 E 7th St Ste 2201 (45202-4453)
PHONE..................513 381-4482
Pat Navin, *Brnch Mgr*
EMP: 132
Web: www.veteransecurity.com
SIC: 7381 Security guard service
PA: Veteran Security Patrol Co.
215 Taylor Ave
Bellevue KY 41073

(G-3627)
VETERANS HEALTH ADMINISTRATION
Also Called: Cincinnati V A Medical Center
3200 Vine St (45220-2213)
PHONE..................513 861-3100
Craig Ryan, *Dir*
EMP: 833
Web: benefits.va.gov
SIC: 8011 9451 Medical centers; Administration of veterans' affairs
HQ: Veterans Health Administration
810 Vermont Ave Nw
Washington DC 20420

(G-3628)
VETERANS OF FOREIGN WARS OF US
3318 E Sharon Rd (45241-1947)
PHONE..................513 563-6830
EMP: 62
SALES (corp-wide): 105.25MM **Privately Held**
SIC: 8641 Veterans' organization

PA: Veterans Of Foreign Wars Of The United States
406 W 34th St Fl 11
Kansas City MO 64111
816 756-3390

(G-3629)
VGP HOLDINGS LLC
3901 River Rd (45204-1033)
PHONE..................513 557-3100
EMP: 288
SIC: 5013 Automotive engines and engine parts
HQ: Vgp Holdings Llc
100 Valvoline Way Pmb 200
Lexington KY 40509
859 357-7777

(G-3630)
VINCENT & VINCENT
3237 Stanhope Ave (45211-6423)
PHONE..................513 617-2089
Tera Vincent, *Owner*
EMP: 50
SALES (est): 780.5K **Privately Held**
Web: www.svdpcincinnati.org
SIC: 8099 7389 Medical services organization; Business Activities at Non-Commercial Site

(G-3631)
VISITING NRSE ASSN OF GRTER CN (PA)
2400 Reading Rd Ste 207 (45202-1429)
PHONE..................513 345-8000
Valerie Landell, *CEO*
Trudy Schwab, *
EMP: 180 **EST:** 1917
SQ FT: 11,492
SALES (est): 8.9MM
SALES (corp-wide): 8.9MM **Privately Held**
Web: www.naiopcincinnati.org
SIC: 8082 Visiting nurse service

(G-3632)
VITAS HEALTHCARE CORPORATION
11500 Northlake Dr Ste 400 (45249-1658)
PHONE..................513 742-6310
Joe Killian, *Genl Mgr*
EMP: 114
SALES (corp-wide): 2.26B **Publicly Held**
Web: www.vitas.com
SIC: 8052 Personal care facility
HQ: Vitas Healthcare Corporation
201 S Bscyne Blvd Ste 400
Miami FL 33131
305 374-4143

(G-3633)
VOLUNTEERS OF AMERICA INC
Also Called: Ohio River Valley
644 Linn St Ste 105 (45203-1733)
PHONE..................513 381-1954
FAX: 513 381-2171
EMP: 80
SALES (corp-wide): 41.61K **Privately Held**
SIC: 8322 8361 Individual and family services; Residential care
PA: Volunteers Of America, Inc.
1660 Duke St Ste 100
Alexandria VA 22314
703 341-5000

(G-3634)
VORA SOLUTION CENTER LLC
100 Tri County Pkwy (45246-3244)
PHONE..................513 867-7277
EMP: 2100 **EST:** 2016
SALES (est): 16.03MM **Privately Held**
Web: www.vorasolutioncenter.com

SIC: 6512 Commercial and industrial building operation

(G-3635)
VORYS SATER SEYMOUR PEASE LLP
301 E 4th St Ste 3500 (45202-4257)
P.O. Box 236 (45201-0236)
PHONE..................513 723-4000
Roger Lautenhiser, *Prin*
EMP: 43
SALES (corp-wide): 133.42MM **Privately Held**
Web: www.vorys.com
SIC: 8111 General practice attorney, lawyer
PA: Vorys, Sater, Seymour And Pease Llp
52 E Gay St
Columbus OH 43215
614 464-6400

(G-3636)
W & H REALTY INC (DH)
Also Called: Holiday Inn
8044 Montgomery Rd Ste 385 (45236-2923)
PHONE..................513 891-1066
J Erik Karnfjord, *Ch Bd*
John J Slaboch, *
EMP: 50 **EST:** 1993
SALES (est): 10.57MM
SALES (corp-wide): 173.43MM **Privately Held**
Web: www.hilton.com
SIC: 7011 Hotels and motels
HQ: Winegardner & Hammons Hotel Group Llc
8044 Montgomery Rd
Cincinnati OH 45236
513 891-1066

(G-3637)
WAD INVESTMENTS OH INC (PA)
11755 Lebanon Rd (45241-2038)
PHONE..................513 891-4477
Wayne Carucci, *CEO*
Dave Neely, *
Benjamin P Kenner, *
Garry Coulier, *
EMP: 40 **EST:** 1990
SQ FT: 100,000
SALES (est): 17MM **Privately Held**
Web: www.gatewaydistribution.net
SIC: 4225 7389 General warehousing and storage; Brokers' services

(G-3638)
WAITE SCHNDER BYLESS CHSLEY LP (PA)
810 Sycamore St Fl 6 (45202-2182)
PHONE..................513 621-0267
Stanley Chesley, *Pr*
EMP: 56 **EST:** 1860
SALES (est): 2.38MM
SALES (corp-wide): 2.38MM **Privately Held**
Web: www.wsbclaw.com
SIC: 8111 General practice attorney, lawyer

(G-3639)
WALT FORD SWEENEY INC (PA)
Also Called: Quick Lane
5400 Glenway Ave (45238-3402)
PHONE..................513 347-2600
Walter J Sweeney Iii, *Pr*
Timothy W Sweeney, *
Joseph P Rouse, *
EMP: 85 **EST:** 1988
SQ FT: 78,000
SALES (est): 27.45MM
SALES (corp-wide): 27.45MM **Privately Held**

Web: www.waltsweeney.com
SIC: 5511 7538 Automobiles, new and used; General automotive repair shops

(G-3640)
WALTON HOME HEALTH CARE LLC
7225 Colerain Ave Ste 205 (45239-5329)
PHONE..................513 270-0555
Ferrah Walton, *CEO*
EMP: 35 **EST:** 2017
SALES (est): 1.16MM **Privately Held**
SIC: 8082 Home health care services

(G-3641)
WARD FINANCIAL GROUP INC
11500 Northlake Dr Ste 305 (45249-1662)
PHONE..................513 791-0303
Jeffrey J Rieder, *Pr*
Bradley C Stegman, *
EMP: 36 **EST:** 1991
SQ FT: 6,000
SALES (est): 983.92K **Privately Held**
Web: ward.aon.com
SIC: 8742 Financial consultant
HQ: Mclagan Partners, Inc.
1600 Summer St Ste 601
Stamford CT 06905
203 359-2878

(G-3642)
WAYNE SIGNER ENTERPRISES INC
Also Called: E-Z Pack
6545 Wiehe Rd (45237-4217)
PHONE..................513 841-1351
Wayne A Signer, *CEO*
Barry Schwartz, *
Barbara Signer, *
Teri Junker, *
EMP: 35 **EST:** 1948
SQ FT: 38,000
SALES (est): 5.25MM **Privately Held**
Web: www.ezpack.com
SIC: 5199 Packaging materials

(G-3643)
WCM HOLDINGS INC
11500 Canal Rd (45241-1862)
PHONE..................513 705-2100
David Herche, *CEO*
Tim Fogarty, *
Melvyn Fisher, *
▲ **EMP:** 120 **EST:** 1978
SALES (est): 10.63MM **Privately Held**
SIC: 5099 2381 3842 Safety equipment and supplies; Gloves, work: woven or knit, made from purchased materials; Clothing, fire resistant and protective

(G-3644)
WEALTH BARTLETT MANAGEMENT
600 Vine St Ste 2100 (45202-2466)
PHONE..................513 345-6217
Reagan Snyder, *Prin*
EMP: 65 **EST:** 2018
SALES (est): 4.32MM **Privately Held**
Web: www.bartlett1898.com
SIC: 6282 Investment advisory service

(G-3645)
WEGMAN COMPANY
1531 Western Ave (45214-2043)
PHONE..................513 381-1111
EMP: 92 **EST:** 2018
SALES (est): 2.3MM **Privately Held**
Web: www.wegmancompany.com
SIC: 1521 Single-family housing construction

(G-3646)
WEGMAN CONSTRUCTION COMPANY

Cincinnati - Hamilton County (G-3647)

Also Called: Wegman Company
1531 Western Ave (45214-2043)
PHONE...................513 381-1111
Scott Wegman, *Pr*
Joseph Wegman, *
Melissa Wegman, *
EMP: 50 **EST:** 1967
SQ FT: 175,000
SALES (est): 9.98MM **Privately Held**
Web: www.wegmancompany.com
SIC: 1799 7389 Office furniture installation; Relocation service

(G-3647)
WELCH HOLDINGS INC
8953 E Miami River Rd (45247-2232)
PHONE...................513 353-3220
James R Welch, *Pr*
Ronnie L Welch, *
EMP: 29 **EST:** 1955
SQ FT: 3,400
SALES (est): 1.33MM **Privately Held**
Web: www.welchsand.com
SIC: 1442 Common sand mining

(G-3648)
WELD PLUS INC
4790 River Rd (45233-1633)
PHONE...................513 941-4411
TOLL FREE: 800
Laurie Rensing, *Ch Bd*
Paul Rensing, *
EMP: 30 **EST:** 1991
SQ FT: 42,000
SALES (est): 9.31MM **Privately Held**
Web: www.weldplus.com
SIC: 5084 Welding machinery and equipment

(G-3649)
WELDCO INC
2121 Spring Grove Ave (45214-1721)
PHONE...................513 744-9353
EMP: 33
SIC: 5084 3264 Welding machinery and equipment; Porcelain electrical supplies

(G-3650)
WELLNESS RESIDENTIAL SVC LLC
260 Northland Blvd Ste 216 (45246-3651)
PHONE...................513 969-4160
Idorenyin Fred, *Prin*
EMP: 49 **EST:** 2020
SALES (est): 2.71MM **Privately Held**
SIC: 8099 Health and allied services, nec

(G-3651)
WELLS FARGO FINCL SEC SVCS INC
Also Called: Wells Fargo
8170 Corporate Park Dr (45242-3313)
PHONE...................513 530-0333
Brad Hughes, *Mgr*
EMP: 447
SALES (corp-wide): 82.86B **Publicly Held**
Web: www.wellsfargo.com
SIC: 6021 National commercial banks
HQ: Wells Fargo Financial Security Services, Inc.
800 Walnut St
Des Moines IA 50309
515 243-2131

(G-3652)
WELTMAN WEINBERG & REIS CO LPA
312 Elm St Ste 1200 (45202-3171)
PHONE...................513 723-2200
Frank Veneziano, *Mgr*
EMP: 190
SALES (corp-wide): 68.52MM **Privately Held**
Web: www.weltman.com

SIC: 8111 General practice law office
PA: Weltman, Weinberg & Reis Co., L.P.A.
965 Keynote Cir
Independence OH 44131
216 685-1000

(G-3653)
WENSMINGER HOLDINGS INC
3330 E Kemper Rd (45241-1538)
PHONE...................513 563-8822
William E Ensminger, *Pr*
Eunice Hemmert, *
Marty Grogan, *
EMP: 59 **EST:** 1961
SQ FT: 30,000
Web: www.arscometals.com
SIC: 6719 Investment holding companies, except banks

(G-3654)
WESLEY COMMUNITY SERVICES LLC
Also Called: MEALS ON WHEELS SOUTHWEST OHIO
2091 Radcliff Dr (45204-1853)
PHONE...................513 661-2777
Jennifer Steele, *Owner*
Jennifer Steele, *Ex Dir*
EMP: 150 **EST:** 1997
SALES (est): 14.04MM **Privately Held**
Web: www.muchmorethanameal.org
SIC: 8322 Senior citizens' center or association

(G-3655)
WEST CHESTER HOLDINGS LLC
Also Called: West Chester Protective Gear
11500 Canal Rd (45241-1862)
PHONE...................513 705-2100
Tim Fogarty, *CEO*
Jim Wilson, *
▲ **EMP:** 134 **EST:** 1995
SQ FT: 200,000
SALES (est): 31.5MM
SALES (corp-wide): 2.8B **Privately Held**
Web: www.westchesterclothing.com
SIC: 3842 5099 2381 5137 Clothing, fire resistant and protective; Safety equipment and supplies; Gloves, work: woven or knit, made from purchased materials; Women's and children's clothing
HQ: Protective Industrial Products, Inc.
25 British American Blvd
Latham NY 12110
518 861-0133

(G-3656)
WEST PARK RETIREMENT COMMUNITY
Also Called: Mercy House Partners
2950 W Park Dr Ofc (45238-3542)
PHONE...................513 451-8900
Kendra Couch, *Pr*
Donald Stinnett, *
EMP: 42 **EST:** 1982
SQ FT: 206,000
SALES (est): 377.82K **Privately Held**
SIC: 8052 8051 Personal care facility; Extended care facility

(G-3657)
WEST SHELL COMMERCIAL INC
Also Called: Colliers International
425 Walnut St Ste 1200 (45202-3993)
PHONE...................513 721-4200
Shenan Murphy, *Pr*
EMP: 55 **EST:** 2000
SQ FT: 11,000
SALES (est): 5.19MM **Privately Held**
SIC: 6531 Real estate agent, commercial

(G-3658)
WEST SIDE PEDIATRICS INC (PA)
663 Anderson Ferry Rd Ste 1 (45238-4798)
PHONE...................513 922-8200
Lee Burroughs Md, *Pr*
R Scott Hunter, *
EMP: 44 **EST:** 1972
SALES (est): 4.92MM **Privately Held**
Web: www.wspcincy.com
SIC: 8011 Pediatrician

(G-3659)
WESTERN & SOUTHERN LF INSUR CO (DH)
Also Called: Western-Southern Life
400 Broadway St Stop G (45202)
P.O. Box 1119 (45201)
PHONE...................513 629-1800
John F Barrett, *Pr*
James Vance, *
Danald J Wuebbling, *Sec*
EMP: 982 **EST:** 1888
SQ FT: 600,000
SALES (est): 62.71MM **Privately Held**
Web: www.westernsouthern.com
SIC: 6211 6311 2511 Investment firm, general brokerage; Life insurance; Play pens, children's: wood
HQ: Western & Southern Financial Group, Inc.
400 Broadway
Cincinnati OH 45202
877 367-9734

(G-3660)
WESTERN BOWL INC
6383 Glenway Ave (45211-6382)
PHONE...................513 574-2200
Erwin Hoinke Junior, *Pr*
Russell Hoinke, *Sec*
EMP: 36 **EST:** 1958
SQ FT: 27,000
SALES (est): 402.43K **Privately Held**
Web: www.strikeandspare.com
SIC: 7933 5813 5812 Ten pin center; Drinking places; Eating places

(G-3661)
WESTERN HILLS CARE CENTER
6210 Cleves Warsaw Pike (45233-4510)
PHONE...................513 941-0099
Barry A Kohn, *Pr*
Sam Boymel, *
Rick Friedman, *
EMP: 83 **EST:** 1986
SQ FT: 150,000
SALES (est): 3.49MM **Privately Held**
Web: www.caringplacehcg.com
SIC: 8051 Convalescent home with continuous nursing care

(G-3662)
WESTERN HILLS COUNTRY CLUB
5780 Cleves Warsaw Pike (45233-4900)
P.O. Box 58644 (45258-0644)
PHONE...................513 922-0011
Dana Cinorell, *COO*
EMP: 75 **EST:** 1912
SQ FT: 20,000
SALES (est): 4.88MM **Privately Held**
Web: www.westernhillscc.com
SIC: 7997 Country club, membership

(G-3663)
WESTERN HILLS SPORTSPLEX INC
Also Called: Western Sports Mall
2323 Ferguson Rd Ste 1 (45238-3500)
PHONE...................513 451-4900
John P Torbeck, *Pr*
Robert Czerwinski, *
John L Torbeck, *

Bobby Farley, *
EMP: 75 **EST:** 1972
SQ FT: 40,000
SALES (est): 1.3MM **Privately Held**
SIC: 7997 7999 Tennis club, membership; Indoor court clubs

(G-3664)
WESTERN SOUTHERN MUTL HOLDG CO (PA)
400 Broadway St (45202)
PHONE...................866 832-7719
EMP: 1450 **EST:** 2000
SALES (est): 3.3B **Privately Held**
Web: www.westernsouthern.com
SIC: 6211 Investment firm, general brokerage

(G-3665)
WESTERN STHERN FINCL GROUP INC (HQ)
Also Called: Western & Southern
400 Broadway St (45202)
P.O. Box 1119 (45201)
PHONE...................877 367-9734
John F Barrett, *Pr*
James N Clark, *
Robert L Walker, *
Herbert R Brown, *
Troy D Brodie, *
EMP: 1800 **EST:** 1888
SALES (est): 1.64B **Privately Held**
Web: www.westernsouthern.com
SIC: 6211 Investment firm, general brokerage
PA: Western & Southern Mutual Holding Company
400 Broadway St
Cincinnati OH 45202

(G-3666)
WESTERN-SOUTHERN LIFE ASRN CO
400 Broadway St (45202-3341)
PHONE...................513 629-1800
John F Barrett, *Pr*
William J Williams, *
James N Clark, *
Ed Hanean, *
EMP: 77 **EST:** 1980
SALES (est): 1.21MM **Privately Held**
Web: www.westernsouthern.com
SIC: 6311 Life insurance
HQ: The Western & Southern Life Insurance Company
400 Broadway Mail Stop G
Cincinnati OH 45202
513 629-1800

(G-3667)
WFTS
Also Called: W C P O - T V
1720 Gilbert Ave (45202-1401)
PHONE...................513 721-9900
Bill Fee, *Genl Mgr*
EMP: 88
SALES (corp-wide): 2.66B **Publicly Held**
Web: www.wcpo.com
SIC: 4833 Television broadcasting stations
HQ: Wfts
4045 N Himes Ave
Tampa FL 33607
813 354-2800

(G-3668)
WHITEHEAD FALANA
2538 Hansford Pl (45214-1178)
PHONE...................513 742-1766
EMP: 34 **EST:** 2020
SALES (est): 510.23K **Privately Held**
SIC: 8351 Child day care services

GEOGRAPHIC SECTION

Cincinnati - Hamilton County (G-3689)

HQ: Ohio Department Of Job And Family Services
30 E Broad St Fl 32
Columbus OH 43215

(G-3669)
WICKSHIRE DEER PARK OPCO LLC
Also Called: Wickshire Deer Park
3801 E Galbraith Rd Ofc (45236-1585)
PHONE..................513 745-7600
Staci Lynn, *Managing Member*
EMP: 29 **EST:** 2000
SQ FT: 20,075
SALES (est): 5.35MM **Privately Held**
SIC: 8059 Domiciliary care

(G-3670)
WIDMERS LLC (HQ)
Also Called: Widmer's Drycleaners
2016 Madison Rd (45208-3238)
PHONE..................513 321-5100
EMP: 200 **EST:** 1910
SQ FT: 33,000
SALES (est): 10.05MM **Privately Held**
Web: www.widmerscleaners.com
SIC: 7216 7217 Cleaning and dyeing, except rugs; Carpet and upholstery cleaning
PA: Zoots Holding Corporation
153 Needham St Bldg 1
Newton MA 02464

(G-3671)
WILKERS INC
Also Called: Robinson Cleaners
11 Wyoming Ave (45215-4303)
PHONE..................513 851-4000
Tom Wilker, *Pr*
EMP: 27
SQ FT: 3,750
Web: www.robinsoncleaners.com
SIC: 7216 Cleaning and dyeing, except rugs
PA: Wilkers, Inc.
5648 Cheviot Rd
Cincinnati OH 45247

(G-3672)
WILLIAM THOMAS GROUP INC
10795 Hughes Rd (45251-4523)
P.O. Box 538703 (45253-8703)
PHONE..................800 582-3107
William Rumpke Junior, *Pr*
Brad Warman, *Prin*
Jason Cozad, *Prin*
Ian Murden, *Prin*
Shawn Meadows, *Prin*
EMP: 85 **EST:** 2007
SALES (est): 11.6MM **Privately Held**
Web: www.william-thomasgroup.com
SIC: 8742 Management consulting services
PA: Rumpke Consolidated Companies, Inc.
3990 Generation Dr
Cincinnati OH 45251

(G-3673)
WILLIAMSBURG OF CINCINNATI MGT
Also Called: Evergreen Kindervelt Gift Shop
230 W Galbraith Rd (45215-5223)
PHONE..................513 948-2308
Lynn Saul, *Ex Dir*
EMP: 285 **EST:** 1984
SALES (est): 51.13MM
SALES (corp-wide): 244.88MM **Privately Held**
Web: www.seniorlifestyle.com
SIC: 8059 5947 Rest home, with health care; Gift, novelty, and souvenir shop
PA: Senior Lifestyle Corporation
303 E Wacker Dr Ste 2400
Chicago IL 60601
312 673-4333

(G-3674)
WINEGRDNER HMMONS HT GROUP LLC (HQ)
Also Called: Radisson Inn
8044 Montgomery Rd (45236-2919)
PHONE..................513 891-1066
Mike Conway, *Ch*
Terry Dammeyer, *Pr*
Brian Perkins, *COO*
Kent Bruggeman, *CFO*
EMP: 120 **EST:** 2015
SALES (est): 25.56MM
SALES (corp-wide): 173.43MM **Privately Held**
Web: www.radissonhotels.com
SIC: 7011 Hotels and motels
PA: Pyramid Advisors Llc
1 Post Office Sq Ste 1900
Boston MA 02109
617 202-2033

(G-3675)
WINGATE PACKAGING INC (PA)
Also Called: Wingate Packaging South
4347 Indeco Ct (45241)
PHONE..................513 745-8600
Robert W Braunschweig, *Ch Bd*
John S Richardson, *
EMP: 36 **EST:** 1983
SQ FT: 44,000
SALES (est): 20.03MM
SALES (corp-wide): 20.03MM **Privately Held**
Web: www.wingate-packaging.com
SIC: 5199 Packaging materials

(G-3676)
WM CCP SOLUTIONS LLC
4228 Airport Rd (45226-1646)
PHONE..................513 871-9733
EMP: 56
SALES (corp-wide): 20.43B **Publicly Held**
SIC: 4953 Hazardous waste collection and disposal
HQ: Wm Ccp Solutions, Llc
1001 Fannin St Ste 4000
Houston TX 77002
713 512-6200

(G-3677)
WNB GROUP LLC
Also Called: Ray Hamilton Company
4817 Section Ave (45212-2118)
P.O. Box 12370 (45212-0370)
PHONE..................513 641-5400
James Wallis, *Pr*
EMP: 49 **EST:** 1892
SALES (est): 9.24MM **Privately Held**
Web: www.rayhamilton.com
SIC: 4212 4214 4731 Moving services; Local trucking with storage; Freight transportation arrangement

(G-3678)
WOOD HERRON & EVANS LLP (PA)
600 Vine St Ste 2800 (45202-2814)
PHONE..................513 241-2324
Bruce Tittel, *Pr*
Donald F Frei, *
David J Josephic, *
David S Stallard, *
J Robert Chambers, *
EMP: 98 **EST:** 1868
SALES (est): 13.15MM
SALES (corp-wide): 13.15MM **Privately Held**
Web: www.whe-law.com
SIC: 8111 General practice law office

(G-3679)
WOOD & LAMPING LLP
Also Called: Wood & Lamping
600 Vine St Ste 2500 (45202-2491)
PHONE..................513 852-6000
Harold G Korbee, *Mgr*
Mark Reckman, *Pt*
EMP: 60 **EST:** 1928
SALES (est): 10.18MM **Privately Held**
Web: www.woodlamping.com
SIC: 8111 General practice attorney, lawyer

(G-3680)
WOOD GRAPHICS INC (PA)
Also Called: United Engraving
8075 Reading Rd Ste 301 (45237-1416)
PHONE..................513 771-6300
Mark Richler, *Pr*
Gaylord H Fill, *
◆ **EMP:** 30 **EST:** 1972
SQ FT: 21,500
SALES (est): 2.44MM
SALES (corp-wide): 2.44MM **Privately Held**
SIC: 3555 7699 2796 Printing trades machinery; Industrial machinery and equipment repair; Platemaking services

(G-3681)
WOODY SANDER FORD INC (PA)
235 W Mitchell Ave (45232-1948)
PHONE..................513 541-5586
William G Sander, *Pr*
James Mullen, *General Sales*
Thomas Paul Sander, *
EMP: 60 **EST:** 1962
SQ FT: 30,000
SALES (est): 4.87MM
SALES (corp-wide): 4.87MM **Privately Held**
Web: www.fordqueencity.com
SIC: 7389 Personal service agents, brokers, and bureaus

(G-3682)
WULCO INC (PA)
Also Called: Jet Machine & Manufacturing
6899 Steger Dr Ste A (45237-3059)
PHONE..................513 679-2600
Richard G Wulfeck, *Pr*
Gary Wulfeck, *
Ken Wulfeck, *
▲ **EMP:** 100 **EST:** 1970
SQ FT: 100,000
SALES (est): 97.32MM **Privately Held**
Web: www.wulco.com
SIC: 5085 3599 Industrial supplies; Machine shop, jobbing and repair

(G-3683)
XAVIER UNIVERSITY
Also Called: Wvxu Radio
3800 Victory Pkwy (45207-1092)
PHONE..................513 745-3335
James King, *Mgr*
EMP: 50
SALES (corp-wide): 321.03MM **Privately Held**
Web: www.xavier.edu
SIC: 4832 8221 Radio broadcasting stations; University
PA: Xavier University
3800 Victory Pkwy Unit 1
Cincinnati OH 45207
513 745-3000

(G-3684)
XLC SRVCES CINCINNATI OHIO INC (HQ)
Also Called: Xlc Services
324 W 9th St Fl 5 (45202-2043)
PHONE..................513 621-3912
David E Foxx, *Pr*
Patricia Foxx, *Sec*
EMP: 27 **EST:** 1989
SALES (est): 10.97MM
SALES (corp-wide): 94.54MM **Privately Held**
Web: welcome.xlcservices.com
SIC: 8742 General management consultant
PA: D.E. Foxx & Associates, Inc.
324 W 9th St Fl 5
Cincinnati OH 45202
513 621-5522

(G-3685)
YORK STREET FRESH FOODS LLC
3465 Hauck Rd (45241-1601)
PHONE..................201 868-9088
EMP: 40 **EST:** 2020
SALES (est): 5.21MM **Privately Held**
SIC: 1541 Food products manufacturing or packing plant construction

(G-3686)
YOUNG & ALEXANDER CO LPA
1 Sheakley Way Ste 125 (45246-3780)
PHONE..................513 326-5555
EMP: 28
SALES (corp-wide): 3.54MM **Privately Held**
Web: www.yandalaw.com
SIC: 8111 General practice attorney, lawyer
PA: Young & Alexander Co., L.P.A.
130 W 2nd St Ste 1500
Dayton OH 45402
937 224-9291

(G-3687)
YOUNG & RUBICAM LLC
Also Called: Sive/Young & Rubicam
36 E 7th St Ste 2500 (45202-4462)
PHONE..................513 345-3400
Dale P Brown, *Brnch Mgr*
EMP: 62
SALES (corp-wide): 18.5B **Privately Held**
Web: www.vml.com
SIC: 7311 Advertising agencies
HQ: Young & Rubicam Llc
175 Greenwich St Fl 28
New York NY 10007
212 210-3017

(G-3688)
YOUNG & RUBICAM LLC
Landor Associates
110 Shillito Pl (45202-2361)
PHONE..................513 419-2300
Marie Zalla, *Mgr*
EMP: 150
SALES (corp-wide): 18.5B **Privately Held**
Web: www.vml.com
SIC: 7311 Advertising consultant
HQ: Young & Rubicam Llc
175 Greenwich St Fl 28
New York NY 10007
212 210-3017

(G-3689)
YOUNG MENS CHRISTIAN ASSOCIATION OF GREATER CINCINNATI (PA)
Also Called: YMCA
1105 Elm St (45202-7513)
PHONE..................513 651-2100
EMP: 40 **EST:** 1853
SALES (est): 44.55MM
SALES (corp-wide): 44.55MM **Privately Held**
Web: www.myy.org
SIC: 8641 Youth organizations

(G-3690)
YOUNG MNS CHRSTN ASSN GRTER CN
Also Called: Powel Crosley Jr Branch
9601 Winton Rd (45231-2637)
PHONE..................513 521-7112
Cindy Tomaszewski, *Mgr*
EMP: 253
SALES (corp-wide): 44.55MM **Privately Held**
Web: www.myy.org
SIC: 8641 7997 Youth organizations; Membership sports and recreation clubs
PA: Young Mens Christian Association Of Greater Cincinnati
1105 Elm St
Cincinnati OH 45202
513 651-2100

(G-3691)
YOUNG MNS CHRSTN ASSN GRTER CN
Also Called: Melrose Branch
2840 Melrose Ave (45206-1214)
PHONE..................513 961-3510
Marcia Smartt, *Dir*
EMP: 95
SALES (corp-wide): 44.55MM **Privately Held**
Web: www.myy.org
SIC: 8641 7991 7997 Youth organizations; Physical fitness facilities; Membership sports and recreation clubs
PA: Young Mens Christian Association Of Greater Cincinnati
1105 Elm St
Cincinnati OH 45202
513 651-2100

(G-3692)
YOUNG MNS CHRSTN ASSN GRTER CN
Also Called: Y M C A
2039 Sherman Ave (45212-2634)
PHONE..................513 731-0115
Alan Geans, *Dir*
EMP: 158
SQ FT: 14,869
SALES (corp-wide): 44.55MM **Privately Held**
Web: www.myy.org
SIC: 8641 8351 7997 7991 Youth organizations; Child day care services; Membership sports and recreation clubs; Athletic club and gymnasiums, membership
PA: Young Mens Christian Association Of Greater Cincinnati
1105 Elm St
Cincinnati OH 45202
513 651-2100

(G-3693)
YOUNG MNS CHRSTN ASSN GRTER CN
Also Called: Ymca/M.e.lions
8108 Clough Pike Fl 1 (45244-2745)
PHONE..................513 474-1400
Jennifer Snyder, *Dir*
EMP: 285
SQ FT: 5,320
SALES (corp-wide): 44.55MM **Privately Held**
Web: www.myy.org
SIC: 8641 8351 7997 7991 Youth organizations; Child day care services; Membership sports and recreation clubs; Physical fitness facilities
PA: Young Mens Christian Association Of Greater Cincinnati
1105 Elm St
Cincinnati OH 45202
513 651-2100

(G-3694)
YOUNG MNS CHRSTN ASSN GRTER CN
Also Called: West End YMCA
1425b Linn St (45214-2605)
PHONE..................513 241-9622
Joseph C Calloway, *Brnch Mgr*
EMP: 95
SALES (corp-wide): 44.55MM **Privately Held**
Web: www.myy.org
SIC: 8641 7991 8351 7032 Youth organizations; Physical fitness facilities; Child day care services; Youth camps
PA: Young Mens Christian Association Of Greater Cincinnati
1105 Elm St
Cincinnati OH 45202
513 651-2100

(G-3695)
YOUNG MNS CHRSTN ASSN GRTER CN
Also Called: William & Clippard YMCA
8920 Cheviot Rd (45251-5910)
PHONE..................513 923-4466
Dirk Langfoss, *Dir*
EMP: 127
SQ FT: 29,230
SALES (corp-wide): 44.55MM **Privately Held**
Web: www.myy.org
SIC: 8641 7991 8351 7032 Youth organizations; Physical fitness facilities; Child day care services; Youth camps
PA: Young Mens Christian Association Of Greater Cincinnati
1105 Elm St
Cincinnati OH 45202
513 651-2100

(G-3696)
YOUNG MNS CHRSTN ASSN GRTER CN
Also Called: YMCA Child Care Center West
112 Findlay St (45202-7710)
PHONE..................513 921-0911
Deborah Rivera, *Mgr*
EMP: 127
SALES (corp-wide): 44.55MM **Privately Held**
Web: www.myy.org
SIC: 8641 7991 8351 7032 Youth organizations; Physical fitness facilities; Child day care services; Youth camps
PA: Young Mens Christian Association Of Greater Cincinnati
1105 Elm St
Cincinnati OH 45202
513 651-2100

(G-3697)
YWCA OF GREATER CINCINNATI (PA)
898 Walnut St Fl 1 (45202-2088)
PHONE..................513 241-7090
Charlene Ventura, *Pr*
Sandra Genco, *
Debbie Brook, *
EMP: 65 **EST:** 1868
SALES (est): 5.81MM
SALES (corp-wide): 5.81MM **Privately Held**
Web: www.ywcacincinnati.org
SIC: 8641 7991 8351 7032 Youth organizations; Physical fitness facilities; Child day care services; Youth camps

(G-3698)
ZIPSCENE LLC
Also Called: Zipscene
615 Main St Fl 5 (45202-2538)
PHONE..................513 201-5174
Rick Lamy, *
EMP: 62 **EST:** 2010
SQ FT: 2,000
SALES (est): 5.08MM **Privately Held**
Web: www.zipscene.com
SIC: 7372 Business oriented computer software

(G-3699)
ZOO CINCINNATI
3400 Vine St (45220-1333)
PHONE..................513 961-0041
Jenny Gainer, *Prin*
EMP: 50 **EST:** 2009
SALES (est): 32.7MM **Privately Held**
Web: www.cincinnatizoo.org
SIC: 8422 Botanical and zoological gardens

(G-3700)
ZOOLOGICAL SOCIETY CINCINNATI
Also Called: CINCINNATI ZOO & BOTANICAL GAR
3400 Vine St (45220-1333)
PHONE..................513 281-4700
Thane Maynard, *Dir*
▲ **EMP:** 320 **EST:** 1875
SALES (est): 73.08MM **Privately Held**
Web: www.cincinnatizoo.org
SIC: 8422 Zoological garden, noncommercial

Circleville
Pickaway County

(G-3701)
1ST CARRIER CORP
177 Neville St (43113-9129)
P.O. Box 911 (43113-0911)
PHONE..................740 477-2587
Jeffrey Lanman, *Pr*
Jeffrey Beaver, *VP*
EMP: 32 **EST:** 1997
SALES (est): 2.46MM **Privately Held**
Web: www.1stcarrier.com
SIC: 4213 4212 Trucking, except local; Local trucking, without storage

(G-3702)
ADENA HEALTH SYSTEM
798 N Court St (43113-1262)
PHONE..................740 420-3000
EMP: 31
SALES (corp-wide): 678.56MM **Privately Held**
Web: www.adena.org
SIC: 8062 Hospital, med school affiliated with nursing and residency
PA: Adena Health System
272 Hospital Rd
Chillicothe OH 45601
740 779-7500

(G-3703)
BROWN MEMORIAL HOME INC
158 E Mound St (43113-1702)
PHONE..................740 474-6238
Luke Conley, *Admn*
Charles Gerhart, *
EMP: 72 **EST:** 1894
SALES (est): 4.01MM **Privately Held**
Web: www.brownmemorialhome.com
SIC: 8052 Personal care facility

(G-3704)
BUCKEYE CHECK CASHING INC
513 E Main St (43113-1873)
PHONE..................740 497-4039
EMP: 35
Web: www.ccfi.com
SIC: 6099 Check cashing agencies
HQ: Buckeye Check Cashing, Inc.
5165 Emerald Pkwy Ste 100
Dublin OH 43017
614 798-5900

(G-3705)
CENTRAL COCA-COLA BTLG CO INC
Also Called: Coca-Cola
387 Walnut St (43113-2225)
PHONE..................740 474-2180
EMP: 29
SALES (corp-wide): 45.75B **Publicly Held**
Web: www.coca-cola.com
SIC: 2086 8741 Bottled and canned soft drinks; Management services
HQ: Central Coca-Cola Bottling Company, Inc.
555 Taxter Rd Ste 550
Elmsford NY 10523
914 789-1100

(G-3706)
DARBY CREEK EXCAVATING INC
19524 London Rd (43113-9614)
PHONE..................740 477-8600
Kevin Steward, *Pr*
Mary Steward, *
Cary Purcell, *
EMP: 90 **EST:** 1992
SQ FT: 7,000
SALES (est): 10.74MM **Privately Held**
Web: www.darbycreekexc.com
SIC: 1794 1623 Excavation and grading, building construction; Sewer line construction

(G-3707)
EATON CONSTRUCTION CO INC
653 Island Rd (43113-9594)
P.O. Box 684 (43113-0684)
PHONE..................740 474-3414
Debbie Manson, *CEO*
EMP: 60 **EST:** 1965
SALES (est): 9.55MM **Privately Held**
SIC: 1611 Highway and street maintenance

(G-3708)
ELECT GENERAL CONTRACTORS INC
27634 Jackson Rd (43113-9039)
P.O. Box 1135 (43113-5135)
PHONE..................740 420-3437
Timothy R Covell, *Pr*
EMP: 30 **EST:** 1989
SALES (est): 5.29MM **Privately Held**
Web: www.electgeneral.com
SIC: 1794 Excavation work

(G-3709)
GOODS HANDS SUPPORTED LIVING
Also Called: GOODS HANDS SUPPORTED LIVING
2489 N Court St (43113-9338)
PHONE..................740 474-2646
EMP: 28
SALES (corp-wide): 4.44MM **Privately Held**
Web: www.ghslohio.org
SIC: 8322 Adult day care center
PA: Goods Hands Supported Living, Ltd.
2491 E Dblin Granville Rd
Columbus OH 43229
614 899-7320

GEOGRAPHIC SECTION

Clayton - Montgomery County (G-3732)

(G-3710)
HEALTH CARE LOGISTICS INC (PA)
450 Town St (43113-2244)
P.O. Box 25 (43113-0025)
PHONE....................740 477-1686
▲ **EMP:** 119 **EST:** 1978
SALES (est): 51.04MM
SALES (corp-wide): 51.04MM **Privately Held**
Web: www.gohcl.com
SIC: 5047 Medical equipment and supplies

(G-3711)
JD MUSIC TILE CO
105 E Ohio St (43113-1917)
PHONE....................740 420-9611
Joe Music, *Pr*
Deana Music, *
EMP: 30 **EST:** 1980
SALES (est): 2.43MM **Privately Held**
SIC: 1752 Ceramic floor tile installation

(G-3712)
LOGAN ELM HEALTH CARE CENTER
370 Tarlton Rd (43113-9136)
PHONE....................740 474-3121
James Farley, *Pr*
Michael Scharfenberger, *
EMP: 320 **EST:** 1973
SALES (est): 10.17MM **Privately Held**
Web: www.loganelm.com
SIC: 8051 Convalescent home with continuous nursing care

(G-3713)
MIDOHIO CRDIOLGY VASCULAR CONS
600 N Pickaway St (43113-1447)
PHONE....................740 420-8174
EMP: 39
SIC: 8062 General medical and surgical hospitals
PA: Midohio Cardiology And Vascular Consultants Inc
3705 Olentngy Rvr Rd
Columbus OH 43214

(G-3714)
NEW HOPE CHRISTIAN ACADEMY
2264 Walnut Creek Pike (43113-8938)
PHONE....................740 477-6427
EMP: 44 **EST:** 1993
SALES (est): 851.69K **Privately Held**
Web: www.nhchristianacademy.org
SIC: 8351 8211 Preschool center; Private elementary and secondary schools

(G-3715)
PICKAWAY AREA RCOVERY SVCS INC
Also Called: FAYETTE RECOVERY CENTER
110 Highland Ave (43113-1208)
PHONE....................740 477-1745
Barry Bennett, *Dir*
Karen Mitchell, *Dir*
EMP: 40 **EST:** 1991
SALES (est): 6.54MM **Privately Held**
Web: www.pickawayarearecoveryservices.com
SIC: 8069 8093 Drug addiction rehabilitation hospital; Alcohol clinic, outpatient

(G-3716)
PICKAWAY CNTY CMNTY ACTION ORG (PA)
Also Called: P I C C A
469 E Ohio St (43113-2034)
PHONE....................740 477-1655
Dave Hannahs, *Ex Dir*
Dave Kline, *

EMP: 50 **EST:** 1965
SQ FT: 6,000
SALES (est): 8.31MM
SALES (corp-wide): 8.31MM **Privately Held**
Web: www.picca.info
SIC: 8322 6513 4121 4119 Social service center; Apartment building operators; Taxicabs; Local passenger transportation, nec

(G-3717)
PICKAWAY MANOR INC
391 Clark Dr (43113-1598)
PHONE....................740 474-5400
Robert Kenworthy, *Pr*
Ned Hardin, *
EMP: 46 **EST:** 1969
SQ FT: 10,000
SALES (est): 7.93MM **Privately Held**
Web: www.optalishealthcare.com
SIC: 8051 8052 Convalescent home with continuous nursing care; Intermediate care facilities

(G-3718)
PRECISION ELECTRICAL SVCS INC
201 W Main St (43113-1621)
P.O. Box 656 (43113-0656)
PHONE....................740 474-4490
John Seyfang Ii, *Pr*
Kelly Seyfang, *
EMP: 35 **EST:** 1989
SQ FT: 12,000
SALES (est): 2.45MM **Privately Held**
Web: www.precisionelectrical.com
SIC: 1731 General electrical contractor

(G-3719)
PROCON PROF CNSTR SVCS INC
2530 Kingston Pike (43113-9599)
P.O. Box 1 (45644-0001)
PHONE....................740 474-5455
Troy Dumm, *Pr*
Dee Minshall Managing, *Prin*
EMP: 31 **EST:** 2000
SQ FT: 2,400
SALES (est): 1.48MM **Privately Held**
SIC: 1542 Commercial and office building contractors

(G-3720)
RHOADS FARM INC
Also Called: Split Rail Nursery
1357 Hitler Road 1 (43113-9706)
PHONE....................740 404-5696
Brett Rhoads, *Prin*
Brent Rhoads, *
Kathy Rhoads, *
Christa Crosier, *
EMP: 60 **EST:** 2005
SALES (est): 2.4MM **Privately Held**
Web: www.rhoadsfarminc.com
SIC: 0191 General farms, primarily crop

(G-3721)
RK FAMILY INC
23625 Us Highway 23 S Lot 3a (43113-9770)
PHONE....................740 474-3874
Tim Lodes, *Prin*
EMP: 146
SALES (corp-wide): 1.22B **Privately Held**
Web: www.ruralking.com
SIC: 5191 Farm supplies
PA: Rk Family, Inc.
4216 Dewitt Ave
Mattoon IL 61938
217 235-7102

(G-3722)
RUMPKE WASTE INC
Also Called: Rumpke Recycling
819 Island Rd (43113-9594)
PHONE....................740 474-9790
Bill Rumpke, *Pr*
EMP: 233
Web: www.rumpke.com
SIC: 4953 Garbage: collecting, destroying, and processing
HQ: Rumpke Waste, Inc.
10795 Hughes Rd
Cincinnati OH 45251
513 851-0122

(G-3723)
SAVINGS BANK (PA)
118 N Court St # 120 (43113-1606)
P.O. Box 310 (43113-0310)
PHONE....................740 474-3191
Steven Gary, *Pr*
Connie Campbell, *
EMP: 35 **EST:** 1912
SQ FT: 8,000
SALES (est): 19.3MM
SALES (corp-wide): 19.3MM **Privately Held**
Web: www.thesavingsbankcircleville.com
SIC: 6022 State trust companies accepting deposits, commercial

(G-3724)
SOFIDEL AMERICA CORP
Also Called: Paper Mill and Converting
25910 Us Highway 23 S (43113-9005)
PHONE....................740 500-1965
Luigi Lazzareschi, *CEO*
EMP: 205
SALES (corp-wide): 2.91B **Privately Held**
Web: www.sofidel.com
SIC: 5113 Industrial and personal service paper
HQ: Sofidel America Corp.
300 Welsh Rd Bldg 1
Horsham PA 19044
215 283-3890

(G-3725)
SUTHERLAND BUILDING PDTS INC
Also Called: Southerland Lumber and Home
460 Lancaster Pike (43113-9272)
PHONE....................740 477-2244
Ryan Taylor, *Brnch Mgr*
EMP: 68
SALES (corp-wide): 10.4MM **Privately Held**
Web: www.sutherlands.com
SIC: 5199 General merchandise, non-durable
PA: Sutherland Building Products, Inc.
4000 Main St
Kansas City MO 64111
816 756-3000

(G-3726)
T-MOBILE
511 E Main St (43113-1873)
PHONE....................740 500-4250
EMP: 42 **EST:** 2019
SALES (est): 108.15K **Privately Held**
Web: www.t-mobile.com
SIC: 4812 Cellular telephone services

(G-3727)
THE BERGER HOSPITAL (HQ)
Also Called: Berger Health System
600 N Pickaway St (43113-1499)
PHONE....................740 474-2126
EMP: 536 **EST:** 1900
SALES (est): 99.03MM
SALES (corp-wide): 4.29B **Privately Held**

SIC: 8062 8082 Hospital, affiliated with AMA residency; Visiting nurse service
PA: Ohiohealth Corporation
3430 Ohhalth Pkwy 5th Flr
Columbus OH 43202
614 788-8860

(G-3728)
UTILITY TRUCK & EQUIPMENT INC
23893 Us Highway 23 S (43113-9003)
P.O. Box 130 (43113-0130)
PHONE....................740 474-5151
Rodney Hill, *Pr*
Ray E Brieker, *
Neal R Anklam, *
Thomas D Yost, *
EMP: 35 **EST:** 1986
SALES (est): 8.18MM **Privately Held**
Web: www.utilitytruck.net
SIC: 5046 Commercial equipment, nec

Clarington
Monroe County

(G-3729)
DIAMOND W LLC
50817 State Route 556 (43915-9639)
PHONE....................970 434-9435
EMP: 52
SALES (corp-wide): 4.56MM **Privately Held**
SIC: 4731 Freight forwarding
PA: Diamond W Llc
3166 Pipe Ct
Grand Junction CO 81504
970 434-9435

Clarksville
Clinton County

(G-3730)
JOY OUTDOOR EDUCATION CTR LLC
Also Called: CAMP JOY
10117 Old 3 C (45113-8670)
P.O. Box 157 (45113-0157)
PHONE....................937 289-2031
Amy Thompson, *
EMP: 40 **EST:** 1945
SALES (est): 3.65MM **Privately Held**
Web: www.camp-joy.org
SIC: 7032 Sporting and recreational camps

Clayton
Montgomery County

(G-3731)
CALVIN ELECTRIC LLC
7272 Pleasant Plain Rd (45315-9718)
P.O. Box 10 (45315-0010)
PHONE....................937 670-2558
EMP: 30 **EST:** 2011
SALES (est): 10.67MM **Privately Held**
Web: www.calvinelectricllc.com
SIC: 1731 General electrical contractor

(G-3732)
ENGLEWOOD TRUCK INC
Also Called: Englewood Trck Towing Recovery
7510 Jacks Ln (45315-8779)
PHONE....................937 836-5109
Frank Cecrle, *Pr*
Brookie Cercle, *
EMP: 45 **EST:** 1947
SQ FT: 12,000

Clayton - Montgomery County (G-3733)   GEOGRAPHIC SECTION

SALES (est): 2.39MM **Privately Held**
Web: www.englewoodtruck.com
SIC: 7549 Towing service, automotive

(G-3733)
IDEAL COMPANY INC (PA)
Also Called: F & M Contractors
8313 Kimmel Rd (45315-8905)
P.O. Box 149 (45315-0149)
PHONE.................................937 836-8683
Kent Filbrun, *Prin*
Fred A Sink, *
Kevin G Filbrun, *
Kenton R Filbrun, *
Bruce Neador, *
EMP: 40 EST: 1960
SQ FT: 2,400
SALES (est): 27.23MM
SALES (corp-wide): 27.23MM **Privately Held**
Web: www.idealco.net
SIC: 1542 Commercial and office building, new construction

(G-3734)
LANDES FRESH MEATS INC
Also Called: Ol' Smokehaus
9476 Haber Rd (45315-9711)
PHONE.................................937 836-3613
Keith Landes, *Pr*
Mark Landes, *
EMP: 29 EST: 1946
SQ FT: 16,000
SALES (est): 2.3MM **Privately Held**
Web: www.landesfreshmeats.com
SIC: 5421 0751 5147 Meat markets, including freezer provisioners; Slaughtering: custom livestock services; Meats, fresh

(G-3735)
MOSS CREEK GOLF COURSE
Also Called: Golf Course Branch
1 Club Dr (45315-7930)
PHONE.................................937 837-4653
TOLL FREE: 800
Steve Lambert, *Owner*
EMP: 50 EST: 1998
SALES (est): 2MM **Privately Held**
Web: www.mosscreekgolfclub.com
SIC: 7992 7999 Public golf courses; Golf driving range

(G-3736)
MOYER INDUSTRIES INC
7555 Jacks Ln (45315-8778)
PHONE.................................937 832-7283
John Moyer, *Pr*
Jane Moyer, *
EMP: 51 EST: 1989
SQ FT: 13,000
SALES (est): 17.68MM **Privately Held**
Web: www.moyerinc.com
SIC: 1521 1611 Single-family housing construction; Surfacing and paving

(G-3737)
TREATMENT TECHNOLOGIES LLC
313 Smith Dr (45315)
PHONE.................................937 802-4883
EMP: 34 EST: 2019
SALES (est): 5.21MM **Privately Held**
SIC: 4952 Sewerage systems
PA: Inframark, Llc
   2002 W Grand Pkwy N # 100
   Katy TX 77449

Cleveland
Cuyahoga County

(G-3738)
127 PS FEE OWNER LLC
1300 Key Tower 127 Public Square (44114)
PHONE.................................216 520-1250
EMP: 99 EST: 2016
SALES (est): 4.96MM **Privately Held**
SIC: 6512 Commercial and industrial building operation

(G-3739)
12985 SNOW HOLDINGS INC
12985 Snow Rd (44130-1006)
PHONE.................................216 267-5000
EMP: 33 EST: 1984
SALES (est): 1.61MM **Privately Held**
Web: www.wbmason.com
SIC: 5112 5044 5021 Stationery and office supplies; Office equipment; Office furniture, nec

(G-3740)
1460 NINTH ST ASSOC LTD PARTNR
Also Called: Brampton Inn
1460 E 9th St (44114-1700)
PHONE.................................216 241-6600
Ray Valle, *Genl Mgr*
EMP: 45 EST: 1996
SQ FT: 18,836
SALES (est): 204.79K **Privately Held**
SIC: 7011 Hotels and motels

(G-3741)
17322 EUCLID AVENUE CO LLC
Also Called: EASTBROOK HEALTHCARE CENTER
17322 Euclid Ave (44112-1210)
PHONE.................................216 486-2280
Andrew Brobbey, *Dir*
EMP: 27 EST: 2015
SALES (est): 9.29MM **Privately Held**
Web: www.eastbrookhealth.com
SIC: 8082 Home health care services

(G-3742)
1ST ALL FILE RECOVERY USA
Also Called: Data Recovery
4400 Renaissance Pkwy # 1 (44128-5794)
PHONE.................................800 399-7150
Dmitry Belkin, *CEO*
EMP: 40 EST: 2009
SALES (est): 2.07MM **Privately Held**
SIC: 7374 Data processing service

(G-3743)
1ST CHOICE ROOFING COMPANY
10311 Berea Rd (44102-2503)
PHONE.................................216 227-7755
Ian Fess, *CEO*
EMP: 37 EST: 2006
SALES (est): 5.07MM **Privately Held**
Web: www.1stchoiceroofing.com
SIC: 1761 Roofing contractor

(G-3744)
21ST CENTURY CON CNSTR INC
2344 Canal Rd (44113-2535)
PHONE.................................216 362-0900
Patrick Butler, *Pr*
EMP: 50 EST: 2001
SALES (est): 8.29MM **Privately Held**
Web: www.21stcenturyconcrete.com
SIC: 1771 Concrete work

(G-3745)
3B HOLDINGS INC (PA)
Also Called: 3b Supply
11470 Euclid Ave Ste 407 (44106-3934)
PHONE.................................800 791-7124
Leonard Dashkin, *Pr*
Robert Dashkin, *
EMP: 35 EST: 2008
SQ FT: 250,000
SALES (est): 21.55MM **Privately Held**
Web: www.3bsupply.com
SIC: 5085 Industrial supplies

(G-3746)
3D SYSTEMS INC
7100 Euclid Ave (44103-4036)
PHONE.................................216 229-2040
William Lewandowski, *
Robert Heinlein, *
EMP: 32 EST: 2014
SALES (est): 987.61K **Privately Held**
Web: www.3dsystems.com
SIC: 7371 Computer software development

(G-3747)
A BEE C SERVICE INC (PA)
Also Called: Service-Tech
7589 First Pl Ste 1 (44146-6727)
PHONE.................................440 735-1505
Alan Sutton, *Pr*
Barbara Sutton, *
Susan Sutton, *
EMP: 42 EST: 1961
SQ FT: 22,000
SALES (est): 9.83MM
SALES (corp-wide): 9.83MM **Privately Held**
Web: www.service-techcorp.com
SIC: 1711 Heating and air conditioning contractors

(G-3748)
A C MANAGEMENT INC
Also Called: Holiday Inn
780 Beta Dr (44143-2328)
PHONE.................................440 461-9200
EMP: 40 EST: 1995
SALES (est): 2.12MM **Privately Held**
Web: www.holidayinn.com
SIC: 7011 5813 5812 Hotels and motels; Drinking places; Eating places

(G-3749)
A D A ARCHITECTS INC
17710 Detroit Ave (44107-3451)
PHONE.................................216 521-5134
Robert Acciarri, *Pr*
EMP: 48 EST: 1981
SQ FT: 1,000
SALES (est): 4.17MM **Privately Held**
Web: www.adaarchitects.com
SIC: 8712 Architectural engineering

(G-3750)
A W S INC
Also Called: Brooklyn Adult Activity Center
10991 Memphis Ave (44144-2055)
PHONE.................................216 941-8800
David Nodge, *Mgr*
EMP: 1273
SALES (corp-wide): 3.95MM **Privately Held**
Web: www.sawinc.org
SIC: 8093 8331 Mental health clinic, outpatient; Job training and related services
PA: A W S Inc
   14775 Broadway Ave
   Maple Heights OH 44137
   216 861-0250

(G-3751)
A W S INC
Also Called: S A W Adult Training Center
4720 Hinckley Industrial Pkwy (44109-6003)
PHONE.................................216 749-0356
William Oliverio, *Mgr*
EMP: 372
SALES (corp-wide): 3.95MM **Privately Held**
Web: www.sawinc.org
SIC: 8331 7331 Vocational training agency; Direct mail advertising services
PA: A W S Inc
   14775 Broadway Ave
   Maple Heights OH 44137
   216 861-0250

(G-3752)
A-1 GENERAL INSURANCE AGENCY (DH)
9700 Rockside Rd Ste 250 (44125-6264)
PHONE.................................216 986-3000
Randy Parker, *Pr*
Randy P Parker, *
Steven Mason, *
Dick Muma, *Prin*
EMP: 80 EST: 1992
SQ FT: 24,000
SALES (est): 23.41MM
SALES (corp-wide): 11.04B **Privately Held**
SIC: 6411 Insurance agents, nec
HQ: Pga Service Corporation
   2636 Elm Hill Pike # 510
   Nashville TN 37214
   615 242-1961

(G-3753)
A-1 HLTHCARE STFFING PLCEMENTS (PA)
Also Called: Beidt Health
11811 Shaker Blvd Ste 330 (44120-1927)
P.O. Box 110782 (44111-0782)
PHONE.................................216 329-3500
Jennifer Sherman, *Managing Member*
Ceda Sherman, *
EMP: 109 EST: 2014
SALES (est): 19.29B
SALES (corp-wide): 19.29B **Privately Held**
Web: www.beidthealth.com
SIC: 7361 8011 8742 Employment agencies; Offices and clinics of medical doctors; Industry specialist consultants

(G-3754)
A1 COMPLETE INC
1383 Sheffield Rd (44121-3649)
PHONE.................................216 691-0363
Don Frombgen, *Pr*
EMP: 33 EST: 2001
SALES (est): 1.73MM **Privately Held**
Web: www.a1cleveland.com
SIC: 1521 General remodeling, single-family houses

(G-3755)
AAA FLEXIBLE PIPE CLG CORP
7277 Bessemer Ave (44127-1815)
P.O. Box 16692 (44116-0692)
PHONE.................................216 341-2900
Margaret Ziegenruecker, *Pr*
Susan Kubach, *
Carol Ann Fisco, *
EMP: 45 EST: 2003
SALES (est): 9.02MM **Privately Held**
Web: www.advancedplumber.com
SIC: 1623 Pipeline construction, nsk

GEOGRAPHIC SECTION

Cleveland - Cuyahoga County (G-3778)

(G-3756)
AAA PIPE CLEANING CORPORATION (PA)
Also Called: AAA Advanced Plbg & Drain Clg
7277 Bessemer Ave (44127-1815)
PHONE..................................216 341-2900
Carol Ann Fisco, *Pr*
Benjamin Fisco Iii, *VP*
Ernest B Fisco, *
Brian D Nix, *
EMP: 103 **EST:** 1935
SQ FT: 90,000
SALES (est): 7.96MM
SALES (corp-wide): 7.96MM **Privately Held**
Web: www.advancedplumber.com
SIC: 7699 1711 Sewer cleaning and rodding; Plumbing, heating, air-conditioning

(G-3757)
ABCO HOLDINGS LLC
Also Called: Abco Fire Protection
4545 W 160th St (44135-2647)
PHONE..................................216 433-7200
▼ **EMP:** 183
Web: www.abcofire.com
SIC: 5099 7389 Safety equipment and supplies; Fire extinguisher servicing

(G-3758)
ABM INDUSTRY GROUPS LLC
Also Called: Ampco System Parking
1459 Hamilton Ave (44114-1105)
PHONE..................................216 621-6600
Steve Brown, *Mgr*
EMP: 50
SALES (corp-wide): 8.1B **Publicly Held**
Web: www.abm.com
SIC: 7521 Parking lots
HQ: Abm Industry Groups, Llc
  14141 Southwest Fwy # 477
  Sugar Land TX 77478
  855 226-3676

(G-3759)
ABM JANITORIAL SERVICES INC
1501 Euclid Ave Ste 320 (44115-2108)
PHONE..................................216 861-1199
Robert J Pfahl, *Mgr*
EMP: 57
SALES (corp-wide): 8.1B **Publicly Held**
Web: www.abm.com
SIC: 7349 Janitorial service, contract basis
HQ: Abm Janitorial Services, Inc.
  1111 Fannin St Ste 1500
  Houston TX 77002
  866 624-1520

(G-3760)
ACCENTURE LLP
1400 W 10th St Ste 401 (44113-1361)
PHONE..................................216 685-1435
James Dickey, *Brnch Mgr*
EMP: 180
Web: www.accenture.com
SIC: 8742 8748 Business management consultant; Business consulting, nec
HQ: Accenture Llp
  500 W Madison St
  Chicago IL 60661
  312 693-5009

(G-3761)
ACD ENTERPRISES INC
Also Called: Decker Forklifts
9601 Granger Rd (44125-5350)
PHONE..................................866 252-4395
Andrew C Decker, *Pr*
◆ **EMP:** 28 **EST:** 1997
SALES (est): 4.62MM **Privately Held**
Web: www.russellconstruction.net

SIC: 5084 Materials handling machinery

(G-3762)
ACE TAXI SERVICE INC
Also Called: Supershuttle
1798 E 55th St (44103-3162)
PHONE..................................216 361-4700
Robert Bavishi, *Pr*
EMP: 68 **EST:** 1997
SQ FT: 10,000
SALES (est): 5.13MM **Privately Held**
Web: www.acetaxi.com
SIC: 4121 Taxicabs

(G-3763)
ACHIEVEMENT CTRS FOR CHILDREN (PA)
4255 Northfield Rd (44128-2811)
PHONE..................................216 292-9700
Bernadette Kerrigan, *CEO*
Patricia Nobili, *
Sally Farwell, *
Scott Peplin, *
EMP: 70 **EST:** 1940
SQ FT: 38,000
SALES (est): 11.08MM
SALES (corp-wide): 11.08MM **Privately Held**
Web: www.achievementcenters.org
SIC: 8322 Social services for the handicapped

(G-3764)
ACOR ORTHOPAEDIC LLC (PA)
18530 S Miles Rd (44128-4200)
PHONE..................................216 662-4500
Joseph Merolla, *Managing Member*
Greg Alaimo, *
Jeff Alaimo, *
▲ **EMP:** 34 **EST:** 1965
SQ FT: 35,000
SALES (est): 8.41MM
SALES (corp-wide): 8.41MM **Privately Held**
Web: www.acor.com
SIC: 3144 3143 3842 3086 Women's footwear, except athletic; Men's footwear, except athletic; Prosthetic appliances; Plastics foam products

(G-3765)
ACT ACQUISITION INC (HQ)
Also Called: Action Stainless
22901 Millcreek Blvd Ste 650 (44122)
PHONE..................................216 292-3800
Richard T Marabito, *CEO*
Lee Martinson, *Pr*
Richard A Manson, *CFO*
Jessica L Burroughs, *VP*
EMP: 44 **EST:** 2020
SALES (est): 24.62MM
SALES (corp-wide): 2.16B **Publicly Held**
SIC: 5051 Steel
PA: Olympic Steel, Inc.
  22901 Mllcreek Blvd Ste 6
  Cleveland OH 44122
  216 292-3800

(G-3766)
ACTION MANAGEMENT SERVICES
6055 Rockside Woods Blvd N Ste 160 (44131-2302)
PHONE..................................216 642-8777
Dale Chorba Senior, *Mng Pt*
Dale Chorba Junior, *Pt*
EMP: 28 **EST:** 1979
SALES (est): 2.2MM **Privately Held**
Web: www.actionmgmt.com
SIC: 7361 Executive placement

(G-3767)
ADALET ENCLOSURE SYSTEMS
4801 W 150th St (44135-3301)
PHONE..................................216 201-2710
EMP: 46 **EST:** 2018
SALES (est): 1.38MM **Privately Held**
Web: www.adalet.com
SIC: 5063 Electrical apparatus and equipment

(G-3768)
ADAMHSCC BOARD
2012 W 25th St Fl 6 (44113-4135)
PHONE..................................216 241-3400
Harvey A Snider, *Ch*
EMP: 29 **EST:** 2011
SALES (est): 687.84K **Privately Held**
Web: www.adamhscc.org
SIC: 8093 Mental health clinic, outpatient

(G-3769)
ADCOM GROUP INC
1468 W 9th St Ste 600 (44113-1299)
PHONE..................................216 574-9100
Joe Kubic, *CEO*
Mark Nuss, *
Steve Dressig, *
Mike Derrick, *
Loren Chylla, *
EMP: 110 **EST:** 1990
SALES (est): 28.51MM **Privately Held**
Web: www.engageadcom.com
SIC: 7336 Graphic arts and related design

(G-3770)
ADVANCE OHIO MEDIA LLC
4800 Tiedeman Rd (44144-2336)
PHONE..................................216 999-3900
Dave Baumgartner, *Dir*
Stephen Hermann, *Prin*
George Halarewicz, *Center Manager*
EMP: 63 **EST:** 2015
SALES (est): 3.48MM **Privately Held**
Web: www.advance-ohio.com
SIC: 4899 Communication services, nec

(G-3771)
AECOM ENERGY & CNSTR INC
Also Called: Washington Group
1300 E 9th St Ste 500 (44114-1503)
PHONE..................................216 622-2300
James Bickford, *Mgr*
EMP: 49
SALES (corp-wide): 14.38B **Publicly Held**
Web: www.aecom.com
SIC: 1622 1611 1629 1623 Bridge construction; General contractor, highway and street construction; Dams, waterways, docks, and other marine construction; Pipeline construction, nsk
HQ: Aecom Energy & Construction, Inc.
  106 Newberry St Sw
  Aiken SC 29801
  213 593-8100

(G-3772)
AFFORDABLE DEM & HLG INC
4980 Mead Ave (44127-1134)
PHONE..................................216 429-1874
Vince Collazo, *Pr*
EMP: 41 **EST:** 2003
SALES (est): 3.6MM **Privately Held**
SIC: 1795 Demolition, buildings and other structures

(G-3773)
AFLAC
4712 E 90th St (44125-1340)
PHONE..................................216 641-8760
EMP: 27 **EST:** 2019

SALES (est): 154.02K **Privately Held**
Web: www.aflac.com
SIC: 6411 Insurance agents and brokers

(G-3774)
AG INTERACTIVE INC (DH)
Also Called: American Greetings
1 American Rd (44144-2354)
PHONE..................................216 889-5000
Josef Mandelbaum, *Ch*
David Ricanati, *
Michael Waxman-lenz, *Sr VP*
Ned Newhouse, *
Kathy Mcconaughy, *Sr VP*
EMP: 120 **EST:** 1999
SQ FT: 34,000
SALES (est): 55.91MM
SALES (corp-wide): 14.52B **Privately Held**
Web: www.americangreetings.com
SIC: 5947 7335 Greeting cards; Commercial photography
HQ: American Greetings Corporation
  1 American Blvd
  Cleveland OH 44145
  216 252-7300

(G-3775)
AGMET LLC (PA)
7800 Medusa Rd (44146-5549)
PHONE..................................440 439-7400
Dana Cassidy, *Pr*
Timothy Andel, *CFO*
▲ **EMP:** 35 **EST:** 1981
SQ FT: 78,000
SALES (est): 21.96MM
SALES (corp-wide): 21.96MM **Privately Held**
Web: www.agmet1.com
SIC: 5093 Ferrous metal scrap and waste

(G-3776)
AIDS TSKFRCE GRTER CLVLAND INC
2829 Euclid Ave (44115-2413)
PHONE..................................216 357-3131
David Postero, *Pr*
EMP: 80 **EST:** 1983
SALES (est): 2.17MM **Privately Held**
Web: www.clevelandtaskforce.org
SIC: 8322 Social service center

(G-3777)
AIM LEASING COMPANY
Also Called: NationaLease
8150 Old Granger Rd (44125-4855)
PHONE..................................216 883-6300
Ben Shaffer, *Mgr*
EMP: 39
SALES (corp-wide): 180.46MM **Privately Held**
Web: www.nationalease.com
SIC: 7389 7538 Purchasing service; Truck engine repair, except industrial
PA: Aim Leasing Company
  1500 Trumbull Ave
  Girard OH 44420
  330 759-0438

(G-3778)
AIR GENERAL INC
6090 Cargo Rd (44135-3112)
PHONE..................................216 501-5643
Ken Derand, *Genl Mgr*
EMP: 41
SALES (corp-wide): 116.9MM **Privately Held**
Web: www.airgeneral.com
SIC: 4581 Airport terminal services
PA: Air General, Inc.
  403 The Hill
  Portsmouth NH 03801

Cleveland - Cuyahoga County (G-3779) GEOGRAPHIC SECTION

800 676-3327

(G-3779)
AIR-TEMP CLIMATE CONTROL INC
Also Called: Air-Temp Mechanical
3013 Payne Ave (44114-4594)
PHONE..................216 579-1552
Allen Krupar, *Pr*
Allen J Krupar, *
Timothy Holmes, *
EMP: 40 **EST:** 1978
SQ FT: 11,000
SALES (est): 5.69MM **Privately Held**
Web: www.air-tempmech.com
SIC: 1711 Warm air heating and air conditioning contractor

(G-3780)
AIRGAS MERCHANT GASES LLC (DH)
6055 Rockside Woods Blvd N Ste 500 (44131-2337)
PHONE..................800 242-0105
Chris Plitnick, *
▲ **EMP:** 31 **EST:** 2003
SALES (est): 99.47MM
SALES (corp-wide): 101.26MM **Privately Held**
SIC: 5084 Welding machinery and equipment
HQ: Airgas, Inc.
259 N Radnor Chester Rd # 100
Radnor PA 19087
610 687-5253

(G-3781)
AKA TEAM INC
1306 E 55th St (44103-1302)
PHONE..................216 751-2000
Ariane Kirkpatrick, *Pr*
EMP: 50 **EST:** 2009
SALES (est): 4.89MM **Privately Held**
Web: www.akateam.com
SIC: 1799 Cleaning new buildings after construction

(G-3782)
ALCYON TCHNCAL SVCS ATS JV LLC
21000 Brookpark Rd (44135-3127)
PHONE..................216 433-2488
EMP: 259
SALES (corp-wide): 10.15MM **Privately Held**
SIC: 8744 Facilities support services
PA: Alcyon Technical Services (Ats) Jv, Llc
360f Quality Cir Nw # 600
Huntsville AL 35806
256 489-3312

(G-3783)
ALEX N SILL COMPANY LLC (HQ)
Also Called: Sill Public Adjusters
6000 Lombardo Ctr Ste 600 (44131)
PHONE..................216 524-9999
TOLL FREE: 800
Michael Perlmuter, *CEO*
EMP: 35 **EST:** 1928
SQ FT: 7,500
SALES (est): 9.69MM
SALES (corp-wide): 59.51MM **Privately Held**
Web: www.sill.com
SIC: 6411 Insurance claim adjusters, not employed by insurance company
PA: Cnl Strategic Capital, Llc
450 S Orange Ave Ste 1400
Orlando FL 32801
407 650-1000

(G-3784)
ALEXANDER MANN SOLUTIONS CORP
1300 E 9th St Ste 400 (44114-1503)
PHONE..................216 336-6756
Rosaleen M Blair, *Ch Bd*
David Leigh, *
Lisa Rea, *Treas*
Selva Naidu, *
Mark Jones, *
EMP: 510 **EST:** 2006
SQ FT: 703,000
SALES (est): 93.35MM
SALES (corp-wide): 584.14K **Privately Held**
Web: www.weareams.com
SIC: 7361 Executive placement
HQ: Alexander Mann Solutions Limited
2nd Floor
London EC2M
207 832-2700

(G-3785)
ALEXIS EPPINGER
Also Called: Sister Sister Cleaning
3878 E 177th St (44128-1617)
PHONE..................216 509-0475
Alexis Eppinger, *Owner*
EMP: 30 **EST:** 2021
SALES (est): 410.57K **Privately Held**
SIC: 7349 7389 Cleaning service, industrial or commercial; Business Activities at Non-Commercial Site

(G-3786)
ALFRED NICKLES BAKERY INC
Also Called: Nickles Bakery
13500 Snow Rd (44142-2544)
PHONE..................216 267-8055
Gary Jerde, *Mgr*
EMP: 46
SALES (corp-wide): 151.88MM **Privately Held**
Web: www.nicklesbakery.com
SIC: 5461 5149 Bread; Bakery products
PA: Alfred Nickles Bakery, Inc.
26 Main St N
Navarre OH 44662
330 879-5635

(G-3787)
ALGART HEALTH CARE INC
8902 Detroit Ave (44102-1840)
PHONE..................216 631-1550
Gary Klein, *Pr*
Garth Ireland, *
Tom Jacobs, *
EMP: 85 **EST:** 1979
SQ FT: 29,000
SALES (est): 6.04MM **Privately Held**
Web: www.algarthealthcare.com
SIC: 8051 Convalescent home with continuous nursing care

(G-3788)
ALL ERECTION & CRANE RENTAL (PA)
4700 Acorn Dr Ste 100 (44131-6942)
P.O. Box 318047 (44131-8047)
PHONE..................216 524-6550
TOLL FREE: 800
Michael C Liptak Junior, *Pr*
Lawrence Liptak, *
Marvine Liptak, *
Wayne C Linson, *
▼ **EMP:** 225 **EST:** 1964
SQ FT: 50,000
SALES (est): 114.83MM
SALES (corp-wide): 114.83MM **Privately Held**
Web: www.allcrane.com

SIC: 7353 7359 Cranes and aerial lift equipment, rental or leasing; Equipment rental and leasing, nec

(G-3789)
ALL ERECTION & CRANE RENTAL
7809 Old Rockside Rd (44131-2384)
PHONE..................216 524-6550
EMP: 50
SALES (corp-wide): 114.83MM **Privately Held**
Web: www.allcrane.com
SIC: 7353 7359 Cranes and aerial lift equipment, rental or leasing; Equipment rental and leasing, nec
PA: All Erection & Crane Rental Corp
4700 Acorn Dr Ste 100
Cleveland OH 44131
216 524-6550

(G-3790)
ALL HEARTS HOME HEALTH CARE
6009 Landerhaven Dr Ste D (44124-4192)
PHONE..................440 342-2026
Kelli Goodrick, *Brnch Mgr*
EMP: 50
SALES (corp-wide): 260.31K **Privately Held**
SIC: 8082 Home health care services
PA: All Hearts Home Health Care Ltd
2577 Overlook Rd
Cleveland OH

(G-3791)
ALL OHIO THREADED ROD CO INC
5349 Saint Clair Ave (44103-1311)
PHONE..................216 426-1800
James Wolford, *CEO*
Rick Fien, *
James Wolford, *VP*
▲ **EMP:** 28 **EST:** 1981
SQ FT: 40,000
SALES (est): 4.38MM **Privately Held**
Web: www.allohiorod.com
SIC: 3312 5085 3316 Bar, rod, and wire products; Industrial supplies; Cold finishing of steel shapes

(G-3792)
ALL-TYPE WELDING & FABRICATION
7690 Bond St (44139-5351)
PHONE..................440 439-3990
Mike Distaulo, *Pr*
Dennis Whitaker, *
EMP: 40 **EST:** 1974
SQ FT: 34,000
SALES (est): 7.64MM **Privately Held**
Web: www.atwf-inc.com
SIC: 3599 7692 1761 Machine and other job shop work; Welding repair; Sheet metal work, nec

(G-3793)
ALLEGION ACCESS TECH LLC
14574 Neo Pkwy (44128-3155)
PHONE..................440 248-2330
Ed Wensing, *Prin*
EMP: 32
Web: www.stanleyaccess.com
SIC: 5031 Doors and windows
HQ: Allegion Access Technologies Llc
65 Scott Swamp Rd
Farmington CT 06032

(G-3794)
ALLENS RONNELL TRNSP LLC
1611 E 79th St Apt 1511 (44103-3452)
PHONE..................440 453-2273
EMP: 28
SALES (est): 1.03MM **Privately Held**

SIC: 4789 Transportation services, nec

(G-3795)
ALORICA CUSTOMER CARE INC
9525 Sweet Valley Dr (44125-4237)
PHONE..................216 525-3311
EMP: 204
SALES (corp-wide): 845.12MM **Privately Held**
SIC: 7389 Telemarketing services
HQ: Alorica Customer Care, Inc.
5085 W Park Blvd Ste 300
Plano TX

(G-3796)
ALPINE NURSING CARE INC
Also Called: Alpine Homehealth Care
4753 Northfield Rd Ste 5 (44128-4540)
PHONE..................216 662-7096
Divyesh C Patel, *Pr*
EMP: 75 **EST:** 2003
SQ FT: 20,000
SALES (est): 2.33MM **Privately Held**
SIC: 8082 Home health care services

(G-3797)
ALS GROUP USA CORP
Als Tribology
6180 Halle Dr Ste D (44125-4636)
PHONE..................281 530-5656
Jim Klippel, *Brnch Mgr*
EMP: 63
SIC: 8734 Testing laboratories
HQ: Als Group Usa, Corp.
10450 Stncliff Rd Ste 210
Houston TX 77099
281 530-5656

(G-3798)
AM INDUSTRIAL GROUP LLC
4680 Grayton Rd (44135-2357)
PHONE..................216 267-6783
EMP: 35
Web: www.amindustrialmachinery.com
SIC: 4225 General warehousing and storage
PA: Am Industrial Group, Llc
16000 Commerce Park Dr
Brookpark OH 44142

(G-3799)
AMERICAN CMPUS COMMUNITIES INC
Also Called: AMERICAN CAMPUS COMMUNITIES, INC.
1983 E 24th St (44115-2403)
PHONE..................216 687-5196
EMP: 46
SALES (corp-wide): 942.41MM **Privately Held**
Web: www.americancampus.com
SIC: 6798 Real estate investment trusts
PA: American Campus Communities Llc
12700 Hill Country Blvd T-200
Austin TX 78738
512 732-1000

(G-3800)
AMERICAN CONSOLIDATED INDS INC (PA)
4650 Johnston Pkwy (44128-3219)
PHONE..................216 587-8000
Josh Kaufman, *Pr*
Joyce Kaufman, *
Steve Lefkowitz, *
◆ **EMP:** 40 **EST:** 1988
SQ FT: 118,000
SALES (est): 46.93MM **Privately Held**
Web: www.monarchsteel.com
SIC: 5051 Steel

GEOGRAPHIC SECTION

Cleveland - Cuyahoga County (G-3822)

(G-3801)
AMERICAN COPY EQUIPMENT INC
Also Called: Online Imaging Solutions
6599 Granger Rd (44131-1415)
PHONE..........................330 722-9555
John Baron, *Pr*
Katherine L Huff, *
EMP: 195 **EST:** 1988
SQ FT: 30,000
SALES (est): 42.53MM
SALES (corp-wide): 92.94MM **Privately Held**
SIC: 5044 Office equipment
PA: Meritech, Inc.
 4577 Hinckley Indus Pkwy
 Cleveland OH 44109
 216 459-8333

(G-3802)
AMERICAN LIVERY SERVICE INC
Also Called: American Limousine Service
11723 Detroit Ave (44107-3001)
PHONE..........................216 221-9330
Robert Mazzarella, *Pr*
Joanne Mazzarella, *
EMP: 45 **EST:** 1953
SQ FT: 2,500
SALES (est): 2.13MM **Privately Held**
Web: www.amerilimo.com
SIC: 4119 Limousine rental, with driver

(G-3803)
AMERICAN MARINE EXPRESS INC
Also Called: Amx
765 E 140th St Ste A (44110-2181)
P.O. Box 32487 (44132-0487)
PHONE..........................216 268-3005
EMP: 30 **EST:** 2007
SALES (est): 10.55MM **Privately Held**
Web: www.amxtrans.com
SIC: 4731 Truck transportation brokers

(G-3804)
AMERICAN MIDWEST MORTGAGE CORP (PA)
6363 York Rd Ste 300 (44130-3031)
PHONE..........................440 882-5210
EMP: 50 **EST:** 1974
SALES (est): 11.54MM **Privately Held**
Web: www.ammcorp.net
SIC: 6162 Mortgage bankers

(G-3805)
AMERICAN NAT FLEET SVC INC
Also Called: American Fleet Services
7714 Commerce Park Oval (44131-2306)
PHONE..........................216 447-6060
Joe Schuerger, *CEO*
EMP: 65 **EST:** 1979
SQ FT: 40,000
SALES (est): 13.13MM **Privately Held**
Web: www.fleetme.com
SIC: 7538 7532 General truck repair; Body shop, automotive

(G-3806)
AMERICAN PRSERVATION BLDRS LLC
127 Public Sq Ste 1300 (44114-1310)
PHONE..........................216 236-2007
Michael Kucera, *Pr*
Harry Lee, *
Dennis Arian, *
Todd Wallace, *
EMP: 68 **EST:** 2007
SALES (est): 20.9MM **Privately Held**
Web: www.americanpreservationbuilders.com
SIC: 1542 Commercial and office building, new construction

(G-3807)
AMERICAN RETIREMENT CORP
Also Called: Homewood Rsdnce At Rchmond Hts
3 Homewood Way (44143-2955)
PHONE..........................216 291-6140
Kim Hutter, *Brnch Mgr*
EMP: 178
SALES (corp-wide): 2.83B **Publicly Held**
Web: www.brookdale.com
SIC: 8051 8052 Skilled nursing care facilities; Intermediate care facilities
HQ: American Retirement Corporation
 111 Westwood Pl Ste 200
 Brentwood TN 37027
 615 221-2250

(G-3808)
AMERICAN TANK & FABRICATING CO (PA)
Also Called: A T & F Co
12314 Elmwood Ave (44111)
PHONE..........................216 252-1500
Terry Ripich, *Ch Bd*
Michael Ripich, *
Kenneth Ripich, *
Brian Spitz, *
Michael Puleo, *HEAVY FABRICATING*
▲ **EMP:** 100 **EST:** 1940
SQ FT: 300,000
SALES (est): 57.84MM
SALES (corp-wide): 57.84MM **Privately Held**
Web: www.atfco.com
SIC: 5051 3443 Metals service centers and offices; Weldments

(G-3809)
AMERIMARK HOLDINGS LLC (HQ)
Also Called: Amerimark Direct
6864 Engle Rd (44130-7910)
PHONE..........................440 325-2000
Mark Ethier, *CEO*
Joe Albanese, *
EMP: 425 **EST:** 2007
SALES (est): 197.32MM
SALES (corp-wide): 890.58MM **Privately Held**
Web: www.amerimarkinteractive.com
SIC: 7331 5961 Direct mail advertising services; Catalog sales
PA: Csc Generation Holdings, Inc.
 8450 Broadway
 Merrillville IN 46410
 219 641-6463

(G-3810)
AML RIGHTSOURCE LLC (PA)
1300 E 9th St Fl 2 (44114)
PHONE..........................216 771-1250
Frank H Ewing, *CEO*
Paul W Linehan, *Pr*
Todd Ayers, *CFO*
EMP: 82 **EST:** 2004
SALES (est): 25.4MM **Privately Held**
Web: www.amlrightsource.com
SIC: 7389 Financial services

(G-3811)
AMOTEC INC (PA)
3133 Chester Ave (44114-4616)
PHONE..........................440 250-4600
Carmine Izzo, *CEO*
EMP: 39 **EST:** 2000
SALES (est): 14.49MM
SALES (corp-wide): 14.49MM **Privately Held**
Web: www.amotecinc.com
SIC: 7361 7363 Executive placement; Temporary help service

(G-3812)
AMROS INDUSTRIES INC
14701 Industrial Pkwy (44135-4547)
PHONE..........................216 433-0010
Gregory Shteyngarts, *Pr*
EMP: 28 **EST:** 1986
SQ FT: 65,000
SALES (est): 1.02MM **Privately Held**
Web: www.clamshellusa.com
SIC: 7389 2821 Packaging and labeling services; Thermoplastic materials

(G-3813)
AMTRUST NORTH AMERICA INC (DH)
Also Called: Amtrust Financial Services
59 Maiden Ln Flr 43 (44114)
PHONE..........................216 328-6100
Barry D Zyskind, *CEO*
Eli Tisser, *Treas*
EMP: 230 **EST:** 2001
SQ FT: 60,000
SALES (est): 1.06B
SALES (corp-wide): 5.96B **Privately Held**
Web: www.amtrustfinancial.com
SIC: 6331 6411 Workers' compensation insurance; Insurance claim processing, except medical
HQ: Amtrust Financial Services, Inc.
 59 Maiden Ln Fl 43
 New York NY 10038

(G-3814)
ANCHOR METAL PROCESSING INC (PA)
11830 Brookpark Rd (44130-1103)
PHONE..........................216 362-1850
Edward Pfaff, *Ch Bd*
Frederick Pfaff, *
Jeff Pfaff, *
Robert Pfaff, *
EMP: 30 **EST:** 1992
SQ FT: 46,000
SALES (est): 4.51MM **Privately Held**
Web: www.anchor-mfg.com
SIC: 3599 1761 3444 Machine shop, jobbing and repair; Sheet metal work, nec; Sheet metalwork

(G-3815)
ANCORA GROUP LLC
6060 Parkland Blvd Ste 200 (44124-4225)
PHONE..........................216 825-4000
Patrick J Berry, *Pr*
EMP: 96 **EST:** 2009
SALES (est): 14.07MM
SALES (corp-wide): 14.52B **Privately Held**
Web: www.ancora.net
SIC: 6282 Investment advisory service
HQ: Focus Financial Partners Inc.
 875 3rd Ave Fl 28
 New York NY 10022
 646 519-2456

(G-3816)
ANESTHESIA ASSOCIATES PLL
835 Ford Rd (44143-3103)
PHONE..........................440 350-0832
John J Fitzgerald, *Pt*
Roy E Ronke, *
William Cress, *
EMP: 101 **EST:** 2012
SALES (est): 5.5MM **Privately Held**
SIC: 8011 Anesthesiologist

(G-3817)
ANGSTROM GRAPHICS INC MIDWEST (HQ)
4437 E 49th St (44125-1005)
PHONE..........................216 271-5300
Wayne R Angstrom, *Ch Bd*
Rachel Malakoff, *
EMP: 249 **EST:** 1917
SQ FT: 230,000
SALES (est): 51.77MM **Privately Held**
Web: www.angstromgraphics.com
SIC: 2752 7331 Offset printing; Direct mail advertising services
PA: Angstrom Graphics Inc
 4437 E 49th St
 Cleveland OH 44125

(G-3818)
ANSELMO RSSIS PREMIER PROD LTD
Also Called: Premiere Produce
4500 Willow Pkwy (44125-1042)
PHONE..........................800 229-5517
Anthony Anselmo, *Pr*
Anthony Rossi, *Pt*
Joe Harvey, *Genl Mgr*
EMP: 43 **EST:** 1997
SALES (est): 10.28MM **Privately Held**
Web: www.premierproduceone.com
SIC: 5148 Fruits, fresh

(G-3819)
APEX TRANSIT SOLUTIONS LLC
805 E 70th St (44103-1705)
PHONE..........................216 938-5606
Susan Rushworth, *Pr*
EMP: 46 **EST:** 2014
SALES (est): 2.45MM **Privately Held**
SIC: 4119 Ambulance service

(G-3820)
APPALACHIAN HARDWOOD LUMBER CO
5433 Perkins Rd (44146-1856)
PHONE..........................440 232-6767
TOLL FREE: 800
Gary S Kaufman, *Pr*
Stephen Kaufman, *
◆ **EMP:** 30 **EST:** 1988
SQ FT: 100,000
SALES (est): 9.42MM **Privately Held**
Web: www.appalachianlumber.com
SIC: 5031 Lumber: rough, dressed, and finished

(G-3821)
APPLEWOOD CENTERS INC (PA)
10427 Detroit Ave (44102-1645)
PHONE..........................216 696-6815
Adam Jacobs, *Ex Dir*
EMP: 60 **EST:** 1832
SQ FT: 17,000
SALES (est): 19.56MM
SALES (corp-wide): 19.56MM **Privately Held**
Web: www.applewoodcenters.org
SIC: 8322 8699 Child related social services; Charitable organization

(G-3822)
APPLEWOOD CENTERS INC
2525 E 22nd St (44115-3266)
PHONE..........................216 696-5800
EMP: 37
SALES (corp-wide): 19.56MM **Privately Held**
Web: www.applewoodcenters.org
SIC: 8322 Child related social services
PA: Applewood Centers, Inc.
 10427 Detroit Ave
 Cleveland OH 44102
 216 696-6815

Cleveland - Cuyahoga County (G-3823)

GEOGRAPHIC SECTION

(G-3823)
APPLEWOOD CENTERS INC
Also Called: Children's Aide Society Campus
10427 Detroit Ave (44102-1645)
PHONE..................216 521-6511
Roberta King, *Mgr*
EMP: 36
SALES (corp-wide): 19.56MM **Privately Held**
Web: www.applewoodcenters.org
SIC: 8322 Child related social services
PA: Applewood Centers, Inc.
    10427 Detroit Ave
    Cleveland OH 44102
    216 696-6815

(G-3824)
APPLEWOOD CENTERS INC
3518 W 25th St (44109-1951)
PHONE..................216 741-2241
J Blumhagen, *Brnch Mgr*
EMP: 98
SALES (corp-wide): 19.56MM **Privately Held**
Web: www.applewoodcenters.org
SIC: 8322 Child related social services
PA: Applewood Centers, Inc.
    10427 Detroit Ave
    Cleveland OH 44102
    216 696-6815

(G-3825)
APPLIED INDUS TECH - CA LLC (HQ)
Also Called: Applied Industrial Tech
1 Applied Plz (44115-2511)
PHONE..................216 426-4000
▲ **EMP:** 307 **EST:** 2002
SALES (est): 343.34MM
SALES (corp-wide): 4.41B **Publicly Held**
Web: www.applied.com
SIC: 5085 Bearings
PA: Applied Industrial Technologies, Inc.
    1 Applied Plz
    Cleveland OH 44115
    216 426-4000

(G-3826)
APPLIED INDUS TECH - DIXIE INC (HQ)
Also Called: Applied Industrial Tech
1 Applied Plz (44115-2511)
P.O. Box 6925 (44101-2193)
PHONE..................216 426-4546
David L Pugh, *Ch Bd*
Richard C Shaw, *
Jeffrey Ramras, *Supply Chain Management Vice-President*
William Purser, *NATIONAL*
James Hopper, *Information Vice President*
▲ **EMP:** 53 **EST:** 1923
SQ FT: 146,000
SALES (est): 1.22B
SALES (corp-wide): 4.41B **Publicly Held**
Web: www.applied.com
SIC: 5172 5169 Lubricating oils and greases; Sealants
PA: Applied Industrial Technologies, Inc.
    1 Applied Plz
    Cleveland OH 44115
    216 426-4000

(G-3827)
APPLIED INDUSTRIAL TECH INC (PA)
1 Applied Plz (44115)
PHONE..................216 426-4000
Neil A Schrimsher, *Pr*
Peter C Wallace, *
David K Wells, *VP*
Kurt W Loring, *Chief Human Resources Officer*
Jon S Ploetz, *VP*
▲ **EMP:** 296 **EST:** 1923
SALES (est): 4.41B
SALES (corp-wide): 4.41B **Publicly Held**
Web: www.applied.com
SIC: 5085 5169 7699 Industrial supplies; Chemicals and allied products, nec; Industrial machinery and equipment repair

(G-3828)
ARAMARK FACILITY SERVICES LLC
Also Called: Aramark
2121 Euclid Ave (44115-2214)
PHONE..................216 687-5000
Pat Underwood, *Off Mgr*
EMP: 104
SIC: 7349 8744 Janitorial service, contract basis; Facilities support services
HQ: Aramark Facility Services, Llc
    2400 Market St Ste 209
    Philadelphia PA 19103
    215 238-3000

(G-3829)
ARBOR CONSTRUCTION CO INC
1350 W 3rd St (44113-1806)
PHONE..................216 360-8989
Robert Stark, *Pr*
Howard Beder, *
EMP: 30 **EST:** 1980
SQ FT: 3,400
SALES (est): 10.58MM **Privately Held**
Web: www.arborconstruction.com
SIC: 1542 Shopping center construction

(G-3830)
ARC DOCUMENT SOLUTIONS INC
Also Called: A R C
3666 Carnegie Ave (44115-2714)
PHONE..................216 281-1234
Tina Lemanomcz, *Brnch Mgr*
EMP: 92
SALES (corp-wide): 281.2MM **Publicly Held**
Web: www.e-arc.com
SIC: 7334 Blueprinting service
PA: Arc Document Solutions, Inc.
    12657 Alcosta Blvd # 200
    San Ramon CA 94583
    925 949-5100

(G-3831)
ARCHITCTRAL INTR RSTRTIONS INC
2401 Train Ave Ste 100 (44113-4254)
PHONE..................216 241-2255
John L Textoris Junior, *Pr*
EMP: 45 **EST:** 1983
SQ FT: 11,000
SALES (est): 3.63MM **Privately Held**
Web: www.air-neo.com
SIC: 1742 Drywall

(G-3832)
ARCONIC WHEEL WHEEL FORGE
5801 Postal Rd (44181-2184)
PHONE..................479 750-6359
EMP: 29 **EST:** 2019
SALES (est): 5.36MM **Privately Held**
SIC: 7822 Motion picture and tape distribution

(G-3833)
AREA TEMPS INC
5805 Pearl Rd (44130-2160)
PHONE..................440 842-2100
Kim Degroff, *Mgr*
EMP: 1849
Web: www.areatemps.com
SIC: 7363 Temporary help service
PA: Area Temps, Inc.
    4511 Rockside Rd Ste 190
    Independence OH 44131

(G-3834)
ARISTOCRAT W NURSING HM CORP
Also Called: Call Traditions
4401 W 150th St (44135-1311)
PHONE..................216 252-7730
Anthony M Coury, *Pr*
EMP: 110
SALES (corp-wide): 5.6MM **Privately Held**
SIC: 8051 Convalescent home with continuous nursing care
PA: Aristocrat West Nursing Home Corporation
    24340 Sperry Dr
    Cleveland OH

(G-3835)
ARTISAN AND TRUCKERS CSLTY CO
6300 Wilson Mills Rd (44143-2109)
PHONE..................440 461-5000
Tricia Griffith, *Pr*
EMP: 69 **EST:** 1994
SALES (est): 102.46MM
SALES (corp-wide): 49.61B **Publicly Held**
Web: www.progressivecommercial.com
SIC: 6331 Automobile insurance
HQ: Progressive Commercial Holdings, Inc.
    6300 Wilson Mills Rd
    Cleveland OH 44143

(G-3836)
ARTWALL LLC
4700 Lakeside Ave E Fl 3 (44114)
PHONE..................216 476-0635
David Aheimer, *Managing Member*
EMP: 32 **EST:** 2011
SALES (est): 4.13MM **Privately Held**
Web: www.4walls.com
SIC: 5023 5091 5141 5092 Decorative home furnishings and supplies; Sporting and recreation goods; Groceries, general line; Toys and hobby goods and supplies

(G-3837)
AT HOLDINGS CORPORATION
23555 Euclid Ave (44117-1703)
PHONE..................216 692-6000
Michael S Lipscomb, *Ch Bd*
Frances S St Clair, *
David Scaife, *
EMP: 736 **EST:** 1990
SQ FT: 1,800,000
SALES (est): 187.9MM **Privately Held**
SIC: 3724 3728 6512 Pumps, aircraft engine; Aircraft parts and equipment, nec; Commercial and industrial building operation
HQ: Eaton Corporation
    1000 Eaton Blvd
    Cleveland OH 44122
    440 523-5000

(G-3838)
ATLANTIS SECURITY COMPANY (PA)
Also Called: Atlantis Company, The
105 Ken Mar Industrial Pkwy (44147-2950)
PHONE..................440 717-7050
▲ **EMP:** 70 **EST:** 1993
SALES (est): 5.29MM **Privately Held**
Web: www.atlantissecurity.com
SIC: 7349 7381 Janitorial service, contract basis; Detective services

(G-3839)
AUSTIN BUILDING AND DESIGN INC (DH)
Also Called: Austin Company, The
6095 Parkland Blvd Ste 100 (44124-6139)
PHONE..................440 544-2600
Michael G Pierce, *Pr*
Noriaki Ohashi, *
Mark Phillips, *
Patrick Flanagan, *
Shinya Urano, *
EMP: 121 **EST:** 2005
SQ FT: 21,869
SALES (est): 156.56MM **Privately Held**
Web: www.theaustin.com
SIC: 1541 1542 8742 8711 Industrial buildings, new construction, nec; Commercial and office building, new construction; Management consulting services; Engineering services
HQ: Kajima U.S.A. Inc.
    3550 Lenox Rd Ne Ste 1850
    Atlanta GA 30326
    404 564-3900

(G-3840)
AUTOGRAPH INC
Also Called: Autograph Foliages
4419 Perkins Ave (44103-3543)
PHONE..................216 881-1911
Thomas M Acklin, *Mgr*
EMP: 45
SALES (corp-wide): 7.85MM **Privately Held**
Web: www.autographfoliages.com
SIC: 5193 Flowers and florists supplies
PA: Autograph, Inc.
    3631 Perkins Ave
    Cleveland OH
    216 426-6151

(G-3841)
AUTOMOTIVE DISTRIBUTORS CO INC
990 Valley Belt Rd (44109)
PHONE..................216 398-2014
EMP: 29
SALES (corp-wide): 42.46MM **Privately Held**
Web: www.adw1.com
SIC: 5013 Automotive supplies and parts
PA: Automotive Distributors Co., Inc.
    2981 Morse Rd
    Columbus OH 43231
    614 476-1315

(G-3842)
AUTOZONE INC
Also Called: Autozone
11414 Kinsman Rd (44104-5045)
PHONE..................216 751-0571
Allen Miller, *Mgr*
EMP: 36
SQ FT: 7,199
SALES (corp-wide): 17.46B **Publicly Held**
Web: www.autozonepro.com
SIC: 5531 5045 5734 Automotive parts; Computer software; Software, business and non-game
PA: Autozone, Inc.
    123 S Front St
    Memphis TN 38103
    901 495-6500

(G-3843)
AUTOZONE INC
Also Called: Autozone
15427 Snow Rd (44142-2346)
PHONE..................216 267-6586
Clint Baeur, *Mgr*
EMP: 32
SQ FT: 7,534
SALES (corp-wide): 17.46B **Publicly Held**
Web: www.autozonepro.com
SIC: 5531 5045 5734 Automotive parts; Computer software; Software, business and non-game
PA: Autozone, Inc.
    123 S Front St
    Memphis TN 38103

GEOGRAPHIC SECTION
Cleveland - Cuyahoga County (G-3865)

901 495-6500

(G-3844)
AUXILIARY BD FAIRVIEW GEN HOSP
Also Called: FAIRVIEW WEST PHYSICIAN CENTER
18101 Lorain Ave (44111-5612)
PHONE..................216 476-7000
EMP: 632 EST: 2011
SALES (est): 12.85MM
SALES (corp-wide): 14.48B Privately Held
Web: www.fairviewhospital.org
SIC: 8062 General medical and surgical hospitals
HQ: Fairview Hospital
18101 Lorain Ave
Cleveland OH 44111
216 476-7000

(G-3845)
AVANTIA INC
9655 Sweet Valley Dr Ste 1 (44125-4271)
PHONE..................216 901-9366
Jennie Zamberlan, Pr
EMP: 35 EST: 2000
SQ FT: 4,500
SALES (est): 31.78K Privately Held
Web: www.avantia-inc.com
SIC: 8748 Business consulting, nec

(G-3846)
B & B WRECKING & EXCVTG INC
4510 E 71st St Ste 6 (44105-5638)
PHONE..................216 429-1700
Pete Boyas, Prin
William A Baumann, *
EMP: 40 EST: 1957
SQ FT: 50,000
SALES (est): 10.33MM Privately Held
Web: www.bbwrecking.net
SIC: 1795 1794 Demolition, buildings and other structures; Excavation and grading, building construction

(G-3847)
BAKER & HOSTETLER LLP (PA)
127 Public Sq Ste 2000 (44114-1214)
PHONE..................216 621-0200
Ronald G Linville, Mng Pt
R Steven Kestner, Executive Partner*
Richard T Fulton, *
Rick L Johnson, *
Katherine Lowry, CIO*
EMP: 274 EST: 1916
SQ FT: 160,000
SALES (est): 309.55K
SALES (corp-wide): 309.55K Privately Held
Web: www.bakerlaw.com
SIC: 8111 General practice attorney, lawyer

(G-3848)
BAKER & HOSTETLER LLP
1375 E 9th St Ste 2100 (44114-1794)
PHONE..................216 430-2960
EMP: 46
SALES (corp-wide): 309.55K Privately Held
Web: www.bakerlaw.com
SIC: 8111 General practice attorney, lawyer
PA: Baker & Hostetler Llp
127 Public Sq Ste 2000
Cleveland OH 44114
216 621-0200

(G-3849)
BARBS GRAFFITI INC (PA)
Also Called: Graffiti Co
3111 Carnegie Ave (44115-2632)
PHONE..................216 881-5550
Abe Miller, Pr
Barbara Miller, *
▲ EMP: 38 EST: 1984
SQ FT: 18,000
SALES (est): 9.07MM
SALES (corp-wide): 9.07MM Privately Held
Web: www.graffiticaps.com
SIC: 2353 2395 5136 5137 Baseball caps; Pleating and stitching; Sportswear, men's and boys'; Sportswear, women's and children's

(G-3850)
BARKLYN HEIGHTS LLC
247 Old Brookpark Rd (44109-5801)
PHONE..................216 577-5960
EMP: 28
Web: www.barklynhts.com
SIC: 7389 Personal service agents, brokers, and bureaus
PA: Barklyn Heights Llc
604 North St
Brooklyn Heights OH 44131
216 404-6036

(G-3851)
BARNES WENDLING CPAS INC (PA)
1350 Euclid Ave Ste 1400 (44115-1830)
PHONE..................216 566-9000
Jeffrey Neuman, Pr
Janine Iacobelli, *
Michael Pappas, AUDITING*
EMP: 45 EST: 1946
SQ FT: 18,500
SALES (est): 10.46MM
SALES (corp-wide): 10.46MM Privately Held
Web: www.barneswendling.com
SIC: 8721 7291 Certified public accountant; Tax return preparation services

(G-3852)
BARRIE G GLVIN OTR/L ASSOC LTD
Also Called: Galvin Edcatn Rsrce Ctr For Fm
25221 Miles Rd Unit F (44128-5494)
PHONE..................216 514-1600
EMP: 30 EST: 1995
SALES (est): 942.43K Privately Held
SIC: 8049 Occupational therapist

(G-3853)
BASF CATALYSTS LLC
Also Called: BASF
23800 Mercantile Rd (44122-5908)
P.O. Box 22126 (44122-0126)
PHONE..................216 360-5005
John Ferek, Brnch Mgr
EMP: 117
SALES (corp-wide): 74.89B Privately Held
Web: catalysts.basf.com
SIC: 2819 8731 Catalysts, chemical; Commercial physical research
HQ: Basf Catalysts Llc
33 Wood Ave S
Iselin NJ 08830
732 205-5000

(G-3854)
BASISTA FURNITURE INC
Also Called: Warehouse
5340 Brookpark Rd (44134-1044)
PHONE..................216 398-5900
Stanley Basista, Brnch Mgr
EMP: 30
SALES (corp-wide): 4.99MM Privately Held
Web: www.basista.com
SIC: 4225 General warehousing and storage
PA: Basista Furniture, Inc.
159 E Aurora Rd
Northfield OH 44067

216 635-1200

(G-3855)
BATTLE BULLYING HOTLINE INC
3185 Warren Rd (44111-1153)
PHONE..................216 731-1976
Michael Prandich, Pr
EMP: 75 EST: 2017
SALES (est): 746.91K Privately Held
SIC: 8322 Hotline

(G-3856)
BAY ADVANCED TECHNOLOGIES LLC
1 Applied Plz (44115-2511)
PHONE..................510 857-0900
EMP: 50
SALES (corp-wide): 4.41B Publicly Held
Web: www.bayat.com
SIC: 5084 Hydraulic systems equipment and supplies
HQ: Bay Advanced Technologies, Llc
8100 Central Ave
Newark CA 94560
510 857-0900

(G-3857)
BAY VILLAGE CITY SCHOOL DST
Also Called: Glenview Ctr For Child Care Lr
28727 Wolf Rd (44140-1351)
PHONE..................440 617-7330
Barbara Manning, Dir
EMP: 51
SALES (corp-wide): 44.78MM Privately Held
Web: www.bayvillageschools.com
SIC: 8211 8351 Public elementary school; Child day care services
PA: Bay Village City School District
377 Dover Center Rd
Cleveland OH 44140
440 617-7300

(G-3858)
BDI INC (HQ)
Also Called: Bearing Distributors
8000 Hub Pkwy (44125-5731)
PHONE..................216 642-9100
Frank L Bystricky, CEO
Bud Thayer, *
Mike Fryz, *
▲ EMP: 171 EST: 1966
SALES (est): 205.13MM
SALES (corp-wide): 1.51B Privately Held
Web: www.bdiexpress.com
SIC: 5085 Bearings
PA: Forge Industries, Inc.
4450 Market St
Youngstown OH 44512
330 960-2468

(G-3859)
BEACHWOOD CITY SCHOOLS
23757 Commerce Park (44122-5825)
PHONE..................216 464-6609
Paul Williams, Superintnt
EMP: 54
SQ FT: 13,600
SALES (corp-wide): 49.62MM Privately Held
Web: www.beachwoodschools.org
SIC: 4151 School buses
PA: Beachwood City Schools
24601 Fairmount Blvd
Cleveland OH 44122
216 464-2600

(G-3860)
BEARING DISTRIBUTORS INC (HQ)
Also Called: Bdi-USA
8000 Hub Pkwy (44125-5788)
P.O. Box 6128 (44194-8000)
PHONE..................216 642-9100
Carl James, Pr
John Ruth, *
Steve Kieffer, *
Dan Maisonville, *
◆ EMP: 200 EST: 1935
SQ FT: 150,000
SALES (est): 518.78MM
SALES (corp-wide): 1.51B Privately Held
Web: www.bdiexpress.com
SIC: 5085 Bearings
PA: Forge Industries, Inc.
4450 Market St
Youngstown OH 44512
330 960-2468

(G-3861)
BECK COMPANY
10701 Broadway Ave (44125-1650)
P.O. Box 25469 (44125-0469)
PHONE..................216 883-0909
Mark Beck, Pr
EMP: 35 EST: 1983
SQ FT: 20,000
SALES (est): 2.46MM Privately Held
Web: www.engineeredroofing.com
SIC: 1761 Roofing contractor

(G-3862)
BELLWETHER
1375 E 9th St Ste 2440 (44114-1731)
PHONE..................949 247-8912
Steven Ferrante, Prin
EMP: 54 EST: 2019
SALES (est): 1.96MM Privately Held
Web: www.bwe.com
SIC: 6531 Real estate brokers and agents

(G-3863)
BELLWETHER ENTP RE CAPITL LLC (PA)
1360 E 9th St Ste 300 (44114)
PHONE..................216 820-4500
Harry Giallourakis, *
Elmer Cole, *
Sara Behrman, *
Bob Momeier, *
EMP: 34 EST: 2008
SQ FT: 7,000
SALES (est): 36.6MM
SALES (corp-wide): 36.6MM Privately Held
Web: www.bwe.com
SIC: 6531 Real estate agent, commercial

(G-3864)
BELMORE LEASING CO LLC
Also Called: Candlewood Park Healthcare Ctr
1835 Belmore Rd (44112-4301)
PHONE..................216 268-3600
Stephen L Rosedale, Managing Member
Ronald S Wilheim, *
Charles R Stoltz, *
EMP: 42 EST: 2004
SQ FT: 28,000
SALES (est): 9.44MM Privately Held
SIC: 8051 Convalescent home with continuous nursing care

(G-3865)
BENESCH FRDLNDER CPLAN ARNOFF
127 Public Sq (44114-1217)
PHONE..................216 363-4686
Jim Hill, Pt
EMP: 32
SALES (corp-wide): 51.22MM Privately Held
Web: www.beneschlaw.com

Cleveland - Cuyahoga County (G-3866) GEOGRAPHIC SECTION

SIC: 8111 General practice attorney, lawyer
PA: Benesch, Friedlander, Coplan & Aronoff Llp
200 Public Sq Ste 2300
Cleveland OH 44114
216 363-4500

(G-3866)
BENESCH FRIEDLANDER COPLAN & ARONOFF LLP (PA)
200 Public Sq Ste 2300 (44114-2309)
PHONE.................................216 363-4500
EMP: 206 EST: 1938
SALES (est): 51.22MM
SALES (corp-wide): 51.22MM Privately Held
Web: www.beneschlaw.com
SIC: 8111 General practice attorney, lawyer

(G-3867)
BENJAMIN ROSE INSTITUTE (PA)
11890 Fairhill Rd (44120-1000)
PHONE.................................216 791-8000
Richard Browdie, Pr
Frank Cardinale, *
EMP: 80 EST: 1908
SQ FT: 31,000
SALES (est): 7.52MM
SALES (corp-wide): 7.52MM Privately Held
Web: www.benrose.org
SIC: 8082 8322 Home health care services; Individual and family services

(G-3868)
BENJAMIN ROSE INSTITUTE
Also Called: Margret Wagner House
2373 Euclid Heights Blvd 2nd Fl (44106-2716)
PHONE.................................216 791-3580
Richard Browdie, CEO
EMP: 119
SQ FT: 27,326
SALES (corp-wide): 7.52MM Privately Held
Web: www.benrose.org
SIC: 8361 8741 8322 Rest home, with health care incidental; Management services; Individual and family services
PA: Benjamin Rose Institute
11890 Fairhill Rd
Cleveland OH 44120
216 791-8000

(G-3869)
BENJAMIN ROSE INSTITUTE
850 Euclid Ave Ste 1100 (44114-3313)
PHONE.................................216 791-8000
Carole Johnson, Prin
EMP: 29
SALES (corp-wide): 7.52MM Privately Held
Web: www.benrose.org
SIC: 8733 Noncommercial research organizations
PA: Benjamin Rose Institute
11890 Fairhill Rd
Cleveland OH 44120
216 791-8000

(G-3870)
BENNETT ADELSON PROF SVCS LLC
6050 Oak Tree Blvd Ste 150 (44131-6927)
PHONE.................................216 369-0140
Nilesh Bandi, Prin
EMP: 50 EST: 2019
SALES (est): 2.25MM Privately Held
Web: www.bennettadelson.com
SIC: 7371 Computer software development

(G-3871)
BEST KARPET KLEAN OHIO LLC
5525 Canal Rd Unit A (44125-4865)
PHONE.................................440 942-2481
Carol Bohr, Managing Member
Linda Bohr, Managing Member
EMP: 50 EST: 2009
SALES (est): 863.57K Privately Held
Web: www.bestkarpetklean.com
SIC: 7217 Carpet and upholstery cleaning

(G-3872)
BEVERAGE DISTRIBUTORS INC
3800 King Ave (44114-3703)
PHONE.................................216 431-1600
James V Conway, Pr
▲ EMP: 150 EST: 1933
SQ FT: 125,000
SALES (est): 44.66MM Privately Held
Web: www.beveragedist.com
SIC: 5181 Beer and other fermented malt liquors

(G-3873)
BIG BANG BAR CLEVELAND LLC
Also Called: Big Bang, The
1163 Front Ave (44113-5821)
P.O. Box 50316 (37205-0316)
PHONE.................................615 264-5650
Meredyth Muller, Managing Member
EMP: 27 EST: 2013
SALES (est): 1MM Privately Held
Web: www.thebigbangbar.com
SIC: 7929 5813 Entertainment service; Bar (drinking places)

(G-3874)
BILLIE LAWLESS
4533 Payne Ave (44103-2332)
PHONE.................................714 851-6372
Billie Lawless, Prin
EMP: 39 EST: 2018
SALES (est): 95.07K Privately Held
Web: www.billielawless.com
SIC: 7822 Motion picture and tape distribution

(G-3875)
BLUE RIBBON MEATS INC (PA)
3316 W 67th Pl (44102-5243)
PHONE.................................216 631-8850
Albert J Radis, Pr
Michael A Radis, VP
Paul Radis, Sec
David Radis, CFO
John Forrester, Prin
EMP: 100 EST: 1952
SQ FT: 8,400
SALES (est): 26.01MM
SALES (corp-wide): 26.01MM Privately Held
Web: www.blueribbonmeats.com
SIC: 5147 5142 Meats, fresh; Meat, frozen: packaged

(G-3876)
BLUE TECH SMART SOLUTIONS LLC
5885 Grant Ave (44105-5607)
PHONE.................................216 271-4800
Paul Hanna, Pr
EMP: 44 EST: 2013
SALES (est): 7.48MM Privately Held
Web: www.btohio.com
SIC: 5045 Computers, peripherals, and software
PA: Blue Technologies, Inc.
5885 Grant Ave
Cleveland OH 44105

(G-3877)
BLUE TECHNOLOGIES INC (PA)
5885 Grant Ave (44105-5607)
P.O. Box 31475 (44131-0475)
PHONE.................................216 271-4800
EMP: 107 EST: 1995
SQ FT: 36,000
SALES (est): 38.38MM Privately Held
Web: www.btohio.com
SIC: 5044 Copying equipment

(G-3878)
BLUE WTR CHAMBER ORCHESTRA INC
3631 Perkins Ave Ste 4c (44114-4707)
PHONE.................................440 781-6215
Carlton R Woods, Admn
Nancy Patterson Admini, Prin
EMP: 44 EST: 2017
SALES (est): 220.92K Privately Held
Web: www.bluewaterorchestra.com
SIC: 7929 Orchestras or bands, nec

(G-3879)
BOEHRINGER INGELHEIM PHARMA
5005 Rockside Rd (44131-2194)
PHONE.................................216 525-0195
Margret Smith, Brnch Mgr
EMP: 227
SALES (corp-wide): 23.34B Privately Held
Web: www.bi-animalhealth.com
SIC: 5122 Drugs, proprietaries, and sundries
HQ: Boehringer Ingelheim Pharmaceuticals, Inc.
900 Ridgebury Rd
Ridgefield CT 06877

(G-3880)
BON SECOURS MERCY HEALTH INC
Also Called: Kaiser Foundation Health Plan
12301 Snow Rd (44130-1002)
PHONE.................................216 362-2000
Geoffrey D Moebius, Mgr
EMP: 34
SALES (corp-wide): 6.92B Privately Held
Web: www.bonsecours.com
SIC: 6324 Hospital and medical service plans
PA: Bon Secours Mercy Health, Inc.
1701 Mercy Health Pl
Cincinnati OH 45237
513 956-3729

(G-3881)
BORDEN DAIRY CO CINCINNATI LLC (DH)
Also Called: H. Meyer Dairy
3068 W 106th St (44111-1801)
PHONE.................................513 948-8811
EMP: 27 EST: 1976
SALES (est): 21.74MM Privately Held
Web: www.bordendairy.com
SIC: 2026 2086 5143 5144 Milk processing (pasteurizing, homogenizing, bottling); Bottled and canned soft drinks; Dairy products, except dried or canned; Poultry and poultry products
HQ: National Dairy, Llc
8750 N Central Expy # 400
Dallas TX 75231
214 459-1100

(G-3882)
BOSTWICK DESIGN PARTNR INC (PA)
2729 Prospect Ave E (44115-2605)
PHONE.................................216 621-7900
Robert Bostwick, Pr
EMP: 28 EST: 1962
SQ FT: 12,500
SALES (est): 5.05MM

SALES (corp-wide): 5.05MM Privately Held
Web: www.bostwickdesign.com
SIC: 8712 Architectural engineering

(G-3883)
BOTTLE SOLUTIONS LLC
12201 Elmwood Ave (44111-5903)
P.O. Box 72107 (44192-0002)
PHONE.................................216 889-3330
EMP: 30 EST: 1855
SALES (est): 4.55MM Privately Held
Web: www.pipelinepackaging.com
SIC: 5085 7336 Glass bottles; Package design

(G-3884)
BOULEVARD MOTEL CORP
Also Called: Comfort Inn
17550 Rosbough Blvd (44130-2580)
PHONE.................................440 234-3131
Lindsey Stoneman, Brnch Mgr
EMP: 101
SQ FT: 21,973
SALES (corp-wide): 96.75MM Privately Held
Web: www.choicehotels.com
SIC: 7011 Hotels and motels
HQ: Boulevard Motel Corp
8171 Maple Lawn Blvd # 380
Fulton MD 20759

(G-3885)
BOXCAST INC
2401 Superior Via Ste 5 (44113-2342)
PHONE.................................888 392-2278
Gordon Daily, CEO
Gordon Daily, Pr
Peter Spaurid, *
Justin Hartman, *
EMP: 35 EST: 2010
SQ FT: 6,000
SALES (est): 4.76MM Privately Held
Web: www.boxcast.com
SIC: 7812 Video production

(G-3886)
BOYAS ENTERPRISES I INC
Also Called: Boyas Excavating, Inc.
11311 Rockside Rd (44125-6208)
PHONE.................................216 524-3620
Michael Boyas, Pr
Stacey Asimou, Treas
Tony Boyas, Admn
EMP: 37 EST: 1947
SQ FT: 6,000
SALES (est): 4.36MM
SALES (corp-wide): 10.06MM Privately Held
Web: www.boyasrecycling.com
SIC: 1795 1542 1794 1799 Wrecking and demolition work; Commercial and office building contractors; Excavation work; Shoring and underpinning work
PA: Pete & Pete Container Service Inc.
4830 Warner Rd
Cleveland OH 44125
216 441-4422

(G-3887)
BP OIL PIPELINE COMPANY
4421 Bradley Rd (44109-3750)
PHONE.................................216 398-8685
Greg Debrock, Mgr
EMP: 1157
SALES (corp-wide): 33.74K Privately Held
SIC: 4612 Crude petroleum pipelines
PA: Bp Oil Pipeline Company
150 W Warrenville Rd
Naperville IL 60563
630 420-5111

GEOGRAPHIC SECTION
Cleveland - Cuyahoga County (G-3910)

(G-3888)
BPI ACQUISITION COMPANY LLC (DH)
127 Public Sq Ste 5110 (44114-1313)
PHONE..................216 589-0198
EMP: 419 **EST:** 2013
SALES (est): 1.65B
SALES (corp-wide): 8.03B **Privately Held**
SIC: 7389 Demonstration service
HQ: First Brands Group, Llc
  127 Public Sq
  Cleveland OH 44114
  248 371-1700

(G-3889)
BRAKE PARTS HOLDINGS INC (DH)
127 Public Sq Ste 5110 (44114-1313)
PHONE..................216 589-0198
EMP: 500 **EST:** 2020
SALES (est): 373.57MM
SALES (corp-wide): 8.03B **Privately Held**
SIC: 6719 Investment holding companies, except banks
HQ: First Brands Group, Llc
  127 Public Sq
  Cleveland OH 44114
  248 371-1700

(G-3890)
BRANDMUSCLE INC (HQ)
1100 Superior Ave E Ste 500 (44114-2548)
PHONE..................216 464-4342
Scott Weeren, *CEO*
Dave Wilson, *
Dan Hickox, *
Evelyn Nugent Exsc, *VP*
Kathy Heflin, *
EMP: 150 **EST:** 2000
SQ FT: 24,000
SALES (est): 64.77MM
SALES (corp-wide): 1.29B **Privately Held**
Web: www.brandmuscle.com
SIC: 7373 8742 Systems software development services; Marketing consulting services
PA: Riverside Partners L.L.C.
  45 Rockefeller Plz # 400
  New York NY 10111
  212 265-6575

(G-3891)
BRAVO WELLNESS LLC (HQ)
20445 Emerald Pkwy Ste 400 (44135-6010)
PHONE..................216 658-9500
Chris Yessayan, *Pr*
Cheryl Tidwell, *Ex VP*
EMP: 47 **EST:** 2008
SQ FT: 7,000
SALES (est): 21.74MM
SALES (corp-wide): 2.75B **Privately Held**
Web: www.bravowell.com
SIC: 8748 8741 Employee programs administration; Administrative management
PA: Medical Mutual Of Ohio
  2060 E 9th St
  Cleveland OH 44115
  216 687-7000

(G-3892)
BRIDGEWAY INC (PA)
2202 Prame Ave (44109-1626)
PHONE..................216 688-4114
Ralph Fee, *Dir*
EMP: 160 **EST:** 1972
SQ FT: 50,000
SALES (est): 4.24MM
SALES (corp-wide): 4.24MM **Privately Held**
Web: www.b-way.com

SIC: 8322 8093 Social service center; Specialty outpatient clinics, nec

(G-3893)
BRIGHTEDGE TECHNOLOGIES INC
Also Called: Brightedge
1500 W 3rd St Ste 405 (44113-1423)
PHONE..................800 578-8023
EMP: 80
Web: www.brightedge.com
SIC: 5045 Computer software
PA: Brightedge Technologies, Inc.
  3 E 3rd Ave Ste 200
  San Mateo CA 94401

(G-3894)
BRIGHTON MANOR COMPANY
Also Called: Holiday Inn
1625 E 31st St (44114)
PHONE..................216 241-3123
Edward S Emerson, *Pr*
Suzanne Emerson, *
Ala Deen, *
EMP: 350 **EST:** 1985
SQ FT: 10,000
SALES (est): 5.25MM **Privately Held**
Web: www.holidayinn.com
SIC: 7011 Hotels and motels

(G-3895)
BRITESKIES LLC
2658 Scranton Rd Ste 3 (44113-5115)
PHONE..................216 369-3600
Michael Berlin, *Managing Member*
EMP: 35 **EST:** 2008
SALES (est): 2.22MM **Privately Held**
Web: www.briteskies.com
SIC: 7371 Computer software development

(G-3896)
BRITTANY RESIDENTIAL INC
Also Called: Highland House
427 Richmond Rd (44143-1498)
PHONE..................216 692-3212
Karen Evley, *Genl Mgr*
EMP: 32
SALES (corp-wide): 3.18MM **Privately Held**
Web: www.brittanyresidential.com
SIC: 8361 Mentally handicapped home
PA: Brittany Residential Inc
  3100 Arcola Rd
  Madison OH 44057
  440 428-6648

(G-3897)
BRITTON-GALLAGHER & ASSOC INC
1375 E 9th St (44114-1797)
PHONE..................216 658-7100
Bruce H Ball, *Ch Bd*
John L Hazen, *
Thomas A Brackett, *
Terry Dragan, *
Ken Ross, *
EMP: 60 **EST:** 1942
SQ FT: 15,000
SALES (est): 16.93MM **Privately Held**
Web: www.acrisure.com
SIC: 6411 Insurance brokers, nec

(G-3898)
BROADBAND EXPRESS LLC
14200 Broadway Ave (44125-1954)
PHONE..................216 712-7505
EMP: 55
SALES (corp-wide): 4.1B **Publicly Held**
Web: recruiting.ultipro.com
SIC: 1731 Communications specialization
HQ: Broadband Express, Llc
  374 Westdale Ave Ste B
  Westerville OH 43082
  614 823-6464

(G-3899)
BROADVUE MOTORS INC
Also Called: Ganley Lincoln Middleburg Hts
6930 Pearl Rd (44130-7832)
PHONE..................440 845-6000
Kenneth Ganley, *Pr*
Lois Ganley, *
Russel W Harris, *
David Robinson, *
Ronald Courey, *
EMP: 70 **EST:** 1947
SQ FT: 26,191
SALES (est): 11.24MM **Privately Held**
Web: www.lincoln.com
SIC: 5511 5012 7538 Automobiles, new and used; Automobiles; General automotive repair shops

(G-3900)
BROKAW INC
1213 W 6th St (44113-1339)
PHONE..................216 241-8003
Bill Brokaw, *Prin*
Tim Brokaw, *
Gregg Brokaw, *
EMP: 35 **EST:** 1987
SQ FT: 11,300
SALES (est): 7.45MM **Privately Held**
Web: www.brokaw.com
SIC: 7311 Advertising consultant

(G-3901)
BROOK BEECH
Also Called: Eech Brook Family Drop-In Ctr
6001 Woodland Ave Ste 2260 (44104)
PHONE..................216 391-4069
Terry Davis, *Prin*
EMP: 250
SALES (corp-wide): 10.39MM **Privately Held**
Web: www.beechbrook.org
SIC: 8322 Family counseling services
PA: Brook Beech
  13201 Granger Rd
  Cleveland OH 44125
  216 831-2555

(G-3902)
BROOK BEECH (PA)
13201 Granger Rd (44125)
PHONE..................216 831-2555
Mario Tonti, *Pr*
Bari E Goggins, *
Gerald Burke, *
EMP: 200 **EST:** 1852
SALES (est): 10.39MM
SALES (corp-wide): 10.39MM **Privately Held**
Web: www.beechbrook.org
SIC: 8322 Child related social services

(G-3903)
BROOKFIELD PROPERTIES LLC
127 Public Sq Ste 3200 (44114-1229)
PHONE..................216 621-6060
EMP: 66
SALES (corp-wide): 816.31MM **Privately Held**
Web: www.brookfieldproperties.com
SIC: 6512 Nonresidential building operators
PA: Brookfield Properties, Llc
  250 Vesey St Fl 11
  New York NY 10281
  212 417-7000

(G-3904)
BROOKS & STAFFORD CO
Also Called: Nationwide
55 Public Sq Ste 1650 (44113-1972)
PHONE..................216 696-3000
Neil Corrigan, *Pr*

John Kunze, *
EMP: 48 **EST:** 1849
SQ FT: 11,000
SALES (est): 4.87MM **Privately Held**
Web: www.brooks-stafford.com
SIC: 6411 Insurance agents, nec

(G-3905)
BROWN GIBBONS LANG LTD PTRSHIP
1111 Superior Ave E # 900 (44114-2522)
PHONE..................216 241-2800
Michael Gibbons, *Pr*
EMP: 30 **EST:** 1991
SALES (est): 855.2K **Privately Held**
SIC: 7519 Utility trailer rental

(G-3906)
BROWNFLYNN LTD (DH)
50 Public Sq Fl 36 (44113-2266)
PHONE..................216 303-6000
EMP: 33 **EST:** 1995
SQ FT: 6,600
SALES (est): 3.94MM
SALES (corp-wide): 673.68MM **Privately Held**
Web: www.erm.com
SIC: 8748 Environmental consultant
HQ: Erm-Delaware, Inc.
  1105 N Market St Ste 1300
  Wilmington DE 19801
  302 651-8300

(G-3907)
BRUNSWICK INSURANCE AGENCY
5309 Transportation Blvd (44125-5333)
P.O. Box 28 (44309-0028)
PHONE..................330 864-8800
EMP: 37 **EST:** 2010
SALES (est): 5.32MM **Privately Held**
Web: www.brunswickcompanies.com
SIC: 6411 Insurance agents, nec

(G-3908)
BUCKEYE HOMECARE SERVICES INC
14077 Cedar Rd Ste 103 (44118-3332)
PHONE..................216 321-9300
Nitesh Patel, *Admn*
Ashfaq Ahmed, *
Farzana Ahmed, *
EMP: 75 **EST:** 2007
SALES (est): 2.59MM **Privately Held**
Web: www.buckeyehcs.com
SIC: 8082 Home health care services

(G-3909)
BUCKINGHAM DLTTLE BRROUGHS LLC
Also Called: Buckingham Doolittle Burroughs
1375 E 9th St Ste 1700 (44114-1790)
PHONE..................216 621-5300
Erin Mccafferty, *Admn*
EMP: 35
SALES (corp-wide): 42.23K **Privately Held**
Web: www.bdblaw.com
SIC: 8111 General practice attorney, lawyer
PA: Buckingham, Doolittle & Burroughs, Llc
  3800 Embassy Pkwy
  Akron OH 44333
  330 376-5300

(G-3910)
BUILDERS EXCHANGE INC (PA)
Also Called: BX OHIO
9555 Rockside Rd Ste 300 (44125-6282)
PHONE..................216 393-6300
Gregg Mazurek, *Ex Dir*
Laurel Screptock, *
EMP: 33 **EST:** 1881

Cleveland - Cuyahoga County (G-3911)

SQ FT: 10,000
SALES (est): 3.86MM
SALES (corp-wide): 3.86MM **Privately Held**
Web: home.bxohio.com
SIC: 8611 Contractors' association

(G-3911)
BURKSHIRE CONSTRUCTION COMPANY
6033 State Rd (44134-2869)
P.O. Box 347248 (44134-7248)
PHONE.................................440 885-9700
Anne M Burkey, *CEO*
EMP: 30 **EST:** 1991
SALES (est): 4.81MM **Privately Held**
SIC: 1541 1542 Industrial buildings, new construction, nec; Nonresidential construction, nec

(G-3912)
BURTON CAROL MANAGEMENT (PA)
Also Called: B C M
4832 Richmond Rd Ste 200 (44128-5993)
PHONE.................................216 464-5130
Robert G Risman, *CEO*
David M King, *General**
Roger Katz, ***
Joy Anzalone, ***
John Petryshin, ***
EMP: 40 **EST:** 2009
SALES (est): 47.4MM
SALES (corp-wide): 47.4MM **Privately Held**
Web: www.burtoncarol.com
SIC: 7011 Hotels and motels

(G-3913)
BUSINESS VOLUNTEERS UNLIMITED
1300 E 9th St Ste 1220 (44114-1513)
PHONE.................................216 736-7711
Brian Broadbent, *Pr*
Elizabeth Hosler Voudouris, *Ex VP*
Ann C Kent, *VP*
EMP: 33 **EST:** 1992
SALES (est): 8.24MM **Privately Held**
Web: www.bvuvolunteers.org
SIC: 8748 Business consulting, nec

(G-3914)
C C F VSCLAR SRGERY AT MRYMUNT
Also Called: Cleveland Clinic
99 Northline Cir Ste 201 (44119-1481)
PHONE.................................216 475-1551
Toby Cosgrove, *Dir*
EMP: 153 **EST:** 1977
SALES (est): 17.48MM **Privately Held**
Web: my.clevelandclinic.org
SIC: 8062 General medical and surgical hospitals

(G-3915)
C C MITCHELL SUPPLY CO INC
3001 E Royalton Rd (44147-2894)
PHONE.................................440 526-2040
Jerome Mitchell, *Ch Bd*
EMP: 35 **EST:** 1954
SQ FT: 48,000
SALES (est): 9.49MM **Privately Held**
Web: www.ccmitchell.net
SIC: 5064 Electrical appliances, major

(G-3916)
C GI VOLUNTARY
3500 Woodridge Rd (44121-1534)
PHONE.................................216 401-0381
Nick Giancola, *Brnch Mgr*
EMP: 28
SALES (corp-wide): 473.56K **Privately Held**
SIC: 6411 Insurance information and consulting services
PA: C Gi Voluntary
3601 Green Rd
Beachwood OH 44122
216 382-2565

(G-3917)
C O HOWARD HANNA MORTGAGE
6000 Parkland Blvd Ste 200 (44124-6120)
PHONE.................................412 967-9000
Donald Latore, *Pr*
EMP: 94 **EST:** 2017
SALES (est): 1.73MM **Privately Held**
Web: www.howardhanna.com
SIC: 6162 Mortgage bankers and loan correspondents

(G-3918)
CALFEE HALTER & GRISWOLD LLP (PA)
Also Called: Calfee
The Calfee Building 1405 E Sixth St (44114)
PHONE.................................216 622-8200
Thomas M Welsh, *Mng Pt*
Thomas F Mckee, *Ch*
Philip M Dawson, *CFO*
Brent D Ballard, *Mng Pt*
Patrick Moennich, *Dir Fin*
EMP: 358 **EST:** 1929
SALES (est): 46.79MM
SALES (corp-wide): 46.79MM **Privately Held**
Web: www.calfee.com
SIC: 8111 General practice attorney, lawyer

(G-3919)
CALVERT WIRE & CABLE CORP (DH)
17909 Cleveland Pkwy Dr Ste 180 (44142)
PHONE.................................216 433-7600
Lorraine Nunez, *Pr*
◆ **EMP:** 38 **EST:** 1979
SQ FT: 12,000
SALES (est): 40.89MM **Publicly Held**
Web: www.wesco.com
SIC: 4899 5063 Data communication services; Wire and cable
HQ: Communications Supply Corp
225 W Station Square Dr # 700
Pittsburgh PA 15219
630 221-6400

(G-3920)
CAMGEN LTD
1621 Euclid Ave Ste 220-314 (44115-2114)
P.O. Box 13141 (44334-8541)
PHONE.................................330 204-8636
EMP: 55 **EST:** 2016
SALES (est): 2.04MM **Privately Held**
SIC: 7371 Computer software development and applications

(G-3921)
CAMPUSEAI INC
1111 Superior Ave E Ste 310 (44114-2522)
PHONE.................................216 589-9626
Anjli Jain, *Ex Dir*
EMP: 120 **EST:** 2007
SALES (est): 14.15MM **Privately Held**
SIC: 7371 Software programming applications

(G-3922)
CANNASURE INSURANCE SVCS LLC
1468 W 9th St Ste 805 (44113-1299)
PHONE.................................800 420-5757
EMP: 27 **EST:** 2010
SALES (est): 12.31MM
SALES (corp-wide): 1.03B **Privately Held**
Web: www.cannasure.com
SIC: 6411 Insurance agents, brokers, and service
HQ: One80 Intermediaries Inc.
160 Federal St Fl 4
Boston MA 02110
216 797-9700

(G-3923)
CANTERBURY GOLF CLUB INC
22000 S Woodland Rd (44122-3061)
PHONE.................................216 561-1914
Edward Kloboves, *Contrlr*
EMP: 80 **EST:** 1920
SQ FT: 50,000
SALES (est): 8.5MM **Privately Held**
Web: www.canterburygc.org
SIC: 7997 5812 Golf club, membership; Eating places

(G-3924)
CAPITAL PROPERTIES MGT LTD
12929 Shaker Blvd (44120-2034)
PHONE.................................216 991-3057
David J Goodman, *Pt*
EMP: 28 **EST:** 1984
SALES (est): 7.99MM **Privately Held**
Web: www.cpm-ltd.com
SIC: 6513 Apartment building operators

(G-3925)
CAR PARTS WAREHOUSE INC
18525 Miles Rd (44128-3444)
PHONE.................................216 581-4800
EMP: 45
SALES (corp-wide): 48.99MM **Privately Held**
Web: www.carpartswarehouse.net
SIC: 5013 Automotive supplies and parts
PA: Car Parts Warehouse, Inc.
5200 W 130th St
Brookpark OH 44142
216 281-4500

(G-3926)
CARDIOVASCULAR CLINIC INC
6525 Powers Blvd Rm 301 (44129-5461)
PHONE.................................440 882-0075
EMP: 29
SALES (est): 2.82MM **Privately Held**
SIC: 8011 Cardiologist and cardio-vascular specialist

(G-3927)
CARE ALLIANCE
2163 Payne Ave (44114)
PHONE.................................216 781-6228
Barbara Clark, *Mgr*
EMP: 33
Web: www.carealliance.org
SIC: 8011 Clinic, operated by physicians
PA: Care Alliance
1530 Saint Clair Ave Ne
Cleveland OH 44114

(G-3928)
CAREERCURVE LLC (HQ)
5005 Rockside Rd Ste 600 (44131-6827)
PHONE.................................800 314-8230
Patricia L Wagoner, *Pr*
EMP: 67 **EST:** 2003
SALES (est): 1.57MM **Privately Held**
Web: www.careercurve.com
SIC: 8742 Human resource consulting services
PA: Careerminds Group Inc.
132 Talbot Dr
Landenberg PA 19350

(G-3929)
CARESOURCE MANAGEMENT GROUP CO
Also Called: CARESOURCE MANAGEMENT GROUP CO.
5900 Landerbrook Dr Ste 300 (44124-4029)
PHONE.................................216 839-1001
Glen Sigel, *Mgr*
EMP: 117
Web: www.caresource.com
SIC: 6324 Health Maintenance Organization (HMO), insurance only
PA: Caresource
230 N Main St
Dayton OH 45402

(G-3930)
CARNEGIE CAPITAL ASSET MGT LLC
Also Called: Carnegie Investment Counsel
30300 Chagrin Blvd (44124-5725)
PHONE.................................216 595-1349
Richard Alt, *CIO*
EMP: 44 **EST:** 2016
SALES (est): 5.1MM **Privately Held**
Web: www.carnegieinvest.com
SIC: 6282 Investment advisory service

(G-3931)
CARTRUCK PACKAGING INC
7315 Associate Ave (44144-1102)
PHONE.................................216 631-7225
Sam Sharaba, *Pr*
EMP: 29 **EST:** 1986
SQ FT: 10,000
SALES (est): 497.29K **Privately Held**
Web: www.cartruckpackaging.com
SIC: 7389 1721 Packaging and labeling services; Industrial painting

(G-3932)
CATHOLIC CHARITIES CORPORATION
Also Called: Matt Talbot Inn
3135 Euclid Ave Ste 202 (44115-2524)
PHONE.................................216 432-0680
Terry Morris, *Dir*
EMP: 79
Web: www.catholiccharitiesusa.org
SIC: 8399 8661 8361 Fund raising organization, non-fee basis; Religious organizations; Residential care
PA: Catholic Charities Corporation
7911 Detroit Ave
Cleveland OH 44102

(G-3933)
CATHOLIC CHARITIES CORPORATION
Also Called: Catholic Chrties Svcs Cyhoga C
7800 Detroit Ave (44102-2814)
PHONE.................................216 939-3713
Edward Carter, *Dir*
EMP: 78
Web: www.catholiccharitiesusa.org
SIC: 8399 8322 Fund raising organization, non-fee basis; General counseling services
PA: Catholic Charities Corporation
7911 Detroit Ave
Cleveland OH 44102

(G-3934)
CATHOLIC CHARITIES CORPORATION
Also Called: Deporres Mrtin Emrgncy Assstnc
1264 E 123rd St (44108-4002)
PHONE.................................216 268-4006
EMP: 78
Web: www.catholiccharitiesusa.org

GEOGRAPHIC SECTION

Cleveland - Cuyahoga County (G-3957)

SIC: 8399 8322 Fund raising organization, non-fee basis; Individual and family services
PA: Catholic Charities Corporation
7911 Detroit Ave
Cleveland OH 44102

(G-3935)
CATHOLIC CHARITIES CORPORATION (PA)
Also Called: CATHOLIC CHARITIES DIOCESE OF
7911 Detroit Ave (44102-2815)
PHONE..................216 334-2900
EMP: 50 EST: 1971
SALES (est): 67.3MM Privately Held
Web: www.ccdocle.org
SIC: 8322 Social service center

(G-3936)
CATHOLIC CMTRIES ASSN OF THE D (PA)
10000 Miles Ave (44105-6130)
P.O. Box 605310 (44105-0310)
PHONE..................216 641-7575
Robert Winnicki, CFO
Andrej Lah, *
EMP: 100 EST: 1893
SALES (est): 11.53MM
SALES (corp-wide): 11.53MM Privately Held
Web: www.clecem.org
SIC: 6553 Cemeteries, real estate operation

(G-3937)
CAVALIERS HOLDINGS LLC (PA)
Also Called: Quicken Loans Arena
1 Center Ct (44115-4001)
PHONE..................216 420-2000
EMP: 430 EST: 2004
SALES (est): 601.5K
SALES (corp-wide): 601.5K Privately Held
Web: www.cavaliersteamshop.com
SIC: 7941 6512 Basketball club; Nonresidential building operators

(G-3938)
CAVALIERS OPERATING CO LLC
Also Called: Q, The
1 Center Ct (44115-4001)
PHONE..................216 420-2000
EMP: 1300 EST: 2005
SALES (est): 601.5K
SALES (corp-wide): 601.5K Privately Held
Web: www.rocketmortgagefieldhouse.com
SIC: 7941 Sports field or stadium operator, promoting sports events
PA: Cavaliers Holdings, Llc
1 Center Ct
Cleveland OH 44115
216 420-2000

(G-3939)
CAVALRY STAFFING LLC
5400 Transportation Blvd Ste 12b (44125)
PHONE..................440 663-9990
EMP: 36 EST: 2008
SALES (est): 239.77K Privately Held
Web: www.cavalrystaffing.com
SIC: 7363 7361 Temporary help service; Labor contractors (employment agency)

(G-3940)
CAVCAPITAL LTD
Also Called: Advance Payroll Funding Ltd.
23000 Millcreek Blvd (44122-5706)
PHONE..................216 831-8900
Joel Adelman, CEO
Adam C Stern, *
Michael Turk, *
EMP: 114 EST: 1998

SQ FT: 4,000
SALES (est): 24.46MM
SALES (corp-wide): 5.01B Publicly Held
Web: www.advancepartners.com
SIC: 8721 Payroll accounting service
PA: Paychex, Inc.
911 Panorama Trl S
Rochester NY 14625
585 385-6666

(G-3941)
CAVITCH FAMILO & DURKIN CO LPA
1300 E 9th St (44114-1501)
PHONE..................216 621-7860
Harvey L Furtkin, Pt
Michael C Cohen, *
EMP: 40 EST: 1899
SQ FT: 16,500
SALES (est): 7.36MM Privately Held
Web: www.cavitch.com
SIC: 8111 General practice law office

(G-3942)
CBIZ INC (PA)
5959 Rockside Woods Blvd N Ste 600 (44131)
PHONE..................216 447-9000
EMP: 1006 EST: 1996
SALES (est): 1.59B Publicly Held
Web: www.cbiz.com
SIC: 7389 6331 8742 Financial services; Fire, marine, and casualty insurance; Management consulting services

(G-3943)
CBIZ ACCNTING TAX ADVSORY WASH
6050 Oak Tree Blvd Ste 500 (44131-6927)
PHONE..................216 447-9000
Jerome P Grisko Junior, Pr
EMP: 40 EST: 2021
SALES (est): 3.56MM Publicly Held
Web: www.cbiz.com
SIC: 7389 6331 8742 Financial services; Fire, marine, and casualty insurance; Management consulting services
PA: Cbiz, Inc.
5959 Rckside Wods Blvd N
Cleveland OH 44131

(G-3944)
CBIZ MHM NORTHERN CAL LLC
6050 Oak Tree Blvd Ste 500 (44131-6927)
PHONE..................216 447-9000
Jerome P Grisko Junior, Pr
EMP: 37 EST: 2021
SALES (est): 9.39MM Publicly Held
Web: cbiz.gcs-web.com
SIC: 6331 8742 Fire, marine, and casualty insurance; Management consulting services
PA: Cbiz, Inc.
5959 Rckside Wods Blvd N
Cleveland OH 44131

(G-3945)
CBTS TECHNOLOGY SOLUTIONS LLC
5910 Landerbrook Dr Ste 250 (44124-6508)
PHONE..................440 569-2300
Theodore H Torbeck, CEO
EMP: 270
SALES (corp-wide): 3.15B Privately Held
Web: www.cbts.com
SIC: 7379 7372 Computer related consulting services; Business oriented computer software
HQ: Cbts Technology Solutions Llc
25 Merchant St
Cincinnati OH 45246

(G-3946)
CCF HEALTH CARE VENTURES INC
Also Called: Cleveland Clinic HM Care Svcs
9775 Rockside Rd Ste 200 (44125-6266)
PHONE..................216 295-1959
Brian Palmer, Dir Fin
EMP: 305 EST: 1986
SALES (est): 11.16MM
SALES (corp-wide): 13.97MM Privately Held
SIC: 8741 Hospital management
PA: Clinic Care Inc
6100 W Creek Rd Ste 25
Cleveland OH 44131
216 986-2680

(G-3947)
CENTAURI HEALTH SOLUTIONS
1457 E 40th St (44103-1103)
PHONE..................216 431-5200
EMP: 61 EST: 2019
SALES (est): 5.94MM Privately Held
Web: www.centaurihs.com
SIC: 8099 Health and allied services, nec

(G-3948)
CENTER FOR ARTS-INSPIRED LRNG
10917 Magnolia Dr (44106-1809)
PHONE..................216 561-5005
Marsha Dobrzynski, Dir
Katherine Solender, Pr
Abigail Sender, Dir
EMP: 27 EST: 2004
SALES (est): 2.1MM Privately Held
Web: www.arts-inspiredlearning.org
SIC: 8999 Art related services

(G-3949)
CENTER FOR COMMUNITY SOLUTIONS
1300 E 9th St Ste 1703 (44114-1504)
PHONE..................216 781-2944
Gregory L Brown, Ex Dir
EMP: 30 EST: 1913
SQ FT: 17,500
SALES (est): 4.12MM Privately Held
Web: www.communitysolutions.com
SIC: 8399 Advocacy group

(G-3950)
CENTER FOR FAMILIES & CHILDREN
Also Called: CENTER FOR FAMILIES AND CHILDREN
3929 Rocky River Dr (44111-4153)
PHONE..................216 252-5800
Charlie Bango, Mgr
EMP: 30
SALES (corp-wide): 29.84MM Privately Held
Web: www.thecentersohio.org
SIC: 8322 8093 Family counseling services; Mental health clinic, outpatient
PA: The Centers For Families And Children
4500 Euclid Ave
Cleveland OH 44103
216 432-7200

(G-3951)
CENTER FOR FAMILIES & CHILDREN
Also Called: East Mental Health
4400 Euclid Ave (44103-3734)
PHONE..................216 671-1919
Jim Penman, Mgr
EMP: 46
SALES (corp-wide): 29.84MM Privately Held
Web: www.thecentersohio.org
SIC: 8322 Individual and family services
PA: The Centers For Families And Children
4500 Euclid Ave
Cleveland OH 44103

216 432-7200

(G-3952)
CENTER FOR HEALTH AFFAIRS
1226 Huron Rd E Ste 2 (44115-1789)
PHONE..................216 696-6900
C Wayne Rice, Pr
Richard Fox, *
EMP: 62 EST: 1918
SQ FT: 30,000
SALES (est): 13.87MM Privately Held
Web: www.neohospitals.org
SIC: 8621 Medical field-related associations

(G-3953)
CENTERS FOR FAMILIES CHILDREN (PA)
Also Called: CENTERS, THE
4500 Euclid Ave (44103-3736)
PHONE..................216 432-7200
Eric L Morse, Pr
Christine Gambatese, *
EMP: 65 EST: 1970
SQ FT: 23,000
SALES (est): 29.84MM
SALES (corp-wide): 29.84MM Privately Held
Web: www.thecentersohio.org
SIC: 8322 Child related social services

(G-3954)
CENTRAL CADILLAC LIMITED
Also Called: Central Cadillac-Hummer
2801 Carnegie Ave (44115-2628)
PHONE..................216 861-5800
Frank H Porter Junior, Pr
EMP: 83 EST: 1943
SQ FT: 40,000
SALES (est): 4.99MM Privately Held
Web: www.centralcadillac.com
SIC: 7538 5521 5511 General automotive repair shops; Used car dealers; Automobiles, new and used

(G-3955)
CENTRAN LOGISTICS INC
6707 Bessemer Ave (44127-1808)
PHONE..................216 271-7100
Thomas Wagner, Pr
Neal Kowalski, *
EMP: 28 EST: 2010
SALES (est): 2.24MM Privately Held
Web: www.centranlogistics.net
SIC: 4789 Car loading

(G-3956)
CENTURY 21 HOMESTAR
Also Called: Century 21
6151 Wilson Mills Rd Ste 110 (44143-2128)
PHONE..................440 449-9100
Gary Giallombardo, Prin
EMP: 50 EST: 2006
SALES (est): 1.87MM Privately Held
Web: www.century21.com
SIC: 6531 Real estate agent, residential

(G-3957)
CERTIFIED CARPET DISTRS INC
9090 Bank St (44125-3426)
PHONE..................216 573-1422
Chris Link, Brnch Mgr
EMP: 45
SALES (corp-wide): 21.09MM Privately Held
Web: www.teamcertified.com
SIC: 5023 Carpets
PA: Certified Carpet Distributors Inc.
231 Haskell Dr Ste 1
Verona PA 15147
412 423-0700

Cleveland - Cuyahoga County (G-3958)

(G-3958)
CGI TECHNOLOGIES SOLUTIONS INC
Also Called: Cgi
1001 Lakeside Ave E Ste 800 (44114-1158)
PHONE..................216 687-1480
Richard Schmitz, *Mgr*
EMP: 108
SALES (corp-wide): 9.87B **Privately Held**
Web: www.lumark.com
SIC: 7379 Computer related consulting services
HQ: Cgi Technologies And Solutions Inc.
11325 Rndom Hills Rd Fl 8 Flr 8
Fairfax VA 22030
703 267-5111

(G-3959)
CHA - COMMUNITY HEALTH AFFAIRS
Also Called: Greater Cleveland Hosp Assn
1226 Huron Rd E (44115-1702)
PHONE..................800 362-2628
William T Ryan, *Pr*
EMP: 78 **EST:** 1997
SALES (est): 9.66MM **Privately Held**
Web: www.neohospitals.org
SIC: 8062 8699 8742 General medical and surgical hospitals; Athletic organizations; Management consulting services

(G-3960)
CHAGRIN VALLEY AUTO PARTS CO
Also Called: NAPA Auto Parts
8550 Brookpark Rd (44129-6806)
PHONE..................216 398-9800
Mike Webster, *Mgr*
EMP: 30
SALES (corp-wide): 5.37MM **Privately Held**
Web: www.napaonline.com
SIC: 5531 5013 Automotive parts; Motor vehicle supplies and new parts
PA: Chagrin Valley Auto Parts Co.
15170 Kinsman Rd
Middlefield OH 44062
440 834-0447

(G-3961)
CHAGRIN VALLEY ENGINEERING LTD
22999 Forbes Rd Ste B (44146-5639)
PHONE..................440 439-1999
EMP: 41 **EST:** 1996
SALES (est): 12.53MM **Privately Held**
Web: www.cvelimited.com
SIC: 8711 Civil engineering

(G-3962)
CHARLES RVER LABS CLVELAND INC
14656 Neo Pkwy (44128-3156)
PHONE..................216 332-1665
Emily Hickey, *Pr*
Jessica Brimecombe, *
Antonio E Lacerda, *
Luke Armstrong, *
David Johst, *
EMP: 55 **EST:** 2007
SQ FT: 27,000
SALES (est): 14.68MM
SALES (corp-wide): 4.13B **Publicly Held**
SIC: 8731 Biotechnical research, commercial
HQ: Charles River Laboratories, Inc.
251 Ballardvale St
Wilmington MA 01887
781 222-6000

(G-3963)
CHARTER ONE BANK NATIONAL ASSOCIATION
Also Called: Charter One
1215 Superior Ave E Ste 245 (44114-3299)
PHONE..................216 277-5326
▲ **EMP:** 5537
SIC: 6021 National commercial banks

(G-3964)
CHECK POINT SOFTWARE TECH INC
6100 Oak Tree Blvd Ste 200 (44131)
PHONE..................440 748-0900
EMP: 37
SALES (corp-wide): 894.19MM **Privately Held**
Web: www.checkpoint.com
SIC: 7372 Prepackaged software
HQ: Check Point Software Technologies, Inc.
100 Oracle Pkwy
Redwood City CA 94065

(G-3965)
CHEMICAL SOLVENTS INC (PA)
3751 Jennings Rd (44109-2889)
PHONE..................216 741-9310
Edward Pavlish, *Ch Bd*
E H Pavlish, *
Gerald J Schill, *
Patricia Pavlish, *
Thos A Mason, *
▲ **EMP:** 45 **EST:** 1970
SQ FT: 30,000
SALES (est): 99.45MM
SALES (corp-wide): 99.45MM **Privately Held**
Web: www.chemicalsolvents.com
SIC: 5169 7349 3471 2992 Detergents and soaps, except specialty cleaning; Chemical cleaning services; Cleaning and descaling metal products; Oils and greases, blending and compounding

(G-3966)
CHEMICAL SOLVENTS INC
1010 Denison Ave (44109-2853)
P.O. Box 931705 (44193-1813)
PHONE..................216 741-9310
Dan Reynolds, *Mgr*
EMP: 65
SALES (corp-wide): 99.45MM **Privately Held**
Web: www.chemicalsolvents.com
SIC: 5169 Industrial chemicals
PA: Chemical Solvents, Inc.
3751 Jennings Rd
Cleveland OH 44109
216 741-9310

(G-3967)
CHESTER AVE HOTEL LLC
Also Called: Residence Inn By Marriott
1914 E 101st St (44106-4136)
PHONE..................216 249-9090
EMP: 31 **EST:** 2019
SALES (est): 678.71K **Privately Held**
Web: residence-inn.marriott.com
SIC: 7011 Hotels and motels

(G-3968)
CHIEFTAIN TRUCKING & EXCAV INC
3926 Valley Rd Ste 300 (44109-3058)
PHONE..................216 485-8034
EMP: 35 **EST:** 1992
SQ FT: 17,500
SALES (est): 5.76MM **Privately Held**
Web: www.chieftaintrucking.com
SIC: 1794 4231 Excavation and grading, building construction; Trucking terminal facilities

(G-3969)
CHILD CARE RESOURCE CENTER (PA)
Also Called: Starting Point
6001 Euclid Ave (44103-3719)
PHONE..................216 575-0061
Bilie Osbourne, *Pr*
EMP: 31 **EST:** 1988
SALES (est): 1.95MM
SALES (corp-wide): 1.95MM **Privately Held**
Web: www.starting-point.org
SIC: 8351 Child day care services

(G-3970)
CHILDRENS MUSEUM OF CLEVELAND
Also Called: CLEVELAND CHILDREN'S MUSEUM
3813 Euclid Ave (44115-2503)
PHONE..................216 791-7114
Jeffrey Saxon, *Dir*
EMP: 49 **EST:** 1981
SQ FT: 11,005
SALES (est): 511.98K **Privately Held**
Web: www.cmcleveland.org
SIC: 8412 Museum

(G-3971)
CHORES UNLIMITED INC
Also Called: Cui
4889 Neo Pkwy (44128-3101)
P.O. Box 46760 (44146-0760)
PHONE..................440 439-5455
Robin Gray, *VP*
Gary Gray, *
Bryan Gray, *
EMP: 85 **EST:** 1983
SALES (est): 9.84MM **Privately Held**
Web: www.cuiservices.com
SIC: 0782 Mowing services, lawn

(G-3972)
CIRCLE HEALTH SERVICES
Also Called: CENTERS, THE
12201 Euclid Ave (44106-4310)
PHONE..................216 721-4010
Eric L Morse, *Pr*
Christine Gambatese, *
EMP: 34 **EST:** 1970
SQ FT: 28,000
SALES (est): 25.32MM **Privately Held**
Web: www.circlehealthservices.org
SIC: 8322 Individual and family services

(G-3973)
CITIZENS CAPITAL MARKETS INC
Also Called: Bowstring Advisors
200 Public Sq Ste 3750 (44114-2321)
PHONE..................216 589-0900
Ralph M Della Ratta, *Genl Mgr*
EMP: 28
SALES (corp-wide): 12.19B **Publicly Held**
Web: www.citizenscapital.com
SIC: 6022 State commercial banks
HQ: Citizens Capital Markets, Inc.
28 State St Fl 13
Boston MA 02109
617 725-5636

(G-3974)
CITY ARCHITECTURE INC
12205 Larchmere Blvd (44120-1101)
PHONE..................216 881-2444
Paul Volpe, *Pr*
Mark Dodds, *
EMP: 27 **EST:** 1989
SALES (est): 7.54MM **Privately Held**
Web: www.cityarch.com

SIC: 8712 Architectural engineering

(G-3975)
CITY LIFE INC (PA)
Also Called: Sammy's
1382 W 9th St Ste 310 (44113-1231)
PHONE..................216 523-5899
Denise M Fugo, *Pr*
Ralph Diorio, *
EMP: 40 **EST:** 1980
SQ FT: 14,550
SALES (est): 5.09MM
SALES (corp-wide): 5.09MM **Privately Held**
Web: www.yfccleveland.org
SIC: 5812 5813 7299 American restaurant; Cocktail lounge; Banquet hall facilities

(G-3976)
CITY MISSION (PA)
5310 Carnegie Ave (44103-4360)
PHONE..................216 431-3510
Richard Trickel, *Ex Dir*
EMP: 42 **EST:** 1910
SALES (est): 353.65K
SALES (corp-wide): 353.65K **Privately Held**
Web: www.thecitymission.org
SIC: 8322 8361 Rehabilitation services; Rehabilitation center, residential: health care incidental

(G-3977)
CITY OF BROOKLYN
7727 Memphis Ave (44144-2100)
PHONE..................216 635-4222
Kay Hutkay, *Brnch Mgr*
EMP: 67
SQ FT: 36,016
SALES (corp-wide): 27.13MM **Privately Held**
Web: www.brooklynohio.gov
SIC: 8322 Senior citizens' center or association
PA: City Of Brooklyn
7619 Memphis Ave Ste B
Cleveland OH 44144
216 351-2133

(G-3978)
CITY OF CLEVELAND
Also Called: Finance Dept
601 Lakeside Ave E Rm 19 (44114-1015)
PHONE..................216 664-2640
EMP: 28
SALES (corp-wide): 972.69MM **Privately Held**
Web: www.clevelandohio.gov
SIC: 8721 9311 Accounting, auditing, and bookkeeping; Finance, taxation, and monetary policy
PA: City Of Cleveland
601 Lakeside Ave E Rm 210
Cleveland OH 44114
216 664-2000

(G-3979)
CITY OF CLEVELAND
Also Called: Parks Recreation & Prpts Dept
21400 Chagrin Blvd (44122-5308)
PHONE..................216 348-7210
EMP: 28
SQ FT: 856
SALES (corp-wide): 972.69MM **Privately Held**
Web: www.clevelandohio.gov
SIC: 6553 9512 Cemetery subdividers and developers; Land, mineral, and wildlife conservation
PA: City Of Cleveland
601 Lakeside Ave E Rm 210

GEOGRAPHIC SECTION
Cleveland - Cuyahoga County (G-4000)

Cleveland OH 44114
216 664-2000

(G-3980)
CITY OF CLEVELAND
Also Called: Port Control
5300 Riverside Dr Ste 15 (44135-3145)
P.O. Box 81009 (44181-0009)
PHONE...................216 265-6000
Ricky Smith Senior, *Dir*
EMP: 1063
SALES (corp-wide): 972.69MM **Privately Held**
Web: www.clevelandairport.com
SIC: 4581 9621 Airport; Aircraft regulating agencies
PA: City Of Cleveland
601 Lakeside Ave E Rm 210
Cleveland OH 44114
216 664-2000

(G-3981)
CITY OF CLEVELAND
Also Called: Public Safety
1708 Southpoint (44109)
PHONE...................216 664-2555
Edward Eckart, *Commsnr*
EMP: 28
SALES (corp-wide): 972.69MM **Privately Held**
Web: www.clevelandohio.gov
SIC: 4119 9229 Ambulance service; Emergency management office, government
PA: City Of Cleveland
601 Lakeside Ave E Rm 210
Cleveland OH 44114
216 664-2000

(G-3982)
CITY OF CLEVELAND
Also Called: Cleveland Emergency Med Svc
2001 Payne Ave (44114-2915)
PHONE...................216 664-2555
Edward Eckart, *Commsnr*
EMP: 35
SALES (corp-wide): 972.69MM **Privately Held**
Web: www.clevelandohio.gov
SIC: 4119 Ambulance service
PA: City Of Cleveland
601 Lakeside Ave E Rm 210
Cleveland OH 44114
216 664-2000

(G-3983)
CITY OF CLEVELAND
Cleveland Public Power
1300 Lakeside Ave E (44114-1135)
PHONE...................216 664-4277
Janet Murphy, *Prin*
EMP: 66
SALES (corp-wide): 972.69MM **Privately Held**
Web: www.cpp.org
SIC: 4911 Distribution, electric power
PA: City Of Cleveland
601 Lakeside Ave E Rm 210
Cleveland OH 44114
216 664-2000

(G-3984)
CITY OF CLEVELAND
Public Works, Dept of
500 Lakeside Ave E (44114)
PHONE...................216 348-2200
Suzi Claytor, *Commsnr*
EMP: 28
SALES (corp-wide): 972.69MM **Privately Held**
Web: www.clevelandohio.gov

SIC: 6512 9512 Nonresidential building operators; Recreational program administration, government
PA: City Of Cleveland
601 Lakeside Ave E Rm 210
Cleveland OH 44114
216 664-2000

(G-3985)
CITY OF CLEVELAND
Also Called: Finance Dept
205 W Saint Clair Ave 4th Fl (44113-1503)
PHONE...................216 664-2430
Doug Divish, *Commsnr*
EMP: 35
SALES (corp-wide): 972.69MM **Privately Held**
Web: www.clevelandohio.gov
SIC: 7374 9199 Data processing and preparation; General government administration
PA: City Of Cleveland
601 Lakeside Ave E Rm 210
Cleveland OH 44114
216 664-2000

(G-3986)
CITY OF CLEVELAND
Division Information Tech Svcs
205 W Saint Clair Ave Fl 4 (44113-1503)
PHONE...................216 664-2941
Doug Davis, *Brnch Mgr*
EMP: 28
SALES (corp-wide): 972.69MM **Privately Held**
Web: www.clevelandohio.gov
SIC: 7376 Computer facilities management
PA: City Of Cleveland
601 Lakeside Ave E Rm 210
Cleveland OH 44114
216 664-2000

(G-3987)
CITY OF CLEVELAND
205 W Saint Clair Ave Fl 5 (44113-1503)
PHONE...................216 664-2625
Calvin Williams, *Chief*
EMP: 53
SALES (corp-wide): 972.69MM **Privately Held**
Web: www.clevelandohio.gov
SIC: 7381 Guard services
PA: City Of Cleveland
601 Lakeside Ave E Rm 210
Cleveland OH 44114
216 664-2000

(G-3988)
CITY OF CLEVELAND
Also Called: Department of Public Utilities
1300 Lakeside Ave E (44114-1135)
PHONE...................216 664-3922
EMP: 32
SALES (corp-wide): 972.69MM **Privately Held**
Web: www.clevelandohio.gov
SIC: 7389 Patrol of electric transmission or gas lines
PA: City Of Cleveland
601 Lakeside Ave E Rm 210
Cleveland OH 44114
216 664-2000

(G-3989)
CITY OF LAKEWOOD
Also Called: Lakewood Community Care Center
2019 Woodward Ave (44107-5635)
PHONE...................216 226-0080
Stephanie Mcmahan, *Prin*
EMP: 27

SALES (corp-wide): 71.48MM **Privately Held**
Web: www.lakewoodoh.gov
SIC: 8351 Child day care services
PA: City Of Lakewood
12650 Detroit Ave
Lakewood OH 44107
216 521-7580

(G-3990)
CITY OF LAKEWOOD
Also Called: Div of Refuse and Recycling
12920 Berea Rd (44111-1626)
PHONE...................216 252-4322
Chris Perry, *Genl Mgr*
EMP: 34
SQ FT: 28,810
SALES (corp-wide): 71.48MM **Privately Held**
Web: www.lakewoodoh.gov
SIC: 4953 9511 Refuse systems; Water control and quality agency, government
PA: City Of Lakewood
12650 Detroit Ave
Lakewood OH 44107
216 521-7580

(G-3991)
CITY OF LAKEWOOD
Also Called: Lakewood Police Dept
12650 Detroit Ave (44107-2832)
PHONE...................216 529-6170
EMP: 45
SALES (corp-wide): 71.48MM **Privately Held**
Web: www.lakewoodnj.gov
SIC: 9221 8111 Police protection, Local government; Legal services
PA: City Of Lakewood
12650 Detroit Ave
Lakewood OH 44107
216 521-7580

(G-3992)
CITY OF LYNDHURST
1341 Parkview Dr Ste 1 (44124-2474)
PHONE...................440 449-5011
Tom Konz, *Dir*
EMP: 32
SALES (corp-wide): 22.76MM **Privately Held**
Web: www.lyndhurst-oh.com
SIC: 8322 Community center
PA: Lyndhurst City Of (Inc)
5301 Mayfield Rd
Cleveland OH 44124
440 442-5777

(G-3993)
CITY OF SOUTH EUCLID
Also Called: Quarry Pool
711 S Belvoir Blvd (44121-2863)
PHONE...................216 381-7674
Kyle Bush, *Mgr*
EMP: 29
SALES (corp-wide): 34.7MM **Privately Held**
Web: www.cityofsoutheuclid.com
SIC: 7999 Swimming pool, non-membership
PA: City Of South Euclid
1349 S Green Rd
South Euclid OH 44121
216 381-1214

(G-3994)
CITY OF WESTLAKE
Also Called: Mayor's Office
27216 Hilliard Blvd (44145-3049)
PHONE...................440 871-3300
Jo Mason, *Dir*
EMP: 28

SALES (corp-wide): 63.98MM **Privately Held**
Web: www.cityofwestlake.org
SIC: 8651 Political organizations
PA: City Of Westlake
27700 Hilliard Blvd
Westlake OH 44145
440 871-3300

(G-3995)
CITY VIEW NURSING & REHAB LLC
Also Called: Cityview Nrsing Rhbltation Ctr
6606 Carnegie Ave (44103-4622)
PHONE...................216 361-1414
EMP: 225 **EST:** 1992
SQ FT: 41,000
SALES (est): 10.33MM **Privately Held**
Web: www.communicarehealth.com
SIC: 8051 Convalescent home with continuous nursing care

(G-3996)
CIULLA SMITH & DALE LLP (PA)
Also Called: Ciulla Smith & Dale
6364 Pearl Rd Ste 4 (44130-3063)
PHONE...................440 884-2036
Joseph Ciulla, *Pt*
Robert Mc Minn, *Pt*
Michael Petrisin, *Pt*
EMP: 28 **EST:** 1960
SQ FT: 5,500
SALES (est): 2.25MM
SALES (corp-wide): 2.25MM **Privately Held**
Web: www.theciullagroup.com
SIC: 8721 Certified public accountant

(G-3997)
CIUNI & PANICHI INC
25201 Chagrin Blvd Ste 200 (44122-5683)
PHONE...................216 831-7171
Vincent Panichi, *Sr Pt*
Charles Ciunini, *
EMP: 60 **EST:** 1973
SQ FT: 20,000
SALES (est): 9.06MM **Privately Held**
Web: www.cp-advisors.com
SIC: 8721 Certified public accountant

(G-3998)
CLASSIC MEDICAL STAFFING LLC
15703 Lorain Ave (44111-5543)
PHONE...................216 688-0900
P Zayas, *Managing Member*
Patty Zayas, *Managing Member*
Sue Mcandrews, *Pt*
EMP: 80 **EST:** 2004
SALES (est): 2.39MM **Privately Held**
SIC: 7363 Medical help service

(G-3999)
CLEARSTEAD ADVISORS LLC
Also Called: Hartland Advsors Llc-Cancelled
1100 Superior Ave E Ste 700 (44114-2530)
PHONE...................216 621-1090
Thomas Hartland, *CEO*
David C Fulton Junior, *Pr*
Tina Sterrett, *CAO*
EMP: 88 **EST:** 1989
SQ FT: 5,181
SALES (est): 13.35MM **Privately Held**
Web: www.clearstead.com
SIC: 8742 6282 Financial consultant; Investment advice

(G-4000)
CLEARSULTING LLC (PA)
1621 Euclid Ave Ste 2150 (44115-2193)
PHONE...................440 488-4274
Marc Ursick, *CEO*
Monica Engelhardt, *

Cleveland - Cuyahoga County (G-4001)　　　GEOGRAPHIC SECTION

EMP: 59 **EST:** 2015
SALES (est): 6.27MM
SALES (corp-wide): 6.27MM **Privately Held**
Web: www.clearsulting.com
SIC: 8742 Management consulting services

(G-4001)
CLEVELAN CLINIC HLTH SYS W REG (HQ)
18101 Lorain Ave (44111-5612)
PHONE..............................216 476-7000
Fred M Degrandis, *CEO*
EMP: 2800 **EST:** 1983
SQ FT: 327,000
SALES (est): 108.15MM
SALES (corp-wide): 14.48B **Privately Held**
Web: my.clevelandclinic.org
SIC: 8741 Hospital management
PA: The Cleveland Clinic Foundation
　9500 Euclid Ave
　Cleveland OH 44195
　216 636-8335

(G-4002)
CLEVELAND AMERICA SCORES
3631 Perkins Ave Ste 2ce (44114-4701)
PHONE..............................216 881-7988
D Pence-meyenberg, *Ex Dir*
Debra Pence-meyenberg, *Ex Dir*
EMP: 35 **EST:** 2003
SALES (est): 775.88K **Privately Held**
Web: www.americascorescleveland.org
SIC: 8699 Charitable organization

(G-4003)
CLEVELAND BROWNS
26500 Curtiss Wright Pkwy (44143-1438)
PHONE..............................216 261-3401
EMP: 57 **EST:** 2009
SALES (est): 109.44K **Privately Held**
Web: www.clevelandbrowns.com
SIC: 7941 Football club

(G-4004)
CLEVELAND CBD HOTEL LLC
Also Called: Radisson Inn
651 Huron Rd E (44115-1116)
PHONE..............................216 377-9000
Kestin Larry, *Pr*
EMP: 45 **EST:** 2019
SALES (est): 2.63MM **Privately Held**
Web: www.getsunmed.com
SIC: 7011 Hotels and motels

(G-4005)
CLEVELAND CHILD CARE INC
3274 W 58th St Fl 1 (44102-5681)
PHONE..............................216 631-3211
Gil Janke Junior, *Pr*
William Mldasi, *
EMP: 38 **EST:** 1980
SQ FT: 5,000
SALES (est): 885.44K **Privately Held**
Web: www.clevelandchild.com
SIC: 8351 Group day care center

(G-4006)
CLEVELAND CHRISTIAN HOME INC
4500 Euclid Ave (44103-3736)
PHONE..............................216 671-0977
Charles Tuttle, *CEO*
James M Mccafferty, *CEO*
Steve Letsky, *CFO*
Katharine Johnson Vinciquerra, *OF Development*
EMP: 38 **EST:** 1943
SALES (est): 5.73MM **Privately Held**
Web: www.cchome.org

SIC: 8322 8331 8361 Social service center; Job training and related services; Residential care

(G-4007)
CLEVELAND CINEMAS MGT CO LTD
13116 Shaker Sq (44120-2313)
PHONE..............................440 528-0355
Tim Hartswick, *Brnch Mgr*
EMP: 50
SALES (corp-wide): 1.97MM **Privately Held**
Web: www.clevelandcinemas.com
SIC: 7832 Motion picture theaters, except drive-in
PA: Cleveland Cinemas Management Co., Ltd.
　2163 Lee Rd Ste 107
　Cleveland OH 44118
　440 349-3306

(G-4008)
CLEVELAND CLINIC CHILDRENS
17800 Jefferson Park Rd Ste 101 (44130-3475)
PHONE..............................440 826-0102
EMP: 3747
SALES (corp-wide): 14.48B **Privately Held**
Web: my.clevelandclinic.org
SIC: 8999 Actuarial consultant
HQ: Cleveland Clinic Children's Hospital For Rehabilitation (Inc)
　2801 Mrtin Lther King Jr
　Cleveland OH 44104
　216 721-5400

(G-4009)
CLEVELAND CLINIC COLE EYE INST
Also Called: Cleveland Clinic
9500 Euclid Ave (44195-0001)
PHONE..............................216 444-4508
Toby Cosgrove, *CEO*
EMP: 28 **EST:** 2015
SALES (est): 5.63MM **Privately Held**
Web: www.clevelandclinic.org
SIC: 8062 General medical and surgical hospitals

(G-4010)
CLEVELAND CLINIC FOUNDATION
Also Called: Cleveland Clinic
2049 E 100th St (44106-2104)
PHONE..............................800 223-2273
Michael P Wascovich, *Dir*
EMP: 303
SALES (corp-wide): 14.48B **Privately Held**
Web: www.clevelandclinic.org
SIC: 8062 General medical and surgical hospitals
PA: The Cleveland Clinic Foundation
　9500 Euclid Ave
　Cleveland OH 44195
　216 636-8335

(G-4011)
CLEVELAND CLINIC FOUNDATION
2111 E 96th St (44106-2917)
PHONE..............................800 223-2273
EMP: 66
SALES (corp-wide): 14.48B **Privately Held**
Web: www.clevelandclinic.org
SIC: 8062 General medical and surgical hospitals
PA: The Cleveland Clinic Foundation
　9500 Euclid Ave
　Cleveland OH 44195
　216 636-8335

(G-4012)
CLEVELAND CLINIC FOUNDATION
Also Called: LL Bulding - Tmsich Pthlogy La
10300 Carnegie Ave Bldg LI (44106)
PHONE..............................216 444-5755
EMP: 57
SALES (corp-wide): 14.48B **Privately Held**
Web: www.clevelandclinic.org
SIC: 8062 General medical and surgical hospitals
PA: The Cleveland Clinic Foundation
　9500 Euclid Ave
　Cleveland OH 44195
　216 636-8335

(G-4013)
CLEVELAND CLINIC FOUNDATION
Also Called: Cleveland Clinic
2035 E 86th St (44106-2963)
PHONE..............................216 444-5715
EMP: 303
SALES (corp-wide): 14.48B **Privately Held**
Web: www.clevelandclinic.org
SIC: 8062 General medical and surgical hospitals
PA: The Cleveland Clinic Foundation
　9500 Euclid Ave
　Cleveland OH 44195
　216 636-8335

(G-4014)
CLEVELAND CLINIC FOUNDATION
Also Called: Cleveland Clnic Lyndhrst Cmpus
1950 Richmond Rd (44124-3719)
PHONE..............................216 448-4325
Scarlet Soriano, *Dir*
EMP: 300
SALES (corp-wide): 14.48B **Privately Held**
Web: my.clevelandclinic.org
SIC: 8062 General medical and surgical hospitals
PA: The Cleveland Clinic Foundation
　9500 Euclid Ave
　Cleveland OH 44195
　216 636-8335

(G-4015)
CLEVELAND CLINIC FOUNDATION
Also Called: Cleveland Clnic Tssig Cncer Ct
10201 Carnegie Ave Ca Bldg (44106-2130)
PHONE..............................866 223-8100
EMP: 41
SALES (corp-wide): 14.48B **Privately Held**
Web: my.clevelandclinic.org
SIC: 8062 General medical and surgical hospitals
PA: The Cleveland Clinic Foundation
　9500 Euclid Ave
　Cleveland OH 44195
　216 636-8335

(G-4016)
CLEVELAND CLINIC FOUNDATION
Also Called: Cleveland Clinic Foundation
9500 Euclid Ave (44195-0002)
PHONE..............................216 444-1764
David S Barnes, *Brnch Mgr*
EMP: 74
SALES (corp-wide): 14.48B **Privately Held**
Web: www.clevelandclinic.org
SIC: 8062 General medical and surgical hospitals
PA: The Cleveland Clinic Foundation
　9500 Euclid Ave
　Cleveland OH 44195
　216 636-8335

(G-4017)
CLEVELAND CLINIC FOUNDATION
315 Euclid Ave (44114-2206)
PHONE..............................216 442-6700

Vanital Patel, *Brnch Mgr*
EMP: 57
SALES (corp-wide): 14.48B **Privately Held**
Web: www.clevelandclinic.org
SIC: 8062 General medical and surgical hospitals
PA: The Cleveland Clinic Foundation
　9500 Euclid Ave
　Cleveland OH 44195
　216 636-8335

(G-4018)
CLEVELAND CLINIC FOUNDATION
Also Called: Cleveland Clinic
2050 E 96th St (44106-2970)
PHONE..............................216 444-5600
EMP: 33
SALES (corp-wide): 14.48B **Privately Held**
Web: www.clevelandclinic.org
SIC: 8062 General medical and surgical hospitals
PA: The Cleveland Clinic Foundation
　9500 Euclid Ave
　Cleveland OH 44195
　216 636-8335

(G-4019)
CLEVELAND CLINIC FOUNDATION
Also Called: Cleveland Clinic
9105 Cedar Ave (44106-2931)
PHONE..............................216 445-4500
EMP: 33
SALES (corp-wide): 14.48B **Privately Held**
Web: my.clevelandclinic.org
SIC: 8062 General medical and surgical hospitals
PA: The Cleveland Clinic Foundation
　9500 Euclid Ave
　Cleveland OH 44195
　216 636-8335

(G-4020)
CLEVELAND CLINIC FOUNDATION (PA)
Also Called: CLEVELAND CLINIC HEALTH SYSTEM
9500 Euclid Ave (44195-0002)
PHONE..............................216 636-8335
Tomislav Mihaljevic, *CEO*
Dennis Laraway, *
Josette Beran, *CSO**
Semih Sen, *Chief Business Development Officer**
Dana Kocsis, *
▲ **EMP:** 1612 **EST:** 1921
SALES (est): 14.48B
SALES (corp-wide): 14.48B **Privately Held**
Web: www.clevelandclinic.org
SIC: 8062 General medical and surgical hospitals

(G-4021)
CLEVELAND CLINIC FOUNDATION
Also Called: Cancer Centre
9500 Euclid Ave Fl 3r35 (44195-0002)
PHONE..............................216 445-6888
Toby Cosgrove, *Owner*
EMP: 30
SALES (corp-wide): 14.48B **Privately Held**
Web: www.clevelandclinic.org
SIC: 8062 General medical and surgical hospitals
PA: The Cleveland Clinic Foundation
　9500 Euclid Ave
　Cleveland OH 44195
　216 636-8335

(G-4022)
CLEVELAND CLINIC FOUNDATION
Also Called: Indepndnce Fmly Hlth RES Cntre
5001 Rockside Rd Fl 1 (44131-2193)

GEOGRAPHIC SECTION
Cleveland - Cuyahoga County (G-4043)

PHONE..................216 986-4000
EMP: 66
SALES (corp-wide): 14.48B **Privately Held**
Web: www.clevelandclinic.org
SIC: 8062 General medical and surgical hospitals
PA: The Cleveland Clinic Foundation
9500 Euclid Ave
Cleveland OH 44195
216 636-8335

(G-4023)
CLEVELAND CLINIC FOUNDATION
Also Called: Cleveland Clinic
9500 Euclid Ave (44195-0002)
PHONE..................216 444-2200
EMP: 336
SALES (corp-wide): 14.48B **Privately Held**
Web: www.clevelandclinic.org
SIC: 8062 General medical and surgical hospitals
PA: The Cleveland Clinic Foundation
9500 Euclid Ave
Cleveland OH 44195
216 636-8335

(G-4024)
CLEVELAND CLINIC FOUNDATION
Also Called: CA Bulding - Tussig Cancer Ctr
10201 Carnegie Ave (44106-2130)
PHONE..................216 442-3412
EMP: 41
SALES (corp-wide): 14.48B **Privately Held**
Web: www.clevelandclinic.org
SIC: 8011 Offices and clinics of medical doctors
PA: The Cleveland Clinic Foundation
9500 Euclid Ave
Cleveland OH 44195
216 636-8335

(G-4025)
CLEVELAND CLINIC FOUNDATION
Also Called: Health Orders
9500 Euclid Ave Ste S51 (44195-0002)
PHONE..................216 444-5540
Floyd Loop, *Brnch Mgr*
EMP: 33
SALES (corp-wide): 14.48B **Privately Held**
Web: www.clevelandclinic.org
SIC: 8011 Medical centers
PA: The Cleveland Clinic Foundation
9500 Euclid Ave
Cleveland OH 44195
216 636-8335

(G-4026)
CLEVELAND CLINIC FOUNDATION
Also Called: Cleveland Clinic Breast Center
9500 Euclid Ave Aq2 (44195-0002)
PHONE..................216 444-6618
Fred Loop, *Brnch Mgr*
EMP: 49
SALES (corp-wide): 14.48B **Privately Held**
Web: www.clevelandclinic.org
SIC: 8011 8062 Clinic, operated by physicians; General medical and surgical hospitals
PA: The Cleveland Clinic Foundation
9500 Euclid Ave
Cleveland OH 44195
216 636-8335

(G-4027)
CLEVELAND CLINIC FOUNDATION
Also Called: Cleveland Clini
9500 Euclid Ave (44195-0002)
PHONE..................216 444-2273
EMP: 33
SALES (corp-wide): 14.48B **Privately Held**
Web: www.clevelandclinic.org
SIC: 8011 Clinic, operated by physicians
PA: The Cleveland Clinic Foundation
9500 Euclid Ave
Cleveland OH 44195
216 636-8335

(G-4028)
CLEVELAND CLINIC FOUNDATION
Also Called: Cleveland Clnic Chld Inptent H
9500 Euclid Ave (44195-0002)
PHONE..................216 444-5437
EMP: 33
SALES (corp-wide): 14.48B **Privately Held**
Web: www.clevelandclinic.org
SIC: 8069 Childrens' hospital
PA: The Cleveland Clinic Foundation
9500 Euclid Ave
Cleveland OH 44195
216 636-8335

(G-4029)
CLEVELAND CLINIC FOUNDATION
Cleveland Clinic
13333 Gerald Dr Ste Nb5 (44130-5716)
PHONE..................216 445-6636
EMP: 49
SALES (corp-wide): 14.48B **Privately Held**
Web: www.clevelandclinic.org
SIC: 8071 Medical laboratories
PA: The Cleveland Clinic Foundation
9500 Euclid Ave
Cleveland OH 44195
216 636-8335

(G-4030)
CLEVELAND CLINIC FOUNDATION
Also Called: Cleveland Clnic HSP Fincl Dept
9500 Euclid Ave (44195-0002)
P.O. Box 931058 (44193-1384)
PHONE..................216 444-5000
Admiral Frank Lauderman, *Brnch Mgr*
EMP: 57
SALES (corp-wide): 14.48B **Privately Held**
Web: www.clevelandclinic.org
SIC: 6733 7389 Trusts, nec; Financial services
PA: The Cleveland Clinic Foundation
9500 Euclid Ave
Cleveland OH 44195
216 636-8335

(G-4031)
CLEVELAND CLINIC FOUNDATION
2045 E 89th St (44106-2972)
PHONE..................216 444-5715
Dave Zarko, *Brnch Mgr*
EMP: 115
SALES (corp-wide): 14.48B **Privately Held**
Web: www.clevelandclinic.org
SIC: 6733 Trusts, nec
PA: The Cleveland Clinic Foundation
9500 Euclid Ave
Cleveland OH 44195
216 636-8335

(G-4032)
CLEVELAND CLNC BCHWD FMLY CTR
26900 Cedar Rd Lbby (44122-1180)
PHONE..................216 839-3100
Andrea Jacobs, *Admn*
Anthony Ruben, *
Michael Rabovsky, *
EMP: 852 EST: 2000
SALES (est): 9.61MM
SALES (corp-wide): 14.48B **Privately Held**
Web: my.clevelandclinic.org
SIC: 8093 Mental health clinic, outpatient
PA: The Cleveland Clinic Foundation
9500 Euclid Ave
Cleveland OH 44195
216 636-8335

(G-4033)
CLEVELAND CLNIC CHLD HOSP FOR (HQ)
2801 Martin Luther King Jr Dr (44104-3815)
PHONE..................216 721-5400
Thomas A Rathbone, *Pr*
EMP: 194 EST: 1895
SQ FT: 120,000
SALES (est): 44.13MM
SALES (corp-wide): 14.48B **Privately Held**
Web: my.clevelandclinic.org
SIC: 8062 General medical and surgical hospitals
PA: The Cleveland Clinic Foundation
9500 Euclid Ave
Cleveland OH 44195
216 636-8335

(G-4034)
CLEVELAND CLNIC EDCTL FNDTION
Also Called: Cleveland Clnic Jurnl Medicine
9500 Euclid Ave (44195-0001)
PHONE..................216 444-1157
Doctor Floyd Loop, *Ex VP*
E Bradley Jones, *Ch Bd*
Kevin Roberts, *Treas*
EMP: 45 EST: 1935
SALES (est): 442.36K **Privately Held**
Web: www.clevelandclinic.org
SIC: 8099 Medical services organization

(G-4035)
CLEVELAND CLNIC HLTH SYSTM-AST
Also Called: Hillcrest Hospital
6780 Mayfield Rd (44124-2203)
PHONE..................440 449-4500
Glen Levy, *Admn*
EMP: 47
SALES (corp-wide): 14.48B **Privately Held**
Web: my.clevelandclinic.org
SIC: 8062 General medical and surgical hospitals
HQ: Cleveland Clinic Health System-East Region
6803 Mayfield Rd Ste 500
Cleveland OH 44124
440 312-6010

(G-4036)
CLEVELAND CLNIC HLTH SYSTM-AST
Also Called: Euclid Hospital
18901 Lake Shore Blvd (44119-1078)
PHONE..................216 692-7555
Warren Rock, *Brnch Mgr*
EMP: 74
SALES (corp-wide): 14.48B **Privately Held**
Web: my.clevelandclinic.org
SIC: 8062 General medical and surgical hospitals
HQ: Cleveland Clinic Health System-East Region
6803 Mayfield Rd Ste 500
Cleveland OH 44124
440 312-6010

(G-4037)
CLEVELAND CLNIC HLTH SYSTM-WST
5555 Transportation Blvd (44125-5371)
PHONE..................216 518-3444
William Wick, *Brnch Mgr*
EMP: 76
SALES (corp-wide): 14.48B **Privately Held**
Web: my.clevelandclinic.org
SIC: 8062 General medical and surgical hospitals
HQ: Cleveland Clinic Health System-Western Region
18101 Lorain Ave
Cleveland OH 44111
216 476-7000

(G-4038)
CLEVELAND CLNIC HLTH SYSTM-WST
Also Called: Hassler Medical Center
18200 Lorain Ave (44111-5605)
PHONE..................216 476-7606
Stevens Flynn, *Dir*
EMP: 105
SALES (corp-wide): 14.48B **Privately Held**
Web: my.clevelandclinic.org
SIC: 8741 8011 Hospital management; General and family practice, physician/surgeon
HQ: Cleveland Clinic Health System-Western Region
18101 Lorain Ave
Cleveland OH 44111
216 476-7000

(G-4039)
CLEVELAND CLNIC LRNER CLLEGE M
9500 Euclid Ave (44195-0001)
PHONE..................216 445-3853
Jacqueline Whatley, *Prin*
EMP: 147 EST: 2003
SALES (est): 3.98MM
SALES (corp-wide): 14.48B **Privately Held**
Web: www.clevelandclinic.org
SIC: 8062 8221 Hospital, medical school affiliation; Colleges and universities
PA: The Cleveland Clinic Foundation
9500 Euclid Ave
Cleveland OH 44195
216 636-8335

(G-4040)
CLEVELAND DENTAL INSTITUTE LLC
4071 Lee Rd Ste 260 (44128-2173)
PHONE..................216 727-0234
EMP: 46 EST: 2018
SALES (est): 1.62MM **Privately Held**
Web: www.cdiohio.org
SIC: 8021 Dentists' office

(G-4041)
CLEVELAND DESTINATION
334 Euclid Ave (44114-2207)
PHONE..................216 875-6652
David Gilbert, *Pr*
EMP: 36 EST: 2018
SALES (est): 2.6MM **Privately Held**
Web: www.thisiscleveland.com
SIC: 7999 Amusement and recreation, nec

(G-4042)
CLEVELAND EAST HOTEL LLC
Also Called: Marriott
26300 Harvard Rd (44122-6146)
PHONE..................216 378-9191
Kenny Didier, *Mgr*
EMP: 99 EST: 2005
SQ FT: 64,509
SALES (est): 9.48MM **Privately Held**
Web: www.marriott.com
SIC: 7011 Hotels and motels

(G-4043)
CLEVELAND EYE LSER SRGERY CTR
22715 Fairview Center Dr (44126-3608)
PHONE..................440 777-8400
Warren Laurita, *Prin*

Cleveland - Cuyahoga County (G-4044)

EMP: 30 **EST:** 2007
SALES (est): 6.49MM **Privately Held**
Web: www.clevelandeyelaser.com
SIC: 8011 Surgeon

(G-4044)
CLEVELAND FOUNDATION
6601 Euclid Ave (44103-3905)
PHONE..................216 861-3810
Ronald B Richard, *CEO*
Constance Hill-johnson, *Ch Bd*
Leslie A Dunford, *
James A Ratner, *
Frank C Sullivan, *Prin*
EMP: 75 **EST:** 1914
SALES (est): 234.72MM **Privately Held**
Web: www.clevelandfoundationrepair.net
SIC: 6732 Charitable trust management

(G-4045)
CLEVELAND FP INC (PA)
12819 Coit Rd (44108-1614)
PHONE..................216 249-4900
Michael Ivany, *Pr*
Martin Eble, *
◆ **EMP:** 90 **EST:** 1984
SQ FT: 103,000
SALES (est): 24.32MM
SALES (corp-wide): 24.32MM **Privately Held**
Web: www.flowpolymers.com
SIC: 5169 Chemicals and allied products, nec

(G-4046)
CLEVELAND GLASS BLOCK INC (PA)
Also Called: Mid America Glass Block
4566 E 71st St (44105-5604)
PHONE..................216 531-6363
Michael Foti, *Pr*
Frank Foti, *
▼ **EMP:** 27 **EST:** 1979
SQ FT: 15,500
SALES (est): 3.12MM
SALES (corp-wide): 3.12MM **Privately Held**
Web: www.innovatebuildingsolutions.com
SIC: 5231 5039 Glass; Glass construction materials

(G-4047)
CLEVELAND GRANITE & MARBLE LLC
4121 Carnegie Ave (44103-4336)
PHONE..................216 291-7637
Kimberly K Lisboa, *Managing Member*
▲ **EMP:** 33 **EST:** 2000
SQ FT: 50,000
SALES (est): 2.42MM **Privately Held**
Web: www.clevelandgranite.com
SIC: 3291 1799 Abrasive metal and steel products; Home/office interiors finishing, furnishing and remodeling

(G-4048)
CLEVELAND GUARDIANS BASBAL LLC (PA)
2401 Ontario St (44115-4003)
PHONE..................216 420-4487
Paul J Dolan, *CEO*
Jon Starret, *
Valerie Arcuri, *
Ken Stefanov, *
Mark Shapiro, *
EMP: 100 **EST:** 1996
SQ FT: 4,000
SALES (est): 51.62MM
SALES (corp-wide): 51.62MM **Privately Held**

Web: www.mlb.com
SIC: 7941 Baseball club, professional and semi-professional

(G-4049)
CLEVELAND HEARTLAB INC
6701 Carnegie Ave Ste 500 (44103-4639)
PHONE..................866 358-9828
▼ **EMP:** 100 **EST:** 2009
SQ FT: 38,000
SALES (est): 24.34MM
SALES (corp-wide): 9.25B **Publicly Held**
Web: www.clevelandheartlab.com
SIC: 8071 Medical laboratories
PA: Quest Diagnostics Incorporated
500 Plaza Dr
Secaucus NJ 07094
973 520-2700

(G-4050)
CLEVELAND HOME TITLE INC
2035 Crocker Rd Ste 201 (44145-2194)
PHONE..................440 788-7100
Brian Cole, *Pr*
EMP: 31 **EST:** 2002
SALES (est): 4.39MM **Privately Held**
Web: www.clevelandhometitle.com
SIC: 6541 Title and trust companies

(G-4051)
CLEVELAND HOPKINS INTL ARPRT
5300 Riverside Dr (44135)
P.O. Box 81009 (44181)
PHONE..................216 265-6000
EMP: 39 **EST:** 2016
SALES (est): 10.29MM **Privately Held**
Web: www.clevelandairport.com
SIC: 4581 Airport

(G-4052)
CLEVELAND INDIANS INC
2401 Ontario St (44115-4003)
PHONE..................216 420-4487
Paul J Dolan, *Ch*
Lawrence J Dolan, *CEO*
Mark Shapiro, *Pr*
Chris Antonetti, *Ex VP*
Dennis Lehman, *Ex VP*
EMP: 256 **EST:** 1962
SALES (est): 10.01MM **Privately Held**
Web: www.mlb.com
SIC: 7941 Baseball club, professional and semi-professional

(G-4053)
CLEVELAND JOB CORPS CENTER
13421 Coit Rd (44110-2269)
PHONE..................216 541-2500
Ramon Serrato, *Pr*
Tom Fitzwater, *
EMP: 160 **EST:** 2007
SALES (est): 12MM **Privately Held**
Web: cleveland.jobcorps.gov
SIC: 8331 Job training and related services

(G-4054)
CLEVELAND MARBLE MOSAIC CO (PA)
4595 Hinckley Industrial Pkwy (44109-6099)
PHONE..................216 749-2840
Robert J Zavagno Junior, *Pr*
Raymond L Zavagno, *
▲ **EMP:** 246 **EST:** 1924
SQ FT: 26,800
SALES (est): 14.72MM
SALES (corp-wide): 14.72MM **Privately Held**
Web: www.clevelandmarble.com

SIC: 1743 1741 Marble installation, interior; Marble masonry, exterior construction

(G-4055)
CLEVELAND METRO BAR ASSN
1375 E 9th St Fl 2 (44114-1724)
PHONE..................216 696-3525
EMP: 30 **EST:** 2010
SALES (est): 2.74MM **Privately Held**
Web: www.clemetrobar.org
SIC: 8111 Legal services

(G-4056)
CLEVELAND METROPARKS (PA)
4101 Fulton Pkwy (44144-1923)
PHONE..................216 635-3200
Brian Zimmerman, *CEO*
Debra K Berry, *
Bruce G Rinker, *
David Whitehead, *
David Kuntz, *
EMP: 292 **EST:** 1917
SQ FT: 9,000
SALES (est): 52.62MM
SALES (corp-wide): 52.62MM **Privately Held**
Web: www.clevelandmetroparks.com
SIC: 7999 Recreation services

(G-4057)
CLEVELAND METROPARKS
Also Called: Cleveland Metroparks Zoo
3900 Wildlife Way (44109-3132)
PHONE..................216 661-6500
Steve Taylor, *Dir*
EMP: 42
SALES (corp-wide): 52.62MM **Privately Held**
Web: www.clevelandmetroparks.com
SIC: 8422 7299 Botanical garden; Banquet hall facilities
PA: Cleveland Metroparks
4101 Fulton Pkwy
Cleveland OH 44144
216 635-3200

(G-4058)
CLEVELAND MSEUM OF NTRAL HSTOR
1 Wade Oval Dr (44106-1701)
PHONE..................216 231-4600
Sonia Winner, *Pr*
Bonnie Cummings, *
Douglas Stelzer, *
▲ **EMP:** 90 **EST:** 1920
SQ FT: 225,000
SALES (est): 27.61MM **Privately Held**
Web: www.cmnh.org
SIC: 8412 Museum

(G-4059)
CLEVELAND MUNICIPAL SCHOOL DST
Also Called: Rhodes Hs-Sch of Leadership
5100 Biddulph Ave (44144-3802)
PHONE..................216 459-4200
Charlene Hilliard, *Prin*
EMP: 64
SALES (corp-wide): 1B **Privately Held**
Web: www.cmsdnet.net
SIC: 8641 8222 8221 8211 Environmental protection organization; Technical institute; Professional schools; Public adult education school
PA: Cleveland Municipal School District Transformation Alliance
1111 Superior Ave E # 180
Cleveland OH 44114
216 838-0000

(G-4060)
CLEVELAND MUNICIPAL SCHOOL DST
Also Called: Children's Aid Society
10427 Detroit Ave (44102-1645)
PHONE..................216 521-6511
Jennifer Blumhagen, *CEO*
EMP: 36
SQ FT: 44,926
SALES (corp-wide): 1B **Privately Held**
Web: www.cmsdnet.net
SIC: 8322 Childrens' aid society
PA: Cleveland Municipal School District Transformation Alliance
1111 Superior Ave E # 180
Cleveland OH 44114
216 838-0000

(G-4061)
CLEVELAND MUNICIPAL SCHOOL DST
Also Called: New Tech West High School
11801 Worthington Ave (44111-5064)
PHONE..................216 838-8700
Shaunamichelle Leonard, *Prin*
EMP: 32
SALES (corp-wide): 1B **Privately Held**
Web: www.cmsdnet.net
SIC: 8211 8399 Public elementary and secondary schools; Advocacy group
PA: Cleveland Municipal School District Transformation Alliance
1111 Superior Ave E # 180
Cleveland OH 44114
216 838-0000

(G-4062)
CLEVELAND MUNICIPAL SCHOOL DST
Also Called: Ridge Road Depot
3832 Ridge Rd (44144-1112)
PHONE..................216 634-7005
Mark Cegelski, *Brnch Mgr*
EMP: 52
SALES (corp-wide): 1B **Privately Held**
Web: www.clevelandmetroschools.org
SIC: 4151 School buses
PA: Cleveland Municipal School District Transformation Alliance
1111 Superior Ave E # 180
Cleveland OH 44114
216 838-0000

(G-4063)
CLEVELAND RESEARCH COMPANY LLC
1375 E 9th St Ste 2700 (44114-1795)
PHONE..................216 649-7250
EMP: 34 **EST:** 2006
SALES (est): 11.56MM **Privately Held**
Web: www.clevelandresearch.com
SIC: 6282 Investment research

(G-4064)
CLEVELAND REST OPER LTD PARTNR
Also Called: TGI Friday's
9700 Rockside Rd Ste 150 (44125-6267)
PHONE..................216 328-1121
EMP: 47 **EST:** 1994
SALES (est): 517.17K **Privately Held**
Web: www.tgifridays.com
SIC: 5812 6794 Eating places; Patent owners and lessors

(G-4065)
CLEVELAND S HOSPITALITY LLC
Also Called: Doubletree Hotel
6200 Quarry Ln (44131-2218)
PHONE..................216 447-1300

Jock Litras, *Managing Member*
EMP: 74 EST: 2005
SQ FT: 59,489
SALES (est): 2.64MM **Privately Held**
Web: www.hilton.com
SIC: 7011 Hotels and motels

(G-4066)
CLEVELAND SKATING CLUB
2500 Kemper Rd (44120-1299)
PHONE..............................216 791-2800
EMP: 90 EST: 1936
SQ FT: 60,000
SALES (est): 4.05MM **Privately Held**
Web: www.clevelandskatingclub.org
SIC: 7997 Country club, membership

(G-4067)
CLEVELAND SOC FOR THE BLIND
Also Called: CLEVELAND SIGHT CENTER
1909 E 101st St (44106-4110)
P.O. Box 1988 (44106-0188)
PHONE..............................216 791-8118
Andrew L Sikorovsky, *Ch*
Thomas J Gibbons, *Vice Chairman**
Stephen Friedman, *
Gary W Poth, *
EMP: 140 EST: 1906
SQ FT: 100,000
SALES (est): 10.39MM **Privately Held**
Web: www.clevelandsightcenter.org
SIC: 8322 5441 Association for the handicapped; Confectionery produced for direct sale on the premises

(G-4068)
CLEVELAND SUPPLYONE INC (DH)
Also Called: Supplyone Retail
26801b Fargo Ave (44146-1338)
PHONE..............................216 514-7000
◆ EMP: 50 EST: 1914
SALES (est): 27.71MM
SALES (corp-wide): 838.82MM **Privately Held**
Web: www.supplyone.com
SIC: 5113 5162 5085 2653 Industrial and personal service paper; Plastics film; Glass bottles; Corrugated and solid fiber boxes
HQ: Supplyone, Inc.
  11 Campus Blvd Ste 150
  Newtown Square PA 19073
  484 582-5005

(G-4069)
CLEVELAND TANK & SUPPLY INC
6560 Juniata Ave (44103-1614)
PHONE..............................216 771-8265
Jack Sattler, *Pr*
EMP: 28 EST: 1992
SQ FT: 10,000
SALES (est): 12.34MM
SALES (corp-wide): 35.45MM **Privately Held**
Web: www.clevelandtank.com
SIC: 5084 Tanks, storage
PA: R B Technologies, Inc.
  16100 Imperial Pkwy
  Strongsville OH 44149
  440 572-3645

(G-4070)
CLEVELAND TEACHERS UNION INC
1228 Euclid Ave Ste 300 (44115-1843)
PHONE..............................216 861-7676
Richard Decolibus, *Pr*
EMP: 40 EST: 1994
SQ FT: 20,000
SALES (est): 3.67MM **Privately Held**
Web: ctu.oh.aft.org
SIC: 8631 8111 Labor union; Legal services

(G-4071)
CLEVELAND THERMAL LLC
1921 Hamilton Ave (44114)
PHONE..............................216 241-3636
Marc G Divis, *Pr*
Linda S Atkins, *
Donald J Hoffman, *
James R Kavalec, *
EMP: 46 EST: 2001
SQ FT: 4,000
SALES (est): 22.96MM **Privately Held**
Web: www.clevelandthermal.com
SIC: 4961 Steam supply systems, including geothermal

(G-4072)
CLEVELAND WATER DEPARTMENT
5953 Deering Ave (44130-2306)
PHONE..............................216 664-3168
Dick Kmetz, *Prin*
B Withers, *OF PU*
Bernardo Garcia, *Commsnr*
EMP: 27 EST: 2011
SALES (est): 556.98K **Privately Held**
Web: www.clevelandwater.com
SIC: 4941 Water supply

(G-4073)
CLEVELAND WESTIN DOWNTOWN
Also Called: Starbucks Licensed Store
777 Saint Clair Ave Ne (44114-1711)
PHONE..............................440 730-4338
Ryan Bunker, *Genl Mgr*
EMP: 51 EST: 2015
SALES (est): 9.73MM **Privately Held**
Web: www.westincleveland.com
SIC: 7011 Hotels

(G-4074)
CLEVELAND YACHTING CLUB INC
200 Yacht Club Dr (44116-1736)
PHONE..............................440 333-1155
Diane May, *Contrlr*
EMP: 60 EST: 1925
SQ FT: 25,000
SALES (est): 4.02MM **Privately Held**
Web: www.cycrr.org
SIC: 7997 Yacht club, membership

(G-4075)
CLEVELAND-CLIFFS INTL HOLDG CO
1100 Superior Ave E Fl 18 (44114-2518)
PHONE..............................216 694-5700
EMP: 95 EST: 2008
SALES (est): 1.34MM
SALES (corp-wide): 22B **Publicly Held**
Web: www.clevelandcliffs.com
SIC: 1011 Iron ores
PA: Cleveland-Cliffs Inc.
  200 Public Sq Ste 3300
  Cleveland OH 44114
  216 694-5700

(G-4076)
CLEVLAND CLINIC FOUNDATION
9500 Uclid Ave Desk 100 (44195-0001)
PHONE..............................216 445-5121
Delos Cosgrove, *CEO*
EMP: 524 EST: 2001
SALES (est): 2.66MM
SALES (corp-wide): 14.48B **Privately Held**
SIC: 8011 Urologist
PA: The Cleveland Clinic Foundation
  9500 Euclid Ave
  Cleveland OH 44195
  216 636-8335

(G-4077)
CLIFFS LOGAN COUNTY COAL LLC
200 Public Sq Ste 3300 (44114-2315)
PHONE..............................216 694-5700
▼ EMP: 108 EST: 2010
SALES (est): 872.46K
SALES (corp-wide): 22B **Publicly Held**
SIC: 5989 1221 Coal; Coal preparation plant, bituminous or lignite
PA: Cleveland-Cliffs Inc.
  200 Public Sq Ste 3300
  Cleveland OH 44114
  216 694-5700

(G-4078)
CLIFFS MINING SERVICES COMPANY
1100 Superior Ave E Ste 1500 (44114)
PHONE..............................218 262-5913
EMP: 171 EST: 1991
SALES (est): 2.48MM
SALES (corp-wide): 22B **Publicly Held**
SIC: 1011 Iron ores
PA: Cleveland-Cliffs Inc.
  200 Public Sq Ste 3300
  Cleveland OH 44114
  216 694-5700

(G-4079)
CLIFFS NATURAL RESOURCES EXPLO
200 Public Sq Ste 3300 (44114-2315)
PHONE..............................216 694-5700
EMP: 114 EST: 2013
SALES (est): 2.46MM
SALES (corp-wide): 22B **Publicly Held**
SIC: 1011 Iron ore mining
PA: Cleveland-Cliffs Inc.
  200 Public Sq Ste 3300
  Cleveland OH 44114
  216 694-5700

(G-4080)
CLIFFS RESOURCES INC (HQ)
200 Public Sq Ste 200 (44114-2301)
PHONE..............................216 694-5700
J S Brinzo, *CEO*
James A Trethewey, *
Cynthia B Bezik, *
EMP: 160 EST: 1978
SQ FT: 65,000
SALES (est): 58.69MM
SALES (corp-wide): 22B **Publicly Held**
SIC: 4011 Railroads, line-haul operating
PA: Cleveland-Cliffs Inc.
  200 Public Sq Ste 3300
  Cleveland OH 44114
  216 694-5700

(G-4081)
CLIFFS UTAC HOLDING LLC
200 Public Sq Ste 3300 (44114-2315)
PHONE..............................216 694-5700
EMP: 57 EST: 2018
SALES (est): 4.19MM
SALES (corp-wide): 22B **Publicly Held**
SIC: 1081 Metal mining services
PA: Cleveland-Cliffs Inc.
  200 Public Sq Ste 3300
  Cleveland OH 44114
  216 694-5700

(G-4082)
CLIMACO WLCOX PECA GROFOLI LPA (PA)
1001 Lakeside Ave E (44114-1158)
PHONE..............................216 621-8484
John R Climaco, *Pt*
EMP: 100 EST: 1971
SALES (est): 5.61MM
SALES (corp-wide): 5.61MM **Privately Held**
Web: www.climacolaw.com
SIC: 8111 General practice law office

(G-4083)
CLIMATE PROS LLC
5309 Hamilton Ave (44114-3909)
PHONE..............................216 881-5200
Todd Ernest, *CEO*
EMP: 85
Web: www.climatepros.com
SIC: 1711 5078 2541 2434 Refrigeration contractor; Commercial refrigeration equipment; Cabinets, except refrigerated: show, display, etc.: wood; Wood kitchen cabinets
PA: Climate Pros, Llc
  2190 Gladstone Ct Ste E
  Glendale Heights IL 60139

(G-4084)
CLINICAL MANAGEMENT CONS INC
1400 W 10th St Ste 301 (44113-1361)
PHONE..............................440 638-5000
Abby Cravotta, *Pr*
EMP: 66
SALES (corp-wide): 4.92MM **Privately Held**
Web: www.clinicalmanagementconsultants.com
SIC: 8999 8741 Scientific consulting; Business management
PA: Clinical Management Consultants, Inc.
  85 Bolinas Rd Ste 18
  Fairfax CA 94930
  415 773-1100

(G-4085)
CLUM MEDIA INC
Also Called: Clum Creative
1419 E 40th St (44103-1103)
PHONE..............................216 239-1525
David B Leitch, *Pr*
EMP: 39 EST: 2016
SALES (est): 1.41MM **Privately Held**
Web: www.clumcreative.com
SIC: 7311 Advertising agencies

(G-4086)
COLEMAN SPOHN CORPORATION (PA)
1775 E 45th St (44103-2318)
PHONE..............................216 431-8070
EMP: 30 EST: 1994
SQ FT: 12,000
SALES (est): 9.31MM **Privately Held**
Web: www.colemanspohn.com
SIC: 1711 Mechanical contractor

(G-4087)
COLLEGE NOW GRTER CLVELAND INC (PA)
1500 W 3rd St Ste 125 (44113-1422)
PHONE..............................216 241-5587
Lee Friedman, *Pr*
EMP: 37 EST: 1967
SALES (est): 24.64MM
SALES (corp-wide): 24.64MM **Privately Held**
Web: www.collegenowgc.org
SIC: 8322 General counseling services

(G-4088)
COLLINWOOD SHALE BRICK SUP CO (PA)
16219 Saranac Rd (44110-2435)
PHONE..............................216 587-2700
Dorothy Strohm, *Ch Bd*

Scott Terhune, *Pr*
Cynthia S Terhune, *Treas*
EMP: 50 **EST:** 1921
SQ FT: 10,000
SALES (est): 40.72MM
SALES (corp-wide): 40.72MM **Privately Held**
SIC: 3273 5032 Ready-mixed concrete; Brick, stone, and related material

(G-4089)
COLUMBIA GAS OF OHIO INC
Also Called: Columbia
7080 Fry Rd (44130-2513)
PHONE...................................440 891-2458
Paul Fackler, *Rgnl Mgr*
EMP: 104
SALES (corp-wide): 5.51B **Publicly Held**
Web: www.columbiagasohio.com
SIC: 4924 Natural gas distribution
HQ: Columbia Gas Of Ohio, Inc.
290 W Nationwide Blvd # 1
Columbus OH 43215
614 460-6000

(G-4090)
COMBER HOLDINGS INC
3304 W 67th Pl (44102-5243)
PHONE...................................216 961-8600
Dean Comber, *Pr*
EMP: 40 **EST:** 1984
SQ FT: 30,000
SALES (est): 6.71MM **Privately Held**
Web: www.shakervalleyfoods.com
SIC: 5141 2011 Food brokers; Meat packing plants

(G-4091)
COMCAST SPOTLIGHT LP
Also Called: Adelphia
3300 Lakeside Ave E (44114-3751)
PHONE...................................216 575-8016
Larry Drake, *Brnch Mgr*
EMP: 28
SALES (corp-wide): 121.57B **Publicly Held**
Web: www.effectv.com
SIC: 7311 Advertising agencies
HQ: Comcast Spotlight, Lp
55 W 46th St Fl 33
New York NY 10036
212 907-8641

(G-4092)
COMEX NORTH AMERICA INC (HQ)
Also Called: Comex Group
101 W Prospect Ave Ste 1020 (44115-1093)
PHONE...................................303 307-2100
Leon Cohen, *Pr*
Christopher Connor, *
◆ **EMP:** 90 **EST:** 2000
SQ FT: 2,900
SALES (est): 132.3MM
SALES (corp-wide): 22.15B **Publicly Held**
SIC: 2851 8742 5198 5231 Paints and paint additives; Corporation organizing consultant; Paints; Paint
PA: The Sherwin-Williams Company
101 W Prospect Ave
Cleveland OH 44115
216 566-2000

(G-4093)
COMMCAPP AMERICA INC
1300 E 9th St Fl 22 (44114-1501)
PHONE...................................678 780-0937
Kareem Lanier, *CEO*
EMP: 45 **EST:** 2020
SALES (est): 1.13MM **Privately Held**

SIC: 8748 Business consulting, nec

(G-4094)
COMMERCIAL ELECTRIC PDTS CORP (PA)
1821 E 40th St (44103-3503)
PHONE...................................216 241-2886
Roger Meyer, *Pr*
Kenneth Culp, *
EMP: 44 **EST:** 1927
SQ FT: 32,000
SALES (est): 17.02MM
SALES (corp-wide): 17.02MM **Privately Held**
Web: www.commercialelectric.com
SIC: 5085 3661 3824 7699 Power transmission equipment and apparatus; Telephones and telephone apparatus; Mechanical and electromechanical counters and devices; Industrial equipment services

(G-4095)
COMMUNICATIONS BUYING GROUP
Also Called: Icg Netcom
6060 Rockside Woods Blvd (44131-7303)
PHONE...................................216 377-3000
William F Beans Junior, *Pr*
H Don Teague, *General*
EMP: 90 **EST:** 1989
SALES (est): 3.62MM **Privately Held**
SIC: 8741 Management services

(G-4096)
COMMUNITY ACTION AGNST ADDCTIO
5209 Euclid Ave (44103)
PHONE...................................216 881-0765
Ronald Winbush, *Dir*
EMP: 35 **EST:** 1971
SQ FT: 24,000
SALES (est): 4.62MM **Privately Held**
Web: www.caaaddiction.org
SIC: 8093 Drug clinic, outpatient

(G-4097)
COMMUNITY ASSSSMENT TRTMNT SVC (PA)
8411 Broadway Ave (44105)
PHONE...................................216 441-0200
Roxanne Wallace, *Dir*
Dan Cratcha, *
William G Malenich, *
EMP: 36 **EST:** 1990
SQ FT: 19,000
SALES (est): 11.97MM **Privately Held**
Web: www.communityassessment.org
SIC: 8093 Substance abuse clinics (outpatient)

(G-4098)
COMMUNITY DIALYSIS CENTER
Also Called: Center For Dialysis Care
11717 Euclid Ave (44106-4350)
PHONE...................................216 295-7000
Diane Wish, *Brnch Mgr*
EMP: 106
Web: www.cdcare.org
SIC: 8092 Kidney dialysis centers
PA: Community Dialysis Center
18720 Chagrin Blvd
Shaker Heights OH 44122

(G-4099)
COMMUNITY DIALYSIS CENTER
Also Called: Center For Dialysis Care
11717 Euclid Ave (44106-4350)
P.O. Box 12220 (44112-0220)
PHONE...................................216 229-6750
Diane Wish, *Ex Dir*

EMP: 125 **EST:** 1974
SQ FT: 25,000
SALES (est): 69.79MM **Privately Held**
Web: www.cdcare.org
SIC: 8092 Kidney dialysis centers

(G-4100)
COMPASS PROFESSIONAL SVCS LLC
1536 Saint Clair Ave Ne # 58 (44114-2004)
PHONE...................................216 705-2233
EMP: 75 **EST:** 2017
SALES (est): 2.2MM **Privately Held**
Web: www.compasssvcs.com
SIC: 7361 Employment agencies

(G-4101)
CONNECTING DOTS CNNCTING TO SL
3030 Euclid Ave (44115-2530)
PHONE...................................216 356-2362
EMP: 42 **EST:** 2019
SALES (est): 2.26MM **Privately Held**
Web: www.ctdcts.com
SIC: 8052 8741 8059 Personal care facility; Nursing and personal care facility management; Personal care home, with health care

(G-4102)
CONNECTIONS IN OHIO INC
8001 Sweet Valley Dr Ste 4 (44125-4218)
PHONE...................................216 228-9760
Joyce Newbacher, *Prin*
EMP: 61 **EST:** 2000
SALES (est): 16.09K **Privately Held**
Web: www.connectionsinohio.com
SIC: 8082 Home health care services

(G-4103)
CONRADS TIRE SERVICE INC (PA)
Also Called: Conrad's Total Car Care
14577 Lorain Ave (44111-3156)
P.O. Box 110584 (44111-0584)
PHONE...................................216 941-3333
John Turk, *Pr*
EMP: 35 **EST:** 1969
SQ FT: 10,000
SALES (est): 43.14MM
SALES (corp-wide): 43.14MM **Privately Held**
Web: www.econrads.com
SIC: 7538 5531 5014 General automotive repair shops; Automotive tires; Automobile tires and tubes

(G-4104)
CONSOLDATED GRAPHICS GROUP INC
Also Called: Consolidated Solutions
1614 E 40th St (44103-2319)
PHONE...................................216 881-9191
▲ **EMP:** 170 **EST:** 1984
SQ FT: 75,000
SALES (est): 43.48MM **Privately Held**
Web: www.csinc.com
SIC: 2752 2759 7331 2791 Offset printing; Commercial printing, nec; Direct mail advertising services; Typesetting

(G-4105)
CONSOLDTED FNDRIES HLDNGS CORP
1621 Euclid Ave Ste 1850 (44115-2126)
PHONE...................................216 772-1041
Newton Portal, *CEO*
EMP: 1000 **EST:** 2005
SALES (est): 690MM
SALES (corp-wide): 822.51MM **Privately Held**

SIC: 6719 8741 Holding companies, nec; Business management
HQ: Cfhc Holdings, Inc.
1621 Euclid Ave Ste 1850
Cleveland OH

(G-4106)
CONSOLIDATED COATINGS CORP
3735 Green Rd (44122-5705)
PHONE...................................216 514-7596
J K Milliken, *Genl Mgr*
Thomas C Sullivan, *
Paul A Granzier, *
EMP: 2047 **EST:** 1904
SQ FT: 4,000
SALES (est): 4.71MM
SALES (corp-wide): 7.26B **Publicly Held**
SIC: 5169 2891 2851 2842 Adhesives and sealants; Adhesives and sealants; Paints and allied products; Polishes and sanitation goods
HQ: Republic Powdered Metals, Inc.
2628 Pearl Rd
Medina OH 44256
330 225-3192

(G-4107)
CONSOLIPLEX HOLDING LLC (PA)
9555 Rockside Rd Ste 300c (44125-6284)
PHONE...................................216 202-3499
George Stadtlander, *Managing Member*
EMP: 37 **EST:** 2013
SALES (est): 2.47MM
SALES (corp-wide): 2.47MM **Privately Held**
Web: www.consoliplex.com
SIC: 8742 Administrative services consultant

(G-4108)
CONSTANT AVIATION LLC (DH)
18601 Cleveland Pkwy Dr Ste 1b (44135)
PHONE...................................800 440-9004
David Davies, *CEO*
Kevin Dillon, *Pr*
Christian Drouin, *COO*
EMP: 200 **EST:** 2006
SALES (est): 99.82MM
SALES (corp-wide): 160.16MM **Privately Held**
Web: www.constantaviation.com
SIC: 7363 4581 Pilot service, aviation; Aircraft maintenance and repair services
HQ: Flexjet, Inc.
26180 Curtiss Wright Pkwy
Cleveland OH 44143
216 261-3880

(G-4109)
CONSTRUCTION LABOR CONTRS LLC
981 Keynote Cir Ste 25 (44131-1842)
PHONE...................................216 741-3351
EMP: 244
Web: www.powerlaborusa.com
SIC: 7361 Labor contractors (employment agency)
HQ: Construction Labor Contractors, Llc
9760 Shepard Rd
Macedonia OH 44056
330 247-1080

(G-4110)
CONSULATE MANAGEMENT CO LLC
Also Called: Mt Royal Villa Care Center
13900 Bennett Rd (44133-3808)
PHONE...................................440 237-7966
Doug Pearson, *Mgr*
EMP: 268
SALES (corp-wide): 491MM **Privately Held**
Web: www.consulatehc.com

GEOGRAPHIC SECTION
Cleveland - Cuyahoga County (G-4131)

SIC: 8051 8052 Skilled nursing care facilities ; Intermediate care facilities
HQ: Consulate Management Company, Llc
800 Concourse Pkwy S # 200
Maitland FL 32751
407 571-1550

(G-4111)
CONSUMER CREDIT COUNSELING SER (PA)
1228 Euclid Ave Ste 390 (44115-1800)
PHONE.................................800 254-4100
Jay Seaton, Pr
EMP: 35 EST: 1964
SQ FT: 1,700
SALES (est): 3.37MM Privately Held
SIC: 8742 Financial consultant

(G-4112)
CONTAINERPORT GROUP INC (HQ)
1340 Depot St Fl 2 (44116-1741)
PHONE.................................440 333-1330
Frederick Hunger, CEO
Richard C Coleman, *
Russell G Graef, *
James R Kramer, *
David N Messer, *
▲ EMP: 57 EST: 1971
SQ FT: 14,000
SALES (est): 167.6MM
SALES (corp-wide): 282.57MM Privately Held
Web: www.containerport.com
SIC: 4731 Brokers, shipping
PA: World Shipping, Inc.
1340 Depot St Ste 200
Cleveland OH 44116
440 356-7676

(G-4113)
CONTROLSOFT INC
5387 Avion Park Dr (44143-1916)
PHONE.................................440 443-3900
Tien Li Chia, Pr
EMP: 50 EST: 1985
SALES (est): 7.16MM Privately Held
Web: www.controlsoftinc.com
SIC: 8748 Systems engineering consultant, ex. computer or professional

(G-4114)
CONVENTION VSTORS BUR OF GRTER
334 Euclid Ave (44114-2207)
PHONE.................................216 875-6600
David Gilbert, Pr
EMP: 28 EST: 1934
SALES (est): 17.43MM Privately Held
Web: www.thisiscleveland.com
SIC: 7371 Computer software development and applications

(G-4115)
CONVENTION VSTORS BUR OF GRTER (PA)
Also Called: CONVENTION & VISITORS BUREAU
50 Public Sq Ste 3100 (44113-2242)
PHONE.................................216 875-6603
Dennis Roche, Pr
EMP: 33 EST: 1934
SQ FT: 7,200
SALES (est): 19.53MM
SALES (corp-wide): 19.53MM Privately Held
Web: www.clevelandconventions.com
SIC: 7389 Convention and show services

(G-4116)
CORPORATE SCREENING SVCS LLC (HQ)
Also Called: Corporate Screening
16530 Commerce Ct Ste 3 (44130-6316)
P.O. Box 361219 (44136-0021)
PHONE.................................440 816-0500
EMP: 63 EST: 1996
SQ FT: 12,900
SALES (est): 10.93MM
SALES (corp-wide): 763.76MM Publicly Held
Web: www.corporatescreening.com
SIC: 7381 Private investigator
PA: First Advantage Corporation
1 Concrse Pkwy Ne Ste 200
Atlanta GA 30328
888 314-9761

(G-4117)
CORPORATE WNGS - CLEVELAND LLC
355 Richmond Rd Ste A (44143-4405)
PHONE.................................216 261-9000
Elizabeth Ricci, CEO
EMP: 51 EST: 2002
SALES (est): 3.78MM Privately Held
Web: www.corporatewings.com
SIC: 4581 Airport control tower operation, except government

(G-4118)
CORRIGAN MOVING SYSTEMS
13900 Keystone Pkwy (44135-5100)
PHONE.................................440 243-5860
EMP: 43
SALES (corp-wide): 1.73MM Privately Held
Web: www.corriganmoving.com
SIC: 4212 Moving services
PA: Corrigan Moving Systems
12875 Corporate Dr Ste B
Cleveland OH 44130
440 243-8560

(G-4119)
CORVEL CORPORATION
Also Called: Corvel
7530 Lucerne Dr Ste 400 (44130-6557)
P.O. Box 3758 (43016-0389)
PHONE.................................800 275-6463
Michael Williams, Mgr
EMP: 43
Web: www.corvel.com
SIC: 8741 Management services
PA: Corvel Corporation
5128 Apache Plume Rd # 4
Fort Worth TX 76109

(G-4120)
COSMIC CONCEPTS LTD
Also Called: Media Star Promotions
5000 Euclid Ave (44103-3749)
PHONE.................................216 696-4230
EMP: 74
SALES (corp-wide): 41.84MM Privately Held
SIC: 8743 Public relations services
PA: Cosmic Concepts, Ltd.
318 Clubhouse Rd
Hunt Valley MD 21031
410 825-8500

(G-4121)
COUNTRY CLUB INC
2825 Lander Rd (44124-4899)
PHONE.................................216 831-9200
Robert C Josey, CEO
EMP: 110 EST: 1889
SQ FT: 112,000
SALES (est): 9.75MM Privately Held
Web: www.thecountryclub.com
SIC: 7997 Country club, membership

(G-4122)
COUNTY OF CUYAHOGA
Also Called: Department Senior Adult S
1701 E 12th St Ste 11 (44114-3237)
PHONE.................................216 420-6750
Susan E Axelrod, Mgr
EMP: 38
Web: www.cuyahogacounty.gov
SIC: 9441 8322 Administration of social and human resources; Senior citizens' center or association
PA: County Of Cuyahoga
1215 W 3rd St
Cleveland OH 44113
216 443-7022

(G-4123)
COUNTY OF CUYAHOGA
Also Called: Child Support Enforcement Agcy
1640 Superior Ave E (44114-2908)
P.O. Box 93318 (44101-5318)
PHONE.................................216 443-5100
Cassondra Mcarthuour, Mgr
EMP: 37
SQ FT: 44,726
Web: www.ccprosecutor.us
SIC: 9441 8322 Administration of social and manpower programs, County government; Child guidance agency
PA: County Of Cuyahoga
1215 W 3rd St
Cleveland OH 44113
216 443-7022

(G-4124)
COUNTY OF CUYAHOGA
Also Called: Activity Training
13231 Euclid Ave (44112-4523)
PHONE.................................216 681-4433
Albert Trefeny, Mgr
EMP: 44
Web: www.cuyahogacounty.gov
SIC: 9441 8322 Administration of social and manpower programs, County government; Individual and family services
PA: County Of Cuyahoga
1215 W 3rd St
Cleveland OH 44113
216 443-7022

(G-4125)
COUNTY OF CUYAHOGA
Also Called: Cuyahoga County Dept Pub Works
2100 Superior Via (44113-2357)
PHONE.................................216 348-3800
Robert C Klaiber, Prin
EMP: 385
Web: www.cuyahogacounty.gov
SIC: 8711 9532 Engineering services; Urban and community development, County government
PA: County Of Cuyahoga
1215 W 3rd St
Cleveland OH 44113
216 443-7022

(G-4126)
COUNTY OF CUYAHOGA
Also Called: Cuyahoga Cnty Bd Dvlpmntal Dsb
1275 Lakeside Ave E (44114-1129)
PHONE.................................216 241-8230
Michael Donzella, Brnch Mgr
EMP: 608
Web: www.cuyahogabdd.org

SIC: 8361 9431 Retarded home; Mental health agency administration, government
PA: County Of Cuyahoga
1215 W 3rd St
Cleveland OH 44113
216 443-7022

(G-4127)
COUNTY OF CUYAHOGA
Also Called: Coroner's Office
11001 Cedar Ave Ste 400 (44106-3043)
PHONE.................................216 698-6526
Elizabeth Balraj, Mgr
EMP: 222
SQ FT: 720
Web: www.cuyahogacounty.gov
SIC: 8049 9431 9111 Coroner; Administration of public health programs, County government; Executive offices, County government
PA: County Of Cuyahoga
1215 W 3rd St
Cleveland OH 44113
216 443-7022

(G-4128)
COUNTY OF CUYAHOGA
5202 Memphis Ave (44144-2231)
PHONE.................................216 941-8800
Barbara Riley, Dir
EMP: 44
Web: www.cuyahogabdd.org
SIC: 8099 8322 Nutrition services; Individual and family services
PA: County Of Cuyahoga
1215 W 3rd St
Cleveland OH 44113
216 443-7022

(G-4129)
COUNTY OF CUYAHOGA
Also Called: Children and Family Services
3955 Euclid Ave (44115-2505)
PHONE.................................216 431-4500
William Denihan, Brnch Mgr
EMP: 82
Web: www.cuyahogacounty.gov
SIC: 8322 9441 Individual and family services; Administration of social and manpower programs, County government
PA: County Of Cuyahoga
1215 W 3rd St
Cleveland OH 44113
216 443-7022

(G-4130)
COUNTY OF CUYAHOGA
Also Called: Department Children Services
3955 Euclid Ave Rm 344 (44115-2505)
PHONE.................................216 432-2621
James Mc Cafferty, Mgr
EMP: 37
Web: www.cuyahogacounty.gov
SIC: 8322 9431 Child related social services; Child health program administration, government
PA: County Of Cuyahoga
1215 W 3rd St
Cleveland OH 44113
216 443-7022

(G-4131)
COUNTY OF CUYAHOGA
Also Called: Central Services Department
2079 E 9th St (44115-1302)
PHONE.................................216 443-6954
Jay Ross, Mgr
EMP: 304
SQ FT: 35,640
Web: www.cuyahogacounty.gov

Cleveland - Cuyahoga County (G-4132)   GEOGRAPHIC SECTION

SIC: 7349 9431 Building maintenance services, nec; Health statistics center, government
PA: County Of Cuyahoga
1215 W 3rd St
Cleveland OH 44113
216 443-7022

(G-4132)
COURTYARD BY MARRIOTT
Also Called: Courtyard Cleveland Beach
3695 Orange Pl (44122-4401)
PHONE..................................216 765-1900
Terri Ball, *Asst Mgr*
EMP: 30 EST: 2008
SALES (est): 2.7MM
SALES (corp-wide): 23.71B Publicly Held
Web: www.marriott.com
SIC: 7011 Hotels and motels
PA: Marriott International, Inc.
7750 Wisconsin Ave
Bethesda MD 20814
301 380-3000

(G-4133)
COURTYARD MANAGEMENT CORP
Also Called: Courtyard By Marriott
5051 W Creek Rd (44131-2165)
PHONE..................................216 901-9988
Scott Arra, *Brnch Mgr*
EMP: 29
SALES (corp-wide): 23.71B Publicly Held
Web: www.marriott.com
SIC: 7011 Hotels and motels
HQ: Courtyard Management Llc
7750 Wisconsin Ave
Bethesda MD 20814

(G-4134)
CPP GROUP HOLDINGS LLC (PA)
1621 Euclid Ave Ste 1850 (44115-2126)
PHONE..................................216 453-4800
James V Stewart, *CEO*
Timothy Trombetta I, *CFO*
EMP: 50 EST: 2019
SALES (est): 822.51MM
SALES (corp-wide): 822.51MM Privately Held
Web: www.cppcorp.com
SIC: 6719 3089 Investment holding companies, except banks; Automotive parts, plastic

(G-4135)
CREATIVE PLAYROOM (PA)
Also Called: Solon Crtive Plyroom Mntessori
16574 Broadway Ave (44137-2602)
PHONE..................................216 475-6464
Joan Wenk, *Pr*
EMP: 60 EST: 1968
SQ FT: 12,000
SALES (est): 1.65MM
SALES (corp-wide): 1.65MM Privately Held
Web: www.creativeplayrooms.com
SIC: 8351 Montessori child development center

(G-4136)
CREDIT FIRST NATIONAL ASSN (DH)
Also Called: GCR TIRES & SERVICE
6275 Eastland Rd (44142-1301)
P.O. Box 81315 (44181-0315)
PHONE..................................216 362-5300
Dean S Miller, *Pr*
Alan K Meier, *CFO*
EMP: 39 EST: 2002
SALES (est): 56.37MM Privately Held
Web: www.cfna.com
SIC: 7389 Financial services

HQ: Bridgestone Americas Tire Operations, Llc
200 4th Ave S Ste 100
Nashville TN 37201
615 937-1000

(G-4137)
CREEKSIDE CARGO INC
15416 Industrial Pkwy (44135-3312)
PHONE..................................216 688-1770
John Kautzman, *Pr*
EMP: 27 EST: 2007
SQ FT: 800
SALES (est): 5.38MM Privately Held
Web: www.creeksidecargo.com
SIC: 4111 4789 Local and suburban transit; Cargo loading and unloading services

(G-4138)
CRESCO LIMITED PARTNERSHIP
3 Summit Park Dr (44131-2599)
PHONE..................................216 520-1200
Joseph Barna, *Pt*
Fred Christie, *Pt*
EMP: 32 EST: 1991
SQ FT: 3,000
SALES (est): 6.04MM Privately Held
Web: www.crescorealestate.com
SIC: 6531 Real estate agent, commercial

(G-4139)
CROSSCOUNTRY MORTGAGE INC
12000 Snow Rd Ste 9 (44130-9314)
PHONE..................................440 845-3700
EMP: 44 EST: 2019
SALES (est): 987.63K Privately Held
Web: www.crosscountrymortgage.com
SIC: 6162 Mortgage bankers and loan correspondents

(G-4140)
CROSSCOUNTRY MORTGAGE LLC
Also Called: American Eagle Mortgage
2160 Superior Ave E (44114-2102)
PHONE..................................440 262-3528
EMP: 56
SALES (corp-wide): 803.24MM Privately Held
Web: www.crosscountrymortgage.com
SIC: 6162 Mortgage bankers and loan correspondents
PA: Crosscountry Mortgage, Llc
6850 Miller Rd
Brecksville OH 44141
440 845-3700

(G-4141)
CROSSROADS HOSPITALITY CO LLC
Also Called: Hampton Inn Cleveland
1460 E 9th St (44114-1700)
PHONE..................................216 241-6600
Jeff Charo, *Mgr*
EMP: 100
Web: www.hilton.com
SIC: 7011 Hotels and motels
HQ: Crossroads Hospitality Company Llc
6430 Rockland Dr
Bethesda MD 20817

(G-4142)
CSA AMERICA STANDARDS INC
Also Called: Csa International Services
8501 E Pleasant Valley Rd (44131-5516)
PHONE..................................216 524-4990
Randall Luecke, *Admn Execs*
EMP: 111
SALES (corp-wide): 367.35MM Privately Held
Web: www.csagroup.org
SIC: 8734 Testing laboratories
HQ: Csa America Standards, Inc.

8501 E Pleasant Valley Rd
Independence OH 44131
216 524-4990

(G-4143)
CT LOGISTICS INC
12487 Plaza Dr (44130-1056)
PHONE..................................216 267-1636
EMP: 150 EST: 2006
SQ FT: 1,000
SALES (est): 22.75MM Privately Held
Web: www.ctlogistics.com
SIC: 4789 7371 Pipeline terminal facilities, independently operated; Computer software development

(G-4144)
CTRAC INC
2222 W 110th St (44102-3512)
PHONE..................................440 572-1000
Susan Williamson, *Pr*
Gary A Seitz, *
EMP: 37 EST: 1972
SQ FT: 15,000
SALES (est): 5.44MM
SALES (corp-wide): 8.35MM Privately Held
Web: www.ctrac.com
SIC: 7331 7374 Mailing service; Data processing service
PA: Pierry, Inc.
557 Grand St
Redwood City CA 94062
800 860-7953

(G-4145)
CUSTOM HDWR ENGRG CNSLTING LLC
Also Called: Che Consulting
5910 Landerbrook Dr Ste 300 (44124-6500)
PHONE..................................636 305-9669
Chris Adams, *Pr*
EMP: 102 EST: 1993
SALES (est): 5.05MM Privately Held
Web: www.parkplacetechnologies.com
SIC: 7378 Computer and data processing equipment repair/maintenance
PA: Park Place Technologies, Llc
5910 Lndrbrook Dr Ste 300
Cleveland OH 44124

(G-4146)
CUYAHOGA COUNTY SANI ENGRG SVC
6100 W Canal Rd (44125-3330)
PHONE..................................216 443-8211
David Reines, *Dir*
EMP: 44 EST: 1921
SALES (est): 1.04MM Privately Held
Web: www.cuyahogacounty.gov
SIC: 4959 Sanitary services, nec

(G-4147)
CWM ENVRONMENTAL CLEVELAND LLC
4450 Johnston Pkwy Ste B (44128-2956)
PHONE..................................216 663-0808
David Kohl, *Managing Member*
EMP: 30 EST: 2005
SQ FT: 15,000
SALES (est): 4.67MM Privately Held
Web: www.metirigroup.com
SIC: 8748 Environmental consultant
PA: Cwm Environmental, Llc
101 Parkview Drive Ext
Kittanning PA 16201

(G-4148)
DAKOTA SOFTWARE CORPORATION (PA)
1375 Euclid Ave Ste 500 (44115-1808)
PHONE..................................216 765-7100
Reginald C Shiverick, *Pr*
EMP: 61 EST: 1988
SALES (est): 7.48MM
SALES (corp-wide): 7.48MM Privately Held
Web: www.dakotasoft.com
SIC: 7372 Prepackaged software

(G-4149)
DATA DEN INC
Also Called: Intercity Line
1901 Train Ave (44113-4203)
PHONE..................................216 622-0900
John E Rose Junior, *Pr*
EMP: 35 EST: 1987
SQ FT: 15,000
SALES (est): 4.3MM Privately Held
SIC: 4731 Truck transportation brokers

(G-4150)
DATAVANTAGE CORPORATION (DH)
Also Called: Micros Retail
30500 Bruce Industrial Pkwy Ste A (44139-3969)
PHONE..................................440 498-4414
Marvin Lader, *CEO*
Bob Walters, *
John E Gularson, *
Jeremy Grunzweig, *
EMP: 270 EST: 1988
SQ FT: 56,400
SALES (est): 35.32MM
SALES (corp-wide): 49.95B Publicly Held
SIC: 5734 5045 8748 7371 Computer and software stores; Computers, peripherals, and software; Business consulting, nec; Custom computer programming services
HQ: Micros Systems, Inc.
7031 Columbia Gateway Dr
Columbia MD 21046
443 285-6000

(G-4151)
DAVIS CONSTRUCTION MANAGEMENT
Also Called: Davis Construction Co
32000 Solon Rd (44139-3589)
PHONE..................................440 248-7770
Jeffrey Davis, *Pr*
Paul Yusko, *VP*
Al Wangenheim, *VP*
EMP: 37 EST: 1958
SQ FT: 14,000
SALES (est): 5.6MM Privately Held
Web: www.davisdevelopmentgroup.com
SIC: 1541 1542 5812 Industrial buildings, new construction, nec; Commercial and office building, new construction; Eating places

(G-4152)
DAVIS YOUNG A LEGAL PROF ASSN (PA)
600 Superior Ave E Ste 1200 (44114-2614)
PHONE..................................216 348-1700
Martin J Murphy, *VP*
Paul D Eklund, *Sec*
EMP: 41 EST: 1972
SQ FT: 12,000
SALES (est): 2.43MM
SALES (corp-wide): 2.43MM Privately Held
Web: www.davisyoung.com
SIC: 8111 General practice law office

Cleveland - Cuyahoga County (G-4175)

(G-4153)
DAYTON HEIDELBERG DISTRG CO
Heidelberg Distributing Co
9101 E Pleasant Valley Rd (44131-5504)
PHONE.................................216 520-2626
Greg Michalec, *VP*
EMP: 233
SALES (corp-wide): 2.07B **Privately Held**
Web: www.heidelbergdistributing.com
SIC: 5181 Beer and other fermented malt liquors
HQ: Dayton Heidelberg Distributing Co., Llc
3601 Dryden Rd
Moraine OH 45439
937 222-8692

(G-4154)
DB CONSULTING GROUP INC
21000 Brookpark Rd Ms142-1 (44135-3127)
PHONE.................................216 433-5132
Rick Stalnacker, *Brnch Mgr*
EMP: 72
SALES (corp-wide): 46.45MM **Privately Held**
Web: www.dbconsultinggroup.com
SIC: 8748 Business consulting, nec
PA: Db Consulting Group, Inc.
3 Bethesda Metro Ctr # 70
Bethesda MD 20814
301 589-4020

(G-4155)
DEALER TIRE LLC (PA)
7012 Euclid Ave (44103-4014)
PHONE.................................216 432-0088
Scott Mueller, *CEO*
Dean Mueller, *
Steve Raguz, *
Cindy Stull, *CSO**
Walter Mueller, *
▲ **EMP:** 450 **EST:** 1918
SQ FT: 50,000
SALES (est): 996.39MM
SALES (corp-wide): 996.39MM **Privately Held**
Web: www.dealertire.com
SIC: 5531 5014 Automotive tires; Automobile tires and tubes

(G-4156)
DEAN A CARMICHAEL
Also Called: Rockside Family Dental Care
6132 W Creek Rd (44131-2130)
PHONE.................................216 524-8481
Val Lundstrom, *Off Mgr*
Richard L Parsanko D.d.s., *Pr*
Dean Carmichael, *VP*
EMP: 39 **EST:** 1975
SQ FT: 3,500
SALES (est): 3.93MM **Privately Held**
Web: www.rocksidefamilydentalcare.com
SIC: 8021 Dentists' office

(G-4157)
DEAN CONTRACTING INC
19100 Holland Rd (44142-1324)
PHONE.................................440 260-7590
Linda A Pontikos, *Pr*
EMP: 30 **EST:** 1983
SALES (est): 1.29MM **Privately Held**
SIC: 1721 Residential painting

(G-4158)
DEANS GREENHOUSE INC
3984 Porter Rd (44145-5298)
PHONE.................................440 871-2050
Larry Dean, *Pr*
Victoria Dean, *VP*
EMP: 38 **EST:** 1924
SQ FT: 1,680
SALES (est): 445.85K **Privately Held**
Web: www.deansgreenhouse.com
SIC: 0181 5992 Flowers: grown under cover (e.g., greenhouse production); Flowers, fresh

(G-4159)
DEHART WORKS LLC
15210 Industrial Pkwy (44135-3308)
PHONE.................................440 600-8003
Gloria Baker, *CEO*
Gloria Baker, *Prin*
EMP: 60 **EST:** 2021
SALES (est): 1MM **Privately Held**
SIC: 7489 Business Activities at Non-Commercial Site

(G-4160)
DELOITTE & TOUCHE LLP
127 Public Sq Ste 3300 (44114-1303)
PHONE.................................216 589-1300
Patrick Mullen, *Pt*
EMP: 1463
Web: www.deloitte.com
SIC: 8721 8742 Certified public accountant; Management consulting services
HQ: Deloitte & Touche Llp
30 Rockefeller Plz # 4350
New York NY 10112
212 492-4000

(G-4161)
DELTA CORPORATE HOLDINGS LLC
Also Called: P A I
12420 Plaza Dr (44130-1057)
PHONE.................................216 433-7700
EMP: 300
Web: www.pai-net.com
SIC: 5085 Fasteners, industrial: nuts, bolts, screws, etc.

(G-4162)
DEPENDABLE PAINTING CO (PA)
4403 Superior Ave (44103-1135)
PHONE.................................216 431-4470
Cindy Friedmann, *Pr*
Donald K Hansen, *Ex VP*
EMP: 49 **EST:** 1928
SQ FT: 20,000
SALES (est): 4.64MM
SALES (corp-wide): 4.64MM **Privately Held**
Web: www.dependableptg.com
SIC: 1721 Exterior commercial painting contractor

(G-4163)
DG3 TOPCO HOLDINGS LLC
25101 Chagrin Blvd Ste 350 (44122-5643)
PHONE.................................216 292-0200
EMP: 53
SALES (est): 620.68K
SALES (corp-wide): 315.22MM **Privately Held**
SIC: 6799 Investors, nec
PA: Resilience Capital Partners Llc
25101 Chgrin Blvd Ste 350
Cleveland OH 44122
216 292-0200

(G-4164)
DI SANTO COMPANIES INC
25111 Emery Rd (44128-5600)
PHONE.................................216 292-7772
George P Di Santo, *Pr*
Catherine G Cogar, *VP*
Derek Di Santo, *VP*
Carolyn Di Santo, *Sec*
EMP: 50 **EST:** 1959
SQ FT: 11,200
SALES (est): 1.45MM **Privately Held**
Web: www.disantocompanies.com
SIC: 0782 Landscape contractors

(G-4165)
DIAMOND METALS DIST INC
4635 W 160th St (44135-2629)
PHONE.................................216 898-7900
EMP: 30 **EST:** 1991
SALES (est): 9.49MM **Privately Held**
Web: www.diamondmetals.com
SIC: 5051 Steel

(G-4166)
DIRECT IMPORT HOME DECOR INC (PA)
Also Called: Cabinet and Granite Direct
4979 W 130th St (44135-5139)
PHONE.................................216 898-9758
Eddie Ni, *Pr*
▲ **EMP:** 32 **EST:** 2003
SQ FT: 50,000
SALES (est): 9.62MM
SALES (corp-wide): 9.62MM **Privately Held**
Web: www.dihusa.com
SIC: 5032 5031 Granite building stone; Kitchen cabinets

(G-4167)
DISTILLATA COMPANY (PA)
1608 E 24th St (44114-4212)
P.O. Box 93845 (44101-5845)
PHONE.................................216 771-2900
TOLL FREE: 800
William E Schroeder, *Pr*
Herbert Buckman, *
J C Little, *
R M Egan, *
Dalphne Axline, *
EMP: 70 **EST:** 1897
SQ FT: 100,000
SALES (est): 15.25MM
SALES (corp-wide): 15.25MM **Privately Held**
Web: www.distillata.com
SIC: 2899 5149 Distilled water; Mineral or spring water bottling

(G-4168)
DIX & EATON INCORPORATED
200 Public Sq Ste 3900 (44114-2322)
PHONE.................................216 241-0405
Chas Withers, *CEO*
Lisa Rose, *
Jim Brown, *CFO*
Kris Dorsey, *Sr VP*
Amy Mcgahan, *Sr VP*
EMP: 50 **EST:** 1952
SQ FT: 23,000
SALES (est): 9.26MM **Privately Held**
Web: www.dix-eaton.com
SIC: 8743 7311 Public relations and publicity; Advertising agencies

(G-4169)
DLR GROUP INC
Also Called: Westlake Reed Leskosky
1422 Euclid Ave Ste 300 (44115-1912)
PHONE.................................216 522-1350
EMP: 60
SALES (corp-wide): 183.73MM **Privately Held**
Web: www.dlrgroup.com
SIC: 8711 8712 Engineering services; Architectural services
HQ: Dlr Group Inc.
6457 Frances St Ste 200
Omaha NE 68106
216 522-1350

(G-4170)
DMD MANAGEMENT INC
Also Called: Legacy Health Services
5520 Broadview Rd (44134-1606)
PHONE.................................216 749-4010
EMP: 238
Web: www.lhshealth.com
SIC: 8741 Management services
PA: Dmd Management, Inc.
12380 Plaza Dr
Cleveland OH 44130

(G-4171)
DMD MANAGEMENT INC (PA)
Also Called: Legacy Health Services
12380 Plaza Dr (44130-1043)
PHONE.................................216 898-8399
Bruce Daskal, *CEO*
Harold Shachter, *
Larry Dancziger, *
Jim Taylor, *
Barry Stump, *
EMP: 50 **EST:** 1990
SQ FT: 28,360
SALES (est): 93.72MM **Privately Held**
Web: www.lhshealth.com
SIC: 8741 Nursing and personal care facility management

(G-4172)
DMD MANAGEMENT INC
12504 Cedar Rd (44106-3217)
PHONE.................................216 371-3600
Bruce Daskal, *Brnch Mgr*
EMP: 238
Web: www.lhshealth.com
SIC: 8322 8051 Adult day care center; Skilled nursing care facilities
PA: Dmd Management, Inc.
12380 Plaza Dr
Cleveland OH 44130

(G-4173)
DODD CAMERA HOLDINGS INC (PA)
Also Called: Dodd Camera
2077 E 30th St (44115-2624)
PHONE.................................216 361-6811
EMP: 38 **EST:** 1891
SALES (est): 12.56MM
SALES (corp-wide): 12.56MM **Privately Held**
Web: www.doddcamera.com
SIC: 5946 5043 5731 Cameras; Photographic cameras, projectors, equipment and supplies; Video cameras and accessories

(G-4174)
DOLLAR PARADISE (PA)
Also Called: United Discount
1240 E 55th St (44103-1029)
PHONE.................................216 432-0421
Amin Alsoussou, *Pr*
EMP: 27 **EST:** 2000
SALES (est): 4.12MM
SALES (corp-wide): 4.12MM **Privately Held**
Web: www.wholesalecloseout.net
SIC: 5199 5331 Gifts and novelties; Variety stores

(G-4175)
DOMINO FOODS INC
Also Called: Domino Sugar
2075 E 65th St (44103-4630)
PHONE.................................216 432-3222
Jeffrey Bender, *Brnch Mgr*
EMP: 172
SALES (corp-wide): 2.16B **Privately Held**
Web: www.asr-group.com

SIC: **2099** 7389 Sugar; Packaging and labeling services
HQ: Domino Foods Inc.
99 Wood Ave S Ste 901
Iselin NJ 08830
732 590-1173

(G-4176)
DONALD MRTENS SONS AMBLNCE SVC (PA)
10830 Brookpark Rd (44130-1119)
PHONE..................................216 265-4211
Dean Martens, *VP*
Donald A Martens Junior, *VP*
Donald S Martens, *Prin*
EMP: 70 **EST:** 1982
SQ FT: 7,410
SALES (est): 20.79MM
SALES (corp-wide): 20.79MM **Privately Held**
Web: www.martensambulance.com
SIC: 4119 Ambulance service

(G-4177)
DONLEN INC
8905 Lake Ave (44102-6315)
PHONE..................................216 961-6767
Donald Strang, *Pr*
EMP: 85 **EST:** 1997
SALES (est): 4.36MM
SALES (corp-wide): 22.51MM **Privately Held**
Web: www.donlen.com
SIC: 7011 Hotels and motels
PA: Strang Corporation
8905 Lake Ave Fl 1
Cleveland OH 44102
216 961-6767

(G-4178)
DONLEYS INC (PA)
5430 Warner Rd (44125-1140)
PHONE..................................216 524-6800
Malcolm M Donley, *Pr*
Terrance K Donley, *Ch Bd*
Don K Dreier, *Ex VP*
Patrick J Powers, *Treas*
EMP: 98 **EST:** 1941
SQ FT: 44,000
SALES (est): 117.62MM
SALES (corp-wide): 117.62MM **Privately Held**
Web: www.donleyinc.com
SIC: 1542 Commercial and office building, new construction

(G-4179)
DORSKY HODGSON + PARTNERS INC (PA)
Also Called: Dorsky Hodgson Parrish Yue
23240 Chagrin Blvd Ste 300 (44122-5405)
PHONE..................................216 464-8600
William Dorsky, *Ch Bd*
Corneila Hodgeson, *
Charles A Cohen, *
Geoffrey J Porter, *
James M Friedman, *
EMP: 60 **EST:** 1958
SALES (est): 5.39MM
SALES (corp-wide): 5.39MM **Privately Held**
SIC: 8712 Architectural engineering

(G-4180)
DORTRONIC SERVICE INC (PA)
Also Called: Action Door
201 E Granger Rd (44131-6728)
PHONE..................................216 739-3667
Michelle Lorello-zoocki, *CEO*
Michael Wittwer, *
Dino Mastanuono, *
Dave Cavasini, *
EMP: 50 **EST:** 1968
SQ FT: 25,000
SALES (est): 17.91MM
SALES (corp-wide): 17.91MM **Privately Held**
Web: www.action-door.com
SIC: 1751 7699 5031 Garage door, installation or erection; Door and window repair; Doors, nec

(G-4181)
DOVETAIL CONSTRUCTION CO INC (PA)
Also Called: Dovetail Solar and Wind
26055 Emery Rd (44128-5765)
P.O. Box 23038 (44023-0038)
PHONE..................................740 592-1800
Alan R Frasz, *Pr*
Matthew Bennett, *Technology*
EMP: 34 **EST:** 1995
SQ FT: 7,200
SALES (est): 4.71MM
SALES (corp-wide): 4.71MM **Privately Held**
Web: www.dovetailsolar.com
SIC: 1731 1711 Electric power systems contractors; Solar energy contractor

(G-4182)
DR TRANSPORTATION INC
3184 E 79th St (44104-4325)
P.O. Box 27469 (44127-0469)
PHONE..................................216 588-6110
EMP: 30 **EST:** 1996
SQ FT: 20,000
SALES (est): 2.1MM **Privately Held**
Web: www.kealytrucking.com
SIC: 4212 Local trucking, without storage

(G-4183)
DRAKE CONSTRUCTION COMPANY (PA)
1545 E 18th St (44114-2923)
PHONE..................................216 664-6500
EMP: 38 **EST:** 1954
SALES (est): 13.74MM
SALES (corp-wide): 13.74MM **Privately Held**
Web: www.drakeconstructionco.com
SIC: 1542 1541 Commercial and office buildings, renovation and repair; Renovation, remodeling and repairs: industrial buildings

(G-4184)
DREISON INTERNATIONAL INC (PA)
4540 W 160th St (44135-2628)
PHONE..................................216 362-0755
John Berger Junior, *Pr*
Theodore Berger Junior, *Pr*
Theodore J Berger Senior, *Ch Bd*
Marilyn J Berger, *
Whitney Slaght, *
◆ **EMP:** 190 **EST:** 1986
SQ FT: 210,000
SALES (est): 61.53MM
SALES (corp-wide): 61.53MM **Privately Held**
Web: www.dreison.com
SIC: 3643 3621 3561 3564 Current-carrying wiring services; Motors, electric; Pumps and pumping equipment; Purification and dust collection equipment

(G-4185)
DRIVE INSURANCE COMPANY
Also Called: Progressive West Insurance Co
6300 Wilson Mills Rd (44143-2109)
PHONE..................................440 446-5100
Kanik Varma, *CEO*
Mark Niehaus, *
Jan Dolohanty, *
Kathleen Scerny, *
Jan Kusner, *
EMP: 98 **EST:** 1970
SQ FT: 750
SALES (est): 49.12MM
SALES (corp-wide): 49.61B **Publicly Held**
Web: www.progressive.com
SIC: 6331 Automobile insurance
HQ: Drive Insurance Holdings, Inc.
6300 Wilson Mills Rd
Cleveland OH 44143

(G-4186)
DRS WEINBERGER AND VISY LLC
3690 Orange Pl Ste 230 (44122-4465)
PHONE..................................216 765-1180
EMP: 43 **EST:** 2001
SALES (est): 2.26MM **Privately Held**
Web: www.weinbergerandvizy.com
SIC: 8011 General and family practice, physician/surgeon

(G-4187)
DTV INC
Also Called: Danny Veghs Home Entertainment
4070 Mayfield Rd (44121-3036)
PHONE..................................216 226-5465
TOLL FREE: 800
Kathy Vegh, *CEO*
Frank Plutt, *
EMP: 35 **EST:** 1963
SALES (est): 9.17MM **Privately Held**
Web: www.dannyveghs.com
SIC: 5046 7699 5962 5091 Vending machines, coin-operated; Billiard table repair; Merchandising machine operators; Billiard equipment and supplies

(G-4188)
DUNBAR ARMORED INC
5505 Cloverleaf Pkwy (44125-4814)
PHONE..................................216 642-5700
EMP: 51
SALES (corp-wide): 4.87B **Publicly Held**
Web: www.dunbarsecurity.com
SIC: 7381 Armored car services
HQ: Dunbar Armored, Inc.
50 Schilling Rd
Hunt Valley MD 21031
410 584-9800

(G-4189)
DUTCH BOY GROUP
101 W Prospect Ave Ste 1020 (44115-1027)
PHONE..................................800 828-5669
EMP: 27 **EST:** 1907
SALES (est): 6.19MM
SALES (corp-wide): 22.15B **Publicly Held**
Web: www.dutchboy.com
SIC: 5198 Paints
PA: The Sherwin-Williams Company
101 W Prospect Ave
Cleveland OH 44115
216 566-2000

(G-4190)
DWELLWORKS LLC (PA)
Also Called: Rss
1317 Euclid Ave (44115-1819)
PHONE..................................216 682-4200
Bob Rosing, *Managing Member*
EMP: 52 **EST:** 2007
SQ FT: 11,000
SALES (est): 25.91MM **Privately Held**
Web: www.dwellworks.com
SIC: 7389 Relocation service

(G-4191)
DWORKEN & BERNSTEIN CO LPA
1468 W 9th St Ste 135 (44113-1220)
PHONE..................................216 230-5170
TOLL FREE: 877
Howard Rebb, *Mgr*
EMP: 40
SALES (corp-wide): 4.27MM **Privately Held**
Web: www.dworkenlaw.com
SIC: 8111 General practice attorney, lawyer
PA: Dworken & Bernstein Co Lpa
60 S Park Pl
Painesville OH 44077
440 316-2664

(G-4192)
DWORKIN INC (PA)
Also Called: Dworkin Trucking
5400 Harvard Ave (44105-4899)
PHONE..................................216 271-5318
Jack E Hankison, *Prin*
Jake Dworkin, *
Otto L Hankison, *
EMP: 50 **EST:** 1939
SQ FT: 15,000
SALES (est): 2.82MM
SALES (corp-wide): 2.82MM **Privately Held**
Web: www.dworkintrucking.com
SIC: 4213 Contract haulers

(G-4193)
E F BOYD & SON INC (PA)
Also Called: Boyd Funeral Home
2165 E 89th St (44106-3420)
PHONE..................................216 791-0770
William F Boyd Ii, *Pr*
Marcella Cox, *
Marina Grant, *
EMP: 34 **EST:** 1906
SQ FT: 20,000
SALES (est): 2.49MM
SALES (corp-wide): 2.49MM **Privately Held**
Web: www.efboyd.com
SIC: 7261 Funeral home

(G-4194)
E-MERGING TECHNOLOGIES GROUP INC
22021 Brookpark Rd Ste 130 (44126-3100)
PHONE..................................440 779-5680
EMP: 95
Web: www.etg1.com
SIC: 7373 Systems integration services

(G-4195)
E-Z ELECTRIC MOTOR SVC CORP
8510 Bessemer Ave (44127-1843)
P.O. Box 22531 (44122-0531)
PHONE..................................216 581-8820
Demetrius Ledgyard, *Pr*
EMP: 29 **EST:** 1965
SQ FT: 15,000
SALES (est): 857.18K **Privately Held**
Web: www.ezelectricmotor.com
SIC: 7694 Electric motor repair

(G-4196)
EARLY CHLDHOOD ENRCHMENT CTR I
19824 Sussex Rd Rm 178 (44122-4917)
PHONE..................................216 991-9761
Lynne Prange, *Dir*
Michelle Block, *Asst Dir*
EMP: 33 **EST:** 1974
SALES (est): 3.52MM **Privately Held**
Web: www.ececshaker.org

GEOGRAPHIC SECTION

Cleveland - Cuyahoga County (G-4218)

SIC: 8351 Preschool center

(G-4197)
EAST OHIO GAS COMPANY (DH)
Also Called: Dominion Energy Ohio
1201 E 55th St (44103-1028)
P.O. Box 26646 (23261-6646)
PHONE.................................800 362-7557
TOLL FREE: 800
Tom D Newland, *Pr*
Michael G Bartels, *VP*
B C Klink Senior, *Res Vice President*
Ron Kovach, *VP*
Brian Brakeman, *VP*
EMP: 1051 EST: 1846
SQ FT: 121,000
SALES (est): 541.91MM
SALES (corp-wide): 39.69B **Privately Held**
Web: www.dominiongaschoice.com
SIC: 4924 Natural gas distribution
HQ: Enbridge Inc.
5400 Westheimer Ct
Houston TX 77056
713 627-5400

(G-4198)
EAST OHIO GAS COMPANY
Also Called: Dominion Energy Ohio
21200 Miles Rd (44128-4502)
PHONE.................................216 736-6959
Bill Armstrong, *Mgr*
EMP: 65
SQ FT: 37,452
SALES (corp-wide): 39.69B **Privately Held**
Web: www.dominiongaschoice.com
SIC: 4924 Natural gas distribution
HQ: The East Ohio Gas Company
1201 E 55th St
Cleveland OH 44103
800 362-7557

(G-4199)
EASTERN EXPRESS LOGISTICS INC (PA)
8777 Rockside Rd (44125-6112)
PHONE.................................800 348-6514
David Ferrante, *Pr*
EMP: 34 EST: 2013
SALES (est): 4.88MM
SALES (corp-wide): 4.88MM **Privately Held**
Web: www.easternexpressinc.com
SIC: 4213 Contract haulers

(G-4200)
EASY2 TECHNOLOGIES INC
Also Called: Easy 2 Technologies
1111 Chester Ave (44114-3545)
PHONE.................................216 479-0482
Ethan Cohen, *CEO*
George Koenig, *Business Development**
Carl Persson Vp Channel Mgt, *Prin*
Matt Walsh, **
EMP: 30 EST: 1996
SQ FT: 9,400
SALES (est): 4.6MM
SALES (corp-wide): 80MM **Privately Held**
Web: www.syndigo.com
SIC: 7373 Systems software development services
HQ: Answers Corporation
6665 Delmar Blvd Ste 3000
Saint Louis MO 63124

(G-4201)
EATON AEROSPACE LLC (HQ)
Also Called: E E M C O
1000 Eaton Blvd (44122-6058)
PHONE.................................216 523-5000
Alexander M Cutler, *CEO*
R H Fearon, *CFO*

▲ EMP: 459 EST: 2000
SALES (est): 80.29MM **Privately Held**
SIC: 5063 Electrical apparatus and equipment
PA: Eaton Corporation Public Limited Company
30 Pembroke Road
Dublin D04Y0

(G-4202) ✪
EATON CORP
1111 Superior Ave E (44114-2522)
PHONE.................................216 523-5000
EMP: 226 EST: 2022
SALES (est): 5.12MM **Privately Held**
SIC: 8742 Marketing consulting services

(G-4203)
EATON CORPORATION
6055 Rockside Woods Blvd N (44131-2301)
PHONE.................................216 265-2799
EMP: 54
Web: www.dix-eaton.com
SIC: 5063 Electrical apparatus and equipment
HQ: Eaton Corporation
1000 Eaton Blvd
Cleveland OH 44122
440 523-5000

(G-4204)
EATON INDUSTRIAL CORPORATION
Also Called: Argo Tech Fluid Elec Dist Div
1000 Eaton Blvd (44122-6058)
PHONE.................................216 692-5456
Heath Monesmith, *Brnch Mgr*
EMP: 101
SIC: 7699 3728 Pumps and pumping equipment repair; Aircraft parts and equipment, nec
HQ: Eaton Industrial Corporation
23555 Euclid Ave
Cleveland OH 44117
216 523-4205

(G-4205)
ECONO LODGE
4353 Northfield Rd (44128-4613)
PHONE.................................216 475-4070
Mike Patel, *Owner*
Binta Patel, *Genl Mgr*
EMP: 56 EST: 1975
SQ FT: 80,000
SALES (est): 224.78K **Privately Held**
Web: www.choicehotels.com
SIC: 7011 Hotels and motels

(G-4206)
EDWARD ALLEN COMPANY
Also Called: Mehler & Hagestrom
1100 Superior Ave E Ste 1820 (44114-2530)
PHONE.................................216 621-4984
Edward Mehler, *Pr*
Pamela Greenfield, **
EMP: 45 EST: 1944
SALES (est): 2.43MM **Privately Held**
Web: www.veritext.com
SIC: 7338 Court reporting service

(G-4207)
EDWARD HOWARD & CO (PA)
1100 Superior Ave E Ste 1600 (44114-2530)
PHONE.................................216 781-2400
Kathleen A Obert, *Ch Bd*
Wayne R Hill, *Pr*
Donald C Hohmeier, *Ex VP*
Nora C Jacobs, *Ex VP*
Mark Grieves, *Ex VP*

EMP: 30 EST: 1925
SALES (est): 2.46MM
SALES (corp-wide): 2.46MM **Privately Held**
Web: www.edwardhoward.com
SIC: 8743 7336 Public relations and publicity ; Graphic arts and related design

(G-4208)
ELECTRA SOUND INC
10779 Brookpark Rd Ste A (44130-1118)
PHONE.................................216 433-1050
Charles Masa, *Pr*
EMP: 167
SALES (corp-wide): 12.2MM **Privately Held**
Web: www.techni-car.com
SIC: 7622 7382 Television repair shop; Security systems services
PA: Electra Sound, Inc.
32483 English Turn
Avon Lake OH 44012
216 433-9600

(G-4209)
ELECTRONIC MERCH SYSTEMS LLC (PA)
Also Called: Electronic Merchant Systems
250 W Huron Rd Ste 300 (44113)
PHONE.................................216 524-0900
James Weiland, *Ch Bd*
Dan Neistadt, *Pr*
Margaret S Weiland, *VP*
Egon P Singerman, *Sec*
EMP: 110 EST: 1987
SQ FT: 23,400
SALES (est): 27.19MM
SALES (corp-wide): 27.19MM **Privately Held**
Web: www.emscorporate.com
SIC: 7359 5044 Business machine and electronic equipment rental services; Office equipment

(G-4210)
ELEMENT MATERIALS TECHNOLOGY CLEVELAND INC (DH)
5405 E Schaaf Rd (44131-1337)
PHONE.................................216 524-1450
EMP: 38 EST: 1911
SALES (est): 10.77MM **Privately Held**
SIC: 8734 Testing laboratories
HQ: Element Materials Technology Group Us Holdings Inc.
15062 Bolsa Chica St
Huntington Beach CA 92649
714 892-1961

(G-4211)
EMERITUS CORPORATION
Also Called: Emeritus At Brookside Estates
15435 Bagley Rd Ste 1 (44130-4827)
PHONE.................................440 201-9200
Chris Belford, *Prin*
EMP: 134
SALES (corp-wide): 2.83B **Publicly Held**
Web: www.emeritus.org
SIC: 8051 Skilled nursing care facilities
HQ: Emeritus Corporation
6737 W Wa St Ste 2300
Milwaukee WI 53214

(G-4212)
EMERY LEASING CO LLC
Also Called: SUBURBAN PAVILION NURSING AND
20265 Emery Rd (44128-4122)
PHONE.................................216 475-8880
Stephen L Rosedale, *Managing Member*
EMP: 270 EST: 1973
SALES (est): 13.4MM **Privately Held**

SIC: 8051 Convalescent home with continuous nursing care

(G-4213)
EMPLOYEE SERVICES LLC
100 American Rd (44144-2322)
PHONE.................................585 593-9870
Jim Walter, *Pr*
EMP: 92 EST: 1986
SALES (est): 2.64MM
SALES (corp-wide): 2.75B **Privately Held**
SIC: 8322 Telephone counseling service
PA: Medical Mutual Of Ohio
2060 E 9th St
Cleveland OH 44115
216 687-7000

(G-4214)
ENERGY HARBOR NUCLEAR CORP
Also Called: Beta Lab & Technical Svcs
6670 Beta Dr (44143-2352)
PHONE.................................440 604-9836
Pete Cena, *Pr*
EMP: 75
SALES (corp-wide): 14.78B **Publicly Held**
Web: www.energyharbor.com
SIC: 8731 8734 Commercial research laboratory; Testing laboratories
HQ: Energy Harbor Nuclear Corp.
168 E Market St
Akron OH 44308
800 646-0400

(G-4215)
ENERGY MGT SPECIALISTS INC
Also Called: Ems
15800 Industrial Pkwy (44135-3320)
PHONE.................................216 676-9045
Alan J Guzik, *Pr*
EMP: 30 EST: 1980
SQ FT: 8,800
SALES (est): 5.55MM **Privately Held**
Web: www.energyman.com
SIC: 1711 Mechanical contractor

(G-4216)
ENGINEERED CON STRUCTURES CORP
14510 Broadway Ave (44125-1960)
EMP: 30 EST: 1970
SALES (est): 2.21MM **Privately Held**
Web: www.ecs1.biz
SIC: 1771 Concrete work

(G-4217)
EQUIPMENT MFRS INTL INC
Also Called: E M I
16151 Puritas Ave (44135-2617)
P.O. Box 94725 (44101-4725)
PHONE.................................216 651-6700
Jerry Senk, *Prin*
R T Mackin, **
Joe Mcfarland, *Prin*
Bill Vondriska, *Prin*
Dave Bowman, *Prin*
▲ EMP: 30 EST: 1982
SQ FT: 65,000
SALES (est): 7.51MM **Privately Held**
Web: www.emi-inc.com
SIC: 3559 5084 Foundry machinery and equipment; Industrial machinery and equipment

(G-4218)
ERNST & YOUNG LLP
Also Called: Ey
950 Main Ave Ste 1800 (44113-7214)
PHONE.................................216 861-5000
Christopher W Smith, *Mgr*
EMP: 65
Web: www.ey.com

(PA)=Parent Co (HQ)=Headquarters
✪ = New Business established in last 2 years

Cleveland - Cuyahoga County (G-4219)

GEOGRAPHIC SECTION

SIC: 8721 Certified public accountant
HQ: Ernst & Young Llp
   1 Manhattan W Fl 6
   New York NY 10001
   703 747-0049

(G-4219)
ERNST & YOUNG LLP
Also Called: Ey
1660 W 2nd St Ste 200 (44113-1446)
PHONE..................216 583-1823
Michelle Settecase, *Prin*
EMP: 35
Web: www.ey.com
SIC: 8721 Certified public accountant
HQ: Ernst & Young Llp
   1 Manhattan W Fl 6
   New York NY 10001
   703 747-0049

(G-4220)
ERNST & YOUNG US LLP
Also Called: Ernst & Young
950 Main Ave Ste 1800 (44113-7214)
PHONE..................216 583-1893
EMP: 63 EST: 2017
SALES (est): 64.28K **Privately Held**
SIC: 8721 Certified public accountant
HQ: Ernst & Young Llp
   1 Manhattan W Fl 6
   New York NY 10001
   703 747-0049

(G-4221)
ERS DIGITAL INC
Also Called: Eblueprints
3666 Carnegie Ave (44115-2714)
PHONE..................216 281-1234
EMP: 80
SIC: 7334 Blueprinting service

(G-4222)
ESI EMPLOYEE ASSISTANCE GROUP
100 American Rd (44144-2322)
PHONE..................800 535-4841
Karen Allen, *VP*
EMP: 107 EST: 2018
SALES (est): 2.1MM
SALES (corp-wide): 2.75B **Privately Held**
Web: www.theeap.com
SIC: 8631 Employees' association
PA: Medical Mutual Of Ohio
   2060 E 9th St
   Cleveland OH 44115
   216 687-7000

(G-4223)
ESOP REALTY INC
Also Called: ESOP
11890 Fairhill Rd (44120-1053)
PHONE..................216 361-0718
EMP: 125 EST: 2018
SALES (est): 169.36K
SALES (corp-wide): 7.52MM **Privately Held**
Web: www.esop-cleveland.org
SIC: 8051 Skilled nursing care facilities
HQ: Empowering And Strengthening Ohio's People, Inc.
   11890 Fairhill Rd
   Cleveland OH 44120

(G-4224)
EURO USA INC (PA)
4481 Johnston Pkwy (44128-2952)
PHONE..................216 714-0500
Joseph D O'donnell, *Pr*
Sean Sullivan, *
William Vardell, *
Nancy A Farmer, *

Doug Speltzer, *
▲ EMP: 100 EST: 1967
SQ FT: 75,000
SALES (est): 31.82MM
SALES (corp-wide): 31.82MM **Privately Held**
Web: www.eurousa.com
SIC: 5149 Specialty food items

(G-4225)
EVARTS-TREMAINE-FLICKER CO
Also Called: Allstate
1111 Superior Ave E Ste 420 (44114-2522)
PHONE..................216 621-7183
J Thomas Hannon, *Pr*
Martin Streigel, *
Thomas Donovan, *
Geraldine Vorasky, *
EMP: 36 EST: 1844
SQ FT: 5,000
SALES (est): 9.44MM **Privately Held**
Web: www.evartstremaine.com
SIC: 6411 Insurance agents, nec

(G-4226)
EVERGREEN COOPERATIVE CORP (PA)
4205 Saint Clair Ave (44103-1121)
PHONE..................216 268-5399
John Mcmicken Junior, *CEO*
EMP: 322 EST: 2008
SALES (est): 3.2MM
SALES (corp-wide): 3.2MM **Privately Held**
Web: www.evgoh.com
SIC: 8748 Business consulting, nec

(G-4227)
EVERGREEN COOPERATIVE LDRY INC
540 E 105th St (44108-4301)
PHONE..................216 268-3548
Craig Forgea, *COO*
Rosalyn Ciulla, *
EMP: 141 EST: 2008
SQ FT: 15,000
SALES (est): 2.3MM **Privately Held**
Web: www.evgoh.com
SIC: 7211 Power laundries, family and commercial

(G-4228)
EVERSTREAM HOLDING COMPANY LLC
1228 Euclid Ave Ste 250 (44115-1831)
PHONE..................216 923-2260
EMP: 141 EST: 2016
SALES (est): 16.83MM **Privately Held**
Web: www.everstream.net
SIC: 8742 Business management consultant

(G-4229)
EXCELAS LLC
387 Golfview Ln Ste 200 (44143-4417)
PHONE..................440 442-7310
Jean C Bourgeois, *Prin*
EMP: 40 EST: 2004
SALES (est): 1.93MM **Privately Held**
Web: www.excelas1.com
SIC: 8099 Medical services organization

(G-4230)
EXCITE IT PARTNERS LLC
Also Called: Excite Health Partners
6133 Rockside Rd Ste 307 (44131-2243)
PHONE..................216 447-9808
Julian Mitchell, *Prin*
EMP: 125
SALES (corp-wide): 41.4MM **Privately Held**
Web: www.excitehealthpartners.com

SIC: 7361 Placement agencies
HQ: Excite It Partners, Llc
   6211 Greenleigh Ave # 320
   Middle River MD 21220

(G-4231)
EXEL GLOBAL LOGISTICS INC
21500 Aerospace Pkwy (44142-1071)
PHONE..................440 243-5900
Bill Krabec, *Brnch Mgr*
EMP: 163
SALES (corp-wide): 88.87B **Privately Held**
SIC: 4731 Freight forwarding
HQ: Exel Global Logistics Inc.
   22879 Glenn Dr Ste 100
   Sterling VA 20164
   877 858-3855

(G-4232)
EXPEDITORS INTL WASH INC
18029 Cleveland Pkwy Dr (44135-3247)
PHONE..................440 243-9900
Robert Gierszal, *Mgr*
EMP: 97
SALES (corp-wide): 9.3B **Publicly Held**
Web: www.expeditors.com
SIC: 4731 Foreign freight forwarding
PA: Expeditors International Of Washington, Inc.
   1015 3rd Ave
   Seattle WA 98104
   206 674-3400

(G-4233)
FABRIZI TRUCKING & PAV CO INC
6751 Eastland Rd (44130-2425)
PHONE..................440 234-1284
Emil Fabrizi, *Owner*
EMP: 70
SQ FT: 1,367
SALES (corp-wide): 23.06MM **Privately Held**
Web: www.fabrizi-inc.com
SIC: 4225 4212 1611 General warehousing; Local trucking, without storage; Highway and street construction
PA: Fabrizi Trucking & Paving Co., Inc.
   20389 1st Ave
   Cleveland OH 44130
   440 973-4929

(G-4234)
FAIRFAX RENAISSANCE DEV CORP
8111 Quincy Ave Ste 100 (44104-2125)
PHONE..................216 361-8400
Vickie E Johnson, *Ex Dir*
EMP: 48 EST: 1992
SQ FT: 80,000
SALES (est): 3.34MM **Privately Held**
Web: www.fairfaxrenaissance.org
SIC: 8399 Community action agency

(G-4235)
FAIRMOUNT MONTESSORI ASSN
Also Called: RUFFING MONTESSORI SCHOOL
3380 Fairmount Blvd (44118)
PHONE..................216 321-7571
Gordon Maas, *Dir*
EMP: 62 EST: 1960
SQ FT: 22,250
SALES (est): 6.27MM **Privately Held**
Web: www.ruffingmontessori.net
SIC: 8351 8211 Montessori child development center; Private elementary and secondary schools

(G-4236)
FAIRVIEW EYE CENTER INC
21375 Lorain Rd (44126-2122)
PHONE..................440 333-3060

Doctor Louis P Caravella, *Pr*
Jeff Terbeck, *
EMP: 87 EST: 1979
SQ FT: 5,000
SALES (est): 7.73MM **Privately Held**
Web: www.fairvieweyecenter.com
SIC: 8011 Opthalmologist

(G-4237)
FAIRVIEW HLTH SYS FDERAL CR UN
18101 Lorain Ave (44111-5612)
PHONE..................216 476-7000
K Gopal, *Owner*
EMP: 398 EST: 2006
SALES (est): 2.43MM
SALES (corp-wide): 14.48B **Privately Held**
SIC: 6061 Federal credit unions
HQ: Fairview Hospital
   18101 Lorain Ave
   Cleveland OH 44111
   216 476-7000

(G-4238)
FAIRVIEW HOSPITAL (HQ)
Also Called: Fairview West Physician Center
18101 Lorain Ave (44111-5612)
PHONE..................216 476-7000
Toby Cosgrove, *CEO*
Louis Caravella Md, *Pr*
Delos Cosgrove, *
Jeffrey A Leimgruber, *CAO*
EMP: 1311 EST: 1894
SQ FT: 327,000
SALES (est): 591.81MM
SALES (corp-wide): 14.48B **Privately Held**
Web: www.fairviewhospital.org
SIC: 8062 8011 General medical and surgical hospitals; Offices and clinics of medical doctors
PA: The Cleveland Clinic Foundation
   9500 Euclid Ave
   Cleveland OH 44195
   216 636-8335

(G-4239)
FALCON PARTNERS LLC
737 Bolivar Rd Ste 4000 (44115-1247)
PHONE..................216 896-1010
Dawn Burdyshaw, *Prin*
EMP: 34 EST: 2019
SALES (est): 2.64MM **Privately Held**
Web: www.falcon-pe.com
SIC: 7363 Help supply services

(G-4240)
FAMILY PHYSICIANS ASSOCIATES (PA)
5187 Mayfield Rd Ste 102 (44124-2467)
PHONE..................440 449-1014
Terrence Isakov, *Pr*
EMP: 50 EST: 1983
SQ FT: 14,179
SALES (est): 4.63MM
SALES (corp-wide): 4.63MM **Privately Held**
Web: www.familyphysicians.org
SIC: 8011 General and family practice, physician/surgeon

(G-4241)
FANTON LOGISTICS INC (PA)
10801 Broadway Ave (44125-1653)
PHONE..................216 341-2400
Mycola Kachaluba, *Pr*
EMP: 52 EST: 2007
SQ FT: 3,700
SALES (est): 8.56MM
SALES (corp-wide): 8.56MM **Privately Held**
Web: www.fantonlogistics.com

GEOGRAPHIC SECTION

Cleveland - Cuyahoga County (G-4265)

SIC: 4213 Trucking, except local

(G-4242)
FASS MANAGEMENT & CONSULTING L
3705 Lee Rd Ste 1 (44120-5100)
PHONE..................................330 405-0545
Akil Hameed, Prin
EMP: 27 EST: 2011
SALES (est): 954.88K Privately Held
Web: www.fass-res.com
SIC: 8748 Business consulting, nec

(G-4243)
FAY SHARPE LLP
1228 Euclid Ave Ste 500 (44115)
PHONE..................................216 363-9000
Patrick Roche, Mng Pt
Patrick Roche, Pt
Thomas E Kocovsky Junior, Pt
Jay F Moldovanyi, Pt
Timothy E Nauman, Pt
EMP: 94 EST: 1884
SQ FT: 40,000
SALES (est): 9.84MM Privately Held
Web: www.faysharpe.com
SIC: 8111 General practice law office

(G-4244)
FEDELI GROUP LLC (PA)
5005 Rockside Rd Ste 500 (44131-2184)
P.O. Box 318003 (44131-8003)
PHONE..................................216 328-8080
Umberto Fedeli, CEO
Nick Fedeli, Ex VP
Andre Lukez, Consulting Officer
Jennifer Tookman, CFO
Ed Kraine, Chief Insurance Officer
EMP: 87 EST: 1975
SQ FT: 25,000
SALES (est): 26.27MM
SALES (corp-wide): 26.27MM Privately Held
Web: www.thefedeligroup.com
SIC: 6411 Insurance agents, nec

(G-4245)
FEDERAL MACHINERY & EQP CO (PA)
Also Called: Federal Equipment Company
8200 Bessemer Ave (44127-1837)
PHONE..................................800 652-2466
Michael Kadis, Pr
Lawrence Kadis, *
Morris I Goldsmith, *
Larry Kadis, *
Adam Covitt, *
◆ EMP: 32 EST: 1957
SQ FT: 350,000
SALES (est): 13.23MM
SALES (corp-wide): 13.23MM Privately Held
Web: www.fedequip.com
SIC: 5084 Materials handling machinery

(G-4246)
FEDERAL RESERVE BANK CLEVELAND (HQ)
Also Called: (Board Of Governors Of The Federal Reserve System, The, Washington, DC)
1455 E 6th St (44114-2566)
P.O. Box 6387 (44101-1387)
PHONE..................................216 579-2000
Loretta J Mester, Pr
Mark Meder, *
Michael Beedles, *
Thomas Dockman, *
William D Fosnight, *
EMP: 760 EST: 1914
SALES (est): 394.78MM Privately Held

Web: www.clevelandfed.org
SIC: 6035 Federal savings banks
PA: Board Of Governors Of The Federal Reserve System
20th St Cnsttution Ave Nw
Washington DC 20551
202 452-3000

(G-4247)
FELI
15105 Saint Clair Ave (44110-3719)
PHONE..................................216 421-6262
Natasya Taylor, Managing Member
EMP: 27 EST: 2014
SALES (est): 331.95K Privately Held
SIC: 8322 Child related social services

(G-4248)
FERENC/LAKESIDE ELECTRIC INC
1192 E 40th St Ste 303/305 (44114-3802)
PHONE..................................216 426-1880
Phillip Ferenc, Pr
EMP: 75 EST: 1987
SALES (est): 4.68MM Privately Held
SIC: 1731 General electrical contractor

(G-4249)
FERRAGON CORPORATION (PA)
Also Called: Ferrous Metal Processing Co.
11103 Memphis Ave (44144-2055)
P.O. Box 74516 (44194-0002)
PHONE..................................216 671-6161
▲ EMP: 72 EST: 1983
SALES (est): 45.54MM
SALES (corp-wide): 45.54MM Privately Held
Web: www.ferragon.com
SIC: 5051 Steel

(G-4250)
FIFTH THIRD BANK OF NORTHEASTERN OHIO
Also Called: Fifth Third Bank
600 Superior Ave E Fl 5 (44114-2621)
PHONE..................................216 274-5533
▲ EMP: 720
SIC: 6021 National commercial banks

(G-4251)
FINELLI ORNAMENTAL IRON CO
Also Called: Finelli Architectural Iron Co
30815 Solon Rd (44139-3485)
PHONE..................................440 248-0050
Frank Finelli, Pr
Angelo Finelli, VP
James Korosec, VP
EMP: 33 EST: 1962
SQ FT: 15,000
SALES (est): 3.45MM Privately Held
Web: www.finelliironworks.com
SIC: 3446 1751 Ornamental metalwork; Carpentry work

(G-4252)
FIREFIGHTERS CMNTY CR UN INC
2300 Saint Clair Ave Ne (44114-4049)
PHONE..................................216 621-4644
William Deighton, Ch Bd
EMP: 49
SALES (corp-wide): 14.61MM Privately Held
Web: www.ffcommunity.com
SIC: 6062 6163 State credit unions, not federally chartered; Loan brokers
PA: Firefighters Community Credit Union, Inc.
4664 E 71st St
Cleveland OH 44125
216 621-4644

(G-4253)
FIRST ALNCE HALTHCARE OHIO INC
11201 Shaker Blvd Ste 308 (44104-3871)
PHONE..................................216 417-8813
David Alexander, CEO
Daisetta Harris, *
Cornell Orr, *
Keisha Pledger, Cons Vice President*
Joenisha Sanders, *
EMP: 80 EST: 2016
SALES (est): 2.55MM Privately Held
Web: www.firstalliancehc.com
SIC: 8093 Mental health clinic, outpatient

(G-4254)
FIRST AMERICAN EQUITY LN SVCS (DH)
1100 Superior Ave E Lbby 3 (44114-2530)
PHONE..................................800 221-8683
Michael B Hopkins, Pr
Michael Cullen Senior, Vice-President Information Systems
John Baumbick, Corporate Counsel*
Sean Conway, *
EMP: 200 EST: 1979
SQ FT: 37,736
SALES (est): 279.16MM Publicly Held
SIC: 6361 Real estate title insurance
HQ: First American Title Insurance Company
1 First American Way
Santa Ana CA 92707
800 854-3643

(G-4255)
FIRST ASSIST HEALTH CARE LLC
5432 Mayfield Rd Ste 205 (44124-2930)
PHONE..................................440 421-9256
Asia Fountain, Managing Member
EMP: 50 EST: 2016
SALES (est): 1MM Privately Held
SIC: 8082 Home health care services

(G-4256)
FIRST CHICE MED STFFING OHIO I (PA)
1457 W 117th St (44107-5101)
PHONE..................................216 521-2222
Charles Slone, Pr
Karen Villalba Md, Dir
EMP: 425 EST: 1998
SALES (est): 6.66MM
SALES (corp-wide): 6.66MM Privately Held
Web: www.firstchoiceohio.com
SIC: 7361 Employment agencies

(G-4257)
FIRST CHOICE MEDICAL STAFFING
1457 W 117th St (44107-5101)
PHONE..................................216 521-2222
Ed Newton, Prin
EMP: 93
SALES (corp-wide): 6.66MM Privately Held
Web: www.firstchoiceohio.com
SIC: 8059 Nursing home, except skilled and intermediate care facility
PA: First Choice Medical Staffing Of Ohio, Inc.
1457 W 117th St
Cleveland OH 44107
216 521-2222

(G-4258)
FIRST INTERSTATE PRPTS LTD
25333 Cedar Rd Ste 300 (44124-3763)
PHONE..................................216 381-2900
Mitchell Schneider, Pr
EMP: 40 EST: 1989

SQ FT: 2,400
SALES (est): 5.1MM Privately Held
Web: www.first-interstate.com
SIC: 6512 Shopping center, property operation only

(G-4259)
FIRST OHIO BANC & LENDING INC
6100 Rockside Woods Blvd N (44131-2366)
PHONE..................................216 642-8900
Kirk Doskocil, Pr
EMP: 52 EST: 2001
SALES (est): 4.34MM Privately Held
SIC: 6162 Mortgage bankers and loan correspondents

(G-4260)
FIRST REALTY PROPERTY MGT LTD
5001 Mayfield Rd (44124-2608)
PHONE..................................440 720-0100
Joseph T Aveni, CEO
Kerri Frankel, VP Opers
James Aveni, VP
Deborah Peterson, Contrlr
EMP: 40 EST: 1997
SALES (est): 4.91MM Privately Held
Web: www.firstrealtypm.com
SIC: 6531 Real estate agent, residential

(G-4261)
FIT TECHNOLOGIES LLC
1375 Euclid Ave (44115-1808)
PHONE..................................216 583-5000
EMP: 48 EST: 1999
SALES (est): 22.11MM Privately Held
Web: www.fittechnologies.com
SIC: 7379 Online services technology consultants

(G-4262)
FITWORKS HOLDING LLC
8555 Day Dr (44129-5614)
PHONE..................................440 842-1499
Chas Comparato, Mgr
EMP: 48
Web: www.fitworks.com
SIC: 7991 Health club
PA: Fitworks Holding, Llc
849 Brainard Rd
Cleveland OH 44143

(G-4263)
FLAGSHIP TRADING CORPORATION
Also Called: Manufacturers Wholesale Lumber
734 Alpha Dr Ste J (44143-2135)
EMP: 35 EST: 1983
SALES (est): 4.96MM Privately Held
SIC: 2491 5031 Structural lumber and timber, treated wood; Lumber, plywood, and millwork

(G-4264)
FLANNERY GEORGALIS LLC
1301 E 9th St Ste 3500 (44114-1838)
PHONE..................................216 367-2095
EMP: 44 EST: 2017
SALES (est): 5.05MM Privately Held
Web: www.flannerygeorgalis.com
SIC: 8111 General practice attorney, lawyer

(G-4265)
FLEXJET LLC (HQ)
Also Called: Flexjet
26180 Curtiss Wright Pkwy (44143-1453)
PHONE..................................216 261-3880
Kenneth Ricci, Managing Member
EMP: 250 EST: 2013
SALES (est): 222.26MM

(PA)=Parent Co (HQ)=Headquarters
✪ = New Business established in last 2 years

Cleveland - Cuyahoga County (G-4266) GEOGRAPHIC SECTION

SALES (corp-wide): 1.09B **Privately Held**
Web: www.flexjet.com
SIC: 7359 Aircraft rental
PA: Directional Capital Llc
  355 Richmond Rd
  Richmond Heights OH 44143
  216 261-3000

(G-4266)
FLIGHT OPTIONS LLC (HQ)
26180 Curtiss Wright Pkwy (44143-1453)
PHONE..................................216 261-3500
James Dauterman, *
Bruce C Boyle, *
Julie Boland, *
EMP: 240 EST: 1998
SQ FT: 119,000
SALES (est): 47.94MM
SALES (corp-wide): 1.09B **Privately Held**
Web: www.flightoptions.com
SIC: 7359 Aircraft rental
PA: Directional Capital Llc
  355 Richmond Rd
  Richmond Heights OH 44143
  216 261-3000

(G-4267)
FOR WOMEN LIKE ME INC
8800 Woodland Ave (44104-3221)
PHONE..................................407 848-7339
Arline Burks, CEO
EMP: 42
SALES (corp-wide): 866.99K **Privately Held**
SIC: 7812 Television film production
PA: For Women Like Me, Inc.
  46 Shopping Plz Ste 155
  Chagrin Falls OH 44022
  407 848-7339

(G-4268)
FOREST CITY COMMERCIAL MGT INC
1228 Euclid Ave Ste 151 (44115-1831)
PHONE..................................216 696-7701
Robert Hanna, Mgr
EMP: 250
SALES (corp-wide): 816.31MM **Privately Held**
SIC: 6531 Real estate managers
HQ: Forest City Commercial Management, Inc.
  50 Public Sq Apt 1410
  Cleveland OH 44113
  216 621-6060

(G-4269)
FOREST CITY COMMERCIAL MGT INC (DH)
50 Public Sq Apt 1410 (44113-2256)
PHONE..................................216 621-6060
Charles Ratner, Pr
Samuel Miller, *
Albert Ratner, *
Robert Prien, *
EMP: 250 EST: 1966
SALES (est): 54.35MM
SALES (corp-wide): 816.31MM **Privately Held**
SIC: 6531 Real estate managers
HQ: Forest City Properties, Llc
  127 Public Sq Ste 3100
  Cleveland OH 44114
  216 621-6060

(G-4270)
FOREST CITY COMMERCIAL MGT INC
Also Called: Tower City Center Management
230 W Huron Rd Ofc Ofc (44113-1431)
PHONE..................................216 623-4750

Lisa Kreiger, Mgr
EMP: 250
SALES (corp-wide): 816.31MM **Privately Held**
Web: www.towercitycenter.com
SIC: 6512 Shopping center, property operation only
HQ: Forest City Commercial Management, Inc.
  50 Public Sq Apt 1410
  Cleveland OH 44113
  216 621-6060

(G-4271)
FOREST CITY ENTERPRISES LP (HQ)
127 Public Sq Ste 3200 (44114-1229)
PHONE..................................216 621-6060
Ketan Patel, Pr
▲ EMP: 350 EST: 1920
SALES (est): 521.79MM
SALES (corp-wide): 816.31MM **Privately Held**
Web: www.forestcityco.com
SIC: 6512 6513 6552 Nonresidential building operators; Apartment building operators; Subdividers and developers, nec
PA: Brookfield Properties, Llc
  250 Vesey St Fl 11
  New York NY 10281
  212 417-7000

(G-4272)
FOREST CITY PROPERTIES LLC (DH)
127 Public Sq Ste 3100 (44114-1228)
PHONE..................................216 621-6060
David La Rue, CEO
Charles Ratner, *
James Ratner, *
Ketan Patel, *
EMP: 130 EST: 1969
SALES (est): 78.49MM
SALES (corp-wide): 816.31MM **Privately Held**
SIC: 6512 6513 Shopping center, property operation only; Apartment hotel operation
HQ: Forest City Enterprises, L.P.
  127 Public Sq Ste 3200
  Cleveland OH 44114
  216 621-6060

(G-4273)
FOREST CITY REALTY TRUST INC
127 Public Sq Ste 3100 (44114-1228)
PHONE..................................216 621-6060
Ketan K Patel, Pr
Charles D Obert, *
EMP: 2909 EST: 2015
SALES (est): 277.76MM
SALES (corp-wide): 816.31MM **Privately Held**
Web: www.brookfieldproperties.com
SIC: 6798 Real estate investment trusts
PA: Brookfield Properties, Llc
  250 Vesey St Fl 11
  New York NY 10281
  212 417-7000

(G-4274)
FOREST CITY RESIDENTIAL DEV
Also Called: Independence Place
9233 Independence Blvd Apt 114 (44130-4781)
PHONE..................................440 888-8664
George Gorman, Mgr
EMP: 37
SALES (corp-wide): 816.31MM **Privately Held**

SIC: 6513 1522 Apartment building operators; Residential construction, nec
HQ: Forest City Residential Development Inc
  1170 Trml Twr 50 Pub Sq 1170
  Terminal Tower
  Cleveland OH 44113
  216 621-6060

(G-4275)
FOREST CITY RESIDENTIAL DEV (DH)
1170 Terminal Tower 50 Public Square (44113)
PHONE..................................216 621-6060
Ronald A Ratner, Ch Bd
Samuel H Miller, *
Albert B Ratner, *
Edward Pelavin, *
Thomas G Smith, *
EMP: 50 EST: 1955
SALES (est): 14.01MM
SALES (corp-wide): 816.31MM **Privately Held**
SIC: 1522 1542 6163 Apartment building construction; Specialized public building contractors; Mortgage brokers arranging for loans, using money of others
HQ: Forest City Enterprises, L.P.
  127 Public Sq Ste 3200
  Cleveland OH 44114
  216 621-6060

(G-4276)
FOREST CY RESIDENTIAL MGT INC (DH)
50 Public Sq Ste 1200 (44113)
PHONE..................................216 621-6060
Ron Ratner, CEO
Charles A Ratner, *
Angelo Pippas, *
James J Prohaska, *
James T Brady, *
EMP: 120 EST: 1930
SQ FT: 25,000
SALES (est): 47.11MM
SALES (corp-wide): 816.31MM **Privately Held**
SIC: 6531 6552 Real estate managers; Subdividers and developers, nec
HQ: Forest City Enterprises, L.P.
  127 Public Sq Ste 3200
  Cleveland OH 44114
  216 621-6060

(G-4277)
FORMFIRE LLC
Also Called: Formfire
1100 Superior Ave E Ste 1650 (44114-2549)
PHONE..................................866 448-2302
Colin Ingram, CEO
EMP: 44 EST: 2006
SALES (est): 5.63MM
SALES (corp-wide): 5.72MM **Privately Held**
Web: www.formfire.com
SIC: 7371 Computer software development
PA: Agencybloc, Llc
  115 E 2nd St
  Cedar Falls IA 50613
  866 338-7075

(G-4278)
FORTUNA CONSTRUCTION CO INC
3133 Waterfall Way (44145-1775)
PHONE..................................440 892-3834
Joyce Fortuna, Pr
Joseph Fortuna, *
Matthew Fortuna, *
EMP: 30 EST: 1985

SALES (est): 2.18MM **Privately Held**
Web: www.fortuna-construction.com
SIC: 1794 1799 7699 1795 Excavation work; Building site preparation; Sewer cleaning and rodding; Wrecking and demolition work

(G-4279)
FOSBEL HOLDING INC (HQ)
20600 Sheldon Rd (44142-1312)
PHONE..................................216 362-3900
Derek Scott, Pr
Kathleen Stevens, *
EMP: 30 EST: 1990
SALES (est): 46.21MM **Privately Held**
Web: www.fosbel.com
SIC: 6719 Investment holding companies, except banks
PA: The Anderson Group Llc
  111 2nd Ave Ne Ste 105
  Saint Petersburg FL 33701

(G-4280)
FOX SPORTS NET OHIO LLC
200 Public Sq Ste 2510 (44114-2309)
PHONE..................................216 415-3300
Francois Mcgillicuddy, Sr VP
Steve Liverani, Prin
Charlie Knudson, VP
Tom Farmer, VP
EMP: 56 EST: 2005
SALES (est): 2.2MM
SALES (corp-wide): 2.71B **Publicly Held**
Web: www.foxsports.com
SIC: 4833 Television broadcasting stations
PA: Amc Networks Inc.
  11 Penn Plz
  New York NY 10001
  212 324-8500

(G-4281)
FOX TELEVISION STATIONS INC
Also Called: Fox 8
5800 S Marginal Rd (44103-1040)
PHONE..................................216 431-8888
Mike Renda, Brnch Mgr
EMP: 250
SALES (corp-wide): 14.91B **Publicly Held**
Web: www.foxla.com
SIC: 4833 Television broadcasting stations
HQ: Fox Television Stations, Inc.
  1999 S Bundy Dr
  Los Angeles CA 90025
  310 584-2000

(G-4282)
FPT CLEVELAND LLC (DH)
Also Called: Ferrous Processing and Trading
8550 Aetna Rd (44105-1607)
PHONE..................................216 441-3800
Andrew M Luntz, *
▲ EMP: 105 EST: 1999
SALES (est): 59.34MM
SALES (corp-wide): 22B **Publicly Held**
Web: www.fptscrap.com
SIC: 4953 5051 5093 3341 Recycling, waste materials; Iron and steel (ferrous) products; Ferrous metal scrap and waste; Secondary nonferrous metals
HQ: Ferrous Processing And Trading Company
  1333 Brewery Park Blvd # 400
  Detroit MI 48207
  313 567-9710

(G-4283)
FRANCISCAN SISTERS OF CHICAGO
Also Called: Mount Alverna Home
6765 State Rd (44134-4581)
PHONE..................................440 843-7800
Patrick Walsh, Mgr
EMP: 315

GEOGRAPHIC SECTION
Cleveland - Cuyahoga County (G-4304)

SALES (corp-wide): 51.72MM **Privately Held**
Web: www.franciscanministries.org
SIC: **8051** Skilled nursing care facilities
PA: Franciscan Sisters Of Chicago
  11500 Theresa Dr
  Lemont IL 60439
  708 647-6500

(G-4284)
FRANCK AND FRIC INCORPORATED
7919 Old Rockside Rd (44131-2300)
P.O. Box 31148 (44131-0148)
PHONE...................................216 524-4451
Donald R Skala Senior, *Pr*
David R Skala, *VP*
Donald C Skala Junior, *VP*
Stacey Carson, *Asst VP*
EMP: 51 **EST:** 1934
SQ FT: 20,000
SALES (est): 4.26MM **Privately Held**
Web: franck-fric-inc.business.site
SIC: **1711** 1761 3441 3444 Ventilation and duct work contractor; Sheet metal work, nec ; Fabricated structural metal; Sheet metalwork

(G-4285)
FRANK NOVAK & SONS INC
Also Called: Flooring Specialties Div
23940 Miles Rd (44128-5425)
PHONE...................................216 475-2495
Gayle Pinchot, *Pr*
Allen J Pinchot, *
Brad Pinchot, *
Mark Pinchot, *
Pamela Bozsvai Pinchot, *
EMP: 100 **EST:** 1912
SQ FT: 12,000
SALES (est): 23.53MM **Privately Held**
Web: www.flooringspecialties.com
SIC: **1721** 1752 1742 Interior commercial painting contractor; Wood floor installation and refinishing; Acoustical and ceiling work

(G-4286)
FRANTZ WARD LLP
200 Public Sq Ste 3020 (44114-1230)
PHONE...................................216 515-1660
Christopher G Keim, *Pt*
Michael J Frantz, *
Daniel A Ward, *
Keith A Ashmus, *
Brett K Bacon, *
EMP: 115 **EST:** 2000
SQ FT: 27,000
SALES (est): 740 **Privately Held**
Web: www.frantzward.com
SIC: **8111** General practice attorney, lawyer

(G-4287)
FREDRICK FRDRICK HLLER ENGNERS
Also Called: F F and H
672 E Royalton Rd (44147-2529)
PHONE...................................440 546-9696
Michael P Long, *Pr*
William T Heller, *VP*
William Gienger, *VP*
Brian Widowski, *VP*
EMP: 43 **EST:** 1940
SALES (est): 2.71MM **Privately Held**
Web: www.imegcorp.com
SIC: **8711** Consulting engineer

(G-4288)
FREEDONIA PUBLISHING LLC
767 Beta Dr (44143-2379)
PHONE...................................440 684-9600
Jeffrey Weiss, *CEO*
EMP: 137 **EST:** 1985
SQ FT: 11,000
SALES (est): 9.1MM
SALES (corp-wide): 24.86MM **Privately Held**
Web: www.freedoniagroup.com
SIC: **8732** Market analysis or research
PA: Marketresearch.Com, Inc.
  6116 Executive Blvd # 550
  Rockville MD 20852
  240 747-3000

(G-4289)
FRIEDMAN DOMIANO SMITH CO LPA
55 Public Sq Ste 1055 (44113-1901)
PHONE...................................216 621-0070
Jeffrey Friedman, *Pr*
David Smith, *
Joseph Domiano, *
EMP: 30 **EST:** 1973
SQ FT: 12,500
SALES (est): 2.51MM **Privately Held**
Web: www.fdslaw.com
SIC: **8111** General practice attorney, lawyer

(G-4290)
FRIENDLY INN SETTLEMENT INC
2386 Unwin Rd (44104-1099)
PHONE...................................216 431-7656
Richgina Jeff-carter, *Dir*
Richgina Jeff, *
EMP: 39 **EST:** 1876
SALES (est): 1.56MM **Privately Held**
Web: www.friendlyinn.org
SIC: **8322** Social service center

(G-4291)
FRIENDS FOR LF RHBLTTION SVCS
6444 Pearl Rd (44130-2900)
PHONE...................................440 558-2859
Kimberly Mehozonek, *Brnch Mgr*
EMP: 34
SALES (corp-wide): 226.3K **Privately Held**
Web: www.fflrehab.com
SIC: **8322** Rehabilitation services
PA: Friends For Life Rehabilitation Services Inc.
  2908 Euclid Ave
  Cleveland OH 44115
  216 600-9181

(G-4292)
FRITO-LAY NORTH AMERICA INC
Also Called: Frito-Lay
4580 Hinckley Industrial Pkwy (44109-6010)
PHONE...................................216 491-4000
Chris Patterson, *Mgr*
EMP: 36
SQ FT: 65,936
SALES (corp-wide): 86.39B **Publicly Held**
Web: www.fritolay.com
SIC: **5145** 5149 Snack foods; Groceries and related products, nec
HQ: Frito-Lay North America, Inc.
  7701 Legacy Dr
  Plano TX 75024

(G-4293)
FRONT STEPS HOUSING & SVCS INC
1545 W 25th St (44113-3158)
PHONE...................................216 781-2250
David Eddy, *Pr*
Sherri Brandon, *Dir*
EMP: 29 **EST:** 1984
SALES (est): 1.44MM **Privately Held**
Web: www.frontstepsservices.org
SIC: **8322** Social service center

(G-4294)
G & S METAL PRODUCTS CO INC
26840 Fargo Ave (44146-1339)
PHONE...................................216 831-2388
Mark Schwartz, *Brnch Mgr*
EMP: 63
SQ FT: 145,964
SALES (corp-wide): 39.36MM **Privately Held**
Web: www.gsmetal.com
SIC: **4225** General warehousing and storage
PA: G & S Metal Products Co., Inc.
  3330 E 79th St
  Cleveland OH 44127
  216 441-0700

(G-4295)
G & S METAL PRODUCTS CO INC (PA)
3330 E 79th St (44127-1831)
P.O. Box 78510 (44105-8510)
PHONE...................................216 441-0700
◆ **EMP:** 165 **EST:** 1949
SALES (est): 39.36MM
SALES (corp-wide): 39.36MM **Privately Held**
Web: www.gsmetal.com
SIC: **3411** 5023 5072 3556 Pans, tinned; Kitchenware; Hardware; Food products machinery

(G-4296)
G AND J AUTOMATIC SYSTEMS INC
Also Called: G & J Packaging
14701 Industrial Pkwy (44135-4547)
PHONE...................................216 741-6070
Gregory Shteyngarts, *Pr*
EMP: 30 **EST:** 1985
SQ FT: 23,000
SALES (est): 1.15MM **Privately Held**
SIC: **7389** 3565 Packaging and labeling services; Packaging machinery

(G-4297)
G J GOUDREAU & CO (PA)
Also Called: Goudreau Management
9701 Brookpark Rd Ste 200 (44129-6824)
PHONE...................................216 351-5233
George J Goudreau Junior, *Pr*
EMP: 28 **EST:** 1940
SQ FT: 12,500
SALES (est): 6.96MM
SALES (corp-wide): 6.96MM **Privately Held**
Web: www.goudreau-management.com
SIC: **1522** 1542 6531 7349 Apartment building construction; Commercial and office building, new construction; Real estate managers; Building maintenance, except repairs

(G-4298)
G M INDUSTRIAL LLC
Also Called: Chemsafe International
1 Zenex Cir (44146-5459)
PHONE...................................440 786-1177
John Mino, *CEO*
George E Kneier, *
▲ **EMP:** 120 **EST:** 1978
SQ FT: 15,120
SALES (est): 22.45MM **Privately Held**
SIC: **5085** Industrial supplies

(G-4299)
G ROBERT TONEY & ASSOC INC (PA)
Also Called: National Liquidators
5401 N Marginal Rd (44114-3925)
PHONE...................................216 391-1900
Jane S Toney, *VP*
Shane Hunt, *VP*
▼ **EMP:** 36 **EST:** 1988
SQ FT: 6,500
SALES (est): 2.48MM
SALES (corp-wide): 2.48MM **Privately Held**
Web: www.yachtauctions.com
SIC: **7389** Repossession service

(G-4300)
GABRIEL PARTNERS LLC
1300 E 9th St Fl 2 (44114-1505)
PHONE...................................216 771-1250
Sam Rosenfeld, *Managing Member*
EMP: 50 **EST:** 2012
SALES (est): 5.92MM **Privately Held**
Web: www.amlrightsource.com
SIC: **7389** Financial services

(G-4301)
GALLAGHER SHARP
1215 Superior Ave E Fl 7 (44114-3282)
PHONE...................................216 241-5310
Todd Haemmerle, *Pt*
William A Viscomi, *Pt*
Alton L Stephens, *Pt*
Joseph W Pappalardo, *Pt*
Alan M Petrov, *Pt*
EMP: 110 **EST:** 1912
SALES (est): 11.19MM **Privately Held**
Web: www.gallaghersharp.com
SIC: **8111** General practice attorney, lawyer

(G-4302)
GARLAND/DBS INC
3800 E 91st St (44105-2103)
PHONE...................................216 641-7500
Dave Sokol, *Pr*
Richard Debacco, *VP*
Melvin Chrostowski, *VP Mktg*
Chuck Ripepi, *CFO*
EMP: 250 **EST:** 2009
SALES (est): 41.27MM
SALES (corp-wide): 715.07MM **Privately Held**
Web: www.dbsgarland.com
SIC: **2952** 6512 8712 Roofing materials; Commercial and industrial building operation; Architectural services
HQ: The Garland Company Inc
  3800 E 91st St
  Cleveland OH 44105
  216 641-7500

(G-4303)
GARRETT DIALYSIS LLC
Also Called: Ridge Park Dialysis
4805 Pearl Rd (44109-5145)
PHONE...................................216 398-6029
James K Hilger, *CAO*
EMP: 64
SIC: **8092** Kidney dialysis centers
HQ: Garrett Dialysis, Llc
  3812 Center Rd
  Brunswick OH 44212
  330 220-4502

(G-4304)
GATEWAY ELECTRIC LLC
4450 Johnston Pkwy Ste A (44128-2956)
PHONE...................................216 518-5500
Rajinder Singh, *Pr*
Satwant Singh, *
Vernon Krieger, *
Brenda Smith, *
Jane Mantz, *
EMP: 110 **EST:** 1985
SQ FT: 5,000
SALES (est): 16.21MM **Privately Held**
Web: www.gatewayelectric.com

Cleveland - Cuyahoga County (G-4305)

(G-4305)
GATEWAY HEALTH CARE CENTER
3 Gateway (44119-2447)
PHONE.................................216 486-4949
Nancy Sugarman, *Admn*
EMP: 53 **EST:** 1988
SQ FT: 42,177
SALES (est): 5.27MM **Privately Held**
SIC: 8051 8052 Skilled nursing care facilities; Intermediate care facilities

(G-4306)
GATEWAY PRODUCTS RECYCLING INC (PA)
Also Called: Gateway Recycling
4223 E 49th St (44125-1001)
PHONE.................................216 341-8777
Tom Sustersic, *Pr*
Cindy Sustersic, *
EMP: 44 **EST:** 1993
SQ FT: 24,000
SALES (est): 16.67MM **Privately Held**
Web: www.gatewayrecycle.com
SIC: 4953 5084 Recycling, waste materials; Recycling machinery and equipment

(G-4307)
GATTO ELECTRIC SUPPLY CO
4501 Willow Pkwy (44125-1047)
PHONE.................................216 641-8400
EMP: 40
SIC: 5063 Electrical supplies, nec

(G-4308)
GCA SERVICES GROUP INC (HQ)
1350 Euclid Ave Ste 1500 (44115-1832)
PHONE.................................800 422-8760
Robert Norton, *Pr*
Randall Twyman, *VF OF Finance*
Barb Hudson, *Chief Human Resources Officer*
Dan Havelka, *Mgr*
EMP: 60 **EST:** 2004
SQ FT: 17,000
SALES (est): 390.55MM
SALES (corp-wide): 8.1B **Publicly Held**
Web: www.gcaservices.com
SIC: 7349 Janitorial service, contract basis
PA: Abm Industries Incorporated
1 Liberty Plz Fl 7
New York NY 10006
212 297-0200

(G-4309)
GEISINGER HEALTH PLAN
10121 Broadway Ave (44125-1638)
PHONE.................................570 271-6211
EMP: 38
SALES (corp-wide): 7.73B **Privately Held**
Web: www.geisinger.org
SIC: 8011 Clinic, operated by physicians
HQ: Geisinger Health Plan
100 N Academy Ave
Danville PA 17822
570 271-8778

(G-4310)
GENERAL ELECTRIC COMPANY
Also Called: GE
4477 E 49th St (44125-1097)
PHONE.................................216 883-1000
Donald Mysliwiec, *Mgr*
EMP: 39
SQ FT: 12,000
SALES (corp-wide): 67.95B **Publicly Held**
Web: www.ge.com

SIC: 7629 3621 3613 3612 Electrical repair shops; Motors and generators; Switchgear and switchboard apparatus; Transformers, except electric
PA: General Electric Company
1 Aviation Way
Cincinnati OH 45215
617 443-3000

(G-4311)
GETINGE USA INC
6559 Wilson Mills Rd Ste 106 (44143-6402)
PHONE.................................440 449-1540
John E Colletta Md, *Brnch Mgr*
EMP: 63
SALES (corp-wide): 7.13B **Privately Held**
Web: www.getinge.com
SIC: 8011 Internal medicine, physician/surgeon
HQ: Getinge Usa, Inc.
45 Barbour Pond Dr
Wayne NJ 07470
973 709-9040

(G-4312)
GIBSON 2021 LLC
181 Oak Leaf Oval (44146-6156)
PHONE.................................440 439-4000
M Lee Gibson, *Managing Member*
Larysa Gibson, *
EMP: 30 **EST:** 2003
SALES (est): 8.1MM **Privately Held**
SIC: 5082 General construction machinery and equipment

(G-4313)
GILLMORE SECURITY SYSTEMS INC
Also Called: Honeywell Authorized Dealer
26165 Broadway Ave (44146-6512)
PHONE.................................440 232-1000
Alan H Gillmore Iii, *Pr*
EMP: 40 **EST:** 1970
SQ FT: 6,000
SALES (est): 8.22MM **Privately Held**
Web: www.gillmoresecurity.com
SIC: 1731 7382 Fire detection and burglar alarm systems specialization; Fire alarm maintenance and monitoring

(G-4314)
GLAUS PYLE SCHMER BRNS DHVEN I
Also Called: Gpd Group
5595 Transportation Blvd (44125-5379)
PHONE.................................216 518-5544
Joseph Ciuni, *Brnch Mgr*
EMP: 31
SALES (corp-wide): 122.1MM **Privately Held**
Web: www.cdcare.org
SIC: 8711 8712 Civil engineering; Architectural services
PA: Glaus, Pyle, Schomer, Burns & Dehaven, Inc.
520 S Main St Ste 2531
Akron OH 44311
330 572-2100

(G-4315)
GLIDDEN HOUSE ASSOCIATES LTD
Also Called: Glidden House Inn
1901 Ford Dr (44106-3923)
PHONE.................................216 231-8900
Joseph Shafran, *Mng Pt*
Thomas Farinacci, *Genl Mgr*
EMP: 37 **EST:** 1987
SALES (est): 4.59MM **Privately Held**
Web: www.gliddenhouse.com
SIC: 7011 Hotels

(G-4316)
GLORIA GADMACK DO
Also Called: Premier Physicians
17800 Shaker Blvd (44120-1748)
PHONE.................................216 363-2353
Gloria Gadmack, *Pt*
EMP: 29 **EST:** 1991
SALES (est): 2.3MM **Privately Held**
SIC: 8011 General and family practice, physician/surgeon

(G-4317)
GMS MANAGEMENT CO INC (PA)
Also Called: Gms Realty
4645 Richmond Rd Ste 101 (44128-5901)
PHONE.................................216 766-6000
Susan Graines, *Pr*
Patty Stegh, *
EMP: 45 **EST:** 1982
SQ FT: 12,000
SALES (est): 5.07MM
SALES (corp-wide): 5.07MM **Privately Held**
SIC: 6513 6512 Apartment building operators; Commercial and industrial building operation

(G-4318)
GOLDEN DRAPERY SUPPLY INC
Also Called: Golden Window Fashions
2500 Brookpark Rd Unit 3 (44134-1450)
PHONE.................................216 351-3283
Bernard Golden Junior, *Pr*
EMP: 28 **EST:** 1983
SQ FT: 25,000
SALES (est): 2.94MM **Privately Held**
SIC: 5023 2591 Window furnishings; Window blinds

(G-4319)
GOOD SAMARITAN HEALTH GROUP INC
4110 Rocky River Dr (44135-1175)
EMP: 225 **EST:** 1963
SALES (est): 10.53MM **Privately Held**
SIC: 8051 Skilled nursing care facilities

(G-4320)
GOODRICH GNNETT NGHBORHOOD CTR
Also Called: Goodrich Gannett Headstart
1801 E 9th St Ste 920 (44114-3103)
PHONE.................................216 432-1717
Allison Wallace, *Dir*
Dave Gunning, *
Stuart Bryan, *
Judith Varn, *
William D Pattie, *
EMP: 37 **EST:** 1963
SALES (est): 2.3MM **Privately Held**
Web: www.ggnc.org
SIC: 8322 7999 Family service agency; Recreation services

(G-4321)
GOVERNORS VILLAGE LLC
Also Called: Governor's Village Assisted Ll
280 N Commons Blvd Apt 101 (44143)
PHONE.................................440 449-8788
Christopher Randall, *Managing Member*
EMP: 51 **EST:** 2001
SQ FT: 33,800
SALES (est): 9.98MM **Privately Held**
Web: www.randallresidence.com
SIC: 8051 Extended care facility

(G-4322)
GOVPLUS LLC
Also Called: GOVPLUS LLC
5907 Ridge Rd (44129-3641)

PHONE.................................440 888-0330
EMP: 31
SALES (corp-wide): 12.19B **Publicly Held**
Web: www.citizensbank.com
SIC: 6022 State commercial banks
HQ: Citizens Bank, National Association
1 Citizens Plz
Providence RI 02903
401 456-7096

(G-4323)
GRACE HOSPICE LLC
16600 W Sprague Rd (44130-6318)
PHONE.................................216 288-7413
Mark Mitchell, *Brnch Mgr*
EMP: 97
Web: www.ghospice.com
SIC: 8052 Personal care facility
PA: Grace Hospice, Llc
500 Kirts Blvd Ste 250
Troy MI 48084

(G-4324)
GRACE HOSPICE LLC
Also Called: Grace Hospice of Middleburg
16600 W Sprague Rd Ste 35 (44130-6318)
PHONE.................................440 826-0350
Michael E Smith, *CEO*
EMP: 109
Web: www.ghospice.com
SIC: 8052 Personal care facility
PA: Grace Hospice, Llc
500 Kirts Blvd Ste 250
Troy MI 48084

(G-4325)
GRACE HOSPITAL
18101 Lorain Ave (44111-5612)
PHONE.................................216 476-2704
David Pelini, *Prin*
EMP: 66
SALES (corp-wide): 9.47MM **Privately Held**
Web: www.gracehospital.org
SIC: 8062 General medical and surgical hospitals
PA: Grace Hospital
2307 W 14th St
Cleveland OH 44113
216 687-1500

(G-4326)
GRANTS PLUS LLC
1422 Euclid Ave Ste 970 (44115-2011)
PHONE.................................216 916-7376
Lauren Steiner, *Managing Member*
EMP: 38 **EST:** 2011
SALES (est): 927.33K **Privately Held**
Web: www.grantsplus.com
SIC: 8742 Management consulting services

(G-4327)
GRAY MEDIA GROUP INC
Also Called: W O I O
1717 E 12th St (44114-3246)
PHONE.................................216 367-7300
Bill Applegate, *VP*
EMP: 77
SALES (corp-wide): 3.28B **Publicly Held**
Web: www.wlbt.com
SIC: 4833 Television broadcasting stations
HQ: Gray Media Group, Inc.
201 Monroe St Fl 20
Montgomery AL 36104

(G-4328)
GRAYBAR ELECTRIC COMPANY INC
6161 Halle Dr (44125-4613)
PHONE.................................216 573-0456
Gerard Musbach, *Mgr*
EMP: 33

GEOGRAPHIC SECTION
Cleveland - Cuyahoga County (G-4348)

SQ FT: 41,949
SALES (corp-wide): 11.04B **Privately Held**
Web: www.graybar.com
SIC: 5063 5065 Electrical supplies, nec; Electronic parts and equipment, nec
PA: Graybar Electric Company, Inc.
34 N Meramec Ave
Saint Louis MO 63105
314 573-9200

(G-4329)
GREAT LAKES GROUP
Also Called: Great Lakes Towing
4500 Division Ave (44102-2228)
PHONE...................216 621-4854
Sheldon Guren, *Ch Bd*
Ronald Rasmus, *
George Sogar, *
EMP: 120 **EST:** 1978
SQ FT: 6,000
SALES (est): 8.67MM **Privately Held**
Web: www.thegreatlakesgroup.com
SIC: 3731 4492 Shipbuilding and repairing; Marine towing services

(G-4330)
GREAT LAKES PUBLISHING COMPANY (PA)
Also Called: Cleveland Magazine
1422 Euclid Ave Ste 730 (44115-2001)
PHONE...................216 771-2833
Lute Harmon Senior, *Ch Bd*
Lute Harmon Junior, *Pr*
Christopher Valantasis, *
Nicole Stoner, *
Geli Valli, *
EMP: 75 **EST:** 1972
SQ FT: 19,000
SALES (est): 10.46MM
SALES (corp-wide): 10.46MM **Privately Held**
Web: www.glpublishing.com
SIC: 2721 7374 Magazines: publishing only, not printed on site; Computer graphics service

(G-4331)
GREATER CLEVELAND FOOD BNK INC
13815 Coit Rd (44110-2201)
PHONE...................216 738-2265
Kristin Warzocha, *Pr*
Kristin Warzocha, *Pr*
Bonnie Barrett, *
EMP: 130 **EST:** 1979
SALES (est): 110.24MM **Privately Held**
Web: www.greaterclevelandfoodbank.org
SIC: 8399 8322 Community development groups; Individual and family services

(G-4332)
GREATER CLEVELAND PARTNERSHIP (PA)
Also Called: CLEVELAND DEVELOPMENT FOUNDATI
1240 Huron Rd E Ste 300 (44115-1722)
PHONE...................216 621-3300
Baiju Shah, *Pr*
William Christopher, *Ch Bd*
Carol Caruso, *Sr VP*
Deb Janik, *Sr VP*
Andrew Jackson, *Sr VP*
EMP: 95 **EST:** 1848
SQ FT: 45,000
SALES (est): 9.58K
SALES (corp-wide): 9.58K **Privately Held**
Web: www.greatercle.com
SIC: 8611 Chamber of Commerce

(G-4333)
GREATER CLEVELAND REGIONAL
1240 W 6th St (44113-1302)
PHONE...................216 575-3932
Joseph A Calabrese, *Brnch Mgr*
EMP: 599
SALES (corp-wide): 30.51MM **Privately Held**
Web: www.riderta.com
SIC: 4111 Local and suburban transit
PA: Greater Cleveland Regional Transit Authority
1240 W 6th St
Cleveland OH 44113
216 566-5100

(G-4334)
GREATER CLEVELAND REGIONAL TRANSIT AUTHORITY (PA)
Also Called: R T A
1240 W 6th St (44113-1302)
PHONE...................216 566-5100
EMP: 300 **EST:** 1900
SALES (est): 30.51MM
SALES (corp-wide): 30.51MM **Privately Held**
Web: www.riderta.com
SIC: 4111 Local and suburban transit

(G-4335)
GREATER CLVLAND RGNAL TRNST AU
Paratransit
4601 Euclid Ave (44103-3737)
PHONE...................216 781-1110
Sylvester Williams, *Prin*
EMP: 599
SALES (corp-wide): 30.51MM **Privately Held**
Web: www.riderta.com
SIC: 4111 Local and suburban transit
PA: Greater Cleveland Regional Transit Authority
1240 W 6th St
Cleveland OH 44113
216 566-5100

(G-4336)
GREATER CLVLAND RGNAL TRNST AU
Also Called: E & C Div
1240 W 6th St 6th Fl (44113-1302)
PHONE...................216 566-5107
Sheryl King Benford, *Mgr*
EMP: 600
SQ FT: 17,000
SALES (corp-wide): 30.51MM **Privately Held**
Web: www.riderta.com
SIC: 4111 Passenger rail transportation
PA: Greater Cleveland Regional Transit Authority
1240 W 6th St
Cleveland OH 44113
216 566-5100

(G-4337)
GREEN CLEAN OHIO LLC
Also Called: Green Clean Janitorial
2580 E 93rd St (44104-2408)
PHONE...................866 853-6337
Akia Booker, *Pr*
EMP: 33 **EST:** 2011
SALES (est): 2.03MM **Privately Held**
Web: www.greencleanohio.com
SIC: 8744 7349 Facilities support services; Janitorial service, contract basis

(G-4338)
GREENBRIER SENIOR LIVING CMNTY
Also Called: Greenbrier Retirement Cmnty
6457 Pearl Rd (44130-2936)
PHONE...................440 888-0400
Debbie Smith, *Mgr*
EMP: 73
SALES (corp-wide): 10.08MM **Privately Held**
Web: www.communicarehealth.com
SIC: 8361 8051 Residential care; Skilled nursing care facilities
PA: Senior Greenbrier Living Community
2 Berea Cmns Ste 1
Berea OH 44017
440 888-5900

(G-4339)
GREENBRIER SENIOR LIVING CMNTY
Also Called: Greenbriar Retirement Center
6455 Pearl Rd (44130-2984)
PHONE...................440 888-5900
Terri Plush, *Mgr*
EMP: 187
SALES (corp-wide): 10.08MM **Privately Held**
Web: www.communicarehealth.com
SIC: 8051 8069 Convalescent home with continuous nursing care; Specialty hospitals, except psychiatric
PA: Senior Greenbrier Living Community
2 Berea Cmns Ste 1
Berea OH 44017
440 888-5900

(G-4340)
GREENS OF LYNDHURST THE INC
Also Called: The Fountain On The Greens
1555 Brainard Rd Apt 305 (44124-6201)
PHONE...................440 460-1000
Liz Gay, *Admn*
EMP: 29 **EST:** 1994
SALES (est): 4.33MM **Privately Held**
Web: www.greensrehab.com
SIC: 8051 8052 Convalescent home with continuous nursing care; Intermediate care facilities

(G-4341)
GROW WELL CLEVELAND CORP
3000 Bridge Ave Ste 4 (44113-3086)
PHONE...................216 282-3838
Peter Finnerty, *Prin*
EMP: 37 **EST:** 2017
SALES (est): 223.5K **Privately Held**
Web: www.growwellcle.com
SIC: 8322 General counseling services

(G-4342)
GUNTON CORPORATION (PA)
Also Called: Pella Window & Door
26150 Richmond Rd (44146-1438)
PHONE...................216 831-2420
William E Gunton, *
Mark Mead, *
Reggie Stacy, *
Howard Hendershott Junior, *Sec*
EMP: 180 **EST:** 1954
SQ FT: 90,000
SALES (est): 93.26MM
SALES (corp-wide): 93.26MM **Privately Held**
Web: www.guntonpella.com
SIC: 5031 Windows

(G-4343)
GYMNASTICS WORLD INC
6630 Harris Rd (44147-2960)
PHONE...................440 526-2970
Ron Ganim, *Pr*
Joan Ganim, *
EMP: 27 **EST:** 1976
SALES (est): 471.56K **Privately Held**
Web: www.gymworldohio.com
SIC: 7999 5699 5136 5137 Gymnastic instruction, non-membership; Sports apparel ; Sportswear, men's and boys'; Sportswear, women's and children's

(G-4344)
H & R BLOCK ESTRN TAX SVCS INC
Also Called: H & R Block
23811 Chagrin Blvd Ste 340 (44122-5525)
PHONE...................216 464-7212
Christine Fuller, *Mgr*
EMP: 46
SALES (corp-wide): 3.47B **Publicly Held**
Web: www.hrblock.com
SIC: 7291 Tax return preparation services
HQ: H & R Block Eastern Tax Services, Inc.
1 H And R Block Way
Kansas City MO 64105

(G-4345)
H T V INDUSTRIES INC
30100 Chagrin Blvd Ste 210 (44124-5705)
PHONE...................216 514-0060
Daniel Harrington, *Ch Bd*
EMP: 100 **EST:** 1982
SALES (est): 4.55MM **Privately Held**
SIC: 8742 Management consulting services

(G-4346)
HAHN LOESER & PARKS LLP (PA)
Also Called: Hahn Loeser
200 Public Sq Ste 2800 (44114-2303)
PHONE...................216 621-0150
John D Rockefeller, *Prin*
Stephen J Knerly Junior, *Pt*
N Herschel Koblenz, *Pt*
Lawrence E Oscar, *Pt*
EMP: 172 **EST:** 1920
SQ FT: 83,400
SALES (est): 37.92MM
SALES (corp-wide): 37.92MM **Privately Held**
Web: www.hahnlaw.com
SIC: 8111 General practice attorney, lawyer

(G-4347)
HANNA COMMERCIAL LLC
Also Called: Hanna Commercial Real Estate
1350 Euclid Ave Ste 700 (44115-1889)
PHONE...................216 861-7200
Mac Biggar Junior, *Pr*
EMP: 65 **EST:** 2016
SALES (est): 9.56MM **Privately Held**
Web: www.hannacre.com
SIC: 6531 Real estate agent, commercial

(G-4348)
HANNA PERKINS SCHOOL
Also Called: Hanna Perkin Center
19910 Malvern Rd (44122)
PHONE...................216 991-4472
Barbara Streeter, *Dir*
Zach France, *Treas*
Burt Griffin, *Bd of Dir*
Karen Baer, *CEO*
EMP: 101 **EST:** 1952
SQ FT: 33,000
SALES (est): 1.35MM **Privately Held**
Web: www.hannaperkins.org
SIC: 8351 8211 Preschool center; Kindergarten

Cleveland - Cuyahoga County (G-4349)   GEOGRAPHIC SECTION

(G-4349)
HANS TRUCK AND TRLR REPR INC
Also Called: Hans' Freightliner Cleveland
14520 Broadway Ave (44125-1960)
PHONE....................216 581-0046
Hans Dabernig, *Pr*
Ilse Dabernig, *
Chris Tench, *Corporate Secretary*
EMP: 53 **EST:** 1971
SQ FT: 20,000
SALES (est): 8.19MM **Privately Held**
Web: www.freightliner.com
SIC: 7539 4173 7699 5511 Trailer repair; Maintenance facilities, buses; Construction equipment repair; Trucks, tractors, and trailers: new and used

(G-4350)
HARLEY-DVIDSON DLR SYSTEMS INC
8555 Sweet Valley Dr Ste Q (44125-4254)
PHONE....................216 573-1393
Dennis Stapleton, *Pr*
Robert Maurer, *
EMP: 54 **EST:** 1987
SALES (est): 12.43MM
SALES (corp-wide): 5.84B **Publicly Held**
SIC: 5734 7371 Computer and software stores; Custom computer programming services
PA: Harley-Davidson, Inc.
     3700 W Juneau Ave
     Milwaukee WI 53208
     414 342-4680

(G-4351)
HARRINGTON ELECTRIC COMPANY
3800 Perkins Ave (44114-4635)
PHONE....................216 361-5101
Thomas A Morgan, *Pr*
James B Morgan Junior, *Ex VP*
James B Morgan Senior, *Stockholder*
EMP: 70 **EST:** 1907
SQ FT: 18,500
SALES (est): 22.41MM **Privately Held**
Web: www.harringtonelectric.com
SIC: 1731 General electrical contractor

(G-4352)
HATZEL AND BUEHLER INC
1200 Resource Dr Ste 10 (44131-1881)
PHONE....................216 777-6000
Anthony Riccelli, *VP*
EMP: 50
SALES (corp-wide): 362.45MM **Privately Held**
Web: www.hatzelandbuehler.com
SIC: 1731 General electrical contractor
HQ: Hatzel And Buehler, Inc.
     3600 Silverside Rd Ste A
     Wilmington DE 19810
     302 478-4200

(G-4353)
HEALTH AID OF OHIO INC (PA)
5230 Hauserman Rd Ste B (44130-1224)
P.O. Box 35107 (44135-0107)
PHONE....................216 252-3900
Carol Gilligan, *Pr*
Cortney B Mcdowell, *VP*
Kristin O'neil, *Mgr*
David Tatka, *
Sheila Harrison, *
EMP: 50 **EST:** 1983
SQ FT: 18,000
SALES (est): 18.94MM
SALES (corp-wide): 18.94MM **Privately Held**
Web: www.healthaidofohio.com

SIC: 5999 7352 3821 Medical apparatus and supplies; Medical equipment rental; Incubators, laboratory

(G-4354)
HEALTH SERVICES (ADAMHS) BRD O
2012 W 25th St Ste 600 (44113-4119)
PHONE....................216 241-3400
Harvey A Snider, *Ch*
EMP: 34 **EST:** 2010
SALES (est): 4.68MM **Privately Held**
Web: www.adamhscc.org
SIC: 8322 Individual and family services

(G-4355)
HEALTHCARE WALTON GROUP LLC
Also Called: Walton Manor Health Care Center
19859 Alexander Rd (44146-5345)
PHONE....................440 439-4433
George S Repchick, *Pr*
William I Weisberg, *VP*
EMP: 89 **EST:** 2012
SALES (est): 4.79MM
SALES (corp-wide): 655.44MM **Privately Held**
SIC: 8051 Convalescent home with continuous nursing care
PA: Saber Healthcare Group, L.L.C.
     23700 Commerce Park
     Beachwood OH 44122
     216 292-5706

(G-4356)
HEARTY HEARTS HOME HEALTH LLC
4161 Ridge Rd (44144-1439)
PHONE....................216 898-5533
Eminelly Garced, *Prin*
EMP: 30 **EST:** 2013
SALES (est): 825.21K **Privately Held**
Web: www.heartyheartshomehealth.com
SIC: 8082 Home health care services

(G-4357)
HELP FOUNDATION INC
Also Called: Nottingham Home
17702 Nottingham Rd (44119-2946)
PHONE....................216 486-5258
Peggy Congdon, *Dir*
EMP: 31
Web: www.helpfoundationinc.org
SIC: 8361 Group foster home
PA: Help Foundation, Inc.
     26900 Euclid Ave
     Euclid OH 44132

(G-4358)
HENRY CALL INC
308 Pines St Ste 100 (44135)
PHONE....................216 433-5609
Clarence Hugh Sneed, *Mgr*
EMP: 152
Web: www.callhenry.com
SIC: 8744 7371 8742 Base maintenance (providing personnel on continuing basis); Computer software development; Management consulting services
PA: Call Henry Inc
     1425 Chaffee Dr Ste 3
     Titusville FL 32780

(G-4359)
HERBST ELECTRIC LLC
Also Called: Herbst Electric Company
5171 Grant Ave (44125-1031)
PHONE....................216 621-5890
John R Benevento, *Pr*
Kenneth Maher, *

Duke Benevento, *
Deborah Benevento, *
EMP: 65 **EST:** 1946
SALES (est): 11.03MM **Privately Held**
Web: www.herbstelectric.com
SIC: 1731 General electrical contractor

(G-4360)
HILEMAN GROUP
1100 W 9th St (44113-1030)
PHONE....................216 926-4365
Tom Hileman, *CEO*
EMP: 42 **EST:** 2019
SALES (est): 4.91MM **Privately Held**
Web: www.globalprairie.com
SIC: 6512 Commercial and industrial building operation

(G-4361)
HILL SIDE PLAZA
Also Called: Hillside Plaza
18220 Euclid Ave (44112-1013)
PHONE....................216 486-6300
Paul Sobel, *Admn*
David Farkas, *
Bob Jones, *
EMP: 51 **EST:** 1963
SQ FT: 14,000
SALES (est): 3.83MM **Privately Held**
Web: www.lhshealth.com
SIC: 8051 8052 Convalescent home with continuous nursing care; Intermediate care facilities

(G-4362)
HILLBROOK CLUB INC
17200 S Woodland Rd (44120-1882)
PHONE....................440 247-4940
Ernest Mishne, *Prin*
EMP: 30 **EST:** 1951
SQ FT: 8,000
SALES (est): 326.55K **Privately Held**
Web: www.clubhillbrook.com
SIC: 7997 5812 Country club, membership; American restaurant

(G-4363)
HILLCREST EGG & CHEESE CO (PA)
Also Called: Hillcrest Foodservice
2735 E 40th St (44115-3510)
PHONE....................216 361-4625
Armin Abraham, *Pr*
Joe Abraham, *
David Abraham, *
Galina Yakobovitch, *
EMP: 79 **EST:** 1974
SQ FT: 95,000
SALES (est): 91.99MM
SALES (corp-wide): 91.99MM **Privately Held**
Web: www.hillcrestfoods.com
SIC: 5143 5142 5147 5144 Dairy products, except dried or canned; Packaged frozen goods; Meats, fresh; Eggs

(G-4364)
HILLCREST HOSPITAL AUXILIARY
6780 Mayfield Rd (44124-2294)
PHONE....................440 449-4500
Harold M Chattman, *Dir*
Gerald B Chattman, *
Gloria D Higgs, *
EMP: 51 **EST:** 1968
SQ FT: 750
SALES (est): 5.6MM **Privately Held**
Web: www.hillcresthospital.org
SIC: 8062 General medical and surgical hospitals

(G-4365)
HILTON GRDN INN - CLEVELAND E
Also Called: Hilton Garden Inns
700 Beta Dr (44143-2376)
PHONE....................440 646-1777
Frank Mancine, *Prin*
EMP: 36 **EST:** 2009
SALES (est): 1.04MM **Privately Held**
Web: www.hilton.com
SIC: 7011 Hotels and motels

(G-4366)
HITCHCOCK CENTER FOR WOMEN INC
Also Called: Hcfw
1227 Ansel Rd (44108)
PHONE....................216 421-0662
Stephen Monto, *Reg Pr*
Sharon Brettas, *
Jeffrey Shafer, *
Tony Kuhel, *
EMP: 45 **EST:** 1978
SQ FT: 20,000
SALES (est): 3.43MM **Privately Held**
Web: www.hcfw.org
SIC: 8361 8093 Rehabilitation center, residential: health care incidental; Alcohol clinic, outpatient

(G-4367)
HKM DRECT MKT CMMNICATIONS INC (PA)
Also Called: H K M
5501 Cass Ave (44102-2121)
PHONE....................800 860-4456
Rob Durham, *Pr*
Scott Durham, *
EMP: 140 **EST:** 1922
SQ FT: 86,000
SALES (est): 26.5MM
SALES (corp-wide): 26.5MM **Privately Held**
Web: www.hkmdirectmarket.com
SIC: 2752 7375 2791 2759 Commercial printing, lithographic; Information retrieval services; Typesetting; Commercial printing, nec

(G-4368)
HLE COMPANY
Also Called: Leff Electric
4700 Spring Rd (44131-1027)
PHONE....................216 325-0941
EMP: 107
SIC: 5063 Electrical supplies, nec

(G-4369)
HNTB CORPORATION
1100 Superior Ave E Ste 1701 (44114-2518)
PHONE....................216 522-1140
Anthony Yacobucci, *Brnch Mgr*
EMP: 41
SALES (corp-wide): 1.9B **Privately Held**
Web: www.hntb.com
SIC: 8711 Consulting engineer
HQ: Hntb Corporation
     715 Kirk Dr
     Kansas City MO 64105
     816 472-1201

(G-4370)
HOB ENTERTAINMENT LLC
308 Euclid Ave (44114-2207)
PHONE....................216 523-2583
EMP: 58
Web: www.houseofblues.com
SIC: 7922 Theatrical producers and services
HQ: Hob Entertainment, Llc
     7060 Hollywood Blvd

Los Angeles CA 90028

(G-4371)
HOBE LCAS CRTIF PUB ACCNTNTS I
4807 Rockside Rd Ste 510 (44131-2161)
PHONE..............................216 524-7167
David Hobe, *Prin*
Jerry Lucas, *
Francis G Bonning Junior, *Prin*
Floyd Trouten, *
EMP: 31 **EST:** 1978
SALES (est): 4.98MM **Privately Held**
Web: www.hobe.com
SIC: 8721 Certified public accountant

(G-4372)
HODELL-NATCO INDUSTRIES INC (PA)
Also Called: Locktooth Division
7825 Hub Pkwy (44125)
PHONE..............................216 447-0165
Otto Reidl, *CEO*
Kevin Reidl, *Pr*
Paul Starr, *VP*
Brandon Liebhard, *VP*
◆ **EMP:** 40 **EST:** 1896
SQ FT: 101,000
SALES (est): 30.19MM
SALES (corp-wide): 30.19MM **Privately Held**
Web: www.hodell-natco.com
SIC: 5072 Bolts

(G-4373)
HOME DEPOT USA INC
Also Called: Home Depot, The
10800 Brookpark Rd (44130)
PHONE..............................216 676-9969
Louis Zager, *Mgr*
EMP: 175
SALES (corp-wide): 152.67B **Publicly Held**
Web: www.homedepot.com
SIC: 5211 7359 Home centers; Tool rental
HQ: Home Depot U.S.A., Inc.
2445 Springfield Ave
Vauxhall NJ 07088

(G-4374)
HOME DEPOT USA INC
Also Called: Home Depot, The
11901 Berea Rd (44111)
PHONE..............................216 251-3091
Kennett Johansson, *Mgr*
EMP: 148
SALES (corp-wide): 152.67B **Publicly Held**
Web: www.homedepot.com
SIC: 5211 7359 Home centers; Tool rental
HQ: Home Depot U.S.A., Inc.
2445 Springfield Ave
Vauxhall NJ 07088

(G-4375)
HOPKINS ACQUISITION INC
127 Public Sq Ste 5300 (44114)
PHONE..............................248 371-1700
Patrick James, *Pr*
Stephen Graham, *CFO*
Edward James, *Ex VP*
Michael Baker, *Sec*
Shekhar Kumar, *Sr VP*
EMP: 651 **EST:** 2011
SALES (corp-wide): 8.03B **Privately Held**
SIC: 6719 Personal holding companies, except banks
HQ: Phnx Acquisition Corp
127 Public Sq Ste 5110
Cleveland OH

(G-4376)
HOPKINS AIRPORT LIMOUSINE SVC (PA)
Also Called: Hopkins Transportation Svcs
13315 Brookpark Rd (44142-1822)
PHONE..............................216 267-8810
Tom Goebel, *Pr*
Jack Goebel, *
Chris Goebel, *
Jeff Goebel, *
Mike Goebel, *
EMP: 200 **EST:** 1964
SQ FT: 1,000
SALES (est): 8.5MM
SALES (corp-wide): 8.5MM **Privately Held**
Web: www.carey.com
SIC: 4119 Limousine rental, with driver

(G-4377)
HOPKINS PARTNERS
Also Called: Sheraton
5300 Riverside Dr Ste 30 (44135-3145)
PHONE..............................216 267-1500
David Mcardle, *Pt*
Kerry Chelm, *Pt*
Richard Watson, *Pt*
EMP: 153 **EST:** 1995
SALES (est): 2.31MM **Privately Held**
Web: four-points.marriott.com
SIC: 7011 Hotels and motels

(G-4378)
HORIZON FREIGHT SYSTEM INC (PA)
8777 Rockside Rd (44125-6112)
PHONE..............................216 341-7410
David Ferrante, *Pr*
James Gifford, *
Robert A Bosak, *
EMP: 50 **EST:** 1982
SQ FT: 15,000
SALES (est): 49.77MM
SALES (corp-wide): 49.77MM **Privately Held**
Web: www.horizonfreightsystem.com
SIC: 4213 Trucking, except local

(G-4379)
HORIZON MID ATLANTIC INC
Also Called: Trx Great Plains, Inc.
8777 Rockside Rd (44125-6112)
PHONE..............................800 480-6829
David Ferrante, *Pr*
Robert A Bosak, *CFO*
James Gifford, *VP*
EMP: 75 **EST:** 2011
SALES (est): 8.59MM
SALES (corp-wide): 49.77MM **Privately Held**
Web: www.horizonfreightsystem.com
SIC: 4213 Trucking, except local
PA: Horizon Freight System, Inc.
8777 Rockside Rd
Cleveland OH 44125
216 341-7410

(G-4380)
HORSESHOE CLEVELAND MGT LLC
Also Called: Jack Entertainment
100 Public Sq Ste 100 (44113-2208)
PHONE..............................216 297-4777
EMP: 60 **EST:** 2010
SALES (est): 4.53MM **Privately Held**
Web: www.cleveland.com
SIC: 7011 Casino hotel

(G-4381)
HOSPICE OF THE WESTERN RESERVE
Also Called: HOSPICE OF THE WESTERN RESERVE, INC
22730 Fairview Center Dr Ste 100 (44126)
PHONE..............................216 227-9048
Nancy Miller, *Brnch Mgr*
EMP: 115
SALES (corp-wide): 76.67MM **Privately Held**
Web: www.hospicewr.org
SIC: 8052 Personal care facility
PA: Hospice Of The Western Reserve, Inc.
17876 Saint Clair Ave
Cleveland OH 44110
216 383-2222

(G-4382)
HOSPICE OF WESTERN RESERVE INC (PA)
17876 Saint Clair Ave (44110-2602)
PHONE..............................216 383-2222
William E Finn, *CEO*
Jeff Kovacs, *
John Mastrojohn Iii, *Ex VP*
EMP: 130 **EST:** 1978
SQ FT: 60,000
SALES (est): 76.67MM
SALES (corp-wide): 76.67MM **Privately Held**
Web: www.hospicewr.org
SIC: 8052 Personal care facility

(G-4383)
HOTEL 1100 CARNEGIE OPCO L P
Also Called: Hilton
1100 Carnegie Ave (44115-2806)
PHONE..............................216 658-6400
Harvey Schach, *Genl Pt*
EMP: 192 **EST:** 1999
SALES (est): 6.55MM **Privately Held**
Web: www.hilton.com
SIC: 7011 Hotels and motels

(G-4384)
HOWARD HANNA REAL ESTATE SVCS
Also Called: Howard Hanna Real Estate
14284 W Sprague Rd (44130-7148)
PHONE..............................440 665-0649
Anita Ripepi, *Prin*
EMP: 38 **EST:** 2018
SALES (est): 244.55K **Privately Held**
Web: www.howardhanna.com
SIC: 6531 Real estate agent, residential

(G-4385)
HOWARD HANNA SMYTHE CRAMER (HQ)
6000 Parkland Blvd (44124)
PHONE..............................216 447-4477
Lucius B Mc Kelvey, *Ch Bd*
David C Paul, *
Alan C Chandler, *
EMP: 250 **EST:** 1972
SQ FT: 16,500
SALES (est): 23.9MM
SALES (corp-wide): 212.06MM **Privately Held**
Web: www.smythecramer.com
SIC: 6531 Real estate agent, residential
PA: Hanna Holdings, Inc.
1090 Freeport Rd Ste 1a
Pittsburgh PA 15238
412 967-9000

(G-4386)
HP MANUFACTURING COMPANY INC (PA)
Also Called: House of Plastics
3705 Carnegie Ave (44115-2750)
PHONE..............................216 361-6500
John R Melchiorre, *Pr*
EMP: 62 **EST:** 1948
SQ FT: 110,000
SALES (est): 10MM
SALES (corp-wide): 10MM **Privately Held**
Web: www.hpmanufacturing.com
SIC: 3089 5162 3993 3082 Injection molding of plastics; Plastics sheets and rods; Signs and advertising specialties; Unsupported plastics profile shapes

(G-4387)
HS FINANCIAL GROUP LLC (PA)
18013 Cleveland Pkwy Dr Ste 170 (44135-3235)
P.O. Box 451193 (44145-0630)
PHONE..............................216 762-1800
Timothy M Sullivan, *Managing Member*
Lauren Summers, *
EMP: 45 **EST:** 2003
SALES (est): 5.23MM
SALES (corp-wide): 5.23MM **Privately Held**
Web: www.hsfgroup.net
SIC: 7322 Collection agency, except real estate

(G-4388)
HUMAN ARC CORPORATION (HQ)
Also Called: Human ARC
1457 E 40th St (44103-1103)
PHONE..............................216 431-5200
EMP: 275 **EST:** 1984
SALES (est): 53.9MM
SALES (corp-wide): 82.13MM **Privately Held**
SIC: 8742 Hospital and health services consultant
PA: Centauri Health Solutions, Inc.
2010 W Whspring Wind Dr S
Phoenix AZ 85085
888 447-8908

(G-4389)
HUNT TIFFANI
17324 Wayne Dr (44128-3371)
PHONE..............................216 258-1923
EMP: 30 **EST:** 2020
SALES (est): 195.95K **Privately Held**
SIC: 8351 Child day care services
HQ: Ohio Department Of Job And Family Services
30 E Broad St Fl 32
Columbus OH 43215

(G-4390)
HUNTINGTON NATIONAL BANK
200 Public Sq Ste 600 (44114-2338)
PHONE..............................216 515-0471
Herb Strong, *Brnch Mgr*
EMP: 36
SALES (corp-wide): 10.84B **Publicly Held**
Web: www.huntington.com
SIC: 6029 Commercial banks, nec
HQ: The Huntington National Bank
41 S High St
Columbus OH 43215
614 480-4293

(G-4391)
HUNTINGTON NATIONAL BANK
Also Called: Huntington National Bank
10001 Chester Ave Ste A (44106-1659)
PHONE..............................216 290-2445
EMP: 31
SALES (corp-wide): 10.84B **Publicly Held**
Web: www.huntington.com
SIC: 6029 Commercial banks, nec
HQ: The Huntington National Bank
41 S High St
Columbus OH 43215
614 480-4293

Cleveland - Cuyahoga County (G-4392) — GEOGRAPHIC SECTION

(G-4392)
HUNTINGTON NATIONAL BANK
917 Euclid Ave 925 (44115-1497)
PHONE..............................216 515-6401
Barrie Christman, *Mgr*
EMP: 41
SALES (corp-wide): 10.84B **Publicly Held**
Web: www.huntington.com
SIC: 6029 6021 Commercial banks, nec; National commercial banks
HQ: The Huntington National Bank
  41 S High St
  Columbus OH 43215
  614 480-4293

(G-4393)
HUNTINGTON NATIONAL BANK
4260 Ridge Rd (44144-1755)
PHONE..............................216 515-0064
EMP: 31
SALES (corp-wide): 10.84B **Publicly Held**
Web: www.huntington.com
SIC: 6029 Commercial banks, nec
HQ: The Huntington National Bank
  41 S High St
  Columbus OH 43215
  614 480-4293

(G-4394)
HWH ARCHTCTS-NGNRS-PLNNERS INC
600 Superior Ave E Ste 1100 (44114-2614)
PHONE..............................216 875-4000
Joseph J Matts, *Pr*
David Lehmer, *
Robert Mccullough, *Ex VP*
Peter P Jancar, *
David R Wismar, *
EMP: 80 **EST:** 1943
SQ FT: 20,000
SALES (est): 10.18MM **Privately Held**
Web: www.hwhaep.com
SIC: 8711 8712 0781 Consulting engineer; Architectural services; Landscape counseling and planning

(G-4395)
HY-GRADE CORPORATION (PA)
3993 E 93rd St (44105-4052)
PHONE..............................216 341-7711
Michael Pemberton, *Pr*
EMP: 35 **EST:** 1951
SQ FT: 25,000
SALES (est): 3.82MM
SALES (corp-wide): 3.82MM **Privately Held**
Web: www.uniquepavingmaterials.com
SIC: 5032 2952 2951 Asphalt mixture; Asphalt felts and coatings; Asphalt paving mixtures and blocks

(G-4396)
HYATT CORPORATION
Also Called: Hyatt Hotel
420 Superior Ave E (44114-1208)
PHONE..............................216 575-1234
Tim Meyer, *Genl Mgr*
EMP: 200
Web: www.hyatt.com
SIC: 7011 5812 Hotels and motels; Eating places
HQ: Hyatt Corporation
  250 Vesey St Fl 15
  New York NY 10281
  312 750-1234

(G-4397)
I & M J GROSS COMPANY (PA)
Also Called: Gross Residential
14300 Ridge Rd Ste 100 (44133-4936)
PHONE..............................440 237-1681
Gary Gross, *Pr*
Harley Gross, *
Sally A Jamieson, *Prin*
EMP: 35 **EST:** 1916
SQ FT: 9,425
SALES (est): 47.07MM
SALES (corp-wide): 47.07MM **Privately Held**
Web: www.grossresidential.com
SIC: 1522 Multi-family dwellings, new construction

(G-4398)
I-X CENTER CORPORATION
Also Called: International Exposition Ctr
6200 Riverside Dr (44135-3189)
PHONE..............................216 265-2675
Robert Peterson, *Pr*
Lisa Vo, *Ex VP*
▲ **EMP:** 125 **EST:** 1975
SQ FT: 2,000,000
SALES (est): 12.6MM
SALES (corp-wide): 367.37MM **Privately Held**
Web: www.ixcenter.com
SIC: 7389 5812 6512 Convention and show services; Eating places; Nonresidential building operators
PA: Park Corporation
  3555 Reserve Commons Dr
  Medina OH 44256
  216 267-4870

(G-4399)
ICP REALTY LLC
4780 Hinckley Industrial Pkwy Ste 100 (44109-6005)
PHONE..............................440 539-1046
Darrell Bossert, *Pr*
EMP: 32 **EST:** 2016
SALES (est): 1.64MM **Privately Held**
Web: www.icpllc.com
SIC: 6531 Real estate agent, commercial

(G-4400)
ICX CORPORATION (DH)
2 Summit Park Dr Ste 105 (44131-2558)
PHONE..............................330 656-3611
Mark Marinik, *Pr*
Gerald F Bender, *
James T Lovins, *
Michael Babbitt, *
Robert Rowland, *
EMP: 50 **EST:** 1988
SQ FT: 14,270
SALES (est): 25.56MM
SALES (corp-wide): 12.19B **Publicly Held**
SIC: 6021 National commercial banks
HQ: Citizens Bank, National Association
  1 Citizens Plz
  Providence RI 02903
  401 456-7096

(G-4401)
IDEASTREAM (PA)
Also Called: WVIZ/PBS HD
1375 Euclid Ave (44115-1826)
PHONE..............................216 916-6100
Larry Pollock, *Ch*
Jerry F Wareham, *
Bob Calsin, *
John Phillips, *
Sylvia Strobel, *
▲ **EMP:** 130 **EST:** 2001
SQ FT: 70,000
SALES (est): 24.6MM
SALES (corp-wide): 24.6MM **Privately Held**
Web: www.ideastream.org
SIC: 4832 Radio broadcasting stations

(G-4402)
IDILLNIRE CNSLTING SLTIONS LLC
1300 E 9th St Ste 800 (44114-1517)
PHONE..............................305 413-8522
Natasha Taylor, *Managing Member*
EMP: 54 **EST:** 2018
SALES (est): 395K **Privately Held**
SIC: 8748 Business consulting, nec

(G-4403)
IEH AUTO PARTS LLC
4565 Hinckley Industrial Pkwy (44109-6009)
PHONE..............................216 351-2560
Chuck Reimel, *Brnch Mgr*
EMP: 44
Web: autoplus1.cypresstg.com
SIC: 4225 General warehousing and storage
HQ: Ieh Auto Parts Llc
  112 Townpark Dr Nw # 300
  Kennesaw GA 30144
  770 701-5000

(G-4404)
ILS TECHNOLOGY LLC
6065 Parkland Blvd (44124-6119)
PHONE..............................800 695-8650
Fred Yentz, *Pr*
EMP: 37 **EST:** 2000
SQ FT: 41,000
SALES (est): 2.09MM
SALES (corp-wide): 1.66B **Publicly Held**
SIC: 7371 Computer software development
HQ: Park-Ohio Industries, Inc.
  6065 Parkland Blvd
  Cleveland OH 44124
  440 947-2000

(G-4405)
INDEPENDENCE BANK
4401 Rockside Rd (44131-2146)
P.O. Box 318048 (44131-8048)
PHONE..............................216 447-1444
Christopher W Mack, *Ch Bd*
Russell G Fortlage, *VP*
Albert E Wainio, *VP*
Dennis A Williams, *VP*
Michael J Occhionaro, *Sec*
EMP: 28 **EST:** 1979
SALES (est): 6.37MM
SALES (corp-wide): 6.37MM **Privately Held**
Web: www.theindebank.com
SIC: 6022 State trust companies accepting deposits, commercial
PA: Independence Bancorp
  4401 Rockside Rd
  Cleveland OH 44131
  216 447-1444

(G-4406)
INDEPENDENT HOTEL PARTNERS LLC
Also Called: Shereton Hotel Independance
5300 Rockside Rd (44131-2118)
PHONE..............................216 524-0700
Ernie Malas, *Managing Member*
EMP: 65 **EST:** 2004
SQ FT: 300,000
SALES (est): 1.15MM **Privately Held**
Web: www.ihg.com
SIC: 7011 Hotels

(G-4407)
INDEPENDENT PERSONNEL SERVICES
Also Called: Clevland Business Consultants
1148 Euclid Ave Ste 405 (44115-1600)
PHONE..............................216 781-5350
Raymond Castelluccio, *Pr*
Tom Corrigan, *VP*
Don Tillery, *VP*
EMP: 55 **EST:** 1984
SALES (est): 2.46MM **Privately Held**
SIC: 7361 Employment agencies

(G-4408)
INDEPNDENCE OFFICE BUS SUP INC
Also Called: Independence Business Supply
4550 Hinckley Industrial Pkwy (44109-6010)
PHONE..............................216 398-8880
Steven Gordon, *Pr*
Tony Angelo, *
James Connelly, *
Phillip Dubiel, *
Larry Norman, *
EMP: 55 **EST:** 1983
SQ FT: 10,250
SALES (est): 29.88MM **Privately Held**
Web: www.orderibs.com
SIC: 5112 5712 Office supplies, nec; Furniture stores

(G-4409)
INDUSTRIAL ORIGAMI INC
6755 Engle Rd Ste A (44130-7947)
PHONE..............................440 260-0000
V Gerry Corrigan, *Pr*
Zach Koekemoer, *
EMP: 29 **EST:** 2004
SALES (est): 1.9MM **Privately Held**
Web: www.industrialorigami.com
SIC: 8711 Industrial engineers

(G-4410)
INDUSTRIAL SECURITY SVC INC (HQ)
4525 W 160th St (44135-2627)
PHONE..............................216 898-9970
John P Andrews, *Pr*
James Hughes, *VP*
EMP: 83 **EST:** 1997
SALES (est): 5.41MM **Privately Held**
SIC: 7381 Security guard service
PA: United American Security, Llc
  1699 S Hanley Rd Ste 350
  Saint Louis MO 63144

(G-4411)
INERTIAL AIRLINE SERVICES INC
Also Called: Inertial Aerospace Services
375 Alpha Park (44143-2237)
PHONE..............................440 995-6555
EMP: 33 **EST:** 1996
SALES (est): 9.47MM **Publicly Held**
SIC: 7699 Nautical and navigational instrument repair
HQ: Heico Aerospace Holdings Corp.
  3000 Taft St
  Hollywood FL 33021
  954 987-4000

(G-4412)
INFOTELECOM LLC
75 Erieview Plz Fl 4 (44114-1839)
PHONE..............................216 373-4600
Eugene Blumin, *COO*
EMP: 397 **EST:** 2005
SALES (est): 231.36K
SALES (corp-wide): 16.05MM **Privately Held**
SIC: 7389 Telephone services
PA: Infotelecom Holdings, Llc
  1 N Wacker Dr
  Chicago IL 60606
  216 373-4811

(G-4413)
INNER CITY NURSING HOME INC
Also Called: Fairfax Health Care Center
9014 Cedar Ave (44106-2932)
PHONE................................216 795-1363
Melvin Pye Junior, *Adm/Dir*
Ethel Pye, *
EMP: 130 **EST:** 1949
SQ FT: 10,000
SALES (est): 9.33MM **Privately Held**
Web: www.fairfaxplace.com
SIC: 8051 Skilled nursing care facilities

(G-4414)
INTEGRATED MEDICAL INC
15627 Neo Pkwy (44128-3150)
PHONE................................216 332-1550
EMP: 38
SIC: 7352 Medical equipment rental

(G-4415)
INTEGRATED POWER SERVICES LLC
Also Called: Monarch
5325 W 130th St (44130-1034)
PHONE................................216 433-7808
Bridgette Gullatta, *Pr*
EMP: 100
Web: www.ips.us
SIC: 7694 Electric motor repair
PA: Integrated Power Services Llc
   250 Exctive Ctr Dr Ste 20
   Greenville SC 29615

(G-4416)
INTEGRATED ROOT SYSTEMS LLC
8400 Sweet Valley Dr Ste 401
(44125-4243)
PHONE................................216 282-7470
EMP: 29 **EST:** 2016
SALES (est): 6.98MM **Privately Held**
Web: www.rootintegration.com
SIC: 7379 Computer related consulting services

(G-4417)
INTERACTIVE PAYER NETWORK LLC
Also Called: Ipn, Interpaynet
5910 Landerbrook Dr Ste 110 (44124-6508)
EMP: 40 **EST:** 1995
SALES (est): 1.58MM **Privately Held**
SIC: 7376 Computer facilities management

(G-4418)
INTERFINISH LLC
9500 Midwest Ave (44125-2463)
PHONE................................216 662-6550
EMP: 29
Web: www.interfinish.net
SIC: 7217 Carpet and upholstery cleaning
PA: Interfinish, Llc
   7471 Candlewood Rd # 104
   Hanover MD 21076

(G-4419)
INTERNTNAL MGT GROUP OVRSEAS L (DH)
Also Called: William Morris Endeavor Entrmt
1360 E 9th St Ste 100 (44114-1730)
PHONE................................216 522-1200
William Prip, *Treas*
Arthur J La Fave Junior, *VP*
Peter Kuhn, *Assistant Chief Financial Officer**
Ian Todd, *
Kevin Lavan, *
◆ **EMP:** 289 **EST:** 1961
SALES (est): 22.2MM
SALES (corp-wide): 5.96B **Publicly Held**
SIC: 7941 7999 7922 Manager of individual professional athletes; Sports instruction, schools and camps; Theatrical producers and services
HQ: William Morris Endeavor
   Entertainment, Llc
   9601 Wilshire Blvd
   Beverly Hills CA 90210
   212 586-5100

(G-4420)
INTERSTATE DIESEL SERVICE INC (PA)
Also Called: American Diesel
5300 Lakeside Ave E (44114-3916)
PHONE................................216 881-0015
Alfred J Buescher, *CEO*
Ann Buescher, *
Brad Buescher, *
◆ **EMP:** 125 **EST:** 1947
SQ FT: 70,000
SALES (est): 25.56MM
SALES (corp-wide): 25.56MM **Privately Held**
Web: www.interstate-mcbee.com
SIC: 5013 3714 Automotive engines and engine parts; Fuel systems and parts, motor vehicle

(G-4421)
INTERSTATE LIFT TRUCKS INC
Also Called: Ilt Toyota-Lift
5667 E Schaaf Rd (44131-1395)
PHONE................................216 328-0970
TOLL FREE: 800
EMP: 45
Web: www.ilttoyotalift.com
SIC: 5084 7353 7699 Lift trucks and parts; Cranes and aerial lift equipment, rental or leasing; Industrial equipment services

(G-4422)
IRONWOOD DEVELOPMENT CORP
20595 Lorain Rd Ste 300 (44126-2062)
PHONE................................440 895-1200
Tom Gowan, *Mgr*
EMP: 235
SALES (corp-wide): 729.16K **Privately Held**
Web: www.ironwood-dev.com
SIC: 8741 Management services
PA: Ironwood Development Corporation
   600 A B Data Dr
   Milwaukee WI 53217
   414 961-1000

(G-4423)
ISAAC FAIR CONSULTING INC
6100 Oak Tree Blvd (44131-2544)
PHONE................................216 643-6790
Roger Hassler, *Mgr*
EMP: 36
SALES (corp-wide): 1.51B **Publicly Held**
SIC: 8742 Management information systems consultant
HQ: Isaac Fair Consulting Inc
   20 W Kinzie St Ste 1600
   Chicago IL 60654

(G-4424)
ISAAC INSTRUMENTS LLC
3121 Bridge Ave (44113)
PHONE................................888 658-7520
Jacques Delarochellire, *CEO*
EMP: 50 **EST:** 2020
SALES (est): 1.19MM **Privately Held**
Web: www.isaacinstruments.com
SIC: 7374 Data processing service

(G-4425)
IVHR LLC
Also Called: Ivhr Inc.
10000 Cedar Ave Ste 2136 (44106-2119)
PHONE................................216 445-4315
Wisam Rizk, *Pr*
EMP: 33 **EST:** 2012
SALES (est): 321.82K
SALES (corp-wide): 14.48B **Privately Held**
SIC: 7379 Computer related services, nec
PA: The Cleveland Clinic Foundation
   9500 Euclid Ave
   Cleveland OH 44195
   216 636-8335

(G-4426)
J L WILSON CO
Also Called: Suntan Supply
3800 Lakeside Ave E Ste 100 (44114)
PHONE................................216 431-4040
Bill Gallagher, *Pr*
EMP: 35 **EST:** 1994
SQ FT: 48,000
SALES (est): 3MM **Privately Held**
SIC: 5087 Service establishment equipment

(G-4427)
J V ENVIROSERVE LIMITED PARTNERSHIP
4600 Brookpark Rd (44134-1012)
PHONE................................216 642-1311
EMP: 40
Web: www.dns.google
SIC: 4212 8748 Hazardous waste transport; Business consulting, nec

(G-4428)
JACK JSEPH MRTON MNDEL FNDTIO
1000 Lakeside Ave E (44114-1117)
PHONE................................216 875-6511
Jehuda Reinharz, *Pr*
Stephen H Hoffman, *Ch Bd*
EMP: 30 **EST:** 2018
SALES (est): 143MM **Privately Held**
Web: www.mandelfoundation.org
SIC: 8641 Civic and social associations

(G-4429)
JACK CLEVELAND CASINO LLC
100 Public Sq (44113-2208)
PHONE................................216 297-4777
EMP: 35 **EST:** 2009
SALES (est): 3.98MM **Privately Held**
Web: www.jackentertainment.com
SIC: 7011 Casino hotel

(G-4430)
JACK ENTERTAINMENT LLC (PA)
100 Public Sq Fl 3 (44113)
PHONE................................313 309-5225
Matthew P Cullen, *CEO*
Glen Tomaszewski, *
Brian Eby, *Sr VP*
Daniel A Reinhard, *
Darlene Monzo, *
EMP: 99 **EST:** 2010
SALES (est): 23.44MM
SALES (corp-wide): 23.44MM **Privately Held**
Web: www.jackentertainment.com
SIC: 7929 7999 5091 Entertainment service; Recreation services; Sharpeners, sporting goods

(G-4431)
JAGI CLVLAND - INDPENDENCE LLC
Also Called: Holiday Inn
6001 Rockside Rd (44131-2209)
PHONE................................216 524-8050
Tom Hibsman, *Genl Mgr*
EMP: 180 **EST:** 1998
SQ FT: 81,713
SALES (est): 4.99MM **Privately Held**
Web: www.hiindependence.com
SIC: 7011 Hotels and motels

(G-4432)
JANIK LLP (PA)
9200 S Hills Blvd Ste 300 (44147-3524)
PHONE................................440 838-7600
Steven Janik, *Managing Member*
EMP: 42 **EST:** 1988
SQ FT: 8,000
SALES (est): 7.21MM
SALES (corp-wide): 7.21MM **Privately Held**
Web: www.janiklaw.com
SIC: 8111 General practice law office

(G-4433)
JANITORIAL SERVICES INC
4830 E 49th St (44125-1014)
PHONE................................216 341-8601
Ronald J Martinez Senior, *Pr*
Ronald J Martinez Junior, *VP*
EMP: 325 **EST:** 1969
SQ FT: 6,000
SALES (est): 14.49MM **Privately Held**
Web: www.jsijanitorial.com
SIC: 7349 Janitorial service, contract basis

(G-4434)
JAVITCH BLOCK LLC (PA)
1100 Superior Ave E (44114-2530)
PHONE................................216 623-0000
Bruce A Block, *Managing Member*
Joel Rathbone, *Managing Member**
EMP: 220 **EST:** 1991
SQ FT: 54,000
SALES (est): 41.42MM
SALES (corp-wide): 41.42MM **Privately Held**
Web: www.jbllc.com
SIC: 8111 General practice law office

(G-4435)
JBK GROUP INC (PA)
Also Called: Event Source
6001 Towpath Dr (44125-4221)
PHONE................................216 901-0000
John Bibbo, *Pr*
Bryan Bibbo, *
EMP: 41 **EST:** 1979
SQ FT: 57,530
SALES (est): 10.75MM
SALES (corp-wide): 10.75MM **Privately Held**
Web: www.eventsource.com
SIC: 7359 Party supplies rental services

(G-4436)
JENNINGS ELIZA HOME INC (HQ)
10603 Detroit Ave (44102-1647)
PHONE................................216 226-0282
Deborah Hiller, *CEO*
Jim Rogerson, *
Joan Lampe, *
EMP: 190 **EST:** 1922
SQ FT: 60,000
SALES (est): 10.29MM **Privately Held**
Web: www.elizajennings.org
SIC: 8051 8052 Convalescent home with continuous nursing care; Intermediate care facilities
PA: Eliza Jennings Senior Care Network
   26376 John Rd Ofc C
   Olmsted Twp OH 44138

Cleveland - Cuyahoga County (G-4437) GEOGRAPHIC SECTION

(G-4437)
JERGENS INC (PA)
Also Called: Tooling Components Division
15700 S Waterloo Rd (44110-3898)
 PHONE................................216 486-5540
 Jack H Schron Junior, *Pr*
 Sue Evans, *
 Kurt Schron, *
 ▲ **EMP:** 195 **EST:** 1942
 SQ FT: 104,000
 SALES (est): 93.96MM
 SALES (corp-wide): 93.96MM **Privately Held**
 Web: www.jergensinc.com
 SIC: 3443 3452 5084 3545 Fabricated plate work (boiler shop); Bolts, nuts, rivets, and washers; Machine tools and accessories; Drill bushings (drilling jig)

(G-4438)
JMA HEALTHCARE LLC
Also Called: Oak Park Health Care Center
24579 Broadway Ave (44146-6338)
 PHONE................................440 439-7976
 Lisa Berkowitz, *Prin*
 EMP: 34 **EST:** 1990
 SQ FT: 33,000
 SALES (est): 2.16MM **Privately Held**
 Web: www.embassyhealthcare.net
 SIC: 8051 Convalescent home with continuous nursing care

(G-4439)
JOHN A HUDEC DDS INC
Also Called: John Hudec DDS & Associates
3329 Broadview Rd (44109-3315)
 PHONE................................216 398-8900
 John A Hudec D.d.s., *Pr*
 EMP: 56 **EST:** 1977
 SQ FT: 2,000
 SALES (est): 953.99K **Privately Held**
 Web: www.hudecdental.com
 SIC: 8021 Dentists' office

(G-4440)
JOHN G JOHNSON CONSTRUCTION CO
1284 Riverbed St (44113-2309)
 PHONE................................216 938-5050
 Marty Weber, *Pr*
 EMP: 57 **EST:** 1943
 SALES (est): 70MM **Privately Held**
 Web: www.johngjohnson.com
 SIC: 1542 Commercial and office building, new construction

(G-4441)
JOHN H KAPPUS CO (PA)
Also Called: Kappus Company
4755 W 150th St (44135-3329)
 PHONE................................216 367-6677
 John Kappus, *Pr*
 Fred Kappus, *
 Ryan Huffman, *Managing Member*
 Michael J Marcis, *
 John Zalenka, *
 EMP: 49 **EST:** 1962
 SALES (est): 23.71MM
 SALES (corp-wide): 23.71MM **Privately Held**
 Web: www.kappuscompany.com
 SIC: 5046 Restaurant equipment and supplies, nec

(G-4442)
JONES DAY LIMITED PARTNERSHIP (PA)
Also Called: Jones Day
901 Lakeside Ave E (44114)
 PHONE................................216 586-3939
 Stephen Brogan, *Pt*
 Erin L Burke, *
 Warren L Nachlis, *
 Dennis Barsky, *
 Bruce Mcdonald, *Pt*
 EMP: 900 **EST:** 1893
 SQ FT: 300,000
 SALES (est): 333.64MM
 SALES (corp-wide): 333.64MM **Privately Held**
 Web: www.jonesday.com
 SIC: 8111 General practice law office

(G-4443)
JTC CONTRACTING INC
Also Called: Jtc Office Services
7635 Hub Pkwy Ste C (44125-5741)
 PHONE................................216 635-0745
 Kathleen Morris, *Pr*
 Ken Morris, *
 EMP: 40 **EST:** 1993
 SALES (est): 4.77MM **Privately Held**
 Web: www.jtcinstall.com
 SIC: 1799 Office furniture installation

(G-4444)
JUDSON (PA)
Also Called: JUDSON UNIVERSITY CIRCLE
2181 Ambleside Dr Apt 411 (44106-7604)
 PHONE................................216 791-2004
 Hong Chae, *CEO*
 Cynthia Dunn, *
 EMP: 80 **EST:** 1906
 SQ FT: 800,000
 SALES (est): 25.9MM
 SALES (corp-wide): 25.9MM **Privately Held**
 Web: www.judsonsmartliving.org
 SIC: 8059 6513 8052 Domiciliary care; Retirement hotel operation; Intermediate care facilities

(G-4445)
JUDSON
Also Called: Judson Manor
1890 E 107th St (44106-2235)
 PHONE................................216 791-2555
 Julie Anderson, *VP*
 EMP: 420
 SALES (corp-wide): 25.9MM **Privately Held**
 Web: www.judsonsmartliving.org
 SIC: 8361 Aged home
 PA: Judson
  2181 Ambleside Dr Apt 411
  Cleveland OH 44106
  216 791-2004

(G-4446)
JUMPORG LLC
12709 Watterson Ave (44105-4539)
 PHONE................................216 250-4678
 Mario Hosea, *Managing Member*
 EMP: 30 **EST:** 2020
 SALES (est): 300K **Privately Held**
 SIC: 8711 Building construction consultant

(G-4447)
K&D MANAGEMENT LLC
Also Called: Reserve Square Apartments
1701 E 12th St Ste 35 (44114-3237)
 PHONE................................216 624-4686
 Lori Brandenberg, *Mgr*
 EMP: 40
 SALES (corp-wide): 47.06MM **Privately Held**
 Web: www.kandd.com
 SIC: 6513 6512 Apartment building operators ; Commercial and industrial building operation
 PA: The K&D Group Inc
  4420 Sherwin Rd Ste 1
  Willoughby OH 44094
  440 946-3600

(G-4448)
KAPLAN TRUCKING COMPANY (PA)
8777 Rockside Rd (44125-6112)
 PHONE................................216 341-3322
 David Ferrante, *Pr*
 James B Gifford, *
 Robert A Bosak, *
 EMP: 75 **EST:** 1934
 SQ FT: 30,000
 SALES (est): 28.49MM
 SALES (corp-wide): 28.49MM **Privately Held**
 Web: www.kaplantrucking.com
 SIC: 4213 Contract haulers

(G-4449)
KARPINSKI ENGINEERING INC (PA)
3135 Euclid Ave Ste 200 (44115-2524)
 PHONE................................216 391-3700
 Jim Cicero, *Pr*
 EMP: 50 **EST:** 1983
 SQ FT: 14,000
 SALES (est): 11.25MM
 SALES (corp-wide): 11.25MM **Privately Held**
 Web: www.karpinskieng.com
 SIC: 8711 Consulting engineer

(G-4450)
KAUFMAN CONTAINER COMPANY (PA)
1000 Keystone Pkwy Ste 100 (44135-5119)
P.O. Box 35902 (44135-0902)
 PHONE................................216 898-2000
 Roger Seid, *Ch*
 Ken Slater, *
 Karen D Melton, *
 Charles Borowiak, *
 Anita Seid, *
 ◆ **EMP:** 118 **EST:** 1910
 SQ FT: 180,000
 SALES (est): 38.96MM
 SALES (corp-wide): 38.96MM **Privately Held**
 Web: www.kaufmancontainer.com
 SIC: 5085 2759 Commercial containers; Screen printing

(G-4451)
KEENE INC
Also Called: Keene Family Holdings Corp
2926 Chester Ave (44114-4414)
 PHONE................................440 605-1020
 EMP: 100 **EST:** 2015
 SALES (est): 500.25K
 SALES (corp-wide): 29.15MM **Privately Held**
 SIC: 8742 Business management consultant
 PA: Keene Building Products Co.
  2926 Chester Ave
  Cleveland OH 44114
  440 605-1020

(G-4452)
KEIS GEORGE LLP (PA)
55 Public Sq Ste 1900 (44113-1906)
 PHONE................................216 241-4100
 William Keis, *Mng Pt*
 Warren Keis, *Pt*
 Herbert L Nussle, *Prin*
 ▲ **EMP:** 40 **EST:** 1985
 SALES (est): 5.04MM **Privately Held**
 Web: www.keisgeorge.com
 SIC: 8111 General practice attorney, lawyer

(G-4453)
KEITH E HUSTON DVM LLC
Also Called: Village Veterinary Clinic
6529 Wilson Mills Rd (44143-3404)
 PHONE................................440 461-2226
 Keith Huston, *Managing Member*
 EMP: 30 **EST:** 2005
 SALES (est): 926.96K **Privately Held**
 Web: www.villageveterinaryclinic.com
 SIC: 0742 Animal hospital services, pets and other animal specialties

(G-4454)
KELLEY FERRARO LLC
950 Main Ave Ste 1300 (44113-7210)
 PHONE................................216 575-0777
 James L Ferraro, *Pt*
 Anthony Gallucci, *Pt*
 Thomas M Wilson, *Pt*
 John M Murphy, *Pt*
 EMP: 52 **EST:** 1997
 SALES (est): 8.52MM **Privately Held**
 Web: www.kelley-ferraro.com
 SIC: 8111 General practice attorney, lawyer

(G-4455)
KELLEY STEEL ERECTORS INC (PA)
7220 Division St (44146-5406)
 PHONE................................440 232-1573
 Dan Gold, *CEO*
 Michael Kelley, *
 Bob Hurley, *
 EMP: 100 **EST:** 1958
 SQ FT: 150,000
 SALES (est): 40.19MM
 SALES (corp-wide): 40.19MM **Privately Held**
 Web: www.kelleysteel.com
 SIC: 1791 7353 Structural steel erection; Cranes and aerial lift equipment, rental or leasing

(G-4456)
KELLISON & CO (PA)
4925 Galaxy Pkwy Ste U (44128-5961)
 PHONE................................216 464-5160
 Kevin Ellison, *Owner*
 EMP: 50 **EST:** 1998
 SALES (est): 9.05MM
 SALES (corp-wide): 9.05MM **Privately Held**
 Web: www.medsphere.com
 SIC: 6411 Insurance brokers, nec

(G-4457)
KEY CAPITAL CORPORATION
127 Public Sq Ste 5600 (44114-1226)
 PHONE................................216 828-8154
 David Given, *Pr*
 Dennis Wagoner, *Treas*
 EMP: 28 **EST:** 1959
 SALES (est): 1.41MM
 SALES (corp-wide): 10.4B **Publicly Held**
 SIC: 6211 Investment bankers
 PA: Keycorp
  127 Public Sq
  Cleveland OH 44114
  216 689-3000

(G-4458)
KEYBANC CAPITAL MARKETS INC (HQ)
Also Called: McDonald Finanacial Group
127 Public Sq (44114)
 PHONE................................800 553-2240
 Randy Paine, *Pr*
 Douglas Preiser, *
 Robert D Moran Junior, *CFO*
 EMP: 400 **EST:** 1983
 SQ FT: 70,000
 SALES (est): 870.68MM

GEOGRAPHIC SECTION
Cleveland - Cuyahoga County (G-4481)

SALES (corp-wide): 10.4B **Publicly Held**
Web: www.key.com
SIC: **6021** 6211 National commercial banks;
  Security brokers and dealers
PA: Keycorp
  127 Public Sq
  Cleveland OH 44114
  216 689-3000

(G-4459)
KEYBANK EB MNGED GRNTEED INV C
Also Called: Magic Fund
  127 Public Sq (44114-1217)
PHONE..............................216 689-3000
Joseph Dedek, *Prin*
EMP: 189 EST: 2009
SALES (est): 24.62MM
SALES (corp-wide): 10.4B **Publicly Held**
SIC: **6722** Money market mutual funds
HQ: Keybank National Association
  127 Public Sq Ste 5600
  Cleveland OH 44114
  800 539-2968

(G-4460)
KEYBANK NATIONAL ASSOCIATION
6912 Pearl Rd (44130-3604)
PHONE..............................440 345-7055
EMP: 32
SALES (corp-wide): 10.4B **Publicly Held**
Web: www.key.com
SIC: **6021** National commercial banks
HQ: Keybank National Association
  127 Public Sq Ste 5600
  Cleveland OH 44114
  800 539-2968

(G-4461)
KEYBANK NATIONAL ASSOCIATION (HQ)
Also Called: Keybank
  127 Public Sq Ste 5600 (44114-1226)
  P.O. Box 92986 (44194-2986)
PHONE..............................800 539-2968
R B Heisler, *Ch*
John Mancuso, *Vice Chairman* *
Christopher Gorman, *
Tom Tulodzieski, *
EMP: 500 EST: 1849
SALES (est): 7.66B
SALES (corp-wide): 10.4B **Publicly Held**
Web: www.key.com
SIC: **6021** 6022 6159 National commercial banks; State commercial banks; Automobile finance leasing
PA: Keycorp
  127 Public Sq
  Cleveland OH 44114
  216 689-3000

(G-4462)
KEYBANK NATIONAL ASSOCIATION
24600 Chagrin Blvd (44122-5666)
PHONE..............................216 464-4727
Linda Himmelini, *Mgr*
EMP: 38
SALES (corp-wide): 10.4B **Publicly Held**
Web: www.key.com
SIC: **6021** National commercial banks
HQ: Keybank National Association
  127 Public Sq Ste 5600
  Cleveland OH 44114
  800 539-2968

(G-4463)
KEYBANK NATIONAL ASSOCIATION
4461 Mayfield Rd (44121-4014)
PHONE..............................216 382-3000
Carl Scalabrino, *Mgr*
EMP: 32

SALES (corp-wide): 10.4B **Publicly Held**
Web: www.key.com
SIC: **6021** National commercial banks
HQ: Keybank National Association
  127 Public Sq Ste 5600
  Cleveland OH 44114
  800 539-2968

(G-4464)
KEYBANK NATIONAL ASSOCIATION
Also Called: Key
  100 Public Sq Ste 600 (44113-2207)
  P.O. Box 94768 (44101-4768)
PHONE..............................216 689-8481
EMP: 540
SALES (corp-wide): 7.56B **Publicly Held**
Web: www.key.com
SIC: **6021** National commercial banks
HQ: Keybank National Association
  127 Public Sq Ste 5600
  Cleveland OH 44114
  800 539-2968

(G-4465)
KEYBANK NATIONAL ASSOCIATION
30200 Chagrin Blvd (44124-5799)
PHONE..............................216 464-6128
Venera Izant, *Mgr*
EMP: 32
SALES (corp-wide): 10.4B **Publicly Held**
Web: www.key.com
SIC: **6021** National trust companies with deposits, commercial
HQ: Keybank National Association
  127 Public Sq Ste 5600
  Cleveland OH 44114
  800 539-2968

(G-4466)
KINDERCARE LEARNING CTRS LLC
Also Called: Kindercare Child Care Network
  5684 Mayfield Rd (44124-2916)
PHONE..............................440 442-8067
Melanie Baisden, *Dir*
EMP: 29
SALES (corp-wide): 967.64MM **Privately Held**
Web: www.kindercare.com
SIC: **8351** Group day care center
HQ: Kindercare Learning Centers, Llc
  650 Ne Holladay St # 1400
  Portland OR 97232

(G-4467)
KINNECT
1427 E 36th St Ste 4203f (44114-4170)
PHONE..............................216 692-1161
EMP: 30 EST: 2008
SALES (est): 1.85MM **Privately Held**
Web: www.kinnect.org
SIC: **8322** Child related social services

(G-4468)
KOHRMAN JACKSON & KRANTZ LLP
1375 E 9th St Fl 29 (44114-1797)
PHONE..............................216 696-8700
Marc C Krantz, *Pt*
S Lee Kohrman, *
Robert H Jackson, *
Byron S Krantz, *
Kevin T O'connor, *Pt*
EMP: 60 EST: 1968
SQ FT: 20,000
SALES (est): 10.98MM **Privately Held**
Web: www.kjk.com
SIC: **8111** General practice attorney, lawyer

(G-4469)
KOINONIA HOMES INC
6161 Oak Tree Blvd Ste 400 (44131-2581)
PHONE..............................216 588-8777

William E Tumney, *Prin*
James C Maher, *
Dineen B Terstage, *
EMP: 500 EST: 1974
SALES (est): 6.93MM **Privately Held**
SIC: **8361** Mentally handicapped home

(G-4470)
KONE INC
6670 W Snowville Rd Ste 7 (44141-4300)
PHONE..............................330 762-8886
David Lytle, *Pr*
EMP: 30
Web: www.kone.us
SIC: **7699** Elevators: inspection, service, and repair
HQ: Kone Inc.
  3333 Warrenville Rd # 700
  Lisle IL 60532
  630 577-1650

(G-4471)
L B & B ASSOCIATES INC
555 E 88th St (44108-1068)
PHONE..............................216 451-2672
Rachel M Rakes, *Brnch Mgr*
EMP: 32
Web: www.lbbassociates.com
SIC: **8744** Facilities support services
PA: L B & B Associates Inc.
  9891 Broken Land Pkwy
  Columbia MD 21046

(G-4472)
LABORERS INTL UN N AMER LCAL 3
Also Called: BUILDING LABORERS LOCAL 310
  3250 Euclid Ave Ste 100 (44115-2599)
PHONE..............................216 881-5901
Terrence Joyce, *Mgr*
Tom Byrne, *Prin*
Micheal Kearny, *Sec*
EMP: 71 EST: 1925
SALES (est): 548.85K **Privately Held**
Web: www.local310.com
SIC: **8631** Labor union

(G-4473)
LABORERS LOCAL UNION NO 860
3334 Prospect Ave E (44115-2616)
PHONE..............................216 432-1022
EMP: 46 EST: 2019
SALES (est): 801.72K **Privately Held**
Web: www.laborers860.com
SIC: **8631** Labor union

(G-4474)
LAKE ERIE CNCIL BOY SCUTS AMER
Also Called: Boy Scouts of America
  2241 Woodland Ave (44115-3214)
  P.O. Box 93388 (44101-5388)
PHONE..............................216 861-6060
Marc Ryan, *CEO*
Paula Swiner, *
EMP: 30 EST: 1912
SQ FT: 20,000
SALES (est): 4.23MM **Privately Held**
Web: www.lecbsa.org
SIC: **8641** Boy Scout organization

(G-4475)
LAKE ERIE MONSTERS
1 Center Ice (44115-4004)
PHONE..............................216 420-0000
EMP: 41 EST: 2009
SALES (est): 566.41K **Privately Held**
Web: www.clevelandmonsters.com
SIC: **7997** Hockey club, except professional and semi-professional

(G-4476)
LAKE HEALTH
7215 Old Oak Blvd Ste A421 (44130-3340)
PHONE..............................440 816-2225
Jerold Gurley, *Prin*
EMP: 33 EST: 2016
SALES (est): 228.52K **Privately Held**
Web: www.uhhospitals.org
SIC: **8011** Offices and clinics of medical doctors

(G-4477)
LAKESIDE SCRAP METALS INC
15000 Miles Ave (44128-2370)
PHONE..............................216 458-7150
Allen Youngman, *Pr*
Ken Ingber, *VP*
David Ingber, *Sec*
◆ EMP: 29 EST: 1984
SQ FT: 45,000
SALES (est): 729.53K **Privately Held**
Web: www.lsminc.net
SIC: **5093** Ferrous metal scrap and waste

(G-4478)
LAKESIDE SUPPLY CO
3000 W 117th St (44111-1667)
PHONE..............................216 941-6800
Ken Mathews, *Pr*
John Joseph Mathews, *
Brian Driscoll, *
EMP: 39 EST: 1932
SQ FT: 35,000
SALES (est): 25.4MM **Privately Held**
Web: www.lakesidesupply.com
SIC: **5074** 5075 5085 Plumbing fittings and supplies; Warm air heating equipment and supplies; Valves and fittings

(G-4479)
LAKEWOOD COUNTRY CLUB COMPANY
2613 Bradley Rd (44145-1799)
PHONE..............................440 871-0400
Brian Pizzimenti, *Genl Mgr*
EMP: 91 EST: 1921
SQ FT: 24,952
SALES (est): 8.47MM **Privately Held**
Web: www.lakewoodcountryclub.com
SIC: **7997** Country club, membership

(G-4480)
LAKEWOOD COUNTRY CLUB PRO SHOP
2613 Bradley Rd (44145-1799)
PHONE..............................440 871-0400
Tom Waitrovich, *Owner*
EMP: 48 EST: 1976
SQ FT: 600
SALES (est): 3.71MM **Privately Held**
Web: www.lakewoodcountryclub.com
SIC: **5941** 7999 Golf goods and equipment; Golf professionals

(G-4481)
LAKEWOOD HOSPITAL ASSOCIATION
1450 Belle Ave (44107-4211)
PHONE..............................216 228-5437
Mary Jo Swartz, *Mgr*
EMP: 109
SALES (corp-wide): 14.48B **Privately Held**
Web: www.lakewoodhospital.org
SIC: **8062** 8011 General medical and surgical hospitals; Offices and clinics of medical doctors
HQ: Lakewood Hospital Association
  14519 Detroit Ave
  Lakewood OH 44107
  216 529-7201

Cleveland - Cuyahoga County (G-4482)   GEOGRAPHIC SECTION

(G-4482)
LALAC ONE LLC
18451 Euclid Ave (44112-1016)
PHONE..................................216 432-4422
EMP: 31 **EST:** 2003
SQ FT: 30,000
SALES (est): 4.74MM **Privately Held**
Web: www.lefcoworthington.com
SIC: 4783 2441 4226 Packing and crating; Boxes, wood; Special warehousing and storage, nec

(G-4483)
LAWRENCE INDUSTRIES INC (PA)
4500 Lee Rd Ste 120 (44128-2959)
PHONE..................................216 518-7000
Lawrence A Kopittke Senior, *Pr*
Richard L Kopittke, *
Arthur Kopittke, *
♦ **EMP:** 50 **EST:** 1969
SQ FT: 160,000
SALES (est): 8.24MM
SALES (corp-wide): 8.24MM **Privately Held**
Web: www.lawrenceindustriesinc.com
SIC: 3599 3541 7699 5084 Machine shop, jobbing and repair; Sawing and cutoff machines (metalworking machinery); Tool repair services; Metalworking tools, nec (such as drills, taps, dies, files)

(G-4484)
LEGACY PROPERTIES INC (HQ)
Also Called: Weston Management Co
29300 Aurora Rd (44139-1810)
PHONE..................................440 349-9000
Anthony Asher, *Pr*
EMP: 28 **EST:** 1964
SQ FT: 10,000
SALES (est): 3.98MM
SALES (corp-wide): 37.76MM **Privately Held**
Web: www.teamweston.com
SIC: 6512 Commercial and industrial building operation
PA: Weston Inc.
4760 Richmond Rd Ste 200
Cleveland OH 44128
440 349-9000

(G-4485)
LEGACY VILLAGE MANAGEMENT LLC
25333 Cedar Rd Ste 303 (44124-3788)
PHONE..................................216 382-3871
Diane Kotowski, *Owner*
EMP: 55 **EST:** 2012
SALES (est): 5.5MM **Privately Held**
Web: www.legacy-village.com
SIC: 8741 Management services

(G-4486)
LEGAL AID SOCIETY OF CLEVELAND (PA)
1223 W 6th St Fl 4 (44113-1354)
PHONE..................................216 861-5500
Colleen Cotter, *Ex Dir*
Bettina Kaplan, *
Tom Mlakar, *
EMP: 60 **EST:** 1905
SQ FT: 25,200
SALES (est): 16.5MM
SALES (corp-wide): 16.5MM **Privately Held**
Web: www.lasclev.org
SIC: 8111 Legal aid service

(G-4487)
LEGAL SUPPORT SIMPLIFIED LLC
7703 Treelawn Dr (44141-1128)
PHONE..................................440 546-3368
EMP: 31 **EST:** 2010
SALES (est): 1.24MM **Privately Held**
SIC: 8111 Legal services

(G-4488)
LEGEND
3111 Carnegie Ave (44115-2632)
PHONE..................................216 534-1541
EMP: 70 **EST:** 2019
SALES (est): 3.62MM **Privately Held**
Web: www.legendheadwear.com
SIC: 5136 Men's and boy's clothing

(G-4489)
LERNER RES INST CLVLAND CLINIC
9500 Euclid Ave (44195-0001)
PHONE..................................216 444-3900
Paul E Dicorleto, *Prin*
EMP: 68 **EST:** 2014
SALES (est): 2.57MM **Privately Held**
Web: www.ccf.org
SIC: 8733 8732 Research institute; Research services, except laboratory

(G-4490)
LESCO INC (HQ)
1385 E 36th St (44114-4114)
PHONE..................................216 706-9250
Jeffrey L Rutherford, *Pr*
J Martin Erbaugh, *Ch Bd*
Bruce K Thorn, *Sr VP*
Michael A Weisbarth, *VP*
Kathleen M Minahan, *VP*
♦ **EMP:** 220 **EST:** 1962
SQ FT: 38,643
SALES (est): 185.05MM
SALES (corp-wide): 4.3B **Publicly Held**
Web: www.lesco.com
SIC: 5191 5083 5261 Grass seed; Lawn machinery and equipment; Retail nurseries
PA: Siteone Landscape Supply, Inc.
300 Colonial Center Pkwy # 6
Roswell GA 30076
470 277-7000

(G-4491)
LEVEL UP CUSTOM CNSTR INC
1588 E 40th St Ste C (44103-2379)
PHONE..................................888 505-9676
Mustafa Khabir, *CEO*
EMP: 28 **EST:** 2018
SALES (est): 1.34MM **Privately Held**
SIC: 1521 Single-family housing construction

(G-4492)
LIFEBANC
4775 Richmond Rd (44128-5919)
PHONE..................................216 752-5433
Gordon Bowen, *Ex Dir*
EMP: 81 **EST:** 1986
SQ FT: 2,100
SALES (est): 55.68MM **Privately Held**
Web: www.lifebanc.org
SIC: 8099 Organ bank

(G-4493)
LIFETIME VALUE LLC
486 Richmond Rd (44143-2746)
PHONE..................................216 544-3215
EMP: 31 **EST:** 2018
SALES (est): 2.02MM **Privately Held**
Web: www.ltvco.com
SIC: 8748 Business consulting, nec

(G-4494)
LIFETOUCH NAT SCHL STUDIOS INC
Also Called: Lifetouch
18683 Sheldon Rd (44130-2471)
P.O. Box 8001 (44811-8001)
PHONE..................................440 234-1337
Sue Cornosh, *Mgr*
EMP: 32
SALES (corp-wide): 2.47B **Privately Held**
Web: www.lifetouch.com
SIC: 7221 Photographer, still or video
HQ: Lifetouch National School Studios Inc.
11000 Viking Dr Ste 300
Eden Prairie MN 55344
952 826-4000

(G-4495)
LIGHT OF HEARTS VILLA INC
283 Union St Ofc (44146-4500)
PHONE..................................440 232-1991
EMP: 52 **EST:** 1987
SALES (est): 3.7MM **Privately Held**
Web: www.lightofheartsvilla.org
SIC: 8322 8052 Emergency shelters; Intermediate care facilities

(G-4496)
LILLIAN AND BETTY RATNER SCHL
27575 Shaker Blvd (44124-5002)
PHONE..................................216 464-0033
Sam Chestnut, *Head of School*
Mary Ann Breisch, *Associate Head of School*
EMP: 40 **EST:** 1982
SQ FT: 32,248
SALES (est): 2.82MM **Privately Held**
Web: www.theratnerschool.org
SIC: 8211 8351 Private elementary school; Montessori child development center

(G-4497)
LINCARE INC
9545 Midwest Ave Ste F (44125-2400)
PHONE..................................216 581-9649
Simone Lester, *Brnch Mgr*
EMP: 35
Web: www.lincare.com
SIC: 7352 5169 5047 Medical equipment rental; Oxygen; Hospital equipment and furniture
HQ: Lincare Inc.
19387 Us Highway 19 N
Clearwater FL 33764
727 530-7700

(G-4498)
LINKING EMPLYMENT ABLTIES PTNT (PA)
Also Called: Leap
2545 Lorain Ave (44113-3412)
PHONE..................................216 696-2716
Beth Glas, *Ex Dir*
Melanie Hogan, *
EMP: 36 **EST:** 1982
SQ FT: 9,000
SALES (est): 1.71MM
SALES (corp-wide): 1.71MM **Privately Held**
Web: www.leapinfo.org
SIC: 8331 Job counseling

(G-4499)
LINSALATA CPITL PRTNERS FUND I
5900 Landerbrook Dr Ste 280 (44124-4020)
PHONE..................................440 684-1400
Frank Linsalata, *Pt*
EMP: 42 **EST:** 2000
SALES (est): 666.35K **Privately Held**
Web: www.linsalatacapital.com
SIC: 6211 Brokers, security

(G-4500)
LITTLE BARK VIEW LIMITED (PA)
8111 Rockside Rd Ste 200 (44125-6135)
PHONE..................................216 520-1250
EMP: 30 **EST:** 1995
SQ FT: 5,480
SALES (est): 4.53MM **Privately Held**
Web: www.expiredwixdomain.com
SIC: 6513 Apartment building operators

(G-4501)
LIZZIES HSE SENIOR HM CARE LLC
48 Alpha Park (44143-2208)
PHONE..................................216 816-4188
Skye Griggs, *CEO*
Skye Griggs, *Managing Member*
EMP: 35 **EST:** 2018
SALES (est): 1.19MM **Privately Held**
SIC: 8082 Home health care services

(G-4502)
LLP GALLAGHER SHARP
1501 Euclid Ave (44115-2113)
PHONE..................................216 241-5310
EMP: 44 **EST:** 1912
SALES (est): 1.27MM **Privately Held**
Web: www.gallaghersharp.com
SIC: 8111 General practice attorney, lawyer

(G-4503)
LLP ZIEGLER METZGER
1111 Superior Ave E Ste 1000 (44114-2568)
PHONE..................................216 781-5470
Robert Metzger, *Mng Pt*
Richard Spotz Junior, *Pt*
Stephen M Darlington, *Pt*
William L Spring, *Pt*
Richard Spotz, *Pt*
EMP: 40 **EST:** 1952
SALES (est): 4.68MM **Privately Held**
Web: www.zieglermetzger.com
SIC: 8111 General practice attorney, lawyer

(G-4504)
LOGAN CLUTCH CORPORATION
Also Called: Lc
28855 Ranney Pkwy (44145-1173)
PHONE..................................440 808-4258
William A Logan, *Pr*
Madelon Logan, *
Elyse Logan, *
▲ **EMP:** 30 **EST:** 1975
SQ FT: 33,000
SALES (est): 8.06MM **Privately Held**
Web: www.loganclutch.com
SIC: 3568 5085 Clutches, except vehicular; Industrial supplies

(G-4505)
LONG TERM CARE OMBUDSMAN
8111 Rockside Rd Ste 250 (44125-6136)
PHONE..................................216 696-2719
Richard Martin, *Dir*
EMP: 33 **EST:** 1977
SALES (est): 1.05MM **Privately Held**
Web: www.ltco.org
SIC: 8322 Social service center

(G-4506)
LOWES HOME CENTERS LLC
Also Called: Lowe's
7327 Northcliff Ave (44144-3249)
PHONE..................................216 351-4723
Mike Hoffmeier, *Brnch Mgr*
EMP: 186
SALES (corp-wide): 86.38B **Publicly Held**
Web: www.lowes.com
SIC: 5211 5031 5722 5064 Home centers; Building materials, exterior; Household appliance stores; Electrical appliances, television and radio
HQ: Lowe's Home Centers, Llc
1000 Lowes Blvd
Mooresville NC 28117
336 658-4000

GEOGRAPHIC SECTION
Cleveland - Cuyahoga County (G-4530)

(G-4507)
LQ MANAGEMENT LLC
Also Called: La Quinta Inn
6161 Quarry Ln (44131-2203)
PHONE..................................216 447-1133
Virginia Klamut, *Brnch Mgr*
EMP: 27
SALES (corp-wide): 1.4B **Publicly Held**
Web: www.lq.com
SIC: 7011 Hotels and motels
HQ: Lq Management L.L.C.
909 Hidden Rdg Ste 600
Irving TX 75038
214 492-6600

(G-4508)
LTV-TRICO INC
25 W Prospect Ave (44115-1066)
PHONE..................................216 622-5000
EMP: 284 **EST:** 1995
SIC: 6719 Investment holding companies, except banks

(G-4509)
LU-JEAN FENG CLINIC LLC
31200 Pinetree Rd (44124-5928)
PHONE..................................216 831-7007
Lu Jean Feng, *Ltd Pt*
EMP: 41 **EST:** 2002
SALES (est): 9.42MM **Privately Held**
Web: www.fengclinic.com
SIC: 8011 Plastic surgeon

(G-4510)
LUTHERAN HOME
2116 Dover Center Rd (44145-3154)
PHONE..................................440 871-0090
Charles H Rinne, *CEO*
Henry Vogel, *
William E Seefeld, *
Carolyn Nyikes, *
Greg Wiechert, *
EMP: 280 **EST:** 1932
SQ FT: 120,000
SALES (est): 16.02MM **Privately Held**
Web: www.lec.org
SIC: 8052 8051 Intermediate care facilities; Skilled nursing care facilities

(G-4511)
LUTHERAN MEDICAL CENTER INC
Also Called: Cleveland Clinic
1730 W 25th St (44113-3108)
PHONE..................................216 696-4300
EMP: 216
SALES (corp-wide): 14.48B **Privately Held**
Web: www.lutheranhospital.org
SIC: 8062 8011 8069 General medical and surgical hospitals; Offices and clinics of medical doctors; Specialty hospitals, except psychiatric
HQ: Lutheran Medical Center Inc.
33001 Solon Rd Ste 112
Solon OH 44139
440 519-6800

(G-4512)
MAB HOME REMODELING LLC
621 Eddy Rd (44108-2337)
PHONE..................................216 761-1360
Michael Brooks, *Prin*
EMP: 29 **EST:** 2008
SALES (est): 1.9MM **Privately Held**
SIC: 1521 General remodeling, single-family houses

(G-4513)
MACDONALD HOSPITAL RESEAR
1110 Euclid Ave (44115-1623)
PHONE..................................216 844-3888
EMP: 45 **EST:** 2011
SALES (est): 690.11K **Privately Held**
SIC: 8062 General medical and surgical hospitals

(G-4514)
MACE PERSONAL DEF & SEC INC (HQ)
4400 Carnegie Ave (44103-4342)
PHONE..................................440 424-5321
Carl Smith, *CFO*
◆ **EMP:** 30 **EST:** 2002
SQ FT: 30,000
SALES (est): 6.79MM
SALES (corp-wide): 37.02MM **Publicly Held**
Web: www.mace.com
SIC: 3999 5065 Self-defense sprays; Security control equipment and systems
PA: Mace Security International, Inc.
4400 Carnegie Ave
Cleveland OH 44103
440 424-5325

(G-4515)
MAGNOLIA CLUBHOUSE INC
11101 Magnolia Dr (44106-1813)
PHONE..................................216 721-3030
Lori D'angelo, *Dir*
EMP: 39 **EST:** 2008
SQ FT: 20,000
SALES (est): 3.45MM **Privately Held**
Web: www.magnoliaclubhouse.org
SIC: 8063 Psychiatric hospitals

(G-4516)
MAINTHIA TECHNOLOGIES INC
Also Called: MTI
21000 Brookpark Rd (44135-3127)
PHONE..................................216 433-2198
Hemant Mainthia, *Pr*
EMP: 80
Web: www.mainthia.com
SIC: 1531 Operative builders
PA: Mainthia Technologies, Inc.
7055 Engle Rd Ste 502
Cleveland OH 44130

(G-4517)
MAJESTIC STEEL USA INC (PA)
Also Called: Majestic Steel Service
31099 Chagrin Blvd Ste 150 (44124-5930)
PHONE..................................440 786-2666
Todd Leebow, *Pr*
Tyler Hall, *
Jonathan Leebow, *
Susan Mahaffee, *
◆ **EMP:** 206 **EST:** 1979
SQ FT: 450,000
SALES (est): 473.49MM
SALES (corp-wide): 473.49MM **Privately Held**
Web: www.majesticsteel.com
SIC: 5051 Steel

(G-4518)
MALONEY + NOVOTNY LLC (PA)
1111 Superior Ave E Ste 700 (44114-2540)
PHONE..................................216 363-0100
Matthew Maloney, *Managing Member*
Peter J Chudyk, *
Timothy Novotny, *
Chris Felice, *
Diane Gallagher, *
EMP: 82 **EST:** 1930
SQ FT: 33,241
SALES (est): 13.49MM
SALES (corp-wide): 13.49MM **Privately Held**
Web: www.maloneynovotny.com
SIC: 8721 Certified public accountant

(G-4519)
MANCAN INC
6341 Pearl Rd (44130-3044)
PHONE..................................440 884-9675
EMP: 1399
SALES (corp-wide): 44.4MM **Privately Held**
Web: www.mancan.com
SIC: 8742 7361 Industrial and labor consulting services; Employment agencies
PA: Mancan, Inc.
48 1st St Nw
Massillon OH 44647
330 832-4595

(G-4520)
MANHEIM AUCTIONS INC
4720 Brookpark Rd (44134-1014)
P.O. Box 34360 (44134-0360)
PHONE..................................216 539-1701
Cleveland Manheim, *Prin*
EMP: 62
SALES (corp-wide): 16.61B **Privately Held**
SIC: 8011 Offices and clinics of medical doctors
HQ: Manheim Auctions, Inc.
6205-A Pchtree Dnwoody Rd
Atlanta GA 30328
866 626-4346

(G-4521)
MANSOUR GAVIN LPA
1001 Lakeside Ave E Ste 1400 (44114)
PHONE..................................216 523-1501
Ernest P Mansour, *Pr*
Jeffrey Embleton, *
Dale E Markworth, *
EMP: 60 **EST:** 1970
SALES (est): 6.76MM **Privately Held**
Web: www.mansourgavin.com
SIC: 8111 General practice attorney, lawyer

(G-4522)
MANUFACTURING ADVOCACY & GROWTH NETWORK INC (PA)
Also Called: MAGNET
1768 E 25th St (44114-4418)
PHONE..................................216 391-7002
EMP: 49 **EST:** 1984
SALES (est): 13.23MM
SALES (corp-wide): 13.23MM **Privately Held**
Web: www.manufacturingsuccess.org
SIC: 8742 Management consulting services

(G-4523)
MARCUS THOMAS LLC
Also Called: Devs United
4781 Richmond Rd (44128-5919)
PHONE..................................216 292-4700
Jim Nash, *Managing Member*
EMP: 99
SALES (corp-wide): 41.11MM **Privately Held**
Web: www.marcusthomasllc.com
SIC: 8742 7373 Management consulting services; Computer integrated systems design
PA: Marcus Thomas, Llc.
4781 Richmond Rd
Cleveland OH 44128
216 292-4700

(G-4524)
MARCUS THOMAS LLC (PA)
4781 Richmond Rd (44128-5919)
PHONE..................................216 292-4700
Jim Nash, *Pr*
Harvey Scholnick, *
James B Nash, *
Joseph J Blaha, *
Ira Thomas, *
EMP: 94 **EST:** 1937
SQ FT: 26,000
SALES (est): 41.11MM
SALES (corp-wide): 41.11MM **Privately Held**
Web: www.marcusthomasllc.com
SIC: 7311 Advertising consultant

(G-4525)
MARRIOTT
7345 Engle Rd (44130-3430)
PHONE..................................440 243-8785
Jerry Clement, *Prin*
EMP: 32 **EST:** 2007
SALES (est): 945.24K **Privately Held**
Web: www.marriott.com
SIC: 7011 Hotels and motels

(G-4526)
MARRIOTT
Also Called: Residence Inn Cleveland Airpor
17525 Rosbough Blvd (44130-2580)
PHONE..................................440 234-6688
Kathy Sellers, *Prin*
EMP: 30 **EST:** 2007
SALES (est): 498.39K **Privately Held**
Web: www.marriott.com
SIC: 7011 Hotels and motels

(G-4527)
MARRIOTT HOTEL SERVICES INC
Also Called: Marriott
4277 W 150th St (44135-1310)
PHONE..................................216 252-5333
Greg Huber, *Genl Mgr*
EMP: 189
SALES (corp-wide): 23.71B **Publicly Held**
Web: www.marriott.com
SIC: 7011 5812 5947 5813 Hotels and motels ; Eating places; Gift, novelty, and souvenir shop; Drinking places
HQ: Marriott Hotel Services, Inc.
10400 Fernwood Rd
Bethesda MD 20817

(G-4528)
MARRIOTT INTERNATIONAL INC
Also Called: Marriott
127 Public Sq Fl 1 (44114-1216)
PHONE..................................216 696-9200
Bob Megazzini, *Mgr*
EMP: 33
SALES (corp-wide): 23.71B **Publicly Held**
Web: www.marriott.com
SIC: 7011 Hotels and motels
PA: Marriott International, Inc.
7750 Wisconsin Ave
Bethesda MD 20814
301 380-3000

(G-4529)
MARS ELECTRIC COMPANY (PA)
6655 Beta Dr Ste 200 (44143-2380)
PHONE..................................440 946-2250
Mark Doris, *Pr*
EMP: 65 **EST:** 1952
SQ FT: 43,000
SALES (est): 111.05MM
SALES (corp-wide): 111.05MM **Privately Held**
Web: www.marselectric.com
SIC: 5063 5719 Electrical supplies, nec; Lighting fixtures

(G-4530)
MARYMOUNT HEALTH CARE SYSTEMS
Also Called: CLEVELAND CLINIC HEALTH SYSTEM

Cleveland - Cuyahoga County (G-4531)   GEOGRAPHIC SECTION

13900 Mccracken Rd (44125-1902)
PHONE.................................216 332-1100
Peggy Matthews, *Admn*
EMP: 975 **EST:** 1983
SQ FT: 411,000
SALES (est): 2.1MM
SALES (corp-wide): 14.48B **Privately Held**
SIC: 8059 8741 Convalescent home; Hospital management
PA: The Cleveland Clinic Foundation
9500 Euclid Ave
Cleveland OH 44195
216 636-8335

(G-4531)
MARYMOUNT HOSPITAL INC (HQ)
9500 Euclid Ave (44195-0001)
PHONE.................................216 581-0500
David Kilarski, *Pr*
▲ **EMP:** 445 **EST:** 1961
SQ FT: 411,000
SALES (est): 149.57MM
SALES (corp-wide): 14.48B **Privately Held**
Web: www.marymount.org
SIC: 8062 8063 8051 8082 General medical and surgical hospitals; Psychiatric hospitals; Skilled nursing care facilities; Home health care services
PA: The Cleveland Clinic Foundation
9500 Euclid Ave
Cleveland OH 44195
216 636-8335

(G-4532)
MAYFIELD CNTRY CLB SCHLRSHIP F
1545 Sheridan Rd (44121-4074)
PHONE.................................216 381-0826
Gina Palich, *Prin*
EMP: 29 **EST:** 2011
SALES (est): 498.72K **Privately Held**
Web: www.mayfieldsandridge.com
SIC: 7997 Country club, membership

(G-4533)
MAZANEC RASKIN & RYDER CO LPA (PA)
Also Called: Mazanec Raskin & Ryder
34305 Solon Rd Ste 100 (44139-2660)
PHONE.................................440 248-7906
Todd M Raskin, *Pr*
Thomas S Mazanec, *
Edward M Ryder, *
EMP: 70 **EST:** 1980
SALES (est): 9.57MM **Privately Held**
Web: www.mrrlaw.com
SIC: 8111 General practice attorney, lawyer

(G-4534)
MAZZELLA HOLDING COMPANY INC (PA)
Also Called: Mazella Companies
21000 Aerospace Pkwy (44142-1000)
PHONE.................................513 772-4466
EMP: 53 **EST:** 2011
SALES (est): 140.8MM **Privately Held**
Web: www.mazzellacompanies.com
SIC: 5051 5085 5088 5072 Rope, wire (not insulated); Industrial supplies; Marine supplies; Builders' hardware, nec

(G-4535)
MC CORMACK ADVISORS INTL
1360 E 9th St Ste 100 (44114-1730)
PHONE.................................216 522-1200
Rodney I Woods, *CEO*
Gerald Gray, *
Raymond G Banta, *
EMP: 47 **EST:** 1973
SALES (est): 2.71MM **Privately Held**
SIC: 6282 Investment counselors

(G-4536)
MCDONALD HOPKINS LLC (PA)
600 Superior Ave E Ste 2100 (44114-2690)
PHONE.................................216 348-5400
John Metzger, *
William J O Neill, *
Steven Harris, *
Shawn M Riley, *
EMP: 175 **EST:** 1933
SQ FT: 80,000
SALES (est): 46.8MM
SALES (corp-wide): 46.8MM **Privately Held**
Web: www.mcdonaldhopkins.com
SIC: 8111 General practice law office

(G-4537)
MCGOWAN & COMPANY INC (PA)
Also Called: McGowan Program Administrators
20595 Lorain Rd Ste 300 (44126)
PHONE.................................800 545-1538
Thomas B Mcgowan Iv, *Pr*
EMP: 61 **EST:** 1958
SQ FT: 48,000
SALES (est): 45.11MM
SALES (corp-wide): 45.11MM **Privately Held**
Web: www.mcgowancompanies.com
SIC: 6411 Insurance agents, nec

(G-4538)
MCGREGOR FOUNDATION
14900 Private Dr (44112-3438)
PHONE.................................216 851-8200
Ann Conn, *CEO*
Robertson Hilton, *
Rob Hilton, *
Sue W Neff, *
Kimberly Henderson, *
EMP: 275 **EST:** 1904
SALES (est): 20.51MM **Privately Held**
Web: www.mcgregoramasa.org
SIC: 8051 Skilled nursing care facilities

(G-4539)
MCGREGOR PACE
2390 E 79th St (44104-2161)
PHONE.................................216 361-0917
EMP: 29
SALES (corp-wide): 56.42MM **Privately Held**
Web: www.mcgregorpace.org
SIC: 8082 Home health care services
PA: Mcgregor Pace
2373 Euclid Heights Blvd
Cleveland OH 44106
216 791-3580

(G-4540)
MCGREGOR PACE
26310 Emery Rd (44128-5735)
PHONE.................................216 791-3580
EMP: 29
SALES (corp-wide): 56.42MM **Privately Held**
Web: www.mcgregorpace.org
SIC: 8082 Home health care services
PA: Mcgregor Pace
2373 Euclid Heights Blvd
Cleveland OH 44106
216 791-3580

(G-4541)
MCI COMMUNICATIONS SVCS LLC
Also Called: Verizon Business
21000 Brookpark Rd (44135-3127)
PHONE.................................216 265-9953
David Fleming, *Brnch Mgr*
EMP: 41
SALES (corp-wide): 136.84B **Publicly Held**
SIC: 4813 Long distance telephone communications
HQ: Mci Communications Services Llc
22001 Loudoun County Pkwy
Ashburn VA 20147
703 886-5600

(G-4542)
MCPHILLIPS PLBG HTG & AC CO
Also Called: Honeywell Authorized Dealer
16115 Waterloo Rd (44110-1665)
PHONE.................................216 481-1400
Sean Mcphillips, *Pr*
EMP: 35 **EST:** 1907
SQ FT: 8,000
SALES (est): 4.48MM **Privately Held**
Web: mcphillips.comuf.com
SIC: 1731 1711 7623 Energy management controls; Boiler maintenance contractor; Refrigeration service and repair

(G-4543)
MEADEN & MOORE LLP (PA)
1375 E 9th St Ste 1800 (44114-2523)
PHONE.................................216 241-3272
James P Carulas, *Pr*
Larry J Holland, *Pr*
David E Daywalt, *VP*
Theodore C Hocevar, *VP*
Roman Kovach, *Contrlr*
EMP: 90 **EST:** 1919
SQ FT: 27,000
SALES (est): 11.13K
SALES (corp-wide): 11.13K **Privately Held**
Web: www.meadenmoore.com
SIC: 8721 Certified public accountant

(G-4544)
MEDICAL ASSESSMENTS LLC
5035 Mayfield Rd Ste 210 (44124-2603)
PHONE.................................216 397-0917
EMP: 45
SIC: 8011 8031 Neurologist; Offices and clinics of osteopathic physicians
PA: Medical Assessments, Llc
4955 Countryside Rd
Cleveland OH 44124

(G-4545)
MEDICAL MUTUAL OF OHIO (PA)
2060 E 9th St (44115-1355)
PHONE.................................216 687-7000
Rick A Chiricosta, *Ch*
Richard A Chiricosta, *
Raymond K Mueller, *
Patricia B Decensi, *
Charles A Bryan, *
EMP: 1400 **EST:** 1934
SQ FT: 381,000
SALES (est): 2.75B
SALES (corp-wide): 2.75B **Privately Held**
Web: www.medmutual.com
SIC: 6411 Insurance agents, nec

(G-4546)
MEDICAL MUTUAL OF OHIO
Also Called: Antares Management Solutions
100 American Rd (44144-2322)
PHONE.................................216 292-0400
Robert Trombly, *Brnch Mgr*
EMP: 118
SALES (corp-wide): 2.75B **Privately Held**
Web: www.medmutual.com
SIC: 6411 6321 Insurance agents, nec; Accident and health insurance carriers
PA: Medical Mutual Of Ohio
2060 E 9th St
Cleveland OH 44115
216 687-7000

(G-4547)
MEDLINK OF OHIO INC (DH)
20600 Chagrin Blvd Ste 290 (44122-5327)
PHONE.................................216 751-5900
Stuart R Russell, *Pr*
Donald G Foster, *
EMP: 400 **EST:** 1988
SQ FT: 1,200
SALES (est): 14.6MM
SALES (corp-wide): 371.62B **Publicly Held**
SIC: 8049 8082 Nurses, registered and practical; Home health care services
HQ: Almost Family, Inc.
9510 Ormsby Station Rd # 300
Louisville KY 40223
502 891-1000

(G-4548)
MEDVET ASSOCIATES LLC
Also Called: Medvet Cleveland West
14000 Keystone Pkwy (44135-5170)
PHONE.................................216 362-6000
Kristen Wagner, *Brnch Mgr*
EMP: 114
Web: www.medvet.com
SIC: 0742 Animal hospital services, pets and other animal specialties
PA: Medvet Associates, Llc
350 E Wilson Bridge Rd
Worthington OH 43085

(G-4549)
MEI HOTELS INCORPORATED
1375 E 9th St Ste 2800 (44114-1795)
PHONE.................................216 589-0441
EMP: 250 **EST:** 1998
SALES (est): 16.4MM **Privately Held**
Web: www.meihotels.com
SIC: 8741 6512 Hotel or motel management; Commercial and industrial building operation

(G-4550)
MENORAH PK CTR FOR SNIOR LVING (PA)
27100 Cedar Rd (44122-1109)
PHONE.................................216 831-6500
Ira Kaplan, *Pr*
Steven Raichilson, *
Enid Roseinberg, *
EMP: 920 **EST:** 1906
SQ FT: 242,000
SALES (est): 39.28MM
SALES (corp-wide): 39.28MM **Privately Held**
Web: www.menorahpark.org
SIC: 8051 6513 8322 Skilled nursing care facilities; Apartment building operators; Outreach program

(G-4551)
MENTAL HLTH SVCS FOR HMLESS PR (PA)
Also Called: FRONTLINE SERVICE
1744 Payne Ave (44114-2910)
PHONE.................................216 623-6555
Steve Friedman, *Ex Dir*
EMP: 163 **EST:** 1989
SQ FT: 7,500
SALES (est): 29.05MM **Privately Held**
Web: www.frontlineservice.org
SIC: 8093 Mental health clinic, outpatient

(G-4552)
MENTOR REM
9775 Rockside Rd Ste 200 (44125-6266)
PHONE.................................216 642-5339
Mary Kay Ziccardi, *Prin*
EMP: 7296 **EST:** 2007

GEOGRAPHIC SECTION
Cleveland - Cuyahoga County (G-4573)

SALES (est): 2.38MM
SALES (corp-wide): 1.64B **Privately Held**
SIC: 8322 Social service center
HQ: Nmh Investment, Llc
  313 Congress St Fl 5
  Boston MA 02210

(G-4553)
MENZIES AVIATION (TEXAS) INC
5921 Cargo Rd (44135-3111)
P.O. Box 81145 (44181-0145)
PHONE..............................216 265-3777
Paul Yagel, *Brnch Mgr*
EMP: 92
SALES (corp-wide): 23.68MM **Privately Held**
Web: www.menziesaviation.com
SIC: 4581 Airports, flying fields, and services
HQ: Menzies Aviation (Texas), Inc.
  3500 William D Tate Ave # 200
  Grapevine TX 76051
  469 281-8200

(G-4554)
MERIT BRASS CO (PA)
Also Called: Merit Brass
  1 Merit Dr (44143-1457)
P.O. Box 43127 (44143-0127)
PHONE..............................216 261-9800
▲ EMP: 236 EST: 1961
SALES (est): 44.19MM
SALES (corp-wide): 44.19MM **Privately Held**
Web: www.meritbrass.com
SIC: 3432 5051 5074 Plumbing fixture fittings and trim; Metals service centers and offices; Plumbing fittings and supplies

(G-4555)
MERIT LEASING CO LLC
Also Called: Grande Pointe Healthcare Cmnty
  3 Merit Dr (44143-1457)
PHONE..............................216 261-9592
Stephen L Rosedale, *Managing Member*
Charles R Stoltz, *MBA CPA CMA*
EMP: 52 EST: 2004
SQ FT: 62,000
SALES (est): 12.96MM **Privately Held**
Web: www.communicarehealth.com
SIC: 8051 Convalescent home with continuous nursing care

(G-4556)
MERITECH INC (PA)
4577 Hinckley Industrial Pkwy (44109)
PHONE..............................216 459-8333
David Duran, *CEO*
Dennis Bednar, *
Mary Ann Bednar, *
EMP: 98 EST: 1983
SQ FT: 30,000
SALES (est): 92.94MM
SALES (corp-wide): 92.94MM **Privately Held**
Web: www.deximaging.com
SIC: 5044 Copying equipment

(G-4557)
MESSINA FLOOR COVERING LLC
Also Called: MFC
  4300 Brookpark Rd Ste 1 (44134-1138)
PHONE..............................216 595-0100
EMP: 75 EST: 1975
SALES (est): 19.35MM **Privately Held**
Web: www.messinaflooring.com
SIC: 5023 1752 Floor coverings; Floor laying and floor work, nec

(G-4558)
METAL FRAMING ENTERPRISES LLC
Also Called: Frameco
  9005 Bank St (44125-3425)
PHONE..............................216 433-7080
EMP: 29 EST: 2007
SQ FT: 3,300
SALES (est): 3MM **Privately Held**
SIC: 1751 Framing contractor

(G-4559)
METLIFE LEGAL PLANS INC
Also Called: Hyatt Legal Plans, Inc.
  1111 Superior Ave E Ste 800 (44114-2541)
PHONE..............................216 241-0022
William H Brooks, *Pr*
Mike Penzner, *Treas*
Andrew Kohn, *VP Opers*
EMP: 96 EST: 1990
SQ FT: 20,000
SALES (est): 26.21MM
SALES (corp-wide): 66.91B **Publicly Held**
Web: www.legalplans.com
SIC: 6411 Insurance brokers, nec
HQ: Metropolitan Life Insurance Company
  200 Park Ave Fl 4
  New York NY 10166
  908 253-1000

(G-4560)
METRO HEALTH DENTAL ASSOCIATES
2500 Metrohealth Dr (44109-1900)
PHONE..............................216 778-4982
Terry White, *CEO*
EMP: 233 EST: 2002
SALES (est): 12.26MM **Privately Held**
Web: www.metrohealth.org
SIC: 8021 Offices and clinics of dentists

(G-4561)
METROHEALTH SYSTEM
Also Called: Metrohealth Buckeye Health Ctr
  2816 E 116th St (44120-2111)
PHONE..............................216 957-4000
E Harry Walker, *Dir*
EMP: 391
SALES (corp-wide): 620.72MM **Privately Held**
Web: www.metrohealth.org
SIC: 8062 4119 Hospital, affiliated with AMA residency; Ambulance service
PA: The Metrohealth System
  2500 Metrohealth Dr
  Cleveland OH 44109
  216 778-7800

(G-4562)
METROHEALTH SYSTEM
Also Called: Metrohealth Broadway Hlth Ctr
  6835 Broadway Ave (44105-1313)
PHONE..............................216 957-1500
Anne C Sowell, *Brnch Mgr*
EMP: 639
SALES (corp-wide): 620.72MM **Privately Held**
Web: www.metrohealth.org
SIC: 8062 8021 General medical and surgical hospitals; Offices and clinics of dentists
PA: The Metrohealth System
  2500 Metrohealth Dr
  Cleveland OH 44109
  216 778-7800

(G-4563)
METROHEALTH SYSTEM
Also Called: Metrohealth
  4229 Pearl Rd (44109-4218)
PHONE..............................216 957-2100
Rob Kubasak, *Brnch Mgr*
EMP: 426
SALES (corp-wide): 620.72MM **Privately Held**
Web: www.metrohealth.org
SIC: 8069 0783 Cancer hospital; Surgery services, ornamental tree
PA: The Metrohealth System
  2500 Metrohealth Dr
  Cleveland OH 44109
  216 778-7800

(G-4564)
METROHEALTH SYSTEM
Also Called: Metrohealth West Park Hlth Ctr
  3838 W 150th St (44111-5805)
PHONE..............................216 957-5000
Thomas Ginley, *Prin*
EMP: 249
SALES (corp-wide): 620.72MM **Privately Held**
Web: www.metrohealth.org
SIC: 8093 8099 9221 Specialty outpatient clinics, nec; Medical rescue squad; Police protection
PA: The Metrohealth System
  2500 Metrohealth Dr
  Cleveland OH 44109
  216 778-7800

(G-4565)
METROHEALTH SYSTEM
Also Called: Ovatient
  2150 W 117th St Ste 1238 (44111-1641)
PHONE..............................216 598-9908
Michael Dalton, *CEO*
EMP: 177
SALES (corp-wide): 620.72MM **Privately Held**
Web: www.metrohealth.org
SIC: 8011 Primary care medical clinic
PA: The Metrohealth System
  2500 Metrohealth Dr
  Cleveland OH 44109
  216 778-7800

(G-4566)
METROHEALTH SYSTEM
Also Called: Department of Ob/Gyn
  2500 Metrohealth Dr (44109-1900)
PHONE..............................216 778-8446
Brian Mercer Md, *Brnch Mgr*
EMP: 106
SALES (corp-wide): 620.72MM **Privately Held**
Web: www.metrohealth.org
SIC: 8011 8093 Obstetrician; Rehabilitation center, outpatient treatment
PA: The Metrohealth System
  2500 Metrohealth Dr
  Cleveland OH 44109
  216 778-7800

(G-4567)
METROHEALTH SYSTEM
Also Called: Metrohealth
  2500 Metrohealth Dr (44109-1900)
PHONE..............................216 778-3867
EMP: 177
SALES (corp-wide): 620.72MM **Privately Held**
Web: www.metrohealth.org
SIC: 4119 6324 8069 Ambulance service; Hospital and medical service plans; Childrens' hospital
PA: The Metrohealth System
  2500 Metrohealth Dr
  Cleveland OH 44109
  216 778-7800

(G-4568)
METROPOLITAN HOTEL LLC
2017 E 9th St (44115-1315)
PHONE..............................216 239-1200
Keith Halfmann, *Prin*
EMP: 65 EST: 2014
SALES (est): 8.47MM **Privately Held**
Web: www.metropolitancleveland.com
SIC: 7011 Hotels

(G-4569)
METROPOLITAN SECURITY SVCS INC
Also Called: Walden Security
  801 W Superior Ave (44113-1829)
PHONE..............................216 298-4076
EMP: 145
Web: www.waldensecurity.com
SIC: 7381 Security guard service
PA: Metropolitan Security Services, Inc.
  100 E 10th St Ste 400
  Chattanooga TN 37402

(G-4570)
MFBUSINESS GROUP
Also Called: Fontaine Bleu'
  3915 Carnegie Ave (44115-2719)
  Rural Route 5214 Thomas St (44137)
PHONE..............................216 609-7297
Manuel Isler-freeman, *CEO*
Manuel Isler-freeman, *Dir*
Donnell Isler-freeman, *Dir*
EMP: 50 EST: 2016
SALES (est): 1.27MM **Privately Held**
SIC: 8741 5812 Business management; Restaurant, family: chain

(G-4571)
MFH PARTNERS INC (PA)
6650 Beta Dr (44143-2352)
P.O. Box 43038 (44143-0045)
PHONE..............................440 461-4100
J D Sullivan, *Ch Bd*
Carron Redena, *
EMP: 279 EST: 2004
SQ FT: 4,000
SALES (est): 32.04MM
SALES (corp-wide): 32.04MM **Privately Held**
SIC: 5084 3535 3568 2296 Industrial machinery and equipment; Belt conveyor systems, general industrial use; Power transmission equipment, nec; Tire cord and fabrics

(G-4572)
MICELI DAIRY PRODUCTS CO (PA)
2721 E 90th St (44104-3396)
PHONE..............................216 791-6222
Joseph D Miceli, *CEO*
John J Miceli Junior, *Ex VP*
Joseph Lograsso, *
Charles Surace, *
Carol Lograsso, *
▲ EMP: 90 EST: 1946
SQ FT: 25,000
SALES (est): 42.47MM
SALES (corp-wide): 42.47MM **Privately Held**
Web: www.miceli-dairy.com
SIC: 2022 0241 Natural cheese; Milk production

(G-4573)
MICHAEL BAKER INTL INC
1111 Superior Ave E Ste 230 (44114-2522)
PHONE..............................412 269-6300
Steven Collar, *Mgr*
EMP: 44
SALES (corp-wide): 1.04B **Privately Held**

Cleveland - Cuyahoga County (G-4574) GEOGRAPHIC SECTION

SIC: **8711** 8741 Civil engineering; Management services
HQ: Michael Baker International, Inc.
500 Grant St Ste 5400
Pittsburgh PA 15219
412 269-6300

(G-4574)
MID-AMERICA CONSULTING GROUP INC
3700 Euclid Ave 2 (44115-2502)
EMP: 85 **EST:** 1988
SALES (est): 4.28MM **Privately Held**
SIC: 7373 8742 Systems software development services; Management consulting services

(G-4575)
MID-AMERICA STEEL CORP
Also Called: Mid-America Stainless
20900 Saint Clair Ave Rear (44117-1130)
PHONE..................800 282-3466
EMP: 50
Web: www.masteel.com
SIC: 5051 3469 3316 3312 Steel; Metal stampings, nec; Cold finishing of steel shapes; Blast furnaces and steel mills

(G-4576)
MID-WEST PRESORT MAILING SERVICES INC (PA)
Also Called: Mid-West Direct
2222 W 110th St (44102-3512)
PHONE..................216 251-2500
EMP: 200 **EST:** 1982
SALES (est): 25.12MM
SALES (corp-wide): 25.12MM **Privately Held**
Web: www.midwestdirect.com
SIC: 7331 Mailing service

(G-4577)
MIDDOUGH INC (PA)
1901 E 13th St Ste 400 (44114-3542)
PHONE..................216 367-6000
Ronald Ledin, *CEO*
Carl Wendell, *
Daniel Lowry Junior, *VP*
Gregory Difrank, *
Richard Hayes, *
EMP: 390 **EST:** 1950
SQ FT: 120,000
SALES (est): 86.29MM
SALES (corp-wide): 86.29MM **Privately Held**
Web: www.middough.com
SIC: 8711 8712 Consulting engineer; Architectural engineering

(G-4578)
MIDLAND TITLE SECURITY INC (DH)
Also Called: First Amrcn Ttle Midland Title
1111 Superior Ave E Ste 700 (44114-2540)
PHONE..................216 241-6045
Diane Davies, *Mgr*
EMP: 100 **EST:** 1955
SALES (est): 159.43MM **Publicly Held**
Web: www.midlandtitle.com
SIC: 6361 Real estate title insurance
HQ: First American Title Insurance Company
1 First American Way
Santa Ana CA 92707
800 854-3643

(G-4579)
MIDTOWN INVESTMENT CO
Also Called: Midtown Towers
5676 Broadview Rd Apt 127 (44134-1639)
PHONE..................216 398-7210
EMP: 53
Web: rent.brookfieldproperties.com
SIC: 6513 Apartment building operators
PA: Midtown Investment Co
2121 S Green Rd Ste 200
Cleveland OH 44121

(G-4580)
MIDWEST CURTAINWALLS INC
5171 Grant Ave (44125-1031)
PHONE..................216 641-7900
Donald F Kelly Junior, *Pr*
EMP: 80 **EST:** 1986
SQ FT: 55,000
SALES (est): 20.39MM
SALES (corp-wide): 21.41MM **Privately Held**
Web: www.midwestcurtainwalls.com
SIC: 3449 3442 1751 Curtain wall, metal; Window and door frames; Window and door (prefabricated) installation
PA: Innovest Global, Inc.
8834 Mayfield Rd
Chesterland OH 44026
216 815-1122

(G-4581)
MILES ALLOYS INC
13800 Miles Ave (44105-5594)
PHONE..................216 295-1000
Michael Shubert, *Pr*
EMP: 30 **EST:** 1966
SQ FT: 30,000
SALES (est): 10MM **Privately Held**
Web: www.milesalloys.com
SIC: 4953 Recycling, waste materials

(G-4582)
MILES CLEANING SERVICES INC
Also Called: Coit
23580 Miles Rd (44128-5433)
PHONE..................216 626-0040
Harvey Siegel, *Pr*
Adrian Siegal, *
EMP: 50 **EST:** 1934
SQ FT: 22,000
SALES (est): 4.1MM **Privately Held**
Web: www.coit.com
SIC: 7217 7216 7349 Carpet and furniture cleaning on location; Drapery, curtain drycleaning; Air duct cleaning

(G-4583)
MILL SUPPLY INC
19801 Miles Rd (44128)
P.O. Box 28750 (44128)
PHONE..................216 518-5072
EMP: 30 **EST:** 1944
SALES (est): 7.29MM **Privately Held**
Web: www.millsupply.com
SIC: 5013 Automotive supplies and parts

(G-4584)
MILLENNIA COMMERCIAL GROUP LTD
127 Public Sq (44114-1217)
PHONE..................216 520-1250
EMP: 99 **EST:** 2018
SALES (est): 5.16MM **Privately Held**
Web: www.themillenniacompanies.com
SIC: 6513 Apartment building operators

(G-4585)
MILLENNIA HOUSING MGT LTD (PA)
4000 Key Tower 127 Public Sq (44114)
PHONE..................216 520-1250
Frank Sinito, *CEO*
John Mcginty, *CFO*
Barry P Weaver, *
Lee J Felgar, *
EMP: 133 **EST:** 1995
SALES (est): 198.28MM
SALES (corp-wide): 198.28MM **Privately Held**
Web: www.mhmltd.com
SIC: 6513 6531 Apartment building operators; Rental agent, real estate

(G-4586)
MILLMAN SURVEYING INC (HQ)
Also Called: Millman National Land Services
950 Main Ave (44113-7201)
PHONE..................330 296-9017
Vincent Macauda, *Pr*
EMP: 44 **EST:** 1996
SALES (est): 8.36MM **Publicly Held**
Web: www.millmanland.com
SIC: 8713 Surveying services
PA: Cbre Group, Inc.
2100 Mcknney Ave Ste 1250
Dallas TX 75201

(G-4587)
MINISTERIAL DAY CARE ASSN (PA)
Also Called: MINISTERIAL DARE CARE
7020 Superior Ave (44103-2638)
PHONE..................216 881-6924
Verneda Bentley, *Ex Dir*
EMP: 30 **EST:** 1970
SQ FT: 15,000
SALES (est): 1.09MM
SALES (corp-wide): 1.09MM **Privately Held**
SIC: 8351 8741 Group day care center; Management services

(G-4588)
MINISTERIAL DAY CARE-HEADSTART
Also Called: MINISTERIAL DAY CARE-HEADSTART
8409 Hough Ave (44103-4248)
PHONE..................216 707-0344
India Perry, *Brnch Mgr*
EMP: 178
SALES (corp-wide): 1.09MM **Privately Held**
SIC: 8351 Head Start center, except in conjunction with school
PA: Day Ministerial Care Association
7020 Superior Ave
Cleveland OH 44103
216 881-6924

(G-4589)
MINUTE MEN INC (PA)
Also Called: Minute Men of FL
3740 Carnegie Ave Ste 201 (44115)
PHONE..................216 426-2225
Samuel Lucarelli, *Pr*
Sam Lucarelli, *
Jason Lucarelli, *
EMP: 60 **EST:** 1967
SQ FT: 5,000
SALES (est): 22.67MM
SALES (corp-wide): 22.67MM **Privately Held**
Web: www.minutemenstaffing.com
SIC: 7363 Temporary help service

(G-4590)
MINUTE MEN SELECT INC
3740 Carnegie Ave Ste 201 (44115-2756)
PHONE..................216 452-0100
Jason S Lucarelli, *CEO*
Matthew Wilkins, *
Steve Sprankel, *
EMP: 50 **EST:** 2009
SALES (est): 2.56MM **Privately Held**
Web: www.minutemenhr.com
SIC: 7363 Temporary help service

(G-4591)
MOBILE HYPERBARIC CENTERS LLC
1375 E 9th St Ste 1850 (44114-1739)
PHONE..................216 443-0430
Charles Cowape, *CEO*
Ronald Gordon, *CEO*
Christy Mattey, *Prin*
EMP: 47 **EST:** 2005
SALES (est): 4.25MM **Privately Held**
SIC: 8082 Home health care services

(G-4592)
MOBILE HYPERBARIC CENTERS LLC
600 Superior Ave E Ste 2400 (44114-2691)
PHONE..................216 443-0430
Charles Cowap, *Pr*
EMP: 33 **EST:** 2015
SALES (est): 6.09MM **Privately Held**
Web: www.mhcenters.com
SIC: 8099 Health and allied services, nec

(G-4593)
MODERN BUILDERS SUPPLY INC
4549 Industrial Pkwy (44135-4541)
PHONE..................216 273-3605
Bryan Blasko, *Mgr*
EMP: 37
SQ FT: 53,842
SALES (corp-wide): 346.23MM **Privately Held**
Web: www.modernbuilderssupply.com
SIC: 5033 5211 Siding, except wood; Lumber and other building materials
PA: Modern Builders Supply, Inc.
3500 Phillips Ave
Toledo OH 43608
419 241-3961

(G-4594)
MODERN BUSINESS ASSOCIATES INC
5801 Postal Rd (44181-2184)
PHONE..................727 563-1500
Mark P Lettelleir, *Pr*
Fred Razook, *
Marjorie Seltzer, *
Paul Wilbur, *
EMP: 100 **EST:** 1900
SALES (est): 8.79MM **Privately Held**
Web: www.decisionhr.com
SIC: 8742 Human resource consulting services

(G-4595)
MODERN HIRE INC (DH)
Also Called: Modern Hire
3201 Enterprise Pkwy Ste 460 (44122)
PHONE..................216 292-0202
Brian Stern, *Pr*
Scott Goodman, *Ex VP*
Michael J Hudy, *Ex VP*
Dennis Deuberry, *CFO*
Tony Anello, *CCO*
EMP: 46 **EST:** 2002
SQ FT: 5,040
SALES (est): 13.29MM
SALES (corp-wide): 2.96B **Publicly Held**
Web: www.hirevue.com
SIC: 8748 Business consulting, nec
HQ: Hirevue, Inc.
10876 S Rver Front Pkwy S
South Jordan UT 84095
801 316-2910

(G-4596)
MONARCH ELECTRIC SERVICE CO (HQ)
5325 W 130th St (44130-1034)

PHONE.....................216 433-7800
John Zuleger, CEO
Tim Jeans, *
George E Roller, *
Brad Roller, *
Kevin George, *
◆ EMP: 80 EST: 1958
SQ FT: 55,000
SALES (est): 11.38MM **Privately Held**
Web: www.monarch-electric.com
SIC: 7699 5063 Industrial machinery and equipment repair; Electrical apparatus and equipment
PA: Integrated Power Services Llc
250 Exctive Ctr Dr Ste 20
Greenville SC 29615

(G-4597)
MONARCH INV & MGT GROUP LLC
Also Called: Brick Loft At Historic W Tech
2201 W 93rd St (44102-3778)
PHONE.....................216 453-3630
EMP: 1100
Web: www.westtech-lofts.com
SIC: 6531 Real estate managers
PA: Monarch Investment & Management Group, Llc
2195 N State Highway 83 # 14
Franktown CO 80116

(G-4598)
MONARCH STEEL COMPANY INC
Also Called: Monarch
4650 Johnston Pkwy (44128-3219)
PHONE.....................216 587-8000
Josh Kaufman, CEO
Robert L Meyer, *
Steve Lefkowitz, *
▲ EMP: 40 EST: 1934
SQ FT: 118,000
SALES (est): 16.75MM **Privately Held**
Web: www.monarchsteel.com
SIC: 5051 5049 3353 Steel; Precision tools; Coils, sheet aluminum
PA: American Consolidated Industries, Inc.
4650 Johnston Pkwy
Cleveland OH 44128

(G-4599)
MORGAN SERVICES INC
Also Called: Morgan Uniforms & Linen Rental
2013 Columbus Rd (44113-3553)
PHONE.....................216 241-3107
Larry Cooper, Genl Mgr
EMP: 134
SQ FT: 15,000
SALES (corp-wide): 72.96MM **Privately Held**
Web: www.morganservices.com
SIC: 7213 7218 Linen supply; Industrial uniform supply
PA: Morgan Services, Inc.
323 N Michigan Ave
Chicago IL 60601
312 346-3181

(G-4600)
MORGAN STNLEY SMITH BARNEY LLC
31099 Chagrin Blvd Fl 3 (44124-5959)
PHONE.....................216 360-4900
EMP: 133
SALES (corp-wide): 54.14B **Publicly Held**
Web: www.morganstanley.com
SIC: 6211 Stock brokers and dealers
HQ: Morgan Stanley Smith Barney, Llc
1585 Broadway
New York NY 10036

(G-4601)
MORGAN STNLEY SMITH BARNEY LLC
200 Public Sq Ste 2600 (44114-2331)
PHONE.....................216 344-8700
Andrew Stover, Brnch Mgr
EMP: 138
SALES (corp-wide): 54.14B **Publicly Held**
Web: www.morganstanley.com
SIC: 6282 Investment advisory service
HQ: Morgan Stanley Smith Barney, Llc
1585 Broadway
New York NY 10036

(G-4602)
MORTGAGE INFORMATION SERVICES (PA)
4877 Galaxy Pkwy Ste I (44128-5952)
PHONE.....................216 514-7480
Leonard R Stein-sapir, Ch Bd
Kenneth Hignett, *
Steven S Kaufman, *
EMP: 60 EST: 1990
SALES (est): 109MM **Privately Held**
Web: www.mtginfo.com
SIC: 6361 6531 Title insurance; Appraiser, real estate

(G-4603)
MORTGAGE NOW INC (PA)
9700 Rockside Rd Ste 295 (44125-6267)
P.O. Box 25502 (44125-0502)
PHONE.....................800 245-1050
James Marchese, Pr
Michael Perry, *
Scott Marinelli, *
EMP: 38 EST: 1997
SQ FT: 6,800
SALES (est): 22.74MM
SALES (corp-wide): 22.74MM **Privately Held**
Web: www.mtgnow.com
SIC: 6162 Mortgage bankers

(G-4604)
MOUNTAIN LAUREL ASSURANCE CO
6300 Wilson Mills Rd (44143)
PHONE.....................440 461-5000
EMP: 370 EST: 1990
SALES (est): 350.62MM
SALES (corp-wide): 49.61B **Publicly Held**
Web: www.progressivecommercial.com
SIC: 6331 Automobile insurance
HQ: Progressive Direct Holdings, Inc.
6300 Wilson Mills Rd
Cleveland OH 44143

(G-4605)
MPC INC
5350 Tradex Pkwy (44102-5887)
PHONE.....................440 835-1405
John Beverstock, Pr
EMP: 47 EST: 1975
SQ FT: 14,000
SALES (est): 2.04MM **Publicly Held**
Web: www.mpcsilentwall.com
SIC: 3296 5044 2493 Acoustical board and tile, mineral wool; Office equipment; Bulletin boards, cork
PA: Ceco Environmental Corp.
14651 Dallas Pkwy Ste 500
Dallas TX 75254

(G-4606)
MRN LIMITED PARTNERSHIP
Also Called: Mrn
629 Euclid Ave Ste 1100 (44114-3009)
P.O. Box 14100 (44114-0100)
PHONE.....................216 589-5631

Richard Maron, Pt
Judith Eigenfeld, *
EMP: 29 EST: 1977
SALES (est): 4.21MM **Privately Held**
Web: www.mrnltd.com
SIC: 6513 Apartment building operators

(G-4607)
MRN-NEWGAR HOTEL LTD
Also Called: Holiday Inn
629 Euclid Ave Lbby 1 (44114-3008)
PHONE.....................216 443-1000
Thomas W Adler, CEO
EMP: 38 EST: 1997
SALES (est): 1.71MM **Privately Held**
Web: www.holidayinn.com
SIC: 7011 Hotels and motels

(G-4608)
MSR LEGACY
1545 Sheridan Rd (44121-4023)
PHONE.....................216 381-0826
Robert Mccreary Iii, Pr
EMP: 90 EST: 1909
SQ FT: 50,000
SALES (est): 34.41K **Privately Held**
Web: www.mayfieldsandridge.com
SIC: 7997 5941 5813 5812 Country club, membership; Sporting goods and bicycle shops; Drinking places; Eating places

(G-4609)
MULTI BUILDERS SUPPLY CO
27800 Cedar Rd (44122-1186)
PHONE.....................216 831-1121
Kevan Millstein, Pr
Norman Millstein, VP
EMP: 42 EST: 1967
SQ FT: 10,000
SALES (est): 4.95MM **Privately Held**
SIC: 5039 5072 5074 5087 Glass construction materials; Hardware; Plumbing and hydronic heating supplies; Janitors' supplies

(G-4610)
MULTI-FUND INC
9700 Rockside Rd Ste 100 (44125-6268)
PHONE.....................216 750-2331
Paul Montigny, Pr
Stuart Montigny, *
EMP: 28 EST: 1990
SQ FT: 6,500
SALES (est): 2.46MM **Privately Held**
SIC: 6163 Mortgage brokers arranging for loans, using money of others

(G-4611)
MURTECH CONSULTING LLC
4700 Rockside Rd Ste 310 (44131-2171)
PHONE.....................216 328-8580
Ailish Murphy, Managing Member
EMP: 95 EST: 2000
SQ FT: 1,600
SALES (est): 10.34MM **Privately Held**
Web: www.murtechstaffing.com
SIC: 8742 7361 General management consultant; Employment agencies

(G-4612)
MUSEUM CNTMPRARY ART CLEVELAND
Also Called: MOCA CLEVELAND
11400 Euclid Ave (44106-3926)
PHONE.....................216 421-8671
Megan Lykins Reich, *
Grace Garver, *
▲ EMP: 27 EST: 1968
SQ FT: 34,000
SALES (est): 3.92MM **Privately Held**
Web: www.mocacleveland.org

SIC: 8412 Museum

(G-4613)
MUSICAL ARTS ASSOCIATION (PA)
Also Called: Cleveland Orchestra, The
11001 Euclid Ave (44106)
PHONE.....................216 231-7300
Gary Hanson, Ex Dir
▲ EMP: 190 EST: 1925
SQ FT: 125,000
SALES (est): 62.14MM
SALES (corp-wide): 62.14MM **Privately Held**
Web: www.clevelandorchestra.com
SIC: 7929 6512 Symphony orchestra; Auditorium and hall operation

(G-4614)
MUTUAL HEALTH SERVICES COMPANY
Also Called: Mutual Holding Company
2060 E 9th St (44115-1313)
PHONE.....................216 687-7000
John Burry Junior, CEO
James W Harless, *
Jerome Rogers, *
Kent Clapp, *
EMP: 333 EST: 1975
SQ FT: 18,600
SALES (est): 45.23MM
SALES (corp-wide): 2.75B **Privately Held**
Web: www.medmutual.com
SIC: 6411 Insurance agents, nec
HQ: Medical Mutual Services, Llc
17800 Royalton Rd
Strongsville OH 44136
440 878-4800

(G-4615)
MZ-RUSSELL INC
3185 E 79th St (44104-4303)
PHONE.....................216 675-2727
Michael Zuchowski, Pr
EMP: 37 EST: 2018
SALES (est): 2.39MM **Privately Held**
SIC: 1795 Demolition, buildings and other structures

(G-4616)
NACCO INDUSTRIES INC (PA)
5875 Landerbrook Dr Ste 220 (44124)
PHONE.....................440 229-5151
J C Butler Junior, Pr
Alfred M Rankin Junior, Non-Executive Chairman of the Board
Elizabeth I Loveman, VP
Thomas A Maxwell, VP
John D Neumann, VP
EMP: 39 EST: 1913
SALES (est): 214.79MM
SALES (corp-wide): 214.79MM **Publicly Held**
Web: www.nacco.com
SIC: 3634 1221 5719 3631 Electric household cooking appliances; Surface mining, lignite, nec; Kitchenware; Household cooking equipment

(G-4617)
NADINE EL ASMAR MD - UH CLVLAN
11100 Euclid Ave Ste 3400 (44106-1716)
PHONE.....................216 844-3400
EMP: 45 EST: 2019
SALES (est): 4.87MM **Privately Held**
Web: www.uhhospitals.org
SIC: 8011 Medical centers

(G-4618)
NATIONAL ASSOCIATES INC
22720 Fairview Center Dr Ste 100 (44126)
PHONE.....................440 333-0222

Cleveland - Cuyahoga County (G-4619) GEOGRAPHIC SECTION

Gerrit Kuechle, *Pr*
EMP: 78 **EST:** 1947
SALES (est): 870.16K
SALES (corp-wide): 255.2MM **Publicly Held**
Web: www.nationalassociates.biz
SIC: 6211 8748 Security brokers and dealers ; Employee programs administration
PA: Farmers National Banc Corp.
20 S Broad St
Canfield OH 44406
330 533-3341

(G-4619)
NATIONAL CITY CAPITAL CORP
1965 E 6th St Fl 8 (44114-2226)
PHONE.................................216 222-2491
William Schecter, *Pr*
EMP: 264 **EST:** 1979
SALES (est): 45.53MM
SALES (corp-wide): 31.88B **Publicly Held**
SIC: 6799 Venture capital companies
PA: The Pnc Financial Services Group Inc
300 5th Ave
Pittsburgh PA 15222
888 762-2265

(G-4620)
NATIONAL CITY CMNTY DEV CORP
1900 E 9th St (44114-3404)
PHONE.................................216 575-2000
Danny Cameran, *Pr*
EMP: 250 **EST:** 1982
SALES (est): 16.61MM
SALES (corp-wide): 31.88B **Publicly Held**
SIC: 8742 Planning consultant
PA: The Pnc Financial Services Group Inc
300 5th Ave
Pittsburgh PA 15222
888 762-2265

(G-4621)
NATIONAL CITY CREDIT CORP
1900 E 9th St Lowr Ll1 (44114-3404)
PHONE.................................216 575-2000
David Daberko, *CEO*
William C Macdonald Lll, *
Thomas A Richlovsky, *
William Mac Donald, *
EMP: 50 **EST:** 1845
SALES (est): 4.43MM
SALES (corp-wide): 31.88B **Publicly Held**
SIC: 6111 Federal and federally sponsored credit agencies
PA: The Pnc Financial Services Group Inc
300 5th Ave
Pittsburgh PA 15222
888 762-2265

(G-4622)
NATIONAL CONCESSION COMPANY
4582 Willow Pkwy (44125-1046)
PHONE.................................216 881-9911
Tuck Axelrod, *Pr*
Christopher Axelrod, *
EMP: 27 **EST:** 1983
SQ FT: 7,500
SALES (est): 1.57MM **Privately Held**
Web: www.nationalconcession.com
SIC: 7999 Concession operator

(G-4623)
NATIONAL CONTINENTAL INSUR CO
6300 Wilson Mills Rd (44143-2109)
PHONE.................................631 320-2405
S Patricia Griffith, *CEO*
EMP: 49 **EST:** 2018
SALES (est): 16.76MM
SALES (corp-wide): 49.61B **Publicly Held**
SIC: 6331 Fire, marine, and casualty insurance
HQ: Progressive Commercial Holdings, Inc.
6300 Wilson Mills Rd
Cleveland OH 44143

(G-4624)
NATIONAL ELECTRO-COATINGS INC
Also Called: National Office Services
15655 Brookpark Rd (44142-1619)
PHONE.................................216 898-0080
Robert W Schneider, *Ch*
Gregory R Schneider, *
Richard Corl, *
▲ **EMP:** 90 **EST:** 1967
SQ FT: 175,000
SALES (est): 19.87MM **Privately Held**
Web: www.natoffice.com
SIC: 2522 7641 1799 5021 Office furniture, except wood; Office furniture repair and maintenance; Office furniture installation; Office and public building furniture

(G-4625)
NATIONAL ENGRG & CONTG CO
Also Called: Netco
50 Public Sq Ste 2175 (44113-2202)
PHONE.................................440 238-3331
Walter Gratz, *CEO*
Anthony Martin, *
Clarke Wilson, *
EMP: 45 **EST:** 1933
SQ FT: 50,000
SALES (est): 2.33MM
SALES (corp-wide): 9.96B **Privately Held**
SIC: 1622 1623 Bridge construction; Sewer line construction
HQ: Balfour Beatty, Llc
1011 Centre Rd Ste 322
Wilmington DE 19805
302 573-3873

(G-4626)
NATIONAL FOODS PACKAGING INC
8200 Madison Ave (44102-2727)
PHONE.................................216 622-2740
John Pallas, *Pr*
▲ **EMP:** 30 **EST:** 2001
SQ FT: 57,261
SALES (est): 9.1MM **Privately Held**
Web: www.nationalfoodsonline.com
SIC: 2099 2035 2045 5149 Seasonings and spices; Pickles, sauces, and salad dressings; Bread and bread type roll mixes: from purchased flour; Breakfast cereals

(G-4627)
NATIONAL GENERAL INSURANCE CO
Also Called: Nationwide
800 Superior Ave E (44114-2613)
PHONE.................................212 380-9462
Kevin Bailey, *Prin*
EMP: 30
Web: www.nationalgeneral.com
SIC: 6411 Insurance agents, nec
HQ: National General Insurance Company
5757 Phantom Dr Ste 200
Hazelwood MO 63042
314 493-8000

(G-4628)
NATIONAL TESTING LABORATORIES (PA)
6571 Wilson Mills Rd Ste 3 (44143-3439)
PHONE.................................440 449-2525
Robert Gelbach, *Pr*
Thomas Zimmerman, *
Steve Tischler, *
EMP: 27 **EST:** 1985
SQ FT: 3,500
SALES (est): 5.06MM
SALES (corp-wide): 5.06MM **Privately Held**
Web: www.watercheck.com
SIC: 8734 Water testing laboratory

(G-4629)
NBW INC
4556 Industrial Pkwy (44135-4542)
PHONE.................................216 377-1700
Burgess J Holt, *Ch*
Thomas Graves, *
Todd Holt, *
Buck L Holt, *
EMP: 48 **EST:** 1935
SQ FT: 25,000
SALES (est): 15.04MM **Privately Held**
Web: www.nbwinc.com
SIC: 1711 1796 7699 3443 Boiler setting contractor; Installing building equipment; Boiler and heating repair services; Fabricated plate work (boiler shop)

(G-4630)
NCS HEALTHCARE INC
3201 Enterprise Pkwy Ste 220 (44122)
PHONE.................................216 514-3350
EMP: 2640
SIC: 5122 8093 8049 8082 Drugs and drug proprietaries; Specialty outpatient clinics, nec; Physical therapist; Oxygen tent service

(G-4631)
NCS INCORPORATED
729 Miner Rd (44143-2117)
PHONE.................................440 684-9455
EMP: 68
SALES (est): 7.61MM **Privately Held**
SIC: 7322 Collection agency, except real estate

(G-4632)
NEAR W SIDE MULTI-SERVICE CORP
Also Called: May Dugan Center
4115 Bridge Ave (44113-3304)
PHONE.................................216 631-5800
Alex Sanchez, *Ch*
EMP: 59 **EST:** 1969
SALES (est): 3.48MM **Privately Held**
Web: www.maydugancenter.org
SIC: 8322 Social service center

(G-4633)
NEIGHBORHOOD HEALTH CARE INC (PA)
Also Called: Neighborhood Family Practice
4115 Bridge Ave # 300 (44113)
PHONE.................................216 281-8945
Jean Polster, *CEO*
Jean Therrien, *
Jim Massey, *
Daniel Gauntner, *
Peggy Keating, *
EMP: 30 **EST:** 1979
SALES (est): 26.47MM
SALES (corp-wide): 26.47MM **Privately Held**
Web: www.nfpmedcenter.org
SIC: 8011 General and family practice, physician/surgeon

(G-4634)
NEPTUNE PLUMBING & HEATING CO
23860 Miles Rd (44128-5464)
PHONE.................................216 475-9100
Scott Wallenstein, *Pr*
EMP: 80 **EST:** 1955
SQ FT: 8,000
SALES (est): 13.86MM **Privately Held**
Web: www.neptuneplumbing.net
SIC: 1711 Plumbing contractors

(G-4635)
NERONE & SONS INC
19501 S Miles Rd Ste 1 (44128-4261)
PHONE.................................216 662-2235
Ton Nerone, *Pr*
Tom Nerone, *
Rick Nerone Senior, *Pr*
Rick Nerone Junior, *Sec*
Carl Nerone, *
EMP: 50 **EST:** 1955
SQ FT: 28,500
SALES (est): 10.49MM **Privately Held**
Web: www.neroneandsons.com
SIC: 1623 1611 Sewer line construction; General contractor, highway and street construction

(G-4636)
NESTAWAY LLC
9100 Bank St Ste 1 (44125-3432)
PHONE.................................216 587-1500
▲ **EMP:** 100
SIC: 1799 2392 Home/office interiors finishing, furnishing and remodeling; Household furnishings, nec

(G-4637)
NEW AVNUES TO INDEPENDENCE INC (PA)
3615 Superior Ave E Ste 4404a (44114-4139)
PHONE.................................216 481-1907
Tom Lewins, *Pr*
Anietta Colemen, *
EMP: 100 **EST:** 1956
SALES (est): 15.06MM
SALES (corp-wide): 15.06MM **Privately Held**
Web: www.newavenues.net
SIC: 8361 Retarded home

(G-4638)
NEW DIRECTIONS INC
30800 Chagrin Blvd (44124-5925)
PHONE.................................216 591-0324
Michael Matoney, *CEO*
EMP: 52 **EST:** 1980
SQ FT: 19,000
SALES (est): 4.78MM **Privately Held**
Web: www.newdirections.co
SIC: 8361 Rehabilitation center, residential: health care incidental

(G-4639)
NEW WORLD COMMUNICATIONS OF OHIO INC
Also Called: Wjw TV
5800 S Marginal Rd (44103-1040)
PHONE.................................216 432-4041
EMP: 200
Web: www.fox8.com
SIC: 4833 Television broadcasting stations

(G-4640)
NEW YORK COMMUNITY BANCORP INC
1801 E 9th St Ste 200 (44114-3103)
PHONE.................................216 736-3480
EMP: 122
SIC: 6036 State savings banks, not federally chartered
PA: New York Community Bancorp, Inc.
615 Merrick Ave
Westbury NY 11801

(G-4641)
NEWMARK & COMPANY RE INC
Also Called: Newmark Grubb Knight Frank
1300 E 9th St Ste 105 (44114-1510)
PHONE.................................216 861-3040

GEOGRAPHIC SECTION
Cleveland - Cuyahoga County (G-4662)

David Hooper, *Mgr*
EMP: 31
SALES (corp-wide): 2.47B **Publicly Held**
Web: www.newmarkrealestate.com
SIC: 6531 6799 Real estate brokers and agents; Investors, nec
HQ: Newmark & Company Real Estate, Inc.
125 Park Ave
New York NY 10017
212 372-2000

(G-4642)
NEXUS ENGINEERING GROUP INC (PA)
1422 Euclid Ave Ste 1400 (44115-2015)
PHONE..................................216 404-7867
Jeffrey O Herzog, *Pr*
Marianne C Corrao, *
EMP: 81 **EST:** 2005
SALES (est): 11.9MM **Privately Held**
Web: www.nexusegroup.com
SIC: 8711 Consulting engineer

(G-4643)
NF II CLEVELAND OP CO LLC
Also Called: Residence Inn By Marriott
527 Prospect Ave E (44115-1113)
PHONE..................................216 443-9043
Steven Rudolph, *Genl Mgr*
EMP: 30 **EST:** 2014
SQ FT: 700,000
SALES (est): 216.67K **Privately Held**
Web: residence-inn.marriott.com
SIC: 7011 Hotels and motels

(G-4644)
NICOLA GUDBRANSON & COOPER LLC
50 Public Sq # 2750 (44113-2202)
PHONE..................................216 621-7227
Robert N Gudbranson Esq, *Managing Member*
EMP: 41 **EST:** 1948
SQ FT: 6,000
SALES (est): 8.04MM **Privately Held**
Web: www.nicola.com
SIC: 8111 General practice attorney, lawyer

(G-4645)
NICOLES CHILD CARE CENTER
12914 Union Ave (44105-1976)
PHONE..................................216 991-2416
EMP: 43
SQ FT: 8,448
SIC: 8351 Child day care services
PA: Nicole's Child Care Center, Inc
4035 E 141st St
Cleveland OH 44128

(G-4646)
NIEDERST MANAGEMENT LTD (PA)
Also Called: NM Residential
22730 Fairview Center Dr Ste 160 (44126)
PHONE..................................440 331-8800
Michael Niederst, *Prin*
EMP: 50 **EST:** 2005
SALES (est): 13.66MM
SALES (corp-wide): 13.66MM **Privately Held**
Web: www.nmresidential.com
SIC: 8741 Management services

(G-4647)
NORRIS BROTHERS CO INC
2138 Davenport Ave (44114-3724)
PHONE..................................216 771-2333
Bernard E Weir Junior, *Pr*
Kenneth Mcbride, *Pr*
Catherine Mcbride, *Sec*
EMP: 120 **EST:** 1867

SQ FT: 60,000
SALES (est): 14.62MM **Privately Held**
Web: www.norrisbr.com
SIC: 1796 1541 7699 1771 Machinery installation; Industrial buildings, new construction, nec; Boiler repair shop; Concrete work

(G-4648)
NORTH COAST CONCRETE INC
6061 Carey Dr (44125-4259)
PHONE..................................216 642-1114
Robert Dalrymple, *Pr*
Linda A Dalrymple, *
EMP: 28 **EST:** 1985
SQ FT: 5,000
SALES (est): 4.98MM **Privately Held**
Web: www.northcoastconcrete.com
SIC: 1771 Concrete pumping

(G-4649)
NORTH OHIO REGIONAL SEWER
3900 Euclid Ave (44115-2506)
PHONE..................................216 299-0312
EMP: 34 **EST:** 2005
SALES (est): 871.08K **Privately Held**
Web: www.neorsd.org
SIC: 4952 Sewerage systems

(G-4650)
NORTH PARK RETIREMENT CMNTY
Also Called: Sovereign Healthcare
14801 Holland Rd Lbby (44142-3080)
PHONE..................................216 267-0555
John Coury Junior, *Pr*
EMP: 50 **EST:** 1988
SALES (est): 4.54MM **Privately Held**
SIC: 8051 Skilled nursing care facilities

(G-4651)
NORTH RANDALL VILLAGE (PA)
21937 Miles Rd (44128-4775)
PHONE..................................216 663-1112
David Smith, *Mayor*
EMP: 48 **EST:** 1905
SQ FT: 6,000
SALES (est): 2.12MM
SALES (corp-wide): 2.12MM **Privately Held**
Web: www.northrandall.com
SIC: 8741 Office management

(G-4652)
NORTHAST OHIO ARWIDE CRDNTING
Also Called: Noaca
1299 Superior Ave E (44114-3204)
PHONE..................................216 621-3055
Howard Maier, *Ex Dir*
William M Grace, *Ch*
EMP: 84 **EST:** 1968
SALES (est): 9.73MM **Privately Held**
Web: www.noaca.org
SIC: 8748 Urban planning and consulting services

(G-4653)
NORTHAST OHIO NGHBRHOOD HLTH S (PA)
4800 Payne Ave (44103-2443)
PHONE..................................216 231-7700
Willie S Austin, *Pr*
EMP: 125 **EST:** 1967
SQ FT: 67,000
SALES (est): 32.93MM
SALES (corp-wide): 32.93MM **Privately Held**
Web: www.neonhealth.org

SIC: 8099 8071 8011 5912 Medical services organization; Medical laboratories; Offices and clinics of medical doctors; Drug stores and proprietary stores

(G-4654)
NORTHAST OHIO NGHBRHOOD HLTH S
Also Called: Superior Health Center
12100 Superior Ave (44106-1444)
PHONE..................................216 851-2600
Patsy Mcclain, *Prin*
EMP: 31
SALES (corp-wide): 32.93MM **Privately Held**
Web: www.neonhealth.org
SIC: 8099 8011 Medical services organization; Clinic, operated by physicians
PA: Northeast Ohio Neighborhood Health Services, Inc.
4800 Payne Ave
Cleveland OH 44103
216 231-7700

(G-4655)
NORTHAST OHIO NGHBRHOOD HLTH S
15201 Euclid Ave (44112-2803)
PHONE..................................216 541-5600
Lee Vesper, *Brnch Mgr*
EMP: 31
SALES (corp-wide): 32.93MM **Privately Held**
Web: www.neonhealth.org
SIC: 8099 Medical services organization
PA: Northeast Ohio Neighborhood Health Services, Inc.
4800 Payne Ave
Cleveland OH 44103
216 231-7700

(G-4656)
NORTHAST OHIO NGHBRHOOD HLTH S
Also Called: Neoh Collinwood Health Center
15322 Saint Clair Ave (44110-3043)
PHONE..................................216 851-1500
EMP: 31
SQ FT: 7,273
SALES (corp-wide): 32.93MM **Privately Held**
Web: www.neonhealth.org
SIC: 8099 8011 Medical services organization; Clinic, operated by physicians
PA: Northeast Ohio Neighborhood Health Services, Inc.
4800 Payne Ave
Cleveland OH 44103
216 231-7700

(G-4657)
NORTHAST OHIO RGONAL SEWER DST
Also Called: Amsc
4747 E 49th St (44125-1011)
PHONE..................................216 641-6000
Bob Gow, *Brnch Mgr*
EMP: 126
SALES (corp-wide): 436.56MM **Privately Held**
Web: www.neorsd.org
SIC: 4952 8734 Sewerage systems; Testing laboratories
PA: Northeast Ohio Regional Sewer District
3900 Euclid Ave
Cleveland OH 44115
216 881-6600

(G-4658)
NORTHAST OHIO RGONAL SEWER DST
Also Called: Southrly Wstwater Trtmnt Plant
6000 Canal Rd (44125-1026)
PHONE..................................216 641-3200
Lowell Eisnaugle, *Mgr*
EMP: 125
SQ FT: 9,916
SALES (corp-wide): 436.56MM **Privately Held**
Web: www.neorsd.org
SIC: 4959 4952 Sanitary services, nec; Sewerage systems
PA: Northeast Ohio Regional Sewer District
3900 Euclid Ave
Cleveland OH 44115
216 881-6600

(G-4659)
NORTHAST OHIO RGONAL SEWER DST (PA)
3900 Euclid Ave (44115-2506)
PHONE..................................216 881-6600
Darnell Brown, *Pr*
Julius Ciaccia, *
Ronald D Sulik, *
EMP: 120 **EST:** 1972
SQ FT: 85,000
SALES (est): 436.56MM
SALES (corp-wide): 436.56MM **Privately Held**
Web: www.neorsd.org
SIC: 4941 Water supply

(G-4660)
NORTHAST OHIO RGONAL SEWER DST
Also Called: Westerly Wstwater Trtmnt Plant
5800 Cleveland Memorial Sh (44102-2122)
PHONE..................................216 961-2187
Andrew Rossiter, *Superintnt*
EMP: 126
SALES (corp-wide): 436.56MM **Privately Held**
Web: www.neorsd.org
SIC: 8711 Civil engineering
PA: Northeast Ohio Regional Sewer District
3900 Euclid Ave
Cleveland OH 44115
216 881-6600

(G-4661)
NORTHAST OHIO TRNCHING SVC INC
17900 Miles Rd Ste 1 (44128-3400)
PHONE..................................216 663-6006
George J Gorup, *Pr*
EMP: 35 **EST:** 1979
SQ FT: 14,422
SALES (est): 2.6MM **Privately Held**
Web: www.ohio-excavating.com
SIC: 1794 Excavation and grading, building construction

(G-4662)
NORTHEAST OHIO ELECTRIC LLC (PA)
Also Called: Doan Pyramid Electric
5069 Corbin Dr (44128-5413)
PHONE..................................216 587-9512
Mike Forlani, *Managing Member*
Lenny Heisler, *
Douglas K Sesnowitz, *
▼ **EMP:** 440 **EST:** 2000
SALES (est): 31.46MM
SALES (corp-wide): 31.46MM **Privately Held**
SIC: 1731 General electrical contractor

Cleveland - Cuyahoga County (G-4663)

(G-4663)
NORTHEAST PROJECTIONS INC
Also Called: N P I Audio Video Solutions
8600 Sweet Valley Dr (44125-4212)
PHONE...............................216 514-5023
Joseph Thompson, *Pr*
Joe Thompson, *
Ted Van Hyning, *
Tracy L Thompson, *
EMP: 50 **EST:** 1992
SQ FT: 4,400
SALES (est): 9.77MM **Privately Held**
Web: www.npiav.com
SIC: 7359 Audio-visual equipment and supply rental

(G-4664)
NORTHERN FROZEN FOODS INC
Also Called: Northern Haserot
21500 Alexander Rd (44146-5511)
PHONE...............................440 439-0600
Douglas Kern, *Pr*
Richard C Speicher, *
Bruce Kern, *
EMP: 200 **EST:** 1950
SQ FT: 105,000
SALES (est): 69.95MM **Privately Held**
Web: www.northernhaserot.com
SIC: 5142 5149 5147 Packaged frozen goods; Canned goods: fruit, vegetables, seafood, meats, etc.; Meats, fresh

(G-4665)
NORTHWESTERLY LTD
Also Called: Northwesterly Assisted Living
1341 Marlowe Ave (44107-2654)
PHONE...............................216 228-2266
EMP: 30 **EST:** 1996
SQ FT: 200
SALES (est): 2.49MM
SALES (corp-wide): 5MM **Privately Held**
Web: www.havenatlakewood.com
SIC: 8051 Skilled nursing care facilities
PA: Kandu Capital Llc
260 E Brown St Ste 315
Birmingham MI 48009
248 642-2914

(G-4666)
NOSTRESS INC
Also Called: Centura X-Ray
4381 Renaissance Pkwy (44128-5759)
PHONE...............................216 593-0226
Douglas Brook, *Pr*
Mark Hale, *
John T Mulligan, *
Mary Luzi, *
EMP: 40 **EST:** 1982
SQ FT: 16,500
SALES (est): 3.95MM **Privately Held**
Web: www.centuraimaging.com
SIC: 5047 Medical equipment and supplies

(G-4667)
NOTTINGHM-SPIRK DSIGN ASSOC IN
2200 Overlook Rd (44106-2326)
PHONE...............................216 800-5782
John Nottingham, *Pr*
John Spirk, *
EMP: 50 **EST:** 1972
SQ FT: 8,000
SALES (est): 12.59MM **Privately Held**
Web: www.nottinghamspirk.com
SIC: 7336 8711 Package design; Designing: ship, boat, machine, and product

(G-4668)
NOVAGARD SOLUTIONS INC (PA)
Also Called: Foam Seal
5109 Hamilton Ave (44114-3907)
PHONE...............................216 881-8111
Sarah Nash, *Ch Bd*
Sarah Nash, *Ch Bd*
Ron Moeller, *
EMP: 104 **EST:** 2002
SQ FT: 250,000
SALES (est): 50MM **Privately Held**
Web: www.novagard.com
SIC: 5169 2822 2869 3567 Adhesives and sealants; Silicone rubbers; Silicones; Incinerators, thermal, fume & catalytic

(G-4669)
NRP HOLDINGS LLC
5309 Transportation Blvd (44125-5333)
PHONE...............................216 475-8900
J David Heller, *Managing Member*
EMP: 150 **EST:** 1995
SALES (est): 100MM **Privately Held**
Web: www.nrpgroup.com
SIC: 1531 Townhouse developers

(G-4670)
NRP MANAGEMENT LLC
5309 Transportation Blvd (44125-5333)
PHONE...............................216 475-8900
J David Heller, *Prin*
EMP: 27 **EST:** 1996
SALES (est): 721.84K **Privately Held**
Web: www.nrpgroup.com
SIC: 8741 Management services

(G-4671)
NSL ANALYTICAL SERVICES INC (PA)
4450 Cranwood Pkwy (44128-4004)
PHONE...............................216 438-5200
Ron Wesel, *CEO*
EMP: 55 **EST:** 1945
SQ FT: 30,877
SALES (est): 18.99MM **Privately Held**
Web: www.nslanalytical.com
SIC: 8734 Testing laboratories

(G-4672)
NU-DI PRODUCTS CO INC
Also Called: Nu-Di
12730 Triskett Rd (44111-2529)
PHONE...............................216 251-9070
Kenneth Bihn, *Pr*
Tim Bihn, *
EMP: 85 **EST:** 1969
SQ FT: 38,000
SALES (est): 9.62MM **Privately Held**
Web: www.nu-di.com
SIC: 3825 5013 Engine electrical test equipment; Testing equipment, electrical: automotive

(G-4673)
NUEVA LUZ URBAN RESOURCE CTR
2226 W 89th St (44102-3863)
PHONE...............................216 651-8236
Max Rodas, *Prin*
EMP: 29 **EST:** 2006
SALES (est): 1.11MM **Privately Held**
Web: www.nlurc.org
SIC: 8322 Social service center

(G-4674)
NURENBERG PRIS HLLER MCCRTHY L
600 Superior Ave E Ste 1200 (44114-2614)
PHONE...............................440 423-0750
TOLL FREE: 800
Leon M Plevin, *Pr*
Marshall I Nurenberg, *
John J Mccarthy, *Sec*
Maurice L Heller, *
EMP: 64 **EST:** 1926
SQ FT: 28,000
SALES (est): 9.19MM **Privately Held**
Web: www.nphm.com
SIC: 8111 General practice law office

(G-4675)
NYMAN CONSTRUCTION CO
23209 Miles Rd Fl 2 (44128-5467)
PHONE...............................216 475-7800
EMP: 30 **EST:** 1995
SQ FT: 16,000
SALES (est): 17.21MM **Privately Held**
Web: www.nymanconstruction.net
SIC: 1541 1542 Industrial buildings and warehouses; Nonresidential construction, nec

(G-4676)
OAK TREE PHYSICIANS INC
Also Called: Oak Tree Woman Health
7255 Old Oak Blvd (44130-3329)
PHONE...............................440 816-8000
Larry Hammerburg, *Ch Bd*
Herb Sharlkhauser, *V Ch Bd*
Clairese Clemmens, *Sec*
EMP: 46 **EST:** 1990
SALES (est): 471.73K **Privately Held**
Web: www.swgeneral.com
SIC: 8062 General medical and surgical hospitals

(G-4677)
OAKWOOD HEALTH CARE SVCS INC
Also Called: Grande Oaks & Grande Pavillion
24579 Broadway Ave (44146-6338)
PHONE...............................440 439-7976
Aaron Handler, *Pr*
EMP: 150 **EST:** 2004
SQ FT: 5,000
SALES (est): 8.46MM **Privately Held**
SIC: 8051 Convalescent home with continuous nursing care

(G-4678)
OAOC ENTERPRISE INC
815 Superior Ave E Ste 1618 (44114-2706)
PHONE...............................216 584-8677
Timothy Dubaniewicz, *CEO*
EMP: 50 **EST:** 2021
SALES (est): 936.66K **Privately Held**
SIC: 0781 Landscape services

(G-4679)
OATEY SUPPLY CHAIN SVCS INC (HQ)
Also Called: Oatey
20600 Emerald Pkwy (44135-6022)
PHONE...............................216 267-7100
John H Mcmillan, *Ch*
Neal Restivo, *CEO*
◆ **EMP:** 200 **EST:** 2001
SQ FT: 165,000
SALES (est): 85.03MM
SALES (corp-wide): 304.6MM **Privately Held**
Web: www.oatey.com
SIC: 3444 5074 Metal roofing and roof drainage equipment; Plumbing and hydronic heating supplies
PA: Oatey Co.
20600 Emerald Pkwy
Cleveland OH 44135
800 203-1155

(G-4680)
OGLEBAY NORTON MAR SVCS CO LLC
1001 Lakeside Ave E 15th Fl (44114-1158)
PHONE...............................216 861-3300
Michael D Lundin, *Pr*
EMP: 1500 **EST:** 1999
SALES (est): 22.31MM **Privately Held**
SIC: 1422 Crushed and broken limestone

(G-4681)
OHIO AEROSPACE INSTITUTE (PA)
Also Called: O A I
22800 Cedar Point Rd (44142)
PHONE...............................440 962-3000
Michael Heil, *Pr*
Salvatore Miraglia, *Ch Bd*
Tony H Smith, *VP Fin*
Jake Breland, *VP*
EMP: 45 **EST:** 1989
SQ FT: 70,000
SALES (est): 8.78MM **Privately Held**
Web: www.oai.org
SIC: 8733 Research institute

(G-4682)
OHIO BLOW PIPE COMPANY (PA)
Also Called: Ohio Blow Pipe
446 E 131st St (44108-1684)
PHONE...............................216 681-7379
Edward Fakeris, *Pr*
William Roberts, *
Lisa Kern, *
EMP: 33 **EST:** 1967
SQ FT: 45,000
SALES (est): 24.37MM
SALES (corp-wide): 24.37MM **Privately Held**
Web: www.innoveyance.com
SIC: 8711 3564 3444 Engineering services; Blowers and fans; Sheet metalwork

(G-4683)
OHIO BUSINESS MACHINES LLC
Also Called: O B M
1111 Superior Ave E Ste 105 (44114-2525)
PHONE...............................216 485-2000
EMP: 50 **EST:** 2002
SALES (est): 25.74MM **Privately Held**
Web: www.ohiobusinessmachines.com
SIC: 5044 7629 5734 Office equipment; Business machine repair, electric; Computer and software stores

(G-4684)
OHIO CHEST PHYSICIANS LTD
15805 Puritas Ave (44135-2611)
PHONE...............................216 267-5139
Linas F Vaitkus Md, *Managing Member*
Patricia Volle, *
EMP: 33 **EST:** 1996
SALES (est): 893.9K **Privately Held**
Web: www.ohiochest.com
SIC: 8011 Pulmonary specialist, physician/ surgeon

(G-4685)
OHIO CITIZEN ACTION (PA)
1511 Brookpark Rd (44109-5802)
PHONE...............................216 861-5200
Alexandra Buchanan, *Ex Dir*
EMP: 30 **EST:** 1976
SALES (est): 777.06K
SALES (corp-wide): 777.06K **Privately Held**
Web: www.ohiocitizen.org
SIC: 8399 Community action agency

(G-4686)
OHIO DEPARTMENT YOUTH SERVICES
Also Called: Toledo Regional Office
615 W Superior Ave (44113-1878)
PHONE...............................419 245-3040
Don Kershner, *Dir*
EMP: 137
Web: dys.ohio.gov

GEOGRAPHIC SECTION
Cleveland - Cuyahoga County (G-4709)

SIC: **9223** 8322 Prison, government; Parole office
HQ: Ohio Department Of Youth Services
4545 Fisher Rd Ste D
Columbus OH 43228

(G-4687)
OHIO DIVERSIFIED SERVICES INC
20226 Detroit Rd (44116-2422)
PHONE.................................440 356-7000
Phyllis Pantona, *Pr*
Kirk Henline, *
EMP: 30 EST: 1985
SQ FT: 10,500
SALES (est): 4.9MM **Privately Held**
SIC: **1542** 8742 Commercial and office building contractors; Construction project management consultant

(G-4688)
OHIO FARMERS WHOLESALE DEALERS INC
Also Called: Ohio Farmers Food Service Dist
2700 E 55th St (44104-2865)
PHONE.................................216 391-9733
EMP: 80
SIC: **5149** 5146 5147 5144 Groceries and related products, nec; Fish and seafoods; Meats and meat products; Poultry products, nec

(G-4689)
OHIO REAL TITLE AGENCY LLC (PA)
1213 Prospect Ave E Ste 200 (44115-1260)
PHONE.................................216 373-9900
Donald Mcfadden, *CEO*
EMP: 40 EST: 2006
SALES (est): 10.12MM **Privately Held**
Web: www.ohiorealtitle.com
SIC: **6541** Title and trust companies

(G-4690)
OHIO RENAL CARE SUPPLY CO LLC
3280 W 25th St (44109-1670)
PHONE.................................216 739-0500
EMP: 33 EST: 1997
SALES (est): 1.21MM
SALES (corp-wide): 21.15B **Privately Held**
SIC: **8092** Kidney dialysis centers
HQ: Fresenius Medical Care Centracare Dialysis, Llc
920 Winter St
Waltham MA 02451
781 699-4191

(G-4691)
OHIO VALLEY FLOORING INC
Also Called: Ohio Valley Flooring
7620 Hub Pkwy Ste 4 (44125-5743)
PHONE.................................216 328-9091
Wayne Fennis, *Brnch Mgr*
EMP: 64
SALES (corp-wide): 49.02MM **Privately Held**
Web: www.ovf.com
SIC: **5023** Carpets
PA: Ohio Valley Flooring, Inc.
5555 Murray Ave
Cincinnati OH 45227
513 271-3434

(G-4692)
OHIOGUIDESTONE
Also Called: Family Life Center Brook Park
17400 Holland Rd (44142-3524)
PHONE.................................216 433-4136
Kathy Dahl, *Mgr*
EMP: 210
SALES (corp-wide): 86.77MM **Privately Held**
Web: www.ohioguidestone.org

SIC: **8351** Child day care services
PA: Ohioguidestone
434 Eastland Rd
Berea OH 44017
440 234-2006

(G-4693)
OHIOGUIDESTONE
Also Called: Pro Kids & Families Program
3500 Carnegie Ave (44115-2641)
PHONE.................................440 260-8900
EMP: 322
SALES (corp-wide): 86.77MM **Privately Held**
Web: www.ohioguidestone.org
SIC: **8322** Social service center
PA: Ohioguidestone
434 Eastland Rd
Berea OH 44017
440 234-2006

(G-4694)
OLD TIME POTTERY LLC
7011 W 130th St Ste 1 (44130-7889)
PHONE.................................440 842-1244
EMP: 55
SALES (corp-wide): 892.49MM **Privately Held**
Web: www.oldtimepottery.com
SIC: **5999** 5023 Art, picture frames, and decorations; Homefurnishings
HQ: Old Time Pottery, Llc
480 River Rock Blvd
Murfreesboro TN 37128
615 890-6060

(G-4695)
OLYMPIC STEEL INC (PA)
Also Called: EZ Dumper
22901 Millcreek Blvd Ste 650 (44122)
PHONE.................................216 292-3800
Richard T Marabito, *CEO*
Michael D Siegal, *
Richard A Manson, *CFO*
Andrew S Greiff, *Pr*
Lisa K Christen, *Corporate Controller*
EMP: 58 EST: 1954
SQ FT: 127,000
SALES (est): 2.16B
SALES (corp-wide): 2.16B **Publicly Held**
Web: www.olysteel.com
SIC: **5051** Steel

(G-4696)
OM PARTNERS LLC
Also Called: Ostendorf-Morris Company
1350 Euclid Ave Ste 700 (44115-1889)
PHONE.................................216 861-7200
EMP: 50
SIC: **6531** Real estate brokers and agents

(G-4697)
ONCODIAGNOSTIC LABORATORY INC
812 Huron Rd E Ste 520 (44115-1126)
P.O. Box 117 (01740-0117)
EMP: 40 EST: 1985
SALES (est): 1.74MM **Privately Held**
Web: www.oncodiagnostic.com
SIC: **8071** Pathological laboratory
PA: Predictive Biosciences, Inc.
128 Spring St 400 Lvel B
Lexington MA 02421

(G-4698)
ONE SKY FLIGHT LLC (HQ)
26180 Curtiss Wright Pkwy (44143-1453)
PHONE.................................877 703-2348
Michael Silvestro, *CEO*
Kenneth Ricci, *Ch*
Michael Rossi, *CFO*

EMP: 31 EST: 2013
SALES (est): 99.82MM
SALES (corp-wide): 160.16MM **Privately Held**
Web: www.flightoptions.com
SIC: **7359** Aircraft rental
PA: Flight Options, Inc.
26180 Curtis Wright Pkwy
Richmond Heights OH 44143
216 261-3880

(G-4699)
ONE WAY EXPRESS INCORPORATED
380 Solon Rd Ste 5 (44146-3809)
PHONE.................................440 439-9182
Cynthia Jackson, *Pr*
Richard Jackson, *
EMP: 40 EST: 1993
SQ FT: 2,500
SALES (est): 2.15MM **Privately Held**
SIC: **4212** 4213 Local trucking, without storage; Trucking, except local

(G-4700)
ONSHIFT INC (PA)
1621 Euclid Ave Ste 1500 (44115-2192)
PHONE.................................216 333-1353
Frank Griffith, *Ex VP*
Ray Desrochers, *Pr*
EMP: 191 EST: 2010
SALES (est): 26.57MM
SALES (corp-wide): 26.57MM **Privately Held**
Web: www.onshift.com
SIC: **7371** Computer software development

(G-4701)
ONX ENTRPRISE SOLUTIONS US INC
5900 Landerbrook Dr Ste 100 (44124-4020)
PHONE.................................440 569-2300
Mike Cox, *CEO*
Rosalind Lehman, *
Brian Nogar, *
EMP: 211 EST: 2009
SALES (est): 2.22MM
SALES (corp-wide): 3.15B **Privately Held**
Web: www.onx.com
SIC: **7379** Computer related consulting services
HQ: Onx Holdings Llc
221 E Fourth St
Cincinnati OH 45202
866 587-2287

(G-4702)
ONYX CREATIVE INC (PA)
Also Called: Bluestreak Consulting
25001 Emery Rd Ste 400 (44128-5627)
PHONE.................................216 223-3200
Mike Crislip, *Pr*
Carole Sanderson, *
EMP: 90 EST: 1974
SQ FT: 20,000
SALES (est): 17.49MM
SALES (corp-wide): 17.49MM **Privately Held**
Web: www.onxycreative.com
SIC: **8712** 8711 Architectural services; Engineering services

(G-4703)
OPTIEM LLC
Also Called: Optiem
1370 W 6th St 3rd Fl (44113-1315)
PHONE.................................216 574-9100
Joe Kubic, *CEO*
EMP: 28 EST: 2000
SQ FT: 5,000
SALES (est): 960.64K **Privately Held**
Web: www.engageadcom.com

SIC: **8742** Marketing consulting services

(G-4704)
OPTIMA 777 LLC
Also Called: Westin Cleveland
777 Saint Clair Ave Ne (44114-1711)
PHONE.................................216 771-7700
EMP: 42 EST: 2014
SALES (est): 6.85MM **Privately Held**
Web: www.westincleveland.com
SIC: **7011** Hotels

(G-4705)
OPTIONS FLIGHT SUPPORT INC
26180 Curtiss Wright Pkwy (44143-1453)
PHONE.................................216 261-3500
Michael Scheerringa, *CEO*
Mark Brody, *
EMP: 720 EST: 1993
SALES (est): 2.28MM
SALES (corp-wide): 160.16MM **Privately Held**
Web: www.flightoptions.com
SIC: **5599** 4522 Aircraft dealers; Air transportation, nonscheduled
PA: Flight Options, Inc.
26180 Curtis Wright Pkwy
Richmond Heights OH 44143
216 261-3880

(G-4706)
ORANGE EARLY CHILDHOOD CENTER
32000 Chagrin Blvd (44124-5922)
PHONE.................................216 831-4909
Sally Hirsch, *Dir*
EMP: 30 EST: 1980
SALES (est): 469.82K **Privately Held**
Web: www.orangerec.com
SIC: **8351** Preschool center

(G-4707)
ORION CARE SERVICES LLC
18810 Harvard Ave (44122-6848)
PHONE.................................216 752-3600
Sally Schwartz Presidnet, *Prin*
Sally Schwartz, *Pr*
Abram Schwartz, *
Chris Ayewoh, *
Keith Yoder, *
EMP: 50 EST: 1978
SALES (est): 1.19MM **Privately Held**
SIC: **8051** 8052 Skilled nursing care facilities ; Intermediate care facilities

(G-4708)
OSBORN ENGINEERING COMPANY (PA)
Also Called: Osborn Engineering Company
1111 Superior Ave E Ste 2100 (44114-2534)
PHONE.................................216 861-2020
E P Baxendale, *Pr*
L V Hooper, *
EMP: 90 EST: 1892
SALES (est): 43.54MM
SALES (corp-wide): 43.54MM **Privately Held**
Web: www.osborn-eng.com
SIC: **8711** 8712 Consulting engineer; Architectural engineering

(G-4709)
OTIS ELEVATOR COMPANY
9800 Rockside Rd Ste 1200 (44125-6270)
PHONE.................................216 573-2333
Gordy Sell, *Mgr*
EMP: 44
SALES (corp-wide): 14.21B **Publicly Held**
Web: www.otis.com

Cleveland - Cuyahoga County (G-4710)

SIC: 5084 1796 3534 Elevators; Elevator installation and conversion; Elevators and equipment
HQ: Otis Elevator Company
  1 Carrier Pl
  Farmington CT 06032
  860 674-3000

(G-4710)
OUTREACH PROFESSIONAL SVCS INC
Also Called: St. Vincent Medical Group
2351 E 22nd St (44115-3111)
PHONE..............................216 472-4094
Beverly Lozar, *COO*
EMP: 83 **EST:** 1989
SQ FT: 3,700
SALES (est): 5.84MM
SALES (corp-wide): 4.3MM **Privately Held**
Web: www.stvincentcharity.com
SIC: 8741 Office management
HQ: St. Vincent Charity Medical Center
  2351 E 22nd St
  Cleveland OH 44115
  216 861-6200

(G-4711)
OVERDRIVE INC (HQ)
1 Overdrive Way (44125-5385)
PHONE..............................216 573-6886
Steven Potash, *Ch Bd*
Erica Lazzaro, *General*
Mike Vantusko, *
Lori Franklin, *
EMP: 98 **EST:** 1986
SQ FT: 10,000
SALES (est): 77.98MM
SALES (corp-wide): 77.98MM **Privately Held**
Web: www.overdrive.com
SIC: 7371 Software programming applications
PA: Overdrive Holdings, Inc.
  1 Overdrive Way
  Cleveland OH 44125
  216 573-6886

(G-4712)
OZANNE CONSTRUCTION CO INC
1635 E 25th St (44114-4214)
PHONE..............................216 696-2876
Dominic L Ozanne, *Pr*
Leroy Ozanne, *
Robert E Fitzgerald, *
Fred Rodgers, *
EMP: 40 **EST:** 1956
SQ FT: 4,000
SALES (est): 22.84MM **Privately Held**
Web: www.ozanne.com
SIC: 1542 Commercial and office building, new construction

(G-4713)
P C GURU INC
Also Called: P C G Computers
23250 Chagrin Blvd Ste 200 (44122-5470)
PHONE..............................216 292-4878
Jonathan Husni, *Pr*
Marie Fahner, *CFO*
EMP: 31 **EST:** 1988
SQ FT: 7,000
SALES (est): 8.05MM **Privately Held**
Web: www.acendex.com
SIC: 8748 Business consulting, nec

(G-4714)
P C VPA
16600 W Sprague Rd Ste 80 (44130-6318)
PHONE..............................440 826-0500
EMP: 30
Web: www.visitingphysicians.com

SIC: 8099 Medical services organization
PA: P C Vpa
  500 Kirts Blvd
  Troy MI 48084

(G-4715)
PANZICA CONSTRUCTION CO
Also Called: Panzica
739 Beta Drive Mayfield Village (44143-2326)
PHONE..............................440 442-4300
EMP: 120 **EST:** 1956
SALES (est): 24.98MM **Privately Held**
Web: www.panzica.com
SIC: 1542 Nonresidential construction, nec

(G-4716)
PARAGON CONSULTING INC
5900 Landerbrook Dr Ste 205 (44124-4029)
PHONE..............................440 684-3101
Carmen Tulino, *Pr*
Mark Atwood, *
Ray Modic, *Stockholder*
EMP: 30 **EST:** 1993
SQ FT: 3,800
SALES (est): 8.67MM **Privately Held**
Web: www.paragon-inc.com
SIC: 8742 General management consultant

(G-4717)
PARAGON TEC INC
3740 Carnegie Ave Ste 302 (44115-2756)
PHONE..............................216 361-5555
Gail Dolman-smith, *Pr*
EMP: 48 **EST:** 1996
SALES (est): 4.16MM **Privately Held**
Web: www.paragon-tec.com
SIC: 8742 General management consultant

(G-4718)
PARAMOUNT DISTILLERS INC
Also Called: Lonz Winery
3116 Berea Rd (44111-1596)
PHONE..............................216 671-6300
▲ **EMP:** 337
SIC: 2084 2085 5182 5812 Wines; Distilled and blended liquors; Wine; Eating places

(G-4719)
PARAN MANAGEMENT COMPANY LTD
2720 Van Aken Blvd Ste 200 (44120-2271)
PHONE..............................216 921-5663
EMP: 47 **EST:** 1975
SQ FT: 3,500
SALES (est): 62.36K **Privately Held**
Web: www.paranmgt.com
SIC: 6531 Real estate managers

(G-4720)
PARK CREEK RTIREMENT CMNTY INC
10064 N Church Dr (44130-4066)
PHONE..............................440 842-5100
John D Spielbuger, *Pr*
Linda Fgoice, *
Jessica Rowland, *
EMP: 29 **EST:** 1987
SQ FT: 40,000
SALES (est): 1.68MM **Privately Held**
Web: www.parkcreekretirement.com
SIC: 8052 Intermediate care facilities

(G-4721)
PARK N FLY LLC
19000 Snow Rd (44142-1412)
PHONE..............................404 264-1000
Judy Behrend, *Brnch Mgr*
EMP: 47

SALES (corp-wide): 165.81MM **Privately Held**
Web: www.pnf.com
SIC: 7521 Parking lots
HQ: Park 'n Fly, Llc.
  2060 Mt Paran Rd
  Atlanta GA 30327
  404 264-1000

(G-4722)
PARK PLACE OPERATIONS INC
Also Called: Airport Pass Park
18899 Snow Rd (44142-1409)
PHONE..............................216 265-0500
Marie Cunningham, *Mgr*
EMP: 29
SALES (corp-wide): 51.29MM **Privately Held**
Web: www.thefastpark.com
SIC: 7521 Parking lots
PA: Park Place Operations, Inc.
  250 W Court St Ste 200e
  Cincinnati OH 45202
  513 241-0415

(G-4723)
PARK PLACE TECHNOLOGIES LLC
Also Called: Park Place
5910 Landerbrook Dr Ste 300 (44124-6500)
PHONE..............................603 617-7123
James Stevens, *Mgr*
EMP: 34
Web: www.parkplacetechnologies.com
SIC: 7378 Computer maintenance and repair
PA: Park Place Technologies, Llc
  5910 Lndrbrook Dr Ste 300
  Cleveland OH 44124

(G-4724)
PARK PLACE TECHNOLOGIES LLC (PA)
5910 Landerbrook Dr Ste 300 (44124)
PHONE..............................877 778-8707
Chris Adams, *Pr*
Hal Malstrom, *
Ted Rieple, *
Mike Knightly, *
Judy Collister, *
EMP: 161 **EST:** 1991
SQ FT: 41,000
SALES (est): 367.44MM **Privately Held**
Web: www.parkplacetechnologies.com
SIC: 7379 3571 7378 3572 Computer related consulting services; Electronic computers; Computer peripheral equipment repair and maintenance; Computer storage devices

(G-4725)
PARKER-HANNIFIN INTL CORP (HQ)
6035 Parkland Blvd (44124-4186)
PHONE..............................216 896-3000
Donald Washkewic, *Pr*
Timothy K Pistell, *
EMP: 450 **EST:** 1967
SALES (est): 76MM
SALES (corp-wide): 19.07B **Publicly Held**
SIC: 8741 Administrative management
PA: Parker-Hannifin Corporation
  6035 Parkland Blvd
  Cleveland OH 44124
  216 896-3000

(G-4726)
PARKWOOD LLC
1000 Lakeside Ave E (44114-1117)
PHONE..............................216 875-6500
EMP: 40
SALES (est): 1.11MM **Privately Held**
Web: www.parkwoodcorp.com

SIC: 6282 Investment advisory service

(G-4727)
PARKWOOD CORPORATION (PA)
1000 Lakeside Ave E (44114-1117)
PHONE..............................216 875-6500
EMP: 42 **EST:** 1977
SQ FT: 13,680
SALES (est): 16.39MM **Privately Held**
Web: www.parkwoodcorp.com
SIC: 6282 Investment advisory service

(G-4728)
PARMA CARE CENTER INC
Also Called: Parma Care Nrsing Rhblttion Ct
5553 Broadview Rd (44134-1604)
PHONE..............................216 661-6800
Eitan Flank, *Owner*
Louis Schonfeld, *
David Farkas, *
Mike Flank, *
Brian Choleran, *
EMP: 159 **EST:** 1957
SQ FT: 55,000
SALES (est): 7.97MM **Privately Held**
Web: www.parmacarecenter.com
SIC: 8052 8051 Intermediate care facilities; Skilled nursing care facilities

(G-4729)
PAT YOUNG SERVICE CO INC (PA)
6100 Hillcrest Dr (44125-4622)
PHONE..............................216 447-8550
Derek W Young, *Pr*
Eugene Resovsky, *
Kirk Young, *
Ernest Mansour, *
Fran Young, *
▲ **EMP:** 49 **EST:** 1925
SQ FT: 35,000
SALES (est): 15.95MM
SALES (corp-wide): 15.95MM **Privately Held**
Web: www.fisherautoparts.com
SIC: 5531 5013 Automotive parts; Automotive supplies and parts

(G-4730)
PAUL A ERTEL
Also Called: Nautica Queen
1153 Main Ave (44113-2324)
PHONE..............................216 696-8888
Paul A Ertel, *Owner*
EMP: 38 **EST:** 1992
SQ FT: 1,000
SALES (est): 1.88MM **Privately Held**
Web: www.ladycaroline.com
SIC: 5812 5813 7999 American restaurant; Cocktail lounge; Beach and water sports equipment rental and services

(G-4731)
PAYCHEX ADVANCE LLC
Also Called: Advance Partners
23000 Millcreek Blvd Fl 2 (44122-5706)
PHONE..............................216 831-8900
EMP: 89 **EST:** 2016
SALES (est): 512.47K
SALES (corp-wide): 5.01B **Publicly Held**
Web: www.advancepartners.com
SIC: 8721 Payroll accounting service
PA: Paychex, Inc.
  911 Panorama Trl S
  Rochester NY 14625
  585 385-6666

(G-4732)
PCC AIRFOILS LLC
16601 Euclid Ave (44112-1405)
PHONE..............................216 692-7900
EMP: 34

Cleveland - Cuyahoga County (G-4753)

SALES (corp-wide): 364.48B Publicly Held
Web: www.pccairfoils.com
SIC: 5099 Brass goods
HQ: Pcc Airfoils, Llc
3401 Entp Pkwy Ste 200
Cleveland OH 44122
216 831-3590

(G-4733)
PEAK NANOSYSTEMS LLC
Also Called: Peak Nano
7700 Hub Pkwy Ste 8 (44125-5744)
PHONE.................................216 264-4818
Chad Lewis, Pr
EMP: 55 EST: 2015
SALES (est): 4.9MM Privately Held
Web: www.peaknano.com
SIC: 8731 Environmental research

(G-4734)
PEASE BELL CPAS LLC (PA)
1422 Euclid Ave Ste 400 (44115-1910)
PHONE.................................216 348-9600
EMP: 34 EST: 1998
SALES (est): 12.12MM Privately Held
Web: www.peasebell.com
SIC: 8721 Certified public accountant

(G-4735)
PEDIATRIC SERVICES INC (PA)
6707 Powers Blvd Ste 203 (44129-5494)
PHONE.................................440 845-1500
Daniel Hostetler Md, Pr
EMP: 38 EST: 1969
SQ FT: 4,000
SALES (est): 4.82MM
SALES (corp-wide): 4.82MM Privately Held
SIC: 8011 Pediatrician

(G-4736)
PEITRO PROPERTIES LTD PARTNR
Also Called: Comfort Inn
6191 Quarry Ln (44131-2203)
PHONE.................................216 328-7777
Teresa Shaley, Mng Pt
Peter Maisano, Pt
EMP: 44 EST: 1988
SQ FT: 1,000
SALES (est): 871.21K Privately Held
Web: www.choicehotels.com
SIC: 7011 Hotels and motels

(G-4737)
PEL LLC
4666 Manufacturing Ave (44135-2638)
PHONE.................................216 267-5775
Michael Sotak, Pr
Jeff Simon, *
EMP: 38 EST: 1949
SQ FT: 45,000
SALES (est): 9.4MM Privately Held
SIC: 5047 Artificial limbs

(G-4738)
PENNSYLVANIA STEEL COMPANY INC
Also Called: Pennsylvania Steel Co Ohio
4521 Willow Pkwy (44125-1041)
PHONE.................................440 243-9800
Robert Noonan, Brnch Mgr
EMP: 54
SALES (corp-wide): 108.8MM Privately Held
Web: www.pasteel.com
SIC: 5051 Steel
PA: Pennsylvania Steel Company, Inc.
1717 Woodhaven Dr
Bensalem PA 19020
215 633-9600

(G-4739)
PEPPER PIKE CLUB COMPANY INC
Also Called: PEPPER PIKE GOLF CLUB
2800 Som Center Rd (44124-4924)
PHONE.................................216 831-9400
Dwayne Collins, Pr
Linda Wasco, *
EMP: 75 EST: 1924
SQ FT: 10,000
SALES (est): 7.27MM Privately Held
Web: www.pepperpike.org
SIC: 7997 8699 Golf club, membership; Charitable organization

(G-4740)
PERIODONTAL ASSOCIATES INC
Also Called: Cole, Benton DDS
29001 Cedar Rd Ste 450 (44124-4051)
PHONE.................................440 461-3400
Howard Kaplan, Pr
Howard M Kaplan D.d.s., Pr
Roger Hess, Sec
EMP: 31 EST: 1974
SALES (est): 6.03MM Privately Held
Web: www.clevelandperio.com
SIC: 8021 Periodontist

(G-4741)
PERK COMPANY INC (PA)
Also Called: Perk Company of Ohio, Inc.
3740 Carnegie Ave Ste 301 Bldg A (44115-2756)
PHONE.................................216 391-1444
Charles Perkins, Pr
Joseph Cifani, *
Anthony Cifani, *
EMP: 44 EST: 1992
SALES (est): 11.93MM Privately Held
Web: www.perkcompany.com
SIC: 1611 General contractor, highway and street construction

(G-4742)
PERMANENT GEN ASRN CORP OHIO
9700 Rockside Rd (44125-6268)
PHONE.................................216 986-3000
Steven Mason, Ch Bd
Randy P Parker, *
David Hettinger, *
Brian Donovan, *
EMP: 45 EST: 1991
SQ FT: 15,000
SALES (est): 34.7MM
SALES (corp-wide): 11.04B Privately Held
SIC: 6331 Fire, marine and casualty insurance and carriers
HQ: Permanent General Companies, Inc.
2636 Elm Hill Pike # 510
Nashville TN 37214
615 242-1961

(G-4743)
PERSONALIZED DATA CORPORATION
Also Called: Personalized Data Entry & Word
26155 Euclid Ave Uppr (44132-3366)
PHONE.................................216 289-2200
Anthony Ruque, Pr
James Horne, *
EMP: 40 EST: 1967
SQ FT: 2,100
SALES (est): 1.35MM Privately Held
SIC: 7374 5734 Tabulating service; Computer peripheral equipment

(G-4744)
PERSPECTUS ARCHITECTURE LLC (PA)
1300 E 9th St Ste 910 (44114-1507)
PHONE.................................216 752-1800

William Ayars, Managing Member
EMP: 39 EST: 2002
SALES (est): 6.26MM
SALES (corp-wide): 6.26MM Privately Held
Web: www.perspectus.com
SIC: 8712 Architectural engineering

(G-4745)
PETE BAUR BUICK GMC INC (PA)
14000 Pearl Rd (44136-8706)
PHONE.................................440 238-5600
Daniel E Baur, Pr
Henry J Baur, *
EMP: 36 EST: 1969
SQ FT: 26,000
SALES (est): 9.19MM
SALES (corp-wide): 9.19MM Privately Held
Web: www.ganleybuickgmc.com
SIC: 5511 5531 7549 Automobiles, new and used; Auto and truck equipment and parts; Automotive maintenance services

(G-4746)
PHILIPS MED SYSTEMS CLVLAND IN (HQ)
Also Called: Philips Healthcare
595 Miner Rd (44143-2131)
PHONE.................................440 483-3000
David A Dripchak, CEO
Jerry C Cirino, Ex VP
William J Cull Senior, VP
Robert Blankenship, CFO
◆ EMP: 500 EST: 1970
SQ FT: 495,000
SALES (est): 665.76MM
SALES (corp-wide): 18.51B Privately Held
Web: www.emergin.com
SIC: 3844 5047 5137 3842 X-ray apparatus and tubes; X-ray film and supplies; Hospital gowns, women's and children's; Surgical appliances and supplies
PA: Koninklijke Philips N.V.
High Tech Campus 52
Eindhoven NB 5656
853015541

(G-4747)
PHOENIX RESIDENTIAL CTRS INC
6465 Pearl Rd Ste 1 (44130-2979)
PHONE.................................440 887-6097
Gary Toth, Brnch Mgr
EMP: 61
SQ FT: 5,845
SALES (corp-wide): 2.27MM Privately Held
Web: www.phoenixresidential.com
SIC: 6513 Apartment building operators
PA: Phoenix Residential Centers Inc.
1954 Hubbard Rd Ste 1
Madison OH 44057
440 428-9082

(G-4748)
PHYSICIAN STAFFING INC
Also Called: Martin Healthcare Group, The
30575 Bainbridge Rd Ste 200 (44139)
PHONE.................................440 542-5000
John S Martin Iii, CEO
Anthony Bernardo, *
Rafik Massouh, Chief Medical Officer*
Sunil Pandya, Chief Strategy Officer*
Jennifer Hayes, *
EMP: 365 EST: 1975
SQ FT: 10,000
SALES (est): 23.32MM
SALES (corp-wide): 43.45MM Privately Held
Web: www.hnihealthcare.com

SIC: 7363 Medical help service
PA: Hospitalists Now, Inc.
7500 Rialto Blvd 1-140
Austin TX 78735
512 730-3053

(G-4749)
PIONEER CLDDING GLZING SYSTEMS
2550 Brookpark Rd (44134-1407)
PHONE.................................216 816-4242
Michael Robinson, Brnch Mgr
EMP: 35
SALES (corp-wide): 50.25MM Privately Held
Web: www.pioneerglazing.com
SIC: 1793 1741 3448 Glass and glazing work; Masonry and other stonework; Prefabricated metal components
PA: Pioneer Cladding And Glazing Systems
4074 Bethany Rd
Mason OH 45040
513 583-5925

(G-4750)
PIONEER MANUFACTURING INC (PA)
Also Called: Pioneer Athletics
4529 Industrial Pkwy (44135-4505)
PHONE.................................216 671-5500
▲ EMP: 99 EST: 1906
SALES (est): 14.63MM
SALES (corp-wide): 14.63MM Privately Held
Web: www.pioneerathletics.com
SIC: 2952 5087 2842 2841 Asphalt felts and coatings; Cleaning and maintenance equipment and supplies; Polishes and sanitation goods; Soap and other detergents

(G-4751)
PIRHL CONTRACTORS LLC
800 W Saint Clair Ave # 4 (44113-1208)
P.O. Box 360619 (44136-0011)
PHONE.................................216 378-9690
EMP: 29 EST: 2005
SALES (est): 4.46MM
SALES (corp-wide): 24.19MM Privately Held
Web: www.pirhl.com
SIC: 1521 Single-family housing construction
PA: Pirhl, Llc
800 W Saint Clair Ave # 4
Cleveland OH 44113
216 378-9690

(G-4752)
PITT-OHIO EXPRESS LLC
5570 Chevrolet Blvd (44130-1497)
PHONE.................................216 433-9000
Mike Todd, Mgr
EMP: 122
SALES (corp-wide): 508.23MM Privately Held
Web: www.pittohioexpress.com
SIC: 4231 4213 4212 Trucking terminal facilities; Trucking, except local; Local trucking, without storage
PA: Pitt-Ohio Express, Llc
15 27th St
Pittsburgh PA 15222
412 232-3015

(G-4753)
PK MANAGEMENT LLC (PA)
26301 Curtiss Wright Pkwy Ste 300 (44143-4413)
PHONE.................................216 472-1870
Gregory F Perlman, Managing Member
Robert A Kriensky, *
Thomas Mc Ginty, *
EMP: 106 EST: 2007

Cleveland - Cuyahoga County (G-4754)

SALES (est): 43.9MM
SALES (corp-wide): 43.9MM **Privately Held**
Web: www.pkmanagement.com
SIC: 6531 Real estate agents and managers

(G-4754)
PLAIN DEALER FEDERAL CR UN INC
5341 Pearl Rd (44129-1503)
PHONE..............................216 999-4270
William Pelger, *CEO*
EMP: 47 **EST:** 1957
SALES (est): 494.26K **Privately Held**
Web: www.plaindealercreditunion.com
SIC: 6061 Federal credit unions

(G-4755)
PLASTIC SAFETY SYSTEMS INC
Also Called: Pss
2444 Baldwin Rd (44104-2505)
PHONE..............................216 231-8590
David E Cowan, *Pr*
Wentworth J Marshall Junior, *Sec*
Janet S Duluc, *
Ben Gascoigne, *General Vice President*
▼ **EMP:** 31 **EST:** 1961
SQ FT: 55,000
SALES (est): 8.51MM **Privately Held**
Web: www.pss-innovations.com
SIC: 8711 Engineering services

(G-4756)
PLATINUMTELE SOLUTIONS LLC
7415 Broadway Ave (44105-2015)
PHONE..............................216 609-5804
Taylor Mercer, *Managing Member*
EMP: 30 **EST:** 2019
SALES (est): 562.98K **Privately Held**
SIC: 8742 Marketing consulting services

(G-4757)
PLAYHOUSE SQUARE FOUNDATION (PA)
Also Called: PLAYHOUSE SQUARE
1501 Euclid Ave Ste 200 (44115-2108)
PHONE..............................216 771-4444
EMP: 245 **EST:** 1973
SALES (est): 24.72MM **Privately Held**
Web: www.playhousesquare.org
SIC: 7922 Legitimate live theater producers

(G-4758)
PLAYHOUSE SQUARE FOUNDATION
Also Called: Crowne Plaza Cleveland
1260 Euclid Ave (44115-1837)
PHONE..............................216 615-7500
EMP: 127
Web: www.ihg.com
SIC: 7011 5812 Hotels and motels; Eating places
PA: Playhouse Square Foundation
1501 Euclid Ave Ste 200
Cleveland OH 44115

(G-4759)
PLAYHOUSE SQUARE HOLDG CO LLC (PA)
Also Called: Prop Shop
1501 Euclid Ave Ste 200 (44115-2108)
PHONE..............................216 771-4444
Art J Falco, *Managing Member*
Darlene Koskinen, *Ex Sec*
EMP: 150 **EST:** 1999
SQ FT: 10,000
SALES (est): 24.27MM
SALES (corp-wide): 24.27MM **Privately Held**
Web: www.playhousesquare.org

SIC: 8399 7922 Fund raising organization, non-fee basis; Performing arts center production

(G-4760)
POLYMER SOLUTIONS GROUP LLC
12819 Coit Rd (44108-1614)
PHONE..............................229 435-8394
EMP: 28 **EST:** 2020
SALES (est): 5.3MM **Privately Held**
Web: www.polymersolutionsgroup.com
SIC: 5169 Chemicals and allied products, nec

(G-4761)
PORTER WRGHT MORRIS ARTHUR LLP
950 Main Ave Ste 500 (44113-7206)
PHONE..............................216 443-2506
Hugh Mckay, *Pt*
EMP: 29
SALES (corp-wide): 47.71MM **Privately Held**
Web: www.porterwright.com
SIC: 8111 General practice law office
PA: Porter, Wright, Morris & Arthur Llp
41 S High St Ste 2900
Columbus OH 43215
614 227-2000

(G-4762)
POSITIVE EDUCATION PROGRAM
Also Called: Hopewell Day Treatment Center
11500 Franklin Blvd (44102-2335)
PHONE..............................216 227-2730
Stephen Sheppard, *Dir*
EMP: 36
SQ FT: 6,764
SALES (corp-wide): 36.7MM **Privately Held**
Web: www.pepcleve.org
SIC: 8211 8322 Specialty education; Self-help organization, nec
PA: Positive Education Program Inc
3100 Euclid Ave
Cleveland OH 44115
216 361-4400

(G-4763)
POSITIVE EDUCATION PROGRAM
Also Called: West Shore Day Treatment Ctr
4320 W 220th St (44126-1818)
PHONE..............................440 471-8200
EMP: 40
SALES (corp-wide): 36.7MM **Privately Held**
Web: www.pepcleve.org
SIC: 8211 8093 Specialty education; Specialty outpatient clinics, nec
PA: Positive Education Program Inc
3100 Euclid Ave
Cleveland OH 44115
216 361-4400

(G-4764)
PRAETORIAN HOLDINGS GROUP LLC
127 Public Sq Ste 4120 (44114-1312)
PHONE..............................440 665-4246
Matt Bahnij, *Managing Member*
EMP: 50 **EST:** 2019
SALES (est): 3.55MM **Privately Held**
Web: www.praetorianvc.com
SIC: 6799 Investors, nec

(G-4765)
PRECISION WELDING CORPORATION
7900 Exchange St (44125-3334)
P.O. Box 25548 (44125-0548)

PHONE..............................216 524-6110
Dennis Nader, *Pr*
Randy Nader, *
EMP: 32 **EST:** 1946
SQ FT: 26,000
SALES (est): 2.31MM **Privately Held**
Web: www.precisionweldingcorp.net
SIC: 7692 3444 3441 Welding repair; Sheet metalwork; Fabricated structural metal

(G-4766)
PREDICTIVE SERVICE LLC (PA)
25200 Chagrin Blvd Ste 300 (44122-5684)
PHONE..............................866 772-6770
John Harman, *
Ralph Delisio, *
EMP: 51 **EST:** 2002
SQ FT: 16,000
SALES (est): 23.37MM
SALES (corp-wide): 23.37MM **Privately Held**
Web: www.seamgroup.com
SIC: 7389 Industrial and commercial equipment inspection service

(G-4767)
PREFERRED ACQUISITION CO LLC (PA)
4871 Neo Pkwy (44128-3101)
PHONE..............................216 587-0957
Craig S Hartman, *CEO*
Justin Valenta, *Managing Member*
Susan Tubbs, *CFO*
Brian Miller, *VP*
EMP: 52 **EST:** 2004
SQ FT: 14,000
SALES (est): 11.99MM
SALES (corp-wide): 11.99MM **Privately Held**
Web: www.preferredllc.net
SIC: 1752 1721 Floor laying and floor work, nec; Commercial painting

(G-4768)
PREMIER TRUCK SLS & RENTL INC
7700 Wall St (44125-3324)
PHONE..............................800 825-1255
Joey Lojek, *Pr*
Brent Humberson, *
Claude Humberson, *
▼ **EMP:** 35 **EST:** 1985
SQ FT: 17,000
SALES (est): 13.12MM **Privately Held**
Web: www.premiertrucksales.com
SIC: 5521 7513 Trucks, tractors, and trailers: used; Truck rental and leasing, no drivers

(G-4769)
PRESSLEY RIDGE FOUNDATION
23701 Miles Rd (44128-5473)
PHONE..............................216 763-0800
EMP: 141
Web: www.pressleyridge.org
SIC: 8322 Individual and family services
PA: Pressley Ridge Foundation
5500 Corporate Dr Ste 400
Pittsburgh PA 15237

(G-4770)
PRETERM FOUNDATION
12000 Shaker Blvd (44120)
PHONE..............................216 991-4577
Chrisse France, *Ex Dir*
EMP: 40 **EST:** 1973
SQ FT: 15,000
SALES (est): 4.93MM **Privately Held**
Web: www.preterm.org
SIC: 8093 8011 Abortion clinic; Offices and clinics of medical doctors

(G-4771)
PRICE FOR PROFIT LLC
6140 Parkland Blvd Ste 250 (44124-6142)
PHONE..............................440 646-9490
Ryan White, *Managing Member*
Keith Hohman, *Managing Member*
Joe Bogner, *
Chris Donnelly, *
EMP: 79 **EST:** 2010
SALES (est): 4.47MM **Privately Held**
Web: www.insight2profit.com
SIC: 8748 Business consulting, nec

(G-4772)
PRODUCTION TOOL SUPPLY OHIO
10801 Brookpark Rd (44130-1197)
PHONE..............................216 265-0000
Terry White, *Pr*
Larry A Wolfe, *Pr*
David D Kahn, *Ex VP*
Mark Kahn, *VP*
EMP: 77 **EST:** 1986
SQ FT: 21,000
SALES (est): 846.14K **Privately Held**
SIC: 5072 5084 Hardware; Metalworking machinery

(G-4773)
PRODUCTS CHEMICAL COMPANY LLC
4005 Clark Ave (44109-1128)
PHONE..............................216 281-1155
Jim Purcoll, *Pr*
EMP: 100 **EST:** 2020
SALES (est): 9.91MM **Privately Held**
Web: www.prod-chem.com
SIC: 5169 Industrial chemicals

(G-4774)
PROFESSIONAL SERVICE INDS INC
Also Called: PSI Testing and Engineering
5555 Canal Rd (44125-4874)
PHONE..............................216 447-1335
Chris Lopez, *Brnch Mgr*
EMP: 33
SALES (corp-wide): 4.15B **Privately Held**
Web: www.intertek.com
SIC: 8711 Consulting engineer
HQ: Professional Service Industries, Inc.
545 E Algonquin Rd
Arlington Heights IL 60005
630 691-1490

(G-4775)
PROGRESSIVE ADJUSTING CO INC
Also Called: Progressive Insurance
6300 Wilson Mills Rd (44143-2109)
PHONE..............................440 461-5000
S Patricia Griffith, *CEO*
Susan Patricia Griffith, *CEO*
EMP: 88 **EST:** 1987
SQ FT: 75,000
SALES (est): 41.72MM
SALES (corp-wide): 49.61B **Publicly Held**
Web: www.progressive.com
SIC: 6331 Fire, marine, and casualty insurance
PA: The Progressive Corporation
6300 Wilson Mills Rd
Mayfield Village OH 44143
440 461-5000

(G-4776)
PROGRESSIVE ADVANCED INSUR CO
Also Called: Progressive Insurance
6300 Wilson Mills Rd (44143-2109)
PHONE..............................440 461-5000
EMP: 299 **EST:** 1926
SALES (est): 619.54MM

GEOGRAPHIC SECTION
Cleveland - Cuyahoga County (G-4797)

SALES (corp-wide): 49.61B **Publicly Held**
Web: www.progressivecommercial.com
SIC: 6411 Insurance agents, nec
HQ: Progressive Direct Holdings, Inc.
6300 Wilson Mills Rd
Cleveland OH 44143

(G-4777)
PROGRESSIVE BAYSIDE INSUR CO (DH)
Also Called: Progressive Insurance
6300 Wilson Mills Rd (44143-2109)
PHONE................................440 395-4460
Susan Patricia Griffith, *CEO*
EMP: 102 EST: 1986
SQ FT: 60,000
SALES (est): 104.11MM
SALES (corp-wide): 49.61B **Publicly Held**
Web: www.progressive.com
SIC: 6331 Fire, marine, and casualty insurance
HQ: Drive Insurance Holdings, Inc.
6300 Wilson Mills Rd
Cleveland OH 44143

(G-4778)
PROGRESSIVE CASUALTY INSUR CO
Progressive Insurance
747 Alpha Dr Ste A21 (44143-2124)
PHONE................................440 603-4033
Bob Flerchinger, *Mgr*
EMP: 46
SALES (corp-wide): 49.61B **Publicly Held**
Web: www.progressive.com
SIC: 6331 6321 Automobile insurance; Accident insurance carriers
HQ: Progressive Casualty Insurance Company
6300 Wilson Mills Rd
Mayfield Village OH 44143
855 347-3939

(G-4779)
PROGRESSIVE CHOICE INSUR CO
Also Called: Progressive Insurance
6300 Wilson Mills Rd (44143-2109)
PHONE................................440 461-5000
Steven A Broz, *Pr*
EMP: 247 EST: 1990
SALES (est): 77.44MM
SALES (corp-wide): 49.61B **Publicly Held**
Web: www.progressive.com
SIC: 6331 Fire, marine, and casualty insurance
HQ: Progressive Direct Holdings, Inc.
6300 Wilson Mills Rd
Cleveland OH 44143

(G-4780)
PROGRESSIVE CLASSIC INSUR CO
Also Called: Progressive Insurance
6300 Wilson Mills Rd (44143-2109)
PHONE................................440 661-5000
Susan Patricia Griffith, *CEO*
EMP: 39 EST: 1988
SALES (est): 624.68MM
SALES (corp-wide): 49.61B **Publicly Held**
Web: www.progressive.com
SIC: 6331 Fire, marine, and casualty insurance
HQ: Drive Insurance Holdings, Inc.
6300 Wilson Mills Rd
Cleveland OH 44143

(G-4781)
PROGRESSIVE COML CSLTY CO
Also Called: Progressive Insurance
6300 Wilson Mills Rd (44143-2109)
PHONE................................440 461-5000
S Patricia Griffith, *CEO*
EMP: 52 EST: 2006
SALES (est): 20.29MM
SALES (corp-wide): 49.61B **Publicly Held**
Web: www.progressivecommercial.com
SIC: 6331 Fire, marine, and casualty insurance
HQ: Drive Insurance Holdings, Inc.
6300 Wilson Mills Rd
Cleveland OH 44143

(G-4782)
PROGRESSIVE EXPRESS INSUR CO
Also Called: Progressive Insurance
6300 Wilson Mills Rd (44143-2109)
PHONE................................440 461-5000
S Patricia Griffith, *Pr*
Susan Patricia Griffith, *
EMP: 144 EST: 1994
SALES (est): 73.67MM
SALES (corp-wide): 49.61B **Publicly Held**
Web: www.progressive.com
SIC: 6411 Insurance agents, nec
HQ: Progressive Commercial Holdings, Inc.
6300 Wilson Mills Rd
Cleveland OH 44143

(G-4783)
PROGRESSIVE FREEDOM INSUR CO
Also Called: Progressive Insurance
6300 Wilson Mills Rd (44143-2109)
PHONE................................440 461-5000
S Patricia Griffith, *CEO*
EMP: 88 EST: 2018
SALES (est): 104.11MM
SALES (corp-wide): 49.61B **Publicly Held**
Web: www.progressivecommercial.com
SIC: 6331 Fire, marine, and casualty insurance
HQ: Progressive Direct Holdings, Inc.
6300 Wilson Mills Rd
Cleveland OH 44143

(G-4784)
PROGRESSIVE GRDN STATE INSUR
Also Called: Progressive Insurance
6300 Wilson Mills Rd (44143-2109)
PHONE................................440 461-5000
EMP: 299 EST: 2005
SALES (est): 82.23MM
SALES (corp-wide): 49.61B **Publicly Held**
Web: www.progressivecommercial.com
SIC: 6411 Property and casualty insurance agent
HQ: Progressive Direct Holdings, Inc.
6300 Wilson Mills Rd
Cleveland OH 44143

(G-4785)
PROGRESSIVE HAWAII INSUR CORP
Also Called: Progressive Insurance
6300 Wilson Mills Rd (44143-2109)
P.O. Box 89490 (44101-6490)
PHONE................................440 461-5000
Geoffrey Thomas Souser, *Pr*
EMP: 72 EST: 1994
SALES (est): 352.14MM
SALES (corp-wide): 49.61B **Publicly Held**
Web: www.progressive.com
SIC: 6411 Insurance agents and brokers
HQ: Drive Insurance Holdings, Inc.
6300 Wilson Mills Rd
Cleveland OH 44143

(G-4786)
PROGRESSIVE PALOVERDE INSUR CO
Also Called: Progressive Insurance
6300 Wilson Mills Rd (44143-2109)
PHONE................................440 461-5000
EMP: 123 EST: 2006
SALES (est): 13.35MM

SALES (corp-wide): 49.61B **Publicly Held**
Web: www.progressive.com
SIC: 6331 Fire, marine, and casualty insurance
HQ: Progressive Direct Holdings, Inc.
6300 Wilson Mills Rd
Cleveland OH 44143

(G-4787)
PROGRESSIVE PREMIER INSUR ILL
Also Called: Progressive Insurance
6300 Wilson Mills Rd W33 (44143)
PHONE................................440 461-5000
S Patricia Griffith, *CEO*
EMP: 97 EST: 1992
SALES (est): 309.77MM
SALES (corp-wide): 49.61B **Publicly Held**
Web: www.progressive.com
SIC: 6411 Insurance agents and brokers
HQ: Progressive Direct Holdings, Inc.
6300 Wilson Mills Rd
Cleveland OH 44143

(G-4788)
PROGRESSIVE RSC INC
Also Called: Progressive Insurance
6300 Wilson Mills Rd (44143-2109)
PHONE................................440 461-5000
S Patricia Griffith, *CEO*
EMP: 95 EST: 2018
SALES (est): 93.45MM
SALES (corp-wide): 49.61B **Publicly Held**
Web: www.progressive.com
SIC: 6331 Fire, marine, and casualty insurance
PA: The Progressive Corporation
6300 Wilson Mills Rd
Mayfield Village OH 44143
440 461-5000

(G-4789)
PROGRESSIVE SELECT INSUR CO
Also Called: Progressive Insurance
6300 Wilson Mills Rd (44143-2109)
PHONE................................440 461-5000
James R Haas, *Prin*
EMP: 846 EST: 1994
SALES (est): 318.15MM
SALES (corp-wide): 49.61B **Publicly Held**
Web: www.progressive.com
SIC: 6411 Insurance agents, nec
HQ: Progressive Direct Holdings, Inc.
6300 Wilson Mills Rd
Cleveland OH 44143

(G-4790)
PROGRESSIVE SPECIALTY INSUR CO
Also Called: Progressive Insurance
6300 Wilson Mills Rd (44143-2109)
PHONE................................440 461-5000
Geoffrey Thomas Souser, *Pr*
EMP: 33040 EST: 1975
SALES (est): 1.46B
SALES (corp-wide): 49.61B **Publicly Held**
Web: www.progressive.com
SIC: 6411 Insurance agents and brokers
HQ: Progressive Casualty Insurance Company
6300 Wilson Mills Rd
Mayfield Village OH 44143
855 347-3939

(G-4791)
PROGRESSIVE UNIVERSAL INSUR CO
Also Called: Progressive Insurance
6300 Wilson Mills Rd (44143-2109)
PHONE................................440 461-5000
S Patricia Griffith, *CEO*
Susan Patricia Griffith, *CEO*

David Schneider, *Sec*
EMP: 211 EST: 2003
SALES (est): 619.54MM
SALES (corp-wide): 49.61B **Publicly Held**
Web: www.progressive.com
SIC: 6331 Fire, marine, and casualty insurance
HQ: Progressive Direct Holdings, Inc.
6300 Wilson Mills Rd
Cleveland OH 44143

(G-4792)
PROGRSSIVE COML ADVNTAGE AGCY
Also Called: Progressive Insurance
6300 Wilson Mills Rd (44143-2109)
PHONE................................440 461-5000
S Patricia Griffith, *CEO*
EMP: 28 EST: 2010
SALES (est): 3.14MM
SALES (corp-wide): 49.61B **Publicly Held**
Web: www.progressivecommercial.com
SIC: 6411 Insurance agents, nec
HQ: Drive Insurance Holdings, Inc.
6300 Wilson Mills Rd
Cleveland OH 44143

(G-4793)
PROGRSSIVE SPCLTY INSUR AGCY I
Also Called: Progressive Insurance
6300 Wilson Mills Rd (44143-2109)
PHONE................................440 461-5000
EMP: 176 EST: 1995
SALES (est): 4.53MM
SALES (corp-wide): 49.61B **Publicly Held**
Web: www.progressivecommercial.com
SIC: 6411 Insurance agents, nec
HQ: Progressive Direct Holdings, Inc.
6300 Wilson Mills Rd
Cleveland OH 44143

(G-4794)
PROVIDENCE HEALTHCARE MGT INC
29225 Chagrin Blvd Ste 230 (44122-4632)
PHONE................................216 200-5917
Eli Gunzburg, *Pr*
EMP: 325 EST: 2008
SALES (est): 24.5MM **Privately Held**
Web: www.providencehcm.com
SIC: 8099 Blood related health services

(G-4795)
PROVIDENCE HOUSE INC
Also Called: Crisis Nursery
2050 W 32nd St (44113)
PHONE................................216 651-5982
Natalie Leek-nelson, *Pr*
Stacy Schiemann, *Program Officer**
EMP: 37 EST: 1981
SQ FT: 5,000
SALES (est): 4.54MM **Privately Held**
Web: www.provhouse.org
SIC: 8322 8361 Child related social services; Residential care

(G-4796)
PS LIFESTYLE LLC
Also Called: Salon PS
55 Public Sq Ste 2075 (44113-1974)
PHONE................................440 600-1595
EMP: 800 EST: 2008
SALES (est): 29.49MM **Privately Held**
Web: shop.pslifestyle.com
SIC: 7231 Unisex hair salons

(G-4797)
PUBCO CORPORATION (PA)
3830 Kelley Ave (44114)
PHONE................................216 881-5300

Cleveland - Cuyahoga County (G-4798) GEOGRAPHIC SECTION

William Dillingham, *Pr*
Stephen R Kalette, *
Maria Szubski, *
◆ **EMP:** 85 **EST:** 1996
SQ FT: 312,000
SALES (est): 121.85MM
SALES (corp-wide): 121.85MM **Privately Held**
Web: www.buckeyebusiness.com
SIC: 3531 3955 6512 Construction machinery; Carbon paper and inked ribbons; Nonresidential building operators

(G-4798)
PULL-A-PART LLC
4433 W 130th St (44135-3011)
PHONE....................330 631-6280
EMP: 32
SALES (corp-wide): 119.55MM **Privately Held**
Web: www.pullapart.com
SIC: 5015 Automotive parts and supplies, used
PA: Pull-A-Part, Llc
   4473 Tilly Mill Rd
   Atlanta GA 30360
   404 607-7000

(G-4799)
QUALITY CONTROL INSPECTION (PA)
9500 Midwest Ave (44125-2463)
PHONE....................440 359-1900
Rick Capone, *Pr*
EMP: 60 **EST:** 1986
SALES (est): 9.83MM
SALES (corp-wide): 9.83MM **Privately Held**
Web: www.qcigroup.com
SIC: 7389 8741 Building inspection service; Construction management

(G-4800)
QUALITY CONTROL SERVICES LLC (PA)
3214 Saint Clair Ave Ne (44114-4008)
PHONE....................216 862-9264
David S Nolan, *Managing Member*
EMP: 34 **EST:** 2004
SALES (est): 2.44MM
SALES (corp-wide): 2.44MM **Privately Held**
Web: www.qcsinspections.com
SIC: 8711 1799 Engineering services; Coating of metal structures at construction site

(G-4801)
QUALITY SOLUTIONS INC
Also Called: QUALITY SOLUTIONS INC
P.O. Box 40147 (44140-0147)
PHONE....................440 933-9946
Francis P Toolan Junior, *Brnch Mgr*
EMP: 27
Web: www.firebrandtech.com
SIC: 2741 8742 8732 Business service newsletters: publishing and printing; Management consulting services; Market analysis or research
HQ: Quality Solutions, Inc.
   44 Merrimac St Ste 22
   Newburyport MA 01950

(G-4802)
QUEENS BEAUTY BAR LLC
4321 Storer Ave (44109-1001)
PHONE....................216 804-0533
EMP: 33 **EST:** 2021
SALES (est): 163.05K **Privately Held**
SIC: 7231 7389 Beauty shops; Business services, nec

(G-4803)
R B C APOLLO EQUITY PARTNERS (DH)
600 Superior Ave E Ste 2300 (44114-2612)
PHONE....................216 875-2626
EMP: 36 **EST:** 1997
SQ FT: 5,000
SALES (est): 29.8MM
SALES (corp-wide): 41.52B **Privately Held**
SIC: 6211 Investment bankers
HQ: Rbc Capital Markets Corporation
   60 S 6th St Ste 700
   Minneapolis MN 55402
   612 371-2711

(G-4804)
R D D INC (PA)
Also Called: Power Direct
4719 Blythin Rd (44125-1209)
PHONE....................216 781-5858
EMP: 120 **EST:** 1994
SQ FT: 15,000
SALES (est): 16.43MM **Privately Held**
Web: www.power-direct.com
SIC: 7389 8742 Telemarketing services; Marketing consulting services

(G-4805)
R L LIPTON DISTRIBUTING CO
9797 Sweet Valley Dr (44125-4241)
PHONE....................216 475-4150
Steve Eisenberg, *Pr*
W Terry Patrick, *
W Bud Biggin, *
C Jack Amstutz, *Stockholder*
▲ **EMP:** 75 **EST:** 1965
SALES (est): 12.5MM **Privately Held**
Web: www.rlliptondist.com
SIC: 5181 5182 5149 Beer and other fermented malt liquors; Wine; Groceries and related products, nec

(G-4806)
RA STAFF COMPANY
Also Called: Staffco-Campisano
16500 W Sprague Rd, Middlebourough Heights (44130-6315)
PHONE....................440 891-9900
Larry Mchale, *Pr*
Heather Kantor, *Off Mgr*
▲ **EMP:** 42 **EST:** 1961
SQ FT: 10,000
SALES (est): 5.31MM **Privately Held**
Web: www.s-cinc.com
SIC: 8743 Sales promotion

(G-4807)
RAE-ANN ENTERPRISES INC
Also Called: Rae-Ann Suburban
27310 W Oviatt Rd (44140-2139)
P.O. Box 40175 (44140-0175)
PHONE....................440 249-5092
Ray Griffiths, *VP*
EMP: 67 **EST:** 1974
SALES (est): 4.86MM **Privately Held**
SIC: 8059 Convalescent home

(G-4808)
RAPID TRANSIT LINE
Also Called: Gcrta
1240 W 6th St (44113-1302)
PHONE....................216 621-9500
Joseph Calabrese, *Owner*
EMP: 34 **EST:** 2000
SALES (est): 3.19MM **Privately Held**
Web: www.riderta.com
SIC: 4111 Bus line operations

(G-4809)
RATHBONE GROUP LLC (PA)
1250 E Granger Rd (44131)
PHONE....................800 870-5521
Kimberly Rathbone, *Managing Member*
EMP: 43 **EST:** 2014
SALES (est): 7.25MM
SALES (corp-wide): 7.25MM **Privately Held**
Web: www.rathbonegroup.com
SIC: 8111 General practice law office

(G-4810)
READER TINNING & ROOFING CO
Also Called: Reader Tinning Roofg & Frnc Co
676 E 152nd St (44110-2395)
PHONE....................216 451-1355
Stuart Reader, *Pr*
Stuart Reader, *Pr*
Michael Reader, *VP*
Roslyn Reader, *Sec*
EMP: 27 **EST:** 1920
SQ FT: 9,042
SALES (est): 975.71K **Privately Held**
Web: www.readerroofing.com
SIC: 1761 1711 Roofing contractor; Heating and air conditioning contractors

(G-4811)
REBIZ LLC
1925 Saint Clair Ave Ne (44114-2028)
PHONE....................844 467-3249
Jumaid Hasan, *Managing Member*
EMP: 50 **EST:** 2014
SALES (est): 5.08MM **Privately Held**
Web: www.rebiz.com
SIC: 7372 7374 Business oriented computer software; Optical scanning data service

(G-4812)
RECOVERY RESOURCES
4269 Pearl Rd Ste 300 (44109-4232)
PHONE....................216 431-4131
EMP: 52
SALES (corp-wide): 620.72MM **Privately Held**
Web: www.recres.org
SIC: 8093 Mental health clinic, outpatient
HQ: Recovery Resources
   3950 Chester Ave
   Cleveland OH 44114
   216 431-4131

(G-4813)
RECOVERY RESOURCES (HQ)
Also Called: METROHEALTH
3950 Chester Ave (44114-4625)
PHONE....................216 431-4131
Debora Rodriguez, *Pr*
Charlotte Rerko, *
William Morgan, *
EMP: 48 **EST:** 1975
SQ FT: 6,800
SALES (est): 9.38MM
SALES (corp-wide): 620.72MM **Privately Held**
Web: www.recres.org
SIC: 8093 Mental health clinic, outpatient
PA: The Metrohealth System
   2500 Metrohealth Dr
   Cleveland OH 44109
   216 778-7800

(G-4814)
RED ROOF INNS INC
Also Called: Red Roof Inn
6020 Quarry Ln (44131-2299)
PHONE....................216 447-0030
EMP: 40
Web: www.redroof.com

SIC: 7011 Hotels and motels
HQ: Red Roof Inns, Inc.
   7815 Walton Pkwy
   New Albany OH 43054
   614 744-2600

(G-4815)
RED ROOF INNS INC
Also Called: Red Roof Inn
29595 Clemens Rd (44145-1056)
PHONE....................440 892-7920
EMP: 40
Web: www.redroof.com
SIC: 7011 Hotels and motels
HQ: Red Roof Inns, Inc.
   7815 Walton Pkwy
   New Albany OH 43054
   614 744-2600

(G-4816)
RED ROOF INNS INC
Also Called: Red Roof Inn
17555 Bagley Rd (44130-2551)
PHONE....................440 202-1521
EMP: 37
Web: www.redroof.com
SIC: 7011 Hotels and motels
HQ: Red Roof Inns, Inc.
   7815 Walton Pkwy
   New Albany OH 43054
   614 744-2600

(G-4817)
REED WESTLAKE LESKOSKY LTD
1422 Euclid Ave Ste 300 (44115-1912)
PHONE....................216 522-0449
EMP: 140
SIC: 8711 8712 Engineering services; Architectural services

(G-4818)
REFRIGERATION SALES COMPANY LLC (DH)
Also Called: Refrigrtion Sls Corp Cleveland
9450 Allen Dr Ste A (44125-4601)
PHONE....................216 525-8200
▲ **EMP:** 47 **EST:** 1945
SALES (est): 46.28MM
SALES (corp-wide): 2.1MM **Privately Held**
Web: www.refrigerationsales.net
SIC: 5078 5075 Refrigeration equipment and supplies; Air conditioning and ventilation equipment and supplies
HQ: Le Groupe Master Inc
   1675 Boul De Montarville
   Boucherville QC J4B 7
   514 527-2301

(G-4819)
REHABCARE GROUP EAST INC
3151 Mayfield Rd (44118-1757)
PHONE....................330 220-8950
Arthur Rothgerber, *Bmch Mgr*
EMP: 206
SALES (corp-wide): 1.09B **Privately Held**
Web: www.kindredhospitals.com
SIC: 8093 Rehabilitation center, outpatient treatment
HQ: Rehabcare Group East, Inc.
   680 S 4th St
   Louisville KY 40202
   314 863-7422

(G-4820)
RELENTLESS RECOVERY INC
1898 Scranton Rd Uppr (44113-2434)
PHONE....................216 621-8333
David Ziebro, *Pr*
Amy Osterling, *
EMP: 60 **EST:** 2002
SALES (est): 22.29MM **Privately Held**

Web: www.relentlessohio.com
SIC: 6153 Credit card services, central agency collection

(G-4821)
RELIABILITY FIRST CORPORATION
3 Summit Park Dr Ste 600 (44131-6900)
PHONE..................................216 503-0600
Timothy R Gallagher, *Pr*
Raymond J Palmieri, *
Larry Bugh, *
Jack Ispvan, *
EMP: 30 EST: 2006
SALES (est): 23.07MM **Privately Held**
SIC: 4911 Transmission, electric power

(G-4822)
RELIANT TECHNOLOGY LLC
Also Called: Go Reliant LLC
5910 Landerbrook Dr Ste 100 (44124-6534)
PHONE..................................404 551-4534
Reid Smith-vaniz, *CEO*
Jennifer Deutsch, *CMO*✱
EMP: 45 EST: 2007
SALES (est): 4.8MM **Privately Held**
Web: www.parkplacetechnologies.com
SIC: 7376 7377 Computer facilities management; Computer hardware rental or leasing, except finance leasing
PA: Park Place Technologies, Llc
  5910 Lndrbrook Dr Ste 300
  Cleveland OH 44124

(G-4823)
RELMEC MECHANICAL LLC
4975 Hamilton Ave (44114-3906)
PHONE..................................216 391-1030
EMP: 180 EST: 2009
SALES (est): 25.65MM **Privately Held**
Web: www.relmecllc.com
SIC: 1711 Mechanical contractor

(G-4824)
REMESH INC
6815 Euclid Ave (44103-3915)
PHONE..................................561 809-9885
Andrew Konya, *CEO*
EMP: 86 EST: 2014
SALES (est): 5.06MM **Privately Held**
Web: www.remesh.ai
SIC: 8742 Management consulting services

(G-4825)
REMINGER CO LPA (PA)
200 Public Sq Ste 1200 (44114-2330)
PHONE..................................216 687-1311
Brian T Gannon, *Pr*
William Meadows, *
Donald Moracz, *
Nick Satullo, *
Richard Rymond, *
EMP: 175 EST: 1958
SALES (est): 49.64MM
SALES (corp-wide): 49.64MM **Privately Held**
Web: www.reminger.com
SIC: 8111 General practice attorney, lawyer

(G-4826)
RENAISSANCE HOTEL OPERATING CO
Also Called: Renaissance Hotel
24 Public Sq Fl 1 (44113-2222)
PHONE..................................216 696-5600
Jerry Mcgauley, *Brnch Mgr*
EMP: 536
SALES (corp-wide): 23.71B **Publicly Held**
Web: renaissance-hotels.marriott.com
SIC: 7011 7389 Hotels and motels; Office facilities and secretarial service rental
HQ: Renaissance Hotel Operating Company
  10400 Fernwood Rd
  Bethesda MD 20817

(G-4827)
RENNER OTTO BOISELLE & SKLAR
1621 Euclid Ave Ste 1900 (44115-2191)
PHONE..................................216 621-1113
Donald Otto, *Pt*
John Renner, *Sr Pt*
Armand Boiselle, *Sr Pt*
Warren Sklar, *Sr Pt*
EMP: 49 EST: 1900
SALES (est): 8.89MM **Privately Held**
Web: www.rennerotto.com
SIC: 8111 General practice law office

(G-4828)
RESEARCH ASSOCIATES INC (PA)
Also Called: R A I
27999 Clemens Rd (44145-1182)
PHONE..................................440 892-1000
Kevin P Prendergast, *Pr*
Dean Kutz, *VP*
Arthur L Sommer, *
Donna Ogle, *
EMP: 70 EST: 1953
SQ FT: 10,800
SALES (est): 5.08MM
SALES (corp-wide): 5.08MM **Privately Held**
Web: www.researchassociatesinc.com
SIC: 7299 Information services, consumer

(G-4829)
RESERVES NETWORK INC (PA)
22021 Brookpark Rd (44126-3100)
PHONE..................................440 779-1400
Neil Stallard, *CEO*
Donald L Stallard, *Ch Bd*
Nicholas Stallard, *CFO*
EMP: 30 EST: 1984
SQ FT: 32,000
SALES (est): 47.53MM
SALES (corp-wide): 47.53MM **Privately Held**
Web: www.trnstaffing.com
SIC: 7363 7361 Temporary help service; Placement agencies

(G-4830)
RESILIENCE FUND III LP (PA)
25101 Chagrin Blvd Ste 350 (44122-5643)
PHONE..................................216 292-0200
David Glickman, *Pt*
Ki Mixon, *Pt*
William Tobin, *Pt*
EMP: 30 EST: 2010
SALES (est): 85.81MM
SALES (corp-wide): 85.81MM **Privately Held**
SIC: 6799 3567 Investors, nec; Industrial furnaces and ovens

(G-4831)
RESOURCE TITLE AGENCY INC (PA)
7100 E Pleasant Valley Rd Ste 100 (44131-5545)
PHONE..................................216 520-0050
Richard Rennell, *Ch*
Leslie Rennell, *
Raymond Bailey, *
EMP: 87 EST: 1984
SQ FT: 24,933
SALES (est): 17.95MM
SALES (corp-wide): 17.95MM **Privately Held**
SIC: 6361 6531 Real estate title insurance; Escrow agent, real estate

(G-4832)
REVENUE ASSISTANCE CORPORATION
Also Called: Revenue Group
3711 Chester Ave (44114-4623)
P.O. Box 93983 (44101-5983)
PHONE..................................216 763-2100
Trey Sheehan, *Pr*
Michael Sheehan, *
Chris Taylor, *
EMP: 200 EST: 1994
SALES (est): 23.32MM **Privately Held**
Web: www.revenuegroup.com
SIC: 7322 Collection agency, except real estate

(G-4833)
REVERE TITLE AGENCY INC
6480 Rockside Woods Blvd S Ste 280 (44131-2222)
PHONE..................................216 447-4070
Thomas A Vacca, *Pr*
EMP: 30 EST: 2002
SALES (est): 2.25MM **Privately Held**
Web: www.reveretitle.com
SIC: 6541 Title and trust companies

(G-4834)
REVITALIZE INDUSTRIES LLC
Also Called: National Commercial Warehouse
4444 Lee Rd (44128-2902)
P.O. Box 470334 (44147-0334)
PHONE..................................440 570-3473
Lisa Oswald, *Managing Member*
EMP: 46 EST: 2012
SALES (est): 2.41MM **Privately Held**
Web: www.kaychem.com
SIC: 4225 General warehousing

(G-4835)
REXEL USA INC
Also Called: Gexpro
5605 Granger Rd (44131-1213)
PHONE..................................216 778-6400
Scott Geraghty, *Mgr*
EMP: 30
SALES (corp-wide): 2.67MM **Privately Held**
Web: www.rexelusa.com
SIC: 5063 Electrical supplies, nec
HQ: Rexel Usa, Inc.
  5429 Lyndon B Jhnson Fwy
  Dallas TX 75240

(G-4836)
RHM REAL ESTATE INC
5845 Landerbrook Dr (44124-4017)
PHONE..................................216 360-8333
John Joyce Junior, *Prin*
EMP: 41 EST: 2015
SALES (est): 716.87K **Privately Held**
Web: www.rhmrealestategroup.com
SIC: 6531 Real estate brokers and agents

(G-4837)
RICCO ENTERPRISES INCORPORATED
6010 Fleet Ave Ste Frnt (44105-7618)
PHONE..................................216 883-7775
Sebastian Ricco, *Pr*
EMP: 28 EST: 1969
SALES (est): 1.01MM **Privately Held**
SIC: 6512 8741 Commercial and industrial building operation; Management services

(G-4838)
RICHARD L BOWEN & ASSOC INC (PA)
13000 Shaker Blvd Ste 1 (44120-2096)
P.O. Box 201685 (44120-8111)
PHONE..................................216 491-9300
Richard L Bowen, *Pr*
Carol Padvorac, *
EMP: 65 EST: 1943
SQ FT: 18,000
SALES (est): 13.12MM
SALES (corp-wide): 13.12MM **Privately Held**
Web: www.rlba.com
SIC: 8712 8741 8711 Architectural engineering; Construction management; Civil engineering

(G-4839)
RICKING HOLDING CO
5800 Grant Ave (44105-5608)
PHONE..................................513 825-3551
Carl Ricking Junior, *Pr*
Joyce Ricking, *
Julie Ricking, *
Carla Droll, *
Preston M Simpson, *
EMP: 33 EST: 1974
SALES (est): 1.26MM **Privately Held**
Web: www.joshen.com
SIC: 5141 2656 5113 Groceries, general line ; Cups, paper: made from purchased material; Bags, paper and disposable plastic

(G-4840)
RIDGE-PLEASANT VALLEY INC (PA)
Also Called: Pleasantview Nursing Home
7377 Ridge Rd (44129-6602)
PHONE..................................440 845-0200
David Farkas, *Admn*
Ester Daskal, *
EMP: 185 EST: 1970
SQ FT: 60,000
SALES (est): 15.3MM
SALES (corp-wide): 15.3MM **Privately Held**
Web: www.lhshealth.com
SIC: 8051 8052 Extended care facility; Intermediate care facilities

(G-4841)
RIPCHO STUDIO INC
7630 Lorain Ave (44102-4297)
PHONE..................................216 631-0664
Bill Ripcho, *Owner*
EMP: 36 EST: 1941
SQ FT: 20,000
SALES (est): 4.81MM **Privately Held**
Web: www.ripchostudio.com
SIC: 7221 Photographer, still or video

(G-4842)
RITZ-CARLTON HOTEL COMPANY LLC
Also Called: Ritz-Carlton
1515 W 3rd St 6th Fl (44113-1450)
PHONE..................................216 623-1300
Kelly Stewart, *Mgr*
EMP: 48
SALES (corp-wide): 23.71B **Publicly Held**
Web: www.ritzcarlton.com
SIC: 7011 Hotels
HQ: The Ritz-Carlton Hotel Company Llc
  7750 Wisconsin Ave
  Bethesda MD 20814
  301 380-3000

(G-4843)
RIVERSIDE COMPANY
127 Public Sq (44114-1217)

Cleveland - Cuyahoga County (G-4844)

GEOGRAPHIC SECTION

PHONE.................216 344-1040
Ali Al Alaf, *VP*
Jennifer Boyce, *CCO*
EMP: 57 **EST:** 1988
SALES (est): 5.67MM **Privately Held**
Web: www.riversidecompany.com
SIC: 6799 Investors, nec

(G-4844)
RIVERSIDE DRIVES INC
Also Called: Riverside Drives
4509 W 160th St (44135-2627)
P.O. Box 35166 (44135-0166)
PHONE.................216 362-1211
Bernard Dillemuth, *Pr*
David Dillemuth, *
Kathleen Dillemuth, *
▼ **EMP:** 28 **EST:** 1985
SQ FT: 7,500
SALES (est): 15.37MM **Privately Held**
Web: www.riversidedrives.com
SIC: 5063 3699 Power transmission equipment, electric; Electrical equipment and supplies, nec

(G-4845)
RIVERSIDE PARTNERS LLC
Also Called: Riverside Company, The
127 Public Sq (44114-1217)
PHONE.................216 344-1040
EMP: 4926
SALES (corp-wide): 1.29B **Privately Held**
Web: www.riversidecompany.com
SIC: 6799 Investors, nec
PA: Riverside Partners L.L.C.
45 Rockefeller Plz # 400
New York NY 10111
212 265-6575

(G-4846)
ROBERT L STARK ENTERPRISES INC
Also Called: Stark Enterprises
629 Euclid Ave Ste 1300 (44114-3003)
PHONE.................216 292-0240
Robert L Stark, *Pr*
Raymond Weiss Junior, *CFO*
Steven Rubin, *
EMP: 50 **EST:** 1982
SALES (est): 10.39MM **Privately Held**
Web: www.starkenterprises.com
SIC: 6552 Land subdividers and developers, commercial

(G-4847)
ROBERT WILEY MD INC
Also Called: Cleveland Eye Clinic
2740 Carnegie Ave (44115-2627)
PHONE.................216 621-3211
Robert G Wiley Md, *Pr*
Thomas Chester O.d., *Prin*
EMP: 47 **EST:** 1964
SQ FT: 1,000
SALES (est): 2.45MM **Privately Held**
Web: www.clevelandeyeclinic.com
SIC: 8011 Opthalmologist

(G-4848)
ROCK HOTEL LTD LLC
Also Called: Hampton Inn
6020 Jefferson Dr (44131-2189)
PHONE.................216 520-2020
Rich Holmes, *Mgr*
Michael Werma, *Managing Member*
EMP: 45 **EST:** 1996
SALES (est): 528.75K **Privately Held**
Web: www.hilton.com
SIC: 7011 Hotels and motels

(G-4849)
ROCK ROLL HALL OF FAME MSEUM I
1100 Rock And Roll Blvd (44114-1023)
PHONE.................216 781-7625
Greg Harris, *CEO*
Gregg Lowe, *
EMP: 100 **EST:** 1985
SQ FT: 150,000
SALES (est): 17.99MM **Privately Held**
Web: www.rockhall.com
SIC: 8412 7922 Museum; Theatrical producers and services

(G-4850)
ROCKET MORTGAGE LLC
100 Public Sq Ste 400 (44113-2207)
PHONE.................216 586-8900
Christopher Mahnen, *Pr*
EMP: 50
SALES (corp-wide): 16.54B **Publicly Held**
Web: www.rocketmortgage.com
SIC: 6162 Mortgage bankers
HQ: Rocket Mortgage, Llc
1050 Woodward Ave
Detroit MI 48226
313 373-7990

(G-4851)
ROCKWOOD EQUITY PARTNERS LLC (PA)
3201 Enterprise Pkwy Ste 370 (44122)
PHONE.................216 342-1760
Brett Keith, *
EMP: 31 **EST:** 2002
SALES (est): 8.38MM
SALES (corp-wide): 8.38MM **Privately Held**
Web: www.rockwoodequity.com
SIC: 6726 Investment offices, nec

(G-4852)
ROEMER UNLIMITED INC
Also Called: R & R Auto Body
15620 Brookpark Rd (44135-3335)
PHONE.................216 267-5454
Ron Roemer, *Pr*
David Roemer, *VP*
Kathleen Roemer, *Sec*
EMP: 30 **EST:** 1973
SQ FT: 25,000
SALES (est): 3.24MM **Privately Held**
Web: www.randrauto-body.com
SIC: 7532 Body shop, automotive

(G-4853)
ROETZEL ANDRESS A LGAL PROF AS
1375 E 9th St Fl 10 (44114-1788)
PHONE.................216 623-0150
EMP: 48
SALES (corp-wide): 43.22MM **Privately Held**
Web: www.ralaw.com
SIC: 8111 General practice attorney, lawyer
PA: Roetzel And Andress, A Legal Professional Association
222 S Main St Ste 400
Akron OH 44308
330 376-2700

(G-4854)
ROSE MARY JOHANNA GRASSELL (PA)
Also Called: CEDAR HOUSE
2346 W 14th St (44113-3613)
PHONE.................216 481-4823
A M Pilla Dd, *Prin*
EMP: 100 **EST:** 1922
SALES (est): 16.31MM
SALES (corp-wide): 16.31MM **Privately Held**
Web: www.rmcle.org
SIC: 8361 8052 Rehabilitation center, residential: health care incidental; Intermediate care facilities

(G-4855)
ROSMANSEARCH INC
30799 Pinetree Rd (44124-5903)
PHONE.................216 256-9020
Judy Rosman, *Prin*
EMP: 43 **EST:** 2008
SALES (est): 987.38K **Privately Held**
Web: www.rosmansearch.com
SIC: 8082 Home health care services

(G-4856)
ROULAN ENTERPRISES INC
Also Called: Carwas, The
4900 Countryside Rd (44124-2515)
PHONE.................440 543-2070
Bob Roulan, *Pr*
EMP: 30 **EST:** 1991
SQ FT: 4,800
SALES (est): 632.69K **Privately Held**
SIC: 7542 Carwash, automatic

(G-4857)
ROULSTON & COMPANY INC (PA)
Also Called: Fairport Asset Management
1350 Euclid Ave Ste 400 (44115-1847)
PHONE.................216 431-3000
Scott D Roulston, *Pr*
EMP: 46 **EST:** 1963
SQ FT: 37,500
SALES (est): 52.37K
SALES (corp-wide): 52.37K **Privately Held**
SIC: 6282 Investment advisory service

(G-4858)
ROYAL LANDSCAPE GARDENING INC
7801 Old Granger Rd (44125-4848)
PHONE.................216 883-7000
Anne M Ali, *Pr*
Benjamin P Ali Junior, *Sr VP*
Benjamin J Ali Senior, *Stockholder*
EMP: 39 **EST:** 1976
SQ FT: 120,000
SALES (est): 2.27MM **Privately Held**
Web: www.royalcompanies.net
SIC: 0781 1629 0782 Landscape planning services; Land preparation construction; Fertilizing services, lawn

(G-4859)
ROYAL MANOR HEALTH CARE INC (PA)
18810 Harvard Ave (44122-6848)
PHONE.................216 752-3600
Abraham Schwartz, *Pr*
Sally Schwartz, *
EMP: 50 **EST:** 1986
SALES (est): 8.6MM **Privately Held**
SIC: 8051 8052 Skilled nursing care facilities ; Intermediate care facilities

(G-4860)
ROYAL OAK NRSING RHBLTTION CTR
Also Called: ROYAL MANOR HOMES
6973 Pearl Rd (44130-7831)
PHONE.................440 884-9191
Margaret Halas, *Dir*
EMP: 48 **EST:** 1992
SALES (est): 7.48MM **Privately Held**
Web: www.embassyhealthcare.net
SIC: 8051 Convalescent home with continuous nursing care

(G-4861)
ROYALTY CARE NURSING LLC
2490 Lee Blvd Ste 200 (44118-1268)
PHONE.................216 386-8762
Napoleon Abner, *CEO*
Jennifer Fox, *
Nicole Abner, *
EMP: 88 **EST:** 2014
SALES (est): 677.04K **Privately Held**
SIC: 8082 Home health care services

(G-4862)
RSM US LLP
1001 Lakeside Ave E Ste 200 (44114-1158)
PHONE.................216 523-1900
John Balick, *Brnch Mgr*
EMP: 34
SALES (corp-wide): 3.71B **Privately Held**
Web: www.rsmus.com
SIC: 8721 Certified public accountant
PA: Rsm Us Llp
30 S Wacker Dr Ste 3300
Chicago IL 60606
312 207-1122

(G-4863)
RUSSELL REAL ESTATE SERVICE
27121 Center Ridge Rd (44145-4024)
PHONE.................440 835-8300
Sue Kenney, *Prin*
EMP: 34 **EST:** 2008
SALES (est): 144.92K **Privately Held**
Web: www.tamarasims.com
SIC: 6531 Real estate agent, residential

(G-4864)
RUSSELL WEISMAN JR MD
11100 Euclid Ave (44106-1716)
PHONE.................216 844-3127
Russell Jr Weisman, *Owner*
EMP: 28 **EST:** 2015
SALES (est): 5.5MM **Privately Held**
SIC: 8011 Physicians' office, including specialists

(G-4865)
RWK SERVICES INC (PA)
Also Called: Ductbreeze
4700 Rockside Rd Ste 330 (44131-2151)
PHONE.................440 526-2144
William Wachs, *Pr*
Kerri Wachs, *Stockholder*
EMP: 48 **EST:** 1989
SQ FT: 2,000
SALES (est): 4.12MM
SALES (corp-wide): 4.12MM **Privately Held**
Web: www.rwkservices.com
SIC: 7349 Janitorial service, contract basis

(G-4866)
RWLP COMPANY
5260 Commerce Pkwy W (44130-1271)
PHONE.................216 883-2424
Bill Giordano, *Pr*
EMP: 30 **EST:** 1979
SALES (est): 2.41MM **Privately Held**
Web: www.advance-door.com
SIC: 7699 5031 1751 Door and window repair; Doors, nec; Window and door (prefabricated) installation

(G-4867)
S&P DATA OHIO LLC
1500 W 3rd St Ste 400 (44113-1438)
PHONE.................216 965-0018
EMP: 400 **EST:** 2010
SALES (est): 31.45MM **Privately Held**
Web: www.spdatadigital.com

GEOGRAPHIC SECTION

Cleveland - Cuyahoga County (G-4890)

SIC: 7389 Telemarketing services

(G-4868)
S-T ACQUISITION COMPANY LLC
Also Called: Service Tech Company
7589 First Pl (44146-6726)
PHONE..................................440 735-1505
Gabriel Chick, *Pr*
Larry Hankinson, *
EMP: 49 **EST:** 2019
SALES (est): 3.76MM **Privately Held**
SIC: 1711 7349 Plumbing, heating, air-conditioning; Janitorial service, contract basis

(G-4869)
SAFEGUARD PROPERTIES LLC (HQ)
7887 Safeguard Cir (44125-5742)
PHONE..................................216 739-2900
Alan Jaffa, *CEO*
Robert Klein, *
George Mehok, *CIO*
Joe lafigliola, *
EMP: 800 **EST:** 1990
SQ FT: 33,600
SALES (est): 55.64MM
SALES (corp-wide): 208.19MM **Privately Held**
Web: www.safeguardproperties.com
SIC: 8741 7382 7381 Management services; Security systems services; Detective and armored car services
PA: Safeguard Properties Management, Llc
7887 Hub Pkwy
Cleveland OH 44125
216 739-2900

(G-4870)
SAFEGUARD PROPERTIES MGT LLC (PA)
Also Called: Safeguard
7887 Hub Pkwy (44125)
PHONE..................................216 739-2900
Alan Jaffa, *Managing Member*
Kathleen Rhubart, *
EMP: 700 **EST:** 2012
SALES (est): 208.19MM
SALES (corp-wide): 208.19MM **Privately Held**
Web: www.safeguardproperties.com
SIC: 1522 Remodeling, multi-family dwellings

(G-4871)
SALINI IMPREGILO/HEALY
786 E 140th St (44110-2176)
PHONE..................................216 539-2050
Jim Carveth, *Prin*
EMP: 228
SALES (corp-wide): 7.95B **Privately Held**
SIC: 1622 Tunnel construction
HQ: Salini Impregilo/Healy Joint Venture Nebt
2600 Independence Ave Se
Washington DC 20003
702 302-6771

(G-4872)
SALON LOFTS
3141 Westgate (44126-1310)
PHONE..................................440 356-1062
Andrienne Worley, *Prin*
EMP: 45 **EST:** 2014
SALES (est): 153.48K **Privately Held**
Web: www.salonlofts.com
SIC: 7231 Hairdressers

(G-4873)
SALVATION ARMY
Also Called: Salvation Army
5005 Euclid Ave (44103-3747)
PHONE..................................330 773-3331
Gregory Cole, *Brnch Mgr*
EMP: 41
SALES (corp-wide): 2.41B **Privately Held**
Web: www.salvationarmyusa.org
SIC: 8069 5932 8741 Specialty hospitals, except psychiatric; Used merchandise stores; Administrative management
HQ: The Salvation Army
440 W Nyack Rd Ofc
West Nyack NY 10994
845 620-7200

(G-4874)
SAM-TOM INC
Also Called: Royce Security Services
4600 Euclid Ave Ste 400 (44103-3761)
PHONE..................................216 426-7752
Joseph W Conley, *Pr*
EMP: 27 **EST:** 2001
SALES (est): 5.4MM **Privately Held**
Web: www.roycesecurity.com
SIC: 7381 Security guard service

(G-4875)
SAMSEL ROPE & MARINE SUPPLY CO (PA)
Also Called: Samsel Supply Company
1285 Old River Rd Uppr (44113-1279)
PHONE..................................216 241-0333
Kathleen A Petrick, *Pr*
F Michael Samsel, *
Wentworth J Marshall, *
Scott Balser, *
Grace F Wilcox, *
▲ **EMP:** 32 **EST:** 1958
SQ FT: 100,000
SALES (est): 8.4MM
SALES (corp-wide): 8.4MM **Privately Held**
Web: www.samselsupply.com
SIC: 2394 5051 4959 5085 Canvas and related products; Rope, wire (not insulated); Environmental cleanup services; Industrial supplies

(G-4876)
SATYAM COMPUTER SERVICES LTD
6000 Fredom Sq Dr Ste 250 (44131)
PHONE..................................216 654-1800
EMP: 150
SIC: 7379 Computer related consulting services

(G-4877)
SAVAGE COMPANIES
Also Called: Enviroserve
4600 Brookpark Rd (44134-1012)
PHONE..................................216 642-1311
M James Kozak, *Brnch Mgr*
EMP: 27
SALES (corp-wide): 1.73B **Privately Held**
Web: www.savageco.com
SIC: 4212 Local trucking, without storage
HQ: Savage Companies
901 W Legacy Center Way
Midvale UT 84047
801 944-6600

(G-4878)
SAVAGE SERVICES CORPORATION
610 E 152nd St (44110-2303)
PHONE..................................216 268-7290
EMP: 49
SALES (corp-wide): 1.73B **Privately Held**
Web: www.savageco.com
SIC: 4212 Animal and farm product transportation services
HQ: Savage Services Corporation
7220 W Legacy Center Way
Midvale UT 84047

(G-4879)
SAVOUR HOSPITALITY LLC
4000 Key Tower 127 Public Sq Fl 40 (44114)
PHONE..................................216 308-0018
Malisse Sinito, *Managing Member*
EMP: 120 **EST:** 2016
SALES (est): 5.91MM **Privately Held**
SIC: 8741 5812 Hotel or motel management; Eating places

(G-4880)
SAW SERVICE AND SUPPLY COMPANY
11925 Zelis Rd (44135-4692)
PHONE..................................216 252-5600
Robert Belock, *Pr*
Linda Belock, *
▲ **EMP:** 50 **EST:** 1953
SQ FT: 30,000
SALES (est): 9.89MM **Privately Held**
Web: www.sawservicesupply.com
SIC: 5072 7699 Power tools and accessories; Power tool repair

(G-4881)
SAY YES CLVLAND SCHLARSHIP INC
Also Called: Say Yes Cleveland
325 Superior Ave E Rm 38 (44114-1205)
PHONE..................................216 273-6350
EMP: 100 **EST:** 2018
SALES (est): 77MM **Privately Held**
Web: www.sayyescleveland.org
SIC: 8641 Civic and social associations

(G-4882)
SCHAFFER PARTNERS INC
Also Called: Partners For Incentives
6545 Carnegie Ave (44103-4619)
PHONE..................................216 881-3000
EMP: 60 **EST:** 1994
SALES (est): 22.98MM **Privately Held**
Web: www.pfi-awards.com
SIC: 5064 5091 5092 Electrical appliances, television and radio; Sporting and recreation goods; Toys and hobby goods and supplies

(G-4883)
SCHNEDER SMLTZ SPIETH BELL LLP
1375 E 9th St Ste 900 (44114-1724)
PHONE..................................216 535-1001
EMP: 44 **EST:** 2018
SALES (est): 4.56MM **Privately Held**
Web: www.sssb-law.com
SIC: 8111 General practice law office

(G-4884)
SCHWEIZER DIPPLE INC
7227 Division St (44146-5405)
PHONE..................................440 786-8090
Michael J Kelley, *Pr*
Lynn E Ulrich, *
Peter A Mcgrogan, *VP*
Roy Page, *
Dennis J Clark, *
EMP: 55 **EST:** 1932
SQ FT: 27,000
SALES (est): 21.1MM
SALES (corp-wide): 40.19MM **Privately Held**
Web: www.schweizer-dipple.com
SIC: 1711 3496 3444 3443 Mechanical contractor; Miscellaneous fabricated wire products; Sheet metalwork; Fabricated plate work (boiler shop)
PA: Kelley Steel Erectors, Inc.
7220 Division St
Cleveland OH 44146

440 232-1573

(G-4885)
SCOTT FETZER COMPANY
Adalet
4801 W 150th St (44135-3301)
PHONE..................................216 267-9000
Fred Lemke, *Brnch Mgr*
EMP: 150
SALES (corp-wide): 226 **Privately Held**
Web: www.scottfetzer.com
SIC: 5063 3469 3357 3613 Wire and cable; Metal stampings, nec; Nonferrous wiredrawing and insulating; Control panels, electric
PA: The Scott Fetzer Company
28800 Clemens Rd
Westlake OH 44145
440 892-3000

(G-4886)
SCOTTCARE CRDVSCULAR SOLUTIONS
4791 W 150th St (44135-3301)
PHONE..................................216 362-0550
EMP: 32 **EST:** 2019
SALES (est): 942.45K **Privately Held**
Web: www.scottcare.com
SIC: 8011 Cardiologist and cardio-vascular specialist

(G-4887)
SEA-LAND CHEMICAL CO (PA)
18013 Cleveland Pkwy Dr Ste 100 (44135)
PHONE..................................440 871-7887
Joseph Clayton, *Pr*
Mark Christeon, *
Ryan Keating, *
Jennifer Altstadt, *
◆ **EMP:** 50 **EST:** 1972
SQ FT: 8,000
SALES (est): 49.03MM
SALES (corp-wide): 49.03MM **Privately Held**
Web: www.sealandchem.com
SIC: 5169 Industrial chemicals

(G-4888)
SEAWAY GAS & PETROLEUM INC
1690 Columbus Rd (44113-2409)
PHONE..................................216 566-9070
Wayne Ecke, *Pr*
EMP: 27 **EST:** 1942
SQ FT: 2,200
SALES (est): 3.16MM **Privately Held**
SIC: 5541 7538 Filling stations, gasoline; General automotive repair shops

(G-4889)
SECURITAS SEC SVCS USA INC
Also Called: East Coast Region
12000 Snow Rd Ste 5 (44130-9314)
PHONE..................................440 887-6800
Scott Fry, *Brnch Mgr*
EMP: 27
SALES (corp-wide): 12.7B **Privately Held**
Web: www.securitasinc.com
SIC: 7381 Security guard service
HQ: Securitas Security Services Usa, Inc.
9 Campus Dr Ste 25
Parsippany NJ 07054
973 267-5300

(G-4890)
SEDLAK MANAGEMENT CONSULTANTS
22901 Millcreek Blvd Ste 600 (44122)
PHONE..................................216 206-4700
Kara Ashby, *Pr*
Joseph A Sedlak, *

Cleveland - Cuyahoga County (G-4891)

Ned N Sedlak, *
Patrick S Sedlak, *
Denise A Longano, *
EMP: 32 **EST:** 1958
SQ FT: 18,500
SALES (est): 6.05MM **Privately Held**
Web: www.jasedlak.com
SIC: 8742 7374 Planning consultant; Data processing and preparation

(G-4891)
SELECT MEDICAL CORPORATION
Also Called: Select Spclty Hosp - Clvland F
11900 Fairhill Rd Ste 100 (44120-1063)
PHONE...................................216 983-8030
EMP: 31
SALES (corp-wide): 6.2B **Publicly Held**
Web: www.selectmedical.com
SIC: 8062 General medical and surgical hospitals
HQ: Select Medical Corporation
4714 Gettysburg Rd
Mechanicsburg PA 17055
717 972-1100

(G-4892)
SELF MPLOYED
6157 Creekhaven Dr Apt 5 (44130-1977)
PHONE...................................216 408-3280
Lee Kamps, *Prin*
EMP: 42 **EST:** 2013
SALES (est): 73.67K **Privately Held**
SIC: 7389 Business Activities at Non-Commercial Site

(G-4893)
SELMAN & COMPANY (DH)
Also Called: Selmanco
1 Integrity Pkwy (44143)
PHONE...................................440 646-9336
John L Selman, *CEO*
David Selman, *
Cheryl M Ahmad, *
Elizabeth M Boettcher, *
James Baum, *
EMP: 52 **EST:** 1954
SQ FT: 26,000
SALES (est): 60.3MM
SALES (corp-wide): 1.03B **Privately Held**
Web: www.selmanco.com
SIC: 6411 Insurance agents, nec
HQ: One80 Intermediaries Inc.
160 Federal St Fl 4
Boston MA 02110
216 797-9700

(G-4894)
SENIOR CITIZENS RESOURCES INC
Also Called: DEACONESS-KRAFFT CENTER
3100 Devonshire Rd (44109-4000)
PHONE...................................216 459-2870
Bernadette Bulanda, *Dir*
Micheal Cole, *
James Havach, *
Jeanne Dover, *
EMP: 27 **EST:** 1971
SALES (est): 762.85K **Privately Held**
Web: www.seniorcitizenresources.org
SIC: 8322 Senior citizens' center or association

(G-4895)
SENIOR TOUCH SOLUTION
Also Called: Homecare
6659 Pearl Rd (44130-3821)
PHONE...................................216 862-4841
Shawnte G Taylor, *CEO*
Shawnta Golston, *
EMP: 40 **EST:** 2020
SALES (est): 915.15K **Privately Held**
Web: www.seniortouchsolutions.com

SIC: 8322 8082 8742 8071 Senior citizens' center or association; Home health care services; Transportation consultant; Testing laboratories

(G-4896)
SEQUOIA INSURANCE COMPANY (DH)
800 Superior Ave E Ste 2100 # 21 (44114-2613)
P.O. Box 1510 (93942-1510)
PHONE...................................831 655-9612
Thomas G Moylan, *Pr*
EMP: 60 **EST:** 1946
SALES (est): 31.32MM
SALES (corp-wide): 5.96B **Privately Held**
Web: www.amtrustfinancial.com
SIC: 6331 Fire, marine and casualty insurance and carriers
HQ: Amtrust Financial Services, Inc.
59 Maiden Ln Fl 43
New York NY 10038

(G-4897)
SERVISAIR LLC (DH)
Also Called: Global Ground
5851 Cargo Rd (44135-3111)
P.O. Box 811150 (44181-1150)
PHONE...................................216 267-9910
Michael J Hancock, *Pr*
Douglas Mc Connell, *
Wes A Bement, *
Timothy R Archer, *
Michael A Albanese, *
EMP: 200 **EST:** 1990
SQ FT: 10,000
SALES (est): 18.19MM
SALES (corp-wide): 2.67M **Privately Held**
SIC: 4581 Airport terminal services
HQ: Servisair Usa & Carribean
6065 Nw 18th St Bldg 716d
Miami FL 33126
305 262-4059

(G-4898)
SHAKER HOUSE
3700 Northfield Rd Ste 3 (44122-5240)
PHONE...................................216 991-6000
Robert Nash, *Mayor*
Robert Nash, *Owner*
Craig Koslan, *
EMP: 54 **EST:** 1956
SQ FT: 7,897
SALES (est): 445.93K **Privately Held**
Web: www.shakerhouseapts.com
SIC: 7011 6513 Hotels; Apartment building operators

(G-4899)
SHANNON ELECTRIC LLC
1400 E 34th St (44114-4113)
PHONE...................................216 378-3620
Mark Shannon, *Pr*
Mike Shannon, *
EMP: 45 **EST:** 2010
SALES (est): 4.27MM **Privately Held**
Web: www.shannonelectric.net
SIC: 1731 General electrical contractor

(G-4900)
SHARON GAY PHLPS - HWARD HNNA
Also Called: Howard Hanna Real Estate
1903 W 25th St (44113-3418)
PHONE...................................216 539-2696
EMP: 73 **EST:** 2017
SALES (est): 148.97K **Privately Held**
Web: sharongayphelps.howardhanna.com

SIC: 6531 Real estate agent, residential

(G-4901)
SHE IS US
10310 Saint Clair Ave (44108-1959)
PHONE...................................863 315-1233
Natasha Taylor, *CEO*
EMP: 100
SALES (est): 150K **Privately Held**
SIC: 7213 Linen supply, clothing

(G-4902)
SHIVE-HATTERY INC
2515 Jay Ave (44113-3091)
PHONE...................................216 532-7143
EMP: 30
SALES (corp-wide): 106.38K **Privately Held**
SIC: 8711 Engineering services
HQ: Shive-Hattery, Inc.
222 3rd Ave Se Ste 300
Cedar Rapids IA 52401
319 364-0227

(G-4903)
SHOREBY CLUB INC
40 Shoreby Dr (44108-1191)
PHONE...................................216 851-2587
Chris Mancusho, *Genl Mgr*
EMP: 68 **EST:** 1988
SALES (est): 4.97MM **Privately Held**
Web: www.shorebyclub.com
SIC: 8699 5812 Personal interest organization; Restaurant, family: independent

(G-4904)
SIERRA LOBO INC
21000 Brookpark Rd (44135)
PHONE...................................419 621-3367
George Satornino, *Brnch Mgr*
EMP: 101
Web: www.sierralobo.com
SIC: 8711 Engineering services
PA: Sierra Lobo, Inc.
102 Pinnacle Dr
Fremont OH 43420

(G-4905)
SIEVERS SECURITY INC (PA)
9775 Rockside Rd Ste 200 (44125-6266)
PHONE...................................216 291-2222
Michael Sievers, *Pr*
Amy Sievers, *Treas*
James F Sievers, *VP*
Robert A Sievers, *Sec*
EMP: 33 **EST:** 1957
SALES (est): 4.69MM
SALES (corp-wide): 4.69MM **Privately Held**
Web: www.guardianalarm.com
SIC: 5999 1731 5211 7699 Alarm signal systems; Fire detection and burglar alarm systems specialization; Garage doors, sale and installation; Garage door repair

(G-4906)
SIEVERS SECURITY SYSTEMS INC
9775 Rockside Rd Ste 200 (44125-6266)
PHONE...................................216 383-1234
Robert Sievers, *Pr*
James Sievers, *
Amy Sievers, *
EMP: 40 **EST:** 1995
SALES (est): 1.85MM **Privately Held**
Web: www.guardianalarm.com
SIC: 7382 Security systems services

(G-4907)
SIGMA-ALDRICH CORPORATION
Research Organics
4353 E 49th St (44125-1003)
P.O. Box 14508 (63178-4508)
PHONE...................................216 206-5424
EMP: 67
SALES (est): 22.82B **Privately Held**
Web: www.sigmaaldrich.com
SIC: 2899 5169 Chemical preparations, nec; Chemicals and allied products, nec
HQ: Sigma-Aldrich Corporation
3050 Spruce St
Saint Louis MO 63103
314 771-5765

(G-4908)
SINGERMAN MLLS DSBERG KNTZ LPA
3333 Richmond Rd Ste 370 (44122-4196)
PHONE...................................216 292-5807
Paul J Singerman, *Pr*
Paul J Singerman, *CEO*
William M Mills, *VP*
Gary S Desberg, *Sec*
Edmund G Kauntz, *Treas*
EMP: 60 **EST:** 2001
SALES (est): 5.68MM **Privately Held**
Web: www.smdklaw.com
SIC: 8111 General practice attorney, lawyer

(G-4909)
SINGLETON HEALTH CARE CTR INC
1867 E 82nd St (44103-4263)
PHONE...................................216 231-0076
Joseph Ireland, *Owner*
Garth Ireland, *
Mary Ireland, *
Channa Ireland, *
EMP: 60 **EST:** 1960
SQ FT: 15,000
SALES (est): 4.18MM **Privately Held**
SIC: 8052 8051 Personal care facility; Skilled nursing care facilities

(G-4910)
SISTERS OF CHARITY
2475 E 22nd St (44115-3221)
PHONE...................................216 696-5560
Terrence Kessler, *Prin*
EMP: 28 **EST:** 2013
SALES (est): 1.91MM **Privately Held**
Web: www.sistersofcharityhealth.org
SIC: 8699 Charitable organization

(G-4911)
SIX CONTINENTS HOTELS INC
Also Called: Intercontinental
9801 Carnegie Ave (44106-2100)
PHONE...................................216 707-4100
Rob Austin, *Mgr*
EMP: 50
Web: www.ihg.com
SIC: 7011 Hotels
HQ: Six Continents Hotels, Inc
35016 Avenue D
Yucaipa CA 92399
770 604-5000

(G-4912)
SKY QUEST LLC
6200 Riverside Dr (44135-3132)
PHONE...................................216 362-9904
Corey Head, *Managing Member*
EMP: 69 **EST:** 2004
SALES (est): 9.61MM **Privately Held**
Web: www.flyskyquest.com
SIC: 4581 Airports, flying fields, and services

GEOGRAPHIC SECTION
Cleveland - Cuyahoga County (G-4936)

(G-4913)
SKYLINE CLVLAND RNAISSANCE LLC
Also Called: Renaissance Cleveland Hotel
24 Public Sq (44113-2213)
PHONE.................216 696-5600
Michael Snegd, *Pr*
Louisa Yeung, *
EMP: 99 **EST:** 2015
SQ FT: 873,000
SALES (est): 9.46MM **Privately Held**
Web: www.renaissancecleveland.com
SIC: 7011 Hotels

(G-4914)
SLMG BRAND LLC
Also Called: Slmg Brand Management Firm
1637 Pleasantdale Rd Apt 2 (44109-6600)
PHONE.................216 333-6468
Samuel Goode, *Managing Member*
EMP: 30 **EST:** 2019
SALES (est): 1.26MM **Privately Held**
Web: www.slmgco-op.org
SIC: 4899 Communication services, nec

(G-4915)
SLOVENE HOME FOR THE AGED
18621 Neff Rd (44119-3018)
PHONE.................216 486-0268
Jeffrey Saf, *Admn*
EMP: 190 **EST:** 1957
SQ FT: 77,000
SALES (est): 8.75MM **Privately Held**
Web: www.slovenehome.org
SIC: 8051 Skilled nursing care facilities

(G-4916)
SOGETI USA LLC
6055 Rockside Woods Blvd N Ste 170 (44131-2301)
PHONE.................216 654-2230
Melinda White, *Prin*
EMP: 62
SALES (corp-wide): 415.14MM **Privately Held**
Web: us.sogeti.com
SIC: 7379 Online services technology consultants
HQ: Sogeti Usa Llc
  10100 Innovation Dr # 200
  Miamisburg OH 45342
  937 291-8100

(G-4917)
SOLIDARITY HEALTH NETWORK INC
4853 Galaxy Pkwy Ste K (44128-5939)
PHONE.................216 831-1220
Anne Glorioso, *Prin*
EMP: 32 **EST:** 1989
SQ FT: 4,500
SALES (est): 2.23MM **Privately Held**
Web: www.shninc.org
SIC: 8399 Health systems agency

(G-4918)
SONKIN & KOBERNA CO LPA
Also Called: Sonkin & Koberna Co, Lpa
3401 Enterprise Pkwy Ste 400 (44112)
PHONE.................216 514-8300
Shale S Sonkin, *Pr*
Rick Sonkin, *VP*
EMP: 28 **EST:** 1975
SQ FT: 3,500
SALES (est): 4.58MM **Privately Held**
Web: www.sklawllc.com
SIC: 8111 General practice law office

(G-4919)
SORBIR INC
Also Called: Marshall Ford Leasing
6200 Mayfield Rd (44124-3203)
P.O. Box 241355 (44124-8355)
PHONE.................440 449-1000
Larry Elk, *Pr*
Jerry Sorkin, *
George Ducas, *
EMP: 75 **EST:** 1934
SQ FT: 40,000
SALES (est): 5.68MM **Privately Held**
Web: www.nickmayerford.com
SIC: 7515 5511 Passenger car leasing; Automobiles, new and used

(G-4920)
SOUTH E HARLEY DAVIDSON SLS CO (PA)
Also Called: Southeast Golf Cars
23105 Aurora Rd (44146-1703)
PHONE.................440 439-5300
Paul Meyers Senior, *CEO*
Paul Meyers Junior, *Pr*
Todd Meyers, *
EMP: 29 **EST:** 1932
SQ FT: 20,000
SALES (est): 22.73MM
SALES (corp-wide): 22.73MM **Privately Held**
Web: www.southeastharley.com
SIC: 5571 7999 Motorcycle dealers; Golf cart, power, rental

(G-4921)
SOUTH SHORE CABLE CNSTR INC
6400 Kolthoff Dr (44142-1310)
PHONE.................440 816-0033
Daniel Geib, *Pr*
James Stack, *
Jay Geib, *
EMP: 70 **EST:** 1989
SALES (est): 13.15MM **Privately Held**
Web: www.southshorecable.com
SIC: 1623 Cable laying construction

(G-4922)
SOUTHWEST FMLY PHYSICIANS INC
7225 Old Oak Blvd Ste D210 (44130-3339)
PHONE.................440 816-2750
David Lash, *Pr*
Steven Tymcio, *
EMP: 48 **EST:** 1975
SQ FT: 10,000
SALES (est): 4MM **Privately Held**
Web: www.southwestfamilyphysicians.com
SIC: 8011 Physicians' office, including specialists

(G-4923)
SOUTHWEST GENERAL HEALTH CTR (PA)
18697 Bagley Rd (44130-3417)
PHONE.................440 816-8000
L Jon Schurmeier, *Pr*
Thomas A Selden Prse, *Prin*
EMP: 2400 **EST:** 1920
SQ FT: 150,000
SALES (est): 414.4MM
SALES (corp-wide): 414.4MM **Privately Held**
Web: www.swgeneral.com
SIC: 8062 General medical and surgical hospitals

(G-4924)
SOUTHWEST UROLOGY LLC (PA)
Also Called: Southwest Urlogy Wmen Cnnctons
6900 Pearl Rd Ste 200 (44130-3640)
PHONE.................440 845-0900
Michael Barkoukis, *Pr*
Tim Sildor Md, *Prin*
Arturo Bossa Md, *Prin*
Laurence Dervasi Md, *Prin*
Michael Barkoukis Md, *Prin*
EMP: 40 **EST:** 1986
SQ FT: 6,000
SALES (est): 3.96MM
SALES (corp-wide): 3.96MM **Privately Held**
Web: www.southwesturology.com
SIC: 8071 8011 Medical laboratories; Pathologist

(G-4925)
SPA PERFORMANCE INC
2701 Park Dr (44120-1708)
PHONE.................216 455-1540
EMP: 40 **EST:** 1993
SALES (est): 6.1MM **Privately Held**
Web: www.sparxiq.com
SIC: 7374 Data processing service

(G-4926)
SPANGENBERG SHIBLEY LIBER LLP
Also Called: Spangenberg Law Firm
1001 Lakeside Ave E Ste 1700 (44114)
PHONE.................216 215-7445
Dennis Lansdowne, *Pt*
William Hawal, *Pt*
Peter H Weinberger, *Pt*
Justin Madden, *Pt*
EMP: 32 **EST:** 1959
SALES (est): 5.03MM **Privately Held**
Web: www.spanglaw.com
SIC: 8111 General practice law office

(G-4927)
SPARKBASE INC
3615 Superior Ave E Ste 4403c (44114-4138)
PHONE.................216 867-0877
EMP: 50 **EST:** 2007
SQ FT: 6,800
SALES (est): 2.73MM **Privately Held**
Web: www.sparkbase.com
SIC: 7389 Financial services

(G-4928)
SPECIALTY CHEMICAL SALES INC (HQ)
Also Called: S C S
4561 W 160th St (44135-2647)
PHONE.................216 267-4248
▲ **EMP:** 27 **EST:** 1995
SALES (est): 18.96MM **Privately Held**
SIC: 4225 5169 General warehousing and storage; Chemicals and allied products, nec
PA: Ravago Holdings America, Inc.
  1900 Smmit Twr Blvd Ste 9
  Orlando FL 32810

(G-4929)
SPECIALTY HOSP CLEVELAND LLC
Also Called: Kindred Hosp - Clveland - Gtwy
2351 E 22nd St Fl 7 (44115-3111)
PHONE.................216 592-2830
Rothgerber L Arthur, *Sr VP*
EMP: 43 **EST:** 1999
SALES (est): 107.62K
SALES (corp-wide): 13.68B **Privately Held**
SIC: 8062 General medical and surgical hospitals
HQ: Kindred Healthcare, Llc
  680 S 4th St
  Louisville KY 40202
  502 596-7300

(G-4930)
SPECIALTY PUMPS GROUP INC (DH)
127 Public Sq Ste 5110 (44114-1313)
PHONE.................216 589-0198
EMP: 37 **EST:** 2018
SALES (est): 49.86MM
SALES (corp-wide): 8.03B **Privately Held**
SIC: 7389 Personal service agents, brokers, and bureaus
HQ: First Brands Group, Llc
  127 Public Sq
  Cleveland OH 44114
  248 371-1700

(G-4931)
SPECTRUM SUPPORTIVE SERVICES
Also Called: Spectrum Supportive Services
4269 Pearl Rd Ste 300 (44109-4232)
PHONE.................216 875-0460
Stephen S Morse, *Ex Dir*
EMP: 43
SALES (corp-wide): 2.2MM **Privately Held**
Web: www.recres.org
SIC: 8331 8322 Vocational rehabilitation agency; Association for the handicapped
PA: Spectrum Of Supportive Services
  2900 Detroit Ave Ste 3
  Cleveland OH 44113
  216 939-2075

(G-4932)
SPEEDEON DATA LLC
5875 Landerbrook Dr Ste 130 (44124-4069)
PHONE.................440 264-2100
Gerard Daher, *Mgr*
Linda Montgomery, *CFO*
Joshua Shale, *COO*
Marc Jerauld, *Ofcr*
EMP: 37 **EST:** 2008
SQ FT: 2,148
SALES (est): 8.94MM **Privately Held**
Web: www.speedeondata.com
SIC: 7374 7379 Data processing service; Computer data escrow service

(G-4933)
SPEND AND SEND
4852 Foxwynde Trl (44143-2756)
PHONE.................216 381-5459
James Vanek, *Prin*
EMP: 27 **EST:** 2010
SALES (est): 89.54K **Privately Held**
SIC: 7389 Business Activities at Non-Commercial Site

(G-4934)
SPIRIT RENT-A-CAR INC
Also Called: Alamo Local Market
29100 Aurora Rd Ste 400 (44139-7213)
PHONE.................440 715-1000
Larry Raemakers, *Pr*
EMP: 2000 **EST:** 1989
SQ FT: 13,000
SALES (est): 9.88MM **Privately Held**
SIC: 7514 Passenger car rental

(G-4935)
SPLASH FINANCIAL INC
812 Huron Rd E Ste 350 (44115-1135)
PHONE.................216 452-0113
EMP: 88 **EST:** 2017
SALES (est): 13.73MM **Privately Held**
Web: www.splashfinancial.com
SIC: 6141 Consumer finance companies

(G-4936)
SPR THERAPEUTICS INC
22901 Millcreek Blvd Ste 500 (44122)
PHONE.................216 378-2658
EMP: 50 **EST:** 2010
SALES (est): 7.77MM **Privately Held**
Web: www.sprtherapeutics.com
SIC: 8731 Biotechnical research, commercial

Cleveland - Cuyahoga County (G-4937)

(G-4937)
SPRINT CORPORATION
Also Called: Sprint
3340 Steelyard Dr (44109-2384)
PHONE..................................216 661-2977
EMP: 112
SALES (corp-wide): 78.56B **Publicly Held**
Web: www.sprint.com
SIC: 4812 Cellular telephone services
HQ: Sprint Llc
   6200 Sprint Pkwy
   Overland Park KS 66251
   855 848-3280

(G-4938)
SQUIRE PATTON BOGGS (US) LLP (PA)
1000 Key Tower 127 Public Sq (44114)
PHONE..................................216 479-8500
EMP: 441 EST: 1890
SALES (est): 458.81MM
SALES (corp-wide): 458.81MM **Privately Held**
Web: www.squirepattonboggs.com
SIC: 8111 General practice law office

(G-4939)
SS KEMP & CO LLC (HQ)
Also Called: Trimark Ss Kemp
4567 Willow Pkwy (44125-1052)
PHONE..................................216 271-7700
TOLL FREE: 800
Mark Fishman, *Pr*
Howard Fishman, *
Steven Fishman, *
EMP: 81 EST: 1926
SQ FT: 70,000
SALES (est): 95.22MM **Privately Held**
Web: www.trimarkusa.com
SIC: 5046 Restaurant equipment and supplies, nec
PA: Trimark Usa, Llc
   9 Hampshire St
   Mansfield MA 02048

(G-4940)
ST VINCENT CHARITY MED CTR (HQ)
Also Called: SISTERS OF CHARITY OF ST. AUGU
2351 E 22nd St (44115-3111)
PHONE..................................216 861-6200
Janice G Murphy, *Pr*
Melvin G Pye Junior, *Ch Bd*
John Rusnaczyk, *
Patrick Mcmahon, *CFO*
Shannan D Ritchie, *
EMP: 80 EST: 1926
SQ FT: 200,000
SALES (est): 89.47MM
SALES (corp-wide): 4.3MM **Privately Held**
Web: www.stvincentcharity.com
SIC: 8062 General medical and surgical hospitals
PA: The Sisters Of Charity Of St Augustine Health System Inc
   2475 E 22nd St
   Cleveland OH 44115
   216 696-5560

(G-4941)
STANDARD WELLNESS COMPANY LLC
425 Literary Rd Apt 100 (44113-4506)
PHONE..................................330 931-1037
Marc Deluca, *CEO*
Kyle Ciccarello, *
Emily Simmerly, *
EMP: 180 EST: 2017
SALES (est): 15.04MM **Privately Held**
Web: www.standardwellness.com

SIC: 2834 7389 Medicines, capsuled or ampuled; Business Activities at Non-Commercial Site

(G-4942)
STANLEY STEEMER INTL INC
Also Called: Cleveland 094
4621 Hinckley Industrial Pkwy Unit 12 (44109-6013)
PHONE..................................614 767-8017
Zackary Jenkins, *Brnch Mgr*
EMP: 34
SALES (corp-wide): 263.72MM **Privately Held**
Web: www.stanleysteemer.com
SIC: 7217 Carpet and furniture cleaning on location
PA: Stanley Steemer International, Inc.
   5800 Innovation Dr
   Dublin OH 43016
   614 764-2007

(G-4943)
STANTEC CONSULTING SVCS INC
1001 Lakeside Ave E Ste 1600 (44114-1158)
PHONE..................................216 621-2407
EMP: 44
SALES (corp-wide): 4.23B **Privately Held**
Web: www.stantec.com
SIC: 8711 Consulting engineer
HQ: Stantec Consulting Services Inc.
   410 17th St Ste 1400
   Denver CO 80202
   303 410-4000

(G-4944)
STATE INDUSTRIAL PRODUCTS CORP (PA)
Also Called: State Chemical Manufacturing
5915 Landerbrook Dr Ste 300 (44124-4039)
PHONE..................................877 747-6986
Harold Uhrman, *Pr*
Robert M San Julian, *
William Barnett, *
Brian Limbert, *
Dan Prugar, *
◆ EMP: 300 EST: 1911
SQ FT: 240,000
SALES (est): 192.96MM
SALES (corp-wide): 192.96MM **Privately Held**
Web: www.stateindustrial.com
SIC: 2841 5072 2842 2992 Soap: granulated, liquid, cake, flaked, or chip; Bolts, nuts, and screws; Polishes and sanitation goods; Lubricating oils and greases

(G-4945)
STEEL WAREHOUSE CLEVELAND LLC (DH)
3193 Independence Rd (44105-1045)
PHONE..................................888 225-3760
Hugh Garvey, *Managing Member*
EMP: 45 EST: 2008
SALES (est): 24.21MM **Privately Held**
Web: www.chesterfieldsteel.com
SIC: 5051 Steel
HQ: Steel Warehouse Company Llc
   2722 Tucker Dr
   South Bend IN 46619
   574 236-5100

(G-4946)
STEEL WAREHOUSE COMPANY LLC
Also Called: Steel Warehouse Ohio
4700 Heidtman Pkwy (44105-1026)
PHONE..................................216 206-2800
EMP: 30

Web: www.steelwarehouse.com
SIC: 5051 Steel
HQ: Steel Warehouse Company Llc
   2722 Tucker Dr
   South Bend IN 46619
   574 236-5100

(G-4947)
STEEL WAREHOUSE OF OHIO LLC
4700 Heidtman Pkwy (44105-1026)
PHONE..................................888 225-3760
Dave Lerman, *CEO*
Mike Lerman, *Pr*
Bill Lerman, *VP*
Ted Lerman, *Sec*
Marc Lerman, *VP*
EMP: 60 EST: 2011
SALES (est): 26.32MM **Privately Held**
Web: www.steelwarehouse.com
SIC: 5051 Steel
PA: Lerman Holding Co. Inc.
   2722 Tucker Dr
   South Bend IN 46619

(G-4948)
STELLA MARIS INC
Also Called: Stella Mris Detoxification Ctr
1320 Washington Ave (44113)
PHONE..................................216 781-0550
Daniel Lettenberger-klein, *Dir*
EMP: 85 EST: 1948
SQ FT: 15,000
SALES (est): 9.93MM **Privately Held**
Web: www.stellamariscleveland.com
SIC: 8069 Alcoholism rehabilitation hospital

(G-4949)
STEP FORWARD (PA)
1801 Superior Ave E Ste 400 (44114-2135)
PHONE..................................216 696-9077
Jacklyn A Chisholm, *Pr*
Derek Cluse, *
Mark C Batson, *
EMP: 100 EST: 1964
SQ FT: 26,000
SALES (est): 69.72MM
SALES (corp-wide): 69.72MM **Privately Held**
Web: www.ceogc.org
SIC: 8399 8322 8351 Antipoverty board; Individual and family services; Child day care services

(G-4950)
STEP FORWARD
Also Called: Carl B Stokes Head Start Ctr
1883 Torbenson Dr (44112-1308)
PHONE..................................216 692-4010
Sonya Dean, *Supervisor*
EMP: 60
SQ FT: 67,962
SALES (corp-wide): 69.72MM **Privately Held**
Web: www.ceogc.org
SIC: 8399 Antipoverty board
PA: Step Forward
   1801 Superior Ave E # 400
   Cleveland OH 44114
   216 696-9077

(G-4951)
STEPFORWARD
Also Called: STEPFORWARD
14209 Euclid Ave (44112-3809)
PHONE..................................216 541-7878
EMP: 59
SALES (corp-wide): 69.72MM **Privately Held**
Web: www.ceogc.org
SIC: 8399 Antipoverty board
PA: Step Forward

1801 Superior Ave E # 400
Cleveland OH 44114
216 696-9077

(G-4952)
STEPFORWARD
Also Called: STEPFORWARD
14402 Puritas Ave (44135-2800)
PHONE..................................216 476-3201
Kelly Demarco, *Ofcr*
EMP: 40
SALES (corp-wide): 69.72MM **Privately Held**
Web: www.ceogc.org
SIC: 8699 Charitable organization
PA: Step Forward
   1801 Superior Ave E # 400
   Cleveland OH 44114
   216 696-9077

(G-4953)
STEPFORWARD
Also Called: William Patrick Day
2421 Community College Ave (44115-3118)
PHONE..................................216 736-2934
Grover Crayton, *Prin*
EMP: 80
SALES (corp-wide): 69.72MM **Privately Held**
Web: www.ceogc.org
SIC: 8351 Head Start center, except in conjunction with school
PA: Step Forward
   1801 Superior Ave E # 400
   Cleveland OH 44114
   216 696-9077

(G-4954)
STEPSTONE GROUP REAL ESTATE LP
127 Public Sq Ste 5050 (44114-1246)
PHONE..................................216 522-0330
EMP: 30
SALES (corp-wide): 4.18MM **Privately Held**
Web: www.stepstonegroup.com
SIC: 8742 6282 Real estate consultant; Investment advice
PA: Stepstone Group Real Estate Lp
   885 3rd Ave Fl 14
   New York NY 10022
   212 351-6100

(G-4955)
STRANG CORPORATION (PA)
Also Called: Don's Lighthouse Inn
8905 Lake Ave Fl 1 (44102-6319)
PHONE..................................216 961-6767
Donald W Strang Junior, *Ch Bd*
Donald W Strang Iii, *Pr*
David Strang, *
Peter Strang, *
Karen Strang, *
EMP: 50 EST: 1942
SQ FT: 20,000
SALES (est): 22.51MM
SALES (corp-wide): 22.51MM **Privately Held**
Web: www.donslighthouse.com
SIC: 7011 Hotels and motels

(G-4956)
STREEM-RSNICK TTELMAN YOUNG PC
29001 Cedar Rd Ste 660 (44124-4041)
PHONE..................................440 461-8200
Richard Streem, *Pr*
Jay Resnick D.d.s., *Prin*
Evan D Tetelman D.d.s., *Prin*
Jeffrey Young, *Prin*
EMP: 32 EST: 1973

GEOGRAPHIC SECTION

Cleveland - Cuyahoga County (G-4978)

SALES (est): 819.78K **Privately Held**
Web: www.wholelifedentistry.com
SIC: 8021 Dentists' office

(G-4957)
STRONGVILLE RECREATION COMPLEX (PA)
Also Called: STRONGSVILLE RECREATION CENTER
18100 Royalton Rd (44136-9500)
PHONE..................440 878-6000
Steve Kilo, *Director Recreation*
EMP: 35 EST: 2004
SALES (est): 72.16K
SALES (corp-wide): 72.16K **Privately Held**
Web: www.strongsville.org
SIC: 7999 Recreation center

(G-4958)
SUMMIT HOTEL TRS 144 LLC
Also Called: Residence Inn By Marriott
527 Prospect Ave E (44115-1113)
PHONE..................216 443-9043
Tracy Sauers, *Prin*
Christopher Eng, *Prin*
EMP: 48 EST: 2017
SALES (est): 5.16MM **Publicly Held**
Web: www.residenceinncleveland.com
SIC: 7011 Hotels and motels
PA: Summit Hotel Properties, Inc.
  13215 Bee Cave Pkwy Ste B
  Austin TX 78738

(G-4959)
SUNRISE DEVELOPMENT CO (DH)
1200 Terminal Tower (44113)
PHONE..................216 621-6060
Samuel Miller, *Pr*
Nathan Shafran, *VP*
Robert G O'brien, *VP*
Albert B Ratner, *
EMP: 400 EST: 1966
SALES (est): 27.89MM
SALES (corp-wide): 816.31MM **Privately Held**
SIC: 6552 Subdividers and developers, nec
HQ: Forest City Enterprises, L.P.
  127 Public Sq Ste 3200
  Cleveland OH 44114
  216 621-6060

(G-4960)
SUNRISE LAND CO (DH)
1250 Terminal Tower 50 Public Sq (44113)
PHONE..................216 621-6060
Robert Monchein, *Pr*
EMP: 39 EST: 1986
SALES (est): 6.31MM
SALES (corp-wide): 816.31MM **Privately Held**
SIC: 6552 Land subdividers and developers, commercial
HQ: Forest City Enterprises, L.P.
  127 Public Sq Ste 3200
  Cleveland OH 44114
  216 621-6060

(G-4961)
SUNRISE SENIOR LIVING LLC
Also Called: Sunrise At Parma
7766 Broadview Rd (44134-6743)
PHONE..................216 447-8909
Rima Hanson, *Mgr*
EMP: 48
SQ FT: 20,703
SALES (corp-wide): 2.92B **Privately Held**
Web: www.sunriseseniorliving.com
SIC: 8051 8361 Skilled nursing care facilities; Residential care
HQ: Sunrise Senior Living, Llc
  7902 Westpark Dr
  Mc Lean VA 22102

(G-4962)
SUNRISE SENIOR LIVING LLC
Also Called: Sunrise At Shaker Heights
16333 Chagrin Blvd (44120-3711)
PHONE..................216 751-0930
EMP: 49
SALES (corp-wide): 2.92B **Privately Held**
Web: www.sunriseseniorliving.com
SIC: 8051 Skilled nursing care facilities
HQ: Sunrise Senior Living, Llc
  7902 Westpark Dr
  Mc Lean VA 22102

(G-4963)
SUNSET MNOR HLTHCARE GROUP INC
Also Called: Crawford Manor Healthcare Ctr
1802 Crawford Rd (44106-2030)
PHONE..................216 795-5710
EMP: 50
SALES (corp-wide): 4.04MM **Privately Held**
Web: www.saberhealth.com
SIC: 8051 Convalescent home with continuous nursing care
PA: Sunset Manor Healthcare Group, Inc.
  26691 Richmond Rd
  Bedford Heights OH 44146
  216 292-5706

(G-4964)
SUPERIOR HOLDING LLC (DH)
3786 Ridge Rd (44144-1127)
PHONE..................216 651-9400
Thomas Farrel, *Pr*
EMP: 36 EST: 2009
SALES (est): 12MM
SALES (corp-wide): 8.44B **Publicly Held**
Web: www.superiorprod.com
SIC: 3494 5085 3492 Valves and pipe fittings, nec; Industrial supplies; Fluid power valves and hose fittings
HQ: Engineered Controls International, Llc
  100 Rego Dr
  Elon NC 27244

(G-4965)
SUPERIOR PRODUCTS LLC
3786 Ridge Rd (44144-1127)
PHONE..................216 651-9400
Donald L Mottinger, *Pr*
Tim Giesse, *
Tim Austin, *
Gregory K Gens, *
EMP: 65 EST: 2009
SQ FT: 75,000
SALES (est): 12MM
SALES (corp-wide): 8.44B **Publicly Held**
Web: www.superiorprod.com
SIC: 3494 5085 3492 Valves and pipe fittings, nec; Industrial fittings; Fluid power valves and hose fittings
HQ: Superior Holding, Llc
  3786 Ridge Rd
  Cleveland OH 44144
  216 651-9400

(G-4966)
SUPPLY TECHNOLOGIES LLC (HQ)
Also Called: I L S
6065 Parkland Blvd Ste 1 (44124)
P.O. Box 248199 (44124)
PHONE..................440 947-2100
Michael Justice, *Managing Member*
Brian Norris, *
◆ EMP: 150 EST: 1998
SQ FT: 7,000
SALES (est): 61.7MM
SALES (corp-wide): 1.66B **Publicly Held**
Web: www.supplytechnologies.com
SIC: 5085 3452 3469 Fasteners, industrial; nuts, bolts, screws, etc.; Bolts, nuts, rivets, and washers; Stamping metal for the trade
PA: Park-Ohio Holdings Corp.
  6065 Parkland Blvd Ste 1
  Cleveland OH 44124
  440 947-2000

(G-4967)
SURESHOT COMMUNICATIONS LLC
3500 Payne Ave Ste Mb (44114-4316)
PHONE..................216 496-6100
Alexander Bolger, *Prin*
Anthony Travick, *
EMP: 58 EST: 2015
SQ FT: 437
SALES (est): 1.25MM **Privately Held**
Web: www.impactcommunications.com
SIC: 8742 Business management consultant

(G-4968)
SURGERY CTR AN OHIO LTD PARTNR
Also Called: Surgery Center, The
19250 Bagley Rd (44130-3347)
PHONE..................440 826-3240
EMP: 111 EST: 2002
SALES (est): 30.7MM
SALES (corp-wide): 20.55B **Publicly Held**
Web: www.accentuatewithin.com
SIC: 8011 Surgeon
HQ: United Surgical Partners International, Inc.
  14201 Dallas Pkwy
  Dallas TX 75254
  972 713-3500

(G-4969)
SUTTER OCONNELL CO
1301 E 9th St Ste 36 (44114-1804)
PHONE..................216 928-4504
EMP: 32
SALES (corp-wide): 967.1K **Privately Held**
Web: www.sutter-law.com
SIC: 8111 General practice attorney, lawyer
PA: Sutter O'connell Co.
  3600 Erieview Tower 1301
  Cleveland OH 44114
  216 928-2200

(G-4970)
SWA INC
Also Called: Century Oak Care Center
7250 Old Oak Blvd (44130-3341)
PHONE..................440 243-7888
Stewart Bossel, *Pr*
EMP: 45 EST: 1986
SQ FT: 48,000
SALES (est): 3.29MM **Privately Held**
SIC: 8051 Convalescent home with continuous nursing care

(G-4971)
SYLVESTER HIGHLAND HOLDING INC
699 Miner Rd (44143-2115)
PHONE..................440 473-1640
▲ EMP: 68
SIC: 5084 Hydraulic systems equipment and supplies

(G-4972)
SYMBA & SNAP GOURMET FOODS INC
Also Called: Snap Gourmet Foods
2275 E 55th St (44103-4452)
PHONE..................407 252-9581
Lincoln Yee, *CEO*
Hong Bongmany, *Admn*
EMP: 40 EST: 2020
SALES (est): 6.72MM **Privately Held**
Web: www.snapgourmetfoods.com
SIC: 1541 Food products manufacturing or packing plant construction

(G-4973)
SYSCO CLEVELAND INC (HQ)
Also Called: Sysco
4747 Grayton Rd (44135-2300)
P.O. Box 94570 (44101-4570)
PHONE..................216 201-3000
Bill Delaney, *CEO*
Chuck Staes, *
EMP: 640 EST: 1989
SQ FT: 990
SALES (est): 195.58MM
SALES (corp-wide): 76.32B **Publicly Held**
Web: www.syscocleveland.com
SIC: 5141 Food brokers
PA: Sysco Corporation
  1390 Enclave Pkwy
  Houston TX 77077
  281 584-1390

(G-4974)
T & F SYSTEMS INC
1599 E 40th St (44103-2389)
EMP: 100 EST: 1963
SALES (est): 7.22MM **Privately Held**
SIC: 1761 Roofing contractor

(G-4975)
T J NEFF HOLDINGS INC
Also Called: Neff & Associates
6405 York Rd (44130-3052)
PHONE..................440 884-3100
Daniel Neff, *Pr*
EMP: 40 EST: 1930
SALES (est): 4.95MM **Privately Held**
Web: www.neff-assoc.com
SIC: 8711 8713 Civil engineering; Surveying services

(G-4976)
T W I INTERNATIONAL INC (DH)
24460 Aurora Rd (44146-1728)
PHONE..................440 439-1830
Armond Waxman, *Ch Bd*
Melvin Waxman, *
Mark Wester, *Finance**
EMP: 110 EST: 1981
SQ FT: 21,000
SALES (est): 47.48MM
SALES (corp-wide): 99.88MM **Privately Held**
SIC: 7389 Packaging and labeling services
HQ: Waxman Usa Inc
  24460 Aurora Rd
  Cleveland OH 44146

(G-4977)
TARGET SYSTEMS INC
7819 Freeway Cir (44130-6308)
PHONE..................440 239-1600
S Allen Deak, *Pr*
Linda D Walter, *VP*
EMP: 27 EST: 1984
SALES (est): 2.42MM **Privately Held**
Web: www.targetsystemsinc.com
SIC: 7377 1731 5045 Computer rental and leasing; Computer installation; Computer peripheral equipment

(G-4978)
TAYLOR MURTIS HUMAN SVCS SYS (PA)
13422 Kinsman Rd (44120-4410)
PHONE..................216 283-4400
Lovell J Custard, *CEO*
Muqit Sabur, *

Cleveland - Cuyahoga County (G-4979)   GEOGRAPHIC SECTION

John Chan, *
Sarah Smith, *
Annetta L Fisher, *
EMP: 70 **EST:** 1954
SQ FT: 35,000
SALES (est): 20.6MM
SALES (corp-wide): 20.6MM **Privately Held**
Web: www.murtistaylor.org
SIC: 8093 8322 Mental health clinic, outpatient; Community center

(G-4979)
TAYLOR MURTIS HUMAN SVCS SYS
12395 Mccracken Rd (44125-2967)
PHONE...................................216 283-4400
Ella Thomas, *Dir*
EMP: 35
SALES (corp-wide): 20.6MM **Privately Held**
Web: www.murtistaylor.org
SIC: 8093 Mental health clinic, outpatient
PA: Murtis Taylor Human Services System
13422 Kinsman Rd
Cleveland OH 44120
216 283-4400

(G-4980)
TBC RETAIL GROUP INC
Also Called: Ntb
5370 W 130th St (44142-1801)
PHONE...................................216 267-8040
Jim Zeuli, *Mgr*
EMP: 30
SALES (corp-wide): 1.8B **Privately Held**
Web: jobs.tbccorp.com
SIC: 7534 5531 Tire retreading and repair shops; Automotive tires
HQ: Tbc Retail Group, Inc.
4280 Prof Ctr Dr Ste 400
Palm Beach Gardens FL 33410
561 383-3000

(G-4981)
TECH ELEVATOR INC
7100 Euclid Ave Ste 140 (44103-4036)
PHONE...................................216 310-3497
Anthony Hughes, *Prin*
EMP: 62 **EST:** 2015
SALES (est): 9.01MM
SALES (corp-wide): 1.84B **Publicly Held**
Web: www.techelevator.com
SIC: 5084 Elevators
PA: Stride, Inc.
11720 Plaza Amer Dr Fl 9
Reston VA 20190
703 483-7000

(G-4982)
TELCO PROS INC
Also Called: Tpi Effiency
2019 Center St Ste 320 (44113-2358)
PHONE...................................877 244-0182
Roger Zona, *CEO*
Roger Zona, *Pr*
Karl Shaw, *
EMP: 38 **EST:** 2009
SALES (est): 8.94MM **Privately Held**
Web: www.tpiefficiency.com
SIC: 8748 Energy conservation consultant

(G-4983)
TEMP TECH LLC
Also Called: Temp Tech
1536 Saint Clair Ave Ne Ste 103 (44114-2004)
PHONE...................................440 805-6037
Juan Mitchell, *Prin*
EMP: 56 **EST:** 2018
SALES (est): 1.21MM **Privately Held**

SIC: 7361 Employment agencies

(G-4984)
TENABLE PROTECTIVE SVCS INC (PA)
2423 Payne Ave (44114)
P.O. Box 828 (44212)
PHONE...................................216 361-0002
Peter Miragliotta, *CEO*
Francis Crish, *
Carl Wagner, *
EMP: 2835 **EST:** 1986
SQ FT: 12,000
SALES (est): 49.63MM **Privately Held**
Web: www.roycesecurity.com
SIC: 7381 Security guard service

(G-4985)
TENSILE TSTG A DIV J T ADAMS I
Also Called: Tensile Tsting Mtllurgical Lab
4520 Willow Pkwy (44125-1042)
PHONE...................................216 641-3290
Tim Adams, *Pr*
S J Arsenault, *Sec*
Tracey Waugaman, *
EMP: 30 **EST:** 1956
SQ FT: 30,000
SALES (est): 4.68MM **Privately Held**
Web: www.tensile.com
SIC: 8734 Metallurgical testing laboratory

(G-4986)
TERRACE CONSTRUCTION CO INC
3965 Pearl Rd (44109-3103)
PHONE...................................216 739-3170
Jeffrey Nock, *Owner*
Mark Edzma, *
EMP: 55 **EST:** 1983
SQ FT: 7,500
SALES (est): 14.84MM **Privately Held**
Web: www.terraceconstruction.com
SIC: 1623 Underground utilities contractor

(G-4987)
TESAR INDUSTRIAL CONTRS INC (PA)
3920 Jennings Rd (44109-2860)
PHONE...................................216 741-8008
James Tesar Junior, *Pr*
Sharon Tesar, *
EMP: 63 **EST:** 1920
SQ FT: 20,000
SALES (est): 7.57MM
SALES (corp-wide): 7.57MM **Privately Held**
Web: www.tesarindustrialcontractors.com
SIC: 1796 4212 4213 Machinery installation; Heavy machinery transport, local; Heavy machinery transport

(G-4988)
TFORCE FREIGHT INC
15775 Industrial Pkwy (44135-3317)
PHONE...................................216 676-4560
John Espe, *Mgr*
EMP: 41
SALES (corp-wide): 8.81B **Privately Held**
Web: www.tforcefreight.com
SIC: 4789 4731 Pipeline terminal facilities, independently operated; Freight forwarding
HQ: Tforce Freight, Inc.
1000 Semmes Ave
Richmond VA 23224
800 333-7400

(G-4989)
TFS FINANCIAL CORPORATION
7007 Broadway Ave (44105)
PHONE...................................216 441-6000
Marc A Stefanski, *Ch Bd*

Ashley H Williams, *
Meredith S Weil, *Corporate Secretary*
Kathleen M Danckers, *CRO*
Susanne N Miller, *CAO*
EMP: 1025 **EST:** 1997
SALES (est): 633.35MM
SALES (corp-wide): 1.05B **Publicly Held**
Web: www.thirdfederal.com
SIC: 6035 Federal savings and loan associations
PA: Third Federal Savings & Loan Association Of Cleveland Mhc
103 Foulk Rd Ste 101
Wilmington DE 19803
302 661-2009

(G-4990)
TH MARTIN INC
8500 Brookpark Rd (44129-6806)
PHONE...................................216 741-2020
Thomas H Martin, *Pr*
EMP: 100 **EST:** 1985
SALES (est): 24.26MM **Privately Held**
Web: www.thmartin.net
SIC: 1711 Ventilation and duct work contractor

(G-4991)
THE ARRAS GROUP INC
1151 N Marginal Rd (44114-3730)
PHONE...................................216 621-1601
EMP: 31
Web: www.engageadcom.com
SIC: 8742 7311 Distribution channels consultant; Advertising agencies

(G-4992)
THE BLONDER COMPANY
Also Called: Blonder Home Accents
3950 Prospect Ave E (44115-2710)
PHONE...................................216 431-3560
◆ **EMP:** 245
Web: www.blonderhome.com
SIC: 5198 2679 5719 Wallcoverings; Wallpaper: made from purchased paper; Housewares, nec

(G-4993)
THE CHAS E PHIPPS COMPANY (PA)
4560 Willow Pkwy (44125-1046)
PHONE...................................216 641-2150
EMP: 28 **EST:** 1921
SALES (est): 12.8MM
SALES (corp-wide): 12.8MM **Privately Held**
Web: www.chasephipps.com
SIC: 5039 Prefabricated structures

(G-4994)
THE CLEVELAND MUSEUM OF ART
11150 East Blvd (44106-1797)
PHONE...................................216 421-7340
▲ **EMP:** 375 **EST:** 1913
SALES (est): 49.18MM **Privately Held**
Web: www.clevelandart.org
SIC: 8412 Museum

(G-4995)
THE CLEVELAND PLANT AND FLOWER COMPANY (PA)
Also Called: Cleveland Plant & Flower Co
12920 Corporate Dr (44130-9312)
PHONE...................................216 898-3500
EMP: 35 **EST:** 1913
SALES (est): 22.39MM
SALES (corp-wide): 22.39MM **Privately Held**
Web: www.cpfco.com
SIC: 5193 Flowers, fresh

(G-4996)
THE CLEVELAND VICON CO INC (PA)
4550 Willow Pkwy (44125-1094)
PHONE...................................216 341-3300
EMP: 40 **EST:** 1961
SALES (est): 9.72MM
SALES (corp-wide): 9.72MM **Privately Held**
Web: www.clevelandvicon.com
SIC: 5031 5072 Doors, nec; Builders' hardware, nec

(G-4997)
THE CLEVELAND-CLIFFS IRON CO
1100 Superior Ave E Ste 1500 (44114-2530)
PHONE...................................216 694-5700
J A Carrabba, *CEO*
D S Gallagher, *
W R Calfee, *
Laurie Brlas, *
EMP: 176 **EST:** 1847
SQ FT: 40,000
SALES (est): 26.54MM
SALES (corp-wide): 22B **Publicly Held**
Web: www.clevelandcliffs.com
SIC: 1011 Iron ore mining
PA: Cleveland-Cliffs Inc.
200 Public Sq Ste 3300
Cleveland OH 44114
216 694-5700

(G-4998)
THE COMMERCIAL TRAFFIC COMPANY
Also Called: CT Logistics
12487 Plaza Dr (44130)
P.O. Box 30382 (44130)
PHONE...................................216 267-2000
Allan Miner, *CEO*
Allan Miner, *Pr*
EMP: 175 **EST:** 1923
SQ FT: 16,000
SALES (est): 23.03MM **Privately Held**
Web: www.ctlogistics.com
SIC: 8721 Accounting, auditing, and bookkeeping

(G-4999)
THE DEAN SUPPLY CO
Also Called: Dean Supply Company
3500 Woodland Ave (44115-3421)
PHONE...................................216 771-3300
EMP: 50 **EST:** 1950
SALES (est): 14.8MM **Privately Held**
Web: www.shopatdean.com
SIC: 5046 5149 5087 5113 Commercial equipment, nec; Canned goods: fruit, vegetables, seafood, meats, etc.; Janitors' supplies; Industrial and personal service paper

(G-5000)
THE GREAT LAKES TOWING COMPANY (PA)
Also Called: Great Lakes Shipyard
4500 Division Ave (44102-2228)
PHONE...................................216 621-4854
EMP: 73 **EST:** 1899
SALES (est): 21.99MM
SALES (corp-wide): 21.99MM **Privately Held**
Web: www.thegreatlakesgroup.com
SIC: 4492 3731 Tugboat service; Shipbuilding and repairing

(G-5001)
THE HATTENBACH COMPANY
Also Called: Hattenbach
5309 Hamilton Ave (44114-3909)

PHONE..................216 881-5200
EMP: 85
Web: www.hattenbach.com
SIC: 1711 5078 2541 2434 Refrigeration contractor; Commercial refrigeration equipment; Cabinets, except refrigerated: show, display, etc.: wood; Wood kitchen cabinets

(G-5002)
THE JAMES B OSWALD COMPANY (PA)
Also Called: Nationwide
1100 Superior Ave E Ste 1500 (44114-2530)
PHONE..................216 367-8787
EMP: 100 EST: 1893
SALES (est): 93.92MM
SALES (corp-wide): 93.92MM Privately Held
Web: www.oswaldcompanies.com
SIC: 6411 Insurance agents, nec

(G-5003)
THE KINDT-COLLINS COMPANY LLC
12651 Elmwood Ave (44111-5994)
PHONE..................216 252-4122
◆ EMP: 72
Web: www.kindt-collins.com
SIC: 5085 2999 3363 3364 Industrial supplies; Waxes, petroleum: not produced in petroleum refineries; Aluminum die-castings; Brass and bronze die-castings

(G-5004)
THE METROHEALTH SYSTEM (PA)
Also Called: Metrohealth
2500 Metrohealth Dr (44109-1900)
PHONE..................216 778-7800
EMP: 4000 EST: 1953
SALES (est): 620.72MM
SALES (corp-wide): 620.72MM Privately Held
Web: www.metrohealth.org
SIC: 8062 Hospital, affiliated with AMA residency

(G-5005)
THE OHIO DESK COMPANY (PA)
Also Called: Ohio Desk
1122 Prospect Ave E (44115-1292)
PHONE..................216 623-0600
EMP: 35 EST: 1908
SALES (est): 27.8MM
SALES (corp-wide): 27.8MM Privately Held
Web: www.ohiodesk.com
SIC: 5021 Office furniture, nec

(G-5006)
THE SANSON COMPANY (PA)
Also Called: Sanson Produce Company
3716 Croton Ave Frnt (44115-3417)
PHONE..................216 431-8560
EMP: 99 EST: 1914
SALES (est): 24.28MM
SALES (corp-wide): 24.28MM Privately Held
Web: www.sansonco.com
SIC: 5148 Fruits, fresh

(G-5007)
THE SISTERS OF CHARITY OF ST AUGUSTINE HEALTH SYSTEM INC (PA)
2475 E 22nd St (44115)
PHONE..................216 696-5560
EMP: 40 EST: 1982
SALES (est): 4.3MM
SALES (corp-wide): 4.3MM Privately Held

Web: www.sistersofcharityhealth.org
SIC: 8661 8733 Nonchurch religious organizations; Noncommercial research organizations

(G-5008)
THIRD FDRAL SAV LN ASSN CLVLAN (HQ)
Also Called: Third Federal
7007 Broadway Ave (44105-1441)
PHONE..................800 844-7333
Marc A Stefanski, Ch Bd
David Huffman, *
Bernard Kobak, *
Ralph M Betters, CIO*
John P Ringenbach, *
EMP: 300 EST: 1938
SALES (est): 414.25MM
SALES (corp-wide): 1.05B Publicly Held
Web: www.trailsidecleveland.com
SIC: 6035 Federal savings and loan associations
PA: Third Federal Savings & Loan Association Of Cleveland Mhc
103 Foulk Rd Ste 101
Wilmington DE 19803
302 661-2009

(G-5009)
THIRD FDRAL SAV LN ASSN CLVLAN
5950 Ridge Rd (44129-3938)
PHONE..................440 885-4900
Donna Walraph, Mgr
EMP: 28
SALES (corp-wide): 1.05B Publicly Held
Web: www.thirdfederal.com
SIC: 6035 Federal savings and loan associations
HQ: Third Federal Savings And Loan Association Of Cleveland
7007 Broadway Ave
Cleveland OH 44105
800 844-7333

(G-5010)
THIRD FDRAL SAV LN ASSN CLVLAN
12594 Rockside Rd (44125-6237)
PHONE..................216 581-0881
Ruby Lyde, Prin
EMP: 28
SALES (corp-wide): 1.05B Publicly Held
Web: www.thirdfederal.com
SIC: 6035 Federal savings and loan associations
HQ: Third Federal Savings And Loan Association Of Cleveland
7007 Broadway Ave
Cleveland OH 44105
800 844-7333

(G-5011)
THIRD FDRAL SAV LN ASSN CLVLAN
8943 Brecksville Rd (44141-2301)
PHONE..................440 526-3001
Sheila Papp, Mgr
EMP: 28
SQ FT: 6,600
SALES (corp-wide): 1.05B Publicly Held
Web: www.thirdfederal.com
SIC: 6035 Federal savings and loan associations
HQ: Third Federal Savings And Loan Association Of Cleveland
7007 Broadway Ave
Cleveland OH 44105
800 844-7333

(G-5012)
THIRD FDRAL SAV LN ASSN CLVLAN
18380 Royalton Rd (44136-5183)
PHONE..................440 238-4333

EMP: 28
SALES (corp-wide): 1.05B Publicly Held
Web: www.thirdfederal.com
SIC: 6035 Federal savings and loan associations
HQ: Third Federal Savings And Loan Association Of Cleveland
7007 Broadway Ave
Cleveland OH 44105
800 844-7333

(G-5013)
THOMPSON HINE LLP (PA)
127 Public Sq Ste 3900 (44114-1291)
PHONE..................216 566-5500
Michael L Hardy, Pt
Frank A Lamanna, COO
Michael Goldberg, CFO
EMP: 370 EST: 1898
SQ FT: 145,000
SALES (est): 209.56MM
SALES (corp-wide): 209.56MM Privately Held
Web: www.thompsonhine.com
SIC: 8111 General practice attorney, lawyer

(G-5014)
THORNHILL FINANCIAL INC
18400 Pearl Rd Ste A (44136-6923)
PHONE..................440 238-0445
Kurt Walcutt, Pr
EMP: 27 EST: 1995
SALES (est): 1.69MM Privately Held
Web: www.thornhillcpa.com
SIC: 8721 7291 Certified public accountant; Tax return preparation services

(G-5015)
THREE VILLAGE CONDOMINIUM
5150 Three Village Dr (44124-3772)
PHONE..................440 461-1483
V S Sagal, Pr
Harrison Fuerst, *
EMP: 37 EST: 1977
SQ FT: 261,000
SALES (est): 1.08MM Privately Held
Web: www.three-village.com
SIC: 8641 Condominium association

(G-5016)
THRIVE LGBT ✪
568 E 101st St Apt 4 (44108-1383)
PHONE..................440 319-5906
Shataila Carter, CEO
EMP: 50 EST: 2022
SALES (est): 1.16MM Privately Held
SIC: 7389 Business services, nec

(G-5017)
THUNDER TECH INC
3635 Perkins Ave Ste 5ne (44114-4610)
PHONE..................216 391-2255
Jason Therrien, Pr
Jason Therrien, Pr
Holly Therrien, *
EMP: 43 EST: 2000
SQ FT: 2,500
SALES (est): 5.38MM Privately Held
Web: www.thundertech.com
SIC: 7374 Computer graphics service

(G-5018)
THYSSENKRUPP MATERIALS NA INC
Also Called: Ken-Mac Metals
17901 Englewood Dr (44130-3454)
PHONE..................440 234-7500
Timothy Yost, Brnch Mgr
EMP: 202
SALES (corp-wide): 40.78B Privately Held
Web: www.thyssenkrupp-materials-na.com

SIC: 5051 Steel
HQ: Thyssenkrupp Materials Na, Inc.
22355 W 11 Mile Rd
Southfield MI 48033
248 233-5600

(G-5019)
TI RESORT LLC
Also Called: Consolidated Management
4832 Richmond Rd Ste 200 (44128-5993)
PHONE..................216 464-5130
EMP: 32 EST: 2000
SALES (est): 437.11K Privately Held
SIC: 7011 Resort hotel

(G-5020)
TILDEN MINING COMPANY LC (HQ)
200 Public Sq Ste 3300 (44114-2315)
PHONE..................216 694-5700
Lourenco Goncalves, Pr
Terry Fedor, Ex VP
Timothy K Flanagan, CFO
James Graham, CLO
EMP: 580 EST: 1995
SALES (est): 369.3MM
SALES (corp-wide): 22B Publicly Held
SIC: 1011 Iron ore mining
PA: Cleveland-Cliffs Inc.
200 Public Sq Ste 3300
Cleveland OH 44114
216 694-5700

(G-5021)
TLC LANDSCAPING LLC
Also Called: Park Place Nursery
38000 Aurora Rd (44139-4619)
PHONE..................440 248-4852
Gary S Stanek, Pr
Kathy Stanek, *
EMP: 47 EST: 1982
SQ FT: 5,000
SALES (est): 2.32MM Privately Held
Web: www.enjoytheview.com
SIC: 0782 4959 Landscape contractors; Snowplowing

(G-5022)
TMT CONSOLIDATED INC
3040 Quigley Rd (44113-4514)
PHONE..................216 781-7016
EMP: 85
SALES (corp-wide): 286.42K Privately Held
SIC: 7389 Automobile recovery service
PA: Tmt Consolidated, Inc
2828 Springboro Rd Pike
Dayton OH
937 294-6355

(G-5023)
TOLEDO INNS INC
Also Called: Crowne Plaza Cleveland Airport
7230 Engle Rd (44130-3427)
PHONE..................440 243-4040
J B Patel, Prin
EMP: 71 EST: 2002
SQ FT: 61,845
SALES (est): 949.21K Privately Held
Web: www.ihg.com
SIC: 7011 Hotels

(G-5024)
TOM PAIGE CATERING COMPANY
2275 E 55th St (44103-4452)
PHONE..................216 431-4236
Thomas E Paige, Pr
Ryan Strickland, *
Roy Manley, *
EMP: 35 EST: 1980
SQ FT: 92,000
SALES (est): 3.74MM Privately Held

Web: www.paigecatering.com
SIC: 8322 Meal delivery program

(G-5025)
TOWARDS EMPLOYMENT INC
1255 Euclid Ave Ste 300 (44115-1807)
PHONE..................................216 696-5750
Jill Rizika, *Ex Dir*
EMP: 40 EST: 1988
SQ FT: 12,500
SALES (est): 5.23MM **Privately Held**
Web: www.towardsemployment.org
SIC: 8322 Social service center

(G-5026)
TOWNPLACE SUITES BY MARRIOTT
Also Called: TownePlace Suites By Marriott
7325 Engle Rd (44130-3430)
PHONE..................................440 816-9300
Jerry Clymond, *Mgr*
Rep Jerry Clymond, *Mgr*
EMP: 30 EST: 1999
SALES (est): 171.06K **Privately Held**
Web: www.marriott.com
SIC: 7011 Hotel, franchised

(G-5027)
TOYOTA MATERIAL HDLG OHIO INC (HQ)
5667 E Schaaf Rd (44131)
PHONE..................................216 328-0970
Daniel Hegler, *Pr*
EMP: 98 EST: 2012
SALES (est): 22.37MM **Privately Held**
Web: www.prolifttoyota.com
SIC: 5084 Materials handling machinery
PA: Toyota Industries Corporation
2-1, Toyodacho
Kariya AIC 448-0

(G-5028)
TRADEONE MARKETING INC
Also Called: Brandmuscle
1500 W 3rd St Ste 325 (44113-1429)
PHONE..................................512 343-2002
Dan Hickox, *Pr*
Evelyn L Nugent, *
Clive Luke, *
EMP: 85 EST: 2000
SQ FT: 22,000
SALES (est): 8.79MM **Privately Held**
Web: www.brandmuscle.com
SIC: 8742 Marketing consulting services

(G-5029)
TRAFFTECH INC
7000 Hubbard Ave (44127-1419)
PHONE..................................216 361-8808
William J Porter, *Pr*
Carol Porter, *
Kim Mc Peak, *
EMP: 50 EST: 1982
SQ FT: 55,000
SALES (est): 9.99MM **Privately Held**
SIC: 1611 General contractor, highway and street construction

(G-5030)
TRANSCON BUILDERS INC (PA)
25250 Rockside Rd Ste 2 (44146)
PHONE..................................440 439-3400
Peter Rzepka, *Ch Bd*
Stanley Freeman, *
Lawrence Apple, *
Fred Rzepka, *
EMP: 30 EST: 1961
SQ FT: 14,000
SALES (est): 26.01MM
SALES (corp-wide): 26.01MM **Privately Held**
Web: www.transconbuilders.com
SIC: 6513 1522 Apartment building operators; Residential construction, nec

(G-5031)
TRANSDIGM GROUP INCORPORATED (PA)
Also Called: Transdigm
1301 E 9th St Ste 3000 (44114-1871)
PHONE..................................216 706-2960
Kevin Stein, *Pr*
W Nicholas Howley, *Ex Ch Bd*
Sarah Wynne, *CAO*
Michael Lisman, *Ex VP*
Joel Reiss, *Ex VP*
EMP: 283 EST: 1993
SQ FT: 20,100
SALES (est): 6.58B
SALES (corp-wide): 6.58B **Publicly Held**
Web: www.transdigm.com
SIC: 3728 5088 Aircraft parts and equipment, nec; Aircraft equipment and supplies, nec

(G-5032)
TRANSPORT SERVICES INC (PA)
10499 Royalton Rd (44133-4432)
PHONE..................................440 582-4900
Albert Therrien, *Ch*
Patricia Therrien, *
Adam Therrien, *
Mike Collins, *
Tom Soggs, *
EMP: 44 EST: 1976
SQ FT: 20,000
SALES (est): 22.27MM
SALES (corp-wide): 22.27MM **Privately Held**
Web: www.transportservices.com
SIC: 5013 7519 7539 Trailer parts and accessories; Trailer rental; Trailer repair

(G-5033)
TRANSPORTATION UNLIMITED INC (PA)
3740 Carnegie Ave Ste 101 (44115-2756)
PHONE..................................216 426-0088
Samuel Lucarelli, *Pr*
Michael Panzarelli, *
Jason Lucarelli, *
EMP: 1450 EST: 1974
SQ FT: 40,000
SALES (est): 48.29MM
SALES (corp-wide): 48.29MM **Privately Held**
SIC: 7363 4213 4212 Truck driver services; Trucking, except local; Local trucking, without storage

(G-5034)
TRANSTAR INDUSTRIES INC
7350 Young Dr (44146-5390)
PHONE..................................855 872-6782
EMP: 67 EST: 2005
SALES (est): 24.68MM **Privately Held**
Web: www.transtar1.com
SIC: 5084 Industrial machinery and equipment

(G-5035)
TRANSTAR INDUSTRIES LLC (DH)
Also Called: Nickels Performance
7350 Young Dr (44146-5390)
PHONE..................................440 232-5100
◆ EMP: 200 EST: 1975
SALES (est): 607.57MM **Privately Held**
Web: www.transtar1.com
SIC: 5013 Automotive supplies and parts
HQ: Linsalata Corp
5900 Lndrbrook Dr Ste 280
Cleveland OH 44124

(G-5036)
TRI ZOB INC
Also Called: West Park Animal Hospital
4117 Rocky River Dr (44135-1107)
PHONE..................................216 252-4500
Borys Pakush, *Pr*
EMP: 29 EST: 1978
SALES (est): 5.44MM **Privately Held**
Web: www.westparkanimalhospital.com
SIC: 0742 Animal hospital services, pets and other animal specialties

(G-5037)
TRIAD ENGINEERING & CONTG CO (PA)
9715 Clinton Rd (44144-1031)
PHONE..................................440 786-1000
Clifford J Kassouf, *Pr*
Paul Kassouf, *
Philip Kassouf, *
Ernest P Mansour, *
EMP: 30 EST: 1987
SQ FT: 5,600
SALES (est): 9.69MM
SALES (corp-wide): 9.69MM **Privately Held**
Web: www.triad-engineering.com
SIC: 8711 Engineering services

(G-5038)
TRICO PRODUCTS CORPORATION (DH)
Also Called: Trico
127 Public Sq (44114-1217)
PHONE..................................248 371-1700
Patrick James, *Pr*
◆ EMP: 150 EST: 1917
SALES (est): 161.69MM
SALES (corp-wide): 8.03B **Privately Held**
Web: www.tricoproducts.com
SIC: 8734 3714 3082 8731 Testing laboratories; Windshield wiper systems, motor vehicle; Tubes, unsupported plastics; Commercial physical research
HQ: Ktri Holdings, Inc.
127 Public Sq Ste 5110
Cleveland OH 44114
216 400-9308

(G-5039)
TUCKER ELLIS LLP (PA)
950 Main Ave Ste 1100 (44113-7213)
PHONE..................................216 592-5000
Robert Tucker, *Pt*
Stephen Ellis, *Pt*
Kim West, *Pt*
EMP: 201 EST: 2003
SQ FT: 100,000
SALES (est): 53.46MM
SALES (corp-wide): 53.46MM **Privately Held**
Web: www.tuckerellis.com
SIC: 8111 General practice attorney, lawyer

(G-5040)
TUDOR ARMS MSTR SUBTENANT LLC
Also Called: Doubletree By Hilton
10660 Carnegie Ave (44106-3019)
P.O. Box 14100 (44114-0100)
PHONE..................................216 696-6611
EMP: 100 EST: 2009
SALES (est): 4.95MM **Privately Held**
Web: www.tudorarmsevents.com
SIC: 7011 Hotels and motels

(G-5041)
TURNER CONSTRUCTION COMPANY
1422 Euclid Ave Ste 200 (44115-1901)
PHONE..................................216 522-1180
Mark Dent, *Brnch Mgr*
EMP: 50
Web: www.turnerconstruction.com
SIC: 1542 Commercial and office building, new construction
HQ: Turner Construction Company Inc
66 Hudson Blvd E
New York NY 10001
212 229-6000

(G-5042)
TUROCY & WATSON LLP ✪
127 Public Sq Fl 57 (44114-1233)
PHONE..................................216 696-8730
EMP: 37 EST: 2023
SALES (est): 955.14K **Privately Held**
SIC: 8111 7389 Legal services; Business services, nec

(G-5043)
TYRONE TOWNHOUSES PA INV LLC
8111 Rockside Rd (44125-6129)
PHONE..................................216 520-1250
EMP: 99 EST: 2014
SALES (est): 4.25MM **Privately Held**
SIC: 6513 Apartment building operators

(G-5044)
U HCMC
11100 Euclid Ave (44106-1716)
PHONE..................................216 721-3405
EMP: 76 EST: 2015
SALES (est): 2.24B **Privately Held**
Web: www.uhhospitals.org
SIC: 8062 General medical and surgical hospitals

(G-5045)
U S XPRESS INC
Also Called: US Xpress
7177 W 130th St (44130-7855)
PHONE..................................440 743-7177
Adam Bolz, *Brnch Mgr*
EMP: 333
Web: www.usxpress.com
SIC: 4213 Contract haulers
HQ: U. S. Xpress, Inc.
4080 Jenkins Rd
Chattanooga TN 37421
866 266-7270

(G-5046)
UHHS/CSAHS - CUYAHOGA INC
2351 E 22nd St (44115-3111)
PHONE..................................440 746-3401
EMP: 70 EST: 2011
SALES (est): 2.67MM **Privately Held**
Web: www.bmsi.net
SIC: 7389 Financial services

(G-5047)
UHMG DEPARTMENT OF UROLOGIST
1611 S Green Rd Ste 106 (44121-4134)
PHONE..................................216 844-3009
Mary Kyanko, *Pr*
EMP: 27
SALES (corp-wide): 4.85MM **Privately Held**
SIC: 8011 Urologist
PA: Uhmg Department Of Urologist
11100 Euclid Ave
Cleveland OH 44106
216 844-3009

(G-5048)
ULLMAN ELECTRIC & TECHNOLOGIES COMPANY
3901 Chester Ave Ste B (44114-4624)
PHONE..................................216 432-5777

EMP: 140 EST: 1982
SALES (est): 25.25MM Privately Held
Web: www.ullmanelectric.com
SIC: 1731 General electrical contractor

(G-5049)
ULMER & BERNE LLP (PA)
Also Called: Ulmer
1660 W 2nd St Ste 1100 (44113-1406)
PHONE.................216 583-7000
Scott P Kadish, Mng Pt
Tia Atchison, CMO
Thomas L Anastos, Pt
Jason P Conte, Pt
Jodi B Rich, Pt
EMP: 284 EST: 1908
SQ FT: 65,000
SALES (est): 50.31MM
SALES (corp-wide): 50.31MM Privately Held
Web: www.ubglaw.com
SIC: 8111 General practice attorney, lawyer

(G-5050)
UNION CLUB COMPANY
1211 Euclid Ave (44115-1865)
PHONE.................216 621-4230
John Wheeler, Pr
John Sherwood, *
Mary Laughlin, *
Mick Bosler, *
EMP: 75 EST: 1872
SQ FT: 75,000
SALES (est): 3.7MM Privately Held
Web: www.theunionclub.org
SIC: 8641 5813 5812 Social club, membership; Drinking places; Eating places

(G-5051)
UNIQUE PAVING MATERIALS CORP
3993 E 93rd St (44105-4096)
PHONE.................216 341-7711
Michael Pemberton, Pr
Jeffrey J Higerd, *
Donna Letizia, *
Don Kautzman, *
EMP: 41 EST: 1998
SQ FT: 25,000
SALES (est): 10.74MM Privately Held
Web: www.uniquepavingmaterials.com
SIC: 1611 Surfacing and paving

(G-5052)
UNITED AGENCIES INC
Also Called: Uai Agency
1422 Euclid Ave Ste 510 (44115-1901)
PHONE.................216 696-8044
John Boyle Iii, Pr
EMP: 48 EST: 1972
SALES (est): 9.16MM Privately Held
Web: www.uainc.com
SIC: 6411 Insurance agents, nec

(G-5053)
UNITED AIRLINES INC
Also Called: Continental Airlines
5970 Cargo Rd (44135-3110)
PHONE.................216 501-4700
Tom Braun, Mgr
EMP: 142
SALES (corp-wide): 53.72B Publicly Held
Web: www.unitedgroundexpress.com
SIC: 4512 Air passenger carrier, scheduled
HQ: United Airlines, Inc.
    233 S Wacker Dr Ste 710
    Chicago IL 60606
    872 825-4000

(G-5054)
UNITED AIRLINES INC
Also Called: Continental Airlines
6090 Cargo Rd (44135-3112)
PHONE.................216 501-5644
EMP: 29
SALES (corp-wide): 53.72B Publicly Held
Web: www.unitedgroundexpress.com
SIC: 4512 Air passenger carrier, scheduled
HQ: United Airlines, Inc.
    233 S Wacker Dr Ste 710
    Chicago IL 60606
    872 825-4000

(G-5055)
UNITED AIRLINES INC
Also Called: Continental Express
5300 Riverside Dr (44135-3182)
PHONE.................216 501-5169
Kathlie Keith, Brnch Mgr
EMP: 28
SALES (corp-wide): 53.72B Publicly Held
Web: www.united.com
SIC: 4512 Air passenger carrier, scheduled
HQ: United Airlines, Inc.
    233 S Wacker Dr Ste 710
    Chicago IL 60606
    872 825-4000

(G-5056)
UNITED CONSUMER FINCL SVCS CO
865 Bassett Rd (44145-1142)
PHONE.................440 835-3230
Cliff Hooley, CEO
William Ciszczon, *
Bill Francis, *
EMP: 200 EST: 1980
SQ FT: 27,000
SALES (est): 43.37MM
SALES (corp-wide): 226 Privately Held
Web: www.ucfs.net
SIC: 6141 Consumer finance companies
PA: The Scott Fetzer Company
    28800 Clemens Rd
    Westlake OH 44145
    440 892-3000

(G-5057)
UNITED CRBRAL PLSY ASSN GRTER (PA)
Also Called: UCP OF GREATER CLEVELAND
10011 Euclid Ave (44106-4701)
PHONE.................216 791-8363
Patricia S Otter, Pr
Randy Simmons, *
EMP: 100 EST: 1950
SQ FT: 40,000
SALES (est): 15.74MM
SALES (corp-wide): 15.74MM Privately Held
Web: www.ucpcleveland.org
SIC: 8361 8331 Rehabilitation center, residential: health care incidental; Vocational rehabilitation agency

(G-5058)
UNITED CRBRAL PLSY ASSN GRTER
Also Called: Edendale House
1374 Edendale St (44121-1627)
PHONE.................216 381-9993
EMP: 45
SALES (corp-wide): 15.74MM Privately Held
Web: www.ucpcleveland.org
SIC: 8361 8052 8059 Rehabilitation center, residential: health care incidental; Intermediate care facilities; Home for the mentally retarded, ex. skilled or intermediate

PA: United Cerebral Palsy Association Of Greater Cleveland, Inc.
    10011 Euclid Ave
    Cleveland OH 44106
    216 791-8363

(G-5059)
UNITED CRBRAL PLSY ASSN GRTER
Also Called: Memphis House
9401 Memphis Ave (44144-2030)
PHONE.................216 351-4888
Frances Diamond, Mgr
EMP: 45
SALES (corp-wide): 15.74MM Privately Held
Web: www.ucpcleveland.org
SIC: 8322 Social service center
PA: United Cerebral Palsy Association Of Greater Cleveland, Inc.
    10011 Euclid Ave
    Cleveland OH 44106
    216 791-8363

(G-5060)
UNITED FINANCIAL CASUALTY CO
6300 Wilson Mills Rd (44143)
PHONE.................440 461-5000
S Patricia Griffith, CEO
Susan Patricia Griffith, CEO
EMP: 93 EST: 1984
SALES (est): 4.31B
SALES (corp-wide): 49.61B Publicly Held
Web: www.progressivecommercial.com
SIC: 6411 Insurance agents, nec
HQ: Progressive Commercial Holdings, Inc.
    6300 Wilson Mills Rd
    Cleveland OH 44143

(G-5061)
UNITED HEALTHCARE OHIO INC
Also Called: United Healthcare
1001 Lakeside Ave E Ste 1000 (44114)
PHONE.................216 694-4080
Lisa Chapman-smith, CEO
EMP: 47
SALES (corp-wide): 371.62B Publicly Held
SIC: 6324 Group hospitalization plans
HQ: United Healthcare Of Ohio, Inc.
    9200 Worthington Rd
    Columbus OH 43085
    614 410-7000

(G-5062)
UNITED LABOR AGENCY INC
737 Bolivar Rd Ste 3000 (44115-1233)
PHONE.................216 664-3446
David Megenhardt, Ex Dir
EMP: 158 EST: 1971
SQ FT: 20,000
SALES (est): 8.05MM Privately Held
Web: www.ulagency.org
SIC: 8399 Community development groups

(G-5063)
UNITED PARCEL SERVICE INC
Also Called: UPS
4300 E 68th St (44105-5797)
PHONE.................800 742-5877
EMP: 258
SALES (corp-wide): 90.96B Publicly Held
Web: www.ups.com
SIC: 4215 Parcel delivery, vehicular
HQ: United Parcel Service, Inc.
    55 Glenlake Pkwy
    Atlanta GA 30328
    404 828-6000

(G-5064)
UNITED PARCEL SERVICE INC
Also Called: UPS
18685 Sheldon Rd (44130-2471)
PHONE.................216 676-4560
EMP: 31
SALES (corp-wide): 90.96B Publicly Held
Web: www.ups.com
SIC: 4215 Parcel delivery, vehicular
HQ: United Parcel Service, Inc.
    55 Glenlake Pkwy
    Atlanta GA 30328
    404 828-6000

(G-5065)
UNITED PARCEL SERVICE INC
Also Called: UPS
17940 Englewood Dr (44130-3463)
PHONE.................440 826-2591
Oscar Vasquez, Mgr
EMP: 31
SALES (corp-wide): 90.96B Publicly Held
Web: www.ups.com
SIC: 4215 Parcel delivery, vehicular
PA: United Parcel Service, Inc.
    55 Glenlake Pkwy Ne
    Atlanta GA 30328
    404 828-6000

(G-5066)
UNITED PARCEL SERVICE INC
Also Called: UPS
947 Englewood Dr (44134-3235)
PHONE.................440 826-2508
Chris Donker, Mgr
EMP: 62
SALES (corp-wide): 90.96B Publicly Held
Web: www.ups.com
SIC: 4513 Parcel delivery, private air
HQ: United Parcel Service, Inc.
    55 Glenlake Pkwy
    Atlanta GA 30328
    404 828-6000

(G-5067)
UNITED WAY GREATER CLEVELAND (PA)
Also Called: United Way
1331 Euclid Ave (44115-1819)
PHONE.................216 436-2100
William Kitson, CEO
Michael E Headen, *
Kenneth L Surratt, INVESTMENT*
Kristen Popelmayer, Chief Marketing*
EMP: 112 EST: 1926
SQ FT: 90,000
SALES (est): 24.53MM
SALES (corp-wide): 24.53MM Privately Held
Web: www.unitedwaycleveland.org
SIC: 8399 United Fund councils

(G-5068)
UNIVERSAL OIL INC
265 Jefferson Ave (44113-2594)
PHONE.................216 771-4300
TOLL FREE: 800
John J Purcell, Pr
EMP: 30 EST: 1875
SQ FT: 25,000
SALES (est): 22.78MM Privately Held
Web: www.universaloil.com
SIC: 5171 2992 Petroleum bulk stations; Lubricating oils

(G-5069)
UNIVERSAL STEEL COMPANY
6600 Grant Ave (44105-5692)
PHONE.................216 883-4972
David P Miller, Ch
Richard W Williams, Pr

Stephen F Ruscher, *VP*
▲ **EMP:** 100 **EST:** 1925
SQ FT: 200,000
SALES (est): 25.69MM
SALES (corp-wide): 79.1MM **Privately Held**
Web: www.univsteel.com
SIC: 3444 5051 Sheet metalwork; Steel
PA: Columbia National Group, Inc.
    6600 Grant Ave
    Cleveland OH 44105
    216 883-4972

(G-5070)
UNIVERSITIES SPACE RES ASSN
Also Called: National Ctr For Space Explrti
10900 Euclid Ave (44106-1712)
PHONE..................216 368-0750
Iwan Alexander, *Dir*
EMP: 32
SALES (corp-wide): 111.29MM **Privately Held**
Web: www.usra.edu
SIC: 8733 Scientific research agency
PA: Universities Space Research Association
    425 3rd St Sw
    Washington DC 20024
    410 730-2656

(G-5071)
UNIVERSITY CIRCLE INCORPORATED (PA)
Also Called: UCI
10831 Magnolia Dr (44106)
PHONE..................216 791-3900
Christopher Ronayne, *Pr*
Daniel J Stahura, *
▲ **EMP:** 30 **EST:** 1957
SQ FT: 10,000
SALES (est): 18.12MM
SALES (corp-wide): 18.12MM **Privately Held**
Web: www.universitycircle.org
SIC: 6531 Real estate agents and managers

(G-5072)
UNIVERSITY HOSPITALS
2915 Ludlow Rd (44120-2308)
P.O. Box 202625 (44120-8127)
PHONE..................216 536-3020
Charles Sullivan, *Prin*
EMP: 99 **EST:** 2015
SALES (est): 9.27MM **Privately Held**
Web: www.uhhospitals.org
SIC: 8062 General medical and surgical hospitals

(G-5073)
UNIVERSITY HOSPITALS CLEVELAND
Also Called: Research Institute Univ Hosp
11100 Euclid Ave (44106-1716)
PHONE..................216 844-1000
Tom Zenty, *Pr*
EMP: 656
SALES (corp-wide): 878.24MM **Privately Held**
Web: www.uhhospitals.org
SIC: 8062 General medical and surgical hospitals
HQ: University Hospitals Cleveland Medical Center
    11100 Euclid Ave
    Cleveland OH 44106

(G-5074)
UNIVERSITY HOSPITALS CLEVELAND
Also Called: UNIVERSITY HOSPITALS OF CLEVELAND
10524 Euclid Avenue, W.O. Walker Center, Suite 3200 Suite 3200 (44106-2205)
PHONE..................216 983-3066
Tamika Williams, *Brnch Mgr*
EMP: 1080
SALES (corp-wide): 878.24MM **Privately Held**
Web: www.uhhospitals.org
SIC: 8093 Substance abuse clinics (outpatient)
HQ: University Hospitals Cleveland Medical Center
    11100 Euclid Ave
    Cleveland OH 44106

(G-5075)
UNIVERSITY HSPTALS CLVLAND MED
Also Called: General Clinical Research Ctr
11100 Euclid Ave Stop Rvc5041 (44106-1716)
PHONE..................216 844-1369
Joyce Dearborn, *Prin*
EMP: 1234
SALES (corp-wide): 878.24MM **Privately Held**
Web: www.uhhospitals.org
SIC: 8062 8071 General medical and surgical hospitals; Medical laboratories
HQ: University Hospitals Cleveland Medical Center
    11100 Euclid Ave
    Cleveland OH 44106

(G-5076)
UNIVERSITY HSPTALS CLVLAND MED
20800 Harvard Rd (44122-7202)
PHONE..................216 358-2346
Mary Ann Koudelka, *Brnch Mgr*
EMP: 1388
SALES (corp-wide): 878.24MM **Privately Held**
Web: www.uhhospitals.org
SIC: 8062 General medical and surgical hospitals
HQ: University Hospitals Cleveland Medical Center
    11100 Euclid Ave
    Cleveland OH 44106

(G-5077)
UNIVERSITY HSPTALS CLVLAND MED
Also Called: Rainbow Pharmacy
5805 Euclid Ave (44103-3715)
PHONE..................216 675-6640
EMP: 1234
SALES (corp-wide): 878.24MM **Privately Held**
Web: www.uhhospitals.org
SIC: 8062 General medical and surgical hospitals
HQ: University Hospitals Cleveland Medical Center
    11100 Euclid Ave
    Cleveland OH 44106

(G-5078)
UNIVERSITY HSPTALS CLVLAND MED (HQ)
Also Called: University Hospitals Hlth Sys
11100 Euclid Ave (44106-1716)
PHONE..................216 844-1000
Thomas Zenty, *CEO*
Daniel Simon, *
Phillip K Chang, *CMO**
▲ **EMP:** 3906 **EST:** 1854
SALES (est): 213.26MM
SALES (corp-wide): 878.24MM **Privately Held**
Web: www.uhhospitals.org
SIC: 8062 8069 General medical and surgical hospitals; Specialty hospitals, except psychiatric
PA: University Hospitals Health System, Inc.
    3605 Warrensville Ctr Rd
    Shaker Heights OH 44122
    216 767-8900

(G-5079)
UNIVERSITY HSPTALS CLVLAND MED
4510 Richmond Rd (44128-5757)
PHONE..................216 844-4663
Mary Havannah, *Mgr*
EMP: 2005
SALES (corp-wide): 878.24MM **Privately Held**
Web: www.uhhospitals.org
SIC: 8062 8082 General medical and surgical hospitals; Home health care services
HQ: University Hospitals Cleveland Medical Center
    11100 Euclid Ave
    Cleveland OH 44106

(G-5080)
UNIVERSITY HSPTALS CLVLAND MED
Also Called: Rainbow Babies & Children
11100 Euclid Ave Rm 737 (44106-1716)
PHONE..................216 844-1767
EMP: 1851
SALES (corp-wide): 878.24MM **Privately Held**
Web: www.uhhospitals.org
SIC: 8062 General medical and surgical hospitals
HQ: University Hospitals Cleveland Medical Center
    11100 Euclid Ave
    Cleveland OH 44106

(G-5081)
UNIVERSITY HSPTALS CLVLAND MED
Rainbow Babies and Chld Hosp
2101 Adelbert Rd (44106-2624)
PHONE..................216 844-3528
EMP: 1851
SALES (corp-wide): 878.24MM **Privately Held**
Web: www.uhhospitals.org
SIC: 8062 8741 General medical and surgical hospitals; Management services
HQ: University Hospitals Cleveland Medical Center
    11100 Euclid Ave
    Cleveland OH 44106

(G-5082)
UNIVERSITY MANOR HLTH CARE CTR
2186 Ambleside Dr (44106-4620)
PHONE..................216 721-1400
Suzanne Fromson, *Pr*
Patricia Weisberg, *
Milton Fromson, *Stockholder**
EMP: 37 **EST:** 1969
SALES (est): 606.02K **Privately Held**
Web: www.saberhealth.com
SIC: 8051 8052 Skilled nursing care facilities; Intermediate care facilities

(G-5083)
UNIVERSITY MNOR HLTHCARE GROUP
Also Called: University Manor Health Care Center
2186 Ambleside Dr (44106-4620)
PHONE..................216 721-1400
George S Repchick, *Pr*
William I Weisberg, *
EMP: 207 **EST:** 2002
SALES (est): 9.64MM
SALES (corp-wide): 655.44MM **Privately Held**
Web: www.saberhealth.com
SIC: 8051 Convalescent home with continuous nursing care
PA: Saber Healthcare Group, L.L.C.
    23700 Commerce Park
    Beachwood OH 44122
    216 292-5706

(G-5084)
UNIVERSITY OPHTHLMLOGY ASSOC I
29001 Cedar Rd Ste 110 (44124-4041)
PHONE..................216 382-8022
William Annable, *Pr*
Ronald Price Md, *Off Mgr*
EMP: 48 **EST:** 1947
SALES (est): 1.66MM **Privately Held**
Web: www.uoaeye.org
SIC: 8011 Opthalmologist

(G-5085)
UNIVERSITY PRIMARY CARE PRAC
11100 Euclid Ave (44106-1716)
PHONE..................216 844-1000
EMP: 99 **EST:** 1994
SALES (est): 5.68MM **Privately Held**
SIC: 8062 General medical and surgical hospitals

(G-5086)
UNIVERSITY SETTLEMENT INC (PA)
4800 Broadway Ave (44127-1071)
PHONE..................216 641-8948
Tracey Mason, *Dir*
EMP: 31 **EST:** 1926
SQ FT: 8,525
SALES (est): 4.78MM
SALES (corp-wide): 4.78MM **Privately Held**
Web: www.universitysettlement.net
SIC: 8322 Social service center

(G-5087)
UNIVERSITY SUBURBAN HEALTH CTR (PA)
1611 S Green Rd (44121-4135)
PHONE..................216 382-8920
Chuck Abbey, *Ex Dir*
John L Naylor Junior, *Prin*
EMP: 195 **EST:** 1973
SQ FT: 27,500
SALES (est): 945.59K **Privately Held**
Web: www.nomshealthcare.com
SIC: 8011 Medical centers

(G-5088)
UPS SUPPLY CHAIN SOLUTIONS INC
Also Called: UPS
18401 Sheldon Rd Ste C (44130-2400)
PHONE..................360 332-5222
Dennis Holmstrom, *Mgr*
EMP: 38
SALES (corp-wide): 90.96B **Publicly Held**
Web: www.ups.com
SIC: 4731 Freight forwarding
HQ: Ups Supply Chain Solutions, Inc.
    12380 Morris Rd
    Alpharetta GA 30005
    678 258-2000

GEOGRAPHIC SECTION

Cleveland - Cuyahoga County (G-5112)

(G-5089)
URBAN LEAG GRTER CLEVELAND INC
2930 Prospect Ave E (44115-2608)
PHONE.................................216 622-0999
Myron F Robinson, *Pr*
Tim Haas, *CFO*
Gregory Johnson, *COO*
Frank Usowell, *VP Opers*
EMP: 32 **EST:** 1917
SQ FT: 1,800
SALES (est): 1.29MM **Privately Held**
Web: www.ulcleveland.org
SIC: 8641 Civic associations

(G-5090)
URS GROUP INC
Also Called: URS
1300 E 9th St Ste 500 (44114-1503)
PHONE.................................216 622-2300
William Laubscher, *Brnch Mgr*
EMP: 404
SALES (corp-wide): 14.38B **Publicly Held**
Web: www.aecom.com
SIC: 8711 Consulting engineer
HQ: Urs Group, Inc.
   300 S Grand Ave Ste 900
   Los Angeles CA 90071
   213 593-8000

(G-5091)
US COMMUNICATIONS AND ELC INC
4933 Neo Pkwy (44128-3103)
PHONE.................................440 519-0880
Patricia Connole, *CEO*
James Connole, *
Robert Williams, *
EMP: 85 **EST:** 1996
SQ FT: 50,000
SALES (est): 26.26MM **Privately Held**
Web: www.uscande.com
SIC: 1731 Telephone and telephone equipment installation

(G-5092)
US FOODS INC
Also Called: Lederer Term 1104
16645 Granite Rd (44137-4301)
PHONE.................................216 475-7400
EMP: 159
Web: www.usfoods.com
SIC: 5149 Dried or canned foods
HQ: Us Foods, Inc.
   9399 W Higgins Rd Ste 500
   Rosemont IL 60018

(G-5093)
USA PARKING SYSTEMS
1124 Bolivar Rd (44115-1206)
PHONE.................................216 621-9255
Delicia Terry, *Mgr*
EMP: 48 **EST:** 2011
SALES (est): 171.8K **Privately Held**
Web: www.usaparking.com
SIC: 7521 Outdoor parking services

(G-5094)
USCG STATION CLEVELAND HARBOR
1055 E 9th St (44114-1003)
PHONE.................................216 937-0141
EMP: 46 **EST:** 2020
SALES (est): 725K **Privately Held**
SIC: 8744 Facilities support services

(G-5095)
UTILICON CORPORATION
6140 Parkland Blvd (44124-6142)
PHONE.................................216 391-8500
Kenneth Lavan, *Pr*
EMP: 44 **EST:** 1978
SALES (est): 1.84MM **Privately Held**
Web: www.utiliconcorp.com
SIC: 1623 Underground utilities contractor

(G-5096)
VALLEJO COMPANY
4000 Brookpark Rd (44134-1132)
PHONE.................................216 741-3933
Katharine Yaroshak, *Pr*
EMP: 42 **EST:** 1993
SALES (est): 11.27MM **Privately Held**
Web: www.vallejoco.com
SIC: 4212 1623 Local trucking, without storage; Oil and gas pipeline construction

(G-5097)
VALLEY FORD TRUCK INC (PA)
Also Called: Valley Sterling of Cleveland
5715 Canal Rd (44125-3494)
PHONE.................................216 524-2400
Brian O'donnell, *Pr*
Michelle Steibner, *
◆ **EMP:** 69 **EST:** 1964
SQ FT: 15,000
SALES (est): 19.19MM
SALES (corp-wide): 19.19MM **Privately Held**
Web: www.valleyfordtruckinc.com
SIC: 5013 5511 5521 5531 Truck parts and accessories; Automobiles, new and used; Trucks, tractors, and trailers: used; Truck equipment and parts

(G-5098)
VENDORS EXCHANGE INTERNATIONAL INC
8700 Brookpark Rd (44129-6810)
PHONE.................................216 432-1800
▲ **EMP:** 70 **EST:** 1963
SALES (est): 10.56MM **Privately Held**
Web: www.vesolutions.co
SIC: 7699 5087 Vending machine repair; Vending machines and supplies

(G-5099)
VERITEXT HOLDING COMPANY
1100 Superior Ave E (44114-2530)
PHONE.................................216 664-0799
EMP: 352
Web: www.veritext.com
SIC: 7338 Court reporting service
PA: Veritext Holding Company
   290 W Mount Pleasant Ave
   Livingston NJ 07039

(G-5100)
VESTIS CORPORATION
Also Called: Aramark
3600 E 93rd St (44105-1620)
PHONE.................................216 341-7400
Douglas Johnson, *Genl Mgr*
EMP: 33
SQ FT: 85,000
SALES (corp-wide): 2.83B **Publicly Held**
Web: www.vestis.com
SIC: 7218 7213 Industrial launderers; Linen supply
PA: Vestis Corporation
   500 Colonial Center Pkwy # 1
   Roswell GA 30076
   470 226-3655

(G-5101)
VETERANS HEALTH ADMINISTRATION
Also Called: Louis Stokes Cleveland Vamc
10701 East Blvd (44106-1702)
PHONE.................................216 791-3800
William Montague, *Dir*
EMP: 3200
Web: benefits.va.gov
SIC: 8011 9451 Medical centers; Administration of veterans' affairs, Federal government
HQ: Veterans Health Administration
   810 Vermont Ave Nw
   Washington DC 20420

(G-5102)
VGS INC
2239 E 55th St (44103-4451)
PHONE.................................216 431-7800
Robert Comben Junior, *Pr*
Donald E Carlton, *
Mick Latkovich, *
James Huduk, *
EMP: 200 **EST:** 1998
SQ FT: 36,000
SALES (est): 3.41MM **Privately Held**
Web: www.vgsjob.org
SIC: 8331 2326 2311 Job training and related services; Work uniforms; Military uniforms, men's and youths': purchased materials

(G-5103)
VICTORIA FIRE & CASUALTY CO
5915 Landerbrook Dr (44124-4039)
PHONE.................................513 648-9888
James Bechtel, *Mgr*
EMP: 28 **EST:** 1986
SALES (est): 1.96MM **Privately Held**
SIC: 6411 Fire Insurance Underwriters' Laboratories

(G-5104)
VICTORY WHITE METAL COMPANY (PA)
6100 Roland Ave (44127-1399)
P.O. Box 605187 (44105-0187)
PHONE.................................216 271-1400
Alex J Stanwick, *Pr*
Jennifer Sturman, *
▲ **EMP:** 60 **EST:** 1920
SQ FT: 60,000
SALES (est): 10.66MM
SALES (corp-wide): 10.66MM **Privately Held**
Web: www.victorywhitemetal.com
SIC: 5085 3356 Valves and fittings; Solder: wire, bar, acid core, and rosin core

(G-5105)
VILLAGE OF CUYAHOGA HEIGHTS (PA)
4863 E 71st St Frnt (44125-1023)
PHONE.................................216 641-7020
Jack Bacci, *Mayor*
Barbara Biro, *
EMP: 97 **EST:** 1918
Web: www.cuyahogaheights.com
SIC: 9111 8641 City and town managers' office; Civic and social associations

(G-5106)
VILLAGE OF VALLEY VIEW
6848 Hathaway Rd (44125-4767)
PHONE.................................216 524-6511
Randall Westfall, *Mayor*
EMP: 32
Web: www.valleyview.net
SIC: 8741 Administrative management
PA: Village Of Valley View
   6848 Hathaway Rd
   Cleveland OH 44125
   216 524-6511

(G-5107)
VILLAGE VETERINARY CLINIC
6529 Wilson Mills Rd (44143-3404)
PHONE.................................440 461-2226
William Sayle, *CEO*
Doctor William Sayle, *Pr*
EMP: 44 **EST:** 1971
SQ FT: 4,009
SALES (est): 3.09MM **Privately Held**
Web: www.villageveterinaryclinic.com
SIC: 0742 Animal hospital services, pets and other animal specialties

(G-5108)
VISCONSI COMPANIES LTD
30050 Chagrin Blvd Ste 360 (44124-5716)
PHONE.................................216 464-5550
Dominic Visconsi Junior, *CEO*
Anthoni Visconsi Ii, *CEO*
EMP: 30 **EST:** 1987
SQ FT: 8,000
SALES (est): 4.53MM **Privately Held**
Web: www.visconsi.com
SIC: 6552 6531 Land subdividers and developers, commercial; Real estate agents and managers

(G-5109)
VISITING NRSE ASSN OF MID-OHIO
Also Called: Vna
2500 E 22nd St (44115-3204)
PHONE.................................216 931-1300
EMP: 32 **EST:** 1999
SALES (est): 6.15MM **Privately Held**
Web: www.vnaohio.org
SIC: 8082 Visiting nurse service
PA: Visiting Nurse Association Health Group, Inc.
   23 Main St 1d
   Holmdel NJ 07733

(G-5110)
VITALYST LLC
3615 Superior Ave E Ste 4406a (44114-4139)
PHONE.................................216 201-9070
EMP: 159
SALES (corp-wide): 20.09MM **Privately Held**
Web: www.vitalyst.com
SIC: 7379 Online services technology consultants
HQ: Vitalyst, Llc
   One Bala Plz Ste 434
   Bala Cynwyd PA 19004

(G-5111)
VITRAN EXPRESS INC
5300 Crayton Ave (44104-2832)
PHONE.................................216 426-8584
Rich Huffman, *Mgr*
EMP: 64
SQ FT: 25,271
Web: www.vitran.com
SIC: 4213 Contract haulers
PA: Vitran Express, Inc.
   12225 Stephens Rd
   Warren MI 48089

(G-5112)
VOCATIONAL GUIDANCE SERVICES (PA)
2239 E 55th St (44103-4451)
PHONE.................................216 431-7800
Robert E Comben Junior, *CEO*
Susie M Barragate, *
Donald E Carlson, *
Michael Latkovich, *
James Hudak, *
EMP: 608 **EST:** 1890
SQ FT: 130,931

Cleveland - Cuyahoga County (G-5113)   GEOGRAPHIC SECTION

SALES (est): 10.41MM
SALES (corp-wide): 10.41MM **Privately Held**
Web: www.vgsjob.org
SIC: **8331** Community service employment training program

(G-5113)
VOCATIONAL SERVICES INC
2239 E 55th St (44103-4451)
PHONE..................216 431-8085
Robert Comben, *Pr*
Donald E Carlson, *
EMP: 48 EST: 1980
SQ FT: 17,541
SALES (est): 596.34K **Privately Held**
Web: www.vsiserve.org
SIC: **2391** 2511 8331 Curtains and draperies; Wood household furniture; Job training and related services

(G-5114)
VOCON DESIGN INC (PA)
3142 Prospect Ave E (44115-2612)
PHONE..................216 588-0800
Debbie Donley, *Pr*
Debbie Mccann, *VP*
Paul G Voinovich, *
Frank Mercuri, *
David M Douglass, *
EMP: 46 EST: 1983
SQ FT: 17,000
SALES (est): 22.01MM
SALES (corp-wide): 22.01MM **Privately Held**
Web: www.vocon.com
SIC: **7389** Interior design services

(G-5115)
VORYS SATER SEYMOUR PEASE LLP
200 Public Sq Ste 1400 (44114-2327)
PHONE..................216 479-6100
F Daniel Balmert, *Pt*
EMP: 61
SALES (corp-wide): 133.42MM **Privately Held**
Web: www.vorys.com
SIC: **8111** General practice attorney, lawyer
PA: Vorys, Sater, Seymour And Pease Llp
52 E Gay St
Columbus OH 43215
614 464-6400

(G-5116)
VOTEM CORP (PA)
2515 Jay Ave Fl 1 (44113-3098)
PHONE..................216 930-4300
Peter Martin, *CEO*
EMP: 80 EST: 2015
SALES (est): 9.72MM
SALES (corp-wide): 9.72MM **Privately Held**
Web: www.votem.com
SIC: **7371** Computer software development

(G-5117)
VSI GLOBAL LLC
Also Called: VSI International
9090 Bank St (44125-3426)
PHONE..................216 642-8778
EMP: 40 EST: 2014
SALES (est): 3.12MM
SALES (corp-wide): 4.26MM **Privately Held**
Web: www.vsiglobal.com
SIC: **7629** 5064 Vacuum cleaner repair; Vacuum cleaners, nec
PA: Lakewood Capital, Llc
7 Old Field Rd
Norwalk CT 06853

203 604-0863

(G-5118)
WABUSH MNES CLFFS MIN MNGING A
200 Public Sq Ste 3300 (44114-2315)
PHONE..................216 694-5700
John Tuomi, *Managing Member*
Terrance Taridei, *CFO*
EMP: 463 EST: 1957
SALES (est): 1.73MM
SALES (corp-wide): 22B **Publicly Held**
SIC: **1011** Iron ore mining
PA: Cleveland-Cliffs Inc.
200 Public Sq Ste 3300
Cleveland OH 44114
216 694-5700

(G-5119)
WACO SCAFFOLDING & EQUIPMENT INC
4545 Spring Rd (44131-1023)
P.O. Box 318028 (44131-8028)
PHONE..................216 749-8900
EMP: 550
SIC: **7359** 3446 5082 1799 Equipment rental and leasing, nec; Scaffolds, mobile or stationary: metal; Scaffolding; Scaffolding

(G-5120)
WADE TRIM
1621 Euclid Ave (44115-2107)
PHONE..................216 363-0300
J Howard Flower, *Pr*
Richard J Allar, *
Kenneth A Tyrpak, *
David Dipietro, *
EMP: 36 EST: 1967
SALES (est): 979.6K **Privately Held**
Web: www.wadetrim.com
SIC: **8711** 8713 Civil engineering; Surveying services

(G-5121)
WALTER HAVERFIELD LLP (PA)
1500 W 3rd St (44113-1467)
PHONE..................216 781-1212
Ralph Cascarilla, *Mng Pt*
Charles T Riehl, *Pt*
Robert S Horbaly, *Pt*
EMP: 66 EST: 1932
SALES (est): 11.68MM
SALES (corp-wide): 11.68MM **Privately Held**
Web: www.walterhav.com
SIC: **8111** General practice attorney, lawyer

(G-5122)
WALTHALL LLP (PA)
6300 Rockside Rd Ste 100 (44131-2221)
PHONE..................216 573-2330
Richard T Lash C.p.a., *Mng Pt*
Charles P Battiato Junior C.p. a., *Pt*
Daniel B Holben C.p.a., *Pt*
James E Sprague C.p.a., *Pt*
Judith A Mondry C.p.a., *Pt*
EMP: 30 EST: 1946
SQ FT: 10,000
SALES (est): 4.32MM
SALES (corp-wide): 4.32MM **Privately Held**
Web: www.walthall.com
SIC: **8721** Certified public accountant

(G-5123)
WE FRESH N REFRESH LLC
1011 Spring Rd (44109-4405)
PHONE..................216 937-9798
Anthony Campbell, *Managing Member*
EMP: 33 EST: 2021

SALES (est): 1.29MM **Privately Held**
SIC: **1799** Paint and wallpaper stripping

(G-5124)
WEGMAN HESSLER VANDERBURG
6055 Rockside Woods Blvd N Ste 200 (44131-2302)
PHONE..................216 642-3342
David J Hessler, *Pr*
Keith Vanderburg, *
Peter A Hessler, *
EMP: 60 EST: 1978
SALES (est): 10.32MM **Privately Held**
Web: www.wegmanlaw.com
SIC: **8111** General practice attorney, lawyer

(G-5125)
WEINBERG CAPITAL GROUP INC (PA)
30195 Chagrin Blvd Ste 222 (44124)
PHONE..................216 503-8307
Ronald E Weinberg Junior, *CEO*
EMP: 96 EST: 2012
SALES (est): 10.48MM
SALES (corp-wide): 10.48MM **Privately Held**
Web: www.weinbergcap.com
SIC: **6799** Investors, nec

(G-5126)
WEINER KEITH D CO L P A INC
Also Called: Keith D Weiner & Assoc Lpa
75 Public Sq Ste 600 (44113-2001)
PHONE..................216 771-6500
Keith D Weiner, *Pr*
Evelyn Schonberg, *
EMP: 45 EST: 1985
SALES (est): 6.41MM **Privately Held**
Web: www.weinerlaw.com
SIC: **8111** General practice attorney, lawyer

(G-5127)
WELDED RING PROPERTIES CO
2180 W 114th St (44102-3516)
PHONE..................216 961-3800
James Janosek, *Pr*
Larry Janosek, *Pt*
EMP: 50 EST: 1983
SQ FT: 196,000
SALES (est): 2.39MM **Privately Held**
Web: www.weldedring.com
SIC: **6512** Commercial and industrial building operation

(G-5128)
WELDING CUTTING TLS & ACC LLC (HQ)
22801 Saint Clair Ave (44117-2524)
PHONE..................216 481-8100
▼ EMP: 35 EST: 2003
SALES (est): 10.3MM
SALES (corp-wide): 4.19B **Publicly Held**
Web: www.lincolnelectric.com
SIC: **5085** Welding supplies
PA: Lincoln Electric Holdings, Inc.
22801 St Clair Ave
Cleveland OH 44117
216 481-8100

(G-5129)
WELTMAN WEINBERG & REIS CO LPA
Also Called: Weltman, Weinberg & Reis Co.,
981 Keynote Cir (44131-1871)
PHONE..................216 459-8633
EMP: 313
SALES (corp-wide): 68.52MM **Privately Held**
Web: www.weltman.com

SIC: **8111** General practice law office
PA: Weltman, Weinberg & Reis Co., L.P.A.
965 Keynote Cir
Independence OH 44131
216 685-1000

(G-5130)
WELTY BUILDING COMPANY LTD
1400 W 10th St (44113-1361)
PHONE..................216 931-2400
Donzell S Taylor, *Brnch Mgr*
EMP: 51
SALES (corp-wide): 47.03MM **Privately Held**
Web: www.thinkwelty.com
SIC: **1799** Athletic and recreation facilities construction
PA: Welty Building Company Ltd.
3421 Ridgewood Rd Ste 200
Fairlawn OH 44333
330 867-2400

(G-5131)
WESCO DISTRIBUTION INC
17909 Cleveland Pkwy Dr Rear (44135)
PHONE..................216 741-0441
Chad Marrison, *Mgr*
EMP: 56
Web: www.wesco.com
SIC: **5063** 5085 Electrical supplies, nec; Industrial supplies
HQ: Wesco Distribution, Inc.
225 W Station Square Dr # 700
Pittsburgh PA 15219

(G-5132)
WEST PARK SHELL
Also Called: Shell
13960 Lorain Ave (44111-3430)
PHONE..................216 252-5086
Ermie Lamanna, *Owner*
Ermie La Manna, *Owner*
EMP: 37 EST: 1967
SQ FT: 1,500
SALES (est): 661.89K **Privately Held**
Web: www.shell.us
SIC: **7011** Motels

(G-5133)
WEST SIDE COMMUNITY HOUSE
9300 Lorain Ave (44102-4725)
PHONE..................216 771-7297
Dawn Kolograf, *Dir*
Terry Weber, *
EMP: 36 EST: 1892
SQ FT: 4,620
SALES (est): 1.3MM **Privately Held**
Web: www.wschouse.org
SIC: **8322** Social service center

(G-5134)
WEST SIDE ECUMENICAL MINISTRY (PA)
Also Called: W S E M
5209 Detroit Ave (44102-2224)
PHONE..................216 325-9369
Phil Buck, *Ex Dir*
EMP: 130 EST: 1966
SQ FT: 29,075
SALES (est): 1.81MM **Privately Held**
Web: www.thecentersohio.org
SIC: **8322** 8661 Individual and family services; Religious organizations

(G-5135)
WESTERN MANAGEMENT INC (PA)
14577 Lorain Ave Rear (44111-3156)
PHONE..................216 941-3333
John Turk, *Pr*
Thomas M Cawley, *
Eric George Turk, *

GEOGRAPHIC SECTION
Cleveland - Cuyahoga County (G-5157)

EMP: 45 **EST:** 1984
SQ FT: 10,000
SALES (est): 3.08MM **Privately Held**
Web: www.econrads.com
SIC: 8741 Management services

(G-5136)
WESTERN RESERVE HISTORICAL SOC (PA)
10825 East Blvd (44106-1777)
PHONE.................................216 721-5722
Kelly Falcone-hall, *CEO*
Gainor B Davis, *
Mary Thoburn, *
EMP: 60 **EST:** 1867
SALES (est): 4.63MM
SALES (corp-wide): 4.63MM **Privately Held**
Web: www.wrhs.org
SIC: 8412 8231 Historical society; Specialized libraries

(G-5137)
WESTERN RESERVE INTERIORS INC
7777 Exchange St Ste 7 (44125-3337)
PHONE.................................216 447-1081
Leslie S Cooke, *Pr*
Tom Cooke, *
Jo Ann Castelli, *
EMP: 30 **EST:** 1979
SQ FT: 25,000
SALES (est): 2.33MM **Privately Held**
Web: www.wri-net.com
SIC: 1742 Plastering, plain or ornamental

(G-5138)
WESTERN RSRVE AREA AGCY ON AGI (PA)
Also Called: WRAAA
1700 E 13th St Ste 114 (44114-3285)
PHONE.................................216 621-0303
E Douglas Beach, *CEO*
Christopher Hall, *
EMP: 189 **EST:** 1974
SALES (est): 79.63MM **Privately Held**
Web: www.areaagingsolutions.org
SIC: 8322 8082 Senior citizens' center or association; Home health care services

(G-5139)
WESTERN RSRVE AREA AGCY ON AGI
Also Called: Passport
1700 E 13th St Ste 114 (44114-3285)
PHONE.................................216 621-0303
EMP: 46
Web: www.psa10a.org
SIC: 8322 Senior citizens' center or association
PA: Western Reserve Area Agency On Aging
1700 E 13th St Ste 114
Cleveland OH 44114

(G-5140)
WESTLAKE VILLAGE INC
Also Called: HOMEWOOD RESIDENCE
28550 Westlake Village Dr (44145-7608)
PHONE.................................440 892-4200
Jeanne Barnard, *Pr*
EMP: 101 **EST:** 1988
SQ FT: 125,000
SALES (est): 18.34MM
SALES (corp-wide): 2.83B **Publicly Held**
SIC: 6513 Retirement hotel operation
HQ: American Retirement Corporation
111 Westwood Pl Ste 200
Brentwood TN 37027
615 221-2150

(G-5141)
WESTON DEVELOPMENT COMPANY LLC
4832 Richmond Rd Ste 100 (44128-5993)
PHONE.................................440 914-8427
Mark K Horton, *Pr*
EMP: 52 **EST:** 2008
SALES (est): 905.18K
SALES (corp-wide): 37.76MM **Privately Held**
Web: www.teamweston.com
SIC: 6531 Real estate agent, commercial
PA: Weston Inc.
4760 Richmond Rd Ste 200
Cleveland OH 44128
440 349-9000

(G-5142)
WESTON HURD LLP (PA)
1301 E 9th St Ste 1900 (44114-1862)
PHONE.................................216 241-6602
EMP: 77 **EST:** 1925
SALES (est): 6.62MM
SALES (corp-wide): 6.62MM **Privately Held**
Web: www.westonhurd.com
SIC: 8111 General practice law office

(G-5143)
WESTON INC (PA)
Also Called: Property 3
4760 Richmond Rd Ste 200 (44128-5979)
PHONE.................................440 349-9000
Ann S Asher, *Pr*
EMP: 29 **EST:** 1964
SALES (est): 37.76MM
SALES (corp-wide): 37.76MM **Privately Held**
Web: www.teamweston.com
SIC: 6512 6541 Commercial and industrial building operation; Title search companies

(G-5144)
WFTS
W E W S - TV
3001 Euclid Ave (44115-2516)
PHONE.................................216 431-5555
Eliot Case, *Brnch Mgr*
EMP: 65
SQ FT: 10,000
SALES (corp-wide): 2.66B **Publicly Held**
Web: www.news5cleveland.com
SIC: 4833 Television broadcasting stations
HQ: Wfts
4045 N Himes Ave
Tampa FL 33607
813 354-2800

(G-5145)
WHITING-TURNER CONTRACTING CO
1001 Lakeside Ave E Ste 100 (44114)
PHONE.................................440 449-9200
Jeff Maeder, *VP*
EMP: 253
SALES (corp-wide): 8.62B **Privately Held**
Web: www.whiting-turner.com
SIC: 1541 1542 1629 Industrial buildings and warehouses; Nonresidential construction, nec; Industrial plant construction
PA: The Whiting-Turner Contracting Company
300 E Joppa Rd
Baltimore MD 21286
410 821-1100

(G-5146)
WHOLE HEALTH MANAGEMENT INC (DH)
1375 E 9th St Ste 2500 (44114-1743)
PHONE.................................216 921-8601
James J Hummer, *Pr*
Randall Twyman, *
Randy Twyman, *
Chuck Siemon, *CIO*
EMP: 40 **EST:** 1981
SQ FT: 5,000
SALES (est): 26.83MM
SALES (corp-wide): 139.08B **Publicly Held**
SIC: 8011 Occupational and industrial specialist, physician/surgeon
HQ: Walgreen Co.
200 Wilmot Rd
Deerfield IL 60015
800 925-4733

(G-5147)
WHS ENGINEERING INC
2012 W 25th St Ste 200 (44113-4131)
PHONE.................................216 227-8505
Bill Shepardson, *Pr*
EMP: 33 **EST:** 2007
SALES (est): 4.34MM **Privately Held**
Web: www.whs-eng.com
SIC: 8711 Professional engineer

(G-5148)
WILLCARE INC
6150 Parkland Blvd Ste 250 (44124-6147)
PHONE.................................216 289-5300
Brason Todd, *Brnch Mgr*
EMP: 141
SALES (corp-wide): 371.62B **Publicly Held**
SIC: 8049 8082 7361 Nurses, registered and practical; Home health care services; Nurses' registry
HQ: Willcare, Inc.
105 Earhart Dr Ste 100
Buffalo NY 14221
716 856-7500

(G-5149)
WINDSTREAM SERVICES LLC
Also Called: WINDSTREAM SERVICES, LLC
1625 Rockwell Ave (44114-2000)
PHONE.................................216 394-0065
Michelle Fortenberry, *Brnch Mgr*
EMP: 29
SALES (corp-wide): 6.77B **Privately Held**
Web: www.windstreamenterprise.com
SIC: 4813 Local and long distance telephone communications
HQ: Windstream Services Pe, Llc
4001 N Rodney Parham Rd
Little Rock AR 72212
501 748-7000

(G-5150)
WINDY HILL LTD INC (PA)
Also Called: Transworld News
3700 Kelley Ave (44114-4533)
PHONE.................................216 391-4800
Joel Kaminsky, *Pr*
Jeffrey Gross, *
EMP: 75 **EST:** 1967
SQ FT: 55,000
SALES (est): 9.88MM
SALES (corp-wide): 9.88MM **Privately Held**
SIC: 5192 5099 Magazines; Video cassettes, accessories and supplies

(G-5151)
WINGATE INC
23775 Commerce Park (44122-5836)
PHONE.................................216 591-1061
EMP: 36 **EST:** 2006
SALES (est): 104.64K **Privately Held**
Web: www.wyndhamhotels.com
SIC: 7011 Hotels and motels

(G-5152)
WIRELESS CENTER INC (PA)
1925 Saint Clair Ave Ne (44114-2028)
PHONE.................................216 503-3777
Azam Kazmi, *Prin*
EMP: 66 **EST:** 2002
SQ FT: 10,000
SALES (est): 61.74MM
SALES (corp-wide): 61.74MM **Privately Held**
Web: www.verizon.com
SIC: 4812 Cellular telephone services

(G-5153)
WISEWEL LLC
32350 S Woodland Rd (44124-5853)
PHONE.................................440 591-4896
Chandika D Jayawardane, *Managing Member*
EMP: 30 **EST:** 2013
SALES (est): 2.26MM **Privately Held**
Web: www.wisewel.com
SIC: 6221 7389 Commodity traders, contracts; Financial services

(G-5154)
WISHING WELL ACQUISITION LTD (PA)
Also Called: Wishing Well Preschool
14574 Ridge Rd (44133-4940)
PHONE.................................440 237-5000
Johanne Wigton, *Pr*
EMP: 50 **EST:** 1993
SQ FT: 11,000
SALES (est): 2.4MM **Privately Held**
Web: www.wishingwellpreschool.com
SIC: 8351 Preschool center

(G-5155)
WKYC-TV INC
Also Called: W K Y C Channel 3
1333 Lakeside Ave E (44114-1159)
PHONE.................................216 344-3300
Brooke Spectorsky, *Pr*
EMP: 220 **EST:** 1948
SALES (est): 65.13MM
SALES (corp-wide): 2.91B **Publicly Held**
Web: www.wkyc.com
SIC: 4833 Television broadcasting stations
PA: Tegna Inc.
8350 Broad St Ste 2000
Tysons VA 22102
703 873-6600

(G-5156)
WM PLOTZ MACHINE AND FORGE CO
Also Called: Peerless Pump Clveland Svc Ctr
2514 Center St (44113-1111)
PHONE.................................216 861-0441
James W Plotz, *Pr*
Thomas D Plotz, *Sec*
EMP: 32 **EST:** 1888
SQ FT: 21,000
SALES (est): 1.33MM **Privately Held**
SIC: 3599 7699 Machine shop, jobbing and repair; Pumps and pumping equipment repair

(G-5157)
WOLF CREEK FEDERAL SVCS INC
Also Called: Chugach
21000 Brookpark Rd Bldg 107-1 (44135-3127)
PHONE.................................216 433-5609
Timothy Tesch, *Mgr*
EMP: 533

Cleveland - Cuyahoga County (G-5158)

(G-5158)
WONG MARGARET W ASSOC CO LPA (PA)
3150 Chester Ave (44114-4617)
PHONE....................313 527-9989
Margaret W Wong, *Pr*
Kathy Hill, *
EMP: 35 **EST:** 1981
SALES (est): 6.55MM
SALES (corp-wide): 6.55MM **Privately Held**
Web: www.imwong.com
SIC: 8111 General practice law office

(G-5159)
WORLD SHIPPING INC (PA)
1340 Depot St Ste 200 (44116-1741)
PHONE....................440 356-7676
Frederick M Hunger, *Pr*
Dennis Mahoney, *
Douglas Denny, *
John E Hunger, *
EMP: 30 **EST:** 1960
SQ FT: 15,000
SALES (est): 282.57MM
SALES (corp-wide): 282.57MM **Privately Held**
Web: www.worldshipping.com
SIC: 4213 4731 Trucking, except local; Agents, shipping

(G-5160)
WORTHINGTON INDUSTRIES INC
Also Called: Worthington Industries, Inc.
4600 Heidtman Pkwy (44105-1023)
PHONE....................216 641-6995
Robert Mann, *Mgr*
EMP: 100
SALES (corp-wide): 4.92B **Publicly Held**
Web: www.worthingtonenterprises.com
SIC: 5051 Steel
PA: Worthington Enterprises, Inc.
200 W Wlson Bridge Rd
Worthington OH 43085
614 438-3210

(G-5161)
WTW DELAWARE HOLDINGS LLC
Also Called: Willis Towers Watson
1001 Lakeside Ave E Ste 1500 (44114)
PHONE....................216 937-4000
EMP: 58
Web: www.wtwco.com
SIC: 8742 8999 7371 7361 Compensation and benefits planning consultant; Actuarial consultant; Computer software systems analysis and design, custom; Employment agencies
HQ: Wtw Delaware Holdings Llc
800 N Glebe Rd
Arlington VA 22203

(G-5162)
WYSE ADVERTISING INC
668 Euclid Ave Ste 100 (44114-3024)
PHONE....................216 696-2424
EMP: 32
Web: www.fallsandco.com
SIC: 7311 Advertising consultant

(G-5163)
X-RAY INDUSTRIES INC
Also Called: Xri Testing
5403 E Schaaf Rd (44131-1337)
PHONE....................216 642-0100
Bob Hensher, *Mgr*
EMP: 87
SALES (corp-wide): 23.29MM **Privately Held**
Web: www.applus.com
SIC: 8071 8734 X-ray laboratory, including dental; Testing laboratories
PA: X-Ray Industries, Inc.
1961 Thunderbird
Troy MI 48084
248 362-5050

(G-5164)
YARDI SYSTEMS
6001 E Royalton Rd Ste 150 (44147-3527)
PHONE....................805 699-2056
Michael Gaeta, *Prin*
EMP: 28 **EST:** 2016
SALES (est): 157.07K **Privately Held**
Web: www.yardi.com
SIC: 7371 Computer software development

(G-5165)
YORKTOWN AUTOMOTIVE CENTER INC
6177 Pearl Rd (44130-3159)
PHONE....................440 885-2803
Douglas Shull, *Pr*
Matthew Hudak, *VP*
Anita Shull, *Sec*
EMP: 41 **EST:** 1968
SQ FT: 9,200
SALES (est): 3.45MM **Privately Held**
Web: www.yorktownserviceplaza.com
SIC: 7538 5541 General automotive repair shops; Filling stations, gasoline

(G-5166)
YOUNG MNS CHRSTN ASSN GRTER CL
Also Called: YMCA
1801 E 12th St Fl 1 (44114-3526)
PHONE....................216 344-7700
Timothy Hilk, *Pr*
EMP: 41 **EST:** 2015
SALES (est): 521.61K **Privately Held**
Web: www.clevelandymca.org
SIC: 8641 Youth organizations

(G-5167)
YOUNG WNS CHRSTN ASSN CLVLAND (PA)
Also Called: YWCA of Cleveland
4019 Prospect Ave (44103)
PHONE....................216 881-6878
Margaret Mitchell, *Pr*
Barbara Danforth, *
EMP: 30 **EST:** 1869
SQ FT: 24,000
SALES (est): 11.08MM
SALES (corp-wide): 11.08MM **Privately Held**
Web: www.ywcaofcleveland.org
SIC: 8641 7991 8351 7032 Youth organizations; Physical fitness facilities; Child day care services; Youth camps

(G-5168)
YOUTH FOR CHRIST/USA INC
Also Called: Campus Life
709 Brookpark Rd Ste 1 (44109-5839)
PHONE....................216 252-9883
Annette Furry, *Mgr*
EMP: 29
SALES (corp-wide): 15.46MM **Privately Held**
Web: www.yfc.net
SIC: 8661 8641 Religious organizations; Civic and social associations
PA: Youth For Christ/Usa, Inc.
7670 S Vaughn Ct
Englewood CO 80112
303 843-9000

(G-5169)
YP LLC
9445 Rockside Rd (44125-6126)
PHONE....................216 642-4000
Kim Gergel, *VP*
EMP: 121
SALES (corp-wide): 916.96MM **Publicly Held**
Web: www.yp.com
SIC: 4813 7319 Local and long distance telephone communications; Distribution of advertising material or sample services
HQ: Yp Llc
2247 Northlake Pkwy Fl 4
Tucker GA 30084
866 570-8863

(G-5170)
YSI MANAGEMENT LLC
6745 Engle Rd Ste 300 (44130-7993)
PHONE....................440 891-4100
William Diefenderfer, *Ch*
EMP: 30 **EST:** 2004
SALES (est): 2.25MM **Publicly Held**
Web: www.ysi.com
SIC: 4225 Warehousing, self storage
HQ: Cubesmart, L.P.
1500 Gateway Blvd Ste 190
Boynton Beach FL 33426
610 535-5700

(G-5171)
Z & SONS LIMITED PARTNERSHIP
7100 E Pleasant Valley Rd # 300 (44131-5544)
PHONE....................440 249-5164
Timothy Zaremba, *Mng Pt*
Nathan Zaremba, *Mng Pt*
EMP: 88 **EST:** 1996
SQ FT: 3,000
SALES (est): 3.67MM **Privately Held**
SIC: 6512 Commercial and industrial building operation

(G-5172)
ZASHIN & RICH CO LPA (PA)
950 Main Ave Fl 4 (44113-7215)
PHONE....................216 696-4441
Andrew Zashin, *Pr*
Stephen Zashin, *
EMP: 35 **EST:** 1980
SALES (est): 5.82MM
SALES (corp-wide): 5.82MM **Privately Held**
Web: www.zrlaw.com
SIC: 8111 General practice attorney, lawyer

(G-5173)
ZAVARELLA BROTHERS CNSTR CO
5381 Erie St Ste B (44146-1739)
P.O. Box 46983 (44146-0983)
PHONE....................440 232-2243
Dan Zavarella, *Pr*
Nicholas Zavarella, *
Chuck Zavarella, *
Daniel Zavarella, *
EMP: 50 **EST:** 1976
SQ FT: 1,000
SALES (est): 4.61MM **Privately Held**
SIC: 1741 Bricklaying

(G-5174)
ZENITH SYSTEMS LLC (PA)
5055 Corbin Dr (44128-5462)
PHONE....................216 587-9510
Paul Francisco, *Managing Member*
Michael Joyce, *
Aldona Nagy, *
EMP: 160 **EST:** 2008
SALES (est): 96.65MM **Privately Held**
Web: www.zenithsystems.com
SIC: 1731 Communications specialization

(G-5175)
ZIEBART OF OHIO INC
Also Called: Ziebart
6754 Pearl Rd (44130-3620)
PHONE....................440 845-6031
Karl Zierow, *Pr*
EMP: 46
SALES (corp-wide): 23.07MM **Privately Held**
Web: www.ziebart.com
SIC: 7549 1799 5531 Lubrication service, automotive; Glass tinting, architectural or automotive; Trailer hitches, automotive
HQ: Ziebart Of Ohio Inc
1290 E Maple Rd
Troy MI 48083

(G-5176)
ZUCKER BUILDING COMPANY
Also Called: State Chemical
5915 Landerbrook Dr Ste 300 (44124-4039)
PHONE....................216 861-7114
Harold Uhrman, *Pr*
Malcolm Zucker, *
EMP: 38 **EST:** 1925
SQ FT: 240,000
SALES (est): 2.22MM **Privately Held**
Web: www.stateindustrial.com
SIC: 6512 Commercial and industrial building operation

Cleveland Heights
Cuyahoga County

(G-5177)
BERKOWITZ KMIN BKATZ MEM CHPEL
1985 S Taylor Rd (44118-2158)
PHONE....................216 932-7900
Stuart Berkowitz, *CEO*
Kirk Berkowitz, *VP*
EMP: 36 **EST:** 1957
SQ FT: 20,000
SALES (est): 363.26K
SALES (corp-wide): 4.1B **Publicly Held**
Web: www.berkowitzkuminbookatzfunerals.com
SIC: 7261 Funeral home
PA: Service Corporation International
1929 Allen Pkwy
Houston TX 77019
713 522-5141

(G-5178)
HEIGHTS LAUNDRY & DRY CLEANING (PA)
1863 Coventry Rd (44118-1610)
PHONE....................216 932-9666
Manning Dishler, *Pr*
Arlene Dishler, *
EMP: 32 **EST:** 1946
SQ FT: 3,000
SALES (est): 948.22K
SALES (corp-wide): 948.22K **Privately Held**
SIC: 7211 7216 Power laundries, family and commercial; Drycleaning plants, except rugs

(G-5179)
HOME DEPOT USA INC
Also Called: Home Depot, The
3460 Mayfield Rd (44118)

GEOGRAPHIC SECTION

Clyde - Sandusky County (G-5200)

PHONE..............................216 297-1303
Timothy E Mccarthy, *Mgr*
EMP: 121
SALES (corp-wide): 152.67B **Publicly Held**
Web: www.homedepot.com
SIC: 5211 7359 Home centers; Tool rental
HQ: Home Depot U.S.A., Inc.
 2445 Springfield Ave
 Vauxhall NJ 07088

(G-5180)
JEWISH EDCATN CTR OF CLEVELAND
2030 S Taylor Rd (44118-2605)
PHONE..............................216 371-0446
Seymour Kopelowitz, *Ex Dir*
EMP: 75 **EST:** 1924
SQ FT: 20,000
SALES (est): 8.29MM **Privately Held**
Web: www.jecc.org
SIC: 8399 Council for social agency

(G-5181)
METROHEALTH SYSTEM
Also Called: Cleveland Heights Medical Ctr
10 Severance Cir (44118-1533)
PHONE..............................216 696-3876
EMP: 177
SALES (corp-wide): 620.72MM **Privately Held**
Web: www.metrohealth.org
SIC: 8062 General medical and surgical hospitals
PA: The Metrohealth System
 2500 Metrohealth Dr
 Cleveland OH 44109
 216 778-7800

(G-5182)
MUSICIANS TOWERS OH TC LP
2727 Lancashire Rd (44106-5518)
PHONE..............................216 520-1250
Frank T Sinito, *Prin*
EMP: 38 **EST:** 2018
SALES (est): 2.57MM **Privately Held**
Web: www.musicianstowersapts.com
SIC: 6513 Apartment building operators

(G-5183)
REILLY PAINTING & CONTG INC
1899 S Taylor Rd (44118-2160)
PHONE..............................216 371-8160
Michael Reilly, *Pr*
Fiona Reilly, *
EMP: 30 **EST:** 1973
SQ FT: 8,063
SALES (est): 2.19MM **Privately Held**
Web: www.reillypainting.com
SIC: 1721 1761 Exterior residential painting contractor; Roofing, siding, and sheetmetal work

(G-5184)
RESOURCE ALLIANCE HOMECARE LLC
2000 Lee Rd Ste 24 (44118-2559)
PHONE..............................216 465-9977
Siana Stewart, *CEO*
EMP: 67 **EST:** 2016
SALES (est): 1.89MM **Privately Held**
Web: www.resourcealliancehomecare.com
SIC: 8082 Home health care services

(G-5185)
RIGHT DRCTION BHVRAL HLTH SVCS
5 Severance Cir Ste 510 (44118-1588)
PHONE..............................216 260-9022

Deandra Evans, *Ex Dir*
EMP: 45 **EST:** 2020
SALES (est): 1.03MM **Privately Held**
Web: www.rdbhs.com
SIC: 8099 Health and allied services, nec

Cleves
Hamilton County

(G-5186)
ANDERSON AUTMTC HTG & AC INC
6085 Hamilton Cleves Rd (45002-9530)
PHONE..............................512 574-0005
Michael E Burg, *Pr*
Glenn Meyer, *VP*
EMP: 36 **EST:** 1929
SQ FT: 8,000
SALES (est): 3.3MM **Privately Held**
Web: www.andersonautomatic.com
SIC: 1711 Warm air heating and air conditioning contractor

(G-5187)
BANTA ELECTRICAL CONTRS INC (PA)
5701 Hamilton Cleves Rd (45002)
P.O. Box 377 (45041)
PHONE..............................513 353-4446
Gale F Banta, *Pr*
Ed Ginter, *
EMP: 35 **EST:** 1985
SQ FT: 12,000
SALES (est): 18.38MM
SALES (corp-wide): 18.38MM **Privately Held**
Web: www.bantaelectric.com
SIC: 1731 General electrical contractor

(G-5188)
EQUIPMENT MAINTENANCE INC
Also Called: Equipment Maintenance & Repair
5885 Hamilton Cleves Rd (45002-9529)
PHONE..............................513 353-3518
Don Holden, *Pr*
EMP: 34 **EST:** 1985
SQ FT: 22,000
SALES (est): 2.29MM **Privately Held**
SIC: 7699 5261 5082 Aircraft and heavy equipment repair services; Lawn and garden equipment; Construction and mining machinery

(G-5189)
KATHMAN ELECTRIC CO INC
8969 Harrison Pike (45002-9757)
PHONE..............................513 353-3365
Raymond E Kathman, *Pr*
Thomas Kathman, *
Gary Kathman, *
EMP: 45 **EST:** 1985
SQ FT: 3,000
SALES (est): 4.89MM **Privately Held**
SIC: 1731 General electrical contractor

(G-5190)
KEN NEYER PLUMBING INC
4895 Hamilton Cleves Rd (45002-9752)
PHONE..............................513 353-3311
James Neyer, *Pr*
Ken Neyer Junior, *VP*
Janet Neyer, *
EMP: 150 **EST:** 1972
SQ FT: 2,500
SALES (est): 22.51MM **Privately Held**
Web: www.neyerplumbing.com
SIC: 1711 Plumbing contractors

(G-5191)
NORTH AMRCN UTLITY SLTIONS LLC
Also Called: Backbone Power Systems
9311 West Rd (45002-9463)
PHONE..............................513 313-2323
EMP: 28 **EST:** 2018
SALES (est): 249.39K
SALES (corp-wide): 5.43MM **Privately Held**
Web: www.backbonenorthamerican.com
SIC: 1711 Plumbing, heating, air-conditioning
PA: Backbone Power Systems, Llc
 9311 West Rd
 Cleves OH 45002
 513 353-0046

(G-5192)
REIS TRUCKING INC
10080 Valley Junction Rd (45002-9406)
PHONE..............................513 353-1960
Paul A Reis, *Pr*
EMP: 28 **EST:** 1980
SQ FT: 7,000
SALES (est): 2.98MM **Privately Held**
Web: www.reistrucking.com
SIC: 4212 Local trucking, without storage

(G-5193)
SEHLHORST EQUIPMENT SVCS INC
8073 Furlong Dr (45002-9117)
P.O. Box 33110 (45233-0110)
PHONE..............................513 353-9300
Douglas Sehlhorst, *Pr*
David Sehlhorst, *
Daniel Sehlhorst Junior, *VP*
Mark Billman, *
EMP: 30 **EST:** 1985
SALES (est): 3.01MM **Privately Held**
Web: www.sehlhorst.com
SIC: 1794 Excavation and grading, building construction

(G-5194)
SEHLHORST EQUIPMENT SVCS LLC
8073 Furlong Dr (45002-9117)
PHONE..............................513 353-9300
Douglas Sehlhorst, *Managing Member*
EMP: 40 **EST:** 2007
SALES (est): 5.84MM **Privately Held**
Web: www.sehlhorst.com
SIC: 1794 Excavation and grading, building construction

(G-5195)
SHOEMAKER MASONRY CNSTR LLC
8856 Harrison Pike (45002-9801)
PHONE..............................989 948-2377
Sara Shoemaker, *Pr*
EMP: 31 **EST:** 2017
SALES (est): 2.38MM **Privately Held**
Web: www.shoemakermasonry.com
SIC: 1521 Single-family housing construction

(G-5196)
WM KRAMER AND SON INC
Also Called: W K S
9171 Harrison Pike Unit 12 (45002-9076)
PHONE..............................513 353-1142
Steven M Kramer, *Pr*
Doug Kramer, *
Bruce Kramer, *
Kevin Kramer, *
Genevieve Kramer, *
EMP: 75 **EST:** 1907
SQ FT: 22,357
SALES (est): 13MM **Privately Held**
Web: www.kramerroofing.com
SIC: 1761 Roofing contractor

Clinton
Summit County

(G-5197)
YOUNG MNS CHRSTN ASSN OF AKRON
Also Called: Camp Y-Noah
815 Mount Pleasant Rd (44216-9621)
PHONE..............................330 376-1335
Michael Ohl, *Ex Dir*
EMP: 51
SQ FT: 10,219
SALES (corp-wide): 21.21MM **Privately Held**
Web: www.akronymca.org
SIC: 7032 8641 Youth camps; Civic and social associations
PA: The Young Men's Christian Association Of Akron Ohio
 50 S Mn St Ste LI100
 Akron OH 44308
 330 376-1335

Clyde
Sandusky County

(G-5198)
ASTORIA PLACE OF CLYDE LLC
Also Called: Heritage Village of Clyde
700 Helen St (43410-2051)
PHONE..............................419 547-9595
Admiral Bonnie Stepanian, *Prin*
Eric Hutchins, *VP Opers*
EMP: 70 **EST:** 2014
SALES (est): 4.58MM
SALES (corp-wide): 19.19MM **Privately Held**
Web: www.certushc.com
SIC: 8051 Skilled nursing care facilities
PA: Certus Healthcare Management, Llc
 20265 Emery Rd
 Cleveland OH 44128
 330 720-0406

(G-5199)
CHANEY ROOFING MAINTENANCE INC
Also Called: C R M
7040 State Route 101 N (43410-9636)
PHONE..............................419 639-2761
Shawn Chaney, *Pr*
Gary S Chaney, *
EMP: 30 **EST:** 1966
SQ FT: 50,000
SALES (est): 6.88MM **Privately Held**
Web: www.crmroofing.com
SIC: 1761 1542 Roofing contractor; Commercial and office building, new construction

(G-5200)
FIRST FINANCIAL
137 W Buckeye St Ste B (43410-1988)
PHONE..............................419 547-7733
Phyllis S Fiser, *Pr*
Marie J Archer, *
Frederick C Bouyack, *
Scott Hicks, *
EMP: 37 **EST:** 1906
SQ FT: 9,000
SALES (est): 5.56MM
SALES (corp-wide): 1.12B **Publicly Held**
Web: www.bankatfirst.com
SIC: 6022 State commercial banks
PA: First Financial Bancorp.
 255 E 5th St Ste 800
 Cincinnati OH 45202
 877 322-9530

Clyde - Sandusky County (G-5201)

(G-5201)
FULTZ & SON INC
Also Called: FSI Disposal
100 S Main St (43410-1633)
PHONE.....................419 547-9365
Larry F Fultz, Pr
Audra Albright, *
EMP: 28 **EST:** 1952
SQ FT: 22,000
SALES (est): 2.34MM **Privately Held**
Web: www.fsidisposal.com
SIC: 4212 4953 Garbage collection and transport, no disposal; Recycling, waste materials

(G-5202)
HOSPICE OF MEMORIAL HOSPITA L
430 S Main St (43410-2142)
PHONE.....................419 334-6626
Anne Shelley, Dir
EMP: 34 **EST:** 2001
SALES (est): 151.26K **Privately Held**
SIC: 8082 Home health care services

(G-5203)
IMPACT CREDIT UNION INC (PA)
1455 W Mcpherson Hwy (43410)
PHONE.....................419 547-7781
Paul Howard, Pr
Kenneth Cobb, *
Scott Hicks, *
EMP: 28 **EST:** 1934
SQ FT: 12,416
SALES (est): 8.49MM
SALES (corp-wide): 8.49MM **Privately Held**
Web: www.impactcu.org
SIC: 6061 6163 Federal credit unions; Loan brokers

(G-5204)
J B HUNT TRANSPORT INC
600 N Woodland Ave (43410-1054)
PHONE.....................419 547-2777
Tracey Walker, Brnch Mgr
EMP: 71
SALES (corp-wide): 12.83B **Publicly Held**
Web: www.jbhunt.com
SIC: 4213 Trucking, except local
HQ: J. B. Hunt Transport, Inc.
615 Jb Hunt Corporate Dr
Lowell AR 72745
479 820-0000

(G-5205)
LAKE ERIE HOSPITALITY LLC
Also Called: Red Roof Inn
1363 W Mcpherson Hwy (43410-1007)
PHONE.....................419 547-6660
Greg Kalski, Mgr
EMP: 71
SALES (corp-wide): 575.81K **Privately Held**
Web: www.redroof.com
SIC: 7011 Hotels and motels
PA: Lake Erie Hospitality, Llc
11303 Us Highway 250 N
Milan OH 44846
419 499-2153

(G-5206)
MEMORIAL HOSPITAL
Memorial Home Health & Hospice
430 S Main St (43410-2142)
PHONE.....................419 547-6419
Anne Shelley, Dir
EMP: 112
SALES (corp-wide): 86.27MM **Privately Held**
Web: www.promedica.org

SIC: 8062 8082 General medical and surgical hospitals; Home health care services
PA: Memorial Hospital
715 S Taft Ave
Fremont OH 43420
419 334-6657

(G-5207)
POLYCHEM LLC
Also Called: Evergreen Plastics
202 Watertower Dr (43410-2154)
PHONE.....................419 547-1400
Mark Jeckering, Genl Mgr
EMP: 75
Web: www.polychem.com
SIC: 3052 4953 Plastic belting; Recycling, waste materials
HQ: Polychem, Llc
6277 Heisley Rd
Mentor OH 44060
440 357-1500

(G-5208)
ROCKWELL SPRINGS TROUT CLUB
1581 County Road 310 (43410-9733)
PHONE.....................419 684-7971
Toni Borchardt, Prin
Kevin Ramsey, *
Jeff Smith, *
EMP: 41 **EST:** 1940
SQ FT: 4,000
SALES (est): 1.24MM **Privately Held**
Web: www.rockwellspringstroutclub.com
SIC: 7032 7041 5812 Fishing camp; Lodging house, organization; Eating places

(G-5209)
SANDCO INDUSTRIES
567 Premier Dr (43410-2157)
PHONE.....................419 547-3273
Donald Nalley, Dir
EMP: 42 **EST:** 1964
SALES (est): 1.39MM **Privately Held**
Web: www.sandcoind.com
SIC: 8331 3639 Sheltered workshop; Major kitchen appliances, except refrigerators and stoves

(G-5210)
SPADER FREIGHT SERVICES INC (PA)
Also Called: S F S
1134 E Mcpherson Hwy (43410-9802)
P.O. Box 246 (43410-0246)
PHONE.....................419 547-1117
EMP: 60 **EST:** 1995
SQ FT: 60,000
SALES (est): 9.5MM **Privately Held**
Web: www.spaderfreight.com
SIC: 4213 Contract haulers

Coal Grove
Lawrence County

(G-5211)
SHAWNEE MENTAL HEALTH CTR INC
Also Called: Shawnee Mental Health
225 Carlton Davidson Ln (45638-2924)
PHONE.....................740 533-6280
Don Thacker, Brnch Mgr
EMP: 34
SALES (corp-wide): 15.31MM **Privately Held**
Web: www.shawneefamilyhealthcenter.com
SIC: 8093 Mental health clinic, outpatient
PA: Shawnee Mental Health Center, Inc.

901 Washington St
Portsmouth OH
740 354-7702

Coldwater
Mercer County

(G-5212)
DICKMAN KETTLER & BRUNER LTD
Also Called: James Dickman & Jillyn Bruner
201 S 2nd St (45828-1747)
P.O. Box 95 (45828-0095)
PHONE.....................419 678-3016
James K Dickman, Pt
EMP: 28 **EST:** 1968
SALES (est): 477.19K **Privately Held**
Web: www.dickmankettlerbruner.com
SIC: 8042 8011 Contact lens specialist optometrist; General and family practice, physician/surgeon

(G-5213)
HCF OF BRIARWOOD INC
Also Called: Briarwood Mano
100 Don Desch Dr (45828-1583)
PHONE.....................419 678-2311
Kristen Wynk, Dir
Liz Schmackers, Business Development*
EMP: 193 **EST:** 2002
SALES (est): 21.02MM
SALES (corp-wide): 305.93MM **Privately Held**
Web: www.briarwood-village.com
SIC: 8051 Extended care facility
PA: Hcf Management, Inc.
1100 Shawnee Rd
Lima OH 45805
419 999-2010

(G-5214)
I-O PROPERTIES LLC
Also Called: Country Butcher, The
4260 Burrville Rd (45828-9773)
PHONE.....................419 852-7836
Riggs Florence, Mgr
EMP: 103
SALES (est): 694.99K **Privately Held**
SIC: 0191 General farms, primarily crop

(G-5215)
LEFELD IMPLEMENT INC
Also Called: John Deere Authorized Dealer
5228 State Route 118 (45828-9702)
PHONE.....................419 678-2375
Steve Layfield, Pr
Paul J Lefeld Junior, VP
Michael Lefeld, *
Dan Lefeld, *
Judy Marbaugh, *
▲ **EMP:** 30 **EST:** 1947
SQ FT: 40,000
SALES (est): 1.02MM **Privately Held**
Web: www.lefeldimp.com
SIC: 5999 5082 Farm machinery, nec; Construction and mining machinery

(G-5216)
LEFELD WELDING & STL SUPS INC (PA)
Also Called: Lefeld Supplies Rental
600 N 2nd St (45828-9777)
PHONE.....................419 678-2397
Stanley E Lefeld, CEO
Gary Lefeld, *
▲ **EMP:** 43 **EST:** 1953
SQ FT: 10,400
SALES (est): 17.78MM
SALES (corp-wide): 17.78MM **Privately Held**

Web: www.lefeld.com
SIC: 5084 7353 1799 3441 Welding machinery and equipment; Heavy construction equipment rental; Welding on site; Fabricated structural metal

(G-5217)
MERCER CNTY JOINT TOWNSHP HOSP
Mercer County Community Hosp
800 W Main St (45828-1613)
PHONE.....................419 678-2341
EMP: 236
SALES (corp-wide): 49.12MM **Privately Held**
Web: www.mercer-health.com
SIC: 8062 General medical and surgical hospitals
PA: Mercer County Joint Township Community Hospital
800 W Main St
Coldwater OH 45828
419 678-2341

(G-5218)
MERCER HEALTH
800 W Main St (45828-1613)
PHONE.....................419 678-4300
Lisa Klenke, CEO
EMP: 100 **EST:** 2015
SALES (est): 25.05MM **Privately Held**
Web: www.mercer-health.com
SIC: 8062 General medical and surgical hospitals

(G-5219)
MIDWEST DAIRIES INC
612 Plum Dr (45828-1141)
PHONE.....................419 678-8059
Mark Abels, Pr
EMP: 79 **EST:** 1990
SIC: 6719 Investment holding companies, except banks

(G-5220)
THE PEOPLES BANK CO INC (PA)
112 W Main St 114 (45828-1701)
P.O. Box 110 (45828-0110)
PHONE.....................419 678-2385
Jack A Hartings, Pr
EMP: 29 **EST:** 1905
SQ FT: 8,000
SALES (est): 22.05MM
SALES (corp-wide): 22.05MM **Privately Held**
Web: www.pbc.bank
SIC: 6022 8721 State trust companies accepting deposits, commercial; Accounting, auditing, and bookkeeping

(G-5221)
WILMER
515 W Sycamore St (45828-1663)
PHONE.....................419 678-6000
Joni Dennis, Prin
EMP: 28 **EST:** 2018
SALES (est): 5.69MM **Privately Held**
Web: www.4wilmer.com
SIC: 5112 Business forms

College Corner
Butler County

(G-5222)
OHIO STATE PARKS INC
Also Called: Hueston Woods Lodge,
5201 Lodge Rd (45003-9038)
PHONE.....................513 664-3504
Tom Arvan, Mgr

GEOGRAPHIC SECTION

Columbus - Delaware County (G-5244)

EMP: 65 EST: 1965
SALES (est): 1.4MM **Privately Held**
Web: www.huestonwoodslodge.com
SIC: 7011 7992 5813 5812 Vacation lodges; Public golf courses; Drinking places; Eating places

Columbia Station
Lorain County

(G-5223)
AMERI-LINE INC
27060 Royalton Rd (44028-9048)
P.O. Box 965 (44028-0965)
PHONE.................................440 316-4500
EMP: 30 EST: 1993
SQ FT: 12,000
SALES (est): 4.66MM **Privately Held**
Web: www.ameri-line.com
SIC: 4213 4731 Contract haulers; Truck transportation brokers

(G-5224)
CLAUST LLC
27457 Royalton Rd (44028-9159)
P.O. Box 1016 (44028-1016)
PHONE.................................440 783-2847
Stelian Hritcu, *Brnch Mgr*
EMP: 29
SALES (corp-wide): 2.88MM **Privately Held**
SIC: 4731 Truck transportation brokers
PA: Claust Llc
28370 Nandina Dr
North Olmsted OH 44070
440 503-5485

(G-5225)
COLUMBIA HILLS COUNTRY CLB INC
16200 East River Rd (44028-9485)
PHONE.................................440 236-5051
Michael Weinhardt, *Pr*
EMP: 66 EST: 1925
SQ FT: 43,000
SALES (est): 12.7MM **Privately Held**
Web: www.columbiahillsgolf.com
SIC: 7997 Country club, membership

(G-5226)
CROSS-ROADS ASPHALT RECYCLING INC
13421 Hawke Rd (44028-9730)
PHONE.................................440 236-5066
EMP: 30 EST: 1983
SALES (est): 1.14MM **Privately Held**
Web: www.crossroadsasphalt.com
SIC: 1771 4953 Blacktop (asphalt) work; Recycling, waste materials

(G-5227)
DISTRIBUTOR MARKETING MGT INC
14147 Station Rd (44028-9760)
PHONE.................................440 236-5534
Loren George, *Pr*
EMP: 38 EST: 1992
SALES (est): 1.3MM **Privately Held**
Web: www.distributormarketing.net
SIC: 7311 8743 Advertising agencies; Sales promotion

(G-5228)
HUNTINGTON NATIONAL BANK
26570 Royalton Rd (44028-9056)
PHONE.................................440 236-5011
Robert Bunsey, *Mgr*
EMP: 31
SALES (corp-wide): 10.84B **Publicly Held**
Web: www.huntington.com

SIC: 6029 Commercial banks, nec
HQ: The Huntington National Bank
41 S High St
Columbus OH 43215
614 480-4293

(G-5229)
MASLYK LANDSCAPING INC
12289 Eaton Commerce Pkwy Ste 2 (44028-9208)
PHONE.................................440 748-3635
Alan Maslyk, *Pr*
EMP: 30 EST: 2005
SALES (est): 1.01MM **Privately Held**
Web: www.maslyklandscaping.com
SIC: 0781 Landscape services

(G-5230)
ZONE SAFETY LLC
Also Called: Zone Safety 365
27100 Royalton Rd Unit 2 (44028-9048)
P.O. Box 508 (44028-0508)
PHONE.................................440 752-9545
Michael Bell, *
EMP: 56 EST: 2017
SALES (est): 2.39MM **Privately Held**
Web: www.zonesafety365.com
SIC: 8748 Business consulting, nec

Columbiana
Columbiana County

(G-5231)
BUCKEYE COMPONENTS LLC
1340 State Route 14 (44408-9648)
PHONE.................................330 482-5163
EMP: 30 EST: 1993
SQ FT: 8,000
SALES (est): 2.47MM **Privately Held**
SIC: 5031 2439 Lumber, plywood, and millwork; Trusses, wooden roof

(G-5232)
CBC GLOBAL
Also Called: Columbiana Boiler Company, LLC
200 W Railroad St (44408-1281)
PHONE.................................330 482-3373
Michael J Sherwin, *Pr*
Thomas F Dougherty, *
Alan G Eckert, *
Gerianne Klepfer, *
Charles R Moore, *
◆ EMP: 45 EST: 1894
SQ FT: 50,000
SALES (est): 16.44MM
SALES (corp-wide): 16.44MM **Privately Held**
Web: www.cbco.com
SIC: 1791 3443 Storage tanks, metal: erection; Process vessels, industrial: metal plate
PA: Columbiana Holding Co Inc
200 W Railroad St
Columbiana OH 44408
330 482-3373

(G-5233)
D & V TRUCKING INC
12803 Columbiana Canfield Rd (44408-9769)
PHONE.................................330 482-9440
Danny W Fowler Junior, *Pr*
EMP: 27 EST: 1981
SQ FT: 20,000
SALES (est): 1.31MM **Privately Held**
SIC: 4212 Dump truck haulage

(G-5234)
DAS DUTCH VILLAGE INN
150 E State Route 14 (44408-8425)
PHONE.................................330 482-5050
Ralph Witmer, *Pt*
Raymond Horst, *Pt*
EMP: 50 EST: 2001
SQ FT: 3,400
SALES (est): 952.72K **Privately Held**
Web: www.dasdutchvillage.com
SIC: 7011 Vacation lodges

(G-5235)
FOUR WHEEL DRIVE HARDWARE LLC
Also Called: 4wd
44488 State Route 14 (44408-9540)
PHONE.................................330 482-4733
George Adler, *CEO*
Eb Peters, *
◆ EMP: 155 EST: 1976
SQ FT: 53,000
SALES (est): 36.74MM
SALES (corp-wide): 8.93B **Publicly Held**
SIC: 5013 5551 Automotive supplies and parts; Automotive parts
HQ: Transamerican Dissolution Company, Llc
400 W Artesia Blvd
Compton CA 90220
310 900-5500

(G-5236)
HEARTLAND CHRISTIAN SCHOOL INC
28 Pittsburgh St (44408-1310)
PHONE.................................330 482-2331
EMP: 103 EST: 1996
SALES (est): 3.43MM **Privately Held**
Web: www.heartlandschool.org
SIC: 8211 8351 Private elementary and secondary schools; Preschool center

(G-5237)
MCMASTER FARMS LLC
345 Old Fourteen Rd (44408-9493)
PHONE.................................330 482-2913
Jon Jesse Mcmaster, *Pt*
David Mcmaster, *Owner*
EMP: 69 EST: 1940
SALES (est): 2.17MM **Privately Held**
Web: www.mcmasterfarmsllc.com
SIC: 0161 0134 0119 Corn farm, sweet; Irish potatoes; Feeder grains

(G-5238)
PHD MANUFACTURING INC
44018 Columbiana Waterford Rd (44408-9481)
PHONE.................................330 482-9256
Anthony A Kopatich, *Pt*
Anthony A Kopatich, *CEO*
Joseph J Corvino, *
EMP: 110 EST: 1971
SQ FT: 131,000
SALES (est): 24.56MM **Privately Held**
Web: www.phd-mfg.com
SIC: 5085 Valves and fittings

(G-5239)
R & L TRANSFER INC
1320 Springfield Rd (44408)
PHONE.................................330 482-5800
EMP: 260
SIC: 4213 4212 Trucking, except local; Local trucking, without storage
HQ: R & L Transfer, Inc.
600 Gilliam Rd
Wilmington OH 45177
937 382-1494

(G-5240)
S-P COMPANY INC (PA)
400 W Railroad St Ste 1 (44408-1294)
PHONE.................................330 782-5651
Gregory Smith, *CEO*
Clarence R Smith Junior, *Ch Bd*
Douglas Hagy, *
Richard Kamperman, *
EMP: 90 EST: 1946
SQ FT: 44,000
SALES (est): 33.46MM
SALES (corp-wide): 33.46MM **Privately Held**
SIC: 3469 3443 3498 6512 Metal stampings, nec; Tanks, standard or custom fabricated: metal plate; Tube fabricating (contract bending and shaping); Commercial and industrial building operation

(G-5241)
SALEM COMMUNITY HOSPITAL
116 Carriage Dr (44408-8306)
PHONE.................................330 482-2265
EMP: 43
SALES (corp-wide): 130.12MM **Privately Held**
Web: www.salemregional.com
SIC: 8011 Medical centers
PA: Salem Community Hospital
1995 E State St
Salem OH 44460
330 332-1551

(G-5242)
YES MANAGEMENT INC
Also Called: Youngstown Electric Supply
44612 State Route 14 (44408-9540)
PHONE.................................330 747-8593
Lee Derose, *Pr*
EMP: 27
SALES (corp-wide): 105.41MM **Privately Held**
Web: www.sydist.com
SIC: 5063 Electrical supplies, nec
HQ: Yes Management Inc.
1142 N Meridian Rd
Youngstown OH 44509
330 747-8593

Columbus
Delaware County

(G-5243)
3SG PLUS LLC
Also Called: 3sg Plus
8415 Pulsar Pl Ste 100 (43240-4032)
PHONE.................................614 652-0019
Nanda Nair, *Pr*
EMP: 37 EST: 2014
SQ FT: 20,000
SALES (est): 4.72MM **Privately Held**
Web: www.3sgplus.com
SIC: 8742 7299 Management information systems consultant; Personal document and information services

(G-5244)
ADENA COMMERCIAL LLC
Also Called: Colliers International
8800 Lyra Dr Ste 650 (43240-2107)
PHONE.................................614 436-9800
EMP: 40 EST: 1997
SQ FT: 7,500
SALES (est): 10.1MM
SALES (corp-wide): 4.46B **Privately Held**
SIC: 6531 Real estate agent, commercial
HQ: Colliers International Property Consultants, Inc.
601 Union St Ste 5300

Columbus - Delaware County (G-5245)

Seattle WA 98101

(G-5245)
AMERICAS HEADQUARTERS
8800 Lyra Dr Ste 350 (43240-2151)
PHONE.................614 339-8200
EMP: 72 **EST:** 2011
SALES (est): 1.33MM **Privately Held**
SIC: 7379 Computer related consulting services

(G-5246)
ANTHEM INSURANCE COMPANIES INC
Also Called: Blue Cross
8940 Lyra Dr (43240-2293)
P.O. Box 182361 (43218-2361)
PHONE.................614 438-3542
Joe Bobey, Brnch Mgr
EMP: 1342
SALES (corp-wide): 171.34B **Publicly Held**
Web: www.anthem.com
SIC: 6324 Hospital and medical service plans
HQ: Anthem Insurance Companies, Inc.
220 Virginia Ave
Indianapolis IN 46204
317 488-6000

(G-5247)
BANC ONE SERVICES CORPORATION (HQ)
Also Called: Banc One
1111 Polaris Pkwy Ste B3 (43240-2031)
P.O. Box 710638 (43271-0001)
PHONE.................614 248-5800
Neil Williams, VP Opers
EMP: 2855 **EST:** 1988
SALES (est): 119.9MM
SALES (corp-wide): 239.43B **Publicly Held**
SIC: 7389 Financial services
PA: Jpmorgan Chase & Co.
383 Madison Ave
New York NY 10179
212 270-6000

(G-5248)
CARFAGNAS INCORPORATED
Also Called: Carfagna's Cleve Meats
1440 Gemini Pl (43240-7001)
PHONE.................614 846-6340
Edward Carfagna, CEO
Dino Carfagna, *
Cecilia Carfagna, *
Sam Carfagna, *
Julie Carfagna Rilley, *
EMP: 50 **EST:** 1946
SALES (est): 6.8MM **Privately Held**
Web: www.carfagnas.com
SIC: 5411 5147 Grocery stores, independent ; Meats and meat products

(G-5249)
CATHCART RAIL LLC (PA)
8940 Lyra Dr Ste 200 (43240-2294)
PHONE.................380 390-2058
Casey Cathcart, Ch
Derek Kissick, COO
Kirk Feiler, CFO
EMP: 27 **EST:** 2019
SALES (est): 114.27MM
SALES (corp-wide): 114.27MM **Privately Held**
Web: www.cathcart-rail.com
SIC: 4789 Railroad car repair

(G-5250)
CATHCART REPAIR FACILITIES LLC (DH)
Also Called: BRC Rail Car Company
8940 Lyra Dr Ste 200 (43240-2294)
EMP: 47 **EST:** 1972
SALES (est): 20.47MM
SALES (corp-wide): 114.27MM **Privately Held**
SIC: 4789 Railroad car repair
HQ: Cathcart Rail Services, Llc
737 Eleanor Industrial Pa
Eleanor WV 25070
304 755-7083

(G-5251)
CGI TECHNOLOGIES SOLUTIONS INC
2000 Polaris Pkwy Ste 110 (43240-2108)
PHONE.................614 880-2200
Joyce Clause, Brnch Mgr
EMP: 58
SALES (corp-wide): 9.87B **Privately Held**
Web: www.lumark.com
SIC: 7379 Computer related consulting services
HQ: Cgi Technologies And Solutions Inc.
11325 Rndom Hills Rd Fl 8 Flr 8
Fairfax VA 22030
703 267-5111

(G-5252)
CHASE EQUIPMENT FINANCE INC (HQ)
1111 Polaris Pkwy Ste A3 (43240-2031)
PHONE.................800 678-2601
Clif H Gottwals, CEO
Gary S Gage, *
▲ **EMP:** 230 **EST:** 1972
SQ FT: 43,000
SALES (est): 53.55MM
SALES (corp-wide): 239.43B **Publicly Held**
SIC: 6021 National commercial banks
PA: Jpmorgan Chase & Co.
383 Madison Ave
New York NY 10179
212 270-6000

(G-5253)
CO HATCH LLC
1554 Polaris Pkwy (43240-4082)
PHONE.................614 368-1810
EMP: 96 **EST:** 2015
SALES (est): 1.14MM **Privately Held**
Web: www.cohatch.com
SIC: 6512 Commercial and industrial building operation

(G-5254)
CORPORATE ONE FEDERAL CR UN (PA)
Also Called: Corporate One
8700 Orion Pl (43240-2078)
P.O. Box 2770 (43216-2770)
PHONE.................614 825-9314
Lee C Butke, CEO
Melissa Ashley, *
Tammy Cantrell, *
Joseph Ghammashi, *
Jim Horlacher, *
EMP: 98 **EST:** 1984
SQ FT: 35,000
SALES (est): 42.08MM
SALES (corp-wide): 42.08MM **Privately Held**
Web: www.corporateone.coop
SIC: 6061 Federal credit unions

(G-5255)
CRANEL INCORPORATED (PA)
Also Called: Cranel Imaging
8999 Gemini Pkwy Ste A (43240-2250)
PHONE.................614 431-8000
Craig Wallace, Pr
James Wallace, *
Michael Tracy, *
Leslie Duff, *
Joseph Jackson, *
EMP: 75 **EST:** 1985
SQ FT: 65,000
SALES (est): 21.83MM
SALES (corp-wide): 21.83MM **Privately Held**
Web: www.cranel.com
SIC: 5045 Computer peripheral equipment

(G-5256)
D & L LIGHTING INC
Also Called: Capital Lighting
901 Polaris Pkwy (43240-2035)
PHONE.................614 841-1200
Larry W King, Pr
David L Winks, VP
▲ **EMP:** 60 **EST:** 1990
SQ FT: 32,000
SALES (est): 9.46MM **Privately Held**
Web: www.capitallightinginc.com
SIC: 5063 5719 Lighting fixtures; Lighting, lamps, and accessories

(G-5257)
DENTALONE PARTNERS INC
Also Called: Dentalworks
1099 Polaris Pkwy (43240-2004)
PHONE.................614 356-7245
EMP: 107
SALES (corp-wide): 85.13MM **Privately Held**
Web: www.dentalworks.com
SIC: 8021 Dental clinic
PA: Dentalone Partners, Inc.
6700 Pinecrest Dr Ste 150
Plano TX 75024
972 755-0800

(G-5258)
DUGAN & MEYERS CNSTR SVCS LTD
8740 Orion Pl Ste 220 (43240-4063)
PHONE.................614 257-7430
Jeffery Kelly, Pr
Lincoln Ketterer, *
Jerome E Meyers, *
Jeffrey Kelly, *
EMP: 40 **EST:** 1997
SQ FT: 2,500
SALES (est): 13.82MM
SALES (corp-wide): 85.83MM **Privately Held**
Web: www.dugan-meyers.com
SIC: 1541 1542 Industrial buildings, new construction, nec; Commercial and office building, new construction
HQ: Dugan & Meyers Construction Co
11110 Kenwood Rd
Blue Ash OH 45242
513 891-4300

(G-5259)
FUSION ALLIANCE LLC
8940 Lyra Dr # 220 (43240-2294)
PHONE.................614 852-8000
Vince Nelson, Brnch Mgr
EMP: 103
SALES (corp-wide): 49.95MM **Privately Held**
Web: digital.neweratech.com
SIC: 7371 Computer software development
HQ: Fusion Alliance, Llc
301 Pnnsylvania Pkwy Ste 2
Carmel IN 46032
317 955-1300

(G-5260)
HDR INC
Also Called: HDR
8890 Lyra Dr Ste 100 (43240-3505)
PHONE.................614 839-5770
Brad Hyre, Brnch Mgr
EMP: 30
SALES (corp-wide): 1.08B **Privately Held**
Web: www.hdrinc.com
SIC: 8711 Engineering services
PA: Hdr, Inc.
1917 S 67th St
Omaha NE 68106
402 399-1000

(G-5261)
HILTON POLARIS
Also Called: Hilton
8700 Lyra Dr (43240-2103)
PHONE.................614 885-1600
Jamie Johnson, Prin
EMP: 42 **EST:** 2008
SALES (est): 4.17MM **Privately Held**
Web: www.hilton.com
SIC: 7011 Hotels

(G-5262)
HUGS HEARTS EARLY LRNG CTR INC
Also Called: Early Learning Center
8989 Antares Ave (43240-2012)
PHONE.................614 848-6777
Pam O'brien, Pr
Tim O'brien, Owner
EMP: 35 **EST:** 1994
SQ FT: 8,700
SALES (est): 799K **Privately Held**
Web: www.hugsnheartselc.com
SIC: 8351 Preschool center

(G-5263)
JPMORGAN CHASE & CO
1000 Polaris Pkwy (43240-2110)
PHONE.................614 248-5800
EMP: 167
SALES (corp-wide): 239.43B **Publicly Held**
Web: www.jpmorganchase.com
SIC: 6021 6162 6141 National commercial banks; Mortgage bankers and loan correspondents; Automobile loans, including insurance
PA: Jpmorgan Chase & Co.
383 Madison Ave
New York NY 10179
212 270-6000

(G-5264)
JPMORGAN CHASE BANK NAT ASSN (HQ)
Also Called: Chase
1111 Polaris Pkwy (43240-2050)
PHONE.................614 436-3055
James Dimon, Ch Bd
Linda B Bammann, *
Crandall C Bowles, *
James S Crown, *
Stephen B Burke, *
◆ **EMP:** 1800 **EST:** 1824
SALES (est): 135.84B
SALES (corp-wide): 239.43B **Publicly Held**
Web: www.chase.com
SIC: 6022 6099 6799 6211 State commercial banks; Travelers' checks issuance; Real estate investors, except property operators; Investment bankers
PA: Jpmorgan Chase & Co.
383 Madison Ave
New York NY 10179
212 270-6000

GEOGRAPHIC SECTION — Columbus - Delaware County (G-5284)

(G-5265)
JPMORGAN INV ADVISORS INC (HQ)
1111 Polaris Pkwy (43240-2031)
P.O. Box 711235 (43271-0001)
PHONE..................614 248-5800
David J Kundert, Pr
EMP: 550 EST: 1985
SQ FT: 50,000
SALES (est): 101.35MM
SALES (corp-wide): 239.43B **Publicly Held**
SIC: 6282 Investment advisory service
PA: Jpmorgan Chase & Co.
383 Madison Ave
New York NY 10179
212 270-6000

(G-5266)
LAWYERS TITLE INSURANCE CORP
8425 Pulsar Pl Ste 310 (43240-4041)
PHONE..................614 221-4523
Sandy Eagon, Brnch Mgr
EMP: 100
Web: www.ltic.com
SIC: 6361 Real estate title insurance
HQ: Lawyers Title Insurance Corporation
601 Riverside Ave
Jacksonville FL 32204
888 866-3684

(G-5267)
LEADING EDJE LLC (PA)
1491 Polaris Pkwy Ste 191 (43240-2041)
PHONE..................614 636-3353
Joelle Brock, CEO
Wendy Ivany, CGO
Erica Krumlauf, COO
EMP: 28 EST: 2007
SALES (est): 9.54MM
SALES (corp-wide): 9.54MM **Privately Held**
Web: www.leadingedje.com
SIC: 7379 Computer related consulting services

(G-5268)
MANTA MEDIA INC
8760 Orion Pl Ste 200 (43240-2109)
PHONE..................888 875-5833
John Swanciger, CEO
George Troutman, *
Dario Ambrosini, CMO*
John Swanciger, Pr
EMP: 48 EST: 1996
SQ FT: 5,000
SALES (est): 10.7MM **Privately Held**
SIC: 7313 Printed media advertising representatives

(G-5269)
MERRILL LYNCH PRCE FNNER SMITH
Also Called: Merrill Lynch
8890 Lyra Dr Ste 500 (43240-3502)
PHONE..................614 225-3000
TOLL FREE: 800
EMP: 210
SALES (corp-wide): 93.85B **Publicly Held**
Web: www.ml.com
SIC: 6211 8742 6282 Security brokers and dealers; Financial consultant; Investment advice
HQ: Merrill Lynch, Pierce, Fenner & Smith Incorporated
111 8th Ave
New York NY 10011
800 637-7455

(G-5270)
METTLER-TOLEDO LLC (HQ)
1900 Polaris Pkwy (43240-4055)
PHONE..................614 438-4511
◆ EMP: 1000 EST: 1901
SALES (est): 2B
SALES (corp-wide): 3.79B **Publicly Held**
Web: www.mt.com
SIC: 3596 5049 7699 3821 Industrial scales; Analytical instruments; Professional instrument repair services; Pipettes, hemocytometer
PA: Mettler-Toledo International Inc.
1900 Polaris Pkwy Fl 6
Columbus OH 43240
614 438-4511

(G-5271)
NATIONAL FINANCIAL SVCS LLC
1324 Polaris Pkwy (43240-2038)
PHONE..................614 841-1790
Dave Cverckl, Mgr
EMP: 805
SALES (corp-wide): 4.35B **Privately Held**
Web: www.mybrokerageinfo.com
SIC: 6799 Investors, nec
HQ: National Financial Services Llc
200 Seaport Blvd Ste 630
Boston MA 02210
800 471-0382

(G-5272)
NEW CINGULAR WIRELESS SVCS INC
Also Called: AT&T Wireless
1495 Polaris Pkwy (43240-2041)
PHONE..................614 847-5880
Jeff Tisone, Brnch Mgr
EMP: 38
SALES (corp-wide): 122.43B **Publicly Held**
SIC: 4812 Cellular telephone services
HQ: New Cingular Wireless Services, Inc.
7277 164th Ave Ne
Redmond WA 98052
425 827-4500

(G-5273)
NEWCOME CORP
Also Called: Newcome Electronic Systems
9005 Antares Ave (43240-2012)
P.O. Box 12247 (43212-0247)
PHONE..................614 848-5688
Timothy W Newcome, Pr
EMP: 33 EST: 1978
SQ FT: 8,500
SALES (est): 676.11K **Privately Held**
SIC: 1731 Fiber optic cable installation

(G-5274)
OHIO BAR TITLE INSURANCE CO
8740 Orion Pl Ste 310 (43240-4063)
PHONE..................614 310-8098
James Stipanovich, Ch Bd
James Stipanovich, Ch Bd
Thomas R Jacklitch Senior, General Vice President
W F Tom Burch Junior, Sr VP
James M Nussbaum Junior, Sr VP
EMP: 52 EST: 1955
SQ FT: 9,000
SALES (est): 10.21MM **Publicly Held**
Web: www.firstam.com
SIC: 6361 Real estate title insurance
PA: First American Financial Corporation
1 First American Way
Santa Ana CA 92707

(G-5275)
OHIO FAIR PLAN UNDWRT ASSN
8800 Lyra Dr (43240-2100)
PHONE..................614 839-6446
TOLL FREE: 800
Norman E Beal, Pt
Ellen Leslie, *
David Engleson, *
David Culler, *
EMP: 38 EST: 1968
SALES (est): 15.96MM **Privately Held**
Web: www.ohiofairplan.com
SIC: 6331 Property damage insurance

(G-5276)
PACIFIC HERITG INN POLARIS LLC
9090 Lyra Dr (43240-2116)
PHONE..................614 880-9080
Rachel Marchant, Managing Member*
Juliann Beatty, *
EMP: 50 EST: 2017
SQ FT: 100,000
SALES (est): 823.95K **Privately Held**
SIC: 7011 Inns

(G-5277)
PFP COLUMBUS LLC
Also Called: Polaris Fashion Place
1500 Polaris Pkwy Ste 2034 (43240-2126)
PHONE..................614 456-0123
EMP: 35 EST: 1998
SALES (est): 3.97MM
SALES (corp-wide): 564.96MM **Privately Held**
Web: www.polarisfashionplace.com
SIC: 6512 Shopping center, property operation only
PA: Washington Prime Group Inc.
180 E Broad St
Columbus OH 43215
614 621-9000

(G-5278)
POLARIS TOWNE CENTER LLC
1500 Polaris Pkwy Ste 3000 (43240-2126)
PHONE..................614 456-0123
EMP: 30 EST: 1998
SALES (est): 4.9MM
SALES (corp-wide): 564.96MM **Privately Held**
Web: www.polarisfashionplace.com
SIC: 6512 Shopping center, property operation only
PA: Washington Prime Group Inc.
180 E Broad St
Columbus OH 43215
614 621-9000

(G-5279)
PRIME AE GROUP INC
8415 Pulsar Pl Ste 300 (43240-4032)
PHONE..................614 839-0250
Kumar Buvanendaran, Pr
EMP: 82
Web: www.primeeng.com
SIC: 8711 8712 Civil engineering; Architectural engineering
PA: Prime Ae Group, Inc.
5521 Res Pk Dr Ste 300
Baltimore MD 21228

(G-5280)
QUICK SOLUTIONS INC
8940 Lyra Dr # 220 (43240-2294)
PHONE..................614 825-8000
Tom Campbell, CEO
Rick Mariotti, *
EMP: 156 EST: 1991
SALES (est): 3.17MM
SALES (corp-wide): 49.95MM **Privately Held**
Web: www.quicksolutions.com
SIC: 7371 Computer software development
PA: Fusion Alliance Holdings, Inc.
301 Pnnsylvnia Pkwy Ste 2
Indianapolis IN 46280
317 955-1300

(G-5281)
ROCKFORD HOMES INC (PA)
999 Polaris Pkwy Ste 200 (43240-2051)
PHONE..................614 785-0015
Robert E Yoakam Senior, CEO
Don Wick, *
Rita Yoakam, *
Robert Yoakam Junior, Pr
EMP: 62 EST: 1985
SALES (est): 15.6MM
SALES (corp-wide): 15.6MM **Privately Held**
Web: www.rockfordhomes.net
SIC: 1521 1522 6552 New construction, single-family houses; Residential construction, nec; Subdividers and developers, nec

(G-5282)
SUNBELT RENTALS INC
1461 Polaris Pkwy (43240-6002)
P.O. Box 410928 (28241-0928)
PHONE..................614 848-4075
Steven Wilson, Brnch Mgr
EMP: 99
SALES (corp-wide): 9.67B **Privately Held**
Web: www.sunbeltrentals.com
SIC: 7353 Heavy construction equipment rental
HQ: Sunbelt Rentals, Inc.
1799 Innovation Pt
Fort Mill SC 29715
803 578-5811

(G-5283)
VEEAM SOFTWARE CORPORATION (PA)
8800 Lyra Dr Ste 350 (43240)
PHONE..................614 339-8200
William H Largent, CEO
Ratmir Timashev, *
Rick Hoffman, WORLDWIDE CHANNELS ALLIANCES*
Carrie Reber, WORLDWIDE Marketing*
Doug Hazelman, Product Strategy Vice President*
EMP: 1274 EST: 2007
SALES (est): 963MM **Privately Held**
Web: www.veeam.com
SIC: 7372 Business oriented computer software

(G-5284)
VENTECH SOLUTIONS INC (PA)
8425 Pulsar Pl Ste 300 (43240-2079)
PHONE..................614 757-1167
Ravi Kunduru, CEO
Ravi Kunduru, Ch
Herb Jones, *
Martin Toomajian Csgo, Prin
Randy Fogle, *
▼ EMP: 85 EST: 2002
SQ FT: 14,000
SALES (est): 50.74MM
SALES (corp-wide): 50.74MM **Privately Held**
Web: www.ventechsolutions.com
SIC: 7371 7373 7379 Computer software development; Systems engineering, computer related; Computer related maintenance services

Columbus - Delaware County

(G-5285)
WINGATE INN
8505 Pulsar Pl (43240-2030)
PHONE..................................614 844-5888
Bashir Ahmed, *Prin*
EMP: 36 EST: 2007
SALES (est): 289.12K **Privately Held**
Web: www.wyndhamhotels.com
SIC: 7011 Hotels and motels

Columbus
Franklin County

(G-5286)
30 LINES
52 E Lynn St Ste 400 (43215-3551)
PHONE..................................614 859-5030
Mike Whaling, *Pr*
EMP: 64 EST: 2013
SALES (est): 1.75MM **Privately Held**
Web: www.30lines.com
SIC: 8742 Marketing consulting services

(G-5287)
3D BUILDING SYSTEMS LLC
Also Called: 3 D Disaster Kleenup Columbus
4110 Perimeter Dr (43228-1049)
PHONE..................................614 351-9695
EMP: 37 EST: 1994
SQ FT: 26,000
SALES (est): 3.2MM **Privately Held**
SIC: 1521 1542 Single-family home remodeling, additions, and repairs; Commercial and office buildings, renovation and repair

(G-5288)
5 STAR HOTEL MANAGEMENT IV LP
Also Called: Residence Inn By Marriott
6191 Quarter Horse Dr (43229-2568)
PHONE..................................614 431-1819
Stephanie Martin, *Prin*
EMP: 47 EST: 2007
SALES (est): 368.04K **Privately Held**
Web: residence-inn.marriott.com
SIC: 7011 Hotels and motels

(G-5289)
500 DEGREES LLC
4030 Easton Sta (43219-7012)
PHONE..................................786 615-8265
EMP: 58
SALES (corp-wide): 6.16MM **Privately Held**
Web: www.weare500degrees.com
SIC: 7389 Personal service agents, brokers, and bureaus
PA: 500 Degrees, Llc
  1166 Dublin Rd Ste 100
  Columbus OH 43215
  614 754-2098

(G-5290)
845 YARD STREET LLC
Also Called: Massage Envy
775 Yard St (43212-3890)
PHONE..................................614 484-6860
Kathleen Turner, *Brnch Mgr*
EMP: 41
SALES (corp-wide): 1.55MM **Privately Held**
Web: www.grandviewyard.com
SIC: 7299 7231 Massage parlor; Facial salons
PA: 845 Yard Street, Llc
  375 N Front St Ste 200
  Columbus OH 43215
  614 857-2330

(G-5291)
A L D PRECAST CORP
1600 Haul Rd (43207-1871)
P.O. Box 398 (43216-0398)
PHONE..................................614 449-3366
Myrna Campbell, *Brnch Mgr*
EMP: 44
Web: www.aldprecast.com
SIC: 7389 Personal service agents, brokers, and bureaus
PA: A L D Precast Corp.
  400 Frank Rd
  Columbus OH 43207

(G-5292)
A T V INC
2047 Leonard Ave (43219-2277)
P.O. Box 307568 (43230-7568)
PHONE..................................614 252-5060
Paul Vellani, *Pr*
EMP: 115 EST: 1981
SQ FT: 7,325
SALES (est): 5.18MM **Privately Held**
SIC: 4141 Local bus charter service

(G-5293)
ABBOT STDIOS ARCHTCTS + PLNNER
471 E Broad St Fl 17 (43215-3842)
PHONE..................................614 461-0101
Michael Lutsch, *Managing Member*
Sean Abbot, *
Keith Fagan, *
Kyle Carpenter, *
Josh Channels, *
EMP: 35 EST: 1995
SALES (est): 13.1MM **Privately Held**
Web: www.abbotstudios.com
SIC: 8712 Architectural engineering

(G-5294)
ABBOTT LABORATORIES
Also Called: Tobal Products
2900 Easton Square Pl (43219-6225)
PHONE..................................847 937-6100
Steven K Williams, *Brnch Mgr*
EMP: 51
SALES (corp-wide): 40.11B **Publicly Held**
Web: www.abbott.com
SIC: 2834 3841 2879 4226 Pharmaceutical preparations; Surgical and medical instruments; Insecticides, agricultural or household; Special warehousing and storage, nec
PA: Abbott Laboratories
  100 Abbott Park Rd
  Abbott Park IL 60064
  224 667-6100

(G-5295)
ABEL-BISHOP & CLARKE REALTY CO
Also Called: Mount Vernon Plaza
1035 Atcheson St Ofc (43203-1302)
PHONE..................................614 253-8627
Frank Damico, *Mgr*
EMP: 89
SALES (corp-wide): 1.14MM **Privately Held**
Web: abcmgt.orleanco.com
SIC: 6513 Apartment building operators
PA: The Abel-Bishop & Clarke Realty Co
  23875 Commerce Park # 120
  Cleveland OH 44122
  216 591-0881

(G-5296)
ABLE ROOFING LLC (PA)
Also Called: Crane Renovation Group
4777 Westerville Rd (43231-6042)
PHONE..................................614 444-2253
Andrew M Hackett, *Pr*
Ryan Huyghe, *Ex VP*
EMP: 57 EST: 2005
SQ FT: 23,000
SALES (est): 26.83MM
SALES (corp-wide): 26.83MM **Privately Held**
Web: www.ableroof.com
SIC: 1741 1761 Chimney construction and maintenance; Roofing contractor

(G-5297)
ABS COASTAL INSULATING LLC
495 S High St Ste 50 (43215-5689)
P.O. Box 2177 (29578-2177)
PHONE..................................843 360-1045
Jeffrey W Edwards, *Pr*
EMP: 46 EST: 2013
SALES (est): 2.38MM
SALES (corp-wide): 2.78B **Publicly Held**
Web: www.abscoastal.com
SIC: 1742 Insulation, buildings
PA: Installed Building Products, Inc.
  495 S High St Ste 50
  Columbus OH 43215
  614 221-3399

(G-5298)
ACADEMIC BHVRAL LRNG ENRCHMENT
20 S 3rd St Ste 210 (43215-4206)
PHONE..................................513 544-4991
EMP: 40
SALES (est): 1.12MM **Privately Held**
Web: www.ablelearningenrichment.com
SIC: 8082 Home health care services

(G-5299)
ACADEMY KIDS LEARNING CTR INC
289 Woodland Ave (43203-1747)
PHONE..................................614 258-5437
David R Weaver, *Pr*
Carol Burns, *
Annett Howell, *
▲ EMP: 40 EST: 1995
SALES (est): 473.96K **Privately Held**
SIC: 8351 Preschool center

(G-5300)
ACCENT DRAPERY CO INC
Also Called: Accent Drapery Supply Co
1180 Goodale Blvd (43212-3793)
PHONE..................................614 488-0741
Patrick Casbarro, *Pr*
Brian Whiteside, *
EMP: 27 EST: 1967
SQ FT: 19,500
SALES (est): 2.35MM **Privately Held**
Web: www.accentdraperies.com
SIC: 5714 5023 2391 Draperies; Draperies; Curtains and draperies

(G-5301)
ACCENTURE LLP
Also Called: Accenture
400 W Nationwide Blvd Ste 100 (43215-2377)
PHONE..................................614 629-2000
John Hrusovsky, *Brnch Mgr*
EMP: 134
Web: www.accenture.com
SIC: 8742 8748 Business management consultant; Business consulting, nec
HQ: Accenture Llp
  500 W Madison St
  Chicago IL 60661
  312 693-5009

(G-5302)
ACCESS INFO HOLDINGS LLC
2500 Charter St (43228-4641)
PHONE..................................614 777-1701
EMP: 724
SALES (corp-wide): 67.1MM **Privately Held**
Web: www.accesscorp.com
SIC: 4226 Document and office records storage
PA: Access Information Holdings, Llc
  500 Unicorn Park Dr # 500
  Woburn MA 01801
  925 583-0100

(G-5303)
ACCESS INFORMATION MGT CORP
Also Called: Access
2500 Charter St Ste B (43228-4641)
PHONE..................................614 777-1701
Andrew Wagner, *Prin*
EMP: 1284
SALES (corp-wide): 116.62MM **Privately Held**
Web: www.accesscorp.com
SIC: 4226 Document and office records storage
PA: Access Information Management Corporation
  4 1st Ave
  Peabody MA 01960
  877 345-3546

(G-5304)
ACCURATE INVNTORY CLCLTING SVC
Also Called: Quantum Services
4284 N High St (43214-3078)
PHONE..................................800 777-9414
Ray Crook Junior, *Pr*
EMP: 355 EST: 1971
SQ FT: 11,600
SALES (est): 13.77MM **Privately Held**
Web: www.quantumservices.com
SIC: 7389 8742 Inventory computing service; Business management consultant

(G-5305)
ACE IRON & METAL COMPANY (PA)
2515 Groveport Rd (43207-3147)
P.O. Box 7813 (43207-0813)
PHONE..................................614 443-5196
EMP: 46 EST: 1962
SALES (est): 9.76MM
SALES (corp-wide): 9.76MM **Privately Held**
Web: www.aceironrecycling.com
SIC: 4953 Recycling, waste materials

(G-5306)
ACLOCHE LLC (PA)
Also Called: Acloche Medical Staffing Svc
1800 Watermark Dr Ste 430 (43215-1397)
PHONE..................................888 608-0889
Kim Shoemaker, *CEO*
EMP: 33 EST: 1968
SQ FT: 12,000
SALES (est): 10.48MM
SALES (corp-wide): 10.48MM **Privately Held**
Web: www.acloche.com
SIC: 7363 8742 Temporary help service; Human resource consulting services

(G-5307)
ACORN DISTRIBUTORS INC
5310 Crosswind Dr (43228-3600)
PHONE..................................614 294-6444
Jennifer Rosenberg, *Pr*
EMP: 40 EST: 2010
SQ FT: 100,000

GEOGRAPHIC SECTION
Columbus - Franklin County (G-5331)

SALES (est): 4.86MM **Privately Held**
Web: www.acorndistributors.com
SIC: **5113** 5087 5046 Disposable plates, cups, napkins, and eating utensils; Janitors' supplies; Commercial equipment, nec

(G-5308)
ACREE-DAILY CORPORATION
771 Dearborn Park Ln Ste N (43085-5720)
PHONE..................................614 452-7300
EMP: 45
Web: www.acreedaily.com
SIC: **1731** 7382 Fire detection and burglar alarm systems specialization; Burglar alarm maintenance and monitoring

(G-5309)
ACS COMPUTER SERVICES CORP
4238 Westview Center Plz (43228-2975)
PHONE..................................614 351-8298
Connie G Angel, *CEO*
David Ferguson, *
EMP: 55 EST: 1990
SQ FT: 5,000
SALES (est): 1.37MM **Privately Held**
Web: www.angelcomputerservice.com
SIC: **7374** Data entry service

(G-5310)
ACTION FOR CHILDREN INC (PA)
78 Jefferson Ave (43215)
PHONE..................................614 224-0222
Diane Bennett, *Ex Dir*
Rhonda Fraas, *
EMP: 38 EST: 1972
SALES (est): 6.34MM
SALES (corp-wide): 6.34MM **Privately Held**
Web: www.actionforchildren.org
SIC: **7299** 8351 8322 Information services, consumer; Child day care services; Individual and family services

(G-5311)
AD INVESTMENTS LLC
375 N Front St Ste 200 (43215-2258)
PHONE..................................614 857-2340
Brian Ellis, *CEO*
EMP: 28 EST: 1999
SALES (est): 4.66MM
SALES (corp-wide): 11.75B **Privately Held**
Web: www.ad4invest.com
SIC: **6512** Commercial and industrial building operation
HQ: Nationwide Realty Investors, Ltd.
   375 N Front St Ste 200
   Columbus OH 43215
   614 857-2330

(G-5312)
ADDUS HEALTHCARE INC
Also Called: Addus Healthcare
1395 E Dublin Granville Rd (43229-3313)
PHONE..................................614 407-0677
EMP: 85
Web: www.addus.com
SIC: **8082** Home health care services
HQ: Addus Healthcare, Inc.
   2300 Warrenville Rd
   Downers Grove IL 60515
   630 296-3400

(G-5313)
ADEPT MARKETING OUTSOURCED LLC
Also Called: Adept
855 Grandview Ave Ste 140 (43215-1189)
PHONE..................................614 360-3132
Justin Spring, *Managing Member*
EMP: 30 EST: 2008
SALES (est): 5.93MM **Privately Held**
Web: www.adeptmarketing.com
SIC: **8742** Marketing consulting services

(G-5314)
ADO PROFESSIONAL SOLUTIONS INC
445 Hutchinson Ave Ste 330 (43235-5677)
PHONE..................................614 681-5050
EMP: 27
Web: www.lhh.com
SIC: **7361** Employment agencies
HQ: Ado Professional Solutions, Inc.
   4800 Deerwood Campus Pkwy # 800
   Jacksonville FL 32246

(G-5315)
ADROIT ASSOC CNSLTING SVCS LLC
Also Called: Aacs Consulting
4809 Moreland Dr W (43220-3121)
PHONE..................................614 966-6925
Mohammad Qasim Nazari, *Prin*
Alamzeb Zarghoon, *Prin*
EMP: 70 EST: 2021
SALES (est): 1.29MM **Privately Held**
SIC: **8742** Management consulting services

(G-5316)
ADS ALLIANCE DATA SYSTEMS INC
Also Called: ADS ALLIANCE DATA SYSTEMS, INC.
3095 Loyalty Cir (43219-3673)
PHONE..................................513 707-6800
EMP: 72
Web: www.breadfinancial.com
SIC: **8322** General counseling services
HQ: Bread Financial Payments, Inc.
   7500 Dallas Pkwy Ste 700
   Plano TX 75024
   214 494-3000

(G-5317)
ADT LLC
Also Called: Protection One
4245 Diplomacy Dr (43228-3803)
PHONE..................................614 793-0861
EMP: 70
SALES (corp-wide): 4.98B **Publicly Held**
Web: www.adt.com
SIC: **7382** Burglar alarm maintenance and monitoring
HQ: Adt Llc
   1501 W Yamato Rd
   Boca Raton FL 33431
   561 988-3600

(G-5318)
ADVANCE HOME CARE LLC (PA)
1191 S James Rd (43227-1800)
PHONE..................................614 436-3611
Abdillahi Yusuf, *
Idil Abdukadir, *
EMP: 80 EST: 2011
SQ FT: 2,000
SALES (est): 4.45MM
SALES (corp-wide): 4.45MM **Privately Held**
Web: www.advancehcare.com
SIC: **8082** Home health care services

(G-5319)
ADVIZEX TECHNOLOGIES LLC
1103 Schrock Rd Ste 100 (43229-1179)
PHONE..................................614 318-0386
C R Howdyshell, *Prin*
EMP: 62
Web: www.advizex.com
SIC: **7373** Value-added resellers, computer systems
PA: Advizex Technologies, Llc
   6480 Rckside Wods Blvd St
   Independence OH 44131

(G-5320)
ADVOCATE SOLUTIONS LLC
762 S Pearl St (43206-2032)
PHONE..................................614 444-5144
EMP: 32 EST: 1995
SQ FT: 5,300
SALES (est): 1.7MM **Privately Held**
Web: www.resultant.com
SIC: **8742** Business management consultant

(G-5321)
AEP ENERGY PARTNERS INC
1 Riverside Plz Fl 1 (43215-2355)
PHONE..................................614 716-1000
Nicholas K Akins, *CEO*
Robert P Powers, *Ex VP*
Brian X Tierney, *CFO*
Lana L Hillebrand, *Sr VP*
EMP: 103 EST: 2007
SALES (est): 474.35K
SALES (corp-wide): 18.98B **Privately Held**
Web: www.aep.com
SIC: **4911** Generation, electric power
PA: American Electric Power Company, Inc.
   1 Riverside Plz Fl 1 # 1
   Columbus OH 43215
   614 716-1000

(G-5322)
AEP GENERATING COMPANY (HQ)
Also Called: Aegco
1 Riverside Plz Ste 1600 (43215)
PHONE..................................614 223-1000
Nick Akins, *Ch*
E L Draper Junior, *Pr*
EMP: 1800 EST: 1982
SALES (est): 311.42MM
SALES (corp-wide): 18.98B **Privately Held**
Web: www.aep.com
SIC: **4911** Generation, electric power
PA: American Electric Power Company, Inc.
   1 Riverside Plz Fl 1 # 1
   Columbus OH 43215
   614 716-1000

(G-5323)
AEP INVESTMENTS HOLDING CO INC
155 W Nationwide Blvd (43215)
PHONE..................................614 583-2900
Stephan T Haynes, *VP*
EMP: 260 EST: 1997
SALES (est): 1.2MM
SALES (corp-wide): 18.98B **Privately Held**
Web: www.aep.com
SIC: **4911** Electric services
PA: American Electric Power Company, Inc.
   1 Riverside Plz Fl 1 # 1
   Columbus OH 43215
   614 716-1000

(G-5324)
AEP POWER MARKETING INC (HQ)
Also Called: America Electric Power Texas
1 Riverside Plz Fl 1 (43215-2355)
PHONE..................................614 716-1000
EMP: 2000 EST: 1996
SALES (est): 28.09MM
SALES (corp-wide): 18.98B **Privately Held**
Web: www.aep.com
SIC: **4911** Distribution, electric power
PA: American Electric Power Company, Inc.
   1 Riverside Plz Fl 1 # 1
   Columbus OH 43215
   614 716-1000

(G-5325)
AEP TEXAS CENTRAL COMPANY
1 Riverside Plz (43215-2355)
PHONE..................................614 716-1000
EMP: 1224
Web: www.aeptexas.com
SIC: **4911** Distribution, electric power

(G-5326)
AEP TEXAS INC (HQ)
Also Called: AEP Texas
1 Riverside Plz (43215-2355)
PHONE..................................614 716-1000
Nicholas K Akins, *Ch Bd*
Julia A Sloat, *
Joseph M Buonaiuto, *CAO*
EMP: 99 EST: 1925
SALES (est): 1.9B
SALES (corp-wide): 18.98B **Privately Held**
Web: www.aep.com
SIC: **4911** Electric services
PA: American Electric Power Company, Inc.
   1 Riverside Plz Fl 1 # 1
   Columbus OH 43215
   614 716-1000

(G-5327)
AEP TEXAS NORTH COMPANY
1 Riverside Plz (43215-2355)
PHONE..................................614 716-1000
EMP: 386
SIC: **4911** Electric services

(G-5328)
AFP 116 CORP
Also Called: Embassy Stes By Hlton Clmbus A
2886 Airport Dr (43219-2240)
PHONE..................................614 536-0500
Anthony Miceli, *CFO*
EMP: 120 EST: 2019
SALES (est): 5.39MM **Privately Held**
Web: www.hilton.com
SIC: **7011** Hotels and motels

(G-5329)
AGGRESSIVE MECHANICAL INC
638 Greenlawn Ave (43223-2635)
PHONE..................................614 443-3280
Kevin Hall, *Pr*
Dan Bosworth, *
Russell Cochenour, *
John Mills, *
EMP: 32 EST: 1997
SQ FT: 8,600
SALES (est): 2.87MM **Privately Held**
Web: www.aggressivemechanical.com
SIC: **1711** Plumbing contractors

(G-5330)
AGILITY PARTNERS LLC
175 S 3rd St Ste 360 (43215-5188)
PHONE..................................740 819-2712
Carly Nauer, *Prin*
EMP: 54 EST: 2018
SALES (est): 6.29MM **Privately Held**
Web: www.agilitypartners.io
SIC: **7371** Computer software development

(G-5331)
AIRNET SYSTEMS INC (DH)
Also Called: Airnet
7250 Star Check Dr (43217-1025)
PHONE..................................614 409-4900
Joan C Makley, *CEO*
Ray L Druseikis, *CAO*
Larry M Glasscock Junior, *EXPRESS SERVICES*
Jeffery B Harris, *Sr VP*
Craig A Leach, *Vice-President Information Systems*

Columbus - Franklin County (G-5332) — GEOGRAPHIC SECTION

EMP: 40 **EST:** 1996
SALES (est): 98.68MM
SALES (corp-wide): 232.5MM **Privately Held**
Web: www.airnet.com
SIC: 4731 4522 Freight transportation arrangement; Air cargo carriers, nonscheduled
HQ: Kalitta Charters, L.L.C.
2820 Tyler Rd
Ypsilanti MI 48198
734 544-3400

(G-5332)
AIRTECH LLC
Also Called: Direct Air
1900 Jetway Blvd (43219-1681)
PHONE..............................614 342-6123
Kurt Lang, Pr
Matt Piatt, *
EMP: 924 **EST:** 1984
SALES (est): 274.01MM
SALES (corp-wide): 1.04B **Privately Held**
Web: www.otcindustrial.com
SIC: 5084 Pumps and pumping equipment, nec
PA: Ohio Transmission Llc
1900 Jetway Blvd
Columbus OH 43219
614 342-6247

(G-5333)
AIRTRON INC
3021 International St (43228-4635)
PHONE..............................614 274-2345
Bill Duecker, Mgr
EMP: 51
Web: www.airtroncolumbus.com
SIC: 1711 5075 Warm air heating and air conditioning contractor; Warm air heating and air conditioning
HQ: Airtron, Inc.
9260 Marketpl Dr
Miamisburg OH 45342
937 898-0826

(G-5334)
ALL CRANE RENTAL CORP (PA)
683 Oakland Park Ave (43224-3936)
PHONE..............................614 261-1800
Michael C Liptak Junior, Pr
Larry Liptak, *
EMP: 60 **EST:** 1983
SQ FT: 46,000
SALES (est): 12.29MM
SALES (corp-wide): 12.29MM **Privately Held**
Web: www.allcrane.com
SIC: 7353 Cranes and aerial lift equipment, rental or leasing

(G-5335)
ALLEGIANT PLUMBING LLC
2162 Mckinley Ave (43204-3417)
PHONE..............................614 824-5002
EMP: 36
SALES (corp-wide): 954.7K **Privately Held**
Web: www.allegiantplumbing.com
SIC: 1711 Plumbing contractors
PA: Allegiant Plumbing Llc
2162 Mckinley Ave
Columbus OH 43204
740 277-6473

(G-5336)
ALLIANCE HM HLTH CARE SVCS LLC
611 E Weber Rd Ste 200 (43211-1097)
PHONE..............................614 928-3053
Hassan Noor, Prin
Mursal Dhudhi, *

EMP: 56 **EST:** 2014
SALES (est): 1.32MM **Privately Held**
Web: www.myalliancehealthohio.com
SIC: 8082 Home health care services

(G-5337)
ALLIANCE HOSPITALITY INC
1221 E Dublin Granville Rd (43229-3301)
PHONE..............................614 885-4334
EMP: 28 **EST:** 1999
SALES (est): 417.16K **Privately Held**
SIC: 7011 Hotels and motels

(G-5338)
ALLIED FABRICATING & WLDG CO
5699 Chantry Dr (43232-4731)
PHONE..............................614 751-6664
Thomas Caminiti, CEO
Joseph Caminiti, *
Jack Burgoon, *
Raymond Cunningham, *
EMP: 34 **EST:** 1971
SQ FT: 30,000
SALES (est): 4.54MM **Privately Held**
Web: www.afaw.net
SIC: 3444 7692 3535 3441 Sheet metal specialties, not stamped; Welding repair; Conveyors and conveying equipment; Fabricated structural metal

(G-5339)
ALPINE INSULATION I LLC
495 S High St Ste 50 (43215-5689)
PHONE..............................614 221-3399
Jeffrey W Edwards, Pr
Michael T Miller, *
Jay P Elliott, *
Todd R Fry, CAO*
EMP: 51 **EST:** 2016
SALES (est): 15.29MM
SALES (corp-wide): 2.78B **Publicly Held**
SIC: 5033 5211 Insulation materials; Insulation material, building
PA: Installed Building Products, Inc.
495 S High St Ste 50
Columbus OH 43215
614 221-3399

(G-5340)
ALRO STEEL CORPORATION
555 Hilliard Rome Rd (43228-9265)
PHONE..............................614 878-7271
Steve White, Mgr
EMP: 32
SALES (corp-wide): 3.43B **Privately Held**
Web: www.alro.com
SIC: 5051 5085 5162 3444 Steel; Industrial supplies; Plastics materials, nec; Sheet metalwork
PA: Alro Steel Corporation
3100 E High St
Jackson MI 49203
517 787-5500

(G-5341)
ALWAYS WITH US CHRTIES AWU CHR
Also Called: Awu Charities
4449 Easton Way Ste 200 (43219-7005)
PHONE..............................800 675-4710
George Reese, CEO
EMP: 30 **EST:** 2015
SALES (est): 99.68K **Privately Held**
Web: www.awucharities.org
SIC: 8322 Social service center

(G-5342)
AMAZON
6366 Downwing Ln (43230-3684)
PHONE..............................951 733-5325
EMP: 38 **EST:** 2018

SALES (est): 214.61K **Privately Held**
SIC: 4225 General warehousing and storage

(G-5343)
AMBER HOME CARE LLC
150 E Campus View Blvd Ste 160 (43235-4648)
PHONE..............................614 523-0668
Bharath Pentyala, CEO
Douglas S Speelman, *
Jason Huxley, *
EMP: 30 **EST:** 2007
SALES (est): 2.32MM **Privately Held**
Web: www.amberhomecare.com
SIC: 8082 Home health care services

(G-5344)
AMBERS DESIGN STUDIO LLC
175 S 3rd St Ste 1090 (43215-5134)
PHONE..............................614 221-1237
EMP: 29 **EST:** 2004
SALES (est): 841.82K **Privately Held**
SIC: 7389 Design services

(G-5345)
AMERICA VOTES
5 E Long St Fl 8 (43215-2996)
PHONE..............................614 236-3410
Khaleh Salehi, Brnch Mgr
EMP: 27
Web: www.americavotes.org
SIC: 8651 Political organizations
PA: America Votes
1155 Conn Ave Nw Ste 600
Washington DC 20036

(G-5346)
AMERICAN BOTTLING COMPANY
Also Called: 7 Up / R C/Canada Dry Btlg Co
950 Stelzer Rd (43219-3740)
PHONE..............................614 237-4201
Mike Stall, Brnch Mgr
EMP: 107
Web: www.keurigdrpepper.com
SIC: 2086 5149 Soft drinks: packaged in cans, bottles, etc.; Groceries and related products, nec
HQ: The American Bottling Company
6425 Hall Of Fame Ln
Frisco TX 75034

(G-5347)
AMERICAN CHEM SOC FDERAL CR UN
2540 Olentangy River Rd (43202-1505)
PHONE..............................614 447-3675
EMP: 1669 **EST:** 1961
SALES (est): 23.54MM **Privately Held**
Web: www.pathwayscu.com
SIC: 6061 Federal credit unions

(G-5348)
AMERICAN ELECTRIC PWR SVC CORP (HQ)
Also Called: American Electric Power
1 Riverside Plz (43215-2373)
P.O. Box 16631 (43216-6631)
PHONE..............................614 716-1000
Nicholas K Akins, Ch Bd
Susan Tomasky, POLICY FIN STRAT PLANNING
Jeffrey D Cross, Deputy General Counsel
J Craig Baker Senior, SVCS
Dale E Heydlauff, Corporate Communication
▲ **EMP:** 500 **EST:** 1937
SQ FT: 800,000
SALES (est): 9.91MM
SALES (corp-wide): 18.98B **Privately Held**
Web: www.aep.com

SIC: 4911 8711 8713 8721 Distribution, electric power; Engineering services; Surveying services; Accounting services, except auditing
PA: American Electric Power Company, Inc.
1 Riverside Plz Fl 1 # 1
Columbus OH 43215
614 716-1000

(G-5349)
AMERICAN ELECTRIC PWR SVC CORP
Also Called: AEP Service
825 Tech Center Dr (43230-6653)
PHONE..............................614 582-1742
James Haunty, Brnch Mgr
EMP: 78
SALES (corp-wide): 18.98B **Privately Held**
Web: www.aep.com
SIC: 4911 Distribution, electric power
HQ: American Electric Power Service Corporation
1 Riverside Plz Fl 1 # 1
Columbus OH 43215
614 716-1000

(G-5350)
AMERICAN FIDELITY ASSURANCE CO
90 Northwoods Blvd Ste B (43235-4719)
PHONE..............................800 437-1011
James Gray, Pr
EMP: 40
Web: www.americanfidelity.com
SIC: 6411 Insurance agents, nec
HQ: American Fidelity Assurance Company
9000 Cameron Pkwy
Oklahoma City OK 73114
405 523-2000

(G-5351)
AMERICAN HEART ASSOCIATION INC
118 Graceland Blvd (43214-1530)
P.O. Box 163549 (43216-3549)
PHONE..............................614 848-6676
Charles Romane, Brnch Mgr
EMP: 46
SALES (corp-wide): 240.32MM **Privately Held**
Web: www.heart.org
SIC: 8621 Professional organizations
PA: American Heart Association, Inc.
7272 Greenville Ave
Dallas TX 75231
214 373-6300

(G-5352)
AMERICAN KIDNEY STONE MGT LTD (PA)
Also Called: Aksm
100 W 3rd Ave Ste 350 (43201-7205)
PHONE..............................800 637-5188
Henry Wise Ii Md, Ch
Ann Stevens, VP Opers
Alan Buergenthal, Corporate Vice President
Ric Hughes, CFO
Theresa Perry, VP
EMP: 30 **EST:** 1984
SQ FT: 11,000
SALES (est): 24.05MM
SALES (corp-wide): 24.05MM **Privately Held**
Web: www.aksm.com
SIC: 8093 Specialty outpatient clinics, nec

(G-5353)
AMERICAN MECHANICAL GROUP INC
Also Called: Honeywell Authorized Dealer

GEOGRAPHIC SECTION

Columbus - Franklin County (G-5374)

5729 Westbourne Ave (43213-1449)
PHONE..................614 575-3720
Brian Yockey, *Pr*
EMP: 32 **EST:** 2005
SALES (est): 4.24MM **Privately Held**
Web: www.amgohio.com
SIC: 1711 Mechanical contractor

(G-5354)
AMERICAN MUNICIPAL POWER INC (PA)
Also Called: AMP
1111 Schrock Rd Ste 100 (43229)
PHONE..................614 540-1111
Marc Gerken, *Pr*
Jon Bisher, *
Robert W Trippe, *
Jolene Thompson, *
Pam Sullivan, *
◆ **EMP:** 218 **EST:** 1971
SQ FT: 100,000
SALES (est): 1.13B
SALES (corp-wide): 1.13B **Privately Held**
Web: www.amppartners.org
SIC: 4911 Distribution, electric power

(G-5355)
AMERICAN NATIONAL RED CROSS
Also Called: American Nat Red Cross - Blood
995 E Broad St (43205-1322)
PHONE..................614 253-2740
EMP: 41
SALES (corp-wide): 3.18B **Privately Held**
Web: www.redcross.org
SIC: 8322 Social service center
PA: The American National Red Cross
431 18th St Nw
Washington DC 20006
202 737-8300

(G-5356)
AMERICAN NATIONAL RED CROSS
Also Called: American Nat Red Cross - Blood
4820 Sawmill Rd (43235-7264)
PHONE..................614 326-2337
Sheryl Powell, *Mgr*
EMP: 41
SALES (corp-wide): 3.18B **Privately Held**
Web: www.redcross.org
SIC: 8322 Social service center
PA: The American National Red Cross
431 18th St Nw
Washington DC 20006
202 737-8300

(G-5357)
AMERICAN NATIONAL RED CROSS
Also Called: American Red Cross
1 W Nationwide Blvd (43215-2752)
PHONE..................800 448-3543
EMP: 31
SALES (corp-wide): 3.18B **Privately Held**
Web: www.redcross.org
SIC: 8322 Social service center
PA: The American National Red Cross
431 18th St Nw
Washington DC 20006
202 737-8300

(G-5358)
AMERICAN NATIONAL RED CROSS
Also Called: American Nat Red Cross - Blood
4327 Equity Dr (43228-3842)
PHONE..................614 334-0425
EMP: 41
SALES (corp-wide): 3.18B **Privately Held**
Web: www.redcross.org
SIC: 8322 Social service center
PA: The American National Red Cross
431 18th St Nw
Washington DC 20006
202 737-8300

(G-5359)
AMERICAN PRECAST REFRACTORIES
2700 Scioto Pkwy (43221-4657)
PHONE..................614 876-8416
John Turner, *Pr*
Suzanne T Deffet, *VP Fin*
EMP: 49 **EST:** 1995
SALES (est): 902.45K
SALES (corp-wide): 91.72MM **Privately Held**
Web: www.alliedmineral.com
SIC: 1611 Concrete construction: roads, highways, sidewalks, etc.
PA: Allied Mineral Products, Llc
2700 Scioto Pkwy
Columbus OH 43221
614 876-0244

(G-5360)
AMERICAN RED CROSS OF GRTR COL (PA)
Also Called: American Red Cross
995 E Broad St (43205-1339)
PHONE..................614 253-7981
Michael Carroll, *CEO*
Michel Schoedinger, *Ch Bd*
EMP: 40 **EST:** 1916
SQ FT: 80,000
SALES (est): 3.21MM
SALES (corp-wide): 3.21MM **Privately Held**
Web: www.redcross.org
SIC: 8322 Social service center

(G-5361)
AMERICAN STRUCTUREPOINT INC
2550 Corporate Exchange Dr Ste 300 (43231-1660)
PHONE..................614 901-2235
EMP: 42
SALES (corp-wide): 84.53MM **Privately Held**
Web: www.structurepoint.com
SIC: 8711 Consulting engineer
PA: American Structurepoint, Inc.
9025 River Rd Ste 200
Indianapolis IN 46240
317 547-5580

(G-5362)
AMERICAN SVCS & PROTECTION LLC
Also Called: American Services
2572 Oakstone Dr Ste 1 (43231-7614)
PHONE..................614 884-0177
Shawn Harper, *Managing Member*
Aaron Harper, *
Philana Harper, *
Lovell Harper, *
EMP: 82 **EST:** 2004
SALES (est): 2.59MM **Privately Held**
Web: www.asapllc.us
SIC: 7381 Security guard service

(G-5363)
AMERICAS FLOOR SOURCE LLC (PA)
3442 Millenium Ct (43219-5551)
P.O. Box 360508 (43236-0508)
PHONE..................614 808-3915
▼ **EMP:** 88 **EST:** 2000
SQ FT: 50,000
SALES (est): 140.05MM **Privately Held**
Web: www.americasfloorsource.com
SIC: 5713 5023 Carpets; Floor coverings

(G-5364)
AMERISOURCE HEALTH SVCS LLC
Also Called: American Health Packaging
2550 John Glenn Ave Ste A (43217)
PHONE..................614 492-8177
▲ **EMP:** 89 **EST:** 1996
SQ FT: 153,000
SALES (est): 49.88MM
SALES (corp-wide): 262.17B **Publicly Held**
Web: www.americanhealthpackaging.com
SIC: 2064 4783 Cough drops, except pharmaceutical preparations; Packing goods for shipping
HQ: Amerisourcebergen Drug Corporation
1 West First Ave
Conshohocken PA 19428
610 727-7000

(G-5365)
AMF BOWLING CENTERS INC
Also Called: AMF
4825 Sawmill Rd (43235-7266)
PHONE..................614 889-0880
EMP: 27
SALES (corp-wide): 1.06B **Publicly Held**
Web: www.amf.com
SIC: 7933 Ten pin center
HQ: Amf Bowling Centers, Inc.
7313 Bell Creek Rd
Mechanicsville VA 23111

(G-5366)
AMLON LTD
Also Called: Best Value Inn
4875 Sinclair Rd (43229-5402)
PHONE..................614 431-3670
Kundan Desai, *Pr*
Alex Adkins, *Prin*
EMP: 38 **EST:** 2004
SALES (est): 641.46K **Privately Held**
SIC: 7011 Inns

(G-5367)
AMUSEMENTS OF AMERICA INC
717 E 17th Ave (43211-2489)
PHONE..................614 297-8863
Karen Salas, *Brnch Mgr*
EMP: 190
SALES (est): 4.89MM **Privately Held**
Web: www.amusementsofamerica.com
SIC: 7999 Amusement ride
PA: Amusements Of America Inc
24 Federal Rd
Monroe Township NJ 08831
305 258-2020

(G-5368)
ANDERSON ALUMINUM CORPORATION
Also Called: Anderson Properties
2816 Morse Rd (43231-6034)
PHONE..................614 476-4877
Helena Anderson, *Pr*
Bradley Anderson, *
EMP: 70 **EST:** 1980
SQ FT: 70,000
SALES (est): 17.46MM **Privately Held**
Web: www.andersoncompanies.com
SIC: 1793 Glass and glazing work

(G-5369)
ANDREW DISTRIBUTION INC
509 Industry Dr (43204-6242)
PHONE..................614 824-3123
Mario Malek, *Prin*
EMP: 305
Web: www.andrewdistribution.com
SIC: 5099 Brass goods
PA: Andrew Distribution, Inc.
2000 Anson Dr
Melrose Park IL 60160

(G-5370)
ANIMAL CARE UNLIMITED INC
2665 Billingsley Rd (43235-1904)
PHONE..................614 766-2317
Donald Burton D.v.m., *Pr*
EMP: 27 **EST:** 1986
SALES (est): 1.67MM **Privately Held**
Web: www.animalcareunlimited.com
SIC: 0742 0752 Veterinarian, animal specialties; Boarding services, kennels

(G-5371)
APCO INDUSTRIES INC
Also Called: Apco Window & Door Company
2030 Dividend Dr (43228-3847)
PHONE..................614 224-2345
TOLL FREE: 800
Bill Clarken Junior, *Pr*
Warren C Gifford, *
Mark M Mason, *WINDOWS & DOORS*
William M Clarkin, *HOME IMP & WHOLESALE*
EMP: 100 **EST:** 1962
SALES (est): 17.33MM **Privately Held**
Web: www.apco.com
SIC: 1761 5033 5039 5031 Gutter and downspout contractor; Siding, except wood; Eavestroughing, parts and supplies; Doors, nec

(G-5372)
APELLES LLC
3700 Corporate Dr Ste 240 (43231)
PHONE..................614 899-7322
EMP: 30 **EST:** 2003
SALES (est): 4.59MM **Privately Held**
Web: www.apellesnow.com
SIC: 7322 Collection agency, except real estate

(G-5373)
APEX MORTGAGE SERVICES LLC
2550 Corporate Exchange Dr Ste 102 (43231-7659)
PHONE..................614 839-2739
Brenton Cline, *Managing Member*
EMP: 78 **EST:** 2003
SQ FT: 16,000
SALES (est): 7.5MM **Privately Held**
Web: www.apexmortgage.cc
SIC: 6162 Mortgage bankers and loan correspondents

(G-5374)
APPALACHIAN POWER COMPANY (HQ)
Also Called: Coalition For Enrgy Ecnmic Rvt
1 Riverside Plz (43215)
PHONE..................614 716-1000
Nicholas K Akins, *Ch Bd*
Brian X Tierney, *
Joseph M Buonaiuto, *CAO*
Lisa M Barton, *Dir*
David M Feinberg, *Dir*
▲ **EMP:** 142 **EST:** 1926
SALES (est): 3.52B
SALES (corp-wide): 18.98B **Privately Held**
Web: www.appalachianpower.com
SIC: 4911 Distribution, electric power
PA: American Electric Power Company, Inc.
1 Riverside Plz Fl 1 # 1
Columbus OH 43215
614 716-1000

Columbus - Franklin County (G-5375)

(G-5375)
APPLIANCE WAREHOUSE AMER INC
536 E Starr Ave (43201-3618)
PHONE.................................614 623-3131
EMP: 58
SALES (corp-wide): 1.97B **Privately Held**
Web: www.appliancewhse.com
SIC: 7629 Electrical household appliance repair
HQ: Appliance Warehouse Of America, Inc.
3201 W Royal Ln Ste 100
Irving TX 75063

(G-5376)
ARA-BEXLEY LLC
1805 E Main St (43205-2207)
PHONE.................................614 253-3300
EMP: 32 **EST:** 2010
SALES (est): 4.55MM
SALES (corp-wide): 822.52MM **Privately Held**
SIC: 8052 Intermediate care facilities
HQ: American Renal Associates Holdings, Inc.
500 Cummings Ctr Ste 6550
Beverly MA 01915

(G-5377)
ARBORS EAST LLC
5500 E Broad St (43213-1497)
PHONE.................................614 575-9003
Stacy Duncan, *Admn*
EMP: 36 **EST:** 1991
SALES (est): 2.24MM **Privately Held**
SIC: 8052 8051 Intermediate care facilities; Skilled nursing care facilities

(G-5378)
ARC INDSTRIES INC FRNKLIN CNTY (PA)
2780 Airport Dr (43219)
PHONE.................................614 479-2500
Geraldine C Nasse, *Prin*
EMP: 143 **EST:** 1971
SQ FT: 8,976
SALES (est): 36.16MM
SALES (corp-wide): 36.16MM **Privately Held**
Web: www.arcind.com
SIC: 8331 Sheltered workshop

(G-5379)
ARC INDSTRIES INC FRNKLIN CNTY
Also Called: ARC Industries North
6633 Doubletree Ave (43229-1112)
PHONE.................................614 436-4800
Nan Burns, *Dir*
EMP: 193
SALES (corp-wide): 36.16MM **Privately Held**
Web: www.arcind.com
SIC: 8331 Sheltered workshop
PA: Arc Industries, Incorporated, Of Franklin County, Ohio
2780 Airport Dr
Columbus OH 43219
614 479-2500

(G-5380)
ARC INDSTRIES INC FRNKLIN CNTY
Also Called: ARC Industreis East
909 Taylor Station Rd (43230-6655)
PHONE.................................614 864-2406
Clarice Pavlick, *Mgr*
EMP: 214
SALES (corp-wide): 36.16MM **Privately Held**
Web: www.arcind.com
SIC: 8331 Sheltered workshop

PA: Arc Industries, Incorporated, Of Franklin County, Ohio
2780 Airport Dr
Columbus OH 43219
614 479-2500

(G-5381)
ARC INDSTRIES INC FRNKLIN CNTY
Also Called: ARC Industries West
250 W Dodridge St (43202-1593)
PHONE.................................614 267-1207
Janet Montgomery, *Dir*
EMP: 214
SALES (corp-wide): 36.16MM **Privately Held**
Web: www.arcind.com
SIC: 8331 Sheltered workshop
PA: Arc Industries, Incorporated, Of Franklin County, Ohio
2780 Airport Dr
Columbus OH 43219
614 479-2500

(G-5382)
ARCADIS A CALIFORNIA PARTNR
8101 N High St Ste 100 (43235-1406)
PHONE.................................614 818-4900
Mike Murray, *Brnch Mgr*
EMP: 50
SALES (corp-wide): 3.14B **Privately Held**
Web: www.ibigroup.com
SIC: 8712 8711 Architectural services; Engineering services
HQ: A Arcadis California Partnership
18401 Von Karman Ave # 3
Irvine CA 92612
949 833-5588

(G-5383)
ARCADIS ENGRG SVCS USA INC (DH)
Also Called: Ibi Group Engrg Svcs USA Inc
8101 N High St Ste 100 (43235-1406)
PHONE.................................614 818-4900
Michael Murray, *CEO*
EMP: 65 **EST:** 1995
SALES (est): 23.26MM
SALES (corp-wide): 3.14B **Privately Held**
Web: www.ibigroup.com
SIC: 8711 Consulting engineer
HQ: Ibi Group Inc
55 St Clair Ave W 7th Fl
Toronto ON M4V 2
416 596-1930

(G-5384)
ARCOS LLC (PA)
445 Hutchinson Ave Ste 600 (43235-5677)
PHONE.................................614 396-5500
Odus Wittenburg, *CEO*
Pete Dorsey, *Pr*
Jason Woods, *CFO*
EMP: 183 **EST:** 2005
SQ FT: 5,200
SALES (est): 23.46MM **Privately Held**
Web: www.arcos-inc.com
SIC: 7371 7379 Computer software development; Online services technology consultants

(G-5385)
ARLEDGE CONSTRUCTION INC
2460 Performance Way (43207-2857)
PHONE.................................614 732-4258
Craig Arledge, *Pr*
EMP: 50 **EST:** 1990
SALES (est): 7.43MM **Privately Held**
Web: www.arledgeconstruction.com
SIC: 1771 Foundation and footing contractor

(G-5386)
ARPITA LLC
Also Called: Village Inn Restaurant
920 S High St (43206-2524)
PHONE.................................614 443-6506
Bill Patel, *Pr*
EMP: 32 **EST:** 1954
SQ FT: 7,500
SALES (est): 452.29K **Privately Held**
Web: www.germanvillageinn.net
SIC: 7011 Hotels

(G-5387)
ARS ALEUT CONSTRUCTION LLC
1071 Fishinger Rd Ste 102& (43221-2356)
PHONE.................................225 381-2991
Steve Martin, *Managing Member*
EMP: 41 **EST:** 2013
SALES (est): 882.46K **Privately Held**
SIC: 1799 Special trade contractors, nec

(G-5388)
ARTHUR G JMES CNCER HOSP RCHAR
460 W 10th Ave (43210-1240)
PHONE.................................614 293-4878
David E Schuller, *Dir*
EMP: 276 **EST:** 1985
SALES (est): 5.6MM
SALES (corp-wide): 8.24B **Privately Held**
Web: www.columbusfoundation.org
SIC: 8733 8731 8069 Medical research; Commercial physical research; Specialty hospitals, except psychiatric
PA: The Ohio State University
281 W Ln Ave
Columbus OH 43210
614 292-6446

(G-5389)
ARTHUR G JMES CNCER HOSP RES I
300 W 10th Ave (43210-1280)
PHONE.................................614 293-3300
Jan A Rupert, *Prin*
EMP: 27 **EST:** 2010
SALES (est): 332.63K **Privately Held**
SIC: 8062 General medical and surgical hospitals

(G-5390)
ARVIND SAGAR INC
Also Called: Homewood Suites
2880 Airport Dr (43219-2240)
PHONE.................................614 428-8800
Arvind Sagar, *Owner*
EMP: 59 **EST:** 2001
SALES (est): 1.18MM **Privately Held**
Web: homewoodsuites3.hilton.com
SIC: 7011 Hotels and motels

(G-5391)
ASC GROUP INC (PA)
Also Called: ASC/Auxano
800 Freeway Dr N Ste 101 (43229-5447)
PHONE.................................614 268-2514
Shaune M Skinner, *Pr*
Elsie Immel Blei, *
EMP: 32 **EST:** 1986
SQ FT: 10,000
SALES (est): 9.94MM
SALES (corp-wide): 9.94MM **Privately Held**
Web: www.ascgroup.net
SIC: 8713 8712 8731 8733 Surveying services; Architectural services; Environmental research; Archeological expeditions

(G-5392)
ASHFORD TRS CLUMBUS EASTON LLC
Also Called: Hampton Inn Stes Clmbs-Ston Ar
4150 Stelzer Rd (43230-4169)
PHONE.................................614 473-9911
EMP: 36 **EST:** 2007
SALES (est): 2.35MM **Privately Held**
Web: www.hilton.com
SIC: 7011 Hotels and motels

(G-5393)
ASHLAND CHEMCO INC
Also Called: Ashland Performance Materials
802 Harmon Ave (43223-2410)
PHONE.................................614 232-8510
Paul W Chellgren, *CEO*
EMP: 75
SQ FT: 19,378
SALES (corp-wide): 2.19B **Publicly Held**
SIC: 5169 Alkalines and chlorine
HQ: Ashland Chemco Inc.
1979 Atlas St
Columbus OH 43228
859 815-3333

(G-5394)
ASHLAND CHEMCO INC
Also Called: Ashland Distribution
1979 Atlas St (43228-9645)
P.O. Box 2219 (43216-2219)
PHONE.................................614 790-3333
Ted Harris, *Distribution Vice President*
EMP: 150
SALES (corp-wide): 2.19B **Publicly Held**
SIC: 2899 5169 Chemical preparations, nec; Chemicals and allied products, nec
HQ: Ashland Chemco Inc.
1979 Atlas St
Columbus OH 43228
859 815-3333

(G-5395)
ASNT CERTIFICATION SVCS LLC
1711 Arlingate Ln (43228-4116)
P.O. Box 28518 (43228-0518)
PHONE.................................614 274-6003
John Kinsey, *Pr*
Danny Keck, *VP*
EMP: 66 **EST:** 2020
SALES (est): 874.25K **Privately Held**
Web: www.asnt.org
SIC: 8734 Product certification, safety or performance

(G-5396)
ASPCA
782 Wager St (43206-1459)
PHONE.................................646 596-0321
EMP: 37 **EST:** 2017
SALES (est): 289.7K **Privately Held**
Web: www.aspca.org
SIC: 8699 Animal humane society

(G-5397)
ASSOCTION FOR DVLPMNTLLY DSBLE
Also Called: Dahlberg Learning Center
1915 E Cooke Rd (43224-2266)
PHONE.................................614 447-0606
Bernice Hagler-cody, *Dir*
EMP: 116
SQ FT: 22,213
SALES (corp-wide): 16.46MM **Privately Held**
Web: www.hattielarlham.org
SIC: 8361 8351 Mentally handicapped home ; Preschool center

PA: Association For The Developmentally Disabled
769 Brooksedge Blvd
Westerville OH 43081
614 486-4361

(G-5398)
ASTORIA PLACE COLUMBUS LLC
Also Called: Columbus Rhbilitation Subacute
44 S Souder Ave (43222-1539)
PHONE.................................614 228-5900
Matthew Macklin, *Managing Member*
Michael Nudell, *
Joseph Brandman, *
Yehudit Goldberg, *
EMP: 99 **EST:** 2014
SQ FT: 52,000
SALES (est): 4.35MM **Privately Held**
SIC: 8051 Mental retardation hospital

(G-5399)
AT&T CORP
Also Called: AT&T
150 E Gay St Ste 4a (43215-3130)
PHONE.................................614 223-8236
Connie Browning, *Pr*
EMP: 31
SALES (corp-wide): 122.43B **Publicly Held**
Web: www.att.com
SIC: 4812 4813 2741 Cellular telephone services; Telephone communication, except radio; Miscellaneous publishing
HQ: At&T Enterprises, Llc
208 S Akard St
Dallas TX 75202
800 403-3302

(G-5400)
ATALIAN US OHIO VALLEY INC (DH)
Also Called: Aetna Integrated Services
646 Parsons Ave (43206-1435)
PHONE.................................614 476-1818
Paul Greenland, *Pr*
EMP: 354 **EST:** 1959
SQ FT: 12,000
SALES (est): 40.3MM
SALES (corp-wide): 5.16MM **Privately Held**
Web: www.gdi.com
SIC: 7349 1711 1731 Janitorial service, contract basis; Plumbing, heating, air-conditioning; Electrical work
HQ: Atalian Global Services, Inc.
417 Fifth Ave
New York NY 10016
212 251-7846

(G-5401)
ATLAS CAPITAL SERVICES INC (PA)
Also Called: Atlas Butler Heating & Cooling
4849 Evanswood Dr (43229-6206)
PHONE.................................614 294-7373
TOLL FREE: 800
Mark Swepston, *Pr*
Larry J Winner, *
George Hoskins, *
EMP: 73 **EST:** 1921
SQ FT: 16,000
SALES (est): 19.84MM **Privately Held**
Web: www.atlasbutler.com
SIC: 1711 Warm air heating and air conditioning contractor

(G-5402)
ATLAS CONSTRUCTION COMPANY
4672 Friendship Dr (43230-4302)
PHONE.................................614 475-2282
Steven Testa, *Pr*
Richard Testa, *
EMP: 60 **EST:** 1945
SQ FT: 4,000
SALES (est): 4.89MM **Privately Held**
SIC: 1771 Concrete work

(G-5403)
ATLAS INDUSTRIAL CONTRS LLC (HQ)
Also Called: Atlas Industrial Contractors
5275 Sinclair Rd (43229-5042)
PHONE.................................614 841-4500
George Ghanem, *Pr*
Timothy Seils, *
EMP: 300 **EST:** 1923
SQ FT: 20,000
SALES (est): 95.55MM **Privately Held**
Web: www.atlascos.com
SIC: 1731 3498 1796 Electrical work; Fabricated pipe and fittings; Machine moving and rigging
PA: Gmg Holdings, Llc
5275 Sinclair Rd
Columbus OH 43229

(G-5404)
ATRIUM CENTERS INC (PA)
2550 Corporate Exchange Dr Ste 200 (43231-1660)
PHONE.................................614 416-0600
EMP: 29 **EST:** 2007
SALES (est): 50.09MM
SALES (corp-wide): 50.09MM **Privately Held**
Web: www.atriumlivingcenters.com
SIC: 8051 Skilled nursing care facilities

(G-5405)
ATRIUM LIVING CENTERS OF EASTERN INDIANA INC (HQ)
Also Called: Atrium Living Ctrs Eastrn In
2780 Airport Dr (43219-2289)
PHONE.................................614 416-2662
EMP: 40 **EST:** 2000
SALES (est): 38.64MM **Privately Held**
SIC: 8741 8052 8051 8361 Nursing and personal care facility management; Intermediate care facilities; Skilled nursing care facilities; Rehabilitation center, residential: health care incidental
PA: Essex Healthcare Corporation
2780 Airport Dr Ste 400
Columbus OH 43219

(G-5406)
AUTO BODY NORTH INC (PA)
Also Called: Auto Body Mill Run
8675 N High St (43235-1003)
P.O. Box 720 (43085-0720)
PHONE.................................614 436-3700
Thomas Carpenter, *Pr*
William L Denney, *
Robert Vance, *
Darryl Patterson, *
EMP: 30 **EST:** 1990
SQ FT: 1,800
SALES (est): 2.18MM **Privately Held**
Web: www.crashchampions.com
SIC: 7532 Collision shops, automotive

(G-5407)
AUTOBODY SUPPLY COMPANY INC
212 N Grant Ave (43215-2691)
PHONE.................................614 228-4328
EMP: 68
SIC: 3563 5013 5198 Air and gas compressors including vacuum pumps; Automotive supplies; Paints, varnishes, and supplies

(G-5408)
AUTOMOTIVE DISTRIBUTORS CO INC (PA)
Also Called: Automotive Distributors Whse
2981 Morse Rd (43231-6098)
PHONE.................................614 476-1315
Robert I Yeoman, *Pr*
Phillip Johnston, *
Frank Schmidt, *
EMP: 65 **EST:** 1985
SQ FT: 70,000
SALES (est): 42.46MM
SALES (corp-wide): 42.46MM **Privately Held**
Web: www.adw1.com
SIC: 5013 Automotive supplies and parts

(G-5409)
AVAAP USA LLC (PA)
1400 Goodale Blvd Ste 100 (43212-3777)
PHONE.................................732 710-3425
Dhiraj Shah, *Pr*
Namrata Shah, *VP*
C K Singla, *Ch*
Indu Singla, *Treas*
EMP: 37 **EST:** 2008
SQ FT: 400
SALES (est): 31.85MM **Privately Held**
Web: www.avaap.com
SIC: 8742 Management consulting services

(G-5410)
AVENTIV RESEARCH INC
Also Called: Aventivs Womens Health RES
3600 Olentangy River Rd Ste A (43214-3437)
PHONE.................................614 495-8970
Samir Arora, *Brnch Mgr*
EMP: 29
Web: www.centricityresearch.com
SIC: 8733 Medical research
PA: Aventiv Research Inc.
99 N Brice Rd Ste 120
Columbus OH 43213

(G-5411)
B & B PLASTICS RECYCLERS INC
3300 Lockbourne Rd (43207-3917)
PHONE.................................614 409-2880
Maria Carreon, *Brnch Mgr*
EMP: 129
SALES (corp-wide): 23.15MM **Privately Held**
Web: www.bbplasticsinc.com
SIC: 4953 Recycling, waste materials
PA: B & B Plastics Recyclers, Inc.
3040 N Locust Ave
Rialto CA 92377
909 829-3606

(G-5412)
BAILEY CAVALIERI LLC (PA)
10 West Broad St Ste 2100 (43215-3455)
PHONE.................................614 221-3258
Michael Mahoney, *Mng Dir*
Michael P Mahoney, *Mng Dir*
EMP: 86 **EST:** 2003
SQ FT: 45,000
SALES (est): 10.13MM
SALES (corp-wide): 10.13MM **Privately Held**
Web: www.baileycav.com
SIC: 8111 General practice attorney, lawyer

(G-5413)
BAIN CAPITAL PRIVATE EQUITY
Also Called: Burlington Coat Factory
6055 E Main St (43213-3356)
PHONE.................................614 751-5315
Dominic Dinnini, *Brnch Mgr*
EMP: 48
SALES (corp-wide): 1.8MM **Privately Held**
Web: www.baincapital.com
SIC: 6799 Investors, nec
HQ: Bain Capital Private Equity, Lp
200 Clarendon St
Boston MA 02116

(G-5414)
BAKER & HOSTETLER LLP
200 Civic Center Dr Ste 12 (43215-7510)
PHONE.................................614 228-1541
EMP: 90
SALES (corp-wide): 309.55K **Privately Held**
Web: www.bakerlaw.com
SIC: 8111 General practice attorney, lawyer
PA: Baker & Hostetler Llp
127 Public Sq Ste 2000
Cleveland OH 44114
216 621-0200

(G-5415)
BAKKT CLEARING LLC
Also Called: Rosenthal Collins Group
1500 Lake Shore Dr Ste 450 (43204-3800)
PHONE.................................614 487-9550
Todd Delay, *Mgr*
EMP: 112
SALES (corp-wide): 780.14MM **Publicly Held**
Web: www.bakkt.com
SIC: 6221 Commodity brokers, contracts
HQ: Bakkt Clearing, Llc
216 W Jackson Blvd # 400
Chicago IL 60606

(G-5416)
BALL BOUNCE AND SPORT INC
3275 Alum Creek Dr (43207-3460)
PHONE.................................614 662-5381
Shaun Davis, *Brnch Mgr*
EMP: 30
SALES (corp-wide): 46.04MM **Privately Held**
Web: www.hedstrom.com
SIC: 5092 Toys and hobby goods and supplies
PA: Ball, Bounce And Sport, Inc.
1 Hedstrom Dr
Ashland OH 44805
419 289-9310

(G-5417)
BALLET METROPOLITAN INC
Also Called: BALLETMET COLUMBUS
322 Mount Vernon Ave (43215-2131)
PHONE.................................614 229-4860
Sue Porter, *Ex Dir*
EMP: 150 **EST:** 1974
SQ FT: 35,000
SALES (est): 7.74MM **Privately Held**
Web: www.balletmet.org
SIC: 7922 7911 Ballet production; Professional dancing school

(G-5418)
BARKAN & NEFF CO LPA (PA)
4200 Regent St Ste 210 (43219-6229)
P.O. Box 1989 (43216-1989)
PHONE.................................614 221-4221
Frank J Neff, *Pr*
Eileen Goodin, *
Sanford Meizlish, *
EMP: 40 **EST:** 1958
SALES (est): 5.9MM
SALES (corp-wide): 5.9MM **Privately Held**
Web: www.barkanmeizlish.com
SIC: 8111 General practice law office

Columbus - Franklin County (G-5419) — GEOGRAPHIC SECTION

(G-5419)
BARKAN MZLISH DROSE WNTZ MCNRV
4200 Regent St Ste 210 (43219-6229)
PHONE..................................614 221-4221
Frank Neff, *Pt*
EMP: 29 **EST:** 2017
SALES (est): 2.32MM **Privately Held**
Web: www.barkanmeizlish.com
SIC: 8111 General practice law office

(G-5420)
BARR ENGINEERING INCORPORATED (PA)
Also Called: National Engrg Archtctral Svcs
2800 Corporate Exchange Dr Ste 240 (43231-7628)
PHONE..................................614 714-0299
Jawdat Siddiqi, *Pr*
Enoch Chipukaizer, *
EMP: 35 **EST:** 1992
SQ FT: 1,500
SALES (est): 8.57MM **Privately Held**
SIC: 8711 8713 8734 1799 Civil engineering; Surveying services; Testing laboratories; Core drilling and cutting

(G-5421)
BATH BDY WRKS LGSTICS SVCS LLC (HQ)
Also Called: Mast Global Logistics
2 Limited Pkwy (43230-1445)
PHONE..................................614 415-7500
Bruce Mosier, *Managing Member*
▲ **EMP:** 116 **EST:** 1986
SALES (est): 97.49MM
SALES (corp-wide): 7.43B **Publicly Held**
Web: www.bathandbodyworks.com
SIC: 5113 Shipping supplies
PA: Bath & Body Works, Inc.
3 Limited Pkwy
Columbus OH 43230
614 415-7000

(G-5422)
BATTELLE MEMORIAL INSTITUTE (PA)
Also Called: Battelle
505 King Ave (43201-2681)
PHONE..................................614 424-6424
John Welch, *Ch Bd*
Lewis Von Thaer, *CEO*
Russell Austin, *Sr VP*
Stephen D Steinour, *Prin*
Chris Boynton, *Ex VP*
▲ **EMP:** 4712 **EST:** 1925
SQ FT: 3,810
SALES (est): 11.02B
SALES (corp-wide): 11.02B **Privately Held**
Web: www.battelle.org
SIC: 8731 Commercial physical research

(G-5423)
BAY STATE GAS COMPANY
200 Civic Center Dr (43215-7510)
PHONE..................................614 460-4292
Steven Jablonski, *Brnch Mgr*
EMP: 82
SALES (corp-wide): 5.51B **Publicly Held**
SIC: 4924 Natural gas distribution
HQ: Bay State Gas Company
4 Technology Dr
Westborough MA 01581
508 836-7000

(G-5424)
BAZEMORE INSURANCE GROUP LLC
Also Called: Nationwide
800 Cross Pointe Rd Ste F (43230-6688)
PHONE..................................614 559-8585
EMP: 42
SALES (corp-wide): 2.31MM **Privately Held**
Web: www.nationwide.com
SIC: 6411 Insurance agents, nec
PA: Bazemore Insurance Group Llc
450 Greenway Dr
Johnstown OH 43031
614 699-5489

(G-5425)
BBI LOGISTICS LLC
80 E Rich St Ste 200 (43215-5249)
PHONE..................................800 809-2172
Brent Bosse, *Managing Member*
EMP: 200 **EST:** 2017
SQ FT: 3,400
SALES (est): 38.85MM **Privately Held**
Web: www.bbilogistics.com
SIC: 4731 Freight transportation arrangement

(G-5426)
BBS PROFESSIONAL CORPORATION
1103 Schrock Rd Bldg Ste 400 (43229-1179)
PHONE..................................614 888-8616
Edward O Vance, *Ch Bd*
Paul R Schlegel, *
Donald F Cuthbert, *
EMP: 80 **EST:** 1937
SQ FT: 19,000
SALES (est): 9.33MM
SALES (corp-wide): 14.92B **Publicly Held**
SIC: 8711 Consulting engineer
HQ: Ch2m Hill, Inc.
6312 S Fiddlers Green Cir 300n
Greenwood Village CO 80111
303 771-0900

(G-5427)
BEAM DENTAL INSURANCE SVCS LLC
226 N 5th St Ste 300 (43215-2780)
PHONE..................................740 262-1409
EMP: 151 **EST:** 2019
SALES (est): 17.2MM **Privately Held**
Web: www.beambenefits.com
SIC: 6324 Dental insurance

(G-5428)
BEAM TECHNOLOGIES INC
80 E Rich St Ste 400 (43215-5286)
PHONE..................................800 648-1179
Alex Frommeyer, *CEO*
Alexander Curry, *
Daniel Dykes, *
EMP: 330 **EST:** 2012
SALES (est): 50.05MM **Privately Held**
Web: www.beambenefits.com
SIC: 3841 6411 Surgical and medical instruments; Insurance agents, brokers, and service

(G-5429)
BEAVER DAM HEALTH CARE CENTER
Also Called: Beverly
1425 Yorkland Rd (43232-1686)
PHONE..................................614 861-6666
Robert Brooks, *Ex Dir*
EMP: 29
SALES (corp-wide): 825.65MM **Privately Held**
Web: www.beaverdamhcc.com
SIC: 8059 8052 8051 Convalescent home; Intermediate care facilities; Skilled nursing care facilities
PA: Golden Living Llc
5220 Tennyson Pkwy # 400
Plano TX 75024
972 372-6300

(G-5430)
BEECHWOLD VETERINARY HOSPITAL (PA)
4590 Indianola Ave (43214-2248)
PHONE..................................614 268-8666
Ed Winderl, *Sec*
Robert Hanson, *
Bruce Wenger, *
Marilyn A Schwab, *
EMP: 40 **EST:** 1952
SQ FT: 6,000
SALES (est): 2.92MM
SALES (corp-wide): 2.92MM **Privately Held**
Web: www.thrivepetcare.com
SIC: 0742 Animal hospital services, pets and other animal specialties

(G-5431)
BELAYUSA CORPORATION
5197 Trabue Rd (43228-9498)
PHONE..................................614 878-8200
Carl Long, *Pr*
EMP: 31 **EST:** 1991
SQ FT: 2,000
SALES (est): 906.75K **Privately Held**
SIC: 7381 Private investigator

(G-5432)
BENESCH FRDLNDER CPLAN ARNOFF
41 S High St Ste 2600 (43215-6164)
PHONE..................................614 223-9300
David Paragas, *Pt*
EMP: 30
SALES (corp-wide): 51.22MM **Privately Held**
Web: www.beneschlaw.com
SIC: 8111 General practice attorney, lawyer
PA: Benesch, Friedlander, Coplan & Aronoff Llp
200 Public Sq Ste 2300
Cleveland OH 44114
216 363-4500

(G-5433)
BEST RESTAURANT EQUIPMENT & DESIGN
4020 Business Park Dr (43204-5023)
PHONE..................................614 488-2378
EMP: 70 **EST:** 1987
SALES (est): 15.03MM **Privately Held**
Web: www.bestrestaurant.com
SIC: 5046 5021 Restaurant equipment and supplies, nec; Restaurant furniture, nec

(G-5434)
BEST SUPPLY INC
1885 Obrien Rd (43228-3866)
PHONE..................................614 527-7000
EMP: 82
SALES (corp-wide): 53.67MM **Privately Held**
Web: www.bestsupply.com
SIC: 5032 Drywall materials
PA: Best Supply, Inc.
33999 Melinz Pkwy
Eastlake OH 44095
440 953-0045

(G-5435)
BEST WESTERN SUITES
Also Called: Best Western
1133 Evans Way Ct (43228-9178)
PHONE..................................614 870-2378
EMP: 61 **EST:** 1996
SALES (est): 1.17MM **Privately Held**
Web: www.bestwestern.com
SIC: 7011 Hotels and motels

(G-5436)
BETTER BUS BUR CENTL OHIO INC
Also Called: Better Bus Bur Centl Ohio I
1169 Dublin Rd (43215-1005)
PHONE..................................614 486-6336
Judy Dollison, *Pr*
EMP: 34 **EST:** 1921
SQ FT: 3,500
SALES (est): 3.25MM **Privately Held**
Web: www.columbus-ohbbb.org
SIC: 8611 Better Business Bureau

(G-5437)
BIG BRTHERS BIG SSTERS CNTL OH (PA)
Also Called: MENTORING CENTER FOR CENTRAL O
1855 E Dublin Granville Rd Fl 1 (43229-3516)
PHONE..................................614 839-2447
Dave Schirner, *VP*
Edward Cohn, *
Heather Campbell, *
Douglas Peterman Junior, *Ch*
Denise Mcconnell, *Treas*
EMP: 44 **EST:** 1933
SQ FT: 11,000
SALES (est): 5.01MM
SALES (corp-wide): 5.01MM **Privately Held**
Web: www.bbbscentralohio.org
SIC: 8322 7033 Helping hand service (Big Brother, etc.); Campgrounds

(G-5438)
BIG LOTS STORES INC
Also Called: Big Lots
300 Phillipi Rd Bldg 500 (43228-1310)
PHONE..................................614 278-6800
EMP: 28
SALES (corp-wide): 4.72B **Publicly Held**
Web: www.biglots.com
SIC: 4225 General warehousing
HQ: Big Lots Stores, Llc
4900 E Dblin Granville Rd
Columbus OH 43081
614 278-6800

(G-5439)
BIG LOTS STORES LLC (HQ)
Also Called: Big Lots
4900 E Dublin Granville Rd (43081-7651)
P.O. Box 28523 (43228-0523)
PHONE..................................614 278-6800
Bruce Thorn, *Pr*
Lisa Bachmann, *Ex VP*
Tim Johnson, *CAO*
Rocky Robins, *Sr VP*
◆ **EMP:** 800 **EST:** 1986
SALES (est): 1.16B
SALES (corp-wide): 4.72B **Publicly Held**
Web: www.biglots.com
SIC: 5331 5021 5044 Variety stores; Furniture; Office equipment
PA: Big Lots, Inc.
4900 E Dblin Granville Rd
Columbus OH 43081
614 278-6800

(G-5440)
BIG RED ROOSTER (HQ)
121 Thurman Ave (43206-2656)
PHONE..................................614 255-0200
Martin J Beck, *CEO*
Aaron Spiess, *
Diane Rambo, *
Vicki Eickelberger, *
Don Hasulak, *
EMP: 44 **EST:** 2009
SALES (est): 34.71MM
SALES (corp-wide): 20.76B **Publicly Held**

GEOGRAPHIC SECTION
Columbus - Franklin County (G-5463)

Web: www.bigredrooster.com
SIC: 8712 8748 7371 Architectural services; Industrial development planning; Computer software systems analysis and design, custom
PA: Jones Lang Lasalle Incorporated
200 E Rndolph St Fl 43-48
Chicago IL 60601
312 782-5800

(G-5441)
BIO-BLOOD COMPONENTS INC
1393 N High St (43201-2459)
PHONE..................................614 294-3183
EMP: 103
SALES (corp-wide): 10.71MM Privately Held
SIC: 8099 2836 Blood bank; Biological products, except diagnostic
PA: Bio-Blood Components, Inc.
5700 Pleasant View Rd
Memphis TN 38134
901 384-6250

(G-5442)
BKG HOLDINGS LLC
Also Called: Bartha Audio Visual
600 N Cassady Ave Ofc (43219-2790)
PHONE..................................614 252-7455
Thomas B Gabbert, Managing Member
John M Killacky, *
Daniel O Bashore, *
EMP: 45 EST: 2005
SQ FT: 48,115
SALES (est): 3.99MM Privately Held
Web: www.bartha.com
SIC: 7812 7359 Audio-visual program production; Audio-visual equipment and supply rental

(G-5443)
BLACK SPPHIRE C CLMBUS UNIV 20
Also Called: Springhill Suites
1421 Olentangy River Rd (43212-1449)
PHONE..................................614 297-9912
Dena St Clair, *
EMP: 100 EST: 2014
SALES (est): 2.62MM Privately Held
Web: springhillsuites.marriott.com
SIC: 7011 Hotels and motels

(G-5444)
BLACKBURNS FABRICATION INC
2467 Jackson Pike (43223-3846)
PHONE..................................614 875-0784
Mark A Blackburn, Pr
Edsel L Blackburn Senior, VP
Carolyn Blackburn, *
Kim Green, *
EMP: 30 EST: 1995
SQ FT: 50,000
SALES (est): 9.2MM Privately Held
Web: www.blackburnsfab.com
SIC: 3441 5051 Fabricated structural metal; Structural shapes, iron or steel

(G-5445)
BLASTMASTER HOLDINGS USA LLC (PA)
Also Called: Blastone International
4510 Bridgeway Ave (43219-1891)
PHONE..................................877 725-2781
Andrew Gooden, *
James Gooden, *
◆ EMP: 100 EST: 2008
SQ FT: 56,000
SALES (est): 34.86MM
SALES (corp-wide): 34.86MM Privately Held
Web: www.blastone.com

SIC: 5084 Industrial machinery and equipment

(G-5446)
BLECKMANN USA LLC
Also Called: Bleckmann Logistics
10 W Broad St Ste 2100 (43215-3455)
PHONE..................................740 809-2645
EMP: 45 EST: 2015
SALES (est): 9.97MM Privately Held
Web: www.bleckmann.com
SIC: 4731 Freight transportation arrangement

(G-5447)
BLOOD SERVICES CENTL OHIO REG (PA)
995 E Broad St (43205-1322)
PHONE..................................614 253-7981
Ambrose Ng, CEO
EMP: 200 EST: 1992
SQ FT: 80,000
SALES (est): 9.98MM Privately Held
Web: www.redcross.org
SIC: 8099 Blood related health services

(G-5448)
BLOWOUT BAR
1378 Grandview Ave (43212-2803)
PHONE..................................614 732-0965
Kristin Dejohn, Prin
EMP: 33 EST: 2012
SALES (est): 665.94K Privately Held
Web: www.theblowoutbar.com
SIC: 7231 Hairdressers

(G-5449)
BLUE FLAG LOGISTICS LLC
5365 Valley Ln E (43231-3114)
PHONE..................................502 975-8473
Ahmed Mahdi, Mgr
EMP: 99 EST: 2021
SALES (est): 2.3MM Privately Held
SIC: 4731 Freight transportation arrangement

(G-5450)
BLUESTONE COUNSELING LLC
3748 Kilmuir Dr (43221-5606)
PHONE..................................614 406-0299
Traci Cahill, Prin
EMP: 28 EST: 2013
SALES (est): 1.73MM Privately Held
Web: www.bluestonecounseling.com
SIC: 8322 General counseling services

(G-5451)
BMI FEDERAL CREDIT UNION (PA)
760 Kinnear Rd Frnt (43212-1487)
P.O. Box 3670 (43016-0340)
PHONE..................................614 298-8527
Sharon Custer, Pr
EMP: 30 EST: 1936
SQ FT: 18,000
SALES (est): 24.27MM
SALES (corp-wide): 24.27MM Privately Held
Web: www.bmifcu.org
SIC: 6061 Federal credit unions

(G-5452)
BOBB AUTOMOTIVE INC
Also Called: Bobb Suzuki
4639 W Broad St (43228-1610)
P.O. Box 28148 (43228-0148)
PHONE..................................614 853-3000
Jeff May, Pr
Thomas O'ryan, VP
EMP: 50 EST: 1924
SQ FT: 15,000
SALES (est): 8.83MM Privately Held
Web: www.bobbsaysyes.com

SIC: 5511 7515 5012 Automobiles, new and used; Passenger car leasing; Automobiles and other motor vehicles

(G-5453)
BOLD PENGUIN INC (HQ)
100 E Broad St Fl 15 (43215-3656)
PHONE..................................614 344-1029
Ilya Bodner, CEO
Dan Gifford, *
Ben Clarke, CDO*
EMP: 60 EST: 2018
SALES (est): 49.87MM
SALES (corp-wide): 11.04B Privately Held
Web: www.boldpenguin.com
SIC: 6411 Insurance agents, brokers, and service
PA: American Family Mutual Insurance Company, S.I.
6000 American Pkwy
Madison WI 53783
608 249-2111

(G-5454)
BOLD PENGUIN COMPANY LLC
Also Called: Bold Penguin
100 E Broad St Fl 15 (43215-3656)
PHONE..................................614 344-1029
EMP: 196 EST: 2016
SALES (est): 4.79MM Privately Held
SIC: 7374 7371 Data processing and preparation; Custom computer programming services

(G-5455)
BONDED CHEMICALS INC (HQ)
Also Called: Chemgroup
2645 Charter St (43228-4605)
PHONE..................................614 777-9240
Marty Wehr, Pr
Sue Wiford, *
▲ EMP: 27 EST: 1945
SALES (est): 47.52MM
SALES (corp-wide): 243.16MM Privately Held
Web: www.chemgroup.com
SIC: 5169 Sanitation preparations
PA: Chemgroup, Inc.
2600 Thunderhawk Ct
Dayton OH 45414
937 898-5566

(G-5456)
BOSS DISPLAY CORPORATION
1975 Galaxie St (43207-1721)
PHONE..................................614 443-9495
David Foster, Pr
David Foster, Prin
David Murphy, *
Evan Trickey, *
EMP: 70 EST: 1934
SQ FT: 20,000
SALES (est): 5.38MM Privately Held
Web: www.bossdisplay.com
SIC: 7389 Exhibit construction by industrial contractors

(G-5457)
BOWEN ENGINEERING CORPORATION
355 E Campus View Blvd Ste 110 (43235-5616)
PHONE..................................614 536-0273
EMP: 100
SALES (corp-wide): 359.35MM Privately Held
Web: www.bowenengineering.com
SIC: 8711 Consulting engineer
PA: Bowen Engineering Corporation
8802 N Meridian St Ste X
Indianapolis IN 46260

219 661-9770

(G-5458)
BOYS GIRLS CLUBS COLUMBUS INC
Also Called: Boys & Girls Club of Columbus
1108 City Park Ave Ste 301 (43206-3686)
PHONE..................................614 221-8830
Drew Dimaccio, Pr
EMP: 46 EST: 1948
SQ FT: 22,000
SALES (est): 4.29MM Privately Held
Web: www.bgccolumbus.org
SIC: 8641 Youth organizations

(G-5459)
BRANDSAFWAY SERVICES LLC
1250 Emig Rd (43223-3354)
PHONE..................................614 443-1314
Trent Galentin, Mgr
EMP: 31
SALES (corp-wide): 2.16B Privately Held
Web: www.brandsafway.com
SIC: 5082 7359 Scaffolding; Equipment rental and leasing, nec
HQ: Brandsafway Services Llc
600 Galleria Pkwy Se # 1100
Atlanta GA 30339

(G-5460)
BREAD FINANCIAL HOLDINGS INC
4590 E Broad St (43213-1301)
PHONE..................................614 729-3000
Bill Salamy, Brnch Mgr
EMP: 114
Web: www.alliancedata.com
SIC: 7389 Credit card service
PA: Bread Financial Holdings, Inc.
3095 Loyalty Cir
Columbus OH 43219

(G-5461)
BREAD FINANCIAL HOLDINGS INC (PA)
3095 Loyalty Cir (43219)
PHONE..................................614 729-4000
Ralph J Andretta, Pr
Roger H Ballou, Non-Executive Chairman of the Board*
Perry S Beberman, Ex VP
Valerie E Greer, CCO
Joseph L Motes Iii, CAO
EMP: 200 EST: 1996
SALES (est): 5.17B Publicly Held
Web: www.alliancedata.com
SIC: 7389 Credit card service

(G-5462)
BREATHING ASSOCIATION
788 Mount Vernon Ave (43203-1408)
PHONE..................................614 457-4570
Joanne Spoth, Prin
Marie E Collart, *
EMP: 35 EST: 1906
SQ FT: 1,800
SALES (est): 2.96MM Privately Held
Web: www.breathingassociation.org
SIC: 8621 Medical field-related associations

(G-5463)
BREEN WINKEL & CO
3752 N High St (43214-3525)
PHONE..................................614 261-1494
Robert A Winkel, Pt
Robert Crabb, Owner
Stephen A Green, Pt
EMP: 28 EST: 1952
SQ FT: 2,400
SALES (est): 1.82MM Privately Held
Web: www.wgcocpas.com

(PA)=Parent Co (HQ)=Headquarters
✿ = New Business established in last 2 years

2024 Harris Ohio Services Directory

SIC: 8721 Accounting services, except auditing

(G-5464)
BREXTON CONSTRUCTION LLC
1123 Goodale Blvd Ste 500 (43212-3780)
PHONE..............................614 441-4110
Mary Beatty, CEO
Timothy P Galvin, *
EMP: 34 EST: 2008
SQ FT: 4,664
SALES (est): 8.71MM Privately Held
Web: www.brextonllc.com
SIC: 1542 Commercial and office building, new construction

(G-5465)
BRICKER & ECKLER LLP (PA)
100 S 3rd St Ste B (43215)
PHONE..............................614 227-2300
Richard C Simpson, Pt
EMP: 311 EST: 1997
SQ FT: 100,000
SALES (est): 49.25MM
SALES (corp-wide): 49.25MM Privately Held
Web: www.brickergraydon.com
SIC: 8111 General practice law office

(G-5466)
BRIGHTVIEW LANDSCAPE SVCS INC
3001 Innis Rd (43224-3741)
PHONE..............................614 478-2085
Joel Korte, Mgr
EMP: 228
SQ FT: 845
SALES (corp-wide): 2.82B Publicly Held
Web: www.brightview.com
SIC: 0781 Landscape services
HQ: Brightview Landscape Services, Inc.
     27001 Agoura Rd Ste 350
     Agoura Hills CA 91301
     818 223-8500

(G-5467)
BROAD STREET HOTEL ASSOC LP
Also Called: Ramada Inn East - Airport
4801 E Broad St (43213-1356)
PHONE..............................614 861-0321
Kevork Toroyian, Pt
Bill Nikolis, *
Patrick Barrett, *
Barkev Kayajian, *
EMP: 78 EST: 1995
SQ FT: 15,000
SALES (est): 462.39K Privately Held
Web: www.wyndhamhotels.com
SIC: 7011 7991 5813 5812 Hotels; Physical fitness facilities; Drinking places; Eating places

(G-5468)
BROOK WILLOW CHRSTN CMMUNITIES
Also Called: Willow Brook Christian Home
55 Lazelle Rd (43235-1402)
PHONE..............................614 885-3300
David Chappell, Admn
EMP: 105
SALES (corp-wide): 7.86MM Privately Held
Web: www.willow-brook.org
SIC: 8052 8051 Intermediate care facilities; Skilled nursing care facilities
PA: Willow Brook Christian Communities, Inc
    100 Willow Brook Way S
    Delaware OH 43015
    740 369-0048

(G-5469)
BROOKSIDE GOLF & CNTRY CLB CO
2770 W Dublin Granville Rd (43235-2785)
PHONE..............................614 889-2581
James Rowlette, Pr
Joseph T Furko Iii, Genl Mgr
EMP: 150 EST: 1927
SQ FT: 75,000
SALES (est): 8.26MM Privately Held
Web: www.brooksidegcc.com
SIC: 7997 Country club, membership

(G-5470)
BROWN AND CALDWELL
445 Hutchinson Ave Ste 540 (43235-5677)
PHONE..............................614 410-6144
Tim Block, Mgr
EMP: 34
SALES (corp-wide): 374.67MM Privately Held
Web: www.brownandcaldwell.com
SIC: 8711 Consulting engineer
PA: Brown And Caldwell
    201 N Civic Dr Ste 115
    Walnut Creek CA 94596
    925 937-9010

(G-5471)
BROWN LOGISTICS SOLUTIONS INC (PA)
Also Called: Inmotion Promotion
2100 Cloverleaf St E (43232-4101)
PHONE..............................614 866-9111
EMP: 37 EST: 1914
SALES (est): 4.23MM
SALES (corp-wide): 4.23MM Privately Held
Web: www.brownls.com
SIC: 4213 Trucking, except local

(G-5472)
BUCKEYE BODY AND EQUIPMENT
Also Called: Buckeye Truck Equipment
939 E Starr Ave (43201-3042)
P.O. Box 1150 (43216-1150)
PHONE..............................614 299-1136
Fred Bongiovanni, Pr
Jeffrey Massey, *
Doug Callahan, *
EMP: 34 EST: 2013
SQ FT: 55,000
SALES (est): 6.3MM Privately Held
Web: www.buckeyebody.com
SIC: 5046 Commercial equipment, nec

(G-5473)
BUCKEYE CMNTY EIGHTY ONE LP
Also Called: Williams Street Apartments
3021 E Dublin Granville Rd (43231-4031)
PHONE..............................614 942-2020
Brenda Jacques, Genl Pt
Steven Boone, Ltd Pt
EMP: 37 EST: 2017
SALES (est): 936.06K Privately Held
SIC: 6513 Apartment building operators

(G-5474)
BUCKEYE CMNTY HOPE FOUNDATION (PA)
3021 E Dublin Granville Rd Ste 200 (43231-4031)
PHONE..............................614 942-2014
Steve J Boone, Pr
Carlisa Saltsman, *
Steven Guthrie, *
Sandy Estep, *
EMP: 100 EST: 1991
SQ FT: 5,000
SALES (est): 13.13MM Privately Held
Web: www.buckeyehope.org

SIC: 1521 Single-family housing construction

(G-5475)
BUCKEYE HOSPITALITY INC
1690 Clara St (43211-2628)
PHONE..............................614 586-1001
EMP: 27 EST: 2008
SALES (est): 193.24K Privately Held
Web: www.buckeyehospitalityconstruction.com
SIC: 7011 Hotels and motels

(G-5476)
BUCKEYE PARTS SERVICES INC
4221 Westward Ave (43228-1045)
PHONE..............................614 274-1888
James R Boucher, Pr
EMP: 40 EST: 1990
SQ FT: 50,000
SALES (est): 8.84MM Privately Held
Web: www.buckeyeparts.com
SIC: 5072 Builders' hardware, nec

(G-5477)
BUCKEYE POWER INC (PA)
Also Called: OHIO RURAL ELECTRIC COOPERATIV
6677 Busch Blvd (43229-1101)
PHONE..............................614 781-0573
Steven Nelson, Ch Bd
Anthony J Ahern, *
Bobby Daniel, *
EMP: 28 EST: 1949
SQ FT: 36,000
SALES (est): 832.7MM
SALES (corp-wide): 832.7MM Privately Held
Web: www.ohioec.org
SIC: 8611 4911 Trade associations; Generation, electric power

(G-5478)
BUCKEYE RANCH INC
Also Called: Cross Creek Day Treatment
2865 W Broad St (43204-2643)
PHONE..............................614 543-1380
John Hiller, Brnch Mgr
EMP: 68
SALES (corp-wide): 58.43MM Privately Held
Web: www.buckeyeranch.org
SIC: 8361 Emotionally disturbed home
PA: The Buckeye Ranch Inc
    5665 Hoover Rd
    Grove City OH 43123
    614 875-2371

(G-5479)
BUCKMAN ENOCHS COSS & ASSOC
4449 Easton Way Ste 130 (43219-7000)
PHONE..............................614 825-6215
Stephen J Enochs, Pr
Ted Coss, VP
EMP: 30 EST: 1978
SALES (est): 2.29MM Privately Held
Web: www.becsearch.com
SIC: 7361 Executive placement

(G-5480)
BUCYRUS RADIO GROUP
4401 Carriage Hill Ln (43220-3837)
PHONE..............................614 451-2191
EMP: 33 EST: 2015
SALES (est): 637.72K Privately Held
Web: www.columbusradiogroup.com
SIC: 4832 Radio broadcasting stations

(G-5481)
BUDROS RUHLIN & ROE INC
1801 Watermark Dr Ste 300 (43215-7088)

PHONE..............................614 481-6900
Kurt Macalpine, CEO
EMP: 59 EST: 1976
SALES (est): 13.65MM
SALES (corp-wide): 1.2B Privately Held
Web: www.corient.com
SIC: 8742 Financial consultant
PA: Ci Financial Corp
    15 York St Suite 2
    Toronto ON M5J 0
    416 364-1145

(G-5482)
BUFFALO-6305 EB ASSOCIATES LLC
Also Called: Holiday Inn Ex Stes Clmbus Arp
6305 E Broad St (43213-1506)
PHONE..............................614 322-8000
Peni Sheedy, Genl Mgr
EMP: 27 EST: 2011
SALES (est): 446.46K Privately Held
Web: www.hiexpress.com
SIC: 7011 Hotels and motels

(G-5483)
BUILDER SERVICES GROUP INC
Also Called: Gale Insulation
2365 Scioto Harper Dr (43204-3495)
PHONE..............................614 263-9378
EMP: 40
SALES (corp-wide): 5.19B Publicly Held
Web: www.truteam.com
SIC: 1742 Insulation, buildings
HQ: Builder Services Group, Inc.
    475 N Williamson Blvd
    Daytona Beach FL 32114
    386 304-2222

(G-5484)
BUREAU WORKERS COMPENSATION
Also Called: Safety and Hygiene
30 W Spring St Fl 25 (43215-2241)
PHONE..............................614 466-5109
Mark Garver, Superintnt
EMP: 60 EST: 1924
SALES (est): 2.96MM Privately Held
SIC: 7382 Security systems services

(G-5485)
BURGESS & NIPLE INC (PA)
330 Rush Aly Ste 700 (43215-3932)
PHONE..............................614 459-2050
Ronald R Schultz Pe, CEO
Kenneth R Davis Junior Pe, Pr
EMP: 275 EST: 1912
SALES (est): 87.59MM
SALES (corp-wide): 87.59MM Privately Held
Web: www.burgessniple.com
SIC: 8711 8712 Consulting engineer; Architectural engineering

(G-5486)
BURGESS & NIPLE INC (HQ)
330 Rush Aly Ste 700 (43215-3932)
PHONE..............................703 631-6041
A L Woods Iii, VP
Arthur L Woods Iii, VP
Julie Connell, *
EMP: 80 EST: 1974
SALES (est): 24.63MM
SALES (corp-wide): 87.59MM Privately Held
Web: www.burgessniple.com
SIC: 8711 8713 0781 8712 Consulting engineer; Surveying services; Landscape architects; Architectural services
PA: Burgess & Niple, Inc.
    330 Rush Aly Ste 700
    Columbus OH 43215
    614 459-2050

GEOGRAPHIC SECTION
Columbus - Franklin County (G-5510)

(G-5487)
BURGESS & NIPLE/HEAPY LLC
330 Rush Aly Ste 700 (43215-3932)
PHONE..................614 459-2050
Karen Anderson, *
EMP: 99 **EST:** 2017
SALES (est): 1.74MM **Privately Held**
Web: www.burgessniple.com
SIC: 8711 8712 7389 Consulting engineer; Architectural services; Business services, nec

(G-5488)
BUSHRA TRANSPORTATION LLC
4200 Westview Center Plz # 101 (43228-2975)
PHONE..................614 745-1584
Badawi Munye, *Prin*
EMP: 28 **EST:** 2012
SALES (est): 1.6MM **Privately Held**
SIC: 4789 Transportation services, nec

(G-5489)
C M R INC
Also Called: Call Management Resources
4449 Easton Way Ste 200 (43219-7005)
PHONE..................614 447-7100
Malcolm Riggle, *Prin*
Elsie Rarey, *Prin*
Howard Newell, *Prin*
EMP: 29 **EST:** 1959
SALES (est): 3.04MM **Privately Held**
SIC: 7389 Telephone answering service

(G-5490)
C V PERRY & CO (PA)
370 S 5th St (43215-5408)
PHONE..................614 221-4131
Brian Vain, *Pr*
EMP: 47 **EST:** 1948
SQ FT: 3,500
SALES (est): 5.25MM
SALES (corp-wide): 5.25MM **Privately Held**
Web: www.cvperry.com
SIC: 1521 6552 6531 New construction, single-family houses; Land subdividers and developers, commercial; Real estate brokers and agents

(G-5491)
C&W FACILITY SERVICES INC
Also Called: Dtz
325 John H Mcconnell Blvd (43215-2672)
PHONE..................614 827-1702
EMP: 1963
SALES (corp-wide): 9.49B **Privately Held**
Web: www.cwservices.com
SIC: 7349 Janitorial service, contract basis
HQ: C&W Facility Services Inc.
140 Kendrick St Ste C120
Needham MA 02494
888 751-9100

(G-5492)
CAHILL CNSTR INC CAHILL CNSTR
6331 Fiesta Dr (43235-5202)
PHONE..................614 442-8570
EMP: 29 **EST:** 2019
SALES (est): 5.1MM **Privately Held**
Web: www.cahillconstruction.com
SIC: 1521 Single-family housing construction

(G-5493)
CALFEE HALTER & GRISWOLD LLP
41 S High St Ste 1200 (43215-3465)
PHONE..................614 621-1500
Karen Scurlock, *Brnch Mgr*
EMP: 45
SALES (corp-wide): 46.79MM **Privately Held**
Web: www.calfee.com
SIC: 8111 General practice attorney, lawyer
PA: Calfee, Halter & Griswold Llp
The Clfee Bldg 1405 E 6th
Cleveland OH 44114
216 622-8200

(G-5494)
CAMERON MITCHELL REST LLC (PA)
Also Called: Ocean Prime
390 W Nationwide Blvd Ste 300 # 3 (43215-2337)
PHONE..................614 621-3663
David Miller, *
EMP: 46 **EST:** 1998
SQ FT: 7,800
SALES (est): 134.21MM
SALES (corp-wide): 134.21MM **Privately Held**
Web: www.cameronmitchell.com
SIC: 8741 5812 Restaurant management; Eating places

(G-5495)
CANYON MEDICAL CENTER INC
5969 E Broad St Ste 200 (43213-1546)
PHONE..................614 864-6010
Stephen D Shell Md, *Pr*
Robert Hershfield Md, *Bd of Dir*
EMP: 48 **EST:** 1976
SQ FT: 18,000
SALES (est): 7.4MM **Privately Held**
Web: www.canyonmc.com
SIC: 8011 Internal medicine, physician/surgeon

(G-5496)
CAP CITY HOTELS LLC
Also Called: Aloft Columbus University Area
1295 Olentangy River Rd (43212-3118)
PHONE..................614 294-7500
Alan Assaf, *
Janet Boissy, *
EMP: 30 **EST:** 2013
SALES (est): 911.03K **Privately Held**
Web: aloft-hotels.marriott.com
SIC: 7011 Hotels

(G-5497)
CAPITAL CITY AVIATION INC
2160 West Case Rd Unit 15 (43235-2539)
PHONE..................614 459-2541
Jason Seavolt, *Pr*
Joseph Makarich, *VP*
Ruben Padro, *Treas*
Brad Guthrie, *Dir*
William Westfall, *Dir*
EMP: 34 **EST:** 2004
SQ FT: 800
SALES (est): 435.25K **Privately Held**
Web: www.capitalcityaviation.com
SIC: 4581 Airports, flying fields, and services

(G-5498)
CAPITAL CITY GROUP INC (HQ)
Also Called: Capital City Crane Rental
2299 Performance Way (43207-2858)
PHONE..................614 278-2120
EMP: 42 **EST:** 1992
SALES (est): 28.53MM
SALES (corp-wide): 61.37MM **Privately Held**
Web: www.ccgroup-inc.com
SIC: 7353 Cranes and aerial lift equipment, rental or leasing
PA: Bay Crane Service, Inc.
1102 43rd Ave
Long Island City NY 11101
718 392-0800

(G-5499)
CAPITAL CITY HOSPICE
2800 Corporate Exchange Dr Ste 170 (43231-7628)
PHONE..................614 441-9300
EMP: 55 **EST:** 2016
SALES (est): 956.52K **Privately Held**
Web: www.capitalcityhospice.com
SIC: 8082 Home health care services

(G-5500)
CAPITAL FIRE PROTECTION CO (PA)
3360 Valleyview Dr (43204-1296)
PHONE..................614 279-9448
William P Jolley, *Pr*
Bryn Haggins, *
Scott Williams, *
Steve Stump, *
EMP: 42 **EST:** 1963
SQ FT: 20,000
SALES (est): 2.08K
SALES (corp-wide): 2.08K **Privately Held**
Web: www.capfire.com
SIC: 1799 Coating, caulking, and weather, water, and fireproofing

(G-5501)
CAPITAL TRANSPORTATION INC
1170 N Cassady Ave (43219-2232)
PHONE..................614 258-0400
Richard M Crockett, *Pr*
EMP: 104 **EST:** 1970
SQ FT: 70,000
SALES (est): 4.91MM **Privately Held**
Web: www.capital-trans.com
SIC: 4119 Limousine rental, with driver

(G-5502)
CAPITAL WHOLESALE DRUG COMPANY
Also Called: Capital Drug
873 Williams Ave (43212-3850)
PHONE..................614 297-8225
George D Richards, *Ch Bd*
George K Richards, *
David L Franklin, *
Linda R Franklin, *
Daniel G Macleod, *
EMP: 55 **EST:** 1927
SQ FT: 45,000
SALES (est): 24.69MM **Privately Held**
Web: www.capital-drug.com
SIC: 5122 Pharmaceuticals

(G-5503)
CAPITOL CITY CARDIOLOGY INC (PA)
5825 Westbourne Ave (43213-1459)
PHONE..................614 464-0884
Charles Noble Md, *Pr*
Ruben Sheares Md, *Stockholder*
Raj Patel Md, *Stockholder*
EMP: 40 **EST:** 1995
SQ FT: 3,000
SALES (est): 4.37MM **Privately Held**
SIC: 8011 Cardiologist and cardio-vascular specialist

(G-5504)
CAPITOL EXPRESS ENTPS INC (PA)
Also Called: Cisco Capitol Express
3815 Twin Creeks Dr (43204-5005)
P.O. Box 462 (43026-0462)
PHONE..................614 279-2819
Kennon Wissinger, *Pr*
Linda Cose, *
EMP: 60 **EST:** 1992
SQ FT: 6,000
SALES (est): 8.45MM **Privately Held**
Web: www.capitolexpress.biz
SIC: 4212 Delivery service, vehicular

(G-5505)
CAPITOL TUNNELING INC
2216 Refugee Rd (43207-2800)
PHONE..................614 444-0255
Kyle Lucas, *Pr*
EMP: 30 **EST:** 1960
SQ FT: 1,200
SALES (est): 9.74MM **Privately Held**
Web: www.capitoltunneling.com
SIC: 1623 Underground utilities contractor

(G-5506)
CARCORP INC
Also Called: Dennis Mitsubishi
2900 Morse Rd (43231-6036)
P.O. Box 29365 (43229-0365)
PHONE..................877 857-2801
Keith Dennis, *Pr*
Aaron Masterson, *
Aaron Casto, *
Jim Tigyer, *
▼ **EMP:** 146 **EST:** 1990
SQ FT: 12,000
SALES (est): 33.49MM **Privately Held**
Web: www.glakeshyundaiofcolumbus.com
SIC: 5511 5521 7515 5571 Automobiles, new and used; Used car dealers; Passenger car leasing; Motorcycle dealers

(G-5507)
CARDINAL BUILDERS INC
4409 E Main St (43213-3061)
PHONE..................614 237-1000
Tim Coady, *Pr*
Tim Kane, *Stockholder**
EMP: 32 **EST:** 1965
SQ FT: 22,000
SALES (est): 679.54K **Privately Held**
SIC: 3541 1521 1522 1761 Machine tool replacement & repair parts, metal cutting types; General remodeling, single-family houses; Hotel/motel and multi-family home renovation and remodeling; Siding contractor

(G-5508)
CARDINAL ORTHOPAEDIC GROUP INC
170 Taylor Station Rd (43213-4491)
PHONE..................614 759-1186
Dale Ingram, *Pr*
EMP: 44 **EST:** 1966
SQ FT: 16,000
SALES (est): 1.59MM **Privately Held**
Web: www.orthopedicone.com
SIC: 8011 Orthopedic physician

(G-5509)
CAREER PARTNERS INTL LLC (PA)
20 S 3rd St Ste 210 (43215-4206)
PHONE..................919 401-4260
Doug Matthews, *Pr*
Karen Romeo, *Sr VP*
Sue Rowley, *Sr VP*
Terry Gillis, *V Ch Bd*
EMP: 30 **EST:** 1987
SALES (est): 52.86MM
SALES (corp-wide): 52.86MM **Privately Held**
Web: www.cpiworld.com
SIC: 8742 General management consultant

(G-5510)
CARET HOLDINGS INC
80 E Rich St Ste 500 (43215-5764)
PHONE..................866 980-9431
Alexander Timm, *CEO*
EMP: 901 **EST:** 2015

(PA)=Parent Co (HQ)=Headquarters
✪ = New Business established in last 2 years

Columbus - Franklin County (G-5511) GEOGRAPHIC SECTION

SQ FT: 109,062
SALES (est): 114.71MM
SALES (corp-wide): 455MM **Publicly Held**
Web: inc.joinroot.com
SIC: 6331 Fire, marine, and casualty insurance
PA: Root, Inc.
80 E Rich St Ste 500
Columbus OH 43215
866 980-9431

(G-5511)
CARGO SOLUTION EXPRESS INC
4540 Fisher Rd (43228-9480)
PHONE..................614 980-0351
EMP: 49
SALES (corp-wide): 102.01MM **Privately Held**
Web: www.cargosolutionexpress.com
SIC: 4213 Trucking, except local
PA: Cargo Solution Express Inc.
14587 Valley Blvd 89
Fontana CA 92335
909 350-1644

(G-5512)
CARLILE PATCHEN & MURPHY LLP (PA)
950 Goodale Blvd Ste 200 (43212-3974)
PHONE..................614 228-6135
Ricky Hollenbaugh, *Pt*
James R Moats, *
Michael Igo, *
EMP: 88 **EST**: 1997
SQ FT: 24,000
SALES (est): 13.61MM
SALES (corp-wide): 13.61MM **Privately Held**
Web: www.cpmlaw.com
SIC: 8111 General practice attorney, lawyer

(G-5513)
CARMENS DIST SYSTEMS INC
4585 Poth Rd (43213-1327)
PHONE..................800 886-8227
Beth Geehring, *CEO*
John Geehring, *
Jeff Gardner, *
▲ **EMP**: 28 **EST**: 1999
SALES (est): 4.59MM **Privately Held**
Web: www.carmensdistributionsystems.com
SIC: 7349 Janitorial service, contract basis

(G-5514)
CARPENTER LIPPS LLP (PA)
280 N High St Ste 1300 (43215-7515)
PHONE..................614 365-4100
Michael H Carpenter, *Mng Pt*
EMP: 54 **EST**: 1994
SALES (est): 5.14MM **Privately Held**
Web: www.carpenterlipps.com
SIC: 8111 General practice attorney, lawyer

(G-5515)
CASLEO CORPORATION
Also Called: Global Meals
2741 E 4th Ave (43219-2824)
PHONE..................614 252-6508
EMP: 120 **EST**: 1994
SALES (est): 2.48MM **Privately Held**
SIC: 8322 Meal delivery program

(G-5516)
CASS INFORMATION SYSTEMS INC
Also Called: Cass Logistics
2675 Corporate Exchange Dr (43231-1662)
P.O. Box 182447 (43218-2447)
PHONE..................614 839-4500
Monique Winston, *Prs Mgr*
EMP: 60
SALES (corp-wide): 197.51MM **Publicly Held**
Web: www.cassinfo.com
SIC: 8742 Business management consultant
PA: Cass Information Systems, Inc.
12444 Pwrscurt Dr Ste 550
Saint Louis MO 63131
314 506-5500

(G-5517)
CASS INFORMATION SYSTEMS INC
2644 Kirkwood Hyw Newark (43218)
PHONE..................614 839-4503
Kathy Callanan, *Brnch Mgr*
EMP: 28
SALES (corp-wide): 197.51MM **Publicly Held**
Web: www.cassinfo.com
SIC: 4813 Telephone communication, except radio
PA: Cass Information Systems, Inc.
12444 Pwrscurt Dr Ste 550
Saint Louis MO 63131
314 506-5500

(G-5518)
CASSIDY TRLEY COML RE SVCS INC
325 John H Mcconnell Blvd Ste 250 (43215-2672)
PHONE..................614 241-4700
Angie Schumacher, *Brnch Mgr*
EMP: 171
SALES (corp-wide): 9.49B **Privately Held**
Web: www.ctmt.com
SIC: 6531 Real estate agent, commercial
HQ: Cassidy Turley Commercial Real Estate Services Inc.
7700 Forsyth Blvd Ste 900
Saint Louis MO 63105
314 862-7100

(G-5519)
CASTO COMMUNITIES CNSTR LTD (PA)
Also Called: Town and Country City
191 W Nationwide Blvd Ste 200 (43215-2568)
PHONE..................614 228-5331
Frank S Benson, *Managing Member*
EMP: 389 **EST**: 1952
SQ FT: 30,000
SALES (est): 4.75MM
SALES (corp-wide): 4.75MM **Privately Held**
Web: www.castocommunities.com
SIC: 6512 Commercial and industrial building operation

(G-5520)
CATHOLIC SOCIAL SERVICES INC
197 E Gay St (43215-3229)
PHONE..................614 221-5891
Rachel Lustig, *Pr*
EMP: 50 **EST**: 2000
SALES (est): 7.78MM **Privately Held**
Web: www.colscss.org
SIC: 8322 Social service center

(G-5521)
CAVALIER TELE MID-ATLANTIC LLC
180 E Broad St Fl 9 (43215-3707)
PHONE..................614 884-0000
Ron Spicer, *Mgr*
EMP: 618
SALES (corp-wide): 6.54B **Privately Held**
SIC: 4813 Long distance telephone communications
HQ: Cavalier Telephone Mid-Atlantic, L.L.C.
2134 W Laburnum Ave
Richmond VA 23227
804 422-4100

(G-5522)
CBC COMPANIES INC (PA)
250 E Broad St Fl 21 (43215-3770)
P.O. Box 1838 (43216-1838)
PHONE..................614 222-4343
EMP: 75 **EST**: 1948
SALES (est): 233.8MM
SALES (corp-wide): 233.8MM **Privately Held**
Web: www.factualdata.com
SIC: 7322 Collection agency, except real estate

(G-5523)
CBCINNOVIS INTERNATIONAL INC (HQ)
Also Called: Cbcinnovis
250 E Broad St Fl 21 (43215-3770)
PHONE..................614 222-4343
Jonathan Price, *Pr*
EMP: 41 **EST**: 2006
SALES (est): 14.62MM
SALES (corp-wide): 233.8MM **Privately Held**
Web: www.factualdata.com
SIC: 7323 Consumer credit reporting bureau
PA: Cbc Companies, Inc.
250 E Broad St Fl 21
Columbus OH 43215
614 222-4343

(G-5524)
CCI ENGINEERING
2323 W 5th Ave Ste 220 (43204-4899)
PHONE..................614 485-0670
EMP: 29 **EST**: 2019
SALES (est): 178.58K **Privately Held**
Web: www.ccitechs.com
SIC: 8621 Engineering association

(G-5525)
CDC MEDICAL
1300 Dublin Rd (43215-1093)
PHONE..................614 504-5511
Brad Infante, *Prin*
EMP: 50 **EST**: 2008
SALES (est): 288.68K **Privately Held**
Web: www.cdcmedical.com
SIC: 5047 Medical equipment and supplies

(G-5526)
CEMS OF OHIO INC
Also Called: MEDFLIGHT OF OHIO
2827 W Dublin Granville Rd (43235-2712)
PHONE..................614 751-6651
Thomas Allenstein, *CEO*
Michael Perkins, *COO*
Jennifer Costello, *CFO*
EMP: 497 **EST**: 2008
SALES (est): 21.43MM **Privately Held**
Web: www.medcareambulance.org
SIC: 4119 Ambulance service
PA: Ohio Medical Transportation, Inc.
2827 W Dblin Granville Rd
Columbus OH 43235

(G-5527)
CENCORA INC
1200 E 5th Ave (43219-2410)
P.O. Box 870 (43085-0870)
PHONE..................610 727-7000
EMP: 28
SALES (corp-wide): 262.17B **Publicly Held**
Web: www.cencora.com
SIC: 5122 Pharmaceuticals
PA: Cencora, Inc.
1 W 1st Ave
Conshohocken PA 19428
610 727-7000

(G-5528)
CENTENE CORPORATION
4349 Easton Way Ste 300 (43219-0001)
PHONE..................513 469-4500
EMP: 48
Web: www.centene.com
SIC: 6324 Hospital and medical service plans
PA: Centene Corporation
7700 Forsyth Blvd
Saint Louis MO 63105

(G-5529)
CENTER FOR CGNTIVE BHVRAL THRA (HQ)
Also Called: Kevin D Arnold
4624 Sawmill Rd (43220-2247)
PHONE..................614 459-4490
EMP: 30 **EST**: 1995
SALES (est): 5.11MM
SALES (corp-wide): 371.62B **Publicly Held**
Web: www.ccbtcolumbus.com
SIC: 8049 Clinical psychologist
PA: Unitedhealth Group Incorporated
9900 Bren Rd E
Minnetonka MN 55343
952 936-1300

(G-5530)
CENTER FOR COGNITV BEHAV PSYCH
4624 Sawmill Rd (43220-2247)
PHONE..................614 459-4490
Sarah Shearer, *Cncil Mbr*
EMP: 30 **EST**: 2015
SALES (est): 979.41K **Privately Held**
Web: www.ccbtcolumbus.com
SIC: 8322 Individual and family services

(G-5531)
CENTER FOR EATING DISORDERS
Also Called: CENTER FOR BALANCED LIVING, TH
8001 Ravines Edge Ct Ste 201 (43235-5423)
PHONE..................614 896-8222
Kelly Trautner, *Pr*
Cheryl Ryland, *
EMP: 42 **EST**: 2000
SALES (est): 2.06MM **Privately Held**
Web: www.centerforbalancedliving.org
SIC: 8052 8731 Home for the mentally retarded, with health care; Medical research, commercial

(G-5532)
CENTER FOR FMLY SAFETY HEALING
655 E Livingston Ave (43205-2618)
PHONE..................614 722-5985
EMP: 28 **EST**: 2018
SALES (est): 422.86K **Privately Held**
Web: www.familysafetyandhealing.org
SIC: 8049 Offices of health practitioner

(G-5533)
CENTER OF VOCTNL ALTRNTVS MNTL (PA)
Also Called: Cova
3770 N High St (43214-3525)
PHONE..................614 294-7117
Judy Braun, *Pr*
EMP: 63 **EST**: 1982
SQ FT: 3,500
SALES (est): 3.83MM
SALES (corp-wide): 3.83MM **Privately Held**
Web: www.covaagua.org
SIC: 8331 Vocational rehabilitation agency

GEOGRAPHIC SECTION — Columbus - Franklin County

(G-5534)
CENTRAL COMMUNITY HSE COLUMBUS (PA)
1150 E Main St (43205)
P.O. Box 7047 (43205)
PHONE.....................614 252-3157
Tamar Forrest, *Ex Dir*
Pamela Mccarthy, *Dir*
Alex Barkley, *Development**
Marci Ryan, **
Tami Hall, **
EMP: 28 **EST:** 1935
SQ FT: 1,500
SALES (est): 3.81MM
SALES (corp-wide): 3.81MM **Privately Held**
Web: www.cchouse.org
SIC: 8322 Social service center

(G-5535)
CENTRAL OHIO AREA AGCY ON AGIN
Also Called: PASSPORT
3776 S High St (43207-4012)
PHONE.....................614 645-7250
Cindy Farson, *Dir*
EMP: 178 **EST:** 1983
SALES (est): 31.41K **Privately Held**
Web: www.coaaa.org
SIC: 8322 Senior citizens' center or association

(G-5536)
CENTRAL OHIO BUILDING CO INC
Also Called: Thor Construction
3756 Agler Rd (43219-3699)
PHONE.....................614 475-6392
Otis Wilbur Ronk, *Pr*
Keith Hupp, **
Shirley Ronk, **
Floyd Swickard, **
C F O'brien, *Prin*
EMP: 35 **EST:** 1971
SQ FT: 2,000
SALES (est): 9.41MM **Privately Held**
SIC: 1542 1541 Institutional building construction; Industrial buildings, new construction, nec

(G-5537)
CENTRAL OHIO DIABETES ASSN
Also Called: Coda
1699 W Mound St (43223-1809)
PHONE.....................614 884-4400
Jeanne Grothaus, *Ex Dir*
Jeanne Grothaus, *Dir*
EMP: 27 **EST:** 1964
SALES (est): 2.39MM **Privately Held**
Web: www.lifecarealliance.org
SIC: 8621 Professional organizations

(G-5538)
CENTRAL OHIO GMING VNTURES LLC
Also Called: Hollywood Casino Columbus
200 Georgesville Rd (43228-2020)
PHONE.....................614 308-3333
Jacques Arragon, *Managing Member*
EMP: 100 **EST:** 2010
SALES (est): 23.62MM
SALES (corp-wide): 6.36B **Publicly Held**
Web: www.hollywoodcolumbus.com
SIC: 7011 Casino hotel
PA: Penn Entertainment, Inc.
825 Brkshire Blvd Ste 200
Wyomissing PA 19610
610 373-2400

(G-5539)
CENTRAL OHIO HOSPITALISTS
3525 Olentangy River Rd Ste 4330 (43214-3937)
PHONE.....................614 255-6900
Joseph A Mack, *Pr*
Nicholas Nelson, ,
EMP: 36 **EST:** 2000
SALES (est): 2.53MM **Privately Held**
Web: www.medonehp.com
SIC: 7363 Medical help service

(G-5540)
CENTRAL OHIO MEDICAL TEXTILES
Also Called: Comtex
575 Harmon Ave (43223-2449)
PHONE.....................614 453-9274
Ken Boock, *Ch*
Myles Noel, **
Becky Davis, **
EMP: 150 **EST:** 2002
SQ FT: 100,000
SALES (est): 15.36MM **Privately Held**
Web: www.comtexlaundry.com
SIC: 7219 Laundry, except power and coin-operated

(G-5541)
CENTRAL OHIO PRIMARY CARE
3535 Olentangy River Rd (43214-3908)
PHONE.....................614 268-8164
Jonathan Matthew Enlow, *Prin*
EMP: 29
Web: www.copcp.com
SIC: 8011 General and family practice, physician/surgeon
PA: Central Ohio Primary Care Physicians, Inc.
655 Africa Rd
Westerville OH 43082

(G-5542)
CENTRAL OHIO PRMRY CARE PHYSCA
4030 Henderson Rd (43220-2287)
PHONE.....................614 442-7550
EMP: 72
Web: www.copcp.com
SIC: 8049 8011 Acupuncturist; Offices and clinics of medical doctors
PA: Central Ohio Primary Care Physicians, Inc.
655 Africa Rd
Westerville OH 43082

(G-5543)
CENTRAL OHIO PRMRY CARE PHYSCA
Also Called: Copc-Radiology
4885 Olentangy River Rd (43214-1952)
PHONE.....................614 451-9229
Tom Jevas, *Mgr*
EMP: 101
Web: www.copcp.com
SIC: 8011 General and family practice, physician/surgeon
PA: Central Ohio Primary Care Physicians, Inc.
655 Africa Rd
Westerville OH 43082

(G-5544)
CENTRAL OHIO PRMRY CARE PHYSCA
Also Called: Capital City Medical Assoc
2489 Stelzer Rd # 101 (43219-4007)
PHONE.....................614 473-1300
Sheryl Moyer, *Mgr*
EMP: 101
Web: www.copcp.com
SIC: 8011 General and family practice, physician/surgeon
PA: Central Ohio Primary Care Physicians, Inc.
655 Africa Rd
Westerville OH 43082

(G-5545)
CENTRAL OHIO TRANSIT AUTHORITY
1333 Fields Ave (43201-2908)
PHONE.....................614 275-5800
Doug Moore, *Brnch Mgr*
EMP: 49
SALES (corp-wide): 103.48MM **Privately Held**
Web: www.cota.com
SIC: 4111 Bus line operations
PA: Central Ohio Transit Authority
33 N High St
Columbus OH 43215
614 275-5800

(G-5546)
CENTRAL OHIO TRANSIT AUTHORITY (PA)
Also Called: Cota
33 N High St (43215)
PHONE.....................614 275-5800
W Curtis Stitt, *Pr*
EMP: 600 **EST:** 1973
SQ FT: 390,000
SALES (est): 103.48MM
SALES (corp-wide): 103.48MM **Privately Held**
Web: www.cota.com
SIC: 4111 Bus line operations

(G-5547)
CENTRAL OHIO TRANSIT AUTHORITY
Also Called: Cota
1600 Mckinley Ave (43222-1002)
PHONE.....................614 228-1776
EMP: 49
SALES (corp-wide): 103.48MM **Privately Held**
Web: www.cota.com
SIC: 4111 Bus line operations
PA: Central Ohio Transit Authority
33 N High St
Columbus OH 43215
614 275-5800

(G-5548)
CENTRAL OHIO TRANSIT AUTHORITY
Also Called: Customer Service
33 N High St Ste 749 (43215-3076)
PHONE.....................614 275-5800
Terry Elder, *Mgr*
EMP: 49
SALES (corp-wide): 103.48MM **Privately Held**
Web: www.cota.com
SIC: 4111 Bus line operations
PA: Central Ohio Transit Authority
33 N High St
Columbus OH 43215
614 275-5800

(G-5549)
CENTRAL PARKING SYSTEM OF OHIO
Also Called: Central Parking System
107 S High St Ste 400 (43215-3456)
PHONE.....................614 224-1320
EMP: 109
SALES (corp-wide): 1.55B **Privately Held**
SIC: 7521 Parking lots
HQ: Central Parking System Of Ohio Inc
507 Mainstream Dr
Nashville TN 37228

(G-5550)
CH RELTY IV/CLMBUS PARTNERS LP
Also Called: Doubletree Columbus Hotel
175 Hutchinson Ave (43235-1413)
PHONE.....................614 885-3334
Dan Ouellette, *Mgr*
EMP: 100
SQ FT: 44,962
Web: www.crowholdings.com
SIC: 7011 6512 5813 5812 Hotels and motels; Nonresidential building operators; Drinking places; Eating places
PA: Ch Realty Iv/Columbus Partners, L.P.
3819 Maple Ave
Dallas TX 75219

(G-5551)
CHARTER COMMUNICATIONS
1600 Dublin Rd Ste 800 (43215-2872)
PHONE.....................614 588-5036
EMP: 33 **EST:** 2018
SALES (est): 674.67K **Privately Held**
Web: corporate.charter.com
SIC: 4841 Cable television services

(G-5552)
CHASE MANHATTAN MORTGAGE CORP
Also Called: Chase Manhattan
200 E Campus View Blvd 3rd Fl (43235-4678)
PHONE.....................614 422-7982
Caidy Patricia, *Brnch Mgr*
EMP: 127
SALES (corp-wide): 239.43B **Publicly Held**
SIC: 6162 Mortgage bankers
HQ: Chase Manhattan Mortgage Corp
343 Thornall St Ste 7
Edison NJ 08837
732 205-0600

(G-5553)
CHASE MANHATTAN MORTGAGE CORP
Also Called: Chase Manhattan
3415 Vision Dr (43219-6009)
PHONE.....................614 422-6900
Beverly Berry, *Brnch Mgr*
EMP: 1219
SALES (corp-wide): 239.43B **Publicly Held**
SIC: 6021 National commercial banks
HQ: Chase Manhattan Mortgage Corp
343 Thornall St Ste 7
Edison NJ 08837
732 205-0600

(G-5554)
CHESROWN OLDSMOBILE GMC INC
Also Called: Chessrown Kia Town
4675 Karl Rd (43229-6456)
P.O. Box 160 (43015-0160)
PHONE.....................614 846-3040
Jim Gill, *Pr*
EMP: 33 **EST:** 1963
SQ FT: 55,000
SALES (est): 1.63MM **Privately Held**
Web: www.gm.com
SIC: 5511 7532 7515 5531 Automobiles, new and used; Top and body repair and paint shops; Passenger car leasing; Auto and home supply stores

Columbus - Franklin County (G-5555) — GEOGRAPHIC SECTION

(G-5555)
CHILD DEV CNCIL FRNKLIN CNTY I
398 S Grant Ave (43215-5549)
PHONE..............................614 221-1694
Mattie James, *Prin*
EMP: 78
SALES (corp-wide): 34.19MM **Privately Held**
Web: www.cdcheadstart.org
SIC: 8351 Head Start center, except in conjunction with school
PA: Child Development Council Of Franklin County, Inc.
999 Crupper Ave
Columbus OH 43229
614 221-1709

(G-5556)
CHILD DEV CNCIL FRNKLIN CNTY I
Also Called: Cdcscn Linden
1718 E Cooke Rd (43224-5213)
PHONE..............................614 262-8190
Mattie James, *Dir*
EMP: 39
SALES (est): 34.19MM **Privately Held**
Web: www.cdcheadstart.org
SIC: 8351 Head Start center, except in conjunction with school
PA: Child Development Council Of Franklin County, Inc.
999 Crupper Ave
Columbus OH 43229
614 221-1709

(G-5557)
CHILD DEV CNCIL FRNKLIN CNTY I (PA)
999 Crupper Ave (43229)
PHONE..............................614 221-1709
Brenda Rivers, *Pr*
Mattie James, *
Greg Watson, *
Staci Kitchen, *
David Bresnen, *
EMP: 60 **EST:** 1985
SALES (est): 34.19MM
SALES (corp-wide): 34.19MM **Privately Held**
Web: www.cdcheadstart.org
SIC: 8351 Head Start center, except in conjunction with school

(G-5558)
CHILD DEV CNCIL FRNKLIN CNTY I
Also Called: Cdc Capital Park Head St Ctr
2150 Agler Rd (43224-4523)
PHONE..............................614 416-5178
EMP: 68
SALES (corp-wide): 34.19MM **Privately Held**
Web: www.cdcheadstart.org
SIC: 8351 Head Start center, except in conjunction with school
PA: Child Development Council Of Franklin County, Inc.
999 Crupper Ave
Columbus OH 43229
614 221-1709

(G-5559)
CHILD DEV CNCIL FRNKLIN CNTY I
Also Called: Cdc Marburn Head Start Ctr
4141 Rudy Rd (43214-2943)
PHONE..............................614 457-2811
EMP: 68
SALES (corp-wide): 34.19MM **Privately Held**
Web: www.cdcheadstart.org
SIC: 8351 Head Start center, except in conjunction with school

PA: Child Development Council Of Franklin County, Inc.
999 Crupper Ave
Columbus OH 43229
614 221-1709

(G-5560)
CHILDHOOD LEAGUE CENT
674 Cleveland Ave (43215-1775)
PHONE..............................614 253-6933
EMP: 40 **EST:** 2018
SALES (est): 3.57MM **Privately Held**
Web: www.childhoodleague.org
SIC: 8699 Charitable organization

(G-5561)
CHILDRENS ANESTHESIA ASSOC INC
700 Childrens Dr (43205-2664)
PHONE..............................614 722-4200
Peter D Winch, *Prin*
EMP: 41 **EST:** 2011
SALES (est): 903.72K **Privately Held**
Web: www.nationwidechildrens.org
SIC: 8011 Pediatrician

(G-5562)
CHILDRENS HOSP REFERENCE LAB
Also Called: Reference Laboratory
525 Kennedy Dr (43215-5528)
PHONE..............................614 722-5477
Sharryl Hamon, *Mgr*
EMP: 49 **EST:** 1985
SALES (est): 3.24MM **Privately Held**
SIC: 8071 8731 Medical laboratories; Commercial physical research

(G-5563)
CHILDRENS HOSPITAL INC
154 W 12th Ave (43210-1302)
PHONE..............................614 355-0616
Mariah Barnes, *Ofcr*
EMP: 59 **EST:** 2014
SALES (est): 39.4MM **Privately Held**
Web: www.nationwidechildrens.org
SIC: 8069 Childrens' hospital

(G-5564)
CHILDRENS HUNGER ALLIANCE (PA)
1105 Schrock Rd Ste 505 (43229-1181)
PHONE..............................614 341-7700
Judy Mobley, *Pr*
EMP: 40 **EST:** 1973
SQ FT: 5,900
SALES (est): 14.77MM
SALES (corp-wide): 14.77MM **Privately Held**
Web: www.childrenshungeralliance.org
SIC: 8322 8399 Social service center; Advocacy group

(G-5565)
CHILDRENS RDIOLOGICAL INST INC
700 Childrens Dr (43205-2664)
PHONE..............................614 722-2363
EMP: 2381 **EST:** 1995
SALES (est): 2.04MM
SALES (corp-wide): 3.6B **Privately Held**
Web: www.nationwidechildrens.org
SIC: 8011 Radiologist
PA: Nationwide Children's Hospital
700 Childrens Dr
Columbus OH 43205
614 722-2000

(G-5566)
CHILLER LLC
200 W Nationwide Blvd (43215-2561)
PHONE..............................614 246-3380

David A Paitson, *Brnch Mgr*
EMP: 38
SALES (corp-wide): 4.89MM **Privately Held**
Web: www.thechiller.com
SIC: 7997 Membership sports and recreation clubs
PA: Chiller Llc
7001 Dublin Park Dr
Dublin OH 43016
614 764-1000

(G-5567)
CHILLER LLC
3600 Chiller Ln (43219-6026)
PHONE..............................614 475-7575
EMP: 39
SALES (corp-wide): 4.89MM **Privately Held**
Web: www.thechiller.com
SIC: 7999 Ice skating rink operation
PA: Chiller Llc
7001 Dublin Park Dr
Dublin OH 43016
614 764-1000

(G-5568)
CHOICE RECOVERY INC
1105 Schrock Rd Ste 700 (43229-1168)
P.O. Box 59013 (37950-9013)
PHONE..............................614 358-9900
Chad Silverstein, *Pr*
EMP: 93 **EST:** 1997
SALES (est): 7.01MM **Privately Held**
Web: www.wakeassoc.com
SIC: 7322 Collection agency, except real estate

(G-5569)
CHRIST KING CATHOLIC CHURCH
Also Called: All Saints Academy Pre School
2855 E Livingston Ave (43209-3041)
PHONE..............................614 236-8838
Tierra Morefield, *Dir*
EMP: 36
SALES (corp-wide): 38.56MM **Privately Held**
Web: www.usccb.org
SIC: 8661 8351 Catholic Church; Preschool center
HQ: King Christ Catholic Church
2777 E Livingston Ave
Columbus OH 43209

(G-5570)
CHRISTIAN MISSIONARY ALLIANCE
Also Called: Sunshine Nursery School
3750 Henderson Rd (43220-2236)
PHONE..............................614 457-4085
Jennifer Rupert, *Dir*
EMP: 28
SALES (corp-wide): 88.61MM **Privately Held**
Web: www.sunshinelearning.center
SIC: 8351 Preschool center
PA: The Christian Missionary Alliance
6421 E Main St
Reynoldsburg OH 43068
380 208-6200

(G-5571)
CHRISTIAN WORTHINGTON VLG INC
165 Highbluffs Blvd (43235-1484)
PHONE..............................614 846-6076
EMP: 56 **EST:** 2010
SALES (est): 3.18MM **Privately Held**
Web: www.wcv.org
SIC: 8361 Aged home

(G-5572)
CINTAS CORPORATION NO 2
Also Called: Cintas
1300 Boltonfield St (43228-3696)
P.O. Box 28246 (43228-0246)
PHONE..............................614 878-7313
John Borak, *Brnch Mgr*
EMP: 72
SALES (corp-wide): 8.82B **Publicly Held**
Web: www.cintas.com
SIC: 5084 7218 Safety equipment; Industrial launderers
HQ: Cintas Corporation No 2
6800 Cintas Blvd
Mason OH 45040

(G-5573)
CIRCLE BUILDING SERVICES INC (PA)
742 Harmon Ave (43223-2450)
P.O. Box 1473 (43216-1473)
PHONE..............................614 228-6090
Daniel M Litzinger, *Pr*
EMP: 43 **EST:** 1969
SALES (est): 2.62MM
SALES (corp-wide): 2.62MM **Privately Held**
Web: www.circlebuildingservices.com
SIC: 7349 Building cleaning service

(G-5574)
CIRCLE BUILDING SERVICES INC
793 Harmon Ave (43223-2411)
PHONE..............................614 228-6090
EMP: 47
SALES (corp-wide): 2.62MM **Privately Held**
Web: www.circlebuildingservices.com
SIC: 7349 Janitorial service, contract basis
PA: Circle Building Services, Inc.
742 Harmon Ave
Columbus OH 43223
614 228-6090

(G-5575)
CITICORP CREDIT SERVICES INC
Also Called: Citicorp
1500 Boltonfield St (43228-3669)
PHONE..............................212 559-1000
Ken Vanderoef, *Mgr*
EMP: 288
SALES (corp-wide): 156.82B **Publicly Held**
Web: www.citigroup.com
SIC: 7389 Credit card service
HQ: Citicorp Credit Services, Inc.
6460 Las Colinas Blvd
Irving TX 75039
469 220-5517

(G-5576)
CITY OF COLUMBUS
Also Called: Dept of Public Utilities
910 Dublin Rd Ste 4050 (43215-1169)
PHONE..............................614 645-7490
Danella Pettenski, *Brnch Mgr*
EMP: 35
SALES (corp-wide): 2.01B **Privately Held**
Web: new.columbus.gov
SIC: 4941 Water supply
PA: City Of Columbus
90 W Broad St Rm B33
Columbus OH 43215
614 645-7671

(G-5577)
CKE ACQUISITION CO LLC
10 W Broad St Ste 2100 (43215-3455)
PHONE..............................614 205-0242
EMP: 36 **EST:** 2021
SALES (est): 1.87MM **Privately Held**

GEOGRAPHIC SECTION
Columbus - Franklin County (G-5600)

SIC: 6799 Investors, nec

(G-5578)
CKS & ASSOCIATES MGT LLC
399 S Grant Ave (43215-5555)
PHONE.................................614 621-9710
EMP: 44
SIC: 8741 Management services
PA: Cks & Associates Management, Llc
4101 Baltimore Ave
Philadelphia PA 19104

(G-5579)
CLAPROOD ROMAN J CO
242 N Grant Ave (43215-2642)
PHONE.................................614 221-5515
Floyd R Claprood Senior, Pr
F Raymond Claprood Junior, VP
EMP: 30 EST: 1939
SQ FT: 25,000
SALES (est): 2.52MM Privately Held
Web: www.rjclaprood.com
SIC: 5193 Flowers, fresh

(G-5580)
CLAREMONT RETIREMENT VILLAGE
7041 Bent Tree Blvd (43235)
PHONE.................................614 761-2011
Clare Kilar, Pt
EMP: 70 EST: 1987
SALES (est): 5MM Privately Held
Web: www.crvillage.com
SIC: 6513 Retirement hotel operation

(G-5581)
CLEAN INNOVATIONS (PA)
Also Called: Columbus Jan Healthnet Svcs
575 E 11th Ave (43211-2605)
P.O. Box 11399 (43211-0399)
PHONE.................................614 299-1187
Howard Cohen, Pr
Annette Cohen, *
Susan Cohen Ungar, *
EMP: 27 EST: 1950
SQ FT: 26,000
SALES (est): 4.98MM
SALES (corp-wide): 4.98MM Privately Held
Web: www.clean-innovations.com
SIC: 5087 Janitors' supplies

(G-5582)
CLEARY COMPANY
989a Old Henderson Rd (43220-3722)
PHONE.................................614 459-4000
George B Cleary, Pr
Catherine Cleary, *
EMP: 27 EST: 1994
SALES (est): 8.53MM Privately Held
Web: www.clearycompany.com
SIC: 1521 7389 General remodeling, single-family houses; Business Activities at Non-Commercial Site

(G-5583)
CLEVELAND CLINIC FOUNDATION
Also Called: Cleveland Clinic Star Imaging
425 Beecher Rd Ste B (43230-6778)
PHONE.................................614 358-4223
George Kafiti, Prin
EMP: 41
SALES (corp-wide): 14.48B Privately Held
Web: www.clevelandclinic.org
SIC: 8099 8031 8011 Blood related health services; Offices and clinics of osteopathic physicians; Offices and clinics of medical doctors
PA: The Cleveland Clinic Foundation
9500 Euclid Ave
Cleveland OH 44195
216 636-8335

(G-5584)
CLEVELAND GLASS BLOCK INC
Also Called: Columbus Glass Block
3091 E 14th Ave (43219-2356)
PHONE.................................614 252-5888
John Krulcik, Mgr
EMP: 32
SALES (corp-wide): 3.12MM Privately Held
Web: www.innovatebuildingsolutions.com
SIC: 5231 5039 Glass; Glass construction materials
PA: Cleveland Glass Block, Inc.
4566 E 71st St
Cleveland OH 44105
216 531-6363

(G-5585)
CLINTNVLLE BCHWOLD CMNTY RSRCE
Also Called: CRC
3222 N High St (43202-1114)
PHONE.................................614 268-3539
Stephanie Baker, Ex Dir
William Owen, *
John H Hamilton, *
Phillip Moots, *
Judith Jones, *
EMP: 50 EST: 1971
SQ FT: 4,000
SALES (est): 5.15MM Privately Held
Web: www.clintonvillecrc.org
SIC: 8322 Community center

(G-5586)
CLM PALLET RECYCLING INC
4311 Janitrol Rd Ste 150 (43228-1389)
PHONE.................................614 272-5761
Steve Foor, Brnch Mgr
EMP: 85
Web: www.clmpallet.com
SIC: 4953 Recycling, waste materials
PA: Clm Pallet Recycling, Inc.
3103 W 1000 N
Fortville IN 46040

(G-5587)
CLOUDBREAK HEALTH LLC
6400 Huntley Rd (43229-1043)
PHONE.................................614 468-6110
Jamey Edwards, CEO
Eric Gombrich, Ex VP
Andy Panos, COO
EMP: 59 EST: 2017
SALES (est): 5.21MM Privately Held
Web: www.cloudbreak.health
SIC: 8099 Health and allied services, nec

(G-5588)
COASTAL RIDGE MANAGEMENT LLC
Also Called: Coastal Ridge Real Estate
80 E Rich St Ste 220 (43215-5764)
PHONE.................................614 339-4608
Mark Yale, CFO
EMP: 363 EST: 2016
SALES (est): 25.85MM Privately Held
Web: www.coastalridgere.com
SIC: 6531 Real estate brokers and agents

(G-5589)
COAXIAL CMMNCTONS OF STHERN OH (PA)
700 Ackerman Rd Ste 280 (43202-1559)
PHONE.................................513 797-3400
W Edward Wood, Pr
W Edward Wood, Pr
Dennis J Mc Gillicuddy, *
D Steven Mc Voy, *
Art Loescher, *
EMP: 55 EST: 1985
SALES (est): 4.42MM
SALES (corp-wide): 4.42MM Privately Held
SIC: 4841 Cable television services

(G-5590)
COBA/SELECT SIRES INC (PA)
1224 Alton Darby Creek Rd (43228-9792)
PHONE.................................614 878-5333
Duane Logan, Pr
Kim M House, *
EMP: 54 EST: 1946
SQ FT: 15,000
SALES (est): 10.25MM
SALES (corp-wide): 10.25MM Privately Held
Web: www.cobaselect.com
SIC: 0752 Artificial insemination services, animal specialties

(G-5591)
CODEX TECHWORKS INC
1500 W 3rd Ave (43212-2843)
PHONE.................................614 486-9900
EMP: 46 EST: 2009
SALES (est): 2.96MM Privately Held
Web: www.codextechworks.com
SIC: 7379 Computer related consulting services

(G-5592)
COLDLINER EXPRESS INC
Also Called: Coldliner Express
4921 Vulcan Ave (43228)
P.O. Box 28767 (43228)
PHONE.................................614 570-0836
Marci S Hinton, Pr
Douglas Abel, *
EMP: 100 EST: 2005
SQ FT: 5,000
SALES (est): 28.57MM Privately Held
Web: www.coldlinerexpress.com
SIC: 4789 Cargo loading and unloading services

(G-5593)
COLDWELL BANKER RESIDENTIAL
Also Called: Coldwell Banker
5975 Cleveland Ave (43231-2256)
PHONE.................................954 771-2600
Mark Ivens, Brnch Mgr
EMP: 33
Web: www.coldwellbanker.com
SIC: 6531 Real estate agent, residential
HQ: Coldwell Banker Residential
5971 Cattleridge Blvd # 202
Sarasota FL 34232
941 487-1400

(G-5594)
COLIA GROUP LLC
3271 Kady Ln (43232-7455)
PHONE.................................614 270-4545
Ibrahim Ibrahim, Prin
Kamil Mohamed, *
EMP: 50 EST: 2017
SALES (est): 1.1MM Privately Held
SIC: 8748 Business consulting, nec

(G-5595)
COLLECTIONS ACQUISITION CO LLC
Also Called: Payliance
2 Easton Oval Ste 210 (43219-6036)
PHONE.................................614 944-5788
John M Cullen Junior, Brnch Mgr
EMP: 103
SALES (corp-wide): 24.24MM Privately Held
Web: www.payliance.com
SIC: 7389 Credit card service
PA: Collections Acquisition Company, Inc.
2 Easton Oval Ste 310
Columbus OH 43219
614 944-5788

(G-5596)
COLLECTOR WELLS INTL INC
6360 Huntley Rd (43229-1008)
PHONE.................................614 888-6263
Sam Stowe, Pr
Mark Nilges, *
Andrew Smith, *
James French, *
Henry Hunt, *
EMP: 65 EST: 1998
SALES (est): 2.75MM Publicly Held
Web: www.graniteconstruction.com
SIC: 1781 Water well drilling
HQ: Layne Christensen Company
9303 New Trls Dr Ste 200
Spring TX 77381
281 475-2600

(G-5597)
COLLIERS INTERNATIONAL
2 Miranova Pl Ste 900 (43215-7054)
PHONE.................................614 436-9800
Kevin James, Prin
EMP: 31 EST: 2014
SALES (est): 4.53MM
SALES (corp-wide): 4.46B Privately Held
SIC: 8742 Real estate consultant
HQ: Colliers International Property Consultants, Inc.
601 Union St Ste 5300
Seattle WA 98101

(G-5598)
COLUMBIA GAS OF OHIO INC (HQ)
Also Called: Columbia
290 W Nationwide Blvd Unit 114 (43215-1082)
P.O. Box 117 (43216-0117)
PHONE.................................614 460-6000
Jack Partridge, Pr
Devit Vajda, CRO
Robert Heidorn, Pr
EMP: 30 EST: 1951
SQ FT: 50,000
SALES (est): 557.39MM
SALES (corp-wide): 5.51B Publicly Held
Web: www.columbiagasohio.com
SIC: 4924 Natural gas distribution
PA: Nisource Inc.
801 E 86th Ave
Merrillville IN 46410
877 647-5990

(G-5599)
COLUMBIA GAS OF OHIO INC
Also Called: Columbia
601 Manor Park Dr (43228-9522)
PHONE.................................614 878-6015
EMP: 81
SALES (corp-wide): 5.51B Publicly Held
Web: www.columbiagasohio.com
SIC: 4924 Natural gas distribution
HQ: Columbia Gas Of Ohio, Inc.
290 W Nationwide Blvd # 1
Columbus OH 43215
614 460-6000

(G-5600)
COLUMBIA GAS OF OHIO INC
Also Called: Columbia
290 W Nationwide Blvd (43215-1082)
P.O. Box 2318 (43216-2318)
PHONE.................................614 481-1000
Gary Schuler, Prin

Columbus - Franklin County (G-5601)

EMP: 149
SALES (corp-wide): 5.51B **Publicly Held**
Web: www.columbiagasohio.com
SIC: 4924 Natural gas distribution
HQ: Columbia Gas Of Ohio, Inc.
290 W Nationwide Blvd # 1
Columbus OH 43215
614 460-6000

(G-5601)
COLUMBIA GAS OF OHIO INC
Also Called: Columbia
200 Civic Center Dr Ste 110 (43215-7510)
PHONE 614 460-6000
EMP: 116
SALES (corp-wide): 5.51B **Publicly Held**
Web: www.columbiagasohio.com
SIC: 4924 Natural gas distribution
HQ: Columbia Gas Of Ohio, Inc.
290 W Nationwide Blvd # 1
Columbus OH 43215
614 460-6000

(G-5602)
COLUMBIA GAS OF OHIO INC
Also Called: Columbia
3550 Johnny Appleseed Ct (43231-4985)
PHONE 614 818-2101
W Frank Davis Junior, *Mgr*
EMP: 98
SALES (corp-wide): 5.51B **Publicly Held**
Web: www.columbiagasohio.com
SIC: 4924 Natural gas distribution
HQ: Columbia Gas Of Ohio, Inc.
290 W Nationwide Blvd # 1
Columbus OH 43215
614 460-6000

(G-5603)
COLUMBIA GAS TRANSMISSION LLC
Also Called: Columbia Energy
290 W Nationwide Blvd Unit 114 (43215-1082)
PHONE 614 460-4704
EMP: 32
SALES (corp-wide): 11.6B **Privately Held**
Web: www.columbiaenergygroup.com
SIC: 4924 Natural gas distribution
HQ: Columbia Gas Transmission, Llc
700 Louisiana St
Houston TX 77002
614 460-6000

(G-5604)
COLUMBIA GULF TRANSMISSION LLC
200 Civic Center Dr (43215-7510)
PHONE 614 460-6991
EMP: 61
SALES (corp-wide): 11.6B **Privately Held**
SIC: 4924 Natural gas distribution
HQ: Columbia Gulf Transmission, Llc
700 Louisiana St
Houston TX 77002
877 287-1782

(G-5605)
COLUMBS/WORTHINGTON HTG AC INC
Also Called: Columbus/Worthington Htg & AC
6363 Fiesta Dr (43235-5202)
PHONE 614 771-5381
Jeff Ford, *Pr*
George Petty, *
EMP: 45 **EST:** 1999
SQ FT: 22,400
SALES (est): 8.43MM
SALES (corp-wide): 1.52B **Privately Held**
Web: www.cwaohio.com
SIC: 1711 7623 7699 Warm air heating and air conditioning contractor; Air conditioning repair; Boiler and heating repair services
PA: American Residential Services Llc
965 Ridge Lake Blvd # 201
Memphis TN 38120
901 271-9700

(G-5606)
COLUMBUS AIRPORT LTD PARTNR
Also Called: Columbus Airport Marriott
1375 N Cassady Ave (43219-1524)
PHONE 614 475-7551
Janet Rhodes, *Prin*
EMP: 160 **EST:** 1988
SQ FT: 220,000
SALES (est): 8.59MM **Privately Held**
Web: www.columbusairportmarriott.com
SIC: 7011 5813 5812 Hotels; Drinking places; Eating places

(G-5607)
COLUMBUS ALZHEIMERS CARE CTR
700 Jasonway Ave (43214-2458)
PHONE 614 459-7050
Monica Wiess, *Admn*
Tonia Hoak, *
EMP: 73 **EST:** 1991
SQ FT: 41,654
SALES (est): 5.96MM **Privately Held**
Web: www.columbusalzheimercenter.com
SIC: 8059 8051 Nursing home, except skilled and intermediate care facility; Skilled nursing care facilities

(G-5608)
COLUMBUS ALZHEIMERS OPER LLC
Also Called: Columbus Alzheimers
700 Jasonway Ave (43214-2458)
PHONE 614 459-7050
Joseph Hazelbaker, *Prin*
Brian Hazelbaker, *Prin*
Ralph Hazelbaker, *Prin*
EMP: 90 **EST:** 2020
SALES (est): 2.6MM **Privately Held**
SIC: 8059 Nursing and personal care, nec

(G-5609)
COLUMBUS ARPRT N CSSADY HT LLC
Also Called: Columbus Airport Marriott
1375 N Cassady Ave (43219-1524)
PHONE 614 475-7551
Christopher Pawelko, *VP*
EMP: 99
SALES (est): 900.37K **Privately Held**
SIC: 7011 Hotels and motels

(G-5610)
COLUMBUS ARTHRITIS CENTER INC
Also Called: Columbus Arthritis Center
1211 Dublin Rd (43215-1077)
P.O. Box 2097 (43086-2097)
PHONE 614 486-5200
Sterling W Hedrick Md, *Pr*
EMP: 54 **EST:** 1995
SALES (est): 9.59MM **Privately Held**
Web: www.columbusarthritis.com
SIC: 8011 Internal medicine, physician/surgeon

(G-5611)
COLUMBUS ASPHALT PAVING INC
5715 Westbourne Ave (43213-1449)
PHONE 614 759-9800
David J Power, *Pr*
Doug Lindsey, *
EMP: 40 **EST:** 1975
SQ FT: 5,200
SALES (est): 8.76MM **Privately Held**
Web: www.columbusasphalt.com
SIC: 1611 Highway and street paving contractor

(G-5612)
COLUMBUS ASSN FOR PRFRMG ARTS (PA)
21 E Main St (43215-5115)
PHONE 614 469-1045
EMP: 48 **EST:** 2010
SALES (est): 2.46MM **Privately Held**
Web: www.capa.com
SIC: 7922 Legitimate live theater producers

(G-5613)
COLUMBUS ASSN FOR THE PRFRMG A (PA)
Also Called: Capa
55 E State St (43215-4203)
PHONE 614 469-1045
William B Conner Junior, *Pr*
Stephanie E Green, *
Barbara B Lach, *
▲ **EMP:** 705 **EST:** 1969
SALES (est): 5.05MM
SALES (corp-wide): 5.05MM **Privately Held**
Web: www.capa.com
SIC: 7922 Legitimate live theater producers

(G-5614)
COLUMBUS ASSN FOR THE PRFRMG A
39 E State St (43215-4203)
PHONE 614 469-0939
William Conner, *Dir*
EMP: 352
SALES (corp-wide): 5.05MM **Privately Held**
Web: www.capa.com
SIC: 7922 7929 Legitimate live theater producers; Entertainers and entertainment groups
PA: The Columbus Association For The Performing Arts
55 E State St
Columbus OH 43215
614 469-1045

(G-5615)
COLUMBUS BAR ASSOCIATION
175 S 3rd St Ste 1100 (43215-5197)
PHONE 614 221-4112
Alex Lagusch, *Dir*
EMP: 46 **EST:** 1869
SALES (est): 2.55MM **Privately Held**
Web: www.cbalaw.org
SIC: 8621 Bar association

(G-5616)
COLUMBUS CANCER CLINIC INC
1699 W Mound St (43223-1809)
PHONE 614 263-5006
Ron Hammond, *Ex Dir*
Charity Hall, *Mgr*
EMP: 29 **EST:** 1921
SALES (est): 427.61K **Privately Held**
Web: www.lifecarealliance.org
SIC: 8011 Oncologist

(G-5617)
COLUMBUS CENTER FOR HUMAN SVCS
Also Called: Columbus Center For Human Serv
540 Industrial Mile Rd (43228-2413)
PHONE 614 278-9362
EMP: 140
SALES (corp-wide): 19.22MM **Privately Held**
SIC: 8052 Intermediate care facilities
PA: Columbus Center For Human Services Inc
540 Industrial Mile Rd
Columbus OH 43228
614 641-2900

(G-5618)
COLUMBUS CHAMBER OF COMMERCE
150 S Front St Ste 220 (43215-7107)
PHONE 614 225-6943
EMP: 43 **EST:** 2017
SALES (est): 1.1MM **Privately Held**
Web: www.columbus.org
SIC: 8611 Chamber of Commerce

(G-5619)
COLUMBUS CHRISTIAN CENTER INC (PA)
Also Called: Faith Christian Accademy
2300 N Cassady Ave (43219-1508)
P.O. Box 24009 (43224-0009)
PHONE 614 416-9673
Pastor David C Forbes, *Prin*
EMP: 40 **EST:** 1990
SALES (est): 2.25MM **Privately Held**
Web: www.faithstadium.org
SIC: 8661 8351 Non-denominational church; Child day care services

(G-5620)
COLUMBUS CITY SCHOOL DISTRICT
Also Called: Heads Start Program
1077 Lexington Ave (43201-2936)
PHONE 614 421-2305
EMP: 35
SALES (corp-wide): 966.92MM **Privately Held**
Web: www.columbus.k12.oh.us
SIC: 8351 Preschool center
PA: Columbus City School District
270 E State St Fl 3
Columbus OH 43215
614 365-5000

(G-5621)
COLUMBUS CITY SCHOOL DISTRICT
Also Called: Cassady Altrntive Elmntary Sch
2500 N Cassady Ave (43219-1514)
PHONE 614 365-5456
Natasha Shaefer, *Prin*
EMP: 68
SALES (corp-wide): 966.92MM **Privately Held**
Web: www.ccsoh.us
SIC: 8211 8351 Public elementary school; Preschool center
PA: Columbus City School District
270 E State St Fl 3
Columbus OH 43215
614 365-5000

(G-5622)
COLUMBUS CITY SCHOOL DISTRICT
Also Called: Columbus Pub Schl Vhcl Maint
889 E 17th Ave (43211-2492)
PHONE 614 365-5263
Phil Downs, *Mgr*
EMP: 34
SALES (corp-wide): 966.92MM **Privately Held**
Web: www.ccsoh.us
SIC: 5013 Automotive servicing equipment
PA: Columbus City School District
270 E State St Fl 3
Columbus OH 43215
614 365-5000

GEOGRAPHIC SECTION

Columbus - Franklin County (G-5644)

(G-5623)
COLUMBUS CITY SCHOOL DISTRICT
Also Called: Columbus Schl Dst Bus Compound
4001 Appian Way (43230-1469)
PHONE..................614 365-6542
EMP: 29
SALES (corp-wide): 966.92MM **Privately Held**
Web: www.ccsoh.us
SIC: 4111 Bus transportation
PA: Columbus City School District
270 E State St Fl 3
Columbus OH 43215
614 365-5000

(G-5624)
COLUMBUS COAL & LIME CO (PA)
Also Called: Granville Builders Supply
1150 Sullivant Ave (43223-1427)
P.O. Box 23156 (43223-0156)
PHONE..................614 224-9241
Katherine N Gatterdam, *CEO*
John Niermeyer, *
Rich Gatterdam, *
Diane Niermeyer, *
June Rees, *
EMP: 30 EST: 1911
SQ FT: 20,000
SALES (est): 9.65MM
SALES (corp-wide): 9.65MM **Privately Held**
Web: www.columbuscoal.com
SIC: 5032 5211 Sand, construction; Brick

(G-5625)
COLUMBUS CONCORD LTD PARTNR
Also Called: Courtyard By Marriott
35 W Spring St (43215-2215)
PHONE..................614 228-3200
Anne Turpin, *Genl Mgr*
Dan Peterson, *Mgr*
Bob Micklash, *CEO*
EMP: 99 EST: 1992
SALES (est): 1.39MM **Privately Held**
Web: courtyard.marriott.com
SIC: 7011 Hotels and motels

(G-5626)
COLUMBUS CTR FOR HUMN SVCS INC (PA)
Also Called: CCHS JOHNSTOWN HOME
540 Industrial Mile Rd (43228-2413)
PHONE..................614 641-2904
Rebecca Sharp, *CEO*
David Mccarty, *Brand President*
Brent Garland, *Board Vice President**
EMP: 145 EST: 1979
SQ FT: 32,000
SALES (est): 21.85MM
SALES (corp-wide): 21.85MM **Privately Held**
Web: www.opendoorcolumbus.org
SIC: 8059 Home for the mentally retarded, ex. skilled or intermediate

(G-5627)
COLUMBUS DERMATOLOGISTS-GRTR
3555 Olentangy River Rd Ste 4000 (43214-3915)
PHONE..................614 268-2748
Laura Crossan, *Off Mgr*
EMP: 27 EST: 2014
SALES (est): 600.01K **Privately Held**
Web: www.docsdermgroup.com
SIC: 8011 Dermatologist

(G-5628)
COLUMBUS DISTRIBUTING COMPANY (PA)
Also Called: Delmar Distributing
4949 Freeway Dr E (43229-5479)
PHONE..................614 846-1000
Paul Jenkins Junior, *Pr*
Paul A Jenkins Junior, *Pr*
Paul A Jenkins Senior, *Ch Bd*
Barbara Jenkins, *
Jeff Jenkins, *Prin*
▲ EMP: 210 EST: 1950
SQ FT: 130,000
SALES (est): 48.9MM
SALES (corp-wide): 48.9MM **Privately Held**
Web: www.columbusdistributing.com
SIC: 5181 Beer and other fermented malt liquors

(G-5629)
COLUMBUS EARLY LEARNING CTRS
East Side Center
162 N Ohio Ave (43203-1567)
PHONE..................614 253-5525
Sharon Graham, *Dir*
EMP: 50
SQ FT: 5,197
SALES (corp-wide): 2.68MM **Privately Held**
Web: www.columbusearlylearning.org
SIC: 8351 Preschool center
PA: Early Columbus Learning Centers
1611 Old Leonard Ave
Columbus OH 43219
614 253-5525

(G-5630)
COLUMBUS EASTON HOTEL LLC
Also Called: Residence Inn By Marriott
3999 Easton Loop W (43219-6152)
PHONE..................614 414-1000
Michael Gouzie, *Brnch Mgr*
EMP: 54
SALES (corp-wide): 24.09MM **Privately Held**
Web: www.hiltoncolumbus.com
SIC: 7011 Hotels and motels
PA: Columbus Easton Hotel Llc
3900 Chagrin Dr Fl 7
Columbus OH 43219
614 414-5000

(G-5631)
COLUMBUS EASTON HOTEL LLC
Also Called: Marriott
3999 Easton Loop W (43219-6152)
PHONE..................614 414-1000
Brad Gester, *Brnch Mgr*
EMP: 35
SALES (corp-wide): 24.09MM **Privately Held**
Web: www.hiltoncolumbus.com
SIC: 7011 Hotels
PA: Columbus Easton Hotel Llc
3900 Chagrin Dr Fl 7
Columbus OH 43219
614 414-5000

(G-5632)
COLUMBUS EASTON HOTEL LLC
3900 Morse Xing (43219-6081)
PHONE..................614 383-2005
Mort Olshan, *Brnch Mgr*
EMP: 63
SALES (corp-wide): 24.09MM **Privately Held**
Web: www.hiltoncolumbus.com
SIC: 7011 Hotels
PA: Columbus Easton Hotel Llc
3900 Chagrin Dr Fl 7
Columbus OH 43219
614 414-5000

(G-5633)
COLUMBUS EQUIPMENT COMPANY (PA)
Also Called: Kubota Authorized Dealer
2323 Performance Way (43207-2473)
PHONE..................614 437-0352
Josh Stivison, *Pr*
Ernie Potter, *
Tim Albright, *
▼ EMP: 43 EST: 1951
SQ FT: 12,000
SALES (est): 78.22MM
SALES (corp-wide): 78.22MM **Privately Held**
Web: www.columbusequipment.com
SIC: 5082 7353 General construction machinery and equipment; Heavy construction equipment rental

(G-5634)
COLUMBUS GREEN CABS INC (PA)
Also Called: Yellow Cabs
1989 Camaro Ave (43207-1716)
PHONE..................614 783-3663
Morgan Kauffman, *CEO*
Jeff Kates, *
Jeff R Glassman, *
EMP: 39 EST: 1928
SQ FT: 26,000
SALES (est): 4.88MM
SALES (corp-wide): 4.88MM **Privately Held**
Web: www.yellowcabofcolumbus.com
SIC: 4121 Taxicabs

(G-5635)
COLUMBUS HEATING & VENT CO
182 N Yale Ave (43222-1127)
PHONE..................614 274-1177
Charles R Gulley, *Pr*
Greogy Yoak, *
Mikel Plythe, *
Michael Blythe, *
EMP: 135 EST: 1874
SALES (est): 9.26MM **Privately Held**
Web: www.columbusheat.com
SIC: 1711 3585 Warm air heating and air conditioning contractor; Furnaces, warm air: electric

(G-5636)
COLUMBUS HILTON DOWNTOWN
401 N High St (43215-2005)
PHONE..................614 384-8600
EMP: 101 EST: 2012
SALES (est): 10.23MM **Privately Held**
Web: columbusdowntown.hilton.com
SIC: 7011 Hotels

(G-5637)
COLUMBUS HOME HEALTH SVCS LLC
1150 Morse Rd Ste 101 (43229-6335)
PHONE..................614 985-1464
EMP: 42 EST: 2010
SALES (est): 1.06MM **Privately Held**
Web: columbushomehealthservices.wordpress.com
SIC: 8082 Home health care services

(G-5638)
COLUMBUS HOSPITALITY LLC
775 Yard St Ste 180 (43212-3857)
PHONE..................614 461-2648
Charles Lagarce, *Managing Member*
EMP: 30 EST: 2001
SALES (est): 9.17MM **Privately Held**
Web: www.columbushospitality.com
Columbus OH 43219
614 414-5000

(G-5639)
COLUMBUS HOTEL PARTNERSHIP LLC
Also Called: Embassy Suites Columbus
2700 Corporate Exchange Dr (43231-1690)
PHONE..................614 890-8600
EMP: 51 EST: 2015
SALES (est): 2.68MM **Privately Held**
Web: www.hilton.com
SIC: 7011 Hotels and motels

(G-5640)
COLUMBUS HOUSING PARTNR INC
Also Called: C.H.P.
3443 Agler Rd Ste 200 (43219-3385)
PHONE..................614 221-8889
Bruce Luecke, *Pr*
Valorie Schwarzmann, *
EMP: 58 EST: 1987
SQ FT: 10,000
SALES (est): 9.89MM **Privately Held**
Web: www.homeportohio.org
SIC: 6552 Land subdividers and developers, residential

(G-5641)
COLUMBUS JEWISH FEDERATION
1175 College Ave (43209-2827)
PHONE..................614 237-7686
Marsha Hurowitz, *Pr*
Mitchell J Orlik, *VP*
Randy Arndt, *Treas*
Robert H Schottenstein, *Sec*
Donald Kelly, *CFO*
EMP: 42 EST: 1955
SQ FT: 15,000
SALES (est): 6.9MM **Privately Held**
Web: www.jewishcolumbus.org
SIC: 8399 Fund raising organization, non-fee basis

(G-5642)
COLUMBUS LEASING LLC
Also Called: Crowne Plaza Columbus North
6500 Doubletree Ave (43229-1111)
PHONE..................614 885-1885
EMP: 57 EST: 2001
SALES (est): 5.72MM **Privately Held**
Web: www.cpcolumbusnorth.com
SIC: 7011 Hotels

(G-5643)
COLUMBUS LITERACY COUNCIL
5825 Chantry Dr (43232-4764)
PHONE..................614 282-7661
Joy D Reyes, *CEO*
Cori Macfarland, *
EMP: 49 EST: 1971
SQ FT: 4,500
SALES (est): 4.54MM **Privately Held**
Web: www.columbusliteracy.org
SIC: 8299 8331 8322 Educational service, nondegree granting: continuing educ.; Job training and related services; Individual and family services

(G-5644)
COLUMBUS MEDICAL ASSOCIATION
1390 Dublin Rd (43215-1009)
PHONE..................614 240-7410
EMP: 53 EST: 1958
SQ FT: 12,432
SALES (est): 251.39K **Privately Held**
Web: www.columbusmedicalassociation.org
SIC: 8621 Health association

Columbus - Franklin County (G-5645) — GEOGRAPHIC SECTION

(G-5645)
COLUMBUS MNTESSORI EDUCATN CTR
979 S James Rd (43227)
PHONE....................614 231-3790
Peggy Fein, *Dir*
EMP: 40 **EST:** 1984
SQ FT: 26,369
SALES (est): 3.33MM **Privately Held**
Web: www.columbusmontessori.org
SIC: 8299 8351 Educational service, nondegree granting: continuing educ.; Montessori child development center

(G-5646)
COLUMBUS MUNICIPAL EMPLOYEES (PA)
365 S 4th St (43215-5422)
PHONE....................614 224-8890
Jim Riederer, *Pr*
Tracy Cera, *
EMP: 31 **EST:** 1935
SQ FT: 5,000
SALES (est): 11.53MM
SALES (corp-wide): 11.53MM **Privately Held**
Web: www.cmefcu.org
SIC: 6061 Federal credit unions

(G-5647)
COLUMBUS MUSEUM OF ART
480 E Broad St (43215)
PHONE....................614 221-6801
Nannette Macjunes, *Dir*
P W Huntington, *
W G Deshler, *
▲ **EMP:** 100 **EST:** 1878
SQ FT: 89,000
SALES (est): 20.31MM **Privately Held**
Web: www.columbusmuseum.org
SIC: 8412 5812 Art gallery; Eating places

(G-5648)
COLUMBUS NEIGHBORHOOD HEALTH C
Also Called: Columbus Neighborhood Health
1905 Parsons Ave (43207-1933)
PHONE....................614 445-0685
EMP: 36
SALES (corp-wide): 24.33MM **Privately Held**
Web: www.primaryonehealth.org
SIC: 8011 Clinic, operated by physicians
PA: Columbus Neighborhood Health Center, Inc.
2780 Airport Dr Ste 100
Columbus OH 43219
614 645-5500

(G-5649)
COLUMBUS NGHBRHOOD HLTH CTR IN
Also Called: Primaryone Health
3433 Agler Rd Ste 2800 (43219-3389)
PHONE....................614 859-1947
EMP: 36
SALES (corp-wide): 24.33MM **Privately Held**
Web: www.primaryonehealth.org
SIC: 8011 Medical centers
PA: Columbus Neighborhood Health Center, Inc.
2780 Airport Dr Ste 100
Columbus OH 43219
614 645-5500

(G-5650)
COLUMBUS NGHBRHOOD HLTH CTR IN
Also Called: Hilltop Health Center

2300 W Broad St (43204-3783)
PHONE....................614 645-2300
Stephanie Ryan, *Mgr*
EMP: 59
SALES (corp-wide): 24.33MM **Privately Held**
Web: www.primaryonehealth.org
SIC: 8361 Residential care
PA: Columbus Neighborhood Health Center, Inc.
2780 Airport Dr Ste 100
Columbus OH 43219
614 645-5500

(G-5651)
COLUMBUS OH 0617 LLC
Also Called: Fairfield Inn Stes Clmbs/New Al
4976 E Dublin Granville Rd (43081-7651)
P.O. Box 958 (45701-0958)
PHONE....................614 855-9766
Jack Bortle, *Prin*
Chad Bortle, *
Michael P Holtz, *
Michael B Holtz, *
Hosh Patel, *
EMP: 30 **EST:** 2018
SALES (est): 1.03MM **Privately Held**
Web: fairfield.marriott.com
SIC: 7011 Hotels and motels

(G-5652)
COLUMBUS REGIONAL AIRPORT AUTH (PA)
4600 International Gtwy Ste 25 (43219-1779)
PHONE....................614 239-4000
Joseph Nardone, *Pr*
EMP: 320 **EST:** 1929
SQ FT: 821,795
SALES (est): 79.8MM **Privately Held**
Web: www.flycolumbus.com
SIC: 4581 Airport

(G-5653)
COLUMBUS SAI MOTORS LLC
Also Called: Hatifield Hyundai
1400 Auto Mall Dr (43228-3657)
PHONE....................614 851-3273
Scott Smith, *COO*
Keith Daniels, *
Dan Hatfield, *
Bud C Hatfield, *
EMP: 50 **EST:** 1987
SQ FT: 24,000
SALES (est): 2.52MM
SALES (corp-wide): 14.37B **Publicly Held**
Web: www.hatfieldhyundai.com
SIC: 7538 5511 7515 5521 General automotive repair shops; Automobiles, new and used; Passenger car leasing; Used car dealers
PA: Sonic Automotive, Inc.
4401 Colwick Rd
Charlotte NC 28211
704 566-2400

(G-5654)
COLUMBUS SPEECH & HEARING CTR
510 E North Broadway St (43214-4114)
PHONE....................614 263-5151
James O Dye, *Pr*
EMP: 79 **EST:** 1923
SQ FT: 40,000
SALES (est): 5.01MM **Privately Held**
Web: www.columbusspeech.org
SIC: 8322 Social services for the handicapped

(G-5655)
COLUMBUS SQ BOWL PALACE INC
5707 Forest Hills Blvd (43231-2990)
PHONE....................614 895-1122
William H Hadler, *Pr*
William George N Hadler, *VP*
EMP: 36 **EST:** 1983
SALES (est): 946.59K **Privately Held**
Web: www.palacelanes.com
SIC: 7933 5813 Ten pin center; Cocktail lounge

(G-5656)
COLUMBUS SYMPHONY ORCHESTRA INC
55 E State St Fl 5 (43215-4203)
PHONE....................614 228-9600
Chad Wintton, *CFO*
EMP: 85 **EST:** 1951
SALES (est): 9.95MM **Privately Held**
Web: www.columbussymphony.com
SIC: 7929 Orchestras or bands, nec

(G-5657)
COLUMBUS TRUCK & EQUIPMENT CENTER LLC (PA)
Also Called: McMahon Truck Center Columbus
1688 E 5th Ave (43219-2599)
P.O. Box 83250 (43203-0250)
PHONE....................614 252-3111
EMP: 60 **EST:** 1949
SALES (est): 14.44MM
SALES (corp-wide): 14.44MM **Privately Held**
Web: ip-198-58-125-100.cloudezapp.io
SIC: 5013 5012 7519 7513 Truck parts and accessories; Trucks, commercial; Trailer rental; Truck leasing, without drivers

(G-5658)
COLUMBUS URBAN LEAGUE
788 Mount Vernon Ave (43203)
PHONE....................614 257-6300
Stephanie Hightower, *Pr*
Gready Pettigrew, *
EMP: 50 **EST:** 1920
SQ FT: 25,000
SALES (est): 13.73MM **Privately Held**
Web: www.cul.org
SIC: 8322 Social service center

(G-5659)
COLUMBUS WORTHINGTON HOSPITALI
Also Called: Double Tree
175 Hutchinson Ave (43235-1413)
PHONE....................614 885-3334
Daniel Ouellette Managing, *Prin*
EMP: 85 **EST:** 2013
SALES (est): 1.95MM **Privately Held**
Web: www.hilton.com
SIC: 7011 Hotel, franchised

(G-5660)
COLUMBUS-RNA-DAVITA LLC
Also Called: Columbus East Dialysis
299 Outerbelt St (43213-1529)
PHONE....................614 501-7224
Alexander Price, *Mgr*
EMP: 30
SIC: 8092 Kidney dialysis centers
HQ: Columbus-Rna-Davita, Llc
601 Hawaii St
El Segundo CA 90245

(G-5661)
COLUMBUS-RNA-DAVITA LLC
Also Called: Columbus Downtown Dialysis
415 E Mound St (43215-5532)

PHONE....................614 228-1773
Shannon Brammer, *Mgr*
EMP: 30
SIC: 8092 Kidney dialysis centers
HQ: Columbus-Rna-Davita, Llc
601 Hawaii St
El Segundo CA 90245

(G-5662)
COLUMBUS-RNA-DAVITA LLC
Also Called: Columbus Dialysis
226 Graceland Blvd Ste 3-09a (43214-1532)
PHONE....................614 985-1732
EMP: 30
SIC: 8092 Kidney dialysis centers
HQ: Columbus-Rna-Davita, Llc
601 Hawaii St
El Segundo CA 90245

(G-5663)
COMENITY CAPITAL BANK
3100 Easton Square Pl (43219-6289)
PHONE....................614 944-3682
EMP: 7275
Web: www.breadfinancial.com
SIC: 6022 State commercial banks
HQ: Comenity Capital Bank
2795 E Cottonwood Pkwy # 100
Salt Lake City UT 84121
801 527-2272

(G-5664)
COMENITY SERVICING LLC
3095 Loyalty Cir (43219-3673)
PHONE....................614 729-4000
Ralph J Andretta, *Managing Member*
EMP: 40 **EST:** 2012
SALES (est): 1.02MM **Publicly Held**
SIC: 7389 Advertising, promotional, and trade show services
PA: Bread Financial Holdings, Inc.
3095 Loyalty Cir
Columbus OH 43219

(G-5665)
COMMERCIAL GROUNDS CARE INC
1901 Dividend Dr (43228-3849)
PHONE....................614 456-3764
EMP: 68
SALES (corp-wide): 24.99MM **Privately Held**
SIC: 7389 Automobile recovery service
PA: Commercial Grounds Care, Inc.
1 Bobcat Ln
Johnson Creek WI 53038
920 699-2000

(G-5666)
COMMERCIAL PARTS & SER
5033 Transamerica Dr (43228-9381)
PHONE....................614 221-0057
Steve Weigel, *Brnch Mgr*
EMP: 55
SALES (corp-wide): 15.62MM **Privately Held**
Web: www.cpsohio.com
SIC: 5087 Restaurant supplies
PA: Commercial Parts & Service Of Cincinnati, Ohio, Inc.
10671 Techwoods Cir
Blue Ash OH 45242
513 984-1900

(G-5667)
COMMERCIAL WORKS INC (PA)
Also Called: Cwi
1299 Boltonfield St (43228-3693)
PHONE....................614 870-2342
EMP: 90 **EST:** 1973
SALES (est): 29.32MM

SALES (corp-wide): 29.32MM **Privately Held**
Web: www.commercial-works.com
SIC: 5021 4214 7389 Office furniture, nec; Furniture moving and storage, local; Interior design services

(G-5668)
COMMUNICARE HEALTH SVCS INC
Also Called: Regency Mnor Rhblttion Sbcute
2000 Regency Manor Cir (43207-1777)
PHONE..................614 443-7210
EMP: 115
SALES (corp-wide): 392.92MM **Privately Held**
Web: www.communicarehealth.com
SIC: 8051 Convalescent home with continuous nursing care
PA: Communicare Health Services, Inc.
  10123 Alliance Rd
  Blue Ash OH 45242
  513 530-1654

(G-5669)
COMMUNITY CRIME PATROL
248 E 11th Ave (43201-2255)
PHONE..................614 247-1765
Ellen Moore, Dir
EMP: 40 EST: 1990
SALES (est): 659.62K **Privately Held**
Web: www.communitycrimepatrol.org
SIC: 7381 Protective services, guard

(G-5670)
COMMUNITY FOR NEW DRCTION INCR
993 E Main St (43205-2342)
PHONE..................614 272-1464
Gregory Jefferson, Pr
John Dawson, Prin
EMP: 40 EST: 1988
SALES (est): 3.67MM **Privately Held**
Web: www.cndcolumbus.org
SIC: 8322 Social service center

(G-5671)
COMMUNITY LIVING EXPERIENCES
2939 Donnylane Blvd (43235-3228)
PHONE..................614 588-0320
William H Campbell, Pr
EMP: 46 EST: 1983
SALES (est): 3.19MM **Privately Held**
Web: www.cleohio.com
SIC: 8361 Mentally handicapped home

(G-5672)
COMMUNITY PRPTS OHIO MGT SVCS
Also Called: Cpo Managment Services
910 E Broad St (43205-1150)
PHONE..................614 253-0984
Isabel Toth, Pr
EMP: 55 EST: 2003
SALES (est): 6.55MM
SALES (corp-wide): 2.01B **Privately Held**
Web: www.cpoms.org
SIC: 6513 Apartment building operators
PA: City Of Columbus
  90 W Broad St Rm B33
  Columbus OH 43215
  614 645-7671

(G-5673)
COMMUNITY RFGEE IMMGRTION SVCS
4645 Executive Dr (43220-3601)
PHONE..................614 235-5747
Angela Plummer, Dir
EMP: 75 EST: 1995
SALES (est): 6.7MM **Privately Held**
Web: www.cris-ohio.com
SIC: 8322 Individual and family services

(G-5674)
COMMUNTIES IN SCHOLS CNTL OHIO
6500 Busch Blvd Ste 105 (43229-1738)
PHONE..................614 268-2472
EMP: 35 EST: 1994
SALES (est): 3.63MM **Privately Held**
Web: www.ciskids.org
SIC: 8641 Youth organizations

(G-5675)
COMPDRUG (PA)
Also Called: Youth To Youth
547 E 11th Ave (43211-2603)
PHONE..................614 224-4506
Robert E Sweet, Pr
Ronald L Pogue, *
Mark Sellers, *
Dustin Mets, *
Dave Bridge, *
EMP: 52 EST: 1970
SQ FT: 15,000
SALES (est): 13.25MM
SALES (corp-wide): 13.25MM **Privately Held**
Web: www.youthtoyouth.net
SIC: 8322 8361 Social service center; Rehabilitation center, residential: health care incidental

(G-5676)
COMPETITOR SWIM PRODUCTS INC
Also Called: Great American Woodies
5310 Career Ct (43213)
P.O. Box 12160 (43212-0160)
PHONE..................800 888-7946
Brad Underwood, Pr
Alan Sprague, VP
EMP: 85 EST: 1987
SQ FT: 60,000
SALES (est): 20.23MM **Privately Held**
Web: www.competitorswim.com
SIC: 5091 Swimming pools, equipment and supplies

(G-5677)
COMPLETE GENERAL CNSTR CO (PA)
1221 E 5th Ave (43219-2493)
PHONE..................614 258-9515
Lee Guzzo, Ch Bd
William Cooper, *
Peter Guzzo, *
Whit Wardell, *
EMP: 150 EST: 1929
SQ FT: 6,000
SALES (est): 98.36MM
SALES (corp-wide): 98.36MM **Privately Held**
Web: www.completegeneral.com
SIC: 1622 Bridge construction

(G-5678)
COMPLETE GENERAL CNSTR CO
1275 E 5th Ave (43219-2411)
PHONE..................614 258-9515
Bill Cooper, Mgr
EMP: 95
SALES (corp-wide): 98.36MM **Privately Held**
Web: www.completegeneral.com
SIC: 8741 Construction management
PA: Complete General Construction Co Inc
  1221 E 5th Ave
  Columbus OH 43219
  614 258-9515

(G-5679)
COMPRODUCTS INC (PA)
Also Called: B & C Communications
1740 Harmon Ave Ste F (43223-3355)
PHONE..................614 276-5552
TOLL FREE: 800
Thomas Harb, CEO
Leland Haydon, *
Steven Stauch, *
EMP: 27 EST: 1963
SQ FT: 12,000
SALES (est): 13.8MM
SALES (corp-wide): 13.8MM **Privately Held**
Web: www.bandccomm.com
SIC: 5065 7622 Radio parts and accessories, nec; Radio repair and installation

(G-5680)
COMRESOURCE INC
1159 Dublin Rd Ste 200 (43215-1874)
PHONE..................614 221-6348
Gary L Potts, Pr
Richard C Hannon Junior, Prin
EMP: 45 EST: 1991
SQ FT: 3,500
SALES (est): 13.08MM **Privately Held**
Web: www.comresource.com
SIC: 7379 Online services technology consultants

(G-5681)
CONFIDENTIAL SERVICES INC
1156 Alum Creek Dr (43209-2720)
P.O. Box 91034 (43209-7034)
PHONE..................614 252-4646
R K Levy, Pr
EMP: 36 EST: 1993
SALES (est): 723.82K **Privately Held**
Web: www.csilocate.com
SIC: 7381 Private investigator

(G-5682)
CONSOLIDATED ELEC DISTRS INC
C E D
265 N Hamilton Rd (43213-1311)
PHONE..................614 445-8871
Danny Willison, Mgr
EMP: 50
SALES (corp-wide): 1.5B **Privately Held**
Web: www.cedcentralohio.com
SIC: 5063 Electrical supplies, nec
PA: Consolidated Electrical Distributors, Inc.
  1920 Westridge Dr
  Irving TX 75038
  972 582-5300

(G-5683)
CONSTRCTION WSTE HLG PRTNERS L
1575 Harmon Ave (43223-3316)
PHONE..................614 683-0001
Michael Brown, Pr
EMP: 38 EST: 2021
SALES (est): 1.65MM **Privately Held**
SIC: 4212 Garbage collection and transport, no disposal

(G-5684)
CONSTRUCTION LABOR CONTRS LLC
Also Called: CLC
6155 Huntley Rd Ste G (43229-1096)
PHONE..................614 932-9937
Steve Dorsey, Genl Mgr
EMP: 244
Web: www.powerlaborusa.com
SIC: 7361 Labor contractors (employment agency)
HQ: Construction Labor Contractors, Llc
  9760 Shepard Rd
  Macedonia OH 44056
  330 247-1080

(G-5685)
CONSTRUCTION ONE INC
Also Called: Construction First
101 E Town St Ste 401 (43215-5247)
PHONE..................614 235-0057
William Moberger, Pr
William A Moberger, *
Steven M Moberger, *
Robert C Moberger, *
Christopher A Moberger, *
EMP: 74 EST: 1980
SQ FT: 7,500
SALES (est): 40.27MM **Privately Held**
Web: www.constructionone.com
SIC: 1521 Single-family housing construction

(G-5686)
CONSTRUCTION SYSTEMS INC (PA)
2865 E 14th Ave (43219-2301)
PHONE..................614 252-0708
Jd Flaherty Junior, Pr
Andrew Poczik, *
Tim Faherty, *
Ted Roshon, *
Randy Swoyer, *
EMP: 99 EST: 1967
SQ FT: 4,500
SALES (est): 24.37MM
SALES (corp-wide): 24.37MM **Privately Held**
Web: www.consysohio.com
SIC: 1742 Drywall

(G-5687)
CONSUMER CR CNSLING SVC OF MDW (PA)
Also Called: APPRISEN
700 Taylor Rd Ste 190 (43230-3318)
PHONE..................614 552-2222
TOLL FREE: 800
Michael Kappas, CEO
Christopher Kallay, *
James Zeier, *
EMP: 43 EST: 1955
SALES (est): 3.35MM
SALES (corp-wide): 3.35MM **Privately Held**
Web: www.apprisen.com
SIC: 7299 Debt counseling or adjustment service, individuals

(G-5688)
CONSUMERS INSURANCE USA INC
471 E Broad St Fl 12 (43215)
P.O. Box 182155 (43218)
PHONE..................615 896-6133
Amanda Farnsworth, Ch Bd
Jimmy Clist, *
William J Wheeler Iii, Pr
Lou Phaten, *
Dennis Kunkel, *
EMP: 60 EST: 1995
SALES (est): 22.54MM
SALES (corp-wide): 1.06B **Privately Held**
Web: www.encova.com
SIC: 6331 Fire, marine, and casualty insurance
HQ: Motorists Mutual Insurance Company
  471 E Broad St
  Columbus OH 43215
  614 225-8211

Columbus - Franklin County (G-5689) — GEOGRAPHIC SECTION

(G-5689)
CONTAINERPORT GROUP INC
Also Called: Cpg
2400 Creekway Dr (43207-3431)
PHONE.................................440 333-1330
Keith Fulk, *Brnch Mgr*
EMP: 40
SALES (corp-wide): 282.57MM **Privately Held**
Web: www.containerport.com
SIC: 4783 4212 4213 Containerization of goods for shipping; Light haulage and cartage, local; Trucking, except local
HQ: Containerport Group, Inc.
 1340 Depot St Fl 2
 Cleveland OH 44116
 440 333-1330

(G-5690)
CONTINENTAL BLDG SYSTEMS LLC
150 E Broad St (43215-3610)
PHONE.................................614 221-1818
Todd Alexander, *Pr*
Gregory Ray, *Ex VP*
Matt Wilhite, *VP*
Brent Baker, *VP*
EMP: 28 **EST:** 2003
SALES (est): 8.91MM **Privately Held**
Web: www.builtbycontinental.com
SIC: 1521 Single-family home remodeling, additions, and repairs

(G-5691)
CONTINENTAL BROADBAND PA
Also Called: Expedient
5000 Arlington Centre Blvd (43220-3075)
PHONE.................................877 570-7827
Charlie Watkins, *Brnch Mgr*
EMP: 87
Web: www.expedient.com
SIC: 7374 Computer graphics service
HQ: Continental Broadband Pennsylvania, Llc
 1 Allegheny Sq Ste 600
 Pittsburgh PA 15212

(G-5692)
CONTINENTAL BUILDING COMPANY
150 E Broad St (43215-3628)
PHONE.................................614 221-1800
Todd Alexander, *CEO*
EMP: 75 **EST:** 2016
SALES (est): 12.33MM **Privately Held**
Web: www.builtbycontinental.com
SIC: 1541 Industrial buildings and warehouses

(G-5693)
CONTINENTAL OFFICE FURN CORP (PA)
Also Called: Continntal Office Environments
5061 Freeway Dr E (43229-5401)
PHONE.................................614 262-5010
Ira Sharfin, *CEO*
Kyle Johnson, *Pr*
◆ **EMP:** 150 **EST:** 1941
SQ FT: 70,000
SALES (est): 53.41MM
SALES (corp-wide): 53.41MM **Privately Held**
Web: www.continentaloffice.com
SIC: 8712 7389 Architectural services; Interior design services

(G-5694)
CONTINENTAL PROPERTIES
150 E Broad St Ste 700 (43215)
P.O. Box 712 (43215)
PHONE.................................614 221-1800
Franklin Kass, *Mng Pt*
John Lucks Junior, *Pt*
EMP: 46 **EST:** 1979
SALES (est): 712.65K **Privately Held**
Web: www.cproperties.com
SIC: 6512 Commercial and industrial building operation

(G-5695)
CONTINENTAL RE COMPANIES (PA)
Also Called: Continental Building Company
150 E Broad St Ste 200 (43215-3644)
PHONE.................................614 221-1800
Franklin Kass, *Ch Bd*
John Lucks Junior, *VP*
James Conway, *
EMP: 140 **EST:** 1979
SALES (est): 24.19MM
SALES (corp-wide): 24.19MM **Privately Held**
Web: www.continental-realestate.com
SIC: 7011 1541 Hotels and motels; Industrial buildings and warehouses

(G-5696)
CONTINENTAL REALTY LTD (HQ)
150 E Gay St (43215-3130)
PHONE.................................614 224-2393
Melissa Johnson, *Prin*
EMP: 54 **EST:** 1989
SALES (est): 8.06MM
SALES (corp-wide): 2.47B **Publicly Held**
Web: www.continental-realestate.com
SIC: 6531 Real estate agent, commercial
PA: Newmark Group, Inc.
 125 Park Ave
 New York NY 10017
 212 372-2000

(G-5697)
CONTINENTAL REALTY LTD
180 E Broad St Ste 1708 (43215-3727)
PHONE.................................614 221-6260
Angel Robbins, *Mgr*
EMP: 38
SALES (corp-wide): 2.47B **Publicly Held**
Web: www.continental-realestate.com
SIC: 6531 Real estate agent, commercial
HQ: Continental Realty Ltd
 150 E Gay St
 Columbus OH 43215

(G-5698)
CONTINENTAL/OLENTANGY HT LLC
1421 Olentangy River Rd (43212-1449)
PHONE.................................614 297-9912
Dena Heinlein, *Dir*
Dena Heinlein, *Mktg Dir*
EMP: 43 **EST:** 2009
SALES (est): 222.64K **Privately Held**
SIC: 7011 Hotels and motels

(G-5699)
CONTINNTAL MSSAGE SOLUTION INC
Also Called: CMS Customer Solutions
41 S Grant Ave Fl 2 (43215-3979)
PHONE.................................614 224-4534
Beau A Hamer, *Pr*
EMP: 65 **EST:** 1997
SALES (est): 6.8MM **Privately Held**
Web: www.continentalmessage.com
SIC: 7299 7389 Personal document and information services; Telephone services

(G-5700)
CONTRACT SWEEPERS & EQP CO (PA)
2137 Parkwood Ave (43219-1145)
PHONE.................................614 221-7441
TOLL FREE: 800
Gerald Kesselring, *Pr*
Mark Dusseau, *
Charles F Glander, *
John C Hartranft, *
Robert E Fultz, *
EMP: 50 **EST:** 1960
SQ FT: 10,000
SALES (est): 22.72MM
SALES (corp-wide): 22.72MM **Privately Held**
Web: www.sweepers.com
SIC: 4959 5084 Sweeping service: road, airport, parking lot, etc.; Cleaning equipment, high pressure, sand or steam

(G-5701)
COPC HOSPITALS
3555 Olentangy River Rd (43214-3912)
PHONE.................................614 268-8164
Timothy Fallon, *Pr*
EMP: 120 **EST:** 2011
SALES (est): 1.24MM **Privately Held**
Web: www.copcp.com
SIC: 8062 General medical and surgical hospitals

(G-5702)
CORPORATE CLEANING INC
1720 Zollinger Rd Ste 99 (43221-2806)
PHONE.................................614 203-6051
Crystal Hughey, *CEO*
Eugene Hughey, *
EMP: 33 **EST:** 2010
SALES (est): 981.62K **Privately Held**
Web: www.corporatecleaning.us
SIC: 7699 7349 7342 1542 Cleaning services; Building and office cleaning services; Rest room cleaning service; Commercial and office building, new construction

(G-5703)
CORPORATE FIN ASSOC CLMBUS INC
671 Camden Yard Ct (43235-3492)
PHONE.................................614 457-9219
Charles E Washbush, *Pr*
EMP: 100 **EST:** 1987
SQ FT: 750
SALES (est): 5.3MM **Privately Held**
Web: www.cfaw.com
SIC: 8742 7389 6211 Business management consultant; Brokers, business: buying and selling business enterprises; Security brokers and dealers

(G-5704)
CORROSION FLUID PRODUCTS CORP (DH)
Also Called: Pumpserve
3000 E 14th Ave (43219-2355)
PHONE.................................248 478-0100
Joseph V Andronaco, *CEO*
Joseph P Andronaco, *
▲ **EMP:** 30 **EST:** 1968
SQ FT: 28,500
SALES (est): 47.66MM
SALES (corp-wide): 4.41B **Publicly Held**
Web: www.corrosionfluid.com
SIC: 5084 5074 Pumps and pumping equipment, nec; Pipes and fittings, plastic
HQ: Fcx Performance, Inc.
 3000 E 14th Ave
 Columbus OH 43219
 614 253-1996

(G-5705)
COSMIC CONCEPTS LTD
Also Called: Cosmic Concepts
399 E Main St Ste 140 (43215-5384)
PHONE.................................614 228-1104
John Riddle, *Brnch Mgr*
EMP: 93
SALES (corp-wide): 42.13MM **Privately Held**
Web: www.mediastarpromo.com
SIC: 8742 Marketing consulting services
PA: Cosmic Concepts, Ltd.
 318 Clubhouse Rd
 Hunt Valley MD 21031
 410 825-8500

(G-5706)
COSTUME SPECIALISTS INC
1801 Lone Eagle St (43228-3647)
PHONE.................................614 464-2115
Wendy C Goldstein, *Pr*
EMP: 36 **EST:** 1979
SALES (est): 5.43MM **Privately Held**
Web: www.costumespecialists.com
SIC: 2389 7299 Theatrical costumes; Costume rental

(G-5707)
COTT SYSTEMS INC
2800 Corporate Exchange Dr Ste 300 (43231-1678)
PHONE.................................614 847-4405
Deborah A Ball, *CEO*
Jodie Bare, *
Karen L Bailey, *
Drew Sheppared, *
Mike Sosh, *
EMP: 95 **EST:** 1888
SQ FT: 20,000
SALES (est): 16.43MM **Privately Held**
Web: www.cottsystems.com
SIC: 7373 7371 2789 Computer integrated systems design; Computer software development and applications; Beveling of cards

(G-5708)
COULTER VENTURES LLC (PA)
Also Called: Rogue Fitness
545 E 5th Ave (43201-2964)
PHONE.................................614 358-6190
William C Henniger, *Managing Member*
Kris Warner, *
◆ **EMP:** 44 **EST:** 2007
SQ FT: 25,000
SALES (est): 54.09MM **Privately Held**
Web: www.roguefitness.com
SIC: 5091 5941 7991 Fitness equipment and supplies; Exercise equipment; Physical fitness facilities

(G-5709)
COUNCIL DEV FIN AGENCIES
100 E Broad St Ste 1200 (43215-3686)
PHONE.................................614 705-1300
Tobias Rittner, *Pr*
Todd Rittner, *Pr*
EMP: 28 **EST:** 1984
SALES (est): 2.45MM **Privately Held**
Web: www.cdfa.net
SIC: 8611 Trade associations

(G-5710)
COUNTY COMMISSIONERS ASSN OHIO
Also Called: CCAO
209 E State St (43215-4309)
PHONE.................................614 220-0636
Larry Long, *Ex Dir*
EMP: 50 **EST:** 1880
SALES (est): 6.47MM **Privately Held**
Web: www.ccao.org
SIC: 8611 Trade associations

(G-5711)
COURTNEY W FLEMING DDS L
3701 N High St (43214-3520)
PHONE.................................614 263-4040

GEOGRAPHIC SECTION — Columbus - Franklin County (G-5735)

Courtney Fleming, *Prin*
EMP: 27 **EST:** 2007
SALES (est): 676.21K **Privately Held**
SIC: 8021 Dentists' office

(G-5712)
COURTYARD BY MRROTT COLUMBUS W
Also Called: Courtyard By Marriott
2350 Westbelt Dr (43228-3822)
PHONE.................614 771-8999
Michelle Anderson, *Prin*
EMP: 33 **EST:** 2007
SALES (est): 866.49K **Privately Held**
Web: courtyard.marriott.com
SIC: 7011 Hotels and motels

(G-5713)
COURTYARD MANAGEMENT CORP
Also Called: Marriott
7411 Vantage Dr (43235-1415)
PHONE.................614 436-7070
Shane Ewald, *Genl Mgr*
EMP: 35
SALES (corp-wide): 23.71B **Publicly Held**
Web: www.marriott.com
SIC: 7011 Hotels and motels
HQ: Courtyard Management Llc
7750 Wisconsin Ave
Bethesda MD 20814

(G-5714)
COURTYARD MANAGEMENT CORP
Also Called: Courtyard By Marriott
2901 Airport Dr (43219-2299)
PHONE.................614 475-8530
Mark Laport, *Mgr*
EMP: 30
SALES (corp-wide): 23.71B **Publicly Held**
Web: www.marriott.com
SIC: 7011 Hotels and motels
HQ: Courtyard Management Llc
7750 Wisconsin Ave
Bethesda MD 20814

(G-5715)
COVENANT TRANSPORT INC
3825 Aries Brook Dr (43207-4696)
PHONE.................423 821-1212
EMP: 504
Web: www.covenantlogistics.com
SIC: 4213 Contract haulers
HQ: Covenant Transport, Inc.
400 Birmingham Hwy
Chattanooga TN 37419
423 821-1212

(G-5716)
COYLE MUSIC CENTERS INC
Also Called: Coyle Music
137 Graceland Blvd (43214-1529)
PHONE.................614 885-6654
Jeffrey A Coyle, *Pr*
EMP: 45 **EST:** 1951
SQ FT: 26,000
SALES (est): 1.48MM **Privately Held**
SIC: 5736 7359 8299 7699 Musical instrument stores; Musical instrument rental services; Musical instrument lessons; Musical instrument repair services

(G-5717)
CP REDI LLC
1030 Freeway Dr N Bldg 6 (43229-5429)
PHONE.................866 682-7462
EMP: 235
SIC: 7629 Electronic equipment repair

(G-5718)
CRABBE BROWN & JAMES LLP (PA)
Also Called: Crabbe, Brown & James
500 S Front St Ste 1200 (43215-7631)
PHONE.................614 229-4509
Larry James, *CEO*
EMP: 44 **EST:** 1918
SALES (est): 4.47MM
SALES (corp-wide): 4.47MM **Privately Held**
Web: www.amundsendavislaw.com
SIC: 8111 General practice law office

(G-5719)
CRANE GROUP CO (PA)
330 W Spring St Ste 200 (43215-2389)
PHONE.................614 754-3000
Tanny Crane, *CEO*
Mike Crane, *Pr*
EMP: 42 **EST:** 1991
SALES (est): 117.63MM **Privately Held**
Web: www.cranegroup.com
SIC: 8741 Management services

(G-5720)
CREATIVE CHILD CARE INC
Also Called: Creative Child Care
1601 Shanley Dr (43224-1203)
PHONE.................614 863-3500
Bernice Hagler-cody, *Dir*
EMP: 34
SQ FT: 5,252
SALES (corp-wide): 49.41K **Privately Held**
Web: www.creativechildcareinc.com
SIC: 8351 Group day care center
PA: Creative Child Care, Inc.
630 Morrison Rd Ste 130
Gahanna OH 43230
614 863-3500

(G-5721)
CREATIVE LIVING INC
150 W 10th Ave (43201-2093)
PHONE.................614 421-1131
Todd D Ackerman, *Pr*
Jody Orsine Geiger, *
Ron Mains, *
Marilyn Frank, *
EMP: 29 **EST:** 1969
SQ FT: 10,000
SALES (est): 722.43K **Privately Held**
Web: www.creative-living.org
SIC: 6513 Retirement hotel operation

(G-5722)
CREATIVE OPTIONS LLC
605 Claycraft Rd (43230-5345)
PHONE.................614 868-1231
Daniel Abel, *CEO*
EMP: 27
SALES (corp-wide): 548.57K **Privately Held**
Web: www.creativeoptions.org
SIC: 8322 Adult day care center
PA: Creative Options, Llc
3753 Attucks Dr
Powell OH 43065
614 769-2499

(G-5723)
CREDIT BUR COLLECTN SVCS INC
Also Called: Cbcs
250 E Broad St Ste 1250 (43215-3708)
PHONE.................614 223-0688
Michael A Smith, *Prin*
EMP: 47 **EST:** 1997
SALES (est): 1.78MM **Privately Held**
Web: www.factualdata.com
SIC: 7322 Adjustment and collection services

(G-5724)
CREDIT BUR COLLECTN SVCS INC (HQ)
Also Called: Cbcs
236 E Town St (43215-4631)
PHONE.................614 223-0688
Larry Ebert, *Pr*
Dirk Cantrell, *
EMP: 50 **EST:** 2003
SQ FT: 60,000
SALES (est): 24.12MM
SALES (corp-wide): 233.8MM **Privately Held**
Web: www.revcosolutions.com
SIC: 7322 Collection agency, except real estate
PA: Cbc Companies, Inc.
250 E Broad St Fl 21
Columbus OH 43215
614 222-4343

(G-5725)
CRESTBROOK INSURANCE COMPANY
1 W Nationwide Blvd (43215-2752)
PHONE.................614 249-7111
Wesley Kim Austen, *Pr*
Carol L Dove, *
Robert W Horner Iii, *VP*
EMP: 642 **EST:** 1985
SALES (est): 25.02MM
SALES (corp-wide): 11.75B **Privately Held**
Web: www.nationwide.com
SIC: 6331 6311 Property damage insurance; Mutual association life insurance
PA: Nationwide Mutual Insurance Company
1 Nationwide Plz
Columbus OH 43215
614 249-7111

(G-5726)
CRETE CARRIER CORPORATION
Also Called: Crete Carrier
5400 Crosswind Dr (43228-3778)
PHONE.................614 853-4500
Scott Clay, *Mgr*
EMP: 195
SALES (corp-wide): 919.75MM **Privately Held**
Web: www.cretecarrier.com
SIC: 4213 Contract haulers
PA: Crete Carrier Corporation
400 Nw 56th St
Lincoln NE 68528
800 998-4095

(G-5727)
CREW SC TEAM COMPANY LLC
Also Called: Columbus Crew SC
1 Black And Gold Blvd (43211-2091)
PHONE.................614 447-2739
EMP: 99 **EST:** 2019
SALES (est): 10.17MM **Privately Held**
Web: www.columbuscrew.com
SIC: 7941 Sports clubs, managers, and promoters

(G-5728)
CREW SOCCER STADIUM LLC
1 Black And Gold Blvd (43211-2091)
PHONE.................614 447-2739
Andy Louthnane, *Pr*
Mark Mccullers, *Pr*
EMP: 52 **EST:** 1998
SALES (est): 2.73MM **Privately Held**
Web: www.columbuscrew.com
SIC: 7941 Soccer club

(G-5729)
CRIMSON DESIGN GROUP LLC
825 Grandview Ave (43215-1123)
PHONE.................614 444-3743
Cheryl Beachy, *Prin*
EMP: 45 **EST:** 2010
SALES (est): 3.91MM **Privately Held**
Web: www.crimsondesigngroup.com
SIC: 7389 Interior designer

(G-5730)
CROSSCHX INC
99 E Main St (43215-5115)
PHONE.................800 501-3161
Sean Lane, *CEO*
Brad Mascho, *
Carlton Fox, *
Jenna Mackey C.p.a., *Prin*
▲ **EMP:** 73 **EST:** 2013
SQ FT: 5,500
SALES (est): 9.43MM **Privately Held**
Web: www.crosschx.com
SIC: 7371 Computer software development

(G-5731)
CROSSCOUNTRY MORTGAGE LLC
2 Miranova Pl Ste 320 (43215-7050)
PHONE.................614 779-0316
EMP: 56
SALES (corp-wide): 803.24MM **Privately Held**
Web: www.crosscountrymortgage.com
SIC: 6162 Mortgage bankers and loan correspondents
PA: Crosscountry Mortgage, Llc
6850 Miller Rd
Brecksville OH 44141
440 845-3700

(G-5732)
CRP CONTRACTING
4477 E 5th Ave (43219-1817)
PHONE.................614 338-8501
James Head, *Pt*
Paul Ondera, *Pt*
EMP: 60
SALES (est): 4.97MM **Privately Held**
SIC: 1611 Airport runway construction

(G-5733)
CS HOTELS LIMITED PARTNERSHIP
Also Called: Courtyard Columbus West
2350 Westbelt Dr (43228-3822)
PHONE.................614 771-8999
Belinda Paterson, *Genl Mgr*
EMP: 75
Web: www.columbiasussex.com
SIC: 7011 Hotels
PA: Cs Hotels Limited Partnership
740 Centre View Blvd
Crestview Hills KY 41017

(G-5734)
CSC DISTRIBUTION LLC
4900 E Dublin Granville Rd (43081-7651)
PHONE.................614 278-6800
Bruce K Thorn, *Pr*
Ronald A Robins Junior, *Sec*
▲ **EMP:** 600 **EST:** 1983
SALES (est): 102.51MM
SALES (corp-wide): 4.72B **Publicly Held**
SIC: 5092 Toys and games
PA: Big Lots, Inc.
4900 E Dblin Granville Rd
Columbus OH 43081
614 278-6800

(G-5735)
CTD INVESTMENTS LLC (PA)
Also Called: Ctd

Columbus - Franklin County (G-5736) — GEOGRAPHIC SECTION

630 E Broad St (43215-3999)
PHONE..................614 570-9949
William Lewis, *
Stephanie Jandik, *
EMP: 50 **EST:** 2015
SQ FT: 6,000
SALES (est): 20MM
SALES (corp-wide): 20MM **Privately Held**
Web: www.verizon.com
SIC: 6799 5999 Investors, nec; Electronic parts and equipment

(G-5736)
CTL ENGINEERING INC (PA)
2860 Fisher Rd (43204-3538)
P.O. Box 44548 (43204-0548)
PHONE..................614 276-8123
C K Satyapriya, *CEO*
David Breitfeller, *
Bipender Jindal, *
Ali Jamshidi, *
EMP: 120 **EST:** 1927
SQ FT: 35,000
SALES (est): 48.4MM
SALES (corp-wide): 48.4MM **Privately Held**
Web: www.ctleng.com
SIC: 8711 8734 8731 8713 Consulting engineer; Metallurgical testing laboratory; Commercial physical research; Surveying services

(G-5737)
DAILY SERVICES LLC (PA)
4 Easton Oval (43219)
PHONE..................614 431-5100
Ryan Mason, *Managing Member*
Ryan Mason, *Pr*
Rick Fazzina, *
EMP: 65 **EST:** 2006
SQ FT: 2,000
SALES (est): 22.38MM **Privately Held**
Web: daily-services-llc-dba-iforce.hub.biz
SIC: 7361 Executive placement

(G-5738)
DANCOR INC
2155 Dublin Rd (43228-9668)
PHONE..................614 340-2155
Dan Fronk, *CEO*
EMP: 35 **EST:** 1994
SQ FT: 20,000
SALES (est): 5.49MM **Privately Held**
Web: www.dancorsolutions.com
SIC: 8748 Business consulting, nec

(G-5739)
DANIS BUILDING CONSTRUCTION CO
777 Goodale Blvd Ste 100 (43212-3862)
PHONE..................614 761-8385
Doug Addis, *Mgr*
EMP: 214
Web: www.danis.com
SIC: 1542 1541 8741 Commercial and office building, new construction; Industrial buildings and warehouses; Construction management
PA: Danis Building Construction Company
3233 Newmark Dr
Miamisburg OH 45342

(G-5740)
DANITE HOLDINGS LTD
Also Called: Danite Sign Co
1640 Harmon Ave (43223-3321)
PHONE..................614 444-3333
Tim Mccord, *Pr*
Shelley Mccord, *Sec*
Calvin Lutz, *Stockholder* *

C William Klausman, *
EMP: 50 **EST:** 1954
SQ FT: 33,500
SALES (est): 9.83MM **Privately Held**
Web: www.danitesign.com
SIC: 3993 1799 Electric signs; Sign installation and maintenance

(G-5741)
DAVEY TREE EXPERT COMPANY
3567 Westerville Rd (43224-2554)
PHONE..................330 673-9511
James Serdy, *Brnch Mgr*
EMP: 60
SALES (corp-wide): 1.51B **Privately Held**
Web: www.davey.com
SIC: 0783 Planting, pruning, and trimming services
PA: The Davey Tree Expert Company
1500 N Mantua St
Kent OH 44240
330 673-9511

(G-5742)
DAVIS-MCMACKIN INC
1880 Mackenzie Dr Ste 101 (43220-2956)
PHONE..................614 824-1587
Robert Davis, *Brnch Mgr*
EMP: 44
SIC: 8712 Architectural services
PA: Davis-Mcmackin Inc
1466 Manning Pkwy
Powell OH 43065

(G-5743)
DAWSON RESOURCES
Also Called: Dawson Personnel
4184 W Broad St (43228-1671)
PHONE..................614 274-8900
Maurine Kenneley, *Brnch Mgr*
EMP: 385
SALES (corp-wide): 47.67MM **Privately Held**
Web: www.dawsoncareers.com
SIC: 7361 Employment agencies
PA: Decapua Enterprises, Inc
1114 Dublin Rd
Columbus OH 43215
614 255-1400

(G-5744)
DAYTON FREIGHT LINES INC
1406 Blatt Blvd (43230-6627)
PHONE..................614 860-1080
Grey Armstrong, *Mgr*
EMP: 176
SALES (corp-wide): 6.59B **Privately Held**
Web: www.daytonfreight.com
SIC: 4213 Trucking, except local
PA: Dayton Freight Lines, Inc.
6450 Poe Ave
Dayton OH 45414
937 264-4060

(G-5745)
DAYTON HEIDELBERG DISTRG CO
Also Called: Dayton Heidelberg Distributing Co.
3801 Parkwest Dr (43228-1457)
PHONE..................614 308-0400
Greg Maurer, *VP*
EMP: 285
SALES (corp-wide): 2.07B **Privately Held**
Web: www.heidelbergdistributing.com
SIC: 5181 Beer and other fermented malt liquors
HQ: Dayton Heidelberg Distributing Co., Llc
3601 Dryden Rd
Moraine OH 45439
937 222-8692

(G-5746)
DAZPAK FLEXIBLE PACKAGING CORP (PA)
2901 E 4th Ave (43219)
PHONE..................614 252-2121
James Rooney, *CEO*
Mike Mc Coy, *CFO*
▲ **EMP:** 102 **EST:** 1964
SQ FT: 50,000
SALES (est): 26.83MM
SALES (corp-wide): 26.83MM **Privately Held**
Web: www.dazpak.com
SIC: 2673 5113 Plastic bags: made from purchased materials; Bags, paper and disposable plastic

(G-5747)
DECAPUA ENTERPRISES INC (PA)
Also Called: Dawson Personnel Systems
1114 Dublin Rd (43215-1039)
PHONE..................614 255-1400
Michael Linton, *Pr*
David Decapua, *
Christopher Decapua, *
Phillip Freeman, *
EMP: 45 **EST:** 2004
SQ FT: 5,000
SALES (est): 47.67MM
SALES (corp-wide): 47.67MM **Privately Held**
Web: www.dawsoncareers.com
SIC: 7361 7363 Placement agencies; Temporary help service

(G-5748)
DEDICATED TECHNOLOGIES INC
175 S 3rd St Ste 200 (43215-5194)
PHONE..................614 460-3200
Jeffrey P Dalton, *Pr*
Patricia Lickliter, *
EMP: 82 **EST:** 1999
SQ FT: 7,000
SALES (est): 7.14MM **Privately Held**
Web: www.dedicatedtech.com
SIC: 8742 7361 8748 Industry specialist consultants; Placement agencies; Business consulting, nec

(G-5749)
DEFABCO INC
3765 E Livingston Ave (43227-2258)
PHONE..................614 231-2700
EMP: 60 **EST:** 1972
SALES (est): 10.01MM **Privately Held**
Web: www.defabco.com
SIC: 1761 3443 3535 3444 Sheet metal work, nec; Pipe, standpipe, and culverts; Conveyors and conveying equipment; Sheet metalwork

(G-5750)
DEFENSE FIN & ACCOUNTING SVC
Also Called: West Entitlement Operations
3990 E Broad St (43213-1152)
PHONE..................614 693-6700
Johnathan Witter, *Dir*
EMP: 2900
Web: www.dfas.mil
SIC: 8721 9711 Accounting services, except auditing; National security
HQ: Defense Finance & Accounting Service
8899 E 56th St
Indianapolis IN 46249

(G-5751)
DELAWARE NORTH-SPORTSERVICE
200 W Nationwide Blvd (43215-2561)
PHONE..................614 246-3203
EMP: 34 **EST:** 2011
SALES (est): 12.15MM

SALES (corp-wide): 2.9B **Privately Held**
Web: www.nationwidearena.com
SIC: 7389 Decoration service for special events
PA: Delaware North Companies Incorporated
250 Delaware Ave Ste 1000
Buffalo NY 14202
716 858-5000

(G-5752)
DELILLE OXYGEN COMPANY (PA)
772 Marion Rd (43207-2595)
P.O. Box 7809 (43207-0809)
PHONE..................614 444-1177
Richard F Carlile, *Prin*
Joseph R Smith, *
Tom Smith, *
Jim Smith, *
EMP: 40 **EST:** 1964
SQ FT: 20,000
SALES (est): 25.92MM
SALES (corp-wide): 25.92MM **Privately Held**
Web: www.delille.com
SIC: 2813 5085 Acetylene; Welding supplies

(G-5753)
DELOITTE & TOUCHE LLP
180 E Broad St Ste 1400 (43215-3611)
PHONE..................614 221-1000
John Mcewan, *Brnch Mgr*
EMP: 632
Web: www.deloitte.com
SIC: 8721 Accounting services, except auditing
HQ: Deloitte & Touche Llp
30 Rockefeller Plz # 4350
New York NY 10112
212 492-4000

(G-5754)
DELPHIA CONSULTING LLC
250 E Broad St Ste 1150 (43215-3773)
PHONE..................614 421-2000
Brian Delphia, *Pr*
Brian Delphia, *CEO*
Alexander Main, *
EMP: 40 **EST:** 1999
SALES (est): 8.63MM **Privately Held**
Web: www.delphiaconsulting.com
SIC: 8742 7372 Human resource consulting services; Business oriented computer software

(G-5755)
DENTAL GROUP AT NORTH HAMILTON
Also Called: Franklinton Dental Group
1531 W Broad St (43222-1043)
PHONE..................614 351-0555
Edward Claeys, *Brnch Mgr*
EMP: 55
SIC: 8021 Dentists' office
PA: Dental Group At North Hamilton
5478 N Hamilton Rd
Columbus OH 43230

(G-5756)
DEPARTMENT OF COMMERCE OHIO
Division Fincl Institutions
77 S High St Fl 21 (43215-6108)
PHONE..................614 728-8400
Charles Dolezal, *Superintnt*
EMP: 64
SIC: 8611 9611 Business associations; Administration of general economic programs, State government
HQ: Department Of Commerce Ohio
6606 Tussing Rd
Reynoldsburg OH 43068

GEOGRAPHIC SECTION

Columbus - Franklin County (G-5780)

(G-5757)
DEPARTMENT OF COMMERCE OHIO
Division of Securities
77 S High St Fl 22 (43215-6108)
PHONE................................614 644-7381
Joe Bishop, *Commsnr*
EMP: 64
SIC: 6211 9311 Security brokers and dealers ; Finance, taxation, and monetary policy, State government
HQ: Department Of Commerce Ohio
  6606 Tussing Rd
  Reynoldsburg OH 43068

(G-5758)
DESIGN CENTRAL INC
6464 Presidential Gtwy (43231-7673)
PHONE................................614 890-0202
Rainer Teufel, *Ch*
EMP: 35 **EST:** 1985
SQ FT: 13,000
SALES (est): 5.06MM **Privately Held**
Web: www.designcentral.com
SIC: 7389 Design, commercial and industrial

(G-5759)
DEVRY UNIVERSITY INC
Also Called: Devry University
2 Easton Oval Ste 310 # 210 (43219-6193)
PHONE................................614 251-6969
Scarlett Howery, *Pr*
EMP: 56
SALES (corp-wide): 266.59MM **Privately Held**
Web: www.devry.edu
SIC: 8742 8221 Human resource consulting services; University
HQ: Devry University, Inc.
  1200 E Diehl Rd
  Naperville IL 60563
  630 515-7700

(G-5760)
DHL HOME CARE LLC
2580 Oakstone Dr Ste A (43231-7693)
PHONE................................614 987-5813
Tom Luft, *Prin*
EMP: 48 **EST:** 2009
SALES (est): 642.36K **Privately Held**
SIC: 8059 Personal care home, with health care

(G-5761)
DIAMOND HILL CAPITAL MGT INC
325 John H Mcconnell Blvd Ste 200 (43215)
PHONE................................614 255-3333
Heather Brilliant, *Pr*
Tom Line, *
EMP: 45 **EST:** 1981
SALES (est): 24.26MM **Publicly Held**
Web: www.diamond-hill.com
SIC: 6282 Investment advisory service
PA: Diamond Hill Investment Group, Inc.
  325 John H Mcconnell Blvd # 200
  Columbus OH 43215

(G-5762)
DIAMOND HILL FUNDS
325 John H Mcconnell Blvd Ste 200 (43215-2677)
PHONE................................614 255-3333
Roderick Dillon, *Pt*
EMP: 38 **EST:** 1997
SQ FT: 8,000
SALES (est): 2.41MM **Privately Held**
Web: www.diamond-hill.com
SIC: 6282 Investment advisory service

(G-5763)
DIAMOND LOGISTICS INC
745 N Wilson Rd (43204-1463)
P.O. Box 28100 (43228-0100)
PHONE................................614 274-9750
EMP: 120
SIC: 4213 Trucking, except local

(G-5764)
DICK MASHETER FORD INC
Also Called: Quick Lane
1100 S Hamilton Rd (43227-1312)
PHONE................................614 861-7150
Robert Masheter, *CEO*
EMP: 100 **EST:** 1967
SALES (est): 25.28MM **Privately Held**
Web: www.masheterford.net
SIC: 5511 7538 Automobiles, new and used; General automotive repair shops

(G-5765)
DICKIE MCCAMEY & CHILCOTE PC (PA)
10 W Broad St Ste 1950 (43215-4793)
PHONE................................412 281-7272
Jeffrey T Wiley, *VP*
John C Conti, *
Steven W Zoffer, *
W Alan Torrance Junior, *Dir*
EMP: 310 **EST:** 1896
SQ FT: 100,000
SALES (est): 56.73MM
SALES (corp-wide): 56.73MM **Privately Held**
Web: www.dmclaw.com
SIC: 8111 General practice law office

(G-5766)
DINSMORE & SHOHL LLP
191 W Nationwide Blvd Ste 300 (43215-2568)
PHONE................................614 628-6880
Peter J Condon, *Prin*
EMP: 77
SALES (corp-wide): 169.43MM **Privately Held**
Web: www.dinsmore.com
SIC: 8111 General practice attorney, lawyer
PA: Dinsmore & Shohl Llp
  255 E 5th St Ste 1900
  Cincinnati OH 45202
  513 977-8200

(G-5767)
DIRECTIONS FOR YOUTH FAMILIES
657 S Ohio Ave (43205-2743)
PHONE................................614 258-8043
John Cervi, *Mgr*
EMP: 34
SALES (corp-wide): 7.45MM **Privately Held**
Web: www.dfyf.org
SIC: 8322 Youth center
PA: Directions For Youth & Families Inc
  1515 Indianola Ave
  Columbus OH 43201
  614 294-2661

(G-5768)
DIRECTIONS FOR YOUTH FAMILIES
3860 Kimberly Pkwy N (43232-4267)
PHONE................................614 694-0203
EMP: 33
SALES (corp-wide): 7.45MM **Privately Held**
Web: www.dfyf.org
SIC: 8322 Social service center
PA: Directions For Youth & Families Inc
  1515 Indianola Ave
  Columbus OH 43201
  614 294-2661

(G-5769)
DIRECTIONS FOR YOUTH FAMILIES (PA)
1515 Indianola Ave (43201-2118)
PHONE................................614 294-2661
Duane Casares, *CEO*
EMP: 50 **EST:** 1983
SQ FT: 1,000
SALES (est): 7.45MM
SALES (corp-wide): 7.45MM **Privately Held**
Web: www.dfyf.org
SIC: 8322 Social service center

(G-5770)
DISMAS DISTRIBUTION SERVICES
450 Mccormick Blvd (43213-1525)
PHONE................................614 861-2525
Bob Parson, *CEO*
EMP: 50 **EST:** 1999
SQ FT: 10,000
SALES (est): 2.68MM **Privately Held**
Web: www.dismas.net
SIC: 7319 Sample distribution

(G-5771)
DISPATCH CONSUMER SERVICES (HQ)
Also Called: Dispatch Color Press
5300 Crosswind Dr (43228-3600)
PHONE................................740 548-5555
John Curtain, *Pr*
EMP: 30 **EST:** 1986
SQ FT: 63,000
SALES (est): 12.34MM
SALES (corp-wide): 450.12MM **Privately Held**
Web: www.dispatchshows.com
SIC: 7319 Distribution of advertising material or sample services
PA: The Dispatch Printing Company
  62 E Broad St
  Columbus OH 43215

(G-5772)
DISPATCH PRODUCTIONS INC
770 Twin Rivers Dr (43215-1127)
PHONE................................614 460-3700
Michael Fiorile, *Pr*
John Butte, *General Vice President*
EMP: 145 **EST:** 1996
SALES (est): 3.67MM
SALES (corp-wide): 450.12MM **Privately Held**
Web: www.dispatchshows.com
SIC: 8999 Radio and television announcing
PA: The Dispatch Printing Company
  62 E Broad St
  Columbus OH 43215

(G-5773)
DIST-TRANS INC
1580 Williams Rd (43207-5183)
PHONE................................614 497-1660
John E Ness, *Pr*
Theodore Waltz, *
Robert E Ness, *
▲ **EMP:** 118 **EST:** 1978
SQ FT: 50,000
SALES (est): 2.49MM **Privately Held**
Web: www.odwlogistics.com
SIC: 4213 Trucking, except local
PA: Jebren, Inc
  1580 Williams Rd
  Columbus OH 43207

(G-5774)
DIVERSIFIED HEALTH MGT INC
3569 Refugee Rd Ste C (43232-9306)
PHONE................................614 338-8888
Alex Phommasathit, *CEO*
Alex Thommasathit, *
EMP: 60 **EST:** 2004
SALES (est): 2.43MM **Privately Held**
Web: www.dhmcorp.net
SIC: 8082 Home health care services

(G-5775)
DIVERSITY SEARCH GROUP LLC
2550 Corporate Exchange Dr Ste 15 (43231-7659)
PHONE................................614 352-2988
Teresa Sherald, *CEO*
EMP: 273 **EST:** 2004
SALES (est): 8.87MM **Privately Held**
Web: www.diversitysearchgroup.com
SIC: 7361 Executive placement

(G-5776)
DIVISION OF GEOLOGICAL SURVEY
2045 Morse Rd Bldg C (43229-6693)
PHONE................................614 265-6576
Thomas Serenko, *Chief*
Michael Angle, *Prin*
EMP: 30 **EST:** 2010
SALES (est): 1.08MM **Privately Held**
Web: www.ohiodnr.gov
SIC: 8713 Surveying services

(G-5777)
DLZ CONSTRUCTION SERVICES INC
6121 Huntley Rd (43229-1003)
PHONE................................614 888-0040
Vikram Rajadhyaksha, *CEO*
EMP: 48 **EST:** 2017
SQ FT: 80,000
SALES (est): 7.67MM **Privately Held**
Web: www.dlz.com
SIC: 8711 Consulting engineer
HQ: Dlz National, Inc.
  6121 Huntley Rd
  Columbus OH 43229

(G-5778)
DLZ OHIO INC (HQ)
6121 Huntley Rd (43229-1003)
PHONE................................614 888-0040
Vikram Raj Rajadhyaksha, *Ch*
A James Siebert, *
David Cutlip, *
Allan C Strange, *
P V Rajadhyaksha, *
EMP: 200 **EST:** 1950
SQ FT: 45,000
SALES (est): 18.43MM **Privately Held**
Web: www.dlz.com
SIC: 8711 1382 8712 8713 Consulting engineer; Geophysical exploration, oil and gas field; Architectural services; Surveying services
PA: Dlz Corporation
  6121 Huntley Rd
  Columbus OH 43229

(G-5779)
DNO INC
3650 E 5th Ave (43219-1805)
PHONE................................614 231-3601
Anthony Dinovo, *Pr*
Carol Dinovo, *
EMP: 80 **EST:** 1989
SQ FT: 10,000
SALES (est): 16.73MM **Privately Held**
Web: www.dnoinc.com
SIC: 2099 5148 Salads, fresh or refrigerated; Fruits, fresh

(G-5780)
DOCTORS OHIOHEALTH CORPORATION
Also Called: Rehabilitation Inst Bus Indust

Columbus - Franklin County (G-5781)

5100 W Broad St (43228-1607)
PHONE..................614 297-4000
Mark Sutter, Pr
EMP: 1950
SALES (corp-wide): 4.29B Privately Held
Web: www.ohiohealth.com
SIC: 8062 General medical and surgical hospitals
HQ: Doctors Ohiohealth Corporation
    5100 W Broad St
    Columbus OH 43228
    614 544-5424

(G-5781)
DOCTORS OHIOHEALTH CORPORATION (HQ)
Also Called: Doctors Hospital North
5100 W Broad St (43228-1607)
PHONE..................614 544-5424
David Blom, CEO
Mike Louge, *
Cheryl Hodges, *
David Morehead, *
Ed Cotter, *
EMP: 1200 EST: 1920
SQ FT: 270,000
SALES (est): 389.57MM
SALES (corp-wide): 4.29B Privately Held
Web: www.ohiohealth.com
SIC: 8062 8011 Hospital, medical school affiliated with residency; Medical insurance plan
PA: Ohiohealth Corporation
    3430 Ohhalth Pkwy 5th Flr
    Columbus OH 43202
    614 788-8860

(G-5782)
DORCY INTERNATIONAL INC (PA)
Also Called: Lifegear
2700 Port Rd (43217-1136)
PHONE..................614 497-5830
◆ EMP: 69 EST: 1985
SALES (est): 10.12MM
SALES (corp-wide): 10.12MM Privately Held
Web: www.dorcy.com
SIC: 5063 Flashlights

(G-5783)
DOUBLE Z CONSTRUCTION COMPANY
2550 Harrison Rd (43204-3510)
PHONE..................614 274-9334
David Guzzo, Pr
John T Stinson, *
Larry Lyons, *
Vincent M Guzzo, *
EMP: 60 EST: 2001
SQ FT: 6,500
SALES (est): 19.38MM Privately Held
Web: www.doublez.co
SIC: 1521 Single-family housing construction

(G-5784)
DOYLE HCM INC
735 Taylor Rd Ste 100 (43230-6274)
PHONE..................614 322-9310
Ryan Doyle, Prin
EMP: 29 EST: 2018
SALES (est): 1.66MM Privately Held
Web: www.doylehcm.com
SIC: 8721 Payroll accounting service

(G-5785)
DR ALXANDER C NNABUE ASSOC PA
825 Dennison Ave (43215-1315)
PHONE..................614 499-7687
EMP: 49
SALES (corp-wide): 6.8MM Privately Held
Web: www.visualeyesgroup.com
SIC: 7336 Commercial art and graphic design
PA: Dr. Alexander C. Nnabue And Associates, Pa
    10240 Lake Arbor Way
    Mitchellville MD 20721
    301 324-9500

(G-5786)
DRIVE CAPITAL
629 N High St (43215-2929)
PHONE..................614 284-9436
EMP: 33 EST: 2018
SALES (est): 1.58MM Privately Held
Web: www.drivecapital.com
SIC: 6799 Investors, nec

(G-5787)
DTAC OF OHIO LLC ◐
Also Called: Hittle House
774 Internet Dr (43207-2589)
PHONE..................614 443-5454
Tiffany Lipschutz, Managing Member
EMP: 50 EST: 2022
SALES (est): 719.04K Privately Held
SIC: 8361 Residential care

(G-5788)
DUBLIN CLEANERS INC (PA)
6845 Caine Rd (43235-4234)
PHONE..................614 764-9934
Gregory J Butler, Pr
EMP: 55 EST: 1946
SQ FT: 12,000
SALES (est): 2.31MM
SALES (corp-wide): 2.31MM Privately Held
Web: www.dublincleaners.com
SIC: 7216 Cleaning and dyeing, except rugs

(G-5789)
DUMMEN NA INC (PA)
Also Called: Ecke Ranch
250 S High St Ste 650 (43215-4630)
PHONE..................614 850-9551
Paul Ecke, Ch Bd
▲ EMP: 32 EST: 1923
SQ FT: 1,500,000
SALES (est): 21.81MM
SALES (corp-wide): 21.81MM Privately Held
SIC: 0181 Flowers, grown in field nurseries

(G-5790)
DUMMEN USA INC (PA)
250 S High St Ste 650 (43215-4630)
PHONE..................614 850-9551
Perry Wismans, Pr
Tobias Dummen, Stockholder
Frank Magneson, Finance
EMP: 27 EST: 1999
SQ FT: 1,250
SALES (est): 4.71MM
SALES (corp-wide): 4.71MM Privately Held
Web: na.dummenorange.com
SIC: 5193 Flowers and florists supplies

(G-5791)
DUNBAR ARMORED INC
2300 Citygate Dr Unit B (43219-3665)
PHONE..................614 475-1969
EMP: 58
SALES (corp-wide): 4.87B Publicly Held
Web: www.dunbarsecurity.com
SIC: 7381 Security guard service
HQ: Dunbar Armored, Inc.
    50 Schilling Rd
    Hunt Valley MD 21031
    410 584-9800

(G-5792)
DUNBAR ARMORED INC
1421 Alpine Dr (43229-2602)
PHONE..................614 848-7833
David Dunbar, Brnch Mgr
EMP: 32
SALES (corp-wide): 4.87B Publicly Held
Web: www.dunbarsecurity.com
SIC: 7381 Armored car services
HQ: Dunbar Armored, Inc.
    50 Schilling Rd
    Hunt Valley MD 21031
    410 584-9800

(G-5793)
DUNCAN SALES INC
Also Called: City Wide Fclty Sltons - Clmbu
350 Mccormick Blvd Ste E (43213-1550)
PHONE..................614 755-6580
Chris Duncan, Pr
EMP: 42 EST: 2002
SALES (est): 1.24MM Privately Held
SIC: 7342 Disinfecting and pest control services

(G-5794)
DURABLE SLATE CO (PA)
Also Called: Durable Materials Company, The
3933 Groves Rd (43232-4138)
PHONE..................614 299-5522
TOLL FREE: 800
Michael Chan, CEO
John Chan, *
Ed Delong, Stockholder*
▲ EMP: 70 EST: 1986
SQ FT: 14,000
SALES (est): 29.99MM Privately Held
Web: www.durableslate.com
SIC: 1761 Roofing contractor

(G-5795)
DURANT DC LLC
4900 E Dublin Granville Rd (43081-7651)
PHONE..................614 278-6800
Bruce Thorn, CEO
EMP: 400 EST: 2018
SALES (est): 35.19MM
SALES (corp-wide): 4.72B Publicly Held
SIC: 4225 Miniwarehouse, warehousing
PA: Big Lots, Inc.
    4900 E Dblin Granville Rd
    Columbus OH 43081
    614 278-6800

(G-5796)
DYNAMIC EDUCTL SYSTEMS INC
329 S Front St (43215-5005)
PHONE..................602 995-0116
EMP: 41
SALES (corp-wide): 57.19MM Privately Held
Web: www.dynamiceducationalsystems.com
SIC: 8331 Job training and related services
HQ: Dynamic Educational Systems, Inc.
    8433 N Black Canyon Hwy
    Phoenix AZ 85021

(G-5797)
DYNAMITE TECHNOLOGIES LLC (PA)
274 Marconi Blvd Ste 300 (43215-2363)
PHONE..................614 538-0095
Matthew Dopkiss, Managing Member
Robert Whitman, Managing Member*
EMP: 38 EST: 2004
SALES (est): 11.91MM Privately Held
Web: www.willowtreeapps.com
SIC: 7371 Computer software development and applications

(G-5798)
E RETAILING ASSOCIATES LLC
Also Called: Customized Girl
2282 Westbrooke Dr (43228-9416)
PHONE..................614 300-5785
Taj Schaffnit, Managing Member
Kurt J Schmalz, *
EMP: 64 EST: 2007
SALES (est): 10.35MM Privately Held
Web: www.eretailing.com
SIC: 8748 5961 2253 Business consulting, nec; Electronic shopping; T-shirts and tops, knit

(G-5799)
EASTON TOWN CENTER II LLC
Also Called: Steiner Associates
160 Easton Town Ctr (43219-6074)
PHONE..................614 416-7000
Roxanne Nally, Mgr
EMP: 60 EST: 2019
SALES (est): 9.84MM Privately Held
Web: www.eastontowncenter.com
SIC: 6512 Shopping center, property operation only

(G-5800)
EASTON TOWN CENTER LLC
Also Called: Easton Town Center Guest Svcs
4016 Townsfair Way Ste 201 (43219-6083)
PHONE..................614 337-2560
Yaromir Steiner, Managing Member
Eddie Bauer, *
EMP: 175 EST: 1997
SQ FT: 10,000
SALES (est): 20.77MM Privately Held
Web: www.eastontowncenter.com
SIC: 6512 Shopping center, regional (300,000-1,000,000) sq. ft.)

(G-5801)
EASTWAY SUPPLIES INC
1561 Alum Creek Dr (43209-2780)
PHONE..................614 252-3650
Gary M Glanzman, Pr
Vanessa Glanzman, Sec
Jason Burton, Treas
EMP: 40 EST: 1971
SQ FT: 10,000
SALES (est): 16.91MM Privately Held
Web: www.eastwaysupplies.com
SIC: 5074 Plumbing fittings and supplies

(G-5802)
EATON CORPORATION
Also Called: Ledger 6031
P.O. Box 182175 (43218-2175)
PHONE..................614 839-4387
EMP: 54
Web: www.dix-eaton.com
SIC: 5063 Electrical apparatus and equipment
HQ: Eaton Corporation
    1000 Eaton Blvd
    Cleveland OH 44122
    440 523-5000

(G-5803)
EBUYS INC
Also Called: Shoemetro
810 Dsw Dr (43219-1828)
PHONE..................858 831-0839
David Tam Duong, CEO
EMP: 50 EST: 2004
SQ FT: 8,700
SALES (est): 28.62MM
SALES (corp-wide): 3.07B Publicly Held
SIC: 5139 Shoes
HQ: Dsw Shoe Warehouse, Inc.
    810 Dsw Dr
    Columbus OH 43219
    614 237-7100

GEOGRAPHIC SECTION
Columbus - Franklin County (G-5826)

(G-5804)
ECLIPSE 3D/PI LLC
825 Taylor Rd (43230-6235)
PHONE..................................614 626-8536
Jeff Burt, *CEO*
Sandra Burt, *
Scott Wolfe, *
EMP: 45 **EST:** 1994
SALES (est): 2.71MM **Privately Held**
Web: www.eclipsecreative.com
SIC: **7335** 2621 Photographic studio, commercial; Printing paper

(G-5805)
ECOHOUSE LLC
Also Called: Ecohouse Solar
4350 Equity Dr (43228-4803)
PHONE..................................614 456-7641
EMP: 30 **EST:** 2008
SALES (est): 1.99MM **Privately Held**
Web: www.ecohousesolar.com
SIC: **1711** Solar energy contractor

(G-5806)
ECONOMIC & CMNTY DEV INST INC
Also Called: ECDI
1655 Old Leonard Ave (43219)
PHONE..................................614 559-0104
Inna Kinney, *Pr*
EMP: 41 **EST:** 1985
SALES (est): 13.82MM **Privately Held**
Web: www.ecdi.org
SIC: **8399** Community development groups

(G-5807)
EDISON WELDING INSTITUTE INC (PA)
Also Called: Buffalo Mfg Works BMW
1250 Arthur E Adams Dr (43221-3585)
PHONE..................................614 688-5000
Henry Cialone, *CEO*
Mark Matson, *
Robert Walter, *
Phil Weisenbach, *
Edward W Ungar, *
▲ **EMP:** 131 **EST:** 1984
SQ FT: 135,000
SALES (est): 26.3MM
SALES (corp-wide): 26.3MM **Privately Held**
Web: www.ewi.org
SIC: **8731** 8711 Commercial physical research; Engineering services

(G-5808)
EDKO LLC
5743 Westbourne Ave (43213-4406)
PHONE..................................614 863-5946
EMP: 49
SALES (corp-wide): 15.4MM **Privately Held**
Web: www.edkollc.com
SIC: **0782** 5191 Lawn care services; Herbicides
PA: Edko, Llc
    4615 Marlena St
    Bossier City LA 71111
    318 425-8671

(G-5809)
EDWARDS MOONEY & MOSES
Also Called: Edwards Mooney & Moses of Ohio
1320 Mckinley Ave Ste B (43222-1115)
PHONE..................................614 351-1439
Randall Hall, *VP*
EMP: 236 **EST:** 1977
SALES (est): 953.11K
SALES (corp-wide): 2.78B **Publicly Held**
Web: www.edwardsmooneyandmoses.com
SIC: **1742** Insulation, buildings
HQ: Installed Building Products Llc
    495 S High St Ste 150
    Columbus OH 43215
    614 221-3399

(G-5810)
ELECTRIC CONNECTION INC
6510 Huntley Rd (43229-1012)
PHONE..................................614 436-1121
Judson G Voorhees, *Pr*
Randy L Harmon, *
EMP: 100 **EST:** 1983
SALES (est): 5.1MM **Privately Held**
Web: www.theelectricconnect.com
SIC: **1731** General electrical contractor

(G-5811)
ELFORD INC
Also Called: Elford Construction Services
1220 Dublin Rd (43215-1008)
PHONE..................................614 488-4000
James W Smith, *CEO*
Edward Straub, *
Michael Fitzpatrick, *
Eric Bull, *
Jeffrey Copeland, *
EMP: 200 **EST:** 1910
SQ FT: 54,000
SALES (est): 115.02MM **Privately Held**
Web: www.elford.com
SIC: **1542** 1541 8741 Commercial and office building, new construction; Industrial buildings, new construction, nec; Construction management

(G-5812)
EMBRACING AUTISM INC
2491 W Dublin Granville Rd (43235-2708)
P.O. Box 29190 (43229-0190)
PHONE..................................614 559-0077
David Rastoka, *Pr*
EMP: 30 **EST:** 2012
SALES (est): 1.06MM
SALES (corp-wide): 166.34MM **Privately Held**
SIC: **8361** Residential care
HQ: Dungarvin Ohio, Llc
    294 E Campus View Blvd
    Columbus OH 43235

(G-5813)
EMC RESEARCH INCORPORATED
3857 N High St (43214-3779)
PHONE..................................614 268-1660
Molly Osahnessy, *Brnch Mgr*
EMP: 28
SALES (corp-wide): 7.79MM **Privately Held**
Web: www.emcresearch.com
SIC: **8732** Market analysis or research
PA: Emc Research, Incorporated
    2001 Broadway Ste 110
    Oakland CA 94612
    972 349-1888

(G-5814)
EMERGENCY SERVICES INC
2323 W 5th Ave Ste 220 (43204-4899)
PHONE..................................614 224-6420
Alen Gora, *Pr*
EMP: 79 **EST:** 1972
SALES (est): 3.14MM **Privately Held**
Web: www.esiohio.com
SIC: **8011** Offices and clinics of medical doctors

(G-5815)
EMPLIFI INC (PA)
Also Called: Emplifi
4400 Easton Cmns (43219-6226)
PHONE..................................614 508-6100
EMP: 49 **EST:** 1995
SQ FT: 12,230
SALES (est): 28.21MM **Privately Held**
Web: www.astutesolutions.com
SIC: **7371** Computer software development

(G-5816)
EMPORA TITLE INC
1362 Cole St (43205-2460)
PHONE..................................937 360-8876
EMP: 35 **EST:** 2020
SALES (est): 1.07MM **Privately Held**
Web: www.emporatitle.com
SIC: **7371** Computer software development and applications

(G-5817)
ENERVISE LLC
6663 Huntley Rd Ste K (43229-1038)
PHONE..................................614 885-9800
EMP: 40
SALES (corp-wide): 16MM **Privately Held**
Web: www.enervise.com
SIC: **1711** Mechanical contractor
HQ: Enervise, Llc
    10226 Alliance Rd
    Blue Ash OH 45242
    513 761-6000

(G-5818)
ENGAGE HEALTHCARE SVCS CORP
Also Called: Ppmc
4619 Kenny Rd Ste 100 (43220-2779)
PHONE..................................614 457-8180
Samuel J Kiehl Iii Md, *CEO*
EMP: 50 **EST:** 1980
SQ FT: 10,000
SALES (est): 4.66MM **Privately Held**
Web: www.engagehbs.com
SIC: **8099** 8742 Blood related health services; Business management consultant

(G-5819)
ENGAUGE HOLDINGS LLC
375 N Front St Ste 400 (43215-2237)
PHONE..................................614 573-1010
EMP: 100
SALES (corp-wide): 5.6MM **Privately Held**
SIC: **7311** 8742 Advertising agencies; Management consulting services
PA: Engauge Holdings, Llc
    437 Grant St Mezz
    Pittsburgh PA 15222
    412 471-5300

(G-5820)
ENVIRNMNTAL SYSTEMS RES INST I
Also Called: Esri
1085 Beecher Xing N Ste A (43230-4563)
PHONE..................................614 933-8698
Steven Kenzie, *Mgr*
EMP: 36
SALES (corp-wide): 490.13MM **Privately Held**
Web: www.esri.com
SIC: **5045** Computer software
PA: Environmental Systems Research Institute, Inc.
    380 New York St
    Redlands CA 92373
    909 793-2853

(G-5821)
ENVIRO IT LLC
Also Called: Accurate It Services
3854 Fisher Rd (43228-1016)
PHONE..................................614 453-0709
Michael Yankelevich, *Managing Member*
Scott Weigand, *
EMP: 30 **EST:** 2003
SALES (est): 2.5MM **Privately Held**
Web: www.accurateit.com
SIC: **7379** 5065 Online services technology consultants; Modems, computer

(G-5822)
ENVISIONWARE INC (PA)
861 Taylor Rd Unit H (43230-6275)
PHONE..................................678 382-6530
Michael J Monk, *CEO*
◆ **EMP:** 43 **EST:** 1998
SALES (est): 9.66MM
SALES (corp-wide): 9.66MM **Privately Held**
Web: www.envisionware.com
SIC: **7371** Computer code authors

(G-5823)
EP FERRIS & ASSOCIATES INC
2130 Quarry Trails Dr # 2 (43228-8981)
PHONE..................................614 299-2999
Edward P Ferris, *Ch Bd*
Matthew Ferris, *Dir*
EMP: 40 **EST:** 1987
SALES (est): 10.01MM **Privately Held**
Web: www.epferris.com
SIC: **8742** 8711 1389 Management consulting services; Construction and civil engineering; Testing, measuring, surveying, and analysis services

(G-5824)
EQUALITY OHIO EDUCATION FUND
370 S 5th St Ste G3 (43215-7436)
PHONE..................................614 224-0400
E Holford, *Ex Dir*
Elyezabeth Holford, *Ex Dir*
EMP: 27 **EST:** 2009
SALES (est): 546.54K **Privately Held**
Web: www.equalityohio.org
SIC: **8699** Charitable organization

(G-5825)
EQUITAS HEALTH INC (PA)
1105 Schrock Rd Ste 400 (43229-1174)
PHONE..................................614 299-2437
William Hardy, *CEO*
Peggy Anderson, *COO*
Fikru Nigusse, *CFO*
Admiral Trent Stechschulte, *Prin*
EMP: 64 **EST:** 1984
SQ FT: 10,000
SALES (est): 72.78MM **Privately Held**
Web: www.equitashealth.com
SIC: **8322** 8093 8011 8049 Individual and family services; Mental health clinic, outpatient; Primary care medical clinic; Nurses and other medical assistants

(G-5826)
ERIE INSUR EXCH ACTVTIES ASSN
445 Hutchinson Ave (43235-5677)
PHONE..................................614 430-8530
EMP: 35
SALES (corp-wide): 1.24B **Privately Held**
Web: www.erieinsurance.com
SIC: **6411** Insurance agents, nec
PA: The Erie Insurance Exchange Activities Association Inc
    100 Erie Insurance Pl
    Erie PA 16530
    800 458-0811

Columbus - Franklin County (G-5827)

(G-5827)
ERNST & YOUNG LLP
Also Called: Ey
800 Yard St Ste 200 (43212-3882)
PHONE..................................614 224-5678
Craig Marshall, *Mng Pt*
EMP: 175
Web: www.ey.com
SIC: 8721 8742 Certified public accountant; Business management consultant
HQ: Ernst & Young Llp
1 Manhattan W Fl 6
New York NY 10001
703 747-0049

(G-5828)
ESCAPE ENTERPRISES INC
Also Called: Steak Escape
222 Neilston St (43215-2636)
PHONE..................................614 224-0300
Kennard Smith, *Ch*
Mark Turner, *
EMP: 94 **EST:** 1982
SQ FT: 10,000
SALES (est): 2.16MM **Privately Held**
Web: www.steakescape.com
SIC: 5812 6794 Steak restaurant; Franchises, selling or licensing

(G-5829)
ESSENDANT CO
1634 Westbelt Dr (43228-3810)
PHONE..................................614 876-7774
Mike Huettel, *Pr*
EMP: 176
SQ FT: 126,000
Web: www.essendant.com
SIC: 5112 5044 Office supplies, nec; Office equipment
HQ: Essendant Co.
1 Pkwy N Blvd Ste 100
Deerfield IL 60015
847 627-7000

(G-5830)
ESSEX HEALTHCARE CORPORATION (PA)
2780 Airport Dr Ste 400 (43219-2289)
PHONE..................................614 416-0600
EMP: 30 **EST:** 1997
SQ FT: 15,000
SALES (est): 38.64MM **Privately Held**
SIC: 6531 Real estate brokers and agents

(G-5831)
ESSILOR LABORATORIES AMER INC
Also Called: Top Network
3671 Interchange Rd (43204-1499)
PHONE..................................614 274-0840
Don Lepore, *Mgr*
EMP: 31
SALES (corp-wide): 2.55MM **Privately Held**
Web: www.essilorinstrumentsusa.com
SIC: 3851 5049 Eyeglasses, lenses and frames; Optical goods
HQ: Essilor Laboratories Of America, Inc.
13515 N Stemmons Fwy
Dallas TX 75234
972 241-4141

(G-5832)
ESTES EXPRESS LINES
Also Called: Estes
1009 Frank Rd (43223-3858)
PHONE..................................614 275-6000
Tom Siefert, *Mgr*
EMP: 99
SQ FT: 4,331
SALES (corp-wide): 3.56B **Privately Held**
Web: www.estes-express.com
SIC: 4213 Contract haulers
PA: Estes Express Lines
3901 W Broad St
Richmond VA 23230
804 353-1900

(G-5833)
EVANS ADHESIVE CORPORATION (HQ)
925 Old Henderson Rd (43220-3779)
PHONE..................................614 451-2665
C Russell Thompson, *Pr*
EMP: 27 **EST:** 1900
SALES (est): 10.19MM
SALES (corp-wide): 84.16MM **Privately Held**
Web: www.evansadhesive.com
SIC: 2891 5085 Adhesives; Abrasives and adhesives
PA: Meridian Adhesives Group Llc
15720 Brixham Hill Ave # 500
Charlotte NC

(G-5834)
EVEREST TECHNOLOGIES INC
1105 Schrock Rd Ste 500 (43229-1174)
PHONE..................................614 436-3120
Vineet Arya, *Pr*
Anil Bakhshi, *
Bob Malik, *
EMP: 30 **EST:** 1997
SALES (est): 5.58MM **Privately Held**
Web: www.everesttech.com
SIC: 7379 Online services technology consultants

(G-5835)
EXCEL DECORATORS INC
3910 Groves Rd Ste A (43232-4162)
PHONE..................................614 522-0056
Sonja Winscott, *Brnch Mgr*
EMP: 77
SALES (corp-wide): 8.56MM **Privately Held**
Web: www.exceldecorators.com
SIC: 7299 Party planning service
PA: Excel Decorators Inc
3748 Kentucky Ave
Indianapolis IN 46221
317 856-1300

(G-5836)
EXCELLENCE HOME HEALTHCARE LLC
2238 S Hamilton Rd Ste 102 (43232-4382)
PHONE..................................614 755-6502
EMP: 50 **EST:** 2011
SALES (est): 817.37K **Privately Held**
SIC: 8082 Home health care services

(G-5837)
EXCLUSIVE LIFESTYLES OHIO LLC
Also Called: Corcoran Global Living
4449 Easton Way (43219-6093)
PHONE..................................740 647-5552
EMP: 32 **EST:** 2021
SALES (est): 63.4K **Privately Held**
SIC: 6531 Buying agent, real estate

(G-5838)
EXEL GLOBAL LOGISTICS INC
2144a John Glenn Ave (43217-1154)
PHONE..................................614 409-4500
Roger Richard, *Brnch Mgr*
EMP: 177
SALES (corp-wide): 88.87B **Privately Held**
SIC: 4731 Domestic freight forwarding
HQ: Exel Global Logistics Inc.
22879 Glenn Dr Ste 100
Sterling VA 20164
877 858-3555

(G-5839)
EXPESITE LLC (DH)
278 N 5th St (43215-2604)
PHONE..................................614 917-1100
EMP: 39 **EST:** 2002
SALES (est): 12.34MM
SALES (corp-wide): 6.07B **Publicly Held**
Web: www.expesite.com
SIC: 7371 Computer software development
HQ: Accruent, Llc
11500 Alterra Pkwy # 110
Austin TX 78758

(G-5840)
EXXCEL PROJECT MANAGEMENT LLC
Also Called: Exxcel
328 Civic Center Dr (43215-5087)
PHONE..................................614 621-4500
F Douglas Reardon, *Pr*
Richard Warren, *
Doug Kaiser, *
Rick Warren, *
James Bach, *
EMP: 28 **EST:** 1991
SQ FT: 10,000
SALES (est): 16.03MM **Privately Held**
Web: www.exxcel.com
SIC: 1542 1541 Commercial and office building, new construction; Industrial buildings, new construction, nec

(G-5841)
FACE FORWARD AESTHETICS LLC
1335 Dublin Rd Ste 110f (43215-1000)
PHONE..................................844 307-5929
Alex Stewart, *CEO*
EMP: 35 **EST:** 2018
SALES (est): 2.12MM **Privately Held**
Web: www.faceforwardaesthetics.com
SIC: 7231 Cosmetology and personal hygiene salons

(G-5842)
FACILITIES MANAGEMENT EX LLC
800 Yard St Ste 115 (43212-3866)
PHONE..................................614 519-2186
Jeffery Wilkins, *CEO*
Brian Gregory, *
Jeffery Wilkins Ceojeffery Wil kins, *CEO*
EMP: 56 **EST:** 2014
SQ FT: 3,200
SALES (est): 5.13MM **Privately Held**
Web: www.gofmx.com
SIC: 7372 Application computer software

(G-5843)
FAHLGREN INC (PA)
Also Called: Fahlgren Mortine
4030 Easton Sta Ste 300 (43219)
PHONE..................................614 383-1500
Neil Mortine, *Pr*
Brent Holbert, *
Aaron Brown, *
EMP: 40 **EST:** 1962
SALES (est): 39.22MM
SALES (corp-wide): 39.22MM **Privately Held**
Web: www.fahlgrenmortine.com
SIC: 7311 Advertising consultant

(G-5844)
FAIRFELD INN STES CLMBUS ARPRT
Also Called: Fairfield Inn
4300 International Gtwy (43219-1749)
PHONE..................................614 237-2100
EMP: 30 **EST:** 2014
SALES (est): 1MM **Privately Held**
Web: www.marriott.com
SIC: 7011 Hotels and motels

(G-5845)
FAIRFIELD INN
Also Called: Fairfield Inn & Suites Columbu
3031 Olentangy River Rd (43202-1572)
PHONE..................................614 267-1111
Frank Stnichols, *Prin*
EMP: 50 **EST:** 2007
SALES (est): 2.16MM **Privately Held**
Web: www.marriott.com
SIC: 7011 Hotels and motels

(G-5846)
FAIRWAY FAMILY PHYSICIANS INC
1171 Fairway Blvd (43213-2581)
PHONE..................................614 861-7051
Joseph Whitlatch Junior Md, *Pr*
Edward Baltes Md, *VP*
EMP: 39 **EST:** 1977
SQ FT: 1,200
SALES (est): 860.57K **Privately Held**
Web: www.copcp.com
SIC: 8011 General and family practice, physician/surgeon

(G-5847)
FAIRWAY INDEPENDENT MRTG CORP
Also Called: Fairway Independent Mortgage
4215 Worth Ave Ste 220 (43219-1546)
PHONE..................................614 930-6552
EMP: 44
Web: www.fairwayindependentmc.com
SIC: 6162 Mortgage bankers
PA: Fairway Independent Mortgage Corporation
4750 S Biltmore Ln
Madison WI 53718

(G-5848)
FAITH MISSION INC
245 N Grant Ave (43215-2641)
PHONE..................................614 224-6617
John Dickey, *Ex Dir*
Susan Villilo, *
EMP: 66 **EST:** 1966
SQ FT: 20,000
SALES (est): 11.18MM
SALES (corp-wide): 24.05MM **Privately Held**
Web: www.lssnetworkofhope.org
SIC: 8322 Social service center
PA: Lutheran Social Services Of Central Ohio
500 W Wilson Bridge Rd
Worthington OH 43085
419 289-3523

(G-5849)
FAMILY PHYSICIANS OF GAHANNA
725 Buckles Ct N (43230-5316)
PHONE..................................614 471-9654
Michael Baehr, *Pt*
John Tyznik, *Pt*
Joseph Lutz, *Pt*
Maria Sammarco, *Pt*
Evan Stathulis, *Pt*
EMP: 38 **EST:** 1987
SALES (est): 2.14MM **Privately Held**
Web: www.copcp.com
SIC: 8011 General and family practice, physician/surgeon

(G-5850)
FARBER CORPORATION
Also Called: Honeywell Authorized Dealer
800 E 12th Ave (43211-2670)
PHONE..................................614 294-1626
Edward A Farber, *Pr*
Tim Farber, *

GEOGRAPHIC SECTION
Columbus - Franklin County (G-5870)

Sandra B Farber, *
▲ **EMP:** 30 **EST:** 1969
SQ FT: 12,000
SALES (est): 15.25MM **Privately Held**
Web: www.farbercorp.com
SIC: 1711 Mechanical contractor

(G-5851)
FARMERS INSURANCE COLUMBUS INC (DH)
Also Called: Farmers Insurance
7400 Skyline Dr E (43235-2706)
P.O. Box 2910 (66201-1310)
PHONE..................614 799-3200
Annette K Schons-thompson, *Pr*
Richard R Weiss, *Treas*
William A Buherer, *Sec*
Martin D Feinstein, *VP*
Russell L Powers, *VP*
EMP: 400 **EST:** 1979
SQ FT: 350,000
SALES (est): 45.95MM **Privately Held**
Web: www.farmers.com
SIC: 6411 Insurance agents, brokers, and service
HQ: Farmers Insurance Exchange
6301 Owensmouth Ave
Woodland Hills CA 91367
888 327-6335

(G-5852)
FAVRET COMPANY
Also Called: Favret Heating & Cooling
1296 Dublin Rd (43215-1008)
PHONE..................614 488-5211
William Favret, *CEO*
Mark Favret, *
Philip Favret, *
EMP: 63 **EST:** 1924
SQ FT: 20,000
SALES (est): 9.9MM **Privately Held**
Web: www.favret.com
SIC: 1711 Warm air heating and air conditioning contractor

(G-5853)
FCX PERFORMANCE INC (HQ)
Also Called: Jh Instruments
3000 E 14th Ave (43219)
PHONE..................614 253-1996
Thomas Cox, *Ch*
Russell S Frazee, *
Chris Hill, *
Theron Neese, *
Brian Miller, *
▲ **EMP:** 40 **EST:** 1999
SQ FT: 44,000
SALES (est): 544.13MM
SALES (corp-wide): 4.41B **Publicly Held**
Web: www.fcxperformance.com
SIC: 5084 5085 3494 Instruments and control equipment; Industrial supplies; Valves and pipe fittings, nec
PA: Applied Industrial Technologies, Inc.
1 Applied Plz
Cleveland OH 44115
216 426-4000

(G-5854)
FD HOLDINGS LLC
250 E Broad St Fl O (43215-3708)
PHONE..................614 228-5775
EMP: 346
SALES (corp-wide): 233.8MM **Privately Held**
Web: www.factualdata.com
SIC: 7323 Credit reporting services
HQ: Fd Holdings Llc
400 Holiday Dr Ste 300
Pittsburgh PA 15220
970 663-5700

(G-5855)
FERGUSON CONSTRUCTION COMPANY
3595 Johnny Appleseed Ct (43231-4985)
PHONE..................614 876-8496
Ben Lindsay, *Brnch Mgr*
EMP: 48
SALES (corp-wide): 73.11MM **Privately Held**
Web: www.ferguson-construction.com
SIC: 1521 Single-family housing construction
PA: Ferguson Construction Company Inc
400 Canal St
Sidney OH 45365
937 498-2381

(G-5856)
FIFTH THIRD BNK OF COLUMBUS OH
Also Called: Fifth Third Bank
21 E State St (43215-4208)
PHONE..................614 744-7595
Jordan Miller, *Pr*
EMP: 900 **EST:** 1985
SALES (est): 57.59MM
SALES (corp-wide): 12.64B **Publicly Held**
SIC: 6022 State trust companies accepting deposits, commercial
PA: Fifth Third Bancorp
38 Fountain Square Plz
Cincinnati OH 45263
800 972-3030

(G-5857)
FINE LINE GRAPHICS CORP
Also Called: Fine Line Graphics
2364 Featherwood Dr (43228-8236)
P.O. Box 163370 (43216-3370)
PHONE..................614 486-0276
James Basch, *Pr*
Mark Carro, *
Gregory Davis, *
▲ **EMP:** 170 **EST:** 1979
SALES (est): 12.15MM **Privately Held**
Web: www.perfectdomain.com
SIC: 2752 7331 Offset printing; Mailing service

(G-5858)
FINITE STATE INC
800 N High St (43215-1430)
PHONE..................614 639-5107
Matthew Wyckhouse, *CEO*
EMP: 65 **EST:** 2017
SALES (est): 5.07MM **Privately Held**
Web: www.finitestate.io
SIC: 7382 Security systems services

(G-5859)
FIRE-SEAL LLC
850 Science Blvd (43230-6609)
PHONE..................614 454-4440
Vince Catalogna, *Owner*
Jamie Hadac, *
EMP: 40 **EST:** 2013
SALES (est): 4.87MM **Privately Held**
Web: www.fireseal-llc.com
SIC: 1799 Fireproofing buildings

(G-5860)
FIRST COMMUNITY CHURCH (PA)
1320 Cambridge Blvd (43212-3200)
PHONE..................614 488-0681
Deborah Lindsay, *Dir*
Ruth Decker, *
Richard Wing, *
Cynthia Harsany, *
EMP: 48 **EST:** 1910
SQ FT: 56,796
SALES (est): 1.34MM

SALES (corp-wide): 1.34MM **Privately Held**
Web: www.fcchurch.com
SIC: 8661 8351 Community Church; Child day care services

(G-5861)
FIRST COMMUNITY VILLAGE
Also Called: National Church Residences First Community Village
1800 Riverside Dr Ofc (43212-1819)
PHONE..................614 324-4455
Tanya Kim Hahn, *Pr*
Diane Tomlinson, *
Edward D Schorr Junior, *Prin*
Harold G Edwards, *
Jane Nash, *
EMP: 300 **EST:** 1963
SQ FT: 1,269
SALES (est): 25.67MM
SALES (corp-wide): 521.67MM **Privately Held**
Web: www.nationalchurchresidences.org
SIC: 8082 8051 8059 8322 Home health care services; Skilled nursing care facilities; Nursing home, except skilled and intermediate care facility; Outreach program
PA: National Church Residences
2335 N Bank Dr
Columbus OH 43220
614 451-2151

(G-5862)
FIRST HOTEL ASSOCIATES LP
Also Called: Westin Hotel
310 S High St (43215-4508)
PHONE..................614 228-3800
EMP: 44 **EST:** 1997
SALES (est): 949.75K **Privately Held**
Web: www.westincolumbus.com
SIC: 7011 5813 5812 Hotels; Drinking places; Eating places

(G-5863)
FIRST LEVEQUE LLC
Also Called: Hotel Leveque
50 W Broad St (43215-3301)
PHONE..................614 224-9500
Stephen L Schwartz, *Managing Member*
EMP: 53 **EST:** 2013
SALES (est): 2.16MM **Privately Held**
Web: www.hotellevequecolumbus.com
SIC: 7011 Hotels

(G-5864)
FIRST MANAGEMENT COMPANY
Also Called: Days Inn
1212 E Dublin Granville Rd (43229-3302)
PHONE..................614 885-9696
Xia Zhang, *Genl Mgr*
Ray Lin, *Pr*
EMP: 72 **EST:** 1987
SQ FT: 3,049
SALES (est): 504.11K **Privately Held**
Web: www.wyndhamhotels.com
SIC: 7011 Hotels and motels

(G-5865)
FIRSTICARE INC
Also Called: FIRSTICARE INC
3280 Morse Rd Ste 213 (43231-6175)
PHONE..................614 721-2273
Oomar Abdi, *Brnch Mgr*
EMP: 40
SALES (corp-wide): 2.1MM **Privately Held**
Web: www.firsticare.net
SIC: 8082 Home health care services
PA: Firsticare Inc.
3280 Morse Rd Ste 213
Columbus OH 43231
614 532-8599

(G-5866)
FIS INVESTOR SERVICES LLC (HQ)
4249 Easton Way Ste 400 (43219-6171)
PHONE..................904 438-6000
Leslie S Brush, *Managing Member*
EMP: 33 **EST:** 2014
SALES (est): 394.59K
SALES (corp-wide): 9.82B **Publicly Held**
SIC: 7389 Financial services
PA: Fidelity National Information Services, Inc.
347 Riverside Ave
Jacksonville FL 32202
904 438-6000

(G-5867)
FISHEL COMPANY
Johnson Brothers Construction
1600 Walcutt Rd (43228-9394)
PHONE..................614 850-4400
Ed Evans, *Mgr*
EMP: 167
SALES (corp-wide): 758.31MM **Privately Held**
Web: www.teamfishel.com
SIC: 1623 8711 1731 3612 Telephone and communication line construction; Engineering services; Electrical work; Transformers, except electric
PA: The Fishel Company
1366 Dublin Rd
Columbus OH 43215
614 274-8100

(G-5868)
FISHEL COMPANY
Also Called: Team Fishel
1600 Walcutt Rd (43228-9394)
PHONE..................614 921-8504
EMP: 90
SALES (corp-wide): 758.31MM **Privately Held**
Web: www.teamfishel.com
SIC: 1623 Underground utilities contractor
PA: The Fishel Company
1366 Dublin Rd
Columbus OH 43215
614 274-8100

(G-5869)
FISHEL COMPANY (PA)
Also Called: Fishel Technologies
1366 Dublin Rd (43215-1093)
PHONE..................614 274-8100
Diane Keeler, *Ch*
John Phillips, *CEO*
Paul Riewe, *VP*
Ken Katz, *Pr*
EMP: 60 **EST:** 1936
SQ FT: 22,000
SALES (est): 758.31MM
SALES (corp-wide): 758.31MM **Privately Held**
Web: www.teamfishel.com
SIC: 8711 1623 1731 Engineering services; Telephone and communication line construction; General electrical contractor

(G-5870)
FITCH INC (DH)
585 S Front St Ste 300 (43215)
PHONE..................614 885-3453
Simon Bolton, *CEO*
Greg Vick, *
Judy Schaefer, *
David B Smith, *Prin*
Deane W Richardson, *Prin*
EMP: 60 **EST:** 1960
SQ FT: 40,000
SALES (est): 25.62MM
SALES (corp-wide): 18.5B **Privately Held**

Columbus - Franklin County (G-5871)   GEOGRAPHIC SECTION

Web: www.landor.com
SIC: 7336 Graphic arts and related design
HQ: Wpp Clapton Square, Llc
   3 World Trade Ctr 175
   New York NY 10007

(G-5871)
FIVE STAR SENIOR LIVING INC
Also Called: Forum At Knightsbridge
4590 Knightsbridge Blvd (43214-4327)
PHONE.................................614 451-6793
Rebecca Converse, *Ex Dir*
EMP: 27
SALES (corp-wide): 934.59MM **Privately Held**
Web: www.fivestarseniorliving.com
SIC: 8051 Skilled nursing care facilities
HQ: Alerislife Inc.
   255 Washington St Ste 300
   Newton MA 02458

(G-5872)
FLAIRSOFT LTD (PA)
7720 Rivers Edge Dr Ste 200 (43235)
PHONE.................................614 888-0700
Dheeraj Kulshrestha, *Pt*
EMP: 48 EST: 2001
SALES (est): 9.54MM
SALES (corp-wide): 9.54MM **Privately Held**
Web: www.flairsoft.net
SIC: 7371 Computer software development

(G-5873)
FLIGHT EXPRESS INC (HQ)
7250 Star Check Dr (43217-1025)
PHONE.................................305 379-8686
Pat Hawk, *Pr*
Stephen Howery, *
EMP: 80 EST: 1985
SALES (est): 25.33MM
SALES (corp-wide): 316.47MM **Privately Held**
SIC: 4512 Air cargo carrier, scheduled
PA: Bayside Capital, Inc.
   1450 Brickell Ave Fl 31
   Miami FL 33131
   305 379-8686

(G-5874)
FLOYD BELL INC (PA)
720 Dearborn Park Ln (43085-5703)
PHONE.................................614 294-4000
▲ EMP: 69 EST: 1971
SALES (est): 7.39MM
SALES (corp-wide): 7.39MM **Privately Held**
Web: www.floydbell.com
SIC: 3669 5065 3661 3651 Emergency alarms; Telephone equipment; Telephone and telegraph apparatus; Household audio and video equipment

(G-5875)
FLOYD BROWNE INTERNATIONAL LTD
Also Called: Floyd Browne Group
7965 N High St Ste 340 (43235-8402)
PHONE.................................740 363-6792
Jay Shutt, *Pr*
Dan Whited, *
John Faber, *
EMP: 85 EST: 1930
SALES (est): 2.84MM **Privately Held**
SIC: 8711 Professional engineer

(G-5876)
FOOD SAFETY NET SERVICES LTD
4130 Fisher Rd (43228-1022)
PHONE.................................614 274-2070
Steve Palmer, *Brnch Mgr*
EMP: 35
SALES (corp-wide): 27.84MM **Privately Held**
Web: www.fsns.com
SIC: 8734 Food testing service
PA: Food Safety Net Services, Ltd.
   199 W Rhapsody Dr
   San Antonio TX 78216
   888 525-9788

(G-5877)
FOR IMPACT SUDDES GRO
1500 Lake Shore Dr (43204-2587)
PHONE.................................614 352-2505
EMP: 28 EST: 2018
SALES (est): 330.43K **Privately Held**
Web: www.forimpact.org
SIC: 8748 Business consulting, nec

(G-5878)
FOREST PARK CHRISTIAN SCHOOL
5600 Karl Rd (43229-3610)
PHONE.................................614 888-5282
Kristina Bundy, *Ex Dir*
Syretta Bates, *Prin*
EMP: 31 EST: 1982
SALES (est): 465.7K **Privately Held**
Web: www.forestparkchristianschool.com
SIC: 8351 8211 Preschool center; Kindergarten

(G-5879)
FORTUNE BRANDS WINDOWS INC (DH)
Also Called: Simonton Windows
3948 Townsfair Way Ste 200 (43219)
PHONE.................................614 532-3500
Mark Savan, *Pr*
Angela M Pla, *
Matthew C Lenz, *
▲ EMP: 244 EST: 2012
SALES (est): 99.47MM
SALES (corp-wide): 5.58B **Privately Held**
Web: www.simonton.com
SIC: 1751 5211 Window and door installation and erection; Door and window products
HQ: Ply Gem Industries, Inc.
   5020 Weston Pkwy Ste 400
   Cary NC 27513
   919 677-3900

(G-5880)
FRANKLIN CNTY BD COMMISSIONERS
Franklin County Facility MGT
373 S High St Fl 2 (43215-4591)
PHONE.................................614 462-3800
Maryann Barnhart, *Dir*
EMP: 144
Web: www.franklincountyohio.gov
SIC: 8744 Facilities support services
PA: Franklin County Board Of Commissioners
   373 S High St 26th Fl
   Columbus OH 43215
   614 525-3322

(G-5881)
FRANKLIN CNTY BD COMMISSIONERS
Also Called: North Community Counseling Ctr
1855 E Dublin Granville Rd Ste 204 (43229-3516)
PHONE.................................614 261-3196
David Kittredge, *Dir*
EMP: 55
Web: www.franklincountyohio.gov
SIC: 9431 8093 Mental health agency administration, government; Mental health clinic, outpatient
PA: Franklin County Board Of Commissioners
   373 S High St 26th Fl
   Columbus OH 43215
   614 525-3322

(G-5882)
FRANKLIN CNTY BD COMMISSIONERS
Also Called: Child Support Enforcement Agcy
80 E Fulton St (43215-5128)
PHONE.................................614 462-3275
Joe Pilat, *Dir*
EMP: 39
Web: www.franklincountyohio.gov
SIC: 8322 Child related social services
PA: Franklin County Board Of Commissioners
   373 S High St 26th Fl
   Columbus OH 43215
   614 525-3322

(G-5883)
FRANKLIN CNTY BD COMMISSIONERS
Also Called: Franklin County Childrens Svcs
4071 E Main St (43213-2952)
PHONE.................................614 229-7100
Chip Spinning, *Dir*
EMP: 500
Web: www.fccs.us
SIC: 8322 Child related social services
PA: Franklin County Board Of Commissioners
   373 S High St 26th Fl
   Columbus OH 43215
   614 525-3322

(G-5884)
FRANKLIN CNTY BD COMMISSIONERS
Franklin County Chld Svcs Bd
855 W Mound St (43223-2208)
PHONE.................................614 275-2571
Chip Spinning, *Dir*
EMP: 200
Web: www.franklincountyohio.gov
SIC: 8322 Childrens' aid society
PA: Franklin County Board Of Commissioners
   373 S High St 26th Fl
   Columbus OH 43215
   614 525-3322

(G-5885)
FRANKLIN CNTY BD COMMISSIONERS
Also Called: Franklin County Sani Engg Dept
280 E Broad St Rm 201 (43215-3745)
PHONE.................................614 525-3100
Thomas D Shockley, *Dir*
EMP: 207
SQ FT: 1,848
Web: www.franklincountyohio.gov
SIC: 4952 Sewerage systems
PA: Franklin County Board Of Commissioners
   373 S High St 26th Fl
   Columbus OH 43215
   614 525-3322

(G-5886)
FRANKLIN COMMUNICATIONS INC
Also Called: Wsny FM
4401 Carriage Hill Ln (43220-3837)
PHONE.................................614 459-9769
Edward K Christian, *CEO*
Alan Goodman, *
EMP: 35 EST: 1945
SQ FT: 10,000
SALES (est): 2.56MM **Publicly Held**
Web: www.rewindcolumbus.com
SIC: 4832 2711 Radio broadcasting stations; Newspapers
HQ: Saga Communications Of New England, Inc.
   73 Kercheval Ave Ste 201
   Grosse Pointe Farms MI 48236
   313 886-7070

(G-5887)
FRANKLIN COUNTY ADAMH BOARD
447 E Broad St (43215-3822)
PHONE.................................614 224-1057
David Royer, *CEO*
EMP: 50 EST: 2014
SALES (est): 4.05MM **Privately Held**
Web: www.adamhfranklin.org
SIC: 8099 Health and allied services, nec

(G-5888)
FRANKLIN COUNTY HISTORICAL SOC
Also Called: Cosi
333 W Broad St (43215)
PHONE.................................614 228-2674
David Chesebrough, *CEO*
Rick Dodsworth, *
Kimberly Pratt, *
◆ EMP: 124 EST: 1964
SQ FT: 200,000
SALES (est): 26.23MM **Privately Held**
Web: www.cosi.org
SIC: 8412 Museum

(G-5889)
FRANKLIN COUNTY PUBLIC HEALTH
280 E Broad St Rm 200 (43215-3745)
PHONE.................................614 525-3160
Ken Farmwald, *Prin*
EMP: 105 EST: 2011
SALES (est): 4.21MM **Privately Held**
Web: www.myfcph.org
SIC: 8099 Health and allied services, nec

(G-5890)
FRANKLIN WORKS INC
1563 Westbelt Dr (43228-3839)
PHONE.................................361 215-2300
EMP: 32
SALES (corp-wide): 112.9K **Privately Held**
SIC: 7389 Personal service agents, brokers, and bureaus
PA: Franklin Works Inc.
   38273 Airport Pkwy
   Willoughby OH 44094
   330 204-9722

(G-5891)
FRATERNAL ORDER OF PLICE OF OH (PA)
222 E Town St Fl 1e (43215-4611)
P.O. Box 112 (43015-0112)
PHONE.................................614 224-5700
Jay Mcdonald, *Pr*
Mark Drum, *
EMP: 30 EST: 1935
SQ FT: 6,500
SALES (est): 62.57K
SALES (corp-wide): 62.57K **Privately Held**
Web: www.fopohio.org
SIC: 8641 Fraternal associations

(G-5892)
FREEDOM RECOVERY LLC
4998 W Broad St Ste 104 (43228-1647)
PHONE.................................614 754-8051

GEOGRAPHIC SECTION

Columbus - Franklin County (G-5916)

Chad Kelly, *Prin*
EMP: 27 **EST:** 2018
SALES (est): 501.68K **Privately Held**
Web: www.freedomrecovery.us
SIC: 8322 General counseling services

(G-5893)
FREEDOM SPECIALTY INSURANCE CO (DH)
Also Called: Travelers Insurance
1 W Nationwide Blvd (43215-2752)
P.O. Box 4120 (85261-4120)
PHONE..................................614 249-1545
Chris Watson, *Pr*
▲ **EMP:** 202 **EST:** 1976
SQ FT: 96,000
SALES (est): 180.73K
SALES (corp-wide): 11.75B **Privately Held**
Web: www.travelers.com
SIC: 6331 Automobile insurance
HQ: Scottsdale Insurance Company
8877 N Gainey Center Dr
Scottsdale AZ 85258
480 365-4000

(G-5894)
FREELAND CONTRACTING CO
2100 Integrity Dr S (43209-2752)
PHONE..................................614 443-2718
James R Fry, *Pr*
Brenda Fry, *
EMP: 32 **EST:** 1990
SQ FT: 19,200
SALES (est): 15.63MM **Privately Held**
Web: www.freelandcc.com
SIC: 1711 Plumbing contractors

(G-5895)
FRESHEALTH LLC
3650 E 5th Ave (43219-1805)
PHONE..................................614 231-3601
Alex Dinovo, *Managing Member*
EMP: 80 **EST:** 2017
SALES (est): 2.17MM **Privately Held**
Web: www.dnoinc.com
SIC: 0723 Fruit crops market preparation services

(G-5896)
FRIENDS OF CASA FRNKLIN CNTY O
Also Called: CASA OF FRANKLIN COUNTY
373 S High St Fl 15 (43215-6320)
PHONE..................................614 525-7450
EMP: 45 **EST:** 1991
SALES (est): 180.57K **Privately Held**
Web: casa.franklincountyohio.gov
SIC: 8322 Child related social services

(G-5897)
FRIENDSHIP VLG OF CLUMBUS OHIO
5757 Ponderosa Dr (43231-3102)
PHONE..................................614 890-8287
Amanda Trzcinski, *Prin*
EMP: 100
SALES (corp-wide): 21.28MM **Privately Held**
Web: www.liveatwesterwood.org
SIC: 8051 Convalescent home with continuous nursing care
PA: Friendship Village Of Columbus Ohio, Inc
5800 Frest Hills Blvd Ofc
Columbus OH 43231
614 890-8282

(G-5898)
FRIENDSHIP VLG OF CLUMBUS OHIO (PA)
5800 Forest Hills Blvd Ofc (43231)
PHONE..................................614 890-8282
Thomas Miller, *Ex Dir*
EMP: 105 **EST:** 1975
SQ FT: 265,000
SALES (est): 21.28MM
SALES (corp-wide): 21.28MM **Privately Held**
Web: www.liveatwesterwood.org
SIC: 8361 8051 Aged home; Skilled nursing care facilities

(G-5899)
FRITO-LAY NORTH AMERICA INC
Also Called: Frito-Lay
6611 Broughton Ave (43213-1523)
PHONE..................................614 508-3004
Don Jacklich, *Mgr*
EMP: 30
SALES (corp-wide): 86.39B **Publicly Held**
Web: www.fritolay.com
SIC: 5145 Snack foods
HQ: Frito-Lay North America, Inc.
7701 Legacy Dr
Plano TX 75024

(G-5900)
FRITZ-RUMER-COOKE CO INC (PA)
1879 Federal Pkwy Fl 2 (43207)
P.O. Box 7884 (43207)
PHONE..................................614 444-8844
TOLL FREE: 800
Clement C Cooke, *Pr*
Karen Cooke, *
EMP: 31 **EST:** 1879
SQ FT: 1,500
SALES (est): 14.49MM
SALES (corp-wide): 14.49MM **Privately Held**
Web: www.frcrail.com
SIC: 1629 Railroad and railway roadbed construction

(G-5901)
FUGEES FAMILY INC
1933 E Dublin Granville Rd Ste 117 (43229-3508)
PHONE..................................678 358-0547
EMP: 27 **EST:** 2018
SALES (est): 3.7MM **Privately Held**
Web: www.fugeesfamily.org
SIC: 8399 Regional planning organization

(G-5902)
FUSIAN INC (PA)
1391 W 5th Ave (43212-2902)
PHONE..................................937 361-7146
Zach Weprin, *CEO*
EMP: 28 **EST:** 2016
SALES (est): 25.38MM
SALES (corp-wide): 25.38MM **Privately Held**
Web: www.fusian.com
SIC: 5812 7371 Japanese restaurant; Computer software development and applications

(G-5903)
G & G CONCRETE CNSTR LLC
2849 Switzer Ave (43219-2313)
PHONE..................................614 475-4151
EMP: 32 **EST:** 2017
SALES (est): 2.44MM **Privately Held**
SIC: 1521 Single-family housing construction

(G-5904)
G D SUPPLY INC (PA)
Also Called: Johnstone Supply
700 Parkwood Ave (43219-2518)
P.O. Box 730 (43216-0730)
PHONE..................................614 258-1111
George Ells Junior, *Pr*
Dorothy Ells, *
George A Ells Senior, *Ch Bd*
EMP: 30 **EST:** 1984
SQ FT: 20,000
SALES (est): 12.71MM
SALES (corp-wide): 12.71MM **Privately Held**
Web: www.johnstonesupply.com
SIC: 5074 5075 5064 Heating equipment (hydronic); Air conditioning and ventilation equipment and supplies; Electric household appliances, nec

(G-5905)
G MECHANICAL INC
6635 Singletree Dr (43229-1120)
PHONE..................................614 844-6750
Christopher Giannetto, *Pr*
EMP: 42 **EST:** 2002
SALES (est): 10.91MM **Privately Held**
Web: www.gmechanical.com
SIC: 1711 Mechanical contractor

(G-5906)
G STEPHENS INC
1175 Dublin Rd Ste 2 (43215-1252)
PHONE..................................614 227-0304
Glenn Stephens, *Brnch Mgr*
EMP: 65
Web: www.gstephensinc.com
SIC: 8741 Construction management
PA: G. Stephens, Inc.
133 N Summit St
Akron OH 44304

(G-5907)
G-COR AUTOMOTIVE CORP (PA)
Also Called: G-Cor
2100 Refugee Rd (43207-2841)
PHONE..................................614 443-6735
Stanley Greenblott, *Pr*
Kenny Greenblott, *
Donald L Feinstein, *
◆ **EMP:** 45 **EST:** 1991
SQ FT: 250,000
SALES (est): 24.96MM **Privately Held**
Web: www.g-corautomotive.com
SIC: 5013 5015 5093 Automotive supplies and parts; Automotive parts and supplies, used; Metal scrap and waste materials

(G-5908)
GALLAGHER GAMS PRYOR TLLAN LTT
471 E Broad St Fl 19 (43215-3864)
PHONE..................................614 228-5151
EMP: 54 **EST:** 1985
SALES (est): 2.29MM **Privately Held**
Web: www.ggptl.com
SIC: 8111 General practice law office

(G-5909)
GANGA HOSPITALITY OHIO LLC
Also Called: Holiday Inn
4530 W Broad St (43228-1644)
PHONE..................................614 870-3700
EMP: 30 **EST:** 1995
SALES (est): 874.17K **Privately Held**
Web: www.hiexpress.com
SIC: 7011 Hotels and motels

(G-5910)
GARDA CL GREAT LAKES INC
Also Called: At Systems
201 Schofield Dr (43213-3831)
PHONE..................................614 863-4044
Ron Drener, *Mgr*
EMP: 33
SALES (corp-wide): 437.24MM **Privately Held**
SIC: 7381 Armored car services
HQ: Garda Cl Great Lakes, Inc.
201 Schofield Dr
Columbus OH 43213
561 939-7000

(G-5911)
GARDA CL GREAT LAKES INC (HQ)
Also Called: United Armored Services
201 Schofield Dr (43213-3831)
PHONE..................................561 939-7000
Stephan Cretier, *Pr*
Chris W Jamroz, *Pr*
EMP: 400 **EST:** 2005
SQ FT: 60,000
SALES (est): 21.9MM
SALES (corp-wide): 437.24MM **Privately Held**
SIC: 7381 7389 7359 Armored car services; Packaging and labeling services; Equipment rental and leasing, nec
PA: Gardaworld Cash Services, Inc.
2000 Nw Corporate Blvd
Boca Raton FL 33431
561 939-7000

(G-5912)
GARDAWORLD SECURITY CORP
Also Called: GARDAWORLD SECURITY CORPORATION
300 Marconi Blvd Ste 310 (43215-2329)
PHONE..................................614 963-2098
EMP: 58
SALES (corp-wide): 21.37MM **Privately Held**
Web: www.garda.com
SIC: 7381 Security guard service
PA: Gardaworld
2000 Nw Corporate Blvd
Boca Raton FL 33431
561 939-7000

(G-5913)
GARDINER ALLEN DRBRTS INSUR LL
Also Called: Nationwide
325 John H Mcconnell Blvd Ste 415 (43215-2672)
PHONE..................................614 221-1500
EMP: 40 **EST:** 1954
SALES (est): 9.66MM **Privately Held**
Web: www.gadinsurance.com
SIC: 6411 Insurance agents, nec

(G-5914)
GARDNER INSURANCE PARTNERS LLC
777 Goodale Blvd Ste 200 (43212-3862)
PHONE..................................614 221-1500
Andi Gardner, *Managing Member*
EMP: 35 **EST:** 2018
SALES (est): 384.12K **Privately Held**
Web: www.gadinsurance.com
SIC: 8742 Business management consultant

(G-5915)
GARDNER-CONNELL LLC
3641 Interchange Rd (43204-1499)
PHONE..................................614 456-4000
EMP: 36
Web: www.gardnerinc.com
SIC: 5191 5083 Farm supplies; Farm and garden machinery
PA: Gardner-Connell Llc
125 Constitution Blvd
Franklin MA 02038

(G-5916)
GARLAND GROUP INC
Also Called: Buckeye Real Estate

Columbus - Franklin County (G-5917)

48 E 15th Ave Frnt (43201-1659)
P.O. Box 8310 (43201-0310)
PHONE..............................614 294-4411
Wayne Garland, *Pr*
Lorie Garland, *
Robert Hendershot, *
EMP: 50 **EST:** 1975
SQ FT: 7,300
SALES (est): 2.73MM **Privately Held**
Web: www.buckeyerealestate.com
SIC: 6513 1522 6531 Apartment building operators; Remodeling, multi-family dwellings; Real estate brokers and agents

(G-5917)
GATES MCDONALD OF OHIO LLC
215 N Front St (43215-2255)
PHONE..............................614 677-3700
EMP: 800
SIC: 6411 Insurance claim processing, except medical

(G-5918)
GATEWAY FILM FOUNDATION
Also Called: GATEWAY FILM CENTER
1550 N High St (43201-1121)
PHONE..............................614 247-4968
EMP: 50 **EST:** 2011
SALES (est): 3.03MM **Privately Held**
Web: www.gatewayfilmcenter.org
SIC: 7832 Motion picture theaters, except drive-in

(G-5919)
GBQ CONSULTING LLC
230 West St Ste 700 (43215-2663)
PHONE..............................614 221-1120
Cara Hounshell, *
EMP: 39 **EST:** 2005
SALES (est): 441.4K
SALES (corp-wide): 20.78MM **Privately Held**
Web: www.gbq.com
SIC: 8742 Management consulting services
PA: Gbq Holdings, Llc
   230 West St Ste 700
   Columbus OH 43215
   614 221-1120

(G-5920)
GBQ HOLDINGS LLC (PA)
230 West St Ste 700 (43215-2663)
PHONE..............................614 221-1120
Darci Congrove, *Managing Member*
Paul Anderson, *
James Bechtel, *
Mark Laplace, *
EMP: 49 **EST:** 2012
SQ FT: 39,178
SALES (est): 20.78MM
SALES (corp-wide): 20.78MM **Privately Held**
Web: www.gbq.com
SIC: 8721 Certified public accountant

(G-5921)
GBQ PARTNERS LLC (PA)
230 West St Ste 700 (43215)
P.O. Box 182108 (43218)
PHONE..............................614 221-1120
Darci Congrove, *Managing Member*
EMP: 58 **EST:** 2005
SALES (est): 14.27MM
SALES (corp-wide): 14.27MM **Privately Held**
Web: www.gbq.com
SIC: 8721 7291 Certified public accountant; Tax return preparation services

(G-5922)
GEBEN COMMUNICATIONS LLC
143 E Main St Apt B (43215-5370)
PHONE..............................614 327-2102
EMP: 78 **EST:** 2018
SALES (est): 5.8MM **Privately Held**
Web: www.gebencommunication.com
SIC: 4899 Communication services, nec

(G-5923)
GEIST LOGISTICS LLC
Also Called: Badl Logistics
3030 Old Horn Lake Rd (43215)
PHONE..............................954 463-6910
EMP: 28
SIC: 4731 Transportation agents and brokers
PA: Geist Logistics, Llc
   8415 Allison Pointe Blvd
   Indianapolis IN 46250

(G-5924)
GEN III INC
2300 Lockbourne Rd (43207-2167)
PHONE..............................614 228-5550
John Mc Cormick, *Pr*
Roger Sparks, *
EMP: 53 **EST:** 1984
SALES (est): 20.28MM
SALES (corp-wide): 378.09MM **Privately Held**
Web: www.wasserstrom.com
SIC: 5046 Restaurant equipment and supplies, nec
HQ: N. Wasserstrom & Sons, Inc.
   2300 Lockbourne Rd
   Columbus OH 43207
   614 228-5550

(G-5925)
GENERAL THEMING CONTRS LLC
Also Called: GTC Artist With Machines
3750 Courtright Ct (43227-2253)
P.O. Box 27173 (43227-0173)
PHONE..............................614 252-6342
Richard D Rogovin, *Prin*
Kim Schanzenbach, *
Rich Witherspoon, *
▲ **EMP:** 105 **EST:** 1999
SQ FT: 60,000
SALES (est): 18.37MM **Privately Held**
Web: www.artistswithmachines.com
SIC: 7389 7336 2759 2396 Sign painting and lettering shop; Commercial art and graphic design; Commercial printing, nec; Automotive and apparel trimmings

(G-5926)
GENERATION HEALTH CORP
Also Called: Broadview Health Center
5151 N Hamilton Rd (43230-1313)
PHONE..............................614 337-1066
George R Powell, *Pr*
Kelly C Mcgee, *Treas*
Renee M Hott, *
Edward Powell Junior, *Sec*
EMP: 47 **EST:** 2001
SQ FT: 57,946
SALES (est): 3.73MM **Privately Held**
Web: www.broadviewhealth.com
SIC: 8051 Skilled nursing care facilities

(G-5927)
GEO BYERS SONS HOLDING INC
Also Called: Hertz
4185 E 5th Ave (43219-1813)
PHONE..............................614 239-1084
Blaine Byers, *Mgr*
EMP: 31
SALES (corp-wide): 98.78MM **Privately Held**
Web: www.hertz.com
SIC: 7514 7513 Rent-a-car service; Truck rental, without drivers
PA: Geo. Byers Sons Holding, Inc.
   427 S Hamilton Rd
   Columbus OH 43213
   614 228-5111

(G-5928)
GEORGE J IGEL & CO INC
2040 Alum Creek Dr (43207-1714)
PHONE..............................614 445-8421
Louis Smoot Senior, *Prin*
Louis Smoot Senior, *Prin*
Brian Van Deventer, *
Jeffrey Fries, *
Ronald L Wallace, *
EMP: 892 **EST:** 1911
SQ FT: 50,000
SALES (est): 86.24MM **Privately Held**
Web: www.buildwithigel.com
SIC: 1794 1623 6552 Excavation and grading, building construction; Sewer line construction; Subdividers and developers, nec

(G-5929)
GEOTEX CONSTRUCTION SVCS INC
1025 Stimmel Rd (43223-2911)
P.O. Box 16331 (43216-6331)
PHONE..............................614 444-5690
EMP: 50 **EST:** 1992
SQ FT: 6,000
SALES (est): 8.72MM **Privately Held**
Web: www.geotexcs.com
SIC: 1623 1794 Underground utilities contractor; Excavation and grading, building construction

(G-5930)
GERLACH JOHN J CTR FOR SNIOR H
Also Called: Ohio Health
180 E Broad St Fl 34 (43215-3707)
PHONE..............................614 566-5858
Michelle Stokes, *Dir*
EMP: 30 **EST:** 1985
SALES (est): 10.18MM **Privately Held**
Web: www.ohiohealth.com
SIC: 8062 General medical and surgical hospitals

(G-5931)
GERMAIN FORD LLC
Also Called: Quick Lane
7250 Sawmill Rd (43235-1942)
PHONE..............................614 889-7777
EMP: 135 **EST:** 1922
SQ FT: 41,000
SALES (est): 28.41MM **Privately Held**
Web: www.germainford.com
SIC: 5511 7539 Automobiles, new and used; Automotive repair shops, nec

(G-5932)
GFL ENVIRONMENTAL SVCS USA INC
Also Called: Heartland Petroleum
4001 E 5th Ave (43219-1812)
PHONE..............................614 441-4001
Sayed Atiyeah, *Manager*
EMP: 45
SALES (corp-wide): 5.03B **Privately Held**
SIC: 2911 5172 Mineral oils, natural; Fuel oil
HQ: Gfl Environmental Services Usa, Inc.
   18927 Hickory Creek Dr
   Mokena IL 60448
   866 579-6900

(G-5933)
GIANT EAGLE INC
Also Called: Giant Eagle
6660 Broughton Ave (43213-1691)
PHONE..............................412 968-5300
EMP: 119
SALES (corp-wide): 1.43B **Privately Held**
Web: www.gianteagle.com
SIC: 5411 5141 5147 5148 Supermarkets, chain; Groceries, general line; Meats, fresh; Fresh fruits and vegetables
PA: Giant Eagle, Inc.
   101 Kappa Dr
   Pittsburgh PA 15238
   866 620-0216

(G-5934)
GILBANE BUILDING COMPANY
145 E Rich St Fl 4 (43215-5253)
PHONE..............................614 948-4000
Walt Mckelvey, *Brnch Mgr*
EMP: 30
SALES (corp-wide): 5.6B **Privately Held**
Web: www.gilbaneco.com
SIC: 8741 1542 Construction management; Nonresidential construction, nec
HQ: Gilbane Building Company
   7 Jackson Walkway Ste 2
   Providence RI 02903
   401 456-5800

(G-5935)
GIRL SCUTS OHIOS HRTLAND CNCIL
Also Called: Girl Scouts
1700 Watermark Dr (43215-1097)
PHONE..............................614 340-8829
Tammy Wharton, *CEO*
EMP: 86
Web: www.gsoh.org
SIC: 8641 Girl Scout organization
PA: Girl Scouts Of Ohio's Heartland Council Inc.
   1700 Watermark Dr
   Columbus OH 43215

(G-5936)
GLAUS PYLE SCHMER BRNS DHVEN I
Also Called: Gpd Group
1801 Watermark Dr Ste 210 (43215-1096)
PHONE..............................614 210-0751
Darrin Kotecki, *Pr*
EMP: 52
SALES (corp-wide): 122.1MM **Privately Held**
Web: www.gpdgroup.com
SIC: 8711 8712 Consulting engineer; Architectural services
PA: Glaus, Pyle, Schomer, Burns & Dehaven, Inc.
   520 S Main St Ste 2531
   Akron OH 44311
   330 572-2100

(G-5937)
GLEN WESLEY INC
Also Called: Wesley Ridge
5155 N High St (43214-1694)
PHONE..............................614 888-7492
Africa Thomas, *Prin*
Margeret Carmany, *
Robert Wehner, *
Lauren Croman, *
Tina Cassady, *
EMP: 100 **EST:** 1967
SQ FT: 279,000
SALES (est): 12.83MM **Privately Held**
Web: www.lec.org
SIC: 8051 6513 8361 Skilled nursing care facilities; Apartment building operators; Geriatric residential care

GEOGRAPHIC SECTION

Columbus - Franklin County (G-5960)

(G-5938)
GLIMCHER REALTY TRUST
180 E Broad St (43215-3714)
PHONE..............................614 621-9000
EMP: 981
SIC: 6512 Commercial and industrial building operation

(G-5939)
GOLD MEDAL PRODUCTS CO
787 Harrison Dr (43204-3507)
PHONE..............................614 228-1155
Thomas Coughlin, *Genl Mgr*
EMP: 40
SALES (corp-wide): 98.56MM **Privately Held**
Web: www.gmpopcorn.com
SIC: 5145 5084 5113 Snack foods; Food industry machinery; Cups, disposable plastic and paper
PA: Gold Medal Products Co.
10700 Medallion Dr
Cincinnati OH 45241
513 769-7676

(G-5940)
GOLDEN ENDNGS GLDEN RTRVER RSC
1043 Elmwood Ave (43212-3255)
PHONE..............................614 486-0773
EMP: 50 EST: 2011
SALES (est): 57.75K **Privately Held**
Web: www.goldenendingsrescue.com
SIC: 6732 Trusts: educational, religious, etc.

(G-5941)
GOODWILL INDS CENTL OHIO INC (PA)
Also Called: Goodwill Columbus
605 S Front St (43215-5777)
PHONE..............................614 294-5181
Ryan Burgess, *Pr*
Hartley Anthony, *
Fred G Pressley, *
Anthony Hartley, *
Michael Goldbeck, *
EMP: 275 EST: 1939
SALES (est): 59.87MM
SALES (corp-wide): 59.87MM **Privately Held**
Web: www.goodwillcolumbus.org
SIC: 8331 5399 Job training services; Surplus and salvage stores

(G-5942)
GOODWILL INDS CENTL OHIO INC
Also Called: Working Community Services
890 N Hague Ave (43204-2174)
PHONE..............................614 274-5296
Timmy Hughes, *Mgr*
EMP: 74
SALES (corp-wide): 59.87MM **Privately Held**
Web: www.goodwillcolumbus.org
SIC: 8331 Job training services
PA: Goodwill Industries Of Central Ohio, Inc.
605 S Front St
Columbus OH 43215
614 294-5181

(G-5943)
GOSH ENTERPRISES INC (PA)
Also Called: Charley's Steakery
5000 Arlington Centre Blvd (43220-3383)
PHONE..............................614 923-4700
Charley Shin, *Pr*
Candra Alisiswanto, *
Bob Wright, *
Brian Hipsher, *CMO**
EMP: 42 EST: 1986
SALES (est): 47.95MM **Privately Held**
Web: www.charleys.com
SIC: 5812 6794 Sandwiches and submarines shop; Franchises, selling or licensing

(G-5944)
GRANDVIEW FAMILY PRACTICE INC
1550 W 5th Ave Lowr (43212-2474)
PHONE..............................740 258-9267
Doctor Charles May, *Pr*
EMP: 41 EST: 1987
SQ FT: 4,000
SALES (est): 2.25MM **Privately Held**
SIC: 8011 Offices and clinics of osteopathic physicians; General and family practice, physician/surgeon

(G-5945)
GRANDVIEW FIFTH AUTO SVC INC
Also Called: Rife's Autobody
2300 Cardigan Ave (43215-1004)
PHONE..............................614 488-6106
Donald H Rife Senior, *Pr*
Donald Rife Junior, *Sec*
EMP: 27 EST: 1943
SQ FT: 3,600
SALES (est): 4.02MM **Privately Held**
Web: www.rifesautobody.com
SIC: 7532 Collision shops, automotive

(G-5946)
GRANGE INDEMNITY INSURANCE CO
Also Called: Grange Mutual Casualty Company
671 S High St (43206)
P.O. Box 1218 (43216)
PHONE..............................614 445-2900
Tom Welch, *Pr*
Randall J Montelone, *
David T Roark, *
Martin J Dinehart, *Mine Operations Vice President**
EMP: 201 EST: 1968
SQ FT: 9,500
SALES (est): 21.29MM
SALES (corp-wide): 889.58MM **Privately Held**
Web: www.grangeinsurance.com
SIC: 6311 6141 Life insurance; Automobile loans, including insurance
PA: Grange Insurance Company
671 S High St
Columbus OH 43206
800 422-0550

(G-5947)
GRANGE INSURANCE COMPANY (PA)
Also Called: Grange Insurance Companies
671 S High St (43206-1072)
P.O. Box 1218 (43216-1218)
PHONE..............................800 422-0550
Tom Welch, *CEO*
J Paul Mccaffrey, *CFO*
Tim Cunningham, *CIO*
Terri Dalenta, *Ex VP*
A C Stone, *Prin*
EMP: 850 EST: 1935
SQ FT: 212,000
SALES (est): 889.58MM
SALES (corp-wide): 889.58MM **Privately Held**
Web: www.grangeinsurance.com
SIC: 6331 Automobile insurance

(G-5948)
GRANGE LIFE INSURANCE COMPANY
671 S High St (43206-1072)
PHONE..............................800 445-3030
Thomas Welch, *CEO*
EMP: 29 EST: 2014
SALES (est): 1.76MM **Privately Held**
Web: www.grangeinsurance.com
SIC: 6411 Insurance agents, nec

(G-5949)
GRAYS TRNSP & LOGISTICS LLC
470 W Broad St Unit 1074 (43215-2759)
P.O. Box 197 (43054-0197)
PHONE..............................614 656-3460
Billy Gray, *Managing Member*
EMP: 30 EST: 2014
SALES (est): 1.23MM **Privately Held**
SIC: 7389 4731 Business Activities at Non-Commercial Site; Transportation agents and brokers

(G-5950)
GREAT HOME HEALTHCARE LLC
2999 E Dublin Granville Rd Ste 215 (43231-4030)
PHONE..............................614 475-4026
Khadra Jama, *Prin*
EMP: 28 EST: 2010
SALES (est): 1.3MM **Privately Held**
Web: www.greathomehealthcare1.com
SIC: 8082 Home health care services

(G-5951)
GREAT NTHRN CNSULTING SVCS INC (PA)
200 E Campus View Blvd Ste 200 (43235-4678)
PHONE..............................614 890-9999
Jeffrey Jones, *CFO*
James C Deboard, *
EMP: 40 EST: 1992
SQ FT: 4,000
SALES (est): 8.56MM **Privately Held**
Web: www.gnorth.com
SIC: 7379 Online services technology consultants

(G-5952)
GREATER CLMBUS CHMBER COMMERCE
150 S Front St Ste 220 (43215-7107)
PHONE..............................614 221-1321
Ty Marsh, *Pr*
Sally A Jackson, *
EMP: 40 EST: 1884
SQ FT: 23,000
SALES (est): 3.59MM **Privately Held**
Web: www.columbusgachamber.com
SIC: 8611 Chamber of Commerce

(G-5953)
GREATER CLMBUS CNVNTION CTR FO
Also Called: Starbucks Licensed Store
400 N High St Fl 4 (43215-2078)
PHONE..............................614 827-2500
Craig Liston, *Genl Mgr*
Art Mcandew, *Asst Mgr*
EMP: 189 EST: 1974
SALES (est): 23.63MM **Privately Held**
Web: www.columbusconventions.com
SIC: 7389 Convention and show services

(G-5954)
GREATER CLMBUS CNVNTION VSTORS (PA)
Also Called: GCCVB
277 W Nationwide Blvd Ste 125 (43215-2853)
PHONE..............................614 221-6623
Paul Astleford, *Pr*
EMP: 38 EST: 1941
SQ FT: 17,000
SALES (est): 18.37MM
SALES (corp-wide): 18.37MM **Privately Held**
Web: www.experiencecolumbus.com
SIC: 7389 Tourist information bureau

(G-5955)
GREENSCAPES LANDSCAPE CO INC
Also Called: Greenscpes Ldscp Archtcts Cntr
4220 Winchester Pike (43232-5612)
PHONE..............................614 837-1869
William A Gerhardt, *Pr*
EMP: 70 EST: 1975
SQ FT: 3,000
SALES (est): 7.96MM **Privately Held**
Web: www.greenscapes.net
SIC: 0782 0781 4959 Landscape contractors ; Landscape architects; Snowplowing

(G-5956)
GREYHOUND LINES INC
111 E Town St (43215-5153)
PHONE..............................614 221-0577
Dole Butterball, *Brnch Mgr*
EMP: 36
SALES (corp-wide): 1.59B **Privately Held**
Web: www.greyhound.com
SIC: 4142 4131 Bus charter service, except local; Intercity and rural bus transportation
HQ: Greyhound Lines, Inc.
350 N Saint Paul St # 300
Dallas TX 75201
214 849-8000

(G-5957)
GRILL REST AT SHERATON SUITES
Also Called: Sheraton
201 Hutchinson Ave (43235-4689)
PHONE..............................614 436-0004
EMP: 47 EST: 1999
SALES (est): 507.62K **Privately Held**
Web: www.sheratonsuitescolumbus.com
SIC: 7011 5812 Hotels; Eating places

(G-5958)
GUARDIAN ELDER CARE COLUMBUS
2425 Kimberly Pkwy E (43232-4271)
PHONE..............................614 868-9306
Brian Rendos, *
Brian Bosak, *
EMP: 73 EST: 2016
SALES (est): 1.66MM **Privately Held**
SIC: 8059 Nursing and personal care, nec

(G-5959)
GUARDIAN ENTERPRISE GROUP INC
3948 Townsfair Way Ste 220 (43219-6095)
P.O. Box 1497 (43086-1497)
PHONE..............................614 416-6080
Richard Schilg, *Pr*
EMP: 42 EST: 2001
SALES (est): 5.89MM
SALES (corp-wide): 5.89MM **Privately Held**
Web: www.guardianenterprisegroup.com
SIC: 7311 Advertising consultant
PA: Guardian Vision International, Inc.
3948 Townsfair Way # 220
Columbus OH 43219
614 416-6080

(G-5960)
GUARDIAN WATER & POWER INC (PA)
1650 Watermark Dr Ste 170 (43215-7006)

Columbus - Franklin County (G-5961) GEOGRAPHIC SECTION

PHONE.................................614 291-3141
Harry Apostolos, *Pr*
Patricia Apostolos, *
Rhonda Neville, *
EMP: 36 **EST:** 1983
SQ FT: 8,000
SALES (est): 9.46MM
SALES (corp-wide): 9.46MM **Privately Held**
Web: www.guardianwp.com
SIC: 7389 7322 Meter readers, remote; Adjustment and collection services

(G-5961)
GUDENKAUF LLC (HQ)
2679 Mckinley Ave (43204-3646)
PHONE.................................614 488-1776
Jeffrey Gudenkauf, *Pr*
Susan Gudenkauf, *
Sanford Potterton, *
Sandy Potterton, *
Mark Rogers, *
EMP: 130 **EST:** 1977
SQ FT: 10,000
SALES (est): 36.57MM
SALES (corp-wide): 350.16MM **Privately Held**
Web: www.congruex.com
SIC: 1623 Telephone and communication line construction
PA: Congruex Llc
  2615 13th St
  Boulder CO 80304
  720 749-2318

(G-5962)
GUTKNECHT CONSTRUCTION COMPANY
Also Called: Gutknecht Construction
2280 Citygate Dr (43219-3588)
PHONE.................................614 532-5410
Jeff Feinman, *Pr*
Jamie Weisent, *
Ben Lindsay, *
Mike Poyer, *
EMP: 44 **EST:** 1975
SQ FT: 7,500
SALES (est): 17.96MM **Privately Held**
Web: www.gutknecht.com
SIC: 1542 Commercial and office building, new construction

(G-5963)
HADLER REALTY COMPANY
Also Called: Hadler Company
2000 Henderson Rd Ste 500 (43220-2496)
PHONE.................................614 457-6650
William N Hadler, *Owner*
EMP: 42 **EST:** 1945
SQ FT: 5,500
SALES (est): 6MM **Privately Held**
Web: www.hadler.com
SIC: 6531 Real estate agent, commercial

(G-5964)
HAGGLUNDS DRIVES INC
2275 International St (43228-4632)
PHONE.................................614 527-7400
◆ **EMP:** 84
SIC: 5084 Hydraulic systems equipment and supplies

(G-5965)
HALO BRANDED SOLUTIONS INC
2550 Corporate Exchange Dr Ste 203 (43231-7659)
PHONE.................................614 434-6275
EMP: 29
SALES (corp-wide): 577.13MM **Privately Held**
Web: www.halo.com

SIC: 5199 Advertising specialties
PA: Halo Branded Solutions, Inc.
  1500 Halo Way
  Sterling IL 61081
  815 625-0980

(G-5966)
HAMILTON CAPITAL LLC
5025 Arlington Centre Blvd Ste 300 (43220-2959)
PHONE.................................614 273-1000
EMP: 68 **EST:** 2018
SALES (est): 4.65MM **Privately Held**
Web: www.hamiltoncapital.com
SIC: 7389 Financial services

(G-5967)
HAMILTON CAPITAL MGT INC
5025 Arlington Centre Blvd Ste 300 (43220-2959)
PHONE.................................614 273-1000
Matthew Hamilton, *Pr*
EMP: 64 **EST:** 1997
SALES (est): 7.62MM **Privately Held**
Web: www.hamiltoncapital.com
SIC: 6282 Investment advisory service

(G-5968)
HAMILTON-PARKER COMPANY (PA)
1865 Leonard Ave (43219-4500)
PHONE.................................614 358-7800
TOLL FREE: 800
Adam Lewin, *Pr*
Connie Tuckerman, *
▲ **EMP:** 83 **EST:** 1934
SQ FT: 50,000
SALES (est): 43.85MM
SALES (corp-wide): 43.85MM **Privately Held**
Web: www.hamiltonparker.com
SIC: 5075 5032 5031 5211 Warm air heating and air conditioning; Brick, stone, and related material; Lumber, plywood, and millwork; Brick

(G-5969)
HANDSON CENTRAL OHIO INC
1105 Schrock Rd Ste 107 (43229-1174)
PHONE.................................614 221-2255
Marilee Chinnici-zuercher, *Pr*
Marilee Zuercher, *Pr*
Bridget Wolf, *CFO*
EMP: 50 **EST:** 1983
SALES (est): 1.76MM **Privately Held**
Web: www.lssnetworkofhope.org
SIC: 8322 8331 Social service center; Job training and related services

(G-5970)
HANLIN-RAINALDI CONSTRUCTION
1060 Kingsmill Pkwy (43229-1143)
PHONE.................................614 436-4204
Grant L Douglass, *Ch Bd*
Ed Rainaldi, *
Michael O Hanlin, *
EMP: 46 **EST:** 1992
SALES (est): 9.78MM **Privately Held**
Web: www.hanlinrainaldi.com
SIC: 1542 Commercial and office building, new construction

(G-5971)
HARD KNOCKS
100 Dillmont Dr (43235-6424)
PHONE.................................614 407-1444
EMP: 28 **EST:** 2018
SALES (est): 982.61K **Privately Held**
Web: www.hardknocksorlando.com
SIC: 7999 Tourist attractions, amusement park concessions and rides

(G-5972)
HAROLD K PHLLIPS RSTRATION INC
972 Harmon Ave (43223-2414)
PHONE.................................614 443-5699
Spike Phillips, *Pr*
Geneva Phillips, *
EMP: 30 **EST:** 1959
SQ FT: 7,000
SALES (est): 2.46MM **Privately Held**
Web: www.phillipsrestoration.com
SIC: 1741 Tuckpointing or restoration

(G-5973)
HAYDOCY AUTOMOTIVE INC
Also Called: Haydocy Automotors
3865 W Broad St (43228-1444)
PHONE.................................614 279-8880
Chris Haydocy, *Pr*
Rita Fitch, *
EMP: 60 **EST:** 1954
SALES (est): 3.5MM **Privately Held**
Web: www.haydocybuickgmccolumbus.com
SIC: 7538 5511 7532 5531 General automotive repair shops; Automobiles, new and used; Top and body repair and paint shops; Auto and home supply stores

(G-5974)
HAYWARD DISTRIBUTING CO (PA)
4061 Perimeter Dr (43228-1048)
PHONE.................................614 272-5953
John M Budde, *Ch Bd*
▲ **EMP:** 35 **EST:** 1947
SQ FT: 36,000
SALES (est): 15.46MM
SALES (corp-wide): 15.46MM **Privately Held**
Web: www.haydist.com
SIC: 5083 Lawn and garden machinery and equipment

(G-5975)
HEAD INC
Also Called: Head Alabama
4477 E 5th Ave (43219-1817)
PHONE.................................614 338-8501
Middleton E Head Junior, *Ch Bd*
James M Head, *
Jim Head, *
Paul Ondera, *
EMP: 50 **EST:** 1927
SQ FT: 6,000
SALES (est): 57.46MM **Privately Held**
Web: www.headinc.com
SIC: 1541 1542 Industrial buildings, new construction, nec; Institutional building construction

(G-5976)
HEALTHLINX INC
1391 W 5th Ave Ste 138 (43212-2902)
P.O. Box 163425 (43216-3425)
PHONE.................................614 542-2228
Matt Berry, *CEO*
Matthew Berry, *
EMP: 47 **EST:** 2007
SALES (est): 7.82MM **Privately Held**
Web: www.healthlinx.com
SIC: 7361 8742 Executive placement; Management consulting services

(G-5977)
HEARTBEAT INTERNATIONAL INC
5000 Arlington Centre Blvd Ste 2241 (43220-3075)
PHONE.................................614 885-7577
EMP: 45 **EST:** 1971
SALES (est): 7.15MM **Privately Held**
Web: www.heartbeatinternational.org

SIC: 8661 8322 Religious organizations; Adoption services

(G-5978)
HEARTLAND BANK (HQ)
430 N Hamilton Rd (43213)
PHONE.................................614 337-4600
G Scott Mccomb, *Pr*
Jay Eggspuehler, *V Ch Bd*
Steve Hines, *Ex VP*
Joe Gottron, *CAO*
EMP: 50 **EST:** 1911
SQ FT: 15,000
SALES (est): 66.93MM **Privately Held**
Web: www.heartland.bank
SIC: 6022 State trust companies accepting deposits, commercial
PA: Heartland Banccorp.
  850 N Hamilton Rd
  Gahanna OH 43230

(G-5979)
HEARTLAND PETROLEUM LLC
4001 E 5th Ave (43219-1812)
PHONE.................................614 441-4001
EMP: 27
Web: www.heartland-petroleum.com
SIC: 5172 Fuel oil

(G-5980)
HEINZERLING COMMUNITY
Also Called: HEINZERLING 1605
1800 Heinzerling Dr (43223-3642)
PHONE.................................614 272-8888
Robert Heinzerling, *Pr*
EMP: 721 **EST:** 1963
SALES (est): 27.06MM **Privately Held**
Web: www.heinzerling.org
SIC: 8322 Individual and family services

(G-5981)
HEINZERLING FOUNDATION (PA)
Also Called: Heinzerling Mem Foundation
1800 Heinzerling Dr (43223-3642)
PHONE.................................614 272-8888
Robert Heninzerli, *Ex Dir*
EMP: 250 **EST:** 1959
SQ FT: 67,000
SALES (est): 25.12MM
SALES (corp-wide): 25.12MM **Privately Held**
Web: www.heinzerling.org
SIC: 8059 8052 Home for the mentally retarded, ex. skilled or intermediate; Intermediate care facilities

(G-5982)
HEINZERLING FOUNDATION
Also Called: Heinzerling Developmental Ctr
1755 Heinzerling Dr (43223-3672)
PHONE.................................614 272-2000
Bob Heinzerling, *Dir*
EMP: 300
SQ FT: 40,300
SALES (corp-wide): 25.12MM **Privately Held**
Web: www.heinzerling.org
SIC: 8059 8361 Home for the mentally retarded, ex. skilled or intermediate; Residential care
PA: Heinzerling Foundation
  1800 Heinzerling Dr
  Columbus OH 43223
  614 272-8888

(G-5983)
HEISER STAFFING SERVICES LLC
330 W Spring St Ste 205 (43215-7300)
P.O. Box 1014 (43085-1014)
PHONE.................................614 800-4188
EMP: 33 **EST:** 2014

GEOGRAPHIC SECTION

Columbus - Franklin County (G-6007)

SALES (est): 2.49MM **Privately Held**
Web: www.heiserstaffing.com
SIC: 7363 Temporary help service

(G-5984)
HENDERSON RD REST SYSTEMS INC (PA)
Also Called: Hyde Park Grille
1615 Old Henderson Rd (43220-3617)
PHONE..................614 442-3310
Richard Hauck, VP
Joseph Soccone, *
EMP: 40 EST: 1988
SQ FT: 6,516
SALES (est): 1.83MM **Privately Held**
Web: www.hydeparkrestaurants.com
SIC: 5812 4119 7542 American restaurant; Limousine rental, with driver; Carwashes

(G-5985)
HER INC (PA)
4261 Morse Rd (43230-1522)
PHONE..................614 221-7400
George W Smith, CEO
Harley E Rouda Senior, Ch Bd
Harley E Rouda Junior, Pr
Geri Van Lent, *
Patricia Halverson, *
EMP: 27 EST: 1956
SQ FT: 9,800
SALES (est): 34.3MM
SALES (corp-wide): 34.3MM **Privately Held**
Web: www.herrealtors.com
SIC: 6531 Real estate agent, residential

(G-5986)
HER MAJESTY MANAGEMENT GROUP ✪
3737 Easton Market Ste 1339 (43219-6023)
PHONE..................614 680-7461
Sarah Walker, CEO
EMP: 55 EST: 2022
SALES (est): 1.25MM **Privately Held**
SIC: 6531 Real estate agents and managers

(G-5987)
HERITAGE DAY HEALTH CENTERS (HQ)
Also Called: National Church Residences Center For Senior Health
2335 N Bank Dr (43220-5423)
PHONE..................614 451-2151
Tanya Kim Hahn, Pr
EMP: 62 EST: 1985
SQ FT: 4,200
SALES (est): 929.74K
SALES (corp-wide): 521.67MM **Privately Held**
Web: www.nationalchurchresidences.org
SIC: 8322 Senior citizens' center or association
PA: National Church Residences
2335 N Bank Dr
Columbus OH 43220
614 451-2151

(G-5988)
HERITAGE HEALTH CARE SERVICES
1625 Bethel Rd Ste 102 (43220-2071)
PHONE..................614 848-6550
Ritch Adams, Mgr
EMP: 103
SALES (corp-wide): 2.44MM **Privately Held**
Web: www.heritage-hcs.com
SIC: 8082 7361 Home health care services; Nurses' registry
PA: Heritage Health Care Services
1100 Shawnee Rd
Lima OH 45805
419 867-2002

(G-5989)
HEXION INC (PA)
Also Called: Hexion
180 E Broad St (43215-3707)
P.O. Box 1310 (43216-1310)
PHONE..................888 443-9466
Michael Lefenfeld, Pr
Mark Bidstrup, Ex VP
Douglas A Johns, Ex VP
Matthew A Sokol, Ex VP
EMP: 243 EST: 1899
SALES (est): 1.26B
SALES (corp-wide): 1.26B **Privately Held**
Web: www.hexion.com
SIC: 8711 2821 5169 4911 Chemical engineering; Epoxy resins; Chemicals, industrial and heavy

(G-5990)
HEXION TOPCO LLC (PA)
180 E Broad St (43215)
PHONE..................614 225-4000
▼ EMP: 68 EST: 2010
SALES (est): 439.43MM **Privately Held**
SIC: 2821 2869 6719 Thermosetting materials; Silicones; Investment holding companies, except banks

(G-5991)
HIGHBANKS CARE CENTER LLC
Also Called: HIGHBANKS CARE CENTER
111 Lazelle Rd (43235-1419)
PHONE..................614 888-2021
Brian Colleran, Managing Member
EMP: 42 EST: 2003
SALES (est): 3.61MM **Privately Held**
Web: www.highbanks-care.net
SIC: 8051 Convalescent home with continuous nursing care

(G-5992)
HIGHLAND SEC INVSTIGATIONS LLC
4197 Shoppers Ln (43228-2035)
PHONE..................614 558-2421
Wayne Sever, Managing Member
Michael Sever, Managing Member*
EMP: 45 EST: 2013
SALES (est): 1.98MM **Privately Held**
Web: www.highlandprotection.net
SIC: 7381 Private investigator

(G-5993)
HIGHLANDS COMMUNITY LRNG CTR
5120 Godown Rd (43220-7202)
PHONE..................614 210-0830
Joshua Harning, Prin
EMP: 28 EST: 2019
SALES (est): 214.65K **Privately Held**
Web: www.hclc.us
SIC: 8322 Community center

(G-5994)
HILTON GARDEN INN
Also Called: Hilton
3232 Olentangy River Rd (43202-1519)
PHONE..................614 263-7200
John Businger, Mgr
EMP: 51 EST: 2007
SALES (est): 2.89MM **Privately Held**
Web: www.hilton.com
SIC: 7011 Hotels and motels

(G-5995)
HILTON GRDN INN CLUMBUS EASTON
3600 Morse Rd Ste A (43219-3012)
PHONE..................877 782-9444
EMP: 35 EST: 2021
SALES (est): 505.48K **Privately Held**
Web: www.hilton.com
SIC: 7011 Resort hotel

(G-5996)
HILTON GRDN INN COLUMBUS ARPRT
Also Called: Hilton Garden Inns
4265 Sawyer Rd (43219-3812)
PHONE..................614 231-2869
Paul Malcolm, Genl Mgr
EMP: 47 EST: 2003
SALES (est): 911.25K **Privately Held**
Web: www.hilton.com
SIC: 7011 Resort hotel

(G-5997)
HOGAN SERVICES INC
1500 Obetz Rd (43207-4477)
PHONE..................614 491-8402
Max Baker, Brnch Mgr
EMP: 30
SALES (corp-wide): 10.54MM **Privately Held**
Web: www.hogan1.com
SIC: 4789 Pipeline terminal facilities, independently operated
PA: Hogan Services, Inc
2150 Schuetz Rd Ste 210
Saint Louis MO 63146
314 421-6000

(G-5998)
HOLIDAY INN EXPRESS
Also Called: Holiday Inn
3045 Olentangy River Rd (43202-1516)
PHONE..................614 447-1212
EMP: 31 EST: 2009
SALES (est): 744.58K **Privately Held**
Web: www.holidayinn.com
SIC: 7011 Hotels and motels

(G-5999)
HOME DEPOT USA INC
Also Called: Home Depot, The
6333 Cleveland Ave (43231)
PHONE..................614 523-0600
Jason Gage, Mgr
EMP: 469
SALES (corp-wide): 152.67B **Publicly Held**
Web: www.homedepot.com
SIC: 5211 7359 Home centers; Tool rental
HQ: Home Depot U.S.A., Inc.
2445 Springfield Ave
Vauxhall NJ 07088

(G-6000)
HOME DEPOT USA INC
Also Called: Home Depot, The
100 S Grener Ave (43228)
PHONE..................614 878-9150
Dan Hernan, Mgr
EMP: 160
SALES (corp-wide): 152.67B **Publicly Held**
Web: www.homedepot.com
SIC: 5211 7359 Home centers; Tool rental
HQ: Home Depot U.S.A., Inc.
2445 Springfield Ave
Vauxhall NJ 07088

(G-6001)
HOME DEPOT USA INC
Also Called: Home Depot, The
5200 N Hamilton Rd (43230)
PHONE..................614 939-5036
Chuck Fry, Mgr
EMP: 192
SALES (corp-wide): 152.67B **Publicly Held**
Web: www.homedepot.com
SIC: 5211 7359 Home centers; Tool rental
HQ: Home Depot U.S.A., Inc.
2445 Springfield Ave
Vauxhall NJ 07088

(G-6002)
HOMELESS FAMILIES FOUNDATION
33 N Grubb St (43215-2748)
P.O. Box 163250 (43216-3250)
PHONE..................614 461-9247
Adrian Corbet, Ex Dir
Jim Hopkins, Ch
EMP: 64 EST: 1986
SALES (est): 3.17MM **Privately Held**
Web: www.homeforfamilies.org
SIC: 8322 Social service center

(G-6003)
HOMEPORT INC
3443 Agler Rd Ste 200 (43219-3385)
PHONE..................614 221-8889
Bruce Luecke, CEO
EMP: 40 EST: 2015
SALES (est): 4.05MM **Privately Held**
Web: www.homeportohio.org
SIC: 6514 Dwelling operators, except apartments

(G-6004)
HOMES AMERICA INC
83 E Stanton Ave (43214-1110)
PHONE..................614 848-8551
EMP: 29
SALES (corp-wide): 2.59MM **Privately Held**
Web: www.americanhomes.bz
SIC: 1521 New construction, single-family houses
PA: Homes America Inc
4604 Dundas Dr
Greensboro NC 27407
336 678-9155

(G-6005)
HOMESTEAD AMERICA
369 E Livingston Ave (43215-5531)
PHONE..................614 221-5400
Dave Anderson, Pr
Marcia Bond, Contrlr
Laura Fprmica, VP
EMP: 280 EST: 2009
SALES (est): 10.97MM **Privately Held**
Web: www.homesteadcos.com
SIC: 6531 Real estate agent, commercial

(G-6006)
HOMETOWN URGENT CARE OF KENTUCKY PSC
1105 Schrock Rd (43229-1146)
PHONE..................614 505-7601
EMP: 31 EST: 2011
SALES (est): 1.31MM **Privately Held**
SIC: 8011 Medical centers

(G-6007)
HOMEWOOD CORPORATION (PA)
Also Called: Homewood Builders
2700 E Dublin Granville Rd Ste 300a (43231-4094)
PHONE..................614 898-7200
John H Bain, CEO
George Anthony Skestos, *
EMP: 120 EST: 1964
SQ FT: 20,000
SALES (est): 46.2MM
SALES (corp-wide): 46.2MM **Privately Held**
Web: www.homewood-homes.com

Columbus - Franklin County (G-6008)

SIC: **1521** New construction, single-family houses

(G-6008)
HORIZON HM HLTH CARE AGCY LLC
3079 W Broad St Ste 6 (43204-1397)
PHONE.................................614 279-2933
Ibrahim Osman, *Managing Member*
EMP: 40 **EST:** 2013
SALES (est): 738.71K **Privately Held**
Web: www.horizon1hhcare.com
SIC: **8082** Home health care services

(G-6009)
HOTEL
337 S Ogden Ave (43204-3148)
PHONE.................................614 373-2002
Shermaine Mason, *Prin*
EMP: 31 **EST:** 2018
SALES (est): 32.59K **Privately Held**
SIC: **7011** Hotels

(G-6010)
HOTEL 50 S FRONT OPCO L P
Also Called: Doubletree Columbus
50 S Front St (43215-4129)
PHONE.................................614 885-3334
Dan Ouellette, *Mgr*
EMP: 100 **EST:** 2006
SALES (est): 2.62MM **Privately Held**
SIC: **7011** 6512 5813 5812 Hotels and motels ; Nonresidential building operators; Drinking places; Eating places

(G-6011)
HOTEL 50 S FRONT OPCO LP
50 S Front St (43215-4129)
PHONE.................................614 228-4600
Raymond Schulte, *Mgr*
EMP: 85 **EST:** 2016
SALES (est): 1.99MM **Privately Held**
SIC: **7011** Resort hotel

(G-6012)
HOTEL 75 E STATE OPCO L P
Also Called: Sheraton Columbus
75 E State St (43215-4203)
PHONE.................................614 365-4500
EMP: 70 **EST:** 2011
SALES (est): 1.11MM **Privately Held**
Web: www.starbucks.com
SIC: **7011** Resort hotel

(G-6013)
HOUSTON INTERESTS LLC
445 Hutchinson Ave Ste 740 (43235-5677)
PHONE.................................614 890-3456
Uday Parekh, *VP*
EMP: 2081
SALES (corp-wide): 795.02MM **Publicly Held**
Web: www.matrixpdm.com
SIC: **8711** Mechanical engineering
HQ: Houston Interests, Llc
    5100 E Skelly Dr Ste 100
    Tulsa OK 74135
    918 496-4400

(G-6014)
HPT TRS IHG-2 INC
Also Called: Sonesta Columbus
33 E Nationwide Blvd (43215-2512)
PHONE.................................614 461-4100
EMP: 36 **EST:** 2012
SALES (est): 585.13K **Privately Held**
SIC: **7011** Hotels

(G-6015)
HUCKLEBERRY HOUSE INC
1421 Hamlet St (43201-2599)

PHONE.................................614 294-5553
Rebecca Westerfelt, *Dir*
EMP: 57 **EST:** 1970
SQ FT: 9,000
SALES (est): 4.52MM **Privately Held**
Web: www.huckhouse.org
SIC: **8322** Crisis center

(G-6016)
HUNTINGTON BANCSHARES INC (PA)
Also Called: Huntington
41 S High St (43287)
PHONE.................................614 480-2265
Stephen D Steinour, *Ch Bd*
Rajeev Syal, *Chief Human Resources Officer*
Paul G Heller, *Chief Technician*
Julie C Tutkovics, *Chief Marketing*
EMP: 1538 **EST:** 1966
SALES (est): 10.84B
SALES (corp-wide): 10.84B **Publicly Held**
Web: www.huntington.com
SIC: **6021** National commercial banks

(G-6017)
HUNTINGTON INSURANCE INC (DH)
Also Called: Nationwide
37 W Broad St Ste 1100 (43215-4132)
PHONE.................................419 720-7900
Paul Baldwin, *Pr*
Ronald L Murray, *Sr VP*
Robert C Hawker Cpcu Arm, *Sr VP*
Pamela M Alspach, *Treas*
Dennis Raab, *CFO*
EMP: 150 **EST:** 1898
SALES (est): 102.97MM
SALES (corp-wide): 10.84B **Publicly Held**
Web: www.nationwide.com
SIC: **6411** Insurance agents, nec
HQ: The Huntington National Bank
    41 S High St
    Columbus OH 43215
    614 480-4293

(G-6018)
HUNTINGTON NATIONAL BANK
3424 Cleveland Ave (43224-2999)
PHONE.................................614 480-0005
Steve Lelonek, *Brnch Mgr*
EMP: 46
SQ FT: 1,762
SALES (corp-wide): 10.84B **Publicly Held**
Web: www.huntington.com
SIC: **6029** 6021 Commercial banks, nec; National commercial banks
HQ: The Huntington National Bank
    41 S High St
    Columbus OH 43215
    614 480-4293

(G-6019)
HUNTINGTON NATIONAL BANK
4661 Reed Rd (43220-3015)
PHONE.................................614 480-0017
Robert Erwin, *Brnch Mgr*
EMP: 46
SALES (corp-wide): 10.84B **Publicly Held**
Web: www.huntington.com
SIC: **6029** 6021 Commercial banks, nec; National commercial banks
HQ: The Huntington National Bank
    41 S High St
    Columbus OH 43215
    614 480-4293

(G-6020)
HUNTINGTON NATIONAL BANK
Also Called: Huntington
3464 S High St (43207-4006)
PHONE.................................614 480-0038

Angie Starcher, *Mgr*
EMP: 51
SQ FT: 2,013
SALES (corp-wide): 10.84B **Publicly Held**
Web: www.huntington.com
SIC: **6029** 6021 Commercial banks, nec; National commercial banks
HQ: The Huntington National Bank
    41 S High St
    Columbus OH 43215
    614 480-4293

(G-6021)
HUNTINGTON NATIONAL BANK (HQ)
41 S High St (43215)
P.O. Box 341470 (43216)
PHONE.................................614 480-4293
Stephen D Steinour, *Ch Bd*
Paul Heller, *
Helga Houston, *CRO*
Jana Litsey, *
Zachary Wasserman, *
▲ **EMP:** 300 **EST:** 1979
SQ FT: 190,000
SALES (est): 7.77B
SALES (corp-wide): 10.84B **Publicly Held**
Web: www.huntington.com
SIC: **6029** Commercial banks, nec
PA: Huntington Bancshares Incorporated
    41 S High St
    Columbus OH 43287
    614 480-2265

(G-6022)
HUNTINGTON NATIONAL BANK
1531 W Lane Ave (43221-3920)
PHONE.................................614 480-0004
Deb Trinkley, *Brnch Mgr*
EMP: 36
SALES (corp-wide): 10.84B **Publicly Held**
Web: www.huntington.com
SIC: **6029** 6021 Commercial banks, nec; National commercial banks
HQ: The Huntington National Bank
    41 S High St
    Columbus OH 43215
    614 480-4293

(G-6023)
HUNTINGTON NATIONAL BANK
1928 N High St (43201-1148)
PHONE.................................614 480-0026
Andrew Bailey, *Brnch Mgr*
EMP: 36
SQ FT: 15,360
SALES (corp-wide): 10.84B **Publicly Held**
Web: www.huntington.com
SIC: **6029** 6021 Commercial banks, nec; National commercial banks
HQ: The Huntington National Bank
    41 S High St
    Columbus OH 43215
    614 480-4293

(G-6024)
HUNTINGTON NATIONAL BANK
1555 W 5th Ave (43212-2494)
PHONE.................................614 480-0020
Frank Nobel, *Mgr*
EMP: 36
SALES (corp-wide): 10.84B **Publicly Held**
Web: www.huntington.com
SIC: **6029** 6021 Commercial banks, nec; National commercial banks
HQ: The Huntington National Bank
    41 S High St
    Columbus OH 43215
    614 480-4293

(G-6025)
HUNTINGTON NATIONAL BANK
Also Called: US Bank
4780 W Broad St (43228-1613)
PHONE.................................800 480-2265
Debra B Krasnow, *Brnch Mgr*
EMP: 31
SALES (corp-wide): 10.84B **Publicly Held**
Web: www.huntington.com
SIC: **6029** Commercial banks, nec
HQ: The Huntington National Bank
    41 S High St
    Columbus OH 43215
    614 480-4293

(G-6026)
HUNTINGTON NATIONAL BANK
5155 N High St (43214-1694)
PHONE.................................614 331-9537
EMP: 51
SALES (corp-wide): 10.84B **Publicly Held**
Web: www.huntington.com
SIC: **6029** Commercial banks, nec
HQ: The Huntington National Bank
    41 S High St
    Columbus OH 43215
    614 480-4293

(G-6027)
HUNTINGTON NATIONAL BANK
7840 Olentangy River Rd (43235-1354)
PHONE.................................614 480-0060
EMP: 31
SALES (corp-wide): 10.84B **Publicly Held**
SIC: **6021** National commercial banks
HQ: The Huntington National Bank
    41 S High St
    Columbus OH 43215
    614 480-4293

(G-6028)
HUNTINGTON NATIONAL BANK
17 S High St Fl 1 (43215-3413)
PHONE.................................614 480-4293
Thomas Hoaglin, *Pr*
EMP: 46
SALES (corp-wide): 10.84B **Publicly Held**
SIC: **6282** Investment advice
HQ: The Huntington National Bank
    41 S High St
    Columbus OH 43215
    614 480-4293

(G-6029)
HUNTINGTON TRUST CO NAT ASSN
41 S High St (43215-6170)
PHONE.................................614 480-5345
Norman Jacobs, *Pr*
Norm Jacobs, *
EMP: 262 **EST:** 1988
SQ FT: 190,000
SALES (est): 24.31MM **Privately Held**
Web: www.huntington.com
SIC: **6733** Trusts, except educational, religious, charity: management

(G-6030)
HY-TEK MATERIAL HANDLING LLC (HQ)
2222 Rickenbacker Pkwy W (43217-5002)
PHONE.................................614 497-2500
TOLL FREE: 800
Samuel Grooms, *Pr*
◆ **EMP:** 76 **EST:** 1989
SQ FT: 55,000
SALES (est): 276.83MM
SALES (corp-wide): 301.53MM **Privately Held**
Web: www.hy-tek.com

GEOGRAPHIC SECTION   Columbus - Franklin County (G-6053)

SIC: **5084** 5013 7538 7513 Materials handling machinery; Truck parts and accessories; Truck engine repair, except industrial; Truck rental, without drivers
PA: Hy-Tek Holdings, Llc
2222 Rickenbacker Pkwy W
Columbus OH 43217
614 497-2500

(G-6031)
HYATT CORPORATION
Also Called: Hyatt Hotel
350 N High St (43215-2006)
PHONE..................614 463-1234
Stephen Stewart, *Genl Mgr*
EMP: 81
Web: www.hyattdevelopment.com
SIC: **7011** 5813 5812 Hotels and motels; Bar (drinking places); Diner
HQ: Hyatt Corporation
250 Vesey St Fl 15
New York NY 10281
312 750-1234

(G-6032)
HYATT CORPORATION
Also Called: Hyatt Hotel
75 E State St (43215-4203)
PHONE..................614 228-1234
Karen Theis, *Brnch Mgr*
EMP: 84
Web: www.hyattdevelopment.com
SIC: **6512** 7011 5812 5813 Nonresidential building operators; Hotels; Eating places; Drinking places
HQ: Hyatt Corporation
250 Vesey St Fl 15
New York NY 10281
312 750-1234

(G-6033)
HYATT REGENCY COLUMBUS
Also Called: Hyatt Hotel
350 N High St (43215-2006)
PHONE..................614 463-1234
Charles Lutrick, *Contrlr*
EMP: 325 EST: 1978
SALES (est): 9.36MM **Privately Held**
Web: www.hyatt.com
SIC: **7011** Hotels and motels

(G-6034)
HYPERION COMPANIES INC
5300 Crosswind Dr (43228-3600)
PHONE..................949 309-2409
EMP: 405
SALES (corp-wide): 15.03MM **Privately Held**
Web: www.hyperion.inc
SIC: **8742** Management consulting services
PA: Hyperion Companies, Inc.
1032 W Taft Ave
Orange CA 92865
949 427-1957

(G-6035)
HYPERLOGISTICS GROUP INC (PA)
9301 Intermodal Ct N (43217-6101)
PHONE..................614 497-0800
Seatta K Layland, *
▲ EMP: 40 EST: 1973
SALES (est): 10.3MM
SALES (corp-wide): 10.3MM **Privately Held**
Web: www.hyperlog.com
SIC: **4225** General warehousing

(G-6036)
I VRABLE INC
Also Called: Heritage Mnor Sklled Nrsing Rh
3248 Henderson Rd (43220-7337)
PHONE..................614 545-5500
EMP: 104 EST: 2006
SALES (est): 1.37MM **Privately Held**
SIC: **8051** Convalescent home with continuous nursing care
PA: Vrable Healthcare, Inc.
3248 Henderson Rd
Columbus OH 43220

(G-6037)
I-FORCE LLC
Also Called: Iforce
4 Easton Oval (43219-6010)
PHONE..................614 431-5100
EMP: 150 EST: 1995
SALES (est): 17.47MM **Privately Held**
Web: www.iforceservices.com
SIC: **7361** Employment agencies

(G-6038)
IBP CORPORATION HOLDINGS INC
495 S High St Ste 50 (43215-5689)
PHONE..................614 692-6360
William Jenkins, *Pr*
Shelley Mcbride, *Sec*
EMP: 2000 EST: 2015
SQ FT: 17,000
SALES (est): 142.91MM
SALES (corp-wide): 2.78B **Publicly Held**
Web: www.installedbuildingproducts.com
SIC: **1742** 6719 Insulation, buildings; Investment holding companies, except banks
PA: Installed Building Products, Inc.
495 S High St Ste 50
Columbus OH 43215
614 221-3399

(G-6039)
IHG MANAGEMENT (MARYLAND) LLC
Also Called: Crowne Plaza Columbus Downtown
33 E Nationwide Blvd (43215-2512)
PHONE..................614 461-4100
Juan Laginia, *Brnch Mgr*
EMP: 145
Web: www.crowneplaza.com
SIC: **7011** Hotels
HQ: Maryland Llc Ihg Management
8844 Columbia 100 Pkwy
Columbia MD 21045

(G-6040)
IJUS LLC (PA)
Also Called: Innovative Joint Utility Svcs
781 Science Blvd # 200 (43230-6921)
PHONE..................614 470-9882
EMP: 85 EST: 2005
SALES (est): 10.83MM
SALES (corp-wide): 10.83MM **Privately Held**
Web: www.trccompanies.com
SIC: **8711** Consulting engineer

(G-6041)
IMEG CONSULTANTS CORP
855 Grandview Ave Ste 300 (43215-1193)
PHONE..................614 443-1178
EMP: 30
SALES (corp-wide): 141.33MM **Privately Held**
SIC: **8711** Engineering services
PA: Imeg Consultants Corp.
623 26th Ave
Rock Island IL 61201
309 788-0673

(G-6042)
IMPACT COMMUNITY ACTION
711 Southwood Ave (43207-1391)
PHONE..................614 252-2799
Robert E Chilton, *CEO*
Sue Petersen, *
Anita Maldonado, *
EMP: 75 EST: 2006
SALES (est): 8.15MM **Privately Held**
Web: www.impactca.org
SIC: **8322** Social service center

(G-6043)
IMPACT FULFILLMENT SVCS LLC
2035 Innis Rd (43224-3646)
PHONE..................614 262-8911
EMP: 120
SALES (corp-wide): 113.86MM **Privately Held**
Web: www.impactfs.com
SIC: **4225** 4783 General warehousing; Packing and crating
PA: Impact Fulfillment Services, Llc
1601 Anthony Rd
Burlington NC 27215
336 227-1130

(G-6044)
IMPROVEIT HOME REMODELING INC (PA)
Also Called: Improveit HM Rmdlg An Ohio Enr
4580 Bridgeway Ave Ste B (43219-1897)
PHONE..................614 297-5121
Seth Cammeyer, *Pr*
Brian Leader, *
Anthony Baird, *
EMP: 58 EST: 1989
SQ FT: 14,000
SALES (est): 34.99MM **Privately Held**
Web: www.improveitusa.com
SIC: **1521** General remodeling, single-family houses

(G-6045)
INDIANA MICHIGAN POWER COMPANY (HQ)
1 Riverside Plz (43215-2355)
PHONE..................614 716-1000
Nicholas K Akins, *Ch Bd*
Paul Chodak Iii, *Pr*
Brian X Tierney, *
Joseph M Buonaiuto, *CAO*
Thomas A Kratt, *Distribution Vice President* *
EMP: 100 EST: 1907
SALES (est): 2.54B
SALES (corp-wide): 18.98B **Privately Held**
Web: www.indianamichiganpower.com
SIC: **4911** Distribution, electric power
PA: American Electric Power Company, Inc.
1 Riverside Plz Fl 1 # 1
Columbus OH 43215
614 716-1000

(G-6046)
INDUS AIRPORT HOTELS I LLC
Also Called: Hilton Grdn Inn Columbus Arprt
4265 Sawyer Rd (43219-3812)
PHONE..................614 231-2869
Janet Boissy, *Prin*
Matthew Shier, *Prin*
EMP: 55 EST: 2016
SALES (est): 1.5MM **Privately Held**
Web: www.indushotels.com
SIC: **7011** Resort hotel

(G-6047)
INDUS AIRPORT HOTELS II LLC
Also Called: Hampton Inn
4280 International Gtwy (43219-1747)
PHONE..................614 235-0717
Janet Boissy, *Prin*
Matthew Shier, *Prin*
EMP: 55 EST: 2016
SALES (est): 2.37MM **Privately Held**
Web: www.hilton.com
SIC: **7011** Hotels and motels

(G-6048)
INDUS HOTEL 77 LLC
77 E Nationwide Blvd (43215-2512)
PHONE..................614 223-1400
EMP: 70
SQ FT: 350,000
SALES (est): 2.4MM **Privately Held**
Web: www.indushotels.com
SIC: **7011** Hotels

(G-6049)
INDUS NEWARK HOTEL LLC (PA)
Also Called: Doubletree By Hilton Newark
4265 Sawyer Rd (43219-3812)
PHONE..................740 322-6455
Janet Boissy, *Prin*
Matthew Shier, *Prin*
EMP: 30 EST: 2016
SALES (est): 1.46MM
SALES (corp-wide): 1.46MM **Privately Held**
Web: www.hilton.com
SIC: **7011** Hotels

(G-6050)
INDUSTRIAL AIR CENTERS LLC
Also Called: Columbus Air Center
2824 Fisher Rd (43204-3553)
PHONE..................614 274-9171
George Burch, *Pr*
EMP: 53
Web: www.iacserv.com
SIC: **5084** Compressors, except air conditioning
PA: Industrial Air Centers Llc
731 E Market St
Jeffersonville IN 47130

(G-6051)
INDUSTRIAL SECURITY SVC INC
2021 E Dublin Granville Rd Ste 130 (43229-3580)
PHONE..................614 785-7046
Carol Johnson, *Prin*
EMP: 48
SIC: **7381** Security guard service
HQ: Industrial Security Service, Inc.
4525 W 160th St
Cleveland OH 44135
216 898-9970

(G-6052)
INGLE-BARR INC
1444 Goodale Blvd (43212-3738)
PHONE..................614 421-0201
EMP: 30
SALES (corp-wide): 19.09MM **Privately Held**
Web: www.4ibi.com
SIC: **1521** 1541 General remodeling, single-family houses; Renovation, remodeling and repairs: industrial buildings
PA: Ingle-Barr, Inc.
20 Plyleys Ln
Chillicothe OH 45601
740 702-6117

(G-6053)
INN HAMPTON AND SUITES
Also Called: Hampton Inn
4100 Regent St Ste G (43219-6160)
PHONE..................614 473-9911
EMP: 36 EST: 2006
SALES (est): 658.42K **Privately Held**

Columbus - Franklin County (G-6054) GEOGRAPHIC SECTION

Web: www.hilton.com
SIC: 7011 Hotels and motels

(G-6054)
INNOVIS DATA SOLUTIONS INC
Also Called: Innovis
250 E Broad St (43215-3708)
PHONE.................................614 222-4343
Jonathan H Price, Pr
Dirk Cantrell, *
Keith Kotrowicsz, *
EMP: 35 EST: 1999
SALES (est): 10.98MM
SALES (corp-wide): 233.8MM Privately Held
Web: www.innovis.com
SIC: 7323 Consumer credit reporting bureau
PA: Cbc Companies, Inc.
250 E Broad St Fl 21
Columbus OH 43215
614 222-4343

(G-6055)
INQUIRY SYSTEMS INC
1195 Goodale Blvd (43212-3730)
PHONE.................................614 464-3800
Carey Hindall, Pr
Carey Bo Hindall, Pr
Kathy Hindall, *
EMP: 30 EST: 1980
SQ FT: 14,000
SALES (est): 2.24MM Privately Held
Web: www.inquirysys.com
SIC: 8742 4783 7311 7389 Marketing consulting services; Packing goods for shipping; Advertising agencies; Subscription fulfillment services: magazine, newspaper, etc.

(G-6056)
INSTALLED BUILDING PDTS II LLC (HQ)
Also Called: Insulation Northwest
495 S High St Ste 50 (43215)
PHONE.................................626 812-6070
Pamela Henson, Pt
EMP: 38 EST: 2008
SALES (est): 10.06MM
SALES (corp-wide): 2.78B Publicly Held
Web: www.installedbuildingproducts.com
SIC: 1742 Insulation, buildings
PA: Installed Building Products, Inc.
495 S High St Ste 50
Columbus OH 43215
614 221-3399

(G-6057)
INSTALLED BUILDING PDTS INC (PA)
Also Called: IBP
495 S High St Ste 50 (43215)
PHONE.................................614 221-3399
Jeffrey W Edwards, Ch Bd
Michael T Miller, *
Todd R Fry, CAO
Brad A Wheeler, COO
Jason R Niswonger, ADMIN SUSTAINABILITY
EMP: 205 EST: 1977
SALES (est): 2.78B
SALES (corp-wide): 2.78B Publicly Held
Web: www.installedbuildingproducts.com
SIC: 1522 5033 5211 Residential construction, nec; Insulation materials; Insulation material, building

(G-6058)
INSTALLED BUILDING PDTS LLC
Also Called: Marsh Building Products
2660 Fisher Rd Ste A (43204-3560)
PHONE.................................614 272-5577
EMP: 197
SALES (corp-wide): 2.78B Publicly Held
Web: www.marshbuild.com
SIC: 5033 5031 Roofing and siding materials; Doors and windows
HQ: Installed Building Products Llc
495 S High St Ste 150
Columbus OH 43215
614 221-3399

(G-6059)
INSTALLED BUILDING PRODUCTS LLC (HQ)
Also Called: Builders Installed Products
495 S High St Ste 150 (43215-5695)
PHONE.................................614 221-3399
EMP: 120 EST: 2001
SALES (est): 579.43MM
SALES (corp-wide): 2.78B Publicly Held
Web: www.installedbuildingproducts.com
SIC: 1742 5211 1761 Plastering, drywall, and insulation; Garage doors, sale and installation; Roofing and gutter work
PA: Installed Building Products, Inc.
495 S High St Ste 50
Columbus OH 43215
614 221-3399

(G-6060)
INSURANCE INTERMEDIARIES INC
Also Called: Nationwide
280 N High St Ste 300 (43215-2535)
PHONE.................................614 846-1111
David S Schmidt, Pr
Larry Bobb, *
Duane Knauer Senv, Pr
EMP: 818 EST: 1975
SQ FT: 14,000
SALES (est): 9.12MM
SALES (corp-wide): 11.75B Privately Held
Web: www.nationwide.com
SIC: 6411 Insurance agents, nec
PA: Nationwide Mutual Insurance Company
1 Nationwide Plz
Columbus OH 43215
614 249-7111

(G-6061)
INSURANCE TECHNOLOGIES CORP
Also Called: Smart Harbor
580 N 4th St Ste 500 (43215-2158)
PHONE.................................866 683-6915
Jason Walker, Mng Pt
EMP: 48
SALES (corp-wide): 173.77MM Privately Held
Web: www.zywave.com
SIC: 7371 Computer software development and applications
HQ: Insurance Technologies Corp
10100 W Innovation Dr # 300
Milwaukee WI 53226
972 245-3660

(G-6062)
INTEGRITY CONCEPTS LLC INC
Also Called: ServiceMaster Elite Janitorial
3500 Millikin Ct Ste A (43228-9196)
PHONE.................................614 529-8332
Daniel Martin, CEO
EMP: 99 EST: 2006
SALES (est): 2.45MM Privately Held
Web: www.servicemaster.com
SIC: 7349 Building maintenance services, nec

(G-6063)
INTEGRITY MUTUAL INSURANCE CO (PA)
Also Called: Integrity
671 S High St (43206-1072)
P.O. Box 539 (54912-0539)
PHONE.................................920 734-4511
Richard J Schinler, Pr
EMP: 91 EST: 1933
SALES (est): 7.82MM
SALES (corp-wide): 7.82MM Privately Held
Web: www.integrityinsurance.com
SIC: 6411 Insurance agents, nec

(G-6064)
INTERBAKE FOODS LLC
Norse Dairy Systems
1700 E 17th Ave (43219-1005)
P.O. Box 1869 (43216-1869)
PHONE.................................614 294-4931
Scott Fullbright, Brnch Mgr
EMP: 137
SALES (corp-wide): 42.47B Privately Held
Web: www.interbake.com
SIC: 5149 Bakery products
HQ: Interbake Foods Llc
1740 Joyce Ave
Columbus OH 43219
614 294-4931

(G-6065)
INTERIM HEALTHCARE INC
784 Morrison Rd (43230-6642)
PHONE.................................614 552-3400
Richard Frederick Nielsen, Prin
EMP: 77
Web: www.interimhealthcare.com
SIC: 8082 Home health care services
PA: Interim Healthcare Inc.
1551 Sawgrs Corp Pkwy # 230
Sunrise FL 33323

(G-6066)
INTERIOR SUPPLY CINCINNATI LLC
481 E 11th Ave (43211-2601)
PHONE.................................614 424-6611
EMP: 30 EST: 1999
SALES (est): 2.33MM Privately Held
Web: www.interiorsupplyinc.com
SIC: 7389 Interior design services

(G-6067)
INTERNAL MDCINE CONS OF CLMBUS
104 N Murray Hill Rd (43228-1524)
PHONE.................................614 878-6413
Robert A Palma, Pr
Doctor Beaver, VP
Thomas E Wanko, Sec
Jeffrey Kaufman, Treas
Peter Pema, VP
EMP: 55 EST: 1968
SQ FT: 5,000
SALES (est): 3.01MM Privately Held
Web: www.imccoh.com
SIC: 8031 8011 Offices and clinics of osteopathic physicians; Internal medicine, physician/surgeon

(G-6068)
INTERNATIONAL DEV ASSN AFRICA
341 S 3rd St Ste 100 (43215-7426)
PHONE.................................314 629-2431
Mohamed Noor, Prin
EMP: 50 EST: 2019
SALES (est): 250.11K Privately Held
SIC: 8641 Civic and social associations

(G-6069)
INTERNATIONAL MASONRY INC
135 Spruce St (43215-1623)
P.O. Box 1598 (43216-1598)
PHONE.................................614 469-8338
John C Casey, Ch
Douglas Casey, *
Brian Casey, *
Mitchell Casey, *
EMP: 48 EST: 1968
SQ FT: 7,500
SALES (est): 1.68MM Privately Held
Web: www.imi-smc.com
SIC: 1741 Bricklaying

(G-6070)
INTERTEK TESTING SVCS NA INC
Also Called: Etl
1717 Arlingate Ln (43228-4116)
PHONE.................................614 279-8090
Andy Gbur, Mgr
EMP: 40
SALES (corp-wide): 4.15B Privately Held
Web: www.intertek.com
SIC: 8734 Testing laboratories
HQ: Intertek Testing Services Na, Inc.
3933 Us Route 11
Cortland NY 13045
607 753-6711

(G-6071)
IRTH SOLUTIONS INC (PA)
5009 Horizons Dr Ste 100 (43220-5284)
PHONE.................................614 459-2328
Jason Adams, CEO
G Brent Bishop, *
EMP: 29 EST: 1985
SQ FT: 12,100
SALES (est): 8.63MM
SALES (corp-wide): 8.63MM Privately Held
Web: www.irthsolutions.com
SIC: 7371 Computer software development

(G-6072)
ISAAC BRANT LEDMAN TEETOR LLP
2 Miranova Pl Ste 700 (43215-3742)
PHONE.................................614 221-2121
Dennis Newman, Pt
EMP: 27 EST: 1987
SALES (est): 7.71MM Privately Held
Web: www.isaacwiles.com
SIC: 8111 General practice law office

(G-6073)
ISAAC WILES & BURKHOLDER LLC
Also Called: Isaac Wiles Burkholder & Teeto
2 Miranova Pl Ste 700 (43215-5098)
PHONE.................................614 221-2121
EMP: 97 EST: 2013
SALES (est): 6.6MM Privately Held
Web: www.isaacwiles.com
SIC: 8111 General practice law office

(G-6074)
ISABELLE RIDGWAY CARE CTR INC
1520 Hawthorne Ave (43203-1762)
PHONE.................................614 252-4931
Patricia Mullins, CEO
John Atala, *
Darrell E Elliott, *
EMP: 79 EST: 1912
SQ FT: 70,400
SALES (est): 8.68MM Privately Held
SIC: 8051 8052 Convalescent home with continuous nursing care; Intermediate care facilities

(G-6075)
ISLAND HOSPITALITY MGT LLC
Also Called: Columbus-Gatehouse Inn
2084 S Hamilton Rd (43232-4302)
PHONE.................................614 864-8844
Bryan Zeitlin, Brnch Mgr
EMP: 40
SALES (corp-wide): 442.84MM Privately Held

GEOGRAPHIC SECTION

Columbus - Franklin County (G-6098)

Web: www.islandhospitality.com
SIC: 8742 7991 7011 Management consulting services; Physical fitness facilities; Hotels
PA: Island Hospitality Management, Llc
    222 Lakeview Ave Ste 200
    West Palm Beach FL 33401
    561 832-6132

(G-6076)
J & D HOME IMPROVEMENT INC (PA)
4400 Easton Cmns (43219-6179)
PHONE.................................800 288-0831
TOLL FREE: 800
Tom Johnston, *Pr*
Ronald Greenbaum, *
EMP: 65 EST: 1987
SALES (est): 5.32MM
SALES (corp-wide): 5.32MM **Privately Held**
SIC: 1799 1771 1521 1741 Waterproofing; Foundation and footing contractor; General remodeling, single-family houses; Foundation building

(G-6077)
J FOOTHILLS LLC
4300 E 5th Ave (43219-1816)
PHONE.................................614 445-8461
EMP: 40 EST: 2010
SALES (est): 390.98K **Privately Held**
SIC: 6513 Apartment building operators
PA: Schottenstein Realty Trust, Inc.
    4300 E 5th Ave
    Columbus OH 43219

(G-6078)
J KUHN ENTERPRISES INC
2200 Mckinley Ave (43204-3417)
PHONE.................................614 481-8838
James Kuhn, *Pr*
EMP: 115 EST: 1989
SALES (est): 4.24MM **Privately Held**
Web: www.ajasphalt.com
SIC: 1771 1611 Blacktop (asphalt) work; Concrete construction: roads, highways, sidewalks, etc.

(G-6079)
JACK BLACK STAFFING LLC
985 Linwood Ave (43206-1674)
PHONE.................................614 629-7614
Brian Bowman, *Managing Member*
Rashawnda Bowman, *
EMP: 50 EST: 2010
SALES (est): 1.35MM **Privately Held**
SIC: 7361 Employment agencies

(G-6080)
JACK CONIE & SONS CORP
Also Called: Conie Construction Company
1340 Windsor Ave (43211-2852)
PHONE.................................614 291-5931
Michael C Conie, *Pr*
Richard P Conie, *
Carol Conie, *
Joseph A Connie, *Stockholder**
EMP: 41 EST: 1971
SQ FT: 10,000
SALES (est): 8.21MM **Privately Held**
Web: www.conie.com
SIC: 1623 1629 Sewer line construction; Earthmoving contractor

(G-6081)
JAG GURU INC
Also Called: Hampton Inn
2093 S Hamilton Rd (43232-4112)
PHONE.................................614 552-2400
Jd Singh, *Pr*

EMP: 51 EST: 2001
SALES (est): 847.91K **Privately Held**
Web: www.hilton.com
SIC: 7011 Hotels and motels

(G-6082)
JAI GURU II INC
Also Called: Holiday Inn
3045 Olentangy River Rd (43202-1516)
PHONE.................................614 920-2400
Alphina Parker, *Genl Mgr*
EMP: 98 EST: 2001
SALES (est): 921.72K **Privately Held**
Web: www.holidayinn.com
SIC: 7011 Hotels and motels

(G-6083)
JAMES CENTER
Also Called: Osu
2050 Kenny Rd (43221-3502)
PHONE.................................614 410-5615
EMP: 182 EST: 2015
SALES (est): 6.65MM **Privately Held**
SIC: 8011 Medical centers

(G-6084)
JAPO INC
3902 Indianola Ave (43214-3156)
P.O. Box 630 (43216-0630)
PHONE.................................614 263-2850
▼ EMP: 47
SIC: 5085 3089 Industrial supplies; Injection molding of plastics

(G-6085)
JEANNE B MCCOY CMNTY CTR FOR A
Also Called: McCoy Center For The Arts
39 E State St (43215-4203)
P.O. Box 508 (43054-0508)
PHONE.................................614 469-0939
EMP: 28
Web: www.mccoycenter.org
SIC: 7922 Ticket agency, theatrical
PA: Jeanne B. Mccoy Community Center For The Arts Corporation
    100 E Dublin Granville Rd
    New Albany OH 43054

(G-6086)
JEGS AUTOMOTIVE INC
Also Called: Buckeye Sales
752 Bonham Ave (43211-2622)
PHONE.................................614 294-5451
Ray Stagg, *Brnch Mgr*
EMP: 390
SALES (corp-wide): 712.86MM **Privately Held**
Web: www.jegs.com
SIC: 5013 Automotive supplies and parts
HQ: Jeg's Automotive, Llc
    101 Jegs Pl
    Delaware OH 43015
    614 294-5050

(G-6087)
JETSELECT LLC
4130 E 5th Ave (43219-1802)
PHONE.................................954 648-0998
EMP: 29
SALES (corp-wide): 27.92MM **Privately Held**
Web: www.flyjetedge.com
SIC: 4522 Flying charter service
HQ: Jetselect Llc
    4131 Worth Ave
    Columbus OH 43219

(G-6088)
JEWISH CMNTY CTR OF GRTER CLMB (PA)
1125 College Ave (43209-7802)
PHONE.................................614 231-2731
Carol Folkerth, *Ex Dir*
Louise Young, *
EMP: 137 EST: 1945
SQ FT: 106,000
SALES (est): 12.7MM
SALES (corp-wide): 12.7MM **Privately Held**
Web: www.columbusjcc.org
SIC: 8641 8699 7999 8351 Social club, membership; Charitable organization; Day camp; Preschool center

(G-6089)
JEWISH FAMILY SERVICE
1070 College Ave Ste A (43209-2489)
PHONE.................................614 231-1890
Chuck Wheiden, *Dir*
EMP: 238 EST: 1958
SALES (est): 4.41MM **Privately Held**
Web: www.jfscolumbus.org
SIC: 8322 8331 Social service center; Vocational rehabilitation agency

(G-6090)
JIFITICOM INC (PA)
1985 Henderson Rd Pmb 63255 (43220-2401)
PHONE.................................914 339-5376
Yaacov Martin, *CEO*
Daniel Tobias, *
EMP: 105 EST: 2011
SALES (est): 6.56MM
SALES (corp-wide): 6.56MM **Privately Held**
Web: www.jifiti.com
SIC: 7371 Computer software development

(G-6091)
JIM KEIM FORD
Also Called: Keim, Jim Ford Sales
5575 Keim Cir (43228-7328)
PHONE.................................614 888-3333
James Keim, *Pr*
L D Pellissier Iii, *Sec*
EMP: 52 EST: 1922
SQ FT: 40,000
SALES (est): 7.35MM **Privately Held**
Web: www.ford.com
SIC: 5511 7538 5521 Automobiles, new and used; General automotive repair shops; Used car dealers

(G-6092)
JMAC INC (PA)
200 W Nationwide Blvd Unit 1 (43215)
PHONE.................................614 436-2418
John P Mcconnell, *Ch Bd*
Michael A Priest, *Pr*
George N Corey, *Prin*
▲ EMP: 28 EST: 1980
SQ FT: 6,000
SALES (est): 94.51MM
SALES (corp-wide): 94.51MM **Privately Held**
SIC: 3325 5198 7999 5511 Steel foundries, nec; Paints; Ice skating rink operation; Automobiles, new and used

(G-6093)
JOBSOHIO
Also Called: Find Your Ohio
41 S High St Ste 1500 (43215-6132)
PHONE.................................614 224-6446
J P Nauseef, *Pr*
EMP: 90 EST: 2011
SALES (est): 294.15MM **Privately Held**

Web: www.jobsohio.com
SIC: 7361 8641 Employment agencies; Civic and social associations

(G-6094)
JOHNSON & FISCHER INCORPORATED
Also Called: J F Painting Co
5303 Trabue Rd (43228-9783)
PHONE.................................614 276-8868
Robert J Johnson, *Pr*
EMP: 45 EST: 1974
SQ FT: 3,000
SALES (est): 4.34MM **Privately Held**
Web: www.thejfcompany.com
SIC: 1721 Commercial painting

(G-6095)
JOHNSONS REAL ICE CREAM LLC
Also Called: Wilcoxon, James H Jr
2728 E Main St (43209-2534)
PHONE.................................614 231-0014
James H Wilcoxon Junior, *Pr*
EMP: 109 EST: 1950
SQ FT: 4,600
SALES (est): 1.11MM **Privately Held**
Web: www.johnsonsrealicecream.com
SIC: 5812 5143 2024 Ice cream stands or dairy bars; Dairy products, except dried or canned; Ice cream and frozen deserts

(G-6096)
JONES DAY LIMITED PARTNERSHIP
325 John H Mcconnell Blvd Ste 600 (43215-2672)
P.O. Box 165017 (43216-5017)
PHONE.................................614 469-3939
Elizabeth P Kessler, *Pt*
EMP: 99
SALES (corp-wide): 333.64MM **Privately Held**
Web: www.jonesday.com
SIC: 8111 General practice law office
PA: Jones Day Limited Partnership
    N Point 901 Lakeside Ave
    Cleveland OH 44114
    216 586-3939

(G-6097)
JONES TRUCK & SPRING REPR INC
350 Frank Rd (43207-2423)
PHONE.................................614 443-4619
John Richard Jones, *Pr*
Jack E Fink, *
EMP: 70 EST: 1978
SQ FT: 12,000
SALES (est): 2.25MM **Privately Held**
Web: www.jonesspring.com
SIC: 7538 General truck repair

(G-6098)
JPMORGAN CHASE BANK NAT ASSN
Also Called: Chase HM Mrtgages Florence Off
3415 Vision Dr (43219-6009)
PHONE.................................212 270-6000
Sharon Hardee, *Prin*
EMP: 53
SALES (corp-wide): 239.43B **Publicly Held**
Web: www.jpmorgan.com
SIC: 6021 National commercial banks
HQ: Jpmorgan Chase Bank, National Association
    1111 Polaris Pkwy
    Columbus OH 43240
    614 436-3055

Columbus - Franklin County (G-6099) — GEOGRAPHIC SECTION

(G-6099)
JUBILEE LIMITED PARTNERSHIP
4300 E 5th Ave (43219-1816)
PHONE.................................614 221-9200
EMP: 5007 EST: 1995
SALES (est): 5.25MM
SALES (corp-wide): 31.53MM **Privately Held**
SIC: 8748 Business consulting, nec
PA: Schottenstein Stores Corporation
    4300 E 5th Ave
    Columbus OH 43219
    614 221-9200

(G-6100)
JULIAN SPEER CO
Also Called: Speer Mechanical
5255 Sinclair Rd (43229-5042)
PHONE.................................614 261-6331
Dennis Shuman, Pr
Michael A Shuman, VP
Dale Witte, VP
John Harper, VP
EMP: 55 EST: 1957
SALES (est): 10.35MM
SALES (corp-wide): 62.38MM **Privately Held**
Web: www.speermechanical.com
SIC: 1711 Mechanical contractor
PA: Speer Industries Incorporated
    5255 Sinclair Rd
    Columbus OH 43229
    614 261-6331

(G-6101)
JUVLY AESTHETIC LLC
40 W Gay St (43215-2811)
PHONE.................................800 254-0188
EMP: 49 EST: 2017
SALES (est): 2.37MM **Privately Held**
Web: www.juvly.com
SIC: 7299 Personal appearance services

(G-6102)
KARL HC LLC
Also Called: Villa Angela Care Center
5700 Karl Rd (43229-3602)
PHONE.................................614 846-5420
James Griffiths, Managing Member
Brian Colleran, Managing Member
Dianna Bozek, Managing Member
EMP: 350 EST: 2001
SQ FT: 102,000
SALES (est): 23.86MM **Privately Held**
SIC: 8051 Skilled nursing care facilities

(G-6103)
KARLSBERGER ARCHITECTURE INC (HQ)
Also Called: Karlsberger & Associates
99 E Main St (43215-5115)
P.O. Box 340130 (43234-0130)
PHONE.................................614 471-1812
Richard Barger, Pr
Karen Plack, Dir
EMP: 51 EST: 1995
SALES (est): 6.01MM
SALES (corp-wide): 18.67MM **Privately Held**
SIC: 8712 8742 7389 Architectural engineering; Planning consultant; Interior decorating
PA: Karlsberger Companies
    99 E Main St
    Columbus OH 43215
    614 461-9500

(G-6104)
KARLSBERGER COMPANIES (PA)
99 E Main St (43215-5115)
PHONE.................................614 461-9500
Michael Tyne, Ch Bd
Richard Barger, *
William O Anderson, *
EMP: 105 EST: 1927
SQ FT: 32,000
SALES (est): 18.67MM
SALES (corp-wide): 18.67MM **Privately Held**
Web: www.karlsberger.com
SIC: 8712 8742 7389 Architectural services; Planning consultant; Interior decorating

(G-6105)
KARRINGTON OPERATING CO INC (DH)
Also Called: Karrington
919 Old Henderson Rd (43220-3722)
PHONE.................................614 324-5951
EMP: 55 EST: 1989
SQ FT: 14,000
SALES (est): 53.12MM
SALES (corp-wide): 2.92B **Privately Held**
Web: www.karrington-charlotte.com
SIC: 8059 Personal care home, with health care
HQ: Sunrise Senior Living, Llc
    7902 Westpark Dr
    Mc Lean VA 22102

(G-6106)
KDM AND ASSOCIATES LLC
5505 Keim Cir (43228-7328)
PHONE.................................614 853-6199
A J Shah, Prin
EMP: 56 EST: 2005
SALES (est): 808.06K **Privately Held**
SIC: 7011 Hotels

(G-6107)
KEGLER BROWN HL RITTER CO LPA (PA)
65 E State St Ste 1800 (43215-4294)
PHONE.................................614 462-5400
Michael E Zatezalo, Mng Pt
Paul R Hess, *
EMP: 138 EST: 1964
SQ FT: 51,000
SALES (est): 26.08MM
SALES (corp-wide): 26.08MM **Privately Held**
Web: www.keglerbrown.com
SIC: 8111 General practice attorney, lawyer

(G-6108)
KELLER GROUP LIMITED
Also Called: Keller Farms Landscape & Nurs
3909 Groves Rd (43232-4138)
PHONE.................................614 866-9551
Lisa Fleming Albers, Managing Member*
EMP: 36 EST: 1978
SQ FT: 11,400
SALES (est): 4.41MM **Privately Held**
Web: www.kellerf.com
SIC: 0782 Landscape contractors

(G-6109)
KELLER WILLIAMS REALTY
Also Called: Keller Williams Realtors
1 Easton Oval Ste 100 (43219-6062)
PHONE.................................614 944-5900
Dean Reiter, Prin
EMP: 43 EST: 2016
SALES (est): 1.02MM **Privately Held**
Web: www.kw.com
SIC: 6531 Real estate agent, residential

(G-6110)
KEMBA FINANCIAL CREDIT UN INC
4311 N High St (43214-2609)
PHONE.................................614 235-2395
Gerald Guy, CEO
EMP: 65
SALES (corp-wide): 95.46MM **Privately Held**
Web: www.kemba.org
SIC: 6062 State credit unions, not federally chartered
PA: Kemba Financial Credit Union, Inc
    555 Officenter Pl Ste 100
    Gahanna OH 43230
    614 235-2395

(G-6111)
KEMBA FINANCIAL CREDIT UNION
4220 E Broad St (43213-1216)
P.O. Box 307370 (43230-7370)
PHONE.................................614 235-2395
Jerry Guy, CEO
EMP: 32 EST: 1976
SQ FT: 1,200
SALES (est): 2.86MM **Privately Held**
Web: www.kemba.org
SIC: 6062 State credit unions, not federally chartered

(G-6112)
KENNETHS HAIR SLONS DAY SPAS I (PA)
Also Called: Kenneth's Design Group
5151 Reed Rd Ste 250b (43220-2594)
PHONE.................................614 457-7712
Kenneth Anders, Pr
EMP: 300 EST: 1977
SQ FT: 46,000
SALES (est): 23.77MM
SALES (corp-wide): 23.77MM **Privately Held**
Web: www.kenneths.com
SIC: 5999 7231 Toiletries, cosmetics, and perfumes; Hair dressing school

(G-6113)
KEY BLUE PRINTS INC (PA)
Also Called: Key Color
195 E Livingston Ave (43215-5793)
PHONE.................................614 228-3285
David M Key Iii, Pr
▲ EMP: 54 EST: 1966
SQ FT: 18,000
SALES (est): 19.53MM
SALES (corp-wide): 19.53MM **Privately Held**
Web: www.keycompanies.com
SIC: 5049 7334 Drafting supplies; Blueprinting service

(G-6114)
KEYBANK NATIONAL ASSOCIATION
88 E Broad St (43215-3506)
PHONE.................................614 460-3415
Gary Weaver, Mgr
EMP: 38
SALES (corp-wide): 10.4B **Publicly Held**
Web: www.key.com
SIC: 6021 National commercial banks
HQ: Keybank National Association
    127 Public Sq Ste 5600
    Cleveland OH 44114
    800 539-2968

(G-6115)
KIDNEY CENTER OF BEXLEY LLC
Also Called: AMERICAN RENAL
1151 College Ave (43209-2827)
PHONE.................................614 231-2200
EMP: 65 EST: 2011
SALES (est): 2.66MM
SALES (corp-wide): 822.52MM **Privately Held**
Web: www.whv.org
SIC: 8092 Kidney dialysis centers
HQ: American Renal Associates Holdings, Inc.
    500 Cummings Ctr Ste 6550
    Beverly MA 01915

(G-6116)
KINDRED NURSING CENTERS E LLC
Also Called: Kindred Trnstnal Care Rhbltton
2770 Clime Rd (43223-3626)
PHONE.................................614 276-8222
Dawn Lewis, Mgr
EMP: 111
SALES (corp-wide): 13.68B **Privately Held**
Web: www.kindredhospitals.com
SIC: 8051 Convalescent home with continuous nursing care
HQ: Kindred Nursing Centers East, L.L.C.
    680 S 4th St
    Louisville KY 40202
    502 596-7300

(G-6117)
KING TUT LOGISTICS LLC
Also Called: Cleopatra Trucking
3600 Enterprise Ave (43228-1047)
PHONE.................................614 538-0509
EMP: 50 EST: 2007
SALES (est): 1.97MM **Privately Held**
Web: www.kingtutlogistics.net
SIC: 4214 4225 7389 Local trucking with storage; General warehousing and storage; Packaging and labeling services

(G-6118)
KLARNA INC
629 N High St Fl 300 (43215-2929)
PHONE.................................614 615-4705
Brian Billingsley, CEO
EMP: 37 EST: 2011
SQ FT: 3,300
SALES (est): 20.7MM
SALES (corp-wide): 1.7B **Privately Held**
Web: www.klarna.com
SIC: 6099 Electronic funds transfer network, including switching
HQ: Klarna Bank Ab
    Sveavagen 46
    Stockholm 111 3

(G-6119)
KLEAN-A-KAR INC (PA)
3383 S High St (43207-3624)
PHONE.................................614 221-3145
Dennis Ramsey, Pr
Doug Ramsey, *
Dan Ramsey, *
EMP: 40 EST: 1961
SALES (est): 2.48MM
SALES (corp-wide): 2.48MM **Privately Held**
SIC: 7542 Washing and polishing, automotive

(G-6120)
KLINGBEIL MANAGEMENT GROUP CO (PA)
21 W Broad St Fl 10 (43215-4172)
PHONE.................................614 220-8900
James D Klingbeil, Pr
EMP: 30 EST: 1974
SALES (est): 2.21MM
SALES (corp-wide): 2.21MM **Privately Held**
Web: www.kcmgt.com
SIC: 6531 1522 8742 8721 Real estate managers; Remodeling, multi-family dwellings; Administrative services consultant; Accounting services, except auditing

GEOGRAPHIC SECTION
Columbus - Franklin County (G-6142)

(G-6121)
KLINGBEIL MULTIFAMILTY FUND IV
21 W Broad St Fl 11 (43215-4100)
PHONE..............................415 398-0106
Paul Rose, *Pr*
EMP: 87
SALES (corp-wide): 9.58MM **Privately Held**
SIC: 6513 Apartment building operators
PA: Klingbeil Multifamilty Fund Iv
   200 California St Ste 300
   San Francisco CA 94111
   415 398-3590

(G-6122)
KM2 SOLUTIONS LLC
Also Called: Technology Hub
2400 Corporate Exchange Dr Ste 120 (43231-7605)
PHONE..............................610 213-1408
EMP: 331
SALES (corp-wide): 42.38MM **Privately Held**
Web: www.km2solutions.com
SIC: 8742 Financial consultant
PA: Km2 Solutions, Llc
   600 Eagleview Blvd Ste 30
   Exton PA 19341
   404 848-8886

(G-6123)
KNAPP VETERINARY HOSPITAL INC
596 Oakland Park Ave (43214-4199)
PHONE..............................614 267-3124
Paul H Knapp D.v.m., *Pr*
John C Munsell, *VP*
Robert Knapp, *VP*
EMP: 33 EST: 1945
SQ FT: 5,000
SALES (est): 866.98K **Privately Held**
Web: www.knappvet.com
SIC: 0742 Animal hospital services, pets and other animal specialties

(G-6124)
KNOWLEDGE MGT INTERACTIVE INC
330 W Spring St Ste 320 (43215-7305)
PHONE..............................614 224-0664
Mark Colasante, *CEO*
Joel Copeland, *
EMP: 35 EST: 2000
SQ FT: 6,800
SALES (est): 2.59MM **Privately Held**
Web: www.kmilearning.com
SIC: 7371 Computer software development

(G-6125)
KONKUS MARBLE & GRANITE INC
Also Called: Konkus Marble & Granite
3737 Zane Trace Dr (43228-3854)
PHONE..............................614 876-4000
Marc Konkus, *Pr*
Annie Konkus, *
▲ EMP: 140 EST: 1997
SQ FT: 99,000
SALES (est): 19MM **Privately Held**
Web: www.konkusmarbleandgranite.com
SIC: 1799 Counter top installation

(G-6126)
KOORSEN FIRE & SECURITY INC
Also Called: Koorsen Fire & Security
727 Manor Park Dr (43228-9522)
PHONE..............................614 878-2228
Dale Underwood, *Brnch Mgr*
EMP: 38
SALES (corp-wide): 150.64MM **Privately Held**
Web: www.koorsen.com
SIC: 7382 Security systems services
PA: Koorsen Fire & Security, Inc.
   2719 N Arlington Ave
   Indianapolis IN 46218
   317 542-1800

(G-6127)
KPMG LLP
191 W Nationwide Blvd Ste 500 (43215-2575)
PHONE..............................614 249-2300
Phillip Smith, *Brnch Mgr*
EMP: 87
SALES (corp-wide): 1.34B **Privately Held**
Web: www.home.kpmg
SIC: 8721 Accounting services, except auditing
PA: Kpmg Llp
   345 Park Ave
   New York NY 10154
   212 758-9700

(G-6128)
KREBER GRAPHICS INC (PA)
2580 Westbell Dr (43228-3827)
PHONE..............................614 529-5701
Jim Kreber, *CEO*
Todd Alexander, *
Stephen Kron, *
EMP: 90 EST: 1947
SQ FT: 86,000
SALES (est): 19.37MM
SALES (corp-wide): 19.37MM **Privately Held**
Web: www.kreber.com
SIC: 7311 Advertising consultant

(G-6129)
KRIEGER FORD INC (PA)
1800 Morse Rd (43229-6691)
PHONE..............................614 888-3320
G Douglas Krieger, *Pr*
John Jeffrey Krieger, *
Brent Ferguson, *
▲ EMP: 140 EST: 1965
SQ FT: 50,000
SALES (est): 47.84MM
SALES (corp-wide): 47.84MM **Privately Held**
Web: www.kriegerford.com
SIC: 5511 7515 7538 7513 Automobiles, new and used; Passenger car leasing; General automotive repair shops; Truck rental and leasing, no drivers

(G-6130)
L BRANDS SERVICE COMPANY LLC (HQ)
3 Limited Pkwy (43230-1467)
PHONE..............................614 415-7000
Leslie H Wexner, *Ch Bd*
▲ EMP: 89 EST: 1982
SALES (est): 8.85MM
SALES (corp-wide): 7.43B **Publicly Held**
SIC: 6512 8743 Nonresidential building operators; Public relations services
PA: Bath & Body Works, Inc.
   3 Limited Pkwy
   Columbus OH 43230
   614 415-7000

(G-6131)
L BRANDS STORE DSIGN CNSTR INC
3 Ltd Pkwy (43230)
PHONE..............................614 415-7000
Gene Torcha, *Pr*
Rick Felice, *
Timothy Faber, *
▲ EMP: 230 EST: 1990
SALES (est): 119.7MM
SALES (corp-wide): 7.43B **Publicly Held**
SIC: 1542 Commercial and office building, new construction
PA: Bath & Body Works, Inc.
   3 Limited Pkwy
   Columbus OH 43230
   614 415-7000

(G-6132)
L V TRUCKING INC
Also Called: L V Trckng
2440 Harrison Rd (43204-3508)
PHONE..............................614 275-4994
Brad Moore, *Pr*
Barbara Moore, *
L Vince Moore, *
EMP: 41 EST: 1972
SQ FT: 3,000
SALES (est): 4.64MM **Privately Held**
Web: www.lvtrucking.com
SIC: 4213 4212 Contract haulers; Local trucking, without storage

(G-6133)
LADAN LEARNING CENTER LLC
6028 Cleveland Ave (43231-2230)
PHONE..............................614 426-4306
Hibo Omar, *Owner*
EMP: 35 EST: 2014
SALES (est): 579.17K **Privately Held**
SIC: 8351 Child day care services

(G-6134)
LANCASTER POLLARD MRTG CO LLC (DH)
10 W Broad St Ste 800 (43215-3476)
PHONE..............................614 224-8800
Thomas R Green, *CEO*
Timothy J Dobyns, *
Kevin J Beerman, *
EMP: 70 EST: 1988
SALES (est): 43.06MM **Privately Held**
SIC: 6159 6162 6282 Intermediate investment banks; Mortgage bankers; Investment advisory service
HQ: Lument Real Estate Capital Holdings, Llc
   10 W Broad St Fl 8
   Columbus OH 43215
   800 837-5100

(G-6135)
LANCE A1 CLEANING SERVICES LLC
342 Hanton Way (43213-4430)
PHONE..............................614 370-0550
EMP: 100 EST: 2015
SALES (est): 764.38K **Privately Held**
SIC: 7699 Cleaning services

(G-6136)
LANDOR & FITCH LLC
191 W Nationwide Blvd Ste 175 (43215-2568)
PHONE..............................614 843-1766
EMP: 40
SALES (corp-wide): 18.5B **Privately Held**
Web: www.landor.com
SIC: 7389 Automobile recovery service
HQ: Landor & Fitch Llc
   175 Greenwich St Fl 31
   New York NY 10007
   415 365-1700

(G-6137)
LANE ALTON & HORST LLC
2 Miranova Pl Ste 220 (43215)
P.O. Box 2289 (43216)
PHONE..............................614 228-6885
EMP: 45 EST: 1935
SQ FT: 24,000
SALES (est): 304.24K **Privately Held**
Web: www.lanealton.com
SIC: 8111 General practice law office

(G-6138)
LANE AVIATION CORPORATION
Also Called: Lane Aviation
4389 International Gtwy Ste 228 (43219-3819)
PHONE..............................614 237-3747
Donna L Earl, *CEO*
Brad Primm, *
EMP: 130 EST: 1935
SQ FT: 172,000
SALES (est): 25.15MM **Privately Held**
Web: www.laneaviationservicescolumbus.com
SIC: 5599 4581 4522 4512 Aircraft, self-propelled; Aircraft servicing and repairing; Air passenger carriers, nonscheduled; Air transportation, scheduled

(G-6139)
LANG STONE COMPANY INC (PA)
4099 E 5th Ave (43219-1812)
P.O. Box 360747 (43236-0747)
PHONE..............................614 235-4099
TOLL FREE: 800
E Dean Coffman, *Pr*
Joann Coffman, *
▲ EMP: 39 EST: 1856
SQ FT: 10,000
SALES (est): 18.28MM
SALES (corp-wide): 18.28MM **Privately Held**
Web: www.langstone.com
SIC: 5032 5211 3281 3272 Granite building stone; Lumber and other building materials; Cut stone and stone products; Concrete products, nec

(G-6140)
LAPHAM-HICKEY STEEL CORP
Lapham-Hickey
753 Marion Rd (43207-2554)
PHONE..............................614 443-4881
Eric Sattler, *Mgr*
EMP: 48
SQ FT: 110,000
SALES (corp-wide): 235.89MM **Privately Held**
Web: www.lapham-hickey.com
SIC: 5051 3443 3441 3398 Steel; Fabricated plate work (boiler shop); Fabricated structural metal; Metal heat treating
PA: Lapham-Hickey Steel Corp.
   5500 W 73rd St
   Bedford Park IL 60638
   708 496-6111

(G-6141)
LARK RESIDENTIAL SUPPORT INC
5026 Sinclair Rd (43229-5431)
PHONE..............................614 582-9721
Jovita Lark, *CEO*
EMP: 31 EST: 2007
SALES (est): 800K **Privately Held**
Web: www.larkresidential.com
SIC: 8322 Adult day care center

(G-6142)
LARRIMER & LARRIMER LLC (PA)
165 N High St Fl 3 (43215-2402)
PHONE..............................614 221-7548
Gavin R Larrimer, *Pt*
Terrence W Larrimer, *Pt*
EMP: 50 EST: 1960
SQ FT: 7,500
SALES (est): 4.6MM
SALES (corp-wide): 4.6MM **Privately Held**

Web: www.larrimer.com
SIC: 8111 General practice law office

(G-6143)
LASTING IMPRSSONS EVENT PTY RN
Also Called: Lasting Imprssions Event Rentl
5080 Sinclair Rd Ste 200 (43229-5412)
PHONE..................................614 252-5400
James P Fritz, Pr
J P Fritz, *
EMP: 78 EST: 1991
SQ FT: 105,000
SALES (est): 4.7MM Privately Held
Web: www.lirents.net
SIC: 7359 Dishes, silverware, tables, and banquet accessories rental

(G-6144)
LATORRE CONCRETE CNSTR INC
850 N Cassady Ave (43219-2298)
PHONE..................................614 257-1401
Mark Latorre, Pr
Anthony Latorre, Sec
EMP: 31 EST: 1972
SQ FT: 11,000
SALES (est): 964.14K Privately Held
Web: www.latorreconcrete.com
SIC: 1771 Concrete work

(G-6145)
LAWHON AND ASSOCIATES INC (PA)
1441 King Ave (43212-2108)
PHONE..................................614 481-8600
Susan Daniels, Pr
Richard Isaly, *
Karrie Bontrager, *
Michele Glinsky, *
EMP: 36 EST: 1985
SQ FT: 16,300
SALES (est): 7.87MM
SALES (corp-wide): 7.87MM Privately Held
Web: www.lawhon-assoc.com
SIC: 8748 Environmental consultant

(G-6146)
LAWRENCE M SHELL DDS
Also Called: Dental Associates
2862 E Main St Ste A (43209-3709)
PHONE..................................614 235-3444
Lawrence M Shell D.d.s., Owner
Cheryl Devore, *
EMP: 40 EST: 1946
SQ FT: 5,000
SALES (est): 688.3K Privately Held
SIC: 8021 Dentists' office

(G-6147)
LAZ KARP ASSOCIATES LLC
245 Marconi Blvd (43215-2314)
PHONE..................................614 227-0356
EMP: 99
Web: www.lazparking.com
SIC: 7521 Parking lots
PA: Laz Karp Associates, Llc
1 Financial Plz
Hartford CT 06103

(G-6148)
LAZEAR CAPITAL PARTNERS LTD (PA)
401 N Front St Ste 250 (43215-2297)
PHONE..................................614 221-1616
Bruce C Lazear, Prin
Bruce Lazear, Pr
EMP: 30 EST: 1998
SALES (est): 23.78MM
SALES (corp-wide): 23.78MM Privately Held

Web: www.lazearcapital.com
SIC: 6799 Investors, nec

(G-6149)
LBI STARBUCKS DC 3
3 Limited Pkwy (43230-1467)
PHONE..................................614 415-6363
Edward Razek, Prin
EMP: 77 EST: 2013
SALES (est): 1.19MM Privately Held
SIC: 8041 Offices and clinics of chiropractors

(G-6150)
LEADER PROMOTIONS INC (PA)
Also Called: Leaderpromos.com
790 E Johnstown Rd (43230)
PHONE..................................614 416-6565
Stephanie Leader, CEO
Kathy Weible, *
▲ EMP: 75 EST: 1995
SQ FT: 14,000
SALES (est): 42.2MM Privately Held
Web: www.leaderpromos.com
SIC: 5199 Advertising specialties

(G-6151)
LEARNING SPECTRUM LTD (PA)
6660 Doubletree Ave Ste 1 (43229-1128)
PHONE..................................614 844-5433
Jill Medley, Pr
EMP: 34 EST: 2005
SALES (est): 4.67MM Privately Held
Web: www.thelearningspectrum.com
SIC: 8748 8351 Educational consultant; Child day care services

(G-6152)
LEGACY MAINTENANCE SVCS LLC
2475 Scioto Harper Dr (43204-3420)
PHONE..................................614 473-8444
Julie Everhart, Prin
EMP: 49 EST: 2012
SALES (est): 3.74MM Privately Held
Web: www.lmsoh.com
SIC: 7349 Janitorial service, contract basis

(G-6153)
LEGAL AID SOCIETY OF COLUMBUS (PA)
1108 City Park Ave Ste 100 (43206-3583)
PHONE..................................614 737-0139
Thomas Weeks, Dir
EMP: 50 EST: 1954
SALES (est): 4.45MM
SALES (corp-wide): 4.45MM Privately Held
Web: www.columbuslegalaid.org
SIC: 8111 Legal aid service

(G-6154)
LEIDOS INC
77 Outerbelt St (43213-1548)
PHONE..................................614 575-4900
EMP: 38
Web: www.leidos.com
SIC: 8731 Commercial physical research
HQ: Leidos, Inc.
1750 Presidents St
Reston VA 20190
571 526-6000

(G-6155)
LEVY & ASSOCIATES LLC
Also Called: Levy & Associates
4645 Executive Dr (43220)
PHONE..................................614 898-5200
EMP: 47 EST: 2006
SQ FT: 12,000
SALES (est): 5.6MM Privately Held
Web: www.levylawllc.com

SIC: 8111 General practice attorney, lawyer

(G-6156)
LIBERTY COMM SFTWR SLTIONS INC
Also Called: Newfound Technologies
1050 Kingsmill Pkwy (43229-1143)
PHONE..................................614 318-5000
EMP: 34 EST: 1993
SQ FT: 8,300
SALES (est): 885.95K Privately Held
Web: www.nfti.com
SIC: 7371 Computer software development

(G-6157)
LIBERTY MORTGAGE COMPANY INC
Also Called: One Nation Mortgages
473 E Rich St (43215-5315)
P.O. Box 918 (43065-0918)
PHONE..................................614 224-4000
Karen Richmond, Pr
Mary Fallieros, *
John Vlahos, *
EMP: 49 EST: 1983
SQ FT: 4,500
SALES (est): 5.21MM Privately Held
Web: www.loansbyliberty.com
SIC: 6162 Mortgage bankers

(G-6158)
LIFE CARE CENTERS AMERICA INC
Also Called: Mayfare Village
3000 Bethel Rd (43220-2262)
PHONE..................................614 889-6320
Julie Klein, Mgr
EMP: 78
SALES (corp-wide): 139.21MM Privately Held
Web: www.lcca.com
SIC: 8051 Convalescent home with continuous nursing care
PA: Life Care Centers Of America, Inc.
3570 Keith St Nw
Cleveland TN 37312
423 472-9585

(G-6159)
LIFE TIME INC
Also Called: Lifetime Fitness
3900 Easton Sta (43219-6064)
PHONE..................................614 428-6000
Rob Zwelling, Mgr
EMP: 95
SALES (corp-wide): 2.22B Publicly Held
Web: www.lifetime.life
SIC: 7991 7299 Health club; Personal appearance services
HQ: Life Time, Inc.
2902 Corporate Pl
Chanhassen MN 55317

(G-6160)
LIFE TIME FITNESS INC
Also Called: Lifetime Fitness
1860 Henderson Rd (43220-2502)
PHONE..................................614 326-1500
Bob Hetzel, Brnch Mgr
EMP: 95
SALES (corp-wide): 2.22B Publicly Held
Web: www.lifetime.life
SIC: 7991 Health club
HQ: Life Time, Inc.
2902 Corporate Pl
Chanhassen MN 55317

(G-6161)
LIFECARE ALLIANCE
Also Called: MEALS ON WHEELS
1699 W Mound St (43223-1855)

PHONE..................................614 278-3130
Joseph W Cole Ii, Ch
Charles W Gehring, *
Robert Click, *
Andrea Albanese Denning, *
John Gregory, *
EMP: 210 EST: 1898
SQ FT: 33,000
SALES (est): 17.52MM Privately Held
Web: www.lifecarealliance.org
SIC: 8082 Home health care services

(G-6162)
LIFESTYLE COMMUNITIES LTD (PA)
230 West St Ste 200 (43215-2655)
PHONE..................................614 918-2000
Michael J Deasecentis Junior, Pt
Michael J Deasecentis Senior, Pt
Richard Miller, *
EMP: 38 EST: 1996
SQ FT: 40,000
SALES (est): 26.74MM
SALES (corp-wide): 26.74MM Privately Held
Web: www.lifestylecommunities.com
SIC: 1522 Multi-family dwellings, new construction

(G-6163)
LIGHTHUSE BHVRAL HLTH SLTONS L
4000 E Main St (43213-3593)
PHONE..................................614 334-6903
EMP: 85 EST: 2019
SALES (est): 5.07MM Privately Held
Web: www.lighthousebhsolutions.com
SIC: 8322 General counseling services

(G-6164)
LIMBACH COMPANY LLC
851 Williams Ave (43212-3849)
PHONE..................................614 299-2175
William Meadows, Brnch Mgr
EMP: 342
SALES (corp-wide): 516.35MM Publicly Held
Web: www.limbachinc.com
SIC: 1711 Mechanical contractor
HQ: Limbach Company Llc
797 Commonwealth Dr
Warrendale PA 15086
412 359-2173

(G-6165)
LIMBACH COMPANY LLC
822 Cleveland Ave (43201-3612)
PHONE..................................614 299-2175
EMP: 110
SALES (corp-wide): 516.35MM Publicly Held
Web: www.limbachinc.com
SIC: 1711 Mechanical contractor
HQ: Limbach Company Llc
797 Commonwealth Dr
Warrendale PA 15086
412 359-2173

(G-6166)
LINCOLN CONSTRUCTION INC
4790 Shuster Rd (43214-1997)
PHONE..................................614 457-6015
EMP: 50 EST: 1971
SALES (est): 15.8MM Privately Held
Web: www.lincolnconstruction.com
SIC: 1542 Commercial and office building, new construction

(G-6167)
LINCOLN POINTE
40 Hutchinson Ave (43235-4759)
PHONE..................................614 253-4602

GEOGRAPHIC SECTION
Columbus - Franklin County (G-6188)

EMP: 45 **EST:** 2018
SALES (est): 259.61K **Privately Held**
Web: www.ardentcommunities.com
SIC: 6513 Apartment building operators

(G-6168)
LINK REAL ESTATE GROUP LLC
2500 Farmers Dr Ste 250 (43235-5840)
PHONE..............................614 686-7775
EMP: 68 **EST:** 2017
SALES (est): 5.35MM **Privately Held**
Web: www.linkapm.com
SIC: 6531 Real estate brokers and agents

(G-6169)
LITTLE DRMERS BIG BLIEVERS LLC
870 Michigan Ave (43215-1109)
PHONE..............................614 824-4666
Sarah Delay, *Dir*
EMP: 45 **EST:** 2008
SALES (est): 1.39MM **Privately Held**
Web: www.littledreamersbigbelievers.com
SIC: 8351 Group day care center

(G-6170)
LIVE MEDIA GROUP HOLDINGS LLC
2091 Arlingate Ln (43228-4113)
PHONE..............................614 297-0001
EMP: 66 **EST:** 2015
SALES (est): 2.75MM **Privately Held**
Web: www.livemediagroup.com
SIC: 7812 Video production

(G-6171)
LIVE TECHNOLOGIES LLC
3445 Millennium Ct (43219-5550)
PHONE..............................614 278-7777
Michael L Ranney Junior, *Pr*
Shawn D Loevenguth, *OF LIVE EVENT DIV*
David Vuppo, *OF SYSTEM INTEGRATION*
Thomas Marks, *CFO*
EMP: 100 **EST:** 2008
SALES (est): 11.85MM
SALES (corp-wide): 11.85MM **Privately Held**
Web: www.gowithlive.com
SIC: 1731 5099 7359 7819 Sound equipment specialization; Video and audio equipment; Audio-visual equipment and supply rental; Sound effects and music production, motion picture
PA: Live Technologies Holdings, Inc.
3445 Millennium Ct
Columbus OH 43219
614 278-7777

(G-6172)
LOEB ELECTRIC COMPANY (PA)
Also Called: Unistrut-Columbus
1800 E 5th Ave Ste A (43219-2592)
PHONE..............................800 686-6351
Charles A Loeb, *Pr*
Jeff Blunt, *CFO*
M J Walsh, *Prin*
Doug Beh, *Ex VP*
Scott Sarno, *Ex Dir*
▲ **EMP:** 95 **EST:** 1911
SQ FT: 220,000
SALES (est): 174.48MM
SALES (corp-wide): 174.48MM **Privately Held**
Web: www.loebelectric.com
SIC: 5063 Electrical supplies, nec

(G-6173)
LOTH INC
Also Called: T W Ruff
855 Grandview Ave Ste 2 (43215-1102)
PHONE..............................614 487-4000
Jason Walaler, *Genl Mgr*
EMP: 32
SALES (corp-wide): 56.34MM **Privately Held**
Web: www.lothinc.com
SIC: 5021 5712 Office furniture, nec; Office furniture
PA: Loth, Inc.
3574 E Kemper Rd
Cincinnati OH 45241
513 554-4900

(G-6174)
LOWES HOME CENTERS LLC
Also Called: Lowe's
1675 Georgesville Square Dr (43228-3689)
PHONE..............................614 853-6200
Billy Houghton, *Mgr*
EMP: 138
SALES (corp-wide): 86.38B **Publicly Held**
Web: www.lowes.com
SIC: 5211 5031 5722 5064 Home centers; Building materials, exterior; Household appliance stores; Electrical appliances, television and radio
HQ: Lowe's Home Centers, Llc
1000 Lowes Blvd
Mooresville NC 28117
336 658-4000

(G-6175)
LSI ADL TECHNOLOGY LLC
2727 Scioto Pkwy (43221-4658)
PHONE..............................614 345-9040
EMP: 45 **EST:** 1993
SQ FT: 56,000
SALES (est): 14.52MM
SALES (corp-wide): 496.98MM **Publicly Held**
Web: www.adltech.com
SIC: 8711 Designing: ship, boat, machine, and product
PA: Lsi Industries Inc.
10000 Alliance Rd
Cincinnati OH 45242
513 793-3200

(G-6176)
LTI INC
3445 Millennium Ct (43219-5550)
PHONE..............................614 278-7777
Michael L Ranney Junior, *Pr*
EMP: 70 **EST:** 1988
SQ FT: 35,000
SALES (est): 7.24MM **Privately Held**
Web: www.gowithlive.com
SIC: 6799 Commodity investors

(G-6177)
LULULEMON USA INC
4085 The Strand W (43219-6128)
PHONE..............................614 418-9127
Carolyn Manning, *Brnch Mgr*
EMP: 102
SIC: 7991 5699 Physical fitness facilities; Sports apparel
HQ: Lululemon Usa Inc.
2201 140th Ave E
Sumner WA 98390
604 732-6124

(G-6178)
LUMENT REAL ESTATE CAPITAL LLC (DH)
Also Called: Hunt Real Estate Capital
10 W Broad St Ste 800 (43215-3476)
PHONE..............................614 586-9380
James P Flynn, *CEO*
Michael Larsen, *COO*
Robert Kirkwood, *CFO*
Nick Gesue, *CCO*
EMP: 50 **EST:** 2010
SALES (est): 149.67MM **Privately Held**
Web: www.lument.com
SIC: 6799 Investors, nec
HQ: Lument Real Estate Capital Holdings, Llc
10 W Broad St Fl 8
Columbus OH 43215
800 837-5100

(G-6179)
LUPER NEIDENTAL & LOGAN A LEG
Also Called: Luper Neidenthal & Logan
1160 Dublin Rd Ste 400 (43215-1052)
PHONE..............................614 221-7663
Frederick M Luper, *Pr*
K Wallace Neidenthal, *
William B Logan Junior, *VP*
Henry P Wickham Junior, *VP*
Roger T Whitaker, *
EMP: 45 **EST:** 1968
SQ FT: 20,000
SALES (est): 5.99MM **Privately Held**
Web: www.lnlattorneys.com
SIC: 8111 General practice law office

(G-6180)
LUTHERAN SENIOR CITY INC (HQ)
Also Called: Lutheran Village Courtyard
935 N Cassady Ave (43219-2283)
PHONE..............................614 228-5200
Reverend Thomas Hudson, *Ch*
Larry Crowell, *
Phil Helser, *
EMP: 299 **EST:** 1962
SQ FT: 121,000
SALES (est): 7.4MM
SALES (corp-wide): 24.05MM **Privately Held**
SIC: 8051 Convalescent home with continuous nursing care
PA: Lutheran Social Services Of Central Ohio
500 W Wilson Bridge Rd
Worthington OH 43085
419 289-3523

(G-6181)
LVD ACQUISITION LLC (HQ)
Also Called: Oasis International
222 E Campus View Blvd (43235-4634)
PHONE..............................614 861-1350
Jeff Chiarugi, *Pr*
Michael Leibold, *
◆ **EMP:** 69 **EST:** 1910
SQ FT: 15,000
SALES (est): 47.04MM
SALES (corp-wide): 652.75MM **Privately Held**
Web: www.oasiscoolers.com
SIC: 3585 3431 5078 Coolers, milk and water: electric; Drinking fountains, metal; Drinking water coolers, mechanical
PA: Culligan International Company
9399 W Higgins Rd # 1100
Rosemont IL 60018
847 430-2800

(G-6182)
LW EQUIPMENT LLC
Also Called: Stealth Auto Recovery
3430 Westerville Rd (43224-3054)
PHONE..............................614 475-7376
Dustin Keller, *Managing Member*
EMP: 30 **EST:** 2018
SALES (est): 5MM **Privately Held**
SIC: 7699 Industrial machinery and equipment repair

(G-6183)
M P DORY CO
2001 Integrity Dr S (43209-2729)
PHONE..............................614 444-2138
Thomas Kuhn, *Pr*
Jeff Kuhn, *
EMP: 80 **EST:** 1984
SQ FT: 11,000
SALES (est): 14.04MM **Privately Held**
Web: www.mpdory.com
SIC: 1611 Guardrail construction, highways

(G-6184)
M/I FINANCIAL LLC (HQ)
4131 Worth Ave Ste 340 (43219-6284)
PHONE..............................614 418-8661
Philip G Creek, *
Derek Klutch, *
EMP: 53 **EST:** 1983
SALES (est): 26.01MM
SALES (corp-wide): 4.03B **Publicly Held**
Web: www.mihomes.com
SIC: 6162 Mortgage brokers, using own money
PA: M/I Homes, Inc.
4131 Worth Ave Ste 500
Columbus OH 43219
614 418-8000

(G-6185)
M/I FINANCIAL CORP
3 Easton Oval Ste 500 (43219-6011)
PHONE..............................614 418-8700
Olin A Jones, *Prin*
EMP: 45 **EST:** 2007
SALES (est): 1.09MM
SALES (corp-wide): 4.03B **Publicly Held**
Web: www.mihomes.com
SIC: 1521 New construction, single-family houses
PA: M/I Homes, Inc.
4131 Worth Ave Ste 500
Columbus OH 43219
614 418-8000

(G-6186)
M/I HOMES INC (PA)
4131 Worth Ave Ste 500 (43219)
PHONE..............................614 418-8000
Robert H Schottenstein, *Ch Bd*
Robert H Schottenstein, *Ch Bd*
Phillip G Creek, *
Susan E Krohne, *CLO*
EMP: 290 **EST:** 1973
SALES (est): 4.03B
SALES (corp-wide): 4.03B **Publicly Held**
Web: www.mihomes.com
SIC: 1531 6162 Speculative builder, single-family houses; Mortgage bankers and loan correspondents

(G-6187)
M/I HOMES CENTRAL OHIO LLC
3 Easton Oval Ste 500 (43219-6011)
PHONE..............................614 418-8000
EMP: 30 **EST:** 2003
SALES (est): 1.75MM
SALES (corp-wide): 4.03B **Publicly Held**
Web: www.mihomes.com
SIC: 1521 New construction, single-family houses
PA: M/I Homes, Inc.
4131 Worth Ave Ste 500
Columbus OH 43219
614 418-8000

(G-6188)
M/I HOMES SERVICE LLC
3 Easton Oval Ste 500 (43219-6011)
PHONE..............................614 418-8300
EMP: 27 **EST:** 2013
SALES (est): 3.21MM
SALES (corp-wide): 4.03B **Publicly Held**
Web: www.mihomes.com

Columbus - Franklin County (G-6189)

SIC: **1521** New construction, single-family houses
PA: M/I Homes, Inc.
4131 Worth Ave Ste 500
Columbus OH 43219
614 418-8000

(G-6189)
MAGNETIC SPRINGS WATER COMPANY (PA)
1917 Joyce Ave (43219-1029)
P.O. Box 182076 (43218-2076)
PHONE..............................614 421-1780
TOLL FREE: 800
James Allison, CEO
James E Allison, *
Jeffrey Allison, *
Sherry Allison, *
Beverly Allison, *
EMP: 70 EST: 1973
SQ FT: 100,000
SALES (est): 36.39MM
SALES (corp-wide): 36.39MM Privately Held
Web: www.magneticsprings.com
SIC: **5149** 5499 Mineral or spring water bottling; Water: distilled mineral or spring

(G-6190)
MAGUIRE & SCHNEIDER LLP
1650 Lake Shore Dr Ste 150 (43204-4942)
PHONE..............................614 224-1222
Patrick Maguire, Pt
Paul Schneider, Pt
EMP: 40 EST: 1994
SALES (est): 4.97MM Privately Held
Web: www.msh-lawfirm.com
SIC: **8111** General practice attorney, lawyer

(G-6191)
MAJIDZADEH ENTERPRISES INC (PA)
Also Called: Resource International
6350 Presidential Gtwy (43231-7653)
PHONE..............................614 823-4949
Farah Majidzadeh, CEO
Kamran Majidzadeh, *
Dominic Maxwell, *
Stasia Vavruska, *
Marcia Limpman, *
EMP: 50 EST: 1983
SALES (est): 53.98MM
SALES (corp-wide): 53.98MM Privately Held
Web: www.resourceinternational.com
SIC: **8711** 8741 Consulting engineer; Construction management

(G-6192)
MANLEY DEAS & KOCHALSKI LLC (PA)
1555 Lake Shore Dr (43204)
P.O. Box 165028 (43216)
PHONE..............................614 220-5611
Brian T Deas, Managing Member
Edward M Kochalski, *
EMP: 110 EST: 2003
SALES (est): 27.87MM
SALES (corp-wide): 27.87MM Privately Held
Web: www.mdklegal.com
SIC: **8111** General practice law office

(G-6193)
MAPSYS INC (PA)
Also Called: Map Systems and Solutions
920 Michigan Ave (43215-1165)
PHONE..............................614 255-7258
Steve Bernard, Pr
Jim Heiberger, *
Terry Payne, *
Paul Neal, *
EMP: 56 EST: 1985
SQ FT: 6,000
SALES (est): 14.09MM
SALES (corp-wide): 14.09MM Privately Held
Web: www.mapsysinc.com
SIC: **7373** 7371 5045 Computer integrated systems design; Custom computer programming services; Computers, peripherals, and software

(G-6194)
MARCUS HOTELS INC
Also Called: Westin Columbus
310 S High St (43215-4508)
PHONE..............................614 228-3800
Tom Baker, Mgr
EMP: 133
SALES (corp-wide): 729.58MM Publicly Held
Web: www.marcushotels.com
SIC: **7011** Resort hotel
HQ: Marcus Hotels Inc
100 E Wscnsin Ave Ste 190
Milwaukee WI 53202

(G-6195)
MARCUS MLLCHAP RE INV SVCS INC
230 West St Ste 100 (43215-2391)
PHONE..............................614 360-9800
Nandy Hart, Brnch Mgr
EMP: 30
SALES (corp-wide): 645.93MM Publicly Held
SIC: **6531** Real estate agent, commercial
HQ: Marcus & Millichap Real Estate Investment Services, Inc.
23975 Park Sorrento # 400
Calabasas CA 91302

(G-6196)
MARCUS THEATRES CORPORATION
Also Called: Crosswoods Ultrascreen Cinema
200 Hutchinson Ave (43235-4687)
PHONE..............................614 436-9818
Tim Burn, Brnch Mgr
EMP: 100
SALES (corp-wide): 729.58MM Publicly Held
Web: www.marcustheatres.com
SIC: **7832** 5813 5812 Motion picture theaters, except drive-in; Tavern (drinking places); Fast food restaurants and stands
HQ: Marcus Theatres Corporation
100 E Wscnsin Ave Ste 190
Milwaukee WI 53202
414 905-1000

(G-6197)
MARFO COMPANY (PA)
Also Called: Trading Corp of America
799 N Hague Ave (43204-1424)
PHONE..............................614 276-3352
Bill Giovanello, CEO
Alan Johnson, *
EMP: 98 EST: 1977
SQ FT: 41,000
SALES (est): 9.97MM
SALES (corp-wide): 9.97MM Privately Held
Web: www.marsala.com
SIC: **5094** 3911 Jewelry; Jewelry apparel

(G-6198)
MARSHALL INFORMATION SVCS LLC
Also Called: Primary Solutions
2780 Airport Dr Ste 120 (43219)
PHONE..............................614 430-0355
Brian Marshall, Pr
Brian Marshall, Managing Member
Joanne Marshall, *
EMP: 40 EST: 1998
SALES (est): 1.9MM Privately Held
Web: www.primarysolutions.net
SIC: **7371** Computer software development

(G-6199)
MARTIN CARPET CLEANING COMPANY
795 S Wall St (43206-1995)
PHONE..............................614 443-4655
John Martin, Ch Bd
Brent Martin, *
Chad Martin, *
EMP: 28 EST: 1890
SQ FT: 8,030
SALES (est): 2.56MM Privately Held
Web: www.martincarpetcleaning.com
SIC: **7217** Carpet and rug cleaning plant

(G-6200)
MARYHAVEN INC (PA)
Also Called: Maryhaven
1791 Alum Creek Dr (43207)
PHONE..............................614 449-1530
EMP: 100 EST: 1959
SQ FT: 100,000
SALES (est): 32.39MM
SALES (corp-wide): 32.39MM Privately Held
Web: www.maryhaven.com
SIC: **8093** Mental health clinic, outpatient

(G-6201)
MARYHAVEN INC
5560 Chantry Dr (43232-4767)
PHONE..............................614 626-2432
Paul Coleman, Prin
EMP: 28
SALES (corp-wide): 32.39MM Privately Held
Web: www.maryhaven.com
SIC: **8322** 8093 8049 Individual and family services; Substance abuse clinics (outpatient); Psychologist, psychotherapist and hypnotist
PA: Maryhaven, Inc.
1791 Alum Creek Dr
Columbus OH 43207
614 449-1530

(G-6202)
MAS INTERNATIONAL MKTG LLC
34 N High St Ste 208 (43215-3088)
PHONE..............................614 556-7083
Mohamed Salad, Managing Member
EMP: 100 EST: 2016
SQ FT: 2,800
SALES (est): 5.06MM Privately Held
SIC: **8742** 5963 Marketing consulting services; Direct sales, telemarketing

(G-6203)
MASON TITLE AGENCY LTD
2800 Delmar Dr (43209-1107)
PHONE..............................614 446-1151
Joe Connoe, Prin
EMP: 44 EST: 2017
SALES (est): 49.35K Privately Held
SIC: **6541** Title and trust companies

(G-6204)
MAST TECHNOLOGY SERVICES INC (HQ)
3 Limited Pkwy (43230-1467)
PHONE..............................614 415-7000
Jon Ricker, Pr
EMP: 34 EST: 1999
SALES (est): 24.46MM
SALES (corp-wide): 7.43B Publicly Held
SIC: **7374** Data processing and preparation
PA: Bath & Body Works, Inc.
3 Limited Pkwy
Columbus OH 43230
614 415-7000

(G-6205)
MATERNOHIO CLINICAL ASSOICATES
1700 Lake Shore Dr (43204-4895)
PHONE..............................614 457-7660
Dan Shemenski, Prin
EMP: 34 EST: 2008
SALES (est): 3.02MM Privately Held
Web: www.moca-obgyns.com
SIC: **8011** Gynecologist

(G-6206)
MATIC INSURANCE SERVICES INC
585 S Front St Ste 300 (43215-5694)
PHONE..............................833 382-1304
Benjamin Madick, CEO
Aaron Schiff, *
Stuart Rhodes, *
EMP: 124 EST: 2014
SALES (est): 46.78MM Privately Held
Web: www.matic.com
SIC: **6331** 7389 Property damage insurance; Business Activities at Non-Commercial Site

(G-6207)
MATRIX MEDIA SERVICES INC
463 E Town St Ste 200 (43215-4706)
PHONE..............................614 228-2200
Charles Mc Crimmon, Pr
EMP: 30 EST: 1988
SQ FT: 15,000
SALES (est): 4.52MM Privately Held
Web: www.matrixmediaservices.com
SIC: **7311** 7312 Advertising consultant; Outdoor advertising services

(G-6208)
MAVEN LLC
620 E Broad St Ste 300 (43215-4037)
PHONE..............................614 353-3873
Venkata Rachuri, CEO
Jenna Morris, *
Edward Chadd, CRO*
EMP: 60 EST: 2010
SALES (est): 5.02MM Privately Held
Web: www.choosemaven.net
SIC: **7379** Computer related consulting services

(G-6209)
MAVENNEXT INC
421 W State St (43215-4008)
PHONE..............................800 850-8708
John Manner, Prin
EMP: 30
SALES (est): 2.45MM Privately Held
SIC: **7379** Computer related consulting services

(G-6210)
MAXIM HEALTHCARE SERVICES INC
Also Called: Columbus Homecare Adult Svcs
445 Hutchinson Ave Ste 720 (43235-8616)
PHONE..............................614 880-1210
David Besancon, Mgr
EMP: 122
Web: www.maximhealthcare.com
SIC: **8322** 8011 Adult day care center; Pediatrician
PA: Maxim Healthcare Services, Inc.
7227 Lee Deforest Dr
Columbia MD 21046

GEOGRAPHIC SECTION
Columbus - Franklin County (G-6233)

(G-6211)
MAXIM HEALTHCARE SERVICES INC
445 Hutchinson Ave Ste 720 (43235-8616)
PHONE.................................740 772-4100
Rachel Fuller, *Brnch Mgr*
EMP: 122
Web: www.maximhealthcare.com
SIC: 8099 8049 Blood related health services
; Nurses and other medical assistants
PA: Maxim Healthcare Services, Inc.
7227 Lee Deforest Dr
Columbia MD 21046

(G-6212)
MAYFAIR NURSING CARE CENTERS
Also Called: Mayfair Village
3000 Bethel Rd (43220-2262)
PHONE.................................614 889-6320
J Edwin Farmer, *Pr*
EMP: 62 **EST:** 1971
SQ FT: 10,000
SALES (est): 6.55MM **Privately Held**
Web: www.lcca.com
SIC: 8051 Convalescent home with continuous nursing care

(G-6213)
MCDANIELS CNSTR CORP INC
1069 Woodland Ave (43219-2177)
PHONE.................................614 252-5852
Dan Moncrief Iii, *Ch*
Eric Girard, *
Rob Laveck, *
EMP: 60 **EST:** 1985
SQ FT: 12,000
SALES (est): 21.92MM **Privately Held**
Web: www.mcdanielsconstruction.com
SIC: 1611 8741 General contractor, highway and street construction; Construction management

(G-6214)
MCDATA SERVICES CORPORATION
265 S Westmoor Ave (43204-2573)
PHONE.................................614 272-5529
Jeff Jordan, *Prin*
EMP: 42
SALES (corp-wide): 35.82B **Publicly Held**
SIC: 7379 Diskette duplicating service
HQ: Mcdata Services Corporation
4 Brocade Pkwy
Broomfield CO 80021
720 558-8000

(G-6215)
MCGILL AIRCLEAN LLC
Also Called: McGill Airclean
1777 Refugee Rd (43207-2119)
PHONE.................................614 829-1200
Paul R Hess, *Managing Member*
Jerry Childress, *
◆ **EMP:** 70 **EST:** 2004
SQ FT: 15,000
SALES (est): 18.29MM
SALES (corp-wide): 126.17MM **Privately Held**
Web: www.mcgillairclean.com
SIC: 3564 1796 Precipitators, electrostatic; Pollution control equipment installation
HQ: United Mcgill Corporation
1 Mission Park
Groveport OH 43125
614 829-1200

(G-6216)
MCJ HOLDINGS INC (PA)
1601 Pemberton Dr (43221-1443)
PHONE.................................937 592-5025
Dwight E Reed, *Pr*
Ann Reed, *
Charles Reed, *
Pam Wasson, *
EMP: 142 **EST:** 1980
SQ FT: 85,000
SALES (est): 21.8MM
SALES (corp-wide): 21.8MM **Privately Held**
Web: www.agilitihealth.com
SIC: 7699 Surgical instrument repair

(G-6217)
MCLANE FOODSERVICE DIST INC
McLane Columbus
4300 Diplomacy Dr (43228-3804)
PHONE.................................614 771-9660
Mike Murphy, *Brnch Mgr*
EMP: 130
SQ FT: 80,000
SALES (corp-wide): 364.48B **Publicly Held**
Web: www.mclaneco.com
SIC: 5141 Food brokers
HQ: Mclane Foodservice Distribution, Inc.
4747 Mclane Pkwy
Temple TX 76504
254 771-7500

(G-6218)
MCNAUGHTON-MCKAY ELC OHIO INC (HQ)
Also Called: McNaughton-Mckay Electric Ohio
2255 Citygate Dr (43219-3567)
PHONE.................................614 476-2800
Donald D Slominski Junior, *CEO*
William Parsons, *
John R Mcnaughton Iii, *Ex VP*
Richard M Dahlstrom, *
John D Kuczmanski, *
▲ **EMP:** 70 **EST:** 1996
SQ FT: 65,000
SALES (est): 102.34MM
SALES (corp-wide): 2.81B **Privately Held**
SIC: 5063 Electrical supplies, nec
PA: Mcnaughton-Mckay Electric Co.
1357 E Lincoln Ave
Madison Heights MI 48071
248 399-7500

(G-6219)
MCR SERVICES INC
340 Forest St (43206-2220)
PHONE.................................614 421-0860
EMP: 32 **EST:** 1992
SALES (est): 7.55MM **Privately Held**
Web: www.mcrservices.com
SIC: 1542 Commercial and office building, new construction

(G-6220)
MEACHAM & APEL ARCHITECTS INC
Also Called: MA Architects
775 Yard St Ste 325 (43212-3890)
PHONE.................................614 764-0407
Mark Daniels, *Pr*
Jim Mitchell, *
John Eymann, *
EMP: 65 **EST:** 1980
SQ FT: 18,000
SALES (est): 11.25MM **Privately Held**
Web: www.designwithma.com
SIC: 8712 Architectural engineering

(G-6221)
MEDIGISTICS INC (PA)
1111 Schrock Rd Ste 200 (43229-1155)
P.O. Box 182255 (43218-2255)
PHONE.................................614 430-5700
Susan Long, *Pr*
Michael Poling, *
Roger Broome, *
Karon Stone, *
Don Kyle, *
EMP: 65 **EST:** 1961
SQ FT: 30,000
SALES (est): 2.25MM
SALES (corp-wide): 2.25MM **Privately Held**
SIC: 7389 8721 Charge account service; Accounting, auditing, and bookkeeping

(G-6222)
MEDONE HEALTH LLC
Also Called: Medone Healthcare Partners
3525 Olentangy River Rd Ste 4330 (43214-3937)
PHONE.................................614 255-6900
EMP: 38 **EST:** 2020
SALES (est): 170K **Privately Held**
SIC: 8099 Health and allied services, nec

(G-6223)
MEDONE HOSPITAL PHYSICIANS
3525 Olentangy River Rd Ste 4330 (43214-3937)
PHONE.................................314 255-6900
EMP: 124 **EST:** 2011
SALES (est): 17.79MM **Privately Held**
Web: www.medonehp.com
SIC: 8062 General medical and surgical hospitals

(G-6224)
MEDVET ASSOCIATES LLC
Also Called: Medvet Hilliard
5230 Renner Rd (43228-9744)
PHONE.................................614 870-0480
Lauren Fuller, *Brnch Mgr*
EMP: 75
Web: www.medvet.com
SIC: 0742 Animal hospital services, pets and other animal specialties
PA: Medvet Associates, Llc
350 E Wilson Bridge Rd
Worthington OH 43085

(G-6225)
MERCANTILE TITLE AGENCY INC
191 W Nationwide Blvd Ste 300 (43215-2568)
PHONE.................................614 628-6880
Donald B Gardiner, *Prin*
EMP: 40 **EST:** 2010
SALES (est): 2.1MM
SALES (corp-wide): 169.43MM **Privately Held**
Web: www.dinsmore.com
SIC: 6361 Title insurance
PA: Dinsmore & Shohl Llp
255 E 5th St Ste 1900
Cincinnati OH 45202
513 977-8200

(G-6226)
MERIEUX NUTRISCIENCES CORP
2057 Builders Pl (43204-4886)
PHONE.................................614 486-0150
EMP: 60
SALES (corp-wide): 7.5MM **Privately Held**
Web: www.merieuxnutrisciences.com
SIC: 8734 Testing laboratories
HQ: Merieux Nutrisciences Corporation
401 N Michigan Ave # 1400
Chicago IL 60611

(G-6227)
MERRY MAIDS LTD PARTNERSHIP
Also Called: Merry Maids
6185 Huntley Rd Ste O (43229-1094)
PHONE.................................614 430-8441
EMP: 44
SALES (corp-wide): 1.1B **Privately Held**
Web: www.merrymaids.com
SIC: 7349 Maid services, contract or fee basis
HQ: Merry Maids Limited Partnership
150 Peabody Pl Ste 100
Memphis TN 38103
901 597-8100

(G-6228)
MESSER CONSTRUCTION CO
3705 Business Park Dr (43204-5007)
PHONE.................................614 275-0141
Erin M Thompson, *VP*
EMP: 105
SALES (corp-wide): 1.35B **Privately Held**
Web: www.messer.com
SIC: 1542 Commercial and office building, new construction
PA: Messer Construction Co.
643 W Court St
Cincinnati OH 45203
513 242-1541

(G-6229)
METHODIST RTRMENT CTR OF CNTL
Also Called: Methodist Eldercare Services
5156 Wesley Way (43214-7502)
PHONE.................................614 888-7492
Margaret Carmany, *CEO*
EMP: 214 **EST:** 1996
SALES (est): 2.57MM **Privately Held**
Web: www.lec.org
SIC: 8361 Aged home

(G-6230)
MEYERS + ASSOCIATES ARCH LLC
232 N 3rd St Ste 300 (43215-2786)
PHONE.................................614 221-9433
EMP: 28 **EST:** 2001
SALES (est): 4.17MM **Privately Held**
Web: www.meyersarchitects.com
SIC: 8712 Architectural engineering

(G-6231)
MICHAELS FINER MEATS LLC
3775 Zane Trace Dr (43228-3854)
P.O. Box 182700 (43218-2700)
PHONE.................................614 527-4900
EMP: 110 **EST:** 1962
SALES (est): 63.15MM **Publicly Held**
Web: shop.chefswarehouse.com
SIC: 5147 5146 5144 Meats, fresh; Seafoods ; Poultry products, nec
PA: The Chefs' Warehouse Inc
100 E Ridge Rd
Ridgefield CT 06877

(G-6232)
MICRO CENTER ONLINE INC
Also Called: Micro Center Online
747 Bethel Rd (43214-1901)
P.O. Box 1143 (43026-6143)
PHONE.................................614 326-8500
John F Baker, *Ch Bd*
T James Koehler, *CFO*
R Dale Brown, *CEO*
EMP: 81 **EST:** 1990
SALES (est): 3.15MM
SALES (corp-wide): 824.57MM **Privately Held**
SIC: 5045 5734 Computer peripheral equipment; Personal computers
PA: Micro Electronics, Inc.
4119 Leap Rd
Hilliard OH 43026
614 850-3000

(G-6233)
MICRO ELECTRONICS INC
Also Called: Microcenter DC
2701 Charter St Ste B (43228-4639)

Columbus - Franklin County (G-6234)

PHONE..................614 334-1430
Steve Lancaster, *Brnch Mgr*
EMP: 372
SALES (corp-wide): 824.57MM **Privately Held**
Web: www.microcenter.com
SIC: 5045 5734 4225 Computer peripheral equipment; Computer and software stores; General warehousing and storage
PA: Micro Electronics, Inc.
4119 Leap Rd
Hilliard OH 43026
614 850-3000

(G-6234)
MID OHIO EMERGENCY SVCS LLC
3525 Olentangy River Rd Ste 4330 (43214-4022)
PHONE..................614 566-5070
Jennifer Bailey, *Prin*
EMP: 42 **EST:** 2010
SALES (est): 776.12K **Privately Held**
Web: www.midohioemergencyservices.com
SIC: 8999 Services, nec

(G-6235)
MID-AMERICAN CLG CONTRS INC
1046 King Ave (43212-2609)
PHONE..................614 291-7170
Tony Cordoso, *Mgr*
EMP: 105
Web: www.macc.net
SIC: 7349 Janitorial service, contract basis
PA: Mid-American Cleaning Contractors, Inc.
447 N Elizabeth St
Lima OH 45801

(G-6236)
MID-OHIO AIR CONDITIONING CORP
Also Called: Mid-Ohio
456 E 5th Ave (43201-2971)
P.O. Box 8397 (43201-0397)
PHONE..................614 291-4664
Rod Burkett, *Pr*
Matthew Trubee, *
EMP: 34 **EST:** 1967
SQ FT: 16,000
SALES (est): 4.44MM **Privately Held**
Web: www.midohioac.com
SIC: 1711 Warm air heating and air conditioning contractor

(G-6237)
MID-OHIO ONCLGY/HEMATOLOGY INC
3100 Plaza Properties Blvd (43219)
PHONE..................614 383-6000
Susan Grubb, *Off Mgr*
EMP: 29
SALES (corp-wide): 9.79MM **Privately Held**
Web: www.zangcenter.com
SIC: 8011 Oncologist
PA: Mid-Ohio Oncology/Hematology, Inc.
3100 Plz Properties Blvd
Columbus OH 43219
614 383-6000

(G-6238)
MID-OHIO ONCOLOGY/ HEMATOLOGY INC (PA)
Also Called: Mark H. Zangmeister Center
3100 Plaza Properties Blvd (43219-1530)
PHONE..................614 383-6000
EMP: 31 **EST:** 1981
SALES (est): 9.79MM
SALES (corp-wide): 9.79MM **Privately Held**
Web: www.zangcenter.com
SIC: 8011 Offices and clinics of medical doctors

(G-6239)
MID-OHIO REGIONAL PLG COMM
111 Liberty St Ste 100 (43215-5850)
PHONE..................614 228-2663
William Murdock, *Ex Dir*
Rory Mcguiness, *Ch*
Karen Angelou, *
Erik Janas, *
EMP: 80 **EST:** 1943
SALES (est): 14.58MM **Privately Held**
Web: www.morpc.org
SIC: 8611 Business associations

(G-6240)
MID-STATE INDUSTRIAL PDTS INC (HQ)
1575 Alum Creek Dr (43209-2712)
PHONE..................614 253-8631
David R Broehm, *Pr*
Stephen English, *VP*
William C Mccullough, *VP*
Curt Mccullough, *VP*
David A Breault, *Treas*
◆ **EMP:** 40 **EST:** 1946
SQ FT: 85,000
SALES (est): 11.03MM
SALES (corp-wide): 85.83MM **Privately Held**
Web: www.msbolt.com
SIC: 5085 5072 Fasteners, industrial: nuts, bolts, screws, etc.; Bolts
PA: Derry Enterprises, Inc.
9883 N Alpine Rd
Machesney Park IL 61115
815 637-9002

(G-6241)
MID-STATE SALES INC (PA)
Also Called: Mid-State Sales
1101 Gahanna Pkwy (43230-6600)
PHONE..................614 864-1811
▲ **EMP:** 56 **EST:** 1969
SALES (est): 13.73MM
SALES (corp-wide): 13.73MM **Privately Held**
Web: www.midstate-sales.com
SIC: 5084 3494 3492 Hydraulic systems equipment and supplies; Pipe fittings; Hose and tube fittings and assemblies, hydraulic/pneumatic

(G-6242)
MIDOHIO CRDIOLGY VASCULAR CONS (PA)
3705 Olentangy River Rd Ste 100 (43214-3467)
PHONE..................614 262-6772
Anthony T Chapekis, *Pr*
EMP: 86 **EST:** 1987
SQ FT: 42,000
SALES (est): 9.31MM **Privately Held**
SIC: 8062 General medical and surgical hospitals

(G-6243)
MIDWEST FRESH FOODS INC
38 N Glenwood Ave (43222-1206)
PHONE..................614 469-1492
Charles Giller, *Pr*
Stan Hunt, *
EMP: 35 **EST:** 1987
SQ FT: 7,000
SALES (est): 4.66MM **Privately Held**
Web: www.midwestfresh.com
SIC: 5148 Fruits, fresh

(G-6244)
MIDWEST MOTOR SUPPLY CO (PA)
Also Called: Kimball Midwest
4800 Roberts Rd (43228-9791)
P.O. Box 2470 (43216-2470)
PHONE..................800 233-1294
Patrick J Mccurdy Junior, *CEO*
Patrick J Mccurdy Junior, *Pr*
Ed Mccurdy, *VP*
David Mccurdy, *VP*
Charles Mccurdy, *VP*
▲ **EMP:** 200 **EST:** 1955
SQ FT: 85,000
SALES (est): 129.4MM
SALES (corp-wide): 129.4MM **Privately Held**
Web: www.kimballmidwest.com
SIC: 3965 3399 8742 Fasteners; Metal fasteners; Materials mgmt. (purchasing, handling, inventory) consultant

(G-6245)
MIDWEST PHYSCANS ANSTHSIA SVCS
5151 Reed Rd Ste 225c (43220-2553)
PHONE..................614 884-0641
Daniel Hiestand, *Pr*
EMP: 98 **EST:** 1992
SALES (est): 9.7MM **Privately Held**
Web: www.mpasohio.com
SIC: 8011 Anesthesiologist

(G-6246)
MIDWEST PROTECTION DIV LLC
2838 Fisher Rd (43204-3555)
PHONE..................844 844-8200
Christian Thomas, *Pr*
EMP: 62 **EST:** 2021
SALES (est): 1.24MM **Privately Held**
Web: www.midwestprotection.net
SIC: 7381 Security guard service

(G-6247)
MILE INC
Also Called: Lions Den
1144 Alum Creek Dr (43209-2701)
PHONE..................614 252-6724
EMP: 127
Web: www.lionsden.com
SIC: 7841 Video disk/tape rental to the general public
PA: Mile, Inc.
110 E Wilson Bridge Rd # 100
Worthington OH 43085

(G-6248)
MILES-MCCLELLAN CNSTR CO INC (PA)
2100 Builders Pl (43204-4885)
PHONE..................614 487-7744
Matthew Q Mcclellan, *Pr*
Dave Mcintosh, *VP*
Ted Tinkler, *
Mike Rodriguez, *
EMP: 39 **EST:** 1978
SQ FT: 19,000
SALES (est): 20.83MM
SALES (corp-wide): 20.83MM **Privately Held**
Web: www.mmbuildings.com
SIC: 1541 1542 Industrial buildings, new construction, nec; Commercial and office building, new construction

(G-6249)
MILLCRAFT PAPER COMPANY
Also Called: Columbus Division
4311 Janitrol Rd Ste 600 (43228-1389)
PHONE..................614 675-4800
Eric Michel, *Brnch Mgr*
EMP: 28
Web: www.millcraft.com
SIC: 5111 5113 Printing paper; Industrial and personal service paper
HQ: The Millcraft Paper Company
9010 Rio Nero Dr
Independence OH 44131

(G-6250)
MILLER TRNSP BUS SVC INC
2510 Park Crescent Dr (43232-4742)
PHONE..................614 915-7211
John Miller, *Mgr*
EMP: 59
Web: www.millertransportation.com
SIC: 4151 School buses
PA: Miller Transportation Bus Service, Inc.
4045 Park 65 Dr
Indianapolis IN 46254

(G-6251)
MINAMYER RSDNTIAL CARE SVCS IN
967 Worthington Woods Loop Rd (43085-5743)
PHONE..................614 802-0190
Darla Minamyer, *Pr*
Dean Minamyer, *
EMP: 31 **EST:** 2002
SALES (est): 5.37MM **Privately Held**
Web: www.beaconspecialized.org
SIC: 8059 Home for the mentally retarded, ex. skilled or intermediate

(G-6252)
MJ BAUMANN CO INC
Also Called: M J Baumann
6400 Broughton Ave (43213-1524)
PHONE..................614 759-7100
Joseph E Baumann, *Pr*
Stephen E Irwin, *
EMP: 72 **EST:** 1970
SQ FT: 7,200
SALES (est): 3.92MM **Privately Held**
SIC: 1711 Plumbing contractors

(G-6253)
MKSK INC (PA)
Also Called: Mksk
462 S Ludlow St (43215-5647)
PHONE..................614 621-2796
Brian Kinzelman, *Managing Member*
Timothy Schmalenberger, *Managing Member*
Chris Hermann, *Managing Member*
Mark Kline, *Managing Member*
Richard Espe, *Managing Member*
EMP: 50 **EST:** 2011
SALES (est): 9.58MM
SALES (corp-wide): 9.58MM **Privately Held**
Web: www.mkskstudios.com
SIC: 0781 Landscape architects

(G-6254)
MKSK INC
462 S Ludlow St (43215-5647)
PHONE..................614 621-2796
Thomas Porto, *Admn*
Brian Kinzelman, *
Timothy Schmalenberger, *
Christopher Hostettler, *
Mark Kline, *
EMP: 81 **EST:** 2018
SALES (est): 997.35K **Privately Held**
Web: www.mkskstudios.com
SIC: 0781 Landscape architects

GEOGRAPHIC SECTION
Columbus - Franklin County (G-6277)

(G-6255)
MODERN FINANCE COMPANY
3449 Great Western Blvd (43204-1235)
PHONE...................614 351-7400
Earl Osborne, *Ex VP*
Brian Hill, *
Carol Hammond, *
Stan R Goodburn, *
EMP: 50 **EST:** 1999
SQ FT: 16,000
SALES (est): 2.72MM **Privately Held**
SIC: 6141 6162 6311 5521 Consumer finance companies; Mortgage brokers, using own money; Life insurance carriers; Automobiles, used cars only

(G-6256)
MOHUN HEALTH CARE CENTER
Also Called: MOHUN HEALTH CARE CENTER GIFT
2320 Airport Dr (43219-2059)
PHONE...................614 416-6132
EMP: 46 **EST:** 1946
SALES (est): 4.95MM **Privately Held**
Web: www.mohun.org
SIC: 8059 5947 Nursing home, except skilled and intermediate care facility; Greeting cards

(G-6257)
MOLINA HEALTHCARE INC
Also Called: Molina Healthcare of Ohio
3000 Corporate Exchange Dr Ste 100 (43231-7689)
PHONE...................800 642-4168
Kathy Mancini, *Brnch Mgr*
EMP: 147
SALES (corp-wide): 34.07B **Publicly Held**
Web: www.molinahealthcare.com
SIC: 6324 Hospital and medical service plans
PA: Molina Healthcare, Inc.
200 Oceangate Ste 100
Long Beach CA 90802
562 435-3666

(G-6258)
MONESI TRUCKING & EQP REPR INC
1715 Atlas St (43228-9648)
PHONE...................614 921-9183
Donald Monesi, *Pr*
Marlene Monesi, *
EMP: 40 **EST:** 1980
SQ FT: 5,000
SALES (est): 5.75MM **Privately Held**
Web: www.monesitrucking.com
SIC: 4212 Dump truck haulage

(G-6259)
MOODY NAT CY DT CLUMBUS MT LLC
Also Called: Courtyard By Mrrott Clmbus Dwn
35 W Spring St (43215-2215)
PHONE...................614 228-3200
Ann Turpin, *Genl Mgr*
EMP: 43 **EST:** 2009
SALES (est): 415.82K **Privately Held**
Web: courtyard.marriott.com
SIC: 7011 Hotels and motels

(G-6260)
MOODY-NOLAN INC (PA)
300 Spruce St Ste 300 (43215-1175)
PHONE...................614 461-4664
Curtis J Moody, *CEO*
Robert K Larimer, *
Paul F Pryor, *
John William Miller, *
Kathleen Ransier, *
EMP: 115 **EST:** 1987
SQ FT: 77,000
SALES (est): 62.45MM **Privately Held**
Web: www.moodynolan.com
SIC: 8712 8711 Architectural engineering; Engineering services

(G-6261)
MOORES ELECTRIC LLC ✪
820 Mansfield Ave (43219-2453)
PHONE...................614 504-2909
Stephanie Moore, *Managing Member*
EMP: 50 **EST:** 2022
SALES (est): 10.03MM **Privately Held**
Web: www.meiohio.com
SIC: 4911 Electric services

(G-6262)
MORGAN TAX SERVICE
5495 Sierra Ridge Dr (43231-3146)
PHONE...................614 948-5296
Rufus Morgan, *Prin*
EMP: 33 **EST:** 2012
SALES (est): 62.58K **Privately Held**
SIC: 7291 Tax return preparation services

(G-6263)
MOST WRSHPFUL EREKA GRND LDGE
124 Stornoway Dr E (43213-2102)
PHONE...................614 626-4076
James Coleman, *Prin*
EMP: 50
SALES (est): 1.67MM **Privately Held**
Web: www.phaohio.org
SIC: 5032 7389 Masons' materials; Business services, nec

(G-6264)
MOTORISTS MUTUAL INSURANCE CO (HQ)
Also Called: Motorists Insurance Group
471 E Broad St Bsmt (43215)
PHONE...................614 225-8211
Gregory Burton, *Ch Bd*
Thomas Obrokta Junior, *Pr*
David Kaufman, *
James Christopher Howat, *
Anne King, *
EMP: 550 **EST:** 1928
SQ FT: 300,000
SALES (est): 1.06B
SALES (corp-wide): 1.06B **Privately Held**
Web: www.encova.com
SIC: 6331 Fire, marine, and casualty insurance; mutual
PA: Encova Mutual Insurance Group, Inc.
471 E Broad St Bsmt
Columbus OH 43215
614 225-8666

(G-6265)
MOUNT CARMEL EAST HOSPITAL
6001 E Broad St (43213-1570)
PHONE...................614 234-6000
TOLL FREE: 800
EMP: 1100 **EST:** 1995
SALES (est): 144.82MM
SALES (corp-wide): 2.49B **Privately Held**
Web: www.mountcarmelhealth.com
SIC: 8062 General medical and surgical hospitals
HQ: Niagara Health Corporation
6150 E Broad St
Columbus OH 43213

(G-6266)
MOUNT CARMEL HEALTH
4171 Arlingate Plz (43228-4115)
PHONE...................614 308-1803
Lisa Brewster, *Mgr*
EMP: 102
SALES (corp-wide): 2.49B **Privately Held**
Web: www.mountcarmelhealth.com
SIC: 8062 General medical and surgical hospitals
HQ: Mount Carmel Health
5300 N Meadows Dr
Grove City OH 43123
614 234-5000

(G-6267)
MOUNT CARMEL HEALTH
6599 E Broad St (43213-1509)
PHONE...................614 986-7752
EMP: 68
SALES (corp-wide): 2.49B **Privately Held**
Web: www.mountcarmelhealth.com
SIC: 8062 General medical and surgical hospitals
HQ: Mount Carmel Health
5300 N Meadows Dr
Grove City OH 43123
614 234-5000

(G-6268)
MOUNT CARMEL HEALTH PLAN INC
6150 E Broad St (43213-1574)
PHONE...................614 546-4300
EMP: 75 **EST:** 1996
SALES (est): 560.05MM **Privately Held**
Web: www.medigold.com
SIC: 8062 General medical and surgical hospitals

(G-6269)
MOUNT CARMEL HEALTH SYSTEM
Also Called: Whitehall Family Health
150 Taylor Station Rd Ste 350 (43213-1157)
PHONE...................614 856-0700
Jennifer A Giersch, *Owner*
EMP: 533
SALES (corp-wide): 2.49B **Privately Held**
Web: www.mountcarmelhealth.com
SIC: 8062 General medical and surgical hospitals
HQ: Mount Carmel Health System
1039 Kingsmill Pkwy
Columbus OH 43229
614 234-6000

(G-6270)
MOUNT CARMEL HEALTH SYSTEM
6150 E Broad St (43213-1574)
P.O. Box 5073 (48007-5073)
PHONE...................734 343-4551
EMP: 37
SALES (est): 22.04MM **Privately Held**
SIC: 8062 General medical and surgical hospitals

(G-6271)
MOUNT CARMEL HEALTH SYSTEM
5723 Westbourne Ave (43213-1449)
PHONE...................614 860-0659
EMP: 436
SALES (corp-wide): 2.49B **Privately Held**
Web: www.mountcarmelhealth.com
SIC: 8062 General medical and surgical hospitals
HQ: Mount Carmel Health System
1039 Kingsmill Pkwy
Columbus OH 43229
614 234-6000

(G-6272)
MOUNT CARMEL HEALTH SYSTEM
6400 E Broad St (43213-2086)
PHONE...................614 234-3355
Richard Brant, *Brnch Mgr*
EMP: 824
SALES (corp-wide): 2.49B **Privately Held**
Web: www.mountcarmelhealth.com
SIC: 8062 General medical and surgical hospitals
HQ: Mount Carmel Health System
1039 Kingsmill Pkwy
Columbus OH 43229
614 234-6000

(G-6273)
MOUNT CARMEL HEALTH SYSTEM
3721 Francine Ct (43232-4843)
PHONE...................614 679-2184
Samba B.a., *Brnch Mgr*
EMP: 533
SALES (corp-wide): 2.49B **Privately Held**
Web: www.mountcarmelhealth.com
SIC: 8062 General medical and surgical hospitals
HQ: Mount Carmel Health System
1039 Kingsmill Pkwy
Columbus OH 43229
614 234-6000

(G-6274)
MOUNT CARMEL HEALTH SYSTEM (HQ)
Also Called: Mount Carmel
1039 Kingsmill Pkwy (43229-1129)
PHONE...................614 234-6000
Michael Englehart, *CEO*
Michael Englehart, *Interim Chief Executive Officer*
Douglas H Stine, *
Andy Priday, *
EMP: 800 **EST:** 1955
SALES (est): 1.39B
SALES (corp-wide): 2.49B **Privately Held**
Web: www.mountcarmelhealth.com
SIC: 8062 General medical and surgical hospitals
PA: Trinity Health Corporation
20555 Victor Pkwy
Livonia MI 48152
734 343-1000

(G-6275)
MOUNT CARMEL HEALTH SYSTEM
750 Mount Carmel Mall (43222-1553)
PHONE...................614 221-1009
EMP: 969
SALES (corp-wide): 2.49B **Privately Held**
Web: www.mountcarmelhealth.com
SIC: 8062 General medical and surgical hospitals
HQ: Mount Carmel Health System
1039 Kingsmill Pkwy
Columbus OH 43229
614 234-6000

(G-6276)
MOUNT CARMEL HEALTH SYSTEM
Also Called: Mount Carmel Behavioral Health
4646 Hilton Corporate Dr (43232-4147)
PHONE...................614 636-6290
EMP: 485
SALES (corp-wide): 2.49B **Privately Held**
Web: www.mountcarmelhealth.com
SIC: 8052 Home for the mentally retarded, with health care
HQ: Mount Carmel Health System
1039 Kingsmill Pkwy
Columbus OH 43229
614 234-6000

(G-6277)
MOUNT CARMEL HEALTH SYSTEM
5965 E Broad St Ste 390 (43213-1565)
PHONE...................614 866-3703
EMP: 291
SALES (corp-wide): 2.49B **Privately Held**
Web: www.mountcarmelhealth.com

Columbus - Franklin County (G-6278) — GEOGRAPHIC SECTION

SIC: 8011 Offices and clinics of medical doctors
HQ: Mount Carmel Health System
1039 Kingsmill Pkwy
Columbus OH 43229
614 234-6000

(G-6278)
MOUNT CARMEL HEALTH SYSTEM
946 Parsons Ave (43206-2346)
PHONE..................614 445-6215
Lisa Richardson, Admn
EMP: 291
SALES (corp-wide): 2.49B Privately Held
Web: www.mountcarmelhealth.com
SIC: 8011 Offices and clinics of medical doctors
HQ: Mount Carmel Health System
1039 Kingsmill Pkwy
Columbus OH 43229
614 234-6000

(G-6279)
MOUNT CARMEL HEALTH SYSTEM
3480 Refugee Rd (43232-4814)
PHONE..................614 235-4039
EMP: 242
SALES (corp-wide): 2.49B Privately Held
Web: www.mountcarmelhealth.com
SIC: 8099 Childbirth preparation clinic
HQ: Mount Carmel Health System
1039 Kingsmill Pkwy
Columbus OH 43229
614 234-6000

(G-6280)
MOVE EZ INC
Also Called: Moveeasy
855 Grandview Ave Ste 140 (43215-1189)
PHONE..................844 466-8339
Venkatesh Ganapathy, CEO
EMP: 57 EST: 2014
SALES (est): 1.52MM Privately Held
Web: www.moveeasy.com
SIC: 7372 6411 4212 Application computer software; Insurance agents, brokers, and service; Moving services

(G-6281)
MT CARMEL EAST URGENT CARE
6435 E Broad St (43213-1507)
PHONE..................614 355-8150
Jim Johnson, Mgr
Mark Hagenberk, Dir
EMP: 85 EST: 2001
SALES (est): 2.35MM Privately Held
Web: www.mountcarmelhealth.com
SIC: 8062 General medical and surgical hospitals

(G-6282)
MUETZEL PLUMBING & HEATING CO
1661 Kenny Rd (43212-2264)
P.O. Box 12489 (43212-0489)
PHONE..................614 299-7700
John R Muetzel, Pr
Thomas C Muetzel, *
Robert Muetzel, *
EMP: 52 EST: 1967
SQ FT: 16,000
SALES (est): 11.77MM Privately Held
Web: www.centralohioplumbingandheating.com
SIC: 1711 Plumbing contractors

(G-6283)
MULTICON BUILDERS INC
Also Called: Multicon Construction
503 S High St (43215-5660)
PHONE..................614 463-1142
EMP: 27
SALES (corp-wide): 3.36MM Privately Held
SIC: 6552 1542 Land subdividers and developers, commercial; Commercial and office building contractors
PA: Multicon Builders, Inc.
495 S High St Ste 150
Columbus OH 43215
614 241-2070

(G-6284)
MWE INVESTMENTS LLC (HQ)
Also Called: Westinghouse
777 Manor Park Dr (43228-9522)
PHONE..................855 944-3571
James H Cline Junior, Managing Member
▲ EMP: 49 EST: 2016
SQ FT: 250,000
SALES (est): 25.89MM Privately Held
Web: www.mwesales.com
SIC: 5063 Generators
PA: Midwest Equipment Sales, Llc
777 Manor Park Dr
Columbus OH 43228

(G-6285)
MYERS/SCHMALENBERGER INC (PA)
Also Called: M S I Design
462 S Ludlow St (43215-5647)
PHONE..................614 621-2796
EMP: 38 EST: 1984
SALES (est): 2.16MM Privately Held
Web: www.mkskstudios.com
SIC: 0781 Landscape architects

(G-6286)
N WASSERSTROM & SONS INC (HQ)
Also Called: Wasserstrom Marketing Division
2300 Lockbourne Rd (43207-6111)
PHONE..................614 228-5550
William Wasserstrom, Pr
John H Mc Cormick, Sr VP
Reid Wasserstrom, Sec
◆ EMP: 250 EST: 1933
SQ FT: 175,000
SALES (est): 100.47MM
SALES (corp-wide): 378.09MM Privately Held
Web: www.wasserstrom.com
SIC: 3556 5046 3444 Food products machinery; Restaurant equipment and supplies, nec; Sheet metalwork
PA: The Wasserstrom Company
4500 E Broad St
Columbus OH 43213
614 228-6525

(G-6287)
NAS VENTURES
4477 E 5th Ave (43219-1817)
PHONE..................614 338-8501
James Head, Pt
Paul Ondera, Pt
EMP: 60
SALES (est): 4.1MM Privately Held
SIC: 1611 Airport runway construction

(G-6288)
NATIONAL AFFRDBL HSING TR INC (PA)
330 Rush Aly Ste 620 (43215-3368)
PHONE..................614 451-9929
James A Bowman, Pr
EMP: 31 EST: 1986
SALES (est): 9.03MM
SALES (corp-wide): 9.03MM Privately Held
Web: www.naht.org
SIC: 8399 Community development groups

(G-6289)
NATIONAL BD OF BLER PRSSURE VS (PA)
1055 Crupper Ave (43229-1108)
PHONE..................614 888-8320
David Douin, Dir
Michael A Mess, *
EMP: 61 EST: 1919
SQ FT: 5,000
SALES (est): 19.52MM
SALES (corp-wide): 19.52MM Privately Held
Web: www.nationalboard.org
SIC: 7389 Inspection and testing services

(G-6290)
NATIONAL BENEFIT PROGRAMS INC
1650 W 5th Ave (43212-2316)
PHONE..................614 481-9000
Joe Concheck, Pr
EMP: 28 EST: 1988
SALES (est): 3.42MM Privately Held
Web: www.assuredpartners.com
SIC: 6411 Insurance brokers, nec
PA: Assuredpartners, Inc.
450 S Orange Ave Fl 4
Orlando FL 32801

(G-6291)
NATIONAL CH RSDNCES PMBROKE GA
2335 Northbank Dr (43220-5423)
PHONE..................614 451-2151
Joe Kasberg, Pr
EMP: 100 EST: 1999
SALES (est): 227.85K Privately Held
Web: www.nationalchurchresidences.org
SIC: 8361 8051 Residential care; Skilled nursing care facilities

(G-6292)
NATIONAL CHURCH RESIDENCES (PA)
2335 N Bank Dr (43220-5423)
PHONE..................614 451-2151
Mark Ricketts, Pr
Joseph R Kasberg, VP
Michelle H Norris, CAO
David A Kayuha, VP
Jerry B Kuyoth, VP
EMP: 193 EST: 1961
SQ FT: 20,000
SALES (est): 521.67MM
SALES (corp-wide): 521.67MM Privately Held
Web: www.nationalchurchresidences.org
SIC: 6513 8051 8059 6531 Apartment building operators; Skilled nursing care facilities; Convalescent home; Real estate agents and managers

(G-6293)
NATIONAL CINEMEDIA LLC
1410 Pennsylvania Ave (43201-2621)
PHONE..................614 297-8933
Tom Lesinski, CEO
Scott Felenstein, *
Ronnie Ng, *
Amy Tunick, CMO*
EMP: 192 EST: 2005
SALES (est): 117.49K
SALES (corp-wide): 25.04MM Privately Held
Web: www.ncm.com
SIC: 7311 Advertising consultant
PA: National Cinemedia, L.L.C.
6300 S Syracuse Way # 30
Centennial CO 80111
303 792-3600

(G-6294)
NATIONAL CNSTR RENTALS INC
Also Called: National Rent A Fence
2177 Mckinley Ave (43204-3418)
PHONE..................614 308-1100
Rob Shriver, Brnch Mgr
EMP: 30
SALES (corp-wide): 123.15MM Privately Held
Web: www.rentnational.com
SIC: 1799 Fence construction
HQ: National Construction Rentals, Inc.
15319 Chatsworth St
Mission Hills CA 91345
818 221-6000

(G-6295)
NATIONAL DISTRIBUTION CENTERS
Also Called: NDC
200 Mccormick Blvd (43213-1535)
PHONE..................419 422-3432
Sid Brown, Pr
▲ EMP: 181 EST: 2001
SALES (est): 1.94MM
SALES (corp-wide): 1.26B Privately Held
SIC: 4225 General warehousing
HQ: National Freight, Inc.
2 Cooper St
Camden NJ 08102
856 691-7000

(G-6296)
NATIONAL ELECTRIC COIL INC (PA)
Also Called: N E C Columbus
800 King Ave (43212-2644)
P.O. Box 370 (43216-0370)
PHONE..................614 488-1151
◆ EMP: 300 EST: 1994
SQ FT: 500,000
SALES (est): 70.69MM Privately Held
Web: www.national-electric-coil.com
SIC: 7694 Electric motor repair

(G-6297)
NATIONAL FEDERATION IND BUS
10 W Broad St Ste 2450 (43215-3487)
PHONE..................614 221-4107
Roger Geiger, VP
EMP: 72
SALES (corp-wide): 52.3MM Privately Held
Web: www.nfib.com
SIC: 8611 Trade associations
PA: National Federation Of Independent Business
53 Century Blvd Ste 250
Nashville TN 37214
615 872-5800

(G-6298)
NATIONAL FREIGHT INC
Also Called: National Distributn Ctr 6
200 Mccormick Blvd (43213-1535)
PHONE..................614 575-8490
Ron Merrill, Brnch Mgr
EMP: 49
SALES (corp-wide): 1.26B Privately Held
Web: www.nfiindustries.com
SIC: 4731 Freight transportation arrangement
HQ: National Freight, Inc.
2 Cooper St
Camden NJ 08102
856 691-7000

(G-6299)
NATIONAL HOUSING CORPORATION (PA)
45 N 4th St Fl 2 (43215-3602)
PHONE..................614 481-8106
H Burkley Showe, Pr
Hugh B Showe Ii, VP

GEOGRAPHIC SECTION
Columbus - Franklin County (G-6320)

Kevin M Showe, *
Andrew Showe, *
David M Showe, *
EMP: 40 **EST:** 1963
SQ FT: 5,000
SALES (est): 42MM
SALES (corp-wide): 42MM **Privately Held**
Web:
www.nationalcorporatehousing.com
SIC: 1522 1542 6513 Apartment building construction; Commercial and office building, new construction; Apartment building operators

(G-6300)
NATIONAL HOUSING TR LTD PARTNR
Also Called: Nht
2335 N Bank Dr (43220)
PHONE.................................614 451-9929
James Bowman, *Pr*
EMP: 46 **EST:** 1987
SQ FT: 800
SALES (est): 742.42K **Privately Held**
SIC: 6726 Management investment funds, closed-end

(G-6301)
NATIONAL RGSTRY OF EMRGNCY MED
Also Called: NATIONAL REGISTRY-EMERGENCY
6610 Busch Blvd (43229-1740)
P.O. Box 29233 (43229-0233)
PHONE.................................614 888-4484
Savero Rodrigo, *Dir*
EMP: 35 **EST:** 1973
SALES (est): 24.89MM **Privately Held**
Web: www.nremt.org
SIC: 8732 8011 Market analysis, business, and economic research; Offices and clinics of medical doctors

(G-6302)
NATIONAL VTRANS MEM MSEUM OPER
300 W Broad St (43215-2761)
PHONE.................................614 362-2800
Matthew D Lutz, *Pr*
EMP: 37 **EST:** 2019
SALES (est): 5.7MM **Privately Held**
Web: www.nationalvmm.org
SIC: 8412 Museum

(G-6303)
NATIONAL YUTH ADVCATE PRGRAM I (PA)
1801 Watermark Dr Ste 200 (43215-7088)
PHONE.................................614 487-8758
Marvena Twigg, *Pr*
Wellington Chimbwanda, *
Dru Whitaker, *Chief Strategy Officer**
Michelle Corry, *
EMP: 42 **EST:** 1983
SALES (est): 98.1MM
SALES (corp-wide): 98.1MM **Privately Held**
Web: www.nyap.org
SIC: 8322 8399 Individual and family services; Advocacy group

(G-6304)
NATIONWIDE AFFINITY INSUR AMER
1 W Nationwide Blvd Ste 100 (43215-2752)
PHONE.................................614 249-2141
EMP: 453 **EST:** 2006
SALES (est): 4.6MM
SALES (corp-wide): 11.75B **Privately Held**
Web: www.nationwide.com
SIC: 6411 Insurance agents, nec
PA: Nationwide Mutual Insurance Company
1 Nationwide Plz
Columbus OH 43215
614 249-7111

(G-6305)
NATIONWIDE ARENA LLC
200 W Nationwide Blvd (43215-2561)
PHONE.................................614 232-8810
EMP: 59 **EST:** 1997
SALES (est): 10.9MM
SALES (corp-wide): 2.9B **Privately Held**
Web: www.nationwidearena.com
SIC: 6512 Nonresidential building operators
PA: Delaware North Companies Incorporated
250 Delaware Ave Ste 1000
Buffalo NY 14202
716 858-5000

(G-6306)
NATIONWIDE ASSET MGT LLC
1 Nationwide Plz (43215-2226)
PHONE.................................614 677-7300
Mark Senff, *Prin*
EMP: 248 **EST:** 2008
SALES (est): 3.26MM
SALES (corp-wide): 11.75B **Privately Held**
Web: www.nationwide.com
SIC: 6722 Money market mutual funds
PA: Nationwide Mutual Insurance Company
1 Nationwide Plz
Columbus OH 43215
614 249-7111

(G-6307)
NATIONWIDE BANK (DH)
Also Called: NATIONWIDE FINANCIAL
1 Nationwide Plz (43215-2226)
P.O. Box 182049 (43218-2049)
PHONE.................................800 882-2822
Steven J Rose, *Pr*
EMP: 149 **EST:** 1998
SALES (est): 255.82MM
SALES (corp-wide): 11.75B **Privately Held**
Web: www.nationwide.com
SIC: 6411 Insurance agents, nec
HQ: Nationwide Financial Services, Inc.
1 Nationwide Plz
Columbus OH 43215

(G-6308)
NATIONWIDE BETTER HEALTH INC
1 Nationwide Plz (43215-2226)
P.O. Box 182171 (43218-2171)
PHONE.................................614 249-7111
EMP: 350
SIC: 6321 Accident and health insurance

(G-6309)
NATIONWIDE CHILDRENS
700 Childrens Dr (43205-2664)
PHONE.................................407 782-0053
Stephanie Cannon, *Prin*
EMP: 45 **EST:** 2019
SALES (est): 50.81MM **Privately Held**
Web: www.nationwidechildrens.org
SIC: 8062 General medical and surgical hospitals

(G-6310)
NATIONWIDE CHILDRENS HOSPITAL
Also Called: Caniano Bsner Pdiatrics Clinic
555 S 18th St Ste 6g (43205-2654)
PHONE.................................614 722-5750
Thomas Hansen, *CEO*
EMP: 431
SALES (corp-wide): 3.6B **Privately Held**
Web: www.nationwidechildrens.org

SIC: 8062 General medical and surgical hospitals
PA: Nationwide Children's Hospital
700 Childrens Dr
Columbus OH 43205
614 722-2000

(G-6311)
NATIONWIDE CHILDRENS HOSPITAL
255 E Main St (43215-5222)
PHONE.................................614 355-1100
EMP: 279
SALES (corp-wide): 3.6B **Privately Held**
Web: www.nationwidechildrens.org
SIC: 8062 General medical and surgical hospitals
PA: Nationwide Children's Hospital
700 Childrens Dr
Columbus OH 43205
614 722-2000

(G-6312)
NATIONWIDE CHILDRENS HOSPITAL
1390 Cleveland Ave Ste 202 (43211-2767)
PHONE.................................614 355-9300
Patricia Feamster, *Mgr*
EMP: 177
SALES (corp-wide): 3.6B **Privately Held**
Web: www.nationwidechildrens.org
SIC: 8062 General medical and surgical hospitals
PA: Nationwide Children's Hospital
700 Childrens Dr
Columbus OH 43205
614 722-2000

(G-6313)
NATIONWIDE CHILDRENS HOSPITAL (PA)
Also Called: Dept of Laboratory Medicine
700 Childrens Dr (43205-2639)
PHONE.................................614 722-2000
Steve Allen, *CEO*
Timothy Robinson, *
Rick Miller, *
Rustin Morse, *CMO**
Ray Bignall Ii, *DIVERSITY HEALTH EQUITY*
◆ **EMP:** 2232 **EST:** 1892
SQ FT: 1,324,000
SALES (est): 3.6B
SALES (corp-wide): 3.6B **Privately Held**
Web: www.nationwidechildrens.org
SIC: 8062 General medical and surgical hospitals

(G-6314)
NATIONWIDE CHILDRENS HOSPITAL
2857 W Broad St (43204-2643)
PHONE.................................614 355-9900
EMP: 101
SALES (corp-wide): 3.6B **Privately Held**
Web: www.nationwidechildrens.org
SIC: 8062 General medical and surgical hospitals
PA: Nationwide Children's Hospital
700 Childrens Dr
Columbus OH 43205
614 722-2000

(G-6315)
NATIONWIDE CHILDRENS HOSPITAL
479 Parsons Ave (43215-5577)
PHONE.................................614 722-5175
Barbara Est, *Prin*
EMP: 127
SALES (corp-wide): 3.6B **Privately Held**
Web: www.nationwidechildrens.org
SIC: 8062 General medical and surgical hospitals
PA: Nationwide Children's Hospital
700 Childrens Dr
Columbus OH 43205
614 722-2000

(G-6316)
NATIONWIDE CHILDRENS HOSPITAL
Also Called: Close To Home Health Care Ctr
6435 E Broad St (43213-1507)
PHONE.................................614 355-8100
Steve Allen, *Brnch Mgr*
EMP: 177
SALES (corp-wide): 3.6B **Privately Held**
Web: www.nationwidechildrens.org
SIC: 8062 General medical and surgical hospitals
PA: Nationwide Children's Hospital
700 Childrens Dr
Columbus OH 43205
614 722-2000

(G-6317)
NATIONWIDE CHILDRENS HOSPITAL
1125 E Main St (43205-1931)
PHONE.................................614 355-9200
Steve Allen, *Brnch Mgr*
EMP: 228
SALES (corp-wide): 3.6B **Privately Held**
Web: www.nationwidechildrens.org
SIC: 8062 General medical and surgical hospitals
PA: Nationwide Children's Hospital
700 Childrens Dr
Columbus OH 43205
614 722-2000

(G-6318)
NATIONWIDE CHILDRENS HOSPITAL
4560 Morse Centre Rd (43229-6602)
PHONE.................................614 355-9400
EMP: 101
SALES (corp-wide): 3.6B **Privately Held**
Web: www.nationwidechildrens.org
SIC: 8062 General medical and surgical hospitals
PA: Nationwide Children's Hospital
700 Childrens Dr
Columbus OH 43205
614 722-2000

(G-6319)
NATIONWIDE CHILDRENS HOSPITAL
Also Called: Steve Cndy Rsmssen Inst For Gn
575 Childrens Xrd (43215-5594)
PHONE.................................614 355-6850
Elaine R Mardis, *Dir*
EMP: 127
SALES (corp-wide): 3.6B **Privately Held**
SIC: 8062 General medical and surgical hospitals
PA: Nationwide Children's Hospital
700 Childrens Dr
Columbus OH 43205
614 722-2000

(G-6320)
NATIONWIDE CHILDRENS HOSPITAL
Also Called: Wexner Research Institute
700 Childrens Dr (43205-2639)
PHONE.................................614 722-2000
Dan Mann, *Admn*
EMP: 228
SALES (corp-wide): 3.6B **Privately Held**
Web: www.nationwidechildrens.org
SIC: 8069 8733 Childrens' hospital; Research institute
PA: Nationwide Children's Hospital
700 Childrens Dr
Columbus OH 43205
614 722-2000

Columbus - Franklin County (G-6321) — GEOGRAPHIC SECTION

(G-6321)
NATIONWIDE CHILDRENS HOSPITAL
Also Called: Columbus Childrens Hospital
655 E Livingston Ave (43205-2618)
PHONE..................................614 722-8200
Karen Days, *Brnch Mgr*
EMP: 355
SALES (corp-wide): 3.6B **Privately Held**
Web: www.nationwidechildrens.org
SIC: 8069 8399 Childrens' hospital;
   Advocacy group
PA: Nationwide Children's Hospital
   700 Childrens Dr
   Columbus OH 43205
   614 722-2000

(G-6322)
NATIONWIDE CHILDRENS HOSPITAL
3433 Agler Rd Ste 1400 (43219-3388)
PHONE..................................614 355-0802
Steve Allen, *Brnch Mgr*
EMP: 127
SALES (corp-wide): 3.6B **Privately Held**
Web: www.nationwidechildrens.org
SIC: 8069 Childrens' hospital
PA: Nationwide Children's Hospital
   700 Childrens Dr
   Columbus OH 43205
   614 722-2000

(G-6323)
NATIONWIDE CHILDRENS HOSPITAL
Also Called: Childrens Hosp Guidance Ctrs
495 E Main St (43215-5679)
PHONE..................................614 355-8000
Linda Wolf, *Dir*
EMP: 228
SALES (corp-wide): 3.6B **Privately Held**
Web: www.nationwidechildrens.org
SIC: 8069 8093 Childrens' hospital; Mental
   health clinic, outpatient
PA: Nationwide Children's Hospital
   700 Childrens Dr
   Columbus OH 43205
   614 722-2000

(G-6324)
NATIONWIDE CHLD HOSP FUNDATION
700 Childrens Dr (43205-2664)
P.O. Box 16810 (43216-6810)
PHONE..................................614 355-5400
James Digan, *Pr*
Kevin Welch, *
Jose Balderrama, *
EMP: 31 **EST:** 1982
SALES (est): 10.71MM
SALES (corp-wide): 3.6B **Privately Held**
Web: www.nationwidechildrens.org
SIC: 8062 General medical and surgical
   hospitals
PA: Nationwide Children's Hospital
   700 Childrens Dr
   Columbus OH 43205
   614 722-2000

(G-6325)
NATIONWIDE CHLD HOSP HOMECARE
Also Called: Children's Homecare Services
455 E Mound St (43215-5595)
PHONE..................................614 355-1100
Heidi Drake, *Dir*
EMP: 2102 **EST:** 1990
SQ FT: 7,000
SALES (est): 5.47MM
SALES (corp-wide): 3.6B **Privately Held**
Web: www.nationwidechildrens.org
SIC: 8082 8322 Home health care services;
   Individual and family services
PA: Nationwide Children's Hospital
   700 Childrens Dr
   Columbus OH 43205
   614 722-2000

(G-6326)
NATIONWIDE CORPORATION (HQ)
Also Called: Nationwide
1 Nationwide Plz (43215-2226)
PHONE..................................614 249-7111
Henry S Ballard, *Prin*
Damon R Mcferson, *Pr*
Steve Rasmussen, *
Philip C Gath, *Chief Actuary**
Robert A Oakley, *
◆ **EMP:** 27 **EST:** 1947
SQ FT: 9,500
SALES (est): 135.44K
SALES (corp-wide): 11.75B **Privately Held**
Web: www.nationwide.com
SIC: 6411 6321 Insurance agents, nec;
   Accident insurance carriers
PA: Nationwide Mutual Insurance Company
   1 Nationwide Plz
   Columbus OH 43215
   614 249-7111

(G-6327)
NATIONWIDE CREDIT UNION
1 Nationwide Plz (43215-2226)
PHONE..................................614 249-6226
Paula Edwards, *Pr*
EMP: 90 **EST:** 1951
SALES (est): 6.21MM **Privately Held**
Web: www.nationwide.com
SIC: 6061 6062 Federal credit unions; State
   credit unions

(G-6328)
NATIONWIDE ENERGY PARTNERS LLC
230 West St Ste 150 (43215-2785)
PHONE..................................614 918-2031
Tj Harper, *Pr*
Dan Lhota, *
Robert Davis, *Senior Financial Executive**
Rick Eurich, *
EMP: 49 **EST:** 1999
SALES (est): 21MM **Privately Held**
Web: www.nationwideenergypartners.com
SIC: 1731 8748 Electrical work; Energy
   conservation consultant

(G-6329)
NATIONWIDE FINANCIAL SVCS INC (DH)
Also Called: Nationwide Financial
1 Nationwide Plz (43215-2226)
P.O. Box 182049 (43218-2049)
PHONE..................................614 249-7111
EMP: 218 **EST:** 1996
SQ FT: 898,000
SALES (est): 754.48MM
SALES (corp-wide): 11.75B **Privately Held**
Web: www.nationwide.com
SIC: 6311 6411 8742 Life insurance;
   Pension and retirement plan consultants;
   Banking and finance consultant
HQ: Nationwide Corporation
   1 Nationwide Plz
   Columbus OH 43215
   614 249-7111

(G-6330)
NATIONWIDE FNCL INSTN DSTRS AG
1 Nationwide Plz 2-05-01 (43215-2226)
PHONE..................................614 249-6825
David L Giertz, *Pr*
Richard Karas, *
Mark R Thresher, *
EMP: 60 **EST:** 1990
SQ FT: 10,000
SALES (est): 17.36MM
SALES (corp-wide): 11.75B **Privately Held**
SIC: 6411 Insurance agents, nec
HQ: Nationwide Corporation
   1 Nationwide Plz
   Columbus OH 43215
   614 249-7111

(G-6331)
NATIONWIDE GENERAL INSUR CO
Also Called: Nationwide
1 W Nationwide Blvd Ste 100 (43215)
PHONE..................................614 249-7111
Dimon Richard Mc Frson, *Pr*
Dimon Richard Mc Ferson, *Pr*
Harold Weihl, *
Richard D Crabtree, *Parent**
Robert Oakley, *Ex VP*
EMP: 1766 **EST:** 1958
SQ FT: 10,000
SALES (est): 183.06MM
SALES (corp-wide): 11.75B **Privately Held**
Web: www.nationwide.com
SIC: 6311 6331 7389 8741 Life insurance;
   Fire, marine, and casualty insurance;
   Financial services; Administrative
   management
PA: Nationwide Mutual Insurance Company
   1 Nationwide Plz
   Columbus OH 43215
   614 249-7111

(G-6332)
NATIONWIDE INSURANCE CO FLA
Also Called: Nationwide
1 W Nationwide Blvd (43215-2752)
PHONE..................................614 249-7111
David Meyer, *Prin*
EMP: 949 **EST:** 1998
SALES (est): 42.26MM
SALES (corp-wide): 11.75B **Privately Held**
Web: www.nationwide.com
SIC: 6331 6311 Property damage insurance;
   Mutual association life insurance
PA: Nationwide Mutual Insurance Company
   1 Nationwide Plz
   Columbus OH 43215
   614 249-7111

(G-6333)
NATIONWIDE INV SVCS CORP
2 Nationwide Plz (43215-2534)
PHONE..................................614 249-7111
Duane Meek, *Pr*
EMP: 289 **EST:** 1974
SALES (est): 9.81MM
SALES (corp-wide): 11.75B **Privately Held**
Web: www.nationwide.com
SIC: 6211 Security brokers and dealers
HQ: Nationwide Life Insurance Company
   1 Nationwide Plz
   Columbus OH 43215
   877 669-6877

(G-6334)
NATIONWIDE LF ANNUITY INSUR CO
Also Called: NW Financial
1 W Nationwide Blvd Ste 100 (43215-2752)
PHONE..................................614 249-7111
Philip Gath, *Prin*
EMP: 788 **EST:** 1982
SALES (est): 3.55B
SALES (corp-wide): 11.75B **Privately Held**
Web: www.nationwide.com
SIC: 6411 Insurance agents, nec
PA: Nationwide Mutual Insurance Company
   1 Nationwide Plz
   Columbus OH 43215
   614 249-7111

(G-6335)
NATIONWIDE LIFE INSUR CO AMER
Also Called: Nationwide
1 Nationwide Plz (43215-2226)
P.O. Box 182928 (43218-2928)
PHONE..................................800 688-5177
Gary D Mcmahan, *Pr*
Alan F Hinkle, *
James G Potter Junior, *Ex VP*
Rosanne Gatta, *
Mary Lynn Finelli, *
◆ **EMP:** 1500 **EST:** 1865
SQ FT: 110,000
SALES (est): 49.95MM
SALES (corp-wide): 11.75B **Privately Held**
Web: www.nationwide.com
SIC: 6411 6211 6719 Insurance agents, nec;
   Brokers, security; Investment holding
   companies, except banks
HQ: Nationwide Financial Services, Inc.
   1 Nationwide Plz
   Columbus OH 43215

(G-6336)
NATIONWIDE LIFE INSURANCE CO (DH)
Also Called: Nationwide
1 Nationwide Plz (43215-2226)
PHONE..................................877 669-6877
Kirt Walker, *Pr*
Timothy Frommeyer, *
Mark Berven, *
Gale King, *
Matt Jauchius, *
EMP: 245 **EST:** 1929
SQ FT: 890,000
SALES (est): 430.48MM
SALES (corp-wide): 11.75B **Privately Held**
Web: www.nationwide.com
SIC: 6411 Property and casualty insurance
   agent
HQ: Nationwide Financial Services, Inc.
   1 Nationwide Plz
   Columbus OH 43215

(G-6337)
NATIONWIDE MUTL FIRE INSUR CO (HQ)
Also Called: Nationwide
1 W Nationwide Blvd Ste 100 (43215-2752)
PHONE..................................614 249-7111
Dimon R Mc Ferson, *Ch Bd*
Richard D Crabtree, *Pr*
Gordon E Mc Cutchan, *Law Vice President*
Robert A Oakley, *Ex VP*
Robert J Woodward Junior, *Ex VP*
EMP: 43 **EST:** 1934
SALES (est): 4.21B
SALES (corp-wide): 11.75B **Privately Held**
Web: www.nationwide.com
SIC: 6411 Insurance agents, nec
PA: Nationwide Mutual Insurance Company
   1 Nationwide Plz
   Columbus OH 43215
   614 249-7111

(G-6338)
NATIONWIDE MUTUAL INSURANCE CO (PA)
Also Called: Nationwide
1 Nationwide Plz (43215-2226)
P.O. Box 182171 (43218-2171)
PHONE..................................614 249-7111
Kirt Walker, *CEO*
Anthony Sharett, *
Mark R Thresher, *
◆ **EMP:** 1247 **EST:** 1925
SQ FT: 1,328,797
SALES (est): 11.75B
SALES (corp-wide): 11.75B **Privately Held**
Web: www.nationwide.com

SIC: 6331 6311 6321 6531 Fire, marine, and casualty insurance: mutual; Life insurance carriers; Accident insurance carriers; Real estate agents and managers

(G-6339)
NATIONWIDE MUTUAL INSURANCE CO
Also Called: Nationwide
275 Marconi Blvd (43215-2314)
PHONE..................................614 249-7654
EMP: 44
SALES (corp-wide): 11.75B **Privately Held**
Web: www.nationwide.com
SIC: 6411 Insurance agents, nec
PA: Nationwide Mutual Insurance Company
1 Nationwide Plz
Columbus OH 43215
614 249-7111

(G-6340)
NATIONWIDE MUTUAL INSURANCE CO
Also Called: Nationwide
5017 Pine Creek Dr (43081-4849)
PHONE..................................614 899-6300
Bill Thompson, *Brnch Mgr*
EMP: 29
SALES (corp-wide): 11.75B **Privately Held**
Web: www.nationwide.com
SIC: 6411 Insurance agents, nec
PA: Nationwide Mutual Insurance Company
1 Nationwide Plz
Columbus OH 43215
614 249-7111

(G-6341)
NATIONWIDE PRPERTY CSLTY INSUR (HQ)
Also Called: Nationwide
1 W Nationwide Blvd Ste 100 (43215-2752)
P.O. Box 182171 (43218-2171)
PHONE..................................614 677-8166
D Richard Mcferson, *Ch*
EMP: 53 **EST:** 1979
SALES (est): 118.56MM
SALES (corp-wide): 11.75B **Privately Held**
Web: www.nationwide.com
SIC: 6411 Insurance agents, nec
PA: Nationwide Mutual Insurance Company
1 Nationwide Plz
Columbus OH 43215
614 249-7111

(G-6342)
NBBJ LLC (HQ)
Also Called: NBBJ Construction Services
250 S High St Ste 300 (43215-4629)
PHONE..................................206 223-5026
EMP: 150 **EST:** 1955
SALES (est): 49.27MM
SALES (corp-wide): 76.56MM **Privately Held**
Web: www.nbbj.com
SIC: 8712 Architectural engineering
PA: Nbbj Lp
223 Yale Ave N
Seattle WA 98109
206 223-5555

(G-6343)
NEACE ASSOC INSUR AGCY OF OHIO
285 Cozzins St (43215-2334)
PHONE..................................614 224-0772
Jeff Kurz, *Mgr*
EMP: 34
SIC: 6411 Insurance agents, nec

PA: Neace & Associates Insurance Agency Of Ohio, Inc
5905 E Galbraith Rd
Cincinnati OH 45236

(G-6344)
NELBUD SERVICES GROUP INC
Also Called: NELBUD SERVICES GROUP, INC.
2168 Cloverleaf St E (43232-4166)
PHONE..................................317 202-0360
EMP: 43
SALES (corp-wide): 279.81MM **Privately Held**
Web: www.nelbud.com
SIC: 7349 Cleaning service, industrial or commercial
HQ: Nelbud Services Llc
51 Koweba Ln
Indianapolis IN 46201
317 202-0360

(G-6345)
NEST TENDERS LIMITED
Also Called: Two Men & A Truck
5083 Westerville Rd (43231-4909)
PHONE..................................614 901-1570
Gail Kelley, *Pr*
John Kelley, *
Steve Barton, *
EMP: 100 **EST:** 1993
SQ FT: 22,000
SALES (est): 9.89MM **Privately Held**
Web: www.twomenandatruck.com
SIC: 4212 Moving services

(G-6346)
NETCARE CORPORATION (PA)
Also Called: NETCARE ACCESS
199 S Cent Ave (43223)
PHONE..................................614 274-9500
A King Stumpp, *Pr*
J A Bonham, *
P G Baynes, *
W Brannon, *
W Colwell, *
EMP: 100 **EST:** 1972
SQ FT: 30,000
SALES (est): 18.02MM
SALES (corp-wide): 18.02MM **Privately Held**
Web: www.netcareaccess.org
SIC: 8093 Mental health clinic, outpatient

(G-6347)
NETJETS ASSN SHRED ARCFT PLOTS
Also Called: Njasap
2740 Airport Dr Ste 330 (43219-2286)
PHONE..................................614 532-0555
John Malmborg, *Pr*
EMP: 36 **EST:** 2008
SALES (est): 8.31MM **Privately Held**
Web: www.njasap-pac.com
SIC: 7363 Pilot service, aviation

(G-6348)
NETJETS AVIATION INC (DH)
4111 Bridgeway Ave (43219-1882)
P.O. Box 369099 (43236-9099)
PHONE..................................614 239-5500
EMP: 500 **EST:** 1964
SALES (est): 222.51MM
SALES (corp-wide): 364.48B **Publicly Held**
Web: www.netjets.com
SIC: 4522 Flying charter service
HQ: Netjets Inc.
4111 Bridgeway Ave
Columbus OH 43219

(G-6349)
NETJETS INTERNATIONAL INC (DH)
4111 Bridgeway Ave (43219-1882)
PHONE..................................614 239-5500
EMP: 665 **EST:** 1995
SQ FT: 22,500
SALES (est): 21.68MM
SALES (corp-wide): 364.48B **Publicly Held**
Web: www.netjets.com
SIC: 4522 Flying charter service
HQ: Netjets Inc.
4111 Bridgeway Ave
Columbus OH 43219

(G-6350)
NETJETS SALES INC
4111 Bridgeway Ave (43219-1882)
P.O. Box 369099 (43236-9099)
PHONE..................................614 239-5500
Bill Noe, *Pr*
EMP: 102 **EST:** 1964
SALES (est): 30.03MM
SALES (corp-wide): 364.48B **Publicly Held**
SIC: 5088 4522 Aircraft and parts, nec; Air transportation, nonscheduled
HQ: Netjets Inc.
4111 Bridgeway Ave
Columbus OH 43219

(G-6351)
NEUROLOGICAL ASSOCIATES INC
931 Chatham Ln (43221-2486)
PHONE..................................614 544-4455
Jeff Ubank, *Pr*
Michele J Meagher, *
Edward J Kosnik, *
EMP: 62 **EST:** 1968
SALES (est): 9.05MM **Privately Held**
Web: www.neuroassociates.com
SIC: 8011 Neurologist

(G-6352)
NEW ALBANY CARE CENTER LLC
5691 Thompson Rd (43230-1345)
PHONE..................................614 855-8866
Melanie O'neil, *Prin*
EMP: 44 **EST:** 1997
SALES (est): 11.37MM **Privately Held**
Web: www.optalishealthcare.com
SIC: 8051 Convalescent home with continuous nursing care

(G-6353)
NEWARK PARCEL SERVICE COMPANY
640 N Cassady Ave (43219-2721)
PHONE..................................614 253-3777
Patrick Sullivan, *Pr*
EMP: 33 **EST:** 1968
SQ FT: 60,000
SALES (est): 4.44MM **Privately Held**
Web: www.newarkparcelservice.com
SIC: 4731 Freight transportation arrangement

(G-6354)
NEXSTAR BROADCASTING INC
Also Called: Wcmh
3165 Olentangy River Rd (43202-1518)
PHONE..................................614 263-4444
Jody Van Fossen, *Mgr*
EMP: 151
SALES (corp-wide): 4.93B **Publicly Held**
Web: www.nexstar.tv
SIC: 4833 Television broadcasting stations
HQ: Nexstar Media Inc.
545 E John Carpenter Fwy
Irving TX 75062
972 373-8800

(G-6355)
NEXTCHAPTER
629 N High St Fl 400 (43215-2929)
PHONE..................................888 861-7122
Janine Sickmeyer, *Prin*
EMP: 48 **EST:** 2015
SQ FT: 300
SALES (est): 560.06K **Privately Held**
Web: www.nextchapterlegal.com
SIC: 8399 Advocacy group

(G-6356)
NF REINSURANCE LTD
1 Nationwide Plz (43215-2226)
PHONE..................................614 249-7111
EMP: 127
SALES (est): 3.22MM
SALES (corp-wide): 11.75B **Privately Held**
SIC: 6311 Life insurance
HQ: Nationwide Financial Services, Inc.
1 Nationwide Plz
Columbus OH 43215

(G-6357)
NIAGARA HEALTH CORPORATION (HQ)
6150 E Broad St (43213-1574)
PHONE..................................614 898-4000
Randall E Moore, *Prin*
Laury Colmann, *
EMP: 200 **EST:** 1989
SALES (est): 439.92MM
SALES (corp-wide): 2.49B **Privately Held**
SIC: 8741 8062 Hospital management; General medical and surgical hospitals
PA: Trinity Health Corporation
20555 Victor Pkwy
Livonia MI 48152
734 343-1000

(G-6358)
NICHOLSON BUILDERS INC
6525 Busch Blvd Ste 101 (43229-1701)
PHONE..................................614 846-7388
William Nicholson, *Owner*
Mike Fought, *
EMP: 47 **EST:** 2003
SALES (est): 9.39MM **Privately Held**
Web: www.nicholsonbuilders.com
SIC: 1521 New construction, single-family houses

(G-6359)
NICKOLAS M SAVKO & SONS INC
4636 Shuster Rd (43214-1934)
PHONE..................................614 451-2242
EMP: 150 **EST:** 1977
SALES (est): 19.35MM **Privately Held**
Web: www.nicksavko.com
SIC: 1623 1611 1794 Underground utilities contractor; Highway and street construction ; Excavation work

(G-6360)
NIRVANA INSURANCE
100 E Campus View Blvd Ste 250 (43235-4647)
PHONE..................................330 217-3079
EMP: 36
SALES (est): 483.25K **Privately Held**
Web: www.nirvanatech.com
SIC: 6411 Insurance agents, nec

(G-6361)
NL OF KY INC
Also Called: Neace Lukens
285 Cozzins St (43215-2334)
PHONE..................................614 224-0772
Jeff Kurz, *Mgr*
EMP: 38

Columbus - Franklin County (G-6362) — GEOGRAPHIC SECTION

SIC: **6411** Insurance agents, nec
HQ: NI Of Ky, Inc.
2305 River Rd
Louisville KY 40206

(G-6362)
NORFOLK SOUTHERN RAILWAY CO
Also Called: Norfolk Southern
4882 Trabue Rd (43228-9391)
PHONE..................................614 771-2183
Mike Braylor, *Prin*
EMP: 134
SALES (corp-wide): 12.16B **Publicly Held**
Web: www.norfolksouthern.com
SIC: **4011** Interurban railways
HQ: Norfolk Southern Railway Company
650 W Peachtree St Nw
Atlanta GA 30308
855 667-3655

(G-6363)
NORSE DAIRY SYSTEMS INC
1700 E 17th Ave (43219-1005)
P.O. Box 1869 (43216-1869)
PHONE..................................614 294-4931
EMP: 201 **EST:** 1995
SQ FT: 850
SALES (corp-wide): 42.47B **Privately Held**
SIC: **6719** 3565 3556 2671 Investment holding companies, except banks; Packaging machinery; Food products machinery; Paper; coated and laminated packaging
PA: George Weston Limited
700-22 St Clair Ave E
Toronto ON M4T 2
226 271-5030

(G-6364)
NORTH AMERICAN BROADCASTING
Also Called: Wrkz
1458 Dublin Rd (43215-1010)
PHONE..................................614 481-7800
Matthew Minich, *Pr*
Nick Reed, *
EMP: 60 **EST:** 1956
SQ FT: 11,000
SALES (est): 7.55MM **Privately Held**
Web: www.nabco-inc.com
SIC: **4832** Radio broadcasting stations

(G-6365)
NORTH BROADWAY CHILDRENS CTR
48 E North Broadway St (43214-4112)
PHONE..................................614 262-6222
Rebecca Mccoy, *Owner*
Rebecca Mccoy, *Dir*
EMP: 30 **EST:** 1924
SALES (est): 1.31MM **Privately Held**
Web: www.north-broadway.org
SIC: **8351** Preschool center

(G-6366)
NORTH CNTL MNTAL HLTH SVCS INC (PA)
Also Called: Ncc Associates
1301 N High St (43201)
PHONE..................................614 227-6865
Don Wood, *CEO*
John Hunter, *
Joseph Niedzwidski, *
EMP: 80 **EST:** 1973
SQ FT: 21,500
SALES (est): 14.38MM
SALES (corp-wide): 14.38MM **Privately Held**
Web: www.ncmhs.org
SIC: **8093** 8361 Mental health clinic, outpatient; Residential care

(G-6367)
NORTHERN AUTOMOTIVE INC (PA)
Also Called: Saturn-West
8600 N High St (43235-1004)
PHONE..................................614 436-2001
TOLL FREE: 800
Thomas Carpenter, *Pr*
William L Denney, *
Robert Vance, *
EMP: 50 **EST:** 1990
SQ FT: 29,000
SALES (est): 22.03MM **Privately Held**
Web: www.northernenterprises.com
SIC: **5511** 7538 5521 Automobiles, new and used; General automotive repair shops; Used car dealers

(G-6368)
NORTHLAND HOTEL INC
Also Called: Super 8 Motel Columbus North
1078 E Dublin Granville Rd (43229-2503)
PHONE..................................614 885-1601
Ray Lin, *Pr*
EMP: 30 **EST:** 1992
SALES (est): 1.47MM **Privately Held**
Web: www.wyndhamhotels.com
SIC: **7011** Hotels

(G-6369)
NORTHPOINTE PROPERTY MGT LLC
3250 Henderson Rd Ste 103 (43220-2398)
PHONE..................................614 579-9712
Aniko Marcy, *Prin*
EMP: 197 **EST:** 2013
SALES (est): 6.8MM **Privately Held**
Web: www.northpointemanagement.com
SIC: **7349** 1799 Building maintenance services, nec; Exterior cleaning, including sandblasting

(G-6370)
NORTHSTAR ANIMAL CARE
2447 North Star Rd (43221-3403)
PHONE..................................614 846-5800
Mandi Justus, *Brnch Mgr*
EMP: 96
SALES (corp-wide): 514.09K **Privately Held**
Web: www.uavethospital.com
SIC: **0742** Animal hospital services, pets and other animal specialties
PA: Northstar Animal Care
1515 W Lane Ave
Columbus OH 43221
614 488-4121

(G-6371)
NORTHWEST BANCSHARES INC (PA)
3 Easton Oval Ste 500 (43219-6011)
P.O. Box 128 (16365-0128)
PHONE..................................800 859-1000
Louis J Torchio, *Pr*
Timothy B Fannin, *Interim Chairman of the Board*
Steven G Fisher, *CRO*
David E Westerburg, *Ex VP*
Michael G Smelko, *CCO*
EMP: 141 **EST:** 2001
SALES (est): 701.75MM **Publicly Held**
Web: www.northwest.bank
SIC: **6021** National commercial banks

(G-6372)
NORTHWEST EYE SURGEONS INC (PA)
2250 N Bank Dr (43220-5420)
PHONE..................................614 451-7550
Robert Lembach, *Pr*
EMP: 46 **EST:** 1970

SALES (est): 5.01MM
SALES (corp-wide): 5.01MM **Privately Held**
Web: www.northwesteyesurgeons.com
SIC: **8011** Opthalmologist

(G-6373)
NOVA CARE
6465 E Broad St Ste B (43213-1576)
PHONE..................................614 864-1089
Rochene Akiatan, *Brnch Mgr*
EMP: 28
Web: www.novacare.com
SIC: **8049** Physical therapist
PA: Nova Care
2906 Island Ave
Philadelphia PA 19153

(G-6374)
NOVA ENGINEERING & ENVMTL LLC
5400 N High St (43214-1117)
PHONE..................................614 325-8092
Kent Adkins, *Business Unit Manager*
EMP: 65
SALES (corp-wide): 1.2B **Privately Held**
Web: www.usanova.com
SIC: **8711** Civil engineering
HQ: Nova Engineering And Environmental, Llc
3900 Kennesaw 75 Pkwy Nw # 100
Kennesaw GA 30144

(G-6375)
NOVOTEC RECYCLING LLC (PA)
3960 Groves Rd (43232-4137)
PHONE..................................614 231-8326
Tom Bolon, *CEO*
EMP: 138 **EST:** 2008
SALES (est): 22MM **Privately Held**
Web: www.novotecrecycling.com
SIC: **4953** 8741 Recycling, waste materials; Management services

(G-6376)
NTK HOTEL GROUP II LLC
Also Called: Hampton Inn
501 N High St (43215-2008)
PHONE..................................614 559-2000
EMP: 60 **EST:** 2000
SALES (est): 2.41MM **Privately Held**
Web: www.hilton.com
SIC: **7011** Hotels and motels

(G-6377)
NURSES HEART PARAMEDICS LLC
2056 Integrity Dr S (43209-2728)
PHONE..................................614 648-5111
James Teague, *CEO*
James Teague, *Managing Member*
Vanessa Garnes, *
Rosaland Berenguer, *
EMP: 40 **EST:** 2013
SALES (est): 2.35MM **Privately Held**
SIC: **7361** Employment agencies

(G-6378)
NUTIS PRESS INC (PA)
Also Called: Printed Resources
3540 E Fulton St (43227-1100)
P.O. Box 27248 (43227-0248)
PHONE..................................614 237-8626
Ira Nutis, *Pr*
Sam Nutis, *
Joey Nutis, *
▼ **EMP:** 107 **EST:** 1961
SQ FT: 95,000
SALES (est): 49.33MM
SALES (corp-wide): 49.33MM **Privately Held**
Web: www.nutis.com

SIC: **5199** Advertising specialties

(G-6379)
O S WALKER COMPANY INC
2195 Wright Brothers Ave (43217-1157)
PHONE..................................614 492-1614
O Walker, *Prin*
EMP: 43
SALES (corp-wide): 55.92MM **Privately Held**
Web: www.drownemachinery.com
SIC: **5084** Industrial machinery and equipment
HQ: O. S. Walker Company, Inc.
600 Day Hill Rd
Windsor CT 06095
508 853-3232

(G-6380)
OAKLAND NURSERY INC (PA)
1156 Oakland Park Ave (43224-3317)
PHONE..................................614 268-3834
Paul S Reiner, *Pr*
John G Reiner, *
▲ **EMP:** 38 **EST:** 1940
SQ FT: 5,000
SALES (est): 12.36MM
SALES (corp-wide): 12.36MM **Privately Held**
Web: www.oaklandnursery.com
SIC: **5261** 0781 Nursery stock, seeds and bulbs; Landscape services

(G-6381)
OBETZ ANIMAL HOSPITAL
3999 Alum Creek Dr (43207-5136)
PHONE..................................614 491-5676
Alec Land, *Pr*
Rona Shapiro D.v.m., *Pt*
EMP: 30 **EST:** 1987
SQ FT: 5,000
SALES (est): 942.47K **Privately Held**
Web: www.obetzah.com
SIC: **0742** Animal hospital services, pets and other animal specialties

(G-6382)
OCALI
Also Called: Ohio Ctr For Atism Low Incdnce
470 Glenmont Ave (43214-3210)
PHONE..................................614 410-0321
Shawn Henry, *Dir*
Shiela Smith, *Prin*
EMP: 47 **EST:** 2005
SALES (est): 3.49MM **Privately Held**
Web: www.ocali.org
SIC: **8322** Social service center

(G-6383)
ODNR
Also Called: Odnr Oil & Gas Resources MGT
2045 Morse Rd (43229-6681)
PHONE..................................614 338-4742
EMP: 28 **EST:** 2013
SALES (est): 8.42MM **Privately Held**
Web: www.ohiodnr.gov
SIC: **0851** Forestry services

(G-6384)
ODW LOGISTICS INC (PA)
Also Called: O D W
400 W Nationwide Blvd Ste 200 (43215-2394)
PHONE..................................614 549-5000
Robert E Ness, *Ch*
John R Ness, *Prin*
Macy A Bergoon, *
Lynn Ness, *
David L Hill, *
◆ **EMP:** 300 **EST:** 1971
SQ FT: 1,000,000

GEOGRAPHIC SECTION

Columbus - Franklin County (G-6406)

SALES (est): 529.12MM
SALES (corp-wide): 529.12MM **Privately Held**
Web: www.odwlogistics.com
SIC: 4731 Freight transportation arrangement

(G-6385)
OFFOR HEALTH INC
Also Called: Smilemd
1103 Schrock Rd Ste 201 (43229-1179)
PHONE.................................877 789-8583
Saket Agrawal, *CEO*
Isaac Brenner, *
EMP: 60 **EST:** 2016
SALES (est): 10MM **Privately Held**
Web: www.smilemdsedation.com
SIC: 8011 Anesthesiologist

(G-6386)
OH-16 CLMBUS WRTHNGTON PRPRTY
Also Called: TownePlace Stes Clmbus Wrthngt
7272 Huntington Park Dr (43235-5718)
PHONE.................................614 885-1557
Greg Moundas, *VP*
EMP: 29 **EST:** 2016
SQ FT: 53,515
SALES (est): 159.01K **Privately Held**
Web: www.marriott.com
SIC: 7011 Hotel, franchised

(G-6387)
OHA HOLDINGS INC (DH)
155 E Broad St Ste 302 (43215-3622)
PHONE.................................614 221-7614
EMP: 64 **EST:** 2003
SALES (est): 96.2K
SALES (corp-wide): 10.07B **Publicly Held**
SIC: 6321 Accident and health insurance carriers
HQ: Fincor Holdings, Inc.
3100 West Rd Ste 200
East Lansing MI 48823
517 323-6198

(G-6388)
OHIC INSURANCE COMPANY (HQ)
300 E Broad St Ste 450 (43215-3614)
PHONE.................................614 221-7777
Jerry Cassidy, *Ch Bd*
Darrell Rainum, *Risk Management Vice-President*
Nancy Libke, *Claims Vice President*
Steve Turover, *VP Fin*
Jim Daldyga, *Underwriting Vice President*
EMP: 80 **EST:** 1978
SALES (est): 34MM
SALES (corp-wide): 662.94MM **Privately Held**
Web: www.thedoctors.com
SIC: 6331 6411 8742 Fire, marine and casualty insurance and carriers; Insurance claim adjusters, not employed by insurance company; Hospital and health services consultant
PA: The Doctors' Company An Interinsurance Exchange
185 Greenwood Rd
Napa CA 94558
707 226-0100

(G-6389)
OHIO ADDICTION RECOVERY CENTER
727 E Main St (43205-1760)
P.O. Box 6353 (43206-0253)
PHONE.................................800 481-8457
Bryan Sacks, *CFO*
EMP: 27 **EST:** 2016
SALES (est): 463.95K **Privately Held**

Web: www.ohioarc.com
SIC: 8322 General counseling services

(G-6390)
OHIO ASSN CMNTY HLTH CTRS INC
2109 Stella Ct Ste 100 (43215-1032)
PHONE.................................614 884-3101
Randy Runyon, *Pr*
Jennifer Bowers, *CFO*
Julie Dirossi-king, *COO*
Ted Wymyslo, *CMO*
Ashley Ballard, *Dir*
EMP: 32 **EST:** 1984
SQ FT: 1,300
SALES (est): 8.24MM **Privately Held**
SIC: 8621 Medical field-related associations

(G-6391)
OHIO ASSN PUB SCHL EMPLOYEES (PA)
Also Called: Oapse-Local 4
6805 Oak Creek Dr Ste 1 (43229-1501)
PHONE.................................614 890-4770
Joe Rugola, *Ex Dir*
EMP: 32 **EST:** 1942
SQ FT: 18,000
SALES (est): 3.01MM
SALES (corp-wide): 3.01MM **Privately Held**
Web: www.oapse.org
SIC: 8631 Labor union

(G-6392)
OHIO ASSOCIATION OF FOODBANKS
100 E Broad St Ste 450 (43215-3638)
PHONE.................................614 221-4336
Lisa Hamler Fugitt, *Ex Dir*
EMP: 66 **EST:** 1985
SALES (est): 60.95MM **Privately Held**
Web: www.ohiofoodbanks.org
SIC: 8322 Social service center

(G-6393)
OHIO AUTO KOLOR INC
3211 W Broad St (43204-1360)
PHONE.................................614 272-2255
Tony Luchini, *Mgr*
EMP: 38
SALES (corp-wide): 18.51MM **Privately Held**
Web: www.ohioautokolor.com
SIC: 5198 5013 Paints; Motor vehicle supplies and new parts
PA: Ohio Auto Kolor, Inc.
2600 Fisher Rd
Columbus OH 43204
614 276-8700

(G-6394)
OHIO AUTO LOAN SERVICES INC
3588 S High St (43207-4007)
PHONE.................................614 434-2397
Jennifer Osborn, *Brnch Mgr*
EMP: 37
SIC: 6141 Automobile loans, including insurance
HQ: Ohio Auto Loan Services, Inc.
8601 Dunwoody Pl Ste 406
Atlanta GA 30350
770 552-9840

(G-6395)
OHIO BELL TELEPHONE COMPANY
Also Called: Ameritech Ohio
96 Normandy Ave (43215)
PHONE.................................614 224-7424
EMP: 7102
SALES (corp-wide): 122.43B **Publicly Held**

SIC: 4813 Local telephone communications
HQ: Ohio Bell Telephone Company
6889 W Snowville Rd
Brecksville OH 44141
216 822-9700

(G-6396)
OHIO BUREAU WKRS COMPENSATION (DH)
30 W Spring St Fl 25 (43215-2216)
PHONE.................................800 644-6292
James Conrad, *Admn*
Barbara Ingram, *
Shawn Crosby, *
EMP: 1500 **EST:** 1911
SALES (est): 1.61B **Privately Held**
Web: info.bwc.ohio.gov
SIC: 6331 9199 Workers' compensation insurance; General government administration
HQ: Executive Office State Of Ohio
77 S High St Fl 30
Columbus OH 43215

(G-6397)
OHIO BUREAU WKRS COMPENSATION
77 S High St (43215-6108)
P.O. Box 15369 (43215-0369)
PHONE.................................614 221-4064
EMP: 27
Web: info.bwc.ohio.gov
SIC: 6411 Insurance agents, brokers, and service
HQ: Ohio Bureau Of Workers' Compensation
30 W Spring St Fl 2-29
Columbus OH 43215

(G-6398)
OHIO COMMUNITY DEV FIN FUND
Also Called: FINANCE FUND
175 S 3rd St Ste 1200 (43215-7102)
PHONE.................................614 221-1114
Randy Runyon, *Ch*
James R Klein, *CEO*
Diana Turoff, *CFO*
Jon Moorehead, *CPO*
Mark Barbash, *COO*
EMP: 46 **EST:** 1987
SALES (est): 9.45MM **Privately Held**
Web: www.financefund.org
SIC: 8399 Neighborhood development group

(G-6399)
OHIO CUSTODIAL MAINTENANCE
Also Called: Ohio Custodial Management
1291 S High St (43206-3472)
PHONE.................................614 443-1232
John Tucker, *CEO*
Scott Tucker, *
EMP: 199 **EST:** 1980
SQ FT: 7,000
SALES (est): 619.91K
SALES (corp-wide): 10.08MM **Privately Held**
Web: www.ohiocustodial.com
SIC: 7349 8742 Janitorial service, contract basis; Management consulting services
PA: Ohio Support Services Corp.
1291 S High St
Columbus OH 43206
614 443-0291

(G-6400)
OHIO DEMOCRATIC PARTY
340 E Fulton St (43215-5418)
PHONE.................................614 221-6563
Chris Redford, *Ch*
EMP: 100 **EST:** 2003
SALES (est): 8.71MM **Privately Held**

Web: www.ohiodems.org
SIC: 8651 Political action committee

(G-6401)
OHIO DEPARTMENT OF MENTAL HEALTH
Also Called: Mhas
30 E Broad St Fl 8 (43215-3414)
PHONE.................................614 466-2337
EMP: 2500
SIC: 8052 Home for the mentally retarded, with health care

(G-6402)
OHIO DEPARTMENT TRANSPORTATION
1600 W Broad St (43223-1202)
PHONE.................................614 275-1300
Jerry Wray, *Dir*
EMP: 40
Web: transportation.ohio.gov
SIC: 9199 8734 General government administration, State government; Automobile proving and testing ground
HQ: Ohio Department Of Transportation
1980 W Broad St
Columbus OH 43223

(G-6403)
OHIO DEPARTMENT YOUTH SERVICES
Also Called: Freedom Center
51 N High St Fl 5 (43215-3008)
PHONE.................................614 466-4314
EMP: 117
Web: dys.ohio.gov
SIC: 9431 8069 Public health agency administration, government; Substance abuse hospitals
HQ: Ohio Department Of Youth Services
4545 Fisher Rd Ste D
Columbus OH 43228

(G-6404)
OHIO DEPT DVLPMNTAL DSBILITIES
Also Called: Youngstown Developmental Ctr
30 E Broad St Fl 8 (43215-3414)
PHONE.................................330 544-2231
Cynthia Renner, *Superintnt*
EMP: 247
SIC: 8361 9431 Retarded home; Administration of public health programs, State government
HQ: Ohio Department Of Developmental Disabilities
30 E Broad St Fl 13
Columbus OH 43215

(G-6405)
OHIO DEPT DVLPMNTAL DSBILITIES
Also Called: Columbus Developmental Center
1601 W Broad St (43222-1054)
PHONE.................................614 272-0509
Charles Flowers, *Mgr*
EMP: 247
SIC: 8063 8052 9431 Psychiatric hospitals; Intermediate care facilities; Administration of public health programs, State government
HQ: Ohio Department Of Developmental Disabilities
30 E Broad St Fl 13
Columbus OH 43215

(G-6406)
OHIO DEPT JOB & FMLY SVCS
Also Called: Bureau Labor Market Info
4300 Kimberly Pkwy N (43232-8296)
PHONE.................................614 752-9494
Keith Ewald, *Dir*
EMP: 30

Columbus - Franklin County (G-6407)

Web: jfs.ohio.gov
SIC: 8331 9441 Community service employment training program; Administration of social and manpower programs, State government
HQ: Ohio Department Of Job And Family Services
30 E Broad St Fl 32
Columbus OH 43215

(G-6407)
OHIO DEPT JOB & FMLY SVCS
Also Called: Office For Children Fmly Svcs
255 E Main St Fl 3 (43215-5222)
PHONE..................................614 466-1213
EMP: 34
Web: jfs.ohio.gov
SIC: 8351 9441 8322 Child day care services ; Administration of social and manpower programs; Individual and family services
HQ: Ohio Department Of Job And Family Services
30 E Broad St Fl 32
Columbus OH 43215

(G-6408)
OHIO DEPT MNTAL HLTH ADDCTION
Also Called: Twin Vly Behavioral Healthcare
2200 W Broad St (43223-1297)
PHONE..................................614 752-0333
Richard Freeland, *Brnch Mgr*
EMP: 160
Web: mha.ohio.gov
SIC: 8063 9431 Psychiatric hospitals; Mental health agency administration, government
HQ: Ohio Department Of Mental Health And Addiction Services
30 E Broad St Fl 36
Columbus OH 43215

(G-6409)
OHIO DEPT MNTAL HLTH ADDCTION
Also Called: Twin Vly Behavioral Hlth Care
2200 W Broad St (43223-1297)
PHONE..................................614 752-0333
Bob Short, *Brnch Mgr*
EMP: 106
Web: www.adamhfranklin.org
SIC: 8062 9431 8093 General medical and surgical hospitals; Administration of public health programs; Mental health clinic, outpatient
HQ: Ohio Department Of Mental Health And Addiction Services
30 E Broad St Fl 36
Columbus OH 43215

(G-6410)
OHIO DEPT MNTAL HLTH ADDCTION
Also Called: Twin Valley
2200 W Broad St (43223-1297)
PHONE..................................614 752-0333
EMP: 93
Web: mha.ohio.gov
SIC: 9431 8063 Mental health agency administration, government; Psychiatric hospitals
HQ: Ohio Department Of Mental Health And Addiction Services
30 E Broad St Fl 36
Columbus OH 43215

(G-6411)
OHIO DEPT RHBILITATION CORECTN
Also Called: Parole & Community Services
770 W Broad St (43222-1419)
PHONE..................................614 274-9000
Jannet Morman, *Chief*
EMP: 69
SIC: 8322 9223 Parole office; Correctional institutions

HQ: Ohio Department Of Rehabilitation And Correction
4545 Fisher Rd Ste D
Columbus OH 43228

(G-6412)
OHIO DEPT RHBILITATION CORECTN
Also Called: Columbus Regional Office
1030 Alum Creek Dr (43209-2701)
PHONE..................................614 752-0800
EMP: 69
SIC: 8322 9223 Parole office; Correctional institutions, State government
HQ: Ohio Department Of Rehabilitation And Correction
4545 Fisher Rd Ste D
Columbus OH 43228

(G-6413)
OHIO DOMESTIC VIOLENCE NETWORK
174 E Long St (43215-1809)
PHONE..................................614 406-7274
Mary O'doherty, *Ex Dir*
EMP: 30 **EST:** 1988
SALES (est): 5.82MM **Privately Held**
Web: www.odvn.org
SIC: 8621 8322 Professional organizations; Individual and family services

(G-6414)
OHIO DSBLITY RGHTS LAW PLICY C
Also Called: DISABILLITY RIGHTS OHIO
200 Civic Center Dr (43215-7510)
PHONE..................................614 466-7264
Michael Kirkman, *Ex Dir*
EMP: 45 **EST:** 2012
SALES (est): 6.27MM **Privately Held**
Web: www.disabilityrightsohio.org
SIC: 8111 Legal services

(G-6415)
OHIO ECOLOGICAL FD & FRM ASSN
41 Croswell Rd Ste D (43214-3062)
PHONE..................................614 421-2022
Carol Goland, *Ex Dir*
John Sowder, *Treas*
Mike Laughlin, *Pr*
EMP: 36 **EST:** 1979
SALES (est): 2MM **Privately Held**
Web: grow.oeffa.org
SIC: 0191 General farms, primarily crop

(G-6416)
OHIO EDUCATION ASSOCIATION (PA)
225 E Broad St Fl 2 (43215-3709)
P.O. Box 2550 (43216-2550)
PHONE..................................614 228-4526
Patricia F Brooks, *Pr*
Larry Wicks, *
Jim Timlin, *
Lori Lee, *
EMP: 60 **EST:** 1924
SQ FT: 5,734
SALES (est): 23.43MM
SALES (corp-wide): 23.43MM **Privately Held**
Web: www.ohea.org
SIC: 8621 Education and teacher association

(G-6417)
OHIO ENVIRONMENTAL COUNCIL
1145 Chesapeake Ave Ste I (43212-2286)
PHONE..................................614 487-7506
Heather Taylor Miesle, *Ex Dir*
Vicki L Deisner, *Dir*
EMP: 42 **EST:** 1969
SQ FT: 1,500
SALES (est): 3.26MM **Privately Held**

Web: www.theoec.org
SIC: 8641 Environmental protection organization

(G-6418)
OHIO EQUITIES LLC
6210 Busch Blvd (43229-1804)
PHONE..................................614 207-1805
EMP: 53
SALES (corp-wide): 25.64MM **Privately Held**
Web: www.ohioequities.com
SIC: 8742 Real estate consultant
PA: Ohio Equities, Llc
605 S Front St Ste 200
Columbus OH 43215
614 224-2400

(G-6419)
OHIO EQUITIES LLC
Also Called: Nai Ohio Equities, Realtors
17 S High St Ste 799 (43215-3450)
PHONE..................................614 469-0058
Lynne Raduege, *Mgr*
EMP: 53
SALES (corp-wide): 25.64MM **Privately Held**
Web: www.ohioequities.com
SIC: 6531 Real estate agent, commercial
PA: Ohio Equities, Llc
605 S Front St Ste 200
Columbus OH 43215
614 224-2400

(G-6420)
OHIO EQUITIES LLC (PA)
Also Called: Nai Ohio Equities
605 S Front St Ste 200 (43215-5777)
PHONE..................................614 224-2400
EMP: 60 **EST:** 1968
SALES (est): 25.64MM
SALES (corp-wide): 25.64MM **Privately Held**
Web: www.ohioequities.com
SIC: 6512 6531 Commercial and industrial building operation; Real estate brokers and agents

(G-6421)
OHIO FARM BUR FEDERATION INC (PA)
Also Called: Our Ohio Communications
280 N High St Fl 6 (43215-2594)
P.O. Box 182383 (43218-2383)
PHONE..................................614 249-2400
Frank Burkett, *Pr*
Steve Hirsch, *
John Fisher, *
Irene Messmer, *
Adam Sharp, *
EMP: 55 **EST:** 1919
SQ FT: 12,700
SALES (est): 1.47MM
SALES (corp-wide): 1.47MM **Privately Held**
Web: www.ofbf.org
SIC: 8699 Farm bureau

(G-6422)
OHIO FUNDATION OF IND COLLEGES
Also Called: O F I C
250 E Broad St Ste 1700 (43215-3722)
PHONE..................................614 469-1950
Jeffrey S Wolf, *Pr*
EMP: 39 **EST:** 1950
SQ FT: 4,400
SALES (est): 4.17MM **Privately Held**
Web: www.ofic.org
SIC: 7389 Fund raising organizations

(G-6423)
OHIO GSTROENTEROLOGY GROUP INC
85 Mcnaughten Rd Ste 320 (43213-5111)
PHONE..................................614 754-5500
Edward Brand, *Prin*
EMP: 29
Web: www.ohiogastro.com
SIC: 8011 Gastronomist
PA: Ohio Gastroenterology Group, Inc.
3400 Olentangy River Rd
Columbus OH 43202

(G-6424)
OHIO GSTROENTEROLOGY GROUP INC (PA)
3400 Olentangy River Rd (43202-1523)
PHONE..................................614 754-5500
Thomas Ransbottom, *Pr*
Christopher Masciola, *
EMP: 43 **EST:** 1995
SALES (est): 21.16MM **Privately Held**
Web: www.ohiogastro.com
SIC: 8011 Gastronomist

(G-6425)
OHIO HEALTH CENTER INC
1000 E Broad St Ste 101 (43205-1333)
PHONE..................................614 252-3636
EMP: 28 **EST:** 1993
SQ FT: 15,042
SALES (est): 6.75MM **Privately Held**
Web: www.ohiohealthcenter.net
SIC: 8011 General and family practice, physician/surgeon

(G-6426)
OHIO HEALTH GROUP LLC
3430 Ohio Health Pkwy (43202-1575)
PHONE..................................614 566-0010
EMP: 34 **EST:** 1995
SALES (est): 16.24MM **Privately Held**
Web: www.themgo.com
SIC: 8011 Medical insurance associations

(G-6427)
OHIO HISTORIC PRESERVATION OFF
1982 Velma Ave (43211-2453)
PHONE..................................614 298-2000
EMP: 47 **EST:** 1950
SALES (est): 348.43K **Privately Held**
Web: www.ohiohistory.org
SIC: 8412 Museum

(G-6428)
OHIO HISTORICAL SOCIETY (PA)
Also Called: OHIO HISTORY CONNECTION
800 E 17th Ave (43211-2497)
PHONE..................................614 297-2300
Lox Logan, *Prin*
Glenda S Greenwood, *
Ronald J Ungvarsky, *
Richard C Simpson, *
Thomas W Johnson, *
EMP: 200 **EST:** 1900
SQ FT: 50,000
SALES (est): 29.62MM
SALES (corp-wide): 29.62MM **Privately Held**
Web: www.ohiohistory.org
SIC: 8412 Museum

(G-6429)
OHIO HOSP FOR PSYCHIATRY LLC
Also Called: Ohio Hospital For Psychiatry
880 Greenlawn Ave (43223-2616)
PHONE..................................614 449-9664
Emily Stroup, *CEO*
EMP: 50 **EST:** 2005
SALES (est): 27.64MM **Publicly Held**

GEOGRAPHIC SECTION
Columbus - Franklin County (G-6451)

Web: www.ohiohospitalforpsychiatry.com
SIC: 8093 Mental health clinic, outpatient
PA: Acadia Healthcare Company, Inc.
6100 Tower Cir Ste 1000
Franklin TN 37067

(G-6430)
OHIO HOSPITAL ASSOCIATION
65 E State St Ste 500 (43215-4227)
PHONE.................................614 221-7614
James R Castle, *Pr*
Mike Abrams, *
Ryan Biles, *
EMP: 62 EST: 1935
SQ FT: 9,000
SALES (est): 16.57MM **Privately Held**
Web: www.ohiohospitals.org
SIC: 8611 Trade associations

(G-6431)
OHIO LIVING
Also Called: Westminster Thurber Community
717 Neil Ave (43215-1609)
PHONE.................................614 228-8888
EMP: 152
Web: www.ohioliving.org
SIC: 8049 Acupuncturist
PA: Ohio Living
9200 Worthington Rd # 300
Westerville OH 43082

(G-6432)
OHIO LIVING COMMUNITIES
Also Called: Ohio Lving Wstmeinster-Thurber
717 Neil Ave (43215-1609)
PHONE.................................614 888-7800
Laurence C Gumina, *Prin*
Donald Edwards, *
Sandra Adam, *
James Joyce, *
Terry White, *
EMP: 80 EST: 1959
SALES (est): 1.93MM **Privately Held**
Web: www.ohioliving.org
SIC: 8051 Skilled nursing care facilities

(G-6433)
OHIO LIVING HOLDINGS
Also Called: Ohio Lving Hspice Grter Clmbus
2740 Airport Dr Ste 140 (43219-2296)
PHONE.................................614 433-0031
Laurence C Gumina, *CEO*
Kevin Futryk, *
Paul Flannery, *
Barbara Sears, *
Raafat Zaki, *
EMP: 99 EST: 2010
SALES (est): 1.12MM **Privately Held**
Web: www.ohioliving.org
SIC: 8051 Skilled nursing care facilities

(G-6434)
OHIO LIVING HOLDINGS
Also Called: Ohio Lving HM Hlth Grter Clmbu
2740 Airport Dr Ste 140 (43219-2296)
PHONE.................................614 433-0031
Laurence C Gumina, *CEO*
Kevin Futryk, *Bd of Dir*
Paul Flannery, *Bd of Dir*
Barbara Sears, *Bd of Dir*
Raafat Zaki, *Bd of Dir*
EMP: 65 EST: 2017
SALES (est): 42.93MM **Privately Held**
Web: www.ohioliving.org
SIC: 8052 Personal care facility

(G-6435)
OHIO MACHINERY CO
Ohio Cat
5252 Walcutt Ct (43228-9641)
PHONE.................................614 878-2287
Kenneth E Taylor, *Brnch Mgr*
EMP: 300
SALES (corp-wide): 185.86MM **Privately Held**
Web: www.ohiocat.com
SIC: 5082 General construction machinery and equipment
PA: Ohio Machinery Co.
3993 E Royalton Rd
Broadview Heights OH 44147
440 526-6200

(G-6436)
OHIO MACHINERY CO
Also Called: Caterpillar
5232 Walcutt Ct (43228-9641)
P.O. Box 28525 (43228-0525)
PHONE.................................614 878-2287
Rick Hensel, *Mgr*
EMP: 28
SALES (corp-wide): 185.86MM **Privately Held**
Web: www.ohiocat.com
SIC: 7538 5082 Truck engine repair, except industrial; Construction and mining machinery
PA: Ohio Machinery Co.
3993 E Royalton Rd
Broadview Heights OH 44147
440 526-6200

(G-6437)
OHIO MEDICAL TRNSP INC (PA)
Also Called: MEDFLIGHT OF OHIO
2827 W Dublin Granville Rd (43235-2712)
PHONE.................................614 791-4400
EMP: 80 EST: 1995
SALES (est): 53.57MM **Privately Held**
Web: www.medflight.com
SIC: 4522 4119 Ambulance services, air; Ambulance service

(G-6438)
OHIO ORTHPD SURGERY INST LLC
4605 Sawmill Rd (43220-2246)
PHONE.................................614 827-8777
EMP: 30 EST: 2002
SALES (est): 3.86MM **Privately Held**
Web: www.orthopedicone.com
SIC: 8011 Orthopedic physician

(G-6439)
OHIO POWER COMPANY (HQ)
Also Called: AEP
1 Riverside Plz (43215-2355)
PHONE.................................614 716-1000
Nicholas K Akins, *Ch Bd*
Brian X Tierney, *
Joseph M Buonaiuto, *CAO*
EMP: 221 EST: 1907
SALES (est): 3.81B
SALES (corp-wide): 18.98B **Privately Held**
Web: www.aepohio.com
SIC: 4911 Electric services
PA: American Electric Power Company, Inc.
1 Riverside Plz Fl 1 # 1
Columbus OH 43215
614 716-1000

(G-6440)
OHIO PUB EMPLYEES RTREMENT SYS
Also Called: EXECUTIVE OFFICE
277 E Town St (43215-4627)
PHONE.................................614 228-8471
Cinthia Sledz, *Ch*
Karen Carraher, *Ex Dir*
Sharon Downs, *Prin*
Blake W Sherry, *COO*
Jenny Starr, *CFO*
EMP: 468 EST: 1935
SQ FT: 145,404
SALES (est): 181.94K **Privately Held**
Web: www.opers.org
SIC: 6371 9441 Pension funds; Administration of social and manpower programs
HQ: Executive Office State Of Ohio
77 S High St Fl 30
Columbus OH 43215

(G-6441)
OHIO REPRODUCTIVE MEDICINE
535 Reach Blvd # 200 (43215-3692)
PHONE.................................614 451-2280
Grant E Schmidt, *Pr*
EMP: 35 EST: 1987
SALES (est): 9.97MM **Privately Held**
Web: www.ohioreproductivemedicine.com
SIC: 8011 Gynecologist

(G-6442)
OHIO RESTAURANT ASSOCIATION
100 E Campus View Blvd Ste 150 (43235-4647)
PHONE.................................614 442-3535
Geoffrey Hetrick, *Pr*
EMP: 34 EST: 1920
SQ FT: 8,880
SALES (est): 2.26MM **Privately Held**
Web: www.ohiorestaurant.org
SIC: 8611 Trade associations

(G-6443)
OHIO SCHOOL BOARDS ASSOCIATION
8050 N High St Ste 100 (43235-6481)
PHONE.................................614 540-4000
Robert M Heard Senior, *Pr*
Rick Lewis, *
▲ EMP: 48 EST: 1955
SALES (est): 29.33K **Privately Held**
Web: www.ohioschoolboards.org
SIC: 8699 Animal humane society

(G-6444)
OHIO SERS
300 E Broad St Ste 100 (43215-3747)
PHONE.................................614 222-5853
James Rossler Junior, *Ch*
EMP: 47 EST: 2011
SALES (est): 9.33MM **Privately Held**
Web: www.ohsers.org
SIC: 6411 Pension and retirement plan consultants

(G-6445)
OHIO SOC OF CRTIF PUB ACCNTNTS
Also Called: Ohio Soceity of Cpas
4249 Easton Way Ste 150 (43219-6163)
PHONE.................................614 764-2727
TOLL FREE: 800
Scott Wiley, *Pr*
Boyd Search, *
Laura Hay, *
EMP: 53 EST: 1903
SQ FT: 13,500
SALES (est): 415.26K **Privately Held**
Web: www.ohiocpa.com
SIC: 8621 Accounting association

(G-6446)
OHIO STATE BAR ASSOCIATION
1700 Lake Shore Dr (43204-4895)
P.O. Box 16562 (43216-6562)
PHONE.................................614 487-2050
EMP: 55 EST: 1984
SALES (est): 8.73MM **Privately Held**
Web: www.ohiobar.org
SIC: 8621 Bar association

(G-6447)
OHIO STATE MEDICAL ASSOCIATION (PA)
Also Called: OSMA
4400 N High St Ste 402 (43214-2635)
PHONE.................................614 527-6762
Richard R Ellison, *Pr*
Brent Mulgrew, *
EMP: 54 EST: 1904
SALES (est): 2.69MM
SALES (corp-wide): 2.69MM **Privately Held**
Web: www.osma.org
SIC: 8621 Medical field-related associations

(G-6448)
OHIO STATE UNIV ALUMNI ASSN
Also Called: ALUMNI ASSOCIATION, THE
2200 Olentangy River Rd (43210-1035)
PHONE.................................614 292-2200
Archie Griffin, *Pr*
EMP: 98 EST: 1910
SQ FT: 9,600
SALES (est): 16.44MM **Privately Held**
Web: www.ohiostatealumni.org
SIC: 8641 8661 Alumni association; Religious organizations

(G-6449)
OHIO STATE UNIV PHYSICIANS INC (HQ)
700 Ackerman Rd Ste 600 (43202-1559)
PHONE.................................614 947-3700
Doug Rund, *Pr*
Pam Edson, *
EMP: 50 EST: 1996
SALES (est): 606.82MM
SALES (corp-wide): 8.24B **Privately Held**
Web: www.osuphysicians.com
SIC: 8011 Clinic, operated by physicians
PA: The Ohio State University
281 W Ln Ave
Columbus OH 43210
614 292-6446

(G-6450)
OHIO STATE UNIV WEXNER MED CTR
Also Called: Division Gstrntrlogy Hptlogy N
410 W 10th Ave (43210-1240)
PHONE.................................614 293-6255
EMP: 142
SALES (corp-wide): 8.24B **Privately Held**
Web: wexnermedical.osu.edu
SIC: 8011 8221 Cardiologist and cardio-vascular specialist; University
HQ: The Ohio State University Wexner Medical Center
410 W 10th Ave
Columbus OH 43210
614 293-8000

(G-6451)
OHIO STATE UNIV WEXNER MED CTR (HQ)
410 W 10th Ave (43210-1240)
PHONE.................................614 293-8000
Michael V Drake, *Pr*
Vincent Tammaro, *
EMP: 1000 EST: 1910
SALES (est): 4.44B
SALES (corp-wide): 8.24B **Privately Held**
Web: wexnermedical.osu.edu
SIC: 8062 General medical and surgical hospitals
PA: The Ohio State University
281 W Ln Ave
Columbus OH 43210
614 292-6446

Columbus - Franklin County (G-6452)

(G-6452)
OHIO STATE UNIV WEXNER MED CTR
320 W 10th Ave (43210-1280)
PHONE..................................614 293-7521
Leona Ayers, *Brnch Mgr*
EMP: 142
SALES (corp-wide): 8.24B **Privately Held**
Web: wexnermedical.osu.edu
SIC: 8221 8011 University; Offices and clinics of medical doctors
HQ: The Ohio State University Wexner Medical Center
410 W 10th Ave
Columbus OH 43210
614 293-8000

(G-6453)
OHIO STATE UNIVERSITY
University Hospitals East
181 Taylor Ave (43203-1779)
PHONE..................................614 257-3000
Thoma Spackman, *Brnch Mgr*
EMP: 111
SALES (corp-wide): 8.24B **Privately Held**
Web: wexnermedical.osu.edu
SIC: 8062 8093 8049 8011 General medical and surgical hospitals; Rehabilitation center, outpatient treatment; Physical therapist; Oncologist
PA: The Ohio State University
281 W Ln Ave
Columbus OH 43210
614 292-6446

(G-6454)
OHIO STATE UNIVERSITY
Also Called: Wosu Public Media
1800 N Pearl St (43201-4533)
PHONE..................................614 292-9678
Tom Rieland, *Genl Mgr*
EMP: 63
SALES (corp-wide): 8.24B **Privately Held**
Web: www.wosu.org
SIC: 4832 4833 Radio broadcasting stations; Television translator station
PA: The Ohio State University
281 W Ln Ave
Columbus OH 43210
614 292-6446

(G-6455)
OHIO STATE UNIVERSITY
Also Called: Ohio State Univ Vtrnarian Hosp
601 Vernon L Tharp St (43210-4007)
PHONE..................................614 292-6661
Doctor Richard M Bednarski, *Dir*
EMP: 28
SALES (corp-wide): 8.24B **Privately Held**
Web: vet.osu.edu
SIC: 0742 8221 Animal hospital services, pets and other animal specialties; University
PA: The Ohio State University
281 W Ln Ave
Columbus OH 43210
614 292-6446

(G-6456)
OHIO STATE UNIVERSITY
Also Called: Medical Center
1375 Perry St (43201-3177)
PHONE..................................614 293-3860
Phil Skinner, *Tax Director*
EMP: 100
SALES (corp-wide): 8.24B **Privately Held**
Web: www.osu.edu
SIC: 8011 8221 Medical centers; University
PA: The Ohio State University
281 W Ln Ave
Columbus OH 43210
614 292-6446

(G-6457)
OHIO STATE UNIVERSITY
Also Called: Student Computer Center
1224 Kinnear Rd (43212-1154)
PHONE..................................614 292-3416
Stanley C Ahalt, *Dir*
EMP: 100
SALES (corp-wide): 8.24B **Privately Held**
Web: www.osu.edu
SIC: 7374 8221 Computer time-sharing; Colleges and universities
PA: The Ohio State University
281 W Ln Ave
Columbus OH 43210
614 292-6446

(G-6458)
OHIO STATE UNIVERSITY
Also Called: Environmental Health & Safety
1314 Kinnear Rd (43212-1156)
PHONE..................................614 292-1284
Cecil Smith, *Mgr*
EMP: 35
SALES (corp-wide): 8.24B **Privately Held**
Web: www.osu.edu
SIC: 8748 8221 Environmental consultant; University
PA: The Ohio State University
281 W Ln Ave
Columbus OH 43210
614 292-6446

(G-6459)
OHIO STATE UNIVERSITY
Also Called: Department Dvelopment-Research
1480 W Lane Ave Rm 255 (43221-3919)
PHONE..................................614 688-0857
Lisa Miller, *Dir*
EMP: 149
SALES (corp-wide): 8.24B **Privately Held**
Web: www.osu.edu
SIC: 8733 8221 Research institute; University
PA: The Ohio State University
281 W Ln Ave
Columbus OH 43210
614 292-6446

(G-6460)
OHIO SUPPORT SERVICES CORP (PA)
1291 S High St (43206-3445)
PHONE..................................614 443-0291
Scott Tucker, *Pr*
John W Tucker, *
EMP: 36 **EST:** 1978
SQ FT: 7,000
SALES (est): 10.08MM
SALES (corp-wide): 10.08MM **Privately Held**
Web: www.ohiosupport.com
SIC: 7381 Security guard service

(G-6461)
OHIO SURGERY CENTER LTD
Also Called: Ohio Surgery Center
930 Bethel Rd (43214-1906)
PHONE..................................614 451-0500
Jeffrey Hiltbrand, *Pt*
EMP: 60 **EST:** 1998
SQ FT: 17,000
SALES (est): 8.91MM **Privately Held**
Web: www.ohiosurgerycenter.com
SIC: 8011 Surgeon

(G-6462)
OHIO TCTCAL ENFRCMENT SVCS LLC
6100 Channingway Blvd Ste 4 (43232-2910)
PHONE..................................614 989-9485
Jessica Walters, *Managing Member*
EMP: 53 **EST:** 2006
SQ FT: 800
SALES (est): 1.66MM **Privately Held**
Web: www.otesllc.com
SIC: 7381 7382 Guard services; Security systems services

(G-6463)
OHIO TRANSMISSION LLC (PA)
Also Called: Otp Industrial Solutions
1900 Jetway Blvd (43219-1681)
PHONE..................................614 342-6247
David Scheer, *CEO*
Kurt Lang, *
Matt Piatt, *
◆ **EMP:** 110 **EST:** 1963
SQ FT: 40,000
SALES (est): 1.04B
SALES (corp-wide): 1.04B **Privately Held**
Web: www.otcindustrial.com
SIC: 5085 5084 Power transmission equipment and apparatus; Materials handling machinery

(G-6464)
OHIO-T-HOME HLTH CARE AGCY LTD
875 N High St Ste 300 (43215-1429)
P.O. Box 12309 (43212-0309)
PHONE..................................614 947-0791
EMP: 80 **EST:** 2011
SALES (est): 4.9MM **Privately Held**
Web: www.ohioathome.com
SIC: 8082 8049 7389 Visiting nurse service; Nurses and other medical assistants; Business Activities at Non-Commercial Site

(G-6465)
OHIOHEALTH CORPORATION (PA)
3430 Ohio Health Pkwy 5th Fl (43202)
PHONE..................................614 788-8860
David Blom, *Pr*
Michael W Louge, *
Robert P Millen, *
Donna Hanly, *
Michael S Bernstein, *
EMP: 1500 **EST:** 1891
SALES (est): 4.29B
SALES (corp-wide): 4.29B **Privately Held**
Web: www.ohiohealth.com
SIC: 8062 8082 8051 General medical and surgical hospitals; Home health care services; Convalescent home with continuous nursing care

(G-6466)
OHIOHEALTH CORPORATION
Also Called: Distrubution Center
2601 Silver Dr (43211-1056)
PHONE..................................614 566-5977
Thomas Sherrin, *Dir*
EMP: 60
SALES (corp-wide): 4.29B **Privately Held**
Web: www.ohiohealth.com
SIC: 8062 General medical and surgical hospitals
PA: Ohiohealth Corporation
3430 Ohhalth Pkwy 5th Flr
Columbus OH 43202
614 788-8860

(G-6467)
OHIOHEALTH GROUP LTD
445 Hutchinson Ave (43235-5677)
PHONE..................................614 566-0056
EMP: 27 **EST:** 1995
SALES (est): 1.87MM **Privately Held**
Web: www.themgo.com

SIC: 8062 General medical and surgical hospitals

(G-6468)
OHIOHLTH RVERSIDE METHDST HOSP
Also Called: Riverside Methodist Hospital
3535 Olentangy River Rd (43214-3908)
PHONE..................................614 566-5000
Brian D Jepson, *Pr*
Steve Markovitch, *
EMP: 944 **EST:** 1884
SQ FT: 327,886
SALES (est): 179.97MM **Privately Held**
Web: www.ohiohealth.com
SIC: 8062 General medical and surgical hospitals

(G-6469)
OLD REPUBLIC NAT TITLE INSUR
Also Called: Old Republic
141 E Town St Ste 100 (43215-5142)
PHONE..................................614 341-1900
Pat Connor, *Mgr*
EMP: 30
SALES (corp-wide): 8.08B **Publicly Held**
Web: www.oldrepublictitle.com
SIC: 6361 6411 Real estate title insurance; Insurance agents, brokers, and service
HQ: Old Republic National Title Insurance Company
3000 Bayport Dr Ste 1000
Tampa FL 33607
800 328-4441

(G-6470)
OLD TIME POTTERY LLC
2200 Morse Rd (43229-5821)
PHONE..................................614 337-1258
EMP: 55
SALES (corp-wide): 892.49MM **Privately Held**
Web: www.oldtimepottery.com
SIC: 5999 5023 Art, picture frames, and decorations; Homefurnishings
HQ: Old Time Pottery, Llc
480 River Rock Blvd
Murfreesboro TN 37128
615 890-6060

(G-6471)
OLOGIE INC
447 E Main St Ste 122 (43215-5661)
PHONE..................................614 221-1107
Beverly Ryan, *CEO*
Beverly Ryan, *Managing Member*
EMP: 78 **EST:** 1987
SALES (est): 13.44MM **Privately Held**
Web: www.ologie.com
SIC: 8742 Marketing consulting services

(G-6472)
OPEN ARMS HEALTH SYSTEMS LLC
868 Freeway Dr N (43229-5420)
PHONE..................................614 385-8354
Christopher Allison, *CEO*
EMP: 100 **EST:** 2011
SALES (est): 9.24MM **Privately Held**
Web: www.oaohio.com
SIC: 8082 Home health care services

(G-6473)
OPHTHLMIC SRGONS CONS OHIO INC
262 Neil Ave Ste 430 (43215-7312)
PHONE..................................614 221-7464
John Burns, *Pr*
David M Lehmann, *
Alice Epitropoulos, *
Doctor N Douglas Baker, *Treas*

GEOGRAPHIC SECTION
Columbus - Franklin County (G-6496)

Doctor Kenneth Cahill, *Sec*
EMP: 49 **EST:** 1969
SQ FT: 14,000
SALES (est): 2.13MM **Privately Held**
Web: www.ohioeyesurgeons.com
SIC: 8011 Opthalmologist

(G-6474)
OPPORTUNITIES FOR OHIOANS (DH)
150 E Campus View Blvd Ste 150
(43235-6608)
PHONE...............................614 438-1200
Kevin Miller, *Ex Dir*
Brenda Cronin, *Chief of Staff**
Erik Williamson, *OF DDD**
Susan Pugh, *OF VR**
Mindy Duncan, *OF BSVI**
EMP: 31 **EST:** 1970
SALES (est): 27.5MM **Privately Held**
Web: ood.ohio.gov
SIC: 8322 Social services for the handicapped
HQ: Executive Office State Of Ohio
77 S High St Fl 30
Columbus OH 43215

(G-6475)
OPTIONS HOME SERVICES LLC
786 Northwest Blvd (43212-3832)
PHONE...............................614 203-6340
Jessica Masternick, *Prin*
EMP: 27 **EST:** 2016
SALES (est): 2.53MM **Privately Held**
Web: www.optionshomeservices.com
SIC: 8082 Home health care services

(G-6476)
ORACLE ELEVATOR COMPANY
Also Called: Oracle Elevator Company
771 Dearborn Park Ln (43085-5720)
PHONE...............................614 781-9731
Paul Belliveau, *Brnch Mgr*
EMP: 29
Web: www.elevatedfacilityservices.com
SIC: 5084 Elevators
PA: Oracle Elevator Holdco, Inc.
8800 Grand Oak Cir # 550
Tampa FL 33617

(G-6477)
ORANGE BARREL MEDIA LLC
250 N Hartford Ave (43222-1100)
PHONE...............................614 294-4898
Pete Scantland, *CEO*
Adam Borchers, ***
EMP: 75 **EST:** 2004
SALES (est): 12.72MM **Privately Held**
Web: www.obm.com
SIC: 3993 7312 Signs and advertising specialties; Outdoor advertising services

(G-6478)
ORCHARD HILTZ & MCCLIMENT INC
580 N 4th St Ste 610 (43215-2157)
PHONE...............................614 418-0600
Gerry Bird, *Ch*
EMP: 44
SALES (corp-wide): 36.76MM **Privately Held**
Web: www.ohm-advisors.com
SIC: 8712 Architectural engineering
PA: Orchard, Hiltz & Mccliment, Inc.
34000 Plymouth Rd
Livonia MI 48150
734 522-6711

(G-6479)
ORDER OF UNTD COML TRVLERS OF (PA)
Also Called: Fraternal Insurance
1801 Watermark Dr Ste 100 (43215-7088)
P.O. Box 159019 (43215-8619)
PHONE...............................614 487-9680
Ron Hunt, *CEO*
Martha Tate Horn, ***
Ron Ives, ***
EMP: 58 **EST:** 1888
SQ FT: 33,000
SALES (est): 16.25MM
SALES (corp-wide): 16.25MM **Privately Held**
Web: www.uct.org
SIC: 6411 Insurance agents, brokers, and service

(G-6480)
ORTHOPEDIC ONE INC
4605 Sawmill Rd (43220-2246)
PHONE...............................614 827-8700
Tom Ellis, *Pr*
EMP: 90
Web: www.orthopedicone.com
SIC: 8011 Orthopedic physician
PA: Orthopedic One, Inc.
170 Taylor Station Rd # 260
Columbus OH 43213

(G-6481)
ORTHOPEDIC ONE INC (PA)
Also Called: Cardinal Orthopaedic Institute
170 Taylor Station Rd (43213-4491)
PHONE...............................614 545-7900
EMP: 28 **EST:** 2003
SALES (est): 38.63MM **Privately Held**
Web: www.orthopedicone.com
SIC: 8011 Orthopedic physician

(G-6482)
ORVEON GLOBAL US LLC
Also Called: Bareminerals
343 N Front St (43215-2266)
PHONE...............................614 348-4994
Lori Jones, *Mgr*
EMP: 273
SALES (corp-wide): 128.12MM **Privately Held**
Web: www.bareminerals.com
SIC: 5122 Cosmetics
PA: Orveon Global Us Llc
579 5th Ave Fl 9
New York NY 10017
332 251-0604

(G-6483)
OSU HARDING HOSPITAL
Also Called: Harding Hospital
1670 Upham Dr (43210-1250)
PHONE...............................614 293-9600
Radu Saveanu, *CEO*
Radu Saveanu, *Prin*
EMP: 33008 **EST:** 1916
SALES (est): 23.54MM
SALES (corp-wide): 8.24B **Privately Held**
Web: wexnermedical.osu.edu
SIC: 8063 8361 8093 Psychiatric hospitals; Residential care; Specialty outpatient clinics, nec
HQ: The Ohio State University Wexner Medical Center
410 W 10th Ave
Columbus OH 43210

(G-6484)
OSU INTERNAL MEDICINE LLC
Also Called: Ohio State Outpatient Care E
543 Taylor Ave (43203-1278)
PHONE...............................614 688-6400
EMP: 62
SALES (corp-wide): 474.46K **Privately Held**
SIC: 8011 Offices and clinics of medical doctors
PA: Osu Internal Medicine Llc
3760 Ridge Mill Dr
Hilliard OH 43026
614 293-2494

(G-6485)
OSU NEPHROLOGY MEDICAL CTR
410 W 10th Ave (43210-1240)
PHONE...............................614 293-8300
Brad Rovin, *Dir*
EMP: 899 **EST:** 1939
SALES (est): 3.78MM **Privately Held**
Web: wexnermedical.osu.edu
SIC: 8062 8299 General medical and surgical hospitals; Educational services

(G-6486)
OSU SPT MDCINE PHYSCIANS INC
2835 Fred Taylor Dr (43202-1552)
PHONE...............................614 293-3600
Chris Kaeding, *Dir*
EMP: 29 **EST:** 1994
SALES (est): 515.72K **Privately Held**
Web: www.osuphysicians.com
SIC: 8011 Orthopedic physician

(G-6487)
OSU SURGERY LLC (PA)
700 Ackerman Rd Ste 350 (43202-1583)
PHONE...............................614 261-1141
Chris Kaiser, ***
EMP: 150 **EST:** 1986
SQ FT: 6,700
SALES (est): 8.29MM
SALES (corp-wide): 8.29MM **Privately Held**
SIC: 8011 Surgeon

(G-6488)
OTHERWORLD INC
5819 Chantry Dr (43232-4764)
PHONE...............................614 868-3631
EMP: 32 **EST:** 2019
SALES (est): 3.04MM **Privately Held**
Web: www.otherworld.com
SIC: 7929 Entertainers and entertainment groups

(G-6489)
OTIS ELEVATOR COMPANY
777 Dearborn Park Ln Ste L (43085-5716)
PHONE...............................614 777-6500
Tim Collins, *Mgr*
EMP: 114
SALES (corp-wide): 14.21B **Publicly Held**
Web: www.otis.com
SIC: 5084 7699 Elevators; Elevators: inspection, service, and repair
HQ: Otis Elevator Company
1 Carrier Pl
Farmington CT 06032
860 674-3000

(G-6490)
OTP HOLDING LLC (HQ)
Also Called: Advanced Industrial Products
1900 Jetway Blvd (43219-1681)
PHONE...............................614 342-6123
Rob Webb, *Managing Member*
EMP: 27 **EST:** 2014
SALES (est): 20.65MM
SALES (corp-wide): 1.04B **Privately Held**
Web: www.otcindustrial.com
SIC: 5085 Industrial fittings
PA: Ohio Transmission Llc
1900 Jetway Blvd
Columbus OH 43219
614 342-6247

(G-6491)
OUR LADY BETHLEHEM SCHOOLS INC
4567 Olentangy River Rd (43214-2499)
PHONE...............................614 459-8285
Marilyn Dono, *Prin*
EMP: 34 **EST:** 1959
SALES (est): 998.93K **Privately Held**
Web: www.ourladyofbethlehem.org
SIC: 8211 8661 8351 Catholic elementary and secondary schools; Catholic Church; Child day care services

(G-6492)
OUR TOWN STUDIOS INC
781 Northwest Blvd (43212-3858)
P.O. Box 163245 (43216-3245)
PHONE...............................614 832-2121
David Robins, *Pr*
David Robins, *Prin*
EMP: 50 **EST:** 2016
SALES (est): 839.77K **Privately Held**
SIC: 8322 Social services for the handicapped

(G-6493)
OUTLET BROADCASTING INC
Also Called: NBC 4
3165 Olentangy River Rd (43202-1518)
PHONE...............................614 263-4444
Douglas Gealy, *Prin*
EMP: 177 **EST:** 1925
SALES (est): 8.87MM **Privately Held**
Web: www.nbc4i.com
SIC: 4833 Television broadcasting stations

(G-6494)
OVERMYER HALL ASSOCIATES
1600 W Lane Ave Ste 200 (43221-3979)
PHONE...............................614 453-4400
Gregory Overmyer, *CEO*
EMP: 47 **EST:** 2012
SALES (est): 13.29MM **Privately Held**
Web: www.oh-ins.com
SIC: 6411 Insurance brokers, nec
HQ: Hub International Limited
150 N Riverside Plz Fl 17
Chicago IL 60606

(G-6495)
P C VPA
Also Called: Visiting Physicians Assn
355 E Campus View Blvd Ste 180 (43235-5616)
PHONE...............................614 840-1688
Beth Pack, *Mgr*
EMP: 30
Web: www.harmonycaresmedicalgroup.com
SIC: 8011 8071 Geriatric specialist, physician/surgeon; Medical laboratories
PA: P C Vpa
500 Kirts Blvd
Troy MI 48084

(G-6496)
PACTIV LLC
2120 Westbelt Dr (43228-3820)
P.O. Box 28147 (43228-0147)
PHONE...............................614 771-5400
Joe Deal, *Opers Mgr*
EMP: 73
Web: www.pactivevergreen.com
SIC: 2631 7389 Paperboard mills; Packaging and labeling services
HQ: Pactiv Llc
1900 W Field Ct
Lake Forest IL 60045
847 482-2000

Columbus - Franklin County (G-6497) — GEOGRAPHIC SECTION

(G-6497)
PANACEA PRODUCTS CORPORATION (PA)
Also Called: J-Mak Industries
2711 International St (43228)
PHONE.................................614 850-7000
Frank A Paniccia, *Pr*
Gregg Paniccia, *
Jim Fancelli, *
Fred Pagura, *
Louis Calderone, *
◆ **EMP:** 40 **EST:** 1967
SALES (est): 49.68MM
SALES (corp-wide): 49.68MM **Privately Held**
Web: www.panaceaproducts.com
SIC: 5051 2542 3496 Metals service centers and offices; Partitions and fixtures, except wood; Miscellaneous fabricated wire products

(G-6498)
PARK & SPRUCE ACQUISITIONS LLC
150 E Broad St (43215-3610)
PHONE.................................614 227-6100
EMP: 60 **EST:** 2021
SALES (est): 2.52MM **Privately Held**
SIC: 7011 Hotels and motels

(G-6499)
PARK PLACE OPERATIONS INC
333 S Front St (43215-5005)
P.O. Box 1353 (43216-1353)
PHONE.................................614 224-3827
Tim Chavez, *Mgr*
EMP: 87
SALES (corp-wide): 51.29MM **Privately Held**
Web: www.parkplaceparking.com
SIC: 7521 Parking lots
PA: Park Place Operations, Inc.
250 W Court St Ste 200e
Cincinnati OH 45202
513 241-0415

(G-6500)
PARKER-HANNIFIN CORPORATION
Also Called: Tube Fittings Division
3885 Gateway Blvd (43228-9723)
PHONE.................................614 279-7070
William Bowman, *Brnch Mgr*
EMP: 120
SALES (corp-wide): 19.07B **Publicly Held**
Web: www.parker.com
SIC: 3494 5074 Pipe fittings; Plumbing fittings and supplies
PA: Parker-Hannifin Corporation
6035 Parkland Blvd
Cleveland OH 44124
216 896-3000

(G-6501)
PARKING SOLUTIONS INC (DH)
Also Called: Parking Sltions For Healthcare
353 W Nationwide Blvd (43215-2311)
PHONE.................................614 469-7000
Aaron D Shocket, *Pr*
EMP: 600 **EST:** 1991
SALES (est): 26.89MM
SALES (corp-wide): 712.86MM **Privately Held**
Web: www.parkingsolutionsinc.com
SIC: 7299 Valet parking
HQ: Towne Park, Llc
555 E North Ln Ste 5020
Conshohocken PA 19428

(G-6502)
PARMAN GROUP INC (PA)
4501 Hilton Corporate Dr (43232-4154)
P.O. Box 360687 (43236-0687)
PHONE.................................513 673-0077
Jamie L Parman, *Pr*
EMP: 35 **EST:** 1992
SQ FT: 22,000
SALES (est): 2.25MM **Privately Held**
Web: www.parman.com
SIC: 8742 Compensation and benefits planning consultant

(G-6503)
PATHWAYS FINANCIAL CR UN INC (PA)
5665 N Hamilton Rd (43230-8326)
PHONE.................................614 416-7588
Jack Radich, *Ch*
Greg Kidwell, *Pr*
Spencer Barton, *Sec*
Mark Lamonte, *Treas*
Deanna Barzak, *Ofcr*
EMP: 85 **EST:** 1973
SALES (est): 30.71MM
SALES (corp-wide): 30.71MM **Privately Held**
Web: www.pathwayscu.com
SIC: 6061 Federal credit unions

(G-6504)
PATRIOT PROTECTION SVCS LLC
433 Industry Dr (43204-6234)
PHONE.................................614 379-1333
Timothy Martin, *Pr*
Rose Likens, *
Timothy Martin, *Mgr*
EMP: 100 **EST:** 2019
SALES (est): 1.29MM **Privately Held**
Web: www.patriotprotectionservices.com
SIC: 7381 Security guard service

(G-6505)
PAUL PETERSON SAFETY DIV INC
950 Dublin Rd (43215-1169)
P.O. Box 1510 (43216-1510)
PHONE.................................614 486-4375
Paul Peterson Junior, *Pr*
Parr Peterson, *
Gary Boylan, *
Colette Peterson, *
EMP: 34 **EST:** 1975
SQ FT: 3,800
SALES (est): 995.53K
SALES (corp-wide): 13.29MM **Privately Held**
SIC: 3993 7359 5999 Signs, not made in custom sign painting shops; Work zone traffic equipment (flags, cones, barrels, etc.) ; Safety supplies and equipment
PA: The Paul Peterson Company
950 Dublin Rd
Columbus OH 43215
614 486-4375

(G-6506)
PEABODY LANDSCAPE CNSTR INC
Also Called: Peabody Landscape Group
2253 Dublin Rd (43228-9629)
PHONE.................................614 488-2877
David G Peabody, *Pr*
EMP: 64 **EST:** 1985
SQ FT: 2,000
SALES (est): 8.32MM **Privately Held**
Web: www.peabodylandscape.com
SIC: 0781 Landscape services

(G-6507)
PEARL INTERACTIVE NETWORK INC
1103 Schrock Rd Ste 109 (43229-1177)
PHONE.................................614 556-4470
Merry Korn, *CEO*
James Caldwell, *
EMP: 350 **EST:** 2006
SALES (est): 25.72MM **Privately Held**
Web: www.pinsourcing.com
SIC: 7371 7361 4813 Custom computer programming services; Employment agencies; Voice telephone communications

(G-6508)
PEDERSEN INSULATION COMPANY
2901 Johnstown Rd (43219-1719)
P.O. Box 30744 (43230-0744)
PHONE.................................614 471-3788
Gregory Pedersen, *Pr*
Valerie Pedersen, *
Jared Goodsite, *
EMP: 40 **EST:** 1963
SQ FT: 7,200
SALES (est): 2.61MM **Privately Held**
Web: www.pedersenco.net
SIC: 1742 1799 Insulation, buildings; Asbestos removal and encapsulation

(G-6509)
PEDIATRIC ADLSCENT MDICINE INC
5072 Reed Rd (43220-7536)
PHONE.................................614 326-1600
Patricia Francis, *Prin*
EMP: 27 **EST:** 2001
SALES (est): 1.86MM **Privately Held**
Web: www.pediatricandadolescentmedicine.net
SIC: 8011 Pediatrician

(G-6510)
PEDIATRIC ASSOCIATES INC (PA)
1021 Country Club Rd Unit A (43213-2479)
PHONE.................................614 501-7337
Malcolm Robbins, *Pr*
Malcolm Robbins Md, *Pr*
William Fernald Md, *Sec*
Sandra Boyle Md, *VP*
Anne Croft Md, *VP*
EMP: 39 **EST:** 1968
SQ FT: 3,000
SALES (est): 10.25MM
SALES (corp-wide): 10.25MM **Privately Held**
Web: www.kidzdoc.com
SIC: 8011 Pediatrician

(G-6511)
PEDIATRIC OPHTHLMLOGY ASSOC IN
555 S 18th St Ste 4c (43205-2654)
PHONE.................................614 224-6222
Gary L Rogers, *Pr*
EMP: 55 **EST:** 1968
SALES (est): 6.31MM **Privately Held**
Web: www.columbuspoa.com
SIC: 8011 Eyes, ears, nose, and throat specialist: physician/surgeon

(G-6512)
PENN NATIONAL GAMING INC
Also Called: Hollywood Casino
200 Georgesville Rd (43228-2020)
PHONE.................................614 308-3333
EMP: 32
SALES (corp-wide): 6.36B **Publicly Held**
Web: www.pngaming.com
SIC: 7011 Casino hotel
PA: Penn Entertainment, Inc.
825 Brkshire Blvd Ste 200
Wyomissing PA 19610
610 373-2400

(G-6513)
PENNEY OPCO LLC
Also Called: JC Penney
5555 Scarborough Blvd Unit 1 (43232-4730)
PHONE.................................614 863-7043
David Thursam, *Mgr*
EMP: 309
SALES (corp-wide): 1.93B **Privately Held**
SIC: 4225 General warehousing and storage
HQ: Penney Opco Llc
6501 Legacy Dr Ste B100
Plano TX 75024
972 431-4746

(G-6514)
PENSION ASSOCIATES INC
Also Called: NW Financial
1 W Nationwide Blvd Ste 100 (43215-2752)
PHONE.................................614 249-7111
Joseph J Gasper, *Prin*
EMP: 277 **EST:** 2000
SALES (est): 4.25MM
SALES (corp-wide): 11.75B **Privately Held**
SIC: 6331 Fire, marine, and casualty insurance: mutual
PA: Nationwide Mutual Insurance Company
1 Nationwide Plz
Columbus OH 43215
614 249-7111

(G-6515)
PEP BOYS - MNNY MOE JACK DEL L
Also Called: Pep Boys
2830 S Hamilton Rd (43232-4906)
PHONE.................................614 864-2092
EMP: 47
SQ FT: 22,400
Web: www.pepboys.com
SIC: 5531 7538 Automotive parts; General automotive repair shops
HQ: Pep Boys - Manny, Moe & Jack Of Delaware Llc
1 Presidential Blvd # 400
Bala Cynwyd PA 19004

(G-6516)
PERFORMANCE SITE COMPANY
2323 Performance Way (43207-2858)
PHONE.................................614 445-7161
EMP: 200
SIC: 1794 Excavation and grading, building construction

(G-6517)
PERSONAL TOUCH HM CARE IPA INC
454 E Main St Ste 227 (43215-5372)
PHONE.................................614 227-6952
Patti Malm, *Mgr*
EMP: 188
SALES (corp-wide): 251.89MM **Privately Held**
Web: www.pthomecare.com
SIC: 8082 Home health care services
PA: Personal Touch Home Care Ipa, Inc.
1985 Marcus Ave Ste 202
New Hyde Park NY 11042
718 468-4747

(G-6518)
PETSMART LLC
Also Called: Petsmart
3713 Easton Market (43219-6023)
PHONE.................................614 418-9389
Craig Samet, *Mgr*
EMP: 34
SALES (corp-wide): 1.03B **Privately Held**
Web: www.petsmart.com
SIC: 5999 0752 0742 Pet food; Grooming services, pet and animal specialties; Veterinary services, specialties
HQ: Petsmart Llc
19601 N 27th Ave
Phoenix AZ 85027
623 580-6100

▲ = Import ▼ = Export
◆ = Import/Export

GEOGRAPHIC SECTION
Columbus - Franklin County (G-6543)

(G-6519)
PGN OP SUMMIT LLC
Also Called: Solivita of Summit's Trace
935 N Cassady Ave (43219-2283)
PHONE..................................614 252-4987
EMP: 41 EST: 2020
SALES (est): 493.42K **Privately Held**
SIC: 8051 Skilled nursing care facilities

(G-6520)
PHANTOM TECHNICAL SERVICES INC
111 Outerbelt St (43213-1548)
PHONE..................................614 868-9920
William G Yates Junior, *Pr*
EMP: 30 EST: 1997
SQ FT: 7,500
SALES (est): 2.04MM **Privately Held**
Web: www.phantomtechnical.com
SIC: 8711 Electrical or electronic engineering

(G-6521)
PHARMSCRIPT LLC
1685 Westbelt Dr (43228-3809)
PHONE..................................908 389-1818
Saul Greenberger, *Managing Member*
EMP: 81
SALES (corp-wide): 256.55MM **Privately Held**
Web: www.pharmscript.com
SIC: 5122 Pharmaceuticals
HQ: Pharmscript L.L.C.
150 Pierce St
Somerset NJ 08873

(G-6522)
PHINNEY INDUSTRIAL ROOFING
700 Hadley Dr (43228-1030)
PHONE..................................614 308-9000
Mike Phinney, *CEO*
Mike Phinney, *Pr*
Kathey Phinney, *
▼ EMP: 65 EST: 1985
SQ FT: 20,000
SALES (est): 13.06MM **Privately Held**
Web: www.phinneyindustrial.com
SIC: 1761 Roofing contractor

(G-6523)
PHYSNA INC
250 West St Ste 100 (43215-7507)
PHONE..................................844 474-9762
Paul Powers, *CEO*
EMP: 74 EST: 2016
SALES (est): 5.3MM **Privately Held**
Web: www.physna.com
SIC: 7371 Computer software development

(G-6524)
PIADA GROUP LLC
1423 Goodale Blvd (43212-3737)
PHONE..................................614 397-1339
Richard Raley, *Prin*
EMP: 52 EST: 2009
SALES (est): 11.34MM **Privately Held**
Web: www.mypiada.com
SIC: 8741 8742 7389 Restaurant management; Business management consultant; Automobile recovery service

(G-6525)
PICK PULL AUTO DISMANTLING INC
2716 Groveport Rd (43207-3149)
PHONE..................................614 497-8858
Della Wilkins, *Brnch Mgr*
EMP: 36
SALES (corp-wide): 2.88B **Publicly Held**
SIC: 5015 Automotive parts and supplies, used
HQ: Pick And Pull Auto Dismantling, Inc.
10850 Gold Center Dr # 325
Rancho Cordova CA 95670
916 689-2000

(G-6526)
PIPE-VALVES INC
1200 E 5th Ave (43219)
P.O. Box 1865 (43216)
PHONE..................................614 294-4971
EMP: 39 EST: 1963
SALES (est): 16.11MM **Privately Held**
Web: www.pipevalves.com
SIC: 5085 Valves and fittings

(G-6527)
PIZZUTI INC (PA)
29 W 3rd Ave (43201-3208)
PHONE..................................614 280-4000
Ronald A Pizzuti, *Ch*
Joel S Pizzuti, *
Scott B West, *
Michael A Chivini, *
William Brennan, *
EMP: 50 EST: 1985
SALES (est): 22.4MM
SALES (corp-wide): 22.4MM **Privately Held**
Web: www.pizzuti.com
SIC: 6552 6531 Subdividers and developers, nec; Real estate managers

(G-6528)
PLANES MVG & STOR CO COLUMBUS
2000 Dividend Dr (43228-3847)
PHONE..................................614 777-9090
John J Planes, *CEO*
John Sabatalo, *
Raymond Gundrum, *
Mark Geis, *
EMP: 51 EST: 1988
SQ FT: 75,000
SALES (est): 5.25MM **Privately Held**
Web: www.teamplanes.com
SIC: 4213 4214 Household goods transport; Local trucking with storage

(G-6529)
PLANNED PRENTHOOD GREATER OHIO (PA)
206 E State St (43215-4311)
PHONE..................................614 224-2235
Stephanie Kight, *CEO*
Lillian Williams, *
EMP: 30 EST: 1966
SALES (est): 44.73MM
SALES (corp-wide): 44.73MM **Privately Held**
Web: www.plannedparenthood.org
SIC: 8093 Family planning clinic

(G-6530)
PLANTE & MORAN PLLC
250 S High St Ste 100 (43215-4629)
PHONE..................................614 849-3000
EMP: 657
SALES (corp-wide): 135.71MM **Privately Held**
Web: www.plantemoran.com
SIC: 8721 8742 Certified public accountant; Business management consultant
HQ: Plante & Moran, Pllc
3000 Town Ctr Ste 100
Southfield MI 48075
248 352-2500

(G-6531)
PLASMACARE INC
3840 E Main St (43213-2947)
PHONE..................................614 231-5322
Douglas Bogue, *Brnch Mgr*
EMP: 89
Web: www.grifols.com
SIC: 8099 Blood bank
HQ: Plasmacare, Inc.
2410 Lillyvale Ave
Los Angeles CA 90032
323 225-2221

(G-6532)
PLAZA PROPERTIES INC (PA)
Also Called: Bexley Plaza Apartments
3016 Maryland Ave (43209-1591)
P.O. Box 9601 (43209-0601)
PHONE..................................614 237-3726
Larry Ruben, *Ch Bd*
Bernard R Ruben, *
Lawrence G Ruben, *
Florine C Ruben, *
EMP: 50 EST: 1958
SQ FT: 5,000
SALES (est): 23.88MM
SALES (corp-wide): 23.88MM **Privately Held**
Web: www.plazaproperties.com
SIC: 6513 6531 Apartment building operators; Real estate managers

(G-6533)
PLUNKETTS PEST CONTROL INC
Also Called: Varment Guard Wildlife
1001 Checkrein Ave (43229-1106)
PHONE..................................614 794-8169
Stacy O'reilly, *Brnch Mgr*
EMP: 51
SALES (corp-wide): 25.97MM **Privately Held**
Web: www.plunketts.net
SIC: 7342 Exterminating and fumigating
PA: Plunkett's Pest Control, Inc.
40 Ne 52nd Wy Fridley
Minneapolis MN
763 571-7100

(G-6534)
POLARIS AUTOMATION INC
Also Called: Electrical Design & Engrg Svcs
6956 E Broad St Pmb 321 (43213-1517)
PHONE..................................614 431-0170
Scott Cooke, *Pr*
James D Cooke, *
Susan Cooke, *
EMP: 40 EST: 1984
SQ FT: 2,573
SALES (est): 5.74MM **Privately Held**
Web: www.polarisautomation.com
SIC: 7389 8711 Design, commercial and industrial; Engineering services

(G-6535)
POMEGRANATE DEVELOPMENT LTD
765 Pierce Dr (43223-2425)
PHONE..................................614 223-1650
EMP: 30 EST: 2010
SALES (est): 987.62K **Privately Held**
SIC: 8093 Mental health clinic, outpatient

(G-6536)
POMEROY IT SOLUTIONS SLS INC
Also Called: ADS
2339 Westbrooke Dr (43228-9557)
PHONE..................................614 876-6521
Tom Schneider, *Mgr*
EMP: 71
Web: www.pomeroy.com
SIC: 1731 Computer installation
HQ: Pomeroy It Solutions Sales Company, Inc.
1020 Petersburg Rd
Hebron KY 41048

(G-6537)
PORTER WRIGHT MORRIS & ARTHUR LLP (PA)
Also Called: Porter Wright
41 S High St Ste 2900 (43215-6165)
PHONE..................................614 227-2000
EMP: 325 EST: 1856
SALES (est): 47.71MM
SALES (corp-wide): 47.71MM **Privately Held**
Web: www.porterwright.com
SIC: 8111 General practice law office

(G-6538)
POURED LLC
1443 Giles Ct (43228-7046)
PHONE..................................614 432-0804
EMP: 29 EST: 2020
SALES (est): 75.02K **Privately Held**
SIC: 1771 Concrete work

(G-6539)
POWER DISTRIBUTORS LLC (PA)
Also Called: Central Power Systems
3700 Paragon Dr (43228-9750)
PHONE..................................614 876-3533
Matthew Finn, *Pr*
▲ EMP: 81 EST: 2012
SALES (est): 87.56MM
SALES (corp-wide): 87.56MM **Privately Held**
Web: www.powerdistributors.com
SIC: 5084 3524 Engines and parts, air-cooled; Lawn and garden equipment

(G-6540)
PPC FLEXIBLE PACKAGING LLC
4041 Roberts Rd (43228-9536)
PHONE..................................614 876-1204
Michael Smith, *Brnch Mgr*
EMP: 133
SALES (corp-wide): 433.54MM **Privately Held**
Web: www.plaspack.com
SIC: 5199 Packaging materials
PA: Ppc Flexible Packaging, Llc
1111 Busch Pkwy
Buffalo Grove IL 60089
847 541-0000

(G-6541)
PREGNANCY DECISION HEALTH CTR
Also Called: PDHC ADMINISTRATIVE OFFICE
665 E Dublin Granville Rd Ste 120 (43229)
PHONE..................................614 888-8774
Jeffrey Silleck, *Dir*
EMP: 27 EST: 1981
SALES (est): 2.71MM **Privately Held**
Web: www.pdhc.org
SIC: 8322 Crisis center

(G-6542)
PRESCRIBE FIT INC
401 W Town St Ste 232 (43215-4034)
PHONE..................................614 598-8788
Brock Leonti, *CEO*
EMP: 50 EST: 2017
SALES (est): 1.96MM **Privately Held**
Web: www.prescribefit.com
SIC: 7991 Physical fitness facilities

(G-6543)
PRESSURE CONNECTIONS CORP
610 Claycraft Rd (43230-5328)
PHONE..................................614 863-6930
◆ EMP: 56 EST: 1981
SALES (est): 8.61MM **Privately Held**
Web: www.pressureconnections.com

Columbus - Franklin County (G-6544) — GEOGRAPHIC SECTION

SIC: 3498 5085 3494 3492 Tube fabricating (contract bending and shaping); Industrial supplies; Valves and pipe fittings, nec; Fluid power valves and hose fittings

(G-6544)
PREVENTION ACTION ALLIANCE
Also Called: DRUG FREE ACTION ALLIANCE
6171 Huntley Rd Ste G (43229-1079)
P.O. Box 340072 (43234-0072)
PHONE..................................614 540-9985
Patricia Harmon, *Ex Dir*
EMP: 54 **EST:** 1991
SALES (est): 5.14MM **Privately Held**
Web: www.preventionactionalliance.org
SIC: 8322 Individual and family services

(G-6545)
PRICED RIGHT CARS INC
Also Called: Miracle Motor Mart
5100 E Main St (43213-2424)
PHONE..................................614 337-0037
Mark Meadows, *Pr*
Jim D Andrea, *
David Mark Meadows, *
EMP: 45 **EST:** 1991
SQ FT: 9,000
SALES (est): 10.01MM **Privately Held**
Web: www.miraclemotormart.com
SIC: 5521 7538 Automobiles, used cars only; General automotive repair shops

(G-6546)
PRIORITY DESIGNS INC
100 S Hamilton Rd (43213-2013)
PHONE..................................614 337-9979
Paul Kolada, *Pr*
Lois Kolada, *
EMP: 65 **EST:** 1990
SQ FT: 55,000
SALES (est): 13MM **Privately Held**
Web: www.prioritydesigns.com
SIC: 7389 Design, commercial and industrial

(G-6547)
PRN NURSE INC
Also Called: Health Care Personnel
6161 Radekin Rd (43232-2921)
PHONE..................................614 864-9292
Sandra K Shane, *Pr*
EMP: 300 **EST:** 1977
SALES (est): 8.14MM **Privately Held**
SIC: 7363 7361 Medical help service; Employment agencies

(G-6548)
PRODUCERS CREDIT CORPORATION
Also Called: PCC
8351 N High St Ste 250 (43235-1440)
PHONE..................................800 641-7522
Dennis Bolling, *Pr*
Irvin Porteus, *
EMP: 149 **EST:** 1932
SALES (est): 3.2MM
SALES (corp-wide): 56.7MM **Privately Held**
Web: www.uproducers.com
SIC: 7389 6159 Financial services; Livestock loan companies
PA: United Producers, Inc.
8351 N High St Ste 250
Columbus OH 43235
614 433-2150

(G-6549)
PROFESSIONAL ELECTRIC PDTS CO
5193 Sinclair Rd (43229-5413)
PHONE..................................614 563-2504
John Borkey Junior, *CEO*
EMP: 27
SALES (corp-wide): 12.53MM **Privately Held**
Web: www.pepconet.com
SIC: 5063 Electrical supplies, nec
HQ: Professional Electric Products Co Inc
33210 Lakeland Blvd
Eastlake OH 44095
800 872-7000

(G-6550)
PROFESSIONALS FOR WOMENS HLTH (PA)
921 Jasonway Ave Ste B (43214-2456)
PHONE..................................614 268-8800
Kevin Hacket Md, *Owner*
Kevin Hackett Md, *Owner*
EMP: 35 **EST:** 1983
SQ FT: 10,000
SALES (est): 7.2MM **Privately Held**
Web: www.pwhealth.com
SIC: 8011 Gynecologist

(G-6551)
PROFUNDS
3435 Stelzer Rd Ste 1000 (43219-6004)
PHONE..................................888 776-5717
EMP: 42
Web: www.profunds.com
SIC: 6722 Money market mutual funds
PA: Profunds
3435 Stelzer Rd Ste 1000
Columbus OH 43219

(G-6552)
PROLOGUE RESEARCH INTL INC
580 N 4th St Ste 270 (43215-2158)
PHONE..................................614 324-1500
Tom Ludlam Junior, *Pr*
EMP: 157 **EST:** 1998
SQ FT: 12,443
SALES (est): 3.21MM **Publicly Held**
Web: www.procro.com
SIC: 8733 Medical research
HQ: Iqvia Biotech Llc
2400 Ellis Rd
Durham NC 27703
984 439-3994

(G-6553)
PROVIDER SERVICES INC
Also Called: High Banks Care Centre
111 Lazelle Rd (43235-1419)
PHONE..................................614 888-2021
Aimee Palmer, *Mgr*
Paula Bourne, *
EMP: 49 **EST:** 1986
SALES (est): 794.77K **Privately Held**
Web: www.highbanks-care.net
SIC: 8399 8059 Social change association; Convalescent home

(G-6554)
PROVIDERS FOR HEALTHY LIVING
8351 N High St Ste 155 (43235-1409)
PHONE..................................614 664-3595
Matthew Lowe, *CEO*
EMP: 55 **EST:** 2011
SALES (est): 2.78MM **Privately Held**
Web: www.providersforhealthyliving.com
SIC: 8322 8093 Family (marriage) counseling; Mental health clinic, outpatient

(G-6555)
PSC METALS LLC
1283 Joyce Ave (43219-2134)
PHONE..................................614 299-4175
Kevin Ringle, *Mgr*
EMP: 38
Web: www.pscmetals.com
SIC: 4953 Recycling, waste materials
HQ: Psc Metals, Llc
2411 N Glassell St
Orange CA 92865
440 753-5400

(G-6556)
QUALITY ASSURED CLEANING INC
6407 Nicholas Dr (43235-5204)
P.O. Box 1250 (43065-1250)
PHONE..................................614 798-1505
Eric Hassen, *VP*
EMP: 43 **EST:** 2003
SALES (est): 2.25MM **Privately Held**
Web: www.goprovantage.com
SIC: 7699 Cleaning services

(G-6557)
QUALITY TOO GOOD MKTG GROUP LL
Also Called: Qtg Marketing
470 W Broad St Ste 21 (43215-2759)
PHONE..................................877 202-6245
EMP: 100 **EST:** 2018
SALES (est): 2.24MM **Privately Held**
Web: www.qualitytoogoodmarketing.com
SIC: 8742 Marketing consulting services

(G-6558)
R DORSEY & COMPANY INC
Also Called: R.dorsey & Company
1250 Arthur E Adams Dr (43221-3560)
P.O. Box 12328 (43212-0328)
PHONE..................................614 486-8900
EMP: 30 **EST:** 1996
SQ FT: 2,000
SALES (est): 4MM **Privately Held**
Web: www.dorseyplus.com
SIC: 7379 Computer related consulting services

(G-6559)
RACQUET CLUB COLUMBUS LTD
1100 Bethel Rd (43220-2699)
PHONE..................................614 457-5671
Jim Hendrix, *Dir*
EMP: 32 **EST:** 1971
SQ FT: 88,000
SALES (est): 960.21K **Privately Held**
Web: www.racquetclub1.com
SIC: 7997 7991 Tennis club, membership; Exercise facilities

(G-6560)
RADHA CORPORATION
Also Called: Hampton Inn West
5625 Trabue Rd (43228-9811)
PHONE..................................614 851-5599
Bikha Patel, *Pr*
EMP: 68 **EST:** 1994
SQ FT: 12,756
SALES (est): 843.11K **Privately Held**
Web: www.hilton.com
SIC: 7011 Hotels and motels

(G-6561)
RAMA INC
Also Called: Staybrdge Sites Columbus Arprt
2890 Airport Dr (43219-2240)
PHONE..................................614 473-9888
Bill Patel, *Pr*
EMP: 56 **EST:** 1996
SALES (est): 964.82K **Privately Held**
Web: www.staybridgesuites.com
SIC: 7011 Hotels and motels

(G-6562)
RB KNOXVILLE LLC
Also Called: Hilton Knoxville
4100 Regent St Ste G (43219-6160)
PHONE..................................865 523-2300
Hadi Kassaee, *Prin*
EMP: 99 **EST:** 2020
SALES (est): 1.53MM **Privately Held**
Web: www.hilton.com
SIC: 7011 Hotels and motels

(G-6563)
RE/MAX PREMIERE CHOICE
Also Called: Re/Max
1214 Middlefield Ct (43235-7597)
PHONE..................................614 436-0330
Dava J, *Prin*
EMP: 42 **EST:** 2018
SALES (est): 177.57K **Privately Held**
Web: www.remax.com
SIC: 6531 Real estate agent, residential

(G-6564)
RECOVERY ONE LLC
3250 Henderson Rd Ste 203 (43220-2398)
PHONE..................................614 336-4207
EMP: 67 **EST:** 2000
SALES (est): 3.17MM
SALES (corp-wide): 1.27B **Publicly Held**
Web: www.recoveryonellc.com
SIC: 7322 8111 Collection agency, except real estate; Legal services
PA: Wsfs Financial Corporation
500 Delaware Ave
Wilmington DE 19801
302 792-6000

(G-6565)
RED ARCHITECTURE LLC
589 W Nationwide Blvd Ste B (43215)
P.O. Box 15247 (43215)
PHONE..................................614 487-8770
EMP: 60 **EST:** 2006
SALES (est): 5.7MM **Privately Held**
Web: www.redarchitecture.com
SIC: 8712 Architectural engineering

(G-6566)
RED CAPITAL MARKETS LLC
10 W Broad St Ste 900 (43215-3449)
PHONE..................................614 857-1400
James Croft, *CEO*
James Murphy, *Pr*
Andrew Steiner, *VP*
EMP: 234 **EST:** 1984
SALES (est): 66.5MM
SALES (corp-wide): 31.88B **Publicly Held**
SIC: 6211 Investment firm, general brokerage
HQ: Pnc Bank, National Association
300 5th Ave
Pittsburgh PA 15222
877 762-2000

(G-6567)
RED ROOF INNS INC
Also Called: Red Roof Inn
441 Ackerman Rd (43202-1569)
PHONE..................................614 267-9941
Todd Jones, *Brnch Mgr*
EMP: 42
Web: www.redroof.com
SIC: 7011 Hotels and motels
HQ: Red Roof Inns, Inc.
7815 Walton Pkwy
New Albany OH 43054
614 744-2600

(G-6568)
RED ROOF INNS INC
Also Called: Red Roof Inn
111 Nationwide Plz (43215)
PHONE..................................614 224-6539
Jeffrey Schwartz, *Mgr*
EMP: 65
Web: www.redroof.com

GEOGRAPHIC SECTION

Columbus - Franklin County (G-6589)

SIC: 7011 Hotels and motels
HQ: Red Roof Inns, Inc.
7815 Walton Pkwy
New Albany OH 43054
614 744-2600

(G-6569)
REDHAWK GLOBAL LLC
Also Called: Redhawk Logistics
2642 Fisher Rd Ste B (43204-3565)
P.O. Box 2946 (43216-2946)
PHONE.............................614 487-8505
Erach N Deboo, *Managing Member*
Michael Tobin, *
◆ EMP: 50 EST: 2002
SQ FT: 200,000
SALES (est): 15.11MM Privately Held
Web: www.redhawklogistics.com
SIC: 4731 4225 Freight forwarding; General warehousing

(G-6570)
REFECTORY RESTAURANT INC
Also Called: Refectory
1092 Bethel Rd (43220-2610)
PHONE.............................614 451-9774
Kamal Boulos, *Pr*
EMP: 48 EST: 1981
SQ FT: 10,000
SALES (est): 1.45MM Privately Held
Web: www.refectory.com
SIC: 5812 7299 French restaurant; Banquet hall facilities

(G-6571)
REFRIGERATION SYSTEMS COMPANY (HQ)
1770 Genessee Ave (43211-1650)
PHONE.............................614 263-0913
Thomas A Leighty, *CEO*
Robert A Appleton, *Pr*
EMP: 63 EST: 1975
SQ FT: 20,000
SALES (est): 4.49MM
SALES (corp-wide): 32.3MM Privately Held
Web: www.refrigerationenergy.biz
SIC: 7623 1541 Refrigeration repair service; Food products manufacturing or packing plant construction
PA: Intercool Usa, Llc
1313 Valwood Pkwy Ste 100
Carrollton TX 75006
972 277-4500

(G-6572)
REGAL HOSPITALITY LLC
Also Called: Sheraton
201 Hutchinson Ave (43235-4689)
PHONE.............................614 436-0004
Elizabeth Procaccianti, *Mgr*
EMP: 102
SALES (corp-wide): 5.01MM Privately Held
Web: www.regalhospitalityinc.com
SIC: 7011 Hotels
PA: Regal Hospitality, Llc
400 Venture Dr Ste B
Lewis Center OH 43035
614 389-1916

(G-6573)
REGENCY HOSPITAL COMPANY LLC
Also Called: Select Spclty Hsptl-Columbus S
1430 S High St (43207-1045)
PHONE.............................614 456-0300
EMP: 188
SALES (corp-wide): 6.2B Publicly Held
Web: www.regencyhospital.com
SIC: 8062 General medical and surgical hospitals

HQ: Regency Hospital Company, L.L.C.
4714 Gettysburg Rd
Mechanicsburg PA 17055
419 318-5700

(G-6574)
REGENCY LEASING CO LLC
Also Called: Regency Manor Rehab
2000 Regency Manor Cir (43207-1777)
PHONE.............................614 542-3100
Jay Hicks, *Pr*
Doug Rowe, *
EMP: 300 EST: 1990
SALES (est): 25.26MM
SALES (corp-wide): 392.92MM Privately Held
SIC: 8051 Skilled nursing care facilities
PA: Communicare Health Services, Inc.
10123 Alliance Rd
Blue Ash OH 45242
513 530-1654

(G-6575)
REITTER STUCCO INC
1100 King Ave (43212-2262)
PHONE.............................614 291-2212
Frederick J Reitter, *Pr*
Robert J Reitter, *
John E Reitter, *
EMP: 40 EST: 1915
SQ FT: 30,000
SALES (est): 8.76MM Privately Held
Web: www.reitterstucco.com
SIC: 1771 5072 Exterior concrete stucco contractor; Hardware

(G-6576)
RELIABLE APPL INSTALLATION INC
3736 Paragon Dr (43228-9750)
PHONE.............................614 246-6840
Randy James, *Brnch Mgr*
EMP: 36
SALES (corp-wide): 2.77MM Privately Held
Web: www.reliableappliance.us
SIC: 4212 Delivery service, vehicular
PA: Reliable Appliance Installation, Inc.
604 Office Pkwy
Westerville OH 43082
614 794-3307

(G-6577)
RENAISSANCE HOTEL OPERATING CO
Also Called: Marriott
50 N 3rd St (43215-3510)
PHONE.............................614 228-5050
Gerie Lonbarob, *Mgr*
EMP: 275
SALES (corp-wide): 23.71B Publicly Held
Web: www.marriott.com
SIC: 7011 Hotels and motels
HQ: Renaissance Hotel Operating Company
10400 Fernwood Rd
Bethesda MD 20817

(G-6578)
RENIER CONSTRUCTION CORP
2164 Citygate Dr (43219-3556)
PHONE.............................614 866-4580
William R Heifner, *Pr*
Thomas Rice, *
Robert Gibbs, *
Neal Bronder, *
EMP: 34 EST: 1980
SQ FT: 8,500
SALES (est): 21.51MM Privately Held
Web: www.renier.com

SIC: 1542 8741 Commercial and office building, new construction; Construction management

(G-6579)
REPUBLCAN STATE CNTL EXEC CMMT
Also Called: Ohio Republican Party
211 S 5th St (43215-5203)
PHONE.............................614 228-2481
Kaye Ayres, *Vice Chairman*
EMP: 30 EST: 1858
SALES (est): 2.24MM Privately Held
Web: www.ohiogop.org
SIC: 8651 Political action committee

(G-6580)
RESEARCH INST AT NTNWIDE CHLD
Also Called: DEPT OF LABORATORY MEDICINE
700 Childrens Dr (43205-2664)
PHONE.............................614 722-2700
John Barnard, *Pr*
Fran Eppich, *Project Officer*
Sherwood L Fawcett, *
Robert Lazarus Junior, *Prin*
William Wise, *
EMP: 140 EST: 1965
SQ FT: 106,000
SALES (est): 230.26MM
SALES (corp-wide): 3.6B Privately Held
Web: www.nationwidechildrens.org
SIC: 8062 8733 General medical and surgical hospitals; Medical research
PA: Nationwide Children's Hospital
700 Childrens Dr
Columbus OH 43205
614 722-2000

(G-6581)
RESIDENCE INN
Also Called: Residence Inn By Marriott
36 E Gay St (43215-3108)
PHONE.............................614 222-2610
Joey Guiyab, *Prin*
EMP: 49 EST: 2009
SALES (est): 1.18MM Privately Held
Web: residence-inn.marriott.com
SIC: 7011 Hotels and motels

(G-6582)
RESIDENCE INN BY MARRIOTT LLC
Also Called: Residence Inn By Marriott
36 E Gay St (43215-3108)
PHONE.............................614 222-2610
Joey Guiyab, *Ofcr*
EMP: 32
SALES (corp-wide): 23.71B Publicly Held
Web: www.marriott.com
SIC: 7011 Hotels and motels
HQ: Residence Inn By Marriott, Llc
10400 Fernwood Rd
Bethesda MD 20817

(G-6583)
RESIDENCE INN BY MARRIOTT LLC
Also Called: Residence Inn By Marriott
7300 Huntington Park Dr (43235-5718)
PHONE.............................614 885-0799
Tim Whitehead, *Genl Mgr*
EMP: 29
SALES (corp-wide): 23.71B Publicly Held
Web: www.marriott.com
SIC: 7011 Hotels and motels
HQ: Residence Inn By Marriott, Llc
10400 Fernwood Rd
Bethesda MD 20817

(G-6584)
RESIDENTIAL FINANCE CORP
1 Easton Oval Ste 400 (43219-6092)
PHONE.............................614 324-4700
EMP: 850
Web: encompass.residentialfinance.com
SIC: 6162 Bond and mortgage companies

(G-6585)
RESIDENTIAL ONE REALTY INC (PA)
Also Called: Prudential
8351 N High St Ste 150 (43235-1409)
PHONE.............................614 436-9830
Joanne Figge, *Pr*
EMP: 40 EST: 1988
SQ FT: 4,500
SALES (est): 1.91MM
SALES (corp-wide): 1.91MM Privately Held
Web: www.castoresidentialrealty.com
SIC: 6531 Real estate agent, residential

(G-6586)
RESOURCE INTERACTIVE
Also Called: Resource
250 S High St Ste 400 (43215-4622)
PHONE.............................614 621-2888
Nancy J Kramer, *CEO*
Kelly Moony, *
EMP: 39 EST: 1981
SALES (est): 2.26MM Privately Held
SIC: 7389 7331 Advertising, promotional, and trade show services; Direct mail advertising services

(G-6587)
RESOURCE INTERNATIONAL INC
Also Called: Rii
6350 Presidential Gtwy (43231-7653)
PHONE.............................614 823-4949
Farah Majidzadeh, *CEO*
Farah B Majidzadeh, *
Kamran Majidzadeh, *
Mark Majidzadeh, *
Stasia Vavruska, *
EMP: 150 EST: 1941
SQ FT: 20,000
SALES (est): 53.98MM
SALES (corp-wide): 53.98MM Privately Held
Web: www.resourceinternational.com
SIC: 1531 8741 8711 8734 ; Management services; Consulting engineer; Testing laboratories
PA: Majidzadeh Enterprises, Inc.
6350 Presidential Gtwy
Columbus OH 43231
614 823-4949

(G-6588)
RIGHTER CO INC
2424 Harrison Rd (43204-3508)
PHONE.............................614 272-9700
Bradley R Nadolson, *Pr*
Jerry Yantes, *
Tracy Ferguson, *
EMP: 45 EST: 1976
SQ FT: 6,400
SALES (est): 9.48MM Privately Held
Web: www.rightercompany.com
SIC: 1622 1542 Bridge construction; Nonresidential construction, nec

(G-6589)
RINGSIDE SEARCH PARTNERS LLC
Also Called: Ringside Talent
266 N 4th St Ste 100 (43215-2565)
PHONE.............................614 643-0700
Chris Fackler, *CEO*
EMP: 38 EST: 2009
SALES (est): 4.11MM Privately Held

(PA)=Parent Co (HQ)=Headquarters
✪ = New Business established in last 2 years

Web: www.ringsidetalent.com
SIC: **7363** 7361 8742 Help supply services; Executive placement; Management consulting services

(G-6590)
RISE BRANDS
134 E Long St (43215-2913)
PHONE..................................614 754-7522
EMP: 46 EST: 2020
SALES (est): 1.71MM **Privately Held**
Web: www.risebrands.com
SIC: **7389** Design services

(G-6591)
RITE RUG CO
5465 N Hamilton Rd (43230-1319)
PHONE..................................614 478-3365
Joel Wood, Mgr
EMP: 37
SALES (corp-wide): 100K **Privately Held**
Web: www.riterug.com
SIC: **7389** 5713 Interior design services; Floor covering stores
PA: Rite Rug Co.
4450 Poth Rd
Columbus OH 43213
614 261-6060

(G-6592)
RIVER CONSULTING LLC (DH)
445 Hutchinson Ave Ste 740 (43235-5677)
PHONE..................................614 797-2480
Gregory Dirfank, Managing Member
Vincent Dimsa, *
John Strayer, *
Ike Patena, *
Walter Martin, *
EMP: 85 EST: 1981
SQ FT: 16,000
SALES (est): 26.82MM **Publicly Held**
SIC: **8711** Consulting engineer
HQ: Kinder Morgan Energy Partners, L.P.
1001 La St Ste 1000
Houston TX 77002
713 369-9000

(G-6593)
RIVER FINANCIAL INC
80 E Rich St Apt 706 (43215-5266)
PHONE..................................415 878-3375
Alex Leishman, CEO
Alexander Leishman, *
Andrew Benson, *
Rod Roudi, *
William Mongan, *
EMP: 35 EST: 2019
SALES (est): 2.33MM **Privately Held**
Web: www.river.com
SIC: **7389** 7299 Financial services; Personal financial services

(G-6594)
RIVER VISTA HLTH WELLNESS LLC
1599 Alum Creek Dr (43209-2596)
PHONE..................................614 643-5454
EMP: 80 EST: 2018
SALES (est): 30.29MM **Privately Held**
Web: www.newvistahealth.com
SIC: **8051** Skilled nursing care facilities

(G-6595)
RIVERSIDE HOSPITAL
3535 Olentangy River Rd (43214-3998)
P.O. Box 9 (43216-0009)
PHONE..................................614 566-5000
Steven Markovich, Pr
EMP: 47 EST: 2006
SALES (est): 6.87MM **Privately Held**
SIC: **8062** General medical and surgical hospitals

(G-6596)
RIVERSIDE NEPHROLOGY ASSOC INC
929 Jasonway Ave Ste A (43214-2330)
PHONE..................................614 538-2250
Kevin Schroeder, Pr
Ronald Deandre Junior, VP
EMP: 52 EST: 1969
SQ FT: 4,000
SALES (est): 2.1MM **Privately Held**
Web: www.ohiokidney.com
SIC: **8011** Nephrologist

(G-6597)
RIVERSIDE PULMONARY ASSOC INC
1679 Old Henderson Rd (43220-3644)
PHONE..................................614 267-8585
Gail Mutchler, Pr
EMP: 33 EST: 1986
SALES (est): 2.35MM **Privately Held**
SIC: **8011** Pulmonary specialist, physician/surgeon

(G-6598)
RIVERSIDE RDLGY INTRVNTNAL ASS (DH)
100 E Campus View Blvd Ste 100 (43235-4647)
PHONE..................................614 340-7747
Marsha Flarghty, Pr
EMP: 45 EST: 1980
SALES (est): 52.25MM
SALES (corp-wide): 52.25MM **Privately Held**
Web: www.riversiderad.com
SIC: **8011** Radiologist
HQ: Lucid Radiology Solutions, Llc
100 E Campus View Blvd
Columbus OH 43235
614 384-2880

(G-6599)
RIVERSIDE SURGICAL ASSOCIATES
3545 Olentangy River Rd Ste 525 (43214-3983)
PHONE..................................614 261-1900
Jonh Matyas, Pr
Charles Gerace Junior Md, Pr
Philip H Taylor Junior Md, VP
EMP: 39 EST: 1953
SQ FT: 1,500
SALES (est): 3.69MM **Privately Held**
Web: www.riversidesurgicalassociates.com
SIC: **8011** Surgeon

(G-6600)
RIVERVIEW HOTEL LLC
Also Called: Hampton Inn
3160 Olentangy River Rd (43202-1517)
PHONE..................................614 268-8700
Andrew Hann, Pr
EMP: 37 EST: 2015
SQ FT: 106,000
SALES (est): 1.71MM **Privately Held**
Web: www.hilton.com
SIC: **7011** Hotels

(G-6601)
RLJ III - EM CLMBUS LESSEE LLC
Also Called: Embassy Suites Columbus
2700 Corporate Exchange Dr (43231-1690)
PHONE..................................614 890-8600
Don Gantt, Genl Mgr
Moly Curnutte, Sls Dir
EMP: 85 EST: 1984
SALES (est): 2.64MM **Privately Held**
Web: columbus.embassysuites.com
SIC: **7011** Hotels and motels

(G-6602)
RLJ MANAGEMENT CO INC (PA)
3021 E Dublin Granville Rd (43231-4031)
PHONE..................................614 942-2020
Steve Boone, Pr
Daniel Slane, *
Bill Harvey, *
Sandy Estep, *
EMP: 207 EST: 1979
SQ FT: 5,200
SALES (est): 24.64MM
SALES (corp-wide): 24.64MM **Privately Held**
Web: www.rljmgt.com
SIC: **6531** 8721 Real estate managers; Accounting services, except auditing

(G-6603)
ROBERT E DAVIS DDS MS INC
5249 W Broad St (43228-5600)
PHONE..................................614 878-7887
Andrew Wade, Pr
EMP: 29 EST: 1978
SQ FT: 5,500
SALES (est): 424.75K **Privately Held**
SIC: **8021** Orthodontist

(G-6604)
ROBERT M NEFF INC
711 Stimmel Rd (43223-2905)
PHONE..................................614 444-1562
Phillip Dante Berkhmeir, Prin
EMP: 40
SQ FT: 2,400
SALES (corp-wide): 2.52MM **Privately Held**
Web: www.rneffinc.com
SIC: **4213** 4215 4212 Contract haulers; Courier services, except by air; Mail carriers, contract
PA: Robert M Neff Inc
1955 James Pkwy
Heath OH 43056
740 928-4393

(G-6605)
ROCKBRIDGE CAPITAL LLC (PA)
4124 Worth Ave (43219)
PHONE..................................614 246-2400
Ronald L Callentine, Ch
Ronald Callentine, *
James Merkel, *
Stephen Denz, *
Kenneth Krebs, *
EMP: 66 EST: 1999
SALES (est): 104.33MM
SALES (corp-wide): 104.33MM **Privately Held**
Web: www.rockbridgecapital.com
SIC: **7011** Hotels and motels

(G-6606)
ROCKHILL HOLDING COMPANY (DH)
Also Called: Rockhill Insurance Company
518 E Broad St (43215)
PHONE..................................816 412-2800
Terry Younghanz, CEO
EMP: 30 EST: 2005
SALES (est): 154.33MM
SALES (corp-wide): 20.63B **Privately Held**
Web: www.stateauto.com
SIC: **6351** Surety insurance
HQ: State Automobile Mutual Insurance Co Inc
518 E Broad St
Columbus OH 43215
833 724-3577

(G-6607)
ROEHRENBECK ELECTRIC INC
2525 English Rd (43207-2899)
PHONE..................................614 443-9709
Richard Roehrenbeck, Pr
EMP: 44 EST: 1964
SQ FT: 10,000
SALES (est): 8.23MM **Privately Held**
Web: www.roehrenbeck.com
SIC: **1731** General electrical contractor

(G-6608)
ROGER D FIELDS ASSOCIATES INC
4588 Kenny Rd Ste 201d (43220-2777)
PHONE..................................614 451-2248
Roger D Fields, Pt
James J O'reilly, Pt
Gregory C Topp, Pt
EMP: 39 EST: 1982
SQ FT: 2,500
SALES (est): 4.56MM **Privately Held**
Web: www.rdfa.com
SIC: **8711** Mechanical engineering

(G-6609)
RONALD MCDNALD HSE CHRTIES CNT
711 E Livingston Ave (43205)
PHONE..................................614 227-3700
Rita Anders, CEO
EMP: 48 EST: 1976
SALES (est): 9.37MM **Privately Held**
Web: www.rmhc-centralohio.org
SIC: **8322** Social service center

(G-6610)
ROOT INC (PA)
Also Called: Root
80 E Rich St Ste 500 (43215-5764)
PHONE..................................866 980-9431
Alexander Timm, CEO
Matt Bonakdarpour, Pr
Megan Binkley, CAO
EMP: 231 EST: 2015
SQ FT: 43,228
SALES (est): 455MM
SALES (corp-wide): 455MM **Publicly Held**
Web: www.joinroot.com
SIC: **6331** Fire, marine, and casualty insurance

(G-6611)
ROSEWIND LIMITED PARTNERSHIP
960 E 5th Ave (43201-3066)
PHONE..................................614 421-6000
Dennis S Guest, Ex Dir
John Hahn, Ofcr
EMP: 150 EST: 1997
SQ FT: 80,000
SALES (est): 4.6MM **Privately Held**
SIC: **8748** Urban planning and consulting services

(G-6612)
ROSSFORD GRTRIC CARE LTD PRTNR
Also Called: Heatherdowns Nursing Center
1496 Old Henderson Rd (43220-3614)
PHONE..................................614 459-0445
Ralph E Hazelbaker, Pt
Carol Campbell, Ltd Pt
Heatherdown Health Care, Cor Gen Pt
EMP: 47 EST: 1988
SALES (est): 6.49MM **Privately Held**
SIC: **8051** Skilled nursing care facilities

(G-6613)
ROTH PRODUCE CO
3882 Agler Rd (43219-3607)
PHONE..................................614 337-2825

GEOGRAPHIC SECTION

Columbus - Franklin County (G-6634)

EMP: 45
Web: www.premierproduceone.com
SIC: 5148 Fruits, fresh

(G-6614)
ROYAL ELECTRIC CNSTR CORP
1250 Memory Ln N Ste B (43209-2749)
PHONE..................614 253-6600
Susan Ernst, *Pr*
Gregory Ernst, *
EMP: 30 **EST:** 1973
SQ FT: 33,000
SALES (est): 2.83MM **Privately Held**
Web: www.royalcorp.com
SIC: 1731 General electrical contractor

(G-6615)
ROYAL F & S HOLDINGS LLC
Also Called: Suitelife
190 S High St Apt 475 (43215-3681)
PHONE..................614 402-8422
Dominique Royal, *Managing Member*
EMP: 52 **EST:** 2018
SALES (est): 650K **Privately Held**
Web: www.staysuitelife.com
SIC: 6513 Apartment hotel operation

(G-6616)
ROYAL PAPER STOCK COMPANY INC (PA)
1300 Norton Rd (43228-3640)
PHONE..................614 851-4714
Michael Radtke, *Pr*
Richard Dahn, *
Martha Radke, *
John Daly, *
EMP: 70 **EST:** 1952
SQ FT: 80,000
SALES (est): 24.2MM
SALES (corp-wide): 24.2MM **Privately Held**
Web: www.royalpaperstock.com
SIC: 4953 Recycling, waste materials

(G-6617)
RTTW LTD
Also Called: Treetree
939 N High St Unit 202 (43201-2555)
PHONE..................614 291-7944
Becca Thompson Apfelstadt, *Pr*
EMP: 28
SALES (est): 8.23MM **Privately Held**
Web: www.treetreeagency.com
SIC: 7311 8742 Advertising consultant; Marketing consulting services

(G-6618)
RTW INC (DH)
518 E Broad St (43215)
P.O. Box 182822 (43218)
PHONE..................952 893-0403
Jeffrey B Murphy, *Pr*
Alfred L Latendresse, *Ex VP*
Keith D Krueger, *VP*
EMP: 78 **EST:** 1983
SQ FT: 31,930
SALES (est): 50.91MM
SALES (corp-wide): 20.63B **Privately Held**
Web: www.stateauto.com
SIC: 6331 Assessment associations: fire, marine and casualty insurance
HQ: Rockhill Holding Company
518 E Broad St
Columbus OH 43215

(G-6619)
RUMMELL DVID G SCHMCHER MIKE R
3600 Olentangy River Rd (43214-3437)
PHONE..................614 451-1110

David Rummel, *Pt*
Mike R Schumacher, *Pt*
EMP: 29 **EST:** 1966
SALES (est): 772.25K **Privately Held**
Web: www.columbusdentists.net
SIC: 8021 Dentists' office

(G-6620)
RUMPKE WASTE INC
1191 Fields Ave (43201-6902)
PHONE..................513 851-0122
Mark Gray, *Mgr*
EMP: 193
SQ FT: 10,416
Web: www.rumpke.com
SIC: 4953 Recycling, waste materials
HQ: Rumpke Waste, Inc.
10795 Hughes Rd
Cincinnati OH 45251
513 851-0122

(G-6621)
RUSH PACKAGE DELIVERY INC
Also Called: Rush Trnsp & Logistics
1733 Mckinley Ave (43222-1050)
PHONE..................937 297-6182
Steve Parker, *CEO*
EMP: 53
SALES (corp-wide): 23.29MM **Privately Held**
SIC: 4212 Local trucking, without storage
PA: Rush Package Delivery, Inc.
2619 Needmore Rd
Dayton OH 45414
937 224-7874

(G-6622)
RUSTYS TOWING SERVICE INC
4845 Obetz Reese Rd (43207-4831)
PHONE..................614 491-6288
Russ Mc Quirt, *Pr*
EMP: 54 **EST:** 1988
SQ FT: 1,200
SALES (est): 6.05MM **Privately Held**
Web: www.rustystowingservice.com
SIC: 7549 Towing service, automotive

(G-6623)
RXP OHIO LLC
Also Called: Verizon
630 E Broad St (43215-3999)
P.O. Box 908 (43054-0908)
PHONE..................614 937-2844
Stephanie Jandik, *Managing Member*
EMP: 80 **EST:** 2015
SQ FT: 15,000
SALES (est): 9.54MM **Privately Held**
Web: www.rxpwireless.com
SIC: 4813 Telephone communications broker

(G-6624)
S & T TRUCK AND AUTO SVC INC
Also Called: Silvan Trucking Company Ohio
3150 Valleyview Dr Rm 8 (43204-2002)
PHONE..................614 272-8163
Brent Greek, *Pr*
Glenda Purdy, *
EMP: 39 **EST:** 1986
SQ FT: 8,000
SALES (est): 6.04MM **Privately Held**
Web: www.silvantrucking.com
SIC: 4212 Local trucking, without storage

(G-6625)
SAFE AND SECURE HOMECARE CORP
1945 North Star Rd (43212-1602)
PHONE..................614 808-0164
Robert J Nicholson, *CEO*
EMP: 52 **EST:** 2013
SALES (est): 1.63MM **Privately Held**

SIC: 8082 Home health care services

(G-6626)
SAFE AUTO INSURANCE COMPANY (DH)
Also Called: S A
4 Easton Oval (43219-6010)
P.O. Box 1623 (27102-1623)
PHONE..................614 231-0200
Ronald H Davies, *CEO*
Mark Lemaster, *
Greg Sutton, *
EMP: 258 **EST:** 1993
SQ FT: 50,000
SALES (est): 360.75MM **Publicly Held**
Web: www.safeauto.com
SIC: 6411 Insurance agents, nec
HQ: Safe Auto Insurance Group, Inc.
4 Easton Oval
Columbus OH 43219
614 231-0200

(G-6627)
SAFE AUTO INSURANCE GROUP INC (HQ)
4 Easton Oval (43219-6010)
PHONE..................614 231-0200
Ronald H Davies, *CEO*
Ari Deshe, *Ch Bd*
Jon P Diamond, *Ch Bd*
Gregory A Sutton, *Treas*
Jon L Trickey, *Sr VP*
EMP: 228 **EST:** 1993
SQ FT: 45,000
SALES (est): 466.18MM **Publicly Held**
SIC: 6331 6411 Automobile insurance; Insurance agents, brokers, and service
PA: The Allstate Corporation
3100 Sanders Rd
Northbrook IL 60062

(G-6628)
SAFEGATE AIRPORT SYSTEMS INC
Also Called: Safegate
700 Science Blvd (43230-6641)
PHONE..................763 535-9299
Per-olof Hammarlund, *Ch*
Thomas Duffy, *Pr*
Michael Leeds, *Sec*
EMP: 44 **EST:** 1992
SALES (est): 1.52MM
SALES (corp-wide): 842.76K **Privately Held**
Web: www.adbsafegate.com
SIC: 4581 Airport
HQ: Adb Safegate Sweden Ab
Djurhagegatan 19
MalmO 213 7
406991700

(G-6629)
SAFELITE AUTOGLASS FOUNDATION
7400 Safelite Way (43235-5086)
P.O. Box 182827 (43218-2827)
PHONE..................614 210-9000
Ryan Trierweiler, *Ch Bd*
EMP: 186 **EST:** 2005
SALES (est): 349.69K
SALES (corp-wide): 3.16B **Privately Held**
Web: www.safelite.com
SIC: 7536 Automotive glass replacement shops
HQ: Safelite Group, Inc.
7400 Safelite Way
Columbus OH 43235
614 210-9000

(G-6630)
SAFELITE BILLING SERVICES CORP
7400 Safelite Way (43235-5086)
P.O. Box 182827 (43218-2827)
PHONE..................614 210-9000
EMP: 118
SALES (est): 288.15K
SALES (corp-wide): 3.16B **Privately Held**
Web: www.safelite.com
SIC: 7536 Automotive glass replacement shops
HQ: Safelite Group, Inc.
7400 Safelite Way
Columbus OH 43235
614 210-9000

(G-6631)
SAFELITE GLASS CORP (DH)
Also Called: Safelite Autoglass
7400 Safelite Way (43235-5086)
P.O. Box 182827 (43218-2827)
PHONE..................614 210-9000
Dan Wislon, *Pr*
Dan H Wilson, *Pr*
George T Haymaker Junior, *Ch Bd*
Douglas A Herron, *Ex VP*
▲ **EMP:** 700 **EST:** 1946
SALES (est): 462.95MM
SALES (corp-wide): 3.16B **Privately Held**
Web: www.safelite.com
SIC: 7536 Automotive glass replacement shops
HQ: Safelite Group, Inc.
7400 Safelite Way
Columbus OH 43235
614 210-9000

(G-6632)
SAFELITE GROUP INC (DH)
Also Called: Safelite Autoglass
7400 Safelite Way (43235)
P.O. Box 182827 (43218)
PHONE..................614 210-9000
Renee Cacchillo, *Pr*
Douglas Herron, *
Tim Spencer, *
Dino Lano, *
Natalie Crede, *
◆ **EMP:** 1000 **EST:** 1947
SALES (est): 1.38B
SALES (corp-wide): 3.16B **Privately Held**
Web: www.safelite.com
SIC: 7536 3231 6411 Automotive glass replacement shops; Windshields, glass: made from purchased glass; Insurance claim processing, except medical
HQ: Belron Group Sa
Boulevard Prince Henri 9b
Luxembourg 1724
27478860

(G-6633)
SAFELITE SOLUTIONS LLC
7400 Safelite Way (43235-5086)
P.O. Box 182827 (43218-2827)
PHONE..................614 210-9000
Dan Wislon, *Pr*
Douglas A Herron, *Ex VP*
EMP: 4052 **EST:** 2003
SALES (est): 24.29MM
SALES (corp-wide): 3.16B **Privately Held**
Web: www.safelitesolutions.com
SIC: 8742 Management consulting services
HQ: Safelite Group, Inc.
7400 Safelite Way
Columbus OH 43235
614 210-9000

(G-6634)
SAFETY SOLUTIONS INC (HQ)
6999 Huntley Rd Ste L (43229-1031)

Columbus - Franklin County (G-6635)

PHONE..................614 799-9900
David L Forsthoffer, *Pr*
John Perrin, *
Mike Boone, *
EMP: 72 **EST:** 1972
SALES (est): 26.71MM
SALES (corp-wide): 15.23B **Publicly Held**
Web: www.grainger.com
SIC: 5084 5136 5139 Safety equipment; Gloves, men's and boys'; Shoes
PA: W.W. Grainger, Inc.
100 Grainger Pkwy
Lake Forest IL 60045
847 535-1000

(G-6635)
SAHARA GLOBAL SECURITY LLC
Also Called: Security
601 S High St (43215-5620)
PHONE..................614 448-7940
Zach C, *Pr*
Zachariah Carper, *
EMP: 80 **EST:** 2021
SALES (est): 2.63MM **Privately Held**
Web: www.saharaglobal.com
SIC: 7382 7381 Security systems services; Security guard service

(G-6636)
SAIA MOTOR FREIGHT LINE LLC
1717 Krieger St (43228-3623)
PHONE..................614 870-8778
EMP: 57
SALES (corp-wide): 2.88B **Publicly Held**
SIC: 4213 Contract haulers
HQ: Saia Motor Freight Line, Llc
11465 Johns Creek Pkwy # 400
Duluth GA 30097
770 232-5067

(G-6637)
SAINT CECILIA CHURCH
Also Called: St Cecilia School
440 Norton Rd (43228-7602)
PHONE..................614 878-5353
Pastor Leo Connolly, *Prin*
EMP: 37 **EST:** 1882
SALES (est): 2.26MM **Privately Held**
Web: www.saintceciliachurch.org
SIC: 8211 8661 8351 Catholic elementary and secondary schools; Religious organizations; Preschool center

(G-6638)
SAINT-GOBAIN GLASS CORPORATION
2779 Westbelt Dr (43228-3862)
PHONE..................614 777-5867
EMP: 86
SALES (corp-wide): 397.78MM **Privately Held**
Web: www.saint-gobain-northamerica.com
SIC: 5039 Exterior flat glass: plate or window
HQ: Saint-Gobain Glass Corporation
20 Moores Rd
Malvern PA 19355
484 595-9430

(G-6639)
SALO INC (PA)
Also Called: Interim Services
300 W Wilson Bridge Rd Ste 250 (43085)
PHONE..................614 436-9404
Kathleen Gilmartin, *CEO*
Michael Hartshorn, *
Christine Oswald, *
Thomas Dimarco, *
Michael Slupecki, *
EMP: 55 **EST:** 1981
SQ FT: 7,500
SALES (est): 52.16MM
SALES (corp-wide): 52.16MM **Privately Held**
Web: www.interim-health.com
SIC: 8082 Home health care services

(G-6640)
SALVATION ARMY
Also Called: Salvation Army
966 E Main St (43205-2339)
PHONE..................614 252-7171
Frank Kirk, *Prin*
EMP: 30
SALES (corp-wide): 2.41B **Privately Held**
Web: www.salvationarmyusa.org
SIC: 8322 8399 Multi-service center; Advocacy group
HQ: The Salvation Army
440 W Nyack Rd Ofc
West Nyack NY 10994
845 620-7200

(G-6641)
SALVATION ARMY
Also Called: Salvation Army
1675 S High St (43207-1863)
P.O. Box 7827 (43207-0827)
PHONE..................800 728-7825
Major Dennis Gensler, *Mgr*
EMP: 27
SALES (corp-wide): 2.41B **Privately Held**
Web: www.saconnects.org
SIC: 8322 8399 Multi-service center; Community development groups
HQ: The Salvation Army
440 W Nyack Rd Ofc
West Nyack NY 10994
845 620-7200

(G-6642)
SANFILLIPO PRODUCE CO INC
Also Called: Sanfillipo Produce Company
4561 E 5th Ave Ste 1 (43219-1896)
PHONE..................614 237-3300
James Sanfillipo, *CEO*
James S Sanfillipo Iii, *CEO*
EMP: 48 **EST:** 1999
SALES (est): 9.91MM **Privately Held**
Web: www.sanfillipoproduce.com
SIC: 5148 Fruits, fresh

(G-6643)
SAR WAREHOUSE STAFFING LLC
1425 E Dublin Granville Rd Ste 109b (43229-3325)
PHONE..................740 963-6235
Amen Soumare, *CEO*
EMP: 57 **EST:** 2021
SALES (est): 3.27MM **Privately Held**
Web: www.sarwarehousestaffing.com
SIC: 7361 7389 Employment agencies; Business Activities at Non-Commercial Site

(G-6644)
SAUER CONSTRUCTION LLC
1105 Schrock Rd (43229-1146)
PHONE..................614 853-2500
Charles Steitz, *Brnch Mgr*
EMP: 75
SALES (corp-wide): 246.72MM **Privately Held**
Web: www.sauerconstruction.com
SIC: 1711 Mechanical contractor
HQ: Sauer Construction, Llc
30 51st St
Pittsburgh PA 15201
412 687-4100

(G-6645)
SAUER GROUP LLC
1105 Schrock Rd (43229-1168)
PHONE..................614 853-2500
Charles D Steitz, *Pr*
Dennis Hartz, *
Terry Kilinay, *
EMP: 200 **EST:** 2007
SALES (est): 44.27MM
SALES (corp-wide): 246.72MM **Privately Held**
Web: www.sauergroup.com
SIC: 1711 Mechanical contractor
PA: Sauer Holdings, Inc.
30 Fifthy First St 1st
Pittsburgh PA 15201
412 687-4100

(G-6646)
SAWMILL ROAD MANAGEMENT CO LLC (PA)
370 S 5th St (43215-5433)
PHONE..................937 342-9071
Judy Ross, *Managing Member*
EMP: 30 **EST:** 1996
SALES (est): 1.94MM
SALES (corp-wide): 1.94MM **Privately Held**
SIC: 6531 2421 Buying agent, real estate; Sawmills and planing mills, general

(G-6647)
SB CAPITAL ACQUISITIONS LLC
Also Called: Jc's 5 Star Outlet
4010 E 5th Ave (43219-1811)
PHONE..................614 443-4080
Jay L Schottenstein, *Prin*
David Bernstein, *Prin*
Scott Bernstein, *Prin*
Kevin Dooley, *Prin*
EMP: 1500 **EST:** 2011
SQ FT: 15,125
SALES (est): 957.24K **Privately Held**
Web: www.sb360.com
SIC: 8742 Retail trade consultant
PA: Sb Capital Group Llc
4300 E 5th Ave
Columbus OH 43219

(G-6648)
SBC ADVERTISING LTD
4030 Easton Sta Ste 300 (43219-7012)
PHONE..................614 891-7070
EMP: 110
Web: www.fahlgrenmortine.com
SIC: 7311 8742 8743 Advertising consultant; Marketing consulting services; Public relations and publicity

(G-6649)
SCHMIDT HSPTALITY CONCEPTS INC
Also Called: Silver Platter Catering
240 E Kossuth St (43206-2119)
PHONE..................614 878-4527
Andrew Schmidt, *Pr*
John Schmidt, *VP*
Geoff Schmidt, *Sec*
EMP: 30 **EST:** 1989
SALES (est): 219.35K **Privately Held**
Web: www.schmidthaus.com
SIC: 5812 7299 Caterers; Banquet hall facilities

(G-6650)
SCHNEIDER DOWNS & CO INC
65 E State St Ste 2000 (43215-4271)
PHONE..................614 621-4060
Joe Patrick, *Mgr*
EMP: 35
SALES (corp-wide): 49.13MM **Privately Held**
Web: www.schneiderdowns.com
SIC: 8721 Certified public accountant
PA: Schneider Downs & Co., Inc.
1 Ppg Pl Ste 1700
Pittsburgh PA 15222
412 261-3644

(G-6651)
SCHOOL EMPLYEES RTRMENT SYS OH
300 E Broad St Ste 100 (43215)
PHONE..................614 222-5853
James R Winfree, *Ex Dir*
Virginia Briszendine, *
Robert Cowman, *OF INVESTMENTS**
EMP: 166 **EST:** 1937
SQ FT: 197,980
SALES (est): 109.02MM **Privately Held**
Web: www.ohsers.org
SIC: 6371 9441 Pension, health, and welfare funds; Administration of social and manpower programs
HQ: Executive Office State Of Ohio
77 S High St Fl 30
Columbus OH 43215

(G-6652)
SCHOOLEY CALDWELL ASSOC INC
300 Marconi Blvd Ste 100 (43215-2329)
PHONE..................614 628-0300
Robert D Loversidge, *Pr*
Terence J Sullivan, *
Vincent A Bednar, *FED GOVN'T**
Jayne M Vandenburgh, *Interim Vice President**
Robert K Smith, *
EMP: 55 **EST:** 1944
SQ FT: 17,255
SALES (est): 9.42MM **Privately Held**
Web: www.schooleycaldwell.com
SIC: 8748 8711 8712 City planning; Consulting engineer; Architectural engineering

(G-6653)
SCHOTTENSTEIN RE GROUP LLC
2 Easton Oval Ste 510 (43219-6013)
PHONE..................614 418-8900
EMP: 38 **EST:** 1979
SQ FT: 15,000
SALES (est): 7.51MM **Privately Held**
Web: www.schottensteinrealestate.com
SIC: 6531 Real estate managers

(G-6654)
SCI SHARED RESOURCES LLC
Also Called: Schoedinger Fnrl & Cremation
229 E State St (43215-4342)
PHONE..................614 224-6105
Robert L Waltrip, *Ch*
EMP: 40
SALES (corp-wide): 4.1B **Publicly Held**
Web: www.sci-corp.com
SIC: 7261 Funeral home
HQ: Sci Shared Resources, Llc
1929 Allen Pkwy
Houston TX 77019
713 522-5141

(G-6655)
SCIOTO DOWNS INC
6000 S High St (43207)
P.O. Box 7823 (43207-0823)
PHONE..................614 295-4700
Edward T Ryan, *Pr*
Rosemarie Williams, *
EMP: 1000 **EST:** 1959
SALES (est): 31.55MM
SALES (corp-wide): 11.53B **Publicly Held**

GEOGRAPHIC SECTION

Columbus - Franklin County (G-6678)

Web: www.sciotodowns.com
SIC: 7948 Horse race track operation
HQ: Mtr Gaming Group, Inc.
    State Route 2 S
    Chester WV 26034
    304 387-8000

(G-6656)
SCRIPTDROP INC
855 Grandview Ave Ste 110 (43215-1102)
PHONE.................................614 641-0648
Nick Potts, *CEO*
Matt Darby, *
Amanda Way, *
EMP: 60 EST: 2016
SALES (est): 8.8MM **Privately Held**
Web: www.scriptdrop.co
SIC: 8082 7371 Home health care services; Computer software development and applications

(G-6657)
SEA LTD (PA)
Also Called: Sea Ltd.
7001 Buffalo Pkwy (43229-1157)
PHONE.................................614 888-4160
Jason Baker, *
Robert K Rupp, *
EMP: 100 EST: 1970
SQ FT: 56,526
SALES (est): 52.89MM **Privately Held**
Web: www.sealimited.com
SIC: 8711 Consulting engineer

(G-6658)
SECURITY CHECK LLC (PA)
Also Called: Security Check
2 Easton Oval Ste 350 (43219-6193)
P.O. Box 1211 (38655-1211)
PHONE.................................614 944-5788
EMP: 150 EST: 1994
SQ FT: 6,000
SALES (est): 4.68MM **Privately Held**
SIC: 7389 7322 Check validation service; Collection agency, except real estate

(G-6659)
SEG OF OHIO INC (PA)
Also Called: Steiner Associates
4016 Townsfair Way Ste 201 (43219-6083)
PHONE.................................614 414-7300
Yaromir Steiner, *CEO*
Barry Rosenberg, *
Beau Arnason, *
Patricia Curry, *
Laura Cooper, *
EMP: 35 EST: 1993
SQ FT: 8,035
SALES (est): 21.81MM **Privately Held**
Web: www.steiner.com
SIC: 6552 Subdividers and developers, nec

(G-6660)
SELECT SPCLTY HOSP - CLMBS/AST
181 Taylor Ave Fl 6 (43203-1779)
PHONE.................................614 293-6931
Michael T Mcgovern, *Pr*
EMP: 251 EST: 1999
SALES (est): 38.65MM
SALES (corp-wide): 6.2B **Publicly Held**
Web: www.selectspecialtyhospitals.com
SIC: 8062 General medical and surgical hospitals
HQ: Select Medical Corporation
    4714 Gettysburg Rd
    Mechanicsburg PA 17055
    717 972-1100

(G-6661)
SELECT SPCLTY HOSP - CLMBUS IN
1087 Dennison Ave (43201-3201)
PHONE.................................614 291-8467
Mary Burkett, *Brnch Mgr*
EMP: 3346
SALES (corp-wide): 6.2B **Publicly Held**
Web: www.selectspecialtyhospitals.com
SIC: 8062 General medical and surgical hospitals
HQ: Select Specialty Hospital - Columbus, Inc.
    4716 Old Gettysburg Rd
    Mechanicsburg PA 17055
    336 718-6300

(G-6662)
SEQUOIA PRO BOWL INC
5501 Sandalwood Blvd (43229-4476)
PHONE.................................614 885-7043
Tim Boss, *Owner*
EMP: 28 EST: 1980
SQ FT: 32,000
SALES (est): 629.3K **Privately Held**
Web: www.sequoiaprobowl.com
SIC: 7933 Ten pin center

(G-6663)
SERENITY CENTER INC
2841 E Dublin Granville Rd (43231-4037)
PHONE.................................614 891-1111
Cynthia Lawes, *Pr*
EMP: 47 EST: 1999
SALES (est): 6.92MM **Privately Held**
Web: www.serenity.center
SIC: 8051 Convalescent home with continuous nursing care

(G-6664)
SERVICE EXPERTS LLC
4247 Diplomacy Dr (43228-3803)
PHONE.................................614 334-3192
EMP: 32
SALES (corp-wide): 17.93B **Privately Held**
Web: www.serviceexperts.com
SIC: 7699 General household repair services
HQ: Service Experts, Llc
    1840 N Grnvlle Ave Ste 12
    Richardson TX 75081
    972 535-3800

(G-6665)
SERVICE PRONET LLC
1535 Georgesville Rd Ste A (43228)
PHONE.................................614 874-4300
Andy Deering, *CEO*
EMP: 35 EST: 2002
SALES (est): 5.28MM
SALES (corp-wide): 23.44MM **Privately Held**
Web: www.theservicepro.net
SIC: 7374 7371 7389 Computer graphics service; Computer software development and applications; Business Activities at Non-Commercial Site
PA: Servicetitan, Inc.
    800 N Brand Blvd Ste 100
    Glendale CA 91203
    855 899-0970

(G-6666)
SETTERLIN BUILDING COMPANY
Also Called: Setterlin
560 Harmon Ave (43223-2406)
PHONE.................................614 459-7077
EMP: 75 EST: 1935
SALES (est): 25.33MM **Privately Held**
Web: www.setterlin.com
SIC: 1541 1542 Industrial buildings and warehouses; Commercial and office building, new construction

(G-6667)
SETTLE MUTER ELECTRIC LTD (PA)
Also Called: S M E
711 Claycraft Rd (43230-6631)
PHONE.................................614 866-7554
Mark Muter, *Pr*
EMP: 113 EST: 1984
SQ FT: 15,000
SALES (est): 21.55MM **Privately Held**
Web: www.settlemuter.com
SIC: 1731 General electrical contractor

(G-6668)
SHADOART PRODUCTIONS INC
Also Called: SHADOWBOX
503 S Front St Ste 260 (43215-5662)
PHONE.................................614 416-7625
Stacie Boord, *Ex Dir*
Steven F Guyer, *
Julie A Klein, *
Tom Cardinal, *
EMP: 68 EST: 2001
SALES (est): 3.61MM **Privately Held**
Web: www.shadowboxlive.org
SIC: 7922 Theatrical companies

(G-6669)
SHALOM HOUSE INC (HQ)
1135 College Ave (43209-7802)
PHONE.................................614 239-1999
David Rosen, *Pr*
EMP: 35 EST: 1990
SALES (est): 2.44MM
SALES (corp-wide): 9.45MM **Privately Held**
SIC: 8361 Residential care
PA: Wexner Heritage Village
    1151 College Ave
    Columbus OH 43209
    614 231-4900

(G-6670)
SHEEDY PAVING INC
730 N Rose Ave (43219-2523)
PHONE.................................614 252-2111
TOLL FREE: 800
James P Sheedy, *Pr*
Michael Sheedy, *
Mark J Sheedy, *
Jean Sheedy, *
EMP: 36 EST: 1941
SQ FT: 3,400
SALES (est): 6.53MM **Privately Held**
Web: www.sheedypaving.com
SIC: 1611 Surfacing and paving

(G-6671)
SHG WHITEHALL HOLDINGS LLC
Also Called: Manor At Whitehall, The
4805 Langley Ave (43213-6125)
PHONE.................................614 501-8271
EMP: 36 EST: 2012
SQ FT: 55,000
SALES (est): 1.95MM **Privately Held**
SIC: 8051 Convalescent home with continuous nursing care

(G-6672)
SHIFTWISE
1263 Ashburnham Dr (43230-1798)
PHONE.................................513 476-1532
EMP: 30 EST: 2018
SALES (est): 49.69K **Privately Held**
Web: www.shiftwise.com
SIC: 7371 Computer software development

(G-6673)
SHOEMAKER ELECTRIC COMPANY
Also Called: Shoemaker Industrial Solutions
831 Bonham Ave (43211-2999)
PHONE.................................614 294-5626
Fred N Kletrovets, *Pr*
Betty Kletrovets, *
Teri Richardson, *
▲ EMP: 29 EST: 1935
SQ FT: 16,000
SALES (est): 5.16MM **Privately Held**
Web: www.shoemakerindustrial.com
SIC: 7694 5063 Electric motor repair; Motors, electric

(G-6674)
SHOWE MANAGEMENT CORPORATION
Also Called: Hamilton Creek Apartments
14 Oak Rd (43217-6003)
PHONE.................................614 492-8111
Cathy Hattin, *Mgr*
EMP: 51
SALES (corp-wide): 42MM **Privately Held**
Web: www.showecompanies.com
SIC: 6513 Apartment building operators
HQ: Showe Management Corporation
    45 N 4th St Fl 2
    Columbus OH 43215
    614 481-8106

(G-6675)
SHRADER TIRE & OIL INC
2021 Harmon Ave (43223-3828)
PHONE.................................614 445-6601
EMP: 37
SALES (corp-wide): 97.58MM **Privately Held**
Web: www.shradertireandoil.com
SIC: 5014 Tires and tubes
PA: Shrader Tire & Oil, Inc.
    2045 W Sylvania Ave # 51
    Toledo OH 43613
    419 472-2128

(G-6676)
SHRI GURU INC
Also Called: Knights Inn
4320 Groves Rd (43232-4103)
PHONE.................................614 552-2071
Jadi Singh, *Pr*
EMP: 48 EST: 1997
SALES (est): 362.49K **Privately Held**
Web: www.sonesta.com
SIC: 7011 Hotels and motels

(G-6677)
SHUMAKER LOOP & KENDRICK LLP
41 S High St Ste 2400 (43215-6150)
PHONE.................................614 463-9441
Michael Born, *Mgr*
EMP: 70
SALES (corp-wide): 68.51MM **Privately Held**
Web: www.shumaker.com
SIC: 8111 General practice attorney, lawyer
PA: Shumaker, Loop & Kendrick, Llp
    1000 Jackson St
    Toledo OH 43604
    419 241-9000

(G-6678)
SIGNATURE CLOSERS LLC
3136 Kingsdale Ctr Ste 117 (43221-2000)
PHONE.................................614 448-7750
Mark Felming Junior, *Pr*
EMP: 32 EST: 2009
SALES (est): 10.62MM
SALES (corp-wide): 2.26B **Publicly Held**

Columbus - Franklin County (G-6679) — GEOGRAPHIC SECTION

Web: www.signatureclosers.com
SIC: 6361 8742 7389 Real estate title insurance; Real estate consultant; Financial services
PA: Stewart Information Services Corporation
1360 Post Oak Blvd Ste 10
Houston TX 77056
713 625-8100

(G-6679)
SIGNATURE CONTROL SYSTEMS LLC
Also Called: Signature Controls
2228 Citygate Dr (43219-3565)
PHONE..................................614 864-2222
TOLL FREE: 877
Tom Foster, *Genl Mgr*
Bryan Roche, *VP Opers*
EMP: 50 EST: 1987
SQ FT: 20,000
SALES (est): 9.01MM
SALES (corp-wide): 9.98MM Privately Held
Web: www.tibaparking.com
SIC: 5063 1799 Control and signal wire and cable, including coaxial; Parking facility equipment installation
PA: Tiba Llc
2228 Citygate Dr
Columbus OH 43219
614 328-2040

(G-6680)
SILLIKER LABORATORIES OHIO INC
2057 Builders Pl (43204-4886)
PHONE..................................614 486-0150
Amitha Miele, *Pr*
EMP: 47 EST: 1989
SQ FT: 4,700
SALES (est): 1.95MM
SALES (corp-wide): 7.5MM Privately Held
SIC: 8734 Food testing service
HQ: Silliker, Inc.
401 N Michigan Ave # 1400
Chicago IL 60611

(G-6681)
SIMON KNTON CNCIL BYSCUTS AMER (PA)
Also Called: BOY SCOUTS OF AMERICA
807 Kinnear Rd (43212-1490)
PHONE..................................614 436-7200
Randy Larson, *Dir*
EMP: 47 EST: 1925
SQ FT: 20,000
SALES (est): 4.84MM
SALES (corp-wide): 4.84MM Privately Held
Web: www.skcscouts.org
SIC: 8641 Boy Scout organization

(G-6682)
SIMOS INSOURCING SOLUTIONS LLC
1356 Cherry Bottom Rd (43230-6771)
PHONE..................................614 470-6088
Tina Inks, *Off Mgr*
EMP: 64
SALES (corp-wide): 1.91B Publicly Held
Web: www.simossolutions.com
SIC: 7361 Employment agencies
HQ: Simos Insourcing Solutions Llc
13010 Morris Rd Ste 650
Alpharetta GA 30004
770 992-3441

(G-6683)
SIMPSON STRONG-TIE COMPANY INC
2600 International St (43228-4617)
PHONE..................................614 876-8060
Dave Williams, *Brnch Mgr*
EMP: 239
SALES (corp-wide): 2.21B Publicly Held
Web: www.strongtie.com
SIC: 5082 3643 3452 Construction and mining machinery; Current-carrying wiring services; Bolts, nuts, rivets, and washers
HQ: Simpson Strong-Tie Company Inc.
5956 W Las Positas Blvd
Pleasanton CA 94588
925 560-9000

(G-6684)
SINCLAIR MEDIA II INC
Also Called: Wsyx and ABC 6
1261 Dublin Rd (43215-7000)
PHONE..................................614 481-6666
Dan Mellon, *Mgr*
EMP: 113
SQ FT: 31,942
SALES (corp-wide): 2.98B Publicly Held
Web: www.abc6onyourside.com
SIC: 4833 Television broadcasting stations
HQ: Sinclair Media Ii, Inc.
10706 Beaver Dam Rd
Hunt Valley MD 21030
513 641-4400

(G-6685)
SKILKENGOLD DEVELOPMENT LLC
Also Called: Skilken
4270 Morse Rd (43230-1523)
PHONE..................................614 418-3100
Ken Gold, *CEO*
Frank Petruziello, *Pr*
Tobi Skilken Gold, *COO*
Steve Stadler, *VP*
Andy Bartz, *VP*
EMP: 46 EST: 2014
SALES (est): 4.99MM Privately Held
Web: www.skilkengold.com
SIC: 6211 1521 Investment firm, general brokerage; Single-family housing construction

(G-6686)
SKINNER DIESEL SERVICES INC (PA)
Also Called: Commercial Radiator
2440 Lockbourne Rd (43207-2168)
PHONE..................................614 491-8785
Mike L Skinner, *Pr*
EMP: 48 EST: 1982
SQ FT: 12,000
SALES (est): 4.62MM
SALES (corp-wide): 4.62MM Privately Held
Web: www.skinnerdieselservice.com
SIC: 7538 7532 Diesel engine repair: automotive; Body shop, trucks

(G-6687)
SKYWAYS LOGISTICS LLC
2122 Lockbourne Rd (43207-2162)
P.O. Box 30911 (43230-0911)
PHONE..................................614 333-0333
Hussnain Ali, *Pr*
EMP: 55 EST: 2012
SALES (est): 2.77MM Privately Held
SIC: 4789 Transportation services, nec

(G-6688)
SLEEP CARE INC
985 Schrock Rd Ste 204 (43229-1139)
PHONE..................................614 901-8989
Craig Pickerill, *Pr*
EMP: 27 EST: 1997
SALES (est): 500.65K Privately Held
Web: www.sleepcareinc.com
SIC: 8093 Biofeedback center

(G-6689)
SMG HOLDINGS LLC
Also Called: Greater Clumbus Convention Ctr
400 N High St Ofc (43215-2076)
PHONE..................................614 827-2500
John Page, *Genl Mgr*
EMP: 32
SALES (corp-wide): 1.13B Privately Held
Web: www.asmglobal.com
SIC: 8741 6512 Management services; Nonresidential building operators
HQ: Smg Holdings, Llc
300 Cnshohckn State Rd # 450
Conshohocken PA 19428

(G-6690)
SMITH & ASSOCIATES EXCAVATING
2765 Drake Rd (43219-1603)
PHONE..................................740 362-3355
Ken Belczak, *Pr*
EMP: 40 EST: 1976
SQ FT: 9,600
SALES (est): 4.75MM Privately Held
Web: www.smithexc.com
SIC: 1794 Excavation and grading, building construction

(G-6691)
SMOOT CONSTRUCTION CO OHIO (HQ)
Also Called: Smoot Construction
1907 Leonard Ave (43219-4503)
PHONE..................................614 253-9000
Lewis R Smoot Senior, *CEO*
Mark Cain, *
Lewis R Smoot Junior, *Sr VP*
Thomas J Fitzpatrick, *
EMP: 50 EST: 1987
SALES (est): 48.16MM
SALES (corp-wide): 48.16MM Privately Held
Web: www.smootconstruction.com
SIC: 1542 Commercial and office building, new construction
PA: The Smoot Corporation
1907 Leonard Ave Ste 200
Columbus OH 43219
614 253-9000

(G-6692)
SONIC AUTOMOTIVE
Also Called: Toyota West
1500 Auto Mall Dr (43228-3660)
PHONE..................................614 870-8200
Jeff Rachor, *Treas*
Thea Wright, *
EMP: 94 EST: 1987
SALES (est): 24.55MM
SALES (corp-wide): 14.37B Publicly Held
Web: www.toyotawest.com
SIC: 5511 7538 7515 5531 Automobiles, new and used; General automotive repair shops; Passenger car leasing; Auto and home supply stores
PA: Sonic Automotive, Inc.
4401 Colwick Rd
Charlotte NC 28211
704 566-2400

(G-6693)
SOUTH SIDE LEARNING & DEV CTR
Also Called: SPROUTFIVE
1621 W 1st Ave Ste 2 (43212)
PHONE..................................614 212-4696
Colin Pagemcginnis, *CEO*
Roberta Bishop, *
EMP: 52 EST: 1922
SALES (est): 3.53MM Privately Held
Web: www.sproutfive.org
SIC: 8351 Preschool center

(G-6694)
SOUTHAST CMNTY MENTAL HLTH CTR (PA)
16 W Long St (43215-2815)
PHONE..................................614 225-0980
Steven Atwood, *CFO*
Sandra Stephenson, *
EMP: 250 EST: 1978
SQ FT: 67,988
SALES (est): 150.84K
SALES (corp-wide): 150.84K Privately Held
Web: www.southeasthc.org
SIC: 8093 8361 8011 Mental health clinic, outpatient; Residential care; Offices and clinics of medical doctors

(G-6695)
SOUTHEAST INC
16 W Long St (43215-2815)
P.O. Box 1809 (43216-1809)
PHONE..................................614 225-0990
EMP: 418 EST: 2011
SALES (est): 49.58MM Privately Held
Web: www.southeasthc.org
SIC: 8069 Specialty hospitals, except psychiatric

(G-6696)
SOUTHERN GLZERS DSTRS OHIO LLC (DH)
Also Called: Glazer's of Ohio
4800 Poth Rd (43213-1332)
PHONE..................................614 552-7900
▲ EMP: 68 EST: 1991
SQ FT: 100,000
SALES (est): 199.75MM
SALES (corp-wide): 7.27B Privately Held
SIC: 5181 5182 Beer and ale; Wine
HQ: Southern Glazer's Wine And Spirits, Llc
2400 Sw 145th Ave Ste 200
Miramar FL 33027
954 680-4600

(G-6697)
SOUTHERN HLLS HLTH RHBLTTION C
Also Called: Vrable II, Inc.
3248 Henderson Rd (43220-7337)
PHONE..................................614 545-5502
EMP: 91 EST: 2006
SQ FT: 40,000
SALES (est): 2.21MM Privately Held
SIC: 8051 Convalescent home with continuous nursing care
PA: Vrable Healthcare, Inc.
3248 Henderson Rd
Columbus OH 43220

(G-6698)
SOUTHWEST LITHOTRIPSY
Also Called: Aksm/Southwest Lithotripsy
100 W 3rd Ave Ste 350 (43201-7205)
PHONE..................................614 447-0281
Ann Stevens, *Dir*
Henry Wise, *CEO*
EMP: 60 EST: 1999
SALES (est): 1.33MM Privately Held
SIC: 8099 Health and allied services, nec

(G-6699)
SOUTHWESTERN ELECTRIC POWER CO (HQ)
1 Riverside Plz (43215)
PHONE..................................614 716-1000
Nicholas K Akins, *Ch Bd*
Malcolm Smoak, *Pr*
Brian X Tierney, *

GEOGRAPHIC SECTION

Joseph M Buonaiuto, *CAO*
EMP: 64 **EST:** 1912
SALES (est): 2.18B
SALES (corp-wide): 18.98B **Privately Held**
Web: www.swepco.com
SIC: 4911 Generation, electric power
PA: American Electric Power Company, Inc.
1 Riverside Plz Fl 1 # 1
Columbus OH 43215
614 716-1000

(G-6700)
SOUTHWESTERN TILE AND MBL CO
1030 Cable Ave (43222-1202)
PHONE.................614 464-1257
Vaughn Fowler, *Pr*
Vaughn Fowler Junior, *Pr*
Robert Fowler, *
Judith Vest, *
Debbie Fuller, *
EMP: 28 **EST:** 1977
SQ FT: 10,000
SALES (est): 1.9MM **Privately Held**
SIC: 1743 Tile installation, ceramic

(G-6701)
SPARTAN WHSE & DIST CO INC (PA)
Also Called: Spartan Logistics
4140 Lockbourne Rd (43207-4221)
PHONE.................614 497-1777
Steve Harmon, *Pr*
Ed Harmon, *
▲ **EMP:** 85 **EST:** 1988
SQ FT: 1,000,000
SALES (est): 90.86MM
SALES (corp-wide): 90.86MM **Privately Held**
Web: www.spartanlogistics.com
SIC: 4225 General warehousing

(G-6702)
SPECTRA HOLDINGS INC
Also Called: Spectra Contract Flooring
3031 International St (43228-4635)
PHONE.................614 921-8493
Robert Mckelvey, *Brnch Mgr*
EMP: 29
SALES (corp-wide): 557.41MM **Privately Held**
Web: www.spectracf.com
SIC: 1752 Floor laying and floor work, nec
HQ: Spectra Holdings, Inc.
616 E Walnut Ave
Dalton GA 30721
706 278-3812

(G-6703)
SPECTRUM MGT HOLDG CO LLC
Also Called: Time Warner
1015 Olentangy River Rd (43212-3148)
PHONE.................614 344-4159
Rhonda Frost, *Pr*
EMP: 45
SALES (corp-wide): 54.61B **Publicly Held**
Web: www.spectrum.com
SIC: 4841 Cable television services
HQ: Spectrum Management Holding Company, Llc
400 Atlantic St
Stamford CT 06901
203 905-7801

(G-6704)
SPEER INDUSTRIES INCORPORATED (PA)
Also Called: Speer Mechanical
5255 Sinclair Rd (43229-5042)
PHONE.................614 261-6331
Samuel A Shuman, *Ch Bd*
Dennis Shuman, *
EMP: 45 **EST:** 1927
SQ FT: 60,000
SALES (est): 62.38MM
SALES (corp-wide): 62.38MM **Privately Held**
Web: www.speermechanical.com
SIC: 1711 Mechanical contractor

(G-6705)
SPORTS MEDICINE GRANT INC (PA)
Also Called: Smgoa
323 E Town St Ste 100 (43215-4774)
PHONE.................614 461-8174
Raymond J Tesner, *Pr*
EMP: 39 **EST:** 1985
SQ FT: 8,600
SALES (est): 4.55MM
SALES (corp-wide): 4.55MM **Privately Held**
SIC: 8031 Offices and clinics of osteopathic physicians

(G-6706)
ST STPHENS CMNTY HMES LTD PRT
Also Called: ST STEPHENS COMMUNITY SERVICE
1500 E 17th Ave (43219-1002)
PHONE.................614 294-6347
Judy Stattmiller, *Ex Dir*
Tim Kelly, *
Ray Thomas, *
Kevin Barnett, *
Vinna Gardner, *
EMP: 80 **EST:** 1919
SQ FT: 41,000
SALES (est): 6.14MM **Privately Held**
Web: www.saintstephensch.org
SIC: 8322 8351 Community center; Child day care services

(G-6707)
ST VINCENT FAMILY SERVICES (PA)
1490 E Main St (43205)
PHONE.................614 252-0731
Anne Ransone, *Pr*
EMP: 132 **EST:** 1967
SALES (est): 14.98MM
SALES (corp-wide): 14.98MM **Privately Held**
Web: www.svfsohio.org
SIC: 8322 8361 8093 Social service center; Residential care for the handicapped; Specialty outpatient clinics, nec

(G-6708)
STAFFING STUDIO LLC
4449 Easton Way Fl 2 (43219-7005)
PHONE.................614 934-1860
EMP: 50 **EST:** 2021
SALES (est): 2.46MM **Privately Held**
Web: www.thestaffingstudio.com
SIC: 7361 Employment agencies

(G-6709)
STAR HOUSE
1220 Corrugated Way (43201-2902)
PHONE.................614 826-5868
Ann Bischoff, *CEO*
Mark Batcheck, *
EMP: 27 **EST:** 2016
SALES (est): 4.59MM **Privately Held**
Web: www.starhouse.us
SIC: 8641 Civic and social associations

(G-6710)
STAR LEASING COMPANY LLC (PA)
4080 Business Park Dr (43204-5023)
PHONE.................614 278-9999
Steve Jackson, *Pr*
Thomas C Copeland Iii, *Prin*
Linda Tulley, *Pr*
Jeffrey H Rosen, *
Michael Hensley, *
EMP: 75 **EST:** 1974
SALES (est): 74.36MM
SALES (corp-wide): 74.36MM **Privately Held**
Web: www.starleasing.com
SIC: 7513 7549 7539 Truck leasing, without drivers; Towing services; Automotive turbocharger and blower repair

(G-6711)
STAR PACKAGING INC
1796 Frebis Ave (43206-3729)
PHONE.................614 564-9936
James R Tata, *Pr*
EMP: 32 **EST:** 1979
SQ FT: 53,000
SALES (est): 6.21MM **Privately Held**
Web: www.starpackaginginc.com
SIC: 5199 4783 Packaging materials; Packing goods for shipping

(G-6712)
STAR SEVEN SIX LTD
2550 Corporate Exchange Dr Ste 109 (43231-7659)
PHONE.................800 669-9623
Eric Hoffmann, *Pr*
Halden Studlien, *Dir*
Bryan Barlow, *COO*
EMP: 30 **EST:** 1999
SALES (est): 5.88MM **Privately Held**
Web: www.sedgwicktech.com
SIC: 7379 Computer related consulting services

(G-6713)
STATE AUTO FINANCIAL CORP (HQ)
Also Called: Stfc
518 E Broad St (43215-3901)
PHONE.................614 464-5000
Michael E Larocco, *Ch*
EMP: 134 **EST:** 1990
SQ FT: 280,000
SALES (est): 1.48B
SALES (corp-wide): 20.63B **Privately Held**
Web: www.stateautolabs.com
SIC: 6331 Fire, marine, and casualty insurance
PA: Liberty Mutual Holding Company Inc.
175 Berkeley St
Boston MA 02117
617 357-9500

(G-6714)
STATE AUTOMOBILE MUTL INSUR CO (DH)
Also Called: State Auto Insurance Companies
518 E Broad St (43215-3901)
P.O. Box 182822 (43218-2822)
PHONE.................833 724-3577
David H Long, *CEO*
EMP: 1500 **EST:** 1921
SQ FT: 270,000
SALES (est): 1.87B
SALES (corp-wide): 20.63B **Privately Held**
Web: www.stateauto.com
SIC: 6331 6411 6351 Fire, marine and casualty insurance and carriers; Insurance agents, brokers, and service; Surety insurance
HQ: Liberty Mutual Insurance Company
175 Berkeley St
Boston MA 02116
617 357-9500

(G-6715)
STATE TCHERS RTREMENT SYS OHIO (HQ)
Also Called: STRS Ohio
275 E Broad St (43215-3703)
PHONE.................614 227-4090
Robert Stein, *Ch*
Michael J Nehf, *
Sandra L Knoesel, *Deputy Executive Director**
Stephen A Mitchell, *Deputy Executive Director**
Robert A Slater, *Deputy Executive Director**
EMP: 232 **EST:** 1919
SQ FT: 176,000
SALES (est): 13.66MM **Privately Held**
Web: www.strsoh.org
SIC: 6371 Pension funds
PA: State Of Ohio
30 E Broad St Fl 40
Columbus OH 43215
614 466-3455

(G-6716)
STATECO FINANCIAL SERVICES INC
518 E Broad St (43215-3901)
P.O. Box 182822 (43218-2822)
PHONE.................614 464-5000
Robert Moone, *Pr*
Urlin G Harris Junior, *VP*
John R Lowther, *
Terry Bowshier, *
EMP: 200 **EST:** 1962
SALES (est): 46.18MM
SALES (corp-wide): 20.63B **Privately Held**
SIC: 6211 Investment firm, general brokerage
HQ: State Auto Financial Corporation
518 E Broad St
Columbus OH 43215

(G-6717)
STAYMOBILE FRANCHISING LLC
1598 N High St (43201-1189)
PHONE.................614 601-3345
EMP: 61
SALES (corp-wide): 29.23MM **Privately Held**
Web: www.staymobile.com
SIC: 6794 Franchises, selling or licensing
PA: Staymobile Franchising, Llc
175 Chstain Meadows Ct Nw
Kennesaw GA 30144
678 695-8535

(G-6718)
STERLING PAPER CO (HQ)
1845 Progress Ave (43207-1726)
PHONE.................614 443-0303
Robert Rosenfeld, *Pr*
Charles R Brown, *Prin*
Roy A Otey, *Prin*
Stephen C Brown, *Prin*
▲ **EMP:** 45 **EST:** 1937
SALES (est): 48.91MM
SALES (corp-wide): 48.91MM **Privately Held**
Web: office.sterling-paper.com
SIC: 5111 5199 Printing paper; Packaging materials
PA: Rosemark Paper, Inc.
1845 Progress Ave
Columbus OH 43207
614 443-0303

(G-6719)
STONEHENGE CAPITAL COMPANY LLC
191 W Nationwide Blvd Ste 600 (43215-2569)
PHONE.................614 246-2456
Thomas Adamak, *Brnch Mgr*
EMP: 28
SALES (corp-wide): 23.58MM **Privately Held**
Web: www.stonehengecapital.com

Columbus - Franklin County (G-6720)

SIC: 6799 Venture capital companies
PA: Stonehenge Capital Company Llc
236 3rd St
Baton Rouge LA 70801
225 408-3000

(G-6720)
STONEHENGE FINCL HOLDINGS INC (PA)
191 W Nationwide Blvd Ste 600 (43215-2568)
PHONE..................................614 246-2500
David R Meuse, *Pr*
Ronald D Brooks, *
Michael J Endres, *
James Henson, *
Brad L Pospichel, *
EMP: 50 **EST:** 1999
SQ FT: 17,000
SALES (est): 4.41MM
SALES (corp-wide): 4.41MM **Privately Held**
SIC: 6799 Venture capital companies

(G-6721)
STRADERS GARDEN CENTERS INC (PA)
Also Called: Strader's Green House
5350 Riverside Dr (43220-1700)
PHONE..................................614 889-1314
Jack D Strader, *Pr*
Mary Brennan, *
Ruth E Strader, *
▲ **EMP:** 125 **EST:** 1953
SQ FT: 30,625
SALES (est): 14.36MM
SALES (corp-wide): 14.36MM **Privately Held**
Web: www.straders.net
SIC: 5261 5193 Retail nurseries; Plants, potted

(G-6722)
STRATEGY NETWORK LLC (PA)
1349 E Broad St (43205-1503)
PHONE..................................614 595-0688
EMP: 35 **EST:** 2001
SALES (est): 21.81MM
SALES (corp-wide): 21.81MM **Privately Held**
Web: www.teamtsn.com
SIC: 8748 8651 Business consulting, nec; Political campaign organization

(G-6723)
STRUTHERS CU A DIV BRDGE CR UN
Also Called: Stecu
1980 W Broad St (43223-1102)
PHONE..................................800 434-7300
Christine Leslie, *Pr*
Jarod Bach, *VP*
EMP: 27 **EST:** 1967
SALES (est): 4.33MM **Privately Held**
Web: www.bridgecu.org
SIC: 6062 6163 State credit unions, not federally chartered; Loan brokers

(G-6724)
STUDENT VOL OPT SERV TO HUMNTY
Also Called: College of Optometry
338 W 10th Ave (43210-1280)
PHONE..................................614 292-9086
EMP: 58 **EST:** 2011
SALES (est): 476.47K **Privately Held**
Web: optometry.osu.edu
SIC: 8042 Offices and clinics of optometrists

(G-6725)
STYLE-LINE INCORPORATED (PA)
Also Called: Chelsea House Fabrics
901 W 3rd Ave Ste A (43212-3131)
P.O. Box 2706 (43216-2706)
PHONE..................................614 291-0600
Laura R Prophater, *Pr*
William H Prophater, *
EMP: 35 **EST:** 1969
SQ FT: 54,000
SALES (est): 4.15MM
SALES (corp-wide): 4.15MM **Privately Held**
Web: www.lookhuman.com
SIC: 5023 5131 2391 1799 Venetian blinds; Drapery material, woven; Curtains, window: made from purchased materials; Drapery track installation

(G-6726)
SULLIVAN BRUCK ARCHITECTS INC
8 S Grant Ave (43215-3954)
PHONE..................................614 464-9800
Gary Bruck, *Pr*
Joseph Sullivan, *VP*
EMP: 30 **EST:** 1985
SQ FT: 10,000
SALES (est): 1.03MM **Privately Held**
Web: www.sbarch.com
SIC: 8712 Architectural engineering

(G-6727)
SUMMIT FINCL STRATEGIES INC
Also Called: Summit Financial Strategies
4111 Worth Ave Ste 510 (43219-3682)
PHONE..................................614 885-1115
Samantha Maccia, *Pr*
Ted Saneholtz, *Advisor**
EMP: 50 **EST:** 1994
SALES (est): 2.29MM **Privately Held**
Web: www.summitfin.com
SIC: 8742 Financial consultant

(G-6728)
SUMTOTAL SYSTEMS LLC
100 E Campus View Blvd Ste 250 (43235-4647)
PHONE..................................352 264-2800
Bruce Duff, *Sr VP*
EMP: 37
SALES (corp-wide): 740.92MM **Privately Held**
Web: www.sumtotalsystems.com
SIC: 7371 Computer software development
HQ: Sumtotal Systems Llc
2850 Nw 43rd St
Gainesville FL 32606
352 264-2800

(G-6729)
SUNBELT RENTALS INC
Also Called: Midwest Reg Columbus
1275 W Mound St (43223-2213)
PHONE..................................614 341-9770
Brad Cahill, *Brnch Mgr*
EMP: 30
SALES (corp-wide): 9.67B **Privately Held**
Web: www.sunbeltrentals.com
SIC: 7353 7359 Heavy construction equipment rental; Equipment rental and leasing, nec
HQ: Sunbelt Rentals, Inc.
1799 Innovation Pt
Fort Mill SC 29715
803 578-5811

(G-6730)
SUNRISE CONNECTICUT AVE ASSN
Also Called: Forum At Knightsbridge
4590 Knightsbridge Blvd (43214-4327)
PHONE..................................614 451-6766
Beckey Converse, *Dir*
EMP: 656
SQ FT: 4,000
SALES (corp-wide): 2.92B **Privately Held**
Web: www.theforumatknightsbridge.com
SIC: 8051 Skilled nursing care facilities
HQ: Sunrise Connecticut Avenue Association
5111 Connecticut Ave Nw
Washington DC 20008
202 966-8020

(G-6731)
SUNRISE SENIOR LIVING MGT INC
2600 E Main St (43209-2446)
PHONE..................................614 235-3900
EMP: 144
SALES (corp-wide): 2.92B **Privately Held**
Web: www.sunriseseniorliving.com
SIC: 7631 8051 Jewelry repair services; Skilled nursing care facilities
HQ: Sunrise Senior Living Management, Inc.
7902 Westpark Dr
Mc Lean VA 22102
703 273-7500

(G-6732)
SUPREME TOUCH HOME HEALTH SVCS
2547 W Broad St (43204-3324)
PHONE..................................614 783-1115
Gbolaga Akinboyede, *Pr*
Sefinat Akinboyede, *
EMP: 42 **EST:** 2010
SALES (est): 2.64MM **Privately Held**
Web: www.supremetouchcare.com
SIC: 8082 Home health care services

(G-6733)
SUPREME VENTURES LLC
Also Called: Columbus Coach Supreme Limosne
3034 Lamb Ave (43219-2311)
PHONE..................................614 372-0355
EMP: 45 **EST:** 2013
SALES (est): 1.45MM **Privately Held**
Web: www.columbuscoach.com
SIC: 4142 Bus charter service, except local

(G-6734)
SURE HOME IMPROVEMENTS LLC
6031 E Main St (43213-3590)
PHONE..................................614 975-7727
EMP: 30 **EST:** 2009
SALES (est): 3.62MM **Privately Held**
Web: www.surehomeimprovements.com
SIC: 1521 General remodeling, single-family houses

(G-6735)
SURGE MANAGEMENT LLC
4 Easton Oval (43219-6010)
PHONE..................................614 431-5100
EMP: 33 **EST:** 2018
SALES (est): 2.7MM **Privately Held**
Web: www.surgestaffing.com
SIC: 8741 Management services

(G-6736)
SURGEFORCE LLC
4 Easton Oval (43219-6010)
PHONE..................................614 431-4991
EMP: 750 **EST:** 2013
SALES (est): 13.32MM **Privately Held**
Web: www.surgeforcegroup.com
SIC: 7361 Employment agencies

(G-6737)
SUTTON & ASSOCIATES INC
2250 Mckinley Ave (43204-3542)
PHONE..................................614 487-9096
Jeff Sutton, *Pr*
Lawrence S Sutton, *Bd of Dir*
Jonathan A Tarbox, *Prin*
EMP: 35 **EST:** 1982
SQ FT: 10,000
SALES (est): 886.05K **Privately Held**
Web: www.suttonandassoc.com
SIC: 1711 8711 Refrigeration contractor; Engineering services

(G-6738)
SW SQUARED LLC
Also Called: Anchor Security and Logistics
1410 Williams Rd (43207-5185)
PHONE..................................614 300-5304
Stacey Walker, *CEO*
EMP: 60 **EST:** 2017
SALES (est): 1.47MM **Privately Held**
Web: www.anchorsecuritylogistics.com
SIC: 7381 Security guard service

(G-6739)
SWITCHBOX INC
4500 Mobile Dr (43220-3782)
PHONE..................................614 334-9517
Joel Stephens, *Pr*
Adam Jackson, *Dir*
EMP: 34 **EST:** 2006
SALES (est): 2MM **Privately Held**
Web: www.switchboxinc.com
SIC: 7371 Computer software development

(G-6740)
SYGMA NETWORK INC
Also Called: Sygma
2400 Harrison Rd (43204-3508)
PHONE..................................614 771-3801
Bob Johnson, *Brnch Mgr*
EMP: 321
SQ FT: 10,000
SALES (corp-wide): 76.32B **Publicly Held**
Web: www.sygmanetwork.com
SIC: 5141 Food brokers
HQ: The Sygma Network Inc
5550 Blazer Pkwy Ste 300
Dublin OH 43017

(G-6741)
SYMPHONY DAGNSTC SVCS NO 1 LLC
Also Called: Mobilexusa
6185 Huntley Rd Ste Q (43229-1094)
PHONE..................................614 888-2226
Bill Glynn, *Mgr*
EMP: 526
SALES (corp-wide): 455.12MM **Privately Held**
SIC: 8071 Medical laboratories
HQ: Symphony Diagnostic Services No. 1, Llc
101 Rock Rd
Horsham PA 19044
215 442-0660

(G-6742)
SYNAPSE TECH SERVICES INC
4449 Easton Way Ste 200 (43219-7005)
PHONE..................................337 592-3205
Manikanta Dunga, *Pr*
EMP: 35 **EST:** 2016
SALES (est): 1.89MM **Privately Held**
Web: www.synapsetechservice.com
SIC: 7371 7379 Custom computer programming services; Computer related consulting services

GEOGRAPHIC SECTION

Columbus - Franklin County (G-6766)

(G-6743)
SYSCO CENTRAL OHIO INC
Also Called: Sysco
2400 Harrison Rd (43204-3508)
P.O. Box 94570 (44101-4570)
EMP: 300 **EST:** 1941
SALES (est): 89.2MM
SALES (corp-wide): 76.32B **Publicly Held**
Web: www.sysco.com
SIC: 5141 5142 Groceries, general line; Packaged frozen goods
PA: Sysco Corporation
1390 Enclave Pkwy
Houston TX 77077
281 584-1390

(G-6744)
T&L GLOBAL MANAGEMENT LLC
Also Called: Pro-Touch
1572 Lafayette Dr (43220-3867)
PHONE..............................614 586-0303
EMP: 86 **EST:** 2011
SALES (est): 2.27MM **Privately Held**
SIC: 7349 5169 Janitorial service, contract basis; Chemicals and allied products, nec

(G-6745)
TABCO CONSULTING SERVICES LLC
700 Morse Rd Ste 210 (43214-1879)
PHONE..............................740 217-0010
James D, *CEO*
James Doublin, *
EMP: 47 **EST:** 2021
SALES (est): 1.27MM **Privately Held**
SIC: 8742 Management consulting services

(G-6746)
TAILORED MANAGEMENT SERVICES (PA)
Also Called: Tailored Management
1165 Dublin Rd (43215-1005)
PHONE..............................614 859-1500
Brad Beach, *Pr*
EMP: 48 **EST:** 1988
SALES (est): 10.55MM **Privately Held**
Web: www.tailoredmanagement.com
SIC: 7361 Employment agencies

(G-6747)
TANGOE US INC
200 E Campus View Blvd (43235-4678)
PHONE..............................614 842-9918
EMP: 165
Web: www.tangoe.com
SIC: 8748 Telecommunications consultant
HQ: Tangoe Us, Inc.
8888 Keystone Xing # 1300
Indianapolis IN 46240
973 257-0300

(G-6748)
TANSKY SALES INC
Also Called: Tanskys Auto Body & Paint Ctr
2475 W Dublin Granville Rd (43235-2708)
PHONE..............................614 793-2080
EMP: 45
SALES (corp-wide): 39.18MM **Privately Held**
Web: www.tanskysawmilltoyota.com
SIC: 7532 Top and body repair and paint shops
PA: Tansky Sales, Inc.
6300 Sawmill Rd
Dublin OH 43017
614 766-4800

(G-6749)
TARRIER FOODS CORP
Also Called: Tarrier
2700 International St (43228-4640)
PHONE..............................614 876-8594
Timothy A Tarrier, *Pr*
Ann Tarrier, *
Julia A Grooms, *
EMP: 42 **EST:** 1978
SQ FT: 54,000
SALES (est): 35.34MM **Privately Held**
Web: www.tarrierfoods.com
SIC: 5149 5145 2099 Dried or canned foods; Nuts, salted or roasted; Food preparations, nec

(G-6750)
TAYLOR STN SURGICAL CTR LTD
Also Called: Taylor Station Surgical Center
275 Taylor Station Rd Unit A (43213-2927)
PHONE..............................614 751-4466
EMP: 80 **EST:** 1996
SQ FT: 1,728
SALES (est): 20.37MM **Privately Held**
Web: www.taylorstation.com
SIC: 8011 Ambulatory surgical center

(G-6751)
TEAM LUBRICATION INC
Also Called: Jiffy Lube
921 Robinwood Ave Ste C (43213-6706)
P.O. Box 13189 (43213-0189)
PHONE..............................614 231-9909
James E Deitz, *Pr*
EMP: 85 **EST:** 1985
SQ FT: 3,900
SALES (est): 1.59MM **Privately Held**
Web: www.jiffylube.com
SIC: 7549 Lubrication service, automotive

(G-6752)
TEAMDYNAMIX SOLUTIONS LLC
Also Called: Teamdynamix
1600 Dublin Rd Ste 200 (43215-2872)
PHONE..............................877 752-6196
Ken Benvenuto, *CEO*
Jessica Newsome Ctrl, *Prin*
EMP: 71 **EST:** 2001
SALES (est): 10.4MM **Privately Held**
Web: www.teamdynamix.com
SIC: 7371 Computer software development

(G-6753)
TEK LOGISTICS LLC
4557 Belvedere Park (43228-6359)
PHONE..............................614 260-9250
EMP: 27 **EST:** 2015
SALES (est): 545.81K **Privately Held**
SIC: 4231 Trucking terminal facilities

(G-6754)
TEK-COLLECT INCORPORATED
871 Park St (43215-1441)
PHONE..............................614 299-2766
Nicole Buhr, *Pr*
Chet Groff, *
Pam Nast, *
Mark Kabbara, *
David Hughes, *
EMP: 163 **EST:** 2001
SQ FT: 5,500
SALES (est): 11.73MM **Privately Held**
Web: www.tekcollect.com
SIC: 7322 Collection agency, except real estate

(G-6755)
TELHIO CREDIT UNION INC (PA)
330 Rush Aly (43215-3368)
P.O. Box 1449 (43216-1449)
PHONE..............................614 221-3233
Leslie Bumgarner, *CEO*
Derrick Bailey, *
EMP: 50 **EST:** 1935
SQ FT: 24,000
SALES (est): 63.04MM
SALES (corp-wide): 63.04MM **Privately Held**
Web: www.telhio.org
SIC: 6061 Federal credit unions

(G-6756)
TFORCE FREIGHT INC
3400 Refugee Rd (43232-4814)
PHONE..............................614 238-2355
Tim Carlyle, *Pr*
EMP: 53
SALES (corp-wide): 8.81B **Privately Held**
Web: www.tforcefreight.com
SIC: 4213 Contract haulers
HQ: Tforce Freight, Inc.
1000 Semmes Ave
Richmond VA 23224
800 333-7400

(G-6757)
TFORCE LOGISTICS EAST LLC
Also Called: Dynamex
2735 Westbelt Dr (43228-3896)
PHONE..............................614 276-6000
William Ewing, *Mgr*
EMP: 34
SALES (corp-wide): 8.81B **Privately Held**
Web: www.tforcelogistics.com
SIC: 4215 4212 Courier services, except by air; Delivery service, vehicular
HQ: Tforce Logistics East, Llc
14881 Quorum Dr Ste 700
Dallas TX 75254

(G-6758)
THE COTTINGHAM PAPER CO
Also Called: Cottingham Party Savers
324 E 2nd Ave (43201-4249)
PHONE..............................614 294-6444
Richard S Cottingham, *Pr*
Craig Cottingham, *
Mary Beth Willis, *
EMP: 37 **EST:** 1932
SQ FT: 48,000
SALES (est): 1.53MM **Privately Held**
SIC: 5046 5113 5087 Restaurant equipment and supplies, nec; Industrial and personal service paper; Janitors' supplies

(G-6759)
THE DAIMLER GROUP INC
1533 Lake Shore Dr (43204-3897)
PHONE..............................614 488-4424
Robert C White, *Ch Bd*
Conrad W Wisinger, *
Herman Ziegler, *
Larry Wendling, *
EMP: 31 **EST:** 1983
SQ FT: 7,000
SALES (est): 15.6MM **Privately Held**
Web: www.daimlergroup.com
SIC: 6552 Land subdividers and developers, commercial

(G-6760)
THE HUNTINGTON INVESTMENT CO (HQ)
41 S High St Fl 7 (43215-6116)
PHONE..............................614 480-3600
Michael Miroballi, *Pr*
Raymond Closz, *COO*
EMP: 105 **EST:** 1985
SQ FT: 110,000
SALES (est): 55.71MM
SALES (corp-wide): 10.84B **Publicly Held**
Web: www.huntington.com
SIC: 6211 Brokers, security
PA: Huntington Bancshares Incorporated
41 S High St
Columbus OH 43287
614 480-2265

(G-6761)
THE OLEN CORPORATION (PA)
4755 S High St (43207-4080)
PHONE..............................614 491-1515
TOLL FREE: 800
EMP: 62 **EST:** 1951
SALES (est): 26.19MM
SALES (corp-wide): 26.19MM **Privately Held**
Web: www.kokosing.biz
SIC: 1442 Construction sand and gravel

(G-6762)
THE YOUNG MENS CHRISTIAN ASSOCIATION OF CENTRAL OHIO (PA)
Also Called: YMCA of Central Ohio
1907 Leonard Ave Ste 150 (43219-4505)
PHONE..............................614 389-4409
EMP: 1500 **EST:** 1855
SALES (est): 63.53MM
SALES (corp-wide): 63.53MM **Privately Held**
Web: www.ymcacolumbus.org
SIC: 8641 Youth organizations

(G-6763)
THOMPSON HINE LLP
10 W Broad St Ste 700 (43215-3476)
PHONE..............................614 469-3200
Anthony C White, *Brnch Mgr*
EMP: 53
SALES (corp-wide): 209.56MM **Privately Held**
Web: www.thompsonhine.com
SIC: 8111 General practice attorney, lawyer
PA: Thompson Hine Llp
127 Public Sq Ste 3900
Cleveland OH 44114
216 566-5500

(G-6764)
THOMPSON HINE LLP
41 S High St Ste 1700 (43215-6157)
PHONE..............................614 469-3200
Anthony White, *Brnch Mgr*
EMP: 53
SALES (corp-wide): 209.56MM **Privately Held**
Web: www.thompsonhine.com
SIC: 8111 General practice attorney, lawyer
PA: Thompson Hine Llp
127 Public Sq Ste 3900
Cleveland OH 44114
216 566-5500

(G-6765)
THREE C BODY SHOP INC (PA)
2300 Briggs Rd (43223-3218)
PHONE..............................614 274-9700
Robert Juniper Junior, *Pr*
EMP: 65 **EST:** 1956
SQ FT: 40,000
SALES (est): 4.69MM
SALES (corp-wide): 4.69MM **Privately Held**
Web: www.threecbodyshop.com
SIC: 7532 7539 Body shop, automotive; Frame repair shops, automotive

(G-6766)
THREE C BODY SHOP INC
8321 N High St (43235-6459)
PHONE..............................614 885-0900
Juniper Bob, *Genl Mgr*
EMP: 39
SALES (corp-wide): 4.69MM **Privately Held**

Columbus - Franklin County (G-6767)

Web: www.threecbodyshop.com
SIC: 7532 Body shop, automotive
PA: Three C Body Shop Inc
  2300 Briggs Rd
  Columbus OH 43223
  614 274-9700

(G-6767)
THRIFTY LLC
Also Called: Dollar Thrifty
2980 Switzer Ave (43219-2372)
PHONE..................................614 237-1500
EMP: 50
SALES (corp-wide): 9.37B Publicly Held
Web: www.thrifty.com
SIC: 7514 Rent-a-car service
HQ: Thrifty, Llc
  8501 Williams Rd
  Estero FL 33928
  239 301-7000

(G-6768)
TIME WARNER CABLE ENTPS LLC
Also Called: Time Warner
1600 Dublin Rd Fl 2 (43215-2098)
PHONE..................................614 255-6289
Rhonda Frost, Pr
EMP: 33
SALES (corp-wide): 54.61B Publicly Held
SIC: 4841 Cable television services
HQ: Time Warner Cable Enterprises Llc
  400 Atlantic St Ste 6
  Stamford CT 06901

(G-6769)
TIME WARNER CABLE ENTPS LLC
Also Called: Time Warner
1125 Chambers Rd (43212-1701)
PHONE..................................614 481-5072
John Uversagtz, Mgr
EMP: 33
SQ FT: 11,813
SALES (corp-wide): 54.61B Publicly Held
SIC: 4841 Cable television services
HQ: Time Warner Cable Enterprises Llc
  400 Atlantic St Ste 6
  Stamford CT 06901

(G-6770)
TITAN LOGISTICS LTD
861 Taylor Rd (43230-6275)
PHONE..................................614 901-4212
Jason Ricci, Pr
EMP: 49 EST: 2005
SALES (est): 2MM Privately Held
Web: www.titanlogisticsofohio.com
SIC: 4789 Transportation services, nec

(G-6771)
TJM CLMBUS LLC TJM CLUMBUS LLC
6500 Doubletree Ave (43229-1111)
PHONE..................................614 885-1885
Steve Petrucelli, Genl Mgr
EMP: 99 EST: 2016
SQ FT: 594,507
SALES (est): 1.91MM Privately Held
SIC: 8741 Hotel or motel management

(G-6772)
TMC MICROGRAPHIC SERVICES INC
2709 Sawbury Blvd (43235-4582)
PHONE..................................614 761-1033
Thomas Harclerode, Mgr
EMP: 40
SIC: 7389 Microfilm recording and developing service
PA: Tmc Micrographic Services Inc
  7575 Tyler Blvd
  Mentor OH

(G-6773)
TOTAL SYSTEM SERVICES
Also Called: Tsys
1500 Boltonfield St (43228-3669)
PHONE..................................614 385-9221
EMP: 48 EST: 2018
SALES (est): 1.09MM Privately Held
SIC: 7389 Design services

(G-6774)
TOWLIFT INC
1200 Milepost Dr (43228-9862)
PHONE..................................614 851-1001
TOLL FREE: 800
Craig Reich, Mgr
EMP: 35
SALES (corp-wide): 246.16MM Privately Held
Web: www.towlift.com
SIC: 5084 7699 Lift trucks and parts; Industrial equipment services
HQ: Towlift, Inc.
  1395 Valley Belt Rd
  Brooklyn Heights OH 44131
  216 749-6800

(G-6775)
TOWN INN CO LLC
Also Called: Holiday Inn
175 E Town St (43215-4609)
PHONE..................................614 221-3281
Gene Calloway, Brnch Mgr
EMP: 77
SQ FT: 124,294
Web: www.hicolumbusdowntown.com
SIC: 7011 Hotels and motels
HQ: Town Inn Co Llc
  3850 Bird Rd Ste 302
  Miami FL 33146
  614 221-3281

(G-6776)
TOWNE PLACE SUITES WORTHINGTON
Also Called: TownePlace Suites By Marriott
7272 Huntington Park Dr (43235-5718)
PHONE..................................614 885-1557
Tim Whitehead, Genl Mgr
EMP: 41 EST: 2007
SALES (est): 342.59K Privately Held
Web: towneplace-suites-columbus-worthington.booked.net
SIC: 7011 Hotel, franchised

(G-6777)
TP MECHANICAL CONTRACTORS INC
Also Called: T P McHncal Cntrs Svc Fbrction
2130 Franklin Rd (43209-2724)
PHONE..................................614 253-8556
Tim Hoover, Mgr
EMP: 95
Web: www.tpmechanical.com
SIC: 1711 Mechanical contractor
HQ: Tp Mechanical Contractors, Llc
  1500 Kemper Meadow Dr
  Cincinnati OH 45240

(G-6778)
TPUSA INC
Also Called: Teleperformance USA
4335 Equity Dr (43228-3842)
PHONE..................................614 621-5512
Trevor Ferger, Ex VP
EMP: 97
SALES (corp-wide): 226.27MM Privately Held
Web: www.teleperformance.com

SIC: 7389 Telemarketing services
HQ: Tpusa, Inc.
  1991 S 4650 W
  Salt Lake City UT 84104
  801 257-5800

(G-6779)
TRACTOR SUPPLY COMPANY
Also Called: Tractor Supply
5525 W Broad St (43228-1119)
PHONE..................................614 878-7170
Tony Daniels, Mgr
EMP: 46
SALES (corp-wide): 14.56B Publicly Held
Web: www.tractorsupply.com
SIC: 5191 Farm supplies
PA: Tractor Supply Company
  5401 Virginia Way
  Brentwood TN 37027
  615 440-4000

(G-6780)
TRADESOURCE INC
1550 Old Henderson Rd (43220-3626)
PHONE..................................614 824-3883
EMP: 57
Web: www.tradesource.com
SIC: 7361 Labor contractors (employment agency)
PA: Tradesource, Inc.
  205 Hallene Rd Ste 211
  Warwick RI 02886

(G-6781)
TRADITIONS AT STYGLER ROAD
Also Called: National Ch Rsdnces Stygler Rd
167 N Stygler Rd (43230-2434)
PHONE..................................614 475-8778
Steve Bodkin, Pr
EMP: 29 EST: 1994
SALES (corp-wide): 521.67MM Privately Held
SIC: 8051 Skilled nursing care facilities
PA: National Church Residences
  2335 N Bank Dr
  Columbus OH 43220
  614 451-2151

(G-6782)
TRANSAMERICA AGENCY NETWRK INC
1650 Watermark Dr Ste 120 (43215-1043)
PHONE..................................614 824-4964
EMP: 320
Web: www.transamerica.com
SIC: 6311 Life insurance
HQ: Transamerica Agency Network, Inc.
  4333 Edgewood Rd Ne
  Cedar Rapids IA 52499

(G-6783)
TRANSAMERICA BUILDING CO
2000 Henderson Rd Ste 500 (43220-2497)
PHONE..................................614 457-8322
William H Hadler, CEO
Russell P Herrold Junior, Sec
William Koniewich, VP
EMP: 45 EST: 1962
SQ FT: 7,000
SALES (est): 2.56MM Privately Held
Web: www.hadler.com
SIC: 1542 Commercial and office building, new construction

(G-6784)
TRANSPORTATION RESOURCES INC
1120 Rarig Ave (43219-2312)
PHONE..................................614 253-7948
Jim Herron, Ex Dir
EMP: 70 EST: 1980
SQ FT: 12,500

SALES (est): 956.56K Privately Held
Web: www.rentalcarsnear.me
SIC: 8399 Community development groups

(G-6785)
TREWBRIC III INC
1701 Moler Rd (43207)
P.O. Box 07847 (43207)
PHONE..................................614 444-2184
Ted Coons, Ch
Ted Coons, CEO
Don Mcnutt, Pr
Lynn Coons, *
◆ EMP: 34 EST: 1948
SQ FT: 37,000
SALES (est): 5MM Privately Held
Web: www.afinitas.com
SIC: 1771 5084 3446 Concrete work; Cement making machinery; Architectural metalwork

(G-6786)
TRI-W GROUP INC
Also Called: Military Spec Packaging
835 Goodale Blvd (43212-3824)
PHONE..................................614 228-5000
▲ EMP: 1241
SIC: 3694 7538 7537 Distributors, motor vehicle engine; Diesel engine repair: automotive; Automotiv e transmission repair shops

(G-6787)
TRIAD ARCHITECTS LTD
172 E State St Ste 600 (43215-4321)
PHONE..................................614 942-1050
David Rice, Owner
David Price, Owner
EMP: 28 EST: 1997
SQ FT: 13,000
SALES (est): 5.36MM Privately Held
Web: www.wearetriad.com
SIC: 8712 Architectural engineering

(G-6788)
TRIAD TRANSPORT INC
1484 Williams Rd (43207-5178)
P.O. Box 818 (74502-0818)
PHONE..................................614 491-9497
Jim Painter, Brnch Mgr
EMP: 44
SALES (corp-wide): 10.24MM Privately Held
SIC: 4213 4953 Trucking, except local; Hazardous waste collection and disposal
PA: Triad Transport, Inc.
  1630 Diesel Ave
  Mcalester OK 74501
  918 421-2429

(G-6789)
TRICONT TRUCKING COMPANY
2200 Westbelt Dr (43228-3820)
PHONE..................................614 527-7398
Jerry Baker, Genl Mgr
EMP: 178
Web: www.triconttrucking.com
SIC: 4212 Local trucking, without storage
HQ: Tricont Trucking Company
  241 Sevilla Ave
  Coral Gables FL 33134
  305 520-8400

(G-6790)
TRINITY HEALTH
120 S Green St (43222-1661)
PHONE..................................614 227-0197
EMP: 48 EST: 2019
SALES (est): 225.83K Privately Held
Web: www.trinity-health.org

GEOGRAPHIC SECTION

Columbus - Franklin County (G-6813)

SIC: 8099 Health and allied services, nec

(G-6791)
TRINITY HEALTH GROUP LTD
Also Called: Nac
827 Yard St (43212)
PHONE..................614 899-4830
Dana Harbuagh, *CEO*
EMP: 42 EST: 1998
SQ FT: 70,000
SALES (est): 5.06MM
SALES (corp-wide): 16MM **Privately Held**
Web: www.trinityhealthgroup.com
SIC: 8712 Architectural services
PA: Nac, Inc.
1203 W Riverside Ave
Spokane WA
509 838-8240

(G-6792)
TRINITY UNITED METHODIST CH
Also Called: United Methodist Church
1581 Cambridge Blvd (43212-2713)
PHONE..................614 488-3659
Pastor Thilit Brooks, *Prin*
Pastor Frank Luchsinger, *Prin*
EMP: 30 EST: 1901
SQ FT: 10,642
SALES (est): 875.7K **Privately Held**
Web: www.trinityumchurch.com
SIC: 8661 8351 Methodist Church; Child day care services

(G-6793)
TROY MOTEL ASSN INC
1690 Clara St (43211-2628)
PHONE..................614 299-4300
Supru Mehta, *Prin*
EMP: 30 EST: 2006
SALES (est): 495.45K **Privately Held**
SIC: 7011 Motels

(G-6794)
TURNER CONSTRUCTION COMPANY
262 Hanover St (43215-2332)
PHONE..................614 984-3000
EMP: 75
Web: www.turnerconstruction.com
SIC: 1542 Commercial and office building, new construction
HQ: Turner Construction Company Inc
66 Hudson Blvd E
New York NY 10001
212 229-6000

(G-6795)
TWENTY FIRST CENTURY COMMUNICATIONS INC
760 Communications Pkwy (43214-1948)
PHONE..................614 442-1215
EMP: 93
SIC: 4899 Data communication services

(G-6796)
TWO MEN & A VACUUM LLC
2025 S High St (43207-2426)
P.O. Box 30062 (43230-0062)
PHONE..................614 300-7970
EMP: 52 EST: 2014
SALES (est): 1.01MM **Privately Held**
Web: www.twomenandavacuum.com
SIC: 7349 7359 Cleaning service, industrial or commercial; Home cleaning and maintenance equipment rental services

(G-6797)
ULMER & BERNE LLP
65 E State St Ste 1100 (43215-4213)
PHONE..................614 229-0000
Alexander Andrews, *Prin*

EMP: 56
SALES (corp-wide): 50.31MM **Privately Held**
Web: www.ubglaw.com
SIC: 8111 General practice attorney, lawyer
PA: Ulmer & Berne Llp
1660 W 2nd St Ste 1100
Cleveland OH 44113
216 583-7000

(G-6798)
UNICO ALLOYS & METALS INC
Also Called: United Alloys and Metals
1177 Joyce Ave (43219-2134)
PHONE..................614 299-0545
Dane Germuska, *Pr*
Frank Santorio, *
John Churley, *
◆ EMP: 76 EST: 1973
SQ FT: 450,000
SALES (est): 22.29MM **Privately Held**
Web: www.uametals.com
SIC: 5093 Ferrous metal scrap and waste
HQ: Cronimet Ferroleg. Gmbh
Sudbeckenstr. 22
Karlsruhe BW 76189
721952250

(G-6799)
UNICON INTERNATIONAL INC (PA)
241 Outerbelt St (43213-1529)
PHONE..................614 861-7070
Peichen Jane Lee, *Pr*
Sherman Lau, *
Michael Mcalear, *VP*
Li-hung David Lee, *VP*
EMP: 75 EST: 1990
SQ FT: 10,000
SALES (est): 20.78MM **Privately Held**
Web: www.unicon-intl.com
SIC: 7371 7379 Computer software systems analysis and design, custom; Computer related consulting services

(G-6800)
UNION FIRST CARE INC ✪
6555 Busch Blvd Ste 104 (43229-1791)
PHONE..................614 396-6192
Abdul Sesay, *CEO*
EMP: 36 EST: 2022
SALES (est): 542.27K **Privately Held**
Web: www.unionfirstcareinc.com
SIC: 8399 Health systems agency

(G-6801)
UNION HEALTHCARE SERVICES INC
2021 E Dublin Granville Rd (43229-3568)
PHONE..................614 686-2322
Ramatou Ismaila, *Pr*
EMP: 50 EST: 2017
SALES (est): 1.6MM **Privately Held**
SIC: 8082 8099 Home health care services; Health and allied services, nec

(G-6802)
UNION MORTGAGE SERVICES INC (PA)
Also Called: First Community Mortgage Svcs
1080 Fishinger Rd (43221-2302)
PHONE..................614 457-4815
James P Simpson, *Pr*
W Matthew Baker, *
EMP: 40 EST: 1990
SQ FT: 1,200
SALES (est): 8.66MM **Privately Held**
SIC: 6163 Mortgage brokers arranging for loans, using money of others

(G-6803)
UNITED ALLOYS & METALS INC
1177 Joyce Ave (43219-2198)
PHONE..................614 299-0545
John Churley, *CEO*
Frank Santoro, *
Brad Moore, *
◆ EMP: 47 EST: 1973
SALES (est): 18.65MM **Privately Held**
Web: www.uametals.com
SIC: 5093 Ferrous metal scrap and waste
HQ: Cronimet Corporation
1 Pilarsky Way
Aliquippa PA 15001
724 375-5004

(G-6804)
UNITED COLLECTION BUREAU INC
4100 Horizons Dr Ste 101 (43220-5283)
P.O. Box 1120 (43537-8120)
PHONE..................614 732-5000
EMP: 47
SALES (corp-wide): 62.18MM **Privately Held**
Web: www.ucbinc.com
SIC: 7322 Collection agency, except real estate
PA: United Collection Bureau, Inc.
5620 Southwyck Blvd
Toledo OH 43614
419 866-6227

(G-6805)
UNITED FD COML WKRS UN LCAL 10
Also Called: UFCW LOCAL 1059
4150 E Main St Fl 2 (43213-2953)
PHONE..................614 235-3635
Rebecca A Berroyer, *Pr*
EMP: 32 EST: 1941
SQ FT: 3,700
SALES (est): 10.2MM **Privately Held**
Web: website.ufcw1059.com
SIC: 8631 Labor union

(G-6806)
UNITED HEALTHCARE OHIO INC (DH)
Also Called: UNITED HEALTHCARE
9200 Worthington Rd (43085)
P.O. Box 1459 (55440-1459)
PHONE..................614 410-7000
Tom Brady, *CEO*
G David Shafer, *
Thomas Sullivan, *
EMP: 350 EST: 1978
SQ FT: 72,000
SALES (est): 70.48K
SALES (corp-wide): 371.62B **Publicly Held**
SIC: 6324 Group hospitalization plans
HQ: United Healthcare Services Inc.
9900 Bren Rd E Ste 300w
Minnetonka MN 55343
952 936-1300

(G-6807)
UNITED MANAGEMENT INC (PA)
Also Called: Casto
250 Civic Center Dr (43215-5086)
PHONE..................614 228-5331
Don M Casto Iii, *Pr*
Frank S Benson Junior, *Prin*
EMP: 75 EST: 1955
SALES (est): 47.75MM
SALES (corp-wide): 47.75MM **Privately Held**
Web: www.castoinfo.com
SIC: 6512 Shopping center, property operation only

(G-6808)
UNITED MTHDST CHLD HM W OHIO C (PA)
Also Called: UNITED METHODIST CHILDREN'S HO
431 E Broad St (43215-4004)
PHONE..................614 885-5020
Sean Reilly, *Ex Dir*
Bill Brownson, *
David Kurtz, *
EMP: 73 EST: 1911
SQ FT: 7,000
SALES (est): 5.99MM
SALES (corp-wide): 5.99MM **Privately Held**
Web: www.umchohio.org
SIC: 8361 8322 Emotionally disturbed home; Adoption services

(G-6809)
UNITED PARCEL SERVICE INC
Also Called: UPS
100 E Campus View Blvd Ste 300 (43235-8602)
PHONE..................614 841-7159
EMP: 93
SALES (corp-wide): 90.96B **Publicly Held**
Web: www.ups.com
SIC: 4215 Package delivery, vehicular
HQ: United Parcel Service, Inc.
55 Glenlake Pkwy
Atlanta GA 30328
404 828-6000

(G-6810)
UNITED PARCEL SERVICE INC
Also Called: UPS
5101 Trabue Rd (43228-9481)
PHONE..................614 870-4111
EMP: 316
SALES (corp-wide): 90.96B **Publicly Held**
Web: www.ups.com
SIC: 4215 Parcel delivery, vehicular
HQ: United Parcel Service, Inc.
55 Glenlake Pkwy
Atlanta GA 30328
404 828-6000

(G-6811)
UNITED PARCEL SERVICE INC
Also Called: UPS
3400 Refugee Rd (43232-4814)
PHONE..................614 237-9171
EMP: 83
SALES (corp-wide): 90.96B **Publicly Held**
Web: www.ups.com
SIC: 4512 Air cargo carrier, scheduled
HQ: United Parcel Service, Inc.
55 Glenlake Pkwy
Atlanta GA 30328
404 828-6000

(G-6812)
UNITED PARCEL SERVICE INC
Also Called: UPS
1711 Georgesville Rd (43228-3619)
PHONE..................614 385-9100
John Cummins, *Brnch Mgr*
EMP: 94
SALES (corp-wide): 90.96B **Publicly Held**
Web: www.ups.com
SIC: 4513 Letter delivery, private air
PA: United Parcel Service, Inc.
55 Glenlake Pkwy Ne
Atlanta GA 30328
404 828-6000

(G-6813)
UNITED PRODUCERS INC (PA)
8351 N High St Ste 250 (43235-1440)
PHONE..................614 433-2150

(PA)=Parent Co (HQ)=Headquarters
✪ = New Business established in last 2 years

Columbus - Franklin County (G-6814)

GEOGRAPHIC SECTION

Mike Bumgarner, *Pr*
Joe Werstak, *
Dennis Bolling, *
EMP: 53 **EST:** 1934
SALES (est): 56.7MM
SALES (corp-wide): 56.7MM **Privately Held**
Web: www.uproducers.com
SIC: 5154 Auctioning livestock

(G-6814)
UNITED RENTALS NORTH AMER INC
Also Called: United Rentals
580 Phillipi Rd (43228-1001)
PHONE...............................614 276-5444
Rich Smith, *Mgr*
EMP: 48
SALES (corp-wide): 14.33B **Publicly Held**
Web: www.unitedrentals.com
SIC: 7353 7359 5082 5083 Heavy construction equipment rental; Equipment rental and leasing, nec; Construction and mining machinery; Farm and garden machinery
HQ: United Rentals (North America), Inc.
100 Frst Strmford Pl Ste 7
Stamford CT 06902
203 622-3131

(G-6815)
UNITED SKATES AMERICA INC
Also Called: USA
4900 Evanswood Dr (43229-6289)
PHONE...............................614 431-2751
Bob Reilly, *Brnch Mgr*
EMP: 35
SALES (corp-wide): 10.65MM **Privately Held**
Web: www.unitedskates.com
SIC: 7999 5812 5941 Roller skating rink operation; Snack shop; Skating equipment
PA: United Skates Of America, Inc.
3362 Refugee Rd
Columbus OH 43232
614 802-2440

(G-6816)
UNITED SKATES OF AMERICA INC (PA)
Also Called: Wow Family Fun Center
3362 Refugee Rd (43232-4810)
PHONE...............................614 802-2440
EMP: 37 **EST:** 1971
SALES (est): 10.65MM
SALES (corp-wide): 10.65MM **Privately Held**
Web: www.unitedskates.com
SIC: 7999 5812 5941 Roller skating rink operation; Snack shop; Skating equipment

(G-6817)
UNITED STATES TROTTING ASSN
800 Michigan Ave (43215-1595)
PHONE...............................614 224-2291
EMP: 88
SALES (corp-wide): 9.83MM **Privately Held**
Web: www.ustrotting.com
SIC: 8743 Public relations and publicity
PA: United States Trotting Association (Inc)
6130 S Sunbury Rd
Westerville OH 43081
614 224-2291

(G-6818)
UNITED STTES SPRTSMENS ALNCE F
Also Called: Sportsmens Alliance Foundation
801 Kingsmill Pkwy (43229-1102)
PHONE...............................614 888-4868
EMP: 45 **EST:** 1978

SQ FT: 7,870
SALES (est): 1.64MM **Privately Held**
Web: www.sportsmensalliance.org
SIC: 8641 Environmental protection organization

(G-6819)
UNITED WAY CENTRAL OHIO INC
Also Called: United Way
360 S 3rd St (43215-5412)
PHONE...............................614 227-2700
Janet E Jackson, *Pr*
Richard Carrick, *
Mike Davis, *
S Dianne Biggs, *
Tobi Furman, *
EMP: 78 **EST:** 1951
SQ FT: 10,000
SALES (est): 22.82MM **Privately Held**
Web: www.liveunitedcentralohio.org
SIC: 8322 Social service center

(G-6820)
UNIVERSAL PALLETS INC
611 Marion Rd (43207-2552)
PHONE...............................614 444-1095
EMP: 27
SALES (corp-wide): 4.01MM **Privately Held**
Web: www.48forty.com
SIC: 5031 2448 Pallets, wood; Cargo containers, wood
PA: Universal Pallets Inc.
659 Marion Rd
Columbus OH 43207
614 444-1095

(G-6821)
UNIVERSAL RECOVERY SYSTEMS INC
Also Called: Stat Communications
850 Harmon Ave (43223-2410)
PHONE...............................614 299-0184
Jeff Saley, *Pr*
EMP: 54 **EST:** 1983
SALES (est): 10.17MM **Privately Held**
Web: www.statcom.net
SIC: 1623 1731 Cable laying construction; Fiber optic cable installation

(G-6822)
UNIVERSAL WINDOWS DIRECT INC
3563 Interchange Rd (43204-1400)
PHONE...............................614 418-5232
Bill Barr, *Prin*
EMP: 100
SALES (corp-wide): 10.22MM **Privately Held**
Web: www.universalwindowsdirect.com
SIC: 5211 1761 Doors, storm: wood or metal; Roofing contractor
PA: Universal Windows Direct, Inc.
23800 Miles Rd
Cleveland OH 44128
216 518-9138

(G-6823)
UNIVERSITY GYN&OB CNSLTNTS INC (PA)
1654 Upham Dr Rm N500 (43210-1250)
PHONE...............................614 293-8697
L Copeland, *Pr*
M Landon, *
Dan Pierce, *
EMP: 30 **EST:** 1975
SALES (est): 2.58MM
SALES (corp-wide): 2.58MM **Privately Held**
SIC: 8011 Gynecologist

(G-6824)
UNIVERSITY OTLRYNGOLOGISTS INC (PA)
Also Called: E N T
810 Mackenzie Dr (43220)
PHONE...............................614 273-2241
David E Schuller Md, *Pr*
David R Kelly Md, *VP*
EMP: 40 **EST:** 1964
SALES (est): 4.28MM
SALES (corp-wide): 4.28MM **Privately Held**
Web: www.sonushearing.com
SIC: 8011 5999 Ears, nose, and throat specialist: physician/surgeon; Hearing aids

(G-6825)
UNTAPPED POTENTIALS LLC
175 S 3rd St Ste 200 (43215-5194)
PHONE...............................888 811-1469
Anthony Baker, *CEO*
EMP: 30 **EST:** 2016
SALES (est): 300K **Privately Held**
Web: www.untappedpotentialsllc.com
SIC: 8742 Business management consultant

(G-6826)
UPH HOLDINGS LLC
Also Called: Marriott Columbus Univ Area
3100 Olentangy River Rd (43202-1517)
PHONE...............................614 447-9777
Dena St Clair, *Dir*
EMP: 99 **EST:** 2015
SALES (est): 4.5MM **Privately Held**
Web: www.universityplazaosu.com
SIC: 7011 Hotels and motels

(G-6827)
UPPER ARLINGTON CITY SCHL DST
Also Called: School Age Child Care
4770 Burbank Dr (43220-2800)
PHONE...............................614 487-5133
EMP: 34
SALES (corp-wide): 158.91MM **Privately Held**
Web: www.uaschools.org
SIC: 8211 8351 Public elementary school; Child day care services
PA: Upper Arlington City School District
1619 Zollinger Rd
Columbus OH 43221
614 487-5000

(G-6828)
UPREACH LLC
4488 Mobile Dr (43220-3713)
PHONE...............................614 442-7702
Melissa Gourley, *Managing Member*
Beth Hunter, *Managing Member*
EMP: 46 **EST:** 2003
SQ FT: 5,937
SALES (est): 8.62MM **Privately Held**
Web: www.upreachgroup.com
SIC: 8322 Social services for the handicapped

(G-6829)
UPS SUPPLY CHAIN SOLUTIONS INC
700 Manor Park Dr Ste 100 (43228-9397)
PHONE...............................614 208-0396
David Abney, *Prin*
EMP: 50 **EST:** 1996
SALES (est): 4.84MM **Privately Held**
SIC: 4731 Agents, shipping

(G-6830)
URBAN FIVE CONSTRUCTION
495 S High St Ste 150 (43215-5695)
PHONE...............................614 241-2070
Randy Williamson, *Brnch Mgr*

EMP: 48
SALES (corp-wide): 3.25MM **Privately Held**
SIC: 1522 Hotel/motel and multi-family home construction
PA: Urban Five Construction
2975 Huron St
Denver CO 80202
614 241-2070

(G-6831)
URGENT CARE SPECIALISTS LLC
2880 Stelzer Rd (43219-3133)
PHONE...............................614 472-2880
George Thomas, *Brnch Mgr*
EMP: 55
SALES (corp-wide): 23.51MM **Privately Held**
Web: www.wellnow.com
SIC: 8011 Clinic, operated by physicians
PA: Urgent Care Specialists Llc
2400 Corp Exch Dr Ste 102
Columbus OH 43231
614 505-7633

(G-6832)
URGENT CARE SPECIALISTS LLC
4300 Clime Rd Ste 110 (43228-6491)
PHONE...............................614 272-1100
Bill Stricker, *Brnch Mgr*
EMP: 55
SALES (corp-wide): 23.51MM **Privately Held**
Web: www.wellnow.com
SIC: 8011 Clinic, operated by physicians
PA: Urgent Care Specialists Llc
2400 Corp Exch Dr Ste 102
Columbus OH 43231
614 505-7633

(G-6833)
URGENT CARE SPECIALISTS LLC
4400 N High St Ste 101 (43214-2635)
PHONE...............................614 263-4400
Wendy Melick, *Brnch Mgr*
EMP: 55
SALES (corp-wide): 23.51MM **Privately Held**
Web: www.wellnow.com
SIC: 8011 Freestanding emergency medical center
PA: Urgent Care Specialists Llc
2400 Corp Exch Dr Ste 102
Columbus OH 43231
614 505-7633

(G-6834)
URGENT CARE SPECIALISTS LLC
Also Called: Accessmd Ancillary Services
2400 Corporate Exchange Dr Ste 102 (43231-7651)
PHONE...............................614 505-7601
Manoj Kumar, *Brnch Mgr*
EMP: 55
SALES (corp-wide): 23.51MM **Privately Held**
Web: www.wellnow.com
SIC: 8011 Physicians' office, including specialists
PA: Urgent Care Specialists Llc
2400 Corp Exch Dr Ste 102
Columbus OH 43231
614 505-7633

(G-6835)
URS GROUP INC
Also Called: URS
277 W Nationwide Blvd (43215-2853)
PHONE...............................614 464-4500
James R Linthicum, *Brnch Mgr*
EMP: 337

GEOGRAPHIC SECTION

Columbus - Franklin County (G-6859)

SALES (corp-wide): 14.38B **Publicly Held**
Web: www.aecom.com
SIC: **8711** 8712 Engineering services; Architectural services
HQ: Urs Group, Inc.
　300 S Grand Ave Ste 900
　Los Angeles CA 90071
　213 593-8000

(G-6836)
US POSTAL SERVICE
374 E 16th Ave (43201-1710)
PHONE.................................614 600-5544
EMP: 33 EST: 2018
SALES (est): 103.48K **Privately Held**
Web: www.usps.com
SIC: **7389** Mailbox rental and related service

(G-6837)
US PROTECTION SERVICE LLC (PA)
Also Called: Now Security Group
5785 Emporium Sq (43231-2802)
PHONE.................................614 794-4950
EMP: 48 EST: 2003
SALES (est): 4.83MM
SALES (corp-wide): 4.83MM **Privately Held**
Web: www.roycesecurityguards.com
SIC: **7381** Security guard service

(G-6838)
US TOGETHER INC
1415 E Dublin Granville Rd Ste 100 (43229-3356)
PHONE.................................614 437-9941
Tatyana Mindlina, *Pr*
Nadia Kasvin, *Dir*
EMP: 128 EST: 2004
SALES (est): 3.7MM **Privately Held**
Web: www.ustogether.us
SIC: **8322** Multi-service center

(G-6839)
USI INSURANCE SERVICES NAT INC
Also Called: Nationwide
580 N 4th St Ste 400 (43215-2153)
PHONE.................................614 228-5565
Patty Woo, *Brnch Mgr*
EMP: 43
Web: www.nationwide.com
SIC: **6411** Insurance agents, nec
HQ: Usi Insurance Services National, Inc.
　150 N Michigan Ave Fl 41
　Chicago IL 60601
　866 294-2571

(G-6840)
VALLEY INTERIOR SYSTEMS INC
Also Called: Price Thrice Supply
3840 Fisher Rd (43228-1016)
PHONE.................................614 351-8440
Jim Melaragno, *Mgr*
EMP: 97
SALES (corp-wide): 54.25MM **Privately Held**
Web: www.buildwithvalley.com
SIC: **1742** Drywall
PA: Valley Interior Systems, Inc.
　2203 Fowler St
　Cincinnati OH 45206
　513 961-0400

(G-6841)
VALUE ADD MANAGEMENT LLC
Also Called: Hometeam Properties
222 E 11th Ave (43201-2547)
PHONE.................................614 291-2600
EMP: 47 EST: 2007
SALES (est): 11.61MM **Privately Held**
Web: www.hometeamproperties.net

SIC: **8741** Business management

(G-6842)
VANGUARD WINES LLC (PA)
1020 W 5th Ave (43212-2630)
PHONE.................................614 291-3493
▲ EMP: 40 EST: 1996
SALES (est): 18.19MM
SALES (corp-wide): 18.19MM **Privately Held**
Web: www.vanguardwines.com
SIC: **5182** Wine

(G-6843)
VECTRA INC
Also Called: Vectra Visual
3950 Business Park Dr (43204-5021)
PHONE.................................614 351-6868
◆ EMP: 200
Web: www.taylor.com
SIC: **2752** 4225 Commercial printing, lithographic; General warehousing and storage

(G-6844)
VERTI INSURANCE COMPANY
3590 Twin Creeks Dr (43204-1628)
PHONE.................................844 448-3784
Marcos March, *Brnch Mgr*
EMP: 60
SALES (corp-wide): 4.38MM **Privately Held**
Web: www.verti.com
SIC: **6331** Automobile insurance
PA: Verti Insurance Company
　211 Main St
　Webster MA 01570
　844 448-3784

(G-6845)
VERTICAL ADVENTURES INC
Also Called: Training Center, The
6513 Kingsmill Ct (43229-1126)
PHONE.................................614 888-8393
Alexis M Roccos, *CEO*
Carrie Roccos, *Sec*
Mattew Roberts, *Pr*
Martha Roberts, *Treas*
EMP: 70 EST: 1994
SQ FT: 6,400
SALES (est): 2.17MM **Privately Held**
Web: www.5.life
SIC: **7997** 7999 Membership sports and recreation clubs; Instruction schools, camps, and services

(G-6846)
VERTIV JV HOLDINGS LLC
1050 Dearborn Dr (43085-1544)
PHONE.................................614 888-0246
Eva M Kalawski, *Sec*
EMP: 6488 EST: 2016
SALES (est): 64.55MM **Privately Held**
SIC: **3679** 3585 6719 Power supplies, all types: static; Air conditioning units, complete: domestic or industrial; Investment holding companies, except banks

(G-6847)
VESTIS CORPORATION
Also Called: Aramark
1900 Progress Ave (43207-1727)
PHONE.................................614 445-8341
TOLL FREE: 800
Joe Carrothers, *Mgr*
EMP: 33
SALES (corp-wide): 2.83B **Publicly Held**
Web: www.vestis.com
SIC: **7218** 7213 Industrial launderers; Uniform supply

PA: Vestis Corporation
　500 Colonial Center Pkwy # 1
　Roswell GA 30076
　470 226-3655

(G-6848)
VETERANS HEALTH ADMINISTRATION
Also Called: Chalmers P Wylie VA Ambltory C
420 N James Rd (43219-1834)
PHONE.................................614 257-5200
EMP: 69
Web: columbus.va.gov
SIC: **8011** 9451 Ambulatory surgical center; Administration of veterans' affairs, Federal government
HQ: Veterans Health Administration
　810 Vermont Ave Nw
　Washington DC 20420

(G-6849)
VETERANS HEALTH ADMINISTRATION
Also Called: Chalmers P Wylie VA Otptent Cl
420 N James Rd (43219-1834)
PHONE.................................614 257-5524
Teri Mzozoyana, *Mgr*
EMP: 196
Web: benefits.va.gov
SIC: **8011** 9451 Clinic, operated by physicians; Administration of veterans' affairs, Federal government
HQ: Veterans Health Administration
　810 Vermont Ave Nw
　Washington DC 20420

(G-6850)
VIDEO DUPLICATION SERVICES INC (PA)
Also Called: Vds
3777 Businceoh Pk Dr Ste A (43204)
PHONE.................................614 871-3827
Peter A Stock, *Pr*
Christian Stock, *
▲ EMP: 37 EST: 1985
SQ FT: 47,000
SALES (est): 1.34MM
SALES (corp-wide): 1.34MM **Privately Held**
SIC: **7812** Video tape production

(G-6851)
VILLA MILANO INC
Also Called: Villa Mlano Bnquet Cnfrnce Ctr
1630 Schrock Rd (43229-8220)
PHONE.................................614 882-2058
Joseph Milano Junior, *Pr*
Dina Milano, *
Joseph Milano Junior, *Pr*
EMP: 30 EST: 1982
SQ FT: 20,000
SALES (est): 1.99MM **Privately Held**
Web: www.villamilano.com
SIC: **7299** Banquet hall facilities

(G-6852)
VITRAN EXPRESS INC
Also Called: Vitran
5075 Krieger Ct (43228-3652)
PHONE.................................614 870-2255
John Swanson, *Brnch Mgr*
EMP: 33
Web: www.vitran.com
SIC: **4213** Trucking, except local
PA: Vitran Express, Inc.
　12225 Stephens Rd
　Warren MI 48089

(G-6853)
VJP HOSPITALITY LTD
Also Called: Four Pnts By Shrton Clmbus Ohi
3030 Plaza Properties Blvd (43219)
PHONE.................................614 475-8383
Paul Patel, *Genl Pt*
EMP: 27 EST: 2009
SALES (est): 738.83K **Privately Held**
Web: four-points.marriott.com
SIC: **7011** Hotels

(G-6854)
VOCATIONAL GUIDANCE SERVICES
200 N High St (43215-2416)
PHONE.................................614 222-2899
EMP: 68
SALES (corp-wide): 10.41MM **Privately Held**
Web: www.vgsjob.org
SIC: **7361** Employment agencies
PA: Vocational Guidance Services Inc
　2239 E 55th St
　Cleveland OH 44103
　216 431-7800

(G-6855)
VOGT SANTER INSIGHTS LTD
Also Called: Vogt Strategic Insights
1310 Dublin Rd (43215-1093)
PHONE.................................614 224-4300
Robert Vogt, *Pt*
EMP: 33 EST: 2010
SALES (est): 4.99MM **Privately Held**
Web: www.vsinsights.com
SIC: **8732** Market analysis or research

(G-6856)
VOLUNTEERS AMERICA OHIO & IND (PA)
1780 E Broad St (43203-2039)
PHONE.................................614 253-6100
Sherry Keyes-hebron, *Pr*
EMP: 120 EST: 1904
SALES (est): 35.53MM
SALES (corp-wide): 35.53MM **Privately Held**
Web: www.voaohin.org
SIC: **8322** 8361 5932 5521 Social service center; Destitute home; Clothing, secondhand; Automobiles, used cars only

(G-6857)
VOLUNTEERS OF AMERICA NW OHIO
Also Called: Volunteers of America
1780 E Broad St (43203-2039)
PHONE.................................419 248-3733
Sue Reamsnyder, *Pr*
EMP: 33 EST: 1994
SALES (est): 1.55MM **Privately Held**
Web: www.voaohin.org
SIC: **8699** 8322 Personal interest organization; Individual and family services

(G-6858)
VORYS SATER SEYMOUR AND PEASE LLP (PA)
52 E Gay St (43215-3161)
P.O. Box 1008 (43216-1008)
PHONE.................................614 464-6400
EMP: 460 EST: 1909
SALES (est): 133.42MM
SALES (corp-wide): 133.42MM **Privately Held**
Web: www.vorys.com
SIC: **8111** General practice attorney, lawyer

(G-6859)
VRABLE HEALTHCARE INC (PA)
3248 Henderson Rd (43220-7337)

Columbus - Franklin County (G-6860) — GEOGRAPHIC SECTION

PHONE.................614 545-5500
EMP: 30 **EST:** 2006
SALES (est): 38.14MM **Privately Held**
Web: www.vrablehealthcare.com
SIC: 8051 Convalescent home with continuous nursing care

(G-6860)
VRABLE IV INC (HQ)
Also Called: Pembroke Pl Sklled Nrsing Rhbl
3248 Henderson Rd (43220-7337)
PHONE.................614 545-5502
Allan Vrable, *Pr*
James Merrill, *
EMP: 89 **EST:** 2006
SQ FT: 52,000
SALES (est): 25.95MM **Privately Held**
SIC: 8051 Convalescent home with continuous nursing care
PA: Vrable Healthcare, Inc.
3248 Henderson Rd
Columbus OH 43220

(G-6861)
VSP VISION CARE
3400 Morse Xing (43219-3093)
PHONE.................614 471-1372
Robin Clark, *Prin*
EMP: 99 **EST:** 2016
SALES (est): 216.58K **Privately Held**
Web: www.vspvision.com
SIC: 6324 Hospital and medical service plans

(G-6862)
W D TIRE WAREHOUSE INC (PA)
Also Called: Convenient Tire Service
3805 E Livingston Ave (43227-2359)
PHONE.................614 461-8944
Doug Reed, *Prin*
Amy Reed, *
Thomas J Brown Junior, *Prin*
▲ **EMP:** 32 **EST:** 1985
SQ FT: 80,000
SALES (est): 8.9MM
SALES (corp-wide): 8.9MM **Privately Held**
Web: www.wdtire.com
SIC: 5014 Automobile tires and tubes

(G-6863)
W NAIL BAR LLC
3697 Corporate Dr (43231-4965)
PHONE.................614 299-9587
Manda Mason, *Managing Member*
EMP: 44 **EST:** 2015
SALES (est): 2.48MM **Privately Held**
Web: www.thewnailbar.com
SIC: 7231 Manicurist, pedicurist

(G-6864)
WALKER NATIONAL INC
2195 Wright Brothers Ave (43217-1157)
PHONE.................614 492-1614
Richard Longo, *Pr*
Deborah Krikorian, *
◆ **EMP:** 30 **EST:** 1988
SALES (est): 7.2MM
SALES (corp-wide): 55.92MM **Privately Held**
SIC: 3499 7699 Magnets, permanent: metallic; Industrial equipment services
PA: Industrial Magnetics, Inc.
1385 M 75 S
Boyne City MI 49712
231 582-3100

(G-6865)
WASHINGTON PRIME ACQSITION LLC
180 E Broad St (43215-3707)
PHONE.................614 621-9000
EMP: 143 **EST:** 2014
SALES (est): 660.56K
SALES (corp-wide): 564.96MM **Privately Held**
Web: www.wpgus.com
SIC: 6798 Real estate investment trusts
HQ: Washington Prime Group, L.P.
180 E Broad St
Columbus OH 43215
614 621-9000

(G-6866)
WASHINGTON PRIME GROUP INC (PA)
Also Called: Glimcher
4900 E Dublin Granville Rd (43215-3707)
PHONE.................614 621-9000
Louis G Conforti, *CEO*
Robert J Laikin, *
Mark E Yale, *Ex VP*
Robert P Demchak, *Corporate Secretary*
Melissa A Indest, *CAO*
EMP: 103 **EST:** 2013
SALES (est): 564.96MM
SALES (corp-wide): 564.96MM **Privately Held**
Web: www.wpgus.com
SIC: 6512 6798 Property operation, retail establishment; Realty investment trusts

(G-6867)
WASSERSTROM COMPANY (PA)
Also Called: National Smallwares
4500 E Broad St (43213-1360)
PHONE.................614 228-6525
Rodney Wasserstrom, *Pr*
Reid Wasserstrom, *
Dennis Blank, *
Alan Wasserstrom, *
David A Tumen, *
◆ **EMP:** 395 **EST:** 1902
SQ FT: 250,000
SALES (est): 378.09MM
SALES (corp-wide): 378.09MM **Privately Held**
Web: www.wasserstrom.com
SIC: 5087 3566 5021 5046 Restaurant supplies; Speed changers, drives, and gears; Office furniture, nec; Commercial cooking and food service equipment

(G-6868)
WASSERSTROM HOLDINGS INC
477 S Front St (43215-5625)
P.O. Box 182056 (43218-2056)
PHONE.................614 228-6525
Alan Wasserstrom, *
EMP: 180 **EST:** 2001
SALES (est): 22.65MM **Privately Held**
Web: www.wasserstrom.com
SIC: 5046 Restaurant equipment and supplies, nec

(G-6869)
WATERSHED DISTILLERY LLC
1145 Chesapeake Ave Ste D (43212-2284)
PHONE.................614 357-1936
EMP: 50 **EST:** 2010
SQ FT: 4,700
SALES (est): 6.9MM **Privately Held**
Web: www.watersheddistillery.com
SIC: 5182 2085 Wine; Distilled and blended liquors

(G-6870)
WATERWORKS LLC
Also Called: Waterworks, The
550 Schrock Rd (43229-1062)
PHONE.................614 253-7246
EMP: 175 **EST:** 1935
SQ FT: 25,000
SALES (est): 24.74MM **Privately Held**
Web: www.thewaterworks.com
SIC: 7699 4212 1711 Sewer cleaning and rodding; Hazardous waste transport; Plumbing, heating, air-conditioning

(G-6871)
WAXXPOT GROUP FRANCHISE LLC
Also Called: Waxxpot
629 N High St Fl 4 (43215-2929)
PHONE.................614 622-3018
EMP: 110 **EST:** 2016
SALES (est): 505.23K **Privately Held**
Web: www.waxxpot.com
SIC: 7231 6794 Cosmetology and personal hygiene salons; Franchises, selling or licensing

(G-6872)
WBNS TV INC
Also Called: Wnbs Channel 10 Weatherline
770 Twin Rivers Dr (43215-1159)
P.O. Box 1010 (43216-1010)
PHONE.................614 460-3700
Rick Rogala, *Pr*
John F Wolfe, *
EMP: 220 **EST:** 1965
SQ FT: 40,000
SALES (est): 38.05MM
SALES (corp-wide): 2.91B **Publicly Held**
Web: www.10tv.com
SIC: 4833 Television broadcasting stations
PA: Tegna Inc.
8350 Broad St Ste 2000
Tysons VA 22102
703 873-6600

(G-6873)
WEILANDS FINE MEATS INC
Also Called: Weiland's Gourmet Market
3600 Indianola Ave (43214-3758)
PHONE.................614 267-9910
John Williams, *Pr*
Tim Teegardin, *
EMP: 27 **EST:** 1961
SQ FT: 15,000
SALES (est): 817.32K **Privately Held**
Web: www.weilandsmarket.com
SIC: 5421 5411 5147 Meat and fish markets; Delicatessen stores; Meats and meat products

(G-6874)
WELCH PACKAGING GROUP INC
Also Called: Welch Packaging Columbus
4700 Alkire Rd (43228-3495)
PHONE.................614 870-2000
EMP: 110
SALES (corp-wide): 457.79MM **Privately Held**
Web: www.welchpkg.com
SIC: 2621 7389 Wrapping and packaging papers; Packaging and labeling services
PA: Welch Packaging Group, Inc.
1020 Herman St
Elkhart IN 46516
574 295-2460

(G-6875)
WELLS FARGO INSURANCE SERVICES OF OHIO LLC
580 N 4th St Ste 400 (43215-2153)
PHONE.................614 324-2820
EMP: 56
SIC: 6411 Insurance agents, brokers, and service

(G-6876)
WENDT-BRISTOL HEALTH SERVICES
921 Jasonway Ave Ste B (43214-2456)
PHONE.................614 403-9966
Sheldon A Gold, *Pr*
Marvin D Kantor, *
EMP: 150 **EST:** 1966
SALES (est): 3MM **Privately Held**
Web: www.pwhealth.com
SIC: 8093 Specialty outpatient clinics, nec

(G-6877)
WESBANCO TITLE AGENCY LLC
1160 Dublin Rd Ste 500 (43215-1085)
PHONE.................866 295-1714
S C Clayton Johnson, *Prin*
John D Kidd, *Prin*
Stephen L Oliver, *Prin*
EMP: 28 **EST:** 2001
SALES (est): 338.81K
SALES (corp-wide): 831.96MM **Publicly Held**
SIC: 7389 Financial services
PA: Wesbanco, Inc.
1 Bank Plz
Wheeling WV 26003
304 234-9000

(G-6878)
WESLEY GLEN RTREMENT CMNTY LLC
5155 N High St (43214-1694)
PHONE.................614 888-7492
EMP: 43 **EST:** 2020
SALES (est): 2.36MM **Privately Held**
Web: www.lec.org
SIC: 8361 Aged home

(G-6879)
WEST ENTERPRISES INC
Also Called: Uniglobe Travel Designers
480 S 3rd St (43215-5702)
PHONE.................614 237-4488
Elizabeth Blount, *Pr*
Leonard Sandine, *
EMP: 44 **EST:** 1981
SALES (est): 9.38MM **Privately Held**
Web: www.uniglobetraveldesigners.com
SIC: 4724 Tourist agency arranging transport, lodging and car rental

(G-6880)
WEST PARK CARE CENTER LLC
Also Called: PICKAWAY MANOR CARE CENTER
1700 Heinzerling Dr (43223-3671)
PHONE.................614 274-4222
Leo Welsh, *Admn*
EMP: 462 **EST:** 2016
SALES (est): 6.59MM **Privately Held**
Web: www.optalishealthcare.com
SIC: 8051 Convalescent home with continuous nursing care
PA: Whetstone Care Center Llc
3863 Trueman Ct
Hilliard OH 43026

(G-6881)
WESTPOST COLUMBUS LLC
6500 Doubletree Ave (43229-1111)
PHONE.................614 885-1885
EMP: 40 **EST:** 2011
SALES (est): 203.94K **Privately Held**
SIC: 7011 Hotels and motels

(G-6882)
WEXNER HERITAGE VILLAGE (PA)
Also Called: HERITAGE HOUSE NURSING HOME
1151 College Ave (43209-2827)
PHONE.................614 231-4900
David Rosen, *Ex Dir*
Chris Christian, *
David Driver, *
Cheryl Howard, *
EMP: 330 **EST:** 1951

GEOGRAPHIC SECTION

Columbus - Franklin County (G-6904)

SQ FT: 224,000
SALES (est): 9.45MM
SALES (corp-wide): 9.45MM **Privately Held**
Web: www.whv.org
SIC: **8052** 8051 Intermediate care facilities; Skilled nursing care facilities

(G-6883)
WHITE CASTLE SYSTEM INC (PA)
Also Called: White Castle
555 Edgar Waldo Way (43215-3070)
P.O. Box 1498 (43216-1498)
PHONE..................................614 228-5781
Edgar W Ingram Iii, *Ch Bd*
Russell J Meyer, *
Nicholas Zuk, *
Elizabeth Ingram, *
Andrew Prakel, *Corporate Controller**
◆ EMP: 275 EST: 1921
SQ FT: 143,000
SALES (est): 538.44MM
SALES (corp-wide): 538.44MM **Privately Held**
Web: www.whitecastle.com
SIC: **5812** 5142 2051 2013 Fast-food restaurant, chain; Meat, frozen: packaged; Bread, cake, and related products; Sausages and other prepared meats

(G-6884)
WHITE LGHT BHVRAL HLTH CLMBUS ✪
4040 E Broad St (43213-1156)
PHONE..................................614 350-4010
Eric Spofford, *Managing Member*
EMP: 100 EST: 2022
SALES (est): 2.85MM **Privately Held**
SIC: **8361** Orphanage

(G-6885)
WHITE OAK INVESTMENTS INC
3730 Lockbourne Rd (43207-5133)
P.O. Box 182022 (43218-2022)
PHONE..................................614 491-1000
Joseph C Bowman, *Pr*
Joseph W Douglass, *
▲ EMP: 65 EST: 1978
SQ FT: 65,000
SALES (est): 4.24MM **Privately Held**
SIC: **7389** Fund raising organizations

(G-6886)
WHITE SWAN INC
100 E Campus Blvd Ste 250, (43215)
PHONE..................................707 615-5005
EMP: 50 EST: 2021
SALES (est): 2.01MM **Privately Held**
SIC: **4212** Local trucking, without storage

(G-6887)
WHITEHALL CITY SCHOOLS
Also Called: C Ray Wllams Erly Chldhood Ctr
4738 Kae Ave (43213-6100)
PHONE..................................614 417-5680
EMP: 40
SALES (corp-wide): 60.11MM **Privately Held**
Web: www.wcsrams.org
SIC: **8351** 8211 Preschool center; Kindergarten
PA: Whitehall City Schools
625 S Yearling Rd
Columbus OH 43213
614 417-5000

(G-6888)
WHITING-TURNER CONTRACTING CO
445 Hutchinson Ave Ste 142 (43235-5677)
PHONE..................................614 459-6515
Tom Garske, *Rgnl Mgr*
EMP: 66
SALES (corp-wide): 8.62B **Privately Held**
Web: www.whiting-turner.com
SIC: **1542** Commercial and office building, new construction
PA: The Whiting-Turner Contracting Company
300 E Joppa Rd
Baltimore MD 21286
410 821-1100

(G-6889)
WIDEOPENWEST NETWORKS LLC
Also Called: Wide Open West
3675 Corporate Dr (43231-4965)
PHONE..................................614 948-4600
Jennifer Moody, *Brnch Mgr*
EMP: 72
SALES (corp-wide): 686.7MM **Publicly Held**
SIC: **8748** Telecommunications consultant
HQ: Wideopenwest Networks, Llc
7887 E Belleview Ave # 10
Englewood CO 80111
720 479-3558

(G-6890)
WIDEPINT INTGRTED SLTIONS CORP
8351 N High St Ste 200 (43235-1501)
PHONE..................................614 410-1587
Todd Mcmillen, *Mgr*
EMP: 82
Web: www.widepoint.com
SIC: **7371** Computer software development
HQ: Widepoint Integrated Solutions Corp.
11250 Waples Mill Rd # 2
Fairfax VA 22030
703 349-5644

(G-6891)
WIL-SITES TRUCK LINES LLC
1250 Walcutt Rd (43228-9349)
PHONE..................................614 444-8873
Richard Wilson, *Prin*
EMP: 37 EST: 2011
SALES (est): 12.14MM **Privately Held**
Web: www.wilsitestrucklines.com
SIC: **4212** Local trucking, without storage

(G-6892)
WILES BOYLE BURKHOLDER &
Also Called: Wiles Doucher
2 Miranova Pl (43215-5098)
PHONE..................................614 221-5216
Daniel Wiles, *
Thomas E Boyle, *
EMP: 67 EST: 1931
SQ FT: 25,000
SALES (est): 7.07MM **Privately Held**
Web: www.isaacwiles.com
SIC: **8111** General practice attorney, lawyer

(G-6893)
WILLGLO SERVICES INC
Also Called: Burge Service
995 Thurman Ave (43206-3133)
P.O. Box 77469 (43207-7469)
PHONE..................................614 443-3020
William Burge, *Pr*
Gloria Burge, *
EMP: 50 EST: 1982
SALES (est): 1.6MM **Privately Held**
Web: www.willgloinc.com
SIC: **8082** Home health care services

(G-6894)
WILLIAMS SCOTSMAN INC
871 Buckeye Park Rd (43207-2586)
PHONE..................................614 449-8675
Sean Roche, *Brnch Mgr*
EMP: 64
SALES (corp-wide): 2.36B **Publicly Held**
Web: www.mobilemini.com
SIC: **3448** 3441 3412 7359 Buildings, portable: prefabricated metal; Fabricated structural metal; Metal barrels, drums, and pails; Equipment rental and leasing, nec
HQ: Williams Scotsman, Inc.
4646 E Van Buren St # 40
Phoenix AZ 85008
480 894-6311

(G-6895)
WILLO SECURITY INC
Also Called: WILLO SECURITY, INC.
1989 W 5th Ave Ste 3 (43212-1912)
PHONE..................................614 481-9456
Steven Alan, *Mgr*
EMP: 118
SALES (corp-wide): 7.28MM **Privately Held**
Web: www.roycesecurity.com
SIC: **7381** Security guard service
PA: Willoughby Services, Inc.
38230 Glenn Ave
Willoughby OH 44094
440 953-9191

(G-6896)
WILSON ENTERPRISES INC
Also Called: Wilson's Turf
900 Buckeye Park Rd (43207)
PHONE..................................614 444-8873
Richard B Wilson, *Pr*
Richard Wilson, *
Daniel Wilson, *
Phil Paolini, *
Janice Smith, *
EMP: 40 EST: 1998
SQ FT: 4,000
SALES (est): 5.76MM **Privately Held**
Web: www.wilsonlandscapeandturf.com
SIC: **0782** Sodding contractor

(G-6897)
WILSON INSULATION COMPANY LLC
Also Called: Custom Glass & Doors
495 S High St Ste 50 (43215-5689)
PHONE..................................626 812-6070
EMP: 93 EST: 2016
SALES (est): 2.46MM
SALES (corp-wide): 2.78B **Publicly Held**
SIC: **1742** Insulation, buildings
PA: Installed Building Products, Inc.
495 S High St Ste 50
Columbus OH 43215
614 221-3399

(G-6898)
WINGLER CONSTRUCTION CORP
Also Called: One Stop Remodeling
771 S Hamilton Rd (43213-3001)
PHONE..................................614 626-8546
Ronald E Wingler, *Pr*
EMP: 34 EST: 1979
SQ FT: 13,000
SALES (est): 1.85MM **Privately Held**
Web: www.winglerconstruction.com
SIC: **1521** 1542 General remodeling, single-family houses; Commercial and office buildings, renovation and repair

(G-6899)
WM COLUMBUS HOTEL LLC
Also Called: Westin Columbus
310 S High St (43215-4508)
PHONE..................................614 228-3800
Nir Liebling, *CIO*
EMP: 250 EST: 2007
SQ FT: 200,000
SALES (est): 25.32MM
SALES (corp-wide): 729.58MM **Publicly Held**
Web: www.westincolumbus.com
SIC: **7011** Hotels
PA: The Marcus Corporation
100 E Wscnsin Ave Ste 190
Milwaukee WI 53202
414 905-1000

(G-6900)
WODA CONSTRUCTION INC
500 S Front St Fl 10 (43215-7628)
PHONE..................................614 396-3200
Jeffrey Woda, *Pr*
David Cooper Junior, *Ex VP*
EMP: 47 EST: 1990
SQ FT: 3,000
SALES (est): 47MM
SALES (corp-wide): 86.58MM **Privately Held**
Web: www.wodagroup.com
SIC: **1522** 1521 Apartment building construction; New construction, single-family houses
PA: Cooper Woda Companies Inc
500 S Front St Fl 10
Columbus OH 43215
614 396-3200

(G-6901)
WODA GROUP INC
500 S Front St Fl 10 (43215-7628)
PHONE..................................614 396-3200
Jeffrey Woda, *Pr*
Joseph M Mccabe, *VP*
David Cooper, *Ex VP*
EMP: 556 EST: 2012
SALES (est): 22.6MM **Privately Held**
Web: www.wodagroup.com
SIC: **6531** Real estate leasing and rentals

(G-6902)
WOODSPRING HOTELS HOLDINGS LLC
2305 Wilson Rd (43228-9594)
PHONE..................................614 272-2170
EMP: 30
SALES (corp-wide): 1.54B **Publicly Held**
Web: www.woodspring.com
SIC: **7011** Hotels
HQ: Woodspring Hotels Holdings Llc
8621 E 21st St N Ste 250
Wichita KS 67206
407 322-4435

(G-6903)
WORKSTATE CONSULTING LLC
30 Spruce St Ste 300 (43215-2260)
PHONE..................................614 559-3904
EMP: 48 EST: 2006
SALES (est): 7.34MM **Privately Held**
Web: www.workstate.com
SIC: **8748** 7371 7379 Business consulting, nec; Custom computer programming services; Computer related consulting services

(G-6904)
WORLDWIDE EQUIPMENT INC
5440 Renner Rd (43228-8941)
PHONE..................................614 876-0336
EMP: 35
SALES (corp-wide): 291.93MM **Privately Held**
Web: www.thetruckpeople.com
SIC: **5012** 5013 Trucks, commercial; Truck parts and accessories
HQ: Worldwide Equipment, Inc.
6416 Asheville Hwy

Columbus - Franklin County (G-6905)

GEOGRAPHIC SECTION

Knoxville TN 37924
606 874-2172

(G-6905)
WORLY PLUMBING SUPPLY INC (PA)
Also Called: Worly Plumbing Supply
400 Greenlawn Ave (43223-2611)
PHONE..................................614 445-1000
Jay Worly, *Pr*
Jeff Worly, *
Judith Tompkins, *
EMP: 54 **EST:** 1952
SQ FT: 96,000
SALES (est): 46.29MM
SALES (corp-wide): 46.29MM **Privately Held**
Web: www.thinkworly.com
SIC: 5074 Plumbing fittings and supplies

(G-6906)
WORTHINGTON INDUSTRIES INC
Worthington Industries, Inc.
1055 Dearborn Dr (43085-1542)
PHONE..................................614 438-3028
Bruce Ruhl, *Mgr*
EMP: 45
SQ FT: 15,000
SALES (corp-wide): 4.92B **Publicly Held**
Web: www.worthingtonenterprises.com
SIC: 7692 3544 Welding repair; Special dies and tools
PA: Worthington Enterprises, Inc.
200 W Old Wlson Bridge Rd
Worthington OH 43085
614 438-3210

(G-6907)
WORTHNGTON CHRSTN VLG CNGRGATE
165 Highbluffs Blvd (43235-1484)
PHONE..................................614 846-6076
Randy Richardson, *Pr*
Joan Yasses, *Mgr*
Dan Spears, *VP*
EMP: 32 **EST:** 1984
SQ FT: 5,861
SALES (est): 4.63MM **Privately Held**
Web: www.wcv.org
SIC: 6513 Apartment building operators

(G-6908)
WORTHNGTON STELPAC SYSTEMS LLC (HQ)
1205 Dearborn Dr (43085-4769)
PHONE..................................614 438-3205
Mark Russell, *CEO*
EMP: 250 **EST:** 1999
SALES (est): 53.23MM
SALES (corp-wide): 4.92B **Publicly Held**
Web: www.worthingtonenterprises.com
SIC: 3325 5051 Steel foundries, nec; Metals service centers and offices
PA: Worthington Enterprises, Inc.
200 W Old Wlson Bridge Rd
Worthington OH 43085
614 438-3210

(G-6909)
WSA STUDIO
982 S Front St (43206-2559)
PHONE..................................614 824-1633
EMP: 47 **EST:** 2018
SALES (est): 1.86MM **Privately Held**
Web: www.wsastudio.com
SIC: 6512 Commercial and industrial building operation

(G-6910)
WWCD LTD
Also Called: Cd102.5
1036 S Front St (43206-3402)
PHONE..................................614 221-9923
EMP: 35 **EST:** 1996
SALES (est): 2.12MM **Privately Held**
Web: www.cd929fm.com
SIC: 4832 Radio broadcasting stations

(G-6911)
X F CONSTRUCTION SVCS INC
Also Called: X F Petroleum Equipment
1120 Claycraft Rd (43230-6640)
PHONE..................................614 575-2700
William R Patrick, *Pr*
James Fairchild, *
Lucille Stallard, *
Robert Patrick, *
Deborah K Smith, *
EMP: 36 **EST:** 1960
SQ FT: 20,000
SALES (est): 2.32MM **Privately Held**
SIC: 1731 1799 5172 General electrical contractor; Service station equipment installation, maint., and repair; Service station supplies, petroleum

(G-6912)
XPO LOGISTICS FREIGHT INC
2625 Westbelt Dr (43228-3828)
PHONE..................................614 876-7100
Freda Hayner, *Mgr*
EMP: 102
SQ FT: 6,460
SALES (corp-wide): 7.74B **Publicly Held**
Web: www.xpo.com
SIC: 4231 4213 4212 Trucking terminal facilities; Trucking, except local; Local trucking, without storage
HQ: Xpo Logistics Freight, Inc.
2211 Old Erhart Rd Ste 10
Ann Arbor MI 48105
800 755-2728

(G-6913)
XTEK PARTNERS INC
Also Called: Xtek Partners
1721 Westbelt Dr (43228-3811)
P.O. Box 6030 (43026-6030)
PHONE..................................614 973-7400
Susan Harrah, *Pr*
Brad Herold, *
EMP: 50 **EST:** 2003
SALES (est): 26.1MM **Privately Held**
Web: www.xtekpartners.com
SIC: 5734 7378 Computer and software stores; Computer maintenance and repair

(G-6914)
XTREME EXPRESS LLC
Also Called: Xtreme Express
6611 Broughton Ave (43213-1523)
PHONE..................................614 735-0291
Fernando Crosa, *Managing Member*
Adam Oakerson, *
Josh Spruill, *
EMP: 134 **EST:** 2014
SALES (est): 12.5MM **Privately Held**
Web: www.goxtremeexpress.com
SIC: 4225 4731 General warehousing and storage; Transportation agents and brokers

(G-6915)
Y M C A HILLTOP EDUCARE INC
Also Called: Day Care Center
1952 W Broad St Ste A (43223-1262)
PHONE..................................614 752-8877
Alex Dawson, *Dir*
EMP: 39 **EST:** 1998
SALES (est): 582.21K **Privately Held**
SIC: 8351 Group day care center

(G-6916)
YORK TEMPLE COUNTRY CLUB
Also Called: YORK GOLF CLUB
7459 N High St (43235-1412)
PHONE..................................614 885-5459
Chuck Dahn, *Genl Mgr*
EMP: 62 **EST:** 1924
SQ FT: 18,000
SALES (est): 2.73MM **Privately Held**
Web: www.yorkgc.com
SIC: 7997 5812 Country club, membership; Eating places

(G-6917)
YOUNG WOMENS CHRISTIAN ASSN (PA)
Also Called: YWCA
65 S 4th St (43215-4356)
PHONE..................................614 224-9121
Christie Angel, *Pr*
EMP: 60 **EST:** 1912
SQ FT: 100,880
SALES (est): 16.19MM
SALES (corp-wide): 16.19MM **Privately Held**
Web: www.ywcacolumbus.org
SIC: 8641 7991 8351 7032 Youth organizations; Physical fitness facilities; Child day care services; Youth camps

(G-6918)
ZANER-BLOSER INC (HQ)
Also Called: Superkids Reading Program
1400 Goodale Blvd Ste 200 (43212-3777)
P.O. Box 16764 (43216-6764)
PHONE..................................614 486-0221
Lisa Carmona, *Pr*
▲ **EMP:** 149 **EST:** 1972
SQ FT: 15,000
SALES (est): 49.81MM
SALES (corp-wide): 109.4MM **Privately Held**
Web: www.zaner-bloser.com
SIC: 5192 5049 8249 2731 Books; School supplies; Correspondence school; Book publishing
PA: Highlights For Children, Inc.
1800 Watermark Dr
Columbus OH 43215
614 486-0631

(G-6919)
ZINK FOODSERVICE GROUP INC
Also Called: Zink Commercial
655 Dearborn Park Ln Ste C (43085-5745)
PHONE..................................800 492-7400
Jim Zink, *Prin*
Mike Mcguire, *Prin*
Tim Zink, *
▲ **EMP:** 135 **EST:** 1975
SQ FT: 32,000
SALES (est): 88MM **Privately Held**
Web: www.zinkfsg.com
SIC: 5082 Construction and mining machinery

(G-6920)
ZIPLINE LOGISTICS LLC (PA)
1600 Dublin Rd Fl 2 (43215)
PHONE..................................888 469-4754
EMP: 50 **EST:** 2007
SALES (est): 112.16MM **Privately Held**
Web: www.ziplinelogistics.com
SIC: 4213 Trucking, except local

Columbus Grove
Putnam County

(G-6921)
CARPE DIEM INDUSTRIES LLC (PA)
Also Called: Colonial Surface Solutions
4599 Campbell Rd (45830-9403)
PHONE..................................419 659-5639
Patricia Langhals, *Pr*
Darren Langhals, *
EMP: 55 **EST:** 1989
SQ FT: 750
SALES (est): 9.25MM
SALES (corp-wide): 9.25MM **Privately Held**
Web: www.colonialsurfacesolutions.com
SIC: 3479 3471 3398 1799 Painting of metal products; Cleaning and descaling metal products; Metal heat treating; Coating of metal structures at construction site

Concord Township
Lake County

(G-6922)
AEROCON PHOTOGRAMMETRIC SVCS (PA)
7294 Hunting Lake Dr (44077-8907)
PHONE..................................440 946-6277
James Liberty, *Prin*
Judith Liberty, *
EMP: 27 **EST:** 1967
SALES (est): 2.31MM
SALES (corp-wide): 2.31MM **Privately Held**
Web: www.ctconsultants.com
SIC: 7389 7335 Photogrammatic mapping; Aerial photography, except mapmaking

(G-6923)
CONCORD BIOSCIENCES LLC
10845 Wellness Way (44077-9041)
PHONE..................................440 357-3200
Clifford W Croley, *CEO*
Michael W Martell, *
EMP: 94 **EST:** 1985
SQ FT: 260,000
SALES (est): 19.57MM **Privately Held**
Web: www.concordbio.com
SIC: 8731 Biotechnical research, commercial
HQ: Frontage Laboratories, Inc.
700 Pennsylvania Dr
Exton PA 19341
610 232-0100

(G-6924)
DE NORA TECH LLC (DH)
7590 Discovery Ln (44077-9190)
PHONE..................................440 710-5334
Paolo Dellacha, *CEO*
Frank J Mcgorty, *COO*
Assunta Rossi, *
Angelo Ferrari, *
◆ **EMP:** 80 **EST:** 1982
SQ FT: 20,000
SALES (est): 99.5MM
SALES (corp-wide): 885.74MM **Privately Held**
Web: business.painesvilleohchamber.org
SIC: 3624 3589 7359 Electrodes, thermal and electrolytic uses: carbon, graphite; Sewage and water treatment equipment; Equipment rental and leasing, nec
HQ: Industrie De Nora Spa
Via Leonardo Bistolfi 35
Milano MI 20134

GEOGRAPHIC SECTION   Copley - Summit County (G-6947)

(G-6925)
DOLBEY SYSTEMS INC (PA)
7280 Auburn Rd (44077-9558)
PHONE..................................440 392-9900
EMP: 37 **EST:** 1994
SQ FT: 26,000
SALES (est): 10.41MM **Privately Held**
Web: www.dolbey.com
SIC: 5044 Office equipment

(G-6926)
EMILY MANAGEMENT INC
Also Called: Quality Plus
10280 Pinecrest Rd (44077-9795)
PHONE..................................440 354-6713
Elizabeth Bauer, *Pr*
EMP: 60 **EST:** 1990
SALES (est): 1.44MM **Privately Held**
SIC: 7363 Temporary help service

(G-6927)
LAKE HOSPITAL SYSTEM INC (HQ)
Also Called: Tripoint Medical Center
7590 Auburn Rd (44077-9176)
PHONE..................................440 375-8100
Robyn Strosaker, *Pr*
EMP: 1200 **EST:** 1902
SQ FT: 150,000
SALES (est): 350.61MM
SALES (corp-wide): 878.24MM **Privately Held**
Web: www.uhhospitals.org
SIC: 8062 Hospital, affiliated with AMA residency
PA: University Hospitals Health System, Inc.
3605 Warrensville Ctr Rd
Shaker Heights OH 44122
216 767-8900

(G-6928)
LAKE HOSPITAL SYSTEM INC
7580 Auburn Rd Ste 314 (44077-9618)
PHONE..................................440 352-0646
Robert B Tracz, *CFO*
EMP: 107
SALES (corp-wide): 878.24MM **Privately Held**
Web: www.uhhospitals.org
SIC: 8031 8011 Offices and clinics of osteopathic physicians; Physicians' office, including specialists
HQ: Lake Hospital System, Inc.
7590 Auburn Rd
Concord Township OH 44077
440 375-8100

(G-6929)
LAKE HOSPITALITY INC
Also Called: Amerihost Inn Suites
7581 Auburn Rd (44077-9176)
PHONE..................................440 579-0300
Sam Shah, *Pr*
EMP: 39 **EST:** 2002
SALES (est): 542.26K **Privately Held**
SIC: 7011 Hotels

(G-6930)
NORTHEAST OHIO HEART ASSOC LLC
7580 Auburn Rd Ste 106 (44077-9616)
PHONE..................................440 352-9554
Kathi Ross, *Brnch Mgr*
EMP: 88
SALES (corp-wide): 1.97MM **Privately Held**
Web: www.uhhospitals.org
SIC: 8062 General medical and surgical hospitals
PA: Northeast Ohio Heart Associates, Llc.
36100 Euclid Ave Ste 120
Willoughby OH 44094
440 951-8360

(G-6931)
OLON USA LLC
7528 Auburn Rd (44077-9176)
PHONE..................................440 357-3300
Paolo Tubertini, *CEO*
Lisa Mothersbaugh, *
EMP: 99 **EST:** 2017
SALES (est): 10.21MM **Privately Held**
Web: www.olonricerca.com
SIC: 8731 Biotechnical research, commercial
HQ: Olon Spa
Strada Provinciale Rivoltana 6/7
Rodano MI 20053
029 523-5111

(G-6932)
QH MANAGEMENT COMPANY LLC
Also Called: Quail Hollow Resort
11080 Concord Hambden Rd (44077-9704)
PHONE..................................440 497-1100
EMP: 27 **EST:** 2007
SALES (est): 2.36MM **Privately Held**
SIC: 7011 Resort hotel

(G-6933)
QUAIL HOLLOW MANAGEMENT INC
Also Called: Quail Hollow Resort Cntry CLB
11295 Quail Hollow Dr (44077-9036)
PHONE..................................440 639-4000
Eric Affeldt, *Pr*
EMP: 103 **EST:** 1972
SQ FT: 17,000
SALES (est): 5.47MM
SALES (corp-wide): 2.44B **Privately Held**
Web: www.invitedclubs.com
SIC: 7997 5812 7992 7011 Golf club, membership; Eating places; Public golf courses; Hotels and motels
HQ: Clubcorp Usa, Inc.
5215 N O Connor Blvd # 2
Irving TX 75039
972 243-6191

(G-6934)
RANPAK CORP (HQ)
7990 Auburn Rd (44077)
P.O. Box 8004 (44077)
PHONE..................................440 354-4445
Omar Asali, *Ch*
◆ **EMP:** 104 **EST:** 1972
SQ FT: 162,000
SALES (est): 165.78MM
SALES (corp-wide): 502.08MM **Publicly Held**
Web: www.ranpak.com
SIC: 5113 Industrial and personal service paper
PA: Js Capital Llc
888 7th Ave Fl 40
New York NY 10016
212 655-7160

(G-6935)
STERILTEK INC (PA)
11910 Briarwyck Woods Dr (44077-9392)
PHONE..................................615 627-0241
EMP: 35 **EST:** 1996
SQ FT: 15,000
SALES (est): 1.43MM **Privately Held**
SIC: 7389 Product sterilization service

(G-6936)
TRIPOINT MEDICAL CENTER
Also Called: Lake Health
7590 Auburn Rd (44077-9176)
PHONE..................................440 375-8100
Donna M Kuta, *Mgr*
EMP: 825 **EST:** 2007
SQ FT: 300,000
SALES (est): 99.87MM **Privately Held**
Web: www.uhhospitals.org
SIC: 8062 General medical and surgical hospitals

Conneaut
Ashtabula County

(G-6937)
AMBOY RIFLE CLUB
100 Hawthorne Dr (44030-2988)
PHONE..................................440 228-9366
Elmer Johnson, *Pr*
Chris Coxon, *
Robert Ziefle, *
Cathy Ezzone, *
EMP: 99 **EST:** 2018
SALES (est): 164.07K **Privately Held**
Web: www.amboyrifleclub.com
SIC: 7991 Physical fitness facilities

(G-6938)
ASHTABULA CNTY RSDNTIAL SVCS C (PA)
29 Parrish Rd (44030-1146)
PHONE..................................440 593-6404
Joy Groel, *Dir*
EMP: 35 **EST:** 1974
SQ FT: 1,000
SALES (est): 3.45MM
SALES (corp-wide): 3.45MM **Privately Held**
SIC: 8361 Mentally handicapped home

(G-6939)
AUTOZONE INC
Also Called: Autozone
199 Gateway Ave Ste D (44030-2352)
PHONE..................................440 593-6934
EMP: 28
SALES (corp-wide): 17.46B **Publicly Held**
Web: www.autozonepro.com
SIC: 5531 5045 5734 Automotive parts; Computer software; Software, business and non-game
PA: Autozone, Inc.
123 S Front St
Memphis TN 38103
901 495-6500

(G-6940)
BESSEMER AND LAKE ERIE RR CO
Also Called: Pittsburgh & Conneaut Dock
950 Ford Ave (44030-1867)
P.O. Box 90 (44030-0090)
PHONE..................................440 593-1102
Robert S Rosati, *Brnch Mgr*
EMP: 75
SALES (corp-wide): 12.74B **Privately Held**
SIC: 6519 Real property lessors, nec
HQ: Bessemer And Lake Erie Railroad Company
17641 Ashland Ave
Homewood IL 60430
708 206-6708

(G-6941)
BEST COMMUNICATIONS INC
213 S Ridge Rd W (44030-8670)
PHONE..................................440 758-5854
Robert Best, *Pr*
EMP: 35 **EST:** 1995
SALES (est): 1.68MM **Privately Held**
SIC: 1794 4813 Excavation work; Telephone communication, except radio

(G-6942)
CONNEAUT TELEPHONE COMPANY
Also Called: Suite224 and Cablesuite541
224 State St (44030-2637)
P.O. Box 579 (44030-0579)
PHONE..................................440 593-7140
Donald Zappitelli, *CEO*
Ray Rapose, *
James Haney, *
P Tom Picard, *
EMP: 34 **EST:** 1897
SQ FT: 8,000
SALES (est): 9.83MM **Privately Held**
Web: www.greatwavecom.com
SIC: 4813 Local telephone communications

(G-6943)
LP OPCO LLC
Also Called: Lake Pnte Rhblttion Nrsing Ctr
22 Parrish Rd (44030-1178)
PHONE..................................440 593-6266
EMP: 55 **EST:** 2016
SALES (est): 2.31MM **Privately Held**
SIC: 8051 Skilled nursing care facilities

(G-6944)
PATTERSON-ERIE CORPORATION
Also Called: Burger King
183 Gateway Ave (44030-2350)
PHONE..................................440 593-6161
EMP: 77
SALES (corp-wide): 45.55MM **Privately Held**
Web: www.bk.com
SIC: 6512 5812 Nonresidential building operators; Fast-food restaurant, chain
PA: Patterson-Erie Corporation
1250 Tower Ln Ste 1
Erie PA 16505
814 455-8031

(G-6945)
UNIVERSITY HSPTALS CNNAUT MED
158 W Main Rd (44030-2039)
PHONE..................................440 593-1131
Tom Zenty, *Prin*
EMP: 78 **EST:** 1919
SALES (est): 35MM **Privately Held**
Web: www.uhhospitals.org
SIC: 8062 General medical and surgical hospitals

Copley
Summit County

(G-6946)
ADVANCED FINANCIAL SERVICES
1234 S Cleveland Massillon Rd (44321-1614)
PHONE..................................800 320-0000
EMP: 28 **EST:** 1993
SALES (est): 1.3MM **Privately Held**
SIC: 7389 Credit card service

(G-6947)
ALLSTAR FINANCIAL GROUP INC
202 Montrose West Ave Ste 200 (44321-2923)
PHONE..................................866 484-2583
EMP: 64
Web: www.starwindins.com
SIC: 8742 Financial consultant
PA: Allstar Financial Group, Inc.
365 Northridge Rd Ste 250
Atlanta GA 30350

Copley - Summit County (G-6948)

(G-6948)
BENEFIT SERVICES INC (PA)
3636 Copley Rd Ste 201 (44321-1602)
P.O. Box 5700 (44101-0700)
PHONE..................................330 666-0337
Connie Frazier, *Pr*
Jerry Newbauer, *
EMP: 100 **EST:** 1993
SQ FT: 18,000
SALES (est): 12.54MM **Privately Held**
Web: www.mutualhealthservices.com
SIC: 6411 Insurance agents, nec

(G-6949)
CHEMICAL ASSOCIATES OF ILLINOIS INC
Also Called: Chemical Associates
1270 S Cleveland Massillon Rd (44321-1683)
PHONE..................................330 666-7200
▲ **EMP:** 45
SIC: 5169 Chemicals and allied products, nec

(G-6950)
CLEVELAND CLINIC FOUNDATION
4389 Medina Rd (44321-1388)
PHONE..................................234 815-5100
EMP: 41
SALES (corp-wide): 14.48B **Privately Held**
Web: www.clevelandclinic.org
SIC: 8062 General medical and surgical hospitals
PA: The Cleveland Clinic Foundation
9500 Euclid Ave
Cleveland OH 44195
216 636-8335

(G-6951)
CONCEPT SERVICES LIMITED
202 Montrose West Ave Ste 100 (44321-2790)
PHONE..................................330 336-2571
Dan Harsh, *Pr*
EMP: 100 **EST:** 2002
SALES (est): 12.86MM **Privately Held**
Web: www.conceptltd.com
SIC: 8742 Sales (including sales management) consultant

(G-6952)
CONCORDIA OF OHIO
Also Called: CONCORDIA AT SUMNER
970 Sumner Pkwy (44321-1693)
PHONE..................................330 664-1000
Charlene Kish, *CEO*
EMP: 42 **EST:** 2012
SALES (est): 16.23MM **Privately Held**
Web: www.concordialm.org
SIC: 8051 Skilled nursing care facilities

(G-6953)
COPLEY HEALTH CENTER INC
155 Heritage Woods Dr (44321-2791)
PHONE..................................330 666-0980
Hollis Garfield, *Pr*
Albert Wiggins, *Treas*
EMP: 175 **EST:** 1989
SQ FT: 100,000
SALES (est): 8.95MM **Privately Held**
Web: www.communicarehealth.com
SIC: 8051 Convalescent home with continuous nursing care

(G-6954)
DEBTNEXT SOLUTIONS LLC
175 Montrose West Ave Ste 170 (44321-3122)
PHONE..................................330 665-0400
EMP: 27 **EST:** 2003
SALES (est): 1.71MM **Privately Held**
Web: www.debtnext.com
SIC: 8742 Financial consultant

(G-6955)
DISINFECTION MGT TECH LLC
Also Called: Dmt Certified
1245 S Cleveland Massillon Rd Ste 1 (44321-1657)
P.O. Box 361273 (44136-0022)
PHONE..................................440 212-1061
Laurie Colagiovanni, *Pr*
EMP: 47 **EST:** 2019
SALES (est): 2.5MM **Privately Held**
SIC: 8744 Facilities support services

(G-6956)
DOWNING ENTERPRISES INC
Also Called: Downing Exhibits
1287 Centerview Cir (44321-1632)
PHONE..................................330 666-3888
William Downing Junior, *CEO*
Michael Carano, *
Karen Gallaher, *
Craig Marsall, *
◆ **EMP:** 100 **EST:** 1972
SQ FT: 144,000
SALES (est): 20MM **Privately Held**
Web: www.downingexhibits.com
SIC: 7389 3999 Trade show arrangement; Barber and beauty shop equipment

(G-6957)
EDWARDS REALTY & INV CORP
Bell Music Company
1314 Centerview Cir (44321-1628)
PHONE..................................330 253-9171
TOLL FREE: 800
EMP: 148
SALES (corp-wide): 4.9MM **Privately Held**
Web: www.thetangier.com
SIC: 7993 Coin-operated amusement devices
PA: Edwards Realty & Investment Corporation
3866 Allard Rd
Medina OH 44256
330 253-9171

(G-6958)
GRAVES LUMBER CO
1315 S Cleveland Massillon Rd (44321-2175)
P.O. Box 14870 (44321-4870)
PHONE..................................330 666-1115
▲ **EMP:** 115 **EST:** 1899
SALES (est): 30.54MM **Privately Held**
Web: www.graveslumber.com
SIC: 5211 5031 Lumber and other building materials; Lumber, plywood, and millwork

(G-6959)
LEWIS LANDSCAPING & NURS INC
3606 Minor Rd (44321-2414)
PHONE..................................330 666-2655
Wilson Lewis, *Pr*
EMP: 30 **EST:** 1983
SALES (est): 2.66MM **Privately Held**
Web: www.lewislandscaping1.com
SIC: 0781 Landscape services

(G-6960)
LORANTFFY CARE CENTER INC
2631 Copley Rd (44321-2198)
P.O. Box 4017 (44321-0017)
PHONE..................................330 666-2631
Elizabeth Domotor, *Pr*
Elizabeth Schmidt, *
EMP: 90 **EST:** 1971
SQ FT: 19,000
SALES (est): 4.9MM **Privately Held**
Web: www.lorantffy.com
SIC: 8051 Convalescent home with continuous nursing care

(G-6961)
MEDVET ASSOCIATES LLC
Also Called: Medvet Akron
1321 Centerview Cir (44321-1627)
PHONE..................................330 665-4996
Amanda Newhouse, *Brnch Mgr*
EMP: 138
Web: www.medvet.com
SIC: 0742 Animal hospital services, pets and other animal specialties
PA: Medvet Associates, Llc
350 E Wilson Bridge Rd
Worthington OH 43085

(G-6962)
RVSHARECOM
155 Montrose West Ave (44321-3121)
PHONE..................................330 907-9479
EMP: 34 **EST:** 2018
SALES (est): 3.26MM **Privately Held**
Web: www.rvshare.com
SIC: 6512 Commercial and industrial building operation

(G-6963)
SHREE HOSPITALITY CORPORATION
Also Called: Radisson Inn 550
200 Montrose West Ave (44321-2788)
PHONE..................................330 666-9300
Himansu Patel, *Pr*
EMP: 29 **EST:** 2006
SALES (est): 204.7K **Privately Held**
Web: www.radissonhotels.com
SIC: 7011 Hotels and motels

(G-6964)
SUMNER HOME FOR THE AGED INC (PA)
Also Called: Sumner On Merriman
4327 Cobblestone Dr (44321-2930)
PHONE..................................330 666-2952
Ted Pappas, *CEO*
EMP: 199 **EST:** 1911
SQ FT: 25,000
SALES (est): 5.05MM
SALES (corp-wide): 5.05MM **Privately Held**
SIC: 8051 Skilled nursing care facilities

(G-6965)
SUN LODGING LLC
Also Called: Best Western
160 Montrose West Ave (44321-1372)
PHONE..................................330 670-0888
Millie Patel, *Prin*
EMP: 33 **EST:** 2008
SALES (est): 903.67K **Privately Held**
Web: www.bestwestern.com
SIC: 7011 Hotels and motels

(G-6966)
THE APOSTOLOS GROUP INC
Also Called: Thomarios
1 Thomarios Rd (44321-1779)
PHONE..................................330 670-9900
EMP: 120 **EST:** 1969
SALES (est): 28.32MM **Privately Held**
Web: www.thomarios.com
SIC: 1542 1541 1721 Commercial and office building, new construction; Industrial buildings, new construction, nec; Bridge painting

(G-6967)
TOWNSHIP OF COPLEY
Road Maintenance
1540 S Cleveland Massillon Rd (44321-1908)
PHONE..................................330 666-1853
EMP: 47
Web: www.copley.oh.us
SIC: 1611 9111 Highway and street construction; Mayors' office
PA: Township Of Copley
1540 S Clvland Mssllon Rd
Copley OH 44321
330 666-1853

Cortland
Trumbull County

(G-6968)
BURNETT POOLS INC (PA)
Also Called: Burnett Pools and Spas
2498 State Route 5 (44410-9339)
PHONE..................................330 372-1725
Alan Burnett, *Pr*
Gary P Burnett, *
Myra May, *
Holly Hess, *
EMP: 40 **EST:** 1948
SQ FT: 8,400
SALES (est): 8.9MM
SALES (corp-wide): 8.9MM **Privately Held**
Web: www.burnettpools.com
SIC: 5999 1799 5941 Swimming pool chemicals, equipment, and supplies; Swimming pool construction; Pool and billiard tables

(G-6969)
CONCORD CARE CTR CORTLAND INC
4250 Sodom Hutchings Rd (44410-9790)
PHONE..................................330 637-7906
Debra A Ifft, *Pr*
EMP: 32 **EST:** 1999
SALES (est): 1.03MM **Privately Held**
Web: www.concordcarecenters.com
SIC: 8051 Skilled nursing care facilities

(G-6970)
CORTLAND HEALTHCARE GROUP INC
Also Called: Cortland Healthcare Center
369 N High St (44410-1022)
PHONE..................................330 638-4015
Dale Sanders, *Admn*
EMP: 156
SALES (corp-wide): 2.67MM **Privately Held**
Web: www.saberhealth.com
SIC: 8051 Convalescent home with continuous nursing care
PA: Cortland Healthcare Group, Inc.
26691 Richmond Rd
Bedford Heights OH 44146
216 292-5706

(G-6971)
DAVID HARNETT DDS INC
Also Called: Cortland Dental Technology Ctr
500 Wakefield Dr Ste 4 (44410-1504)
PHONE..................................330 638-3065
David L Harnett D.d.s., *Pr*
EMP: 39 **EST:** 1974
SQ FT: 9,000
SALES (est): 561.86K **Privately Held**
Web: www.cortlanddentaltechnology.com
SIC: 8021 Dental clinics and offices

(G-6972)
MARK THOMAS FORD INC
3098 State Route 5 (44410-9207)

GEOGRAPHIC SECTION

Coshocton - Coshocton County (G-6994)

PHONE..................................330 638-1010
Tom Levak, *Pr*
EMP: 44 **EST:** 1997
SQ FT: 27,700
SALES (est): 21.92MM **Privately Held**
Web: www.markthomasford.net
SIC: 5511 7538 7532 5521 Automobiles, new and used; General automotive repair shops; Top and body repair and paint shops; Used car dealers

(G-6973)
MILLER YOUNT PAVING INC
2295 Hoagland Blackstub Rd (44410-9318)
PHONE..................................561 951-7416
David A Grayson, *VP*
Herbert Cottrell, *
Nate Schaeffer, *
EMP: 40 **EST:** 1987
SALES (est): 3.46MM **Privately Held**
SIC: 1794 1771 1522 Excavation work; Blacktop (asphalt) work; Hotel/motel and multi-family home construction

(G-6974)
OHIO LIVING
303 N Mecca St (44410-1074)
PHONE..................................330 638-2420
EMP: 228
Web: www.ohioliving.org
SIC: 6519 Real property lessors, nec
PA: Ohio Living
   9200 Worthington Rd # 300
   Westerville OH 43082

(G-6975)
OVER RAINBOW ADULT DAYCARE
110 Windsor Dr (44410-2701)
PHONE..................................330 638-9599
Donna Fye, *Owner*
EMP: 30 **EST:** 1997
SALES (est): 423.38K **Privately Held**
SIC: 8322 Adult day care center

(G-6976)
TRUMBLL-MAHONING MED GROUP INC
Also Called: Trumbll-Mhoning Med Group Phrm
2600 State Route 5 (44410-9393)
PHONE..................................330 372-8800
EMP: 50 **EST:** 1980
SALES (est): 7.68MM **Privately Held**
Web: www.trumbullmahoning.com
SIC: 8011 5912 Medical centers; Drug stores

Coshocton
Coshocton County

(G-6977)
BUCKEYE CHECK CASHING INC
Also Called: Checksmart
105 S 2nd Street (43812-1517)
PHONE..................................740 575-4314
EMP: 35
Web: www.ccfi.com
SIC: 6099 Check cashing agencies
HQ: Buckeye Check Cashing, Inc.
   5165 Emerald Pkwy Ste 100
   Dublin OH 43017
   614 798-5900

(G-6978)
COLLEGE PARK INC
Also Called: College Park HM Hlth Care Plus
380 Browns Ln Ste 7 (43812-2075)
PHONE..................................740 623-4607
Tim Postlewaite, *Pr*
EMP: 196

SALES (corp-wide): 4.95MM **Privately Held**
Web: www.collegeparkinc.com
SIC: 8361 Geriatric residential care
PA: College Park, Inc
   21990 Orchard St
   West Lafayette OH
   740 623-4612

(G-6979)
COLUMBUS & OHIO RIVER RR CO
47849 Papermill Rd (43812-9724)
PHONE..................................740 622-8092
EMP: 28 **EST:** 1988
SALES (est): 2.02MM
SALES (corp-wide): 9.7MM **Privately Held**
SIC: 4011 Railroads, line-haul operating
PA: Summit View, Inc.
   47849 Papermill Rd
   Coshocton OH

(G-6980)
COSHOCTON CNTY EMRGNCY MED SVC
Also Called: Ccems
513 Chestnut St (43812-1210)
PHONE..................................740 622-4294
Todd Shroyer, *Dir*
EMP: 164 **EST:** 1976
SQ FT: 2,500
SALES (est): 555.08K **Privately Held**
Web: www.coshoctonbeacontoday.com
SIC: 4119 Ambulance service
PA: County Of Coshocton
   401 1/2 Main St
   Coshocton OH 43812
   740 622-1753

(G-6981)
COSHOCTON CNTY HEAD START INC
3201 County Road 16 (43812-9123)
PHONE..................................740 622-3667
Patricia Bachert, *Dir*
Suzy Lapp, *
EMP: 30 **EST:** 1971
SALES (est): 3.13MM **Privately Held**
Web: www.brackenquarterhorses.com
SIC: 8351 Head Start center, except in conjunction with school

(G-6982)
COUNTY OF COSHOCTON
Also Called: Child Support Agency
725 Pine St (43812-2318)
PHONE..................................740 622-1020
Melinda Fehrman, *Dir*
EMP: 28
Web: www.coshoctonbeacontoday.com
SIC: 8322 9111 Child related social services; County supervisors' and executives' office
PA: County Of Coshocton
   401 1/2 Main St
   Coshocton OH 43812
   740 622-1753

(G-6983)
DOCTORS OFFICE
Also Called: Urgent Care
1460 Orange St (43812-2229)
P.O. Box 457 (43812-0457)
PHONE..................................740 622-3016
Greg Golden, *Mgr*
EMP: 28 **EST:** 1999
SALES (est): 225.45K **Privately Held**
Web: www.coshoctonhospital.org
SIC: 8011 Freestanding emergency medical center

(G-6984)
FAMILY PHYSICIANS OF COSHOCTON
440 Browns Ln (43812-2071)
PHONE..................................740 622-0332
Jerold A Meyer, *Pr*
EMP: 91 **EST:** 1973
SQ FT: 2,400
SALES (est): 1.7MM **Privately Held**
Web: www.coshoctonhospital.org
SIC: 8062 General medical and surgical hospitals

(G-6985)
FRONTIER POWER COMPANY
770 S 2nd St (43812-1978)
P.O. Box 280 (43812-0280)
PHONE..................................740 622-6755
Robert E Wise, *Pr*
Martin Daugherty, *
Blair Porteus, *
John Powell, *
EMP: 34 **EST:** 1936
SQ FT: 8,000
SALES (est): 18.11MM **Privately Held**
Web: www.frontier-power.com
SIC: 4911 Distribution, electric power

(G-6986)
HILSCHER-CLARKE ELECTRIC CO
572 S 3rd St (43812-2057)
P.O. Box 877 (43812-0877)
PHONE..................................740 622-5557
Ted Foster, *Mgr*
EMP: 170
SALES (corp-wide): 65.49MM **Privately Held**
Web: www.hilscher-clarke.com
SIC: 1731 General electrical contractor
PA: Hilscher-Clarke Electric Company
   519 4th St Nw
   Canton OH 44703
   330 452-9806

(G-6987)
INTERIM HLTHCARE CAMBRIDGE INC
232 Chestnut St (43812-1164)
PHONE..................................740 623-2949
Thomas J Dimarco, *Brnch Mgr*
EMP: 89
Web: www.interimhealthcare.com
SIC: 8082 Home health care services
PA: Interim Healthcare Of Cambridge, Inc.
   300 W Wilson Bridge Rd
   Worthington OH 43085

(G-6988)
ITM MARKETING INC
Also Called: Intellitarget Marketing Svcs
331 Main St (43812-1510)
PHONE..................................740 295-3575
EMP: 124 **EST:** 1996
SALES (est): 6.18MM **Privately Held**
Web: www.itmmarketing.com
SIC: 8742 7374 2741 7322 Marketing consulting services; Data processing and preparation; Telephone and other directory publishing; Adjustment and collection services

(G-6989)
J & R DOOR LLC
46700 County Road 405 (43812-8701)
P.O. Box 391 (43812-0391)
PHONE..................................740 623-2782
EMP: 27 **EST:** 2006
SALES (est): 2.51MM **Privately Held**
Web: www.j-rdoor.com

SIC: 1751 Garage door, installation or erection

(G-6990)
LANDSTAR GLOBAL LOGISTICS INC
1247 E Main St (43812-1742)
PHONE..................................740 575-4700
Donovan Shivers, *Brnch Mgr*
EMP: 62
Web: www.landstar.com
SIC: 4213 4214 4731 Trucking, except local; Local trucking with storage; Freight transportation arrangement
HQ: Landstar Global Logistics, Inc.
   13410 Sutton Park Dr S
   Jacksonville FL 32224

(G-6991)
LP COSHOCTON LLC
Also Called: Signature Healthcare Coshocton
100 S Whitewoman St (43812-1068)
PHONE..................................470 622-1220
Admiral Melody Shannon, *Prin*
EMP: 48 **EST:** 2014
SALES (est): 10.29MM **Privately Held**
Web: www.shcofcoshocton.com
SIC: 8051 Skilled nursing care facilities
PA: Signature Healthcare, Llc
   12201 Bluegrass Pkwy
   Louisville KY 40299

(G-6992)
MCWANE INC
Clow Water Systems Company
2266 S 6th St (43812-8906)
P.O. Box 6001 (43812-6001)
PHONE..................................740 622-6651
Jeff Otterstedt, *Mgr*
EMP: 400
SALES (corp-wide): 970.37MM **Privately Held**
Web: www.mcwaneductile.com
SIC: 3321 5085 5051 3444 Cast iron pipe and fittings; Industrial supplies; Pipe and tubing, steel; Sheet metalwork
PA: Mcwane, Inc.
   2900 Highway 280 S # 300
   Birmingham AL 35223
   205 414-3100

(G-6993)
NGO DEVELOPMENT CORPORATION
Also Called: Energy Corportive
504 N 3rd St (43812-1113)
P.O. Box 662 (43812-0662)
PHONE..................................740 622-9560
Scott Kees, *Mgr*
EMP: 453
SALES (corp-wide): 24.14MM **Privately Held**
Web: www.myenergycoop.com
SIC: 1382 4923 5984 Oil and gas exploration services; Gas transmission and distribution; Propane gas, bottled
HQ: Ngo Development Corporation
   1500 Granville Rd
   Newark OH 43055
   740 344-3790

(G-6994)
NOVELTY ADVERTISING CO INC
Also Called: Kenyon Co
1148 Walnut St (43812-1769)
PHONE..................................740 622-3113
Gregory Coffman, *Pr*
James Mcconnel, *VP*
◆ **EMP:** 50 **EST:** 1895
SQ FT: 100,000
SALES (est): 4.39MM **Privately Held**
Web: www.noveltyadv.com

Coshocton - Coshocton County (G-6995)

SIC: 2752 5199 Calendars, lithographed; Advertising specialties

(G-6995)
OHIO DEPT JOB & FMLY SVCS
725 Pine St (43812-2318)
PHONE....................740 295-7516
EMP: 34
Web: jfs.ohio.gov
SIC: 8322 Social service center
HQ: Ohio Department Of Job And Family Services
30 E Broad St Fl 32
Columbus OH 43215

(G-6996)
OXFORD MINING COMPANY - KY LLC
544 Chestnut St (43812-1209)
PHONE....................740 622-6302
EMP: 33 **EST:** 2010
SALES (est): 6.04MM
SALES (corp-wide): 814.89MM **Privately Held**
SIC: 1221 Strip mining, bituminous
HQ: Oxford Mining Company, Llc
544 Chestnut St
Coshocton OH 43812

(G-6997)
PRIME HEALTHCARE FOUNDATION
Also Called: Breast Health Center
1460 Orange St (43812-2229)
PHONE....................740 623-4178
EMP: 304
SALES (corp-wide): 878.52MM **Privately Held**
Web: www.coshoctonhospital.org
SIC: 8062 General medical and surgical hospitals
HQ: Prime Healthcare Foundation-Coshocton, Llc
1460 Orange St
Coshocton OH 43812
740 622-6411

(G-6998)
PRIME HLTHCARE FNDTN-CSHCTON L
1397 Walnut St (43812-2238)
PHONE....................740 623-4013
Larry Cahill, *Brnch Mgr*
EMP: 183
SALES (corp-wide): 878.52MM **Privately Held**
Web: www.coshoctonhospital.org
SIC: 8062 General medical and surgical hospitals
HQ: Prime Healthcare Foundation-Coshocton, Llc
1460 Orange St
Coshocton OH 43812
740 622-6411

(G-6999)
RESIDNTIAL HM FOR DVLPMNTLLY D (PA)
Also Called: Rhdd
925 Chestnut St (43812-1302)
P.O. Box 997 (43812-0997)
PHONE....................740 622-9778
Lisa Reed, *CEO*
Michael Dennis, *
Marylin Shroyer, *
James Nelson, *
Rita Shaw, *
EMP: 140 **EST:** 1976
SQ FT: 1,200
SALES (est): 9.71MM
SALES (corp-wide): 9.71MM **Privately Held**
Web: www.rhddinc.org

SIC: 8361 Mentally handicapped home

(G-7000)
ROSCOE VILLAGE FOUNDATION
Also Called: Village Inn Restaurant
200 N Whitewoman St (43812-1059)
PHONE....................740 622-2222
Joel Hampton, *CEO*
EMP: 56
SALES (corp-wide): 586.34K **Privately Held**
Web: www.roscoevillage.com
SIC: 5812 7299 5813 Restaurant, family: chain; Banquet hall facilities; Tavern (drinking places)
PA: Roscoe Village Foundation, Inc
600 N Whitewoman St
Coshocton OH 43812
740 622-7644

(G-7001)
SALO INC
232 Chestnut St (43812-1164)
PHONE....................740 623-2331
EMP: 140
SALES (corp-wide): 52.16MM **Privately Held**
Web: www.interim-health.com
SIC: 8082 Home health care services
PA: Salo, Inc.
300 W Wlson Brdge Rd Ste
Columbus OH 43085
614 436-9404

(G-7002)
SALO INC
Also Called: Interim Services
450 N 3rd St (43812-1111)
PHONE....................877 759-2106
Cindi Harriman, *Mgr*
EMP: 50
SALES (corp-wide): 52.16MM **Privately Held**
Web: www.interimhealthcare.com
SIC: 7363 7361 Medical help service; Nurses' registry
PA: Salo, Inc.
300 W Wlson Brdge Rd Ste
Columbus OH 43085
614 436-9404

(G-7003)
THOMPKINS CHILD ADLESCENT SVCS
1199 S 2nd St (43812-1920)
PHONE....................740 622-4470
Charles Larrick, *Dir*
EMP: 86
SALES (corp-wide): 5.05MM **Privately Held**
Web: www.thompkinstreatment.org
SIC: 8093 Mental health clinic, outpatient
PA: Thompkins Child And Adolescent Services
2845 Bell St
Zanesville OH 43701
740 454-0738

(G-7004)
WESTMORELAND RESOURCES GP LLC
544 Chestnut St (43812-1209)
PHONE....................740 622-6302
Martin Purvis, *CEO*
EMP: 81 **EST:** 2007
SALES (est): 24.31MM
SALES (corp-wide): 814.89MM **Privately Held**
SIC: 1221 Bituminous coal and lignite-surface mining
PA: Westmoreland Mining Llc

10375 Pk Mdows Dr Ste 400
Lone Tree CO 80124
303 922-6463

(G-7005)
WILEY COMPANIES (PA)
Also Called: Organic Technologies
545 Walnut St (43812-1656)
P.O. Box 1665 (43812-6665)
PHONE....................740 622-0755
▲ **EMP:** 130 **EST:** 1981
SALES (est): 45.49MM
SALES (corp-wide): 45.49MM **Privately Held**
Web: www.wileyco.com
SIC: 2087 8731 2869 Concentrates, flavoring (except drink); Commercial physical research; Industrial organic chemicals, nec

Coventry Township
Summit County

(G-7006)
ANR ELECTRIC LLC
3783 State Rd (44203)
PHONE....................330 644-4454
Nicholas Gotto, *Prin*
EMP: 60 **EST:** 2012
SALES (est): 9.79MM **Privately Held**
Web: www.anrelectricco.com
SIC: 1731 Electrical work

(G-7007)
ECHOLS HEATING AND AC INC
85 Hanna Pkwy (44319-1166)
PHONE....................330 773-3500
Jim Echols, *Pr*
Elaine Echols, *Sec*
EMP: 31 **EST:** 1989
SQ FT: 18,480
SALES (est): 1.29MM **Privately Held**
Web: www.echolsheating.com
SIC: 1711 Warm air heating and air conditioning contractor

(G-7008)
FRED W ALBRECHT GROCERY CO
Also Called: Acme
3235 Manchester Rd Unit A (44319-1459)
PHONE....................330 645-6222
Bernie King, *Brnch Mgr*
EMP: 109
SALES (corp-wide): 455.09K **Privately Held**
Web: www.acmestores.com
SIC: 5912 5411 7384 5992 Drug stores and proprietary stores; Grocery stores; Photofinish laboratories; Florists
PA: The Fred W Albrecht Grocery Company
2700 Gilchrist Rd Ste A
Akron OH 44305
330 733-2263

(G-7009)
GLAUS PYLE SCHMER BRNS DHVEN I
Also Called: Gpd Group
470 Portage Lakes Dr Ste 212 (44319-2290)
PHONE....................330 645-2131
David B Granger, *Pr*
EMP: 27
SALES (corp-wide): 122.1MM **Privately Held**
Web: www.gpdgroup.com
SIC: 8711 Consulting engineer

PA: Glaus, Pyle, Schomer, Burns & Dehaven, Inc.
520 S Main St Ste 2531
Akron OH 44311
330 572-2100

(G-7010)
HI-WAY DISTRIBUTING CORP AMER
3716 E State St (44203-4548)
PHONE....................330 645-6633
Jeff Hornak, *Pr*
Mark Hornak, *Sec*
Dominic A Musitano Junior, *Prin*
J L Miller, *Prin*
Joseph P Mueller, *Prin*
▲ **EMP:** 60 **EST:** 1975
SQ FT: 48,000
SALES (est): 22.18MM **Privately Held**
SIC: 5199 5731 General merchandise, non-durable; Automotive sound equipment

(G-7011)
INTERVAL BROTHERHOOD HOMES INC
Also Called: IBH
3445 S Main St (44319-3028)
P.O. Box 26203 (44319-6203)
PHONE....................330 644-4095
Father Samuel Ciccolini, *Dir*
EMP: 75 **EST:** 1970
SQ FT: 1,626
SALES (est): 8.91MM **Privately Held**
Web: www.ibh.org
SIC: 8361 8211 Rehabilitation center, residential: health care incidental; Elementary and secondary schools

(G-7012)
K COMPANY INCORPORATED
Also Called: Honeywell Authorized Dealer
2234 S Arlington Rd (44319-1929)
PHONE....................330 773-5125
Thomas Bauer, *CEO*
Christopher Martin, *Pr*
Susan Popovich, *Sec*
Carmen Dempsey, *Treas*
EMP: 110 **EST:** 1972
SQ FT: 43,000
SALES (est): 44.77MM **Privately Held**
Web: www.thekcompany.com
SIC: 1711 Warm air heating and air conditioning contractor

(G-7013)
LEGACY ROOFING SERVICES LLC
Also Called: Legacy Commercial Roofing
800 Killian Rd (44319-2555)
P.O. Box 26635 (44319-6635)
PHONE....................330 645-6000
Kevin Burgess, *
EMP: 65 **EST:** 2019
SALES (est): 5.01MM **Privately Held**
Web: www.legacyroofing.com
SIC: 1761 Roofing contractor

(G-7014)
OHIO HCKRY HRVEST BRND PDTS IN
Also Called: Hickory Harvest Foods
90 Logan Pkwy (44319-1177)
PHONE....................330 644-6266
Joe Swiatkowski, *Pr*
Michael Swiatkowski, *
EMP: 32 **EST:** 1972
SQ FT: 32,000
SALES (est): 15.78MM **Privately Held**
Web: www.hickoryharvest.com
SIC: 5145 5149 2099 Nuts, salted or roasted; Fruits, dried; Food preparations, nec

GEOGRAPHIC SECTION

Cuyahoga Falls - Summit County (G-7035)

(G-7015)
REM-OHIO INC
470 Portage Lakes Dr Ste 207
(44319-2296)
PHONE.................330 644-9730
EMP: 32
SALES (corp-wide): 19.17MM **Privately Held**
Web: www.rem-oh.com
SIC: 8361 8721 Retarded home; Accounting, auditing, and bookkeeping
PA: Rem-Ohio, Inc
   6921 York Ave S
   Minneapolis MN 55435
   952 925-5067

(G-7016)
TERIK ROOFING INC
72 Hanna Pkwy (44319-1165)
PHONE.................330 785-0060
Eric Gelal, *Pr*
Terry Clark, *
Eric Gelal, *VP*
EMP: 30 EST: 2002
SQ FT: 4,000
SALES (est): 2.75MM **Privately Held**
Web: www.terikroofing.com
SIC: 1761 Roofing contractor

Covington
Miami County

(G-7017)
APPLE FARM SERVICE INC (PA)
Also Called: Apple Farm Service Infc
10120 W Versailles Rd (45318-9618)
PHONE.................937 526-4851
William Apple, *Pr*
Ina Pearl Apple, *VP*
Linda Apple, *
EMP: 40 EST: 1956
SQ FT: 16,875
SALES (est): 22.52MM
SALES (corp-wide): 22.52MM **Privately Held**
Web: www.applefarmservice.com
SIC: 5083 7699 Agricultural machinery, nec; Farm machinery repair

(G-7018)
GM MECHANICAL INC (PA)
4263 N State Route 48 (45318)
P.O. Box 190 (45318)
PHONE.................937 473-3006
EMP: 74 EST: 1975
SALES (est): 9.96MM
SALES (corp-wide): 9.96MM **Privately Held**
SIC: 1794 1711 3498 3444 Excavation work; Plumbing contractors; Fabricated pipe and fittings; Sheet metalwork

(G-7019)
UVMC NURSING CARE INC
Also Called: Covington Care Center
75 Mote Dr (45318-1245)
PHONE.................937 473-2075
Brenda Lewis, *Brnch Mgr*
EMP: 103
SQ FT: 30,672
Web: www.premierhealth.com
SIC: 8059 8069 8051 Nursing home, except skilled and intermediate care facility; Specialty hospitals, except psychiatric; Skilled nursing care facilities
PA: Uvmc Nursing Care, Inc.
   3130 N County Road 25a
   Troy OH 45373

Crestline
Crawford County

(G-7020)
CONSULATE MANAGEMENT CO LLC
Also Called: Crestline Nursing Center
327 W Main St (44827-1434)
PHONE.................419 683-3255
Joseph Conte, *Prin*
EMP: 222
SALES (corp-wide): 491MM **Privately Held**
Web: www.consulatehc.com
SIC: 8051 Convalescent home with continuous nursing care
HQ: Consulate Management Company, Llc
   800 Concourse Pkwy S # 200
   Maitland FL 32751
   407 571-1550

(G-7021)
CRESTLINE NURSING CENTER LLC
327 W Main St (44827-1434)
PHONE.................419 683-3255
EMP: 50 EST: 2017
SALES (est): 2.55MM **Privately Held**
Web: www.crestlinenwh.com
SIC: 8051 Convalescent home with continuous nursing care

(G-7022)
EDGAR TRENT CNSTR CO LLC
Also Called: Edgar Trent Construction Co
1301 Freese Works Pl (44827)
PHONE.................419 683-4939
Edgar Trent, *Owner*
EMP: 57 EST: 1994
SALES (est): 4.95MM **Privately Held**
Web: www.edgartrentconstruction.com
SIC: 1623 Cable laying construction

(G-7023)
GOLDEN HAWK INC
4594 Lincoln Hwy 30 (44827-9685)
PHONE.................419 683-3304
Raymond Miller, *Pr*
EMP: 64 EST: 1976
SALES (est): 473.29K **Privately Held**
SIC: 4212 Local trucking, without storage
PA: Golden Hawk Transportation Co.
   4594 Lincoln Hwy
   Crestline OH 44827

(G-7024)
GOLDEN HAWK TRANSPORTATION CO (PA)
4594 Lincoln Hwy (44827-9685)
PHONE.................419 683-3304
EMP: 70 EST: 1992
SQ FT: 10,000
SALES (est): 9.06MM **Privately Held**
Web: www.goldenhawktransportation.com
SIC: 4213 Heavy hauling, nec

(G-7025)
MEDCENTRAL HEALTH SYSTEM
Also Called: Crestline Hospital
291 Heiser Ct (44827-1453)
PHONE.................419 683-1040
Susan Brown, *Admn*
EMP: 258
SALES (corp-wide): 4.29B **Privately Held**
Web: www.medcentral.org
SIC: 8062 8093 8049 General medical and surgical hospitals; Rehabilitation center, outpatient treatment; Physical therapist
HQ: Medcentral Health System
   335 Glessner Ave
   Mansfield OH 44903
   419 526-8000

(G-7026)
SUNRISE COOPERATIVE INC
Also Called: Crestline Agronomy
3000 W Bucyrus St (44827-1674)
PHONE.................419 683-7340
Steve Niese, *Brnch Mgr*
EMP: 27
SALES (corp-wide): 515.25MM **Privately Held**
Web: www.sunriseco-op.com
SIC: 5191 Farm supplies
PA: Sunrise Cooperative, Inc.
   2025 W State St
   Fremont OH 43420
   419 332-6468

(G-7027)
UNITED BANK NATIONAL ASSN
245 N Seltzer St (44827-1423)
P.O. Box 186 (44827-0186)
PHONE.................419 683-1010
Wanda Massey, *Mgr*
EMP: 28
SALES (corp-wide): 564.3MM **Publicly Held**
Web: www.parknationalbank.com
SIC: 6021 National commercial banks
HQ: United Bank National Association (Inc)
   401 S Sandusky Ave
   Bucyrus OH 44820
   419 562-3040

Cridersville
Auglaize County

(G-7028)
CRIDERSVILLE HEALTH CARE CTR
Also Called: CRIDERSVILLE NURSING HOME
603 E Main St Frnt (45806-2411)
PHONE.................419 645-4468
Greg Costello, *Dir*
EMP: 55 EST: 1961
SALES (est): 2.06MM **Privately Held**
Web: www.cridersvillehealthcare.com
SIC: 8052 8051 Intermediate care facilities; Skilled nursing care facilities

(G-7029)
OTTERBEIN HOMES
Also Called: Otterbein Cridersville
100 Red Oak Dr (45806-9618)
PHONE.................419 645-5114
Susan Chandler, *Ex Dir*
EMP: 73
SQ FT: 50,000
SALES (corp-wide): 74.71MM **Privately Held**
Web: www.otterbein.org
SIC: 8361 8051 Aged home; Skilled nursing care facilities
PA: Otterbein Homes
   3855 Lower Market St # 300
   Lebanon OH 45036
   513 933-5400

Croton
Licking County

(G-7030)
HARTFORD FARMS LLC
Also Called: Buckeye Egg Farm Lp-Main Off
11212 Croton Rd (43013-9725)
PHONE.................740 893-7200
Matt Doyle, *CFO*
Bill Leininger, *Dir*
Don Hershey, *Genl Mgr*
EMP: 600 EST: 1979
SALES (est): 23.57MM **Privately Held**
SIC: 5144 Eggs

Curtice
Ottawa County

(G-7031)
MENTOR 67 LLC
300 W Mill St (43412-7704)
P.O. Box 565 (44061-0565)
PHONE.................800 589-5842
James R Gardner, *Pr*
Raymond W Layman, *Care Vice President**
EMP: 60 EST: 2017
SALES (est): 4.84MM **Privately Held**
Web: www.ncltinc.com
SIC: 5084 Materials handling machinery

Cuyahoga Falls
Summit County

(G-7032)
ADO STAFFING INC
Also Called: Flux Staffing
3773 State Rd (44223-2603)
PHONE.................330 922-2077
Shawn Lynch, *Mgr*
EMP: 400
Web: www.olsten.com
SIC: 7363 Temporary help service
HQ: Ado Staffing, Inc.
   4800 Deerwood Campus Pkwy # 800
   Jacksonville FL 32246
   631 844-7800

(G-7033)
AJAX COMMERCIAL CLEANING INC
3566 State Rd 5 (44223-2600)
P.O. Box 4031 (44223-4031)
PHONE.................330 928-4543
William J Berger, *Pr*
EMP: 99 EST: 2003
SALES (est): 3.5MM **Privately Held**
Web: www.ajaxcommercialcleaning.com
SIC: 7349 Cleaning service, industrial or commercial

(G-7034)
AL SPITZER FORD INC
Also Called: Quick Lane
3737 State Rd (44223-2603)
PHONE.................330 929-6546
Allen Spitzer, *Pr*
EMP: 32 EST: 1973
SQ FT: 30,000
SALES (est): 6.49MM
SALES (corp-wide): 16.64K **Privately Held**
Web: www.alspitzerford.com
SIC: 5511 7538 Automobiles, new and used; General automotive repair shops
PA: Spitzer Management, Inc.
   150 E Bridge St
   Elyria OH 44035
   440 323-4671

(G-7035)
ALRO STEEL CORPORATION
Also Called: Alro Steel
4787 State Rd (44223)
P.O. Box 3555 (44223-7555)
PHONE.................330 929-4660
Todd Rumler, *Mgr*
EMP: 48
SQ FT: 77,094
SALES (corp-wide): 3.43B **Privately Held**

Cuyahoga Falls - Summit County (G-7036)

GEOGRAPHIC SECTION

Web: www.alro.com
SIC: 5051 Steel
PA: Alro Steel Corporation
3100 E High St
Jackson MI 49203
517 787-5500

(G-7036)
ALSIDE INC (HQ)
Also Called: Alside Window Company
3773 State Rd (44223-2603)
P.O. Box 2010 (44309-2010)
PHONE.................................330 929-1811
Brian Strauss, *Pr*
EMP: 40 EST: 1947
SALES (est): 101.57MM
SALES (corp-wide): 1.18B **Privately Held**
Web: www.alside.com
SIC: 5031 Windows
PA: Associated Materials, Llc
3773 State Rd
Cuyahoga Falls OH 44223
330 929-1811

(G-7037)
ALTERCARE INC
2728 Bailey Rd (44221-2236)
PHONE.................................330 929-4231
EMP: 27
SALES (corp-wide): 6.9MM **Privately Held**
Web: www.altercareonline.com
SIC: 8361 8322 8059 8051 Aged home; Rehabilitation services; Nursing home, except skilled and intermediate care facility; Skilled nursing care facilities
PA: Altercare, Inc.
35990 Westminister Ave
North Ridgeville OH 44039
440 327-5285

(G-7038)
AMERICAN DE ROSA LAMPARTS LLC (HQ)
Also Called: Luminance
370 Falls Commerce Pkwy (44224-1062)
◆ EMP: 85 EST: 1951
SALES (est): 29.4MM
SALES (corp-wide): 31.1MM **Privately Held**
Web: luminance.us.com
SIC: 5063 3364 3229 Lighting fixtures; Brass and bronze die-castings; Bulbs for electric lights
PA: Luminance Acquisition, Llc
25101 Chagrin Blvd # 350
Cleveland OH

(G-7039)
AMERICAN EX TRVL RLTED SVCS IN
Also Called: American Express
911 Graham Rd Ste 24 (44221-1160)
PHONE.................................330 922-5700
EMP: 37
SALES (corp-wide): 67.36B **Publicly Held**
Web: consumer-travel.americanexpress.com
SIC: 4724 Travel agencies
HQ: American Express Travel Related Services Company, Inc.
200 Vesey St
New York NY 10285
212 640-2000

(G-7040)
APPELGREN LTD
3772 Wyoga Lake Rd (44224-4946)
PHONE.................................330 945-6402
Lasse Knudsen, *Pr*
Jeannette Knudsen, *
EMP: 30 EST: 1994
SALES (est): 1.7MM **Privately Held**

SIC: 1741 Masonry and other stonework

(G-7041)
ASSOCIATED MATERIALS LLC (PA)
Also Called: Alside Supply Center
3773 State Rd (44223-2603)
P.O. Box 2010 (44309-2010)
PHONE.................................330 929-1811
James Drexinger, *CEO*
Erik D Ragatz, *
Brian C Strauss, *
Scott F Stephens, *
William L Topper, *
▲ EMP: 1003 EST: 1947
SQ FT: 63,000
SALES (est): 1.18B
SALES (corp-wide): 1.18B **Privately Held**
Web: www.associatedmaterials.com
SIC: 3089 5033 5031 3442 Plastics hardware and building products; Roofing and siding materials; Windows; Metal doors, sash, and trim

(G-7042)
ASSOCIATED MATERIALS FIN INC
3773 State Rd (44223-2603)
P.O. Box 2010 (44309-2010)
PHONE.................................330 922-7624
Thomas Chieffe, *CEO*
Kieth Lavanway, *Pr*
EMP: 85 EST: 2008
SALES (est): 52.99MM
SALES (corp-wide): 1.18B **Privately Held**
Web: www.associatedmaterials.com
SIC: 1799 Window treatment installation
PA: Associated Materials, Llc
3773 State Rd
Cuyahoga Falls OH 44223
330 929-1811

(G-7043)
ASSOCIATED MATERIALS GROUP INC (PA)
3773 State Rd (44223-2603)
PHONE.................................330 929-1811
EMP: 183 EST: 2010
SALES (est): 542.5MM **Privately Held**
Web: www.associatedmaterials.com
SIC: 3089 5033 5031 3442 Plastics hardware and building products; Roofing and siding materials; Windows; Metal doors, sash, and trim

(G-7044)
ASSOCIATED MTLS HOLDINGS LLC
3773 State Rd (44223-2603)
P.O. Box 2010 (44309-2010)
PHONE.................................330 929-1811
Ira D Kleinman, *Ch Bd*
EMP: 2000 EST: 1947
SALES (est): 139.53MM **Privately Held**
Web: www.associatedmaterials.com
SIC: 5033 5031 5063 3442 Roofing and siding materials; Windows; Wire and cable; Metal doors, sash, and trim
PA: Associated Materials Group, Inc.
3773 State Rd
Cuyahoga Falls OH 44223

(G-7045)
AUTO PARTS CENTER-CUYAHOGA FLS
Also Called: Federated Auto Parts
2990 Oakwood Dr (44221-1647)
PHONE.................................330 928-2149
Glenn Fresh, *Pr*
EMP: 35 EST: 1975
SQ FT: 10,000
SALES (est): 935.03K
SALES (corp-wide): 15.95MM **Privately Held**

Web: www.fisherautoparts.com
SIC: 5013 5531 Automotive supplies and parts; Automotive parts
PA: Pat Young Service Co Inc
6100 Hillcrest Dr
Cleveland OH 44125
216 447-8550

(G-7046)
BADILAD LLC
1015 Howe Ave Apt 11 (44221-5170)
PHONE.................................330 805-3173
Adebola Adewumi, *Managing Member*
EMP: 30 EST: 2019
SALES (est): 440K **Privately Held**
SIC: 4213 Trucking, except local

(G-7047)
BARRETT & ASSOCIATES INC (PA)
Also Called: B & A
1060 Graham Rd Ste C (44224-2960)
PHONE.................................330 928-2323
Gerald Barrett Ph.d., *Prin*
Gerald Barrett, *Pr*
Patricia Barrett, *
EMP: 42 EST: 1973
SQ FT: 5,220
SALES (est): 2.04MM **Privately Held**
Web: www.barrett-associates.com
SIC: 8742 Business management consultant

(G-7048)
BAYADA HOME HEALTH CARE INC
2251 Front St Ste 202 (44221-2578)
PHONE.................................330 929-5512
EMP: 80
SALES (corp-wide): 694.21MM **Privately Held**
Web: www.bayada.com
SIC: 8082 Visiting nurse service
PA: Bayada Home Health Care, Inc.
1 W Main St
Moorestown NJ 08057
856 231-1000

(G-7049)
BECKER PUMPS CORPORATION
100 E Ascot Ln (44223-3768)
PHONE.................................330 928-9966
Doctor Dorothee Becker, *Pr*
Eva M Bell, *
Ann M Ormsby, *
▲ EMP: 46 EST: 1975
SQ FT: 33,400
SALES (est): 23.79MM **Privately Held**
Web: www.beckerpumps.com
SIC: 5084 Compressors, except air conditioning

(G-7050)
BLACK HORSE BROTHERS INC
141 Broad Blvd Ste 108 (44221-3804)
PHONE.................................267 265-0013
EMP: 35
SALES (est): 1.61MM **Privately Held**
SIC: 4213 Trucking, except local

(G-7051)
BP OIL SUPPLY COMPANY
Also Called: B P Products North America
1205 Main St (44221-4949)
PHONE.................................330 945-4132
Moira Roth, *Mgr*
EMP: 45
SQ FT: 5,008
SALES (corp-wide): 296.92MM **Privately Held**
Web: www.bp.com
SIC: 5172 Crude oil
HQ: Bp Oil Supply Company
28100 Torch Pkwy

Warrenville IL 60555
630 836-5000

(G-7052)
CARDINAL RETIREMENT VILLAGE
171 Graham Rd (44223-1773)
PHONE.................................330 928-7888
Scott Phillips, *Pt*
Kim Richards, *Prin*
EMP: 30 EST: 1985
SALES (est): 1.03MM **Privately Held**
Web: www.titansenquest.com
SIC: 6513 8052 8361 Retirement hotel operation; Intermediate care facilities; Residential care

(G-7053)
CARING FOR KIDS INC
650 Graham Rd Ste 101 (44221-1051)
PHONE.................................330 928-0044
Jill Davies, *Ex Dir*
Patricia Ameling, *
Jill Davis, *
EMP: 64 EST: 1995
SALES (est): 6.09MM **Privately Held**
Web: www.cfkadopt.org
SIC: 8322 Adoption services

(G-7054)
CIRCLE PRIME MANUFACTURING
2114 Front St (44221)
P.O. Box 112 (44221)
PHONE.................................330 923-0019
James Mothersbaugh, *Pr*
Robert Mothersbaugh, *
EMP: 27 EST: 1989
SQ FT: 50,000
SALES (est): 6.28MM **Privately Held**
Web: www.circleprime.com
SIC: 3672 8731 3663 3812 Printed circuit boards; Commercial physical research; Radio broadcasting and communications equipment; Antennas, radar or communications

(G-7055)
CITY OF CUYAHOGA FALLS
Also Called: Electric Services
2550 Bailey Rd (44221-2950)
PHONE.................................330 971-8000
Robert L Bye, *Superintnt*
EMP: 45
SALES (corp-wide): 65.73MM **Privately Held**
Web: www.cityofcf.com
SIC: 4911 Distribution, electric power
PA: City Of Cuyahoga Falls
2310 2nd St
Cuyahoga Falls OH 44221
330 971-8230

(G-7056)
CITY OF CUYAHOGA FALLS
Also Called: Water Department
2310 2nd St (44221-2583)
PHONE.................................330 971-8130
EMP: 28
SALES (corp-wide): 65.73MM **Privately Held**
Web: www.cityofcf.com
SIC: 4941 Water supply
PA: City Of Cuyahoga Falls
2310 2nd St
Cuyahoga Falls OH 44221
330 971-8230

(G-7057)
CITY OF CUYAHOGA FALLS
Also Called: Quirk Cultural Center
1201 Grant Ave (44223-2314)
PHONE.................................330 971-8425

GEOGRAPHIC SECTION

Cuyahoga Falls - Summit County (G-7078)

Janet Verchio, *Mgr*
EMP: 37
SALES (corp-wide): 65.73MM **Privately Held**
Web: www.cityofcf.com
SIC: 8322 9111 Senior citizens' center or association; Mayors' office
PA: City Of Cuyahoga Falls
2310 2nd St
Cuyahoga Falls OH 44221
330 971-8230

(G-7058)
CITY OF CUYAHOGA FALLS
Also Called: Sewage Department
2560 Bailey Rd (44221-2950)
PHONE...................330 971-8005
EMP: 55
SALES (corp-wide): 65.73MM **Privately Held**
Web: www.cityofcf.com
SIC: 4952 Sewerage systems
PA: City Of Cuyahoga Falls
2310 2nd St
Cuyahoga Falls OH 44221
330 971-8230

(G-7059)
CITY OF CUYAHOGA FALLS
Also Called: Building/Engineering Dept
2310 2nd St (44221-2583)
PHONE...................330 971-8230
EMP: 37
SALES (corp-wide): 65.73MM **Privately Held**
Web: www.cityofcf.com
SIC: 8711 Engineering services
PA: City Of Cuyahoga Falls
2310 2nd St
Cuyahoga Falls OH 44221
330 971-8230

(G-7060)
CITY OF CUYAHOGA FALLS
Also Called: Street Department
2560 Bailey Rd (44221-2950)
PHONE...................330 971-8030
EMP: 28
SALES (corp-wide): 65.73MM **Privately Held**
Web: www.cityofcf.com
SIC: 1611 Highway and street construction
PA: City Of Cuyahoga Falls
2310 2nd St
Cuyahoga Falls OH 44221
330 971-8230

(G-7061)
CITY OF CUYAHOGA FALLS
Also Called: Brookledge Golf Club
1621 Bailey Rd (44221-5209)
PHONE...................330 971-8416
Steve Black, *Mgr*
EMP: 37
SALES (corp-wide): 65.73MM **Privately Held**
Web: www.brookledgegc.com
SIC: 7992 9111 Public golf courses; Mayors' office
PA: City Of Cuyahoga Falls
2310 2nd St
Cuyahoga Falls OH 44221
330 971-8230

(G-7062)
CLEVELAND CLINIC FOUNDATION
857 Graham Rd (44221-1170)
PHONE...................330 923-9585
EMP: 33
SALES (corp-wide): 14.48B **Privately Held**
Web: www.clevelandclinic.org
SIC: 8062 General medical and surgical hospitals
PA: The Cleveland Clinic Foundation
9500 Euclid Ave
Cleveland OH 44195
216 636-8335

(G-7063)
COLTENE/WHALEDENT INC (HQ)
235 Ascot Pkwy (44223-3701)
PHONE...................330 916-8800
Jerry Sullivan, *Pr*
Martin Schaufelberger, *
Joseph Fasano, *
Nick Huber, *
Gerhard Mahrle, *
▲ **EMP:** 222 **EST:** 1990
SQ FT: 89,000
SALES (est): 107.17MM **Privately Held**
Web: www.coltene.com
SIC: 5047 Dental equipment and supplies
PA: Coltene Holding Ag
Feldwiesenstrasse 20
AltstAtten SG 9450

(G-7064)
COMDOC INC
220 Ascot Pkwy (44223-3346)
PHONE...................330 920-3900
EMP: 68
SALES (corp-wide): 6.89B **Publicly Held**
Web: www.comdoc.com
SIC: 7334 5999 5943 Photocopying and duplicating services; Photocopy machines; Stationery stores
HQ: Comdoc, Inc.
8247 Pittsburg Ave Nw
North Canton OH 44720
330 896-2346

(G-7065)
CRAIN COMMUNICATIONS INC
Also Called: Rubber & Plastics News
2291 Riverfront Pkwy Ste 1000 (44221-2580)
PHONE...................330 836-9180
Robert S Simmons, *VP*
EMP: 36
SALES (corp-wide): 249.16MM **Privately Held**
Web: www.tirebusiness.com
SIC: 2711 2721 7389 Newspapers: publishing only, not printed on site; Periodicals; Advertising, promotional, and trade show services
PA: Crain Communications, Inc.
1155 Gratiot Ave
Detroit MI 48207
313 446-6000

(G-7066)
CRYSTAL CLINIC INC
Also Called: Crystal Clnic Orthpdic Ctr - F
437 Portage Trl (44221-3227)
PHONE...................330 929-9136
EMP: 41
SALES (corp-wide): 54.91MM **Privately Held**
Web: www.crystalclinic.com
SIC: 8011 Orthopedic physician
PA: Crystal Clinic, Inc.
3975 Embassy Pkwy Ste A
Akron OH 44333
330 668-4040

(G-7067)
CUYAHOGA FALLS GENERAL HOSPITAL
1900 23rd St (44223-1404)
P.O. Box 2090 (44224-0090)
PHONE...................330 971-7000
EMP: 825
Web: www.summahealth.org
SIC: 8062 Hospital, affiliated with AMA residency

(G-7068)
DANBURY WOODS LTD
Also Called: Danbury Woods Cuyahoga Falls
1691 Queens Gate Cir (44221-5542)
PHONE...................330 928-6757
William J Lemmon, *Prin*
EMP: 33 **EST:** 2011
SALES (est): 1.25MM **Privately Held**
Web: www.storypoint.com
SIC: 6513 Retirement hotel operation

(G-7069)
DAVIS EYE CENTER INC
789 Graham Rd (44221-1045)
PHONE...................330 923-5676
Charles H Davis, *Owner*
EMP: 62 **EST:** 1997
SALES (est): 14.23MM **Privately Held**
Web: www.daviseyecenter.com
SIC: 8031 8011 Offices and clinics of osteopathic physicians; Offices and clinics of medical doctors

(G-7070)
DENTRONIX INC
235 Ascot Pkwy (44223-3701)
PHONE...................330 916-7300
Jerry Sullivan, *Pr*
Joseph Fasano, *
EMP: 53 **EST:** 1976
SQ FT: 16,000
SALES (est): 2.51MM **Privately Held**
Web: www.diatechusa.com
SIC: 3843 5047 3842 3841 Orthodontic appliances; Dental equipment and supplies; Surgical appliances and supplies; Surgical and medical instruments
HQ: Coltene/Whaledent Inc.
235 Ascot Pkwy
Cuyahoga Falls OH 44223

(G-7071)
EDWIN SHAW REHAB LLC
405 Tallmadge Rd Ste 1 (44221-3342)
PHONE...................330 436-0910
Rita Green, *Prin*
Skip Paris, *Fin Mgr*
EMP: 99 **EST:** 2005
SALES (est): 8.17MM **Privately Held**
SIC: 8069 Specialty hospitals, except psychiatric

(G-7072)
FALLS FAMILY PRACTICE INC (PA)
Also Called: Falls Dermatology
857 Graham Rd (44221-1170)
PHONE...................330 923-9585
A Hugh Mclaughlin, *Pr*
EMP: 30 **EST:** 1982
SALES (est): 2.91MM **Privately Held**
Web: www.fallsfamilypractice.com
SIC: 8062 General medical and surgical hospitals

(G-7073)
FALLS HEATING & COOLING INC
Also Called: Honeywell Authorized Dealer
461 Munroe Falls Ave (44221-3407)
PHONE...................330 929-8777
Larry Burris, *Pr*
Paul Burris, *
Marge Laria, *
EMP: 35 **EST:** 1987
SQ FT: 4,069
SALES (est): 4.58MM
SALES (corp-wide): 36.34MM **Privately Held**
Web: www.fallsheating.com
SIC: 1711 Warm air heating and air conditioning contractor
PA: User Friendly Home Services, Llc
10200 Grogans Mill Rd
The Woodlands TX 77380
281 465-5400

(G-7074)
FALLS MOTOR CITY INC
Also Called: Falls Chrysler Jeep Dodge
4100 State Rd (44223-2612)
PHONE...................330 929-3066
Paul Hrnchar, *Pr*
EMP: 50 **EST:** 1994
SALES (est): 10.56MM **Privately Held**
Web: www.valleymotorcity.com
SIC: 5511 7514 Automobiles, new and used; Rent-a-car service

(G-7075)
FALLS STAMPING & WELDING CO (PA)
2900 Vincent St (44221-1954)
PHONE...................330 928-1191
Rick Boettner, *Ch*
David Cesar, *
Jason Taft, *
EMP: 125 **EST:** 1919
SQ FT: 95,000
SALES (est): 23.36MM
SALES (corp-wide): 23.36MM **Privately Held**
Web: www.falls-stamping.com
SIC: 3465 3469 3544 3711 Automotive stampings; Stamping metal for the trade; Special dies, tools, jigs, and fixtures; Chassis, motor vehicle

(G-7076)
FALLS VLG RETIREMENT CMNTY LTD
330 Broadway St E (44221-3312)
PHONE...................330 945-9797
Micahel Francis, *Mng Dir*
EMP: 100 **EST:** 2001
SQ FT: 77,000
SALES (est): 9.44MM **Privately Held**
Web: www.fallsvillagesnr.com
SIC: 8051 8052 Convalescent home with continuous nursing care; Intermediate care facilities

(G-7077)
GARDENS WESTERN RESERVE INC
45 Chart Rd (44223-2821)
PHONE...................330 928-4500
Rich Piekarski, *Brnch Mgr*
EMP: 33
SALES (corp-wide): 7.41MM **Privately Held**
Web: www.gardensofwesternreserve.com
SIC: 8361 Aged home
PA: Gardens Of Western Reserve, Inc.
9975 Greentree Pkwy
Streetsboro OH 44241
330 342-9100

(G-7078)
HOME DEPOT USA INC
Also Called: Home Depot, The
325 Howe Ave (44221)
PHONE...................330 922-3448
Daniel Berend, *Mgr*
EMP: 202
SALES (corp-wide): 152.67B **Publicly Held**
Web: www.homedepot.com
SIC: 5211 7359 Home centers; Tool rental
HQ: Home Depot U.S.A., Inc.

Cuyahoga Falls - Summit County (G-7079)   GEOGRAPHIC SECTION

2445 Springfield Ave
Vauxhall NJ 07088

(G-7079)
HOMETOWN CARE LLC
2040 Front St (44221-3218)
PHONE..................330 926-1118
Tim Boyer, *Brnch Mgr*
EMP: 36
SALES (corp-wide): 5.62MM **Privately Held**
Web: www.commcareinc.org
SIC: 8082 Home health care services
PA: Hometown Care, Llc
2291 Riverfront Pkwy # 20
Cuyahoga Falls OH 44221
330 926-1118

(G-7080)
HOOVER KACYON LLC
527 Portage Trl (44221-3295)
PHONE..................330 922-4491
Tyler Six, *Prin*
EMP: 28 **EST:** 2019
SALES (est): 2.43MM **Privately Held**
Web: www.hooverkacyon.com
SIC: 8111 General practice attorney, lawyer

(G-7081)
HUNTINGTON NATIONAL BANK
2305 2nd St (44221-2529)
PHONE..................330 920-6190
Laurie Wesolowski, *Brnch Mgr*
EMP: 36
SALES (corp-wide): 10.84B **Publicly Held**
Web: www.huntington.com
SIC: 6029 Commercial banks, nec
HQ: The Huntington National Bank
41 S High St
Columbus OH 43215
614 480-4293

(G-7082)
JJ&PL SERVICES-CONSULTING LLC
1474 Main St (44221-4927)
PHONE..................330 923-5783
Hans R Leitner, *CEO*
EMP: 38 **EST:** 2010
SALES (est): 4.69MM **Privately Held**
Web: www.mach3machining.com
SIC: 3441 7699 Building components, structural steel; Industrial machinery and equipment repair

(G-7083)
JULIUS ZORN INC
Also Called: Juzo USA
3690 Zorn Dr (44223-3580)
P.O. Box 1088 (44223-1088)
PHONE..................330 923-4999
Anne Rose Zorn, *Pr*
Petra Zorn, *
Uwe Schettler, *
▲ **EMP:** 75 **EST:** 1980
SQ FT: 30,000
SALES (est): 27.4MM
SALES (corp-wide): 118.66MM **Privately Held**
Web: www.juzousa.com
SIC: 5047 3842 Medical equipment and supplies; Hosiery, support
PA: Julius Zorn Gmbh
Juliusplatz 1
Aichach BY 86551
82519010

(G-7084)
KENTIX DEVELOPMENTAL HLTH INC
3439 Atterbury St (44221-1115)
PHONE..................330 949-0131
Jennifer Spitaleri, *Prin*

EMP: 33 **EST:** 2011
SALES (est): 468.33K **Privately Held**
Web: www.kentixdh.com
SIC: 8082 Home health care services

(G-7085)
KEUCHEL & ASSOCIATES INC
Also Called: Spunfab
175 Muffin Ln (44223)
P.O. Box 3435 (44223)
PHONE..................330 945-9455
Ken Keuchel, *Pr*
Herb Keuchel, *Stockholder**
Herbert W Keuchel, *
Richard W Staehle, *
◆ **EMP:** 50 **EST:** 1979
SQ FT: 40,000
SALES (est): 4.65MM **Privately Held**
Web: www.spunfab.com
SIC: 2241 8711 Narrow fabric mills; Consulting engineer

(G-7086)
KYOCERA SGS PRECISION TLS INC (PA)
Also Called: Kyocera Precision Tools
150 Marc Dr (44223-2630)
P.O. Box 187 (44262-0187)
PHONE..................330 688-6667
Thomas Haag, *Pr*
Jeff Burton, *Prin*
Aaron Holb, *
▲ **EMP:** 50 **EST:** 1961
SALES (est): 58.68MM
SALES (corp-wide): 58.68MM **Privately Held**
Web: www.kyocera-sgstool.com
SIC: 3545 5084 Cutting tools for machine tools; Industrial machinery and equipment

(G-7087)
LINDEN-TWO INC
137 Ascot Pkwy (44223)
PHONE..................330 928-4064
Peter Tilgner, *Pr*
Ken Erwin, *
Bob Hughey, *
EMP: 42 **EST:** 1985
SQ FT: 26,000
SALES (est): 8.48MM **Privately Held**
Web: www.lindenindustries.com
SIC: 3559 5084 Plastics working machinery; Industrial machinery and equipment

(G-7088)
MICNAN INC (PA)
Also Called: Ace Mitchell Bowlers Mart
3365 Cavalier Trl (44224-4905)
P.O. Box 3168 (44223-0468)
PHONE..................330 920-6200
David Grau, *Pr*
Karen Grau, *
Mary E Limbach, *
▲ **EMP:** 46 **EST:** 1973
SQ FT: 26,000
SALES (est): 22.68MM
SALES (corp-wide): 22.68MM **Privately Held**
Web: www.acemitchell.com
SIC: 5091 Bowling equipment

(G-7089)
MILL POND FAMILY PHYSICIANS
265 Portage Trail Ext W Ste 200 (44223-3613)
PHONE..................330 928-3111
Donald A Dahlen, *Pr*
Dawn Hubbard, *
Ross Black, *
EMP: 38 **EST:** 1990
SALES (est): 2.41MM **Privately Held**

SIC: 8062 General medical and surgical hospitals

(G-7090)
NORTH COAST CAPITAL FUNDING (PA)
1727 Portage Trl (44223-1738)
PHONE..................330 923-5333
EMP: 55 **EST:** 1996
SQ FT: 8,600
SALES (est): 5.26MM **Privately Held**
Web: www.nccfinc.com
SIC: 6163 Mortgage brokers arranging for loans, using money of others

(G-7091)
NSK INDUSTRIES INC (PA)
150 Ascot Pkwy (44223-3354)
P.O. Box 1089 (44223-0089)
PHONE..................330 923-4112
◆ **EMP:** 67 **EST:** 1980
SALES (est): 14.81MM
SALES (corp-wide): 14.81MM **Privately Held**
Web: www.nskind.com
SIC: 5085 3479 3451 Fasteners, industrial: nuts, bolts, screws, etc.; Coating of metals and formed products; Screw machine products

(G-7092)
PORTAGE PATH BEHAVORIAL HEALTH
Also Called: Portage Path Behavioral Health
792 Graham Rd Ste C (44221-1000)
PHONE..................330 928-2324
EMP: 27
SALES (corp-wide): 12.13MM **Privately Held**
Web: www.portagepath.org
SIC: 8093 Mental health clinic, outpatient
PA: Portage Path Behavioral Health
340 S Broadway St
Akron OH 44308
330 253-3100

(G-7093)
PRC MEDICAL LLC (PA)
111 Stow Ave Ste 200 (44221-2560)
PHONE..................330 493-9004
Harry Curley, *Pr*
EMP: 75 **EST:** 1988
SQ FT: 10,000
SALES (est): 6.58MM
SALES (corp-wide): 6.58MM **Privately Held**
Web: www.prcmedical.com
SIC: 7322 Collection agency, except real estate

(G-7094)
PREMIERE MEDICAL RESOURCES INC
2750 Front St (44221-1969)
PHONE..................330 923-5899
Joseph Chase, *Pr*
EMP: 28 **EST:** 2013
SALES (est): 2.95MM **Privately Held**
Web: www.unityhealthnetwork.org
SIC: 8742 8721 7379 Hospital and health services consultant; Accounting services, except auditing; Computer related maintenance services

(G-7095)
RITE AID OF OHIO INC
Also Called: Rite Aid
1914 Bailey Rd (44221-4312)
PHONE..................330 922-4466
EMP: 47

SALES (corp-wide): 24.09B **Publicly Held**
Web: www.riteaid.com
SIC: 5912 7384 Drug stores; Photofinishing laboratory
HQ: Rite Aid Of Ohio, Inc.
1200 Intrepid Ave Ste 2
Philadelphia PA 19112

(G-7096)
RIVERFRONT STFFING SLTIONS INC
2121 Front St Ste A (44221-3219)
PHONE..................330 929-3002
Amy M Rose, *Pr*
EMP: 40 **EST:** 1998
SALES (est): 1.45MM **Privately Held**
SIC: 7361 Employment agencies

(G-7097)
RIVERFRONT YMCA SCHL AGE - ECH
544 Broad Blvd (44221-3836)
PHONE..................330 733-2551
Rebecca Baker, *Dir*
EMP: 36 **EST:** 2019
SALES (est): 233.83K **Privately Held**
Web: www.akronymca.org
SIC: 8641 Youth organizations

(G-7098)
RON MARHOFER AUTO FAMILY
257 Huddleston Ave (44221-4901)
PHONE..................330 940-4422
Chuck Tepus, *Prin*
EMP: 27 **EST:** 2016
SALES (est): 539.43K **Privately Held**
Web: www.marhofer.com
SIC: 7538 5531 5511 General automotive repair shops; Auto and home supply stores; New and used car dealers

(G-7099)
RON MARHOFER AUTOMALL INC
1260 Main St (44221-4923)
PHONE..................330 835-6707
Ronald L Marhofer, *Brnch Mgr*
EMP: 132
SALES (corp-wide): 53.93MM **Privately Held**
Web: www.hyundaiofakron.com
SIC: 7532 5511 Body shop, automotive; Automobiles, new and used
PA: Ron Marhofer Automall, Inc
1350 Main St
Cuyahoga Falls OH 44221
330 923-5059

(G-7100)
RON MARHOFER AUTOMALL INC (PA)
Also Called: Ron Mrhfer Lncoln Mrcury Hynda
1350 Main St (44221-4925)
PHONE..................330 923-5059
Ron Marhofer, *Pr*
EMP: 50 **EST:** 1979
SQ FT: 20,000
SALES (est): 53.93MM
SALES (corp-wide): 53.93MM **Privately Held**
Web: www.hyundaiofakron.com
SIC: 5511 7538 7532 7515 Automobiles, new and used; General automotive repair shops; Top and body repair and paint shops; Passenger car leasing

(G-7101)
STREAMLINEMD LLC
111 Stow Ave Ste 200 (44221-2560)
PHONE..................330 564-2627
EMP: 88 **EST:** 2010
SALES (est): 1.67MM **Privately Held**

GEOGRAPHIC SECTION

Dayton - Greene County (G-7125)

Web: www.streamlinemd.com
SIC: 6531 Real estate agent, commercial

(G-7102)
SUMMA HEALTH
Also Called: SUMMA HEALTH
2345 4th St (44221-2573)
PHONE...................330 926-0384
EMP: 75
SALES (corp-wide): 1.78B Privately Held
Web: www.summahealth.org
SIC: 8062 General medical and surgical hospitals
PA: Summa Health System
1077 Gorge Blvd
Akron OH 44310
330 375-3000

(G-7103)
SUMMA WESTERN RESERVE HOSP LLC
Also Called: Rehab At The Nat
2345 4th St (44221-2573)
PHONE...................330 926-0384
EMP: 31
SALES (corp-wide): 155.93MM Privately Held
Web: www.westernreservehospital.org
SIC: 8062 Hospital, AMA approved residency
HQ: Western Reserve Hospital, Llc
1900 23rd St
Cuyahoga Falls OH 44223

(G-7104)
SUNRISE SENIOR LIVING LLC
Also Called: Sunrise of Cuyahoga Falls
1500 State Rd (44223-1302)
PHONE...................330 929-8500
Bethany Hall, Mgr
EMP: 45
SALES (corp-wide): 2.92B Privately Held
Web: www.sunriseseniorliving.com
SIC: 8051 Skilled nursing care facilities
HQ: Sunrise Senior Living, Llc
7902 Westpark Dr
Mc Lean VA 22102

(G-7105)
TESTA ENTERPRISES INC
2335 2nd St Ste A (44221-2529)
PHONE...................330 926-9060
Paul Testa, Pr
Ryan Landi, *
EMP: 35 EST: 1978
SALES (est): 9.19MM Privately Held
SIC: 1541 Industrial buildings, new construction, nec

(G-7106)
THAYER PWR COMM LINE CNSTR LLC
3432 State Rd Ste A (44223-3791)
PHONE...................330 922-4950
Matt Luden, Prin
EMP: 58
SALES (corp-wide): 200.7MM Privately Held
Web: www.thayerpc.com
SIC: 1623 Communication line and transmission tower construction
HQ: Thayer Power & Communication Line Construction Company, Llc
12345 Worthington Rd Nw
Pataskala OH 43062
740 927-0021

(G-7107)
THE W L TUCKER SUPPLY COMPANY (PA)
2800 2nd St (44221-1998)
PHONE...................330 928-2155
EMP: 28 EST: 1915
SALES (est): 7.18MM
SALES (corp-wide): 7.18MM Privately Held
Web: www.wltucker.com
SIC: 5032 5211 Plastering materials; Masonry materials and supplies

(G-7108)
TOP NOTCH TRUCKERS INC
113 Portage Trl Ste E (44221-3244)
PHONE...................540 787-7777
Jakhongir Fayziev, Pr
EMP: 84 EST: 2020
SALES (est): 2.41MM Privately Held
SIC: 4213 Trucking, except local

(G-7109)
TRADITIONS AT BATH RD INC
Also Called: National Church
300 E Bath Rd (44223-2510)
PHONE...................330 929-6272
EMP: 93 EST: 1991
SALES (est): 1.8MM Privately Held
SIC: 8051 8361 Skilled nursing care facilities ; Residential care

(G-7110)
TRAFFIC SAFETY SOLUTIONS LLC
572 Scenic Valley Way (44223-2988)
PHONE...................216 214-3735
Maria Lignos Brajdich, Managing Member
Maria Jacobozzi, *
EMP: 48 EST: 2018
SALES (est): 2.22MM Privately Held
SIC: 7389 Flagging service (traffic control)

(G-7111)
TRIAD COMMUNICATIONS INC
1701 Front St (44221-4711)
PHONE...................330 237-3531
Rick Krochka, Pr
EMP: 83 EST: 1994
SQ FT: 1,400
SALES (est): 3.48MM Privately Held
Web: www.triadadv.com
SIC: 7311 Advertising consultant

(G-7112)
TRILLIUM FAMILY SOLUTIONS INC
Also Called: Family Cnsling Svcs Cntl Stark
111 Stow Ave Ste 100 (44221-2560)
PHONE...................330 454-7066
Cathy Trubisay, CEO
EMP: 33 EST: 1896
SALES (est): 1.74MM Privately Held
Web: www.trilliumfs.org
SIC: 8322 General counseling services

(G-7113)
ULTRA TECH MACHINERY INC
297 Ascot Pkwy (44223-3701)
PHONE...................330 929-5544
Don Hagarty, Pr
Robert Hagarty, *
Jim Hagarty, *
▲ EMP: 30 EST: 1986
SQ FT: 11,000
SALES (est): 8.44MM Privately Held
Web: www.utmachinery.com
SIC: 3599 7389 Machine shop, jobbing and repair; Design, commercial and industrial

(G-7114)
WESTERN RESERVE HEALTH SYS LLC
2750 Front St (44221-1969)
PHONE...................330 923-8660
Jeffrey Schiciano, Managing Member

EMP: 27 EST: 2010
SALES (est): 1.49MM Privately Held
Web: www.westernreservehospital.org
SIC: 8099 Blood related health services

(G-7115)
WESTERN RESERVE HOSPITAL LLC (HQ)
1900 23rd St (44223-1404)
PHONE...................330 971-7000
EMP: 678 EST: 2009
SALES (est): 155.93MM
SALES (corp-wide): 155.93MM Privately Held
Web: www.westernreservehospital.org
SIC: 8062 Hospital, AMA approved residency
PA: Western Reserve Hospital Partners, Llc
1900 23rd St
Cuyahoga Falls OH 44223
330 971-7000

(G-7116)
WESTERN RSRVE HOSP PRTNERS LLC (PA)
1900 23rd St (44223-1404)
PHONE...................330 971-7000
Robert A Kent, Managing Member
EMP: 175 EST: 2017
SALES (est): 155.93MM
SALES (corp-wide): 155.93MM Privately Held
Web: www.westernreservehospital.org
SIC: 8062 Hospital, AMA approved residency

(G-7117)
WINGS OF CHANGE THERAPY INC
1909 3rd St (44221-3807)
PHONE...................330 715-6046
Jordye Joyce, Pr
EMP: 38 EST: 2010
SALES (est): 536.96K Privately Held
Web: www.wingsofchangetherapyinc.com
SIC: 8049 Occupational therapist

(G-7118)
WINSTON BRDCSTG NETWRK INC
Also Called: Wbnx TV 55
2690 State Rd (44223-1644)
PHONE...................330 928-5711
Eddie Brown, Pr
Eddie Brown Present, Prin
EMP: 150 EST: 1979
SQ FT: 10,000
SALES (est): 7.88MM Privately Held
Web: www.wbnx.com
SIC: 4833 Television broadcasting stations

(G-7119)
YOUNG MNS CHRSTN ASSN OF AKRON
Also Called: YMCA Cuyahoga Falls Branch
544 Broad Blvd (44221-3836)
PHONE...................330 923-5223
Adam Clutts, Ex Dir
EMP: 51
SQ FT: 36,237
SALES (corp-wide): 21.21MM Privately Held
Web: www.akronymca.org
SIC: 8641 7991 8351 7032 Youth organizations; Physical fitness facilities; Child day care services; Youth camps
PA: The Young Men's Christian Association Of Akron Ohio
50 S Mn St Ste Ll100
Akron OH 44308
330 376-1335

Dalton
Wayne County

(G-7120)
GERBER FEED SERVICE INC
3094 Moser Rd (44618-9074)
P.O. Box 509 (44618-0509)
PHONE...................330 857-4421
Brad Gerber, Pr
John Nussbaum, *
Fae Gerber, *
Michelle Nussbaum, *
Harley Gerber, *
EMP: 45 EST: 1965
SQ FT: 250,000
SALES (est): 6.83MM Privately Held
Web: www.gerberfeed.com
SIC: 5191 Feed

(G-7121)
PROVIDE-A-CARE INC
Also Called: Shady Lawn Nursing Home
15028 Old Lincoln Way (44618-9731)
PHONE...................330 828-2278
David J Lipins, Pr
Nathan Levitansky, *
Reuven Dessler, *
EMP: 150 EST: 1961
SQ FT: 50,000
SALES (est): 7.82MM Privately Held
SIC: 8052 8051 Intermediate care facilities; Skilled nursing care facilities

(G-7122)
WENGER EXCAVATING INC
26 N Cochran St (44618-9808)
P.O. Box 499 (44618-0499)
PHONE...................330 837-4767
Howard J Wenger, Pr
Clair Good, *
Sandra Wenger, *
EMP: 28 EST: 1965
SQ FT: 6,000
SALES (est): 4.91MM Privately Held
Web: www.wengerexcavating.com
SIC: 1794 1623 Excavation and grading, building construction; Sewer line construction

Dayton
Greene County

(G-7123)
1ST ADVNCE SEC INVSTGTIONS INC
1675 Woodman Dr (45432-3336)
P.O. Box 61128 (45406-9128)
PHONE...................937 210-9010
Darryl Johnson, CEO
EMP: 60 EST: 2015
SALES (est): 1.88MM Privately Held
Web: www.1stadvancesecurity.com
SIC: 7381 Security guard service

(G-7124)
823 DAYTON HOTEL TENANT LLC
Also Called: Hope Hotel & Conference Center
10823 Chidlaw Rd (45433-1102)
PHONE...................937 879-2696
David Meyer, Owner
EMP: 49 EST: 1989
SALES (est): 4.56MM Privately Held
Web: www.hopehotel.com
SIC: 7011 Hotels

(G-7125)
AEROSPACE CORPORATION
4180 Watson Way (45433-5648)
PHONE...................937 657-9634

Dayton - Greene County (G-7126)   **GEOGRAPHIC SECTION**

EMP: 39
SALES (corp-wide): 1.2B **Privately Held**
Web: www.aerospace.org
SIC: **8733** 8711 8731 Scientific research agency; Engineering services; Commercial physical research
PA: The Aerospace Corporation
    14745 Lee Rd
    Chantilly VA 20151
    310 336-5000

(G-7126)
AIR FRCE MUSEUM FOUNDATION INC
1100 Spaatz St Bldg 489 (45433)
P.O. Box 33624 (45433)
PHONE....................937 258-1218
Michael Imhoff, *Ex Dir*
EMP: 40 EST: 1960
SQ FT: 5,500
SALES (est): 7.5MM **Privately Held**
Web: www.afmuseum.com
SIC: **8412** Museum

(G-7127)
BUTT CONSTRUCTION COMPANY INC
3858 Germany Ln (45431-1607)
P.O. Box 31306 (45437-0306)
PHONE....................937 426-1313
Rachel Butt, *Pr*
Bill Butt, *
David Butt, *
EMP: 50 EST: 1927
SQ FT: 4,400
SALES (est): 27.62MM **Privately Held**
Web: www.buttconstruction.com
SIC: **1542** 1541 Institutional building construction; Industrial buildings, new construction, nec

(G-7128)
CDO TECHNOLOGIES INC (PA)
Also Called: C D O
5200 Springfield St Ste 320 (45431)
PHONE....................937 258-0022
Alphonso Wofford, *Pr*
Don Ertel, *
Greg Greening, *
Grant Richardson, *
Mary Tingle, *
▲ EMP: 75 EST: 1990
SQ FT: 6,000
SALES (est): 49.74MM **Privately Held**
Web: www.cdotech.com
SIC: **7371** 7373 Computer software systems analysis and design, custom; Computer integrated systems design

(G-7129)
DAYTON POWER AND LIGHT COMPANY (DH)
Also Called: AES Ohio
1065 Woodman Dr (45432-1423)
P.O. Box 1247 (45401-1247)
PHONE....................937 331-3900
TOLL FREE: 800
Ken Zagzebski, *CEO*
Tom Raga, *Pr*
Andrew M Vesey, *Ch Bd*
Kurt A Tornquist Ctrl, *CAO*
Lisa Krueger, *Dir Opers*
EMP: 200 EST: 1911
SALES (est): 852MM
SALES (corp-wide): 12.67B **Publicly Held**
Web: www.aes-ohio.com
SIC: **4911** 4931 Generation, electric power; Electric and other services combined
HQ: Dpl Inc.
    1065 Woodman Dr
    Dayton OH 45432
    937 259-7215

(G-7130)
DPL INC (HQ)
Also Called: AES
1065 Woodman Dr (45432-1438)
PHONE....................937 259-7215
Lisa Krueger, *Ofcr*
Karin M Nyhuis, *Contrlr*
Gustavo Garavaglia, *CFO*
EMP: 219 EST: 1911
SALES (est): 861MM
SALES (corp-wide): 12.67B **Publicly Held**
Web: www.aes-ohio.com
SIC: **4911** Generation, electric power
PA: The Aes Corporation
    4300 Wilson Blvd Ste 1100
    Arlington VA 22203
    703 522-1315

(G-7131)
DUNCAN OIL CO (PA)
Also Called: Duncan Oil Co.
849 Factory Rd (45434-6134)
PHONE....................937 426-5945
Roger Mcdaniel, *Pr*
Judy Mc Daniel, *
Steven A Wells, *
Steven Heck, *
Ryan Mcdaniel, *COO*
EMP: 28 EST: 1960
SQ FT: 5,000
SALES (est): 59.45MM
SALES (corp-wide): 59.45MM **Privately Held**
Web: www.duncan-oil.com
SIC: **5172** 5411 5983 1542 Gasoline; Convenience stores; Fuel oil dealers; Service station construction

(G-7132)
EAST DAYTON CHRISTIAN SCHOOL
999 Spinning Rd (45431-2847)
PHONE....................937 252-5400
Stacey Auvil, *Prin*
Karen Winnett, *
Norman Hartman, *
Stan Ellingson, *
EMP: 40 EST: 1978
SALES (est): 4.55MM **Privately Held**
Web: www.eastdaytonchristian.org
SIC: **8211** 8351 Private combined elementary and secondary school; Preschool center
PA: New Life Fellowship, Inc.
    365 W 36th Street Ext
    Shadyside OH 43947

(G-7133)
HIDY MOTORS INC (PA)
Also Called: Hidy Honda
2300 Heller Drive Beaver Creek (45434)
PHONE....................937 426-9564
David Hidy, *Pr*
Rita Mayes, *
EMP: 88 EST: 1973
SQ FT: 33,000
SALES (est): 9.73MM
SALES (corp-wide): 9.73MM **Privately Held**
Web: www.honda.com
SIC: **5511** 5012 7515 Automobiles, new and used; Automobiles and other motor vehicles; Passenger car leasing

(G-7134)
HOME CARE NETWORK INC
Also Called: Pedianet
4130 Linden Ave Ste 350 (45432-3065)
PHONE....................937 258-1111
Holly Nugnet, *Prin*
EMP: 144
Web: www.hcnmidwest.net
SIC: **8082** Home health care services
PA: Home Care Network, Inc.
    1191 Lyons Rd
    Dayton OH 45458

(G-7135)
INNOVATIVE TECHNOLOGIES CORP (PA)
Also Called: Itc
1020 Woodman Dr Ste 100 (45432-1410)
PHONE....................937 252-2145
Ramesh K Mehan, *Pr*
Ramesh Mehan, *
Renee Mehan, *
EMP: 70 EST: 1987
SQ FT: 16,000
SALES (est): 9.87MM
SALES (corp-wide): 9.87MM **Privately Held**
Web: www.itc-1.com
SIC: **8742** 7375 Management consulting services; Information retrieval services

(G-7136)
MECHANICAL SYSTEMS DAYTON INC
Also Called: Msd
4401 Springfield St (45431-1040)
PHONE....................937 254-3235
Beverly Stewart, *CEO*
Mark Turvene, *
John Stewart, *
EMP: 100 EST: 1984
SQ FT: 40,000
SALES (est): 100.5K **Privately Held**
Web: www.msdinc.net
SIC: **1711** Mechanical contractor

(G-7137)
P E SYSTEMS INC
5100 Springfield St Ste 510 (45431)
PHONE....................937 258-0141
Larry Bogemann, *Brnch Mgr*
EMP: 142
Web: www.pesystems.com
SIC: **8711** Consulting engineer
PA: P E Systems, Inc.
    10201 Fairfax Blvd # 400
    Fairfax VA 22030

(G-7138)
PAIN MANAGEMENT ASSOCIATES INC
Also Called: Dayton Outpatien Practice
1010 Woodman Dr Ste 100 (45432-1429)
PHONE....................937 252-2000
EMP: 285 EST: 1994
SQ FT: 36,000
SALES (est): 4.86MM
SALES (corp-wide): 3.6B **Privately Held**
SIC: **8093** Specialty outpatient clinics, nec
HQ: Team Health Holdings, Inc.
    265 Brkview Cntre Way Ste
    Knoxville TN 37919
    865 693-1000

(G-7139)
PARALLAX ADVANCED RES CORP
3640 Colonel Glenn Hwy (45435-0001)
PHONE....................937 775-2620
EMP: 53
SALES (corp-wide): 40.73MM **Privately Held**
Web: www.wright.edu
SIC: **8641** Alumni association
PA: Parallax Advanced Research Corporation
    4035 Colonel Glenn Hwy
    Beavercreek Township OH 45431
    937 705-1000

(G-7140)
R&L HERO DELIVERY LLC
3830 Linden Ave (45432-3002)
PHONE....................937 824-0291
Rolania Lee, *Managing Member*
EMP: 60 EST: 2019
SALES (est): 300K **Privately Held**
SIC: **4731** Freight forwarding

(G-7141)
RELX INC
9393 Springboro Pike (45432)
PHONE....................937 865-1012
EMP: 150
SALES (corp-wide): 11.42B **Privately Held**
Web: www.lexisnexis.com
SIC: **7375** Information retrieval services
HQ: Relx Inc.
    230 Park Ave Ste 700
    New York NY 10169
    212 309-8100

(G-7142)
THE UNITED STATES DEPT A FORCE
Also Called: National Museum Usaf
1100 Spaatz St (45433)
PHONE....................937 255-3286
John Hudson, *Brnch Mgr*
EMP: 468
Web: nationalmuseum.af.mil
SIC: **8412** 9711 Museum; Air Force
HQ: The United States Department Of Air Force
    10690 Air Force Pentagon
    Washington DC 20330

(G-7143)
UNISON INDUSTRIES LLC
2455 Dayton Xenia Rd (45434-7148)
PHONE....................904 667-9904
Belinda Kidwell, *Mgr*
EMP: 400
SALES (corp-wide): 67.95B **Publicly Held**
Web: www.unisonindustries.com
SIC: **3728** 4581 3714 3498 Aircraft parts and equipment, nec; Aircraft servicing and repairing; Motor vehicle parts and accessories; Fabricated pipe and fittings
HQ: Unison Industries, Llc
    7575 Baymeadows Way
    Jacksonville FL 32256
    904 739-4000

(G-7144)
WINGS OF LOVE SERVICES LLC
4130 Linden Ave Ste 180 (45432-3058)
PHONE....................937 789-8192
Janon White, *Prin*
EMP: 29 EST: 2014
SALES (est): 1.45MM **Privately Held**
SIC: **4789** 8059 8322 Transportation services, nec; Personal care home, with health care; Adult day care center

Dayton
Montgomery County

(G-7145)
1ST ADVNCE SEC INVSTGTIONS INC
111 W 1st St Ste 101 (45402-1137)
P.O. Box 61128 (45406-9128)
PHONE....................937 317-4433
Darryl Johnson, *Pr*
EMP: 49 EST: 2013
SALES (est): 2.18MM **Privately Held**
Web: www.1stadvancesecurity.com
SIC: **7381** 8742 Security guard service; Training and development consultant

GEOGRAPHIC SECTION

Dayton - Montgomery County (G-7168)

(G-7146)
1WORLDSYNC INC
7777 Washington Village Dr Ste 360 (45459-3958)
PHONE..................866 280-4013
EMP: 51
SALES (corp-wide): 78.29MM Privately Held
Web: www.1worldsync.com
SIC: 7371 Computer software development
HQ: 1worldsync, Inc.
  300 S Riverside Plz # 1400
  Chicago IL 60606
  866 280-4013

(G-7147)
2 J SUPPLY LLC (PA)
1456 N Keowee St (45404)
PHONE..................937 223-0811
EMP: 28 **EST:** 1962
SALES (est): 51.63MM
SALES (corp-wide): 51.63MM Privately Held
Web: www.2jsupply.com
SIC: 5075 Warm air heating equipment and supplies

(G-7148)
937 DELIVERS COOPERATIVE
840 Germantown St (45402-8311)
PHONE..................937 802-0709
Shanon Morgan, *Managing Member*
EMP: 32 **EST:** 2020
SALES (est): 1.22MM Privately Held
SIC: 4212 Delivery service, vehicular

(G-7149)
A PLUS EXPEDITING & LOGISTICS
2947 Boulder Ave (45414-4846)
P.O. Box 570 (45404-0570)
PHONE..................937 424-0220
EMP: 32 **EST:** 2008
SALES (est): 7.61MM Privately Held
Web: www.aplusexpediting.com
SIC: 4731 Freight forwarding

(G-7150)
AAA MIAMI VALLEY (PA)
Also Called: AAA Travel Agency
825 S Ludlow St (45402-2612)
PHONE..................937 224-2896
Gus Geil, *Ch Bd*
John E Horn, *
James Eikenberry, *Vice Chairman*
Raymond Keyton, *
Richard Harris, *
EMP: 80 **EST:** 1920
SQ FT: 15,000
SALES (est): 22.9MM
SALES (corp-wide): 22.9MM Privately Held
Web: www.cruisesunlimited.com
SIC: 4724 8699 Travel agencies; Automobile owners' association

(G-7151)
AABEL EXTERMINATING CO
440 Congress Park Dr (45459-4125)
PHONE..................937 434-4343
John R Moran, *Pr*
Charles R Norman, *Ch Bd*
EMP: 34 **EST:** 1937
SQ FT: 4,000
SALES (est): 937.3K Privately Held
Web: www.a-abel.com
SIC: 7342 Pest control in structures

(G-7152)
ABN FINANCIAL GROUP
8911 Shadycreek Dr (45458-3342)
PHONE..................937 522-0101
Alex Abuyuan, *Prin*
EMP: 35 **EST:** 2017
SALES (est): 447.84K Privately Held
Web: www.abnfinancial.com
SIC: 6282 Investment advice

(G-7153)
ACCESS HOSPITAL DAYTON LLC
Also Called: ACCESS HOSPITAL FOR PSYCHIATRY DAYTON
2611 Wayne Ave Bldg 61 (45420-1833)
PHONE..................937 228-0579
John A Johnson, *Prin*
EMP: 96 **EST:** 2010
SALES (est): 4.08MM
SALES (corp-wide): 17.79MM Privately Held
Web: www.accesshospital.com
SIC: 8093 Mental health clinic, outpatient
PA: Access Ohio Llc
  6400 E Broad St Ste 400
  Columbus OH 43213
  614 655-3345

(G-7154)
ACTIVE ELECTRIC INCORPORATED
1885 Southtown Blvd (45439-1931)
PHONE..................937 299-1885
EMP: 69 **EST:** 1983
SALES (est): 9.48MM Privately Held
Web: www.active-electric.com
SIC: 1731 Electrical work

(G-7155)
ADAMS-ROBINSON ENTERPRISES INC (PA)
Also Called: Adams Robinson Construction
2735 Needmore Rd (45414-4207)
PHONE..................937 274-5318
Michael Adams, *CEO*
M Bradley Adams, *
David Miller, *
Kimberly Adams-connors, *Corporate Secretary*
EMP: 35 **EST:** 1983
SQ FT: 10,324
SALES (est): 88.19MM
SALES (corp-wide): 88.19MM Privately Held
Web: www.adamsrobinson.com
SIC: 1542 Commercial and office building, new construction

(G-7156)
ADAPTIVE DEVELOPMENT CORP
6060 Milo Rd (45414-3418)
PHONE..................937 890-3388
EMP: 28
SALES (est): 985.43K Privately Held
Web: www.adaptivedevcorp.com
SIC: 8741 Management services

(G-7157)
ADVANCE HOME CARE LLC
1250 W Dorothy Ln (45409-1317)
PHONE..................937 723-6335
EMP: 60
SALES (corp-wide): 4.45MM Privately Held
Web: www.advancehcare.com
SIC: 8082 Home health care services
PA: Advance Home Care Llc
  1191 S James Rd
  Columbus OH 43227
  614 436-3611

(G-7158)
AEROSEAL LLC
Also Called: Aerobarrier
1851 S Metro Pkwy (45459-2523)
PHONE..................937 428-9300
Amit Gupta, *Brnch Mgr*
EMP: 30
SALES (corp-wide): 31.78MM Privately Held
Web: www.aeroseal.com
SIC: 8748 3679 Energy conservation consultant; Hermetic seals, for electronic equipment
PA: Aeroseal Llc
  225 Byers Rd 1
  Miamisburg OH 45342
  937 428-9300

(G-7159)
AGAPE FOR YOUTH INC
2300 S Edwin C Moses Blvd Ste 140 (45417-4667)
PHONE..................937 439-4406
Stephen Geib, *Ex Dir*
Arloa Thomas, *Ex Dir*
Stephen Branham, *Prin*
EMP: 34 **EST:** 1989
SALES (est): 3.72MM Privately Held
Web: www.agapeforyouth.com
SIC: 8322 Child related social services

(G-7160)
AHF OHIO INC
264 Wilmington Ave (45420-1989)
PHONE..................937 256-4663
Rick Cordonnier, *Admn*
EMP: 89
SALES (corp-wide): 25.83MM Privately Held
Web: www.ahfohio.com
SIC: 8051 8361 Skilled nursing care facilities; Residential care
PA: Ahf Ohio, Inc.
  5920 Venture Dr Ste 100
  Dublin OH 43017
  614 760-7352

(G-7161)
ALCOHOL DRG ADDCTION MNTAL SVC
Also Called: Adamhs Bd For Montgomery Cnty
409 E Monument Ave Ste 102 (45402-1260)
PHONE..................937 443-0416
EMP: 28 **EST:** 1960
SALES (est): 1.09MM Privately Held
Web: www.mentalhealthservicesdayton.com
SIC: 8069 8093 Drug addiction rehabilitation hospital; Mental health clinic, outpatient

(G-7162)
ALL ABOUT HOME CARE SVCS LLC
70 Birch Aly Ste 240 (45440-1477)
PHONE..................937 222-2980
EMP: 37 **EST:** 2012
SALES (est): 916.8K Privately Held
SIC: 8082 Home health care services

(G-7163)
ALLIED BUILDERS INC (PA)
Also Called: Allied Fence Builders
1644 Kuntz Rd (45404)
P.O. Box 94 (45404)
PHONE..................937 226-0311
Linda S Helton, *Pr*
Bill Helton Junior, *VP*
EMP: 47 **EST:** 1972
SQ FT: 25,500
SALES (est): 9.28MM
SALES (corp-wide): 9.28MM Privately Held
Web: www.alliedperimetersecurity.com
SIC: 1799 Fence construction

(G-7164)
ALLIED SUPPLY COMPANY INC (PA)
Also Called: Johnson Contrls Authorized Dlr
1100 E Monument Ave (45402-1343)
PHONE..................937 224-9833
William V Homan, *Ch Bd*
Thomas E Homan, *
Scott Gibbons, *
J W Van De Grift, *
EMP: 40 **EST:** 1948
SQ FT: 65,000
SALES (est): 23.68MM
SALES (corp-wide): 23.68MM Privately Held
Web: www.alliedsupply.com
SIC: 5078 5075 5085 Refrigeration equipment and supplies; Warm air heating equipment and supplies; Mill supplies

(G-7165)
ALPHA & OMEGA BLDG SVCS INC (PA)
2843 Culver Ave Ste A (45429-3720)
PHONE..................937 298-2125
James Baker, *CEO*
EMP: 38 **EST:** 1986
SQ FT: 7,000
SALES (est): 16.61MM
SALES (corp-wide): 16.61MM Privately Held
Web: www.aobuildingservices.com
SIC: 7349 Janitorial service, contract basis

(G-7166)
ALPHA MEDIA LLC
Also Called: Wing-FM
717 E David Rd (45429-5218)
PHONE..................937 294-5858
John King, *Genl Mgr*
EMP: 46
SALES (corp-wide): 441.62MM Privately Held
Web: www.alphamediausa.com
SIC: 4832 Radio broadcasting stations
HQ: Alpha Media Llc
  1211 Sw 5th Ave Ste 600
  Portland OR 97204

(G-7167)
ALRO STEEL CORPORATION
821 Springfield St (45403-1252)
PHONE..................937 253-6121
TOLL FREE: 800
Tim Elliott, *Mgr*
EMP: 40
SQ FT: 120,000
SALES (corp-wide): 3.43B Privately Held
Web: www.alro.com
SIC: 5051 3441 3317 3316 Steel; Fabricated structural metal; Steel pipe and tubes; Cold finishing of steel shapes
PA: Alro Steel Corporation
  3100 E High St
  Jackson MI 49203
  517 787-5500

(G-7168)
ALTERNATE SLTONS HLTH NTWRK LL (PA)
1050 Forrer Blvd (45420-3640)
PHONE..................937 681-9269
David Ganszarto, *CEO*
EMP: 65 **EST:** 2002
SALES (est): 49.74MM
SALES (corp-wide): 49.74MM Privately Held
Web: www.ashealthnet.com
SIC: 7363 Temporary help service

Dayton - Montgomery County (G-7169)

GEOGRAPHIC SECTION

(G-7169)
ALTERNATE SOLUTIONS FIRST LLC
1251 E Dorothy Ln (45419-2106)
PHONE..............................937 298-1111
EMP: 200 **EST:** 1999
SQ FT: 2,000
SALES (est): 4.83MM **Privately Held**
Web: www.ashomecare.com
SIC: 8082 7361 Home health care services; Nurses' registry

(G-7170)
AMERICAN CITY BUS JOURNALS INC
Also Called: Dayton Business Journal
40 N Main St Ste 810 (45423-1053)
PHONE..............................937 528-4400
EMP: 268
SALES (corp-wide): 2.88B **Privately Held**
Web: www.acbj.com
SIC: 2711 7313 Newspapers: publishing only, not printed on site; Newspaper advertising representative
HQ: American City Business Journals, Inc.
120 W Morehead St Ste 400
Charlotte NC 28202
704 973-1000

(G-7171)
AMERICAN INSURANCE STRATEGIES ✪
78 Marco Ln (45458-3817)
PHONE..............................937 221-8896
EMP: 50 **EST:** 2023
SALES (est): 1.2MM
SALES (corp-wide): 19.63MM **Privately Held**
Web: www.aiscorporate.com
SIC: 6411 Insurance agents, brokers, and service
PA: Twfg Holding Company, Llc
1201 Lk Wdlnds Dr Ste 402
The Woodlands TX 77380
281 367-3424

(G-7172)
AMERICAN NURSING CARE INC
6450 Poe Ave Ste 118 (45414-2646)
PHONE..............................937 438-3844
TOLL FREE: 800
Kitty Makley, *Brnch Mgr*
EMP: 325
Web: www.americannursingcare.com
SIC: 8051 8082 Skilled nursing care facilities; Home health care services
HQ: American Nursing Care, Inc.
6281 Tri Ridge Blvd # 300
Loveland OH 45140
513 576-0262

(G-7173)
AMG INC (PA)
Also Called: AMG-Eng
1497 Shoup Mill Rd (45414-3903)
PHONE..............................937 274-0376
Alberto G Mendez, *Pr*
Julieta Davis, *
John Haas, *
Scott Feller, *
Maria C Mendez, *
EMP: 45 **EST:** 1980
SQ FT: 26,796
SALES (est): 16.15MM
SALES (corp-wide): 16.15MM **Privately Held**
Web: www.amg-eng.com
SIC: 8711 Consulting engineer

(G-7174)
ANDREW CASEY ELECTRIC LLC
4008 N Dixie Dr (45414-5241)
PHONE..............................937 765-4210
Andrew Casey, *Pr*
EMP: 28 **EST:** 2016
SALES (est): 11.95MM **Privately Held**
Web: www.electriciandaytonohio.com
SIC: 4911 Electric services

(G-7175)
ANESTHESIOLOGY SVCS NETWRK LTD
1 Wyoming St (45409-2722)
P.O. Box 632317 (45263-2317)
PHONE..............................937 208-6173
Charles Cardone, *Pr*
EMP: 41 **EST:** 1996
SALES (est): 17.28MM **Privately Held**
Web: www.asndayton.org
SIC: 8011 Anesthesiologist

(G-7176)
APPLIED MECHANICAL SYSTEMS INC (PA)
Also Called: AMS
5598 Wolf Creek Pike (45426-2400)
PHONE..............................937 854-3073
EMP: 126 **EST:** 1974
SALES (est): 33.51MM
SALES (corp-wide): 33.51MM **Privately Held**
Web: www.appliedmechanicalsys.com
SIC: 1711 Plumbing contractors

(G-7177)
APPLIED RESEARCH SOLUTIONS INC
51 Plum St Ste 240 (45440-1397)
PHONE..............................937 912-6100
Gary Wittlinger, *CEO*
Gary Wittlinger, *
Kevin Sullivan, *
EMP: 85 **EST:** 2012
SALES (est): 26.76MM
SALES (corp-wide): 139.33MM **Privately Held**
Web: www.appliedres.com
SIC: 8733 Research institute
PA: Riverside Research Institute
100 William St
New York NY 10038
212 563-4545

(G-7178)
ARDENT TECHNOLOGIES INC
6234 Far Hills Ave (45459-1927)
PHONE..............................937 312-1345
Srinivas Appalaneni, *Pr*
EMP: 98 **EST:** 2000
SALES (est): 11.35MM **Privately Held**
Web: www.ardentinc.com
SIC: 8748 8711 Business consulting, nec; Consulting engineer

(G-7179)
AREA AGCY ON AGING PLG SVC ARE
Also Called: AREA AGENCY ON AGING P S A 2
40 W 2nd St Ste 400 (45402-1873)
PHONE..............................800 258-7277
Doug Mcgarry, *Ex Dir*
EMP: 126 **EST:** 1984
SALES (est): 51.35MM **Privately Held**
Web: www.info4seniors.org
SIC: 8322 8082 Senior citizens' center or association; Home health care services

(G-7180)
ARROW WINE STORES INC
Also Called: Arrow Wine & Spirits
615 Lyons Rd (45459-3978)
PHONE..............................937 433-6778
Dennis Freyvogel, *Owner*
EMP: 29
SALES (corp-wide): 3.32MM **Privately Held**
Web: www.arrowwineandspirits.com
SIC: 5921 5993 5194 5182 Wine; Tobacco stores and stands; Tobacco and tobacco products; Wine and distilled beverages
PA: Arrow Wine Stores, Inc.
2950 Far Hills Ave
Dayton OH
937 298-1456

(G-7181)
ARTEMIS CTR FOR ALTRNTVES TO D (PA)
310 W Monument Ave (45402-3000)
PHONE..............................937 461-5091
Patti Schwartvauber, *Ex Dir*
EMP: 29 **EST:** 1998
SALES (est): 1.7MM
SALES (corp-wide): 1.7MM **Privately Held**
Web: www.artemiscenter.org
SIC: 8322 Family counseling services

(G-7182)
ASSOCTED SPCLSTS OF INTRNAL MD
7707 Paragon Rd Ste 101 (45459-4070)
PHONE..............................937 208-7272
Roger H Griffin Md, *Pr*
EMP: 27 **EST:** 1984
SALES (est): 945.66K **Privately Held**
Web: www.premierhealth.com
SIC: 8011 Internal medicine, physician/surgeon

(G-7183)
ATLAS PARTNERS LLC
7750 Paragon Rd (45459-4050)
PHONE..............................937 439-7970
EMP: 150
SIC: 7375 7319 Information retrieval services; Media buying service

(G-7184)
ATRIUM MEDICAL CENTER
40 W 4th St Ste 525 (45402-1841)
PHONE..............................513 424-2111
Michael Ashworth, *Prin*
EMP: 46 **EST:** 2008
SALES (est): 1.94MM **Privately Held**
Web: www.premierhealth.com
SIC: 8011 Medical centers

(G-7185)
BAE SYSTEMS IAP RESEARCH LLC
2763 Culver Ave (45429-3723)
PHONE..............................937 296-1806
EMP: 40
Web: www.iap.com
SIC: 8731 Commercial research laboratory

(G-7186)
BATH & BODY WORKS LLC
Also Called: Bath & Body Works
2700 Miamisburg Centerville Rd Unit 1 (45459)
PHONE..............................937 439-0350
Christiane Michaels, *Pr*
EMP: 60
SALES (corp-wide): 7.43B **Publicly Held**
Web: www.bathandbodyworks.com
SIC: 5999 7313 Toiletries, cosmetics, and perfumes; Radio advertising representative
HQ: Bath & Body Works, Llc
7 Limited Pkwy E
Reynoldsburg OH 43068

(G-7187)
BAYMARK HEALTH SERVICES LA INC
4201 N Main St (45405-1624)
PHONE..............................937 203-2017
EMP: 115
SALES (corp-wide): 106.29MM **Privately Held**
Web: www.medmark.com
SIC: 8093 Substance abuse clinics (outpatient)
PA: Baymark Health Services Of Louisiana, Inc.
1720 Lakepointe Dr # 117
Lewisville TX 75057
214 379-3300

(G-7188)
BEACON CAPITAL MANAGEMENT INC
7777 Washington Village Dr Ste 280 (45459-3976)
PHONE..............................937 203-4025
Esfand Dinshaw, *CEO*
EMP: 850 **EST:** 1998
SALES (est): 2.02MM
SALES (corp-wide): 1.64B **Privately Held**
Web: www.beaconinvesting.com
SIC: 6282 Investment advisory service
HQ: Sammons Financial Group, Inc.
8300 Mills Civic Pkwy
West Des Moines IA 50266
515 221-4836

(G-7189)
BEHAVIOR KEY SERVICES LLC
5963a Kentshire Dr (45440-4253)
PHONE..............................937 952-6379
Hal Housewarth, *Prin*
EMP: 58 **EST:** 2013
SALES (est): 1.1MM **Privately Held**
Web: www.keyaba.com
SIC: 8099 Health and allied services, nec

(G-7190)
BERRIEHILL RESEARCH CORP
7735 Paragon Rd (45459-4051)
PHONE..............................937 435-1016
Jeffery A Berrie, *Pr*
EMP: 30 **EST:** 2005
SALES (est): 4.84MM
SALES (corp-wide): 418.64MM **Privately Held**
Web: www.ara.com
SIC: 8731 Commercial physical research
HQ: Applied Research Associates, Inc.
4300 San Mateo Blvd Ne
Albuquerque NM 87110
505 883-3636

(G-7191)
BERRY NETWORK
6 N Main St Ste 610 (45402-1908)
PHONE..............................513 702-3373
EMP: 94 **EST:** 2018
SALES (est): 2.43MM **Privately Held**
Web: www.berrynetwork.com
SIC: 7311 Advertising agencies

(G-7192)
BIESER GREER & LANDIS LLP
6 N Main St Ste 400 (45402-1914)
PHONE..............................937 223-3277
Charles Shook, *Pt*

GEOGRAPHIC SECTION
Dayton - Montgomery County (G-7215)

Edward Shank, *Pt*
David Greer, *Pt*
Irvin Bieser, *Pt*
Leo Krebs, *Pt*
EMP: 80 **EST:** 1961
SALES (est): 5.3MM **Privately Held**
Web: www.bieisergreer.com
SIC: 8111 General practice attorney, lawyer

(G-7193)
BIG HILL REALTY CORP (PA)
Also Called: Federer Homes and Gardens RE
5580 Far Hills Ave (45429-2285)
PHONE..................937 435-1177
William Ryan, *CEO*
Jeffrey Owens, *
George Long, *
Jeff Owens, *
EMP: 35 **EST:** 1968
SQ FT: 3,500
SALES (est): 9.87MM
SALES (corp-wide): 9.87MM **Privately Held**
Web: www.bighill.com
SIC: 6531 Real estate agent, residential

(G-7194)
BIGGER ROAD VETERINARY CLINIC (PA)
5655 Bigger Rd (45440-2714)
PHONE..................937 435-3262
E Eugene Snyder D.v.m., *Pr*
Christine Snyder, *Sec*
EMP: 32 **EST:** 1976
SQ FT: 2,200
SALES (est): 2.24MM
SALES (corp-wide): 2.24MM **Privately Held**
Web: www.biggervet.com
SIC: 0742 Animal hospital services, pets and other animal specialties

(G-7195)
BLUE TOOTH DENTAL
2198 Hewitt Ave (45440-4242)
PHONE..................937 432-6677
EMP: 74
Web: www.bluetoothdental.com
SIC: 8021 Dentists' office
PA: Blue Tooth Dental
9201 N Dixie Dr
Dayton OH

(G-7196)
BONBRIGHT DISTRIBUTORS INC (PA)
Also Called: Bonbright
1 Arena Park Dr (45417-4678)
PHONE..................937 222-1001
H Brock Anderson, *Pr*
Jim Brown, *
John Dimario, *
Richard B Pohl Junior, *Sec*
▲ **EMP:** 84 **EST:** 1983
SQ FT: 70,000
SALES (est): 21.41MM
SALES (corp-wide): 21.41MM **Privately Held**
Web: www.bonbright.com
SIC: 5181 Beer and other fermented malt liquors

(G-7197)
BOOST ENGAGEMENT LLC
Also Called: Shumsky Promotional
811 E 4th St (45402-2227)
PHONE..................937 223-2203
Anita Emoff, *Ch*
Dawn Conway, *
Michael J Emoff Cvo, *Prin*
◆ **EMP:** 50 **EST:** 1953

SQ FT: 19,500
SALES (est): 24.1MM **Privately Held**
Web: www.engageboost.com
SIC: 5199 Advertising specialties

(G-7198)
BOWSER-MORNER INC (PA)
4518 Taylorsville Rd (45424-2440)
P.O. Box 51 (45401-0051)
PHONE..................937 236-8805
EMP: 130 **EST:** 1955
SALES (est): 17.99MM
SALES (corp-wide): 17.99MM **Privately Held**
Web: www.bowser-morner.com
SIC: 8734 8748 8711 Testing laboratories; Business consulting, nec; Engineering services

(G-7199)
BP OIL SUPPLY COMPANY
1580 Miamisburg Centerville Rd (45459)
PHONE..................937 434-7008
Wanda Taylor, *Mgr*
EMP: 53
SALES (corp-wide): 296.92MM **Privately Held**
Web: www.bp.com
SIC: 5172 Crude oil
HQ: Bp Oil Supply Company
28100 Torch Pkwy
Warrenville IL 60555
630 836-5000

(G-7200)
BRACKETT BUILDERS INC (PA)
418 E 1st St (45402)
PHONE..................937 339-7505
Eric Stahl, *Pr*
Vern Hoying, *
Thomas Hoying, *
Janet Hieatt, *
EMP: 27 **EST:** 1983
SALES (est): 16.02MM
SALES (corp-wide): 16.02MM **Privately Held**
Web: www.brackettbuilders.com
SIC: 1542 Commercial and office buildings, renovation and repair

(G-7201)
BROWER INSURANCE AGENCY LLC
409 E Monument Ave Ste 400 (45402)
PHONE..................937 228-4135
EMP: 125
SIC: 6411 Insurance agents and brokers

(G-7202)
BUCKEYE CHARTER SERVICE INC
Also Called: Buckeye Charters
8240 Expansion Way (45424-6382)
PHONE..................937 879-3000
EMP: 30
Web: www.buckeyecharters.com
SIC: 4142 Bus charter service, except local
PA: Buckeye Charter Service, Inc.
1235 E Hanthorn Rd
Lima OH 45804

(G-7203)
BUCKEYE POOLS INC
671 Miamisburg Centerville Rd (45459)
P.O. Box 750548 (45475-0548)
PHONE..................937 434-7916
Gary Aiken, *Pr*
EMP: 28 **EST:** 1959
SALES (est): 2.35MM **Privately Held**
Web: www.buckeyepools.com
SIC: 7389 1799 Swimming pool and hot tub service and maintenance; Swimming pool construction

(G-7204)
BUCKEYE TRILS GIRL SCOUT CNCIL (PA)
450 Shoup Mill Rd (45415-3518)
PHONE..................937 275-7601
TOLL FREE: 800
Barbara Bonisas, *CEO*
EMP: 41 **EST:** 1921
SQ FT: 40,000
SALES (est): 721.88K
SALES (corp-wide): 721.88K **Privately Held**
Web: www.gswo.org
SIC: 8641 Girl Scout organization

(G-7205)
BUCKINGHAM & COMPANY
Also Called: Buckingham Financial Group
6856 Loop Rd (45459-2159)
PHONE..................937 435-2742
Jay A Buckingham, *Pr*
EMP: 43 **EST:** 1982
SQ FT: 15,000
SALES (est): 5.46MM **Privately Held**
Web: www.mybuckingham.com
SIC: 7291 8742 6282 Tax return preparation services; Financial consultant; Investment advisory service

(G-7206)
BURD BROTHERS INC
1789 Stanley Ave (45404-1116)
PHONE..................513 708-7787
Tyler Burdick, *Brnch Mgr*
EMP: 33
Web: www.burdbrothers.com
SIC: 4213 Trucking, except local
PA: Burd Brothers, Inc.
4294 Armstrong Blvd
Batavia OH 45103

(G-7207)
BUSINESS FURNITURE LLC
Also Called: Steelcase Authorized Dealer
607 E 3rd St Ste 200 (45402-2219)
PHONE..................937 293-1010
Debra M Oakes, *Brnch Mgr*
EMP: 50
SALES (corp-wide): 51.46MM **Privately Held**
Web: www.businessfurniture.net
SIC: 5021 7641 5023 Office furniture, nec; Furniture repair and maintenance; Carpets
PA: Business Furniture, Llc
8421 Bearing Dr Ste 200
Indianapolis IN 46268
317 216-4844

(G-7208)
BUTLER HEATING COMPANY
Also Called: Butler Heating & AC
120 Springfield St (45403-1110)
PHONE..................937 253-8871
Donald Probst, *CEO*
Steven Scothorn, *
EMP: 40 **EST:** 1949
SQ FT: 15,400
SALES (est): 2.14MM **Privately Held**
Web: www.butlerheating.com
SIC: 1711 Warm air heating and air conditioning contractor

(G-7209)
C K FRANCHISING INC
111 W 1st St Ste 910 (45402-1134)
PHONE..................937 264-1933
EMP: 76 **EST:** 2019
SALES (est): 1.91MM **Privately Held**
Web: www.comfortkeepersfranchise.com

SIC: 8082 Home health care services

(G-7210)
CARE ONE LLC
Also Called: Spring Creek Nursing Center
5440 Charlesgate Rd (45424-1049)
PHONE..................937 236-6707
EMP: 34
SALES (corp-wide): 907.2MM **Privately Held**
Web: www.care-one.com
SIC: 8051 Convalescent home with continuous nursing care
PA: Care One, Llc
173 Bridge Plz N
Fort Lee NJ 07024
201 242-4000

(G-7211)
CARESOURCE (PA)
230 N Main St (45402)
P.O. Box 8738 (45401)
PHONE..................937 224-3300
Erhardt Preitauer, *Pr*
David Goltz, *
David Finkel, *
Jeff Myers, *
Fred A Schulz, *
EMP: 800 **EST:** 1989
SALES (est): 1.04B **Privately Held**
Web: www.caresource.com
SIC: 6321 Health insurance carriers

(G-7212)
CARESOURCE OHIO INC (HQ)
Also Called: CareSource USA Holding
230 N Main St (45402-1263)
P.O. Box 8738 (45401-8738)
PHONE..................937 224-3300
EMP: 142 **EST:** 1985
SALES (est): 10.06B **Privately Held**
Web: www.caresource.com
SIC: 8621 Health association
PA: Caresource
230 N Main St
Dayton OH 45402

(G-7213)
CARRIAGE INN RTRMENT CMNTY OF
Also Called: Carriage Inn of Dayton
5040 Philadelphia Dr (45415-3604)
PHONE..................937 278-0404
Robert L Huff, *Pr*
EMP: 74 **EST:** 1986
SALES (est): 6.07MM **Privately Held**
Web: www.carriageinnofdayton.com
SIC: 8051 Convalescent home with continuous nursing care

(G-7214)
CARRIAGE INN TROTWOOD INC
Also Called: Shiloh Springs Care Center
5020 Philadelphia Dr (45415-3653)
PHONE..................937 854-1180
Ken Bernsen, *Pr*
EMP: 47 **EST:** 2007
SQ FT: 6,500
SALES (est): 4.99MM **Privately Held**
SIC: 8051 Convalescent home with continuous nursing care

(G-7215)
CASSANOS INC (PA)
Also Called: Cassano's Pizza & Subs
1700 E Stroop Rd (45429-5095)
PHONE..................937 294-8400
Vic Cassano Junior, *Ch Bd*
EMP: 45 **EST:** 1949
SQ FT: 37,500
SALES (est): 30.98K
SALES (corp-wide): 30.98K **Privately Held**

Dayton - Montgomery County (G-7216) — GEOGRAPHIC SECTION

Web: www.cassanos.com
SIC: **5812** 5149 6794 2045 Pizzeria, chain; Baking supplies; Franchises, selling or licensing; Pizza doughs, prepared: from purchased flour

(G-7216)
CATALYST PAPER (USA) INC
7777 Washington Village Dr Ste 210 (45459-3995)
PHONE...................................937 528-3800
Linda Mcclinchy, *VP*
EMP: 50
SIC: **5111** Fine paper
HQ: Catalyst Paper (Usa) Inc.
   2200 6th Ave Ste 800
   Seattle WA 98121
   206 838-2070

(G-7217)
CATERPLLAR TRMBLE CTRL TECH LL
Also Called: Caterpillar Authorized Dealer
5475 Kellenburger Rd (45424-1013)
PHONE...................................937 233-8921
▲ **EMP**: 99 **EST**: 2002
SALES (est): 22.45MM **Privately Held**
Web: www.caterpillar.com
SIC: **8731** 5082 Biotechnical research, commercial; Construction and mining machinery

(G-7218)
CATHOLIC SCIAL SVCS OF MAMI VL (PA)
Also Called: Miami Valley Family Care Ctr
922 W Riverview Ave (45402-6424)
PHONE...................................937 223-7217
Ronald Eckerle Ex, *Dir*
EMP: 30 **EST**: 1922
SALES (est): 21.57MM
SALES (corp-wide): 21.57MM **Privately Held**
Web: www.cssmv.org
SIC: **8322** 8351 Family service agency; Child day care services

(G-7219)
CENTERVILLE LANDSCAPING INC
1082 W Spring Valley Pike (45458-3106)
PHONE...................................937 433-5395
Thomas C Shields, *Pr*
EMP: 31 **EST**: 1972
SQ FT: 4,800
SALES (est): 1.8MM **Privately Held**
Web: www.centervillelandscape.com
SIC: **0782** 1711 Seeding services, lawn; Irrigation sprinkler system installation

(G-7220)
CENTRIC CONSULTING LLC (PA)
Also Called: Practical Solution
1215 Lyons Rd # F (45458-1858)
PHONE...................................888 781-7567
Dave Rosevelt, *Managing Member*
Dave Rosevelt, *Managing Member*
Larry English, *
Eric Van Luven, *
Jim Schaller, *
EMP: 78 **EST**: 1999
SQ FT: 1,000
SALES (est): 24.22MM
SALES (corp-wide): 24.22MM **Privately Held**
Web: www.centricconsulting.com
SIC: **8748** Systems engineering consultant, ex. computer or professional

(G-7221)
CHAPEL ELECTRIC CO LLC
1985 Founders Dr (45420-4012)
PHONE...................................937 222-2290
Dennis F Quebe, *Ch*
Gregory P Ross, *
Roger Van Der Horst, *
Richard E Penewit, *
EMP: 280 **EST**: 1946
SQ FT: 40,000
SALES (est): 27.11MM
SALES (corp-wide): 12.58B **Publicly Held**
Web: www.quebeholdingsinc.com
SIC: **1731** General electrical contractor
HQ: Quebe Holdings, Inc.
   1985 Founders Dr
   Dayton OH 45420
   937 222-2290

(G-7222)
CHEMINEER INC
Also Called: Kenics
5870 Poe Ave (45414-3442)
P.O. Box 1123 (45401-1123)
PHONE...................................937 454-3200
◆ **EMP**: 160
Web: www.nov.com
SIC: **3559** 3556 3554 3531 Chemical machinery and equipment; Food products machinery; Paper industries machinery; Construction machinery

(G-7223)
CHILDRENS HOME CARE DAYTON
Also Called: CHILDREN'S HOME CARE
18 Childrens Plz (45404-1867)
PHONE...................................937 641-4663
EMP: 65 **EST**: 1992
SALES (est): 19.12MM **Privately Held**
Web: www.childrensdayton.org
SIC: **7361** 8082 Nurses' registry; Home health care services

(G-7224)
CHILDRENS LAB SCHOOLS INC
Also Called: GLORIA DEI MONTESSORI SCHOOL
615 Shiloh Dr (45415-3452)
PHONE...................................937 274-7195
Christina Allen, *Dir*
EMP: 31 **EST**: 1962
SQ FT: 5,500
SALES (est): 662.97K **Privately Held**
Web: www.gloriadeimontessori.org
SIC: **8351** 8211 Preschool center; Elementary and secondary schools

(G-7225)
CHOICES IN COMMUNITY LIVING (PA)
1651 Needmore Rd Ste B (45414-3801)
PHONE...................................937 898-3655
W Thomas Weaver, *Pr*
EMP: 120 **EST**: 1985
SQ FT: 2,000
SALES (est): 14.1MM
SALES (corp-wide): 14.1MM **Privately Held**
Web: www.partnersohio.com
SIC: **8361** 8052 Retarded home; Intermediate care facilities

(G-7226)
CINCINNATI AML REFL EMER C LLC
Also Called: Dayton Care Center
6405 Clyo Rd (45459-2763)
PHONE...................................937 610-0414
EMP: 29 **EST**: 2008
SALES (est): 249.82K **Privately Held**
Web: www.carecentervets.com
SIC: **8082** Home health care services

(G-7227)
CITY OF CENTERVILLE
Also Called: Golf Course At Yankee Trace
10000 Yankee St (45458-3520)
PHONE...................................937 438-3585
EMP: 51
Web: www.centervilleohio.gov
SIC: **5812** 7299 Eating places; Banquet hall facilities
PA: City Of Centerville
   100 W Spring Valley Rd
   Dayton OH 45458
   937 433-7151

(G-7228)
CITY OF DAYTON
Also Called: Dayton City Water Department
3210 Chuck Wagner Ln (45414-4401)
PHONE...................................937 333-6070
EMP: 84
SALES (corp-wide): 283.1MM **Privately Held**
Web: www.daytonohio.gov
SIC: **4941** Water supply
PA: City Of Dayton
   101 W 3rd St
   Dayton OH 45402
   937 333-3333

(G-7229)
CITY OF DAYTON
Also Called: Dayton Wastewater Trtmnt Plant
2800 Guthrie Rd Ste A (45417-6700)
PHONE...................................937 333-1837
Chris Clark, *Brnch Mgr*
EMP: 72
SALES (corp-wide): 283.1MM **Privately Held**
Web: www.daytonohio.gov
SIC: **4952** Sewerage systems
PA: City Of Dayton
   101 W 3rd St
   Dayton OH 45402
   937 333-3333

(G-7230)
CITY OF DAYTON
Also Called: City Dayton Waste Collection
1010 Ottawa St Bldg 7 (45402-1317)
PHONE...................................937 333-4860
Tom Ritchie, *Mgr*
EMP: 80
SALES (corp-wide): 283.1MM **Privately Held**
Web: www.daytonohio.gov
SIC: **4953** 4212 Refuse systems; Local trucking, without storage
PA: City Of Dayton
   101 W 3rd St
   Dayton OH 45402
   937 333-3333

(G-7231)
CITY OF DAYTON
Also Called: City Dayton Water Distribution
945 Ottawa St (45402-1365)
PHONE...................................937 333-7138
EMP: 49
SALES (corp-wide): 283.1MM **Privately Held**
Web: www.daytonohio.gov
SIC: **4971** Water distribution or supply systems for irrigation
PA: City Of Dayton
   101 W 3rd St
   Dayton OH 45402
   937 333-3333

(G-7232)
CITY OF DAYTON
Also Called: Water Department
320 W Monument Ave (45402-3017)
PHONE...................................937 333-3725
William Zilli, *Brnch Mgr*
EMP: 40
SQ FT: 14,000
SALES (corp-wide): 283.1MM **Privately Held**
Web: www.daytonohio.gov
SIC: **1623** 4941 Water, sewer, and utility lines ; Water supply
PA: City Of Dayton
   101 W 3rd St
   Dayton OH 45402
   937 333-3333

(G-7233)
CITY OF KETTERING
Also Called: Parks Maintenance
3170 Valleywood Dr (45429-3938)
PHONE...................................937 296-2486
F Postle, *Mgr*
EMP: 30
SALES (corp-wide): 98.01MM **Privately Held**
Web: www.ketteringoh.org
SIC: **8743** Public relations and publicity
PA: City Of Kettering
   3600 Shroyer Rd
   Kettering OH 45429
   937 296-2400

(G-7234)
CITY OF MORAINE
Also Called: Moraine Natatorium
3800 Main St (45439-1467)
PHONE...................................937 535-1100
Roger Jeffers, *Dir*
EMP: 40
Web: www.moraine.oh.us
SIC: **7999** Swimming pool, non-membership
PA: City Of Moraine
   4200 Dryden Rd
   Moraine OH 45439
   937 535-1000

(G-7235)
CLEAN HRBORS ES INDUS SVCS INC
6151 Executive Blvd (45424-1440)
PHONE...................................937 425-0512
Mike Webb, *Brnch Mgr*
EMP: 96
SALES (corp-wide): 5.41B **Publicly Held**
Web: www.cleanharbors.com
SIC: **4953** Hazardous waste collection and disposal
HQ: Clean Harbors Es Industrial Services, Inc.
   4760 World Hstn Pkwy
   Houston TX 77032
   713 672-8004

(G-7236)
CLIFF VIESSMAN INC
5560 Brentlinger Dr (45414-3510)
PHONE...................................937 454-6490
Brian Malin, *Mgr*
EMP: 92
SALES (corp-wide): 79.41MM **Privately Held**
Web: www.viessmantrucking.com
SIC: **4213** Contract haulers
PA: Cliff Viessman, Inc.
   215 1st Ave
   Gary SD 57237
   605 272-3222

GEOGRAPHIC SECTION　　　　　　　　　　　　　　　　　　　　　　　Dayton - Montgomery County (G-7258)

(G-7237)
CNI THL OPS LLC
Also Called: Courtyard Dayton
7087 Miller Ln (45414-2653)
PHONE.................................937 890-6112
Keon Marvasti, Mgr
EMP: 30
SALES (corp-wide): 18MM Privately Held
Web: www.marriott.com
SIC: 7011 Hotels and motels
PA: Cni Thl Ops, Llc
　　515 S Flower St Fl 44
　　Los Angeles CA

(G-7238)
COLDWELL BNKR HRITG RLTORS LLC (PA)
Also Called: Coldwell Banker
4486 Indian Ripple Rd (45440-3203)
PHONE.................................937 434-7600
EMP: 40 EST: 1967
SALES (est): 8.98MM
SALES (corp-wide): 8.98MM Privately Held
Web: www.coldwellbankerishome.com
SIC: 6531 6512 Real estate agent, residential; Commercial and industrial building operation

(G-7239)
COLUMBIA SUSSEX CORPORATION
Also Called: Days Inn-Dayton North
7470 Miller Ln (45414-2442)
PHONE.................................937 898-4946
Rob Zarza, Brnch Mgr
EMP: 37
SALES (corp-wide): 493.85MM Privately Held
Web: www.columbiasussex.com
SIC: 7011 Hotels and motels
PA: Columbia Sussex Corporation
　　740 Centre View Blvd
　　Crestview Hills KY 41017
　　859 578-1100

(G-7240)
COMBINED TECH GROUP INC
6061 Milo Rd (45414-3417)
PHONE.................................937 274-4866
Chad Kuhns, Managing Member
Kurtis Vanburen, *
Tina Vanburen, *
EMP: 28 EST: 1998
SQ FT: 50,000
SALES (est): 9.87MM Privately Held
Web: www.comtechgrp.com
SIC: 5084 Industrial machinery and equipment

(G-7241)
COMMSYS INC
7887 Washington Village Dr Ste 220 (45459-3957)
PHONE.................................937 220-4990
Robert S Turner, Pr
EMP: 42 EST: 1989
SALES (est): 4.98MM Privately Held
Web: www.commsys.com
SIC: 7373 7371 Systems integration services; Computer software systems analysis and design, custom

(G-7242)
COMMUNITY HLH CTR OF GTR DATON
Also Called: Charles Drew Health Center
1323 W 3rd St (45402-6714)
PHONE.................................937 461-4336
EMP: 27
Web: www.communityhealthdayton.org
SIC: 8011 Clinic, operated by physicians
PA: Community Health Centers Of Greater Dayton
　　1323 W 3rd St
　　Dayton OH 45402

(G-7243)
COMMUNITY HLTH CTRS GRTER DYTO
165 S Edwin C Moses Blvd (45402)
PHONE.................................937 558-0180
James Gross, Brnch Mgr
EMP: 27
Web: www.communityhealthdayton.org
SIC: 8011 Clinic, operated by physicians
PA: Community Health Centers Of Greater Dayton
　　1323 W 3rd St
　　Dayton OH 45402

(G-7244)
COMPUNET CLINICAL LABS LLC
2508 Sandridge Dr (45439)
PHONE.................................937 208-3555
Ed Doucette, Brnch Mgr
EMP: 48
SALES (corp-wide): 2.41MM Privately Held
Web: www.compunetlab.com
SIC: 8071 Medical laboratories
HQ: Compunet Clinical Laboratories, Llc
　　2308 Sandridge Dr
　　Moraine OH 45439
　　937 296-0844

(G-7245)
CONCORD DAYTON HOTEL II LLC
Also Called: Dayton Marriott
1414 S Patterson Blvd (45409-2105)
PHONE.................................937 223-1000
Dena St Clair, Managing Member
EMP: 38 EST: 2014
SALES (est): 1.94MM Privately Held
SIC: 5812 7011 American restaurant; Hotels and motels

(G-7246)
CONNOR CONCEPTS INC
Also Called: Chop House Restaurant
7727 Washington Village Dr (45459-3954)
PHONE.................................937 291-1661
EMP: 28
Web: www.connorconcepts.com
SIC: 5812 7299 American restaurant; Banquet hall facilities
PA: Connor Concepts, Inc.
　　10911 Turkey Dr
　　Knoxville TN 37934

(G-7247)
COOLIDGE WALL CO LPA (PA)
33 W 1st St Ste 600 (45402-1289)
PHONE.................................937 223-8177
J Stephen Herbert, Pr
EMP: 91 EST: 1853
SQ FT: 30,000
SALES (est): 12.82MM
SALES (corp-wide): 12.82MM Privately Held
Web: www.coollaw.com
SIC: 8111 General practice attorney, lawyer

(G-7248)
CORBUS LLC (HQ)
9059 Springboro Pike Ste B (45449)
PHONE.................................937 226-7724
Rajesh K Soin, Ch Bd
Vishal Soin, *
Paul Daloia, *
Chris Collins, *
Patrick Sepate, Vice President Business*
EMP: 669 EST: 1998
SQ FT: 12,500
SALES (est): 4.62K
SALES (corp-wide): 51.58MM Privately Held
Web: www.corbus.com
SIC: 8748 8742 Business consulting, nec; Marketing consulting services
PA: Soin International, Llc
　　1129 Mmsburg Cntrvlle Rd Ste
　　Dayton OH 45449
　　937 427-7646

(G-7249)
CORDELL TRANSPORTATION CO LLC
Also Called: Cordell Transportation Co.
2942 Boulder Ave (45414-4847)
PHONE.................................937 277-7271
Lori Van Opstal, Pr
EMP: 237 EST: 1999
SALES (est): 12.63MM Privately Held
Web: www.cordelltransportation.com
SIC: 4214 Local trucking with storage

(G-7250)
COUNTY OF MONTGOMERY
Also Called: Transportation Improvement Dst
451 W 3rd St (45422-0001)
P.O. Box P.O Box 972 (45422-0001)
PHONE.................................937 225-6140
EMP: 60 EST: 2010
SALES (est): 12.04MM
SALES (corp-wide): 603.13MM Privately Held
Web: www.mcohio.org
SIC: 4789 Transportation services, nec
PA: County Of Montgomery
　　451 W 3rd St
　　Dayton OH 45422
　　937 225-4000

(G-7251)
COUNTY OF MONTGOMERY
Also Called: Montgomery Sanitary Engrg
451 W 3rd St (45422-0001)
PHONE.................................937 225-6294
EMP: 35
SALES (corp-wide): 603.13MM Privately Held
Web: www.mcohio.org
SIC: 1731 Electrical work
PA: County Of Montgomery
　　451 W 3rd St
　　Dayton OH 45422
　　937 225-4000

(G-7252)
COUNTY OF MONTGOMERY
Also Called: Miami Vly Regional Crime Lab
361 W 3rd St (45402-1418)
PHONE.................................937 225-4990
Kenneth Betz, Dir
EMP: 154
SALES (corp-wide): 603.13MM Privately Held
Web: www.mcohio.org
SIC: 8743 Sales promotion
PA: County Of Montgomery
　　451 W 3rd St
　　Dayton OH 45422
　　937 225-4000

(G-7253)
COUNTY OF MONTGOMERY
Also Called: Engineering Department
5625 Little Richmond Rd (45426-3219)
PHONE.................................937 854-4576
Mark Hartung, Mgr
EMP: 64
SQ FT: 5,000
SALES (corp-wide): 603.13MM Privately Held
Web: www.mcohio.org
SIC: 8711 Engineering services
PA: County Of Montgomery
　　451 W 3rd St
　　Dayton OH 45422
　　937 225-4000

(G-7254)
COUNTY OF MONTGOMERY
Also Called: Treasurers Office
451 W 3rd St Fl 2 (45422-0001)
P.O. Box 972 (45422)
PHONE.................................937 225-4010
Hugh Quill, Treas
EMP: 114
SALES (corp-wide): 603.13MM Privately Held
Web: www.mcohio.org
SIC: 9111 8611 County supervisors' and executives' office; Business associations
PA: County Of Montgomery
　　451 W 3rd St
　　Dayton OH 45422
　　937 225-4000

(G-7255)
COUNTY OF MONTGOMERY
Also Called: Sheriff's Office
345 W 2nd St (45422-6401)
PHONE.................................937 225-4192
EMP: 74
SALES (corp-wide): 603.13MM Privately Held
Web: www.mcohio.org
SIC: 9221 8399 Sheriffs' office; Community action agency
PA: County Of Montgomery
　　451 W 3rd St
　　Dayton OH 45422
　　937 225-4000

(G-7256)
COUNTY OF MONTGOMERY
Also Called: Coroner
361 W 3rd St (45402-1418)
PHONE.................................937 225-4156
EMP: 35
SALES (corp-wide): 603.13MM Privately Held
Web: www.mcohio.org
SIC: 8011 Pathologist
PA: County Of Montgomery
　　451 W 3rd St
　　Dayton OH 45422
　　937 225-4000

(G-7257)
COUNTY OF MONTGOMERY
Also Called: Stillwater Center
8100 N Main St (45415-1702)
PHONE.................................937 264-0460
Michelle Pierce Mobley, Dir
EMP: 238
SQ FT: 108,000
SALES (corp-wide): 603.13MM Privately Held
Web: www.mcohio.org
SIC: 8051 8052 Mental retardation hospital; Home for the mentally retarded, with health care
PA: County Of Montgomery
　　451 W 3rd St
　　Dayton OH 45422
　　937 225-4000

(G-7258)
COURTYARD BY MRROTT DYTN-NVRSI
Also Called: Courtyard By Marriott

2006 S Edwin C Moses Blvd (45417-4675)
PHONE..................937 220-9060
Karen Younce, *Prin*
EMP: 42 **EST:** 2007
SALES (est): 1.21MM **Privately Held**
Web: www.marriott.com
SIC: 7011 Hotels and motels

(G-7259)
COX ARBORTEUM
Also Called: 5 Rivers Park
6733 Springboro Pike (45449-3496)
PHONE..................937 434-9005
R Edgington, *Genl Mgr*
EMP: 179 **EST:** 1974
SQ FT: 1,000
SALES (est): 173.59K
SALES (corp-wide): 603.13MM **Privately Held**
Web: www.coxarboretumfoundation.org
SIC: 8422 Arboretum
PA: County Of Montgomery
451 W 3rd St
Dayton OH 45422
937 225-4000

(G-7260)
CPCA MANUFACTURING LLC
Also Called: Composite Advantage
750 Rosedale Dr (45402-5758)
PHONE..................937 723-9031
Shane Weyant, *Pr*
EMP: 85 **EST:** 2018
SALES (est): 8.13MM
SALES (corp-wide): 1.03B **Privately Held**
Web: www.creativecompositesgroup.com
SIC: 8741 Management services
HQ: Creative Pultrusions, Inc.
214 Industrial Ln
Alum Bank PA 15521
814 839-4186

(G-7261)
CRN HEALTHCARE INC
519 Xenia Ave (45410-1823)
PHONE..................937 250-1412
Keith Vukasinovich, *CEO*
EMP: 70 **EST:** 2017
SALES (est): 2MM **Privately Held**
Web: www.crnhealth.com
SIC: 8099 Blood related health services

(G-7262)
CROSWELL OF WILLIAMSBURG LLC
4828 Wolf Creek Pike (45417-9438)
PHONE..................800 782-8747
John W Croswell, *Brnch Mgr*
EMP: 65
SALES (corp-wide): 9.27MM **Privately Held**
Web: www.gocroswell.com
SIC: 4142 Bus charter service, except local
PA: Croswell Of Williamsburg Llc
975 W Main St
Williamsburg OH 45176
513 724-2206

(G-7263)
CROWN PACKAGING CORPORATION (PA)
Also Called: CROWN
1885 Woodman Center Dr (45420-1157)
PHONE..................937 294-6580
▼ **EMP:** 150 **EST:** 1967
SALES (est): 46.06MM
SALES (corp-wide): 46.06MM **Privately Held**
Web: www.crownpkg.com
SIC: 5199 Packaging materials

(G-7264)
CSA ANIMAL NUTRITION LLC
Also Called: Csa Animal Nutrition
6640 Poe Ave Ste 225 (45414-2678)
PHONE..................866 615-8084
Charles Schininger, *Managing Member*
EMP: 30 **EST:** 2017
SQ FT: 11,000
SALES (est): 4.93MM **Privately Held**
Web: www.csaanimalnutrition.com
SIC: 0752 Animal specialty services

(G-7265)
CWCC INC
5030 Nebraska Ave (45424-6126)
PHONE..................937 236-6116
Zondra Seltner, *Dir*
EMP: 68
SALES (corp-wide): 2.81MM **Privately Held**
Web: www.inspirechildren.com
SIC: 8351 Preschool center
PA: Cwcc, Inc.
7677 Paragon Rd Ste D
Dayton OH 45459
937 938-1235

(G-7266)
CYCLE-LOGIK LLC
Also Called: Logik
4242 Clyo Rd (45440-6101)
PHONE..................937 381-7055
James Radbin, *CEO*
EMP: 70 **EST:** 2015
SALES (est): 2.4MM **Privately Held**
Web: www.cycle-logik.com
SIC: 7991 Physical fitness facilities

(G-7267)
DARCIE R CLARK LPCC LLC
Also Called: Riverscape Counseling
11 W Monument Ave Ste 100 (45402-1293)
PHONE..................937 319-4448
Darcie Clark, *Managing Member*
EMP: 38 **EST:** 2012
SALES (est): 647.36K **Privately Held**
Web: www.riverscapecounseling.com
SIC: 8322 7371 General counseling services; Computer software development and applications

(G-7268)
DAY AIR CREDIT UNION INC (PA)
3501 Wilmington Pike (45429-4840)
P.O. Box 292980 (45429-8980)
PHONE..................937 643-2160
William J Burke, *Pr*
Paul Hauck, *
Don Mccauley, *Ch*
EMP: 43 **EST:** 1945
SQ FT: 16,000
SALES (est): 34.11MM
SALES (corp-wide): 34.11MM **Privately Held**
Web: www.dayair.org
SIC: 6061 Federal credit unions

(G-7269)
DAYBREAK INC (PA)
605 S Patterson Blvd (45402-2649)
PHONE..................937 395-4600
Linda Kramer, *CEO*
EMP: 31 **EST:** 1975
SQ FT: 53,681
SALES (est): 7.28MM
SALES (corp-wide): 7.28MM **Privately Held**
Web: www.daybreakdayton.org
SIC: 8322 Social service center

(G-7270)
DAYTON APPLIANCE PARTS LLC (DH)
122 Sears St (45402-1765)
PHONE..................937 224-0487
Timothy Houtz, *Pr*
James Houtz, *VP*
Brian Baker, *Contrlr*
EMP: 35 **EST:** 2021
SQ FT: 15,000
SALES (est): 13.25MM
SALES (corp-wide): 1.1B **Privately Held**
Web: www.encompass.com
SIC: 5064 5722 Appliance parts, household; Appliance parts
HQ: Pt Intermediate Holdings Iii, Llc
1200 N Greenbriar Dr
Addison IL 60101
630 889-0172

(G-7271)
DAYTON AREA CHAMBER COMMERCE
8 N Main St # 100 (45402-1904)
PHONE..................937 226-1444
Phil Parker, *Pr*
Chris Kershner, *
EMP: 28 **EST:** 1907
SALES (est): 1.23MM **Privately Held**
Web: www.daytonchamber.org
SIC: 8611 Chamber of Commerce

(G-7272)
DAYTON BAG & BURLAP CO (PA)
Also Called: Dayton Bag & Burlap
322 Davis Ave (45403-2900)
P.O. Box 8 (45401-0008)
PHONE..................937 258-8000
Samuel W Lumby, *Pr*
Lisa Pierce, *
Charlie Cretcher, *
Jeffery S Rutter, *
◆ **EMP:** 46 **EST:** 1910
SQ FT: 140,000
SALES (est): 46.25MM
SALES (corp-wide): 46.25MM **Privately Held**
Web: www.daybag.com
SIC: 5199 Burlap

(G-7273)
DAYTON CHILDRENS CARDIOLOGY
1 Childrens Plz (45404-1873)
PHONE..................937 641-3418
Joseph E Ross, *Pr*
Doctor Joseph E Ross, *Pr*
Doctor Michael A Ralston, *VP*
EMP: 49 **EST:** 1964
SQ FT: 800
SALES (est): 3.79MM **Privately Held**
Web: www.childrensdayton.org
SIC: 8062 General medical and surgical hospitals

(G-7274)
DAYTON CHILDRENS HOSPITAL
4475 Far Hills Ave (45429-2405)
PHONE..................937 641-5760
Nancy Droze, *Brnch Mgr*
EMP: 65
SALES (corp-wide): 639.25MM **Privately Held**
Web: www.childrensdayton.org
SIC: 8062 General medical and surgical hospitals
PA: Dayton Children's Hospital
1 Childrens Plz
Dayton OH 45404
937 641-3000

(G-7275)
DAYTON CHILDRENS HOSPITAL
730 Valley St Ste C (45404-1958)
PHONE..................937 641-3500
Maria Nanagas, *Dir*
EMP: 70
SALES (corp-wide): 639.25MM **Privately Held**
Web: www.childrensdayton.org
SIC: 8062 General medical and surgical hospitals
PA: Dayton Children's Hospital
1 Childrens Plz
Dayton OH 45404
937 641-3000

(G-7276)
DAYTON CHILDRENS HOSPITAL (PA)
Also Called: Children's Medical Center
1 Childrens Plz (45404-1815)
PHONE..................937 641-3000
Deborah Feldman, *CEO*
Matt Graybill Fache, *
David Miller, *
▲ **EMP:** 2800 **EST:** 1919
SQ FT: 345,000
SALES (est): 639.25MM
SALES (corp-wide): 639.25MM **Privately Held**
Web: www.childrensdayton.org
SIC: 8069 Childrens' hospital

(G-7277)
DAYTON CORRUGATED PACKAGING CORP (PA)
Also Called: Commomwealth Container
1300 Wayne Ave (45410-1495)
PHONE..................937 254-8422
EMP: 36 **EST:** 1978
SALES (est): 9.27MM
SALES (corp-wide): 9.27MM **Privately Held**
Web: www.daytoncorrugated.com
SIC: 5199 Packaging materials

(G-7278)
DAYTON COUNTRY CLUB COMPANY
555 Kramer Rd (45419-3399)
PHONE..................937 294-3352
Steven Gongola, *Genl Mgr*
Jeffrey Grant, *
EMP: 90 **EST:** 1897
SALES (est): 4.71MM **Privately Held**
Web: www.daytoncountryclub.com
SIC: 7997 Country club, membership

(G-7279)
DAYTON DEV COALITION INC
900 Kettering Tower (45402)
PHONE..................937 222-4422
Jeff Hoagland, *CEO*
EMP: 34 **EST:** 2002
SALES (est): 6.19MM **Privately Held**
Web: www.daytonregion.com
SIC: 8742 Business planning and organizing services

(G-7280)
DAYTON DOOR SALES INC (PA)
Also Called: Overhead Door Co of Dayton
1112 Springfield St (45403-1405)
P.O. Box 134 (45404-0134)
PHONE..................937 253-9181
Dean Monnin, *Pr*
Kenneth F Monnin, *
Lawrence J Becker, *
EMP: 40 **EST:** 1960
SQ FT: 8,800
SALES (est): 13.42MM **Privately Held**
Web: www.daytondoorsales.com

GEOGRAPHIC SECTION
Dayton - Montgomery County (G-7302)

SIC: **1751** 7699 5031 Garage door, installation or erection; Garage door repair; Doors, garage

(G-7281)
DAYTON EYE SURGERY CENTER
81 Sylvania Dr (45440-3237)
PHONE.................................937 431-9531
Charles Kidwell Junior, *Prin*
EMP: 42 **EST:** 1998
SALES (est): 6.24MM **Privately Held**
Web: www.daytoneyes.com
SIC: **8011** Opthalmologist

(G-7282)
DAYTON FMLY PRACTICE ASSOC INC
3328 S Smithville Rd (45420-1569)
PHONE.................................937 254-5661
David Denka, *Pr*
Cynthia Kallet, *VP*
Arvin Nanda, *Treas*
EMP: 29 **EST:** 1958
SQ FT: 6,400
SALES (est): 2.52MM **Privately Held**
Web: www.daytonfpa.com
SIC: **8031** 8011 Offices and clinics of osteopathic physicians; General and family practice, physician/surgeon

(G-7283)
DAYTON FREIGHT LINES INC
6265 Executive Blvd Ste A (45424-1439)
PHONE.................................937 236-4880
Brian Gratch, *Mgr*
EMP: 374
SALES (corp-wide): 6.59B **Privately Held**
Web: www.daytonfreight.com
SIC: **4213** 4731 4231 Less-than-truckload (LTL); Freight consolidation; Trucking terminal facilities
PA: Dayton Freight Lines, Inc.
6450 Poe Ave
Dayton OH 45414
937 264-4060

(G-7284)
DAYTON FREIGHT LINES INC (PA)
Also Called: Dayton Freight
6450 Poe Ave Ste 311 (45414)
P.O. Box 340 (45377)
PHONE.................................937 264-4060
EMP: 250 **EST:** 1981
SALES (est): 6.59B
SALES (corp-wide): 6.59B **Privately Held**
Web: www.daytonfreight.com
SIC: **4213** 4212 Trucking, except local; Local trucking, without storage

(G-7285)
DAYTON GASTROENTEROLOGY LLC
75 Sylvania Dr (45440-3237)
PHONE.................................937 320-5050
EMP: 86 **EST:** 1983
SALES (est): 24.71MM
SALES (corp-wide): 24.71MM **Privately Held**
Web: www.daytongastro.com
SIC: **8011** Gastronomist
PA: One Gi Llc
65 Germantown Ct Ste 300
Cordova TN 38018
901 682-1203

(G-7286)
DAYTON HEART CENTER INC (PA)
1530 Needmore Rd Ste 300 (45414-3980)
PHONE.................................937 277-4274
Davic Joffe, *Pr*

C David Joffe, *
Joel H Tobiansky, *
Timothy D Markus, *Pt*
Enayatollah Tabesh, *
EMP: 60 **EST:** 1983
SQ FT: 38,000
SALES (est): 8.7MM **Privately Held**
Web: www.premierhealth.com
SIC: **8011** Cardiologist and cardio-vascular specialist

(G-7287)
DAYTON HISTORY
Also Called: CARILLON HISTORICAL PARK
1000 Carillon Blvd (45409)
PHONE.................................937 293-2841
Brady Kress, *CEO*
Eric Cluxton, *
Ron Rollins, *Vice Chairman**
Alexandra Ollinger, *
Ginny Strausburg, *
EMP: 125 **EST:** 1940
SALES (est): 9.18MM **Privately Held**
Web: www.daytonhistory.org
SIC: **8412** 7999 Museum; Tourist attractions, amusement park concessions and rides

(G-7288)
DAYTON HOSPICE INCORPORATED (PA)
Also Called: HOSPICE OF BUTLER AND WARREN C
324 Wilmington Ave (45420-1890)
PHONE.................................937 256-4490
Deborah Dailey, *Pr*
Jerry Durst, *
William H Macbeth, *
EMP: 275 **EST:** 1978
SQ FT: 85,000
SALES (est): 88.83MM
SALES (corp-wide): 88.83MM **Privately Held**
Web: www.hospiceofdayton.org
SIC: **8052** Personal care facility

(G-7289)
DAYTON HOTELS LLC
AC Hotel By Marriott Dayton
124 Madison St (45402-1712)
PHONE.................................937 965-7500
Ian Legros, *Brnch Mgr*
EMP: 100
SALES (corp-wide): 2.29MM **Privately Held**
Web: ac-hotels.marriott.com
SIC: **7011** Hotels
HQ: Dayton Hotels, Llc
20 Rockridge Rd
Englewood OH

(G-7290)
DAYTON MEDICAL IMAGING
Also Called: U S Diagnostics
7901 Schatz Pointe Dr (45459-3826)
PHONE.................................937 439-0390
Jeffrey Sergent, *Mgr*
EMP: 35
SQ FT: 3,372
SALES (est): 2MM **Privately Held**
SIC: **8011** 8071 Radiologist; X-ray laboratory, including dental

(G-7291)
DAYTON ORTHPDIC SRGERY SPT MDC
5491 Far Hills Ave (45429-2325)
PHONE.................................937 436-5763
EMP: 30 **EST:** 1996
SALES (est): 2.35MM **Privately Held**
Web: www.daytonorthopedicsurgery.com

SIC: **8011** Orthopedic physician

(G-7292)
DAYTON OSTEOPATHIC HOSPITAL
Also Called: Victor J Cassano Health Center
165 S Edwin C Moses Blvd (45402-8472)
PHONE.................................937 558-0200
Victor Cassano, *Prin*
EMP: 31
SALES (corp-wide): 2.46B **Privately Held**
Web: www.ketteringhealth.org
SIC: **8062** General medical and surgical hospitals
HQ: Dayton Osteopathic Hospital
405 W Grand Ave
Dayton OH 45405
937 762-1629

(G-7293)
DAYTON OSTEOPATHIC HOSPITAL (HQ)
Also Called: Grandview Hospital & Med Ctr
405 W Grand Ave (45405-7538)
PHONE.................................937 762-1629
Russell J Wetherell, *Pr*
Todd Anderson, *
Edward Mann, *
EMP: 1134 **EST:** 1926
SQ FT: 700,000
SALES (est): 729.64MM
SALES (corp-wide): 2.46B **Privately Held**
Web: www.ketteringhealth.org
SIC: **8062** General medical and surgical hospitals
PA: Kettering Adventist Healthcare
3535 Southern Blvd
Dayton OH 45429
937 298-4331

(G-7294)
DAYTON OSTEOPATHIC HOSPITAL
Also Called: Sugarcreek Health Center
6438 Wilmington Pike (45459-7022)
PHONE.................................937 558-3800
EMP: 27
SALES (corp-wide): 2.46B **Privately Held**
Web: www.ketteringhealth.org
SIC: **8062** General medical and surgical hospitals
HQ: Dayton Osteopathic Hospital
405 W Grand Ave
Dayton OH 45405
937 762-1629

(G-7295)
DAYTON OSTEOPATHIC HOSPITAL
Also Called: Southview Hosp & Fmly Hlth Ctr
1997 Miamisburg Centerville Rd (45459)
PHONE.................................937 439-6000
Greg Henderson, *Brnch Mgr*
EMP: 35
SQ FT: 2,070
SALES (corp-wide): 2.46B **Privately Held**
Web: www.ketteringhealth.org
SIC: **8062** 5912 General medical and surgical hospitals; Drug stores
HQ: Dayton Osteopathic Hospital
405 W Grand Ave
Dayton OH 45405
937 762-1629

(G-7296)
DAYTON OSTEOPATHIC HOSPITAL
7677 Yankee St (45459-3475)
PHONE.................................937 401-6503
EMP: 27
SALES (corp-wide): 2.46B **Privately Held**
Web: www.ketteringhealth.org
SIC: **8062** General medical and surgical hospitals
HQ: Dayton Osteopathic Hospital
405 W Grand Ave
Dayton OH 45405
937 762-1629

(G-7297)
DAYTON PERFORMING ARTS ALIANCE
126 N Main St Ste 210 (45402-1766)
PHONE.................................937 224-3521
Paul Helfrich, *Ex Dir*
Wendy Campbell, *
Davis Reed, *Vice Chairman**
Daniel Deitz, *
Julie Smallwood, *
EMP: 46 **EST:** 1933
SQ FT: 2,022
SALES (est): 8.23MM **Privately Held**
Web: www.daytonperformingarts.org
SIC: **7922** Performing arts center production

(G-7298)
DAYTON PHYSICIANS LLC (PA)
6680 Poe Ave Ste 200 (45414-2855)
PHONE.................................937 280-8400
EMP: 84 **EST:** 2005
SQ FT: 5,000
SALES (est): 22.86MM
SALES (corp-wide): 22.86MM **Privately Held**
Web: www.daytonphysicians.com
SIC: **8011** Oncologist

(G-7299)
DAYTON PHYSICIANS LLC
8881 N Main St (45415-1333)
PHONE.................................937 208-2636
Robert Baird, *Prin*
EMP: 43 **EST:** 2005
SALES (est): 5.19MM **Privately Held**
Web: www.daytonphysicians.com
SIC: **8011** Oncologist

(G-7300)
DAYTON PROF BASBAL CLB LLC
Also Called: Dayton Dragons Baseball
220 N Patterson Blvd 1st Fl (45402-1279)
P.O. Box 2107 (45401-2107)
PHONE.................................937 228-2287
Robert Murphy, *Pr*
Eric Deutsch, *
EMP: 28 **EST:** 1999
SALES (est): 141.04K
SALES (corp-wide): 2.6MM **Privately Held**
Web: www.daytondragons.com
SIC: **7941** Baseball club, professional and semi-professional
PA: Palisades Arcadia Baseball Llc
50 W Broad St Ste 1330
Columbus OH

(G-7301)
DAYTON REALTORS
1515 S Main St (45409-2644)
P.O. Box 111 (45401-0111)
PHONE.................................937 223-0900
Carlton Jackson, *CEO*
EMP: 30 **EST:** 1909
SQ FT: 18,000
SALES (est): 3.14MM **Privately Held**
Web: www.daytonrealtors.com
SIC: **8611** 6531 Real estate board; Real estate agents and managers

(G-7302)
DAYTON SYNCHRNOUS SPPORT CTR I
Also Called: Dssc
1700 E Monument Ave (45402-1364)
PHONE.................................937 226-1559
Dan Schreirer, *Pr*

Dayton - Montgomery County (G-7303)

GEOGRAPHIC SECTION

Norm S Klein, *Pr*
EMP: 27 **EST**: 1991
SQ FT: 45,000
SALES (est): 4.13MM
SALES (corp-wide): 77.69MM **Privately Held**
SIC: 4789 4212 4731 Freight car loading and unloading; Local trucking, without storage; Freight forwarding
PA: Fcs Industries, Inc.
9850 Pelham Rd
Taylor MI 48180
313 295-0505

(G-7303)
DAYTON V LW LLC
33 E 5th St (45402-2403)
PHONE....................937 229-9836
Charles Everhardt, *Mgr*
EMP: 47
SALES (est): 2.35MM **Privately Held**
SIC: 7011 Hotels

(G-7304)
DAYTON VTREO-RETINAL ASSOC INC
301 W 1st St Ste 300 (45402-3038)
PHONE....................937 228-5015
Jeffrey A Horwitz Md, *Pr*
Steven A Miller Md, *Sec*
EMP: 36 **EST**: 1976
SALES (est): 1.25MM **Privately Held**
SIC: 8011 Opthalmologist

(G-7305)
DAYTON WALLS & CEILINGS INC
4328 Webster St (45414-4936)
P.O. Box 13561 (45413-0561)
PHONE....................937 277-0531
Eric Peterson, *Pr*
John Peterson, *
Robert Coyle, *
EMP: 82 **EST**: 1986
SQ FT: 14,000
SALES (est): 8.12MM **Privately Held**
Web: www.dwceiling.com
SIC: 1742 Drywall

(G-7306)
DAYTON WINDUSTRIAL CO
137 E Helena St (45404-1052)
P.O. Box 931112 (31193-1112)
PHONE....................937 461-2603
Greg Jackson, *Pr*
EMP: 30 **EST**: 1910
SALES (est): 10.54MM
SALES (corp-wide): 3.02B **Privately Held**
Web: www.winsupplyinc.com
SIC: 5085 Valves and fittings
PA: Winsupply Inc.
3110 Kettering Blvd
Moraine OH 45439
937 294-5331

(G-7307)
DDC GROUP INC
Also Called: Brightstar Care
10536 Success Ln (45458-3561)
PHONE....................937 619-3111
Patrick Luers, *Pr*
Kelly Luers, *
EMP: 170 **EST**: 2009
SALES (est): 4.28MM **Privately Held**
Web: www.brightstarcare.com
SIC: 8082 Home health care services

(G-7308)
DELOITTE & TOUCHE LLP
220 E Monument Ave Ste 500 (45402)
PHONE....................937 223-8821
Edward T Bentley, *Mgr*
EMP: 43
Web: www.deloitte.com
SIC: 8721 8742 Certified public accountant; Management consulting services
HQ: Deloitte & Touche Llp
30 Rockefeller Plz # 4350
New York NY 10112
212 492-4000

(G-7309)
DELOITTE CONSULTING LLP
711 E Monument Ave Ste 201 (45402)
PHONE....................937 223-8821
EMP: 43
SIC: 8742 8748 Management consulting services; Business consulting, nec
HQ: Deloitte Consulting Llp
30 Rockefeller Plz
New York NY 10112
212 492-4000

(G-7310)
DERMATLGISTS OF SOUTHWEST OHIO (PA)
5300 Far Hills Ave Ste 100 (45429-2323)
PHONE....................937 435-2094
Stephen B Levitt Md, *Pr*
Thomas G Olsen Md, *VP*
EMP: 45 **EST**: 1978
SQ FT: 3,000
SALES (est): 10.62MM
SALES (corp-wide): 10.62MM **Privately Held**
Web: www.docsdermgroup.com
SIC: 8011 Dermatologist

(G-7311)
DESIGN HOMES & DEVELOPMENT CO
Also Called: Dhdc
8534 Yankee St Ste A (45458-1889)
PHONE....................937 438-3667
Shery Oakes, *Pr*
EMP: 35 **EST**: 1987
SALES (est): 5MM **Privately Held**
Web: www.designhomesco.com
SIC: 8711 1542 1521 6531 Civil engineering; Commercial and office building contractors; Single-family housing construction; Real estate agents and managers

(G-7312)
DIALYSIS CENTERS DAYTON LLC
Also Called: Dialysis Center Dayton- North
455 Turner Rd (45415-3630)
PHONE....................937 208-7900
Deanna Shaffer, *Brnch Mgr*
EMP: 68
SALES (corp-wide): 9.59MM **Privately Held**
Web: www.renalphysicians.com
SIC: 8092 Kidney dialysis centers
PA: Dialysis Centers Of Dayton, L.L.C.
110 N Main St Ste 500
Dayton OH 45402
937 499-9866

(G-7313)
DIGESTIVE CARE INC
75 Sylvania Dr (45440-3237)
PHONE....................937 320-5050
Jonhathan Saxe Md, *Pr*
William Wilson, *
Richard C Cammerer Md, *VP*
Giti Rostami Md, *Physician*
EMP: 53 **EST**: 1984
SALES (est): 6.88MM **Privately Held**
Web: www.daytongastro.com
SIC: 8011 Gastronomist

(G-7314)
DIGESTIVE SPECIALISTS INC
Also Called: Digestive Endoscopy Center
999 Brubaker Dr Ste 1 (45429-3505)
PHONE....................937 534-7330
Ramesh Gandhi, *Pr*
Harold Fishman, *
▲ **EMP**: 30 **EST**: 1969
SALES (est): 7.7MM **Privately Held**
Web: www.digestivespecialists.com
SIC: 8011 Physicians' office, including specialists

(G-7315)
DINSMORE & SHOHL LLP
1 S Main St Ste 1300 (45402-2058)
PHONE....................937 449-6400
Cliff Rowe, *Mgr*
EMP: 48
SALES (corp-wide): 169.43MM **Privately Held**
Web: www.dinsmore.com
SIC: 8111 General practice attorney, lawyer
PA: Dinsmore & Shohl Llp
255 E 5th St Ste 1900
Cincinnati OH 45202
513 977-8200

(G-7316)
DOMESTIC RELATIONS
301 W 3rd St Ste 500 (45402-1446)
PHONE....................937 225-4063
Mike Howley, *Dir*
EMP: 37 **EST**: 1800
SALES (est): 460K **Privately Held**
Web: www.mcohio.org
SIC: 8743 Public relations and publicity

(G-7317)
DRT HOLDINGS INC (PA)
618 Greenmount Blvd (45419-3271)
PHONE....................937 298-7391
EMP: 60 **EST**: 2008
SALES (est): 177.41MM **Privately Held**
Web: www.drtholdingsllc.com
SIC: 6719 3599 3728 Investment holding companies, except banks; Machine shop, jobbing and repair; Aircraft parts and equipment, nec

(G-7318)
DRURY HOTELS COMPANY LLC
Also Called: Drury Inn & Suites Dayton N
6616 Miller Ln (45414-2663)
PHONE....................937 454-5200
Steven Patton, *Mgr*
EMP: 45
SALES (corp-wide): 555.12MM **Privately Held**
Web: www.druryhotels.com
SIC: 7011 Hotels
PA: Drury Hotels Company, Llc
13075 Manchester Rd # 100
Saint Louis MO 63131
314 429-2255

(G-7319)
DYER GRFALO MANN SCHLTZ A LGA (PA)
131 N Ludlow St Ste 1400 (45402-1110)
PHONE....................937 223-8888
Carmine Garofalo, *Pr*
Michael E Dyer, *
Douglas A Mann, *
EMP: 56 **EST**: 1992
SALES (est): 12.58MM **Privately Held**
Web: www.ohiotiger.com
SIC: 8111 General practice law office

(G-7320)
E-MEK TECHNOLOGIES LLC (PA)
Also Called: E-Mek Technologies
7410 Webster St (45414-5816)
PHONE....................937 424-3166
Larry Crossley, *Managing Member*
Larry Crossley, *Pr*
▲ **EMP**: 40 **EST**: 2006
SALES (est): 11.1MM **Privately Held**
Web: www.e-mek.com
SIC: 7379 Online services technology consultants

(G-7321)
EAGLE CERTIFICATION GROUP
40 N Main St (45423-1021)
PHONE....................937 293-2000
Becki Kauscher, *Prin*
EMP: 55 **EST**: 2019
SALES (est): 1.32MM **Privately Held**
Web: www.eaglecertificationgroup.com
SIC: 8748 Environmental consultant

(G-7322)
EARLY EXPRESS SERVICES INC
Also Called: Early Express Mail Services
1333 E 2nd St (45403-1020)
P.O. Box 2422 (45401-2422)
PHONE....................937 223-5801
Cindy Woodward, *Pr*
Karen Sensel, *
EMP: 29 **EST**: 1977
SQ FT: 17,000
SALES (est): 2.36MM **Privately Held**
Web: www.earlyexpress.com
SIC: 7331 4212 7374 Mailing service; Delivery service, vehicular; Data processing service

(G-7323)
EAST WAY BEHAVIORAL HLTH CARE
600 Wayne Ave (45410-1122)
PHONE....................937 222-4900
Jonh Strahm, *Pr*
Jonh Strahm, *CEO*
Bob Groskops, *
EMP: 97 **EST**: 1957
SQ FT: 25,000
SALES (est): 5.14MM
SALES (corp-wide): 29.94MM **Privately Held**
Web: www.eastway.org
SIC: 8093 8742 8249 Mental health clinic, outpatient; Hospital and health services consultant; Medical training services
PA: Eastway Corporation
600 Wayne Ave
Dayton OH 45410
937 496-2000

(G-7324)
EASTWAY CORPORATION (PA)
Also Called: EASTWAY BEHAVORIAL HEALTHCARE
600 Wayne Ave (45410-1199)
P.O. Box 983 (45401-0983)
PHONE....................937 496-2000
John F Strahm, *CEO*
Mary K Norman, *
James D Sherman, *
Helen A Bailey, *Corporate Secretary**
Robert J Groskopf, *
EMP: 115 **EST**: 1957
SALES (est): 29.94MM
SALES (corp-wide): 29.94MM **Privately Held**
Web: www.eastway.org
SIC: 8063 8322 Mental hospital, except for the mentally retarded; Individual and family services

GEOGRAPHIC SECTION
Dayton - Montgomery County (G-7347)

(G-7325)
ECHOING HILLS VILLAGE INC
3400 Stop 8 Rd (45414-3428)
PHONE..................800 419-6513
EMP: 31
SALES (corp-wide): 39.8MM **Privately Held**
Web: www.ehvi.org
SIC: 8699 Charitable organization
PA: Echoing Hills Village, Inc.
36272 County Road 79
Warsaw OH 43844
740 327-2311

(G-7326)
ECHOING HILLS VILLAGE INC
Also Called: Echoing Wood Residential Cntr
5455 Salem Bend Dr (45426-1609)
PHONE..................937 854-5151
Rose Barber, Mgr
EMP: 77
SALES (corp-wide): 39.8MM **Privately Held**
Web: www.ehvi.org
SIC: 7032 8051 Sporting and recreational camps; Skilled nursing care facilities
PA: Echoing Hills Village, Inc.
36272 County Road 79
Warsaw OH 43844
740 327-2311

(G-7327)
ECHOING HILLS VILLAGE INC
Also Called: Echoing Valley
7040 Union Schoolhouse Rd (45424-5207)
PHONE..................937 237-7881
Rose Barber, Mgr
EMP: 71
SALES (corp-wide): 39.8MM **Privately Held**
Web: www.ehvi.org
SIC: 7032 8059 Sporting and recreational camps; Home for the mentally retarded, ex. skilled or intermediate
PA: Echoing Hills Village, Inc.
36272 County Road 79
Warsaw OH 43844
740 327-2311

(G-7328)
ECONOMY LINEN & TOWEL SERVICE INC (PA)
Also Called: Ecomed Medical Linen Service
80 Mead St (45402-2395)
PHONE..................937 222-4625
EMP: 175 EST: 1931
SALES (est): 19.82MM
SALES (corp-wide): 19.82MM **Privately Held**
Web: www.economylinen.com
SIC: 7213 7211 Linen supply; Power laundries, family and commercial

(G-7329)
EDAPTIVE COMPUTING INC
1245 Lyons Rd Ste G (45458-1818)
PHONE..................937 433-0477
Anju Chawla, CEO
Praveen Chawla, *
EMP: 70 EST: 1997
SQ FT: 10,000
SALES (est): 9.55MM **Privately Held**
Web: www.edaptive.com
SIC: 7371 Computer software development

(G-7330)
EFIX IT SOLUTIONS LLC
Also Called: It Services
3920 Kittyhawk Dr (45403-2842)
PHONE..................937 476-7533
Edwin Kariuki, Managing Member
EMP: 45 EST: 2013
SALES (est): 896.12K **Privately Held**
Web: www.computerrepairindaytonoh.com
SIC: 7378 Computer and data processing equipment repair/maintenance

(G-7331)
ELIZABETH PLACE HOLDINGS LLC
1 Elizabeth Pl (45417-3445)
PHONE..................323 300-3700
EMP: 30 EST: 2003
SALES (est): 2.36MM **Privately Held**
SIC: 8011 Physicians' office, including specialists

(G-7332)
ELIZABETHS NEW LIFE CENTER INC
Also Called: ELIZABETH'S NEW LIFE WOMEN'S C
2201 N Main St (45405-3528)
PHONE..................937 226-7414
Vivian Koob, Ex Dir
EMP: 54 EST: 1989
SALES (est): 5.72MM **Privately Held**
Web: www.enlc.life
SIC: 8322 Individual and family services

(G-7333)
ELLIOTT TOOL TECHNOLOGIES LTD (PA)
Also Called: Elliott
1760 Tuttle Ave (45403-3428)
PHONE..................937 253-6133
EMP: 66 EST: 1892
SQ FT: 37,000
SALES (est): 11.87MM **Privately Held**
Web: www.elliott-tool.com
SIC: 7359 3542 5072 3541 Equipment rental and leasing, nec; Machine tools, metal forming type; Hand tools; Machine tools, metal cutting type

(G-7334)
ELLIPSE SOLUTIONS LLC
7917 Washington Woods Dr (45459-4026)
PHONE..................937 312-1547
EMP: 31 EST: 2010
SALES (est): 3.9MM **Privately Held**
Web: www.ellipsesolutions.com
SIC: 8748 Systems engineering consultant, ex. computer or professional

(G-7335)
EMS TEAM LLC
Also Called: Buckeye Ambulance
1371 W Rahn Rd (45459-1431)
PHONE..................800 735-8190
Dereck Pristas, CEO
Dereck Pristas, Managing Member
Donald Butts, *
EMP: 40 EST: 2011
SQ FT: 12,000
SALES (est): 4.53MM **Privately Held**
Web: www.emsteam.net
SIC: 4119 Ambulance service

(G-7336)
ENVIRNMENTAL ENGRG SYSTEMS INC
Also Called: Honeywell Authorized Dealer
17 Creston Ave (45404-1701)
PHONE..................937 228-6492
Eric Miske, Pr
Thomas J Miske, *
Jeredythe Miske, *
Martin Stewart, *
EMP: 30 EST: 1975
SQ FT: 10,000
SALES (est): 2.31MM **Privately Held**
Web: www.eesfacilityservices.com
SIC: 1711 Mechanical contractor

(G-7337)
ENVIROCONTROL SYSTEMS INC
165 E Helena St (45404)
P.O. Box 247 (45409)
PHONE..................937 275-4718
Lisa E Crosley, Pr
Doug Crosley, *
EMP: 34 EST: 1997
SQ FT: 1,200
SALES (est): 6.08MM **Privately Held**
Web: www.envirocontrolsystems.com
SIC: 1711 Mechanical contractor

(G-7338)
EQUITAS HEALTH INC
Also Called: Dayton Pharmacy
1222 S Patterson Blvd Ste 110 (45402-2657)
PHONE..................937 424-1440
Matthew Insley, Brnch Mgr
EMP: 28
Web: www.equitashealth.com
SIC: 8062 General medical and surgical hospitals
PA: Equitas Health, Inc.
1105 Schrock Rd Ste 400
Columbus OH 43229

(G-7339)
ERIE CONSTRUCTION MID-WEST INC
Also Called: Erie Construction Co
3520 Sudachi Dr (45414-2435)
PHONE..................937 898-4688
Jeff Block, Mgr
EMP: 87
SALES (corp-wide): 139.2MM **Privately Held**
Web: www.eriehome.com
SIC: 1521 5211 1799 1761 General remodeling, single-family houses; Door and window products; Kitchen and bathroom remodeling; Siding contractor
PA: Erie Construction Mid-West, Llc
3516 Granite Cir
Toledo OH 43617
567 408-2145

(G-7340)
EVANGLCAL RTRMENT VLLGES INC D
Also Called: Friendship Village of Dayton
5790 Denlinger Rd (45426-1838)
PHONE..................937 837-5581
Reverend Henry Gathagan, Pr
EMP: 230 EST: 1972
SQ FT: 439,000
SALES (est): 4.3MM **Privately Held**
Web: www.trousdalelc.org
SIC: 6513 Retirement hotel operation

(G-7341)
EXCELLENCE IN MOTIVATION INC
6 N Main St Ste 370 (45402-1908)
PHONE..................763 445-3000
Robert Miller, Pr
John Kernan, *
EMP: 160 EST: 1993
SALES (est): 9.68MM
SALES (corp-wide): 49.87MM **Privately Held**
SIC: 8748 8741 Business consulting, nec; Management services
PA: One10 L.L.C.
11055 Wayzata Blvd # 900
Minnetonka MN 55305
763 445-3000

(G-7342)
EXTERMITAL CHEMICALS INC
Also Called: Extermital Pest Control
1026 Wayne Ave (45410-1404)
P.O. Box 1533 (45401-1533)
PHONE..................937 253-6144
Terry Teague, Pr
Lee Schroeder, VP
Walter Moore, Treas
Frederick Young, Sec
EMP: 28 EST: 1935
SQ FT: 6,000
SALES (est): 2.48MM **Privately Held**
Web: www.extermital.com
SIC: 7342 Pest control in structures

(G-7343)
EXTRACT LLC
425 N Findlay St Ste 218 (45404-2287)
PHONE..................937 732-9495
Nadine Jackson, Prin
EMP: 70 EST: 2016
SALES (est): 849.77K **Privately Held**
SIC: 7389 7381 Personal investigation service; Security guard service

(G-7344)
EYE LASER & SURGERY CENTER
4235 Indian Ripple Rd (45440-3284)
PHONE..................937 427-7800
Robert Rich, Prin
EMP: 28 EST: 2010
SALES (est): 1.53MM **Privately Held**
Web: www.stahlvision.com
SIC: 8011 Surgeon

(G-7345)
FAI ELECTRONICS CORP
Also Called: Future Active Industrial Elec
4407 Walnut St Ste 250 (45440-1493)
PHONE..................937 426-0090
Ted Smith, Mgr
EMP: 49
SALES (corp-wide): 3.15B **Privately Held**
SIC: 5065 Electronic parts
HQ: Fai Electronics Corp
41 Main St
Bolton MA 01740

(G-7346)
FAR HILLS OPEN MRI INC
5529 Far Hills Ave (45429-2225)
PHONE..................937 435-6674
Ron Fiesta, Pr
EMP: 75 EST: 2002
SALES (est): 1.88MM
SALES (corp-wide): 12.07MM **Privately Held**
SIC: 8011 Radiologist
PA: Inmed Diagnostics Services Of Sc, Llc
126 S Assembly St
Columbia SC 29201
803 988-0082

(G-7347)
FAR HILLS SURGICAL CENTER LLC (PA)
2400 Miami Valley Dr # 2000 (45459-4774)
PHONE..................937 208-8000
Donald Ames Md, Ch
Michael Galvin, Admn
EMP: 30 EST: 1998
SALES (est): 4.78MM
SALES (corp-wide): 4.78MM **Privately Held**
Web: www.farhillssurgical.com
SIC: 8011 Surgeon

Dayton - Montgomery County (G-7348) GEOGRAPHIC SECTION

(G-7348)
FAR OAKS ORTHOPEDISTS INC (PA)
6438 Wilmington Pike Ste 220 (45459-7021)
PHONE.....................937 433-5309
Daniel Dunaway Md, *Pr*
Timothy Quinn Md, *VP*
Steven Klenhenz Md, *VP*
Donald Ames Md, *VP*
John Lochner Md, *VP*
EMP: 35 **EST:** 1961
SALES (est): 3.2MM
SALES (corp-wide): 3.2MM **Privately Held**
Web: www.faroaksorthopedists.com
SIC: 8062 General medical and surgical hospitals

(G-7349)
FAR OAKS ORTHOPEDISTS INC
3737 Southern Blvd Ste 2100 (45429)
PHONE.....................937 433-5309
Daniel J Dunaway Md, *Prin*
EMP: 32
SALES (corp-wide): 3.2MM **Privately Held**
Web: www.faroaksorthopedists.com
SIC: 8011 Sports medicine specialist, physician
PA: Far Oaks Orthopedists, Inc.
6438 Wilmington Pike # 220
Dayton OH 45459
937 433-5309

(G-7350)
FERGUSON CONSTRUCTION COMPANY
825 S Ludlow St (45402-2612)
PHONE.....................937 274-1173
Jay T Gearon, *Brnch Mgr*
EMP: 37
SALES (corp-wide): 73.11MM **Privately Held**
Web: www.ferguson-construction.com
SIC: 1541 1542 Industrial buildings, new construction, nec; Nonresidential construction, nec
PA: Ferguson Construction Company Inc
400 Canal St
Sidney OH 45365
937 498-2381

(G-7351)
FERGUSON HILLS INC (PA)
Also Called: Caesar Creek Flea Market
7812 Mcewen Rd Ste 200 (45459-4069)
PHONE.....................513 539-4497
Louis Levin, *CEO*
Allen Levin, *VP*
EMP: 76 **EST:** 1979
SQ FT: 3,000
SALES (est): 1.93MM
SALES (corp-wide): 1.93MM **Privately Held**
SIC: 7389 Flea market

(G-7352)
FIRST DAY FINCL FEDERAL CR UN (PA)
1030 N Main St (45405-4212)
P.O. Box 407 (45405-0407)
PHONE.....................937 222-4546
Ben Roth, *Pr*
EMP: 30 **EST:** 1934
SQ FT: 6,000
SALES (est): 1.98MM
SALES (corp-wide): 1.98MM **Privately Held**
SIC: 6061 6162 Federal credit unions; Mortgage bankers and loan correspondents

(G-7353)
FIRST PRIORITY URGENT CARE LLC
1 Elizabeth Pl Ste 100 (45417-3445)
PHONE.....................937 723-7230
Jenny V Wariboko, *CEO*
EMP: 42
SALES (corp-wide): 419.17K **Privately Held**
Web: www.firstpriorityurgentcare.com
SIC: 8011 Freestanding emergency medical center
PA: First Priority Urgent Care Llc
5130 Salem Ave
Trotwood OH 45426
937 529-4443

(G-7354)
FIRST STUDENT INC
301 Gaddis Blvd (45403-1314)
P.O. Box 49 (43040-0049)
PHONE.....................937 645-0201
Kim Scharf, *Mgr*
EMP: 415
Web: www.firststudentinc.com
SIC: 4151 School buses
PA: First Student, Inc.
191 Rosa Parks St Ste 800
Cincinnati OH 45202

(G-7355)
FISHEL COMPANY
7651 Center Point 70 Blvd (45424-5193)
PHONE.....................937 233-2268
Chris Sands, *Mgr*
EMP: 42
SALES (corp-wide): 758.31MM **Privately Held**
Web: www.teamfishel.com
SIC: 1623 1794 Gas main construction; Excavation work
PA: The Fishel Company
1366 Dublin Rd
Columbus OH 43215
614 274-8100

(G-7356)
FISK KINNE HOLDINGS INC
Also Called: Acculube
403 Homestead Ave (45417-3921)
P.O. Box 3807 (45401-3807)
PHONE.....................937 461-9906
EMP: 40
SIC: 5169 5172 Industrial chemicals; Lubricating oils and greases

(G-7357)
FIVE RIVERS METROPARKS
2222 N James H Mcgee Blvd (45417-9544)
PHONE.....................937 278-2601
EMP: 43
Web: www.metroparks.org
SIC: 7999 Recreation services
PA: Five Rivers Metroparks
409 E Monument Ave # 300
Dayton OH 45402

(G-7358)
FIVE RIVERS METROPARKS
600 E 2nd St (45402-1381)
PHONE.....................937 228-2088
Jim Harless, *Brnch Mgr*
EMP: 43
Web: www.metroparks.org
SIC: 7999 Recreation services
PA: Five Rivers Metroparks
409 E Monument Ave # 300
Dayton OH 45402

(G-7359)
FLANAGAN LBERMAN HOFFMAN SWAIM
10 N Ludlow St Ste 200 (45402-1856)
PHONE.....................937 223-5200
Patrick A Flanagan, *Pt*
James E Swaim, *Pt*
Wayne P Stephan, *Pt*
Bradley C Smith, *Pt*
Dennis Lieberman, *Pt*
EMP: 32 **EST:** 1930
SALES (est): 4.34MM **Privately Held**
Web: www.flrlegal.com
SIC: 8111 General practice attorney, lawyer

(G-7360)
FOODBANK INC
56 Armor Pl (45417-1187)
PHONE.....................937 461-0265
Burma Thomas, *CEO*
Michelle Riley, *
EMP: 29 **EST:** 2009
SALES (est): 34.02MM **Privately Held**
Web: www.thefoodbankdayton.org
SIC: 8322 Social service center

(G-7361)
FOODLINER INC
5560 Brentlinger Dr (45414-3510)
PHONE.....................937 898-0075
Lowell Stepp, *Brnch Mgr*
EMP: 64
SALES (corp-wide): 114.96MM **Privately Held**
Web: www.foodliner.com
SIC: 4213 Contract haulers
PA: Foodliner, Inc.
2099 Southpark Ct Ste 1
Dubuque IA 52003
563 584-2670

(G-7362)
FORNEY INDUSTRIES INC
3435 Stop 8 Rd (45414-3427)
PHONE.....................937 494-6102
Kyle Pettine, *COO*
EMP: 54
SALES (corp-wide): 43.61MM **Privately Held**
Web: www.forneyind.com
SIC: 5084 Welding machinery and equipment
PA: Forney Industries, Inc.
2057 Vermont Dr
Fort Collins CO 80525
800 521-6038

(G-7363)
FOUNDTION FOR CMNTY BLOOD CNTR (PA)
Also Called: Community Tissue Services
349 S Main St (45402)
PHONE.....................937 461-3450
David M Smith, *CEO*
Julia M Belden, *
Jodi L Minneman, *
Diane L Wilson, *
Don Frericks, *CAO*
EMP: 250 **EST:** 1964
SQ FT: 110,000
SALES (est): 210
SALES (corp-wide): 210 **Privately Held**
Web: www.solvita.org
SIC: 8099 Blood bank

(G-7364)
FOX CLEANERS INC (PA)
4333 N Main St (45405-5035)
PHONE.....................937 276-4171
John Roberts, *Pr*
EMP: 50 **EST:** 1945
SQ FT: 30,000
SALES (est): 1.01MM
SALES (corp-wide): 1.01MM **Privately Held**
Web: www.thefoxcleaners.com
SIC: 7216 7215 Drycleaning plants, except rugs; Laundry, coin-operated

(G-7365)
FRANCISCAN AT ST LEONARD
8100 Clyo Rd (45458-2720)
PHONE.....................937 433-0480
Timothy Dressman, *Ex Dir*
EMP: 89 **EST:** 1985
SALES (est): 3.38MM **Privately Held**
Web: www.chilivingcommunities.org
SIC: 8059 8052 Personal care home, with health care; Intermediate care facilities

(G-7366)
FRANKLIN EQUIPMENT LLC
Also Called: Franklin Equipment
1500 Kuntz Rd (45404-1233)
PHONE.....................937 951-3819
EMP: 48
SALES (corp-wide): 14.33B **Publicly Held**
Web: www.unitedrentals.com
SIC: 5083 5084 Tractors, agricultural; Industrial machinery and equipment
HQ: Franklin Equipment, Llc
4141 Hamilton Square Blvd
Groveport OH 43125

(G-7367)
FRANKLIN IRON & METAL CORP
1939 E 1st St (45403-1131)
PHONE.....................937 253-8184
Jack Edelman, *Pr*
Debra Edelman, *
▲ **EMP:** 105 **EST:** 1961
SQ FT: 60,000
SALES (est): 22.21MM **Privately Held**
Web: www.franklin-iron.com
SIC: 5093 3341 3312 Ferrous metal scrap and waste; Secondary nonferrous metals; Blast furnaces and steel mills

(G-7368)
FREUND FREZE ARNOLD A LGAL PRO (PA)
Also Called: Freund, Freeze & Arnold
10 N Ludlow St (45402-1854)
PHONE.....................937 222-2424
Neil F Freund, *CEO*
Stephen V Freeze, *
Thomas B Bruns, *
Wayne E Waite, *
John J Garvey Junior, *Sec*
EMP: 90 **EST:** 1984
SALES (est): 18.45MM
SALES (corp-wide): 18.45MM **Privately Held**
Web: www.ffalaw.com
SIC: 8111 General practice attorney, lawyer

(G-7369)
FRIENDS FIVE RIVERS METROPARKS (PA)
1375 E Siebenthaler Ave (45414-5357)
PHONE.....................937 275-7275
Charles Shoemaker, *Ex Dir*
EMP: 247 **EST:** 1963
SQ FT: 9,400
SALES (est): 2.48MM
SALES (corp-wide): 2.48MM **Privately Held**
Web: www.metroparks.org
SIC: 7999 Recreation services

GEOGRAPHIC SECTION
Dayton - Montgomery County (G-7395)

(G-7370)
FRYE MECHANICAL INC
1500 Humphrey Ave (45410-3307)
PHONE................................937 222-8750
Rodney Frye, *Pr*
Naomi Frye, *
Melissa Frye, *
EMP: 80 **EST:** 2002
SALES (est): 15.16MM **Privately Held**
Web: www.fryemechanical.com
SIC: 1711 Mechanical contractor

(G-7371)
FRYMAN-KUCK GENERAL CONTRS INC
5150 Webster St (45414-4228)
P.O. Box 13655 (45413-0655)
PHONE................................937 274-2892
Paul Kuck, *Pr*
Randy Kuck, *
Kent Kuck, *
Kurt Kuck, *
EMP: 50 **EST:** 1945
SALES (est): 10.57MM **Privately Held**
SIC: 1542 1541 1629 1622 Commercial and office buildings, renovation and repair; Renovation, remodeling and repairs; industrial buildings; Waste water and sewage treatment plant construction; Highway construction, elevated

(G-7372)
G7 SERVICES INC
Also Called: ServiceMaster By Angler
1524 E 2nd St (45403-1025)
PHONE................................937 256-3473
Mark Gerken, *VP*
Geoffrey Ganz, *
EMP: 40 **EST:** 2017
SALES (est): 2.54MM **Privately Held**
Web: www.servicemasterrestore.com
SIC: 7349 Building maintenance services, nec

(G-7373)
GEM CITY CHEMICALS INC
1287 Air City Ave (45404-1203)
P.O. Box 251 (45404-0251)
PHONE................................937 224-0711
Thomas Weber, *Pr*
EMP: 100 **EST:** 1957
SQ FT: 8,000
SALES (est): 2.69MM **Privately Held**
SIC: 7389 5169 Packaging and labeling services; Industrial chemicals

(G-7374)
GEM CITY HOME CARE LLC (HQ)
Also Called: AMEDISYS
8534 Yankee St Ste 2a (45458-1889)
PHONE................................937 438-9100
EMP: 36 **EST:** 2000
SALES (est): 13.34MM **Publicly Held**
Web: www.gemcityhc.com
SIC: 7361 Nurses' registry
PA: Amedisys, Inc.
3854 American Way Ste A
Baton Rouge LA 70816

(G-7375)
GILLSON SOLUTIONS INC
3100 Research Blvd Ste 260 (45420)
PHONE................................937 751-0119
EMP: 31
SALES (corp-wide): 761.64K **Privately Held**
SIC: 4213 Trucking, except local
PA: Gillson Solutions Inc
1801 E Dr Mrtn Lther King
Stockton CA 95205
925 400-9094

(G-7376)
GLOBAL ASSOCIATES INC
7106 Corporate Way (45459-4227)
PHONE................................937 312-1204
EMP: 35
SQ FT: 17,000
SALES (est): 4.36MM **Privately Held**
Web: www.gassociates.com
SIC: 7379 Computer related consulting services

(G-7377)
GOHYPERSONIC INCORPORATED
Also Called: Ghi
848 E Monument Ave (45402-1312)
PHONE................................937 331-9460
Lance Jacobsen, *Pr*
EMP: 32 **EST:** 2006
SALES (est): 4.15MM **Privately Held**
Web: www.gohypersonic.com
SIC: 8711 Engineering services

(G-7378)
GOOD SAMARITAN HOSPITAL
2222 Philadelphia Dr (45406-1813)
PHONE................................937 278-2612
EMP: 2000
Web: www.premierhealth.com
SIC: 8062 Hospital, affiliated with AMA residency

(G-7379)
GOODWILL ESTER SEALS MIAMI VLY (PA)
660 S Main St (45402-2708)
PHONE................................937 461-4800
Lance W Detrick, *Pr*
Leo E Dugdale Iii, *CFO*
EMP: 210 **EST:** 1934
SQ FT: 105,000
SALES (est): 95.69MM
SALES (corp-wide): 95.69MM **Privately Held**
Web: www.gesmv.org
SIC: 8322 Social service center

(G-7380)
GOODWILL ESTER SEALS MIAMI VLY
Goodwill Inds of Miami Vly
660 S Main St (45402-2708)
PHONE................................937 461-4800
EMP: 300
SALES (corp-wide): 95.69MM **Privately Held**
Web: www.gesmv
SIC: 4225 General warehousing and storage
PA: Easter Goodwill Seals Miami Valley
660 S Main St
Dayton OH 45402
937 461-4800

(G-7381)
GOSIGER HOLDINGS INC (PA)
Also Called: Gosiger
108 Mcdonough St (45402-2267)
P.O. Box 533 (45401-0533)
PHONE................................937 228-5174
Peter G Haley, *Pr*
EMP: 180 **EST:** 2012
SALES (est): 142.92MM
SALES (corp-wide): 142.92MM **Privately Held**
Web: www.gosiger.com
SIC: 5084 Machine tools and accessories

(G-7382)
GOSIGER INC
108 Mcdonough St (45402-2267)
P.O. Box 533 (45401-0533)
PHONE................................937 228-5174
◆ **EMP:** 435
Web: www.gosiger.com
SIC: 5084 Machine tools and accessories

(G-7383)
GRACEWORKS LUTHERAN SERVICES (PA)
6430 Inner Mission Way (45459-7400)
PHONE................................937 433-2140
Willis O Serr Ii, *Pr*
Michael W Allen, *VP Fin*
EMP: 550 **EST:** 1926
SQ FT: 250,000
SALES (est): 57.32MM
SALES (corp-wide): 57.32MM **Privately Held**
Web: www.graceworks.org
SIC: 8051 Skilled nursing care facilities

(G-7384)
GREATER DAYTON PUBLIC TV INC
Also Called: THINK TV
110 S Jefferson St (45402-2402)
PHONE................................937 220-1600
David M Fogarty, *Pr*
EMP: 90 **EST:** 1975
SQ FT: 24,500
SALES (est): 5.27MM **Privately Held**
Web: www.thinktv.org
SIC: 4833 Television broadcasting stations

(G-7385)
GREATER DAYTON SURGERY CTR LLC
1625 Delco Park Dr (45420-1391)
PHONE................................937 535-2200
Todd Evans, *Ex Dir*
EMP: 50 **EST:** 2005
SQ FT: 15,000
SALES (est): 17.83MM **Privately Held**
Web: www.daytonsurgerycenter.com
SIC: 8011 Surgeon

(G-7386)
GREATER DYTON RGNAL TRNST AUTH (PA)
Also Called: R T A
4 S Main St Ste C (45402-2052)
PHONE................................937 425-8310
Mark Donaghy, *CEO*
Mary K Stanforth, *
EMP: 100 **EST:** 1971
SALES (est): 86MM
SALES (corp-wide): 86MM **Privately Held**
Web: www.iriderta.org
SIC: 4111 Bus line operations

(G-7387)
GREATER DYTON RGNAL TRNST AUTH
Also Called: Recruiting Department
600 Campus 600 Longworth St (45401)
PHONE................................937 425-8400
EMP: 614
SALES (corp-wide): 86MM **Privately Held**
Web: www.iriderta.org
SIC: 4111 Bus line operations
PA: Greater Dayton Regional Transit Authority
4 S Main St Ste C
Dayton OH 45402
937 425-8310

(G-7388)
GREENTREE GROUP INC (PA)
1360 Technology Ct Ste 100 (45430)
PHONE................................937 490-5500
EMP: 65 **EST:** 1993
SQ FT: 25,000
SALES (est): 19.35MM **Privately Held**
Web: www.greentreegroup.com
SIC: 7379 8742 Computer related maintenance services; Management consulting services

(G-7389)
GS1 US INC
7887 Washington Village Dr Ste 300 (45459-3988)
PHONE................................609 620-0200
EMP: 181
SALES (corp-wide): 81.19MM **Privately Held**
Web: www.gs1us.org
SIC: 8611 Trade associations
PA: Gs1 Us, Inc.
300 Charles Ewing Blvd
Ewing NJ 08628
937 435-3870

(G-7390)
GYPC INC
Also Called: Marquette Group
475 Stonehaven Rd (45429-1645)
PHONE................................309 677-0405
EMP: 225
SIC: 7311 Advertising consultant

(G-7391)
HAMMERMAN GRAF HUGHES & CO INC
4486 Indian Ripple Rd (45440-3203)
PHONE................................937 320-1262
Richard P Graf, *Prin*
Dennis Hughes, *Prin*
Thomas J Mikos, *Prin*
Andrew Scholes, *Prin*
Donald E Stewart, *Prin*
EMP: 42 **EST:** 1939
SQ FT: 4,000
SALES (est): 4.86MM **Privately Held**
Web: www.hghcpa.com
SIC: 8721 Certified public accountant

(G-7392)
HAMPTON INN
7043 Miller Ln (45414-2653)
PHONE................................937 387-0598
Larry Bhog, *Prin*
EMP: 41 **EST:** 2008
SALES (est): 452.35K **Privately Held**
Web: www.hilton.com
SIC: 7011 Hotels and motels

(G-7393)
HAMPTON INN OF HUBER HEIGHTS
Also Called: Hampton Inn
5588 Merily Way (45424-2029)
PHONE................................937 233-4300
Ballu Patel, *Mng Pt*
Neil Patel, *Pt*
EMP: 29 **EST:** 2000
SALES (est): 501.32K **Privately Held**
Web: www.hilton.com
SIC: 7011 Hotels and motels

(G-7394)
HAND & RECONSTRUCTIVE SURGEONS
2400 Miami Valley Dr (45459-4774)
PHONE................................937 298-2262
EMP: 37
SALES (est): 461.27K **Privately Held**
Web: www.premierhealth.com
SIC: 8011 Surgeon

(G-7395)
HAND RCNSTRUCTIVE SURGEONS INC

Dayton - Montgomery County (G-7396) GEOGRAPHIC SECTION

2400 Miami Valley Dr (45459-4774)
PHONE...................................937 435-4263
Rannie Alsamkari, *Prin*
Peter S Barre, *Prin*
Beth A Berrettoni, *Prin*
Christopher J Danis, *Prin*
EMP: 44 **EST:** 1988
SALES (est): 1.76MM **Privately Held**
Web: www.premierhealth.com
SIC: 8011 General and family practice, physician/surgeon

(G-7396)
HARBORSIDE DAYTON LTD PARTNR
Also Called: Forest View Care Rhbltition Ctr
323 Forest Ave (45405-4599)
PHONE...................................937 224-0793
EMP: 955
SALES (corp-wide): 5.86B **Publicly Held**
SIC: 8051 Convalescent home with continuous nursing care
HQ: Harborside Of Dayton Limited Partnership
155 Federal St Ste 1100
Boston MA

(G-7397)
HARBORSIDE HEALTHCARE LLC
Also Called: Laurelwood, The
3797 Summit Glen Dr Frnt (45449-3657)
PHONE...................................937 436-6155
Deborah Schott, *Brnch Mgr*
EMP: 221
SALES (corp-wide): 5.86B **Publicly Held**
Web: www.genesishcc.com
SIC: 8051 Skilled nursing care facilities
HQ: Harborside Healthcare, Llc
5100 Sun Ave Ne
Albuquerque NM 87109

(G-7398)
HAROLD J BECKER COMPANY INC
3946 Indian Ripple Rd (45440-3450)
PHONE...................................614 279-1414
Kevin L Bechtel, *Pr*
Nicholas Bechtel, *
Naomi Terry, *
EMP: 30 **EST:** 1949
SQ FT: 12,000
SALES (est): 8.8MM **Privately Held**
Web: www.hjbecker.com
SIC: 1761 1799 Roofing contractor; Waterproofing

(G-7399)
HAVEN BHAVIORAL HEALTHCARE INC
Also Called: Haven Behavioral Hosp Dayton
1 Elizabeth Pl Ste A (45417-3445)
PHONE...................................937 234-0100
EMP: 114
Web: www.havenbehavioral.com
SIC: 8322 Senior citizens' center or association
PA: Haven Behavioral Healthcare, Inc.
3102 West End Ave # 1000
Nashville TN 37203

(G-7400)
HEALING TOUCH AGENCY LLC
201 Riverside Dr Ste 1d (45405-4956)
PHONE...................................937 813-8333
Vicki Harris, *CEO*
EMP: 38 **EST:** 2011
SALES (est): 879.4K **Privately Held**
SIC: 8082 Home health care services

(G-7401)
HEALTH AT HOME LLC
6445 Far Hills Ave (45459-2725)
PHONE...................................937 436-7717
Judy Budi, *Prin*
Bonnie Smith, *
Tina Gregory, *
EMP: 45 **EST:** 2008
SALES (est): 816.24K **Privately Held**
SIC: 8099 Health and allied services, nec

(G-7402)
HEAPY ENGINEERING INC (PA)
1400 W Dorothy Ln (45409-1310)
PHONE...................................937 224-0861
EMP: 115 **EST:** 1945
SALES (est): 24.65MM
SALES (corp-wide): 24.65MM **Privately Held**
Web: www.heapy.com
SIC: 8711 Consulting engineer

(G-7403)
HEARTSPRING HOME HLTH CARE LLC
1251 E Dorothy Ln (45419-2106)
PHONE...................................937 531-6920
Al Lefeld, *CFO*
EMP: 90 **EST:** 2011
SALES (est): 2.21MM **Privately Held**
SIC: 8099 Health and allied services, nec

(G-7404)
HEIL BROTHERS INCORPORATED
Also Called: Heil Brothers Lawn & Grdn Eqp
2218 Wilmington Pike (45420-1433)
PHONE...................................937 256-3500
Jerry D Heil, *Owner*
Jerome D Heil, *Pr*
Kenneth Heil, *Sec*
EMP: 27 **EST:** 1979
SQ FT: 9,000
SALES (est): 2.36MM **Privately Held**
Web: www.heilbrothers.com
SIC: 5261 7699 Lawnmowers and tractors; Lawn mower repair shop

(G-7405)
HENRY JERGENS CONTRACTOR INC
1280 Brandt Pike (45404-2468)
PHONE...................................937 233-1830
Charles F Jergens, *Pr*
Patricia Jergens, *
EMP: 27 **EST:** 1939
SQ FT: 1,500
SALES (est): 978.33K **Privately Held**
SIC: 7353 1794 Heavy construction equipment rental; Excavation work

(G-7406)
HIGH VOLTAGE MAINTENANCE CORP (DH)
Also Called: Vertiv
5100 Energy Dr (45414-3525)
PHONE...................................937 278-0811
Charles S Helldoerfer, *Pr*
Thomas E Nation, *
EMP: 35 **EST:** 1966
SQ FT: 10,000
SALES (est): 24.75MM
SALES (corp-wide): 6.86B **Publicly Held**
Web: www.hvmcorp.com
SIC: 8734 8711 Testing laboratories; Electrical or electronic engineering
HQ: Vertiv Group Corporation
505 N Cleveland Ave
Westerville OH 43082
614 888-0246

(G-7407)
HOLIDAY INN EXPRESS
Also Called: Holiday Inn
5655 Wilmington Pike (45459-7102)
PHONE...................................937 424-5757
Angela Shockley, *Dir*
EMP: 39 **EST:** 2003
SALES (est): 837.87K **Privately Held**
Web: www.holidayinn.com
SIC: 7011 Hotels and motels

(G-7408)
HOME CARE NETWORK INC (PA)
1191 Lyons Rd (45458-1857)
PHONE...................................800 600-3974
EMP: 89 **EST:** 1994
SALES (est): 23.32MM **Privately Held**
Web: www.hcnmidwest.net
SIC: 8082 7361 Visiting nurse service; Nurses' registry

(G-7409)
HOME DEPOT USA INC
Also Called: Home Depot, The
345 Springboro Pike (45449)
PHONE...................................937 312-9053
Darryl Sanders, *Mgr*
EMP: 175
SALES (corp-wide): 152.67B **Publicly Held**
Web: www.homedepot.com
SIC: 5211 7359 Home centers; Tool rental
HQ: Home Depot U.S.A., Inc.
2445 Springfield Ave
Vauxhall NJ 07088

(G-7410)
HOME DEPOT USA INC
Also Called: Home Depot, The
5860 Wilmington Pike (45459)
PHONE...................................937 312-9076
Kelly Cassidy, *Mgr*
EMP: 100
SALES (corp-wide): 152.67B **Publicly Held**
Web: www.homedepot.com
SIC: 5211 7359 Home centers; Tool rental
HQ: Home Depot U.S.A., Inc.
2445 Springfield Ave
Vauxhall NJ 07088

(G-7411)
HOME DEPOT USA INC
Also Called: Home Depot, The
5200 Salem Ave Unit A (45426)
PHONE...................................937 837-1551
Julie Bradley, *Mgr*
EMP: 206
SALES (corp-wide): 152.67B **Publicly Held**
Web: www.homedepot.com
SIC: 5211 7359 Home centers; Tool rental
HQ: Home Depot U.S.A., Inc.
2445 Springfield Ave
Vauxhall NJ 07088

(G-7412)
HOME EXPERTS REALTY
93 W Franklin St Ste 106 (45459-4761)
PHONE...................................937 435-6000
Clyde Corle, *Mgr*
EMP: 33 **EST:** 2018
SALES (est): 1.23MM **Privately Held**
Web: www.homeexpertsrealty.net
SIC: 6531 Real estate agent, residential

(G-7413)
HORENSTEIN NCHLSON BLMNTHAL A
124 E 3rd St Fl 5 (45402-2186)
PHONE...................................937 224-7200
Steven V Hornstein, *Pt*
Bruce Nicholson, *Pt*
Gary Blumenthal, *Pt*
Wilbur S Lang, *Prin*
EMP: 40 **EST:** 1980
SALES (est): 4.33MM **Privately Held**
Web: www.hnb-law.com
SIC: 8111 General practice law office

(G-7414)
HORIZON PAYROLL SERVICES INC
2700 Miamisburg Centerville Rd Ste 580 (45459)
P.O. Box 751053 (45475-1053)
PHONE...................................937 434-8244
Marilynne Saliwanchik, *Pr*
Alan Saliwanchik, *
EMP: 300 **EST:** 1981
SQ FT: 3,000
SALES (est): 6.97MM **Privately Held**
Web: www.horizonpayrollsolutions.com
SIC: 7371 5045 Custom computer programming services; Computers, peripherals, and software

(G-7415)
HOSS VALUE CARS & TRUCKS INC (PA)
Also Called: Voss Hyundai
766 Miamisburg Centerville Rd (45459)
PHONE...................................937 428-2400
EMP: 49 **EST:** 1997
SALES (est): 18.46MM **Privately Held**
Web: www.vosshyundai.com
SIC: 5511 7538 Automobiles, new and used; General automotive repair shops

(G-7416)
HUMANE SOCIETY GREATER DAYTON
1661 Nicholas Rd (45417-6714)
PHONE...................................937 268-7387
Kevin Usilton, *Dir*
Brian Weltge, *Dir*
EMP: 31 **EST:** 1902
SALES (est): 3.03MM **Privately Held**
Web: www.hsdayton.org
SIC: 8699 Animal humane society

(G-7417)
HUNTINGTON NATIONAL BANK
500 Miamisburg Centerville Rd (45459-4757)
PHONE...................................937 428-7400
Kim Hartwell, *Mgr*
EMP: 31
SALES (corp-wide): 10.84B **Publicly Held**
Web: www.huntington.com
SIC: 6029 6021 Commercial banks, nec; National commercial banks
HQ: The Huntington National Bank
41 S High St
Columbus OH 43215
614 480-4293

(G-7418)
IMDT ACQUISITION LLC
Also Called: Ross Medical Education Center
4490 Brandt Pike (45424-6049)
PHONE...................................937 235-0510
Beth Millard, *Dir*
EMP: 52
SALES (corp-wide): 851.73K **Privately Held**
SIC: 6799 Investors, nec
PA: Imdt Acquisition, Llc
22800 Hall Rd Ste 800
Clinton Township MI 48036
810 637-6100

(G-7419)
IMPACT SALES INC
2501 Neff Rd (45414-5001)
PHONE...................................937 274-1905

GEOGRAPHIC SECTION   **Dayton - Montgomery County (G-7440)**

Carl Pennington, *Mgr*
EMP: 95
SALES (corp-wide): 26.16MM **Privately Held**
Web: www.acosta.com
SIC: 5141 Food brokers
PA: Impact Sales, Inc.
6600 Corporate Ctr Pkwy
Jacksonville FL 32216
208 343-5800

(G-7420)
IMPROVEIT HOME REMODELING INC
Also Called: Improveit Hme Rmdlng OH Enrgy
7200 Poe Ave Ste 102 (45414-2798)
PHONE..............................937 204-1551
EMP: 29
Web: www.improveitusa.com
SIC: 1521 General remodeling, single-family houses
PA: Improveit Home Remodeling, Inc.
4580 Bridgeway Ave Ste B
Columbus OH 43219

(G-7421)
INDUSTRIAL FIBERGLASS SPC INC
Also Called: Fiber Systems
351 Deeds Ave (45404)
PHONE..............................937 222-9000
Theodore Morton, *Ch Bd*
Janice Morton, *
Valerie Cline, *
Karen Ramsey, *
Melanie Shockey, *
EMP: 35 **EST:** 1978
SALES (est): 4.47MM **Privately Held**
Web: www.ifs-frp.com
SIC: 3229 1799 Glass fiber products; Service station equipment installation, maint., and repair

(G-7422)
INTEGRATED DATA SERVICES INC
111 Harries St Apt 202 (45402-1889)
PHONE..............................937 656-5496
Jerry W Murray, *Prin*
EMP: 50
SALES (corp-wide): 15.13MM **Privately Held**
Web: www.get-integrated.com
SIC: 7374 Data processing service
PA: Integrated Data Services, Inc.
2831 Saint Rose Pkwy # 200
Henderson NV 89052
310 647-3439

(G-7423)
INTERIM HEALTHCARE OF DAYTON
Also Called: Interim Services
30 W Rahn Rd Ste 2 (45429-2238)
PHONE..............................937 291-5330
Thomas J Dimarco, *Pr*
Craig Smith Attorney, *Prin*
EMP: 1686 **EST:** 1974
SQ FT: 2,500
SALES (est): 876.07K
SALES (corp-wide): 52.16MM **Privately Held**
Web: www.interimhealthcare.com
SIC: 8082 Home health care services
PA: Salo, Inc.
300 W Wlson Brdge Rd Ste
Columbus OH 43085
614 436-9404

(G-7424)
INTERNAL REVENUE SERVICE
3100 Big Hill Rd (45419-1207)
PHONE..............................937 643-1494
EMP: 93
Web: www.irs.gov

SIC: 8011 Internal medicine, physician/surgeon
HQ: Internal Revenue Service
1111 Constitution Ave, Nw
Washington DC 20220
202 803-9000

(G-7425)
INTERNTNAL QLTY HALTHCARE CORP (PA)
Also Called: International Qulty Healthcare
6927 N Main St Ste 101 (45415-2507)
PHONE..............................513 731-3338
EMP: 28 **EST:** 1997
SALES (est): 5.12MM **Privately Held**
Web: www.iqhc.org
SIC: 8082 7361 5047 Home health care services; Nurses' registry; Medical equipment and supplies

(G-7426)
IRONGATE INC
1353 Lyons Rd (45458-1822)
PHONE..............................937 432-3432
Steven Brown, *Pr*
EMP: 53
SALES (corp-wide): 24.13MM **Privately Held**
Web: www.irongaterealtors.com
SIC: 6531 Real estate agent, residential
PA: Irongate, Inc
122 N Main St
Centerville OH 45459
937 433-3300

(G-7427)
JEWISH FDRTION GRTER DYTON INC
Also Called: Boonshoft Ctr For Jwish Clture
525 Versailles Dr (45459-6074)
PHONE..............................937 830-7904
Marc Jacob, *Brnch Mgr*
EMP: 63
SALES (corp-wide): 4.77MM **Privately Held**
Web: www.jewishdayton.org
SIC: 8322 Community center
PA: Jewish Federation Of Greater Dayton, Inc.
525 Versailles Dr
Dayton OH 45459
937 610-1555

(G-7428)
JEWISH FDRTION GRTER DYTON INC
Also Called: Covenant House
4911 Covenant House Dr (45426-2007)
PHONE..............................937 837-2651
Arthur Cohn, *Mgr*
EMP: 82
SALES (corp-wide): 4.77MM **Privately Held**
Web: www.jewishdayton.org
SIC: 8322 8051 Community center; Skilled nursing care facilities
PA: Jewish Federation Of Greater Dayton, Inc.
525 Versailles Dr
Dayton OH 45459
937 610-1555

(G-7429)
JJR SOLUTIONS LLC
Also Called: Jjr Solutions
607 E 3rd St Ste 400 (45402-2219)
PHONE..............................937 912-0288
David L Judson Junior, *Managing Member*
Linda Skinner, *
EMP: 35 **EST:** 2009
SALES (est): 5.58MM **Privately Held**

Web: www.jjrsolutions.com
SIC: 8742 7371 7376 8711 Management information systems consultant; Computer software development and applications; Computer facilities management; Engineering services

(G-7430)
JOHNSON RESTORATION LLC
9411 Oak Brook Dr (45458-3021)
PHONE..............................937 907-5056
EMP: 34 **EST:** 2017
SALES (est): 977.02K **Privately Held**
Web: www.johnsonrestoration.net
SIC: 1799 Special trade contractors, nec

(G-7431)
JYG INNOVATIONS LLC
6450 Poe Ave Ste 103 (45414-2667)
PHONE..............................937 630-3858
EMP: 58 **EST:** 2009
SQ FT: 3,000
SALES (est): 6.22MM **Privately Held**
Web: www.jyginnovations.com
SIC: 8742 8748 7371 7379 Management consulting services; Systems engineering consultant, ex. computer or professional; Custom computer programming services; Computer related maintenance services

(G-7432)
KAIYUH SERVICES LLC
4123 Arcadia Blvd (45420-2817)
PHONE..............................907 569-9599
EMP: 97 **EST:** 2010
SALES (est): 3.68MM **Privately Held**
SIC: 1522 Hotel/motel and multi-family home construction

(G-7433)
KBR WYLE SERVICES LLC
2700 Indian Ripple Rd (45440-3638)
PHONE..............................937 320-2713
Mike Gilkey, *Brnch Mgr*
EMP: 150
Web: www.kbr.com
SIC: 8731 Commercial physical research
HQ: Kbr Wyle Services, Llc
601 Jefferson St Ste 7911
Houston TX 77002

(G-7434)
KEROAM TRANSPORTATION INC (PA)
4518 Webster St (45414-4940)
PHONE..............................937 274-7033
Kevin Burch, *Pr*
Archie Crawford, *
Greg Atkinson, *
Roger Atkinson Junior, *VP*
Amy Hogan, *
EMP: 60 **EST:** 1983
SQ FT: 36,000
SALES (est): 6.94MM
SALES (corp-wide): 6.94MM **Privately Held**
SIC: 4212 4213 Local trucking, without storage; Trucking, except local

(G-7435)
KETTERING ADVENTIST HEALTHCARE (PA)
Also Called: Kettering Health Network
3535 Southern Blvd (45429-1221)
PHONE..............................937 298-4331
Michael Gentry, *CEO*
Roy Chew, *
Russ Wethell, *
EMP: 1097 **EST:** 1982
SQ FT: 500,000

SALES (est): 2.46B
SALES (corp-wide): 2.46B **Privately Held**
Web: www.ketteringhealth.org
SIC: 8062 General medical and surgical hospitals

(G-7436)
KETTERING ANESTHESIA ASSOC
3533 Southern Blvd Ste 3400 (45429)
PHONE..............................937 225-3429
Laurence Holland, *Pr*
Roy Haines, *VP*
EMP: 49 **EST:** 1969
SALES (est): 1.79MM **Privately Held**
Web: www.kaaohio.com
SIC: 8011 Anesthesiologist

(G-7437)
KETTERING CITY SCHOOL DISTRICT
Also Called: Transportation Dept
2640 Wilmington Pike (45419-2455)
PHONE..............................937 499-1770
Dan Girbin, *Genl Mgr*
EMP: 37
SALES (corp-wide): 139.07MM **Privately Held**
Web: www.ketteringschools.org
SIC: 8211 4789 Public elementary and secondary schools; Cargo loading and unloading services
PA: Kettering City School District
580 Lincoln Park Blvd # 100
Dayton OH 45429
937 499-1400

(G-7438)
KETTERING CITY SCHOOL DISTRICT
Also Called: Kettering School Maintainence
2636 Wilmington Pike (45419-2455)
PHONE..............................937 297-1990
Tom Lee, *Mgr*
EMP: 37
SALES (corp-wide): 139.07MM **Privately Held**
Web: www.ketteringschools.org
SIC: 8211 7349 Public elementary school; Building maintenance services, nec
PA: Kettering City School District
580 Lincoln Park Blvd # 100
Dayton OH 45429
937 499-1400

(G-7439)
KETTERING MEDICAL CENTER
Also Called: Kettering Health Network
1251 E Dorothy Ln (45419-2106)
PHONE..............................937 384-8750
Christine Turner, *Dir*
EMP: 30
SALES (corp-wide): 2.46B **Privately Held**
Web: www.ketteringhealth.org
SIC: 8062 Hospital, professional nursing school
HQ: Kettering Medical Center
3535 Southern Blvd
Kettering OH 45429
937 298-4331

(G-7440)
KETTERING PATHOLOGY ASSOC INC
Also Called: Kpa
3535 Southern Blvd (45429-1221)
PHONE..............................937 298-4331
Patricia Mcdowell, *Pr*
Richard Pelstring, *VP*
Doctor Hsing-ming Meng, *Treas*
Yvonne Dowdy, *Sec*
Diann Snider, *Acctg Mgr*
EMP: 75 **EST:** 1964
SALES (est): 1.7MM **Privately Held**

Web: www.ketteringhealth.org
SIC: 8071 8062 Medical laboratories; General medical and surgical hospitals

(G-7441)
KIDNEY CARE SPECIALISTS LLC
1362 E Stroop Rd (45429-4926)
PHONE..................................937 643-0015
EMP: 33 EST: 2009
SALES (est): 1.92MM Privately Held
Web: www.kidneycareohio.com
SIC: 8011 Nephrologist

(G-7442)
KINDRED HEALTHCARE LLC
Also Called: Kindred Hospital-Dayton
601 S Edwin C Moses Blvd (45417-3424)
PHONE..................................937 222-5963
Christina Stover, CEO
EMP: 30
SALES (corp-wide): 13.68B Privately Held
Web: www.kindredhospitals.com
SIC: 8062 General medical and surgical hospitals
HQ: Kindred Healthcare, Llc
    680 S 4th St
    Louisville KY 40202
    502 596-7300

(G-7443)
KINDRED HEALTHCARE LLC
Also Called: Kindred Hospital
707 S Edwin C Moses Blvd (45417-3462)
PHONE..................................937 222-5963
Susan Davis, Mgr
EMP: 34
SALES (corp-wide): 13.68B Privately Held
Web: www.kindredhospitals.com
SIC: 8062 8051 8011 General medical and surgical hospitals; Skilled nursing care facilities; Dispensary, operated by physicians
HQ: Kindred Healthcare, Llc
    680 S 4th St
    Louisville KY 40202
    502 596-7300

(G-7444)
KMH SYSTEMS INC (PA)
6900 Poe Ave (45414-2531)
PHONE..................................800 962-3178
▲ EMP: 40 EST: 1975
SALES (est): 23.04MM
SALES (corp-wide): 23.04MM Privately Held
Web: www.kmhsystems.com
SIC: 5084 7359 Materials handling machinery; Equipment rental and leasing, nec

(G-7445)
KOHLER FOODS INC (PA)
Also Called: Kohler Catering
4572 Presidential Way (45429-5751)
PHONE..................................937 291-3600
Erwin Kohler Junior, Pr
Betty Kohler, *
Craig Kohler, *
EMP: 50 EST: 1959
SQ FT: 9,000
SALES (est): 2.67MM
SALES (corp-wide): 2.67MM Privately Held
Web: www.kohlercatering.net
SIC: 7299 5812 Banquet hall facilities; Caterers

(G-7446)
KRISH HOSPITALITY LLC
3661 Maxton Rd (45414-2433)
PHONE..................................859 351-1060
EMP: 83
SALES (corp-wide): 577.29K Privately Held
SIC: 7011 Hotels and motels
PA: Krish Hospitality Llc
    70 Chris Perry Ln
    Columbus OH 43213
    614 604-6400

(G-7447)
L R G INC
Also Called: G.L.R., Inc. Alabama Division
3795 Wyse Rd (45414-2540)
PHONE..................................937 890-0510
Brandon Shoup, Pr
Heath Peters, *
Philip Bayer, *
EMP: 53 EST: 1987
SQ FT: 9,870
SALES (est): 114.37MM Privately Held
Web: www.glrinc.net
SIC: 1542 1522 Commercial and office building, new construction; Residential construction, nec

(G-7448)
LABORATORY OF DERMATOPATHOLOGY
7835 Paragon Rd (45459-4021)
PHONE..................................937 434-2351
Thomas G Olsen, Prin
EMP: 40 EST: 1984
SQ FT: 3,000
SALES (est): 4.95MM Privately Held
Web: www.dermpathlab.com
SIC: 8071 Testing laboratories

(G-7449)
LANCO GLOBAL SYSTEMS INC
1430c Yankee Park Pl (45458-1829)
PHONE..................................937 660-8090
Venkat Kadiyala, Brnch Mgr
EMP: 98
SALES (corp-wide): 9.59MM Privately Held
Web: www.lancogs.com
SIC: 7379 Online services technology consultants
PA: Lanco Global Systems, Inc.
    21515 Ridgetop Cir # 150
    Sterling VA 20166
    703 953-2157

(G-7450)
LAPHAM-HICKEY STEEL CORP
3911 Dayton Park Dr (45414-4411)
PHONE..................................937 236-6940
EMP: 52
SALES (corp-wide): 235.89MM Privately Held
Web: www.lapham-hickey.com
SIC: 5051 Steel
PA: Lapham-Hickey Steel Corp.
    5500 W 73rd St
    Bedford Park IL 60638
    708 496-6111

(G-7451)
LEGRAND NORTH AMERICA LLC
Also Called: C2g
6500 Poe Ave (45414-2527)
PHONE..................................937 224-0639
EMP: 420
Web: www.legrand.us
SIC: 1731 5063 5045 3643 Communications specialization; Cable conduit; Computer peripheral equipment; Current-carrying wiring services
HQ: Legrand North America, Llc
    60 Woodlawn St
    West Hartford CT 06110
    860 233-6251

(G-7452)
LENZ INC
Also Called: Lenz Company
3301 Klepinger Rd (45406-1823)
P.O. Box 1044 (45401-1044)
PHONE..................................937 277-9364
Robert Wagner, Pr
▲ EMP: 50 EST: 1955
SQ FT: 15,000
SALES (est): 6.28MM Privately Held
Web: www.lenzinc.com
SIC: 6531 3089 Real estate brokers and agents; Fittings for pipe, plastics

(G-7453)
LEWIS & MICHAEL INC (PA)
3920 Image Dr (45414-2524)
P.O. Box 97 (45401-0097)
PHONE..................................937 252-6683
David Lewis, Pr
Charles M Lewis, *
◆ EMP: 30 EST: 1941
SQ FT: 40,000
SALES (est): 10.35MM
SALES (corp-wide): 10.35MM Privately Held
Web: www.atlaslm.com
SIC: 4213 4214 4225 Household goods transport; Household goods moving and storage, local; General warehousing

(G-7454)
LIFESTGES SMRTAN CTRS FOR WMEN
Also Called: Lifestgs-Smrtan Ctrs For Women
2200 Philadelphia Dr # 101 (45406-1813)
PHONE..................................937 277-8988
Bruce Bernie, Prin
Samaritan Health Parners, Prin
EMP: 40 EST: 1997
SQ FT: 5,220
SALES (est): 463.48K Privately Held
Web: www.premierhealth.com
SIC: 8099 8011 Medical services organization; Offices and clinics of medical doctors

(G-7455)
LINCOLN PARK ASSOCIATES II LP
Also Called: Lincoln Park Manor
694 Isaac Prugh Way (45429-3481)
PHONE..................................937 297-4300
Charles Osborn Junior, Pt
Miami Valley Hospital, Ltd Pt
EMP: 70 EST: 1989
SQ FT: 40,000
SALES (est): 18.68MM Privately Held
Web: www.lincolnpark-manor.com
SIC: 8051 8059 8052 Convalescent home with continuous nursing care; Nursing home, except skilled and intermediate care facility; Intermediate care facilities

(G-7456)
LION FIRST RESPONDER PPE INC
7200 Poe Ave Ste 400 (45414-2798)
PHONE..................................937 898-1949
Steve Schwartz, CEO
David Cook, *
EMP: 57 EST: 2015
SALES (est): 24.98MM
SALES (corp-wide): 13.99MM Privately Held
SIC: 2311 3842 5047 Firemen's uniforms: made from purchased materials; Clothing, fire resistant and protective; Medical equipment and supplies
HQ: Lion Safety Resources Group, Inc.
    7200 Poe Ave Ste 400
    Dayton OH 45414
    937 898-1949

(G-7457)
LION GROUP INC (HQ)
7200 Poe Ave Ste 400 (45414)
PHONE..................................937 898-1949
Steve Schwartz, CEO
Andrew Schwartz, *
James Disanto, *
Richard Musick, *
EMP: 90 EST: 2014
SQ FT: 3,700
SALES (est): 327.39MM
SALES (corp-wide): 13.99MM Privately Held
Web: www.lionprotects.com
SIC: 6719 2311 5047 Investment holding companies, except banks; Firemen's uniforms: made from purchased materials; Medical equipment and supplies
PA: Lion Protects B.V.
    Rheastraat 14
    Tilburg NB 5047
    135076800

(G-7458)
LION-VALLEN LTD PARTNERSHIP (DH)
Also Called: L V I
7200 Poe Ave Ste 400 (45414)
PHONE..................................937 898-1949
▼ EMP: 111 EST: 1996
SALES (est): 75.52MM
SALES (corp-wide): 13.99MM Privately Held
SIC: 5136 5137 Uniforms, men's and boys'; Uniforms, women's and children's
HQ: Lion Group, Inc.
    7200 Poe Ave Ste 400
    Dayton OH 45414
    937 898-1949

(G-7459)
LORENZ CORPORATION (PA)
Also Called: Show What You Know
501 E 3rd St (45402-2280)
P.O. Box 802 (45401-0802)
PHONE..................................937 228-6118
Reiff Lorenz, Pr
Reiff Lorenz, Ch Bd
Geoffrey R Lorenz, *
John Schimtz, *
Kris Kropff, *
▲ EMP: 60 EST: 1890
SQ FT: 55,000
SALES (est): 9.68MM
SALES (corp-wide): 9.68MM Privately Held
Web: www.lorenz.com
SIC: 2759 5049 2721 2741 Music, sheet: printing, nsk; School supplies; Periodicals, publishing only; Music, sheet: publishing only, not printed on site

(G-7460)
LOWES HOME CENTERS LLC
Also Called: Lowe's
8421 Troy Pike (45424-1029)
PHONE..................................937 235-2920
Rob Kalp, Mgr
EMP: 115
SALES (corp-wide): 86.38B Publicly Held
Web: www.lowes.com
SIC: 5211 5031 5722 5064 Home centers; Building materials, exterior; Household appliance stores; Electrical appliances, television and radio
HQ: Lowe's Home Centers, Llc
    1000 Lowes Blvd
    Mooresville NC 28117
    336 658-4000

GEOGRAPHIC SECTION
Dayton - Montgomery County (G-7484)

(G-7461)
LOWES HOME CENTERS LLC
Also Called: Lowe's
2900 Martins Dr (45449-3602)
PHONE..........................937 438-4900
EMP: 138
SALES (corp-wide): 86.38B **Publicly Held**
Web: www.lowes.com
SIC: 5211 5031 5722 5064 Home centers; Building materials, exterior; Household appliance stores; Electrical appliances, television and radio
HQ: Lowe's Home Centers, Llc
1000 Lowes Blvd
Mooresville NC 28117
336 658-4000

(G-7462)
LOWES HOME CENTERS LLC
Also Called: Lowe's
5252 Salem Ave (45426-1702)
PHONE..........................937 854-8200
EMP: 138
SALES (corp-wide): 86.38B **Publicly Held**
Web: www.lowes.com
SIC: 5211 5031 5722 5064 Home centers; Building materials, exterior; Household appliance stores; Electrical appliances, television and radio
HQ: Lowe's Home Centers, Llc
1000 Lowes Blvd
Mooresville NC 28117
336 658-4000

(G-7463)
MAACO FRANCHISING INC
3474 Needmore Rd (45414-4314)
PHONE..........................937 236-6700
Jerry Ptasky, *Brnch Mgr*
EMP: 41
SALES (corp-wide): 2.3B **Publicly Held**
Web: www.maaco.com
SIC: 7532 Paint shop, automotive
HQ: Maaco Franchising, Inc.
440 S Church St Ste 700
Charlotte NC 28202
704 377-8855

(G-7464)
MAD RIVER LOCAL SCHOOL DST
Also Called: Building & Grounds Maintenance
1841 Harshman Rd (45424-5019)
PHONE..........................937 237-4275
Ron Atkins, *Mgr*
EMP: 37
SALES (corp-wide): 48.94MM **Privately Held**
Web: www.madriverschools.org
SIC: 4151 School buses
PA: Mad River Local School District
801 Old Harshman Rd
Dayton OH 45431
937 259-6606

(G-7465)
MANCO REAL ESTATE MGT INC
1905 Salem Ave (45406-4906)
PHONE..........................937 277-9551
Julius Rastikis, *Pr*
Robert Flory, *Treas*
EMP: 27 EST: 1985
SQ FT: 600
SALES (est): 977.76K **Privately Held**
Web: www.mancopropertyservices.com
SIC: 6531 Real estate managers

(G-7466)
MARSH & MCLENNAN AGENCY LLC
Also Called: Marsh
309 Webster St (45402-1569)
PHONE..........................937 228-4135
Karen Harker, *Brnch Mgr*
EMP: 125
SALES (corp-wide): 22.74B **Publicly Held**
Web: www.marshmma.com
SIC: 6411 Insurance brokers, nec
HQ: Marsh & Mclennan Agency Llc
9850 Nw 41st St Ste 100
Miami FL 33178

(G-7467)
MARY C ENTERPRISES INC (PA)
Also Called: Dots Market
2274 Patterson Rd (45420-3061)
PHONE..........................937 253-6169
Rob Bernhard, *Pr*
EMP: 80 EST: 1950
SQ FT: 18,000
SALES (est): 9.31MM **Privately Held**
Web: www.dotsmarket.com
SIC: 5411 6099 5421 Supermarkets, independent; Electronic funds transfer network, including switching; Meat markets, including freezer provisioners

(G-7468)
MARY SCOTT NURSING HOME INC
3109 Campus Dr (45406-4100)
PHONE..........................937 278-0761
Kenneth Crawford, *Ex Dir*
EMP: 98 EST: 1913
SALES (est): 5.01MM **Privately Held**
SIC: 8051 Skilled nursing care facilities
PA: Mary Scott Centers Inc
3109 Campus Dr
Dayton OH 45406

(G-7469)
MAXWELL LIGHTNING PROTECTION
621 Pond St (45402-1348)
PHONE..........................937 228-7250
TOLL FREE: 800
Wayne Maxwell, *Pr*
Wayne S Maxwell, *
Lynn Maxwell-busse, *VP*
EMP: 38 EST: 1963
SQ FT: 7,200
SALES (est): 2.82MM **Privately Held**
Web: www.maxwell-lp.com
SIC: 1731 General electrical contractor

(G-7470)
MBI SOLUTIONS INC
332 Congress Park Dr (45459-4133)
PHONE..........................937 619-4000
Paul Kolodzik Md, *CEO*
Tom Grile, *
Terry Heineman, *
Steve Broughton, *
EMP: 541 EST: 1984
SQ FT: 22,000
SALES (est): 4.64MM **Privately Held**
Web: www.mbi-digital.com
SIC: 8721 Billing and bookkeeping service
PA: Premier Health Care System, Inc.
332 Congress Park Dr
Dayton OH

(G-7471)
MBP HOLDINGS INC
2030 Winners Cir (45404-1130)
TOLL FREE: 800
EMP: 60 EST: 1989
SQ FT: 15,000
Web: www.marshbuild.com
SIC: 6719 Investment holding companies, except banks

(G-7472)
MCAFEE HEATING & AC CO INC
Also Called: McAfee Air Duct Cleaning
4750 Hempstead Station Dr (45429-5164)
PHONE..........................937 438-1976
Gregory K Mcafee, *Pr*
Naomi Mcafee, *VP*
EMP: 27 EST: 1990
SQ FT: 3,500
SALES (est): 8.1MM **Privately Held**
Web: www.mcair.com
SIC: 1711 Warm air heating and air conditioning contractor

(G-7473)
MCH SERVICES INC
190 E Spring Valley Pike (45458-3803)
PHONE..........................260 432-9699
EMP: 168
SALES (corp-wide): 34.4MM **Privately Held**
Web: www.mchservicesinc.com
SIC: 8082 Home health care services
HQ: Mch Services Inc
108 Lundy Ln
Hattiesburg MS

(G-7474)
MECHANICAL CNSTR MANAGERS LLC (PA)
Also Called: Rieck Services
5245 Wadsworth Rd (45414-3507)
P.O. Box 13565 (45413-0565)
PHONE..........................937 274-1987
EMP: 190 EST: 1949
SQ FT: 50,000
SALES (est): 39.47MM
SALES (corp-wide): 39.47MM **Privately Held**
Web: www.rieckservices.com
SIC: 1711 1761 Mechanical contractor; Sheet metal work, nec

(G-7475)
MED AMERICA HLTH SYSTEMS CORP (PA)
1 Wyoming St (45409-2722)
PHONE..........................937 223-6192
T G Breitenbach, *Pr*
Dale Creech, *
Timothy Jackson, *
EMP: 4700 EST: 1982
SQ FT: 1,000,000
SALES (est): 1.48B
SALES (corp-wide): 1.48B **Privately Held**
Web: www.premierhealth.com
SIC: 8062 8741 8082 General medical and surgical hospitals; Management services; Home health care services

(G-7476)
MED-PASS INCORPORATED
1 Reynolds Way (45430-1586)
PHONE..........................937 438-8884
Lisa Hanauer, *Pr*
Kim Buckingham, *
Susan Spiegel, *
Doug Harlow, *
Valerie Crider-hill, *Dir*
EMP: 41 EST: 1989
SQ FT: 40,000
SALES (est): 6.5MM **Privately Held**
Web: www.med-pass.com
SIC: 5112 8742 Computer and photocopying supplies; Management consulting services

(G-7477)
MEDICINE MIDWEST LLC
Also Called: Primed At Congress Park
979 Congress Park Dr (45459-4009)
PHONE..........................937 435-8786
Leslie Schrager, *Mgr*
EMP: 29
SALES (corp-wide): 2.91MM **Privately Held**
SIC: 8043 Offices and clinics of podiatrists
PA: Medicine Midwest Llc
4700 Smith Rd Ste A
Cincinnati OH 45212
513 533-1199

(G-7478)
MEDISYNC MIDWEST LTD LBLTY CO
Also Called: Medisync
3080 Ackerman Blvd (45429-3555)
PHONE..........................513 533-1199
EMP: 85 EST: 1996
SALES (est): 17.62MM **Privately Held**
Web: www.medisync.com
SIC: 8742 Hospital and health services consultant

(G-7479)
MEMORIAL HALL
125 E 1st St (45402-1214)
PHONE..........................937 293-2841
EMP: 65 EST: 2017
SALES (est): 108.88K **Privately Held**
SIC: 7299 Banquet hall facilities

(G-7480)
MERCHNTS SEC SVC DYTON OHIO IN
2015 Wayne Ave (45410-2134)
P.O. Box 432 (45409-0432)
PHONE..........................937 256-9373
James Houpt, *Pr*
EMP: 104 EST: 1901
SQ FT: 1,500
SALES (est): 5.13MM **Privately Held**
Web: www.merchantssecurity.com
SIC: 7381 Security guard service

(G-7481)
MERCO GROUP INC
6528 Poe Ave (45414-2527)
PHONE..........................937 890-5841
Robert Folkerth, *Brnch Mgr*
EMP: 60
SIC: 5099 Firearms and ammunition, except sporting
PA: The Merco Group Inc
7711 N 81st St
Milwaukee WI 53223

(G-7482)
MESSER CONSTRUCTION CO
4801 Hempstead Station Dr Unit A (45429-5171)
PHONE..........................937 291-1300
Matthew R Schnelle, *VP*
EMP: 105
SALES (corp-wide): 1.35B **Privately Held**
Web: www.messer.com
SIC: 1542 Commercial and office building, new construction
PA: Messer Construction Co.
643 W Court St
Cincinnati OH 45203
513 242-1541

(G-7483)
METCON LTD (PA)
5150 Webster St (45414-4228)
P.O. Box 13607 (45413-0607)
PHONE..........................937 447-9200
EMP: 27 EST: 1996
SALES (est): 9.39MM **Privately Held**
Web: www.metconltd.com
SIC: 1771 Foundation and footing contractor

(G-7484)
MFH INC (PA)
Also Called: Media Group At Michael's, The
241 E Alex Bell Rd (45459-2706)

Dayton - Montgomery County (G-7485) GEOGRAPHIC SECTION

PHONE..................937 435-4701
Michael Schuh Junior, *Pr*
EMP: 39 **EST:** 1984
SQ FT: 3,000
SALES (est): 2.39MM
SALES (corp-wide): 2.39MM **Privately Held**
Web: www.michaelssalon.com
SIC: 7231 7241 Hairdressers; Barber shops

(G-7485)
MFH INC
Also Called: Michaels For Hair
241 E Alex Bell Rd (45459-2706)
PHONE..................937 435-4701
Kathleen Lee, *Mgr*
EMP: 61
SALES (corp-wide): 2.39MM **Privately Held**
Web: www.michaelssalon.com
SIC: 7231 Hairdressers
PA: Mfh, Inc.
  241 E Alex Bell Rd
  Dayton OH 45459
  937 435-4701

(G-7486)
MIAMI VALLEY BROADCASTING CORP (HQ)
Also Called: Oldies 95
1611 S Main St (45409-2547)
PHONE..................937 259-2111
Edrew Fichser, *Pr*
James Hatcher, *
EMP: 162 **EST:** 1964
SQ FT: 54,000
SALES (est): 35.98MM
SALES (corp-wide): 16.61B **Privately Held**
Web: www.whio.com
SIC: 4833 Television broadcasting stations
PA: Cox Enterprises, Inc.
  6305 Pachtree Dunwoody Rd
  Atlanta GA 30328
  678 645-0000

(G-7487)
MIAMI VALLEY GOLF CLUB (PA)
3311 Salem Ave (45406-2699)
PHONE..................937 278-7381
Mel Cloud, *Mgr*
EMP: 75 **EST:** 1919
SQ FT: 35,000
SALES (est): 1.32MM
SALES (corp-wide): 1.32MM **Privately Held**
Web: www.miamivalleygolfclub.com
SIC: 7992 Public golf courses

(G-7488)
MIAMI VALLEY HOSPITAL
Also Called: Belmont Physicians
2451 Wayne Ave (45420-1893)
PHONE..................937 208-7396
Lisa Garrison, *Brnch Mgr*
EMP: 448
SALES (corp-wide): 1.48B **Privately Held**
Web: www.premierhealth.com
SIC: 8011 8062 Offices and clinics of medical doctors; General medical and surgical hospitals
HQ: Miami Valley Hospital
  1 Wyoming St
  Dayton OH 45409
  937 208-8000

(G-7489)
MIAMI VALLEY HOSPITAL
Also Called: Sports Medicine Center
1525 E Stroop Rd (45429-5065)
PHONE..................937 208-7450
John Connoly, *Mgr*
EMP: 403
SALES (corp-wide): 1.48B **Privately Held**
Web: www.premierhealth.com
SIC: 8041 Offices and clinics of chiropractors
HQ: Miami Valley Hospital
  1 Wyoming St
  Dayton OH 45409
  937 208-8000

(G-7490)
MIAMI VALLEY HOSPITAL
Miami Valley South Health Ctr
5801 Clyo Rd (45459-2782)
PHONE..................937 208-4076
Goodwin Grant, *Mgr*
EMP: 493
SALES (corp-wide): 1.48B **Privately Held**
Web: www.premierhealth.com
SIC: 8062 General medical and surgical hospitals
HQ: Miami Valley Hospital
  1 Wyoming St
  Dayton OH 45409
  937 208-8000

(G-7491)
MIAMI VALLEY HOSPITAL
Also Called: Miami Valley South Campus
2400 Miami Valley Dr (45459-4774)
PHONE..................937 438-2400
Joanne Ringer, *Mgr*
EMP: 583
SALES (corp-wide): 1.48B **Privately Held**
Web: www.premierhealth.com
SIC: 8062 General medical and surgical hospitals
HQ: Miami Valley Hospital
  1 Wyoming St
  Dayton OH 45409
  937 208-8000

(G-7492)
MIAMI VALLEY HOSPITAL (HQ)
Also Called: Premier Health
1 Wyoming St (45409-2711)
PHONE..................937 208-8000
Jenny M Lewis, *Pr*
Mark Shaker, *
Makkie Clancy, *
Lisa Bishop, *
Barbara Johnson, *
EMP: 5000 **EST:** 1890
SQ FT: 1,000,000
SALES (est): 1.35B
SALES (corp-wide): 1.48B **Privately Held**
Web: www.premierhealth.com
SIC: 8062 General medical and surgical hospitals
PA: Med America Health Systems Corporation
  1 Wyoming St
  Dayton OH 45409
  937 223-6192

(G-7493)
MIAMI VALLEY HOSPITAL
122 S Patterson Blvd Ste 390 (45402-2409)
PHONE..................937 208-4673
Mary Fischer, *Prin*
EMP: 448
SALES (corp-wide): 1.48B **Privately Held**
Web: www.premierhealth.com
SIC: 8062 General medical and surgical hospitals
HQ: Miami Valley Hospital
  1 Wyoming St
  Dayton OH 45409
  937 208-8000

(G-7494)
MIAMI VALLEY HOSPITAL
Also Called: Child Care Center
1816 Harvard Blvd (45406-4539)
PHONE..................937 224-3916
Angela Collins, *Dir*
EMP: 403
SALES (corp-wide): 1.48B **Privately Held**
Web: www.premierhealth.com
SIC: 8351 Group day care center
HQ: Miami Valley Hospital
  1 Wyoming St
  Dayton OH 45409
  937 208-8000

(G-7495)
MIAMI VALLEY HOSPITALIST GROUP
30 E Apple St Ste 3300 (45409-2939)
PHONE..................937 208-8394
Angela Black, *Prin*
EMP: 100 **EST:** 2013
SALES (est): 7.66MM **Privately Held**
Web: www.premierhealth.com
SIC: 6324 Hospital and medical service plans

(G-7496)
MIAMI VALLEY HSING ASSN I INC
907 W 5th St (45402-8306)
PHONE..................937 263-4449
EMP: 44 **EST:** 1993
SQ FT: 1,000
SALES (est): 47.94K **Privately Held**
Web: www.mvfairhousing.com
SIC: 8052 Home for the mentally retarded, with health care

(G-7497)
MIAMI VALLEY MEMORY GRDNS ASSN (DH)
1639 E Lytle 5 Points Rd (45458-5203)
PHONE..................937 885-7779
Lona Jones, *Genl Mgr*
EMP: 30 **EST:** 1956
SALES (est): 4.01MM
SALES (corp-wide): 4.1B **Publicly Held**
Web: www.miamivalleymemory.com
SIC: 6553 0782 Cemetery association; Lawn and garden services
HQ: Sci Ohio Funeral Services, Inc.
  1985 S Taylor Rd
  Cleveland Heights OH 44118

(G-7498)
MIAMI VALLEY REGIONAL PLG COMM
10 N Ludlow St Ste 700 (45402-1855)
PHONE..................937 223-6323
Donald R Spang, *Dir*
▲ **EMP:** 44 **EST:** 1964
SQ FT: 11,000
SALES (est): 9.25MM **Privately Held**
Web: www.mvrpc.org
SIC: 8748 Economic consultant

(G-7499)
MIAMI VALLEY SCHOOL
5151 Denise Dr (45429-1999)
PHONE..................937 434-4444
Jay Scheurle, *Prin*
Peter B Benedict Ii, *Prin*
EMP: 93 **EST:** 1964
SALES (est): 11.11MM **Privately Held**
Web: www.mvschool.com
SIC: 8351 8211 Preschool center; Elementary and secondary schools

(G-7500)
MIAMI VLY CHILD DEV CTRS INC (PA)
Also Called: MVCDC
215 Horace St (45402-8318)
PHONE..................937 226-5664
Marry Burn, *Pr*
David Marker, *
Dayvenia Chesney, *
EMP: 85 **EST:** 1964
SQ FT: 22,000
SALES (est): 43.26MM
SALES (corp-wide): 43.26MM **Privately Held**
Web: www.mvcdc.org
SIC: 8351 Head Start center, except in conjunction with school

(G-7501)
MIAMI VLY CHILD DEV CTRS INC
Also Called: Miami View Head Start
215 Horace St (45402-8318)
PHONE..................937 228-1644
EMP: 38
SALES (corp-wide): 43.26MM **Privately Held**
Web: www.mvcdc.org
SIC: 8351 Head Start center, except in conjunction with school
PA: Miami Valley Child Development Centers, Inc.
  215 Horace St
  Dayton OH 45402
  937 226-5664

(G-7502)
MIAMI VLY CHILD DEV CTRS INC
Also Called: Twin Towers Head Start
517 Noel Ct (45410-1865)
PHONE..................937 258-2470
Sandy Beard, *Mgr*
EMP: 49
SALES (corp-wide): 43.26MM **Privately Held**
Web: www.mvcdc.org
SIC: 8351 Preschool center
PA: Miami Valley Child Development Centers, Inc.
  215 Horace St
  Dayton OH 45402
  937 226-5664

(G-7503)
MIAMI VLY CMNTY ACTION PARTNR (PA)
Also Called: MVCAP
719 S Main St (45402-2709)
PHONE..................937 222-1009
Lisa Stempler, *Pr*
Stephen V Pipenger, *
Joyce E Price, *
EMP: 60 **EST:** 1964
SQ FT: 21,000
SALES (est): 14.59MM
SALES (corp-wide): 14.59MM **Privately Held**
Web: www.miamivalleycap.org
SIC: 8399 8322 6732 Community action agency; Individual and family services; Trusts: educational, religious, etc.

(G-7504)
MIKE-SELLS POTATO CHIP CO (HQ)
333 Leo St (45404-1007)
P.O. Box 13749 (45413-0749)
PHONE..................937 228-9400
D W Mikesell, *
Martha J Mikesell, *
EMP: 30 **EST:** 1910
SQ FT: 95,000
SALES (est): 34.32MM
SALES (corp-wide): 47.84MM **Privately Held**
Web: www.mikesells.com
SIC: 2096 5145 Potato chips and other potato-based snacks; Snack foods

GEOGRAPHIC SECTION
Dayton - Montgomery County (G-7526)

PA: Mike-Sell's West Virginia, Inc.
333 Leo St
Dayton OH 45404
937 228-9400

(G-7505)
MIKE-SELLS WEST VIRGINIA INC (PA)
333 Leo St (45404)
P.O. Box 115 (45404)
PHONE.................937 228-9400
EMP: 75 EST: 1910
SALES (est): 47.84MM
SALES (corp-wide): 47.84MM **Privately Held**
SIC: 2096 5145 Potato chips and other potato-based snacks; Pretzels

(G-7506)
MILLER-VALENTINE PARTNERS LTD
Also Called: M-V Rlty Mller Valentine Group
409 E Monument Ave Ste 200 (45402)
PHONE.................513 588-1000
Jack Goodwin, Mgr
EMP: 45
SALES (corp-wide): 23.33MM **Privately Held**
Web: www.millervalentine.com
SIC: 6531 Real estate agents and managers
PA: Miller-Valentine Partners Ltd.
9349 Waterstone Blvd # 20
Cincinnati OH 45249
937 293-0900

(G-7507)
MILLER-VLENTINE OPERATIONS INC (PA)
Also Called: Miller Valentine Group
409 E Monument Ave Ste 200 (45402)
PHONE.................937 293-0900
Bill Krul, CEO
William Krul, *
Jack Goodwin, *
Arleen Dudash, *
Edward Blake, *
EMP: 35 EST: 2004
SALES (est): 49.82MM
SALES (corp-wide): 49.82MM **Privately Held**
Web: www.millervalentine.com
SIC: 6531 6552 Real estate managers; Subdividers and developers, nec

(G-7508)
MILLER-VLENTINE OPERATIONS INC
Also Called: Miller Valentine Group
9435 Waterstone Blvd (45409)
PHONE.................513 771-0900
EMP: 383
SALES (corp-wide): 49.82MM **Privately Held**
Web: www.millervalentine.com
SIC: 6552 6531 Subdividers and developers, nec; Real estate managers
PA: Miller-Valentine Operations, Inc.
409 E Monu Ave Ste 200
Dayton OH 45402
937 293-0900

(G-7509)
MINI UNIVERSITY INC (PA)
115 Harbert Dr Ste A (45440-5127)
PHONE.................937 426-1414
Julie Thorner, Pr
EMP: 55 EST: 1987
SALES (est): 5.16MM
SALES (corp-wide): 5.16MM **Privately Held**
Web: www.miniuniversity.net
SIC: 8351 Group day care center

(G-7510)
MODERN OFFICE METHODS INC
Also Called: Mom
7485 Paragon Rd (45459-5315)
PHONE.................937 436-2295
Scott Meredith, Brnch Mgr
EMP: 34
SALES (corp-wide): 45.16MM **Privately Held**
Web: www.momnet.com
SIC: 7699 5999 Professional instrument repair services; Photocopy machines
PA: Modern Office Methods, Inc.
4747 Lake Forest Dr
Cincinnati OH 45242
513 791-0909

(G-7511)
MONTAQUE CLEANING SERVICES LLC
520 Liscum Dr (45417-8803)
PHONE.................937 705-0429
EMP: 50
SALES (est): 1.16MM **Privately Held**
SIC: 7389 7349 Business Activities at Non-Commercial Site; Janitorial service, contract basis

(G-7512)
MOONLIGHT SECURITY INC
4977 Northcutt Pl (45414-3839)
PHONE.................937 252-1600
John Pawelski, Pr
EMP: 85 EST: 1995
SALES (est): 2.5MM **Privately Held**
Web: www.moonlightsecurityinc.com
SIC: 7381 Security guard service

(G-7513)
MORAINE COUNTRY CLUB
4075 Southern Blvd (45429-1199)
PHONE.................937 294-6200
Jack E King, Pr
Jack Proud, *
John Giering, *
EMP: 35 EST: 1929
SQ FT: 20,000
SALES (est): 6.79MM **Privately Held**
Web: www.morainecountryclub.com
SIC: 7997 Country club, membership

(G-7514)
MORGAN SERVICES INC
817 Webster St (45404-1529)
PHONE.................937 223-5241
Mike Gardner, Brnch Mgr
EMP: 118
SALES (corp-wide): 72.96MM **Privately Held**
Web: www.morganservices.com
SIC: 7213 7211 Linen supply; Power laundries, family and commercial
PA: Morgan Services, Inc.
323 N Michigan Ave
Chicago IL 60601
312 346-3181

(G-7515)
MOTION INDUSTRIES INC
Also Called: Motion Industries
7400 Webster St (45414-5816)
P.O. Box 24335 (45424-0335)
PHONE.................937 236-7711
Frank Harrall, Mgr
EMP: 28
SQ FT: 12,000
SALES (corp-wide): 22.1B **Publicly Held**
Web: www.motion.com
SIC: 5085 Industrial supplies
HQ: Motion Industries, Inc.
1605 Alton Rd
Birmingham AL 35210
205 956-1122

(G-7516)
MOTO FRANCHISE CORPORATION (PA)
Also Called: Motophoto
7086 Corporate Way Ste 2 (45459-4298)
PHONE.................937 291-1900
Harry D Loyle, Pr
Joseph M O'hara, VP
Ron Mohney, *
EMP: 32 EST: 2002
SQ FT: 3,500
SALES (est): 5.22MM
SALES (corp-wide): 5.22MM **Privately Held**
SIC: 6794 Franchises, selling or licensing

(G-7517)
MUHA CONSTRUCTION INC
Also Called: Midwest Painting
855 Congress Park Dr Ste 101 (45459-4096)
PHONE.................937 435-0678
David J Muha, Pr
Chuck Albert, *
EMP: 46 EST: 1985
SQ FT: 40,000
SALES (est): 5.82MM **Privately Held**
Web: www.muhaconstruction.com
SIC: 1721 1542 Commercial painting; Commercial and office building contractors

(G-7518)
MURFBOOKS LLC
1825 Webster St (45404-1147)
PHONE.................937 260-3741
Greg Murphy, Brnch Mgr
EMP: 29
SALES (corp-wide): 367.14K **Privately Held**
Web: www.murfbooks.com
SIC: 5192 Books
PA: Murfbooks Llc
1723 Webster St
Dayton OH 45404
937 212-9165

(G-7519)
MUTUAL ELECTRIC COMPANY
3660 Dayton Park Dr (45414-4406)
P.O. Box 131222 (45413-1222)
PHONE.................937 254-6211
Ted Michel, Pr
Belinda Michel, *
Robert Kreitzer, *
EMP: 32 EST: 1944
SQ FT: 7,000
SALES (est): 1.87MM **Privately Held**
Web: www.mutual-electric.com
SIC: 1731 General electrical contractor

(G-7520)
MVHE INC (HQ)
110 N Main St Ste 370 (45402-3729)
PHONE.................937 499-8211
Ken Prunier, Pr
Joseph Mendhall, *
David Sturgeon, *
EMP: 40 EST: 1986
SQ FT: 2,100
SALES (est): 54.89MM
SALES (corp-wide): 1.48B **Privately Held**
SIC: 8099 8011 Medical services organization; Offices and clinics of medical doctors
PA: Med America Health Systems Corporation
1 Wyoming St
Dayton OH 45409

937 223-6192

(G-7521)
MVHE INC
Also Called: Beavercreek Fmly Mdcine Obsttr
111 Harbert Dr (45440-5117)
PHONE.................937 208-7575
EMP: 229
SALES (corp-wide): 1.48B **Privately Held**
SIC: 8011 Physicians' office, including specialists
HQ: Mvhe, Inc.
110 N Main St Ste 370
Dayton OH 45402

(G-7522)
MW METALS GROUP LLC
461 Homestead Ave (45417-3921)
P.O. Box 546 (45401-0546)
PHONE.................937 222-5992
Joel Frydman, CEO
Farley Frydman, Pr
EMP: 65 EST: 1955
SQ FT: 150,000
SALES (est): 18.57MM **Privately Held**
Web: www.mwmetals.com
SIC: 3341 5093 Secondary nonferrous metals; Scrap and waste materials

(G-7523)
MYTEAM1 LLC
Also Called: One Call Now
6450 Poe Ave Ste 500 (45414-2648)
P.O. Box 596 (45373-0596)
PHONE.................877 698-3262
EMP: 34
Web: www.onsolve.com
SIC: 4813 Data telephone communications

(G-7524)
N C R EMPLOYEES BENEFIT ASSN
Also Called: NCR Country Club
4435 Dogwood Trl (45429-1239)
PHONE.................937 299-3571
Steve Scarpino, Pr
EMP: 150 EST: 1953
SQ FT: 44,000
SALES (est): 10.49MM **Privately Held**
Web: www.ncrcountryclub.com
SIC: 7997 7991 5812 Country club, membership; Physical fitness facilities; Eating places

(G-7525)
NATIONAL HERITG ACADEMIES INC
Also Called: Emerson Academy
501 Hickory St (45410-1232)
PHONE.................937 223-2889
Alison Foreman, Brnch Mgr
EMP: 29
Web: www.nhaschools.com
SIC: 8741 Management services
PA: National Heritage Academies, Inc.
3850 Broadmoor Ave Se # 201
Grand Rapids MI 49512

(G-7526)
NATIONAL HERITG ACADEMIES INC
Also Called: North Dayton School Discovery
3901 Turner Rd (45415-3654)
PHONE.................937 278-6671
Ron Albino, Brnch Mgr
EMP: 29
Web: www.nhaschools.com
SIC: 8741 Management services
PA: National Heritage Academies, Inc.
3850 Broadmoor Ave Se # 201
Grand Rapids MI 49512

Dayton - Montgomery County (G-7527)

(G-7527)
NATIONAL HOSPICE COOPERATIVE
7575 Paragon Rd (45459-5316)
PHONE..................................937 256-9507
Kent Anderson, *CEO*
EMP: 40 **EST:** 2018
SALES (est): 972.68K **Privately Held**
Web:
www.nationalhospicecooperative.org
SIC: 8011 Health maintenance organization

(G-7528)
NCT RETAIL
7 Dayton Wire Pkwy (45404-1242)
PHONE..................................937 236-8000
EMP: 47 **EST:** 2019
SALES (est): 1.39MM **Privately Held**
Web: www.ncttech.com
SIC: 7311 Advertising agencies

(G-7529)
NELSON TREE SERVICE INC (DH)
Also Called: Nelson
3300 Office Park Dr (45439-2394)
PHONE..................................937 294-1313
Lou Nekola, *Pr*
Jeff Jones, *
EMP: 35 **EST:** 1919
SQ FT: 4,000
SALES (est): 17.93MM
SALES (corp-wide): 1.16B **Privately Held**
Web: www.nelsontree.com
SIC: 0783 Tree trimming services for public utility lines
HQ: Utility Vegetation Services, Inc.
   708 Blair Mill Rd
   Willow Grove PA 19090

(G-7530)
NICHOLAS E DAVIS
Also Called: Taft Law
40 N Main St Ste 1700 (45423-1029)
PHONE..................................937 228-2838
Nicholas Davis, *Pt*
EMP: 48 **EST:** 2016
SALES (est): 2.47MM **Privately Held**
SIC: 8111 General practice law office

(G-7531)
NORTHROP GRMMN SPCE & MSSN SYS
1900 Founders Dr Ste 202 (45420-1182)
PHONE..................................937 259-4956
EMP: 60
SIC: 7372 7374 Prepackaged software; Data processing and preparation
HQ: Northrop Grumman Space & Mission Systems Corp.
   6379 San Ignacio Ave
   San Jose CA 95119
   703 280-2900

(G-7532)
NORTHWEST CHILD DEVELOPMENT AN
2823 Campus Dr (45406-4103)
PHONE..................................937 559-9565
EMP: 40 **EST:** 2017
SALES (est): 331.86K **Privately Held**
SIC: 8351 Child day care services

(G-7533)
OAK CREEK TERRACE INC
2316 Springmill Rd (45440-2504)
PHONE..................................937 439-1454
Barry A Kohn, *Pr*
Samuel Boymel, *
Harold J Sosna, *
EMP: 101 **EST:** 1985
SALES (est): 6.42MM **Privately Held**
Web: www.caringplacehcg.com
SIC: 8051 Convalescent home with continuous nursing care

(G-7534)
OHIO PEDIATRICS INC (PA)
1775 Delco Park Dr (45420-1398)
PHONE..................................937 299-2743
James Bryant, *Pr*
EMP: 45 **EST:** 1986
SALES (est): 5.21MM **Privately Held**
Web: www.ohiopediatrics.com
SIC: 8011 Pediatrician

(G-7535)
OHIOS HOSPICE INC
7575 Paragon Rd (45459)
PHONE..................................937 256-4490
John L Green, *Prin*
EMP: 99 **EST:** 2018
SALES (est): 24.49MM **Privately Held**
Web: www.hospiceofdayton.org
SIC: 8052 Personal care facility

(G-7536)
OHIOS HOSPICE FOUNDATION 0
324 Wilmington Ave (45420-1890)
PHONE..................................937 256-4490
EMP: 28 **EST:** 2011
SALES (est): 6.33MM **Privately Held**
Web: www.hospiceofdayton.org
SIC: 8052 Personal care facility

(G-7537)
OLECO INC
137 N Main St Ste 722 (45402-1862)
PHONE..................................937 223-3000
Colleen Diefenbacher, *Brnch Mgr*
EMP: 29
SALES (corp-wide): 25MM **Privately Held**
Web: www.globaltec.com
SIC: 8731 Electronic research
PA: Oleco, Inc.
   18683 Trimble Ct
   Spring Lake MI 49456
   616 842-6790

(G-7538)
ONE LINCOLN PARK
590 Isaac Prugh Way (45429-3482)
PHONE..................................937 298-0594
Miller Valentine, *Pt*
Charles A Osborn Junior Ldt, *Pt*
EMP: 33 **EST:** 1986
SALES (est): 10.29MM **Privately Held**
Web: www.lincolnparkseniors.com
SIC: 6513 6531 Retirement hotel operation; Real estate agents and managers

(G-7539)
ONEFIFTEEN RECOVERY
601 S Edwin C Moses Blvd (45417-3424)
PHONE..................................937 223-5609
EMP: 30 **EST:** 2019
SALES (est): 1.86MM **Privately Held**
Web: www.onefifteen.org
SIC: 8742 Business management consultant

(G-7540)
ORBIT MOVERS & ERECTORS INC
1101 Negley Pl (45402-6258)
PHONE..................................937 277-8080
James Arnett Junior, *Ch*
Jay Hahn, *
David Grayson, *
Donald Roberts, *
EMP: 42 **EST:** 1975
SQ FT: 125,000
SALES (est): 946.41K **Privately Held**
Web: www.orbitsdo.com
SIC: 1796 1791 Millwright; Iron work, structural
PA: Unitize Company, Inc.
   1101 Negley Pl
   Dayton OH 45402

(G-7541)
ORTHOPEDIC ASSOCIATES DAYTON
7980 N Main St (45415-2328)
PHONE..................................937 280-4988
Thomas Cook, *Prin*
Melinda Scott, *
Julie Shott, *
Lance Tigyer, *
EMP: 45 **EST:** 2010
SALES (est): 6.38MM **Privately Held**
Web: www.orthodayton.net
SIC: 8011 Orthopedic physician

(G-7542)
OTTERBEIN SNIOR LFSTYLE CHICES
Also Called: OTTERBEIN SENIOR LIFESTYLE CHOICES
9320 Avalon Cir (45458-4989)
PHONE..................................937 885-5426
Amy Kincaid, *Brnch Mgr*
EMP: 39
SALES (corp-wide): 74.71MM **Privately Held**
Web: www.otterbein.org
SIC: 8059 8051 Nursing home, except skilled and intermediate care facility; Skilled nursing care facilities
PA: Otterbein Homes
   3855 Lower Market St # 300
   Lebanon OH 45036
   513 933-5400

(G-7543)
P & R COMMUNICATIONS SVC INC (PA)
Also Called: First Page
731 E 1st St (45402-1302)
PHONE..................................937 512-8100
Katherine Ward, *CEO*
Steve Reeves, *
David Reeves, *
EMP: 39 **EST:** 1964
SQ FT: 30,000
SALES (est): 8.96MM
SALES (corp-wide): 8.96MM **Privately Held**
Web: www.pandrcommunications.com
SIC: 7622 5065 Radio repair shop, nec; Radio parts and accessories, nec

(G-7544)
PAE & ASSOCIATES INC
7925 Paragon Rd (45459-4090)
PHONE..................................937 833-0013
EMP: 75 **EST:** 1992
SQ FT: 5,700
SALES (est): 1.62MM **Privately Held**
SIC: 1629 Industrial plant construction

(G-7545)
PAIN EVLATION MGT CTR OHIO INC
Also Called: Pain Evaluation & MGT Ctr O
1550 Yankee Park Pl Ste A (45458-1838)
PHONE..................................937 439-4949
Richard M Donnini, *Pr*
EMP: 47 **EST:** 1989
SALES (est): 4.22MM **Privately Held**
Web: www.daytonpain.com
SIC: 8011 Orthopedic physician

(G-7546)
PARADIGM INDUSTRIAL LLC
Also Called: Paradigm Industrial
730 Lorain Ave (45410-2425)
PHONE..................................937 224-4415
Ashley Webb, *Pr*
EMP: 40 **EST:** 1999
SALES (est): 6.39MM **Privately Held**
Web: www.vulcantoolcompany.com
SIC: 7699 7363 Industrial machinery and equipment repair; Employee leasing service

(G-7547)
PATRICIA A DICKERSON MD
1299 E Alex Bell Rd (45459-2658)
PHONE..................................937 436-1117
Patricia A Dickerson, *Owner*
EMP: 28 **EST:** 1991
SALES (est): 1.13MM **Privately Held**
Web: www.caringderms.com
SIC: 8011 Dermatologist

(G-7548)
PEOPLFRST HMCARE HSPICE OHIO L (DH)
Also Called: Acclaim Hspice Plltive Care Dy
7887 Washington Village Dr Ste 135 (45459-3959)
PHONE..................................937 433-2400
Cindy Henderson, *Prin*
EMP: 50 **EST:** 2007
SALES (est): 1.14MM
SALES (corp-wide): 13.68B **Privately Held**
SIC: 8082 Home health care services
HQ: Kindred Healthcare, Llc
   680 S 4th St
   Louisville KY 40202
   502 596-7300

(G-7549)
PEPSI-COLA METRO BTLG CO INC
Also Called: Pepsi-Cola
526 Milburn Ave (45404-1678)
PHONE..................................937 461-4664
Tim Trant, *Genl Mgr*
EMP: 49
SQ FT: 115,000
SALES (corp-wide): 86.39B **Publicly Held**
Web: www.pepsico.com
SIC: 2086 5149 Soft drinks: packaged in cans, bottles, etc.; Groceries and related products, nec
HQ: Pepsi-Cola Metropolitan Bottling Company, Inc.
   700 Anderson Hill Rd
   Purchase NY 10577
   914 767-6000

(G-7550)
PERI NATAL PARTNERS LLC
7707 Paragon Rd Ste 103 (45459-4070)
PHONE..................................937 208-6970
Terry Stuerman, *Brnch Mgr*
EMP: 99
SALES (corp-wide): 317.93K **Privately Held**
Web: www.premierhealth.com
SIC: 8011 Offices and clinics of medical doctors
PA: Peri Natal Partners Llc
   1 Berry Dr
   Dayton OH 45426
   937 208-2516

(G-7551)
PHOENIX GROUP HOLDING CO
509 Windsor Park Dr (45459-4112)
PHONE..................................937 704-9850
George Coates, *CEO*
Robert D Gray, *
EMP: 140 **EST:** 1990
SALES (est): 8.46MM **Privately Held**
Web: www.thephxway.com

GEOGRAPHIC SECTION
Dayton - Montgomery County (G-7574)

SIC: 8711 Consulting engineer

(G-7552)
PICKREL BROS INC
Also Called: Pickrel Brothers
901 S Perry St (45402-2526)
PHONE..................937 461-5960
Thomas Pickrel, *CEO*
James L Pickrel, *
James L Rohl, *
EMP: 50 EST: 1953
SQ FT: 25,000
SALES (est): 17.6MM **Privately Held**
Web: www.pickrelbros.com
SIC: 5074 Plumbing fittings and supplies

(G-7553)
PICKREL SCHAEFFER EBELING LPA
40 N Main St Ste 2700 (45423-2700)
PHONE..................937 223-1130
Paul Zimmer, *Pr*
Jon Rosmeyer, *
EMP: 55 EST: 1915
SQ FT: 16,000
SALES (est): 10.26MM **Privately Held**
Web: www.pselaw.com
SIC: 8111 General practice law office

(G-7554)
PIQUA FAMILY PRACTICE
110 N Main St Ste 350 (45402-3735)
PHONE..................937 773-6314
EMP: 28 EST: 1992
SALES (est): 440.45K **Privately Held**
Web: www.premierhealth.com
SIC: 8011 General and family practice, physician/surgeon

(G-7555)
PLANNED PARENTHOOD ASSOCIATION (PA)
Also Called: Planned Prnthood of Grter Mami
224 N Wilkinson St (45402-3096)
PHONE..................937 226-0780
EMP: 33 EST: 1964
SQ FT: 14,000
SALES (est): 3.89MM
SALES (corp-wide): 3.89MM **Privately Held**
Web: www.plannedparenthood.org
SIC: 8093 8322 Family planning clinic; Individual and family services

(G-7556)
PLASTIC SRGERY INST DAYTON INC
Also Called: Maupin Johnson & Schmidt Md's
9985 Dayton Lebanon Pike (45458-4231)
PHONE..................937 886-2980
Gregory E Maupin Md, *Pr*
Doctor Steven Shmidt, *Pt*
EMP: 35 EST: 1979
SQ FT: 1,000
SALES (est): 4.61MM **Privately Held**
Web: www.daytonplasticsurgery.com
SIC: 8011 Plastic surgeon

(G-7557)
PLATINUM EXPRESS INC
2549 Stanley Ave (45404-2730)
PHONE..................937 235-9540
Mina Burba, *Pr*
EMP: 38 EST: 1999
SALES (est): 5.82MM **Privately Held**
Web: www.platinumexpressinc.com
SIC: 4213 Trucking, except local

(G-7558)
PORTER WRGHT MORRIS ARTHUR LLP
Also Called: Attorneys-At-Law
1 S Main St Ste 1600 (45402-2088)
P.O. Box 1805 (45401-1805)
PHONE..................937 449-6810
R Bruce Snyder, *Mng Pt*
EMP: 29
SQ FT: 25,500
SALES (corp-wide): 47.71MM **Privately Held**
Web: www.porterwright.com
SIC: 8111 General practice law office
PA: Porter, Wright, Morris & Arthur Llp
  41 S High St Ste 2900
  Columbus OH 43215
  614 227-2000

(G-7559)
PRECISION MTAL FABRICATION INC (PA)
191 Heid Ave (45404-1217)
PHONE..................937 235-9261
Jim Hackenberger, *Pr*
John Limberg, *
EMP: 57 EST: 1984
SQ FT: 30,000
SALES (est): 9.02MM
SALES (corp-wide): 9.02MM **Privately Held**
Web: www.premetfab.com
SIC: 7692 3444 Welding repair; Sheet metalwork

(G-7560)
PREMIER HEALTH PARTNERS (PA)
Also Called: MIAMI VALLEY
110 N Main St Ste 450 (45402-3712)
PHONE..................937 499-9596
James R Pancoast, *Pr*
Mark Shaker, *
Mary H Boosalis, *
William E Linesch, *
Thomas M Duncan, *
EMP: 636 EST: 1995
SALES (est): 2.41MM
SALES (corp-wide): 2.41MM **Privately Held**
Web: www.premierhealth.com
SIC: 8082 Home health care services

(G-7561)
PREMIER INTEGRATED MED ASSOC (PA)
Also Called: Primed Physicians
6551 Centerville Business Pkwy Ste 110 (45459)
PHONE..................937 291-6813
Mark Couch, *Pr*
EMP: 67 EST: 1959
SALES (est): 18.68MM
SALES (corp-wide): 18.68MM **Privately Held**
Web: www.primedphysicians.com
SIC: 8011 Internal medicine, physician/surgeon

(G-7562)
PRIMARY CARE NTWRK PRMIER HLTH
Also Called: Perinatal Partners
2350 Miami Valley Dr Ste 410 (45459-4785)
PHONE..................937 424-9800
Terri L Stuerman, *VP*
EMP: 41
SALES (corp-wide): 25.36MM **Privately Held**
Web: www.premierhealth.com
SIC: 8011 General and family practice, physician/surgeon
PA: Primary Care Network Of Premier Health Partners
  110 N Main St Ste 350
  Dayton OH 45402
  937 226-7085

(G-7563)
PRIMARY CR NTWRK PRMR HLTH PRT (PA)
Also Called: Samanritan Family Care
110 N Main St Ste 350 (45402-3735)
PHONE..................937 226-7085
Ken Prunier, *Pr*
Dave Sturgeon, *
EMP: 30 EST: 1996
SALES (est): 25.36MM
SALES (corp-wide): 25.36MM **Privately Held**
Web: www.premierhealth.com
SIC: 8011 General and family practice, physician/surgeon

(G-7564)
PRIMARY CR NTWRK PRMR HLTH PRT
1222 S Patterson Blvd Ste 120 (45402-2684)
PHONE..................937 208-9090
EMP: 31
SALES (corp-wide): 25.36MM **Privately Held**
Web: www.premierhealth.com
SIC: 8011 General and family practice, physician/surgeon
PA: Primary Care Network Of Premier Health Partners
  110 N Main St Ste 350
  Dayton OH 45402
  937 226-7085

(G-7565)
PRIMARY DAYTON INNKEEPERS LLC
7701 Washington Village Dr (45459-3954)
PHONE..................937 938-9550
EMP: 27 EST: 2011
SALES (est): 892.67K **Privately Held**
SIC: 7011 Hotels

(G-7566)
PRIMED KETTERING PEDIATRICS
5250 Far Hills Ave Ste 110 (45429-2382)
PHONE..................937 433-7991
Debra Bockhorn, *Prin*
EMP: 34 EST: 2005
SALES (est): 399.53K **Privately Held**
Web: www.primedphysicians.com
SIC: 8011 Internal medicine, physician/surgeon

(G-7567)
PRIMED PHYSICIANS
8501 Troy Pike # 1 (45424-1054)
PHONE..................937 237-4945
EMP: 76 EST: 2019
SALES (est): 737.05K **Privately Held**
Web: www.primedphysicians.com
SIC: 8011 Internal medicine, physician/surgeon

(G-7568)
PRIMED PHYSICIANS
6551 Centerville Business Pkwy Ste 110 (45459)
PHONE..................937 298-8058
John E Mauer Md, *Pt*
Tamara Togliatti, *Pt*
Malak Adib, *Pt*
EMP: 44 EST: 2007
SALES (est): 2.26MM **Privately Held**
Web: www.primedphysicians.com
SIC: 8011 General and family practice, physician/surgeon

(G-7569)
PRODUCE ONE INC
904 Woodley Rd (45403-1444)
PHONE..................931 253-4749
Gary Pavlofsky, *Pr*
Ervin Pavlofsky, *
EMP: 75 EST: 1920
SQ FT: 14,000
SALES (est): 18.58MM
SALES (corp-wide): 18.58MM **Privately Held**
Web: www.premierproduceone.com
SIC: 5148 5142 5147 5149 Fruits, fresh; Fish, frozen: packaged; Meats, fresh; Canned goods: fruit, vegetables, seafood, meats, etc.
PA: Premier Produce Properties, Ltd.
  4500 Willow Pkwy
  Cleveland OH 44125
  800 229-5517

(G-7570)
PROJECT CURE INC
200 Daruma Pkwy (45439-7909)
PHONE..................937 262-3500
Zel Skelton, *Dir*
EMP: 50 EST: 1970
SQ FT: 14,280
SALES (est): 2.41MM **Privately Held**
Web: www.projectcureinc.org
SIC: 8093 Substance abuse clinics (outpatient)

(G-7571)
PROJECTS UNLIMITED INC (PA)
6300 Sand Lake Rd (45414-2649)
PHONE..................937 918-2200
EMP: 170 EST: 1954
SALES (est): 38.25MM
SALES (corp-wide): 38.25MM **Privately Held**
Web: www.pui.com
SIC: 3672 3679 3643 3625 Printed circuit boards; Harness assemblies, for electronic use: wire or cable; Current-carrying wiring services; Relays and industrial controls

(G-7572)
PROTECTIVE COATINGS INC
4321 Webster St (45414-4935)
PHONE..................937 275-7711
EMP: 30 EST: 1993
SQ FT: 4,000
SALES (est): 2.4MM **Privately Held**
Web: www.pci-corp.biz
SIC: 1721 1761 1752 1741 Interior commercial painting contractor; Roofing, siding, and sheetmetal work; Floor laying and floor work, nec; Foundation building

(G-7573)
PULMONARY CRTCAL CARE CONS INC
Also Called: Thakore, Gnan N MD
1520 S Main St Ste 2 (45409-2643)
PHONE..................937 461-5815
Gnan Thakore Md, *Pr*
Michael W Craig, *Pr*
Doctor Eduardo Casalmir, *VP*
Doctor James Graham, *Sec*
EMP: 37 EST: 1984
SALES (est): 9.37MM **Privately Held**
Web: www.pulmcare.com
SIC: 8011 Pulmonary specialist, physician/surgeon

(G-7574)
PURE HEALTHCARE
324 Wilmington Ave (45420-1890)
PHONE..................937 668-7873
Amy Kemper, *Prin*

Dayton - Montgomery County (G-7575) — **GEOGRAPHIC SECTION**

EMP: 30 EST: 2014
SALES (est): 857.54K Privately Held
Web: www.purehealthcare.org
SIC: 8082 Home health care services

(G-7575)
QUEBE HOLDINGS INC (HQ)
Also Called: Chapel Electric Co.
1985 Founders Dr (45420-4012)
P.O. Box 1294 (45401-1294)
PHONE.................937 222-2290
Dennis F Quebe, Pr
Gregory P Ross, *
Roger Vanderhorst, *
Richard E Penewit, *
EMP: 100 EST: 2002
SQ FT: 40,000
SALES (est): 102.18MM
SALES (corp-wide): 12.58B Publicly Held
Web: www.quebe.com
SIC: 1731 Lighting contractor
PA: Emcor Group, Inc.
    301 Merritt 7
    Norwalk CT 06851
    203 849-7800

(G-7576)
R L FENDER CONSTRUCTION CO
Also Called: Fender Construction
362 Huffman Ave (45403-2459)
PHONE.................937 258-9604
Dennis Schimpf, Pr
John Schimpf, VP
Kimball Birdseye, CFO
EMP: 27 EST: 1983
SQ FT: 10,000
SALES (est): 2.23MM Privately Held
Web: www.rlfender.com
SIC: 1542 1541 Commercial and office building, new construction; Industrial buildings, new construction, nec

(G-7577)
R L O INC (PA)
Also Called: Great Clips
466 Windsor Park Dr (45459-4111)
P.O. Box 750250 (45475-0250)
PHONE.................937 620-9998
Clara Osterhage, Pr
Raymond Osterhage, *
EMP: 35 EST: 1995
SALES (est): 2.34MM
SALES (corp-wide): 2.34MM Privately Held
Web: www.greatclips.com
SIC: 7231 Unisex hair salons

(G-7578)
R S STOLL AND COMPANY
Also Called: Stoll & Co
1801 S Metro Pkwy (45459-2523)
PHONE.................937 434-7800
Ronald S Stoll, Pr
EMP: 38 EST: 1983
SQ FT: 12,000
SALES (est): 981.26K Privately Held
Web: www.americaswatchmaker.com
SIC: 7631 Watch repair

(G-7579)
RAHN DENTAL GROUP INC
5660 Far Hills Ave (45429-2206)
PHONE.................937 435-0324
Douglas Patton, Pr
Doctor Paul Unverferth, VP
Doctor Richard C Quinttus, Sec
EMP: 45 EST: 1975
SALES (est): 2.56MM Privately Held
Web: www.rahndentalgroup.com
SIC: 8021 Dentists' office

(G-7580)
RAM RESTORATION LLC
Also Called: Ram Resources
11125 Yankee St (45458-3698)
PHONE.................937 347-7418
EMP: 36 EST: 2012
SQ FT: 2,500
SALES (est): 2.61MM Privately Held
Web: www.ramrestorationusa.com
SIC: 1799 1521 1522 Home/office interiors finishing, furnishing and remodeling; Single-family home remodeling, additions, and repairs; Hotel/motel and multi-family home renovation and remodeling

(G-7581)
REAL ART DESIGN GROUP INC (PA)
520 E 1st St (45402-1221)
PHONE.................937 223-9955
Christopher Wire, Pr
EMP: 54 EST: 1984
SQ FT: 25,000
SALES (est): 9.16MM
SALES (corp-wide): 9.16MM Privately Held
Web: www.realart.com
SIC: 7336 7311 Graphic arts and related design; Advertising consultant

(G-7582)
REALMARK PROPERTY INVESTORS
Also Called: Fox Hunt Apts
2095 Valley Greene Dr (45440)
PHONE.................937 434-7242
Dona Anderson, Mgr
EMP: 27
SIC: 6513 Apartment building operators
PA: Realmark Property Investors Limited Partnership - li
    2350 N Forest Rd
    Getzville NY 14068

(G-7583)
RELIABLE CONTRACTORS INC
Also Called: Rave - Rlable Audio Video Elec
94 Compark Rd Ste 200 (45459-4853)
PHONE.................937 433-0262
Joe Ryan, Pr
EMP: 60 EST: 1942
SQ FT: 12,500
SALES (est): 13.16MM Privately Held
Web: www.reliable-contractors.com
SIC: 1731 General electrical contractor

(G-7584)
RELIABLE HOME HEALTHCARE LLC
50 Chestnut St Ste 224 (45440-1489)
PHONE.................937 274-2900
Farhiya Ibrahim, Prin
EMP: 30 EST: 2015
SALES (est): 333.32K Privately Held
Web: www.bluesummitcare.com
SIC: 8082 Home health care services

(G-7585)
RENTHOTEL DAYTON LLC
Also Called: Doubletree Hotel
11 S Ludlow St (45402-1810)
PHONE.................937 461-4700
Robert Holsten, Prin
▲ EMP: 87 EST: 1997
SQ FT: 184,000
SALES (est): 506.31K Privately Held
Web: www.hilton.com
SIC: 7011 Hotels

(G-7586)
RES CARE HOME CARE
Also Called: Rest Care
8265 Mcewen Rd (45458-2040)
PHONE.................937 436-3966
EMP: 79
SALES (corp-wide): 231.97K Privately Held
SIC: 8082 Home health care services
PA: Res. Care Home Care
    1930 Commerce Center Blvd
    Fairborn OH 45324
    937 439-7500

(G-7587)
RESCUE91 HEALTHCARE SVCS LLC
1715 Springfield St Ste 4 (45403-1431)
PHONE.................937 500-5371
Kelvin Afful, Managing Member
EMP: 35 EST: 2018
SALES (est): 1.2MM Privately Held
Web: www.rescue91healthcareservices.com
SIC: 8082 Home health care services

(G-7588)
RESIDENT HM ASSN GRTER DYTON I
3661 Salem Ave (45406-1627)
PHONE.................937 278-0791
Brenda Whitney, Dir
EMP: 65 EST: 1966
SQ FT: 4,582
SALES (est): 5.24MM Privately Held
Web: www.rhadayton.com
SIC: 8361 Mentally handicapped home

(G-7589)
RESIDENTIAL CARE INC
Also Called: Temporary Health Care Service
1250 W Dorothy Ln Ste 304 (45409-1312)
PHONE.................937 299-8090
Mary Kostick, Pr
EMP: 256 EST: 1990
SQ FT: 1,300
SALES (est): 4.61MM Privately Held
SIC: 7361 7363 Employment agencies; Help supply services

(G-7590)
REYNOLDS AND REYNOLDS HOLDINGS
Also Called: Managed Marketing Solutions
1 Reynolds Way (45430-1586)
PHONE.................937 485-8125
EMP: 41 EST: 2015
SALES (est): 26.08MM Privately Held
Web: www.reyrey.com
SIC: 5112 Business forms

(G-7591)
RITE AID OF OHIO INC
Also Called: Rite Aid
3875 Salem Ave (45406-1633)
PHONE.................937 277-1611
Alan Kreinbihl, Brnch Mgr
EMP: 47
SALES (corp-wide): 24.09B Publicly Held
Web: www.riteaid.com
SIC: 5912 7384 Drug stores; Photofinishing laboratory
HQ: Rite Aid Of Ohio, Inc.
    1200 Intrepid Ave Ste 2
    Philadelphia PA 19112

(G-7592)
RITE AID OF OHIO INC
Also Called: Rite Aid
2532 E 3rd St (45403-2019)
PHONE.................937 258-8101
Larue Brogan, Mgr
EMP: 47
SALES (corp-wide): 24.09B Publicly Held
Web: www.riteaid.com
SIC: 5912 7384 Drug stores; Photofinishing laboratory
HQ: Rite Aid Of Ohio, Inc.
    1200 Intrepid Ave Ste 2
    Philadelphia PA 19112

(G-7593)
RITE AID OF OHIO INC
Also Called: Rite Aid
2916 Linden Ave (45410-3027)
PHONE.................937 256-3111
John Nash, Mgr
EMP: 47
SALES (corp-wide): 24.09B Publicly Held
Web: www.riteaid.com
SIC: 5912 7384 Drug stores; Photofinishing laboratory
HQ: Rite Aid Of Ohio, Inc.
    1200 Intrepid Ave Ste 2
    Philadelphia PA 19112

(G-7594)
RIVERSIDE COMPUTING INC
Also Called: Agilit
8613 N Dixie Dr (45414-2403)
PHONE.................937 440-9199
Wesley Gipe, Pr
David Gipe, Proj Mgr
EMP: 36 EST: 1997
SQ FT: 3,600
SALES (est): 4.34MM Privately Held
Web: www.propoint.net
SIC: 7379 Computer related consulting services

(G-7595)
RIVERVIEW HEALTH INSTITUTE
1 Elizabeth Pl (45417-3445)
PHONE.................937 222-5390
Ethan Fallang, CEO
EMP: 64 EST: 2003
SALES (est): 19.42MM Privately Held
Web: www.riverviewhealthinstitute.com
SIC: 8011 Medical centers

(G-7596)
ROSE HEALTH CARE SERVICES LTD
419 Grafton Ave (45406-5202)
PHONE.................937 277-7518
C Hamilton, Owner
EMP: 30 EST: 1999
SALES (est): 830K Privately Held
SIC: 8082 Home health care services

(G-7597)
RUMPKE TRANSPORTATION CO LLC
Also Called: Rumpke Container Service
1932 E Monument Ave (45402-1359)
PHONE.................937 461-0004
Kyle Aughe, Mgr
EMP: 263
Web: www.rumpke.com
SIC: 4953 7359 Refuse collection and disposal services; Portable toilet rental
HQ: Rumpke Transportation Company, Llc
    10795 Hughes Rd
    Cincinnati OH 45251
    513 851-0122

(G-7598)
RUSH EXPEDITING INC
2619 Needmore Rd (45414-4205)
PHONE.................937 885-0894
Jan E Parker, Pr
EMP: 30 EST: 2003
SALES (est): 2.71MM Privately Held
Web: www.rush-delivery.com
SIC: 4729 Carpool/vanpool arrangement

GEOGRAPHIC SECTION
Dayton - Montgomery County (G-7620)

(G-7599)
RUSH TRUCK LEASING INC
Also Called: Daytonidealease
7655 Poe Ave (45414-2552)
PHONE..............................937 264-2365
EMP: 32
SALES (corp-wide): 7.93B **Publicly Held**
Web: www.rushenterprises.com
SIC: 5012 7538 5531 5014 Automobiles and other motor vehicles; General automotive repair shops; Auto and home supply stores; Tires and tubes
HQ: Rush Truck Leasing, Inc.
11777 Highway Dr
Cincinnati OH 45241
513 733-8510

(G-7600)
S & G 3 LLC
5161 Cornerstone North Blvd (45440-2274)
PHONE..............................937 988-0050
EMP: 30 EST: 2016
SALES (est): 2.56MM **Privately Held**
SIC: 1522 Hotel/motel, new construction

(G-7601)
S & S MANAGEMENT INC
Also Called: Holiday Inn
5612 Merily Way (45424-2065)
PHONE..............................937 235-2000
Brian Mckenzie, *Mgr*
EMP: 53
SALES (corp-wide): 9.26MM **Privately Held**
Web: www.holidayinn.com
SIC: 7011 Hotels and motels
PA: S & S Management Inc
550 Folkerth Ave 100
Sidney OH 45365
937 498-9645

(G-7602)
S&D/OSTERFELD MECH CONTRS INC
1101 Negley Pl (45402-6258)
PHONE..............................937 277-1700
Jeff Arthur, *CEO*
James Arnett Junior, *CEO*
Lisa Schneider, *
David Grayson, *
Donald Roberts, *
EMP: 58 EST: 1908
SQ FT: 125,000
SALES (est): 2.36MM **Privately Held**
Web: www.unitize.com
SIC: 1711 Mechanical contractor
PA: Unitize Company, Inc.
1101 Negley Pl
Dayton OH 45402

(G-7603)
SABO INC
Also Called: Submarine House
1137 Brown St (45409-2603)
PHONE..............................937 222-7939
Greg Sabo, *Pr*
EMP: 28 EST: 1973
SQ FT: 1,400
SALES (est): 441.01K **Privately Held**
Web: www.submarinehouse.com
SIC: 5812 6794 Sandwiches and submarines shop; Franchises, selling or licensing

(G-7604)
SAIA MOTOR FREIGHT LINE LLC
Also Called: Saia
3154 Transportation Rd (45404-2359)
PHONE..............................937 237-0140
Bob Arbogasp, *Mgr*
EMP: 57
SALES (corp-wide): 2.88B **Publicly Held**
SIC: 4213 Contract haulers
HQ: Saia Motor Freight Line, Llc
11465 Johns Creek Pkwy # 400
Duluth GA 30097
770 232-5067

(G-7605)
SAINT JOSEPH ORPHANAGE
6680 Poe Ave Ste 450 (45414-2857)
PHONE..............................937 643-0398
Annette Kingery, *Brnch Mgr*
EMP: 76
SALES (corp-wide): 18.19MM **Privately Held**
Web: www.newpath.org
SIC: 8361 Group foster home
PA: Saint Joseph Orphanage
5400 Edalbert Dr
Cincinnati OH 45239
513 741-3100

(G-7606)
SALVATION ARMY
Also Called: Salvation Army
1000 N Keowee St (45404-1520)
P.O. Box 10007 (45402-7007)
PHONE..............................937 528-5100
Thomas Depreis, *Brnch Mgr*
EMP: 27
SALES (corp-wide): 2.41B **Privately Held**
Web: www.salvationarmyusa.org
SIC: 8322 8661 Family service agency; Miscellaneous denomination church
HQ: The Salvation Army
440 W Nyack Rd Ofc
West Nyack NY 10994
845 620-7200

(G-7607)
SAMARITAN BEHAVIORAL HLTH INC (DH)
601 S Edwin C Moses Blvd (45417-3424)
PHONE..............................937 734-8333
Sue Mcgatha, *CEO*
Marilyn Houser, *VP*
Janet Rogers, *Treas*
EMP: 38 EST: 2002
SALES (est): 21.19MM **Privately Held**
Web: www.sbhihelp.org
SIC: 8093 Mental health clinic, outpatient
HQ: Samaritan Health Partners
2222 Philadelphia Dr
Dayton OH 45406
937 208-8400

(G-7608)
SAMARITAN HEALTH PARTNERS (HQ)
2222 Philadelphia Dr (45406-1813)
PHONE..............................937 208-8400
K Douglas Deck, *Pr*
Thomas M Duncan, *
EMP: 2165 EST: 1985
SQ FT: 1,000,000
SALES (est): 26.91MM **Privately Held**
Web: www.premierhealth.com
SIC: 8062 General medical and surgical hospitals
PA: Commonspirit Health
444 W Lake St Ste 2500
Chicago IL 60606

(G-7609)
SAMPLE MACHINING INC
Also Called: Bitec
220 N Jersey St (45403-1220)
PHONE..............................937 258-3338
Beverly Bleicher, *Pr*
Kevin Bleicher, *
EMP: 45 EST: 1985
SQ FT: 19,000
SALES (est): 9.71MM **Privately Held**
Web: www.bitecsmi.com
SIC: 3599 8734 Custom machinery; Testing laboratories

(G-7610)
SANDYS TOWING
1541 S Broadway St (45417-4616)
PHONE..............................937 228-6832
EMP: 39
Web: www.sandystowing.com
SIC: 7549 Towing service, automotive
PA: Sandys Towing
3053 Springboro W
Moraine OH 45439

(G-7611)
SATURN ELECTRIC INC
2628 Nordic Rd (45414-3424)
P.O. Box 13830 (45413-0830)
PHONE..............................937 278-2580
Doug Kash, *Pr*
EMP: 50 EST: 1989
SQ FT: 10,000
SALES (est): 7.9MM **Privately Held**
Web: www.saturn-electric.com
SIC: 1731 General electrical contractor

(G-7612)
SCOTT INDUSTRIAL SYSTEMS INC (PA)
4433 Interpoint Blvd (45424-5708)
P.O. Box 1387 (45401-1387)
PHONE..............................937 233-8146
Randall Scott, *Ch Bd*
Chuck Volpe, *
Mark Bryan, *
Charles Volpe, *
Paul Sellati, *
EMP: 75 EST: 1986
SQ FT: 63,000
SALES (est): 48.63MM
SALES (corp-wide): 48.63MM **Privately Held**
Web: www.scottindustrialsystems.com
SIC: 5084 Hydraulic systems equipment and supplies

(G-7613)
SCREEN WORKS INC (PA)
3970 Image Dr (45414-2524)
PHONE..............................937 264-9111
Jeff Cottrell, *Prin*
Jeff Cottrell, *Prin*
Ron Witters, *Prin*
EMP: 48 EST: 1987
SQ FT: 42,000
SALES (est): 2.67MM
SALES (corp-wide): 2.67MM **Privately Held**
Web: www.screenworksinc.com
SIC: 7336 5199 7389 3993 Silk screen design; Advertising specialties; Embroidery advertising; Signs and advertising specialties

(G-7614)
SEBALY SHLLITO DYER A LGAL PRO (PA)
1900 Kettering Tower 40 N Main St Lbby 11 (45423)
PHONE..............................937 222-2500
Jon M Sebaly, *Mng Pt*
Jon M Sebaly, *Pr*
Beverly Shillito, *
James Dyer, *
Gale S Finley, *
EMP: 63 EST: 1986
SALES (est): 7.75MM
SALES (corp-wide): 7.75MM **Privately Held**
Web: www.ssdlaw.com
SIC: 8111 General practice attorney, lawyer

(G-7615)
SENIOR RESOURCE CONNECTION (PA)
Also Called: MEALS ON WHEELS
222 Salem Ave (45406-5805)
PHONE..............................937 223-8246
Chuck Comp, *VP*
EMP: 195 EST: 1956
SQ FT: 25,000
SALES (est): 6.6MM
SALES (corp-wide): 6.6MM **Privately Held**
Web: www.seniorresourceconnection.com
SIC: 8322 Senior citizens' center or association

(G-7616)
SERCO SERVICES INC
2217 Acorn Dr (45419-2745)
PHONE..............................937 369-4066
Kyle Snow, *Brnch Mgr*
EMP: 153
SALES (corp-wide): 6.07B **Privately Held**
SIC: 8741 Management services
HQ: Serco Services, Inc.
12930 Worldgate Dr # 600
Herndon VA 20170
703 939-6000

(G-7617)
SHOOK NATIONAL CORPORATION
Also Called: Shook Construction
4977 Northcutt Pl (45414-3839)
P.O. Box 138806 (45413-8806)
PHONE..............................937 276-6666
EMP: 250
SIC: 8741 1542 1629 1541 Construction management; Commercial and office building, new construction; Waste water and sewage treatment plant construction; Industrial buildings, new construction, nec

(G-7618)
SHRED-IT US JV LLC
Also Called: Shred-It
903 Brandt St (45404-2231)
PHONE..............................937 401-4224
Todd Garula, *District General Manager*
EMP: 1298
SALES (corp-wide): 2.66B **Publicly Held**
Web: www.shredit.com
SIC: 7389 Document and office record destruction
HQ: Shred-It Us Jv Llc
11311 Cornell Park Dr # 125
Blue Ash OH 45242
513 245-8659

(G-7619)
SHRINERS INTERNATIONAL
Also Called: Shriners Children's Ohio
1 Childrens Plz 2 (45404-1873)
PHONE..............................855 206-2096
EMP: 107
Web: www.shrinerschildrens.org
SIC: 8641 Fraternal associations
PA: Shriners Hospitals For Children
2900 N Rocky Point Dr
Tampa FL 33607

(G-7620)
SIBCY CLINE INC
8353 Yankee St (45458-1809)
PHONE..............................937 610-3404
Irma Wise, *Brnch Mgr*
EMP: 121
SALES (corp-wide): 98.72MM **Privately Held**

Dayton - Montgomery County (G-7621) — GEOGRAPHIC SECTION

Web: www.sibcycline.com
SIC: 6531 Real estate agent, residential
PA: Sibcy Cline, Inc.
    8044 Montgomery Rd # 300
    Cincinnati OH 45236
    513 984-4100

(G-7621)
SIEMENS MED SOLUTIONS USA INC
651 Skyview Dr (45449-1632)
PHONE.................................937 859-5413
Edward Ballard, *Prin*
EMP: 257
SALES (corp-wide): 84.48B **Privately Held**
Web: www.siemens.com
SIC: 7699 X-ray equipment repair
HQ: Siemens Medical Solutions Usa, Inc.
    40 Liberty Blvd
    Malvern PA 19355
    888 826-9702

(G-7622)
SILVER SPRUCE HOLDING LLC
Also Called: Growthplay
3123 Research Blvd Ste 250 (45420)
PHONE.................................937 259-1200
Bruce Sevy, *Mgr*
EMP: 39
SALES (corp-wide): 5.67MM **Privately Held**
SIC: 8742 Management consulting services
PA: Silver Spruce Holding, Llc
    17 E Erie St
    Chicago IL

(G-7623)
SNOW TRANSPORT & BROKERAGE
308 Fernwood Ave (45405-2623)
PHONE.................................937 474-8058
EMP: 38
SALES (corp-wide): 5.1MM **Privately Held**
SIC: 4789 Pipeline terminal facilities, independently operated
PA: Snow Transport & Brokerage, Inc
    3972 Egypt Rd
    Snellville GA 30039
    855 469-7669

(G-7624)
SOGETI USA LLC
6494 Centerville Business Pkwy (45459-2633)
PHONE.................................937 433-3334
EMP: 92
SALES (corp-wide): 415.14MM **Privately Held**
Web: us.sogeti.com
SIC: 7379 Online services technology consultants
HQ: Sogeti Usa Llc
    10100 Innovation Dr # 200
    Miamisburg OH 45342
    937 291-8100

(G-7625)
SOUTH COMMUNITY INC
Also Called: Youth Partial Hospitalization
2745 S Smithville Rd Ste 14 (45420)
PHONE.................................937 252-0100
Melissa Buck, *Prin*
EMP: 44
SALES (corp-wide): 22.07MM **Privately Held**
Web: www.southcommunity.com
SIC: 8093 Mental health clinic, outpatient
PA: South Community Inc.
    3095 Kettering Blvd Ste 1
    Moraine OH 45439
    937 293-8300

(G-7626)
SOUTH COMMUNITY INC
1349 E Stroop Rd (45429-4929)
PHONE.................................937 293-1115
Lori Bachman, *Brnch Mgr*
EMP: 45
SALES (corp-wide): 22.07MM **Privately Held**
Web: www.southcommunity.com
SIC: 8093 Mental health clinic, outpatient
PA: South Community Inc.
    3095 Kettering Blvd Ste 1
    Moraine OH 45439
    937 293-8300

(G-7627)
SOUTH DAYTON FAMILY PHYSICIANS
1525 E Stroop Rd Ste 200 (45429-5057)
PHONE.................................937 208-7400
Eric M Mchenry, *Prin*
EMP: 29 EST: 1972
SALES (est): 487.03K **Privately Held**
Web: www.premierhealth.com
SIC: 8011 Urologist

(G-7628)
SOUTH DYTON ACUTE CARE CONS IN
Also Called: Acute Care Consultants
33 W Rahn Rd (45429-2219)
PHONE.................................937 433-8990
Robert L Barker, *Pr*
Doctor George Crespo, *VP*
Doctor Shachi Rattan, *VP*
Doctor Jeffrey Weinstein, *Sec*
EMP: 107 EST: 1987
SQ FT: 10,000
SALES (est): 9.43MM **Privately Held**
Web: www.sdacc.com
SIC: 8011 Physicians' office, including specialists

(G-7629)
SOUTH DYTON URLGCAL ASSCATIONS (PA)
10 Southmoor Cir Nw Ste 1 (45429-2444)
PHONE.................................937 294-1489
Ralph M Cruz Md, *Treas*
Sammy Hemway Md, *VP*
Sharat C Kalvakota Md, *Sec*
Juan M Palomar Md, *Pr*
EMP: 30 EST: 1975
SQ FT: 5,000
SALES (est): 2.37MM
SALES (corp-wide): 2.37MM **Privately Held**
SIC: 8011 Urologist

(G-7630)
SOUTHERN EXPRESS LUBES INC
3781 Salem Ave (45406-1651)
PHONE.................................937 278-5807
Dwayne Mowen, *Mgr*
EMP: 38
SIC: 7549 Lubrication service, automotive
PA: Southern Express Lubes, Inc.
    8520 Conn Ave Ste 200
    Chevy Chase MD

(G-7631)
SPACE & ASSET MANAGEMENT INC (PA)
Also Called: Elements IV Interiors
3680 Wyse Rd (45414-2539)
PHONE.................................937 918-1000
EMP: 30 EST: 1990
SALES (est): 10.36MM **Privately Held**
Web: www.elementsiv.com
SIC: 5021 7389 Furniture; Interior design services

(G-7632)
SPACEPOINTE INC
1231 Lyons Rd (45458-1858)
PHONE.................................937 886-7995
Sayu Abend, *CEO*
Nathan Gooden, *
Osato Osayande, *
EMP: 50 EST: 2014
SALES (est): 2.37MM **Privately Held**
SIC: 7371 Custom computer programming services

(G-7633)
SPEARS TRANSFER & EXPEDITING
Also Called: SPEARS TRANSFER & EXPEDITING
2637 Nordic Rd (45414-3423)
PHONE.................................937 275-2443
Mike Spears, *Brnch Mgr*
EMP: 87
SALES (corp-wide): 44.89MM **Privately Held**
Web: www.spearsexpedite.com
SIC: 4212 4214 Local trucking, without storage; Local trucking with storage
HQ: Spears Transfer & Expediting, Inc.
    303 Corporate Center Dr # 10
    Vandalia OH 45377

(G-7634)
SPRING HILLS HEALTH CARE LLC
Also Called: Spring Hills At Singing Woods
140 E Woodbury Dr (45415-2841)
PHONE.................................937 274-1400
John Steiner, *Prin*
EMP: 65
Web: www.springhills.com
SIC: 8051 Convalescent home with continuous nursing care
PA: Spring Hills Health Care Llc
    515 Plainfield Ave
    Edison NJ 08817

(G-7635)
SPRINGFIELD CARTAGE LLC
1615 Springfield St (45403-1429)
P.O. Box 1263 (45401-1263)
PHONE.................................937 222-2120
EMP: 35 EST: 2004
SQ FT: 133,000
SALES (est): 3.62MM **Privately Held**
Web: www.springfieldcartage.us
SIC: 4212 Light haulage and cartage, local

(G-7636)
SPRINGHILLS LLC
Also Called: SPRINGHILLS LLC
51 Plum St (45440-1395)
PHONE.................................937 705-5002
Unanda Bell, *Prin*
EMP: 47
Web: www.springhills.com
SIC: 8059 Personal care home, with health care
PA: Spring Hills Health Care Llc
    515 Plainfield Ave
    Edison NJ 08817

(G-7637)
STAFFTECH INC
8534 Yankee St Ste 1c (45458-1889)
PHONE.................................937 228-2667
Allen Stephen, *Prin*
EMP: 70 EST: 2019
SALES (est): 1.87MM **Privately Held**
Web: www.stafftechservices.com
SIC: 7363 Temporary help service

(G-7638)
STAHL VISION LASER SURGERY CTR
4235 Indian Ripple Rd Ste 100 (45440-3284)
PHONE.................................937 643-2020
Brian Stahl, *Owner*
EMP: 35 EST: 2000
SALES (est): 4.17MM **Privately Held**
Web: www.stahlvision.com
SIC: 8011 Opthalmologist

(G-7639)
STARWIN INDUSTRIES LLC
3387 Woodman Dr (45429-4100)
PHONE.................................937 293-8568
Matthew Eberhardt, *CEO*
Rick Little, *
EMP: 50 EST: 1973
SQ FT: 30,000
SALES (est): 13.46MM
SALES (corp-wide): 18.89MM **Privately Held**
Web: www.starwin-ind.com
SIC: 7372 3728 3663 3599 Prepackaged software; Aircraft parts and equipment, nec; Radio and t.v. communications equipment; Machine and other job shop work
PA: Eti Mission Controls, Llc
    3387 Woodman Dr
    Dayton OH 45429
    937 832-4200

(G-7640)
STATE FARM LIFE INSURANCE CO
Also Called: State Farm Insurance
1436 Needmore Rd (45414-3965)
PHONE.................................937 276-1900
Jim Mcghee, *Mgr*
EMP: 48
SALES (corp-wide): 27.88B **Privately Held**
Web: www.statefarm.com
SIC: 6411 Insurance agents and brokers
HQ: State Farm Life Insurance Company Inc
    1 State Farm Plz
    Bloomington IL 61701
    309 766-2311

(G-7641)
STEPHENS INVESTMENTS LLC
417 E Stroop Rd (45429-2829)
PHONE.................................937 299-4993
EMP: 34 EST: 2016
SALES (est): 216.68K **Privately Held**
Web: www.stephensdirect.com
SIC: 6799 Investors, nec

(G-7642)
STEVE BROWN
1353 Lyons Rd (45458-1822)
PHONE.................................937 436-2700
Steve Brown, *Pt*
EMP: 60 EST: 2007
SALES (est): 2.24MM **Privately Held**
SIC: 6531 Real estate agent, residential

(G-7643)
STIFEL IND ADVISORS LLC
Also Called: Centruy Securities Associates
1250 W Dorothy Ln Ste 307 (45409-1326)
PHONE.................................937 293-1220
Robert Harris, *Mgr*
EMP: 47
SALES (corp-wide): 4.35B **Publicly Held**
Web: www.stifelindependence.com
SIC: 6211 Security brokers and dealers
HQ: Stifel Independent Advisors, Llc
    1 Fnncial Plz 501 N Brd
    Saint Louis MO 63102

GEOGRAPHIC SECTION
Dayton - Montgomery County (G-7667)

(G-7644)
STIFEL IND ADVISORS LLC
28 E Rahn Rd Ste 112 (45429-5460)
PHONE.....................937 312-0111
David Harris, *Brnch Mgr*
EMP: 47
SALES (corp-wide): 4.35B **Publicly Held**
Web: www.stifelindependence.com
SIC: 7389 Brokers' services
HQ: Stifel Independent Advisors, Llc
1 Fnncial Plz 501 N Brd
Saint Louis MO 63102

(G-7645)
STONESPRING TRNSTNAL CARE CTR
4000 Singing Hills Blvd (45414-3238)
PHONE.....................937 415-8000
EMP: 29
SALES (corp-wide): 84.56MM **Privately Held**
Web: www.carespring.com
SIC: 8741 Nursing and personal care facility management
HQ: Stonespring Transitional Care Center, Llc
390 Wards Rd
Loveland OH 45140

(G-7646)
STRATACACHE INC (PA)
Also Called: Stratacache Products
40 N Main St Ste 2600 (45423)
PHONE.....................937 224-0485
Chris Riegel, *CEO*
Kevin Mcgree, *CFO*
Russell Young, *
John Rau, *
▲ EMP: 110 EST: 1990
SQ FT: 65,000
SALES (est): 249.08MM **Privately Held**
Web: www.stratacache.com
SIC: 5734 4822 Software, business and non-game; Nonvocal message communications

(G-7647)
STRESS CARE/BRIDGES
Also Called: GRANDVIEW HOSPITAL
405 W Grand Ave (45405-7538)
PHONE.....................937 723-3200
Peggy Mann, *Prin*
EMP: 52 EST: 2000
SALES (est): 650.97MM **Privately Held**
Web: www.ketteringhealth.org
SIC: 8062 General medical and surgical hospitals

(G-7648)
STUDEBAKER ELECTRIC COMPANY
8459 N Main St Ste 106 (45415-1324)
PHONE.....................937 890-9510
David L Studebaker, *CEO*
Phillip Lahrmer, *
EMP: 100 EST: 1954
SALES (est): 9.86MM **Privately Held**
Web: www.studebakerelectric.com
SIC: 1731 General electrical contractor

(G-7649)
SUBURBAN VETERINARIAN CLINIC
102 E Spring Valley Pike (45458-3803)
PHONE.....................937 433-2160
Dan Lokai, *Owner*
EMP: 28 EST: 1969
SQ FT: 6,200
SALES (est): 1.53MM **Privately Held**
Web: www.suburbanvetclinic.com
SIC: 0742 Animal hospital services, pets and other animal specialties

(G-7650)
SUMMIT SOLUTIONS INC
Also Called: Summit Quest
446 Windsor Park Dr (45459-4111)
P.O. Box 751735 (45475-1735)
PHONE.....................937 291-4333
Jeff S Lafave, *CEO*
EMP: 40 EST: 1998
SALES (est): 1.52MM **Privately Held**
Web: www.summitqwest.com
SIC: 8748 Business consulting, nec

(G-7651)
SUMMITT OHIO LEASING CO LLC
Also Called: COMMUNICARE HEALTH SERVICES
3800 Summit Glen Dr (45449-3647)
PHONE.....................937 436-2273
EMP: 54 EST: 2005
SALES (est): 13.84MM
SALES (corp-wide): 392.92MM **Privately Held**
SIC: 8051 Convalescent home with continuous nursing care
PA: Communicare Health Services, Inc.
10123 Alliance Rd
Blue Ash OH 45242
513 530-1654

(G-7652)
SUN YER BUNZ LLC
Also Called: Digi Satellite
235 W Grand Ave (45405-4543)
PHONE.....................937 222-3474
Daryl J Williams, *
EMP: 83 EST: 2001
SALES (est): 1.71MM **Privately Held**
SIC: 4841 Direct broadcast satellite services (DBS)

(G-7653)
SUNRISE SENIOR LIVING LLC
Also Called: Brighton Gardens Wash Township
6800 Paragon Rd Ofc (45459-3164)
PHONE.....................937 438-0054
Rose Marie Caldwell, *Mgr*
EMP: 50
SALES (corp-wide): 2.92B **Privately Held**
Web: www.sunriseseniorliving.com
SIC: 8051 Skilled nursing care facilities
HQ: Sunrise Senior Living, Llc
7902 Westpark Dr
Mc Lean VA 22102

(G-7654)
SUPERIOR DENTAL CARE INC
6683 Centerville Business Pkwy (45459-2634)
PHONE.....................937 438-0283
Traci Harrell, *CEO*
Richard W Portune D.d.s., *Pr*
Douglas R Hoefling D.d.s., *Treas*
James R Miller D.d.s., *Sec*
EMP: 59 EST: 1985
SQ FT: 7,878
SALES (est): 10.23MM **Privately Held**
Web: www.superiordental.com
SIC: 6321 Health insurance carriers

(G-7655)
SUPERNOVA LGSTIC SOLUTIONS LLC
5850 Shady Cove Ln (45426-2118)
PHONE.....................937 369-8618
Deonna M Chambers, *CEO*
EMP: 33 EST: 2017
SALES (est): 972.73K **Privately Held**
SIC: 8742 Personnel management consultant

(G-7656)
SUPPLY TECHNOLOGIES LLC
6675 Homestretch Rd (45414-2513)
PHONE.....................937 898-5795
John Spradlang, *Mgr*
EMP: 100
SALES (corp-wide): 1.66B **Publicly Held**
Web: www.supplytechnologies.com
SIC: 5085 Fasteners, industrial: nuts, bolts, screws, etc.
HQ: Supply Technologies Llc
6065 Parkland Blvd
Cleveland OH 44124
440 947-2100

(G-7657)
SYNERGY HOMECARE
Also Called: Synergy Homecare South Dayton
501 Windsor Park Dr (45459-4112)
PHONE.....................937 610-0555
EMP: 95 EST: 2010
SQ FT: 1,000
SALES (est): 4.05MM **Privately Held**
Web: www.synergyhomecare.com
SIC: 8082 Home health care services

(G-7658)
SYSTEMAX MANUFACTURING INC
6450 Poe Ave Ste 200 (45414-2655)
PHONE.....................937 368-2300
Curt Rush, *Sec*
▲ EMP: 54 EST: 1980
SQ FT: 185,000
SALES (est): 6.18MM **Publicly Held**
SIC: 5961 7373 3577 3571 Computers and peripheral equipment, mail order; Systems integration services; Computer peripheral equipment, nec; Electronic computers
PA: Global Industrial Company
11 Harbor Park Dr
Port Washington NY 11050

(G-7659)
TANGRAM FLEX INC
607 E 3rd St Ste 500 (45402-2219)
PHONE.....................937 985-3199
Ricky Peters, *CEO*
John Launchbury, *
Jodee Leroux, *
EMP: 33 EST: 2018
SALES (est): 2.56MM **Privately Held**
Web: www.tangramflex.com
SIC: 7371 7373 Computer software systems analysis and design, custom; Systems engineering, computer related

(G-7660)
TEAM HEALTH HOLDINGS INC
6229 Troy Pike (45424-3646)
PHONE.....................937 252-2000
Suresh Gupta, *Brnch Mgr*
EMP: 29
SALES (corp-wide): 3.6B **Privately Held**
Web: www.teamhealth.com
SIC: 8059 Rest home, with health care
HQ: Team Health Holdings, Inc.
265 Brkview Cntre Way Ste
Knoxville TN 37919
865 693-1000

(G-7661)
TEKNOL INC (PA)
Also Called: Rubber Seal Products
5751 Webster St (45414-3520)
P.O. Box 13387 (45413-0387)
PHONE.....................937 264-0190
Kent Von Behren, *Pr*
R Von Behren, *Stockholder**
▲ EMP: 57 EST: 1976
SQ FT: 60,000
SALES (est): 9.75MM
SALES (corp-wide): 9.75MM **Privately Held**
Web: www.medallionrefinish.com
SIC: 2899 2891 5198 2851 Chemical preparations, nec; Sealants; Paints, varnishes, and supplies; Paints and allied products

(G-7662)
TERADATA INTERNATIONAL INC (HQ)
10000 Innovation Dr (45449)
PHONE.....................866 548-8348
EMP: 163 EST: 2007
SALES (est): 1.53MM **Publicly Held**
SIC: 8742 Business management consultant
PA: Teradata Corporation
17095 Via Del Campo
San Diego CA 92127

(G-7663)
TESTECH INC
10051 Beaufort Run (45458-9260)
PHONE.....................937 435-8584
EMP: 88
Web: www.testech.com
SIC: 8711 8713 7389 Engineering services; Surveying services; Building inspection service

(G-7664)
TFORCE FREIGHT INC
3730 Valley St (45424-5144)
PHONE.....................937 236-4700
Scott Gettys, *Mgr*
EMP: 30
SALES (corp-wide): 8.81B **Privately Held**
Web: www.tforcefreight.com
SIC: 4213 4212 Contract haulers; Local trucking, without storage
HQ: Tforce Freight, Inc.
1000 Semmes Ave
Richmond VA 23224
800 333-7400

(G-7665)
THE F A REQUARTH COMPANY
Also Called: Requarth Lumber Co.
447 E Monument Ave (45402-1226)
P.O. Box 38 (45401-0038)
PHONE.....................937 224-1141
EMP: 30 EST: 1860
SALES (est): 4.98MM **Privately Held**
Web: www.requarth.com
SIC: 2431 2491 5211 2421 Millwork; Wood preserving; Lumber and other building materials; Sawmills and planing mills, general

(G-7666)
THE JOHN A BECKER CO
Also Called: Becker Electric Supply
1341 E 4th St (45402-2235)
P.O. Box 247 (45401-0247)
PHONE.....................937 226-1341
EMP: 231
SIC: 5063 Electrical construction materials

(G-7667)
THE MARIA-JOSEPH CENTER
4830 Salem Ave (45416-1716)
PHONE.....................937 278-2692
Sharon Thornton, *Pr*
EMP: 400 EST: 1930
SQ FT: 500,000
SALES (est): 22.8MM **Privately Held**
Web: www.maria-joseph.net
SIC: 8052 8051 Intermediate care facilities; Skilled nursing care facilities
PA: Commonspirit Health
444 W Lake St Ste 2500

Dayton - Montgomery County (G-7668)

GEOGRAPHIC SECTION

Chicago IL 60606

(G-7668)
THE MEDICAL CENTER AT ELIZABETH PLACE LLC
Also Called: McEp
7970 N Main St (45415-2328)
PHONE.....................937 223-6237
EMP: 120
Web: www.mcep.us
SIC: 8062 General medical and surgical hospitals

(G-7669)
TIPP MACHINE & TOOL INC
4201 Little York Rd (45414-2507)
PHONE.....................937 890-8428
EMP: 124
SIC: 3544 3599 7389 Special dies and tools; Machine shop, jobbing and repair; Grinding, precision: commercial or industrial

(G-7670)
TIPTON GROUP INC
10554 Success Ln Ste D (45458-3657)
PHONE.....................937 885-6300
Richard D Tipton, Pr
▲ EMP: 27 EST: 1981
SQ FT: 3,600
SALES (est): 1.22MM Privately Held
Web: www.tiptongroupinc.com
SIC: 6531 Real estate managers

(G-7671)
TM CAPTURE SERVICES LLC
Also Called: Macalogic
4380 Buckeye Ln Ste 222 (45440-7300)
PHONE.....................937 728-1781
EMP: 70 EST: 2012
SALES (est): 2.95MM Privately Held
Web: www.macalogic.com
SIC: 8741 7389 8742 Administrative management; Business Activities at Non-Commercial Site; Sales (including sales management) consultant

(G-7672)
TOGA-PAK INC
2208 Sandridge Dr (45439)
P.O. Box Rr&Box363 (45409)
PHONE.....................937 294-7311
EMP: 40 EST: 1981
SALES (est): 5.69MM Privately Held
Web: www.ipack.com
SIC: 3081 5084 5199 Unsupported plastics film and sheet; Packaging machinery and equipment; Packaging materials

(G-7673)
TOPS ROOFING INC
1116 W Stewart St (45417-3970)
P.O. Box 2336 (45401-2336)
PHONE.....................937 228-6074
Sidney Thomas, CEO
James L Gibson, *
Edward R Thomas, *
EMP: 30 EST: 1983
SQ FT: 450
SALES (est): 1.22MM Privately Held
SIC: 1761 Roofing contractor

(G-7674)
TOWNEPLACE SUITES DAYTON NORTH
Also Called: TownePlace Suites By Marriott
3642 Maxton Rd (45414-2834)
PHONE.....................937 898-5700
Randy Dee, Prin
EMP: 37 EST: 2007
SALES (est): 784.25K Privately Held

Web: www.marriott.com
SIC: 7011 Hotel, franchised

(G-7675)
TOYOTA INDUSTRIES N AMER INC
Also Called: Prolift Industrial Equipment
6254 Executive Blvd (45424-1423)
PHONE.....................937 237-0976
Stephen Ford, Mgr
EMP: 82
Web: www.toyota.com
SIC: 5511 7699 Automobiles, new and used; Industrial truck repair
HQ: Toyota Industries North America, Inc.
3030 Barker Dr
Columbus IN 47201
812 341-3810

(G-7676)
TRANSFREIGHT LLC
98 Quality Ln (45449-2141)
PHONE.....................937 865-9270
Chris Tucker, Mgr
EMP: 383
SALES (corp-wide): 2.11B Privately Held
SIC: 4789 Pipeline terminal facilities, independently operated
HQ: Transfreight, Llc
3940 Olympic Blvd Ste 500
Erlanger KY 41018
859 372-5930

(G-7677)
TRANSOFT INC
7333 Paragon Rd Ste 250 (45459-4157)
PHONE.....................937 427-6200
Wayne Spalding, Mgr
EMP: 86
Web: www.oneadvanced.com
SIC: 5045 Computers, peripherals, and software
HQ: Transoft, Inc
1165 Nrthchase Pkwy Se St
Marietta GA 30067

(G-7678)
TRIANGLE PRECISION INDUSTRIES
1650 Delco Park Dr (45420-1392)
PHONE.....................937 299-6776
Gerald D Schriml, Pr
Paul S Holzinger, *
EMP: 57 EST: 1982
SQ FT: 23,400
SALES (est): 6.55MM Privately Held
Web: www.triangleprecision.com
SIC: 3599 7692 3446 3444 Machine shop, jobbing and repair; Welding repair; Architectural metalwork; Sheet metalwork

(G-7679)
TURNER PROPERTY SVCS GROUP INC
3199 Klepinger Rd # 200 (45406-1837)
PHONE.....................937 461-7474
Sean Turner, Pr
John S Turner, *
Debolin Biza, Corporate Secretary*
EMP: 42 EST: 2005
SQ FT: 5,000
SALES (est): 8.68MM Privately Held
Web: www.turnerpsg.com
SIC: 6512 Nonresidential building operators

(G-7680)
UNITED ART AND EDUCATION INC
799 Lyons Rd (45459-3980)
PHONE.....................800 322-3247
Kelly Warnen, Dir
EMP: 27
SALES (corp-wide): 22.67MM Privately Held

Web: www.unitednow.com
SIC: 5999 7389 5943 Artists' supplies and materials; Laminating service; School supplies
PA: United Art And Education, Inc.
4413 Airport Expy
Fort Wayne IN 46809
260 478-1121

(G-7681)
UNITED BUILDING MATERIALS INC
Also Called: United
1509 Stanley Ave (45404-1112)
PHONE.....................937 222-4444
EMP: 30
Web: www.unitedbuildingmaterials.com
SIC: 5211 5032 Lumber products; Drywall materials

(G-7682)
UNITED CHURCH HOMES INC
Also Called: Trinity Community Beavercreek
3218 Indian Ripple Rd (45440-3637)
PHONE.....................937 426-8481
Laura Farrell, Dir
EMP: 104
SALES (corp-wide): 115.52MM Privately Held
Web: www.unitedchurchhomes.org
SIC: 8051 8052 8361 Convalescent home with continuous nursing care; Intermediate care facilities; Geriatric residential care
PA: United Church Homes, Inc.
170 E Center St
Marion OH 43302
800 837-2211

(G-7683)
UNITED RHBLTTION SVCS GRTER DY
4710 Troy Pike (45424-5740)
PHONE.....................937 233-1230
Dennis G Grant, Ex Dir
Dennis G Grant, Dir
EMP: 74 EST: 1956
SQ FT: 37,000
SALES (est): 6.09MM Privately Held
Web: www.ursdayton.org
SIC: 8351 8322 8093 8049 Child day care services; Individual and family services; Rehabilitation center, outpatient treatment; Speech pathologist

(G-7684)
UNITED STTES DEPT OF HMLAND SE
Also Called: Usdhsa
2748 Symphony Way (45449-3315)
PHONE.....................937 821-5543
Brian B Kardos, Ch Bd
Elisabeta Kardos, Corporate Secretary
Attila Molnar, Pr
Nora Molname, Treas
Andrea Kardos, Ex Dir
EMP: 58 EST: 2004
SALES (est): 997.63K Privately Held
SIC: 7381 Detective and armored car services

(G-7685)
UNITED TELEMANAGEMENT CORP
6640 Poe Ave (45414-2678)
PHONE.....................937 454-1888
Jim Hague, Managing Member
Terry L Henley, *
Don Campbell, *
Barry Brooks, *
Margaret Isaacs, *
EMP: 45 EST: 1991
SALES (est): 2.16MM Privately Held
Web: www.utccares.com

SIC: 8741 Management services

(G-7686)
UNITED WAY OF THE GRTER DYTON (PA)
Also Called: UNITED WAY
409 E Monument Ave (45402-1260)
P.O. Box 634625 (45263-4625)
PHONE.....................937 225-3060
Tom Maultsby, Pr
EMP: 33 EST: 1914
SALES (est): 4.24MM
SALES (corp-wide): 4.24MM Privately Held
Web: www.dayton-unitedway.org
SIC: 8399 8322 United Fund councils; Individual and family services

(G-7687)
UNIVERSAL 1 CREDIT UNION INC (PA)
1 River Park Dr (45409-2104)
P.O. Box 467 (45409-0467)
PHONE.....................800 762-9555
Loren A Rush, Pr
Ann Parrish, *
Steve Shore, OF LOANS*
Shannon Maloney, V PRESCORP SERVICES AND MIS*
Glenn Kershner, Executive Business Development Vice President*
EMP: 73 EST: 1937
SALES (est): 20.54MM
SALES (corp-wide): 20.54MM Privately Held
Web: www.u1cu.org
SIC: 6061 Federal credit unions

(G-7688)
UNIVERSAL EXPRESS LLC
129 Mcclure St (45403-2431)
PHONE.....................404 642-4747
EMP: 31
SALES (corp-wide): 331.21K Privately Held
SIC: 7363 Truck driver services
PA: Universal Express Llc
250 Woodstream Dr
Springboro OH 45066
502 296-3167

(G-7689)
UNIVERSITY OF DAYTON (PA)
300 College Park Ave (45469)
PHONE.....................937 229-1000
Doctor Daniel J Curran, Pr
Gurvinder Rekhi, CIO*
▲ EMP: 2000 EST: 1850
SQ FT: 25,000
SALES (est): 669.42MM
SALES (corp-wide): 669.42MM Privately Held
Web: www.udayton.edu
SIC: 8221 8733 University; Noncommercial research organizations

(G-7690)
UNIVERSITY OF DAYTON
Also Called: University of Dyton Schl Engrg
300 College St (45402-8002)
PHONE.....................937 229-2113
Doctor John E Leyland, Dir
EMP: 250
SALES (corp-wide): 669.42MM Privately Held
Web: www.udayton.edu
SIC: 8733 8221 Research institute; University
PA: The University Of Dayton
300 College Park
Dayton OH 45469
937 229-1000

GEOGRAPHIC SECTION
Dayton - Montgomery County (G-7713)

(G-7691)
UNIVERSITY OF DAYTON
Also Called: University Dayton RES Inst
711 E Monument Ave Ste 101
(45469-0001)
PHONE.................................937 229-3822
John Leland, *Dir*
EMP: 400
SALES (corp-wide): 669.42MM **Privately Held**
Web: www.udayton.edu
SIC: 8733 8221 Research institute; University
PA: The University Of Dayton
   300 College Park
   Dayton OH 45469
   937 229-1000

(G-7692)
UNIVERSITY OF DAYTON
300 College Park Dr (45469-0002)
PHONE.................................937 255-3141
Bernard Ploeger, *Brnch Mgr*
EMP: 52
SALES (corp-wide): 669.42MM **Privately Held**
Web: www.udayton.edu
SIC: 8742 8221 Management consulting services; University
PA: The University Of Dayton
   300 College Park
   Dayton OH 45469
   937 229-1000

(G-7693)
UNIVERSITY OF DAYTON
Also Called: Research Institute
1529 Brown St (45469-7000)
PHONE.................................937 229-3913
EMP: 319
SALES (corp-wide): 669.42MM **Privately Held**
Web: www.udayton.edu
SIC: 8742 8221 Management consulting services; University
PA: The University Of Dayton
   300 College Park
   Dayton OH 45469
   937 229-1000

(G-7694)
UPPER VALLEY MEDICAL CENTER
110 N Main St Ste 450 (45402-3712)
PHONE.................................937 440-7107
J Michael Sims, *Brnch Mgr*
EMP: 430
SALES (corp-wide): 2.41MM **Privately Held**
Web: www.premierhealth.com
SIC: 8011 Clinic, operated by physicians
HQ: Upper Valley Medical Center
   3130 N County Road 25a
   Troy OH 45373

(G-7695)
URBAN RETAIL PROPERTIES LLC
Also Called: Glimsher Retail Properties
2700 Miamisburg Centerville Rd (45459)
PHONE.................................937 433-0957
EMP: 40
SALES (corp-wide): 49.26MM **Privately Held**
Web: www.urbanretail.com
SIC: 8741 Management services
HQ: Urban Retail Properties, Llc
   925 Suth Fdral Hwy Ste 70
   Boca Raton FL 33432

(G-7696)
URGENT CARE SPECIALISTS LLC
6210 Brandt Pike (45424-4019)
PHONE.................................937 236-8630
Lisa Kay, *Brnch Mgr*
EMP: 55
SALES (corp-wide): 23.51MM **Privately Held**
Web: www.wellnow.com
SIC: 8011 Freestanding emergency medical center
PA: Urgent Care Specialists Llc
   2400 Corp Exch Dr Ste 102
   Columbus OH 43231
   614 505-7633

(G-7697)
US INSPECTION SERVICES INC (DH)
Also Called: Acuren Inspection
7333 Paragon Rd Ste 240 (45459-4157)
PHONE.................................937 660-9879
Peter Scannell, *Pr*
▲ **EMP:** 50 **EST:** 1994
SQ FT: 18,000
SALES (est): 20.89MM
SALES (corp-wide): 1.5B **Privately Held**
Web: www.acuren.com
SIC: 8734 Testing laboratories
HQ: Acuren Inspection, Inc.
   30 Main St Ste 402
   Danbury CT 06810
   203 702-8740

(G-7698)
VALICOR ENVIRONMENTAL SVCS LLC
300 Cherokee Dr (45417-8113)
PHONE.................................937 268-6501
Mitch George, *Mgr*
EMP: 55
SALES (corp-wide): 683.99MM **Privately Held**
Web: www.valicor.com
SIC: 4953 Recycling, waste materials
HQ: Valicor Environmental Services, Llc
   1045 Reed Dr
   Monroe OH 45050
   513 733-4666

(G-7699)
VALLEY INTERIOR SYSTEMS INC
2760 Thunderhawk Ct (45414-3464)
PHONE.................................937 890-7319
Terry Gyetvai, *Brnch Mgr*
EMP: 54
SALES (corp-wide): 54.25MM **Privately Held**
Web: www.buildwithvalley.com
SIC: 1742 Drywall
PA: Valley Interior Systems, Inc.
   2203 Fowler St
   Cincinnati OH 45206
   513 961-0400

(G-7700)
VANDALIA BLCKTOP SLCOATING INC
6740 Webster St (45414-2613)
PHONE.................................937 454-0571
H David Brusman Junior, *Pr*
EMP: 50 **EST:** 1976
SQ FT: 2,000
SALES (est): 10.2MM **Privately Held**
Web: www.vandaliablacktop.com
SIC: 1611 1794 Highway and street paving contractor; Excavation work

(G-7701)
VERIZON WIRELESS INC
Also Called: Verizon Wireless
2340 Miamisburg Centerville Rd (45459)
PHONE.................................937 434-2355
Bridget Gerber, *Mgr*
EMP: 55
SALES (corp-wide): 133.97B **Publicly Held**
Web: www.verizonwireless.com
SIC: 4812 Cellular telephone services
HQ: Verizon Wireless, Inc.
   1 Verizon Way
   Basking Ridge NJ 07920

(G-7702)
VERTNEYS LLC
70 Birch Aly Ste 240-7347 (45440-1479)
PHONE.................................937 272-0585
Jared White, *Pr*
EMP: 30 **EST:** 2017
SALES (est): 1.07MM **Privately Held**
SIC: 1799 7699 Cleaning new buildings after construction; Cleaning services

(G-7703)
VESTIS CORPORATION
Also Called: Aramark
1200 Webster St (45404-1557)
P.O. Box 139 (45404-0139)
PHONE.................................937 223-6667
TOLL FREE: 800
Jarrod Burch, *Genl Mgr*
EMP: 33
SALES (corp-wide): 2.83B **Publicly Held**
Web: www.vestis.com
SIC: 7218 7213 7216 Industrial uniform supply; Uniform supply; Drycleaning plants, except rugs
PA: Vestis Corporation
   500 Colonial Center Pkwy # 1
   Roswell GA 30076
   470 226-3655

(G-7704)
VETERAN SECURITY PATROL CO
601 S Edwin C Moses Blvd Ste 170 (45417-3424)
PHONE.................................937 222-7333
Roy Belcher, *Brnch Mgr*
EMP: 131
Web: www.veteransecurity.com
SIC: 7381 Security guard service
PA: Veteran Security Patrol Co.
   215 Taylor Ave
   Bellevue KY 41073

(G-7705)
VETERANS HEALTH ADMINISTRATION
Also Called: Dayton V A Medical Center
4100 W 3rd St (45428-9000)
PHONE.................................937 268-6511
Jodi Cokl, *Brnch Mgr*
EMP: 903
Web: dayton.va.gov
SIC: 8011 9451 Medical centers; Administration of veterans' affairs
HQ: Veterans Health Administration
   810 Vermont Ave Nw
   Washington DC 20420

(G-7706)
VICTORIA THEATRE ASSOCIATION
Also Called: Dayton Live
138 N Main St (45402-1776)
PHONE.................................937 461-8190
EMP: 154 **EST:** 1976
SALES (est): 8.79MM **Privately Held**
Web: www.daytonlive.org
SIC: 6512 Nonresidential building operators

(G-7707)
VINEBROOK HOMES LLC
3500 Park Center Dr Ste 100 (45414)
PHONE.................................855 513-5678
Mike Fannon, *Dir*
EMP: 302 **EST:** 2012
SALES (est): 13.55MM **Privately Held**
Web: www.vinebrookhomes.com
SIC: 6531 4731 Real estate leasing and rentals; Customhouse brokers

(G-7708)
VINEBROOK IL LLC
5550 Huber Rd (45424-2001)
PHONE.................................614 783-5573
EMP: 83 **EST:** 2016
SALES (est): 851K **Privately Held**
Web: www.vinebrookhomes.com
SIC: 6531 Real estate brokers and agents

(G-7709)
VOCALINK INC
405 W 1st St Ste A (45402-3007)
PHONE.................................937 223-1415
Amelia Rodriguez, *Pr*
EMP: 405 **EST:** 1995
SALES (est): 23.79MM **Privately Held**
Web: www.vocalink.net
SIC: 7389 Translation services

(G-7710)
VOLVO BMW DYTON EVANS VOLKSWAG
Also Called: Evans Motor Works
7124 Poe Ave (45414-2546)
PHONE.................................937 890-6200
Jim Evans, *Pr*
Jims Evans, *Pr*
EMP: 50 **EST:** 2009
SALES (est): 11.2MM **Privately Held**
Web: www.bmwofdayton.com
SIC: 5511 7538 Automobiles, new and used; General automotive repair shops

(G-7711)
VOSS AUTO NETWORK INC (PA)
Also Called: Hoss
766 Miamisburg Centerville Rd (45459)
PHONE.................................937 428-2447
Teresa Haynes, *Prin*
John Voss, *
EMP: 50 **EST:** 1972
SQ FT: 45,288
SALES (est): 51.4MM
SALES (corp-wide): 51.4MM **Privately Held**
Web: www.vossauto.com
SIC: 5511 7538 7513 5521 Automobiles, new and used; General automotive repair shops; Truck rental and leasing, no drivers; Used car dealers

(G-7712)
VOSS AUTO NETWORK INC
100 Loop Rd (45459-2142)
PHONE.................................937 433-1444
John Voss, *Mgr*
EMP: 430
SALES (corp-wide): 51.4MM **Privately Held**
Web: www.vossauto.com
SIC: 7532 5521 Body shop, automotive; Automobiles, used cars only
PA: Voss Auto Network, Inc.
   766 Mmsburg Cnterville Rd
   Dayton OH 45459
   937 428-2447

(G-7713)
VOSS CHEVROLET INC
100 Loop Rd (45459-2197)
PHONE.................................937 428-2500
John E Voss, *Pr*
EMP: 190 **EST:** 1962
SQ FT: 55,000
SALES (est): 21.2MM **Privately Held**
Web: www.vosschevy.com

Dayton - Montgomery County (G-7714) **GEOGRAPHIC SECTION**

SIC: **5511** 5521 5012 Automobiles, new and used; Used car dealers; Automobiles and other motor vehicles

(G-7714)
VOSS DODGE (PA)
90 Loop Rd (45459-2140)
PHONE..............................937 435-7800
EMP: 50 EST: 1972
SQ FT: 26,000
SALES (est): 5.43MM **Privately Held**
Web: www.dodge.com
SIC: **5511** 5521 5012 Automobiles, new and used; Used car dealers; Automobiles and other motor vehicles

(G-7715)
WASHINGTON TWNSHIP MNTGMERY CN
Also Called: Washington Twnship Rcrtion Ctr
895 Miamisburg Centerville Rd (45459)
PHONE..............................937 433-0130
David Paice, *Dir*
EMP: 44
SQ FT: 20,000
Web: www.washingtontwp.org
SIC: **7999** 7991 Recreation center; Physical fitness facilities
PA: Washington Township, Montgomery County
8200 Mcewen Rd
Dayton OH 45458
937 435-2376

(G-7716)
WELLNOW URGENT CARE PC
Also Called: Wellnow Urgent Care and RES
6210 Brandt Pike Ste 102 (45424-4019)
PHONE..............................937 236-8630
Gretchen Jackson, *Brnch Mgr*
EMP: 53
SALES (corp-wide): 21MM **Privately Held**
Web: www.wellnow.com
SIC: **8011** Clinic, operated by physicians
PA: Wellnow Urgent Care, P.C.
13448 Cicero Ave
Crestwood IL 60418
708 682-3384

(G-7717)
WENZLER DAY LEARNING CTR INC
Also Called: Wenzler Daycare & Learning Ctr
4535 Presidential Way (45429-5752)
PHONE..............................937 435-8200
Brenda Wenzler, *Pr*
Benita Wenzler, *
EMP: 37 EST: 1989
SALES (est): 437.31K **Privately Held**
Web: www.wenzlerlearningcenter.com
SIC: **8351** Group day care center

(G-7718)
WESTCARE OHIO INC
Also Called: East End Community Services
624 Xenia Ave (45410-1826)
PHONE..............................937 259-1898
Jan Lepore-jentleson, *Ex Dir*
EMP: 42 EST: 1998
SQ FT: 3,706
SALES (est): 2.37MM **Privately Held**
Web: www.east-end.org
SIC: **8322** 8399 Social service center; Community development groups

(G-7719)
WESTMNSTER FNCL SECURITIES INC
Also Called: Westminster Fincl Companies
50 Chestnut St (45440-1398)
PHONE..............................937 898-5010

Miles Brazie, *CEO*
Lawrence Miles Brazie, *
Ken Warnick, *
EMP: 29 EST: 1985
SALES (est): 9.57MM **Privately Held**
Web: www.westminsterfinancial.com
SIC: **6211** Brokers, security

(G-7720)
WHITE FAMILY COMPANIES INC
Also Called: White Allen Chevrolet
442 N Main St (45405-4923)
PHONE..............................937 222-3701
Howard Monk, *Genl Mgr*
EMP: 31
SALES (corp-wide): 95.84MM **Privately Held**
Web: www.whiteallenchevy.com
SIC: **5511** 7513 5012 Automobiles, new and used; Truck rental and leasing, no drivers; Automobiles and other motor vehicles
PA: The White Family Companies Inc
2 River Pl Ste 444
Dayton OH 45405
937 220-6394

(G-7721)
WIDOWS HOME OF DAYTON OHIO
50 S Findlay St (45403-2091)
PHONE..............................937 252-1661
Antonette Flohre, *Pr*
Everett Telljohann, *
Paul Heinrich, *
Gloria Ross, *
Dale Heinz, *
EMP: 70 EST: 1875
SQ FT: 50,000
SALES (est): 6.59MM **Privately Held**
Web: www.widowshome.org
SIC: **8051** 8361 Convalescent home with continuous nursing care; Aged home

(G-7722)
WIGGINS CLG & CRPT SVC INC (PA)
4699 Salem Ave Ste 2 (45416-1724)
PHONE..............................937 279-9080
Jewel Wiggins, *Pr*
Brenda Wiggins, *
EMP: 62 EST: 1990
SQ FT: 2,400
SALES (est): 2.19MM **Privately Held**
Web: www.wigginscleaning.com
SIC: **7349** 7217 Cleaning service, industrial or commercial; Carpet and furniture cleaning on location

(G-7723)
WILLIAM J HAGERTY DDS INC
7058 Corporate Way Ste 2 (45459-4243)
PHONE..............................937 434-3987
William J Hagerty D.d.s., *Prin*
EMP: 47
SALES (corp-wide): 2.19MM **Privately Held**
Web: www.williamjhagertydds.com
SIC: **8021** Dentists' office
PA: William J Hagerty Dds Inc
321 N Broadway St
Trotwood OH 45426
937 434-3987

(G-7724)
WILLIAMS LAST MILE HM LGSTICS
6510 Semmes Ln (45424-7117)
PHONE..............................937 313-9096
Joseph K Williams, *Prin*
EMP: 50 EST: 2019
SALES (est): 1.75MM **Privately Held**
SIC: **4789** Transportation services, nec

(G-7725)
WOOLPERT INC (PA)
4454 Idea Center Blvd (45430)
PHONE..............................937 461-5660
EMP: 228 EST: 1935
SALES (est): 166.22MM
SALES (corp-wide): 166.22MM **Privately Held**
Web: www.woolpert.com
SIC: **8711** Consulting engineer

(G-7726)
WORKFLOWONE LLC
220 E Monument Ave (45402-1287)
P.O. Box 1167 (45401-1167)
PHONE..............................877 735-4966
◆ EMP: 2000
SIC: **2754** 2791 4225 4731 Forms, business; gravure printing; Typesetting; General warehousing and storage; Freight transportation arrangement

(G-7727)
WRIGHT STATE PHYSCANS DRMTLOGY
2350 Miami Valley Dr Ste 210 (45459-4785)
PHONE..............................937 401-1100
EMP: 85
SALES (corp-wide): 2.48MM **Privately Held**
Web: www.wrightstatephysicians.org
SIC: **8011** General and family practice, physician/surgeon
PA: Wright State Physicians Dermatology
725 University Blvd
Beavercreek OH 45324
937 224-7546

(G-7728)
WRIGHT STATE PHYSICIANS INC
30 E Apple St Ste 6257 (45409-2939)
PHONE..............................937 208-3999
Gregory Barbour, *Pr*
EMP: 169
SALES (corp-wide): 29.3MM **Privately Held**
Web: www.wrightstatephysicians.org
SIC: **8011** Internal medicine, physician/surgeon
PA: Wright State Physicians , Inc.
725 University Blvd
Fairborn OH 45324
937 245-7200

(G-7729)
WRIGHT STATE UNIVERSITY
Also Called: Department of Surgery
1 Wyoming St 128 E Apple St 7th Fl (45409)
PHONE..............................937 208-2177
Mary Mccarthy, *Ch*
EMP: 58
SALES (corp-wide): 159.41MM **Privately Held**
Web: www.wright.edu
SIC: **8221** 8011 University; General and family practice, physician/surgeon
PA: Wright State University
3640 Colonel Glenn Hwy
Dayton OH 45435
937 775-3333

(G-7730)
XPO LOGISTICS FREIGHT INC
3410 Stop 8 Rd (45414-3428)
PHONE..............................937 898-9808
John Crawley, *Mgr*
EMP: 54
SQ FT: 18,920
SALES (corp-wide): 7.74B **Publicly Held**

Web: www.xpo.com
SIC: **4213** Contract haulers
HQ: Xpo Logistics Freight, Inc.
2211 Old Erhart Rd Ste 10
Ann Arbor MI 48105
800 755-2728

(G-7731)
YODER INDUSTRIES INC (PA)
2520 Needmore Rd (45414-4204)
PHONE..............................937 278-5769
Charles W Slicer, *Ch*
Ron Zeverka, *
Pam Stewart, *
Charles W Slicer, *Prin*
J B Yoder, *
EMP: 110 EST: 1956
SQ FT: 32,000
SALES (est): 9.1MM
SALES (corp-wide): 9.1MM **Privately Held**
Web: www.yoderindustries.com
SIC: **3363** 3369 3471 3365 Aluminum die-castings; Nonferrous foundries, nec; Plating and polishing; Aluminum foundries

(G-7732)
YOUNG MNS CHRSTN ASSN GRTER DY
Also Called: YMCA Crayon Club Chld Care
316 N Wilkinson St (45402-3060)
PHONE..............................937 228-9622
Nancy Hudecek, *Dir*
EMP: 105
SALES (corp-wide): 36.75MM **Privately Held**
Web: www.daytonymca.org
SIC: **8641** 8351 7997 7991 Youth organizations; Child day care services; Membership sports and recreation clubs; Physical fitness facilities
PA: Young Men's Christian Association Of Greater Dayton
118 W 1st St Ste 300
Dayton OH 45402
937 223-5201

(G-7733)
YOUNG MNS CHRSTN ASSN GRTER DY
Also Called: South Cmty Family YMCA Cdc
4545 Marshall Rd (45429-5716)
PHONE..............................937 312-1810
Kelley Ingram, *Dir*
EMP: 176
SALES (corp-wide): 36.75MM **Privately Held**
Web: www.daytonymca.org
SIC: **8641** 7991 8351 7032 Youth organizations; Physical fitness facilities; Child day care services; Youth camps
PA: Young Men's Christian Association Of Greater Dayton
118 W 1st St Ste 300
Dayton OH 45402
937 223-5201

(G-7734)
YOUNG MNS CHRSTN ASSN GRTER DY
Also Called: Beavercreek YMCA Sch's Out I
111 W 1st St Ste 207 (45402-1154)
PHONE..............................937 426-9622
Stacy Wentzell, *Dir*
EMP: 70
SALES (corp-wide): 36.75MM **Privately Held**
Web: www.daytonymca.org
SIC: **8641** 7997 Youth organizations; Membership sports and recreation clubs

GEOGRAPHIC SECTION   Defiance - Defiance County (G-7756)

PA: Young Men's Christian Association Of Greater Dayton
118 W 1st St Ste 300
Dayton OH 45402
937 223-5201

(G-7735)
ZAPPIA ENTERPRISES LLC
3210 Early Rd (45415-2705)
PHONE..................937 277-3010
Daniel Zappia, *Prin*
EMP: 36 **EST:** 2015
SALES (est): 1.76MM **Privately Held**
Web: www.zappiafoods.com
SIC: 8748 Business consulting, nec

(G-7736)
ZIEHLER LANDSCAPING
1045 E Centerville Station Rd (45459-5500)
PHONE..................937 312-9575
Andrew Ziehler, *Owner*
EMP: 36 **EST:** 1999
SALES (est): 2.34MM **Privately Held**
Web: www.discoverziehler.com
SIC: 0782 Landscape contractors

(G-7737)
ZIKS FAMILY PHARMACY 100
1130 W 3rd St (45402-6812)
PHONE..................937 225-9350
EMP: 30 **EST:** 2005
SQ FT: 5,500
SALES (est): 3MM **Privately Held**
Web: www.ziksrx.com
SIC: 5912 5047 8082 Drug stores; Medical and hospital equipment; Home health care services

(G-7738)
ZIKS HOME HEALTHCARE LLC
1130 W 3rd St (45402-6812)
PHONE..................937 225-9350
Nnenna Iheme, *Pr*
EMP: 55 **EST:** 2016
SALES (est): 887.37K **Privately Held**
SIC: 8082 Home health care services

De Graff
Logan County

(G-7739)
SCHINDEWOLF EXPRESS INC
200 S Boggs St (43318-7905)
PHONE..................937 585-5919
EMP: 52 **EST:** 1991
SALES (est): 9.83MM **Privately Held**
Web: www.schindewolfexpress.com
SIC: 4213 4212 Contract haulers; Local trucking, without storage

Deerfield
Portage County

(G-7740)
DEERFIELD FARMS
9041 State Route 224 (44411-8715)
P.O. Box 155 (44411-0155)
PHONE..................330 584-4715
B William Wallbrown, *Pr*
John Wallbrown, *VP*
EMP: 34 **EST:** 1979
SQ FT: 5,000
SALES (est): 3.86MM **Privately Held**
Web: www.deerfieldagservices.com
SIC: 0191 1799 1521 General farms, primarily crop; Fence construction; Patio and deck construction and repair

(G-7741)
DEERFIELD FARMS SERVICE INC
9041 State Route 224 (44411-8715)
P.O. Box 155 (44411-0155)
PHONE..................330 584-4715
EMP: 75
Web: www.deerfieldagservices.com
SIC: 5153 5191 4221 5083 Grain elevators; Fertilizer and fertilizer materials; Grain elevator, storage only; Agricultural machinery and equipment

Defiance
Defiance County

(G-7742)
BROOKVIEW HEALTHCARE CTR
Also Called: Brookview Healthcare Center
214 Harding St (43512-1381)
PHONE..................419 784-1014
Paul Dauerman, *Pr*
EMP: 89 **EST:** 1991
SALES (est): 15.69MM **Privately Held**
Web: www.brookviewhealthcare.com
SIC: 8059 8051 Convalescent home; Skilled nursing care facilities

(G-7743)
DEFIANCE CNTY BD COMMISSIONERS
Also Called: Defiance County Senior Center
140 E Broadway St (43512-1639)
PHONE..................419 782-3233
Tina Hiler, *Dir*
EMP: 30
SALES (corp-wide): 44.65MM **Privately Held**
Web: www.defiance-county.com
SIC: 8322 Individual and family services
PA: Defiance County Board Of Commissioners
500 Court St Ste A
Defiance OH 43512
419 782-4761

(G-7744)
DEFIANCE FAMILY PHYSICIANS LTD
1250 Ralston Ave Ste 104 (43512-5308)
PHONE..................419 785-3281
Robert Barnett Md, *Pt*
EMP: 29 **EST:** 1982
SALES (est): 592.89K **Privately Held**
SIC: 8011 General and family practice, physician/surgeon

(G-7745)
FAMILY FARM & HOME INC
1500 N Clinton St (43512-4100)
PHONE..................419 783-1702
EMP: 35
SALES (corp-wide): 220MM **Privately Held**
Web: www.familyfarmandhome.com
SIC: 0191 General farms, primarily crop
PA: Family Farm & Home, Inc.
900 3rd St Ste 302
Muskegon MI 49440
231 722-8335

(G-7746)
FAUSTER-CAMERON INC (PA)
Also Called: Defiance Clinic
1400 E 2nd St (43512-9905)
PHONE..................419 784-1414
TOLL FREE: 800
Chad L Peter, *CEO*
Allen Gaspar, *
John Racciato, *
Nathan Fogt, *

EMP: 280 **EST:** 1962
SQ FT: 101,908
SALES (est): 23.83MM
SALES (corp-wide): 23.83MM **Privately Held**
SIC: 8011 Medical centers

(G-7747)
FITZENRIDER INC
Also Called: Honeywell Authorized Dealer
827 Perry St (43512-2738)
PHONE..................419 784-0828
John Jacob, *Pr*
Philip Fitzenrider, *
EMP: 30 **EST:** 1955
SQ FT: 15,000
SALES (est): 2.42MM **Privately Held**
Web: www.fitzenriderhvac.com
SIC: 1711 Warm air heating and air conditioning contractor

(G-7748)
HEATHERS DAY CARE LLC
121 Hopkins St (43512-2220)
PHONE..................419 784-9600
Heather Mcmonigal, *CEO*
EMP: 36 **EST:** 2008
SALES (est): 995.43K **Privately Held**
Web: www.heathersdaycare.org
SIC: 8351 Group day care center

(G-7749)
HOWARD PAINTING INC
1740 Spruce St (43512-2457)
P.O. Box 3 (43512-0003)
PHONE..................419 782-7786
Joseph W Howard, *Pr*
EMP: 31 **EST:** 1954
SQ FT: 8,500
SALES (est): 793.93K **Privately Held**
Web: www.howardpainting.com
SIC: 1721 Exterior commercial painting contractor

(G-7750)
HUBBARD COMPANY
612 Clinton St (43512-2637)
P.O. Box 100 (43512-0100)
PHONE..................419 784-4455
E Keith Hubbard, *Ch Bd*
Thomas K Hubbard, *
Stephen F Hubbard, *
Jean A Hubbard, *
EMP: 44 **EST:** 1906
SQ FT: 20,000
SALES (est): 2.24MM **Privately Held**
Web: www.friendsoffice.com
SIC: 5943 5192 2752 2732 Office forms and supplies; Books; Offset printing; Book printing

(G-7751)
KELLER LOGISTICS GROUP INC (PA)
24862 Elliott Rd Ste 101 (43512-9237)
PHONE..................866 276-9486
Bryan Keller, *CEO*
Aaron Keller, *VP*
John Weinberg, *CFO*
Beth Woodbury, *Prin*
Nate Schaublin, *Prin*
EMP: 39 **EST:** 1978
SALES (est): 96.92MM **Privately Held**
Web: www.kellerlogistics.com
SIC: 4731 7389 4225 Freight transportation arrangement; Packaging and labeling services; General warehousing and storage

(G-7752)
LAUREL HEALTHCARE
Also Called: LAURRELS OF DEFIANCE
1701 Jefferson Ave (43512-3493)
PHONE..................419 782-7879
Dennis G Sherman, *Pr*
EMP: 85 **EST:** 1978
SALES (est): 9.18MM **Privately Held**
Web: www.cienahealthcare.com
SIC: 8051 Convalescent home with continuous nursing care

(G-7753)
LOWES HOME CENTERS LLC
Also Called: Lowe's
1831 N Clinton St (43512-8555)
PHONE..................419 782-9000
EMP: 148
SALES (corp-wide): 86.38B **Publicly Held**
Web: www.lowes.com
SIC: 5211 5031 5722 5064 Home centers; Building materials, exterior; Household appliance stores; Electrical appliances, television and radio
HQ: Lowe's Home Centers, Llc
1000 Lowes Blvd
Mooresville NC 28117
336 658-4000

(G-7754)
MAMMOTH TECH INC (PA)
Also Called: Credit Adjustments
1250 Geneva Blvd (43512-4303)
P.O. Box 180 (44045-0180)
PHONE..................419 782-3709
Jason Osborne, *CEO*
Jason Osborn, *
Lisa Bloomfield, *
Michael Osborne, *
David Weisner, *
EMP: 102 **EST:** 1955
SQ FT: 40,000
SALES (est): 42.53MM
SALES (corp-wide): 42.53MM **Privately Held**
Web: www.credit-adjustments.com
SIC: 7322 Collection agency, except real estate

(G-7755)
MAUMEE VALLEY GUIDANCE CTR INC (PA)
211 Biede Ave (43512-2497)
PHONE..................419 782-8856
William Bierie, *Ex Dir*
EMP: 40 **EST:** 1960
SQ FT: 6,000
SALES (est): 4.92MM
SALES (corp-wide): 4.92MM **Privately Held**
Web: www.maumeevalleyguidancecenter.org
SIC: 8093 Mental health clinic, outpatient

(G-7756)
MCNAUGHTON-MCKAY ELC OHIO INC
Also Called: McNaughton-Mckay Electric Co
188 Fox Run Dr (43512-1394)
PHONE..................419 784-0295
William Parsons, *Mgr*
EMP: 30
SALES (corp-wide): 2.81B **Privately Held**
SIC: 5063 Electrical supplies, nec
HQ: Mcnaughton-Mckay Electric Company Of Ohio, Inc.
2255 Citygate Dr
Columbus OH 43219
614 476-2800

Defiance - Defiance County (G-7757)

(G-7757)
MERCY HLTH - DEFIANCE HOSP LLC
Also Called: Mercy Hospital of Defiance
1404 E 2nd St (43512-2440)
PHONE.................................419 782-8444
Bob Baxter, *Pr*
EMP: 156 **EST:** 2005
SALES (est): 53.21MM
SALES (corp-wide): 6.92B **Privately Held**
Web: www.mercyweb.org
SIC: 8062 General medical and surgical hospitals
PA: Bon Secours Mercy Health, Inc.
   1701 Mercy Health Pl
   Cincinnati OH 45237
   513 956-3729

(G-7758)
NORTHWSTERN OHIO CMNTY ACTION (PA)
1933 E 2nd St (43512-2503)
PHONE.................................419 784-2150
Deborah Gerken, *Ex Dir*
Dean Genter, *
EMP: 150 **EST:** 1965
SQ FT: 8,000
SALES (est): 16MM
SALES (corp-wide): 16MM **Privately Held**
Web: www.nocac.org
SIC: 8399 8322 Community action agency; Individual and family services

(G-7759)
OHIO DEPT RHBILITATION CORECTN
Also Called: Parole & Community Services
418 Auglaize St (43512)
PHONE.................................419 782-3385
Connie Maaffel, *Brnch Mgr*
EMP: 49
SIC: 8322 9223 Social service center; Correctional institutions
HQ: Ohio Department Of Rehabilitation And Correction
   4545 Fisher Rd Ste D
   Columbus OH 43228

(G-7760)
PERSON CENTERED SERVICES INC
197 A Park Island Ave (43512)
PHONE.................................419 782-7274
EMP: 37
Web: www.activeday.com
SIC: 8999 Actuarial consultant
PA: Person Centered Services, Inc.
   1421 N Court St
   Circleville OH 43113

(G-7761)
PIONEER QUICK LUBES INC
1166 S Clinton St (43512-2707)
P.O. Box 363 (48624-0363)
PHONE.................................419 782-2213
EMP: 48 **EST:** 1995
SQ FT: 5,000
SALES (est): 1.19MM **Privately Held**
Web: www.pioneerql.com
SIC: 7549 Lubrication service, automotive

(G-7762)
PREMIER FINANCIAL CORP (PA)
Also Called: Premier
601 Clinton St (43512)
PHONE.................................419 782-5015
EMP: 55 **EST:** 1995
SALES (est): 456.36MM **Publicly Held**
Web: www.premierfincorp.com
SIC: 6035 6331 6321 6311 Federal savings and loan associations; Fire, marine, and casualty insurance; Accident and health insurance; Life insurance

(G-7763)
PROMEDICA HEALTH SYSTEM INC
1200 Ralston Ave (43512-9908)
PHONE.................................419 783-6802
EMP: 126
SALES (corp-wide): 187.07MM **Privately Held**
Web: www.promedica.org
SIC: 8062 General medical and surgical hospitals
PA: Promedica Health System, Inc.
   100 Madison Ave
   Toledo OH 43604
   567 585-9600

(G-7764)
QUADCO REHABILITATION CENTER
Also Called: QUADCO REHABILITATION CENTER INC
1838 E 2nd St (43512-2502)
PHONE.................................419 782-0389
EMP: 35
SALES (corp-wide): 1.38MM **Privately Held**
Web: www.quadcorehab.org
SIC: 8093 Rehabilitation center, outpatient treatment
PA: Quadco Rehabilitation Center, Inc.
   427 N Defiance St
   Stryker OH 43557
   419 682-1011

(G-7765)
RELIANCE FINANCIAL SERVICES NA
401 Clinton St (43512-2632)
P.O. Box 467 (43512-0467)
PHONE.................................419 783-8007
Jeffrey D Sewell, *CEO*
Gregory Marquiss, *
EMP: 30 **EST:** 1997
SALES (est): 4.37MM
SALES (corp-wide): 75.87MM **Publicly Held**
Web: www.yourstatebank.com
SIC: 7389 Financial services
HQ: The State Bank And Trust Company
   401 Clinton St
   Defiance OH 43512
   419 783-8950

(G-7766)
RICHLAND CO & ASSOCIATES INC (PA)
101 Clinton St Ste 2200 (43512-2173)
P.O. Box 385 (43512-0385)
PHONE.................................419 782-0141
Douglas A Mc Donald, *Pr*
Kevin R Mcdonald, *VP*
Brenda Mathewson, *
Ann Westrick, *
EMP: 40 **EST:** 1953
SQ FT: 3,500
SALES (est): 1.98MM
SALES (corp-wide): 1.98MM **Privately Held**
Web: www.richlandroofing.com
SIC: 1761 Roofing contractor

(G-7767)
RURBANC DATA SERVICES INC
Also Called: Rdsi Banking Systems
7622 N State Route 66 (43512-6715)
P.O. Box 467 (43512-0467)
PHONE.................................419 782-2530
Kurt Kratzer, *Pr*
Gary Saxman, *
Karen Oskey, *
Gwen Anderson, *
EMP: 60 **EST:** 2003
SALES (est): 2.39MM
SALES (corp-wide): 75.87MM **Publicly Held**
Web: ir.yourstatebank.com
SIC: 7374 Data processing service
PA: Sb Financial Group, Inc.
   401 Clinton St
   Defiance OH 43512
   419 783-8950

(G-7768)
SB FINANCIAL GROUP INC (PA)
401 Clinton St (43512)
P.O. Box 467 (43512)
PHONE.................................419 783-8950
Mark A Klein, *Ch Bd*
Anthony V Cosentino, *Ex VP*
Ernesto Gaytan, *Chief Technician*
Keeta J Diller, *Ex VP*
EMP: 192 **EST:** 1983
SALES (est): 75.87MM
SALES (corp-wide): 75.87MM **Publicly Held**
Web: ir.yourstatebank.com
SIC: 6022 State trust companies accepting deposits, commercial

(G-7769)
STATE BANK AND TRUST COMPANY (HQ)
Also Called: State Bank
401 Clinton St (43512-2662)
P.O. Box 467 (43512-0467)
PHONE.................................419 783-8950
Mark A Klein, *CEO*
Mark A Soukup, *
Steven D Vandemark, *
Rodger G Martin, *
Dean J Miller, *Stockholder*
◆ **EMP:** 35 **EST:** 1902
SQ FT: 10,000
SALES (est): 61.04MM
SALES (corp-wide): 75.87MM **Publicly Held**
Web: www.yourstatebank.com
SIC: 6022 6163 State trust companies accepting deposits, commercial; Loan brokers
PA: Sb Financial Group, Inc.
   401 Clinton St
   Defiance OH 43512
   419 783-8950

(G-7770)
STYKEMAIN-BUICK-GMC LTD (PA)
25124 Elliott Rd (43512-9003)
PHONE.................................419 784-5252
Joseph Stykemain, *
EMP: 77 **EST:** 1992
SQ FT: 30,000
SALES (est): 39.26MM **Privately Held**
Web: www.stykemain.com
SIC: 5511 5012 Automobiles, new and used; Automobiles

(G-7771)
TAS AVIATION DEFIANCE INC
20399 Airport Rd (43512-6763)
PHONE.................................419 658-4444
Anthony Saxton, *Pr*
EMP: 32 **EST:** 1976
SQ FT: 22,000
SALES (est): 1.07MM **Privately Held**
Web: www.tas-aviation.com
SIC: 4581 Airport

(G-7772)
THOMAS E KELLER TRUCKING INC
24862 Elliott Rd (43512-9217)
PHONE.................................419 784-4805
Bryan Keller, *Pr*
EMP: 367 **EST:** 1978
SALES (est): 26.91MM **Privately Held**
Web: www.kellerlogistics.com
SIC: 4213 Contract haulers

(G-7773)
UNITED PARCEL SERVICE INC
Also Called: UPS
820 Carpenter Rd (43512-1726)
PHONE.................................419 782-3552
Mike Kenneth, *Mgr*
EMP: 31
SALES (corp-wide): 90.96B **Publicly Held**
Web: www.ups.com
SIC: 4215 4513 Package delivery, vehicular; Air courier services
HQ: United Parcel Service, Inc.
   55 Glenlake Pkwy
   Atlanta GA 30328
   404 828-6000

(G-7774)
WAGNER METALS LLC
Also Called: Wagner Roofg & Cnstr Solutions
1340 W High St Ste E (43512-5307)
PHONE.................................419 594-7445
Brett T Wagner, *Managing Member*
EMP: 30 **EST:** 2010
SALES (est): 4.73MM **Privately Held**
Web: www.trustwagner.com
SIC: 1761 Roofing contractor

(G-7775)
WERLOR INC
Also Called: Werlor Waste Control
1420 Ralston Ave (43512-1380)
PHONE.................................419 784-4285
Casey Wertz, *Pr*
Gerald Wertz, *
Mark Hageman, *
Tom Taylor, *
Casey Wertz, *VP*
EMP: 36 **EST:** 1969
SQ FT: 8,000
SALES (est): 3.57MM **Privately Held**
Web: www.werlor.com
SIC: 2875 4212 4953 Compost; Garbage collection and transport, no disposal; Recycling, waste materials

Delaware
Delaware County

(G-7776)
ACI INDUSTRIES LTD (PA)
970 Pittsburgh Dr Frnt (43015-3872)
PHONE.................................740 368-4160
Ralph Paglieri, *Pt*
Scott H Fischer, *
Helen Harper, *
◆ **EMP:** 49 **EST:** 1984
SQ FT: 225,000
SALES (est): 10MM
SALES (corp-wide): 10MM **Privately Held**
Web: www.aci-industries.com
SIC: 3341 5093 3339 Secondary nonferrous metals; Scrap and waste materials; Primary nonferrous metals, nec

(G-7777)
AFTERMARKET PARTS COMPANY LLC (HQ)
Also Called: New Flyer
3229 Sawmill Pkwy (43015-7541)
PHONE.................................740 369-1056
Jim Marcotuli, *Pr*
▲ **EMP:** 85 **EST:** 2013
SALES (est): 16.12MM
SALES (corp-wide): 2.05B **Privately Held**
SIC: 5013 Automotive brakes
PA: Nfi Group Inc
   711 Kernaghan Ave

Winnipeg MB R2C 3
204 224-1251

(G-7778)
ALPHA GROUP OF DELAWARE INC
Also Called: Ergon
1000 Alpha Dr (43015-8642)
PHONE.................................740 368-5820
EMP: 58
SALES (corp-wide): 4.65MM **Privately Held**
Web: www.alphagroup.net
SIC: 8331 9111 Job training and related services; County supervisors' and executives' office
PA: The Alpha Group Of Delaware Inc
1000 Alpha Dr
Delaware OH 43015
740 368-5810

(G-7779)
ALPHA GROUP OF DELAWARE INC (PA)
1000 Alpha Dr (43015-8642)
PHONE.................................740 368-5810
Dave Nuscher, *CEO*
Joseph Leonard, *
EMP: 55 **EST:** 1970
SALES (est): 4.65MM
SALES (corp-wide): 4.65MM **Privately Held**
Web: www.alphagroup.net
SIC: 8331 9111 Sheltered workshop; County supervisors' and executives' office

(G-7780)
BRIDGES TO INDEPENDENCE INC (PA)
106 Stover Dr (43015-8601)
PHONE.................................740 362-1996
Chris Ritchie, *Pr*
EMP: 120 **EST:** 1999
SALES (est): 2.41MM
SALES (corp-wide): 2.41MM **Privately Held**
Web: www.bridgestoindependence.com
SIC: 8322 Social service center

(G-7781)
BUNS OF DELAWARE INC
Also Called: Buns Restaurant & Bakery
14 W Winter St (43015-1919)
PHONE.................................740 363-2867
Vasili Konstantinidis, *Pr*
EMP: 28 **EST:** 1864
SQ FT: 11,184
SALES (est): 471.15K **Privately Held**
Web: www.bunsrestaurant.com
SIC: 5812 5461 7299 2051 Eating places; Retail bakeries; Banquet hall facilities; Bread, cake, and related products

(G-7782)
CAC GROUP LLC
2097 London Rd (43015-8470)
PHONE.................................740 369-4328
EMP: 43
SALES (corp-wide): 4.84MM **Privately Held**
Web: www.customairco.com
SIC: 7623 1711 Refrigeration service and repair; Septic system construction
PA: Cac Group Llc
935 Claycraft Rd
Columbus OH 43230
614 552-4822

(G-7783)
CARPENTER & LEE CONSULTING LLC
2237 Hyatts Rd (43015-7989)
PHONE.................................614 766-8670
Bruce M Carpenter, *Pt*
Bruce M Carpenter, *Managing Member*
EMP: 43 **EST:** 2007
SALES (est): 2.38MM **Privately Held**
SIC: 7379 Computer related consulting services

(G-7784)
CENTRAL OHIO CONTRACTORS INC
888 Us Highway 42 N (43015-9014)
PHONE.................................740 369-7700
EMP: 70
SALES (corp-wide): 3.3MM **Privately Held**
Web: www.centralohiocontractor.com
SIC: 1522 4953 Residential construction, nec; Refuse collection and disposal services
PA: Central Ohio Contractors, Inc.
2879 Jackson Pike
Grove City OH 43123
614 539-2579

(G-7785)
CENTRAL OHIO MENTAL HEALTH CTR (PA)
250 S Henry St (43015-2978)
PHONE.................................740 368-7837
Neil Tolbert, *CFO*
Tom Sefcik, *
EMP: 70 **EST:** 1956
SQ FT: 6,000
SALES (est): 4.42MM
SALES (corp-wide): 4.42MM **Privately Held**
Web: www.comhc.net
SIC: 8093 Mental health clinic, outpatient

(G-7786)
COMFORT EXPRESS INC
Also Called: Honeywell Authorized Dealer
3527 State Route 37 W (43015-8619)
PHONE.................................740 389-4400
Maureen Mathews, *Genl Mgr*
EMP: 38 **EST:** 1990
SQ FT: 2,400
SALES (est): 738.61K **Privately Held**
Web: www.comfortxpress.com
SIC: 1711 Warm air heating and air conditioning contractor

(G-7787)
COUNTY OF DELAWARE
50 Channing St (43015-2050)
P.O. Box 8006 (43015-8006)
PHONE.................................740 833-2240
Chad Antel, *Mgr*
EMP: 49
SALES (corp-wide): 208.3MM **Privately Held**
Web: www.delawaregop.org
SIC: 1623 Water, sewer, and utility lines
PA: County Of Delaware
91 N Sandusky St
Delaware OH 43015
740 368-1800

(G-7788)
COUNTY OF DELAWARE
Also Called: Delaware County Engineers
50 Channing St (43015-2050)
P.O. Box 8006 (43015-8006)
PHONE.................................740 833-2400
Chris Bauserman, *Mgr*
EMP: 165
SALES (corp-wide): 208.3MM **Privately Held**
Web: www.delawaregop.org
SIC: 8711 1611 Engineering services; Highway and street construction
PA: County Of Delaware
91 N Sandusky St
Delaware OH 43015
740 368-1800

(G-7789)
COUNTY OF DELAWARE
Also Called: Delaware General Health Dst
1 W Winter St 2nd Fl (43015-1918)
P.O. Box 570 (43015-0570)
PHONE.................................740 203-2040
EMP: 70 **EST:** 1920
SQ FT: 15,000
SALES (est): 14.43MM **Privately Held**
Web: www.delawarehealth.org
SIC: 8011 Clinic, operated by physicians

(G-7790)
CREATIVE FOUNDATIONS INC (PA)
20 Troy Rd (43015-4501)
P.O. Box 1508 (43015-8508)
PHONE.................................877 345-6733
David Robins, *CEO*
David Robbins, *
EMP: 35 **EST:** 2001
SQ FT: 6,000
SALES (est): 10.97MM
SALES (corp-wide): 10.97MM **Privately Held**
Web: www.creativefoundations.org
SIC: 8322 Social service center

(G-7791)
CREATIVE FOUNDATIONS INC
20 Troy Rd (43015-4501)
PHONE.................................614 832-2121
EMP: 55
SALES (corp-wide): 10.97MM **Privately Held**
Web: www.creativefoundations.org
SIC: 8051 Mental retardation hospital
PA: Creative Foundations, Inc.
20 Troy Rd
Delaware OH 43015
877 345-6733

(G-7792)
CSX TRANSPORTATION INC
Also Called: CSX
770 Hills Miller Rd (43015-9760)
PHONE.................................740 362-7924
EMP: 75
SALES (corp-wide): 11.07B **Publicly Held**
SIC: 4011 Railroads, line-haul operating
HQ: Csx Transportation, Inc.
500 Water St
Jacksonville FL 32202
904 359-3100

(G-7793)
DEL-CO WATER COMPANY INC (PA)
6658 Olentangy River Rd (43015)
PHONE.................................740 548-7746
Timothy D Mcnamara, *Pr*
Kenneth Zarbaugh, *
Robert Jenkins, *
EMP: 75 **EST:** 1969
SQ FT: 8,000
SALES (est): 48.18MM
SALES (corp-wide): 48.18MM **Privately Held**
Web: www.delcowater.org
SIC: 4941 Water supply

(G-7794)
DELAWARE CITY SCHOOL DISTRICT
Also Called: Delaware City School Garage
2462 Liberty Rd (43015-8810)
PHONE.................................740 363-5901
EMP: 57
SALES (corp-wide): 91.75MM **Privately Held**
Web: www.dcs.k12.oh.us
SIC: 8211 7538 Public elementary school; General automotive repair shops
PA: Delaware City School District
74 W William St
Delaware OH 43015
740 833-1100

(G-7795)
EQUITY RESOURCES INC
15 W Central Ave Ste 103 (43015-1953)
PHONE.................................740 363-7300
Bob Mckarin, *Genl Mgr*
EMP: 29
Web: www.callequity.net
SIC: 6162 Mortgage bankers and loan correspondents
PA: Equity Resources, Inc.
25 S Park Pl
Newark OH 43055

(G-7796)
EVOLUTION AG LLC
Also Called: Kubota Authorized Dealer
5565 State Route 37 E (43015-9464)
PHONE.................................740 363-1341
James R Henkel, *Ch Bd*
Thomas M Hill, *
David P Shipley, *
Douglas D Loudenslager, *
EMP: 36 **EST:** 2012
SALES (est): 9.18MM **Privately Held**
Web: www.evolutionagllc.com
SIC: 5083 Farm implements

(G-7797)
FIRSTENTERPRISES INC
2000 Nutter Farms Ln (43015-9195)
PHONE.................................740 369-5100
Mike Doyle, *Prin*
EMP: 301
SALES (corp-wide): 682.92MM **Privately Held**
SIC: 4213 Trucking, except local
PA: Firstenterprises, Inc.
202 Heritage Park Dr
Murfreesboro TN 37129
615 890-9229

(G-7798)
FOOR CONCRETE CO INC (PA)
5361 State Route 37 E (43015-9684)
PHONE.................................740 513-4346
Archie E Foor Junior, *Pr*
EMP: 48 **EST:** 1990
SALES (est): 4.66MM
SALES (corp-wide): 4.66MM **Privately Held**
Web: www.foorconcrete.com
SIC: 1771 Concrete pumping

(G-7799)
FRANCHISE GROUP INC (HQ)
109 Innovation Ct Ste J (43015)
PHONE.................................740 363-2222
Andy Laurence, *CEO*
Eric F Seeton, *CFO*
Kenneth Todd Evans Chief Franc hising, *Ofcr*
Andrew F Kaminsky, *Ex VP*
Lee Wright, *CCO*
EMP: 386 **EST:** 1996
SALES (est): 4.4B
SALES (corp-wide): 4.4B **Privately Held**
Web: www.franchisegrp.com
SIC: 6794 7291 5961 Patent owners and lessors; Tax return preparation services; Catalog and mail-order houses
PA: Freedom Vcm Inc.
109 Innovation Ct Ste J
Delaware OH 43015

Delaware - Delaware County (G-7800)

740 363-2222

(G-7800)
GANZFAIR INVESTMENT INC
Also Called: Shamrock Golf Club
231 Clubhouse Dr (43015-8490)
PHONE.................................614 792-6630
Gary Bachinski, *Pr*
EMP: 29 **EST:** 1992
SQ FT: 5,000
SALES (est): 857.51K **Privately Held**
SIC: 7992 7997 Public golf courses; Membership sports and recreation clubs

(G-7801)
GEOAMPS LLC
1707 Hyatts Rd (43015-9215)
PHONE.................................614 389-4872
EMP: 34 **EST:** 2011
SALES (est): 4.45MM **Privately Held**
Web: www.irthsolutions.com
SIC: 7371 Computer software development

(G-7802)
GRADY MEMORIAL HOSPITAL (PA)
561 W Central Ave (43015-1489)
PHONE.................................740 615-1000
David Blom, *CEO*
Johnni Beckel, *
EMP: 325 **EST:** 1904
SQ FT: 124,740
SALES (est): 30.99MM
SALES (corp-wide): 30.99MM **Privately Held**
Web: www.ohiohealth.com
SIC: 8062 General medical and surgical hospitals

(G-7803)
HELPLINE DEL MRROW CUNTIES INC
Also Called: Helpline
11 N Franklin St (43015-1913)
PHONE.................................740 369-3316
Susan Hanson, *Ex Dir*
EMP: 45 **EST:** 1972
SQ FT: 3,187
SALES (est): 3.18MM **Privately Held**
Web: www.helplinedelmor.org
SIC: 8322 Social service center

(G-7804)
HERITAGE COOPERATIVE INC (PA)
Also Called: Heritage Cooperative
59 Greif Pkwy Ste 200 (43015-7205)
PHONE.................................877 240-4393
Jeffrey Osentoski, *CEO*
Ronald Angelilli, *
EMP: 59 **EST:** 2009
SALES (est): 461.99MM **Privately Held**
Web: www.heritagecooperative.com
SIC: 5153 5261 4925 4932 Grains; Fertilizer; Liquefied petroleum gas, distribution through mains; Gas and other services combined

(G-7805)
HUNTINGTON NATIONAL BANK
95 E William St (43015-2148)
PHONE.................................740 363-9343
Ann Healy, *Brnch Mgr*
EMP: 36
SALES (corp-wide): 10.84B **Publicly Held**
Web: www.huntington.com
SIC: 6029 Commercial banks, nec
HQ: The Huntington National Bank
41 S High St
Columbus OH 43215
614 480-4293

(G-7806)
INN AT OLENTANGY TRAIL
36 Corduroy Rd (43015-7879)
PHONE.................................740 417-9287
Carrie Mccarter, *Prin*
EMP: 28 **EST:** 2011
SALES (est): 4.01MM **Privately Held**
Web: www.olentangytrail.com
SIC: 7011 Bed and breakfast inn

(G-7807)
INNO-PAK LLC (PA)
100 Founders Ct (43015-4460)
PHONE.................................740 363-0090
Chris Sanzone, *CEO*
▲ **EMP:** 73 **EST:** 1992
SALES (est): 47.06MM **Privately Held**
Web: www.innopak.com
SIC: 5199 Packaging materials

(G-7808)
JEGS AUTOMOTIVE LLC (HQ)
Also Called: Jeg's High-Performance Center
101 Jegs Pl (43015)
PHONE.................................614 294-5050
Jeffrey R Hennion, *CEO*
◆ **EMP:** 150 **EST:** 1960
SQ FT: 200,000
SALES (est): 100.86MM
SALES (corp-wide): 712.86MM **Privately Held**
Web: www.jegs.com
SIC: 5013 5961 5531 Automotive supplies and parts; Automotive supplies and equipment, mail order; Automotive parts
PA: Equity Greenbriar Group L P
1 Greenwich Plz
Greenwich CT 06830
914 925-9600

(G-7809)
JP MORGAN PARTNERS LLC
Also Called: Chase
61 N Sandusky St (43015-1925)
P.O. Box 24696 (43224-0696)
PHONE.................................800 848-9136
Donald Alecci, *Prin*
EMP: 29 **EST:** 2000
SALES (est): 5.08MM **Privately Held**
Web: locator.chase.com
SIC: 6022 State commercial banks

(G-7810)
JPMORGAN CHASE BANK NAT ASSN
61 N Sandusky St (43015-1925)
P.O. Box 710573 (43271-0001)
PHONE.................................740 363-8032
Mindy Hoffman, *Mgr*
EMP: 44
SALES (corp-wide): 239.43B **Publicly Held**
Web: www.chase.com
SIC: 6021 National commercial banks
HQ: Jpmorgan Chase Bank, National Association
1111 Polaris Pkwy
Columbus OH 43240
614 436-3055

(G-7811)
KHEMPCO BLDG SUP CO LTD PARTNR (PA)
Also Called: Arlington-Blaine Lumber Co
130 Johnson Dr (43015-8699)
PHONE.................................740 549-0465
James D Klingbeil Junior, *Genl Pt*
Richard Robinson, *Pt*
Donny Bowman, *Pt*
EMP: 100 **EST:** 1963

SALES (est): 22.54MM
SALES (corp-wide): 22.54MM **Privately Held**
Web: www.khempco.com
SIC: 5031 5211 2439 2431 Lumber: rough, dressed, and finished; Lumber and other building materials; Trusses, except roof: laminated lumber; Doors, wood

(G-7812)
KROGER CO
2000 Nutter Farms Ln (43015-9195)
PHONE.................................859 630-6959
Lisa Allen, *Mgr*
EMP: 600
SALES (corp-wide): 150.04B **Publicly Held**
Web: www.thekrogerco.com
SIC: 4225 General warehousing
PA: The Kroger Co
1014 Vine St
Cincinnati OH 45202
513 762-4000

(G-7813)
KROGER COMPANY
Also Called: Kroger
2000 Nutter Farms Ln (43015-9195)
PHONE.................................740 657-2124
Bruce Macaulay, *Pr*
▲ **EMP:** 1000 **EST:** 2003
SALES (est): 178MM
SALES (corp-wide): 150.04B **Publicly Held**
Web: www.kroger.com
SIC: 4225 General warehousing and storage
PA: The Kroger Co
1014 Vine St
Cincinnati OH 45202
513 762-4000

(G-7814)
LIBERTY COMMUNITY CENTER
Also Called: LIBERTY COMMUNITY CHILDRENS CE
207 London Rd (43015-2585)
PHONE.................................740 369-3876
EMP: 29 **EST:** 1947
SALES (est): 791.31K **Privately Held**
Web: www.delawarelcc.org
SIC: 8351 Preschool center

(G-7815)
LIBERTY TECHNOLOGY COMPANY LLC
620 Liberty Rd (43015-9387)
PHONE.................................740 363-1941
Vera Maruli, *CFO*
EMP: 40 **EST:** 2014
SALES (est): 1.16MM
SALES (corp-wide): 25.37MM **Privately Held**
Web: www.libertycasting.com
SIC: 8741 Management services
PA: Liberty Casting Company Llc
550 Liberty Rd
Delaware OH 43015
740 363-1941

(G-7816)
MARYHAVEN INC
88 N Sandusky St (43015-1756)
PHONE.................................740 203-3800
Charles Williams, *Brnch Mgr*
EMP: 28
SALES (corp-wide): 32.39MM **Privately Held**
Web: www.maryhaven.com
SIC: 8093 Alcohol clinic, outpatient
PA: Maryhaven, Inc.
1791 Alum Creek Dr
Columbus OH 43207
614 449-1530

(G-7817)
MEDIU INC
106 Stover Dr (43015-8601)
PHONE.................................614 332-7410
Paul Timmerman, *CEO*
Michael Berichon, *
EMP: 27 **EST:** 2003
SALES (est): 7.14MM **Privately Held**
Web: www.mediu.com
SIC: 7371 Computer software development

(G-7818)
MEDQUEST HEALTH CENTER INC
Also Called: Healthsource of Delaware
840 Sunbury Rd Ste 506 (43015-7207)
PHONE.................................740 417-4567
Shauna K Hart, *Prin*
EMP: 28
SALES (corp-wide): 201.42K **Privately Held**
Web: www.medquesthc.com
SIC: 8041 Offices and clinics of chiropractors
PA: Medquest Health Center Inc
33 Lexngton Sprngmill Rd
Ontario OH 44906
419 529-5544

(G-7819)
NATIONAL LIME AND STONE CO
Also Called: National Lime Stone Clmbus Reg
2406 S Section Line Rd (43015-9518)
P.O. Box 537 (43015-0537)
PHONE.................................740 548-4206
Carolyn Coder, *Off Mgr*
EMP: 28
SALES (corp-wide): 167.89MM **Privately Held**
Web: www.natlime.com
SIC: 1422 Crushed and broken limestone
PA: The National Lime And Stone Company
551 Lake Cascade Pkwy
Findlay OH 45840
419 422-4341

(G-7820)
OCCUPATIONAL HEALTH LINK (PA)
557 Sunbury Rd (43015-8410)
PHONE.................................614 885-0039
EMP: 28 **EST:** 1996
SALES (est): 9.84MM **Privately Held**
Web: www.oehpmco.com
SIC: 6331 8399 Workers' compensation insurance; Health systems agency

(G-7821)
PROFESSIONAL PAVEMENT SVCS LLC
152 Troutman Rd (43015-8998)
PHONE.................................740 726-2222
Matthew Kinney, *Managing Member*
EMP: 45 **EST:** 2010
SALES (est): 6MM **Privately Held**
Web: www.professionalpavement.net
SIC: 1771 0781 7349 Concrete work; Landscape services; Cleaning service, industrial or commercial

(G-7822)
RADIOLOGY PHYSICIANS INC
3769 Kingman Hill Dr Ste 220 (43015-7711)
P.O. Box 1026 (43065-1026)
PHONE.................................614 717-9840
Michael Gregg Md, *Prin*
Michael Gregg, *Pr*
EMP: 28 **EST:** 1984
SALES (est): 261.94K **Privately Held**
Web: www.rpidayton.com

SIC: 8011 Radiologist

(G-7823)
RECOVERY PREVENTION RESOURCES
118 Stover Dr (43015-8601)
PHONE.................................740 369-6811
Tony Williams, *CEO*
EMP: 29 EST: 1975
SQ FT: 20,000
SALES (est): 1.58MM **Privately Held**
Web: www.escuelavaldez.org
SIC: 8093 Mental health clinic, outpatient

(G-7824)
SARAH MOORE HLTH CARE CTR INC
Also Called: Sarah Moore Community
26 N Union St (43015-1922)
PHONE.................................740 362-9641
Ronald White, *Pr*
Thomas W Hess, *
EMP: 59 EST: 1893
SQ FT: 30,000
SALES (est): 5.51MM **Privately Held**
SIC: 8059 8052 Nursing home, except skilled and intermediate care facility; Intermediate care facilities

(G-7825)
SCHNEIDER NAT CARRIERS INC
600 London Rd (43015-3839)
PHONE.................................740 362-6910
Jerry Jackson, *Mgr*
EMP: 1943
SALES (corp-wide): 5.5B **Publicly Held**
Web: www.schneider.com
SIC: 4731 4213 Truck transportation brokers ; Trucking, except local
HQ: Schneider National Carriers, Inc.
    3101 Packerland Dr
    Green Bay WI 54313
    920 592-2000

(G-7826)
SKY CLIMBER TWR SOLUTIONS LLC
Also Called: Sky Climber Telecom
1800 Pittsburgh Dr (43015-3870)
PHONE.................................740 203-3900
Thomas Warchol, *Genl Mgr*
EMP: 30 EST: 2013
SQ FT: 10,000
SALES (est): 2.55MM **Privately Held**
Web: www.skyclimbertelecom.com
SIC: 1623 Transmitting tower (telecommunication) construction

(G-7827)
SOURCEPOINT
800 Cheshire Rd (43015-6038)
PHONE.................................740 363-6677
Fara Waugh, *Ex Dir*
Kimberly Clewell, *
Fara Waugh, *Dir*
EMP: 90 EST: 1992
SQ FT: 58,000
SALES (est): 12.38MM **Privately Held**
Web: www.mysourcepoint.org
SIC: 8322 Senior citizens' center or association

(G-7828)
STARTUPSCOM LLC
7691 Perry Rd (43015-9117)
PHONE.................................800 799-6998
Wil Schroter, *CEO*
EMP: 66 EST: 2011
SALES (est): 2.98MM **Privately Held**
Web: www.startups.com
SIC: 8742 Marketing consulting services

(G-7829)
STRATEGY GROUP FOR MEDIA INC
7669 Stagers Loop (43015-7010)
PHONE.................................740 201-5500
Rex Elsass, *CEO*
Scott Schweitzer, *COO*
EMP: 39 EST: 2000
SALES (est): 1.3MM **Privately Held**
Web: www.tsgco.com
SIC: 7812 Audio-visual program production

(G-7830)
THORSENS GREENHOUSE LLC
2069 Hyatts Rd (43015-9215)
PHONE.................................740 363-5069
Doug Thorsen, *Pt*
▲ EMP: 35 EST: 2000
SQ FT: 140,000
SALES (est): 4.07MM **Privately Held**
Web: www.thorsensgreenhouse.com
SIC: 0181 5193 Flowers: grown under cover (e.g., greenhouse production); Nursery stock

(G-7831)
TRUCCO CONSTRUCTION CO INC
3531 Airport Rd (43015-9467)
PHONE.................................740 417-9010
Mark Trucco, *CEO*
Mitchell Trucco, *
Ken Carr, *
EMP: 155 EST: 1990
SQ FT: 24,470
SALES (est): 56.28MM **Privately Held**
Web: www.truccoconstruction.com
SIC: 1623 1771 1794 1611 Underground utilities contractor; Concrete work; Excavation and grading, building construction; Highway and street construction

(G-7832)
U S XPRESS INC
2000 Nutter Farms Ln (43015-9195)
PHONE.................................740 363-0700
Scott Cluff, *Brnch Mgr*
EMP: 399
Web: www.usxpress.com
SIC: 4213 Contract haulers
HQ: U. S. Xpress, Inc.
    4080 Jenkins Rd
    Chattanooga TN 37421
    866 266-7270

(G-7833)
V & P HYDRAULIC PRODUCTS LLC
1700 Pittsburgh Dr (43015-3869)
PHONE.................................740 203-3600
Brad Scott, *Managing Member*
Scott Braumiller, *Managing Member**
Judd Scott, *Managing Member**
EMP: 70 EST: 1937
SQ FT: 45,000
SALES (est): 19.03MM **Privately Held**
Web: www.vphyd.com
SIC: 5084 Hydraulic systems equipment and supplies

(G-7834)
WILLOW BROOK CHRISTIAN SVCS
100 Delaware Xing W (43015-7853)
PHONE.................................740 201-5640
EMP: 43 EST: 2010
SALES (est): 23.58MM **Privately Held**
Web: www.willow-brook.org
SIC: 8051 Skilled nursing care facilities

(G-7835)
WILLOW BROOK CHRSTN CMMUNITIES (PA)
Also Called: WILLOW BROOK CHRISTIAN VILLAGE
100 Willow Brook Way S (43015-3249)
PHONE.................................740 369-0048
Larry Harris, *CEO*
EMP: 60 EST: 1972
SQ FT: 21,780
SALES (est): 7.86MM
SALES (corp-wide): 7.86MM **Privately Held**
Web: www.willow-brook.org
SIC: 8052 8051 Intermediate care facilities; Skilled nursing care facilities

Delphos
Allen County

(G-7836)
ALL TEMP REFRIGERATION INC
Also Called: Tdk Refrigeration Leasing
18996 State Route 66 (45833-9326)
PHONE.................................419 692-5016
Keith Pohlman, *Pr*
EMP: 50 EST: 1986
SQ FT: 11,900
SALES (est): 10.42MM **Privately Held**
Web: www.atrcontractors.com
SIC: 1711 7359 Refrigeration contractor; Equipment rental and leasing, nec

(G-7837)
BUNGE NORTH AMERICA EAST LLC
234 S Jefferson St (45833-1820)
P.O. Box 485 (45833-0485)
PHONE.................................419 692-6010
Tim Hodson, *Mgr*
EMP: 1567
SALES (corp-wide): 687.86MM **Privately Held**
Web: www.bunge.com
SIC: 5153 Grains
PA: Bunge North America (East), L.L.C.
    1391 Tmbrlake Mnor Pkwy S
    Chesterfield MO 63017
    314 292-2000

(G-7838)
CITIZENS BANK OF DELPHOS
Also Called: Citizens Bank
114 E 3rd St (45833-1761)
PHONE.................................419 692-2010
TOLL FREE: 800
John Miller, *Pr*
Joe Reinemeyer, *Pr*
EMP: 65 EST: 1893
SALES (est): 722.5K **Publicly Held**
SIC: 6035 Federal savings institutions
PA: United Bancshares, Inc.
    105 Progressive Dr
    Columbus Grove OH 45830

(G-7839)
COMMUNITY HLTH PRFSSIONALS INC
1500 E 5th St (45833-9145)
PHONE.................................419 695-8101
EMP: 40
SALES (corp-wide): 12.27MM **Privately Held**
Web: www.comhealthpro.org
SIC: 8082 Visiting nurse service
PA: Community Health Professionals, Inc.
    1159 Westwood Dr
    Van Wert OH 45891
    419 238-9223

(G-7840)
DOUBLE A TRAILER SALES INC (PA)
1750 E 5th St (45833-9138)
P.O. Box 129 (45833-0129)
PHONE.................................419 692-7626
Mark A Wannemacher, *Pr*
Charles Wannemacher, *
Mary Ann Wannemacher, *
▲ EMP: 29 EST: 1965
SQ FT: 14,000
SALES (est): 5.28MM
SALES (corp-wide): 5.28MM **Privately Held**
Web: www.doubleatrailer.com
SIC: 5084 7539 Industrial machine parts; Trailer repair

(G-7841)
JWJ INVESTMENTS INC
Also Called: Richland Manor
800 Ambrose Dr (45833-9146)
PHONE.................................419 643-3161
William J Mc Clellan, *Pr*
EMP: 173
SALES (corp-wide): 4.77MM **Privately Held**
SIC: 8059 8051 Nursing home, except skilled and intermediate care facility; Skilled nursing care facilities
PA: Jwj Investments, Inc.
    300 Cherry St
    Genoa OH 43430
    419 855-7755

(G-7842)
NR LEE RESTORATION LTD
7470 Grone Rd (45833-9107)
PHONE.................................419 692-2233
Nathan Lee, *Pr*
Nathan R Lee, *
EMP: 28 EST: 1998
SALES (est): 2.47MM **Privately Held**
Web: www.nrlee.com
SIC: 1761 1741 Roofing contractor; Tuckpointing or restoration

(G-7843)
PALMER-DONAVIN MFG CO
Lima Div
911 Spencerville Rd (45833-2351)
PHONE.................................419 692-5000
Jerry Miner, *Mgr*
EMP: 49
SALES (corp-wide): 292.82MM **Privately Held**
Web: www.palmerdonavin.com
SIC: 5039 5074 Prefabricated structures; Heating equipment (hydronic)
PA: The Palmer-Donavin Manufacturing Company
    3210 Centerpoint Dr
    Urbancrest OH 43123
    800 652-1234

(G-7844)
SPECILZED ALTRNTVES FOR FMLIES (PA)
Also Called: SAFY
10100 Elida Rd (45833-9056)
PHONE.................................419 695-8010
Tonya Brooks-thomas, *Dir*
Karen Niese, *
EMP: 59 EST: 1983
SALES (est): 22.34MM
SALES (corp-wide): 22.34MM **Privately Held**
Web: www.safy.org
SIC: 8322 Child related social services

(G-7845)
SPECILZED ALTRNTVES FOR FMLIES (PA)
Also Called: S A F Y
10100 Elida Rd (45833-9056)

Delphos - Allen County (G-7846)

PHONE..................................419 695-8010
Scott Spangler, *Pr*
Norman Pfaadt, *
Jim Sherman, *
Marc Bloomingdale, *
Jane Wintz, *
EMP: 50 **EST:** 1983
SQ FT: 4,800
SALES (est): 7.25MM **Privately Held**
Web: www.safy.org
SIC: 8322 Child related social services

(G-7846)
TOLEDO MOLDING & DIE LLC
Also Called: Delphos Plant 2
24086 State Route 697 (45833-9203)
P.O. Box 393 (45833-0393)
PHONE..................................419 692-6022
Keith Riegle, *Mgr*
EMP: 256
Web: www.tmdinc.com
SIC: 5031 3714 Molding, all materials; Motor vehicle parts and accessories
HQ: Toledo Molding & Die, Llc
1429 Coining Dr
Toledo OH 43612

(G-7847)
VANCREST LTD
Also Called: Vancrest Healthcare Cntr
1425 E 5th St (45833-9142)
PHONE..................................419 695-2871
Cindy Langenkamp, *Mgr*
EMP: 27
SQ FT: 1,306
SALES (corp-wide): 28.02MM **Privately Held**
Web: www.vancrest.com
SIC: 8051 Convalescent home with continuous nursing care
PA: Vancrest, Ltd.
120 W Main St Ste 200
Van Wert OH 45891
419 238-0715

(G-7848)
VNA COMPREHENSIVE SERVICES INC
602 E 5th St (45833-1510)
PHONE..................................419 695-8101
Amy Zalar, *Mgr*
EMP: 63
SALES (corp-wide): 12.27MM **Privately Held**
Web: www.comhealthpro.org
SIC: 8082 Visiting nurse service
HQ: Vna Comprehensive Services, Inc.
1157 Westwood Dr
Van Wert OH 45891

Delta
Fulton County

(G-7849)
BLUESCOPE RECYCLING & MTLS LLC
7300 State Route 109 (43515-9450)
PHONE..................................816 968-3000
EMP: 180
Web: www.bluescoperecycling.com
SIC: 5093 Scrap and waste materials
HQ: Bluescope Recycling And Materials Llc
295 S Commerce Dr
Waterloo IN 46793
419 540-4355

(G-7850)
FARMERS MERCHANTS BANCORP INC
Also Called: Farmers & Merchants State Bank
101 Main St (43515-1309)
PHONE..................................419 822-9510
Deborah Kauffman, *Mgr*
EMP: 52
SALES (corp-wide): 155.85MM **Publicly Held**
Web: www.fm.bank
SIC: 6035 6029 Federal savings institutions; Commercial banks, nec
PA: Farmers & Merchants Bancorp, Inc.
307 N Defiance St
Archbold OH 43502
419 446-2501

(G-7851)
INDUSTRIAL REPAIR AND MFG (PA)
1140 E Main St (43515-9406)
PHONE..................................419 822-4232
TOLL FREE: 877
▲ **EMP:** 42 **EST:** 1995
SQ FT: 48,000
SALES (est): 4.92MM **Privately Held**
Web: www.irmworldwide.com
SIC: 7699 7363 3443 Industrial machinery and equipment repair; Truck driver services; Containers, shipping (bombs, etc.): metal plate

(G-7852)
METALX LLC
7300 State Route 109 (43515-9450)
PHONE..................................260 232-3000
Jon Brown, *Brnch Mgr*
EMP: 60
SALES (corp-wide): 110.6MM **Privately Held**
Web: www.metalx.net
SIC: 5093 Metal scrap and waste materials
PA: Metalx, Llc
9910 Dupont Circle Dr E # 200
Fort Wayne IN 46825
260 232-3000

(G-7853)
NATURE FRESH FARMS USA INC
7445 State Route 109 (43515-9450)
PHONE..................................419 330-5080
Peter Quiring, *Pr*
EMP: 36 **EST:** 2015
SALES (est): 9.78MM
SALES (corp-wide): 83.56MM **Privately Held**
Web: www.naturefresh.ca
SIC: 0191 General farms, primarily crop
HQ: Nature Fresh Farms Inc
525 Essex Rd 14
Leamington ON N8H 3
519 326-8603

(G-7854)
NORTH STAR BLUESCOPE STEEL LLC
6767 County Road 9 (43515-9449)
PHONE..................................419 822-2200
Conrad Winkler, *Pr*
Laeek Afzal, *
Jeff Joldrichsen, *
Kristin Malosh, *HSE*
Ashley Kotowski, *
◆ **EMP:** 345 **EST:** 1995
SQ FT: 600,000
SALES (est): 221.89MM **Privately Held**
Web: www.nsbsl.com
SIC: 5051 Steel
PA: Bluescope Steel Limited
L 24 181 William St
Melbourne VIC 3000

Dennison
Tuscarawas County

(G-7855)
FIRST NATIONAL BNK OF DENNISON (HQ)
Also Called: First National Bank
105 Grant St (44621-1247)
P.O. Box 31 (44621-0031)
PHONE..................................740 922-2532
Blair Hillyer, *Pr*
Larry J Mosher, *
John S Bartles, *
R E Wise, *
EMP: 40 **EST:** 1933
SQ FT: 6,200
SALES (est): 10.6MM
SALES (corp-wide): 8.77MM **Privately Held**
Web: www.fnbdennison.com
SIC: 6021 National commercial banks
PA: Fnb, Inc.
105 Grant St
Dennison OH 44621
740 922-2532

(G-7856)
FNB INC (PA)
105 Grant St (44621-1247)
P.O. Box 31 (44621-0031)
PHONE..................................740 922-2532
Blair Hillyer, *Pr*
Linda Clouse, *
EMP: 30 **EST:** 1989
SALES (est): 8.77MM
SALES (corp-wide): 8.77MM **Privately Held**
Web: www.fnbdennison.com
SIC: 6021 National commercial banks

(G-7857)
HARCATUS TR-CNTY CMNTY ACTION
108 N 2nd St (44621-1264)
PHONE..................................740 922-3600
Michelle Lucas, *Brnch Mgr*
EMP: 43
SALES (corp-wide): 10.01MM **Privately Held**
Web: www.harcatus.org
SIC: 8322 Social service center
PA: Harcatus Tri-County Community Action Organization
821 Anola St
Dover OH 44622
740 922-0933

(G-7858)
TRINITY HOSPITAL TWIN CITY
819 N 1st St (44621-1003)
PHONE..................................740 922-2800
EMP: 263 **EST:** 2011
SQ FT: 52,127
SALES (est): 26.5MM **Privately Held**
Web: www.trinitytwincity.org
SIC: 8011 8062 Medical centers; Hospital, AMA approved residency
HQ: Sylvania Franciscan Health
1715 Indian Wood Cir # 200
Maumee OH

(G-7859)
TUSCO GROCERS INC
30 S 4th St (44621-1412)
PHONE..................................740 922-8721
Gregory W Kimble, *CEO*
Jayn Devney, *
Hudson Hillyer, *
Mike Oberholzer, *
Fred Bollon, *
▼ **EMP:** 65 **EST:** 1990
SQ FT: 259,000
SALES (est): 21MM
SALES (corp-wide): 276.35MM **Privately Held**
SIC: 5141 Groceries, general line
PA: Laurel Grocery Company Llc
129 Barbourville Rd
London KY 40744
606 878-6601

(G-7860)
TWIN CITY HOSPITAL
Also Called: Physical Therapy Dept
6408 Mckee Rd (44621-9010)
PHONE..................................740 922-6675
Richard Price, *Dir*
EMP: 33 **EST:** 1996
SALES (est): 2.42MM **Privately Held**
Web: www.trinitytwincity.org
SIC: 8062 General medical and surgical hospitals

(G-7861)
UTICA EAST OHIO MIDSTREAM LLC
8349 Azalea Rd Sw (44621-9100)
PHONE..................................740 431-4168
EMP: 408 **EST:** 2012
SALES (est): 1.93MM
SALES (corp-wide): 10.91B **Publicly Held**
SIC: 1382 Oil and gas exploration services
HQ: Utica Gas Services, L.L.C.
525 Central Park Dr # 1005
Oklahoma City OK 73105
877 413-1023

(G-7862)
VALLEY MINING INC
4412 Pleasant Valley Rd Se (44621-9038)
P.O. Box 152 (44683-0152)
PHONE..................................740 922-3942
EMP: 130
SIC: 1221 1629 Auger mining, bituminous; Land preparation construction

Derwent
Guernsey County

(G-7863)
BI-CON ENGINEERING LLC
Also Called: B C E
10901 Clay Pike Rd (43733-9900)
PHONE..................................740 685-9217
EMP: 33 **EST:** 2012
SALES (est): 4.97MM **Privately Held**
Web: www.bi-conengineering.com
SIC: 8711 Consulting engineer

(G-7864)
BI-CON SERVICES INC
Also Called: BSI Group, The
10901 Clay Pike Rd (43733-9900)
P.O. Box 10 (43733-0010)
PHONE..................................740 685-2542
EMP: 400 **EST:** 1971
SALES (est): 171.41MM **Privately Held**
Web: www.bi-conservices.com
SIC: 1623 3498 3443 Water, sewer, and utility lines; Fabricated pipe and fittings; Fabricated plate work (boiler shop)

Deshler
Henry County

(G-7865)
CORE & MAIN INC
300 S Chestnut St Ste C (43516-1049)

GEOGRAPHIC SECTION

Dover - Tuscarawas County (G-7884)

PHONE......................419 278-2000
Steve Leclair, *CEO*
EMP: 392
SALES (corp-wide): 6.7B **Publicly Held**
Web: www.coreandmain.com
SIC: 5039 Soil erosion control fabrics
PA: Core & Main, Inc.
  1830 Craig Park Ct
  Saint Louis MO 63146
  314 432-4700

(G-7866)
EAST WATER LEASING CO LLC
Also Called: Communicare Health Services
620 E Water St (43516-1327)
PHONE......................419 278-6921
EMP: 32 **EST:** 2010
SALES (est): 2.41MM
SALES (corp-wide): 392.92MM **Privately Held**
SIC: 8051 Convalescent home with continuous nursing care
PA: Communicare Health Services, Inc.
  10123 Alliance Rd
  Blue Ash OH 45242
  513 530-1654

Dexter City
Noble County

(G-7867)
B&N COAL INC
38455 Marietta Rt (45727-6500)
P.O. Box 100 (45727-0100)
PHONE......................740 783-3575
Carl Baker, *Pr*
Roger Osborne, *
Bob Cunningham, *
EMP: 36 **EST:** 1962
SQ FT: 21,000
SALES (est): 5.44MM **Privately Held**
SIC: 1221 8711 Strip mining, bituminous; Engineering services

(G-7868)
WARREN DRILLING CO INC
Also Called: Warren Trucking
305 Smithson St (45727-9749)
P.O. Box 103 (45727-0103)
PHONE......................740 783-2775
Dan R Warren, *Pr*
Randy C Warren, *
Emily Warren, *
Lewis D Warren, *
Paul H Warren, *
EMP: 110 **EST:** 1939
SALES (est): 12.53MM **Privately Held**
Web: www.warrendrillingandtrucking.com
SIC: 1381 Directional drilling oil and gas wells

Dillonvale
Jefferson County

(G-7869)
COLAIANNI CONSTRUCTION INC
2141 State Route 150 (43917-7889)
PHONE......................740 769-2362
Vincent Colaianni, *Pr*
Vincent Colaianni, *VP*
Mary Ann Colaianni, *
EMP: 40 **EST:** 1961
SALES (est): 9.25MM **Privately Held**
Web: www.colaianniconst.com
SIC: 1542 Commercial and office building, new construction

Donnelsville
Clark County

(G-7870)
VARTEK SERVICES INC
Also Called: Vartek
17 S Hampton Rd (45319-1000)
PHONE......................937 438-3550
Michael Hosford, *CEO*
Darlene Waite, *
EMP: 35 **EST:** 1989
SALES (est): 9.59MM **Privately Held**
Web: www.vartek.com
SIC: 8742 Management information systems consultant

Dover
Tuscarawas County

(G-7871)
ABBOTT ELECTRIC INC
610 S Tuscarawas Ave Rear (44622-2346)
PHONE......................330 343-8941
Brent Fatzinger, *Brnch Mgr*
EMP: 55
SALES (corp-wide): 25.29MM **Privately Held**
Web: www.abbottelectric.com
SIC: 1731 General electrical contractor
PA: Abbott Electric, Inc.
  1935 Allen Ave Se
  Canton OH 44707
  330 452-6601

(G-7872)
BERNER TRUCKING INC
5885 Crown Rd Nw (44622-9610)
P.O. Box 660 (44622-0660)
PHONE......................330 343-5812
James E Knisely, *Pr*
John M Berner, *
Adrienne M Berner, *
EMP: 150 **EST:** 1959
SQ FT: 22,500
SALES (est): 19.39MM **Privately Held**
Web: www.bernertrucking.com
SIC: 4212 Dump truck haulage

(G-7873)
BFC INC (PA)
Also Called: Farmer Smiths Market
1213 E 3rd St (44622-1227)
PHONE......................330 364-6645
William Barkett, *CEO*
James Barkett, *
Thomas Barkett, *
Ronald Barkett, *
EMP: 36 **EST:** 1924
SQ FT: 20,000
SALES (est): 3.71MM
SALES (corp-wide): 3.71MM **Privately Held**
Web: www.barkettfruit.com
SIC: 5148 5143 5144 2099 Vegetables; Dairy products, except dried or canned; Eggs; Salads, fresh or refrigerated

(G-7874)
BUEHLER FOOD MARKETS INC
Also Called: Buehler 10
3000 N Wooster Ave (44622-9469)
PHONE......................330 364-3079
Doug Wills, *Mgr*
EMP: 150
SALES (corp-wide): 399.12MM **Privately Held**
Web: www.buehlers.com
SIC: 5411 7384 5992 5912 Grocery stores, independent; Photofinish laboratories; Florists; Drug stores and proprietary stores
HQ: Buehler Food Markets Incorporated
  1401 Old Mansfield Rd
  Wooster OH 44691
  330 264-4355

(G-7875)
CONWED PLAS ACQUISITION V LLC
Also Called: Filtrexx International
2243 State Route 516 Nw (44622-7242)
PHONE......................877 542-7699
Chris Hatzenbuhler, *CEO*
Ray Swartzwelder, *Pr*
EMP: 99 **EST:** 2014
SALES (est): 7.79MM **Publicly Held**
SIC: 8731 Environmental research
PA: Mativ Holdings, Inc.
  100 Kimball Pl Ste 600
  Alpharetta GA 30009

(G-7876)
COUNTRY CLUB CENTER HOMES INC
Also Called: Country Club Retirement Ctr IV
860 E Iron Ave (44622-2082)
PHONE......................330 343-6351
Michael Hohman, *Admn*
Jeffrey Holland, *
John Jack E Holland, *Treas*
EMP: 96 **EST:** 1976
SALES (est): 10.02MM **Privately Held**
Web: www.countryclubretirementcampus.com
SIC: 8051 8059 8052 Convalescent home with continuous nursing care; Convalescent home; Intermediate care facilities

(G-7877)
COUNTY OF TUSCARAWAS
Also Called: Health Dept
897 E Iron Ave (44622-2030)
P.O. Box 443 (44622-0443)
PHONE......................330 343-5555
Linda J Fanning, *Prin*
EMP: 71
Web: www.tusccourtsouthern.com
SIC: 8399 9111 Health and welfare council; County supervisors' and executives' office
PA: County Of Tuscarawas
  125 E High Ave
  New Philadelphia OH 44663
  330 364-8811

(G-7878)
CS TRUCKING LLC
6531 Mckracken Dr Nw (44622-7682)
PHONE......................330 878-1990
Kathy Weickeo, *Brnch Mgr*
EMP: 108
SALES (corp-wide): 13.07MM **Privately Held**
Web: www.cstruckingllc.com
SIC: 4212 Local trucking, without storage
PA: Cs Trucking, Llc
  366 Travelers Rd
  East Freedom PA 16637
  814 224-0395

(G-7879)
DISCOUNT DRUG MART INC
3015 N Wooster Ave (44622-9491)
PHONE......................330 343-7700
Mike Lantree, *Mgr*
EMP: 32
SALES (corp-wide): 497.8MM **Privately Held**
Web: www.discount-drugmart.com
SIC: 5912 7384 Drug stores; Photofinishing laboratory
HQ: Discount Drug Mart, Inc.
  211 Commerce Dr
  Medina OH 44256
  330 725-2340

(G-7880)
DOVER CHEMICAL CORPORATION (HQ)
3676 Davis Rd Nw (44622-9771)
PHONE......................330 343-7711
Jack Teat Junior, *Pr*
Chuck Fletcher, *
Darren Schwede, *
Don Stevenson, *
Tom Freeman, *
◆ **EMP:** 170 **EST:** 1975
SQ FT: 260,000
SALES (est): 202.07MM
SALES (corp-wide): 2.03B **Privately Held**
Web: www.doverchem.com
SIC: 2819 2869 2899 5169 Industrial inorganic chemicals, nec; Industrial organic chemicals, nec; Chemical preparations, nec; Chemicals and allied products, nec
PA: Icc Industries Inc.
  725 5th Ave
  New York NY 10022
  212 521-1700

(G-7881)
DOVER CITY SCHOOLS
Also Called: New Dawn Child Care Center
865 1/2 E Iron Ave (44622-2099)
PHONE......................330 343-8880
Sue Mathews, *Dir*
EMP: 40
SALES (corp-wide): 33.83MM **Privately Held**
Web: www.dovertornadoes.com
SIC: 8211 8351 Public elementary and secondary schools; Child day care services
PA: Dover City Schools
  228 W 6th St
  Dover OH 44622
  330 364-1906

(G-7882)
DOVER HYDRAULICS INC (PA)
Also Called: Dover Hydraulics South
2996 Progress St (44622)
P.O. Box 2239 (44622)
PHONE......................330 364-1617
Robert D Sensel, *Pr*
Eric Kinsey, *
▲ **EMP:** 61 **EST:** 1982
SQ FT: 25,000
SALES (est): 12.58MM
SALES (corp-wide): 12.58MM **Privately Held**
Web: www.doverhydraulics.com
SIC: 7699 Hydraulic equipment repair

(G-7883)
DOVER NURSING CENTER LLC
Also Called: Park Village Health Care Ctr
1525 N Crater Ave (44622-9558)
PHONE......................330 364-4436
Robert J O'donnell, *CEO*
EMP: 81 **EST:** 1955
SQ FT: 32,000
SALES (est): 5.13MM **Privately Held**
Web: www.parkvillagehealthcare.com
SIC: 8052 8051 Intermediate care facilities; Skilled nursing care facilities

(G-7884)
DOVER PHILA FEDERAL CREDIT UN (PA)
119 Fillmore Ave (44622-2061)
PHONE......................330 364-8874
Jack Dooling, *Pr*

Jason Garner, *
EMP: 40 **EST:** 1953
SQ FT: 6,000
SALES (est): 13.73MM
SALES (corp-wide): 13.73MM **Privately Held**
Web: www.dover-philafcu.org
SIC: 6061 Federal credit unions

(G-7885)
GIANT EAGLE INC
Also Called: Giant Eagle
515 Union Ave Ste 243 (44622-3000)
PHONE.................................330 364-5301
Jason Lanzer, *Mgr*
EMP: 100
SALES (corp-wide): 1.43B **Privately Held**
Web: www.gianteagle.com
SIC: 5411 5912 5193 Supermarkets, chain; Drug stores; Flowers and florists supplies
PA: Giant Eagle, Inc.
    101 Kappa Dr
    Pittsburgh PA 15238
    866 620-0216

(G-7886)
GREER STEEL COMPANY
1 Boat St (44622-2076)
P.O. Box 1900 (26507-1900)
PHONE.................................330 343-8811
John R Raese, *Pr*
James M Troy, *
◆ **EMP:** 150 **EST:** 1991
SALES (est): 46.37MM
SALES (corp-wide): 84.57MM **Privately Held**
Web: www.greersteel.com
SIC: 5051 Steel
PA: Greer Industries, Inc.
    570 Canyon Rd
    Morgantown WV 26508
    304 296-2549

(G-7887)
HARCATUS TR-CNTY CMNTY ACTION (PA)
Also Called: Harcatus Tr-Cnty Cmnty Action
821 Anola St (44622)
PHONE.................................740 922-0933
Alison Kerns, *Ex Dir*
Sandra Edwards, *
Robert Baker, *
Elmer Leeper, *
EMP: 46 **EST:** 1965
SQ FT: 1,500
SALES (est): 10.01MM
SALES (corp-wide): 10.01MM **Privately Held**
Web: www.harcatus.org
SIC: 8322 Social service center

(G-7888)
HARRY HUMPHRIES AUTO CITY INC
Also Called: Ford
311 Commercial Pkwy (44622-3123)
PHONE.................................330 343-6681
Glenn Mears, *Pr*
EMP: 27 **EST:** 1956
SQ FT: 28,000
SALES (est): 4.98MM **Privately Held**
Web: www.harryhumphriesautocity.com
SIC: 5511 7538 Automobiles, new and used; General automotive repair shops

(G-7889)
HENNIS NURSING HOME
Also Called: Hennis Care Centre At Dover
1720 N Cross St (44622-1044)
PHONE.................................330 364-8849
Harry Hennis II, *Pr*
Harry Hennis Ii, *Pr*
Patricia Hennis, *
EMP: 180 **EST:** 1950
SALES (est): 9.61MM **Privately Held**
Web: www.henniscarecentre.com
SIC: 8051 8052 Convalescent home with continuous nursing care; Intermediate care facilities

(G-7890)
HUNTINGTON NATIONAL BANK
232 W 3rd St Ste 207 (44622-2969)
P.O. Box 100 (44622-0100)
PHONE.................................330 343-6611
Katherine Fausnight, *Prin*
EMP: 41
SALES (corp-wide): 10.84B **Publicly Held**
Web: www.huntington.com
SIC: 6029 6021 Commercial banks, nec; National commercial banks
HQ: The Huntington National Bank
    41 S High St
    Columbus OH 43215
    614 480-4293

(G-7891)
KIMBLE COMPANY (PA)
Also Called: Kimble Clay & Limestone
3596 State Route 39 Nw (44622-7232)
PHONE.................................330 343-1226
EMP: 160 **EST:** 1952
SALES (est): 78.85MM
SALES (corp-wide): 78.85MM **Privately Held**
Web: www.kimblecompanies.com
SIC: 1221 Bituminous coal and lignite-surface mining

(G-7892)
KIMBLE RECYCL & DISPOSAL INC (PA)
Also Called: Ace Disposal
3596 State Route 39 Nw (44622-7232)
P.O. Box 448 (44622-0448)
PHONE.................................330 343-1226
Keith Kimble, *Pr*
Greg Kimble, *
Rick Kimble, *
EMP: 121 **EST:** 1987
SQ FT: 2,300
SALES (est): 57.76MM **Privately Held**
Web: www.kimblecompanies.com
SIC: 4953 Garbage: collecting, destroying, and processing

(G-7893)
MID-OHIO CONTRACTING INC
1817 Horns Ln Nw (44622)
P.O. Box 708 (44622)
PHONE.................................330 343-2925
D W Zimmerman, *Prin*
Francis G Fitzpatrick, *Prin*
EMP: 41 **EST:** 1981
SQ FT: 3,200
SALES (est): 1.35MM **Privately Held**
SIC: 1623 Pipeline construction, nsk

(G-7894)
MINNESOTA LIMITED LLC
2198 Donald Dr (44622-7493)
PHONE.................................330 343-4612
Gary Hawk, *Brnch Mgr*
EMP: 134
SALES (corp-wide): 2.13B **Privately Held**
Web: www.otisminnesota.com
SIC: 1623 Oil and gas pipeline construction
HQ: Minnesota Limited, Llc
    18640 200th St Nw
    Big Lake MN 55309
    763 262-7000

(G-7895)
NEW DAWN HEALTH CARE INC
Also Called: New Dawn Retirement Community
865 E Iron Ave (44622-2099)
PHONE.................................330 343-5521
Daniel Hershberger, *Pr*
Perry Hershberger, *
Sandra Hershberger, *
Harry Hershberger, *
EMP: 187 **EST:** 1976
SQ FT: 73,000
SALES (est): 9.77MM **Privately Held**
Web: www.newdawnrehabcare.com
SIC: 8051 8361 8351 8052 Skilled nursing care facilities; Aged home; Child day care services; Intermediate care facilities

(G-7896)
NICK STRIMBU INC
303 Oxford St (44622-1976)
PHONE.................................330 448-4046
EMP: 140
SALES (corp-wide): 27.55MM **Privately Held**
Web: www.nickstrimbu.com
SIC: 4213 Trucking, except local
PA: Nick Strimbu, Inc.
    3500 Parkway Dr
    Brookfield OH 44403
    330 448-4046

(G-7897)
NOVOGRADAC & COMPANY LLP
3025 N Wooster Ave (44622-9491)
PHONE.................................415 356-8000
Daniel J Smith, *Pt*
EMP: 38
Web: www.novoco.com
SIC: 8721 Certified public accountant
PA: Novogradac & Company Llp
    1160 Btry St E Bldg Ste 2
    San Francisco CA 94111

(G-7898)
OLYMPIC STEEL INC
555 Commercial Pkwy (44622-3127)
PHONE.................................330 602-6279
Chad Butcher, *Brnch Mgr*
EMP: 67
SALES (corp-wide): 2.16B **Publicly Held**
Web: www.olysteel.com
SIC: 5051 Steel
PA: Olympic Steel, Inc.
    22901 Mllcreek Blvd Ste 6
    Cleveland OH 44122
    216 292-3800

(G-7899)
PARK VLG ASSISTED LIVING LLC
1525 N Crater Ave (44622-9500)
PHONE.................................330 364-4436
Rose Anne O Donnell, *Prin*
EMP: 27 **EST:** 2009
SALES (est): 1.84MM **Privately Held**
Web: www.parkvillagehealthcare.com
SIC: 8051 Skilled nursing care facilities

(G-7900)
SMITH AMBULANCE SERVICE INC (PA)
214 W 3rd St (44622-2965)
PHONE.................................330 602-0050
Robert L Smith, *Pr*
EMP: 30 **EST:** 1993
SALES (est): 2MM **Privately Held**
Web: www.smithambulance.com
SIC: 4119 Ambulance service

(G-7901)
SMITH CONCRETE CO (PA)
Also Called: Division of Selling Materials
2301 Progress St (44622-9641)
P.O. Box 356 (45750-0356)
PHONE.................................740 373-7441
Mike Murphy, *Genl Mgr*
EMP: 50 **EST:** 1922
SQ FT: 2,000
SALES (est): 5.07MM
SALES (corp-wide): 5.07MM **Privately Held**
Web: www.shellyco.com
SIC: 3272 3273 1442 Dry mixture concrete; Ready-mixed concrete; Construction sand and gravel

(G-7902)
SPRINGVALE HEALTH CENTERS INC (PA)
201 Hospital Dr (44622)
PHONE.................................330 343-6631
Jj Boroski, *Dir*
EMP: 40 **EST:** 1969
SQ FT: 10,841
SALES (est): 10.28MM
SALES (corp-wide): 10.28MM **Privately Held**
Web: www.cmhdover.org
SIC: 8093 Mental health clinic, outpatient

(G-7903)
TEATER ORTHOPEDIC SURGEONS
Also Called: Teater, Thomas L MD
515 Union Ave Ste 167 (44622-3005)
PHONE.................................330 343-3335
Scott F Holder, *Pr*
EMP: 47 **EST:** 1985
SQ FT: 4,879
SALES (est): 2.37MM **Privately Held**
Web: my.clevelandclinic.org
SIC: 8062 General medical and surgical hospitals

(G-7904)
TUSCARWAS AMBLTORY SRGERY CTR
320 Oxford St (44622-1963)
PHONE.................................330 365-2101
Kelly Theodosopoulous, *Managing Member*
EMP: 51 **EST:** 1997
SQ FT: 15,337
SALES (est): 4.61MM **Privately Held**
SIC: 8093 Specialty outpatient clinics, nec

(G-7905)
UNION COUNTRY CLUB
1000 N Bellevue Ave (44622-9457)
PHONE.................................330 343-5544
Jim Miller, *Pr*
EMP: 49 **EST:** 1911
SQ FT: 1,092
SALES (est): 1.48MM **Privately Held**
Web: www.unioncountryclub.net
SIC: 7997 Country club, membership

(G-7906)
UNION HOSPITAL ASSOCIATION
500 Medical Park Dr (44622-3204)
PHONE.................................330 602-0719
EMP: 43
SALES (corp-wide): 14.48B **Privately Held**
Web: www.unionhospital.org
SIC: 8062 General medical and surgical hospitals
HQ: Union Hospital Association
    659 Boulevard St
    Dover OH 44622
    330 343-3311

GEOGRAPHIC SECTION

Dublin - Franklin County (G-7928)

(G-7907)
UNION HOSPITAL ASSOCIATION (HQ)
Also Called: Union Hospital
659 Boulevard St (44622-2077)
PHONE..................................330 343-3311
William W Harding, *CEO*
EMP: 957 **EST:** 1906
SQ FT: 280,000
SALES (est): 106.03MM
SALES (corp-wide): 14.48B **Privately Held**
Web: www.unionhospital.org
SIC: 8062 8011 General medical and surgical hospitals; Offices and clinics of medical doctors
PA: The Cleveland Clinic Foundation
9500 Euclid Ave
Cleveland OH 44195
216 636-8335

(G-7908)
UPS FAMILY HEALTH CENTER NORTH
110 Dublin Dr (44622-7805)
PHONE..................................330 364-8038
EMP: 57 **EST:** 2017
SALES (est): 811.28K
SALES (corp-wide): 14.48B **Privately Held**
Web: www.upsnorth.com
SIC: 8011 Pediatrician
PA: The Cleveland Clinic Foundation
9500 Euclid Ave
Cleveland OH 44195
216 636-8335

(G-7909)
WAYNE GAR DOOR SLS & SVC INC (PA)
Also Called: Wayne Garage Door Sales & Svc
2150 State Route 39 Nw (44622-7419)
P.O. Box 98 (44622-0098)
PHONE..................................330 343-6679
TOLL FREE: 800
Luke Yoder, *Pr*
David Hershberger, *
EMP: 33 **EST:** 1973
SQ FT: 22,000
SALES (est): 6.42MM
SALES (corp-wide): 6.42MM **Privately Held**
Web: www.waynedoor.com
SIC: 1751 Garage door, installation or erection

(G-7910)
WEAVER APPLIANCE SLS & SVC LLC
2613 N Wooster Ave (44622-8805)
PHONE..................................330 852-4555
EMP: 55
SALES (corp-wide): 801.84K **Privately Held**
Web: www.weaverappliance.com
SIC: 7629 5722 Electrical household appliance repair; Household appliance stores
PA: Weaver Appliance Sales & Service Llc
715 Commercial Pkwy
Dover OH 44622
330 852-4555

(G-7911)
ZIEGLER TIRE AND SUPPLY CO
Also Called: Ziegler Oil Co
411 Commercial Pkwy (44622-3125)
PHONE..................................330 343-7739
Tom West, *Mgr*
EMP: 29
SQ FT: 100,000
SALES (corp-wide): 111.76MM **Privately Held**
Web: www.zieglertire.com
SIC: 5531 7534 Automotive tires; Rebuilding and retreading tires
PA: The Ziegler Tire And Supply Company
4150 Millennium Blvd Se
Massillon OH 44646
330 834-3332

Doylestown
Wayne County

(G-7912)
AKRON CHILDREN S HOSPITAL
105 Franklin Dr (44230-1528)
PHONE..................................330 310-0157
EMP: 53 **EST:** 2010
SALES (est): 413.04K **Privately Held**
Web: www.akronchildrens.org
SIC: 8062 General medical and surgical hospitals

(G-7913)
CHIPPEWA GOLF CORP
Also Called: Chippewa Golf Club
12147 Shank Rd (44230-9707)
PHONE..................................330 658-2566
Kevin Larizza, *Pr*
EMP: 48 **EST:** 1963
SQ FT: 4,800
SALES (est): 1.84MM **Privately Held**
Web: www.chippewagolfclub.com
SIC: 7992 Public golf courses

(G-7914)
CHIPPEWA SCHOOL DISTRICT
Also Called: SC Chippewa Preschool
165 Brooklyn Ave (44230-1204)
PHONE..................................330 658-4868
Ronna Haer, *Prin*
EMP: 31
SALES (corp-wide): 18.3MM **Privately Held**
Web: www.chippewa.k12.oh.us
SIC: 8351 Preschool center
PA: Chippewa School District
56 N Portage St
Doylestown OH 44230
330 658-6700

(G-7915)
DOYLESTOWN TELEPHONE COMPANY (PA)
Also Called: Doylestown Communications
81 N Portage St (44230-1349)
PHONE..................................330 658-2121
Tom Brockman, *Pr*
Sandra Brockman, *
EMP: 38 **EST:** 1899
SQ FT: 4,400
SALES (est): 4.33MM
SALES (corp-wide): 4.33MM **Privately Held**
Web: www.doylestowntelephone.com
SIC: 4813 Local telephone communications

(G-7916)
THE GALEHOUSE COMPANIES INC
Also Called: Galehouse Lumber
12667 Portage St (44230-9735)
P.O. Box 267 (44230-0267)
PHONE..................................330 658-2023
EMP: 30 **EST:** 1968
SALES (est): 10.79MM **Privately Held**
Web: www.galehouse.com
SIC: 5031 5211 1531 1521 Lumber: rough, dressed, and finished; Millwork and lumber; Condominium developers; New construction, single-family houses

Dresden
Muskingum County

(G-7917)
DAG-DELL INC
507 Main St (43821-1110)
P.O. Box 70 (43023-0070)
PHONE..................................740 754-2600
Maura Mantell, *CEO*
EMP: 30 **EST:** 1984
SQ FT: 6,000
SALES (est): 672.83K **Privately Held**
SIC: 8361 Mentally handicapped home

Dublin
Franklin County

(G-7918)
3SG CORPORATION
344 Cramer Creek Ct (43017-2585)
PHONE..................................614 761-8394
EMP: 302
Web: www.3sgplus.com
SIC: 7379 Online services technology consultants

(G-7919)
AC HOTEL COLUMBUS DUBLIN
Also Called: AC Hotels
6540 Riverside Dr (43017-1464)
PHONE..................................614 798-8652
EMP: 100 **EST:** 2017
SALES (est): 2.28MM **Privately Held**
Web: ac-hotels.marriott.com
SIC: 7011 Hotels

(G-7920)
ADVANCED PRGRM RESOURCES INC (PA)
Also Called: Touchmark
2715 Tuller Pkwy (43017-2310)
PHONE..................................614 761-9994
EMP: 47 **EST:** 1989
SQ FT: 5,100
SALES (est): 3.62MM **Privately Held**
SIC: 7379 7373 8742 7372 Computer related consulting services; Systems integration services; Management consulting services; Application computer software

(G-7921)
ADVOCATE RCM LLC
Also Called: Cmdm
5475 Rings Rd Ste 300 (43017-7537)
PHONE..................................614 210-1885
Todd Walker, *CEO*
Kirk Reinitz, *Chief Development Officer*
Becky Enderle, *
EMP: 65 **EST:** 2003
SQ FT: 22,000
SALES (est): 3.04MM
SALES (corp-wide): 25.33MM **Privately Held**
SIC: 8721 Billing and bookkeeping service
PA: Ventra Health, Inc.
5001 Lyndon B Johnson Fwy
Dallas TX 75244
972 861-1270

(G-7922)
AFFILIATED RESOURCE GROUP INC
5700 Perimeter Dr Ste H (43017-3247)
P.O. Box 491 (43017-0491)
PHONE..................................614 889-6555
Mike Moran, *Pr*
EMP: 51 **EST:** 1993
SQ FT: 7,500
SALES (est): 8.46MM **Privately Held**
Web: www.aresgrp.com
SIC: 7379 Computer related consulting services

(G-7923)
AHF OHIO INC
4880 Tuttle Rd (43017-7566)
PHONE..................................614 760-8870
Justin Moore, *Admn*
EMP: 97
SALES (corp-wide): 25.83MM **Privately Held**
Web: www.ahfohio.com
SIC: 8051 8361 Skilled nursing care facilities ; Residential care
PA: Ahf Ohio, Inc.
5920 Venture Dr Ste 100
Dublin OH 43017
614 760-7352

(G-7924)
AHF/CENTRAL STATES INC
Also Called: Belcourt Terracenursing Home
5920 Venture Dr Ste 100 (43017-2236)
PHONE..................................724 941-7150
Brian Vermillion, *Dir*
EMP: 135
SQ FT: 23,780
SALES (corp-wide): 9.84MM **Privately Held**
Web: www.mcmurrayhillsmanor.com
SIC: 8051 Skilled nursing care facilities
PA: Ahf/Central States, Inc.
249 W Mcmurray Rd
Canonsburg PA 15317
724 941-7150

(G-7925)
AHIP OH COLUMBUS ENTPS LLC
Also Called: Embassy Suites Columbus Dublin
5100 Upper Metro Pl (43017-3384)
PHONE..................................614 790-9000
EMP: 60 **EST:** 2017
SALES (est): 1.15MM **Privately Held**
Web: www.hilton.com
SIC: 7011 Hotels and motels

(G-7926)
AIR FORCE ONE INC (PA)
Also Called: Honeywell Authorized Dealer
5810 Shier Rings Rd Ste B (43016-6239)
PHONE..................................614 889-0121
EMP: 65 **EST:** 1984
SALES (est): 49.27MM
SALES (corp-wide): 49.27MM **Privately Held**
Web: www.airforceone.com
SIC: 1711 Mechanical contractor

(G-7927)
AKKODIS INC
Also Called: Modis
495 Metro Pl S Ste 200 (43017-5329)
PHONE..................................614 781-6070
Monty Ragland, *Mgr*
EMP: 183
Web: www.modis.com
SIC: 8748 Systems engineering consultant, ex. computer or professional
HQ: Akkodis,
4800 Deerwood Campus Pkwy
Jacksonville FL 32246
904 360-2300

(G-7928)
ALEXSON SERVICES INC
Also Called: Via Quest
525 Metro Pl N Ste 300 (43017-5320)

Dublin - Franklin County (G-7929)

PHONE..............................614 889-5837
Richard Johnson, Pr
EMP: 59 EST: 1988
SALES (est): 11.75MM Privately Held
SIC: 8082 Home health care services

(G-7929)
ALLEGIANCE ADMINISTRATORS LLC
Also Called: Allegiance Select
5500 Frantz Rd Ste 100 (43017-3545)
PHONE..............................877 895-1414
Haytham Elzayn, CEO
Joe Ryan, *
Nicole Blackburn, *
Paul Miles, Chief Actuary*
EMP: 50 EST: 2010
SALES (est): 26.01MM Privately Held
Web: www.renascentps.com
SIC: 5511 8748 New and used car dealers; Telecommunications consultant

(G-7930)
ALLIANCE MEDICAL INC
Also Called: Allmed
5000 Tuttle Crossing Blvd (43016-1534)
P.O. Box 8023 (43016-2023)
PHONE..............................800 890-3092
EMP: 45
SIC: 5192 5047 Books; Medical equipment and supplies

(G-7931)
ALLIED COMMUNICATIONS CORP
4300 Tuller Rd (43017-5008)
PHONE..............................614 588-3370
Hassan Ayoub, Pr
David Morrow, Prin
EMP: 30 EST: 2018
SALES (est): 887.97K Privately Held
Web: www.alliedcommunications.org
SIC: 4899 Communication services, nec

(G-7932)
AMERICAN CLLEGE CRDLGY FNDTION
Also Called: Accf Accreditation
5600 Blazer Pkwy Ste 220 # 320 (43017-3554)
PHONE..............................614 442-5950
Abe Joseph, Brnch Mgr
EMP: 40
SALES (corp-wide): 106.88MM Privately Held
Web: www.acc.org
SIC: 8621 Medical field-related associations
PA: American College Of Cardiology Foundation
2400 N St Nw
Washington DC 20037
202 375-6000

(G-7933)
AMERICAN HEALTH NETWORK INC
5900 Parkwood Pl (43016-1216)
PHONE..............................614 794-4500
Kim Rittenhouse, Mgr
EMP: 44
SALES (corp-wide): 371.62B Publicly Held
Web: www.ahni.com
SIC: 8011 Offices and clinics of medical doctors
HQ: American Health Network, Inc.
7440 Woodland Dr
Indianapolis IN 46278

(G-7934)
AMERICAN HLTH NETWRK OHIO LLC (DH)
Also Called: Pediatric Physicians of Newark
5900 Parkwood Pl (43016-1216)
PHONE..............................614 794-4500
Ben Park, CEO
EMP: 80 EST: 1987
SALES (est): 239.45MM
SALES (corp-wide): 371.62B Publicly Held
Web: www.ahni.com
SIC: 8011 Offices and clinics of medical doctors
HQ: Optum, Inc.
11000 Optum Cir
Eden Prairie MN 55344
952 936-1300

(G-7935)
AMERICAN MULTI-CINEMA INC
Also Called: AMC
6700 Village Pkwy (43017-2073)
PHONE..............................614 889-0580
Stephanie Mcclullan, Genl Mgr
EMP: 27
Web: www.amctheatres.com
SIC: 7832 Exhibitors, itinerant: motion picture
HQ: American Multi-Cinema, Inc.
11500 Ash St
Leawood KS 66211
913 213-2000

(G-7936)
AMERICAN MUTL SHARE INSUR CORP (PA)
Also Called: AMERICAN SHARE INSURANCE
5656 Frantz Rd (43017-2552)
PHONE..............................614 764-1900
Theresa Mason, Pr
G Duane Welsh, *
Curtis L Robson, *
EMP: 32 EST: 1974
SQ FT: 10,000
SALES (est): 14.37MM
SALES (corp-wide): 14.37MM Privately Held
Web: www.americanshare.com
SIC: 6411 Insurance agents, nec

(G-7937)
AMERIFIRST FINANCIAL CORP
Also Called: Ameriprise Financial Services
5930 Venture Dr (43017-2240)
PHONE..............................614 766-5709
EMP: 51
SALES (corp-wide): 306.62MM Privately Held
Web: www.ameriprise.com
SIC: 6162 Mortgage bankers
HQ: Amerifirst Financial Corporation
3125 W Main St
Kalamazoo MI 49006
269 324-4240

(G-7938)
ANDREW INSURANCE ASSOCIATES
Also Called: Nationwide
545 Metro Pl S Ste 150 (43017-5453)
PHONE..............................614 336-8030
Michael J Clark, Pr
EMP: 89 EST: 1969
SALES (est): 2.49MM
SALES (corp-wide): 10.07B Publicly Held
Web: www.andrewins.com
SIC: 6411 6311 6321 6331 Insurance agents, nec; Life insurance carriers; Accident and health insurance carriers; Fire, marine and casualty insurance and carriers
PA: Arthur J. Gallagher & Co.
2850 Golf Rd
Rolling Meadows IL 60008
630 773-3800

(G-7939)
APPALACHIAN FUELS LLC (PA)
6375 Riverside Dr Ste 200 (43017-5045)
PHONE..............................606 928-0460
EMP: 247 EST: 2001
SALES (est): 19.87MM
SALES (corp-wide): 19.87MM Privately Held
SIC: 1241 Coal mining services

(G-7940)
ASHLAND AQUALON FUNCTIONAL INGREDIENTS
5200 Blazer Pkwy (43017-3309)
PHONE..............................614 790-3333
EMP: 30
SIC: 7389 Business Activities at Non-Commercial Site

(G-7941)
ASPEN ENERGY CORPORATION
4789 Rings Rd Ste 100 (43017-1883)
PHONE..............................614 884-5300
Jonathan Peele, Pr
EMP: 33 EST: 2000
SQ FT: 4,800
SALES (est): 9.31MM Privately Held
Web: www.aspenenergy.com
SIC: 6221 Commodity brokers, contracts

(G-7942)
BARRINGTON SCHOOL
6046 Tara Hill Dr (43017-3804)
PHONE..............................614 336-3000
Jessica Hoffman, Prin
EMP: 37 EST: 2014
SALES (est): 2.08MM Privately Held
Web: www.thebarringtonschool.com
SIC: 8351 Preschool center

(G-7943)
BBC&M ENGINEERING INC (PA)
6190 Enterprise Ct (43016-7297)
PHONE..............................614 793-2226
Stephen C Pasternack, Pr
Timothy A Van Echo, *
Ronald T Erb, *
David L Monroe, *
Stephen L Loskota, *
EMP: 65 EST: 1957
SQ FT: 25,000
SALES (est): 5.22MM
SALES (corp-wide): 5.22MM Privately Held
Web: sell.sawbrokers.com
SIC: 8711 Consulting engineer

(G-7944)
BMI FEDERAL CREDIT UNION
6165 Emerald Pkwy (43016-3248)
P.O. Box 3670 (43016-0340)
PHONE..............................614 707-4000
William Allender, Pr
Sharon Custer, *
EMP: 100 EST: 1934
SQ FT: 44,000
SALES (est): 3.31MM Privately Held
Web: www.bmifcu.org
SIC: 6061 Federal credit unions

(G-7945)
BMW FINANCIAL SERVICES NA LLC
5515 Parkcenter Cir (43017-3541)
PHONE..............................614 718-6900
John Christman, Mgr
EMP: 96
SALES (corp-wide): 169.02B Privately Held
Web: www.bmwcollaborationlab.com
SIC: 6159 Automobile finance leasing
HQ: Bmw Financial Services Na, Llc
5550 Britton Pkwy
Hilliard OH 43026

(G-7946)
BOUND TREE MEDICAL LLC (DH)
5000 Tuttle Crossing Blvd (43016-1534)
P.O. Box 8023 (43016-2023)
PHONE..............................614 760-5000
Matt Walter, Managing Member
▲ EMP: 80 EST: 2000
SQ FT: 30,000
SALES (est): 107.48MM
SALES (corp-wide): 6.03B Privately Held
Web: www.boundtree.com
SIC: 5047 Medical equipment and supplies
HQ: Sarnova, Inc.
5000 Tuttle Crossing Blvd
Dublin OH 43016

(G-7947)
BRENTLINGER ENTERPRISES
Also Called: Midwestern Auto Group
6335 Perimeter Loop Rd (43017-3207)
PHONE..............................614 889-2571
Mark Brentlinger, Pt
▲ EMP: 160 EST: 1967
SQ FT: 100,000
SALES (est): 60.06MM Privately Held
Web: www.magcars.com
SIC: 5511 7538 Automobiles, new and used; General automotive repair shops

(G-7948)
BUCKEYE CHECK CASHING INC (HQ)
Also Called: First Virginia
5165 Emerald Pkwy Ste 100 (43017-1095)
PHONE..............................614 798-5900
Ted Saunders, CEO
Kyle Hanson, *
EMP: 200 EST: 1987
SALES (est): 341.31MM Privately Held
Web: www.ccfi.com
SIC: 6099 Check cashing agencies
PA: Community Choice Financial Inc.
6785 Bobcat Way Ste 200
Dublin OH 43016

(G-7949)
CAMERON MITCHELL REST LLC
6644 Riverside Dr (43017-9503)
PHONE..............................724 824-7558
EMP: 72
SALES (corp-wide): 134.21MM Privately Held
Web: www.cameronmitchell.com
SIC: 8741 Management services
PA: Cameron Mitchell Restaurants, Llc
390 W Nationwide Blvd # 300
Columbus OH 43215
614 621-3663

(G-7950)
CARDINAL HEALTH INC (PA)
Also Called: Cardinalhealth
7000 Cardinal Pl (43017)
PHONE..............................614 757-5000
Jason M Hollar, CEO
Gregory B Kenny, Non-Executive Chairman of the Board*
Aaron E Alt, *
Ola M Snow, Chief Human Resources Officer*
Jessica L Mayer, CLO CCO*
◆ EMP: 2800 EST: 1979
SALES (est): 205.01B
SALES (corp-wide): 205.01B Publicly Held

GEOGRAPHIC SECTION
Dublin - Franklin County (G-7971)

Web: www.cardinalhealth.com
SIC: 5122 5047 8741 3842 Pharmaceuticals; Surgical equipment and supplies; Management services; Surgical appliances and supplies

(G-7951)
CARDINAL HEALTH 100 INC (HQ)
Also Called: Bindley Western Drug
7000 Cardinal Pl (43017-1091)
PHONE..............................614 757-5000
William E Bindley, *Ch Bd*
Michael D Mc Cormick, *Executive President**
Keith W Burks, *
Gregory S Beyerl, *
Michael L Shinn, *
EMP: 280 EST: 1968
SQ FT: 70,000
SALES (est): 448.71MM
SALES (corp-wide): 205.01B **Publicly Held**
SIC: 5122 5047 Drugs, proprietaries, and sundries; Medical and hospital equipment
PA: Cardinal Health, Inc.
    7000 Cardinal Pl
    Dublin OH 43017
    614 757-5000

(G-7952)
CARDINAL HEALTH 110 INC
Also Called: Cardinal Health
7000 Cardinal Pl (43017-1091)
PHONE..............................614 717-5000
Robert Walter, *Pr*
EMP: 28 EST: 1988
SALES (est): 22.8MM
SALES (corp-wide): 205.01B **Publicly Held**
SIC: 5047 Instruments, surgical and medical
PA: Cardinal Health, Inc.
    7000 Cardinal Pl
    Dublin OH 43017
    614 757-5000

(G-7953)
CARDINAL HEALTH 200 LLC (HQ)
7000 Cardinal Pl (43017-1091)
PHONE..............................614 757-5000
◆ EMP: 50 EST: 1996
SALES (est): 562.61MM
SALES (corp-wide): 205.01B **Publicly Held**
Web: www.cardinalhealth.com
SIC: 5122 Pharmaceuticals
PA: Cardinal Health, Inc.
    7000 Cardinal Pl
    Dublin OH 43017
    614 757-5000

(G-7954)
CARDINAL HEALTH 201 INC (HQ)
7000 Cardinal Pl (43017-1091)
PHONE..............................614 757-5000
EMP: 43 EST: 1996
SALES (est): 47MM
SALES (corp-wide): 205.01B **Publicly Held**
SIC: 5122 Pharmaceuticals
PA: Cardinal Health, Inc.
    7000 Cardinal Pl
    Dublin OH 43017
    614 757-5000

(G-7955)
CARDINAL HEALTH 301 LLC (HQ)
Also Called: Pyxis Data Systems
7000 Cardinal Pl (43017-1091)
PHONE..............................614 757-5000
R Kerry Clark, *CEO*
▲ EMP: 600 EST: 1987

SALES (est): 178.6MM
SALES (corp-wide): 205.01B **Publicly Held**
SIC: 5122 Pharmaceuticals
PA: Cardinal Health, Inc.
    7000 Cardinal Pl
    Dublin OH 43017
    614 757-5000

(G-7956)
CARDINAL HEALTH 414 LLC (HQ)
7000 Cardinal Pl (43017-1091)
PHONE..............................614 757-5000
Jason Hollar, *CEO*
Steve Mason Ceo Medical Segmen t, *Prin*
Debbie Weitzman Ceo Pharmaceut ical Segment, *Prin*
Ben Brinker, *
Brad Cochran, *
▲ EMP: 155 EST: 1971
SQ FT: 60,967
SALES (est): 1.04B
SALES (corp-wide): 205.01B **Publicly Held**
SIC: 2835 2834 8052 Radioactive diagnostic substances; Pharmaceutical preparations; Home for the mentally retarded, with health care
PA: Cardinal Health, Inc.
    7000 Cardinal Pl
    Dublin OH 43017
    614 757-5000

(G-7957)
CARDIO PARTNERS INC (DH)
5000 Tuttle Crossing Blvd (43016)
P.O. Box 8023 (43016)
PHONE..............................614 760-5000
Mark Dougherty, *Pr*
EMP: 50 EST: 2012
SALES (est): 37.28MM
SALES (corp-wide): 6.03B **Privately Held**
Web: www.sarnova.com
SIC: 5047 7389 Medical equipment and supplies; Business Activities at Non-Commercial Site
HQ: Sarnova, Inc.
    5000 Tuttle Crossing Blvd
    Dublin OH 43016

(G-7958)
CAREWORKS OF OHIO INC
Also Called: Vocworks
5555 Glendon Ct Ste 300 (43016-3302)
P.O. Box 1040 (43017-6040)
PHONE..............................614 792-1085
EMP: 700
SIC: 8059 7361 8741 6411 Personal care home, with health care; Employment agencies; Management services; Insurance agents, brokers, and service

(G-7959)
CAROLINAS IT LLC
5747 Perimeter Dr (43017)
PHONE..............................919 856-2300
EMP: 75 EST: 1996
SALES (est): 4.27MM
SALES (corp-wide): 118.88MM **Privately Held**
SIC: 7373 7379 Systems integration services; Computer related consulting services
PA: Winxnet, Llc
    63 Marginal Way Ste 400
    Portland ME 04101
    207 780-0497

(G-7960)
CBRE INC
5175 Emerald Pkwy (43017-1063)
PHONE..............................614 764-4798

EMP: 29
SALES (corp-wide): 13.07B **Publicly Held**
SIC: 6531 Real estate agent, commercial
HQ: Cbre, Inc.
    400 S Hope St Ste 25
    Los Angeles CA 75201
    310 477-5876

(G-7961)
CHECKSMART FINCL HOLDINGS CORP (HQ)
6785 Bobcat Way Ste 200 (43016)
PHONE..............................614 798-5900
Daniel Yaussy, *Prin*
EMP: 32 EST: 2006
SALES (est): 20.28MM **Privately Held**
SIC: 6099 Check cashing agencies
PA: Community Choice Financial Inc.
    6785 Bobcat Way Ste 200
    Dublin OH 43016

(G-7962)
CHILLER LLC (PA)
Also Called: Chiller
7001 Dublin Park Dr (43016-8340)
PHONE..............................614 764-1000
Wendy Herb, *Pr*
David A Paitson, *
EMP: 75 EST: 1997
SQ FT: 76,000
SALES (est): 4.89MM
SALES (corp-wide): 4.89MM **Privately Held**
Web: www.thechiller.com
SIC: 7999 Ice skating rink operation

(G-7963)
CHY HOTEL LLC
Also Called: Dublin Sprnghill Stes By Mrrot
4475 Bridge Park Ave (43017-2225)
PHONE..............................614 766-7255
EMP: 40 EST: 2018
SALES (est): 1.06MM **Privately Held**
Web: www.marriott.com
SIC: 7011 Hotels

(G-7964)
CITY OF DUBLIN
Also Called: Division Streets & Utilities
6555 Shier Rings Rd (43016-8716)
PHONE..............................614 410-4750
Ron Burns, *Dir*
EMP: 85
SQ FT: 3,052
SALES (corp-wide): 153.11MM **Privately Held**
Web: www.dublinohiousa.gov
SIC: 4911 Electric services
PA: City Of Dublin
    5555 Perimeter Dr
    Dublin OH 43017
    614 410-4400

(G-7965)
CLINIX HEALTHCARE LLC
5080 Tuttle Crossing Blvd Ste 300 (43016)
PHONE..............................614 792-5422
Olga Magyar, *Managing Member*
EMP: 44 EST: 1999
SALES (est): 2.67MM **Privately Held**
Web: www.clinixhealthcare.com
SIC: 8099 Medical services organization

(G-7966)
COLUMBUS DNV INC
5777 Frantz Rd (43017-1886)
PHONE..............................614 761-1214
EMP: 134
Web: www.dnvcolumbus.com

SIC: 5084 8711 1799 8731 Instruments and control equipment; Consulting engineer; Corrosion control installation; Commercial physical research

(G-7967)
COMMAND ALKON INCORPORATED
6750 Crosby Ct (43016-7644)
PHONE..............................614 799-0600
Randy Willaman, *Brnch Mgr*
EMP: 40
SALES (corp-wide): 86.02MM **Privately Held**
Web: www.commandalkon.com
SIC: 3823 7371 3625 Industrial process measurement equipment; Custom computer programming services; Relays and industrial controls
PA: Command Alkon Incorporated
    1800 Intl Pk Dr Ste 400
    Birmingham AL 35243
    205 879-3282

(G-7968)
COMMUNITY CHOICE FINANCIAL INC (PA)
Also Called: Easy Money
6785 Bobcat Way Ste 200 (43016-1443)
PHONE..............................614 798-5900
EMP: 197 EST: 2011
SALES (est): 1.02B **Privately Held**
Web: www.ccfi.com
SIC: 6099 Check cashing agencies

(G-7969)
COMPASS CONSTRUCTION INC
7670 Fishel Dr S (43016-8820)
PHONE..............................614 761-7800
Larry Mirgon, *Pr*
Frank Reynolds, *
EMP: 80 EST: 1983
SQ FT: 14,400
SALES (est): 4.98MM **Privately Held**
Web: www.ccidw.com
SIC: 1742 Drywall

(G-7970)
COMPMANAGEMENT INC (HQ)
6377 Emerald Pkwy (43016-3272)
P.O. Box 884 (43017-6884)
PHONE..............................614 376-5300
Stephen Brown, *CEO*
Jonathan Wagner, *
Richard Kurth, *
Daniel Sullivan, *
EMP: 40 EST: 1984
SALES (est): 105.98MM **Privately Held**
Web: www.compmgt.com
SIC: 6411 Insurance agents, brokers, and service
PA: Sedgwick Cms Holdings, Inc.
    1100 Rdgway Loop Rd Ste 2
    Memphis TN 38120

(G-7971)
CON-WAY MULTIMODAL INC (DH)
5165 Emerald Pkwy (43017-1092)
PHONE..............................614 923-1400
John Beckett, *Sr VP*
Gregory Orr, *
David Dietrich, *
Gregory L Orr, *
EMP: 64 EST: 2000
SALES (est): 22.23MM
SALES (corp-wide): 3.63B **Privately Held**
Web: www.xpo.com
SIC: 4731 Transportation agents and brokers
HQ: Stg Intermodal, Inc.
    5165 Emerald Pkwy Ste 300
    Dublin OH 43017
    614 923-1400

Dublin - Franklin County (G-7972) — GEOGRAPHIC SECTION

(G-7972)
CONSOLIDATED LEARNING CTRS INC
Also Called: Jelly Bean Junction Lrng Ctr
7100 Muirfield Dr Ste 200 (43017-2864)
PHONE..................................614 791-0050
Jeffry Roby, *CEO*
Bonnie Roby, *
EMP: 36 **EST:** 1997
SQ FT: 4,000
SALES (est): 332.57K **Privately Held**
SIC: 8351 Preschool center

(G-7973)
CORAZON COUNTRY CLUB LLC
7155 Corazon Dr (43016-6151)
PHONE..................................614 504-5250
John Crackenfeld, *Prin*
EMP: 35 **EST:** 2012
SALES (est): 1.21MM **Privately Held**
Web: www.clubatcorazon.com
SIC: 7991 Health club

(G-7974)
COUNTRY CLUB AT MUIRFIELD VLG
Also Called: COUNTRY CLUB, THE
8715 Muirfield Dr (43017-9600)
PHONE..................................614 764-1714
Jim Hughes, *CEO*
John Blute, *
EMP: 30 **EST:** 1980
SQ FT: 35,000
SALES (est): 3.38MM **Privately Held**
Web: www.tccmv.com
SIC: 7997 Country club, membership

(G-7975)
COVETRUS NORTH AMERICA LLC (HQ)
Also Called: Covetrus North America
400 Metro Pl N Ste 100 (43017)
PHONE..................................614 761-9095
Matt Yordy, *Pr*
Sean Henderson, *
◆ **EMP:** 170 **EST:** 2005
SALES (est): 967.04MM
SALES (corp-wide): 4.58B **Privately Held**
Web: software.covetrus.com
SIC: 5047 5122 Veterinarians' equipment and supplies; Biologicals and allied products
PA: Covetrus North America, Llc
12 Mountfort St
Portland ME 04101
888 280-2221

(G-7976)
CP DUBLIN LLC
Also Called: Columbus Marriott Northwest
5605 Blazer Pkwy (43017-3301)
PHONE..................................614 791-1000
William J Yung Iii, *Pr*
EMP: 97 **EST:** 2019
SALES (est): 2.8MM **Privately Held**
Web: www.marriott.com
SIC: 7011 Hotels

(G-7977)
CPS MEDMANAGEMENT LLC
Also Called: McKesson Medmanagement
655 Metro Pl S Ste 450 (43017-3388)
PHONE..................................901 748-0470
EMP: 56 **EST:** 2008
SALES (est): 2.03MM
SALES (corp-wide): 302.11MM **Privately Held**
SIC: 8741 Management services
HQ: Cps Solutions, Llc
655 Metro Pl S Ste 450
Dublin OH 43017
901 748-0470

(G-7978)
CPS SOLUTIONS LLC (HQ)
655 Metro Pl S Ste 450 (43017-3388)
PHONE..................................901 748-0470
Calvin Johnson, *CEO*
Don Nickleson, *Ch Bd*
Karl Bedwell, *CIO*
Glenn Etow, *Pr*
Sam Daniel, *CFO*
EMP: 119 **EST:** 2000
SALES (est): 243.96MM
SALES (corp-wide): 302.11MM **Privately Held**
Web: www.cps.com
SIC: 8742 8741 Management consulting services; Management services
PA: Pps Holdings, Inc.
6409 N Quail Hollow Rd
Memphis TN 38120
901 748-0470

(G-7979)
CRAWFORD HOYING LTD (PA)
6640 Riverside Dr Ste 500 (43017-9534)
PHONE..................................614 335-2020
Mark Mayers, *COO*
Chris Lanning, *Pr*
EMP: 102 **EST:** 2002
SALES (est): 40.67K
SALES (corp-wide): 40.67K **Privately Held**
Web: www.crawfordhoying.com
SIC: 6531 Real estate agents and managers

(G-7980)
CUTLER REAL ESTATE INC
6375 Riverside Dr Ste 210 (43017-5241)
PHONE..................................614 339-4664
Doug Green, *Genl Mgr*
EMP: 45 **EST:** 2013
SALES (est): 1.97MM **Privately Held**
Web: the-hursh-group.westwoodohio.com
SIC: 6531 6519 Real estate agent, residential ; Real property lessors, nec

(G-7981)
DASH TECHNOLOGIES INC
565 Metro Pl S Ste 400 (43017-5380)
PHONE..................................614 593-3274
Amitkumar Bhavsar, *Pr*
EMP: 180 **EST:** 2010
SALES (est): 17.25MM **Privately Held**
Web: www.dashtechinc.com
SIC: 7371 Custom computer programming services

(G-7982)
DATA SYSTEMS INTGRTION GROUP I
485 Metro Pl S Ste 101 (43017-5374)
PHONE..................................614 344-4600
EMP: 130 **EST:** 2006
SALES (est): 17.32MM **Privately Held**
Web: www.dsiginc.com
SIC: 7371 Software programming applications

(G-7983)
DATAECONOMY INC
565 Metro Pl S (43017-5351)
PHONE..................................614 356-8153
Ravi Kopuri, *CEO*
EMP: 46 **EST:** 2018
SALES (est): 1.38MM **Privately Held**
Web: www.dataeconomy.io
SIC: 8742 Management information systems consultant

(G-7984)
DATALYSYS LLC
5200 Upper Metro Pl Ste 120 # 125 (43017-5377)
PHONE..................................614 495-0260
EMP: 40 **EST:** 2007
SALES (est): 4.19MM **Privately Held**
Web: www.datalysys.com
SIC: 7379 Online services technology consultants

(G-7985)
DAVE THMAS FNDTION FOR ADPTION
4900 Tuttle Crossing Blvd (43016-1532)
PHONE..................................614 764-8454
Rita Soronen, *CEO*
Dennis Lynch, *
EMP: 41 **EST:** 1992
SALES (est): 52.42MM **Privately Held**
Web: www.davethomasfoundation.org
SIC: 8322 Adoption services

(G-7986)
DEDICATED TECH SERVICES INC
545 Metro Pl S Ste 100 (43017-5353)
PHONE..................................614 309-0059
Patricia E Lickliter, *Pr*
EMP: 28 **EST:** 2008
SQ FT: 2,300
SALES (est): 2.34MM **Privately Held**
Web: www.dtsdelivers.com
SIC: 7371 7373 7376 7379 Computer software development; Local area network (LAN) systems integrator; Computer facilities management; Computer related maintenance services

(G-7987)
DIMENSION SERVICE CORPORATION
Also Called: D S C
5500 Frantz Rd Ste 100 (43017-3545)
P.O. Box 2082 (43017-7082)
PHONE..................................614 226-7455
Bradley Hunter, *Pr*
Alan Weiner, *
EMP: 125 **EST:** 1985
SQ FT: 25,000
SALES (est): 22.38MM **Privately Held**
Web: www.dimensionservice.com
SIC: 6399 Warranty insurance, automobile

(G-7988)
DOT NET FACTORY LLC
Also Called: TELEPHONY & DATA SOLUTIONS
4393 Tuller Rd Ste A (43017)
PHONE..................................614 792-0645
Patrick Parker, *CEO*
Bradford Mandell, *
Benjamin S Zacks, *
EMP: 80 **EST:** 2005
SALES (est): 16.15MM
SALES (corp-wide): 19.69MM **Privately Held**
Web: www.empowerid.com
SIC: 7371 Computer software development
PA: Microman, Inc.
4393 Tuller Rd A
Dublin OH 43017
614 923-8000

(G-7989)
DUBLIN BUILDING SYSTEMS CO
6233 Avery Rd (43016-8788)
P.O. Box 370 (43017-0370)
PHONE..................................614 760-5831
Thomas W Irelan, *Pr*
Victor D Irelan, *
Kevin J Morris, *
Robert J Howe, *
Richard W Irelan, *
EMP: 44 **EST:** 1966
SQ FT: 5,000
SALES (est): 10.18MM **Privately Held**
Web: www.dublinbuilding.com
SIC: 1791 1521 Structural steel erection; Single-family housing construction

(G-7990)
DUBLIN CITY SCHOOLS
6371 Shier Rings Rd (43016-9498)
PHONE..................................614 764-5926
Victor Dodds, *Dir*
EMP: 51
SALES (corp-wide): 306.12MM **Privately Held**
Web: www.dublinschools.net
SIC: 4151 School buses
PA: Dublin City Schools
5175 Emerald Pkwy
Dublin OH 43017
614 764-5913

(G-7991)
DUBLIN CNVLARIUM OPERATING LLC
6430 Post Rd (43016-1226)
PHONE..................................614 761-1188
Joseph Hazelbaker, *Prin*
Brian Hazelbaker, *Prin*
Ralph Hazelbaker, *Prin*
EMP: 72 **EST:** 2020
SALES (est): 1.97MM **Privately Held**
Web: www.theconvalarium.com
SIC: 8059 Nursing and personal care, nec

(G-7992)
DUBLIN FAMILY CARE INC
250 W Bridge St (43017-1172)
PHONE..................................614 761-2244
James J Barr Md, *Pr*
Doctor Joseph Carducci, *VP*
EMP: 30 **EST:** 1986
SALES (est): 1.39MM **Privately Held**
Web: www.dublinfamilycare250.com
SIC: 8011 General and family practice, physician/surgeon

(G-7993)
DUBLIN GERIATRIC CARE CO LP
Also Called: Convalarium At Indian Run
6430 Post Rd (43016-1226)
PHONE..................................614 761-1188
Ralph E Hazelbaker, *Pt*
Dublin Health Care, *Cor Gen Pt*
EMP: 44 **EST:** 1988
SALES (est): 5.45MM **Privately Held**
SIC: 8059 8051 Convalescent home; Skilled nursing care facilities

(G-7994)
DUBLIN HOTEL LTD LIABILITY CO
Also Called: Columbus-Marriott NW
5605 Paul G Blazer Memorial Pkwy (43017)
PHONE..................................513 891-1066
EMP: 42 **EST:** 1997
SALES (est): 447.13K **Privately Held**
SIC: 7011 Hotels and motels

(G-7995)
DUBLIN INTERNAL MEDICINE INC
5070 Bradenton Ave (43017-3520)
PHONE..................................614 764-1777
Elden Apling, *Pr*
EMP: 28 **EST:** 1982
SALES (est): 741.35K **Privately Held**
Web: www.copcp.com
SIC: 8011 General and family practice, physician/surgeon

GEOGRAPHIC SECTION
Dublin - Franklin County (G-8019)

(G-7996)
DUBLIN LATCHKEY
5970 Venture Dr Ste A (43017-2263)
PHONE..............................614 793-0871
EMP: 28 EST: 1983
SALES (est): 1.91MM **Privately Held**
Web: www.dublinlatchkey.org
SIC: 8351 Preschool center

(G-7997)
DUBLIN SPRINGS LLC
Also Called: DUBLIN SPRINGS
7625 Hospital Dr (43016-9649)
PHONE..............................614 717-1800
Garry Hoyes, *CEO*
EMP: 140 EST: 2011
SALES (est): 36.74MM **Privately Held**
Web: www.columbusspringsdublin.com
SIC: 8069 Drug addiction rehabilitation hospital

(G-7998)
DUBLIN SURGERY CENTER LLC
5005 Parkcenter Ave (43017-3582)
PHONE..............................614 932-9548
EMP: 28 EST: 2010
SALES (est): 4.35MM **Privately Held**
Web: www.dublinsurgicalcenter.com
SIC: 8011 Ambulatory surgical center

(G-7999)
EASE LOGISTICS SERVICES LLC
Also Called: Ease Logistics
5725 Avery Rd (43016-8756)
PHONE..............................614 553-7007
Peter Coratola Junior, *Managing Member*
EMP: 200 EST: 2014
SALES (est): 25.25MM **Privately Held**
Web: www.easelogistics.com
SIC: 4731 Freight transportation arrangement

(G-8000)
ECI MACOLA/MAX LLC (DH)
5455 Rings Rd Ste 100 (43017)
PHONE..............................978 539-6186
Alex Braverman, *
James A Workman, *
Lisa Wise, *
EMP: 170 EST: 1971
SQ FT: 30,000
SALES (est): 28.12MM **Privately Held**
Web: www.ecisolutions.com
SIC: 7371 7372 5045 2759 Computer software development; Prepackaged software; Computer software; Letterpress printing
HQ: Exact Holding B.V.
  Molengraaffsingel 33
  Delft ZH 2629
  157115000

(G-8001)
ECI MACOLA/MAX HOLDING LLC
Also Called: Eclipse Midco
5455 Rings Rd Ste 400 (43017-7531)
PHONE..............................614 410-2712
Ron Brooks, *CEO*
EMP: 30 EST: 2004
SIC: 6719 Personal holding companies, except banks

(G-8002)
EMERALD PEDIATRICS
5695 Innovation Dr (43016-3312)
PHONE..............................614 932-5050
Donna Hickel, *Mgr*
EMP: 30 EST: 2004
SALES (est): 2.6MM **Privately Held**
Web: www.emeraldpediatrics.com
SIC: 8011 Pediatrician

(G-8003)
EMPIRE FOOD BROKERS INC
Also Called: T S G
6131 Avery Rd (43016-8761)
P.O. Box 485 (43017-0485)
PHONE..............................614 889-2322
EMP: 36
SALES (corp-wide): 19.29MM **Privately Held**
Web: www.empirefoods.com
SIC: 5141 Food brokers
PA: Empire Food Brokers, Inc.
  1837 Harbor Ave
  Cordova TN 38088
  901 756-8681

(G-8004)
ENCORE REHABILITATION SERVICES
6479 Reflections Dr Ste 230 (43017-2374)
PHONE..............................614 459-6901
EMP: 45 EST: 2007
SALES (est): 919.96K **Privately Held**
SIC: 8093 Rehabilitation center, outpatient treatment

(G-8005)
EPCON CMMNTIES FRANCHISING INC
500 Stonehenge Pkwy (43017-7572)
PHONE..............................614 761-1010
EMP: 87 EST: 1995
SQ FT: 10,000
SALES (est): 16.88MM **Privately Held**
Web: www.epconfranchising.com
SIC: 1531 6794 Condominium developers; Franchises, selling or licensing

(G-8006)
EQUITY RESOURCES INC
7251 Sawmill Rd Ste 100 (43016-7407)
P.O. Box 5177 (43058-5177)
PHONE..............................614 389-4462
Paul Bufta, *VP*
EMP: 29
Web: www.callequity.net
SIC: 6162 6141 Mortgage bankers and loan correspondents; Personal credit institutions
PA: Equity Resources, Inc.
  25 S Park Pl
  Newark OH 43055

(G-8007)
ERP ANALYSTS INC
425 Metro Pl N Ste 510 (43017-7328)
PHONE..............................614 718-9222
Srikanth Gaddam, *Pr*
EMP: 499 EST: 2003
SALES (est): 75.1MM **Privately Held**
Web: www.erpa.com
SIC: 7379 Computer related consulting services

(G-8008)
EVERFAST INC
6315 Sawmill Rd (43017-1471)
PHONE..............................614 789-0900
Michelle Stimer, *Mgr*
EMP: 34
SALES (corp-wide): 83.93MM **Privately Held**
Web: www.calicocorners.com
SIC: 5949 5131 Fabric stores piece goods; Piece goods and other fabrics
PA: Everfast, Inc.
  203 Gale Ln
  Kennett Square PA 19348
  610 444-9700

(G-8009)
EVERHART ADVISORS
535 Metro Pl S (43017-5302)
PHONE..............................614 717-9705
Scott Everhart, *Pr*
EMP: 57 EST: 2002
SALES (est): 3.7MM **Privately Held**
Web: www.everhartadvisors.com
SIC: 6282 Investment advisory service

(G-8010)
FANNING/HOWEY ASSOCIATES INC
4930 Bradenton Ave Ste 200 (43017-7502)
PHONE..............................614 764-4661
Alan Esparza, *Mgr*
EMP: 96
SALES (corp-wide): 23.29MM **Privately Held**
Web: www.fhai.com
SIC: 8712 Architectural engineering
PA: Fanning/Howey Associates, Inc.
  1200 Irmscher Blvd
  Celina OH 45822
  419 586-2292

(G-8011)
FAST SWITCH LTD
4900 Blazer Pkwy (43017-3305)
P.O. Box 99 (43017-0099)
PHONE..............................614 336-1122
Mark Pukita, *CEO*
EMP: 300 EST: 1996
SQ FT: 1,200
SALES (est): 23.3MM **Privately Held**
Web: www.fastswitch.com
SIC: 7361 Executive placement

(G-8012)
FIREFLY AGENCY LLC
Also Called: Nationwide
655 Metro Pl S Ste 330 (43017-5459)
PHONE..............................614 507-7847
EMP: 42 EST: 2018
SALES (est): 2.38MM **Privately Held**
Web: www.fireflyagency.com
SIC: 6411 Insurance agents, brokers, and service

(G-8013)
FORESIGHT CORPORATION
655 Metro Pl S Ste 900 (43017)
PHONE..............................614 791-1600
Robert Fisher, *Pr*
Douglas Spence, *
Kristin Maxwell, *
Edward Hafner, *
EMP: 43 EST: 1990
SALES (est): 4.95MM
SALES (corp-wide): 4.38B **Privately Held**
SIC: 7371 Computer software development
HQ: Cloud Software Group, Inc.
  851 W Cypress Creek Rd
  Fort Lauderdale FL 33309

(G-8014)
FRANK GATES SERVICE COMPANY (DH)
Also Called: Avizent
5000 Bradenton Ave Ste 100 (43017-3520)
P.O. Box 182364 (43218-2364)
PHONE..............................614 793-8000
Daniel R Sullivan, *Pr*
Robert Zamary, *
Madeleine Melancon, *
Harrison W Smith, *
Frank Gates, *
EMP: 300 EST: 1995
SQ FT: 66,000
SALES (est): 92.89MM **Privately Held**
SIC: 8742 Compensation and benefits planning consultant
HQ: York Risk Services Group, Inc.
  1 Upper Pond Rd Bldg F
  Parsippany NJ 07054
  973 404-1200

(G-8015)
FRANKLIN EQUIPMENT LLC
7570 Fishel Dr S (43016-8819)
PHONE..............................614 389-2161
Troy Gabriel, *Brnch Mgr*
EMP: 48
SALES (corp-wide): 14.33B **Publicly Held**
Web: www.unitedrentals.com
SIC: 7359 Equipment rental and leasing, nec
HQ: Franklin Equipment, Llc
  4141 Hamilton Square Blvd
  Groveport OH 43125

(G-8016)
FRIENDSHIP VLG OF DUBLIN OHIO
Also Called: Friendship Village of Dublin
6000 Riverside Dr Ofc (43017-5073)
PHONE..............................614 764-1600
John Schwarck, *Ex Dir*
EMP: 250 EST: 1978
SALES (est): 35.26MM **Privately Held**
Web: www.fvdublin.org
SIC: 8059 8051 Rest home, with health care; Skilled nursing care facilities

(G-8017)
FST BROKERAGE SERVICES INC (HQ)
5025 Bradenton Ave Ste B (43017-3506)
PHONE..............................614 529-7900
Fred M Campbell, *Prin*
EMP: 52 EST: 1991
SQ FT: 42,000
SALES (est): 23.63MM
SALES (corp-wide): 100.02MM **Privately Held**
Web: www.fstlogistics.com
SIC: 4212 Local trucking, without storage
PA: Fst Logistics, Inc.
  1727 Georgesville Rd
  Columbus OH 43228
  614 529-7900

(G-8018)
G2O LLC
Also Called: Clutch Interactive
5455 Rings Rd Ste 500 (43017-7527)
PHONE..............................614 523-3070
Kelly Gratz, *Pr*
Dave Dieterle, *
Mike Keegan, *
Blane Walter, *
EMP: 500 EST: 1978
SQ FT: 50,000
SALES (est): 42.5MM **Privately Held**
Web: www.meetclutch.com
SIC: 7379 Online services technology consultants

(G-8019)
GARDEN CITY GROUP LLC (DH)
Also Called: Gcg Loudoun Co
5151 Blazer Pkwy Ste A (43017-9306)
P.O. Box 2899 (11746-0911)
PHONE..............................631 470-5000
EMP: 200 EST: 1994
SALES (est): 47.1MM
SALES (corp-wide): 618.42MM **Privately Held**
Web: www.skinderclassaction.net
SIC: 8111 Specialized legal services
HQ: Epiq Class Action & Claims Solutions, Inc.
  10300 Sw Allen Blvd

Dublin - Franklin County (G-8020) — GEOGRAPHIC SECTION

Beaverton OR 97005

(G-8020)
GEMINI PROPERTIES
Also Called: G P M C
6470 Post Rd Ofc (43016-7206)
PHONE.................614 764-2800
EMP: 31
SALES (corp-wide): 4.67MM **Privately Held**
Web: www.seniorstar.com
SIC: 6513 Retirement hotel operation
PA: Gemini Properties
   1516 S Boston Ave Ste 301
   Tulsa OK 74119
   918 592-4400

(G-8021)
GOKEN AMERICA LLC
Also Called: Goken America
5100 Parkcenter Ave Ste 100 (43017)
PHONE.................614 495-8104
Taksunori Nakamura, *
EMP: 100 **EST:** 2005
SQ FT: 2,500
SALES (est): 22.38MM **Privately Held**
Web: www.goken-global.com
SIC: 8742 Management consulting services

(G-8022)
GOLDEN RESERVE LLC
270 Bradenton Ave (43017-7516)
PHONE.................614 563-2818
EMP: 45 **EST:** 2016
SALES (est): 5.77MM **Privately Held**
Web: www.goldenreserve.com
SIC: 6799 Investors, nec

(G-8023)
GUILD ASSOCIATES INC (PA)
5750 Shier Rings Rd (43016-1234)
PHONE.................614 798-8215
Henry Berns, *CEO*
Dominic Dinovo, *
Dolores Dinovo, *
▲ **EMP:** 65 **EST:** 1981
SQ FT: 53,000
SALES (est): 24.49MM
SALES (corp-wide): 24.49MM **Privately Held**
Web: www.guildassociates.com
SIC: 3559 8731 Chemical machinery and equipment; Chemical laboratory, except testing

(G-8024)
H N S SPORTS GROUP LTD
6085 Memorial Dr (43017-8218)
PHONE.................614 764-4653
Dan Sullivan, *Mng Pt*
Steve Nicklaus, *Pt*
John Hines, *Pt*
EMP: 32 **EST:** 2002
SALES (est): 1.83MM **Privately Held**
Web: www.hnssports.com
SIC: 8699 Professional golf association

(G-8025)
HAGERTY INSURANCE AGENCY LLC
555 Metro Pl N (43017-5362)
PHONE.................877 922-9701
EMP: 55
SALES (corp-wide): 171.66MM **Privately Held**
Web: www.hagertyagent.com
SIC: 6411 Insurance agents, nec
PA: Hagerty Insurance Agency, Llc
   121 Drivers Edge
   Traverse City MI 49684
   877 922-9701

(G-8026)
HARDAGE HOTELS I LLC
Also Called: Chase Suite Hotel
4130 Tuller Rd (43017-9502)
PHONE.................614 766-7762
William Quigley, *Mgr*
EMP: 96
Web: www.hardagehospitality.com
SIC: 7011 Hotel, franchised
PA: Hardage Hotels I, Llc
   12555 High Bluff Dr # 330
   San Diego CA 92130

(G-8027)
HASLETT HEATING & COOLING INC
Also Called: Honeywell Authorized Dealer
7686 Fishel Dr N # A (43016-8746)
PHONE.................614 299-2133
Jeff Florer, *Pr*
Bruce Ames, *
EMP: 27 **EST:** 2003
SALES (est): 1.73MM **Privately Held**
Web: www.haslettmechanical.com
SIC: 1711 Plumbing contractors

(G-8028)
HEALTHSPOT INC
545 Metro Pl S Ste 430 (43017-3386)
PHONE.................614 361-1193
EMP: 60
Web: www.healthspot.net
SIC: 8621 Health association

(G-8029)
HOLO PUNDITS INC
425 Metro Pl N Ste 440 (43017-5325)
PHONE.................614 707-5225
Vinod Dega, *CEO*
EMP: 50 **EST:** 2013
SALES (est): 2.38MM **Privately Held**
Web: www.holopundits.com
SIC: 7371 Computer software writing services

(G-8030)
HOME INSPECTIONS
715 Shawan Falls Dr Unit 1954 (43017-6700)
PHONE.................800 241-0133
EMP: 48 **EST:** 2016
SALES (est): 1.01MM **Privately Held**
Web: www.hcinspectors.com
SIC: 7389 Building inspection service

(G-8031)
HOTEL 2345 LLC
Also Called: Cloverleaf Suites
4130 Tuller Rd (43017-9502)
PHONE.................614 766-7762
EMP: 30 **EST:** 2016
SALES (est): 1.03MM **Privately Held**
Web: www.cloverleafsuites.com
SIC: 7011 Inns

(G-8032)
HR BUTLER LLC
63 Corbins Mill Dr Ste A (43017-8314)
PHONE.................614 923-2900
Thomas Hedge, *Pr*
EMP: 38 **EST:** 2000
SALES (est): 5.06MM **Privately Held**
Web: www.hrbutler.com
SIC: 8721 8742 Payroll accounting service; Human resource consulting services

(G-8033)
HUSKY MARKETING AND SUPPLY CO
Also Called: Husky Energy
5550 Blazer Pkwy Ste 200 (43017-3478)
PHONE.................614 210-2300
Jonathan Mckenzie, *CFO*
EMP: 40 **EST:** 2007
SALES (est): 76.47MM
SALES (corp-wide): 40.39B **Privately Held**
Web: hmsc.huskyenergy.com
SIC: 1321 1382 Natural gasoline production; Oil and gas exploration services
PA: Cenovus Energy Inc
   225 6 Ave Sw
   Calgary AB T2P 1
   403 766-2000

(G-8034)
IGS SOLAR LLC
6100 Emerald Pkwy (43016-3248)
PHONE.................844 447-7652
Scott H White, *Pr*
EMP: 81 **EST:** 2014
SALES (est): 2.38MM **Privately Held**
Web: www.igs.com
SIC: 1711 Solar energy contractor

(G-8035)
IGS VENTURES INC
6100 Emerald Pkwy (43016-3248)
PHONE.................614 659-5000
Scott White, *Pr*
EMP: 150 **EST:** 1989
SALES (est): 12.14MM **Privately Held**
Web: www.igs.com
SIC: 6799 Venture capital companies
PA: Interstate Gas Supply, Llc
   6100 Emerald Pkwy
   Dublin OH 43016

(G-8036)
INEOS HYGIENICS LLC
5220 Blazer Pkwy (43017-3494)
PHONE.................614 790-5428
EMP: 60 **EST:** 2020
SALES (est): 3.57MM **Privately Held**
SIC: 5047 Medical equipment and supplies

(G-8037)
INFOVERITY LLC (PA)
5131 Post Rd Ste 220 (43017-2194)
PHONE.................614 327-5173
Adam Sigg, *
Steve Ruff, *
EMP: 38 **EST:** 2011
SQ FT: 2,500
SALES (est): 7.07MM
SALES (corp-wide): 7.07MM **Privately Held**
Web: www.infoverity.com
SIC: 8748 7389 Business consulting, nec; Business services, nec

(G-8038)
INFOVISION21 INC
6077 Frantz Rd Ste 105 (43017-3373)
PHONE.................614 761-8844
Bapaiah Koneru, *Pr*
EMP: 44 **EST:** 1996
SQ FT: 2,500
SALES (est): 3.46MM **Privately Held**
Web: www.infovision21.com
SIC: 7374 7371 7379 Data processing and preparation; Computer software development; Computer related consulting services

(G-8039)
INNOVATIVE THERAPIES LLC
7000 Cardinal Pl (43017-1091)
PHONE.................866 484-6798
Donald Casey, *CEO*
Michael Duffy, *
Michael Kauffman, *
Stephen Falk, *
Samer Samad, *
▲ **EMP:** 62 **EST:** 2006
SALES (est): 42.91MM
SALES (corp-wide): 205.01B **Publicly Held**
Web: www.andelynbio.com
SIC: 5047 Medical equipment and supplies
PA: Cardinal Health, Inc.
   7000 Cardinal Pl
   Dublin OH 43017
   614 757-5000

(G-8040)
INTEGRA CNCINNATI/COLUMBUS INC
Also Called: Dublin
6241 Riverside Dr (43017-5068)
PHONE.................614 764-8040
Bruce Daubner, *Pr*
Gary Wright, *
EMP: 30 **EST:** 2011
SALES (est): 1.81MM **Privately Held**
SIC: 6531 Real estate agents and managers

(G-8041)
INTERSTATE GAS SUPPLY LLC (PA)
Also Called: Interstate Gas Supply
6100 Emerald Pkwy (43016-3248)
P.O. Box 9060 (43017-0960)
PHONE.................877 995-4447
Scott White, *Pr*
Doug Austin, *
Jim Baich, *
Tami Wilson Cfro, *Prin*
EMP: 267 **EST:** 1989
SQ FT: 100,000
SALES (est): 302.94MM **Privately Held**
Web: www.igs.com
SIC: 1311 Natural gas production

(G-8042)
JACKSON I-94 LTD PARTNERSHIP
Also Called: Rodeway Inn
6059 Frantz Rd Ste 205 (43017-3368)
PHONE.................614 793-2244
EMP: 77 **EST:** 1993
SQ FT: 2,400
SALES (est): 176.99K **Privately Held**
Web: www.choicehotels.com
SIC: 7011 5812 Hotels and motels; Eating places

(G-8043)
JOE KNOWS ENERGY LLC
5880 Venture Dr Ste D (43017-6141)
PHONE.................614 989-2228
Daniel Lorenz, *Managing Member*
EMP: 50 **EST:** 2013
SALES (est): 2.85MM **Privately Held**
Web: www.joeknowsenergy.com
SIC: 7361 Employment agencies

(G-8044)
K&R NETWORK SOLUTIONS
5747 Perimeter Dr (43017-3245)
PHONE.................858 292-5766
Chris Claudio, *CEO*
Michael Williams, *
Jeremy Kurth, *
EMP: 40 **EST:** 2002
SALES (est): 5.26MM
SALES (corp-wide): 118.88MM **Privately Held**
Web: www.logically.com
SIC: 7379 7373 7376 Online services technology consultants; Local area network (LAN) systems integrator; Computer facilities management
PA: Winxnet, Llc
   63 Marginal Way Ste 400
   Portland ME 04101

207 780-0497

(G-8045)
KAPPA KAPPA GAMMA FOUNDATION (PA)
Also Called: KAPPA KAPPA GAMMA FRATERNITY
6640 Riverside Dr Ste 200 (43017-9535)
P.O. Box 38 (43216-0038)
PHONE..................614 228-6515
Maggie Sims Coons, *Ex Dir*
EMP: 35 **EST:** 1870
SALES (est): 7.99MM
SALES (corp-wide): 7.99MM **Privately Held**
Web: www.kappakappagamma.org
SIC: 8641 University club

(G-8046)
KASSEL EQUITY GROUP LLC (PA)
7686 Fishel Dr N Ste B (43016-8746)
PHONE..................614 310-4060
Thomas Werner, *CEO*
Felipe Gonzalez, *Project MGT*
Brenda Werner, *COO*
EMP: 29 **EST:** 2010
SALES (est): 107.51MM
SALES (corp-wide): 107.51MM **Privately Held**
Web: www.kasselequity.com
SIC: 6799 Investors, nec

(G-8047)
KE GUTRIDGE LLC
7686 Fishel Dr N Apt A (43016-8746)
PHONE..................614 299-2133
EMP: 94
SALES (corp-wide): 107.51MM **Privately Held**
Web: www.gutridge.com
SIC: 1711 Plumbing contractors
HQ: Ke Gutridge, Llc
  88 S 2nd St
  Newark OH 43055
  740 349-9411

(G-8048)
KE GUTRIDGE LLC
Also Called: Titan Electric
7686 Fishel Dr N # B (43016-8746)
PHONE..................614 885-5200
EMP: 125
SALES (corp-wide): 107.51MM **Privately Held**
Web: www.gutridge.com
SIC: 5063 Electrical apparatus and equipment
HQ: Ke Gutridge, Llc
  88 S 2nd St
  Newark OH 43055
  740 349-9411

(G-8049)
KINETICS NOISE CONTROL INC (PA)
Also Called: Hammond Kinetics
6300 Irelan Pl (43016-1278)
P.O. Box 655 (43017-0655)
PHONE..................614 889-0480
◆ **EMP:** 135 **EST:** 1958
SALES (est): 38.42MM
SALES (corp-wide): 38.42MM **Privately Held**
Web: www.kineticsnoise.com
SIC: 3829 3625 3446 5084 Vibration meters, analyzers, and calibrators; Noise control equipment; Acoustical suspension systems, metal; Industrial machinery and equipment

(G-8050)
KK ASSOCIATES LLC (PA)
Also Called: Kk Associates
555 Metro Pl N Ste 100 (43017-1389)
PHONE..................614 783-7966
Maheswara Kasa, *Managing Member*
EMP: 46 **EST:** 2004
SALES (est): 5MM
SALES (corp-wide): 5MM **Privately Held**
Web: www.kksoftwareassociates.com
SIC: 7371 Computer software development and applications

(G-8051)
KURTZ BROS CENTRAL OHIO LLC
6279 Houchard Rd (43016-8817)
P.O. Box 207 (43086-0207)
PHONE..................614 873-2000
EMP: 50 **EST:** 2006
SQ FT: 2,500
SALES (est): 9.7MM
SALES (corp-wide): 27.73MM **Privately Held**
Web: www.kbcolumbus.com
SIC: 0782 Mulching services, lawn
PA: Kurtz Bros., Inc.
  6415 Granger Rd
  Independence OH 44131
  216 986-7000

(G-8052)
L&T TECHNOLOGY SERVICES LTD
5550 Blazer Pkwy Ste 125 (43017-3482)
PHONE..................732 688-4402
Feroz Reza, *Mgr*
EMP: 496
Web: www.ltts.com
SIC: 8711 Acoustical engineering
HQ: L&T Technology Services Limited
  West Block Ii, L&T Knowledge City,
  Vadodara GJ 39001

(G-8053)
LEADING EDJE LLC
5555 Perimeter Dr Ste 101 (43017-3219)
PHONE..................614 636-3353
Erica Krumlaus, *Brnch Mgr*
EMP: 42
SALES (corp-wide): 9.54MM **Privately Held**
Web: www.leadingedje.com
SIC: 7379 Computer related consulting services
PA: Leading Edje Llc
  1491 Polaris Pkwy Ste 191
  Columbus OH 43240
  614 636-3353

(G-8054)
LIFE TIME INC
3825 Hard Rd (43016-8335)
PHONE..................614 789-7824
EMP: 76
SALES (corp-wide): 2.22B **Publicly Held**
Web: www.lifetime.life
SIC: 7991 Health club
HQ: Life Time, Inc.
  2902 Corporate Pl
  Chanhassen MN 55317

(G-8055)
LINEBRGER GGGAN BLAIR SMPSON L
5080 Tuttle Crossing Blvd Ste 340 (43016-3540)
PHONE..................614 210-8100
George Calloway, *Owner*
EMP: 36
SALES (corp-wide): 167.16MM **Privately Held**
Web: www.lgbs.com

SIC: 8111 Specialized law offices, attorneys
PA: Linebarger Goggan Blair & Sampson, Llp
  2700 Via Fortuna Ste 500
  Austin TX 78746
  512 447-6675

(G-8056)
LODGING FIRST LLC
94 N High St Ste 250 (43017-1110)
PHONE..................614 792-2770
EMP: 50 **EST:** 2004
SALES (est): 912.82K **Privately Held**
SIC: 7021 Rooming and boarding houses

(G-8057)
LOGIC SOFT INC
Also Called: Www.logicsoftusa.com
5900 Sawmill Rd Ste 200 (43017-2588)
PHONE..................614 884-5544
Ketan Shah, *CEO*
Satish Barapatre, *
Harish Kukreja, *
EMP: 55 **EST:** 1997
SQ FT: 3,000
SALES (est): 5.03MM **Privately Held**
Web: www.logicsoftusa.com
SIC: 7371 Computer software development

(G-8058)
LOWES HOME CENTERS LLC
Also Called: Lowe's
6555 Dublin Center Dr (43017-5016)
PHONE..................614 659-0530
Shane Thompson, *Mgr*
EMP: 148
SALES (corp-wide): 86.38B **Publicly Held**
Web: www.lowes.com
SIC: 5211 5031 5722 5064 Home centers; Building materials, exterior; Household appliance stores; Electrical appliances, television and radio
HQ: Lowe's Home Centers, Llc
  1000 Lowes Blvd
  Mooresville NC 28117
  336 658-4000

(G-8059)
MANAGEMENT AND NETWRK SVCS LLC
Also Called: Management & Network Services
6500 Emerald Pkwy Ste 310 (43016-7460)
PHONE..................800 949-2159
Brian Deeley, *CEO*
John Hoffman, *
EMP: 81 **EST:** 1996
SALES (est): 5.8MM
SALES (corp-wide): 357.78B **Publicly Held**
Web: www.mnsnetwork.com
SIC: 8741 Nursing and personal care facility management
HQ: Management & Network Services, Inc.
  201 E 4th St Ste 900
  Cincinnati OH 45202
  513 719-2600

(G-8060)
MANNYS CLEANING CO
6605 Longshore St (43017-2773)
PHONE..................614 596-1919
Manuel Amaya, *Owner*
EMP: 40 **EST:** 2003
SALES (est): 281.56K **Privately Held**
SIC: 7699 Cleaning services

(G-8061)
MEDCO HEALTH SOLUTIONS INC
Also Called: Express Script
5151 Blazer Pkwy Ste B (43017-5405)
PHONE..................614 822-2000

William Kelly, *Mgr*
EMP: 243
SALES (corp-wide): 195.26B **Publicly Held**
Web: www.express-scripts.com
SIC: 5961 8742 Pharmaceuticals, mail order; Management consulting services
HQ: Medco Health Solutions, Inc.
  100 Parsons Pond Dr
  Franklin Lakes NJ 07417
  201 269-3400

(G-8062)
MEDICAL MUTUAL OF OHIO
545 Metro Pl S (43017-3386)
PHONE..................614 621-4585
John Stofa, *Mgr*
EMP: 39
SALES (corp-wide): 2.75B **Privately Held**
Web: www.medmutual.com
SIC: 8011 Medical insurance plan
PA: Medical Mutual Of Ohio
  2060 E 9th St
  Cleveland OH 44115
  216 687-7000

(G-8063)
MEEDER ASSET MANAGEMENT INC
6125 Memorial Dr (43017)
P.O. Box 7177 (43017-0777)
PHONE..................614 760-2112
Robert S Meeder Junior, *Pr*
Donald F Meeder, *
EMP: 58 **EST:** 1974
SQ FT: 10,000
SALES (est): 4.82MM **Privately Held**
Web: www.meederinvestment.com
SIC: 6282 Investment counselors

(G-8064)
MICROMAN INC (PA)
Also Called: Telephony & Data Solutions
4393 Tuller Rd Ste A (43017)
PHONE..................614 923-8000
Bradford Mandell, *COO*
EMP: 42 **EST:** 1987
SQ FT: 23,873
SALES (est): 19.69MM
SALES (corp-wide): 19.69MM **Privately Held**
Web: www.microman.com
SIC: 7373 5734 Computer integrated systems design; Computer peripheral equipment

(G-8065)
MITSUBSHI INTL FD INGRDNTS INC (DH)
5475 Rings Rd Ste 450 (43017-7564)
PHONE..................614 652-1111
Koji Shimizu, *Pr*
Montgomery Emmanuel, *
Michael Fortescue, *
◆ **EMP:** 35 **EST:** 2004
SQ FT: 10,800
SALES (est): 76.43MM **Privately Held**
Web: www.mifiusa.com
SIC: 5169 5122 Food additives and preservatives; Vitamins and minerals
HQ: Mitsubishi Corporation (Americas)
  151 W 42nd St Fl 34
  New York NY 10036
  212 605-2000

(G-8066)
MUIRFIELD VILLAGE GOLF CLUB
Also Called: Memorial Tournament, The
5750 Memorial Dr (43017-9742)
PHONE..................614 889-6700
Jack Nicklaus, *Pr*
John G Hines, *

David Sherman, *
Dan Maher, *
EMP: 50 **EST:** 1972
SQ FT: 40,000
SALES (est): 22.75MM **Privately Held**
Web: www.mvgc.org
SIC: 7997 Golf club, membership

(G-8067)
N S INTERNATIONAL LTD
Also Called: N. S. International, Ltd.
5910 Venture Dr Ste.D (43017-6146)
PHONE.................................248 251-1600
EMP: 67
Web: www.nsna.com
SIC: 5013 Motor vehicle supplies and new parts
HQ: N.S. International Ltd.
600 Wilshire Dr
Troy MI 48084
248 251-1600

(G-8068)
NATIONAL SHUNT SERVICE LLC
Also Called: Nssl
6375 Riverside Dr Ste 200 (43017-5045)
PHONE.................................978 637-2293
Darren Fitzgerald, *Managing Member*
Carrie Hood, *
Serge Rouleau, *
Tj Campbell, *
Graeme Noble, *
EMP: 400 **EST:** 2014
SALES (est): 10.58MM **Privately Held**
Web: www.nationalshunt.com
SIC: 4214 Local trucking with storage

(G-8069)
NATIONWIDE CHILDRENS HOSPITAL
5680 Venture Dr (43017-2190)
PHONE.................................614 355-8737
L Kluchurosky, *Prgrm Mgr*
EMP: 33 **EST:** 2013
SALES (est): 2.77MM **Privately Held**
Web: www.nationwidechildrens.org
SIC: 8062 General medical and surgical hospitals

(G-8070)
NATIONWIDE CHILDRENS HOSPITAL
7450 Hospital Dr (43016-9642)
PHONE.................................614 355-7000
EMP: 101
SALES (corp-wide): 3.6B **Privately Held**
Web: www.nationwidechildrens.org
SIC: 8322 8093 8049 8011 Individual and family services; Specialty outpatient clinics, nec; Acupuncturist; Offices and clinics of medical doctors
PA: Nationwide Children's Hospital
700 Childrens Dr
Columbus OH 43205
614 722-2000

(G-8071)
NATIONWIDE MUTUAL INSURANCE CO
Also Called: Nationwide
5455 Rings Rd (43017-3573)
PHONE.................................614 734-1276
Terry Austin, *Mgr*
EMP: 29
SALES (corp-wide): 11.75B **Privately Held**
Web: www.nationwide.com
SIC: 6411 Insurance agents, nec
PA: Nationwide Mutual Insurance Company
1 Nationwide Plz
Columbus OH 43215
614 249-7111

(G-8072)
NATIONWIDE RTRMENT SLTIONS INC (DH)
5900 Parkwood Pl (43016-1216)
P.O. Box 182171 (43218-2171)
PHONE.................................614 854-8300
Duane Meek, *Pr*
Chris Cole, *
EMP: 125 **EST:** 1973
SQ FT: 7,000
SALES (est): 95.92MM
SALES (corp-wide): 11.75B **Privately Held**
Web: www.nrsforu.com
SIC: 6371 8748 8742 6411 Pension funds; Employee programs administration; Management consulting services; Insurance agents, brokers, and service
HQ: Nationwide Corporation
1 Nationwide Plz
Columbus OH 43215
614 249-7111

(G-8073)
NESTLE USA INC
Also Called: Nestle Quality Assurance Ctr
6625 Eiterman Rd (43016-8727)
PHONE.................................614 526-5300
EMP: 278
Web: www.nestleusa.com
SIC: 8734 Food testing service
HQ: Nestle Usa, Inc.
1812 N Moore St
Arlington VA 22209
703 682-4600

(G-8074)
NETSMART TECHNOLOGIES INC
5455 Rings Rd (43017-3573)
PHONE.................................800 434-2642
Alistair Deakin, *Brnch Mgr*
EMP: 468
SALES (corp-wide): 509.9MM **Privately Held**
Web: www.ntst.com
SIC: 7371 8742 5045 7373 Custom computer programming services; Management consulting services; Computers, peripherals, and software; Value-added resellers, computer systems
HQ: Netsmart Technologies, Inc.
11100 Nall Ave
Overland Park KS 66211

(G-8075)
NETWAVE CORPORATION
Also Called: Netwave
8242 Inistork Ct (43017-8638)
PHONE.................................614 850-6300
EMP: 36 **EST:** 1994
SALES (est): 2.48MM **Privately Held**
Web: www.netwavecorp.com
SIC: 7379 5045 Computer related consulting services; Computers, peripherals, and software

(G-8076)
NEW YORK LF INSUR JOE STICH RG
5455 Rings Rd Ste 300 (43017-7521)
PHONE.................................614 793-2121
EMP: 28 **EST:** 2016
SALES (est): 405.38K **Privately Held**
SIC: 6411 Insurance agents, brokers, and service

(G-8077)
NOKIA OF AMERICA CORPORATION
5475 Rings Rd Ste 101 (43017-7564)
PHONE.................................614 860-2000
Linn Jones, *Mgr*
EMP: 59
SALES (corp-wide): 24.19B **Privately Held**
Web: www.nokia.com
SIC: 8731 Commercial physical research
HQ: Nokia Of America Corporation
600 Mountain Ave Ste 700
New Providence NJ 07974

(G-8078)
OAKLAND PK CNSERVATION CLB INC
3138 Strathaven Ct (43017-1913)
PHONE.................................614 989-8739
Steve Hiser, *Trst*
Charles Hooker, *
EMP: 56 **EST:** 1954
SALES (est): 193.78K **Privately Held**
Web: www.oaklandparkconservation.org
SIC: 7997 Membership sports and recreation clubs

(G-8079)
OCLC INC (PA)
Also Called: Oclc
6565 Kilgour Pl (43017-3395)
PHONE.................................614 764-6000
Skip Prichard, *Pr*
Bill Rozek, *CFO*
EMP: 860 **EST:** 1967
SQ FT: 350,000
SALES (est): 208.36MM
SALES (corp-wide): 208.36MM **Privately Held**
Web: www.oclc.org
SIC: 7375 On-line data base information retrieval

(G-8080)
OHIO GSTROENTEROLOGY GROUP INC
6670 Perimeter Dr Ste 200 (43016-8065)
PHONE.................................614 754-5500
EMP: 29
Web: www.ohiogastro.com
SIC: 8011 Gastronomist
PA: Ohio Gastroenterology Group, Inc.
3400 Olentangy River Rd
Columbus OH 43202

(G-8081)
OHIOHEALTH CORPORATION
Also Called: Dublin Methodist Hospital
7500 Hospital Dr (43016-8518)
PHONE.................................614 544-8000
Cheryl Herbert, *Pr*
EMP: 500
SALES (corp-wide): 4.29B **Privately Held**
Web: www.ohiohealth.com
SIC: 8062 General medical and surgical hospitals
PA: Ohiohealth Corporation
3430 Ohhalth Pkwy 5th Flr
Columbus OH 43202
614 788-8860

(G-8082)
ORAL FCIAL SRGONS OHIO RCHARD
5155 Bradenton Ave Ste 100 (43017-7558)
PHONE.................................614 764-9455
Doctor Richard E Scheetz, *Prin*
EMP: 29 **EST:** 2001
SALES (est): 90.44K **Privately Held**
Web: www.omfso.com
SIC: 8021 Dental surgeon

(G-8083)
ORTHOPEDIC ONE INC
4945 Bradenton Ave (43017-3521)
PHONE.................................614 570-4419
EMP: 32
Web: www.orthopedicone.com
SIC: 8011 Orthopedic physician
PA: Orthopedic One, Inc.
170 Taylor Station Rd # 260
Columbus OH 43213

(G-8084)
OSU INTERNAL MEDICINE LLC (PA)
6700 University Blvd # 4c (43016-3508)
PHONE.................................614 293-0080
Earnest Mazzaferri Md, *Pr*
Earl Metz Md, *VP*
John Fromkes Md, *Treas*
EMP: 55 **EST:** 1984
SALES (est): 2.63MM
SALES (corp-wide): 2.63MM **Privately Held**
Web: wexnermedical.osu.edu
SIC: 8741 Business management

(G-8085)
PACER TRANSPORT INC
Also Called: Pacer
5165 Emerald Pkwy (43017-1092)
PHONE.................................614 923-1400
EMP: 90
SIC: 4213 4731 Trucking, except local; Freight forwarding

(G-8086)
PAIN CARE SPECIALISTS LLC
Also Called: St Anne Mercy Hospital
6397 Emerald Pkwy Ste 100 (43016-2231)
PHONE.................................614 865-2120
Rao Lingam, *Pt*
Adil Katabay, *Pt*
Michael Orzo, *Pt*
Nikesh Batra, *Pt*
Kim Chowdhury, *Pt*
EMP: 27 **EST:** 2001
SALES (est): 2.16MM **Privately Held**
Web: www.americanpainconsortium.com
SIC: 8011 Orthopedic physician

(G-8087)
PARALLEL TECHNOLOGIES INC
4868 Blazer Pkwy (43017-3302)
PHONE.................................614 798-9700
Joseph Redman, *Pr*
Martin B Jacobs, *
EMP: 80 **EST:** 1984
SQ FT: 8,500
SALES (est): 34.75MM
SALES (corp-wide): 34.75MM **Privately Held**
Web: www.paralleltech.com
SIC: 1623 7372 Telephone and communication line construction; Business oriented computer software
PA: R C I Communications Inc
4868 Blazer Pkwy
Dublin OH 43017
614 798-9700

(G-8088)
PASSPORT HEALTH LLC
5650 Blazer Pkwy Ste 174 (43017-3562)
PHONE.................................614 453-3920
Doug Shackell, *Brnch Mgr*
EMP: 114
SALES (corp-wide): 181.98MM **Privately Held**
Web: www.passporthealthusa.com
SIC: 8011 Clinic, operated by physicians
HQ: Passport Health, Llc
8324 E Hartford Dr # 200
Scottsdale AZ 85255
480 345-6800

GEOGRAPHIC SECTION

Dublin - Franklin County (G-8112)

(G-8089)
PERMEDION INC
5475 Rings Rd Ste 200 (43017-7565)
PHONE..................614 895-9900
William Lucia, *Pr*
Thomas A Schultz, *
EMP: 205 **EST:** 2007
SALES (est): 1.02MM
SALES (corp-wide): 8.69B **Privately Held**
Web: www.gainwelltechnologies.com
SIC: 8741 Hospital management
HQ: Health Management Systems Inc
5615 High Point Dr # 100
Irving TX 75038
214 453-3000

(G-8090)
PERSISTENT SYSTEMS INC
5080 Tuttle Crossing Blvd Ste 150 (43016)
PHONE..................614 763-6500
EMP: 46
Web: www.persistent.com
SIC: 7389 Personal service agents, brokers, and bureaus
HQ: Persistent Systems Inc.
2055 Laurelwood Rd # 210
Santa Clara CA 95054
408 216-7010

(G-8091)
PHYSICIANS PROFESSIONAL MGT
Also Called: P P M C
5475 Rings Rd (43017-7537)
P.O. Box 1849 (04241-1849)
PHONE..................207 782-7494
TOLL FREE: 800
EMP: 40 **EST:** 1996
SALES (est): 2.42MM **Privately Held**
Web: www.advocatercm.com
SIC: 8721 Billing and bookkeeping service

(G-8092)
PMI SUPPLY INC
Also Called: Progressive Medical Intl
5000 Tuttle Crossing Blvd (43016-1534)
P.O. Box 8023 (43016-2023)
PHONE..................760 598-1128
▲ **EMP:** 60
SIC: 5047 Medical equipment and supplies

(G-8093)
POWER ACQUISITION LLC (HQ)
5025 Bradenton Ave Ste 130 (43017-3506)
PHONE..................614 228-5000
John B Simmons, *CEO*
J Michael Kirksey, *CFO*
EMP: 55 **EST:** 2016
SALES (est): 598.3MM
SALES (corp-wide): 1.47B **Privately Held**
SIC: 3694 7538 7537 Distributors, motor vehicle engine; Diesel engine repair; automotive; Automotiv e transmission repair shops
PA: Oep Capital Advisors, L.P.
510 Madison Ave Fl 19
New York NY 10022
212 277-1500

(G-8094)
PRATER ENGINEERING ASSOC INC
6130 Wilcox Rd (43016-1265)
PHONE..................614 766-4896
EMP: 57 **EST:** 1996
SQ FT: 1,250
SALES (est): 4.66MM **Privately Held**
Web: www.praterengineering.com
SIC: 8711 Consulting engineer

(G-8095)
PRESIDIO INFRSTRCTURE SLTONS L
5025 Bradenton Ave Ste B (43017-3506)
PHONE..................614 381-1400
Tom Montes, *Brnch Mgr*
EMP: 50
SALES (corp-wide): 3.03B **Privately Held**
Web: www.presidio.com
SIC: 7373 Computer integrated systems design
HQ: Presidio Infrastructure Solutions Llc
6355 E Paris Ave Se
Caledonia MI 49316
616 871-1500

(G-8096)
PRIMARY CARE NURSING SERVICES
3140 Lilly Mar Ct (43017-5075)
PHONE..................614 764-0960
Susan M Sharpe, *Pr*
EMP: 50 **EST:** 1985
SALES (est): 1.9MM **Privately Held**
Web: www.primarycarenursing.com
SIC: 8082 8011 Visiting nurse service; Offices and clinics of medical doctors

(G-8097)
PROFESSIONAL REVIEW NETWRK INC
5126 Blazer Pkwy (43017-1339)
P.O. Box 675 (43348-0675)
PHONE..................614 791-2700
Darlene Almand, *Pr*
EMP: 40 **EST:** 1989
SALES (est): 1.69MM **Privately Held**
SIC: 8742 Hospital and health services consultant

(G-8098)
PROGRESSIVE MEDICAL INTL INC
Also Called: Progressive Medical Intl
5000 Tuttle Crossing Blvd (43016-1534)
PHONE..................760 957-5500
Marc Lawrence, *Pr*
▲ **EMP:** 36 **EST:** 1992
SQ FT: 35,000
SALES (est): 1.41MM **Privately Held**
SIC: 5047 Medical equipment and supplies

(G-8099)
PROLINK STAFFING SERVICES LLC
4700 Lakehurst Ct Ste 200 (43016-2230)
PHONE..................614 405-9810
EMP: 805
SALES (corp-wide): 45.57MM **Privately Held**
Web: www.prolinkworks.com
SIC: 7363 Temporary help service
PA: Prolink Staffing Services, Llc
4600 Montgomery Rd # 300
Cincinnati OH 45212
513 489-5300

(G-8100)
PSI SUPPLY CHAIN SOLUTIONS LLC
5050 Bradenton Ave (43017-3520)
P.O. Box 130 (43017-0130)
PHONE..................614 389-4717
EMP: 370 **EST:** 2010
SALES (est): 436.65K
SALES (corp-wide): 302.11MM **Privately Held**
Web: www.chroniclecm.com
SIC: 8742 Hospital and health services consultant
HQ: Pharmacy Systems, Inc.
5050 Bradenton Ave
Dublin OH
614 766-0101

(G-8101)
QUALITY SUPPLY CHAIN CO-OP INC
1 Dave Thomas Blvd (43017-5452)
PHONE..................614 764-3124
EMP: 40 **EST:** 2010
SALES (est): 6.29MM **Privately Held**
Web: www.wqscc.com
SIC: 8741 Business management

(G-8102)
QUANTUM HEALTH INC
5240 Blazer Pkwy (43017-3309)
PHONE..................800 257-2038
Kara J Trott, *CEO*
Randy Gebhardt, *
Peter Bridges, *CCO**
Wayne R Lorgus, *
Jim Stark, *
EMP: 1300 **EST:** 1999
SQ FT: 25,000
SALES (est): 562.16K **Privately Held**
Web: www.quantum-health.com
SIC: 8082 Home health care services

(G-8103)
QUEST SOFTWARE INC
Aeilita Div
6500 Emerald Pkwy Ste 400 (43016-6234)
PHONE..................614 336-9223
Ratmir Timashev, *Mgr*
EMP: 46
SALES (corp-wide): 647.68MM **Privately Held**
Web: www.quest.com
SIC: 7372 Prepackaged software
PA: Quest Software Inc.
20 Enterprise Ste 100
Aliso Viejo CA 92656
949 754-8000

(G-8104)
QWEST CORPORATION
Also Called: Qwest
4650 Lakehurst Ct (43016-3254)
PHONE..................614 793-9258
Tom Wynne, *Brnch Mgr*
EMP: 65
SALES (corp-wide): 14.56MM **Publicly Held**
Web: www.centurylink.com
SIC: 4813 Telephone communication, except radio
HQ: Qwest Corporation
100 Centurylink Dr
Monroe LA 71203
318 388-9000

(G-8105)
RANDALL MORTGAGE SERVICES (PA)
655 Metro Pl S Ste 600 (43017-3394)
PHONE..................614 336-7948
Robert R Shepherd, *Pr*
Thomas A Clarkson, *
Eric D Anderson, *
EMP: 123 **EST:** 1991
SALES (est): 18.18MM **Privately Held**
SIC: 6163 Mortgage brokers arranging for loans, using money of others

(G-8106)
REAL PROPERTY MANAGEMENT INC (PA)
5550 Blazer Pkwy Ste 175 (43017-3495)
PHONE..................614 766-6500
Matt Steele, *Pr*
EMP: 27 **EST:** 1979
SQ FT: 10,000
SALES (est): 5.77MM
SALES (corp-wide): 5.77MM **Privately Held**
Web: www.rpmanagement.com
SIC: 6531 8721 Real estate managers; Billing and bookkeeping service

(G-8107)
RENAISSANCETECH
5880 Venture Dr Ste B (43017-6141)
PHONE..................419 569-3999
Benjamin Karam, *Pr*
EMP: 30 **EST:** 2015
SALES (est): 1.37MM **Privately Held**
Web: www.renaissancetech.com
SIC: 7371 Computer software development

(G-8108)
RETAIL SERVICE SYSTEMS INC
Also Called: Midwest Furniture & Mat Outl
6221 Riverside Dr Ste 2n (43017-5070)
PHONE..................614 203-6126
Carlton Scott Andrew, *Pr*
EMP: 75 **EST:** 2013
SALES (est): 19.51MM **Privately Held**
Web: www.retailservicesystems.com
SIC: 5021 Furniture

(G-8109)
REVEL IT INC
4900 Blazer Pkwy (43017-3305)
PHONE..................614 336-1122
Randy Dean, *Pr*
EMP: 64 **EST:** 2019
SALES (est): 7.19MM **Privately Held**
Web: www.revelit.com
SIC: 7379 Computer related consulting services

(G-8110)
ROTO GROUP LLC (PA)
Also Called: Roto
7001 Discovery Blvd Fl 2 (43017-3261)
PHONE..................614 760-8690
Joseph Wisne, *Pr*
Allen Boerger, *
Neil Baker, *
Bridgette Mariea, *
Steve Langsdorf, *
EMP: 76 **EST:** 2004
SQ FT: 60,000
SALES (est): 14.96MM
SALES (corp-wide): 14.96MM **Privately Held**
Web: www.roto.com
SIC: 7999 Exhibition operation

(G-8111)
RUSCILLI CONSTRUCTION CO INC (PA)
5815 Wall St Ste 1 (43017-3265)
PHONE..................614 876-9484
L Jack Ruscilli, *Ch Bd*
Louis V Ruscilli, *
Robert A Ruscilli Junior, *Pr*
EMP: 80 **EST:** 1945
SQ FT: 35,000
SALES (est): 77.07MM
SALES (corp-wide): 77.07MM **Privately Held**
Web: www.ruscilli.com
SIC: 1541 8741 1542 Industrial buildings, new construction, nec; Construction management; Commercial and office building, new construction

(G-8112)
SANCTUARY AT TUTTLE CROSSING
4880 Tuttle Rd Ofc (43017-7566)
PHONE..................614 408-0182
Robert Banasik, *Pr*
EMP: 68 **EST:** 1998
SALES (est): 6.06MM **Privately Held**
Web: www.ahfohio.com

Dublin - Franklin County (G-8113) — GEOGRAPHIC SECTION

SIC: 8051 Skilled nursing care facilities

(G-8113)
SARNOVA INC (HQ)
5000 Tuttle Crossing Blvd (43016-1534)
P.O. Box 8023 (43016-2023)
PHONE..............................614 760-5000
Dan Connors, *Ch*
Mark Dougherty, *
EMP: 80 EST: 2008
SALES (est): 340.05MM
SALES (corp-wide): 6.03B **Privately Held**
Web: www.sarnova.com
SIC: 5999 5047 Medical apparatus and supplies; Medical equipment and supplies
PA: Investor Ab
   Arsenalsgatan 8c
   Stockholm 111 4
   86142000

(G-8114)
SARNOVA HOLDINGS INC
5000 Tuttle Crossing Blvd (43016-1534)
PHONE..............................614 760-5000
Jeff Prestel, *CEO*
EMP: 495 EST: 2016
SALES (corp-wide): 6.03B **Privately Held**
Web: www.sarnova.com
SIC: 6719 5047 Investment holding companies, except banks; Medical equipment and supplies
HQ: Patricia Industries Ab
   Arsenalsgatan 8c
   Stockholm

(G-8115)
SB HOTEL LLC (PA)
Also Called: Ramada Inn
5775 Perimeter Dr Ste 290 (43017-3224)
PHONE..............................614 793-2244
Kenneth J Castrop, *Managing Member*
William W Wolfe, *
EMP: 50 EST: 1971
SQ FT: 100,000
SALES (est): 2.19MM
SALES (corp-wide): 2.19MM **Privately Held**
Web: www.wyndhamhotels.com
SIC: 7011 5812 5813 Hotels and motels; Family restaurants; Cocktail lounge

(G-8116)
SCANA ENERGY MARKETING LLC
6100 Emerald Pkwy (43016)
P.O. Box 12427 (29211)
PHONE..............................803 217-1322
George Bullwinkel, *Pr*
Robert Edwards, *
EMP: 92 EST: 1977
SQ FT: 5,300
SALES (est): 46.9MM **Privately Held**
Web: www.igsenergymarketing.com
SIC: 4924 4911 Natural gas distribution; Electric services
PA: Interstate Gas Supply, Llc
   6100 Emerald Pkwy
   Dublin OH 43016

(G-8117)
SEDGWICK CMS HOLDINGS INC
6377 Emerald Pkwy (43016-3272)
PHONE..............................800 825-6755
Robert Bossart, *Brnch Mgr*
EMP: 357
Web: www.sedgwick.com
SIC: 6411 Insurance agents, nec
PA: Sedgwick Cms Holdings, Inc.
   1100 Rdgway Loop Rd Ste 2
   Memphis TN 38120

(G-8118)
SHEPHERD EXCAVATING INC
6295 Cosgray Rd (43016-8737)
PHONE..............................614 889-1115
Jerry Semon, *Pr*
Robert Toombs, *
EMP: 47 EST: 1972
SQ FT: 4,000
SALES (est): 9.91MM **Privately Held**
Web: www.shepherdexcavating.com
SIC: 1771 Foundation and footing contractor

(G-8119)
SIGNATURE INC (PA)
7689 Birch Ln (43016-7735)
P.O. Box 3128 (43016-0061)
PHONE..............................614 766-5101
Steve Wolever, *Pr*
Jeffrey Scholes, *COO*
EMP: 40 EST: 1985
SALES (est): 8.36MM **Privately Held**
Web: www.signatureworldwide.com
SIC: 8741 Management services

(G-8120)
SIGNATURE INC
Also Called: Signature Worldwide
7689 Birch Ln (43016-7735)
P.O. Box 3128 (43016-0061)
PHONE..............................614 766-5101
Amy White, *Pr*
EMP: 59
Web: www.signatureworldwide.com
SIC: 8742 Marketing consulting services
PA: Signature, Inc.
   7689 Birch Ln
   Dublin OH 43016

(G-8121)
SIMON PROPERTY GROUP
Also Called: Tuttle Crossing Associates
5043 Tuttle Crossing Blvd Ste 200 (43016)
PHONE..............................614 798-3015
Peter Cooper, *Genl Mgr*
EMP: 49 EST: 1995
SALES (est): 2.4MM **Privately Held**
Web: www.simon.com
SIC: 6512 Shopping center, property operation only

(G-8122)
SMILEY SAMUEL E DDS PC
Also Called: Seikel, Daniel D DDS
5156 Blazer Pkwy Ste 200 (43017-7318)
PHONE..............................614 889-0726
Samuel E Smiley D.d.s., *Pr*
EMP: 27 EST: 1985
SALES (est): 670.14K **Privately Held**
Web: www.smileydentalgroup.com
SIC: 8021 Dental clinic

(G-8123)
SOCIUS1 LLC
Also Called: Socius
5747 Perimeter Dr Ste 200 (43017-3258)
PHONE..............................614 280-9880
EMP: 60
Web: www.velosio.com
SIC: 8742 Business management consultant

(G-8124)
STANLEY STEEMER INTL INC (PA)
Also Called: Stanley Steemer Carpet Cleaner
5800 Innovation Dr (43016-3271)
P.O. Box 8004 (43016-2004)
PHONE..............................614 764-2007
Wesley C Bates, *CEO*
Justin Bates, *
Eric Smith, *
Philip P Ryser, *
Mark Bunner C.p.a., *VP*
▲ EMP: 250 EST: 1947
SQ FT: 55,000
SALES (est): 263.72MM
SALES (corp-wide): 263.72MM **Privately Held**
Web: www.stanleysteemer.com
SIC: 7217 3635 6794 5713 Carpet and furniture cleaning on location; Household vacuum cleaners; Franchises, selling or licensing; Carpets

(G-8125)
STERLING COMMERCE (AMERICA) LLC
Also Called: Sterling Commerce Group
4600 Lakehurst Ct (43016-2248)
P.O. Box 8000 (43016-2000)
PHONE..............................614 793-7000
EMP: 650
SIC: 7373 Systems software development services

(G-8126)
STERLING COMMERCE LLC
4600 Lakehurst Ct (43016-2248)
PHONE..............................614 798-2192
EMP: 2500
SIC: 7372 Business oriented computer software

(G-8127)
STG CARTAGE LLC
Also Called: Xpo Logistics Cartage, LLC
5165 Emerald Pkwy Ste 300 (43017-1097)
PHONE..............................614 923-1400
Paul Svindland, *CEO*
EMP: 2000 EST: 1998
SALES (est): 88.94MM
SALES (corp-wide): 3.63B **Privately Held**
SIC: 4731 Freight forwarding
HQ: Stg Intermodal, Inc.
   5165 Emerald Pkwy Ste 300
   Dublin OH 43017
   614 923-1400

(G-8128)
STG CARTAGE LLC
5165 Emerald Pkwy Ste 300 (43017-1097)
PHONE..............................614 923-1400
EMP: 30
SALES (est): 10.17MM **Privately Held**
Web: www.stgusa.com
SIC: 4731 Freight forwarding

(G-8129)
STG INTERMODAL INC (DH)
5165 Emerald Pkwy Ste 300 (43017-1097)
PHONE..............................614 923-1400
Paul Svindland, *CEO*
Antonino Arlotta, *
John J Hardig, *
◆ EMP: 80 EST: 1974
SALES (est): 2B
SALES (corp-wide): 3.63B **Privately Held**
Web: www.stgusa.com
SIC: 4731 Freight transportation arrangement
HQ: Stg Logistics, Inc.
   951 Thorndale Ave
   Bensenville IL 60106
   630 581-0519

(G-8130)
STG INTERMODAL SOLUTIONS INC (DH)
Also Called: STG Intermodal Solutions
5165 Emerald Pkwy (43017-1092)
PHONE..............................614 923-1400
Antonino Arlotta, *VP*
◆ EMP: 109 EST: 1984
SQ FT: 107,000
SALES (est): 6.89K
SALES (corp-wide): 3.63B **Privately Held**
Web: www.stgusa.com
SIC: 4731 Agents, shipping
HQ: Stg Intermodal, Inc.
   5165 Emerald Pkwy Ste 300
   Dublin OH 43017
   614 923-1400

(G-8131)
STG STACKTRAIN LLC (DH)
Also Called: Pacer Stacktrain
5165 Emerald Pkwy Ste 300 (43017-1097)
PHONE..............................614 923-1400
Daniel W Avramovich, *Pr*
Antinino Arlotta, *Treas*
◆ EMP: 103 EST: 2009
SALES (est): 100.68MM
SALES (corp-wide): 3.63B **Privately Held**
SIC: 4731 Freight transportation arrangement
HQ: Stg Intermodal, Inc.
   5165 Emerald Pkwy Ste 300
   Dublin OH 43017
   614 923-1400

(G-8132)
STRATEGIC SYSTEMS INC
475 Metro Pl S Ste 450 (43017-3532)
PHONE..............................614 717-4774
Jyothsna Vadada, *CEO*
Sankar Mangapuram, *
EMP: 116 EST: 2004
SALES (est): 14.73MM **Privately Held**
Web: www.strsi.com
SIC: 7379 Online services technology consultants

(G-8133)
STRIVE ENTERPRISES INC (PA) ○
6555 Longshore St Ste 220 (43017-2944)
PHONE..............................614 593-2840
Matt Cole, *CEO*
Anson Frericks, *Pr*
Ben Pham, *COO*
Rachel Paulose, *Sec*
James Mcquade Ctrl, *Prin*
EMP: 40 EST: 2022
SALES (est): 1.74MM
SALES (corp-wide): 1.74MM **Privately Held**
Web: www.strivefunds.com
SIC: 7389 Financial services

(G-8134)
SUMMIT NW CORPORATION (DH)
Also Called: Summit NW
5165 Emerald Pkwy (43017-1097)
PHONE..............................503 255-3826
Robert C Hodson, *Pr*
Matthew Hodson, *
EMP: 60 EST: 1999
SALES (est): 26.69MM
SALES (corp-wide): 3.63B **Privately Held**
Web: www.stgusa.com
SIC: 4731 4225 4212 Customhouse brokers; General warehousing and storage; Liquid haulage, local
HQ: Stg Logistics, Inc.
   951 Thorndale Ave
   Bensenville IL 60106
   630 581-0519

(G-8135)
SUNRISE SENIOR LIVING LLC
Also Called: Sunrise of Dublin
4175 Stoneridge Ln (43017-2080)
PHONE..............................614 718-2062
EMP: 40
SALES (corp-wide): 2.92B **Privately Held**
Web: www.sunriseseniorliving.com

GEOGRAPHIC SECTION

Dublin - Franklin County (G-8157)

SIC: 8051 Skilled nursing care facilities
HQ: Sunrise Senior Living, Llc
7902 Westpark Dr
Mc Lean VA 22102

(G-8136)
SUTPHEN CORPORATION (PA)
Also Called: Sutphen
6450 Eiterman Rd (43016-8711)
P.O. Box 158 (43002-0158)
PHONE.................................800 726-7030
Drew Sutphen, *Pr*
Thomas C Sutphen, *
Julie S Phelps, *
Robert M Sutphen, *Stockholder*
Greg Mallon, *
▼ EMP: 180 EST: 1962
SQ FT: 90,000
SALES (est): 173.19MM
SALES (corp-wide): 173.19MM **Privately Held**
Web: www.sutphen.com
SIC: 3711 5087 Fire department vehicles (motor vehicles), assembly of; Firefighting equipment

(G-8137)
SYGMA NETWORK INC (HQ)
Also Called: Sygma
5550 Blazer Pkwy Ste 300 (43017)
P.O. Box 7327 (43017)
PHONE.................................614 734-2500
Thomas Russell, *CEO*
Steven Deasey, *
Bob Kotula, *Finance & Operations*
Michael Bain, *
▲ EMP: 150 EST: 1969
SQ FT: 30,000
SALES (est): 1.87B
SALES (corp-wide): 76.32B **Publicly Held**
Web: www.sygmanetwork.com
SIC: 5141 Food brokers
PA: Sysco Corporation
1390 Enclave Pkwy
Houston TX 77077
281 584-1390

(G-8138)
T & R PROPERTIES (PA)
Also Called: T & R Property Management
3895 Stoneridge Ln (43017-2152)
PHONE.................................614 923-4000
P Ronald Sabatino, *Pr*
Tamra L Potts, *
Cathy Saporito, *Prin*
EMP: 30 EST: 1983
SQ FT: 1,200
SALES (est): 22.09MM
SALES (corp-wide): 22.09MM **Privately Held**
Web: www.trprop.com
SIC: 6531 Real estate managers

(G-8139)
T-CETRA LLC
7240 Muirfield Dr Ste 200 (43017-2902)
PHONE.................................877 956-2359
EMP: 202 EST: 2007
SALES (est): 14.96MM **Privately Held**
Web: www.tcetra.co
SIC: 7371 Computer software development

(G-8140)
TARTAN FIELDS GOLF CLUB LTD
8070 Tartan Fields Dr (43017-8780)
PHONE.................................614 792-0900
Britney Shafley, *Rlshp*
Britney Shafley, *Member Relations*
Jim Russell Membership, *Dir*
Marcus Dekeyser, *Head Golf Professional*
EMP: 67 EST: 1996

SALES (est): 2.47MM **Privately Held**
Web: www.tartanfields.com
SIC: 7997 5941 5813 5812 Golf club, membership; Sporting goods and bicycle shops; Drinking places; Eating places

(G-8141)
THORSON BAKER & ASSOC INC
Also Called: THORSON BAKER & ASSOC, INC
525 Metro Pl N Ste 440 (43017-5356)
PHONE.................................614 389-3144
Mike Thorson, *Pt*
EMP: 32
Web: www.thorsonbaker.com
SIC: 8711 Consulting engineer
PA: Baker Thorson & Associates Inc
3030 W Streetsboro Rd
Richfield OH 44286

(G-8142)
TOOGANN TECHNOLOGIES LLC
Also Called: Racar Engineering
555 Metro Pl N Ste 500 (43017-1303)
PHONE.................................614 973-9266
EMP: 80 EST: 2015
SALES (est): 4.94MM **Privately Held**
Web: www.toogann.com
SIC: 8711 Engineering services

(G-8143)
TRI-ANIM HEALTH SERVICES INC (DH)
5000 Tuttle Crossing Blvd (43016-1534)
P.O. Box 8023 (43016-2023)
PHONE.................................614 760-5000
Jeff Prestel, *Pr*
Dale Clendon, *
Dan L Pister, *
Eddie Avanessians, *
◆ EMP: 103 EST: 1975
SQ FT: 38,600
SALES (est): 91.07MM
SALES (corp-wide): 6.03B **Privately Held**
Web: www.tri-anim.com
SIC: 5047 Medical equipment and supplies
HQ: Sarnova, Inc.
5000 Tuttle Crossing Blvd
Dublin OH 43016

(G-8144)
TUTTLE INN DEVELOPERS LLC
Also Called: Holiday Inn
5500 Tuttle Crossing Blvd (43016-1247)
PHONE.................................614 793-5500
Tim Dehnart, *Mgr*
EMP: 29
Web: www.holidayinn.com
SIC: 7011 Hotels and motels
PA: Tuttle Inn Developers, Llc
9904 N By Northeast Blvd
Fishers IN 46037

(G-8145)
TYSON GROUP
5650 Blazer Pkwy (43017-3562)
PHONE.................................800 659-1080
Lisa Tyson, *Prin*
EMP: 33 EST: 2018
SALES (est): 304.24K **Privately Held**
Web: www.tysongroup.com
SIC: 6531 Real estate brokers and agents

(G-8146)
UNIVENTURE INC (PA)
Also Called: Univenture CD Packg & Systems
4266 Tuller Rd (43017-5007)
PHONE.................................937 645-4600
Ross O Youngs, *CEO*
Michele Cole, *
Larry George, *

▲ EMP: 95 EST: 1996
SQ FT: 100,000
SALES (est): 24.43MM **Privately Held**
Web: www.univenture.com
SIC: 7389 7336 Packaging and labeling services; Package design

(G-8147)
VARGO LLC (PA)
Also Called: Vargo Whse Exction Systems LLC
5555 Frantz Rd (43017-1880)
PHONE.................................614 876-1163
J Michael Vargo, *CEO*
EMP: 27 EST: 1976
SALES (est): 14.15MM
SALES (corp-wide): 14.15MM **Privately Held**
Web: www.vargosolutions.com
SIC: 5084 Conveyor systems

(G-8148)
VARGO SOLUTIONS INC
Also Called: Vargo Solutions
5555 Frantz Rd (43017)
PHONE.................................614 876-1163
Bart Cera, *CEO*
Carlos Ysasi, *
Gary Condit, *
EMP: 92 EST: 2021
SQ FT: 16,000
SALES (est): 13.89MM **Privately Held**
Web: www.vargosolutions.com
SIC: 5084 Conveyor systems

(G-8149)
VARO ENGINEERS INC (HQ)
Also Called: Varo Engineers A Salas Obrien
2751 Tuller Pkwy (43017-2317)
PHONE.................................614 459-0424
EMP: 65 EST: 1948
SALES (est): 10.47MM
SALES (corp-wide): 110.61MM **Privately Held**
Web: www.salasobrien.com
SIC: 8711 Consulting engineer
PA: Salas O'brien Engineers, Inc.
305 S 11th St
San Jose CA 95112
408 282-1500

(G-8150)
VELOSIO LLC (PA)
5747 Perimeter Dr Ste 200 (43017-3258)
PHONE.................................614 280-9880
Jeff Geisler, *CEO*
Jim Bowman, *CRO*
Joseph Longo, *COO*
EMP: 30 EST: 2017
SALES (est): 25.67MM
SALES (corp-wide): 25.67MM **Privately Held**
Web: www.velosio.com
SIC: 8748 Business consulting, nec

(G-8151)
VERDANTAS LLC (PA)
6397 Emerald Pkwy Ste 200 (43016-2231)
PHONE.................................614 793-8777
Jesse Kropelnicki, *CEO*
Pat Sheridan, *
Christopher Lee, *
John Hull, *
David Richards, *
EMP: 125 EST: 1987
SQ FT: 9,180
SALES (est): 172.75MM
SALES (corp-wide): 172.75MM **Privately Held**
Web: www.hullinc.com

SIC: 8711 8748 Consulting engineer; Environmental consultant

(G-8152)
VIAQUEST LLC (PA)
525 Metro Pl N Ste 300 (43017-5320)
PHONE.................................614 889-5837
Richard Johnson, *Pr*
Janet Pell, *
EMP: 29 EST: 1999
SALES (est): 46.33MM
SALES (corp-wide): 46.33MM **Privately Held**
Web: www.viaquestinc.com
SIC: 8741 Business management

(G-8153)
VIAQUEST BEHAVIORAL HEALTH LLC (HQ)
Also Called: Summit Quest Academy
525 Metro Pl N Ste 450 (43017-5321)
PHONE.................................614 339-0868
Richard Johnson, *Pr*
EMP: 33 EST: 1995
SQ FT: 1,500
SALES (est): 25.29MM
SALES (corp-wide): 46.33MM **Privately Held**
Web: www.viaquestinc.com
SIC: 8082 Home health care services
PA: Viaquest, Llc
525 Metro Pl N Ste 300
Dublin OH 43017
614 889-5837

(G-8154)
VIAQUEST RESIDENTIAL SVCS LLC (PA)
Also Called: Supportcare Ohio
525 Metro Pl N Ste 350 (43017-5451)
PHONE.................................614 889-5837
Richard Johnson, *Pr*
EMP: 35 EST: 1993
SALES (est): 6.08MM **Privately Held**
Web: www.viaquestinc.com
SIC: 8082 Home health care services

(G-8155)
VIBO CONSTRUCTION INC
4140 Tuller Rd Ste 112 (43017-5013)
PHONE.................................614 210-6780
Tania Prespia, *Pr*
EMP: 35 EST: 2011
SQ FT: 2,500
SALES (est): 2.68MM **Privately Held**
SIC: 1521 Single-family housing construction

(G-8156)
VITAS HEALTHCARE CORP MIDWEST
655 Metro Pl S (43017-3380)
PHONE.................................614 822-2700
EMP: 200
SALES (corp-wide): 2.26B **Publicly Held**
SIC: 8052 Personal care facility
HQ: Vitas Healthcare Corporation Midwest
8527 Bluejacket St
Overland Park KS 66214
913 722-1631

(G-8157)
VRABLE HEALTHCARE INC
Also Called: Grand, The
4500 John Shields Pkwy (43017-2669)
PHONE.................................614 889-8585
EMP: 46
Web: www.grandofdublin.com
SIC: 8051 Convalescent home with continuous nursing care
PA: Vrable Healthcare, Inc.

Dublin - Franklin County (G-8158)

3248 Henderson Rd
Columbus OH 43220

(G-8158)
W W WILLIAMS COMPANY LLC (DH)
400 Metro Pl N (43017-3577)
PHONE.................614 228-5000
John Simmons, *CEO*
Andy Gasser, *
EMP: 60 **EST:** 2016
SALES (est): 522.02MM
SALES (corp-wide): 1.47B **Privately Held**
Web: www.wwwilliams.com
SIC: 3694 7538 7537 Distributors, motor vehicle engine; Diesel engine repair: automotive; Automotive transmission repair shops
HQ: Power Acquisition Llc
5025 Bradenton Ave # 130
Dublin OH 43017
614 228-5000

(G-8159)
WA BUTLER COMPANY (DH)
Also Called: Covetrus North America
400 Metro Pl N Ste 100 (43017-3340)
P.O. Box 7153 (43017-0753)
PHONE.................614 761-9095
Leo Mcneil, *CFO*
EMP: 33 **EST:** 2009
SALES (est): 160.12MM
SALES (corp-wide): 4.58B **Privately Held**
SIC: 5149 5047 5122 Pet foods; Veterinarians' equipment and supplies; Biologicals and allied products
HQ: Covetrus Animal Health Holdings Limited
College Mains Road
Dumfries DG2 0
138 726-2626

(G-8160)
WD PARTNERS INC (PA)
Also Called: Cjm Technologies
7007 Discovery Blvd (43017-3218)
PHONE.................614 634-7000
EMP: 400 **EST:** 1968
SALES (est): 48.6MM
SALES (corp-wide): 48.6MM **Privately Held**
Web: www.wdpartners.com
SIC: 8712 Architectural services

(G-8161)
WEASTEC INCORPORATED
6195 Enterprise Ct (43016-3293)
PHONE.................614 734-9645
Craig Miley, *Brnch Mgr*
EMP: 42
Web: www.weastec.com
SIC: 5531 8711 Automotive parts; Engineering services
HQ: Weastec, Incorporated
1600 N High St
Hillsboro OH 45133
937 393-6800

(G-8162)
WELTMAN WEINBERG & REIS CO LPA
5000 Bradenton Ave Ste 100 (43017-3574)
PHONE.................614 801-2600
Allen Reis, *Brnch Mgr*
EMP: 340
SALES (corp-wide): 68.52MM **Privately Held**
Web: www.weltman.com
SIC: 8111 General practice law office
PA: Weltman, Weinberg & Reis Co., L.P.A.
965 Keynote Cir
Independence OH 44131

216 685-1000

(G-8163)
WENDYS COMPANY (PA)
Also Called: Wendy's
1 Dave Thomas Blvd (43017)
PHONE.................614 764-3100
Kirk Tanner, *CEO*
Nelson Peltz, *Non-Executive Chairman of the Board*
Peter W May, *Non-Executive Vice Chairman of the Board*
Gunther Plosch, *CFO*
Coley O'brien, *CPO*
◆ **EMP:** 475 **EST:** 1929
SQ FT: 324,025
SALES (est): 2.18B
SALES (corp-wide): 2.18B **Publicly Held**
Web: www.wendys.com
SIC: 5812 6794 Fast-food restaurant, chain; Franchises, selling or licensing

(G-8164)
WENDYS RESTAURANTS LLC (HQ)
Also Called: Wendy's
1 Dave Thomas Blvd (43017-5452)
PHONE.................614 764-3100
Emil J Brolick, *Pr*
Emil Brolick, *
Todd Pengor, *
Steven B Graham, *Chief Accounting Officer*
EMP: 31 **EST:** 2008
SQ FT: 249,025
SALES (est): 521.06MM
SALES (corp-wide): 2.18B **Publicly Held**
Web: www.wendys.com
SIC: 5812 6794 Fast-food restaurant, chain; Franchises, selling or licensing
PA: The Wendy's Company
1 Dave Thomas Blvd
Dublin OH 43017
614 764-3100

(G-8165)
WHITEBOARD MARKETING
5950 Venture Dr Ste D (43017-2256)
PHONE.................614 562-1912
Sean White, *CEO*
EMP: 35 **EST:** 2016
SALES (est): 1.24MM **Privately Held**
Web: www.whiteboard-mktg.com
SIC: 8742 Marketing consulting services

(G-8166)
XPO CARTAGE INC
5165 Emerald Pkwy Ste 300 (43017-1097)
PHONE.................614 766-6111
EMP: 50 **EST:** 2015
SALES (est): 12.48MM **Privately Held**
Web: www.xpo.com
SIC: 4731 Freight transportation arrangement

(G-8167)
ZAPS TECHNOCRATS INC
545 Metro Pl S Ste 100 (43017-5353)
PHONE.................614 664-3199
Zafar Abid, *CEO*
Zerqa Abid, *
Mohammad Ahmed, *
EMP: 75 **EST:** 2005
SALES (est): 2.43MM **Privately Held**
Web: www.zapstechnocrats.com
SIC: 7371 7379 Computer software development and applications; Computer related consulting services

Dundee
Tuscarawas County

(G-8168)
CBTK GROUP INC
Also Called: Springhill Construction
17201 Dover Rd (44624-9445)
PHONE.................330 359-9111
Craig Cox, *CEO*
EMP: 35 **EST:** 2012
SALES (est): 2.29MM **Privately Held**
SIC: 1521 1522 Single-family housing construction; Residential construction, nec

East Canton
Stark County

(G-8169)
KNIGHT MATERIAL TECH LLC (PA)
5385 Orchardview Dr Se (44730-9568)
P.O. Box 30070 (44730-0070)
PHONE.................330 488-1651
Kevin Brooks, *Pr*
◆ **EMP:** 72 **EST:** 2001
SALES (est): 30.8MM
SALES (corp-wide): 30.8MM **Privately Held**
Web: www.knightmaterials.com
SIC: 2911 5172 5169 4922 Petroleum refining; Petroleum products, nec; Chemicals and allied products, nec; Natural gas transmission

(G-8170)
MID-EAST TRUCK & TRACTOR SERVICE INC
831 Nassau St W (44730-1156)
P.O. Box 30124 (44730-0124)
PHONE.................330 488-0398
EMP: 100 **EST:** 1973
SALES (est): 13.76MM **Privately Held**
Web: www.mideasttrucking.com
SIC: 4212 Heavy machinery transport, local

East Liberty
Logan County

(G-8171)
CLARK TRUCKING INC
11590 Township Road 157 (43319-8500)
PHONE.................937 642-0335
▲ **EMP:** 151
SIC: 4214 4213 Local trucking with storage; Contract haulers

(G-8172)
HONDA LOGISTICS NORTH AMER INC (DH)
11590 Township Road 298 (43319-9487)
PHONE.................937 642-0335
Tamaki Hashimoto, *Pr*
EMP: 1338 **EST:** 2013
SALES (est): 1.09B **Privately Held**
Web: www.hlna.com
SIC: 4226 Special warehousing and storage, nec
HQ: Honda Logistics Inc.
6, Ichibancho
Chiyoda-Ku TKY 102-0

(G-8173)
MIDWEST EXPRESS INC (DH)
11590 Township Road 298 (43319-9450)
PHONE.................937 642-0335
Tamaki Hashimoto, *Pr*
Robert Overbaugh, *
Ed Allison, *
Tadao Endo, *
▲ **EMP:** 950 **EST:** 1986
SQ FT: 1,833,902
SALES (est): 153.56MM **Privately Held**
Web: www.midwestexpinc.com
SIC: 4226 Special warehousing and storage, nec
HQ: Honda Logistics North America, Inc.
11590 Township Road 298
East Liberty OH 43319
937 642-0335

(G-8174)
NX AUTMOTIVE LOGISTICS USA INC (DH)
13900 State Route 287 (43319)
PHONE.................937 642-8333
Tosaki Watanabe, *Pr*
Teizo Kanda, *VP*
Fumio Moriyama, *Pr*
Toshiaki Watanabe, *Pr*
Tomie Mori, *Ex VP*
EMP: 220 **EST:** 1989
SQ FT: 400,000
SALES (est): 39.3MM **Privately Held**
Web: www.nxal-usa.com
SIC: 4226 Special warehousing and storage, nec
HQ: Nippon Express U.S.A., Inc.
800 N Il Route 83
Wood Dale IL 60191
708 304-9800

(G-8175)
RELIANT MECHANICAL INC
Also Called: Building Management Services
3271 County Rd 154 (43319-9458)
P.O. Box 239 (43319-0239)
PHONE.................937 644-0074
EMP: 76 **EST:** 1986
SALES (est): 19.26MM **Privately Held**
Web: www.reliantmechanicalinc.com
SIC: 1711 Plumbing contractors

(G-8176)
TRANSPORTATION RESEARCH CENTER INC
10820 State Route 347 (43319)
P.O. Box B67 (43319)
PHONE.................937 666-2011
EMP: 550 **EST:** 1974
SALES (est): 55.7MM **Privately Held**
Web: www.trcpg.com
SIC: 8734 Automobile proving and testing ground

(G-8177)
VALEO NORTH AMERICA INC
12979 County Road 153 (43319-9431)
PHONE.................248 550-6054
EMP: 50
SALES (corp-wide): 2.67MM **Privately Held**
SIC: 7389 Automobile recovery service
HQ: Valeo North America, Inc.
150 Stephenson Hwy
Troy MI 48083

East Liverpool
Columbiana County

(G-8178)
AT&T TELEHOLDINGS INC
Also Called: SBC
214 W 5th St (43920-2834)
PHONE.................330 385-9967
Jim Protzman, *Mgr*
EMP: 152

GEOGRAPHIC SECTION

East Sparta - Stark County (G-8199)

SALES (corp-wide): 122.43B **Publicly Held**
Web: www.att.com
SIC: **4813** 8721 Telephone communication, except radio; Accounting, auditing, and bookkeeping
HQ: At&T Teleholdings, Inc.
30 S Wacker Dr Fl 34
Chicago IL 60606
800 288-2020

(G-8179)
CITY HOSPITAL ASSOCIATION
Also Called: EAST LIVERPOOL CITY HOSPITAL
425 W 5th St (43920-2405)
PHONE..................................330 385-7200
Kenneth J Cochran, *CEO*
Patrick Beaver, *
Pamela Smith, *
Kyle Johnson, *
EMP: 600 **EST:** 1896
SQ FT: 226,660
SALES (est): 82.37MM **Privately Held**
Web: www.elch.org
SIC: **8062** General medical and surgical hospitals

(G-8180)
COMPREHENSIVE BEHAVIORAL HLTH
Also Called: COMPREHENSIVE BEHAVIORAL HEALTH
321 W 5th St (43920-2849)
PHONE..................................330 385-8800
K Kaza, *Brnch Mgr*
EMP: 236
SALES (corp-wide): 9.68MM **Privately Held**
Web: www.compcareohio.com
SIC: **8093** Mental health clinic, outpatient
PA: Comprehensive Behavioral Health Associates, Inc.
104 Javit Ct Ste A
Youngstown OH 44515
330 797-4050

(G-8181)
EAST LIVERPOOL COUNTRY CLUB
2485 Park Way (43920-1426)
P.O. Box 16 (43920-5016)
PHONE..................................330 385-7197
Joseph H Smith, *Pr*
Gary Weekley, *VP*
Dale Meller, *Treas*
EMP: 27 **EST:** 1920
SQ FT: 10,000
SALES (est): 1.18MM **Privately Held**
Web: www.elcountryclub.org
SIC: **7997** Country club, membership

(G-8182)
EAST LVERPOOL CONVALESCENT CTR (PA)
Also Called: Orchards of East Liverpool
709 Armstrong Ln (43920-1245)
PHONE..................................330 382-0101
Geraldine Adkins, *Pr*
Steve Zdinak, *Admn*
EMP: 60 **EST:** 1966
SALES (est): 4.57MM
SALES (corp-wide): 4.57MM **Privately Held**
SIC: **8052** Intermediate care facilities

(G-8183)
HERITAGE VALLEY HEALTH SYS INC
48462 Bell School Rd Ste C (43920-9625)
PHONE..................................724 773-8209
Jay Zdunek, *Brnch Mgr*
EMP: 51

Web: www.heritagevalley.org
SIC: **8031** 8011 Offices and clinics of osteopathic physicians; Medical centers
HQ: Heritage Valley Health System, Inc.
1000 Dutch Ridge Rd
Beaver PA 15009
724 728-7000

(G-8184)
HERITAGE VALLEY HEALTH SYS INC
16280 Dresden Ave (43920-9024)
PHONE..................................724 773-1995
Robin Mediate, *Mgr*
EMP: 39
Web: www.heritagevalley.org
SIC: **8099** Childbirth preparation clinic
HQ: Heritage Valley Health System, Inc.
1000 Dutch Ridge Rd
Beaver PA 15009
724 728-7000

(G-8185)
HILL INTL TRCKS NA LLC (PA)
47866 Y & O Rd (43920-8724)
P.O. Box 2170 (43920-0170)
PHONE..................................330 386-6440
▼ **EMP:** 100 **EST:** 1890
SQ FT: 30,000
SALES (est): 51.73MM
SALES (corp-wide): 51.73MM **Privately Held**
Web: www.hillintltrucks.com
SIC: **5511** 5531 7538 Trucks, tractors, and trailers: new and used; Truck equipment and parts; General automotive repair shops

(G-8186)
MIKE PUSATERI EXCAVATING INC
16363 Saint Clair Ave (43920-9129)
P.O. Box 2136 (43920-0136)
PHONE..................................330 385-5221
Michael J Pusateri, *Pr*
James V Pusateri, *
Debra Smith, *
Michael Pusateri, *
EMP: 35 **EST:** 1960
SQ FT: 4,800
SALES (est): 5.26MM **Privately Held**
SIC: **1794** Excavation work

(G-8187)
NENTWICK CONVALESCENT HOME
500 Selfridge St (43920-1997)
PHONE..................................330 385-5001
Reverend John Nentwick, *Pr*
Alfred Tambellini, *
Mary Nentwick Tambellini, *
EMP: 47 **EST:** 1951
SQ FT: 28,000
SALES (est): 4.19MM **Privately Held**
Web: www.valleyoakscare.com
SIC: **8059** 8051 Convalescent home; Skilled nursing care facilities

(G-8188)
NORTH STAR CRITICAL CARE LLC
16356 State Route 267 (43920-3932)
P.O. Box 2011 (43920-0011)
PHONE..................................330 386-9110
Christine Lerussi, *Mgr*
Christine Lerussi, *Managing Member*
EMP: 28 **EST:** 2006
SALES (est): 2.18MM **Privately Held**
Web: www.northstar-critical-care.com
SIC: **4119** Ambulance service

(G-8189)
OHIO MINORITY MEDICAL
517 Broadway St Ste 500 (43920-3167)
PHONE..................................513 400-5011
Michael Ward Ii, *Pr*

EMP: 50 **EST:** 2018
SALES (est): 480.81K **Privately Held**
SIC: **8011** Offices and clinics of medical doctors

(G-8190)
P N P INC
Also Called: Calcutta Health Care Center
48444 Bell School Rd (43920-9646)
PHONE..................................330 386-1231
Joseph Cilone, *Pr*
EMP: 51 **EST:** 2011
SQ FT: 144
SALES (est): 8.98MM
SALES (corp-wide): 9.95MM **Privately Held**
Web: www.inspirahealthgroup.com
SIC: **8099** Health screening service
PA: Jcth Holdings, Inc.
48444 Bell School Rd
East Liverpool OH 43920
330 386-1231

(G-8191)
PRIME HLTHCARE FNDTON- E LVRPO (DH)
Also Called: River Valley Health Partners
425 W 5th St (43920-2405)
PHONE..................................330 385-7200
Prem Reddy, *Pr*
EMP: 78 **EST:** 2015
SALES (est): 49.26MM
SALES (corp-wide): 878.52MM **Privately Held**
Web: www.elch.org
SIC: **8742** Hospital and health services consultant
HQ: Prime Healthcare Services Inc
3480 E Guasti Rd
Ontario CA 91761

(G-8192)
RIVER VALLEY PHYSICIANS LLC
15655 State Route 170 Ste H (43920-9672)
P.O. Box 2396 (43920-0396)
PHONE..................................330 386-3610
Linda Crawford, *Mgr*
Sarah Stafford, *Admn*
EMP: 58 **EST:** 2013
SALES (est): 2.52MM **Privately Held**
Web: www.elch.org
SIC: **8099** Childbirth preparation clinic

(G-8193)
SH BELL COMPANY
2217 Michigan Ave (43920-3637)
PHONE..................................412 963-9910
Rusty Davis, *Mgr*
EMP: 39
SALES (corp-wide): 20.28MM **Privately Held**
Web: www.shbellco.com
SIC: **3479** 4226 4225 Aluminum coating of metal products; Special warehousing and storage, nec; General warehousing and storage
PA: S.H. Bell Company
644 Alpha Dr
Pittsburgh PA 15238
412 963-9910

(G-8194)
YOUNG MNS CHRSTN ASSN OF E LVR
Also Called: YMCA
500 E 4th St (43920-3404)
PHONE..................................330 385-0663
EMP: 79
SALES (corp-wide): 1.82MM **Privately Held**
Web: www.ymca.org

SIC: **8641** Youth organizations
PA: The Young Men's Christian Association Of East Liverpool Ohio
15655 State Route 170 A2
East Liverpool OH 43920
330 385-6400

East Palestine
Columbiana County

(G-8195)
ELDER SALES & SERVICE INC
Also Called: John Deere Authorized Dealer
49290 State Route 14 (44413-9725)
PHONE..................................330 426-2166
C H Mccutcheon, *Mgr*
EMP: 40
SALES (corp-wide): 10.93MM **Privately Held**
Web: www.deere.com
SIC: **5999** 5082 Farm equipment and supplies; Contractor's materials
PA: Elder Sales & Service, Inc.
4488 Grnville Sandy Lk Rd
Stoneboro PA 16153
724 376-3390

(G-8196)
JASAR RECYCLING INC
183 Edgeworth Ave (44413-1554)
P.O. Box 115 (44408-0115)
PHONE..................................864 233-5421
Ed Mcnee, *Pr*
▼ **EMP:** 70 **EST:** 1999
SQ FT: 240,000
SALES (est): 22.15MM **Privately Held**
Web: www.jasarrecycling.com
SIC: **4953** Recycling, waste materials

(G-8197)
NORFOLK SOUTHERN RAILWAY CO
248 N Market St (44413-2152)
PHONE..................................855 667-3655
EMP: 110
SALES (corp-wide): 12.16B **Publicly Held**
Web: www.norfolksouthern.com
SIC: **4111** Local railway passenger operation
HQ: Norfolk Southern Railway Company
650 W Peachtree St Nw
Atlanta GA 30308
855 667-3655

(G-8198)
PREMIUM UTILITY CONTRACTOR INC
50263 State Route 14 (44413-1027)
PHONE..................................951 313-0808
Alyssa Cowley, *Dir*
EMP: 40
SALES (est): 3.03MM **Privately Held**
SIC: **1623** Electric power line construction

East Sparta
Stark County

(G-8199)
WILLIAMS SUPER SERVICE INC
Also Called: Williams Toyota Lift
9462 Main Ave Se (44626-9583)
P.O. Box 359 (44626-0359)
PHONE..................................330 733-7750
Paul Williams, *Pr*
EMP: 27 **EST:** 1946
SQ FT: 6,000
SALES (est): 4.61MM **Privately Held**
Web: www.williamstoyotalift.com

SIC: **7699** 5084 Industrial machinery and equipment repair; Lift trucks and parts

Eastlake
Lake County

(G-8200)
BEVCORP LLC (HQ)
37200 Research Dr (44095-1869)
PHONE..............................440 954-3500
Michael Connelly, *Managing Member*
Donald Albert, *
Vicki Connelly, *
▲ **EMP:** 64 **EST:** 2002
SQ FT: 40,000
SALES (est): 41.55MM **Publicly Held**
Web: www.bevcorp.com
SIC: **5084** Industrial machinery and equipment
PA: John Bean Technologies Corporation
    70 W Madison St Ste 4400
    Chicago IL 60602

(G-8201)
DUNBAR MECHANICAL INC
1884 E 337th St (44095-5232)
PHONE..............................440 220-2000
EMP: 50
SALES (corp-wide): 51.9MM **Privately Held**
Web: www.dunbarinc.com
SIC: **1711** Mechanical contractor
PA: Dunbar Mechanical, Inc.
    2806 N Reynolds Rd
    Toledo OH 43615
    419 537-1900

(G-8202)
EASTLAKE LODGING LLC
Also Called: Radisson Eastlake
35000 Curtis Blvd (44095-4019)
PHONE..............................440 953-8000
Mike Madonna, *Genl Mgr*
EMP: 909 **EST:** 1997
SALES (est): 2.53MM
SALES (corp-wide): 364.48B **Publicly Held**
Web: www.eastlakelocksmiths.com
SIC: **7011** Resort hotel
HQ: Concord Hospitality Enterprises Company, Llc
    11410 Common Oaks Dr
    Raleigh NC 27614

(G-8203)
JOBBERS AUTOMOTIVE LLC
34600 Lakeland Blvd (44095-5240)
PHONE..............................216 524-2229
Bill Gryzenia, *Managing Member*
John Gemperline, *
EMP: 44 **EST:** 2003
SALES (est): 9.87MM
SALES (corp-wide): 24.35MM **Privately Held**
SIC: **5013** Automotive supplies and parts
PA: Dealershop, Inc.
    35980 Woodward Ave # 210
    Bloomfield Hills MI 48304
    248 599-1891

(G-8204)
JOHN F GALLAGHER PLUMBING CO
36360 Lakeland Blvd (44095-5314)
PHONE..............................440 946-4256
Michael J Gallagher, *Pr*
John Gallagher Ii, *Stockholder*
Patrick F Gallagher, *Stockholder**
Thomas E Gallagher, *Stockholder**
EMP: 52 **EST:** 1963

SQ FT: 10,000
SALES (est): 20.8MM **Privately Held**
Web: www.jfgallagherco.com
SIC: **1711** 1794 Mechanical contractor; Excavation work

(G-8205)
MILLENIUM CONTROL SYSTEMS LLC
34525 Melinz Pkwy Ste 205 (44095-4037)
PHONE..............................440 510-0050
Joseph Chuhran, *
Joel Conklin, *
Toni Chuhran, *
EMP: 37 **EST:** 1997
SQ FT: 12,000
SALES (est): 10.63MM **Privately Held**
Web: www.m-controls.com
SIC: **7373** Systems integration services

(G-8206)
NATIONAL TOOL LEASING INC
Also Called: Rental Tools Online
33801 Curtis Blvd Ste 114 (44095-4045)
P.O. Box 1905 (22313-1905)
PHONE..............................866 952-8665
Nathaniel Grant, *Mgr*
EMP: 28
SALES (corp-wide): 437.26K **Privately Held**
Web: www.rentaltoolsonline.com
SIC: **5251** 5084 7359 7353 Tools; Pneumatic tools and equipment; Tool rental; Heavy construction equipment rental
PA: National Tool Leasing Incorporated
    46122 Geneva Ter
    Sterling VA 20165
    866 952-8665

(G-8207)
PROFESSIONAL ELECTRIC PRODUCTS CO INC (DH)
Also Called: Pepco
33210 Lakeland Blvd (44095-5205)
P.O. Box 1570 (44096-1570)
PHONE..............................800 872-7000
EMP: 55 **EST:** 1968
SALES (est): 143.25MM
SALES (corp-wide): 12.53MM **Privately Held**
Web: www.pepconet.com
SIC: **5063** Electrical supplies, nec
HQ: Sonepar Usa Holdings, Inc.
    4400 Leeds Ave Ste 500
    Charleston SC 29405
    843 872-3500

(G-8208)
SERVICE MASTER CO
Also Called: Service Mstr By Disaster Recon
33851 Curtis Blvd Ste 202 (44095-4003)
PHONE..............................330 864-7300
EMP: 50 **EST:** 2014
SALES (est): 890.69K **Privately Held**
Web: www.servicemaster.com
SIC: **7349** Building maintenance services, nec

(G-8209)
SREE SAI HOTELS LLC
35000 Curtis Blvd (44095-4019)
PHONE..............................630 440-0765
Surender Pampati, *Admn*
EMP: 27 **EST:** 2015
SALES (est): 523.18K **Privately Held**
SIC: **7011** Hotels

Eaton
Preble County

(G-8210)
COLONIAL BANC CORP (PA)
110 W Main St (45320-1746)
P.O. Box 309 (45320-0309)
PHONE..............................937 456-5544
Joan Kreitzer, *Pr*
EMP: 36 **EST:** 1875
SALES (est): 5.64MM
SALES (corp-wide): 5.64MM **Privately Held**
SIC: **6021** 7291 National commercial banks; Tax return preparation services

(G-8211)
COUNTY OF PREBLE
116 E Main St Ste B (45320-1763)
PHONE..............................937 456-2085
Dawna Simpson, *Brnch Mgr*
EMP: 37
SALES (corp-wide): 35.63MM **Privately Held**
Web: www.prebco.org
SIC: **8322** Probation office
PA: County Of Preble
    101 E Main St
    Eaton OH 45320
    937 456-8143

(G-8212)
DAYTON OSTEOPATHIC HOSPITAL
Also Called: Dayton Sports Medicine Preble
450b Washington Jackson Rd (45320-7600)
PHONE..............................937 456-8300
EMP: 27
SALES (corp-wide): 2.46B **Privately Held**
Web: www.ketteringhealth.org
SIC: **8062** General medical and surgical hospitals
HQ: Dayton Osteopathic Hospital
    405 W Grand Ave
    Dayton OH 45405
    937 762-1629

(G-8213)
EATON GRDNS RHBLTTION HLTH CAR
Also Called: MAPLE GARDENS REHABILITATION A
515 S Maple St (45320-9413)
PHONE..............................937 456-5537
EMP: 85 **EST:** 2015
SALES (est): 6.31MM **Privately Held**
Web: www.maplehc.com
SIC: **8051** Convalescent home with continuous nursing care

(G-8214)
L & M PRODUCTS INC
1308 N Maple St (45320-1127)
PHONE..............................937 456-7141
Ben Hollinger, *Pr*
EMP: 31 **EST:** 1973
SALES (est): 1.15MM **Privately Held**
Web: www.lmproducts.org
SIC: **8331** Vocational rehabilitation agency

(G-8215)
MEDPRO LLC
251 W Lexington Rd (45320-9282)
PHONE..............................937 336-5586
Gina Hatmaker, *CEO*
Patrick Caylor, *
Ernest Hatmaker, *
EMP: 75 **EST:** 2014
SALES (est): 1.78MM **Privately Held**

SIC: **4119** Ambulance service

(G-8216)
NAMI OF PREBLE COUNTY OHIO
800 E Saint Clair St (45320-2433)
PHONE..............................937 456-4947
Shelly Ratliff, *Dir*
EMP: 50 **EST:** 2013
SALES (est): 920.05K **Privately Held**
Web: www.preblecountyohio.com
SIC: **8322** 8699 Old age assistance; Charitable organization

(G-8217)
NORFOLK SOUTHERN CORPORATION
6716 Crawfordsville Campbellstown Rd (45320)
PHONE..............................937 472-0067
EMP: 43
SALES (corp-wide): 12.16B **Publicly Held**
Web: www.norfolksouthern.com
SIC: **4011** Railroads, line-haul operating
PA: Norfolk Southern Corporation
    650 W Peachtree St Nw
    Atlanta GA 30308
    855 667-3655

(G-8218)
OCTOBER ENTERPRISES INC
Also Called: Greenbriar Nursing Center, The
501 W Lexington Rd (45320-9274)
PHONE..............................937 456-9535
Paul De Palma, *Pr*
EMP: 72 **EST:** 1990
SQ FT: 27,660
SALES (est): 4.19MM **Privately Held**
Web: www.greenbriarcampus.com
SIC: **8051** 8052 Convalescent home with continuous nursing care; Intermediate care facilities

(G-8219)
PARKER-HANNIFIN CORPORATION
Tube Fittings Division
725 N Beech St (45320-1499)
PHONE..............................937 456-5571
William Bowman, *Brnch Mgr*
EMP: 71
SALES (corp-wide): 19.07B **Publicly Held**
Web: www.parker.com
SIC: **3494** 5074 3498 3492 Pipe fittings; Plumbing fittings and supplies; Tube fabricating (contract bending and shaping); Fluid power valves and hose fittings
PA: Parker-Hannifin Corporation
    6035 Parkland Blvd
    Cleveland OH 44124
    216 896-3000

(G-8220)
PREBLE CNTY BD DVLPMNTAL DSBLT (PA)
Also Called: Preble County Board of Dd
200 Eaton Lewisburg Rd (45320-1190)
PHONE..............................937 456-5891
Eva Howard, *Pr*
EMP: 27 **EST:** 1967
SALES (est): 2.42MM
SALES (corp-wide): 2.42MM **Privately Held**
Web: www.prebledd.org
SIC: **8211** 8051 School for retarded, nec; Mental retardation hospital

(G-8221)
PREBLE COUNTY HEAD START
Also Called: Capo Preble County
304 Eaton Lewisburg Rd (45320-1105)
PHONE..............................937 456-2800

GEOGRAPHIC SECTION

Elyria - Lorain County (G-8240)

Tim Donnellan, *CEO*
Rita Daily County Headstart, *Dir*
EMP: 127 **EST:** 1974
SQ FT: 3,000
SALES (est): 377.49K
SALES (corp-wide): 14.59MM **Privately Held**
Web: www.preblecountyesc.org
SIC: 8351 Head Start center, except in conjunction with school
PA: Miami Valley Community Action Partnership
719 S Main St
Dayton OH 45402
937 222-1009

(G-8222)
REID PHYSICIAN ASSOCIATES INC
Also Called: Reid Physicians Associates
109 E Washington Jackson Rd Ste B (45320-9793)
PHONE.................................937 456-4400
Joellen Tapalman, *Mgr*
EMP: 390
SALES (corp-wide): 99.52MM **Privately Held**
Web: www.reidhealth.org
SIC: 8011 General and family practice, physician/surgeon
PA: Reid Physician Associates, Inc.
1100 Reid Pkwy
Richmond IN 47374
765 983-3000

(G-8223)
SAMARITAN BEHAVIORAL HLTH INC
2172 Us Route 127 N (45320-9289)
P.O. Box 267 (45320-0267)
PHONE.................................937 456-1915
Sue Mcgatha, *Prin*
EMP: 132
Web: www.sbhihelp.org
SIC: 8093 Mental health clinic, outpatient
HQ: Samaritan Behavioral Health, Inc.
601 S Edwin C Moses Blvd
Dayton OH 45417
937 734-8333

(G-8224)
STEINKE TRACTOR SALES INC
707 S Barron St (45320-9335)
P.O. Box 148 (45320-0148)
PHONE.................................937 456-4271
Dale Donderhaar, *Pr*
Madonna Creager, *Sec*
EMP: 30 **EST:** 1978
SQ FT: 16,000
SALES (est): 894.01K **Privately Held**
SIC: 5261 7699 5083 Lawn and garden equipment; Farm machinery repair; Agricultural machinery and equipment

(G-8225)
VANCREST LTD
Also Called: Vancrest Healthcare Cntr Eaton
1600 Park Ave (45320-9674)
PHONE.................................937 456-3010
EMP: 27
SALES (corp-wide): 28.02MM **Privately Held**
Web: www.vancrest.com
SIC: 8051 Convalescent home with continuous nursing care
PA: Vancrest, Ltd.
120 W Main St Ste 200
Van Wert OH 45891
419 238-0715

Edgerton
Williams County

(G-8226)
ADAMS HLPING HANDS HM CARE LLC
Also Called: Visiting Angels of NW Ohio
143 N Michigan Ave (43517-9322)
PHONE.................................419 298-0034
Michael Adams, *Prin*
EMP: 45 **EST:** 2021
SALES (est): 449.15K **Privately Held**
SIC: 8082 Home health care services

(G-8227)
AIR-WAY MANUFACTURING COMPANY
Also Called: Final Assembly and Whse Fcilty
303 W River St (43517-9670)
P.O. Box 485 (43517-0485)
PHONE.................................419 298-2366
Kim De Young, *Genl Mgr*
EMP: 130
SALES (corp-wide): 94.32MM **Privately Held**
Web: www.air-way.com
SIC: 5084 Hydraulic systems equipment and supplies
PA: Air-Way Manufacturing Company Inc
586 N Main St
Olivet MI 49076
269 749-2161

(G-8228)
LIECHTY INC
Also Called: John Deere Authorized Dealer
2773 Us Highway 6 (43517-9704)
PHONE.................................419 298-2302
Brad Warner, *Mgr*
EMP: 35
SALES (corp-wide): 33.49MM **Privately Held**
Web: www.deere.com
SIC: 7699 5999 5082 Farm machinery repair; Farm machinery, nec; Construction and mining machinery
HQ: Liechty, Inc.
1701 S Defiance St
Archbold OH 43502
419 445-1565

Edon
Williams County

(G-8229)
SLATTERY OIL COMPANY INC
Also Called: Marathon Oil
107 W Indiana St (43518-8612)
P.O. Box 484 (43518)
PHONE.................................419 272-3305
Mitch Slattery, *Owner*
EMP: 35
SALES (corp-wide): 9.85MM **Privately Held**
Web: www.slatteryoil.com
SIC: 5171 Petroleum bulk stations
PA: Slattery Oil Company Inc
204 4th St
Defiance OH 43512
419 542-7676

Elmore
Ottawa County

(G-8230)
HASSELKUS FARMS INC
2673 Hessville Rd (43416-9516)
PHONE.................................419 862-3735
Elaine Hasselkus, *Pr*
EMP: 40 **EST:** 1947
SALES (est): 863.23K **Privately Held**
SIC: 0191 General farms, primarily crop

Elyria
Lorain County

(G-8231)
ABBEWOOD LIMITED PARTNERSHIP
Also Called: The Abbewood
1210 Abbe Rd S Ofc (44035-7276)
PHONE.................................440 366-8980
Logan Sexton, *Genl Pt*
EMP: 29 **EST:** 1985
SALES (est): 8.15MM **Privately Held**
Web: www.centurypa.com
SIC: 8361 Aged home

(G-8232)
ABRAHAM FORD LLC
Also Called: Elyria Ford
1115 E Broad St (44035-6305)
PHONE.................................440 233-7402
Nick Abraham, *Pr*
EMP: 30 **EST:** 1920
SQ FT: 16,000
SALES (est): 890.19K **Privately Held**
Web: www.elyriaford.com
SIC: 7389 7538 5531 5521 Personal service agents, brokers, and bureaus; General automotive repair shops; Auto and home supply stores; Used car dealers

(G-8233)
ACCUCALL LLC
144 Keep Ct (44035-2215)
PHONE.................................440 522-8681
Steven Schroeder, *Pr*
EMP: 50 **EST:** 2008
SALES (est): 1.07MM **Privately Held**
SIC: 7389 Telephone answering service

(G-8234)
BUCKEYE COMMUNITY BANK
42935 N Ridge Rd (44035-1052)
PHONE.................................440 233-8800
Ben Norton, *CEO*
Bruce E Stevens, *Pr*
David L Croston, *CFO*
Stephen C Wright, *Prin*
Ben Norton, *Sr VP*
EMP: 114 **EST:** 1999
SALES (est): 9.24MM **Privately Held**
Web: www.buckeyebank.com
SIC: 6022 State commercial banks
PA: Buckeye Bancshares, Inc.
105 Sheffield Ctr
Lorain OH 44055

(G-8235)
CENTRO PROPERTIES GROUP LLC
3343 Midway Mall (44035-9003)
P.O. Box 7674 (22116-7674)
PHONE.................................440 324-6610
Mark Bressler, *Mgr*
EMP: 31
SALES (corp-wide): 1.97MM **Privately Held**
SIC: 5311 6512 Department stores; Nonresidential building operators
PA: Centro Properties Group Llc
1 Fayette St Ste 300
Conshohocken PA 19428
610 941-9304

(G-8236)
CLEVELAND CLINIC
Also Called: Elyria Fmly Hlth & Surgery Ctr
303 Chestnut Commons Dr (44035-9607)
PHONE.................................440 366-9444
John Secrist, *Pt*
EMP: 1106 **EST:** 1974
SALES (est): 8.19MM
SALES (corp-wide): 14.48B **Privately Held**
Web: my.clevelandclinic.org
SIC: 8011 Clinic, operated by physicians
PA: The Cleveland Clinic Foundation
9500 Euclid Ave
Cleveland OH 44195
216 636-8335

(G-8237)
COMPRHNSIVE HLTH CARE OHIO INC (HQ)
Also Called: Emh Regional Healthcare System
630 E River St (44035-5902)
PHONE.................................440 329-7500
Donald Sheldon, *Pr*
EMP: 1200 **EST:** 1985
SQ FT: 450,000
SALES (est): 194.86MM
SALES (corp-wide): 878.24MM **Privately Held**
SIC: 8741 Hospital management
PA: University Hospitals Health System, Inc.
3605 Warrensville Ctr Rd
Shaker Heights OH 44122
216 767-8900

(G-8238)
COUNTY OF LORAIN
Also Called: Lorain Cnty Bd Mntal Rtrdtion
1091 Infirmary Rd (44035-4804)
PHONE.................................440 329-3734
Amber Fisher Ph.d., *Superintnt*
EMP: 88
SALES (corp-wide): 253.29MM **Privately Held**
Web: www.loraincounty.us
SIC: 8322 8361 Social service center; Mentally handicapped home
PA: County Of Lorain
226 Middle Ave
Elyria OH 44035
440 329-5201

(G-8239)
COUNTY OF LORAIN
Also Called: Lake Erie Eductl Cmpt Assn
1885 Lake Ave (44035-2551)
PHONE.................................440 324-5777
Lloyd Wright, *Dir*
EMP: 66
SALES (corp-wide): 253.29MM **Privately Held**
Web: www.loraincounty.us
SIC: 8299 4813 Educational services; Internet connectivity services
PA: County Of Lorain
226 Middle Ave
Elyria OH 44035
440 329-5201

(G-8240)
COUNTY OF LORAIN
Also Called: Lorain County Childrens Svcs
226 Middle Ave 4th Fl (44035-5629)

Elyria - Lorain County (G-8241) — GEOGRAPHIC SECTION

PHONE.............................440 329-5340
EMP: 95
SALES (corp-wide): 253.29MM **Privately Held**
Web: www.loraincounty.us
SIC: 8322 8361 Adoption services; Group foster home
PA: County Of Lorain
226 Middle Ave
Elyria OH 44035
440 329-5201

(G-8241)
COUNTY OF LORAIN
Also Called: Adult Probation Department
308 2nd St (44035-5506)
PHONE.............................440 326-4700
Bart Hobart, *Dir*
EMP: 37
SALES (corp-wide): 253.29MM **Privately Held**
Web: www.loraincounty.us
SIC: 8322 Probation office
PA: County Of Lorain
226 Middle Ave
Elyria OH 44035
440 329-5201

(G-8242)
DOT DIAMOND CORE DRILLING INC (PA)
780 Sugar Ln (44035-6312)
P.O. Box 683 (44036-0683)
PHONE.............................440 322-6466
Jeannie Nolan, *Pr*
Pat Nolan, *
Ryan Nolan, *
EMP: 28 **EST:** 1974
SQ FT: 7,200
SALES (est): 8.32MM
SALES (corp-wide): 8.32MM **Privately Held**
Web: www.dotdrilling.com
SIC: 1771 Concrete work

(G-8243)
ECHOING HILLS VILLAGE INC
Also Called: Engram Home
175 Chadwick Ct (44035-4669)
PHONE.............................440 323-0915
EMP: 39
SALES (corp-wide): 39.8MM **Privately Held**
Web: www.ehvi.org
SIC: 7032 8059 Sporting and recreational camps; Home for the mentally retarded, ex. skilled or intermediate
PA: Echoing Hills Village, Inc.
36272 County Road 79
Warsaw OH 43844
740 327-2311

(G-8244)
EDUCATONAL SVC CTR LORAIN CNTY (PA)
1885 Lake Ave (44035-2551)
PHONE.............................440 244-1659
Thomas Rockwell, *Superintnt*
EMP: 101 **EST:** 1914
SALES (est): 4.46MM
SALES (corp-wide): 4.46MM **Privately Held**
Web: www.loraincountyesc.org
SIC: 8741 8211 Administrative management; Elementary and secondary schools

(G-8245)
ELYRIA COUNTRY CLUB COMPANY
41625 Oberlin Elyria Rd (44035-7599)
PHONE.............................440 322-6391
Kimberly Violo, *Mgr*
Eric Toth, *
EMP: 91 **EST:** 1905
SQ FT: 19,892
SALES (est): 3.53MM **Privately Held**
Web: elyriacountryclub.clubhouseonline-e3.com
SIC: 7997 Country club, membership

(G-8246)
ELYRIA FOUNDRY COMPANY LLC
745 Leo Bullocks Pkwy (44035-4882)
PHONE.............................440 322-4657
EMP: 65
SALES (corp-wide): 49.84MM **Privately Held**
Web: www.elyriafoundry.com
SIC: 4225 General warehousing and storage
PA: Elyria Foundry Company Llc
120 Filbert St
Elyria OH 44035
440 322-4657

(G-8247)
ELYRIA FOUNDRY HOLDINGS LLC
120 Filbert St (44035-5357)
PHONE.............................440 322-4657
EMP: 300 **EST:** 2006
Web: www.elyriafoundry.com
SIC: 6719 Investment holding companies, except banks

(G-8248)
ELYRIA-LORAIN BROADCASTING CO (HQ)
Also Called: Elts Broadcasting
538 Broad St Ste 400 (44035-5508)
PHONE.............................440 322-3761
George Hudnutt, *Pr*
Philip Kelly, *
EMP: 50 **EST:** 1945
SQ FT: 3,000
SALES (est): 4.71MM
SALES (corp-wide): 17.95MM **Privately Held**
Web: www.northcoastnow.com
SIC: 4832 Radio broadcasting stations
PA: Lorain County Printing & Publishing Co Inc
225 East Ave
Elyria OH
440 329-7000

(G-8249)
EMH REGIONAL MEDICAL CENTER (DH)
630 E River St (44035-5902)
PHONE.............................440 329-7500
EMP: 1612 **EST:** 1907
SALES (est): 188.32MM
SALES (corp-wide): 878.24MM **Privately Held**
SIC: 8062 General medical and surgical hospitals
HQ: Comprehensive Health Care Of Ohio, Inc.
630 E River St
Elyria OH 44035
440 329-7500

(G-8250)
FIRST STUDENT INC
42242 Albrecht Rd (44035-4702)
PHONE.............................440 284-8030
Cheri Lengel, *Mgr*
EMP: 111
Web: www.firststudentinc.com
SIC: 4151 School buses
PA: First Student, Inc.
191 Rosa Parks St Ste 800
Cincinnati OH 45202

(G-8251)
FIRST TRANSIT INC
530 Abbe Rd S (44035-6302)
PHONE.............................440 365-0224
EMP: 76
SALES (corp-wide): 4.23MM **Privately Held**
Web: www.transdevna.com
SIC: 4111 Local and suburban transit
HQ: First Transit, Inc.
600 Vine St Ste 1400
Cincinnati OH 45202
513 241-2200

(G-8252)
FOREVERGREEN LAWN CARE INC
1313 Taylor St (44035-6249)
PHONE.............................440 376-7515
EMP: 35 **EST:** 2019
SALES (est): 2.07MM **Privately Held**
Web: www.4evergreenlawn.com
SIC: 0782 Lawn care services

(G-8253)
GROSS PLUMBING INCORPORATED
Also Called: Gross Supply
6843 Lake Ave (44035-2149)
PHONE.............................440 324-9999
Daniel Gross, *Pr*
Edward J Gross, *
Guy Gross, *
Martha Taylor, *
EMP: 50 **EST:** 1956
SQ FT: 25,000
SALES (est): 9.3MM **Privately Held**
Web: www.grossplumbing.com
SIC: 1711 5999 Plumbing contractors; Plumbing and heating supplies

(G-8254)
GTRADVANCE LLC
366 Chestnut Commons Dr (44035-9604)
PHONE.............................440 365-1670
EMP: 250 **EST:** 2011
SALES (est): 5.28MM **Privately Held**
SIC: 7361 Employment agencies

(G-8255)
HEMATOLOGY ONCOLOGY CENTER
41201 Schadden Rd Ste 2 (44035-2249)
PHONE.............................440 324-0401
Lisa Dumpskey, *Mgr*
EMP: 27 **EST:** 1998
SALES (est): 2.19MM **Privately Held**
SIC: 8011 Oncologist

(G-8256)
HOME DEPOT USA INC
Also Called: Home Depot, The
150 Market Dr (44036)
PHONE.............................440 324-7222
James Meiden, *Mgr*
EMP: 119
SALES (corp-wide): 152.67B **Publicly Held**
Web: www.homedepot.com
SIC: 5211 7359 Home centers; Tool rental
HQ: Home Depot U.S.A., Inc.
2445 Springfield Ave
Vauxhall NJ 07088

(G-8257)
HORIZON EDUCATION CENTERS
Also Called: Horizon Education Centers
233 Bond St (44035-3507)
PHONE.............................440 322-0288
Louise Reuter, *Brnch Mgr*
EMP: 27
SALES (corp-wide): 19.97MM **Privately Held**
Web: www.horizoneducationcenters.org
SIC: 8351 Preschool center
PA: Horizon Education Centers
25300 Lorain Rd Fl 2
North Olmsted OH 44070
440 779-1930

(G-8258)
HORIZON EDUCATION CENTERS
Also Called: Allen Horizon Center
10347 Dewhurst Rd (44035-8403)
PHONE.............................440 458-5115
Donna Trent, *Brnch Mgr*
EMP: 27
SALES (corp-wide): 19.97MM **Privately Held**
Web: www.horizoneducationcenters.org
SIC: 8351 Preschool center
PA: Horizon Education Centers
25300 Lorain Rd Fl 2
North Olmsted OH 44070
440 779-1930

(G-8259)
HUNTINGTON NATIONAL BANK
111 Antioch Dr (44035-9104)
PHONE.............................440 406-5070
Matt Clark, *Brnch Mgr*
EMP: 36
SALES (corp-wide): 10.84B **Publicly Held**
Web: www.huntington.com
SIC: 6029 Commercial banks, nec
HQ: The Huntington National Bank
41 S High St
Columbus OH 43215
614 480-4293

(G-8260)
HUNTINGTON NATIONAL BANK
248 Abbe Rd N (44035-3799)
PHONE.............................440 365-1890
Renee Gafton, *Mgr*
EMP: 31
SALES (corp-wide): 10.84B **Publicly Held**
Web: www.huntington.com
SIC: 6029 Commercial banks, nec
HQ: The Huntington National Bank
41 S High St
Columbus OH 43215
614 480-4293

(G-8261)
I E R INC
Also Called: SERVPRO
6856 Lake Ave (44035-2150)
PHONE.............................440 324-2620
William C Mikolic, *Pr*
William C Mikolic, *Pr*
Don Mikolic, *VP*
EMP: 37 **EST:** 1986
SQ FT: 9,000
SALES (est): 803.68K **Privately Held**
Web: www.servprothenorthcoast.com
SIC: 7349 Building maintenance services, nec

(G-8262)
INN HAMPTON AND SUITES
1795 Lorain Blvd (44035-2849)
PHONE.............................440 324-7755
Aakruti Chandat, *Genl Mgr*
EMP: 42 **EST:** 2013
SALES (est): 552.53K **Privately Held**
Web: www.hilton.com
SIC: 7011 Hotels and motels

(G-8263)
INVACARE RESPIRATORY CORP
Also Called: Invacare
899 Cleveland St (44035-4107)
PHONE.............................440 329-6000

GEOGRAPHIC SECTION
Elyria - Lorain County (G-8285)

Dale A La Porte, *Sec*
◆ **EMP:** 54 **EST:** 1981
SALES (est): 7.95MM
SALES (corp-wide): 741.73MM **Publicly Held**
Web: global.invacare.com
SIC: **5047** Medical equipment and supplies
PA: Invacare Corporation
1 Invacare Way
Elyria OH 44035
440 329-6000

(G-8264)
K & M NEWSPAPER SERVICES INC
827 Walnut St (44035-3352)
PHONE.................................845 782-3817
Mark Jacobs, *Pr*
▲ **EMP:** 80 **EST:** 1984
SALES (est): 5.38MM **Privately Held**
Web: www.kmnewspaper.com
SIC: **5084** Printing trades machinery, equipment, and supplies

(G-8265)
KOKOSING CONSTRUCTION CO INC
1539 Lowell St (44035-4868)
PHONE.................................440 322-2685
W Brian Burgett, *CEO*
EMP: 87
SALES (corp-wide): 1.17B **Privately Held**
Web: www.kokosing.biz
SIC: **8711** Civil engineering
HQ: Kokosing Construction Company, Inc.
6235 Westerville Rd
Westerville OH 43081
614 228-1029

(G-8266)
KS ASSOCIATES INC
260 Burns Rd Ste 100 (44035-1513)
PHONE.................................440 365-4730
Lynn Miggins, *Pr*
Mark Skellenger, *
EMP: 96 **EST:** 1973
SALES (est): 9.86MM **Privately Held**
Web: www.ksassociates.com
SIC: **8711** 8713 Civil engineering; Surveying services

(G-8267)
LEGAL AID SOCIETY OF CLEVELAND
1530 W River Rd N (44035-2791)
PHONE.................................440 324-1121
Marley Eiger, *Brnch Mgr*
EMP: 31
SALES (corp-wide): 16.5MM **Privately Held**
Web: www.lasclev.org
SIC: **8111** Legal aid service
PA: The Legal Aid Society Of Cleveland
1223 W 6th St Fl 2
Cleveland OH 44113
216 861-5500

(G-8268)
LIFE CARE CENTERS AMERICA INC
1212 Abbe Rd S (44035-7269)
PHONE.................................440 365-5200
Douglas Mcdermott, *Brnch Mgr*
EMP: 83
SALES (corp-wide): 139.21MM **Privately Held**
Web: www.lcca.com
SIC: **8051** Convalescent home with continuous nursing care
PA: Life Care Centers Of America, Inc.
3570 Keith St Nw
Cleveland TN 37312
423 472-9585

(G-8269)
LIFECARE AMBULANCE INC
598 Cleveland St (44035-4144)
PHONE.................................440 323-2527
Peter De La Porte, *Brnch Mgr*
EMP: 45
SALES (corp-wide): 10.51MM **Privately Held**
Web: www.lifecareambulance.com
SIC: **4119** Ambulance service
PA: Lifecare Ambulance Inc.
640 Cleveland St
Elyria OH 44035
440 323-6111

(G-8270)
LIFESHARE CMNTY BLOOD SVCS INC (PA)
105 Cleveland St (44035-6137)
PHONE.................................440 322-5700
Richard Cluck, *Pr*
Michael Dash, *VP*
EMP: 35 **EST:** 1948
SQ FT: 10,000
SALES (est): 5.47MM
SALES (corp-wide): 5.47MM **Privately Held**
Web: www.lifeshare.cc
SIC: **8099** Blood bank

(G-8271)
LORAIN CNTY BD DVLPMNTAL DSBLT
1091 Infirmary Rd (44035-4804)
PHONE.................................440 329-3734
Amber Fisher, *Superintnt*
Heather Gurchik, *
EMP: 49 **EST:** 2003
SALES (est): 1.46MM **Privately Held**
Web: www.murrayridgecenter.org
SIC: **8093** 8331 Mental health clinic, outpatient; Sheltered workshop

(G-8272)
LOWES HOME CENTERS LLC
Also Called: Lowe's
646 Midway Blvd (44035-2442)
PHONE.................................440 324-5004
EMP: 138
SALES (corp-wide): 86.38B **Publicly Held**
Web: www.lowes.com
SIC: **5211** 5031 5722 Home centers; Building materials, exterior; Household appliance stores
HQ: Lowe's Home Centers, Llc
1000 Lowes Blvd
Mooresville NC 28117
336 658-4000

(G-8273)
MATIA MOTORS INC
Also Called: Jack Matia Honda
823 Leona St (44035-2300)
PHONE.................................440 365-7311
Jack Matia, *Pr*
Barbara Matia, *
EMP: 47 **EST:** 1984
SQ FT: 10,000
SALES (est): 8.11MM **Privately Held**
Web: www.jackmatiahonda.com
SIC: **5511** 7538 7532 5531 Automobiles, new and used; General automotive repair shops; Top and body repair and paint shops ; Auto and home supply stores

(G-8274)
METRO DESIGN INC
10740 Middle Ave (44035-7816)
P.O. Box 248 (44036-0248)
PHONE.................................440 458-4200

Jeffery Kraps, *Pr*
EMP: 29 **EST:** 1982
SQ FT: 10,000
SALES (est): 903.98K **Privately Held**
Web: www.metrodesigninc.com
SIC: **3599** 7699 3844 Custom machinery; X-ray equipment repair; X-ray apparatus and tubes

(G-8275)
MONARCH DENTAL CORP
435 Griswold Rd (44035-2304)
PHONE.................................440 324-2310
Janet Davis, *Mgr*
EMP: 34
SALES (corp-wide): 303.67MM **Privately Held**
Web: www.monarchdental.com
SIC: **8021** Dental clinic
HQ: Monarch Dental Corp
7989 Belt Line Rd Ste 90
Dallas TX 75248

(G-8276)
MULTILINK INC
Also Called: Multifab
580 Ternes Ln (44035-6252)
PHONE.................................440 366-6966
Steven Kaplan, *Pr*
Kathy Kaplan, *
Steve Cannon, *
◆ **EMP:** 140 **EST:** 1983
SQ FT: 110,000
SALES (est): 51.75MM **Privately Held**
Web: www.gomultilink.com
SIC: **5063** 3829 Wire and cable; Cable testing machines

(G-8277)
MURRAY RIDGE PROD CTR INC
1091 Infirmary Rd (44035-4804)
PHONE.................................440 329-3734
Amber Fischer, *Superintnt*
EMP: 104 **EST:** 1970
SQ FT: 100,000
SALES (est): 1.06MM **Privately Held**
Web: www.mrpcinc.com
SIC: **8331** 8322 Vocational rehabilitation agency; Social services for the handicapped

(G-8278)
NATIONAL MENTOR HOLDINGS INC
1530 W River Rd N Ste 300 (44035-2788)
PHONE.................................440 657-5658
EMP: 270
SALES (corp-wide): 1.64B **Privately Held**
Web: www.sevitahealth.com
SIC: **8361** Residential care
HQ: National Mentor Holdings, Inc.
313 Congress St Fl 5
Boston MA 02210
617 790-4800

(G-8279)
NC HHA INC
Also Called: INTREPID USA HEALTHCARE SERVIC
1170 E Broad St Ste 101 (44035-6351)
PHONE.................................216 593-7750
Adrienne Adkins, *Prin*
Cecellia Callis, *
EMP: 246 **EST:** 1982
SALES (est): 1.61MM
SALES (corp-wide): 1.17K **Privately Held**
SIC: **8082** Home health care services
HQ: Intrepid U.S.A., Inc.
14841 Dallas Pkwy Ste 625
Dallas TX 75254
214 445-3750

(G-8280)
NEW CINGULAR WIRELESS SVCS INC
Also Called: AT&T
1547 W River Rd N (44035-2713)
PHONE.................................440 324-7200
Troy Bagshaw, *Brnch Mgr*
EMP: 33
SALES (corp-wide): 122.43B **Publicly Held**
SIC: **4812** Cellular telephone services
HQ: New Cingular Wireless Services, Inc.
7277 164th Ave Ne
Redmond WA 98052
425 827-4500

(G-8281)
NORTH OHIO HEART CENTER INC (PA)
125 E Broad St Ste 305 (44035-6447)
PHONE.................................440 204-4000
John W Schaeffer, *Pr*
EMP: 50 **EST:** 1976
SALES (est): 24.11MM **Privately Held**
Web: www.nohc.com
SIC: **8011** Cardiologist and cardio-vascular specialist

(G-8282)
NORTHERN OHIO ROOFG SHTMTL INC
Also Called: Norfab
880 Infirmary Rd (44035-4884)
PHONE.................................440 322-8262
David Phiel, *Pr*
Joseph A Blaszak, *
EMP: 27 **EST:** 1972
SQ FT: 12,000
SALES (est): 2.02MM **Privately Held**
Web: www.northernohioroofing.com
SIC: **1761** Roofing contractor

(G-8283)
OPEN DOOR CHRISTN SCHOOLS INC
8287 W Ridge Rd (44035-4498)
PHONE.................................440 322-6386
Denver Daniel, *Dir*
Angie Lowe, *
Tarrell Dunckel, *
EMP: 98 **EST:** 1976
SQ FT: 42,000
SALES (est): 5.8MM **Privately Held**
Web: www.odcs.org
SIC: **8211** 8351 Private combined elementary and secondary school; Preschool center

(G-8284)
PACIFIC MGT HOLDINGS LLC
Also Called: Pharmacy-Lite Packaging
250 Warden Ave (44035-2650)
P.O. Box 775 (44036-0775)
PHONE.................................440 324-3339
Ian Brennan, *
▼ **EMP:** 30 **EST:** 1990
SQ FT: 90,000
SALES (est): 16.32MM **Privately Held**
Web: www.pharmacylite.com
SIC: **5199** Packaging materials

(G-8285)
PARKER-HANNIFIN CORPORATION
Gresen Hydraulics
520 Ternes Ln (44035-6266)
P.O. Box 4026 (44036-2026)
PHONE.................................440 366-5100
Andy Ross, *Brnch Mgr*
EMP: 78
SALES (corp-wide): 19.07B **Publicly Held**

Elyria - Lorain County (G-8286)

Web: www.parker.com
SIC: 5084 Hydraulic systems equipment and supplies
PA: Parker-Hannifin Corporation
6035 Parkland Blvd
Cleveland OH 44124
216 896-3000

(G-8286)
PLATINUM RESTORATION INC
104 Reaser Ct (44035-6285)
PHONE..................................440 327-0699
Wayne Hudspath, *Pr*
Michelle Brooks, *
EMP: 30 EST: 2002
SQ FT: 5,000
SALES (est): 2.9MM **Privately Held**
Web: www.callplatinumrestoration.net
SIC: 1741 1629 Tuckpointing or restoration; Waste water and sewage treatment plant construction

(G-8287)
PLATINUM RSTORATION CONTRS INC
104 Reaser Ct (44035-6285)
PHONE..................................440 327-0699
Michelle Brooks, *Pr*
EMP: 33 EST: 2010
SALES (est): 8.38MM **Privately Held**
Web: www.callplatinumrestoration.net
SIC: 6331 Property damage insurance

(G-8288)
PROFESSIONAL ELECTRIC PDTS CO
Also Called: Pepco
1190 E Broad St (44035-6306)
PHONE..................................800 379-3790
EMP: 27
SALES (corp-wide): 12.53MM **Privately Held**
Web: www.pepconet.com
SIC: 5063 Electrical supplies, nec
HQ: Professional Electric Products Co Inc
33210 Lakeland Blvd
Eastlake OH 44095
800 872-7000

(G-8289)
RAKESH RANJAN MD & ASSOC INC
Also Called: Charak Ctr For Hlth & Wellness
347 Midway Blvd Ste 210 (44035-2496)
PHONE..................................440 324-5555
Anish Ranjan, *Mgr*
EMP: 70
SALES (corp-wide): 23.02MM **Privately Held**
Web: www.charakcenter.com
SIC: 8011 Psychiatrist
PA: Rakesh Ranjan, M.D. & Associates, Inc.
12395 Mccracken Rd A-U
Cleveland OH 44125
216 375-9897

(G-8290)
RAMADA ELYRIA RSRVTONS WRLD WI
Also Called: Ramada By Wyndham
1825 Lorain Blvd (44035-2406)
PHONE..................................440 324-5411
April Bartosch, *Mgr*
EMP: 32 EST: 2012
SALES (est): 306.69K **Privately Held**
Web: www.wyndhamhotels.com
SIC: 7011 Inns

(G-8291)
RAYMOND H VECCHIO
1288 Abbe Rd N Ste C (44035-1679)

PHONE..................................440 365-9580
Raymond H Vecchio, *Pr*
EMP: 27 EST: 1973
SQ FT: 4,000
SALES (est): 446.78K **Privately Held**
Web: www.vecchiodds.com
SIC: 8021 Dentists' office

(G-8292)
S B S TRANSIT INC
Also Called: First Student
42242 Albrecht Rd (44035-4702)
PHONE..................................440 288-2222
Kenneth Van Wagnen, *Pr*
EMP: 36 EST: 2006
SALES (est): 1.9MM
SALES (corp-wide): 5.71B **Privately Held**
Web: www.sbstransit.com
SIC: 4151 4142 4493 5551 School buses; Bus charter service, except local; Marinas; Boat dealers
PA: Firstgroup Plc
395 King Street
Aberdeen AB24
122 421-9225

(G-8293)
SCHOOL EMPLYEES LRAIN CNTY CR
340 Griswold Rd (44035-2301)
PHONE..................................440 324-3400
Edward Enyedi, *CEO*
EMP: 27 EST: 1958
SALES (est): 6.08MM **Privately Held**
Web: www.selccu.org
SIC: 6061 Federal credit unions

(G-8294)
SHREE SAVA LTD
739 Leona St (44035-2350)
PHONE..................................440 324-7676
Sam Patel, *Pt*
Ratilalbhai G Patel, *Pt*
Mahesh Patidar, *Pt*
Ramesh Patel, *Pt*
Naran Patel, *Pt*
EMP: 31 EST: 1990
SQ FT: 29,000
SALES (est): 499.39K **Privately Held**
SIC: 7011 Hotels and motels

(G-8295)
SIBLEY INC
Also Called: Sibley Door Company
41530 Schadden Rd (44035-2227)
P.O. Box 655 (44036-0655)
PHONE..................................440 233-5836
Daniell Brian, *Pr*
EMP: 33 EST: 1928
SQ FT: 11,000
SALES (est): 1.12MM **Privately Held**
Web: www.sibleyinc.com
SIC: 1761 Roofing contractor

(G-8296)
SOUTH SHORE ELECTRIC INC
Also Called: South Shore Electric
589 Ternes Ln (44035-6251)
P.O. Box 321 (44036-0321)
PHONE..................................440 366-6289
Paul Zielazienski, *Pr*
Kathryn Zielazienski, *
Karen M Hughes, *
EMP: 40 EST: 1984
SQ FT: 11,000
SALES (est): 7.22MM **Privately Held**
Web: www.southshoreelectricinc.com
SIC: 1731 General electrical contractor

(G-8297)
THE HC COMPANIES INC
1400 Lowell St (44035-4867)
PHONE..................................440 313-4712
EMP: 55
SALES (corp-wide): 447.38MM **Privately Held**
Web: www.hc-companies.com
SIC: 1541 Industrial buildings and warehouses
HQ: The Hc Companies Inc
2450 Edison Blvd Ste 3
Twinsburg OH 44087
440 632-3333

(G-8298)
VANTAGE AGING
42495 N Ridge Rd (44035-1045)
PHONE..................................440 324-3588
Mary Ensman, *Prin*
EMP: 417
SALES (corp-wide): 11.1MM **Privately Held**
Web: www.vantageaging.org
SIC: 8322 Senior citizens' center or association
PA: Vantage Aging
388 S Main St Ste 325
Akron OH 44311
330 253-4597

(G-8299)
VITALANT
333 E Bridge St (44035-5222)
PHONE..................................440 322-8720
EMP: 40 EST: 2018
SALES (est): 277.49K **Privately Held**
Web: www.vitalant.org
SIC: 8099 Blood bank

(G-8300)
VOCATIONAL GUIDANCE SERVICES
Also Called: Vocational Services
359 Lowell St (44035-4935)
PHONE..................................440 322-1123
Lynn Merholz, *Mgr*
EMP: 309
SALES (corp-wide): 10.41MM **Privately Held**
Web: www.vgsjob.org
SIC: 8331 Vocational training agency
PA: Vocational Guidance Services Inc
2239 E 55th St
Cleveland OH 44103
216 431-7800

(G-8301)
WILLIAMS BROS BUILDERS INC
686 Sugar Ln (44035-6310)
PHONE..................................440 365-3261
Bart Williams, *Pr*
Jonathan R Traut, *
EMP: 30 EST: 1959
SQ FT: 2,000
SALES (est): 6.3MM **Privately Held**
Web: www.williamsbrothersbuilders.com
SIC: 1541 1542 Industrial buildings, new construction, nec; Commercial and office building contractors

Englewood
Montgomery County

(G-8302)
ALLENDEVAUX & COMPANY LLC
35 Rockridge Rd (45322-2749)
PHONE..................................937 657-1270
Rebekah Allendevaux, *CEO*
EMP: 32 EST: 2014

SALES (est): 2.51MM **Privately Held**
Web: www.allendevaux.com
SIC: 8748 Business consulting, nec

(G-8303)
ANALYTICAL PACE SERVICES LLC
25 Holiday Dr (45322-2706)
PHONE..................................937 832-8242
Brooke Chandler, *Mgr*
EMP: 66
Web: www.pacelabs.com
SIC: 8734 Soil analysis
HQ: Pace Analytical Services, Llc
2665 Long Lake Rd Ste 300
Roseville MN 55113

(G-8304)
CREATIVE MICROSYSTEMS INC
Also Called: Civica CMI
52 Hillside Ct (45322-2745)
PHONE..................................937 836-4499
Lin Mallott, *CEO*
Arvind Kohli, *
EMP: 80 EST: 1979
SQ FT: 14,400
SALES (est): 9.46MM **Privately Held**
Web: www.civica.com
SIC: 7373 7372 Systems integration services ; Prepackaged software

(G-8305)
DAYTON SURGEONS INC
Also Called: Miami Valley Hospital
9000 N Main St Ste 233 (45415-1184)
PHONE..................................937 228-4126
Phillip C Williams, *Pr*
EMP: 66 EST: 1989
SALES (est): 4.91MM **Privately Held**
Web: www.daytonsurgeons.com
SIC: 8011 Surgeon

(G-8306)
GARBER ELECTRICAL CONTRS INC
Also Called: Garber Connect
100 Rockridge Rd (45322-2737)
PHONE..................................937 771-5202
Gary A Garber, *Pr*
EMP: 60 EST: 2009
SALES (est): 21.91MM **Privately Held**
Web: www.garberelectric.com
SIC: 1731 General electrical contractor

(G-8307)
GEM CITY SURGICAL ASSOCIATES
Also Called: Dutro, John A MD
9000 N Main St Ste 233 (45415-1184)
PHONE..................................254 400-1783
Jennifer Plack, *Pt*
John A Dutro Md, *Pt*
Thomas Heck Md, *Pt*
Douglas Paul, *Prin*
Walter A Riely Junior, *Prin*
EMP: 36 EST: 2001
SALES (est): 1.68MM **Privately Held**
Web: www.premierhealth.com
SIC: 8011 Surgeon

(G-8308)
GEM CITY UROLOGIST INC (PA)
9000 N Main St Ste 333 (45415-1185)
PHONE..................................937 832-8400
Jan Bernie Md, *Ex VP*
Ahmad Abouhossein Md, *Prin*
Howard B Abromowitz, *
EMP: 27 EST: 1974
SALES (est): 1.91MM
SALES (corp-wide): 1.91MM **Privately Held**
SIC: 8011 Urologist

GEOGRAPHIC SECTION

Etna - Licking County (G-8332)

(G-8309)
GRACE BRETHREN VILLAGE
1010 Taywood Rd Ofc (45322-2415)
PHONE..............................937 836-4011
Mike Montgomery, *Admn*
EMP: 48 **EST:** 1969
SALES (est): 4.72MM **Privately Held**
Web: www.gbvillage.com
SIC: 8051 Convalescent home with continuous nursing care

(G-8310)
IRONGATE INC
Also Called: Iron Gate Realtors
16 W Wenger Rd Ste E (45322-2724)
PHONE..............................937 890-4880
EMP: 53
SALES (corp-wide): 24.13MM **Privately Held**
Web: www.irongaterealtors.com
SIC: 6531 Real estate agent, residential
PA: Irongate, Inc
122 N Main St
Centerville OH 45459
937 433-3300

(G-8311)
KING KOLD INC
331 N Main St (45322-1333)
PHONE..............................937 836-2731
Douglas Smith, *Pr*
Robert L Smith, *Sec*
EMP: 31 **EST:** 1968
SQ FT: 5,210
SALES (est): 1.06MM **Privately Held**
Web: www.kingkoldinc.com
SIC: 2038 2013 2011 5142 Frozen specialties, nec; Cooked meats, from purchased meat; Meat packing plants; Fish, frozen: packaged

(G-8312)
KLEPTZ EARLY LEARNING CENTER
1100 W National Rd (45315-9508)
PHONE..............................937 832-6750
Beth Wyandt, *Prin*
EMP: 100 **EST:** 2015
SALES (est): 423.05K **Privately Held**
Web: www.northmontschools.net
SIC: 8351 Preschool center

(G-8313)
LIBERTY NURSING CENTER
Also Called: Englewood Manor
425 Lauricella Ct (45322)
P.O. Box 340 (45322-0340)
PHONE..............................937 836-5143
Linda Black-kurek, *Pr*
Linda Black Kurek, *
EMP: 49 **EST:** 1962
SALES (est): 1.75MM **Privately Held**
Web: www.libertynursingcenters.com
SIC: 8051 8052 Convalescent home with continuous nursing care; Intermediate care facilities

(G-8314)
LIFESTAGES BOUTIQUE FOR WOMEN
9000 N Main St Ste 232 (45415-1184)
PHONE..............................937 274-5420
Stephanie Pilgrim, *Mgr*
EMP: 56 **EST:** 1998
SALES (est): 923.05K **Privately Held**
Web: www.premierhealth.com
SIC: 8011 5699 5632 Offices and clinics of medical doctors; Wigs, toupees, and wiglets ; Lingerie and corsets (underwear)

(G-8315)
LITTLE LEAG BSBAL ENGLWOOD INC
700 Arcadia Blvd (45322-1839)
PHONE..............................937 545-2670
EMP: 28
SALES (est): 113.72K **Privately Held**
SIC: 7997 Outdoor field clubs

(G-8316)
ODW LOGISTICS INC ✪
301 Lau Pkwy (45315-8803)
PHONE..............................614 549-5000
Grant Baker, *Contrlr*
EMP: 50 **EST:** 2024
SALES (est): 2.57MM **Privately Held**
Web: www.odwlogistics.com
SIC: 4789 Transportation services, nec

(G-8317)
PARADISE HOTELS LLC
Also Called: Red Roof Inn
9325 N Main St (45415-1128)
PHONE..............................937 836-8339
EMP: 48 **EST:** 2003
SALES (est): 670K **Privately Held**
Web: www.redroof.com
SIC: 7011 Hotels and motels

(G-8318)
PARK VIEW MANOR INC (PA)
425 Lauricella Ct (45322)
PHONE..............................937 296-1550
James A Lauricella Senior, *Pr*
Lena M Lauricella, *
EMP: 90 **EST:** 1997
SALES (est): 7.11MM
SALES (corp-wide): 7.11MM **Privately Held**
SIC: 8052 8051 Intermediate care facilities; Skilled nursing care facilities

(G-8319)
PRIMARY CARE NTWRK PRMIER HLTH
Also Called: Samaritan N Fmly Physicians
9000 N Main St Ste 202 (45415-1165)
PHONE..............................937 836-5170
Susan Smith, *Mgr*
EMP: 41
SALES (corp-wide): 25.36MM **Privately Held**
Web: www.premierhealth.com
SIC: 8011 General and family practice, physician/surgeon
PA: Primary Care Network Of Premier Health Partners
110 N Main St Ste 350
Dayton OH 45402
937 226-7085

(G-8320)
PRISTINE SNIOR LVING ENGLEWOOD
425 Lauricella Ct (45322)
PHONE..............................937 836-5143
EMP: 200 **EST:** 2016
SALES (est): 2.85MM **Privately Held**
Web: www.pristinesrenglewood.com
SIC: 8361 Aged home

(G-8321)
RITE AID OF OHIO INC
Also Called: Rite Aid
900 Union Blvd (45322-2221)
PHONE..............................937 836-5204
Nadine Poake, *Mgr*
EMP: 47
SALES (corp-wide): 24.09B **Publicly Held**
Web: www.riteaid.com
SIC: 5912 7384 Drug stores; Photofinishing laboratory
HQ: Rite Aid Of Ohio, Inc.
1200 Intrepid Ave Ste 2
Philadelphia PA 19112

(G-8322)
SAMARITAN N SURGERY CTR LTD
9000 N Main St (45415-1180)
PHONE..............................937 567-6100
EMP: 41 **EST:** 1998
SALES (est): 4.33MM **Privately Held**
Web: www.premierhealth.com
SIC: 8062 General medical and surgical hospitals

(G-8323)
SUNRISE SENIOR LIVING LLC
95 W Wenger Rd (45322-2723)
PHONE..............................937 836-9617
Jennifer Tibbettgrady, *Brnch Mgr*
EMP: 50
SALES (corp-wide): 2.92B **Privately Held**
Web: www.sunriseseniorliving.com
SIC: 8051 Skilled nursing care facilities
HQ: Sunrise Senior Living, Llc
7902 Westpark Dr
Mc Lean VA 22102

(G-8324)
TV MINORITY COMPANY INC
Dayton Origin Distribution Ctr
30 Lau Pkwy (45315-8777)
PHONE..............................937 832-9350
Brad Eib, *Brnch Mgr*
EMP: 48
SALES (corp-wide): 28.76MM **Privately Held**
SIC: 4731 8742 Freight forwarding; Transportation consultant
PA: T.V. Minority Company, Inc.
9400 Pelham Rd
Taylor MI 48180
313 386-1048

(G-8325)
VECTREN ENERGY DLVRY OHIO LLC
175 W Wenger Rd (45322-2726)
PHONE..............................937 331-3080
Maria Bubp, *Brnch Mgr*
EMP: 36
SALES (corp-wide): 8.7B **Publicly Held**
SIC: 4924 Natural gas distribution
HQ: Vectren Energy Delivery Of Ohio, Llc
1300 Experiment Farm Rd
Troy OH 45373
800 227-1376

(G-8326)
WEIFFENBACH MARBLE & TILE CO
150 Lau Pkwy (45315-8787)
PHONE..............................937 832-7055
Craig Lindsey, *Pr*
EMP: 40 **EST:** 2010
SALES (est): 4.41MM **Privately Held**
Web: www.weiffenbachmarble-tile.com
SIC: 1743 Tile installation, ceramic

(G-8327)
YOUNG MNS CHRSTN ASSN GRTER DY
Also Called: Metropolitan YMCA
1200 W National Rd (45315-9504)
P.O. Box 38 (45322-0038)
PHONE..............................937 836-9622
April Turner, *Dir*
EMP: 175
SALES (corp-wide): 36.75MM **Privately Held**
Web: www.daytonymca.org
SIC: 8641 8661 7997 Community membership club; Religious organizations; Membership sports and recreation clubs
PA: Young Men's Christian Association Of Greater Dayton
118 W 1st St Ste 300
Dayton OH 45402
937 223-5201

Etna
Franklin County

(G-8328)
BASEMENT DCTOR HM IMPRV CTR CP
13659 National Rd Sw (43068-3352)
PHONE..............................800 880-8324
Sarah Witt, *Brnch Mgr*
EMP: 78
SALES (corp-wide): 9.52MM **Privately Held**
Web: www.mybasementdoctor.com
SIC: 1799 Waterproofing
PA: Basement Doctor Home Improvement Center Copyright
7369 E Livingston Ave
Reynoldsburg OH 43068
614 349-3435

(G-8329)
FIVE SEASONS LANDSCAPE MGT INC
9886 Mink St Sw Rear (43068-3812)
PHONE..............................740 964-2915
EMP: 100 **EST:** 1997
SQ FT: 5,000
SALES (est): 11.81MM **Privately Held**
Web: www.fiveseasonslandscape.com
SIC: 0781 Landscape services

(G-8330)
HARRIS & HEAVENER EXCVTG INC
149 Humphries Dr (43068-6801)
PHONE..............................740 927-1423
EMP: 28 **EST:** 1996
SALES (est): 4.21MM **Privately Held**
Web: www.harrisheavener.com
SIC: 1794 Excavation and grading, building construction

(G-8331)
TRINITY HOME BUILDERS LLC
14099 Sunladen Dr Sw (43068)
PHONE..............................614 898-7200
George Skestos, *Mgr*
EMP: 50
Web: www.trinity-homes.com
SIC: 1521 New construction, single-family houses
PA: Trinity Home Builders, Llc
2700 E Dblin Grnvlle Rd S
Columbus OH 43231

Etna
Licking County

(G-8332)
BEST LIGHTING PRODUCTS INC (HQ)
Also Called: Best Lighting Products
1213 Etna Pkwy (43062-8041)
PHONE..............................740 964-1198
Jeffrey S Katz, *CEO*
George Jue, *
◆ **EMP:** 55 **EST:** 1997
SQ FT: 60,000
SALES (est): 44.25MM **Privately Held**

Web: www.bestlighting.net
SIC: 5063 3646 Electrical apparatus and equipment; Commercial lighting fixtures
PA: Corinthian Capital Group, Llc
  601 Lexington Ave Rm 5901
  New York NY 10022

(G-8333)
LADY WARRIORS SUMMER SOFTBALL
8868 Watkins Rd Sw (43062-9053)
P.O. Box 169 (43062-0169)
PHONE.................................614 668-6329
Scott Schindler, Pr
EMP: 120 EST: 2011
SALES (est): 223.84K Privately Held
SIC: 8641 Youth organizations

(G-8334)
PROGRESSIVE FLOORING SVCS INC
100 Heritage Dr (43062-8042)
PHONE.................................614 868-9005
Richard A South, CEO
Richard J South, *
Nino A Cervi, *
EMP: 28 EST: 1978
SQ FT: 45,300
SALES (est): 7.4MM Privately Held
Web: www.progressiveflooring.com
SIC: 1752 Carpet laying

Euclid
Cuyahoga County

(G-8335)
A W S INC
Also Called: Euclid Adult Training Center
1490 E 191st St (44117-1321)
PHONE.................................216 486-0600
Daisy Maleckar, Genl Mgr
EMP: 50
SALES (corp-wide): 3.95MM Privately Held
Web: www.sawinc.org
SIC: 8331 8322 Vocational rehabilitation agency; Rehabilitation services
PA: A W S Inc
  14775 Broadway Ave
  Maple Heights OH 44137
  216 861-0250

(G-8336)
AGHAPY PLUS INC
25451 Euclid Ave (44117-2611)
PHONE.................................216 820-3996
Monir Mikhaiel, Brnch Mgr
EMP: 52
SALES (corp-wide): 90.57K Privately Held
SIC: 7389 Personal service agents, brokers, and bureaus
PA: Aghapy Plus Inc.
  4501 Tuxedo Ave
  Cleveland OH 44134
  216 351-5170

(G-8337)
AMERATHON LLC
26300 Euclid Ave Ste 810 (44132-3718)
PHONE.................................419 230-9108
Sara Simpson, Opers Mgr
EMP: 50
SIC: 8071 Medical laboratories
HQ: Amerathon, Llc
  671 Ohio Pike Ste K
  Cincinnati OH 45245
  513 752-3200

(G-8338)
BUCKEYE CHECK CASHING INC
22641 Euclid Ave # 5 (44117-1622)
PHONE.................................216 486-3434
EMP: 35
Web: www.ccfi.com
SIC: 6099 Check cashing agencies
HQ: Buckeye Check Cashing, Inc.
  5165 Emerald Pkwy Ste 100
  Dublin OH 43017
  614 798-5900

(G-8339)
BUCKEYE CHECK CASHING INC
22318a Lake Shore Blvd (44123-1717)
PHONE.................................216 289-8462
EMP: 35
Web: www.ccfi.com
SIC: 6099 Check cashing agencies
HQ: Buckeye Check Cashing, Inc.
  5165 Emerald Pkwy Ste 100
  Dublin OH 43017
  614 798-5900

(G-8340)
DEACON 10 LLC
Also Called: Premier Protective Security
1353 E 260th St Ste 110 (44132-2818)
PHONE.................................216 731-4000
Neal Alexander, CEO
Debra Fikaris, *
EMP: 99 EST: 2011
SALES (est): 2.03MM Privately Held
SIC: 7381 Security guard service

(G-8341)
EUCLID HOSPITAL (HQ)
Also Called: CLEVELAND CLINIC HEALTH SYSTEM
18901 Lake Shore Blvd (44119-1078)
PHONE.................................216 531-9000
Tom Selden, CEO
Mark Froimson, Pr
Lauren Rock, COO
Cheryl Pecon, Ex Sec
EMP: 287 EST: 1951
SQ FT: 14,144
SALES (est): 113.54MM
SALES (corp-wide): 14.48B Privately Held
Web: www.euclidhospital.org
SIC: 8062 General medical and surgical hospitals
PA: The Cleveland Clinic Foundation
  9500 Euclid Ave
  Cleveland OH 44195
  216 636-8335

(G-8342)
EUCLIDEAN SUPPORT SERVICES INC
26250 Euclid Ave (44132-3305)
PHONE.................................330 405-8501
Brian M Dean, Owner
EMP: 50 EST: 2019
SALES (est): 1.18MM Privately Held
SIC: 7389 Business Activities at Non-Commercial Site

(G-8343)
FIRST STUDENT INC
393 Babbitt Rd (44123-1645)
PHONE.................................216 767-7600
EMP: 96
Web: www.firststudentinc.com
SIC: 4151 School buses
PA: First Student, Inc.
  191 Rosa Parks St Ste 800
  Cincinnati OH 45202

(G-8344)
HANI ASHQAR DDS & PARTNERS LLC
19551 Euclid Ave (44117-1409)
PHONE.................................203 560-3131
EMP: 39
SALES (corp-wide): 181.02K Privately Held
Web: www.angel-dentalcare.com
SIC: 8021 Offices and clinics of dentists
PA: Hani Ashqar Dds And Partners Llc
  29836 Tamarack Trl
  Westlake OH 44145
  216 387-7488

(G-8345)
HELP FOUNDATION INC
27348 Oak Ct (44132-2114)
PHONE.................................216 289-7710
EMP: 31
Web: www.helpfoundationinc.org
SIC: 8641 Civic and social associations
PA: Help Foundation, Inc.
  26900 Euclid Ave
  Euclid OH 44132

(G-8346)
HELP FOUNDATION INC (PA)
26900 Euclid Ave (44132-3404)
PHONE.................................216 432-4810
Daniel J Rice, CEO
EMP: 45 EST: 1989
SALES (est): 10.54MM Privately Held
Web: www.helpfoundationinc.org
SIC: 8741 Administrative management

(G-8347)
HGR INDUSTRIAL SURPLUS INC (PA)
Also Called: H G R
20001 Euclid Ave (44117-1480)
PHONE.................................216 486-4567
Brian Krueger, CEO
Paul Betori, *
Jeff Mclain, Prin
▼ EMP: 45 EST: 1998
SQ FT: 250,000
SALES (est): 24.12MM
SALES (corp-wide): 24.12MM Privately Held
Web: www.hgrinc.com
SIC: 5084 Materials handling machinery

(G-8348)
HUNTINGTON NATIONAL BANK
Also Called: US Bank
1545 E 260th St (44132-3102)
PHONE.................................440 943-3389
EMP: 31
SALES (corp-wide): 10.84B Publicly Held
Web: www.usbank.com
SIC: 6029 Commercial banks, nec
HQ: The Huntington National Bank
  41 S High St
  Columbus OH 43215
  614 480-4293

(G-8349)
INDELCO CUSTOM PRODUCTS INC
25861 Tungsten Rd (44132-2817)
PHONE.................................216 797-7300
Mitchell Opalich, Pr
Lorraine Simer, VP
EMP: 36 EST: 1964
SQ FT: 21,500
SALES (est): 917.12K Privately Held
Web: www.indelco.com

SIC: 3599 3498 3561 3089 Machine shop, jobbing and repair; Tube fabricating (contract bending and shaping); Pumps and pumping equipment; Fittings for pipe, plastics

(G-8350)
INDIAN HLLS HLTHCARE GROUP INC
Also Called: Willows Health & Rehab Center, The
1500 E 191st St (44117-1398)
PHONE.................................216 486-8880
George S Repchick, Pr
William I Weisberg, *
EMP: 674 EST: 1983
SALES (est): 6.5MM
SALES (corp-wide): 655.44MM Privately Held
Web: www.saberhealth.com
SIC: 8051 8052 Skilled nursing care facilities; Intermediate care facilities
PA: Saber Healthcare Group, L.L.C.
  23700 Commerce Park
  Beachwood OH 44122
  216 292-5706

(G-8351)
JLJI ENTERPRISES INC
21711 Tungsten Rd (44117-1116)
PHONE.................................216 481-2175
John Torres, Brnch Mgr
EMP: 128
Web: www.jljiinc.com
SIC: 1542 Commercial and office building, new construction
PA: J.L.J.I. Enterprises, Inc.
  5620 Broadway Ave
  Cleveland OH 44127

(G-8352)
KEYBANK NATIONAL ASSOCIATION
22481 Lake Shore Blvd (44123-1312)
PHONE.................................216 289-7670
Fran Tomba, Brnch Mgr
EMP: 38
SALES (corp-wide): 10.4B Publicly Held
Web: www.key.com
SIC: 6021 National commercial banks
HQ: Keybank National Association
  127 Public Sq Ste 5600
  Cleveland OH 44114
  800 539-2968

(G-8353)
LAKE ERIE ABRASIVE & TOOL INC
24811 Rockwell Dr (44117-1243)
PHONE.................................216 692-2778
▲ EMP: 27
SIC: 5085 Abrasives

(G-8354)
LANDMARK RECOVERY OHIO LLC
19350 Euclid Ave (44117-1425)
PHONE.................................855 950-5035
Trenette Hewett, Brnch Mgr
EMP: 272
SALES (corp-wide): 14.71MM Privately Held
Web: www.landmarkrecovery.com
SIC: 8093 Substance abuse clinics (outpatient)
PA: Landmark Recovery Of Ohio, Llc
  720 Cool Springs Blvd # 500
  Franklin TN 37067
  888 448-0302

(G-8355)
LINCOLN ELECTRIC COMPANY
26250 Bluestone Blvd (44132-2824)
PHONE.................................216 481-8100
Christopher L Mapes, Prin

GEOGRAPHIC SECTION — Fairborn - Greene County (G-8376)

EMP: 30
SALES (corp-wide): 4.19B **Publicly Held**
Web: ir.lincolnelectric.com
SIC: 5085 Welding supplies
HQ: Lincoln Electric Company
  22801 St Clair Ave
  Cleveland OH 44117
  216 481-8100

(G-8356)
LINCOLN ELECTRIC INTL HOLDG CO (HQ)
22801 Saint Clair Ave (44117-2524)
PHONE..................216 481-8100
John Stropki, *Ch*
◆ **EMP:** 92 **EST:** 1987
SALES (est): 26.62MM
SALES (corp-wide): 4.19B **Publicly Held**
Web: www.lincolnelectric.com
SIC: 5085 Welding supplies
PA: Lincoln Electric Holdings, Inc.
  22801 St Clair Ave
  Cleveland OH 44117
  216 481-8100

(G-8357)
LIONS GATE SEC SOLUTIONS INC
Also Called: Lion's Gate Trning SEC Sltions
2073 E 221st St (44117-2103)
PHONE..................440 539-8382
Charisse Montgomery, *Pr*
Richard Montgomery, *
Joeseph Hodges, *
EMP: 50 **EST:** 2017
SALES (est): 849.73K **Privately Held**
SIC: 7389 Business Activities at Non-Commercial Site

(G-8358)
MULTICARE HLTH EDUCTL SVCS INC
Also Called: Multicare Home Health Services
27691 Euclid Ave Ste B-1 (44132-3546)
PHONE..................216 731-8900
Lorenza Henderson, *Pr*
EMP: 27 **EST:** 1997
SALES (est): 3.95MM **Privately Held**
Web: www.multicarehomehealthservices.com
SIC: 8082 Home health care services

(G-8359)
NATIONAL PREMIER PROTECTIVE (PA)
Also Called: Premier Security
1353 E 260th St Ste 1 (44132-2818)
PHONE..................216 731-4000
Neal Alexander, *Managing Member*
Deb Fikaris, *Prin*
Aurther Brown, *Contrlr*
EMP: 70 **EST:** 2004
SALES (est): 4.62MM
SALES (corp-wide): 4.62MM **Privately Held**
Web: www.thepremierteam.net
SIC: 8748 Business consulting, nec

(G-8360)
QUALCHOICE HEALTH PLAN INC (HQ)
Also Called: University Hospitals Hlth Sys
24701 Euclid Ave (44117-1714)
PHONE..................440 544-2800
TOLL FREE: 888
Thomas A Sullivan, *Pr*
Karen Fifer Ferry, *
Rebecca Nedelkoff Holland, *
EMP: 245 **EST:** 1993
SALES (est): 2.13MM
SALES (corp-wide): 878.24MM **Privately Held**

SIC: 6324 Health Maintenance Organization (HMO), insurance only
PA: University Hospitals Health System, Inc.
  3605 Warrensville Ctr Rd
  Shaker Heights OH 44122
  216 767-8900

(G-8361)
SHECONNA L DANIELS
24370 Garden Dr Apt 1206 (44123-2466)
PHONE..................216 370-0256
Sheconna Daniels, *Prin*
EMP: 81 **EST:** 2016
SALES (est): 288.02K **Privately Held**
Web: www.arcschenectady.org
SIC: 8322 Individual and family services

(G-8362)
SISTERS OF ST JSEPH ST MARK PR
Also Called: Mount St Joseph Nursing Home
21800 Chardon Rd (44117-2125)
PHONE..................216 531-7426
Mother M Raphael, *Admn*
Raphael Gregg, *
Sister Mary Raphael Gregg, *Admn*
Sister Paschal Yap, *Sec*
EMP: 255 **EST:** 1942
SQ FT: 90,000
SALES (est): 8.8MM **Privately Held**
Web: www.mountstjoseph.net
SIC: 8051 Convalescent home with continuous nursing care

(G-8363)
UNIVERSITY MEDNET (PA)
18599 Lake Shore Blvd (44119-1093)
PHONE..................216 383-0100
Richard Hammond, *Pr*
Seth Eisengart Md, *Ch Bd*
Arnold Rozensweig Md, *Sec*
Kenneth Spano Md, *Treas*
EMP: 300 **EST:** 1987
SQ FT: 124,000
SALES (est): 10.47MM
SALES (corp-wide): 10.47MM **Privately Held**
SIC: 8069 8082 5999 Specialty hospitals, except psychiatric; Home health care services; Medical apparatus and supplies

(G-8364)
WINDSTREAM SERVICES LLC
Also Called: WINDSTREAM SERVICES, LLC
25900 Lakeland Blvd (44132-2637)
PHONE..................216 242-6315
EMP: 29
SALES (corp-wide): 6.77B **Privately Held**
Web: www.windstreamenterprise.com
SIC: 4813 Telephone communication, except radio
HQ: Windstream Services Pe, Llc
  4001 N Rodney Parham Rd
  Little Rock AR 72212
  501 748-7000

Fairborn
Greene County

(G-8365)
ADAPT-A-PAK INC
678 Yellow Springs Fairfield Rd Ste 100 (45324)
PHONE..................937 845-0386
TOLL FREE: 800
EMP: 37 **EST:** 1987
SALES (est): 5.75MM **Privately Held**
Web: www.adaptapak.com

SIC: 2653 5113 Boxes, corrugated: made from purchased materials; Shipping supplies

(G-8366)
ADVANCED MECHANICAL SVCS INC
Also Called: Honeywell Authorized Dealer
575 Sports St (45324)
P.O. Box 68 (45324)
PHONE..................937 879-7426
William Burrowes, *Pr*
William D Parsons, *
▲ **EMP:** 32 **EST:** 1989
SALES (est): 4.99MM **Privately Held**
Web: www.honeywell.com
SIC: 1711 Warm air heating and air conditioning contractor

(G-8367)
BRILLIGENT SOLUTIONS LLC (PA)
1130 Channingway Dr (45324-9240)
PHONE..................937 879-4148
David Geloneck, *Managing Member*
David Geloneck, *Pr*
Doug Henry, *
Brian Oskey, *
Chad Pettit, *
EMP: 27 **EST:** 2007
SQ FT: 7,400
SALES (est): 4.88MM **Privately Held**
Web: www.brilligent.com
SIC: 8711 8731 Consulting engineer; Commercial physical research

(G-8368)
CACI-CMS INFO SYSTEMS LLC
2600 Paramount Pl Ste 300 (45324-6816)
PHONE..................937 986-3600
J P London, *Ch Bd*
EMP: 197
SALES (corp-wide): 6.7B **Publicly Held**
Web: www.caci.com
SIC: 7373 Computer integrated systems design
HQ: Caci-Cms Information Systems, Llc
  1100 N Glebe Rd Ste 200
  Arlington VA 22201
  703 841-7800

(G-8369)
COMBS INTERIOR SPECIALTIES INC
475 W Funderburg Rd (45324-2359)
PHONE..................937 879-2047
EMP: 75 **EST:** 2007
SALES (est): 9.68MM **Privately Held**
Web: www.combsinterior.com
SIC: 1542 1751 1521 Nonresidential construction, nec; Carpentry work; Single-family housing construction

(G-8370)
COVENANT CARE OHIO INC
Wright Nursing Center
829 Yellow Springs Fairfield Rd (45324)
PHONE..................937 878-7046
Greg Nijack, *Admn*
EMP: 90
Web: www.wrightrehabcenter.com
SIC: 8052 8069 8051 Intermediate care facilities; Specialty hospitals, except psychiatric; Skilled nursing care facilities
HQ: Covenant Care Ohio, Inc.
  120 Vantis Dr Ste 200
  Aliso Viejo CA 92656
  949 349-1200

(G-8371)
CURTISS-WRIGHT CONTROLS
Also Called: Curtiss-Wright Controls
2600 Paramount Pl Ste 200 (45324-6816)
PHONE..................937 252-5601
EMP: 50

SALES (corp-wide): 2.85B **Publicly Held**
Web: www.curtisswright.com
SIC: 8711 8731 3769 3625 Consulting engineer; Commercial physical research; Space vehicle equipment, nec; Relays and industrial controls
HQ: Curtiss-Wright Controls Electronic Systems, Inc.
  28965 Avenue Penn
  Santa Clarita CA 91355
  661 257-4430

(G-8372)
DAVE MARSHALL INC (PA)
Also Called: Ziebart
1448 Kauffman Ave (45324-3108)
PHONE..................937 878-9135
David Marshall, *Pr*
Susan Marshall, *
EMP: 44 **EST:** 1966
SALES (est): 2.24MM
SALES (corp-wide): 2.24MM **Privately Held**
Web: www.ziebart.com
SIC: 7549 Undercoating/rustproofing cars

(G-8373)
DAYSPRING HEALTH CARE CENTER
8001 Dayton Springfield Rd (45324-1907)
PHONE..................937 864-5800
Matt Walters, *Pr*
Barry Bortz, *
EMP: 45 **EST:** 1998
SALES (est): 5.53MM
SALES (corp-wide): 84.56MM **Privately Held**
SIC: 8051 8052 Skilled nursing care facilities; Intermediate care facilities
PA: Carespring Health Care Management, Llc
  390 Wards Corner Rd
  Loveland OH 45140
  513 943-4000

(G-8374)
FAIRBORN BUICK-GMC TRUCK INC
Also Called: Fairborn Pontiac
1105 N Central Ave (45324-5668)
P.O. Box 432 (45324-0432)
PHONE..................937 878-7371
TOLL FREE: 888
EMP: 65
SIC: 5511 7538 7532 Automobiles, new and used; General automotive repair shops; Top and body repair and paint shops

(G-8375)
FAIRBORN CITY SCHOOL DISTRICT
200 N Wright Ave (45324-5074)
PHONE..................937 878-1772
Charlotte Tingelstad, *Dist Mgr*
EMP: 36
SALES (corp-wide): 75.85MM **Privately Held**
Web: www.fairborn.k12.oh.us
SIC: 4119 Local passenger transportation, nec
PA: Fairborn City School District
  306 E Whittier Ave
  Fairborn OH 45324
  937 878-3961

(G-8376)
HOME DEPOT USA INC
Also Called: Home Depot, The
3775 Presidential Dr (45324)
PHONE..................937 431-7346
Tiffany A Collinsworth, *Mgr*
EMP: 129
SALES (corp-wide): 152.67B **Publicly Held**

Fairborn - Greene County (G-8377)   **GEOGRAPHIC SECTION**

Web: www.homedepot.com
SIC: 5211 7359 Home centers; Tool rental
HQ: Home Depot U.S.A., Inc.
2445 Springfield Ave
Vauxhall NJ 07088

(G-8377)
I SUPPLY CO
1255 Spangler Rd (45324-9768)
P.O. Box 1739 (45324-7739)
PHONE..................................937 878-5240
Jerry Parisi, *Ch*
Gerald Parisi, *
Mario Parisi, *
Joe Parisi, *
Joseph Parisi, *
EMP: 175 EST: 1974
SQ FT: 109,000
SALES (est): 98.97MM Privately Held
Web: www.isupplyco.com
SIC: 5087 5113 Janitors' supplies; Industrial and personal service paper

(G-8378)
LOGTEC INC
1825 Commerce Center Blvd (45324-6336)
PHONE..................................937 878-8450
EMP: 143
SALES (corp-wide): 6.07B Privately Held
SIC: 8748 Business consulting, nec
HQ: Logtec, Inc.
12930 Worldgate Dr # 600
Herndon VA 20170
703 939-6000

(G-8379)
MENARD INC
1277 E Dayton Yellow Springs Rd (45324-6327)
PHONE..................................937 318-2831
EMP: 57
SALES (corp-wide): 1.7B Privately Held
Web: www.menards.com
SIC: 8742 Management consulting services
PA: Menard, Inc.
5101 Menard Dr
Eau Claire WI 54703
715 876-2000

(G-8380)
PREMIER HOTEL GROUP LLC
Also Called: Baymont Inn & Suites
730 E Xenia Dr (45324-5149)
PHONE..................................937 754-9109
William E Parker, *Managing Member*
EMP: 61 EST: 2001
SALES (est): 991.36K Privately Held
Web: www.wyndhamhotels.com
SIC: 7011 7389 Inns; Convention and show services

(G-8381)
TAITECH INC
Wright Patterson Afb (45324)
PHONE..................................937 255-4141
EMP: 39
Web: www.taitech.com
SIC: 8731 Commercial physical research
PA: Taitech, Inc.
1430 Oak Ct Ste 301
Beavercreek OH 45430

(G-8382)
UNITED CHURCH HOMES INC
Also Called: Trinity Community At Fairborn
789 Stoneybrook Trl (45324-6021)
PHONE..................................937 878-0262
Jeremy Lemon, *Admn*
EMP: 69
SALES (corp-wide): 115.52MM Privately Held

Web: www.unitedchurchhomes.org
SIC: 8052 8051 Intermediate care facilities; Skilled nursing care facilities
PA: United Church Homes, Inc.
170 E Center St
Marion OH 43302
800 837-2211

(G-8383)
VECTREN ENERGY DLVRY OHIO LLC
1335 E Dayton Yellow Springs Rd (45324-6349)
PHONE..................................937 259-7400
Jerry Pfiefer, *Brnch Mgr*
EMP: 36
SALES (corp-wide): 8.7B Publicly Held
SIC: 4911 Distribution, electric power
HQ: Vectren Energy Delivery Of Ohio, Llc
1300 Experiment Farm Rd
Troy OH 45373
800 227-1376

(G-8384)
VETERANS OF FOREIGN WARS OF US
5075 Enon Xenia Rd Ste B (45324-9613)
PHONE..................................937 864-2361
EMP: 64
SALES (corp-wide): 105.25MM Privately Held
SIC: 8641 Veterans' organization
PA: Veterans Of Foreign Wars Of The United States
406 W 34th St Fl 11
Kansas City MO 64111
816 756-3390

(G-8385)
VISICON INC
Also Called: Hope Hotel & Conference Center
Bldg 823 Area A (45324)
PHONE..................................937 879-2696
David Meyers, *Pr*
Micki Witter, *Genl Mgr*
EMP: 47 EST: 1988
SQ FT: 132,000
SALES (est): 424.75K Privately Held
Web: www.visicon.com
SIC: 7011 Hotels

(G-8386)
VMETRO INC (DH)
Also Called: V Metro
2600 Paramount Pl Ste 200 (45324-6816)
PHONE..................................281 584-0728
James H Gerberman, *Pr*
▲ EMP: 51 EST: 1987
SQ FT: 18,371
SALES (est): 938.06K
SALES (corp-wide): 2.85B Publicly Held
SIC: 3825 3672 3577 5065 Test equipment for electronic and electric measurement; Printed circuit boards; Computer peripheral equipment, nec; Electronic parts and equipment, nec
HQ: Curtiss-Wright Controls, Inc.
15801 Brixham Hill Ave # 200
Charlotte NC 28277
704 869-4600

(G-8387)
WASTE MANAGEMENT OHIO INC (HQ)
Also Called: Waste Management
1700 N Broad St (45324)
P.O. Box 4648 (60197)
PHONE..................................800 343-6047
EMP: 37 EST: 1985
SALES (est): 47.01MM
SALES (corp-wide): 20.43B Publicly Held

SIC: 4953 Garbage: collecting, destroying, and processing
PA: Waste Management, Inc.
800 Capitol St Ste 3000
Houston TX 77002
713 512-6200

Fairfield
Butler County

(G-8388)
ALBA MANUFACTURING INC
8950 Seward Rd (45011-9109)
PHONE..................................513 874-0551
Tom Moon, *Pr*
Thomas N Inderhees, *
Mike Kroger, *
EMP: 52 EST: 1973
SQ FT: 67,000
SALES (est): 11.39MM Privately Held
Web: www.albamfg.com
SIC: 3535 5084 3312 Conveyors and conveying equipment; Conveyor systems; Blast furnaces and steel mills

(G-8389)
ALEXSON SERVICES INC
Also Called: Fairfield Center
350 Kolb Dr (45014-5357)
PHONE..................................513 874-0423
Andrea Levenson, *CEO*
EMP: 60 EST: 1990
SALES (est): 2.47MM
SALES (corp-wide): 2.47MM Privately Held
SIC: 8361 8052 8051 Retarded home; Intermediate care facilities; Skilled nursing care facilities
PA: Manor Home Ownership Of Facilities, Inc.
246 N Broadway
Geneva OH 44041
513 531-3826

(G-8390)
AURGROUP FINANCIAL CR UN INC (PA)
Also Called: Aurgroup Financial Credit Un
8811 Holden Blvd (45014-2109)
PHONE..................................513 942-4422
Tim Boellner, *CEO*
EMP: 29 EST: 1936
SALES (est): 8.54MM
SALES (corp-wide): 8.54MM Privately Held
Web: www.aurgroup.org
SIC: 6061 Federal credit unions

(G-8391)
BAKEMARK USA LLC
Bakemark Cincinnati
9250 Seward Rd # D (45014-5457)
PHONE..................................513 870-0880
TOLL FREE: 800
Doug Townsend, *Brnch Mgr*
EMP: 100
SALES (corp-wide): 578.75MM Privately Held
Web: www.yourbakemark.com
SIC: 5149 5046 Baking supplies; Commercial equipment, nec
PA: Bakemark Usa Llc
7351 Crider Ave
Pico Rivera CA 90660
562 949-1054

(G-8392)
BANSAL CONSTRUCTION INC
3263 Homeward Way Ste A (45014-4237)

P.O. Box 132 (45071-0132)
PHONE..................................513 874-5410
Anurag Bansal, *Pr*
Ambrish K Bansal, *
EMP: 35 EST: 1989
SQ FT: 5,000
SALES (est): 6.03MM Privately Held
Web: www.bansalconstruction.com
SIC: 1731 1794 General electrical contractor; Excavation work

(G-8393)
BELFLEX STAFFING NETWORK LLC
4757 Dixie Hwy (45014-1847)
PHONE..................................513 939-3444
EMP: 571
SALES (corp-wide): 112.31MM Privately Held
Web: www.belflex.com
SIC: 7363 Temporary help service
HQ: Belflex Staffing Network, Llc
11591 Goldcoast Dr
Cincinnati OH 45249
513 488-8588

(G-8394)
BIG OKI LLC
Also Called: Rnr Tire Express
6500 Dixie Hwy # 4 (45014-5424)
PHONE..................................513 874-1111
EMP: 36
SALES (corp-wide): 432.06K Privately Held
Web: www.rnrtires.com
SIC: 7534 Tire repair shop
PA: Big Oki Llc
7141 Manderlay Dr
Florence KY 41042
859 657-5200

(G-8395)
BROCK & SONS INC
8731 N Gilmore Rd (45014-2105)
PHONE..................................513 874-4555
Linda Brock, *Pr*
Geoffrey Brock, *
EMP: 34 EST: 1937
SQ FT: 1,500
SALES (est): 1.68MM Privately Held
Web: www.brockandsons.com
SIC: 1623 1611 Water main construction; General contractor, highway and street construction

(G-8396)
BUTLER CNTY BD DVLPMNTAL DSBLT
Also Called: Community Supports Services
441 Patterson Blvd (45014-2511)
PHONE..................................513 867-5913
EMP: 51
SALES (corp-wide): 12.86MM Privately Held
Web: www.butlerdd.org
SIC: 8361 9111 8052 Retarded home; County supervisors' and executives' office; Intermediate care facilities
PA: Butler County Board Of Developmental Disabilities
282 N Fair Ave
Hamilton OH 45011
513 785-2815

(G-8397)
BYRON PRODUCTS INC
3781 Port Union Rd (45014-2207)
PHONE..................................513 870-9111
Mark Byron, *Ch*
Rick Henry, *
▲ EMP: 70 EST: 1982
SQ FT: 44,000

GEOGRAPHIC SECTION

Fairfield - Butler County (G-8416)

SALES (est): 12.92MM **Privately Held**
Web: www.byronproducts.com
SIC: 7692 Welding repair

(G-8398)
CALVARY INDUSTRIES INC (PA)
9233 Seward Rd (45014-5407)
PHONE......................513 874-1113
John P Morelock Junior, *CEO*
Ivan Byers, *
Thomas Rielage, *
▲ EMP: 48 EST: 1983
SQ FT: 100,000
SALES (est): 200.07K
SALES (corp-wide): 200.07K **Privately Held**
Web: www.calvaryindustries.com
SIC: 2819 5169 Industrial inorganic chemicals, nec; Chemicals and allied products, nec

(G-8399)
CFC INVESTMENT COMPANY
6200 S Gilmore Rd (45014-5141)
P.O. Box 145496 (45250-5496)
PHONE......................513 870-2203
Kenneth S Miller, *Pr*
Kevin Guilfoyle, *Sr VP*
Kenneth W Stecher, *Dir*
James Denoski, *Dir*
Steven J Johnston, *Pr*
EMP: 48 EST: 1970
SQ FT: 383,000
SALES (est): 2.4MM
SALES (corp-wide): 10.01B **Publicly Held**
Web: www.cinfin.com
SIC: 7359 Equipment rental and leasing, nec
PA: Cincinnati Financial Corporation
    6200 S Gilmore Rd
    Fairfield OH 45014
    513 870-2000

(G-8400)
CHILDRENS HOSPITAL MEDICAL CTR
Also Called: Cincinatti Chld Hosp Med Ctr
3050 Mack Rd Ste 105 (45014-5375)
PHONE......................513 636-6400
John Linser, *Brnch Mgr*
EMP: 284
SALES (corp-wide): 2.94B **Privately Held**
Web: www.cincinnatichildrens.org
SIC: 8733 8071 Medical research; Medical laboratories
PA: Children's Hospital Medical Center
    3333 Burnet Ave
    Cincinnati OH 45229
    513 636-4200

(G-8401)
CINCINNATI CASUALTY COMPANY
6200 S Gilmore Rd (45014-5141)
P.O. Box 145496 (45250-5496)
PHONE......................513 870-2000
Larry Plum, *Pr*
Thomas A Joseph, *Pr*
Robert B Morgan, *Sr VP*
Robert J Driehaus, *Sec*
Ted Elchynski, *Sr VP*
EMP: 103 EST: 1973
SQ FT: 370,000
SALES (est): 25.48MM
SALES (corp-wide): 10.01B **Publicly Held**
Web: www.cinfin.com
SIC: 6411 Insurance agents, nec
HQ: Cincinnati Insurance Company
    6200 S Gilmore Rd
    Fairfield OH 45014
    513 870-2000

(G-8402)
CINCINNATI FINANCIAL CORP (PA)
6200 S Gilmore Rd (45014-5141)
P.O. Box 145496 (45250-5496)
PHONE......................513 870-2000
Steven J Johnston, *Ch Bd*
Stephen M Spray, *
Michael J Sewell, *Ex VP*
Lisa A Love, *CLO*
Steven A Soloria, *Ex VP*
EMP: 3214 EST: 1968
SQ FT: 1,508,200
SALES (est): 10.01B
SALES (corp-wide): 10.01B **Publicly Held**
Web: www.cinfin.com
SIC: 6311 6411 6211 7389 Life insurance carriers; Property and casualty insurance agent; Investment firm, general brokerage; Financial services

(G-8403)
CINCINNATI INDEMINTY CO
6200 S Gilmore Rd (45014-5141)
P.O. Box 145496 (45250-5496)
PHONE......................513 870-2000
John Schiff, *Pr*
T F Elchynski, *
James E Benoski, *
EMP: 94 EST: 1988
SALES (est): 14.71MM
SALES (corp-wide): 10.01B **Publicly Held**
Web: www.cinfin.com
SIC: 6411 Insurance agents, nec
HQ: Cincinnati Insurance Company
    6200 S Gilmore Rd
    Fairfield OH 45014
    513 870-2000

(G-8404)
CINCINNATI INSURANCE COMPANY (HQ)
Also Called: Cincinnati Insurance
6200 S Gilmore Rd (45014-5141)
P.O. Box 145496 (45250-5496)
PHONE......................513 870-2000
EMP: 2750 EST: 1950
SALES (est): 1.48B
SALES (corp-wide): 10.01B **Publicly Held**
Web: www.cinfin.com
SIC: 6311 6331 6321 6211 Life insurance carriers; Fire, marine and casualty insurance and carriers; Accident and health insurance; Security brokers and dealers
PA: Cincinnati Financial Corporation
    6200 S Gilmore Rd
    Fairfield OH 45014
    513 870-2000

(G-8405)
CINCINNATI LIFE INSURANCE CO
6200 S Gilmore Rd (45014-5141)
P.O. Box 145496 (45250-5496)
PHONE......................513 870-2000
David M Popplewell, *Pr*
David M Popplewell, *Pr*
Robert J Driehaus, *
Kenneth W Stecher, *
EMP: 950 EST: 1988
SQ FT: 383,000
SALES (est): 101.65MM
SALES (corp-wide): 10.01B **Publicly Held**
Web: www.cinfin.com
SIC: 6411 Insurance agents, nec
HQ: Cincinnati Insurance Company
    6200 S Gilmore Rd
    Fairfield OH 45014
    513 870-2000

(G-8406)
COMMUNITY HEALTH ALLIANCE (PA)
1020 Symmes Rd (45014)
PHONE......................513 896-3458
Scott Gehring, *CEO*
Kelly Hibner-kald, *COO*
Marc Seifert, *CFO*
EMP: 31 EST: 2016
SALES (est): 12.43MM
SALES (corp-wide): 12.43MM **Privately Held**
Web: www.communityhealthalliance.com
SIC: 8069 8063 Alcoholism rehabilitation hospital; Mental hospital, except for the mentally retarded

(G-8407)
DNA DIAGNOSTICS CENTER INC (DH)
Also Called: Ddc
1 Ddc Way (45014-2281)
PHONE......................513 881-7800
EMP: 76 EST: 1994
SQ FT: 66,000
SALES (est): 46.78MM
SALES (corp-wide): 220.81K **Privately Held**
Web: www.dnacenter.com
SIC: 8734 Testing laboratories
HQ: Eurofins Clinical Testing Us Holdings, Inc.
    2200 Rittenhouse St # 175
    Des Moines IA 50321
    717 656-2300

(G-8408)
DVA HLTHCARE - STHWEST OHIO LL
Also Called: Fairfield Dialysis
1210 Hicks Blvd (45014-1921)
PHONE......................513 939-1110
John Winstel, *Brnch Mgr*
EMP: 35
SIC: 8092 Kidney dialysis centers
HQ: Dva Healthcare - Southwest Ohio, Llc
    2000 16th St
    Denver CO 80202
    253 733-4501

(G-8409)
EAGLE INDUSTRIES OHIO INC
Also Called: Allgood Home Improvements
275 Commercial Dr (45014-5565)
PHONE......................513 247-2900
Edward Grant, *Pr*
EMP: 35 EST: 1995
SQ FT: 5,114
SALES (est): 2.14MM **Privately Held**
Web: www.myallgoodhome.com
SIC: 7299 Home improvement and renovation contractor agency

(G-8410)
ELEMENT MTLS TECH CNCNNATI INC (DH)
Also Called: Element
3701 Port Union Rd (45014-2200)
PHONE......................513 984-4112
Charles Noall, *CEO*
Steven Etter, *
Bob Neugebauer, *
Charles Noall, *Pr*
Jo Wetz, *Ex VP*
EMP: 45 EST: 1970
SQ FT: 11,000
SALES (est): 112.01MM **Privately Held**
Web: www.element.com
SIC: 8734 Testing laboratories
HQ: Element Materials Technology Group Limited
    Davidson Building, 5 Southampton Street
    London WC2E
    800 470-3598

(G-8411)
EMBASSY HEALTHCARE INC
Also Called: Parkside Nrsing Rehabilitation
908 Symmes Rd (45014-1842)
PHONE......................513 868-6500
Aaron Handler, *Pr*
EMP: 40 EST: 2008
SALES (est): 14.31MM **Privately Held**
Web: www.embassyhealthcare.net
SIC: 8051 Convalescent home with continuous nursing care

(G-8412)
ERIC BOEPPLER FMLY LTD PARTNR
Also Called: Empire Transportation
9331 Seward Rd Ste A (45014-2272)
PHONE......................513 860-3324
Eric Boeppler, *Pt*
EMP: 60 EST: 2005
SALES (est): 1.53MM **Privately Held**
Web: www.empire-transportation.com
SIC: 4119 Limousine rental, with driver

(G-8413)
ESJ CARRIER CORPORATION
3240 Production Dr (45014-4230)
P.O. Box 181060 (45018-1060)
PHONE......................513 728-7388
Eva Ambrose, *CEO*
Sandra Ambrose, *
EMP: 40 EST: 1998
SALES (est): 8.22MM **Privately Held**
Web: www.esjcarrier.com
SIC: 4731 Truck transportation brokers

(G-8414)
FOX SERVICES INC
4660 Industry Dr (45014-1923)
PHONE......................513 858-2022
Gary Fox Senior, *Ch*
Kelly Fox, *Pr*
Patty Fox, *Treas*
Jane Fox, *VP*
EMP: 30 EST: 1980
SQ FT: 3,750
SALES (est): 4.35MM **Privately Held**
SIC: 1611 1794 1795 5261 Grading; Excavation and grading, building construction; Wrecking and demolition work; Top soil

(G-8415)
FOXTAIL FOODS LLC
6880 Fairfield Business Ctr (45014)
PHONE......................973 582-4613
EMP: 2767 EST: 2019
SALES (est): 43.04MM
SALES (corp-wide): 434.51MM **Privately Held**
Web: www.foxtailfoods.com
SIC: 5141 Groceries, general line
PA: Fairfield Gourmet Food Corp.
    11 Cliffside Dr
    Cedar Grove NJ 07009
    973 575-4365

(G-8416)
GATEWAY TO GRACE FUNDATION INC
1260 Hicks Blvd (45014-1921)
PHONE......................513 869-4645
EMP: 46 EST: 2010
SALES (est): 273.57K **Privately Held**
Web: www.gateway2grace.org

Fairfield - Butler County (G-8417)

GEOGRAPHIC SECTION

SIC: 8351 Child day care services

(G-8417)
GREAT MIAMI VALLEY YMCA
Also Called: Fairfield YMCA Pre-School
5220 Bibury Rd (45014-3665)
PHONE...............513 829-3091
Julia Brant, *Dir*
EMP: 84
SALES (corp-wide): 13.47MM **Privately Held**
Web: www.gmvymca.org
SIC: 8641 7991 8351 7032 Youth organizations; Physical fitness facilities; Child day care services; Youth camps
PA: The Great Miami Valley Young Men's Christian Association
105 N 2nd St
Hamilton OH 45011
513 887-0001

(G-8418)
HOGAN TRUCK LEASING INC
2001 Ddc Way (45014-2285)
PHONE...............513 454-3500
Jeff Buhraw, *Mgr*
EMP: 28
SALES (corp-wide): 127.28MM **Privately Held**
Web: www.hogan1.com
SIC: 7513 7363 Truck rental and leasing, no drivers; Truck driver services
PA: Hogan Truck Leasing, Inc.
2150 Schuetz Rd Ste 210
Saint Louis MO 63146
314 421-6000

(G-8419)
HOLIDAY INN EXPRESS
Also Called: Holiday Inn
6755 Fairfield Business Ctr (45014)
PHONE...............513 860-2900
Diana Eynon, *Mgr*
EMP: 33 EST: 1997
SALES (est): 471.19K **Privately Held**
Web: www.holidayinn.com
SIC: 7011 Hotels and motels

(G-8420)
INTERNISTS OF FAIRFIELD INC
5150 Sandy Ln (45014-2738)
PHONE...............513 896-9595
Edward Herzig, *Pr*
EMP: 46 EST: 1978
SQ FT: 2,400
SALES (est): 421.92K **Privately Held**
SIC: 8062 General medical and surgical hospitals

(G-8421)
JACO WATERPROOFING LLC
4350 Wade Mill Rd (45014-5853)
P.O. Box 865 (45061-0865)
PHONE...............513 738-0084
EMP: 27 EST: 1995
SALES (est): 6.7MM **Privately Held**
Web: www.jacowaterproofing.com
SIC: 1799 Waterproofing

(G-8422)
JAMISON CNSTR SOLUTIONS INC
96 Arndt Ct (45014-1942)
PHONE...............513 377-0705
Jamie Lemire, *Pr*
EMP: 30 EST: 2011
SALES (est): 8.96MM **Privately Held**
Web: www.jcsolutionsinc.com
SIC: 1611 1771 1794 Surfacing and paving; Concrete work; Excavation and grading, building construction

(G-8423)
JTF CONSTRUCTION INC
4235 Mulhauser Rd (45014-5450)
PHONE...............513 860-9835
Gregory W Fisher, *Pr*
EMP: 70 EST: 1997
SQ FT: 6,900
SALES (est): 10.43MM **Privately Held**
Web: www.jtfconstruction.com
SIC: 1521 General remodeling, single-family houses

(G-8424)
JUST CANDY LLC
6820 Fairfield Business Ctr Dr (45014)
PHONE...............201 805-8562
Erik Mandell, *Managing Member*
EMP: 38 EST: 2015
SALES (est): 2.03MM **Privately Held**
Web: www.justcandy.com
SIC: 5199 Candy making goods and supplies

(G-8425)
KELLEY BROTHERS ROOFING INC
4905 Factory Dr (45014-1916)
PHONE...............513 829-7717
Robert Kelley, *Pr*
Michael Kelley, *
John Newlon, *
Steven Gebing, *
EMP: 100 EST: 1978
SQ FT: 25,000
SALES (est): 20.7MM **Privately Held**
Web: www.kbroof.com
SIC: 1761 Roofing contractor

(G-8426)
LESAINT LOGISTICS TRNSP INC
200 Northpointe Dr (45014-2231)
PHONE...............513 942-3056
Bob Mitz, *Brnch Mgr*
EMP: 46
SALES (corp-wide): 4.2B **Publicly Held**
Web: www.hubgroup.com
SIC: 4731 Freight transportation arrangement
HQ: Lesaint Logistics Transportation, Inc.
4487 Le Saint Ct
West Chester OH 45014

(G-8427)
LOVELAND EXCAVATING INC
Also Called: Loveland Excavating and Paving
260 Osborne Dr (45014-2246)
PHONE...............513 965-6600
Matthew J Brennan, *CEO*
Donald L Brennan, *Stockholder*
William Peters, *Stockholder*
EMP: 45 EST: 1996
SQ FT: 3,000
SALES (est): 10.21MM
SALES (corp-wide): 10.21MM **Privately Held**
Web: www.lovelandexcavatingandpaving.com
SIC: 1794 Excavation and grading, building construction
PA: Ohio Heavy Equipment Leasing, Llc
9520 Le Saint Dr
Fairfield OH 45014
513 965-6600

(G-8428)
MCCLOY ENGINEERING LLC
Also Called: Accutek Testing Laboratory
3701 Port Union Rd (45014-2200)
PHONE...............513 984-4112
John Mccloy, *Pr*
EMP: 45 EST: 2002
SALES (est): 6.08MM **Privately Held**
SIC: 8734 Product testing laboratories

HQ: Element Materials Technology Huntington Beach Llc
15062 Bolsa Chica St
Huntington Beach CA 92649
714 892-1961

(G-8429)
MEDER ELECTRONIC INC
4150 Thunderbird Ln (45014-2235)
PHONE...............508 295-0771
Bernard Meder, *Ch Bd*
John Beigel, *
Craig Holes, *
Robert Serdy, *
Greg Holmes, *
▲ EMP: 75 EST: 1999
SALES (est): 22.58MM
SALES (corp-wide): 741.05MM **Publicly Held**
Web: www.standexelectronics.com
SIC: 5065 Electronic parts and equipment, nec
HQ: Standexmeder Electronics Gmbh
Friedrich-List-Str. 15
Engen BW 78234
77339253200

(G-8430)
MERCY HAMILTON HOSPITAL
3000 Mack Rd (45014-5335)
PHONE...............513 603-8600
Dave Ferrell, *Pr*
EMP: 29 EST: 1800
SALES (est): 2.57MM **Privately Held**
SIC: 8062 General medical and surgical hospitals

(G-8431)
MIDDLETOWN INNKEEPERS INC
Also Called: Hampton Inn Cncnnati Nrthwst/F
430 Kolb Dr (45014-5361)
PHONE...............513 942-3440
Har S Bharnagar, *Pr*
EMP: 32 EST: 1998
SALES (est): 627.84K **Privately Held**
Web: www.hilton.com
SIC: 7011 Hotels and motels

(G-8432)
MINDFULLY LLC
1251 Nilles Rd Ste 5 (45014-7205)
PHONE...............513 939-0300
Melvin S Shotten, *Prin*
EMP: 87 EST: 2006
SALES (est): 2.41MM **Privately Held**
Web: www.mindfully.com
SIC: 8099 Health and allied services, nec

(G-8433)
MOXIE PEST CONTROL LP
7060 Fairfield Business Ctr (45014)
PHONE...............513 216-1804
EMP: 27
SALES (corp-wide): 247.71K **Privately Held**
Web: www.moxieservices.com
SIC: 7342 Pest control in structures
PA: Moxie Pest Control, Lp
6867 Nancy Ridge Dr Ste E
San Diego CA 92121
858 547-9900

(G-8434)
MULTICARE MANAGEMENT GROUP INC
Also Called: Parkside Nrsing Rhbltation Ctr
908 Symmes Rd (45014-1842)
PHONE...............513 868-6500
Aaron B Handler, *Adm/Dir*
EMP: 61 EST: 1978
SQ FT: 27,000

SALES (est): 10.43MM **Privately Held**
Web: www.embassyhealthcare.net
SIC: 8051 Convalescent home with continuous nursing care

(G-8435)
OSBORNE TRUCKING COMPANY (PA)
325 Osborne Dr (45014-2250)
PHONE...............513 874-2090
Brad Osborne, *Pr*
EMP: 50 EST: 1959
SQ FT: 510,000
SALES (est): 11.69MM
SALES (corp-wide): 11.69MM **Privately Held**
Web: www.osborneho.com
SIC: 4213 Trucking, except local

(G-8436)
RAY ST CLAIR ROOFING INC
3810 Port Union Rd (45014-2202)
PHONE...............513 874-1234
Raymond J St Clair, *Pr*
Kevin St Clair, *
EMP: 35 EST: 1956
SQ FT: 7,000
SALES (est): 4.8MM **Privately Held**
Web: www.raystclair.com
SIC: 1761 1751 1741 Roofing contractor; Window and door (prefabricated) installation; Chimney construction and maintenance

(G-8437)
RIEMAN ARSZMAN CSTM DISTRS INC
Also Called: Custom Distributors
9190 Seward Rd (45014-5406)
PHONE...............513 874-5444
Ken Rieman, *Pr*
EMP: 34 EST: 1985
SQ FT: 15,000
SALES (est): 14.36MM **Privately Held**
Web: www.customdistributors.com
SIC: 5064 Electrical appliances, major

(G-8438)
SCHIFF JOHN J & THOMAS R & CO
Also Called: Schiff Agency
6200 S Gilmore Rd (45014-5141)
P.O. Box 145496 (45250-5496)
PHONE...............513 870-2580
Raymond E Broerman, *Pr*
John J Schiff Junior, *Ch Bd*
EMP: 40 EST: 1939
SALES (est): 2.59MM **Privately Held**
Web: www.schiffinsurance.com
SIC: 6411 Property and casualty insurance agent

(G-8439)
SHIP-PAQ INC
Also Called: Ship-Paq
3845 Port Union Rd (45014-2208)
PHONE...............513 860-0700
James R Jarboe, *CEO*
Randy Jarboe, *Pr*
Nancy L Jarboe, *VP*
Kyle Jarboe, *VP*
▲ EMP: 34 EST: 1987
SQ FT: 46,500
SALES (est): 11.42MM **Privately Held**
Web: www.ship-paq.com
SIC: 5199 Packaging materials

(G-8440)
SIBCY CLINE INC
600 Wessel Dr (45014-3600)
PHONE...............513 385-3330
Rob Stix, *Mgr*

EMP: 81
SALES (corp-wide): 98.72MM **Privately Held**
Web: www.sibcycline.com
SIC: **6531** Real estate agent, residential
PA: Sibcy Cline, Inc.
8044 Montgomery Rd # 300
Cincinnati OH 45236
513 984-4100

(G-8441)
SKYLINE CEM HOLDINGS LLC (PA)
Also Called: Skyline Chili
4180 Thunderbird Ln (45014-2235)
PHONE..................................513 874-1188
Dick Williams, *Interim Chief Executive Officer*
▲ EMP: 137 EST: 1949
SQ FT: 42,000
SALES (est): 58.14MM
SALES (corp-wide): 58.14MM **Privately Held**
Web: www.skylinechili.com
SIC: **5812** 2038 6794 5149 Restaurant, family: chain; Frozen specialties, nec; Franchises, selling or licensing; Groceries and related products, nec

(G-8442)
SOUTHERN GLZERS WINE SPRITS TX
Also Called: Just Cheking Cash
4305 Mulhauser Rd Ste 4 (45014-2265)
PHONE..................................513 755-7082
John Roberts, *Mgr*
EMP: 50
SALES (corp-wide): 7.27B **Privately Held**
Web: www.southernglazers.com
SIC: **5182** Wine
HQ: Southern Glazer's Wine And Spirits Of Texas, Llc
2001 Diplomat Dr
Farmers Branch TX 75234
972 277-2000

(G-8443)
STANDEX ELECTRONICS INC (HQ)
Also Called: Standex-Meder Electronics
4150 Thunderbird Ln (45014-2235)
PHONE..................................513 871-3777
John Meeks, *CEO*
Robert Lintz, *VP*
▲ EMP: 98 EST: 1999
SQ FT: 22,022
SALES (est): 43MM
SALES (corp-wide): 741.05MM **Publicly Held**
Web: www.standexelectronics.com
SIC: **3625** 5065 Motor controls and accessories; Electronic parts and equipment, nec
PA: Standex International Corporation
23 Keewaydin Dr
Salem NH 03079
603 893-9701

(G-8444)
SUNESIS ENVIRONMENTAL LLC
325 Commercial Dr (45014-5567)
PHONE..................................513 326-6000
Richard E Jones Junior, *Pr*
Andrea Strunk, *
EMP: 92 EST: 2015
SALES (est): 5.69MM **Privately Held**
Web: www.sunesisenvironmental.com
SIC: **1629** 1795 1623 Dams, waterways, docks, and other marine construction; Wrecking and demolition work; Sewer line construction

(G-8445)
TGM ASSOCIATES LP
Also Called: Camelot East Apartments
1400 Sherwood Dr (45014-4120)
PHONE..................................513 829-8383
EMP: 28
Web: www.tgmassociates.com
SIC: **6513** Apartment hotel operation
PA: Tgm Associates L.P.
650 5th Ave Fl 28
New York NY 10019

(G-8446)
THE ELLENBEE-LEGGETT COMPANY INC
3765 Port Union Rd (45014-2207)
P.O. Box 8025 (45014)
PHONE..................................513 874-3200
EMP: 110
Web: www.performancefoodservice.com
SIC: **5141** 5147 5142 2015 Groceries, general line; Meats and meat products; Meat, frozen: packaged; Poultry slaughtering and processing

(G-8447)
THERMAL SOLUTIONS INC
9491 Seward Rd (45014-5411)
PHONE..................................513 742-2836
EMP: 55
SALES (corp-wide): 14.37MM **Privately Held**
Web: www.thermalsolutions.com
SIC: **1742** Insulation, buildings
PA: Thermal Solutions, Inc.
9329 County Rd 107
Proctorville OH 45669
740 886-2861

(G-8448)
TREW LLC (PA)
10045 International Blvd (45014-2347)
PHONE..................................800 571-8739
EMP: 92 EST: 2019
SALES (est): 54.68MM
SALES (corp-wide): 54.68MM **Privately Held**
Web: www.trewautomation.com
SIC: **5084** Materials handling machinery

(G-8449)
TRI COUNTY EXTENDED CARE CTR
5200 Camelot Dr (45014-4009)
P.O. Box 18040 (45018-0040)
PHONE..................................513 829-3555
Samuel Boymel, *Pr*
Samuel Boymel, *Ch*
Rachel Boymel, *
Gidon Eltad, *
Peggy Morris, *
EMP: 250 EST: 1978
SQ FT: 120,000
SALES (est): 11.49MM **Privately Held**
Web: www.tricountyextendedcare.com
SIC: **8051** Extended care facility

(G-8450)
UNIVERSAL TRANSPORTATION SYSTE (PA)
Also Called: Uts
5284 Winton Rd (45014-3912)
PHONE..................................513 829-1287
EMP: 200 EST: 1976
SQ FT: 1,200
SALES (est): 18.64MM **Privately Held**
Web: www.uts-ohio.com
SIC: **4111** 8742 Local and suburban transit; Transportation consultant

(G-8451)
US FOODS INC
Also Called: Cinc Transit Whs 1103
4487 Le Saint Ct (45014)
PHONE..................................513 874-3900
EMP: 159
Web: www.usfoods.com
SIC: **5149** Dried or canned foods
HQ: Us Foods, Inc.
9399 W Higgins Rd Ste 500
Rosemont IL 60018

(G-8452)
VERITIV OPERATING COMPANY
Also Called: International Paper
6120 S Gilmore Rd Ste 400 (45014-5163)
PHONE..................................513 285-0999
Jim Baumer, *Brnch Mgr*
EMP: 133
SALES (corp-wide): 14.52B **Privately Held**
Web: www.veritiv.com
SIC: **5113** Industrial and personal service paper
HQ: Veritiv Operating Company
1000 Abrnthy Rd Ne Bldg 4
Atlanta GA 30328
770 391-8200

(G-8453)
WCA GROUP LLC
Also Called: Thomas Glbraith Htg Coolg Plbg
9520 Le Saint Dr (45014)
PHONE..................................513 540-2761
EMP: 174
SALES (corp-wide): 215.03MM **Privately Held**
Web: www.thomasgalbraith.com
SIC: **1711** Warm air heating and air conditioning contractor
HQ: Wca Group, Llc
10640 E 59th St
Indianapolis IN 46236
317 957-0071

(G-8454)
WILLIAMS SCOTSMAN INC
4444 Dixie Hwy (45014-1114)
PHONE..................................978 228-0305
Jason Clemons, *Brnch Mgr*
EMP: 29
SALES (corp-wide): 2.36B **Publicly Held**
Web: www.mobilemini.com
SIC: **4225** General warehousing and storage
HQ: Williams Scotsman, Inc.
4646 E Van Buren St # 40
Phoenix AZ 85008
480 894-6311

(G-8455)
ZEBEC OF NORTH AMERICA INC
210 Donald Dr (45014-3007)
P.O. Box 181570 (45018-1570)
PHONE..................................513 829-5533
Ed Synder, *Pr*
Scott Snyder, *
Chris Snyder, *
◆ EMP: 35 EST: 1992
SQ FT: 7,000
SALES (est): 4.02MM **Privately Held**
Web: www.zebec.com
SIC: **3949** 5091 Sporting and athletic goods, nec; Sporting and recreation goods

Fairfield Township
Butler County

(G-8456)
BETHESDA HOSPITAL INC
Also Called: Bethesda Butler Hospital
3125 Hamilton Mason Rd (45011-5307)
PHONE..................................513 894-8888
Greg Owens, *Dir*
EMP: 140
Web: www.trihealth.com
SIC: **8062** General medical and surgical hospitals
HQ: Bethesda Hospital, Inc.
4750 Wesley Ave
Cincinnati OH 45212
513 569-6100

(G-8457)
BUTLER CNTY BD DVLPMNTAL DSBLT
Liberty Center
5645 Liberty Fairfield Rd (45011-2251)
PHONE..................................513 785-2870
Sherry Dillon, *Mgr*
EMP: 51
SALES (corp-wide): 12.86MM **Privately Held**
Web: www.butlerdd.org
SIC: **8361** 9111 8331 Retarded home; County supervisors' and executives' office; Job training services
PA: Butler County Board Of Developmental Disabilities
282 N Fair Ave
Hamilton OH 45011
513 785-2815

(G-8458)
BUTLER TECH
Also Called: Southwest Ohio Computer Assn
3611 Hamilton Middletown Rd (45011-2241)
PHONE..................................513 867-1028
Mike Crumley, *Superintnt*
EMP: 38
SALES (corp-wide): 78.28K **Privately Held**
Web: www.butlertech.org
SIC: **8211** 7372 Public combined elementary and secondary school; Educational computer software
PA: Butler Technology & Career Development Schools
3603 Hmlton Middletown Rd
Hamilton OH 45011
513 868-1911

(G-8459)
CREEKSIDE GOLF LTD
Also Called: Walden Ponds Golf Club
6090 Golf Club Ln (45011-7816)
PHONE..................................513 785-2999
EMP: 27 EST: 1996
SALES (est): 632.06K **Privately Held**
Web: www.waldenponds.com
SIC: **7992** Public golf courses

(G-8460)
GLENWARD INC
Also Called: GLEN MEADOWS
3472 Hamilton Mason Rd (45011-5437)
PHONE..................................513 863-3100
Glyndon Powell, *Pr*
Chuck Powell, *
EMP: 50 EST: 1974
SQ FT: 4,000
SALES (est): 6.61MM **Privately Held**
Web: www.glen-meadows.net
SIC: **8051** Skilled nursing care facilities

(G-8461)
GREAT MIAMI VALLEY YMCA
Also Called: East Butler County YMCA
6645 Morris Rd (45011-5417)
PHONE..................................513 892-9622
Cindy Koenig, *Brnch Mgr*
EMP: 84

Fairfield Township - Butler County (G-8462)

SALES (corp-wide): 13.47MM **Privately Held**
Web: www.gmvymca.org
SIC: 8641 7991 8351 7032 Youth organizations; Physical fitness facilities; Child day care services; Youth camps
PA: The Great Miami Valley Young Men's Christian Association
105 N 2nd St
Hamilton OH 45011
513 887-0001

(G-8462)
HEALTH AND SAFETY SCIENCES LLC
3189 Princeton Rd (45011-5338)
PHONE.................513 488-1952
Steve Ludwig, *Brnch Mgr*
EMP: 34
SALES (corp-wide): 8.17MM **Privately Held**
Web: www.healthandsafetysciences.com
SIC: 8742 Management consulting services
PA: Health And Safety Sciences, Llc
3224 Winchester Ave
Ashland KY 41101
606 393-3036

(G-8463)
MENARD INC
2865 Princeton Rd (45011-5342)
PHONE.................513 737-2204
EMP: 70
SALES (corp-wide): 1.7B **Privately Held**
Web: www.menards.com
SIC: 5211 1521 Home centers; Single-family home remodeling, additions, and repairs
PA: Menard, Inc.
5101 Menard Dr
Eau Claire WI 54703
715 876-2000

(G-8464)
ROBIDEN INC
Also Called: Red Squirrel
6059 Creekside Way (45011-7882)
PHONE.................513 421-0000
Dennis Kurlas, *Pr*
EMP: 27 **EST:** 1988
SALES (est): 942.47K **Privately Held**
SIC: 0782 Lawn and garden services

(G-8465)
TRANSITIONAL LIVING LLC (HQ)
Also Called: Transitional Living Inc
2052 Princeton Rd (45011-4746)
PHONE.................513 863-6383
Sheri Bartles, *Ex Dir*
David F Craft, *
Mike Francis, *
EMP: 65 **EST:** 1978
SQ FT: 20,000
SALES (est): 10.4MM
SALES (corp-wide): 12.43MM **Privately Held**
Web: www.tliving.org
SIC: 8069 Alcoholism rehabilitation hospital
PA: Community Health Alliance
1020 Symmes Road
Fairfield OH 45014
513 896-3458

(G-8466)
TRIHEALTH INC
Also Called: Heritage Butlr Fmly Physicians
3145 Hamilton Mason Rd Ste 300 (45011-8556)
PHONE.................513 867-0015
EMP: 122
Web: www.cgha.com
SIC: 8011 Physicians' office, including specialists
HQ: Trihealth, Inc.
625 Eden Park Dr
Cincinnati OH 45202
513 569-5400

Fairlawn
Summit County

(G-8467)
BOBER MARKEY FEDOROVICH & CO (PA)
Also Called: Bmf
3421 Ridgewood Rd Ste 300 (44333-3180)
PHONE.................330 762-9785
Stanley M Bober, *Pr*
Allen Markey, *VP*
M Richard Bendel, *VP*
Richard C Fedorovich, *Mng Pt*
Dale Reuther, *VP*
EMP: 78 **EST:** 1959
SQ FT: 11,000
SALES (est): 10.58MM
SALES (corp-wide): 10.58MM **Privately Held**
Web: www.bmf.cpa
SIC: 8721 Certified public accountant

(G-8468)
CADNA RUBBER COMPANY INC
Also Called: Cadna Automotive
703 S Cleveland Massillon Rd (44333-3023)
PHONE.................901 566-9090
◆ **EMP:** 30
SIC: 5013 Automotive engines and engine parts

(G-8469)
CELLCO PARTNERSHIP
Also Called: Verizon Wireless
3750 W Market St Unit A (44333-4803)
PHONE.................330 697-2211
EMP: 71
SALES (corp-wide): 133.97B **Publicly Held**
Web: www.verizonwireless.com
SIC: 4812 Cellular telephone services
HQ: Cellco Partnership
1 Verizon Way
Basking Ridge NJ 07920

(G-8470)
CHIMA TRAVEL BUREAU INC (PA)
55 Merz Blvd Unit B (44333-2895)
PHONE.................330 867-4770
Craig P Chima, *Pr*
Lance Chima, *
Derek Chima, *
EMP: 28 **EST:** 1918
SQ FT: 2,000
SALES (est): 4.63MM
SALES (corp-wide): 4.63MM **Privately Held**
Web: www.chima.travel
SIC: 4724 Tourist agency arranging transport, lodging and car rental

(G-8471)
CLEVELAND CLINIC FOUNDATION
Also Called: Cleveland Clnic Akron Gen Smmi
3600 W Market St Ste 200 (44333-4540)
PHONE.................833 427-5634
EMP: 41
SALES (corp-wide): 14.48B **Privately Held**
Web: my.clevelandclinic.org
SIC: 8062 General medical and surgical hospitals
PA: The Cleveland Clinic Foundation
9500 Euclid Ave
Cleveland OH 44195
216 636-8335

(G-8472)
CUTLER REAL ESTATE (PA)
2800 W Market St (44333-4007)
P.O. Box 3076 (44223-0376)
PHONE.................330 836-9141
Jay Cutler, *Pr*
William H Marting, *
Dana E Gechoff, *
EMP: 80 **EST:** 1949
SQ FT: 10,000
SALES (est): 6.01MM
SALES (corp-wide): 6.01MM **Privately Held**
Web: jmills.cutlerhomes.com
SIC: 6531 Real estate agent, residential

(G-8473)
DEEDSCOM INC
3094 W Market St Ste 242 (44333-3624)
PHONE.................330 606-0119
Shawn Shepherd, *Owner*
EMP: 28 **EST:** 2015
SALES (est): 86.25K **Privately Held**
Web: www.deeds.com
SIC: 8111 Legal services

(G-8474)
DENTAL HEALTH SERVICES
110 N Miller Rd Ste 200 (44333-3787)
PHONE.................330 864-9090
Franchesk Dearlo, *Owner*
Marvin D Cohen D.d.s., *Owner*
▲ **EMP:** 35 **EST:** 1979
SALES (est): 868.93K **Privately Held**
Web: www.dentalhealthservices.com
SIC: 8021 Dentists' office

(G-8475)
DIALAMERICA MARKETING INC
3090 W Market St Ste 210 (44333-3616)
PHONE.................330 836-5293
Ted Herik, *Mgr*
EMP: 320
SALES (corp-wide): 101.12MM **Privately Held**
Web: www.aucera.com
SIC: 7389 Telemarketing services
PA: Dialamerica Marketing, Inc.
960 Macarthur Blvd
Mahwah NJ 07430
201 327-0200

(G-8476)
EMERALD HEALTH NETWORK INC (HQ)
3320 W Market St # 100 (44333-3306)
PHONE.................216 479-2030
Peter Osner, *Pr*
EMP: 65 **EST:** 1983
SQ FT: 26,000
SALES (est): 4.93MM **Privately Held**
SIC: 8742 Hospital and health services consultant
PA: Ehn Holdings, Incorporated
1301 E 9th St Ste 24
Cleveland OH 44114

(G-8477)
ENGINEERING CONS GROUP INC
3394 W Market St (44333-3306)
P.O. Box 13375 (44334-8775)
PHONE.................330 869-9949
Michael Santucci, *Pr*
James Scavuzzo, *VP*
Deborah Patton, *Mgr*
EMP: 63 **EST:** 1992
SQ FT: 5,000
SALES (est): 4.43MM **Privately Held**
Web: www.ecg-inc.com
SIC: 7371 Computer software development

(G-8478)
FAIRLAWN ASSOCIATES LTD
Also Called: Hilton Akron Fairlawn
3180 W Market St (44333-3314)
PHONE.................330 867-5000
EMP: 150 **EST:** 1978
SQ FT: 250,000
SALES (est): 6.56MM **Privately Held**
Web: www.akronhilton.com
SIC: 7011 5812 6519 6512 Hotels and motels ; Restaurant, family: chain; Real property lessors, nec; Commercial and industrial building operation

(G-8479)
FAIRLAWN OPCO LLC
Also Called: Arbors At Fairlawn
575 S Cleveland Massillon Rd (44333-3019)
PHONE.................502 429-8062
Robert Norcross, *CEO*
EMP: 99 **EST:** 2014
SQ FT: 60,000
SALES (est): 6.25MM **Privately Held**
Web: www.arborsatfairlawn.com
SIC: 8051 Convalescent home with continuous nursing care

(G-8480)
FIRST CHICE MED STFFING OHIO I
3200 W Market St Ste 1 (44333-3315)
PHONE.................330 867-1409
Cammy Davis, *Brnch Mgr*
EMP: 66
SALES (corp-wide): 6.66MM **Privately Held**
Web: www.firstchoiceohio.com
SIC: 8099 Medical services organization
PA: First Choice Medical Staffing Of Ohio, Inc.
1457 W 117th St
Cleveland OH 44107
216 521-2222

(G-8481)
FIRST COMMUNICATIONS LLC (PA)
Also Called: First Communications
3340 W Mkt St (44333-3381)
PHONE.................330 835-2323
TOLL FREE: 888
Raymond Hexamer, *Managing Member*
Joseph Morris, *
Marvin Sharpless, *
Margi Shaw, *
Mark Sollenberger, *
▲ **EMP:** 85 **EST:** 1998
SALES (est): 49.95MM
SALES (corp-wide): 49.95MM **Privately Held**
Web: www.firstcomm.com
SIC: 8748 Telecommunications consultant

(G-8482)
FULLY ACCOUNTABLE LLC
2725 Abington Rd Ste 100 (44333-4042)
PHONE.................330 940-1440
Christopher Giorgio, *Prin*
EMP: 30 **EST:** 2016
SALES (est): 1.3MM **Privately Held**
Web: www.fullyaccountable.com
SIC: 8721 Accounting, auditing, and bookkeeping

GEOGRAPHIC SECTION

Findlay - Hancock County (G-8505)

(G-8483)
HOSPICE CARE OHIO
Also Called: Hospice Visiting Nurse Service
3358 Ridgewood Rd (44333-3118)
PHONE.................................330 665-1455
EMP: 98 EST: 1994
SALES (est): 4.36MM **Privately Held**
SIC: 8082 Visiting nurse service

(G-8484)
HUNTINGTON NATIONAL BANK
2700 W Market St (44333-4236)
PHONE.................................330 867-2828
Dave Coduto, *Brnch Mgr*
EMP: 41
SALES (corp-wide): 10.84B **Publicly Held**
Web: www.huntington.com
SIC: 6029 Commercial banks, nec
HQ: The Huntington National Bank
    41 S High St
    Columbus OH 43215
    614 480-4293

(G-8485)
INNOVAIRRE COMMUNICATIONS LLC
3200 W Market St Ste 302 (44333-3326)
PHONE.................................330 869-8500
EMP: 226
SALES (corp-wide): 447.95MM **Privately Held**
Web: www.innovairre.com
SIC: 7389 Fund raising organizations
PA: Innovairre Communications, Llc
    2 Executive Campus # 200
    Cherry Hill NJ 08002
    856 663-2500

(G-8486)
INTERIM HALTHCARE COLUMBUS INC
Also Called: Interim Services
3040 W Market St Ste 1 (44333-3642)
PHONE.................................330 836-5571
Jan Pike, *Mgr*
EMP: 262
SALES (corp-wide): 52.16MM **Privately Held**
Web: www.interimhealthcare.com
SIC: 7363 7361 Temporary help service; Nurses' registry
HQ: Interim Healthcare Of Columbus, Inc.
    784 Morrison Rd
    Gahanna OH 43230
    614 888-3130

(G-8487)
JCK RECYCLING LLC
3090 W Market St (44333)
PHONE.................................419 698-1153
◆ EMP: 30 EST: 2002
SALES (est): 5.23MM
SALES (corp-wide): 47.82MM **Privately Held**
Web: www.omnisource.com
SIC: 7389 Scrap steel cutting
HQ: Protrade Steel Company, Ltd.
    5700 Darrow Rd Ste 114
    Hudson OH 44236

(G-8488)
KAISER FOUNDATION HOSPITALS
Also Called: Fairlawn Medical Offices
4055 Embassy Pkwy Ste 110 (44333-1781)
PHONE.................................800 524-7371
EMP: 29
SALES (corp-wide): 70.8B **Privately Held**
Web: www.kaisercenter.com
SIC: 8011 Offices and clinics of medical doctors
HQ: Kaiser Foundation Hospitals Inc
    1 Kaiser Plz
    Oakland CA 94612
    510 271-6611

(G-8489)
KUMHO TIRE CO INC
711 Kumho Dr (44333-5101)
PHONE.................................330 666-4030
Robert Loeser, *Genl Mgr*
EMP: 45 EST: 1992
SQ FT: 30,000
SALES (est): 3.02MM **Privately Held**
Web: www.kumhotireusa.com
SIC: 8733 Research institute
PA: Kumho Tire
    69 Banpo-Daero 9-Gil Seocho-Gu
    Seoul

(G-8490)
MIRACLE PATH STAFFING AGCY INC
123 S Miller Rd Ste 225 (44333-4181)
PHONE.................................234 205-3541
Amena Barnes, *Pr*
EMP: 50 EST: 2017
SALES (est): 850K **Privately Held**
Web: www.miraclepathstaffingagency.com
SIC: 8742 7361 Management consulting services; Employment agencies

(G-8491)
MONTROSE FORD INC (PA)
Also Called: MTA Leasing
3960 Medina Rd (44333-2495)
P.O. Box 5260 (44334-0260)
PHONE.................................330 666-0711
TOLL FREE: 800
Michael Thompson, *Ch Bd*
Joseph Stefanini,   *
Chris Mills,   *
Mary Lou Taylor,   *
EMP: 103 EST: 1980
SQ FT: 20,000
SALES (est): 97.63MM
SALES (corp-wide): 97.63MM **Privately Held**
Web: www.montrosefordakron.com
SIC: 5511 5521 7515 7513 Automobiles, new and used; Used car dealers; Passenger car leasing; Truck rental and leasing, no drivers

(G-8492)
OLYMPIC UROGYNECOLOGY LLC
3009 Smith Rd Ste 400 (44333-2670)
PHONE.................................330 953-3414
EMP: 30
SALES (corp-wide): 891.38K **Privately Held**
Web: www.summiturogyn.com
SIC: 8011 Gynecologist
PA: Olympic Urogynecology, Llc
    925 Trailwood Dr
    Youngstown OH 44512
    330 953-3414

(G-8493)
PAC ASSOCIATES INC
Also Called: Doubletree
3150 W Market St (44333-3314)
PHONE.................................330 869-9000
Rennick Andreoli, *CEO*
EMP: 75 EST: 1991
SALES (est): 1.41MM **Privately Held**
Web: www.pacassociates.com
SIC: 7011 Hotels

(G-8494)
PRO-MODEL & TALENT MGMT INC
3421 Ridgewood Rd (44333-3164)
PHONE.................................330 665-0723
EMP: 36 EST: 2015
SALES (est): 421.64K **Privately Held**
Web: www.pmtm.com
SIC: 8741 Management services

(G-8495)
SALO INC
Also Called: Interim Healthcare
3040 W Market St Ste 1 (44333-3642)
PHONE.................................330 836-5571
Joyce Macy, *Mgr*
EMP: 234
SALES (corp-wide): 52.16MM **Privately Held**
Web: www.interimhealthcare.com
SIC: 8082 Home health care services
PA: Salo, Inc.
    300 W Wlson Brdge Rd Ste
    Columbus OH 43085
    614 436-9404

(G-8496)
SANCTUARY SOFTWARE STUDIO INC
3090 W Market St Ste 300 (44333-3623)
PHONE.................................330 666-9690
EMP: 49 EST: 1993
SALES (est): 2.15MM **Privately Held**
Web: www.sancsoft.com
SIC: 7372 7371 Application computer software; Computer software development

(G-8497)
SCOTT S DUKO ATTORNEY AT LAW
3560 W Market St (44333-2664)
PHONE.................................800 593-6676
EMP: 31
SALES (corp-wide): 574.94K **Privately Held**
SIC: 8111 General practice attorney, lawyer
PA: Scott S. Duko, Attorney At Law, Ltd
    3685 Stutz Dr Ste 100
    Canfield OH 44406
    330 550-5428

(G-8498)
SEIBERT-KECK INSURANCE AGENCY (PA)
2950 W Market St Ste A (44333-3600)
PHONE.................................330 867-3140
EMP: 38 EST: 1910
SQ FT: 17,000
SALES (est): 10.61MM
SALES (corp-wide): 10.61MM **Privately Held**
Web: www.ip-sk.com
SIC: 6411 Insurance agents, nec

(G-8499)
SENTIENT STUDIOS LTD
2894 Chamberlain Rd Apt 6 (44333-3468)
P.O. Box 13141 (44334-8541)
PHONE.................................330 204-8636
William Genkin, *Managing Member*
EMP: 41 EST: 2016
SALES (est): 1.04MM **Privately Held**
SIC: 7373 3569 Computer integrated systems design; Robots, assembly line: industrial and commercial

(G-8500)
ST EDWARD HOME
Also Called: VILLAGE AT SAINT EDWARD
3131 Smith Rd (44333-2697)
PHONE.................................330 668-2828
EMP: 200 EST: 1964
SQ FT: 210,000
SALES (est): 22.78MM **Privately Held**
Web: www.vsecommunities.org
SIC: 8051 8361 Skilled nursing care facilities ; Residential care

(G-8501)
STOUFFER REALTY INC (PA)
130 N Miller Rd Ste A (44333-3728)
PHONE.................................330 835-4900
Gary D Stouffer, *Pr*
EMP: 47 EST: 1987
SALES (est): 9.74MM
SALES (corp-wide): 9.74MM **Privately Held**
Web: www.stoufferrealty.com
SIC: 6531 Real estate agent, residential

(G-8502)
SUMMA HEALTH
Also Called: Summa Rehabilitation Services
3378 W Market St # B (44333-3306)
PHONE.................................330 836-9023
EMP: 60
SALES (corp-wide): 1.78B **Privately Held**
Web: www.summahealth.org
SIC: 8062 General medical and surgical hospitals
PA: Summa Health System
    1077 Gorge Blvd
    Akron OH 44310
    330 375-3000

(G-8503)
WELTY BUILDING COMPANY LTD (PA)
3421 Ridgewood Rd Ste 200 (44333-3165)
PHONE.................................330 867-2400
Donzell Taylor, *CEO*
Donzell S Taylor,   *
Jeffrey W Floyd,   *
Mary Taylor,   *
EMP: 48 EST: 1945
SQ FT: 2,400
SALES (est): 47.03MM
SALES (corp-wide): 47.03MM **Privately Held**
Web: www.thinkwelty.com
SIC: 1542 8741 1522 Commercial and office building, new construction; Construction management; Hotel/motel and multi-family home construction

Findlay
Hancock County

(G-8504)
631 SOUTH MAIN STREET DEV LLC
Also Called: Hancock Hotel
631 S Main St (45840-3127)
PHONE.................................419 423-0631
Rodney Nichols, *Managing Member*
EMP: 70 EST: 2018
SALES (est): 4.88MM **Publicly Held**
Web: www.hancockhotel.com
SIC: 7011 Hotels
PA: Marathon Petroleum Corporation
    539 S Main St
    Findlay OH 45840

(G-8505)
A B M INC
119 E Sandusky St (45840)
PHONE.................................419 421-2292
Wayne Mitrick, *Mgr*
EMP: 1494
Web: www.abm.com
SIC: 7349 Cleaning service, industrial or commercial

Findlay - Hancock County (G-8506)

PA: A B M, Inc.
180 N Lasalle St Ste 1700
Chicago IL 60601

(G-8506)
ACT I TEMPORARIES FINDLAY INC
2017 Tiffin Ave (45840-9502)
PHONE..............................419 423-0713
Angela Robinson, *Pr*
William Robinson, *
EMP: 30 **EST:** 1959
SQ FT: 750
SALES (est): 1.01MM **Privately Held**
SIC: 7363 Temporary help service
PA: The Act 1 Group Inc
1999 W 190th St
Torrance CA 90504

(G-8507)
ADP RPO
Also Called: ADP
3401 Technology Dr (45840-9547)
PHONE..............................419 420-1830
Terry Terhark, *CEO*
EMP: 44 **EST:** 2015
SALES (est): 3.84MM
SALES (corp-wide): 18.01B **Publicly Held**
Web: www.adp.com
SIC: 7374 Data processing service
PA: Automatic Data Processing, Inc.
1 Adp Blvd
Roseland NJ 07068
973 974-5000

(G-8508)
ALVADA CONST INC
Also Called: Alvada Construction
1700 Fostoria Ave Ste 800 (45840-6222)
P.O. Box 390 (45839-0390)
PHONE..............................419 595-4224
Richard Kirk, *Pr*
Kevin Kurtz, *Prin*
Scott Gross, *Prin*
Jean Rogier, *Prin*
Roger Bishop, *Prin*
EMP: 150 **EST:** 1987
SQ FT: 1,500
SALES (est): 25.28MM **Privately Held**
Web: www.alvadaconstruction.com
SIC: 1542 Commercial and office building, new construction

(G-8509)
APPRAISAL RESEARCH CORPORATION (PA)
101 E Sandusky St Ste 408 (45840-3257)
P.O. Box 1002 (45839-1002)
PHONE..............................419 423-3582
Richard Hoffman, *Pr*
Janice A Hoffman, *
EMP: 100 **EST:** 1978
SQ FT: 3,600
SALES (est): 5.28MM
SALES (corp-wide): 5.28MM **Privately Held**
Web: www.vgsi.com
SIC: 6531 Appraiser, real estate

(G-8510)
APTIM CORP
16406 E Us Route 224 (45840-9761)
PHONE..............................419 423-3526
EMP: 260
SALES (corp-wide): 2.2B **Privately Held**
SIC: 8748 Environmental consultant
HQ: Aptim Corp.
10001 Woodloch Forest Dr # 450
The Woodlands TX 70802
832 823-2700

(G-8511)
BENCHMARK NATIONAL CORPORATION
1800 Industrial Dr (45840-5439)
PHONE..............................419 424-0900
EMP: 29
SALES (corp-wide): 5.73MM **Privately Held**
Web: www.benchmarknational.com
SIC: 7389 Inspection and testing services
PA: Benchmark National Corporation
3161 N Republic Blvd
Toledo OH 43615
419 843-6691

(G-8512)
BIRCHAVEN VILLAGE (PA)
15100 Birchaven Ln Ofc C (45840-9779)
P.O. Box 1425 (45839-1425)
PHONE..............................419 424-3000
Tim Storer, *Admn*
EMP: 88 **EST:** 1956
SQ FT: 75,000
SALES (est): 35.25MM
SALES (corp-wide): 35.25MM **Privately Held**
Web: www.birchaven.org
SIC: 8051 6514 Skilled nursing care facilities ; Dwelling operators, except apartments

(G-8513)
BIRCHAVEN VILLAGE
415 College St (45840-3619)
PHONE..............................419 424-3000
Robert Benson, *Prin*
EMP: 196
SALES (corp-wide): 35.25MM **Privately Held**
Web: www.birchaven.org
SIC: 8059 Convalescent home
PA: Birchaven Village
15100 Birchaven Ln Ofc C
Findlay OH 45840
419 424-3000

(G-8514)
BLANCHARD VALLEY HEALTH SYSTEM (PA)
1900 S Main St (45840-1214)
PHONE..............................419 423-4500
Scott Malaney, *Pr*
John Bookmyer, *
Duane Jebbett, *
Kurt Geisheimer, *
Karen Klassen Harder, *
EMP: 1196 **EST:** 1891
SQ FT: 50,000
SALES (est): 32.58MM
SALES (corp-wide): 32.58MM **Privately Held**
Web: www.bvhealthsystem.org
SIC: 8741 7349 Hospital management; Building maintenance, except repairs

(G-8515)
BLANCHARD VALLEY MED ASSOC INC
200 W Pearl St (45840-1332)
PHONE..............................419 424-0380
Gary E Hirschfeld Md, *Pr*
EMP: 90 **EST:** 1971
SQ FT: 14,000
SALES (est): 13.04MM **Privately Held**
Web: www.bvma.com
SIC: 8011 Internal medicine, physician/ surgeon

(G-8516)
BLANCHARD VLY RGIONAL HLTH CTR (HQ)
Also Called: Blanchard Valley Hospital
1900 S Main St (45840-1214)
PHONE..............................419 423-4500
Scott Malaney, *Pr*
William D Watkins Cpo Bluffton Campus, *Prin*
▲ **EMP:** 750 **EST:** 1891
SQ FT: 50,000
SALES (est): 383.49MM
SALES (corp-wide): 32.58MM **Privately Held**
Web: www.bvhealthsystem.org
SIC: 8062 Hospital, affiliated with AMA residency
PA: Blanchard Valley Health System
1900 S Main St
Findlay OH 45840
419 423-4500

(G-8517)
BLANCHARD VLY RSDNTIAL SVCS IN
Also Called: BVRSI
1701 E Main Cross St (45840-7064)
PHONE..............................419 422-6503
Tammy Bonifas, *CEO*
Michelle Post, *COO*
Kendra Greene, *Dir Fin*
EMP: 70 **EST:** 2014
SALES (est): 3.8MM **Privately Held**
Web: www.bvrsi.org
SIC: 8322 Individual and family services

(G-8518)
BOB MILLER RIGGING INC
Also Called: Hrm Leasing
11758 Township Road 100 (45840-9730)
P.O. Box 1445 (45839-1445)
PHONE..............................419 422-7477
H Robert Miller, *Pr*
EMP: 30 **EST:** 1988
SALES (est): 2.39MM **Privately Held**
Web: www.millerrigginginc.com
SIC: 4212 Heavy machinery transport, local

(G-8519)
BULLDAWG HOLDINGS LLC (PA)
Also Called: Flag City Mack
151 Stanford Pkwy (45840-1731)
PHONE..............................419 423-3131
Alex B Clarke, *Pr*
Alex B Clarke, *Prin*
Greg Jack, *
EMP: 46 **EST:** 1980
SQ FT: 36,900
SALES (est): 20MM
SALES (corp-wide): 20MM **Privately Held**
Web: www.flagcitymack.com
SIC: 5012 5531 Truck tractors; Truck equipment and parts

(G-8520)
CARMIKE CINEMAS LLC
Also Called: Carmike Cinemas
906 Interstate Dr (45840-1927)
P.O. Box 1403 (45839-1403)
PHONE..............................419 423-7414
Alice Couch, *Brnch Mgr*
EMP: 39
Web: www.amctheatres.com
SIC: 7832 Exhibitors, itinerant: motion picture
HQ: Carmike Cinemas, Llc
11500 Ash St
Leawood KS 66211
913 213-2000

(G-8521)
CASCADE CORPORATION
2000 Production Dr (45840-5449)
P.O. Box 841 (45839-0841)
PHONE..............................419 425-3675
EMP: 32
Web: www.cascorp.com
SIC: 5084 3569 Materials handling machinery; Assembly machines, non-metalworking
HQ: Cascade Corporation
2201 Ne 201st Ave
Fairview OR 97024
503 669-6300

(G-8522)
CENTURY HEALTH INC (PA)
1918 N Main St (45840-3818)
PHONE..............................419 425-5050
Colleen Schlea, *CEO*
Carletta Capes, *
Nida Rider, *
EMP: 51 **EST:** 1976
SQ FT: 11,700
SALES (est): 5.09MM
SALES (corp-wide): 5.09MM **Privately Held**
Web: www.centuryhealth.net
SIC: 8093 Alcohol clinic, outpatient

(G-8523)
COLUMBIA GAS OF OHIO INC
Also Called: Columbia
1800 Broad Ave (45840-2722)
P.O. Box 2318 (43216-2318)
PHONE..............................419 435-7725
H R Rowe, *Brnch Mgr*
EMP: 122
SALES (corp-wide): 5.51B **Publicly Held**
Web: www.columbiagasohio.com
SIC: 4924 Natural gas distribution
HQ: Columbia Gas Of Ohio, Inc.
290 W Nationwide Blvd # 1
Columbus OH 43215
614 460-6000

(G-8524)
CREATIVE HAIR DESIGNS
212 E Sandusky St (45840-4903)
PHONE..............................419 425-4247
Mark Creighton, *Owner*
EMP: 44 **EST:** 1989
SALES (est): 384.56K **Privately Held**
Web: www.creative-hair-designs.com
SIC: 7231 Hairdressers

(G-8525)
DENOVO CONSTRUCTORS INC
853 Tarra Oaks Dr (45840-0927)
P.O. Box 766 (45839-0766)
PHONE..............................419 265-8888
EMP: 83
SALES (corp-wide): 24.44MM **Privately Held**
Web: www.denovogrp.com
SIC: 6512 Nonresidential building operators
PA: Denovo Constructors, Inc.
100 S Wacker Dr Ll1-50
Chicago IL 60606
312 733-9370

(G-8526)
DRURY HOTELS COMPANY LLC
Also Called: Drury Inn & Suites Findlay
820 Trenton Ave (45840-2645)
PHONE..............................419 422-9700
Rebecca Scott, *Brnch Mgr*
EMP: 27
SALES (corp-wide): 555.12MM **Privately Held**
Web: www.druryhotels.com
SIC: 7011 Hotels
PA: Drury Hotels Company, Llc
13075 Manchester Rd # 100
Saint Louis MO 63131
314 429-2255

GEOGRAPHIC SECTION

Findlay - Hancock County (G-8548)

(G-8527)
ENTERPRISE RENT-A-CAR
Also Called: Enterprise Rent-A-Car
2028 Tiffin Ave (45840-9501)
PHONE..................419 424-9626
Rex Bibler, *Prin*
EMP: 34 EST: 2016
SALES (est): 130.87K **Privately Held**
Web: www.enterprise.com
SIC: 7514 Rent-a-car service

(G-8528)
FINDLAY COUNTRY CLUB
1500 Country Club Dr (45840-6369)
PHONE..................419 422-9263
James Price, *COO*
Chad Bain, *
EMP: 40 EST: 1908
SQ FT: 5,000
SALES (est): 2.73MM **Privately Held**
Web: www.findlaycc.com
SIC: 7997 7991 5813 5812 Country club, membership; Physical fitness facilities; Drinking places; Eating places

(G-8529)
FINDLAY INN & CONFERENCE CTR
200 E Main Cross St (45840)
PHONE..................419 422-5682
Ralph Russo, *Pt*
Todd Mccracken, *Genl Mgr*
EMP: 35 EST: 1989
SALES (est): 3.53MM **Privately Held**
Web: www.findlayinn.com
SIC: 7011 7299 6512 5812 Resort hotel; Banquet hall facilities; Nonresidential building operators; Eating places

(G-8530)
FINDLAY SURGERY CENTER LTD
1709 Medical Blvd (45840-1398)
PHONE..................419 421-4845
EMP: 38 EST: 1998
SALES (est): 6.55MM
SALES (corp-wide): 32.58MM **Privately Held**
Web: www.findlaysurgerycenter.com
SIC: 8062 General medical and surgical hospitals
PA: Blanchard Valley Health System
    1900 S Main St
    Findlay OH 45840
    419 423-4500

(G-8531)
FINDLAY TRUCK LINE INC
106 W Front St (45840-3408)
P.O. Box 1362 (45839-1362)
PHONE..................419 422-1945
Gregory J Cassidy, *Pr*
EMP: 86 EST: 1939
SQ FT: 10,000
SALES (est): 2.28MM **Privately Held**
Web: www.findlaywarehousing.com
SIC: 4212 Local trucking, without storage

(G-8532)
FIRST CHOICE SOURCING SOLUTION
15757 Forest Ln (45840-8612)
P.O. Box 723 (45839-0723)
PHONE..................419 359-4002
Lou Fontana, *CEO*
Joshua Benson, *VP*
EMP: 50 EST: 2018
SALES (est): 1.38MM **Privately Held**
Web: www.gofcss.com
SIC: 8748 Business consulting, nec

(G-8533)
FLEETMASTER EXPRESS INC
1531 Harvard Ave (45840-1738)
PHONE..................419 420-1835
Paul Fricke, *Brnch Mgr*
EMP: 30
SALES (corp-wide): 81.91MM **Privately Held**
Web: www.fleetmasterexpress.com
SIC: 4213 Contract haulers
PA: Fleetmaster Express, Incorporated
    1814 Hollins Rd Ne Ste A
    Roanoke VA 24012
    540 344-8834

(G-8534)
FRIENDS SERVICE CO INC (PA)
Also Called: Friends Business Source
2300 Bright Rd (45840-5432)
PHONE..................419 427-1704
Kenneth J Schroeder, *CEO*
Kenneth J Schroeder, *Pr*
Dale Alt, *CIO**
Margaret Schroeder, *
Dennis Mitchell, *
EMP: 73 EST: 1991
SQ FT: 65,000
SALES (est): 48.82MM **Privately Held**
Web: www.friendsoffice.com
SIC: 5021 5044 5087 2752 Furniture; Office equipment; Janitors' supplies; Photolithographic printing

(G-8535)
GARNER TRNSP GROUP INC
9231 County Rd 313 (45840-9005)
P.O. Box 1506 (45839-1506)
PHONE..................419 422-5742
Sherri Garner Brumbaugh, *Pr*
David A Ferris, *
Pamela R Johnson, *
EMP: 136 EST: 1997
SALES (est): 2.16MM **Privately Held**
Web: www.garnertrucking.com
SIC: 4213 Trucking, except local

(G-8536)
GARNER TRUCKING INC (PA)
Also Called: Garner Transportation Group
9291 County Road 313 (45839)
P.O. Box 1506 (45839)
PHONE..................419 422-5742
Jean Garner, *Ch*
Sherri Brumbaugh, *
Don Perkins, *
Lewis S Witherspoon, *
Regina R Garner, *
EMP: 99 EST: 1967
SQ FT: 19,000
SALES (est): 17.97MM
SALES (corp-wide): 17.97MM **Privately Held**
Web: www.garnertrucking.com
SIC: 4213 4731 4212 Contract haulers; Truck transportation brokers; Local trucking, without storage

(G-8537)
GENERATIVE GROWTH II LLC (PA)
317 W Main Cross St (45840-3314)
PHONE..................419 422-8090
EMP: 287 EST: 2017
SALES (est): 96.66MM
SALES (corp-wide): 96.66MM **Privately Held**
Web: www.remkes.com
SIC: 5141 Groceries, general line

(G-8538)
GILMORE JASION MAHLER LTD
Also Called: Pry Professional Group
551 Lake Cascade Pkwy (45840-1388)
P.O. Box 1106 (45839-1106)
PHONE..................419 423-4481
Roger Criblez, *CEO*
EMP: 44
SALES (corp-wide): 8.03MM **Privately Held**
Web: www.gjmltd.com
SIC: 8721 Certified public accountant
PA: Gilmore Jasion Mahler, Ltd
    1715 Indian Wood Cir # 100
    Maumee OH 43537
    419 794-2000

(G-8539)
GRAHAM PACKG PLASTIC PDTS LLC (DH)
170 Stanford Pkwy (45840-1732)
PHONE..................419 423-3271
John Lindy, *Manager*
EMP: 32 EST: 2005
SALES (est): 54.08MM **Publicly Held**
SIC: 5199 Packaging materials
HQ: Graham Packaging Company, L.P.
    700 Indian Springs Dr
    Lancaster PA 17601
    717 849-8500

(G-8540)
HANCO AMBULANCE INC
417 6th St (45840-5198)
PHONE..................419 423-2912
Duane Donaldson, *Pr*
Rob Martin, *
EMP: 36 EST: 1971
SQ FT: 4,200
SALES (est): 455.97K **Privately Held**
Web: www.bvhealthsystem.org
SIC: 4119 Ambulance service

(G-8541)
HANCOCK CNTY BD DVLPMNTAL DSBL
Also Called: Blanchard Valley Center
1700 E Sandusky St (45840-6463)
PHONE..................419 422-6387
Steve Harper, *Prin*
Steve Harper, *Dir*
Kelli Grisham, *
EMP: 65 EST: 2009
SALES (est): 9.33MM **Privately Held**
Web: www.blanchardvalley.org
SIC: 6311 Life insurance

(G-8542)
HANCOCK FEDERAL CREDIT UNION
1701 E Melrose Ave (45840-4415)
P.O. Box 1623 (45839-1623)
PHONE..................419 420-0338
Joyce Mohr, *CEO*
Suzzette Boyd, *Sr VP*
John Holzwart, *VP*
Donna Litchle, *Prin*
EMP: 28 EST: 1938
SALES (est): 4.79MM **Privately Held**
Web: www.hancockfcu.com
SIC: 6061 Federal credit unions

(G-8543)
HANCOCK-HRDN-WYNDT-PTNAM CMNTY (PA)
Also Called: HHWPCAC
1637 Tiffin Ave (45840-6848)
P.O. Box 179 (45839-0179)
PHONE..................419 423-3755
Dennis La Rocco, *Ex Dir*
Dave Salucci, *
EMP: 125 EST: 1965
SQ FT: 6,300
SALES (est): 14.92MM
SALES (corp-wide): 14.92MM **Privately Held**
Web: www.hhwpcac.org
SIC: 8399 Community action agency

(G-8544)
HARDIN STREET MARINE LLC
200 E Hardin St (45840-4969)
PHONE..................419 672-6500
EMP: 66 EST: 2014
SALES (est): 82.94MM **Publicly Held**
SIC: 4612 Crude petroleum pipelines
HQ: Mplx Lp
    200 E Hardin St
    Findlay OH 45840
    419 421-2121

(G-8545)
HCF OF FINDLAY INC
Also Called: Fox Run Manor
11745 Township Road 145 (45840-1093)
PHONE..................419 999-2010
Barbara Masella, *VP*
EMP: 137 EST: 2012
SALES (est): 6.37MM
SALES (corp-wide): 305.93MM **Privately Held**
Web: www.foxrunmanor.com
SIC: 8051 Convalescent home with continuous nursing care
PA: Hcf Management, Inc.
    1100 Shawnee Rd
    Lima OH 45805
    419 999-2010

(G-8546)
HELTON ENTERPRISES INC (PA)
151 Stanford Pkwy (45840-1731)
PHONE..................419 423-4180
Charles D Walter, *Ch Bd*
James Hoffman, *
Dan Campling, *
EMP: 38 EST: 1970
SQ FT: 39,600
SALES (est): 2.49MM
SALES (corp-wide): 2.49MM **Privately Held**
Web: www.nationalease.com
SIC: 7513 5012 5531 Truck leasing, without drivers; Truck tractors; Truck equipment and parts

(G-8547)
HUNTINGTON NATIONAL BANK
Also Called: Home Mortgage
236 S Main St (45840-3352)
P.O. Box 300 (45839-0300)
PHONE..................419 429-4627
James Burwell, *Pr*
EMP: 36
SALES (corp-wide): 10.84B **Publicly Held**
Web: www.huntington.com
SIC: 6029 6022 Commercial banks, nec; State commercial banks
HQ: The Huntington National Bank
    41 S High St
    Columbus OH 43215
    614 480-4293

(G-8548)
HYWAY TRUCKING COMPANY
10060 W Us Route 224 (45840-1914)
P.O. Box 416 (45839-0416)
PHONE..................419 423-7145
Matt Lenhart, *Pr*
EMP: 100 EST: 1986
SALES (est): 20.26MM
SALES (corp-wide): 100.02MM **Privately Held**

Findlay - Hancock County (G-8549) GEOGRAPHIC SECTION

Web: www.hywaytrucking.com
SIC: 4213 4212 Contract haulers; Local trucking, without storage
PA: Fst Logistics, Inc.
   1727 Georgesville Rd
   Columbus OH 43228
   614 529-7900

(G-8549)
INTELLIHARTX LLC (PA)
129 E Crawford St (45840-4802)
P.O. Box 360 (45839-0360)
PHONE..................................419 949-5040
Philip Gower, *Pr*
John Kunysz, *CEO*
Philip Gower, *COO*
EMP: 37 EST: 2012
SQ FT: 32,000
SALES (est): 10.38MM
SALES (corp-wide): 10.38MM **Privately Held**
Web: www.itxcompanies.com
SIC: 8742 6324 Hospital and health services consultant; Hospital and medical service plans

(G-8550)
INTERIM HLTH CARE OF NRTHWSTER
Also Called: Interim Services
2129 Stephen Avnue Ste 3 (45840)
PHONE..................................419 422-5328
Krista Finsto, *Mgr*
EMP: 98
SALES (corp-wide): 52.16MM **Privately Held**
Web: www.interimhealthcare.com
SIC: 8082 Home health care services
HQ: Interim Health Care Of Northwestern Ohio, Inc
   3100 W Central Ave # 250
   Toledo OH 43606

(G-8551)
ITX HEALTHCARE LLC
129 E Crawford St Ste 360 (45840-4802)
PHONE..................................844 489-2273
Philip Robert Gower, *Prin*
EMP: 39 EST: 2016
SALES (est): 1.08MM **Privately Held**
SIC: 8099 Health and allied services, nec

(G-8552)
JK-CO LLC
16960 E State Route 12 (45840-9744)
PHONE..................................419 422-5240
Joseph L Kurtz, *Managing Member*
C Leon Thornton, *
▼ EMP: 45 EST: 2002
SQ FT: 40,000
SALES (est): 9.57MM **Privately Held**
Web: www.jk-co.com
SIC: 3743 4789 Railroad car rebuilding; Railroad car repair

(G-8553)
KANDU GROUP
318 W Main Cross St (45840-3315)
PHONE..................................419 425-2638
Mike Chiarelli, *CEO*
EMP: 80 EST: 1988
SALES (est): 3.08MM **Privately Held**
Web: www.kandugroup.org
SIC: 7361 Employment agencies

(G-8554)
KOHLS DEPARTMENT STORES INC
Also Called: Findlay Distribution Center
7855 County Road 140 (45840-1818)
PHONE..................................419 421-5301
Mike Morgan, *Mgr*
EMP: 30
Web: corporate.kohls.com
SIC: 4225 General warehousing and storage
HQ: Kohl's, Inc.
   N56w17000 Ridgewood Dr
   Menomonee Falls WI 53051
   262 703-7000

(G-8555)
KRAMER ENTERPRISES INC (PA)
Also Called: City Laundry & Dry Cleaning Co
1800 Westfield Dr (45840-1780)
PHONE..................................419 422-7924
TOLL FREE: 800
Paul T Kramer, *Pr*
Pamela E Kramer, *
Carl P Kramer, *
EMP: 70 EST: 1944
SQ FT: 6,500
SALES (est): 10.66MM
SALES (corp-wide): 10.66MM **Privately Held**
Web: www.cityuniformsandlinen.com
SIC: 7213 7216 Uniform supply; Drycleaning plants, except rugs

(G-8556)
LARICHE CHEVROLET-CADILLAC INC
Also Called: Lariche Chevrolet-Cadillac
215 E Main Cross St (45840-4878)
PHONE..................................419 422-1855
TOLL FREE: 800
Lou Lariche, *Pr*
John Lariche, *General Vice President*
Scott Lariche, *
EMP: 72 EST: 1981
SQ FT: 25,000
SALES (est): 10.61MM **Privately Held**
Web: www.larichecars.com
SIC: 5511 5521 7515 7538 Automobiles, new and used; Used car dealers; Passenger car leasing; General automotive repair shops

(G-8557)
LEADFIRSTAI LLC (PA)
1219 W Main Cross St Ste 205 (45840-0707)
PHONE..................................419 424-6647
Gary Harpst, *Managing Member*
EMP: 28 EST: 2001
SALES (est): 9.41MM
SALES (corp-wide): 9.41MM **Privately Held**
Web: www.leadfirst.ai
SIC: 8748 Business consulting, nec

(G-8558)
LEGACY NTRAL STONE SRFACES LLC
Also Called: Legacy Marble and Granite
235 Stanford Pkwy (45840-1733)
PHONE..................................419 420-7440
EMP: 40 EST: 2008
SALES (est): 4.39MM **Privately Held**
Web: www.legacynss.com
SIC: 1743 Marble installation, interior

(G-8559)
LOWES HOME CENTERS LLC
Also Called: Lowe's
1077 Bright Rd (45840-6978)
PHONE..................................419 420-7531
Mary Parkins, *Brnch Mgr*
EMP: 138
SALES (corp-wide): 86.38B **Publicly Held**
Web: www.lowes.com
SIC: 5211 5031 5722 5064 Home centers; Building materials, exterior; Household appliance stores; Electrical appliances, television and radio
HQ: Lowe's Home Centers, Llc
   1000 Lowes Blvd
   Mooresville NC 28117
   336 658-4000

(G-8560)
MANLEYS MANOR NURSING HOME INC
Also Called: HERITAGE, THE
2820 Greenacre Dr (45840-4157)
PHONE..................................419 424-0402
L Don Manley, *Adm/Dir*
Karen Manley, *
EMP: 47 EST: 1967
SQ FT: 1,200,000
SALES (est): 13.16MM **Privately Held**
Web: www.trilogyhs.com
SIC: 8051 6512 Convalescent home with continuous nursing care; Commercial and industrial building operation

(G-8561)
MARATHON PETROLEUM CORPORATION (PA)
Also Called: Marathon Petroleum
539 S Main St (45840-3229)
PHONE..................................419 422-2121
▲ EMP: 1055 EST: 1887
SALES (est): 150.31B **Publicly Held**
Web: www.marathonpetroleum.com
SIC: 2911 5172 Petroleum refining; Gasoline

(G-8562)
MARATHON PETROLEUM SUPPLY LLC
539 S Main St (45840-3229)
PHONE..................................419 422-2121
Kevin Michael Henning, *Managing Member*
EMP: 49 EST: 1997
SALES (est): 98.8MM **Publicly Held**
SIC: 5172 Petroleum products, nec
PA: Marathon Petroleum Corporation
   539 S Main St
   Findlay OH 45840

(G-8563)
MARATHON PIPE LINE LLC (HQ)
539 S Main St Ste 7614 (45840)
PHONE..................................419 422-2121
▲ EMP: 107 EST: 1997
SQ FT: 25,000
SALES (est): 799.62MM **Publicly Held**
Web: www.marathonpipeline.com
SIC: 4612 4613 Crude petroleum pipelines; Refined petroleum pipelines
PA: Marathon Petroleum Corporation
   539 S Main St
   Findlay OH 45840

(G-8564)
MCNAUGHTON-MCKAY ELC OHIO INC
1950 Industrial Dr (45840-5441)
PHONE..................................419 422-2984
Timothy J Krucki, *Prin*
EMP: 30
SQ FT: 35,000
SALES (corp-wide): 2.81B **Privately Held**
SIC: 5063 Electrical supplies, nec
HQ: Mcnaughton-Mckay Electric Company Of Ohio, Inc.
   2255 Citygate Dr
   Columbus OH 43219
   614 476-2800

(G-8565)
MED1CARE LTD (PA)
116 S Main St (45840-3424)
PHONE..................................419 866-0555
Michelle L Barlow, *Prin*
EMP: 98 EST: 2001
SALES (est): 7.76MM
SALES (corp-wide): 7.76MM **Privately Held**
Web: www.med1care.org
SIC: 7363 Medical help service

(G-8566)
MEDCORP INC
330 N Cory St (45840-3566)
PHONE..................................419 425-9700
EMP: 243
SIC: 4119 8082 Ambulance service; Home health care services
PA: Medcorp, Inc.
   745 Medcorp Dr
   Toledo OH 43608

(G-8567)
MIAMI INDUSTRIAL TRUCKS INC
130 Stanford Pkwy (45840-1732)
PHONE..................................419 424-0042
Michael Wechta, *Mgr*
EMP: 37
SALES (corp-wide): 48.64MM **Privately Held**
Web: www.mitlift.com
SIC: 5084 Materials handling machinery
PA: Miami Industrial Trucks, Inc.
   2830 E River Rd
   Moraine OH 45439
   937 293-4194

(G-8568)
MID-AMERICAN CLG CONTRS INC
1648 Tiffin Ave (45840-6849)
PHONE..................................419 429-6222
John Whitaker, *Brnch Mgr*
EMP: 105
Web: www.macc.net
SIC: 7349 Janitorial service, contract basis
PA: Mid-American Cleaning Contractors, Inc.
   447 N Elizabeth St
   Lima OH 45801

(G-8569)
MIDWEST COMMUNICATIONS LLC
Also Called: Comwavz
16380 E Us Route 224 (45840-7743)
P.O. Box 2891 (43606-0891)
PHONE..................................419 420-8000
EMP: 30 EST: 2000
SQ FT: 12,000
SALES (est): 1.34MM **Privately Held**
SIC: 4813 Online service providers

(G-8570)
MILLSTREAM AREA CREDIT UN INC
1007 Western Ave (45840-2347)
PHONE..................................419 422-5626
Karen Reams, *CEO*
Karen Reams, *
EMP: 27 EST: 1966
SALES (est): 3.89MM **Privately Held**
Web: www.millstreamcu.com
SIC: 6061 6163 Federal credit unions; Loan brokers

(G-8571)
MPLX LP (HQ)
200 E Hardin St (45840-4969)
PHONE..................................419 421-2121
Michael J Hennigan, *Pr*
C Kristopher Hagedorn, *Ex VP*

GEOGRAPHIC SECTION
Findlay - Hancock County (G-8594)

EMP: 30 EST: 2012
SALES (est): 11.28B **Publicly Held**
Web: www.mplx.com
SIC: **4612** 4613 Crude petroleum pipelines; Refined petroleum pipelines
PA: Marathon Petroleum Corporation
539 S Main St
Findlay OH 45840

(G-8572)
NAPOLEON WASH-N-FILL INC
Also Called: Flag City Exterior Wash
1035 Croy Dr (45840-6737)
PHONE.................................419 424-1726
Galen Ratliff, *Mgr*
EMP: 117
Web: www.washnfill.com
SIC: **7542** Washing and polishing, automotive
PA: Napoleon Wash-N-Fill, Inc.
339 E Main Cross St
Findlay OH 45840

(G-8573)
NORTHWEST OHIO ORTHPDICS SPT M
7595 County Road 236 (45840-8738)
PHONE.................................419 427-1984
James D Egleston, *Pr*
EMP: 110 EST: 2001
SALES (est): 7.88MM **Privately Held**
Web: www.nwomedicine.com
SIC: **8011** Orthopedic physician

(G-8574)
OHIO MACHINERY CO
Also Called: International Fuel Systems
3541 Speedway Dr (45840-7213)
PHONE.................................419 423-1447
Jim Hemminger, *Brnch Mgr*
EMP: 28
SALES (corp-wide): 185.86MM **Privately Held**
Web: www.ohiocat.com
SIC: **5084** 7538 Engines and parts, diesel; Diesel engine repair: automotive
PA: Ohio Machinery Co.
3993 E Royalton Rd
Broadview Heights OH 44147
440 526-6200

(G-8575)
PARTITIONS PLUS INCORPORATED
12517 County Road 99 (45840-9771)
PHONE.................................419 422-2600
Brian Robinson, *Admn*
EMP: 40 EST: 2011
SQ FT: 40,000
SALES (est): 5.1MM **Privately Held**
Web: www.partitions.plus
SIC: **5046** 2541 5021 Partitions; Wood partitions and fixtures; Racks

(G-8576)
PLUMBLINE CONSULTING LLC
2498 Bluestone Dr (45840-7318)
PHONE.................................419 581-2973
EMP: 29 EST: 2008
SALES (est): 544.48K **Privately Held**
Web: www.plumblineconsulting.com
SIC: **7379** Computer related consulting services

(G-8577)
PLUMBLINE SOLUTIONS INC
Also Called: Solomon Cloud Solutions
1219 W Main Cross St Ste 101 (45840-0702)
PHONE.................................419 581-2963
Gary Harpst, *Ch*
Vern Strong, *

EMP: 27 EST: 2004
SALES (est): 3.72MM **Privately Held**
Web: www.solomoncloudsolutions.com
SIC: **7371** Computer software development

(G-8578)
PRIMROSE RTRMENT CMMNTIES LLC
Also Called: Findlay Retirement Community
8580 Township Road 237 (45840-8507)
PHONE.................................419 422-6200
Kim Remily, *Prin*
EMP: 60
Web: www.primroseretirement.com
SIC: **8361** Aged home
PA: Primrose Retirement Communities Llc
815 N 2nd St
Aberdeen SD 57401

(G-8579)
PRIMROSE SENIOR HOLDINGS LLC
Also Called: Primrose Rtrment Cmnty Findlay
8580 Township Road 237 (45840-8507)
PHONE.................................605 226-3300
James L Thares, *Managing Member*
EMP: 71 EST: 2018
SALES (est): 1.7MM **Privately Held**
Web: www.primroseretirement.com
SIC: **8361** Aged home

(G-8580)
QUALITY LINES INC
2440 Bright Rd (45840-5436)
P.O. Box 904 (45839-0904)
PHONE.................................740 815-1165
Ronald Smith, *Pr*
EMP: 122 EST: 1997
SQ FT: 6,000
SALES (est): 20MM **Privately Held**
SIC: **1623** 7389 Pipeline construction, nsk; Business services, nec

(G-8581)
RENAISSANCE HOUSE INC
1665 Tiffin Ave Ste E (45840-6853)
PHONE.................................419 425-0633
Connie Phillips, *Mgr*
EMP: 58
SALES (corp-wide): 3.75MM **Privately Held**
Web: www.renaissancehouseinc.org
SIC: **8361** Mentally handicapped home
PA: Renaissance House, Inc.
103 N Washington St
Tiffin OH 44883
419 447-7901

(G-8582)
RIDGE & ASSOCIATES INC
9747 W Us Route 224 (45840-9374)
P.O. Box 1091 (45839-1091)
PHONE.................................419 423-3641
Larry J Hoover, *Pr*
Gerald C Lieb, *Sec*
Patty Rall, *Off Mgr*
EMP: 34 EST: 1976
SQ FT: 3,600
SALES (est): 1.13MM **Privately Held**
Web: www.ridgeassociates.com
SIC: **8711** Consulting engineer

(G-8583)
RIGHTTHING LLC (HQ)
Also Called: Rightthing, The
3401 Technology Dr (45840-9547)
PHONE.................................419 420-1830
Terry Terhark, *CEO*
EMP: 360 EST: 2003
SQ FT: 43,000
SALES (est): 54.55MM
SALES (corp-wide): 18.01B **Publicly Held**

Web: www.adp.com
SIC: **7361** Employment agencies
PA: Automatic Data Processing, Inc.
1 Adp Blvd
Roseland NJ 07068
973 974-5000

(G-8584)
SMITHFIELD DIRECT LLC
1124 E Lincoln St (45840-6436)
PHONE.................................419 422-2233
EMP: 93
Web: carando.sfdbrands.com
SIC: **5147** Meats, fresh
HQ: Smithfield Direct, Llc
4225 Naperville Rd # 600
Lisle IL 60532

(G-8585)
SPECTRUM EYE CARE INC
15840 Medical Dr S Ste A (45840-7833)
PHONE.................................419 423-8665
Paul Armstrong, *Pr*
Paul Armstrong, *VP*
Jack G Hendershot Junior, *Pr*
Candice Hendershot, *
EMP: 50 EST: 1973
SQ FT: 2,000
SALES (est): 4.7MM **Privately Held**
Web: www.spectrumeyecareinc.com
SIC: **8011** Opthalmologist

(G-8586)
SPHERION OF LIMA INC
7746 County Road 140 (45840-1792)
PHONE.................................567 208-5471
EMP: 4468
SALES (corp-wide): 22.59MM **Privately Held**
Web: www.applyohio.com
SIC: **7363** Temporary help service
PA: Spherion Of Lima, Inc.
216 N Elizabeth St
Lima OH 45801
419 224-8367

(G-8587)
ST CATHERINES CARE CTR FINDLAY
8455 County Road 140 (45840-1828)
PHONE.................................419 422-3978
Albert E Jenkins Iii, *Pr*
EMP: 41 EST: 1965
SQ FT: 8,500
SALES (est): 1.37MM **Privately Held**
SIC: **8051** Convalescent home with continuous nursing care

(G-8588)
STONECO INC (DH)
1700 Fostoria Ave Ste 200 (45840-6218)
P.O. Box 865 (45839-0865)
PHONE.................................419 422-8854
John T Bearss, *Pr*
Don Weber, *VP*
Jack Zouhary, *Sec*
EMP: 33 EST: 1972
SQ FT: 34,000
SALES (est): 50.04MM
SALES (corp-wide): 32.72B **Privately Held**
Web: www.shellyco.com
SIC: **2951** 1411 Asphalt and asphaltic paving mixtures (not from refineries); Limestone, dimension-quarrying
HQ: Shelly Company
80 Park Dr
Thornville OH 43076
740 246-6315

(G-8589)
STREACKER TRACTOR SALES INC
Also Called: Kubota Authorized Dealer
1218 Trenton Ave (45840-1922)
PHONE.................................419 422-6973
Joe Streacker, *Mgr*
EMP: 38
SALES (corp-wide): 6.63MM **Privately Held**
Web: www.streackertractor.com
SIC: **5999** 5083 Farm equipment and supplies; Farm and garden machinery
PA: Streacker Tractor Sales, Inc.
1400 N 5th St
Fremont OH 43420
419 334-9775

(G-8590)
SUNRISE SENIOR LIVING LLC
Also Called: Sunrise of Findlay
401 Lake Cascade Pkwy (45840-1378)
PHONE.................................419 425-3440
Charles Latta, *Ex Dir*
EMP: 47
SALES (corp-wide): 2.92B **Privately Held**
Web: www.sunriseseniorliving.com
SIC: **8051** 8361 Skilled nursing care facilities ; Residential care
HQ: Sunrise Senior Living, Llc
7902 Westpark Dr
Mc Lean VA 22102

(G-8591)
TESORO REFINING & MKTG CO LLC
539 S Main St (45840-3229)
PHONE.................................419 421-2159
EMP: 162
SIC: **5172** Petroleum products, nec
HQ: Tesoro Refining & Marketing Company Llc
19100 Ridgewood Pkwy
San Antonio TX 78259
210 626-6000

(G-8592)
THE HERCULES TIRE & RUBBER COMPANY (DH)
Also Called: Tire Dealers Warehouse
1995 Tiffin Ave Ste 205 (45840-0311)
PHONE.................................800 677-9535
◆ EMP: 35 EST: 1950
SALES (est): 144.87MM
SALES (corp-wide): 1.82B **Privately Held**
Web: www.herculestire.com
SIC: **5014** Tires and tubes
HQ: American Tire Distributors, Inc.
12200 Herbert Wayne Ct # 150
Huntersville NC 28078
704 992-2000

(G-8593)
THE NATIONAL LIME AND STONE COMPANY (PA)
551 Lake Cascade Pkwy (45840-1388)
P.O. Box 120 (45839-0120)
PHONE.................................419 422-4341
EMP: 30 EST: 1903
SALES (est): 167.89MM
SALES (corp-wide): 167.89MM **Privately Held**
Web: www.natlime.com
SIC: **1422** 1442 3273 1423 Crushed and broken limestone; Sand mining; Ready-mixed concrete; Crushed and broken granite

(G-8594)
TOWNEPLACE SUITES BY MARRIOTT
Also Called: TownePlace Suites By Marriott

Findlay - Hancock County (G-8595)

2501 Tiffin Ave (45840-9512)
PHONE..................419 425-9545
Traci Binkley, *Prin*
EMP: 30 EST: 2007
SALES (est): 602.72K **Privately Held**
Web: www.marriott.com
SIC: 7011 Hotel, franchised

(G-8595)
UNITED PARCEL SERVICE INC
Also Called: UPS
1301 Commerce Pkwy (45840-1971)
PHONE..................419 424-9494
EMP: 41
SALES (corp-wide): 90.96B **Publicly Held**
Web: www.ups.com
SIC: 4215 7521 Parcel delivery, vehicular; Automobile storage garage
HQ: United Parcel Service, Inc.
55 Glenlake Pkwy
Atlanta GA 30328
404 828-6000

(G-8596)
VCA ANIMAL HOSPITALS INC
Also Called: VCA Findlay Animal Hospital
2141 Bright Rd (45840-5433)
PHONE..................419 423-7232
Annette Augsberger, *Brnch Mgr*
EMP: 30
SALES (corp-wide): 42.84B **Privately Held**
Web: www.vcahospitals.com
SIC: 0742 Animal hospital services, pets and other animal specialties
HQ: Vca Animal Hospitals, Inc.
12401 W Olympic Blvd
Los Angeles CA 90064

(G-8597)
WARNER BUICK-NISSAN INC
Also Called: Warner Nissan
1060 County Road 95 (45840)
PHONE..................419 423-7161
Larry R Warner, *Pr*
Chris Phillips, *
EMP: 42 EST: 1971
SQ FT: 17,000
SALES (est): 4.73MM **Privately Held**
Web: www.nissanusa.com
SIC: 5511 7538 7532 5521 Automobiles, new and used; General automotive repair shops; Top and body repair and paint shops; Used car dealers

(G-8598)
WOODSON OPERATIONS ONE LTD
Also Called: Holiday Inn
941 Interstate Dr (45840-1926)
PHONE..................419 420-1776
George Woodson, *CEO*
EMP: 44 EST: 1997
SALES (est): 490.04K **Privately Held**
Web: www.holidayinn.com
SIC: 7011 7991 Hotels and motels; Physical fitness facilities

(G-8599)
YOUNG MNS CHRISTN ASSN FINDLAY (PA)
Also Called: YMCA OF FINDLAY
300 E Lincoln St (45840-4943)
PHONE..................419 422-4424
Bent Finlay, *Ex Dir*
EMP: 100 EST: 1888
SQ FT: 70,000
SALES (est): 4.66MM
SALES (corp-wide): 4.66MM **Privately Held**
Web: www.findlayymca.org

SIC: 8641 7997 7991 Youth organizations; Membership sports and recreation clubs; Physical fitness facilities

Flat Rock
Seneca County

(G-8600)
FLAT ROCK CARE CENTER
7353 County Rd 29 (44828)
PHONE..................419 483-7330
Reverend Nancy S Hull, *Pr*
Jason Grant, *
EMP: 92 EST: 1866
SALES (est): 5.31MM **Privately Held**
Web: www.flatrockhomes.org
SIC: 8361 8741 Mentally handicapped home; Management services

Flushing
Belmont County

(G-8601)
RES-CARE INC
41743 Mount Hope Rd (43977-9777)
PHONE..................740 968-0181
EMP: 34
SALES (corp-wide): 8.83B **Publicly Held**
Web: www.rescare.com
SIC: 8361 Residential care
HQ: Res-Care, Inc.
805 N Whittington Pkwy
Louisville KY 40222
502 394-2100

Forest
Hardin County

(G-8602)
WAMPUM HARDWARE CO
Also Called: Northern Ohio Explosives
17507 Township Road 50 (45843-9602)
P.O. Box 155 (45843-0155)
PHONE..................419 273-2542
Gerald Davis, *Pr*
EMP: 28
SALES (corp-wide): 24.8MM **Privately Held**
Web: www.wampumhardware.com
SIC: 5169 Explosives
PA: Wampum Hardware Co.
636 Paden Rd
New Galilee PA 16141
724 336-4501

Fort Loramie
Shelby County

(G-8603)
AVIATION AUTO TRNSP SPCLSTS IN
Also Called: Aatsi
1100 Tower Dr (45845-8719)
PHONE..................502 785-4657
James Burke, *Pr*
Susan Burke, *VP*
EMP: 42 EST: 2020
SALES (est): 1.24MM **Privately Held**
SIC: 4225 4214 General warehousing; Local trucking with storage

(G-8604)
HICKORY HILL LAKES INC
Also Called: Country Concert
7103 State Route 66 (45845-9756)
PHONE..................937 295-3000

Paul Barhorst, *Prin*
James Prenger, *Prin*
EMP: 50 EST: 1979
SALES (est): 856.7K **Privately Held**
Web: www.countryconcert.com
SIC: 7999 Amusement and recreation, nec

(G-8605)
LINCOLN ELECTRIC AUTOMTN INC (HQ)
Also Called: Tennessee Rand
407 S Main St (45845-8716)
PHONE..................937 295-2120
David M Knapke, *Pr*
EMP: 281 EST: 1962
SQ FT: 82,000
SALES (est): 137.07MM
SALES (corp-wide): 4.19B **Publicly Held**
Web: www.waynetrail.com
SIC: 3728 3599 7692 3544 Aircraft parts and equipment, nec; Tubing, flexible metallic; Welding repair; Special dies, tools, jigs, and fixtures
PA: Lincoln Electric Holdings, Inc.
22801 St Clair Ave
Cleveland OH 44117
216 481-8100

Fort Recovery
Mercer County

(G-8606)
COOPER FARMS INC (PA)
2321 State Route 49 (45846-9501)
P.O. Box 339 (45846-0339)
PHONE..................419 375-4116
James R Cooper, *Pr*
Gary A Cooper, *
Dianne L Cooper, *
Anada E Cooper, *
Neil Diller, *
EMP: 100 EST: 1940
SQ FT: 38,000
SALES (est): 106.74MM
SALES (corp-wide): 106.74MM **Privately Held**
Web: www.cooperfarms.com
SIC: 2048 5191 Poultry feeds; Feed

(G-8607)
COOPER HATCHERY INC
Also Called: Cooper Farms Liquid Egg Pdts
2360 Wabash Rd (45846-9586)
PHONE..................419 375-5800
Jim Cooper, *Prin*
EMP: 50 EST: 2014
SALES (est): 5.14MM **Privately Held**
Web: www.cooperfarms.com
SIC: 5144 Eggs

(G-8608)
FORT RECOVERY EQUITY INC
Also Called: St Anthony Feed Mill
5458 State Route 49 (45846-9551)
PHONE..................419 942-1148
Eldo Wendell, *Mgr*
EMP: 122
SALES (corp-wide): 10.47MM **Privately Held**
Web: www.fortrecoveryindustries.com
SIC: 5153 5191 Grain elevators; Farm supplies
PA: Fort Recovery Equity, Inc.
2351 Wabash Rd
Fort Recovery OH 45846
419 375-4119

(G-8609)
FORT RECOVERY EQUITY INC (PA)
2351 Wabash Rd (45846-9586)
PHONE..................419 375-4119
William Glass, *CEO*
Arnie Sumner, *
EMP: 33 EST: 1919
SQ FT: 15,000
SALES (est): 10.47MM
SALES (corp-wide): 10.47MM **Privately Held**
Web: www.fortrecoveryindustries.com
SIC: 2015 5153 Egg processing; Grain elevators

(G-8610)
HULL BROS INC
Also Called: Kubota Authorized Dealer
520 E Boundary St (45846)
P.O. Box 634 (45846)
PHONE..................419 375-2827
Richard D Hull, *Pr*
Norman F Hull Junior, *VP*
EMP: 27 EST: 1896
SQ FT: 30,000
SALES (est): 4.08MM **Privately Held**
Web: www.hullbros.com
SIC: 5999 5261 5722 5083 Farm equipment and supplies; Lawn and garden equipment; Household appliance stores; Farm and garden machinery

(G-8611)
V H COOPER & CO INC (HQ)
Also Called: Cooper Foods
2321 State Route 49 (45846-9501)
P.O. Box 339 (45846-0339)
PHONE..................419 375-4116
James R Cooper, *Pr*
Gary A Cooper, *
Dianne L Cooper, *
Anada E Cooper, *
Neil Diller, *
EMP: 150 EST: 1975
SQ FT: 4,400
SALES (est): 44.54MM
SALES (corp-wide): 93.22MM **Privately Held**
SIC: 0253 2015 2011 Turkeys and turkey eggs; Chicken slaughtering and processing; Pork products, from pork slaughtered on site
PA: Cooper Hatchery, Inc.
22348 Road 140
Oakwood OH 45873
419 594-3325

(G-8612)
ZUMSTEIN INC (PA)
Also Called: Cheeseman
2200 State Route 119 (45846-9713)
PHONE..................419 375-4132
EMP: 68 EST: 1946
SALES (est): 52.15MM
SALES (corp-wide): 52.15MM **Privately Held**
Web: www.cheeseman.com
SIC: 4213 Trucking, except local

Fostoria
Seneca County

(G-8613)
BODIE ELECTRIC INC
1109 N Main St (44830-1979)
P.O. Box 1043 (44830-1043)
PHONE..................419 435-3672
Marianne Bodie, *Pr*
R Scott Bodie, *
Pete Finch, *

GEOGRAPHIC SECTION

Franklin - Warren County (G-8634)

EMP: 40 EST: 1964
SQ FT: 8,200
SALES (est): 3.17MM **Privately Held**
Web: www.bodieelectric.com
SIC: 1731 General electrical contractor

(G-8614)
BOWLING TRANSPORTATION INC (PA)
1827 Sandusky St (44830-2754)
PHONE.....................419 436-9590
Bill J Bowling, *Pr*
Don Bowling, *
Jo Ann May, *
EMP: 80 EST: 1987
SQ FT: 4,250
SALES (est): 18.9MM
SALES (corp-wide): 18.9MM **Privately Held**
Web: www.bowlingtransportation.com
SIC: 4213 4212 Contract haulers; Local trucking, without storage

(G-8615)
FIRST OHIO CREDIT UNION (PA)
1650 N Countyline St (44830)
PHONE.....................419 435-8513
Stephen Favor, *Pr*
EMP: 41 EST: 1947
SQ FT: 14,000
SALES (est): 4.37MM
SALES (corp-wide): 4.37MM **Privately Held**
Web: www.firstohiocu.org
SIC: 6061 Federal credit unions

(G-8616)
FOSTORIA HOSPITAL ASSOCIATION
Also Called: PROMEDICA
501 Van Buren St (44830-1534)
PHONE.....................419 435-7734
Arturo Polizzi, *Pr*
EMP: 254 EST: 1931
SQ FT: 68,000
SALES (est): 46.16MM
SALES (corp-wide): 187.07MM **Privately Held**
Web: www.promedica.org
SIC: 8062 Hospital, affiliated with AMA residency
PA: Promedica Health System, Inc.
    100 Madison Ave
    Toledo OH 43604
    567 585-9600

(G-8617)
GEARY FMLY YUNG MNS CHRSTN ASS
154 W Center St (44830-2201)
PHONE.....................419 435-6608
Eric Stinehelfer, *Dir*
EMP: 45 EST: 1909
SALES (est): 1.23MM **Privately Held**
Web: www.gearyfamilyymca.org
SIC: 8641 8351 Recreation association; Child day care services

(G-8618)
GOOD SHEPHERD HOME
725 Columbus Ave (44830-3255)
PHONE.....................419 937-1801
Chris Widman, *Dir*
EMP: 145 EST: 1902
SQ FT: 75,000
SALES (est): 12.78MM **Privately Held**
Web: www.goodshepherdhome.com
SIC: 8052 8051 Intermediate care facilities; Skilled nursing care facilities

(G-8619)
HCF MANAGEMENT INC
Also Called: Hcf Management
25 Christopher Dr (44830-3318)
PHONE.....................419 435-8112
Paula Kirkpatrick, *Brnch Mgr*
EMP: 28
SALES (corp-wide): 305.93MM **Privately Held**
Web: www.hcfinc.com
SIC: 8051 Convalescent home with continuous nursing care
PA: Hcf Management, Inc.
    1100 Shawnee Rd
    Lima OH 45805
    419 999-2010

(G-8620)
INDEPENDENCE CARE COMMUNITY
Also Called: Independence House
1000 Independence Ave (44830-9614)
PHONE.....................419 435-8505
Cheryl Buckland, *Pr*
Larry D Manley, *
Darlene Delarosa, *
EMP: 38 EST: 1991
SQ FT: 40,000
SALES (est): 3.85MM **Privately Held**
Web: www.independence-house.com
SIC: 8051 Skilled nursing care facilities

(G-8621)
NATIONAL MENTOR HOLDINGS INC
526 Plaza Dr (44830-1352)
PHONE.....................419 443-0867
EMP: 323
SALES (corp-wide): 1.64B **Privately Held**
Web: www.sevitahealth.com
SIC: 8082 8361 Home health care services; Mentally handicapped home
HQ: National Mentor Holdings, Inc.
    313 Congress St Fl 5
    Boston MA 02210
    617 790-4800

(G-8622)
REINEKE FORD INC
Also Called: Ford Rental System
1303 Perrysburg Rd (44830-1394)
PHONE.....................888 691-8175
Thomas A Reineke, *Pr*
William F Reineke, *
EMP: 28 EST: 1960
SQ FT: 15,000
SALES (est): 2.49MM **Privately Held**
Web: www.reinekefamilydealerships.com
SIC: 5511 7515 7513 5521 Automobiles, new and used; Passenger car leasing; Truck rental and leasing, no drivers; Used car dealers

(G-8623)
RES-CARE INC
Also Called: Dillon Group Homes
1016 Dillon Cir (44830-3395)
PHONE.....................419 435-6620
Denise Tucker, *Mgr*
EMP: 82
SALES (corp-wide): 8.83B **Publicly Held**
Web: www.rescare.com
SIC: 8052 Home for the mentally retarded, with health care
HQ: Res-Care, Inc.
    805 N Whittington Pkwy
    Louisville KY 40222
    502 394-2100

(G-8624)
ROAD & RAIL SERVICES INC
3101 N Township Road 47 (44830-9381)
PHONE.....................502 365-5361
Davis Sell, *Brnch Mgr*
EMP: 71
SALES (corp-wide): 104.11MM **Privately Held**
Web: www.roadandrail.com
SIC: 4789 4013 Railroad maintenance and repair services; Railroad switching
PA: Road & Rail Services, Inc.
    4233 Bardstown Rd Ste 200
    Louisville KY 40218
    502 495-6688

(G-8625)
SENECA COUNTY
602 S Corporate Dr W (44830-9456)
PHONE.....................419 435-0729
Kathy Nye, *Mgr*
EMP: 35
SALES (corp-wide): 61.95MM **Privately Held**
Web: www.seneca-county.com
SIC: 8331 Sheltered workshop
PA: Seneca County
    111 Madison St
    Tiffin OH 44883
    419 447-4550

(G-8626)
ST CTHRNES CARE CTRS FSTRIA I
Also Called: St Catherine's Manor
25 Christopher Dr (44830-3318)
PHONE.....................419 435-8112
Jim Unverferth, *Pr*
EMP: 50 EST: 1964
SQ FT: 34,000
SALES (est): 2.35MM **Privately Held**
Web: www.stcatherinesfostoria.com
SIC: 8051 Convalescent home with continuous nursing care

(G-8627)
VAUGHN INDUSTRIES LLC
21934 Twp Rd 218 (44830)
PHONE.....................419 396-3900
EMP: 100
SALES (corp-wide): 88.39MM **Privately Held**
Web: www.vaughnindustries.com
SIC: 1731 Electric power systems contractors
PA: Vaughn Industries, Llc
    1201 E Findlay St
    Carey OH 43316
    419 396-3900

Fowler
Trumbull County

(G-8628)
MEADOWBROOK MANOR OF HARTFORD
Also Called: Concord Health Center Hartford
3090 Five Points Hartford Rd (44418-9726)
PHONE.....................330 772-5253
Alexander Sherman, *Pr*
Jeffrey Goldstein, *
Samuel Sherman, *
EMP: 50 EST: 1954
SQ FT: 15,000
SALES (est): 2.41MM **Privately Held**
SIC: 8051 Convalescent home with continuous nursing care

Frankfort
Ross County

(G-8629)
DAVID W MILLIKEN (PA)
Also Called: Milliken's Dairy Cone
2 S Main St (45628-8018)
P.O. Box 427 (45628-0427)
PHONE.....................740 998-5023
David W Milliken, *Owner*
EMP: 30 EST: 1968
SALES (est): 924.33K
SALES (corp-wide): 924.33K **Privately Held**
SIC: 5812 1521 Ice cream, soft drink and soda fountain stands; New construction, single-family houses

(G-8630)
VALLEY VIEW MNOR NRSING HM INC
Also Called: VALLEY VIEW ALZHEIMER'S CARE C
3363 Ragged Ridge Rd (45628-9551)
PHONE.....................740 998-2948
Judith Heimerl-brown, *Pr*
Marge Poyner, *
Tammy Robertson, *
EMP: 38 EST: 1968
SALES (est): 4.32MM **Privately Held**
SIC: 8059 8051 Rest home, with health care; Skilled nursing care facilities

Franklin
Warren County

(G-8631)
AMPLE INDUSTRIES INC
4000 Commerce Center Dr (45005-1897)
PHONE.....................937 746-9700
EMP: 210
Web: www.resourcelabel.com
SIC: 5199 Packaging materials

(G-8632)
CARINGTON HEALTH SYSTEMS
Also Called: Franklin Ridge Care Facility
421 Mission Ln (45005-2327)
PHONE.....................937 743-2754
Sylvia Sipe, *Brnch Mgr*
EMP: 312
SALES (corp-wide): 58.43MM **Privately Held**
Web: www.carington.com
SIC: 8051 8052 Convalescent home with continuous nursing care; Intermediate care facilities
PA: Carington Health Systems
    8200 Beckett Park Dr
    Hamilton OH 45011
    513 682-2700

(G-8633)
DAYTON HOSPICE INCORPORATED
5940 Long Meadow Dr (45005-9689)
PHONE.....................513 422-0300
Vicky Forrest, *Brnch Mgr*
EMP: 225
SALES (corp-wide): 88.83MM **Privately Held**
Web: www.hospiceofdayton.org
SIC: 8052 Personal care facility
PA: Hospice Of Dayton, Incorporated
    324 Wilmington Ave
    Dayton OH 45420
    937 256-4490

(G-8634)
DRURY HOTELS COMPANY LLC
Also Called: Drury Inn & Suites Middletown
3320 Village Dr (45005-5602)
PHONE.....................513 425-6650
Allison Less, *Brnch Mgr*
EMP: 27
SALES (corp-wide): 555.12MM **Privately Held**

Franklin - Warren County (G-8635)

Web: www.druryhotels.com
SIC: 7011 Hotels
PA: Drury Hotels Company, Llc
13075 Manchester Rd # 100
Saint Louis MO 63131
314 429-2255

(G-8635)
EAGLE EQUIPMENT CORPORATION
Also Called: Fluid Power Components
245 Industrial Dr (45005-4429)
PHONE...................................937 746-0510
Jeff Fronk, *Pr*
EMP: 44
SQ FT: 7,000
SALES (corp-wide): 10.67MM **Privately Held**
Web: www.eagleequip.com
SIC: 5084 Hydraulic systems equipment and supplies
PA: Eagle Equipment Corporation
666 Brooksedge Blvd
Westerville OH 43081
614 882-9200

(G-8636)
FAMILY PRACTICE ASSOCIATES
5275 State Route 122 # 100 (45005-9617)
PHONE...................................513 424-7291
Thomas Furlong, *Prin*
Matthew Stone, *Prin*
John Ryan Prinicpal, *Prin*
Jean Murphy, *Prin*
EMP: 32 EST: 1979
SALES (est): 839.09K **Privately Held**
Web: www.premierhealth.com
SIC: 8011 Physicians' office, including specialists

(G-8637)
FRANKLIN CITY SCHOOLS
Also Called: Bus Garage
136 E 6th St (45005-2598)
PHONE...................................937 743-8670
Ruth Staggs, *Dir*
EMP: 36
SALES (corp-wide): 46.34MM **Privately Held**
Web: www.franklincityschools.com
SIC: 8211 7521 Public elementary and secondary schools; Parking garage
PA: Franklin City Schools
754 E 4th St
Franklin OH 45005
937 743-8603

(G-8638)
GAME HAUS LLC
3455 Renaissance Blvd (45005-9677)
PHONE...................................513 490-1799
Robert Hanes, *Prin*
EMP: 30 EST: 2016
SALES (est): 114.3K **Privately Held**
Web: www.thegamehaus.com
SIC: 7997 Membership sports and recreation clubs

(G-8639)
H7 NETWORK
610 Harpwood Dr (45005-6504)
PHONE...................................513 526-5139
Angel Hicks, *Prin*
EMP: 28 EST: 2016
SALES (est): 338.09K **Privately Held**
Web: www.h7network.com
SIC: 8742 Marketing consulting services

(G-8640)
HENDERSON TURF FARM INC
2969 Beal Rd (45005-4603)
PHONE...................................937 748-1559
Marvin N Kolstein, *Pr*
Reita C Henderson, *
EMP: 40 EST: 1961
SQ FT: 1,600
SALES (est): 4.62MM **Privately Held**
Web: www.hendersonturf.com
SIC: 0191 0181 0782 0711 General farms, primarily crop; Sod farms; Lawn services; Fertilizer application services

(G-8641)
HUNTINGTON NATIONAL BANK
340 S Main St (45005-2228)
P.O. Box 245 (45005-0245)
PHONE...................................937 746-9904
Robert Knipper, *Mgr*
EMP: 36
SQ FT: 3,000
SALES (corp-wide): 10.84B **Publicly Held**
Web: www.huntington.com
SIC: 6029 6021 Commercial banks, nec; National trust companies with deposits, commercial
HQ: The Huntington National Bank
41 S High St
Columbus OH 43215
614 480-4293

(G-8642)
I-75 PIERSON AUTOMOTIVE INC
Also Called: Guyler Automotive
5001 Sebald Dr (45005-5300)
PHONE...................................513 424-1881
Brenda Pierson, *Pr*
J Michael Guyler, *
EMP: 40 EST: 1947
SALES (est): 7.66MM **Privately Held**
Web: www.i75piersonauto.com
SIC: 5511 7538 7532 Automobiles, new and used; General automotive repair shops; Top and body repair and paint shops

(G-8643)
KOEHLKE COMPONENTS INC
1201 Commerce Center Dr (45005-7206)
PHONE...................................937 435-5435
Tom Koehlke, *Pr*
▲ EMP: 54 EST: 1976
SQ FT: 10,000
SALES (est): 17.72MM **Privately Held**
Web: www.koehlke.com
SIC: 5065 8711 Electronic parts; Engineering services

(G-8644)
LAKE ERIE ELECTRIC INC
360 Industrial Dr (45005-4432)
PHONE...................................937 743-1220
EMP: 117
SALES (corp-wide): 111.7MM **Privately Held**
Web: www.lakeerieelectric.com
SIC: 1731 General electrical contractor
PA: Lake Erie Electric, Inc.
25730 1st St
Westlake OH 44145
440 835-5565

(G-8645)
OHIO-KENTUCKY STEEL CORP
2001 Commerce Center Dr (45005-1478)
PHONE...................................937 743-4600
EMP: 30
SIC: 5051 Steel

(G-8646)
OHIO-KENTUCKY STEEL LLC
2001 Commerce Center Dr (45005-1478)
PHONE...................................937 743-4600
EMP: 30 EST: 2018
SQ FT: 84,000
SALES (est): 10.73MM
SALES (corp-wide): 10.73MM **Privately Held**
Web: www.ohkysteel.com
SIC: 5051 Steel
PA: American Posts, Llc
810 Chicago St
Toledo OH 43611
419 720-0652

(G-8647)
PRIMARY CARE NTWRK PRMIER HLTH
8401 Claude Thomas Rd (45005-1497)
PHONE...................................937 743-5965
Jerome Yount, *Brnch Mgr*
EMP: 29
SALES (corp-wide): 25.36MM **Privately Held**
Web: www.premierhealth.com
SIC: 8011 General and family practice, physician/surgeon
PA: Primary Care Network Of Premier Health Partners
110 N Main St Ste 350
Dayton OH 45402
937 226-7085

(G-8648)
ROMITECH INC (HQ)
321 Conover Dr (45005-1957)
PHONE...................................937 297-9529
Dan Hutcheson, *Pr*
Rob Banerjee, *
Mike Sheppard, *
EMP: 32 EST: 1991
SQ FT: 45,000
SALES (est): 8.38MM
SALES (corp-wide): 1.69B **Privately Held**
SIC: 5999 8748 Fiberglass materials, except insulation; Business consulting, nec
PA: Milliken & Company
920 Milliken Rd
Spartanburg SC 29303
864 503-2020

(G-8649)
SIGHTLESS CHILDREN CLUB INC
Also Called: SIGHTLESS CHILDREN CLUB INC
1028 E 4th St (45005-1834)
PHONE...................................937 671-9162
EMP: 29
SALES (corp-wide): 8.46K **Privately Held**
Web: www.theenvisionfoundation.org
SIC: 7997 Membership sports and recreation clubs
PA: Sightless Children Club
950 Helke Rd
Vandalia OH 45377
937 671-9171

(G-8650)
SLN NURSERY LLC
Also Called: Ohio Nursery Exchange
2969 Beal Rd (45005-4603)
PHONE...................................937 845-3130
Brandon Hunt, *
EMP: 40 EST: 2020
SALES (est): 1.05MM **Privately Held**
SIC: 0181 Ornamental nursery products

(G-8651)
UNIFIRST CORPORATION
Also Called: Unifirst
265 Industrial Dr (45005-4429)
PHONE...................................937 746-0531
John Leugers, *Brnch Mgr*
EMP: 45
SQ FT: 38,000
SALES (corp-wide): 2.23B **Publicly Held**
Web: www.unifirst.com
SIC: 7218 7213 Industrial uniform supply; Uniform supply
PA: Unifirst Corporation
68 Jonspin Rd
Wilmington MA 01887
978 658-8888

(G-8652)
WALTER F STEPHENS JR INC
415 South Ave (45005-3647)
PHONE...................................937 746-0521
Carla Baker, *VP*
Walter F Stephens Junior, *Pr*
Ruth Ann Stephens, *Ch Bd*
Diane Stephens Maloney, *Sec*
Patty Gleason, *VP*
EMP: 50 EST: 1940
SQ FT: 45,000
SALES (est): 2.39MM **Privately Held**
Web: www.stephenscatalogs.com
SIC: 5999 2389 5122 5023 Police supply stores; Uniforms and vestments; Toiletries; Kitchenware

Franklin Furnace
Scioto County

(G-8653)
BIG SANDY FURNITURE INC (HQ)
Also Called: Big Sandy Service Company
8375 Gallia Pike (45629)
PHONE...................................740 574-2113
Robert W Vanhoose Iii, *CEO*
Julie Hudson, *
▲ EMP: 100 EST: 1956
SQ FT: 250,000
SALES (est): 39.82MM **Privately Held**
Web: www.bigsandysuperstore.com
SIC: 4225 5712 5995 5999 General warehousing and storage; Furniture stores; Optical goods stores; Toiletries, cosmetics, and perfumes
PA: Big Sandy Distribution, Inc.
8375 Gallia Pike
Franklin Furnace OH 45629

(G-8654)
G & J PEPSI-COLA BOTTLERS INC
Also Called: Pepsico
4587 Gallia Pike (45629-8777)
P.O. Box 299 (45629-0299)
PHONE...................................740 354-9191
Robert Ross, *Brnch Mgr*
EMP: 350
SALES (corp-wide): 404.54MM **Privately Held**
Web: www.pepsico.com
SIC: 2086 5149 Carbonated soft drinks, bottled and canned; Groceries and related products, nec
PA: G & J Pepsi-Cola Bottlers Inc
9435 Waterstone Blvd # 390
Cincinnati OH 45249
513 785-6060

(G-8655)
HAVERHILL COKE COMPANY LLC
Also Called: Sun Coke Energy
2446 Gallia Pike (45629-8837)
PHONE...................................740 355-9819
▲ EMP: 65 EST: 1998
SALES (est): 50.61MM **Publicly Held**
Web: www.haverhillwindows.net
SIC: 5051 Steel
HQ: Suncoke Energy Partners, L.P.
1011 Warrenville Rd # 600
Lisle IL 60532
630 824-1000

GEOGRAPHIC SECTION

Frazeysburg
Muskingum County

(G-8656)
REM CORP
26 E 3rd St (43822-9651)
P.O. Box 3 (43822-0003)
PHONE..................................740 828-2601
Faith Oleary, *Mgr*
EMP: 148
SALES (corp-wide): 682.18K **Privately Held**
SIC: 8082 Home health care services
PA: Rem Corp.
265 S Pioneer Blvd
Springboro OH 45066
800 990-0302

(G-8657)
RIDGE CORPORATION
5777 Raiders Rd (43822-7512)
PHONE..................................740 513-9880
EMP: 44
SALES (corp-wide): 31.14MM **Privately Held**
Web: www.ridgecorp.com
SIC: 5084 Industrial machinery and equipment
PA: Ridge Corporation
1201 Etna Pkwy
Etna OH 43062
614 421-7434

Fredericksburg
Wayne County

(G-8658)
BOTHA TRUCKING LLC
5421 County Road 229 (44627-9698)
P.O. Box 254 (44627-0254)
PHONE..................................330 695-2296
Phillip Botha, *Managing Member*
EMP: 63 **EST:** 2014
SALES (est): 2.05MM **Privately Held**
SIC: 4212 Baggage transfer

Fredericktown
Knox County

(G-8659)
FIRST-KNOX NATIONAL BANK
137 N Main St (43019-1109)
P.O. Box 1270 (43050-1270)
PHONE..................................740 694-2015
Patty Frazee, *Mgr*
EMP: 39
SALES (corp-wide): 564.3MM **Publicly Held**
Web: www.parknationalbank.com
SIC: 6021 National commercial banks
HQ: The First-Knox National Bank
1 S Main St
Mount Vernon OH 43050
740 399-5500

(G-8660)
INTEGRITY KKSING PPLINE SVCS L
Also Called: Ikps
17531 Waterford Rd (43019-9561)
P.O. Box 226 (43019-0226)
PHONE..................................740 694-6315
Marsha Rinehart, *CEO*
Timothy Seibert, *
Adams Potes, *
EMP: 175 **EST:** 2012
SQ FT: 16,000
SALES (est): 54.45MM
SALES (corp-wide): 1.17B **Privately Held**
Web: www.kokosing.biz
SIC: 4613 Gasoline pipelines (common carriers)
PA: Kokosing, Inc.
6235 Wstrville Rd Ste 200
Westerville OH 43081
614 212-5700

(G-8661)
KCC SUPPLY LLC (DH)
700 Salem Ave Ext (43019-9188)
PHONE..................................740 694-6315
EMP: 27 **EST:** 2013
SALES (est): 5.75MM
SALES (corp-wide): 1.17B **Privately Held**
SIC: 5099 Durable goods, nec
HQ: Kokosing Construction Company, Inc.
6235 Westerville Rd
Westerville OH 43081
614 228-1029

(G-8662)
KOKOSING CONSTRUCTION CO INC
17531 Waterford Rd (43019-9159)
PHONE..................................740 694-6315
Carl Uhinck, *Brnch Mgr*
EMP: 100
SALES (corp-wide): 1.17B **Privately Held**
Web: www.kokosing.biz
SIC: 1611 1622 General contractor, highway and street construction; Bridge construction
HQ: Kokosing Construction Company, Inc.
6235 Westerville Rd
Westerville OH 43081
614 228-1029

Freeport
Harrison County

(G-8663)
ROSEBUD MINING COMPANY
28490 Birmingham Rd (43973-9754)
PHONE..................................740 658-4217
EMP: 60
SALES (corp-wide): 221.86MM **Privately Held**
Web: www.rosebudmining.com
SIC: 1241 Coal mining services
PA: Rosebud Mining Company
301 Market St
Kittanning PA 16201
724 545-6222

Fremont
Sandusky County

(G-8664)
ADVANTAGE FORD LINCOLN MERCURY
885 Hagerty Dr (43420-9162)
P.O. Box 1167 (43420-8167)
PHONE..................................419 334-9751
Merlton Brandenburg, *Pr*
Herbert D Stump, *
EMP: 40 **EST:** 1995
SQ FT: 23,000
SALES (est): 9.38MM **Privately Held**
Web: www.advantagefordfremont.com
SIC: 5511 7538 7532 Automobiles, new and used; General automotive repair shops; Top and body repair and paint shops

(G-8665)
ALKON CORPORATION (PA)
728 Graham Dr (43420-4073)
PHONE..................................419 355-9111
Mark Winter, *Pr*
▲ **EMP:** 60 **EST:** 1968
SQ FT: 40,000
SALES (est): 27.26MM
SALES (corp-wide): 27.26MM **Privately Held**
Web: www.alkoncorp.com
SIC: 3491 3082 5084 5085 Valves, nuclear; Tubes, unsupported plastics; Industrial machinery and equipment; Hydraulic and pneumatic pistons and valves

(G-8666)
AMCOR FLEXIBLES NORTH AMER INC
Also Called: Bermis
730 Industrial Dr (43420-8678)
PHONE..................................419 334-9465
EMP: 51
SALES (corp-wide): 14.69B **Privately Held**
Web: www.amcor.com
SIC: 5199 Packaging materials
HQ: Amcor Flexibles North America, Inc.
2200 Badger Ave
Oshkosh WI 54904
920 727-4100

(G-8667)
ASSISTED LIVING CONCEPTS LLC
Also Called: Rutherford House
805 S Buchanan St Ofc (43420-4999)
PHONE..................................419 334-6962
Andrew Connors, *Dir*
EMP: 28
SALES (corp-wide): 571.18MM **Privately Held**
SIC: 8051 8052 Skilled nursing care facilities; Intermediate care facilities
HQ: Assisted Living Concepts, Llc
141 W Jackson Blvd # 2650
Chicago IL 60604

(G-8668)
CARITAS INC
Also Called: PARKVIEW CARE CENTER
1406 Oak Harbor Rd (43420-1025)
PHONE..................................419 332-2589
Patrick Kriner, *Pr*
EMP: 36 **EST:** 1975
SQ FT: 15,000
SALES (est): 2.59MM **Privately Held**
SIC: 8051 8361 Convalescent home with continuous nursing care; Aged home

(G-8669)
CENTURY 21 PREMIERE PROPERTIES
Also Called: Century 21
308 E State St (43420-4152)
PHONE..................................419 334-2121
Annette Wilcox, *Ofcr*
EMP: 34 **EST:** 2018
SALES (est): 173.01K **Privately Held**
Web: www.c21bolterealestate.com
SIC: 6531 Real estate agent, residential

(G-8670)
COLUMBIA GAS OF OHIO INC
Also Called: Columbia
1208 Dickinson St (43420-1647)
PHONE..................................419 332-9951
Lisa Carmean, *Brnch Mgr*
EMP: 79
SALES (corp-wide): 5.51B **Publicly Held**
Web: www.columbiagasohio.com
SIC: 4924 Natural gas distribution
HQ: Columbia Gas Of Ohio, Inc.
290 W Nationwide Blvd # 1
Columbus OH 43215
614 460-6000

(G-8671)
COMMUNITY AND RURAL HLTH SVCS (PA)
Also Called: COMMUNITY HEALTH SERVICES
2221 Hayes Ave (43420-2632)
PHONE..................................419 334-8943
J Liszak, *Pr*
Tyson Bouyack, *
EMP: 70 **EST:** 1970
SQ FT: 28,000
SALES (est): 13.02MM
SALES (corp-wide): 13.02MM **Privately Held**
Web: www.chsohio.com
SIC: 8011 Clinic, operated by physicians

(G-8672)
COUNTY OF SANDUSKY
Also Called: School of Hope
1001 Castalia St (43420-4015)
PHONE..................................419 637-2243
Jayne Repp, *Prin*
EMP: 100
SALES (corp-wide): 63.91MM **Privately Held**
Web: www.sanduskycounty.org
SIC: 8331 Sheltered workshop
PA: County Of Sandusky
622 Croghan St
Fremont OH 43420
419 334-6100

(G-8673)
CROGHAN COLONIAL BANK (HQ)
323 Croghan St (43420-3088)
P.O. Box C (43420-0557)
PHONE..................................419 332-7301
Kendall Rieman, *Pr*
Allan Mehlow, *
Barry F Luse, *
Jodi A Albright, *
Don W Miller, *
EMP: 45 **EST:** 1984
SQ FT: 39,500
SALES (est): 46.83MM **Publicly Held**
Web: www.croghan.com
SIC: 6022 State trust companies accepting deposits, commercial
PA: Croghan Bancshares, Inc.
323 Croghan St
Fremont OH 43420

(G-8674)
DAMSCHRODER ROOFING INC
2625 E State St (43420-8523)
PHONE..................................419 332-5000
Dana Howell, *Pr*
EMP: 27 **EST:** 2005
SALES (est): 6.69MM **Privately Held**
Web: www.damschroderroofing.com
SIC: 1761 Roofing contractor

(G-8675)
DJ ROOFING & IMPRVS LLC
1043 County Road 99 (43420-9314)
PHONE..................................419 307-5712
EMP: 36
SALES (est): 1.03MM **Privately Held**
SIC: 7389 1761 Business Activities at Non-Commercial Site; Roofing, siding, and sheetmetal work

(G-8676)
FIRST CHOICE PACKAGING INC (PA)
Also Called: First Choice Packg Solutions
1501 W State St (43420-1629)
PHONE..................................419 333-4100
Paul W Tomick, *Ch*
Frank Wolfinger, *
▲ **EMP:** 105 **EST:** 1985

Fremont - Sandusky County (G-8677)

SALES (est): 23.18MM
SALES (corp-wide): 23.18MM **Privately Held**
Web: www.firstchoicepackaging.com
SIC: 3089 7389 Thermoformed finished plastics products, nec; Packaging and labeling services

(G-8677)
FLEX-TEMP EMPLOYMENT SVCS INC
Also Called: Pagan
524 W State St (43420-2532)
PHONE: 419 355-9675
Larry Aaron, *Mgr*
EMP: 143
SALES (corp-wide): 4.74MM **Privately Held**
Web: www.flextemp.com
SIC: 7363 Temporary help service
PA: Flex-Temp Employment Services, Inc.
1514 E Farwell St Frnt Unit
Sandusky OH 44870
419 625-3470

(G-8678)
FOSBEL WAHL HOLDINGS LLC
Also Called: Wahl Refractory Solutions
767 S State Route 19 (43420-9260)
PHONE: 419 334-2650
EMP: 52 **EST:** 2020
SALES (est): 5.04MM **Privately Held**
Web: www.fosbel.com
SIC: 5085 Refractory material

(G-8679)
FREMONT CITY SCHOOLS
Also Called: Fremont City Schools
1100 North St (43420-1132)
PHONE: 419 332-6454
Lloyd Gracy, *Brnch Mgr*
EMP: 89
SALES (corp-wide): 62.58MM **Privately Held**
Web: www.fremontschools.net
SIC: 4151 School buses
PA: Fremont City Schools
500 W State St Ste A
Fremont OH 43420
419 334-5442

(G-8680)
FREMONT LOGISTICS LLC
1301 Heinz Rd (43420-8584)
PHONE: 419 333-0669
EMP: 32 **EST:** 2003
SALES (est): 1.75MM
SALES (corp-wide): 15.34B **Privately Held**
SIC: 4225 General warehousing and storage
HQ: Es3, Llc
6 Optical Ave
Keene NH 03431
603 354-6100

(G-8681)
GARNER TRUCKING INC
Also Called: Ron's Truck Trlr & Auto Repr
2673 E State St (43420-9257)
PHONE: 419 334-4040
Barry Meade, *Owner*
EMP: 37
SALES (corp-wide): 17.97MM **Privately Held**
Web: www.garnertrucking.com
SIC: 7538 General truck repair
PA: Garner Trucking, Inc.
9291 County Rd 313
Findlay OH 45839
419 422-5742

(G-8682)
GOODNIGHT INN INC
Also Called: Days Inn
3701 N State Route 53 (43420-9318)
PHONE: 419 334-9551
Kerri Henry, *Mgr*
EMP: 33
SALES (corp-wide): 2.97MM **Privately Held**
Web: www.wyndhamhotels.com
SIC: 7011 Hotels and motels
PA: Goodnight Inn, Inc.
11313 Us Highway 250 N
Milan OH 44846
419 626-3610

(G-8683)
GOODWILL INDS ERIE HRON OTTAWA
Also Called: Fremont Plant Operations
1597 Pontiac Ave (43420-9792)
PHONE: 419 334-7566
T Burnsderter, *Brnch Mgr*
EMP: 76
SALES (corp-wide): 11.58MM **Privately Held**
Web: www.goodwillsandusky.org
SIC: 8322 Individual and family services
PA: Goodwill Industries Of Erie, Huron, Ottawa And Sandusky Counties, Inc.
419 W Market St
Sandusky OH 44870
419 625-4744

(G-8684)
GREAT LKES CMNTY ACTION PARTNR (PA)
127 S Front St (43420-3021)
P.O. Box 590 (43420-0590)
PHONE: 419 333-6068
Ruthann House, *CEO*
David R Kipplen, *
EMP: 70 **EST:** 1965
SQ FT: 17,000
SALES (est): 53.21MM
SALES (corp-wide): 53.21MM **Privately Held**
Web: www.glcap.org
SIC: 8351 8322 8331 Head Start center, except in conjunction with school; Individual and family services; Job training services

(G-8685)
GREAT LKES CMNTY ACTION PARTNR
Also Called: Fremont TMC Head Start
765 S Buchanan St (43420-4903)
PHONE: 419 334-8511
Brenda Barton, *Dir*
EMP: 32
SALES (corp-wide): 53.21MM **Privately Held**
Web: www.glcap.org
SIC: 8351 8331 Head Start center, except in conjunction with school; Job training services
PA: Great Lakes Community Action Partnership
127 S Front St
Fremont OH 43420
419 333-6068

(G-8686)
GREAT LKES CMNTY ACTION PARTNR
Also Called: Trips
1071 N 5th St (43420-3931)
P.O. Box 590 (43420-0590)
PHONE: 419 332-8089
Robin Richter, *Brnch Mgr*
EMP: 31
SALES (corp-wide): 53.21MM **Privately Held**
Web: www.glcap.org
SIC: 7389 8331 Personal service agents, brokers, and bureaus; Job training services
PA: Great Lakes Community Action Partnership
127 S Front St
Fremont OH 43420
419 333-6068

(G-8687)
INOAC EXTERIOR SYSTEMS LLC
Also Called: Automotive Part Supplier
1410 Motor Ave (43420-1437)
PHONE: 419 334-8951
Anthony Nadeau, *Mgr*
EMP: 190
Web: www.inoacusa.com
SIC: 5013 Body repair or paint shop supplies, automotive
HQ: Inoac Exterior Systems, Llc
1410 Motor Ave
Fremont OH 43420
419 334-8951

(G-8688)
INOAC EXTERIOR SYSTEMS LLC (DH)
1410 Motor Ave (43420-1437)
PHONE: 419 334-8951
Rob Depotter, *Pr*
EMP: 50 **EST:** 2011
SQ FT: 3,000
SALES (est): 116.61MM **Privately Held**
Web: www.inoacusa.com
SIC: 5013 Body repair or paint shop supplies, automotive
HQ: Inoac Usa, Inc.
1515 Equity Dr Ste 200
Troy MI 48084
248 619-7031

(G-8689)
KELLER OCHS KOCH INC
Also Called: SCI
416 S Arch St (43420-2965)
PHONE: 419 332-8288
John P Keller, *Pr*
Lawrence L Koch, *
EMP: 35 **EST:** 1947
SQ FT: 20,000
SALES (est): 456.05K
SALES (corp-wide): 4.1B **Publicly Held**
SIC: 7261 Funeral home
PA: Service Corporation International
1929 Allen Pkwy
Houston TX 77019
713 522-5141

(G-8690)
LOWES HOME CENTERS LLC
Also Called: Lowe's
1952 N State Route 53 (43420-8637)
PHONE: 419 355-0221
EMP: 143
SALES (corp-wide): 86.38B **Publicly Held**
Web: www.lowes.com
SIC: 5211 5031 5722 5064 Home centers; Building materials, exterior; Household appliance stores; Electrical appliances, television and radio
HQ: Lowe's Home Centers, Llc
1000 Lowes Blvd
Mooresville NC 28117
336 658-4000

(G-8691)
LUTHERAN HOMES SOCIETY INC
Also Called: Genacross Lthran Svcs Bthany P
916 North St (43420-1154)
PHONE: 419 334-5500
EMP: 165
SALES (corp-wide): 54.58MM **Privately Held**
Web: www.genacrosslutheranservices.org
SIC: 8361 Aged home
PA: Lutheran Homes Society, Inc.
2021 N Mccord Rd
Toledo OH 43615
419 861-4990

(G-8692)
LUTZ PTO
1929 Buckland Ave (43420-3505)
PHONE: 419 332-0091
EMP: 35 **EST:** 2011
SALES (est): 212.76K **Privately Held**
Web: www.fremontschools.net
SIC: 8641 Parent-teachers' association

(G-8693)
MEMORIAL HOSPITAL (PA)
Also Called: MEMORIAL HOSPITAL HEALTHLINK
715 S Taft Ave (43420-3296)
PHONE: 419 334-6657
Pamella Jensen, *CEO*
John Al Gorman, *
EMP: 420 **EST:** 1915
SQ FT: 197,000
SALES (est): 86.27MM
SALES (corp-wide): 86.27MM **Privately Held**
Web: www.promedica.org
SIC: 8062 General medical and surgical hospitals

(G-8694)
MOSSER CONSTRUCTION INC (HQ)
122 S Wilson Ave (43420-2725)
P.O. Box D (43420-0558)
PHONE: 419 334-3801
EMP: 150 **EST:** 1948
SALES (est): 53.97MM
SALES (corp-wide): 101.73MM **Privately Held**
Web: www.mosserconstruction.com
SIC: 1541 1542 Industrial buildings, new construction, nec; Commercial and office building, new construction
PA: Wmog, Inc.
122 S Wilson Ave
Fremont OH 43420
419 334-3801

(G-8695)
MOTION CONTROLS ROBOTICS INC
1500 Walter Ave (43420-1449)
PHONE: 419 334-5886
EMP: 63 **EST:** 1995
SQ FT: 57,000
SALES (est): 10.31MM **Privately Held**
Web: www.motioncontrolsrobotics.com
SIC: 8742 Automation and robotics consultant

(G-8696)
OHIO DEPT JOB & FMLY SVCS
Also Called: Sandusky Cnty Job & Fmly Svcs
2511 Countryside Dr (43420-9016)
PHONE: 419 334-3891
Peter Cantu, *Brnch Mgr*
EMP: 34
Web: jfs.ohio.gov

GEOGRAPHIC SECTION

Gahanna - Franklin County (G-8717)

SIC: 9441 7363 Administration of social and manpower programs, State government; Help supply services
HQ: Ohio Department Of Job And Family Services
30 E Broad St Fl 32
Columbus OH 43215

(G-8697)
PROMEDICA HEALTH SYSTEM INC
Also Called: Heartland HM Hlth Care Hospice
907 W State St Ste A (43420-2548)
PHONE..............................419 355-9209
EMP: 63
SALES (corp-wide): 187.07MM **Privately Held**
Web: www.promedicaseniorcare.org
SIC: 6324 Health Maintenance Organization (HMO), insurance only
PA: Promedica Health System, Inc.
100 Madison Ave
Toledo OH 43604
567 585-9600

(G-8698)
RK FAMILY INC
1800 E State St (43420-4000)
PHONE..............................419 355-8230
Tim Lodes, *Prin*
EMP: 195
SALES (corp-wide): 1.22B **Privately Held**
Web: www.ruralking.com
SIC: 5191 Farm supplies
PA: Rk Family, Inc.
4216 Dewitt Ave
Mattoon IL 61938
217 235-7102

(G-8699)
RTHRFORD B HAYES PRSDNTIAL CTR
Also Called: RUTHERFORD B HAYES PRESIDENTIA
Spiegel Grove (43420)
PHONE..............................419 332-2081
Christy Weininger, *Ex Dir*
Christie Weininger, *
EMP: 43 EST: 1916
SALES (est): 2.14MM **Privately Held**
Web: www.rbhayes.org
SIC: 8231 8412 Libraries; Museum

(G-8700)
S A COMUNALE CO INC
1524 Oak Harbor Rd (43420-1027)
PHONE..............................419 334-3841
Bob Waskielis, *Mgr*
EMP: 82
SALES (corp-wide): 12.58B **Publicly Held**
Web: www.sacomunale.com
SIC: 1711 Fire sprinkler system installation
HQ: S. A. Comunale Co., Inc.
2900 Newpark Dr
Barberton OH 44203
330 706-3040

(G-8701)
SEAL AFTERMARKET PRODUCTS LLC
1110 Napoleon St (43420-2328)
PHONE..............................419 355-1200
Fred Burkhart, *Brnch Mgr*
EMP: 50
Web: www.sealaftermarketproducts.com
SIC: 5082 Construction and mining machinery
PA: Seal Aftermarket Products, Llc
2315 Sw 32nd Ave
Pembroke Park FL 33023

(G-8702)
SIERRA LOBO INC (PA)
Also Called: Sierra Lobo
102 Pinnacle Dr (43420-7400)
PHONE..............................419 332-7101
EMP: 32 EST: 1993
SALES (est): 48.53MM **Privately Held**
Web: www.sierralobo.com
SIC: 8711 Consulting engineer

(G-8703)
SISTERS OF MRCY OF THE AMRCAS
Also Called: Sisters of Mercy Fremont, Ohio
1220 Tiffin St (43420-3562)
PHONE..............................419 332-8208
Janette Tahy, *Mgr*
EMP: 88
SALES (corp-wide): 26.99MM **Privately Held**
Web: www.mercymontessori.org
SIC: 8361 Aged home
HQ: Sisters Of Mercy Of The Americas South Central Community, Inc
2335 Grandview Ave
Cincinnati OH
513 221-1800

(G-8704)
SPRINGLEAF FINCL HOLDINGS LLC
2200 Sean Dr Ste 10 (43420-9772)
PHONE..............................419 334-9748
EMP: 376
SALES (corp-wide): 1.89B **Privately Held**
Web: www.onemainfinancial.com
SIC: 7389 Financial services
PA: Springleaf Financial Holdings, Llc
601 Nw 2nd St Ste 300
Evansville IN 47708
800 961-5577

(G-8705)
STYLE CREST ENTERPRISES INC (PA)
2450 Enterprise St (43420)
P.O. Box A (43420)
PHONE..............................419 355-8586
Thomas L Kern, *CEO*
Phillip Burton, *VP*
Henry Valle, *
Bryan T Kern, *Operations**
Tyrone G Frantz, *
EMP: 58 EST: 1996
SQ FT: 40,000
SALES (est): 167.61MM
SALES (corp-wide): 167.61MM **Privately Held**
Web: www.stylecrestinc.com
SIC: 3089 5075 Plastics hardware and building products; Warm air heating and air conditioning

(G-8706)
TITAN PROPANE LLC
2145 Napoleon Rd (43420-1502)
PHONE..............................419 332-9832
Arnold Cafkey, *Mgr*
EMP: 219
SALES (corp-wide): 8.93B **Publicly Held**
Web: www.amerigas.com
SIC: 4925 5984 Gas production and/or distribution; Propane gas, bottled
HQ: Titan Propane Llc
460 N Gulph Rd Ste 100
King Of Prussia PA 19406
610 337-7000

(G-8707)
VOLUNTERS AMER CARE FACILITIES
Also Called: Bethesda Care Center
600 N Brush St (43420-1402)
PHONE..............................419 334-9521
Roger Wyman, *Ex Dir*
EMP: 120
SALES (corp-wide): 56.23MM **Privately Held**
SIC: 8322 Social service center
PA: Volunteers Of America Care Facilities
7530 Market Place Dr
Eden Prairie MN 55344
952 941-0305

(G-8708)
WARNER MECHANICAL CORPORATION
1609 Dickinson St (43420-1119)
P.O. Box 747 (43420-0747)
PHONE..............................419 332-7116
Trent Bloomfield, *CEO*
James Krock, *VP*
EMP: 30 EST: 1946
SQ FT: 10,000
SALES (est): 9.8MM **Privately Held**
Web: www.warnermech.com
SIC: 1711 Mechanical contractor

(G-8709)
WMOG INC (PA)
Also Called: Mosser Group, The
122 S Wilson Ave (43420-2767)
P.O. Box D (43420-0558)
PHONE..............................419 334-3801
Robert H Moyer, *Ch*
J P Boyle, *VP*
Al Mehlow, *Sec*
Joe Luzar, *VP*
EMP: 50 EST: 1948
SALES (est): 101.73MM
SALES (corp-wide): 101.73MM **Privately Held**
Web: www.quarrylakes.com
SIC: 1541 7359 1611 Industrial buildings, new construction, nec; Equipment rental and leasing, nec; Highway and street construction

Gahanna
Franklin County

(G-8710)
AMERICAN NATIONAL RED CROSS
Also Called: American Red Cross
337 Stoneridge Ln (43230-6783)
PHONE..............................614 473-3783
EMP: 31
SALES (corp-wide): 3.18B **Privately Held**
Web: www.redcross.org
SIC: 8322 Social service center
PA: The American National Red Cross
431 18th St Nw
Washington DC 20006
202 737-8300

(G-8711)
BENCHMARK INDUSTRIAL INC (PA)
Also Called: Plasco Safety Products
950 Claycraft Rd (43230-6634)
P.O. Box 367 (45501-0367)
PHONE..............................614 695-6500
Jim Reid, *Pr*
EMP: 99 EST: 1946
SQ FT: 35,000
SALES (est): 47.34MM
SALES (corp-wide): 47.34MM **Privately Held**
Web: www.benchmarkindustrial.com
SIC: 5085 Industrial supplies

(G-8712)
BUCKEYE ELM CONTRACTING LLC
1333 Research Rd (43230-6624)
PHONE..............................888 315-8663
EMP: 35 EST: 2017
SALES (est): 6.31MM **Privately Held**
Web: www.buckeye-elm.com
SIC: 8742 Construction project management consultant

(G-8713)
COLUMBUS WOMENS WELLNESS
4625 Morse Rd Ste 200 (43230-8355)
PHONE..............................614 532-8370
Jennifer Jones, *Pr*
EMP: 31 EST: 2017
SALES (est): 955.73K **Privately Held**
Web: www.columbuswomenswellness.com
SIC: 8099 Health and allied services, nec

(G-8714)
CUSTOM AC & HTG CO
Also Called: Honeywell Authorized Dealer
935 Claycraft Rd (43230-6650)
PHONE..............................614 552-4822
Patrick Halaiko, *Pr*
Jeff Reed, *
Steve Wistler, *
Leon Blalock, *
EMP: 75 EST: 1976
SQ FT: 7,500
SALES (est): 17.16MM **Privately Held**
Web: www.customairco.com
SIC: 1711 Warm air heating and air conditioning contractor

(G-8715)
DEEMSYS INC (PA)
800 Cross Pointe Rd Ste A (43230-6687)
PHONE..............................614 322-9928
Vijiayarani Benjamin, *Ch Bd*
Jacob Benjamin, *
Dexter Benjamin, *
EMP: 52 EST: 2002
SQ FT: 5,100
SALES (est): 4.55MM
SALES (corp-wide): 4.55MM **Privately Held**
Web: www.deemsysinc.com
SIC: 8748 2741 7373 8299 Business consulting, nec; Internet publishing and broadcasting; Systems software development services; Educational service, nondegree granting: continuing educ.

(G-8716)
ESTATE INFORMATION SVCS LLC
Also Called: Eis
670 Morrison Rd Ste 300 (43230-5324)
PHONE..............................614 729-1700
J C Gunnell, *CEO*
Janet Gennail, *
John Pickens, *
Michael Lame, *
Victoria Edwards, *
EMP: 60 EST: 2000
SQ FT: 20,000
SALES (est): 10.82MM **Privately Held**
Web: www.eismgmt.com
SIC: 7322 Collection agency, except real estate

(G-8717)
GULF SOUTH MEDICAL SUPPLY INC
915 Taylor Rd Unit A (43230-3292)
PHONE..............................614 501-9080
EMP: 48
SALES (corp-wide): 308.95B **Publicly Held**

Gahanna - Franklin County (G-8718)

SIC: **5047** Medical equipment and supplies
HQ: Gulf South Medical Supply Inc
4345 Sthpint Blvd Ste 100
Jacksonville FL 32216
904 332-3000

(G-8718)
HEART CARE
765 N Hamilton Rd Ste 120 (43230-8707)
PHONE..................................614 533-5000
EMP: 40
SALES (est): 1.12MM **Privately Held**
Web: www.ohiohealth.com
SIC: **8062** General medical and surgical hospitals

(G-8719)
INTERIM HALTHCARE COLUMBUS INC (HQ)
Also Called: INTERIM SERVICES
784 Morrison Rd (43230-6642)
PHONE..................................614 888-3130
Thomas J Dimarco, *Pr*
Michael W Hartshorn, *
Richard Nielsen, *
EMP: 30 EST: 1971
SQ FT: 3,400
SALES (est): 3.63MM
SALES (corp-wide): 52.16MM **Privately Held**
Web: www.interimhealthcare.com
SIC: **8082** Home health care services
PA: Salo, Inc.
300 W Wlson Brdge Rd Ste
Columbus OH 43085
614 436-9404

(G-8720)
KOGNETICS LLC
147 N High St (43230-3028)
PHONE..................................614 591-4416
Inder Thukral, *Prin*
Rajeev Vaid, *
Benjamin Pollock, *
EMP: 40 EST: 2018
SALES (est): 1.62MM **Privately Held**
Web: www.kognetics.com
SIC: **7371** Computer software development

(G-8721)
MAGNIT APC I LLC
471 Morrison Rd Unit N (43230-3365)
PHONE..................................614 252-7300
Mark D Brady, *COO*
EMP: 50
SIC: **7363** Labor resource services
HQ: Magnit Apc I, Llc
420 S Orange Ave Ste 900
Orlando FL 32801
407 770-6161

(G-8722)
MARK-L INC
Also Called: Mark-L Construction
1180 Claycraft Rd (43230-6640)
PHONE..................................614 863-8832
Mark A Laivins, *Senior President*
Mark A Laivins Senior, *Pr*
EMP: 32 EST: 1981
SQ FT: 8,000
SALES (est): 16.06MM **Privately Held**
Web: www.marklconstruction.com
SIC: **1542** Commercial and office building, new construction

(G-8723)
MAXIM HEALTHCARE SERVICES INC
735 Taylor Rd (43230-6274)
PHONE..................................614 986-3001
EMP: 153
Web: www.maximhealthcare.com
SIC: **8082** Home health care services
PA: Maxim Healthcare Services, Inc.
7227 Lee Deforest Dr
Columbia MD 21046

(G-8724)
MEDASSIST INCORPORATED
735 Taylor Rd Ste 140 (43230-6274)
PHONE..................................614 367-9416
John Wolfe, *Mgr*
EMP: 162
Web: www.gomedassist.com
SIC: **8322** Individual and family services
HQ: Medassist, Incorporated
10400 Linn Station Rd # 100
Louisville KY 40223

(G-8725)
NESCO INC
81 Mill St Ste 200 (43230-1718)
PHONE..................................614 785-9675
EMP: 970
SALES (corp-wide): 514.23MM **Privately Held**
Web: www.nescoresource.com
SIC: **7361** Employment agencies
PA: Nesco, Inc.
6140 Parkland Blvd # 110
Cleveland OH 44124
440 461-6000

(G-8726)
RELIANT CAPITAL SOLUTIONS LLC (PA)
Also Called: Reliant Recovery Solutions
670 Cross Pointe Rd (43230)
P.O. Box 30469 (43230)
PHONE..................................614 452-6100
Margie Brickner, *Owner*
David Shull, *CFO*
EMP: 185 EST: 2006
SQ FT: 20,000
SALES (est): 23.68MM **Privately Held**
Web: www.reliantcapitalsolutions.com
SIC: **7322** Collection agency, except real estate

(G-8727)
ROCKY FORK HUNT AND CNTRY CLB
Also Called: Rocky Fork Country Club
5189 Clark State Rd (43230-2207)
PHONE..................................614 471-7828
Tom Wheat, *Genl Mgr*
EMP: 51 EST: 1912
SALES (est): 3.43MM **Privately Held**
Web: www.rockyforkhcc.com
SIC: **7997** 5812 Country club, membership; Eating places

(G-8728)
ROMANOFF ELC RESIDENTIAL LLC
1288 Research Rd (43230-6625)
PHONE..................................614 755-4500
Matthew Romanoff, *CEO*
EMP: 99 EST: 2011
SALES (est): 5.82MM
SALES (corp-wide): 52.63MM **Privately Held**
Web: www.romanoffgroup.cc
SIC: **1731** General electrical contractor
PA: The Romanoff Group Llc
1288 Research Rd
Gahanna OH 43230
614 755-4500

(G-8729)
ROMANOFF ELECTRIC INC (PA)
1288 Research Rd (43230-6625)
PHONE..................................614 755-4500
Matthew Romanoff, *Pr*
EMP: 234 EST: 1982
SQ FT: 14,000
SALES (est): 53.66MM
SALES (corp-wide): 53.66MM **Privately Held**
Web: www.romanoffgroup.cc
SIC: **1731** General electrical contractor

(G-8730)
ROMANOFF GROUP LLC (PA)
1288 Research Rd (43230-6625)
PHONE..................................614 755-4500
Matthew Romanoff, *CEO*
EMP: 28 EST: 2000
SALES (est): 52.63MM
SALES (corp-wide): 52.63MM **Privately Held**
Web: www.romanoffgroup.cc
SIC: **1711** 1731 Plumbing, heating, air-conditioning; General electrical contractor

(G-8731)
SUNRISE SENIOR LIVING LLC
Also Called: Sunrise of Gahanna
775 E Johnstown Rd (43230-2115)
PHONE..................................614 418-9775
Todd Gable, *Mgr*
EMP: 48
SALES (corp-wide): 2.92B **Privately Held**
Web: www.sunriseseniorliving.com
SIC: **8051** 8361 Skilled nursing care facilities; Residential care
HQ: Sunrise Senior Living, Llc
7902 Westpark Dr
Mc Lean VA 22102

(G-8732)
TERRACON CONSULTANTS INC
Also Called: Terracon Consultants N4
800 Morrison Rd (43230-6643)
PHONE..................................614 863-3113
Kevin Ernst, *Mgr*
EMP: 93
Web: www.terracon.com
SIC: **8711** 8731 Consulting engineer; Environmental research
HQ: Terracon Consultants, Inc.
10841 S Ridgeview Rd
Olathe KS 66061

(G-8733)
THE H T HACKNEY CO
875 Taylor Station Rd (43230-6655)
P.O. Box 30371 (43230-0371)
PHONE..................................614 751-5100
Joe Wackerly, *Genl Mgr*
EMP: 40
SALES (corp-wide): 24.07MM **Privately Held**
Web: www.hthackney.com
SIC: **5141** Food brokers
PA: The H T Hackney Co
502 S Gay St Ste 300
Knoxville TN 37902
865 546-1291

(G-8734)
WINN-SCAPES INC
Also Called: Winnscapes Inc/Schmidt Nurs Co
6079 Taylor Rd (43230-3211)
PHONE..................................614 866-9466
Richard Winnestaffer, *CEO*
Carl Morris Junior, *Pr*
EMP: 45 EST: 1981
SQ FT: 6,000
SALES (est): 5.8MM **Privately Held**
Web: www.winnscapes.com
SIC: **0782** Landscape contractors

Galena
Delaware County

(G-8735)
BRISKEY CONCRETE INC
100 B's And K Rd (43021)
PHONE..................................517 403-9869
EMP: 44
SALES (corp-wide): 897.01K **Privately Held**
SIC: **1771** Concrete work
PA: Briskey Concrete, Inc.
Sunbury OH 43074
517 424-6519

(G-8736)
IRONSITE INC
72 Holmes St (43021)
P.O. Box 304 (43074)
PHONE..................................740 965-4616
EMP: 30 EST: 2000
SALES (est): 2.34MM **Privately Held**
Web: www.ironsiteinc.com
SIC: **0781** Landscape services

(G-8737)
MIDWEST INVESTORS GROUP INC
Also Called: Metro Staffing
11619 Trenton Rd (43021-9511)
P.O. Box 705 (53177-0705)
PHONE..................................270 887-8888
Joe Mickunas, *Pr*
EMP: 123 EST: 2007
SALES (est): 2.44MM **Privately Held**
SIC: **8331** 8742 7389 Manpower training; General management consultant; Business services, nec

(G-8738)
OHIO ARSON SCHOOL INC
5600 Hughes Rd (43021-9541)
PHONE..................................740 881-4467
John Bernans, *Dir*
Pastor Steven Stolartzyk, *Prin*
Tom Houston, *
EMP: 30 EST: 1961
SALES (est): 512.03K **Privately Held**
Web: www.ohioarsonschoolinc.org
SIC: **8331** 8211 Skill training center; Elementary and secondary schools

(G-8739)
PLANE DETAIL LLC
2720 S 3 Bs And K Rd (43021-9785)
PHONE..................................614 734-1201
EMP: 35 EST: 2008
SALES (est): 962.89K **Privately Held**
Web: www.planedetail.com
SIC: **4581** Aircraft cleaning and janitorial service

Galion
Crawford County

(G-8740)
A & G MANUFACTURING CO INC (PA)
Also Called: A G Mercury
280 Gelsanliter Rd (44833-2234)
P.O. Box 935 (44833-0935)
PHONE..................................419 468-7433
Arvin Shifley, *Pr*
Doug Shifley, *
Glen E Shifley Junior, *Sec*
Glen Shifley Senior, *Prin*
▲ EMP: 40 EST: 1970
SQ FT: 100,000
SALES (est): 9.98MM
SALES (corp-wide): 9.98MM **Privately Held**

Web: www.agmercury.com
SIC: **3599** 7692 3446 3444 Machine shop, jobbing and repair; Welding repair; Architectural metalwork; Sheet metalwork

(G-8741)
A M COMMUNICATIONS LTD (PA)
5707 State Route 309 (44833-9541)
PHONE.............................419 528-3051
EMP: 67 **EST:** 2002
SQ FT: 8,000
SALES (est): 23.75MM
SALES (corp-wide): 23.75MM **Privately Held**
Web: www.amcable.com
SIC: **4899** Data communication services

(G-8742)
AVITA HEALTH SYSTEM
Also Called: Robert L Dawson M.D., James
955 Hosford Rd (44833-9325)
PHONE.............................419 468-7059
James H Wurm, *Pt*
EMP: 96
SALES (corp-wide): 444.64K **Privately Held**
Web: www.avitahealth.org
SIC: **8011** Internal medicine, physician/surgeon
PA: Avita Health System
269 Portland Way S
Galion OH 44833
419 468-4841

(G-8743)
AVITA HEALTH SYSTEM (PA)
Also Called: Avita Health System
269 Portland Way S (44833-2312)
PHONE.............................419 468-4841
Jerry Morasko, *CEO*
EMP: 71 **EST:** 2010
SALES (est): 444.64K
SALES (corp-wide): 444.64K **Privately Held**
Web: www.avitahealth.org
SIC: **8011** Internal medicine, physician/surgeon

(G-8744)
AVITA HOME HEALTH AND HOSPICE
1220 N Market St (44833-1443)
PHONE.............................419 468-7985
Catherine Sapp, *Ex Dir*
EMP: 50
SALES (est): 1.05MM **Privately Held**
Web: www.avitahomehealth.org
SIC: **8082** Home health care services

(G-8745)
BAILLIE LUMBER CO LP
3953 County Road 51 (44833-9630)
PHONE.............................419 462-2000
Russel Jones, *Brnch Mgr*
EMP: 40
SALES (corp-wide): 595.03MM **Privately Held**
Web: www.baillie.com
SIC: **5031** 2426 2421 Lumber: rough, dressed, and finished; Hardwood dimension and flooring mills; Sawmills and planing mills, general
PA: Baillie Lumber Co., L.P.
4002 Legion Dr
Hamburg NY 14075
800 950-2850

(G-8746)
CRAWFORD CNTY SHARED HLTH SVCS
1220 N Market St (44833-1443)
P.O. Box 327 (44833-0327)
PHONE.............................419 468-7985
Bert Maglott, *Ex Dir*
EMP: 45 **EST:** 1985
SALES (est): 5.48MM **Privately Held**
SIC: **8082** Home health care services

(G-8747)
FIRST FEDERAL BANK OF OHIO (PA)
140 N Columbus St (44833)
P.O. Box 957 (44833)
PHONE.............................419 468-1518
Joseph Clime, *Pr*
Eric S Geyer, *
Thomas Moore, *
Rodney J Vose, *
David Schockman, *
EMP: 39 **EST:** 1891
SQ FT: 12,000
SALES (est): 8.59MM
SALES (corp-wide): 8.59MM **Privately Held**
Web: www.firstfederalbankofohio.bank
SIC: **6035** Federal savings and loan associations

(G-8748)
FLICK LUMBER CO INC
Also Called: Flick Packaging
340 S Columbus St (44833-2624)
P.O. Box 296 (44833-0296)
PHONE.............................419 468-6278
Gary G Flick, *Pr*
George Flick, *
EMP: 30 **EST:** 1936
SQ FT: 35,200
SALES (est): 5.09MM **Privately Held**
Web: www.flickpackaging.com
SIC: **4783** Packing goods for shipping

(G-8749)
HUNTINGTON NATIONAL BANK
Also Called: Firstmerit Bank
260 Portland Way N (44833-1631)
PHONE.............................419 468-6868
Sherry Clevenger, *Mgr*
EMP: 31
SALES (corp-wide): 10.84B **Publicly Held**
Web: www.huntington.com
SIC: **6029** Commercial banks, nec
HQ: The Huntington National Bank
41 S High St
Columbus OH 43215
614 480-4293

(G-8750)
PAIN MANAGEMENT GROUP LLC
269 Portland Way S (44833-2312)
PHONE.............................419 462-4547
EMP: 34
SALES (corp-wide): 9.01MM **Privately Held**
Web: www.painmgmtgroup.com
SIC: **8011** Internal medicine, physician/surgeon
PA: Pain Management Group Llc
123 E Crawford St
Findlay OH 45840
419 722-6645

(G-8751)
SURFSIDE MOTORS INC (PA)
Also Called: Craig Smith Auto Group
7459 State Route 309 (44833-9735)
P.O. Box 850 (44833-0850)
PHONE.............................419 419-4776
TOLL FREE: 866
Craig A Smith, *Pr*
Bonnie J Heston, *
EMP: 42 **EST:** 1994
SQ FT: 21,000
SALES (est): 21.83MM
SALES (corp-wide): 21.83MM **Privately Held**
Web: www.craigsmithautogroup.com
SIC: **5511** 5521 7538 7532 Automobiles, new and used; Used car dealers; General automotive repair shops; Top and body repair and paint shops

Gallipolis
Gallia County

(G-8752)
AREA AGENCY ON AGING DST 7 INC
Also Called: Galia County Council On Aging
1167 State Route 160 (45631-8407)
P.O. Box 441 (45631-0441)
PHONE.............................740 446-7000
Shirley Doff, *Brnch Mgr*
EMP: 74
SALES (corp-wide): 63.29MM **Privately Held**
Web: www.aaa7.org
SIC: **8322** Senior citizens' center or association
PA: Area Agency On Aging District 7, Inc.
160 Dorsey Dr
Rio Grande OH 45674
800 582-7277

(G-8753)
COUNTY OF GALLIA
Also Called: Gallia County Human Services
848 3rd Ave (45631-1625)
P.O. Box 339 (45631-0339)
PHONE.............................740 446-3222
Kathy Mccalla, *Dir*
EMP: 28
SALES (corp-wide): 48.25MM **Privately Held**
Web: www.gallianet.net
SIC: **6371** 9111 Pension, health, and welfare funds; County supervisors' and executives' office
PA: County Of Gallia
18 Locust St Ste 1292
Gallipolis OH 45631
740 446-4612

(G-8754)
COUNTY OF GALLIA
Also Called: Gallia County Engineer
1167 State Route 160 (45631-8407)
PHONE.............................740 446-4009
Bret Boothe, *County Engineer*
EMP: 37
SALES (corp-wide): 48.25MM **Privately Held**
Web: www.galliacounty.org
SIC: **8711** Engineering services
PA: County Of Gallia
18 Locust St Ste 1292
Gallipolis OH 45631
740 446-4612

(G-8755)
COUNTY OF GALLIA
77 Mill Creek Rd (45631-8423)
PHONE.............................740 446-6902
Crystal Double, *Brnch Mgr*
EMP: 27
SALES (corp-wide): 48.25MM **Privately Held**
Web: www.gallianet.net
SIC: **8999** Artists and artists' studios
PA: County Of Gallia
18 Locust St Ste 1292
Gallipolis OH 45631
740 446-4612

(G-8756)
GALLIPOLIS HOSPITALITY INC
Also Called: Holiday Inn
577 State Route 7 N (45631-5921)
PHONE.............................740 446-0090
Anthony Etnyre, *Pr*
Gary Kilgore, *
EMP: 120 **EST:** 1972
SQ FT: 50,000
SALES (est): 262.6K **Privately Held**
Web: www.holidayinn.com
SIC: **7011** 5813 5812 Hotels and motels; Drinking places; Eating places

(G-8757)
HOLZER CLINIC LLC
Also Called: Holzer Hospital
90 Jackson Pike (45631-1562)
PHONE.............................740 446-5412
EMP: 33
SALES (corp-wide): 337.52MM **Privately Held**
Web: www.holzerclinic.com
SIC: **8011** 7991 Clinic, operated by physicians; Health club
HQ: Holzer Clinic Llc
90 Jackson Pike
Gallipolis OH 45631
740 446-5411

(G-8758)
HOLZER CLINIC LLC
1086 Jackson Pike (45631-1396)
PHONE.............................740 446-5074
Theresa Remy, *VP*
EMP: 34
SALES (corp-wide): 337.52MM **Privately Held**
Web: www.holzerclinic.com
SIC: **8052** Personal care facility
HQ: Holzer Clinic Llc
90 Jackson Pike
Gallipolis OH 45631
740 446-5411

(G-8759)
HOLZER CLINIC LLC (HQ)
Also Called: HOLZER CONSOLIDATED HEALTH SYS
90 Jackson Pike (45631-1562)
PHONE.............................740 446-5411
Christopher T Meyer, *CEO*
Craig Strafford, *
EMP: 566 **EST:** 1949
SQ FT: 95,000
SALES (est): 110.59MM
SALES (corp-wide): 337.52MM **Privately Held**
Web: www.holzerclinic.com
SIC: **8011** 8741 Physicians' office, including specialists; Management services
PA: Holzer Health System
100 Jackson Pike
Gallipolis OH 45631
740 446-5000

(G-8760)
HOLZER CLINIC LLC
100 Jackson Pike (45631-1560)
PHONE.............................304 746-3701
Matt Johnson, *Brnch Mgr*
EMP: 36
SALES (corp-wide): 337.52MM **Privately Held**
Web: www.holzerclinic.com
SIC: **8062** General medical and surgical hospitals
HQ: Holzer Clinic Llc
90 Jackson Pike
Gallipolis OH 45631
740 446-5411

(PA)=Parent Co (HQ)=Headquarters
✪ = New Business established in last 2 years

Gallipolis - Gallia County (G-8761)

(G-8761)
HOLZER HEALTH SYSTEM (PA)
Also Called: Holzer
100 Jackson Pike (45631-1560)
PHONE.................................740 446-5000
Michael Canady, *CEO*
Brent Saundrs, *
Troy Miller, *
EMP: 552 **EST:** 1985
SALES (est): 337.52MM
SALES (corp-wide): 337.52MM **Privately Held**
Web: www.holzer.org
SIC: 8062 General medical and surgical hospitals

(G-8762)
HOLZER HOSPITAL FOUNDATION (HQ)
Also Called: Holzer Medical Center
100 Jackson Pike (45631-1560)
PHONE.................................740 446-5000
Brent A Saunders, *Ch Bd*
Christopher T Meyer, *
Michael R Canady, *CMO*
Mister John S Cunningham, *Ex VP*
EMP: 898 **EST:** 1929
SQ FT: 254,000
SALES (est): 212.03MM
SALES (corp-wide): 337.52MM **Privately Held**
SIC: 8062 General medical and surgical hospitals
PA: Holzer Health System
 100 Jackson Pike
 Gallipolis OH 45631
 740 446-5000

(G-8763)
MEDI HOME HEALTH AGENCY INC
392 Silver Bridge Plz (45631-1833)
PHONE.................................740 441-1779
John Kerns, *Prin*
EMP: 32
SALES (corp-wide): 14.21MM **Privately Held**
SIC: 8082 Home health care services
HQ: Medi Home Health Agency, Inc.
 105 Main St
 Steubenville OH 43953

(G-8764)
OHIO DEPT DVLPMNTAL DSBILITIES
Also Called: Gallipolis Developmental Ctr
2500 Ohio Ave (45631-1656)
PHONE.................................740 446-1642
Don Walker, *Bmch Mgr*
EMP: 247
SIC: 8063 8052 9431 Psychiatric hospitals; Intermediate care facilities; Administration of public health programs, State government
HQ: Ohio Department Of Developmental Disabilities
 30 E Broad St Fl 13
 Columbus OH 43215

(G-8765)
OHIO VALLEY BANC CORP (PA)
420 3rd Ave (45631-1135)
P.O. Box 240 (45631-0240)
PHONE.................................740 446-2631
Larry E Miller, *CEO*
Larry E Miller Ii, *Pr*
Thomas E Wiseman, *Ch Bd*
Scott W Shockey, *Sr VP*
Ryan J Jones, *Chief Operations*
EMP: 42 **EST:** 1992
SALES (est): 74.49MM **Publicly Held**
Web: www.ovbc.com
SIC: 6022 State commercial banks

(G-8766)
OHIO VALLEY BANK COMPANY (HQ)
Also Called: Ohio Valley Bank
420 3rd Ave (45631)
P.O. Box 240 (45631)
PHONE.................................740 446-2631
Larry E Miller Ii, *Pr*
Scott W Shockey, *Ex VP*
Bryan F Stepp, *CLO*
Katrinka V Hart-harris, *Sr VP*
Allen W Elliott, *Sr VP*
EMP: 188 **EST:** 1872
SALES (est): 56.33MM **Publicly Held**
Web: www.ovbc.com
SIC: 6022 State trust companies accepting deposits, commercial
PA: Ohio Valley Banc Corp.
 420 3rd Ave
 Gallipolis OH 45631

(G-8767)
OHIO VALLEY HOME HEALTH INC (PA)
Also Called: FAMILY HOME HEALTH PLUS
1480 Jackson Pike (45631-2602)
P.O. Box 274 (45631-0274)
PHONE.................................740 441-1393
Don Corbin, *CEO*
Michael Valley, *
EMP: 28 **EST:** 2000
SALES (est): 4.05MM
SALES (corp-wide): 4.05MM **Privately Held**
Web: www.yourchoicehealthcare.net
SIC: 8082 Home health care services

(G-8768)
RES-CARE INC
240 3rd Ave (45631-1026)
PHONE.................................740 446-7549
Roberta Vangundy, *Mgr*
EMP: 82
SALES (corp-wide): 8.83B **Publicly Held**
Web: www.rescare.com
SIC: 8082 Home health care services
HQ: Res-Care, Inc.
 805 N Whittington Pkwy
 Louisville KY 40222
 502 394-2100

(G-8769)
THOMAS DO-IT CENTER INC (PA)
Also Called: Thomas Rental
176 Mccormick Rd (45631-8745)
PHONE.................................740 446-2002
Autumn Thomas, *Ex Dir*
Jim Thomas, *
Marlene Hall, *
Lee Cyrus, *
Jay Hall, *
▲ **EMP:** 45 **EST:** 1988
SALES (est): 9.63MM
SALES (corp-wide): 9.63MM **Privately Held**
Web: www.thomasdoit.com
SIC: 7359 2439 5211 5251 Equipment rental and leasing, nec; Trusses, wooden roof; Lumber products; Hardware stores

(G-8770)
WOODLAND CENTERS INC (PA)
3086 State Route 160 (45631)
PHONE.................................740 446-5500
David Tener, *Dir*
EMP: 55 **EST:** 1974
SQ FT: 18,000
SALES (est): 123.1K
SALES (corp-wide): 123.1K **Privately Held**
Web: www.hopewellhealth.org
SIC: 8093 Mental health clinic, outpatient

Galloway
Franklin County

(G-8771)
HEALTH CARE LOGISTICS INC
6106 Bausch Rd (43119-9382)
PHONE.................................800 848-1633
Susan Egelhoff, *Prin*
EMP: 65
SALES (corp-wide): 51.04MM **Privately Held**
Web: www.gohcl.com
SIC: 4789 Pipeline terminal facilities, independently operated
PA: Health Care Logistics, Inc.
 450 Town St
 Circleville OH 43113
 740 477-1686

(G-8772)
JOSHUA M HALDERMAN DDS LLC
1101 Norton Rd (43119-8956)
PHONE.................................614 309-1474
EMP: 37
SALES (corp-wide): 227.7K **Privately Held**
Web: www.gallowaysmiles.com
SIC: 8021 Dentists' office
PA: Joshua M Halderman Dds Llc
 4844 Calloway Ct
 Dublin OH

(G-8773)
MIKES TRUCKING LTD
570 Plain City Georgesville Rd Se (43119)
PHONE.................................614 879-8808
Mike Culbertson, *Pt*
EMP: 29 **EST:** 1985
SALES (est): 3.88MM **Privately Held**
Web: www.mikestrucking.com
SIC: 4212 Dump truck haulage

Gambier
Knox County

(G-8774)
KENYON COLLEGE
Also Called: Kenyon Inn
100 W Wegan St (43022)
P.O. Box 273 (43022-0273)
PHONE.................................740 427-2202
EMP: 32
SALES (corp-wide): 124.31MM **Privately Held**
Web: www.knoxcountyohiohotelrestaurant.com
SIC: 7011 8221 Hotels and motels; College, except junior
PA: Kenyon College
 1 Kenyon College
 Gambier OH 43022
 740 427-5000

Garfield Heights
Cuyahoga County

(G-8775)
JENNINGS ASSISTED LIVING
10204 Granger Rd (44125-3106)
PHONE.................................216 581-2900
Allison Q Salopeck, *CEO*
EMP: 50 **EST:** 2020
SALES (est): 701.15K **Privately Held**
Web: www.jenningsohio.org
SIC: 8099 Health and allied services, nec

(G-8776)
LOVING CARE HOME HLTH AGCY LLC
9545 Midwest Ave Ste I (44125-2400)
PHONE.................................216 322-9316
EMP: 58 **EST:** 2017
SALES (est): 872.93K **Privately Held**
SIC: 8099 Health and allied services, nec

(G-8777)
NCBW GRTER CLVLAND CHPTER WMEN
12680 Rockside Rd (44125-4525)
PHONE.................................216 232-2992
Yvonne M Conwell, *Pr*
EMP: 60 **EST:** 2021
SALES (est): 970.75K **Privately Held**
SIC: 6732 Trusts: educational, religious, etc.

(G-8778)
PLATINUM CARRIERS LLC
12325 Broadway Ave (44125-1847)
P.O. Box 188 (44233-0188)
PHONE.................................877 318-9607
EMP: 65 **EST:** 2015
SALES (est): 2.54MM **Privately Held**
Web: www.platinumcarriers.com
SIC: 4213 Trucking, except local

Garrettsville
Portage County

(G-8779)
RITE AID OF OHIO INC
Also Called: Rite Aid
10764 North St (44231-1016)
PHONE.................................330 527-2828
Louis Harr, *Mgr*
EMP: 47
SALES (corp-wide): 24.09B **Publicly Held**
Web: www.riteaid.com
SIC: 5912 7384 Drug stores; Photofinishing laboratory
HQ: Rite Aid Of Ohio, Inc.
 1200 Intrepid Ave Ste 2
 Philadelphia PA 19112

(G-8780)
SKYLANE LLC
Also Called: Sky Lane Drive-Thru
8311 Windham St (44231-9406)
PHONE.................................330 527-9999
EMP: 36 **EST:** 2007
SQ FT: 120,000
SALES (est): 472.77K **Privately Held**
Web: www.skylanebowling.com
SIC: 5812 7933 Restaurant, family: chain; Bowling centers

Gates Mills
Cuyahoga County

(G-8781)
ARBOR REHABILITATION & HEALTCR
45125 Fairmount Blvd (44040)
P.O. Box 99 (44040-0099)
PHONE.................................440 423-0206
Robert Vadas, *Pr*
EMP: 275 **EST:** 2005
SALES (est): 19.54MM **Privately Held**
Web: www.arborrehab.com
SIC: 8322 Rehabilitation services

GEOGRAPHIC SECTION

Georgetown - Brown County (G-8802)

(G-8782)
CHAGRIN VALLEY HUNT CLUB
7620 Old Mill Rd (44040-9700)
P.O. Box 159 (44040-0159)
PHONE..............................440 423-4414
Fred Floyd, *Pr*
EMP: 40 **EST:** 1909
SQ FT: 7,463
SALES (est): 1.71MM **Privately Held**
Web: www.cvhuntclub.org
SIC: 7997 Country club, membership

Geneva
Ashtabula County

(G-8783)
599 W MAIN CORPORATION
Also Called: Homestead
599 W Main St (44041-1252)
PHONE..............................440 466-1079
Jamie Miller, *Pr*
EMP: 48 **EST:** 1965
SALES (est): 981.61K **Privately Held**
SIC: 8052 Home for the mentally retarded, with health care

(G-8784)
CONTINING HLTHCARE SLTIONS INC
Also Called: Esther Marie Nursing Home
60 West St (44041-9723)
PHONE..............................440 466-1181
Susan Knowson, *Owner*
EMP: 363
SALES (corp-wide): 134.65MM **Privately Held**
Web: www.continuinghc.com
SIC: 8051 Skilled nursing care facilities
PA: Continuing Healthcare Solutions, Inc.
2875 Center Rd Ste 6
Brunswick OH 44212
216 772-1105

(G-8785)
GENEVA AREA RCRTL EDCTL ATHC T
Also Called: Gareat Sports Complex
1822 S Broadway (44041-7129)
P.O. Box 316 (44041-0316)
PHONE..............................440 466-1002
Ronald W Clutter, *Ch Bd*
EMP: 31 **EST:** 2008
SQ FT: 750,000
SALES (est): 4.69MM **Privately Held**
Web: www.spireacademy.com
SIC: 7997 Membership sports and recreation clubs

(G-8786)
HOMELIFE RESIDENTIAL SVCS INC
4933 N Myers Rd (44041-7703)
PHONE..............................440 964-2419
Paul Mikulin, *Pr*
EMP: 35 **EST:** 1987
SALES (est): 518.16K **Privately Held**
SIC: 8322 Individual and family services

(G-8787)
NEIGHBORHOOD LOGISTICS CO INC
Also Called: Truckmen
5449 Bishop Rd (44041-9600)
PHONE..............................440 466-0020
Bruce Fleischmann, *Pr*
David Jewell, *
Jeff Jenks,. *
Julie Lefelhoc, *
▲ **EMP:** 34 **EST:** 1991
SQ FT: 110,000
SALES (est): 4.97MM **Privately Held**
Web: www.truckmen.com
SIC: 4225 4214 4212 General warehousing and storage; Local trucking with storage; Local trucking, without storage

(G-8788)
RAE-ANN CENTER INC
Also Called: Rae-Ann Gneva Sklled Nrsing Rh
839 W Main St (44041-1218)
PHONE..............................440 466-5733
John Griffiths, *Mgr*
EMP: 37
SQ FT: 12,000
SALES (corp-wide): 9.01MM **Privately Held**
Web: www.rae-ann.net
SIC: 8052 8051 Intermediate care facilities; Skilled nursing care facilities
PA: Rae-Ann Center, Inc.
29505 Detroit Rd
Westlake OH 44145
440 871-5181

(G-8789)
TEGAM INC (HQ)
Also Called: Tegam
10 Tegam Way (44041-1144)
PHONE..............................440 466-6100
Andrew Brush, *Genl Mgr*
Adam Fleder, *
EMP: 43 **EST:** 1979
SQ FT: 28,600
SALES (est): 13.43MM
SALES (corp-wide): 1.66B **Publicly Held**
Web: www.tegam.com
SIC: 3829 7629 Measuring and controlling devices, nec; Electrical measuring instrument repair and calibration
PA: Advanced Energy Industries, Inc.
1595 Wynkoop St Ste 800
Denver CO 80202
970 407-6626

(G-8790)
THIRD DIMENSION INC (HQ)
633 Pleasant Ave (44041-1176)
PHONE..............................440 466-4040
Louie Dejesus, *Pr*
▲ **EMP:** 50 **EST:** 1984
SQ FT: 180,000
SALES (est): 23.37MM
SALES (corp-wide): 1.87B **Privately Held**
Web: www.thirdinc.com
SIC: 7389 5199 7336 Packaging and labeling services; Packaging materials; Graphic arts and related design
PA: Green Bay Packaging Inc.
1700 N Webster Ave
Green Bay WI 54302
920 433-5111

(G-8791)
UHHS-MEMORIAL HOSP OF GENEVA
870 W Main St (44041-1219)
PHONE..............................440 466-1141
William Lawrence, *Admn*
Laurie Lewis, *
EMP: 294 **EST:** 1903
SQ FT: 56,391
SALES (est): 16.47MM **Privately Held**
Web: www.uhhs.com
SIC: 8062 General medical and surgical hospitals

(G-8792)
UNIVERSITY HOSP GENEVA MED CTR
870 W Main St (44041-1219)
PHONE..............................440 415-0159
Krishnan Sundararajan, *Prin*
EMP: 77 **EST:** 2000
SALES (est): 56.61MM **Privately Held**
Web: www.uhhospitals.org
SIC: 8062 General medical and surgical hospitals

Genoa
Ottawa County

(G-8793)
CIMARRON EXPRESS INC
21611 State Route 51 W (43430-1245)
P.O. Box 185 (43430-0185)
PHONE..............................419 855-7713
Glenn Grady, *Pr*
James Shepperd, *
Denise Hoyles, *
EMP: 65 **EST:** 1984
SQ FT: 800
SALES (est): 9.98MM **Privately Held**
Web: www.cimarronexpress.com
SIC: 4213 Contract haulers

(G-8794)
GENOA BANKING COMPANY (HQ)
Also Called: Genoa Bank
801 Main St (43430-1637)
P.O. Box 98 (43430-0098)
PHONE..............................419 855-8381
Martin Sutter, *Pr*
Douglas Jergens, *
Richard Hillman, *Senior Loan Officer**
Todd Marsh, *
Ron Gladieux, *
EMP: 29 **EST:** 1902
SQ FT: 10,000
SALES (est): 21.12MM **Privately Held**
Web: www.genoabank.com
SIC: 6022 State trust companies accepting deposits, commercial
PA: Genbanc, Inc.
801 Main St
Genoa OH 43430

(G-8795)
MCCLELLAN MANAGEMENT INC
Also Called: Genoa Care Center
300 Cherry St (43430-1823)
PHONE..............................419 855-7755
William Mc Clellan, *Pr*
EMP: 47 **EST:** 1985
SQ FT: 20,000
SALES (est): 1.39MM **Privately Held**
Web: www.trilogyhs.com
SIC: 8051 8052 Convalescent home with continuous nursing care; Intermediate care facilities

Georgetown
Brown County

(G-8796)
ABCAP FOUNDATION
406 W Plum St (45121-1056)
PHONE..............................937 378-6041
Alvin Norris, *Prin*
EMP: 37 **EST:** 2004
SALES (est): 1.09MM **Privately Held**
Web: www.abcap.net
SIC: 8082 Home health care services

(G-8797)
ADAMS BROWN CNTIES ECNMIC OPPR
9262 Mount Orab Pike (45121-9311)
PHONE..............................937 378-3431
Dan Wickerham, *Brnch Mgr*
EMP: 49
SALES (corp-wide): 19.1MM **Privately Held**
Web: www.abcap.net
SIC: 4953 Recycling, waste materials
PA: Adams & Brown Counties Economic Opportunities, Inc.
406 W Plum St
Georgetown OH 45121
937 378-6041

(G-8798)
BROWN CNTY BD MNTAL RTARDATION
325 W State St Bldg A (45121-1229)
PHONE..............................937 378-4891
Theresa Armstrong, *Prin*
Lena Bradford, *
EMP: 46 **EST:** 1966
SQ FT: 100,000
SALES (est): 322.86K **Privately Held**
Web: www.browncbdd.org
SIC: 8331 3993 2396 Sheltered workshop; Signs and advertising specialties; Automotive and apparel trimmings

(G-8799)
BROWN CO ED SERVICE CENTER
9231b Hamer Rd (45121-1527)
PHONE..............................937 378-6118
James D Fraizer, *Superintnt*
Robin Tore, *
EMP: 42 **EST:** 1923
SALES (est): 2.24MM **Privately Held**
Web: www.brownesc.us
SIC: 8211 8741 Specialty education; Management services

(G-8800)
COVENANT CARE OHIO INC
Also Called: Villa Georgetown
8065 Doctor Faul Rd (45121-8811)
PHONE..............................937 378-0188
Sandra Leedy, *Mgr*
EMP: 75
SIC: 8051 Convalescent home with continuous nursing care
HQ: Covenant Care Ohio, Inc.
120 Vantis Dr Ste 200
Aliso Viejo CA 92656
949 349-1200

(G-8801)
RUMPKE WASTE INC
9427 Beyers Rd (45121-9301)
PHONE..............................937 378-4126
TOLL FREE: 800
Ronda Yates, *Mgr*
EMP: 213
Web: www.rumpke.com
SIC: 4953 4212 Refuse collection and disposal services; Local trucking, without storage
HQ: Rumpke Waste, Inc.
10795 Hughes Rd
Cincinnati OH 45251
513 851-0122

(G-8802)
SOUTHWEST HLTHCARE BROWN CNTY
Also Called: Southwest Regional Medical Ctr
425 Home St (45121-1407)
P.O. Box 62609 (45262-0609)
PHONE..............................937 378-7800
TOLL FREE: 800
Kathy Wolf, *Asstg*
EMP: 126 **EST:** 1952
SQ FT: 120,000
SALES (est): 9.7MM **Privately Held**
SIC: 8062 General medical and surgical hospitals

Germantown
Montgomery County

(G-8803)
ASTORIA HEALTHCARE GROUP LLC
Also Called: Astoria Health & Rehab Center
300 Astoria Rd (45327-1712)
PHONE..................................937 855-2363
George S Repchick, *Pr*
William I Weisberg, *VP*
EMP: 96 **EST:** 2012
SALES (est): 5.55MM
SALES (corp-wide): 655.44MM **Privately Held**
Web: www.saberhealth.com
SIC: 8051 Convalescent home with continuous nursing care
PA: Saber Healthcare Group, L.L.C.
23700 Commerce Park
Beachwood OH 44122
216 292-5706

(G-8804)
SCHOOL TRANSPORTATION
59 Peffley St (45327-1021)
PHONE..................................937 855-3897
Rick Wharton, *Genl Mgr*
Sherry Parr, *Superintnt*
Rick Wharton, *Mgr*
Frances Wagner, *Mgr*
EMP: 50 **EST:** 2010
SALES (est): 1.01MM **Privately Held**
SIC: 4789 Transportation services, nec

(G-8805)
SMYRNA READY MIX CONCRETE LLC
9151 Township Park Dr (45327-8711)
PHONE..................................937 855-0410
Hank Ernst, *Brnch Mgr*
EMP: 37
SALES (corp-wide): 1.05B **Privately Held**
Web: www.smyrnareadymix.com
SIC: 5211 5032 3273 Cement; Concrete and cinder building products; Ready-mixed concrete
PA: Smyrna Ready Mix Concrete, Llc
1000 Hollingshead Cir
Murfreesboro TN 37129
615 355-1028

Gibsonburg
Sandusky County

(G-8806)
REINO LINEN SERVICE INC (HQ)
Also Called: Reino Cleaners
119 S Main St (43431-1336)
PHONE..................................419 637-2151
EMP: 93 **EST:** 1943
SALES (est): 10.54MM
SALES (corp-wide): 147.62MM **Privately Held**
Web: www.healthcarelinensg.com
SIC: 7211 Power laundries, family and commercial
PA: Healthcare Linen Services Group
255 38th Ave Ste M
Saint Charles IL 60174
888 873-4740

(G-8807)
WESTFIELD ELECTRIC INC
2995 State Route 51 (43431-9710)
P.O. Box 93 (43431-0093)
PHONE..................................419 862-0078
Sheri M Busdeker, *CEO*
Thomas R Busdeker, *
EMP: 35 **EST:** 1999
SQ FT: 10,000
SALES (est): 5.28MM **Privately Held**
Web: www.westfieldgroups.com
SIC: 1731 5063 General electrical contractor; Electrical construction materials

Girard
Trumbull County

(G-8808)
AIM INTEGRATED LOGISTICS INC
Also Called: NationaLease
1500 Trumbull Ave (44420-3453)
PHONE..................................330 759-0438
EMP: 400 **EST:** 1984
SALES (est): 30.81MM
SALES (corp-wide): 180.46MM **Privately Held**
Web: www.aimntls.com
SIC: 4212 7513 8741 7699 Truck rental with drivers; Truck leasing, without drivers; Management services; Industrial truck repair
PA: Aim Leasing Company
1500 Trumbull Ave
Girard OH 44420
330 759-0438

(G-8809)
AIM LEASING COMPANY (PA)
Also Called: NationaLease
1500 Trumbull Ave (44420)
PHONE..................................330 759-0438
Thomas Fleming, *Pr*
Terry Dimascio, *
Rick Fox, *
EMP: 60 **EST:** 1962
SQ FT: 10,000
SALES (est): 180.46MM
SALES (corp-wide): 180.46MM **Privately Held**
Web: www.aimntls.com
SIC: 7513 7538 5983 4212 Truck leasing, without drivers; General truck repair; Fuel oil dealers; Truck rental with drivers

(G-8810)
BOARDMAN MEDICAL SUPPLY CO (HQ)
Also Called: Innovative Concept
300 N State St (44420-2595)
PHONE..................................330 545-6700
Felix S Savon, *Pr*
Robin S Ivany, *
Christine E Savon, *
▲ **EMP:** 130 **EST:** 1982
SQ FT: 3,400
SALES (est): 25.53MM
SALES (corp-wide): 25.53MM **Privately Held**
Web: www.boardmanmedicalsupply.com
SIC: 5999 7352 Hospital equipment and supplies; Medical equipment rental
PA: Sateri Home, Inc.
7246 Ronjoy Pl
Youngstown OH 44512
330 758-8106

(G-8811)
FIRE FOE CORP
999 Trumbull Ave (44420-3448)
P.O. Box 128 (44410-0128)
PHONE..................................330 759-9834
Earnest M Nicholas, *Pr*
Mary Nicholas, *
EMP: 35 **EST:** 1978
SQ FT: 18,000
SALES (est): 4.22MM **Privately Held**
Web: www.firefoe.com
SIC: 3569 7699 Sprinkler systems, fire: automatic; Fire control (military) equipment repair

(G-8812)
FLEMING LEASING LLC
1500 Trumbull Ave (44420-3453)
PHONE..................................703 842-1358
C Thomas Steele Junior, *Admn*
EMP: 239
SALES (corp-wide): 180.46MM **Privately Held**
Web: www.aimntls.com
SIC: 7359 Equipment rental and leasing, nec
HQ: Fleming Leasing, L.L.C.
7397 Ward Park Ln
Springfield VA 22153
703 842-1358

(G-8813)
GIRARD CITY SCHOOL DISTRICT
Also Called: Bus Garage
130 W Broadway Ave (44420-2501)
PHONE..................................330 545-6407
EMP: 37
SALES (corp-wide): 25.94MM **Privately Held**
Web: www.girardcityschools.org
SIC: 4151 School buses
PA: Girard City School District
100 W Main St Ste 2
Girard OH 44420
330 545-2596

(G-8814)
GIRARD EQUIPMENT CO
1745 N State St (44420-1027)
P.O. Box 4176 (44515-0176)
PHONE..................................330 545-2575
John P Cerni Ii, *Pr*
EMP: 50 **EST:** 1987
SQ FT: 6,000
SALES (est): 4.51MM
SALES (corp-wide): 357.54MM **Privately Held**
Web: www.girardequip.com
SIC: 7539 5012 Trailer repair; Trailers for trucks, new and used
PA: Trivista Companies, Inc.
3311 Adventureland Dr
Altoona IA 50009
515 967-3300

(G-8815)
HOSPICE OF VALLEY INC (PA)
979 Tibbetts Wick Rd Ste A (44420-1182)
PHONE..................................330 788-1992
Terry Kilbury, *Dir*
EMP: 74 **EST:** 1979
SALES (est): 14.04MM **Privately Held**
Web: www.mercy.com
SIC: 8069 8322 Specialty hospitals, except psychiatric; Individual and family services

(G-8816)
INDUSTRIAL INSUL COATINGS LLC
142 E 2nd St (44420-2905)
P.O. Box 154 (44420-0154)
PHONE..................................800 506-1399
Richard Marchese, *Pr*
John Zajac, *
Edward Zajac, *
EMP: 28 **EST:** 2015
SALES (est): 2.11MM **Privately Held**
Web: www.iicinsulation.com
SIC: 1742 7389 Insulation, buildings; Business Activities at Non-Commercial Site

(G-8817)
INTERSTATE SHREDDING LLC
27 Furnace Ln (44420-3214)
P.O. Box 29 (44420-0029)
PHONE..................................330 545-5477
▲ **EMP:** 40
Web: www.interstateshreddingllc.com
SIC: 4953 Recycling, waste materials

(G-8818)
LIFELINE PARTNERS INC
1825 Tibbetts Wick Rd (44420-1222)
PHONE..................................330 501-6316
Kathleen Burgdorf, *Pr*
Bruce Burgdorf, *
EMP: 36 **EST:** 2000
SALES (est): 2.58MM **Privately Held**
Web: www.lifelinepartners.com
SIC: 8322 Rehabilitation services

(G-8819)
MAHONING COUNTRY CLUB INC
710 E Liberty St (44420-2310)
PHONE..................................330 545-2517
John Ezzo, *Pr*
Dave Ezzo, *
Susan Siguiee, *
EMP: 38 **EST:** 1952
SQ FT: 50,000
SALES (est): 409.7K **Privately Held**
Web: www.mahoningcountryclub.com
SIC: 5812 7992 5941 Eating places; Public golf courses; Sporting goods and bicycle shops

(G-8820)
MEDVET ASSOCIATES LLC
Also Called: Medvet Mahoning Valley
2680 W Liberty St (44420-3113)
PHONE..................................330 530-8387
Sandy Post, *Brnch Mgr*
EMP: 41
Web: www.medvet.com
SIC: 0742 Animal hospital services, pets and other animal specialties
PA: Medvet Associates, Llc
350 E Wilson Bridge Rd
Worthington OH 43085

(G-8821)
OMNI MANOR INC (PA)
101 W Liberty St (44420-2844)
PHONE..................................330 545-1550
John Masternick, *Pr*
Leo Grimes, *
Dorothy Masternick, *
EMP: 200 **EST:** 1980
SALES (est): 23.03MM
SALES (corp-wide): 23.03MM **Privately Held**
Web: www.windsorhouseinc.com
SIC: 8051 Convalescent home with continuous nursing care

(G-8822)
PATRIOT HOMECARE INC
986 Tibbetts Wick Rd (44420-1138)
PHONE..................................330 306-9651
Craig K Colton, *Prin*
EMP: 220 **EST:** 2011
SALES (est): 15.49MM **Privately Held**
Web: www.patriothc.org
SIC: 8082 Visiting nurse service

(G-8823)
PRISMA INTEGRATION CORP
50 Harry St (44420-1709)
PHONE..................................330 545-8690
EMP: 28 **EST:** 2017
SALES (est): 11.37MM

GEOGRAPHIC SECTION   Grafton - Lorain County (G-8844)

SALES (corp-wide): 11.79MM **Privately Held**
Web: www.prismaintegration.com
SIC: **7374** Data processing and preparation
PA: Prisma Impianti Spa
    Via Asti 7
    Basaluzzo AL 15060
    014 348-9891

(G-8824)
SHEPHERD OF VLY LTHRAN RTRMENT
1501 Tibbetts Wick Rd (44420-1206)
PHONE.................................330 544-0771
Don Kalmar, *Brnch Mgr*
EMP: 31
SALES (corp-wide): 42.58MM **Privately Held**
Web: www.shepherdofthevalley.com
SIC: **8361** Aged home
PA: Shepherd Of The Valley Lutheran
    Retirement Services, Inc.
    5525 Silica Rd
    Youngstown OH 44515
    330 530-4038

(G-8825)
SHIR-SATH INC
Also Called: Days Inn
1615 E Liberty St (44420-2419)
PHONE.................................330 759-9820
Krupal Desai, *Pr*
EMP: 52 **EST:** 2009
SQ FT: 18,000
SALES (est): 449.5K **Privately Held**
Web: www.wyndhamhotels.com
SIC: **7011** Hotels and motels

(G-8826)
SOFT TOUCH WOOD LLC
Also Called: Soft Tuch Furn Repr Rfinishing
1560 S State St (44420-3315)
PHONE.................................330 545-4204
Terry Chudakoff, *Pr*
Bob Leer, *
EMP: 40 **EST:** 2000
SQ FT: 5,000
SALES (est): 4.83MM **Privately Held**
Web: www.softtouchfurniture.com
SIC: **7641** 2531 Furniture refinishing; Public building and related furniture

(G-8827)
SOUTHERNTIER TELECOM INC (PA)
5555 Sampson Dr (44420-3508)
PHONE.................................330 550-2733
Marina Miller, *CEO*
Alex Borodyanskiy, *
EMP: 40 **EST:** 2016
SALES (est): 9.38MM
SALES (corp-wide): 9.38MM **Privately Held**
SIC: **4813** Telephone communication, except radio

(G-8828)
UNITED PARCEL SERVICE INC
Also Called: UPS
800 Trumbull Ave (44420-3445)
PHONE.................................330 545-0177
Paul Hammond, *Mgr*
EMP: 52
SALES (corp-wide): 90.96B **Publicly Held**
Web: www.ups.com
SIC: **4215** Parcel delivery, vehicular
HQ: United Parcel Service, Inc.
    55 Glenlake Pkwy
    Atlanta GA 30328
    404 828-6000

(G-8829)
UNIVERSAL DEVELOPMENT MGT INC (PA)
Also Called: Howard Johnson
1607 Motor Inn Dr Ste 1 (44420-2496)
PHONE.................................330 759-7017
Ronald R Anderson, *Pr*
Harold J Anderson, *
EMP: 30 **EST:** 1973
SQ FT: 12,000
SALES (est): 5.54MM
SALES (corp-wide): 5.54MM **Privately Held**
Web: www.universaldevelopment.net
SIC: **7011** 1542 Hotels and motels; Nonresidential construction, nec

(G-8830)
VEC INC
977 Tibbetts Wick Rd (44420-1133)
PHONE.................................330 539-4044
Rex A Ferry, *Pr*
Rachel Barber, *
EMP: 72 **EST:** 1965
SALES (est): 69.26MM **Privately Held**
Web: www.vecohio.com
SIC: **1731** General electrical contractor

(G-8831)
YOUNGSTOWN WLCOME HSPTLITY LLC
1620 Motor Inn Dr (44420-2422)
PHONE.................................330 759-6600
EMP: 108 **EST:** 2007
SALES (est): 2.28MM **Privately Held**
SIC: **7011** Hotels and motels

Glenford
Perry County

(G-8832)
WASTE MANAGEMENT MICHIGAN INC
Also Called: Waste Management
3415 Township Rd Ste 447 (43739)
PHONE.................................740 787-2327
Frank Fello, *Genl Mgr*
EMP: 52
SALES (corp-wide): 20.43B **Publicly Held**
SIC: **4953** Garbage: collecting, destroying, and processing
HQ: Waste Management Of Michigan, Inc.
    48797 Alpha Dr Ste 100
    Wixom MI 48393
    586 574-2760

(G-8833)
WASTE MANAGEMENT OHIO INC
Also Called: Waste Management
3415 Township Road 447 (43739-9704)
PHONE.................................740 787-2327
EMP: 49
SALES (corp-wide): 20.43B **Publicly Held**
SIC: **4953** Recycling, waste materials
HQ: Waste Management Of Ohio, Inc.
    1700 N Broad St
    Fairborn OH 45324

Glenwillow
Cuyahoga County

(G-8834)
METRO DECOR LLC
Also Called: Mdesign
30320 Emerald Valley Pkwy (44139)
P.O. Box 39606 (44139)
PHONE.................................855 498-5899
Susan Lizan-immerman, *Managing Member*
EMP: 200 **EST:** 2015
SALES (est): 63.34MM
SALES (corp-wide): 101.36MM **Privately Held**
Web: www.mdesignhomedecor.com
SIC: **5023** Decorative home furnishings and supplies
PA: Interdesign, Inc.
    30725 Solon Indus Pkwy
    Solon OH 44139
    440 248-0178

Glouster
Athens County

(G-8835)
HOCKINGTHENSPERRY CMNTY ACTION (PA)
3 Cardaras Dr (45732-8011)
P.O. Box 220 (45732-0220)
PHONE.................................740 767-4500
Doug Stanley, *Ex Dir*
EMP: 40 **EST:** 1966
SQ FT: 7,400
SALES (est): 30.74MM
SALES (corp-wide): 30.74MM **Privately Held**
Web: www.hapcap.org
SIC: **8399** 8331 8322 Community action agency; Job training and related services; Individual and family services

(G-8836)
US HOTEL OSP VENTURES LLC
Also Called: Burr Oak State Park Lodge
10660 Burr Oak Lodge Rd (45732-8909)
PHONE.................................740 767-2112
Kyle Scholten, *Prin*
EMP: 60 **EST:** 2011
SALES (est): 992.35K **Privately Held**
Web: www.stayburroak.com
SIC: **7011** Resort hotel

Goshen
Clermont County

(G-8837)
NORTHERN PLUMBING SYSTEMS
1708 State Route 28 (45122-9754)
PHONE.................................513 831-5111
EMP: 31 **EST:** 2004
SALES (est): 4.51MM **Privately Held**
Web: www.nplgs.com
SIC: **1711** Plumbing contractors

Grafton
Lorain County

(G-8838)
BECHTOLD ENTERPRISES INC
Also Called: ABC
951 Main St (44044-1447)
PHONE.................................440 791-7177
James Bechtold, *Pr*
Christi Bechtold, *
EMP: 50 **EST:** 2012
SALES (est): 2.23MM **Privately Held**
SIC: **8748** Business consulting, nec

(G-8839)
GRAFTON READY MIX CONCRET INC
1155 Elm St (44044-1303)
P.O. Box 823 (44052-0823)
PHONE.................................440 926-2911
Jeffrey Riddell, *Pr*
EMP: 120 **EST:** 1987
SQ FT: 15,000
SALES (est): 828.67K **Privately Held**
SIC: **3273** 5032 5211 Ready-mixed concrete; Brick, stone, and related material; Masonry materials and supplies
PA: Consumeracq, Inc.
    2509 N Ridge Rd E
    Lorain OH 44055

(G-8840)
KELCO ENTERPRISES INC
Also Called: Pop A Lock of Ohio
36300 Grafton Eastern Rd (44044-9637)
PHONE.................................440 926-4357
Kelly Waddell, *Pr*
Sandra Waddell, *
EMP: 32 **EST:** 2001
SALES (est): 203.03K **Privately Held**
Web: www.popalock.com
SIC: **7699** Locksmith shop

(G-8841)
ROSS CONSOLIDATED CORP (PA)
36790 Giles Rd (44044-9125)
PHONE.................................440 748-5800
Maureen Cromling, *Pr*
EMP: 70 **EST:** 1948
SQ FT: 3,008
SALES (est): 104.49MM
SALES (corp-wide): 104.49MM **Privately Held**
Web: www.rossenvironmental.com
SIC: **4953** 4212 8741 Incinerator operation; Local trucking, without storage; Management services

(G-8842)
ROSS INCINERATION SERVICES INC
36790 Giles Rd (44044-9125)
PHONE.................................440 366-2000
Arthur Hargate, *CEO*
Maureen M Cromling, *
James Larson, *
William E Cromling Ii, *VP*
▼ **EMP:** 115 **EST:** 1981
SALES (est): 56.22MM
SALES (corp-wide): 104.49MM **Privately Held**
Web: www.rossenvironmental.com
SIC: **4953** Incinerator operation
PA: Ross Consolidated Corp.
    36790 Giles Rd
    Grafton OH 44044
    440 748-5800

(G-8843)
ROSS TRANSPORTATION SVCS INC
36790 Giles Rd (44044-9125)
PHONE.................................440 748-5900
William E Cromling Ii, *Pr*
EMP: 250 **EST:** 1981
SALES (est): 21.24MM
SALES (corp-wide): 104.49MM **Privately Held**
Web: www.rossenvironmental.com
SIC: **4213** Contract haulers
PA: Ross Consolidated Corp.
    36790 Giles Rd
    Grafton OH 44044
    440 748-5800

(G-8844)
SHAMA EXPRESS LLC
1014 Commerce Dr (44044-1276)
PHONE.................................216 925-6530
Mafil Askarov, *Pr*
Kamran Askarov, *
EMP: 92 **EST:** 2011
SALES (est): 5.56MM **Privately Held**
Web: www.shamaexpress.com

Grand Rapids
Wood County

(G-8845)
HERTZFELD POULTRY FARMS INC
15799 Milton Rd (43522-9761)
PHONE......................419 832-2070
Dave Hertzfeld, *Owner*
EMP: 80
SALES (corp-wide): 5.75MM **Privately Held**
Web: www.hpfeggs.com
SIC: 0191 0751 0119 General farms, primarily crop; Poultry services; Popcorn farm
PA: Hertzfeld Poultry Farms Inc.
   8525 Schadel Rd
   Waterville OH

(G-8846)
RAPIDS NURSING HOMES INC
Also Called: Grand Rapids Care Center
24201 W 3rd St (43522-8702)
PHONE......................216 292-5706
Robert Tebeau, *Pr*
Ronald Tebeau, *
Ernest Tebeau, *
EMP: 47
SALES (est): 5.2MM **Privately Held**
Web: www.saberhealth.com
SIC: 8051 Convalescent home with continuous nursing care

(G-8847)
ROBERT BETTINGER INC
21211 W State Route 65 (43522-9818)
PHONE......................419 832-6033
EMP: 50 **EST:** 1991
SQ FT: 2,796
SALES (est): 1.04MM **Privately Held**
SIC: 7299 Banquet hall facilities

Grand River
Lake County

(G-8848)
101 RIVER INC
Also Called: Grand River Seafood Supply
101 River St (44045-8212)
P.O. Box 120 (44045-0120)
PHONE......................440 352-6343
Gerald Powell, *Pr*
EMP: 47 **EST:** 1985
SQ FT: 7,000
SALES (est): 414.89K **Privately Held**
Web: www.picklebills.com
SIC: 5812 5146 Steak and barbecue restaurants; Fish and seafoods

Granville
Licking County

(G-8849)
BUXTON INN INC
Also Called: Buxton Inn
313 Broadway E (43023-1307)
PHONE......................740 587-0001
Orville O Orr, *Mgr*
Orville O Orr, *Pr*
Audrey V Orr, *
EMP: 40 **EST:** 1812
SQ FT: 20,000
SALES (est): 346.94K **Privately Held**
Web: www.buxtoninn.com
SIC: 5812 7011 Eating places; Hotels

(G-8850)
CENTRAL OHIO GERIATRICS LLC
590 Newark Granville Rd (43023-1436)
PHONE......................614 530-4077
John Weigand, *CEO*
EMP: 36 **EST:** 2009
SALES (est): 2.3MM **Privately Held**
Web: www.cog-med.com
SIC: 8011 Primary care medical clinic

(G-8851)
CHAMPION FEED AND PET SUP LLC
400 S Main St (43023-1470)
PHONE......................740 369-3020
EMP: 30 **EST:** 2009
SALES (est): 946.4K **Privately Held**
Web: www.championfeedandpet.com
SIC: 5153 Grains
PA: Heritage Cooperative, Inc.
   59 Greif Pkwy Ste 200
   Delaware OH 43015

(G-8852)
CLGT SOLUTIONS LLC
Also Called: Clovehitch
1670 Columbus Rd Ste C (43023-1232)
PHONE......................740 920-4795
EMP: 39 **EST:** 2010
SQ FT: 150
SALES (est): 2.49MM **Privately Held**
Web: www.clgtsolutions.com
SIC: 7389 8748 8742 Translation services; Testing service, educational or personnel; Management consulting services

(G-8853)
GRANVILLE HOSPITALITY LLC
314 Broadway E (43023-1308)
PHONE......................740 587-3333
Brian Newkirk, *
Jerry Martin, *
EMP: 52 **EST:** 2003
SQ FT: 50,000
SALES (est): 4.15MM **Privately Held**
Web: www.granvilleinn.com
SIC: 5812 7011 5813 Restaurant, family; independent; Hotels; Drinking places

(G-8854)
REVLOCAL (PA)
4009 Columbus Rd (43023-8612)
P.O. Box 511 (43050-0511)
PHONE......................800 456-7470
Aaron Boggs, *VP*
EMP: 82 **EST:** 2011
SALES (est): 10.33MM
SALES (corp-wide): 10.33MM **Privately Held**
Web: www.revlocal.com
SIC: 8742 Marketing consulting services

(G-8855)
TIMBUK FARMS INC
2030 Timbuk Rd (43023-9785)
PHONE......................740 587-2178
James Gibson, *Pr*
Lavonda Gibson, *
EMP: 66 **EST:** 1952
SQ FT: 100,000
SALES (est): 5.59MM **Privately Held**
Web: www.timbuk.com
SIC: 0181 0811 Flowers: grown under cover (e.g., greenhouse production); Christmas tree farm

(G-8856)
VARO ENGINEERS INC
2790 Columbus Rd (43023-1252)
PHONE......................740 587-2228
Dane Cox, *Brnch Mgr*
EMP: 48
SALES (corp-wide): 110.61MM **Privately Held**
Web: www.salasobrien.com
SIC: 8711 Consulting engineer
HQ: Varo Engineers, Inc.
   2751 Tuller Pkwy
   Dublin OH 43017
   614 459-0424

Green
Summit County

(G-8857)
PROFESSIONAL ELECTRIC PDTS CO
3729 Boettler Oaks Drive (44232)
P.O. Box 1570 (44096-1570)
PHONE......................330 896-3790
EMP: 27
SALES (corp-wide): 12.53MM **Privately Held**
Web: www.pepconet.com
SIC: 5063 Electrical supplies, nec
HQ: Professional Electric Products Co Inc
   33210 Lakeland Blvd
   Eastlake OH 44095
   800 872-7000

Green Springs
Seneca County

(G-8858)
ELMWOOD CENTERS INC (PA)
Also Called: Elm Springs
441 N Broadway St (44836-9689)
PHONE......................419 332-3378
Kathy Hunt, *CEO*
EMP: 67 **EST:** 1937
SQ FT: 4,000
SALES (est): 8.61MM
SALES (corp-wide): 8.61MM **Privately Held**
Web: www.elmwoodcommunities.com
SIC: 8051 Skilled nursing care facilities

(G-8859)
GREAT LKES CMNTY ACTION PARTNR
Also Called: Quilter Cvlian Cnsrvation Camp
1518 E County Road 113 (44836-9606)
P.O. Box 590 (43420-0590)
PHONE......................419 639-2802
Tim Havice, *Brnch Mgr*
EMP: 47
SALES (corp-wide): 53.21MM **Privately Held**
Web: www.glcap.org
SIC: 8399 Community action agency
PA: Great Lakes Community Action Partnership
   127 S Front St
   Fremont OH 43420
   419 333-6068

(G-8860)
KENNETH G MYERS CNSTR CO INC
201 Smith St (44836-9669)
P.O. Box 37 (44836-0037)
PHONE......................419 639-2051
Todd E Myers, *Pr*
Ronald Rowe, *
Brent Myers, *
Dan Willey, *
EMP: 100 **EST:** 1958
SQ FT: 3,200
SALES (est): 11.44MM **Privately Held**
Web: www.kgmyers.com
SIC: 1623 Underground utilities contractor

(G-8861)
MILLER CABLE COMPANY
210 S Broadway St (44836)
P.O. Box 68 (44836)
PHONE......................419 639-2091
Don W Miller, *Ch Bd*
Jim Chamberlin, *
James Chamberlin Junior, *VP*
John Hartley, *
Thomas Sprow, *
EMP: 62 **EST:** 1973
SQ FT: 2,500
SALES (est): 8.71MM **Privately Held**
Web: www.millercable.com
SIC: 1731 General electrical contractor

(G-8862)
WYNN-REETH INC
Also Called: Remote Support Services
137 S Broadway St (44836-9319)
P.O. Box 785 (44836-0785)
PHONE......................419 639-2094
Bruce Hunt, *Pr*
Jarrod Hunt, *
EMP: 50 **EST:** 1994
SALES (est): 5.47MM **Privately Held**
Web: www.wynn-reeth.com
SIC: 8361 Mentally handicapped home

Greenfield
Highland County

(G-8863)
ADENA HEALTH SYSTEM
Also Called: Adena Fmly Medicine-Greenfield
1075 N Washington St (45123-9780)
PHONE......................937 981-9444
Keith Coleman, *Brnch Mgr*
EMP: 31
SALES (corp-wide): 678.56MM **Privately Held**
Web: www.adena.org
SIC: 8062 Hospital, med school affiliated with nursing and residency
PA: Adena Health System
   272 Hospital Rd
   Chillicothe OH 45601
   740 779-7500

(G-8864)
GREENFIELD AREA MEDICAL CTR
Also Called: ADENA REGIONAL MEDICAL CENTER
550 Mirabeau St (45123-1617)
PHONE......................937 981-9400
Mark Shuter, *CEO*
EMP: 305 **EST:** 1945
SQ FT: 32,000
SALES (est): 24.44MM
SALES (corp-wide): 678.56MM **Privately Held**
Web: www.adena.org
SIC: 8062 General medical and surgical hospitals
PA: Adena Health System
   272 Hospital Rd
   Chillicothe OH 45601
   740 779-7500

(G-8865)
GREENFIELD PRODUCTS INC
1230 N Washington St (45123-9783)
P.O. Box 99 (45123-0099)
PHONE......................937 981-2696
Ann Gessner Pence, *Pr*
Wesley Pence, *

GEOGRAPHIC SECTION
Greenville - Darke County (G-8886)

◆ **EMP:** 51 **EST:** 1959
SQ FT: 12,000
SALES (est): 14.27MM **Privately Held**
Web: www.greenfieldproducts.com
SIC: 5088 Transportation equipment and supplies

(G-8866)
HIGHLAND HEALTH PROVIDERS CORP
1092 Jefferson St (45123-8319)
PHONE..........................937 981-1121
Amanda Warix, *Ex Dir*
EMP: 67
SALES (corp-wide): 9.75MM **Privately Held**
Web: www.hhproviders.org
SIC: 8011 General and family practice, physician/surgeon
PA: Highland Health Providers Corporation
1487 N High St Ste 102
Hillsboro OH 45133
937 840-6575

Greenville
Darke County

(G-8867)
CHAMBERS LEASING SYSTEMS CORP
5187 Childrens Home Bradford Rd (45331)
PHONE..........................937 547-9777
Curt Betts, *Brnch Mgr*
EMP: 30
Web: www.ventureexpress.com
SIC: 4213 Contract haulers
PA: Chambers Leasing Systems Corp
3100 N Summit St
Toledo OH 43611

(G-8868)
DARKE COUNTY SHERIFFS PATROL
5185 County Home Rd (45331-9753)
PHONE..........................937 548-3399
EMP: 33 **EST:** 2010
SALES (est): 318.45K **Privately Held**
Web: www.darkecountysheriff.org
SIC: 7381 Protective services, guard

(G-8869)
DAVE KNAPP FORD LINCOLN INC (PA)
500 Wagner Ave (45331-2539)
PHONE..........................937 547-3000
David O Knapp, *Pr*
Karen S Knapp, *
EMP: 40 **EST:** 1993
SALES (est): 11.89MM **Privately Held**
Web: www.daveknappford.com
SIC: 5511 5531 5012 Automobiles, new and used; Auto and home supply stores; Automobiles and other motor vehicles

(G-8870)
DAYTON PHYSICIANS LLC
1111 Sweitzer St Ste C (45331-1189)
PHONE..........................937 547-0563
Pilar Gonzalez-monk, *Brnch Mgr*
EMP: 78
SALES (corp-wide): 22.86MM **Privately Held**
Web: www.daytonphysicians.com
SIC: 8011 Primary care medical clinic
PA: Dayton Physicians, Llc
6680 Poe Ave Ste 200
Dayton OH 45414
937 280-8400

(G-8871)
DIALYSIS CENTERS DAYTON LLC
Also Called: Dialysis Ctr Dyton- Darke Cnty
1111 Sweitzer St Ste B (45331-1189)
PHONE..........................937 548-7019
Kari Lee, *Brnch Mgr*
EMP: 69
SALES (corp-wide): 9.59MM **Privately Held**
Web: www.renalphysicians.com
SIC: 8092 Kidney dialysis centers
PA: Dialysis Centers Of Dayton, L.L.C.
110 N Main St Ste 500
Dayton OH 45402
937 499-9866

(G-8872)
DREW AG-TRANSPORT INC
5450 Sebring Warner Rd (45331-8800)
PHONE..........................937 548-3200
Rod Drew, *Pr*
EMP: 53 **EST:** 1998
SALES (est): 4.04MM **Privately Held**
Web: www.drewagtransportinc.net
SIC: 4213 Contract haulers

(G-8873)
FAMILY HLTH SVCS DRKE CNTY INC (PA)
Also Called: FAMILY HEALTH
5735 Meeker Rd (45331-1180)
PHONE..........................937 548-3806
Jean Young, *Ex Dir*
Mitch Eiting, *
Michael Rieman, *
Kent James, *
Janice Anderson, *
EMP: 120 **EST:** 1973
SQ FT: 43,000
SALES (est): 39.96MM
SALES (corp-wide): 39.96MM **Privately Held**
Web: www.familyhealthservices.org
SIC: 8011 Clinic, operated by physicians

(G-8874)
GREENVILLE FEDERAL
690 Wagner Ave (45331-2649)
PHONE..........................937 548-4158
Jeff Knisi, *CEO*
Susan Allread, *
EMP: 30 **EST:** 1883
SQ FT: 11,000
SALES (est): 9.45MM **Privately Held**
Web: www.greenvillefederal.com
SIC: 6035 Federal savings and loan associations
HQ: Greenville Federal Financial Corporation
690 Wagner Ave
Greenville OH 45331

(G-8875)
GREENVILLE INN INC
Also Called: Mad Anthony's Lounge
851 Martin St Unit 1 (45331-1800)
PHONE..........................937 548-3613
Mike Perkins, *Pr*
EMP: 28 **EST:** 1985
SALES (est): 265K **Privately Held**
Web: www.thegreenvilleinn.com
SIC: 7011 5812 Hotels; Eating places

(G-8876)
GREENVILLE NATIONAL BANCORP (PA)
446 S Broadway St (45331-1926)
PHONE..........................937 548-1114
Steve Burns, *Pr*
Kent A James, *VP*
Douglas M Custenborder, *VP*
EMP: 48 **EST:** 1934
SQ FT: 7,500
SALES (est): 21.37MM
SALES (corp-wide): 21.37MM **Privately Held**
Web: www.bankgnb.bank
SIC: 6712 Bank holding companies

(G-8877)
GREENVILLE NATIONAL BANK (HQ)
Also Called: GNB Banking Centers
446 S Broadway St (45331-1960)
P.O. Box 190 (45331-0190)
PHONE..........................937 548-1114
Kent A James, *Pr*
Michael Randall, *
Steven A Burns, *
Douglas M Custenborder, *
EMP: 50 **EST:** 1934
SQ FT: 7,500
SALES (est): 21.58MM
SALES (corp-wide): 21.37MM **Privately Held**
Web: www.bankgnb.bank
SIC: 6021 National commercial banks
PA: Greenville National Bancorp Inc
446 S Broadway St
Greenville OH 45331
937 548-1114

(G-8878)
HOSPICE OF DARKE COUNTY INC (PA)
Also Called: STATE OF THE HEART HOSPICE
1350 N Broadway St (45331-2461)
PHONE..........................937 548-2999
Ted Bauer, *Ex Dir*
EMP: 40 **EST:** 1981
SQ FT: 5,000
SALES (est): 10.89MM **Privately Held**
Web: www.stateoftheheartcare.org
SIC: 8052 Personal care facility

(G-8879)
LANDMARK STAR PROPERTIES INC
Also Called: Comfort Inn Greenville
1190 E Russ Rd (45331-2769)
PHONE..........................937 316-5252
Chan Patel, *Pr*
EMP: 28 **EST:** 1997
SQ FT: 30,000
SALES (est): 335.72K **Privately Held**
Web: www.choicehotels.com
SIC: 7011 Hotels and motels

(G-8880)
LOWES HOME CENTERS LLC
Also Called: Lowe's
1550 Wagner Ave (45331-2892)
PHONE..........................937 547-2400
Gerald Carroll, *Brnch Mgr*
EMP: 157
SALES (corp-wide): 86.38B **Publicly Held**
Web: www.lowes.com
SIC: 5211 5031 5722 5064 Home centers; Building materials, exterior; Household appliance stores; Electrical appliances, television and radio
HQ: Lowe's Home Centers, Llc
1000 Lowes Blvd
Mooresville NC 28117
336 658-4000

(G-8881)
MOTE AND ASSOCIATES INC
214 W 4th St (45331-1480)
PHONE..........................937 548-7511
Richard T Mote, *Pr*
Jerry Mcclannan, *VP*
EMP: 31 **EST:** 1972
SQ FT: 900
SALES (est): 1.94MM **Privately Held**
Web: www.moteassociates.com
SIC: 8711 8713 Civil engineering; Surveying services

(G-8882)
REST HAVEN NURSING HOME INC
1096 N Ohio St (45331-2999)
PHONE..........................937 548-1138
Michelle Bruns, *Admn*
EMP: 92 **EST:** 1953
SQ FT: 20,000
SALES (est): 5.42MM **Privately Held**
Web: www.vancrest.com
SIC: 8052 8059 8051 Intermediate care facilities; Rest home, with health care; Skilled nursing care facilities

(G-8883)
RUMPKE WASTE INC
5474 Jaysville Saint Johns Rd (45331-9704)
PHONE..........................937 548-1939
Bruce Truman, *Mgr*
EMP: 239
Web: www.rumpke.com
SIC: 4953 7359 4212 Recycling, waste materials; Equipment rental and leasing, nec; Local trucking, without storage
HQ: Rumpke Waste, Inc.
10795 Hughes Rd
Cincinnati OH 45251
513 851-0122

(G-8884)
SECOND NATIONAL BANK (HQ)
499 S Broadway St (45331-1961)
P.O. Box 130 (45331-0130)
PHONE..........................937 548-2122
Ray Lear, *Ch*
Marvin J Stammen, *
Alan W Greiner, *
John Swallow, *
Thomas Copp, *
EMP: 40 **EST:** 1883
SQ FT: 7,500
SALES (est): 4.7MM
SALES (corp-wide): 564.3MM **Publicly Held**
Web: www.parknationalbank.com
SIC: 6021 6163 National commercial banks; Loan brokers
PA: Park National Corporation
50 N 3rd St
Newark OH 43055
740 349-8451

(G-8885)
SECOND NATIONAL BANK
1302 Wagner Ave (45331-2704)
PHONE..........................937 548-5068
Brian Wagner, *Mgr*
EMP: 43
SALES (corp-wide): 564.3MM **Publicly Held**
Web: www.parknationalbank.com
SIC: 6021 National commercial banks
HQ: Second National Bank
499 S Broadway St
Greenville OH 45331
937 548-2122

(G-8886)
SPIRIT MEDICAL TRANSPORT LLC
5484 S State Route 49 (45331-1032)
PHONE..........................937 548-2800
EMP: 72 **EST:** 2007
SALES (est): 6.28MM **Privately Held**
Web: www.spiritmedicaltransport.com

Greenville - Darke County (G-8887)

SIC: **4119** Ambulance service

(G-8887)
THE ANDERSONS MARATHON ETHANOL LLC
5728 Sebring Warner Rd N (45331-9800)
PHONE...............................937 316-3700
EMP: 40
Web: www.andersonsgrain.com
SIC: 5153 Grains

(G-8888)
VALVOLINE INSTANT OIL CHANGE
Also Called: Valvoline Instant Oil Change
661 Wagner Ave (45331-2648)
PHONE...............................937 548-0123
EMP: 190
SALES (corp-wide): 6.65MM **Privately Held**
Web: www.valvoline.com
SIC: 7549 Lubrication service, automotive
PA: Valvoline Instant Oil Change Inc
7391 Bltmore Annplis Blvd
Glen Burnie MD 21061
410 760-5344

(G-8889)
VILLAGE GREEN HEALTHCARE CTR
Also Called: Gade Nursing Home 2
405 Chestnut St (45331-1306)
PHONE...............................937 548-1993
Martha Gade, *Pr*
Cheryl Stump, *
EMP: 47 **EST:** 1961
SALES (est): 1.72MM **Privately Held**
SIC: 8051 Convalescent home with continuous nursing care

(G-8890)
WAYNE HEALTH CORPORATION (PA)
835 Sweitzer St (45331)
P.O. Box 8001 (27533)
PHONE...............................919 736-1110
William Paugh, *Pr*
EMP: 1190 **EST:** 1985
SQ FT: 250,000
SALES (est): 618.07K
SALES (corp-wide): 618.07K **Privately Held**
Web: www.waynehealthcare.org
SIC: 8062 General medical and surgical hospitals

(G-8891)
WAYNE HEALTHCARE (PA)
Also Called: WAYNE HEALTHCARE
835 Sweitzer St (45331-1007)
PHONE...............................937 548-1141
Wayne Deschambeau, *Pr*
E G Husted, *
S A Hawes, *
EMP: 384 **EST:** 1920
SALES (est): 74.06MM
SALES (corp-wide): 74.06MM **Privately Held**
Web: www.waynehealthcare.org
SIC: 8062 General medical and surgical hospitals

Greenwich
Huron County

(G-8892)
JOHNSON BROS RUBBER CO INC
Also Called: Johnson Bros Greenwich
41 Center St (44837-1049)
PHONE...............................419 752-4814
Ken Bostic, *Mgr*
EMP: 30
SALES (corp-wide): 21.76MM **Privately Held**
Web: www.johnsonbrosrubbercompany.com
SIC: 5199 3743 3634 3545 Foams and rubber; Railroad equipment; Electric housewares and fans; Machine tool accessories
PA: Johnson Bros. Rubber Co.
42 W Buckeye St
West Salem OH 44287
419 853-4122

Grove City
Franklin County

(G-8893)
AFG INDUSTRIES INC
Also Called: AGC Automotive Americas
4000 Gantz Rd Ste A (43123-4844)
PHONE...............................614 322-4580
▲ **EMP:** 66
SIC: 7549 1793 1799 3231 Automotive customizing services, nonfactory basis; Glass and glazing work; Glass tinting, architectural or automotive; Products of purchased glass

(G-8894)
ALADDIN TEMPLE
Also Called: ALADDIN SHRINE TEMPLE
1801 Gateway Cir (43123-7629)
PHONE...............................614 475-2609
Martin Nash, *Prin*
Gene Steineman, *Ex Dir*
EMP: 28 **EST:** 1905
SQ FT: 87,120
SALES (est): 583.71K **Privately Held**
Web: www.aladdinshrine.org
SIC: 8641 Fraternal associations

(G-8895)
AMERICAN AIR FURNACE COMPANY
Also Called: American Air Comfort Tech
3945 Brookham Dr (43123)
PHONE...............................614 876-1702
Steve Sliemers, *Pr*
Michael Sliemers, *
EMP: 63 **EST:** 1989
SQ FT: 24,000
SALES (est): 10.25MM **Privately Held**
Web: www.americanairheating.com
SIC: 1711 Warm air heating and air conditioning contractor

(G-8896)
AMERICAN MULTI-CINEMA INC
Also Called: AMC
4218 Buckeye Pkwy (43123-8377)
PHONE...............................614 801-9130
EMP: 29
Web: www.amctheatres.com
SIC: 7832 Exhibitors, itinerant: motion picture
HQ: American Multi-Cinema, Inc.
11500 Ash St
Leawood KS 66211
913 213-2000

(G-8897)
BLISSFUL CORPORATION
Also Called: Comfort Inn
4197 Marlane Dr (43123-2937)
PHONE...............................614 539-3500
EMP: 53 **EST:** 1997
SQ FT: 10,986
SALES (est): 908.66K **Privately Held**
Web: www.choicehotels.com
SIC: 7011 Hotels and motels

(G-8898)
BOSCH REXROTH CORPORATION
3940 Gantz Rd Ste F (43123-4845)
PHONE...............................614 527-7400
Ted Bojanowski, *Pr*
EMP: 50
SALES (corp-wide): 230.19MM **Privately Held**
Web: www.boschrexroth-us.com
SIC: 5084 Hydraulic systems equipment and supplies
HQ: Bosch Rexroth Corporation
14001 S Lkes Dr S Pt Bus
Charlotte NC 28273
704 583-4338

(G-8899)
BRIAR-GATE REALTY INC (PA)
Also Called: Fireproof Record Center
3827 Brookham Dr (43123-4827)
P.O. Box 1150 (43123-6150)
PHONE...............................614 299-2121
C M Gibson, *Prin*
Michael James, *
Edward F James, *
Susan Eichinger, *
Helen M Watkins, *
EMP: 83 **EST:** 1944
SQ FT: 80,000
SALES (est): 22.02MM
SALES (corp-wide): 22.02MM **Privately Held**
Web: www.vitalrecordscontrol.com
SIC: 4226 Document and office records storage

(G-8900)
BROCON CONSTRUCTION INC
2120 Hardy Parkway St (43123-1240)
PHONE...............................614 871-7300
George Brobst, *Pr*
George M Brobst Junior, *Pr*
EMP: 45 **EST:** 1988
SALES (est): 9.37MM **Privately Held**
Web: www.brocon.net
SIC: 1742 Drywall

(G-8901)
BUCK EQUIPMENT INC
1720 Feddern Ave (43123-1206)
PHONE...............................614 539-3039
Dennis Hamilton, *CEO*
◆ **EMP:** 35 **EST:** 1934
SQ FT: 60,000
SALES (est): 9.44MM **Privately Held**
Web: www.buckequipment.com
SIC: 3531 3743 3441 5088 Logging equipment; Railroad equipment; Fabricated structural metal; Railroad equipment and supplies

(G-8902)
BUCKEYE RANCH INC (PA)
5665 Hoover Rd (43123-9280)
PHONE...............................614 875-2371
Vickie Thomps-sandy, *CEO*
D Nicholas Rees, *
Richard Rieser, *
Gary Stammler, *
Roger Minner, *
EMP: 250 **EST:** 1961
SQ FT: 182,023
SALES (est): 58.43MM
SALES (corp-wide): 58.43MM **Privately Held**
Web: www.buckeyeranch.org
SIC: 8361 Emotionally disturbed home

(G-8903)
BUCKEYE RANCH FOUNDATION INC
5665 Hoover Rd (43123-9280)
PHONE...............................614 875-2371
EMP: 43 **EST:** 2011
SALES (est): 4.73MM **Privately Held**
Web: www.buckeyeranch.org
SIC: 8093 Mental health clinic, outpatient

(G-8904)
C H BRADSHAW CO
2004 Hendrix Dr (43123-1278)
PHONE...............................614 871-2087
Robert Slack, *Pr*
Jeanne Slack, *
EMP: 27 **EST:** 1954
SQ FT: 22,000
SALES (est): 4.7MM **Privately Held**
Web: www.chbradshaw.com
SIC: 5084 7699 Petroleum industry machinery; Tank repair

(G-8905)
CARRIAGE COURT COMPANY INC
Also Called: Carriage Crt Snior Communities
2320 Sonora Dr (43123-2423)
PHONE...............................614 871-8000
Patricia Williams, *Admn*
EMP: 147
SIC: 8059 8361 Personal care home, with health care; Residential care
PA: Carriage Court Corporation
2041 Riverside Dr Ste 100
Columbus OH

(G-8906)
CATHOLIC HEALTH INITIATIVES
2160 Southwest Blvd (43123-1893)
PHONE...............................614 871-3047
EMP: 5001
Web: www.catholichealth.net
SIC: 8099 Blood related health services
HQ: Catholic Health Initiatives
1700 Edison Dr
Milford OH 45150
513 576-0262

(G-8907)
CENTRAL OHIO CONTRACTORS INC (PA)
2879 Jackson Pike (43123-9737)
PHONE...............................614 539-2579
Ralph D Loewendick, *Pr*
Luanne Sigman, *
EMP: 70 **EST:** 1977
SALES (est): 3.3MM
SALES (corp-wide): 3.3MM **Privately Held**
Web: www.centralohiocontractor.com
SIC: 4953 Sanitary landfill operation

(G-8908)
CENTRAL OHIO SURGICAL ASSOC (PA)
5500 N Meadows Dr Ste 210 (43123-7688)
PHONE...............................614 222-8000
Jeff Turner, *Pr*
EMP: 40 **EST:** 1983
SALES (est): 4.62MM
SALES (corp-wide): 4.62MM **Privately Held**
Web: www.cosadocs.com
SIC: 8011 Cardiologist and cardio-vascular specialist

(G-8909)
CJ MAHAN CONSTRUCTION CO LLC (PA)
Also Called: C.J. Mahan Construction Co
3458 Lewis Centre Way (43123)
PHONE...............................614 277-4545

Douglas R Mccrea, *Managing Member*
C Jeffrey Mahan, *Managing Member**
EMP: 51 **EST:** 2003
SALES (est): 43.17MM
SALES (corp-wide): 43.17MM **Privately Held**
Web: www.cjmahan.com
SIC: 1622 Bridge, tunnel, and elevated highway construction

(G-8910)
COLUMBUS CARDIOLOGY CONS INC
5350 N Meadows Dr (43123-2546)
PHONE..................................614 224-2281
F Kevin Hackett Md, *Pr*
EMP: 220 **EST:** 1986
SALES (est): 6.42MM **Privately Held**
SIC: 8062 General medical and surgical hospitals

(G-8911)
COLUMBUS LINTEL INC
Also Called: Days Inn
1849 Stringtown Rd (43123-3956)
PHONE..................................614 871-0440
EMP: 39 **EST:** 1992
SQ FT: 11,755
SALES (est): 483.76K **Privately Held**
Web: www.wyndhamhotels.com
SIC: 7011 5813 Hotels and motels; Drinking places

(G-8912)
CONVERSE ELECTRIC INC
3783 Gantz Rd (43123-1892)
PHONE..................................614 808-4377
Jerry Converse, *Pr*
Diane Lutsko, *
Chris Converse, *
Dave Novontny, *
Bill Mount, *
EMP: 100 **EST:** 1960
SALES (est): 16.49MM **Privately Held**
Web: www.converseelectric.com
SIC: 1731 General electrical contractor

(G-8913)
CST UTILITIES L L C
2136 Hardy Parkway St (43123-1240)
PHONE..................................614 801-9600
EMP: 64 **EST:** 2020
SALES (est): 5.66MM **Privately Held**
Web: www.cstutilities.com
SIC: 1623 Underground utilities contractor

(G-8914)
DELTA SHIPPING INC
3971 Hoover Rd Ste 254 (43123-2839)
PHONE..................................619 261-7456
Sameer Trehan, *CEO*
EMP: 33 **EST:** 2019
SALES (est): 850K **Privately Held**
SIC: 4231 Trucking terminal facilities

(G-8915)
DENIER ELECTRIC CO INC
Also Called: Denier
4000 Gantz Rd Ste C (43123-4844)
PHONE..................................614 338-4664
Mike Kallmeyer, *Brnch Mgr*
EMP: 62
SALES (corp-wide): 54.98MM **Privately Held**
Web: www.denier.com
SIC: 1731 General electrical contractor
PA: Denier Electric Co., Inc.
7266 New Haven Rd
Harrison OH 45030
513 738-2641

(G-8916)
DHANLAXMI LLC
Also Called: Red Roof Inn
4055 Jackpot Rd (43123-9739)
PHONE..................................614 871-9617
EMP: 62 **EST:** 2004
SQ FT: 9,216
SALES (est): 1.31MM **Privately Held**
Web: www.redroof.com
SIC: 7011 Hotels and motels

(G-8917)
DSI SYSTEMS INC
3650 Brookham Dr Ste K (43123-4929)
PHONE..................................614 871-1456
Traci Fusner, *Mgr*
Donna Bocox, *Sec*
▲ **EMP:** 40 **EST:** 1988
SALES (est): 991.91K **Privately Held**
SIC: 5065 Electronic parts and equipment, nec

(G-8918)
ESEC CORPORATION
Also Called: Columbus Peterbilt
6240 Enterprise Pkwy (43123-9286)
P.O. Box 69 (43123-0069)
PHONE..................................614 875-3732
Tim Darr, *Mgr*
EMP: 29
SQ FT: 26,480
SALES (corp-wide): 4.66MM **Privately Held**
Web: www.ohiopeterbilt.com
SIC: 5084 5012 5531 Industrial machinery and equipment; Trucks, commercial; Truck equipment and parts
PA: Esec Corporation
44 Victoria Rd
Youngstown OH 44515
330 799-1536

(G-8919)
FEDEX GROUND PACKAGE SYS INC
Also Called: Fedex
6120 S Meadows Dr (43123-9298)
PHONE..................................800 463-3339
EMP: 80
SALES (corp-wide): 90.16B **Publicly Held**
Web: www.fedex.com
SIC: 4213 4212 Contract haulers; Local trucking, without storage
HQ: Fedex Ground Package System, Inc.
1000 Fedex Dr
Coraopolis PA 15108
800 463-3339

(G-8920)
FRESENIUS MED CARE S GROVE CY
Also Called: Fresenius Kdney Care S Grove C
5775 N Meadows Dr Ste B (43123-7300)
PHONE..................................614 801-2505
EMP: 31
SALES (corp-wide): 361.08K **Privately Held**
SIC: 8092 Kidney dialysis centers
PA: Fresenius Medical Care South Grove City, Llc
920 Winter St
Waltham MA 02451
781 699-9000

(G-8921)
GRAND ARIE OF THE FRTNRL ORDER (PA)
1623 Gateway Cir (43123-9309)
PHONE..................................614 883-2200
David Tice, *Pr*
Edgar L Bollenbacher Ed, *Ch Bd*
Chris Lainas Junior, *Ch*
Donald R Jim West, *

EMP: 42 **EST:** 1898
SALES (est): 12.76MM
SALES (corp-wide): 12.76MM **Privately Held**
Web: www.foe.com
SIC: 8641 University club

(G-8922)
GROVE CITY CTR FOR DENTISTRY
4104 Broadway (43123-3065)
PHONE..................................614 875-3141
Bryan Simone, *CEO*
EMP: 30 **EST:** 1956
SALES (est): 599.92K **Privately Held**
Web: www.grovecitycenterfordentistry.com
SIC: 8021 Dentists' office

(G-8923)
GXO LOGISTICS SUPPLY CHAIN INC
3650 Brooklyn Dr Ste B2 (43123)
PHONE..................................614 305-1705
John Hunter, *Brnch Mgr*
EMP: 32
SALES (corp-wide): 9.78B **Publicly Held**
Web: www.gxo.com
SIC: 4731 Freight forwarding
HQ: Gxo Logistics Supply Chain, Inc.
4043 Piedmont Pkwy
High Point NC 27265
336 232-4100

(G-8924)
HAWKEYE HOTELS INC
Courtyard Columbus Grove City
1668 Buckeye Pl (43123-1519)
PHONE..................................614 782-8292
Dale Nysetvold, *Brnch Mgr*
EMP: 32
SALES (corp-wide): 84.56MM **Privately Held**
Web: www.hawkeyehotels.com
SIC: 7011 Hotels
PA: Hawkeye Hotels Inc.
2681 James St
Coralville IA 52241
319 752-7400

(G-8925)
HILTON GARDEN INN
Also Called: Hilton
3928 Jackpot Rd (43123-8636)
PHONE..................................614 539-8944
Kevin Jeans, *Genl Mgr*
EMP: 43 **EST:** 2001
SALES (est): 1.05MM **Privately Held**
Web: www.hilton.com
SIC: 7011 Hotels and motels

(G-8926)
HKT TELESERVICES INC (PA)
Also Called: Hkt Teleservices
3400 Southpark Pl Ste F (43123-4857)
P.O. Box 159 (43123-0159)
PHONE..................................614 652-6300
EMP: 175 **EST:** 1994
SALES (est): 38.13MM **Privately Held**
Web: www.hktteleservices.com
SIC: 7299 7389 Personal financial services; Telemarketing services

(G-8927)
HOKUTO USA INC
2200 Southwest Blvd Ste K (43123-2854)
PHONE..................................614 782-6200
Robin Hughes, *CEO*
Yoshimasa Sekiguchi, *
EMP: 42 **EST:** 2008
SALES (est): 9.62MM **Privately Held**
Web: www.hokutousa.com

SIC: 8711 Engineering services

(G-8928)
INSTANTWHIP-COLUMBUS INC (HQ)
3855 Marlane Dr (43123-9224)
P.O. Box 249 (43123-0249)
PHONE..................................614 871-9447
Douglas A Smith, *Pr*
Vinson Lewis, *
Tom G Michaelides, *
G Fredrick Smith, *
EMP: 32 **EST:** 1936
SQ FT: 10,300
SALES (est): 6.32MM
SALES (corp-wide): 97.42MM **Privately Held**
Web: www.instantwhip.com
SIC: 2026 5143 2023 8741 Whipped topping, except frozen or dry mix; Dairy products, except dried or canned; Dietary supplements, dairy and non-dairy based; Management services
PA: Instantwhip Foods, Inc.
2200 Cardigan Ave
Columbus OH 43215
614 488-2536

(G-8929)
KARRINGTON OPERATING CO INC
Also Called: Enrichment Center
4200 Kelnor Dr (43123-2944)
PHONE..................................614 875-0514
Bridget Baldwin, *Dir*
EMP: 252
SALES (corp-wide): 2.92B **Privately Held**
Web: www.todayschildlearning.com
SIC: 8059 8051 Personal care home, with health care; Skilled nursing care facilities
HQ: Karrington Operating Company, Inc.
919 Old Henderson Rd
Columbus OH 43220

(G-8930)
KERN INC (HQ)
3940 Gantz Rd Ste A (43123-4845)
PHONE..................................614 317-2600
Richard Stepp, *CEO*
▲ **EMP:** 36 **EST:** 1997
SQ FT: 30,000
SALES (est): 26.09MM
SALES (corp-wide): 26.09MM **Privately Held**
Web: www.kerninc.com
SIC: 7359 Office machine rental, except computers
PA: Kern Usa Llc
3940 Gantz Rd Ste A
Grove City OH 43123
614 317-2600

(G-8931)
KIRK WILLIAMS COMPANY INC
2734 Home Rd (43123-1701)
PHONE..................................614 875-9023
James K Williams Junior, *Pr*
James K Williams Iii, *Sec*
EMP: 80 **EST:** 1949
SQ FT: 40,000
SALES (est): 22.21MM **Privately Held**
Web: www.kirkwilliamsco.com
SIC: 1711 3564 3444 Mechanical contractor; Blowers and fans; Sheet metalwork

(G-8932)
KIRK WILLIAMS PIPING & PLBG CO
2734 Home Rd (43123-1701)
P.O. Box 189 (43123-0189)
PHONE..................................614 875-9023
James K Williams Iii, *Pr*
James K Williams Junior, *VP*
EMP: 50 **EST:** 1993

Grove City - Franklin County (G-8933)

SQ FT: 40,000
SALES (est): 5.35MM **Privately Held**
SIC: **1711** 1623 Plumbing contractors; Pipeline construction, nsk

(G-8933)
MCKNIGHT DEVELOPMENT CORP
Also Called: Mc Knight Group
3351 Mcdowell Rd (43123-2907)
P.O. Box 370 (43123-0370)
PHONE.................................614 875-1689
Homer R Mcknight, *CEO*
David K Mcknight, *Prin*
Hal Pieper, *
Philip J Tipton,   *
EMP: 47 EST: 1970
SQ FT: 12,000
SALES (est): 25.49MM **Privately Held**
Web: www.mcknightgroup.com
SIC: **1542** 1541 Commercial and office building, new construction; Industrial buildings, new construction, nec

(G-8934)
MICROTEL INN
Also Called: Microtel
1800 Stringtown Rd (43123-9049)
PHONE.................................614 277-0705
Nick Patel, *Pr*
EMP: 51 EST: 1997
SALES (est): 494.43K **Privately Held**
Web: www.wyndhamhotels.com
SIC: **7011** Hotels and motels

(G-8935)
MID-OHIO FOODBANK
3960 Brookham Dr (43123-9741)
PHONE.................................614 277-3663
Mathew Habash, *Pr*
Marilyn Tomasi, *
Sharon Grunwell, *
Lyn Hang, *
Nick Davis, *CPO*
EMP: 118 EST: 1975
SQ FT: 204,500
SALES (est): 115.17MM **Privately Held**
Web: www.mofc.org
SIC: **8322** 8699 Meal delivery program; Athletic organizations

(G-8936)
MOUNT CARMEL HEALTH (DH)
5300 N Meadows Dr (43123-2546)
PHONE.................................614 234-5000
Marcia Ladue, *Prin*
EMP: 1600 EST: 1886
SALES (est): 278.53MM
SALES (corp-wide): 2.49B **Privately Held**
Web: www.mountcarmelhealth.com
SIC: **8062** Hospital, professional nursing school
HQ: Niagara Health Corporation
      6150 E Broad St
      Columbus OH 43213

(G-8937)
MOUNT CARMEL HEALTH SYSTEM
Also Called: Mount Carmel Grove City
300 N Meadows Dr (43123)
PHONE.................................614 663-5300
EMP: 35 EST: 1995
SALES (est): 2.95MM **Privately Held**
Web: www.mountcarmelhealth.com
SIC: **8062** General medical and surgical hospitals

(G-8938)
MYERS MACHINERY MOVERS INC
2210 Hardy Parkway St (43123-1243)
PHONE.................................614 871-5052
Gary Myers, *Pr*
Butch Myers, *
Stacie Cope, *
EMP: 50 EST: 1979
SQ FT: 10,000
SALES (est): 5.23MM **Privately Held**
Web: www.myersmachinerymovers.com
SIC: **4213** 1796 4212 Heavy machinery transport; Machine moving and rigging; Local trucking, without storage

(G-8939)
N & E LEARNING LLC
1239 Lamplighter Dr (43123-8170)
PHONE.................................614 270-1559
Ehab Eskander, *Prin*
EMP: 28 EST: 2010
SALES (est): 119.65K **Privately Held**
SIC: **8351** Child day care services

(G-8940)
NATRAJ CORPORATION
Also Called: Best Western
4026 Jackpot Rd (43123-9700)
PHONE.................................614 875-7770
Anilkumar Patel, *Pr*
EMP: 45 EST: 1993
SQ FT: 10,080
SALES (est): 508.06K **Privately Held**
Web: www.bestwestern.com
SIC: **7011** Hotels and motels

(G-8941)
NIPPON EXPRESS USA INC
Also Called: Air Cargo Department
3705 Urbancrest Industrial Dr (43123-1772)
PHONE.................................614 295-0030
Yuji Isoyama, *Mgr*
EMP: 42
Web: www.nipponexpress.com
SIC: **4731** Domestic freight forwarding
HQ: Nippon Express U.S.A., Inc.
      800 N Il Route 83
      Wood Dale IL 60191
      708 304-9800

(G-8942)
NORTHEAST OBGYN
2399 Old Stringtown Rd (43123-2919)
PHONE.................................614 875-4191
EMP: 38 EST: 2019
SALES (est): 230.08K **Privately Held**
Web: www.avinawomenscare.com
SIC: **8011** Gynecologist

(G-8943)
ORTHOPDIC SPINE CTR AT PLRIS L
4092 Gantz Rd (43123-4816)
PHONE.................................937 707-4662
EMP: 33 EST: 2004
SALES (est): 2MM **Privately Held**
SIC: **8011** Orthopedic physician

(G-8944)
PAVEMENT PROTECTORS INC
Also Called: M & D Blacktop Sealing
2020 Longwood Ave (43123-1218)
PHONE.................................614 875-9989
Steve Bernsdorf, *Pr*
Chad Bernsdorf, *
EMP: 27 EST: 1964
SQ FT: 10,000
SALES (est): 5.12MM **Privately Held**
Web: www.mdblacktop.com
SIC: **1611** Surfacing and paving

(G-8945)
PHOENIX CARGO LLC
1679 Gateway Cir (43123)
PHONE.................................614 407-3322
Samandar Umrzokov, *Pr*
Samandar Umrzokov, *Managing Member*
EMP: 168 EST: 2017
SQ FT: 5,000
SALES (est): 27.39MM **Privately Held**
Web: www.phoenixcargollc.com
SIC: **4213** Trucking, except local

(G-8946)
PITT-OHIO EXPRESS LLC
2101 Hardy Parkway St (43123-1213)
PHONE.................................614 801-1064
Rich Hassit, *Genl Mgr*
EMP: 148
SALES (corp-wide): 508.23MM **Privately Held**
Web: www.pittohioexpress.com
SIC: **4213** Contract haulers
PA: Pitt-Ohio Express, Llc
      15 27th St
      Pittsburgh PA 15222
      412 232-3015

(G-8947)
R R DONNELLEY & SONS COMPANY
Also Called: Wallace
3801 Gantz Rd Ste A (43123-4915)
PHONE.................................614 539-5527
Jeremy Liening, *Mgr*
EMP: 41
SALES (corp-wide): 4.99B **Privately Held**
Web: www.rrd.com
SIC: **4225** General warehousing and storage
HQ: R. R. Donnelley & Sons Company
      35 W Wacker Dr
      Chicago IL 60601
      312 326-8000

(G-8948)
RED BULL MEDIA HSE N AMER INC
2101 Southwest Blvd (43123-2100)
PHONE.................................614 801-5193
Rochelle Lewis, *Brnch Mgr*
EMP: 250
SALES (corp-wide): 10.06B **Privately Held**
SIC: **5099** Firearms and ammunition, except sporting
HQ: Red Bull Media House North America, Inc.
      1740 Stewart St
      Santa Monica CA 90404
      310 393-4647

(G-8949)
RYDER INTEGRATED LOGISTICS INC
Also Called: Ryder
3750 Brookham Dr Ste A (43123-4850)
PHONE.................................614 801-0224
Gorin Radivojevic, *Mgr*
EMP: 36
SALES (corp-wide): 11.78B **Publicly Held**
Web: lms.ryder.com
SIC: **4731** Freight forwarding
HQ: Ryder Integrated Logistics, Inc.
      2333 Ponce De Leon Blvd
      Coral Gables FL 33134
      786 247-1987

(G-8950)
SAFETY TODAY INC (HQ)
Also Called: Midwest Service Center
3287 Southwest Blvd (43123-2210)
PHONE.................................614 409-7200
Edward Gustafson, *Prin*
Anthony Spearing, *
▲ EMP: 30 EST: 1946
SQ FT: 90,000
SALES (est): 24.94MM **Privately Held**
Web: www.safetytoday.com
SIC: **5084** 5047 5099 Safety equipment; Industrial safety devices: first aid kits and masks; Safety equipment and supplies

PA: Volk Enterprises, Inc.
      1335 Ridgeland Pkwy # 120
      Alpharetta GA 30004

(G-8951)
SAXTON REAL ESTATE CO (PA)
3703 Broadway (43123-2201)
PHONE.................................614 875-2327
William E Saxton, *Pr*
EMP: 35 EST: 1959
SQ FT: 1,500
SALES (est): 4.33MM
SALES (corp-wide): 4.33MM **Privately Held**
Web: www.saxtonrealestate.com
SIC: **6531** Real estate agent, residential

(G-8952)
SCI SHARED RESOURCES LLC
Also Called: Schoednger Fnrl HM - Nrris Gro
4242 Hoover Rd (43123-3625)
PHONE.................................614 875-6333
EMP: 1851
SALES (corp-wide): 4.1B **Publicly Held**
Web: www.sci-corp.com
SIC: **7261** Funeral service and crematories
HQ: Sci Shared Resources, Llc
      1929 Allen Pkwy
      Houston TX 77019
      713 522-5141

(G-8953)
SECURITAS SEC SVCS USA INC
Also Called: East Central Region
2180 Southwest Blvd (43123-1893)
PHONE.................................614 871-6051
Wayne Bailey, *Mgr*
EMP: 47
SALES (corp-wide): 12.7B **Privately Held**
Web: www.securitasinc.com
SIC: **7381** Security guard service
HQ: Securitas Security Services Usa, Inc.
      9 Campus Dr Ste 25
      Parsippany NJ 07054
      973 267-5300

(G-8954)
SGB MANAGEMENT INC
Also Called: Hampton Inn
4017 Jackpot Rd (43123-9739)
PHONE.................................614 539-1177
EMP: 48 EST: 1997
SQ FT: 15,562
SALES (est): 684.5K **Privately Held**
Web: www.hilton.com
SIC: **7011** Hotels and motels

(G-8955)
SMITHFIELD DIRECT LLC
6130 Enterprise Pkwy (43123-9286)
PHONE.................................614 539-9600
Gene Adams, *Prin*
EMP: 120
Web: carando.sfdbrands.com
SIC: **5147** Meats, fresh
HQ: Smithfield Direct, Llc
      4225 Naperville Rd # 600
      Lisle IL 60532

(G-8956)
SOLID WASTE AUTH CENTL OHIO
Also Called: Swaco
4239 London Groveport Rd (43123)
PHONE.................................614 871-5100
David J Bush, *Ch*
Ronald J Mills, *
Paul Koehler, *
EMP: 120 EST: 1989
SQ FT: 7,500
SALES (est): 65.17MM **Privately Held**
Web: www.swaco.org

GEOGRAPHIC SECTION

Groveport - Franklin County (G-8979)

SIC: 4953 Sanitary landfill operation

(G-8957)
SUN DEVELOPMENT & MGT CORP
Also Called: Holiday Inn
3951 Jackpot Rd (43123-8637)
PHONE..........................614 801-9000
Stephanie Robson, *Mgr*
EMP: 104
SALES (corp-wide): 28.08MM **Privately Held**
Web: www.sun-companies.com
SIC: 7011 Hotels and motels
PA: Sun Development & Management Corporation
5701 Progress Rd
Indianapolis IN 46241
317 247-5500

(G-8958)
SUPERIOR AR-GRUND AMBLNCE SVC
Also Called: Community Mobile Health
2160 Southwest Blvd (43123-1893)
PHONE..........................630 832-2000
David B Hill Iii, *Pr*
EMP: 104 EST: 2005
SALES (est): 1.68MM **Privately Held**
SIC: 4119 Ambulance service

(G-8959)
TOSOH AMERICA INC (HQ)
3600 Gantz Rd (43123-1895)
PHONE..........................614 539-8622
Jan Top, *Pr*
◆ EMP: 350 EST: 1989
SQ FT: 250,000
SALES (est): 687.43MM **Privately Held**
Web: www.tosohamerica.com
SIC: 5169 3564 5047 5052 Industrial chemicals; Blowers and fans; Diagnostic equipment, medical; Coal and other minerals and ores
PA: Tosoh Corporation
2-2-1, Yaesu
Chuo-Ku TKY 104-0

(G-8960)
TURN-KEY INDUSTRIAL SVCS LLC
4512 Harrisburg Pike (43123)
PHONE..........................614 274-1128
Gregory Less, *Managing Member*
EMP: 52 EST: 2017
SALES (est): 2.79MM **Privately Held**
Web: www.turn-keyind.com
SIC: 7692 3441 Automotive welding; Building components, structural steel

(G-8961)
TVC GROUP LLC
2802 London Groveport Rd (43123-9590)
PHONE..........................919 241-7830
EMP: 31 EST: 2016
SALES (est): 246.92K **Privately Held**
Web: www.totalveterinarycare.com
SIC: 8742 Marketing consulting services

(G-8962)
USHER TRANSPORT INC
Also Called: Usher Transport
2040 Hendrix Dr (43123-1215)
PHONE..........................614 875-0528
EMP: 58
SALES (corp-wide): 51.55MM **Privately Held**
Web: www.ushertransport.com
SIC: 4213 Contract haulers
PA: Usher Transport, Inc.
3801 Shanks Ln
Louisville KY 40216
502 449-4000

(G-8963)
VALUE INN INC
1947 Stringtown Rd (43123-2935)
PHONE..........................888 315-2378
Fu Ih Chu, *Pr*
EMP: 37 EST: 1999
SQ FT: 1,950
SALES (est): 139.26K **Privately Held**
SIC: 7011 Motels

(G-8964)
VRC COMPANIES LLC
3827 Brookham Dr (43123-4827)
PHONE..........................614 299-2122
EMP: 51
SALES (corp-wide): 131.52MM **Privately Held**
Web: www.vitalrecordscontrol.com
SIC: 4226 8741 Document and office records storage; Management services
HQ: Vrc Companies, Llc
5384 Poplar Ave Ste 500
Memphis TN 38119
901 310-2005

(G-8965)
WATERBEDS N STUFF INC (PA)
Also Called: Beds N Stuff
3933 Brookham Dr (43123-9295)
PHONE..........................614 871-1171
Gerald Spero, *Pr*
▲ EMP: 35 EST: 1972
SQ FT: 25,500
SALES (est): 10.63MM
SALES (corp-wide): 10.63MM **Privately Held**
Web: www.waterbedsnstuff.com
SIC: 5947 5712 5199 Gift shop; Waterbeds and accessories; Gifts and novelties

(G-8966)
WELSPUN USA INC
3901 Gantz Rd Ste A (43123-4914)
PHONE..........................614 945-5100
Devesh Shriv, *Brnch Mgr*
EMP: 30
Web: www.welspunusa.com
SIC: 5131 Textiles, woven, nec
HQ: Welspun Usa, Inc.
10 W 33rd St Rm 1221
New York NY 10001
212 620-2000

Groveport
Franklin County

(G-8967)
AGILITI INC
4391 Professional Pkwy (43125-9035)
PHONE..........................614 409-2734
EMP: 86
SALES (corp-wide): 1.17B **Privately Held**
Web: www.agilitihealth.com
SIC: 5047 Medical equipment and supplies
HQ: Agiliti, Inc.
11095 Viking Dr Ste 300
Eden Prairie MN 55344
952 893-3200

(G-8968)
ALMO DISTRIBUTING PA INC
6500 Port Rd (43125-9103)
PHONE..........................267 350-2726
EMP: 624
Web: www.almo.com
SIC: 8621 Professional organizations
HQ: Almo Distributing Pennsylvania, Inc.
2709 Commerce Way
Philadelphia PA 19154
800 345-2566

(G-8969)
AMSTED INDUSTRIES INCORPORATED
Griffin Wheel
3900 Bixby Rd (43125-9510)
PHONE..........................614 836-2323
Joe Cuske, *Manager*
EMP: 54
SALES (corp-wide): 3.96B **Privately Held**
Web: www.amsted.com
SIC: 3321 5088 3743 3714 Railroad car wheels and brake shoes, cast iron; Railroad equipment and supplies; Railroad equipment; Motor vehicle parts and accessories
PA: Amsted Industries Incorporated
111 S Wacker Dr Ste 4400
Chicago IL 60606
312 645-1700

(G-8970)
ARC INDSTRIES INC FRNKLIN CNTY
Also Called: Bixby Living Skills Center
4200 Bixby Rd (43125-9509)
PHONE..........................614 836-6050
EMP: 107
SALES (corp-wide): 36.16MM **Privately Held**
Web: www.arcind.com
SIC: 8399 Council for social agency
PA: Arc Industries, Incorporated, Of Franklin County, Ohio
2780 Airport Dr
Columbus OH 43219
614 479-2500

(G-8971)
ARC INDSTRIES INC FRNKLIN CNTY
Also Called: ARC Industries South
4395 Marketing Pl (43125-9556)
PHONE..........................614 836-0700
EMP: 150
SALES (corp-wide): 36.16MM **Privately Held**
Web: www.arcind.com
SIC: 8322 8331 Social services for the handicapped; Job training and related services
PA: Arc Industries, Incorporated, Of Franklin County, Ohio
2780 Airport Dr
Columbus OH 43219
614 479-2500

(G-8972)
AVNET INTEGRATED INC
Also Called: Avnet
5300 Centerpoint Pkwy (43125-2501)
PHONE..........................614 851-8700
EMP: 50
SIC: 7378 Computer maintenance and repair

(G-8973)
AVT TECHNOLOGY SOLUTIONS LLC
5350 Centerpoint Pkwy (43125-2501)
PHONE..........................727 539-7429
Robert M Dutkowsky, *CEO*
EMP: 92 EST: 2016
SALES (est): 10.12MM
SALES (corp-wide): 57.56B **Publicly Held**
SIC: 7372 Prepackaged software
HQ: Tech Data Corporation
5350 Tech Data Dr
Clearwater FL 33760
727 539-7429

(G-8974)
BATH BDY WRKS LGSTICS SVCS LLC
Also Called: Mast Global Logistics
4400 S Hamilton Rd (43125-9559)
PHONE..........................513 435-1643
Alex Hass, *Brnch Mgr*
EMP: 36
SALES (corp-wide): 7.43B **Publicly Held**
Web: waitingroom.bathandbodyworks.com
SIC: 5113 Shipping supplies
HQ: Bath & Body Works Logistics Services, Llc
2 Limited Pkwy
Columbus OH 43230
614 415-7500

(G-8975)
C & R INC (PA)
5600 Clyde Moore Dr (43125-1081)
PHONE..........................614 497-1130
Ronald E Murphy, *Pr*
Phillip Lee Mc Kitrick, *
Christina M Murphy, *
EMP: 47 EST: 1972
SALES (est): 9.11MM
SALES (corp-wide): 9.11MM **Privately Held**
Web: www.crproducts.com
SIC: 3444 7692 3443 3312 Sheet metal specialties, not stamped; Welding repair; Fabricated plate work (boiler shop); Blast furnaces and steel mills

(G-8976)
CARDINAL HEALTH INC
5995 Commerce Center Dr (43125-1099)
PHONE..........................614 409-6770
Arnie Randall, *Dir*
EMP: 93
SALES (corp-wide): 205.01B **Publicly Held**
Web: www.cardinalhealth.com
SIC: 5122 Pharmaceuticals
PA: Cardinal Health, Inc.
7000 Cardinal Pl
Dublin OH 43017
614 757-5000

(G-8977)
CEVA LOGISTICS LLC
Also Called: Ceva Logistics
2727 London Groveport Rd (43125-9304)
PHONE..........................614 482-5000
Robert Harper, *Brnch Mgr*
EMP: 121
SALES (corp-wide): 31.16K **Privately Held**
Web: www.cevalogistics.com
SIC: 4731 Freight forwarding
HQ: Ceva Logistics, Llc
15350 Vickery Dr
Houston TX 77032
281 618-3100

(G-8978)
COMMERCIAL WAREHOUSE & CARTAGE
6295 Commerce Center Dr (43125-1137)
PHONE..........................614 409-3901
EMP: 65
SALES (corp-wide): 28.79MM **Privately Held**
Web: www.cwclogon.com
SIC: 4225 General warehousing
PA: Commercial Warehouse & Cartage Inc
3402 Meyer Rd
Fort Wayne IN 46803
260 426-7825

(G-8979)
CONCORD EXPRESS INC (HQ)
5905 Green Pointe Dr S Ste D (43125-2007)
PHONE..........................718 656-7821

Groveport - Franklin County (G-8980) GEOGRAPHIC SECTION

Joseph Chang, *Ch Bd*
◆ **EMP:** 31 **EST:** 1976
SQ FT: 100
SALES (est): 11.99MM **Privately Held**
SIC: 4731 Foreign freight forwarding
PA: Concord Express Limited
Rm 8 36/F Skyline Twr
Kowloon Bay KLN

(G-8980)
CRAFT WHOLESALERS INC
Also Called: Kp Creek Gifts
4600 S Hamilton Rd (43125-9636)
PHONE.................................740 964-6210
Tara Parker, *Pr*
Karen Piper, *
▼ **EMP:** 108 **EST:** 1981
SQ FT: 50,000
SALES (est): 24.72MM **Privately Held**
Web: www.shopcwi.com
SIC: 5092 5961 Arts and crafts equipment and supplies; Arts and crafts equipment and supplies, mail order

(G-8981)
CUTHBERT GREENHOUSE INC (PA)
4900 Hendron Rd (43125-9506)
PHONE.................................614 836-3866
Wayne Cuthbert, *Pr*
David Cuthbert, *
Brett Cuthbert, *
Grogery Cuthbert, *
▲ **EMP:** 30 **EST:** 1952
SQ FT: 518,000
SALES (est): 3.44MM
SALES (corp-wide): 3.44MM **Privately Held**
Web: www.cuthbertgreenhouse.com
SIC: 0181 Flowers: grown under cover (e.g., greenhouse production)

(G-8982)
DECKERS NURSERY INC
6239 Rager Rd (43125-9266)
PHONE.................................614 836-2130
Brian M Decker, *Pr*
Patricia D Decker, *Sec*
EMP: 40 **EST:** 1982
SQ FT: 10,000
SALES (est): 2.27MM **Privately Held**
Web: www.deckersnursery.com
SIC: 0181 Nursery stock, growing of

(G-8983)
EDDIE BAUER LLC
Also Called: Eddie Bauer
6600 Alum Creek Dr (43125-9100)
PHONE.................................614 497-8200
EMP: 33
SALES (corp-wide): 3.08B **Privately Held**
Web: stores.eddiebauer.com
SIC: 4225 General warehousing and storage
HQ: Eddie Bauer Llc
2200 1st Ave S Ste 400
Seattle WA 98134

(G-8984)
EDDIE BUER FLFILLMENT SVCS INC
6600 Alum Creek Dr (43125-9420)
PHONE.................................614 497-8200
Richard Lauer, *Pr*
Anthony Miller, *
Louis Fratturo, *
▼ **EMP:** 700 **EST:** 1994
SQ FT: 1,500,000
SALES (est): 10.2MM **Privately Held**
SIC: 4225 General warehousing and storage

(G-8985)
EMERITUS CORPORATION
Also Called: Emeritus At Lakeview
4000 Lakeview Xing (43125-9059)
PHONE.................................614 836-5990
EMP: 164
SALES (corp-wide): 2.83B **Publicly Held**
Web: www.emeritus.org
SIC: 8051 Skilled nursing care facilities
HQ: Emeritus Corporation
6737 W Wa St Ste 2300
Milwaukee WI 53214

(G-8986)
ESSILOR OF AMERICA INC
2400 Spiegel Dr Ste A (43125-9132)
PHONE.................................614 492-0888
Den Lucas, *Mgr*
EMP: 47
SALES (corp-wide): 2.55MM **Privately Held**
Web: www.essilor.com
SIC: 7389 4225 Personal service agents, brokers, and bureaus; General warehousing and storage
HQ: Essilor Of America, Inc.
13555 N Stemmons Fwy
Dallas TX 75234

(G-8987)
EXEL INC
6390 Commerce Ct (43125-1158)
PHONE.................................614 836-1265
EMP: 60
SALES (corp-wide): 88.87B **Privately Held**
Web: www.onestoporderform.com
SIC: 4731 Freight forwarding
HQ: Exel Inc.
360 Westar Blvd Fl 4
Westerville OH 43082
614 865-5819

(G-8988)
FARO SERVICES INC (PA)
7070 Pontius Rd (43125-7504)
PHONE.................................614 497-1700
Rich Ashton, *Pr*
▲ **EMP:** 200 **EST:** 1993
SQ FT: 322,000
SALES (est): 51.81MM **Privately Held**
Web: www.farousa.com
SIC: 4225 4731 General warehousing; Freight transportation arrangement

(G-8989)
FRANK BRUNCKHORST CO LLC
2225 Spiegel Dr (43125-9036)
PHONE.................................614 662-5300
EMP: 130
SALES (corp-wide): 359.27MM **Privately Held**
Web: www.boarshead.com
SIC: 5147 Meats, fresh
PA: Frank Brunckhorst Co., L.L.C.
1819 Main St Ste 800
Sarasota FL 34236
941 955-0994

(G-8990)
FRANKLIN EQUIPMENT LLC (HQ)
4141 Hamilton Square Blvd (43125-9084)
PHONE.................................614 228-2014
EMP: 51 **EST:** 2007
SQ FT: 20,000
SALES (est): 52MM
SALES (corp-wide): 14.33B **Publicly Held**
Web: www.franklinequipmentllc.com
SIC: 3524 5083 Lawn and garden equipment; Tractors, agricultural
PA: United Rentals, Inc.
100 1st Stmford Pl Ste 70
Stamford CT 06902
203 622-3131

(G-8991)
GEMINI SOLAR LLC
4433 Professional Pkwy (43125-9228)
PHONE.................................833 339-2097
Robert Holland, *Managing Member*
EMP: 27 **EST:** 2018
SALES (est): 1.21MM **Privately Held**
SIC: 1711 Solar energy contractor

(G-8992)
ISOMEDIX OPERATIONS INC
Also Called: Steris Isomedix
4405 Marketing Pl (43125-9556)
PHONE.................................614 836-5757
John M Schweers, *Prin*
EMP: 54
SQ FT: 2,197
Web: www.steris.com
SIC: 8734 Industrial sterilization service
HQ: Isomedix Operations Inc.
5960 Heisley Rd
Mentor OH 44060

(G-8993)
MOUNT CARMEL HEALTH
Also Called: Mount Carmel Home Medical Eqp
4473 Professional Pkwy (43125-9229)
PHONE.................................614 234-0034
Walter Finnigan, *Dir*
EMP: 136
SALES (corp-wide): 2.49B **Privately Held**
Web: www.mountcarmelhealth.com
SIC: 8062 General medical and surgical hospitals
HQ: Mount Carmel Health
5300 N Meadows Dr
Grove City OH 43123
614 234-5000

(G-8994)
OWENS & MINOR DISTRIBUTION INC
2820 Global Dr (43125-7508)
PHONE.................................614 491-8465
EMP: 871
Web: www.owens-minor.com
SIC: 5047 Medical equipment and supplies
HQ: Owens & Minor Distribution, Inc.
9120 Lockwood Blvd
Mechanicsville VA 23116
804 723-7000

(G-8995)
PINNACLE DATA SYSTEMS INC
Also Called: Pdsi
6600 Port Rd (43125-9129)
PHONE.................................614 748-1150
▲ **EMP:** 148
SIC: 3575 3572 7378 7373 Computer terminals; Computer auxiliary storage units; Computer maintenance and repair; Systems software development services

(G-8996)
PRO HEALTH CARE SERVICES LTD
270 Main St Ste A (43125-1180)
P.O. Box 472 (43125-0472)
PHONE.................................614 856-9111
Maria Delaluz-munoz, *Genl Pt*
Marco A Quezada, *Pt*
EMP: 117 **EST:** 1999
SALES (est): 3.13MM **Privately Held**
Web: phcsinhomeware.bitrix24.site
SIC: 8082 Visiting nurse service

(G-8997)
RADIAL SOUTH LP
6360 Port Rd 6440 (43125-9488)
PHONE.................................678 584-4047
EMP: 418
SALES (corp-wide): 2.34B **Privately Held**
Web: www.radial.com
SIC: 5045 4226 Computers, peripherals, and software; Special warehousing and storage, nec
HQ: Radial South, L.P.
935 1st Ave
King Of Prussia PA 19406
610 491-7000

(G-8998)
RAYMOND STORAGE CONCEPTS INC
4333 Directors Blvd (43125-9504)
PHONE.................................614 275-3494
Steve Mullarkey, *Pr*
EMP: 45
SALES (corp-wide): 75.94MM **Privately Held**
Web: www.raymondsci.com
SIC: 5084 7699 Materials handling machinery; Industrial equipment services
PA: Raymond Storage Concepts, Inc.
5480 Creek Rd Unit 1
Blue Ash OH 45242
513 891-7290

(G-8999)
RENTOKIL NORTH AMERICA INC
Also Called: Initial Tropical Plant Svcs
6300 Commerce Center Dr Ste G (43125-1183)
PHONE.................................614 837-0099
Monica Desch, *Mgr*
EMP: 50
SALES (corp-wide): 6.7B **Privately Held**
Web: www.jcehrlich.com
SIC: 5193 0781 Flowers and nursery stock; Landscape services
HQ: Rentokil North America, Inc.
1125 Berkshire Blvd # 15
Wyomissing PA 19610
470 643-3300

(G-9000)
RICART FORD INC
Also Called: Ricart Automotive
4255 S Hamilton Rd (43125-9332)
PHONE.................................614 836-5321
Rhett C Ricart, *Pr*
Paul F Ricart Junior, *VP*
Rob Crauthers, *
▲ **EMP:** 460 **EST:** 1953
SQ FT: 13,000
SALES (est): 98.99MM **Privately Held**
Web: www.ricart.com
SIC: 5511 7538 Automobiles, new and used; General automotive repair shops

(G-9001)
SK FOOD GROUP INC
3301 Toy Rd (43125-9363)
PHONE.................................614 409-0666
Barry Fischetto, *Admn*
EMP: 327
SALES (corp-wide): 4.49B **Privately Held**
Web: www.skfoodgroup.com
SIC: 8748 Business consulting, nec
HQ: Sk Food Group Inc.
790 S 75th Ave Ste 100
Tolleson AZ 85353
206 935-8100

GEOGRAPHIC SECTION

(G-9002)
SPRINGS WINDOW FASHIONS LLC
6295 Commerce Center Dr (43125-1137)
PHONE..................614 492-6770
Mike Mehring, *Mgr*
EMP: 47
SALES (corp-wide): 1.56B **Privately Held**
Web: www.springswindowfashions.com
SIC: 4225 General warehousing and storage
PA: Springs Window Fashions, Llc
7549 Graber Rd
Middleton WI 53562
608 836-1011

(G-9003)
STARTECHCOM USA LLP
Also Called: Startech.com USA
4490 S Hamilton Rd (43125-9563)
PHONE..................800 265-1844
Paul Seed, *CEO*
Ken Kalopsis, *Vice Chairman*
Bill Bouwmeester, *CFO*
▲ **EMP:** 391 **EST:** 2002
SQ FT: 24,000
SALES (est): 79.49MM
SALES (corp-wide): 128.48MM **Privately Held**
Web: www.startech.com
SIC: 5045 Computer peripheral equipment
PA: Startech.Com Ltd
45 Artisans Cres
London ON N5V 5

(G-9004)
THURMAN SCALE COMPANY
4025 Lakeview Xing (43125-9039)
PHONE..................614 221-9077
Neal Copley, *Prin*
EMP: 119 **EST:** 2001
SALES (est): 2.07MM
SALES (corp-wide): 166.77MM **Privately Held**
Web: www.thurmanscale.com
SIC: 5046 Scales, except laboratory
PA: Fancor, Inc.
6800 W 64th St Ste 102
Mission KS 66202
816 471-0231

(G-9005)
TRILOGY FULFILLMENT LLC
6600 Alum Creek Dr (43125-9420)
PHONE..................614 491-0553
EMP: 79 **EST:** 2010
SALES (est): 18.96MM
SALES (corp-wide): 343.05MM **Privately Held**
Web: www.trilogyff.com
SIC: 8742 Distribution channels consultant
PA: Golden Gate Private Equity Incorporated
1 Embarcadero Ctr Fl 39
San Francisco CA 94111
415 983-2706

(G-9006)
TROWBRIDGE STORAGE COMPANY
Also Called: Trowbridge Mvg Relocation Svcs
5825 Green Pointe Dr S (43125-1084)
P.O. Box 308 (43125-0308)
PHONE..................614 766-0116
TOLL FREE: 800
FAX: 614 836-0527
EMP: 35 **EST:** 1892
SQ FT: 35,000
SALES (est): 3.65MM **Privately Held**
Web: www.trowbridgemoving.com
SIC: 4213 4214 Household goods transport; Furniture moving and storage, local

(G-9007)
UNITED MCGILL CORPORATION (HQ)
1 Mission Park (43125-1100)
PHONE..................614 829-1200
James D Mcgill, *Pr*
Jayne F Mcgill, *Sec*
▲ **EMP:** 30 **EST:** 1951
SQ FT: 13,000
SALES (est): 126.17MM
SALES (corp-wide): 126.17MM **Privately Held**
Web: www.unitedmcgill.com
SIC: 3444 3564 5169 3567 Ducts, sheet metal; Precipitators, electrostatic; Sealants; Industrial furnaces and ovens
PA: The Mcgill Corporation
One Mission Park
Groveport OH 43125
614 829-1200

(G-9008)
UNITED PARCEL SERVICE INC
Also Called: UPS
2250 Spiegel Dr (43125-9131)
PHONE..................800 742-5877
EMP: 31
SALES (corp-wide): 90.96B **Publicly Held**
Web: www.ups.com
SIC: 4789 Pipeline terminal facilities, independently operated
HQ: United Parcel Service, Inc.
55 Glenlake Pkwy
Atlanta GA 30328
404 828-6000

(G-9009)
URGENT CARE SPECIALISTS LLC
3813 S Hamilton Rd (43125-9330)
PHONE..................614 835-0400
EMP: 55
SALES (corp-wide): 23.51MM **Privately Held**
Web: www.wellnow.com
SIC: 8011 Freestanding emergency medical center
PA: Urgent Care Specialists Llc
2400 Corp Exch Dr Ste 102
Columbus OH 43231
614 505-7633

(G-9010)
USAVINYL LLC
Also Called: Weatherables
5795 Green Pointe Dr S (43125-1083)
PHONE..................614 771-4805
Julie Foster, *
◆ **EMP:** 80 **EST:** 2002
SALES (est): 12.4MM **Privately Held**
Web: www.weatherables.com
SIC: 5211 5031 Fencing; Building materials, exterior

(G-9011)
UTILITY TECHNOLOGIES INTL CORP
Also Called: Uti
4700 Homer Ohio Ln (43125-9230)
PHONE..................614 879-7624
EMP: 50 **EST:** 1992
SALES (est): 9.98MM **Privately Held**
Web: www.uti-corp.com
SIC: 8711 Consulting engineer

(G-9012)
WABASH NATIONAL TRLR CTRS INC
5825 Green Pointe Dr S (43125-1084)
PHONE..................614 878-6088
Chuck Sells, *Mgr*
EMP: 55
SALES (corp-wide): 2.54B **Publicly Held**
Web: www.onewabash.com

SIC: 5013 5012 7539 5599 Motor vehicle supplies and new parts; Automobiles and other motor vehicles; Automotive repair shops, nec; Utility trailers
HQ: Wabash National Trailer Centers, Inc.
1000 Sagamore Pkwy S
Lafayette IN 47905
765 771-5300

(G-9013)
WAXMAN CONSUMER PDTS GROUP INC
5920 Green Pointe Dr S Ste A (43125-1182)
PHONE..................614 491-0500
Jeff Willey, *Mgr*
EMP: 45
SALES (corp-wide): 99.88MM **Privately Held**
Web: www.spraysensations.com
SIC: 5074 5072 Plumbing fittings and supplies; Casters and glides
HQ: Waxman Consumer Products Group Inc.
24460 Aurora Rd
Bedford Heights OH 44146

(G-9014)
WILLIAM R HAGUE INC
Also Called: Hague Quality Water Intl
4343 S Hamilton Rd (43125-9332)
PHONE..................614 836-2115
Robert Hague, *Pr*
◆ **EMP:** 100 **EST:** 1960
SQ FT: 90,000
SALES (est): 24.32MM
SALES (corp-wide): 3.85B **Publicly Held**
Web: www.haguewater.com
SIC: 5999 7389 3589 Water purification equipment; Water softener service; Water filters and softeners, household type
PA: A. O. Smith Corporation
11270 W Park Pl Ste 170
Milwaukee WI 53224
414 359-4000

Hamilton
Butler County

(G-9015)
80 ACRES URBAN AGRICULTURE INC
7415 Hamilton Enterprise Park Dr, (45011-4571)
PHONE..................888 547-1569
Dan Barnett, *Brnch Mgr*
EMP: 83
SALES (corp-wide): 28.81MM **Privately Held**
Web: www.80acresfarms.com
SIC: 0182 Food crops grown under cover
PA: 80 Acres Urban Agriculture, Inc.
345 High St Fl 7
Hamilton OH 45011
513 218-4387

(G-9016)
ACPI SYSTEMS INC
Also Called: Automated Control & Power
3445 Hamilton New London Rd (45013-9459)
P.O. Box 368 (45061-0368)
PHONE..................513 738-3840
EMP: 45
Web: www.acpi-systems.com
SIC: 1731 8711 Electrical work; Electrical or electronic engineering

(G-9017)
ATLAS MACHINE AND SUPPLY INC
8556 Trade Center Dr # 250 (45011-9354)
PHONE..................502 584-7262
Sonny Welker, *Mgr*
EMP: 27
SALES (corp-wide): 52.44MM **Privately Held**
Web: www.atlasmachine.com
SIC: 5084 3599 Compressors, except air conditioning; Machine shop, jobbing and repair
PA: Atlas Machine And Supply, Inc.
7000 Global Dr
Louisville KY 40258
502 584-7262

(G-9018)
BORREGO DIALYSIS LLC
Also Called: West Hamilton Dialysis
1532 Main St (45013-1078)
PHONE..................513 737-0158
James K Hilger, *CAO*
EMP: 41
Web: www.khccares.com
SIC: 8092 Kidney dialysis centers
HQ: Borrego Dialysis, Llc
10475 Harrison Ave
Harrison OH 45030
513 202-0373

(G-9019)
BUILDER SERVICES GROUP INC
Also Called: Gale Insulation
28 Kiesland Ct (45015)
PHONE..................513 942-2204
Russ Miller, *Brnch Mgr*
EMP: 40
SALES (corp-wide): 5.19B **Publicly Held**
SIC: 1742 Insulation, buildings
HQ: Builder Services Group, Inc.
475 N Williamson Blvd
Daytona Beach FL 32114
386 304-2222

(G-9020)
BUTLER COUNTY OF OHIO
Also Called: Butler County Care Facility
315 High St (45011-6056)
PHONE..................513 887-3728
Charles Demidovich, *Dir*
EMP: 70
Web: www.bcohio.gov
SIC: 8052 9111 8322 8051 Intermediate care facilities; County supervisors' and executives' office; Individual and family services; Skilled nursing care facilities
PA: Butler, County Of Ohio
315 High St Fl 6
Hamilton OH 45011
513 887-3278

(G-9021)
BUTLER BHAVIORAL HLTH SVCS INC (PA)
Also Called: HAMILTON COUNSELING CENTER T/S
1502 University Blvd (45011)
PHONE..................513 896-7887
Kimball Stricklin, *CEO*
EMP: 28 **EST:** 1960
SALES (est): 8.1MM
SALES (corp-wide): 8.1MM **Privately Held**
Web: www.bbhs.org
SIC: 8093 Mental health clinic, outpatient

(G-9022)
BUTLER CNTY BD DVLPMNTAL DSBLT
Also Called: Janat Clemmons Center

Hamilton - Butler County (G-9023)

282 N Fair Ave (45011-4222)
PHONE.................................513 785-2815
Mary May, *Prin*
EMP: 51
SALES (corp-wide): 12.86MM **Privately Held**
Web: www.butlerdd.org
SIC: 8361 8351 Retarded home; Preschool center
PA: Butler County Board Of Developmental Disabilities
282 N Fair Ave
Hamilton OH 45011
513 785-2815

(G-9023)
BUTLER CNTY CMNTY HLTH CNSRTIU
Also Called: PRIMARY HEALTH SOLUTIONS
300 High St Fl 4 (45011-6078)
P.O. Box 837 (45012-0837)
PHONE.................................513 454-1468
Marc Bellisario, *CEO*
Donald Reimer, *
Julia Belden, *
EMP: 250 **EST:** 2000
SQ FT: 22,000
SALES (est): 31.93MM **Privately Held**
Web: www.bcchcinc.org
SIC: 8011 General and family practice, physician/surgeon

(G-9024)
BUTLER CNTY RGIONAL TRNST AUTH
Also Called: Bcrta
3045 Moser Ct (45011-5373)
PHONE.................................513 785-5237
Carla Lakatos, *Ex Dir*
Robert Ruzinsky, *
EMP: 102 **EST:** 2014
SALES (est): 8.64MM **Privately Held**
Web: www.butlercountyrta.com
SIC: 4111 Local and suburban transit

(G-9025)
CARINGTON HEALTH SYSTEMS (PA)
Also Called: Franklin Ridge Care Facility
8200 Beckett Park Dr (45011)
PHONE.................................513 682-2700
Glyndon Powell, *Pr*
Edward Byington, *
EMP: 35 **EST:** 2004
SALES (est): 58.43MM
SALES (corp-wide): 58.43MM **Privately Held**
Web: www.carington.com
SIC: 8741 8051 Hospital management; Skilled nursing care facilities

(G-9026)
CHACO CREDIT UNION INC (PA)
601 Park Ave (45013-3064)
PHONE.................................513 785-3500
Ronald Lang, *Pr*
Dan Daily, *
Kurt Winkler, *
EMP: 50 **EST:** 1938
SALES (est): 5.48MM
SALES (corp-wide): 5.48MM **Privately Held**
Web: www.telhio.org
SIC: 6061 Federal credit unions

(G-9027)
CINCINNATI & OHIO RLWY SVC LLC
561 Main St (45013-3221)
PHONE.................................513 371-3377
EMP: 35 **EST:** 1992
SALES (est): 1.25MM **Privately Held**
SIC: 4789 Railroad maintenance and repair services

(G-9028)
CITY OF HAMILTON
2210 S Erie Hwy (45011-4128)
PHONE.................................513 785-7551
Bob Sutton, *Superintnt*
EMP: 27
SALES (corp-wide): 116.27MM **Privately Held**
Web: www.hamilton-oh.gov
SIC: 4952 9621 Sewerage systems; Transportation department: government, nonoperating
PA: City Of Hamilton
345 High St Fl 3
Hamilton OH 45011
513 785-7000

(G-9029)
CLOSSMAN CATERING INCORPORATED
3725 Symmes Rd (45015-3305)
PHONE.................................513 942-7744
EMP: 40 **EST:** 1995
SALES (est): 2.29MM **Privately Held**
Web: www.clossmancatering.net
SIC: 8322 Meal delivery program

(G-9030)
COLONIAL SENIOR SERVICES INC
Also Called: Berkeley Square Retirement Ctr
100 Berkley Dr (45013-1787)
PHONE.................................513 856-8600
Jim Mayer, *Brnch Mgr*
EMP: 95
Web: www.community-first.org
SIC: 8741 8211 8399 8351 Management services; Kindergarten; Fund raising organization, non-fee basis; Preschool center
PA: Colonial Senior Services, Inc.
230 Ludlow St
Hamilton OH 45011

(G-9031)
COLONIAL SENIOR SERVICES INC
Also Called: Westover Preparatory School
855 Stahlheber Rd (45013-1963)
PHONE.................................513 867-4006
EMP: 47
Web: www.community-first.org
SIC: 8741 8211 8351 Management services; Kindergarten; Preschool center
PA: Colonial Senior Services, Inc.
230 Ludlow St
Hamilton OH 45011

(G-9032)
COLONIAL SENIOR SERVICES INC
Also Called: Westover Retirement Community
855 Stahlheber Rd (45013-1963)
PHONE.................................513 844-8004
EMP: 94
Web: www.community-first.org
SIC: 8741 Management services
PA: Colonial Senior Services, Inc.
230 Ludlow St
Hamilton OH 45011

(G-9033)
COMMUNITY BEHAVIORAL HLTH INC
824 S Martin Luther King Jr Blvd (45011-3216)
PHONE.................................513 887-8500
Mark Zoellner, *Brnch Mgr*
EMP: 160
SALES (corp-wide): 9.55MM **Privately Held**
Web: www.community-first.org
SIC: 8093 Mental health clinic, outpatient
PA: Community Behavioral Health, Inc.
442 S 2nd St
Hamilton OH 45011
513 785-4783

(G-9034)
CONCORD HMLTNIAN RVRFRONT HT L
Also Called: Courtyard By Marriott
1 Riverfront Plz (45011-2712)
PHONE.................................513 896-6200
Carmam Johnson, *Prin*
EMP: 43 **EST:** 2006
SALES (est): 2.97MM **Privately Held**
Web: courtyard.marriott.com
SIC: 7011 Hotels and motels

(G-9035)
CONNECTOR MANUFACTURING CO (DH)
Also Called: C M C
3501 Symmes Rd (45015-1369)
PHONE.................................513 860-4455
William J Boehm, *Ch Bd*
Joe Klenk, *Pr*
Frank Privett, *VP Sls*
James Boehm, *VP Mfg*
▲ **EMP:** 172 **EST:** 1940
SQ FT: 103,000
SALES (est): 92.62MM
SALES (corp-wide): 5.37B **Publicly Held**
Web: www.cmclugs.com
SIC: 5063 Electrical apparatus and equipment
HQ: Burndy Llc
47 E Industrial Park Dr
Manchester NH 03109

(G-9036)
DARANA HYBRID INC (PA)
903 Belle Ave (45015-1605)
PHONE.................................513 860-4490
▲ **EMP:** 92 **EST:** 1985
SQ FT: 20,000
SALES (est): 70MM **Privately Held**
Web: www.daranahybrid.com
SIC: 1731 3444 General electrical contractor ; Sheet metalwork

(G-9037)
DUBOIS CHEMICALS INC
Also Called: Eagle Chemicals
2550 Bobmeyer Rd (45015-1366)
PHONE.................................513 868-9662
Tisha Adette, *Mgr*
EMP: 49
SALES (corp-wide): 5.31MM **Privately Held**
Web: www.duboischemicals.com
SIC: 5169 Chemicals and allied products, nec
HQ: Dubois Chemicals, Inc.
3630 E Kemper Rd
Sharonville OH 45241

(G-9038)
ELLISON TECHNOLOGIES INC
5333 Mulhauser Rd (45011-9349)
PHONE.................................513 874-2736
EMP: 27
Web: www.ellisontechnologies.com
SIC: 5084 Machine tools and accessories
HQ: Ellison Technologies, Inc.
9828 Arlee Ave
Santa Fe Springs CA 90670
562 949-8311

(G-9039)
FITTON CTR FOR CREATIVE ARTS
101 S Monument Ave (45011-2833)
PHONE.................................513 863-8873
Rick H Jones, *Dir*
EMP: 38 **EST:** 1993
SQ FT: 45,000
SALES (est): 1.4MM **Privately Held**
Web: www.fittoncenter.org
SIC: 8699 Charitable organization

(G-9040)
FLEXENTIAL CORP
5307 Mulhauser Rd (45011-9349)
PHONE.................................513 645-2900
Ernest Leffler, *Brnch Mgr*
EMP: 36
SALES (corp-wide): 513.25MM **Privately Held**
Web: www.flexential.com
SIC: 8748 Systems engineering consultant, ex. computer or professional
HQ: Flexential Corp.
8809 Lenox Pointe Dr G
Charlotte NC 28273

(G-9041)
FORT HAMILTON HOSPITAL (DH)
Also Called: CHARLES F KETTERING MEMORIAL H
630 Eaton Ave (45013-2767)
PHONE.................................513 867-2000
Bob Weber, *Sec*
EMP: 65 **EST:** 1925
SQ FT: 350,000
SALES (est): 163.17MM
SALES (corp-wide): 2.46B **Privately Held**
Web: www.ketteringhealth.org
SIC: 8062 General medical and surgical hospitals
HQ: Kettering Medical Center
3535 Southern Blvd
Kettering OH 45429
937 298-4331

(G-9042)
FORT HAMILTON HOSPITAL
Also Called: Kbec Fort Hamilton Hospital
630 Eaton Ave (45013-2767)
PHONE.................................513 867-2382
EMP: 234
SALES (corp-wide): 2.46B **Privately Held**
Web: www.ketteringhealth.org
SIC: 8062 General medical and surgical hospitals
HQ: The Fort Hamilton Hospital
630 Eaton Ave
Hamilton OH 45013
513 867-2000

(G-9043)
FORT HAMILTON HOSPITAL
Horizon Service
630 Eaton Ave (45013-2767)
PHONE.................................513 867-2280
EMP: 426
SALES (corp-wide): 2.46B **Privately Held**
Web: www.ketteringhealth.org
SIC: 8062 8093 General medical and surgical hospitals; Specialty outpatient clinics, nec
HQ: The Fort Hamilton Hospital
630 Eaton Ave
Hamilton OH 45013
513 867-2000

(G-9044)
FRESENIUS MED CARE BUTLER CTY
Also Called: Fresenius Kdney Care W Hmilton
890 Nw Washington Blvd (45013-1281)
PHONE.................................513 737-1415

Michelle Smallwood, *Brnch Mgr*
EMP: 30
SALES (corp-wide): 4.29MM **Privately Held**
Web: www.fmcna.com
SIC: 8092 Kidney dialysis centers
PA: Fresenius Medical Care Butler County, Llc
920 Winter St
Waltham MA 02451
781 699-9000

(G-9045)
GOLDEN YEARS NURSING HOME INC
Also Called: Golden Years Health Care
2436 Old Oxford Rd (45013-9332)
PHONE...................513 893-0471
Kyra Hornsby, *Admn*
EMP: 244 **EST:** 1964
SQ FT: 15,000
SALES (est): 7.79MM
SALES (corp-wide): 58.43MM **Privately Held**
Web: www.goldenyears-care.net
SIC: 8051 Extended care facility
PA: Carington Health Systems
8200 Beckett Park Dr
Hamilton OH 45011
513 682-2700

(G-9046)
GREAT MAMI VLY YUNG MNS CHRSTN (PA)
Also Called: Fairfield YMCA
105 N 2nd St (45011)
PHONE...................513 887-0001
Daven W Fippon, *Pr*
EMP: 60 **EST:** 1889
SQ FT: 60,000
SALES (est): 13.47MM
SALES (corp-wide): 13.47MM **Privately Held**
Web: www.gmvymca.org
SIC: 8641 7991 8351 7032 Youth organizations; Physical fitness facilities; Child day care services; Youth camps

(G-9047)
GREAT MIAMI VALLEY YMCA
Also Called: YMCA Camp Campbell Gard
4803 Augspurger Rd (45011-9547)
PHONE...................513 867-0600
Rick Taylor, *Brnch Mgr*
EMP: 84
SALES (corp-wide): 13.47MM **Privately Held**
Web: www.ccgymca.org
SIC: 8641 7033 Youth organizations; Campsite
PA: The Great Miami Valley Young Men's Christian Association
105 N 2nd St
Hamilton OH 45011
513 887-0001

(G-9048)
GREAT MIAMI VALLEY YMCA
Also Called: Central Hamilton YMCA
105 N 2nd St (45011-2701)
PHONE...................513 887-0014
Angela Howard, *Brnch Mgr*
EMP: 84
SALES (corp-wide): 13.47MM **Privately Held**
Web: www.gmvymca.org
SIC: 8641 7991 8351 7032 Youth organizations; Physical fitness facilities; Child day care services; Youth camps

PA: The Great Miami Valley Young Men's Christian Association
105 N 2nd St
Hamilton OH 45011
513 887-0001

(G-9049)
GREAT MIAMI VALLEY YMCA
Also Called: Fitton Family YMCA
1307 Nw Washington Blvd (45013-1207)
PHONE...................513 868-9622
Ron Thunderhouse, *Ex Dir*
EMP: 84
SALES (corp-wide): 13.47MM **Privately Held**
Web: www.gmvymca.org
SIC: 8641 7991 8351 7032 Youth organizations; Physical fitness facilities; Child day care services; Youth camps
PA: The Great Miami Valley Young Men's Christian Association
105 N 2nd St
Hamilton OH 45011
513 887-0001

(G-9050)
HAMILTON CITY SCHOOL DISTRICT
1315 Chestnut St (45011-3738)
PHONE...................513 887-5055
Lee Wallace, *Dir*
EMP: 30
SALES (corp-wide): 156.73MM **Privately Held**
Web: www.hamiltoncityschools.com
SIC: 8211 7349 Public senior high school; School custodian, contract basis
PA: Hamilton City School District
533 Dayton St
Hamilton OH 45011
513 887-5000

(G-9051)
HERITAGE FAMILY MEDICAL INC
435 Park Ave (45013-3053)
PHONE...................513 867-9000
Chad H Dunkle Md, *Treas*
Daniel Niehaus Md, *VP*
Gregory Savage Md, *Pr*
EMP: 30 **EST:** 1975
SALES (est): 715.3K **Privately Held**
SIC: 8011 General and family practice, physician/surgeon

(G-9052)
HHD AVIATION LLC
Also Called: United Sttes Trining Tstg Ctrs
2820 Bobmeyer Rd Hngr C7-210 (45015-1783)
PHONE...................513 426-8378
Darrin Wargacki, *Pr*
EMP: 81 **EST:** 2010
SALES (est): 2.97MM **Privately Held**
SIC: 4581 5999 8748 Airports, flying fields, and services; Educational aids and electronic training materials; Testing service, educational or personnel

(G-9053)
HOME DEPOT USA INC
Also Called: Home Depot, The
6562 Winford Ave (45011)
PHONE...................513 887-1450
Michael Yudt, *Mgr*
EMP: 90
SALES (corp-wide): 152.67B **Publicly Held**
Web: www.homedepot.com
SIC: 5211 7359 Home centers; Tool rental
HQ: Home Depot U.S.A., Inc.
2445 Springfield Ave
Vauxhall NJ 07088

(G-9054)
INLOES MECHANICAL INC
Also Called: Inloes Heating and Cooling
157 N B St (45013-3102)
PHONE...................513 896-9499
Ryan Inloes, *Pr*
Richard A Inloes, *
EMP: 28 **EST:** 1979
SQ FT: 32,000
SALES (est): 2.37MM **Privately Held**
Web: www.inloesheatingandcooling.com
SIC: 1711 Warm air heating and air conditioning contractor

(G-9055)
INTEGRATED POWER SERVICES LLC
2175a Schlichter Dr (45015-1482)
PHONE...................513 863-8816
Jason Reynolds, *Brnch Mgr*
EMP: 28
SQ FT: 20,500
Web: www.ips.us
SIC: 7694 Electric motor repair
PA: Integrated Power Services Llc
250 Exctive Ctr Dr Ste 20
Greenville SC 29615

(G-9056)
KETTERING HEALTH HAMILTON (HQ)
630 Eaton Ave (45013)
PHONE...................513 867-2000
James A Kingsbury, *Pr*
EMP: 1100 **EST:** 1985
SQ FT: 350,000
SALES (est): 10.33MM
SALES (corp-wide): 2.46B **Privately Held**
Web: www.ketteringhealth.org
SIC: 8062 General medical and surgical hospitals
PA: Kettering Adventist Healthcare
3535 Southern Blvd
Dayton OH 45429
937 298-4331

(G-9057)
KETTERING HEALTH NETWORK
630 Eaton Ave (45013-2767)
PHONE...................513 585-6000
EMP: 33 **EST:** 2019
SALES (est): 722.15K **Privately Held**
Web: www.ketteringhealth.org
SIC: 8099 Health and allied services, nec

(G-9058)
KNOSE CONCRETE CONSTRUCTN INC
4926 Cincinnati Brookville Rd (45013-9210)
P.O. Box 502 (45041-0502)
PHONE...................513 738-8200
Dennis Knose Press, *Prin*
EMP: 35 **EST:** 2015
SALES (est): 2.18MM **Privately Held**
Web: www.knoseconcrete.com
SIC: 1521 Single-family housing construction

(G-9059)
LCD AGENCY SERVICES LLC
Also Called: Lcd Nrse Aide Acdemy HM Hlth A
6 S 2nd St Ste 409 (45011-2865)
PHONE...................513 497-0441
Lamonda Dye, *Managing Member*
EMP: 29 **EST:** 2010
SQ FT: 1,500
SALES (est): 2.4MM **Privately Held**
SIC: 8059 8249 Convalescent home; Practical nursing school

(G-9060)
LIFESPAN INCORPORATED (PA)
Also Called: LIFESPAN
1900 Fairgrove Ave (45011-1966)
PHONE...................513 868-3210
Cynthia Stever, *CEO*
EMP: 74 **EST:** 1945
SQ FT: 21,000
SALES (est): 4.69MM
SALES (corp-wide): 4.69MM **Privately Held**
Web: www.community-first.org
SIC: 8322 Family service agency

(G-9061)
LOWES HOME CENTERS LLC
Also Called: Lowe's
1495 Main St (45013-1075)
PHONE...................513 737-3700
EMP: 115
SALES (corp-wide): 86.38B **Publicly Held**
Web: www.lowes.com
SIC: 5211 5031 5722 5064 Home centers; Building materials, exterior; Household appliance stores; Electrical appliances, television and radio
HQ: Lowe's Home Centers, Llc
1000 Lowes Blvd
Mooresville NC 28117
336 658-4000

(G-9062)
M A FOLKES COMPANY INC
3095 Mcbride Ct (45011-5203)
P.O. Box 425 (45012-0425)
PHONE...................513 785-4200
Michael Folkes, *Pr*
EMP: 45 **EST:** 1997
SQ FT: 200,000
SALES (est): 4.84MM **Privately Held**
Web: www.mafolkes.com
SIC: 7389 4225 8741 Packaging and labeling services; General warehousing and storage; Management services

(G-9063)
MATANDY STEEL & METAL PDTS LLC
Also Called: Matandy Steel Sales
1200 Central Ave (45011-3825)
P.O. Box 1186 (45012-1186)
PHONE...................513 844-2277
Andrew Schuster, *Pr*
Frank Pfirman, *
Aaron Higdon, *
EMP: 100 **EST:** 1999
SQ FT: 125,000
SALES (est): 24.68MM **Privately Held**
Web: www.matandy.com
SIC: 5051 Metals service centers and offices

(G-9064)
MCCULLOUGH-HYDE MEM HOSP INC
1390 Eaton Ave (45013-1407)
PHONE...................513 863-2215
Peter Towne, *Owner*
EMP: 27
SALES (corp-wide): 52.1MM **Privately Held**
Web: www.trihealth.com
SIC: 8062 General medical and surgical hospitals
PA: The Mccullough-Hyde Memorial Hospital Incorporated
110 N Poplar St
Oxford OH 45056
513 523-2111

Hamilton - Butler County (G-9065)

GEOGRAPHIC SECTION

(G-9065)
MIDLAND TITLE SECURITY INC
300 High St Ste 404 (45011-6078)
PHONE..................513 863-7600
Frank Froelke, *Mgr*
EMP: 177
Web: www.aptitles.com
SIC: 6541 Title and trust companies
HQ: Midland Title Security, Inc
  1111 Superior Ave E # 700
  Cleveland OH 44114
  216 241-6045

(G-9066)
MILLIKIN AND FITTON LAW FIRM (PA)
Also Called: Millikin & Fitton
232 High St (45011-2711)
P.O. Box 598 (45012-0598)
PHONE..................513 863-6700
John J Reister, *Pt*
Michele Gressell, *Prin*
Michael A Fulton, *Pt*
John G Rosmarin, *Pt*
Stanley D Rullman, *Pt*
EMP: 29
SALES (est): 4.43MM
SALES (corp-wide): 4.43MM **Privately Held**
Web: www.mfitton.com
SIC: 8111 General practice attorney, lawyer

(G-9067)
NATIONWIDE INSURANCE
633 High St (45011-6082)
PHONE..................513 341-7221
EMP: 27 **EST:** 2017
SALES (est): 1.61MM **Privately Held**
Web: www.nationwide.com
SIC: 6331 6311 Associated factory mutuals, fire and marine insurance; Life insurance

(G-9068)
NEW LONDON HILLS CLUB INC
1400 Hamilton New London Rd (45013-4016)
PHONE..................513 868-9026
Steve Timmer, *Pr*
EMP: 50 **EST:** 1957
SALES (est): 489.69K **Privately Held**
Web: www.newlondonhills.com
SIC: 7997 Country club, membership

(G-9069)
ODW LOGISTICS INC
345 High St Ste 600 (45011-6072)
PHONE..................513 785-4980
John Guggenbiller, *Pr*
EMP: 66
SALES (corp-wide): 529.12MM **Privately Held**
Web: www.odwlogistics.com
SIC: 4731 Freight transportation arrangement
PA: Odw Logistics, Inc.
  400 W Nationwide Blvd # 200
  Columbus OH 43215
  614 549-5000

(G-9070)
ODW LTS LLC
Also Called: Odw LTS
345 High St (45011-6071)
PHONE..................800 978-3168
John Guggenbiller, *Pr*
John Ness, *
Joe Keller, *
EMP: 125 **EST:** 2009
SQ FT: 2,600
SALES (est): 9.88MM **Privately Held**
Web: www.odwlogistics.com

SIC: 4731 Transportation agents and brokers

(G-9071)
PARTNERS IN PRIME (PA)
Also Called: Prime Club
230 Ludlow St (45011-2903)
PHONE..................513 867-1998
Stephen Schnabl, *CEO*
Shelley Ratliff, *
EMP: 50 **EST:** 1954
SQ FT: 30,000
SALES (est): 2.08MM
SALES (corp-wide): 2.08MM **Privately Held**
Web: www.community-first.org
SIC: 8322 4119 Old age assistance; Local passenger transportation, nec

(G-9072)
PERSONAL TOUCH HM CARE IPA INC
7924 Jessies Way Ste C (45011-1336)
PHONE..................513 868-2272
Jenny Justice, *Mgr*
EMP: 165
SALES (corp-wide): 251.89MM **Privately Held**
Web: www.pthomecare.com
SIC: 8082 Home health care services
PA: Personal Touch Home Care Ipa, Inc.
  1985 Marcus Ave Ste 202
  New Hyde Park NY 11042
  718 468-4747

(G-9073)
PRESSLEY RIDGE FOUNDATION
734 Dayton St (45011-3460)
PHONE..................513 737-0400
EMP: 141
Web: www.pressleyridge.org
SIC: 8322 Individual and family services
PA: Pressley Ridge Foundation
  5500 Corporate Dr Ste 400
  Pittsburgh PA 15237

(G-9074)
PRIMETECH COMMUNICATIONS INC
4505 Mulhauser Rd (45011)
P.O. Box 531730 (45253)
PHONE..................513 942-6000
Brad Shoemaker, *Pr*
Marcia Shoemaker, *
EMP: 86 **EST:** 1996
SQ FT: 17,000
SALES (est): 17.06MM
SALES (corp-wide): 258.79MM **Privately Held**
Web: www.adbcompanies.com
SIC: 1731 Cable television installation
HQ: Adb Companies, Llc
  18777 Us Highway 66
  Eureka MO 63069

(G-9075)
PTC TRANSPORT LTD
1849 Sky Meadow Dr (45013-9624)
PHONE..................513 738-0900
Ted Case, *Pr*
EMP: 40 **EST:** 1994
SALES (est): 2.31MM **Privately Held**
SIC: 4731 Truck transportation brokers

(G-9076)
PULMONARY CRITICAL CARE AND SL
25 Office Park Dr (45013-1496)
PHONE..................513 893-5764
Muhammad Nizar Orfahli, *Prin*
EMP: 28 **EST:** 2007
SALES (est): 2.1MM **Privately Held**

Web: www.pccsm.com
SIC: 8011 Pulmonary specialist, physician/surgeon

(G-9077)
RACK & BALLAUER EXCVTG CO INC
Also Called: Rack & Ballauer Excavating
11321 Paddys Run Rd (45013-9403)
PHONE..................513 738-7000
Larry Ballauer, *Pr*
Randy Rack, *
Scot Rack, *
EMP: 50 **EST:** 1983
SQ FT: 4,000
SALES (est): 10.25MM **Privately Held**
Web: www.rackballauer.com
SIC: 1794 Excavation work

(G-9078)
RESIDENCE AT KENSINGTON PLACE
Also Called: Residence At Huntington Court
350 Hancock Ave (45011-4448)
PHONE..................513 863-4218
Larry Schindler, *Mgr*
EMP: 120
SALES (corp-wide): 9.63MM **Privately Held**
Web: www.huntington-court.net
SIC: 8051 Convalescent home with continuous nursing care
PA: The Residence At Kensington Place
  751 Kensington St
  Middletown OH 45044
  513 424-3511

(G-9079)
RK FAMILY INC
1416 Main St (45013-1004)
PHONE..................513 737-0436
David Pfeiffer, *Prin*
EMP: 146
SALES (corp-wide): 1.22B **Privately Held**
Web: www.ruralking.com
SIC: 5191 Farm supplies
PA: Rk Family, Inc.
  4216 Dewitt Ave
  Mattoon IL 61938
  217 235-7102

(G-9080)
SALVAGNINI AMERICA INC (DH)
27 Bicentennial Ct (45015-1382)
PHONE..................513 874-8284
Andrea Scarpari, *CEO*
Eugenio Bassan, *
Vicente Undurraga, *
Doug Johnson, *
▲ **EMP:** 40 **EST:** 1984
SQ FT: 60,000
SALES (est): 111.23MM **Privately Held**
Web: www.salvagnini.com
SIC: 5084 Machine tools and accessories
HQ: Salvagnini Italia Spa
  Via Ingegnere Guido Salvagnini 51
  Sarego VI 36040
  044 483-4250

(G-9081)
SMALL WORLD CHILDRENS CENTER
Also Called: Community Christian School
3100 Hamilton Princeton Rd (45011-9630)
PHONE..................513 867-9963
Dulcie Bushhorn, *Dir*
Marsha Gebhart, *Dir*
EMP: 38 **EST:** 1975
SALES (est): 217.71K **Privately Held**
Web: www.smallworldchildrenscenter.org
SIC: 8351 8211 Group day care center; Private elementary and secondary schools

(G-9082)
SOJOURNER RECOVERY SVCS LLC (PA)
Also Called: Sojourner Recovery Services
515 Dayton St (45011-3455)
PHONE..................513 868-7654
Scott Dehring, *CEO*
EMP: 30 **EST:** 1985
SALES (est): 9.39MM **Privately Held**
Web: www.sojournerrecovery.com
SIC: 8093 Substance abuse clinics (outpatient)

(G-9083)
STRAWSER CONSTRUCTION INC
Also Called: STRAWSER CONSTRUCTION INC
8600 Bilstein Blvd (45015-2204)
PHONE..................513 874-6192
EMP: 111
SALES (corp-wide): 55.3MM **Privately Held**
Web: www.strawserconstruction.com
SIC: 1521 Single-family housing construction
HQ: Strawser Construction Inc.
  1392 Dublin Rd
  Columbus OH 43215

(G-9084)
SUNRISE SENIOR LIVING LLC
Also Called: Sunrise of Hamilton
896 Nw Washington Blvd (45013-1281)
PHONE..................513 893-9000
Jamie Cianciolo, *Ex Dir*
EMP: 40
SALES (corp-wide): 2.92B **Privately Held**
Web: www.sunriseseniorliving.com
SIC: 8051 Skilled nursing care facilities
HQ: Sunrise Senior Living, Llc
  7902 Westpark Dr
  Mc Lean VA 22102

(G-9085)
THYSSENKRUPP BILSTEIN AMER INC
3033 Symmes Rd (45015-1330)
PHONE..................513 881-7600
Andrew Guthridge, *CFO*
EMP: 100
SALES (corp-wide): 40.78B **Privately Held**
Web: www.bilstein.com
SIC: 5014 Automobile tires and tubes
HQ: Thyssenkrupp Bilstein Of America, Inc.
  8685 Bilstein Blvd
  Hamilton OH 45015
  513 881-7600

(G-9086)
THYSSENKRUPP BILSTEIN AMER INC (HQ)
8685 Bilstein Blvd (45015-2205)
PHONE..................513 881-7600
Fabian Schmahl, *Pr*
▲ **EMP:** 212 **EST:** 1972
SQ FT: 115,000
SALES (est): 510.8MM
SALES (corp-wide): 40.78B **Privately Held**
Web: www.bilsteinrocks.com
SIC: 3714 5013 Shock absorbers, motor vehicle; Springs, shock absorbers and struts
PA: Thyssenkrupp Ag
  Thyssenkrupp Allee 1
  Essen NW 45143
  2018440

(G-9087)
TRIHEALTH INC
Also Called: Bethesda Care Butler County
8500 Bilstein Blvd Ste 100 (45015-2218)
PHONE..................513 874-3990

GEOGRAPHIC SECTION

Becky Harris, *Pr*
EMP: 122
Web: www.trihealth.com
SIC: 8011 Occupational and industrial specialist, physician/surgeon
HQ: Trihealth, Inc.
 625 Eden Park Dr
 Cincinnati OH 45202
 513 569-5400

(G-9088)
ULTRAEDIT INC
Also Called: IDM Computer Solutions
5559 Eureka Dr Ste B (45011-4267)
PHONE.....................216 464-7465
Derek Holder, *Dir*
EMP: 79
SALES (corp-wide): 284.59MM **Privately Held**
Web: www.ultraedit.com
SIC: 7372 Prepackaged software
HQ: Ultraedit, Inc.
 10801 N Mpac Expy Bldg 1
 Austin TX 78759
 713 523-4433

(G-9089)
UNITED PARCEL SERVICE INC
Also Called: UPS
1951 Logan Ave (45015-1020)
PHONE.....................513 863-1681
Bryan Zelen, *Mgr*
EMP: 31
SALES (corp-wide): 90.96B **Publicly Held**
Web: www.ups.com
SIC: 4215 Parcel delivery, vehicular
HQ: United Parcel Service, Inc.
 55 Glenlake Pkwy
 Atlanta GA 30328
 404 828-6000

(G-9090)
UNITED PERFORMANCE METALS LLC (HQ)
Also Called: United Performance Metals
3475 Symmes Rd (45015-1363)
PHONE.....................513 860-6500
Peter Neuberger, *Pr*
Craft O'neal, *Ch*
Greg Chase, *
Jeffrey Liesch, *
◆ **EMP:** 260 **EST:** 1982
SQ FT: 110,000
SALES (est): 158.59MM
SALES (corp-wide): 2.41B **Privately Held**
Web: www.upmet.com
SIC: 5051 Steel
PA: O'neal Industries, Inc.
 2311 Highland Ave S # 20
 Birmingham AL 35205
 205 721-2880

(G-9091)
WATSON GRAVEL INC (PA)
2728 Hamilton Cleves Rd (45013-9452)
PHONE.....................513 863-0070
Ronald E Watson, *Pr*
Michael T Watson, *
Janet L Meyers, *
EMP: 37 **EST:** 1970
SQ FT: 2,000
SALES (est): 9.82MM
SALES (corp-wide): 9.82MM **Privately Held**
Web: www.watsongravel.com
SIC: 1442 Gravel mining

(G-9092)
WILLIAMS SCOTSMAN INC
Also Called: Williams Scotsman - Cincinnati
125 Distribution Dr (45014-4257)
PHONE.....................513 874-1280
Jack Kubica, *Brnch Mgr*
EMP: 35
SALES (corp-wide): 2.36B **Publicly Held**
Web: info.willscot.ca
SIC: 5039 Mobile offices and commercial units
HQ: Williams Scotsman, Inc.
 4646 E Van Buren St # 40
 Phoenix AZ 85008
 480 894-6311

(G-9093)
WULCO INC
Also Called: Cima
1010 Eaton Ave Ste B # B (45013-4640)
PHONE.....................513 379-6115
Richard G Wulfeck, *Pr*
EMP: 95
Web: www.wulco.com
SIC: 5085 3599 Industrial supplies; Machine shop, jobbing and repair
PA: Wulco, Inc.
 6899 Steger Dr Ste A
 Cincinnati OH 45237

(G-9094)
ZARTRAN LLC
3035 Symmes Rd (45015-1330)
PHONE.....................513 870-4800
Donald Browning, *CEO*
EMP: 75 **EST:** 2008
SALES (est): 2.52MM **Privately Held**
Web: www.zartran.com
SIC: 4213 Refrigerated products transport

Hanoverton
Columbiana County

(G-9095)
SPREAD EAGLE TAVERN INC
10150 Plymouth St (44423-9630)
PHONE.....................330 223-1583
David Johnson, *Pr*
Mark Webb, *Sec*
EMP: 142 **EST:** 1988
SALES (est): 946.98K
SALES (corp-wide): 24.79MM **Privately Held**
Web: www.spreadeagletavern.com
SIC: 7011 5812 Bed and breakfast inn; Eating places
PA: Summitville Tiles, Inc
 15364 State Rte 644
 Summitville OH 43962
 330 223-1511

Harrison
Hamilton County

(G-9096)
AERO PROPULSION SUPPORT INC
Also Called: Aero Propulsion Support Group
108 May Dr Ste A (45030-2005)
PHONE.....................513 367-9452
Allan Slattery, *Pr*
Rose Slattery, *
EMP: 49 **EST:** 1992
SQ FT: 25,000
SALES (est): 9.33MM **Privately Held**
Web: www.aeropropulsion.com
SIC: 4581 Aircraft maintenance and repair services

(G-9097)
ALTAQUIP LLC (HQ)
100 Production Dr (45030-1477)
PHONE.....................513 674-6464
Mike King, *Managing Member*
EMP: 50 **EST:** 2003
SALES (est): 32.28MM
SALES (corp-wide): 226 **Privately Held**
Web: www.altaquip.com
SIC: 7699 Lawn mower repair shop
PA: The Scott Fetzer Company
 28800 Clemens Rd
 Westlake OH 44145
 440 892-3000

(G-9098)
CINCINNATI ASPHALT CORPORATION
6000 Madden Way (45030-2260)
P.O. Box 757 (45030-0757)
PHONE.....................513 367-0250
Joey Madden, *Pr*
EMP: 52 **EST:** 2013
SALES (est): 11.44MM **Privately Held**
Web: www.cincyasphalt.com
SIC: 1611 1794 1771 Concrete construction: roads, highways, sidewalks, etc.; Excavation work; Concrete work

(G-9099)
CINCINNATI EARLY LEARNING CTR
498 S State St (45030-1446)
PHONE.....................513 367-2129
EMP: 70
SALES (corp-wide): 5.06MM **Privately Held**
Web: www.celcinc.org
SIC: 8351 Preschool center
PA: Early Cincinnati Learning Center Inc
 1301 E Mcmillan St
 Cincinnati OH 45206
 513 961-2690

(G-9100)
CRONIN AUTOMOTIVE CO LLC
10700 New Haven Rd (45030-1646)
PHONE.....................513 202-5812
Emily Whalbring, *Admn*
EMP: 28 **EST:** 2017
SALES (est): 3.37MM **Privately Held**
Web: www.croninauto.com
SIC: 7538 General automotive repair shops

(G-9101)
DENIER ELECTRIC CO INC (PA)
Also Called: Denier Technologies Div
7266 New Haven Rd (45030-9278)
PHONE.....................513 738-2641
Dennis J Denier, *CEO*
Diane K Herbort, *
George D Roberts, *
Jeffry A Heitker, *
Sandra Feldhaus, *
EMP: 215 **EST:** 1942
SQ FT: 40,000
SALES (est): 54.98MM
SALES (corp-wide): 54.98MM **Privately Held**
Web: www.denier.com
SIC: 1731 General electrical contractor

(G-9102)
DITTMAN-ADAMS COMPANY
10080 Crosby Rd (45030-9272)
PHONE.....................513 870-7530
Garry Adams, *Pr*
Ryan Smith, *
EMP: 43 **EST:** 1945
SALES (est): 4.41MM **Privately Held**
Web: www.dittman-adams.com
SIC: 5194 Cigarettes

(G-9103)
ECHOS HAVEN LLC
114 Broadway St (45030-1317)
PHONE.....................513 715-1189
Dixie E Shumway, *Managing Member*
EMP: 35 **EST:** 2015
SALES (est): 468.22K **Privately Held**
SIC: 8361 Residential care for the handicapped

(G-9104)
F & M MAFCO INC (HQ)
9149 Dry Fork Rd (45030-1901)
P.O. Box 11013 (45211-0013)
PHONE.....................513 367-2151
Gary Bernardez, *CEO*
◆ **EMP:** 186 **EST:** 1946
SQ FT: 85,000
SALES (est): 97.61MM
SALES (corp-wide): 180.37MM **Privately Held**
Web: www.ameco.com
SIC: 5085 5072 7353 5082 Welding supplies; Hardware; Heavy construction equipment rental; General construction machinery and equipment
PA: American Equipment Company, Inc.
 2106 Anderson Rd
 Greenville SC 29611
 864 295-7800

(G-9105)
F & M MAFCO INC
651 Enterprise Dr (45030-1691)
PHONE.....................513 367-2151
Wendy Welder, *Mgr*
EMP: 29
SALES (corp-wide): 180.37MM **Privately Held**
Web: www.ameco.com
SIC: 5085 1541 Welding supplies; Industrial buildings and warehouses
HQ: F & M Mafco, Inc.
 9149 Dry Fork Rd
 Harrison OH 45030
 513 367-2151

(G-9106)
FCN BANK CORP
590 Ring Rd (45030-1694)
P.O. Box 511 (45030-0511)
PHONE.....................513 367-6111
EMP: 30
SALES (corp-wide): 25.93MM **Privately Held**
Web: www.fcnbank.com
SIC: 6021 National commercial banks
HQ: Fcn Bank Corp
 501 Main St
 Brookville IN 47012
 765 647-4116

(G-9107)
HARRISON AVENUE ASSEMBLY GOD
Also Called: Hilltop Nursery School
949 Harrison Ave (45030-1520)
PHONE.....................513 367-6109
Doctor John Hembree, *Pastor*
EMP: 30 **EST:** 1961
SQ FT: 10,000
SALES (est): 772.37K **Privately Held**
SIC: 8661 8351 8211 Churches, temples, and shrines; Nursery school; Elementary and secondary schools

(G-9108)
HARRISON BUILDING AND LN ASSN (PA)
10490 New Haven Rd (45030-1657)
P.O. Box 590 (45030-0590)
PHONE.....................513 367-2015

Randall Grubbs, *Pr*
EMP: 28 **EST:** 1916
SALES (est): 9.02MM
SALES (corp-wide): 9.02MM **Privately Held**
Web: www.bankhbl.com
SIC: 6036 6035 Savings and loan associations, not federally chartered; Federal savings and loan associations

(G-9109)
HINSON ROOFING & SHTMTL INC
6191 Kilby Rd (45030-9416)
PHONE................................513 367-4477
EMP: 32 **EST:** 1994
SQ FT: 4,800
SALES (est): 2.29MM **Privately Held**
SIC: 1761 Roofing contractor

(G-9110)
HUBERT COMPANY LLC (DH)
Also Called: Hubert
9555 Dry Fork Rd (45030-1994)
PHONE................................513 367-8600
Mark Rudy, *Pr*
◆ **EMP:** 306 **EST:** 1946
SQ FT: 453,000
SALES (est): 108.32MM
SALES (corp-wide): 4.39B **Privately Held**
Web: www.hubert.com
SIC: 5046 Store fixtures
HQ: Takkt Ag
   Presselstr. 12
   Stuttgart BW 70191
   711346580

(G-9111)
KAPLAN INDUSTRIES INC
Also Called: Midwest Cylinder
6255 Kilby Rd (45030-9440)
PHONE................................856 779-8181
Dean Kaplan, *Pr*
Rita Kaplan, *
Jim Johnston, *
◆ **EMP:** 70 **EST:** 1959
SQ FT: 6,000
SALES (est): 22.87MM **Privately Held**
Web: www.kaplanindustries.com
SIC: 3491 8734 Compressed gas cylinder valves; Hydrostatic testing laboratory

(G-9112)
MODERN DAY CONCRETE CNSTR INC
9773 Crosby Rd (45030-9707)
PHONE................................513 738-1026
Frank Klosterman, *Ch*
Thomas Weisman, *
David Sellet, *
Gail Evans, *Sec*
EMP: 35 **EST:** 1964
SQ FT: 2,500
SALES (est): 844.17K **Privately Held**
SIC: 1771 Concrete work

(G-9113)
PAVEMENT PRTNERS CNCINNATI LLC ✪
6000 Madden Way (45030-2260)
PHONE................................513 367-0250
Jeff Payne, *Pr*
Jeff Payne, *Managing Member*
EMP: 47 **EST:** 2022
SALES (est): 11.67MM
SALES (corp-wide): 71.78MM **Privately Held**
SIC: 1611 Highway and street construction
PA: Pavement Partners Holding, Llc
   7861 David Williams Way
   Bristow VA

(G-9114)
RGT MANAGEMENT INC
10554 Harrison Ave (45030-1944)
PHONE................................513 715-4640
EMP: 37
Web: www.tacobell.com
SIC: 8741 Business management
PA: R.G.T. Management, Inc.
   116 Mc Davis Blvd # 216
   Santa Rosa Beach FL 32459

(G-9115)
RODEM INC (PA)
Also Called: Rodem Process Equipment
10001 Martins Way (45030-2259)
PHONE................................513 922-6140
Christopher Diener, *Pr*
Christopher A Diener, *
Jeffrey L Diener, *
Nancy D Finke, *
Susan D Kerr, *
▲ **EMP:** 40 **EST:** 1971
SALES (est): 46.35MM
SALES (corp-wide): 46.35MM **Privately Held**
Web: www.rodem.com
SIC: 5084 Dairy products manufacturing machinery, nec

(G-9116)
TAKKT FOODSERVICES LLC (PA)
9555 Dry Fork Rd (45030-1906)
PHONE................................513 367-8600
▲ **EMP:** 187 **EST:** 2008
SQ FT: 576,715
SALES (est): 25.64MM **Privately Held**
Web: hubertnorthamericaservice.openfos.com
SIC: 5046 Store fixtures

(G-9117)
TITAN MECHANICAL SOLUTIONS LLC
11003 State Route 128 (45030-9710)
PHONE................................513 738-5800
EMP: 37 **EST:** 2011
SALES (est): 13.05MM **Privately Held**
Web: www.titan-ms.com
SIC: 1711 Mechanical contractor

(G-9118)
TRIUMPH ENERGY CORPORATION
9171 Dry Fork Rd (45030-1901)
PHONE................................513 367-9900
Ronald Wittekind, *Ch*
Gerry Francis, *
EMP: 199 **EST:** 1963
SQ FT: 14,500
SALES (est): 29.37MM
SALES (corp-wide): 42.31MM **Privately Held**
Web: www.triumphenergy.com
SIC: 5172 5541 Petroleum products, nec; Gasoline service stations
PA: Hawkstone Associates, Inc.
   9171 Dry Fork Rd
   Harrison OH
   513 367-9900

(G-9119)
WAYNE/SCOTT FETZER COMPANY
Also Called: Wayne Water Systems
101 Production Dr (45030-1477)
PHONE................................800 237-0987
Duane Johnson, *Pr*
▲ **EMP:** 200 **EST:** 1985
SQ FT: 160,000
SALES (est): 52.15MM
SALES (corp-wide): 226 **Privately Held**
Web: www.waynepumps.com
SIC: 3561 5074 Pumps, domestic: water or sump; Water purification equipment
PA: The Scott Fetzer Company
   28800 Clemens Rd
   Westlake OH 44145
   440 892-3000

(G-9120)
WILLIAM HENRY HARRISON JR HS
9830 West Rd (45030-1929)
PHONE................................513 367-4831
Christian Tracy, *Prin*
EMP: 50 **EST:** 2019
SALES (est): 212.73K **Privately Held**
SIC: 7997 Membership sports and recreation clubs

(G-9121)
WORLD GROUP SECURITIES INC
1010 Harrison Ave (45030-1793)
PHONE................................513 367-5900
Gregg Bien, *Brnch Mgr*
EMP: 53
SALES (corp-wide): 21.08MM **Privately Held**
Web: www.worldfinancialgroup.com
SIC: 6211 Security brokers and dealers
PA: World Group Securities Inc
   11315 Johns Creek Pkwy
   Duluth GA 30097
   770 246-9889

Harrod
Allen County

(G-9122)
R D JONES EXCAVATING INC
10225 Alger Rd (45850-9792)
P.O. Box 127 (45850-0127)
PHONE................................419 648-5870
Randy Jones, *Pr*
Dana Jones, *
EMP: 50 **EST:** 1971
SQ FT: 1,200
SALES (est): 9.7MM **Privately Held**
Web: www.rdjonesexcavatinginc.com
SIC: 1794 Excavation and grading, building construction

Hartford
Trumbull County

(G-9123)
STANWADE METAL PRODUCTS INC
Also Called: Stanwade Tanks and Equipment
6868 State Rt 305 (44424)
P.O. Box 10 (44424-0010)
PHONE................................330 772-2421
EMP: 44 **EST:** 1947
SALES (est): 5.25MM **Privately Held**
Web: www.stanwade.com
SIC: 3443 5084 Fuel tanks (oil, gas, etc.), metal plate; Petroleum industry machinery

Hartville
Stark County

(G-9124)
CONGRESS LAKE CLUB COMPANY
Also Called: CONGRESS LAKE CLUB
1 East Dr Ne (44632-8890)
P.O. Box 370 (44632-0370)
PHONE................................330 877-9318
Fred Zollinger Iii, *Pr*
EMP: 40 **EST:** 1896
SQ FT: 40,000
SALES (est): 3.85MM **Privately Held**
Web: www.congresslakeclub.com
SIC: 7997 Golf club, membership

(G-9125)
GENTLEBROOK INC (PA)
880 Sunnyside St Sw (44632-9087)
PHONE................................330 877-3694
Norman Wengerd, *CEO*
Mike Sleutz, *
EMP: 78 **EST:** 1974
SALES (est): 21.11MM
SALES (corp-wide): 21.11MM **Privately Held**
Web: www.gentlebrook.org
SIC: 8361 8741 Retarded home; Management services

(G-9126)
GFS LEASING INC
Also Called: Altercare Hartville
1420 Smith Kramer St Ne (44632-8730)
PHONE................................330 877-2666
Chelle Sink, *Admn*
EMP: 100
SALES (corp-wide): 9.34MM **Privately Held**
Web: www.altercareonline.com
SIC: 8051 Convalescent home with continuous nursing care
PA: Gfs Leasing Inc
   1463 Tallmadge Rd
   Kent OH 44240
   330 296-6415

(G-9127)
HRM ENTERPRISES INC (PA)
Also Called: True Value
1015 Edison St Nw Ste 3 (44632-8510)
PHONE................................330 877-9353
William J Howard, *Pr*
Wayne Miller, *
◆ **EMP:** 160 **EST:** 1955
SQ FT: 85,000
SALES (est): 45.74MM
SALES (corp-wide): 45.74MM **Privately Held**
Web: www.hartvillehardware.com
SIC: 5947 5812 7389 Gift shop; American restaurant; Flea market

(G-9128)
KINGSWAY FARM & STORAGE INC
1555 Andrews St Ne (44632-9018)
PHONE................................330 877-6241
Kevin King, *Brnch Mgr*
EMP: 35
Web: www.kingswaypumpkinfarm.com
SIC: 0161 Pumpkin farm
PA: Kingsway Farm & Storage, Inc.
   9888 Gans Ave Ne
   Canton OH 44721

(G-9129)
SCHONER CHEVROLET INC
720 W Maple St (44632-8504)
P.O. Box 9 (44632-0009)
PHONE................................330 877-6731
Mark E Hanlon, *Pr*
Dorothy Hanlon, *
EMP: 30 **EST:** 1936
SQ FT: 20,000
SALES (est): 2.8MM **Privately Held**
Web: www.schonerchevrolet.com
SIC: 5511 7514 7538 7515 Automobiles, new and used; Rent-a-car service; General automotive repair shops; Passenger car leasing

GEOGRAPHIC SECTION

Hebron - Licking County (G-9149)

(G-9130)
SOMMERS MARKET LLC (PA)
Also Called: Grocery Outlet Supermarket
214 Market Ave Sw (44632-8545)
PHONE..................................330 352-7470
Roland Sommers, *Managing Member*
David J Sommers, *
Phil Weidler, *
EMP: 51 **EST:** 2007
SQ FT: 6,000
SALES (est): 2.62MM
SALES (corp-wide): 2.62MM **Privately Held**
Web: www.sommersmarket.com
SIC: 5411 5141 Grocery stores, independent; Groceries, general line

(G-9131)
WHOLESALE DECOR LLC
650 S Prospect Ave Ste 200 (44632-8904)
PHONE..................................330 587-7100
Philip Daetwyler, *CEO*
EMP: 27
SALES (corp-wide): 9.33MM **Privately Held**
Web: www.ohiowholesale.com
SIC: 5023 Homefurnishings
PA: Wholesale Decor Llc
   286 W Greenwich Rd
   Seville OH 44273
   877 745-5050

Haviland
Paulding County

(G-9132)
MCK TRUCKING INC
2952 Road 107 (45851-9638)
PHONE..................................419 622-1111
Michael Keysor, *Pr*
EMP: 30 **EST:** 2014
SALES (est): 4.74MM **Privately Held**
Web: www.customassembly.net
SIC: 4212 Local trucking, without storage

Heath
Licking County

(G-9133)
GUMMER WHOLESALE INC (PA)
1945 James Pkwy (43056-4000)
P.O. Box 2288 (43056-0288)
PHONE..................................740 928-0415
Chad Gummer, *Pr*
Michael Gummer, *
Lillian Gummer, *
EMP: 67 **EST:** 1953
SQ FT: 50,000
SALES (est): 44.52MM
SALES (corp-wide): 44.52MM **Privately Held**
Web: www.gummerwholesale.net
SIC: 5194 5145 5199 5141 Cigarettes; Candy; Novelties, paper; Groceries, general line

(G-9134)
INTERIM HALTHCARE COLUMBUS INC
Also Called: Interim Services
675 Hopewell Dr (43056-1579)
PHONE..................................740 349-8700
Susan Hamann, *Brnch Mgr*
EMP: 262
SALES (corp-wide): 52.16MM **Privately Held**
Web: www.interimhealthcare.com

SIC: 8082 Home health care services
HQ: Interim Healthcare Of Columbus, Inc.
   784 Morrison Rd
   Gahanna OH 43230
   614 888-3130

(G-9135)
LICKING MEMORIAL HOSPITAL
Also Called: Licking Mem Frmly Prctice Heath
687 Hopewell Dr Ste 2 (43056-1579)
PHONE..................................740 348-7915
EMP: 347
Web: www.lmhealth.org
SIC: 8062 General medical and surgical hospitals
HQ: Licking Memorial Hospital
   1320 W Main St
   Newark OH 43055
   740 348-4137

(G-9136)
MISTRAS GROUP INC
1480 James Pkwy (43056-4018)
PHONE..................................740 788-9188
Mike Jones, *Brnch Mgr*
EMP: 176
SQ FT: 13,000
Web: www.mistrasgroup.com
SIC: 8734 Testing laboratories
PA: Mistras Group, Inc.
   195 Clarksville Rd
   Princeton Junction NJ 08550

(G-9137)
ROBERTSON CNSTR SVCS INC
1801 Thornwood Dr (43056-9311)
PHONE..................................740 929-1000
Christian H Robertson, *Pr*
Michele Robertson, *
EMP: 100 **EST:** 1997
SQ FT: 6,000
SALES (est): 45.56MM **Privately Held**
Web: www.robertsonconstruction.net
SIC: 1542 Commercial and office building, new construction

(G-9138)
SAMUEL SON & CO (USA) INC
Samuel Packaging Systems Group
1455 James Pkwy (43056-4007)
PHONE..................................740 522-2500
Jay Jones, *Mgr*
EMP: 100
SALES (corp-wide): 504.18MM **Privately Held**
Web: www.samuel.com
SIC: 3089 5085 5084 5199 Plastics processing; Industrial supplies; Industrial machinery and equipment; Packaging materials
PA: Samuel, Son & Co. (Usa) Inc.
   1401 Davey Rd Ste 300
   Woodridge IL 60517
   800 323-4424

(G-9139)
SHRADER TIRE & OIL INC
433 Hopewell Dr (43056-1577)
PHONE..................................740 788-8032
EMP: 37
SALES (corp-wide): 97.58MM **Privately Held**
Web: www.shradertireandoil.com
SIC: 5014 Tires and tubes
PA: Shrader Tire & Oil, Inc.
   2045 W Sylvania Ave # 51
   Toledo OH 43613
   419 472-2128

(G-9140)
SNS HOSPITALITY LLC
Also Called: Holiday Inn
773 Hebron Rd (43056-1355)
PHONE..................................740 522-8499
Champak Shah, *Mng Pt*
Thomas Shaw, *Prin*
EMP: 34 **EST:** 2007
SALES (est): 296.64K **Privately Held**
Web: www.holidayinn.com
SIC: 7011 Hotels and motels

Hebron
Licking County

(G-9141)
CARTCOM INC
200 Arrowhead Blvd (43025-9466)
PHONE..................................740 644-0912
Omair Tariq, *Brnch Mgr*
EMP: 100
SALES (corp-wide): 260MM **Privately Held**
SIC: 4225 General warehousing and storage
PA: Cart.Com, Inc.
   1334 Brittmoore Rd # 225
   Houston TX 77043
   713 545-8130

(G-9142)
DDM-DGTAL IMGING DATA PROC MLI
Also Called: Ddm Direct of Ohio
190 Milliken Dr (43025-9657)
PHONE..................................740 928-1110
Eill Hillard, *Brnch Mgr*
EMP: 97
SALES (corp-wide): 4.99B **Privately Held**
SIC: 7331 Mailing service
HQ: Ddm-Digital Imaging, Data Processing And Mailing Services, L C
   1223 William St
   Buffalo NY 14206
   716 893-8671

(G-9143)
HENDRICKSON INTERNATIONAL CORP
Also Called: Hendrickson Auxiliary Axles
277 N High St (43025-8008)
PHONE..................................740 929-5600
Mike Keeler, *Genl Mgr*
EMP: 78
SALES (corp-wide): 758.84MM **Privately Held**
Web: www.hendrickson-intl.com
SIC: 3714 3493 3089 5084 Motor vehicle parts and accessories; Steel springs, except wire; Plastics containers, except foam; Industrial machinery and equipment
HQ: Hendrickson International Corporation
   840 S Frontage Rd
   Woodridge IL 60517

(G-9144)
INTEGRIS COMPOSITES INC
1051 O Neill Dr (43025)
PHONE..................................740 928-0326
Erick Johnson, *Brnch Mgr*
EMP: 65
Web: www.integriscomposites.com
SIC: 3229 3795 8711 Yarn, fiberglass; Tanks and tank components; Engineering services
HQ: Integris Composites, Inc.
   8075 Leesburg Pike # 210
   Vienna VA 22182

(G-9145)
LEGEND SMELTING AND RECYCL INC (HQ)

Also Called: L S R
717 O Neill Dr (43025)
PHONE..................................740 928-0139
Randy Hess, *Pr*
Mark Sasko, *
Paul Leary, *
▲ **EMP:** 60 **EST:** 1989
SQ FT: 90,000
SALES (est): 23.52MM
SALES (corp-wide): 2.19MM **Privately Held**
Web: www.legendsmeltingrecycling.com
SIC: 5093 Nonferrous metals scrap
PA: Elemental Global Services S A
   Ul. Traugutta 42a
   Grodzisk Mazowiecki 05-82
   223909135

(G-9146)
MAXIM HEALTHCARE SERVICES INC
96 Integrity Dr Ste A (43025-7013)
PHONE..................................740 526-2222
EMP: 216
Web: www.maximhealthcare.com
SIC: 8082 Home health care services
PA: Maxim Healthcare Services, Inc.
   7227 Lee Deforest Dr
   Columbia MD 21046

(G-9147)
MCNAUGHTON-MCKAY ELC OHIO INC
107 Capital Dr (43025-9489)
P.O. Box 399 (43025-0399)
PHONE..................................740 929-2727
Jeff Robinson, *Mgr*
EMP: 30
SQ FT: 20,000
SALES (corp-wide): 2.81B **Privately Held**
SIC: 5063 Electrical supplies, nec
HQ: Mcnaughton-Mckay Electric Company Of Ohio, Inc.
   2255 Citygate Dr
   Columbus OH 43219
   614 476-2800

(G-9148)
MID STATE SYSTEMS INC
9455 Lancaster Rd (43025-9640)
P.O. Box 926 (43025-0926)
PHONE..................................740 928-1115
Leon Zazworsky, *Pr*
Judy K Zazworsky, *
EMP: 44 **EST:** 1970
SQ FT: 11,500
SALES (est): 2.25MM **Privately Held**
Web: www.midstatesystems.com
SIC: 4225 General warehousing and storage

(G-9149)
MPW INDUSTRIAL SERVICES INC (HQ)
Also Called: MPW
9711 Lancaster Rd (43025-9764)
PHONE..................................800 827-8790
Monte Black, *CEO*
▲ **EMP:** 600 **EST:** 1972
SQ FT: 75,000
SALES (est): 213.53MM
SALES (corp-wide): 213.53MM **Privately Held**
Web: www.mpwservices.com
SIC: 7349 Cleaning service, industrial or commercial
PA: Mpw Industrial Services Group, Inc.
   9711 Lancaster Rd
   Hebron OH 43025
   740 927-8790

(G-9150)
MPW INDUSTRIAL SVCS GROUP INC (PA)
9711 Lancaster Rd (43025-9764)
PHONE.................................740 927-8790
Monte R Black, *CEO*
Jared Black, *
Sarah D Pemberton, *
EMP: 255 **EST:** 1972
SQ FT: 24,000
SALES (est): 213.53MM
SALES (corp-wide): 213.53MM **Privately Held**
Web: www.mpwservices.com
SIC: 7349 8744 3589 Cleaning service, industrial or commercial; Facilities support services; Commercial cleaning equipment

(G-9151)
MPW INDUSTRIAL WATER SVCS INC
9711 Lancaster Rd (43025-9764)
P.O. Box 10 (43025-0010)
PHONE.................................800 827-8790
Monte R Black, *Pr*
EMP: 174 **EST:** 1998
SALES (est): 5.85MM
SALES (corp-wide): 213.53MM **Privately Held**
Web: www.mpwservices.com
SIC: 4499 Water transportation cleaning services
HQ: Mpw Management Services Corp.
9711 Lancaster Rd
Hebron OH 43025

(G-9152)
NFI INDUSTRIES INC
522 Milliken Dr (43025-9657)
PHONE.................................740 527-9060
Patrick Milton, *Brnch Mgr*
EMP: 42
SALES (corp-wide): 1.26B **Privately Held**
Web: www.nfiindustries.com
SIC: 4731 Freight transportation arrangement
PA: Nfi Industries, Inc.
Triad1828 2 Cooper St 1828 Triad
Camden NJ 08102
877 634-3777

(G-9153)
S R DOOR INC (PA)
Also Called: Seal-Rite Door
1120 O Neill Dr (43025-9409)
P.O. Box 2109 (43216-2109)
PHONE.................................740 927-3558
Scott A Miller, *Pr*
Glen Miller, *
EMP: 80 **EST:** 1980
SQ FT: 75,000
SALES (est): 9.96MM
SALES (corp-wide): 9.96MM **Privately Held**
Web: www.palmerdonavin.com
SIC: 2431 3442 3211 5031 Doors, wood; Metal doors; Construction glass; Lumber, plywood, and millwork

(G-9154)
STATE INDUSTRIAL PRODUCTS CORP
Also Called: State Chemical Manufacturing
383 N High St (43025-9436)
PHONE.................................740 929-6370
Kale Moberg, *Brnch Mgr*
EMP: 76
SALES (corp-wide): 192.96MM **Privately Held**
Web: www.stateindustrial.com
SIC: 2841 5072 Soap: granulated, liquid, cake, flaked, or chip; Bolts, nuts, and screws
PA: State Industrial Products Corporation
5915 Landerbrook Dr # 300
Cleveland OH 44124
877 747-6986

(G-9155)
TRUCKOMAT CORPORATION
Also Called: Iowa 80 Group
10707 Lancaster Rd Ste 37 (43025-9622)
P.O. Box 837 (43025-0837)
PHONE.................................740 467-2818
Jeff Corley, *Genl Mgr*
EMP: 31
SALES (corp-wide): 513.63MM **Privately Held**
Web: www.truckomat.com
SIC: 7542 5013 Truck wash; Motor vehicle supplies and new parts
HQ: Truckomat Corporation
515 Sterling Dr
Walcott IA 52773
563 284-6965

(G-9156)
TRULITE GL ALUM SOLUTIONS LLC
160 N High St (43025-9011)
P.O. Box 220 (43025-0220)
PHONE.................................740 929-2443
EMP: 60
SIC: 3211 5039 3231 Tempered glass; Exterior flat glass: plate or window; Products of purchased glass
PA: Trulite Glass & Aluminum Solutions, Llc
403 Westpark Ct Ste 201
Peachtree City GA 30009

Helena
Sandusky County

(G-9157)
TECHNIQUE ROOFING SYSTEMS LLC
290 Main St (43435-9803)
P.O. Box 180 (43435-0180)
PHONE.................................419 680-2025
Keith Timmons, *Prin*
EMP: 30 **EST:** 2019
SALES (est): 1.57MM **Privately Held**
Web: www.techniqueroofing.com
SIC: 1761 Roofing contractor

Hicksville
Defiance County

(G-9158)
HICKORY CREEK HLTHCARE FNDTION
Also Called: Creek At Hicksburg
401 Fountain St (43526-1337)
PHONE.................................419 542-7795
Bill Langschiet, *Mgr*
EMP: 48
SALES (corp-wide): 7.98MM **Privately Held**
Web: www.hickorycreekhealthcare.org
SIC: 8051 Skilled nursing care facilities
PA: Hickory Creek Healthcare Foundation, Inc.
5 Concourse Pkwy Ste 2575
Atlanta GA 30328
678 990-7262

(G-9159)
HICKSVILLE BANK INC (HQ)
144 E High St (43526-1163)
P.O. Box 283 (43526-0283)
PHONE.................................419 542-7726
Anthony Primack, *Pr*
Lucy Hilbert, *Sr VP*
Greg Mohr, *VP*
Chad Yoder, *CFO*
Larry Coburn, *Pr*
EMP: 32 **EST:** 1910
SQ FT: 5,000
SALES (est): 6.39MM **Privately Held**
Web: www.thb.bank
SIC: 6022 State trust companies accepting deposits, commercial
PA: Empire Bancshares, Inc.
144 E High St
Hicksville OH 43526

(G-9160)
MARK MLFORD HCKSVLLE JINT TWN (PA)
Also Called: COMMUNITY MEMORIAL HOSPITAL
208 Columbus St (43526-1250)
PHONE.................................419 542-6692
Jane Zachrich, *CEO*
Susan Hobeck, *
Michelle Waggoner, *
Chuck Bohlmann, *
EMP: 200 **EST:** 1953
SQ FT: 100,000
SALES (est): 23.63MM
SALES (corp-wide): 23.63MM **Privately Held**
Web: www.cmhosp.com
SIC: 8062 Hospital, affiliated with AMA residency

(G-9161)
NEMCO INC
Also Called: Nemco Food Equipment
301 Meuse Argonne St (43526-1169)
P.O. Box 305 (43526-0305)
PHONE.................................419 542-7751
Stan Guillam, *Pr*
Kenny Moffatt, *
EMP: 70 **EST:** 1976
SALES (est): 5.01MM **Privately Held**
Web: www.nemcofoodequip.com
SIC: 5046 Restaurant equipment and supplies, nec

(G-9162)
WHOLESALE HOUSE INC (PA)
Also Called: Twh
503 W High St (43526-1037)
P.O. Box 268 (43526-0268)
PHONE.................................419 542-1315
Marcy Keesbury, *Pr*
Stephen D Height, *
◆ **EMP:** 70 **EST:** 1978
SQ FT: 74,000
SALES (est): 49.24MM
SALES (corp-wide): 49.24MM **Privately Held**
Web: www.twhouse.com
SIC: 5065 Electronic parts and equipment, nec

Highland Heights
Cuyahoga County

(G-9163)
C & S ASSOCIATES INC
Also Called: National Lien Digest
729 Miner Rd (44143-2117)
P.O. Box 24101 (44124-0101)
PHONE.................................440 461-9661
Mary B Cowan, *Pr*
Delores A Cowan, *
Greg Powelson, *
Bernie Cowan, *
Bernard J Cowan, *
EMP: 50 **EST:** 1974
SQ FT: 9,000
SALES (est): 9.06MM **Privately Held**
Web: www.ncscredit.com
SIC: 7322 2721 Collection agency, except real estate; Periodicals, publishing only

(G-9164)
COMPASSNATE HNDS STFFING SLTON
675 Alpha Dr Ste E (44143-2139)
PHONE.................................216 710-6736
Tanesha Hardy, *CEO*
Tanesha Hardy, *Managing Member*
EMP: 40 **EST:** 2020
SALES (est): 1.11MM **Privately Held**
Web: www.compassionatehandsstaffing.org
SIC: 7361 Labor contractors (employment agency)

(G-9165)
EIGHTH DAY SOUND SYSTEMS INC
5450 Avion Park Dr (44143-1919)
PHONE.................................440 995-2647
Tom Arko, *Pr*
Catherine Bellante, *
Jack Boessneck, *
▲ **EMP:** 27 **EST:** 1980
SQ FT: 27,500
SALES (est): 10.2MM
SALES (corp-wide): 51.05MM **Privately Held**
Web: www.8thdaysound.com
SIC: 1731 Sound equipment specialization
PA: Clair Global Corp.
1 Ellen Ave
Lititz PA 17543
717 626-4000

(G-9166)
HOME DEPOT USA INC
Also Called: Home Depot, The
6199 Wilson Mills Rd (44143)
PHONE.................................440 684-1343
Rick Evans, *Mgr*
EMP: 156
SALES (corp-wide): 152.67B **Publicly Held**
Web: www.homedepot.com
SIC: 5211 7359 Home centers; Tool rental
HQ: Home Depot U.S.A., Inc.
2445 Springfield Ave
Vauxhall NJ 07088

(G-9167)
KEMPER HSE HGHLAND HTS OPER LL
407 Golfview Ln (44143-4414)
PHONE.................................440 461-0600
Matthew Majher, *Contrlr*
EMP: 75 **EST:** 2014
SQ FT: 50,000
SALES (est): 3.58MM **Privately Held**
Web: www.kemperhouse.com
SIC: 8361 Aged home

(G-9168)
LAKE BUSINESS PRODUCTS INC (PA)
653 Miner Rd (44143-2115)
PHONE.................................440 953-1199
EMP: 140 **EST:** 1962
SALES (est): 20.75MM
SALES (corp-wide): 20.75MM **Privately Held**
Web: www.lakebusinessproducts.com
SIC: 5044 5065 5112 Copying equipment; Facsimile equipment; Stationery and office supplies

GEOGRAPHIC SECTION
Hilliard - Franklin County (G-9193)

(G-9169)
PHILIPS HEALTHCARE CLEVELAND
595 Miner Rd (44143-2131)
PHONE..................................440 483-3235
◆ EMP: 49 EST: 2010
SALES (est): 4.99MM Privately Held
SIC: 5047 X-ray machines and tubes

(G-9170)
RPC ELECTRONICS INC (PA)
749 Miner Rd (44143-2145)
PHONE..................................440 461-4700
Lenord Applebaum, Pr
Ira Dryer, *
▲ EMP: 33 EST: 1931
SALES (est): 9.48MM
SALES (corp-wide): 9.48MM Privately Held
Web: www.rpcelectronics.com
SIC: 5065 Electronic parts

(G-9171)
S A COMUNALE CO INC
Also Called: S.A. Comunale Co.
135 Alpha Park (44143-2224)
PHONE..................................440 684-9325
EMP: 82
SALES (corp-wide): 12.58B Publicly Held
Web: www.sacomunale.com
SIC: 1711 Mechanical contractor
HQ: S. A. Comunale Co., Inc.
2900 Newpark Dr
Barberton OH 44203
330 706-3040

(G-9172)
THINGS REMEMBERED INC
Also Called: Things Remembered
5500 Avion Park Dr (44143-1911)
PHONE..................................440 473-2000
▲ EMP: 4000
SIC: 7389 5947 Engraving service; Gift shop

(G-9173)
WINGSPAN CARE GROUP (PA)
463 Lowell Dr (44143-3619)
PHONE..................................216 932-2800
Adam G Jacobs Ph.d., Pr
EMP: 44 EST: 2002
SALES (est): 12.58MM Privately Held
Web: www.wingspancg.org
SIC: 8621 Medical field-related associations

Hilliard
Franklin County

(G-9174)
3C TECHNOLOGY SOLUTIONS LLC
2786 Walcutt Rd (43026-9209)
P.O. Box 816 (43026-0816)
PHONE..................................614 319-4681
Jeremy Fultz, Prin
EMP: 33 EST: 2010
SALES (est): 5.94MM Privately Held
Web: www.3ctechs.com
SIC: 7373 Computer systems analysis and design

(G-9175)
ACCELERATED HEALTH SYSTEMS LLC
3780 Ridge Mill Dr (43026-7458)
PHONE..................................614 334-5135
EMP: 32
Web: www.athletico.com
SIC: 8049 Physical therapist
HQ: Accelerated Health Systems, Llc
2122 York Rd Ste 300
Oak Brook IL 60523
630 575-6200

(G-9176)
ALL TRUCKS INC
5185 Tarlton Blvd (43026-2656)
PHONE..................................614 800-4595
Jatinder Bhamgu, CEO
EMP: 30 EST: 2012
SALES (est): 2.15MM Privately Held
SIC: 4212 Local trucking, without storage

(G-9177)
AMAZON DATA SERVICES INC
5101 Hayden Run Rd (43026-9457)
PHONE..................................206 617-0149
EMP: 34
SIC: 7379 Computer related consulting services
HQ: Amazon Data Services, Inc.
410 Terry Ave N
Seattle WA 98109

(G-9178)
AMERICAN REGENT INC
4150 Lyman Dr (43026-1230)
PHONE..................................614 436-2222
Joseph Kenneth Keller, CEO
EMP: 100
Web: www.americanregent.com
SIC: 2834 5122 Pharmaceutical preparations; Pharmaceuticals
HQ: American Regent, Inc.
5 Ramsay Rd
Shirley NY 11967
631 924-4000

(G-9179)
ARAMARK
Also Called: Aramark
2800 Walker Rd (43026-8313)
PHONE..................................614 921-7495
EMP: 69 EST: 2015
SALES (est): 259.8K Privately Held
Web: aramark.dejobs.org
SIC: 8733 Medical research

(G-9180)
ARCTIC EXPRESS INC
4277 Lyman Dr (43026-1227)
P.O. Box 129 (43026-0129)
PHONE..................................614 876-4008
Richard E Durst, CEO
EMP: 111 EST: 1981
SQ FT: 12,100
SALES (est): 15.14MM Privately Held
Web: www.arcticexpress.com
SIC: 4213 Contract haulers

(G-9181)
BAESMAN GROUP INC (PA)
4477 Reynolds Dr (43026-1261)
PHONE..................................614 771-2300
EMP: 91 EST: 1952
SALES (est): 22.34MM
SALES (corp-wide): 22.34MM Privately Held
Web: www.baesman.com
SIC: 2752 7331 2791 2789 Commercial printing, lithographic; Direct mail advertising services; Typesetting; Bookbinding and related work

(G-9182)
BALAJI D LOGANATHAN
Also Called: Spritle Software
6352 Pinefield Dr (43026-7704)
PHONE..................................614 918-0411
Balaji D Loganathan, Prin
EMP: 130 EST: 2021
SALES (est): 1.69MM Privately Held
SIC: 7371 7389 Software programming applications; Business Activities at Non-Commercial Site

(G-9183)
BLESSING HOME HEALTH CARE INC
5214 Tarlmeadows Ln (43026-2649)
PHONE..................................614 329-2086
Mohamed Warmahaye, Pr
EMP: 30 EST: 2019
SALES (est): 764.01K Privately Held
Web: www.blessinghhc.com
SIC: 8082 7389 Home health care services; Business Activities at Non-Commercial Site

(G-9184)
BMW FINANCIAL SERVICES NA LLC (DH)
Also Called: Alphera Financial Services
5550 Britton Pkwy (43026)
PHONE..................................614 718-6900
Ed Robinson, CEO
EMP: 45 EST: 1984
SQ FT: 118,000
SALES (est): 456.49MM
SALES (corp-wide): 169.02B Privately Held
Web: www.bmwusa.com
SIC: 6159 Automobile finance leasing
HQ: Bmw Of North America, Llc
300 Chestnut Ridge Rd
Woodcliff Lake NJ 07677
800 831-1117

(G-9185)
BRUNER CORPORATION (PA)
Also Called: Honeywell Authorized Dealer
3637 Lacon Rd (43026-1202)
PHONE..................................614 334-9000
Randy Sleeper, CEO
Mark Wenger, *
EMP: 175 EST: 1958
SQ FT: 4,200
SALES (est): 45.91MM
SALES (corp-wide): 45.91MM Privately Held
Web: www.honeywell.com
SIC: 1711 Plumbing contractors

(G-9186)
BUCK AND SONS LDSCP SVC INC
7147 Hayden Run Rd (43026-7792)
P.O. Box 1119 (43026-6119)
PHONE..................................614 876-5359
Charles William Buck, CEO
Steven A Buck, *
Mark Meyers, *
EMP: 40 EST: 1972
SQ FT: 20,000
SALES (est): 2.48MM Privately Held
Web: www.buckandsons.com
SIC: 0782 1711 Landscape contractors; Irrigation sprinkler system installation

(G-9187)
CARDINAL ORTHOPEDIC INSTITUTE
Also Called: Greater Ohio Orthpd Surgeons
3777 Trueman Ct (43026-2496)
PHONE..................................614 488-1816
Jaren Bombach Md, Pr
Beth Locket, Mgr
EMP: 27 EST: 1960
SQ FT: 1,500
SALES (est): 605.32K Privately Held
Web: www.orthopedicone.com
SIC: 8011 Orthopedic physician

(G-9188)
CARESOURCE MANAGEMENT GROUP CO
3455 Mill Run Dr (43026-9078)
PHONE..................................614 221-3370
EMP: 40
SIC: 6321 Health insurance carriers
PA: Caresource Management Group Co.
230 N Main St
Dayton OH 45402

(G-9189)
COLUMBUS HUMANE
3015 Scioto Darby Executive Ct (43026-8990)
PHONE..................................614 777-7387
Dan C Knapp, Dir
EMP: 118 EST: 1883
SQ FT: 32,000
SALES (est): 5.34MM Privately Held
Web: www.columbushumane.org
SIC: 8699 Animal humane society

(G-9190)
CREDIT UNION OF OHIO INC (PA)
5500 Britton Pkwy (43026-7456)
PHONE..................................614 487-6650
Susan Birkhimer, CEO
EMP: 30 EST: 1967
SQ FT: 10,000
SALES (est): 9.34MM
SALES (corp-wide): 9.34MM Privately Held
Web: www.cuofohio.org
SIC: 6061 Federal credit unions

(G-9191)
DEDICATED NURSING ASSOC INC
3535 Fishinger Blvd Ste 140 (43026-7505)
PHONE..................................866 450-5550
EMP: 124
Web: www.dedicatednurses.com
SIC: 7361 7363 8051 Nurses' registry; Medical help service; Skilled nursing care facilities
PA: Dedicated Nursing Associates, Inc.
6536 State Route 22
Delmont PA 15626

(G-9192)
DFS CORPORATE SERVICES LLC
Also Called: Discover Card Services
3311 Mill Meadow Dr (43026-9088)
P.O. Box 3025 (43054-3025)
PHONE..................................614 777-7020
Mike Devario, Mgr
EMP: 50
SALES (corp-wide): 20.61B Publicly Held
Web: www.discoverglobalnetwork.com
SIC: 7389 7322 Credit card service; Adjustment and collection services
HQ: Dfs Corporate Services Llc
2500 Lake Cook Rd 2
Riverwoods IL 60015
224 405-0900

(G-9193)
EASTERSALS CNTL SOUTHEAST OHIO
Also Called: Easter Sals Cntl Sthast Ohio I
3830 Trueman Ct (43026-2496)
PHONE..................................614 228-5523
Pandora Shaw-dupras, CEO
Joanie Johnson, *
EMP: 110 EST: 1945
SALES (est): 6.07MM
SALES (corp-wide): 57.97MM Privately Held
Web: www.easterseals.com
SIC: 8322 Social service center
PA: Easter Seals, Inc.
141 W Jackson Blvd 1400a
Chicago IL 60604
312 726-6200

Hilliard - Franklin County (G-9194)

GEOGRAPHIC SECTION

(G-9194)
ECOPLUMBERS LLC
4691 Northwest Pkwy (43026-1126)
PHONE..................................614 299-9903
Aaron Gynor, *Managing Member*
Michael Barnhart, *CFO*
EMP: 34 **EST:** 2007
SALES (est): 10.68MM **Privately Held**
Web: www.geteco.com
SIC: 1711 Plumbing contractors

(G-9195)
EQUITY CNSTR SOLUTIONS LLC (PA)
Also Called: Equity Real Estate
4653 Trueman Blvd Ste 100 (43026-2490)
PHONE..................................614 802-2900
Steve Wathen, *CEO*
Patrick Wathen, *OF ECH*
Dave Jones, *OF ECS*
Ryan Moore, *CFO*
EMP: 45 **EST:** 1989
SQ FT: 9,000
SALES (est): 57.68MM **Privately Held**
Web: www.equity.net
SIC: 1542 1541 6552 Commercial and office building, new construction; Industrial buildings, new construction, nec; Subdividers and developers, nec

(G-9196)
EQUITY LLC
4653 Trueman Blvd Ste 100 (43026-2490)
PHONE..................................614 802-2900
Steve Wathen, *CEO*
Patrick Wathen, *Pr*
Ryan Moore, *CFO*
EMP: 70 **EST:** 2015
SALES (est): 8.75MM **Privately Held**
SIC: 1542 1541 6552 Commercial and office building, new construction; Industrial buildings, new construction, nec; Subdividers and developers, nec

(G-9197)
GREENIX HOLDINGS LLC
4635 Oracle Ln (43026-7488)
PHONE..................................614 961-7378
EMP: 70
SALES (corp-wide): 61.55MM **Privately Held**
Web: www.greenixpc.com
SIC: 7342 Pest control in structures
PA: Greenix Holdings, Llc
  1280 S 800 E Ste 200
  Orem UT 84097
  801 820-4619

(G-9198)
HI-WAY PAVING INC
4343 Weaver Ct N (43026-1193)
P.O. Box 550 (43026-0550)
PHONE..................................614 876-1700
Charles L Keith, *CEO*
James Taylor, *
Brad Allison, *
Mark Lamonte, *
Dustin P Keith, *
EMP: 100 **EST:** 1969
SQ FT: 9,500
SALES (est): 21.63MM **Privately Held**
Web: www.hiwaypaving.com
SIC: 1611 Concrete construction: roads, highways, sidewalks, etc.

(G-9199)
HILLIARD FAMILY MEDICINE INC
Also Called: Hilliard Family Dentistry
3958 Leap Rd Ste 101 (43026-3107)
PHONE..................................614 876-8989
Joseph M Jeu Md, *Pr*
EMP: 31 **EST:** 1984
SALES (est): 3.46MM **Privately Held**
Web: www.hilliardfamilydentistry.com
SIC: 8011 General and family practice, physician/surgeon

(G-9200)
HILLIARD HLTH RHBILITATION INC
Also Called: DARBY GLENN NURSING AND REHABI
4787 Tremont Club Dr (43026-5034)
PHONE..................................614 777-6001
Dionne Nicol, *Owner*
EMP: 52 **EST:** 2010
SALES (est): 8.97MM **Privately Held**
Web: www.darbyglenn.com
SIC: 8051 Convalescent home with continuous nursing care

(G-9201)
HILLIARD OPERATOR LLC
Also Called: Hilliard Asssted Lving Mmory C
4303 Trueman Blvd (43026-2631)
PHONE..................................614 503-4414
EMP: 1199
SALES (corp-wide): 108.41MM **Privately Held**
Web: www.spectrumretirement.com
SIC: 8361 Aged home
HQ: Hilliard Operator, Llc
  4600 S Syracuse St Fl 11
  Denver CO 80237
  303 360-8812

(G-9202)
HUNTINGTON NATIONAL BANK
1880 Hilliard Rome Rd (43026-7565)
PHONE..................................614 480-4500
Robert Gray, *Brnch Mgr*
EMP: 36
SALES (corp-wide): 10.84B **Publicly Held**
Web: www.huntington.com
SIC: 6029 6021 Commercial banks, nec; National trust companies with deposits, commercial
HQ: The Huntington National Bank
  41 S High St
  Columbus OH 43215
  614 480-4293

(G-9203)
HYO OK INC
4315 Cosgray Rd (43026-7786)
PHONE..................................614 876-7644
Yun Kin, *Pr*
EMP: 30 **EST:** 2009
SALES (est): 159.81K **Privately Held**
SIC: 7219 Garment alteration and repair shop

(G-9204)
INDUS HILLIARD HOTEL LLC
Also Called: Hampton Inn Stes Clmbus Hllard
3950 Lyman Dr (43026-1210)
PHONE..................................614 334-1800
Janet Boissy, *Prin*
David Patel, *Prin*
EMP: 50 **EST:** 2016
SALES (est): 1.14MM **Privately Held**
Web: www.hilton.com
SIC: 7011 Hotels

(G-9205)
INTERNTNAL PDTS SRCING GROUP I (HQ)
Also Called: Ipsg / Micro Center
4119 Leap Rd (43026-1117)
P.O. Box 910 (43026-0910)
PHONE..................................614 850-3000
Richard Mershad, *Pr*
▲ **EMP:** 56 **EST:** 2003
SQ FT: 125,000
SALES (est): 49.66MM
SALES (corp-wide): 824.57MM **Privately Held**
SIC: 5045 Computers, peripherals, and software
PA: Micro Electronics, Inc.
  4119 Leap Rd
  Hilliard OH 43026
  614 850-3000

(G-9206)
JMD ARCHITECTURAL PDTS INC
Also Called: J.M.D. Architectural Products
2240 Venus Dr (43026-8124)
PHONE..................................614 527-0306
Darren Taylor, *VP*
EMP: 28
SALES (corp-wide): 3.83MM **Privately Held**
Web: www.jmdinc.com
SIC: 1793 Glass and glazing work
PA: J.M.D. Architectural Products, Inc.
  8200 Flick Rd
  Tipp City OH 45371
  937 667-5806

(G-9207)
JOHN ERAMO & SONS INC
3670 Lacon Rd (43026-1223)
PHONE..................................614 777-0020
Christopher Eramo, *CEO*
Rocco A Eramo, *
Anthony J Eramo, *
John T Eramo, *
Christopher D Eramo, *
EMP: 70 **EST:** 1966
SQ FT: 6,000
SALES (est): 13.98MM **Privately Held**
Web: www.eramo.com
SIC: 1794 Excavation and grading, building construction

(G-9208)
KELLER WILLIAMS REALTY ATLANTA
Also Called: Keller Williams Realtors
3535 Fishinger Blvd Ste 100 (43026-7504)
PHONE..................................614 406-5461
Ava Cooper, *Ch*
EMP: 47 **EST:** 2019
SALES (est): 165.16K **Privately Held**
Web: www.kw.com
SIC: 6531 Real estate agent, residential

(G-9209)
LASERFLEX CORPORATION (HQ)
Also Called: Laserflex
3649 Parkway Ln (43026-1214)
PHONE..................................614 850-9600
Ken Kinkopf, *Pr*
EMP: 62 **EST:** 1992
SQ FT: 75,000
SALES (est): 22.35MM **Publicly Held**
Web: www.customlasercuttingservices.com
SIC: 7389 7699 7692 3599 Metal cutting services; Industrial machinery and equipment repair; Welding repair; Machine shop, jobbing and repair
PA: Ryerson Holding Corporation
  227 W Monroe St Fl 27
  Chicago IL 60606

(G-9210)
LOWES HOME CENTERS LLC
Also Called: Lowe's
3600 Park Mill Run Dr (43026-8123)
PHONE..................................614 529-5900
EMP: 138
SALES (corp-wide): 86.38B **Publicly Held**
Web: www.lowes.com
SIC: 5211 5031 5722 5064 Home centers; Building materials, exterior; Household appliance stores; Electrical appliances, television and radio
HQ: Lowe's Home Centers, Llc
  1000 Lowes Blvd
  Mooresville NC 28117
  336 658-4000

(G-9211)
METRO FITNESS HILLIARD
3440 Heritage Club Dr (43026-3326)
PHONE..................................614 850-0070
EMP: 43 **EST:** 2019
SALES (est): 443.56K **Privately Held**
Web: www.metrofitnessgymhilliardoh.com
SIC: 7991 Health club

(G-9212)
METRO HEATING AND AC CO
Also Called: Metro Air
4731 Northwest Pkwy (43026-3102)
PHONE..................................614 777-1237
Frank J Tate Junior, *Pr*
EMP: 35 **EST:** 1990
SQ FT: 5,000
SALES (est): 5.84MM **Privately Held**
Web: www.metroheatingandair.com
SIC: 1711 Warm air heating and air conditioning contractor

(G-9213)
METROPOLITAN ENVMTL SVCS INC
5055 Nike Dr (43026-9692)
PHONE..................................614 771-1881
Rick Gaffey, *Pr*
Rick Gaffey, *Pr*
Erick Zeigler, *
James Aman, *
EMP: 90 **EST:** 1993
SQ FT: 10,000
SALES (est): 10.1MM
SALES (corp-wide): 191.56MM **Privately Held**
Web: www.metenviro.com
SIC: 7349 1794 1629 Cleaning service, industrial or commercial; Excavation work; Dredging contractor
PA: Carylon Corporation
  2000 Palm Bch Lkes Blvd S
  West Palm Beach FL 33409
  561 323-4737

(G-9214)
MICRO CENTER INC (HQ)
4119 Leap Rd (43026-1117)
PHONE..................................614 850-3000
Richard Mershad, *CEO*
EMP: 34 **EST:** 1979
SALES (est): 39.23MM
SALES (corp-wide): 824.57MM **Privately Held**
Web: www.microcenter.com
SIC: 5734 5045 Computer and software stores; Computers, peripherals, and software
PA: Micro Electronics, Inc.
  4119 Leap Rd
  Hilliard OH 43026
  614 850-3000

(G-9215)
MICRO ELECTRONICS INC
Also Called: Micro Thinner
4055 Leap Rd (43026-1115)
P.O. Box 848 (43026-0848)
PHONE..................................614 850-3410
Jim Koehler, *Mgr*
EMP: 79

GEOGRAPHIC SECTION
Hilliard - Franklin County (G-9239)

SALES (corp-wide): 824.57MM **Privately Held**
Web: www.microcenter.com
SIC: **5734** 5045 Personal computers; Computer peripheral equipment
PA: Micro Electronics, Inc.
4119 Leap Rd
Hilliard OH 43026
614 850-3000

(G-9216)
MILL RUN CARE CENTER LLC
Also Called: MILL RUN GARDENS & CARE CENTER
3399 Mill Run Dr (43026-9078)
PHONE.................614 527-3000
EMP: 49 EST: 1997
SALES (est): 6.84MM **Privately Held**
Web: www.optalishealthcare.com
SIC: **8059** 8052 8051 Nursing home, except skilled and intermediate care facility; Intermediate care facilities; Skilled nursing care facilities

(G-9217)
MILLS/JAMES INC
Also Called: Mills James Productions
3545 Fishinger Blvd (43026-9550)
PHONE.................614 777-9333
Cameron James, *CEO*
Ken Mills, *
EMP: 130 EST: 1984
SQ FT: 47,000
SALES (est): 24.33MM **Privately Held**
Web: www.millsjames.com
SIC: **7819** 7812 Services allied to motion pictures; Motion picture production and distribution

(G-9218)
MOUNT CARMEL HEALTH
4674 Britton Pkwy (43026-9823)
PHONE.................614 527-8674
EMP: 102
SALES (corp-wide): 2.49B **Privately Held**
Web: www.mountcarmelhealth.com
SIC: **8062** General medical and surgical hospitals
HQ: Mount Carmel Health
5300 N Meadows Dr
Grove City OH 43123
614 234-5000

(G-9219)
MOUNT CARMEL HEALTH SYSTEM
3617 Heritage Club Dr (43026-1313)
PHONE.................614 876-1260
EMP: 242
SALES (corp-wide): 2.49B **Privately Held**
Web: www.mountcarmelhealth.com
SIC: **8011** Offices and clinics of medical doctors
HQ: Mount Carmel Health System
1039 Kingsmill Pkwy
Columbus OH 43229
614 234-6000

(G-9220)
NATIONWIDE CHILDRENS HOSPITAL
Also Called: Children's Hospital Outpatient
3955 Brown Park Dr Ste C (43026-3137)
PHONE.................614 355-8200
EMP: 127
SALES (corp-wide): 3.6B **Privately Held**
Web: www.nationwidechildrens.org
SIC: **8069** 8071 Childrens' hospital; Medical laboratories
PA: Nationwide Children's Hospital
700 Childrens Dr
Columbus OH 43205
614 722-2000

(G-9221)
NORTHWEST OBSTTRICS GYNCLOGY A
Also Called: Northwest Ob Gyn
3841 Trueman Ct (43026-2496)
PHONE.................614 777-4801
Karen G King, *Pr*
Alyson H Leeman, *Sec*
EMP: 38 EST: 1997
SALES (est): 5.8MM **Privately Held**
Web: www.obgynhilliardohio.com
SIC: **8011** Gynecologist

(G-9222)
OHIO HEALTH INFO PARTNR INC
3455 Mill Run Dr Ste 315 (43026-9491)
PHONE.................614 664-2600
Dan Paoletti, *CEO*
Frank Schoffler, *
Frederick Richards, *
Kathleen M Farrell, *
EMP: 29 EST: 2010
SALES (est): 8.02MM **Privately Held**
Web: www.clinisync.org
SIC: **8742** Hospital and health services consultant

(G-9223)
OHIO STATE HOME SERVICES INC
Everdry Waterproofing Columbus
4271 Weaver Ct N (43026-1132)
PHONE.................614 850-5600
Ken Barnett, *Mgr*
EMP: 80
SQ FT: 1,700
SALES (corp-wide): 48.55MM **Privately Held**
Web: www.everdrycolumbus.com
SIC: **1799** 1794 1741 Waterproofing; Excavation and grading, building construction; Foundation building
PA: Ohio State Home Services, Inc.
365 Highland Rd E
Macedonia OH 44056
330 467-1055

(G-9224)
OPEN TEXT INC
Also Called: Open Text
3671 Ridge Mill Dr (43026-7752)
PHONE.................614 658-3588
Anik Ganguly, *Mgr*
EMP: 50
SALES (corp-wide): 832.31MM **Privately Held**
Web: www.opentext.com
SIC: **7372** Prepackaged software
HQ: Open Text Inc.
2440 Sand Hill Rd Ste 302
Menlo Park CA 94025
650 645-3000

(G-9225)
ORTHOPEDIC ONE INC
Also Called: Orthopedic One
3777 Trueman Ct (43026-2496)
PHONE.................614 488-1816
Jenelle Wood, *Brnch Mgr*
EMP: 40
Web: www.orthopedicone.com
SIC: **8011** Orthopedic physician
PA: Orthopedic One, Inc.
170 Taylor Station Rd # 260
Columbus OH 43213

(G-9226)
PARKINS INCORPORATED
Also Called: Hampton Inn
3950 Lyman Dr (43026-1210)
PHONE.................614 334-1800
EMP: 44 EST: 2006
SALES (est): 486.3K **Privately Held**
Web: www.hilton.com
SIC: **7011** Hotels and motels

(G-9227)
PREMIUM BEVERAGE SUPPLY LTD
3701 Lacon Rd (43026-1202)
PHONE.................614 777-1007
Ron Wilson, *Prin*
▲ EMP: 92 EST: 1995
SALES (est): 5.36MM **Privately Held**
Web: www.premiumbeveragesupply.com
SIC: **5921** 5182 Beer (packaged); Wine and distilled beverages

(G-9228)
RDP FOODSERVICE LTD
4200 Parkway Ct (43026-1200)
P.O. Box 14866 (43214-0866)
PHONE.................614 261-5661
EMP: 72 EST: 1995
SQ FT: 30,000
SALES (est): 58.81MM **Privately Held**
Web: www.rdpfoodservice.com
SIC: **5149** 5087 Pizza supplies; Restaurant supplies

(G-9229)
SCIOTO DARBY CONCRETE INC
4540 Edgewyn Ave (43026-1222)
PHONE.................614 876-3114
David M Hamilton, *Pr*
EMP: 70 EST: 1978
SQ FT: 20,000
SALES (est): 7.05MM **Privately Held**
Web: www.sciotodarby.com
SIC: **1771** Concrete pumping

(G-9230)
SEDGWICK CMS HOLDINGS INC
Also Called: Sedgwick CMS
3455 Mill Run Dr (43026-9078)
PHONE.................614 658-0900
Mary Heyineman, *Mgr*
EMP: 714
Web: www.sedgwick.com
SIC: **6411** Insurance claim adjusters, not employed by insurance company
PA: Sedgwick Cms Holdings, Inc.
1100 Rdgway Loop Rd Ste 2
Memphis TN 38120

(G-9231)
SIGNATURE DERMATOLOGY LLC
3853 Trueman Ct (43026-2496)
PHONE.................614 777-1200
Marya Cassandra, *Prin*
Andrea Costanza, *Prin*
EMP: 34 EST: 2008
SALES (est): 4.61MM **Privately Held**
Web: www.signaturedermatology.com
SIC: **8011** Dermatologist

(G-9232)
SIMPLE BATH LTD
4235 Leap Rd (43026-1125)
PHONE.................614 888-2284
William R Mcmaster, *Pr*
EMP: 35 EST: 2011
SALES (est): 3.2MM **Privately Held**
Web: www.simplebathohio.net
SIC: **1521** Single-family home remodeling, additions, and repairs

(G-9233)
SPIRES MOTORS INC
Also Called: Buckeye Honda
3820 Parkway Ln (43026-1217)
P.O. Box 189 (43130-0189)
PHONE.................614 771-2345
Gerald J Spires, *Pr*
Dennis E Spires, *
Tim Spires, *
William B Schuck, *
EMP: 42 EST: 1984
SQ FT: 10,000
SALES (est): 6.31MM **Privately Held**
Web: www.buckeyenissan.com
SIC: **5511** 7538 Automobiles, new and used; General automotive repair shops

(G-9234)
SUTPHEN TOWERS INC
4500 Sutphen Ct (43026)
P.O. Box 158 (43002)
PHONE.................614 876-1262
EMP: 81 EST: 1978
SALES (est): 19.23MM **Privately Held**
Web: www.sutphen.com
SIC: **3713** 7538 Truck bodies and parts; Truck engine repair, except industrial

(G-9235)
TALX CORPORATION
3455 Mill Run Dr (43026-8673)
PHONE.................614 527-9404
Kathy Couglin, *Mgr*
EMP: 63
SALES (corp-wide): 5.27B **Publicly Held**
Web: workforce.equifax.com
SIC: **7373** Systems software development services
HQ: Talx Corporation
11432 Lackland Rd
Saint Louis MO 63146
314 214-7000

(G-9236)
TEAM RAHAL INC
Also Called: Rahal Land and Racing
4601 Lyman Dr (43026-1249)
PHONE.................614 529-7000
◆ EMP: 65 EST: 1995
SQ FT: 30,000
SALES (est): 5.07MM **Privately Held**
Web: www.rahal.com
SIC: **7948** Motor vehicle racing and drivers

(G-9237)
TEN PIN ALLEY
5499 Ten Pin Aly (43026-1042)
PHONE.................614 876-2475
Brent Garland, *Prin*
EMP: 43 EST: 2006
SQ FT: 15,000
SALES (est): 611.26K **Privately Held**
Web: www.bowlero.com
SIC: **5813** 7933 Cocktail lounge; Ten pin center

(G-9238)
UPPER ARLINGTON LUTHERAN CH
3500 Mill Run Dr (43026-7770)
PHONE.................614 451-3736
Pastor Paul Uring, *Prin*
EMP: 35 EST: 1956
SALES (est): 2.62MM **Privately Held**
Web: www.ualc.org
SIC: **8661** 8351 Lutheran Church; Preschool center

(G-9239)
VANNER INC
4282 Reynolds Dr (43026-1297)
PHONE.................614 771-2718
Chris Collet, *VP*
EMP: 73 EST: 1996
SALES (est): 18.59MM **Privately Held**
Web: www.vanner.com
SIC: **8711** Electrical or electronic engineering

Hilliard - Franklin County (G-9240) — GEOGRAPHIC SECTION

(G-9240)
VERIZON NEW YORK INC
Also Called: Verizon
5000 Britton Pkwy (43026-9445)
PHONE..................614 301-2498
Joseph Barbarita, *Brnch Mgr*
EMP: 1844
SALES (corp-wide): 133.97B **Publicly Held**
Web: www.verizon.com
SIC: 4812 Cellular telephone services
HQ: Verizon New York Inc.
140 West St
New York NY 10007
212 395-1000

(G-9241)
W W WILLIAMS COMPANY LLC
Also Called: Williams Dtroit Diesel-Allison
3535 Parkway Ln (43026-1214)
PHONE..................614 527-9400
Jason Milligan, *Genl Mgr*
EMP: 35
SALES (corp-wide): 1.47B **Privately Held**
Web: www.wwwilliams.com
SIC: 7538 General truck repair
HQ: The W W Williams Company Llc
400 Metro Pl N Ste 201
Dublin OH 43017
614 228-5000

(G-9242)
WHITE GORILLA CORPORATION
6218 Lampton Pond Dr (43026-7188)
PHONE..................202 384-6486
Rondell Earvin, *Sec*
EMP: 28 **EST:** 2018
SALES (est): 180.97K **Privately Held**
SIC: 8699 Charitable organization

(G-9243)
WILLIS SPANGLER STARLING
4635 Trueman Blvd (43026-2491)
PHONE..................614 586-7900
EMP: 51 **EST:** 2019
SALES (est): 4.59MM **Privately Held**
Web: www.willisattorneys.com
SIC: 8111 General practice attorney, lawyer

(G-9244)
WIRELESS MASTER LLC ⬧
Also Called: Wireless Masters
4340 Lyman Dr (43026-1243)
PHONE..................877 995-5888
Mike Abulaban, *Managing Member*
EMP: 85 **EST:** 2022
SALES (est): 4.17MM **Privately Held**
SIC: 4899 Data communication services

(G-9245)
WIRELESS PARTNERS LLC
4485 Cemetery Rd (43026-1120)
PHONE..................614 850-0040
EMP: 121
Web: www.wirelesspartners.org
SIC: 4812 Cellular telephone services

(G-9246)
WOLF AND WOOF LLC
Also Called: Camp Bow Wow
5100 Nike Dr Ste B (43026-7462)
PHONE..................614 527-2267
Lori L Thelen, *Prin*
EMP: 30 **EST:** 2009
SALES (est): 641.63K **Privately Held**
Web: www.campbowwow.com
SIC: 0752 Grooming services, pet and animal specialties

(G-9247)
YASHCO SYSTEMS INC
3974 Brown Park Dr (43026-1168)
PHONE..................614 467-4600
Simren Datta, *Pr*
Sheetal Datta, *Sr VP*
EMP: 92 **EST:** 2000
SALES (est): 7.44MM **Privately Held**
Web: www.yashco.com
SIC: 8748 7371 Business consulting, nec; Custom computer programming services

Hillsboro
Highland County

(G-9248)
ADENA HEALTH SYSTEM
Also Called: Urgent Care-Hillsboro
160 Roberts Ln Ste A (45133-7616)
P.O. Box 985 (45177-0985)
PHONE..................937 383-1040
Michael Choo, *Prin*
EMP: 31
SALES (corp-wide): 678.56MM **Privately Held**
Web: www.adena.org
SIC: 8062 Hospital, med school affiliated with nursing and residency
PA: Adena Health System
272 Hospital Rd
Chillicothe OH 45601
740 779-7500

(G-9249)
BEAZER EAST INC
Plum Run Stone Division
4281 Roush Rd (45133-9147)
PHONE..................937 364-2311
J Craig Morgan, *Mgr*
EMP: 35
SALES (corp-wide): 23.02B **Privately Held**
SIC: 3281 3273 1422 Stone, quarrying and processing of own stone products; Ready-mixed concrete; Crushed and broken limestone
HQ: Beazer East, Inc.
600 River Ave Ste 200
Pittsburgh PA 15212
412 428-9407

(G-9250)
BUCKEYE CHECK CASHING INC
583 Harry Sauner Rd (45133-9507)
PHONE..................937 393-9087
EMP: 35
Web: www.ccfi.com
SIC: 6099 Check cashing agencies
HQ: Buckeye Check Cashing, Inc.
5165 Emerald Pkwy Ste 100
Dublin OH 43017
614 798-5900

(G-9251)
CONGREGATE LIVING OF AMERICA
Also Called: Crestwood Rdge Sklled Nrsing R
141 Willetsville Pike (45133-9476)
PHONE..................937 393-6700
Ramona Stapleton, *Admn*
EMP: 59
SALES (corp-wide): 8.88MM **Privately Held**
SIC: 8052 8051 Intermediate care facilities; Skilled nursing care facilities
PA: Congregate Living Of America, Inc
463 E Pike St
Morrow OH 45152
513 899-2801

(G-9252)
CVS REVCO DS INC
Also Called: CVS
1400 N High St (45133-8514)
PHONE..................937 393-4218
Winnie Jeffries, *Mgr*
EMP: 110
SALES (corp-wide): 357.78B **Publicly Held**
Web: www.cvs.com
SIC: 5912 7384 Drug stores; Photofinishing laboratory
HQ: Cvs Revco D.S., Inc.
1 Cvs Dr
Woonsocket RI 02895
401 765-1500

(G-9253)
FIFTH THIRD BNK OF STHERN OH I (HQ)
Also Called: Fifth Third Bank
511 N High St (45133-1134)
PHONE..................937 840-5353
Raymond Webb, *Pr*
EMP: 27 **EST:** 1907
SQ FT: 18,000
SALES (est): 18.26MM
SALES (corp-wide): 12.64B **Publicly Held**
SIC: 6022 6162 State trust companies accepting deposits, commercial; Mortgage bankers and loan correspondents
PA: Fifth Third Bancorp
38 Fountain Square Plz
Cincinnati OH 45263
800 972-3030

(G-9254)
GENESIS RESPIRATORY SVCS INC
109 W Main St (45133-1452)
PHONE..................937 393-4423
EMP: 29
SALES (corp-wide): 11.03MM **Privately Held**
Web: www.genesisoxygen.com
SIC: 5047 Medical equipment and supplies
PA: Genesis Respiratory Services, Inc.
4132 Gallia St
Portsmouth OH 45662
740 354-4363

(G-9255)
HIGHLAND CNTY CMNTY ACTION ORG (PA)
Also Called: HCCAO
1487 N High St Ste 500 (45133-6812)
PHONE..................937 393-3060
Fred Berry, *Pr*
Greg Barr, *
Richard Graves, *
Julia Wise, *
Jennifer Baker, *Finance*
EMP: 35 **EST:** 1965
SALES (est): 12.51MM
SALES (corp-wide): 12.51MM **Privately Held**
Web: www.hccao.org
SIC: 8322 Social service center

(G-9256)
HIGHLAND CNTY JINT TWNSHP DST
Also Called: Highland District Hospital
1275 N High St (45133-8273)
PHONE..................937 393-6100
Jim Baer, *CEO*
Randy Lennartz, *
Paula Detterman, *
Thomas Degen, *
Eddy Maillot, *
EMP: 400 **EST:** 1914
SALES (est): 63.02MM **Privately Held**
Web: www.hdh.org

SIC: 8062 Hospital, affiliated with AMA residency

(G-9257)
HIGHLAND COMPUTER FORMS INC (PA)
Also Called: R & S Data Products
1025 W Main St (45133)
P.O. Box 831 (45133)
PHONE..................937 393-4215
Robert D Wilson, *Pr*
Philip D Wilson, *
EMP: 56 **EST:** 1979
SQ FT: 70,000
SALES (est): 22.01MM
SALES (corp-wide): 22.01MM **Privately Held**
Web: www.hcf.com
SIC: 2752 5112 Commercial printing, lithographic; Business forms

(G-9258)
HIGHLAND HEALTH PROVIDERS CORP
1402 N High St (45133-8514)
PHONE..................937 393-4899
Amanda Warix, *Ex Dir*
EMP: 67
SALES (corp-wide): 9.75MM **Privately Held**
Web: www.hhproviders.org
SIC: 8011 General and family practice, physician/surgeon
PA: Highland Health Providers Corporation
1487 N High St Ste 102
Hillsboro OH 45133
937 840-6575

(G-9259)
HOSPITAL HM HLTH SVCS HGHLAND
1275 N High St (45133-8273)
PHONE..................937 393-6371
EMP: 36 **EST:** 1994
SALES (est): 1.71MM **Privately Held**
Web: www.hdh.org
SIC: 8082 Home health care services

(G-9260)
ITW FOOD EQUIPMENT GROUP LLC
Also Called: Hobart
1495 N High St (45133-8203)
PHONE..................937 393-4271
Bill Zinno, *Mgr*
EMP: 241
SALES (corp-wide): 15.93B **Publicly Held**
Web: www.itwfoodequipment.com
SIC: 5046 Restaurant equipment and supplies, nec
HQ: Itw Food Equipment Group Llc
701 S Ridge Ave
Troy OH 45374

(G-9261)
JERRY HAAG MOTORS INC
1475 N High St (45133-9473)
PHONE..................937 402-2090
Steven R Haag, *Pr*
EMP: 32 **EST:** 1953
SQ FT: 17,700
SALES (est): 5.07MM **Privately Held**
Web: www.jerryhaagmotors.com
SIC: 5511 7538 5531 Automobiles, new and used; General automotive repair shops; Auto and home supply stores

(G-9262)
LANGSTONMC KENNA LESIA
Also Called: Langston Family Dental Clinic
321 Chillicothe Ave (45133-7378)
P.O. Box 400 (45133-0400)

GEOGRAPHIC SECTION

Holland - Lucas County (G-9283)

PHONE..................937 393-1472
Lesia Langston-mckenna, *Owner*
EMP: 33 **EST:** 1984
SQ FT: 680
SALES (est): 497.11K **Privately Held**
Web: www.langstondentalhillsboro.com
SIC: 8021 Dentists' office

(G-9263)
MERCHANTS NATIONAL BANK (HQ)
100 N High St (45133-1152)
P.O. Box 10 (45133-0010)
PHONE..................937 393-1134
Paul W Pence Junior, *CEO*
Don Fender, *
Jacob Dehart, *
EMP: 50 **EST:** 1879
SALES (est): 49.21MM
SALES (corp-wide): 28.88MM **Privately Held**
Web: www.merchantsnat.com
SIC: 6022 State commercial banks
PA: Merchants Bancorp, Inc.
100 N High St
Hillsboro OH 45133
937 393-1993

(G-9264)
OHIO HELPING HANDS CLG SVC LLC
5356 Griffith Rd (45133-8737)
PHONE..................937 402-0733
Laura Goolsby, *Prin*
EMP: 35 **EST:** 2004
SALES (est): 499.1K **Privately Held**
Web: www.ohiohelpinghands.com
SIC: 7349 Cleaning service, industrial or commercial

(G-9265)
ORTHOPEDIC CONS CINCINNATI
1275 N High St (45133-8273)
PHONE..................937 393-6169
EMP: 33
SALES (corp-wide): 20.42MM **Privately Held**
Web: www.orthocincy.com
SIC: 8011 Orthopedic physician
PA: Orthopedic Consultants Of Cincinnati
7798 Discovery Dr Ste A
West Chester OH 45069
513 733-8894

(G-9266)
PAS TECHNOLOGIES INC
Also Called: Standardaero
214 Hobart Dr (45133-9487)
PHONE..................937 840-1053
Mark Greene, *Mgr*
EMP: 100
Web: www.standardaerocomponents.com
SIC: 3724 7699 Aircraft engines and engine parts; Aircraft and heavy equipment repair services
HQ: Pas Technologies Inc.
1234 Atlantic Ave
North Kansas City MO 64116

(G-9267)
PIKE NATURAL GAS COMPANY
144 Bowers Ave (45133-1532)
P.O. Box 249 (45133-0249)
PHONE..................937 393-4602
Robert Seeling, *VP*
EMP: 67 **EST:** 1954
SQ FT: 7,500
SALES (est): 2.43MM
SALES (corp-wide): 8.21MM **Privately Held**
Web: www.utilitypipelineltd.com

SIC: 4924 Natural gas distribution
PA: Clearfield Ohio Holdings Inc
Radnor Corp Ctr Bldg 5 St
Radnor PA 19087
610 293-0410

(G-9268)
XPO LOGISTICS FREIGHT INC
5215 Us Highway 50 (45133-9166)
PHONE..................937 364-2361
James New, *Mgr*
EMP: 28
SALES (corp-wide): 7.74B **Publicly Held**
Web: www.xpo.com
SIC: 4213 Contract haulers
HQ: Xpo Logistics Freight, Inc.
2211 Old Erhart Rd Ste 10
Ann Arbor MI 48105
800 755-2728

Hinckley
Medina County

(G-9269)
DUTCH VALLEY HOME INC
222 Concord Ln (44233-9662)
P.O. Box 53 (44233-0053)
PHONE..................330 273-8322
EMP: 185 **EST:** 1994
SALES (est): 8.46MM **Privately Held**
Web: www.dutchvalleyhomes.com
SIC: 1521 New construction, single-family houses

(G-9270)
ICON GOVERNMENT (HQ)
1265 Ridge Rd Ste A (44233-9801)
PHONE..................330 278-2643
EMP: 356 **EST:** 2015
SALES (est): 55.34MM **Privately Held**
SIC: 8731 8732 Medical research, commercial; Commercial nonphysical research
PA: Icon Public Limited Company
Legal Department
Dublin 18

(G-9271)
PINE HILLS GOLF CLUB INC
433 W 130th St (44233-9566)
PHONE..................330 225-4477
William Gertrack, *Pr*
Scott Forester, *
EMP: 27 **EST:** 1955
SQ FT: 5,820
SALES (est): 259.88K **Privately Held**
SIC: 7992 Public golf courses

(G-9272)
THE GREAT LAKES CONSTRUCTION CO
Also Called: Tglcc
2608 Great Lakes Way (44233-9590)
PHONE..................330 220-3900
EMP: 125 **EST:** 1946
SALES (est): 52.25MM
SALES (corp-wide): 96.25MM **Privately Held**
Web: www.greatlakesway.com
SIC: 1611 1629 General contractor, highway and street construction; Land preparation construction
PA: Great Lakes Companies Inc
2608 Great Lakes Way
Hinckley OH
330 220-3900

(G-9273)
WILLIAMS SCOTSMAN INC
2643 Great Lakes Way (44233-9590)
PHONE..................216 399-6285
Justin Bryant, *Brnch Mgr*
EMP: 29
SALES (corp-wide): 2.36B **Publicly Held**
Web: www.mobilemini.com
SIC: 5085 Bins and containers, storage
HQ: Williams Scotsman, Inc.
4646 E Van Buren St # 40
Phoenix AZ 85008
480 894-6311

Hiram
Portage County

(G-9274)
GREAT LAKES CHEESE CO INC (PA)
17825 Great Lakes Pkwy (44234-9677)
P.O. Box 1806 (44234-1806)
PHONE..................440 834-2500
Gary Vanic, *Pr*
John Epprecht, *
Albert Z Meyers, *
Marcel Dasen, *
Hans Epprecht, *
◆ **EMP:** 500 **EST:** 1958
SQ FT: 218,000
SALES (est): 1.69B
SALES (corp-wide): 1.69B **Privately Held**
Web: www.greatlakescheese.com
SIC: 5143 2022 Cheese; Natural cheese

(G-9275)
PINES ALF INC
18144 Claridon Troy Rd (44234-9520)
PHONE..................330 856-4232
Michael P Slyk, *Prin*
Time Chesney, *
EMP: 35 **EST:** 2018
SALES (est): 821.33K **Privately Held**
Web: www.pinesalf.com
SIC: 8361 Aged home

Holland
Lucas County

(G-9276)
ADAMS ELEVATOR EQUIPMENT CO (DH)
Also Called: Schindler Logistics Center
1530 Timber Wolf Dr (43528-9129)
PHONE..................847 581-2900
Robert Schreck, *CEO*
▲ **EMP:** 62 **EST:** 1930
SALES (est): 13.41MM **Privately Held**
Web: www.adamselevator.com
SIC: 3312 3825 3534 5084 Locomotive wheels, rolled; Signal generators and averagers; Elevators and equipment; Materials handling machinery
HQ: Schindler Enterprises Inc.
20 Whippany Rd
Morristown NJ 07960
973 397-6500

(G-9277)
AIR TRANSPORT INTL LTD LBLTY
1750 Eber Rd Ste A (43528-7896)
PHONE..................501 615-3500
Dick Hickey, *Mgr*
EMP: 606
SIC: 4731 Freight transportation arrangement
HQ: Air Transport International Limited Liability Company
2800 Cantrell Rd Ste 500
Little Rock AR 72202

(G-9278)
ANNE GRADY CORPORATION (PA)
1525 Eber Rd (43528)
P.O. Box 1297 (43528)
PHONE..................419 380-8985
Roger Fortener, *Ex Dir*
Steve King, *
EMP: 250 **EST:** 1976
SQ FT: 70,000
SALES (est): 20.72MM
SALES (corp-wide): 20.72MM **Privately Held**
Web: www.annegrady.org
SIC: 8361 8052 Retarded home; Intermediate care facilities

(G-9279)
ANNE GRADY CORPORATION
1645 Trade Rd (43528-8204)
PHONE..................419 867-7501
David A Boston, *Ex Dir*
EMP: 140
SQ FT: 20,000
SALES (corp-wide): 20.72MM **Privately Held**
Web: www.annegrady.org
SIC: 8331 Job training and related services
PA: Anne Grady Corporation
1525 Eber Rd
Holland OH 43528
419 380-8985

(G-9280)
BLACK SWAMP STEEL INC
1761 Commerce Rd (43528-9789)
P.O. Box 1180 (43528-1180)
PHONE..................419 867-8050
Dave Coronado, *Pr*
Steve Sieracke, *
Brad Carpenter, *
Jon West, *
EMP: 27 **EST:** 1991
SALES (est): 5.36MM **Privately Held**
Web: www.blackswampsteel.com
SIC: 1791 Structural steel erection

(G-9281)
BOSTLEMAN CORP
7142 Nightingale Dr Ste 1 (43528-7851)
EMP: 50 **EST:** 1946
SALES (est): 11.68MM **Privately Held**
Web: www.bostleman.com
SIC: 1542 6552 8741 Commercial and office building, new construction; Subdividers and developers, nec; Construction management

(G-9282)
BRENNAN EQUIPMENT SERVICES CO
Also Called: Brennan Equipment Services
6940 Hall St (43528-9485)
PHONE..................419 867-6000
TOLL FREE: 800
James H Brennan, *Pr*
James H Brennan Junior, *Pr*
Thomas J Backoff, *
EMP: 30 **EST:** 1957
SQ FT: 35,000
SALES (est): 8.99MM **Privately Held**
Web: www.gobrennan.com
SIC: 5084 7359 Materials handling machinery; Industrial truck rental

(G-9283)
COUNTY OF LUCAS
Also Called: Lucas County Engineer
1049 S Mccord Rd Bldg A (43528-7020)
PHONE..................419 213-2892
Keith G Earley, *Dir*
EMP: 196
SALES (corp-wide): 569.39MM **Privately Held**

Holland - Lucas County (G-9284) — GEOGRAPHIC SECTION

Web: co.lucas.oh.us
SIC: 8711 Engineering services
PA: County Of Lucas
   1 Government Ctr Ste 600
   Toledo OH 43604
   419 213-4406

(G-9284)
COURTYARD MANAGEMENT CORP
Also Called: Courtyard By Marriott
1435 E Mall Dr (43528-9490)
PHONE...............................419 866-1001
Jamie Talberth, *Mgr*
EMP: 30
SALES (corp-wide): 23.71B **Publicly Held**
Web: courtyard.marriott.com
SIC: 7011 Hotels and motels
HQ: Courtyard Management Llc
   7750 Wisconsin Ave
   Bethesda MD 20814

(G-9285)
GLEASON CONSTRUCTION CO INC
540 S Centennial Rd (43528-8400)
PHONE...............................419 865-7480
James F Gleason, *Pr*
Carol S Gleason, *
EMP: 33 EST: 1985
SQ FT: 20,000
SALES (est): 2.84MM **Privately Held**
SIC: 1623 Underground utilities contractor

(G-9286)
HABITEC SECURITY INC (PA)
Also Called: Habitec
1545 Timber Wolf Dr (43528)
P.O. Box 352497 (43635)
PHONE...............................419 537-6768
John Smythe, *Pr*
Nancy Smythe, *
EMP: 75 EST: 1972
SQ FT: 9,000
SALES (est): 8.89MM
SALES (corp-wide): 8.89MM **Privately Held**
Web: www.habitecsecurity.com
SIC: 7382 Security systems services

(G-9287)
HAMILTON MANUFACTURING CORP
1026 Hamilton Dr (43528-8210)
PHONE...............................419 867-4858
Robin Ritz, *CEO*
Bonnie Osborne, *
Steve Alt, *
Laura Harris, *
▲ EMP: 45 EST: 1921
SQ FT: 32,000
SALES (est): 8.81MM **Privately Held**
Web: www.hamiltonmfg.com
SIC: 3172 8711 Coin purses; Designing; ship, boat, machine, and product

(G-9288)
HOBBY LOBBY STORES INC
6645 Airport Hwy (43528-8419)
PHONE...............................419 861-1862
EMP: 48
SALES (corp-wide): 1.92B **Privately Held**
Web: www.hobbylobby.com
SIC: 6794 5945 Patent owners and lessors; Children's toys and games, except dolls
PA: Hobby Lobby Stores, Inc.
   7707 Sw 44th St
   Oklahoma City OK 73119
   405 745-1100

(G-9289)
I AND T HOLDINGS INV GROUP INC
7050 Spring Meadows Dr W Ste A (43528-7203)
PHONE...............................269 207-7773
Hope Gleaves, *Prin*
EMP: 30 EST: 2020
SALES (est): 511.19K **Privately Held**
SIC: 8742 Financial consultant

(G-9290)
ITS TECHNOLOGIES INC (PA)
7060 Spring Meadows Dr W Ste D (43528-8061)
PHONE...............................419 842-2100
Roger L Radeloff, *Pr*
Barrie Howell, *
Charles M Tarband, *
EMP: 100 EST: 1985
SALES (est): 13.77MM
SALES (corp-wide): 13.77MM **Privately Held**
Web: www.wehirepeople.com
SIC: 7363 7361 Temporary help service; Employment agencies

(G-9291)
JML HOLDINGS INC
Also Called: Bassett Nut Company
6210 Merger Rd (43528-9593)
PHONE...............................419 866-7500
Jon M Levine, *Pr*
Larry J Robbins, *VP*
Jeff Williams, *COO*
◆ EMP: 33 EST: 1928
SQ FT: 12,000
SALES (est): 1.57MM **Privately Held**
Web: www.bassettnut.com
SIC: 5441 5145 2064 Nuts; Nuts, salted or roasted; Popcorn balls or other treated popcorn products

(G-9292)
KLUMM BROS
9241 W Bancroft St (43528-9731)
PHONE...............................419 829-3166
EMP: 40 EST: 2015
SALES (est): 3.17MM **Privately Held**
Web: www.klummbros.com
SIC: 1794 Excavation and grading, building construction

(G-9293)
LAKE ERIE MED SURGICAL SUP INC
6920 Hall St (43528-9485)
P.O. Box 1267 (43528-1267)
PHONE...............................734 847-3847
Jeannie Sieren, *Brnch Mgr*
EMP: 44
SALES (corp-wide): 9.12MM **Privately Held**
SIC: 5047 Medical equipment and supplies
PA: Lake Erie Medical & Surgical Supply, Inc.
   7560 Lewis Ave
   Temperance MI 48182
   734 847-3847

(G-9294)
LUTHERAN HOMES SOCIETY INC
1905 Perrysburg Holland Rd (43528-9582)
PHONE...............................419 724-1525
EMP: 165
SALES (corp-wide): 54.58MM **Privately Held**
Web: www.genacrosslutheranservices.org
SIC: 8361 Residential care
PA: Lutheran Homes Society, Inc.
   2021 N Mccord Rd
   Toledo OH 43615
   419 861-4990

(G-9295)
LUTHERAN HOMES SOCIETY INC
Also Called: Genacross Lthran Svcs - Wolf C
2001 Perrysburg Holland Rd (43528-7005)
PHONE...............................419 861-2233
EMP: 165
SALES (corp-wide): 54.58MM **Privately Held**
Web: www.genacrosslutheranservices.org
SIC: 8051 Skilled nursing care facilities
PA: Lutheran Homes Society, Inc.
   2021 N Mccord Rd
   Toledo OH 43615
   419 861-4990

(G-9296)
LUTHERAN VILLAGE AT WOLF CREEK
Also Called: CREEKSIDE CONDOMINIUMS
2001 Perrysburg Holland Rd Ofc (43528-8001)
PHONE...............................419 861-2233
Mark Gavorski, *Prin*
EMP: 46 EST: 1996
SQ FT: 113,154
SALES (est): 7.98MM **Privately Held**
Web: www.genacrosslutheranservices.org
SIC: 8059 8361 8052 8051 Rest home, with health care; Residential care; Intermediate care facilities; Skilled nursing care facilities

(G-9297)
MIDWEST CONTRACTING INC
1428 Albon Rd (43528-8683)
PHONE...............................419 866-4560
Aaron Koder, *Pr*
EMP: 45 EST: 1996
SALES (est): 12.51MM **Privately Held**
Web: www.midwest-contracting.com
SIC: 1542 Commercial and office building, new construction

(G-9298)
MILLER FIREWORKS COMPANY INC (PA)
Also Called: Miller Fireworks Novelty
501 Glengary Rd (43528-9416)
PHONE...............................419 865-7329
John F Miller Iii, *Pr*
▲ EMP: 33 EST: 1948
SQ FT: 2,520
SALES (est): 2.18MM
SALES (corp-wide): 2.18MM **Privately Held**
Web: www.millerfireworks.com
SIC: 5092 5999 Fireworks; Fireworks

(G-9299)
PAGE PLUS CELLULAR
1615 Timber Wolf Dr (43528-8304)
P.O. Box 351415 (43635-1415)
PHONE...............................800 550-2436
EMP: 56 EST: 2018
SALES (est): 550.78K **Privately Held**
Web: d11ouvxgl3fqi0.cloudfront.net
SIC: 4812 Cellular telephone services

(G-9300)
PLASTIC TECHNOLOGIES INC (PA)
Also Called: Pti
1440 Timber Wolf Dr (43528)
P.O. Box 964 (43528)
PHONE...............................419 867-5400
Tom Brady, *Ch*
Craig S Barrow, *
Elizabeth Brady, *
Sumit Mukherjee, *
▲ EMP: 92 EST: 1985
SQ FT: 46,000
SALES (est): 17.09MM
SALES (corp-wide): 17.09MM **Privately Held**
Web: www.plastictechnologies.com
SIC: 8734 8731 Product testing laboratory, safety or performance; Commercial physical research

(G-9301)
QUALITY INN TOLEDO AIRPORT
Also Called: Quality Inn
1401 E Mall Dr (43528-9490)
PHONE...............................419 867-1144
Debra Friedman, *Prin*
EMP: 27 EST: 2005
SALES (est): 871.95K **Privately Held**
Web: www.choicehotels.com
SIC: 7011 Hotels and motels

(G-9302)
RDH OHIO LLC
Also Called: Etchen Co, The
1255 Corporate Dr (43528-9590)
PHONE...............................419 475-8621
Richard Herman, *Pr*
David Berland, *VP*
▲ EMP: 28 EST: 1948
SQ FT: 2,400
SALES (est): 2.03MM **Privately Held**
Web: www.lhbrands.com
SIC: 5199 Advertising specialties

(G-9303)
SCHINDLER ELEVATOR CORPORATION
Millar Elevator Service
1530 Timber Wolf Dr (43528-9161)
P.O. Box 960 (43528-0960)
PHONE...............................419 867-5100
Tim Shaey, *Mgr*
EMP: 110
SQ FT: 2,000
Web: www.schindler.com
SIC: 7699 Elevators: inspection, service, and repair
HQ: Schindler Elevator Corporation
   20 Whippany Rd
   Morristown NJ 07960
   973 397-6500

(G-9304)
SPONSELLER GROUP INC (PA)
1600 Timber Wolf Dr (43528-8303)
PHONE...............................419 861-3000
Harold P Sponseller, *Ch*
Keith Sponseller, *Pr*
David Nowak, *VP*
Kevin R Nevius, *VP*
EMP: 44 EST: 1973
SQ FT: 8,900
SALES (est): 11.2MM
SALES (corp-wide): 11.2MM **Privately Held**
Web: www.sponsellergroup.com
SIC: 8711 3599 Consulting engineer; Machine shop, jobbing and repair

(G-9305)
SPRING MDOW EXTNDED CARE CTR F (PA)
1125 Clarion Ave (43528-8107)
PHONE...............................419 866-6124
John H Stone, *Pr*
EMP: 95 EST: 1975
SQ FT: 50,000
SALES (est): 9.61MM
SALES (corp-wide): 9.61MM **Privately Held**
Web: www.springmeadowsvhc.com
SIC: 8052 8051 Intermediate care facilities; Skilled nursing care facilities

GEOGRAPHIC SECTION

Hudson - Summit County (G-9327)

(G-9306)
STONE OAK COUNTRY CLUB
100 Stone Oak Blvd (43528-9131)
PHONE....................419 867-0969
Keith Olander, *Pr*
EMP: 100 **EST:** 2003
SQ FT: 25,517
SALES (est): 3.84MM **Privately Held**
Web: www.stoneoakcountryclub.org
SIC: 7997 Golf club, membership

(G-9307)
TEKNI-PLEX INC
Also Called: Global Technology Center
1445 Timber Wolf Dr (43528-8302)
PHONE....................419 491-2399
Paul J Young, *CEO*
Phil Bourgeois, *VP*
EMP: 41 **EST:** 1967
SALES (est): 5.16MM **Privately Held**
Web: www.tekni-plex.com
SIC: 2679 7389 2672 Egg cartons, molded pulp: made from purchased material; Packaging and labeling services; Cloth lined paper: made from purchased paper

(G-9308)
TOLEDO CLINIC INC
6135 Trust Dr Ste 230 (43528-9360)
PHONE....................419 865-3111
Robin Graham, *Brnch Mgr*
EMP: 84
SALES (corp-wide): 119.13MM **Privately Held**
Web: www.toledoclinic.com
SIC: 8099 Blood related health services
PA: Toledo Clinic, Inc.
    4235 Secor Rd
    Toledo OH 43623
    419 473-3561

(G-9309)
TOTAL FLEET SOLUTIONS LLC
7050 Spring Meadows Dr W Ste A (43528)
PHONE....................419 868-8853
Todd W Roberts, *Managing Member*
Brent Parent, *
Chris Grubbs, *
▲ **EMP:** 50 **EST:** 2018
SQ FT: 5,000
SALES (est): 37.64MM
SALES (corp-wide): 596.1MM **Privately Held**
SIC: 5084 Materials handling machinery
HQ: Tfs, Ltd.
    3235 Levis Commons Blvd
    Perrysburg OH 43551
    419 868-8853

(G-9310)
UNITED ROOFING & SHEET METAL
7255 Progress St (43528-9682)
P.O. Box 107 (43528-0107)
PHONE....................419 865-5576
Thomas E Seiple, *Pr*
Gary L Grup, *VP*
EMP: 32 **EST:** 1967
SQ FT: 20,000
SALES (est): 910.88K **Privately Held**
Web: www.unitedrsm.com
SIC: 1761 Roofing contractor

(G-9311)
VELOCITY A MANAGED SVCS CO INC (PA)
6936 Spring Valley Dr (43528-9488)
P.O. Box 1179 (43528-1179)
PHONE....................419 868-9983
Gregory Kiley, *Ch*
Edward J Kiley Junior, *Dir*
William Werner, *Sec*

Betty Ong, *CFO*
Mark Walker, *Pr*
EMP: 125 **EST:** 2005
SALES (est): 57.15MM **Privately Held**
Web: www.velocitymsc.com
SIC: 7373 4899 Computer system selling services; Data communication services

(G-9312)
VELOCITY A MANAGED SVCS CO INC
7130 Spring Meadows Dr W (43528-9296)
P.O. Box 990 (43528-0990)
PHONE....................281 221-4444
EMP: 53
SALES (est): 1.68MM **Privately Held**
Web: www.velocitymsc.com
SIC: 7011 Hotels and motels

(G-9313)
VINYL DESIGN CORPORATION
7856 Hill Ave (43528-9181)
PHONE....................419 283-4009
Patrick J Trompeter, *Pr*
EMP: 29 **EST:** 1988
SQ FT: 36,000
SALES (est): 4.72MM **Privately Held**
Web: www.vinyldesigncorp.com
SIC: 3089 5033 2452 Windows, plastics; Siding, except wood; Prefabricated wood buildings

(G-9314)
WAREHOUSE SVCS GROUP LTD LBLTY
6145 Merger Dr (43528-8430)
P.O. Box 965 (43528-0965)
PHONE....................419 868-6400
EMP: 45 **EST:** 1994
SQ FT: 70,000
SALES (est): 1.34MM **Privately Held**
SIC: 4225 General warehousing and storage

(G-9315)
WOODSAGE CORPORATION
7400 Airport Hwy (43528-9545)
P.O. Box 1040 (43528-1040)
PHONE....................419 866-8000
Jim Cannaley, *Pr*
EMP: 78 **EST:** 1998
SALES (est): 7.85MM **Privately Held**
Web: www.woodsage.com
SIC: 6282 Investment advice

Holmesville
Holmes County

(G-9316)
ACTION COUPLING & EQP INC
8248 County Road 245 (44633-9724)
P.O. Box 99 (44633-0099)
PHONE....................330 279-4242
Scott Eliot, *Pr*
▲ **EMP:** 80 **EST:** 1991
SQ FT: 75,000
SALES (est): 10.74MM **Privately Held**
Web: www.actioncoupling.com
SIC: 3569 5087 3429 Firefighting and related equipment; Firefighting equipment; Hardware, nec

Hooven
Hamilton County

(G-9317)
GOZAL INCORPORATED
Also Called: Borderless Logistics

4450 Monroe Ave (45033-7640)
PHONE....................833 603-0303
Khusnitdin Abdullayev, *CEO*
EMP: 40 **EST:** 2014
SALES (est): 5.22MM **Privately Held**
SIC: 4731 Freight transportation arrangement

Hopedale
Harrison County

(G-9318)
GABLES CARE CENTER INC
351 Lahm Dr (43976-9761)
PHONE....................740 937-2900
EMP: 46 **EST:** 1992
SQ FT: 26,000
SALES (est): 8.47MM **Privately Held**
SIC: 8051 Convalescent home with continuous nursing care

Hubbard
Trumbull County

(G-9319)
BLUE BEACON USA LP
Also Called: Blue Beacon Truck Wash
7044 Truck World Blvd (44425-3253)
PHONE....................330 534-4419
Bill Rigley, *Mgr*
EMP: 53
SALES (corp-wide): 38MM **Privately Held**
Web: www.bluebeacon.com
SIC: 7542 Truck wash
PA: Blue Beacon U.S.A., L.P.
    500 Graves Blvd
    Salina KS 67401
    785 825-2221

(G-9320)
CONNIE PARKS (PA)
Also Called: Biomedical Laboratory
4504 Logan Way Ste B (44425-3345)
PHONE....................330 759-8334
Connie Parks, *Owner*
EMP: 35 **EST:** 1975
SALES (est): 2.15MM
SALES (corp-wide): 2.15MM **Privately Held**
SIC: 8071 Testing laboratories

(G-9321)
DESALVO CONSTRUCTION COMPANY
1491 W Liberty St (44425-3310)
PHONE....................330 759-8145
Joseph K Desalvo, *Pr*
Sandra S Algoe, *
Cammie E Desalvo, *
EMP: 30 **EST:** 1984
SQ FT: 12,320
SALES (est): 9.49MM **Privately Held**
Web: www.dccgc.com
SIC: 1541 1542 Industrial buildings, new construction, nec; Commercial and office building, new construction

(G-9322)
OHIO STEEL SHEET AND PLATE INC
7845 Chestnut Ridge Rd (44425-9702)
P.O. Box 1146 (44482-1146)
PHONE....................800 827-2401
John Rebhan, *Pr*
Eric Rebhan, *
Mike Link, *
EMP: 45 **EST:** 1987
SQ FT: 320,000
SALES (est): 7.47MM **Privately Held**
Web: www.ohiosteelplate.com

SIC: 3312 5051 3444 Sheet or strip, steel, hot-rolled; Metals service centers and offices; Sheet metalwork

Huber Heights
Montgomery County

(G-9323)
AMAZING GRACE HM HLTH CARE LLC
7039 Taylorsville Rd (45424-3182)
PHONE....................937 825-4862
EMP: 71 **EST:** 2014
SQ FT: 424
SALES (est): 660.1K **Privately Held**
Web: www.amazinggracehomecare.org
SIC: 8082 8322 Home health care services; Homemakers' service

(G-9324)
KHN PHARMACY HUBER
Also Called: Leader Drug Store
8701 Troy Pike Ste 4 (45424-1055)
PHONE....................937 558-3333
EMP: 113 **EST:** 2009
SALES (est): 6.64MM
SALES (corp-wide): 2.46B **Privately Held**
Web: www.ketteringhealth.org
SIC: 8062 General medical and surgical hospitals
HQ: Dayton Osteopathic Hospital
    405 W Grand Ave
    Dayton OH 45405
    937 762-1629

(G-9325)
MJO INDUSTRIES INC (PA)
Also Called: Hughes-Peters
8000 Technology Blvd (45424-1573)
PHONE....................800 590-4055
EMP: 88 **EST:** 1923
SALES (est): 42.32MM
SALES (corp-wide): 42.32MM **Privately Held**
Web: www.hughespeters.com
SIC: 5063 5065 3679 Wire and cable; Connectors, electronic; Electronic circuits

(G-9326)
PRIMARY CARE NTWRK PRMIER HLTH
Also Called: Samaritan Family Care
6251 Good Samaritan Way Ste 210a (45424-5253)
PHONE....................937 237-9575
EMP: 55
SALES (corp-wide): 25.36MM **Privately Held**
Web: www.premierhealth.com
SIC: 8062 General medical and surgical hospitals
PA: Primary Care Network Of Premier
    Health Partners
    110 N Main St Ste 350
    Dayton OH 45402
    937 226-7085

Hudson
Summit County

(G-9327)
AKRON GENERAL HEALTH SYSTEM
1310 Corporate Dr (44236-4430)
PHONE....................330 344-3030
Thomas Schmidlin Md, *Pt*
EMP: 705
SALES (corp-wide): 14.48B **Privately Held**
Web: www.akrongeneral.org

Hudson - Summit County (G-9328)

SIC: **8099** 8011 Physical examination and testing services; Clinic, operated by physicians
HQ: Akron General Health System
1 Akron General Ave
Akron OH 44307
330 344-6000

(G-9328)
ALBERT GUARNIERI & CO
7481 Herrick Park Dr (44236-2367)
PHONE...................................330 794-9834
EMP: 51
SALES (corp-wide): 9.51MM **Privately Held**
Web: www.albertguarnieri.com
SIC: **5194** 5145 5141 Tobacco and tobacco products; Confectionery; Groceries, general line
PA: Albert Guarnieri & Co.
1133 E Market St
Warren OH 44483
330 394-5636

(G-9329)
ALL OHIO LANDSCAPING INC
5649 Akron Cleveland Rd (44236-2611)
PHONE...................................330 650-2226
Mark Malbin, *Pr*
EMP: 65 **EST:** 2005
SALES (est): 926.32K **Privately Held**
SIC: **0781** Landscape services

(G-9330)
ALLSTATE INSURANCE COMPANY
Also Called: Allstate
75 Milford Dr Ste 222 (44236-2778)
PHONE...................................330 650-2917
Tracy L Mc Kenica, *Prin*
Tracy L Mc Kenica, *Prin*
EMP: 30 **EST:** 1973
SALES (est): 2.48MM **Privately Held**
Web: www.allstate.com
SIC: **6411** 6311 7389 Insurance agents, brokers, and service; Life insurance; Financial services

(G-9331)
ALPHA TECHNOLOGIES SVCS LLC (DH)
6279 Hudson Crossing Pkwy Ste 200 (44236)
PHONE...................................330 745-1641
◆ **EMP:** 60 **EST:** 1996
SALES (est): 48.18MM
SALES (corp-wide): 223.55MM **Privately Held**
Web: www.alpha-technologies.com
SIC: **3823** 8748 Process control instruments; Testing services
HQ: Dynisco Instruments Llc
38 Forge Pkwy
Franklin MA 02038
508 541-9400

(G-9332)
ASCENT GLOBAL LOGISTICS LLC
5876 Darrow Rd (44236-3864)
PHONE...................................330 342-8700
Brian Pollock, *Dir Opers*
EMP: 133
SALES (corp-wide): 1.6B **Privately Held**
Web: www.ascentlogistics.com
SIC: **4731** Freight forwarding
HQ: Ascent Global Logistics, Llc
427 E Stewart St Ste 2
Milwaukee WI 53207
414 615-1500

(G-9333)
ASCENT GLOBL LGSTICS HLDNGS IN (PA)
Also Called: GTS
5876 Darrow Rd (44236-3864)
PHONE...................................603 881-3350
Michael Valentine, *Pr*
Paul Kithcart, *
EMP: 40 **EST:** 1995
SQ FT: 24,780
SALES (est): 43.4MM **Privately Held**
Web: www.ascentlogistics.com
SIC: **4731** Freight forwarding

(G-9334)
BOXOUT LLC (PA)
Also Called: Meyerpt
6333 Hudson Crossing Pkwy (44236-4346)
PHONE...................................833 462-7746
Ron Harrington, *CEO*
◆ **EMP:** 219 **EST:** 1948
SQ FT: 50,000
SALES (est): 58.63MM
SALES (corp-wide): 58.63MM **Privately Held**
Web: www.meyerpt.com
SIC: **5122** 5047 3843 8041 Vitamins and minerals; Medical and hospital equipment; Dental equipment and supplies; Offices and clinics of chiropractors

(G-9335)
BROWN DERBY ROADHOUSE
72 N Main St Ste 208 (44236-2883)
PHONE...................................330 528-3227
Parris Girvas, *Pr*
Leo Carmelli, *
EMP: 45 **EST:** 2000
SALES (est): 425.68K **Privately Held**
Web: www.brownderbyusa.com
SIC: **5812** 7299 Steak restaurant; Banquet hall facilities

(G-9336)
C M M INC
546 Meadowridge Way (44236-1182)
PHONE...................................216 789-7480
Ronald Mamula, *Pr*
EMP: 33 **EST:** 1999
SALES (est): 5.24MM **Privately Held**
Web: www.cmm-inc.com
SIC: **8741** Construction management

(G-9337)
CATASTROPHE MGT SOLUTIONS INC
280 Executive Pkwy W (44236-1695)
PHONE...................................800 959-2630
EMP: 95
SALES (est): 5.09MM **Privately Held**
Web: www.pilotcat.com
SIC: **8741** Management services
PA: Catastrophe Management Solutions, Inc.
1055 Hillcrest Rd Ste A1
Mobile AL 36695
251 607-7771

(G-9338)
CHASE TRANSCRIPTIONS INC (PA)
1737 Georgetown Rd Ste G (44236-5013)
PHONE...................................330 656-3980
Michael C Geaney, *Pr*
EMP: 34 **EST:** 1980
SQ FT: 4,000
SALES (est): 3.45MM
SALES (corp-wide): 3.45MM **Privately Held**
Web: www.chaseclinicaldocumentation.com
SIC: **7338** Secretarial and typing service

(G-9339)
CHILDRENS HOSP MED CTR AKRON
5655 Hudson Dr (44236-4451)
PHONE...................................330 342-5437
EMP: 54
SALES (corp-wide): 1.4B **Privately Held**
Web: www.akronchildrens.org
SIC: **8011** Freestanding emergency medical center
PA: Childrens Hospital Medical Center Of Akron
1 Perkins Sq
Akron OH 44308
330 543-1000

(G-9340)
COMPMED ANALYSIS LLC (PA)
1742 Georgetown Rd Ste G (44236-5007)
P.O. Box 671 (44236-0671)
PHONE...................................330 650-0888
EMP: 29 **EST:** 2005
SALES (est): 2.89MM
SALES (corp-wide): 2.89MM **Privately Held**
Web: www.enablecomp.com
SIC: **6411** Medical insurance claim processing, contract or fee basis

(G-9341)
COUNTRY CLUB OF HUDSON
2155 Middleton Rd (44236-1434)
P.O. Box 533 (44236-0533)
PHONE...................................330 650-1188
Karen Twedell, *Mgr*
EMP: 98 **EST:** 1966
SQ FT: 2,000
SALES (est): 7.13MM **Privately Held**
Web: www.cchudson.com
SIC: **7997** 5812 Country club, membership; Eating places

(G-9342)
DAEDALUS BOOKS INC
Also Called: Daedalus Books Warehouse Outl
5581 Hudson Industrial Pkwy (44236-5019)
P.O. Box 6000 (21046-6000)
PHONE...................................800 395-2665
◆ **EMP:** 170 **EST:** 1980
SALES (est): 18.75MM **Privately Held**
Web: www.daedalusbooks.com
SIC: **5192** 5942 Books; Book stores

(G-9343)
DREW MEDICAL INC (PA)
75 Milford Dr Ste 201 (44236-2778)
PHONE...................................407 363-6700
Michael Dinkel, *Pr*
EMP: 30 **EST:** 1991
SALES (est): 4.7MM **Privately Held**
SIC: **8071** Medical laboratories

(G-9344)
EDWARDS HEALTH CARE SERVICES (PA)
Also Called: Direct Health Care Supply
5640 Hudson Industrial Pkwy (44236-5011)
P.O. Box 429 (44236-0429)
PHONE...................................330 342-9555
EMP: 33 **EST:** 1994
SQ FT: 5,500
SALES (est): 9.88MM **Privately Held**
Web: www.myehcs.com
SIC: **5047** Medical equipment and supplies

(G-9345)
ESSENDANT CO
100 E Highland Rd (44236)
PHONE...................................330 650-9361
Dave Martin, *Mgr*
EMP: 29
Web: www.essendant.com
SIC: **5112** Office supplies, nec
HQ: Essendant Co.
1 Pkwy N Blvd Ste 100
Deerfield IL 60015
847 627-7000

(G-9346)
EVOLV LLC
5171 Hudson Dr (44236-3735)
PHONE...................................440 994-9115
EMP: 41
SALES (corp-wide): 1.02MM **Privately Held**
Web: www.evolvapor.com
SIC: **7371** Computer software development
PA: Evolv, Llc
1741 W 47th St
Ashtabula OH 44004
440 998-5697

(G-9347)
FAMILY MEDICAL CARE INC
1320 Corporate Dr Ste 200 (44236-4442)
PHONE...................................330 633-3883
William Kedia Md, *Pr*
Mark Apte Md, *Prin*
Martin Saunders D.o.s., *Prin*
EMP: 38 **EST:** 2000
SALES (est): 2.3MM **Privately Held**
Web: www.fmcplus.com
SIC: **8011** General and family practice, physician/surgeon

(G-9348)
FEDEX SUPPLYCHAIN SYSTEMS INC
Also Called: Fedex
5455 Darrow Rd (44236-4082)
▲ **EMP:** 1800 **EST:** 1989
SALES (est): 51.4MM
SALES (corp-wide): 90.16B **Publicly Held**
SIC: **8742** 4213 8741 4731 Transportation consultant; Trucking, except local; Management services; Freight transportation arrangement
PA: Fedex Corporation
942 Shady Grove Rd S
Memphis TN 38120
901 818-7500

(G-9349)
FORTEC FIBERS INC
6245 Hudson Crossing Pkwy (44236-4348)
PHONE...................................800 963-7101
EMP: 29 **EST:** 2001
SQ FT: 69,000
SALES (est): 1.21MM **Privately Held**
Web: www.fortecmedical.com
SIC: **5047** Medical equipment and supplies

(G-9350)
FORTEC MEDICAL INC (PA)
6245 Hudson Crossing Pkwy (44236-4348)
PHONE...................................330 463-1265
Drew Forhan, *Pr*
John Voyzey, *
EMP: 30 **EST:** 1988
SQ FT: 69,000
SALES (est): 44.9MM **Privately Held**
Web: www.fortecmedical.com
SIC: **5047** Medical equipment and supplies

GEOGRAPHIC SECTION

Hudson - Summit County (G-9374)

(G-9351)
FORVIS LLP
102 1st St Ste 201 (44236-5386)
PHONE.............................330 650-1752
Craig Anderson, *Mgr*
EMP: 47
SALES (corp-wide): 392MM **Privately Held**
Web: www.forvis.com
SIC: 8721 Certified public accountant
PA: Forvis, Llp
  910 E Saint Louis St # 400
  Springfield MO 65806
  417 831-8293

(G-9352)
GEM EDWARDS INC
Also Called: Gemco Medical
5640 Hudson Industrial Pkwy (44236-5011)
P.O. Box 429 (44236-0429)
PHONE.............................330 342-8300
Toni Edwards, *Pr*
▲ **EMP:** 100 **EST:** 1992
SQ FT: 80,000
SALES (est): 43.47MM **Privately Held**
Web: www.gemedwardspharmacy.com
SIC: 5122 5961 5999 5047 Medicinals and botanicals; Food, mail order; Alarm and safety equipment stores; Hospital equipment and furniture

(G-9353)
GEMCARE WELLNESS INC
5640 Hudson Industrial Pkwy (44236-5011)
P.O. Box 429 (44236-0429)
PHONE.............................800 294-9176
EMP: 78 **EST:** 2018
SALES (est): 1.11MM **Privately Held**
Web: www.gemcarewellness.com
SIC: 8049 Dietician

(G-9354)
GIAMBRONE MASONRY INC
10000 Aurora Hudson Rd (44236-2520)
P.O. Box 810 (44202-0810)
EMP: 34 **EST:** 1977
SQ FT: 2,500
SALES (est): 1.12MM **Privately Held**
Web: www.as-av.com
SIC: 1741 Bricklaying

(G-9355)
HUDSON ELMS OPCO LLC
Also Called: Hudson Elms Nrsing HM Asssted
563 W Streetsboro St (44236-2050)
PHONE.............................330 650-0436
EMP: 30 **EST:** 2020
SALES (est): 2.42MM **Privately Held**
Web: www.hudsonelms.com
SIC: 8059 Nursing home, except skilled and intermediate care facility

(G-9356)
HUDSON MONTESSORI ASSOCIATION
Also Called: Hudson Montessori School
7545 Darrow Rd (44236-1305)
PHONE.............................330 650-0424
Mat Virgil, *Prin*
Julia Brown, *
EMP: 40 **EST:** 1962
SALES (est): 4.56MM **Privately Held**
Web: www.hudsonmontessori.org
SIC: 8351 8211 Preschool center; Private elementary school

(G-9357)
HUNTINGTON NATIONAL BANK
116 W Streetsboro St Ste 1 (44236-2756)
PHONE.............................330 653-5161
Margaret Haines, *Mgr*
EMP: 36
SALES (corp-wide): 10.84B **Publicly Held**
Web: www.huntington.com
SIC: 6029 Commercial banks, nec
HQ: The Huntington National Bank
  41 S High St
  Columbus OH 43215
  614 480-4293

(G-9358)
J-NAN ENTERPRISES LLC
Also Called: Goddard Schools
5601 Darrow Rd (44236-4087)
PHONE.............................330 653-3766
Jeffery A Lutz, *Owner*
Jeffery A Lutz, *Pr*
Nancy E Lutz, *VP*
EMP: 32 **EST:** 2006
SQ FT: 8,000
SALES (est): 482.36K **Privately Held**
Web: www.goddardschool.com
SIC: 8351 Preschool center

(G-9359)
JE CARSTEN COMPANY (PA)
Also Called: Vita Pup
7481 Herrick Park Dr (44236-2367)
PHONE.............................330 794-4440
J M Carsten, *Pr*
Peter Carsten, *
James E Carsten, *
EMP: 34 **EST:** 1947
SALES (est): 2.75MM
SALES (corp-wide): 2.75MM **Privately Held**
SIC: 5194 5145 Cigarettes; Confectionery

(G-9360)
KAULIG CAPITAL LLC
1521 Georgetown Rd Ste 101 (44236-4078)
PHONE.............................330 968-1110
Tim Clepper, *Pr*
Paul Martin, *CFO*
Chad Luckie, *COO*
EMP: 42 **EST:** 2016
SALES (est): 2.52MM **Privately Held**
Web: www.kauligcapital.com
SIC: 6799 Investors, nec

(G-9361)
KAULIG RACING INC (PA)
1521 Georgetown Rd (44236-4066)
P.O. Box 1627 (27374-1627)
PHONE.............................815 382-8007
Matthew Kaulig, *Pr*
EMP: 55 **EST:** 2015
SALES (est): 5.05MM
SALES (corp-wide): 5.05MM **Privately Held**
Web: www.kauligracing.com
SIC: 7948 Racing, including track operation

(G-9362)
LEAF HOME LLC (PA)
Also Called: Thiel's Home Solutions
1595 Georgetown Rd (44236-4055)
PHONE.............................800 290-6106
Jeffrey Housenbold, *Pr*
Scarlett O'sullivan, *CFO*
EMP: 28 **EST:** 2016
SALES (est): 68.14MM
SALES (corp-wide): 68.14MM **Privately Held**
Web: www.leafhome.com
SIC: 1799 Kitchen and bathroom remodeling

(G-9363)
LIFECENTER PLUS INC
5133 Darrow Rd (44236-4003)
PHONE.............................330 342-9021
David L Hall, *Pr*
Martin Spector, *
Lorel Rubins, *
Jan Rubins, *
Lauren Saulino, *
EMP: 46 **EST:** 1987
SQ FT: 58,000
SALES (est): 4.93MM **Privately Held**
Web: www.lifecenterplus.com
SIC: 7991 Health club

(G-9364)
MEYER DECORATIVE SURFACES USA INC
Also Called: Mayer Laminates MA
300 Executive Pkwy W Ste 100 (44236-1603)
PHONE.............................800 776-3900
▲ **EMP:** 220
SIC: 5031 Building materials, interior

(G-9365)
ON SEARCH PARTNERS LLC
102 1st St Ste 201 (44236-5386)
PHONE.............................440 318-1006
Joshua Nathanson, *Prin*
EMP: 66 **EST:** 2019
SALES (est): 4.48MM **Privately Held**
Web: www.onpartners.com
SIC: 7361 Executive placement

(G-9366)
OPEN PRACTICE SOLUTIONS LTD
300 Executive Pkwy W Ste 300 (44236-1603)
PHONE.............................234 380-8345
Michael Teutsch, *CEO*
Ryan Arnold, *Pr*
EMP: 30 **EST:** 2005
SALES (est): 2.12MM **Privately Held**
Web: www.openpracticesolutions.com
SIC: 7371 Computer software development

(G-9367)
PASCO INC
Also Called: G M A C Insurance Center
5600 Hudson Industrial Pkwy Ste 200 (44236-3798)
PHONE.............................330 650-0613
EMP: 33 **EST:** 1986
SALES (est): 6.58MM **Privately Held**
Web: www.pasco-group.com
SIC: 6411 7323 Insurance information and consulting services; Credit reporting services

(G-9368)
PIPELINE PACKAGING CORPORATION (HQ)
100 Executive Pkwy (44236-1630)
PHONE.............................440 349-3200
Christopher Nelson, *Pr*
Dennis T Puening, *
Daniel Herbert, *
▲ **EMP:** 30 **EST:** 1986
SQ FT: 85,000
SALES (est): 104.29MM
SALES (corp-wide): 138.41MM **Privately Held**
Web: www.pipelinepackaging.com
SIC: 5199 Packaging materials
PA: Cleveland Steel Container Corporation
  100 Executive Pkwy
  Hudson OH 44236
  440 349-8000

(G-9369)
PRINTERS DEVIL INC
77 Maple Dr (44236-3037)
PHONE.............................330 650-1218
William Stemple, *Pr*
EMP: 27 **EST:** 1977
SQ FT: 800
SALES (est): 581.35K **Privately Held**
Web: www.printersdevilinc.com
SIC: 2752 7334 Offset printing; Photocopying and duplicating services

(G-9370)
RENTAL CONCEPTS INC (PA)
Also Called: Fleet Response
695 Boston Mills Rd (44236-1100)
PHONE.............................216 525-3870
Ronald E Mawaka, *CEO*
Myron S Zadony, *
Ronald E Mawaka, *Ch*
Scott Mawaka, *
Claude E Nolty, *
EMP: 50 **EST:** 1986
SALES (est): 9.11K
SALES (corp-wide): 9.11K **Privately Held**
Web: www.fleetresponse.com
SIC: 7514 Rent-a-car service

(G-9371)
RESTORATION RESOURCES INC
Also Called: SERVPRO
1546 Georgetown Rd (44236-4067)
PHONE.............................330 650-4486
Bruce Johnson, *Pr*
Terri Johnson, *
EMP: 39 **EST:** 1986
SQ FT: 2,700
SALES (est): 4.81MM **Privately Held**
Web: www.servpronorthernsummitcounty.com
SIC: 7349 Building maintenance services, nec

(G-9372)
ROCK MEDICAL ORTHOPEDICS INC
571 Boston Mills Rd Ste 100 (44236-1164)
PHONE.............................216 496-3168
EMP: 61 **EST:** 2018
SALES (est): 4.2MM **Privately Held**
Web: www.rock-med.com
SIC: 8099 Health and allied services, nec

(G-9373)
SETON CATHOLIC SCHOOL HUDSON
6923 Stow Rd (44236-3240)
PHONE.............................330 342-4200
Sister Marie Damicone, *Prin*
Paula Worhatch, *
EMP: 52 **EST:** 1997
SQ FT: 20,624
SALES (est): 7.14MM **Privately Held**
Web: www.setoncatholicschool.org
SIC: 8211 8351 Private elementary and secondary schools; Child day care services

(G-9374)
SUMMA WESTERN RESERVE HOSP LLC
Also Called: Hudson Specialty Center
5655 Hudson Dr (44236-4454)
PHONE.............................330 650-5110
EMP: 31
SALES (corp-wide): 155.93MM **Privately Held**
Web: www.westernreservehospital.org
SIC: 8062 Hospital, AMA approved residency
HQ: Western Reserve Hospital, Llc
  1900 23rd St
  Cuyahoga Falls OH 44223

Hudson - Summit County (G-9375)

(G-9375)
UNITY HEALTH NETWORK LLC
5655 Hudson Dr Ste 110 (44236-4454)
PHONE..................................330 655-3820
Laurie Swinehart, *Brnch Mgr*
EMP: 27
SALES (corp-wide): 51.74MM **Privately Held**
Web: www.unityhealthnetwork.org
SIC: 8099 Blood related health services
PA: Unity Health Network, Llc
2750 Front St
Cuyahoga Falls OH 44221
330 923-5899

(G-9376)
US TELERADIOLOGY LLC (HQ)
5655 Hudson Dr Ste 210 (44236-4455)
PHONE..................................678 904-2599
Frank Ferraro, *CEO*
Robert Roche, *
EMP: 40 **EST:** 2002
SALES (est): 7.61MM
SALES (corp-wide): 9.33MM **Privately Held**
SIC: 8011 Radiologist
PA: Aris Radiology Professionals Of Michigan, Pc
118 W Streetsboro St
Hudson OH 44236
330 655-3800

(G-9377)
WATERWAY GAS & WASH COMPANY
5611 Darrow Rd (44236-4013)
PHONE..................................636 537-1111
EMP: 27
SALES (corp-wide): 381.21MM **Privately Held**
Web: www.waterway.com
SIC: 7542 Washing and polishing, automotive
PA: Waterway Gas & Wash Company
727 Goddard Ave
Chesterfield MO 63005
636 537-1111

(G-9378)
WOLTERS KLUWER CLINICAL DRUG INFORMATION INC
1100 Terex Rd (44236-3771)
P.O. Box 1560 (21741-1560)
PHONE..................................330 650-6506
EMP: 65
Web: www.wolterskluwer.com
SIC: 2731 2791 7379 Books, publishing only ; Typesetting, computer controlled; Computer related maintenance services

(G-9379)
WONDERWORKER INC
Also Called: Sky Zone Boston Heights
6217 Chittenden Rd (44236-2021)
PHONE..................................234 249-3030
Charles Hallis, *Pr*
Ivana Matyas, *
EMP: 80 **EST:** 2012
SQ FT: 24,000
SALES (est): 1.13MM **Privately Held**
SIC: 7999 Trampoline operation

Huntsburg
Geauga County

(G-9380)
ARMS TRUCKING CO INC (PA)
14818 Mayfield Rd (44046-8770)
PHONE..................................800 362-1343
TOLL FREE: 800

Howard W Bates, *Pr*
Brian Bates, *
Patricia Bates, *
Abbie Logan, *Corporate Secretary*
EMP: 40 **EST:** 1953
SQ FT: 21,000
SALES (est): 16.51MM
SALES (corp-wide): 16.51MM **Privately Held**
Web: www.thearmsgroup.us
SIC: 4213 4214 Contract haulers; Local trucking with storage

(G-9381)
BLOSSOM HILLS NURSING HOME
Also Called: Blossom Hill Care Center
12496 Princeton Rd (44046-9792)
P.O. Box 369 (44046-0369)
PHONE..................................440 635-5567
Donald Gray, *Pr*
Charles Ohman, *
George Ohman, *
EMP: 36 **EST:** 1976
SQ FT: 18,500
SALES (est): 9.15MM **Privately Held**
Web: www.blossomhillhealthcare.com
SIC: 8051 8052 Convalescent home with continuous nursing care; Intermediate care facilities

(G-9382)
HERSHEY MONTESSORI SCHOOL INC
11530 Madison Rd (44046-9707)
PHONE..................................440 357-0918
Paula Leigh-doyle, *Headmaster*
EMP: 96
SALES (corp-wide): 4.69MM **Privately Held**
Web: www.hershey-montessori.org
SIC: 8351 Montessori child development center
PA: Hershey Montessori School Inc
10229 Prouty Rd
Concord Township OH 44077
440 357-0918

Huntsville
Logan County

(G-9383)
COLOMA EMERGENCY AMBULANCE INC (PA)
Also Called: Pride Care Ambulance
3771 Township Road 221 (43324-9579)
P.O. Box 2288 (49003-2288)
PHONE..................................269 343-2224
Brian Balow, *CEO*
Marie Eisbrenner, *COO*
Roger Schaefer, *CFO*
EMP: 82 **EST:** 1967
SALES (est): 9.19MM **Privately Held**
SIC: 4119 Ambulance service

Huron
Erie County

(G-9384)
BARNES NURSERY INC (PA)
3511 Cleveland Rd W (44839-1025)
PHONE..................................800 421-8722
TOLL FREE: 800
Robert Barnes, *Pr*
Jarret Barnes, *
Julie Barnes, *
EMP: 49 **EST:** 1950
SQ FT: 5,000
SALES (est): 4.83MM

SALES (corp-wide): 4.83MM **Privately Held**
Web: www.barnesnursery.com
SIC: 0782 0181 5261 Landscape contractors ; Nursery stock, growing of; Garden supplies and tools, nec

(G-9385)
CHEFS GARDEN INC
9009 Huron Avery Rd (44839-2448)
PHONE..................................419 433-4947
Barbara Jones, *Pr*
Bob L Jones, *
Lee Jones, *
Robert N Jones, *
EMP: 130 **EST:** 1981
SQ FT: 1,684
SALES (est): 23.67MM **Privately Held**
Web: www.chefs-garden.com
SIC: 2099 5148 0161 Ready-to-eat meals, salads, and sandwiches; Fresh fruits and vegetables; Market garden

(G-9386)
COUNTY OF ERIE
Also Called: Erie County Care Facility
3916 Perkins Ave (44839-1059)
PHONE..................................419 627-8733
Marian Hill, *Dir*
EMP: 41
SALES (corp-wide): 77.73MM **Privately Held**
Web: eriecounty.oh.gov
SIC: 8051 9111 Convalescent home with continuous nursing care; County supervisors' and executives' office
PA: County Of Erie
2900 Columbus Ave
Sandusky OH 44870
419 627-7682

(G-9387)
ERIE METROPARKS GENERAL INFO
3109 Hull Rd (44839-2165)
PHONE..................................419 621-4220
Stephen Dice, *Brnch Mgr*
EMP: 33
SALES (corp-wide): 182.39K **Privately Held**
Web: www.eriemetroparks.org
SIC: 7999 Recreation services
PA: Erie Metroparks General Information
3910 Perkins Ave
Huron OH 44839
419 625-7783

(G-9388)
FIRELANDS TECH VENTURES LLC
Also Called: Firelands Scientific
2300 University Dr E (44839-9173)
PHONE..................................419 616-5115
EMP: 39 **EST:** 2018
SALES (est): 5.98MM **Privately Held**
Web: www.firelandsscientific.com
SIC: 5122 Vitamins and minerals

(G-9389)
HUMANTICS INNVTIVE SLTIONS INC
Also Called: Humanetics
900 Denton Dr (44839-8922)
PHONE..................................567 265-5200
Chris O'connor, *Owner*
EMP: 150
SALES (corp-wide): 117.39MM **Privately Held**
Web: www.humaneticsgroup.com
SIC: 8748 Business consulting, nec
HQ: Humanetics Innovative Solutions, Inc.
23300 Haggerty Rd
Farmington Hills MI 48335

(G-9390)
HURON CEMENT PRODUCTS COMPANY (PA)
Also Called: H & C Building Supplies
617 Main St (44839-2593)
PHONE..................................419 433-4161
John Caporini, *Pr*
EMP: 38 **EST:** 1914
SQ FT: 37,800
SALES (est): 4.66MM
SALES (corp-wide): 4.66MM **Privately Held**
Web: www.terminalreadymix.com
SIC: 5032 3273 3546 3272 Cement; Ready-mixed concrete; Power-driven handtools; Concrete products, nec

(G-9391)
HURON HEALTH CARE CENTER INC
Also Called: Admirals Pnte Nrsing Rhblttion
1920 Cleveland Rd W (44839-1211)
PHONE..................................419 433-4990
Amy Donaldson, *Admn*
EMP: 41 **EST:** 1993
SALES (est): 4.55MM **Privately Held**
Web: www.admirals-pointe.net
SIC: 8051 Convalescent home with continuous nursing care

(G-9392)
SAW MILL CREEK LTD
Also Called: Lodge At Saw Mill Creek, The
400 Sawmill Creek Dr W (44839-2261)
PHONE..................................419 433-3800
Greg Hill, *Pt*
Tom Bleile, *Pt*
EMP: 76 **EST:** 1974
SALES (est): 549.55K **Privately Held**
Web: www.sawmillcreekresort.com
SIC: 7011 6512 5813 5812 Hotels and motels ; Nonresidential building operators; Drinking places; Eating places

(G-9393)
SC RESORT LTD
Also Called: Sawmill Creek Resort, Ltd.
400 Sawmill Creek Dr W (44839-2261)
PHONE..................................419 433-3800
Richard Zimmermann, *Pr*
EMP: 170 **EST:** 1996
SALES (est): 24.67MM
SALES (corp-wide): 1.8B **Publicly Held**
Web: www.sawmillcreekresort.com
SIC: 5812 7011 Eating places; Resort hotel
PA: Cedar Fair, L.P.
1 Cedar Point Dr
Sandusky OH 44870
419 627-2344

Independence
Cuyahoga County

(G-9394)
ACCEL PERFORMANCE GROUP LLC (DH)
6100 Oak Tree Blvd Ste 200 (44131)
PHONE..................................216 658-6413
Robert Tobey, *CEO*
Robert Romanelli, *
Andrew Mazzarella, *
◆ **EMP:** 180 **EST:** 1993
SQ FT: 200,000
SALES (est): 53.05MM
SALES (corp-wide): 659.7MM **Publicly Held**
Web: www.airsoftswat.com

GEOGRAPHIC SECTION

Independence - Cuyahoga County (G-9417)

SIC: **3714** 5013 3053 Motor vehicle parts and accessories; Automotive supplies and parts; Gaskets; packing and sealing devices
HQ: Msdp Group Llc
1350 Pullman Dr Dock #14
El Paso TX 79936
915 857-5200

(G-9395)
ACCURATE GROUP HOLDINGS INC (PA)
6000 Freedom Square Dr Ste 300 (44131)
PHONE..................................216 520-1740
Paul Doman, *Pr*
Michael Lynch, *
EMP: 59 **EST:** 2012
SALES (est): 72.64MM **Privately Held**
Web: www.accurategroup.com
SIC: 6361 6411 Real estate title insurance; Title insurance agents

(G-9396)
ADO PROFESSIONAL SOLUTIONS INC
6150 Oak Tree Blvd Ste 490 (44131-6917)
PHONE..................................216 328-0888
EMP: 27
Web: www.lhh.com
SIC: 7361 Employment agencies
HQ: Ado Professional Solutions, Inc.
4800 Deerwood Campus Pkwy # 800
Jacksonville FL 32246

(G-9397)
ADVIZEX TECHNOLOGIES LLC (PA)
Also Called: Advizex Technologies
6480 Rockside Woods Blvd S Ste 190 (44131-2233)
PHONE..................................216 901-1818
Fred Traversi, *CEO*
John Brier, *
Marc Sarazin, *
Patrick Fettuccia, *
Mark Woelke, *
EMP: 39 **EST:** 1975
SQ FT: 6,600
SALES (est): 106.52MM **Privately Held**
Web: www.advizex.com
SIC: 7373 Value-added resellers, computer systems

(G-9398)
AGILE GLOBAL SOLUTIONS INC
5755 Granger Rd Ste 610 (44131-1458)
PHONE..................................916 655-7745
EMP: 29
SALES (corp-wide): 6.65MM **Privately Held**
Web: www.agileglobalsolutions.com
SIC: 7372 Business oriented computer software
PA: Agile Global Solutions, Inc.
193 Blue Ravine Rd # 160
Folsom CA 95630
916 353-1780

(G-9399)
AIRGAS USA LLC
6055 Rockside Woods Blvd N Ste 500 (44131-2301)
PHONE..................................216 642-6600
EMP: 287
SALES (corp-wide): 101.26MM **Privately Held**
Web: www.airgas.com
SIC: 5169 5084 5087 Compressed gas; Welding machinery and equipment; Janitors' supplies
HQ: Airgas Usa, Llc
259 N Radnor Chester Rd
Radnor PA 19087
216 642-6600

(G-9400)
AKKODIS INC
Also Called: Modis
6150 Oak Tree Blvd Ste 490 (44131-6917)
PHONE..................................216 447-1909
Andy Brouse, *Brnch Mgr*
EMP: 183
Web: www.modis.com
SIC: 7361 Executive placement
HQ: Akkodis, Inc.
4800 Deerwood Campus Pkwy
Jacksonville FL 32246
904 360-2300

(G-9401)
ALLIANCE LEGAL SOLUTIONS LLC
Also Called: Major Legal Services
6161 Oak Tree Blvd Ste 300 (44131-2581)
PHONE..................................216 525-0100
Matt Lyon, *CFO*
Amanda Stepowoy, *
EMP: 71 **EST:** 2014
SQ FT: 2,000
SALES (est): 3.8MM **Privately Held**
Web: www.alliancesolutionsgrp.com
SIC: 7361 Labor contractors (employment agency)

(G-9402)
ALLIANCE SOLUTIONS GROUP LLC (PA)
Also Called: Talentlaunch
6161 Oak Tree Blvd Ste 130 (44131-2581)
PHONE..................................216 503-1690
Aaron Grossman, *Pr*
Matt Lyon, *
Doug Dandurand, *
EMP: 39 **EST:** 2001
SQ FT: 7,000
SALES (est): 25.11MM
SALES (corp-wide): 25.11MM **Privately Held**
Web: www.mytalentlaunch.com
SIC: 7363 7361 Temporary help service; Employment agencies

(G-9403)
ALLIANCE TCHNCAL SOLUTIONS LLC
6161 Oak Tree Blvd Ste 300 (44131-2516)
PHONE..................................216 548-2290
EMP: 35 **EST:** 2012
SALES (est): 1.6MM **Privately Held**
Web: www.alliancetechnical.jobs
SIC: 7361 Executive placement

(G-9404)
ALS ASSCTION NTHRN OHIO CHPTER
6155 Rockside Rd Ste 403 (44131-2217)
PHONE..................................216 592-2572
Mary Wheelock, *Ex Dir*
EMP: 27 **EST:** 1986
SALES (est): 1.11MM **Privately Held**
Web: www.als.org
SIC: 8322 8699 Individual and family services; Charitable organization

(G-9405)
AP/AIM INDPNDNCE SITES TRS LLC
Also Called: Embassy Suites
5800 Rockside Woods Blvd N (44131-2346)
PHONE..................................216 986-9900
EMP: 51 **EST:** 2008
SALES (est): 2.6MM **Privately Held**
Web: www.hilton.com
SIC: 7011 Hotels and motels

(G-9406)
APPROVED NETWORKS LLC
Also Called: Champion One
7575 E Pleasant Valley Rd (44131-5567)
PHONE..................................216 831-1800
Michael Rapp, *CEO*
EMP: 30
Web: www.approvednetworks.com
SIC: 5049 Optical goods
HQ: Approved Networks Llc
6 Orchard Ste 150
Lake Forest CA 92630
800 590-9535

(G-9407)
AREA TEMPS INC (PA)
Also Called: Area Temps
4511 Rockside Rd Ste 190 (44131-2157)
PHONE..................................216 781-5350
Raymond Castelluccio, *CEO*
Kent Castelluccio, *
EMP: 40 **EST:** 1986
SALES (est): 27.42MM **Privately Held**
Web: www.areatemps.com
SIC: 7363 Temporary help service

(G-9408)
AW FABER-CASTELL USA INC
Also Called: Creativity For Kids
9000 Rio Nero Dr (44131-5502)
PHONE..................................216 643-4660
▲ **EMP:** 79 **EST:** 1996
SALES (est): 46.1MM
SALES (corp-wide): 687.1MM **Privately Held**
Web: www.fabercastell.com
SIC: 5092 5112 3944 Arts and crafts equipment and supplies; Stationery and office supplies; Games, toys, and children's vehicles
HQ: Faber-Castell Ag
Nurnberger Str. 2
Stein BY 90547
91199650

(G-9409)
BEACON HILL STAFFING GROUP LLC
Also Called: Beacon Hill Technologies
6155 Rockside Rd Ste 305 (44131-2217)
PHONE..................................216 447-8900
Jeff Rosen, *Mgr*
EMP: 137
SALES (corp-wide): 105.41MM **Privately Held**
Web: www.beaconhillstaffing.com
SIC: 7361 Employment agencies
PA: Beacon Hill Staffing Group, Llc
20 Ashburton Pl
Boston MA 02108
617 326-4000

(G-9410)
BEAR COMMUNICATIONS INC
900 Resource Dr Ste 8 (44131-1884)
PHONE..................................216 642-1670
EMP: 73
SALES (corp-wide): 601.04MM **Privately Held**
Web: www.bearcom.com
SIC: 5065 Communication equipment
HQ: Bear Communications, Inc.
4009 Dist Dr Ste 200
Garland TX 75041

(G-9411)
BLUE CHIP CONSULTING GROUP
6050 Oak Tree Blvd Ste 290 (44131-6927)
PHONE..................................216 503-6000
EMP: 28 **EST:** 2018
SALES (est): 493.59K **Privately Held**

SIC: **8748** Business consulting, nec

(G-9412)
BOBBY TRIPODI FOUNDATION INC (PA)
Also Called: Cornerstone Hope Bravement Ctr
5905 Brecksville Rd (44131-1517)
P.O. Box 31555 (44131-0555)
PHONE..................................216 524-3787
Mark Tripodi, *Ex Dir*
EMP: 50 **EST:** 2008
SALES (est): 4.76MM
SALES (corp-wide): 4.76MM **Privately Held**
Web: www.cornerstoneofhope.org
SIC: 8322 General counseling services

(G-9413)
BSL - APPLIED LASER TECH LLC (PA)
Also Called: Alt
1100 Resource Dr (44131-1888)
P.O. Box 25623 (44125-0623)
PHONE..................................216 663-8181
EMP: 30 **EST:** 1989
SALES (est): 11.65MM **Privately Held**
Web: www.altconnect.com
SIC: 5045 7378 Printers, computer; Computer maintenance and repair

(G-9414)
C & K INDUSTRIAL SERVICES INC (PA)
5617 E Schaaf Rd (44131-1334)
PHONE..................................216 642-0055
Arthur Karas, *Pr*
George Karas, *
Chris Karas, *Stockholder**
EMP: 100 **EST:** 1980
SQ FT: 8,000
SALES (est): 47.3MM
SALES (corp-wide): 47.3MM **Privately Held**
Web: www.ckindustrial.com
SIC: 4959 7349 Sweeping service: road, airport, parking lot, etc.; Building maintenance services, nec

(G-9415)
CANON SOLUTIONS AMERICA INC
6000 Freedom Square Dr Ste 240 (44131)
PHONE..................................216 446-3830
Craig Palmer, *Brnch Mgr*
EMP: 30
Web: csa.canon.com
SIC: 5044 Office equipment
HQ: Canon Solutions America, Inc.
1 Canon Park
Melville NY 11747
631 330-5000

(G-9416)
CANON SOLUTIONS AMERICA INC
Also Called: Dps
6161 Oak Tree Blvd Ste 301 (44131-2516)
PHONE..................................216 750-2980
EMP: 30
Web: csa.canon.com
SIC: 5044 Office equipment
HQ: Canon Solutions America, Inc.
1 Canon Park
Melville NY 11747
631 330-5000

(G-9417)
CBIZ TECHNOLOGIES LLC
6050 Oak Tree Blvd Ste 500 (44131-6927)
PHONE..................................216 447-9000
Jim King, *Managing Member*
Mary Jane Mcgrew, *Financial Operations Vice President*

Independence - Cuyahoga County (G-9418)   **GEOGRAPHIC SECTION**

EMP: 50 **EST:** 1992
SQ FT: 6,000
SALES (est): 10.78MM **Publicly Held**
Web: www.cbiz.com
SIC: 7379 Online services technology consultants
PA: Cbiz, Inc.
   5959 Rckside Wods Blvd N
   Cleveland OH 44131

(G-9418)
CHRONIC CARE MANAGEMENT INC
Also Called: Cosan Group
6505 Rockside Rd Ste 200 (44131-2386)
P.O. Box 2640 (44241-0640)
PHONE..................................440 248-6500
David Hunt, *Pr*
Daniel Dzina, *
EMP: 240 **EST:** 2015
SALES (est): 15.08MM **Privately Held**
Web: www.cosangroup.com
SIC: 8741 Business management

(G-9419)
CLEVELAND ANESTHESIA GROUP
6161 Oak Tree Blvd (44131-2581)
P.O. Box 94908 (44101-4908)
PHONE..................................216 901-5706
John Bastulli, *Pr*
Keith Levendorf, *
Joyce Hardaway Md, *Prin*
Robert Rogoff Md, *Prin*
EMP: 48 **EST:** 1971
SALES (est): 8.97MM **Privately Held**
SIC: 8062 General medical and surgical hospitals

(G-9420)
CLEVELAND CLINIC FOUNDATION
Also Called: Cleveland Clinic Health System
6801 Brecksville Rd Ste 10 (44131-5058)
PHONE..................................216 636-7400
Bertram Sue, *Brnch Mgr*
EMP: 85
SALES (corp-wide): 14.48B **Privately Held**
Web: www.clevelandclinic.org
SIC: 8042 Offices and clinics of optometrists
PA: The Cleveland Clinic Foundation
   9500 Euclid Ave
   Cleveland OH 44195
   216 636-8335

(G-9421)
CLEVELAND CLINIC FOUNDATION
5001 Rockside Rd Ste 700 (44131-6803)
PHONE..................................216 986-4312
Cynthia Deyling, *Brnch Mgr*
EMP: 90
SALES (corp-wide): 14.48B **Privately Held**
Web: www.clevelandclinic.org
SIC: 8011 Clinic, operated by physicians
PA: The Cleveland Clinic Foundation
   9500 Euclid Ave
   Cleveland OH 44195
   216 636-8335

(G-9422)
CLEVELAND UNLIMITED INC
Also Called: Revol Communications
7165 E Pleasant Valley Rd (44131-5541)
P.O. Box 31810 (44131-0810)
EMP: 389
Web: www.cui-flatrate.com
SIC: 4812 Radiotelephone communication

(G-9423)
CONSUMER SUPPORT SERVICES INC
6505 Rockside Rd Ste 400 (44131-2386)
PHONE..................................216 447-1521
Kim Wosotowsky, *Mgr*

EMP: 66
SALES (corp-wide): 29.01MM **Privately Held**
Web: www.cssohio.org
SIC: 8322 Social service center
PA: Consumer Support Services Inc
   2040 Cherry Valley Rd # 1
   Newark OH 43055
   740 788-8257

(G-9424)
COOK PAVING AND CNSTR CO
4545 Spring Rd (44131-1023)
PHONE..................................216 267-7705
Linda Fletcher, *Pr*
Michael Alex, *
Jim Matheos, *
Keith L Rogers, *Corporate Secretary**
EMP: 50 **EST:** 1941
SQ FT: 12,000
SALES (est): 10.47MM **Privately Held**
Web: www.cookpaving.com
SIC: 1623 8741 1795 1611 Sewer line construction; Construction management; Wrecking and demolition work; Highway and street construction

(G-9425)
CORAL COMPANY (PA)
4401 Rockside Rd Ste 390 (44131-2147)
PHONE..................................216 932-8822
Peter Rubin, *Pr*
EMP: 48 **EST:** 1987
SALES (est): 9.92MM
SALES (corp-wide): 9.92MM **Privately Held**
Web: www.thecoralcompany.com
SIC: 6552 Land subdividers and developers, commercial

(G-9426)
COVIA HOLDINGS LLC (PA)
3 Summit Park Dr Ste 700 (44131-6901)
PHONE..................................800 255-7263
◆ **EMP:** 90 **EST:** 1970
SALES (est): 1.6B
SALES (corp-wide): 1.6B **Privately Held**
Web: www.coviacorp.com
SIC: 1446 Silica mining

(G-9427)
CSA AMRICA TSTG CRTFCATION LLC
Also Called: Csa Group
8501 E Pleasant Valley Rd (44131-5516)
PHONE..................................216 524-4990
EMP: 340 **EST:** 2018
SALES (est): 8.5MM **Privately Held**
SIC: 7389 Inspection and testing services

(G-9428)
DENTALCARE PARTNERS INC
Also Called: Sears Dental Center
6200 Oak Tree Blvd Ste 200 (44131-6933)
PHONE..................................216 584-1000
EMP: 1000
Web: www.dentalonepartners.com
SIC: 8021 Dentists' office

(G-9429)
EINHEIT ELECTRIC CO
240 Tuxedo Ave (44131-1142)
PHONE..................................216 661-6000
Jerome Mraz, *Prin*
EMP: 30 **EST:** 2011
SALES (est): 20.75MM **Privately Held**
Web: www.einheitelectric.com
SIC: 1521 Single-family housing construction

(G-9430)
ENTITLE DIRECT GROUP INC
6100 Oak Tree Blvd Ste 200 (44131-6914)
PHONE..................................216 236-7800
Timothy Dwyer, *CEO*
Lee Baskey, *
EMP: 32 **EST:** 2006
SALES (est): 4.74MM **Publicly Held**
Web: orders.mytitlegenius.com
SIC: 6361 Guarantee of titles
PA: Radian Group Inc.
   550 E Swdsford Rd Ste 350
   Wayne PA 19087

(G-9431)
ESC OF CUYAHOGA COUNTY
6393 Oak Tree Blvd Ste 300 (44131-6957)
PHONE..................................216 524-3000
Doctor B Menderink, *Superintnt*
Doctor Bob Menderink, *Superintnt*
EMP: 45 **EST:** 2012
SALES (est): 477.65K **Privately Held**
Web: www.escneo.org
SIC: 8331 Manpower training

(G-9432)
FIRST HOSPITAL LABS LLC
Also Called: Fssolutions
6150 Oak Tree Blvd (44131-6917)
P.O. Box 649 (19090-0649)
PHONE..................................215 396-5500
Meredith Vadis, *Pr*
Beth Dozoretz, *
Mary Ellen Petti, *
Stephen Haller, *
Gloria Nuss, *
EMP: 185 **EST:** 1988
SQ FT: 12,000
SALES (est): 24.52MM
SALES (corp-wide): 719.64MM **Publicly Held**
Web: www.vaulthealth.com
SIC: 8741 7389 8748 Management services; Business consulting, nec
PA: Sterling Check Corp.
   6150 Oak Tree Blvd Ste 49
   Independence OH 44131
   212 736-5100

(G-9433)
GEEKS ON CALL
7100 E Pleasant Valley Rd Ste 300 (44131-5544)
PHONE..................................800 905-4335
Amanda Spivey, *Owner*
EMP: 59 **EST:** 2015
SALES (est): 620.59K **Privately Held**
Web: www.geeksoncall.com
SIC: 7378 Computer and data processing equipment repair/maintenance

(G-9434)
GRAFTECH HOLDINGS INC
6100 Oak Tree Blvd Ste 300 (44131)
PHONE..................................216 676-2000
Joel L Hawthorne, *CEO*
Erick R Asmussen, *VP*
John D Moran, *VP*
EMP: 98 **EST:** 1993
SALES (est): 9.13MM **Publicly Held**
Web: www.graftechaet.com
SIC: 1499 3624 Graphite mining; Carbon and graphite products
PA: Graftech International Ltd.
   982 Keynote Cir
   Brooklyn Heights OH 44131

(G-9435)
HALEY & ALDRICH INC
6500 Rockside Rd Ste 200 (44131-2319)
PHONE..................................216 739-0555

David Hagen, *Mgr*
EMP: 69
SALES (corp-wide): 78.95MM **Privately Held**
Web: www.haleyaldrich.com
SIC: 8711 8748 Consulting engineer; Environmental consultant
PA: Haley & Aldrich, Inc.
   70 Blanchard Rd Ste 204
   Burlington MA 01803
   781 685-2115

(G-9436)
IHS ENTERPRISE LLC (PA)
Also Called: PWC International
5755 Granger Rd Ste 905 (44131-1461)
PHONE..................................216 588-9078
Ansir Junaid, *Pr*
Liaz Shah, *
EMP: 150 **EST:** 1997
SQ FT: 75,000
SALES (est): 42.36MM **Privately Held**
SIC: 4731 Domestic freight forwarding

(G-9437)
INDEPENDENCE EXCAVATING INC (PA)
Also Called: Independence Excavating
5720 E Schaaf Rd (44131-1396)
PHONE..................................216 524-1700
Victor Digeronimo Junior, *CEO*
Robert D Digeronimo, *
Richard Digeronimo, *
Gregory T Digeronimo, *
▲ **EMP:** 50 **EST:** 1956
SQ FT: 35,000
SALES (est): 220.53MM
SALES (corp-wide): 220.53MM **Privately Held**
Web: www.indexc.com
SIC: 1629 1794 1611 1771 Land preparation construction; Excavation work; General contractor, highway and street construction; Concrete repair

(G-9438)
JAGI SPRINGHILL LLC
Also Called: Springhill Suites Independence
6060 Rockside Pl (44131-2225)
PHONE..................................216 264-4190
Michael Nanosky, *Pr*
EMP: 34 **EST:** 2016
SALES (est): 590.66K **Privately Held**
SIC: 7011 Hotels and motels

(G-9439)
K & M INTERNATIONAL INC (PA)
Also Called: Wild Republic
7711 E Pleasant Valley Rd (44131)
PHONE..................................330 425-2550
Gopala B Pillai, *Pr*
Vishnu Chandran, *
Kamala Pillai, *
Daniel Davis, *
◆ **EMP:** 65 **EST:** 1979
SALES (est): 24.5MM
SALES (corp-wide): 24.5MM **Privately Held**
Web: www.wildrepublic.com
SIC: 5092 5199 Toys, nec; Gifts and novelties

(G-9440)
KEYFACTOR INC (PA)
6150 Oak Tree Blvd Ste 200 (44131)
PHONE..................................216 785-2986
Jordan Rackie, *CEO*
Kevin Von Keyserling, *
Ken Keeler, *CFO*
Pete Rosvall, *Ch Bd*
John Harris, *

GEOGRAPHIC SECTION

Independence - Cuyahoga County (G-9463)

EMP: 105 EST: 2003
SQ FT: 6,000
SALES (est): 16.73MM
SALES (corp-wide): 16.73MM Privately Held
Web: www.keyfactor.com
SIC: 7371 Computer software development

(G-9441)
KNOWLEDGE SUPPORT SYSTEMS INC (PA)
Also Called: Kalibrate Technologies
6133 Rockside Rd Ste 302 (44131-2243)
PHONE.....................973 408-9157
Bob Stein, *Pr*
Gregg Budoi, *CFO*
EMP: 32 EST: 2000
SALES (est): 4.88MM
SALES (corp-wide): 4.88MM Privately Held
SIC: 7371 Computer software development

(G-9442)
KURTZ BROS INC (PA)
6415 Granger Rd (44131-1413)
P.O. Box 31179 (44131-0179)
PHONE.....................216 986-7000
EMP: 50 EST: 1974
SALES (est): 27.73MM
SALES (corp-wide): 27.73MM Privately Held
Web: www.kurtz-bros.com
SIC: 5031 5211 Lumber, plywood, and millwork; Lumber and other building materials

(G-9443)
LIBERTY HOME MORTGAGE CORP
6225 Oak Tree Blvd (44131)
PHONE.....................440 644-0001
Khash Saghafi, *Prin*
EMP: 139 EST: 2013
SALES (est): 11.81MM Privately Held
Web: www.libertyhomemortgage.org
SIC: 6162 7371 Mortgage brokers, using own money; Computer software development and applications

(G-9444)
LIFE LINE SCREENING AMER LTD
6150 Oak Tree Blvd Ste 200 (44131)
PHONE.....................216 581-6556
Mike Nicoletti, *Prin*
EMP: 161
Web: www.lifelinescreening.com
SIC: 8099 Health screening service
PA: Life Line Screening Of America Ltd.
    901 S Mopac Expy Ste 130
    Austin TX 78746

(G-9445)
LIGHTHOUSE INSURANCE GROUP LLC (HQ)
Also Called: Lig Solutions
6100 Rockside Woods Blvd N Ste 300 (44131)
PHONE.....................216 503-2439
Jason Farro, *CEO*
EMP: 50 EST: 2009
SALES (est): 10.41MM
SALES (corp-wide): 10.07B Publicly Held
Web: www.ligsolutions.com
SIC: 6411 Insurance agents, nec
PA: Arthur J. Gallagher & Co.
    2850 Golf Rd
    Rolling Meadows IL 60008
    630 773-3800

(G-9446)
LJB INCORPORATED
6480 Rockside Woods Blvd S Ste 290 (44131-2222)
PHONE.....................440 683-4504
Brian Frantz, *Brnch Mgr*
EMP: 35
SALES (corp-wide): 241.37K Privately Held
Web: www.ljbinc.com
SIC: 8713 8712 8711 Surveying services; Architectural services; Consulting engineer
PA: Ljb Incorporated
    2133 University Park Dr # 250
    Okemos MI 48864
    517 349-9280

(G-9447)
LOCUM MEDICAL GROUP LLC
6100 Oak Tree Blvd Ste 110 (44131-2544)
PHONE.....................216 464-2125
EMP: 55
SIC: 7363 Medical help service

(G-9448)
LONGBOW RESEARCH LLC (PA)
6100 Oak Tree Blvd Ste 440 (44131-6949)
PHONE.....................216 986-0700
EMP: 60 EST: 2003
SALES (est): 8.5MM
SALES (corp-wide): 8.5MM Privately Held
Web: www.longbowresearch.com
SIC: 6282 Investment research

(G-9449)
MAI CAPITAL MANAGEMENT LLC (PA)
Also Called: MAI Wealth Advisors
6050 Oak Tree Blvd Ste 500 (44131)
PHONE.....................216 920-4800
Richard J Buoncore, *Managing Member*
EMP: 54 EST: 2021
SALES (est): 10K
SALES (corp-wide): 10K Privately Held
Web: www.mai.capital
SIC: 6282 Investment advisory service

(G-9450)
MAXIM HEALTHCARE SERVICES INC
6155 Rockside Rd (44131-2200)
PHONE.....................216 606-3000
EMP: 92
Web: www.maximhealthcare.com
SIC: 7363 Medical help service
PA: Maxim Healthcare Services, Inc.
    7227 Lee Deforest Dr
    Columbia MD 21046

(G-9451)
MEDIQUANT LLC (PA)
6200 Oak Tree Blvd (44131-6945)
PHONE.....................440 746-2300
James Jacobs Junior, *CEO*
EMP: 128 EST: 1999
SALES (est): 28.52MM
SALES (corp-wide): 28.52MM Privately Held
Web: www.mediquant.com
SIC: 5045 Computer software

(G-9452)
MILLCRAFT GROUP LLC (PA)
Also Called: Deltacraft
9000 Rio Nero Dr (44131-5502)
PHONE.....................216 441-5500
▲ EMP: 75 EST: 1995
SALES (est): 388.34MM Privately Held
Web: www.millcraft.com
SIC: 5111 5113 2679 Printing paper; Industrial and personal service paper; Paper products, converted, nec

(G-9453)
MILLCRAFT PAPER COMPANY (HQ)
Also Called: Millcraft
9010 Rio Nero Dr (44131-5502)
▲ EMP: 52 EST: 1920
SALES (est): 388.34MM Privately Held
Web: www.millcraft.com
SIC: 5111 5113 Printing paper; Industrial and personal service paper
PA: The Millcraft Group Llc
    9000 Rio Nero Dr
    Independence OH 44131

(G-9454)
MMI-CPR LLC (HQ)
Also Called: Cpr
7100 E Pleasant Valley Rd Ste 300 (44131-5544)
PHONE.....................216 674-0645
Alan B Colberg, *Pr*
EMP: 37 EST: 2013
SQ FT: 15,000
SALES (est): 4.84MM
SALES (corp-wide): 11.13B Publicly Held
Web: www.merrymtggroup.com
SIC: 7629 Telephone set repair
PA: Assurant, Inc.
    260 Interstate N Cir Se
    Atlanta GA 30339
    770 763-1000

(G-9455)
MOLINA HEALTHCARE INC
Also Called: Molina Healthcare of Ohio
6161 Oak Tree Blvd (44131-2516)
PHONE.....................216 606-1400
EMP: 37
SALES (corp-wide): 34.07B Publicly Held
Web: www.molinahealthcare.com
SIC: 8099 Blood related health services
PA: Molina Healthcare, Inc.
    200 Oceangate Ste 100
    Long Beach CA 90802
    562 435-3666

(G-9456)
NATIONS LENDING CORPORATION
4 Summit Park Dr Ste 200 (44131-2583)
PHONE.....................877 816-1220
EMP: 77
SALES (corp-wide): 164.99MM Privately Held
Web: www.nationslending.com
SIC: 6162 Mortgage bankers
PA: Nations Lending Corporation
    4 Summit Park Dr Ste 200
    Independence OH 44131
    216 363-6901

(G-9457)
NATIONS LENDING CORPORATION (PA)
Also Called: N L C
4 Summit Park Dr Ste 200 (44131-2583)
PHONE.....................216 363-6901
Jeremy E Sopko, *CEO*
William Lee Osborne Junior, *Pr*
EMP: 195 EST: 2003
SQ FT: 8,500
SALES (est): 164.99MM
SALES (corp-wide): 164.99MM Privately Held
Web: www.nationslending.com
SIC: 6162 6163 Mortgage bankers; Mortgage brokers arranging for loans, using money of others

(G-9458)
NEW CINGULAR WIRELESS SVCS INC
Also Called: AT&T
6901 Rockside Rd Ste 10 (44131-2379)
PHONE.....................216 901-1296
Tim Hoag, *Brnch Mgr*
EMP: 27
SALES (corp-wide): 122.43B Publicly Held
SIC: 4812 Cellular telephone services
HQ: New Cingular Wireless Services, Inc.
    7277 164th Ave Ne
    Redmond WA 98052
    425 827-4500

(G-9459)
NEXTLINK WIRELESS LLC
3 Summit Park Dr Ste 750 (44131-6966)
PHONE.....................216 619-3200
Michelle Moran, *Brnch Mgr*
EMP: 1580
SALES (corp-wide): 133.97B Publicly Held
SIC: 4812 Cellular telephone services
HQ: Nextlink Wireless, Llc
    13865 Sunrise Valley Dr # 4
    Herndon VA 20171

(G-9460)
NORTHAST SRGCAL WOUND CARE INC (PA)
6100 Rockside Woods Blvd N Ste 425 (44131-2366)
PHONE.....................216 643-2780
Keith Warner, *Pr*
Shukri Elkhariri, *
Ivan Tewarson, *
Seung Kwon Lee, *
EMP: 43 EST: 1998
SALES (est): 9.31MM
SALES (corp-wide): 9.31MM Privately Held
Web: www.neswc.com
SIC: 8011 Surgeon

(G-9461)
NUONOSYS INC
Also Called: Onosys
5005 Rockside Rd Ste 1100 (44131-6800)
P.O. Box 68 (27302-0068)
PHONE.....................888 666-7976
Chris Anderle, *Pr*
EMP: 32 EST: 2016
SALES (est): 2.57MM Privately Held
Web: www.onosys.com
SIC: 7371 5734 Computer software development and applications; Software, business and non-game

(G-9462)
NVP WARRANTY
5755 Granger Rd Ste 777 (44131-1459)
PHONE.....................888 270-5835
EMP: 57 EST: 2017
SALES (est): 4.24MM Privately Held
Web: www.nvpwarranty.com
SIC: 7538 General automotive repair shops

(G-9463)
OHIO MENTOR INC (DH)
Also Called: Ohio Mentor
6200 Rockside Woods Blvd N Ste 305 (44131-2343)
PHONE.....................216 525-1885
William Mckinney, *CEO*
Edward Murphy, *
Elizabeth Hopper, *
Arthur Shea, *
Peter E Gladitsch, *

Independence - Cuyahoga County (G-9464)

EMP: 110 EST: 1984
SALES (est): 45.61MM
SALES (corp-wide): 1.64B Privately Held
Web: www.oh-mentor.com
SIC: 8059 8322 Home for the mentally retarded, ex. skilled or intermediate; General counseling services
HQ: National Mentor, Inc.
313 Congress St Fl 5
Boston MA 02210
617 790-4800

(G-9464)
OLD RPBLIC TTLE NTHRN OHIO LLC
Also Called: Old Republic
6480 Rockside Woods Blvd S Ste 170 (44131-2233)
PHONE.................................216 524-5700
EMP: 112 EST: 2002
SALES (est): 4.94MM
SALES (corp-wide): 8.08B Publicly Held
Web: www.oldrepublictitle.com
SIC: 6411 6162 6211 Insurance agents, brokers, and service; Mortgage bankers; Underwriters, security
HQ: Old Republic National Title Insurance Company
3000 Bayport Dr Ste 1000
Tampa FL 33607
800 328-4441

(G-9465)
PANTEK INCORPORATED
4401 Rockside Rd Ste 205 (44131-2144)
P.O. Box 1553 (44309-1553)
PHONE.................................216 344-1614
EMP: 42 EST: 1995
SQ FT: 3,200
SALES (est): 2.13MM Privately Held
Web: www.pantek.com
SIC: 7373 4813 Computer integrated systems design; Online service providers

(G-9466)
PFG VENTURES LP (PA)
Also Called: Proforma
8800 E Pleasant Valley Rd Ste 1 (44131-5558)
PHONE.................................216 520-8400
Greg Muzzillo, Prin
Brian Smith, Pr
Tom Rizzi, Sr VP
EMP: 100 EST: 1999
SQ FT: 30,000
SALES (est): 51.16MM Privately Held
Web: www.proforma.com
SIC: 5112 6794 Stationery and office supplies; Franchises, selling or licensing

(G-9467)
PLUMBERS LCAL 55 FEDERAL CR UN
980 Keynote Cir (44131-1828)
PHONE.................................216 459-0099
Doreen Cannon, Pr
EMP: 27 EST: 2015
SALES (est): 935.49K Privately Held
Web: www.plumbers55.com
SIC: 8631 Labor union

(G-9468)
POLYMER ADDITIVES INC (HQ)
Also Called: Valtris Specialty Chemicals
7500 E Pleasant Valley Rd (44131-5536)
PHONE.................................216 875-7200
Simon Medley, CEO
Ron Masterson, COO
◆ EMP: 75 EST: 2014
SQ FT: 30,000
SALES (est): 465.61MM
SALES (corp-wide): 465.61MM Privately Held

Web: www.valtris.com
SIC: 5169 Chemicals and allied products, nec
PA: Polymer Additives Holdings, Inc.
7500 E Pleasant Valley Rd
Independence OH 44131
216 875-7200

(G-9469)
POLYMER ADDITIVES HOLDINGS INC (PA)
Also Called: Valtris
7500 E Pleasant Valley Rd (44131-5536)
PHONE.................................216 875-7200
Paul Angus, Pr
Andy Gehrlein, *
Jim Mason, *
Steve Hughes, Comm Vice President*
EMP: 200 EST: 2014
SALES (est): 465.61MM
SALES (corp-wide): 465.61MM Privately Held
Web: www.valtris.com
SIC: 5169 2899 Chemicals and allied products, nec; Chemical preparations, nec

(G-9470)
PRECISION ENVIRONMENTAL CO (HQ)
5500 Old Brecksville Rd (44131-1508)
PHONE.................................216 642-6040
Tony Digeronimo, Pr
Jim Reeves, *
EMP: 296 EST: 1987
SALES (est): 57.3MM Privately Held
Web: www.precision-env.com
SIC: 1799 Asbestos removal and encapsulation
PA: Integrated Solutions, Inc.
215 S Laura Ave
Wichita KS 67211

(G-9471)
PRECISION METALFORMING ASSN
6363 Oak Tree Blvd (44131-2556)
PHONE.................................216 901-8800
William E Gaskin, CEO
Doug Johnson, *
David C Klotz, *
Daniel E Ellashek, *
Bill Smith, *
▲ EMP: 41 EST: 1942
SQ FT: 20,000
SALES (est): 75.76K Privately Held
Web: www.pma.org
SIC: 8611 2731 Trade associations; Book publishing

(G-9472)
PROFORMA INC (PA)
Also Called: Proforma Worldwide Support Ctr
8800 E Pleasant Valley Rd Ste 1 (44131)
PHONE.................................800 825-1525
Greg Muzzillo, CEO
Vera Muzzillo, *
Brian Smith, *
Greg Armstrong, *
Charity Gibson, CMO*
EMP: 141 EST: 1978
SQ FT: 30,000
SALES (est): 55.19MM
SALES (corp-wide): 55.19MM Privately Held
Web: www.proforma.com
SIC: 5112 Stationery and office supplies

(G-9473)
PROGRSSIVE FGHTING SYSTEMS LLC
Also Called: Strong Style Mma Training Ctr
6900 Granger Rd (44131-1414)

PHONE.................................216 520-0271
Marcus A Marinelli, Managing Member
EMP: 50 EST: 2007
SALES (est): 1.07MM Privately Held
Web: www.strongstyle.com
SIC: 7999 7991 Martial arts school, nec; Physical fitness facilities

(G-9474)
PROTEGIS LLC (DH)
Also Called: Protegis Fire & Safety
6155 Rockside Rd Ste 400 (44131-2217)
PHONE.................................216 377-3044
Don Combs, *
EMP: 32 EST: 1985
SQ FT: 17,000
SALES (est): 26MM
SALES (corp-wide): 559.39MM Privately Held
Web: www.protegis.com
SIC: 7382 Security systems services
HQ: Summit Fire & Security Llc
1025 Telegraph St
Reno NV 89502

(G-9475)
REHMANN ROBSON LLC
Also Called: Rehmann
6060 Rockside Woods Blvd N Ste 125 (44131-7303)
PHONE.................................248 952-5000
Adam Williams, Brnch Mgr
EMP: 31
SALES (corp-wide): 102.74MM Privately Held
Web: www.rehmann.com
SIC: 8721 7381 Certified public accountant; Private investigator
HQ: Rehmann Robson Llc
5800 Gratiot Rd Ste 201
Saginaw MI 48638
989 799-9580

(G-9476)
RESOURCE TITLE NAT AGCY INC
7100 E Pleasant Valley Rd Ste 100 (44131-5544)
PHONE.................................216 520-0050
EMP: 64 EST: 2010
SQ FT: 9,000
SALES (est): 18.24MM Privately Held
Web: www.rtnai.com
SIC: 6361 6531 Real estate title insurance; Escrow agent, real estate

(G-9477)
ROCKSIDE HOSPITALITY LLC
Also Called: Crowne Plz Clvland Sth/Ndpndnc
5300 Rockside Rd (44131-2118)
PHONE.................................216 524-0700
Gloria Maciak, Contrlr
EMP: 81 EST: 2009
SALES (est): 2.47MM Privately Held
Web: www.ihg.com
SIC: 7011 Hotels

(G-9478)
ROE DENTAL LABORATORY INC
7165 E Pleasant Valley Rd (44131)
PHONE.................................216 663-2233
Bruce Kowalski, Pr
Dana Kowalski, *
EMP: 57 EST: 1930
SQ FT: 8,500
SALES (est): 10.92MM Privately Held
Web: www.roedentallab.com
SIC: 8072 Crown and bridge production

(G-9479)
ROSE COMMUNITY MANAGEMENT LLC (PA)
6000 Freedom Square Dr Ste 500 (44131)
PHONE.................................917 542-3600
Angelo Pimpas, Pr
EMP: 195 EST: 2003
SQ FT: 11,000
SALES (est): 20.97MM
SALES (corp-wide): 20.97MM Privately Held
Web: www.rosecommunity.com
SIC: 6531 Real estate managers

(G-9480)
ROSS BRITTAIN SCHONBERG LPA
6480 Rockside Woods Blvd S Ste 350 (44131-2224)
PHONE.................................216 447-1551
Alan Ross, Pr
Lynn Schonberg, *
Brian Brittain, *
Richard Walters, *
Patrick Harrington, *
EMP: 34 EST: 1991
SQ FT: 11,257
SALES (est): 5.48MM Privately Held
Web: www.rbslaw.com
SIC: 8111 Labor and employment law

(G-9481)
RWK SERVICES INC CCI
4700 Rockside Rd Ste 330 (44131-2151)
PHONE.................................216 387-3754
EMP: 28 EST: 2020
SALES (est): 230.14K Privately Held
Web: www.rwkservices.com
SIC: 7349 Janitorial service, contract basis

(G-9482)
SEARCH MASTERS INC
2 Summit Park Dr (44131-6919)
PHONE.................................216 532-8660
Tom Soko, Pr
John Venesile, VP
Tom Maine, VP
EMP: 47 EST: 1973
SALES (est): 6.23MM Privately Held
Web: www.searchmasters.com
SIC: 7361 Executive placement

(G-9483)
SIRVA MORTGAGE INC
Also Called: CMS Mortgage Services
6200 Oak Tree Blvd Ste 300 (44131-6934)
PHONE.................................800 531-3837
Paul Klemme, Pr
EMP: 99 EST: 1992
SALES (est): 9.67MM
SALES (corp-wide): 1.63B Privately Held
Web: myrewards.sirvahomebenefits.com
SIC: 6162 Mortgage bankers
HQ: Cms Holding, Llc
700 Oakmont Ln
Westmont IL 60559

(G-9484)
SIRVA RELOCATION LLC (DH)
Also Called: Sirva Worldwide Relocation Mvg
6200 Oak Tree Blvd Ste 300 (44131-6934)
PHONE.................................216 606-4000
Deborah L Balli, Pr
Katrina Lea, *
Douglas V Gathany, *
Steve Uveges, *
Eryk J Spytek, *
EMP: 385 EST: 1981
SALES (est): 40.11MM
SALES (corp-wide): 1.63B Privately Held
Web: www.sirva.com

GEOGRAPHIC SECTION

Ironton - Lawrence County (G-9505)

SIC: 7389 Relocation service
HQ: North American Van Lines, Inc.
101 E Wash Blvd Ste 1100
Fort Wayne IN 46802
800 348-3746

(G-9485)
STERLING CHECK CORP (PA)
6150 Oak Tree Blvd Ste 490 (44131)
PHONE..................212 736-5100
Joshua Peirez, *CEO*
Michael Grebe, *Ch Bd*
Lou Paglia, *Pr*
Peter Walker, *Ex VP*
Steven Barnett, *Legal RISK*
EMP: 56 **EST:** 2015
SALES (est): 719.64MM
SALES (corp-wide): 719.64MM **Publicly Held**
Web: www.sterlingcheck.com
SIC: 8742 Human resource consulting services

(G-9486)
STERLING INFOSYSTEMS INC (DH)
Also Called: Sterlingbackcheck
6150 Oak Tree Blvd Ste 490 (44131-6976)
PHONE..................212 736-5100
Josh Peirez, *CEO*
Lou Paglia, *
Steve Barnett, *RISK Legal**
Peter Walker, *
EMP: 352 **EST:** 1975
SQ FT: 40,000
SALES (est): 404.76MM
SALES (corp-wide): 719.64MM **Publicly Held**
Web: www.sterlingcheck.com
SIC: 8742 Human resource consulting services
HQ: Sterling Intermediate Corp
6150 Oak Tree Blvd Ste 49
Independence OH 44131
212 736-5100

(G-9487)
STERLING INFOSYSTEMS INC
Also Called: Occupational Hlth Safety Dept
4511 Rockside Rd Fl 4 (44131-2199)
PHONE..................216 685-7600
Kurt Schwall, *Prin*
EMP: 352
SALES (corp-wide): 719.64MM **Publicly Held**
Web: www.sterlingcheck.com
SIC: 7381 7389 Private investigator; Personal investigation service
HQ: Sterling Infosystems, Inc.
6150 Oak Tree Blvd # 490
Independence OH 44131
212 736-5100

(G-9488)
STRATEGIC WEALTH PARTNERS
5005 Rockside Rd Ste 1200 (44131-6829)
PHONE..................216 800-9000
Mark Tepper, *Prin*
EMP: 28 **EST:** 2009
SALES (est): 5.93MM **Privately Held**
Web: www.swpconnect.com
SIC: 6282 6722 Investment advisory service; Management investment, open-end

(G-9489)
TALERIS CREDIT UNION INC
6111 Oak Tree Blvd Ste 110 (44131-2589)
P.O. Box 318072 (44131-8072)
PHONE..................216 739-2300
Robin D Thomas, *Pr*
James Mckenzie, *VP Opers*
Harley Hill, *
EMP: 45 **EST:** 1935
SALES (est): 2.94MM **Privately Held**
Web: www.taleriscu.org
SIC: 6061 Federal credit unions

(G-9490)
THYSSENKRUPP MATERIALS NA INC
6050 Oak Tree Blvd Ste 110 (44131-6927)
PHONE..................216 883-8100
Randy Pacelli, *Brnch Mgr*
EMP: 60
SQ FT: 65,000
SALES (corp-wide): 40.78B **Privately Held**
Web: www.thyssenkrupp-materials-na.com
SIC: 5051 3341 Steel; Secondary nonferrous metals
HQ: Thyssenkrupp Materials Na, Inc.
22355 W 11 Mile Rd
Southfield MI 48033
248 233-5600

(G-9491)
TRADES EQUIPMENT LLC
8200 E Pleasant Valley Rd (44131-5523)
PHONE..................419 625-4444
James Eble, *Pr*
▲ **EMP:** 50 **EST:** 1994
SQ FT: 4,000
SALES (est): 9.87MM **Privately Held**
Web: www.mrrooter.com
SIC: 1711 Plumbing contractors

(G-9492)
UNITED STTES PRTCTIVE SVCS COR (PA)
Also Called: U S Protective Services
750 W Resource Dr Ste 200 (44131-1879)
P.O. Box 28222 (44128-0222)
PHONE..................216 475-8550
Theodore Cohen Junior, *Pr*
Gilda Cohen, *
EMP: 50 **EST:** 1988
SQ FT: 48,000
SALES (est): 5.08MM **Privately Held**
Web: www.usprotective.net
SIC: 7382 Burglar alarm maintenance and monitoring

(G-9493)
UNITED TRNSP UN INSUR ASSN (PA)
Also Called: SMART - TRANSPORTATION DIVISIO
6060 Rockside Woods Blvd N (44131-7303)
PHONE..................216 228-9400
John Previsich, *Pr*
Dan Johnson, *
C F Lane, *
Charles Luna, *
◆ **EMP:** 120 **EST:** 1969
SALES (est): 17.68MM
SALES (corp-wide): 17.68MM **Privately Held**
Web: www.utuia.org
SIC: 8631 6411 Labor union; Insurance agents, brokers, and service

(G-9494)
VALASSIS DIRECT MAIL INC
Also Called: Valassis
3 Summit Park Dr Ste 430 (44131-2582)
PHONE..................216 573-1400
Rick Brouse, *Mgr*
EMP: 56
Web: www.vericast.com
SIC: 7331 Mailing service
HQ: Valassis Direct Mail, Inc.
15955 La Cantera Pkwy
San Antonio TX 78256
800 437-0479

(G-9495)
VALIC FINANCIAL ADVISOR
2 Summit Park Dr (44131-2553)
PHONE..................216 643-6340
Donald Koller, *Reg Dir*
EMP: 31 **EST:** 2015
SALES (est): 470.72K **Privately Held**
Web: www.corebridgefinancial.com
SIC: 6311 Life insurance

(G-9496)
VIAQUEST RESIDENTIAL SVCS LLC
4700 Rockside Rd Ste 100 (44131-2148)
PHONE..................216 446-2650
Regan Eveland, *Admn*
EMP: 215
Web: www.viaquestinc.com
SIC: 8082 Home health care services
PA: Viaquest Residential Services, Llc
525 Metro Pl N Ste 350
Dublin OH 43017

(G-9497)
VISITING NRSE ASSN HLTHCARE PR
Also Called: Visiting Nurse
925 Keynote Cir Ste 300 (44131-1869)
PHONE..................216 931-1300
EMP: 104 **EST:** 2010
SALES (est): 513.06K **Privately Held**
Web: www.vnaohio.org
SIC: 8082 Visiting nurse service

(G-9498)
WEDRON SILICA LLC
3 Summit Park Dr Ste 700 (44131)
P.O. Box 119 (60557)
PHONE..................815 433-2449
William Conway, *Ch*
Charles Fowler, *
Jennifer Deckard, *
Joseph Fodo, *
David Crandall, *
EMP: 90 **EST:** 1984
SQ FT: 4,500
SALES (est): 17.45MM
SALES (corp-wide): 1.6B **Privately Held**
SIC: 1446 Industrial sand
HQ: Covia Solutions Inc.
3 Summit Park Dr Ste 700
Independence OH 44131
404 214-3200

(G-9499)
WELLNESS IQ INC
6450 Rockside Woods Blvd S Ste 220 (44131-2237)
PHONE..................216 264-2727
Lisa M Theis, *Prin*
EMP: 34 **EST:** 2013
SALES (est): 5.68MM **Privately Held**
Web: www.wellnessiq.net
SIC: 8099 Health and allied services, nec

(G-9500)
WELTMAN WEINBERG & REIS CO LPA (PA)
Also Called: WW&r
965 Keynote Cir (44131-1829)
PHONE..................216 685-1000
Robert B Weltman, *Pr*
Alan Weinberg, *
Theresa Fortunato, *
Terrence Heffernan, *
Alan Hochheiser, *
EMP: 170 **EST:** 1951
SALES (est): 68.52MM
SALES (corp-wide): 68.52MM **Privately Held**
Web: www.weltman.com

SIC: 8111 General practice law office

Ironton
Lawrence County

(G-9501)
AHF OHIO INC
Also Called: Sanctuary At The Ohio Valley
2932 S 5th St (45638-2865)
PHONE..................740 532-6188
Brian Eichenlaub, *Admn*
EMP: 68
SALES (corp-wide): 25.83MM **Privately Held**
Web: www.ahfohio.com
SIC: 8051 Skilled nursing care facilities
PA: Ahf Ohio, Inc.
5920 Venture Dr Ste 100
Dublin OH 43017
614 760-7352

(G-9502)
AMERICAN HYDRAULIC SVCS INC
1912 S 1st St (45638-2478)
P.O. Box 624 (41129-0624)
PHONE..................606 739-8680
Jeremiah Fulks, *Pr*
Randall Blankenship, *
▲ **EMP:** 41 **EST:** 2001
SALES (est): 9.14MM **Privately Held**
Web: www.americanhydraulic.net
SIC: 3593 7699 Fluid power cylinders, hydraulic or pneumatic; Hydraulic equipment repair

(G-9503)
BLAST-ALL INC
541 Private Road 908 (45638-8602)
P.O. Box 603 (45638-0603)
PHONE..................606 393-5786
Katerine Nieman, *CEO*
Tim Price, *
James Price, *
Rob Marshall, *
EMP: 40 **EST:** 2014
SALES (est): 1.28MM **Privately Held**
Web: www.blast-all.com
SIC: 7349 Cleaning service, industrial or commercial

(G-9504)
BRYANT HEALTH CENTER INC
Also Called: Sanctuary of The Ohio Valley
2932 S 5th St (45638-2865)
P.O. Box 683 (45638-0683)
PHONE..................740 532-6188
Robert Banasik, *Pr*
EMP: 69 **EST:** 1983
SALES (est): 9.36MM
SALES (corp-wide): 14.06MM **Privately Held**
SIC: 8059 8051 Nursing home, except skilled and intermediate care facility; Skilled nursing care facilities
PA: Omnilife Health Care Systems, Inc.
50 W 5th Ave
Columbus OH 43201
614 299-3100

(G-9505)
BWC TRUCKING COMPANY INC
164 State Route 650 (45638)
P.O. Box 267 (45638)
PHONE..................740 532-5188
EMP: 50 **EST:** 1993
SQ FT: 1,020
SALES (est): 8.22MM **Privately Held**
Web: www.bwctrucking.com

Ironton - Lawrence County (G-9506)

SIC: 4213 Trucking, except local

(G-9506)
COAL GROVE LONG TERM CARE INC
Also Called: Sunset Nursing Center
813 1/2 Marion Pike (45638-3070)
PHONE...............................740 532-0449
David Dixon, *Admn*
EMP: 27
SALES (est): 1.74MM **Privately Held**
SIC: 8051 Convalescent home with continuous nursing care

(G-9507)
HECLA WATER ASSOCIATION (PA)
3190 State Route 141 (45638-8486)
PHONE...............................740 533-0526
Ray Howard, *CEO*
EMP: 33 **EST:** 1969
SQ FT: 8,000
SALES (est): 8.26MM
SALES (corp-wide): 8.26MM **Privately Held**
Web: www.heclawater.com
SIC: 4941 Water supply

(G-9508)
IRONTON LWRNCE CNTY AREA CMNTY (PA)
305 N 5th St (45638-1578)
PHONE...............................740 532-3534
Doctor Gossett, *Ex Dir*
EMP: 260 **EST:** 1965
SQ FT: 4,500
SALES (est): 40.69MM
SALES (corp-wide): 40.69MM **Privately Held**
Web: www.ilcao.org
SIC: 4111 8099 8351 8331 Local and suburban transit; Nutrition services; Preschool center; Job training and related services

(G-9509)
J & J GENERAL MAINTENANCE INC
2430 S 3rd St (45638-2637)
PHONE...............................740 533-9729
Jackie Fields, *Pr*
Jackie Fields, *Pr*
Jeffery Fields, *
EMP: 80 **EST:** 2008
SQ FT: 1,800
SALES (est): 12.08MM **Privately Held**
Web: www.jjgmi.com
SIC: 1731 1711 1794 1623 General electrical contractor; Plumbing, heating, air-conditioning; Excavation and grading, building construction; Water and sewer line construction

(G-9510)
JO-LIN HEALTH CENTER INC
1050 Clinton St (45638-2876)
P.O. Box 329 (45638-0329)
PHONE...............................740 532-0860
Jo L Heaberlin, *Pr*
Jo Linda Heaberlin, *Pr*
Richard Heaberlin, *
Delores Jean Dalton, *
EMP: 48 **EST:** 1974
SQ FT: 20,000
SALES (est): 2.01MM **Privately Held**
SIC: 8361 8051 Rehabilitation center, residential: health care incidental; Skilled nursing care facilities

(G-9511)
MENDED REEDS SERVICES INC
Also Called: MENDED REEDS MENTAL HEALTH
700 Park Ave (45638-1502)
P.O. Box 108 (45638-0108)
PHONE...............................740 532-6220
David Lambert, *Ex Dir*
Ed Carpenter, *
EMP: 115 **EST:** 2014
SALES (est): 883.24K **Privately Held**
Web: www.mendedreedsservices.com
SIC: 8322 Adoption services

(G-9512)
MI - DE - CON INC
3331 S 3rd St (45638-2863)
P.O. Box 4450 (45638-4450)
PHONE...............................740 532-2277
Michael L Floyd, *Pr*
Dennis L Salyers, *
Michael L Floyd, *Pr*
EMP: 99 **EST:** 1999
SALES (est): 25.59MM **Privately Held**
Web: www.midecon-inc.com
SIC: 1542 Nonresidential construction, nec

(G-9513)
SHERMAN THOMPSON OH TC LP
275 N 3rd St (45638-1469)
PHONE...............................216 520-1250
Frank Sinito, *Genl Pt*
EMP: 99
SALES (est): 2.03MM **Privately Held**
Web: www.shermanthompsontowers.com
SIC: 6513 Apartment building operators

(G-9514)
SOUTHERN OHIO BHVORAL HLTH LLC
2113 S 7th St (45638-2538)
P.O. Box 327 (45638-0327)
PHONE...............................740 533-0055
EMP: 45 **EST:** 2004
SQ FT: 1,500
SALES (est): 1.09MM **Privately Held**
Web: www.sobhforyou.com
SIC: 8093 Mental health clinic, outpatient

Jackson
Jackson County

(G-9515)
A J STOCKMEISTER INC (PA)
702 E Main St (45640-2131)
P.O. Box 667 (45640-0667)
PHONE...............................740 286-2106
Alan Stockmeister, *Ch Bd*
Tom Geiger, *
Seth Stockmeister, *
Kay Howe, *
EMP: 30 **EST:** 1947
SQ FT: 5,000
SALES (est): 6.56MM
SALES (corp-wide): 6.56MM **Privately Held**
Web: www.stockmeister.com
SIC: 1711 Mechanical contractor

(G-9516)
BRENMAR CONSTRUCTION INC
900 Morton St (45640-1089)
PHONE...............................740 286-2151
Todd Ghearing, *Pr*
Tim Ousley, *
Andy Graham, *
EMP: 68 **EST:** 1988
SQ FT: 5,000
SALES (est): 22.06MM **Privately Held**
Web: www.brenmarconstruction.com
SIC: 1542 3312 Commercial and office building contractors; Structural shapes and pilings, steel

(G-9517)
CHILD DEV CTR JACKSON CNTY
692 Pattonsville Rd (45640)
P.O. Box 431 (45640)
PHONE...............................740 286-3995
Marlene D Ray, *Ex Dir*
EMP: 35 **EST:** 1972
SQ FT: 4,000
SALES (est): 828.66K **Privately Held**
Web: www.cdcjackson.com
SIC: 8351 Group day care center

(G-9518)
GEIGER BROTHERS INC
Also Called: Geiger Brothers
317 Ralph St (45640-2036)
P.O. Box 469 (45640-0469)
PHONE...............................740 286-0800
EMP: 400 **EST:** 1909
SALES (est): 140.15MM **Privately Held**
Web: www.geigerbrothers.com
SIC: 1541 8711 1731 1711 Industrial buildings, new construction, nec; Construction and civil engineering; Electric power systems contractors; Mechanical contractor

(G-9519)
HOLZER HOME CARE SERVICES
100 Jackson Hill Rd (45640)
PHONE...............................740 288-4287
Ramona Jenkins, *Dir*
Patty Snider, *Mgr*
EMP: 77 **EST:** 2002
SALES (est): 5.82MM
SALES (corp-wide): 337.52MM **Privately Held**
SIC: 8082 Home health care services
HQ: Holzer Hospital Foundation Inc
100 Jackson Pike
Gallipolis OH 45631
740 446-5000

(G-9520)
HOLZER MEDICAL CTR - JACKSON
500 Burlington Rd (45640-9360)
PHONE...............................740 288-4625
Ross A Matlack, *Pr*
Rhonda Dailey, *
EMP: 100 **EST:** 2000
SALES (est): 29.91MM **Privately Held**
SIC: 8062 General medical and surgical hospitals

(G-9521)
HOSSER ASSISTED LIVING
101 Markham Dr (45640-8697)
PHONE...............................740 286-8785
Jami Gross, *Admn*
EMP: 34 **EST:** 2000
SQ FT: 36,000
SALES (est): 2.5MM **Privately Held**
SIC: 8051 Skilled nursing care facilities

(G-9522)
JACKSON COUNTY BD ON AGING INC (PA)
Also Called: JACKSON COUNTY SENIOR CITIZENS
25 E Mound St (45640-1223)
PHONE...............................740 286-2909
Anglea Harrisison, *Dir*
Rose Henson, *
EMP: 40 **EST:** 1973
SALES (est): 1.22MM
SALES (corp-wide): 1.22MM **Privately Held**
Web: transportation.jvcai.org
SIC: 8322 Old age assistance

(G-9523)
OAK HILL FINANCIAL INC
14621 State Route 93 (45640-9767)
PHONE...............................740 286-3283
EMP: 459 **EST:** 1981
SALES (est): 8.82MM **Privately Held**
SIC: 7389 Personal service agents, brokers, and bureaus

(G-9524)
RED ROOF INNS INC
Also Called: Red Roof Inn
1000 Acy Ave (45640-9536)
P.O. Box 667 (45640-0667)
PHONE...............................740 288-1200
EMP: 31
Web: www.redroof.com
SIC: 7011 Hotels and motels
HQ: Red Roof Inns, Inc.
7815 Walton Pkwy
New Albany OH 43054
614 744-2600

(G-9525)
STOCKMEISTER ENTERPRISES INC
700 E Main St (45640-2131)
P.O. Box 684 (45640-0684)
PHONE...............................740 286-1619
Alan Stockmeister, *CEO*
EMP: 27 **EST:** 1972
SQ FT: 5,300
SALES (est): 9.94MM **Privately Held**
Web: www.stockmeister.com
SIC: 1542 Commercial and office building, new construction

(G-9526)
TRACTOR SUPPLY COMPANY
Also Called: Tractor Supply 673
780 E Main St (45640-2131)
PHONE...............................740 288-1079
Joyce Mcdonald, *Mgr*
EMP: 38
SALES (corp-wide): 14.56B **Publicly Held**
Web: www.tractorsupply.com
SIC: 5191 Farm supplies
PA: Tractor Supply Company
5401 Virginia Way
Brentwood TN 37027
615 440-4000

(G-9527)
UNITED CHURCH HOMES INC
Also Called: Four Winds Nursing Facility
215 Seth Ave (45640-9405)
PHONE...............................740 286-7551
John Evans, *Admn*
EMP: 47
SALES (corp-wide): 115.52MM **Privately Held**
Web: www.unitedchurchhomes.org
SIC: 8052 8051 Intermediate care facilities; Skilled nursing care facilities
PA: United Church Homes, Inc.
170 E Center St
Marion OH 43302
800 837-2211

(G-9528)
WALMART INC
Also Called: Walmart
100 Walmart Dr (45640-8692)
PHONE...............................740 286-8203
Danny Tharpe, *Brnch Mgr*
EMP: 29
SQ FT: 188,222
SALES (corp-wide): 648.13B **Publicly Held**

GEOGRAPHIC SECTION

Web: corporate.walmart.com
SIC: **5311** 5411 5912 5048 Department stores, discount; Supermarkets, greater than 100,000 square feet (hypermarket); Drug stores and proprietary stores; Ophthalmic goods
PA: Walmart Inc.
702 Sw 8th St
Bentonville AR 72716
479 273-4000

(G-9529)
WATERLOO COAL COMPANY INC (PA)
Also Called: Madison Mine Supply Co
235 E Main St (45640-1715)
P.O. Box 626 (45640-0626)
PHONE..............................740 286-0004
EMP: 70 **EST:** 1934
SALES (est): 23.4MM
SALES (corp-wide): 23.4MM **Privately Held**
Web: www.waterloocoal.com
SIC: **1221** 1411 1459 Strip mining, bituminous; Limestone, dimension-quarrying ; Clays (common) quarrying

(G-9530)
YOUNG MNS CHRSTN ASSN MTRO LOS
Also Called: Jackson Area YMCA
594 E Main St (45640-2163)
PHONE..............................740 286-7008
Heather Hill, *Dir*
EMP: 52
SALES (corp-wide): 73.8MM **Privately Held**
Web: www.jacksonareaymca.org
SIC: **7991** 7997 Athletic club and gymnasiums, membership; Membership sports and recreation clubs
PA: Young Men's Christian Association Of Metropolitan Los Angeles
625 S New Hampshire Ave
Los Angeles CA 90005
213 380-6448

Jackson Center
Shelby County

(G-9531)
EMI CORP (PA)
Also Called: E M I Plastic Equipment
801 W Pike St (45334-6037)
P.O. Box 590 (45334-0590)
PHONE..............................937 596-5511
James E Andraitis, *Pr*
Brad Wren, *
Linda Andraitis-varljen, *Treas*
▲ **EMP:** 85 **EST:** 1980
SQ FT: 80,000
SALES (est): 38.37MM
SALES (corp-wide): 38.37MM **Privately Held**
Web: www.emicorp.com
SIC: **3544** 5084 Special dies, tools, jigs, and fixtures; Industrial machinery and equipment

(G-9532)
PLASTIPAK PACKAGING INC
300 Washington St (45334-4013)
PHONE..............................937 596-5166
William P Young, *Brnch Mgr*
EMP: 51
SALES (corp-wide): 2.9B **Privately Held**
Web: www.plastipak.com
SIC: **5199** Packaging materials
HQ: Plastipak Packaging, Inc.
41605 Ann Arbor Rd E
Plymouth MI 48170
734 455-3600

(G-9533)
RISING SUN EXPRESS LLC
1003 S Main St (45334-1123)
P.O. Box 610 (45334-0610)
PHONE..............................937 596-6167
Herman Mcbride, *Managing Member*
Barbara Howerton, *
EMP: 90 **EST:** 1981
SALES (est): 8.69MM **Privately Held**
Web: www.risingsunexpress.com
SIC: **4213** 4212 Trucking, except local; Local trucking, without storage

Jamestown
Greene County

(G-9534)
CLINTON ALUMINUM DIST INC
5120 Waynesville Jamestown Rd (45335)
PHONE..............................866 636-7640
EMP: 44
SALES (corp-wide): 78.78MM **Privately Held**
Web: www.clintonaluminum.com
SIC: **5051** Steel
PA: Clinton Aluminum Distribution, Inc.
2811 Eastern Rd
Norton OH 44203
330 882-6743

(G-9535)
LIBERTY NRSING CTR OF JMESTOWN
4960 Old Us Route 35 E (45335-1712)
PHONE..............................937 675-3311
Linda Black-kurck, *Pr*
Linda Blackkurck, *
EMP: 34 **EST:** 2001
SALES (est): 727.27K **Privately Held**
Web: www.libertynursingcenters.com
SIC: **8051** Convalescent home with continuous nursing care

(G-9536)
TWIST AERO LLC
5100 Waynesville Jamestown Rd (45335)
P.O. Box 177 (45335-0177)
PHONE..............................937 675-9581
EMP: 45 **EST:** 2018
SALES (est): 2.9MM **Privately Held**
Web: www.twistaero.com
SIC: **7363** Pilot service, aviation

Jefferson
Ashtabula County

(G-9537)
AMERICAN POWER TOWER LLC
538 Goodale Rd (44047-9546)
PHONE..............................440 261-2245
Cole Bryson, *Managing Member*
Michael Bryson, *Genl Mgr*
EMP: 28 **EST:** 2021
SALES (est): 5.19MM **Privately Held**
SIC: **1623** Transmitting tower (telecommunication) construction

(G-9538)
COUNTY OF ASHTABULA
Also Called: Ashtabula County Highway Dept
186 E Satin St (44047-1419)
PHONE..............................440 576-2816
Timothy Martin, *Mgr*
EMP: 182
SQ FT: 250
Web: www.ashtabulacounty.us

SIC: **1611** Highway and street maintenance
PA: County Of Ashtabula
25 W Jefferson St
Jefferson OH 44047

(G-9539)
RAGS BROOMS & MOPS INC
790 State Route 307 E (44047)
PHONE..............................440 969-0164
Michele Simmen, *Pr*
EMP: 75 **EST:** 1999
SALES (est): 777.13K **Privately Held**
Web: www.ragsbroomsandmops.com
SIC: **7349** Cleaning service, industrial or commercial

Jeffersonville
Fayette County

(G-9540)
MEANDER HSPITALITY GROUP V LLC
Also Called: Fairfield Inn
11349 Allen Rd (43128-9773)
PHONE..............................740 948-9305
Janet Perry, *of Optns*
EMP: 49 **EST:** 2013
SQ FT: 41,810
SALES (est): 935.31K **Privately Held**
Web: fairfield.marriott.com
SIC: **7011** Hotels and motels

(G-9541)
OMSAGAR HOTELS LTD
11431 Allen Rd (43128-9773)
PHONE..............................703 675-7785
Joshue Hudson, *Brnch Mgr*
EMP: 80
SALES (corp-wide): 262.58K **Privately Held**
SIC: **7011** Hotels
PA: Omsagar Hotels, Ltd.
300 S 2nd St Fl 2
Columbus OH

(G-9542)
PRIME OUTLETS ACQUISITION LLC
Also Called: Prime Otlets At Jffrsonville I
8000 Factory Shops Blvd (43128-9600)
PHONE..............................740 948-9090
EMP: 28
SIC: **6512** 8611 Shopping center, property operation only; Business associations
HQ: Prime Outlets Acquisition Llc
225 W Washington St
Indianapolis IN 46204

Jewett
Harrison County

(G-9543)
MARKWEST UTICA EMG LLC
46700 Giacobbi Rd (43986-9553)
PHONE..............................740 942-4810
Frank M Semple, *Brnch Mgr*
EMP: 175
Web: www.markwest.com
SIC: **1321** Natural gas liquids
HQ: Markwest Utica Emg, L.L.C.
1515 Arapahoe St
Denver CO 80202
303 925-9200

Johnstown
Licking County

(G-9544)
ATRIUM APPAREL CORPORATION
188 Commerce Blvd (43031-9011)
PHONE..............................740 966-8200
Douglas Tu, *Pr*
Dave Hirsch, *
Jason Tu, *
EMP: 65 **EST:** 1996
SQ FT: 80,000
SALES (est): 8.04MM **Privately Held**
Web: www.atriumco.com
SIC: **7389** Apparel designers, commercial

(G-9545)
CARLISLE MSNRY/CNSTRUCTION INC
6300 Van Fossen Rd (43031-9414)
PHONE..............................740 966-5045
Tim Carlisle, *Pr*
EMP: 35 **EST:** 1989
SQ FT: 5,022
SALES (est): 2.48MM **Privately Held**
SIC: **1741** Masonry and other stonework

(G-9546)
HEIMERL FARMS LTD
3891 Mink St (43031-9529)
PHONE..............................740 967-0063
James Heimerl, *CEO*
Brad Heimerl, *
Matt Heimerl, *
EMP: 40 **EST:** 1975
SALES (est): 2.62MM **Privately Held**
Web: www.heimerlfarms.com
SIC: **0191** General farms, primarily crop

(G-9547)
KNOWLTON DEVELOPMENT CORP
8825 Smiths Mill Rd (43031)
PHONE..............................614 656-1130
Nick Whitley, *CEO*
EMP: 28 **EST:** 2013
SALES (est): 510.8K
SALES (corp-wide): 1.7B **Privately Held**
Web: kdc-companies.com.bitverzo.com
SIC: **8741** Management services
PA: Corporation Developpement Knowlton Inc.
210-375 Boul Roland-Therrien
Longueuil QC J4H 4
450 243-2000

(G-9548)
PETERMANN LTD
6097 Johnstown Utica Rd (43031-9408)
PHONE..............................740 967-7533
EMP: 173
Web: www.petermannbus.com
SIC: **4119** Local passenger transportation, nec
HQ: Petermann Ltd
1861 Section Rd
Cincinnati OH 45237

(G-9549)
TECHNICAL RUBBER COMPANY INC (PA)
Also Called: Tech International
200 E Coshocton St (43031)
P.O. Box 486 (43031)
PHONE..............................740 967-9015
Dan Layne, *Pr*
Robert Overs, *
Jeff Sellers, *
Gary Armstrong, *
Nikki Layne, *

Johnstown - Licking County (G-9550)

◆ **EMP:** 197 **EST:** 1939
SQ FT: 10,000
SALES (est): 47.18MM
SALES (corp-wide): 47.18MM **Privately Held**
Web: www.trc4r.com
SIC: 3011 5014 2891 Tire sundries or tire repair materials, rubber; Tire and tube repair materials; Sealing compounds, synthetic rubber or plastic

(G-9550)
ZANDEX HEALTH CARE CORPORATION
Also Called: Northview Senior Living Center
267 N Main St (43031-1018)
PHONE....................740 454-1400
Karen Baltzell, *Mgr*
EMP: 170
Web: www.cedarhillcare.org
SIC: 8052 8059 Intermediate care facilities; Rest home, with health care
PA: Zandex Health Care Corporation
1122 Taylor St
Zanesville OH 43701

Kalida
Putnam County

(G-9551)
TRILOGY HEALTHCARE PUTNAM LLC
755 Ottawa St (45853-2096)
P.O. Box 388 (45853-0388)
PHONE....................419 532-2961
Randal J Bufford, *Managing Member*
Kevin Kidd, *Ex Dir*
EMP: 2891 **EST:** 2005
SALES (est): 1.75MM
SALES (corp-wide): 146.9MM **Privately Held**
Web: www.trilogyhs.com
SIC: 8051 Skilled nursing care facilities
PA: Trilogy Rehab Services, Llc
303 N Hurstbourne Pkwy # 200
Louisville KY 40222
800 335-1060

Kelleys Island
Erie County

(G-9552)
CAMP PATMOS INC
920 Monaghan Rd (43438-5502)
P.O. Box 1920 (43438-1920)
PHONE....................419 746-2214
Ed Miller, *Ex Dir*
EMP: 50 **EST:** 1951
SALES (est): 730.63K **Privately Held**
Web: www.camppatmos.com
SIC: 7032 Summer camp, except day and sports instructional

(G-9553)
KELLSTONE INC
Also Called: Kellstone
Lake Shore Drive (43438)
P.O. Box 31 (43438-0031)
PHONE....................419 746-2396
Ralph Kunar, *Mgr*
EMP: 40
SALES (corp-wide): 29.28MM **Privately Held**
SIC: 3281 1422 Cut stone and stone products; Crushed and broken limestone
HQ: Kellstone, Inc.
3203 Harvard Ave
Newburgh Heights OH 44105

Kensington
Columbiana County

(G-9554)
M3 MIDSTREAM LLC
Also Called: Kensington Plant
11543 State Route 644 (44427)
PHONE....................330 223-2220
EMP: 34
SALES (corp-wide): 57MM **Privately Held**
Web: www.momentummidstream.com
SIC: 1382 Oil and gas exploration services
PA: M3 Midstream Llc
600 Travis St Ste 5600
Houston TX 77002
713 783-3000

Kent
Portage County

(G-9555)
AERO INDUSTRIES INC
4240 Sunnybrook Rd (44240-7320)
PHONE....................330 626-3246
Jim Tuerk, *Brnch Mgr*
EMP: 74
SALES (corp-wide): 47.72MM **Privately Held**
Web: www.aeroindustries.com
SIC: 7532 5199 Top and body repair and paint shops; Tarpaulins
PA: Aero Industries, Inc.
4243 W Bradbury Ave
Indianapolis IN 46241
317 244-2433

(G-9556)
ALPHAMICRON INCORPORATED
1950 State Route 59 Ste 100 (44240-4118)
PHONE....................330 676-0648
Bahman Taheri, *CEO*
Tamas Kosa, *CSO*
EMP: 40 **EST:** 2001
SQ FT: 30,000
SALES (est): 4.42MM **Privately Held**
Web: www.alphamicron.com
SIC: 8732 Research services, except laboratory

(G-9557)
ALSICO USA INC (PA)
Also Called: Euclid Vidaro Mfg. Co.
333 Martinel Dr (44240-4370)
P.O. Box 550 (44240-0010)
PHONE....................330 673-7413
Charles Rosenblatt, *Pr*
Edward Davis, *
Howard Fleischmann, *
▲ **EMP:** 80 **EST:** 1870
SQ FT: 29,000
SALES (est): 19.16MM
SALES (corp-wide): 19.16MM **Privately Held**
Web: www.vidaro.com
SIC: 5136 Men's and boy's clothing

(G-9558)
ALTERCARE INC
1463 Tallmadge Rd (44240-6664)
PHONE....................330 677-4550
John Goodman, *Prin*
EMP: 27
SALES (corp-wide): 6.9MM **Privately Held**
Web: www.altercareonline.com
SIC: 8322 Rehabilitation services
PA: Altercare, Inc.
35990 Westminister Ave
North Ridgeville OH 44039

440 327-5285

(G-9559)
AMETEK TCHNICAL INDUS PDTS INC (HQ)
Also Called: Ametek Electromechanical Group
100 E Erie St Ste 130 (44240-3587)
PHONE....................330 673-3451
David A Zapico, *Ch Bd*
Matt French, *
Peter Smith, *
Todd Schlegel, *
Kathryn E Sena, *
EMP: 65 **EST:** 2009
SALES (est): 85.66MM
SALES (corp-wide): 6.6B **Publicly Held**
Web: www.ametektip.com
SIC: 3621 5063 3566 Motors, electric; Motors, electric; Speed changers, drives, and gears
PA: Ametek, Inc.
1100 Cassatt Rd
Berwyn PA 19312
610 647-2121

(G-9560)
CARTER-JONES COMPANIES INC (PA)
Also Called: Carter Lumber
601 Tallmadge Rd (44240-7331)
P.O. Box 5194 (44240-5194)
PHONE....................330 673-6100
Neil Sackett, *CEO*
Neil Sackett, *Pr*
Jeffrey S Donley, *
Judy Lee, *
Brian Horning Ctrl, *Prin*
EMP: 50 **EST:** 1934
SQ FT: 60,000
SALES (est): 2.57B
SALES (corp-wide): 2.57B **Privately Held**
Web: www.doitbest.com
SIC: 5251 6552 5211 Hardware stores; Subdividers and developers, nec; Millwork and lumber

(G-9561)
CARTER-JONES LUMBER COMPANY (HQ)
Also Called: Carter Lumber
601 Tallmadge Rd (44240-7331)
PHONE....................330 673-6100
Neil Sackett, *Ch*
Jeffrey S Donley, *
Judy Lee, *
W E Carter, *Prin*
T Neil Jones, *Prin*
▲ **EMP:** 156 **EST:** 1932
SQ FT: 60,000
SALES (est): 415.55MM
SALES (corp-wide): 2.57B **Privately Held**
Web: www.carterlumber.com
SIC: 5211 5031 Lumber products; Lumber: rough, dressed, and finished
PA: Carter-Jones Companies, Inc.
601 Tallmadge Rd
Kent OH 44240
330 673-6100

(G-9562)
CHILDRENS HOSP MED CTR AKRON
1951 State Route 59 Ste A (44240-8128)
PHONE....................330 676-1020
Carrie Gavriloff, *Prin*
EMP: 54
SALES (corp-wide): 1.4B **Privately Held**
Web: www.akronchildrens.org
SIC: 8062 General medical and surgical hospitals

PA: Childrens Hospital Medical Center Of Akron
1 Perkins Sq
Akron OH 44308
330 543-1000

(G-9563)
CITY OF AKRON
Also Called: Municipal Water Supply
1570 Ravenna Rd (44240-6111)
PHONE....................330 678-0077
Jeff Bronowski, *Mgr*
EMP: 54
SALES (corp-wide): 395.24MM **Privately Held**
Web: www.akronohio.gov
SIC: 4941 Water supply
PA: City Of Akron
166 S High St Rm 502
Akron OH 44308
330 375-2720

(G-9564)
CLEVELAND CLNIC AKRON GEN VSTI
4080 Brimfield Plz (44240-6902)
PHONE....................330 677-4666
Deb Damon, *Dir*
EMP: 100
SALES (corp-wide): 16.73MM **Privately Held**
Web: www.vnsi.org
SIC: 8082 Visiting nurse service
PA: Cleveland Clinic Akron General Visiting Nurse Service
1 Home Care Pl
Akron OH 44320
330 745-1601

(G-9565)
COLEMAN PROFESSIONAL SVCS INC (PA)
Also Called: Coleman Data Solutions
5982 Rhodes Rd (44240)
PHONE....................330 673-1347
Nelson Burns, *CEO*
EMP: 110 **EST:** 1978
SALES (est): 67.31MM
SALES (corp-wide): 67.31MM **Privately Held**
Web: www.colemanservices.org
SIC: 8093 7349 7374 7371 Mental health clinic, outpatient; Janitorial service, contract basis; Data entry service; Custom computer programming services

(G-9566)
COUNTY FIRE PROTECTION LLC
4620 Crystal Pkwy (44240-8020)
PHONE....................330 633-1014
Jeff Wyatt, *Prin*
John Ludwig, *
Robert Bradley, *
John Mckernan, *Prin*
EMP: 64 **EST:** 2019
SALES (est): 5.27MM **Privately Held**
Web: www.county-fire.com
SIC: 7389 Fire protection service other than forestry or public

(G-9567)
CVS REVCO DS INC
Also Called: CVS
500 S Water St (44240-3548)
PHONE....................330 678-4009
EMP: 62
SALES (corp-wide): 357.78B **Publicly Held**
Web: www.cvs.com
SIC: 5912 7384 Drug stores and proprietary stores; Photofinishing laboratory

GEOGRAPHIC SECTION

Kent - Portage County (G-9588)

HQ: Cvs Revco D.S., Inc.
 1 Cvs Dr
 Woonsocket RI 02895
 401 765-1500

(G-9568)
DAVEY RESOURCE GROUP INC (HQ)
Also Called: Land Management Group
295 S Water St Ste 300 (44240-3590)
PHONE..................330 673-5685
Patrick Covey, *CEO*
Thea Sears, *
EMP: 45 **EST:** 2017
SALES (est): 31.72MM
SALES (corp-wide): 1.51B **Privately Held**
Web: www.davey.com
SIC: 0783 Planting, pruning, and trimming services
PA: The Davey Tree Expert Company
 1500 N Mantua St
 Kent OH 44240
 330 673-9511

(G-9569)
DAVEY TREE EXPERT COMPANY
1550 Franklin Ave (44240-3771)
PHONE..................330 678-5818
EMP: 87
SALES (corp-wide): 1.51B **Privately Held**
Web: www.davey.com
SIC: 0783 Planting, pruning, and trimming services
PA: The Davey Tree Expert Company
 1500 N Mantua St
 Kent OH 44240
 330 673-9511

(G-9570)
DAVEY TREE EXPERT COMPANY (PA)
1500 N Mantua St (44240-2399)
P.O. Box 5193 (44240-5193)
PHONE..................330 673-9511
Karl J Warnke, *Chief Executive Officer PAS*
Karl J Warnke, *Ch Bd*
Patrick M Covey, *COO*
Joseph R Paul, *CFO*
Nicholas R Sucic, *VP*
EMP: 175 **EST:** 1909
SALES (est): 1.51B
SALES (corp-wide): 1.51B **Privately Held**
Web: www.davey.com
SIC: 0783 0782 0811 0181 Removal services, bush and tree; Lawn care services ; Tree farm; Nursery stock, growing of

(G-9571)
DAYTON FREIGHT LINES INC
280 Progress Blvd (44240-8015)
PHONE..................330 346-0750
Robert Kantorowski, *Prin*
EMP: 91
SALES (corp-wide): 6.59B **Privately Held**
Web: www.daytonfreight.com
SIC: 4213 Contract haulers
PA: Dayton Freight Lines, Inc.
 6450 Poe Ave
 Dayton OH 45414
 937 264-4060

(G-9572)
DON WARTKO CONSTRUCTION CO
Also Called: Design Concrete Surfaces
975 Tallmadge Rd (44240-6474)
PHONE..................330 673-5252
Thomas Wartko, *Pr*
David Wartko, *
Mike Wartko, *
Doris Wartko, *
Ron Wartko, *
EMP: 60 **EST:** 1967

SQ FT: 15,000
SALES (est): 12.73MM **Privately Held**
Web: www.donwartkoconstruction.com
SIC: 1623 1794 3732 Oil and gas line and compressor station construction; Excavation work; Boatbuilding and repairing

(G-9573)
EAST END WELDING LLC
357 Tallmadge Rd (44240-7201)
PHONE..................330 677-6000
Tim Rosengarten, *CEO*
▲ **EMP:** 120 **EST:** 1967
SQ FT: 146,500
SALES (est): 16.96MM
SALES (corp-wide): 376.52MM **Privately Held**
Web: www.eastendwelding.com
SIC: 7692 3599 Welding repair; Custom machinery
PA: Connell Limited Partnership
 1 International Pl Fl 31
 Boston MA 02110
 617 737-2700

(G-9574)
FAIRCHILD MD LEASING CO LLC
Also Called: KENT HEALTHCARE CENTER
1290 Fairchild Ave (44240-1814)
PHONE..................330 678-4912
EMP: 150 **EST:** 2000
SALES (est): 5.67MM **Privately Held**
SIC: 8051 Skilled nursing care facilities

(G-9575)
FRANKLIN CROSSING OH LP
1214 Anita Dr (44240)
PHONE..................216 520-1250
Frank Sinito, *Genl Pt*
EMP: 99 **EST:** 2017
SALES (est): 3.74MM **Privately Held**
Web: www.villagesatfranklincrossing.com
SIC: 6513 Apartment building operators

(G-9576)
GERMAN FAMILY SOCIETY INC
Also Called: German American Family Society
3871 Ranfield Rd (44240-6760)
PHONE..................330 678-8229
Joseph Geiser, *Pr*
Jim Resnick, *
Hilda Resnick, *
Jim Armbrust, *
Carl Townhauser, *
EMP: 40 **EST:** 1958
SALES (est): 58.86K **Privately Held**
Web: www.germanfamilysociety.com
SIC: 7997 7299 Membership sports and recreation clubs; Banquet hall facilities

(G-9577)
GFS LEASING INC (PA)
Also Called: Altercare of Ravenna
1463 Tallmadge Rd (44240-6664)
PHONE..................330 296-6415
Gerald F Schroer, *Pr*
EMP: 80 **EST:** 1959
SQ FT: 23,000
SALES (est): 9.34MM
SALES (corp-wide): 9.34MM **Privately Held**
Web: www.altercareonline.com
SIC: 8051 Convalescent home with continuous nursing care

(G-9578)
HOMETOWN BANK (PA)
142 N Water St (44240-2419)
P.O. Box 310 (44240-0006)
PHONE..................330 673-9827

Timothy J Mcfarlane, *Ch*
Timothy J Mcfarlane, *OF*
Jeffrey Donovan, *Dir*
Thomas J, *Grp Exec*
Jeffrey J Knauf, *Dir*
EMP: 27 **EST:** 1898
SQ FT: 6,000
SALES (est): 11.23MM
SALES (corp-wide): 11.23MM **Privately Held**
Web: www.ht.bank
SIC: 6022 State commercial banks

(G-9579)
HUNTINGTON NATIONAL BANK
1729 E Main St (44240-2573)
PHONE..................330 677-8200
Karen Duffy, *Mgr*
EMP: 36
SALES (corp-wide): 10.84B **Publicly Held**
Web: www.huntington.com
SIC: 6029 6021 Commercial banks, nec; National commercial banks
HQ: The Huntington National Bank
 41 S High St
 Columbus OH 43215
 614 480-4293

(G-9580)
INDUSTRIAL TUBE AND STEEL CORP (PA)
4658 Crystal Pkwy (44240-8020)
PHONE..................330 474-5530
Dick Siess, *Pr*
Diane Saulino, *
Frederick H Gillen, *
H William Kranz Junior, *Prin*
▲ **EMP:** 35 **EST:** 1956
SQ FT: 30,000
SALES (est): 48.35MM
SALES (corp-wide): 48.35MM **Privately Held**
Web: www.industrialtube.com
SIC: 5051 Steel

(G-9581)
INTERIM HEALTHCARE INC
Also Called: Interim Services
184 Currie Hall Pkwy Ste 1 (44240-4388)
PHONE..................330 677-8010
Jan Pajk, *VP*
EMP: 77
Web: www.interimhealthcare.com
SIC: 8082 Home health care services
PA: Interim Healthcare Inc.
 1551 Sawgrs Corp Pkwy # 230
 Sunrise FL 33323

(G-9582)
KAISER FOUNDATION HOSPITALS
Also Called: Kent Medical Offices
2500 State Route 59 (44240-7105)
PHONE..................800 524-7377
EMP: 29
SALES (corp-wide): 70.8B **Privately Held**
Web: www.kaisercenter.com
SIC: 8011 Offices and clinics of medical doctors
HQ: Kaiser Foundation Hospitals Inc
 1 Kaiser Plz
 Oakland CA 94612
 510 271-6611

(G-9583)
KENT ADHESIVE PRODUCTS CO
Also Called: K A P C O
1000 Cherry St (44240-7501)
P.O. Box 626 (44240-0011)
PHONE..................330 678-1626
Edward Small, *Pr*
Philip M Zavracky, *

Jenifer Codrea, *
◆ **EMP:** 80 **EST:** 1974
SQ FT: 100,000
SALES (est): 23.36MM **Privately Held**
Web: www.kapco.com
SIC: 2679 2672 2675 7389 Paper products, converted, nec; Adhesive papers, labels, or tapes: from purchased material; Die-cut paper and board; Laminating service

(G-9584)
KENTRIDGE AT GOLDEN POND LTD
5241 Sunnybrook Rd (44240-7383)
PHONE..................330 677-4040
EMP: 30 **EST:** 2007
SALES (est): 6.06MM **Privately Held**
Web: www.thegablesofkentridge.com
SIC: 8361 Aged home

(G-9585)
KLABEN LINCOLN FORD INC (PA)
Also Called: Klaben Auto Group
1080 W Main St (44240-2006)
PHONE..................330 593-6800
Albert Klaben, *Pr*
Richard Klaben, *
EMP: 98 **EST:** 1981
SALES (est): 23.26MM
SALES (corp-wide): 23.26MM **Privately Held**
Web: www.klaben.com
SIC: 5511 7515 5012 7538 Automobiles, new and used; Passenger car leasing; Automobiles and other motor vehicles; General automotive repair shops

(G-9586)
MAAG AUTOMATIK INC
Also Called: Maag Reduction Engineering
235 Progress Blvd (44240-8055)
PHONE..................330 677-2225
EMP: 35
SALES (corp-wide): 8.44B **Publicly Held**
Web: www.maag.com
SIC: 3532 5084 Crushing, pulverizing, and screening equipment; Pulverizing machinery and equipment
HQ: Maag Reduction, Inc.
 9401 Sthrn Pine Blvd
 Charlotte NC 28273

(G-9587)
METIS CONSTRUCTION SVCS LLC
175 E Erie St Ste 303 (44240-3595)
PHONE..................330 677-7333
Julieann Brandle, *Pr*
Julie Brandle, *
Donna Komar, *
Katie Wright, *
Steve Brandle, *
EMP: 63 **EST:** 2009
SALES (est): 24.28MM **Privately Held**
Web: www.metisconstruction.com
SIC: 1542 Commercial and office building contractors

(G-9588)
MJM MANAGEMENT CORPORATION
Also Called: Silver Meadows
1214 Anita Dr Apt 101 (44240-1763)
PHONE..................330 678-0761
John Daltorio, *Mgr*
EMP: 34
SALES (corp-wide): 2.24MM **Privately Held**
Web: www.mjmmanagement.com
SIC: 6531 Real estate managers
PA: M.J.M. Management Corporation
 2425 W 11th St Ste 3
 Cleveland OH 44113
 216 566-7676

(PA)=Parent Co (HQ)=Headquarters
✪ = New Business established in last 2 years

Kent - Portage County (G-9589)

(G-9589)
NORTHASTERN EDUCTL TV OHIO INC
Also Called: Western Reserve Public Media
1750 W Campus Center Dr (44240-3820)
P.O. Box 5191 (44240-5191)
PHONE................................330 677-4549
Trina Cutter, *Pr*
EMP: 35
SALES (corp-wide): 5.52MM **Privately Held**
Web: www.pbswesternreserve.org
SIC: 4833 Television broadcasting stations
PA: Northeastern Educational Television Of Ohio, Inc.
1750 W Campus Center Dr
Kent OH
330 677-4549

(G-9590)
PALESTINE CHLD RELIEF FUND
Also Called: Pcrf, The
1340 Morris Rd (44240-4518)
P.O. Box 861716 (90086-1716)
PHONE................................330 678-2645
Steve Sosebee, *CEO*
EMP: 56 **EST:** 1991
SALES (est): 10.71MM **Privately Held**
Web: www.pcrf.net
SIC: 8099 Medical services organization

(G-9591)
PORTAGE AREA RGONAL TRNSP AUTH
Also Called: Parta
2000 Summit Rd (44240-7140)
PHONE................................330 678-1287
Rick Bissler, *Pr*
EMP: 100 **EST:** 1970
SQ FT: 41,905
SALES (est): 16.09MM **Privately Held**
Web: www.partaonline.org
SIC: 4111 Local and suburban transit

(G-9592)
QUALITY IP LLC
145 River St Ste 101 (44240-3580)
PHONE................................330 931-4141
EMP: 77 **EST:** 2004
SALES (est): 9.9MM **Privately Held**
Web: www.qualityip.com
SIC: 7371 Custom computer programming services

(G-9593)
REDUCTION ENGINEERING INC
Also Called: Accu Grind
235 Progress Blvd (44240-8055)
PHONE................................330 677-2225
◆ **EMP:** 45
Web: www.maag.com
SIC: 5084 3532 Industrial machinery and equipment; Crushing, pulverizing, and screening equipment

(G-9594)
ROBINSON HEALTH SYSTEM INC
Also Called: Robinson Memorial Training Ctr
408 Devon Pl Ste B (44240-6479)
PHONE................................330 677-3434
Mike Walker, *Mgr*
EMP: 3542
SALES (corp-wide): 878.24MM **Privately Held**
Web: www.robinsonmemorial.org
SIC: 8062 General medical and surgical hospitals
HQ: Robinson Health System, Inc.
6847 N Chestnut St
Ravenna OH 44266
330 297-0811

(G-9595)
ROBINSON HEALTH SYSTEM INC
Also Called: Kent Mammography Center
401 Devon Pl Ste 115 (44240-6481)
PHONE................................330 678-0900
EMP: 3542
SALES (corp-wide): 878.24MM **Privately Held**
Web: www.robinsonmemorial.org
SIC: 8062 General medical and surgical hospitals
HQ: Robinson Health System, Inc.
6847 N Chestnut St
Ravenna OH 44266
330 297-0811

(G-9596)
ROBINSON HEALTH SYSTEM INC
Med Center One
1993 State Route 59 (44240-7609)
PHONE................................330 297-0811
Jack Monda, *Dir*
EMP: 3542
SALES (corp-wide): 878.24MM **Privately Held**
Web: www.uhhospitals.org
SIC: 8062 General medical and surgical hospitals
HQ: Robinson Health System, Inc.
6847 N Chestnut St
Ravenna OH 44266
330 297-0811

(G-9597)
ROBINSON HEALTH SYSTEM INC
Also Called: Robinson Surgery Center
411 Devon Pl (44240-6480)
PHONE................................330 678-4100
Janis Barnes, *Dir*
EMP: 3542
SALES (corp-wide): 878.24MM **Privately Held**
Web: www.robinsonmemorial.org
SIC: 8062 8093 General medical and surgical hospitals; Specialty outpatient clinics, nec
HQ: Robinson Health System, Inc.
6847 N Chestnut St
Ravenna OH 44266
330 297-0811

(G-9598)
STOW-KENT ANIMAL HOSPITAL INC (PA)
4559 Kent Rd (44240-5298)
PHONE................................330 673-0049
Thomas Albers D.v.m., *Pr*
Carmella Albers, *
EMP: 27 **EST:** 1967
SALES (est): 4.67MM
SALES (corp-wide): 4.67MM **Privately Held**
Web: www.wetreatpets.com
SIC: 0742 Animal hospital services, pets and other animal specialties

(G-9599)
STOW-KENT ANIMAL HOSPITAL INC
Also Called: Portage Animal Clinic
4148 State Route 43 (44240-6916)
PHONE................................330 673-1002
EMP: 27
SALES (corp-wide): 4.67MM **Privately Held**
Web: www.wetreatpets.com
SIC: 0742 Animal hospital services, pets and other animal specialties
PA: Stow-Kent Animal Hospital Inc
4559 Kent Rd
Kent OH 44240
330 673-0049

(G-9600)
SUMMA WESTERN RESERVE HOSP LLC
Also Called: Laboratory Services
307 W Main St Ste B (44240-2400)
PHONE................................330 926-3337
EMP: 31
SALES (corp-wide): 155.93MM **Privately Held**
Web: www.westernreservehospital.org
SIC: 8062 Hospital, AMA approved residency
HQ: Western Reserve Hospital, Llc
1900 23rd St
Cuyahoga Falls OH 44223

(G-9601)
TALLMADGE ASPHALT AND PAVING COMPANY INC
741 Tallmadge Rd (44240-7329)
PHONE................................330 677-0000
EMP: 60 **EST:** 1980
SALES (est): 9.93MM **Privately Held**
Web: www.tallmadgeasphalt.com
SIC: 1771 Blacktop (asphalt) work

(G-9602)
TAYLOR COMPANIES OHIO INC
4200 Mogadore Rd (44240-7258)
PHONE................................330 677-8380
Brian E Taylor, *Pr*
EMP: 50 **EST:** 2014
SALES (est): 5.79MM **Privately Held**
Web: www.taylorcompaniesofohio.com
SIC: 1522 Residential construction, nec

(G-9603)
TOWNHALL 2
Also Called: Townhall 2 24 Hour Helpline
155 N Water St (44240-2418)
PHONE................................330 678-3006
Sue Whitehurst, *Ex Dir*
EMP: 40 **EST:** 2002
SALES (est): 3.69MM **Privately Held**
Web: www.townhall2.com
SIC: 8322 Social service center

(G-9604)
U S DEVELOPMENT CORP
Also Called: Akro-Plastics
900 W Main St (44240-2285)
PHONE................................330 673-6900
Jerold Ramsey, *Pr*
EMP: 80 **EST:** 1985
SQ FT: 185,000
SALES (est): 10.75MM **Privately Held**
Web: www.rotomold.net
SIC: 3089 6512 Molding primary plastics; Commercial and industrial building operation

(G-9605)
UNITY HEALTH NETWORK LLC
307 W Main St (44240-2400)
PHONE................................330 678-7782
Robert A Kent Junior, *Admn*
EMP: 27
SALES (corp-wide): 51.74MM **Privately Held**
Web: www.unityhealthnetwork.org
SIC: 8011 Internal medicine practitioners
PA: Unity Health Network, Llc
2750 Front St
Cuyahoga Falls OH 44221
330 923-5899

(G-9606)
WILBUR REALTY INC
Also Called: Century 21
548 S Water St (44240-3548)
P.O. Box 624 (44240-0011)
PHONE................................330 673-5883
Steve Boyles, *Pr*
EMP: 51 **EST:** 1950
SQ FT: 3,000
SALES (est): 1.57MM **Privately Held**
Web: www.century21.com
SIC: 6531 Real estate agent, residential

(G-9607)
WINE-ART OF OHIO INC
Also Called: Carlson, L D Company
463 Portage Blvd (44240-7286)
PHONE................................330 678-7733
Ronald Hartman, *CEO*
Ann Carst, *
Bruce B Laybourne, *
Laurence D Carlson, *
◆ **EMP:** 45 **EST:** 1971
SQ FT: 40,000
SALES (est): 23.3MM **Privately Held**
Web: www.ldcarlson.com
SIC: 5149 Wine makers' equipment and supplies

(G-9608)
YOUNG AND ASSOCIATES INC
121 E Main St (44240-2524)
P.O. Box 711 (44240-0013)
PHONE................................330 678-0524
Gary J Young, *Ch*
James Kleinfelter, *
EMP: 38 **EST:** 1978
SQ FT: 2,500
SALES (est): 7.04MM **Privately Held**
Web: www.younginc.com
SIC: 8742 Marketing consulting services

Kenton
Hardin County

(G-9609)
BAPTIST HEALTH HARDIN (HQ)
Also Called: Hardin Memorial Hospital
921 E Franklin St (43326-2020)
PHONE................................419 673-0761
David Blom, *CEO*
Michael W Louge, *
Mark Seckinger, *
Ron Snyder, *
EMP: 190 **EST:** 1943
SQ FT: 91,678
SALES (est): 31.23MM
SALES (corp-wide): 4.29B **Privately Held**
Web: www.ohiohealth.com
SIC: 8062 General medical and surgical hospitals
PA: Ohiohealth Corporation
3430 Ohhalth Pkwy 5th Flr
Columbus OH 43202
614 788-8860

(G-9610)
BKP AMBULANCE DISTRICT
439 S Main St (43326-1946)
PHONE................................419 674-4574
Allen Barrett, *Pr*
Alan Long, *
Randy Scharf, *
EMP: 30 **EST:** 1975
SALES (est): 1.52MM **Privately Held**
Web: www.bkpambulance.com
SIC: 4119 Ambulance service

(G-9611)
BRIMS IMPORTS
Also Called: Brims Imports Auto Salvage
County 140 E (43326)
P.O. Box 471 (43326-0471)
PHONE................................419 675-1099

GEOGRAPHIC SECTION
Kettering - Montgomery County (G-9633)

Matt Brim, *Mgr*
EMP: 32
SALES (corp-wide): 4.49MM **Privately Held**
Web: www.brimsimports.biz
SIC: 5015 Automotive parts and supplies, used
PA: Brim's Imports
370 W Franklin St
Kenton OH 43326
419 674-4137

(G-9612)
CITY OF KENTON (PA)
111 W Franklin St (43326-1972)
PHONE..................419 674-4850
Randy Manns, *Mayor*
EMP: 27 **EST:** 1856
Web: www.cityofkenton.com
SIC: 9111 8611 Mayors' office; Business associations

(G-9613)
COUNTY OF HARDIN
Also Called: Hardin Cnty Dept Mntal Rtrdtio
705 N Ida St (43326-1060)
PHONE..................419 674-4158
Mark Kieffer, *Prin*
EMP: 31
Web: www.hardincourts.com
SIC: 8331 Vocational training agency
PA: County Of Hardin
1 Courthouse Sq Ste 100
Kenton OH 43326
419 674-2205

(G-9614)
H & H GREEN LLC
13670 Us Highway 68 (43326-9302)
PHONE..................419 674-4152
William Hall, *Managing Member*
EMP: 43 **EST:** 2009
SQ FT: 43,000
SALES (est): 2.53MM **Privately Held**
SIC: 5087 Service establishment equipment

(G-9615)
HARDIN CNTY CNCIL ON AGING INC
100 Memorial Dr (43326-2089)
PHONE..................419 673-1102
Bette Bibler, *Dir*
EMP: 42 **EST:** 1978
SALES (est): 1.8MM **Privately Held**
Web: www.hardincoa.net
SIC: 8322 Senior citizens' center or association

(G-9616)
HARDIN COUNTY HOME
Also Called: HARDIN HILLS HEALTH CENTER
1211 W Lima St (43326-8846)
PHONE..................419 673-0961
Debbie Lamb, *Pr*
EMP: 95 **EST:** 1900
SALES (est): 6.07MM **Privately Held**
Web: co.hardin.oh.us
SIC: 8059 Nursing home, except skilled and intermediate care facility

(G-9617)
HEALTH PARTNERS WESTERN OHIO
Also Called: Kenton Community Health Center
111 W Espy St (43326-2117)
PHONE..................419 679-5994
Liza Frantz, *Dir*
EMP: 27
SALES (corp-wide): 70.67MM **Privately Held**
Web: www.hpwohio.org
SIC: 8099 Blood related health services
PA: Health Partners Of Western Ohio
329 N West St
Lima OH 45801
419 221-3072

(G-9618)
HIGH POINT HOME HEALTH LTD
118 S Main St (43326-1942)
PHONE..................419 674-4090
EMP: 42
SALES (corp-wide): 1.98MM **Privately Held**
Web: www.highpointhomehealth.com
SIC: 8099 Childbirth preparation clinic
PA: High Point Home Health Ltd
180 Reynolds Ave
Bellefontaine OH 43311
937 592-9800

(G-9619)
HOME SAV & LN CO KENTON OHIO
Also Called: Home Savings & Loan
116 E Franklin St (43326-1924)
P.O. Box 117 (43326-0117)
PHONE..................419 673-1117
Chuck Dixon, *Pr*
EMP: 41 **EST:** 1888
SALES (est): 5.9MM **Privately Held**
Web: www.hslc.bank
SIC: 6036 6035 Savings and loan associations, not federally chartered; Federal savings institutions

(G-9620)
KENTON NRSING RHBLTTION CTR LL
117 Jacob Parrot Rd (43326-9506)
PHONE..................419 674-4197
Brenda Lewis, *Admn*
EMP: 32 **EST:** 2017
SALES (est): 9.9MM **Privately Held**
Web: www.kentonnursingandrehab.com
SIC: 8051 Convalescent home with continuous nursing care

(G-9621)
MID-OHIO ENERGY COOP INC
Also Called: MIDOHIO ENERGY COOPERATIVE
1210 W Lima St (43326)
P.O. Box 224 (43326)
PHONE..................419 568-5321
John Metcalf, *Pr*
EMP: 28 **EST:** 1938
SQ FT: 10,000
SALES (est): 25.84MM **Privately Held**
Web: www.midohioenergy.com
SIC: 4911 Distribution, electric power

(G-9622)
PRECISION STRIP INC
190 Bales Rd (43326-8909)
PHONE..................419 674-4186
Don Bornhorst, *Brnch Mgr*
EMP: 52
SALES (corp-wide): 14.81B **Publicly Held**
Web: www.precision-strip.com
SIC: 4225 3341 General warehousing and storage; Secondary nonferrous metals
HQ: Precision Strip Inc.
86 S Ohio St
Minster OH 45865
419 628-2343

(G-9623)
TRACTOR SUPPLY COMPANY
948 E Columbus St (43326-1683)
PHONE..................419 673-8900
Ben Smith, *Pr*
EMP: 27
SALES (corp-wide): 14.56B **Publicly Held**
Web: www.tractorsupply.com
SIC: 5191 Farm supplies
PA: Tractor Supply Company
5401 Virginia Way
Brentwood TN 37027
615 440-4000

(G-9624)
UNITED CH RSDNCES KNTON OHIO I
Also Called: CHAPEL HILL COMMUNITY
900 E Columbus St (43326-1758)
P.O. Box 1806 (43301-1806)
PHONE..................740 382-4885
Mark Seckinger, *Pr*
Robert Hart, *
Brian Allen, *
Cheryl Wickersham, *
Ronald Beach, *
EMP: 43 **EST:** 1989
SQ FT: 28,000
SALES (est): 480.62K
SALES (corp-wide): 115.52MM **Privately Held**
Web: www.unitedchurchhomes.org
SIC: 6513 Retirement hotel operation
PA: United Church Homes, Inc.
170 E Center St
Marion OH 43302
800 837-2211

Kettering
Montgomery County

(G-9625)
ALTERNATE SLTONS HMCARE DYTON
1050 Forrer Blvd (45420-3640)
PHONE..................937 298-1111
EMP: 1042 **EST:** 2000
SALES (est): 49.74MM
SALES (corp-wide): 49.74MM **Privately Held**
Web: www.ashealthnet.com
SIC: 7363 Temporary help service
PA: Alternate Solutions Health Network, Llc
1050 Forrer Blvd
Dayton OH 45420
937 681-9269

(G-9626)
BLU DIAMOND HOME CARE LLC
3481 Office Park Dr Ste 120 (45439-2299)
PHONE..................937 723-7836
EMP: 35 **EST:** 2017
SALES (est): 178K **Privately Held**
Web: www.bludiamondhomecare.com
SIC: 8082 Home health care services

(G-9627)
COMMUNITY BLOOD CENTER
Also Called: Solvita
2900 College Dr (45420-2972)
PHONE..................800 684-7783
Christopher Graham, *CEO*
EMP: 67
SALES (corp-wide): 906.51K **Privately Held**
SIC: 8071 Medical laboratories
PA: Community Blood Center
349 S Main St
Dayton OH 45402
937 528-5506

(G-9628)
COMMUNITY TISSUE SERVICES
2900 College Dr (45420-2972)
PHONE..................937 222-0228
David M Smith Md, *CEO*
EMP: 34 **EST:** 2012
SALES (est): 185.36K **Privately Held**
Web: www.solvita.org
SIC: 8621 Professional organizations

(G-9629)
KETTERING MEDICAL CENTER (HQ)
Also Called: KETTERING HEALTH NETWORK
3535 Southern Blvd (45429-1298)
PHONE..................937 298-4331
Jarrod Mcnaughton, *CEO*
Fred Manchur, *
Roy Chew, *
Walter Sackett, *
Russell Wetherell, *
EMP: 901 **EST:** 1959
SQ FT: 500,000
SALES (est): 1.08B
SALES (corp-wide): 2.46B **Privately Held**
Web: www.ketteringhealth.org
SIC: 8062 Hospital, professional nursing school
PA: Kettering Adventist Healthcare
3535 Southern Blvd
Dayton OH 45429
937 298-4331

(G-9630)
LADD DISTRIBUTION LLC (DH)
4849 Hempstead Station Dr (45429-5156)
PHONE..................937 438-2646
Scott Leichtling, *Managing Member*
▲ **EMP:** 80 **EST:** 2007
SQ FT: 48,000
SALES (est): 25.56MM **Privately Held**
Web: www.te.com
SIC: 5065 Connectors, electronic
HQ: Te Connectivity Corporation
1050 Westlakes Dr
Berwyn PA 19312
610 893-9800

(G-9631)
OOVOO LLC
Also Called: Krush Technology
1700 S Patterson Blvd Ste 300 (45409-2141)
P.O. Box 340488 (45434-0488)
PHONE..................917 515-2074
EMP: 75 **EST:** 2006
SALES (est): 6.12MM **Privately Held**
SIC: 4899 Data communication services

(G-9632)
REYNOLDS AND REYNOLDS COMPANY (HQ)
Also Called: Reynolds and Reynolds
1 Reynolds Way (45430-1586)
PHONE..................937 485-2000
Tommy Barras, *CEO*
Rob Nalley, *Vice Chairman*
Chris Walsh, *Pr*
Willie Daughters, *COO*
▲ **EMP:** 1000 **EST:** 1889
SQ FT: 60,000
SALES (est): 911.08MM
SALES (corp-wide): 1.54B **Privately Held**
Web: www.reyrey.com
SIC: 7373 6159 Computer integrated systems design; Machinery and equipment finance leasing
PA: Universal Computer Systems, Inc.
6700 Hollister St
Houston TX 77040
713 718-1800

(G-9633)
STAMPER STAFFING LLC
2812 Purdue Dr (45420-3458)
PHONE..................937 938-7010

Mary Stamper, *
EMP: 49 **EST:** 2018
SALES (est): 1.14MM **Privately Held**
SIC: 7361 Placement agencies

(G-9634)
WRIGHT STATE UNIVERSITY
Also Called: Cox Institute
3525 Southern Blvd (45429-1221)
PHONE.................................937 298-4331
Diane Myers, *Brnch Mgr*
EMP: 70
SALES (corp-wide): 159.41MM **Privately Held**
Web: www.wright.edu
SIC: 8733 8221 Medical research; University
PA: Wright State University
3640 Colonel Glenn Hwy
Dayton OH 45435
937 775-3333

Kidron
Wayne County

(G-9635)
CHRISTIAN SCHOOLS INC
Also Called: Central Christian School
3970 Kidron Rd (44636)
P.O. Box 9 (44636)
PHONE.................................330 857-7311
Eugene Miller, *Superintnt*
Bethany Nussbaum, *
EMP: 89 **EST:** 1961
SALES (est): 3.81MM **Privately Held**
Web: www.ccscomets.org
SIC: 8211 8351 Private combined elementary and secondary school; Preschool center

(G-9636)
JILCO INDUSTRIES INC (PA)
Also Called: Preferred Airparts
11234 Hackett Rd (44636)
P.O. Box 12 (44636-0012)
PHONE.................................330 698-0280
Ken Stoltzfus Junior, *Pr*
Brian Stoltzfus, *
Colby Stoltfus, *
◆ **EMP:** 28 **EST:** 1982
SQ FT: 78,000
SALES (est): 10.04MM
SALES (corp-wide): 10.04MM **Privately Held**
Web: www.preferredairparts.com
SIC: 5088 5599 4522 Aircraft and parts, nec; Aircraft instruments, equipment or parts; Nonscheduled charter services

(G-9637)
KIDRON ELECTRIC INC
Also Called: Kidron Electric & Mech Contrs
5358 Kidron Rd (44636)
P.O. Box 248 (44636)
PHONE.................................330 857-2871
Carrie Neuenschwander, *Prin*
Paul A Neuenschwander, *Prin*
EMP: 30 **EST:** 1938
SQ FT: 50,000
SALES (est): 6.71MM **Privately Held**
Web: www.kidronelectric.com
SIC: 1731 1711 General electrical contractor ; Warm air heating and air conditioning contractor

Killbuck
Holmes County

(G-9638)
KILLBUCK SAVINGS BANK COMPANY (HQ)
165 N Main St (44637)
P.O. Box 407 (44637)
PHONE.................................330 276-4881
Craig Lawhead, *Pr*
Marion Troyer, *
Vic Weaver, *
Lawrence Cardinal, *
EMP: 40 **EST:** 1900
SQ FT: 12,000
SALES (est): 26.51MM **Publicly Held**
Web: www.killbuckbank.com
SIC: 6022 State trust companies accepting deposits, commercial
PA: Killbuck Bancshares, Inc.
165 N Main St
Killbuck OH 44637

(G-9639)
OHIO STATE TAXIDERMY SUPPLY
20 Straits Ln (44637-9581)
PHONE.................................330 674-8600
Rudy Eppley, *Owner*
EMP: 27 **EST:** 2017
SALES (est): 1.99MM **Privately Held**
Web: www.ohiotaxidermysupply.com
SIC: 7699 Taxidermists

Kimbolton
Guernsey County

(G-9640)
CARDIDA CORPORATION
74978 Broadhead Rd (43749-9747)
PHONE.................................740 439-4359
Carl Larue, *Pr*
Bill La Rue, *
Dan La Rue, *
Karen Striff, *
EMP: 75 **EST:** 1988
SALES (est): 1.54MM **Privately Held**
SIC: 7011 6552 Resort hotel; Land subdividers and developers, commercial

(G-9641)
SALT FORK RESORT CLUB INC
74978 Broadhead Rd (43749-9747)
PHONE.................................740 498-8116
Karl Larue, *Pr*
EMP: 40 **EST:** 2010
SALES (est): 2.01MM **Privately Held**
SIC: 7011 7997 Resort hotel; Membership sports and recreation clubs

Kings Mills
Warren County

(G-9642)
KINGS ISLAND COMPANY
6300 Kings Island Dr (45034)
PHONE.................................513 754-5700
Carl Lindner, *Pr*
◆ **EMP:** 220 **EST:** 1984
SALES (est): 24.34MM
SALES (corp-wide): 1.8B **Publicly Held**
Web: www.visitkingsisland.com
SIC: 7996 Theme park, amusement
PA: Cedar Fair, L.P.
1 Cedar Point Dr
Sandusky OH 44870
419 627-2344

(G-9643)
KINGS ISLAND PARK LLC
Also Called: Kings Island
6300 Kings Island Dr (45034)
P.O. Box 901 (45034-0901)
PHONE.................................513 754-5901
Greg Scheid, *Brnch Mgr*
EMP: 200
SALES (corp-wide): 1.8B **Publicly Held**
Web: www.visitkingsisland.com
SIC: 7996 Theme park, amusement
HQ: Kings Island Park Llc
1 Cedar Point Dr
Sandusky OH 44870
419 626-0830

Kinsman
Trumbull County

(G-9644)
BAYLOFF STMPED PDTS KNSMAN INC
8091 State Route 5 (44428-9628)
P.O. Box 289 (44428-0289)
PHONE.................................330 876-4511
Richard Bayer, *Pr*
Kevin Jordan, *
Dan Moore, *
Dixon Morgan, *
M E Newcomer, *
EMP: 80 **EST:** 1948
SQ FT: 115,000
SALES (est): 6.4MM **Privately Held**
Web: www.bayloff.com
SIC: 3469 7692 3444 3315 Stamping metal for the trade; Welding repair; Sheet metalwork; Steel wire and related products

Kirtland
Lake County

(G-9645)
LAKE METROPARKS
Also Called: Lake Farm Park
8800 Euclid Chardon Rd (44094-9520)
PHONE.................................440 256-2122
Andrew Baker, *Mgr*
EMP: 27
SQ FT: 28,107
SALES (corp-wide): 23.35MM **Privately Held**
Web: www.lakemetroparks.com
SIC: 7999 Recreation services
PA: Lake Metroparks
11211 Spear Rd
Painesville OH 44077
440 639-7275

(G-9646)
MR EXCAVATOR INC
8616 Euclid Chardon Rd (44094-9586)
PHONE.................................440 256-2008
William A Flesher, *Pr*
Tim Flesher, *
Patricia Flesher, *
EMP: 85 **EST:** 1962
SALES (est): 25.41MM **Privately Held**
Web: www.mrexcavator.com
SIC: 1794 Excavation and grading, building construction

Kitts Hill
Lawrence County

(G-9647)
FIELDS EXCAVATING INC
177 Township Road 191 (45645-8730)
PHONE.................................740 532-1780
EMP: 65 **EST:** 1967
SALES (est): 8.93MM **Privately Held**
Web: www.fields-excavating.com
SIC: 1623 Water and sewer line construction

La Rue
Marion County

(G-9648)
OHIO FRESH EGGS LLC
2845 Larue Marseilles Rd (43332-8917)
PHONE.................................740 499-2352
Troy Holcomb, *Mgr*
EMP: 105
SALES (corp-wide): 25.27MM **Privately Held**
SIC: 5144 Eggs
PA: Ohio Fresh Eggs, Llc
11212 Croton Rd
Croton OH 43013
740 893-7200

(G-9649)
STOFCHECK AMBULANCE SVC INC (PA)
220 S High St (43332-8881)
P.O. Box 333 (43332-0333)
PHONE.................................740 499-2200
Edward Stofcheck, *Pr*
Edward Stofcheck Senior, *Pr*
EMP: 30 **EST:** 1987
SALES (est): 1.61MM **Privately Held**
Web: www.stofcheck-ballinger.com
SIC: 4119 Ambulance service

Lagrange
Lorain County

(G-9650)
RURAL LORAIN COUNTY WATER AUTH
42401 State Route 303 (44050-9717)
P.O. Box 567 (44050-0567)
PHONE.................................440 355-5121
George Green, *Pr*
Tim Mahoney, *
EMP: 60 **EST:** 1977
SALES (est): 18.23MM **Privately Held**
Web: www.rlcwa.org
SIC: 4941 Water supply

(G-9651)
WEST DEVELOPMENT GROUP LLC (DH)
Also Called: Wdg
300 Commerce Dr (44050-9493)
P.O. Box 646 (44050-0646)
PHONE.................................440 355-4682
Richard West, *Pr*
EMP: 67 **EST:** 2000
SQ FT: 12,000
SALES (est): 3.04MM
SALES (corp-wide): 4.59B **Publicly Held**
Web: www.henry.com
SIC: 5033 Roofing, asphalt and sheet metal
HQ: Henry Company Llc
999 N Pcf Cast Hwy Ste 80
El Segundo CA 90245
310 955-9200

GEOGRAPHIC SECTION

(G-9652)
WEST ROOFING SYSTEMS INC (PA)
121 Commerce Dr (44050-9491)
PHONE.................................800 356-5748
Chris West, *Pr*
Jeff Johnson, *
Daniel Patete, *
▲ **EMP:** 39 **EST:** 1980
SQ FT: 10,700
SALES (est): 16.1MM
SALES (corp-wide): 16.1MM **Privately Held**
Web: www.westroofingsystems.com
SIC: 1761 1542 Roofing contractor; Commercial and office building, new construction

Lake Waynoka
Brown County

(G-9653)
LAKE WYNOKA PRPRTY OWNERS ASSN
1 Waynoka Dr (45171-8728)
PHONE.................................937 446-3774
Vickie Johnson, *Prin*
EMP: 46 **EST:** 1970
SQ FT: 1,100
SALES (est): 1.68MM **Privately Held**
Web: www.lakewaynoka.com
SIC: 8641 Homeowners' association

Lakeside
Ottawa County

(G-9654)
LAKESIDE ASSOCIATION
236 Walnut Ave (43440-1400)
PHONE.................................419 798-4461
Kevin Sibbring, *Ex Dir*
Thomas Derby, *
EMP: 42 **EST:** 1873
SQ FT: 3,500
SALES (est): 10.82MM **Privately Held**
Web: www.lakesideohio.com
SIC: 8621 Professional organizations

Lakeview
Logan County

(G-9655)
INDIAN LK HEALTHCARE GROUP LLC
Also Called: Indian Lake Rehabilitation Center
14442 Us Highway 33 (43331-9284)
PHONE.................................937 843-4929
George S Repchick, *Pr*
William Weisberg, *
EMP: 114 **EST:** 2016
SALES (est): 3.04MM
SALES (corp-wide): 655.44MM **Privately Held**
Web: www.saberhealth.com
SIC: 8051 Convalescent home with continuous nursing care
PA: Saber Healthcare Group, L.L.C.
  23700 Commerce Park
  Beachwood OH 44122
  216 292-5706

Lakeville
Holmes County

(G-9656)
ROUND LK CHRISTN ASSEMBLY INC
114 State Route 3 (44638-9699)
PHONE.................................419 827-2018
Ralph Eichelberger, *Pr*
Carolyn Eichelberger, *Admn*
Carl Bruce, *Treas*
EMP: 27 **EST:** 1950
SQ FT: 35,000
SALES (est): 1.55MM **Privately Held**
Web: www.roundlake.org
SIC: 7032 Sporting and recreational camps

Lakewood
Cuyahoga County

(G-9657)
AMERIFIRST FINANCIAL CORP
14701 Detroit Avenue Ste 750 (44107-4109)
PHONE.................................216 452-5120
EMP: 51
SALES (corp-wide): 306.62MM **Privately Held**
Web: www.uhm.com
SIC: 6162 Mortgage bankers and loan correspondents
HQ: Amerifirst Financial Corporation
  3125 W Main St
  Kalamazoo MI 49006
  269 324-4240

(G-9658)
AREA TEMPS INC
14801 Detroit Ave (44107-3909)
PHONE.................................216 227-8200
Gail Enders, *Prin*
EMP: 669
Web: www.areatemps.com
SIC: 7363 Temporary help service
PA: Area Temps, Inc.
  4511 Rockside Rd Ste 190
  Independence OH 44131

(G-9659)
BECK CENTER FOR ARTS
17801 Detroit Ave (44107-3499)
PHONE.................................216 521-2540
Lucinda Einhouse, *CEO*
Frederick B Unger, *
William J Backus Junior, *Treas*
Jerry Mcthersom, *Dir Fin*
EMP: 127 **EST:** 1933
SQ FT: 60,000
SALES (est): 3.02MM **Privately Held**
Web: www.beckcenter.org
SIC: 7922 Performing arts center production

(G-9660)
CITY OF LAKEWOOD
Also Called: Senior Center West
16024 Madison Ave (44107-5616)
PHONE.................................216 521-1515
EMP: 34
SALES (corp-wide): 71.48MM **Privately Held**
Web: www.lakewoodoh.gov
SIC: 8322 Senior citizens' center or association
PA: City Of Lakewood
  12650 Detroit Ave
  Lakewood OH 44107
  216 521-7580

(G-9661)
CLEVELAND CLINIC
1508 Lauderdale Ave (44107-3608)
PHONE.................................216 374-0239
EMP: 52 **EST:** 2013
SALES (est): 130.81K **Privately Held**
Web: www.ccf.org
SIC: 8099 Health and allied services, nec

(G-9662)
CORNUCOPIA INC
Also Called: Natures Bin
18120 Sloane Ave (44107-3108)
PHONE.................................216 521-4600
Nancy Cuttler, *Ex Dir*
Scott Duennes, *
EMP: 36 **EST:** 1975
SQ FT: 6,000
SALES (est): 4.45MM **Privately Held**
Web: www.cornucopia-inc.org
SIC: 8331 5499 Vocational rehabilitation agency; Health foods

(G-9663)
CRESTMONT NURSING HOME N CORP
Also Called: Crestmont North
13330 Detroit Ave (44107-2850)
PHONE.................................216 228-9550
Elias J Coury, *Pr*
Norman Fox, *Sec*
EMP: 110 **EST:** 1986
SALES (est): 4.47MM **Privately Held**
Web: www.crestmontnorth.com
SIC: 8051 Convalescent home with continuous nursing care

(G-9664)
DEEP MIND MUSIC LLC
11850 Edgewater Dr Apt 904 (44107-1799)
PHONE.................................440 829-6401
David Fahrland, *Prin*
EMP: 54 **EST:** 2018
SALES (est): 339.9K **Privately Held**
SIC: 7371 Computer software development and applications

(G-9665)
FERRY CAP & SET SCREW COMPANY
2180 Halstead Ave (44107-6226)
PHONE.................................440 315-9291
EMP: 88
SALES (corp-wide): 15.78B **Publicly Held**
SIC: 4225 General warehousing and storage
HQ: Ferry Cap & Set Screw Company
  13300 Bramley Ave
  Lakewood OH 44107
  216 649-7400

(G-9666)
FERRY CAP & SET SCREW COMPANY (HQ)
Also Called: Stanley Engineered Fastening
13300 Bramley Ave (44107-6248)
PHONE.................................216 649-7400
David Ballou, *Genl Mgr*
▲ **EMP:** 175 **EST:** 1906
SQ FT: 130,000
SALES (est): 53.35MM
SALES (corp-wide): 15.78B **Publicly Held**
SIC: 5085 Fasteners, industrial: nuts, bolts, screws, etc.
PA: Stanley Black & Decker, Inc.
  1000 Stanley Dr
  New Britain CT 06053
  860 225-5111

(G-9667)
FIRST FDRAL SAV LN ASSN LKWOOD (PA)
14806 Detroit Ave (44107-3910)
PHONE.................................216 221-7300
Timothy E Phillips, *Pr*
W Charles Geiger Iii, *Ch Bd*
Judy Platek, *
Paul Capka, *
Richard Smith, *
EMP: 130 **EST:** 1935
SQ FT: 12,000
SALES (est): 76.35MM
SALES (corp-wide): 76.35MM **Privately Held**
Web: www.ffl.net
SIC: 6035 Federal savings and loan associations

(G-9668)
HANSON SERVICES INC (PA)
17017 Madison Ave (44107-3501)
P.O. Box 771222 (44107-0051)
PHONE.................................216 226-5425
Mary Ann Hanson, *Pr*
Kanchan Adhikary, *
EMP: 125 **EST:** 1996
SQ FT: 2,200
SALES (est): 5.72MM
SALES (corp-wide): 5.72MM **Privately Held**
Web: www.hansonservices.com
SIC: 8082 Visiting nurse service

(G-9669)
INVESTMENT PDTS FFL INV SVCS
14806 Detroit Ave (44107-3910)
PHONE.................................216 529-2700
James D Lechko, *Prin*
EMP: 35 **EST:** 2015
SALES (est): 397.76K **Privately Held**
Web: www.fflinvestments.com
SIC: 6411 Insurance agents, brokers, and service

(G-9670)
JMO & DSL LLC
Also Called: Synergy Homecare of Westlake
13702 Detroit Ave (44107-4620)
PHONE.................................216 785-9375
Daphne Slawski, *Prin*
EMP: 50 **EST:** 2019
SALES (est): 994.79K **Privately Held**
Web: www.synergyhomecare.com
SIC: 8082 Home health care services

(G-9671)
KEYBANK NATIONAL ASSOCIATION
1435 Warren Rd (44107-3946)
PHONE.................................216 226-0850
John Keating, *Mgr*
EMP: 38
SQ FT: 6,586
SALES (corp-wide): 10.4B **Publicly Held**
Web: www.key.com
SIC: 6021 National commercial banks
HQ: Keybank National Association
  127 Public Sq Ste 5600
  Cleveland OH 44114
  800 539-2968

(G-9672)
LAKEWOOD CATHOLIC ACADEMY
Also Called: Holy Family
14808 Lake Ave (44107-1352)
PHONE.................................216 521-4352
Kathleen Ogrin, *Dir*
EMP: 28
Web: www.lakewoodcatholicacademy.com

Lakewood - Cuyahoga County (G-9673)

GEOGRAPHIC SECTION

SIC: 8351 Child day care services
PA: Lakewood Catholic Academy
   14808 Lake Ave
   Lakewood OH 44107

(G-9673)
LAKEWOOD HEALTH CARE CENTER
Also Called: ENNIS COURT
13315 Detroit Ave (44107-2849)
   PHONE.....................216 226-3103
Patrice Campbell, *Pr*
EMP: 54 **EST:** 1981
SQ FT: 20,000
SALES (est): 9.49MM **Privately Held**
Web: www.enniscourt.com
SIC: 8051 Extended care facility

(G-9674)
LAKEWOOD HOSPITAL ASSOCIATION (HQ)
14519 Detroit Ave (44107-4316)
   PHONE.....................216 529-7201
Fred Degrandis, *CEO*
Jack Gustin, *CAO**
EMP: 530 **EST:** 1907
SQ FT: 100,000
SALES (est): 94.02MM
SALES (corp-wide): 14.48B **Privately Held**
Web: www.lakewoodhospital.org
SIC: 8062 General medical and surgical hospitals
PA: The Cleveland Clinic Foundation
   9500 Euclid Ave
   Cleveland OH 44195
   216 636-8335

(G-9675)
LAKEWOOD RECREATION DEPARTMENT
13701 Lake Ave (44107-1440)
   PHONE.....................216 529-4081
Ms. Emma Petrie Barcelona, *Pr*
EMP: 31 **EST:** 2010
SALES (est): 672.66K **Privately Held**
Web: www.lakewoodrecreation.com
SIC: 8322 Community center

(G-9676)
LAKEWOOD RNGERS EDCATN FNDTION
14100 Franklin Blvd (44107-4516)
   PHONE.....................216 521-2100
EMP: 34 **EST:** 1984
SALES (est): 140.17K **Privately Held**
Web: www.lakewoodcityschools.org
SIC: 4832 Educational

(G-9677)
LAKEWOOD SENIOR CAMPUS LLC
13900 Detroit Ave (44107-4624)
   PHONE.....................216 228-7650
EMP: 46 **EST:** 2007
SALES (est): 11.91MM **Privately Held**
Web: www.oneillhc.com
SIC: 8051 Skilled nursing care facilities

(G-9678)
MAPLE RETAIL LTD PARTNERSHIP
14600 Detroit Ave # 1500 (44107-4207)
   PHONE.....................216 221-6600
Walter Zaremba, *Pt*
EMP: 100 **EST:** 1997
SQ FT: 48,628
SALES (est): 4.73MM **Privately Held**
SIC: 6512 Shopping center, property operation only

(G-9679)
MERIDIAN CONDOMINIUMS INC
12550 Lake Ave (44107-1575)
   PHONE.....................216 228-4211
Ellie Seligman, *Mgr*
EMP: 27 **EST:** 1974
SALES (est): 712.67K **Privately Held**
Web: www.themeridiancondos.net
SIC: 8641 Condominium association

(G-9680)
OSTER SERVICES LLC
17415 Northwood Ave Ste 100 (44107-2268)
   PHONE.....................440 596-8489
Alexis S Oster, *Prin*
Tom Ream, *Prin*
EMP: 35 **EST:** 2011
SALES (est): 4.32MM **Privately Held**
Web: www.osterservices.net
SIC: 1521 New construction, single-family houses

(G-9681)
PALLET DISTRIBUTORS INC (PA)
Also Called: E-Pallet
14701 Detroit Ave Ste 750 (44107-4109)
   PHONE.....................888 805-9670
Greg Fronk, *Pr*
Sandy Riedel, *
EMP: 50 **EST:** 1996
SALES (est): 22.47MM **Privately Held**
Web: www.epalletinc.com
SIC: 5031 5085 Pallets, wood; Plastic pallets

(G-9682)
ROBERT C BARNEY DVM INC
Also Called: Lakewood Animal Hospital
14587 Madison Ave (44107-4325)
   PHONE.....................216 221-5380
Robert C Barney, *Pr*
EMP: 31 **EST:** 1982
SALES (est): 1.09MM **Privately Held**
Web: www.vcahospitals.com
SIC: 0742 Animal hospital services, pets and other animal specialties

(G-9683)
ROUNDSTONE MANAGEMENT LTD
15422 Detroit Ave (44107-3830)
   PHONE.....................440 617-0333
EMP: 130 **EST:** 2009
SALES (est): 7.27MM **Privately Held**
Web: www.roundstoneinsurance.com
SIC: 8741 Business management

(G-9684)
SACRED HOUR INC
Also Called: Sacred Hour Wellness Spas
17917 Detroit Ave (44107-3415)
   PHONE.....................216 228-9750
Tabitha Baker, *Pr*
EMP: 55 **EST:** 2004
SALES (est): 659.5K **Privately Held**
Web: www.sacredhour.com
SIC: 7991 7371 7389 Spas; Computer software development and applications; Business Activities at Non-Commercial Site

(G-9685)
SECURITY HUT INC (PA)
Also Called: Secura Fact
18614 Detroit Ave (44107-3202)
   PHONE.....................216 226-0461
Charles Brooks, *Pr*
EMP: 100 **EST:** 1995
SALES (est): 2.13MM **Privately Held**
Web: www.securityhut.com
SIC: 7381 7375 Private investigator; Information retrieval services

(G-9686)
VANGUARD PROPERTY MANAGEMENT
18900 Detroit Ext Unit 800 (44107-3255)
P.O. Box 367 (44107-0367)
   PHONE.....................216 521-8222
EMP: 36 **EST:** 2009
SALES (est): 1.14MM **Privately Held**
Web: www.vanguardcleveland.net
SIC: 8741 Business management

(G-9687)
WITHIN3 INC (PA)
17415 Northwood Ave Ste 300 (44107-2268)
P.O. Box 450679 (44145-0613)
   PHONE.....................855 948-4463
Lance P Hill, *CEO*
Stephen Mathey, *
EMP: 258 **EST:** 2006
SQ FT: 3,500
SALES (est): 30.76MM **Privately Held**
Web: www.within3.com
SIC: 8733 Educational research agency

(G-9688)
YOUNG MNS CHRSTN ASSN GRTER CL
Also Called: Lakewood Y
16915 Detroit Ave (44107-3620)
   PHONE.....................216 521-8400
Gary Brick, *Dir*
EMP: 89
SQ FT: 21,781
SALES (corp-wide): 25.51MM **Privately Held**
Web: www.clevelandymca.org
SIC: 8641 7991 8351 7032 Youth organizations; Physical fitness facilities; Child day care services; Youth camps
PA: Young Men's Christian Association Of Greater Cleveland
   1301 E 9th St Fl 9
   Cleveland OH 44114
   216 781-1337

(G-9689)
ZAREMBA GROUP LLC
14600 Detroit Ave (44107-4207)
   PHONE.....................216 221-6600
David Zaremba, *CEO*
Joseph J Urbancic, *
Robert Steadley, *
EMP: 64 **EST:** 1997
SQ FT: 12,000
SALES (est): 15.35MM **Privately Held**
Web: www.zarembagroup.com
SIC: 6552 8111 6531 Land subdividers and developers, commercial; Legal services; Real estate managers

Lancaster
Fairfield County

(G-9690)
ACCURATE MECHANICAL INC
566 Mill Park Dr (43130-7744)
   PHONE.....................740 681-1332
EMP: 58
SALES (corp-wide): 21.57MM **Privately Held**
Web: www.accuratehvac.com
SIC: 5074 5063 3499 1711 Heating equipment (hydronic); Electrical supplies, nec; Aerosol valves, metal; Septic system construction
PA: Accurate Mechanical, Inc.
   3001 River Rd
   Chillicothe OH
   740 775-5005

(G-9691)
AG-PRO OHIO LLC
Also Called: John Deere Authorized Dealer
1200 Delmont Rd Sw (43130-9550)
   PHONE.....................740 653-6951
Ed Smith, *Prin*
EMP: 38
SALES (corp-wide): 204.78MM **Privately Held**
Web: www.agprocompanies.com
SIC: 5261 5511 5999 7359 Lawnmowers and tractors; Trucks, tractors, and trailers: new and used; Farm equipment and supplies; Rental store, general
HQ: Ag-Pro Ohio, Inc.
   19595 Us Highway 84 E
   Boston GA 31626
   229 498-8833

(G-9692)
AIR EVAC EMS INC
Also Called: Air Evac Lifeteam
2929 Lancaster Thornville Rd Ne (43130-8547)
   PHONE.....................417 274-6754
Mike Jackson, *Prin*
EMP: 126
Web: www.lifeteam.net
SIC: 4522 Ambulance services, air
HQ: Air Evac Ems, Inc.
   1001 Boardwalk Springs Pl
   O Fallon MO 63368

(G-9693)
ALLERGY & ASTHMA INC
2405 N Columbus St Ste 270 (43130-8185)
   PHONE.....................740 654-8623
H C Nataraj, *Brnch Mgr*
EMP: 48
SALES (corp-wide): 1.02MM **Privately Held**
Web: www.premierallergyohio.com
SIC: 8011 Allergist
PA: Allergy & Asthma, Inc.
   9800 Shelbyville Rd # 220
   Louisville KY 40223
   614 864-6649

(G-9694)
ANCHOR HOCKING HOLDINGS INC
519 N Pierce Ave (43130-2969)
   PHONE.....................800 562-7511
EMP: 50
SALES (corp-wide): 697.24MM **Privately Held**
Web: www.theoneidagroup.com
SIC: 5046 Commercial cooking and food service equipment
PA: Anchor Hocking Holdings, Inc.
   1600 Dublin Rd Ste 200
   Columbus OH 43215
   740 687-2500

(G-9695)
ARBOR VIEW FAMILY MEDICINE INC
1941 W Fair Ave (43130-9671)
   PHONE.....................740 687-3386
David Scoggin, *Prin*
EMP: 30 **EST:** 1997
SALES (est): 1.58MM **Privately Held**
Web: www.arborviewfamilymedicine.com
SIC: 8071 Medical laboratories

(G-9696)
BMU77 LLC
10 Whiley Rd (43130-8147)
   PHONE.....................740 652-1679
Matt Upp, *CFO*
EMP: 40 **EST:** 2015

GEOGRAPHIC SECTION
Lancaster - Fairfield County (G-9718)

SALES (est): 4.92MM **Privately Held**
SIC: 1623 Underground utilities contractor

(G-9697)
BOB-BOYD FORD INC (PA)
Also Called: Bobboyd Auto Family
2840 N Columbus St (43130)
P.O. Box 767 (43130)
PHONE..................614 860-0606
Robert G Dawes, *Pr*
Robert G Dawes, *Pr*
Boyd Fackler, *
Virginia H Robb, *
Michael D Bornstein, *
EMP: 56 EST: 1946
SALES (est): 21.61MM
SALES (corp-wide): 21.61MM **Privately Held**
Web: www.bobboyd.com
SIC: 5511 7538 Automobiles, new and used; General automotive repair shops

(G-9698)
CARLETON REALTY INC
826 N Memorial Dr (43130-2567)
PHONE..................740 653-5200
Renee Schmelzer, *Brnch Mgr*
EMP: 28
SALES (corp-wide): 8.16MM **Privately Held**
Web: www.carletonrealty.com
SIC: 6531 Real estate agent, residential
PA: Carleton Realty Inc
   580 W Schrock Rd
   Westerville OH 43081
   614 431-5700

(G-9699)
CARPEDIEM MANAGEMENT COMPANY
Also Called: Rax Restaurant
800 E Main St (43130-3939)
PHONE..................740 687-1563
Bill Hess, *Mgr*
EMP: 35
Web: www.raxroastbeef.com
SIC: 5812 8741 Sandwiches and submarines shop; Restaurant management
PA: Carpediem Management Company
   5017 Pine Creek Dr
   Westerville OH 43081

(G-9700)
CIRBA SOLUTIONS US INC (PA)
Also Called: Lithchem
265 Quarry Rd Se (43130-8271)
PHONE..................740 653-6290
Steven Kinsbursky, *CEO*
▲ EMP: 29 EST: 2013
SALES (est): 46.81MM
SALES (corp-wide): 46.81MM **Privately Held**
Web: www.cirbasolutions.com
SIC: 2819 4953 3341 Industrial inorganic chemicals, nec; Recycling, waste materials; Recovery and refining of nonferrous metals

(G-9701)
CITY OF LANCASTER
Also Called: Lancaster Municipal Gas
1424 Campground Rd (43130-9503)
PHONE..................740 687-6670
Michael R Pettit, *Superintnt*
EMP: 46
SALES (corp-wide): 52.07MM **Privately Held**
Web: ci.lancaster.oh.us
SIC: 1311 4924 Crude petroleum and natural gas; Natural gas distribution
PA: City Of Lancaster
   104 E Main St
   Lancaster OH 43130
   740 687-6600

(G-9702)
CLAYPOOL ELECTRIC INC
Also Called: Claypool Electrical Contg
1275 Lancaster Kirkersville Rd Nw (43130-8969)
PHONE..................740 653-5683
Greg Davis, *Pr*
Barbara Claypool, *
Tucker Brady, *
Charles Claypool, *
EMP: 160 EST: 1955
SQ FT: 20,000
SALES (est): 32.16MM **Privately Held**
Web: www.claypoolelectric.com
SIC: 1731 General electrical contractor

(G-9703)
CMS BUSINESS SERVICES LLC
Also Called: Servicmster Coml Clg Advantage
416 N Mount Pleasant Ave (43130-3134)
PHONE..................740 687-0577
Teresa Marshall, *Managing Member*
Dan Marshall, *Managing Member*
EMP: 80 EST: 2008
SALES (est): 1.02MM **Privately Held**
Web: www.servicemaster.com
SIC: 7349 Janitorial service, contract basis

(G-9704)
COMMUNITY ACTION PRGRAM COMM O (PA)
Also Called: LANCASTER-FAIRFIELD COMMUNITY
1743 E Main St (43130-9838)
P.O. Box 768 (43130-0768)
PHONE..................740 653-1711
Kellie Ailes, *Ex Dir*
EMP: 100 EST: 1965
SQ FT: 3,000
SALES (est): 14.41MM
SALES (corp-wide): 14.41MM **Privately Held**
Web: www.faircaa.org
SIC: 8322 Social service center

(G-9705)
COMMUNITY BANK
201 N Columbus St (43130-3006)
PHONE..................740 654-0900
Alan Hooker, *Pr*
Thomas E Buck, *Sr VP*
Ida M Neely, *Treas*
Judith Williams, *VP*
EMP: 40 EST: 1945
SALES (est): 2.78MM
SALES (corp-wide): 40.9MM **Publicly Held**
Web: www.unifiedbank.com
SIC: 6022 State trust companies accepting deposits, commercial
PA: United Bancorp, Inc.
   201 S 4th St
   Martins Ferry OH 43935
   740 633-0445

(G-9706)
CRESTVIEW MANOR NURSING HOME (PA)
Also Called: Crestview Manor II
957 Becks Knob Rd (43130-8800)
PHONE..................740 654-2634
Winfield S Eckert, *Pr*
Jo Ann Eckert, *
EMP: 110 EST: 1958
SQ FT: 52,000
SALES (est): 13.26MM
SALES (corp-wide): 13.26MM **Privately Held**
Web: www.crestviewrehab.com
SIC: 8051 6513 Extended care facility; Apartment building operators

(G-9707)
DAGGER JHNSTON MLLER OGLVIE HM (PA)
144 E Main St (43130-3712)
P.O. Box 667 (43130-0667)
PHONE..................740 653-6464
Norman J Ogilvie Junior, *Prin*
Mark Bibler, *Pt*
James W Miller, *Pt*
Randy Happeney, *Pt*
Robert E Johnston, *Pt*
EMP: 30 EST: 1904
SQ FT: 2,200
SALES (est): 4.65MM
SALES (corp-wide): 4.65MM **Privately Held**
Web: www.daggerlaw.com
SIC: 8111 General practice attorney, lawyer

(G-9708)
DREW VENTURES INC (PA)
Also Called: Drew Shoe
252 Quarry Rd Se (43130-8054)
PHONE..................740 653-4271
Dennis B Tishkoff, *CEO*
Marc Tishkoff, *Pr*
Peter Struzzi, *CFO*
▲ EMP: 43 EST: 1875
SQ FT: 60,000
SALES (est): 11.82MM
SALES (corp-wide): 11.82MM **Privately Held**
Web: www.drewshoe.com
SIC: 5139 Shoes

(G-9709)
FAIRFIELD CNTY JOB & FMLY SVCS
239 W Main St (43130-3739)
PHONE..................800 450-8845
Michael Orlando, *Prin*
Jamie Fauble, *Prin*
EMP: 35 EST: 2007
SALES (est): 4.51MM **Privately Held**
Web: www.fcjfs.org
SIC: 8399 Council for social agency

(G-9710)
FAIRFIELD COMMUNITY HEALTH CTR
Also Called: Fchc
220 E Walnut St (43130-4464)
PHONE..................740 277-6043
Clinton G Kuntz, *CEO*
Micheal Horn Berger, *
EMP: 39 EST: 2009
SALES (est): 9.13MM **Privately Held**
Web: www.fairfieldchc.org
SIC: 8082 Home health care services

(G-9711)
FAIRFIELD DIAGNSTC IMAGING LLC
Also Called: Fairfield Medical Center
1241 River Valley Blvd (43130-1653)
PHONE..................740 654-6312
Sky Gettys, *CEO*
EMP: 40 EST: 1998
SALES (est): 3.81MM **Privately Held**
SIC: 8062 General medical and surgical hospitals

(G-9712)
FAIRFIELD FEDERAL SAV LN ASSN (PA)
111 E Main St (43130-3713)
P.O. Box 728 (43130-0728)
PHONE..................740 653-3863
Ronald Keaton, *Pr*
EMP: 50 EST: 1895
SQ FT: 22,500
SALES (est): 9.69MM
SALES (corp-wide): 9.69MM **Privately Held**
Web: www.fairfieldfederal.com
SIC: 6035 8111 Federal savings and loan associations; Legal services

(G-9713)
FAIRFIELD HOMES INC (PA)
Also Called: Gorsuch Management
603 W Wheeling St (43130-3630)
PHONE..................740 653-3583
Leonard F Gorsuch, *Pr*
Jackie Evans, *
EMP: 30 EST: 1992
SALES (est): 2.38MM **Privately Held**
Web: www.fairfieldhomesohio.com
SIC: 6513 Apartment building operators

(G-9714)
FAIRFIELD HOMES INC (PA)
Also Called: Gorsuch Management
603 W Wheeling St (43130-3630)
P.O. Box 190 (43130-0190)
PHONE..................740 653-3583
Leonard F Gorsuch, *CEO*
Ronald P Burson, *
EMP: 30 EST: 1947
SQ FT: 7,000
SALES (est): 25.24MM
SALES (corp-wide): 25.24MM **Privately Held**
Web: www.fairfieldhomesohio.com
SIC: 6531 1522 Real estate managers; Multi-family dwelling construction, nec

(G-9715)
FAIRFIELD INSUL & DRYWALL LLC
1655 Election House Rd Nw (43130-9059)
PHONE..................740 654-8811
Paul Moentmann, *Pr*
EMP: 49 EST: 2016
SQ FT: 10,000
SALES (est): 10K **Privately Held**
Web: www.fairfieldid.com
SIC: 1742 1751 Acoustical and ceiling work; Lightweight steel framing (metal stud) installation

(G-9716)
FAIRFIELD INTERNAL MEDICINE
135 N Ewing St Ste 305 (43130-3379)
PHONE..................740 681-9447
Nancy Alspach, *Mgr*
EMP: 29 EST: 2005
SALES (est): 1.79MM **Privately Held**
Web: www.copcp.com
SIC: 8011 General and family practice, physician/surgeon

(G-9717)
FAIRFIELD MEDICAL ASSOCIATES
1781 Countryside Dr (43130-1186)
PHONE..................740 687-8377
Scott R Baker, *Pt*
Agnes M Laus, *Pt*
Sarah Alley, *Pt*
EMP: 27 EST: 2001
SQ FT: 4,767
SALES (est): 7.3MM **Privately Held**
Web: www.fmchealth.org
SIC: 8062 General medical and surgical hospitals

(G-9718)
FAIRFIELD MEDICAL CENTER (PA)
401 N Ewing St (43130-3371)
PHONE..................740 687-8000

Lancaster - Fairfield County (G-9719)

Sky Gettys, *CEO*
Julie Grow, *CFO*
EMP: 2000 **EST:** 1914
SQ FT: 380,000
SALES (est): 344.62MM
SALES (corp-wide): 344.62MM **Privately Held**
Web: www.fmchealth.org
SIC: 8062 7352 5999 General medical and surgical hospitals; Medical equipment rental ; Medical apparatus and supplies

(G-9719)
FAIRFIELD NATIONAL BANK
1280 N Memorial Dr (43130-1625)
PHONE.................................740 653-1422
Linda Harris, *Mgr*
EMP: 88
SALES (corp-wide): 564.3MM **Publicly Held**
Web: www.parknationalbank.com
SIC: 6021 National commercial banks
HQ: Fairfield National Bank
143 W Main St
Lancaster OH 43130
740 653-7242

(G-9720)
FAIRFIELD NATIONAL BANK (HQ)
143 W Main St (43130-3700)
P.O. Box 607 (43130-0607)
PHONE.................................740 653-7242
Stephen Wells, *Pr*
EMP: 50 **EST:** 1872
SQ FT: 5,000
SALES (est): 6.47MM
SALES (corp-wide): 564.3MM **Publicly Held**
Web: www.parknationalbank.com
SIC: 6021 National commercial banks
PA: Park National Corporation
50 N 3rd St
Newark OH 43055
740 349-8451

(G-9721)
FAIRHOPE HSPICE PLLTIVE CARE I
282 Sells Rd (43130-3461)
PHONE.................................740 654-7077
Denise Bauer, *CEO*
EMP: 100 **EST:** 1984
SALES (est): 13.36MM **Privately Held**
Web: www.fairhopehospice.org
SIC: 8051 8082 Skilled nursing care facilities ; Home health care services

(G-9722)
FAMILY YMCA LNCSTER FRFELD CNT (PA)
Also Called: ROBERT K FOX FAMILY WIDE
465 W 6th Ave (43130-2597)
PHONE.................................740 654-0616
Mike Lieber, *CEO*
Steve Murry, *
EMP: 46 **EST:** 1985
SALES (est): 2.48MM
SALES (corp-wide): 2.48MM **Privately Held**
Web: www.ymcalancaster.org
SIC: 7991 7997 Physical fitness facilities; Membership sports and recreation clubs

(G-9723)
FAMILY YMCA OF LANCSTR&FAIRFLD
1180 E Locust St (43130-4044)
PHONE.................................740 277-1373
Mike Lieber, *Brnch Mgr*
EMP: 64
SALES (corp-wide): 2.48MM **Privately Held**
Web: www.ymcalancaster.org
SIC: 8641 7991 8351 7032 Youth organizations; Physical fitness facilities; Child day care services; Youth camps
PA: Family Ymca Of Lancaster And Fairfield County
465 W 6th Ave
Lancaster OH 43130
740 654-0616

(G-9724)
GRANDVLLE PIKE FMLY PHYSICIANS
1800 Granville Pike (43130-1043)
PHONE.................................740 687-0793
Ralph R Romaker, *Prin*
Mark Aebi, *Prin*
Joeseph Ginty, *Prin*
EMP: 31 **EST:** 1994
SALES (est): 435.66K **Privately Held**
Web: www.copcp.com
SIC: 8011 General and family practice, physician/surgeon

(G-9725)
HOME HEALTH CONNECTION INC
3062 Columbus Lancaster Rd Nw (43130-8126)
PHONE.................................614 839-4545
Shirine Mafi, *Pr*
Shawn Mafi, *VP*
EMP: 33 **EST:** 2000
SALES (est): 3.24MM **Privately Held**
Web: www.hhc-oh.com
SIC: 8059 8011 Personal care home, with health care; Offices and clinics of medical doctors

(G-9726)
JANESSA INC
Also Called: Knights Inn
1327 River Valley Blvd (43130-1600)
PHONE.................................740 687-4823
Kirtesh Patel, *VP*
Sangita Patel, *Pr*
EMP: 100 **EST:** 1987
SQ FT: 20,736
SALES (est): 365.87K **Privately Held**
Web: www.sonesta.com
SIC: 7011 Hotels and motels

(G-9727)
JONES COCHENOUR & CO INC (PA)
125 W Mulberry St (43130-3064)
PHONE.................................740 653-9581
EMP: 41 **EST:** 1949
SALES (est): 2.57MM **Privately Held**
Web: www.jcccpa.com
SIC: 8721 Certified public accountant

(G-9728)
KUMLER COLLISION INC
Also Called: Kumler Automotive
2313 E Main St (43130-9350)
PHONE.................................740 653-4301
Dean De Rolph, *Pr*
Cathie De Rolph, *
EMP: 28 **EST:** 1928
SQ FT: 24,000
SALES (est): 1.24MM **Privately Held**
Web: www.kumler.com
SIC: 7532 Body shop, automotive

(G-9729)
LANCASTER BINGO COMPANY LLC
200 Quarry Rd Se (43130-9304)
PHONE.................................800 866-5001
EMP: 175 **EST:** 2021
SALES (est): 12.92MM **Privately Held**
SIC: 5092 Bingo games and supplies

(G-9730)
LANCASTER COUNTRY CLUB
3100 Country Club Rd Sw (43130-8937)
P.O. Box 1098 (43130-0818)
PHONE.................................740 654-3535
Richard Waibel, *Genl Pt*
Jim Aranda, *
EMP: 64 **EST:** 1909
SQ FT: 4,000
SALES (est): 784.15K **Privately Held**
Web: www.lancastercc.com
SIC: 7997 5941 5812 Swimming club, membership; Golf goods and equipment; Eating places

(G-9731)
LANCASTER HOST LLC
Also Called: Holiday Inn Ex Ht & Suites
1861 Riverway Dr (43130-1494)
P.O. Box 54465 (40555-4465)
PHONE.................................740 654-4445
Phil Greer, *CEO*
EMP: 34 **EST:** 1998
SALES (est): 464.7K **Privately Held**
Web: www.lancasterhostgolf.com
SIC: 7011 Hotels and motels

(G-9732)
LANCASTER RADIATION ONCOLOGY
401 N Ewing St (43130-3372)
PHONE.................................740 687-8554
Joseph Mc Kelvey, *Pr*
EMP: 45 **EST:** 2001
SALES (est): 2.12MM **Privately Held**
Web: www.fmchealth.org
SIC: 8011 Radiologist

(G-9733)
LOWES HOME CENTERS LLC
Also Called: Lowe's
2240 Lowes Dr (43130-5700)
PHONE.................................740 681-3464
Dave Taylor, *Mgr*
EMP: 172
SALES (corp-wide): 86.38B **Publicly Held**
Web: www.lowes.com
SIC: 5211 5031 5722 5064 Home centers; Building materials, exterior; Household appliance stores; Electrical appliances, television and radio
HQ: Lowe's Home Centers, Llc
1000 Lowes Blvd
Mooresville NC 28117
336 658-4000

(G-9734)
MAIN STREET TERRACE CARE CTR
1318 E Main St (43130-4004)
PHONE.................................740 653-8767
Ed Telle, *Pr*
Peggy S Dupler, *
EMP: 56 **EST:** 1952
SQ FT: 5,182
SALES (est): 4.39MM **Privately Held**
Web: www.mainstreetterracecarecenter.com
SIC: 8052 8051 Intermediate care facilities; Skilled nursing care facilities

(G-9735)
MID-OHIO PSYCHLOGICAL SVCS INC (PA)
106 Starret St Ste 100 (43130-3993)
PHONE.................................740 687-0042
Kimberly Blair, *Ex Dir*
EMP: 32 **EST:** 1990
SALES (est): 2.99MM **Privately Held**
Web: www.mopsohio.com
SIC: 8322 8093 General counseling services ; Mental health clinic, outpatient

(G-9736)
NEW HRZONS MNTAL HLTH SVCS INC (PA)
Also Called: Pickerngton Area Cunseling Ctr
230 N Columbus St Ste B (43130-3093)
PHONE.................................740 901-3150
Anthony Motta, *CEO*
Patrick Fleming, *CFO*
EMP: 62 **EST:** 1971
SALES (est): 7.2MM **Privately Held**
Web: www.newhorizonsmentalhealth.org
SIC: 8322 General counseling services

(G-9737)
PRIMROSE RTRMENT CMMNITIES LLC
1481 Wesley Way (43130-7756)
PHONE.................................740 653-3900
Kim Remily, *Brnch Mgr*
EMP: 60
Web: www.primroseretirement.com
SIC: 8361 Aged home
PA: Primrose Retirement Communities Llc
815 N 2nd St
Aberdeen SD 57401

(G-9738)
RECOVERY CENTER
201 S Columbus St (43130)
PHONE.................................740 687-4500
Trisha Farrar, *Ex Dir*
EMP: 28 **EST:** 1973
SQ FT: 12,500
SALES (est): 1.34MM **Privately Held**
Web: www.therecoverycenter.org
SIC: 8699 8093 Charitable organization; Rehabilitation center, outpatient treatment

(G-9739)
RIVERVIEW SURGERY CENTER
Also Called: River View Surgery Center
2401 N Columbus St (43130-8190)
PHONE.................................740 681-2700
EMP: 33 **EST:** 1997
SALES (est): 3.25MM **Privately Held**
Web: www.fmchealth.org
SIC: 8062 General medical and surgical hospitals

(G-9740)
SALO INC
Also Called: Interim Services
2680 N Columbus St Ste A (43130-8411)
PHONE.................................740 653-5990
Paul Sprouse, *Brnch Mgr*
EMP: 187
SALES (corp-wide): 52.16MM **Privately Held**
Web: www.interimhealthcare.com
SIC: 8082 7363 Home health care services; Help supply services
PA: Salo, Inc.
300 W Wlson Brdge Rd Ste
Columbus OH 43085
614 436-9404

(G-9741)
SINGLETON CONSTRUCTION LLC
Also Called: ADM Facilities
4730 Wilson Rd Nw (43130-9582)
P.O. Box 309 (43110-0309)
PHONE.................................740 756-7331
Denise Doczy-delong, *CEO*
Nancy Doczy, *
EMP: 82 **EST:** 1995
SALES (est): 27.4MM **Privately Held**
Web: www.singletonconstruction.net

GEOGRAPHIC SECTION

Lebanon - Warren County (G-9764)

SIC: **1542** Commercial and office building contractors

(G-9742)
SOUTH CENTRAL POWER COMPANY (PA)
720 Mill Park Dr (43130)
PHONE..................740 653-4422
TOLL FREE: 800
Rick Lemonds, *Pr*
Tom Musick, *
Cathy Bitler, *
Kenneth Davis, *
Rebecca Witt, *
▲ **EMP:** 110 **EST:** 1936
SALES (est): 369.45MM
SALES (corp-wide): 369.45MM **Privately Held**
Web: www.southcentralpower.com
SIC: **4911** Distribution, electric power

(G-9743)
SOUTH CENTRAL POWER COMPANY
720 Mill Park Dr (43130-7933)
PHONE..................614 837-4351
EMP: 31
SALES (corp-wide): 338.8MM **Privately Held**
Web: www.southcentralpower.com
SIC: **4911** Distribution, electric power
PA: South Central Power Company Inc
720 Mill Park Dr
Lancaster OH 43130
740 653-4422

(G-9744)
STANDING STONE NATIONAL BANK (PA)
137 W Wheeling St (43130-3708)
P.O. Box 310 (43113-0310)
PHONE..................740 653-5115
Barry Ritchey, *Pr*
Albert Horvath, *VP*
EMP: 48 **EST:** 1989
SQ FT: 7,500
SALES (est): 5.17MM **Privately Held**
SIC: **6021** National commercial banks

(G-9745)
STIFEL IND ADVISORS LLC
109 E Main St (43130-3744)
PHONE..................740 653-9222
Kathy Kittredge, *Brnch Mgr*
EMP: 47
SALES (corp-wide): 4.35B **Publicly Held**
Web: www.stifelindependence.com
SIC: **7381** Guard services
HQ: Stifel Independent Advisors, Llc
1 Fnncial Plz 501 N Brd
Saint Louis MO 63102

(G-9746)
TAYLOR CHEVROLET INC
Also Called: Taylor Dealership
1164 Stone Run Ct (43130-2778)
PHONE..................740 653-2091
Martin N Taylor, *Pr*
Milton Taylor Junior, *VP*
EMP: 28 **EST:** 1960
SALES (est): 4.84MM **Privately Held**
Web: www.visittaylorchevy.com
SIC: **5511** 7538 7514 Automobiles, new and used; General automotive repair shops; Passenger car rental

(G-9747)
TIKI BOWLING LANES INC
Also Called: Tiki Lounge & Restaurant
1521 Tiki Ln (43130-8793)
PHONE..................740 654-4513
James Shaner, *Pr*
EMP: 29 **EST:** 1962
SALES (est): 470.14K **Privately Held**
Web: www.tikilanes.com
SIC: **7933** 5812 Ten pin center; Eating places

(G-9748)
VETERANS OF FOREIGN WARS OF US
116 Perry St (43130-4445)
P.O. Box 2508 (43130-5508)
PHONE..................740 653-1516
EMP: 65
SALES (corp-wide): 105.25MM **Privately Held**
SIC: **8641** Veterans' organization
PA: Veterans Of Foreign Wars Of The United States
406 W 34th St Fl 11
Kansas City MO 64111
816 756-3390

(G-9749)
WEST AFTER SCHOOL CENTER
Also Called: AFTERSCHOOL PROGRAMS OF LANCAS
625 Garfield Ave (43130-2432)
PHONE..................740 653-5678
Ruth Petrovay, *Dir*
EMP: 30 **EST:** 2008
SALES (est): 1.32MM **Privately Held**
Web: www.westafterschoolcenter.org
SIC: **8351** Head Start center, except in conjunction with school

(G-9750)
WINDSOR COMPANIES (PA)
1430 Collins Rd Nw (43130-8815)
PHONE..................740 653-8822
Thomas W Moore, *Pt*
Melvin L Moore, *Pt*
EMP: 33 **EST:** 1973
SQ FT: 2,200
SALES (est): 7MM
SALES (corp-wide): 7MM **Privately Held**
Web: www.thewindsorcompanies.com
SIC: **6552** Subdividers and developers, nec

Leavittsburg
Trumbull County

(G-9751)
SOH TRUMBUL CO HELP ME GROW
3688 Nelson Mosier Rd (44430-9760)
PHONE..................330 675-6610
Denise Allen, *Brnch Mgr*
EMP: 31
SIC: **7389** Personal service agents, brokers, and bureaus
PA: Soh Trumbul Co Help Me Grow
176 Chestnut Ave Ne
Warren OH 44483

Lebanon
Warren County

(G-9752)
ADDITION MANUFACTURING TECHNOLOGIES LLC
Also Called: Addisonmckee
1637 Kingsview Dr (45036-8395)
PHONE..................513 228-7000
▲ **EMP:** 175
Web: www.numalliance.com
SIC: **3542** 3599 5084 3549 Bending machines; Machine shop, jobbing and repair ; Industrial machinery and equipment; Metalworking machinery, nec

(G-9753)
ALLEN FIELDS ASSOC INC
3525 Grant Ave Ste D (45036-6431)
PHONE..................513 228-1010
Raymond Watson, *Owner*
EMP: 34 **EST:** 2004
SALES (est): 1.56MM **Privately Held**
Web: www.fieldselectric.com
SIC: **3699** 5063 Electrical equipment and supplies, nec; Electrical apparatus and equipment

(G-9754)
ANISHIV INC
Also Called: Knights Inn
725 E Main St (45036-1917)
PHONE..................513 932-3034
Alkeff Patl, *Pr*
Pete Patel, *VP*
EMP: 31 **EST:** 1989
SALES (est): 231.62K **Privately Held**
Web: www.sonesta.com
SIC: **7011** Hotels and motels

(G-9755)
ASC OF CINCINNATI INC
4028 Binion Way (45036-9367)
P.O. Box 230 (41001-0230)
PHONE..................513 886-7100
Steven Stortz, *Pr*
Stain Smith, *
EMP: 34 **EST:** 2004
SQ FT: 3,000
SALES (est): 2.32MM **Privately Held**
SIC: **4841** Cable and other pay television services

(G-9756)
BEACH AT MASON LTD PARTNERSHIP
Also Called: Beach Waterpark
3000 Henkle Dr (45036-9258)
PHONE..................513 398-7946
Michael T Schueler, *Genl Pt*
▲ **EMP:** 41 **EST:** 1985
SALES (est): 602.33K **Privately Held**
Web: www.schuelergroup.com
SIC: **7996** Theme park, amusement

(G-9757)
BOB PULTE CHEVROLET INC
909 Columbus Ave (45036-1401)
P.O. Box 814 (45036-0814)
PHONE..................513 932-0303
TOLL FREE: 800
Robert Pulte, *Pr*
EMP: 49 **EST:** 1987
SQ FT: 19,000
SALES (est): 14.54MM **Privately Held**
Web: www.bobpulte.com
SIC: **5511** 7515 5551 Automobiles, new and used; Passenger car leasing; Boat dealers

(G-9758)
CCH HEALTHCARE OH LLC
Also Called: Cedarview Rhbltion Nrsing Car
115 Oregonia Rd (45036-1983)
PHONE..................513 932-1121
EMP: 31 **EST:** 2014
SALES (est): 5.34MM **Privately Held**
Web: www.cedarviewhc.com
SIC: **8051** Convalescent home with continuous nursing care

(G-9759)
CITY OF LEBANON
Also Called: Electric Department
125 S Sycamore St (45036-2129)
PHONE..................513 228-3200
Shawn Coffey, *Dir*
EMP: 31
SALES (corp-wide): 31.58MM **Privately Held**
Web: www.lebanonohio.gov
SIC: **4911** 9111 Electric services; Executive offices, Local government
PA: City Of Lebanon
50 S Brdwy St
Lebanon OH 45036
513 933-7210

(G-9760)
CONGER CONSTRUCTION GROUP INC
2020 Mckinley Blvd (45036-6425)
P.O. Box 1069 (45036-5069)
PHONE..................513 932-1206
Larry Conger, *Pr*
Jacob Conger, *
Joseph Litvin, *
Jeremy Bolling, *
EMP: 30 **EST:** 1992
SQ FT: 12,000
SALES (est): 18.43MM **Privately Held**
Web: www.congerbuilt.com
SIC: **1542** Commercial and office building, new construction

(G-9761)
CORNERSTONE HLTHCARE SLTONS LL
301 S Mechanic St (45036-2213)
PHONE..................937 985-4011
Jason Roller, *Prin*
EMP: 60 **EST:** 2013
SALES (est): 958.09K **Privately Held**
SIC: **8099** Medical services organization

(G-9762)
COUNTY OF WARREN
Also Called: Warren County Wtr & Sewer Dept
903 N Broadway St (45036-1308)
P.O. Box 530 (45036-0530)
PHONE..................513 925-1377
Chris Brausch, *Mgr*
EMP: 60
SQ FT: 1,940
SALES (corp-wide): 196MM **Privately Held**
Web: www.wcauditor.org
SIC: **4941** 4952 Water supply; Sewerage systems
PA: County Of Warren
406 Justice Dr Rm 323
Lebanon OH 45036
513 695-1242

(G-9763)
DAYTON OSTEOPATHIC HOSPITAL
Also Called: Corwin M. Nixon Health Center
1470 N Broadway St (45036-1744)
PHONE..................513 696-1200
EMP: 27
SALES (corp-wide): 2.46B **Privately Held**
Web: www.ketteringhealth.org
SIC: **8062** General medical and surgical hospitals
HQ: Dayton Osteopathic Hospital
405 W Grand Ave
Dayton OH 45405
937 762-1629

(G-9764)
EASTGATE GROUP LTD
Also Called: Eastgate Graphics
611 Norgal Dr (45036-9275)
PHONE..................513 228-5522
EMP: 31 **EST:** 2004
SALES (est): 7.02MM **Privately Held**
Web: www.eastgategraphics.com

Lebanon - Warren County (G-9765)　　　GEOGRAPHIC SECTION

SIC: 5199 Packaging materials

(G-9765)
EQUIPMENT DEPOT OHIO INC
Cleaning Division
1000 Kingsview Dr (45036-9572)
PHONE.................513 934-2121
EMP: 44
Web: www.eqdepot.com
SIC: 5084 7359 Processing and packaging equipment; Home cleaning and maintenance equipment rental services
HQ: Equipment Depot Ohio, Inc.
4331 Rossplain Dr
Blue Ash OH 45236
513 891-0600

(G-9766)
GEORGE STEEL FABRICATING INC
1207 Us Route 42 S (45036-8198)
PHONE.................513 932-2887
John George, *Pr*
Kevin Nickell, *
Brad Frost, *
EMP: 35 EST: 1960
SQ FT: 32,100
SALES (est): 5.02MM Privately Held
Web: www.georgesteel.com
SIC: 7692 3441 3599 Welding repair; Fabricated structural metal; Machine shop, jobbing and repair

(G-9767)
GOLDEN LAMB
Also Called: Golden Lamb Rest Ht & Gift Sp
27 S Broadway St (45036-1705)
PHONE.................513 932-5065
Bill Kilimnik, *Genl Mgr*
N Lee Comisar, *
EMP: 76 EST: 1803
SALES (est): 3.24MM Privately Held
Web: www.goldenlamb.com
SIC: 5812 5947 7011 American restaurant; Gift shop; Hotels

(G-9768)
HEALTH CARE OPPORTUNITIES INC (PA)
Also Called: Cedars of Lebanon Nursing Home
102 E Silver St (45036-1812)
PHONE.................513 932-0300
Bernard Moscowitz, *Pr*
EMP: 47 EST: 1981
SQ FT: 12,000
SALES (est): 3.37MM
SALES (corp-wide): 3.37MM Privately Held
Web: www.cedarsoflebanonhc.com
SIC: 8051 Skilled nursing care facilities

(G-9769)
IRONS FRUIT FARM
1640 Stubbs Mill Rd (45036-9657)
PHONE.................513 932-2853
Ron Irons, *Owner*
EMP: 30 EST: 1942
SALES (est): 917.62K Privately Held
Web: www.ironsfruitfarm.com
SIC: 0175 Apple orchard

(G-9770)
JBM PACKAGING COMPANY
Also Called: Jbm Packaging
2850 Henkle Dr (45036-8894)
P.O. Box 828 (45036-0828)
PHONE.................513 933-8333
▲ EMP: 150 EST: 1985
SALES (est): 23.84MM Privately Held
Web: www.jbmpackaging.com

SIC: 2677 5112 Envelopes; Envelopes

(G-9771)
JIT PACKAGING CINCINNATI INC (PA)
Also Called: J I T
1550 Kingsview Dr (45036-8389)
PHONE.................513 933-0250
Jeff Jones, *Pr*
EMP: 37 EST: 1997
SALES (est): 4.93MM
SALES (corp-wide): 4.93MM Privately Held
SIC: 5199 Packaging materials

(G-9772)
KWEEN INDUSTRIES INC
Also Called: King's Electric Services
2964 S Us Route 42 (45036-8887)
P.O. Box 382 (45036-0382)
PHONE.................513 932-2293
Louis Schuler, *Pr*
Kingsley M Wientge Iii, *Pr*
Kelly Wientge, *
Michael Schuler, *
EMP: 85 EST: 1983
SQ FT: 4,000
SALES (est): 11.67MM Privately Held
Web: www.kingselectric.co
SIC: 1731 General electrical contractor

(G-9773)
LCNB CORP (PA)
2 N Broadway St (45036-1787)
P.O. Box 59 (45036-0059)
PHONE.................513 932-1414
Eric J Meilstrup, *Pr*
Spencer S Cropper, *Ch Bd*
Robert C Haines Ii, *Ex VP*
Lawrence P Mulligan Junior, *Ex VP*
Matthew P Layer, *Ex VP*
EMP: 50 EST: 1998
SQ FT: 28,000
SALES (est): 95.01MM
SALES (corp-wide): 95.01MM Publicly Held
Web: www.lcnb.com
SIC: 6021 National commercial banks

(G-9774)
LCNB NATIONAL BANK (HQ)
2 N Broadway St Lowr (45036-1787)
P.O. Box 59 (45036-0059)
PHONE.................513 932-1414
Steve Foster, *Ex VP*
Spencer S Cropper, *Ch Bd*
Ben Jackson, *Ex VP*
Bernard Wright Junior, *Ex VP*
Eric J Meilstrup, *Ex VP*
EMP: 80 EST: 1877
SALES (est): 81.91MM
SALES (corp-wide): 95.01MM Publicly Held
Web: www.lcnb.com
SIC: 6021 National commercial banks
PA: Lcnb Corp.
2 N Broadway St
Lebanon OH 45036
513 932-1414

(G-9775)
LEBANON FORD INC
Also Called: Lebanon Ford
770 Columbus Ave (45036-1608)
P.O. Box 118 (45036-0118)
PHONE.................513 932-1010
Winston R Pittman Senior, *Pr*
Lisa A Cryder, *
Bonnie A Kasik, *
EMP: 70 EST: 1979
SQ FT: 21,000

SALES (est): 20.72MM Privately Held
Web: www.lebanonford.com
SIC: 5511 5521 7538 Automobiles, new and used; Used car dealers; General automotive repair shops

(G-9776)
LUCAS SUMITOMO BRAKES INC
1650 Kingsview Dr (45036-8390)
PHONE.................513 934-0024
Paul C Hirt, *Prin*
EMP: 46 EST: 2005
SALES (est): 580.83K Privately Held
Web: www.advics-ohio.com
SIC: 3714 5013 5015 Motor vehicle brake systems and parts; Automotive brakes; Motor vehicle parts, used

(G-9777)
MASTERS DRUG COMPANY INC
Also Called: Masters Pharmaceutical
3600 Pharma Way (45036-9479)
PHONE.................800 982-7922
Nick Loporcaro, *Prin*
EMP: 279 EST: 2017
SALES (est): 89.95MM
SALES (corp-wide): 308.95B Publicly Held
Web: www.mastersrx.com
SIC: 5122 Pharmaceuticals
PA: Mckesson Corporation
6555 State Highway 161
Irving TX 75039
972 446-4800

(G-9778)
MIAMI VALLEY GAMING & RACG LLC
6000 W State Route 63 (45036-7900)
PHONE.................513 934-7070
Domenic Mancini, *Pr*
EMP: 213 EST: 2011
SALES (est): 21.82MM
SALES (corp-wide): 2.46B Publicly Held
Web: www.miamivalleygaming.com
SIC: 7999 0971 Gambling and lottery services; Game services
PA: Churchill Downs Incorporated
600 N Hrstbrne Pkwy Ste 4
Louisville KY 40222
502 636-4400

(G-9779)
ONPOWER INC
3525 Grant Ave Ste A (45036)
PHONE.................513 228-2100
Larry D Davis, *Pr*
Tom Mergy, *
EMP: 27 EST: 2001
SQ FT: 41,350
SALES (est): 8MM Privately Held
Web: www.onpowerinc.com
SIC: 3511 8711 Gas turbines, mechanical drive; Consulting engineer

(G-9780)
OTTERBEIN HOMES
585 N State Route 741 (45036-9551)
PHONE.................513 696-8565
EMP: 33 EST: 2018
SALES (est): 18.05MM Privately Held
Web: www.otterbein.org
SIC: 8051 Skilled nursing care facilities

(G-9781)
OTTERBEIN HOMES (PA)
Also Called: OTTERBEIN SENIOR LIFESTYLE CHO
3855 Lower Market St Ste 300 (45036-7653)
PHONE.................513 933-5400
Jill Hreben, *CEO*

Donald L Gilmore, *
Jim Tunstill, *
Jill Hreben, *Pr*
Tammy Cassidy, *
EMP: 400 EST: 1912
SALES (est): 74.71MM
SALES (corp-wide): 74.71MM Privately Held
Web: www.otterbein.org
SIC: 8361 8051 8052 1522 Aged home; Skilled nursing care facilities; Intermediate care facilities; Residential construction, nec

(G-9782)
PFB MANUFACTURING LLC
Also Called: Plasti-Fab Eps PDT Solutions
2725 Henkle Dr (45036-8247)
PHONE.................513 836-3232
EMP: 50
SALES (corp-wide): 9.45MM Privately Held
Web: www.plastifab.com
SIC: 5033 Insulation materials
PA: Pfb Manufacturing, Llc
116 Pine St S
Lester Prairie MN 55354
952 445-4089

(G-9783)
PRODUCTION SVCS UNLIMITED INC
Also Called: WARREN COUNTY OF PRODUCTION SE
575 Columbus Ave (45036-1603)
PHONE.................513 695-1658
Heather Moore, *Dir*
EMP: 30 EST: 1969
SQ FT: 30,000
SALES (est): 2.8MM Privately Held
Web: www.psuinc.org
SIC: 8331 Sheltered workshop

(G-9784)
QUANTUM METALS INC
3675 Taft Rd (45036-6424)
PHONE.................513 573-0144
◆ EMP: 40 EST: 1994
SQ FT: 100,000
SALES (est): 11.61MM Privately Held
Web: www.quantummetals.com
SIC: 5093 Ferrous metal scrap and waste

(G-9785)
RIVER VALLEY DIALYSIS LLC
Also Called: Lebanon Dialysis Center
918b Columbus Ave (45036-1402)
PHONE.................513 934-0272
Sue Greene, *Bmch Mgr*
EMP: 35
SIC: 8092 Kidney dialysis centers
HQ: River Valley Dialysis, Llc
601 Hawaii St
El Segundo CA 90245

(G-9786)
RK FAMILY INC
1879 Deerfield Rd (45036-9946)
PHONE.................513 934-0015
EMP: 170
SALES (corp-wide): 1.22B Privately Held
Web: www.ruralking.com
SIC: 5191 Farm supplies
PA: Rk Family, Inc.
4216 Dewitt Ave
Mattoon IL 61938
217 235-7102

(G-9787)
SIBCY CLINE INC
Also Called: Sibcy, Cline Realtors
103 Oregonia Rd (45036-1983)
PHONE.................513 932-6334

GEOGRAPHIC SECTION
Lewis Center - Delaware County (G-9808)

Amy Davis, *Mgr*
EMP: 120
SALES (corp-wide): 98.72MM **Privately Held**
Web: www.sibcycline.com
SIC: 6531 Real estate agent, residential
PA: Sibcy Cline, Inc.
   8044 Montgomery Rd # 300
   Cincinnati OH 45236
   513 984-4100

(G-9788)
SIEMENS INDUSTRY INC
4170 Columbia Rd (45036-9588)
PHONE..............................800 879-8079
Tony Telfer, *Mgr*
EMP: 40
SALES (corp-wide): 84.48B **Privately Held**
Web: www.siemens.com
SIC: 7699 Industrial equipment services
HQ: Siemens Industry, Inc.
   100 Technology Dr
   Alpharetta GA 30005
   847 215-1000

(G-9789)
SITE WORX LLC
Also Called: Siteworx
3800 Turtlecreek Rd (45036-8642)
PHONE..............................513 229-0295
Matt Smith, *Pr*
Joe Smith, *
Mike Smith, *General*
EMP: 95 **EST:** 2010
SALES (est): 34.83MM **Privately Held**
Web: www.siteworxohio.com
SIC: 1542 Commercial and office building, new construction

(G-9790)
SPARTAN SUPPLY CO
942 Old 122 Rd (45036-8632)
PHONE..............................513 932-6954
Robert Hill, *Ch Bd*
Tim Carpenter, *
Joann Hill, *
EMP: 40 **EST:** 1979
SQ FT: 50,000
SALES (est): 2.66MM **Privately Held**
Web: www.spartanpallets.com
SIC: 7699 Pallet repair

(G-9791)
SUMMIT ENTERPRISES CONTG CORP
640 N Broadway St (45036-1724)
PHONE..............................513 426-1623
Jerry Tarrab, *Ch Bd*
EMP: 30 **EST:** 2010
SALES (est): 2.8MM **Privately Held**
SIC: 1761 Siding contractor

(G-9792)
TALBERT HOUSE
Also Called: Community Correctional Center
5234 W State Route 63 (45036-8202)
PHONE..............................513 933-9304
Jennifer Burnside, *Mgr*
EMP: 66
SALES (corp-wide): 75.69MM **Privately Held**
Web: www.talberthouse.org
SIC: 8322 Substance abuse counseling
PA: Talbert House
   2600 Victory Pkwy
   Cincinnati OH 45206
   513 872-5863

(G-9793)
TESTERMAN DENTAL
767 Columbus Ave Ste 1 (45036-1749)
PHONE..............................513 932-4806
Gregg Testerman D.d.s., *Pr*
Cherie Testerman, *VP*
Gregg Testerman, *Pr*
EMP: 36 **EST:** 1946
SALES (est): 440.25K **Privately Held**
Web: www.testermandental.com
SIC: 8021 Dentists' office

(G-9794)
TRIHEALTH INC
Also Called: Deerfield Family Practice
100 Arrow Springs Blvd Ste 2800 (45036-7002)
PHONE..............................513 282-7300
EMP: 122
Web: www.trihealth.com
SIC: 8011 General and family practice, physician/surgeon
HQ: Trihealth, Inc.
   625 Eden Park Dr
   Cincinnati OH 45202
   513 569-5400

(G-9795)
TRIPLE Q FOUNDATIONS CO INC
139 Harmon Ave (45036-9511)
PHONE..............................513 932-3121
Darren Poore, *Pr*
Jeannie Szellinger, *
EMP: 35 **EST:** 1997
SALES (est): 2.18MM **Privately Held**
SIC: 1771 Foundation and footing contractor

(G-9796)
TRUE WING AVIATION LLC
2061 Tumbleweed Ln (45036-9076)
PHONE..............................937 657-3990
James Struewing, *Prin*
EMP: 35 **EST:** 2015
SALES (est): 105.5K **Privately Held**
Web: www.wing.com
SIC: 4581 Airports, flying fields, and services

(G-9797)
VEGA AMERICAS INC
3877 Mason Research Pkwy (45036-9435)
PHONE..............................513 272-0524
EMP: 999
SALES (corp-wide): 1.94MM **Privately Held**
Web: www.vega.com
SIC: 5047 Medical equipment and supplies
HQ: Vega Americas, Inc.
   3877 Mason Research Pkwy
   Lebanon OH 45036
   513 272-0131

(G-9798)
WARREN CNTY BD DVLPMNTAL DSBLT
42 Kings Way (45036-9593)
PHONE..............................513 925-1813
Megan Manuel, *Superintnt*
Michele Swearingen, *
EMP: 127 **EST:** 1966
SALES (est): 10.72MM **Privately Held**
Web: www.warrencountydd.org
SIC: 8052 Home for the mentally retarded, with health care

(G-9799)
WARREN COUNTY CMNTY SVCS INC (PA)
Also Called: WCCS
645 Oak St Ste A (45036-1751)
PHONE..............................513 695-2100
Doctor Charles Peckham, *Ch*
Larry Sargeant, *
EMP: 175 **EST:** 1966
SQ FT: 24,000
SALES (est): 13.26MM
SALES (corp-wide): 13.26MM **Privately Held**
Web: www.wccsi.org
SIC: 8399 Antipoverty board

(G-9800)
YOUNG MNS CHRSTN ASSN GRTER CN
Also Called: YMCA
1699 Deerfield Rd (45036-9215)
PHONE..............................513 932-1424
Mike Carroll, *CEO*
EMP: 824
SALES (corp-wide): 44.55MM **Privately Held**
Web: www.countrysideymca.org
SIC: 8641 7991 8351 7032 Youth organizations; Physical fitness facilities; Child day care services; Youth camps
PA: Young Mens Christian Association Of Greater Cincinnati
   1105 Elm St
   Cincinnati OH 45202
   513 651-2100

Leipsic
Putnam County

(G-9801)
OTTERBEIN HOMES
Also Called: Oherbein Kpsic Rtirement Cmnty
901 E Main St (45856-9342)
PHONE..............................419 943-4376
Jason Mcclellan, *Ex Dir*
EMP: 37
SALES (corp-wide): 74.71MM **Privately Held**
Web: www.meadowsofleipsic.com
SIC: 8051 Skilled nursing care facilities
PA: Otterbein Homes
   3855 Lower Market St # 300
   Lebanon OH 45036
   513 933-5400

(G-9802)
PRETIUM PACKAGING LLC
Also Called: Patrick's
150 S Werner St (45856-1363)
PHONE..............................419 943-3733
EMP: 145
SALES (corp-wide): 868.81MM **Privately Held**
Web: www.pretiumpkg.com
SIC: 5199 Packaging materials
PA: Pretium Packaging, L.L.C.
   1555 Page Industrial Blvd
   Saint Louis MO 63132
   314 727-8200

Lewis Center
Delaware County

(G-9803)
ABUSE REFUGE INC
Also Called: Abuse Refuge Org
928 Polaris Grand Dr Apt G (43035-7619)
PHONE..............................614 686-2121
Michael Gibson, *Prin*
Kelly Dehn, *
EMP: 99 **EST:** 2020
SALES (est): 668.52K **Privately Held**
Web: www.abuserefuge.org

SIC: 8322 General counseling services

(G-9804)
AMERICAN BUS SOLUTIONS INC
8850 Whitney Dr (43035-8297)
PHONE..............................614 888-2227
Rajeev Kumar, *Pr*
Manisha Dixit, *
Mark Heidkamp, *
EMP: 58 **EST:** 1998
SQ FT: 2,000
SALES (est): 7.87MM **Privately Held**
Web: www.absi-usa.com
SIC: 7379 Computer related consulting services

(G-9805)
AMERICAN NATIONAL RED CROSS
Also Called: American Red Cross
1327 Cameron Ave (43035-9662)
PHONE..............................614 436-3862
EMP: 31
SALES (corp-wide): 3.18B **Privately Held**
Web: www.redcross.org
SIC: 8322 Social service center
PA: The American National Red Cross
   431 18th St Nw
   Washington DC 20006
   202 737-8300

(G-9806)
APTOS LLC
400 Venture Dr (43035-9275)
PHONE..............................614 840-1400
EMP: 60
SALES (corp-wide): 36.83MM **Privately Held**
Web: www.aptos.com
SIC: 5044 5045 7378 7699 Cash registers; Accounting machines using machine readable programs; Computer and data processing equipment repair/maintenance; Cash register repair
HQ: Aptos Llc
   11175 Cicero Dr Ste 650
   Alpharetta GA 30022
   866 493-7037

(G-9807)
ATS CAROLINA INC
Also Called: Automation Tooling Systems
425 Enterprise Dr (43035-9424)
PHONE..............................803 324-9300
Stew Wiatersprecher, *CEO*
▲ **EMP:** 135 **EST:** 1997
SALES (est): 1.08MM
SALES (corp-wide): 1.9B **Privately Held**
Web: www.atsautomation.com
SIC: 7373 Systems integration services
PA: Ats Corporation
   730 Fountain St N Bldg 2
   Cambridge ON N3H 4
   604 332-2666

(G-9808)
ATS SYSTEMS OREGON INC
425 Enterprise Dr (43035-9424)
PHONE..............................541 738-0932
Anthony Caputo, *CEO*
Maria Perrella, *
Stewart Mccvaig, *Sec*
▲ **EMP:** 214 **EST:** 1966
SQ FT: 85,000
SALES (est): 4.13MM
SALES (corp-wide): 1.9B **Privately Held**
Web: www.atsautomation.com
SIC: 3569 5084 Robots, assembly line: industrial and commercial; Industrial machinery and equipment
PA: Ats Corporation
   730 Fountain St N Bldg 2

Cambridge ON N3H 4
604 332-2666

(G-9809)
AUGUST MACK ENVIRONMENTAL INC
7830 N Central Dr Ste B (43035-8773)
PHONE.................................740 548-1500
Bennett Thayer, *Mgr*
EMP: 115
SALES (corp-wide): 25.48MM **Privately Held**
Web: www.augustmack.com
SIC: 8748 Environmental consultant
PA: August Mack Environmental, Inc.
   1302 N Meridian St # 300
   Indianapolis IN 46202
   317 916-8000

(G-9810)
AUTOMATION TOOLING SYSTEMS (HQ)
Also Called: Ats Ohio
425 Enterprise Dr (43035-9424)
PHONE.................................614 781-8063
Joe Moreno, *Prin*
▲ **EMP:** 140 **EST:** 1987
SQ FT: 150,000
SALES (est): 448.64MM
SALES (corp-wide): 1.9B **Privately Held**
Web: www.atsautomation.com
SIC: 5084 Industrial machinery and equipment
PA: Ats Corporation
   730 Fountain St N Bldg 2
   Cambridge ON N3H 4
   604 332-2666

(G-9811)
BLENDON GARDENS INC
Also Called: Blendon Gardens
9590 S Old State Rd (43035-9492)
PHONE.................................614 840-0500
Loren L Brelsford, *Pr*
EMP: 44 **EST:** 1968
SQ FT: 1,979
SALES (est): 8.1MM **Privately Held**
Web: www.blendongardens.com
SIC: 0781 Landscape architects

(G-9812)
CARE HEATING AND COOLING INC
397 Venture Dr Ste B (43035-9519)
PHONE.................................614 841-1555
EMP: 35 **EST:** 1994
SQ FT: 1,000
SALES (est): 788.05K **Privately Held**
Web: www.careheatingcooling.com
SIC: 1711 Warm air heating and air conditioning contractor

(G-9813)
CENTRAL BEVERAGE GROUP LTD
Also Called: Superior Bev Group Centl Ohio
8133 Highfield Dr (43035-9673)
PHONE.................................614 294-3555
John Antonucci, *Pt*
▲ **EMP:** 140 **EST:** 1946
SQ FT: 116,000
SALES (est): 22.36MM **Privately Held**
Web: www.superiorbeveragegroup.com
SIC: 5181 Beer and other fermented malt liquors

(G-9814)
CHILLER LLC
8144 Highfield Dr (43035-9673)
PHONE.................................740 549-0009
Jason Beebee, *Mgr*
EMP: 39

SALES (corp-wide): 4.89MM **Privately Held**
Web: www.thechiller.com
SIC: 7999 Ice skating rink operation
PA: Chiller Llc
   7001 Dublin Park Dr
   Dublin OH 43016
   614 764-1000

(G-9815)
DCB FINANCIAL CORP
110 Riverbend Ave (43035)
PHONE.................................740 657-7000
EMP: 164
Web: www.webdcb.com
SIC: 6022 State commercial banks

(G-9816)
DELAWARE CNTY BD DVLPMNTAL DSB
7991 Columbus Pike (43035-9611)
PHONE.................................740 201-3600
Robert R Morgan, *Superintnt*
EMP: 109 **EST:** 2006
SALES (est): 21.02MM **Privately Held**
Web: www.dcbdd.org
SIC: 8322 Child related social services

(G-9817)
DEXXXON DIGITAL STORAGE INC
7611 Green Meadows Dr (43035-9445)
PHONE.................................740 548-7179
Simon N Garneau, *Pr*
Babak Sarshar, *
Dave Burke, *
Leon Rijnbeek, *
Sassan Shafiee, *
▲ **EMP:** 35 **EST:** 2003
SQ FT: 60,000
SALES (est): 17.33MM **Privately Held**
Web: www.digitalstorage.com
SIC: 5112 7371 Computer and photocopying supplies; Custom computer programming services
PA: Dexxon Groupe
   79 Avenue Louis Roche
   Gennevilliers 92230

(G-9818)
DIETARY SOLUTIONS INC
171 Green Meadows Dr S (43035-9458)
P.O. Box 684 (43035-0684)
PHONE.................................614 985-6567
Kay Lachi, *Pr*
EMP: 80 **EST:** 2002
SALES (est): 3.42MM **Privately Held**
Web: www.dietarysolutions.net
SIC: 8049 Dietician

(G-9819)
DIGITEK SOFTWARE INC
650 Radio Dr (43035-7111)
PHONE.................................614 764-8875
EMP: 40 **EST:** 1994
SQ FT: 3,000
SALES (est): 4.82MM **Privately Held**
Web: www.digiteksoftware.com
SIC: 7371 Computer software development

(G-9820)
FIRST COMMONWEALTH BANK
110 Riverbend Ave (43035)
PHONE.................................740 657-7000
EMP: 166
SALES (corp-wide): 626.61MM **Publicly Held**
Web: www.fcbanking.com
SIC: 6021 National commercial banks
HQ: First Commonwealth Bank
   601 Philadelphia St
   Indiana PA 15701
   724 349-7220

(G-9821)
FIVE CFC INC
6416 Pullman Dr (43035-7377)
PHONE.................................937 578-3271
EMP: 48
SALES (corp-wide): 288.19K **Privately Held**
SIC: 7389 Personal service agents, brokers, and bureaus
PA: Five Cfc, Inc.
   18552 Barker Rd
   Marysville OH

(G-9822)
GERMANN BROS LLC
Also Called: Green Lawn Specialists
774 Peachblow Rd (43035-9101)
PHONE.................................614 905-7314
Philip Germann, *Managing Member*
Kyle Germann, *Prin*
EMP: 40 **EST:** 2019
SALES (est): 3.5MM **Privately Held**
SIC: 0782 Lawn care services

(G-9823)
GILSON COMPANY INC (PA)
7975 N Central Dr (43035-9409)
P.O. Box 200 (43035-0200)
PHONE.................................740 548-7298
▲ **EMP:** 41 **EST:** 1939
SALES (est): 22.23MM
SALES (corp-wide): 22.23MM **Privately Held**
Web: www.globalgilson.com
SIC: 5049 3829 3821 Analytical instruments; Measuring and controlling devices, nec; Laboratory apparatus and furniture

(G-9824)
INSIDE OUTFITTERS INC
Also Called: S O S Shades
8333 Green Meadows Dr N Ste B (43035-8497)
PHONE.................................614 798-3500
▲ **EMP:** 46
SIC: 5023 2591 2221 2211 Draperies; Drapery hardware and window blinds and shades; Draperies and drapery fabrics, manmade fiber and silk; Draperies and drapery fabrics, cotton

(G-9825)
LEARNING SPECTRUM LTD
2630 Aikin Cir N (43035-8068)
PHONE.................................614 316-1160
Jill Medley, *Brnch Mgr*
EMP: 35
Web: www.thelearningspectrum.com
SIC: 8351 Child day care services
PA: The Learning Spectrum Ltd
   6660 Doubletree Ave Ste 1
   Columbus OH 43229

(G-9826)
LIBERTY TWNSHIP POWELL Y M C A
814 Shanahan Rd Ste 100 (43035-9192)
PHONE.................................740 938-2007
Dave Patterson, *Brnch Mgr*
EMP: 70
Web: www.ymcacolumbus.org
SIC: 8641 Youth organizations
PA: Liberty Township Powell Y M C A
   7798 Liberty Rd N
   Powell OH 43065

(G-9827)
LUMENOMICS INC
Also Called: Inside Outfitters
8333 Green Meadows Dr N Ste B (43035-8496)

PHONE.................................614 798-3500
Carlee Swihart, *VP Opers*
EMP: 46
Web: www.insideoutfitters.com
SIC: 5023 2591 2221 2211 Draperies; Drapery hardware and window blinds and shades; Draperies and drapery fabrics, manmade fiber and silk; Draperies and drapery fabrics, cotton
PA: Lumenomics, Inc.
   7800 7th Ave S
   Seattle WA 98108

(G-9828)
MEYERS LDSCP SVCS & NURS INC
6081 Columbus Pike (43035-9008)
P.O. Box 697 (43035-0697)
PHONE.................................614 210-1194
Michael Meyers, *Pr*
EMP: 45 **EST:** 1998
SQ FT: 2,400
SALES (est): 4.18MM **Privately Held**
Web: www.meyerslandscapeservices.com
SIC: 0781 Landscape services

(G-9829)
MIX TALENT LLC
1051 Evadell Dr (43035-6078)
PHONE.................................614 572-9452
EMP: 68 **EST:** 2019
SALES (est): 6.91MM **Privately Held**
Web: www.mix-talent.com
SIC: 7299 Miscellaneous personal service

(G-9830)
NATIONWIDE MUTUAL INSURANCE CO
Also Called: Nationwide
9243 Columbus Pike (43035-8278)
PHONE.................................614 430-3047
Steve Falker, *Mgr*
EMP: 58
SQ FT: 4,032
SALES (corp-wide): 11.75B **Privately Held**
Web: www.nationwide.com
SIC: 6411 Insurance agents, nec
PA: Nationwide Mutual Insurance Company
   1 Nationwide Plz
   Columbus OH 43215
   614 249-7111

(G-9831)
NEUMERIC TECHNOLOGIES CORP
590 Enterprise Dr (43035-9427)
PHONE.................................614 610-4999
Sudheer Gaddam, *CEO*
EMP: 65 **EST:** 1999
SQ FT: 1,300
SALES (est): 5.56MM **Privately Held**
Web: www.ntc-us.com
SIC: 7371 Computer software development

(G-9832)
NORTH CENTRAL INSULATION INC
Also Called: North Central Insulation
5542 Columbus Pike Ste C (43035-9602)
PHONE.................................740 548-8125
Brent Dudgeon, *Ofcr*
EMP: 65
SALES (corp-wide): 24.79MM **Privately Held**
Web: www.nci-ins.com
SIC: 1742 Insulation, buildings
PA: North Central Insulation, Inc.
   7539 State Route 13
   Bellville OH 44813
   419 886-2030

GEOGRAPHIC SECTION

Liberty Township - Butler County (G-9854)

(G-9833)
ORECO INC
110 Riverbend Ave (43035)
PHONE.....................724 349-7220
EMP: 150 EST: 2017
SALES (est): 1.82MM
SALES (corp-wide): 626.61MM Publicly Held
SIC: 6021 National commercial banks
PA: First Commonwealth Financial Corporation
    601 Philadelphia St
    Indiana PA 15701
    724 349-7220

(G-9834)
QUINTUS TECHNOLOGIES LLC
8270 Green Meadows Dr N (43035-9450)
PHONE.....................614 891-2732
Ed Williams, *Managing Member*
EMP: 50 EST: 2014
SALES (est): 7.38MM Privately Held
Web: www.quintustechnologies.com
SIC: 7699 7389 3443 Industrial equipment services; Industrial and commercial equipment inspection service; Industrial vessels, tanks, and containers

(G-9835)
SARCOM INC
8337a Green Meadows Dr N (43035-9451)
PHONE.....................614 854-1300
▲ EMP: 960
SIC: 5045 7373 7374 7372 Computers, peripherals, and software; Computer integrated systems design; Data processing and preparation; Prepackaged software

(G-9836)
SUDHI INFOMATICS INC
590 Enterprise Dr (43035-9427)
PHONE.....................855 200-6650
EMP: 29 EST: 2008
SALES (est): 2.39MM Privately Held
Web: www.sudhi-infomatics.com
SIC: 7379 Computer related consulting services

(G-9837)
SVATS INC
589 Carle Ave (43035-8296)
PHONE.....................614 214-4115
Baby Suseela Maganti, *CEO*
EMP: 45 EST: 2014
SALES (est): 1.79MM Privately Held
Web: www.svatsinc.com
SIC: 7379 Computer related consulting services

(G-9838)
THE DELAWARE COUNTY BANK INC
Also Called: Delaware County Bank & Tr Co
110 Riverbend Ave (43035)
P.O. Box 1001 (43035-1001)
PHONE.....................740 657-7000
EMP: 166
SIC: 6022 State trust companies accepting deposits, commercial

(G-9839)
TRIPLE T TRANSPORT INC (PA)
433 Lewis Center Rd (43035-9049)
P.O. Box 649 (43035-0649)
PHONE.....................740 657-3244
Darin Puppel, *Pr*
Wade Amelung, *
EMP: 124 EST: 1987
SQ FT: 12,000
SALES (est): 361.76MM Privately Held
Web: www.triplettransport.com

SIC: 4213 Trucking, except local

(G-9840)
VAUGHN INDUSTRIES LLC
7749 Green Meadows Dr (43035-9445)
PHONE.....................740 548-7100
Kelli Kitzler, *Mgr*
EMP: 100
SALES (corp-wide): 88.39MM Privately Held
Web: www.vaughnindustries.com
SIC: 1731 1711 General electrical contractor ; Mechanical contractor
PA: Vaughn Industries, Llc
    1201 E Findlay St
    Carey OH 43316
    419 396-3900

Lewisburg
Preble County

(G-9841)
NUTRITION TRNSP SVCS LLC
6531 State Route 503 N (45338-6713)
PHONE.....................937 962-2661
Scott Rutgers, *Managing Member*
EMP: 75 EST: 2000
SALES (est): 7.75MM
SALES (corp-wide): 176.74B Privately Held
SIC: 4731 Freight forwarding
HQ: Provimi North America, Inc.
    6571 State Route 503 N
    Lewisburg OH 45338
    937 770-2400

(G-9842)
PROVIMI NORTH AMERICA INC (HQ)
Also Called: Cargill Premix and Nutrition
6571 State Route 503 N (45338-6713)
PHONE.....................937 770-2400
Thomas Taylor, *Pr*
▲ EMP: 253 EST: 1973
SALES (est): 7.75MM
SALES (corp-wide): 176.74B Privately Held
Web: www.provimius.com
SIC: 5191 2048 Animal feeds; Prepared feeds, nec
PA: Cargill, Incorporated
    15407 Mcginty Rd W
    Wayzata MN 55391
    800 227-4455

Lewistown
Logan County

(G-9843)
MID-STATES PACKAGING INC
Also Called: Mid-States Packaging
12163 St Rt 274 (43333-9707)
PHONE.....................937 843-3243
Jeffrey C Davidson, *Pr*
Larry Winner, *
EMP: 50 EST: 1998
SQ FT: 80,000
SALES (est): 9.27MM Privately Held
Web: www.midstatespackaging.com
SIC: 5199 Packaging materials

Lexington
Richland County

(G-9844)
MEADE CONSTRUCTION INC (PA)
Also Called: Meade Construction Company

13 N Mill St (44904-1200)
PHONE.....................740 694-5525
Andrew Meade, *CEO*
Chris Mortimer, *
Chris Thornton, *
Philip Meade, *
EMP: 30 EST: 1991
SALES (est): 8.94MM
SALES (corp-wide): 8.94MM Privately Held
Web: www.meaderoofingservices.com
SIC: 1761 Roofing contractor

(G-9845)
SUPERIOR BEVERAGE GROUP LTD
32 Eagle Dr Unit A (44904-1369)
PHONE.....................419 529-0702
Mike Caffrey, *Brnch Mgr*
EMP: 188
Web: www.superiorbeveragegroup.com
SIC: 5499 5149 Beverage stores; Beverages, except coffee and tea
PA: The Superior Beverage Group Ltd
    31031 Diamond Pkwy
    Solon OH 44139

Liberty Center
Henry County

(G-9846)
OHIO DEPARTMENT YOUTH SERVICES
Also Called: Maumee Youth Center
Township Rd 1 D U 469 (43532)
PHONE.....................419 875-6965
Nan Hoff, *Mgr*
EMP: 117
Web: dys.ohio.gov
SIC: 9223 8322 Prison, government; Youth center
HQ: Ohio Department Of Youth Services
    4545 Fisher Rd Ste D
    Columbus OH 43228

Liberty Township
Butler County

(G-9847)
AS LOGISTICS INC (DH)
Also Called: Amstan Logistics
7570 Bales St Ste 310 (45069-0003)
PHONE.....................513 863-4627
Dan Dunham, *Pr*
Bruce Proctor, *
◆ EMP: 70 EST: 1974
SQ FT: 28,000
SALES (est): 75.42MM Privately Held
Web: www.amstan.com
SIC: 4213 Trucking, except local
HQ: As America, Inc.
    30 Knightsbridge Rd # 301
    Piscataway NJ 08854

(G-9848)
CHILDRENS HOSPITAL MEDICAL CTR
7777 Yankee Rd (45044-3500)
PHONE.....................513 803-9600
Mark Mumford, *CFO*
EMP: 1105
SALES (corp-wide): 2.94B Privately Held
Web: www.cincinnatichildrens.org
SIC: 8062 8011 General medical and surgical hospitals; Medical centers
PA: Children's Hospital Medical Center
    3333 Burnet Ave
    Cincinnati OH 45229
    513 636-4200

(G-9849)
CHRIST HOSPITAL
Also Called: Christ Hosp Physcans - Obsttri
7335 Yankee Rd Ste 202 (45044-1253)
PHONE.....................513 648-7950
Kelly L Christian, *Brnch Mgr*
EMP: 66
SALES (corp-wide): 1.3B Privately Held
Web: www.thechristhospital.com
SIC: 8062 General medical and surgical hospitals
PA: The Christ Hospital
    2139 Auburn Ave
    Cincinnati OH 45219
    513 585-2000

(G-9850)
CHRIST HOSPITAL
6939 Cox Rd (45069-7595)
PHONE.....................513 648-7800
EMP: 66
SALES (corp-wide): 1.3B Privately Held
Web: www.thechristhospital.com
SIC: 8062 General medical and surgical hospitals
PA: The Christ Hospital
    2139 Auburn Ave
    Cincinnati OH 45219
    513 585-2000

(G-9851)
CRYPTIC VECTOR LLC
7570 Bales St Ste 400 (45069-0004)
PHONE.....................513 318-9061
Sean Olding, *Managing Member*
Christopher Dattilo, *
Jonathan Elchison, *
Cory Fowler, *
Michael Trueblood, *
EMP: 92 EST: 2019
SALES (est): 15.84MM Privately Held
Web: www.crypticvector.com
SIC: 7371 Custom computer programming services

(G-9852)
FOUR BRIDGES COUNTRY CLUB LTD
Also Called: Liberty Township
8300 Four Bridges Dr (45044-8489)
PHONE.....................513 759-4620
Ron Townsend, *Pt*
EMP: 100 EST: 2001
SALES (est): 5.1MM Privately Held
Web: www.fourbridges.com
SIC: 7997 Country club, membership

(G-9853)
LAKOTA LOCAL SCHOOL DISTRICT
Also Called: Bus Garage
6947 Yankee Rd (45044-9719)
PHONE.....................513 777-2150
Doug Lantz, *Brnch Mgr*
EMP: 49
SALES (corp-wide): 239.02MM Privately Held
Web: www.lakotaonline.com
SIC: 4151 4225 4173 School buses; General warehousing and storage; Bus terminal and service facilities
PA: Lakota Local School District
    5572 Princeton Rd
    Liberty Township OH 45011
    513 874-5505

(G-9854)
LIBERTY CTR LODGING ASSOC LLC
Also Called: Liberty Center AC By Marriott
7505 Gibson St (45069-7517)
PHONE.....................608 833-4100
Cj Raymond, *Managing Member*

Liberty Township - Butler County (G-9855)

EMP: 30 **EST:** 1985
SQ FT: 109,457
SALES (est): 1.05MM **Privately Held**
Web: www.marriott.com
SIC: 7011 Hotels

(G-9855)
ON DECK SERVICES INC
8263 Kyles Station Rd Ste 1 (45044-9573)
PHONE.................................513 759-2854
EMP: 36 **EST:** 1985
SQ FT: 5,000
SALES (est): 4.06MM **Privately Held**
Web: www.ondeckservices.com
SIC: 1521 Patio and deck construction and repair

(G-9856)
ORTHOPEDIC ASSOCIATES
7117 Dutchland Pkwy (45044-9096)
PHONE.................................800 824-9861
EMP: 69
Web: www.oadoctors.com
SIC: 8011 Orthopedic physician
PA: Orthopedic Associates Of Sw Ohio, Inc.
7677 Yankee St Ste 110
Centerville OH 45459

(G-9857)
PNC BANC CORP OHIO
7355 N Liberty Dr (45044-9182)
PHONE.................................513 981-2420
Debbie Williams, *Brnch Mgr*
EMP: 86
SALES (corp-wide): 31.88B **Publicly Held**
Web: www.pnc.com
SIC: 6021 National commercial banks
HQ: Pnc Banc Corp, Ohio
201 E 5th St
Cincinnati OH 45202
513 651-8738

(G-9858)
VIGILANT DEFENSE
Also Called: Vigilant Technology Solutions
7570 Bales St Ste 250 (45069-7750)
PHONE.................................513 309-0672
Chris Nyhuis, *Pr*
Chris Nyhuis, *Owner*
Katherine Nyhuis, *
EMP: 40 **EST:** 2009
SALES (est): 4.78MM **Privately Held**
SIC: 7382 Security systems services

(G-9859)
VIGILANT LLC
7570 Bales St Ste 250 (45069-7750)
PHONE.................................513 300-1460
EMP: 55 **EST:** 2019
SALES (est): 5.83MM **Privately Held**
Web: www.vigilantnow.com
SIC: 7379 Computer related consulting services

Lima
Allen County

(G-9860)
AERCO SANDBLASTING COMPANY
429 N Jackson St (45801-4121)
PHONE.................................419 224-2464
Cynthia Wallace, *Pr*
Pearl Miller, *
Norma Miller, *
EMP: 35 **EST:** 1974
SQ FT: 1,296
SALES (est): 4.3MM **Privately Held**
Web: www.aerco-sandblasting.com

SIC: 1799 Sandblasting of building exteriors

(G-9861)
ALDELANO CORPORATION (PA)
2050 Spencerville Rd (45805-3322)
PHONE.................................909 861-3970
Alfred Hollingsworth, *Pr*
Hattie Hollingsworth, *Sec*
Nicole Smith, *COO*
EMP: 31 **EST:** 1989
SALES (est): 23.8MM **Privately Held**
Web: www.aldelanosolarsolutions.com
SIC: 4225 8742 7389 General warehousing and storage; Transportation consultant; Packaging and labeling services

(G-9862)
ALL GODS GRACES INC (PA)
Also Called: Home Instead Senior Care
1142 W North St (45805-2462)
P.O. Box 634 (45802-0634)
PHONE.................................419 222-8109
TOLL FREE: 888
Dana Kortokrax Press, *Prin*
Beth Kortokrax, *Treas*
EMP: 87 **EST:** 2014
SALES (est): 4.56MM
SALES (corp-wide): 4.56MM **Privately Held**
Web: www.homeinstead.com
SIC: 8082 Home health care services

(G-9863)
ALLEN COUNTY EDUCTL SVC CTR
1920 Slabtown Rd (45801-3309)
PHONE.................................419 222-1836
Donald Smith, *Superintnt*
EMP: 47 **EST:** 1914
SALES (est): 1.01MM **Privately Held**
Web: www.allencountyesc.org
SIC: 8299 8351 Educational services; Preschool center

(G-9864)
ALLIED ENVIRONMENTAL SVCS INC
585 Liberty Commons Pkwy (45804-1829)
PHONE.................................419 227-4004
TOLL FREE: 800
Kay E Rauch, *Pr*
Clyde R Rauch, *
EMP: 45 **EST:** 1987
SQ FT: 5,000
SALES (est): 8.7MM **Privately Held**
Web: www.allied-environmental.com
SIC: 8748 1799 Environmental consultant; Asbestos removal and encapsulation

(G-9865)
ANHEUSER-BUSCH LLC
Also Called: Anheuser-Busch
3535 Saint Johns Rd (45804-4016)
PHONE.................................419 221-2337
Molly Ramage, *Mgr*
EMP: 35
SALES (corp-wide): 1.31B **Privately Held**
Web: www.budweisertours.com
SIC: 5181 Beer and other fermented malt liquors
HQ: Anheuser-Busch, Llc
1 Busch Pl
Saint Louis MO 63118
800 342-5283

(G-9866)
AUTO-OWNERS LIFE INSURANCE CO
2325 N Cole St (45801-2305)
P.O. Box 4570 (45802-4570)
PHONE.................................419 227-1452
Scott Wilder, *Mgr*
EMP: 38

SALES (corp-wide): 2.41B **Privately Held**
Web: www.auto-owners.com
SIC: 6411 Insurance agents, nec
HQ: Auto-Owners Life Insurance Company
6101 Anacapri Blvd
Lansing MI 48917

(G-9867)
BEAVER DAM HEALTH CARE CENTER
Also Called: Beverly
599 S Shawnee St (45804-1461)
PHONE.................................419 227-2154
Peggy Stewart, *Mgr*
EMP: 29
SALES (corp-wide): 825.65MM **Privately Held**
Web: www.beaverdamhcc.com
SIC: 8059 8052 8051 Convalescent home; Intermediate care facilities; Convalescent home with continuous nursing care
PA: Golden Living Llc
5220 Tennyson Pkwy # 400
Plano TX 75024
972 372-6300

(G-9868)
BEST ONE TIRE & SVC LIMA INC (PA)
701 E Hanthorn Rd (45804-3823)
PHONE.................................419 229-2380
David Mitchell, *Pr*
Sheila Mitchell, *
▲ **EMP:** 45 **EST:** 1933
SQ FT: 100,000
SALES (est): 14.67MM
SALES (corp-wide): 14.67MM **Privately Held**
Web: www.bestonetire.com
SIC: 7534 5531 5014 Tire recapping; Automotive tires; Truck tires and tubes

(G-9869)
BITTERSWEET INC
4640 Fort Amanda Rd (45805-4412)
PHONE.................................419 999-9174
EMP: 71
SALES (corp-wide): 6.89MM **Privately Held**
SIC: 8049 Physiotherapist
PA: Bittersweet Inc
12660 Archbold Whthuse Rd
Whitehouse OH 43571
419 875-6986

(G-9870)
BON SECOURS MERCY HEALTH INC
2875 W Elm St (45805-2510)
PHONE.................................419 991-7805
EMP: 28
SALES (corp-wide): 6.92B **Privately Held**
Web: www.bonsecours.com
SIC: 8062 General medical and surgical hospitals
PA: Bon Secours Mercy Health, Inc.
1701 Mercy Health Pl
Cincinnati OH 45237
513 956-3729

(G-9871)
BUCKEYE CHARTER SERVICE INC (PA)
1235 E Hanthorn Rd (45804-3996)
P.O. Box 627 (45802-0627)
PHONE.................................419 222-2455
William Harnishfeger, *Pr*
Frank Harnishfeger, *
EMP: 40 **EST:** 1989
SALES (est): 4.87MM **Privately Held**
Web: www.buckeyecharterservice.com
SIC: 4142 Bus charter service, except local

(G-9872)
BUCKEYE CHECK CASHING INC
1980 Elida Rd (45805-1515)
PHONE.................................567 371-3497
EMP: 35
Web: www.ccfi.com
SIC: 6099 Check cashing agencies
HQ: Buckeye Check Cashing, Inc.
5165 Emerald Pkwy Ste 100
Dublin OH 43017
614 798-5900

(G-9873)
CHANDNI INC
Also Called: Comfort Inn
1210 Neubrecht Rd Ste 106206 (45801-3118)
PHONE.................................419 228-4251
EMP: 29 **EST:** 1995
SALES (est): 503.22K **Privately Held**
Web: www.choicehotels.com
SIC: 7011 Hotels and motels

(G-9874)
CITY OF LIMA
Sanitary Engineer
50 Town Sq 3rd Fl (45801-4948)
P.O. Box 1198 (45802-1198)
PHONE.................................419 221-5294
EMP: 29
SALES (corp-wide): 46.19MM **Privately Held**
Web: www.limaohio.gov
SIC: 4959 Sanitary services, nec
PA: City Of Lima
50 Town Sq
Lima OH 45801
419 228-5462

(G-9875)
COLUMBIA PROPERTIES LIMA LLC
Also Called: Holiday Inn
1920 Roschman Ave (45804-3444)
PHONE.................................419 222-0004
Sharron Snider, *Sls Dir*
EMP: 106 **EST:** 2006
SALES (est): 178.11K **Privately Held**
Web: www.holidayinn.com
SIC: 7011 Hotels and motels

(G-9876)
COMFORT KEEPERS
Also Called: Kin Care
1726 Allentown Rd (45805-1856)
PHONE.................................419 229-1031
Peggy J Kincaid, *Pr*
Walter Kincaid Junior, *VP*
EMP: 49 **EST:** 1999
SALES (est): 366.36K **Privately Held**
Web: www.comfortkeepers.com
SIC: 8082 Visiting nurse service

(G-9877)
CORPORATE SUPPORT INC (PA)
2262 Baton Rouge (45805-1132)
PHONE.................................419 221-3838
Harold Breidenbach, *CEO*
Troy Breidenbach, *
William Schroeder, *
Marsha Fisher, *
John Whittaker, *Stockholder*
EMP: 50 **EST:** 1988
SALES (est): 2.48MM
SALES (corp-wide): 2.48MM **Privately Held**
Web: www.corporatesupport.us
SIC: 7389 Packaging and labeling services

GEOGRAPHIC SECTION
Lima - Allen County (G-9900)

(G-9878)
COUNTY OF ALLEN
Also Called: Allen County Childrens Svcs Bd
123 W Spring St (45801-4833)
PHONE......................419 227-8590
Mike Mullins, *Dir*
EMP: 45
SALES (corp-wide): 98.9MM **Privately Held**
Web: www.allencsb.com
SIC: 8322 Child related social services
PA: County Of Allen
    301 N Main St
    Lima OH 45801
    419 228-3700

(G-9879)
COUNTY OF ALLEN
Also Called: Information & Referral Center
951 Commerce Pkwy Ste 100
(45804-4040)
P.O. Box 4506 (45802-4506)
PHONE......................419 228-2120
Lynn Shock, *Dir*
EMP: 38
SALES (corp-wide): 98.9MM **Privately Held**
Web: www.allencountyohio.com
SIC: 8322 Social service center
PA: County Of Allen
    301 N Main St
    Lima OH 45801
    419 228-3700

(G-9880)
COUNTY OF ALLEN
Also Called: Allen Metro Housinig Auth
600 S Main St (45804-1242)
PHONE......................419 228-6065
Cindy Ring, *Dir*
EMP: 50
SALES (corp-wide): 98.9MM **Privately Held**
Web: www.allencountyohio.com
SIC: 6531 Housing authority operator
PA: County Of Allen
    301 N Main St
    Lima OH 45801
    419 228-3700

(G-9881)
COUNTY OF ALLEN
Also Called: Allen County Health Care Ctr
3125 Ada Rd (45801-3328)
PHONE......................419 221-1103
Jerome O'neal, *Admn*
EMP: 38
SALES (corp-wide): 98.9MM **Privately Held**
Web: www.allencountyohio.com
SIC: 8361 8051 Aged home; Skilled nursing care facilities
PA: County Of Allen
    301 N Main St
    Lima OH 45801
    419 228-3700

(G-9882)
CROWN GROUP INCORPORATED
1340 Neubrecht Rd (45801-3120)
PHONE......................586 558-5311
William F Baer, *Pr*
Robert G Howse, *
Michael Kaleel, *
EMP: 35 **EST:** 1965
SALES (est): 2.1MM **Privately Held**
SIC: 8741 Management services

(G-9883)
DE HAVEN HOME AND GARDEN CENTERS INC
775 Shawnee Rd (45805-3435)
PHONE......................419 227-7003
▲ **EMP:** 50
SIC: 0782 5251 5261 Lawn care services; Hardware stores; Garden supplies and tools, nec

(G-9884)
DEGEN EXCAVATING INC
1920 Bible Rd (45801-2295)
PHONE......................419 225-6871
Josh Barhorst, *Pr*
Fritz W Degen, *
William F Degen, *
Dennis Gesler, *
EMP: 55 **EST:** 1960
SQ FT: 10,000
SALES (est): 8.57MM **Privately Held**
Web: www.degenex.com
SIC: 1623 1794 Sewer line construction; Excavation work

(G-9885)
EAST OF CHICAGO PIZZA INC (PA)
121 W High St Fl 12 (45801-4349)
PHONE......................419 225-7116
Anthony Collins, *Pr*
EMP: 69 **EST:** 1982
SALES (est): 24.41MM
SALES (corp-wide): 24.41MM **Privately Held**
Web: www.eastofchicago.com
SIC: 6794 5812 Franchises, selling or licensing; Pizzeria, chain

(G-9886)
ENCOMPASS CARE INC
1100 Shawnee Rd (45805-3529)
PHONE......................419 999-2030
Gary Sommer, *Prin*
EMP: 114 **EST:** 2007
SALES (est): 1.95MM **Privately Held**
Web: www.ec-rehab.com
SIC: 8049 Physical therapist

(G-9887)
ERIC W WARNOCK
Also Called: Whole Health Dentistry
230 N Eastown Rd (45807-2211)
PHONE......................419 228-2233
Eric W Warnock, *Owner*
EMP: 30 **EST:** 1975
SALES (est): 1.13MM **Privately Held**
Web: www.wholehealthdentistry.com
SIC: 8021 Dentists' office

(G-9888)
FAMILY BIRTH CENTER LIMA MEM
1001 Bellefontaine Ave (45804-2800)
PHONE......................419 998-4570
Kathy Davis, *Dir*
EMP: 42 **EST:** 1998
SALES (est): 386.98K **Privately Held**
Web: www.limamemorial.org
SIC: 8062 General medical and surgical hospitals

(G-9889)
FAMILY RSOURCE CTR NW OHIO INC (PA)
Also Called: Northwest Fmly Svcs Dda Fmly R
530 S Main St (45804-1240)
PHONE......................419 222-1168
John Bindas, *Pr*
EMP: 50 **EST:** 1973
SQ FT: 23,000
SALES (est): 14.08MM
SALES (corp-wide): 14.08MM **Privately Held**
Web: www.frcohio.com
SIC: 8093 Mental health clinic, outpatient

(G-9890)
FORT AMANDA SPECIALTIES LLC
1747 Fort Amanda Rd (45804-1864)
PHONE......................419 229-0088
▲ **EMP:** 85 **EST:** 2004
SALES (est): 48.08MM
SALES (corp-wide): 11.26B **Privately Held**
Web: www.nouryon.com
SIC: 5169 Industrial chemicals
PA: Akzo Nobel N.V.
    Amsterdam NH
    889697555

(G-9891)
GENERAL AUDIT CORPORATION
Also Called: Keybridge Medical Revenue MGT
2348 Baton Rouge Ste A (45805-1167)
P.O. Box 1568 (45802-1568)
PHONE......................419 993-2900
Ned E Koenig, *Ch*
N Jean Koenig, *
Scott G Koenig, *
EMP: 54 **EST:** 1981
SQ FT: 6,300
SALES (est): 4.3MM **Privately Held**
Web: www.keybridgemed.com
SIC: 7322 8111 Collection agency, except real estate; Legal services

(G-9892)
GRAND AERIE OF THE FRATERNAL
Also Called: Foe 370
800 W Robb Ave (45801-2760)
P.O. Box 1108 (45802-1108)
PHONE......................419 227-1566
Ron Morris, *Brnch Mgr*
EMP: 41
SALES (corp-wide): 12.76MM **Privately Held**
Web: www.foe.com
SIC: 8641 Fraternal associations
PA: Grand Aerie Of The Fraternal Order Of Eagles
    1623 Gateway Cir
    Grove City OH 43123
    614 883-2200

(G-9893)
GRAYBAR ELECTRIC COMPANY INC
990 W Grand Ave (45801-3428)
PHONE......................419 228-7441
Dennis Altenburger, *Brnch Mgr*
EMP: 35
SALES (corp-wide): 11.04B **Privately Held**
Web: www.graybar.com
SIC: 5063 Electrical supplies, nec
PA: Graybar Electric Company, Inc.
    34 N Meramec Ave
    Saint Louis MO 63105
    314 573-9200

(G-9894)
GREENFIELD HTS OPER GROUP LLC
1318 Chestnut St (45804-2542)
PHONE......................312 877-1153
EMP: 50 **EST:** 2017
SALES (est): 2.04MM **Privately Held**
SIC: 5122 Pharmaceuticals

(G-9895)
HAWTHORNE HILLS CNTRY CLB INC
1000 Fetter Rd (45801-3320)
PHONE......................419 221-1891
Mat Otto, *Mgr*
EMP: 50 **EST:** 1961
SALES (est): 765.43K **Privately Held**
SIC: 7992 Public golf courses

(G-9896)
HCF MANAGEMENT INC (PA)
Also Called: Health Care Facilities
1100 Shawnee Rd (45805-3583)
PHONE......................419 999-2010
Kerri Romes, *Pr*
Fred J Rinehart, *
Robert Wilson, *
Robert Noft, *
Michalynn Wilson, *
EMP: 60 **EST:** 1968
SQ FT: 15,000
SALES (est): 305.93MM
SALES (corp-wide): 305.93MM **Privately Held**
Web: www.hcfinc.com
SIC: 8051 6513 Convalescent home with continuous nursing care; Apartment building operators

(G-9897)
HCF MANAGEMENT INC
Also Called: Shawnee Manor Nursing Home
2535 Fort Amanda Rd (45804-3728)
PHONE......................419 999-2055
Kevin Kidd, *Dir*
EMP: 57
SALES (corp-wide): 305.93MM **Privately Held**
Web: www.hcfinc.com
SIC: 8361 8051 Geriatric residential care; Skilled nursing care facilities
PA: Hcf Management, Inc.
    1100 Shawnee Rd
    Lima OH 45805
    419 999-2010

(G-9898)
HCF OF CELINA INC
1100 Shawnee Rd (45805-3583)
PHONE......................419 999-2010
EMP: 281
SALES (corp-wide): 305.93MM **Privately Held**
Web: www.celinamanor.com
SIC: 8051 Convalescent home with continuous nursing care
HQ: Hcf Of Celina, Inc.
    1001 Myers Rd
    Celina OH 45822
    419 586-6645

(G-9899)
HCF OF LIMA INC
Also Called: Lima Manor
1100 Shawnee Rd (45805-3583)
PHONE......................419 999-2010
EMP: 57
SALES (corp-wide): 8.11MM **Privately Held**
Web: www.limamanor.com
SIC: 8051 Convalescent home with continuous nursing care
PA: Hcf Of Lima, Inc.
    750 Brower Rd
    Lima OH 45801
    419 227-2611

(G-9900)
HCF OF LIMA INC (PA)
Also Called: LIMA MANOR
750 Brower Rd (45801-2515)
PHONE......................419 227-2611
Scott Unverferth, *Prin*
Barbara Masella, *VP*
Carrie Van Oss, *Adm/Asst*
EMP: 42 **EST:** 2004

Lima - Allen County (G-9901) GEOGRAPHIC SECTION

SALES (est): 8.11MM
SALES (corp-wide): 8.11MM **Privately Held**
Web: www.limamanor.com
SIC: 8051 Convalescent home with continuous nursing care

(G-9901)
HCF OF SHAWNEE INC
Also Called: SHAWNEE MANOR
2535 Fort Amanda Rd (45804-3728)
PHONE..............................419 999-2055
David Walsh, VP
EMP: 48 EST: 2008
SALES (est): 12.51MM **Privately Held**
Web: www.shawneemanor.com
SIC: 8051 Convalescent home with continuous nursing care

(G-9902)
HEALTH PARTNERS WESTERN OHIO
329 Nw St 2nd Fl (45801-4331)
PHONE..............................419 221-3072
Bill Stolly, Pr
EMP: 41 EST: 2015
SALES (est): 1.46MM **Privately Held**
Web: www.hpwohio.org
SIC: 8082 Oxygen tent service

(G-9903)
HEALTH PARTNERS WESTERN OHIO (PA)
Also Called: LIMA COMMUNITY HEALTH CENTER
329 N West St (45801)
PHONE..............................419 221-3072
Janis Sunderhaus, CEO
EMP: 38 EST: 2003
SALES (est): 70.67MM
SALES (corp-wide): 70.67MM **Privately Held**
Web: www.hpwohio.org
SIC: 8399 Health systems agency

(G-9904)
HEALTHPRO MEDICAL BILLING INC
4132 Elida Rd (45807)
P.O. Box 1524 (45802)
PHONE..............................419 223-2717
John Stiles, Pr
EMP: 55 EST: 1981
SALES (est): 5.01MM **Privately Held**
Web: www.healthpromedical.com
SIC: 8721 Billing and bookkeeping service

(G-9905)
HERITAGE HEALTH CARE SERVICES (PA)
1100 Shawnee Rd (45805-3529)
PHONE..............................419 867-2002
Rich Adams, Pr
EMP: 150 EST: 1994
SALES (est): 2.44MM
SALES (corp-wide): 2.44MM **Privately Held**
Web: www.heritage-hcs.com
SIC: 8082 Home health care services

(G-9906)
HOSPITALITY INC
1250 Neubrecht Rd (45801-3118)
PHONE..............................419 227-0112
Mike Patel, Pr
Ushee Patel, VP
Andy Patel, Prin
Bulla Bhbbai Patel, Prin
Randi Henric, Ex Dir
EMP: 84 EST: 1983
SALES (est): 360.1K **Privately Held**

SIC: 7011 Hotels and motels

(G-9907)
HR SERVICES INC
675 W Market St Ste 200 (45801-4603)
P.O. Box 1155 (45802-1155)
PHONE..............................419 224-2462
Robert Schulte, Pr
EMP: 47 EST: 1999
SQ FT: 8,500
SALES (est): 7.28MM
SALES (corp-wide): 5.01B **Publicly Held**
Web: www.mystaffingpro.com
SIC: 7363 7361 Employee leasing service; Employment agencies
PA: Paychex, Inc.
911 Panorama Trl S
Rochester NY 14625
585 385-6666

(G-9908)
HUNTINGTON NATIONAL BANK
Also Called: Home Mortgage
631 W Market St (45801-4603)
PHONE..............................419 226-8200
Rick Kortokrax, Mgr
EMP: 36
SALES (corp-wide): 10.84B **Publicly Held**
Web: www.huntington.com
SIC: 6029 6162 6021 Commercial banks, nec ; Mortgage bankers; National commercial banks
HQ: The Huntington National Bank
41 S High St
Columbus OH 43215
614 480-4293

(G-9909)
IHS SERVICES INC
3225 W Elm St Ste D (45805-2520)
PHONE..............................419 224-8811
EMP: 51
Web: www.ihsservices.info
SIC: 6531 Real estate managers
PA: Ihs Services, Inc.
5888 Cleveland Ave # 201
Columbus OH

(G-9910)
INCREDIBLE PRODUCTS LLC
Also Called: Concrete Protector The
1221 Stewart Rd (45801-3223)
PHONE..............................567 297-3700
Larry Quick, Managing Member
EMP: 35 EST: 2015
SALES (est): 3.3MM **Privately Held**
Web: www.theconcreteprotector.com
SIC: 1771 Blacktop (asphalt) work

(G-9911)
INTERNATIONAL BRAKE INDS INC (DH)
Also Called: Carlson Quality Brake
1840 Mccullough St (45801-3000)
PHONE..............................419 227-4421
Gary Cohen, CEO
Teresa Holden, *
▲ EMP: 32 EST: 1967
SQ FT: 91,000
SALES (est): 49.13MM
SALES (corp-wide): 8.03B **Privately Held**
Web: www.internationalbrakeindustries.com
SIC: 5013 Motor vehicle supplies and new parts
HQ: Qualitor, Inc.
127 Public Sq Ste 5300
Cleveland OH 44114
248 204-8600

(G-9912)
JEFFERS CRANE SERVICE INC
Also Called: Crane Service Div
1119 S Metcalf St (45804-1144)
PHONE..............................419 223-9010
TOLL FREE: 888
Richard Hosmer, Mgr
EMP: 41
SALES (corp-wide): 114.83MM **Privately Held**
Web: www.allcrane.com
SIC: 7389 7353 Crane and aerial lift service; Cranes and aerial lift equipment, rental or leasing
HQ: Jeffers Crane Service, Inc.
5421 Navarre Ave
Oregon OH 43616
419 693-0421

(G-9913)
KIDNEY SERVICES W CENTL OHIO
750 W High St Ste 100 (45801-3959)
PHONE..............................419 227-0918
Dodi West, CEO
EMP: 31 EST: 2002
SALES (est): 1.07MM **Privately Held**
SIC: 8092 Kidney dialysis centers

(G-9914)
KINDRED HEALTHCARE LLC
Also Called: Kindred Hospital Lima
730 W Market St (45801-4602)
PHONE..............................419 224-1888
Gwen Taulbee, Brnch Mgr
EMP: 36
SALES (corp-wide): 13.68B **Privately Held**
Web: www.kindredhospitals.com
SIC: 8062 General medical and surgical hospitals
HQ: Kindred Healthcare, Llc
680 S 4th St
Louisville KY 40202
502 596-7300

(G-9915)
KIRBY RISK CORPORATION
Kirby Risk Electrical Supply
1249 Stewart Rd (45801-3223)
P.O. Box 1684 (45802-1684)
PHONE..............................419 221-0123
TOLL FREE: 800
Chris Britt, Brnch Mgr
EMP: 62
SALES (corp-wide): 501.02MM **Privately Held**
Web: www.kirbyrisk.com
SIC: 5063 5085 Electrical supplies, nec; Mill supplies
PA: Kirby Risk Corporation
1815 Sagamore Pkwy N
Lafayette IN 47904
765 448-4567

(G-9916)
KLEMAN SERVICES LLC
Also Called: ServiceMaster
2150 Baty Rd (45807-1957)
PHONE..............................419 339-0871
Michael C Kleman, Managing Member
EMP: 55 EST: 1965
SQ FT: 7,500
SALES (est): 1.74MM **Privately Held**
Web: www.smyourservice.com
SIC: 7349 Building maintenance services, nec

(G-9917)
LIBERTY RETIREMENT CMNTY LIMA
2440 Baton Rouge (45805-5104)
PHONE..............................419 331-2273
Linda M Black-kurek, Pr

EMP: 27 EST: 2017
SALES (est): 7.06MM **Privately Held**
Web: www.libertynursingcenters.com
SIC: 8051 Skilled nursing care facilities

(G-9918)
LIMA AUTO MALL INC
Also Called: Lima Cdllac Pntiac Olds Nissan
2200 N Cable Rd (45807-1792)
P.O. Box 1649 (45802-1649)
PHONE..............................419 993-6000
William C Timmermeister, Pr
Rodger L Mc Clain, *
Susan B Timmermeister, *
EMP: 100 EST: 1921
SQ FT: 21,000
SALES (est): 24.53MM **Privately Held**
Web: www.limaautomall.com
SIC: 5511 7538 7532 7515 Automobiles, new and used; General automotive repair shops; Top and body repair and paint shops ; Passenger car leasing

(G-9919)
LIMA CITY SCHOOL DISTRICT
Also Called: Lima City School Central Svcs
600 E Wayne St (45801-4182)
PHONE..............................419 996-3400
Tim Haller, Prin
EMP: 29
SALES (corp-wide): 67.77MM **Privately Held**
Web: www.limacityschools.org
SIC: 8211 4151 7538 Public elementary school; School buses; General automotive repair shops
PA: Lima City School District
755 St Johns Ave
Lima OH 45804
419 996-3400

(G-9920)
LIMA CNVLSCENT HM FNDATION INC (PA)
Also Called: LIMA CONVALESCENT HOME
1650 Allentown Rd (45805)
PHONE..............................419 227-5450
Randy Cox, Ex Dir
EMP: 84 EST: 1958
SQ FT: 41,886
SALES (est): 13.58MM
SALES (corp-wide): 13.58MM **Privately Held**
Web: www.limaconvalescenthome.com
SIC: 8059 8051 Convalescent home; Skilled nursing care facilities

(G-9921)
LIMA COMMUNICATIONS CORP
Also Called: Wlio Television-Channel 35
1424 Rice Ave (45805-1949)
PHONE..............................419 228-8835
Kevin Creamer, Pr
David E Plaugher, *
EMP: 75 EST: 1951
SQ FT: 5,000
SALES (est): 12.48MM
SALES (corp-wide): 910.95MM **Privately Held**
Web: www.hometownstations.com
SIC: 4833 Television broadcasting stations
PA: Block Communications, Inc.
405 Madison Ave Ste 2100
Toledo OH 43604
419 724-6212

(G-9922)
LIMA FAMILY YMCA (PA)
345 S Elizabeth St (45801-4805)
PHONE..............................419 223-6045
William Blewit, Pr

GEOGRAPHIC SECTION
Lima - Allen County (G-9942)

Clyde Raush, *
EMP: 74 **EST:** 1888
SQ FT: 111,000
SALES (est): 1.68MM
SALES (corp-wide): 1.68MM **Privately Held**
Web: www.limaymca.net
SIC: 8641 8351 8322 7991 Civic associations; Child day care services; Individual and family services; Physical fitness facilities

(G-9923)
LIMA FAMILY YMCA
Also Called: Y. M. C. A. of Lima
136 S West St (45801-4851)
PHONE..................................419 223-6055
John Smith, *Dir*
EMP: 71
SALES (corp-wide): 1.68MM **Privately Held**
Web: www.limaymca.net
SIC: 8641 7991 8351 7032 Youth organizations; Physical fitness facilities; Child day care services; Youth camps
PA: Lima Family Ymca
345 S Elizabeth St
Lima OH 45801
419 223-6045

(G-9924)
LIMA MEDICAL SUPPLIES INC
770 W North St (45801-3923)
PHONE..................................419 226-9581
TOLL FREE: 800
Ron Drees, *Dir*
EMP: 39 **EST:** 1964
SQ FT: 13,000
SALES (est): 7.91MM
SALES (corp-wide): 6.92B **Privately Held**
SIC: 5047 Medical equipment and supplies
HQ: Mcauley Management Services, Inc.
730 W Market St
Lima OH 45801
419 226-9684

(G-9925)
LIMA MEMORIAL HOSPITAL (HQ)
Also Called: Lima Memorial Health System
1001 Bellefontaine Ave (45804-2899)
P.O. Box 932842 (44193-0023)
PHONE..................................419 228-3335
Michael Swick, *Pr*
Bob Armstrong, *
EMP: 612 **EST:** 1899
SALES (est): 234.63MM
SALES (corp-wide): 240.6MM **Privately Held**
Web: www.limamemorial.org
SIC: 8062 General medical and surgical hospitals
PA: Lima Memorial Joint Operating Company
1001 Bellefontaine Ave
Lima OH 45804
419 228-5165

(G-9926)
LIMA MEMORIAL JOINT OPER CO (PA)
1001 Bellefontaine Ave (45804-2800)
P.O. Box 932842 (44193-0023)
PHONE..................................419 228-5165
Michael Swick, *Pr*
Eric Pohjala, *
EMP: 1500 **EST:** 1998
SALES (est): 240.6MM
SALES (corp-wide): 240.6MM **Privately Held**
Web: www.limamemorial.org
SIC: 8062 General medical and surgical hospitals

(G-9927)
LIMA SHEET METAL MACHINE & MFG
Also Called: Lima Sheet Metal
1001 Bowman Rd (45804-3409)
PHONE..................................419 229-1161
Michael R Emerick, *Pr*
Thomas Emerick, *
Ann Emerick, *
EMP: 31 **EST:** 1974
SQ FT: 26,250
SALES (est): 2.49MM **Privately Held**
Web: www.limasheetmetal.com
SIC: 3589 3599 7349 7692 Commercial cooking and foodwarming equipment; Machine shop, jobbing and repair; Building maintenance, except repairs; Welding repair

(G-9928)
LIPPINCOTT PLMBNG-HTING AC INC
872 Saint Johns Ave (45804-1567)
PHONE..................................419 222-0856
Michael Ray Lawrence, *Pr*
Richard Michael Lyons, *
Rebecca Sue Lawrence, *
EMP: 28 **EST:** 1963
SQ FT: 2,000
SALES (est): 2.43MM **Privately Held**
Web: www.lippincottplumbing.com
SIC: 1731 1711 Electrical work; Plumbing contractors

(G-9929)
LOST CREEK HLTH CARE RHBLTTION
804 S Mumaugh Rd (45804-3569)
PHONE..................................419 225-9040
EMP: 157 **EST:** 2010
SALES (est): 3.5MM **Privately Held**
SIC: 8051 Skilled nursing care facilities
PA: Guardian Healthcare Home Office I, Llc
8796 Route 219
Brockway PA 15824

(G-9930)
LOWES HOME CENTERS LLC
Also Called: Lowe's
2411 N Eastown Rd (45807-1618)
PHONE..................................419 331-3598
Jason Carhorn, *Mgr*
EMP: 157
SALES (corp-wide): 86.38B **Publicly Held**
Web: www.lowes.com
SIC: 5211 5031 5722 5064 Home centers; Building materials, exterior; Household appliance stores; Electrical appliances, television and radio
HQ: Lowe's Home Centers, Llc
1000 Lowes Blvd
Mooresville NC 28117
336 658-4000

(G-9931)
LUCKEY TRANSFER LLC
401 E Robb Ave (45801-2952)
PHONE..................................800 435-4371
EMP: 56
SALES (corp-wide): 6.77MM **Privately Held**
Web: www.luckeylogistics.com
SIC: 4213 Contract haulers
PA: Luckey Transfer, Llc
29988 N 00 East Rd
Streator IL 61364
815 672-2931

(G-9932)
M & W CONSTRUCTION ENTPS LLC
1201 Crestwood Dr (45805-1669)
PHONE..................................419 227-2000
Steven W Roebuck, *Pr*
Brad Beining, *Genl Mgr*
EMP: 27 **EST:** 1973
SALES (est): 5.22MM **Privately Held**
Web: www.mandwconst.com
SIC: 1541 1542 1761 Industrial buildings and warehouses; Nonresidential construction, nec; Roofing contractor

(G-9933)
MARIMOR INDUSTRIES INC
2450 Ada Rd (45801-3342)
PHONE..................................419 221-1226
Angela Herzog, *Ex Dir*
EMP: 77 **EST:** 1968
SQ FT: 31,000
SALES (est): 3.54MM **Privately Held**
Web: www.marimorindustries.org
SIC: 8331 Vocational rehabilitation agency

(G-9934)
MERCY HLTH - ST RTAS MED CTR L (HQ)
Also Called: Putnam Cnty Amblatory Care Ctr
730 W Market St (45801-4602)
PHONE..................................419 227-3361
Steve Walter, *Ch Bd*
John Renner, *
EMP: 1700 **EST:** 1970
SQ FT: 563,000
SALES (est): 488.57MM
SALES (corp-wide): 6.92B **Privately Held**
Web: www.mercy.com
SIC: 8062 7352 General medical and surgical hospitals; Medical equipment rental
PA: Bon Secours Mercy Health, Inc.
1701 Mercy Health Pl
Cincinnati OH 45237
513 956-3729

(G-9935)
MID-AMERICAN CLG CONTRS INC (PA)
447 N Elizabeth St (45801-4336)
PHONE..................................419 229-3899
John Whittacker, *Pr*
William Schroeder, *Stockholder*
Harold Breidenbach, *
Marsha Fisher, *
Kermit Nuesmeyer, *
EMP: 100 **EST:** 1991
SQ FT: 8,000
SALES (est): 10.51MM **Privately Held**
Web: www.macc.net
SIC: 7349 Janitorial service, contract basis

(G-9936)
MODERN BUILDERS SUPPLY INC
1245 Neubrecht Rd (45801-3117)
PHONE..................................419 224-4627
EMP: 30
SALES (corp-wide): 346.23MM **Privately Held**
Web: www.modernbuilderssupply.com
SIC: 5033 Roofing and siding materials
PA: Modern Builders Supply, Inc.
3500 Phillips Ave
Toledo OH 43608
419 241-3961

(G-9937)
NATIONAL LIME AND STONE CO
1314 Findlay Rd (45801-3106)
PHONE..................................419 228-3434
Nick Morris, *Mgr*
EMP: 28
SQ FT: 1,200
SALES (corp-wide): 167.89MM **Privately Held**
Web: www.natlime.com
SIC: 1422 Crushed and broken limestone
PA: The National Lime And Stone Company
551 Lake Cascade Pkwy
Findlay OH 45840
419 422-4341

(G-9938)
NATIONWIDE CHILDRENS HOSPITAL
830 W High St (45801-3971)
PHONE..................................419 221-3177
EMP: 76
SALES (corp-wide): 3.6B **Privately Held**
Web: www.nationwidechildrens.org
SIC: 8062 General medical and surgical hospitals
PA: Nationwide Children's Hospital
700 Childrens Dr
Columbus OH 43205
614 722-2000

(G-9939)
NELSON PACKAGING COMPANY INC
Also Called: Nelson
1801 Reservoir Rd (45804-3152)
PHONE..................................419 229-3471
Sharon Faza, *Pr*
Issam Faza, *
Stephen L Becker, *
▲ **EMP:** 65 **EST:** 1980
SQ FT: 70,000
SALES (est): 12.86MM **Privately Held**
Web: www.nelsonpackagingco.com
SIC: 7389 Packaging and labeling services

(G-9940)
NICHOLAS D STARR INC (PA)
Also Called: Master Maintenance Co
301 W Elm St (45801-4813)
P.O. Box 5092 (45802-5092)
PHONE..................................419 229-3192
Nicholas D Starr, *Pr*
EMP: 120 **EST:** 1981
SQ FT: 25,000
SALES (est): 4.96MM **Privately Held**
Web: www.master-maintenance.com
SIC: 7349 Janitorial service, contract basis

(G-9941)
NORTHWEST OHIO SRGCAL SPCALIST
Also Called: Northwest Ohio Srgcal Spcalist
1003 Bellefontaine Ave Ste 150 (45804-2868)
PHONE..................................419 998-8207
Jay Franklin Oaks Md, *Pr*
EMP: 47 **EST:** 1983
SALES (est): 481.7K **Privately Held**
Web: www.limamemorial.org
SIC: 8062 General medical and surgical hospitals

(G-9942)
NORTHWESTERN OHIO SEC SYSTEMS (PA)
121 E High St (45801-4417)
P.O. Box 869 (45802-0869)
PHONE..................................419 227-1655
Trell Yocum, *Pr*
EMP: 47 **EST:** 1972
SQ FT: 36,000
SALES (est): 8.93MM
SALES (corp-wide): 8.93MM **Privately Held**
Web: www.nwoss.com
SIC: 5999 1731 7382 Alarm signal systems; Access control systems specialization; Security systems services

Lima - Allen County (G-9943)

GEOGRAPHIC SECTION

(G-9943)
NOURYON CHEMICALS LLC
1747 Fort Amanda Rd (45804-1864)
PHONE..............................419 229-0088
EMP: 38
Web: www.nouryon.com
SIC: 5169 Organic chemicals, synthetic
HQ: Nouryon Chemicals Llc
  131 S Dearborn St # 1000
  Chicago IL 60603
  312 544-7000

(G-9944)
OB-GYN SPECIALISTS LIMA INC
Also Called: Ryan, Charles R MD Facog
830 W High St Ste 101 (45801-3968)
PHONE..............................419 227-0610
James L Kahn, *Pr*
EMP: 42 **EST:** 1976
SQ FT: 6,900
SALES (est): 6.67MM **Privately Held**
Web: www.obgynlimaohio.com
SIC: 8011 Gynecologist

(G-9945)
ORTHOPAEDIC INSTITUTE OHIO INC (PA)
801 Medical Dr Ste A (45804-4030)
PHONE..............................419 222-6622
John Duggan, *Pr*
James O'neil, *VP*
David L Davis, *
Roger Terry, *
Steven Calte, *
EMP: 100 **EST:** 1997
SQ FT: 4,335
SALES (est): 10.65MM
SALES (corp-wide): 10.65MM **Privately Held**
Web: www.orthoohio.com
SIC: 8011 Orthopedic physician

(G-9946)
PAJKA EYE CENTER INC
855 W Market St Ste A (45805-2764)
P.O. Box 1692 (45802-1692)
PHONE..............................419 228-7432
John Pajka, *Pr*
EMP: 38 **EST:** 1974
SALES (est): 7.25MM **Privately Held**
Web: www.pajkaeyecenter.com
SIC: 8011 Opthalmologist

(G-9947)
PAYCHEX INC
My Staffing Pro
675 W Market St (45801-4603)
PHONE..............................800 939-2462
Jamie Roof, *Brnch Mgr*
EMP: 60
SALES (corp-wide): 5.01B **Publicly Held**
Web: www.paychex.com
SIC: 8721 Payroll accounting service
PA: Paychex, Inc.
  911 Panorama Trl S
  Rochester NY 14625
  585 385-6666

(G-9948)
PERRY PRO TECH INC (PA)
265 Commerce Pkwy (45804-4011)
PHONE..............................419 228-1360
TOLL FREE: 800
Barry Clark, *Pr*
Paulette Borges, *
Frank B Cory, *
David Zimerle, *
Don Katalenas, *
EMP: 80 **EST:** 1965
SQ FT: 45,000
SALES (est): 47.78MM
SALES (corp-wide): 47.78MM **Privately Held**
Web: www.perryprotech.com
SIC: 5999 5044 7378 Typewriters and business machines; Office equipment; Computer maintenance and repair

(G-9949)
PLUS MANAGEMENT SERVICES INC
Also Called: Villa At Baton Rouge, The
2440 Baton Rouge Ofc (45805-5105)
PHONE..............................419 331-2273
Gerome Oneal, *Mgr*
EMP: 45
Web: www.plusmanagement.com
SIC: 8742 8741 Management consulting services; Management services
PA: Plus Management Services, Inc.
  2905 Oak Hill Ct
  Lima OH 45805

(G-9950)
PLUS MANAGEMENT SERVICES INC (PA)
2905 Oak Hill Ct (45805-4475)
PHONE..............................419 225-9018
Jerome O'neal, *Pr*
EMP: 112 **EST:** 1992
SALES (est): 9.03MM **Privately Held**
Web: www.plusmanagement.com
SIC: 8742 8741 Hospital and health services consultant; Management services

(G-9951)
POWELL COMPANY INC
Also Called: Rightway Food Service
3255 Saint Johns Rd (45804-4022)
PHONE..............................419 228-3552
Ronald Lee Williams, *Pr*
EMP: 65 **EST:** 2021
SALES (est): 11.16MM **Privately Held**
SIC: 5149 5148 5142 5087 Canned goods: fruit, vegetables, seafood, meats, etc.; Fruits, fresh; Fruits, frozen; Janitors' supplies

(G-9952)
PRIMROSE RTRMENT CMMNITIES LLC
3500 W Elm St (45807-2296)
PHONE..............................419 224-1200
Carla Dysert, *Ex Dir*
EMP: 67
Web: www.primroseretirement.com
SIC: 8361 Aged home
PA: Primrose Retirement Communities Llc
  815 N 2nd St
  Aberdeen SD 57401

(G-9953)
R & K GORBY LLC
Also Called: Howard Johnson Lima
1920 Roschman Ave (45804-3444)
PHONE..............................419 222-0004
EMP: 36 **EST:** 1958
SALES (est): 484.19K **Privately Held**
Web: www.hojolima.com
SIC: 7011 Hotels and motels

(G-9954)
ROEDER CARTAGE COMPANY INC (PA)
1979 N Dixie Hwy (45801-3253)
PHONE..............................419 221-1600
Calvin E Roeder, *CEO*
EMP: 55 **EST:** 1974
SQ FT: 21,000
SALES (est): 5.59MM
SALES (corp-wide): 5.59MM **Privately Held**
Web: www.roedercartage.com
SIC: 4213 Contract haulers

(G-9955)
ROSCHMANS RESTAURANT ADM
Also Called: Hampton Inn
1933 Roschman Ave (45804-3496)
PHONE..............................419 225-8300
Robert Roschman, *Pr*
EMP: 34 **EST:** 1997
SALES (est): 509.38K **Privately Held**
Web: www.hilton.com
SIC: 7011 Hotels and motels

(G-9956)
ROSENS INC
Also Called: Rosens, Inc
1132 E Hanthorn Rd (45804-3930)
PHONE..............................419 225-7382
Iven Wells, *Pr*
EMP: 89
Web: www.rosensdiversifiedinc.com
SIC: 5191 Fertilizers and agricultural chemicals
HQ: Rosen's, Inc.
  1120 Lake Ave
  Fairmont MN 56031
  507 238-4201

(G-9957)
RUSH TRUCK LEASING INC
Also Called: Limaidealease
2655 Saint Johns Rd (45804-4006)
PHONE..............................419 224-6045
EMP: 32
SALES (corp-wide): 7.93B **Publicly Held**
Web: www.rushenterprises.com
SIC: 5012 7538 5531 5014 Automobiles and other motor vehicles; General automotive repair shops; Auto and home supply stores; Tires and tubes
HQ: Rush Truck Leasing, Inc.
  11777 Highway 39
  Cincinnati OH 45241
  513 733-8510

(G-9958)
S&S / SUPERIOR COACH CO INC
2550 Central Point Pkwy (45804-3890)
PHONE..............................888 324-7895
Mike Mckiernan, *VP*
EMP: 45 **EST:** 2017
SALES (est): 4.69MM **Privately Held**
Web: www.ss-superior.com
SIC: 7532 Body shop, automotive

(G-9959)
SEWER RODDING EQUIPMENT CO
Also Called: Sreco Flexible
3434 S Dixie Hwy (45804-3756)
PHONE..............................419 991-2065
Larry Drain, *Mgr*
EMP: 140
SALES (corp-wide): 9.75MM **Privately Held**
SIC: 5032 3546 3423 Sewer pipe, clay; Power-driven handtools; Hand and edge tools, nec
PA: Sewer Rodding Equipment Co Inc
  3217 Carter Ave
  Marina Del Rey CA 90292
  310 301-9009

(G-9960)
SHAWNEE COUNTRY CLUB
1700 Shawnee Rd (45805-3899)
PHONE..............................419 227-7177
Elliot Burke, *Club House Manager*
EMP: 75 **EST:** 1904
SQ FT: 37,000
SALES (est): 2.69MM **Privately Held**
Web: www.shawneecountryclub.com
SIC: 7997 5812 Country club, membership; Eating places

(G-9961)
SMITH-BOUGHAN INC
Also Called: Smith-Boughan Mechanical Svcs
777 S Copus Rd (45801-4169)
P.O. Box 1235 (45802-1235)
PHONE..............................419 991-8040
EMP: 80 **EST:** 1927
SALES (est): 24.41MM **Privately Held**
Web: www.sbmech.com
SIC: 1711 Plumbing, heating, air-conditioning

(G-9962)
SPALLINGER MILLWRIGHT SVC CO
Also Called: Spallnger Atclave Systms/US MI
1155 E Hanthorn Rd (45804-3929)
PHONE..............................419 225-5830
Scott Spallinger, *Pr*
▲ **EMP:** 42 **EST:** 1989
SQ FT: 80,000
SALES (est): 9.61MM **Privately Held**
Web: www.spallinger.com
SIC: 3446 1796 Stairs, staircases, stair treads: prefabricated metal; Machinery installation

(G-9963)
SPECIALIZED ALTERNATIVES FOR F
Also Called: Safy Behavioral Health of Lima
658 W Market St Ste 101 (45801-5604)
PHONE..............................419 222-1527
EMP: 132
SALES (corp-wide): 22.34MM **Privately Held**
Web: www.safy.org
SIC: 8322 Child related social services
PA: Specialized Alternatives For Families And Youth Of Ohio, Inc.
  10100 Elida Rd
  Delphos OH 45833
  419 695-8010

(G-9964)
SPHERION OF LIMA INC (PA)
216 N Elizabeth St (45801-4350)
P.O. Box 1155 (45802-1155)
PHONE..............................419 224-8367
Grace Schulte, *Pr*
Robert Schulte, *
EMP: 30 **EST:** 1972
SQ FT: 4,400
SALES (est): 22.59MM
SALES (corp-wide): 22.59MM **Privately Held**
Web: www.applyohio.com
SIC: 7363 Temporary help service

(G-9965)
SPRINGVIEW MANOR NURSING HOME
Also Called: SPRINGVIEW MANOR
883 W Spring St (45805-3228)
PHONE..............................419 227-3661
Josh Mcclellan, *Owner*
EMP: 47 **EST:** 1963
SQ FT: 20,000
SALES (est): 5.42MM **Privately Held**
Web: www.springviewmanorhc.com
SIC: 8051 Extended care facility

(G-9966)
STOLLY INSURANCE AGENCY INC
Also Called: Nationwide
1730 Allentown Rd (45805-1856)
P.O. Box 5067 (45802-5067)
PHONE..............................419 227-2570
Mark E Stolly, *Pr*
Timothy J Stolly, *

GEOGRAPHIC SECTION

Lima - Allen County (G-9988)

William R Stolly, *
Janet K Wade, *
EMP: 50 **EST:** 1904
SQ FT: 4,600
SALES (est): 9.01MM **Privately Held**
Web: www.stolly.com
SIC: 6411 Insurance agents, nec

(G-9967)
STOOPS OF LIMA INC
598 E Hanthorn Rd (45804-3822)
PHONE.............................419 228-4334
Jeffrey Stoops, *CEO*
John Frigge, *
EMP: 52 **EST:** 1983
SALES (est): 1.46MM **Privately Held**
Web: www.truckcountry.com
SIC: 5012 5511 Trucks, commercial; Trucks, tractors, and trailers: new and used

(G-9968)
SWD CORPORATION
Also Called: Superior Wholesale Distrs
435 N Main St (45801-4314)
P.O. Box 340 (45802-0340)
PHONE.............................419 227-2436
Carl Berger Junior, *Pr*
David L Cockerell, *
Kenneth Simmers, *
EMP: 50 **EST:** 1884
SQ FT: 85,000
SALES (est): 47.59MM **Privately Held**
Web: www.swdcorporation.com
SIC: 5194 5142 Tobacco and tobacco products; Packaged frozen goods

(G-9969)
T AND D INTERIORS INCORPORATED
3626 Allentown Rd (45807-2138)
PHONE.............................419 331-4372
Brad Selover, *Pr*
William Timothy Estes, *
Kim Selover, *
Marsha Estes, *
EMP: 40 **EST:** 1981
SQ FT: 14,800
SALES (est): 5.21MM **Privately Held**
Web: www.tdinteriorsinc.com
SIC: 1742 1752 Acoustical and ceiling work; Floor laying and floor work, nec

(G-9970)
THE LOCHHAVEN COMPANY
Also Called: Lockhaven Apts
1640 Allentown Rd Ofc (45805-1876)
PHONE.............................419 227-5450
Mary Jo Horstman, *Mgr*
Sara Music, *Asst Mgr*
EMP: 56 **EST:** 1986
SALES (est): 873.38K
SALES (corp-wide): 13.58MM **Privately Held**
Web: www.limaconvalescenthome.com
SIC: 6513 8361 Retirement hotel operation; Geriatric residential care
PA: Lima Convalescent Home Foundation, Inc.
1650 Allentown Rd
Lima OH 45805
419 227-5450

(G-9971)
TOM AHL CHRYSLR-PLYMOUTH-DODGE
617 King Ave (45805-1793)
PHONE.............................419 227-0202
Thomas W Ahl, *Pr*
Andrea Ahl, *
EMP: 150 **EST:** 1953
SQ FT: 4,000
SALES (est): 23.32MM **Privately Held**
Web: www.tomahlchryslerdodge.com
SIC: 5511 7515 Automobiles, new and used; Passenger car leasing

(G-9972)
TOP LINE EXPRESS INC
1805 N Dixie Hwy (45801-3255)
P.O. Box 5277 (45802-5277)
PHONE.............................419 221-1705
EMP: 30
Web: www.toplineexpress.com
SIC: 4213 Trucking, except local

(G-9973)
TRISCO SYSTEMS INCORPORATED
2000 Baty Rd (45807-1955)
PHONE.............................419 339-3906
Steven W Walter, *Pr*
Brian U Walter, *
EMP: 130 **EST:** 1990
SQ FT: 15,000
SALES (est): 25.8MM **Privately Held**
Web: www.triscosystems.com
SIC: 1541 1542 Renovation, remodeling and repairs: industrial buildings; Commercial and office buildings, renovation and repair

(G-9974)
TUTTLE CONSTRUCTION INC
880 Shawnee Rd (45805-3466)
PHONE.............................419 228-6262
EMP: 160 **EST:** 1928
SALES (est): 29.25MM **Privately Held**
SIC: 1541 1542 4932 Industrial buildings, new construction, nec; Commercial and office building, new construction; Gas and other services combined

(G-9975)
UNITED PARCEL SERVICE INC
Also Called: UPS
801 Industry Ave (45804-4169)
PHONE.............................419 222-7399
John Smith, *Mgr*
EMP: 31
SALES (corp-wide): 90.96B **Publicly Held**
Web: www.ups.com
SIC: 4215 4513 Parcel delivery, vehicular; Air courier services
HQ: United Parcel Service, Inc.
55 Glenlake Pkwy
Atlanta GA 30328
404 828-6000

(G-9976)
UNITED STATES PLASTIC CORP
Also Called: Neatlysmart
1390 Neubrecht Rd (45801-3120)
PHONE.............................419 228-2242
EMP: 100 **EST:** 1962
SALES (est): 4MM
SALES (corp-wide): 49.68MM **Privately Held**
Web: www.usplastic.com
SIC: 5162 3089 Plastics materials and basic shapes; Plastics processing
HQ: Stanita Foundation
941 Fry Rd
Greenwood IN 46142
317 881-6751

(G-9977)
UNITED TELEPHONE COMPANY OHIO
122 S Elizabeth St (45801-4802)
P.O. Box 2001 (45806-0001)
PHONE.............................419 227-1660
James D Gadd, *Mgr*
EMP: 187
SALES (corp-wide): 5.96B **Privately Held**
SIC: 4813 Telephone communication, except radio
HQ: United Telephone Company Of Ohio
100 Centurylink Dr
Monroe LA 71203
318 388-9000

(G-9978)
VOLUNTERS AMER CARE FACILITIES
Also Called: Lost Creek Care Center
804 S Mumaugh Rd (45804-3569)
PHONE.............................419 225-9040
Shelley Kendick, *Mgr*
EMP: 116
SALES (corp-wide): 56.23MM **Privately Held**
SIC: 8051 8052 Skilled nursing care facilities ; Intermediate care facilities
PA: Volunteers Of America Care Facilities
7530 Market Place Dr
Eden Prairie MN 55344
952 941-0305

(G-9979)
WANNEMACHER ENTERPRISES INC (PA)
Also Called: Wannemacher Total Logistics
400 E Hanthorn Rd (45804-2460)
PHONE.............................419 225-9060
Greg Wannemacher, *Pr*
Donna Wannemacher, *Sec*
Andy Wannemacher, *VP*
Randy Fetter, *VP*
Beth Nickles, *VP*
EMP: 46 **EST:** 1991
SQ FT: 1,000,450
SALES (est): 24.83MM
SALES (corp-wide): 24.83MM **Privately Held**
Web: www.wanntl.com
SIC: 4225 4213 General warehousing and storage; Trucking, except local

(G-9980)
WASTE MANAGEMENT OHIO INC
1550 E 4th St (45804-2710)
PHONE.............................419 221-2029
EMP: 49
SALES (corp-wide): 14.91B **Publicly Held**
SIC: 4953 Refuse systems
HQ: Waste Management Of Ohio, Inc.
1700 N Broad St
Fairborn OH 45324

(G-9981)
WEST CENTRAL OHIO GROUP LTD
Also Called: Institute For Orthpdic Surgery
801 Medical Dr Ste B (45804-4030)
PHONE.............................419 224-7586
Mark G Mcdonald, *CEO*
EMP: 75 **EST:** 1998
SALES (est): 55.78MM **Privately Held**
Web: www.ioshospital.com
SIC: 8011 Orthopedic physician

(G-9982)
WEST CNTL OHIO SRGERY ENDSCOPY
770 W High St Ste 100 (45801-5900)
PHONE.............................419 226-8700
EMP: 45 **EST:** 1998
SQ FT: 17,000
SALES (est): 1.65MM **Privately Held**
Web: www.gastrohealth.com
SIC: 8011 Gastronomist

(G-9983)
WEST MARKET ST FMLY PHYSICIANS
Also Called: Neidhardt, David MD
915 W Market St Ste E (45805-2769)
PHONE.............................419 229-4747
Edward Tremoulis, *Pr*
Doctor David Neidhardt, *VP*
Deborah Tremoulis, *Sec*
EMP: 28 **EST:** 1986
SQ FT: 4,900
SALES (est): 749.6K **Privately Held**
SIC: 8011 General and family practice, physician/surgeon

(G-9984)
WEST OHIO CMNTY ACTION PARTNR (PA)
Also Called: Head Start
540 S Central Ave (45804)
PHONE.............................419 227-2586
EMP: 114 **EST:** 1994
SALES (est): 8.9MM **Privately Held**
Web: www.wocap.org
SIC: 8399 8322 8351 Community action agency; Individual and family services; Child day care services

(G-9985)
WEST OHIO CMNTY ACTION PARTNR
Also Called: Lacca
540 S Central Ave (45804-1306)
PHONE.............................419 227-2586
EMP: 46
Web: www.lacca.org
SIC: 8322 Social service center
PA: West Ohio Community Action Partnership
540 S Central Ave
Lima OH 45804

(G-9986)
WESTGATE LANES INCORPORATED
721 N Cable Rd (45805-1738)
PHONE.............................419 229-3845
Andy Johnston, *Pr*
Wes Johnston, *
Keith Callahan, *
EMP: 39 **EST:** 1958
SQ FT: 50,000
SALES (est): 824.87K **Privately Held**
Web: www.westgateentertainmentcenter.com
SIC: 5812 7933 Cafeteria; Bowling centers

(G-9987)
WIECHART ENTERPRISES INC
Also Called: All Service Glass
4511 Elida Rd (45807-1151)
PHONE.............................419 227-0027
TOLL FREE: 800
Eric Wiechart, *Pr*
EMP: 30 **EST:** 1975
SQ FT: 12,000
SALES (est): 4.71MM **Privately Held**
Web: www.allservglass.com
SIC: 7536 1793 Automotive glass replacement shops; Glass and glazing work

(G-9988)
WRIGHT MULCH INC
1227 E Hanthorn Rd (45804-3931)
PHONE.............................419 228-1173
Aaron Wright, *Bmch Mgr*
EMP: 43
SALES (corp-wide): 34.4K **Privately Held**
SIC: 0782 Mulching services, lawn
PA: Wright Mulch, Inc.
1601 E 4th St
Lima OH 45804
419 228-1173

Lima
Auglaize County

(G-9989)
COMMUNITY HLTH PRFSSIONALS INC
Also Called: Helping Hands
3739 Shawnee Rd # A (45806-1618)
PHONE..................................419 991-1822
Claudia Crawfford, *Dir*
EMP: 48
SALES (corp-wide): 12.27MM **Privately Held**
Web: www.comhealthpro.org
SIC: 8082 Visiting nurse service
PA: Community Health Professionals, Inc.
1159 Westwood Dr
Van Wert OH 45891
419 238-9223

(G-9990)
ENDOSCOPY CTR OF W CNTL OHIO L
2793 Shawnee Rd (45806-1444)
PHONE..................................419 879-3636
EMP: 32 **EST:** 2007
SALES (est): 5.72MM
SALES (corp-wide): 371.62B **Publicly Held**
Web: www.gastrohealth.com
SIC: 8011 Gastronomist
PA: Unitedhealth Group Incorporated
9900 Bren Rd E
Minnetonka MN 55343
952 936-1300

(G-9991)
GASTRO-INTESTINAL ASSOC INC
Also Called: Endoscopy Center W Centl Ohio
2793 Shawnee Rd (45806-1444)
PHONE..................................419 227-8209
Mark Leifer, *Pr*
Richard Capone Md, *Pr*
Charles W Brunelli Md, *VP*
EMP: 45 **EST:** 1977
SALES (est): 2.49MM **Privately Held**
Web: www.gastrohealth.com
SIC: 8011 Gastronomist

(G-9992)
HUME SUPPLY INC
2685 Summer Rambo Ct (45806-1667)
PHONE..................................419 991-5751
Daven Stedke, *Pr*
John E Stedke, *
Janice Stedke, *
EMP: 42 **EST:** 1948
SALES (est): 19.47MM **Privately Held**
Web: www.humecontractingllc.com
SIC: 1541 Industrial buildings, new construction, nec

(G-9993)
INTERIM HLTH CARE OF NRTHWSTER
Also Called: Interim Services
3745 Shawnee Rd Ste 108 (45806-1665)
PHONE..................................419 228-9345
Tammy Bergfield, *Admn*
EMP: 98
SALES (corp-wide): 52.16MM **Privately Held**
Web: www.interimhealthcare.com
SIC: 8082 Home health care services
HQ: Interim Health Care Of Northwestern Ohio, Inc
3100 W Central Ave # 250
Toledo OH 43606

(G-9994)
OFFICE WORLD INC (PA)
Also Called: Virtual Pc's
3820 S Dixie Hwy (45806-1848)
PHONE..................................419 991-4694
Chuck Greeley, *Pr*
EMP: 41 **EST:** 1962
SQ FT: 20,000
SALES (est): 7.67MM
SALES (corp-wide): 7.67MM **Privately Held**
SIC: 5045 5044 7374 5734 Computers, nec; Office equipment; Data processing service; Computer and software stores

Lindsey
Sandusky County

(G-9995)
LUCKEY FARMERS INC
154 Dewey St (43442-3002)
P.O. Box 305 (43442-0305)
PHONE..................................419 665-2322
Phil Bodey, *Mgr*
EMP: 40
SALES (corp-wide): 37.96MM **Privately Held**
Web: www.luckeyfarmers.com
SIC: 4221 Grain elevator, storage only
PA: Luckey Farmers, Inc.
1200 W Main St
Woodville OH 43469
419 849-2711

Lisbon
Columbiana County

(G-9996)
ALBCO SALES INC (PA)
230 Maple St (44432-1274)
PHONE..................................330 424-9446
Joe Stafeld, *Pr*
Gary Staffald, *
Tim Redovian, *
William Mullane Junior, *Sec*
EMP: 40 **EST:** 1985
SQ FT: 1,000
SALES (est): 4.81MM
SALES (corp-wide): 4.81MM **Privately Held**
Web: www.albco.com
SIC: 5051 Steel

(G-9997)
BUCKEYE TRANSFER LLC
Also Called: Signal Terminal, The
44626 State Rte 154 (44432-9393)
PHONE..................................330 719-0375
Lee Stoneburner, *Mgr*
EMP: 54
SALES (corp-wide): 1.38MM **Privately Held**
Web: www.buckeyetransfer.com
SIC: 4731 Freight forwarding
PA: Buckeye Transfer Llc
41738 Esterly Dr
Columbiana OH 44408
330 482-7070

(G-9998)
COLUMBANA CNTY FOR DVLPMNTAL D
Also Called: Service and Support ADM
35947 State Route 172 (44432-9404)
PHONE..................................330 424-0404
EMP: 184
SALES (corp-wide): 90.8MM **Privately Held**
Web: www.ccbdd.net
SIC: 8059 Home for the mentally retarded, ex. skilled or intermediate
HQ: Columbiana County Board Of Developmental Disabilities/Robert Bycroft School
7675 State Route 45
Lisbon OH 44432

(G-9999)
COMMUNITY ACTION AGCY CLMBANA (PA)
7880 Lincole Pl (44432-8324)
PHONE..................................330 424-7221
Carol Bretz, *Ex Dir*
EMP: 90 **EST:** 1965
SQ FT: 12,600
SALES (est): 21.1MM
SALES (corp-wide): 21.1MM **Privately Held**
Web: www.caaofcc.org
SIC: 8351 Head Start center, except in conjunction with school

(G-10000)
COMMUNITY EDUCATION CTRS INC
8473 County Home Rd (44432-9418)
PHONE..................................330 424-4065
Michael L Caltabiano, *Brnch Mgr*
EMP: 30
Web: www.geogroup.com
SIC: 8744 Correctional facility
HQ: Community Education Centers, Inc.
4955 Technology Way
Boca Raton FL 33431
561 893-0101

(G-10001)
D W DICKEY AND SON INC (PA)
Also Called: D W Dickey
7896 Dickey Dr (44432)
P.O. Box 189 (44432)
PHONE..................................330 424-1441
Gary Neville, *Pr*
Timothy Dickey, *
David Dickey, *
Janet Blosser, *
EMP: 128 **EST:** 1948
SALES (est): 43.61MM
SALES (corp-wide): 43.61MM **Privately Held**
Web: www.dwdickey.com
SIC: 5169 3273 5172 Explosives; Ready-mixed concrete; Fuel oil

(G-10002)
EMPLOYMENT DEVELOPMENT INC
8330 County Home Rd (44432-9418)
PHONE..................................330 424-7711
Phil Carter, *Dir*
EMP: 30 **EST:** 1969
SQ FT: 8,000
SALES (est): 2.82MM **Privately Held**
Web: www.employment-development.com
SIC: 8331 Sheltered workshop

(G-10003)
HUNTINGTON NATIONAL BANK
24 N Park Ave (44432-1240)
PHONE..................................330 424-7226
Dave Thilibin, *Mgr*
EMP: 31
SALES (corp-wide): 10.84B **Publicly Held**
Web: www.huntington.com
SIC: 6029 6022 Commercial banks, nec; State commercial banks
HQ: The Huntington National Bank
41 S High St
Columbus OH 43215
614 480-4293

(G-10004)
MAHONING CLMBANA TRAINING ASSN
7989 Dickey Dr Ste 4 (44432-8393)
PHONE..................................330 420-9675
EMP: 48
SALES (corp-wide): 2.47MM **Privately Held**
Web: www.mctaworkforce.org
SIC: 8331 Job training and related services
PA: Mahoning & Columbiana Training Association
721 Boardman Poland Rd
Youngstown OH 44512
330 747-5639

(G-10005)
MIKOUIS ENTERPRISE INC
Also Called: Sunrise Homes
38655 Saltwell Rd (44432-8348)
PHONE..................................330 424-1418
EMP: 55 **EST:** 1995
SALES (est): 4.27MM
SALES (corp-wide): 4.27MM **Privately Held**
Web: www.sunrisehomes-oh.com
SIC: 8059 Nursing home, except skilled and intermediate care facility
PA: Empowering People Workshop, Inc.
2460 Elm Rd Ne Ste 500
Warren OH 44483
330 393-5929

(G-10006)
NAFFAH SOUTH LLC
Also Called: Days Inn
40952 State Route 154 (44432-9545)
PHONE..................................330 420-0111
EMP: 30 **EST:** 2008
SALES (est): 440.52K **Privately Held**
Web: www.wyndhamhotels.com
SIC: 7011 Hotels and motels

(G-10007)
VISTA CENTRE
100 Vista Dr (44432-1010)
PHONE..................................330 424-5852
Mary Rice, *Pr*
EMP: 38 **EST:** 1985
SALES (est): 5.26MM **Privately Held**
Web: www.continuinghc.com
SIC: 8052 8051 Home for the mentally retarded, with health care; Skilled nursing care facilities

Little Hocking
Washington County

(G-10008)
DSV SOLUTIONS LLC
251 Arrowhead Rd (45742-5394)
P.O. Box 452 (45742-0452)
PHONE..................................740 989-1200
Larry Hawkins, *Off Mgr*
EMP: 151
SALES (corp-wide): 21.99B **Privately Held**
Web: www.go2uti.com
SIC: 4731 Freight forwarding
HQ: Dsv Solutions, Llc
200 Wood Ave S Ste 300
Iselin NJ 08830
732 850-8000

GEOGRAPHIC SECTION

Lockbourne
Franklin County

(G-10009)
AG CONTAINER TRANSPORT LLC
433 London Groveport Rd (43137)
P.O. Box 268 (43137)
PHONE..............................740 862-8866
David Landis Iii, *Prin*
EMP: 82 **EST:** 2010
SALES (est): 7.53MM **Privately Held**
Web: www.pappastrucking.com
SIC: 4213 Trucking, except local

(G-10010)
COLUMBUS SUTHEAST HT GROUP LLC
5950 S High St (43137-9275)
PHONE..............................614 491-3800
Evan Studder, *CEO*
Zena Smith, *Mgr*
EMP: 27 **EST:** 2016
SALES (est): 2.01MM
SALES (corp-wide): 11.53B **Publicly Held**
SIC: 7011 Casino hotel
PA: Caesars Entertainment, Inc.
  100 W Liberty St Fl 12
  Reno NV 89501
  775 328-0100

(G-10011)
DEALERS SUPPLY NORTH INC (HQ)
Also Called: Dsn
2315 Creekside Pkwy Ste 500 (43137-9313)
PHONE..............................614 274-6285
Kim R Holm, *Pr*
Ed Wiethe, *
▲ **EMP:** 30 **EST:** 2002
SQ FT: 56,000
SALES (est): 14.17MM
SALES (corp-wide): 686.34MM **Privately Held**
Web: mannington.my.site.com
SIC: 5023 Carpets
PA: Mannington Mills Inc.
  75 Mannington Mills Rd
  Salem NJ 08079
  800 356-6787

(G-10012)
MCLANE FOODSERVICE DIST INC
Also Called: McLane Lockbourne
2240 Creekside Parkway (43137-9314)
PHONE..............................614 662-7700
Aaron Alexander, *Brnch Mgr*
EMP: 43
SALES (corp-wide): 364.48B **Publicly Held**
Web: www.mclaneco.com
SIC: 5141 Food brokers
HQ: Mclane Foodservice Distribution, Inc.
  4747 Mclane Pkwy
  Temple TX 76504
  254 771-7500

(G-10013)
ODW LOGISTICS INC
1533 Rohr Rd (43137-9251)
PHONE..............................614 549-5000
EMP: 35
SALES (corp-wide): 529.12MM **Privately Held**
Web: www.odwlogistics.com
SIC: 4225 General warehousing and storage
PA: Odw Logistics, Inc.
  400 W Nationwide Blvd # 200
  Columbus OH 43215
  614 549-5000

(G-10014)
QUAKER SALES & DIST INC
2155 Rohr Rd (43137-9323)
PHONE..............................914 767-7010
EMP: 1304
SALES (corp-wide): 86.39B **Publicly Held**
SIC: 4225 Miniwarehouse, warehousing
HQ: Quaker Sales & Distribution, Inc.
  433 W Van Buren St
  Chicago IL 60607
  312 821-1000

(G-10015)
S P RICHARDS COMPANY
1815 Beggrow St (43137-7578)
PHONE..............................614 497-2270
Dennis Reid, *Genl Mgr*
EMP: 45
SALES (corp-wide): 2.35B **Privately Held**
Web: www.sprichards.com
SIC: 5112 5021 Office supplies, nec; Office furniture, nec
HQ: S. P. Richards Company
  4300 Wildwood Pkwy # 100
  Atlanta GA 30339
  770 436-6881

(G-10016)
STREAMLINE TECHNICAL SVCS LLC
4555 Creekside Pkwy (43137-9287)
PHONE..............................614 441-7448
EMP: 80 **EST:** 2016
SALES (est): 1.53MM **Privately Held**
Web: www.sts-us.net
SIC: 7373 Computer integrated systems design

(G-10017)
WALMART INC
Also Called: Walmart
2525 Rohr Rd Ste A (43137-9296)
PHONE..............................614 409-5500
EMP: 50
SALES (corp-wide): 648.13B **Publicly Held**
Web: corporate.walmart.com
SIC: 4225 General warehousing and storage
PA: Walmart Inc.
  702 Sw 8th St
  Bentonville AR 72716
  479 273-4000

Lodi
Medina County

(G-10018)
CLEVELAND CLINIC FOUNDATION
Also Called: Akron General Lodi Hospital
225 Elyria St (44254-1031)
PHONE..............................330 948-5523
EMP: 49
SALES (corp-wide): 14.48B **Privately Held**
Web: www.clevelandclinic.org
SIC: 8062 General medical and surgical hospitals
PA: The Cleveland Clinic Foundation
  9500 Euclid Ave
  Cleveland OH 44195
  216 636-8335

(G-10019)
LODI COMMUNITY HOSPITAL (HQ)
225 Elyria St (44254-1096)
PHONE..............................330 948-1222
TOLL FREE: 800
Tom Whelan, *Admn*
Barb Fish, *
Cindy Dennison, *
EMP: 80 **EST:** 1920
SQ FT: 30,118
SALES (est): 28.77MM
SALES (corp-wide): 14.48B **Privately Held**
Web: www.lodihospital.org
SIC: 8062 General medical and surgical hospitals
PA: The Cleveland Clinic Foundation
  9500 Euclid Ave
  Cleveland OH 44195
  216 636-8335

(G-10020)
MAPLE MOUNTAIN INDUSTRIES INC
312 Bank St (44254-1006)
PHONE..............................330 948-2510
Aileen Mcdowell, *Prin*
EMP: 33
SIC: 5084 Industrial machinery and equipment
PA: Maple Mountain Industries Inc
  1820 Mulligan Hill Rd
  New Florence PA 15944

Logan
Hocking County

(G-10021)
BAZELL OIL CO INC
14371 State Route 328 (43138-9449)
P.O. Box 2 (43138-0002)
PHONE..............................740 385-5420
Joseph Michael Bazell, *Pr*
Donald D Poling, *
EMP: 35 **EST:** 1972
SQ FT: 7,500
SALES (est): 9.05MM **Privately Held**
Web: www.bazellracefuels.com
SIC: 5172 5983 Fuel oil; Fuel oil dealers

(G-10022)
HOCKING VALLEY INDUSTRIES INC
1369 E Front St (43138-9031)
P.O. Box 64 (43138-0064)
PHONE..............................740 385-2118
Janet Flanagan, *Mgr*
EMP: 47 **EST:** 1971
SQ FT: 12,000
SALES (est): 1.2MM **Privately Held**
Web: www.hockingdd.org
SIC: 8331 Sheltered workshop

(G-10023)
HOCKING VLY CMNTY HOSP MEM FUN (PA)
Also Called: Hocking Valley Community Hosp
601 State Route 664 N (43138-8541)
P.O. Box 966 (43138-0966)
PHONE..............................740 380-8389
Stacey Gabriel, *CEO*
Julie Stuck, *
Leeann Helber, *
Randy Montgomery, *
EMP: 342 **EST:** 1966
SQ FT: 69,000
SALES (est): 40.29MM
SALES (corp-wide): 40.29MM **Privately Held**
Web: www.hvch.org
SIC: 8062 Hospital, affiliated with AMA residency

(G-10024)
HOCKINGTHENSPERRY CMNTY ACTION
1005 C I C Dr (43138-9245)
PHONE..............................740 385-6813
Dick Stevens, *Brnch Mgr*
EMP: 50
SALES (corp-wide): 30.74MM **Privately Held**
Web: www.hapcap.org
SIC: 8322 Social service center
PA: Hocking.Athens.Perry Community Action
  3 Cardaras Dr
  Glouster OH 45732
  740 767-4500

(G-10025)
HOLIDAY INN EXPRESS
Also Called: Holiday Inn
12916 Grey St (43138-9632)
PHONE..............................740 385-7700
Kristin Jones, *Managing Member*
EMP: 33 **EST:** 2003
SALES (est): 269.94K **Privately Held**
Web: www.hiexpress.com
SIC: 7011 Tourist camps, cabins, cottages, and courts

(G-10026)
HOPEWELL HEALTH CENTERS INC
Also Called: Hopewell Health Centers
460 E 2nd St (43138-1492)
PHONE..............................740 385-8468
Kimberly Andrews, *Prin*
EMP: 48
SALES (corp-wide): 66.73MM **Privately Held**
Web: www.hopewellhealth.org
SIC: 8093 Mental health clinic, outpatient
PA: Hopewell Health Centers, Inc.
  1049 Western Ave
  Chillicothe OH 45601
  740 773-1006

(G-10027)
HOPEWELL HEALTH CENTERS INC
541 State Route 664 N Ste C (43138-8541)
P.O. Box 1145 (43138-4145)
PHONE..............................740 385-6594
Tom Odell, *Dir*
EMP: 83
SALES (corp-wide): 66.73MM **Privately Held**
Web: www.hopewellhealth.org
SIC: 8093 Mental health clinic, outpatient
PA: Hopewell Health Centers, Inc.
  1049 Western Ave
  Chillicothe OH 45601
  740 773-1006

(G-10028)
HOPEWELL HEALTH CENTERS INC
1383 W Turner St (43138)
PHONE..............................740 385-2555
Julieta Wine, *Brnch Mgr*
EMP: 35
SALES (corp-wide): 66.73MM **Privately Held**
Web: www.hopewellhealth.org
SIC: 8093 Mental health clinic, outpatient
PA: Hopewell Health Centers, Inc.
  1049 Western Ave
  Chillicothe OH 45601
  740 773-1006

(G-10029)
INTEGRTED SVCS FOR BHVRAL HLTH
33 W 2nd St (43138-1886)
PHONE..............................740 216-4093
EMP: 61
Web: www.isbh.org
SIC: 8322 8399 8331 Individual and family services; Health systems agency; Job training and related services
PA: Integrated Services For Behavioral Health, Inc.
  1950 Mount Saint Marys Dr
  Nelsonville OH 45764

Logan - Hocking County (G-10030)

(G-10030)
KEYNES BROS INC
1 W Front St (43138-1825)
P.O. Box 628 (43138-0628)
PHONE...................740 385-6824
EMP: 65
Web: www.keynesbros.com
SIC: 2041 5191 Flour mills, cereal (except rice); Feed

(G-10031)
KILBARGER CONSTRUCTION INC
Also Called: C & L Supply
450 Gallagher Ave (43138-1893)
P.O. Box 946 (43138-0946)
PHONE...................740 385-6019
Edward Kilbarger, CEO
James E Kilbarger, *
Anthony Kilbarger, *
Ann Kilbarger, *
EMP: 120 EST: 1958
SQ FT: 2,500
SALES (est): 21.74MM Privately Held
Web: www.kilbarger.com
SIC: 1381 Drilling oil and gas wells

(G-10032)
LOGAN HEALTHCARE LEASING LLC
300 Arlington Ave (43138-1708)
PHONE...................216 367-1214
Eli Gunzburg, Mgr
EMP: 99 EST: 2017
SQ FT: 42,100
SALES (est): 1.96MM Privately Held
SIC: 8051 Mental retardation hospital

(G-10033)
LOGAN-HOCKING SCHOOL DISTRICT
Also Called: Maintenance Department
13483 Maysville Williams Rd (43138-8971)
PHONE...................740 385-7844
Keith Brown, Mgr
EMP: 36
SALES (corp-wide): 60.48MM Privately Held
Web: www.loganhocking.school
SIC: 8211 7349 Public elementary school; School custodian, contract basis
PA: Logan-Hocking School District
2019 E Front St
Logan OH 43138
740 385-8517

(G-10034)
MENNEL MILLING COMPANY
Also Called: Mennel Milling Logan
1 W Front St (43138-1825)
PHONE...................740 385-6824
Larry Hawkins, Opers
EMP: 37
SALES (corp-wide): 211.12MM Privately Held
Web: www.mennel.com
SIC: 5191 2041 Feed; Flour mills, cereal (except rice)
PA: The Mennel Milling Company
319 S Vine St
Fostoria OH 44830
419 435-8151

(G-10035)
MNM HOTELS INC
Also Called: Baymont Inn & Suites
12819 State Route 664 S (43138-9533)
PHONE...................740 385-1700
Brock Boyle, Genl Mgr
EMP: 78 EST: 2007
SALES (est): 491.32K Privately Held
Web: www.wyndhamhotels.com
SIC: 7011 Inns

(G-10036)
ROTARY INTERNATIONAL INC
11153 Walnut Dowler Rd (43138-9091)
PHONE...................740 385-8575
Andrew Mcghee, CEO
EMP: 35 EST: 1998
SALES (est): 117.45K Privately Held
Web: www.loganohiorotary.org
SIC: 8699 Charitable organization

London
Madison County

(G-10037)
ARMALY LLC
Also Called: Armaly Brands
110 W 1st St (43140-1484)
PHONE...................740 852-3621
Annmarie Armaly, Treas
▼ EMP: 40 EST: 2010
SALES (est): 13.98MM
SALES (corp-wide): 14.92MM Privately Held
Web: www.armalybrands.com
SIC: 3089 5199 3086 Floor coverings, plastics; Sponges (animal); Plastics foam products
PA: Armaly Sponge Company
1900 Easy St
Commerce Township MI 48390
248 669-2100

(G-10038)
BUCKEYE FORD INC
Also Called: Quick Lane
110 Us Highway 42 Se (43140)
P.O. Box 677 (43140-0677)
PHONE...................740 852-7842
TOLL FREE: 800
James E Hunt, Pr
John Sawyer, *
Timothy A Sheerin, *
EMP: 45 EST: 1986
SQ FT: 30,000
SALES (est): 11.48MM Privately Held
Web: www.buckeyefordlondon.com
SIC: 5511 7538 Automobiles, new and used; General automotive repair shops

(G-10039)
CHAMPAIGN RESIDENTIAL SVCS INC
Also Called: Champaign Residential
117 W High St Ste 104 (43140-1300)
PHONE...................740 852-3850
Barbara Lambert, Ex Dir
EMP: 1016
SALES (corp-wide): 40.28MM Privately Held
Web: www.crsi-oh.com
SIC: 8361 Retarded home
PA: Champaign Residential Services, Inc.
1150 Scioto St Ste 201
Urbana OH 43078
937 653-1320

(G-10040)
COUGHLIN CHEVROLET INC
255 Lafayette St (43140-9071)
P.O. Box 438 (43140-0438)
PHONE...................740 852-1122
TOLL FREE: 800
Todd Hardy, Mgr
EMP: 40
SALES (corp-wide): 75.69MM Privately Held
Web: www.coughlinpataskala.com
SIC: 5511 7532 5521 5083 Automobiles, new and used; Body shop, automotive; Automobiles, used cars only; Livestock equipment
PA: Coughlin Chevrolet, Inc.
9000 Broad St Sw
Pataskala OH 43062
740 964-9191

(G-10041)
DAYSTAR TRANSPORTATION LLC
271 W High St (43140-1703)
PHONE...................740 852-9202
Ron Grant, Genl Mgr
Keith Howard, Mgr
◆ EMP: 31 EST: 2000
SQ FT: 2,000
SALES (est): 3.86MM Privately Held
SIC: 4212 Delivery service, vehicular

(G-10042)
HUNTINGTON NATIONAL BANK
2 E High St (43140-1209)
PHONE...................740 852-1234
Joyce Baurle, Mgr
EMP: 31
SALES (corp-wide): 10.84B Publicly Held
Web: www.huntington.com
SIC: 6029 Commercial banks, nec
HQ: The Huntington National Bank
41 S High St
Columbus OH 43215
614 480-4293

(G-10043)
HUNTINGTON NATIONAL BANK
Also Called: Home Mortgage
61 S Main St (43140-1268)
PHONE...................740 852-1234
Steve Lelonek, Mgr
EMP: 31
SALES (corp-wide): 10.84B Publicly Held
Web: www.huntington.com
SIC: 6029 6162 6021 Commercial banks, nec; Mortgage bankers; National commercial banks
HQ: The Huntington National Bank
41 S High St
Columbus OH 43215
614 480-4293

(G-10044)
JD EQUIPMENT INC
Also Called: John Deere Authorized Dealer
1660 Us Highway 42 Ne (43140-9337)
PHONE...................614 879-6620
TOLL FREE: 800
◆ EMP: 200
Web: www.agprocompanies.com
SIC: 5999 5083 Farm equipment and supplies; Agricultural machinery and equipment

(G-10045)
LONDON HEALTH & REHAB CTR LLC
218 Elm St (43140-2130)
PHONE...................740 852-3100
George S Repchick, Pr
William Weisberg, *
EMP: 151 EST: 2014
SALES (est): 4.8MM
SALES (corp-wide): 655.44MM Privately Held
Web: www.saberhealth.com
SIC: 8051 Convalescent home with continuous nursing care
PA: Saber Healthcare Group, L.L.C.
23700 Commerce Park
Beachwood OH 44122
216 292-5706

(G-10046)
MADISON COUNTY COMMUNITY HOSPITAL (PA)
Also Called: Madison County Hospital
210 N Main St (43140-1115)
PHONE...................740 845-7000
EMP: 301 EST: 1962
SALES (est): 53.48MM
SALES (corp-wide): 53.48MM Privately Held
Web: www.madison-health.com
SIC: 8062 General medical and surgical hospitals

(G-10047)
MADISON FAMILY HEALTH CORP
Also Called: MADISON COUNTY HOSPITAL
210 N Main St (43140-1115)
PHONE...................740 845-7000
Dana Engle, CEO
EMP: 39 EST: 1997
SALES (est): 13.58MM
SALES (corp-wide): 53.48MM Privately Held
Web: www.madison-health.com
SIC: 8062 General medical and surgical hospitals
PA: Madison County Community Hospital
210 N Main St
London OH 43140
740 845-7000

(G-10048)
NATIONWIDE INSRNCE SPNNING INS
Also Called: Nationwide
11 S Union St (43140-1215)
PHONE...................408 520-6420
EMP: 37 EST: 2020
SALES (est): 204.25K Privately Held
Web: www.nationwide.com
SIC: 6411 Insurance agents, nec

(G-10049)
PETERS MAIN STREET PHOTOGRAPHY (PA)
Also Called: Main Street Photography
314 N Main St (43140-9339)
P.O. Box 587 (43140-0587)
PHONE...................740 852-2731
Larry Peters, Pr
EMP: 28 EST: 1990
SQ FT: 4,500
SALES (est): 2.48MM
SALES (corp-wide): 2.48MM Privately Held
Web: www.petersphotography.com
SIC: 7221 Photographer, still or video

(G-10050)
SABER HEALTHCARE GROUP LLC
Also Called: Arbors At London
218 Elm St (43140-2130)
PHONE...................740 852-3100
Pam Degroodt, Brnch Mgr
EMP: 63
SALES (corp-wide): 655.44MM Privately Held
Web: www.saberhealth.com
SIC: 8051 Convalescent home with continuous nursing care
PA: Saber Healthcare Group, L.L.C.
23700 Commerce Park
Beachwood OH 44122
216 292-5706

(G-10051)
STAPLES CONTRACT & COML LLC
500 E High St (43140-9303)
PHONE...................740 845-5600
Ross Neaffer, Mgr

GEOGRAPHIC SECTION
Lorain - Lorain County (G-10071)

EMP: 40
Web: www.staplesadvantage.com
SIC: 5943 5112 Stationery stores; Stationery and office supplies
HQ: Staples Contract & Commercial Llc
500 Staples Dr
Framingham MA 01702
508 253-5000

Lorain
Lorain County

(G-10052)
ABSOLUTE MACHINE TOOLS INC (PA)
Also Called: Absolute Prfmce For Abslute VI
7420 Industrial Parkway Dr (44053-2064)
PHONE..................440 960-6911
Steve Ortner, *Pr*
Hayden Wellman, *VP*
▲ **EMP:** 34 **EST:** 1988
SQ FT: 18,000
SALES (est): 22.61MM **Privately Held**
Web: www.absolutemachine.com
SIC: 5084 Machine tools and accessories

(G-10053)
ANCHOR LODGE LTD PARTNERSHIP
3756 W Erie Ave (44053-1292)
PHONE..................440 244-2019
Nicole Sprenger, *Prin*
Michael Sprenger, *Prin*
Kenneth Malanowski, *Prin*
EMP: 80 **EST:** 1995
SALES (est): 1.19MM **Privately Held**
SIC: 6513 Apartment building operators

(G-10054)
ANCHOR LODGE NURSING HOME INC
Also Called: SPRENGER HEALTH CARE SYSTEMS
3756 W Erie Ave Ofc (44053-1298)
PHONE..................440 244-2019
Scott Springer, *Pr*
Donel L Springer, *
EMP: 46 **EST:** 1962
SQ FT: 20,000
SALES (est): 9.36MM
SALES (corp-wide): 43.05MM **Privately Held**
Web: www.sprengerhealthcare.com
SIC: 8052 8051 Intermediate care facilities; Skilled nursing care facilities
PA: Bluesky Healthcare Inc.
3885 Oberlin Ave
Lorain OH 44053
440 989-5200

(G-10055)
APPLEWOOD CENTERS INC
1865 N Ridge Rd E Ste A (44055-3359)
PHONE..................440 324-1300
Mary Munn, *Brnch Mgr*
EMP: 67
SALES (corp-wide): 19.56MM **Privately Held**
Web: www.applewoodcenters.org
SIC: 8093 Mental health clinic, outpatient
PA: Applewood Centers, Inc.
10427 Detroit Ave
Cleveland OH 44102
216 696-6815

(G-10056)
AUTUMN AEGIS INC
Also Called: Assisted Living Apartments
1130 Tower Blvd Ste A (44052-5200)
PHONE..................440 282-6768
Anthony Sprenger, *Pr*
EMP: 404 **EST:** 1948
SALES (est): 6.77MM **Privately Held**
Web: www.sprengerhealthcare.com
SIC: 8051 Convalescent home with continuous nursing care
PA: Sprenger Enterprises, Inc.
3905 Oberlin Ave Ste 1
Lorain OH 44053

(G-10057)
AVIVA METALS INC
5311 W River Rd (44055-3735)
PHONE..................440 277-1226
EMP: 55
Web: www.avivametals.com
SIC: 5051 Steel
HQ: Aviva Metals, Inc.
2929 W 12th St
Houston TX 77008
713 869-9600

(G-10058)
BAY MECHANICAL & ELEC CORP
2221 W Park Dr (44053-1158)
PHONE..................440 282-6816
Terry Burns, *Ch Bd*
Robin Newberry, *
Mark Huston, *
EMP: 51 **EST:** 1948
SQ FT: 22,000
SALES (est): 14.01MM **Privately Held**
Web: www.baymec.com
SIC: 1711 1731 7389 Plumbing contractors; Electrical work; Crane and aerial lift service

(G-10059)
BEAVER PARK MARINA INC
6101 W Erie Ave (44053-1698)
PHONE..................440 282-6308
William Schaeffer, *Pr*
Gayle Schaeffer, *VP*
David Herzer, *Sec*
EMP: 37 **EST:** 1945
SQ FT: 9,300
SALES (est): 1.07MM **Privately Held**
Web: www.beaverpark.com
SIC: 5551 4493 Motor boat dealers; Marinas

(G-10060)
BERKEBILE RUSSELL & ASSOCIATES
1720 Cooper Foster Park Rd W Ste B (44053-4200)
PHONE..................440 989-4480
Lawrence G Thorley Md, *Pr*
Stephen Ticich Md, *Sec*
EMP: 33
SQ FT: 4,000
SALES (est): 2.3MM **Privately Held**
Web: www.rbarad.com
SIC: 8071 X-ray laboratory, including dental

(G-10061)
BLUESKY HEALTHCARE INC (PA)
Also Called: Sprenger Health Care Systems
3885 Oberlin Ave (44053-2813)
PHONE..................440 989-5200
Nicole Sprenger, *CEO*
EMP: 27 **EST:** 2001
SALES (est): 43.05MM
SALES (corp-wide): 43.05MM **Privately Held**
Web: www.sprengerhealthcare.com
SIC: 8051 Skilled nursing care facilities

(G-10062)
CENTURY TEL OF ODON INC (HQ)
Also Called: Centurylink
203 W 9th St (44052-1906)
PHONE..................440 244-8544
Glen Post, *Ch Bd*
Karen Pucket, *
EMP: 250 **EST:** 1984
SALES (est): 68.22MM
SALES (corp-wide): 14.56MM **Publicly Held**
Web: www.verizon.com
SIC: 4813 Telephone communication, except radio
PA: Lumen Technologies, Inc.
100 Centurylink Dr
Monroe LA 71203
318 388-9000

(G-10063)
CHURCH ON NORTH COAST (PA)
4125 Leavitt Rd (44053-2300)
PHONE..................440 960-1100
Pastor Louis Kayatin, *Prin*
Sharon Maszton, *Treas*
EMP: 33 **EST:** 1975
SQ FT: 30,000
SALES (est): 2.26MM
SALES (corp-wide): 2.26MM **Privately Held**
Web: www.cnclove.org
SIC: 8661 8211 8351 Non-denominational church; Private elementary school; Preschool center

(G-10064)
CITY OF LORAIN
Water Div
1106 W 1st St (44052-1434)
PHONE..................440 204-2500
Robert De Santis, *Dir*
EMP: 53
SALES (corp-wide): 66.11MM **Privately Held**
Web: www.cityoflorain.org
SIC: 4941 4952 4939 Water supply; Sewerage systems; Combination utilities, nec
PA: Lorain, City Of (Inc)
200 W Erie Ave Ste 714
Lorain OH 44052
440 204-2090

(G-10065)
CLEVELAND CLINIC FOUNDATION
Also Called: Lorain Family Hlth & RES Ctrs
5700 Cooper Foster Park Rd W Ste A (44053-4152)
PHONE..................440 988-5651
Floyd D Loop, *Brnch Mgr*
EMP: 49
SALES (corp-wide): 14.48B **Privately Held**
Web: my.clevelandclinic.org
SIC: 8093 8062 Specialty outpatient clinics, nec; General medical and surgical hospitals
PA: The Cleveland Clinic Foundation
9500 Euclid Ave
Cleveland OH 44195
216 636-8335

(G-10066)
CLEVELAND CLINIC FOUNDATION
5172 Leavitt Rd Ste B (44053-2385)
PHONE..................440 282-7420
EMP: 33
SALES (corp-wide): 14.48B **Privately Held**
Web: www.clevelandclinic.org
SIC: 8062 General medical and surgical hospitals
PA: The Cleveland Clinic Foundation
9500 Euclid Ave
Cleveland OH 44195
216 636-8335

(G-10067)
CMS & CO MANAGEMENT SVCS INC
Also Called: Sprenger Retirement Centers
3905 Oberlin Ave (44053-2853)
PHONE..................440 989-5200
Nita Anderson, *Pr*
EMP: 76 **EST:** 2001
SALES (est): 31.73MM
SALES (corp-wide): 43.05MM **Privately Held**
Web: www.sprengerretirementcenters.com
SIC: 8051 Skilled nursing care facilities
PA: Bluesky Healthcare Inc.
3885 Oberlin Ave
Lorain OH 44053
440 989-5200

(G-10068)
COMMUNITY HLTH PRTNERS RGNAL F (HQ)
3700 Kolbe Rd (44053-1611)
PHONE..................440 960-4000
Brian Lockwood, *Pr*
Heather Nickum, *
Everett Taylor, *
EMP: 1520 **EST:** 1985
SALES (est): 61.03MM
SALES (corp-wide): 6.92B **Privately Held**
SIC: 8062 General medical and surgical hospitals
PA: Bon Secours Mercy Health, Inc.
1701 Mercy Health Pl
Cincinnati OH 45237
513 956-3729

(G-10069)
COUNTY OF LORAIN
Also Called: Board of Mental Health
1173 N Ridge Rd E Ste 101 (44055-3032)
PHONE..................440 233-2020
EMP: 29
SALES (corp-wide): 253.29MM **Privately Held**
Web: www.loraincounty.us
SIC: 9199 8322 General government administration, County government; General counseling services
PA: County Of Lorain
226 Middle Ave
Elyria OH 44035
440 329-5201

(G-10070)
CSX TRANSPORTATION INC
Also Called: CSX
311 Broadway Rear (44052-1631)
PHONE..................440 245-3930
Lucius Clanhard, *Brnch Mgr*
EMP: 150
SALES (corp-wide): 14.66B **Publicly Held**
Web: www.csx.com
SIC: 4011 Railroads, line-haul operating
HQ: Csx Transportation, Inc.
500 Water St #15
Jacksonville FL 32202
904 359-3100

(G-10071)
ECHOING HILLS VILLAGE INC
Also Called: Echoing Lake Residential Home
3295 Leavitt Rd (44053-2203)
PHONE..................440 989-1400
EMP: 71
SALES (corp-wide): 39.8MM **Privately Held**
Web: www.ehvi.org
SIC: 7032 8052 8051 Sporting and recreational camps; Intermediate care facilities; Skilled nursing care facilities
PA: Echoing Hills Village, Inc.

Lorain - Lorain County (G-10072) GEOGRAPHIC SECTION

36272 County Road 79
Warsaw OH 43844
740 327-2311

(G-10072)
ELECTRICAL CORP AMERICA INC
3807 W Erie Ave (44053-1239)
PHONE..................................440 245-3007
Mark Benco, *Mgr*
EMP: 168
SALES (corp-wide): 53.52MM **Privately Held**
Web: www.ecahq.com
SIC: 1731 General electrical contractor
PA: Electrical Corporation Of America, Inc.
7320 Arlington Ave
Raytown MO 64133
816 737-3206

(G-10073)
EXOCHEM CORPORATION
2421 E 28th St (44055-2198)
PHONE..................................440 277-1246
Randall Miraldi, *Pr*
Lois Miraldi, *
Kathleen Roark, *
▲ **EMP:** 54 **EST:** 1968
SQ FT: 21,000
Web: www.exochem.com
SIC: 6719 Investment holding companies, except banks

(G-10074)
FABRIZI TRUCKING & PAV CO INC
Also Called: Fabrizi Trucking & Paving Co
2140 E 28th St (44055-1933)
PHONE..................................440 277-0127
EMP: 70
SALES (corp-wide): 23.06MM **Privately Held**
Web: www.fabrizi-inc.com
SIC: 4213 1611 1522 Trucking, except local; Surfacing and paving; Residential construction, nec
PA: Fabrizi Trucking & Paving Co., Inc.
20389 1st Ave
Cleveland OH 44130
440 973-4929

(G-10075)
FIRST FDRAL SAV LN ASSN LORAIN (PA)
3721 Oberlin Ave (44053-2761)
PHONE..................................440 282-6188
Michael Brosky, *Pr*
John Malanski, *Pr*
EMP: 75 **EST:** 1921
SQ FT: 28,000
SALES (est): 14.41MM
SALES (corp-wide): 14.41MM **Privately Held**
Web: www.fflorain.bank
SIC: 6035 Federal savings and loan associations

(G-10076)
GERGELYS MINT KING SUPS SVC IN
947 Broadway Ste 201 (44052-1988)
PHONE..................................440 244-4446
John Gergely, *Pr*
Michael Gergely, *
Maggie Gergely, *
Lori Gergely, *
EMP: 49 **EST:** 1970
SQ FT: 12,000
SALES (est): 3.95MM **Privately Held**
Web: www.gergelys.net
SIC: 7349 5169 5113 Cleaning service, industrial or commercial; Specialty cleaning and sanitation preparations; Industrial and personal service paper

(G-10077)
HORIZON EDUCATION CENTERS
Also Called: Horizon Activities Center
4911 Grove Ave (44055-3615)
PHONE..................................440 277-5437
EMP: 27
SALES (corp-wide): 19.97MM **Privately Held**
Web: www.horizoneducationcenters.org
SIC: 8322 8351 Geriatric social service; Child day care services
PA: Horizon Education Centers
25300 Lorain Rd Fl 2
North Olmsted OH 44070
440 779-1930

(G-10078)
JIFFY PRODUCTS AMERICA INC
5401 Baumhart Rd Ste B (44053-2078)
PHONE..................................440 282-2818
Aarstein Knutson, *Ch Bd*
Ornulf Sjursen, *Ch Bd*
Daniel Schrodt, *Pr*
Stanton Kessler, *Sec*
◆ **EMP:** 67 **EST:** 1985
SQ FT: 12,000
SALES (est): 41.9MM **Privately Held**
Web: www.jiffygroup.com
SIC: 5191 Farm supplies
HQ: Jiffy International As
Skippergata 2a
Kristiansand S

(G-10079)
KOHLMYER SPORTING GOODS INC
Also Called: Kohlmyer Sports
5000 Grove Ave (44055-3659)
PHONE..................................440 277-8296
Mike Molnar, *Pr*
Richard Boesger, *
Dale Hoffman, *
▲ **EMP:** 29 **EST:** 1971
SQ FT: 13,000
SALES (est): 620.94K **Privately Held**
SIC: 5941 5091 Sporting goods and bicycle shops; Sporting and recreation goods

(G-10080)
KOLCZUN KLCZUN ORTHPD ASSOC IN
Also Called: Cleveland Clinic
5800 Cooper Foster Park Rd W (44053-4131)
PHONE..................................440 985-3113
Michael Kolczun Junior Md, *Pr*
Donald Blanford, *
EMP: 959 **EST:** 1941
SQ FT: 11,000
SALES (est): 4.64MM
SALES (corp-wide): 14.48B **Privately Held**
Web: my.clevelandclinic.org
SIC: 8011 Orthopedic physician
PA: The Cleveland Clinic Foundation
9500 Euclid Ave
Cleveland OH 44195
216 636-8335

(G-10081)
KUNO CREATIVE GROUP INC
Also Called: Kuno Creative
3248 W Erie Ave (44053-1228)
PHONE..................................440 261-5002
Christopher Knipper, *CEO*
Shannon Barnes, *OF ENTERPRISE ACCOUNTS*
Jarrick Cooper, *OF WEB Operations*
Shaun Kanary, *OF GROWTH STRATEGIES*
Vanessa Knipper, *OF CLIENT SUCCESS*
EMP: 43 **EST:** 2000
SALES (est): 5.13MM **Privately Held**
Web: www.kunocreative.com

SIC: 8742 Marketing consulting services

(G-10082)
LAKELAND GLASS CO (PA)
4994 Grove Ave (44055-3614)
PHONE..................................440 277-4527
Scott Kosman, *Pr*
EMP: 29 **EST:** 1984
SQ FT: 40,000
SALES (est): 2.38MM
SALES (corp-wide): 2.38MM **Privately Held**
Web: www.lakelandglass.com
SIC: 1793 Glass and glazing work

(G-10083)
LNB BANCORP INC
457 Broadway (44052-1739)
PHONE..................................440 244-6000
EMP: 267
Web: www.4lnb.com
SIC: 6022 State commercial banks

(G-10084)
LORAIN CNTY ALCHOL DRG ABUSE S
Also Called: Lcada
1882 E 32nd St (44055-1812)
PHONE..................................440 323-6122
Vesta Warner, *Mgr*
EMP: 61
SQ FT: 1,384
SALES (corp-wide): 10.49MM **Privately Held**
Web: www.thelcadaway.org
SIC: 8093 Substance abuse clinics (outpatient)
PA: Lorain County Alcohol And Drug Abuse Services, Inc.
2115 W Park Dr
Lorain OH 44053
440 989-4900

(G-10085)
LORAIN CNTY CMNTY ACTION AGCY
Also Called: Lccaa-Hopkins Locke-Head Start
1050 Reid Ave (44052-1962)
PHONE..................................440 246-0480
Shauna Matelski, *Prin*
EMP: 106
SALES (corp-wide): 16.55MM **Privately Held**
Web: www.lccaa.net
SIC: 8351 Head Start center, except in conjunction with school
PA: Lorain County Community Action Agency, Inc.
936 Broadway
Lorain OH 44052
440 245-2009

(G-10086)
LORAIN COUNTY ALCOHOL AND DRUG
Also Called: LORAIN COUNTY ALCOHOL AND DRUG
305 W 20th St (44052-3726)
PHONE..................................440 246-0109
Sami Sfeir, *Owner*
EMP: 60
SALES (corp-wide): 9.94MM **Privately Held**
Web: www.thelcadaway.org
SIC: 8093 Substance abuse clinics (outpatient)
PA: Lorain County Alcohol And Drug Abuse Services, Inc.
2115 W Park Dr
Lorain OH 44053
440 989-4900

(G-10087)
LORAIN MANOR INC
Also Called: Lorain Manor Nursing Home
1882 E 32nd St (44055-1812)
PHONE..................................440 277-8173
Anthony Sprenger, *Pr*
Donel Sprenger, *
EMP: 70 **EST:** 1949
SQ FT: 10,000
SALES (est): 3.81MM **Privately Held**
SIC: 8051 8052 Skilled nursing care facilities; Intermediate care facilities
PA: Sprenger Enterprises, Inc.
3905 Oberlin Ave Ste 1
Lorain OH 44053

(G-10088)
LORAIN NATIONAL BANK (HQ)
457 Broadway (44052-1769)
PHONE..................................440 244-6000
James R Herrick, *Ch Bd*
James F Kidd, *V Ch Bd*
Dan Klimas, *CEO*
Kevin W Nelson, *Ex VP*
Thomas P Ryan, *Ex VP*
EMP: 125 **EST:** 1961
SQ FT: 50,000
SALES (est): 46.35MM **Publicly Held**
Web: www.morningjournal.com
SIC: 6021 National trust companies with deposits, commercial
PA: Northwest Bancshares, Inc.
3 Easton Oval Ste 500
Columbus OH 43219

(G-10089)
LORAIN NATIONAL BANK
200 W 6th St (44052-1704)
PHONE..................................440 244-7242
Chuck D'angeles, *Mgr*
EMP: 57
Web: www.morningjournal.com
SIC: 6021 National trust companies with deposits, commercial
HQ: The Lorain National Bank
457 Broadway
Lorain OH 44052
440 244-6000

(G-10090)
LOWES HOME CENTERS LLC
Also Called: Lowe's
7500 Oak Point Rd (44053-4149)
PHONE..................................440 985-5700
Dave Summers, *Brnch Mgr*
EMP: 138
SALES (corp-wide): 86.38B **Publicly Held**
Web: www.lowes.com
SIC: 5211 5031 5722 5064 Home centers; Building materials, exterior; Household appliance stores; Electrical appliances, television and radio
HQ: Lowe's Home Centers, Llc
1000 Lowes Blvd
Mooresville NC 28117
336 658-4000

(G-10091)
LUCAS PLUMBING & HEATING INC
2125 W Park Dr (44053-1195)
PHONE..................................440 282-4567
Frank J Lucas, *Pr*
Bruce Mc Cartney, *
EMP: 50 **EST:** 1958
SQ FT: 9,800
SALES (est): 5.93MM **Privately Held**
Web: www.lucasplumbing.com
SIC: 1711 Plumbing contractors

GEOGRAPHIC SECTION

Louisville - Stark County (G-10112)

(G-10092)
MERCY HLTH - RGNAL MED CTR LLC
3700 Kolbe Rd (44053-1611)
PHONE.....................440 960-4000
EMP: 2200 **EST:** 2010
SALES (est): 101.44MM
SALES (corp-wide): 6.92B **Privately Held**
Web: www.mercy.com
SIC: 8011 Medical centers
PA: Bon Secours Mercy Health, Inc.
 1701 Mercy Health Pl
 Cincinnati OH 45237
 513 956-3729

(G-10093)
MONARCH DENTAL CORP
Also Called: Bright Now Dental
4785 Leavitt Rd (44053-2136)
PHONE.....................440 282-6677
Edwin Reyes D.d.s., *Mgr*
EMP: 29
SALES (corp-wide): 303.67MM **Privately Held**
Web: www.brightnow.com
SIC: 8021 Dental clinic
HQ: Monarch Dental Corp
 7989 Belt Line Rd Ste 90
 Dallas TX 75248

(G-10094)
NATIONAL BRONZE MTLS OHIO INC
Also Called: Aviva Metals
5311 W River Rd (44055-3735)
PHONE.....................440 277-1226
Michael Greathead, *Pr*
Norman M Lazarus, *
Jill Conyer, *
Phil Meehan, *Sr VP*
▲ **EMP:** 27 **EST:** 1997
SALES (est): 11.02MM **Privately Held**
Web: www.avivametals.com
SIC: 3366 3341 5051 Copper foundries; Secondary nonferrous metals; Copper
PA: Metchem Anstalt
 C/O Feger Treuunternehmen Reg.
 Vaduz

(G-10095)
NEW LIFE HOSPICE INC
3500 Kolbe Rd (44053-1632)
PHONE.....................440 934-1458
Jon Hanson, *Dir*
EMP: 115 **EST:** 1993
SQ FT: 21,000
SALES (est): 8.58MM
SALES (corp-wide): 6.92B **Privately Held**
SIC: 8082 8051 Home health care services; Skilled nursing care facilities
HQ: Community Health Partners Regional Foundation
 3500 Kolbe Rd
 Lorain OH 44053
 440 960-4000

(G-10096)
NORCARE ENTERPRISES INC (PA)
Also Called: NORTH CENTER, THE
6140 S Broadway (44053)
PHONE.....................440 233-7232
Amy Denger, *CEO*
Bernadek Stchick, *
EMP: 250 **EST:** 1948
SQ FT: 55,000
SALES (est): 823.51K
SALES (corp-wide): 823.51K **Privately Held**
Web: www.nordcenter.org
SIC: 8093 Mental health clinic, outpatient

(G-10097)
NORD CENTER
6140 S Broadway (44053-3891)
PHONE.....................440 233-7232
EMP: 32 **EST:** 1960
SALES (est): 19.42MM **Privately Held**
Web: www.nordcenter.org
SIC: 8093 Mental health clinic, outpatient

(G-10098)
NORD CENTER ASSOCIATES INC (HQ)
Also Called: NORTH CENTER, THE
6140 S Broadway (44053)
PHONE.....................440 233-7232
Amy Denger, *CEO*
▲ **EMP:** 185 **EST:** 1947
SQ FT: 46,371
SALES (est): 17.86MM
SALES (corp-wide): 823.51K **Privately Held**
Web: www.nordcenter.org
SIC: 8093 Mental health clinic, outpatient
PA: Norcare Enterprises, Inc.
 6140 S Broadway
 Lorain OH 44053
 440 233-7232

(G-10099)
R & J TRUCKING INC
5250 Baumhart Rd (44053-2046)
PHONE.....................440 960-1508
EMP: 34
Web: www.americanbulkcommodities.com
SIC: 4212 Dump truck haulage
HQ: R & J Trucking, Inc.
 8063 Southern Blvd
 Youngstown OH 44512
 800 262-9365

(G-10100)
RDF LOGISTICS INC
7425 Industrial Parkway Dr (44053-2064)
PHONE.....................440 282-9060
Rosario Boscarello, *Pr*
Dino Boscarello, *
▲ **EMP:** 150 **EST:** 2001
SQ FT: 110,000
SALES (est): 21.82MM **Privately Held**
Web: www.rdflogistics.com
SIC: 4213 Trucking, except local

(G-10101)
RDF TRUCKING CORPORATION
Also Called: RDF Logistics
7425 Industrial Parkway Dr (44053-2064)
PHONE.....................440 282-9060
Rosario Boscarello, *Pr*
Dino Boscarello, *
EMP: 70 **EST:** 1984
SALES (est): 5.43MM **Privately Held**
Web: www.rdflogistics.com
SIC: 4213 Trucking, except local

(G-10102)
SPRENGER ENTERPRISES INC (PA)
3905 Oberlin Ave Ste 1 (44053-2853)
P.O. Box 88126 (60188-0126)
PHONE.....................630 529-0700
Kenneth Malanowski, *Pr*
Nicole Sprenger, *
Mark A Sprenger, *
Chris Mallett, *
Sandra Kaiser, *
EMP: 100 **EST:** 1989
SALES (est): 48.07MM **Privately Held**
SIC: 8741 Nursing and personal care facility management

(G-10103)
TERMINAL READY-MIX INC
524 Colorado Ave (44052-2198)
PHONE.....................440 288-0181
Theresa Pelton, *Pr*
John Falbo, *
Diane Gale, *
Pete Falbo, *
▲ **EMP:** 45 **EST:** 1954
SQ FT: 1,000
SALES (est): 9.12MM **Privately Held**
Web: www.terminalreadymix.com
SIC: 3273 1611 Ready-mixed concrete; Highway and street paving contractor

(G-10104)
TRADEMARK GLOBAL LLC (HQ)
Also Called: Trademark Games
7951 W Erie Ave (44053)
PHONE.....................440 960-6200
John Snowden, *CEO*
Jim Sustar, *
Jason Dietz, *
Abdul Khan, *CIO*
▲ **EMP:** 39 **EST:** 1999
SQ FT: 300,000
SALES (est): 54.09MM
SALES (corp-wide): 54.09MM **Privately Held**
Web: www.trademarkglobal.com
SIC: 5199 5961 General merchandise, non-durable; Electronic shopping
PA: Trademark Games Holdings, Llc
 7951 W Erie Ave
 Lorain OH 44053
 440 960-6200

(G-10105)
UNITED STATES STEEL CORP
Lorain Pipe Mill
2199 E 28th St (44055-1932)
PHONE.....................440 240-2500
Sarah Casalla, *Mgr*
EMP: 550
SALES (corp-wide): 21.07B **Publicly Held**
Web: www.ussteel.com
SIC: 5051 Steel
PA: United States Steel Corp
 600 Grant St
 Pittsburgh PA 15219
 412 433-1121

(G-10106)
UNITEDHEALTHCARE INSURANCE CO
Also Called: United Healthcare
2022 W 29th St (44052-4206)
PHONE.....................440 282-1357
EMP: 1437
SALES (corp-wide): 371.62B **Publicly Held**
Web: www.uhc.com
SIC: 6324 Health Maintenance Organization (HMO), insurance only
HQ: Unitedhealthcare Insurance Company
 185 Asylum St
 Hartford CT 06103

(G-10107)
VERTIV ENERGY SYSTEMS INC
Also Called: Vertiv
1510 Kansas Ave (44052-3364)
PHONE.....................440 288-1122
◆ **EMP:** 800
SIC: 3661 3644 7629 Telephone and telegraph apparatus; Noncurrent-carrying wiring devices; Telecommunication equipment repair (except telephones)

Loudonville
Ashland County

(G-10108)
COLONIAL MNOR HLTH CARE CTR IN
747 S Mount Vernon Ave (44842-1416)
PHONE.....................419 994-4191
Jack Snowbarger, *Pr*
Linda Snowbarger, *
EMP: 46 **EST:** 1975
SQ FT: 32,000
SALES (est): 8.54MM **Privately Held**
SIC: 8051 Convalescent home with continuous nursing care

(G-10109)
H & H CUSTOM HOMES LLC
16573 State Route 3 (44842-9735)
P.O. Box 409 (44842-0409)
PHONE.....................419 994-4070
Eddie Troyer, *
EMP: 45 **EST:** 2004
SQ FT: 2,000
SALES (est): 2.54MM **Privately Held**
Web: www.hhcustomhomes.com
SIC: 1521 New construction, single-family houses

(G-10110)
R D THOMPSON PAPER PDTS CO INC
1 Madison St (44842-9786)
P.O. Box 88 (44842-0088)
PHONE.....................419 994-3614
Thomas Thompson, *Pr*
EMP: 35 **EST:** 1953
SQ FT: 25,000
SALES (est): 4.81MM **Privately Held**
Web: www.rdthompsonpaper.com
SIC: 5199 Packaging materials

Louisville
Stark County

(G-10111)
ALLIANCE CRANE & RIGGING INC
Also Called: Dirtworks Drainage
2321 Energy Dr (44641-9189)
P.O. Box 338 (44201-0338)
PHONE.....................330 823-8823
Kurt Ryan Klingelhofer, *CEO*
Kurt Ryan Klingelhofer, *Pr*
Charles Klingelhofer, *Operating Officer*
EMP: 39 **EST:** 2007
SALES (est): 4.31MM **Privately Held**
Web: www.dwdrainage.com
SIC: 1794 Excavation and grading, building construction

(G-10112)
ALTERCARE LSVLLE CTR FOR RHBLT
7187 Saint Francis St (44641-9050)
PHONE.....................330 875-4224
Gerald Schroer, *Pr*
Gary Dubin, *
Glenn Wickes, *
EMP: 43 **EST:** 1960
SQ FT: 12,000
SALES (est): 5.84MM **Privately Held**
Web: louisville.altercareonline.com
SIC: 8051 Convalescent home with continuous nursing care

Louisville - Stark County (G-10113)

(G-10113)
AULTMAN HEALTH FOUNDATION
1925 Williamsburg Way Ne (44641-8781)
PHONE.................................330 875-6050
EMP: 243
SALES (corp-wide): 77.49MM **Privately Held**
Web: www.aultman.org
SIC: **8062** General medical and surgical hospitals
PA: Aultman Health Foundation
2600 6th St Sw
Canton OH 44710
330 452-9911

(G-10114)
CITY OF LOUISVILLE (PA)
215 S Mill St (44641-1665)
PHONE.................................330 875-3321
Cynthia Kerchner, *Mayor*
Thomas Ault, *
EMP: 35 EST: 1834
SQ FT: 50,000
Web: www.louisvilleohio.gov
SIC: **9111** 8611 City and town managers' office; Business associations

(G-10115)
COON CAULKING & SEALANTS INC
Also Called: Coon Caulking & Restoration
7349 Ravenna Ave (44641-9788)
P.O. Box 259 (44641-0259)
PHONE.................................330 875-2100
Stephen Coon, *Pr*
Joseph Kreinbrink, *
Jennifer Coon, *
Carolyn M Buckridge, *
EMP: 60 EST: 1983
SQ FT: 50,000
SALES (est): 10.54MM **Privately Held**
Web: www.coonrestoration.com
SIC: **1799** Caulking (construction)

(G-10116)
ESLICH WRECKING COMPANY
3525 Broadway Ave (44641-8902)
PHONE.................................330 488-8300
John Eslich, *Pr*
Richard Eslich, *
Elizabeth Eslich, *
EMP: 50 EST: 1964
SQ FT: 30,000
SALES (est): 5.28MM **Privately Held**
Web: www.eslichwrecking.com
SIC: **1795** 1794 Demolition, buildings and other structures; Excavation work

(G-10117)
OAK HILLS MANOR LLC
4466 Lynnhaven Ave (44641-9513)
PHONE.................................330 875-5060
Connie Brandt, *Prin*
EMP: 28 EST: 2008
SALES (est): 4.81MM **Privately Held**
SIC: **8361** Geriatric residential care

(G-10118)
OAKHILL MANOR CARE CENTER
4466 Lynnhaven Ave (44641-9513)
PHONE.................................330 875-5060
Ana Schaefer, *Pr*
EMP: 49 EST: 1981
SALES (est): 2.15MM **Privately Held**
SIC: **8051** Skilled nursing care facilities

(G-10119)
PERFORMANCE TECHNOLOGIES LLC
3690 Tulane Ave (44641-7960)
PHONE.................................330 875-1216
Andy Connolly, *Brnch Mgr*
EMP: 52
SALES (corp-wide): 4.15B **Publicly Held**
Web: www.patenergy.com
SIC: **1389** Pumping of oil and gas wells
HQ: Performance Technologies Llc
3715 S Radio Rd
El Reno OK 73036

(G-10120)
PROGRESSIVE GREEN MEADOWS LLC
Also Called: Green Madows Hlth Wellness Ctr
7770 Columbus Rd Ne (44641-9773)
PHONE.................................330 875-1456
Julie Esack, *Managing Member*
EMP: 71 EST: 2000
SALES (est): 8.91MM **Privately Held**
Web: www.greenmeadowscarecenter.com
SIC: **8051** Convalescent home with continuous nursing care

(G-10121)
PROGRESSIVE QUALITY CARE INC
7770 Columbus Rd Ne (44641-9773)
PHONE.................................330 875-7866
Daniel Shiller, *Brnch Mgr*
EMP: 40
SALES (corp-wide): 35.53MM **Privately Held**
Web: www.progressivequalitycare.com
SIC: **7389** Personal service agents, brokers, and bureaus
PA: Progressive Quality Care, Inc.
5553 Broadview Rd
Parma OH 44134
216 661-6800

(G-10122)
ROMAN CTHLIC DOCESE YOUNGSTOWN
Also Called: St Joseph Care Center
2308 Reno Dr (44641-9083)
PHONE.................................330 875-5562
John Banks, *Superintnt*
EMP: 160
SALES (corp-wide): 54.72MM **Privately Held**
Web: www.saintjosephseniorliving.org
SIC: **8361** 8052 8051 Rest home, with health care incidental; Intermediate care facilities; Skilled nursing care facilities
PA: Roman Catholic Diocese Of Youngstown
144 W Wood St
Youngstown OH 44503
330 744-8451

(G-10123)
TODDS ENVIROSCAPES INC
7727 Paris Ave (44641-9598)
PHONE.................................330 875-0768
Todd Pugh, *Pr*
EMP: 225 EST: 1987
SALES (est): 23.55MM **Privately Held**
Web: www.growinggood.com
SIC: **0782** Landscape contractors

(G-10124)
YOUNG MNS CHRSTN ASSN CNTL STA
Also Called: Louisville YMCA
1421 S Nickelplate St (44641-2647)
PHONE.................................330 875-1611
Donna Kuehner, *Dir*
EMP: 95
SALES (corp-wide): 20.07MM **Privately Held**
Web: www.ymcastark.org
SIC: **8641** 7991 8351 7032 Youth organizations; Physical fitness facilities; Child day care services; Youth camps
PA: Young Mens Christian Association Of Central Stark County, Inc.
4700 Dressler Rd Nw
Canton OH 44718
330 491-9622

Loveland
Clermont County

(G-10125)
AAA EMERGENCY SERVICE
1279 Lebnon (45140)
PHONE.................................513 554-6473
EMP: 37 EST: 1994
SALES (est): 1.89MM **Privately Held**
SIC: **1521** 1799 Repairing fire damage, single-family houses; Special trade contractors, nec

(G-10126)
AMERICAN NURSING CARE INC (DH)
6281 Tri Ridge Blvd Ste 300 (45140-8345)
PHONE.................................513 576-0262
Thomas J Karpinski, *Pr*
EMP: 65 EST: 1976
SALES (est): 102.1MM **Privately Held**
Web: www.americannursingcare.com
SIC: **8051** Convalescent home with continuous nursing care
HQ: Chi Health At Home
1700 Edison Dr Ste 300
Milford OH 45150

(G-10127)
AMS CONSTRUCTION INC (PA)
10670 Loveland Madeira Rd (45140-8964)
P.O. Box 42068 (45242-0068)
PHONE.................................513 794-0410
EMP: 65 EST: 1991
SALES (est): 24.25MM **Privately Held**
Web: www.amsdigs.com
SIC: **1731** Electrical work

(G-10128)
BOY-KO MANAGEMENT INC
Also Called: LODGE NURSING & REHAB CENTER
9370 Union Cemetery Rd (45140-9577)
PHONE.................................513 677-4900
Richard Friedmann, *CFO*
Richard J Friedmann, *
EMP: 50 EST: 2001
SALES (est): 10.08MM **Privately Held**
Web: www.caringplacehcg.com
SIC: **8059** Convalescent home

(G-10129)
BRYAN EQUIPMENT SALES INC
6300 Smith Rd (45140-1588)
PHONE.................................513 248-2000
EMP: 66 EST: 1948
SALES (est): 21.11MM **Privately Held**
Web: www.bryanequipment.com
SIC: **5083** Farm and garden machinery

(G-10130)
CARESPRING HEALTH CARE MGT LLC (PA)
Also Called: Carespring
390 Wards Corner Rd (45140-6969)
PHONE.................................513 943-4000
Chris Chirumbolo, *CEO*
David Eppers, *
Debbie Berling, *
Henry Schneider, *Stockholder**
Cathy Hamblen, *
EMP: 40 EST: 2007
SALES (est): 84.56MM
SALES (corp-wide): 84.56MM **Privately Held**
Web: www.carespring.com
SIC: **8741** 8099 Hospital management; Blood related health services

(G-10131)
CHI NATIONAL HOME CARE (DH)
6281 Tri Ridge Blvd Ste 300 (45140-8345)
PHONE.................................513 576-0262
Daniel Dietz, *Dir*
EMP: 92 EST: 2012
SALES (est): 121.31MM **Privately Held**
Web: www.chihealthathome.com
SIC: **8082** Home health care services
HQ: Chi Health At Home
1700 Edison Dr Ste 300
Milford OH 45150

(G-10132)
COLD JET LLC (PA)
Also Called: Cold Jet
6283 Tri Ridge Blvd Pmb 100 (45140-8318)
PHONE.................................513 831-3211
Eugene L Cooke Iii, *CEO*
Scott Gatje, *
◆ EMP: 130 EST: 1986
SQ FT: 40,000
SALES (est): 53.68MM
SALES (corp-wide): 53.68MM **Privately Held**
Web: www.coldjet.com
SIC: **5084** Industrial machinery and equipment

(G-10133)
CREEKSIDE LTD LLC
Also Called: Oasis Golf Club
902 Loveland Miamiville Rd (45140-6952)
PHONE.................................513 583-4977
Lew Rosenbloom, *Genl Mgr*
EMP: 58
Web: www.oasisgolfclub.com
SIC: **7992** Public golf courses
PA: Creekside, Ltd, Llc
5 Glosser Richardson Rd
Lebanon OH 45036

(G-10134)
CUSTOM CHEMICAL SOLUTIONS LLC
167 Commerce Dr (45140-7727)
PHONE.................................800 291-1057
EMP: 45 EST: 2018
SALES (est): 2.34MM **Privately Held**
Web: www.washingsystems.com
SIC: **5169** Industrial chemicals

(G-10135)
DILL-ELAM INC
Also Called: City Service
1461 State Route 28 (45140)
PHONE.................................513 575-0017
Gary Dill, *Pr*
Steve Elam, *
EMP: 48 EST: 1982
SALES (est): 4.58MM **Privately Held**
SIC: **4213** 4212 Trucking, except local; Local trucking, without storage

(G-10136)
DR GERALD F JOHNSON DDS INC
11050 S Lebanon Rd (45140-9393)
PHONE.................................513 683-8333
EMP: 53
Web: www.johnson-orthodontics.com
SIC: **8021** Orthodontist
PA: Dr Gerald F Johnson Dds Inc

GEOGRAPHIC SECTION
Loveland - Clermont County (G-10159)

6499 S Mason Montgomery
Mason OH 45040

(G-10137)
FISCHER PUMP & VALVE COMPANY (PA)
Also Called: Fischer Process Industries
155 Commerce Dr (45140-7727)
PHONE..................513 583-4800
Ken Fischer, *Pr*
Ray Didonato, *
▲ **EMP:** 38 **EST:** 1964
SQ FT: 18,000
SALES (est): 24.46MM
SALES (corp-wide): 24.46MM **Privately Held**
Web: www.fischerprocess.com
SIC: 5085 5084 Hydraulic and pneumatic pistons and valves; Pumps and pumping equipment, nec

(G-10138)
GLOBE AMERICAN CASUALTY CO
Also Called: Gre Insurance Group
6281 Tri Ridge Blvd Unit 1 (45140-8345)
PHONE..................513 576-3200
V M Yerrill, *Ch Bd*
H Haskowitz, *Sr VP*
Thomas Gardner, *Sec*
Charles Ruzicka, *Sr VP*
Mark Fiebrink, *Ex VP*
EMP: 220 **EST:** 1951
SALES (est): 64.79MM
SALES (corp-wide): 20.63B **Privately Held**
SIC: 6331 Fire, marine, and casualty insurance: stock
HQ: Liberty-Usa Corporation
464 West St
Keene NH 03431
603 352-3221

(G-10139)
GRAIL
Also Called: GRAILVILLE
931 Obannonville Rd (45140-9741)
P.O. Box 36162 (45236-0162)
PHONE..................513 683-2340
Terrie Puckett, *Prin*
Martha Heidkamp, *
EMP: 40 **EST:** 1944
SALES (est): 498.75K **Privately Held**
Web: www.grail-us.org
SIC: 5942 8299 8699 Book stores; Educational services; Charitable organization

(G-10140)
HEALTHSOURCE OF OHIO INC
Also Called: Goshen Family Practice
1507 State Route 28 (45140-8413)
PHONE..................513 575-1444
David Coffey Md, *Dir*
EMP: 27
SALES (corp-wide): 67.96MM **Privately Held**
Web: www.healthsourceofohio.org
SIC: 8093 8011 Specialty outpatient clinics, nec; Offices and clinics of medical doctors
PA: Healthsource Of Ohio, Inc.
424 Wards Corner Rd # 200
Loveland OH 45140
513 576-7700

(G-10141)
HEALTHSOURCE OF OHIO INC (PA)
Also Called: PEEBLES FAMILY HEALTH & DENTAL
424 Wards Corner Rd Ste 200 (45140-6908)
PHONE..................513 576-7700
▲ **EMP:** 40 **EST:** 1976
SALES (est): 67.96MM
SALES (corp-wide): 67.96MM **Privately Held**
Web: www.healthsourceofohio.org
SIC: 8093 Specialty outpatient clinics, nec

(G-10142)
HICKORY WOODS GOLF COURSE INC
1240 Hickory Woods Dr (45140-9488)
PHONE..................513 575-3900
Dennis Acomb, *Pr*
EMP: 39 **EST:** 1983
SALES (est): 907.66K **Privately Held**
Web: www.hickorywoods.com
SIC: 7992 Public golf courses

(G-10143)
J DANIEL & COMPANY INC
1975 Phoenix Drive (45140-9241)
PHONE..................513 575-3100
James Danella, *Pr*
Daniel Deranski, *
Robert Kearns, *
EMP: 90 **EST:** 1981
SALES (est): 24.37MM
SALES (corp-wide): 545.12MM **Privately Held**
Web: www.jdanielco.com
SIC: 1623 Communication line and transmission tower construction
PA: Danella Companies, Inc.
2290 Butler Pike
Plymouth Meeting PA 19462
610 828-6200

(G-10144)
J L G CO INC
419 Wards Corner Rd (45140-9027)
PHONE..................513 248-1755
Steven C Stille Senior, *Pr*
EMP: 27 **EST:** 1965
SQ FT: 12,000
SALES (est): 838.38K **Privately Held**
Web: www.jlgfloors.com
SIC: 1752 5713 Carpet laying; Carpets

(G-10145)
KINGS VETERINARY HOSPITAL
3335 W State Route 22 3 (45140-1568)
PHONE..................513 697-0400
Doctor Paul Lecompte, *Pr*
EMP: 44 **EST:** 2013
SALES (est): 381.09K **Privately Held**
Web: www.kingsvethospital.com
SIC: 0742 Animal hospital services, pets and other animal specialties

(G-10146)
LEFKE TREE EXPERTS LLC
10900 Loveland Madeira Rd (45140-8969)
PHONE..................513 325-1783
Nicholas Lefke, *Managing Member*
EMP: 47 **EST:** 2015
SQ FT: 650
SALES (est): 2.14MM **Privately Held**
Web: www.treeservicelovelandoh.com
SIC: 0783 Planting, pruning, and trimming services

(G-10147)
LODGE CARE CENTER INC
9370 Union Cemetery Rd (45140-9577)
PHONE..................513 683-9966
Barry A Kohn, *Pr*
Sam Boymel, *VP*
EMP: 43 **EST:** 1992
SALES (est): 8.8MM **Privately Held**
Web: www.caringplacehcg.com
SIC: 8051 Convalescent home with continuous nursing care

(G-10148)
LOVELAND HEALTH CARE CENTER
Also Called: Loveland Hlth Care Nrsing Rhab
501 N 2nd St (45140-6667)
PHONE..................513 605-6000
Steve Boymel, *Pr*
EMP: 110 **EST:** 1979
SQ FT: 20,000
SALES (est): 7.94MM **Privately Held**
Web: www.hcmg.com
SIC: 8051 Convalescent home with continuous nursing care
PA: Central Accounting Systems, Inc.
12500 Reed Hartman Hwy
Cincinnati OH 45241

(G-10149)
MCCLUSKEY CHEVROLET INC (PA)
Also Called: McCluskey Automotive
179 Commerce Dr (45140-7727)
P.O. Box 7911 (45140-7911)
PHONE..................513 761-1111
Keith Mccluskey, *CEO*
Daniel Mccluskey, *CEO*
Keith P Mccluskey, *Pr*
Gina Owens, *
EMP: 140 **EST:** 1927
SQ FT: 100,000
SALES (est): 45.86MM
SALES (corp-wide): 45.86MM **Privately Held**
Web: www.mccluskeychevrolet.com
SIC: 5511 7515 7513 5521 Automobiles, new and used; Passenger car leasing; Truck rental and leasing, no drivers; Used car dealers

(G-10150)
MCCORMICK EQUIPMENT CO INC (PA)
112 Northeast Dr (45140-7144)
PHONE..................513 677-8888
R Peter Kimener, *Pr*
Bruce A Buckley, *
EMP: 33 **EST:** 1964
SQ FT: 30,000
SALES (est): 26.43MM
SALES (corp-wide): 26.43MM **Privately Held**
Web: www.mccequip.com
SIC: 5084 Materials handling machinery

(G-10151)
MIKES CARWASH INC (PA)
100 Northeast Dr (45140-7144)
PHONE..................513 677-4700
Mike Dahm, *Pr*
Greg Reis, *
Andrew Dowden, *
Belinda Anders, *
EMP: 35 **EST:** 2014
SALES (est): 25.8MM
SALES (corp-wide): 25.8MM **Privately Held**
Web: www.mikescarwash.com
SIC: 7542 Washing and polishing, automotive

(G-10152)
MIKESCAR WASH
100 Northeast Dr (45140-7144)
PHONE..................513 672-6440
EMP: 35
SALES (est): 4.74MM **Privately Held**
Web: www.mikescarwash.com
SIC: 7542 Washing and polishing, automotive

(G-10153)
NORMANDY SWIM & TENNIS CLUB
9595 Union Cemetery Rd (45140-7185)
PHONE..................513 683-0232
Paul Swift, *Mgr*
EMP: 30 **EST:** 2001
SQ FT: 1,331
SALES (est): 212.59K **Privately Held**
Web: www.normandyswim.org
SIC: 7997 Swimming club, membership

(G-10154)
NURTUR HOLDINGS LLC (PA)
6279 Tri Ridge Blvd Ste 250 (45140-8301)
PHONE..................614 487-3033
EMP: 32 **EST:** 2004
SALES (est): 7.56MM **Privately Held**
Web: www.nurtur.com
SIC: 7231 Cosmetology school

(G-10155)
NUTUR HOLDINGS LLC
6281 Tri Ridge Blvd Ste 140 (45140)
PHONE..................513 576-9333
EMP: 150 **EST:** 2004
SALES (est): 642.29K **Privately Held**
SIC: 7231 Cosmetology school

(G-10156)
OBANNON CREEK GOLF CLUB
6842 Oakland Rd (45140-9723)
PHONE..................513 683-5657
Marianne Fahms, *Genl Mgr*
EMP: 46 **EST:** 1975
SQ FT: 17,000
SALES (est): 2.75MM **Privately Held**
Web: www.obannoncreek.com
SIC: 7997 5941 5813 5812 Golf club, membership; Golf goods and equipment; Bar (drinking places); Grills (eating places)

(G-10157)
PARAMOUNT LAWN SERVICE INC
8900 Glendale Milford Rd Unit A1 (45140)
PHONE..................513 984-5200
Joseph Tekulve, *Pr*
EMP: 28 **EST:** 1988
SQ FT: 3,750
SALES (est): 1.4MM **Privately Held**
Web: www.paramountlandscaping.com
SIC: 0782 4959 Landscape contractors; Snowplowing

(G-10158)
SERVER SUITES LLC
Also Called: Erp Suites
6281 Tri Ridge Blvd Ste 10 (45140-8345)
PHONE..................513 831-5528
Mike Moorman, *CEO*
Mike Moorman, *Managing Member*
David A Reynolds, *Managing Member*
Mike Kelleher, *VP*
Liam Oconnor, *VP*
EMP: 103 **EST:** 2006
SQ FT: 2,800
SALES (est): 18.02MM **Privately Held**
Web: www.erpsuites.com
SIC: 4813 7379 Wire telephone; Computer related consulting services

(G-10159)
SHAWCOR PIPE PROTECTION LLC
Also Called: Dsg Canusa
173 Commerce Dr (45140-7727)
P.O. Box 498830 (45249-8830)
PHONE..................513 683-7800
Jim Huntebrinker, *Brnch Mgr*
EMP: 30
SIC: 5084 Industrial machinery and equipment

(PA)=Parent Co (HQ)=Headquarters
✪ = New Business established in last 2 years

Loveland - Clermont County (G-10160)

HQ: Shawcor Pipe Protection Llc
5875 N Sam Houston Pkwy W S
Houston TX 77086

(G-10160)
SHAWNEESPRING HLTH CRE CNTR RL
390 Wards Corner Rd (45140-6969)
PHONE.................................513 943-4000
Barry Bortz, *Prin*
EMP: 86 **EST:** 2007
SALES (est): 4.73MM
SALES (corp-wide): 84.56MM **Privately Held**
SIC: 8011 Offices and clinics of medical doctors
HQ: Shawneespring Health Care Center, Llc
10111 Simonson Rd
Harrison OH 45030
513 367-7780

(G-10161)
SOTTILE & BARILE LLC
394 Wards Corner Rd Ste 180 (45140-8362)
PHONE.................................513 345-0592
Tony Sottile, *Pr*
EMP: 30 **EST:** 2015
SALES (est): 3MM **Privately Held**
Web: www.sottileandbarile.com
SIC: 8111 General practice attorney, lawyer

(G-10162)
SST BEARING CORPORATION (HQ)
Also Called: Sst
154 Commerce Dr (45140-7781)
PHONE.................................513 583-5500
▲ **EMP:** 88 **EST:** 1957
SALES (est): 23.92MM **Privately Held**
Web: www.sstbearingcorp.com
SIC: 5085 Bearings, bushings, wheels, and gears
PA: Solve Industrial Motion Group Llc
3945 Westinghouse Blvd
Charlotte NC 28273

(G-10163)
THE GARRETSON FIRM RESOLUTION GROUP INC
Also Called: Garretson Resolution Group
6281 Tri Ridge Blvd Ste 300 (45140-8345)
PHONE.................................513 794-0400
EMP: 200
SIC: 8111 Bankruptcy law

(G-10164)
THE ROBERT MCCABE COMPANY INC (PA)
Also Called: McCabe Do It Center
118 Northeast Dr (45140-7144)
PHONE.................................513 683-2662
EMP: 60 **EST:** 1971
SALES (est): 20.51MM
SALES (corp-wide): 20.51MM **Privately Held**
Web: www.mccabelumber.com
SIC: 5211 5251 5072 Lumber products; Hardware stores; Hardware

(G-10165)
TRIAGE LLC
Also Called: Talemed
6279 Tri Ridge Blvd Ste 110 (45140-8396)
PHONE.................................513 774-7300
Randy Baker, *
EMP: 260 **EST:** 2006
SALES (est): 18.87MM **Privately Held**
Web: www.triagestaff.com
SIC: 7361 Nurses' registry

(G-10166)
WASHING SYSTEMS LLC (HQ)
167 Commerce Dr (45140-7727)
PHONE.................................800 272-1974
John Walroth, *CEO*
Jonathan C Dill, *Ex VP*
▼ **EMP:** 110 **EST:** 1989
SALES (est): 49.48MM **Privately Held**
Web: www.washingsystems.com
SIC: 5169 2841 Detergents; Soap and other detergents
PA: Kao Corporation
1-14-10, Nihombashikayabacho
Chuo-Ku TKY 103-0

Lowellville
Mahoning County

(G-10167)
CRICKET CONSTRUCTION LTD
400 E Water St (44436-1247)
PHONE.................................330 536-8773
Barbara J Slaven, *Pr*
EMP: 30 **EST:** 1999
SALES (est): 1.98MM **Privately Held**
SIC: 1521 Single-family housing construction

(G-10168)
ENERTECH ELECTRICAL INC
101 Youngstown Lowellville Rd (44436-1010)
PHONE.................................330 536-2131
Gregory T Haren, *CEO*
John Donofrio Junior, *Pr*
John A Wilaj, *
▲ **EMP:** 30 **EST:** 1981
SQ FT: 8,000
SALES (est): 9.78MM **Privately Held**
Web: www.enertechelectrical.com
SIC: 1731 General electrical contractor

(G-10169)
LYCO CORPORATION
Also Called: Pilorusso Construction Div
1089 N Hubbard Rd (44436-9737)
PHONE.................................412 973-9176
Patsy Pilorusso, *Pr*
Elio Massullo, *Owner*
W C Pilorusso, *VP*
Mike Pallotto, *VP*
EMP: 33 **EST:** 1947
SQ FT: 25,000
SALES (est): 1.15MM **Privately Held**
Web: www.lyco-mfg.com
SIC: 7699 3441 Welding equipment repair; Fabricated structural metal

(G-10170)
M & M WINE CELLAR INC
Also Called: L'U Vabella
259 Bedford Rd (44436-9547)
PHONE.................................330 536-6450
Frank Sergi, *Pr*
EMP: 30 **EST:** 2006
SALES (est): 2.39MM **Privately Held**
Web: www.luvabella.com
SIC: 5499 5149 5182 Juices, fruit or vegetable; Juices; Wine

(G-10171)
S E T INC
Also Called: S.E.T. Inc.of Ohio
235 E Water St Ste C (44436-1273)
PHONE.................................330 536-6724
Douglas Susany, *Pr*
EMP: 50 **EST:** 1988
SQ FT: 3,500
SALES (est): 17MM **Privately Held**
Web: www.setinc.biz

SIC: 1794 Excavation work

Lucas
Richland County

(G-10172)
WORTHINGTON ANALYTICAL SVCS
2657 Pleasant Valley Rd (44843-9744)
PHONE.................................614 599-5254
David J Reznik, *Pr*
EMP: 76 **EST:** 1992
SQ FT: 2,200
SALES (est): 336.79K **Privately Held**
SIC: 7699 Laboratory instrument repair

Lucasville
Scioto County

(G-10173)
CAMELOT REALTY INVESTMENTS
10689 Us-23 (45648)
P.O. Box 1312 (45648-1312)
PHONE.................................740 357-5291
EMP: 30 **EST:** 2010
SALES (est): 1.38MM **Privately Held**
SIC: 6799 Investors, nec

(G-10174)
CONSULATE MANAGEMENT CO LLC
Also Called: Edgewood Manor of Lucasville
10098 Big Bear Creek Rd (45648-9168)
PHONE.................................740 259-2351
Mike Bubinsky, *Mgr*
EMP: 261
SALES (corp-wide): 491MM **Privately Held**
Web: www.consulatehc.com
SIC: 8059 8051 Nursing home, except skilled and intermediate care facility; Skilled nursing care facilities
HQ: Consulate Management Company, Llc
800 Concourse Pkwy S # 200
Maitland FL 32751
407 571-1550

(G-10175)
EDGEWOOD MANOR LUCASVILLE LLC
Also Called: Edgewood Manor Lucasville II
10098a Big Bear Creek Rd (45648-9168)
P.O. Box 789 (45648-0789)
PHONE.................................740 259-5536
Tom Barr, *Managing Member*
EMP: 100 **EST:** 2019
SALES (est): 3.08MM **Privately Held**
Web: www.edgewoodmanoroflucasville.com
SIC: 8059 Nursing home, except skilled and intermediate care facility

(G-10176)
EDGEWOOD MANOR OF LUCASVILLE
Also Called: Convalescent Center Lucasville
10098 Big Bear Creek Rd (45648-9168)
PHONE.................................740 259-5536
Tom Barr, *Admn*
EMP: 50 **EST:** 1982
SALES (est): 4.72MM **Privately Held**
Web: www.edgewoodmanoroflucasville.com
SIC: 8051 Convalescent home with continuous nursing care

(G-10177)
EDGEWOOD MNOR LUCASVILLE I LLC
10098 Big Bear Creek Rd (45648-9168)
PHONE.................................740 259-5536
EMP: 80 **EST:** 2017
SALES (est): 7.09MM **Privately Held**
Web: www.edgewoodmanoroflucasville.com
SIC: 8051 Convalescent home with continuous nursing care

(G-10178)
FRIENDS OF GOOD SHEPHERD MANOR
Also Called: GOOD SHEPHERD MANOR
374 Good Manor Rd (45648-9606)
PHONE.................................740 289-2861
Normand Tremblay, *Dir*
Helen Dovenbarger, *
EMP: 46 **EST:** 1965
SQ FT: 30,593
SALES (est): 205.01K **Privately Held**
SIC: 8361 8052 Retarded home; Intermediate care facilities

(G-10179)
PORK CHAMP LLC
1136 Coldicott Hill Rd (45648-9595)
PHONE.................................740 493-2164
Bryan Mc Coy, *Mgr*
EMP: 48
SALES (corp-wide): 1.7MM **Privately Held**
SIC: 0219 0291 General livestock, nec; Livestock farm, general
PA: Pork Champ Llc
5170 Blazer Pkwy
Dublin OH 43017
419 253-0637

(G-10180)
SCIOTO COUNTY REGION WTR DST 1
Also Called: Water 1
326 Robert Lucas Rd (45648-9204)
P.O. Box 310 (45648-0310)
PHONE.................................740 259-2301
Johnathan King, *Genl Mgr*
EMP: 29 **EST:** 1968
SALES (est): 10.81MM **Privately Held**
Web: www.water1.org
SIC: 4941 Water supply

(G-10181)
SOUTHERN OHIO MEDICAL CENTER
10 Thomas Hollow Rd (45648-8889)
PHONE.................................740 259-5699
EMP: 90
SALES (corp-wide): 546.1MM **Privately Held**
Web: www.somc.org
SIC: 8062 General medical and surgical hospitals
PA: Southern Ohio Medical Center
1805 27th St
Portsmouth OH 45662
740 354-5000

Luckey
Wood County

(G-10182)
EXCHANGE BANK INC (HQ)
235 Main St (43443)
PHONE.................................419 833-3401
FAX: 419 833-3663
EMP: 30
SQ FT: 1,000
SALES (est): 5.29MM
SALES (corp-wide): 46.94MM **Publicly Held**

GEOGRAPHIC SECTION

Macedonia - Summit County (G-10205)

SIC: 6022 State commercial banks
PA: Sb Financial Group, Inc.
401 Clinton St
Defiance OH 43512
419 783-8950

Lynchburg
Highland County

(G-10183)
BLUE CREEK ENTERPRISES INC
(PA)
316 N Main St (45142)
P.O. Box 517 (45142-0517)
PHONE.................................937 364-2920
Ralph Captain, *Pr*
▲ **EMP:** 50 **EST:** 1997
SQ FT: 4,500
SALES (est): 23.68MM
SALES (corp-wide): 23.68MM **Privately Held**
Web: www.miracllc.com
SIC: 7371 7373 Computer software systems analysis and design, custom; Systems software development services

(G-10184)
CCC CONTRACTORS LLC
6951 State Route 134 (45142-9705)
PHONE.................................937 579-5100
EMP: 30 **EST:** 2006
SQ FT: 3,000
SALES (est): 1.79MM **Privately Held**
SIC: 5082 General construction machinery and equipment

(G-10185)
HIGHLAND HEALTH PROVIDERS CORP
8900 State Route 134 (45142-9272)
PHONE.................................937 364-2346
Amanda Warix, *Ex Dir*
EMP: 67
SALES (corp-wide): 9.75MM **Privately Held**
Web: www.hhproviders.org
SIC: 8011 General and family practice, physician/surgeon
PA: Highland Health Providers Corporation
1487 N High St Ste 102
Hillsboro OH 45133
937 840-6575

(G-10186)
SKW MANAGEMENT LLC
3841 Panhandle Rd (45142-9449)
PHONE.................................937 382-7938
Samuel K Wilkin, *Managing Member*
EMP: 42 **EST:** 2009
SQ FT: 1,200
SALES (est): 2.27MM **Privately Held**
SIC: 6513 Apartment building operators

Lyons
Fulton County

(G-10187)
B W GRINDING CO
Also Called: Bw Supply Co.
15048 County Rd 10-3 (43533-9713)
P.O. Box 307 (43533-0307)
PHONE.................................419 923-1376
Martin Welch, *Pr*
EMP: 35 **EST:** 1978
SQ FT: 30,000
SALES (est): 7.64MM **Privately Held**
Web: www.bwsupplyco.com

SIC: 5085 3324 Industrial tools; Commercial investment castings, ferrous

Macedonia
Summit County

(G-10188)
AGS CUSTOM GRAPHICS INC
Also Called: A G S Ohio
8107 Bavaria Dr E (44056)
PHONE.................................330 963-7770
John Green, *Pr*
Mark Edgar, *
EMP: 74 **EST:** 1993
SQ FT: 70,000
SALES (est): 23.96MM
SALES (corp-wide): 4.99B **Privately Held**
Web: www.rrd.com
SIC: 2752 2721 7375 2791 Offset printing; Periodicals; Information retrieval services; Typesetting
HQ: R. R. Donnelley & Sons Company
35 W Wacker Dr
Chicago IL 60601
312 326-8000

(G-10189)
AWE HOSPITALITY GROUP LLC
9652 N Bedford Rd (44056-1008)
PHONE.................................330 888-8836
Anthony Budroe, *Pr*
Rochelle Budroe, *Sec*
EMP: 30 **EST:** 2011
SALES (est): 409.48K **Privately Held**
SIC: 7011 Hotels and motels

(G-10190)
CHAMPION OPCO LLC
9011 Freeway Dr (44056-1524)
PHONE.................................440 249-6768
EMP: 30
Web: www.championwindow.com
SIC: 5031 Windows
HQ: Champion Opco, Llc
12121 Champion Way
Cincinnati OH 45241
513 327-7338

(G-10191)
DUN RITE HOME IMPROVEMENT INC
8601 Freeway Dr (44056-1535)
PHONE.................................330 650-5322
EMP: 30 **EST:** 1989
SQ FT: 5,400
SALES (est): 2.28MM **Privately Held**
Web: www.calldunrite.com
SIC: 4959 1761 5211 1521 Snowplowing; Roofing contractor; Door and window products; Single-family home remodeling, additions, and repairs

(G-10192)
GENERAL CRANE RENTAL LLC
9680 Freeway Dr (44056-1035)
PHONE.................................330 908-0001
Dan Manos, *Pr*
EMP: 35 **EST:** 1988
SQ FT: 10,000
SALES (est): 4.67MM **Privately Held**
Web: www.generalcranerental.com
SIC: 7353 Cranes and aerial lift equipment, rental or leasing

(G-10193)
GIRL SCOUTS NORTH EAST OHIO
(PA)
1 Girl Scout Way (44056-2156)
PHONE.................................330 864-9933
Jane Christyson, *CEO*

John Graves, *
Brittany Zaehringer, *
EMP: 88 **EST:** 1962
SQ FT: 35,000
SALES (est): 16.37MM **Privately Held**
Web: www.gsneo.org
SIC: 8641 Girl Scout organization

(G-10194)
JA HTL LLC
240 Highland Rd E (44056-2102)
PHONE.................................330 467-1981
Umesh Patel, *Prin*
EMP: 28 **EST:** 2009
SALES (est): 472.19K **Privately Held**
SIC: 7011 Hotels

(G-10195)
JUMBO LOGISTICS LLC ✪
1229 Deepwood Dr (44056-2419)
PHONE.................................216 662-5420
EMP: 48 **EST:** 2022
SALES (est): 1.8MM **Privately Held**
SIC: 4789 7389 Transportation services, nec; Business Activities at Non-Commercial Site

(G-10196)
KAIVAL CORPORATION
Also Called: Knights Inn
240 Highland Rd E (44056-2102)
PHONE.................................330 467-1981
Umesh Patel, *Pr*
EMP: 41 **EST:** 2000
SQ FT: 29,850
SALES (est): 237.49K **Privately Held**
Web: www.sonesta.com
SIC: 7011 Hotels and motels

(G-10197)
KEYBANK NATIONAL ASSOCIATION
640 E Aurora Rd Ste A (44056-1859)
PHONE.................................330 748-8010
EMP: 32
SALES (corp-wide): 10.4B **Publicly Held**
Web: www.key.com
SIC: 6021 National commercial banks
HQ: Keybank National Association
127 Public Sq Ste 5600
Cleveland OH 44114
800 539-2968

(G-10198)
LAKIREDDY DENTAL LLC
Also Called: Aspen Dental
545 E Aurora Rd (44056-1837)
PHONE.................................330 439-0355
Shirisha Madulapally, *Mgr*
EMP: 54
SALES (corp-wide): 574.86K **Privately Held**
Web: www.aspendental.com
SIC: 8021 Dentists' office
PA: Lakireddy Dental Llc
12576 S Churchill Way
Strongsville OH 44149
216 661-8077

(G-10199)
LOGISTICAL RESOURCE GROUP INC
573 Highland Rd E Ste 2 (44056-2148)
PHONE.................................330 283-3733
EMP: 100 **EST:** 2020
SALES (est): 3.42MM **Privately Held**
Web: www.logisticalrg.com
SIC: 8742 Business planning and organizing services

(G-10200)
NEWTOWN NINE INC (PA)
Also Called: Ohio Materials Handling
8155 Roll And Hold Pkwy (44056-2146)
PHONE.................................440 781-0623
James P Orenga, *Pr*
Antoinette Orenga, *
▲ **EMP:** 57 **EST:** 1976
SQ FT: 38,000
SALES (est): 10.35MM
SALES (corp-wide): 10.35MM **Privately Held**
Web: www.burnslift.com
SIC: 5084 Lift trucks and parts

(G-10201)
OHIO STATE HOME SERVICES INC
(PA)
Also Called: Ohio State Waterproofing
365 Highland Rd E (44056-2103)
PHONE.................................330 467-1055
TOLL FREE: 800
Nick Di Cello, *Pr*
EMP: 170 **EST:** 1977
SQ FT: 15,000
SALES (est): 48.55MM
SALES (corp-wide): 48.55MM **Privately Held**
Web: www.ohiostatewaterproofing.com
SIC: 1799 Waterproofing

(G-10202)
PRO QUIP INC
850 Highland Rd E (44056-2190)
PHONE.................................330 468-1850
Harry J Abraham, *CEO*
Rosalyn Abraham, *
George Braun, *
▲ **EMP:** 55 **EST:** 1969
SQ FT: 26,000
SALES (est): 12.54MM **Privately Held**
Web: www.proquipinc.com
SIC: 5084 Industrial machinery and equipment

(G-10203)
PROGRESSIVE MACEDONIA LLC
Also Called: Avenue At Macedonia, The
9730 Valley View Rd (44056-2040)
PHONE.................................330 748-8800
Admiral Robyn Doerr, *Prin*
EMP: 50 **EST:** 2015
SQ FT: 79,000
SALES (est): 7.65MM **Privately Held**
Web: www.avenueatmacedonia.com
SIC: 8051 Skilled nursing care facilities

(G-10204)
SHEFFIELD STEEL PRODUCTS COMPANY
355 Ledge Rd (44056-1017)
P.O. Box 560254 (44056-0254)
PHONE.................................330 468-0091
EMP: 32 **EST:** 1955
SALES (est): 9.76MM **Privately Held**
Web: www.sheffieldsteel.net
SIC: 5051 Steel

(G-10205)
SPECIALTY LUBRICANTS CORP
Also Called: SLC Custom Packaging
8300 Corporate Park Dr (44056-2300)
PHONE.................................330 425-2567
Robin Bugenske, *CEO*
Sherry Bugenske, *
◆ **EMP:** 42 **EST:** 1979
SQ FT: 64,000
SALES (est): 11.24MM **Privately Held**
Web: www.speclubes.com

Macedonia - Summit County (G-10206)

SIC: **7389** 5172 Packaging and labeling services; Lubricating oils and greases

(G-10206)
STG ELECTRIC SERVICES LLC
360 Highland Rd E (44056-2169)
PHONE..............................330 650-0513
Chris Jaskiewicz, *Managing Member*
Mark Muzzana, *
EMP: 50 EST: 2017
SALES (est): 17.96MM **Privately Held**
Web: www.stgelectricservices.com
SIC: **4911** Electric services

(G-10207)
SYSTEMS PACK INC
649 Highland Rd E (44056-2109)
PHONE..............................330 467-5729
Ray Attwell, *Pr*
Dennis Kay, *
Laurene Neval, *
EMP: 30 EST: 1977
SQ FT: 62,131
SALES (est): 8MM **Privately Held**
Web: www.systemspackinc.com
SIC: **5199** 7389 5113 2653 Packaging materials; Packaging and labeling services; Shipping supplies; Corrugated and solid fiber boxes

(G-10208)
TPC WIRE & CABLE CORP (HQ)
Also Called: Hoffman Products
9600 Valley View Rd (44056-2059)
PHONE..............................800 211-4542
R Adam Norwitt, *Pr*
▲ EMP: 107 EST: 2009
SQ FT: 129,000
SALES (est): 188.88MM
SALES (corp-wide): 12.55B **Publicly Held**
Web: www.tpcwire.com
SIC: **5063** Electronic wire and cable
PA: Amphenol Corporation
    358 Hall Ave
    Wallingford CT 06492
    203 265-8900

(G-10209)
W W GRAINGER INC
Also Called: Grainger 165
8211 Bavaria Dr E (44056)
PHONE..............................330 425-8388
Bob Holzer, *Brnch Mgr*
EMP: 30
SALES (corp-wide): 15.23B **Publicly Held**
Web: www.johnsoncontrols.com
SIC: **4225** 5085 General warehousing and storage; Industrial supplies
PA: W.W. Grainger, Inc.
    100 Grainger Pkwy
    Lake Forest IL 60045
    847 535-1000

(G-10210)
YOUNG MNS CHRSTN ASSN OF AKRON
Also Called: Longwood Family YMCA
8761 Shepard Rd (44056-1990)
PHONE..............................330 467-8366
John Herman, *Dir*
EMP: 38
SALES (corp-wide): 21.11MM **Privately Held**
Web: www.akronymca.org
SIC: **8641** 7991 8351 7032 Youth organizations; Physical fitness facilities; Child day care services; Youth camps
PA: The Young Men's Christian Association Of Akron Ohio
    50 S Mn St Ste Ll100
    Akron OH 44308

330 376-1335

Madison
Lake County

(G-10211)
AMERICAN EAGLE HLTH CARE SVCS
Also Called: Cardinal Wds Skilled Nursing
6831 Chapel Rd (44057-2255)
PHONE..............................440 428-5103
Joyce Humphrey, *Pr*
EMP: 53 EST: 1991
SQ FT: 2,237
SALES (est): 2.17MM **Privately Held**
Web: www.cardinalwoodsrehab.com
SIC: **8051** Convalescent home with continuous nursing care

(G-10212)
CLEVELAND CLINIC FOUNDATION
2999 Mcmackin Rd Ste Ec1 (44057-2330)
PHONE..............................440 428-1111
EMP: 33
SALES (corp-wide): 14.48B **Privately Held**
Web: www.clevelandclinic.org
SIC: **8062** General medical and surgical hospitals
PA: The Cleveland Clinic Foundation
    9500 Euclid Ave
    Cleveland OH 44195
    216 636-8335

(G-10213)
CLEVELAND MOTOR CARRIER INC
204 Parkway Blvd (44057-3277)
PHONE..............................440 901-9192
EMP: 66
SALES (corp-wide): 1.16MM **Privately Held**
SIC: **4731** Freight transportation arrangement
PA: Cleveland Motor Carrier Inc.
    7665 Mentor Ave
    Mentor OH 44060
    888 330-7576

(G-10214)
CW OPCO LLC
Also Called: Cardinal Wds Sklled Nrsing Rh
6831 Chapel Rd (44057-2255)
PHONE..............................440 428-5103
EMP: 48 EST: 2017
SALES (est): 8.39MM **Privately Held**
Web: www.cardinalwoodsrehab.com
SIC: **8051** Convalescent home with continuous nursing care

(G-10215)
EASTWOOD RESIDENTIAL SVCS INC (PA)
6455 N Ridge Rd # 1 (44057-2516)
PHONE..............................440 428-8169
James Victor, *Pr*
EMP: 32 EST: 1975
SALES (est): 1.61MM
SALES (corp-wide): 1.61MM **Privately Held**
SIC: **8361** Residential care

(G-10216)
FAMILY FARM & HOME INC
6600 N Ridge Rd (44057-2554)
PHONE..............................440 307-1030
EMP: 35
SALES (corp-wide): 220MM **Privately Held**
Web: www.familyfarmandhome.com
SIC: **5191** Farm supplies
PA: Family Farm & Home, Inc.

900 3rd St Ste 302
Muskegon MI 49440
231 722-8335

(G-10217)
HUNTINGTON NATIONAL BANK
6565 N Ridge Rd (44057-2555)
PHONE..............................440 428-1124
Jackie Evangelista, *Brnch Mgr*
EMP: 31
SALES (corp-wide): 10.84B **Publicly Held**
Web: www.huntington.com
SIC: **6029** Commercial banks, nec
HQ: The Huntington National Bank
    41 S High St
    Columbus OH 43215
    614 480-4293

(G-10218)
J P JENKS INC
4493 S Madison Rd (44057-9422)
P.O. Box 370 (44057-0370)
PHONE..............................440 428-4500
Ray Kennedy, *Pr*
EMP: 76 EST: 1972
SQ FT: 20,000
SALES (est): 849.22K
SALES (corp-wide): 83.57MM **Privately Held**
Web: www.jpjenks.com
SIC: **4213** 4212 Contract haulers; Local trucking, without storage
PA: R. W. Sidley Incorporated
    436 Casement Ave
    Painesville OH 44077
    440 352-9343

(G-10219)
LAKE COUNTY YMCA
Also Called: East End YMCA Pre School
730 N Lake St (44057-3153)
PHONE..............................440 428-5125
Michele Kuester, *Dir*
EMP: 143
SALES (corp-wide): 13.16MM **Privately Held**
Web: www.lakecountyymca.org
SIC: **8641** 7991 8351 7032 Youth organizations; Physical fitness facilities; Child day care services; Youth camps
PA: Lake County Young Men's Christian Association
    933 Mentor Ave Fl 2
    Painesville OH 44077
    440 352-3303

(G-10220)
MADISON CARE INC
Also Called: FRANKLIN RIDGE CARE FACILITY
7600 S Ridge Rd (44057-9746)
PHONE..............................440 428-1492
Susan Knowlson, *Dir*
EMP: 273 EST: 1966
SQ FT: 69,000
SALES (est): 8.75MM
SALES (corp-wide): 58.43MM **Privately Held**
Web: www.embassyhealthcare.net
SIC: **8051** Convalescent home with continuous nursing care
PA: Carington Health Systems
    8200 Beckett Park Dr
    Hamilton OH 45011
    513 682-2700

(G-10221)
MADISON MEDICAL CAMPUS
Also Called: Lake Hospital Systems
6270 N Ridge Rd (44057-2567)
PHONE..............................440 428-6800

Rick Kondas, *Dir*
EMP: 52 EST: 1987
SALES (est): 1.7MM **Privately Held**
Web: www.uhhospitals.org
SIC: **8062** General medical and surgical hospitals

(G-10222)
MADISON VILLAGE MANOR INC
731 N Lake St (44057-3152)
PHONE..............................440 428-1519
Admiral Lisa Griesmer, *Prin*
EMP: 35 EST: 1976
SALES (est): 951.02K **Privately Held**
Web: www.mvmgables.com
SIC: **8052** Intermediate care facilities

Magnolia
Stark County

(G-10223)
AXIOM WIRELESS LLC
3323 Magnolia Rd Nw (44643-9528)
PHONE..............................330 863-4410
EMP: 50 EST: 2010
SQ FT: 15,000
SALES (est): 5.91MM **Privately Held**
Web: www.axiomwireless.net
SIC: **4812** Cellular telephone services

Maineville
Warren County

(G-10224)
AMS CONSTRUCTION INC
Also Called: Estephenson Brenda & John
7431 Windsor Park Dr (45039-9193)
PHONE..............................513 398-6689
John K Stephenson, *Brnch Mgr*
EMP: 85
Web: www.amsdigs.com
SIC: **1731** Electrical work
PA: Ams Construction, Inc.
    10670 Loveland Madeira Rd
    Loveland OH 45140

(G-10225)
BILL DELORD AUTOCENTER INC
Also Called: Pontiac Bill Delord Autocenter
5455 Grandin Pass Ct (45039-8428)
PHONE..............................513 932-3000
William Delord, *Pr*
Julie Spencer, *
EMP: 51 EST: 1993
SALES (est): 9.23MM **Privately Held**
Web: www.jakesweeney.com
SIC: **5511** 7538 Automobiles, new and used; General automotive repair shops

(G-10226)
CHARLES H HAMILTON CO
5875 S State Route 48 (45039-9798)
P.O. Box 99 (45039-0099)
PHONE..............................513 683-2442
Charles H Hamilton Junior, *Pr*
EMP: 85 EST: 1964
SQ FT: 8,000
SALES (est): 9.87MM **Privately Held**
Web: www.charleshhamiltonco.com
SIC: **1794** 1623 1771 Excavation and grading, building construction; Water, sewer, and utility lines; Curb construction

(G-10227)
COUNTRYSIDE YUNG MNS CHRSTN AS
Also Called: YMCA

GEOGRAPHIC SECTION
Mansfield - Richland County (G-10247)

6246 Turning Leaf Way (45039-7802)
PHONE..................513 677-3702
Ronda Jones, *Brnch Mgr*
EMP: 51
SALES (corp-wide): 17.03MM **Privately Held**
Web: www.countrysideymca.org
SIC: 8641 7991 8351 7032 Youth organizations; Physical fitness facilities; Child day care services; Youth camps
PA: Countryside Young Mens Christian Association Of Warren County, Lebanon, Ohio (Inc)
1699 Deerfield Rd
Lebanon OH 45036
513 932-1424

(G-10228)
MIKE WARD LANDSCAPING LLC
Also Called: Eastgate Sod
424 E Us Highway 22 And 3 (45039-9650)
PHONE..................513 683-6436
Kenneth Michael Ward, *Pr*
EMP: 30 **EST:** 1979
SQ FT: 15,441
SALES (est): 4.08MM **Privately Held**
Web: www.wardthorntonlandscapes.com
SIC: 0181 0782 Sod farms; Lawn services

(G-10229)
OXFORD PHYSCL THRAPY RHBLTTION
5988 S State Route 48 (45039-8845)
PHONE..................513 549-1927
EMP: 35
Web: www.oxfordphysicaltherapy.com
SIC: 8049 Physical therapist
PA: Oxford Physical Therapy And Rehabilitation, Inc.
345 S College Ave
Oxford OH 45056

(G-10230)
PRIME HOME CARE LLC (HQ)
Also Called: OXFORD HEALTHCARE
2775 W Us Highway 22 And 3 Ste 1b (45039)
PHONE..................513 340-4183
EMP: 35 **EST:** 2006
SALES (est): 9.33MM **Privately Held**
Web: www.primehomecarellc.com
SIC: 8082 Visiting nurse service
PA: Help At Home, Llc
33 S State St Ste 500
Chicago IL 60603

Malta
Morgan County

(G-10231)
COMMUNITY ACTION PRGRAM CORP O
Also Called: Play & Learn School
320 S Main St (43758-9058)
P.O. Box 309 (43758-0309)
PHONE..................740 962-3792
Mary Robertson, *Dir*
EMP: 102
SALES (corp-wide): 17.72MM **Privately Held**
Web: www.wmcap.org
SIC: 8399 8351 Community action agency; Child day care services
PA: Community Action Program Corp, Of Washington-Morgan County Ohio, Inc
218 Putnam St
Marietta OH 45750
740 373-3745

(G-10232)
EZ GROUT CORPORATION INC
Also Called: Ezg Manufacturing
1833 N Riverview Rd (43758-9303)
PHONE..................740 962-2024
Damian Lang, *Owner*
EMP: 40 **EST:** 2007
SALES (est): 6.62MM **Privately Held**
Web: www.ezgmfg.com
SIC: 5082 3499 3549 Masonry equipment and supplies; Chests, fire or burglary resistive: metal; Wiredrawing and fabricating machinery and equipment, ex. die

Malvern
Carroll County

(G-10233)
GREEN LINES TRANSPORTATION INC (PA)
7089 Alliance Rd Nw (44644-9428)
P.O. Box 377 (44644-0377)
PHONE..................330 863-2111
Roger A Bettis, *Pr*
Brad Yoder, *
EMP: 50 **EST:** 1981
SQ FT: 17,000
SALES (est): 12.91MM
SALES (corp-wide): 12.91MM **Privately Held**
Web: www.greenlines.net
SIC: 4213 Contract haulers

(G-10234)
HOPPES CONSTRUCTION LLC
4036 Coral Rd Nw (44644-9468)
P.O. Box 604 (44644-0604)
PHONE..................580 310-0090
Lynn Hoppe, *Brnch Mgr*
EMP: 53
Web: www.hoppesconstruction.com
SIC: 1521 Single-family housing construction
PA: Hoppe"s Construction, Llc
12580 County Road 1538
Ada OK 74820

(G-10235)
ROBERTSON PLUMBING & HEATING
Also Called: Robertson's Building Center
7389 Canton Rd Nw (44644-9463)
PHONE..................330 863-0611
William Robertson, *Pr*
EMP: 27 **EST:** 1898
SQ FT: 40,000
SALES (est): 3.94MM **Privately Held**
Web: www.doitbest.com
SIC: 5251 1711 5031 Hardware stores; Plumbing contractors; Building materials, exterior

(G-10236)
ROGER BETTIS TRUCKING INC
7089 Alliance Rd Nw (44644-9428)
P.O. Box 396 (44644-0396)
PHONE..................330 863-2111
EMP: 36 **EST:** 1985
SQ FT: 14,000
SALES (est): 2.99MM **Privately Held**
Web: www.greenlines.net
SIC: 4213 Trucking, except local

(G-10237)
SHECKLER EXCAVATING INC
6203 Alliance Rd Nw (44644-9203)
P.O. Box 340 (44644-0340)
PHONE..................330 866-1999
Cheryl Sheckler, *Pr*
Bill Sheckler, *
▲ **EMP:** 65 **EST:** 1983
SALES (est): 3.6MM **Privately Held**
Web: www.shecklerexc.com
SIC: 1794 Excavation work

Manchester
Adams County

(G-10238)
A LOVING HART HM HLTH CARE LLC
255 Cabin Creek Rd (45144-9312)
PHONE..................937 549-4484
Jessika Rena Saunders, *Pr*
EMP: 60 **EST:** 2016
SALES (est): 2.22MM **Privately Held**
Web: www.alovinghearthhc.com
SIC: 8082 Home health care services

(G-10239)
DAYTON POWER AND LIGHT COMPANY
Also Called: DPL
745 Us Highway 52 Unit 1 (45144-8450)
PHONE..................937 549-2641
Ron Rodrique, *Brnch Mgr*
EMP: 189
SQ FT: 1,040
SALES (corp-wide): 12.67B **Publicly Held**
Web: www.aes-ohio.com
SIC: 4911 Fossil fuel electric power generation
HQ: The Dayton Power And Light Company
1065 Woodman Dr
Dayton OH 45432
937 331-3900

(G-10240)
DAYTON POWER AND LIGHT COMPANY
14869 Us Highway 52 (45144-9332)
PHONE..................937 549-2641
Dave Orme, *Manager*
EMP: 72
SALES (corp-wide): 12.67B **Publicly Held**
Web: www.aes-ohio.com
SIC: 4931 4932 4911 Electric and other services combined; Gas and other services combined; Fossil fuel electric power generation
HQ: The Dayton Power And Light Company
1065 Woodman Dr
Dayton OH 45432
937 331-3900

Mansfield
Richland County

(G-10241)
1-888-OHIOCOMP INC
1495 W Longview Ave (44906-1872)
PHONE..................888 644-6266
Dan Neubert, *CEO*
EMP: 74
SALES (corp-wide): 3.81MM **Privately Held**
Web: www.minutemenmco.com
SIC: 8082 Home health care services
PA: 1-888-Ohiocomp, Inc.
2900 Carnegie Ave
Cleveland OH 44115
216 426-0646

(G-10242)
A TOUCH OF GRACE INC
787 Lexington Ave Ste 303 (44907-1998)
PHONE..................567 560-2350
EMP: 37
SALES (corp-wide): 2.33MM **Privately Held**
Web: www.atouchofgracehomehealth.com
SIC: 8082 Home health care services
PA: A Touch Of Grace, Inc.
809 Coshocton Ave Ste B
Mount Vernon OH 43050
740 397-7971

(G-10243)
AMBROSE ASPHALT INC
2251 Marion Avenue Rd (44903-9411)
P.O. Box 167 (44862-0167)
PHONE..................419 774-1780
Matthew Ambrose, *Pr*
Cheryl Ambrose, *Sec*
EMP: 27 **EST:** 2001
SALES (est): 1.94MM **Privately Held**
Web: www.ambryasphalt.net
SIC: 1611 Highway and street paving contractor

(G-10244)
ASSOCIATED CREDIT SERVICE INC
6 Plymouth St (44904-1122)
P.O. Box 9041 (44904-9041)
PHONE..................419 524-6446
Linda Caudell, *Pr*
EMP: 30 **EST:** 1985
SALES (est): 1.1MM **Privately Held**
SIC: 7322 Collection agency, except real estate

(G-10245)
BLACK RIVER GROUP INC (PA)
Also Called: Black River Display Group
195 E 4th St (44902-1519)
PHONE..................419 524-6699
Terry Neff, *Pr*
EMP: 47 **EST:** 1960
SQ FT: 74,000
SALES (est): 11.55MM
SALES (corp-wide): 11.55MM **Privately Held**
Web: www.blackriverconnect.com
SIC: 7311 2752 2791 2789 Advertising agencies; Commercial printing, lithographic; Typesetting; Bookbinding and related work

(G-10246)
BLACK RIVER GROUP INC
Also Called: Black River Display
195 E 4th St (44902-1519)
PHONE..................419 524-4312
Greg Tritt, *Brnch Mgr*
EMP: 40
SALES (corp-wide): 11.55MM **Privately Held**
Web: www.blackriverconnect.com
SIC: 5023 5039 Floor coverings; Ceiling systems and products
PA: Black River Group, Inc.
195 E 4th St
Mansfield OH 44902
419 524-6699

(G-10247)
BLUESCOPE RECYCLING & MTLS LLC
2384 Springmill Rd (44903-8009)
PHONE..................419 747-6522
Mark Vassella, *Brnch Mgr*
EMP: 60
Web: www.bluescoperecycling.com
SIC: 4953 Recycling, waste materials
HQ: Bluescope Recycling And Materials Llc
295 S Commerce Dr
Waterloo IN 46793
419 540-4355

Mansfield - Richland County (G-10248)

(G-10248)
BREITINGER COMPANY
595 Oakenwaldt St (44905-1900)
PHONE..................................419 526-4255
Milo Breitinger, *Pr*
EMP: 120 **EST:** 1954
SQ FT: 106,000
SALES (est): 13.94MM **Privately Held**
Web: www.breitingercompany.com
SIC: 3441 3469 7692 3444 Fabricated structural metal; Metal stampings, nec; Welding repair; Sheet metalwork

(G-10249)
BUCKEYE CHECK CASHING INC
Also Called: Checksmart
801 N Lexington Springmill Rd (44906-3316)
PHONE..................................419 528-1315
EMP: 35
Web: www.ccfi.com
SIC: 6099 Check cashing agencies
HQ: Buckeye Check Cashing, Inc.
5165 Emerald Pkwy Ste 100
Dublin KY 43017
614 798-5900

(G-10250)
CAMBRIDGE HOME HEALTH CARE
780 Park Ave W Unit B (44906-3022)
PHONE..................................419 775-1253
Sue Dezort, *Mgr*
EMP: 831
SALES (corp-wide): 371.62B **Publicly Held**
Web: www.cambridgehomehealth.com
SIC: 8082 Home health care services
HQ: Cambridge Home Health Care Inc
9510 Ormsby Station Rd # 300
Louisville KY 40223
330 270-8661

(G-10251)
CENTER FOR INDVDUAL FMLY SVCS (PA)
Also Called: Catalyst Life Services
741 Scholl Rd (44907)
PHONE..................................419 522-4357
Laura Montgomery, *Pr*
Veronica L Groff, *
EMP: 110 **EST:** 1952
SQ FT: 30,000
SALES (est): 15.86MM
SALES (corp-wide): 15.86MM **Privately Held**
Web: www.catalystlifeservices.org
SIC: 8093 8322 Mental health clinic, outpatient; Individual and family services

(G-10252)
CHILDRENS CMPRHENSIVE SVCS INC
1451 Lucas Rd (44903-8682)
P.O. Box 2226 (44905-0226)
PHONE..................................419 589-5511
Steven Covington, *Brnch Mgr*
EMP: 90
SALES (corp-wide): 14.28B **Publicly Held**
SIC: 8322 8361 Individual and family services; Residential care
HQ: Children's Comprehensive Services, Inc.
3401 West End Ave Ste 400
Nashville TN 37203
615 250-0000

(G-10253)
CHILDRENS HOSP MED CTR AKRON
371 Cline Ave (44907-1021)
PHONE..................................419 521-2900
Jonas Bronk, *Pr*
EMP: 54
SALES (corp-wide): 1.4B **Privately Held**
Web: www.akronchildrens.org
SIC: 8062 General medical and surgical hospitals
PA: Childrens Hospital Medical Center Of Akron
1 Perkins Sq
Akron OH 44308
330 543-1000

(G-10254)
CONTINENTAL HOME HEALTH CARE
1495 W Longview Ave Ste 103 (44906-1872)
PHONE..................................419 521-2470
EMP: 50
Web: www.continentalhhc.net
SIC: 8082 Visiting nurse service
PA: Continental Home Health Care Inc
5898 Cleveland Ave # 100
Columbus OH 43231

(G-10255)
COUNTY OF RICHLAND
Also Called: New Hope Center
314 Cleveland Ave (44902-8623)
PHONE..................................419 774-4200
EMP: 350
SALES (corp-wide): 122.09MM **Privately Held**
Web: www.rnewhope.org
SIC: 8059 9111 Home for the mentally retarded, ex. skilled or intermediate; County supervisors' and executives' office
PA: County Of Richland
50 Park Ave E Ste 3
Mansfield OH 44902
419 774-5501

(G-10256)
CRYSTAL CARE CENTERS INC (PA)
Also Called: Crystal Care of Mansfield
1159 Wyandotte Ave (44906)
PHONE..................................419 747-2666
Jerry Smith, *Pr*
EMP: 90 **EST:** 1992
SALES (est): 5.87MM **Privately Held**
Web: www.crystalcarecenters.com
SIC: 8051 8059 Convalescent home with continuous nursing care; Rest home, with health care

(G-10257)
DAYTON FREIGHT LINES INC
103 Cairns Rd (44903-8992)
PHONE..................................419 589-0350
Justin Sharky, *Brnch Mgr*
EMP: 51
SALES (corp-wide): 6.59B **Privately Held**
Web: www.daytonfreight.com
SIC: 4213 Trucking, except local
PA: Dayton Freight Lines, Inc.
6450 Poe Ave
Dayton OH 45414
937 264-4060

(G-10258)
DISCOVERY SCHOOL
855 Millsboro Rd (44903-1997)
PHONE..................................419 756-8880
Amy Oswalt, *Prin*
EMP: 39 **EST:** 1975
SALES (est): 1.27MM **Privately Held**
Web: www.discovery-school.net
SIC: 8211 8351 Private elementary school; Preschool center

(G-10259)
DTE INC
110 Baird Pkwy (44903-7909)
PHONE..................................419 522-3428
Dean Russell, *Pr*
Burke Melching, *
Rob Nelson, *
EMP: 30 **EST:** 1990
SQ FT: 45,000
SALES (est): 2.43MM **Privately Held**
Web: www.dteinc.com
SIC: 7629 3661 Telephone set repair; Telephone and telegraph apparatus

(G-10260)
EDGE PLASTICS INC
Also Called: Jobs On Site
449 Newman St (44902-1123)
PHONE..................................419 522-6696
Diana White, *Mgr*
EMP: 50
Web: www.edgeplasticsinc.com
SIC: 7363 Help supply services
PA: Edge Plastics, Inc.
449 Newman St
Mansfield OH 44902

(G-10261)
ELITE EXCAVATING COMPANY INC
Also Called: Elite Excavating Ohio Company
4500 Snodgrass Rd (44903)
P.O. Box 290 (44862)
PHONE..................................419 683-4200
Micheal Scott Fulmer, *Pr*
Patricia Fulmer, *
EMP: 28 **EST:** 1999
SQ FT: 8,000
SALES (est): 5.33MM **Privately Held**
SIC: 1794 Excavation work

(G-10262)
ELIXIR VI LLC
3117 Kings Corners Rd W (44904-9506)
PHONE..................................419 884-9808
EMP: 145
SIC: 8059 Nursing home, except skilled and intermediate care facility
PA: Elixir Vi, Llc
561 Leeds Gate
Wadsworth OH 44281

(G-10263)
FIRST ASSEMBLY CHILD CARE
Also Called: Assembly Child Care
1000 Mcpherson St (44903-7145)
PHONE..................................419 529-6501
Kim Mccoy, *Dir*
Ilona J Director, *Dir*
Kim Glavic, *Asst Dir*
EMP: 27 **EST:** 1972
SALES (est): 509.65K **Privately Held**
Web: www.mansfieldfirst.com
SIC: 8351 8661 Child day care services; Religious organizations

(G-10264)
FIRST CHICE MED STFFING OHIO I
Also Called: First Choice Medical Staffing
90 W 2nd St (44902-1917)
PHONE..................................419 521-2700
Charles Slone, *Brnch Mgr*
EMP: 106
SALES (corp-wide): 6.66MM **Privately Held**
Web: www.firstchoiceohio.com
SIC: 7361 Employment agencies
PA: First Choice Medical Staffing Of Ohio, Inc.
1457 W 117th St
Cleveland OH 44107
216 521-2222

(G-10265)
FREEDOM CAREGIVERS
1069 Lexington Ave # B (44907-2265)
PHONE..................................567 560-8277
Lisa Graham, *Mgr*
EMP: 27 **EST:** 2018
SALES (est): 98.17K **Privately Held**
Web: www.freedom-caregivers.com
SIC: 8082 Home health care services

(G-10266)
GAASH HOME HEALTH CARE LLC
Also Called: Health Care
911 S Main St (44907-2037)
PHONE..................................419 775-4823
Omar Qalinle, *CEO*
EMP: 60 **EST:** 2009
SALES (est): 2.48MM **Privately Held**
Web: www.gaashhomehealthcare.com
SIC: 8082 Home health care services

(G-10267)
GLOBAL ENERGY PARTNERS LLC
Also Called: Gofs
3401 State Route 13 (44904-9394)
PHONE..................................419 756-8027
Jim Jackson, *Pr*
Annette Jones, *Sec*
EMP: 27 **EST:** 2013
SALES (est): 15.22MM **Privately Held**
Web: www.globalenergypartnersllc.com
SIC: 1389 5082 1623 Oil field services, nec; Oil field equipment; Oil and gas line and compressor station construction

(G-10268)
HEALING HRTS CUNSELING CTR INC
680 Park Ave W Ste 204 (44906-3706)
PHONE..................................419 528-5993
Maja-lisa Anderson, *Pr*
EMP: 35 **EST:** 2015
SALES (est): 31.99K **Privately Held**
Web: www.healingheartscc.com
SIC: 8322 General counseling services

(G-10269)
HOME DEPOT USA INC
Also Called: Home Depot, The
2000 August Dr (44906)
PHONE..................................419 529-0015
Rob Haner, *Mgr*
EMP: 196
SALES (corp-wide): 152.67B **Publicly Held**
Web: www.homedepot.com
SIC: 5211 7359 Home centers; Tool rental
HQ: Home Depot U.S.A., Inc.
2445 Springfield Ave
Vauxhall NJ 07088

(G-10270)
HUNTINGTON NATIONAL BANK
Also Called: Firstmerit
1277 Ashland Rd (44905-2252)
PHONE..................................419 589-3111
Lorri Mullins, *Genl Mgr*
EMP: 31
SALES (corp-wide): 10.84B **Publicly Held**
Web: www.huntington.com
SIC: 6029 Commercial banks, nec
HQ: The Huntington National Bank
41 S High St
Columbus OH 43215
614 480-4293

(G-10271)
HURSH DRUGS INC
Also Called: Hursh Drug
90 N Diamond St (44902-1392)

GEOGRAPHIC SECTION
Mansfield - Richland County (G-10292)

PHONE.............................419 524-0521
Robert H Knowlton, *Pr*
EMP: 41 EST: 1898
SQ FT: 20,000
SALES (est): 1.43MM **Privately Held**
Web: www.hurshdrugs.com
SIC: **5912** 5047 Drug stores; Instruments, surgical and medical

(G-10272)
INSTALLED BUILDING PDTS LLC
Also Called: Mooney and Moses
303 E Main St (44904-1336)
PHONE.............................419 884-0676
Mike Stricklin, *Mgr*
EMP: 49
SALES (corp-wide): 2.78B **Publicly Held**
Web: www.installedbuildingproducts.com
SIC: **1742** Insulation, buildings
HQ: Installed Building Products Llc
495 S High St Ste 150
Columbus OH 43215
614 221-3399

(G-10273)
J & B ACOUSTICAL INC
Also Called: Classical Glass & Mirror
2750 Lexington Ave (44904)
P.O. Box 3015 (44904)
PHONE.............................419 884-1155
EMP: 75 EST: 1957
SALES (est): 9.62MM **Privately Held**
Web: www.jb-ohio.com
SIC: **1742** Acoustical and ceiling work

(G-10274)
J-TRAC INC
Also Called: Dearman Moving and Storage
961 N Main St (44903-8124)
P.O. Box 1992 (44901-1992)
PHONE.............................419 524-3456
Tim Cambell, *Pr*
Chris Cambell, *
EMP: 50 EST: 1991
SALES (est): 2.32MM **Privately Held**
Web: www.dearmanmoving.com
SIC: **4225** 4214 4213 4212 General warehousing; Local trucking with storage; Trucking, except local; Local trucking, without storage

(G-10275)
JACKSON & SONS DRILLING & PUMP
Also Called: Ohio Geothermal
3401 State Route 13 (44904-9394)
PHONE.............................419 756-2758
TOLL FREE: 800
James D Jackson, *Pr*
EMP: 30 EST: 1979
SALES (est): 1.03MM **Privately Held**
SIC: **4911** 7389 7335
; Water softener service; Commercial photography

(G-10276)
JONES POTATO CHIP CO (PA)
823 Bowman St (44903-4107)
PHONE.............................419 529-9424
Robert Jones, *Pr*
Regina Jones, *
Charles K Hellinger, *
Frederick W Jones, *
EMP: 46 EST: 1940
SQ FT: 50,000
SALES (est): 9.05MM
SALES (corp-wide): 9.05MM **Privately Held**
Web: www.joneschips.com

SIC: **2096** 5145 Potato chips and other potato-based snacks; Potato chips

(G-10277)
KADEMENOS WISEHART HINES (PA)
6 W 3rd St Ste 200 (44902-1200)
PHONE.............................419 524-6011
Troy Wisehart, *Pr*
Victor P Kademenos, *
EMP: 40 EST: 1956
SALES (est): 2.25MM
SALES (corp-wide): 2.25MM **Privately Held**
Web: www.ckclawyers.com
SIC: **8111** General practice attorney, lawyer

(G-10278)
KHODIYAR INC
880 Laver Rd (44905-2341)
PHONE.............................419 589-2200
Paresh Patel, *Prin*
EMP: 29 EST: 2007
SALES (est): 476.86K **Privately Held**
SIC: **7011** Hotels and motels

(G-10279)
KOKOSING CONSTRUCTION CO INC
606 N Main St (44902-7337)
PHONE.............................419 524-5656
W Brian Burgett, *CEO*
EMP: 102
SALES (corp-wide): 1.17B **Privately Held**
Web: www.kokosing.biz
SIC: **1611** General contractor, highway and street construction
HQ: Kokosing Construction Company, Inc.
6235 Westerville Rd
Westerville OH 43081
614 228-1029

(G-10280)
KOORSEN FIRE & SECURITY INC
100 Swarn Pkwy (44903-6515)
PHONE.............................419 526-2212
Randy Koorsen, *Pr*
EMP: 30
SALES (corp-wide): 150.64MM **Privately Held**
Web: www.koorsen.com
SIC: **7382** Protective devices, security
PA: Koorsen Fire & Security, Inc.
2719 N Arlington Ave
Indianapolis IN 46218
317 542-1800

(G-10281)
LEXINGTON COURT CARE CENTER
Also Called: BURNS INTERNATIONAL STAFFING
250 Delaware Ave (44904-1215)
PHONE.............................419 884-2000
Toni Marone, *Admn*
EMP: 42 EST: 1982
SALES (est): 7.1MM **Privately Held**
Web: www.atriumlivingcenters.com
SIC: **8052** 8051 Intermediate care facilities; Skilled nursing care facilities

(G-10282)
LIND OUTDOOR ADVERTISING CO
Also Called: Lind Media Company
409 N Main St 411 (44902)
P.O. Box 5601 (44901-5601)
PHONE.............................419 522-2600
EMP: 35 EST: 1991
SQ FT: 24,000
SALES (est): 3.25MM **Privately Held**
Web: www.lindmedia.com

SIC: **7312** 7311 Billboard advertising; Advertising agencies

(G-10283)
LQ MANAGEMENT LLC
Also Called: La Quinta Inn
120 Stander Ave (44903-9405)
PHONE.............................419 774-0005
Stephanie Lee, *Mgr*
EMP: 27
SALES (corp-wide): 1.4B **Publicly Held**
Web: www.lq.com
SIC: **7011** Hotels and motels
HQ: Lq Management L.L.C.
909 Hidden Rdg Ste 600
Irving TX 75038
214 492-6600

(G-10284)
MADISON LOCAL SCHOOL DISTRICT
Also Called: Madison Child Care Center
103 Bahl Ave (44905-2804)
PHONE.............................419 589-7851
Natasha Repp, *Dir*
EMP: 40
SALES (corp-wide): 43.74MM **Privately Held**
Web: www.mlsd.net
SIC: **8211** 8351 Preparatory school; Child day care services
PA: Madison Local School District
1379 Grace St
Mansfield OH 44905
419 589-2600

(G-10285)
MAJOR METALS COMPANY
844 Kochheiser Rd (44904-8637)
PHONE.............................419 886-4600
Jeffrey C Mason, *Pr*
Wayne Riffe, *
EMP: 30 EST: 1973
SQ FT: 60,000
SALES (est): 10MM **Privately Held**
Web: www.majormetals.net
SIC: **3312** 5051 3317 Plate, sheet and strip, except coated products; Iron or steel flat products; Steel pipe and tubes

(G-10286)
MANSFIELD CEMENT FLOORING INC
11 N Mill St (44904-1200)
P.O. Box 3212 (44904-0212)
PHONE.............................419 884-3733
FAX: 419 884-1473
EMP: 50 EST: 1968
SQ FT: 7,000
SALES (est): 8MM **Privately Held**
SIC: **1771** Flooring contractor

(G-10287)
MANSFIELD HOTEL PARTNERSHIP (PA)
Also Called: Quality Inn
500 N Trimble Rd (44906-2102)
PHONE.............................419 529-1000
Sandy Kiser, *Mgr*
Ronald Fewster, *Pt*
Doctor When Fu Chin, *Pt*
Patrick Mc Allister, *Pt*
EMP: 38 EST: 1987
SQ FT: 44,000
SALES (est): 2.07MM
SALES (corp-wide): 2.07MM **Privately Held**
Web: www.choicehotels.com
SIC: **7011** 7991 Hotels and motels; Physical fitness facilities

(G-10288)
MANSFIELD MEMORIAL HOMES
Also Called: Robert Sturges Memorial Homes
55 Wood St (44903-2251)
P.O. Box 966 (44901-0966)
PHONE.............................419 774-5100
EMP: 125 EST: 2011
SALES (est): 4.33MM **Privately Held**
Web: www.mansfieldmh.com
SIC: **6513** Retirement hotel operation

(G-10289)
MANSFIELD MEMORIAL HOMES LLC (PA)
Also Called: GERIATRICS CENTER OF MANSFIELD
50 Blymyer Ave (44903-2343)
P.O. Box 966 (44901-0966)
PHONE.............................419 774-5100
Raymond Loughman, *
EMP: 129 EST: 1953
SALES (est): 5.47MM
SALES (corp-wide): 5.47MM **Privately Held**
Web: www.mansfieldmh.com
SIC: **8051** 8052 Convalescent home with continuous nursing care; Intermediate care facilities

(G-10290)
MANSFIELD TRUCK SLS & SVC INC
85 Longview Ave E (44903-4205)
P.O. Box 1516 (44901-1516)
PHONE.............................419 522-9811
TOLL FREE: 800
Fred Bollon, *Pr*
EMP: 65 EST: 1996
SALES (est): 2.3MM
SALES (corp-wide): 15.49MM **Privately Held**
SIC: **5012** 5511 7538 Trucks, commercial; Trucks, tractors, and trailers: new and used; General truck repair
PA: Truck Sales & Service, Inc.
3429 Brightwood Rd
Midvale OH
740 922-3412

(G-10291)
MECHANICS BANK (HQ)
2 S Main St (44902-2931)
PHONE.............................419 524-0831
Mark Masters, *Pr*
Jason Painley, *
Nicholas Gesouras, *Corporate Secretary**
EMP: 35 EST: 1886
SQ FT: 5,000
SALES (est): 29.34MM **Privately Held**
Web: www.mymechanics.com
SIC: **6022** State commercial banks
PA: Mechanics Financial Corporation
2 S Main St
Mansfield OH 44902

(G-10292)
MEDCENTRAL HEALTH SYSTEM
Also Called: Med Central HM Hlth & Hospice
335 Glessner Ave (44903-2269)
PHONE.............................419 526-8442
Marte Alsleben, *Owner*
EMP: 215
SALES (corp-wide): 4.29B **Privately Held**
Web: www.medcentral.org
SIC: **8062** 8082 8093 General medical and surgical hospitals; Home health care services; Specialty outpatient clinics, nec
HQ: Medcentral Health System
335 Glessner Ave
Mansfield OH 44903
419 526-8000

Mansfield - Richland County (G-10293) GEOGRAPHIC SECTION

(G-10293)
MEDCENTRAL HEALTH SYSTEM (HQ)
Also Called: Ohiohealth Mansfield Hospital
335 Glessner Ave (44903-2269)
PHONE.................................419 526-8000
Beth Hildreth, *VP*
EMP: 1060 EST: 1911
SQ FT: 300,000
SALES (est): 328.79MM
SALES (corp-wide): 4.29B **Privately Held**
Web: www.medcentral.org
SIC: **8062** General medical and surgical hospitals
PA: Ohiohealth Corporation
3430 Ohhalth Pkwy 5th Flr
Columbus OH 43202
614 788-8860

(G-10294)
MEDCENTRAL HEALTH SYSTEM
770 Balgreen Dr Ste 105 (44906-4106)
PHONE.................................419 526-8970
James Meyer, *Brnch Mgr*
EMP: 215
SALES (corp-wide): 4.29B **Privately Held**
Web: www.medcentral.org
SIC: **8062** General medical and surgical hospitals
HQ: Medcentral Health System
335 Glessner Ave
Mansfield OH 44903
419 526-8000

(G-10295)
MEDIC RSPNSE AMBULANCE SVC INC (PA)
98 S Diamond St (44902-7564)
PHONE.................................419 522-1998
Thomas F Wappner, *Pr*
William C Wappner, *
EMP: 30 EST: 1988
SQ FT: 1,600
SALES (est): 2.15MM
SALES (corp-wide): 2.15MM **Privately Held**
SIC: **4119** Ambulance service

(G-10296)
MERRILL SWANSON DDS LLC
355 W Main St (44904-9543)
PHONE.................................419 884-3411
Lisa S Swanson, *Prin*
EMP: 30 EST: 2008
SALES (est): 527.73K **Privately Held**
SIC: **8021** Dentists' office

(G-10297)
MID-OHIO HEART CLINIC INC
335 Glessner Ave (44903-2269)
PHONE.................................419 524-8151
William Polinsky Md, *Pr*
Gregory Vigesaa Md, *VP*
Michael Amalfitano Md, *VP*
EMP: 35 EST: 1988
SALES (est): 3.84MM **Privately Held**
Web: www.midohioheart.com
SIC: **8062** General medical and surgical hospitals

(G-10298)
MID-OHIO PIPELINE COMPANY INC
Also Called: Mid-Ohio Pipeline Services
2270 Eckert Rd (44904-9742)
PHONE.................................419 884-3772
Jordan Yates, *Pr*
EMP: 40 EST: 1970
SALES (est): 10.97MM
SALES (corp-wide): 6.93B **Publicly Held**
Web: www.mopipeline.com

SIC: **1623** Oil and gas pipeline construction
PA: Api Group Corporation
1100 Old Highway 8 Nw
New Brighton MN 55112
651 636-4320

(G-10299)
MID-OHIO PIPELINE SERVICES LLC
4244 State Route 546 (44904-9327)
P.O. Box 3049 (44904-0049)
PHONE.................................419 884-3772
Brent Yates, *CEO*
Jordan Yates, *Pr*
Thomas A Lyndon, *CFO*
Emily Keinath, *Sec*
Mark Polovitz, *Asst Tr*
EMP: 42 EST: 2010
SALES (est): 57.46MM
SALES (corp-wide): 6.93B **Publicly Held**
Web: www.mopipeline.com
SIC: **7389** Pipeline and power line inspection service
HQ: Api Group, Inc.
1100 Old Highway 8 Nw
New Brighton MN 55112
651 636-4320

(G-10300)
MT BUSINESS TECHNOLOGIES INC (DH)
1150 National Pkwy (44906-1911)
P.O. Box 37 (44901-0037)
PHONE.................................419 529-6100
TOLL FREE: 800
Chuck Rounds, *Pr*
EMP: 130 EST: 1930
SQ FT: 64,000
SALES (est): 51.28MM
SALES (corp-wide): 6.89B **Publicly Held**
Web: www.mtbt.com
SIC: **5044** 7378 7379 Copying equipment; Computer peripheral equipment repair and maintenance; Computer related consulting services
HQ: Xerox Business Solutions Inc
8701 Florida Mining Blvd
Tampa FL 33624

(G-10301)
NANOGATE NORTH AMERICA LLC
Also Called: Kronis Coatings
1575 W Longview Ave (44906-1806)
PHONE.................................419 747-6639
EMP: 300
SALES (corp-wide): 193.63MM **Privately Held**
Web: www.jayindinc.com
SIC: **5198** Paints
HQ: Nanogate North America Llc
150 Longview Ave E
Mansfield OH 44903
419 524-3778

(G-10302)
NANOGATE NORTH AMERICA LLC (HQ)
Also Called: A Techniplas Company
150 Longview Ave E (44903-4206)
PHONE.................................419 524-3778
Ali El-haj, *CEO*
David Culton, *
EMP: 194 EST: 2016
SALES (est): 128.58MM
SALES (corp-wide): 193.63MM **Privately Held**
Web: www.jayindinc.com
SIC: **1799** Coating of concrete structures with plastic
PA: Techniplas Us Llc
N44 W33341 Wtrtown Plank
Nashotah WI 53058

262 369-5555

(G-10303)
NATIONWIDE CHILDRENS HOSPITAL
536 S Trimble Rd (44906-3418)
PHONE.................................419 528-3140
EMP: 51
SALES (corp-wide): 3.6B **Privately Held**
Web: www.nationwidechildrens.org
SIC: **8071** 8062 Medical laboratories; General medical and surgical hospitals
PA: Nationwide Children's Hospital
700 Childrens Dr
Columbus OH 43205
614 722-2000

(G-10304)
NEW MERCY OUTREACH INC
1221 S Trimble Rd (44907-2200)
PHONE.................................567 560-9021
Ashantia Ginn, *Ex Dir*
EMP: 28
SALES (est): 1.46MM **Privately Held**
Web: www.newmercyoutreach.com
SIC: **8361** Group foster home

(G-10305)
NEXT GENERATION BAG INC
230 Industrial Dr (44904-1346)
PHONE.................................419 884-1327
John D Frecka, *CEO*
EMP: 29 EST: 2001
SALES (est): 403.78K **Privately Held**
SIC: **5199** Packaging materials

(G-10306)
OAK GROVE MANOR INC
1670 Crider Rd (44903-9268)
PHONE.................................419 589-6222
Med Velasco, *Admn*
EMP: 45 EST: 1980
SALES (est): 5.15MM **Privately Held**
Web: www.oakgrovemansfield.com
SIC: **8051** Convalescent home with continuous nursing care

(G-10307)
OHIO EYE ASSOCIATES INC
Also Called: Marquardt, Richard F Od
466 S Trimble Rd (44906-3416)
PHONE.................................800 423-0694
TOLL FREE: 800
John L Marquardt, *Pr*
Leonard D Quick, *
EMP: 96 EST: 1973
SQ FT: 32,000
SALES (est): 13.11MM **Privately Held**
Web: www.ohioeyeassociates.com
SIC: **8011** Opthalmologist

(G-10308)
OHIO SKI SLOPES INC
Also Called: Snow Trails Ski Resort
3100 Possum Run Rd (44903-7524)
P.O. Box 1456 (44901-1456)
PHONE.................................419 774-9818
David L Carto, *Pr*
EMP: 98 EST: 1961
SQ FT: 54,500
SALES (est): 9.3MM **Privately Held**
Web: www.snowtrails.com
SIC: **5812** 7999 5941 Eating places; Ski instruction; Skiing equipment

(G-10309)
OHIOHEALTH PHYSICIAN GROUP INC (HQ)
Also Called: Ohio Hlth Hart Vsclar Physcans
335 Glessner Ave (44903-2269)
PHONE.................................567 241-7000

Robert L Perkins, *Prin*
EMP: 50 EST: 1992
SALES (est): 19.71MM
SALES (corp-wide): 4.29B **Privately Held**
Web: www.ohiohealth.com
SIC: **8062** General medical and surgical hospitals
PA: Ohiohealth Corporation
3430 Ohhalth Pkwy 5th Flr
Columbus OH 43202
614 788-8860

(G-10310)
PARK HOSPITALITY LLC
Also Called: Holiday Inn
116 Park Ave W (44902-1607)
PHONE.................................419 525-6000
Joe Puhl, *Admn*
Christina Mansfield, *
Dharmendra Patel, *
EMP: 34 EST: 2014
SALES (est): 2.42MM **Privately Held**
Web: www.holidayinn.com
SIC: **7011** Hotels and motels

(G-10311)
RICHLAND NEWHOPE INDS INC
Also Called: Richland Newhope
314 Cleveland Ave (44902-8623)
PHONE.................................419 774-4200
Jan Arnold, *Ex Dir*
EMP: 40
SALES (corp-wide): 8.39MM **Privately Held**
Web: www.rniinc.com
SIC: **8331** Job training and related services
PA: Richland Newhope Industries, Inc.
150 E 4th St
Mansfield OH 44902
419 774-4400

(G-10312)
RICHLAND NEWHOPE INDS INC
985 W Longview Ave (44906-2133)
PHONE.................................419 774-4496
Marsha Madden, *Prin*
EMP: 40
SALES (corp-wide): 8.39MM **Privately Held**
Web: www.rniinc.com
SIC: **8331** Job training and related services
PA: Richland Newhope Industries, Inc.
150 E 4th St
Mansfield OH 44902
419 774-4400

(G-10313)
RICHLAND NEWHOPE INDS INC (PA)
150 E 4th St (44902-1520)
P.O. Box 916 (44901-0916)
PHONE.................................419 774-4400
Elizabeth Prather, *Ex Dir*
EMP: 250 EST: 1963
SQ FT: 63,000
SALES (est): 8.39MM
SALES (corp-wide): 8.39MM **Privately Held**
Web: www.rniinc.com
SIC: **0782** 2448 7349 8331 Lawn and garden services; Wood pallets and skids; Building maintenance services, nec; Job training and related services

(G-10314)
RICHLAND TRUST COMPANY
3 N Main St Ste 1 (44902-1740)
PHONE.................................419 525-8700
Timothy J Lehman, *Pr*
Jerrold Coon, *
Ray Piar, *
EMP: 163 EST: 1898

GEOGRAPHIC SECTION
Maple Heights - Cuyahoga County (G-10335)

SALES (est): 7.04MM
SALES (corp-wide): 564.3MM **Publicly Held**
Web: www.parknationalbank.com
SIC: **6022** 8721 State trust companies accepting deposits, commercial; Accounting, auditing, and bookkeeping
PA: Park National Corporation
50 N 3rd St
Newark OH 43055
740 349-8451

(G-10315)
SALVANALLE INC
Also Called: Everdry Waterproofing
2760 Crider Rd (44903-8721)
PHONE..............................419 529-4700
TOLL FREE: 800
EMP: 35 EST: 1995
SQ FT: 6,500
SALES (est): 2.55MM **Privately Held**
Web: www.basementwaterproofer.com
SIC: **1799** Waterproofing

(G-10316)
SKYBOX INVESTMENTS INC
Also Called: Brasspack Packing Supply
1275 Pollock Pkwy (44905-1374)
P.O. Box 1567 (44901-1567)
PHONE..............................419 525-6013
James Miller, *CEO*
Rodney Robertson, *
Marc Miller, *
Marty Rice, *
Joseph R Murach, *
EMP: 45 EST: 1996
SQ FT: 60,000
SALES (est): 9.16MM **Privately Held**
Web: www.skyboxpackaging.com
SIC: **5199** Packaging materials

(G-10317)
SKYBOX PACKAGING LLC
Also Called: Mr Box
1275 Pollock Pkwy (44905-1374)
P.O. Box 1567 (44901-1567)
PHONE..............................419 525-7209
Marc Miller, *Pr*
EMP: 152 EST: 2001
SALES (est): 27.06MM
SALES (corp-wide): 882.33MM **Privately Held**
Web: www.skyboxpackaging.com
SIC: **3086** 5199 2653 5162 Packaging and shipping materials, foamed plastics; Packaging materials; Boxes, corrugated: made from purchased materials; Plastics materials and basic shapes
PA: Atlantic Packaging Products Ltd
111 Progress Ave
Scarborough ON
416 298-8101

(G-10318)
SPRING MEADOW EXTENDED CARE CE
105 S Main St (44902-7901)
PHONE..............................419 866-6124
Donald D Graber, *Brnch Mgr*
EMP: 33
SALES (corp-wide): 9.61MM **Privately Held**
Web: www.springmeadowsvhc.com
SIC: **8052** Intermediate care facilities
PA: Spring Meadow Extended Care Center Facility, Inc.
1125 Clarion Ave
Holland OH 43528
419 866-6124

(G-10319)
THE MAPLE CITY ICE COMPANY
Mansfield Distributing Co Div
1245 W Longview Ave (44906-1907)
PHONE..............................419 747-4777
Michael J Berry, *Brnch Mgr*
EMP: 37
SQ FT: 16,463
SALES (corp-wide): 16.72MM **Privately Held**
Web: www.maplecityice.net
SIC: **5181** Beer and other fermented malt liquors
PA: The Maple City Ice Company
371 Cleveland Rd
Norwalk OH 44857
419 668-2531

(G-10320)
UNITED PARCEL SERVICE INC
Also Called: UPS
875 W Longview Ave (44906-2131)
PHONE..............................419 747-3080
Chuck Kastor, *Mgr*
EMP: 31
SALES (corp-wide): 90.96B **Publicly Held**
Web: www.ups.com
SIC: **4215** Package delivery, vehicular
HQ: United Parcel Service, Inc.
55 Glenlake Pkwy
Atlanta GA 30328
404 828-6000

(G-10321)
VALVOLINE INSTANT OIL CHNGE FR
Also Called: Valvoline Instant Oil Change
1439 Ashland Rd (44905-2256)
PHONE..............................419 589-5396
Michael Wilzcinski, *Mgr*
EMP: 45
SQ FT: 4,000
Web: www.valvoline.com
SIC: **7549** Automotive maintenance services
HQ: Valvoline Instant Oil Change Franchising, Inc.
100 Valvoline Way
Lexington KY 40509

(G-10322)
VISITING NRSE ASSN OF CLVELAND
Also Called: Vna of Mid Ohio
40 W 4th St (44902-1206)
P.O. Box 1742 (44901-1742)
PHONE..............................419 522-4969
Cortney Swihart, *Ex Dir*
Dana Traxler, *
EMP: 40 EST: 1904
SALES (est): 691.28K **Privately Held**
Web: www.vnaohio.org
SIC: **8082** Visiting nurse service

(G-10323)
W WILLIAM SCHMIDT & ASSOCIATES
Also Called: Schmidt SEC & Investigations
514 Airport Rd Hanger 6 (44903-8993)
PHONE..............................419 526-4747
EMP: 137
SALES (corp-wide): 12.93MM **Privately Held**
Web: www.schmidtsecurity.com
SIC: **7381** Security guard service
PA: W. William Schmidt And Associates, Inc.
241 Industrial Pkwy
Mansfield OH 44903
419 526-4747

(G-10324)
WEDGEWOOD ESTATES
Also Called: Casto Health Care
600 S Trimble Rd (44906-3420)
PHONE..............................419 756-7400
William Casto, *Owner*
EMP: 30 EST: 1997
SALES (est): 2.51MM **Privately Held**
Web: www.wedgewoodseniorliving.com
SIC: **8059** 8052 Convalescent home; Intermediate care facilities

(G-10325)
WESTERN INVENTORY SERVICE INC
1251 Lexington Ave Ste 4 (44907-2666)
PHONE..............................419 756-7071
Greg Yurga, *Mgr*
EMP: 195
SIC: **7389** Inventory computing service
HQ: Western Inventory Service, Inc.
665 Rodi Rd Ste 500
Pittsburgh PA 15235
412 256-9008

(G-10326)
WOMENS CARE INC
500 S Trimble Rd (44906-4103)
PHONE..............................419 756-6000
TOLL FREE: 800
Thomas H Croghan, *Pr*
Edroy L Mc Millan, *
EMP: 49 EST: 1970
SQ FT: 8,500
SALES (est): 2.47MM **Privately Held**
Web: www.wcareinc.com
SIC: **8011** Gynecologist

(G-10327)
YOUNG MNS CHRSTN ASSN OF MNSFE
Also Called: Mansfield Area Y
750 Scholl Rd (44907-1570)
PHONE..............................419 522-3511
Cristen Gilbert, *CEO*
EMP: 30 EST: 1870
SALES (est): 4.15MM **Privately Held**
Web: www.ymcanco.org
SIC: **8641** Youth organizations

Mantua
Portage County

(G-10328)
AWL TRANSPORT INC
Also Called: Tlx
4626 State Route 82 (44255-9654)
PHONE..............................330 899-3444
Jerry W Carlton, *Pr*
EMP: 82 EST: 2008
SALES (est): 17.28MM **Privately Held**
Web: www.awltransport.com
SIC: **4213** Contract haulers

(G-10329)
COMPASS PACKAGING LLC
10585 Main St (44255-9600)
P.O. Box 739 (44080-0739)
PHONE..............................330 274-2001
▲ EMP: 41 EST: 2003
SQ FT: 24,000
SALES (est): 13.98MM **Privately Held**
Web: www.compasspackaging.com
SIC: **5199** Packaging materials

(G-10330)
HATTIE LARLHAM COMMUNITY SVCS
Also Called: DOGGY DAY CARE
9772 Diagonal Rd (44255-9160)
PHONE..............................330 274-2272
Dennis Allen, *Ex Dir*
EMP: 49 EST: 1998
SALES (est): 1.81MM
SALES (corp-wide): 3.56MM **Privately Held**
Web: www.hattielarlham.org
SIC: **8322** Association for the handicapped
PA: Hattie Larlham Community Living
7996 Darrow Rd
Twinsburg OH 44087
330 274-2272

(G-10331)
HATTIE LRLHAM CTR FOR CHLDREN (PA)
Also Called: HATTIE'S PRE-SCHOOL
9772 Diagonal Rd (44255-9128)
PHONE..............................330 274-2272
Dennis Allen, *CEO*
Darryl E Mast, *
Michelle Anderson, *
Sandy Neal, *
Dotty Grexa, *
EMP: 246 EST: 1963
SQ FT: 120,000
SALES (est): 61.41MM
SALES (corp-wide): 61.41MM **Privately Held**
Web: www.hattielarlham.org
SIC: **8361** 8322 8052 Retarded home; Individual and family services; Intermediate care facilities

(G-10332)
LARLHAM CARE HATTIE GROUP
9772 Diagonal Rd (44255-9128)
PHONE..............................330 274-2272
Dennis Allen, *CEO*
EMP: 53 EST: 2001
SALES (est): 4.35MM **Privately Held**
Web: www.hattielarlham.org
SIC: **8099** Medical services organization

Maple Heights
Cuyahoga County

(G-10333)
AREA TEMPS INC
15689 Broadway Ave (44137-1121)
PHONE..............................216 518-2000
EMP: 668
Web: www.areatemps.com
SIC: **7363** Temporary help service
PA: Area Temps, Inc.
4511 Rockside Rd Ste 190
Independence OH 44131

(G-10334)
CITY OF MAPLE HEIGHTS
Also Called: Senior Services
15901 Libby Rd (44137-1215)
PHONE..............................216 587-5451
EMP: 46
Web: www.citymapleheights.com
SIC: **8322** Social service center
PA: City Of Maple Heights
5353 Lee Rd
Cleveland OH 44137
216 662-6000

(G-10335)
CLIFTON STEEL COMPANY
Also Called: Clifton Heat Treating
16500 Rockside Rd (44137-4324)
PHONE..............................216 662-6111
Larry Crissman, *Brnch Mgr*
EMP: 37
SALES (corp-wide): 54.37MM **Privately Held**

Web: www.cliftonsteel.com
SIC: 5051 Steel
HQ: Clifton Steel Company
16500 Rockside Rd
Maple Heights OH 44137
216 662-6111

(G-10336)
CLIFTON STEEL COMPANY (HQ)
16500 Rockside Rd (44137-4324)
PHONE..................................216 662-6111
Herbert C Neides, *Pr*
Howard Feldenkris, *
Bruce Goodman, *CUST SERVCS*
◆ EMP: 58 EST: 1971
SQ FT: 160,000
SALES (est): 49.36MM
SALES (corp-wide): 54.37MM **Privately Held**
Web: www.cliftonsteel.com
SIC: 5051 3441 3443 3398 Steel; Fabricated structural metal; Metal parts; Metal heat treating
PA: Clifton Capital Holdings, Llc
16500 Rockside Rd
Maple Heights OH 44137
330 562-9000

(G-10337)
DAYNAS HOMECARE LLC
14616 Tabor Ave (44137-3859)
PHONE..................................216 323-0323
EMP: 30 EST: 2005
SALES (est): 1.04MM **Privately Held**
SIC: 8082 Home health care services

(G-10338)
FLAWLESS JANITORIAL LLC
5165 Joseph St (44137-1531)
PHONE..................................216 266-1425
EMP: 30 EST: 2021
SALES (est): 819.71K **Privately Held**
SIC: 7349 7389 Cleaning service, industrial or commercial; Business services, nec

(G-10339)
HARVEST SHERWOOD FD DISTRS INC
16625 Granite Rd (44137-4301)
PHONE..................................216 662-8000
Darby Murphy, *Brnch Mgr*
EMP: 500
SALES (corp-wide): 547.82MM **Privately Held**
Web: www.harvestsherwood.com
SIC: 5147 Meats, fresh
HQ: Harvest Sherwood Food Distributors, Inc.
12499 Evergreen Ave
Detroit MI 48228
313 659-7300

(G-10340)
HOME DEPOT USA INC
Also Called: Home Depot, The
21000 Libby Rd (44137)
PHONE..................................216 581-6611
Randy Behm, *Mgr*
EMP: 58
SALES (corp-wide): 152.67B **Publicly Held**
Web: www.homedepot.com
SIC: 5211 7359 Home centers; Tool rental
HQ: Home Depot U.S.A., Inc.
2445 Springfield Ave
Vauxhall NJ 07088

(G-10341)
IN TERMINAL SERVICES CORP
5300 Greenhurst Ext (44137-1139)
PHONE..................................216 518-8407

Bill Donahue, *Brnch Mgr*
EMP: 198
SALES (corp-wide): 10.92MM **Privately Held**
Web: www.conglobal.com
SIC: 7389 Crane and aerial lift service
PA: In Terminal Services Corporation
3111 167th St
Hazel Crest IL 60429
708 225-2400

(G-10342)
KOINONIA PARTNERS HOLDINGS LLC
Also Called: Lee House
5041 Lee Rd (44137-1227)
PHONE..................................216 588-8777
Diane Beastrom, *Brnch Mgr*
EMP: 29
SALES (corp-wide): 146.62K **Privately Held**
SIC: 7389 Business Activities at Non-Commercial Site
PA: Koinonia Partners Holdings, Llc
7051 State Rd
Parma OH 44134
216 588-8777

(G-10343)
PECK DISTRIBUTORS INC
Also Called: Peck Food Service
17000 Rockside Rd (44137-4345)
PHONE..................................216 587-6814
Stephen Peck Junior, *Pr*
Kenneth Peck, *
David Peck, *
Scott Peck, *
▲ EMP: 35 EST: 1983
SQ FT: 50,000
SALES (est): 23.19MM **Privately Held**
Web: www.peckfoodservice.com
SIC: 5113 5149 5142 Industrial and personal service paper; Canned goods: fruit, vegetables, seafood, meats, etc.; Packaged frozen goods

(G-10344)
REVITALIZE INDUSTRIES LLC
Also Called: National Commercial Warehouse
17000 Rockside Rd (44137-4345)
P.O. Box 470334 (44147-0334)
PHONE..................................440 570-3473
Lisa Oswald, *Managing Member*
EMP: 46 EST: 2012
SALES (est): 2.28MM **Privately Held**
SIC: 4225 Miniwarehouse, warehousing

(G-10345)
SAJOVIE BROTHERS LDSCPG INC
7991 Pennsylvania Ave (44137-4340)
PHONE..................................216 662-4983
EMP: 30 EST: 1999
SALES (est): 1.38MM **Privately Held**
Web: www.sajoviebros.com
SIC: 0781 Landscape services

(G-10346)
SHERWOOD FOOD DISTRIBUTORS LLC
Also Called: Sherwood Fd Dstrs Clveland Div
16625 Granite Rd (44137-4301)
PHONE..................................216 662-8000
EMP: 88
SALES (corp-wide): 547.82MM **Privately Held**
Web: www.sherwoodfoods.com
SIC: 5147 5144 5146 Meats, fresh; Poultry: live, dressed or frozen (unpackaged); Fish, frozen, unpackaged
HQ: Sherwood Food Distributors, L.L.C.
12499 Evergreen Ave

Detroit MI 48228
313 659-7300

(G-10347)
ST LAWRENCE HOLDINGS LLC
16500 Rockside Rd (44137-4324)
PHONE..................................330 562-9000
Herbert Neides, *Pr*
Jonh Zanin, *
EMP: 34 EST: 2017
SALES (est): 5.01MM
SALES (corp-wide): 54.37MM **Privately Held**
Web: www.stlawrencesteel.com
SIC: 5051 3443 3441 Steel; Fabricated plate work (boiler shop); Fabricated structural metal
PA: Clifton Capital Holdings, Llc
16500 Rockside Rd
Maple Heights OH 44137
330 562-9000

(G-10348)
ST LAWRENCE STEEL CORPORATION
16500 Rockside Rd (44137-4324)
PHONE..................................330 562-9000
◆ EMP: 34
Web: www.stlawrencesteel.com
SIC: 5051 3443 3441 Steel; Fabricated plate work (boiler shop); Fabricated structural metal

(G-10349)
SUNRISE HEALTHCARE GROUP LLC
Also Called: Sunrise Pnte Care Rhblttion Ct
19900 Clare Ave (44137-1806)
PHONE..................................216 662-3343
George S Repchick, *Pr*
William I Weisberg, *
EMP: 181 EST: 2012
SALES (est): 10.48MM
SALES (corp-wide): 655.44MM **Privately Held**
Web: www.phxhealthohio.com
SIC: 8051 Convalescent home with continuous nursing care
PA: Saber Healthcare Group, L.L.C.
23700 Commerce Park
Beachwood OH 44122
216 292-5706

(G-10350)
SUNTWIST CORP
Also Called: Post-Up Stand
5461 Dunham Rd (44137-3644)
PHONE..................................800 935-3534
Ram Tamir, *Pr*
Alon Weimer, *
▲ EMP: 76 EST: 2001
SQ FT: 2,600
SALES (est): 7.44MM **Privately Held**
SIC: 7336 Graphic arts and related design

Marblehead
Ottawa County

(G-10351)
BAY PINT RESORT OPERATIONS LLC
Also Called: Bay Point Yacht Club
10948 E Bayshore Rd (43440-2303)
PHONE..................................419 798-4434
George Durkin, *Pr*
Brooke Brown, *VP*
Ed Durkin, *Sec*
Tom Redinger, *Prin*
EMP: 33 EST: 1950
SQ FT: 1,200

SALES (est): 4.2MM **Privately Held**
Web: www.baypointresorthomes.com
SIC: 7011 Resort hotel

Marengo
Morrow County

(G-10352)
DEARTH MANAGEMENT COMPANY
Also Called: Bennington Glen Nursing Home
825 State Route 61 (43334-9215)
P.O. Box 10 (43334-0010)
PHONE..................................419 253-0144
TOLL FREE: 888
Jim Deel, *Admn*
EMP: 62
SALES (corp-wide): 24.94MM **Privately Held**
Web: www.benningtonglen.com
SIC: 8051 8052 Skilled nursing care facilities; Intermediate care facilities
PA: Dearth Management Company
134 Northwoods Blvd Ste C
Columbus OH
614 847-1070

Maria Stein
Mercer County

(G-10353)
BROOKSIDE HOLDINGS LLC (PA)
Also Called: Brookside Trucking
8022 State Route 119 (45860-8708)
P.O. Box 68 (45860-0068)
PHONE..................................419 925-4457
EMP: 43 EST: 1978
SQ FT: 9,800
SALES (est): 2.28MM
SALES (corp-wide): 2.28MM **Privately Held**
Web: www.brooksidetrucking.com
SIC: 4212 4213 Local trucking, without storage; Trucking, except local

(G-10354)
MOELLER TRUCKING INC
8100 Industrial Dr (45860-9544)
PHONE..................................419 925-4799
Gary Moeller, *Pr*
Art Moeller Junior, *VP*
Terry Moeller, *
EMP: 90 EST: 1970
SQ FT: 3,500
SALES (est): 26.07MM **Privately Held**
Web: www.moellertrucking.com
SIC: 4213 4212 Contract haulers; Local trucking, without storage

Marietta
Washington County

(G-10355)
AMERICAN PRODUCERS SUP CO INC (PA)
119 2nd St (45750-3102)
P.O. Box 1050 (45750-6050)
PHONE..................................740 373-5050
Christopher L Brunton, *Pr*
Rick Blizzard, *
Joseph Wesel, *
Carol Lindamood, *
Mark Magers, *
▲ EMP: 54 EST: 1963
SQ FT: 50,000
SALES (est): 62.42MM
SALES (corp-wide): 62.42MM **Privately Held**

GEOGRAPHIC SECTION
Marietta - Washington County (G-10378)

Web: www.americanproducers.com
SIC: 5082 5085 Contractor's materials;
Abrasives

(G-10356)
ANTERO RESOURCES CORPORATION
27841 State Route 7 (45750-9060)
PHONE..................740 760-1000
EMP: 60
Web: www.anteroresources.com
SIC: 1382 Oil and gas exploration services
PA: Antero Resources Corporation
1615 Wynkoop St
Denver CO 80202

(G-10357)
BD OIL GATHERING CORP
649 Mitchells Ln (45750-6865)
PHONE..................740 374-9355
EMP: 29 EST: 1993
SALES (est): 2.26MM Privately Held
Web: www.bdoil.com
SIC: 1382 Oil and gas exploration services

(G-10358)
BUCKEYE CHECK CASHING INC
234 Pike St (45750-3322)
PHONE..................740 374-6005
EMP: 35
Web: www.ccfi.com
SIC: 6099 Check cashing agencies
HQ: Buckeye Check Cashing, Inc.
5165 Emerald Pkwy Ste 100
Dublin OH 43017
614 798-5900

(G-10359)
BUCKEYE HEALTH STAFFING LLC
Also Called: Buckeye Hlth Stffng/Bckeye Src
125 Putnam St Ste 110 (45750-2936)
PHONE..................614 706-9337
Justin Tolliver, Prin
Bryan Casey, *
Scott Powell, *
EMP: 50 EST: 2020
SALES (est): 1.27MM Privately Held
Web: www.buckeyehealthstaffing.com
SIC: 7361 Employment agencies

(G-10360)
BUCKEYE HILLS-HCK VLY REG DEV (HQ)
Also Called: Area Agency On Aging
1400 Pike St (45750-5196)
P.O. Box 520 (45773-0520)
PHONE..................740 373-0087
Misty Casto, CEO
EMP: 48 EST: 1968
SALES (est): 183.87K
SALES (corp-wide): 255.55K Privately Held
Web: www.buckeyehills.org
SIC: 8748 Urban planning and consulting services
PA: Appalachian Development Corporation
1400 Pike St
Marietta OH 45750
740 374-9436

(G-10361)
CDK PERFORATING LLC
2167 State Route 821 (45750-1196)
PHONE..................817 862-9834
EMP: 59
SALES (corp-wide): 609.53MM Publicly Held
Web: www.nineenergyservice.com
SIC: 1389 Oil field services, nec
HQ: Cdk Perforating, Llc

6500 West Fwy Ste 600
Fort Worth TX 76116
817 945-1051

(G-10362)
COMMUNITY ACTION PRGRAM CORP O (PA)
218 Putnam St (45750-3014)
P.O. Box 144 (45750-0144)
PHONE..................740 373-3745
David E Brightbill, *
EMP: 85 EST: 1967
SQ FT: 9,700
SALES (est): 17.72MM
SALES (corp-wide): 17.72MM Privately Held
Web: www.wmcap.org
SIC: 8399 Community action agency

(G-10363)
COMMUNITY ACTION PRGRAM CORP O
Also Called: Norwood School
205 Phillips St (45750-3427)
PHONE..................740 373-6016
EMP: 103
SALES (corp-wide): 17.72MM Privately Held
Web: www.wmcap.org
SIC: 8399 8322 Community action agency; Individual and family services
PA: Community Action Program Corp, Of Washington-Morgan County Ohio, Inc
218 Putnam St
Marietta OH 45750
740 373-3745

(G-10364)
COUNTY OF WASHINGTON
Also Called: Washington Cnty Engineers Off
103 Westview Ave (45750-9403)
PHONE..................740 376-7430
Roger Wright, Engr
EMP: 29
Web: www.washingtongov.org
SIC: 8711 Engineering services
PA: County Of Washington
205 Putnam St
Marietta OH 45750
740 373-6623

(G-10365)
DAVIS PICKERING & COMPANY INC
Also Called: American Procomm
165 Enterprise Dr (45750-8051)
PHONE..................740 373-5896
Jeffrey A Williamson, CEO
Dustin W Flinn, *
Daniel M Fliehman, *
Kelly A Fisher, *
EMP: 80 EST: 1989
SQ FT: 6,000
SALES (est): 24.99MM
SALES (corp-wide): 1.91B Privately Held
Web: www.davispickering.com
SIC: 1731 General electrical contractor
PA: The Day & Zimmermann Group Inc
1500 Spring Garden St
Philadelphia PA 19130
215 299-8000

(G-10366)
DIVERSIFIED PRODUCTION LLC
111 Industry Rd Unit 206 (45750-9315)
P.O. Box 141 (45773-0141)
PHONE..................740 373-8771
Martin Miller, Brnch Mgr
EMP: 142
SALES (corp-wide): 99.2MM Privately Held
Web: ir.div.energy

SIC: 1382 Oil and gas exploration services
HQ: Diversified Production Llc
4150 Belden Village St Nw
Canton OH 44718

(G-10367)
FARM CREDIT SVCS MID-AMERICA
470 Pike St (45750-3328)
PHONE..................740 373-8211
Steve Reed, Brnch Mgr
EMP: 1060
SALES (corp-wide): 26MM Privately Held
Web: www.fcma.com
SIC: 6159 Farm mortgage companies
PA: Farm Credit Services Of Mid-America
1540 Us Highway 62 Sw
Wshngtn Ct Hs OH 43160
740 335-3306

(G-10368)
FIRST SETTLEMENT ORTHOPAEDICS (PA)
Also Called: Nayak, Naresh K MD
611 2nd St Ste A (45750-2167)
PHONE..................740 373-8756
Gregory Krivchenia Ii, Pr
Naresh K Nayak, *
Jesse R Ada, *
Gary W Miller, *
John Henry, Stockholder*
EMP: 32 EST: 1971
SQ FT: 17,500
SALES (est): 7.05MM Privately Held
Web: www.visitfso.com
SIC: 8011 8049 Sports medicine specialist, physician; Physical therapist

(G-10369)
GREEN VALLEY CO-OP INC
219 3rd St (45750-3002)
P.O. Box 369 (44406-0369)
PHONE..................740 374-7741
EMP: 63
SIC: 5191 Farm supplies

(G-10370)
HEALTH CARE PLUS
Also Called: Marden Companies, The
125 Putnam St Ste 300 (45750-2935)
P.O. Box 941 (45750-0941)
PHONE..................740 373-9446
Randy Mason, Owner
EMP: 118
Web: www.mardencompanies.com
SIC: 8082 Visiting nurse service
HQ: Health Care Plus
470 Olde Worthington Rd # 200
Westerville OH 43082

(G-10371)
HUNTINGTON NATIONAL BANK
Marietta Savings Bank
226 3rd St (45750-3001)
P.O. Box 775 (45750-0775)
PHONE..................740 373-2886
Mike Laderosa, Pr
EMP: 36
SALES (corp-wide): 10.84B Publicly Held
Web: www.huntington.com
SIC: 6029 Commercial banks, nec
HQ: The Huntington National Bank
41 S High St
Columbus OH 43215
614 480-4293

(G-10372)
IDDINGS TRUCKING INC
741 Blue Knob Rd (45750-8275)
PHONE..................740 568-1780
EMP: 105
Web: www.iddingstrucking.com

SIC: 4212 4213 Coal haulage, local; Heavy hauling, nec

(G-10373)
IEH AUTO PARTS LLC
Also Called: Auto Plus
123 Tennis Center Dr (45750-9765)
PHONE..................740 373-8327
Scott Reynolds, Brnch Mgr
EMP: 44
Web: www.autoplus.biz
SIC: 5013 Automotive supplies and parts
HQ: Ieh Auto Parts Llc
112 Townpark Dr Nw # 300
Kennesaw GA 30144
770 701-5000

(G-10374)
IEH AUTO PARTS LLC
121 Tennis Center Dr (45750-9765)
PHONE..................740 373-8151
EMP: 52
Web: www.autoplus.biz
SIC: 5013 Automotive supplies and parts
HQ: Ieh Auto Parts Llc
112 Townpark Dr Nw # 300
Kennesaw GA 30144
770 701-5000

(G-10375)
INN AT MARIETTA LTD
150 Browns Rd Ofc (45750-9086)
PHONE..................740 373-9600
Charlotte Forsyth, Pt
Deb Patrick, Admn
Charlotte Forsyth, Admn
EMP: 50 EST: 1996
SALES (est): 463.48K Privately Held
SIC: 7011 8052 Inns; Intermediate care facilities

(G-10376)
JANI-SOURCE LLC
478 Bramblewood Heights Rd (45750-8501)
PHONE..................740 374-6298
TOLL FREE: 877
Bryan Waller, Managing Member
Judy Waller, Managing Member*
EMP: 50 EST: 1991
SQ FT: 2,400
SALES (est): 2.19MM Privately Held
Web: www.janisource.com
SIC: 7349 5999 Janitorial service, contract basis; Cleaning equipment and supplies

(G-10377)
KELLY PAVING INC
20220 State Rte 7 (45750)
P.O. Box 366 (26187-0366)
PHONE..................740 373-6495
Gerald Little, Pr
Roger Thomas, *
EMP: 45 EST: 1978
SALES (est): 8.88MM
SALES (corp-wide): 433.35MM Privately Held
Web: www.shellyandsands.com
SIC: 1611 Highway and street paving contractor
PA: Shelly And Sands, Inc.
3570 S River Rd
Zanesville OH 43701
740 453-0721

(G-10378)
KEMRON ENVIRONMENTAL SVCS INC
2343 State Route 821 (45750-5464)
PHONE..................740 373-4071
David Vandenberg, Brnch Mgr

Marietta - Washington County (G-10379) — GEOGRAPHIC SECTION

EMP: 28
SALES (corp-wide): 45.95MM **Privately Held**
Web: www.kemron.com
SIC: 8711 8748 8731 8734 Consulting engineer; Environmental consultant; Commercial physical research; Testing laboratories
PA: Kemron Environmental Services, Inc.
1359-A Ellswrth Indus Blv
Atlanta GA 30318
404 601-6930

(G-10379)
KOROSEAL INTERIOR PRODUCTS LLC
700 Bf Goodrich Rd (45750-7849)
PHONE..................................855 753-5474
EMP: 207
SALES (corp-wide): 116.19MM **Privately Held**
Web: www.koroseal.com
SIC: 1541 Warehouse construction
PA: Koroseal Interior Products, Llc
7929 National Tpke
Louisville KY 40214
330 668-7600

(G-10380)
LESLIE EQUIPMENT CO
Also Called: John Deere Authorized Dealer
105 Tennis Center Dr (45750-9765)
P.O. Box 37 (45750-0037)
PHONE..................................740 373-5255
Torque Setterstrom, *Mgr*
EMP: 44
SALES (corp-wide): 43.04MM **Privately Held**
Web: www.deere.com
SIC: 5083 Farm and garden machinery
PA: Leslie Equipment Co.
6248 Webster Rd
Cowen WV 26206
304 226-3299

(G-10381)
LOWES HOME CENTERS LLC
Also Called: Lowe's
842 Pike St (45750-3503)
PHONE..................................740 374-2151
Paul Rea, *Brnch Mgr*
EMP: 138
SALES (corp-wide): 86.38B **Publicly Held**
Web: www.lowes.com
SIC: 5211 5031 5722 5064 Home centers; Building materials, exterior; Household appliance stores; Electrical appliances, television and radio
HQ: Lowe's Home Centers, Llc
1000 Lowes Blvd
Mooresville NC 28117
336 658-4000

(G-10382)
MARCH INVESTORS LTD
Also Called: Hampton Inn
508 Pike St (45750-3332)
PHONE..................................740 373-5353
EMP: 33 **EST:** 2004
SALES (est): 899.89K **Privately Held**
Web: www.hilton.com
SIC: 7011 Hotels and motels

(G-10383)
MARIETTA HLTH CARE PHYSICIANS
400 Matthew St Ste 220 (45750-1656)
PHONE..................................740 376-5044
Michael Brockett, *Mng Pt*
Kenneth Leopold, *Pt*
EMP: 38 **EST:** 1982
SALES (est): 253.11K **Privately Held**

Web: www.mhsystem.org
SIC: 8011 General and family practice, physician/surgeon

(G-10384)
MARIETTA MEMORIAL HOSPITAL (PA)
Also Called: Memorial Health System
401 Matthew St (45750-1635)
PHONE..................................740 374-1400
TOLL FREE: 800
Tom Tucker, *Ch Bd*
J Stott Cantley, *
Orive E Fischer, *
Eric Young, *
Colleen Cook, *
EMP: 900 **EST:** 1921
SQ FT: 100,000
SALES (est): 454.22MM
SALES (corp-wide): 454.22MM **Privately Held**
Web: www.mhsystem.org
SIC: 8062 8069 General medical and surgical hospitals; Alcoholism rehabilitation hospital

(G-10385)
MARIETTA OCCPTNAL HLTH PRTNERS
401 Matthew St (45750-1635)
PHONE..................................740 374-9954
Joni Washburn, *Admn*
EMP: 64 **EST:** 2003
SALES (est): 1.48MM
SALES (corp-wide): 454.22MM **Privately Held**
Web: www.mhsystem.org
SIC: 8011 Occupational and industrial specialist, physician/surgeon
PA: Marietta Memorial Hospital Inc
401 Matthew St
Marietta OH 45750
740 374-1400

(G-10386)
MARIETTA SILOS LLC
2417 Waterford Rd (45750-7828)
PHONE..................................740 373-2822
Dennis Blauser, *CEO*
EMP: 50 **EST:** 1916
SQ FT: 50,000
SALES (est): 11.02MM **Privately Held**
Web: www.mariettasilos.com
SIC: 1542 Silo construction, agricultural

(G-10387)
MARIETTA SURGERY CENTER
611 2nd St Ste A (45750-2167)
PHONE..................................740 373-7207
Shirley Thomas, *Prin*
EMP: 29 **EST:** 2010
SALES (est): 6.12MM **Privately Held**
Web: www.mariettasurgicalcenter.com
SIC: 8011 Surgeon

(G-10388)
MARTEL LODGING LTD
329 S 7th St (45750-3346)
P.O. Box 30 (45750-0030)
PHONE..................................740 373-7373
Terry L St Peter, *Prin*
EMP: 33 **EST:** 2010
SALES (est): 688.34K **Privately Held**
SIC: 7011 Vacation lodges

(G-10389)
MICROBAC LABORATORIES INC
158 Starlite Dr (45750-5279)
PHONE..................................740 373-4071
EMP: 44

SALES (corp-wide): 81.36MM **Privately Held**
Web: www.microbac.com
SIC: 8734 Water testing laboratory
PA: Microbac Laboratories, Inc.
2009 Mackenzie Way # 100
Cranberry Township PA 16066
412 459-1060

(G-10390)
MID OHIO VLY BULK TRNSPT INC
16380 State Route 7 (45750-8246)
P.O. Box 734 (45750-0734)
PHONE..................................740 373-2481
Mayeeta Merrill, *Pr*
Charles Merrill, *
EMP: 30 **EST:** 1994
SALES (est): 6.23MM
SALES (corp-wide): 11.68MM **Privately Held**
Web: www.mid-ohiovalleybulk.com
SIC: 4731 Freight transportation arrangement
PA: Mid-Ohio Valley Lime, Inc.
State Rt 7 S
Marietta OH 45750
740 373-1006

(G-10391)
MONDO POLYMER TECHNOLOGIES INC
27620 State Route 7 (45750-5146)
P.O. Box 250 (45773-0250)
PHONE..................................740 376-9396
EMP: 40 **EST:** 1999
SQ FT: 3,200
SALES (est): 12.11MM **Privately Held**
Web: www.mondopolymer.com
SIC: 4953 2822 Recycling, waste materials; Synthetic rubber

(G-10392)
MORRISON INC
Also Called: Honeywell Authorized Dealer
410 Colegate Dr (45750-9549)
PHONE..................................740 373-5869
Kenneth Morrison, *Pr*
David M Haas, *
EMP: 45 **EST:** 1955
SQ FT: 6,000
SALES (est): 9.52MM **Privately Held**
Web: www.morrisonhvac.com
SIC: 1711 5722 Refrigeration contractor; Electric household appliances

(G-10393)
MOTEL INVESTMENTS MARIETTA INC
Also Called: Quality Inn
700 Pike St (45750-3501)
PHONE..................................740 374-8190
EMP: 32 **EST:** 1996
SALES (est): 1.67MM **Privately Held**
Web: www.choicehotels.com
SIC: 7011 Hotels and motels

(G-10394)
MOVEMENT FITNESS LLC
315 Gross St (45750-2038)
PHONE..................................419 410-5733
Brant Whited, *Pr*
EMP: 30 **EST:** 2017
SALES (est): 279.44K **Privately Held**
Web: www.movementmarietta.com
SIC: 7991 Physical fitness facilities

(G-10395)
NICHOLAS AUTO ELEC RBLDING LLC
Also Called: Nicholas Auto Electrical Rebuilding, LLC

202 Gibbons St (45750-9449)
PHONE..................................740 373-3861
Charles G Nicholas, *Prin*
EMP: 76
SALES (corp-wide): 242.85K **Privately Held**
SIC: 7538 General automotive repair shops
PA: Nicholas Auto Electrical Rebuilders, Llc
111 Industry Rd Unit 201
Marietta OH 45750
740 376-0213

(G-10396)
PEOPLES BANCORP INC (PA)
138 Putnam St (45750-2923)
P.O. Box 738 (45750-0738)
PHONE..................................740 373-3155
Charles W Sulerzyski, *Pr*
David L Mead, *Non-Executive Chairman of the Board*
George W Broughton, *Non-Executive Vice Chairman of the Board*
John C Rogers, *Ex VP*
Douglas V Wyatt, *Chief Commercial Lending Officer*
EMP: 103 **EST:** 1980
SALES (est): 526.82MM
SALES (corp-wide): 526.82MM **Publicly Held**
Web: www.peoplesbancorp.com
SIC: 6022 State commercial banks

(G-10397)
PEOPLES BANK (HQ)
138 Putnam St (45750)
P.O. Box 738 (45750)
PHONE..................................740 373-3155
Chuck Sulerziski, *Pr*
Susan D Rector, *Ch Bd*
EMP: 76 **EST:** 1914
SALES (est): 349.7MM
SALES (corp-wide): 526.82MM **Publicly Held**
Web: www.peoplesbancorp.com
SIC: 6022 State commercial banks
PA: Peoples Bancorp Inc.
138 Putnam St
Marietta OH 45750
740 373-3155

(G-10398)
PHYSICIANS CARE OF MARIETTA (PA)
Also Called: Physicians Care of Marrita
800 Pike St Ste 2 (45750-3507)
PHONE..................................740 373-2519
EMP: 75 **EST:** 1996
SALES (est): 4.67MM **Privately Held**
Web: www.mhsystem.org
SIC: 8011 Clinic, operated by physicians

(G-10399)
PIONEER PIPE INC
Also Called: Pioneer Group
2021 Hanna Rd (45750-8255)
PHONE..................................740 376-2400
David M Archer, *Pr*
Arlene M Archer, *
▲ **EMP:** 600 **EST:** 1981
SQ FT: 24,800
SALES (est): 79.66MM **Privately Held**
Web: www.pioneergroup.us
SIC: 3498 1711 3443 3441 Pipe sections, fabricated from purchased pipe; Plumbing contractors; Fabricated plate work (boiler shop); Fabricated structural metal

(G-10400)
PLATINUM RECOVERY LLC
Also Called: Regional Collection Services
2019 State Route 821 (45750-5494)

GEOGRAPHIC SECTION

Marion - Marion County (G-10421)

PHONE..................740 373-8811
Sean Sward, *Pr*
Sean Sward, *CEO*
Sabrina Leiter, *
EMP: 30 **EST:** 2021
SALES (est): 971.44K **Privately Held**
Web: www.platinumcompaniesinc.com
SIC: 7322 Collection agency, except real estate

(G-10401)
POWER SYSTEM ENGINEERING INC
Also Called: Pse
2349a State Route 821 (45750-3530)
PHONE..................740 568-9220
Bruce Lane, *Brnch Mgr*
EMP: 28
SALES (corp-wide): 14.27MM **Privately Held**
Web: www.powersystem.org
SIC: 8711 Consulting engineer
PA: Power System Engineering, Inc.
  2424 Rimrock Rd Ste 300
  Fitchburg WI 53713
  608 268-3528

(G-10402)
R & J TRUCKING INC
14530 State Route 7 (45750)
PHONE..................740 374-3050
Dennis Coe, *Mgr*
EMP: 34
Web: www.americanbulkcommodities.com
SIC: 4212 4213 Dump truck haulage; Heavy hauling, nec
HQ: R & J Trucking, Inc.
  8063 Southern Blvd
  Youngstown OH 44512
  800 262-9365

(G-10403)
REHABLTTION CTR AT MRIETTA MEM
Also Called: Rehabltion Ctr At Mrtta Mmori
401 Matthew St (45750-1635)
PHONE..................740 374-1407
Carol Mcauley, *Dir*
EMP: 41 **EST:** 1993
SALES (est): 986.53K **Privately Held**
Web: www.mhsystem.org
SIC: 8093 8361 Rehabilitation center, outpatient treatment; Residential care

(G-10404)
RICHARDSON PRINTING CORP (PA)
Also Called: Zip Center, The-Division
201 Acme St (45750-3404)
P.O. Box 663 (45750-0663)
PHONE..................800 848-9752
TOLL FREE: 800
Dennis E Valentine, *Pr*
Charles E Schwab, *
Robert Richardson Junior, *Stockholder*
▲ **EMP:** 60 **EST:** 1944
SQ FT: 100,000
SALES (est): 2.1MM
SALES (corp-wide): 2.1MM **Privately Held**
Web: www.rpcprint.com
SIC: 7389 2752 Mailing and messenger services; Offset printing

(G-10405)
SELBY GENERAL HOSPITAL (PA)
1106 Colegate Dr (45750-1323)
PHONE..................740 568-2000
Steve Smith, *Pr*
Thomas Tucker, *Ch Bd*
Scott Cantley, *Pr*
Eric Young, *CFO*
EMP: 243 **EST:** 1928
SQ FT: 65,000
SALES (est): 77.72MM
SALES (corp-wide): 77.72MM **Privately Held**
Web: www.selbygeneralhospital.com
SIC: 8062 Hospital, affiliated with AMA residency

(G-10406)
UNITED CHURCH HOMES INC
Also Called: Harmer Place
401 Harmar St (45750-2732)
PHONE..................740 376-5600
Kenneth Daniel, *CEO*
James Henry, *
EMP: 49 **EST:** 1969
SALES (est): 6.8MM **Privately Held**
Web: www.unitedchurchhomes.org
SIC: 8361 8051 Aged home; Skilled nursing care facilities

(G-10407)
UNITED PARCEL SERVICE INC
Also Called: UPS
105 Industry Rd (45750-9355)
PHONE..................740 373-0772
EMP: 31
SALES (corp-wide): 90.96B **Publicly Held**
Web: www.ups.com
SIC: 4215 Package delivery, vehicular
HQ: United Parcel Service, Inc.
  55 Glenlake Pkwy
  Atlanta GA 30328
  404 828-6000

(G-10408)
VADAKIN INC
Also Called: Vadakin Industrial Services
110 Industry Rd (45750-9355)
P.O. Box 565 (45750-0565)
PHONE..................740 373-7518
Sara Hooper, *Pr*
Gregory Grose, *Sec*
Mark Whiteley, *
EMP: 50 **EST:** 1931
SQ FT: 16,000
SALES (est): 3.29MM **Privately Held**
Web: www.vadakininc.com
SIC: 7349 Cleaning service, industrial or commercial

(G-10409)
VALLEY HOSPITALITY INC
Also Called: Holiday Inn
701 Pike St (45750-3502)
PHONE..................740 374-9660
Andy Benson, *Pr*
Rita H Stephan, *
EMP: 60 **EST:** 1988
SQ FT: 50,000
SALES (est): 549.85K **Privately Held**
Web: www.holidayinn.com
SIC: 7011 5812 5813 7299 Hotels and motels; Family restaurants; Bars and lounges; Banquet hall facilities

(G-10410)
WARREN BROS & SONS INC (PA)
Also Called: Warrens IGA
108 S 7th St B (45750-3338)
PHONE..................740 373-1430
Kin Brewer, *Pr*
Lisa G Brewer, *
EMP: 50 **EST:** 1950
SALES (est): 2.48MM
SALES (corp-wide): 2.48MM **Privately Held**
Web: www.marathonoil.com
SIC: 8721 Certified public accountant

(G-10411)
WASCO INC (PA)
340 Muskingum Dr (45750-1435)
PHONE..................740 373-3418
Joseph Faires, *CEO*
Tara Meeks, *Mgr*
EMP: 64 **EST:** 1971
SQ FT: 22,000
SALES (est): 2.52MM
SALES (corp-wide): 2.52MM **Privately Held**
Web: www.wascoinc.org
SIC: 8331 Sheltered workshop

(G-10412)
WAYNE STREET DEVELOPMENT LLC
424 2nd St (45750-2115)
PHONE..................740 373-5455
Abraham Sellers, *Prin*
EMP: 30 **EST:** 2010
SALES (est): 913.16K **Privately Held**
SIC: 8741 Management services

(G-10413)
WESTFALL TOWING LLC
1024 Pike St (45750-3521)
PHONE..................740 371-5185
Steve Griffith, *Mgr*
EMP: 29 **EST:** 2016
SALES (est): 496.1K **Privately Held**
SIC: 7549 Towing services

(G-10414)
WESTLAKE DIMEX LLC
Also Called: Dimex LLC
28305 State Route 7 (45750-5151)
P.O. Box 337 (45773-0337)
PHONE..................740 374-3100
Andy Antil, *CEO*
Dan Allan, *
▲ **EMP:** 160 **EST:** 1991
SQ FT: 224,000
SALES (est): 52.85MM **Publicly Held**
Web: www.dimexcorp.com
SIC: 6726 3089 3069 Investment offices, nec; Plastics hardware and building products; Mats or matting, rubber, nec
PA: Westlake Corporation
  2801 Post Oak Blvd Ste 60
  Houston TX 77056

(G-10415)
YOUNG MENS CHRISTIAN ASSN
Also Called: Marietta Family YMCA
1303 Colegate Dr Ste B (45750-1367)
PHONE..................740 373-2250
Suzy Zumwalde, *Ex Dir*
Al Miller, *
Roger Pitasky, *
Robert Ferguson, *
Dennis Cooke, *
EMP: 65 **EST:** 1902
SALES (est): 977.71K **Privately Held**
Web: www.mariettaymca.org
SIC: 8641 8351 Recreation association; Child day care services

---

Marion
Marion County

(G-10416)
AG-PRO OHIO LLC
219 Columbus Sandusky Rd N (43302-8911)
PHONE..................740 389-5458
EMP: 42
SALES (corp-wide): 204.78MM **Privately Held**
Web: www.agprocompanies.com
SIC: 5083 Agricultural machinery and equipment
HQ: Ag-Pro Ohio, Llc
  19595 Us Highway 84 E
  Boston GA 31626
  229 498-8833

(G-10417)
AQUA TECH ENVMTL LABS INC (PA)
Also Called: Atel
1776 Marion Waldo Rd (43302-7428)
PHONE..................740 389-5991
Paul Crerar, *Pr*
EMP: 29 **EST:** 1978
SQ FT: 5,000
SALES (est): 2.51MM
SALES (corp-wide): 2.51MM **Privately Held**
Web: www.alloway.com
SIC: 8734 Hazardous waste testing

(G-10418)
ARCELRMTTAL TBLAR PDTS MRION I
Also Called: Arcelormittal Tubular Pdts USA
686 W Fairground St (43302-1706)
PHONE..................740 382-3979
Edward Vore, *CEO*
▲ **EMP:** 100 **EST:** 2002
SQ FT: 410,000
SALES (est): 29.14MM
SALES (corp-wide): 2.74B **Privately Held**
Web: www.arcelormittal-oh.com
SIC: 5051 Steel
HQ: Arcelormittal Tubular Products Usa Llc
  4 Gateway Ctr
  Pittsburgh PA 15222
  419 342-1200

(G-10419)
BOISE CASCADE COMPANY
Also Called: Boise Cascade
3007 Harding Hwy E Bldg 203b (43302-2575)
PHONE..................740 382-6766
Jeff Wiska, *Brnch Mgr*
EMP: 105
SALES (corp-wide): 8.39B **Publicly Held**
Web: www.bc.com
SIC: 5031 Building materials, exterior
PA: Boise Cascade Company
  1111 W Jffrson St Ste 300
  Boise ID 83702
  208 384-6161

(G-10420)
BUCKEYE COLLISION SERVICE INC
Also Called: Buckeye Collision Towing
1770 Harding Hwy E (43302-8527)
PHONE..................740 387-5313
Brian Reed, *Pr*
Robert Reed, *Pr*
Sharon Reed, *VP*
EMP: 39 **EST:** 1975
SQ FT: 1,800
SALES (est): 2.1MM **Privately Held**
Web: www.buckeyecollision.us
SIC: 7532 Body shop, automotive

(G-10421)
CENTER STREET CMNTY CLINIC INC
136 W Center St (43302-3704)
PHONE..................740 751-6380
Cliff Edwards, *CEO*
EMP: 29 **EST:** 2005
SALES (est): 8.36MM **Privately Held**
Web: www.centerstreetclinic.org
SIC: 8059 Personal care home, with health care

Marion - Marion County (G-10422) — GEOGRAPHIC SECTION

(G-10422)
COMMUNITY CNSLING WLLNESS CTRS (PA)
320 Executive Dr (43302)
PHONE...............................740 387-5210
Brett Mutchler, *Admn*
Martin Gaudiose, *
Beverly Young, *
EMP: 46 **EST:** 1974
SQ FT: 2,500
SALES (est): 2.41MM
SALES (corp-wide): 2.41MM **Privately Held**
Web: www.maccsite.com
SIC: 8322 8093 General counseling services; Specialty outpatient clinics, nec

(G-10423)
CONCERNED CTZENS AGNST VLNCE A
Also Called: TURNING POINT
330 Barks Rd W (43302-7304)
P.O. Box 875 (43301-0875)
PHONE...............................740 382-8988
Paula Roller, *Ex Dir*
Gary Pendleton, *Brand President*
Brenda Harden, *Board Vice President*
EMP: 27 **EST:** 1979
SALES (est): 2.18MM **Privately Held**
Web: www.turningpoint6.org
SIC: 8322 Social service center

(G-10424)
CVS REVCO DS INC
Also Called: CVS
137 Mcmahan Blvd (43302-5656)
PHONE...............................740 389-1122
Joyce Smith, *Mgr*
EMP: 50
SALES (corp-wide): 357.78B **Publicly Held**
Web: www.cvs.com
SIC: 5912 7384 Drug stores; Photofinishing laboratory
HQ: Cvs Revco D.S., Inc.
 1 Cvs Dr
 Woonsocket RI 02895
 401 765-1500

(G-10425)
CVS REVCO DS INC
Also Called: CVS
535 Delaware Ave (43302-5051)
PHONE...............................740 383-6244
EMP: 50
SALES (corp-wide): 357.78B **Publicly Held**
Web: www.cvs.com
SIC: 5912 7384 Drug stores; Photofinishing laboratory
HQ: Cvs Revco D.S., Inc.
 1 Cvs Dr
 Woonsocket RI 02895
 401 765-1500

(G-10426)
FAHEY BANKING COMPANY
Also Called: East Side Branch
949 E Center St (43302-4350)
P.O. Box 333 (43301-0333)
PHONE...............................740 382-8232
Robert Fanner, *Brnch Mgr*
EMP: 35
SALES (corp-wide): 11.4MM **Privately Held**
Web: www.faheybank.bank
SIC: 6022 State trust companies accepting deposits, commercial
PA: The Fahey Banking Company
 127 N Main St
 Marion OH 43302
 740 382-8231

(G-10427)
FREDERICK C SMITH CLINIC INC (HQ)
Also Called: Marion Area Health Center
1040 Delaware Ave (43302-6416)
P.O. Box 1800 (43301-1800)
PHONE...............................740 383-7000
Dalsukh Madia, *Pr*
J Charles Garvin Md, *VP*
Michael P Coyne, *
Ronald J Waldheger, *
EMP: 400 **EST:** 1925
SQ FT: 100,000
SALES (est): 46.36MM
SALES (corp-wide): 4.29B **Privately Held**
Web: www.ohiohealth.com
SIC: 8062 General medical and surgical hospitals
PA: Ohiohealth Corporation
 3430 Ohhalth Pkwy 5th Flr
 Columbus OH 43202
 614 788-8860

(G-10428)
GLAUS PYLE SCHMER BRNS DHVEN I
Also Called: Gpd Group
286 Summit St (43302-5226)
PHONE...............................740 382-6840
Darrin Kotecki, *Pr*
EMP: 27
SALES (corp-wide): 122.1MM **Privately Held**
Web: www.gpdgroup.com
SIC: 8711 Consulting engineer
PA: Glaus, Pyle, Schomer, Burns & Dehaven, Inc.
 520 S Main St Ste 2531
 Akron OH 44311
 330 572-2100

(G-10429)
GRAHAM INVESTMENT CO (PA)
Also Called: Casod Industrial Properties
3007 Harding Hwy Bldg 203 (43302-2575)
PHONE...............................740 382-0902
Ted Graham, *Pr*
EMP: 100 **EST:** 1969
SALES (est): 9.21MM
SALES (corp-wide): 9.21MM **Privately Held**
SIC: 6512 4225 Commercial and industrial building operation; General warehousing and storage

(G-10430)
HOLBROOK & MANTER (PA)
181 E Center St (43302-3813)
P.O. Box 437 (43301-0437)
PHONE...............................740 387-8620
Brad Idge, *Pt*
Thomas Kalb, *
EMP: 30 **EST:** 1919
SQ FT: 6,270
SALES (est): 4.59MM
SALES (corp-wide): 4.59MM **Privately Held**
Web: www.holbrookmanter.com
SIC: 8721 Certified public accountant

(G-10431)
INTERIM HALTHCARE COLUMBUS INC
298 E Center St Ste D (43302-4148)
PHONE...............................740 387-0301
Anthony Vogele, *Brnch Mgr*
EMP: 237
SALES (corp-wide): 52.16MM **Privately Held**
Web: www.interimhealthcare.com
SIC: 8082 Home health care services
HQ: Interim Healthcare Of Columbus, Inc.
 784 Morrison Rd
 Gahanna OH 43230
 614 888-3130

(G-10432)
KA WANNER INC
Also Called: Robotworx
370 W Fairground St (43302-1728)
PHONE...............................740 251-4636
Keith Wanner, *Pr*
EMP: 30 **EST:** 1992
SQ FT: 75,000
SALES (est): 6.07MM **Privately Held**
SIC: 5084 Industrial machinery and equipment

(G-10433)
LOWES HOME CENTERS LLC
Also Called: Lowe's
1840 Marion Mount Gilead Rd (43302-5826)
PHONE...............................740 389-9737
Rhonda Walker, *Mgr*
EMP: 148
SALES (corp-wide): 86.38B **Publicly Held**
Web: www.lowes.com
SIC: 5211 5031 5722 5064 Home centers; Building materials, exterior; Household appliance stores; Electrical appliances, television and radio
HQ: Lowe's Home Centers, Llc
 1000 Lowes Blvd
 Mooresville NC 28117
 336 658-4000

(G-10434)
MARCA INDUSTRIES INC
2387 Harding Hwy E (43302-8531)
PHONE...............................740 387-1035
Liz Owens, *Dir*
EMP: 51 **EST:** 1967
SQ FT: 50,000
SALES (est): 2.55MM **Privately Held**
Web: www.marcaindustries.org
SIC: 8331 Sheltered workshop

(G-10435)
MARION ANCILLARY SERVICES LLC
1040 Delaware Ave (43302-6416)
PHONE...............................740 383-7983
Michael P Coyne, *Prin*
EMP: 33 **EST:** 2000
SALES (est): 2.46MM **Privately Held**
SIC: 8011 Pathologist

(G-10436)
MARION CARE LEASING LLC
Also Called: Community Care Rehabilitation
175 Community Dr (43302-6487)
PHONE...............................740 387-7537
EMP: 80 **EST:** 2017
SALES (est): 7.39MM **Privately Held**
SIC: 8051 Convalescent home with continuous nursing care

(G-10437)
MARION CNTY BD DEV DSABILITIES
Also Called: Marion County Board of Mr Dd
2387 Harding Hwy E (43302-8529)
PHONE...............................740 387-1035
Lee Wedemeyer, *Superintnt*
EMP: 83 **EST:** 2001
SALES (est): 4.55MM **Privately Held**
Web: www.marioncountydd.org
SIC: 8322 Social service center

(G-10438)
MARION FAMILY YMCA
Also Called: YMCA
645 Barks Rd E (43302-6517)
PHONE...............................740 725-9622
Bob Houston, *Pr*
EMP: 60 **EST:** 1900
SALES (est): 2.67MM **Privately Held**
Web: www.marionymca.org
SIC: 8322 8641 Youth center; Youth organizations

(G-10439)
MARION GENERAL HOSPITAL INC (HQ)
1000 Mckinley Park Dr (43302-6397)
PHONE...............................740 383-8400
John Sanders, *Pr*
EMP: 719 **EST:** 1955
SQ FT: 247,000
SALES (est): 155.59MM
SALES (corp-wide): 4.29B **Privately Held**
Web: www.ohiohealth.com
SIC: 8062 Hospital, AMA approved residency
PA: Ohiohealth Corporation
 3430 Ohhalth Pkwy 5th Flr
 Columbus OH 43202
 614 788-8860

(G-10440)
MARION LODGE
Also Called: Holiday Inn
1842 Marion Mount Gilead Rd (43302-5826)
PHONE...............................740 389-4300
Andrea Shoaf, *Managing Member*
Bruce Jenkins, *Genl Mgr*
EMP: 46 **EST:** 1998
SALES (est): 925.84K **Privately Held**
Web: www.holidayinn.com
SIC: 7011 Hotels and motels

(G-10441)
MARION MANOR
195 Executive Dr (43302-6343)
PHONE...............................740 387-9545
L Bruce Levering, *
EMP: 48 **EST:** 1967
SQ FT: 30,000
SALES (est): 947.77K **Privately Held**
Web: www.marionmanornursing.com
SIC: 8059 8051 Nursing home, except skilled and intermediate care facility; Skilled nursing care facilities

(G-10442)
MARYHAVEN INC
333 E Center St Ste 102 (43302-4142)
PHONE...............................740 375-5550
Shawn Holt, *CEO*
EMP: 28
SALES (corp-wide): 32.39MM **Privately Held**
Web: www.maryhaven.com
SIC: 8069 Alcoholism rehabilitation hospital
PA: Maryhaven, Inc.
 1791 Alum Creek Dr
 Columbus OH 43207
 614 449-1530

(G-10443)
MATHEWS DDGE CHRYSLER JEEP INC
1866 Marion Waldo Rd (43302-7430)
PHONE...............................740 389-2341
Thurman Matthews, *Pr*
EMP: 28 **EST:** 1985
SALES (est): 4.76MM **Privately Held**
Web: www.mathewsdodgechryslerjeep.com

GEOGRAPHIC SECTION

Marion - Marion County (G-10463)

SIC: 5511 7538 7515 Automobiles, new and used; General automotive repair shops; Passenger car leasing

(G-10444)
MATHEWS KENNEDY FORD L-M INC (PA)
Also Called: Mathews Auto Group
1155 Delaware Ave (43302)
PHONE.................................740 387-3673
TOLL FREE: 800
Thurman R Mathews, *Pr*
Thomas Mathews, *Lawyer*
Jean Mitchell, *
EMP: 75 **EST:** 1961
SQ FT: 35,000
SALES (est): 21.33MM
SALES (corp-wide): 21.33MM **Privately Held**
Web: www.mathewsfordmarion.com
SIC: 5511 7538 7532 7515 Automobiles, new and used; General automotive repair shops; Top and body repair and paint shops ; Passenger car leasing

(G-10445)
METROPLTAN EDCTL TCHNICAL ASSN
Also Called: Meta Solutions
100 Executive Dr (43302-6306)
PHONE.................................740 389-4798
Jamie Grube, *CEO*
EMP: 203 **EST:** 2016
SALES (est): 23.88MM **Privately Held**
Web: www.metasolutions.net
SIC: 8748 Educational consultant

(G-10446)
NATIONAL LIME AND STONE CO
700 Likens Rd (43302-8601)
P.O. Box 144 (43301-0144)
PHONE.................................740 387-3485
Scott Silver, *Mgr*
EMP: 28
SALES (corp-wide): 167.89MM **Privately Held**
Web: www.natlime.com
SIC: 1422 5999 Limestones, ground; Rock and stone specimens
PA: The National Lime And Stone Company
    551 Lake Cascade Pkwy
    Findlay OH 45840
    419 422-4341

(G-10447)
NEW HORIZONS SURGERY CTR LLC
1167 Independence Ave (43302-6360)
PHONE.................................740 375-5854
Brian Hempstead, *CEO*
EMP: 35 **EST:** 1999
SALES (est): 5.98MM
SALES (corp-wide): 20.55B **Publicly Held**
Web: www.newhorizonsc.com
SIC: 8011 General and family practice, physician/surgeon
PA: Tenet Healthcare Corporation
    14201 Dallas Pkwy
    Dallas TX 75254
    469 893-2200

(G-10448)
NUCOR STEEL MARION INC (HQ)
912 Cheney Ave (43302-6208)
P.O. Box 1801 (43301-1801)
PHONE.................................740 383-4011
◆ **EMP:** 375 **EST:** 1981
SALES (est): 63.75MM
SALES (corp-wide): 34.71B **Publicly Held**
Web: www.nucorhighway.com

SIC: 3316 3441 3312 5051 Cold finishing of steel shapes; Fabricated structural metal; Iron and steel products, hot-rolled; Iron and steel (ferrous) products
PA: Nucor Corporation
    1915 Rexford Rd
    Charlotte NC 28211
    704 366-7000

(G-10449)
OHIO-AMERICAN WATER CO INC (HQ)
Also Called: Marion District
365 E Center St (43302-4155)
PHONE.................................740 382-3993
TOLL FREE: 800
John E Eckart, *Pr*
T Wilkes Coleman, *
Dwayne D Cole, *
Christine J Doron, *
Stephen B Givens, *
EMP: 45 **EST:** 1800
SQ FT: 8,500
SALES (est): 10.45MM
SALES (corp-wide): 4.23B **Publicly Held**
SIC: 4941 Water supply
PA: American Water Works Company, Inc.
    1 Water St
    Camden NJ 08102
    856 955-4001

(G-10450)
PRIYA PVT LTD
Also Called: Super 8 Motel
2117 Marion Mount Gilead Rd (43302-8990)
P.O. Box 102 (45839-0102)
PHONE.................................740 389-1998
Dinesh Patel, *Mng Pt*
EMP: 64 **EST:** 1998
SQ FT: 45,000
SALES (est): 305.64K **Privately Held**
Web: www.wyndhamhotels.com
SIC: 7011 Hotels and motels

(G-10451)
RESIDENTIAL HM ASSN MARION INC (PA)
Also Called: RHAM
205 Center St Ste 100 (43302-3700)
PHONE.................................740 387-9999
Shirley Russell, *Dir*
EMP: 105 **EST:** 1974
SALES (est): 3.44MM
SALES (corp-wide): 3.44MM **Privately Held**
Web: www.marionstar.com
SIC: 8742 8361 6531 Management consulting services; Retarded home; Real estate agents and managers

(G-10452)
RK FAMILY INC
233 America Blvd (43302-7805)
PHONE.................................740 389-2674
Tim Lodes, *Prin*
EMP: 122
SALES (corp-wide): 1.22B **Privately Held**
Web: www.ruralking.com
SIC: 5191 Farm supplies
PA: Rk Family, Inc.
    4216 Dewitt Ave
    Mattoon IL 61938
    217 235-7102

(G-10453)
SACK N SAVE INC
Also Called: King Saver
725 Richmond Ave (43302-1935)
PHONE.................................740 382-2464
David Fass, *Mgr*

EMP: 48
Web: www.freshencounter.com
SIC: 5411 6099 Grocery stores, chain; Money order issuance
HQ: Sack 'n Save, Inc.
    317 W Main Cross St
    Findlay OH 45840
    419 422-8090

(G-10454)
SIMS BROS INC (PA)
Also Called: Sims Brothers Recycling
1011 S Prospect St (43302-6217)
P.O. Box 1170 (43301-1170)
PHONE.................................740 387-9041
TOLL FREE: 800
▲ **EMP:** 95 **EST:** 1965
SALES (est): 32.93MM
SALES (corp-wide): 32.93MM **Privately Held**
Web: www.simsbros.com
SIC: 5051 5013 5093 3341 Iron and steel (ferrous) products; Automotive supplies and parts; Waste paper; Secondary nonferrous metals

(G-10455)
STEAM TRBINE ALTRNTIVE RSRCES
Also Called: Star
370 W Fairground St (43302)
P.O. Box 862 (43301)
PHONE.................................740 387-5535
Sue B Flaherty, *Ch Bd*
Tammy Flaherty, *
Ken Kubinski, *
Donna Macgregor Rambin, *
EMP: 45 **EST:** 1988
SALES (est): 8.4MM **Privately Held**
Web: www.starturbine.com
SIC: 3511 5085 Steam turbines; Industrial supplies

(G-10456)
SUNBRIDGE MARION HLTH CARE LLC
Also Called: Partners Mrion Care Rhbltton
524 James Way (43302-7801)
PHONE.................................740 389-6306
Shannon Kellogg, *Mgr*
EMP: 91
SALES (corp-wide): 5.86B **Publicly Held**
Web: www.kingstonhealthcare.com
SIC: 8051 8093 Skilled nursing care facilities ; Rehabilitation center, outpatient treatment
HQ: Sunbridge Marion Health Care Llc
    101 Sun Ave Ne
    Albuquerque NM 87109
    505 821-3355

(G-10457)
TURBO PARTS LLC
1676 Cascade Dr (43302-8509)
PHONE.................................740 223-1695
Tony Mitola, *Brnch Mgr*
EMP: 98
Web: www.mdaturbines.com
SIC: 5013 Automotive supplies and parts
PA: Turbo Parts, Llc
    767 Pierce Rd Ste 2
    Clifton Park NY 12065

(G-10458)
UCC IX DBA BARRINGTON SQUARE
Also Called: CHAPEL HILL COMMUNITY
170 E Center St (43302-3815)
P.O. Box 1806 (43301-1806)
PHONE.................................740 382-4885
EMP: 65 **EST:** 1995
SALES (est): 382.62K
SALES (corp-wide): 115.52MM **Privately Held**

SIC: 8361 Residential care
PA: United Church Homes, Inc.
    170 E Center St
    Marion OH 43302
    800 837-2211

(G-10459)
UNITED CH RESIDENCES GOSHEN
Also Called: CHAPEL HILL COMMUNITY
170 E Center St (43302-3815)
P.O. Box 1806 (43301-1806)
PHONE.................................740 382-4885
EMP: 65 **EST:** 2011
SALES (est): 422.28K
SALES (corp-wide): 115.52MM **Privately Held**
Web: www.unitedchurchhomes.org
SIC: 8361 Residential care
PA: United Church Homes, Inc.
    170 E Center St
    Marion OH 43302
    800 837-2211

(G-10460)
UNITED CH RSDNCES IMMKLEE CYPR
Also Called: CHAPEL HILL COMMUNITY
170 E Center St (43302-3815)
P.O. Box 1806 (43301-1806)
PHONE.................................740 382-4885
EMP: 60 **EST:** 2011
SALES (est): 319.93K
SALES (corp-wide): 115.52MM **Privately Held**
Web: www.unitedchurchhomes.org
SIC: 8361 Aged home
PA: United Church Homes, Inc.
    170 E Center St
    Marion OH 43302
    800 837-2211

(G-10461)
UNITED CH RSDNCES IMMKLEE FLA
Also Called: Cypress Run
170 E Center St (43302-3815)
PHONE.................................740 382-4885
EMP: 82 **EST:** 2011
SALES (est): 368.76K
SALES (corp-wide): 115.52MM **Privately Held**
Web: www.unitedchurchhomes.org
SIC: 8361 Aged home
PA: United Church Homes, Inc.
    170 E Center St
    Marion OH 43302
    800 837-2211

(G-10462)
UNITED CHURCH HOMES INC (PA)
Also Called: Chapel Hill Community
170 E Center St (43302-3815)
P.O. Box 1806 (43301-1806)
PHONE.................................800 837-2211
Reverend Kenneth Daniel, *CEO*
Brian S Allen, *Pr*
Timothy Hackett, *VP*
Pam White, *VP*
Edwin Allen, *VP*
EMP: 60 **EST:** 1920
SQ FT: 20,000
SALES (est): 115.52MM
SALES (corp-wide): 115.52MM **Privately Held**
Web: www.unitedchurchhomes.org
SIC: 8361 Residential care

(G-10463)
UNITED PARCEL SERVICE INC
Also Called: UPS
1476 Likens Rd (43302-8788)
PHONE.................................614 383-4580

Marion - Marion County (G-10464)

GEOGRAPHIC SECTION

EMP: 31
SALES (corp-wide): 90.96B **Publicly Held**
Web: www.ups.com
SIC: 4215 Parcel delivery, vehicular
HQ: United Parcel Service, Inc.
55 Glenlake Pkwy
Atlanta GA 30328
404 828-6000

(G-10464)
WHIRLPOOL CORPORATION
Whirlpool
1300 Marion Agosta Rd (43302-9577)
PHONE.................................740 383-7122
Stan Kenneth, *VP*
EMP: 45
SALES (corp-wide): 19.45B **Publicly Held**
Web: www.whirlpoolcorp.com
SIC: 3633 5064 3632 Laundry dryers, household or coin-operated; Washing machines; Household refrigerators and freezers
PA: Whirlpool Corporation
2000 N M-63
Benton Harbor MI 49022
269 923-5000

Martins Ferry
Belmont County

(G-10465)
COLERAIN TOWNSHIP
53979 Colerain Pike (43935-1143)
PHONE.................................740 633-5778
William J Nagel, *Prin*
EMP: 40 **EST:** 2009
SALES (est): 200.87K **Privately Held**
Web: www.nwlsd.org
SIC: 6733 Trusts, nec

(G-10466)
COMMUNITY MENTAL HEALTH SVC
301 Walnut St (43935-1429)
PHONE.................................740 633-2161
Mary Denoble, *Ex Dir*
EMP: 27
SALES (corp-wide): 4.97MM **Privately Held**
Web: www.southeasthc.org
SIC: 8093 Mental health clinic, outpatient
PA: Community Mental Health Service
68353 Bannock Rd
Saint Clairsville OH 43950
740 695-9344

(G-10467)
EAST OHIO HOSPITAL LLC
Also Called: Joint Implant Surgeons
90 N 4th St (43935-1648)
PHONE.................................740 633-1100
Lex Reddy, *Pr*
EMP: 131
SALES (corp-wide): 50.49MM **Privately Held**
Web: www.eohospital.com
SIC: 8062 General medical and surgical hospitals
PA: East Ohio Hospital, Llc
90 N 4th St
Martins Ferry OH 43935
740 633-1100

(G-10468)
EAST OHIO HOSPITAL LLC (PA)
90 N 4th St (43935-1648)
PHONE.................................740 633-1100
Bernie Albertini, *COO*
EMP: 29 **EST:** 2020
SALES (est): 50.49MM

SALES (corp-wide): 50.49MM **Privately Held**
Web: www.eohospital.com
SIC: 8062 General medical and surgical hospitals

(G-10469)
N F MANSUETTO & SONS INC
Also Called: Mansuetto Roofing Company
116 Wood St (43935-1710)
PHONE.................................740 633-7320
Matthew Mansuetto, *Pr*
Eugene Ochap, *
Francis M Mansuetto, *
EMP: 30 **EST:** 1966
SQ FT: 10,000
SALES (est): 5.6MM **Privately Held**
Web: www.mansuettoroofing.com
SIC: 1761 Roofing contractor

(G-10470)
STONEY HOLLOW TIRE INC
7 N 1st St (43935)
P.O. Box 310 (43935)
PHONE.................................740 635-5200
Earl Buono, *Pr*
Jeff Sterling, *
▲ **EMP:** 90 **EST:** 1987
SQ FT: 80,000
SALES (est): 10.09MM **Privately Held**
Web: www.stoneyhollowtire.com
SIC: 5014 Automobile tires and tubes

(G-10471)
TURF CARE SUPPLY CORP
Also Called: TURF CARE SUPPLY CORP.
100 Picoma Rd (43935-9700)
PHONE.................................740 633-8247
Chris Musser, *Mgr*
EMP: 74
Web: www.turfcaresupply.com
SIC: 0782 Turf installation services, except artificial
PA: Turf Care Supply, Llc
50 Pearl Rd Ste 200
Brunswick OH 44212

(G-10472)
UNIFIED BANK (HQ)
Also Called: CITIZENS BANK
201 S 4th St (43935-1311)
P.O. Box 10 (43935-0010)
PHONE.................................740 633-0445
James W Everson, *CEO*
Scott Everson, *
Randall M Greenwood, *
James Lodes, *Senior Vice President Lending*
Michael A Lloyd, *Senior Vice President Management Information Systems*
EMP: 40 **EST:** 1902
SQ FT: 20,000
SALES (est): 31.74MM
SALES (corp-wide): 40.9MM **Publicly Held**
Web: www.unifiedbank.com
SIC: 6022 State trust companies accepting deposits, commercial
PA: United Bancorp, Inc.
201 S 4th St
Martins Ferry OH 43935
740 633-0445

Marysville
Union County

(G-10473)
ADVANCED SURGICAL ASSOCIATES
388 Damascus Rd (43040-5535)
PHONE.................................937 578-2650
Chris Brock, *Prin*
EMP: 36 **EST:** 2017
SALES (est): 379.82K **Privately Held**
SIC: 8011 Offices and clinics of medical doctors

(G-10474)
BASINGER LFE ENHNCMNT SPRT SVC (PA)
Also Called: Bless
941 E 5th St (43040-1703)
PHONE.................................614 557-5461
Robert Basinger, *Managing Member*
EMP: 93 **EST:** 2014
SALES (est): 2.86MM
SALES (corp-wide): 2.86MM **Privately Held**
Web: www.blessllc.org
SIC: 8361 Residential care for the handicapped

(G-10475)
BOB FORD CHAPMAN INC
Also Called: Bob Chapman Ford
1255 Columbus Ave (43040)
P.O. Box 315 (43040)
PHONE.................................937 642-0015
Robert G Chapman, *Pr*
Linda Chapman, *
EMP: 36 **EST:** 1936
SQ FT: 28,200
SALES (est): 5.59MM **Privately Held**
Web: www.chapmanford.com
SIC: 5511 7538 Automobiles, new and used; General automotive repair shops

(G-10476)
BONNIE PLANTS LLC
21109 Cotton Slash Rd (43040-8985)
PHONE.................................937 642-7764
EMP: 123
SALES (corp-wide): 11.78MM **Privately Held**
Web: www.bonnieplants.com
SIC: 5992 5261 5085 Plants, potted; Nursery stock, seeds and bulbs; Industrial supplies
PA: Bonnie Plants, Llc
1727 Highway 223
Union Springs AL 36089
334 738-3104

(G-10477)
BY-LINE TRANSIT INC
16505 Springdale Rd (43040-8941)
PHONE.................................937 642-2500
Deborah Bywater, *Pr*
Ronald P Bywater, *
EMP: 49 **EST:** 1985
SALES (est): 1.28MM **Privately Held**
Web: www.bylinetransit.com
SIC: 4213 Contract haulers

(G-10478)
CARRIAGE CRT-MRYSVLLE LTD PRTN
717 S Walnut St (43040-1639)
PHONE.................................937 642-2202
Rita Orahood, *Ex Dir*
Jeffrey Johns, *Prin*
EMP: 30 **EST:** 1994
SALES (est): 1.3MM **Privately Held**
SIC: 8361 8052 Aged home; Intermediate care facilities

(G-10479)
CHAMBERS LEASING SYSTEMS CORP
23198 Northwest Pkwy (43040-8100)
PHONE.................................937 642-4260

Ed Lee, *Brnch Mgr*
EMP: 30
Web: www.ventureexpress.com
SIC: 4213 Contract haulers
PA: Chambers Leasing Systems Corp
3100 N Summit St
Toledo OH 43611

(G-10480)
CONTINENTAL
13601 Industrial Pkwy (43040-8890)
PHONE.................................937 644-8940
EMP: 49
SALES (est): 1.19MM **Privately Held**
Web: www.continental.com
SIC: 5085 Industrial supplies

(G-10481)
CONTITECH USA INC
Also Called: Continental Contitech
13601 Industrial Pkwy (43040-8890)
PHONE.................................937 644-8900
Ken Kontely, *Mgr*
EMP: 78
SALES (corp-wide): 45.02B **Privately Held**
Web: www.continental-industry.com
SIC: 5084 3399 3496 Industrial machinery and equipment; Metal fasteners; Mats and matting
HQ: Contitech Usa, Inc.
703 S Clvland Mssillon Rd
Fairlawn OH 44333

(G-10482)
DAYTON POWER AND LIGHT COMPANY
1201 W 5th St (43040-9291)
PHONE.................................937 642-9100
Steve Hall, *Mgr*
EMP: 54
SALES (corp-wide): 12.67B **Publicly Held**
Web: www.aes-ohio.com
SIC: 4911 Generation, electric power
HQ: The Dayton Power And Light Company
1065 Woodman Dr
Dayton OH 45432
937 331-3900

(G-10483)
DISABLED AMERICAN VETERANS
Also Called: Chapter 55
209 Prairie Dr (43040-9095)
PHONE.................................937 644-1907
Rowland Seymour, *Treas*
EMP: 100
SALES (corp-wide): 147.45MM **Privately Held**
Web: www.dav.org
SIC: 8641 Veterans' organization
PA: Disabled American Veterans
860 Dolwick Dr
Erlanger KY 41018
859 441-7300

(G-10484)
ELITE SOUTHERN CNSTR LLC
480 Emmaus Rd (43040-5558)
PHONE.................................614 441-1285
Ronald L Itnyre Junior, *Brnch Mgr*
EMP: 92
SALES (corp-wide): 495.76K **Privately Held**
SIC: 1521 General remodeling, single-family houses
PA: Elite Southern Construction Llc
154 Timber Creek Dr Ste 5
Cordova TN 38018
901 871-7663

GEOGRAPHIC SECTION
Marysville - Union County (G-10506)

(G-10485)
GABLES AT GREEN PASTURES
390 Gables Dr (43040-9582)
PHONE.............................937 642-3893
Lorie Whittington, *Dir*
EMP: 27 EST: 2001
SALES (est): 5.35MM **Privately Held**
Web: www.memorialohio.com
SIC: 8051 Convalescent home with continuous nursing care

(G-10486)
GENRIC INC
883 London Ave Ste A (43040-9166)
PHONE.............................937 553-9250
Philip C Drake, *CEO*
Paul Attwood, *
EMP: 399 EST: 1996
SALES (est): 20MM **Privately Held**
Web: www.genric.com
SIC: 1731 7381 7382 Safety and security specialization; Security guard service; Security systems services

(G-10487)
HEALTH CARE RTREMENT CORP AMER
Also Called: Heartland of Marysville
755 S Plum St (43040-1631)
PHONE.............................937 644-8836
Charlie George, *Genl Mgr*
EMP: 91
SQ FT: 26,000
SALES (corp-wide): 187.07MM **Privately Held**
Web: www.promedicaseniorcare.org
SIC: 8051 Convalescent home with continuous nursing care
HQ: Health Care And Retirement
    Corporation Of America
    333 N Summit St Ste 103
    Toledo OH 43604
    419 252-5500

(G-10488)
HONDA DEV & MFG AMER LLC
Also Called: Honda Support Office
19900 State Route 739 (43040-9256)
PHONE.............................937 644-0724
EMP: 200
Web: www.honda.com
SIC: 5511 3711 3465 8742 Automobiles, new and used; Motor vehicles and car bodies; Automotive stampings; Training and development consultant
HQ: Honda Development & Manufacturing
    Of America, Llc
    24000 Honda Pkwy
    Marysville OH 43040
    937 642-5000

(G-10489)
HONDA FEDERAL CREDIT UNION
24000 Honda Pkwy (43040-9251)
PHONE.............................937 642-6000
Joe Mattera, *Brnch Mgr*
EMP: 34
SALES (corp-wide): 51.81MM **Privately Held**
Web: www.hondafcu.org
SIC: 6061 Federal credit unions
PA: Honda Federal Credit Union
    19701 Hamilton Ave # 130
    Torrance CA 90502
    310 217-0509

(G-10490)
HONDA FEDERAL CREDIT UNION
17655 Echo Dr (43040-9793)
PHONE.............................937 642-6000
Carrie Strausser, *Mgr*
EMP: 37
SALES (corp-wide): 51.81MM **Privately Held**
Web: www.hondafcu.org
SIC: 6061 Federal credit unions
PA: Honda Federal Credit Union
    19701 Hamilton Ave # 130
    Torrance CA 90502
    310 217-0509

(G-10491)
HOSPITLIST SVCS MED GROUP OF M
Also Called: Hospitlst Srvcs Med Grp Mrysvl
500 London Ave (43040-3570)
PHONE.............................937 644-6115
EMP: 870 EST: 2011
SALES (est): 12.77MM **Privately Held**
SIC: 8099 Health and allied services, nec

(G-10492)
LOWES HOME CENTERS LLC
Also Called: Lowe's
15775 Us Highway 36 (43040-9484)
PHONE.............................937 578-4440
EMP: 138
SALES (corp-wide): 86.38B **Publicly Held**
Web: www.lowes.com
SIC: 5211 5031 5722 5064 Home centers; Building materials, exterior; Household appliance stores; Electrical appliances, television and radio
HQ: Lowe's Home Centers, Llc
    1000 Lowes Blvd
    Mooresville NC 28117
    336 658-4000

(G-10493)
MARYHAVEN INC
715 S Plum St (43040-1631)
PHONE.............................937 644-9192
Paul Coleman, *Brnch Mgr*
EMP: 28
SALES (corp-wide): 32.39MM **Privately Held**
Web: www.maryhaven.com
SIC: 8069 Alcoholism rehabilitation hospital
PA: Maryhaven, Inc.
    1791 Alum Creek Dr
    Columbus OH 43207
    614 449-1530

(G-10494)
MARYSVILLE STEEL INC
323 E 8th St (43040)
P.O. Box 383 (43040-0383)
PHONE.............................937 642-5971
Steven J Clayman, *CEO*
EMP: 31 EST: 1951
SQ FT: 50,000
SALES (est): 4.09MM **Privately Held**
SIC: 3441 1791 5039 Fabricated structural metal; Structural steel erection; Joists

(G-10495)
MARYSVLLE EXMPTED VLG SCHL DST
1280 Charles Ln (43040-9797)
PHONE.............................937 645-6733
Sue Lamendola, *Brnch Mgr*
EMP: 49
SALES (corp-wide): 77.56MM **Privately Held**
Web: www.ucbdd.org
SIC: 7389 Personal service agents, brokers, and bureaus
PA: Marysville Exempted Village School
    District
    212 Chestnut St
    Marysville OH 43040
    937 644-8105

(G-10496)
MARYSVLLE OHIO SRGICAL CTR LLC
17853 State Route 31 (43040-8520)
PHONE.............................937 578-4200
R Mark Stover, *Brnch Mgr*
EMP: 152
SALES (corp-wide): 3.16MM **Privately Held**
SIC: 8011 Orthopedic physician
PA: Marysville Ohio Surgical Center, L.L.C.
    122 Professional Pkwy
    Marysville OH

(G-10497)
MEMORIAL HOSP AUX UN CNTY OHIO (PA)
Also Called: Memorial Health
500 London Ave (43040-5512)
PHONE.............................937 644-6115
Chip Hubbs, *Pr*
Spence Fisher, *
Jeff Ehlers, *
EMP: 600 EST: 1952
SQ FT: 132,000
SALES (est): 157.54MM
SALES (corp-wide): 157.54MM **Privately Held**
Web: www.memorialohio.com
SIC: 8062 Hospital, affiliated with AMA residency

(G-10498)
MEMORIAL HOSPITAL UNION COUNTY
Also Called: MEMORIAL HOSPITAL OF UNION COUNTY
660 London Ave (43040-1515)
PHONE.............................937 644-1001
Chip Hubbs, *Brnch Mgr*
EMP: 195
SALES (corp-wide): 157.54MM **Privately Held**
Web: www.memorialohio.com
SIC: 8062 General medical and surgical hospitals
PA: Memorial Hospital Auxiliary Of Union
    County, Ohio, Inc.
    500 London Ave
    Marysville OH 43040
    937 644-6115

(G-10499)
MILCREST HEALTHCARE INC
Also Called: Monarch Skilled Nursing Rehab
730 Millcrest Dr (43040-1833)
PHONE.............................937 642-0218
Janet Harris, *Pr*
Donna Crawford, *Prin*
EMP: 60 EST: 2001
SALES (est): 3.67MM **Privately Held**
SIC: 8051 Convalescent home with continuous nursing care

(G-10500)
NISSIN INTL TRNSPT USA INC
Also Called: Nissin International Transport
16940 Square Dr (43040-9616)
PHONE.............................937 644-2644
EMP: 75
Web: www.nitusa.com
SIC: 4731 Freight forwarding
HQ: Nissin International Transport U.S.A.,
    Inc.
    1540 W 190th St
    Torrance CA 90501
    310 222-8500

(G-10501)
PARKER-HANNIFIN CORPORATION
Also Called: Hydraulic Pump Pwr Systems Div
14249 Industrial Pkwy (43040-9504)
PHONE.............................937 644-3915
Charles Hawkins, *VP*
EMP: 35
SALES (corp-wide): 19.07B **Publicly Held**
Web: www.parker.com
SIC: 5084 Hydraulic systems equipment and supplies
PA: Parker-Hannifin Corporation
    6035 Parkland Blvd
    Cleveland OH 44124
    216 896-3000

(G-10502)
PARKWAY PIZZA INCORPORATED
Also Called: Benny's Pizza
968 Columbus Ave (43040-9501)
PHONE.............................937 303-8800
Fred Neumier, *Pr*
EMP: 95 EST: 2005
SALES (est): 2.28MM **Privately Held**
Web: www.bennyspizza.com
SIC: 5812 6794 Pizza restaurants; Franchises, selling or licensing

(G-10503)
R & D NESTLE CENTER INC (HQ)
Also Called: Nestle Product Technology Ctr
809 Collins Ave (43040-1308)
PHONE.............................937 642-7015
Mark Schneider, *CEO*
Gillian Anantharaman, *
Kenneth G Boehm, *
▲ EMP: 52 EST: 1986
SALES (est): 46.45MM **Privately Held**
SIC: 8731 Biotechnical research, commercial
PA: Nestle S.A.
    Avenue Nestle 55
    Vevey VD 1800

(G-10504)
RMI INTERNATIONAL INC
Also Called: Rodbat Security Services
24500 Honda Pkwy (43040)
PHONE.............................937 642-5032
Marco Norman, *Mgr*
EMP: 38
SALES (corp-wide): 20.44MM **Privately Held**
Web: www.rmiintl.com
SIC: 7381 Security guard service
PA: Rmi International, Inc.
    8125 Somerset Blvd
    Paramount CA 90723
    562 806-9098

(G-10505)
ROAD & RAIL SERVICES INC
24500 Honda Pkwy (43040-9140)
PHONE.............................937 578-0089
Bill Mason, *Mgr*
EMP: 71
SALES (corp-wide): 104.11MM **Privately Held**
Web: www.roadandrail.com
SIC: 4789 Railroad maintenance and repair services
PA: Road & Rail Services, Inc.
    4233 Bardstown Rd Ste 200
    Louisville KY 40218
    502 495-6688

(G-10506)
RYAN LOGISTICS INC
648 Clymer Rd (43040-1659)
PHONE.............................937 642-4158
Tracy Yoesting, *Pr*
Matt Price, *Prin*

Marysville - Union County (G-10507)

EMP: 80 **EST:** 2000
SALES (est): 21.23MM **Privately Held**
Web: www.ryanlogistics.com
SIC: 4731 Freight forwarding

(G-10507)
SCIOTO LLC (HQ)
Also Called: Scioto Services
405 S Oak St (43040-1756)
PHONE.................................937 644-0888
TOLL FREE: 800
Thomas C Kruse, *Pr*
David Anderson, *CFO*
EMP: 266 **EST:** 1975
SALES (est): 10.58MM
SALES (corp-wide): 290.16MM **Privately Held**
Web: www.sciotoservices.com
SIC: 7349 1711 5085 Janitorial service, contract basis; Mechanical contractor; Industrial supplies
PA: Marsden Holding, L.L.C.
2124 University Ave W
Saint Paul MN 55114
651 641-1717

(G-10508)
SCOTTS COMPANY LLC (HQ)
Also Called: Scotts Miracle-Gro Products
14111 Scottslawn Rd (43040-7801)
P.O. Box 418 (43040-0418)
PHONE.................................937 644-0011
Michael P Kelty, *
Christopher L Nagel, *
David M Aronowitz, *
◆ **EMP:** 143 **EST:** 1969
SALES (est): 1.59B
SALES (corp-wide): 3.55B **Publicly Held**
Web: www.scotts.com
SIC: 2873 2874 2879 0782 Fertilizers: natural (organic), except compost; Phosphates; Fungicides, herbicides; Lawn services
PA: The Scotts Miracle-Gro Company
14111 Scottslawn Rd
Marysville OH 43040
937 644-0011

(G-10509)
SCOTTS MIRACLE-GRO COMPANY (PA)
Also Called: Scotts Miracle-Gro
14111 Scottslawn Rd (43040-7801)
PHONE.................................937 644-0011
James Hagedorn, *Ch Bd*
James Hagedorn, *Ch Bd*
Nate Baxter, *COO*
Matthew E Garth, *CAO*
Dimiter Todorov, *Corporate Secretary*
▲ **EMP:** 343 **EST:** 1868
SALES (est): 3.55B
SALES (corp-wide): 3.55B **Publicly Held**
Web: www.scottsmiraclegro.com
SIC: 2873 7342 2879 Nitrogenous fertilizers; Pest control services; Insecticides and pesticides

(G-10510)
ST JHNS EVANG LTHRAN CH MRYSV
Also Called: St John's Lutheran School
12809 State Route 736 (43040-9056)
PHONE.................................937 644-5540
Herbert Mock, *Prin*
Ted Howard, *V Ch Bd*
Pastor Thomas Hackett, *Prin*
Pastor Jack Heino, *Prin*
EMP: 37 **EST:** 1843
SALES (est): 2.26MM **Privately Held**
Web: www.sjsmarysville.org

SIC: 8661 8211 8351 Lutheran Church; Elementary and secondary schools; Preschool center

(G-10511)
STRAIGHT 72 INC
Also Called: MAI Manufacturing
20078 State Route 4 (43040-9723)
PHONE.................................740 943-5730
EMP: 60 **EST:** 1995
SALES (est): 9.25MM **Privately Held**
Web: www.maimfg.com
SIC: 8711 3544 Acoustical engineering; Special dies, tools, jigs, and fixtures

(G-10512)
STRAUSS GERALD DDS INC
123 N Court St (43040-1101)
P.O. Box 433 (43040-0433)
PHONE.................................937 642-8500
Gerald Strauss, *Pr*
EMP: 32 **EST:** 1973
SQ FT: 2,749
SALES (est): 558.53K **Privately Held**
SIC: 8021 Dentists' office

(G-10513)
U-CO INDUSTRIES INC
16900 Square Dr Ste 110 (43040-8948)
PHONE.................................937 644-3021
Teresa O'connell, *Admn*
Teresa O'connell, *Adult Service Director*
EMP: 51 **EST:** 1974
SQ FT: 6,500
SALES (est): 788.32K **Privately Held**
Web: www.ucoindustries.com
SIC: 8331 Sheltered workshop

(G-10514)
UNION COUNTY PHYSICIAN CORP
500 London Ave (43040-3570)
PHONE.................................800 686-4677
Olas A Hubbs Iii, *Pr*
EMP: 122 **EST:** 2008
SALES (est): 21.17MM **Privately Held**
SIC: 8011 Offices and clinics of medical doctors

(G-10515)
UNION RURAL ELECTRIC COOP INC (PA)
15461 Us Highway 36 (43040)
P.O. Box 393 (43040)
PHONE.................................937 642-1826
Roger Yoder, *Pr*
EMP: 38 **EST:** 1926
SQ FT: 4,000
SALES (est): 63.18MM
SALES (corp-wide): 63.18MM **Privately Held**
Web: www.ure.com
SIC: 4911 8611 Distribution, electric power; Business associations

(G-10516)
UNIVENTURE INC
Also Called: Univenture CD Packg & Systems
16710 Square Dr (43040-9616)
PHONE.................................877 831-9428
EMP: 56
Web: www.univenture.com
SIC: 7336 Package design
PA: Univenture, Inc.
4266 Tuller Rd
Dublin OH 43017

Mason
Warren County

(G-10517)
AERO FULFILLMENT SERVICES CORP (PA)
3900 Aero Dr (45040-8840)
PHONE.................................800 225-7145
Jon T Gimpel, *Pr*
Jon T Gimpel, *Pr*
Brenda Conaway, *
▲ **EMP:** 100 **EST:** 1986
SQ FT: 125,000
SALES (est): 47.77MM
SALES (corp-wide): 47.77MM **Privately Held**
Web: www.aerofulfillment.com
SIC: 4225 7374 7331 2759 General warehousing; Data processing service; Mailing service; Commercial printing, nec

(G-10518)
AFIDENCE INC
5412 Courseview Dr Ste 122 (45040)
PHONE.................................513 234-5822
Bryan Hogan, *Pr*
Barbara Hogan, *
EMP: 28 **EST:** 2009
SALES (est): 4.83MM **Privately Held**
Web: www.afidence.com
SIC: 7373 Computer integrated systems design

(G-10519)
ALTIX CORPORATION
6402 Thornberry Ct (45040-7846)
PHONE.................................513 216-8386
Yannick Schilly, *Pr*
EMP: 43 **EST:** 2018
SALES (est): 4.42MM **Privately Held**
Web: www.altixconsulting.com
SIC: 8748 Business consulting, nec

(G-10520)
ARMOR CONSOLIDATED INC (PA)
4600 N Mason Montgomery Rd (45040-9176)
PHONE.................................513 923-5260
David K Schmitt, *CEO*
EMP: 510 **EST:** 1996
SALES (est): 23.51MM
SALES (corp-wide): 23.51MM **Privately Held**
Web: www.thearmorgroup.com
SIC: 3441 3446 3443 6719 Fabricated structural metal; Architectural metalwork; Fabricated plate work (boiler shop); Investment holding companies, except banks

(G-10521)
ATOS IT SOLUTIONS AND SVCS INC
4705 Duke Dr (45040-7645)
PHONE.................................513 336-1000
Brandy Wilhite, *Mgr*
EMP: 451
SALES (corp-wide): 129.21MM **Privately Held**
Web: www.unify.com
SIC: 7379 Computer related maintenance services
HQ: Atos It Solutions And Services Inc.
5920 Wndhven Pkwy Ste 120
Plano TX 75093
682 978-8622

(G-10522)
BAYER & BECKER INC (PA)
Also Called: Bayer Becker

6900 Tylersville Rd Ste A (45040-1593)
PHONE.................................513 492-7401
Keith Becker, *Pr*
EMP: 36 **EST:** 1978
SQ FT: 2,000
SALES (est): 8.28MM
SALES (corp-wide): 8.28MM **Privately Held**
Web: www.bayerbecker.com
SIC: 8713 8711 Surveying services; Civil engineering

(G-10523)
BENCHMARK DIGITAL PARTNERS LLC (PA)
5181 Natorp Blvd Ste 610 (45040-5910)
PHONE.................................513 774-1000
R Mukund, *Managing Member*
Natasha Porter, *
▲ **EMP:** 87 **EST:** 2008
SQ FT: 16,000
SALES (est): 34.72MM
SALES (corp-wide): 34.72MM **Privately Held**
Web: www.benchmarkgensuite.com
SIC: 7371 Computer software systems analysis and design, custom

(G-10524)
BROOKSIDE EXTENDED CARE CENTER
780 Snider Rd (45040-1391)
PHONE.................................513 398-1020
Mike Levenson, *CEO*
Rich Johnson, *
Becky Meister, *
EMP: 40 **EST:** 1980
SQ FT: 37,000
SALES (est): 2.14MM **Privately Held**
Web: www.brooksideextendedcare.net
SIC: 8059 Home for the mentally retarded, ex. skilled or intermediate

(G-10525)
CANON SOLUTIONS AMERICA INC
4900 Parkway Dr Ste 170 (45040-9702)
PHONE.................................513 229-8020
Gregory Coles, *Mgr*
EMP: 32
Web: csa.canon.com
SIC: 5044 Copying equipment
HQ: Canon Solutions America, Inc.
1 Canon Park
Melville NY 11747
631 330-5000

(G-10526)
CARING HEARTS HM HLTH CARE INC (PA)
6677 Summer Field Dr (45040-7332)
PHONE.................................513 339-1237
Gloria Hayes, *Pr*
Tyrone Spears, *
Ronnell Spears, *
EMP: 250 **EST:** 1988
SALES (est): 8.49MM **Privately Held**
SIC: 8082 Home health care services

(G-10527)
CENGAGE LEARNING INC
South-Western
5191 Natorp Blvd Lowr (45040-7599)
PHONE.................................513 229-1000
EMP: 500
Web: www.cengage.com
SIC: 7371 Computer software development and applications
HQ: Cengage Learning, Inc.
5191 Natorp Blvd
Mason OH 45040

GEOGRAPHIC SECTION

(G-10528)
CHARD SNYDER & ASSOCIATES LLC
Also Called: Chard Synder
6867 Cintas Blvd (45040)
PHONE...................513 459-9997
Joyce Snyder, Pr
Kenneth Chard, *
EMP: 165 EST: 1988
SQ FT: 24,600
SALES (est): 14.46MM
SALES (corp-wide): 947.08MM Privately Held
Web: www.chard-snyder.com
SIC: 8721 Payroll accounting service
PA: Ascensus, Llc
  200 Dryden Rd E Ste 1000
  Dresher PA 19025
  215 648-8000

(G-10529)
CHILDRENS HOSPITAL MEDICAL CTR
Also Called: Children's Outpatient North
9560 Children Dr (45040-9362)
PHONE...................513 636-6800
Char Mason, Brnch Mgr
EMP: 379
SALES (corp-wide): 2.94B Privately Held
Web: www.cincinnatichildrens.org
SIC: 8733 8093 8011 8069 Medical research; Specialty outpatient clinics, nec; Offices and clinics of medical doctors; Childrens' hospital
PA: Children's Hospital Medical Center
  3333 Burnet Ave
  Cincinnati OH 45229
  513 636-4200

(G-10530)
CHRIST HOSPITAL
Also Called: Christ Hosp Spcial Chmstry Lab
7450 S Mason Montgomery Rd (45040)
PHONE...................513 648-7900
EMP: 57
SALES (corp-wide): 1.3B Privately Held
SIC: 8062 Hospital, med school affiliated with nursing and residency
PA: The Christ Hospital
  2139 Auburn Ave
  Cincinnati OH 45219
  513 585-2000

(G-10531)
CINCI HOSPITALITIES INC
5589 State Route 741 (45040)
PHONE...................513 398-8075
Gurwinder Singh, Mgr
EMP: 31 EST: 2008
SALES (est): 440.05K Privately Held
SIC: 7011 Hotels and motels

(G-10532)
CINCINNATI AESTHETICS LLC
8381 Oakdale Ct (45040-5010)
PHONE...................513 204-3490
Erhan Erdeger, Brnch Mgr
EMP: 39
SALES (corp-wide): 501.71K Privately Held
Web: www.cincinnati-aesthetics.com
SIC: 8011 Dermatologist
PA: Cincinnati Aesthetics, Llc
  7558 Central Parke Blvd
  Mason OH 45040
  513 807-0351

(G-10533)
CINTAS CORPORATION NO 1 (HQ)
6800 Cintas Blvd (45040-9151)
PHONE...................513 459-1200
Richard T Farmer, Ch Bd
Robert Kohlhepp, *
Karen L Carnahan, *
Michael Thompson, *
◆ EMP: 1500 EST: 1987
SQ FT: 75,000
SALES (est): 103.67MM
SALES (corp-wide): 8.82B Publicly Held
Web: www.cintas.com
SIC: 5137 5136 7213 7549 Uniforms, women's and children's; Uniforms, men's and boys'; Uniform supply; Automotive maintenance services
PA: Cintas Corporation
  6800 Cintas Blvd
  Cincinnati OH 45262
  513 459-1200

(G-10534)
CINTAS CORPORATION NO 2
Also Called: Cintas
5800 Cintas Blvd (45040)
P.O. Box 636525 (45263-6525)
PHONE...................513 459-1200
EMP: 1000
SALES (corp-wide): 8.82B Publicly Held
Web: www.cintas.com
SIC: 5084 Safety equipment
HQ: Cintas Corporation No. 2
  6800 Cintas Blvd
  Mason OH 45040

(G-10535)
CINTAS CORPORATION NO 2 (HQ)
Also Called: Cintas Fire Protection
6800 Cintas Blvd (45040-9151)
P.O. Box 625737 (45262-5737)
PHONE...................513 459-1200
▲ EMP: 2000 EST: 2000
SALES (est): 1.75B
SALES (corp-wide): 8.82B Publicly Held
Web: www.cintas.com
SIC: 5084 Safety equipment
PA: Cintas Corporation
  6800 Cintas Blvd
  Cincinnati OH 45262
  513 459-1200

(G-10536)
CINTAS CORPORATION NO 3 (HQ)
6800 Cintas Blvd (45040-9151)
P.O. Box 625737 (45262-5737)
PHONE...................513 459-1200
EMP: 61 EST: 1995
SALES (est): 75.38MM
SALES (corp-wide): 8.82B Publicly Held
Web: www.cintas.com
SIC: 7218 Industrial uniform supply
PA: Cintas Corporation
  6800 Cintas Blvd
  Cincinnati OH 45262
  513 459-1200

(G-10537)
CINTAS DOCUMENT MANAGEMENT LLC (HQ)
6800 Cintas Blvd (45040-9151)
PHONE...................800 914-1960
Scott D Farmer, CEO
EMP: 30 EST: 2007
SALES (est): 9.49MM
SALES (corp-wide): 8.82B Publicly Held
Web: www.cintas.com
SIC: 7299 Personal document and information services
PA: Cintas Corporation
  6800 Cintas Blvd
  Cincinnati OH 45262
  513 459-1200

(G-10538)
CINTAS-RUS LP (HQ)
6800 Cintas Blvd (45040-9151)
P.O. Box 625737 (45262-5737)
PHONE...................513 459-1200
EMP: 38 EST: 2000
SALES (est): 10.47MM
SALES (corp-wide): 8.82B Publicly Held
SIC: 7218 Industrial uniform supply
PA: Cintas Corporation
  6800 Cintas Blvd
  Cincinnati OH 45262
  513 459-1200

(G-10539)
CLEVELAND CONSTRUCTION INC
5390 Courseview Dr Ste 200 (45040)
PHONE...................440 255-8000
David Kurilko, Mgr
EMP: 141
SALES (corp-wide): 426.33MM Privately Held
Web: www.clevelandconstruction.com
SIC: 1542 1721 1742 1521 Commercial and office building, new construction; Commercial wallcovering contractor; Plastering, drywall, and insulation; Single-family housing construction
PA: Cleveland Construction, Inc.
  8620 Tyler Blvd
  Mentor OH 44060
  440 255-8000

(G-10540)
CLOPAY CORPORATION (HQ)
8585 Duke Blvd (45040-3100)
PHONE...................800 282-2260
Franklin Smith Junior, CFO
Gary Abyad, Sr VP
Ellen Shoemaker, Sr VP
Eugene Colleran, Sr VP
◆ EMP: 231 EST: 1889
SQ FT: 130,587
SALES (est): 935.67MM
SALES (corp-wide): 2.69B Publicly Held
Web: www.clopaydoor.com
SIC: 3081 3442 2431 1796 Plastics film and sheet; Garage doors, overhead: metal; Garage doors, overhead, wood; Power generating equipment installation
PA: Griffon Corporation
  712 5th Ave Fl 18
  New York NY 10019
  212 957-5000

(G-10541)
COBB MOTEL COMPANY LLC
Also Called: Ramada Inn
9665 S Mason Montgomery Rd (45040-9397)
PHONE...................513 336-8871
Janet Foster, Prin
EMP: 27 EST: 2003
SALES (est): 210.15K Privately Held
Web: www.wyndhamhotels.com
SIC: 7011 Hotels and motels

(G-10542)
COMMUNITY CONCEPTS INC (PA)
Also Called: Community Concepts & Options
6699 Tri Way Dr (45040-2604)
PHONE...................513 398-8181
EMP: 110 EST: 1990
SALES (est): 10.6MM Privately Held
Web: www.cciohio.com
SIC: 8059 8082 Home for the mentally retarded, ex. skilled or intermediate; Home health care services

(G-10543)
CP MASON LLC
Also Called: Cincinnati Marriott Northeast
9664 S Mason Montgomery Rd (45040-9397)
PHONE...................513 459-9800
EMP: 87 EST: 2019
SALES (est): 1.86MM Privately Held
SIC: 7011 Hotels

(G-10544)
DIRECT EXPEDITING LLC
5311 Bentley Oak Dr (45040-8780)
P.O. Box 317 (45040-0317)
PHONE...................877 880-3400
EMP: 35
SQ FT: 10,000
SALES (est): 2MM Privately Held
SIC: 4119 Local rental transportation

(G-10545)
EVOKES LLC
8118 Corporate Way Ste 212 (45040)
PHONE...................513 947-8433
Daniel Lincoln, Pr
Tony Leslie, *
EMP: 50 EST: 2015
SQ FT: 900
SALES (est): 5.06MM Privately Held
Web: www.evokesllc.com
SIC: 3822 8011 Building services monitoring controls, automatic; Surgeon

(G-10546)
FAIRBORN EQUIPMENT MIDWEST INC
5155 Financial Way (45040-0055)
PHONE...................513 492-9422
Bill Mcbrayer, Pr
EMP: 76 EST: 2000
SALES (est): 13.27MM Privately Held
Web: www.fairbornequipmentmidwest.com
SIC: 5084 Materials handling machinery

(G-10547)
FDS BANK
9111 Duke Blvd Ste 100 (45040)
PHONE...................513 573-2265
Jack Brown, Pr
EMP: 3232 EST: 2001
SALES (est): 973.33MM
SALES (corp-wide): 23.87B Publicly Held
SIC: 6029 Commercial banks, nec
PA: Macy's, Inc.
  151 W 34th St
  New York NY 10001
  212 494-1621

(G-10548)
FESTO CORPORATION
7777 Columbia Rd (45039-1203)
PHONE...................513 486-1050
EMP: 250
SALES (corp-wide): 3.96B Privately Held
Web: www.festo.com
SIC: 5085 Industrial supplies
HQ: Festo Corporation
  1377 Motor Pkwy Ste 310
  Islandia NY 11749
  800 993-3786

(G-10549)
FORD MOTOR COMPANY
Also Called: Ford
4680 Parkway Dr Ste 420 (45040-8117)
PHONE...................513 573-1101
EMP: 30
SALES (corp-wide): 160.34B Publicly Held

Mason - Warren County (G-10550)   **GEOGRAPHIC SECTION**

SIC: **6159** Automobile finance leasing
PA: Ford Motor Company
1 American Rd
Dearborn MI 48126
313 322-3000

(G-10550)
FORTE INDUSTRIAL EQUIPMENT SYSTEMS INC
Also Called: Forte Industries
6037 Commerce Ct (45040-8819)
PHONE.................................513 398-2800
EMP: 32
SIC: **5084 8711 3537** Materials handling machinery; Consulting engineer; Industrial trucks and tractors

(G-10551)
FUJITEC AMERICA INC (HQ)
Also Called: Fujitec
7258 Innovation Way (45040-8015)
PHONE.................................513 755-6100
Takakazu Uchiyama, *CEO*
Katsuji Okuda, *
Masashi Tsuchihata, *
Ray Gibson, *
Melissa Kawahara, *
▲ EMP: 200 EST: 1977
SQ FT: 300,000
SALES (est): 205.47MM **Privately Held**
Web: www.fujitecamerica.com
SIC: **5084** Elevators
PA: Fujitec Co., Ltd.
591-1, Miyatacho
Hikone SGA 522-0

(G-10552)
G&K SERVICES LLC (HQ)
6800 Cintas Blvd (45040-9151)
PHONE.................................513 459-1200
Scott D Farmer, *CEO*
J Michael Hansen, *
Thomas E Frooma, *
◆ EMP: 300 EST: 1902
SALES (est): 102.73MM
SALES (corp-wide): 8.82B **Publicly Held**
Web: www.cintas.com
SIC: **7218 7213 7219** Industrial uniform supply; Apron supply; Garment making, alteration, and repair
PA: Cintas Corporation
6800 Cintas Blvd
Cincinnati OH 45262
513 459-1200

(G-10553)
GATESAIR INC (HQ)
5300 Kings Island Dr Ste 101 (45040-2668)
PHONE.................................513 459-3400
Barbara Spicek, *CEO*
Joseph Mack, *
Jeff Hills, *
▲ EMP: 80 EST: 1922
SQ FT: 30,000
SALES (est): 43.1MM
SALES (corp-wide): 1.81B **Privately Held**
Web: www.gatesair.com
SIC: **1731** 3663 Communications specialization; Radio broadcasting and communications equipment
PA: The Gores Group Llc
9800 Wilshire Blvd
Beverly Hills CA 90212
310 209-3010

(G-10554)
GENERAL REVENUE CORPORATION
Also Called: G R C
4660 Duke Dr Ste 200 (45040-8466)
PHONE.................................513 469-1472
Jonathan Finley, *Pr*
EMP: 133 EST: 1981
SQ FT: 100,000
SALES (est): 13.04MM
SALES (corp-wide): 2.22MM **Privately Held**
Web: www.generalrevenue.com
SIC: **7322** Collection agency, except real estate
PA: Single-Point Group International Inc
400-255 Consumers Rd
Toronto ON M2J 1
416 491-1313

(G-10555)
GLOBAL EDM INC
Also Called: Global E.D.M. Supplies, Inc
7697 Innovation Way (45040-9605)
PHONE.................................513 701-0468
▲ EMP: 81
SIC: **5084** Industrial machinery and equipment

(G-10556)
GREATER CINCINNATI CREDIT UN
Also Called: GREATER CINCINNATI CREDIT UNION
7948 S Mason Montgomery Rd (45040-8249)
PHONE.................................513 559-1234
Ben Sawyer, *Brnch Mgr*
EMP: 27
SALES (corp-wide): 5.57MM **Privately Held**
Web: www.gccu.org
SIC: **6061** Federal credit unions
PA: Greater Cincinnati Credit Union, Inc.
7221 Montgomery Rd Ste 1
Cincinnati OH 45236
513 559-1234

(G-10557)
GRIZZLY GOLF CENTER INC
Also Called: Golf Center At Kings Island
6042 Fairway Dr (45040-2006)
PHONE.................................513 398-5200
Peter Ryan, *Genl Mgr*
EMP: 300 EST: 1971
SQ FT: 5,000
SALES (est): 4.81MM **Publicly Held**
Web: www.masongrizzly.com
SIC: **7992 5812 5941 0782** Public golf courses; Eating places; Golf goods and equipment; Landscape contractors
HQ: Great American Insurance Company
301 E 4th St
Cincinnati OH 45202
513 369-5000

(G-10558)
HAAG-SREIT USA INC
3535 Kings Mills Rd (45040-2303)
PHONE.................................513 336-7255
EMP: 140
SIC: **5047 5048** Surgical equipment and supplies; Ophthalmic goods

(G-10559)
HAAG-STREIT USA INC (DH)
Also Called: Reliance Medical Products
3535 Kings Mills Rd (45040)
PHONE.................................513 398-3937
Ernest Cavin, *CEO*
◆ EMP: 85 EST: 1898
SQ FT: 100,000
SALES (est): 48.83MM **Privately Held**
Web: us.haag-streit.com
SIC: **3841 5048** Surgical and medical instruments; Ophthalmic goods
HQ: Haag-Streit Holding Ag
Gartenstadtstrasse 10
KOniz BE 3098

(G-10560)
HERITAGE CLUB
6690 Heritage Club Dr (45040-4649)
PHONE.................................513 459-7711
EMP: 100 EST: 1995
SQ FT: 11,600
SALES (est): 5.23MM **Privately Held**
Web: www.heritageclub.com
SIC: **7997** Country club, membership

(G-10561)
HI-FIVE DEVELOPMENT SVCS INC
202 W Main St Ste C (45040-1882)
PHONE.................................513 336-9280
Mark Davis, *Pr*
Brian Zilch, *
EMP: 27 EST: 2001
SQ FT: 1,200
SALES (est): 44.53MM **Privately Held**
Web: www.hifive1.com
SIC: **1542** Commercial and office building, new construction

(G-10562)
HI-TEK MANUFACTURING INC
Also Called: System EDM of Ohio
6050 Hi Tek Ct (45040-2602)
PHONE.................................513 459-1094
Cletis Jackson, *Pr*
Teresa Stang, *VP*
▲ EMP: 180 EST: 1979
SQ FT: 71,000
SALES (est): 41.41MM **Privately Held**
Web: www.hitekmfg.com
SIC: **3599 7692 3724 3714** Machine shop, jobbing and repair; Welding repair; Aircraft engines and engine parts; Motor vehicle parts and accessories

(G-10563)
ICR INC
Also Called: Icr Engineering
4770 Duke Dr Ste 300 (45040-9873)
PHONE.................................513 900-7007
EMP: 133
SALES (est): 58MM **Privately Held**
Web: www.icr-team.com
SIC: **8711 7371** Engineering services; Software programming applications
PA: Icr, Inc.
6200 S Main St Ste 200
Aurora CO 80016
720 728-7030

(G-10564)
INDUSTRIAL AIR CENTERS INC
Also Called: INDUSTRIAL AIR CENTERS INC.
6428 Castle Dr (45040-9412)
PHONE.................................513 770-4161
David Suder, *Mgr*
EMP: 35
Web: www.iacserv.com
SIC: **5084** Compressors, except air conditioning
PA: Industrial Air Centers Llc
731 E Market St
Jeffersonville IN 47130

(G-10565)
INTELLIGRATED SYSTEMS INC (HQ)
Also Called: Honeywell Intelligrated
7901 Innovation Way (45040-9498)
PHONE.................................866 936-7300
Chris Cole, *CEO*
Jim Mccarthy, *Pr*
Ed Puisis, *CFO*
▲ EMP: 800 EST: 1996
SQ FT: 390,000
SALES (est): 1.69B
SALES (corp-wide): 36.66B **Publicly Held**
Web: sps.honeywell.com
SIC: **3535 5084 7371** Conveyors and conveying equipment; Industrial machinery and equipment; Computer software development
PA: Honeywell International Inc.
855 S Mint St
Charlotte NC 28202
704 627-6200

(G-10566)
INTELLIGRATED SYSTEMS LLC
7901 Innovation Way (45040-9498)
PHONE.................................513 701-7300
Bryan Jones, *
Ed Puisis, *
Jim Mcknight, *Sr VP*
EMP: 2300 EST: 2001
SQ FT: 260,000
SALES (est): 365.17MM
SALES (corp-wide): 36.66B **Publicly Held**
SIC: **3535 5084 7371** Conveyors and conveying equipment; Materials handling machinery; Computer software development
HQ: Intelligrated Systems, Inc.
7901 Innovation Way
Mason OH 45040
866 936-7300

(G-10567)
INTELLIGRATED SYSTEMS OHIO LLC (DH)
7901 Innovation Way (45040-9498)
PHONE.................................513 701-7300
TOLL FREE: 800
Jim Mccarthy, *Pr*
Stephen Ackerman, *
Stephen Causey, *
◆ EMP: 600 EST: 2010
SQ FT: 332,000
SALES (est): 528.2MM
SALES (corp-wide): 36.66B **Publicly Held**
SIC: **3535 5084 3537** Conveyors and conveying equipment; Industrial machinery and equipment; Palletizers and depalletizers
HQ: Intelligrated Systems, Inc.
7901 Innovation Way
Mason OH 45040
866 936-7300

(G-10568)
INTERSTATE CONTRACTORS LLC
Also Called: Ic Roofing
762 Reading Rd # G (45040-1362)
PHONE.................................513 372-5393
EMP: 40 EST: 2010
SALES (est): 2.37MM **Privately Held**
Web: www.ic-roofing.com
SIC: **8611 3444** Business associations; Metal roofing and roof drainage equipment

(G-10569)
JEWISH HOME CINCINNATI INC
Also Called: Cedar Village
5467 Cedar Village Dr (45040-8693)
PHONE.................................513 754-3100
Dan Fagan, *CEO*
EMP: 275 EST: 1883
SQ FT: 257,000
SALES (est): 18MM **Privately Held**
Web: www.ajas.org
SIC: **8049 8051** Physical therapist; Skilled nursing care facilities

(G-10570)
JUSTIN DOYLE HOMES
5378a Cox Smith Rd (45040-6803)
PHONE.................................513 623-1418
EMP: 27 EST: 2018
SALES (est): 2.68MM **Privately Held**
Web: www.justindoylehomes.com

GEOGRAPHIC SECTION

Mason - Warren County (G-10593)

SIC: 1521 New construction, single-family houses

(G-10571)
L-3 CMMNCATIONS NOVA ENGRG INC
4393 Digital Way (45040-7604)
P.O. Box 16850 (84116-0850)
PHONE..................877 282-1168
Mark Fischer, *Pr*
EMP: 101 EST: 1990
SQ FT: 80,000
SALES (est): 3.8MM
SALES (corp-wide): 19.42B **Publicly Held**
SIC: 8711 3663 Electrical or electronic engineering; Carrier equipment, radio communications
HQ: L3 Technologies, Inc.
600 3rd Ave Fl 34
New York NY 10016
321 727-9100

(G-10572)
LEEF BROS INC
Also Called: Leef Services
6800 Cintas Blvd (45040-9151)
PHONE..................952 912-5500
Dan French, *Prin*
EMP: 48 EST: 1908
SALES (est): 1.94MM
SALES (corp-wide): 8.82B **Publicly Held**
SIC: 7218 Industrial uniform supply
HQ: G&K Services, Llc
6800 Cintas Blvd
Mason OH 45040
513 459-1200

(G-10573)
LH TRUCKING INC
6589 Bunker Oak Trl (45040-1038)
PHONE..................513 398-1682
EMP: 35 EST: 1987
SQ FT: 15,000
SALES (est): 1.71MM **Privately Held**
SIC: 4213 Trucking, except local

(G-10574)
LIFE TIME INC
Also Called: Lifetime
8310 Wilkens Blvd (45040-7364)
PHONE..................513 234-0660
Schuana Lynn Doyle, *Prin*
EMP: 114
SALES (corp-wide): 2.22B **Publicly Held**
Web: www.lifetime.life
SIC: 7991 Health club
HQ: Life Time, Inc.
2902 Corporate Pl
Chanhassen MN 55317

(G-10575)
LOWES HOME CENTERS LLC
Also Called: Lowe's
9380 S Mason Montgomery Rd (45040-8827)
PHONE..................513 336-9741
Kathleen Barefield, *Brnch Mgr*
EMP: 143
SALES (corp-wide): 86.38B **Publicly Held**
Web: www.lowes.com
SIC: 5211 5031 5722 5064 Home centers; Building materials, exterior; Household appliance stores; Electrical appliances, television and radio
HQ: Lowe's Home Centers, Llc
1000 Lowes Blvd
Mooresville NC 28117
336 658-4000

(G-10576)
MACYS CR & CUSTOMER SVCS INC
9111 Duke Blvd (45040-8999)
PHONE..................513 398-5221
Michael Gatio, *Pr*
EMP: 3000 EST: 1994
SALES (est): 121.82MM
SALES (corp-wide): 23.87B **Publicly Held**
SIC: 7389 7322 6141 Credit card service; Adjustment and collection services; Personal credit institutions
HQ: Macy's Retail Holdings, Llc
151 W 34th St
New York NY 10001

(G-10577)
MASON FAMILY RESORTS LLC
Also Called: Great Wolf Lodge
2501 Great Wolf Dr (45040-8085)
PHONE..................608 237-5871
John Emery, *
Jim Calder, *
Alex Lombardo, *
EMP: 450 EST: 2005
SALES (est): 35.11MM
SALES (corp-wide): 8.02B **Publicly Held**
Web: www.greatwolf.com
SIC: 5812 7011 7299 Family restaurants; Hotels and motels; Banquet hall facilities
HQ: Great Wolf Resorts Holdings, Inc.
1255 Fourier Dr Ste 201
Madison WI 53717
608 662-4700

(G-10578)
MASON HEALTH CARE CENTER
5640 Cox Smith Rd (45040-2210)
PHONE..................513 398-2881
Shelley Owens, *Dir*
EMP: 35 EST: 2004
SALES (est): 13.98MM **Privately Held**
Web: www.masonhc.com
SIC: 8051 8361 Convalescent home with continuous nursing care; Aged home

(G-10579)
MASTERS PHARMACEUTICAL LLC
Also Called: Masters Pharmaceutical
3600 Pharma Way (45036-9479)
PHONE..................800 982-7922
Dennis Smith, *Pr*
Kevin Moore, *CFO*
▲ EMP: 180 EST: 2000
SQ FT: 40,000
SALES (est): 22.63MM **Privately Held**
Web: www.mastersrx.com
SIC: 5122 Pharmaceuticals

(G-10580)
MCV HEALTH CARE FACILITIES INC
411 Western Row Rd (45040-1438)
PHONE..................513 398-1486
Donald Sams, *Pr*
Roger H Schwartz, *
EMP: 47 EST: 1988
SQ FT: 79,000
SALES (est): 9.35MM **Privately Held**
Web: www.christianvillages.org
SIC: 8051 8059 8052 Extended care facility; Rest home, with health care; Intermediate care facilities

(G-10581)
MEDPLUS INC
4690 Parkway Dr (45040-8172)
PHONE..................513 229-5500
EMP: 370
Web: www.medpluspro.com
SIC: 8011 Offices and clinics of medical doctors

(G-10582)
MVD COMMUNICATIONS LLC (PA)
Also Called: Mvd Connect
5188 Cox Smith Rd (45040)
P.O. Box 815 (45040)
PHONE..................513 683-4711
Jeff Black, *Managing Member*
Thad Edmonds, *
EMP: 65 EST: 1992
SQ FT: 16,000
SALES (est): 21.9MM
SALES (corp-wide): 21.9MM **Privately Held**
Web: www.mvdconnect.com
SIC: 4813 Data telephone communications

(G-10583)
NAVIENT SOLUTIONS LLC
4660 Duke Dr Ste 300 (45040-8466)
PHONE..................513 605-7530
EMP: 204
SALES (corp-wide): 4.83B **Publicly Held**
Web: www.navient.com
SIC: 6111 Student Loan Marketing Association
HQ: Navient Solutions, Llc
123 S Justison St Ste 300
Wilmington DE 19801
703 810-3000

(G-10584)
NEXTRX LLC
Also Called: Wellpoint Health Networks
8990 Duke Blvd (45040-8943)
PHONE..................317 532-6000
EMP: 846 EST: 2000
SALES (est): 16.38MM
SALES (corp-wide): 195.26B **Publicly Held**
Web: www.wellpointnextrx.com
SIC: 6324 5961 Group hospitalization plans; Pharmaceuticals, mail order
HQ: Express Scripts, Inc.
1 Express Way
Saint Louis MO 63121
314 996-0900

(G-10585)
NSC GLBAL MNAGED RESOURCES LLC
4705 Duke Dr Ste 250 (45040-7645)
P.O. Box 7 (43160-0007)
PHONE..................646 499-9113
Christian Lopez, *Managing Member*
EMP: 43 EST: 2014
SALES (est): 4.28MM **Privately Held**
Web: www.nscglobal.com
SIC: 7361 Employment agencies

(G-10586)
OMYA INDUSTRIES INC (HQ)
Also Called: Omya
4605 Duke Dr (45040-7626)
PHONE..................513 387-4600
Rainer Seidler, *CEO*
Patrick Preussner, *
Athanasios Katsilometes, *
Paul Thimons, *
◆ EMP: 85 EST: 1977
SALES (est): 193.55MM **Privately Held**
SIC: 1422 Crushed and broken limestone
PA: Omya Ag
Baslerstrasse 42
Oftringen AG 4665

(G-10587)
OXFORD PHYSCL THRAPY RHBLTTION
7567 Central Parke Blvd Ste B (45040)
PHONE..................513 229-7560

Peter S Zulia, *Mgr*
EMP: 46
Web: www.oxfordphysicaltherapy.com
SIC: 8049 Physical therapist
PA: Oxford Physical Therapy And Rehabilitation, Inc.
345 S College Ave
Oxford OH 45056

(G-10588)
OXFORD PHYSICAL THERAPY INC
Also Called: OXFORD PHYSICAL THERAPY INC
7567 Central Parke Blvd (45040-2242)
PHONE..................513 229-7560
Ben Sherman, *Mgr*
EMP: 35
Web: www.oxfordphysicaltherapy.com
SIC: 8049 Physical therapist
PA: Oxford Physical Therapy And Rehabilitation, Inc.
345 S College Ave
Oxford OH 45056

(G-10589)
P J & R J CONNECTION INC
Also Called: Goddard School, The
754 Reading Rd (45040-1362)
PHONE..................513 398-2777
EMP: 36 EST: 1996
SALES (est): 2.17MM **Privately Held**
Web: www.goddardschool.com
SIC: 8351 Preschool center

(G-10590)
PARAMOUNTS KINGS ISLAND
6300 Kings Island Dr (45040-9665)
PHONE..................513 754-5700
Jane Cooper, *Prin*
EMP: 212 EST: 2010
SALES (est): 2.36MM **Privately Held**
Web: www.visitkingsisland.com
SIC: 7996 Theme park, amusement

(G-10591)
PETSMART INC
Also Called: Petsmart
8175 Arbor Square Dr (45040-5003)
PHONE..................513 336-0365
Rodney Cramer, *Brnch Mgr*
EMP: 28
SALES (corp-wide): 1.03B **Privately Held**
Web: www.petsmart.com
SIC: 5999 0752 Pet supplies; Training services, pet and animal specialties (not horses)
HQ: Petsmart Llc
19601 N 27th Ave
Phoenix AZ 85027
623 580-6100

(G-10592)
PG
3900 Aero Dr (45040-8840)
PHONE..................513 698-6901
EMP: 80 EST: 2019
SALES (est): 2.55MM **Privately Held**
Web: www.pgcareers.com
SIC: 8748 Business consulting, nec

(G-10593)
PIONEER CLDDING GLZING SYSTEMS (PA)
4074 Bethany Rd (45040-9047)
PHONE..................513 583-5925
Tom Heinold, *Prin*
Tim Hoh, *Prin*
Roger Kramer, *
▲ EMP: 90 EST: 1999
SQ FT: 215,000
SALES (est): 50.25MM

Mason - Warren County (G-10594) GEOGRAPHIC SECTION

SALES (corp-wide): 50.25MM **Privately Held**
Web: www.pioneerglazing.com
SIC: **1793** Glass and glazing work

(G-10594)
PRIMARY CR NTWRK PRMR HLTH PRT
7450 S Mason Montgomery Rd (45040-7802)
PHONE.................................513 204-5785
EMP: 41
SALES (corp-wide): 25.36MM **Privately Held**
Web: www.premierhealth.com
SIC: **8099** Childbirth preparation clinic
PA: Primary Care Network Of Premier Health Partners
110 N Main St Ste 350
Dayton OH 45402
937 226-7085

(G-10595)
PRIMARY CR NTWRK PRMR HLTH PRT
4859 Nixon Park Dr Ste A (45040-8106)
PHONE.................................513 492-5940
EMP: 29
SALES (corp-wide): 25.36MM **Privately Held**
Web: www.premierhealth.com
SIC: **8011** General and family practice, physician/surgeon
PA: Primary Care Network Of Premier Health Partners
110 N Main St Ste 350
Dayton OH 45402
937 226-7085

(G-10596)
PROFESSNAL PSYCHATRIC SVCS LLC
6402 Thornberry Ct (45040-7846)
P.O. Box 808 (45040-0808)
PHONE.................................513 229-7585
Mohamed Aziz, *Prin*
EMP: 34 EST: 2007
SALES (est): 1.04MM **Privately Held**
Web: www.ppsych.com
SIC: **8011** Psychiatrist

(G-10597)
PURE CONCEPT SALON INC
Also Called: Pure Concept Ecosalon & Spa
5625 Deerfield Cir (45040-1484)
PHONE.................................513 770-2120
Renee Hydrich, *Brnch Mgr*
EMP: 44
Web: www.pureconceptsalon.com
SIC: **7231** Hairdressers
PA: Pure Concept Salon, Inc.
8740 Montgomery Rd Ste 7
Cincinnati OH 45236

(G-10598)
QUEEN CITY HOSPICE LLC
Also Called: ADDUS
4605 Duke Dr Ste 220 (45040-1553)
PHONE.................................513 510-4406
Tony Izquierdo, *Prin*
EMP: 1093 EST: 2014
SALES (est): 951.46MM **Publicly Held**
Web: www.queencityhospice.com
SIC: **8082** Home health care services
PA: Addus Homecare Corporation
6303 Cowboys Way Ste 600
Frisco TX 75034

(G-10599)
REDKEY EXPRESS LLC
123 E Main St (45040-1917)
PHONE.................................859 393-3221
Brian Gray, *Managing Member*
Mary Johnson, *Prin*
EMP: 30 EST: 2012
SALES (est): 1.04MM **Privately Held**
Web: www.redkeyexpress.com
SIC: **7389** Courier or messenger service

(G-10600)
REMTEC AUTOMATION LLC
6049 Hi Tek Ct (45040-2603)
PHONE.................................877 759-8151
EMP: 30 EST: 1981
SALES (est): 11.28MM
SALES (corp-wide): 12.7MM **Privately Held**
Web: www.remtecautomation.com
SIC: **8742** Automation and robotics consultant
PA: The C M Paula Company
6049 Hi Tek Ct
Mason OH 45040
513 759-7473

(G-10601)
REMTEC ENGINEERING
Also Called: Mbs Acquisition
6049 Hi Tek Ct (45040-2603)
PHONE.................................513 860-4299
Keith Rosnell, *CEO*
EMP: 30 EST: 1981
SQ FT: 25,000
SALES (est): 1.04MM **Privately Held**
Web: www.remtecautomation.com
SIC: **3569** 5084 Assembly machines, non-metalworking; Robots, industrial

(G-10602)
ROYALMONT ACADEMY
200 Northcrest Dr (45040)
PHONE.................................513 754-0555
Chris Willertz, *Prin*
Matt Schlotman, *Prin*
EMP: 34 EST: 1996
SQ FT: 23,362
SALES (est): 1.51MM **Privately Held**
Web: www.royalmontacademy.org
SIC: **8211** 8351 Private elementary and secondary schools; Preschool center

(G-10603)
ROYALTY TRUCKING INC
4836 Tylersville Rd (45040-2500)
P.O. Box 1878 (45071-1878)
PHONE.................................513 771-1860
Handy Royalty, *Pr*
Rodeney Dennison, *
EMP: 138 EST: 1940
SQ FT: 100,000
SALES (est): 23.04MM
SALES (corp-wide): 23.04MM **Privately Held**
Web: www.royaltytruckinginc.com
SIC: **4214** Local trucking with storage
PA: Cincinnati Packaging & Distribution, Inc.
3023 Kemper Rd Bldg 6
Cincinnati OH 45241
513 771-1860

(G-10604)
RXCROSSROADS 3PL LLC
4200 Binion Way Ste 200 (45036-9469)
PHONE.................................866 447-9758
Michele Lau, *Managing Member*
EMP: 150 EST: 2020
SALES (est): 25MM **Privately Held**
SIC: **5122** Pharmaceuticals

(G-10605)
SECURITY NAT AUTO ACCPTNCE LLC
6951 Cintas Blvd (45040-8923)
P.O. Box 76809 (90076-0809)
PHONE.................................513 459-8118
Grant Skeens, *CEO*
Adam Catino, *CFO*
EMP: 162 EST: 1986
SQ FT: 24,000
SALES (est): 21.56MM **Privately Held**
SIC: **6141** 6159 Personal credit institutions; Automobile finance leasing

(G-10606)
SELECT HOTELS GROUP LLC
Also Called: Hyatt Pl Cincinnati-Northeast
5070 Natorp Blvd (45040-8263)
PHONE.................................513 754-0003
Chris Larmour, *Brnch Mgr*
EMP: 51
Web: www.hyatt.com
SIC: **7011** 8741 6519 Hotels and motels; Hotel or motel management; Real property lessors, nec
HQ: Select Hotels Group, L.L.C.
71 South Wacker Dr
Chicago IL 60606
312 750-1234

(G-10607)
SHIVER SECURITY SYSTEMS LLC
Also Called: Sonitrol of South West Ohio
6404 Thornberry Ct Ste 410 (45040-3502)
PHONE.................................513 719-4000
Chip Shizer Senior, *Owner*
EMP: 40
SALES (corp-wide): 532.87MM **Privately Held**
Web: www.shiversecurity.com
SIC: **7382** Burglar alarm maintenance and monitoring
HQ: Shiver Security Systems, Llc
15 Pinnacle Point Dr
Miamisburg OH
937 228-7301

(G-10608)
SIEMENS GOVERNMENT TECH INC
8114 Indian Summer Way (45040-9405)
PHONE.................................513 492-7759
EMP: 84
SALES (corp-wide): 84.48B **Privately Held**
Web: www.siemensgovt.com
SIC: **8999** Artists and artists' studios
HQ: Siemens Government Technologies, Inc.
1881 Cmpus Cmmons Dr Ste
Reston VA 20191
703 480-8901

(G-10609)
STOCKTON MORTGAGE CORPORATION
5155 Financial Way Ste 8 (45040-0055)
PHONE.................................513 486-4140
EMP: 45
SALES (corp-wide): 216.88K **Privately Held**
Web: www.stockton.com
SIC: **6162** Mortgage bankers and loan correspondents
PA: Stockton Mortgage Corporation
1246 Old State Route 74
Batavia OH 45103
513 384-8751

(G-10610)
STRESS ENGINEERING SVCS INC
7030 Stress Engineering Way (45040-7386)
PHONE.................................513 336-6701
Kate Harvey, *Brnch Mgr*
EMP: 60
SALES (corp-wide): 88.19MM **Privately Held**
Web: www.stress.com
SIC: **8711** Consulting engineer
PA: Stress Engineering Services, Inc.
13800 Westfair East Dr
Houston TX 77041
281 955-2900

(G-10611)
SUBURBAN OIL COMPANY
4291 State Route 741 S (45040-1970)
PHONE.................................513 459-8100
EMP: 40 EST: 1966
SALES (est): 17.58MM
SALES (corp-wide): 712.86MM **Privately Held**
Web: www.suburbanoil.com
SIC: **5172** 5983 Lubricating oils and greases; Fuel oil dealers
HQ: Tri County Petroleum Inc.
Rr 103
Riddlesburg PA 16672
814 928-1034

(G-10612)
SUGAR & SPICE SPA LLC
4635 Court Yard Dr (45040-2926)
PHONE.................................513 319-0112
Theresa Baker Gordon, *Prin*
Theresa Baker Gordon, *CEO*
Debra Wright, *
Donald Gordon, *
EMP: 55 EST: 2015
SQ FT: 4,000
SALES (est): 319.22K **Privately Held**
SIC: **7996** 7231 7929 7299 Amusement parks; Cosmetology and personal hygiene salons; Entertainment service; Facility rental and party planning services

(G-10613)
SUMMIT FUNDING GROUP INC (HQ)
4680 Parkway Dr Ste 300 (45040-7979)
PHONE.................................513 489-1222
Richard Ross, *Pr*
Carlton Zwilling, *
Louis Beck, *Stockholder**
Harry Yeaggy, *Stockholder**
EMP: 50 EST: 1993
SQ FT: 19,395
SALES (est): 25.97MM
SALES (corp-wide): 1.12B **Publicly Held**
Web: www.summit-funding.com
SIC: **6159** Equipment and vehicle finance leasing companies
PA: First Financial Bancorp.
255 E 5th St Ste 800
Cincinnati OH 45202
877 322-9530

(G-10614)
TELEDYNE INSTRUMENTS INC
Also Called: Teledyne Tekmar
4736 Socialville Foster Rd (45040-8265)
PHONE.................................513 229-7000
EMP: 28
SALES (corp-wide): 5.64B **Publicly Held**
Web: www.teledynelabs.com
SIC: **5049** 3826 3829 3821 Laboratory equipment, except medical or dental; Analytical instruments; Measuring and controlling devices, nec; Laboratory apparatus and furniture

GEOGRAPHIC SECTION

Massillon - Stark County (G-10637)

HQ: Teledyne Instruments, Inc.
16830 Chestnut St
City Of Industry CA 91748
626 934-1500

(G-10615)
TENSURE CONSULTING LLC
5325 Deerfield Blvd Ste 144 (45040)
PHONE..................513 428-4493
Justin Billig, *CEO*
EMP: 88 **EST:** 2019
SALES (est): 10.33MM **Privately Held**
Web: www.tensure.io
SIC: 7371 Computer software development

(G-10616)
TO SCALE SOFTWARE LLC
Also Called: Stack Constructyion Technology
6398 Thornberry Ct (45040-7816)
PHONE..................513 253-0053
Phillip Ogilby, *Managing Member*
Jane Baysore, *
EMP: 35 **EST:** 2007
SALES (est): 4.1MM **Privately Held**
Web: www.cloudtakeoff.com
SIC: 7372 Prepackaged software

(G-10617)
TOUCHSTONE MDSE GROUP LLC (PA)
7200 Industrial Row Dr (45040-1386)
PHONE..................513 741-0400
Derek Block, *Pr*
Bill Bok, *Pr*
Chris Berger, *Sr VP*
Andrew Backen, *Sr VP*
▲ **EMP:** 64 **EST:** 2003
SQ FT: 12,000
SALES (est): 39.08MM
SALES (corp-wide): 39.08MM **Privately Held**
Web: www.tmgideas.com
SIC: 5199 Advertising specialties

(G-10618)
TRAYAK INC
7577 Central Parke Blvd Ste 317 (45040)
P.O. Box 577 (45040-0577)
PHONE..................513 252-8089
Prashant Jagtap, *Pr*
EMP: 50 **EST:** 2010
SALES (est): 2.29MM **Privately Held**
Web: www.trayak.com
SIC: 7371 Computer software development and applications

(G-10619)
TRIHEALTH G LLC
Also Called: Health First Physicians - Masn
7423 S Mason Montgomery Rd (45040-7828)
PHONE..................513 398-3445
EMP: 27
Web: www.trihealth.com
SIC: 8011 General and family practice, physician/surgeon
HQ: Trihealth G, Llc
4600 Wesley Ave Ste N
Cincinnati OH 45212
513 732-0700

(G-10620)
TRIHEALTH HF LLC
7423 S Mason Montgomery Rd Ste B (45040-7828)
PHONE..................513 398-3445
Brian Hoffman, *Managing Member*
EMP: 27 **EST:** 2012
SALES (est): 966.9K **Privately Held**
Web: www.trihealth.com

SIC: 8099 Health and allied services, nec

(G-10621)
TRIPLEFIN LLC (HQ)
8990 Duke Blvd (45040-8943)
PHONE..................855 877-5346
Rick Randall, *
Michael Eckstein, *
Joseph Conda, *
▲ **EMP:** 100 **EST:** 1983
SALES (est): 49.07MM
SALES (corp-wide): 240.09MM **Privately Held**
SIC: 5122 Pharmaceuticals
PA: Eversana Life Science Services, Llc
7045 College Blvd Ste 300
Overland Park KS 66211
866 336-1336

(G-10622)
UC HEALTH LLC
Also Called: Uc Health Primary Care Mason
9313 S Mason Montgomery Rd Ste 200 (45040-8009)
PHONE..................513 584-6999
EMP: 51
Web: www.uchealth.com
SIC: 8011 Internal medicine, physician/surgeon
PA: Uc Health, Llc.
3200 Burnet Ave
Cincinnati OH 45229

(G-10623)
VERNOVIS LTD
4770 Duke Dr Ste 180 (45040-9376)
PHONE..................513 234-7201
EMP: 54 **EST:** 2015
SALES (est): 8.47MM **Privately Held**
Web: www.vernovis.com
SIC: 7363 Help supply services

(G-10624)
VET PATH SERVICES INC
Also Called: Vps
6450 Castle Dr (45040-9412)
PHONE..................513 469-0777
Christopher Johnson, *Pr*
Philip Long, *
EMP: 35 **EST:** 2005
SQ FT: 13,000
SALES (est): 3.02MM **Privately Held**
Web: www.vetpathservicesinc.com
SIC: 8071 Pathological laboratory

(G-10625)
VNDLY LLC
4900 Parkway Dr Ste 125 (45040-8430)
PHONE..................513 572-2500
Shashank Saxena, *CEO*
EMP: 50 **EST:** 2017
SQ FT: 5,483
SALES (est): 11.56MM **Publicly Held**
Web: www.workday.com
SIC: 7372 7374 Application computer software; Data processing service
PA: Workday, Inc.
6110 Stoneridge Mall Rd
Pleasanton CA 94588

Massillon
Stark County

(G-10626)
3-D SERVICE LTD (PA)
Also Called: Magnetech
800 Nave Rd Se (44646-9476)
PHONE..................330 830-3500
Bernie Dewees, *Pr*

▲ **EMP:** 120 **EST:** 2002
SQ FT: 85,000
SALES (est): 4.3MM
SALES (corp-wide): 4.3MM **Privately Held**
Web: www.magnetech.com
SIC: 7694 7699 Electric motor repair; Industrial equipment services

(G-10627)
A A HAMMERSMITH INSURANCE INC (PA)
210 Erie St N (44646-8400)
P.O. Box 591 (44648-0591)
PHONE..................330 832-7411
Robert Mcafee, *Pr*
Richard Snyder, *
Phillip Fox, *
Frank Sauser, *
Herold Weatherbee, *
EMP: 27 **EST:** 1874
SQ FT: 6,000
SALES (est): 4.88MM
SALES (corp-wide): 4.88MM **Privately Held**
Web: www.aahammersmith.com
SIC: 6411 Insurance agents, nec

(G-10628)
A P & P DEV & CNSTR CO (PA)
2851 Lincoln Way E (44646)
PHONE..................330 833-8886
Nichkolas Maragas, *Pr*
EMP: 35 **EST:** 1967
SQ FT: 2,000
SALES (est): 10.97MM
SALES (corp-wide): 10.97MM **Privately Held**
SIC: 1542 6513 Commercial and office building, new construction; Apartment building operators

(G-10629)
ADVANCED INDUSTRIAL ROOFG INC
1330 Erie St S (44646-7906)
PHONE..................330 837-1999
Fred Horner, *Pr*
Jeff Rupert, *
EMP: 75 **EST:** 1988
SQ FT: 12,140
SALES (est): 13.01MM **Privately Held**
Web: www.airoofing.com
SIC: 1761 Roofing contractor

(G-10630)
ALTERNATIVE RESIDENCES TWO INC
1865 Tremont Ave Se (44646-6940)
PHONE..................330 833-5564
Gerri Addessi, *Prin*
EMP: 71
SALES (corp-wide): 2.27MM **Privately Held**
SIC: 8361 Mentally handicapped home
PA: Alternative Residences Two, Inc.
100 W Main St Lowr
Saint Clairsville OH 43950
740 526-0514

(G-10631)
ARE INC
400 Nave Rd Sw (44646)
P.O. Box 1100 (44648-1100)
PHONE..................330 830-7800
EMP: 518
SIC: 3713 3714 3792 5013 Truck bodies and parts; Motor vehicle body components and frame; Travel trailers and campers; Motor vehicle supplies and new parts

(G-10632)
BILL HAWK INC
2200 Venture Cir Se (44646-8632)
PHONE..................330 833-5558
EMP: 70
SIC: 1623 Pipe laying construction

(G-10633)
C-N-D INDUSTRIES INC
Also Called: Cnd Machine
359 State Ave Nw (44647-4269)
PHONE..................330 478-8811
Clyde Shetler, *Pr*
Don Rossbach, *
EMP: 40 **EST:** 1989
SQ FT: 28,000
SALES (est): 2.36MM **Privately Held**
SIC: 3441 3599 7692 3444 Fabricated structural metal; Machine shop, jobbing and repair; Welding repair; Sheet metalwork

(G-10634)
CANTON ERECTORS INC
Also Called: C E I
1369 Sanders Ave Sw (44647-7632)
PHONE..................330 453-7363
Brian Selinsky, *Pr*
Bryan Grove, *
Susan Smith, *
▲ **EMP:** 30 **EST:** 1964
SALES (est): 6.17MM **Privately Held**
Web: www.ceicrane.com
SIC: 1796 7353 Machine moving and rigging ; Cranes and aerial lift equipment, rental or leasing

(G-10635)
CHRISTIAN RIVERTREE SCHOOL
Also Called: Rivertreechristian
7373 Portage St Nw (44646-9315)
PHONE..................330 494-1860
Pamela Clevenger, *Dir*
EMP: 53 **EST:** 1980
SALES (est): 1.27MM **Privately Held**
Web: www.rivertreejackson.com
SIC: 8351 Preschool center

(G-10636)
CONSULATE MANAGEMENT CO LLC
Also Called: Legends Care Center
2311 Nave Rd Sw (44646)
PHONE..................330 837-1001
Tara Price, *Mgr*
EMP: 405
SALES (corp-wide): 491MM **Privately Held**
Web: www.consulatehc.com
SIC: 8051 Skilled nursing care facilities
HQ: Consulate Management Company, Llc
800 Concourse Pkwy S # 200
Maitland FL 32751
407 571-1550

(G-10637)
DEERFIELD AG SERVICES INC
Also Called: Deerfield AG Services, Inc.
411 Oberlin Ave Sw (44647-7826)
PHONE..................330 584-4715
EMP: 35
SALES (corp-wide): 53.24MM **Privately Held**
Web: www.deerfieldagservices.com
SIC: 5153 5191 4221 5083 Grain elevators; Fertilizer and fertilizer materials; Grain elevator, storage only; Agricultural machinery and equipment
PA: Deerfield Ag Services Inc
9041 State Route 224
Deerfield OH 44411
330 507-7811

Massillon - Stark County (G-10638)

(G-10638)
EMSCO INC (HQ)
Also Called: Electric Melting Services Co
1000 Nave Rd Se (44646-9478)
P.O. Box 607 (44648-0607)
PHONE.................................330 830-7125
James J Dyer, *Pr*
▲ **EMP:** 31 **EST:** 1983
SQ FT: 55,000
SALES (est): 15.01MM
SALES (corp-wide): 645.5MM **Privately Held**
Web: www.emsco.com
SIC: 7699 Industrial machinery and equipment repair
PA: Inductotherm Group, Llc
 10 Indel Ave
 Rancocas NJ 08073
 609 267-9000

(G-10639)
FAMILY PRACTICE ASSOCIATES
2300 Wales Ave Nw Ste 100 (44646-2323)
PHONE.................................330 832-3188
M Terrance Simon, *VP*
Doctor Wayne Lutzke, *Prin*
Eugene Pogorelec, *Prin*
EMP: 28 **EST:** 1979
SQ FT: 20,000
SALES (est): 1.43MM **Privately Held**
Web: www.pioneerphysicians.com
SIC: 8011 General and family practice, physician/surgeon

(G-10640)
FRESH MARK INC
950 Cloverleaf St Se (44646-9647)
PHONE.................................330 833-9870
Mike Portilla, *Brnch Mgr*
EMP: 264
SALES (corp-wide): 1.38B **Privately Held**
Web: www.freshmark.com
SIC: 4222 Warehousing, cold storage or refrigerated
PA: Fresh Mark, Inc.
 1888 Southway St Sw
 Massillon OH 44646
 330 832-7491

(G-10641)
FRESH MARK INC (PA)
Also Called: Superior's Brand Meats
1888 Southway St Sw (44646-9429)
PHONE.................................330 832-7491
Neil Genshaft, *Ch*
Tim Cranor, *
Tom Cicarella, *
David Cochenour, *
◆ **EMP:** 500 **EST:** 1932
SQ FT: 80,000
SALES (est): 1.38B
SALES (corp-wide): 1.38B **Privately Held**
Web: www.freshmark.com
SIC: 2013 5147 2011 Prepared beef products, from purchased beef; Meats and meat products; Meat packing plants

(G-10642)
HANOVER HOUSE INC
435 Avis Ave Nw (44646-3599)
PHONE.................................330 837-1741
EMP: 40 **EST:** 1972
SALES (est): 4.78MM **Privately Held**
SIC: 8051 Convalescent home with continuous nursing care

(G-10643)
HEALTH PLAN OF OHIO INC
Also Called: Massillon Cmnty Hosp Hlth Plan
100 Lillian Gish Blvd Sw Ste 301
(44647-6588)
PHONE.................................330 837-6880
William Epling, *Pr*
EMP: 160 **EST:** 1985
SALES (est): 23.53MM
SALES (corp-wide): 192.59MM **Privately Held**
Web: www.healthplan.org
SIC: 6324 Health Maintenance Organization (HMO), insurance only
PA: Health Plan Of West Va Inc
 1110 Main St
 Wheeling WV 26003
 740 695-3585

(G-10644)
HEALTH SERVICES INC
Also Called: Complete Home Care
2520 Wales Ave Nw Ste 120 (44646-2398)
PHONE.................................330 837-7678
James Budiscak, *Pr*
Mervin Strine, *
Richard Leffler, *
EMP: 41 **EST:** 1983
SQ FT: 5,500
SALES (est): 156.53K
SALES (corp-wide): 11MM **Privately Held**
Web: www.completehcohio.com
SIC: 8049 5999 Physical therapist; Hospital equipment and supplies
PA: The Health Group
 5425 High Mill Ave Nw
 Massillon OH 44646
 330 833-3174

(G-10645)
HEARTLAND BHAVIORAL HEALTHCARE
3000 Erie St S (44646-7976)
PHONE.................................330 833-3135
Helen Stevens, *CEO*
EMP: 77 **EST:** 1895
SALES (est): 8.28MM **Privately Held**
Web: www.heartlandbehavioral.com
SIC: 8063 Psychiatric hospitals

(G-10646)
HUNTINGTON NATIONAL BANK
Also Called: Noble's Pond Branch
5338 Wales Ave Nw (44646-9381)
PHONE.................................330 830-1200
Debbie Secrest, *Brnch Mgr*
EMP: 36
SALES (corp-wide): 10.84B **Publicly Held**
Web: www.huntington.com
SIC: 6029 Commercial banks, nec
HQ: The Huntington National Bank
 41 S High St
 Columbus OH 43215
 614 480-4293

(G-10647)
HYDRO-DYNE INC
225 Wetmore Ave Se (44646-6788)
P.O. Box 318 (44648-0318)
PHONE.................................330 832-5076
Rose Ann Dare, *Pr*
Lynn Neel, *
Sherri Mcmillen, *Mgr*
Ken Yeaman, *
Jean Holiday, *
▲ **EMP:** 50 **EST:** 1967
SQ FT: 130,000
SALES (est): 1.46MM **Privately Held**
Web: www.hydrodyneinc.com
SIC: 3585 8711 Evaporative condensers, heat transfer equipment; Engineering services

(G-10648)
IDENTITEK SYSTEMS INC
Also Called: Adams Signs
1100 Industrial Ave Sw (44647-7608)
P.O. Box 347 (44648-0347)
PHONE.................................330 832-9844
Joseph Pugliese, *Pr*
EMP: 53 **EST:** 1943
SQ FT: 70,000
SALES (est): 9.74MM **Privately Held**
Web: www.adamsigns.com
SIC: 1799 3993 Sign installation and maintenance; Signs and advertising specialties

(G-10649)
KENMORE CONSTRUCTION CO INC
Also Called: American Sand & Gravel Div
9500 Forty Corners Rd Nw (44647-9309)
PHONE.................................330 832-8888
Chris Scala, *Mgr*
EMP: 75
SALES (corp-wide): 44.06MM **Privately Held**
Web: www.kenmorecompanies.com
SIC: 1611 1442 General contractor, highway and street construction; Construction sand and gravel
PA: Kenmore Construction Co., Inc.
 700 Home Ave
 Akron OH 44310
 330 762-8936

(G-10650)
LOWES HOME CENTERS LLC
Also Called: Lowe's
101 Massillon Marketplace Dr Sw
(44646-2015)
PHONE.................................330 832-1901
Ron Vyof, *Brnch Mgr*
EMP: 186
SALES (corp-wide): 86.38B **Publicly Held**
Web: www.lowes.com
SIC: 5211 5031 5722 5064 Home centers; Building materials, exterior; Household appliance stores; Electrical appliances, television and radio
HQ: Lowe's Home Centers, Llc
 1000 Lowes Blvd
 Mooresville NC 28117
 336 658-4000

(G-10651)
MAGNETECH INDUSTRIAL SVCS INC (DH)
Also Called: Magnetech Industrial Services
800 Nave Rd Se (44646-9476)
PHONE.................................330 830-3500
Michael P Moore, *Pr*
William Wisniewveski, *
James I Depew, *
▲ **EMP:** 80 **EST:** 2000
SALES (est): 74MM **Publicly Held**
Web: www.magnetech.com
SIC: 7694 Electric motor repair
HQ: les Subsidiary Holdings, Inc
 5433 Westheimer Rd # 500
 Houston TX 77056
 713 860-1500

(G-10652)
MASSILLON CABLE TV INC (PA)
814 Cable Ct Nw (44647-4284)
P.O. Box 1000 (44648-1000)
PHONE.................................330 833-4134
Richard W Gessner, *Ch*
Robert B Gessner, *
Elizabeth Mcallister, *VP*
Richard Gessner Junior, *VP*
Susan R Gessner, *
EMP: 75 **EST:** 1965
SQ FT: 10,000
SALES (est): 28.82MM
SALES (corp-wide): 28.82MM **Privately Held**
Web: www.mctvohio.com
SIC: 4841 8748 4813 Cable television services; Telecommunications consultant; Internet host services

(G-10653)
MASSILLON SENIOR LIVING LTD
Also Called: Danbury Massillon
2550 University Dr Se (44646-7414)
PHONE.................................330 833-7229
William J Lemmon, *Prin*
EMP: 50 **EST:** 2014
SALES (est): 1.4MM **Privately Held**
Web: www.storypoint.com
SIC: 6513 Retirement hotel operation

(G-10654)
MATRIX SYS AUTO FINISHES LLC
600 Nova Dr Se (44646-8884)
PHONE.................................248 668-8135
W Kent Gardner, *Pr*
Sean Hook, *Director of Information*
EMP: 412 **EST:** 1983
SQ FT: 26,000
SALES (est): 5.94MM
SALES (corp-wide): 60.04MM **Privately Held**
Web: www.matrixsystem.com
SIC: 5198 2851 Paints; Paints and allied products
PA: Quest Specialty Chemicals, Inc.
 225 Sven Farms Dr Ste 204
 Charleston SC 29492
 800 966-7580

(G-10655)
MCTV INC
814 Cable Ct Nw (44647-4284)
PHONE.................................330 833-4134
Katherine Gessner, *Pr*
EMP: 62 **EST:** 1998
SALES (est): 2.65MM **Privately Held**
Web: www.mctvohio.com
SIC: 4841 Cable television services

(G-10656)
MEADOW WIND HLTH CARE CTR INC
300 23rd St Ne (44646-4996)
PHONE.................................330 833-2026
Robert Buchanan, *Pr*
John Faust, *
EMP: 52 **EST:** 1982
SQ FT: 32,000
SALES (est): 5.24MM **Privately Held**
Web: www.meadowwind.net
SIC: 8051 Convalescent home with continuous nursing care

(G-10657)
MIDWEST HEALTH SERVICES INC (PA)
107 Tommy Henrich Dr Nw (44647-5402)
PHONE.................................330 828-0779
Joseph Knetzer, *Pr*
Kristine Knetzer, *OF HEALTH**
EMP: 125 **EST:** 1998
SALES (est): 10.13MM
SALES (corp-wide): 10.13MM **Privately Held**
Web: www.midwestfamilyofcompanies.com
SIC: 8361 Halfway group home, persons with social or personal problems

GEOGRAPHIC SECTION — Masury - Trumbull County (G-10678)

(G-10658)
MISCOR GROUP LTD
800 Nave Rd Se (44646-9476)
PHONE..................................330 830-3500
▲ EMP: 269
SIC: 7629 7539 3519 Electrical equipment repair services; Electrical services; Diesel, semi-diesel, or duel-fuel engines, including marine

(G-10659)
MOCHO LTD
Also Called: Kozmos Grille
37 1st St Sw (44647-6641)
PHONE..................................330 832-8807
Chuck Thompson, *Prin*
EMP: 30 EST: 2007
SALES (est): 629.8K Privately Held
Web: www.kozmosgrille.com
SIC: 5812 7299 Pizza restaurants; Banquet hall facilities

(G-10660)
OHIO PACKAGING
777 3rd St Nw (44647-4203)
P.O. Box 850 (44648-0850)
PHONE..................................330 833-2884
Dale Kiaski Managing, *Prin*
Dale Kiaski, *Managing Member*
Rick Hazen, *
▲ EMP: 95 EST: 1964
SQ FT: 1,800
SALES (est): 28.84MM
SALES (corp-wide): 5.22B Publicly Held
Web: www.greif.com
SIC: 5199 Packaging materials
HQ: Greif Packaging Llc
    5800 Cane Run Rd
    Louisville KY 40258

(G-10661)
PEOPLES CARTAGE INC
8045 Navarre Rd Sw (44648)
PHONE..................................330 833-8571
Joseph Chevreau, *Prin*
EMP: 49
Web: www.peoplesservices.com
SIC: 4225 General warehousing
HQ: People's Cartage, Inc.
    2207 Kimball Rd Se
    Canton OH 44707
    330 453-3709

(G-10662)
REPUBLIC SERVICES INC
Also Called: Republic Services
2800 Erie St S (44646-7915)
PHONE..................................330 830-9050
Pete Gutwin, *Brnch Mgr*
EMP: 27
SQ FT: 11,000
SALES (corp-wide): 14.96B Publicly Held
Web: www.republicservices.com
SIC: 4953 Refuse collection and disposal services
PA: Republic Services, Inc.
    18500 N Allied Way
    Phoenix AZ 85054
    480 627-2700

(G-10663)
RJ MATTHEWS COMPANY
2780 Richville Dr Se (44646-8396)
PHONE..................................330 834-3000
Tammy Zimmerman, *Prin*
EMP: 30 EST: 2013
SALES (est): 3.68MM Privately Held
Web: www.rjmatthews.com
SIC: 5191 Feed

(G-10664)
ROBERT J MATTHEWS COMPANY (PA)
Also Called: P B S Animal Health
2780 Richville Dr Se (44646-8396)
PHONE..................................330 834-3000
Della L Matthews, *Ch Bd*
John D Matthews, *
J Stephen Matthews, *
Robert K Matthews, *
Edward Cutcher, *
◆ EMP: 60 EST: 1950
SQ FT: 40,000
SALES (est): 24.8MM
SALES (corp-wide): 24.8MM Privately Held
Web: www.rjmatthews.com
SIC: 5122 Pharmaceuticals

(G-10665)
ROSE LN HLTH RHABILITATION INC
Also Called: Rose Lane Health Center
5425 High Mill Ave Nw (44646-9005)
PHONE..................................330 833-3174
Dennis Potts, *Pr*
Karren Talbot, *
EMP: 196 EST: 2010
SQ FT: 34,000
SALES (est): 14.66MM
SALES (corp-wide): 11MM Privately Held
Web: www.sprengerhealthcare.com
SIC: 8051 Extended care facility
PA: The Health Group
    5425 High Mill Ave Nw
    Massillon OH 44646
    330 833-3174

(G-10666)
ROUND ROOM LLC
3 Massillon Marketplace Dr Sw (44646-2014)
PHONE..................................330 880-0660
EMP: 29
Web: www.tccrocks.com
SIC: 4813 Local and long distance telephone communications
PA: Round Room, Llc
    525 Congressional Blvd
    Carmel IN 46032

(G-10667)
SEIFERT TECHNOLOGIES INC (PA)
2323 Nave Rd Se (44646-8822)
PHONE..................................330 833-2700
Timothy Seifert, *Pr*
Matthew D Ashton, *VP*
Richard T Kettler, *VP*
EMP: 65 EST: 1985
SQ FT: 8,900
SALES (est): 10.58MM
SALES (corp-wide): 10.58MM Privately Held
Web: www.seifert.com
SIC: 7389 Drafting service, except temporary help

(G-10668)
SHADY HOLLOW CNTRY CLB CO INC
4865 Wales Ave Nw (44646-9396)
PHONE..................................330 832-1581
Keith Baklarc, *Mgr*
EMP: 93 EST: 1964
SALES (est): 4.49MM Privately Held
Web: www.shadyhollowcc.com
SIC: 7997 7992 7991 5941 Country club, membership; Public golf courses; Physical fitness facilities; Sporting goods and bicycle shops

(G-10669)
SHEARERS FOODS LLC (HQ)
Also Called: Shearer's Snacks
100 Lincoln Way E (44646)
PHONE..................................800 428-6843
Mark Mcneil, *CEO*
Montgomery Pooley, *
Fritz Kohmann, *
Alan Fritts, *Corporate Controller*
C J Fraleigh, *
◆ EMP: 700 EST: 1980
SQ FT: 200,000
SALES (est): 712.7MM
SALES (corp-wide): 14.52B Privately Held
Web: www.shearers.com
SIC: 2096 5145 Potato chips and similar snacks; Snack foods
PA: Clayton, Dubilier & Rice, Inc.
    375 Park Ave Fl 18
    New York NY 10152
    212 407-5200

(G-10670)
SHEARERS FOODS PHOENIX LLC
100 Lincoln Way E (44646-6634)
PHONE..................................330 834-4330
William Nictakis, *Pr*
EMP: 35
SALES (corp-wide): 14.52B Privately Held
SIC: 5145 Snack foods
HQ: Shearer's Foods Phoenix, Llc
    616 S 55th Ave Ste 102
    Phoenix AZ 85043
    330 834-4330

(G-10671)
SMITHERS GROUP INC
1845 Harsh Ave Se (44646-7123)
PHONE..................................330 833-8548
Michael J Hochschwender, *CEO*
EMP: 60
SALES (corp-wide): 115.78MM Privately Held
Web: www.smithers.com
SIC: 3829 8734 8071 Testing equipment: abrasion, shearing strength, etc.; Product testing laboratory, safety or performance; Medical laboratories
PA: The Smithers Group Inc
    121 S Main St Ste 300
    Akron OH 44308
    330 762-7441

(G-10672)
WESTON AND ASSOCIATES LLC
295 Wetmore Ave Se (44646-6788)
PHONE..................................330 791-7118
Andrew Feucht, *Pr*
Andrew Feucht, *Managing Member*
EMP: 125 EST: 2017
SALES (est): 10.92MM Privately Held
Web: www.westonandassociates.com
SIC: 8741 Management services

(G-10673)
WHISLER PLUMBING & HEATING INC
Also Called: Plumbing & Heating
2521 Lincoln Way E (44646-5099)
PHONE..................................330 833-2875
W Stuart Kraft, *Pr*
Sharon Kannel, *
Jack Sponseller, *
Tammy Duplain, *
EMP: 62 EST: 1930
SQ FT: 2,500
SALES (est): 10.29MM Privately Held
Web: www.whislerph.com
SIC: 1711 Plumbing contractors

(G-10674)
YMCA OF MASSILLON (PA)
Also Called: YMCA OF WESTERN STARK COUNTY
131 Tremont Ave Se (44646-6637)
PHONE..................................330 837-5116
Jim Stamford, *Dir*
EMP: 87 EST: 1920
SQ FT: 16,342
SALES (est): 3.13MM
SALES (corp-wide): 3.13MM Privately Held
Web: www.weststarky.org
SIC: 8641 Youth organizations

(G-10675)
YOUNG MNS CHRSTN ASSN CNTL STA
Also Called: Jackson Community YMCA
7389 Caritas Cir Nw (44646-9118)
PHONE..................................330 830-6275
Jean Campbell, *Brnch Mgr*
EMP: 192
SALES (corp-wide): 20.07MM Privately Held
Web: www.ymcastark.org
SIC: 8641 7991 8351 7032 Youth organizations; Physical fitness facilities; Child day care services; Youth camps
PA: Young Mens Christian Association Of Central Stark County, Inc.
    4700 Dressler Rd Nw
    Canton OH 44718
    330 491-9622

(G-10676)
ZIEGLER TIRE AND SUPPLY CO (PA)
Also Called: Ziegler Tire
4150 Millennium Blvd Se (44646-7449)
PHONE..................................330 834-3332
Nate Clements, *Pr*
John Ziegler Junior, *VP*
William Ziegler, *
EMP: 35 EST: 1919
SQ FT: 112,000
SALES (est): 111.76MM
SALES (corp-wide): 111.76MM Privately Held
Web: www.zieglertire.com
SIC: 5531 5014 Automotive tires; Truck tires and tubes

Masury
Trumbull County

(G-10677)
ADDISON LEASING CO LLC
Also Called: Addison Healthcare Center
8055 Addison Rd (44438-1204)
PHONE..................................513 530-1600
Richard Odenthal, *Prin*
Sandra Smiddy, *
EMP: 50 EST: 2018
SALES (est): 6.54MM Privately Held
Web: www.communicarehealth.com
SIC: 8051 Convalescent home with continuous nursing care

(G-10678)
GONDA LAWN CARE LLC
7822 2nd St (44438-1435)
PHONE..................................330 701-7232
Steven Gonda, *CEO*
EMP: 50 EST: 2016
SALES (est): 766.57K Privately Held
SIC: 0782 Lawn care services

(G-10679)
P I & I MOTOR EXPRESS INC (PA)
908 Broadway St (44438-1356)
P.O. Box 685 (16146-0685)
PHONE..................................330 448-4035
Joseph Kerola, *Pr*
William Kerola, *
EMP: 128 **EST:** 1951
SQ FT: 76,000
SALES (est): 44.18MM
SALES (corp-wide): 44.18MM **Privately Held**
Web: www.piimx.com
SIC: 8741 4213 4212 Management services; Trucking, except local; Local trucking, without storage

(G-10680)
PENN-OHIO ELECTRICAL COMPANY
Also Called: Penn Ohio Electrical Contrs
1370 Sharon Hogue Rd (44438-8710)
PHONE..................................330 448-1234
Chris O'brien, *Pr*
John P O'brien, *VP*
Kirt J O'brien, *Sec*
Daniel O'brien, *Treas*
EMP: 30 **EST:** 1968
SQ FT: 5,000
SALES (est): 8.81MM **Privately Held**
Web: www.pennohioelectric.com
SIC: 1731 General electrical contractor

(G-10681)
TFORCE FREIGHT INC
7945 3rd St (44438-1336)
PHONE..................................330 448-0440
Ike Henry, *Mgr*
EMP: 35
SALES (corp-wide): 8.81B **Privately Held**
Web: www.tforcefreight.com
SIC: 4213 Contract haulers
HQ: Tforce Freight, Inc.
1000 Semmes Ave
Richmond VA 23224
800 333-7400

Maumee
Lucas County

(G-10682)
1 NATURAL WAY LLC
4064 Technology Dr Ste B (43537-9739)
PHONE..................................888 977-2229
Ryan Wright, *Managing Member*
EMP: 27 **EST:** 2011
SALES (est): 4.53MM **Privately Held**
Web: www.1naturalway.com
SIC: 5137 Baby goods

(G-10683)
ABOUTGOLF LIMITED (PA)
352 Tomahawk Dr (43537-1612)
PHONE..................................419 482-9095
William Bales, *CEO*
Bill Bales, *Prin*
▲ **EMP:** 38 **EST:** 2002
SQ FT: 20,000
SALES (est): 9.71MM
SALES (corp-wide): 9.71MM **Privately Held**
Web: www.aboutgolf.com
SIC: 7992 Public golf courses

(G-10684)
ACCELERANT TECHNOLOGIES LLC
Also Called: Accelerant Solutions
1715 Indian Wood Cir Ste 200 (43537-4055)
PHONE..................................419 236-8768
Billy Mack, *Pr*
Tyler Ball, *
Michael Cadden, *
EMP: 58 **EST:** 2003
SALES (est): 3.58MM **Privately Held**
Web: www.discoveraccelerant.com
SIC: 8999 8742 8711 Nuclear consultant; Management consulting services; Energy conservation engineering

(G-10685)
ADVANCED CNSTR GROUP INC
Also Called: Advanced Roofing Services
205 W Sophia St (43537-2166)
P.O. Box 1150 (43537-8150)
PHONE..................................419 891-1505
Sam Scamardo, *Pr*
EMP: 30 **EST:** 1992
SQ FT: 8,000
SALES (est): 8.3MM **Privately Held**
Web: www.advancedroofingservices.net
SIC: 1761 Roofing contractor

(G-10686)
AKTION ASSOCIATES INCORPORATED (PA)
1687 Woodlands Dr (43537-4018)
PHONE..................................419 893-7001
EMP: 40 **EST:** 1979
SALES (est): 51.16MM
SALES (corp-wide): 51.16MM **Privately Held**
Web: www.aktion.com
SIC: 5045 7371 Computers, peripherals, and software; Custom computer programming services

(G-10687)
ALSIDE INC
3510 Briarfield Blvd (43537-9504)
PHONE..................................419 865-0934
Todd Anderson, *Brnch Mgr*
EMP: 55
SALES (corp-wide): 1.18B **Privately Held**
Web: www.alside.com
SIC: 5211 5033 3089 1751 Windows, storm: wood or metal; Siding, except wood; Siding, plastics; Window and door (prefabricated) installation
HQ: Alside, Inc.
3773 State Rd
Cuyahoga Falls OH 44223
330 929-1811

(G-10688)
ALTA360 RESEARCH INC
Also Called: Ritter & Associates, Inc.
1690 Woodlands Dr Ste 103 (43537-4165)
PHONE..................................419 535-5757
EMP: 50 **EST:** 1990
SQ FT: 5,000
SALES (est): 5.67MM
SALES (corp-wide): 17.48MM **Privately Held**
Web: www.alta360research.com
SIC: 8732 Market analysis or research
HQ: Brand Equity Builders, Inc.
31 Bailey Ave Ste 1
Ridgefield CT 06877

(G-10689)
AMERICAN BROADBAND TELECOM CO
1480 Ford St (43537-1731)
PHONE..................................419 824-5800
Jeff Ansted, *Pr*
EMP: 36 **EST:** 2003
SALES (est): 5.56MM **Privately Held**
Web: www.ambt.net
SIC: 8748 Telecommunications consultant

(G-10690)
AMERICAN FRAME CORPORATION (PA)
400 Tomahawk Dr (43537)
PHONE..................................419 893-5595
Laura Jajko, *Pr*
Ronald J Mickel, *
Dana Dunbar, *
Larry Haddad, *
Michael Cromly, *
▲ **EMP:** 63 **EST:** 1967
SQ FT: 33,000
SALES (est): 10.36MM
SALES (corp-wide): 10.36MM **Privately Held**
Web: www.americanframe.com
SIC: 5961 5023 3444 7699 Mail order house, nec; Homefurnishings; Sheet metalwork; Picture framing, custom

(G-10691)
ANATRACE PRODUCTS LLC (HQ)
Also Called: Calibre Scientific
434 W Dussel Dr (43537-1624)
PHONE..................................800 252-1280
Ben Travis, *CEO*
Mike Drury, *
Connie Cupilary, *
James Schmalz, *
EMP: 30 **EST:** 2013
SALES (est): 17.03MM **Privately Held**
Web: www.anatrace.com
SIC: 5169 Detergents and soaps, except specialty cleaning
PA: Stonecalibre, Llc
2049 Century Park E # 2550
Los Angeles CA 90067

(G-10692)
ANDERSONS INC (PA)
Also Called: Andersons, The
1947 Briarfield Blvd (43537-1690)
P.O. Box 119 (43537-0119)
PHONE..................................419 893-5050
Michael J Anderson Senior, *Ch Bd*
Patrick E Bowe, *Pr*
William E Krueger, *COO*
Brian A Valentine, *Ex VP*
Christine M Castellano, *Corporate Secretary*
EMP: 150 **EST:** 1947
SALES (est): 14.75B
SALES (corp-wide): 14.75B **Publicly Held**
Web: www.andersonsinc.com
SIC: 0723 5191 2874 4789 Crop preparation services for market; Farm supplies; Phosphatic fertilizers; Railroad car repair

(G-10693)
ANDERSONS INC
Also Called: Retail Distribution Center
1380 Ford St (43537-1733)
P.O. Box 119 (43537-0119)
PHONE..................................419 891-6479
Mike Anderson, *Mgr*
EMP: 28
SALES (corp-wide): 14.75B **Publicly Held**
Web: www.andersonsinc.com
SIC: 4225 General warehousing
PA: The Andersons Inc
1947 Briarfield Blvd
Maumee OH 43537
419 893-5050

(G-10694)
ANDERSONS AGRICULTURE GROUP LP (HQ)
Also Called: Anderson's Farm
1947 Briarfield Blvd (43537-1690)
P.O. Box 119 (43537-0119)
PHONE..................................419 893-5050
Hal Reed, *Pt*
◆ **EMP:** 45 **EST:** 2000
SALES (est): 47.7MM
SALES (corp-wide): 14.75B **Publicly Held**
Web: www.andersonsinc.com
SIC: 5153 Grains
PA: The Andersons Inc
1947 Briarfield Blvd
Maumee OH 43537
419 893-5050

(G-10695)
ARROWHEAD BEHAVIORAL HLTH LLC
1725 Timber Line Rd (43537-4015)
PHONE..................................419 891-9333
Theresa Contreras, *CEO*
Cathy Longacre, *
EMP: 120 **EST:** 2019
SALES (est): 8.84MM **Privately Held**
Web: www.arrowheadbehavioral.com
SIC: 8063 Psychiatric hospitals

(G-10696)
AUTO-OWNERS LIFE INSURANCE CO
1645 Indian Wood Cir Ste 202 (43537-4400)
PHONE..................................419 887-1218
EMP: 28
SALES (corp-wide): 2.41B **Privately Held**
Web: www.auto-owners.com
SIC: 6411 Insurance agents, nec
HQ: Auto-Owners Life Insurance Company
6101 Anacapri Blvd
Lansing MI 48917

(G-10697)
AUXILIARY ST LUKES HOSPITAL
Also Called: St Lukes Gift Shop
5901 Monclova Rd (43537-1841)
PHONE..................................419 893-5911
Irene Wolff, *Mgr*
EMP: 61 **EST:** 1972
SQ FT: 500
SALES (est): 2.8MM **Privately Held**
SIC: 5947 8699 Gift shop; Charitable organization

(G-10698)
BARNES GROUP INC
370 W Dussel Dr Ste A (43537)
PHONE..................................419 891-9292
Tracy Allison, *Contrlr*
EMP: 172
SALES (corp-wide): 1.26B **Publicly Held**
Web: www.onebarnes.com
SIC: 5072 3495 Hardware; Wire springs
PA: Barnes Group Inc.
123 Main St
Bristol CT 06010
860 583-7070

(G-10699)
BENNETT ENTERPRISES INC
Also Called: Hampton Inn
1409 Reynolds Rd (43537-1625)
PHONE..................................419 893-1004
Ken Brandt, *Mgr*
EMP: 165
SQ FT: 3,613
SALES (corp-wide): 29.45MM **Privately Held**
Web: www.hilton.com
SIC: 7011 Hotels and motels
PA: Bennett Enterprises, Inc.
27476 Holiday Ln
Perrysburg OH 43551
419 874-1933

GEOGRAPHIC SECTION

Maumee - Lucas County (G-10722)

(G-10700)
BIG VILLAGE INSIGHTS INC
1900 Indian Wood Cir Ste 200 (43537-4033)
PHONE..................419 893-0029
Debi Jankowski, *Brnch Mgr*
EMP: 92
SALES (corp-wide): 44.55MM **Publicly Held**
Web: www.big-village.com
SIC: 8732 Survey service: marketing, location, etc.
HQ: Big Village Insights, Inc.
  301 Carnegie Ctr Ste 301 # 301
  Princeton NJ 08540

(G-10701)
BIONIX LLC
1670 Indian Wood Cir (43537-4004)
PHONE..................419 727-8421
EMP: 76 **EST**: 2020
SALES (est): 6.14MM **Privately Held**
Web: www.bionix.com
SIC: 5047 Medical equipment and supplies

(G-10702)
BIONIX SAFETY TECHNOLOGIES LTD (HQ)
1670 Indian Wood Cir (43537-4004)
PHONE..................419 727-0552
Andrew Milligan, *Pr*
Doctor James Huttner, *VP*
EMP: 41 **EST**: 1988
SALES (est): 10.55MM **Privately Held**
Web: www.bionix.com
SIC: 3825 3826 5084 3829 Test equipment for electronic and electric measurement; Analytical instruments; Industrial machinery and equipment; Measuring and controlling devices, nec
PA: M&H Medical Holdings, Inc.
  1670 Indian Wood Cir
  Maumee OH 43537

(G-10703)
BPREX CLOSURES LLC
Also Called: Research & Development
1695 Indian Circle Ste 116 (43537)
PHONE..................812 424-2904
Michael Wenerd, *Manager*
EMP: 100
Web: www.berryglobal.com
SIC: 5199 Packaging materials
HQ: Bprex Closures, Llc
  101 Oakley St
  Evansville IN 47710
  812 424-2904

(G-10704)
BRIDGEPOINT RISK MGT LLC
Also Called: Nationwide
1440 Arrowhead Dr (43537-4016)
PHONE..................419 794-1075
EMP: 36
SALES (corp-wide): 1.15B **Privately Held**
Web: www.bridgepointrm.com
SIC: 8741 6411 Management services; Insurance agents, brokers, and service
HQ: Bridgepoint Risk Management Llc
  5 Greenwich Office Park # 5
  Greenwich CT 06831
  203 274-8010

(G-10705)
BRONDES ALL MAKES AUTO LEASING
Also Called: BRONDES ALL MAKES AUTO LEASING INC
1511 Reynolds Rd (43537-1601)
PHONE..................419 887-1511
Phillip Brondes Junior, *Pr*
EMP: 61
SALES (corp-wide): 23.61MM **Privately Held**
Web: www.brondesfordtoledo.com
SIC: 7515 Passenger car leasing
PA: Ford Brondes
  5545 Secor Rd
  Toledo OH 43623
  419 473-1411

(G-10706)
BUEHRER GROUP ARCH & ENGRG
314 Conant St (43537-3358)
PHONE..................419 893-9021
Kent Buehrer, *Pr*
Brent Buehrer, *VP*
Hubert Buehrer, *Treas*
EMP: 48 **EST**: 1984
SQ FT: 5,000
SALES (est): 5.19MM **Privately Held**
Web: www.buehrergroup.com
SIC: 8712 8711 Architectural engineering; Engineering services

(G-10707)
CANON SOLUTIONS AMERICA INC
1724 Indian Wood Cir Ste F (43537-4415)
PHONE..................419 897-9244
John Thomas, *Brnch Mgr*
EMP: 30
Web: csa.canon.com
SIC: 5044 Office equipment
HQ: Canon Solutions America, Inc.
  1 Canon Park
  Melville NY 11747
  631 330-5000

(G-10708)
CENTAUR MAIL INC
Also Called: Centaur Associates
4064 Technology Dr Ste A (43537-9739)
PHONE..................419 887-5857
Michael J Walters, *Pr*
Dennise Kamcza, *
EMP: 30 **EST**: 1995
SQ FT: 10,500
SALES (est): 991.1K **Privately Held**
Web: www.centaurassociates.com
SIC: 4215 Parcel delivery, vehicular

(G-10709)
CENTERWELL HEALTH SERVICES INC
1900 Indian Wood Cir Ste 100 (43537-4033)
PHONE..................419 482-6519
Michele Hrovat, *Mgr*
EMP: 51
SALES (corp-wide): 7.62MM **Privately Held**
Web: www.gentivahs.com
SIC: 8082 Home health care services
PA: Centerwell Health Services, Inc.
  3350 Rvrwood Pkwy Se # 140
  Atlanta GA 30339
  770 951-6450

(G-10710)
CHECKER NOTIONS COMPANY INC (PA)
Also Called: Checker Distributors
400 W Dussel Dr Ste B (43537-1653)
PHONE..................419 893-3636
J Robert Krieger Iii, *Pr*
Bradley Krieger, *
▲ **EMP**: 105 **EST**: 1948
SQ FT: 120,000
SALES (est): 57.9MM
SALES (corp-wide): 57.9MM **Privately Held**
Web: www.checkerdist.com
SIC: 5131 5199 5949 5162 Sewing supplies and notions; Art goods and supplies; Quilting materials and supplies; Plastics basic shapes

(G-10711)
CONSULATE HEALTHCARE INC (PA)
Also Called: PARKSIDE MANOR
3231 Manley Rd (43537-9680)
PHONE..................419 865-1248
Jeff Orloski, *Ex Dir*
Lynn Buchlee, *
Patrick C, *
EMP: 50 **EST**: 1971
SALES (est): 7MM
SALES (corp-wide): 7MM **Privately Held**
Web: www.consulatehc.com
SIC: 8051 8052 Skilled nursing care facilities; Intermediate care facilities

(G-10712)
CONSULATE MANAGEMENT CO LLC
Also Called: Swan Point Care Center
3600 Butz Rd (43537-9691)
PHONE..................419 867-7926
EMP: 222
SALES (corp-wide): 491MM **Privately Held**
Web: www.consulatehc.com
SIC: 8051 Skilled nursing care facilities
HQ: Consulate Management Company, Llc
  800 Concourse Pkwy S # 200
  Maitland FL 32751
  407 571-1550

(G-10713)
COURTYARD MANAGEMENT CORP
Also Called: Courtyard By Marriott
415 W Dussel Dr (43537-1667)
PHONE..................419 897-2255
Roxanne Collins, *Brnch Mgr*
EMP: 28
SALES (corp-wide): 23.71B **Publicly Held**
Web: www.marriott.com
SIC: 7011 Hotels and motels
HQ: Courtyard Management Llc
  7750 Wisconsin Ave
  Bethesda MD 20814

(G-10714)
CRAIG TRANSPORTATION CO
819 Kingsbury St Ste 102 (43537-1861)
P.O. Box 1010 (43552-1010)
PHONE..................419 874-7981
Lance C Craig, *Prin*
Chris Simmons, *
Phil Jacks, *
John Craig, *
Gail M Craig, *
EMP: 40 **EST**: 1929
SQ FT: 14,000
SALES (est): 16.03MM **Privately Held**
Web: www.craigtransport.com
SIC: 4731 4213 Freight transportation arrangement; Trucking, except local

(G-10715)
DANA CREDIT CORPORATION
3939 Technology Dr (43537-9194)
PHONE..................419 887-3000
Paul J Bishop, *Pr*
Latitia D Marth, *VP*
Dennis Greenwald, *VP*
Dean L Wilson, *VP*
EMP: 409 **EST**: 1980
SQ FT: 55,000
SALES (est): 150.75MM **Publicly Held**
SIC: 6159 Machinery and equipment finance leasing
HQ: Dana Limited
  3939 Technology Dr
  Maumee OH 43537

(G-10716)
DANBERRY CO
3555 Briarfield Blvd (43537-9383)
PHONE..................419 866-8888
Dan Mcquillen, *Brnch Mgr*
EMP: 39
SALES (corp-wide): 23.49MM **Privately Held**
Web: www.luxionhomes.com
SIC: 6531 Real estate agent, residential
PA: The Danberry Co
  3242 Executive Pkwy # 203
  Toledo OH 43606
  419 534-6592

(G-10717)
DARI PIZZA ENTERPRISES II INC
1683 Woodlands Dr Ste A (43537-4052)
PHONE..................419 534-3000
Suzan Dari, *Pr*
Omar Dari, *
EMP: 150 **EST**: 2002
SALES (est): 3.03MM **Privately Held**
SIC: 5812 8742 6531 Lunchrooms and cafeterias; New business start-up consultant; Real estate agents and managers

(G-10718)
DESIGN ENGNERS CNSULTING ASSOC
415 Conant St (43537-3388)
PHONE..................419 891-0022
EMP: 27 **EST**: 1992
SQ FT: 1,700
SALES (est): 948.11K **Privately Held**
Web: www.kleinfelder.com
SIC: 8711 Consulting engineer

(G-10719)
EATON CORPORATION
1660 Indian Wood Cir (43537-4004)
PHONE..................419 891-7627
Charles M Stoneberg, *Mgr*
EMP: 47
Web: www.dix-eaton.com
SIC: 5063 Electrical apparatus and equipment
HQ: Eaton Corporation
  1000 Eaton Blvd
  Cleveland OH 44122
  440 523-5000

(G-10720)
ELITE INVESTMENTS LLC
644 Dussel Dr (43537-2412)
PHONE..................419 350-8949
EMP: 57 **EST**: 2007
SALES (est): 1.8MM **Privately Held**
SIC: 6799 Investors, nec

(G-10721)
ENTELCO CORPORATION
6528 Weatherfield Ct (43537-9468)
PHONE..................419 872-4620
Stephen Stranahan, *Pr*
EMP: 63 **EST**: 1981
SQ FT: 3,000
Web: www.baycontrols.com
SIC: 6719 Investment holding companies, except banks

(G-10722)
EPILEPSY CTR OF NRTHWSTERN OHI
1701 Holland Rd (43537-1699)
PHONE..................419 867-5950
TOLL FREE: 800

Chad Bringman, *Dir*
Roy J Cherry, *
EMP: 47 **EST:** 1977
SALES (est): 4.36MM **Privately Held**
Web: www.epilepsycenter.org
SIC: 8322 Social service center

(G-10723)
ERIE SHORES CREDIT UNION INC (PA)
1688 Woodlands Dr (43537-4019)
P.O. Box 9037 (43537-9037)
PHONE..............................419 897-8110
Jim Troknya, *Ch Bd*
Ralph Kubacki, *
EMP: 31 **EST:** 1945
SQ FT: 8,536
SALES (est): 4.87MM **Privately Held**
Web: www.escu.net
SIC: 6061 Federal credit unions

(G-10724)
FELLER FINCH & ASSOCIATES INC (PA)
1683 Woodlands Dr Ste A (43537-4052)
PHONE..............................419 893-3680
Donald L Feller, *Pr*
Gregory N Feller, *
Chris Crisenbery, *
EMP: 40 **EST:** 1984
SQ FT: 5,000
SALES (est): 4.99MM
SALES (corp-wide): 4.99MM **Privately Held**
Web: www.fellerfinch.com
SIC: 8713 8711 Surveying services; Civil engineering

(G-10725)
FOCUS HEALTHCARE OF OHIO LLC
1725 Timber Line Rd (43537-4015)
PHONE..............................419 891-9333
TOLL FREE: 800
EMP: 37 **EST:** 1998
SALES (est): 2.42MM
SALES (corp-wide): 4.29MM **Privately Held**
Web: www.focushealthcare.com
SIC: 8063 Psychiatric hospitals
PA: Focus Healthcare Of Tennessee, Llc
7429 Shallowford Rd
Chattanooga TN 37421
423 308-2560

(G-10726)
GALLON TKACS BSSNULT SCHFFER L (PA)
1450 Arrowhead Dr (43537-4016)
P.O. Box 352018 (43635-2018)
PHONE..............................419 843-2001
Jack E Gallon, *Pr*
William E Takacs, *
Jeffrey Julius, *
EMP: 90 **EST:** 1967
SQ FT: 30,728
SALES (est): 9.5MM
SALES (corp-wide): 9.5MM **Privately Held**
Web: www.gallonlaw.com
SIC: 8111 General practice attorney, lawyer

(G-10727)
GENIUS SOLUTIONS ENGRG CO (HQ)
Also Called: Gs Engineering
6421 Monclova Rd (43537-9760)
PHONE..............................419 794-9914
Grigoriy Grinberg, *Pr*
Matthew Shade, *
EMP: 39 **EST:** 2004
SALES (est): 9.47MM

SALES (corp-wide): 741.05MM **Publicly Held**
Web: www.mold-tech.com
SIC: 8711 2821 7389 Mechanical engineering; Thermoplastic materials; Engraving service
PA: Standex International Corporation
23 Keewaydin Dr
Salem NH 03079
603 893-9701

(G-10728)
GILMORE JASION MAHLER LTD (PA)
1715 Indian Wood Cir Ste 100 (43537-4055)
PHONE..............................419 794-2000
Kevin M Gilmore, *Mng Pt*
Adele Jasion, *Pt*
Andrew Mahler, *Pt*
EMP: 44 **EST:** 1996
SALES (est): 8.03MM
SALES (corp-wide): 8.03MM **Privately Held**
Web: www.gjmltd.com
SIC: 8721 Certified public accountant

(G-10729)
GIRL SCOUTS OF WESTERN OHIO
Also Called: Girl Scuts Wstn Ohio Tledo Div
460 W Dussel Dr # A (43537-4205)
PHONE..............................567 225-3557
EMP: 44
SALES (corp-wide): 13.28MM **Privately Held**
Web: www.gswo.org
SIC: 8641 Girl Scout organization
PA: Girl Scouts Of Western Ohio
4930 Cornell Rd
Blue Ash OH 45242
513 489-1025

(G-10730)
HEALTH MANAGEMENT SOLUTIONS
1901 Indian Wood Cir (43537-4002)
PHONE..............................419 536-5690
Katie Leaventon, *Mgr*
EMP: 45 **EST:** 2019
SALES (est): 930.56K **Privately Held**
Web: www.promedica.org
SIC: 6411 Insurance agents, nec

(G-10731)
HELM AND ASSOCIATES INC
501 W Sophia St Unit 8 (43537-1884)
PHONE..............................419 893-1480
Keith Helminski, *Pr*
Jerry Helminski, *
John Schrein, *
Maria Iwinski, *Stockholder*
EMP: 29 **EST:** 1982
SQ FT: 6,900
SALES (est): 435.73K **Privately Held**
Web: www.helmtest.com
SIC: 1711 1731 1541 Warm air heating and air conditioning contractor; Electrical work; Industrial buildings and warehouses

(G-10732)
HEMATOGY ONCOLOGY TOLEDO CLINC
5805 Monclova Rd (43537-1839)
PHONE..............................419 794-7720
EMP: 49
SALES (corp-wide): 268.5K **Privately Held**
Web: www.toledoclinic.com
SIC: 8011 Oncologist
PA: Toledo Clinc Hematogy Oncology
4235 Secor Rd
Toledo OH 43623
419 479-5605

(G-10733)
JDI GROUP INC
360 W Dussel Dr (43537-1631)
PHONE..............................419 725-7161
Timothy Fry, *Pr*
Matthew Davis, *
EMP: 78 **EST:** 2001
SQ FT: 27,000
SALES (est): 15.09MM **Privately Held**
Web: www.thejdigroup.com
SIC: 8712 8711 Architectural engineering; Engineering services

(G-10734)
JOHNSON CNTRLS SEC SLTIONS LLC
1722 Indian Wood Cir Ste F (43537-4044)
PHONE..............................419 243-8400
Steve Carlson, *Genl Mgr*
EMP: 37
Web: datasource.johnsoncontrols.com
SIC: 7382 Burglar alarm maintenance and monitoring
HQ: Johnson Controls Security Solutions Llc
6600 Congress Ave
Boca Raton FL 33487
561 264-2071

(G-10735)
KEYBANK NATIONAL ASSOCIATION
409 Conant St (43537-3359)
PHONE..............................419 893-7696
Linda Mcneal, *Brnch Mgr*
EMP: 44
SALES (corp-wide): 10.4B **Publicly Held**
Web: www.key.com
SIC: 6021 National commercial banks
HQ: Keybank National Association
127 Public Sq Ste 5600
Cleveland OH 44114
800 539-2968

(G-10736)
KEYSTONE AUTO GLASS INC
2255 Linden Ct (43537-2338)
PHONE..............................419 509-0497
Neal Golding, *Pr*
Alan Golding, *
Andrew K Golding, *
Brian Silver, *
EMP: 100 **EST:** 1953
SQ FT: 20,000
SALES (est): 5.44MM **Privately Held**
SIC: 3714 7536 5531 5013 Motor vehicle parts and accessories; Automotive glass replacement shops; Auto and home supply stores; Motor vehicle supplies and new parts

(G-10737)
KUHLMAN CORPORATION (PA)
Also Called: Kuhlman Construction Products
1845 Indian Wood Cir (43537-4072)
P.O. Box 714 (43697-0714)
PHONE..............................419 897-6000
Timothy L Goligoski, *Pr*
Kenneth Kuhlman, *
Terry Schaefer, *
▲ **EMP:** 32 **EST:** 1901
SQ FT: 18,000
SALES (est): 42.49MM
SALES (corp-wide): 42.49MM **Privately Held**
Web: www.gerkencompanies.com
SIC: 4226 5032 3273 Special warehousing and storage, nec; Brick, stone, and related material; Ready-mixed concrete

(G-10738)
LANTZ DENTAL PROSTHETICS INC
6490 Wheatstone Ct (43537-9402)
PHONE..............................419 866-1515
Tom Lantz, *Pr*
Martha Lantz, *VP*
Sherry Morrin, *Sec*
EMP: 28 **EST:** 1984
SQ FT: 6,000
SALES (est): 785.35K **Privately Held**
Web: www.lantzdental.com
SIC: 8072 Crown and bridge production

(G-10739)
LEANTRAK INC
1645 Indian Wood Cir Ste 101 (43537-4419)
PHONE..............................419 482-0797
Bob Wadas, *CEO*
Dave Steer, *
EMP: 30 **EST:** 2002
SALES (est): 4.74MM **Privately Held**
Web: www.leantrak.com
SIC: 8711 Consulting engineer

(G-10740)
LIFE CONNECTION OF OHIO (PA)
3661 Briarfield Blvd Ste 105 (43537)
PHONE..............................419 893-4891
Matthew Wadsworth, *Pr*
John Emmerich, *
EMP: 92 **EST:** 1981
SQ FT: 52,000
SALES (est): 30.22MM **Privately Held**
Web: www.lifeconnection.org
SIC: 8099 Organ bank

(G-10741)
LOTT INDUSTRIES INCORPORATED
Also Called: Lott Industries
1645 Holland Rd (43537-1622)
PHONE..............................419 891-5215
Robert Stebbins, *Mgr*
EMP: 495
SALES (corp-wide): 4.4MM **Privately Held**
Web: www.lottserves.org
SIC: 8331 Sheltered workshop
PA: Lott Industries Incorporated
3350 Hill Ave
Toledo OH 43607
419 534-4980

(G-10742)
LTCCORP GOVERNMENT SERVICES-OH INC
Also Called: Toltest
1480 Ford St (43537-1731)
PHONE..............................419 794-3500
◆ **EMP:** 300
Web: www.ltccorp.com
SIC: 1542 8744 Nonresidential construction, nec; Facilities support services

(G-10743)
LUPO & KOCZKUR PC
1690 Woodlands Dr (43537-4045)
PHONE..............................419 897-7931
Robin Lupo, *Mgr*
EMP: 43
SALES (corp-wide): 2.43MM **Privately Held**
Web: www.lupokoczkur.com
SIC: 8111 General practice attorney, lawyer
PA: Lupo & Koczkur Pc
17000 Kercheval Ave # 200
Grosse Pointe MI 48230
586 532-5000

GEOGRAPHIC SECTION
Maumee - Lucas County (G-10768)

(G-10744)
MANNIK & SMITH GROUP INC (HQ)
Also Called: M S G
1800 Indian Wood Cir (43537-4086)
PHONE.................................419 891-2222
Dean Niese, *CEO*
C Michael Smith, *Pr*
Dean Niese, *Sr VP*
Rich Bertz, *Prin*
Mark Smoley, *Prin*
EMP: 105 **EST:** 1955
SQ FT: 36,500
SALES (est): 39.58MM
SALES (corp-wide): 350.6MM **Privately Held**
Web: www.manniksmithgroup.com
SIC: 8711 8748 Consulting engineer; Business consulting, nec
PA: Trilon Group, Llc
  1200 17th St Ste 860
  Denver CO 80202
  833 487-4566

(G-10745)
MATRIX TECHNOLOGIES INC (PA)
Also Called: MTI Engineering
1760 Indian Wood Cir (43537-4070)
PHONE.................................419 897-7200
David L Bishop, *Pr*
David J Blaida, *
Donald J Krompak, *
EMP: 100 **EST:** 1980
SQ FT: 39,000
SALES (est): 56.59MM
SALES (corp-wide): 56.59MM **Privately Held**
Web: www.matrixti.com
SIC: 8711 Consulting engineer

(G-10746)
MAUMEE EYE CLINIC INC
Also Called: Hawkins, Terrence Do
5655 Monclova Rd Ste 2 (43537-1870)
PHONE.................................419 893-4883
Clark D Weidaw, *Pr*
EMP: 36 **EST:** 1978
SQ FT: 1,200
SALES (est): 2.16MM **Privately Held**
Web: www.mecrecordsrequests.com
SIC: 8011 Opthalmologist

(G-10747)
MCNAUGHTON-MCKAY ELC OHIO INC
355 Tomahawk Dr Unit 1 (43537-1757)
PHONE.................................419 891-0262
Timothy J Krucki, *Brnch Mgr*
EMP: 36
SQ FT: 38,000
SALES (corp-wide): 2.81B **Privately Held**
SIC: 5063 Electrical supplies, nec
HQ: Mcnaughton-Mckay Electric Company Of Ohio, Inc.
  2255 Citygate Dr
  Columbus OH 43219
  614 476-2800

(G-10748)
MEYER HILL LYNCH CORPORATION
1771 Indian Wood Cir (43537-4009)
PHONE.................................419 897-9797
D Stuart Lovee, *Pr*
D Stuart Love, *
Robert Shick, *
Kathleen Casey, *
▼ **EMP:** 40 **EST:** 1989
SQ FT: 20,000
SALES (est): 10.13MM **Privately Held**
Web: www.neweratech.com
SIC: 7379 Computer related consulting services

(G-10749)
MOSSER CONSTRUCTION INC
1613 Henthorne Dr (43537-1300)
PHONE.................................419 861-5100
Chuck Moyer, *Brnch Mgr*
EMP: 50
SALES (corp-wide): 101.73MM **Privately Held**
Web: www.mosserconstruction.com
SIC: 1542 1541 Commercial and office building, new construction; Industrial buildings, new construction, nec
HQ: Mosser Construction, Inc.
  122 S Wilson Ave
  Fremont OH 43420
  419 334-3801

(G-10750)
NORTHWEST OHIO CHAPTER CFMA
145 Chesterfield Ln (43537-2209)
PHONE.................................419 891-1040
EMP: 49 **EST:** 2011
SALES (est): 2.34MM **Privately Held**
SIC: 6022 State commercial banks

(G-10751)
NURSENOW LLC
644 Dussel Dr (43537-2412)
PHONE.................................812 868-7732
David Kissinger, *CEO*
EMP: 76 **EST:** 2020
SALES (est): 4.58MM **Privately Held**
Web: www.nursenowstaffing.com
SIC: 7363 Temporary help service

(G-10752)
OCCUPATIONAL SERVICES
5901 Monclova Rd (43537-1841)
PHONE.................................419 891-8003
EMP: 37 **EST:** 1992
SALES (est): 731.65K **Privately Held**
SIC: 8011 Offices and clinics of medical doctors

(G-10753)
OWENS INTERMODAL LLC
1415 Holland Rd Ste A (43537-1646)
PHONE.................................419 365-2704
Robert Owens, *Pr*
Robert Owens, *Managing Member*
Karen Owens, *Managing Member**
EMP: 32 **EST:** 2017
SALES (est): 2.26MM **Privately Held**
Web: www.owensiml.com
SIC: 4731 Brokers, shipping

(G-10754)
PARAMONT CARE OF MICHIGAN
Also Called: Promedica Medicare Plan
1901 Indian Wood Cir (43537-4002)
P.O. Box 981 (43697-0981)
PHONE.................................419 887-2728
EMP: 79
Web: www.paramounthealthcare.com
SIC: 8099 Blood related health services
PA: Paramount Care Of Michigan
  214 E Elm Ave Ste 107
  Monroe MI 48162

(G-10755)
PARAMOUNT CARE INC (DH)
Also Called: Paramount Health Care
1901 Indian Wood Cir (43537-4002)
P.O. Box 928 (43697-0928)
PHONE.................................419 887-2500
John C Randolph, *Pr*
Robert J Kolodzy, *
Mark Moser, *
Jeffrey C Kuhn, *
EMP: 365 **EST:** 1987

SQ FT: 59,900
SALES (est): 259.67MM
SALES (corp-wide): 187.07MM **Privately Held**
Web: www.paramounthealthcare.com
SIC: 6321 Accident insurance carriers
HQ: Promedica Insurance Corp
  1901 Indian Wood Cir
  Maumee OH 43537
  419 887-2500

(G-10756)
PONTOON SOLUTIONS INC
1695 Indian Wood Cir Ste 200 (43537-4083)
PHONE.................................855 881-1533
EMP: 510
Web: www.pontoonsolutions.com
SIC: 7363 Temporary help service
HQ: Pontoon Solutions, Inc.
  4800 Deerwood Campus Pkwy # 800
  Jacksonville FL 32246
  855 881-1533

(G-10757)
PROMEDICA HEALTH SYSTEM INC
Also Called: Promediccal Heath Syytem
660 Beaver Creek Cir Ste 200 (43537-1745)
PHONE.................................419 891-6201
EMP: 126
SALES (corp-wide): 187.07MM **Privately Held**
Web: www.promedica.org
SIC: 8062 General medical and surgical hospitals
PA: Promedica Health System, Inc.
  100 Madison Ave
  Toledo OH 43604
  567 585-9600

(G-10758)
RECYCLING SERVICES INC (PA)
Also Called: Allshred Services
3940 Technology Dr (43537-9264)
PHONE.................................419 381-7762
Willie Geiser, *Pr*
EMP: 37 **EST:** 1989
SQ FT: 47,000
SALES (est): 6.91MM **Privately Held**
Web: www.vitalrecordscontrol.com
SIC: 7389 Document and office record destruction

(G-10759)
REDWOOD LIVING INC
Also Called: Redwood
1520 Market Place Dr W8 (43537)
PHONE.................................216 360-9441
EMP: 172 **EST:** 1990
SALES (est): 97.61MM **Privately Held**
SIC: 8742 Management consulting services

(G-10760)
RESIDENCE INN TOLEDO MAUMEE
1370 Arrowhead Dr (43537-1728)
PHONE.................................419 891-2233
EMP: 33 **EST:** 2010
SALES (est): 484.82K **Privately Held**
SIC: 7011 Hotel, franchised

(G-10761)
RESOLUTE BANK
3425 Briarfield Blvd Ste 100 (43537)
PHONE.................................419 868-1750
Kevin Rahe, *CEO*
G Mark Loreto, *
Susan Martin, *
EMP: 34 **EST:** 2006
SALES (est): 8.33MM **Privately Held**
Web: www.jnanabhumiap.in

SIC: 6035 Federal savings and loan associations

(G-10762)
RICHFIELD INN INC
Also Called: Courtyard Toledo Maumee
415 W Dussel Dr (43537-1667)
PHONE.................................248 946-5838
Jitendra B Patel, *CEO*
EMP: 46 **EST:** 2008
SALES (est): 481.12K **Privately Held**
Web: www.wyndhamhotels.com
SIC: 7011 Hotels and motels

(G-10763)
ROBEX LLC (PA)
1745 Indian Wood Cir (43537-4042)
PHONE.................................419 270-0770
Jon Parker, *CEO*
EMP: 28 **EST:** 2017
SALES (est): 37MM
SALES (corp-wide): 37MM **Privately Held**
Web: www.robex.us
SIC: 8742 Automation and robotics consultant

(G-10764)
SAVAGE AND ASSOCIATES INC (PA)
655 Beaver Creek Cir (43537-1738)
PHONE.................................419 475-8665
Ralph E Toland Iii, *Pr*
Phil Johnson, *
Mark Smigelski, *
Russell Karban, *
Nick Camp, *
EMP: 102 **EST:** 1960
SALES (est): 23.47MM
SALES (corp-wide): 23.47MM **Privately Held**
Web: www.savageandassociates.com
SIC: 6411 Life insurance agents

(G-10765)
SHREE SHIV LLC
Also Called: Comfort Inn
1702 Toll Gate Dr (43537-1674)
PHONE.................................419 897-5555
Henry Desai, *Genl Mgr*
EMP: 37 **EST:** 2001
SALES (est): 954.09K **Privately Held**
Web: www.choicehotels.com
SIC: 7011 Hotels and motels

(G-10766)
SKEYE WHOLESALE INC
Also Called: Skeye Wholesale
6630 Maumee Western Rd (43537-9368)
PHONE.................................419 720-4440
EMP: 68 **EST:** 2007
SALES (est): 6.38MM **Privately Held**
Web: www.skeyewholesale.com
SIC: 5099 Brass goods

(G-10767)
SOUTHWEST ANESTHESIA SVCS INC
5901 Monclova Rd (43537-1841)
PHONE.................................419 897-8370
Thomas Andersen, *CEO*
EMP: 27 **EST:** 2008
SALES (est): 851.18K **Privately Held**
SIC: 8011 Anesthesiologist

(G-10768)
SPARTAN CHEMICAL COMPANY INC
Also Called: Spartan
1110 Spartan Dr (43537-1725)
PHONE.................................419 897-5551
Stephen H Swigart, *CEO*
John Swigart, *

Maumee - Lucas County (G-10769)

Jim Lenardson, *
James R Lenardson, *
Kenneth G Ford, *
◆ **EMP:** 231 **EST:** 1956
SQ FT: 450,000
SALES (est): 92.49MM **Privately Held**
Web: www.spartanchemical.com
SIC: 5169 Chemicals and allied products, nec

(G-10769)
ST LUKES HOSPITAL (DH)
Also Called: BON SECURE MERCY HEALTH
5901 Monclova Rd (43537-1899)
PHONE..................419 893-5911
Jennifer Montgomery, Pr
EMP: 269 **EST:** 1906
SQ FT: 324,324
SALES (corp-wide): 6.92B **Privately Held**
Web: www.mclaren.org
SIC: 8062 5912 Hospital, affiliated with AMA residency; Drug stores
HQ: Mercy Health
12621 Eckel Junction Rd
Perrysburg OH 43551
513 639-2800

(G-10770)
STLUKES MEDICAL IMAGERY
5757 Monclova Rd (43537-1863)
PHONE..................419 893-4856
Stephen A Eldridge, Prin
EMP: 40 **EST:** 2010
SALES (est): 755.88K **Privately Held**
SIC: 8062 General medical and surgical hospitals

(G-10771)
STONECO INC
Also Called: Shelley Company
1360 Ford St (43537-1733)
PHONE..................419 893-7645
Lee Wehner, Mgr
EMP: 40
SALES (corp-wide): 32.72B **Privately Held**
Web: www.shellyco.com
SIC: 1422 5032 Crushed and broken limestone; Stone, crushed or broken
HQ: Stoneco, Inc.
1700 Fostoria Ave Ste 200
Findlay OH 45840
419 422-8854

(G-10772)
SUN FEDERAL CREDIT UNION (PA)
1625 Holland Rd (43537)
PHONE..................800 786-0945
Gary C Moritz, Pr
Don Kruger, *
Marcia Bourdo, OK Vice President*
Mark Deyoung, OK Vice President*
Francesca Vogel, OF BUYS Development*
EMP: 40 **EST:** 1950
SQ FT: 21,000
SALES (est): 31.63MM
SALES (corp-wide): 31.63MM **Privately Held**
Web: sunfederalcu.locatorsearch.com
SIC: 6061 Federal credit unions

(G-10773)
SUNSHINE COMMUNITIES (PA)
Also Called: Sunshine Inc. Northwest Ohio
7223 Maumee Western Rd (43537-9755)
PHONE..................419 865-0251
Elizabeth J Holland, Ex Dir
Tyson Stuckey, *
Steffanie Brumett, *
Ronie Regent, *
EMP: 280 **EST:** 1949

SQ FT: 150,000
SALES (est): 51.72K
SALES (corp-wide): 51.72K **Privately Held**
Web: www.sunshine.org
SIC: 8361 8052 8322 Retarded home; Intermediate care facilities; Individual and family services

(G-10774)
TOLEDO MEDICAL EQUIPMENT CO (PA)
Also Called: Young Medical Services
4060 Technology Dr (43537-9263)
PHONE..................419 866-7120
TOLL FREE: 800
Timothy D Pontius, Pr
Kathy Mikolajczak, *
EMP: 48 **EST:** 1974
SQ FT: 20,000
SALES (est): 2.14MM
SALES (corp-wide): 2.14MM **Privately Held**
Web: www.darahmedical.com
SIC: 7352 5999 Medical equipment rental; Medical apparatus and supplies

(G-10775)
TONY PACKOS TOLEDO LLC (PA)
Also Called: Tony Packo's Food Company
1412 Arrowhead Dr (43537-4016)
PHONE..................419 691-6054
Tony Packo, CEO
Emily Bennett, *
Steve Peoo, *
EMP: 28 **EST:** 1932
SALES (est): 8.24MM
SALES (corp-wide): 8.24MM **Privately Held**
Web: www.tonypacko.com
SIC: 5812 5149 Carry-out only (except pizza) restaurant; Pickles, preserves, jellies, and jams

(G-10776)
UNITED COLLECTION BUREAU INC
1345 Ford St (43537-1732)
PHONE..................419 866-6227
Ka W Tsui, Brnch Mgr
EMP: 47
SALES (corp-wide): 62.18MM **Privately Held**
Web: www.ucbinc.com
SIC: 7322 Collection agency, except real estate
PA: United Collection Bureau, Inc.
5620 Southwyck Blvd
Toledo OH 43614
419 866-6227

(G-10777)
UNITED PARCEL SERVICE INC
Also Called: UPS
1550 Holland Rd (43537-1657)
PHONE..................419 891-6776
Karen Park, Mgr
EMP: 2228
SALES (corp-wide): 90.96B **Publicly Held**
Web: www.ups.com
SIC: 4215 Package delivery, vehicular
HQ: United Parcel Service, Inc.
55 Glenlake Pkwy
Atlanta GA 30328
404 828-6000

(G-10778)
VRC COMPANIES LLC
3940 Technology Dr (43537-9264)
PHONE..................419 381-7762
EMP: 32
SALES (corp-wide): 131.52MM **Privately Held**

Web: www.vitalrecordscontrol.com
SIC: 4226 8741 Document and office records storage; Management services
HQ: Vrc Companies, Llc
5384 Poplar Ave Ste 500
Memphis TN 38119
901 310-2005

(G-10779)
WELLCARE PHYSICIANS GROUP LLC
5901 Monclova Rd (43537-1841)
PHONE..................419 891-8541
Dennis M Wagner, Prin
EMP: 37 **EST:** 2007
SALES (est): 701.29K **Privately Held**
SIC: 8011 Physicians' office, including specialists

(G-10780)
WHITEHURST COMPANY (PA)
6325 Garden Rd (43537-1271)
P.O. Box 286 (43552-0286)
PHONE..................419 534-6022
Herb Fultz, Pr
James Mc Innis, *
EMP: 43 **EST:** 1983
SALES (est): 1.88MM
SALES (corp-wide): 1.88MM **Privately Held**
SIC: 6531 6513 Real estate managers; Apartment building operators

(G-10781)
WILLIAM VAUGHAN COMPANY
Also Called: Northwest Ohio Prctice MGT Con
145 Chesterfield Ln (43537-2209)
PHONE..................419 891-1040
William J Horst, Pr
Gregory J Arndt, *
Michelle M Clement, *
Aaron D Swiggum, *
David J Baymiller, *
EMP: 63 **EST:** 1957
SQ FT: 1,600
SALES (est): 10.24MM **Privately Held**
Web: www.wvco.com
SIC: 8721 Certified public accountant

(G-10782)
YOUNG MNS CHRSTN ASSN OF GRTER
Also Called: YMCA
2100 S Holland Sylvania Rd (43537)
PHONE..................419 866-9622
Vicki Coleman, Mgr
EMP: 105
SALES (corp-wide): 29.37MM **Privately Held**
Web: www.ymcatoledo.org
SIC: 8641 7991 8351 7032 Youth organizations; Physical fitness facilities; Child day care services; Youth camps
PA: The Young Men's Christian Association Of Greater Toledo
6465 Sylvania Ave
Sylvania OH 43560
419 729-8135

(G-10783)
YOUNG MNS CHRSTN ASSN OF GRTER
Also Called: YMCA
716 Askin St (43537-3602)
PHONE..................419 794-7304
EMP: 64
SALES (corp-wide): 29.37MM **Privately Held**
Web: www.ymcatoledo.org

SIC: 8641 Youth organizations
PA: The Young Men's Christian Association Of Greater Toledo
6465 Sylvania Ave
Sylvania OH 43560
419 729-8135

Mayfield Heights
Cuyahoga County

(G-10784)
AMERIWOUND
5800 Landerbrook Dr Ste 100 (44124-4083)
PHONE..................216 273-9800
Samson Fixler, Prin
EMP: 67 **EST:** 2012
SALES (est): 10.02MM **Privately Held**
Web: www.ameriwound.com
SIC: 8011 Offices and clinics of medical doctors

(G-10785)
BECK ALUMINUM CORPORATION
6150 Parkland Blvd Ste 260 (44124-6147)
PHONE..................440 684-4848
◆ **EMP:** 87
Web: www.beckaluminum.com
SIC: 5051 Aluminum bars, rods, ingots, sheets, pipes, plates, etc.

(G-10786)
ELK & ELK CO LPA (PA)
6105 Parkland Blvd Ste 200 (44124-4258)
PHONE..................800 355-6446
David J Elk, Pt
Arthur M Elk, Pt
EMP: 48 **EST:** 1984
SALES (est): 10.09MM
SALES (corp-wide): 10.09MM **Privately Held**
Web: www.elkandelk.com
SIC: 8111 General practice law office

(G-10787)
JOHN RBRTS HAIR STUDIO SPA INC (PA)
6727 Eastgate Dr (44124-2021)
PHONE..................216 839-1430
EMP: 73 **EST:** 1993
SQ FT: 7,000
SALES (est): 4.88MM **Privately Held**
Web: www.jrspa.com
SIC: 7231 Hairdressers

(G-10788)
LINSALATA CAPITAL PARTNERS INC
5900 Landerbrook Dr Ste 280 (44124-4029)
PHONE..................440 684-1400
Frank Linsalata, Pr
EMP: 402 **EST:** 2008
SALES (est): 43.9MM **Privately Held**
Web: www.linsalatacapital.com
SIC: 6799 Venture capital companies

(G-10789)
MATERION BRUSH INTL INC
6070 Parkland Blvd Ste 3 (44124-4191)
PHONE..................216 486-4200
Richard Trate, Pr
William Laditak, *
EMP: 100 **EST:** 2000
SQ FT: 16,000
SALES (est): 28.15MM **Publicly Held**
Web: www.materion.com
SIC: 5051 Metals service centers and offices
PA: Materion Corporation
6070 Parkland Blvd

GEOGRAPHIC SECTION

Medina - Medina County (G-10808)

Mayfield Heights OH 44124

(G-10790)
MATERION CERAMICS INC
6070 Parkland Blvd (44124-4191)
PHONE..................................216 486-4200
EMP: 275 EST: 2000
SALES (est): 15.64MM Privately Held
Web: www.materion.com
SIC: 5051 Metals service centers and offices

(G-10791)
ONX ACQUISITION LLC
Also Called: Onx Enterprise Solutions
5910 Landerbrook Dr Ste 250
(44124-6508)
PHONE..................................440 569-2300
EMP: 300
SIC: 7372 7379 Business oriented computer software; Computer related consulting services

(G-10792)
PARK PLACE TECHNOLOGIES LLC
Also Called: AMI
5910 Landerbrook Dr Ste 300
(44124-6500)
PHONE..................................610 544-0571
EMP: 390
Web: www.parkplacetechnologies.com
SIC: 7378 Computer maintenance and repair
PA: Park Place Technologies, Llc
    5910 Lndrbrook Dr Ste 300
    Cleveland OH 44124

(G-10793)
TRIMBLE TRNSP ENTP SLTIONS INC (HQ)
6085 Parkland Blvd (44124-4184)
PHONE..................................216 831-6606
David Wangler, Pr
David Mook, *
Jeffrey Ritter, *
Scott Vanselous, *
David Schildmeyer, *
EMP: 125 EST: 1986
SQ FT: 32,500
SALES (est): 93.8MM
SALES (corp-wide): 3.8B Publicly Held
Web: transportation.trimble.com
SIC: 7372 Business oriented computer software
PA: Trimble Inc.
    10368 Westmoor Dr
    Westminster CO 80021
    720 887-6100

Mayfield Village
Cuyahoga County

(G-10794)
MARCUM LLP
6685 Beta Dr (44143-2320)
PHONE..................................440 459-5700
Dani Gisondo, Brnch Mgr
EMP: 41
SALES (corp-wide): 379.94MM Privately Held
Web: www.marcumwealth.com
SIC: 8721 Certified public accountant
PA: Marcum Llp
    730 3rd Ave Fl 11
    New York NY 10017
    212 485-5500

(G-10795)
PROGRESSIVE CASUALTY INSUR CO (DH)
Also Called: Progressive Insurance
6300 Wilson Mills Rd (44143-2109)
PHONE..................................855 347-3939
Tricia Griffith, Pr
John P Sauerland, *
▼ EMP: 3300 EST: 1956
SALES (est): 10.2B
SALES (corp-wide): 49.61B Publicly Held
Web: www.progressive.com
SIC: 6351 6411 6321 6331 Surety insurance ; Insurance agents, brokers, and service; Accident and health insurance; Fire, marine and casualty insurance and carriers
HQ: Drive Insurance Holdings, Inc.
    6300 Wilson Mills Rd
    Cleveland OH 44143

(G-10796)
SECUREDATA LLC
700 Beta Dr Ste 100 (44143-2378)
PHONE..................................323 944-0822
Sergey Gulyayev, Managing Member
EMP: 28 EST: 2019
SALES (est): 1.01MM Privately Held
Web: www.securedatarecovery.com
SIC: 7379 Computer related maintenance services

(G-10797)
WIRELESS ENVIRONMENT LLC
Also Called: Mr. Beams
600 Beta Dr Ste 100 (44143-2355)
PHONE..................................216 455-0192
David Levine, Pr
Mark Plush, CFO
▲ EMP: 29 EST: 2006
SQ FT: 1,000
SALES (est): 4.65MM Publicly Held
Web: www.mrbeams.com
SIC: 1731 Lighting contractor
HQ: Ring Llc
    12515 Cerise Ave
    Hawthorne CA 90250
    310 929-7085

Mc Arthur
Vinton County

(G-10798)
HOPEWELL HEALTH CENTERS INC
Also Called: Tri County Mental Health
313 1/2 W Main St (45651-1014)
PHONE..................................740 596-4809
George Wigley, Prin
EMP: 35
SALES (corp-wide): 66.73MM Privately Held
Web: www.hopewellhealth.org
SIC: 8093 8322 Mental health clinic, outpatient; General counseling services
PA: Hopewell Health Centers, Inc.
    1049 Western Ave
    Chillicothe OH 45601
    740 773-1006

(G-10799)
VINTON COUNTY NATIONAL BANK (HQ)
Also Called: VINTON CO NATIONAL BANK
112 W Main St (45651-1200)
P.O. Box 460 (45651-0460)
PHONE..................................800 223-4031
Mark Erslan, Pr
Ron Collins, *
EMP: 43 EST: 1900
SQ FT: 13,239
SALES (est): 54.53MM
SALES (corp-wide): 54.53MM Privately Held
Web: www.vcnbfamily.bank
SIC: 6162 6029 Mortgage bankers and loan correspondents; Commercial banks, nec
PA: Community Bancshares, Inc.
    112 W Main St
    Mc Arthur OH 45651
    740 596-4561

Mc Dermott
Scioto County

(G-10800)
VOIERS ENTERPRISES INC
Also Called: REST HAVEN NURSING HOME
2274 Mc Dermott Pond Creek Rd
(45652-9192)
P.O. Box 156 (45652-0156)
PHONE..................................740 259-2838
Sarah E Voiers, Pr
Deborah Akers, *
Anna Clarke, *
Steven Akers, *
EMP: 30 EST: 1968
SALES (est): 1.9MM Privately Held
SIC: 8052 Personal care facility

Mc Donald
Trumbull County

(G-10801)
PREDATOR TRUCKING COMPANY (PA)
3181 Trumbull Ave (44437-1313)
P.O. Box 315 (44437-0315)
PHONE..................................330 530-0712
Charles Haselow, CEO
Russell Golden, *
James Golden, *
Gary Golden, *
EMP: 33 EST: 1992
SQ FT: 1,000
SALES (est): 7.2MM Privately Held
Web: web.predatortrucking.com
SIC: 4213 Trucking, except local

Mc Guffey
Hardin County

(G-10802)
ROHRS FARMS
810 Courtright St (45859-8022)
P.O. Box 300 (45859-0300)
PHONE..................................419 757-0110
Jason Rohrs, *
EMP: 30 EST: 2012
SALES (est): 2.42MM Privately Held
Web: www.rohrsfarms.com
SIC: 0191 General farms, primarily crop

Mcconnelsville
Morgan County

(G-10803)
MIBA BEARINGS US LLC
5037 N State Route 60 Nw (43756-9218)
PHONE..................................740 962-4242
F Peter Mitterbauer, Ch Bd
Markus Hofer, *
▲ EMP: 300 EST: 2001
SQ FT: 182,000
SALES (est): 95.82MM
SALES (corp-wide): 242.12K Privately Held
Web: www.miba.com
SIC: 5085 3365 3471 3511 Bearings; Aluminum foundries; Plating and polishing; Turbines and turbine generator sets
HQ: Mitterbauer Beteiligungs Gmbh
    Dr. Mitterbauer-StraBe 3
    Laakirchen 4663
    76132541

(G-10804)
SALO INC
109 E Main St (43756-1125)
PHONE..................................740 651-5209
EMP: 140
SALES (corp-wide): 52.16MM Privately Held
Web: www.interim-health.com
SIC: 8082 Home health care services
PA: Salo, Inc.
    300 W Wlson Brdge Rd Ste
    Columbus OH 43085
    614 436-9404

Medina
Medina County

(G-10805)
AHF OHIO INC
Also Called: Samaritan Care Center & Villa
806 E Washington St (44256)
PHONE..................................330 725-4123
Brad Willmore, Admn
EMP: 64
SALES (corp-wide): 25.83MM Privately Held
Web: www.ahfohio.com
SIC: 8051 8361 Skilled nursing care facilities ; Residential care
PA: Ahf Ohio, Inc.
    5920 Venture Dr Ste 100
    Dublin OH 43017
    614 760-7352

(G-10806)
AMERICAN SALON GROUP LLC
4081 N Jefferson St (44256-5622)
PHONE..................................330 975-0085
EMP: 65 EST: 2019
SALES (est): 740.27K Privately Held
SIC: 7231 Beauty shops

(G-10807)
AMF BOWLING CENTERS INC
Also Called: AMF
201 Harding St (44256-1636)
PHONE..................................330 725-4548
EMP: 27
SALES (corp-wide): 1.06B Publicly Held
Web: www.amf.com
SIC: 7933 Ten pin center
HQ: Amf Bowling Centers, Inc.
    7313 Bell Creek Rd
    Mechanicsville VA 23111

(G-10808)
ARMSTRONG UTILITIES INC
Also Called: Armstrong Cable Service
1141 Lafayette Rd (44256-2421)
PHONE..................................330 723-3536
Karen Troxell, Mgr
EMP: 58
Web: www.agoc.com
SIC: 1731 4841 7375 Cable television installation; Cable television services; Information retrieval services
HQ: Armstrong Utilities, Inc.
    1 Armstrong Pl
    Butler PA 16001
    724 283-0925

Medina - Medina County (G-10809) GEOGRAPHIC SECTION

(G-10809)
ATLAS TRANSPORTATION LLC
799 N Court St Ste 16 (44256-1766)
PHONE.............................202 963-4241
Diliyor Yusupov, *Managing Member*
EMP: 35 **EST:** 2018
SALES (est): 4MM **Privately Held**
SIC: 4213 Trucking, except local

(G-10810)
AUTOMTIVE RFNISH CLOR SLTONS I
2771 Sunburst Dr (44256-6494)
PHONE.............................330 461-6067
Strath Wood, *Pr*
EMP: 50 **EST:** 2016
SALES (est): 853.04K **Privately Held**
SIC: 3999 7538 Atomizers, toiletry; General automotive repair shops

(G-10811)
AVENUE AT MEDINA
699 E Smith Rd (44256-2639)
PHONE.............................330 721-7001
Deb Lougheed, *Admn*
EMP: 28 **EST:** 2014
SALES (est): 7.29MM **Privately Held**
Web: www.avenueatmedina.com
SIC: 8051 Convalescent home with continuous nursing care

(G-10812)
AVERTEST LLC
Also Called: American Court & DRG Tstg Svcs
124 N Court St (44256-1923)
PHONE.............................330 591-7219
EMP: 32
SALES (corp-wide): 12.1MM **Privately Held**
Web: www.averhealth.com
SIC: 8071 7371 Testing laboratories; Computer software development and applications
PA: Avertest, Llc
2916 W Marshall St Ste A
Richmond VA 23230
866 680-3106

(G-10813)
BACKYARD STORAGE SOLUTIONS LLC
2648 Medina Rd Unit 13 (44256-9322)
PHONE.............................330 723-4412
EMP: 68
Web: www.heartlandsheds.com
SIC: 4225 General warehousing and storage
HQ: Backyard Storage Solutions, Llc
317 S Main St Ste 600
Ann Arbor MI 48104
734 242-6900

(G-10814)
BATTERED WOMENS SHELTER
Also Called: Hope Hling Srvvor Resource Ctr
696 E Washington St Ste 1a (44256-3319)
PHONE.............................330 723-3900
Kathy Henninger, *Mgr*
EMP: 49
SALES (corp-wide): 6.35MM **Privately Held**
Web: www.hopeandhealingresources.org
SIC: 8322 Social service center
PA: Battered Women's Shelter
974 E Market St
Akron OH 44305
330 374-0740

(G-10815)
BRIDGESHOME HEALTH CARE INC
Also Called: Bridgeshome Health Care
5075 Windfall Rd (44256-8613)
PHONE.............................330 764-1000
Chris Baker, *Dir*
EMP: 267 **EST:** 2012
SALES (est): 3.39MM
SALES (corp-wide): 76.67MM **Privately Held**
SIC: 8062 8082 General medical and surgical hospitals; Home health care services
HQ: Hospice Of Medina County
5075 Windfall Rd
Medina OH 44256

(G-10816)
CAMBRIDGE HOME HEALTH CARE
Also Called: Almost Family
750 E Washington St Ste B1 (44256-2196)
PHONE.............................330 725-1968
Elaine Kithcart, *Brnch Mgr*
EMP: 713
SALES (corp-wide): 371.62B **Publicly Held**
Web: www.cambridgehomehealth.com
SIC: 8082 7361 Home health care services; Nurses' registry
HQ: Cambridge Home Health Care Inc
9510 Ormsby Station Rd # 300
Louisville KY 40223
330 270-8661

(G-10817)
CATHOLIC CHARITIES CORPORATION
Also Called: Catholic Charities
4210 N Jefferson St (44256-5639)
PHONE.............................330 723-9615
Timothy Putka, *Dir*
EMP: 79
Web: www.ccdocle.org
SIC: 8322 Social service center
PA: Catholic Charities Corporation
7911 Detroit Ave
Cleveland OH 44102

(G-10818)
CELLCO PARTNERSHIP
Also Called: Verizon
1231 N Court St (44256-1581)
PHONE.............................330 764-7380
Stacy Armstrong, *Brnch Mgr*
EMP: 71
SALES (corp-wide): 133.97B **Publicly Held**
Web: www.verizonwireless.com
SIC: 4812 Cellular telephone services
HQ: Cellco Partnership
1 Verizon Way
Basking Ridge NJ 07920

(G-10819)
CHICK MASTER INCUBATOR COMPANY (PA)
Also Called: Jamesway Chick Mstr Incubator
1093 Medina Rd (44256-8352)
PHONE.............................330 722-5591
Robert Holzer, *CEO*
Alan Shandler, *
Michael Hurd, *
Chad Daniels, *
◆ **EMP:** 89 **EST:** 1944
SALES (est): 24.34MM
SALES (corp-wide): 24.34MM **Privately Held**
Web: www.chickmaster.com
SIC: 3523 1711 Incubators and brooders, farm; Plumbing, heating, air-conditioning

(G-10820)
CHU MANAGEMENT CO INC (PA)
2875 Medina Rd (44256-9672)
PHONE.............................330 725-4571
Ding-shu Chu, *Pr*
EMP: 40 **EST:** 1984
SQ FT: 45,000
SALES (est): 9.2MM
SALES (corp-wide): 9.2MM **Privately Held**
Web: www.wyndhamhotels.com
SIC: 8741 Hotel or motel management

(G-10821)
CLARK BRANDS LLC
427 N Court St (44256-1869)
PHONE.............................330 723-9886
Al Carmen, *Prin*
EMP: 1542
SALES (corp-wide): 72.54MM **Privately Held**
Web: www.clarkbrands.com
SIC: 6794 Franchises, selling or licensing
PA: Clark Brands Llc
750 Warrenville Rd # 301
Lisle IL 60532
877 462-5275

(G-10822)
CLEVELAND EAR NOSE THROAT CTR
970 E Washington St Ste 6a (44256-2181)
PHONE.............................330 723-6673
EMP: 39
SALES (corp-wide): 4.91MM **Privately Held**
Web: my.clevelandclinic.org
SIC: 8011 Ears, nose, and throat specialist: physician/surgeon
PA: Cleveland Ear, Nose, Throat Center Inc
5400 Trnsp Blvd Ste 8
Cleveland OH 44125
216 662-3373

(G-10823)
CLEVELAND JAZZ ORCHESTRA
6027 Triple Crown Dr (44256-7475)
PHONE.............................419 908-8858
EMP: 35 **EST:** 1996
SALES (est): 252.41K **Privately Held**
Web: www.clevelandjazz.org
SIC: 7929 Orchestras or bands, nec

(G-10824)
CMBF PRODUCTS INC
111 S Elmwood Ave (44256-2207)
PHONE.............................330 725-4941
Matt Dietrich, *Pr*
EMP: 215
SALES (corp-wide): 669.66MM **Privately Held**
Web: www.carlislecbf.com
SIC: 8748 Business consulting, nec
HQ: Cmbf Products, Inc.
920 Lake Rd
Medina OH 44256

(G-10825)
CONSUMER SUPPORT SERVICES INC
2575 Medina Rd Ste A (44256-6606)
PHONE.............................330 764-4785
Barbie Knoll, *Mgr*
EMP: 74
SALES (corp-wide): 29.01MM **Privately Held**
Web: www.cssohio.org
SIC: 8059 8322 Personal care home, with health care; Individual and family services
PA: Consumer Support Services Inc
2040 Cherry Valley Rd # 1
Newark OH 43055
740 788-8257

(G-10826)
CUSTOM PERSONNEL INC
190 Highland Dr (44256-3199)
PHONE.............................330 723-4131
William A Schoenstein Junior, *CEO*
Robert Zufra, *
Nancy Normile, *
EMP: 308 **EST:** 1985
SALES (est): 8.72MM **Privately Held**
SIC: 7363 Employee leasing service

(G-10827)
CUSTOM-PAK INC
Also Called: Custompak
885 W Smith Rd (44256-2424)
PHONE.............................330 725-0800
Ronald P Camaglia, *Pr*
Frederick Camaglia, *VP*
◆ **EMP:** 65 **EST:** 1971
SQ FT: 55,000
SALES (est): 5.19MM
SALES (corp-wide): 23.28MM **Privately Held**
Web: www.custom-pak.com
SIC: 7389 Packaging and labeling services
PA: Industrial Chemical Corp.
885 W Smith Rd
Medina OH 44256
330 725-0800

(G-10828)
DIPROINDUCA (USA) LIMITED LLC
Also Called: Diproinduca USA
2528 Medina Rd (44256-8144)
PHONE.............................330 722-4442
Efrain Riera, *Pr*
Mark Heuschkel, *
▼ **EMP:** 80 **EST:** 2012
SQ FT: 4,300
SALES (est): 8.25MM **Privately Held**
Web: www.diproinduca.com
SIC: 5093 8999 4959 Metal scrap and waste materials; Earth science services; Environmental cleanup services

(G-10829)
DISCOUNT DRUG MART INC (HQ)
Also Called: Drug Mart
211 Commerce Dr (44256-1331)
PHONE.............................330 725-2340
Donald Boodjeh, *CEO*
Parviz Boodjeh, *
John Gains, *
Thomas Mcconnell, *Sr VP*
Dough Boodjeh, *
▲ **EMP:** 250 **EST:** 1968
SQ FT: 500,000
SALES (est): 497.8MM
SALES (corp-wide): 497.8MM **Privately Held**
Web: www.discount-drugmart.com
SIC: 5912 5331 5411 5451 Drug stores; Variety stores; Grocery stores; Dairy products stores
PA: Gentry Health Services, Inc.
33381 Walker Rd Ste A
Avon Lake OH 44012
330 721-1077

(G-10830)
DIVERSFIED EMPLYEE SLTIONS INC
3745 Medina Rd (44256-9510)
PHONE.............................330 764-4125
Thomas L Skeen, *Prin*
EMP: 30 **EST:** 1998
SALES (est): 2.25MM **Privately Held**
Web: www.des4you.com

GEOGRAPHIC SECTION
Medina - Medina County (G-10853)

SIC: **7361** Employment agencies

(G-10831)
DO IT BEST CORP
Also Called: Do It Best
444 Independence Dr (44256-2407)
PHONE.................................330 725-3859
Mike Patalita, *Mgr*
EMP: 251
SALES (corp-wide): 3.48B **Privately Held**
Web: www.doitbestonline.com
SIC: **5072** 5211 5251 Builders' hardware, nec
; Lumber and other building materials;
Hardware stores
PA: Do It Best Corp.
1626 Broadway Ste 100
Fort Wayne IN 46802
260 748-5300

(G-10832)
DP MEDINA HOLDINGS INC
1291 Medina Rd (44256-8135)
PHONE.................................216 254-7883
Don Peyatt, *CEO*
EMP: 35 EST: 2019
SALES (est): 2.67MM **Privately Held**
SIC: **5013** 7699 Truck parts and accessories
; Service station equipment repair

(G-10833)
FBC CHEMICAL CORPORATION
900 W Smith Rd (44256-2485)
PHONE.................................330 723-7780
Dennis Kelm, *Brnch Mgr*
EMP: 27
SALES (corp-wide): 43.14MM **Privately Held**
Web: www.fbcchem.com
SIC: **5169** Industrial chemicals
PA: Fbc Chemical Corporation
634 Route 228
Mars PA 16046
724 625-3116

(G-10834)
FECHKO EXCAVATING INC
865 W Liberty St Ste 120 (44256-1332)
PHONE.................................330 722-2890
John Fechko, *Pr*
Matthew Honigman, *
Dean Fechko, *
EMP: 70 EST: 1977
SQ FT: 4,000
SALES (est): 9.94MM **Privately Held**
Web: www.fechko.com
SIC: **1794** Excavation and grading, building construction

(G-10835)
FECHKO EXCAVATING LLC
865 W Liberty St Ste 120 (44256-1332)
PHONE.................................330 722-2890
John Fechko, *
EMP: 82 EST: 2017
SALES (est): 9.9MM **Privately Held**
Web: www.fechko.com
SIC: **1794** Excavation and grading, building construction

(G-10836)
FIORILLI CONSTRUCTION CO INC
Also Called: Fiorilli Construction
1247 Medina Rd (44256-8135)
P.O. Box 836 (44212-0836)
PHONE.................................216 696-5845
Carmen Fiorilli, *Pr*
Carmen Fiorilli, *Pr*
Jeff Troxell, *
EMP: 36 EST: 2001
SALES (est): 18.67MM **Privately Held**
Web: www.fio-con.com

SIC: **1542** Commercial and office building, new construction

(G-10837)
G J SHUE INC
Also Called: Citgo
2855 Medina Rd (44256-9672)
PHONE.................................330 722-0082
Greg J Shue, *Pr*
Christine Shue, *Sec*
EMP: 28 EST: 1980
SQ FT: 1,800
SALES (est): 2.38MM **Privately Held**
Web: www.citgo.com
SIC: **5541** 5921 7513 Filling stations, gasoline; Beer (packaged); Truck rental, without drivers

(G-10838)
GENES RFRGN HTG & AC INC
Also Called: Gene's Refrigeration
6222 Norwalk Rd (44256-9454)
PHONE.................................330 723-4104
Ralph E Tolliver, *Pr*
Emily M Berberich, *
Richard L Laribee, *
Carolyn S Byrd, *
Gene Tolliver, *
EMP: 43 EST: 1981
SQ FT: 8,600
SALES (est): 11.08MM **Privately Held**
Web: www.genesrefrigeration.com
SIC: **1711** Warm air heating and air conditioning contractor

(G-10839)
HARIOM ASSOCIATES MEDINA LLC
Also Called: Holiday Inn
2850 Medina Rd (44256-8275)
PHONE.................................330 723-4994
EMP: 88 EST: 1995
SALES (est): 370.26K **Privately Held**
Web: www.holidayinn.com
SIC: **7011** Hotels and motels

(G-10840)
HOSPICE OF MEDINA COUNTY (HQ)
Also Called: Robertson Bereavement Center
5075 Windfall Rd (44256-8613)
PHONE.................................330 725-1900
EMP: 56 EST: 1981
SALES (est): 21.16MM
SALES (corp-wide): 76.67MM **Privately Held**
Web: www.hospicewr.org
SIC: **8069** 8082 Geriatric hospital; Home health care services
PA: Hospice Of The Western Reserve, Inc.
17876 Saint Clair Ave
Cleveland OH 44110
216 383-2222

(G-10841)
HOSPICE OF THE WESTERN RESERVE
Also Called: HOSPICE OF THE WESTERN RESERVE, INC
5075 Windfall Rd (44256-8613)
PHONE.................................330 800-2240
William E Finn, *CEO*
EMP: 31
SALES (corp-wide): 76.67MM **Privately Held**
Web: www.hospicewr.org
SIC: **8082** 8069 Home health care services; Specialty hospitals, except psychiatric
PA: Hospice Of The Western Reserve, Inc.
17876 Saint Clair Ave
Cleveland OH 44110
216 383-2222

(G-10842)
HUNTINGTON NATIONAL BANK
Also Called: Firstmerit Bank
39 Public Sq Ste 100 (44256-2297)
PHONE.................................330 721-5555
Michael James, *Brnch Mgr*
EMP: 41
SALES (corp-wide): 10.84B **Publicly Held**
Web: www.huntington.com
SIC: **6029** Commercial banks, nec
HQ: The Huntington National Bank
41 S High St
Columbus OH 43215
614 480-4293

(G-10843)
HUNTINGTON NATIONAL BANK
3460 Medina Rd (44256-8296)
PHONE.................................330 723-6666
Erin Weber, *Mgr*
EMP: 36
SQ FT: 5,600
SALES (corp-wide): 10.84B **Publicly Held**
Web: www.huntington.com
SIC: **6029** Commercial banks, nec
HQ: The Huntington National Bank
41 S High St
Columbus OH 43215
614 480-4293

(G-10844)
HUNTINGTON NATIONAL BANK
125 W Washington St (44256-2232)
PHONE.................................330 722-6762
EMP: 31
SALES (corp-wide): 10.84B **Publicly Held**
Web: www.huntington.com
SIC: **6029** Commercial banks, nec
HQ: The Huntington National Bank
41 S High St
Columbus OH 43215
614 480-4293

(G-10845)
HUNTINGTON NATIONAL BANK
975 N Court St (44256-1503)
P.O. Box 805 (44258-0805)
PHONE.................................330 725-0593
Robin Robinson, *Mgr*
EMP: 31
SALES (corp-wide): 10.84B **Publicly Held**
Web: www.huntington.com
SIC: **6029** Commercial banks, nec
HQ: The Huntington National Bank
41 S High St
Columbus OH 43215
614 480-4293

(G-10846)
INDUSTRIAL CHEMICAL CORP (PA)
Also Called: Custom Pak
885 W Smith Rd (44256-2424)
PHONE.................................330 725-0800
Ron Camaglia, *Pr*
Frederick Camaglia, *
▲ EMP: 50 EST: 1946
SQ FT: 55,000
SALES (est): 23.28MM
SALES (corp-wide): 23.28MM **Privately Held**
SIC: **5169** 7389 Chemicals, industrial and heavy; Packaging and labeling services

(G-10847)
INTEGRES GLOBAL LOGISTICS INC (DH)
Also Called: Integres Fast Forward Shipping
84 Medina Rd (44256-9616)
PHONE.................................866 347-2101
R Louis Schneeberger, *Pr*
EMP: 79 EST: 2001

SQ FT: 20,954
SALES (est): 9.44MM
SALES (corp-wide): 4.43B **Publicly Held**
Web: www.arcb.com
SIC: **4213** Trucking, except local
HQ: Panther Ii Transportation, Inc.
84 Medina Rd
Medina OH 44256

(G-10848)
INTERVENTION FOR PEACE INC
Also Called: Peace Foundation
689 W Liberty St Ste 7 (44256)
PHONE.................................330 725-1298
Rick Davidson, *Mgr*
Pattie Henighan, *
EMP: 28 EST: 1999
SALES (est): 1.96MM **Privately Held**
Web: www.ifpeace.com
SIC: **8082** Visiting nurse service

(G-10849)
K & M CONSTRUCTION COMPANY
230 E Smith Rd (44256-2623)
PHONE.................................330 723-3681
Jerry A Schwab, *Pr*
David Schwab, *
Donna L Schwab, *
Mary Lynn Hites, *
EMP: 94 EST: 1944
SQ FT: 2,000
SALES (est): 2.38MM
SALES (corp-wide): 32.72B **Privately Held**
SIC: **1611** 1771 Resurfacing contractor; Driveway, parking lot, and blacktop contractors
HQ: Medina Supply Company
230 E Smith Rd
Medina OH 44256
330 723-3681

(G-10850)
KAISER FOUNDATION HOSPITALS
Also Called: Medina Medical Offices
3443 Medina Rd (44256-5360)
PHONE.................................800 524-7377
Marvin Baker, *Brnch Mgr*
EMP: 36
SALES (corp-wide): 70.8B **Privately Held**
Web: www.akronchildrens.org
SIC: **8011** Offices and clinics of medical doctors
HQ: Kaiser Foundation Hospitals Inc
1 Kaiser Plz
Oakland CA 94612
510 271-6611

(G-10851)
LANDER HOTEL GROUP LLC
387 Medina Rd Ste 600 (44256-9674)
PHONE.................................330 590-8040
Joseph C Moffa, *Prin*
EMP: 34 EST: 2007
SALES (est): 749.39K **Privately Held**
Web: www.rileyhotelgroup.com
SIC: **7011** Hotels

(G-10852)
MARK D SANDRIDGE INC
133 Commerce Dr (44256-1333)
PHONE.................................330 764-6106
Mark D Sandridge, *Pr*
EMP: 29 EST: 1984
SALES (est): 5.02MM **Privately Held**
Web: www.sandridge.com
SIC: **4213** Trucking, except local

(G-10853)
MARVIN W MIELKE INC
Also Called: Mw Mielke
1040 Industrial Pkwy (44256-2449)

PHONE....................330 725-8845
David A Mielke, Pr
Mary Anne Mielke, *
Terry Mielke, *
EMP: 100 **EST:** 1980
SQ FT: 20,000
SALES (est): 24.91MM **Privately Held**
Web: www.mwmielke.com
SIC: 1711 Plumbing contractors

(G-10854)
MEDIN-SMMIT AMBLTORY SRGERY CT
Also Called: Medina Surgery Center, The
3780 Medina Rd Ste 120 (44256-9312)
PHONE....................330 952-0014
Mister Bill Gauvignon, Pr
EMP: 27 **EST:** 2010
SALES (est): 1.42MM **Privately Held**
SIC: 8011 Physical medicine, physician/surgeon

(G-10855)
MEDINA COUNTRY CLUB LLC
5588 Wedgewood Rd (44256-8800)
PHONE....................330 725-6621
Michael J Cavey, Pt
Doctor Robert Agee, Pt
EMP: 71 **EST:** 1962
SQ FT: 15,000
SALES (est): 4.91MM **Privately Held**
Web: www.medinacc.com
SIC: 7997 Country club, membership

(G-10856)
MEDINA COUNTY
Also Called: Medina County Home
6144 Wedgewood Rd (44256-7860)
PHONE....................330 723-9553
Greg Brown, Brnch Mgr
EMP: 33
SQ FT: 33,504
SALES (corp-wide): 162.22MM **Privately Held**
Web: www.medinaco.org
SIC: 8361 9111 Rest home, with health care incidental; County supervisors' and executives' office
PA: Medina County
144 N Broadway St Ste 201
Medina OH 44256
330 723-3641

(G-10857)
MEDINA COUNTY
Also Called: Medina County Health Dept
4800 Ledgewood Dr (44256-7666)
PHONE....................330 722-9511
Krista Wasowski, Brnch Mgr
EMP: 135
SALES (corp-wide): 162.22MM **Privately Held**
Web: www.medinahealth.org
SIC: 8399 9111 Health systems agency; County supervisors' and executives' office
PA: Medina County
144 N Broadway St Ste 201
Medina OH 44256
330 723-3641

(G-10858)
MEDINA COUNTY PARK DISTRICT
6364 Deerview Ln (44256-8008)
PHONE....................330 722-9364
Nathan D Eppink, Dir
EMP: 35 **EST:** 2020
SALES (est): 2.29MM **Privately Held**
Web: www.medinacountyparks.com
SIC: 8999 Natural resource preservation service

(G-10859)
MEDINA FIBER LLC
1671 Medina Rd (44256-9655)
PHONE....................330 366-2008
Brian Snider, Prin
Rene Co Gonzalez, Prin
Lauren Co Bender, Prin
EMP: 40 **EST:** 2019
SALES (est): 2.37MM **Privately Held**
Web: www.lit-fiber.com
SIC: 4813 Internet connectivity services

(G-10860)
MEDINA HOSPITAL (PA)
1000 E Washington St (44256-2167)
PHONE....................330 725-1000
EMP: 843 **EST:** 1942
SALES (est): 39.67MM
SALES (corp-wide): 39.67MM **Privately Held**
Web: my.clevelandclinic.org
SIC: 8062 General medical and surgical hospitals

(G-10861)
MEDINA HOSPITAL
Life Support Team
1000 E Washington St (44256-2167)
PHONE....................330 723-3117
Ken Milligan, Brnch Mgr
EMP: 30
SALES (corp-wide): 39.67MM **Privately Held**
Web: my.clevelandclinic.org
SIC: 8062 General medical and surgical hospitals
PA: Medina Hospital
1000 E Washington St
Medina OH 44256
330 725-1000

(G-10862)
MEDINA MEADOWS
550 Miner Dr (44256-1472)
PHONE....................330 725-1550
Sharona Grunspan, Pr
Sam Krichevsky, *
EMP: 48 **EST:** 1981
SQ FT: 28,000
SALES (est): 4.98MM **Privately Held**
SIC: 8051 Convalescent home with continuous nursing care

(G-10863)
MEDINA MEDICAL INVESTORS LTD
Also Called: Life Care Center of Medina
2400 Columbia Rd (44256-9414)
PHONE....................330 483-3131
Forrest I Preston, Genl Pt
EMP: 89 **EST:** 1960
SQ FT: 70,000
SALES (est): 10.25MM **Privately Held**
Web: www.lcca.com
SIC: 8051 8059 Convalescent home with continuous nursing care; Rest home, with health care

(G-10864)
MEDINA SUPPLY COMPANY
820 W Smith Rd (44256-2425)
PHONE....................330 364-4411
Daryl Albright, Mgr
EMP: 45
SALES (corp-wide): 32.72B **Privately Held**
Web: www.shellyco.com
SIC: 1429 Igneus rock, crushed and broken-quarrying
HQ: Medina Supply Company
230 E Smith Rd
Medina OH 44256
330 723-3681

(G-10865)
MH LOGISTICS CORP
Also Called: M H Equipment
2575 Medina Rd (44256-6606)
PHONE....................330 425-2476
TOLL FREE: 800
Harry Bruno, Brnch Mgr
EMP: 80
SALES (corp-wide): 309.83MM **Privately Held**
Web: www.mhequipment.com
SIC: 5084 7359 Materials handling machinery; Equipment rental and leasing, nec
PA: M.H. Logistics Corp.
8901 N Industrial Rd
Peoria IL 61615
309 579-8020

(G-10866)
MIELKE HOLDINGS LLC
1040 Industrial Pkwy (44256-2449)
PHONE....................330 725-8845
EMP: 72 **EST:** 2019
SALES (est): 4.82MM **Privately Held**
Web: www.mwmielke.com
SIC: 1711 Mechanical contractor

(G-10867)
NATIONS LENDING CORPORATION
303 E Washington St (44256-2116)
PHONE....................440 785-0963
EMP: 70
SALES (corp-wide): 164.99MM **Privately Held**
Web: www.nationslending.com
SIC: 6162 Mortgage bankers
PA: Nations Lending Corporation
4 Summit Park Dr Ste 200
Independence OH 44131
216 363-6901

(G-10868)
NORTH AMERICAN DENTAL MGT LLC
2736 Medina Rd Ste 114 (44256-9801)
PHONE....................330 721-0606
EMP: 1061
SALES (corp-wide): 62.77MM **Privately Held**
Web: www.nadentalgroup.com
SIC: 8021 Dental clinic
PA: North American Dental Management, Llc
125 Enterprise Dr Ste 200
Pittsburgh PA 15275
724 698-2500

(G-10869)
NORTH GATEWAY TIRE COMPANY INC
4001 Pearl Rd (44256-9000)
PHONE....................330 725-8473
Robert H Dunlap, CEO
Darrell Hill, *
G E Mc Kittrick, *
EMP: 41 **EST:** 1979
SQ FT: 40,000
SALES (est): 2.82MM
SALES (corp-wide): 114.34MM **Privately Held**
Web: www.northgatewaytire.com
SIC: 5531 5014 Automotive tires; Automobile tires and tubes
PA: Dunlap & Kyle Company, Inc.
280 Eureka St
Batesville MS 38606
662 563-7601

(G-10870)
NURTURY
250 N Spring Grove St (44256-1921)
PHONE....................330 723-1800
Mary Kubasta, Pr
Kent Kubasta, *
EMP: 36 **EST:** 1977
SQ FT: 7,500
SALES (est): 462.06K **Privately Held**
Web: www.thenurturyschool.com
SIC: 8351 Preschool center

(G-10871)
OHIO EYE CARE CONSULTANTS LLC
3583 Reserve Commons Dr (44256-8180)
PHONE....................330 722-8300
EMP: 43 **EST:** 2003
SALES (est): 4.35MM **Privately Held**
Web: www.neohioeyes.com
SIC: 8011 Opthalmologist

(G-10872)
PANTHER II TRANSPORTATION INC (DH)
Also Called: Panther
84 Medina Rd (44256-9616)
PHONE....................800 685-0657
R Louis Schneeberger, CEO
Edward Wadel, *
David Buss, *
David Sosnowski, *
Allen Motter, *
EMP: 185 **EST:** 1992
SQ FT: 33,000
SALES (est): 51.99MM
SALES (corp-wide): 4.43B **Publicly Held**
SIC: 4213 4212 4522 Trucking, except local; Local trucking, without storage; Air transportation, nonscheduled
HQ: Panther Premium Logistics, Inc.
84 Medina Rd
Medina OH 44256

(G-10873)
PANTHER PREMIUM LOGISTICS INC (HQ)
84 Medina Rd (44256)
PHONE....................800 685-0657
R Louis Schneeberger, Pr
David Buss, *
Frank Ilacqua, *
Bob Businger, *
Edward Wadel, CIO*
EMP: 300 **EST:** 2005
SQ FT: 50,000
SALES (est): 100.75MM
SALES (corp-wide): 4.43B **Publicly Held**
Web: www.arcb.com
SIC: 4213 4212 Trucking, except local; Local trucking, without storage
PA: Arcbest Corporation
8401 Mcclure Dr
Fort Smith AR 72916
479 785-6000

(G-10874)
PARK CORPORATION (PA)
Also Called: Charleston Ordnance Center
3555 Reserve Commons Dr (44256-5900)
P.O. Box 8678 (25303-0678)
PHONE....................216 267-4870
Raymond P Park, Ch Bd
Daniel K Park, *
Shelva J Davis, *
Tim Geharing, *
Ricky L Bertrem, *
◆ **EMP:** 300 **EST:** 1948
SALES (est): 367.37MM
SALES (corp-wide): 367.37MM **Privately Held**

GEOGRAPHIC SECTION
Medina - Medina County (G-10897)

Web: www.parkcorp.com
SIC: 5084 3547 6512 7999 Industrial machinery and equipment; Rolling mill machinery; Commercial and industrial building operation; Exposition operation

(G-10875)
PEACOCK HOTELS LLC
Also Called: Red Roof Inn
5021 Eastpointe Dr (44256-8234)
PHONE..................................330 725-1395
EMP: 38 EST: 2003
SQ FT: 500
SALES (est): 928.98K **Privately Held**
Web: www.redroof.com
SIC: 7011 Hotels and motels

(G-10876)
PLASTIPAK PACKAGING INC
850 W Smith Rd (44256-2425)
PHONE..................................330 725-0205
Robert Jedreski, *Mgr*
EMP: 200
SQ FT: 60,000
SALES (corp-wide): 2.9B **Privately Held**
Web: www.plastipak.com
SIC: 5199 Packaging materials
HQ: Plastipak Packaging, Inc.
  41605 Ann Arbor Rd E
  Plymouth MI 48170
  734 455-3600

(G-10877)
PLEASANT VALLEY CNSTR CO
1093 Medina Rd Ste 100 (44256-8352)
PHONE..................................330 239-0176
Gino P Faciana, *Pr*
Barbara E Faciana, *VP*
Joseph C Tramonte, *VP*
Michael A Ricciuti, *VP*
EMP: 97 EST: 1982
SALES (est): 44.1MM **Privately Held**
Web: www.pleasantvalleycorporation.com
SIC: 1542 Commercial and office building contractors

(G-10878)
PLEASANT VALLEY CORPORATION
Also Called: National Pleasant Valley
1093 Medina Rd Ste 100 (44256-8352)
PHONE..................................330 239-0176
Gino Faciana, *CEO*
Gino P Faciana, *Pr*
Barbara E Faciana, *VP*
Joseph C Tramonte, *VP*
Michael A Ricciuti, *VP*
EMP: 85 EST: 2009
SALES (est): 7.89MM **Privately Held**
Web: www.pleasantvalleycorporation.com
SIC: 1731 1711 Electrical work; Plumbing contractors

(G-10879)
PROFESSIONAL RESTORATION SVC
Also Called: Serv Pro of Barberton/Norton
1170 Industrial Pkwy (44256-2486)
PHONE..................................330 825-1803
Michal Fosdick, *Pr*
EMP: 42 EST: 1996
SQ FT: 36,500
SALES (est): 2.21MM **Privately Held**
Web: www.servprobarbertonnorton.com
SIC: 7349 Building maintenance services, nec

(G-10880)
PSE CREDIT UNION INC
3845 Pearl Rd (44256-9001)
PHONE..................................330 661-0160
Janice L Thomas, *Brnch Mgr*
EMP: 27
SALES (corp-wide): 9.02MM **Privately Held**
Web: www.psecreditunion.org
SIC: 6061 Federal credit unions
PA: Pse Credit Union, Inc.
  5255 Regency Dr
  Cleveland OH 44129
  440 843-8300

(G-10881)
QUICKINSURED BROKERAGE
Also Called: Quickinsured Brkg A Ritter Co
1684 Medina Rd (44256-9314)
PHONE..................................330 722-7070
Lincoln T Lafayette, *Pr*
EMP: 41 EST: 2017
SALES (est): 930.74K **Privately Held**
Web: www.ritterim.com
SIC: 6282 Investment advisory service
PA: Ritter Insurance Marketing, Llc
  2605 Interstate Dr
  Harrisburg PA 17110

(G-10882)
REC CENTER
Also Called: Medina Community Recrtl Ctr
855 Weymouth Rd (44256-2039)
PHONE..................................330 721-6900
Mike Wright, *Dir*
EMP: 40 EST: 2011
SALES (est): 436.48K **Privately Held**
Web: www.medinaoh.org
SIC: 7999 Recreation center

(G-10883)
REDEFINE ENTERPRISES LLC
Also Called: Rise Fitness
3839 Pearl Rd (44256-9001)
PHONE..................................330 952-2024
Andrew Hamlin, *Managing Member*
EMP: 28 EST: 2016
SQ FT: 12,500
SALES (est): 460.23K **Privately Held**
Web: www.rise.fit
SIC: 7991 Physical fitness facilities

(G-10884)
RILEY HOTEL GROUP LLC
387 Medina Rd Ste 400 (44256-9674)
PHONE..................................330 590-8040
EMP: 37 EST: 2004
SALES (est): 2.29MM **Privately Held**
Web: www.rileyhotelgroup.com
SIC: 7011 Hotels

(G-10885)
ROMEOS PIZZA FRANCHISE LLC
Also Called: Romeo's Pizza
1113 Medina Rd Ste 200 (44256-9326)
P.O. Box 1103 (44258-1103)
PHONE..................................234 248-4549
Aubree Shockley, *Prin*
EMP: 204 EST: 2014
SALES (est): 602.75K **Privately Held**
Web: www.romeospizza.com
SIC: 5812 6794 Pizzeria, independent; Franchises, selling or licensing

(G-10886)
S&V INDUSTRIES INC (PA)
5054 Paramount Dr (44256-5363)
PHONE..................................330 666-1986
Senthil K Sundarapandian, *CEO*
Joan Owens, *
Mahesh Douglas, *
✪ EMP: 35 EST: 1993
SQ FT: 1,618
SALES (est): 12.47MM **Privately Held**
Web: www.svindustries.com

SIC: 5049 3089 3312 Engineers' equipment and supplies, nec; Casting of plastics; Forgings, iron and steel

(G-10887)
SAMARITAN CARE CENTER INC
Also Called: Samaritan Care Center
806 E Washington St (44256-2194)
PHONE..................................330 725-4123
Amy Donaldson, *Admn*
Kirk Hartline, *
Bob Banasik, *
EMP: 61 EST: 1988
SALES (est): 4.69MM
SALES (corp-wide): 14.06MM **Privately Held**
Web: www.ahfohio.com
SIC: 8059 8051 8052 Nursing home, except skilled and intermediate care facility; Skilled nursing care facilities; Intermediate care facilities
PA: Omnilife Health Care Systems, Inc.
  50 W 5th Ave
  Columbus OH 43201
  614 299-3100

(G-10888)
SANCTUARY MEDINA LLC
555 Springbrook Dr (44256-3651)
PHONE..................................330 725-3393
EMP: 28 EST: 2016
SALES (est): 4.78MM **Privately Held**
Web: www.sanctuaryhealthnetwork.com
SIC: 8051 Convalescent home with continuous nursing care

(G-10889)
SIMMONS BROTHERS CORPORATION
780 W Smith Rd Ste A (44256-3513)
PHONE..................................330 722-1415
Donald Simmons, *CEO*
William Simmons, *
David Simmons, *
EMP: 32 EST: 1959
SQ FT: 14,336
SALES (est): 6.48MM **Privately Held**
Web: www.simmonsbrothers.net
SIC: 1541 Industrial buildings, new construction, nec

(G-10890)
SISLER HEATING & COOLING INC
249 S State Rd (44256-2430)
P.O. Box 308 (44258-0308)
PHONE..................................330 722-7101
Dennis Sisler, *Pr*
Christy Meadows, *
EMP: 29 EST: 1979
SQ FT: 7,500
SALES (est): 925.8K **Privately Held**
Web: www.callgoldendays.com
SIC: 1711 1794 Ventilation and duct work contractor; Excavation work

(G-10891)
SOCIETY HANDICAPPED CITZ MEDIN
Also Called: SOCIETY FOR HANDICAPPED CITIZENS OF MEDINA COUNTY
5810 Deerview Ln (44256-8003)
PHONE..................................330 722-1710
EMP: 199
SALES (corp-wide): 9.62MM **Privately Held**
Web: www.thesocietylink.org
SIC: 1521 New construction, single-family houses
PA: Society For Handicapped Citizens Of Medina County (Inc)
  4283 Paradise Rd
  Seville OH 44273

  330 722-1900

(G-10892)
SPRAY PRODUCTS CORPORATION
1000 Lake Rd (44256-2760)
PHONE..................................610 277-1010
EMP: 52
SALES (corp-wide): 103.14MM **Privately Held**
Web: www.sprayproducts.com
SIC: 7822 Motion picture and tape distribution
PA: Spray Products Corporation
  1323 Conshohocken Rd
  Plymouth Meeting PA 19462
  610 277-1010

(G-10893)
STEINGASS MECHANICAL CONTG LLC
754 S Progress Dr (44256-1368)
PHONE..................................330 725-6090
Charles S S Slaybaugh, *CEO*
William Steingass, *Prin*
William Lesure, *Prin*
Richard Mann, *Prin*
Linda Steingass, *
EMP: 30 EST: 2018
SQ FT: 12,000
SALES (est): 9.44MM **Privately Held**
Web: www.steingassmechanical.com
SIC: 1794 1711 Excavation and grading, building construction; Plumbing contractors

(G-10894)
SUMMA HEALTH CENTER LK MEDINA
3780 Medina Rd Ste 220 (44256-9312)
PHONE..................................330 952-0014
Victoria J Meshekow, *Prin*
EMP: 62 EST: 2010
SALES (est): 9.82MM **Privately Held**
Web: www.summahealth.org
SIC: 8062 General medical and surgical hospitals

(G-10895)
SUMMIT MANAGEMENT SERVICES INC
201 Northland Dr Ofc (44256-1528)
PHONE..................................330 723-0864
EMP: 41
SALES (corp-wide): 10.56MM **Privately Held**
Web: www.summitmanagementliving.com
SIC: 6513 Apartment building operators
PA: Summit Management Services, Inc.
  730 W Market St
  Akron OH 44303
  330 762-4011

(G-10896)
SWINGLE J AND P PLUMBING & HTG
Also Called: Swingle Mechanical Contractors
645 Lafayette Rd (44256-2341)
PHONE..................................330 723-4840
John Swingle, *Pr*
Barbara Swingle, *Sec*
EMP: 32 EST: 1970
SQ FT: 13,659
SALES (est): 590.19K **Privately Held**
Web: www.swingleplumbingmedinacounty.com
SIC: 1711 Septic system construction

(G-10897)
T L C PACKAGING INC
1077 Ty Dr (44256-3061)
PHONE..................................330 722-7622

Medina - Medina County (G-10898)

Tom Cahalan, *Pr*
EMP: 35 **EST:** 1994
SQ FT: 24,000
SALES (est): 1.73MM **Privately Held**
SIC: 4783 Packing goods for shipping

(G-10898)
TEKNOBILITY LLC
3013 Gary Kyle Ct (44256-6854)
PHONE..............................216 255-9433
Carmen D Melillo, *Prin*
Carmen Melillo, *Pr*
Jeffrey Lammers, *Prin*
EMP: 45 **EST:** 2010
SALES (est): 2.34MM **Privately Held**
Web: www.teknobility.com
SIC: 7373 Computer systems analysis and design

(G-10899)
TELCOM CONSTRUCTION SVCS INC
5067 Paramount Dr (44256-5364)
PHONE..............................330 239-6900
Joe Anello, *Pr*
EMP: 85 **EST:** 1998
SQ FT: 5,000
SALES (est): 9.55MM **Privately Held**
Web: www.telcomcs.com
SIC: 4899 Communication signal enhancement network services

(G-10900)
TRUE NORTH ENERGY LLC
241 S State Rd (44256-2430)
PHONE..............................330 722-2031
Mark E Lyden, *Pr*
EMP: 84
SALES (corp-wide): 265.72MM **Privately Held**
Web: www.truenorthstores.com
SIC: 5172 5541 Gasoline; Gasoline service stations
PA: True North Energy, Llc
 10346 Brecksville Rd
 Brecksville OH 44141
 877 245-9336

(G-10901)
WELLERT CORPORATION
5136 Beach Rd (44256-9610)
PHONE..............................330 239-2699
TOLL FREE: 888
Robert L Wellert, *Pr*
EMP: 31 **EST:** 1980
SQ FT: 3,500
SALES (est): 534.83K **Privately Held**
Web: www.wellert.com
SIC: 8713 8748 8711 Surveying services; Environmental consultant; Civil engineering

(G-10902)
WERKS KRAFT ENGINEERING LLC
935 Heritage Dr (44256-2404)
PHONE..............................330 721-7374
Kris Klingmann, *Pr*
EMP: 45 **EST:** 2018
SQ FT: 60,000
SALES (est): 4.63MM **Privately Held**
Web: www.kraftwerks.com
SIC: 8711 3566 3535 3441 Engineering services; Speed changers (power transmission equipment), except auto; Conveyors and conveying equipment; Fabricated structural metal

(G-10903)
WESTERN RSRVE MSONIC CMNTY INC
4931 Nettleton Rd Apt 4318 (44256-5353)
PHONE..............................330 721-3000
EMP: 150 **EST:** 1996

SALES (est): 3.98MM
SALES (corp-wide): 9.1MM **Privately Held**
Web: www.omcoh.org
SIC: 8059 8052 8051 Rest home, with health care; Intermediate care facilities; Skilled nursing care facilities
PA: Browning Mesonic Community Inc
 8883 Browning Dr
 Waterville OH 43566
 419 878-4055

(G-10904)
WOLFF BROS SUPPLY INC (PA)
6078 Wolff Rd (44256-9499)
P.O. Box 508 (44258-0508)
PHONE..............................330 725-3451
EMP: 137 **EST:** 1950
SALES (est): 119.09MM
SALES (corp-wide): 119.09MM **Privately Held**
Web: www.wolffbros.com
SIC: 5063 5074 5075 Electrical apparatus and equipment; Plumbing fittings and supplies; Air conditioning and ventilation equipment and supplies

(G-10905)
WOOD INVESTMENT PROPERTY LLC
Also Called: Dynamerican
1011 Lake Rd (44256-2450)
PHONE..............................330 644-5100
EMP: 38 **EST:** 1957
SQ FT: 5,200
SALES (est): 1.68MM **Privately Held**
Web: www.godynamerican.com
SIC: 7699 7389 Septic tank cleaning service; Sewer inspection service

(G-10906)
ZIMOHANA LLC
1213 Medina Rd (44256-5408)
PHONE..............................330 922-4721
Amy K Zimmerman, *Prin*
EMP: 60 **EST:** 2017
SALES (est): 1.61MM **Privately Held**
SIC: 8082 Home health care services

Medway
Clark County

(G-10907)
AMERICAN SUNCRAFT CO INC
Also Called: American Suncraft Cnstr Co
10836 Schiller Rd (45341-9743)
PHONE..............................937 849-9475
Ronnie Boling, *Pr*
EMP: 41 **EST:** 1976
SQ FT: 16,500
SALES (est): 12.31MM **Privately Held**
Web: www.asuncraft.com
SIC: 7699 1521 Tank repair and cleaning services; New construction, single-family houses

Mentor
Lake County

(G-10908)
ADVANCED SOLUTIONS FOR EDUCATN
Also Called: Ivy League Academy
8303 Tyler Blvd (44060-4220)
PHONE..............................224 518-3111
Ozgur Balsoy, *CEO*
EMP: 35 **EST:** 2009
SALES (est): 1.3MM **Privately Held**
Web: www.as4ed.com

SIC: 8748 8351 Educational consultant; Child day care services

(G-10909)
AIR TECHNICAL INDUSTRIES INC
7501 Clover Ave (44060-5297)
PHONE..............................440 951-5191
Pero Novak, *CEO*
Vida Novak, *
◆ **EMP:** 40 **EST:** 1964
SQ FT: 80,000
SALES (est): 9.7MM **Privately Held**
Web: www.airtechnical.com
SIC: 3569 3536 3535 5084 Robots, assembly line: industrial and commercial; Hoists, cranes, and monorails; Bulk handling conveyor systems; Materials handling machinery

(G-10910)
ALTERCARE OF MNTOR CTR FOR RHB
9901 Johnnycake Ridge Rd (44060-6739)
PHONE..............................440 953-4421
Gerald Schroer, *Pr*
EMP: 43 **EST:** 2001
SALES (est): 403.9K **Privately Held**
Web: www.altercareonline.com
SIC: 8051 Convalescent home with continuous nursing care

(G-10911)
ANGELS IN WAITING HOME CARE
8336 Tyler Blvd (44060-4221)
PHONE..............................440 946-0349
EMP: 28
Web: www.aiwhomecare.com
SIC: 8082 Home health care services
PA: Angels In Waiting Home Care
 38052 Euclid Ave Ste 280
 Willoughby OH 44094

(G-10912)
AQUA OHIO INC
8644 Station St (44060-4316)
PHONE..............................440 255-3984
Lou Kreider, *Mgr*
EMP: 92
SALES (corp-wide): 2.05B **Publicly Held**
SIC: 4941 Water supply
HQ: Aqua Ohio, Inc.
 6650 South Ave
 Youngstown OH 44512
 330 726-8151

(G-10913)
AREA TEMPS INC
7288 Mentor Ave (44060-7578)
PHONE..............................440 975-4400
Lisa Mccoy, *Mgr*
EMP: 1547
Web: www.areatemps.com
SIC: 7363 Temporary help service
PA: Area Temps, Inc.
 4511 Rockside Rd Ste 190
 Independence OH 44131

(G-10914)
BEACON HEALTH
9220 Mentor Ave (44060-6412)
PHONE..............................440 354-9924
Spencer Kline, *CEO*
EMP: 150 **EST:** 1969
SQ FT: 14,000
SALES (est): 5.09MM **Privately Held**
Web: www.crossroadshealth.org
SIC: 8093 Mental health clinic, outpatient

(G-10915)
BUYERS PRODUCTS COMPANY (PA)
9049 Tyler Blvd (44060-4800)
PHONE..............................440 974-8888
Mark Saltzman, *Pr*
Rhonda Carder, *CFO*
◆ **EMP:** 150 **EST:** 1947
SQ FT: 172,000
SALES (est): 128.77MM
SALES (corp-wide): 128.77MM **Privately Held**
Web: www.buyersproducts.com
SIC: 5013 3714 Truck parts and accessories; Motor vehicle parts and accessories

(G-10916)
BUYERS PRODUCTS COMPANY
8200 Tyler Blvd (44060-4252)
PHONE..............................440 974-8888
EMP: 150
SALES (corp-wide): 128.77MM **Privately Held**
Web: www.buyersproducts.com
SIC: 5013 Truck parts and accessories
PA: Buyers Products Company
 9049 Tyler Blvd
 Mentor OH 44060
 440 974-8888

(G-10917)
CARDINAL COMMERCECOM INC
6119 Heisley Rd (44060-1837)
PHONE..............................440 352-8444
EMP: 50
SIC: 4813 Online service providers

(G-10918)
CARDINALCOMMERCE CORPORATION
Also Called: C C
8100 Tyler Blvd Ste 100 (44060-4887)
PHONE..............................877 352-8444
Michael Keresman Iii, *CEO*
Chandra Balasubramanian, *
Francis Sherwin, *
Eric Goodman, *
Jeffrey Neville, *
EMP: 60 **EST:** 2009
SALES (est): 21.03MM **Privately Held**
Web: www.cardinalcommerce.com
SIC: 7361 Employment agencies

(G-10919)
CBKB INC
Also Called: Hvac
8669 Twinbrook Rd (44060-4340)
P.O. Box 661 (44061-0661)
PHONE..............................440 946-6019
Cary Burrier, *Pr*
Kevin Barry, *
EMP: 30 **EST:** 1976
SQ FT: 6,400
SALES (est): 2MM **Privately Held**
Web: www.burrierservice.com
SIC: 1711 Warm air heating and air conditioning contractor

(G-10920)
CHARTER HOTEL GROUP LTD PARTNR (PA)
Also Called: Courtyard By Marriott
5966 Heisley Rd (44060-1886)
PHONE..............................216 772-4538
EMP: 35 **EST:** 1994
SQ FT: 2,500
SALES (est): 2.22MM **Privately Held**
Web: courtyard.marriott.com
SIC: 7011 5812 Hotels and motels; Eating places

GEOGRAPHIC SECTION
Mentor - Lake County (G-10943)

(G-10921)
CHILDRENS DNTL SPCLSTS LK CNTY
8484 Market St (44060-4169)
PHONE..................................440 266-1740
Dennis Beeson, *Pr*
EMP: 35 **EST:** 1969
SALES (est): 642.86K **Privately Held**
SIC: 8021 Dentists' office

(G-10922)
CLASSIC AUTOMOTIVE GROUP INC
Also Called: Classic Chevrolet
6877 Center St (44060-4233)
P.O. Box 300 (44061-0300)
PHONE..................................440 255-5511
EMP: 33
Web: www.bmwgroup.com
SIC: 5511 7538 7515 Automobiles, new and used; General automotive repair shops; Passenger car leasing
PA: Classic Automotive Group Inc.
2571 Some Ctr
Wellington OH 44090

(G-10923)
CLEVELAND CONSTRUCTION INC (PA)
Also Called: CCI
8620 Tyler Blvd (44060-4348)
PHONE..................................440 255-8000
Jon Small, *Pr*
Mark T Small, *
Keith Ziegler, *
James Small, *
▲ **EMP:** 50 **EST:** 1980
SQ FT: 42,500
SALES (est): 426.33MM
SALES (corp-wide): 426.33MM **Privately Held**
Web: www.clevelandconstruction.com
SIC: 1542 1742 1752 Commercial and office building contractors; Plastering, plain or ornamental; Floor laying and floor work, nec

(G-10924)
CLS FACILITIES MGT SVCS INC
Also Called: Cls Facilities Management Svcs
8061 Tyler Blvd (44060-4809)
PHONE..................................440 602-4600
Robert A Waldrip, *Pr*
Bill Brodnick, *
EMP: 37 **EST:** 1987
SQ FT: 10,000
SALES (est): 12.71MM **Privately Held**
Web: www.clsfacilityservices.com
SIC: 5063 1731 Lighting fixtures, commercial and industrial; Lighting contractor

(G-10925)
COMPONENT REPAIR TECHNOLOGIES INC
Also Called: C R T
8507 Tyler Blvd (44060-4231)
P.O. Box 305 (44061-0305)
PHONE..................................440 255-1793
EMP: 400 **EST:** 1985
SALES (est): 31.25MM **Privately Held**
Web: www.componentrepair.com
SIC: 7699 Aircraft and heavy equipment repair services

(G-10926)
CONVENIENT FOOD MART INC (HQ)
Also Called: Convenient Food Mart
6078 Pinecone Dr (44060-1865)
PHONE..................................800 860-8844
John Call, *Pr*
EMP: 30 **EST:** 1958
SQ FT: 12,000
SALES (est): 10.42MM **Privately Held**
Web: www.convenientfoodmart.com
SIC: 5411 5541 6794 Convenience stores, chain; Filling stations, gasoline; Franchises, selling or licensing
PA: Wanacs Corp.
467 N State St
Painesville OH 44077

(G-10927)
COUNTY OF LAKE
Also Called: Deepwood Center
8121 Deepwood Blvd (44060-7703)
PHONE..................................440 350-5100
Elfriede Roman, *Superintnt*
EMP: 87
SALES (corp-wide): 219.71MM **Privately Held**
Web: www.lakebdd.org
SIC: 8331 Job training and related services
PA: County Of Lake
8 N State St Ste 215
Painesville OH 44077
440 350-2500

(G-10928)
CROSSCOUNTRY MORTGAGE LLC
9179 Mentor Ave Ste H (44060-6476)
PHONE..................................440 413-0867
EMP: 56
SALES (corp-wide): 803.24MM **Privately Held**
Web: www.crosscountrymortgage.com
SIC: 6162 Mortgage bankers and loan correspondents
PA: Crosscountry Mortgage, Llc
6850 Miller Rd
Brecksville OH 44141
440 845-3700

(G-10929)
CROSSROADS HEALTH (PA)
8445 Munson Rd (44060-2410)
PHONE..................................440 255-1700
Shayna Jackson, *Pr*
Kenneth Iwashita, *
EMP: 100 **EST:** 1984
SALES (est): 8.28MM
SALES (corp-wide): 8.28MM **Privately Held**
Web: www.crossroadshealth.org
SIC: 8093 8322 8011 Mental health clinic, outpatient; Individual and family services; Offices and clinics of medical doctors

(G-10930)
CT CONSULTANTS INC (PA)
8150 Sterling Ct (44060-5698)
PHONE..................................440 951-9000
David Wiles, *Pr*
EMP: 128 **EST:** 1922
SQ FT: 24,000
SALES (est): 34.37MM
SALES (corp-wide): 34.37MM **Privately Held**
Web: www.ctconsultants.com
SIC: 8713 8711 8712 Surveying services; Civil engineering; Architectural services

(G-10931)
D & S CUSTOM VAN INC
Also Called: D & S Auto Collision Restyling
7588 Tyler Blvd (44060-4871)
PHONE..................................440 946-2178
Carmen Paterniti, *Pr*
EMP: 31 **EST:** 1977
SQ FT: 34,000
SALES (est): 4.39MM **Privately Held**
Web: www.dsautomotive.com
SIC: 7538 General automotive repair shops

(G-10932)
DCR SYSTEMS LLC (PA)
Also Called: Classic Accident Repair Center
8697 Tyler Blvd (44060-4346)
PHONE..................................440 205-9900
EMP: 40 **EST:** 2004
SALES (est): 8.83MM
SALES (corp-wide): 8.83MM **Privately Held**
Web: www.dcrsystems.com
SIC: 7538 General automotive repair shops

(G-10933)
DEEPWOOD INDUSTRIES INC
8121 Deepwood Blvd (44060-7703)
PHONE..................................440 350-5231
EMP: 181 **EST:** 1962
SALES (est): 1.04MM **Privately Held**
Web: www.deepwoodindustries.com
SIC: 8322 8331 7331 Settlement house; Job training and related services; Direct mail advertising services

(G-10934)
E2B TEKNOLOGIES INC (PA)
Also Called: Anytime Collect
9325 Progress Pkwy # A (44060-1855)
PHONE..................................440 352-4700
William Henslee, *Pr*
EMP: 44 **EST:** 2001
SALES (est): 9.8MM
SALES (corp-wide): 9.8MM **Privately Held**
Web: www.e2btek.com
SIC: 7379 Computer related consulting services

(G-10935)
ELECTRO-ANALYTICAL INC
Also Called: E A Group
7118 Industrial Park Blvd (44060-5314)
PHONE..................................440 951-3514
Patrick G Herbert, *Pr*
Jeffrey A Herbert, *
Timothy S Bowen, *
EMP: 31 **EST:** 1982
SQ FT: 7,700
SALES (est): 4.87MM **Privately Held**
Web: www.eagroupohio.com
SIC: 8734 Testing laboratories

(G-10936)
EMPIRE DENTAL ARTS LLC (PA)
9140 Lake Shore Blvd (44060-1637)
PHONE..................................216 410-1331
Todd Russell, *CEO*
EMP: 27 **EST:** 2017
SALES (est): 2.32MM
SALES (corp-wide): 2.32MM **Privately Held**
Web: www.empiredentalarts.com
SIC: 8021 Dentists' office

(G-10937)
ENTERPRISE DOOR & SUPPLY INC
Also Called: Enterprise Door & Supply Co.
7673 Saint Clair Ave (44060-5235)
P.O. Box 360 (44061-0360)
PHONE..................................440 942-3478
Timothy Evanko, *Managing Member*
Timothy Evanko, *Pr*
Carl Loebig, *
EMP: 30 **EST:** 1980
SALES (est): 5.18MM **Privately Held**
Web: www.enterprisedoor.com
SIC: 5031 Windows

(G-10938)
EUCLID FISH COMPANY
7839 Enterprise Dr (44060-5386)
P.O. Box 180 (44061-0180)
PHONE..................................440 951-6448
Charles L Young, *Ch Bd*
John Young, *
Marilyn G Young, *
EMP: 66 **EST:** 1944
SQ FT: 18,000
SALES (est): 23.43MM **Privately Held**
Web: www.euclidfish.com
SIC: 5141 5142 5143 5144 Food brokers; Packaged frozen goods; Dairy products, except dried or canned; Poultry and poultry products

(G-10939)
EYE LIGHTING INTL N AMER INC
9150 Hendricks Rd (44060-2146)
P.O. Box 150 (44061-0150)
PHONE..................................440 350-7000
Greg Barry, *Pr*
Tom Salpietra, *
Marcus Tuttle, *
▲ **EMP:** 170 **EST:** 1991
SQ FT: 100,000
SALES (est): 46.99MM
SALES (corp-wide): 2.96B **Publicly Held**
SIC: 5063 Lighting fixtures
HQ: Iwasaki Electric Co., Ltd.
1-1-7, Higashinihombashi
Chuo-Ku TKY 103-0

(G-10940)
FULTON & ASSOC BALANCE CO LLC
9045 Osborne Dr (44060-4326)
PHONE..................................440 943-9450
EMP: 44 **EST:** 2000
SALES (est): 1.97MM **Privately Held**
Web: www.integratesting.com
SIC: 8711 Heating and ventilation engineering

(G-10941)
GENERATOR ONE LLC
7487 Tyler Blvd (44060-5401)
PHONE..................................440 942-8449
EMP: 50 **EST:** 2013
SALES (est): 7.05MM **Privately Held**
Web: www.protectingyourpower.com
SIC: 5063 7629 1731 Generators; Generator repair; Electric power systems contractors

(G-10942)
GENOMONCOLOGY LLC
4790 Farley Dr (44060-1000)
PHONE..................................440 617-6087
Bradley Wertz, *Dir*
Victor Peroni, *CFO*
Garreth Hippe, *CCO*
Manuel J Glynias, *CEO*
Ian Maurer, *VP*
EMP: 36 **EST:** 2012
SALES (est): 4.97MM **Privately Held**
Web: www.genomoncology.com
SIC: 7371 Computer software systems analysis and design, custom

(G-10943)
GREAT LAKES POWER PRODUCTS INC (PA)
Also Called: John Deere Authorized Dealer
7455 Tyler Blvd (44060-8389)
PHONE..................................440 951-5111
Harry Allen Junior, *CEO*
Harry L Allen Junior, *Ch Bd*
Richard J Pennza, *
David Bell, *
Sam Profio, *
▲ **EMP:** 60 **EST:** 1973
SQ FT: 55,000
SALES (est): 27.96MM
SALES (corp-wide): 27.96MM **Privately Held**

Mentor - Lake County (G-10944)

Web: www.glpower.com
SIC: 5085 5084 3566 Power transmission equipment and apparatus; Materials handling machinery; Speed changers (power transmission equipment), except auto

(G-10944)
GREAT LAKES-RAMCO INC
7455 Tyler Blvd (44060-5401)
PHONE...................586 759-5500
Harry L Allen Junior, *Pr*
Harry L Allen Iii, *VP*
Richard J Pennza, *
EMP: 44 **EST:** 1958
SQ FT: 22,000
SALES (est): 3.67MM
SALES (corp-wide): 23.26MM **Privately Held**
Web: www.glpower.com
SIC: 5013 7699 Automotive supplies and parts; Industrial truck repair
PA: Great Lakes Power Service Co.
7455 Tyler Blvd
Mentor OH 44060
440 951-5111

(G-10945)
HANK BLOOM SERVICES INC
Also Called: Environmental Conditioning Sys
7567 Tyler Blvd (44060-4869)
PHONE...................440 946-7823
EMP: 30
SIC: 1711 Warm air heating and air conditioning contractor

(G-10946)
HENRY J FIORITTO DDS INC
6303 Center St (44060-2467)
PHONE...................440 951-5511
Henry J Fioritto D.d.s., *Pr*
EMP: 48 **EST:** 1970
SALES (est): 2.19MM **Privately Held**
Web: www.fiorittodental.com
SIC: 8021 Dentists' office

(G-10947)
HOLIDAY INN
7701 Reynolds Rd (44060-5320)
PHONE...................440 951-7333
Robert Mangano, *Prin*
EMP: 39 **EST:** 2009
SALES (est): 426.92K **Privately Held**
Web: www.holidayinn.com
SIC: 7011 Hotels and motels

(G-10948)
HOLIDAY INN EX HT STES LAMALFA
Also Called: Holiday Inn
5785 Heisley Rd (44060-1883)
PHONE...................440 357-0384
FAX: 440 357-0560
EMP: 30
SQ FT: 111,000
SALES (est): 1.54MM **Privately Held**
SIC: 7011 Hotels and motels

(G-10949)
HOME DEPOT USA INC
Also Called: Home Depot, The
9615 Diamond Centre Dr (44060)
PHONE...................440 357-0428
Gregory L Loney, *Store Mgr*
EMP: 135
SALES (corp-wide): 152.67B **Publicly Held**
Web: www.homedepot.com
SIC: 5211 7359 Home centers; Tool rental
HQ: Home Depot U.S.A., Inc.
2445 Springfield Ave
Vauxhall NJ 07088

(G-10950)
HZW ENVIRONMENTAL CONS LLC (PA)
6105 Heisley Rd (44060-1837)
PHONE...................800 804-8484
Phillip Shrout, *
Seline Griffith, *
EMP: 27 **EST:** 1987
SQ FT: 4,400
SALES (est): 4.11MM **Privately Held**
Web: www.hzwenv.com
SIC: 8748 Environmental consultant

(G-10951)
INSIGHT CUNSELING WELLNESS LLC
8031 Middlesex Rd (44060-7621)
PHONE...................330 635-0638
Shellie Rozic, *Prin*
EMP: 35 **EST:** 2018
SALES (est): 610.74K **Privately Held**
Web: www.insightcounselingoh.com
SIC: 8099 Health and allied services, nec

(G-10952)
INTEGRA SVCS INTERMEDIATE LLC
9045 Osborne Dr (44060-4326)
PHONE...................317 409-2130
Travis Nichols, *Managing Member*
EMP: 301 **EST:** 2021
SALES (est): 50MM **Privately Held**
SIC: 1711 Heating systems repair and maintenance

(G-10953)
ISOMEDIX OPERATIONS INC (DH)
5960 Heisley Rd (44060-1834)
PHONE...................877 783-7497
Walter Rosebrough, *CEO*
Karen L Burton, *VP*
Michael J Tokich, *VP*
Ronald E Snyder, *Sec*
Dennis P Patton, *Sec*
EMP: 99 **EST:** 1986
SQ FT: 5,000
SALES (est): 112.23MM **Privately Held**
Web: www.steris.com
SIC: 8734 Testing laboratories
HQ: Steris Corporation
5960 Heisley Rd
Mentor OH 44060
440 354-2600

(G-10954)
JANCE & COMPANY INCORPORATED
8666 Tyler Blvd (44060-4327)
PHONE...................440 255-5800
Paul A Jance, *Pr*
Evelyn Kuzilla, *
EMP: 35 **EST:** 1970
SQ FT: 6,000
SALES (est): 1.67MM **Privately Held**
SIC: 8741 1541 1542 Construction management; Industrial buildings and warehouses; Nonresidential construction, nec

(G-10955)
JIM BROWN CHEVROLET INC (PA)
6877 Center St (44060-4233)
P.O. Box 300 (44061-0300)
PHONE...................440 255-5511
James Brown, *Pr*
Frank Lakava, *
Jeff Fortuna, *
EMP: 175 **EST:** 1979
SQ FT: 47,000
SALES (est): 32.23MM
SALES (corp-wide): 32.23MM **Privately Held**

Web: www.chevrolet.com
SIC: 5511 7515 Automobiles, new and used; Passenger car leasing

(G-10956)
JTO CLUB CORP
Also Called: Mentor Hsley Rcquet Fitnes CLB
6011 Heisley Rd (44060-1867)
PHONE...................440 352-1900
Maureen Osborne, *CEO*
Jerome Osborne, *
EMP: 32 **EST:** 1971
SQ FT: 70,000
SALES (est): 942.89K
SALES (corp-wide): 34.91MM **Privately Held**
Web: www.jtoinc.com
SIC: 7991 Health club
PA: T O J Inc
6011 Heisley Rd
Mentor OH 44060
440 352-1900

(G-10957)
JUST IN TIME STAFFING INC
8130 Tyler Blvd (44060-4852)
PHONE...................440 205-2002
EMP: 115
Web: www.jits.jobs
SIC: 7361 Employment agencies
PA: Just In Time Staffing, Inc.
8200 Tyler Blvd
Mentor OH 44060

(G-10958)
KAISER FOUNDATION HOSPITALS
Also Called: Mentor Medical Offices
7695 Mentor Ave (44060-5540)
PHONE...................800 524-7377
EMP: 33
SALES (corp-wide): 70.8B **Privately Held**
Web: www.kaisercenter.com
SIC: 8011 Offices and clinics of medical doctors
HQ: Kaiser Foundation Hospitals Inc
1 Kaiser Plz
Oakland CA 94612
510 271-6611

(G-10959)
LAKE COUNTY COUNCIL ON AGING (PA)
8520 East Ave (44060-4302)
PHONE...................440 205-8111
Joseph R Tomsick, *CEO*
Edgar Barnett Junior, *Ex Dir*
EMP: 35 **EST:** 1972
SALES (est): 2.74MM
SALES (corp-wide): 2.74MM **Privately Held**
Web: www.lccoa.org
SIC: 8322 Senior citizens' center or association

(G-10960)
LAKE COUNTY GENERAL HEALTH DST
5966 Heisley Rd (44060-5849)
PHONE...................440 350-2543
EMP: 58
SALES (est): 6.42MM **Privately Held**
Web: www.lcghd.org
SIC: 8621 Health association

(G-10961)
LAKE HOSPITAL SYSTEM INC
9485 Mentor Ave (44060-4597)
PHONE...................440 255-8133
EMP: 107
SALES (corp-wide): 878.24MM **Privately Held**

Web: www.macyfamilydentistry.com
SIC: 8021 Dentists' office
HQ: Lake Hospital System, Inc.
7590 Auburn Rd
Concord Township OH 44077
440 375-8100

(G-10962)
LAKE HOSPITAL SYSTEM INC
8316 Yellowbrick Rd (44060-4960)
PHONE...................440 205-8818
Harold Thomas, *Pr*
EMP: 107
SALES (corp-wide): 878.24MM **Privately Held**
Web: www.uhhospitals.org
SIC: 8062 General medical and surgical hospitals
HQ: Lake Hospital System, Inc.
7590 Auburn Rd
Concord Township OH 44077
440 375-8100

(G-10963)
LAWNFIELD MENTOR LLC
Also Called: Lawnfield Inn and Suites
8434 Mentor Ave (44060-5817)
PHONE...................440 205-7378
EMP: 50 **EST:** 1999
SQ FT: 1,375
SALES (est): 968.83K **Privately Held**
SIC: 7011 Hotels and motels

(G-10964)
LIFESERVICES MANAGEMENT CORP
Also Called: Salidawoods
7685 Lake Shore Blvd (44060-3359)
PHONE...................440 257-3866
Karen Harrell, *Genl Mgr*
EMP: 85
Web: www.npseniorliving.com
SIC: 8399 8052 Community development groups; Intermediate care facilities
PA: Lifeservices Management Corporation
1625 Lowell Ave
Erie PA 16505

(G-10965)
LOWES HOME CENTERS LLC
Also Called: Lowe's
9600 Mentor Ave (44060-4529)
PHONE...................440 392-0027
Brian Braunstien, *Mgr*
EMP: 143
SALES (corp-wide): 86.38B **Publicly Held**
Web: www.lowes.com
SIC: 5211 5031 5722 5064 Home centers; Building materials, exterior; Household appliance stores; Electrical appliances, television and radio
HQ: Lowe's Home Centers, Llc
1000 Lowes Blvd
Mooresville NC 28117
336 658-4000

(G-10966)
MATERIALS MGT MICROSYSTEMS
Also Called: Microsystems
5960 Heisley Rd (44060-1834)
PHONE...................262 240-9900
Ed Becker, *Pr*
Janet Becker, *
EMP: 70 **EST:** 1991
SALES (est): 11.65MM **Privately Held**
Web: www.steris.com
SIC: 7371 Computer software development

(G-10967)
MCDOWELL HOMES LLC
Also Called: McDowell Homes RE Svcs
6272 Center St (44060-8608)

GEOGRAPHIC SECTION
Mentor - Lake County (G-10989)

PHONE..............................440 205-2000
Kayleen Mcdowell, *Prin*
EMP: 45 **EST:** 2015
SALES (est): 985.91K **Privately Held**
Web: www.mcdhomes.com
SIC: 6531   Real estate agent, residential

(G-10968)
MENTOR EXEMPTED VLG SCHL DST
Also Called: Mentor School Service Trnsp
7060 Hopkins Rd (44060-4487)
PHONE..............................440 974-5260
Karen Gerardi, *Dir*
EMP: 56
SALES (corp-wide): 95.62MM **Privately Held**
Web: www.mentorschools.net
SIC: 4151   School buses
PA: Mentor Exempted Village School District
  6451 Center St
  Mentor OH 44060
  440 255-4444

(G-10969)
MENTOR HOSPITALITY LLC
Also Called: Holiday Inn Clvland Nrthst-Mnt
7701 Reynolds Rd (44060-5320)
PHONE..............................440 951-7333
Kiran Patel, *Prin*
EMP: 40 **EST:** 2016
SALES (est): 1.05MM **Privately Held**
Web: www.holidayinn.com
SIC: 7011   Hotels and motels

(G-10970)
MENTOR LUMBER AND SUPPLY CO (PA)
Also Called: Mentor Wholesale Lumber
7180 Center St (44060)
P.O. Box 599 (44061)
PHONE..............................440 255-8814
Reed H Martin, *Pr*
Jerome T Osborne, *
Mack Stewart, *
Barbie Rita, *
EMP: 120 **EST:** 1922
SQ FT: 100,000
SALES (est): 43.83MM
SALES (corp-wide): 43.83MM **Privately Held**
Web: www.mentorlumber.com
SIC: 5031 5211   Lumber: rough, dressed, and finished; Lumber and other building materials

(G-10971)
MENTOR SENIOR LIVING LLC
Also Called: Danbury Mentor
9150 Lake Shore Blvd (44060-1672)
PHONE..............................440 701-4560
William J Lemmon, *Prin*
EMP: 67 **EST:** 2017
SALES (est): 1.15MM **Privately Held**
SIC: 8361   Residential care

(G-10972)
MENTOR SURGERY CENTER LTD
9485 Mentor Ave Ste 1 (44060-8711)
PHONE..............................440 205-5725
EMP: 50 **EST:** 1995
SALES (est): 9.33MM **Privately Held**
Web: www.mentorsurgery.com
SIC: 8011   Ambulatory surgical center

(G-10973)
MICHAELS INC
Also Called: Lamalfa Party Center
5783 Heisley Rd (44060-1883)
PHONE..............................440 357-0384
Michael Lamalfa Senior, *Pr*
Martin Lamalfa, *
EMP: 77 **EST:** 1972
SQ FT: 36,000
SALES (est): 3.31MM **Privately Held**
Web: www.lamalfa.com
SIC: 7299   Banquet hall facilities

(G-10974)
MILL ROSE LABORATORIES INC
7310 Corp Blvd (44060)
PHONE..............................440 974-6730
Paul M Miller, *Pr*
Stephen W Kovalcheck Junior, *CFO*
Lawrence W Miller, *
▲ **EMP:** 40 **EST:** 1977
SQ FT: 59,000
SALES (est): 6.27MM
SALES (corp-wide): 24.82MM **Privately Held**
Web: www.millroselabs.com
SIC: 3991 5047   Brooms and brushes; Medical equipment and supplies
PA: The Mill-Rose Company
  7995 Tyler Blvd
  Mentor OH 44060
  440 255-9171

(G-10975)
MILL-ROSE COMPANY (PA)
Also Called: Mill-Rose
7995 Tyler Blvd (44060-4896)
PHONE..............................440 255-9171
Paul M Miller, *Pr*
Lawrence W Miller, *
Diane Miller, *
▲ **EMP:** 160 **EST:** 1920
SQ FT: 61,000
SALES (est): 24.82MM
SALES (corp-wide): 24.82MM **Privately Held**
Web: www.millrose.com
SIC: 3841 5085 3991 3624   Surgical instruments and apparatus; Industrial supplies; Brushes, household or industrial; Carbon and graphite products

(G-10976)
MONODE MARKING PRODUCTS INC (PA)
Also Called: Lectroetch Company, The
9200 Tyler Blvd (44060-1882)
PHONE..............................440 975-8802
Tom Mackey, *Pr*
EMP: 45 **EST:** 1956
SQ FT: 15,000
SALES (est): 9.29MM
SALES (corp-wide): 9.29MM **Privately Held**
Web: www.monode.com
SIC: 3542 5084   Marking machines; Printing trades machinery, equipment, and supplies

(G-10977)
MOVING SOLUTIONS INC
Also Called: Great Lakes Record Center
8001 Moving Way (44060-4898)
PHONE..............................440 946-9300
William Tyers, *Pr*
Lynne Mazeika, *
Verne Mccelland, *Sec*
▲ **EMP:** 60 **EST:** 1976
SQ FT: 100,000
SALES (est): 14.48MM **Privately Held**
Web: www.yourmovingsolutions.com
SIC: 4214 4731   Local trucking with storage; Freight transportation arrangement

(G-10978)
MWD LOGISTICS INC
7236 Justin Way (44060-4881)
PHONE..............................440 266-2500
Rob Dibble, *Prin*
EMP: 35
SALES (corp-wide): 24.64MM **Privately Held**
Web: www.mwdlogistics.com
SIC: 4225   General warehousing
PA: Mwd Logistics, Inc.
  222 Tappan Dr N
  Ontario OH 44906
  419 522-3510

(G-10979)
NEW CINGULAR WIRELESS SVCS INC
Also Called: AT&T
7701 Mentor Ave (44060-5446)
PHONE..............................440 975-8304
Stephen Babbitt, *Mgr*
EMP: 38
SALES (corp-wide): 122.43B **Publicly Held**
SIC: 4812   Cellular telephone services
HQ: New Cingular Wireless Services, Inc.
  7277 164th Ave Ne
  Redmond WA 98052
  425 827-4500

(G-10980)
NORTHWEST COUNTRY PLACE INC
7177 Industrial Park Blvd (44060-5327)
PHONE..............................440 488-2700
Thomas A Armagno, *Brnch Mgr*
EMP: 159
Web: www.nwcpinc.com
SIC: 8742   Management consulting services
PA: Northwest Country Place Inc
  9223 Amber Wood Dr
  Willoughby OH 44094

(G-10981)
OMNI CART SERVICES INC
Also Called: Ohio Carts
7370 Production Dr (44060-4859)
P.O. Box 366 (44061-0366)
PHONE..............................440 205-8363
Keith Woolf, *Pr*
Joel Levin, *Stockholder*
William Jacobson, *
EMP: 35 **EST:** 1983
SQ FT: 10,000
SALES (est): 4.79MM **Privately Held**
Web: www.ocserv.com
SIC: 7699   Shopping cart repair

(G-10982)
PAG MENTOR A1 INC
Also Called: Audi Willoughby
8599 Market St (44060-4124)
PHONE..............................440 951-1040
TOLL FREE: 800
Jerry Severin, *
▲ **EMP:** 29 **EST:** 1957
SQ FT: 22,000
SALES (est): 14.21MM **Privately Held**
Web: www.stoddard.com
SIC: 5511 5013   Automobiles, new and used; Automotive supplies and parts

(G-10983)
PALADINA HEALTH LLC
Also Called: PALADINA HEALTH, LLC
7695 Mentor Ave (44060-5540)
PHONE..............................440 368-0900
EMP: 30
SALES (corp-wide): 478.59MM **Privately Held**
Web: www.eversidehealth.com
SIC: 8099   Childbirth preparation clinic
HQ: Everside Health, Llc
  1400 Wewatta St Ste 350
  Denver CO 80202
  866 808-6005

(G-10984)
PLATFORM CEMENT INC
Also Called: Platform Contracting
7503 Tyler Blvd (44060-5403)
PHONE..............................440 602-9750
Jason Klar, *Pr*
Elizabeth Bechkowiak, *
Sally Murphy, *
EMP: 35 **EST:** 1991
SQ FT: 1,000
SALES (est): 4.86MM **Privately Held**
Web: www.platformcontracting.com
SIC: 1771   Concrete work

(G-10985)
PRINCETON TOOL INC (PA)
Also Called: Princeton Precision Group
7830 Division Dr (44060)
P.O. Box 508 (44061)
PHONE..............................440 290-8666
Kenneth Bevington Iii, *CEO*
▲ **EMP:** 135 **EST:** 1997
SALES (est): 20.3MM
SALES (corp-wide): 20.3MM **Privately Held**
Web: www.princetontool.com
SIC: 3599 5084   Machine shop, jobbing and repair; Tool and die makers equipment

(G-10986)
PRUDENTIAL SELECT PROPERTIES (PA)
Also Called: Century 21
7395 Center St (44060-5801)
PHONE..............................440 255-1111
Frank Kaim, *Pr*
Jane Kaim, *
EMP: 65 **EST:** 1975
SQ FT: 6,000
SALES (est): 2.07MM
SALES (corp-wide): 2.07MM **Privately Held**
Web: www.century21.com
SIC: 6531   Real estate agent, residential

(G-10987)
RAYMOND A GREINER DDS INC
Also Called: Greiner Dental & Associates
7553 Center St (44060-6001)
PHONE..............................440 951-6688
Marcia Tupa D.d.s., *Mgr*
James N Greiner D.d.s., *VP*
Steven H Greiner D.d.s., *VP*
EMP: 28 **EST:** 1954
SQ FT: 4,000
SALES (est): 270.14K **Privately Held**
Web: www.drgv.net
SIC: 8021   Dentists' office

(G-10988)
RB SIGMA LLC
6111 Heisley Rd (44060-1837)
PHONE..............................440 290-0577
EMP: 85 **EST:** 2016
SALES (est): 34.04MM **Privately Held**
Web: www.rbsigma.com
SIC: 8741 5047 3999 5734   Management services; Medical equipment and supplies; Barber and beauty shop equipment; Software, business and non-game

(G-10989)
RED GROUP LIMITED
7314 Lake Shore Blvd (44060-3030)
P.O. Box 60 (44061-0060)
PHONE..............................440 256-1268
EMP: 30
SALES (est): 1.07MM **Privately Held**
SIC: 7389   Business services, nec

Mentor - Lake County (G-10990)

(G-10990)
REGISTERED CONTRACTORS INC
8425 Station St (44060-4924)
PHONE..............................440 205-0873
Edward A Krevas, *CEO*
Livio Stipcic, *Pr*
EMP: 28 **EST:** 1992
SQ FT: 7,000
SALES (est): 1.22MM **Privately Held**
Web: www.registeredcontractors.com
SIC: 1541 1542 1521 Industrial buildings and warehouses; Commercial and office building contractors; Single-family housing construction

(G-10991)
RELIABLE RNNERS CURIER SVC INC
8624 Station St (44060-4316)
PHONE..............................440 578-1011
Marc P Coben, *Pr*
EMP: 40 **EST:** 1985
SQ FT: 2,800
SALES (est): 5.5MM **Privately Held**
Web: www.rrunners.com
SIC: 4225 General warehousing and storage

(G-10992)
RESIDENCE INN BY MARRIOTT LLC
Also Called: Marriott
5660 Emerald Ct (44060-1869)
PHONE..............................440 392-0800
EMP: 31
SALES (corp-wide): 23.71B **Publicly Held**
Web: www.marriott.com
SIC: 7011 Hotels and motels
HQ: Residence Inn By Marriott, Llc
10400 Fernwood Rd
Bethesda MD 20817

(G-10993)
RUNYON & SONS ROOFING INC
8745 Munson Rd (44060-4323)
PHONE..............................440 974-6810
Clyde Runyon Junior, *Pr*
Tom Runyon, *
EMP: 60 **EST:** 1977
SALES (est): 18.21MM **Privately Held**
Web: www.runyonroofing.com
SIC: 1522 1542 1521 Multi-family dwelling construction, nec; Commercial and office building contractors; Single-family home remodeling, additions, and repairs

(G-10994)
RUSTIC PATHWAYS LLC
6082 Pinecone Dr (44060-1865)
PHONE..............................440 497-4166
Shayne Fitz-coy, *Managing Member*
EMP: 59 **EST:** 2019
SALES (est): 787.2K **Privately Held**
Web: www.rusticpathways.com
SIC: 7389 Design services

(G-10995)
SIGNATURE HEALTH INC
7232 Justin Way (44060-4881)
PHONE..............................440 578-8200
EMP: 150 **EST:** 2019
SALES (est): 20.77MM **Privately Held**
Web: www.signaturehealthinc.org
SIC: 8099 Health and allied services, nec

(G-10996)
SOLV-ALL LLC
9142 Tyler Blvd (44060-1881)
PHONE..............................888 765-8255
EMP: 100
SIC: 5087 7349 Service establishment equipment; Building maintenance services, nec

(G-10997)
SOURCEONE HEALTHCARE TECH INC (HQ)
Also Called: Mxr Imaging
8020 Tyler Blvd (44060-4825)
PHONE..............................440 701-1200
Leo Zuckerman, *CEO*
Larry Lawson, *
EMP: 27 **EST:** 1994
SQ FT: 42,000
SALES (est): 46.02MM
SALES (corp-wide): 109.03MM **Privately Held**
Web: www.sourceonehealth.com
SIC: 5047 Medical laboratory equipment
PA: Mxr Imaging, Inc.
4909 Murphy Canyon Rd # 120
San Diego CA 92123
858 565-4472

(G-10998)
SOUTH SHORE CONTROLS INC
9395 Pinecone Dr (44060-1862)
PHONE..............................440 259-2500
John Ovsek, *VP*
Chris Langmack, *
EMP: 45 **EST:** 1995
SQ FT: 22,000
SALES (est): 10.23MM **Privately Held**
Web: www.southshorecontrols.com
SIC: 3549 5084 Metalworking machinery, nec; Instruments and control equipment

(G-10999)
STERIS ISOMEDIX SERVICES INC
Also Called: Steris Isomedix
5960 Heisley Rd (44060-1834)
PHONE..............................440 354-2600
♦ **EMP:** 335
Web: www.steris-ast.com
SIC: 8734 8742 Industrial sterilization service; Industry specialist consultants

(G-11000)
SUMMERVILLE SENIOR LIVING INC
Also Called: Summerville At Mentor
5700 Emerald Ct (44060-1870)
PHONE..............................440 354-5499
Russell Ragland, *Pr*
EMP: 39
SALES (corp-wide): 2.83B **Publicly Held**
SIC: 8051 Skilled nursing care facilities
HQ: Summerville Senior Living, Inc.
3131 Elliott Ave Ste 500
Seattle WA 98121
206 298-2909

(G-11001)
SYNERGY HEALTH NORTH AMERICA INC
5960 Heisley Rd (44060-1834)
PHONE..............................813 891-9550
EMP: 799
SIC: 5047 7213 Surgical equipment and supplies; Linen supply

(G-11002)
T O J INC (PA)
6011 Heisley Rd (44060-1867)
PHONE..............................440 352-1900
Maureen Osborne, *Pr*
Jerry Osborne Iii, *Pr*
Timothy Posar, *
EMP: 38 **EST:** 1966
SQ FT: 32,000
SALES (est): 34.91MM
SALES (corp-wide): 34.91MM **Privately Held**
Web: www.jtoinc.com

SIC: 1542 1522 6552 4959 Commercial and office building, new construction; Condominium construction; Land subdividers and developers, commercial; Snowplowing

(G-11003)
THIRD FDRAL SAV LN ASSN CLVLAN
Also Called: Third Federal
7339 Mentor Ave (44060-7523)
PHONE..............................440 946-9040
Michelle Hayes, *Mgr*
EMP: 28
SALES (corp-wide): 1.05B **Publicly Held**
Web: www.thirdfederal.com
SIC: 6035 Federal savings and loan associations
HQ: Third Federal Savings And Loan Association Of Cleveland
7007 Broadway Ave
Cleveland OH 44105
800 844-7333

(G-11004)
TOWLIFT INC
7520 Clover Ave Ste A (44060-5200)
PHONE..............................440 951-9519
Kirk Smee, *Mgr*
EMP: 35
SALES (corp-wide): 246.16MM **Privately Held**
Web: www.towlift.com
SIC: 5084 7353 7699 Materials handling machinery; Heavy construction equipment rental; Industrial machinery and equipment repair
HQ: Towlift, Inc.
1395 Valley Belt Rd
Brooklyn Heights OH 44131
216 749-6800

(G-11005)
TRI-COUNTY AMBULANCE SVC INC
7000 Spinach Dr (44060-4958)
PHONE..............................440 951-4600
Kevin Farrell, *Pr*
John F Farrell, *
Beth Farrell, *
EMP: 41 **EST:** 1985
SQ FT: 8,000
SALES (est): 4.5MM **Privately Held**
Web: www.tricountyambulance.com
SIC: 4119 Ambulance service

(G-11006)
UNITED WAY OF LAKE COUNTY INC
Also Called: UNITED WAY
9285 Progress Pkwy (44060-1854)
PHONE..............................440 639-4420
Dione Demitro, *Pr*
David Munson, *VP*
EMP: 28 **EST:** 1958
SQ FT: 8,800
SALES (est): 1.8MM **Privately Held**
Web: www.uwlc.org
SIC: 8322 Social service center

(G-11007)
UNIVERSITY HSPTALS CLVLAND MED
Also Called: Lake Univ Ireland Cancer Ctr
9485 Mentor Ave Ste 102 (44060-8722)
PHONE..............................440 205-5755
Staton Gerson Md, *Dir*
EMP: 1851
SQ FT: 1,269
SALES (corp-wide): 878.24MM **Privately Held**
Web: www.uhhospitals.org
SIC: 8062 8011 General medical and surgical hospitals; Oncologist

HQ: University Hospitals Cleveland Medical Center
11100 Euclid Ave
Cleveland OH 44106

(G-11008)
UNIVERSITY MEDNET
9000 Mentor Ave Ste 101 (44060-4496)
PHONE..............................440 255-0800
Evelyn Havrillo, *Mgr*
EMP: 150
SALES (corp-wide): 10.47MM **Privately Held**
SIC: 8011 8093 Clinic, operated by physicians; Specialty outpatient clinics, nec
PA: University Mednet
18599 Lake Shore Blvd
Euclid OH 44119
216 383-0100

(G-11009)
VECMAR CORPORATION
Also Called: Vecmar Computer Solutions
7595 Jenther Dr (44060-4872)
PHONE..............................440 953-1119
Greg Pluscusky, *Pr*
Brian Dipasquale, *
Philip R Pagon Ii, *VP*
James Matonis, *
Nick Zitnik, *
▲ **EMP:** 30 **EST:** 1990
SQ FT: 25,000
SALES (est): 6.49MM **Privately Held**
Web: www.vecmar.com
SIC: 5045 Computers, nec

(G-11010)
VOLK OPTICAL INC
Also Called: Volk Optical
7893 Enterprise Dr (44060-5309)
PHONE..............................440 942-6161
Jyoti Gupta, *Pr*
Gary Webel, *
▲ **EMP:** 70 **EST:** 1974
SQ FT: 18,000
SALES (est): 19.28MM
SALES (corp-wide): 2.23B **Privately Held**
Web: www.volk.com
SIC: 8011 3851 3827 Offices and clinics of medical doctors; Lenses, ophthalmic; Optical instruments and lenses
HQ: Halma Holdings Inc.
535 Sprngfeld Ave Ste 110
Summit NJ 07901
513 772-5501

(G-11011)
W TEAM COMPANY (PA)
Also Called: Willoughby Supply
7433 Clover Ave (44060-5211)
PHONE..............................440 942-7939
Albert Romanini, *Pr*
EMP: 37 **EST:** 1983
SQ FT: 85,000
SALES (est): 27.12MM
SALES (corp-wide): 27.12MM **Privately Held**
Web: www.willoughbysupply.com
SIC: 5033 Roofing and siding materials

(G-11012)
WPMI INC
9325 Progress Pkwy (44060-1855)
PHONE..............................440 392-2171
Stephanie Molnar, *CEO*
Lori Ware, *
EMP: 33 **EST:** 2003
SALES (est): 2.17MM **Privately Held**
SIC: 8742 Marketing consulting services

GEOGRAPHIC SECTION

(G-11013)
ZAPPYS AUTO WASHES
8806 Mentor Ave (44060-6264)
PHONE..........................844 927-9274
Aj Zappitelli, *Pt*
EMP: 30 **EST:** 2010
SALES (est): 376.63K **Privately Held**
Web: www.zappysautowashes.com
SIC: 7542 5015 Washing and polishing, automotive; Automotive supplies, used: wholesale and retail

Mentor On The Lake
Lake County

(G-11014)
COMPANION CARE SERVICES INC (PA)
7618 Miami Rd (44060-3227)
PHONE..........................440 257-0075
Marie Joseph, *Pr*
Debbie Scott, *
EMP: 40 **EST:** 1994
SQ FT: 1,600
SALES (est): 1.89MM **Privately Held**
SIC: 8082 Home health care services

(G-11015)
MAIN SEQUENCE TECHNOLOGY INC (PA)
5370 Pinehill Dr (44060-1434)
PHONE..........................440 946-5214
Martin Snyder, *Pr*
Michael H Snyder, *CIO**
William F Kubicek, *
Gretchen Kubicek, *
EMP: 30 **EST:** 1998
SALES (est): 6.58MM
SALES (corp-wide): 6.58MM **Privately Held**
Web: www.pcrecruiter.net
SIC: 7371 Computer software development

Metamora
Fulton County

(G-11016)
ANDERZACK-PITZEN CNSTR INC
424 E Main St (43540-9753)
P.O. Box H (43540-0207)
PHONE..........................419 644-2111
EMP: 100 **EST:** 1992
SQ FT: 6,000
SALES (est): 35.63MM **Privately Held**
Web: www.wecandigit.com
SIC: 1623 1794 Underground utilities contractor; Excavation work

Miamisburg
Montgomery County

(G-11017)
21ST CENTURY SOLUTIONS LTD (PA)
Also Called: Gokeyless
955 Mound Rd (45342-3263)
PHONE..........................877 439-5377
Josh Stamps, *Managing Member*
EMP: 42 **EST:** 2003
SQ FT: 30,000
SALES (est): 7.8MM
SALES (corp-wide): 7.8MM **Privately Held**
Web: www.gokeyless.com
SIC: 7699 Locksmith shop

(G-11018)
7NT ENTERPRISES LLC (PA)
Also Called: 7nt
3090 S Tech Blvd (45342-4860)
PHONE..........................614 961-2026
Travis Burr, *
EMP: 45 **EST:** 2008
SALES (est): 2.32MM **Privately Held**
Web: www.7nteng.com
SIC: 8711 8713 Consulting engineer; Surveying services

(G-11019)
A-1 SPRINKLER COMPANY INC
2383 Northpointe Dr (45342-2989)
PHONE..........................937 859-6198
Bill Hausmann, *CEO*
EMP: 68 **EST:** 1982
SQ FT: 15,000
SALES (est): 14.17MM **Privately Held**
Web: www.a1ssi.com
SIC: 3569 5087 Firefighting and related equipment; Firefighting equipment

(G-11020)
ADVANCED MEDICAL EQUIPMENT INC (PA)
426 Alexandersville Rd (45342)
PHONE..........................937 534-1080
Randy Willhelm, *Pr*
Andrew Willhelm, *
Todd Wright, *
EMP: 37 **EST:** 1982
SALES (est): 4.42MM
SALES (corp-wide): 4.42MM **Privately Held**
Web: www.pediatrichomeservice.com
SIC: 5999 5047 Medical apparatus and supplies; Medical equipment and supplies

(G-11021)
AEROSEAL LLC (PA)
225 Byers Rd # 1 (45342-3614)
PHONE..........................937 428-9300
Amit Gupta, *CEO*
Vijay Kollepara, *VP*
Daniel Crowe, *CFO*
Chris Gibson, *VP Mktg*
Tim Burnette, *Commercial Vice President*
▲ **EMP:** 32 **EST:** 2011
SALES (est): 24.7MM
SALES (corp-wide): 24.7MM **Privately Held**
Web: www.aeroseal.com
SIC: 8748 3679 Energy conservation consultant; Hermetic seals, for electronic equipment

(G-11022)
AIRTRON INC
2485 Belvo Rd (45342-3909)
PHONE..........................859 371-7780
Alan Mcwilliams, *Mgr*
EMP: 38
Web: www.delmonde.com
SIC: 1711 Warm air heating and air conditioning contractor
HQ: Airtron, Inc.
    9260 Marketpl Dr
    Miamisburg OH 45342
    937 898-0826

(G-11023)
ALDRICH CHEMICAL
Also Called: Sigma-Aldrich
3858 Benner Rd (45342-4304)
PHONE..........................937 859-1808
Diane Szydell, *Mgr*
EMP: 74
SQ FT: 30,000
SALES (corp-wide): 22.82B **Privately Held**
SIC: 2819 5084 2899 2869 Isotopes, radioactive; Chemical process equipment; Chemical preparations, nec; Industrial organic chemicals, nec
HQ: Aldrich Chemical
    3050 Spruce St
    Saint Louis MO 63103
    314 771-5765

(G-11024)
AMSIVE OH LLC
3303 W Tech Blvd (45342)
PHONE..........................937 885-8000
Don Landrum, *Managing Member*
Jim Wisnionski, *Managing Member**
Gordon Anderson, *Managing Member**
Mike Dolan, *Managing Member**
EMP: 70 **EST:** 1965
SQ FT: 140,000
SALES (est): 25.06MM
SALES (corp-wide): 147.04MM **Privately Held**
Web: www.amsive.com
SIC: 7331 7374 2752 Direct mail advertising services; Data processing service; Commercial printing, lithographic
HQ: Amsive Aq Llc
    1224 Poinsett Hwy
    Greenville SC 29609

(G-11025)
BELL VAULT AND MONU WORKS INC
1019 S Main St (45342-3148)
PHONE..........................937 866-2444
Timothy Bell, *Pr*
Greg Bell, *Sec*
EMP: 28 **EST:** 1928
SQ FT: 17,000
SALES (est): 3.44MM **Privately Held**
Web: www.bellvaultandmonument.com
SIC: 3272 5999 7261 3281 Burial vaults, concrete or precast terrazzo; Monuments, finished to custom order; Funeral service and crematories; Cut stone and stone products

(G-11026)
BRADY WARE & SCHOENFELD INC (DH)
Also Called: Brady Ware & Company
3601 Rigby Rd Ste 400 (45342-5039)
PHONE..........................937 223-5247
Brian Carr, *Pr*
Brian Carr, *CEO*
Jeffrey A Jackson, *Treas*
Tom Gmeiner, *VP*
Michael Stover, *VP*
EMP: 60 **EST:** 1962
SQ FT: 16,000
SALES (est): 12.63MM
SALES (corp-wide): 1.12B **Publicly Held**
Web: www.bradyware.com
SIC: 8721 Certified public accountant
HQ: First Financial Bank, National Association
    255 E 5th St Ste 700
    Cincinnati OH 45202
    877 322-9530

(G-11027)
BRIXEY AND MEYER INC (PA)
Also Called: Brixey & Meyer
2991 Newmark Dr (45342-5416)
PHONE..........................937 291-4110
Dave Brixey, *Prin*
EMP: 49 **EST:** 2015
SALES (est): 5.05MM
SALES (corp-wide): 5.05MM **Privately Held**
Web: www.brixeyandmeyer.com

SIC: 8721 Certified public accountant

(G-11028)
BUCKEYE ECOCARE
2550 Belvo Rd (45342-3969)
PHONE..........................937 435-4727
Mark Grunkemeyer, *Pr*
EMP: 32 **EST:** 1984
SALES (est): 8.63MM **Privately Held**
Web: www.buckeyeecocare.com
SIC: 0782 Landscape contractors

(G-11029)
C & E SALES LLC
Also Called: C & E Advanced Technologies
2400 Technical Dr (45342-6136)
P.O. Box 736405 (75373-6405)
PHONE..........................937 434-8830
EMP: 94 **EST:** 1978
SALES (est): 49.47MM
SALES (corp-wide): 149.21MM **Privately Held**
Web: www.ceadvancedtech.com
SIC: 5063 Electrical fittings and construction materials
PA: Eis Intermediate Holdings, Llc
    2018 Powers Ferry Rd
    Atlanta GA 30339
    678 255-3600

(G-11030)
C B MFG & SLS CO INC (PA)
4455 Infirmary Rd (45342-1299)
PHONE..........................937 866-5986
Charles S Biehn Junior, *CEO*
Richard Porter, *
Merle Wilberding, *
Donald M Cain, *
▲ **EMP:** 67 **EST:** 1967
SQ FT: 90,000
SALES (est): 22.18MM
SALES (corp-wide): 22.18MM **Privately Held**
Web: www.americancuttingedge.com
SIC: 5085 3423 Knives, industrial; Knives, agricultural or industrial

(G-11031)
CANON SOLUTIONS AMERICA INC
1 Prestige Pl (45342-3794)
PHONE..........................937 260-4495
Todd Kostkan, *Brnch Mgr*
EMP: 27
Web: csa.canon.com
SIC: 5044 5045 Copying equipment; Computer software
HQ: Canon Solutions America, Inc.
    1 Canon Park
    Melville NY 11747
    631 330-5000

(G-11032)
CAPGEMINI AMERICA INC
Also Called: Sogeti
10100 Innovation Dr Ste 200 (45342-4966)
PHONE..........................678 427-6642
Adam Guediri, *Account Executive*
EMP: 300
SALES (corp-wide): 415.14MM **Privately Held**
Web: www.capgemini.com
SIC: 7379 Online services technology consultants
HQ: Capgemini America, Inc.
    79 Fifth Ave Fl 3
    New York NY 10003
    212 314-8000

Miamisburg - Montgomery County (G-11033)

(G-11033)
CAPITAL HEALTH SERVICES INC (PA)
Also Called: Capital Health Services
3015 Newmark Dr (45342-5418)
PHONE.................................937 277-0505
Ken Bernsen, *CEO*
Joshua Huff, *
Sarah Manning, *
Kara Bernsen, *
EMP: 34 **EST:** 2004
SALES (est): 7.96MM **Privately Held**
Web: www.capitalhealthhomecare.com
SIC: 8051 8059 Skilled nursing care facilities ; Personal care home, with health care

(G-11034)
CARRIAGE INN OF TROTWOOD INC
Also Called: Shiloh Springs Care Center
3015 Newmark Dr (45342)
PHONE.................................937 277-0505
Ken Bernsen, *Pr*
EMP: 44 **EST:** 2008
SALES (est): 7.35MM **Privately Held**
SIC: 8051 Convalescent home with continuous nursing care

(G-11035)
CESO INC (PA)
Also Called: Ceso
3601 Rigby Rd Ste 300 (45342-5047)
PHONE.................................937 435-8584
David Oakes, *Pr*
James I Weprin, *
Kathleen Cyphert, *
EMP: 29 **EST:** 1987
SALES (est): 26.41MM
SALES (corp-wide): 26.41MM **Privately Held**
Web: www.cesoinc.com
SIC: 8711 3674 8712 Civil engineering; Light emitting diodes; Architectural services

(G-11036)
CLARK SCHAEFER HACKETT & CO (PA)
10100 Innovation Dr Ste 400 (45342-4965)
PHONE.................................937 226-0070
Carl R Coburn, *Pr*
Paul A Bendik, *VP*
Kevin T Davis, *VP*
William G Edwards, *VP*
Thomas L Hackett, *VP*
EMP: 45 **EST:** 1937
SALES (est): 26.49MM
SALES (corp-wide): 26.49MM **Privately Held**
Web: www.cshco.com
SIC: 8721 Certified public accountant

(G-11037)
CONCEPT IMAGING GROUP INC
Also Called: Innomark Communications
3233 S Tech Blvd (45342-0843)
PHONE.................................888 466-6627
EMP: 45 **EST:** 1991
SALES (est): 3.92MM
SALES (corp-wide): 96.09MM **Privately Held**
SIC: 7336 Commercial art and graphic design
PA: Innomark Communications Llc
420 Distribution Cir
Fairfield OH 45014
888 466-6627

(G-11038)
CONNOR GROUP A RE INV FIRM LLC
10510 Springboro Pike (45342-4956)
PHONE.................................937 434-3095
Lawrence Connor, *Managing Member*
Brock Wright, *CIO*
EMP: 475 **EST:** 1996
SALES (est): 14.22MM **Privately Held**
Web: www.connorgroup.com
SIC: 6531 Real estate agents and managers

(G-11039)
CORNERSTONE RESEARCH GROUP INC
Also Called: C R G
510 Earl Blvd (45342-6411)
PHONE.................................937 320-1877
Patrick J Hood, *Pr*
Chrysa Theodore, *
Jeffrey Bennett, *
EMP: 112 **EST:** 1997
SQ FT: 20,979
SALES (est): 28.89MM **Privately Held**
Web: www.crgrp.com
SIC: 8733 Scientific research agency

(G-11040)
COURTYARD BY MARRIOTT
Also Called: Courtyard By Marriott
100 Prestige Pl (45342-5340)
PHONE.................................937 433-3131
Bob Tate, *Genl Mgr*
EMP: 27 **EST:** 2007
SALES (est): 1MM **Privately Held**
Web: courtyard.marriott.com
SIC: 7011 Hotels and motels

(G-11041)
CRANE AMERICA SERVICES INC
Also Called: Terex Services
1027 Byers Rd (45342-5487)
P.O. Box 39245 (45342)
PHONE.................................937 293-6526
EMP: 380
SIC: 7699 Industrial machinery and equipment repair

(G-11042)
DANIS BUILDING CONSTRUCTION CO (PA)
Also Called: Danis
3233 Newmark Dr (45342-5422)
PHONE.................................937 228-1225
John Danis, *Pr*
Thomas P Hammelrath, *
Tim Carlson, *
EMP: 50 **EST:** 1916
SQ FT: 29,000
SALES (est): 215.57MM **Privately Held**
Web: www.danis.com
SIC: 1542 1541 Commercial and office building, new construction; Industrial buildings and warehouses

(G-11043)
DANIS COMPANIES
3233 Newmark Dr (45342-5422)
PHONE.................................937 228-1225
Thomas J Danis, *Ch Bd*
Glenn P Schimpf, *V Ch Bd*
Richard C Russell, *Pr*
Gregory L Mccann, *Sr VP*
EMP: 500 **EST:** 1988
SQ FT: 42,784
SALES (est): 20.4MM **Privately Held**
Web: www.danis.com
SIC: 1629 Industrial plant construction

(G-11044)
DANIS INDUSTRIAL CNSTR CO
3233 Newmark Dr (45342-5422)
PHONE.................................937 228-1225
John Danis, *CEO*
EMP: 75 **EST:** 2002
SALES (est): 8.41MM **Privately Held**
Web: www.danis.com
SIC: 1522 Residential construction, nec
PA: Danis Building Construction Company
3233 Newmark Dr
Miamisburg OH 45342

(G-11045)
DAVIS H ELLIOT CNSTR CO INC
1 S Gebhart Church Rd (45342-3646)
PHONE.................................937 847-8025
Eliot Davis, *Brnch Mgr*
EMP: 33
SALES (corp-wide): 173.15MM **Privately Held**
Web: www.dhec.com
SIC: 1731 General electrical contractor
HQ: Davis H. Elliot Construction Company , Inc.
673 Blue Sky Pkwy
Lexington KY 40509
859 263-5148

(G-11046)
DAYTON CHILDRENS HOSPITAL
Also Called: Dayton Childrens - S Campus
3333 W Tech Blvd (45342-0955)
PHONE.................................937 641-3000
EMP: 88
SALES (corp-wide): 639.25MM **Privately Held**
Web: www.childrensdayton.org
SIC: 8099 Blood related health services
PA: Dayton Children's Hospital
1 Childrens Plz
Dayton OH 45404
937 641-3000

(G-11047)
DAYTON POWER AND LIGHT COMPANY
1 S Gebhart Church Rd (45342-3646)
PHONE.................................937 331-3032
Madonna Nessle, *Prin*
EMP: 45
SALES (corp-wide): 12.67B **Publicly Held**
Web: www.aes-ohio.com
SIC: 4911 4932 4931 Generation, electric power; Gas and other services combined; Electric and other services combined
HQ: The Dayton Power And Light Company
1065 Woodman Dr
Dayton OH 45432
937 331-3900

(G-11048)
DOUBLETREE GUEST SUITES DAYTON
300 Prestige Pl (45342-5300)
PHONE.................................937 436-2400
Jennifer Brown, *Genl Mgr*
Kelly Brown, *
EMP: 40 **EST:** 2005
SALES (est): 452.9K **Privately Held**
SIC: 7011 Hotel, franchised

(G-11049)
EIS INTERMEDIATE HOLDINGS LLC
Also Called: C&E Advanced Technologies
2400 Technical Dr (45342-6136)
PHONE.................................800 228-2790
Shannah Plaugher Acctsuperviso r, *Brnch Mgr*
EMP: 100
SALES (corp-wide): 149.21MM **Privately Held**
Web: www.ceadvancedtech.com
SIC: 5063 Electrical apparatus and equipment
PA: Eis Intermediate Holdings, Llc
2018 Powers Ferry Rd
Atlanta GA 30339
678 255-3600

(G-11050)
EMERGENCY MEDICINE SPECIALISTS
3131 Newmark Dr Ste 210 (45342-5400)
PHONE.................................937 438-8910
Richard Garrson, *Pr*
EMP: 57 **EST:** 2005
SALES (est): 1.86MM **Privately Held**
Web: www.em-specialists.org
SIC: 8011 Freestanding emergency medical center

(G-11051)
ESKO-GRAPHICS INC (HQ)
Also Called: Eskoartwork
8535 Gander Creek Dr (45342-5436)
PHONE.................................937 454-1721
Stefaan Deveen, *CEO*
Frank Mcfaden, *CFO*
James O'reilly, *Sec*
◆ **EMP:** 70 **EST:** 1997
SQ FT: 27,000
SALES (est): 78.44MM
SALES (corp-wide): 1.73B **Publicly Held**
Web: www.esko.com
SIC: 5084 7372 Printing trades machinery, equipment, and supplies; Prepackaged software
PA: Veralto Corporation
225 Wyman St Ste 250
Waltham MA 02451
202 828-0850

(G-11052)
EUBEL BRADY STTMAN ASSET MGT I
Also Called: Ebs Asset Management
10100 Innovation Dr Ste 410 (45342-4966)
PHONE.................................937 291-1223
Robert J Suttman, *Pr*
Ronald L Eubel, *CIO*
Mark E Brady, *
William Hazel, *
Bernard J Holtgreive, *
EMP: 50 **EST:** 1993
SQ FT: 12,000
SALES (est): 10.05MM **Privately Held**
Web: www.ebsinvests.com
SIC: 6282 Investment advisory service

(G-11053)
EVENFLO COMPANY INC (DH)
Also Called: Evenflo
3131 Newmark Dr Ste 300 (45342-5400)
PHONE.................................937 415-3300
Dave Taylor, *CEO*
Peter Banat, *
Josh Korth, *
David Mcgillivary, *Treas*
◆ **EMP:** 48 **EST:** 1920
SQ FT: 1,250,000
SALES (est): 272.16MM **Privately Held**
Web: www.evenflo.com
SIC: 5099 2531 Baby carriages, strollers and related products; Seats, automobile
HQ: Goodbaby International Holdings Limited
Rm 2502 25/F Tung Chiu Coml Ctr
Wan Chai HK

(G-11054)
EXPEDIENT TECH SOLUTIONS LLC
8561 Gander Creek Dr (45342)
P.O. Box 302 (45327)
PHONE.................................937 535-4300
Marcus Thompson, *CEO*
EMP: 39 **EST:** 2004
SALES (est): 5.27MM **Privately Held**

GEOGRAPHIC SECTION

Miamisburg - Montgomery County (G-11076)

Web: www.expedienttechnology.com
SIC: 7379 Computer related consulting services

(G-11055)
FIRST MOBILE TRUST LLC
2835 Miami Village Dr Ste 203 (45342-4916)
PHONE................855 270-3592
Jeff Hack, *Prin*
Glenn Renzulli, *
Ben Weiner, *
EMP: 34 **EST:** 2012
SALES (est): 2.57MM
SALES (corp-wide): 843.32MM **Privately Held**
SIC: 7371 Computer software development
HQ: Paya Holdings Inc.
  303 Perimeter Ctr N # 600
  Atlanta GA 30346
  800 261-0240

(G-11056)
FRICKERS USA LLC (PA)
Also Called: Fricker's Restaurant
228 Byers Rd Ste 100 (45342-3675)
PHONE................937 865-9242
Ray Frick, *Pr*
Ray Frick, *Pr*
Karen Smith, *
EMP: 27 **EST:** 2006
SQ FT: 2,300
SALES (est): 7.07MM
SALES (corp-wide): 7.07MM **Privately Held**
Web: www.frickers.com
SIC: 5812 6794 American restaurant; Franchises, selling or licensing

(G-11057)
GAYSTON CORPORATION
Also Called: Mulch Masters of Ohio
721 Richard St (45342-1840)
P.O. Box 523 (45343-0523)
PHONE................937 743-6050
Adam Stone, *CEO*
Andrew Sheldrick, *
◆ **EMP:** 125 **EST:** 1951
SQ FT: 280,000
SALES (est): 23.81MM **Privately Held**
Web: www.gayston.com
SIC: 1794 3999 2819 2499 Excavation and grading, building construction; Military insignia; Aluminum compounds; Mulch, wood and bark

(G-11058)
HAHN AUTOMATION GROUP US INC
10909 Industry Ln (45342-0818)
PHONE................937 886-3232
John C Hanna, *CEO*
Thomas Hahn, *
EMP: 60 **EST:** 1993
SQ FT: 63,000
SALES (est): 24.97MM
SALES (corp-wide): 2.27B **Privately Held**
Web: www.invotec.com
SIC: 8711 3599 Machine tool design; Custom machinery
HQ: Hahn Automation Group Holding Gmbh
  Liebshausener Str. 3
  Rheinbollen RP 55494
  676490220

(G-11059)
HCL OF DAYTON INC
4000 Miamisburg Centerville Rd Ste 410 (45342)
PHONE................937 384-8300
Phillip Douglas, *CEO*
EMP: 203 **EST:** 2000

SALES (est): 4.86MM
SALES (corp-wide): 444.19MM **Privately Held**
SIC: 8062 General medical and surgical hospitals
HQ: Lifecare Holdings, Llc
  5340 Legacy Dr Ste 150
  Plano TX 75024

(G-11060)
HEARTLAND MIAMISBURG OH LLC
Also Called: Promedica Sklled Nrsing Rhbltt
450 Oak Ridge Blvd (45342-3673)
PHONE................937 866-8885
EMP: 38 **EST:** 2007
SALES (est): 6.06MM **Privately Held**
SIC: 8051 Convalescent home with continuous nursing care

(G-11061)
HILTON GARDEN INNS MGT LLC
Also Called: Hilton
12000 Innovation Dr (45342-4970)
PHONE................937 247-5850
EMP: 272
SALES (corp-wide): 10.23B **Publicly Held**
Web: www.hilton.com
SIC: 7011 Hotels and motels
HQ: Hilton Garden Inns Management Llc
  7930 Jones Branch Dr
  Mc Lean VA 22102
  703 883-1000

(G-11062)
HOTEL DAYTON OPCO L P
Also Called: Homewood Suites Hotel Dayton S
3100 Contemporary Ln (45342-5399)
PHONE................937 432-9161
Miller P Membr, *Prin*
EMP: 59 **EST:** 1999
SALES (est): 1.01MM **Privately Held**
Web: homewoodsuites3.hilton.com
SIC: 7011 Hotels and motels

(G-11063)
INDUS VALLEY CONSULTANTS INC (PA)
9049 Springboro Pike (45342-5057)
PHONE................937 660-4748
Srikanth Paladugu, *Pr*
EMP: 35 **EST:** 1996
SALES (est): 8.19MM **Privately Held**
Web: www.indusvalley.com
SIC: 7379 Online services technology consultants

(G-11064)
INNMARK COMMUNICATIONS LLC
3005 W Tech Blvd (45342-0824)
PHONE................888 466-6627
EMP: 106
SALES (corp-wide): 96.09MM **Privately Held**
Web: www.innmarkcom.com
SIC: 7379 Online services technology consultants
PA: Innmark Communications Llc
  420 Distribution Cir
  Fairfield OH 45014
  888 466-6627

(G-11065)
INTERSTATE FORD INC
Also Called: Quick Lane
125 Alexandersville Rd (45342)
PHONE................937 866-0781
EMP: 130 **EST:** 1981
SALES (est): 21.15MM **Privately Held**
Web: www.interstateford.com

SIC: 5511 5521 7538 Automobiles, new and used; Used car dealers; General automotive repair shops

(G-11066)
KETTERING MEDICAL CENTER
Also Called: Sycamore Medical Center
4000 Miamisburg Centerville Rd (45342)
PHONE................937 866-0551
Clifton D Patten, *CFO*
EMP: 350
SQ FT: 110,000
SALES (corp-wide): 2.46B **Privately Held**
Web: www.ketteringhealth.org
SIC: 8062 General medical and surgical hospitals
HQ: Kettering Medical Center
  3535 Southern Blvd
  Kettering OH 45429
  937 298-4331

(G-11067)
KINGSTON OF MIAMISBURG LLC
1120 Dunaway St (45342-3839)
PHONE................937 866-9089
EMP: 52 **EST:** 1976
SQ FT: 35,000
SALES (est): 10.75MM **Privately Held**
Web: www.kingstonhealthcare.com
SIC: 8051 Skilled nursing care facilities

(G-11068)
LEXISNEXIS GROUP
4700 Lyons Rd (45342-6453)
PHONE................937 865-6900
EMP: 187
SALES (corp-wide): 11.42B **Privately Held**
Web: www.lexisnexis.co.in
SIC: 7375 Data base information retrieval
HQ: Lexisnexis Group
  9443 Springboro Pike
  Miamisburg OH 45342
  937 865-6800

(G-11069)
LEXISNEXIS GROUP (DH)
Also Called: Lexisnexis Group
9443 Springboro Pike (45342)
PHONE................937 865-6900
Kurt Sanford, *CEO*
Joe Eberhardt Gcno, *Prin*
▲ **EMP:** 162 **EST:** 2004
SALES (est): 359.22MM
SALES (corp-wide): 11.42B **Privately Held**
Web: www.lexisnexis.co.in
SIC: 7375 2741 Data base information retrieval; Miscellaneous publishing
HQ: Relx Inc.
  230 Park Ave Ste 700
  New York NY 10169
  212 309-8100

(G-11070)
LJB INC (PA)
2500 Newmark Dr (45342-5407)
PHONE................937 259-5000
EMP: 130 **EST:** 1966
SALES (est): 27.44MM
SALES (corp-wide): 27.44MM **Privately Held**
Web: www.ljbinc.com
SIC: 8712 Architectural engineering

(G-11071)
MARXENT LABS LLC (PA)
Also Called: Marxent
10170 Penny Ln Ste 200 (45342-5014)
PHONE................727 851-9522
Beck Besecker, *CEO*
Barry Besecker, *
Rick Hanley, *

EMP: 40 **EST:** 2012
SALES (est): 10.02MM
SALES (corp-wide): 10.02MM **Privately Held**
Web: www.marxentlabs.com
SIC: 7371 Computer software development and applications

(G-11072)
MENARD INC
8480 Springboro Pike (45342-4407)
PHONE................937 630-3550
Dennis Dixon, *Brnch Mgr*
EMP: 76
SALES (corp-wide): 1.7B **Privately Held**
Web: www.menards.com
SIC: 5211 1521 Home centers; Single-family home remodeling, additions, and repairs
PA: Menard, Inc.
  5101 Menard Dr
  Eau Claire WI 54703
  715 876-2000

(G-11073)
MONARCH DENTAL CORP
Also Called: Monarch Dental - Dayton
36 Fiesta Ln (45342-5301)
PHONE................937 684-4845
Michael Smith, *Mgr*
EMP: 46
SQ FT: 2,400
SALES (corp-wide): 303.67MM **Privately Held**
Web: www.monarchdental.com
SIC: 8021 Dental clinic
HQ: Monarch Dental Corp
  7989 Belt Line Rd Ste 90
  Dallas TX 75248

(G-11074)
MOODYS OF DAYTON INC (PA)
Also Called: Moody's
4359 Infirmary Rd (45342-1231)
P.O. Box 509 (45343-0509)
PHONE................614 443-3898
John Wagner, *Pr*
Douglas F Wagner, *
EMP: 29 **EST:** 1961
SQ FT: 12,500
SALES (est): 5.22MM
SALES (corp-wide): 5.22MM **Privately Held**
Web: www.moodysofdayton.com
SIC: 1781 Water well drilling

(G-11075)
NATIONAL CITY MORTGAGE INC (HQ)
3232 Newmark Dr (45342-5433)
PHONE................937 910-1200
Leo E Knight Junior, *Ch Bd*
Rick A Smalldon, *
Todd A Householder, *
Gregory A Davis, *
Jack Case, *
EMP: 1600 **EST:** 1955
SQ FT: 500,000
SALES (est): 1.04B
SALES (corp-wide): 31.88B **Publicly Held**
Web: www.national-citymortgage.com
SIC: 6162 Mortgage bankers and loan correspondents
PA: The Pnc Financial Services Group Inc
  300 5th Ave
  Pittsburgh PA 15222
  888 762-2265

(G-11076)
NURSES CARE INC (PA)
9009 Springboro Pike (45342-4418)
PHONE................513 424-1141

Miamisburg - Montgomery County (G-11077)

GEOGRAPHIC SECTION

Sheila Rush, *CEO*
EMP: 100 **EST:** 1991
SALES (est): 3.83MM
SALES (corp-wide): 3.83MM **Privately Held**
Web: www.nursescareinc.com
SIC: 8082 Home health care services

(G-11077)
OBERER DEVELOPMENT CO (PA)
Also Called: Oberer Companies
3445 Newmark Dr (45342-5426)
PHONE....................937 910-0851
George R Oberer Senior, *Ch*
EMP: 40 **EST:** 1971
SALES (est): 22.02MM
SALES (corp-wide): 22.02MM **Privately Held**
Web: www.oberer.com
SIC: 6552 1521 1522 1542 Land subdividers and developers, commercial; Single-family housing construction; Residential construction, nec; Nonresidential construction, nec

(G-11078)
OBERER RESIDENTIAL CNSTR LTD
Also Called: Gold Key Homes
3445 Newmark Dr (45342-5426)
PHONE....................937 278-0851
George Oberer Junior, *Pr*
EMP: 95 **EST:** 1997
SALES (est): 2.31MM
SALES (corp-wide): 22.02MM **Privately Held**
Web: www.obererlanddevelopers.com
SIC: 1521 6531 1522 New construction, single-family houses; Real estate agents and managers; Residential construction, nec
PA: Oberer Development Co.
3445 Newmark Dr
Miamisburg OH 45342
937 910-0851

(G-11079)
ONEIL & ASSOCIATES INC (PA)
Also Called: Oneil
495 Byers Rd (45342-3798)
PHONE....................937 865-0800
Hernan Olivas, *CEO*
Hernan Olivas, *Pr*
Joe Stevens, *
David Stackhouse, *CIO*
Cindy Schneider Ctrl, *Prin*
EMP: 176 **EST:** 1947
SQ FT: 75,000
SALES (est): 39.18MM
SALES (corp-wide): 39.18MM **Privately Held**
Web: www.oneil.com
SIC: 2741 8999 7336 Technical manuals: publishing only, not printed on site; Technical manual preparation; Commercial art and illustration

(G-11080)
PAM SPECIALTY HOSP DAYTON LLC
Also Called: Pam Specialty Hospital Dayton
4000 Miamisburg Centerville Rd (45342)
PHONE....................937 384-8300
Chris Lafontsee, *CEO*
EMP: 293 **EST:** 2019
SALES (est): 10.4MM **Privately Held**
Web: www.pamhealth.com
SIC: 8062 General medical and surgical hospitals
PA: Post Acute Medical, Llc
1828 Good Hope Rd Ste 102
Enola PA 17025

(G-11081)
PANINI NORTH AMERICA INC
1229 Byers Rd (45342-5770)
PHONE....................937 291-2195
▲ **EMP:** 37 **EST:** 1996
SALES (est): 14.21MM
SALES (corp-wide): 94.3K **Privately Held**
Web: www.panini.com
SIC: 5049 Bank equipment and supplies
HQ: D21 Holding Spa
Via Po 39
Torino TO

(G-11082)
PATENTED ACQUISITION CORP (PA)
Also Called: Think Patented
2490 Cross Pointe Dr (45342-3584)
PHONE....................937 353-2299
Ken Mcnerney, *Ch*
David Mcnerney, *Pr*
▲ **EMP:** 93 **EST:** 2006
SALES (est): 46.97MM **Privately Held**
Web: www.thinkpatented.com
SIC: 7389 7331 Printers' services: folding, collating, etc.; Mailing service

(G-11083)
PEQ SERVICES + SOLUTIONS INC (HQ)
1 Prestige Pl Ste 900 (45342-6103)
PHONE....................937 610-4800
Jason Evans, *Pr*
David Senseman, *
Robert Butcher, *
EMP: 60 **EST:** 2001
SALES (est): 21.26MM **Privately Held**
SIC: 8748 Business consulting, nec
PA: Buchanan Technologies, Inc.
1026 Texan Trl Ste 200
Grapevine TX 76051

(G-11084)
PIONEER AUTOMOTIVE TECH INC (DH)
10100 Innovation Dr (45342-4966)
PHONE....................937 746-2293
◆ **EMP:** 175 **EST:** 1981
SALES (est): 90.78MM **Privately Held**
SIC: 5013 3714 3651 Automotive supplies and parts; Motor vehicle parts and accessories; Household audio and video equipment
HQ: Pioneer North America, Inc.
970 W 190th St Ste 360
Torrance CA 90502
310 952-2000

(G-11085)
PNC MORTGAGE COMPANY (DH)
Also Called: PNC
3232 Newmark Dr Bldg 2 (45342-5433)
PHONE....................412 762-2000
Robert Crowl, *Prin*
EMP: 45 **EST:** 2009
SALES (est): 25.95MM
SALES (corp-wide): 31.88B **Publicly Held**
Web: www.pnc.com
SIC: 6162 Mortgage bankers and loan correspondents
HQ: Pnc Bank, National Association
300 5th Ave
Pittsburgh PA 15222
877 762-2000

(G-11086)
PRECISION IMPACTS LLC
721 Richard St (45342-1840)
PHONE....................937 530-8254
EMP: 89 **EST:** 2021
SALES (est): 7.95MM **Privately Held**

SIC: 3449 1761 Miscellaneous metalwork; Sheet metal work, nec

(G-11087)
PREMIER GROUPE LLC
6045 Manning Rd (45342-1609)
PHONE....................937 272-1520
Bobby Boyer, *Pr*
EMP: 30 **EST:** 2017
SALES (est): 2.47MM **Privately Held**
Web: www.premiergroupohio.com
SIC: 1521 General remodeling, single-family houses

(G-11088)
RED ROOF INNS INC
Also Called: Red Roof Inn
222 Byers Rd (45342-3615)
PHONE....................937 866-0705
Gerald Shulze, *Mgr*
EMP: 40
Web: www.redroof.com
SIC: 7011 Hotels and motels
HQ: Red Roof Inns, Inc.
7815 Walton Pkwy
New Albany OH 43054
614 744-2600

(G-11089)
RETALIX INC
2490 Technical Dr (45342-6136)
PHONE....................937 384-2277
Barry Shaked, *Pr*
Karen Weaver, *
Barry Shake, *
EMP: 47 **EST:** 1979
SQ FT: 72,000
SALES (est): 2.32MM **Privately Held**
Web: www.ncr.com
SIC: 5734 7372 Software, business and non-game; Prepackaged software
HQ: Ncr Global Ltd
9 Dafna
Raanana 43662

(G-11090)
RHEA ARYAN INC
Also Called: Quality Inn
250 Byers Rd (45342-3615)
PHONE....................937 865-0077
Rick Chobres, *Mgr*
EMP: 132
SALES (corp-wide): 1.69MM **Privately Held**
Web: www.choicehotels.com
SIC: 7011 Hotels and motels
PA: Rhea Aryan Inc
330 Glensprings Dr
Cincinnati OH 45246
513 349-3913

(G-11091)
RIVERAIN TECHNOLOGIES INC
Also Called: Riverain Medical
3130 S Tech Blvd (45342-4882)
PHONE....................937 425-6811
Steve Worrell, *CEO*
San Finkelstein, *
EMP: 30 **EST:** 2004
SALES (est): 9MM **Privately Held**
Web: www.riveraintech.com
SIC: 5047 X-ray machines and tubes

(G-11092)
SGI MATRIX LLC (PA)
1041 Byers Rd (45342-5487)
PHONE....................937 438-9033
James Young, *
Jeffrey S Young, *
John Schomburg, *
Joseph Jenkins, *

EMP: 68 **EST:** 1977
SQ FT: 12,000
SALES (est): 18.53MM
SALES (corp-wide): 18.53MM **Privately Held**
Web: www.matrixsys.com
SIC: 8711 7373 3873 Engineering services; Computer integrated systems design; Watches, clocks, watchcases, and parts

(G-11093)
SHAWNTECH COMMUNICATIONS INC (PA)
Also Called: SCI
8521 Gander Creek Dr (45342-5436)
PHONE....................937 898-4900
Lance Fancher, *Pr*
Amelia Fancher, *
Winifred Labomme, *
EMP: 46 **EST:** 1987
SALES (est): 25.22MM **Privately Held**
Web: www.shawntech.com
SIC: 5065 5999 1731 Mobile telephone equipment; Communication equipment; Electrical work

(G-11094)
SOGETI USA LLC (DH)
10100 Innovation Dr Ste 200 (45342-4966)
PHONE....................937 291-8100
Matthew Huber, *Sec*
EMP: 150 **EST:** 1971
SQ FT: 18,332
SALES (est): 236.78MM
SALES (corp-wide): 415.14MM **Privately Held**
Web: us.sogeti.com
SIC: 7379 Online services technology consultants
HQ: Capgemini North America, Inc.
623 5th Ave Fl 33
New York NY 10022
212 314-8000

(G-11095)
STEINER EOPTICS INC (PA)
Also Called: Sensor Technology Systems
3475 Newmark Dr (45342-5426)
PHONE....................937 426-2341
Alan Page, *Dir*
EMP: 80 **EST:** 1991
SQ FT: 50,000
SALES (est): 16.24MM **Privately Held**
Web: www.steiner-defense.com
SIC: 8731 3851 Electronic research; Ophthalmic goods

(G-11096)
SUPPLEMENTAL HEALTHCARE
10050 Innovation Dr Ste 320 (45342-4931)
PHONE....................937 247-0169
Matt Stierwalt, *Brnch Mgr*
EMP: 39
SALES (corp-wide): 37.62MM **Privately Held**
SIC: 7363 Temporary help service
PA: Supplemental Healthcare
1640 Redstone Center Dr # 2
Park City UT 84098
813 673-8848

(G-11097)
THINKPATH ENGINEERING SVCS LLC (PA)
9080 Springboro Pike Ste 300 (45342-4669)
PHONE....................937 291-8374
Robert Trick, *
Robert Trick, *Pr*
Kelly Hankinson, *
EMP: 33 **EST:** 2008

SQ FT: 6,330
SALES (est): 8.96MM Privately Held
Web: www.thinkpath.com
SIC: 7373 7361 8999 8711 Computer-aided engineering (CAE) systems service; Executive placement; Technical writing; Mechanical engineering

(G-11098)
THOMPSON HINE LLP
10050 Innovation Dr Ste 400 (45342-4934)
P.O. Box 8801 (45401-8801)
PHONE..............................937 443-6859
Jessica Sachs, *Brnch Mgr*
EMP: 70
SALES (corp-wide): 209.56MM Privately Held
Web: www.thompsonhine.com
SIC: 8111 General practice attorney, lawyer
PA: Thompson Hine Llp
   127 Public Sq Ste 3900
   Cleveland OH 44114
   216 566-5500

(G-11099)
ULLIMAN SCHUTTE CNSTR LLC (PA)
Also Called: U S C
9111 Springboro Pike (45342-4420)
PHONE..............................937 247-0375
Matthew S Ulliman, *
EMP: 30 EST: 1998
SQ FT: 4,000
SALES (est): 2.63MM
SALES (corp-wide): 2.63MM Privately Held
Web: www.ullimanschutte.com
SIC: 1542 Commercial and office building, new construction

(G-11100)
UNITED GRINDING NORTH AMER INC (DH)
2100 United Grinding Blvd (45342-6804)
PHONE..............................937 859-1975
Markus Stolmar, *Pr*
Rodger Pinney, *
▲ EMP: 66 EST: 1984
SALES (est): 50.13MM Privately Held
Web: www.grinding.com
SIC: 5084 Industrial machinery and equipment
HQ: Bz Bank Aktiengesellschaft
   Egglirain 15
   Wilen Bei Wollerau SZ 8832

(G-11101)
UNITED WHEELS INC
8877 Gander Creek Dr (45342-5432)
PHONE..............................937 865-2813
EMP: 47 EST: 2017
SALES (est): 1.88MM Privately Held
SIC: 5013 Wheels, motor vehicle

(G-11102)
VEOLIA ES TCHNCAL SLUTIONS LLC
4301 Infirmary Rd (45342-1231)
PHONE..............................937 859-6101
Bob Luzanski, *Mgr*
EMP: 30
Web: www.veolianorthamerica.com
SIC: 4953 Recycling, waste materials
HQ: Onyx Environmental Services Llc
   53 State St Ste 14
   Boston MA 02109
   617 849-6600

(G-11103)
WALKER AUTO GROUP INC
Also Called: Walker Mitsubishi
8457 Springboro Pike (45342-4403)
PHONE..............................937 433-4950
John V H Walker Junior, *Ch*
John Walker Iii, *Pr*
Beverly Walker, *
Jeff Walker, *
Cathleen Crotty, *
EMP: 90 EST: 1950
SQ FT: 65,000
SALES (est): 24.85MM Privately Held
Web: www.walkertoyota.com
SIC: 5511 7538 7532 5531 Automobiles, new and used; General automotive repair shops; Top and body repair and paint shops ; Auto and home supply stores

(G-11104)
WURTH ELECTRONICS ICS INC
Also Called: Wurth Elecktronik
1982 Byers Rd (45342-3249)
PHONE..............................937 415-7700
Brad Weaver, *CEO*
EMP: 27 EST: 2010
SALES (est): 11.87MM
SALES (corp-wide): 20.7B Privately Held
Web: www.we-online.com
SIC: 5065 3672 Electronic parts; Printed circuit boards
HQ: Wurth Group Of North America Inc.
   93 Grant St
   Ramsey NJ 07446

(G-11105)
YASKAWA AMERICA INC
Motoman Robotics Division
100 Automation Way (45342-4962)
PHONE..............................937 847-6200
Steve Barhorst, *Div Pres*
EMP: 180
SQ FT: 304,815
Web: www.yaskawa.com
SIC: 7694 Armature rewinding shops
HQ: Yaskawa America, Inc.
   2121 S Norman Dr
   Waukegan IL 60085
   847 887-7000

Miamitown
Hamilton County

(G-11106)
GATEWAY CON FORMING SVCS INC
5938 Hamilton-Cleves Rd (45041)
P.O. Box 130 (45041-0130)
PHONE..............................513 353-2000
Robert Bilz, *Pr*
Tim Hughey, *
Brandon Erfman, *
Jean C Hughey, *
J Robert Hughey, *Stockholder*
EMP: 75 EST: 1960
SQ FT: 3,000
SALES (est): 8.8MM
SALES (corp-wide): 8.8MM Privately Held
Web: www.gatewayconcreteforming.com
SIC: 1771 3449 3496 3429 Foundation and footing contractor; Bars, concrete reinforcing: fabricated steel; Miscellaneous fabricated wire products; Hardware, nec
PA: Imcon Corp.
   5938 State Route 128
   Miamitown OH 45041
   513 353-2000

(G-11107)
MERCHANDISE INC
Also Called: MI
5929 State Rte 128 (45041-2501)
P.O. Box 10 (45041-0010)
PHONE..............................513 353-2200
Donald W Karches, *
Elizabeth Ann Karches, *
Nick Bachus, *Prin*
▼ EMP: 70 EST: 1963
SQ FT: 50,000
SALES (est): 20.17MM Privately Held
Web: www.merchandiseinc.com
SIC: 5085 5099 5122 5199 Industrial supplies; Video and audio equipment; Drugs, proprietaries, and sundries; General merchandise, non-durable

Miamiville
Clermont County

(G-11108)
AIM MRO HOLDINGS LLC (PA)
Also Called: T&B Manufacturing
375 Center St 175 (45147-5000)
PHONE..............................513 831-2938
Scott Wandtke, *Pr*
Jaclyn Holloway, *CFO*
◆ EMP: 42 EST: 1993
SQ FT: 20,000
SALES (est): 25.39MM Privately Held
Web: www.aimmro.com
SIC: 5088 Aircraft engines and engine parts

(G-11109)
CARTER SITE DEVELOPMENT LLC
106 Glendale Milford Rd (45147)
P.O. Box 20 (45147-0020)
PHONE..............................513 831-8843
David Carter, *Managing Member*
Mark Carter, *
EMP: 30 EST: 2011
SALES (est): 3.69MM Privately Held
Web: www.carterohio.com
SIC: 1611 Grading

Middle Point
Van Wert County

(G-11110)
OGLETHORPE MIDDLEPOINT LLC
Also Called: Ridgeview Hospital
17872 Lincoln Hwy (45863-9700)
PHONE..............................419 968-2950
EMP: 33 EST: 2011
SALES (est): 16.88MM Privately Held
Web: www.ridgeviewhospital.net
SIC: 8063 Psychiatric hospitals

(G-11111)
THE E AND R TRAILER SALES AND SERVICES INC (PA)
20186 Lincoln Hwy (45863-9784)
PHONE..............................419 968-2115
TOLL FREE: 800
EMP: 28 EST: 1959
SALES (est): 5.14MM
SALES (corp-wide): 5.14MM Privately Held
Web: www.ertrailer.com
SIC: 5013 Truck parts and accessories

Middlebranch
Stark County

(G-11112)
HENDERSON ROOFING & CNSTR INC
8045 Dawnwood Ave Ne (44652-9008)
PHONE..............................330 323-1500
Ken Henderson, *Prin*
EMP: 42 EST: 2014
SALES (est): 3.13MM Privately Held
Web: www.hendersonohio.com
SIC: 1761 Roofing contractor

Middleburg Heights
Cuyahoga County

(G-11113)
BREWER-GARRETT COMPANY (PA)
6800 Eastland Rd (44130-2402)
PHONE..............................440 243-3535
Lou Joseph, *CEO*
EMP: 145 EST: 1959
SQ FT: 31,500
SALES (est): 47.66MM
SALES (corp-wide): 47.66MM Privately Held
Web: www.brewer-garrett.com
SIC: 1711 4961 8711 Mechanical contractor; Steam and air-conditioning supply; Engineering services

(G-11114)
COMPASS HEALTH BRANDS CORP (PA)
Also Called: Compass Health
6753 Engle Rd Ste A (44130-7935)
PHONE..............................800 376-7263
Stuart J Straus, *Pr*
Henry Lin, *
Jim Hileman, *
Ryan Moore, *
Jeff Swain, *
◆ EMP: 110 EST: 2014
SQ FT: 20,000
SALES (est): 122.32MM Privately Held
Web: www.compasshealthbrands.com
SIC: 5047 Medical equipment and supplies

(G-11115)
FOUNDTION SRGERY AFFLATE MDDLB
Also Called: Big Creek Surgery Center
15345 Bagley Rd (44130-4825)
PHONE..............................440 743-8400
James Holfinger, *Bd of Dir*
EMP: 33 EST: 2004
SALES (est): 11.02MM Privately Held
Web: www.swgeneral.com
SIC: 8062 General medical and surgical hospitals

(G-11116)
HAMPTON INN & SUITE INC
Also Called: Hampton Inn
7074 Engle Rd (44130-3423)
PHONE..............................440 234-0206
Mark Cspell, *Mgr*
Mark Cseplo, *
EMP: 46 EST: 1998
SALES (est): 382.73K Privately Held
Web: www.hilton.com
SIC: 7011 Hotels and motels

(G-11117)
HY-TEK MATERIAL HANDLING INC
Also Called: HY-TEK MATERIAL HANDLING, INC.
7550 Lucerne Dr Ste 204 (44130-6503)
PHONE..............................440 239-9852
Mark Santos, *Brnch Mgr*
EMP: 42
SALES (corp-wide): 301.53MM Privately Held
Web: www.hy-tek.com
SIC: 5084 Materials handling machinery
HQ: Hy-Tek Material Handling, Llc
   2222 Rickenbacker Pkwy W
   Columbus OH 43217
   614 497-2500

Middleburg Heights - Cuyahoga County (G-11118)

(G-11118)
KELLER WILLIAMS BRUCE
7087 Pearl Rd D (44130-4940)
PHONE..................................440 888-6800
Bruce Trammell, *Owner*
EMP: 35 **EST:** 2010
SALES (est): 468.98K **Privately Held**
SIC: 6531 Real estate agent, residential

(G-11119)
MARSDEN HOLDING LLC
6751 Engle Rd Ste H (44130-7900)
PHONE..................................440 973-7774
Linda Simek, *Brnch Mgr*
EMP: 30
SALES (corp-wide): 290.16MM **Privately Held**
Web: www.marsden.com
SIC: 8999 Artists and artists' studios
PA: Marsden Holding, L.L.C.
   2124 University Ave W
   Saint Paul MN 55114
   651 641-1717

(G-11120)
PATTERSON DENTAL SUPPLY INC
Also Called: Patterson Dental 632
6920 Engle Rd Ste Bb (44130-8493)
PHONE..................................440 891-1050
Rex Plemann, *Mgr*
EMP: 27
SQ FT: 8,300
SALES (corp-wide): 6.47B **Publicly Held**
Web: www.pattersoncompanies.com
SIC: 5047 Dental equipment and supplies
HQ: Patterson Dental Supply, Inc.
   1031 Mendota Heights Rd
   Saint Paul MN 55120
   651 686-1600

(G-11121)
QUADAX INC (PA)
7500 Old Oak Blvd (44130-3343)
PHONE..................................440 777-6300
Thomas Hockman, *CEO*
R Ralph Daugstrup, *
John Leskiw, *
Anthony Petras, *
Gene Calai, *
EMP: 35 **EST:** 1973
SQ FT: 2,000
SALES (est): 40.39MM
SALES (corp-wide): 40.39MM **Privately Held**
Web: www.quadax.com
SIC: 8721 Billing and bookkeeping service

(G-11122)
REGENCY HOSPITAL COMPANY LLC
6990 Engle Rd (44130-3420)
PHONE..................................440 202-4200
David Kern, *Brnch Mgr*
EMP: 97
SALES (corp-wide): 6.2B **Publicly Held**
Web: www.regencyhospital.com
SIC: 8062 General medical and surgical hospitals
HQ: Regency Hospital Company, L.L.C.
   4714 Gettysburg Rd
   Mechanicsburg PA 17055
   419 318-5700

(G-11123)
RESIDENCE INN BY MARRIOTT LLC
Also Called: Residence Inn By Marriott
19149 Bagley Rd (44130-3302)
PHONE..................................440 638-5856
EMP: 28
SALES (corp-wide): 23.71B **Publicly Held**
Web: www.marriott.com
SIC: 7011 Hotels and motels
HQ: Residence Inn By Marriott, Llc
   10400 Fernwood Rd
   Bethesda MD 20817

(G-11124)
RICHS TOWING & SERVICE INC (PA)
20531 1st Ave (44130-2437)
PHONE..................................440 234-3435
Michael Tomasko, *Pr*
Sandy Saponari, *
EMP: 47 **EST:** 1961
SQ FT: 5,000
SALES (est): 4.88MM
SALES (corp-wide): 4.88MM **Privately Held**
Web: www.richstowing.net
SIC: 7549 Towing service, automotive

(G-11125)
RIVALS SPORTS GRILLE LLC
6710 Smith Rd (44130-2656)
PHONE..................................216 267-0005
EMP: 48 **EST:** 2007
SQ FT: 4,368
SALES (est): 1.81MM **Privately Held**
Web: www.rivalscleveland.com
SIC: 5812 7372 Grills (eating places); Application computer software

(G-11126)
ROSCOE MEDICAL INC (HQ)
6753 Engle Rd Ste A (44130-7935)
PHONE..................................440 572-1962
◆ **EMP:** 27 **EST:** 2005
SALES (est): 2.57MM **Privately Held**
Web: www.compasshealthbrands.com
SIC: 5047 Medical equipment and supplies
PA: Compass Health Brands Corp.
   6753 Engle Rd Ste A
   Middleburg Heights OH 44130

(G-11127)
SAVINO DEL BENE USA INC
7043 Pearl Rd Ste 230 (44130-4976)
PHONE..................................347 960-5568
EMP: 196
SALES (corp-wide): 4.67B **Privately Held**
Web: www.savinodelbene.com
SIC: 4731 Freight transportation arrangement
HQ: Savino Del Bene U.S.A., Inc.
   34 Engelhard Ave
   Avenel NJ 07001

(G-11128)
SOUTHWEST COMMUNITY HEALTH SYS
Also Called: Southwest General Hospital
18697 Bagley Rd (44130-3417)
PHONE..................................440 816-8000
William Young, *CEO*
Vasu Pandrangi, *
Thomas A Selden, *
Stanley Trupo, *
James Bastian, *
EMP: 3000 **EST:** 1920
SQ FT: 567,121
SALES (est): 11.52K **Privately Held**
Web: www.swgeneral.com
SIC: 8062 General medical and surgical hospitals

(G-11129)
SOUTHWEST GENERAL MED GROUP
18697 Bagley Rd (44130-3417)
PHONE..................................440 816-8000
EMP: 2000 **EST:** 1990
SALES (est): 17.57MM **Privately Held**
Web: www.swgeneral.com
SIC: 8062 General medical and surgical hospitals

(G-11130)
TAZMANIAN FREIGHT FWDG INC (PA)
Also Called: Tazmanian Freight Systems
6640 Engle Rd Ste H (44130-7948)
P.O. Box 811090 (44181-1090)
PHONE..................................216 265-7881
Robert Rossbach, *CEO*
▲ **EMP:** 40 **EST:** 1987
SALES (est): 100.53MM **Privately Held**
Web: www.tazmanian.com
SIC: 4731 Freight forwarding

(G-11131)
THE INTERLAKE STEAMSHIP CO
7300 Engle Rd (44130-3429)
PHONE..................................440 260-6900
James R Barker, *Ch*
Mark W Barker, *
Paul R Tregurtha, *
Robert F Dorn, *
William M Thornton, *
EMP: 275 **EST:** 1876
SQ FT: 22,330
SALES (est): 141.28MM **Privately Held**
Web: www.interlakesteamship.com
SIC: 4432 Freight transportation on the great lakes
PA: Interlake Holding Company
   1 Landmark Sq Ste 710
   Stamford CT 06901

(G-11132)
UNITED PARCEL SERVICE INC
Also Called: UPS
18401 Sheldon Rd (44130-2400)
PHONE..................................216 676-1570
EMP: 41
SALES (corp-wide): 90.96B **Publicly Held**
Web: www.ups.com
SIC: 4512 Air cargo carrier, scheduled
HQ: United Parcel Service, Inc.
   55 Glenlake Pkwy
   Atlanta GA 30328
   404 828-6000

(G-11133)
VERANTIS CORPORATION (PA)
7251 Engle Rd Ste 300 (44130-3400)
PHONE..................................440 243-0700
Don Day, *CEO*
William Jackson, *
▼ **EMP:** 30 **EST:** 2009
SALES (est): 25.41MM **Privately Held**
Web: www.verantis.com
SIC: 5075 3564 Air pollution control equipment and supplies; Blowers and fans

(G-11134)
WADSWORTH SERVICE INC
7851 Freeway Cir (44130-6308)
PHONE..................................419 861-8181
EMP: 45
SALES (corp-wide): 9.24MM **Privately Held**
Web: www.wadsworthsolutions.com
SIC: 1711 Refrigeration contractor
PA: Wadsworth Service, Inc.
   1500 Michael Owens Way
   Perrysburg OH 43551
   216 391-7263

(G-11135)
WORLD EX SHIPG TRNSP FWDG SVCS (PA)
Also Called: Westainer Lines
17851 Jefferson Park Rd Ste 101 (44130-3461)
PHONE..................................440 826-5055
Brian Buckholz, *Pr*
John Morgan, *
Jeff Ryer, *
◆ **EMP:** 30 **EST:** 1987
SQ FT: 2,800
SALES (est): 4.5MM
SALES (corp-wide): 4.5MM **Privately Held**
SIC: 4731 Freight forwarding

(G-11136)
XNGAGE LLC
16900 Bagley Rd (44130-2542)
PHONE..................................440 990-5767
EMP: 35 **EST:** 2016
SALES (est): 531.76K **Privately Held**
Web: www.xngage.com
SIC: 7371 Computer software development

(G-11137)
ZIN TECHNOLOGIES INC (HQ)
6745 Engle Rd Ste 105 (44130-7993)
PHONE..................................440 625-2200
Daryl Z Laisure, *Pr*
Gary W Mynchenberg, *
Carlos Grodsinsky, *
EMP: 38 **EST:** 1957
SQ FT: 60,000
SALES (est): 48.9MM **Privately Held**
Web: www.zin-tech.com
SIC: 8731 8711 7379 Engineering laboratory, except testing; Consulting engineer; Computer related consulting services
PA: Voyager Space Holdings, Inc.
   1225 17th St Ste 1100
   Denver CO 80202
   303 500-6985

Middlefield
Geauga County

(G-11138)
BRIAR HL HLTH CARE RSDENCE INC
Also Called: Ohman Family Living At Briar
15950 Pierce St (44062-9577)
P.O. Box 277 (44062-0277)
PHONE..................................440 632-5241
George Ohman, *Pr*
Charles Ohman, *
Donald Gray, *
Andy Ohman, *
EMP: 95 **EST:** 1962
SQ FT: 10,000
SALES (est): 6.56MM **Privately Held**
Web: www.ohmanfamilyliving.com
SIC: 8051 Convalescent home with continuous nursing care

(G-11139)
CARTER-JONES LUMBER COMPANY
Also Called: Carter Lumber
14601 Kinsman Rd (44062-9245)
PHONE..................................440 834-8164
Lenny Barciskoi, *Mgr*
EMP: 30
SALES (corp-wide): 2.57B **Privately Held**
Web: www.carterlumber.com
SIC: 2452 5074 5211 Prefabricated buildings, wood; Plumbing and hydronic heating supplies; Lumber products
HQ: The Carter-Jones Lumber Company
   601 Tallmadge Rd
   Kent OH 44240
   330 673-6100

(G-11140)
HANS ROTHENBUHLER & SON INC
15815 Nauvoo Rd (44062-8501)

PHONE..............................440 632-6000
John Rothenbuhler, *Pr*
▲ **EMP:** 40 **EST:** 1956
SALES (est): 6.97MM **Privately Held**
Web: www.rothenbuhlercheesemakers.com
SIC: 2022 5451 5143 2023 Natural cheese; Dairy products stores; Dairy products, except dried or canned; Dry, condensed and evaporated dairy products

(G-11141)
HOPEWELL (PA)
Also Called: HOPEWELL THERAPEUTIC FARM
9637 State Route 534 (44062-9516)
P.O. Box 193 (44439-0193)
PHONE..............................440 426-2000
EMP: 29 **EST:** 1995
SQ FT: 3,600
SALES (est): 7.55MM **Privately Held**
Web: www.hopewellcommunity.org
SIC: 8361 Mentally handicapped home

(G-11142)
KRAFTMAID TRUCKING INC (PA)
16052 Industrial Pkwy (44062-9382)
P.O. Box 1055 (44062-1055)
PHONE..............................440 632-2531
EMP: 100 **EST:** 1989
SQ FT: 12,000
SALES (est): 10.48MM
SALES (corp-wide): 10.48MM **Privately Held**
Web: www.kraftmaid.com
SIC: 4813 2517 Telephone communication, except radio; Wood television and radio cabinets

(G-11143)
OLD MEADOW FARMS INC
Also Called: Middlefield Farm & Garden
15980 Georgia Rd (44062-8236)
P.O. Box 309 (44062-0309)
PHONE..............................440 632-5590
Pierre Hodgins, *Pr*
EMP: 33 **EST:** 1932
SQ FT: 11,000
SALES (est): 6.05MM **Privately Held**
Web: www.mfgkubota.com
SIC: 5999 5261 5599 5571 Farm equipment and supplies; Lawn and garden equipment; Snowmobiles; All-terrain vehicle parts and accessories

(G-11144)
PREMIER NURSING NETWORK LLC
15561 W High St Ste 3 (44062-9455)
PHONE..............................440 563-1586
Dakotah Fetty, *Managing Member*
EMP: 100 **EST:** 2018
SALES (est): 3.83MM **Privately Held**
Web: www.premiernursingnetwork.com
SIC: 8099 7371 Health and allied services, nec; Computer software development and applications

(G-11145)
RAVENWOOD MENTAL HLTH CTR INC
16030 E High St (44062-9474)
P.O. Box 246 (44062-0246)
PHONE..............................440 632-5355
Dave Boyle, *Brnch Mgr*
EMP: 72
SALES (corp-wide): 11.31MM **Privately Held**
Web: www.ravenwoodhealth.com
SIC: 8093 Mental health clinic, outpatient
PA: Ravenwood Mental Health Center, Inc.
12557 Ravenwood Dr
Chardon OH 44024
440 285-3568

(G-11146)
WESTERN RESERVE FARM COOPERATIVE INC
Also Called: Do It Best
16003 E High St (44062-7234)
P.O. Box 339 (44062-0339)
PHONE..............................440 632-0271
TOLL FREE: 800
EMP: 95
Web: www.wrfc.com
SIC: 5191 5983 5211 Farm supplies; Fuel oil dealers; Lumber and other building materials

Middleport
Meigs County

(G-11147)
COUNTY OF MEIGS
Also Called: Meigs Cnty Dept Jobs Fmly Svcs
175 Race St (45760-1078)
P.O. Box 191 (45760-0191)
PHONE..............................740 992-2117
Michael Swisher, *Mgr*
EMP: 45
Web: www.meigscountyclerkofcourts.com
SIC: 8322 9111 Social service center; County supervisors' and executives' office
PA: County Of Meigs
100 E 2nd St Rm 201
Pomeroy OH 45769
740 992-5290

(G-11148)
MEIGS COUNTY CARE CENTER LLC
Also Called: Overbrook Center
333 Page St (45760-1391)
PHONE..............................740 992-6472
Charla Brown, *Pt*
David Snyder, *Admn*
EMP: 150 **EST:** 1988
SQ FT: 36,000
SALES (est): 6.76MM **Privately Held**
Web: www.overbrookcenter.com
SIC: 8051 8052 8093 Extended care facility; Personal care facility; Rehabilitation center, outpatient treatment

Middletown
Butler County

(G-11149)
ABILITIES FIRST FOUNDATION INC (PA)
4710 Timber Trail Dr (45044-5399)
PHONE..............................513 423-9496
Tom Wheeler, *Ex Dir*
J Thomas Wheeler, *
Elaine Garver, *
Karen Smith, *
Ray Debrosse, *
EMP: 86 **EST:** 1958
SQ FT: 31,200
SALES (est): 2.6MM
SALES (corp-wide): 2.6MM **Privately Held**
Web: www.abilitiesfirst.org
SIC: 8211 8361 8049 8351 School for retarded, nec; Mentally handicapped home; Physical therapist; Child day care services

(G-11150)
ADS MANUFACTURING OHIO LLC
1701 Reinartz Blvd (45042-2127)
PHONE..............................513 217-4502
Mark Booker, *Managing Member*
EMP: 70 **EST:** 2011
SALES (est): 3.03MM
SALES (corp-wide): 19.21MM **Privately Held**
Web: www.advancedds.ca
SIC: 7389 Design services
PA: Advanced Design Solutions Inc
1-533 Romeo St S
Stratford ON N5A 4
519 271-7810

(G-11151)
ALL MAKE SOLUTIONS LLC
Also Called: AMS Construction Parts
2710 S Main St (45044)
P.O. Box 1651 (45042)
PHONE..............................800 255-6253
Daniel Million, *Managing Member*
EMP: 55 **EST:** 2010
SQ FT: 1,000
SALES (est): 10.21MM **Privately Held**
Web: www.amsconstructionparts.com
SIC: 5082 General construction machinery and equipment

(G-11152)
ARCHDIOCESE OF CINCINNATI
Also Called: Mother Teresa Elementary Sch
6085 Jackie Dr (45044-8867)
PHONE..............................513 779-6585
Anne Schulz, *Prin*
EMP: 40
SALES (corp-wide): 222.98MM **Privately Held**
Web: www.catholicaoc.org
SIC: 8611 Business associations
PA: Archdiocese Of Cincinnati
100 E 8th St Fl 8
Cincinnati OH 45202
513 421-3131

(G-11153)
ATRIUM MEDICAL CENTER (DH)
1 Medical Center Dr (45044)
PHONE..............................513 424-2111
EMP: 1108 **EST:** 1913
SALES (est): 248.37MM
SALES (corp-wide): 2.41MM **Privately Held**
Web: www.premierhealth.com
SIC: 8062 General medical and surgical hospitals
HQ: Atrium Health System
1 Medical Center Dr
Middletown OH 45005

(G-11154)
BROWNS RUN COUNTRY CLUB
6855 Sloebig Rd (45042-9448)
PHONE..............................513 423-6291
David Baril, *Genl Mgr*
Todd Dodge, *
Gerg Martin, *
Jennifer Fuller, *
EMP: 29 **EST:** 1956
SALES (est): 835.8K **Privately Held**
Web: www.brownsruncc.com
SIC: 7997 Country club, membership

(G-11155)
CATALYST COUNSELING LLC
5104 Sandhurst Ct (45044-7870)
PHONE..............................937 219-7770
Christian Thurman, *Prin*
EMP: 46 **EST:** 2014
SALES (est): 835.45K **Privately Held**
Web: www.catalystcounselingllc.org
SIC: 8322 Individual and family services

(G-11156)
CHURCH OF GOD RETIREMENT CMNTY
Also Called: Willow Knoll Nursing Center
4400 Vannest Ave (45042-2770)
PHONE..............................513 422-5600
Pamela Van Nest, *Admn*
Brenda Lewis, *
Diane Kloenne, *
West Johnson, *
Dee Allen, *
EMP: 41 **EST:** 1982
SQ FT: 28,000
SALES (est): 2.05MM **Privately Held**
Web: www.pristinesrmiddletown.com
SIC: 8051 8052 8361 Convalescent home with continuous nursing care; Intermediate care facilities; Residential care

(G-11157)
CITY OF MIDDLETOWN
Also Called: Water Treatment
805 Columbia Ave (45042-1907)
PHONE..............................513 425-7781
Scott Belcher, *Mgr*
EMP: 68
SALES (corp-wide): 64.88MM **Privately Held**
Web: www.cityofmiddletown.org
SIC: 3589 4941 Water treatment equipment, industrial; Water supply
PA: City Of Middletown
1 Donham Plz
Middletown OH 45042
513 425-7766

(G-11158)
COHEN BROTHERS INC (PA)
1520 14th Ave (45044-5801)
P.O. Box 957 (45044-0957)
PHONE..............................513 422-3696
TOLL FREE: 800
Wilbur Cohen, *Ch Bd*
Kenneth Cohen, *
Donald Zulanch, *
Robert Dumes, *
Neil Cohen, *
EMP: 50 **EST:** 1924
SQ FT: 90,000
SALES (est): 138.63MM
SALES (corp-wide): 138.63MM **Privately Held**
Web: www.cohenusa.com
SIC: 5093 3441 3341 3312 Ferrous metal scrap and waste; Fabricated structural metal; Secondary nonferrous metals; Blast furnaces and steel mills

(G-11159)
COHEN ELECTRONICS INC
Also Called: Cohen Middletown
3120 S Verity Pkwy (45044-7443)
PHONE..............................513 425-6911
David Dellostritto, *Dir*
Amy E Brown, *
EMP: 99 **EST:** 2015
SALES (est): 11.52MM
SALES (corp-wide): 138.63MM **Privately Held**
Web: www.cohenusa.com
SIC: 5093 Ferrous metal scrap and waste
PA: Cohen Brothers, Inc.
1520 14th Ave
Middletown OH 45044
513 422-3696

(G-11160)
CRANE CONSUMABLES INC
155 Wright Dr (45044-3311)
PHONE..............................513 539-9980
Robert Crane, *CEO*

Middletown - Butler County (G-11161)

EMP: 45 EST: 2007
SALES (est): 5.47MM Privately Held
Web: www.craneconsumables.com
SIC: 7389 2241 Packaging and labeling services; Labels, woven

(G-11161)
EASTERN EXPRESS INC
Also Called: EASTERN EXPRESS INC
30 Enterprise Dr (45044-8925)
PHONE..................513 267-1212
EMP: 201
SALES (corp-wide): 4.88MM Privately Held
Web: www.easternexpressinc.com
SIC: 4213 Contract haulers
PA: Eastern Express Logistics, Inc.
8777 Rockside Rd
Cleveland OH 44125
800 348-6514

(G-11162)
ENTERPRISE PDTS PARTNERS LP
3590 Yankee Rd (45044-8932)
PHONE..................513 423-2122
Christopher Ingram, Brnch Mgr
EMP: 64
SALES (corp-wide): 49.72B Publicly Held
Web: www.enterpriseproducts.com
SIC: 7822 Motion picture and tape distribution
PA: Enterprise Products Partners L.P.
1100 Louisiana St Fl 10
Houston TX 77002
713 381-6500

(G-11163)
EOSYS GROUP INC
2660 Towne Blvd (45044-8986)
PHONE..................513 217-7294
EMP: 36
Web: www.eosysgroup.com
SIC: 7373 Systems integration services
PA: The Eosys Group Inc
140 Weakley Ln
Smyrna TN 37167

(G-11164)
GARDEN MANOR EXTENDED CARE CEN
6898 Hamilton Middletown Rd (45044-7851)
PHONE..................513 420-5972
Sam Boymel, Pr
Rachel Mrs S Boymel, Treas
EMP: 250 EST: 1950
SQ FT: 10,000
SALES (est): 9.7MM Privately Held
SIC: 8051 8361 Convalescent home with continuous nursing care; Residential care

(G-11165)
HART INDUSTRIES INC (PA)
Also Called: Hart Industrial Products Div
931 Jeanette St (45042)
PHONE..................513 541-4278
Herman E Hart, CEO
Roger Hart, *
Christopher Hart, *
▲ EMP: 34 EST: 1966
SQ FT: 47,000
SALES (est): 26.71MM
SALES (corp-wide): 26.71MM Privately Held
Web: www.hose.com
SIC: 5085 Hose, belting, and packing

(G-11166)
INTERSCOPE MANUFACTURING INC
2901 Carmody Blvd (45042)
PHONE..................513 423-8866
John Michael Brill, CEO
◆ EMP: 50 EST: 1988
SQ FT: 175,000
SALES (est): 8.72MM Privately Held
Web: www.interscopemfg.com
SIC: 3599 7389 Custom machinery; Repossession service

(G-11167)
J P TRANSPORTATION CO INC
2518 Oxford State Rd (45044-8909)
P.O. Box 66 (45042-0066)
PHONE..................513 424-6978
Kenneth Henderson, Pr
Donald Henderson, *
EMP: 45 EST: 1958
SQ FT: 3,200
SALES (est): 1.95MM Privately Held
Web: www.jptco.com
SIC: 4213 4212 Contract haulers; Local trucking, without storage

(G-11168)
KINETIC RENOVATIONS LLC
616 Moore St (45044-4515)
PHONE..................937 321-1576
Mark Ernst, Managing Member
EMP: 40 EST: 2017
SALES (est): 777.06K Privately Held
Web: www.kineticrenovations.com
SIC: 7299 Home improvement and renovation contractor agency

(G-11169)
LINCARE INC
4765 Emerald Way (45044-8963)
PHONE..................513 705-4250
EMP: 47
Web: www.lincare.com
SIC: 8082 Home health care services
HQ: Lincare Inc.
19387 Us Highway 19 N
Clearwater FL 33764
727 530-7700

(G-11170)
LOWES HOME CENTERS LLC
Also Called: Lowe's
3125 Towne Blvd (45044-6299)
PHONE..................513 727-3900
EMP: 138
SALES (corp-wide): 86.38B Publicly Held
Web: www.lowes.com
SIC: 5211 5031 5722 5064 Home centers; Building materials, exterior; Household appliance stores; Electrical appliances, television and radio
HQ: Lowe's Home Centers, Llc
1000 Lowes Blvd
Mooresville NC 28117
336 658-4000

(G-11171)
MARTIN GREG EXCAVATING INC
1501 S University Blvd (45044-5967)
PHONE..................513 727-9300
Gregory L Martin, Pr
Herbert Martin, *
Rebecca Martin, *
EMP: 31 EST: 1954
SQ FT: 27,500
SALES (est): 4.93MM Privately Held
Web: www.martinexcavating.com
SIC: 1794 Excavation and grading, building construction

(G-11172)
MIAMI UNIVERSITY
Also Called: Miami University-Middletown
4200 E University Blvd (45042)
PHONE..................513 727-3200
Kelly Cowan, Ex Dir
EMP: 350
SALES (corp-wide): 394.64MM Privately Held
Web: www.miamioh.edu
SIC: 8221 8742 8331 University; Training and development consultant; Job training services
PA: Miami University
501 E High St
Oxford OH 45056
513 529-1809

(G-11173)
MIDDLETOWN TUBE WORKS INC
2201 Trine St (45044-5766)
PHONE..................513 727-0080
Angela Phillips, Pr
EMP: 80 EST: 1993
SQ FT: 230,000
SALES (est): 25.35MM
SALES (corp-wide): 37.42MM Privately Held
Web: www.phillipstube.com
SIC: 5051 Steel
PA: Phillips Mfg. And Tower Co.
5578 State Rte 61 N
Shelby OH 44875
419 347-1720

(G-11174)
MIDDLTOWN AREA SNIOR CTZENS IN
3907 Central Ave (45044-5006)
P.O. Box 421668 (45044-7966)
PHONE..................513 423-1734
Ralph Conner, Pr
Alesia Childress, *
Alicia Chambers, *
Basil Fleming, *
EMP: 31 EST: 1956
SQ FT: 22,000
SALES (est): 2.5MM Privately Held
Web: www.middletownseniorcenter.com
SIC: 8322 Senior citizens' center or association

(G-11175)
MIDUSA CREDIT UNION (PA)
1201 Crawford St (45044-4575)
PHONE..................513 420-8640
Chris Johnson, Pr
EMP: 40 EST: 1934
SQ FT: 6,000
SALES (est): 8.4MM
SALES (corp-wide): 8.4MM Privately Held
Web: www.myusacu.com
SIC: 6061 Federal credit unions

(G-11176)
MOORES FITNESS WORLD INC
Also Called: Store N
413 S Breiel Blvd (45044-5109)
PHONE..................513 424-0000
Shane Burns, Mgr
EMP: 109
SALES (corp-wide): 921.4K Privately Held
SIC: 7991 Exercise facilities
PA: Moore's Fitness World, Inc.
651 Congress Park Dr
Dayton OH

(G-11177)
NU WAVES LTD
Also Called: Nuwaves Engineering
132 Edison Dr (45044-3269)
PHONE..................513 360-0800
Jeff Wells, CEO
Tim Wurth, *
EMP: 43 EST: 2000
SQ FT: 30,200
SALES (est): 12MM Privately Held
Web: www.nuwaves.com
SIC: 8711 Electrical or electronic engineering

(G-11178)
OXYMED INC (PA)
Also Called: Wrencare
4765 Emerald Way (45044-8963)
PHONE..................513 705-4250
Richard Wren, Pr
Ronald Ferguson, *
Gerald Fitzgerald, *
EMP: 30 EST: 1999
SQ FT: 1,100
SALES (est): 24.7MM
SALES (corp-wide): 24.7MM Privately Held
SIC: 5047 Medical equipment and supplies

(G-11179)
PAC WORLDWIDE HOLDING COMPANY
3131 Cincinnati Dayton Rd (45044-8965)
PHONE..................513 217-3200
Steve Foster, VP
EMP: 29
Web: www.pac.com
SIC: 5112 Envelopes
PA: Pac Worldwide Holding Company
15435 Ne 92nd St
Redmond WA 98052

(G-11180)
PHOENIX CORPORATION
Also Called: Phoenix Metals
1401 Made Dr (45044-9846)
PHONE..................513 727-4763
Mike Gara, Prin
EMP: 36
SALES (corp-wide): 14.81B Publicly Held
Web: www.phoenixmetals.com
SIC: 5051 Steel
HQ: Phoenix Corporation
4685 Buford Hwy
Peachtree Corners GA 30071
770 447-4211

(G-11181)
PRECISION STRIP INC
4400 Oxford State Rd (45044-8914)
PHONE..................513 423-4166
EMP: 65
SALES (corp-wide): 14.81B Publicly Held
Web: www.precision-strip.com
SIC: 5051 Steel
HQ: Precision Strip Inc.
86 S Ohio St
Minster OH 45865
419 628-2343

(G-11182)
QUALITY TEAM MANAGEMENT INC
Also Called: Ramada Inn
4430 Stratford Dr (45042-2957)
PHONE..................937 490-2000
Nayeem Aziz, Pr
EMP: 47 EST: 1993
SQ FT: 45,000
SALES (est): 497.65K Privately Held
Web: www.wyndhamhotels.com
SIC: 7011 Hotels and motels

(G-11183)
RITTENHOUSE
3000 Mcgee Ave (45044-4991)
PHONE..................513 423-2322
Lisa Rice, Ex Dir
EMP: 37 EST: 1999
SQ FT: 4,800
SALES (est): 2.67MM Privately Held

GEOGRAPHIC SECTION

SIC: 8059 Personal care home, with health care

(G-11184)
ROBINSON HTG AIR-CONDITIONING
1208 2nd Ave (45044-4210)
PHONE.....................513 422-6812
TOLL FREE: 800
Stuart Robinson, *Pr*
Zereda Robinson, *
EMP: 27 EST: 1945
SQ FT: 4,000
SALES (est): 2.22MM **Privately Held**
Web: www.robinsonheating.com
SIC: 1711 1731 Warm air heating and air conditioning contractor; Electrical work

(G-11185)
ROOSEVELT SURGICAL ASSOCIATES
4040 Roosevelt Blvd (45044-6619)
PHONE.....................513 424-0941
Gary A Cobb Md, *Pr*
EMP: 33 EST: 1990
SALES (est): 2.19MM **Privately Held**
Web: www.premierhealth.com
SIC: 8011 General and family practice, physician/surgeon

(G-11186)
SOUTHWEST OHIO AMBLTORY SRGERY
295 N Breiel Blvd (45042-3807)
PHONE.....................513 425-0930
Eugene D Herrmann, *Pr*
Jerry Magone, *VP*
Gary Cobb, *Treas*
Jeffrey Nicolai, *Dir*
EMP: 36 EST: 1997
SQ FT: 11,500
SALES (est): 1.53MM **Privately Held**
SIC: 8011 Ambulatory surgical center

(G-11187)
SSI FABRICATED INC
2860 Cincinnati Dayton Rd (45044-9802)
PHONE.....................513 217-3535
Richard Hall, *Pr*
Mark Franks, *
Joel K Elkin, *
EMP: 33 EST: 1990
SQ FT: 6,000
SALES (est): 4.83MM **Privately Held**
Web: www.ssifabricated.com
SIC: 7699 5074 Industrial equipment services; Heating equipment (hydronic)

(G-11188)
SUNCOKE ENERGY INC
Also Called: Mto Suncoke
3353 Yankee Rd (45044-8927)
PHONE.....................513 727-5571
Frederick Henderson, *Brnch Mgr*
EMP: 40
Web: www.suncoke.com
SIC: 1241 Coal mining services
PA: Suncoke Energy, Inc.
  1011 Wrrnville Rd Ste 600
  Lisle IL 60532

(G-11189)
SUNRISE TREATMENT CENTER LLC
160 N Breiel Blvd (45042-3806)
PHONE.....................513 217-4676
EMP: 27
SALES (corp-wide): 20.38MM **Privately Held**
Web: www.sunrisetreatmentcenter.net
SIC: 8093 Detoxification center, outpatient
PA: Sunrise Treatment Center, Llc

6460 Harrison Ave Ste 100
Cincinnati OH 45247
513 941-4999

(G-11190)
SUPER SHINE INC
1549 S Breiel Blvd Ste A (45044-6861)
P.O. Box 146 (45042-0146)
PHONE.....................513 423-8999
EMP: 35 EST: 1987
SALES (est): 500K **Privately Held**
Web: brianlorenztelehea.wixsite.com
SIC: 7349 7363 Janitorial service, contract basis; Domestic help service

(G-11191)
VALVOLINE INSTANT OIL CHNGE FR
1321 S Breiel Blvd (45044-6205)
PHONE.....................513 422-4980
James Maupin, *Brnch Mgr*
EMP: 37
Web: www.valvoline.com
SIC: 7549 Lubrication service, automotive
HQ: Valvoline Instant Oil Change Franchising, Inc.
  100 Valvoline Way
  Lexington KY 40509

(G-11192)
VOLUNTEERS OF AMERICA INC
Also Called: Woodlands
2101 S Main St Apt 312 (45044-2604)
PHONE.....................513 420-1887
Rhonda Brandenburg, *Brnch Mgr*
EMP: 181
SALES (corp-wide): 152.62K **Privately Held**
Web: www.voa.org
SIC: 8322 Social service center
PA: Volunteers Of America, Inc.
  1660 Duke St Ste 100
  Alexandria VA 22314
  703 341-5000

Middletown
Warren County

(G-11193)
ACCESS COUNSELING SERVICES LLC
4464 S Dixie Hwy (45005-5464)
PHONE.....................513 649-8008
Debra Cotter, *
Judith Freeland, *
Lynn Harris, *
EMP: 101 EST: 2011
SALES (est): 8.88MM **Privately Held**
Web: www.acscounseling.com
SIC: 8093 Mental health clinic, outpatient

(G-11194)
DAYS INN MIDDLETOWN
Also Called: Red Carpet Inn
3458 Commerce Dr (45005-5229)
PHONE.....................513 420-9378
EMP: 71 EST: 1991
SQ FT: 26,144
SALES (est): 183.82K **Privately Held**
Web: www.wyndhamhotels.com
SIC: 7011 Hotels and motels

(G-11195)
DAYTON CHILDRENS HOSPITAL
100 Campus Loop Rd (45005-5187)
PHONE.....................513 424-2850
Carol Driscoll, *Prin*
EMP: 98
SALES (corp-wide): 639.25MM **Privately Held**

Web: www.childrensdayton.org
SIC: 8062 8031 8011 General medical and surgical hospitals; Offices and clinics of osteopathic physicians; Offices and clinics of medical doctors
PA: Dayton Children's Hospital
  1 Childrens Plz
  Dayton OH 45404
  937 641-3000

(G-11196)
DVA HLTHCARE - STHWEST OHIO LL
Also Called: Butler County Dialysis
3497 S Dixie Hwy (45005-5717)
PHONE.....................513 422-1467
John Winstel, *Brnch Mgr*
EMP: 35
SIC: 8092 Kidney dialysis centers
HQ: Dva Healthcare - Southwest Ohio, Llc
  2000 16th St
  Denver CO 80202
  253 733-4501

(G-11197)
ERMC II LP
Also Called: Towne Mall
3461 Towne Blvd Unit 250 (45005-5555)
PHONE.....................513 424-8517
Emerson Russell, *Mgr*
EMP: 85
Web: www.aus.com
SIC: 7349 Janitorial service, contract basis
PA: Ermc Ii, L.P.
  1 Park Pl 6148
  Chattanooga TN 37421

(G-11198)
GREAT MAMI VLY YUNG MNS CHRSTN
5750 Innovation Dr (45005-5189)
PHONE.....................513 217-5501
Donna Keith, *Dir*
EMP: 85
SALES (corp-wide): 13.47MM **Privately Held**
Web: www.gmvymca.org
SIC: 8641 Youth organizations
PA: The Great Miami Valley Young Men's Christian Association
  105 N 2nd St
  Hamilton OH 45011
  513 887-0001

(G-11199)
HIGHTOWERS PETROLEUM COMPANY
Also Called: Hightowers Petroleum Company
3577 Commerce Dr (45005-5232)
PHONE.....................513 423-4272
Stephen L Hightower, *CEO*
Yudell Hightower, *
Gary Visher, *
EMP: 50 EST: 1985
SQ FT: 132,000
SALES (est): 23.75MM **Privately Held**
Web: www.hightowerspetroleum.com
SIC: 5172 Diesel fuel

(G-11200)
OTTERBEIN HOMES
105 Atrium Dr (45005-5166)
PHONE.....................513 260-7690
EMP: 38
SALES (corp-wide): 74.71MM **Privately Held**
Web: www.otterbein.org
SIC: 8361 8059 8051 Aged home; Nursing home, except skilled and intermediate care facility; Skilled nursing care facilities
PA: Otterbein Homes
  3855 Lower Market St # 300

Lebanon OH 45036
513 933-5400

(G-11201)
PRIMARY CR NTWRK PRMR HLTH PRT
Also Called: Anne Camm, Psy.d., Company
1 Medical Center Dr (45005-2584)
PHONE.....................513 420-5233
Christopher Danis, *CEO*
EMP: 43
SALES (corp-wide): 25.36MM **Privately Held**
Web: www.premierhealth.com
SIC: 8011 General and family practice, physician/surgeon
PA: Primary Care Network Of Premier Health Partners
  110 N Main St Ste 350
  Dayton OH 45402
  937 226-7085

(G-11202)
SPRING HILLS HEALTH CARE LLC
Also Called: Spring Hills At Middletown
3851 Towne Blvd (45005-5595)
PHONE.....................513 424-9999
Charlene Himes, *Mgr*
EMP: 71
Web: www.springhills.com
SIC: 8051 Skilled nursing care facilities
PA: Spring Hills Health Care Llc
  515 Plainfield Ave
  Edison NJ 08817

Midvale
Tuscarawas County

(G-11203)
AMKO SERVICE COMPANY (DH)
Also Called: Dover Cryogenics
3211 Brightwood Rd (44653)
P.O. Box 280 (44653-0280)
PHONE.....................330 364-8857
Darren Nippard, *Pr*
Duane R Yant, *Prin*
▲ EMP: 50 EST: 1965
SALES (est): 2.55MM **Privately Held**
Web: www.amkotech.com
SIC: 7699 3443 7629 Tank repair and cleaning services; Cryogenic tanks, for liquids and gases; Electrical repair shops
HQ: Linde Inc.
  10 Riverview Dr
  Danbury CT 06810
  203 837-2000

(G-11204)
KLX ENERGY SERVICES LLC
3571 Brighwood Rd (44653)
PHONE.....................740 922-1155
EMP: 35
SALES (corp-wide): 888.4MM **Publicly Held**
Web: www.klx.com
SIC: 1389 Fishing for tools, oil and gas field
HQ: Klx Energy Services Llc
  3040 Post Oak Blvd # 1500
  Houston TX 77056
  832 844-1015

Milan
Erie County

(G-11205)
FISHER - TITUS AFFILIATED SVCS
Also Called: North Central EMS
12513 Us Highway 250 N (44846-9546)

Milan - Erie County (G-11206)

PHONE.................................419 663-1367
Ashley Ballah, *Ex Dir*
Patrick Martin, *
Paul Douglas, *
EMP: 300 **EST:** 1985
SALES (est): 4.27MM
SALES (corp-wide): 41.4MM **Privately Held**
SIC: 4119 Ambulance service
PA: Fisher - Titus Health
   272 Benedict Ave
   Norwalk OH 44857
   419 668-8101

(G-11206)
FREUDENBERG-NOK GENERAL PARTNR
Transtec
11617 State Route 13 (44846)
P.O. Box 556 (44846-0556)
PHONE.................................419 499-2502
EMP: 193
SALES (corp-wide): 12.23B **Privately Held**
Web: www.fst.com
SIC: 7389 5013 Packaging and labeling services; Automotive supplies and parts
HQ: Freudenberg-Nok General Partnership
   47774 W Anchor Ct
   Plymouth MI 48170
   734 451-0020

(G-11207)
LINCARE INC
11001 Us Highway 250 N Ste E15 (44846-9300)
PHONE.................................419 499-1188
EMP: 29
Web: www.lincare.com
SIC: 7352 Medical equipment rental
HQ: Lincare Inc.
   19387 Us Highway 19 N
   Clearwater FL 33764
   727 530-7700

(G-11208)
MILAN SKILLED NURSING LLC
Also Called: Continuing Healthcare of Milan
185 S Main St (44846-9765)
PHONE.................................216 727-3996
Brian Haylor, *CFO*
Mark Sprenger, *VP*
Scott Sprenger, *COO*
Benjamin Parsons, *Dir*
Jeff Bunner, *Ex Dir*
EMP: 70 **EST:** 2015
SALES (est): 1.08MM **Privately Held**
SIC: 8049 Nurses and other medical assistants

(G-11209)
NORTHERN OHIO ANIMAL HEALTHCAR
2502 State Route 113 E (44846-9419)
PHONE.................................419 499-4949
Lynn Arnold, *Pr*
EMP: 35
SALES (corp-wide): 490.27K **Privately Held**
Web: www.noahpetclinic.com
SIC: 0742 Animal hospital services, pets and other animal specialties
PA: Northern Ohio Animal Healthcar
   2405 E Perkins Ave
   Sandusky OH 44870
   419 625-2484

(G-11210)
PACKAGING & PADS R US LLC (PA)
12406 Us Highway 250 N (44846-9382)
PHONE.................................419 499-2905
Harry Perdue Junior, *Managing Member*
Lisa Brownell, *
EMP: 30 **EST:** 2007
SQ FT: 40,000
SALES (est): 12.04MM
SALES (corp-wide): 12.04MM **Privately Held**
Web: www.pandprus.com
SIC: 5199 Packaging materials

(G-11211)
PRECISION PAVING INC
3414 State Route 113 E (44846-9426)
PHONE.................................419 499-7283
Mike Kegarise, *Pr*
Jeff Crecelius, *
Matt Kluding, *
EMP: 33 **EST:** 2002
SQ FT: 10,000
SALES (est): 4.62MM **Privately Held**
Web: www.ppaving.com
SIC: 1611 Surfacing and paving

(G-11212)
SIERRA LOBO INC
11401 Hoover Rd (44846-9711)
PHONE.................................301 345-1386
Daniel Lowe, *Pr*
EMP: 27 **EST:** 2013
SALES (est): 2.8MM **Privately Held**
Web: www.sierralobo.com
SIC: 8111 Administrative and government law

(G-11213)
XPO LOGISTICS FREIGHT INC
Also Called: Xpo Logistics
12518 Us Highway 250 N (44846-9540)
PHONE.................................419 499-8888
Jeffrey Mount, *Mgr*
EMP: 37
SALES (corp-wide): 7.74B **Publicly Held**
Web: www.xpo.com
SIC: 4731 Freight transportation arrangement
HQ: Xpo Logistics Freight, Inc.
   2211 Old Erhart Rd Ste 10
   Ann Arbor MI 48105
   800 755-2728

Milford
Clermont County

(G-11214)
1 TOM PLUMBER LLC
Also Called: 1 866 Plumber
24 Whitney Dr Ste A (45150-9521)
PHONE.................................866 758-6237
Larry Dell Hensley, *Owner*
EMP: 45 **EST:** 2018
SALES (est): 3.55MM **Privately Held**
Web: www.1tomplumber.com
SIC: 1711 Plumbing contractors

(G-11215)
A W FARRELL & SON INC
745 Us Route 50 (45150-9510)
PHONE.................................513 334-0715
Craig Miller, *Brnch Mgr*
EMP: 29
SALES (corp-wide): 53.34MM **Privately Held**
Web: www.awfarrell.com
SIC: 1761 Roofing contractor
PA: A. W. Farrell & Son, Inc.
   3649 Lake Shore Dr E
   Dunkirk NY 14048
   716 366-4950

(G-11216)
APPLE SVEN HOSPITALITY MGT INC
Also Called: Homewood Suties - Milford
600 Chamber Dr (45150-1444)
PHONE.................................513 248-4663
Andrea Farias, *Genl Mgr*
Pat Ross, *Genl Mgr*
EMP: 32 **EST:** 2008
SALES (est): 380.89K **Privately Held**
Web: homewoodsuites3.hilton.com
SIC: 7011 Hotels and motels

(G-11217)
BERKHEIMER ENTERPRISES LLC
Also Called: Beneficial Talent Source
2 Crestview Dr (45150-1701)
PHONE.................................513 884-8702
EMP: 28 **EST:** 2017
SALES (est): 2.99MM **Privately Held**
Web: www.beneficialtalentsource.com
SIC: 7361 Employment agencies

(G-11218)
BETHESDA HOSPITAL INC
Also Called: Bethesda Group Practice
5861 Cinema Dr (45150-1489)
PHONE.................................513 248-8800
Loretta Clark, *Mgr*
EMP: 54
Web: www.trihealth.com
SIC: 8011 General and family practice, physician/surgeon
HQ: Bethesda Hospital, Inc.
   4750 Wesley Ave
   Cincinnati OH 45212
   513 569-6100

(G-11219)
BUCKHORN INC (HQ)
Also Called: Buckhorn
400 Techne Center Dr Ste 215 (45150-9779)
PHONE.................................513 831-4402
Joel Grant, *Sr VP*
◆ **EMP:** 37 **EST:** 1981
SALES (est): 96.56MM
SALES (corp-wide): 813.07MM **Publicly Held**
Web: www.buckhorninc.com
SIC: 5199 Packaging materials
PA: Myers Industries, Inc.
   1293 S Main St
   Akron OH 44301
   330 253-5592

(G-11220)
BURKE INC
Also Called: Burke Milford
25 Whitney Dr Ste 110 (45150-8400)
PHONE.................................513 576-5700
Ron Tatham, *Brnch Mgr*
EMP: 66
Web: www.burke.com
SIC: 8732 Market analysis or research
PA: Burke, Inc.
   500 W 7th St
   Cincinnati OH 45203

(G-11221)
CHI HEALTH AT HOME (DH)
1700 Edison Dr Ste 300 (45150-2729)
PHONE.................................513 576-0262
Dan Dietz, *Pr*
Lieutenant Wilburn Junior, *Pr*
Rich Smith, *
EMP: 50 **EST:** 1993
SALES (est): 223.41MM **Privately Held**
Web: www.chihealthathome.com
SIC: 7363 8093 Medical help service; Specialty outpatient clinics, nec
HQ: Bethesda, Inc.
   619 Oak St 7 N
   Cincinnati OH 45206
   513 569-6400

(G-11222)
CHRISTIAN FAMILY CREDIT UNION
410 Chamber Dr (45150-3098)
PHONE.................................513 528-1521
Kimberly Mcmillan, *Prin*
EMP: 128
Web: www.christianfamilycu.com
SIC: 6061 Federal credit unions
PA: Christian Family Credit Union, Inc
   8800 Cleveland Ave Nw
   North Canton OH 44720

(G-11223)
CINTAS CORPORATION NO 2
Also Called: Cintas
27 Whitney Dr (45150-9784)
PHONE.................................513 965-0800
Scott Wolfe, *Mgr*
EMP: 180
SALES (corp-wide): 8.82B **Publicly Held**
Web: www.cintas.com
SIC: 5084 7213 Safety equipment; Uniform supply
HQ: Cintas Corporation No. 2
   6800 Cintas Blvd
   Mason OH 45040

(G-11224)
CONEY ISLAND INC
502 Techne Center Dr (45150-8774)
PHONE.................................513 232-8230
Victor W Nolting, *CEO*
Linda Layton, *
Jennifer Reder, *
Brenda Walker, *Stockholder**
▲ **EMP:** 36 **EST:** 1886
SALES (est): 9.77MM **Privately Held**
Web: www.coneyislandpark.com
SIC: 7999 Tourist attractions, amusement park concessions and rides

(G-11225)
DOWNING DISPLAYS INC (PA)
550 Techne Center Dr (45150-2763)
PHONE.................................513 248-9800
Michael J Scherer, *Pr*
Catherine H Downing, *
Wesley Jacobs, *
Peter O Toole, *
William N Kirkham, *
▲ **EMP:** 65 **EST:** 1967
SQ FT: 110,000
SALES (est): 14.5MM
SALES (corp-wide): 14.5MM **Privately Held**
Web: www.downingdisplays.com
SIC: 7319 Display advertising service

(G-11226)
EPSILON
Also Called: Colloquy
1000 Summit Dr Unit 200 (45150-2724)
PHONE.................................513 248-2882
Brian Kennedy, *CEO*
EMP: 190 **EST:** 1981
SQ FT: 38,000
SALES (est): 4.85MM **Publicly Held**
SIC: 7371 Computer software development
PA: Bread Financial Holdings, Inc.
   3095 Loyalty Cir
   Columbus OH 43219

(G-11227)
FAIRWAY INDEPENDENT MRTG CORP
5989 Meijer Dr Ste 1 (45150-1544)
PHONE.................................513 833-1973
EMP: 45
Web: www.fairwayindependentmc.com

GEOGRAPHIC SECTION

Milford - Clermont County (G-11250)

SIC: 6162 Mortgage bankers
PA: Fairway Independent Mortgage Corporation
4750 S Biltmore Ln
Madison WI 53718

(G-11228)
FRESENIUS MED CARE MILFORD LLC
Also Called: FRESENIUS KIDNEY CARE MILFORD
5890 Meadow Creek Dr (45150-3087)
PHONE..................513 248-1690
William Valle, *
EMP: 30 EST: 2016
SALES (est): 3.04MM **Privately Held**
SIC: 8092 Kidney dialysis centers

(G-11229)
FRONTLINE NATIONAL LLC
502 Techne Center Dr Ste G (45150-8780)
PHONE..................513 528-7823
EMP: 62 EST: 2004
SALES (est): 5.44MM **Privately Held**
Web: www.frontlinenational.com
SIC: 7363 Medical help service

(G-11230)
HOMETEAM INSPECTION SERVICE
575 Chamber Dr (45150-1498)
PHONE..................513 831-1300
Paul Spires, *Pr*
EMP: 210 EST: 1991
SQ FT: 6,764
SALES (est): 3.36MM **Privately Held**
Web: www.hometeam.com
SIC: 7389 6794 Building inspection service; Franchises, selling or licensing

(G-11231)
HOMETOWN URGENT CARE
Also Called: HOMETOWN URGENT CARE
1068 State Route 28 Ste C (45150-2095)
PHONE..................513 831-5900
EMP: 37
SALES (corp-wide): 23.51MM **Privately Held**
Web: www.wellnow.com
SIC: 8049 8011 Occupational therapist; Medical centers
PA: Urgent Care Specialists Llc
2400 Corp Exch Dr Ste 102
Columbus OH 43231
614 505-7633

(G-11232)
HOPEBRIDGE LLC
Also Called: Hopebridge Autism Therapy Ctr
1001 Ford Cir Ste A (45150-2740)
PHONE..................513 831-2578
EMP: 32
SALES (corp-wide): 598.8MM **Privately Held**
Web: www.hopebridge.com
SIC: 8093 Mental health clinic, outpatient
HQ: Hopebridge, Llc
3500 Depauw Blvd Ste 3070
Indianapolis IN 46268

(G-11233)
INTERNATIONAL TECHNEGROUP INC (HQ)
5303 Dupont Cir (45150-2734)
PHONE..................513 576-3900
Thomas A Gregory, *CEO*
EMP: 100 EST: 1983
SQ FT: 28,000
SALES (est): 25.81MM **Privately Held**
Web: www.iti-global.com

SIC: 7371 Computer software development
PA: Wipro Limited
Doddakannelli, Sarjapur Road,
Bengaluru KA 56003

(G-11234)
JACKSON BLUFORD AND SON INC (PA)
910 Us Route 50 (45150-9703)
PHONE..................513 831-6231
EMP: 70 EST: 1920
SALES (est): 9.34MM
SALES (corp-wide): 9.34MM **Privately Held**
Web: www.blufordjackson.com
SIC: 4212 1752 Coal haulage, local; Wood floor installation and refinishing

(G-11235)
KROGER CO
Also Called: Kroger Seasonal - Spa DC
401 Milford Pkwy (45150-1298)
PHONE..................859 630-6959
Lisa Allen, *Mgr*
EMP: 75
SALES (corp-wide): 150.04B **Publicly Held**
Web: www.thekrogerco.com
SIC: 4225 General warehousing and storage
PA: The Kroger Co
1014 Vine St
Cincinnati OH 45202
513 762-4000

(G-11236)
LIBERTY INSULATION CO INC
5782 Deerfield Rd (45150-2657)
PHONE..................513 621-0108
Denver Smith, *Pr*
Nancy Smith, *
Laura Meo, *
EMP: 60 EST: 1975
SALES (est): 4.23MM **Privately Held**
Web: www.libertyinsulation.com
SIC: 1742 Insulation, buildings

(G-11237)
LOWES HOME CENTERS LLC
Also Called: Lowe's
5694 Romar Dr (45150-8505)
PHONE..................513 965-3280
EMP: 143
SALES (corp-wide): 86.38B **Publicly Held**
Web: www.lowes.com
SIC: 5211 5031 5722 5064 Home centers; Building materials, exterior; Household appliance stores; Electrical appliances, television and radio
HQ: Lowe's Home Centers, Llc
1000 Lowes Blvd
Mooresville NC 28117
336 658-4000

(G-11238)
LYKINS COMPANIES INC (PA)
Also Called: Lykins Energy Solutions
5163 Wolfpen Pleasant Hill Rd (45150)
P.O. Box 643875 (45264)
PHONE..................513 831-8820
Jeff Lykins, *CEO*
Robert J Manning, *
EMP: 40 EST: 1948
SQ FT: 10,000
SALES (est): 94.22MM
SALES (corp-wide): 94.22MM **Privately Held**
Web: www.lykinscompanies.com
SIC: 4213 5172 5411 Trucking, except local; Gasoline; Convenience stores, chain

(G-11239)
LYKINS OIL COMPANY (HQ)
5163 Wolfpen Pleasant Hill Rd (45150)
PHONE..................513 831-8820
D Jeff Lykins, *Pr*
Ronald Lykins, *
Robert J Manning, *
EMP: 30 EST: 1948
SQ FT: 12,000
SALES (est): 53.64MM
SALES (corp-wide): 94.22MM **Privately Held**
SIC: 5172 5983 Gasoline; Fuel oil dealers
PA: Lykins Companies, Inc.
5163 Wlfpen Plasant Hl Rd
Milford OH 45150
513 831-8820

(G-11240)
LYKINS TRANSPORTATION INC
5163 Wolfpen Pleasant Hill Rd (45150-9632)
PHONE..................513 831-8820
Donald F Lykins, *CEO*
Robert J Manning, *
Jeff Lykins, *
Ron Lykins, *
EMP: 60 EST: 1996
SQ FT: 10,000
SALES (est): 4.57MM
SALES (corp-wide): 94.22MM **Privately Held**
SIC: 4213 Liquid petroleum transport, non-local
PA: Lykins Companies, Inc.
5163 Wlfpen Plasant Hl Rd
Milford OH 45150
513 831-8820

(G-11241)
MADISON TREE CARE & LDSCPG INC
636 Round Bottom Rd (45150-9568)
PHONE..................513 576-6391
Frederick J Butcher, *Pr*
Dora Mae Butcher, *
Richard L E Butcher, *
Darlene Girouard, *
John Butcher, *
EMP: 43 EST: 1946
SALES (est): 5.25MM **Privately Held**
Web: www.madisontreecincy.com
SIC: 0783 Planting, pruning, and trimming services

(G-11242)
MELINK CORPORATION
5140 River Valley Rd (45150-9108)
PHONE..................513 685-0958
Stephen K Melink, *Pr*
EMP: 68 EST: 1997
SQ FT: 36,000
SALES (est): 20.82MM **Privately Held**
Web: www.melinkcorp.com
SIC: 8711 8748 3822 Heating and ventilation engineering; Energy conservation consultant; Appliance controls,except air-conditioning and refrigeration

(G-11243)
MIKE CASTRUCCI FORD
1020 Business 28 (45150-2002)
PHONE..................513 831-7010
Mike Castrucci, *Owner*
EMP: 150 EST: 1987
SQ FT: 1,152
SALES (est): 20.79MM **Privately Held**
Web: www.mikecastrucciford.com

SIC: 5511 7538 7532 5521 Automobiles, new and used; General automotive repair shops; Top and body repair and paint shops; Used car dealers

(G-11244)
MOHAMMAD SHOAIB
301 Old Bank Rd (45150-1997)
PHONE..................513 831-7829
Mohammad Shoaib, *Prin*
EMP: 32 EST: 2007
SQ FT: 4,170
SALES (est): 550.19K **Privately Held**
SIC: 7011 Hotels and motels

(G-11245)
MOTOR SYSTEMS INCORPORATED
Also Called: MSI
460 Milford Pkwy (45150-9104)
PHONE..................513 576-1725
EMP: 32 EST: 1996
SQ FT: 16,000
SALES (est): 10.62MM **Privately Held**
Web: www.motorsystems.com
SIC: 5063 Electrical apparatus and equipment

(G-11246)
MRP INC
Also Called: Medical Radiation Physics
5632 Sugar Camp Rd (45150-9673)
PHONE..................513 965-9700
John Freshcorn, *Pr*
EMP: 39 EST: 1988
SQ FT: 6,200
SALES (est): 4.21MM **Privately Held**
Web: www.mrpinc.com
SIC: 8011 Radiologist

(G-11247)
NURSES CARE INC
201 Mound Ave (45150-3520)
PHONE..................513 791-0233
Tammy Stover, *Brnch Mgr*
EMP: 85
SALES (corp-wide): 3.83MM **Privately Held**
Web: www.nursescareinc.com
SIC: 7361 Nurses' registry
PA: Nurses Care, Inc.
9009 Springboro Pike
Miamisburg OH 45342
513 424-1141

(G-11248)
PETER A WIMBERG COMPANY INC
Also Called: Wimberg Lansdscaping
1354 Us Route 50 (45150)
PHONE..................513 271-2332
Peter A Wimberg, *Pr*
John Wimberg, *
EMP: 40 EST: 1980
SALES (est): 2.22MM **Privately Held**
Web: www.wimberglandscaping.com
SIC: 0782 Landscape contractors

(G-11249)
PINNACLE PAVING & SEALING LLC
793 Round Bottom Rd (45150-9509)
PHONE..................513 474-4900
Alan Vahumensky, *Pr*
EMP: 40 EST: 1997
SALES (est): 5.04MM **Privately Held**
Web: www.pinnaclepaving.com
SIC: 1611 Surfacing and paving

(G-11250)
PIVOTEK LLC
910 Lila Ave Rear (45150-1631)
PHONE..................513 372-6205

Milford - Clermont County (G-11251)

Kent Hodson, *Pr*
James Foley, *
Tracy Snyder, *
◆ **EMP:** 35 **EST:** 2011
SALES (est): 8.14MM **Privately Held**
Web: www.pivotek.net
SIC: 1542 1522 Commercial and office building contractors; Residential construction, nec

(G-11251)
PROFESSIONAL LAMINATE MLLWK INC
Also Called: Pro-Lam
1003 Tech Dr (45150-9780)
PHONE..........................513 891-7858
Shannon P Bitzer, *CEO*
Scott W Bitzer, *
▲ **EMP:** 42 **EST:** 1986
SQ FT: 22,000
SALES (est): 9.85MM **Privately Held**
Web: www.thepligroup.com
SIC: 5031 5712 Kitchen cabinets; Customized furniture and cabinets

(G-11252)
RIDGE OHIO
25 Whitney Dr Ste 120 (45150-8400)
PHONE..........................513 804-2204
John Mckay, *Prin*
EMP: 28 **EST:** 2019
SALES (est): 2.46MM **Privately Held**
Web: www.theridgeohio.com
SIC: 8093 Substance abuse clinics (outpatient)

(G-11253)
RINALDI ORTHODONTICS INC
5987 Meijer Dr (45150-2191)
PHONE..........................513 831-6160
Anthony Lawrence Rinaldi, *Prin*
EMP: 33
SALES (corp-wide): 866.91K **Privately Held**
Web: www.rinaldiorthodontics.com
SIC: 8021 Orthodontist
PA: Rinaldi Orthodontics, Inc.
6406 Thornberry Ct 220a
Mason OH 45040
513 234-7890

(G-11254)
ROCKWELL AUTOMATION OHIO LLC (HQ)
1700 Edison Dr (45150-2729)
PHONE..........................513 576-6151
Ralph Delisio, *Genl Mgr*
EMP: 75 **EST:** 1981
SALES (est): 15.28MM **Publicly Held**
SIC: 7373 7379 Systems software development services; Computer related consulting services
PA: Rockwell Automation, Inc.
1201 S 2nd St
Milwaukee WI 53204

(G-11255)
SI LIQUIDATING INC
Also Called: Sensource Global Sourcing
5405 Dupont Cir Ste A (45150-2798)
PHONE..........................513 388-2076
Andrew Martin, *Pr*
▲ **EMP:** 37 **EST:** 1995
SQ FT: 4,000
SALES (est): 2.23MM **Privately Held**
Web: www.senco-international.com
SIC: 8711 Engineering services

(G-11256)
SIEMENS INDUSTRY SOFTWARE INC
2000 Eastman Dr (45150-2712)
PHONE..........................513 576-2400
Tony Asfusso, *Pr*
EMP: 31
SALES (corp-wide): 84.48B **Privately Held**
Web: new.siemens.com
SIC: 7371 Computer software development
HQ: Siemens Industry Software Inc.
5800 Granite Pkwy Ste 600
Plano TX 75024
972 987-3000

(G-11257)
SILER EXCAVATION SERVICES
6025 Catherine Dr (45150-2203)
PHONE..........................513 400-8628
EMP: 40 **EST:** 2007
SALES (est): 1.93MM **Privately Held**
SIC: 1794 1389 Excavation work; Construction, repair, and dismantling services

(G-11258)
SPA LLC (DH)
Also Called: S P A
401 Milford Pkwy (45150-1298)
PHONE..........................513 733-8800
▼ **EMP:** 30 **EST:** 1986
SALES (est): 23.2MM
SALES (corp-wide): 573.33MM **Privately Held**
Web: www.softpack.com
SIC: 7389 Personal service agents, brokers, and bureaus
HQ: Schwarz Partners Packaging, Llc
10 W Carmel Dr Ste 300
Carmel IN 46032
317 290-1140

(G-11259)
TATA AMERICA INTL CORP
Also Called: Tata Consultancy Services
1000 Summit Dr Unit 1 (45150-2724)
PHONE..........................513 677-6500
Sumanta Roy, *Rgnl Mgr*
EMP: 300
Web: www.tcs.com
SIC: 7372 7373 7371 Prepackaged software; Computer integrated systems design; Custom computer programming services
HQ: Tata America International Corporation
101 Park Ave Fl 2603
New York NY 10178
212 557-8038

(G-11260)
TERRACE PARK COUNTRY CLUB INC
5341 S Milford Rd (45150-9744)
PHONE..........................513 965-4061
Al Washvill, *Genl Mgr*
EMP: 75 **EST:** 1910
SQ FT: 17,000
SALES (est): 4.53MM **Privately Held**
Web: www.terraceparkcc.com
SIC: 7997 Country club, membership

(G-11261)
TOTAL QUALITY LOGISTICS LLC
Also Called: Tql
1701 Edison Dr (45150-2728)
PHONE..........................513 831-2600
Ken Oaks, *CEO*
EMP: 40
SALES (corp-wide): 8.85B **Privately Held**
Web: www.tql.com
SIC: 4731 Truck transportation brokers
HQ: Total Quality Logistics, Llc
4289 Ivy Pointe Blvd
Cincinnati OH 45245

(G-11262)
TRIPACK LLC
401 Milford Pkwy Ste C (45150-9119)
PHONE..........................513 248-1255
Tom S Linz, *Managing Member*
Nick Linz, *
▲ **EMP:** 40 **EST:** 2006
SQ FT: 6,000
SALES (est): 11.12MM **Privately Held**
Web: www.tripack.net
SIC: 5084 7389 Packaging machinery and equipment; Labeling bottles, cans, cartons, etc.

(G-11263)
TRUCRAFT ROOFING LLC
807 Round Bottom Rd (45150-9519)
PHONE..........................513 965-9200
EMP: 40 **EST:** 2010
SALES (est): 9.63MM **Privately Held**
Web: www.trucraftroofing.com
SIC: 1761 Roofing contractor

(G-11264)
UC HEALTH LLC
300 Chamber Dr (45150-1734)
PHONE..........................513 475-8050
EMP: 51
Web: www.uchealth.com
SIC: 8099 8011 Childbirth preparation clinic; Offices and clinics of medical doctors
PA: Uc Health, Llc.
3200 Burnet Ave
Cincinnati OH 45229

Milford Center
Union County

(G-11265)
FORUM MANUFACTURING INC
77 Brown St (43045-8900)
PHONE..........................937 349-8685
Nancy Kovacs, *Pr*
Jim J Kraus, *Prin*
Gerald Shannon, *Prin*
▲ **EMP:** 33 **EST:** 1990
SQ FT: 19,000
SALES (est): 1.28MM **Privately Held**
Web: www.forummfg.com
SIC: 1751 Cabinet building and installation

Millbury
Wood County

(G-11266)
BEST AIRE COMPRESSOR SERVICE (DH)
Also Called: Best Aire
3648 Rockland Cir (43447-9804)
PHONE..........................419 726-0055
Tracy D Paglary, *Prin*
EMP: 100 **EST:** 2008
SQ FT: 37,100
SALES (est): 25.69MM
SALES (corp-wide): 6.88B **Publicly Held**
Web: www.best-aire.com
SIC: 5075 5251 7699 Compressors, air conditioning; Pumps and pumping equipment; Compressor repair
HQ: G. Denver And Co., Llc
800 Beaty St
Davidson NC 28036

(G-11267)
DELVENTHAL COMPANY
3796 Rockland Cir (43447-9651)
PHONE..........................419 244-5570
Steve Delventhal, *Pr*
James Hahn, *
Sharon Delventhal, *
EMP: 30 **EST:** 2002
SQ FT: 12,000
SALES (est): 14.29MM **Privately Held**
Web: www.thedelventhalco.com
SIC: 1541 1542 Industrial buildings, new construction, nec; Commercial and office building contractors

(G-11268)
FORMLABS OHIO INC
Also Called: Spectra Photopolymers
27800 Lemoyne Rd Ste J (43447-9683)
PHONE..........................419 837-9783
Alex Mejiritski, *Pr*
EMP: 45 **EST:** 2017
SALES (est): 10.33MM
SALES (corp-wide): 179.32MM **Privately Held**
Web: www.formlabs.com
SIC: 2899 5169 Chemical preparations, nec; Chemicals and allied products, nec
PA: Formlabs Inc.
35 Medford St Ste 201
Somerville MA 02143
617 932-5227

(G-11269)
GETGO TRANSPORTATION CO LLC
28500 Lemoyne Rd (43447-9431)
PHONE..........................419 666-6850
EMP: 39 **EST:** 2001
SQ FT: 14,000
SALES (est): 5.79MM **Privately Held**
Web: www.getgotransportation.com
SIC: 4214 4225 Local trucking with storage; General warehousing

(G-11270)
LAKE TOWNSHIP TRUSTEES
3800 Ayers Rd (43447-9745)
PHONE..........................419 836-1143
Dan Mclargin, *Mgr*
EMP: 30
Web: www.laketwpohio.com
SIC: 9111 7997 3531 City and town managers' office; Baseball club, except professional and semi-professional; Road construction and maintenance machinery
PA: Lake Township Trustees
27975 Cummings Rd
Millbury OH 43447

(G-11271)
T S EXPEDITING SERVICES INC (PA)
Also Called: Tri-State Expedited Service
27681 Cummings Rd (43447-9762)
P.O. Box 307 (43552-0307)
PHONE..........................419 837-2401
EMP: 82 **EST:** 1983
SALES (est): 26.66MM
SALES (corp-wide): 26.66MM **Privately Held**
Web: www.tstate.com
SIC: 4731 Freight forwarding

Millersburg
Holmes County

(G-11272)
B & L TRANSPORT INC (PA)
3149 State Route 39 (44654-8805)
P.O. Box 130 (44654-0130)

GEOGRAPHIC SECTION

Millersburg - Holmes County (G-11294)

PHONE.....................866 848-2888
Ben Mast, *Pr*
Jon Mast, *
EMP: 28 **EST:** 1980
SQ FT: 4,500
SALES (est): 8.72MM **Privately Held**
Web: www.bl-transport.com
SIC: 4213 Trucking, except local

(G-11273)
BERLIN TRANSPORTATION LLC
7576 State Rte 241 (44654-8822)
PHONE.....................330 674-3395
Ken Wengard, *
Marlin Wengerd, *
EMP: 30 **EST:** 1969
SQ FT: 6,000
SALES (est): 2.3MM **Privately Held**
Web: www.berlintransportation.com
SIC: 4213 Contract haulers

(G-11274)
BIJOE DEVELOPMENT INC
7188 State Rte 62 & 39 (44654)
PHONE.....................330 674-5981
William Baker, *Pr*
Joseph Cross, *
EMP: 40 **EST:** 1989
SQ FT: 4,000
SALES (est): 1.01MM **Privately Held**
SIC: 1389 1311 Oil field services, nec; Crude petroleum and natural gas production

(G-11275)
CHEESE HOLDINGS INC
Also Called: Troyer Cheese, Inc.
6597 County Road 625 (44654-9071)
PHONE.....................330 893-2479
James A Troyer, *Pr*
John Troyer, *Sec*
EMP: 45 **EST:** 1959
SQ FT: 59,500
SALES (est): 21.22MM
SALES (corp-wide): 320.05MM **Privately Held**
Web: www.liparifoods.com
SIC: 5147 2032 5143 5149 Meats, cured or smoked; Ethnic foods, canned, jarred, etc.; Cheese; Specialty food items
PA: Lipari Foods Operating Company Llc
26661 Bunert Rd
Warren MI 48089
586 447-3500

(G-11276)
CHRISTIAN AID MINISTRIES (PA)
Also Called: GOOD SAMARITAN, THE
4464 State Route 39 (44654-9677)
P.O. Box 360 (44610-0360)
PHONE.....................330 893-2428
David N Troyer, *Pr*
Roman Mullet, *
Paul Weaver, *
▼ **EMP:** 50 **EST:** 1981
SQ FT: 8,160
SALES (est): 148.82MM
SALES (corp-wide): 148.82MM **Privately Held**
Web: www.christianaidministries.org
SIC: 5999 8322 Religious goods; Disaster service

(G-11277)
COBLENTZ DISTRIBUTING INC (PA)
Also Called: Walnut Creek Foods
3850 State Route 39 (44654-9683)
P.O. Box 240 (44687-0240)
PHONE.....................330 893-3895
EMP: 192 **EST:** 1977
SALES (est): 57.23MM
SALES (corp-wide): 57.23MM **Privately Held**

Web: www.walnutcreekfoods.com
SIC: 5143 5451 Cheese; Cheese

(G-11278)
CSB BANCORP INC (PA)
Also Called: CSB
91 N Clay St (44654-1117)
P.O. Box 232 (44654-0232)
PHONE.....................330 674-9015
Eddie L Steiner, *Pr*
Robert K Baker, *
Paula J Meiler, *Sr VP*
EMP: 40 **EST:** 1991
SALES (est): 52.76MM
SALES (corp-wide): 52.76MM **Publicly Held**
Web: www.csb1.com
SIC: 6022 State commercial banks

(G-11279)
HOLMES LUMBER & BLDG CTR INC (PA)
Also Called: Holmes Lumber & Supply
6139 S R 39 (44654)
PHONE.....................330 674-9060
Paul Miller, *Pr*
Harry A Shaw, *Prin*
James H Estill, *Prin*
Elmo M Estill, *Prin*
EMP: 104 **EST:** 1952
SQ FT: 16,000
SALES (est): 32.18MM
SALES (corp-wide): 32.18MM **Privately Held**
Web: www.holmeslumber.com
SIC: 5031 5211 2439 2434 Lumber, plywood, and millwork; Lumber and other building materials; Structural wood members, nec; Wood kitchen cabinets

(G-11280)
HOLMES SIDING CONTRACTORS LTD (PA)
Also Called: Mrv Siding Supply
6767 County Road 624 (44654-8840)
PHONE.....................330 674-3382
Jeremy Yoder, *Managing Member*
EMP: 48 **EST:** 1984
SQ FT: 100,000
SALES (est): 11.42MM
SALES (corp-wide): 11.42MM **Privately Held**
Web: www.holmessiding.com
SIC: 1761 Siding contractor

(G-11281)
HOLMES-WAYNE ELECTRIC COOP (PA)
6060 State Route 83 (44654)
P.O. Box 112 (44654)
PHONE.....................330 674-1055
Glenn Miller, *Pr*
EMP: 35 **EST:** 1935
SQ FT: 25,000
SALES (est): 20.25MM
SALES (corp-wide): 20.25MM **Privately Held**
Web: www.hwecoop.com
SIC: 4911 Distribution, electric power

(G-11282)
KEIM LUMBER COMPANY (PA)
4465 State Route 557 (44654-9479)
P.O. Box 40 (44617-0040)
PHONE.....................330 893-2251
TOLL FREE: 800
▲ **EMP:** 90 **EST:** 1890
SALES (est): 49.38MM
SALES (corp-wide): 49.38MM **Privately Held**
Web: www.keimlumber.com

SIC: 5211 5031 Lumber and other building materials; Lumber: rough, dressed, and finished

(G-11283)
LIFECARE HOSPICE
1263 Glen Dr Ste B (44654-8958)
PHONE.....................330 674-8448
EMP: 45
Web: www.ohiohospicelifecare.org
SIC: 8052 Personal care facility
PA: Lifecare Hospice
1900 Akron Rd
Wooster OH 44691

(G-11284)
LIPARI FOODS OPERATING CO LLC
Also Called: Troyer Manufacturing
6597 County Road 625 (44654-9071)
PHONE.....................330 893-2479
Jonas Yoder, *Brnch Mgr*
EMP: 40
SALES (corp-wide): 320.05MM **Privately Held**
Web: www.liparifoods.com
SIC: 8721 2022 2099 2013 Accounting, auditing, and bookkeeping; Cheese; natural and processed; Food preparations, nec; Sausages and other prepared meats
PA: Lipari Foods Operating Company Llc
26661 Bunert Rd
Warren MI 48089
586 447-3500

(G-11285)
MAST TRUCKING INC
6471 County Road 625 (44654-8833)
PHONE.....................330 674-8913
Willis Mast, *Pr*
Elsie Mast, *
Kevin Mast, *
EMP: 100 **EST:** 1969
SALES (est): 28.63MM **Privately Held**
Web: www.masttruckinginc.com
SIC: 4213 Contract haulers

(G-11286)
MILLERSBURG TIRE SERVICE INC
7375 State Route 39 (44654-8319)
PHONE.....................330 674-1085
Brad Schmuker, *Pr*
▲ **EMP:** 30 **EST:** 1953
SQ FT: 7,000
SALES (est): 6.69MM **Privately Held**
Web: www.millersburgtireservice.com
SIC: 5014 5531 Automobile tires and tubes; Automotive tires

(G-11287)
MULTI PRODUCTS COMPANY
7188 State Route 39 (44654-9204)
P.O. Box 1597 (76241-1597)
PHONE.....................330 674-5981
Jeff Berlin, *CEO*
William T Baker, *
Greg Guthrie, *
Bud Doty, *
◆ **EMP:** 29 **EST:** 1965
SQ FT: 30,000
SALES (est): 2.24MM **Privately Held**
Web: www.plungerlift.com
SIC: 3533 5084 Oil field machinery and equipment; Industrial machinery and equipment

(G-11288)
PIONEER TRAILS INC
7572 State Route 241 (44654-8822)
PHONE.....................330 674-1234
TOLL FREE: 800
David Swartzentruber, *Pr*

EMP: 35 **EST:** 1985
SQ FT: 16,000
SALES (est): 2.44MM **Privately Held**
Web: www.pioneertrailsbus.com
SIC: 4142 Bus charter service, except local

(G-11289)
POMERENE HOSPITAL (PA)
981 Wooster Rd (44654-1536)
PHONE.....................330 674-1015
P W Smith Junior, *CEO*
EMP: 270 **EST:** 1937
SQ FT: 45,000
SALES (est): 39.48MM
SALES (corp-wide): 39.48MM **Privately Held**
Web: www.pomerenehospital.org
SIC: 8062 General medical and surgical hospitals

(G-11290)
PRECISION GEOPHYSICAL INC (PA)
2695 State Route 83 (44654-9455)
P.O. Box 152 (44654-0152)
PHONE.....................330 674-2198
Steven Mc Crossin, *Pr*
EMP: 32 **EST:** 1990
SALES (est): 4.77MM **Privately Held**
Web: www.precisiongeophysical.com
SIC: 1382 Oil and gas exploration services

(G-11291)
ROCKWOOD PRODUCTS LTD
Also Called: Rockwood Door & Millwork
5264 Township Road 401 (44654-8740)
PHONE.....................330 893-2392
EMP: 30 **EST:** 1986
SALES (est): 3.1MM **Privately Held**
Web: www.rockwooddoor.com
SIC: 5211 2431 5031 Door and window products; Doors and door parts and trim, wood; Doors and windows

(G-11292)
SAFE-N-SOUND SECURITY INC
5555 County Road 203 Unit B2 (44654-8291)
PHONE.....................330 491-1148
Ryan Torrence, *Pr*
EMP: 60 **EST:** 1998
SALES (est): 2.35MM **Privately Held**
Web: www.safensoundsecurity.net
SIC: 7382 Burglar alarm maintenance and monitoring

(G-11293)
TGS INTERNATIONAL INC
4464 State Route 39 (44654-9677)
P.O. Box 355 (44610-0355)
PHONE.....................330 893-4828
David Troyer, *Ex Dir*
Paul Weaver, *
Roman Mullet, *
EMP: 50 **EST:** 1986
SALES (est): 6.43MM
SALES (corp-wide): 148.82MM **Privately Held**
Web: www.cambooks.org
SIC: 4731 2731 Freight forwarding; Book publishing
PA: Christian Aid Ministries
4464 State Route 39
Millersburg OH 44654
330 893-2428

(G-11294)
UNIVERSAL WELL SERVICES INC
11 S Washington St (44654-1341)
PHONE.....................814 333-2656
EMP: 93
SALES (corp-wide): 4.15B **Publicly Held**

Web: www.patenergy.com
SIC: **1389** Oil field services, nec
HQ: Universal Well Services, Inc.
13549 S Mosiertown Rd
Meadville PA 16335
814 337-1983

(G-11295)
VILLAGE MOTORS INC
Also Called: Village Chrysler-Dodge
784 Wooster Rd (44654-1031)
PHONE..............................330 674-2055
Thomas Green, *Pr*
Marc Miller, *
EMP: **67** EST: 1955
SQ FT: 11,200
SALES (est): **9MM Privately Held**
Web: www.villagemotorsinc.com
SIC: **5511** 5521 5012 Automobiles, new and used; Used car dealers; Automobiles and other motor vehicles

(G-11296)
WEAVER LEATHER LLC (HQ)
7540 County Road 201 (44654-9296)
P.O. Box 68 (44660-0068)
PHONE..............................330 674-7548
▲ EMP: **86** EST: 1973
SALES (est): **44.29MM**
SALES (corp-wide): **469.89MM Privately Held**
Web: www.weaverleather.com
SIC: **3199** 5199 3172 3161 Harness or harness parts; Leather and cut stock; Personal leather goods, nec; Luggage
PA: Blue Point Capital Partners Llc
127 Public Sq Ste 5100
Cleveland OH 44114
216 535-4700

Millersport
Fairfield County

(G-11297)
ASPLUNDH TREE EXPERT LLC
Also Called: Asplundh
12488 Lancaster St Bldg 94 (43046-8076)
PHONE..............................740 467-1028
Debbie Tooper, *Mgr*
EMP: **27**
SALES (corp-wide): **1.16B Privately Held**
Web: www.asplundh.com
SIC: **0783** Tree trimming services for public utility lines
PA: Asplundh Tree Expert, Llc
708 Blair Mill Rd
Willow Grove PA 19090
215 784-4200

(G-11298)
PRE-FORE INC
Also Called: Professional Rfrgn & AC
410 Blacklick Eastern Rd Ne (43046-9527)
P.O. Box 518 (43046-0518)
PHONE..............................740 467-2206
Gary Kendrick, *Pr*
John Callow Senior, *Sec*
Keith Schooley, *
EMP: **32** EST: 1997
SALES (est): **2.25MM Privately Held**
Web: www.professionalrefrigerationac.com
SIC: **1711** Warm air heating and air conditioning contractor

(G-11299)
TWC ENTRPRISES ELEC CONTRS LLC
Also Called: TWC Enterprises

2438 Blacklick Eastern Rd Ne (43046-1103)
PHONE..............................740 467-9004
Thomas Cumbow, *Pr*
EMP: **36** EST: 1996
SALES (est): **2.53MM Privately Held**
Web: www.twcenterprisesec.com
SIC: **1731** General electrical contractor

(G-11300)
WHETSTONE MEDICAL CLINIC INC
12135 Lancaster St (43046-8063)
P.O. Box 218 (43046-0218)
PHONE..............................740 467-2787
James W Whetstone, *Pr*
EMP: **29** EST: 1991
SALES (est): **3.06MM Privately Held**
Web: www.fmchealth.org
SIC: **8062** General medical and surgical hospitals

Mineral City
Tuscarawas County

(G-11301)
MUSKINGUM WTRSHED CNSRVNCY DST
Also Called: Atwood Lake Park
4956 Shop Rd Ne (44656-8851)
PHONE..............................330 343-6780
J Anthony Luther, *Superintnt*
EMP: **119**
SALES (corp-wide): **78.16K Privately Held**
Web: www.mwcd.org
SIC: **7996** 7033 Amusement parks; Trailer parks and campsites
PA: Muskingum Watershed Conservancy District
1319 3rd St Nw
New Philadelphia OH 44663
330 343-6647

Mineral Ridge
Trumbull County

(G-11302)
JACKSON INTERNATIONAL INC
Also Called: Jaxon
3714 Union St (44440-9004)
PHONE..............................866 379-2009
Robert Jackson, *CEO*
Barbara Jackson, *Sec*
▲ EMP: **37** EST: 1989
SALES (est): **3.67MM Privately Held**
Web: www.jaxonusa.com
SIC: **5084** Industrial machinery and equipment

(G-11303)
MAHONING VALLEY SANITARY DST
1181 Ohltown Mcdonald Rd (44440-9322)
P.O. Box 4119 (44515-0119)
PHONE..............................330 799-6315
Jack Vaughn, *Pr*
Alan Tatalovich, *
Thomas Holloway, *
EMP: **53** EST: 1926
SALES (est): **17.14MM Privately Held**
Web: www.meanderwater.org
SIC: **4941** Water supply

(G-11304)
ROOD TRUCKING COMPANY INC (PA)
3505 Union St (44440-9007)
PHONE..............................330 652-3519
George H Rood, *Pr*
Diane E Rood, *

EMP: **121** EST: 1965
SQ FT: 10,000
SALES (est): **9.75MM**
SALES (corp-wide): **9.75MM Privately Held**
Web: www.roodtrucking.com
SIC: **4212** 4213 Mail carriers, contract; Trucking, except local

Minerva
Stark County

(G-11305)
CONSUMERS NATIONAL BANK (HQ)
614 E Lincolnway (44657-2096)
P.O. Box 256 (44657-0256)
PHONE..............................330 868-7701
Ralf Lober, *Pr*
EMP: **45** EST: 1965
SQ FT: 6,000
SALES (est): **40.59MM Publicly Held**
Web: www.consumers.bank
SIC: **6021** National commercial banks
PA: Consumers Bancorp, Inc.
614 E Lincoln Way
Minerva OH 44657

(G-11306)
EDGEWATER GOLF INC
Also Called: Edgewater Golf Club
2401 Fox Ave Se (44657-9146)
PHONE..............................330 862-2630
Diane Simms, *Pr*
EMP: **27** EST: 1970
SQ FT: 9,973
SALES (est): **398.66K Privately Held**
Web: www.golfedgewater18.com
SIC: **7992** Public golf courses

(G-11307)
INTERNAL MEDICAL PHYSICIANS
1168 Alliance Rd Nw (44657-8736)
PHONE..............................330 868-3711
EMP: **72**
Web: www.impdoctors.com
SIC: **8011** Internal medicine, physician/surgeon
PA: Internal Medical Physicians
1207 W State St Ste N
Alliance OH 44601

(G-11308)
LIBERTY TIRE SERVICES LLC
14864 Lincoln St Se (44657-8548)
PHONE..............................330 868-0097
George Nolan, *Mgr*
EMP: **28**
SALES (corp-wide): **302.95MM Privately Held**
Web: www.libertytire.com
SIC: **4953** Recycling, waste materials
HQ: Liberty Tire Services, Llc
600 River Ave Ste 3
Pittsburgh PA 15212
412 562-1700

(G-11309)
MINERVA ELDER CARE INC
Also Called: Minerva Elderly Care
1035 E Lincolnway (44657-1297)
PHONE..............................330 868-4147
Renee Forester, *Admn*
Pat Moschgat, *
Edward Martell Senior, *Pr*
Martha Martell, *
Tracy Randall, *
EMP: **41** EST: 1971
SQ FT: 12,000
SALES (est): **2.82MM Privately Held**

SIC: **8051** Extended care facility

(G-11310)
MINERVA WELDING AND FABG INC
22133 Us Route 30 (44657-9401)
P.O. Box 369 (44657-0369)
PHONE..............................330 868-7731
James A Gram, *Pr*
Stephen J Gram, *
Daniel E Gram, *
EMP: **40** EST: 1949
SQ FT: 20,000
SALES (est): **9.72MM Privately Held**
Web: www.minervawelding.com
SIC: **5084** 3599 Industrial machinery and equipment; Machine shop, jobbing and repair

(G-11311)
YOUNG MNS CHRSTN ASSN CNTL STA
Also Called: Minerva Area YMCA
687 Lynnwood Dr (44657-1250)
PHONE..............................330 868-5988
Teresa Arrasmith, *Mgr*
EMP: **182**
SALES (corp-wide): **20.07MM Privately Held**
Web: www.ymcastark.org
SIC: **8641** Youth organizations
PA: Young Mens Christian Association Of Central Stark County, Inc.
4700 Dressler Rd Nw
Canton OH 44718
330 491-9622

Minford
Scioto County

(G-11312)
SOUTHERN OHIO MEDICAL CENTER
Also Called: Somc Minford Family Practice
8792 State Route 335 (45653-8698)
PHONE..............................740 820-2141
EMP: **90**
SALES (corp-wide): **546.1MM Privately Held**
Web: www.somc.org
SIC: **8062** General medical and surgical hospitals
PA: Southern Ohio Medical Center
1805 27th St
Portsmouth OH 45662
740 354-5000

Mingo Junction
Jefferson County

(G-11313)
JEFFERSON BEHAVIORAL HLTH SYS
220 Murdock St (43938-1062)
PHONE..............................740 535-1314
EMP: **71**
SALES (corp-wide): **3.52MM Privately Held**
Web: www.jbhsohio.org
SIC: **8621** Health association
PA: Jefferson Behavioral Health System
1 Ross Park Blvd Ste 201
Steubenville OH 43952
740 264-7751

(G-11314)
JSW STEEL USA OHIO INC
Also Called: Jsw USA
1500 Commercial St (43938-1096)
P.O. Box 99 (43938-0099)
PHONE..............................740 535-8172

Mark Bush, CEO
Cynthia L Woolheater, *
Jonathan Shank, *
Rahul Singh, *
EMP: 347 **EST:** 2016
SALES (est): 166.04MM **Privately Held**
Web: www.jswsteel.us
SIC: 5051 3312 Steel; Pipes, iron and steel
PA: Jsw Steel Limited
   Jsw Centre, Bandra Kurla Complex,
   Mumbai MH 40005

Minster
Auglaize County

(G-11315)
ARROWHEAD PARK GOLF CLUB INC
2211 Dirksen Rd (45865-9348)
P.O. Box 73 (45865-0073)
PHONE.................................419 628-2444
Mike Griner, *Pr*
Tom Griner, *Sec*
Bruce Bernhole, *Treas*
EMP: 31 **EST:** 1967
SALES (est): 320.16K **Privately Held**
Web: www.arrowhead-golf.com
SIC: 7992 5941 Public golf courses; Golf goods and equipment

(G-11316)
GARMANN/MILLER & ASSOC INC (PA)
Also Called: Garmann Miller Architects
38 S Lincoln Dr (45865-1220)
P.O. Box 71 (45865-0071)
PHONE.................................419 628-4240
Bruce Miller, *Pr*
Brad Garmann, *VP*
EMP: 38 **EST:** 1993
SQ FT: 2,800
SALES (est): 5.84MM **Privately Held**
Web: www.creategm.com
SIC: 8712 8711 0781 Architectural engineering; Engineering services; Landscape architects

(G-11317)
H A DORSTEN INC
146 N Main St (45865-1120)
P.O. Box 156 (45865-0156)
PHONE.................................419 628-2327
Ronald A Dorsten, *Pr*
Frank P Connaughton, *
H A Dersten, *
James E Weger, *
EMP: 50 **EST:** 1953
SQ FT: 2,500
SALES (est): 27.3MM **Privately Held**
Web: www.hadorsteninc.com
SIC: 1541 1542 Industrial buildings, new construction, nec; Commercial and office building, new construction

(G-11318)
MINSTER BANK (HQ)
95 W 4th St (45865-1060)
P.O. Box 90 (45865-0090)
PHONE.................................419 628-2351
Mark Henschen, *CEO*
Kenneth Wuebker, *
Phyllis Rose, *
Dale Luebke, *
Daniel Heitmeyer, *
EMP: 42 **EST:** 1914
SQ FT: 33,000
SALES (est): 25.83MM **Privately Held**
Web: www.minsterbank.com

SIC: 6022 State trust companies accepting deposits, commercial
PA: Minster Financial Corp.
   95 W 4th St
   Minster OH 45865

(G-11319)
MINSTER FARMERS COOP EXCH
Also Called: Minster Farmers Co-Op Exchange
292 W 4th St (45865-1024)
P.O. Box 100 (45865-0100)
PHONE.................................419 628-4705
Kevin Doseck, *Genl Mgr*
EMP: 55 **EST:** 1920
SQ FT: 4,800
SALES (est): 8.89MM **Privately Held**
SIC: 5191 5153 5172 2041 Farm supplies; Grain elevators; Engine fuels and oils; Flour and other grain mill products

(G-11320)
PRECISION STRIP INC (HQ)
86 S Ohio St (45865-1246)
P.O. Box 104 (45865-0104)
PHONE.................................419 628-2343
Joe Wolf, *Pr*
Thomas A Compton, *
▲ **EMP:** 200 **EST:** 1977
SQ FT: 300,000
SALES (est): 284.47MM
SALES (corp-wide): 14.81B **Publicly Held**
Web: www.precision-strip.com
SIC: 5051 Steel
PA: Reliance, Inc.
   16100 N 71st St Ste 400
   Scottsdale AZ 85254
   480 564-5700

(G-11321)
PRECISION STRIP TRANSPORT INC (HQ)
86 S Ohio St (45865)
P.O. Box 104 (45865)
PHONE.................................419 628-2343
Marie Eiting, *Pr*
EMP: 37 **EST:** 1988
SQ FT: 9,000
SALES (est): 9.13MM
SALES (corp-wide): 14.81B **Publicly Held**
Web: www.precision-strip.com
SIC: 4212 Local trucking, without storage
PA: Reliance, Inc.
   16100 N 71st St Ste 400
   Scottsdale AZ 85254
   480 564-5700

Mogadore
Portage County

(G-11322)
ASW GLOBAL LLC (PA)
3375 Gilchrist Rd (44260-1253)
PHONE.................................330 733-6291
Andre Thornton, *Managing Member*
Nick Mihyov, *
Robert Glenn Sims, *
George Hand, *
▲ **EMP:** 70 **EST:** 2006
SQ FT: 1,500,000
SALES: 50.24MM
SALES (corp-wide): 50.24MM **Privately Held**
Web: www.aswglobal.com
SIC: 4225 General warehousing

(G-11323)
ASW GLOBAL LLC
Also Called: Asw Supply Chain Service

3325 Gilchrist Rd (44260-1253)
PHONE.................................330 798-5184
EMP: 70
SALES (corp-wide): 50.24MM **Privately Held**
Web: www.aswglobal.com
SIC: 4225 General warehousing
PA: Asw Global, Llc
   3375 Gilchrist Rd
   Mogadore OH 44260
   330 733-6291

(G-11324)
BICO AKRON INC
Also Called: Bico Steel Service Centers
3100 Gilchrist Rd (44260-1246)
PHONE.................................330 794-1716
Michael A Ensminger, *Pr*
▲ **EMP:** 65 **EST:** 1988
SQ FT: 90,000
SALES (est): 23.91MM
SALES (corp-wide): 84.25MM **Privately Held**
Web: www.bicosteel.com
SIC: 5051 3443 Steel; Fabricated plate work (boiler shop)
PA: Bico Buyer, Inc.
   3100 Gilchrist Rd
   Mogadore OH 44260
   330 794-1716

(G-11325)
CORNWELL QUALITY TOOLS COMPANY
Also Called: Cornwell Quality Tools
200 N Cleveland Ave (44260-1205)
PHONE.................................330 628-2627
Bill Nobley, *Brnch Mgr*
EMP: 77
SQ FT: 3,000
SALES (corp-wide): 55.65MM **Privately Held**
Web: www.cornwelltools.com
SIC: 3423 5085 Hand and edge tools, nec; Industrial supplies
PA: The Cornwell Quality Tools Company
   667 Seville Rd
   Wadsworth OH 44281
   330 336-3506

(G-11326)
EMPIRE ONE LLC
1532 State Route 43 (44260-8900)
PHONE.................................330 628-9310
Brian Taylor, *Prin*
EMP: 40 **EST:** 2006
SALES (est): 1.76MM **Privately Held**
SIC: 7389 Water softener service

(G-11327)
H M MILLER CONSTRUCTION CO
1225 Waterloo Rd (44260-9598)
P.O. Box 131 (44260-0131)
PHONE.................................330 628-4811
John Smith, *Pr*
Patrick Smith, *
Mike Smith, *
EMP: 55 **EST:** 1972
SQ FT: 20,000
SALES (est): 9.74MM **Privately Held**
Web: www.hmmillercc.com
SIC: 1623 7353 Sewer line construction; Heavy construction equipment rental

(G-11328)
HENRYS KING TOURING COMPANY
1369 Burbridge Dr (44260-1601)
PHONE.................................330 628-1886
Timothy Walsh, *Prin*
EMP: 35 **EST:** 2010
SALES (est): 181.73K **Privately Held**

SIC: 7929 Entertainers and entertainment groups

(G-11329)
KIDS-PLAY INC
Also Called: Kids Play Green
2096 Creeks Crossing Trl (44260-9365)
PHONE.................................330 896-2400
EMP: 27
SALES (corp-wide): 990.2K **Privately Held**
SIC: 8351 Group day care center
PA: Kids-Play, Inc.
   195 S Main St Ste 202b
   Akron OH 44308
   234 571-5505

(G-11330)
OMEGA LABORATORIES INC
400 N Cleveland Ave (44260-1209)
PHONE.................................330 628-5748
John C Vitullo, *CEO*
Jay Davis, *
Bill Corl, *
EMP: 61 **EST:** 2000
SQ FT: 44,709
SALES (est): 9.47MM **Privately Held**
Web: www.omegalaboratories.com
SIC: 8734 Testing laboratories

(G-11331)
PTAO SFFELD ELEM OHIO CONGRESS
Also Called: National Cngress Prnts Tachers
1128 Waterloo Rd (44260-9577)
PHONE.................................330 628-3430
EMP: 32 **EST:** 2011
SALES (est): 178.95K **Privately Held**
Web: www.pto.org
SIC: 8641 Parent-teachers' association

(G-11332)
TAYLOR CJ DEVELOPMENT INC
3470 Gilchrist Rd (44260-1215)
PHONE.................................330 628-5501
Sherry Taylor, *Pr*
Chris Taylor, *
Tam Taylor, *
Joe Taylor, *
EMP: 95 **EST:** 1981
SQ FT: 4,000
SALES (est): 12.12MM **Privately Held**
Web: www.veritacorp.com
SIC: 1731 Fiber optic cable installation

Monroe
Butler County

(G-11333)
BAKER EQUIPMENT AND MTLS LTD
990 N Garver Rd (45050-1278)
P.O. Box 526 (45050-0526)
PHONE.................................513 422-6697
Cynthia S Baker, *Managing Member*
EMP: 30 **EST:** 1996
SALES (est): 24.55MM
SALES (corp-wide): 582.21MM **Privately Held**
SIC: 1771 Concrete work
HQ: Baker Concrete Construction, Inc.
   900 N Garver Rd
   Monroe OH 45050
   513 539-4000

(G-11334)
BENEDICT ENTERPRISES INC (PA)
750 Lakeview Rd (45050-1707)
P.O. Box 370 (45050-0370)
PHONE.................................513 539-9216
Arnold Benedict, *Pr*

Monroe - Butler County (G-11335)

Elizabeth Benedict, *
EMP: 28 **EST:** 1957
SQ FT: 20,528
SALES (est): 4.68MM
SALES (corp-wide): 4.68MM **Privately Held**
Web: www.bei-benedict.com
SIC: 7513 7519 5511 7538 Truck rental, without drivers; Trailer rental; Trucks, tractors, and trailers: new and used; General truck repair

(G-11335)
BRUNK EXCAVATING INC
Also Called: Brunk Excavating
301 Breaden Dr (45050-1428)
PHONE..................513 360-0308
Jason Brunk, *Pr*
EMP: 27 **EST:** 1994
SALES (est): 8.1MM **Privately Held**
Web: www.brunkexcavating.com
SIC: 1629 1794 1795 4959 Pond construction; Excavation work; Wrecking and demolition work; Snowplowing

(G-11336)
CIPTED CORP
301 Lawton Ave (45050-1215)
PHONE..................412 829-2120
EMP: 75
SALES (est): 4.52MM **Privately Held**
SIC: 3713 5012 Truck bodies (motor vehicles); Trucks, noncommercial

(G-11337)
CONSTRUCTION LABOR CONTRS LLC
60 American Way Ste B (45050-1718)
PHONE..................513 539-2904
Greg Colle, *Mgr*
EMP: 244
Web: www.powerlaborusa.com
SIC: 7361 Labor contractors (employment agency)
HQ: Construction Labor Contractors, Llc
  9760 Shepard Rd
  Macedonia OH 44056
  330 247-1080

(G-11338)
DUGAN & MEYERS INDUSTRIAL LLC
900 N Garver Rd (45050-1241)
PHONE..................513 539-4000
Steven Klinker, *Pr*
Jerome Meyers, *
EMP: 75 **EST:** 2019
SALES (est): 8.35MM **Privately Held**
Web: www.dugan-meyers.com
SIC: 1542 Commercial and office building, new construction

(G-11339)
DUGAN & MEYERS LLC
900 N Garver Rd (45050-1241)
PHONE..................513 891-4300
EMP: 181
SALES (corp-wide): 53.77MM **Privately Held**
Web: www.dugan-meyers.com
SIC: 1542 Nonresidential construction, nec
PA: Dugan & Meyers Llc
  11110 Kenwood Rd
  Blue Ash OH 45242
  513 891-4300

(G-11340)
DUKE ENERGY OHIO INC
593 Todhunter Rd (45050-1026)
PHONE..................513 287-4622
Jim Morgan, *Brnch Mgr*
EMP: 4498

SALES (corp-wide): 29.06B **Publicly Held**
Web: www.duke-energy.com
SIC: 4911 4932 Electric services; Gas and other services combined
HQ: Duke Energy Ohio, Inc.
  139 E 4th St
  Cincinnati OH 45202
  704 382-3853

(G-11341)
HAYNEEDLE INC
1003 Logistics Way (45044-3218)
PHONE..................402 715-3000
Ash Eldifrawi, *Prin*
EMP: 300
SALES (corp-wide): 648.13B **Publicly Held**
Web: www.hayneedle.com
SIC: 8742 Retail trade consultant
HQ: Hayneedle, Inc.
  10810 Farnam Dr Ste 300
  Omaha NE 68154
  402 715-3000

(G-11342)
KAISER LOGISTICS LLC
201 Lawton Ave (45050-1213)
PHONE..................937 534-0213
EMP: 81 **EST:** 2005
SALES (est): 512.01K
SALES (corp-wide): 57.25B **Publicly Held**
SIC: 8741 Business management
PA: Performance Food Group Company
  12500 West Creek Pkwy
  Richmond VA 23238
  804 484-7700

(G-11343)
LITHKO RESTORATION TECH LLC (PA)
Also Called: Lrt Restoration Technologies
990 N Main St (45050)
P.O. Box 569 (45050-0569)
PHONE..................513 863-5500
Mike Pellegrini, *
EMP: 50 **EST:** 1979
SALES (est): 24.1MM
SALES (corp-wide): 24.1MM **Privately Held**
Web: www.lrtrestoration.com
SIC: 1771 Concrete repair

(G-11344)
MCGRAW/KOKOSING INC
101 Clark Blvd (45044-3216)
PHONE..................614 212-5700
Daniel B Walker, *Pr*
Chris A Bergs, *
Tim Freed, *
EMP: 500 **EST:** 1992
SQ FT: 232,000
SALES (est): 106.35MM
SALES (corp-wide): 1.17B **Privately Held**
Web: www.kokosing.biz
SIC: 1541 Renovation, remodeling and repairs: industrial buildings
PA: Kokosing, Inc.
  6235 Wstrville Rd Ste 200
  Westerville OH 43081
  614 212-5700

(G-11345)
OHIO LIVING
Also Called: Ohio Presbt Retirement Vlg
225 Britton Ln (45050-1154)
PHONE..................513 539-7391
TOLL FREE: 800
Stan Kappers, *Brnch Mgr*
EMP: 254
Web: www.ohioliving.org

SIC: 8361 8052 8051 Rest home, with health care incidental; Intermediate care facilities; Skilled nursing care facilities
PA: Ohio Living
  9200 Worthington Rd # 300
  Westerville OH 43082

(G-11346)
OHIO PIZZA PRODUCTS LLC (DH)
Also Called: Performnce Fodservice - Presto
201 Lawton Ave (45050-1213)
P.O. Box 549 (45050-0549)
PHONE..................937 294-6969
Phil Weeda Senior, *Ch*
Vito P Weeda, *
Jeff Schrand, *
Dewey Weeda, *
Dale Lipa, *
EMP: 80 **EST:** 1951
SQ FT: 80,000
SALES (est): 52.32MM
SALES (corp-wide): 57.25B **Publicly Held**
Web: www.prestofoods.com
SIC: 5149 Pizza supplies
HQ: Institution Food House, Inc.
  543 12th Street Dr Nw
  Hickory NC 28601
  804 869-9151

(G-11347)
PAC WORLDWIDE CORPORATION
Also Called: Pac Manufacturing
575 Gateway Blvd (45050-2586)
PHONE..................800 535-0039
EMP: 37
Web: www.pac.com
SIC: 5112 2677 Envelopes; Envelopes
HQ: Pac Worldwide Corporation
  15435 Ne 92nd St
  Redmond WA 98052
  425 202-4000

(G-11348)
PAC WORLDWIDE CORPORATION
Also Called: Copac
575 Gateway Blvd (45050-2586)
PHONE..................800 535-0039
Lance Fletcher, *Brnch Mgr*
EMP: 89
Web: www.pac.com
SIC: 5199 Packaging materials
HQ: Pac Worldwide Corporation
  15435 Ne 92nd St
  Redmond WA 98052
  425 202-4000

(G-11349)
PETERMANN LTD
505 Yankee Rd (45050-1069)
PHONE..................513 539-0324
Peter Settle, *Brnch Mgr*
EMP: 139
Web: www.petermannbus.com
SIC: 4151 School buses
HQ: Petermann Ltd
  1861 Section Rd
  Cincinnati OH 45237

(G-11350)
ROB RICHTER LANDSCAPING INC
240 Senate Dr (45050-1715)
PHONE..................513 539-0300
Richard Richter, *Managing Member*
EMP: 30 **EST:** 1978
SQ FT: 19,280
SALES (est): 2.43MM **Privately Held**
SIC: 0782 Landscape contractors

(G-11351)
SIMPLE JOURNEY INC
913 Lebanon St (45050-1448)
PHONE..................513 360-2678
Rachelle R Hepperly, *Pr*
EMP: 77 **EST:** 2007
SALES (est): 3.91MM
SALES (corp-wide): 46.97MM **Privately Held**
Web: www.otsinc.org
SIC: 8361 Retarded home
PA: Caregiver Behavioral Services, Inc.
  4800 Overton Plz Ste 440
  Fort Worth TX 76109
  800 299-5161

(G-11352)
TITAN REINFORCING LLC
990 N Garver Rd (45050-1278)
PHONE..................513 539-4000
Cindy Baker, *Managing Member*
Britney Higginbotham, *Managing Member*
EMP: 28 **EST:** 2002
SALES (est): 871.97K **Privately Held**
Web: www.titanresteel.com
SIC: 1522 Apartment building construction

(G-11353)
VALICOR ENVIRONMENTAL SVCS LLC (HQ)
Also Called: Valicor
1045 Reed Dr (45050-1717)
PHONE..................513 733-4666
Steve Hopper, *CEO*
Dave Brown, *
Dustin Mcdulin, *CFO*
▲ **EMP:** 50 **EST:** 1982
SQ FT: 16,000
SALES (est): 91.53MM
SALES (corp-wide): 683.99MM **Privately Held**
Web: www.valicor.com
SIC: 8748 Environmental consultant
PA: Ppc Investment Partners Lp
  110 N Wacker Dr Ste 4400
  Chicago IL 60606
  312 447-6050

(G-11354)
VALLEN DISTRIBUTION INC
673 Gateway Blvd (45050-2587)
EMP: 45
Web: www.vallen.com
SIC: 5085 Industrial supplies
HQ: Vallen Distribution, Inc.
  2100 The Oaks Pkwy
  Belmont NC 28012

(G-11355)
WORTHINGTON ENTERPRISES INC
350 Lawton Ave (45050-1216)
PHONE..................513 539-9291
David Kleimeyer, *Mgr*
EMP: 97
SQ FT: 120,000
SALES (corp-wide): 4.92B **Publicly Held**
Web: www.worthingtonenterprises.com
SIC: 3325 5051 3471 3441 Steel foundries, nec; Metals service centers and offices; Plating and polishing; Fabricated structural metal
PA: Worthington Enterprises, Inc.
  200 W Wlson Bridge Rd
  Worthington OH 43085
  614 438-3210

Monroeville
Huron County

(G-11356)
JHI GROUP INC (PA)
Also Called: Janotta & Herner
309 Monroe St (44847-9406)
PHONE...................419 465-4611
James Limbird, *Pr*
James Shelley, *
Jason Ott, *
Steve Durbin, *
Seth Herrnstein, *
EMP: 165 **EST:** 1962
SALES (est): 50.67MM **Privately Held**
Web: www.janottaherner.com
SIC: 1542 Commercial and office building, new construction

(G-11357)
MIDWAY INC (PA)
Also Called: Midway Truck Center
220 Sandusky St (44847-9506)
P.O. Box 188 (44847-0188)
PHONE...................419 465-2551
▼ **EMP:** 60 **EST:** 1944
SALES (est): 9.64MM
SALES (corp-wide): 9.64MM **Privately Held**
Web: www.monroevillefreightliner.com
SIC: 5013 5012 7538 Automotive supplies and parts; Trucks, commercial; General automotive repair shops

(G-11358)
PLOGER TRANSPORTATION LLC
149 Sandusky St (44847-9460)
PHONE...................419 465-2100
Jerron Morrow, *Brnch Mgr*
EMP: 49
SALES (corp-wide): 15MM **Privately Held**
Web: www.plogertrans.com
SIC: 4731 Freight transportation arrangement
PA: Ploger Transportation, Llc
   300 Cleaveland Rd
   Norwalk OH 44857
   419 465-2100

(G-11359)
TUSING BUILDERS LTD
2596 Us Highway 20 E (44847)
PHONE...................419 465-3100
Jason Tusing, *Pt*
EMP: 28 **EST:** 1998
SALES (est): 8.69MM **Privately Held**
Web: www.trusttusing.com
SIC: 1542 1521 Commercial and office building, new construction; Single-family housing construction

(G-11360)
UNDERGROUND UTILITIES INC
416 Monroe St (44847)
P.O. Box 428 (44847)
PHONE...................419 465-2587
John A Bores, *CEO*
Joseph Hossler, *
Thomas Mclaughlin, *VP Fin*
Michael Prinatt, *
Greg Schafer, *
EMP: 96 **EST:** 1978
SQ FT: 12,000
SALES (est): 22.77MM **Privately Held**
Web: www.undergroundutilitiesinc.com
SIC: 1623 Underground utilities contractor

Montgomery
Hamilton County

(G-11361)
BETHESDA FOUNDATION INC
10500 Montgomery Rd (45242-4402)
PHONE...................513 745-1616
Ed Osossky, *Pr*
Gary Algie, *Dir*
EMP: 36 **EST:** 1974
SQ FT: 2,200
SALES (est): 567K **Privately Held**
Web: www.bethesdafoundation.com
SIC: 7389 Fund raising organizations

(G-11362)
BETHESDA HOSPITAL INC
Also Called: Bethesda Corp Communications
10700 Montgomery Rd Ste 315 (45242-3255)
PHONE...................513 247-0224
L Thomas Wilburn, *Pr*
EMP: 43
Web: www.trihealth.com
SIC: 8741 Administrative management
HQ: Bethesda Hospital, Inc.
   4750 Wesley Ave
   Cincinnati OH 45212
   513 569-6100

(G-11363)
BETHESDA HOSPITAL INC
Also Called: Bethesda North Hospital
10500 Montgomery Rd (45242-4402)
P.O. Box 422410 (45242-2410)
PHONE...................513 745-1111
John Prout, *Pr*
EMP: 452
Web: www.trihealth.com
SIC: 8062 General medical and surgical hospitals
HQ: Bethesda Hospital, Inc.
   4750 Wesley Ave
   Cincinnati OH 45212
   513 569-6100

(G-11364)
CARDIOLOGY CTR OF CINCINNATI (PA)
Also Called: Cardiology Center Cincinnati
10525 Montgomery Rd # A (45242-4401)
P.O. Box 631834 (45263-0001)
PHONE...................513 745-9800
Edward J Loughery, *Pr*
EMP: 30 **EST:** 1977
SALES (est): 4.08MM **Privately Held**
Web: www.thecardiologycenter.com
SIC: 8011 Cardiologist and cardio-vascular specialist

(G-11365)
CINCINNATI HAND SURGERY CONS (PA)
10700 Montgomery Rd Ste 150 (45242-3255)
PHONE...................513 961-4263
Peter Stern, *Pr*
Doctor John Mc Donough, *VP*
Doctor Thomas Kiefhaber, *Sec*
EMP: 30 **EST:** 1986
SQ FT: 9,000
SALES (est): 107.23K
SALES (corp-wide): 107.23K **Privately Held**
Web: www.handsurg.com
SIC: 8011 Surgeon

(G-11366)
DAYMARK WEALTH PARTNERS LLC ✪
9675 Montgomery Rd (45242-7263)
PHONE...................513 838-2524
Michael Quin, *Managing Member*
EMP: 30 **EST:** 2022
SALES (est): 1.91MM **Privately Held**
SIC: 6282 Investment advice

(G-11367)
EQUITY DIAMOND BROKERS INC (PA)
Also Called: Eddie Lane's Diamond Showroom
9563 Montgomery Rd Bsmt (45242-0208)
PHONE...................513 793-4760
Edmund Lane, *Pr*
Patrick Higgins, *
Ted Bevis, *
EMP: 35 **EST:** 1969
SALES (est): 2.37MM
SALES (corp-wide): 2.37MM **Privately Held**
Web: www.eddielanes.com
SIC: 5094 5944 Jewelry; Jewelry stores

(G-11368)
F C FRANCHISING SYSTEMS INC
Also Called: Fresh Coat Painters
10700 Montgomery Rd Ste 300 (45242-3255)
PHONE...................513 563-8339
EMP: 38 **EST:** 2005
SALES (est): 2.64MM **Privately Held**
Web: www.freshcoatpainters.com
SIC: 1721 Painting and paper hanging

(G-11369)
MORRIS KENT ORTHODONTICS INC
9573 Montgomery Rd (45242-7211)
PHONE...................513 226-0459
EMP: 43
SALES (corp-wide): 489.39K **Privately Held**
Web: www.kentmorrisorthodontics.com
SIC: 8021 Orthodontist
PA: Morris Kent Orthodontics Inc
   425 Walnut St Ste 2400
   Cincinnati OH 45202
   513 226-0459

(G-11370)
OHIO HEART HEALTH CENTER INC
10506 Montgomery Rd Ste 504 (45242-4400)
PHONE...................513 792-7800
EMP: 165
SIC: 8011 Cardiologist and cardio-vascular specialist
PA: Ohio Heart Health Center, Inc
   237 Wlliam Howard Taft Rd
   Cincinnati OH 45219

(G-11371)
OHIO NATIONAL LIFE ASRN CORP
1 Financial Way Ste 100 (45242-5800)
P.O. Box 237 (45201-0237)
PHONE...................513 794-6100
David B Omaley, *CEO*
Gates Smith, *
EMP: 791 **EST:** 1979
SALES (est): 21.09MM
SALES (corp-wide): 2.2MM **Privately Held**
Web: www.constellationinsurance.com
SIC: 6311 6321 Mutual association life insurance; Disability health insurance
HQ: Augustar Life Insurance Company
   1 Financial Way Ste 100
   Montgomery OH 45242

(G-11372)
ORAL & FACIAL SURGERY ASSOC
10506 Montgomery Rd Ste 203 (45242-4400)
PHONE...................513 791-0550
James D Morrison, *Prin*
EMP: 27 **EST:** 1990
SALES (est): 6.85MM **Privately Held**
Web: www.omscincinnati.com
SIC: 8021 Dental surgeon

(G-11373)
PROLINK HEALTHCARE STAFFING
10700 Montgomery Rd Ste 1 (45242-3260)
PHONE...................513 489-5300
Tony A Munafo, *Prin*
EMP: 90 **EST:** 2012
SALES (est): 2.55MM **Privately Held**
Web: www.prolinkworks.com
SIC: 7363 Temporary help service

(G-11374)
SIBCY CLINE INC
9979 Montgomery Rd (45242-5311)
PHONE...................513 793-2700
Tim Mahoney, *Mgr*
EMP: 120
SALES (corp-wide): 98.72MM **Privately Held**
Web: www.sibcycline.com
SIC: 6531 Real estate agent, residential
PA: Sibcy Cline, Inc.
   8044 Montgomery Rd # 300
   Cincinnati OH 45236
   513 984-4100

(G-11375)
SYCAMORE BOARD OF EDUCATION
YMCA Child Care-Montgomery
9609 Montgomery Rd (45242-7205)
PHONE...................513 489-3937
Charles Day, *Dir*
EMP: 151
SALES (corp-wide): 113.13MM **Privately Held**
Web: www.sycamoreschools.org
SIC: 8211 7991 8351 7032 Public elementary and secondary schools; Physical fitness facilities; Child day care services; Youth camps
PA: Sycamore Board Of Education
   5959 Hagewa Dr
   Blue Ash OH 45242
   513 686-1700

(G-11376)
TRIHEALTH INC
10600 Montgomery Rd Ste 300 (45242-4463)
PHONE...................513 794-5600
EMP: 366
Web: www.trihealth.com
SIC: 8062 General medical and surgical hospitals
HQ: Trihealth, Inc.
   625 Eden Park Dr
   Cincinnati OH 45202
   513 569-5400

(G-11377)
TRIHEALTH INC
Also Called: Bethesda North Hospital
10506 Montgomery Rd (45242-4400)
PHONE...................513 865-1111
Jason Niehaus, *Sr VP*
EMP: 407
Web: www.trihealth.com
SIC: 8741 Hospital management
HQ: Trihealth, Inc.
   625 Eden Park Dr
   Cincinnati OH 45202
   513 569-5400

(G-11378)
TRIHEALTH INC
Also Called: Trihealth Fitnes Hlth Pavilion
6200 Pfeiffer Rd Ste 330 (45242-5864)
PHONE.................................513 985-0900
EMP: 773
Web: www.trihealth.com
SIC: 8741 8011 Hospital management; Offices and clinics of medical doctors
HQ: Trihealth, Inc.
  625 Eden Park Dr
  Cincinnati OH 45202
  513 569-5400

(G-11379)
TRIHEALTH OS LLC
Also Called: Trihealth Orthpd & Spine Inst
10547 Montgomery Rd Ste 400a
(45242-4418)
PHONE.................................513 791-6611
EMP: 3091
Web: www.trihealth.com
SIC: 8069 Orthopedic hospital
HQ: Trihealth Os, Llc
  8311 Montgomery Rd
  Cincinnati OH 45236
  513 985-3700

(G-11380)
TWIN LAKES SENIOR LIVING CMNTY
9840 Montgomery Rd (45242-6272)
PHONE.................................360 933-0741
EMP: 66 **EST:** 2017
SALES (est): 464.42K **Privately Held**
Web: www.lec.org
SIC: 8361 Aged home

Montpelier
Williams County

(G-11381)
BOB-MOR INC
Also Called: Quality Inn
13508 State Route 15 (43543-9737)
PHONE.................................419 485-5555
John P Kidston, *Pr*
Hal R Hendricks, *
EMP: 130 **EST:** 1978
SQ FT: 150,000
SALES (est): 2.3MM **Privately Held**
Web: www.choicehotels.com
SIC: 7011 5812 Hotels and motels; Eating places

(G-11382)
BRYAN TRUCK LINE INC
Also Called: Bryan Systems
14020 Us Hwy 20 Ste A (43543)
PHONE.................................419 485-8373
Ronald W Dean, *Ch Bd*
Larry H Dean, *
Cindy Dennis, *
Buck Muhlford, *
EMP: 100 **EST:** 1949
SQ FT: 16,000
SALES (est): 11.06MM
SALES (corp-wide): 25.12MM **Privately Held**
Web: www.bryansystems.com
SIC: 4212 4213 Local trucking, without storage; Trucking, except local
PA: Best Way Motor Lines, Inc.
  14020 Us Highway 20a
  Montpelier OH 43543
  419 485-8373

(G-11383)
COMMUNITY HSPTALS WLLNESS CTRS
Also Called: Montpelier Hospital
909 E Snyder Ave (43543-1251)
PHONE.................................419 485-3154
Phil Ennen, *CEO*
EMP: 34
SALES (corp-wide): 77.07MM **Privately Held**
Web: www.chwcshospital.org
SIC: 8062 General medical and surgical hospitals
PA: Community Hospitals And Wellness Centers
  433 W High St
  Bryan OH 43506
  419 636-1131

(G-11384)
DECORATIVE PAINT INCORPORATED
700 Randolph St (43543-1464)
PHONE.................................419 485-0632
EMP: 83 **EST:** 2010
SALES (est): 8.91MM **Privately Held**
Web: www.decorativepaintinc.com
SIC: 7532 Paint shop, automotive

(G-11385)
MONTPELIER EXEMPTED VLG SCHL (PA)
1015 E Brown Rd (43543-2026)
P.O. Box 193 (43543-0193)
PHONE.................................419 485-3676
Jamison Grime, *Superintnt*
EMP: 30 **EST:** 1999
SALES (est): 14.54MM
SALES (corp-wide): 14.54MM **Privately Held**
Web: www.montpelier.k12.oh.us
SIC: 8211 7371 Public elementary and secondary schools; Computer software development and applications

(G-11386)
ROBINAIR LEASING CO LLC
Also Called: Evergreen Healthcare Center
924 Charlies Way (43543-1904)
PHONE.................................513 530-1600
Richard Odenthal, *CEO*
Sandra Smiddy, *
EMP: 50 **EST:** 2018
SALES (est): 4.95MM **Privately Held**
Web: www.communicarehealth.com
SIC: 7359 Equipment rental and leasing, nec

(G-11387)
WIELAND CHASE LLC (HQ)
14212 Selwyn Dr (43543-9595)
PHONE.................................419 485-3193
Devin Denner, *Pr*
Daniel Goehler, *
James Palmour, *
◆ **EMP:** 59 **EST:** 1837
SQ FT: 129,000
SALES (est): 44.89MM
SALES (corp-wide): 233.23MM **Privately Held**
Web: www.wieland-chase.com
SIC: 5051 Metals service centers and offices
PA: Wieland Corporation
  4162 English Oak Dr
  Lansing MI 48911
  517 372-8650

Moraine
Montgomery County

(G-11388)
AIRGAS INC
Also Called: Airgas
2400 Sandridge Dr (45439-1849)
PHONE.................................937 222-8312
EMP: 70
SALES (corp-wide): 101.26MM **Privately Held**
Web: www.airgas.com
SIC: 5169 5084 Compressed gas; Welding machinery and equipment
HQ: Airgas, Inc.
  259 N Radnor Chester Rd # 100
  Radnor PA 19087
  610 687-5253

(G-11389)
APRIL ENTERPRISES INC
Also Called: Walnut Creek Nursing Facility
5070 Lamme Rd (45439-3266)
PHONE.................................937 293-7703
Admiral John Hochwalt, *Prin*
EMP: 101 **EST:** 1991
SALES (est): 22.08MM **Privately Held**
Web: www.walnutcreekcampus.com
SIC: 8051 Skilled nursing care facilities

(G-11390)
BATTELLE RIPPE KINGSTON LLP
2000 W Dorothy Ln (45439-1820)
PHONE.................................937 853-1470
EMP: 105
Web: www.rsmus.com
SIC: 8721 Accounting, auditing, and bookkeeping

(G-11391)
BERRY NETWORK LLC (DH)
3100 Kettering Blvd (45439-1924)
P.O. Box 8818 (45401-8818)
PHONE.................................800 366-1264
Joni Arison, *Pr*
Frank Mcnaulty, *VP*
EMP: 196 **EST:** 1987
SQ FT: 55,000
SALES (est): 21.51K
SALES (corp-wide): 916.96MM **Publicly Held**
Web: www.berrynetwork.com
SIC: 7319 Distribution of advertising material or sample services
HQ: Yp Holdings Llc
  2247 Northlake Pkwy Fl 10
  Tucker GA 30084
  866 570-8863

(G-11392)
BRIGIDS PATH INC
3601 S Dixie Dr (45439-2307)
PHONE.................................937 350-1785
Jill Kingston, *Ex Dir*
Megan Zarnitz, *
EMP: 50 **EST:** 2014
SALES (est): 3.06MM **Privately Held**
Web: www.brigidspath.org
SIC: 8011 Offices and clinics of medical doctors

(G-11393)
BUSINESSPLANS INCORPORATED
Also Called: Mycafeteriaplan
1 Tyler Way (45439-7503)
PHONE.................................937 865-6501
EMP: 46 **EST:** 1978
SALES (est): 11.13MM **Privately Held**
Web: www.businessplansinc.com
SIC: 6411 Pension and retirement plan consultants
PA: Navia Benefit Solutions, Inc.
  600 Naches Ave Sw Ste 100
  Renton WA 98057

(G-11394)
BWI CHASSIS DYNAMICS NA INC
2582 E River Rd (45439-1514)
PHONE.................................937 455-5230
Jeff Zhao, *Brnch Mgr*
EMP: 50
SIC: 8734 Testing laboratories
HQ: Bwi Chassis Dynamics (Na), Inc.
  12501 Grand River Rd
  Brighton MI 48116
  937 455-5308

(G-11395)
BWI NORTH AMERICA INC
Also Called: Bwi Group NA
2582 E River Rd (45439-1514)
PHONE.................................937 212-2892
Greg Bowman, *Mgr*
EMP: 50
SALES (corp-wide): 32.41MM **Privately Held**
Web: www.bwigroup.com
SIC: 8734 Product testing laboratories
HQ: Bwi North America Inc.
  3100 Res Blvd Ste 240
  Kettering OH 45420

(G-11396)
CAVU GROUP
Also Called: Latent Heat Solution
2400 E River Rd (45439-1530)
PHONE.................................937 429-2114
EMP: 27
SALES (est): 1.73MM **Privately Held**
Web: www.cavugroup.com
SIC: 8748 Business consulting, nec

(G-11397)
CHEMSTATION INTERNATIONAL INC (PA)
Also Called: Chemstation
3400 Encrete Ln (45439-1946)
PHONE.................................937 294-8265
EMP: 45 **EST:** 1982
SALES (est): 59.59MM
SALES (corp-wide): 59.59MM **Privately Held**
Web: www.chemstation.com
SIC: 6794 2842 2899 2841 Franchises, selling or licensing; Cleaning or polishing preparations, nec; Chemical preparations, nec; Soap and other detergents

(G-11398)
COMMAND ROOFING CO
2485 Arbor Blvd (45439-1776)
PHONE.................................937 298-1155
Jessica Phlipot, *CEO*
Michael R Davis, *
EMP: 110 **EST:** 1984
SQ FT: 50,000
SALES (est): 11.77MM **Privately Held**
Web: www.commandroofing.com
SIC: 1761 1751 Roofing contractor; Carpentry work

(G-11399)
COMPUNET CLINICAL LABS LLC (HQ)
Also Called: Compunet Clinical Labs
2308 Sandridge Dr (45439-1856)
PHONE.................................937 296-0844
Ed Doucette, *CEO*
Teresa Williams, *
Jan Wooles, *
EMP: 250 **EST:** 1986
SALES (est): 115.32MM
SALES (corp-wide): 2.41MM **Privately Held**
Web: www.compunetlab.com

GEOGRAPHIC SECTION

Moraine - Montgomery County (G-11420)

SIC: 8071 Medical laboratories
PA: Premier Health Partners
   110 N Main St Ste 450
   Dayton OH 45402
   937 499-9596

(G-11400)
DAYTON EWS INC
Also Called: Everybodys Workplace Solutions
3050 Springboro Pike (45439-1812)
PHONE.................................937 293-1010
Bill Kasch, Pr
Thomas Shafer, *
Scot Freeman, *
EMP: 50 EST: 1984
SQ FT: 80,000
SALES (est): 7.38MM Privately Held
SIC: 5021 7641 5023 Office furniture, nec; Furniture repair and maintenance; Carpets

(G-11401)
DAYTON HEIDELBERG DISTRG CO
Service Distributing Div
3601 Dryden Rd (45439-1411)
PHONE.................................937 220-6450
Chris Rammel, VP
EMP: 331
SALES (corp-wide): 2.07B Privately Held
Web: www.heidelbergdistributing.com
SIC: 5181 5182 5149 5921 Beer and other fermented malt liquors; Wine; Groceries and related products, nec; Beer (packaged)
HQ: Dayton Heidelberg Distributing Co., Llc
   3601 Dryden Rd
   Moraine OH 45439
   937 222-8692

(G-11402)
DAYTON HEIDELBERG DISTRG LLC (HQ)
3601 Dryden Rd (45439-1411)
PHONE.................................937 222-8692
Joe Noll, Pr
◆ EMP: 329 EST: 1959
SQ FT: 165,000
SALES (est): 472.84MM
SALES (corp-wide): 2.07B Privately Held
Web: www.heidelbergdistributing.com
SIC: 5181 Beer and other fermented malt liquors
PA: Redwood Holdings, Llc
   7301 Parkway Dr
   Hanover MD 21076
   410 579-4140

(G-11403)
DDW CONSULTING INC (PA)
3176 Kettering Blvd (45439-1924)
PHONE.................................937 299-9920
EMP: 53 EST: 1976
SALES (est): 12.97MM
SALES (corp-wide): 12.97MM Privately Held
Web: www.wilconcorp.com
SIC: 1541 1542 Industrial buildings, new construction, nec; Commercial and office building, new construction

(G-11404)
DONNELLON MC CARTHY INC
Also Called: DONNELLON MC CARTHY, INC.
2580 Lance Dr (45409-1512)
PHONE.................................937 299-0200
EMP: 39
SALES (corp-wide): 24.97MM Privately Held
Web: dme.us.com
SIC: 5999 5065 Photocopy machines; Facsimile equipment
PA: Donnellon Mccarthy, Inc.
   10855 Medallion Dr
   Cincinnati OH 45241
   513 769-7800

(G-11405)
E S I INC
Also Called: Esi Electrical Contractors
3178 Encrete Ln (45439-1902)
P.O. Box 55 (45401-0055)
PHONE.................................937 298-7481
EMP: 120
SALES (corp-wide): 4.66B Publicly Held
Web: www.esielectrical.com
SIC: 1731 Electrical work
HQ: E. S. I., Inc.
   4696 Devitt Dr
   West Chester OH 45246
   513 454-3741

(G-11406)
ELASTIZELL SYSTEMS INC
2475 Arbor Blvd (45439-1754)
PHONE.................................937 298-1313
Donald L Phlipot, Pr
Jeannine E Phlipot, *
EMP: 50 EST: 1972
SQ FT: 6,000
SALES (est): 4.56MM Privately Held
Web: www.elastizell-systems.com
SIC: 1771 Concrete work

(G-11407)
ENTING WATER CONDITIONING INC (PA)
Also Called: Superior Water Conditioning Co
3211 Dryden Rd Frnt (45439-1400)
PHONE.................................937 294-5100
TOLL FREE: 800
Mel Entingh, CEO
Dan Entingh, *
Doris Entingh, *
Karen Entingh, *
▲ EMP: 31 EST: 1965
SQ FT: 43,440
SALES (est): 2.89MM
SALES (corp-wide): 2.89MM Privately Held
Web: www.enting.com
SIC: 3589 5999 5074 Water filters and softeners, household type; Water purification equipment; Water purification equipment

(G-11408)
FAMILY SERVICE ASSOCIATION
Also Called: FAMILY SERVICES AND COMMUNITY
2211 Arbor Blvd (45439-1521)
PHONE.................................937 222-9481
Bonnie Parrish, Ex Dir
EMP: 33 EST: 1896
SQ FT: 7,700
SALES (est): 1.46MM Privately Held
Web: www.fsadayton.org
SIC: 8322 Social service center

(G-11409)
FIDELITY HEALTH CARE
Also Called: Premier Health Pharmacy Fidelity
3170 Kettering Blvd (45439-1924)
PHONE.................................937 208-6400
TOLL FREE: 800
Paula Thompson, Pr
Renee Mock, VP
EMP: 13578 EST: 1983
SQ FT: 30,000
SALES (est): 49.59MM
SALES (corp-wide): 1.48B Privately Held
Web: www.premierhealth.com
SIC: 8082 Home health care services
PA: Med America Health Systems Corporation
   1 Wyoming St
   Dayton OH 45409
   937 223-6192

(G-11410)
FIELDSTONE LIMITED PARTNERSHIP (PA)
Also Called: Fox Run Apartments
4000 Miller Valentine Ct (45439-1465)
PHONE.................................937 293-0900
Dan Keller, Prin
EMP: 200 EST: 1997
SALES (est): 7.44MM
SALES (corp-wide): 7.44MM Privately Held
Web: www.fieldstone.com
SIC: 6513 Apartment building operators

(G-11411)
FLAGEL HUBER FLAGEL & CO (PA)
3400 S Dixie Dr (45439-2304)
PHONE.................................937 299-3400
Randal Kuvin, Managing Member
Randal Kuvin, Pt
James R Harkwall, *
EMP: 43 EST: 1933
SQ FT: 13,200
SALES (est): 6.4MM
SALES (corp-wide): 6.4MM Privately Held
Web: www.fhf-cpa.com
SIC: 8721 Certified public accountant

(G-11412)
FUYAO GLASS AMERICA INC
800 Fuyao Ave (45439-7500)
PHONE.................................937 951-9263
EMP: 814
Web: www.fuyaousa.com
SIC: 1793 Glass and glazing work
HQ: Fuyao Glass America Inc.
   2801 W Stroop Rd
   Dayton OH 45439
   937 496-5777

(G-11413)
GLOBE FOOD EQUIPMENT COMPANY
2153 Dryden Rd (45439-1739)
PHONE.................................937 299-5493
Hilton Garner, Pr
◆ EMP: 39 EST: 1991
SALES (est): 13.65MM
SALES (corp-wide): 4.04B Publicly Held
Web: www.globefoodequip.com
SIC: 5046 Restaurant equipment and supplies, nec
PA: The Middleby Corporation
   1400 Toastmaster Dr
   Elgin IL 60120
   847 741-3300

(G-11414)
GRACE HOSPICE LLC
3033 Kettering Blvd Ste 210 (45439-1948)
PHONE.................................937 293-1381
Janice Urke, Admn
EMP: 109
Web: www.ghospice.com
SIC: 8052 Personal care facility
PA: Grace Hospice, Llc
   500 Kirts Blvd Ste 250
   Troy MI 48084

(G-11415)
GROUNDSYSTEMS INC
Also Called: GROUNDSYSTEMS, INC.
2929 Northlawn Ave (45439-1647)
PHONE.................................937 903-5325
Steve Barhorst, Brnch Mgr
EMP: 30
SALES (corp-wide): 17.09MM Privately Held
Web: www.groundsystems.net
SIC: 0782 Lawn care services
PA: Groundsystems, Llc
   11315 Williamson Rd
   Blue Ash OH 45241
   800 570-0213

(G-11416)
HEADING4WARD INVESTMENT CO (PA)
Also Called: Miracle
2425 W Dorothy Ln (45439-1827)
PHONE.................................937 293-9994
William M Sherk Junior, Pr
◆ EMP: 66 EST: 1988
SQ FT: 11,500
SALES (est): 17.01MM Privately Held
Web: www.bngmiraclepet.com
SIC: 3999 0752 5999 Pet supplies; Animal specialty services; Pet supplies

(G-11417)
HOGAN TRUCK LEASING INC
1860 Cardington Rd (45409-1503)
PHONE.................................937 293-0033
EMP: 28
SALES (corp-wide): 127.28MM Privately Held
Web: www.hogan1.com
SIC: 7513 7363 Truck rental and leasing, no drivers; Help supply services
PA: Hogan Truck Leasing, Inc.
   2150 Schuetz Rd Ste 210
   Saint Louis MO 63146
   314 421-6000

(G-11418)
HOMEFULL
2621 Dryden Rd # 302 (45439-1670)
PHONE.................................937 293-1945
Tina Patterson, Ex Dir
Candace High, *
Maureen Pero, *
EMP: 70 EST: 1987
SALES (est): 5.41MM Privately Held
Web: www.homefull.org
SIC: 8322 Emergency shelters

(G-11419)
KASTLE ELECTRIC COMPANY
4501 Kettering Blvd (45439-2137)
P.O. Box 1451 (45401-1451)
PHONE.................................937 254-2681
K Andrew Stuhlmiller, CEO
Gregory P Brush, *
William S Page, *
EMP: 120 EST: 1925
SALES (est): 4.85MM Privately Held
Web: www.quebeholdingsinc.com
SIC: 1731 General electrical contractor

(G-11420)
LINCARE INC
1948 W Dorothy Ln (45439-1818)
PHONE.................................937 299-1141
James Warden, Mgr
EMP: 35
Web: www.lincare.com
SIC: 7352 Medical equipment rental
HQ: Lincare Inc.
   19387 Us Highway 19 N
   Clearwater FL 33764
   727 530-7700

(PA)=Parent Co (HQ)=Headquarters
✪ = New Business established in last 2 years

Moraine - Montgomery County (G-11421) — GEOGRAPHIC SECTION

(G-11421)
MCGOHAN/BRABENDER AGENCY INC (PA)
Also Called: McGohan Brabender
3931 S Dixie Dr (45439-2313)
PHONE..................937 293-1600
Scott Mcgohan, *CEO*
Patrick L Mcgohan, *CEO*
Tim Brabender, *
Rodney L Miller, *
EMP: 39 **EST:** 1972
SQ FT: 1,400
SALES (est): 49.31MM
SALES (corp-wide): 49.31MM **Privately Held**
Web: www.mcgohanbrabender.com
SIC: 6411 Insurance agents, nec

(G-11422)
MCON INDS INC (HQ)
Also Called: Miller Consolidated Inds Inc
2221 Arbor Blvd (45439-1521)
PHONE..................937 294-2681
Thomas Miller, *CEO*
Kelly Henderson, *
EMP: 49 **EST:** 1982
SQ FT: 55,000
SALES (est): 44.45MM
SALES (corp-wide): 44.45MM **Privately Held**
Web: www.millerconsolidated.com
SIC: 5051 3398 Steel; Metal heat treating
PA: Wilse, Inc.
938 W County Road 250 S
Greensburg IN

(G-11423)
MEDVET ASSOCIATES INC
Also Called: MEDVET ASSOCIATES, INC
2714 Springboro W (45439-1710)
PHONE..................937 293-2714
EMP: 78
Web: www.medvet.com
SIC: 0742 Animal hospital services, pets and other animal specialties
PA: Medvet Associates, Llc
350 E Wilson Bridge Rd
Worthington OH 43085

(G-11424)
MEDVET ASSOCIATES LLC
Also Called: Medvet Dayton
2714 Springboro W (45439-1710)
PHONE..................937 293-2714
Kristen Wagner, *Brnch Mgr*
EMP: 133
Web: www.medvet.com
SIC: 0742 Animal hospital services, pets and other animal specialties
PA: Medvet Associates, Llc
350 E Wilson Bridge Rd
Worthington OH 43085

(G-11425)
MIAMI INDUSTRIAL TRUCKS INC (PA)
Also Called: Miami Industrial Trucks
2830 E River Rd (45439-1500)
PHONE..................937 293-4194
TOLL FREE: 800
Mark Jones, *CEO*
George Malacos, *Ch*
EMP: 75 **EST:** 1956
SQ FT: 43,000
SALES (est): 48.64MM
SALES (corp-wide): 48.64MM **Privately Held**
Web: www.mitlift.com
SIC: 5084 7359 7699 Materials handling machinery; Equipment rental and leasing, nec; Industrial equipment services

(G-11426)
MICROTEK LABORATORIES INC
Also Called: Microtek
2400 E River Rd (45439-1530)
PHONE..................937 236-2213
Timothy Riazzi, *Pr*
Marvin L Kidd, *
Trent Matthews, *
Rosie Kidd, *Stockholder*
Marvin Kidd Tkhldr, *Prin*
◆ **EMP:** 30 **EST:** 1985
SQ FT: 80,000
SALES (est): 5.29MM **Privately Held**
Web: www.cavugroup.com
SIC: 8734 Testing laboratories

(G-11427)
NEW DIMENSION METALS CORP
3050 Dryden Rd (45439-1620)
PHONE..................937 299-2233
John Gray, *Pr*
Jeff Schroder, *
▲ **EMP:** 40 **EST:** 1986
SQ FT: 110,000
SALES (est): 24.47MM
SALES (corp-wide): 56.04MM **Privately Held**
Web: www.ndmetals.com
SIC: 5051 Steel
PA: Gray America Corp
3050 Dryden Rd
Moraine OH 45439
937 293-9313

(G-11428)
NOLAND COMPANY (HQ)
Also Called: Winsupply St Petersburg FL Co.
3110 Kettering Blvd (45439-1924)
PHONE..................937 396-7980
Arjay Hoggard, *Pr*
Monte Salsman, *
James Adcox, *
Sharon Vanausdal, *
David Metzger, *
◆ **EMP:** 224 **EST:** 1922
SALES (est): 274.44K
SALES (corp-wide): 3.02B **Privately Held**
SIC: 5074 5075 5063 5085 Plumbing fittings and supplies; Air conditioning equipment, except room units, nec; Electrical supplies, nec; Industrial supplies
PA: Winsupply Inc.
3110 Kettering Blvd
Moraine OH 45439
937 294-5331

(G-11429)
PRIME TIME PTY EVENT RENTL LLC
5225 Springboro Pike (45439-2970)
PHONE..................937 296-9262
Bart A Nye, *Pr*
EMP: 45 **EST:** 1997
SQ FT: 17,000
SALES (est): 12.96MM **Privately Held**
Web: www.primetimepartyrental.com
SIC: 7359 Party supplies rental services

(G-11430)
PROVIDENCE MEDICAL GROUP INC
2912 Springboro W Ste 201 (45439-1674)
PHONE..................937 297-8999
Susan Becker, *COO*
EMP: 43 **EST:** 2002
SALES (est): 3.84MM **Privately Held**
Web: www.provmedgroup.com
SIC: 8741 Administrative management

(G-11431)
QUALSTL CORP
2221 Arbor Blvd (45439-1521)
PHONE..................937 294-4133
Thomas Miller, *Pr*
Alice Miller, *
EMP: 30 **EST:** 1927
SQ FT: 42,000
SALES (est): 21.7MM
SALES (corp-wide): 44.45MM **Privately Held**
Web: www.qualitysteels.com
SIC: 5051 Steel
HQ: Mcon Inds, Inc.
2221 Arbor Blvd
Moraine OH 45439
937 294-2681

(G-11432)
R G SELLERS COMPANY (PA)
Also Called: R G Seller Co
3185 Elbee Rd (45439-1919)
PHONE..................937 299-1545
TOLL FREE: 800
Doug Sellers, *CEO*
Tom Sellers, *
Barbara Sellers, *
EMP: 37 **EST:** 1959
SQ FT: 10,500
SALES (est): 2.6MM
SALES (corp-wide): 2.6MM **Privately Held**
Web: www.rgsellers.com
SIC: 5141 Food brokers

(G-11433)
RES-CARE INC
Also Called: Rescare
2012 Springboro W (45439-1648)
PHONE..................937 298-6276
EMP: 61
SALES (corp-wide): 8.83B **Publicly Held**
Web: www.rescare.com
SIC: 8052 Home for the mentally retarded, with health care
HQ: Res-Care, Inc.
805 N Whittington Pkwy
Louisville KY 40222
502 394-2100

(G-11434)
RES-CARE INC
3033 Kettering Blvd Ste 325 (45439-1962)
PHONE..................419 523-4981
Angela Hannahs, *Dir*
EMP: 96
SALES (corp-wide): 8.83B **Publicly Held**
Web: www.rescare.com
SIC: 8059 Home for the mentally retarded, ex. skilled or intermediate
HQ: Res-Care, Inc.
805 N Whittington Pkwy
Louisville KY 40222
502 394-2100

(G-11435)
RLS & ASSOCIATES INC
Also Called: Robbie L Sarles and Associates
3131 S Dixie Dr Ste 545 (45439-2223)
PHONE..................937 299-5007
Robbie Sarles, *Pr*
Opal Sarles, *Sec*
Alex Schule, *VP*
Andrew Schule, *VP*
EMP: 40 **EST:** 1987
SQ FT: 4,152
SALES (est): 5.32MM **Privately Held**
Web: www.rlsandassoc.com
SIC: 8742 Transportation consultant

(G-11436)
SANDYS AUTO & TRUCK SVC INC
3053 Springboro W (45439-1811)
PHONE..................937 461-4980
Ted Durig, *Pr*
Doug Thomas, *
EMP: 60 **EST:** 1997
SQ FT: 14,000
SALES (est): 5.04MM **Privately Held**
Web: www.sandystowing.com
SIC: 7549 Towing service, automotive

(G-11437)
SETECH INCORPORATED
Also Called: Setech Dayton OH
3100 Dryden Rd (45439-1622)
PHONE..................937 425-9482
EMP: 210
SALES (corp-wide): 48.43MM **Privately Held**
Web: www.setech.com
SIC: 8742 8748 5085 Management consulting services; Business consulting, nec; Industrial supplies
PA: Setech Supply Chain Solutions, Llc
151 Heritage Park Dr # 301
Murfreesboro TN 37129
877 673-8324

(G-11438)
SHOOK CONSTRUCTION CO (PA)
2000 W Dorothy Ln (45439-1820)
PHONE..................937 276-6666
EMP: 100 **EST:** 1925
SALES (est): 99.22MM
SALES (corp-wide): 99.22MM **Privately Held**
Web: www.shookconstruction.com
SIC: 1629 1542 8741 Waste water and sewage treatment plant construction; Commercial and office building, new construction; Construction management

(G-11439)
SOUTH COMMUNITY INC (PA)
3095 Kettering Blvd Ste 1 (45439-1983)
PHONE..................937 293-8300
Carol Smerz, *Pr*
EMP: 116 **EST:** 1972
SQ FT: 40,883
SALES (est): 22.07MM
SALES (corp-wide): 22.07MM **Privately Held**
Web: www.southcommunity.com
SIC: 8093 Mental health clinic, outpatient

(G-11440)
SPACE MANAGEMENT INC
Also Called: Professional Building Maint
2601 W Dorothy Ln (45439-1831)
PHONE..................937 254-6622
Kevin Ray Findlay, *Pr*
EMP: 100 **EST:** 1978
SQ FT: 5,000
SALES (est): 2.41MM **Privately Held**
Web: www.spacemanagement.com
SIC: 7349 Janitorial service, contract basis

(G-11441)
SUNSONG NORTH AMERICA INC
3535 Kettering Blvd (45439-2014)
PHONE..................919 365-3825
Scott Hanks, *Prin*
Yue Zhou, *
▲ **EMP:** 35 **EST:** 2014
SALES (est): 5.4MM **Privately Held**
Web: www.sunsongusa.com
SIC: 5085 Industrial supplies

(G-11442)
TANNER HEATING & AC INC
2238 E River Rd (45439-1520)
PHONE..................937 299-2500
Robert F Tanner, *Pr*
Thomas Tanner, *
David M Tanner, *
EMP: 29 **EST:** 1986

SQ FT: 17,500
SALES (est): 2.01MM **Privately Held**
Web: www.tannerhvac.com
SIC: **1711** Warm air heating and air conditioning contractor

(G-11443)
THE ELDER-BEERMAN STORES CORP
Also Called: El-Bee
3155 Elbee Rd (45439-2046)
P.O. Box 20159 (17402-0140)
PHONE.................................937 296-2700
▲ EMP: 6053
SIC: **5311** 5661 7389 Department stores, non-discount; Shoe stores; Credit card service

(G-11444)
THE WAGNER-SMITH COMPANY
3201 Encrete Ln (45439-1903)
P.O. Box 127 (45401-0127)
PHONE.................................866 338-0398
EMP: 490 EST: 1917
SALES (est): 28MM
SALES (corp-wide): 4.66B **Publicly Held**
Web: www.wagnersmith.com
SIC: **1731** 3531 5082 7353 General electrical contractor; Construction machinery; Construction and mining machinery; Heavy construction equipment rental
HQ: Mdu Construction Services Group, Inc.
1150 W Century Ave
Bismarck ND 58503
701 530-1000

(G-11445)
VAN MAYBERRYS & STORAGE INC
1850 Cardington Rd (45409-1503)
PHONE.................................937 298-8800
William Mayberry Junior, *Pr*
Victoria Voehringer, *
EMP: 35 EST: 1945
SQ FT: 35,000
SALES (est): 2.34MM **Privately Held**
Web: www.mayberrysvan.com
SIC: **4213** 4214 Household goods transport; Local trucking with storage

(G-11446)
VITAS HEALTHCARE CORPORATION
3055 Kettering Blvd Ste 218 (45439-1989)
PHONE.................................937 299-5379
EMP: 71
SALES (corp-wide): 2.26B **Publicly Held**
Web: www.vitas.com
SIC: **8052** Personal care facility
HQ: Vitas Healthcare Corporation
201 S Bscyne Blvd Ste 400
Miami FL 33131
305 374-4143

(G-11447)
WALNUT CREEK SNIOR LVING CMPUS
5070 Lamme Rd (45439-3266)
PHONE.................................937 293-7703
EMP: 34 EST: 2019
SALES (est): 844.06K **Privately Held**
Web: www.walnutcreekcampus.com
SIC: **8051** Skilled nursing care facilities

(G-11448)
WEILER WELDING COMPANY INC
2400 Sandridge Dr (45439-1849)
PHONE.................................937 222-8312
EMP: 71
Web: www.airgas.com

SIC: **5169** 5084 Compressed gas; Welding machinery and equipment

(G-11449)
WINE TRENDS
3601 Dryden Rd (45439-1411)
PHONE.................................937 222-8692
EMP: 48 EST: 2016
SALES (est): 433.89K **Privately Held**
Web: www.winetrendsinc.com
SIC: **5182** Wine

(G-11450)
WINSUPPLY INC (PA)
Also Called: Wss-Dayton
3110 Kettering Blvd (45439-1924)
PHONE.................................937 294-5331
John Mckenzie, *Pr*
Richard Schwartz, *
Gary Benaszeski, *
Bruce Anderson, *
Philip Kremer, *
EMP: 100 EST: 1956
SQ FT: 20,000
SALES (est): 3.02B
SALES (corp-wide): 3.02B **Privately Held**
Web: www.winsupplyinc.com
SIC: **1542** 5085 5074 Commercial and office building contractors; Industrial supplies; Plumbing fittings and supplies

(G-11451)
YOWELL TRANSPORTATION SVC INC
1840 Cardington Rd (45409-1503)
PHONE.................................937 294-5933
Neil T Yowell Iii, *Prin*
Victor Yowell, *
Joe Ford, *
EMP: 75 EST: 1977
SQ FT: 22,000
SALES (est): 9.2MM **Privately Held**
Web: www.yowelltransportation.com
SIC: **4213** 4214 Contract haulers; Local trucking with storage

Moreland Hills
Cuyahoga County

(G-11452)
GALT ENTERPRISES INC
Also Called: Galt
34555 Chagrin Blvd Ste 100 (44022-1056)
P.O. Box 22189 (44122-0189)
PHONE.................................216 464-6744
Lee M Hoffman, *Pr*
William T Davis, *
EMP: 35 EST: 1977
SQ FT: 5,000
SALES (est): 9.1MM **Privately Held**
Web: www.galtenterprises.com
SIC: **6411** Insurance agents, nec

Morral
Marion County

(G-11453)
FETTER SON FARMS LTD LBLTY CO
2421 Morral Kirkpatrick Rd W (43337)
P.O. Box 38 (43337)
PHONE.................................740 465-2961
EMP: 35 EST: 2000
SALES (est): 2.35MM **Privately Held**
Web: www.fetter-trucking.com
SIC: **4213** Contract haulers

(G-11454)
MORRAL COMPANIES LLC (HQ)
132 Postle Ave (43337-7505)
P.O. Box 26 (43337-0026)
PHONE.................................740 465-3251
Daryl Gates, *CEO*
Joe Cunningham, *CFO*
EMP: 46 EST: 1963
SQ FT: 15,000
SALES (est): 176.58MM **Privately Held**
Web: www.morralcompanies.com
SIC: **4783** 5191 Packing and crating; Fertilizer and fertilizer materials
PA: Central Ohio Farmers Co-Op, Inc.
751 E Farming St
Marion OH 43302

Morrow
Warren County

(G-11455)
CONGREGATE LIVING OF AMERICA (PA)
463 E Pike St (45152-1221)
PHONE.................................513 899-2801
Oscar Jarnicki, *Pr*
Cynthia Jarnicki, *
EMP: 60 EST: 1962
SALES (est): 8.88MM
SALES (corp-wide): 8.88MM **Privately Held**
SIC: **8051** 8052 Skilled nursing care facilities; Intermediate care facilities

(G-11456)
VALLEY MACHINE TOOL INC
9773 Morrow Cozaddale Rd (45152-8589)
PHONE.................................513 899-2737
Larry R Wilson, *Pr*
Ralph Wilson, *
Douglas Wilson, *
EMP: 40 EST: 1967
SQ FT: 11,000
SALES (est): 3.03MM **Privately Held**
SIC: **3599** 7692 Machine shop, jobbing and repair; Welding repair

Moscow
Clermont County

(G-11457)
VISTRA CORP
Also Called: William H Zimmer Power Station
1781 Us Highway 52 (45153-9617)
PHONE.................................513 467-5289
Paul King, *Brnch Mgr*
EMP: 250
SALES (corp-wide): 14.78B **Publicly Held**
Web: www.vistracorp.com
SIC: **4911** Distribution, electric power
PA: Vistra Corp.
6555 Sierra Dr
Irving TX 75039
214 812-4600

Mount Eaton
Wayne County

(G-11458)
QUALITY BLOCK & SUPPLY INC (DH)
Rte 250 (44659)
PHONE.................................330 364-4411
Jerry A Schwab, *Pr*
David Schwab, *
Donna Schwab, *

Mary Lynn Hites, *Treas*
EMP: 27 EST: 1973
SQ FT: 4,000
SALES (est): 5.91MM
SALES (corp-wide): 32.72B **Privately Held**
SIC: **3271** 3273 5032 Blocks, concrete or cinder: standard; Ready-mixed concrete; Concrete and cinder block
HQ: Schwab Industries, Inc.
2301 Progress St
Dover OH 44622
330 364-4411

Mount Gilead
Morrow County

(G-11459)
CONSOLIDATED COOPERATIVE
Also Called: CONSOLIDATED COOPERATIVE
5255 State Route 95 (43338-9763)
P.O. Box 111 (43338-0111)
PHONE.................................419 947-3055
Richard Carter, *Ch Bd*
Brian Newton, *
Tom Myser, *
Wes Reinhardt, *
H R Gearhiser, *Vice Chairman*
EMP: 55 EST: 1936
SQ FT: 18,000
SALES (est): 62.84MM **Privately Held**
Web: www.consolidated.coop
SIC: **4911** 8611 Distribution, electric power; Business associations

(G-11460)
FINGLES HOLDINGS LLC
Also Called: Finley's Facilities Services
5707 State Route 61 (43338)
PHONE.................................419 468-5321
EMP: 33 EST: 2016
SALES (est): 4.58MM
SALES (corp-wide): 3.63B **Privately Held**
SIC: **5078** Refrigerators, commercial (reach-in and walk-in)
HQ: Eec Acquisition, Llc
370 Wabasha St N Ste 1700
Saint Paul MN 55102
800 822-2303

(G-11461)
HPM AMERICA LLC
820 W Marion Rd (43338-1095)
PHONE.................................419 946-0222
EMP: 60 EST: 2008
SALES (est): 2.29MM **Privately Held**
SIC: **8748** Business consulting, nec

(G-11462)
MARYHAVEN INC
245 Neal Ave Ste A (43338-9372)
PHONE.................................419 946-6734
Mike Durham, *Brnch Mgr*
EMP: 28
SALES (corp-wide): 32.39MM **Privately Held**
Web: www.maryhaven.com
SIC: **8093** Mental health clinic, outpatient
PA: Maryhaven, Inc.
1791 Alum Creek Dr
Columbus OH 43207
614 449-1530

(G-11463)
MORROW COUNTY HOSPITAL
Also Called: Morrow County Hospital MCH At
651 W Marion Rd (43338-1096)
PHONE.................................419 949-3085
Christopher Truax, *Pr*

EMP: 300
SALES (corp-wide): 22.13MM **Privately Held**
Web: www.morrowcountyhospital.com
SIC: 8062 General medical and surgical hospitals
PA: Morrow County Hospital
651 W Marion Rd
Mount Gilead OH 43338
419 946-5015

(G-11464)
PAM JOHNSONIDENT
Also Called: McDonald's
535 W Marion Rd (43338-1025)
PHONE 419 946-4551
Pam Johnson, *Pr*
EMP: 37 **EST:** 1994
SALES (est): 120.25K **Privately Held**
Web: www.mcdonalds.com
SIC: 5812 7221 Fast-food restaurant, chain; Photographic studios, portrait

(G-11465)
WOODSIDE VILLAGE CARE CENTER
841 W Marion Rd (43338-1094)
PHONE 419 947-2015
William Casto, *Pt*
William R Casto, *Pt*
Gary Casto, *Pt*
EMP: 78 **EST:** 1979
SQ FT: 28,000
SALES (est): 6.61MM **Privately Held**
Web: www.atriumlivingcenters.com
SIC: 8052 8051 Intermediate care facilities; Skilled nursing care facilities

Mount Hope
Holmes County

(G-11466)
GMI HOLDINGS INC (DH)
Also Called: Genie Company, The
1 Door Dr (44660-2503)
P.O. Box 67 (44660-0067)
PHONE 800 354-3643
Mike Kridel, *Pr*
Craig Smith, *
◆ **EMP:** 350 **EST:** 1990
SQ FT: 230,000
SALES (est): 142.14MM **Privately Held**
Web: www.geniecompany.com
SIC: 5064 3699 Vacuum cleaners, nec; Door opening and closing devices, electrical
HQ: Overhead Door Corporation
2501 S State Hwy 121 Ste
Lewisville TX 75067
469 549-7100

(G-11467)
MT HOPE AUCTION INC (PA)
Also Called: Farmers Produce Auction
8076 State Rte 241 (44660)
P.O. Box 82 (44660-0082)
PHONE 330 674-6188
Steven Mullett, *Pr*
EMP: 30 **EST:** 1980
SALES (est): 2.42MM
SALES (corp-wide): 2.42MM **Privately Held**
Web: www.mthopeauction.com
SIC: 5154 7389 Auctioning livestock; Auctioneers, fee basis

(G-11468)
OVERHEAD DOOR CORPORATION
One Door Dr (44660-2503)
P.O. Box 67 (44660-0067)
PHONE 330 674-7015

EMP: 54
Web: www.overheaddoor.com
SIC: 1751 Garage door, installation or erection
HQ: Overhead Door Corporation
2501 S State Hwy 121 Ste
Lewisville TX 75067
469 549-7100

Mount Orab
Brown County

(G-11469)
CHILD FOCUS INC
710 N High St (45154-8349)
PHONE 937 444-1613
Jim Carter, *Pr*
EMP: 43
SALES (corp-wide): 20.97MM **Privately Held**
Web: www.child-focus.org
SIC: 8322 8351 Child related social services; Child day care services
PA: Child Focus, Inc.
4629 Aicholtz Rd
Cincinnati OH 45244
513 752-1555

(G-11470)
EVERYDAY HOMECARE LLC
711 S High St (45154-8947)
P.O. Box 367 (45154-0367)
PHONE 937 444-1672
Vicky Cirley, *Owner*
EMP: 27 **EST:** 2002
SALES (est): 9.29MM **Privately Held**
Web: www.everydayhomecare.com
SIC: 8082 Home health care services

(G-11471)
HOSPICE OF HOPE INC
215 Hughes Blvd (45154-8356)
PHONE 937 444-4900
Kavin Cartmell, *Brnch Mgr*
EMP: 92
Web: www.hospiceofhope.com
SIC: 8052 Personal care facility
PA: Hospice Of Hope, Inc.
909 Kenton Station Dr B
Maysville KY 41056

(G-11472)
MT ORAB FIRE DEPARTMENT INC
Also Called: Mount Orab Ems
113 Spice St (45154-8932)
P.O. Box 454 (45154-0454)
PHONE 937 444-3945
Lisa Reeves, *Chief*
EMP: 27
Web: www.mtoraboh.us
SIC: 4119 Ambulance service
PA: Mt Orab Fire Department Inc
105 Spice St
Mount Orab OH 45154
800 962-1484

(G-11473)
RESCARE OHIO INC (DH)
Also Called: Willimsburg Rsdntial Altrntves
613 W Main St (45154-8265)
PHONE 513 724-1177
EMP: 50 **EST:** 1994
SALES (est): 7.67MM
SALES (corp-wide): 8.83B **Publicly Held**
SIC: 8361 8052 Self-help group home; Intermediate care facilities
HQ: Res-Care, Inc.
805 N Whittington Pkwy
Louisville KY 40222
502 394-2100

Mount Sterling
Madison County

(G-11474)
MAHLE BEHR MT STERLING INC
10500 Oday Harrison Rd (43143-9474)
PHONE 740 869-3333
◆ **EMP:** 367 **EST:** 2011
SALES (est): 94.17MM
SALES (corp-wide): 3.75MM **Privately Held**
SIC: 5013 3714 Automotive engines and engine parts; Motor vehicle engines and parts
HQ: Mahle Behr Japan K.K.
1-9-12, Kitaotsuka
Toshima-Ku TKY 170-0

(G-11475)
STEPHENS PIPE & STEEL LLC
10732 Schadel Ln (43143-9731)
P.O. Box 237 (43143-0237)
PHONE 740 869-2257
Rick Redman, *Prin*
EMP: 135
Web: www.spsfence.com
SIC: 3523 3496 3494 3446 Farm machinery and equipment; Miscellaneous fabricated wire products; Valves and pipe fittings, nec; Architectural metalwork
HQ: Stephens Pipe & Steel, Llc
2224 E Highway 619
Russell Springs KY 42642
270 866-3331

Mount Vernon
Knox County

(G-11476)
BEHAVRIAL HLTHCARE PRTNERS CNT
Also Called: BEHAVORIAL HEALTHCARE PARTNERS OF CENTRAL OHIO, INC.
8402 Blackjack Road Ext (43050-9193)
PHONE 740 397-0442
Francis Deutschle, *Dir*
EMP: 44
SALES (corp-wide): 10.91MM **Privately Held**
Web: www.bhcpartners.org
SIC: 8093 Mental health clinic, outpatient
PA: Behavioral Healthcare Partners Of Central Ohio, Inc.
65 Messimer Dr Unit 2
Newark OH 43055
740 522-8477

(G-11477)
BUCKEYE ORAL & MAXILLOFACIAL
1650 Coshocton Ave Ste D (43050-1548)
PHONE 740 392-2000
Jack Mcewan, *Brnch Mgr*
EMP: 36
SALES (corp-wide): 192.78K **Privately Held**
Web: www.buckeyeomfs.com
SIC: 8021 Dental surgeon
PA: Buckeye Oral & Maxillofacial Surgery Llc
110 Polaris Pkwy Ste 125
Westerville OH 43082
614 794-9700

(G-11478)
C E S CREDIT UNION INC (PA)
1215 Yauger Rd (43050-9233)
P.O. Box 631 (43050-0631)
PHONE 740 397-1136

James Depue, *Pr*
James Depue, *Pr*
Kelly Schermerhorn, *
EMP: 45 **EST:** 1952
SQ FT: 7,800
SALES (est): 8.11MM
SALES (corp-wide): 8.11MM **Privately Held**
Web: www.cescu.com
SIC: 6061 Federal credit unions

(G-11479)
COUNTRY CLUB CENTER II LTD
Also Called: COUNTRY CLUB RETIREMENT CAMPUS
1350 Yauger Rd (43050-9233)
PHONE 740 397-2350
John Holland, *Pt*
Tonia Ressing, *Pt*
EMP: 109 **EST:** 1977
SQ FT: 50,000
SALES (est): 6.09MM **Privately Held**
Web: www.countryclubretirementcampus.com
SIC: 8051 8052 Convalescent home with continuous nursing care; Intermediate care facilities

(G-11480)
COUNTRY COURT
Also Called: DELAWARE COURT
1076 Coshocton Ave (43050-1474)
PHONE 740 397-4125
L Bruce Levering, *Pr*
EMP: 461 **EST:** 1971
SQ FT: 30,000
SALES (est): 5.91MM
SALES (corp-wide): 26.43MM **Privately Held**
Web: www.countrycourt.com
SIC: 8051 Convalescent home with continuous nursing care
PA: Levering Management, Inc.
201 N Main St
Mount Vernon OH 43050
740 397-3897

(G-11481)
COYNE GRAPHIC FINISHING INC
Also Called: Coyne Finishing
1301 Newark Rd (43050-4730)
PHONE 740 397-6232
Robert Coyne, *Ch*
Kevin Coyne, *
Alice Ann Coyne, *
EMP: 28 **EST:** 1926
SQ FT: 57,000
SALES (est): 2.95MM **Privately Held**
Web: www.coynefinishing.com
SIC: 7336 2752 Graphic arts and related design; Commercial printing, lithographic

(G-11482)
DAILY SERVICES LLC
Also Called: DAILY SERVICES LLC
12 E Gambier St (43050-3316)
PHONE 740 326-6130
Ryan Mason, *Brnch Mgr*
EMP: 185
Web: www.surgestaffing.com
SIC: 8999 Artists and artists' studios
PA: Daily Services, Llc
4 Easton Oval
Columbus OH 43219

(G-11483)
DECOSKY MOTOR HOLDINGS INC
Also Called: Decosky GM Center
510 Harcourt Rd # 550 (43050-3920)
P.O. Box 351 (43050-0351)
PHONE 740 397-9122

GEOGRAPHIC SECTION
Mount Vernon - Knox County (G-11507)

John Decosky, *Pr*
EMP: 35 **EST:** 1956
SALES (est): 4.13MM **Privately Held**
SIC: 5511 7538 Automobiles, new and used; General automotive repair shops

(G-11484)
DMS RECYCLING LLC
350 Pittsburgh Ave (43050-3928)
PHONE......................740 397-0790
Xiao Dong Qu, *
EMP: 30 **EST:** 2014
SALES (est): 2.4MM **Privately Held**
Web: www.dmsrecycling.com
SIC: 4953 Recycling, waste materials

(G-11485)
EMMETT DAN HOUSE LTD PARTNR
Also Called: Amerihost Mt. Vernon
150 Howard St (43050-3596)
PHONE......................740 392-6886
EMP: 45 **EST:** 2002
SQ FT: 50,000
SALES (est): 275.79K **Privately Held**
SIC: 7011 6512 5812 Bed and breakfast inn; Nonresidential building operators; Eating places

(G-11486)
EUROLINK INC
106 W Ohio Ave (43050-2442)
PHONE......................740 392-1549
Mark Hauberg, *Pr*
Elaine Hauberg, *
▲ **EMP:** 30 **EST:** 1996
SALES (est): 2.81MM **Privately Held**
Web: www.innovativeproductivitytechnologies.com
SIC: 5084 Machine tools and accessories

(G-11487)
EWERS UTILITY SERVICE LLC
Also Called: Telecommunications Contractor
301 Columbus Rd (43050-4427)
Rural Route 301 (43050)
PHONE......................740 326-4451
Jason Ewers, *Prin*
EMP: 30 **EST:** 2007
SALES (est): 4.75MM **Privately Held**
Web: www.ewersutility.com
SIC: 1623 Underground utilities contractor

(G-11488)
FIRST-KNOX NATIONAL BANK (HQ)
Also Called: First-Knox National Division
1 S Main St (43050-3223)
PHONE......................740 399-5500
Gordon E Yance, *Pr*
Carlos E Watkins, *Vice Chairman**
David L Trautman, *
EMP: 140 **EST:** 1847
SQ FT: 58,000
SALES (est): 10.14MM
SALES (corp-wide): 564.3MM **Publicly Held**
Web: www.parknationalbank.com
SIC: 6021 8721 National trust companies with deposits, commercial; Accounting, auditing, and bookkeeping
PA: Park National Corporation
50 N 3rd St
Newark OH 43055
740 349-8451

(G-11489)
HOSPICE OF KNOX COUNTY
17700 Coshocton Rd (43050-9218)
PHONE......................740 397-5188
Austin Swallow, *Dir*
EMP: 46 **EST:** 1983
SQ FT: 2,300
SALES (est): 1.16MM **Privately Held**
Web: www.hospiceofnorthcentralohio.org
SIC: 8082 8322 Home health care services; Individual and family services

(G-11490)
KNOX AUTO LLC
Also Called: Chevrolet Buick GMC Mt Vernon
510 Harcourt Rd (43050-3920)
PHONE......................330 701-5266
EMP: 35 **EST:** 2018
SALES (est): 5.02MM **Privately Held**
Web: www.mountvernongm.com
SIC: 5511 5013 7538 Automobiles, new and used; Trailer parts and accessories; General automotive repair shops

(G-11491)
KNOX CARDIOLOGY ASSOCIATES
7 Woodlake Trl Ste A (43050-8103)
PHONE......................740 397-0108
Jawahar Palaniappan, *Pr*
EMP: 35 **EST:** 1981
SQ FT: 5,400
SALES (est): 1.86MM **Privately Held**
SIC: 8062 General medical and surgical hospitals

(G-11492)
KNOX COMMUNITY HOSPITAL (PA)
1330 Coshocton Ave (43050-1495)
PHONE......................740 393-9000
Bruce White, *CEO*
Michael Ambrosiani, *CFO*
EMP: 607 **EST:** 1977
SQ FT: 160,000
SALES (est): 211.62MM
SALES (corp-wide): 211.62MM **Privately Held**
Web: www.kch.org
SIC: 8062 General medical and surgical hospitals

(G-11493)
KNOX COUNTY
Also Called: Knox Cnty Dept Wtr Waste Waste
17602 Coshocton Rd (43050-9218)
PHONE......................740 397-7041
John W Hunt, *Mgr*
EMP: 86
SALES (corp-wide): 61.17MM **Privately Held**
Web: www.knoxchamber.com
SIC: 4941 9111 Water supply; County supervisors' and executives' office
PA: Knox County
117 E High St Rm 161
Mount Vernon OH 43050
740 393-6703

(G-11494)
KNOX COUNTY
Also Called: Knox County Health Department
11660 Upper Gilchrist Rd (43050-9084)
PHONE......................740 392-2200
Dennis Murray, *Mgr*
EMP: 49
SALES (corp-wide): 61.17MM **Privately Held**
Web: www.knoxchamber.com
SIC: 9431 8082 Administration of public health programs, County government; Home health care services
PA: Knox County
117 E High St Rm 161
Mount Vernon OH 43050
740 393-6703

(G-11495)
KNOX COUNTY HEAD START INC (PA)
11700 Upper Gilchrist Rd Ste B (43050-9232)
P.O. Box 1225 (43050-8225)
PHONE......................740 397-1344
Margaret Tazewell, *Ex Dir*
EMP: 33 **EST:** 1965
SQ FT: 4,000
SALES (est): 5.1MM
SALES (corp-wide): 5.1MM **Privately Held**
Web: www.knoxheadstart.org
SIC: 8351 Head Start center, except in conjunction with school

(G-11496)
KNOX NEW HOPE INDUSTRIES INC
1375 Newark Rd (43050-4779)
PHONE......................740 397-4601
Clare Bartlett, *Dir*
EMP: 150 **EST:** 1965
SQ FT: 30,000
SALES (est): 2.2MM **Privately Held**
Web: www.newhopeind.com
SIC: 8331 Sheltered workshop

(G-11497)
LABELLE HMHEALTH CARE SVCS LLC
314 S Main St Ste B (43050-3333)
PHONE......................740 392-1405
Eva Ingram, *Mgr*
EMP: 67
SALES (corp-wide): 9.17MM **Privately Held**
SIC: 8082 Home health care services
PA: Labelle Homehealth Care Services Llc
1653 Brice Rd
Reynoldsburg OH 43068
614 367-0881

(G-11498)
LOWES HOME CENTERS LLC
Also Called: Lowe's
1010 Coshocton Ave (43050-1411)
PHONE......................740 393-5350
Ken Kaiser, *Mgr*
EMP: 143
SALES (corp-wide): 86.38B **Publicly Held**
Web: www.lowes.com
SIC: 5211 5031 5722 5064 Home centers; Building materials, exterior; Household appliance stores; Electrical appliances, television and radio
HQ: Lowe's Home Centers, Llc
1000 Lowes Blvd
Mooresville NC 28117
336 658-4000

(G-11499)
MAUSER USA LLC
Also Called: Mauser
219 Commerce Dr (43050-4645)
PHONE......................740 397-1762
Chuck Sesco, *Mgr*
EMP: 62
Web: www.mauserpackaging.com
SIC: 5085 Packing, industrial
HQ: Mauser Usa, Llc
1515 W 22nd St Ste 1100
Oak Brook IL 60523

(G-11500)
MOUNT VERNON COUNTRY CLUB CO
8927 Martinsburg Rd (43050-9504)
P.O. Box 347 (43050-0347)
PHONE......................740 392-4216
Henry Labrun, *Pr*
EMP: 68 **EST:** 1915
SQ FT: 7,000
SALES (est): 945.49K **Privately Held**
Web: www.mtvcountryclub.com
SIC: 7997 5812 5813 7992 Country club, membership; Eating places; Drinking places ; Public golf courses

(G-11501)
MOUNT VERNON ELDERLY SVCS LLC
1350 Yauger Rd (43050-9233)
PHONE......................740 397-2350
EMP: 80 **EST:** 1979
SALES (est): 3.44MM **Privately Held**
SIC: 8051 Skilled nursing care facilities

(G-11502)
MT VERNON STAR PROPERTIES INC
Also Called: Holiday Inn Express Mt. Vernon
11555 Upper Gilchrist Rd (43050-9084)
PHONE......................740 392-1900
EMP: 37 **EST:** 2010
SALES (est): 528.57K **Privately Held**
Web: www.hiexpress.com
SIC: 7011 Hotels and motels

(G-11503)
OAK HLTH CARE INVSTORS OF MT V
Also Called: Laurels of Mt Vernon
13 Avalon Rd (43050-1403)
PHONE......................740 397-3200
EMP: 95
Web: www.cienahealthcare.com
SIC: 8051 8052 Convalescent home with continuous nursing care; Intermediate care facilities
HQ: Oak Health Care Investors Of Mt Vernon, Inc
8181 Worthington Rd
Westerville OH 43082

(G-11504)
RANDS TRUCKING INC
1201 Gambier Rd (43050-3844)
PHONE......................740 397-1144
EMP: 39
SALES (corp-wide): 23.52MM **Privately Held**
Web: www.randstrucking.com
SIC: 4213 Trucking, except local
PA: Rands Trucking, Inc.
W8527 Gokey Rd
Ladysmith WI 54848
800 268-3933

(G-11505)
RICHARD WOLFE TRUCKING INC
7203 Newark Rd (43050-9552)
PHONE......................740 392-2445
Richard J Wolfe, *Pr*
EMP: 41 **EST:** 1990
SALES (est): 5.04MM **Privately Held**
Web: www.richardwolfetrucking.com
SIC: 4213 Contract haulers

(G-11506)
ROLLS-ROYCE ENERGY SYSTEMS INC
105 N Sandusky St (43050-2447)
PHONE......................703 834-1700
◆ **EMP:** 1000
SIC: 3511 5084 8711 Turbines and turbine generator sets; Compressors, except air conditioning; Engineering services

(G-11507)
S AND S GILARDI INC
Also Called: Lannings Foods
1033 Newark Rd (43050-4640)

Mount Vernon - Knox County (G-11508)

PHONE..................740 397-2751
Sam Gilardi, *Pr*
Brenda Giraldi, *
Steve Gilardi, *
Shelly Giraldi, *
EMP: 90 **EST:** 1980
SQ FT: 20,000
SALES (est): 10.37MM **Privately Held**
Web: www.lannings.com
SIC: 5147 5421 5451 5143 Meats, fresh; Meat markets, including freezer provisioners; Dairy products stores; Dairy products, except dried or canned

(G-11508)
SIEMENS ENERGY INC
105 N Sandusky St (43050-2447)
PHONE..................740 393-8897
EMP: 32
SALES (corp-wide): 33.81B **Privately Held**
Web: www.siemens.com
SIC: 1629 1731 3511 Power plant construction; Energy management controls; Turbines and turbine generator sets
HQ: Siemens Energy, Inc.
4400 N Alafaya Trl
Orlando FL 32826
407 736-2000

(G-11509)
YOUNG MNS CHRSTN ASSN GRTER NY
Also Called: Young Mens Christian Assn
103 N Main St (43050-2407)
PHONE..................740 392-9622
EMP: 140
SALES (corp-wide): 164.13MM **Privately Held**
Web: www.ymcanyc.org
SIC: 8641 7991 8351 7032 Youth organizations; Physical fitness facilities; Child day care services; Youth camps
PA: Young Men's Christian Association Of Greater New York
5 W 63rd St Fl 6
New York NY 10023
212 630-9600

(G-11510)
YOUNG MNS CHRSTN ASSN OF MT VR
Also Called: YMCA
103 N Main St (43050-2407)
PHONE..................740 392-9622
Wayne Uhrig, *Dir*
EMP: 60 **EST:** 1907
SQ FT: 53,000
SALES (est): 1.77MM **Privately Held**
Web: www.mtvymca.org
SIC: 8641 7991 8351 7032 Youth organizations; Physical fitness facilities; Child day care services; Youth camps

(G-11511)
ZANDEX HEALTH CARE CORPORATION
Also Called: Apple Tree Homes
1133 Gambier Rd # 1139 (43050-3839)
PHONE..................740 392-1099
Terry Mack, *Prin*
EMP: 97
Web: www.cedarhillcare.org
SIC: 8052 Intermediate care facilities
PA: Zandex Health Care Corporation
1122 Taylor St
Zanesville OH 43701

Mount Victory
Hardin County

(G-11512)
PLAZA INN FOODS INC
Also Called: Plaza Inn Restaurant
491 S Main St (43340-8869)
P.O. Box 257 (43340-0257)
PHONE..................937 354-2181
Joan Wagner, *Pr*
EMP: 27 **EST:** 1965
SQ FT: 9,600
SALES (est): 939.63K **Privately Held**
Web: www.plazainn.net
SIC: 5812 7011 Caterers; Inns

Munroe Falls
Summit County

(G-11513)
BELL & BLAIRE LLC
103 S Main St (44262-1637)
PHONE..................330 794-5647
EMP: 30 **EST:** 2012
SALES (est): 5.73MM **Privately Held**
Web: www.bellandblaire.com
SIC: 1711 Mechanical contractor

(G-11514)
THOMPSON ELECTRIC INC
49 Northmoreland Ave (44262-1717)
PHONE..................330 686-2300
Larry Thompson, *Pr*
Bill Anderson, *
Roland Sequin, *
Worth Thompson Junior, *Stockholder*
EMP: 250 **EST:** 1977
SQ FT: 33,000
SALES (est): 41.22MM **Privately Held**
Web: www.thompsonelectric.com
SIC: 1731 General electrical contractor

Napoleon
Henry County

(G-11515)
AMERICOLD LOGISTICS LLC
1175 Independence Dr (43545-9718)
PHONE..................419 599-5015
Tony Castle, *Brnch Mgr*
EMP: 75
SALES (corp-wide): 2.67B **Publicly Held**
Web: www.americold.com
SIC: 4222 Warehousing, cold storage or refrigerated
HQ: Americold Logistics, Llc
10 Glenlake Pkwy Ste 600
Atlanta GA 30328
678 441-1400

(G-11516)
AMERICOLD LOGISTICS LLC
1800 Industrial Dr (43545-9736)
PHONE..................419 599-5015
Tony Castle, *Brnch Mgr*
EMP: 35
SALES (corp-wide): 2.67B **Publicly Held**
Web: www.americold.com
SIC: 4222 Warehousing, cold storage or refrigerated
HQ: Americold Logistics, Llc
10 Glenlake Pkwy Ste 600
Atlanta GA 30328
678 441-1400

(G-11517)
AUTOMATIC FEED CO (HQ)
Also Called: Automatic Feed Company
476 E Riverview Ave (43545-1899)
PHONE..................419 592-0050
Peter Beck, *VP*
William L Beck, *
▲ **EMP:** 86 **EST:** 1949
SQ FT: 160,000
SALES (est): 26.83MM **Privately Held**
Web: www.automaticfeed.com
SIC: 5084 Industrial machinery and equipment
PA: Nidec Corporation
338, Kuzetonoshirocho, Minami-Ku
Kyoto KYO 601-8

(G-11518)
CIVISTA BANK
122 E Washington St (43545-1646)
PHONE..................419 599-1065
EMP: 50
Web: www.civista.bank
SIC: 6022 6163 State commercial banks; Loan brokers
HQ: Civista Bank
100 E Water St
Sandusky OH 44870
419 625-4121

(G-11519)
CLOVERLEAF TRANSPORT CO
1165 Independence Dr (43545-9718)
PHONE..................419 599-5015
Dale Lilleholm, *Genl Mgr*
EMP: 54
SALES (corp-wide): 1.98MM **Privately Held**
SIC: 4119 Local passenger transportation, nec
PA: Cloverleaf Transport Co.
2800 Cloverleaf Ct
Sioux City IA 51111
712 279-8044

(G-11520)
CUSTAR STONE CO
9072 County Road 424 (43545)
P.O. Box 607 (43545)
PHONE..................419 669-4327
Brent Gerken, *Pr*
Mike Gerken, *VP*
Jon Myers, *Sec*
Julian Gerken, *Stockholder*
EMP: 33 **EST:** 1994
SQ FT: 3,000
SALES (est): 1.15MM **Privately Held**
Web: www.gerkencompanies.com
SIC: 1422 Crushed and broken limestone

(G-11521)
CUSTOM AGRI SYSTEMS INC (PA)
Also Called: C A S
255 County Road R (43545-5748)
PHONE..................419 599-5180
EMP: 40 **EST:** 1982
SALES (est): 35.63MM
SALES (corp-wide): 35.63MM **Privately Held**
Web: www.casindustries.com
SIC: 5191 Farm supplies

(G-11522)
FILLING MEMORIAL HOME OF MERCY (PA)
N160 State Route 108 (43545-9278)
PHONE..................419 592-6451
Paul E Oehrtman, *Prin*
Paul Oehrtman, *
EMP: 280 **EST:** 1958
SQ FT: 53,000
SALES (est): 11.98MM
SALES (corp-wide): 11.98MM **Privately Held**
Web: www.fillinghome.org
SIC: 8052 Home for the mentally retarded, with health care

(G-11523)
GAZETTE PUBLISHING COMPANY
Also Called: Fulton County Expositor
595 E Riverview Ave (43545-1865)
P.O. Box 376 (43567-0376)
PHONE..................419 335-2010
Janice May, *Mgr*
EMP: 69
SALES (corp-wide): 4.39MM **Privately Held**
Web: www.northwestsignal.net
SIC: 7313 5994 2711 Newspaper advertising representative; Newsstand; Newspapers
PA: The Gazette Publishing Company
42 S Main St
Oberlin OH

(G-11524)
GERKEN MATERIALS INC (PA)
9072 County Road 424 (43545-9732)
P.O. Box 607 (43545-0607)
PHONE..................419 533-2421
EMP: 50 **EST:** 1959
SALES (est): 46.53MM
SALES (corp-wide): 46.53MM **Privately Held**
Web: www.gerkencompanies.com
SIC: 1611 2951 Highway and street paving contractor; Asphalt and asphaltic paving mixtures (not from refineries)

(G-11525)
HENRY COUNTY HOSPITAL INC
1600 E Riverview Ave Frnt (43545-9399)
PHONE..................419 592-4015
Kim Bordenkircher, *CEO*
Michelle Rychener, *
Jim Nowaczyk, *
Kelley Wachtman, *
EMP: 308 **EST:** 1920
SQ FT: 100,000
SALES (est): 35.75MM **Privately Held**
Web: www.henrycountyhospital.org
SIC: 8062 General medical and surgical hospitals

(G-11526)
LIECHTY INC
20 Interstate Dr (43545-9713)
PHONE..................419 592-3075
EMP: 35
SALES (corp-wide): 33.49MM **Privately Held**
Web: www.liechtyfarmequip.com
SIC: 5083 Agricultural machinery and equipment
HQ: Liechty, Inc.
1701 S Defiance St
Archbold OH 43502
419 445-1565

(G-11527)
LUTHERAN HOMES SOCIETY INC
1036 S Perry St (43545-2172)
PHONE..................419 591-4060
Nicole Giesige, *COO*
EMP: 166
SALES (corp-wide): 54.58MM **Privately Held**
Web: www.genacrosslutheranservices.org
SIC: 8361 Aged home
PA: Lutheran Homes Society, Inc.
2021 N Mccord Rd

GEOGRAPHIC SECTION
Nelsonville - Athens County (G-11549)

Toledo OH 43615
419 861-4990

(G-11528)
MEL LANZER CO
2266 Scott St (43545-1064)
PHONE.................................419 592-2801
Charlotte Zgela, *Pr*
Matthew Lanzer, *
Cheryl Huffman, *
Margaret Lanzer, *
Dan Follett, *
EMP: 33 **EST:** 1950
SQ FT: 5,000
SALES (est): 10.88MM **Privately Held**
Web: www.mellanzer.com
SIC: 1541 1542 Industrial buildings, new construction, nec; Commercial and office building contractors

(G-11529)
MIDWEST CMNTY FEDERAL CR UN
1429 Scott St (43545-1073)
PHONE.................................419 599-5522
EMP: 43
SALES (corp-wide): 6.99MM **Privately Held**
Web: www.midwestcommunity.org
SIC: 6061 Federal credit unions
PA: Midwest Community Federal Credit Union
087780 State Routs 66
Defiance OH 43512
419 783-6500

(G-11530)
NAPOLEON MACHINE LLC
476 E Riverview Ave (43545-1855)
PHONE.................................419 591-7010
EMP: 35 **EST:** 2010
SALES (est): 5.59MM **Privately Held**
Web: www.napoleonmachine.com
SIC: 1721 3599 Commercial painting; Machine and other job shop work

(G-11531)
NORTHCREST NURSING & REHAB
240 Northcrest Dr (43545-7737)
PHONE.................................419 599-4070
Jennifer Rohrf, *Pr*
EMP: 34 **EST:** 2007
SALES (est): 5.44MM **Privately Held**
Web: www.northcrestnursinghc.com
SIC: 8051 8052 8059 Convalescent home with continuous nursing care; Personal care facility; Nursing home, except skilled and intermediate care facility

(G-11532)
SAFETY GROOVING & GRINDING LP
13226 County Road R (43545-5966)
P.O. Box 675 (21009-0675)
EMP: 40 **EST:** 1983
SALES (est): 5.63MM
SALES (corp-wide): 45.52MM **Privately Held**
SIC: 1771 Concrete work
PA: Swank Construction Company, Llc
632 Hunt Valley Cir
New Kensington PA 15068
724 727-3497

(G-11533)
TREP LTD
Also Called: Petrolube
900 American Rd (43545-6498)
PHONE.................................419 717-5624
Wayne Hitchcock, *Genl Mgr*
EMP: 30 **EST:** 2016
SALES (est): 1.65MM **Privately Held**

SIC: 1711 5541 Mechanical contractor; Gasoline Stations with convenience stores

(G-11534)
VERNON NAGEL INC
O154 County Road 11c (43545)
PHONE.................................419 592-3861
EMP: 70 **EST:** 1947
SALES (est): 14.96MM **Privately Held**
Web: www.nagelinc.com
SIC: 1622 1623 Bridge construction; Underground utilities contractor

Nashport
Muskingum County

(G-11535)
HANBY FARMS INC
10790 Newark Rd (43830-9066)
P.O. Box 97 (43830-0097)
PHONE.................................740 763-3554
Ralph Hanby, *Pr*
Doug Hanby, *
David R Hanby, *
Carol Hanby, *
EMP: 40 **EST:** 1960
SQ FT: 10,000
SALES (est): 5.16MM **Privately Held**
Web: www.performancefeed.com
SIC: 2048 5153 5191 Livestock feeds; Corn; Fertilizer and fertilizer materials

Navarre
Stark County

(G-11536)
ALTERCARE OF OHIO INC
7222 Day Ave Sw (44662-9502)
P.O. Box 2279 (44720-0279)
PHONE.................................330 767-3458
Gerald F Schroer, *Pr*
EMP: 57 **EST:** 1983
SALES (est): 21.26MM **Privately Held**
Web: www.altercareonline.com
SIC: 8051 Convalescent home with continuous nursing care

(G-11537)
GENCRAFT DESIGNS LLC
7412 Massillon Rd Sw (44662-9318)
PHONE.................................330 359-6251
Paul Swartzentruber, *Prin*
EMP: 27 **EST:** 1988
SQ FT: 7,200
SALES (est): 1.06MM **Privately Held**
Web: www.gencraftdesigns.com
SIC: 2511 7389 Wood household furniture; Design services

(G-11538)
HODGES TRUCKING COMPANY LLC
5368 Biery St Sw (44662-9743)
PHONE.................................405 947-7764
EMP: 41
SALES (corp-wide): 1.57B **Privately Held**
Web: www.hodgestruckingcompany.com
SIC: 4213 Heavy machinery transport
HQ: Hodges Trucking Company, L.L.C.
4050 W I40
Oklahoma City OK 73108
405 947-7764

(G-11539)
ROBERT G OWEN TRUCKING INC (PA)
9260 Erie Ave Sw (44662)
P.O. Box 187 (44662)

PHONE.................................330 756-1013
Steven Owen, *Pr*
Christopher Owen, *
Patricia Owen, *
EMP: 28 **EST:** 1938
SQ FT: 8,000
SALES (est): 3.62MM
SALES (corp-wide): 3.62MM **Privately Held**
SIC: 4213 Contract haulers

Negley
Columbiana County

(G-11540)
A M & O TOWING INC
11341 State Route 170 (44441-9713)
PHONE.................................330 385-0639
Mary Price, *Pr*
EMP: 40 **EST:** 1971
SALES (est): 2.14MM **Privately Held**
Web: www.amotowing.com
SIC: 4492 Towing and tugboat service

Nelsonville
Athens County

(G-11541)
DAN SECHKAR SECH KAR C
4831 2nd St (45764-9568)
PHONE.................................740 753-9955
Dan Sech-kar, *Pr*
EMP: 43
Web: www.sechkar.com
SIC: 8322 Social service center
PA: Dan Sechkar Sech Kar C
311 S Main St
New Lexington OH 43764

(G-11542)
DOCTORS HOSPITAL CLEVELAND INC
Also Called: Ohio Health
11 John Lloyd Evans Memorial Dr (45764-2523)
PHONE.................................740 753-7300
Steve Swart, *Pr*
Lemar Wyse, *Pr*
EMP: 101 **EST:** 1950
SQ FT: 15,000
SALES (est): 8.04MM **Privately Held**
Web: www.ohiohealth.com
SIC: 8051 8062 Skilled nursing care facilities ; General medical and surgical hospitals

(G-11543)
ED MAP INC
296 S Harper St Ste 1 (45764-1600)
PHONE.................................740 753-3439
Michael Mark, *CEO*
Micah Zimmerman, *
Gregory Smith, *
Kerry Stoessel Pigman, *
Greg Smith, *
EMP: 83 **EST:** 2001
SQ FT: 7,000
SALES (est): 15.07MM **Privately Held**
Web: www.perfectdomain.com
SIC: 5192 Books

(G-11544)
FIRST NAT BNK OF NELSONVILLE (PA)
Also Called: First National Bank
11 Public Sq (45764-1132)
P.O. Box 149 (45764-0149)
PHONE.................................740 753-1941
Steven Cox, *Pr*

Mary Jane Lax, *
Eric Courtney, *
Suzie Witmann, *
EMP: 32 **EST:** 1916
SALES (est): 4.19MM
SALES (corp-wide): 4.19MM **Privately Held**
Web: www.first-national.com
SIC: 6021 National commercial banks

(G-11545)
GEORGIA-BOOT INC
Also Called: Durango Boot
39 E Canal St (45764-1247)
PHONE.................................740 753-1951
Gerald M Cohn, *CEO*
Thomas R Morrison, *Pr*
EMP: 100 **EST:** 1937
SALES (est): 16.82MM **Privately Held**
Web: www.georgiaboot.com
SIC: 5139 3144 3143 3021 Shoes; Women's footwear, except athletic; Men's footwear, except athletic; Rubber and plastics footwear

(G-11546)
HOCKINGTHENSPERRY CMNTY ACTION
Also Called: Headstart
40 Saint Charles St (45764-1504)
PHONE.................................740 753-9404
Angie Smith, *Mgr*
EMP: 51
SALES (corp-wide): 30.74MM **Privately Held**
Web: www.hapcap.org
SIC: 8351 Head Start center, except in conjunction with school
PA: Hocking.Athens.Perry Community Action
3 Cardaras Dr
Glouster OH 45732
740 767-4500

(G-11547)
HOCKINS ATHENS PRRY CMNTY ACTI
50 Saint Charles St (45764-1504)
PHONE.................................740 753-3062
Greg Andrews, *Prin*
EMP: 189
SALES (corp-wide): 35.22MM **Privately Held**
Web: www.hapcap.org
SIC: 8322 Social service center
PA: Hockins Athens Perry Community Action
11100 State Route 550
Athens OH 45701
740 385-3644

(G-11548)
INTEGRTED SVCS FOR BHVRAL HLTH (PA)
1950 Mount Saint Marys Dr (45764-1280)
P.O. Box 132 (45701-0132)
PHONE.................................740 300-0225
EMP: 38 **EST:** 1995
SQ FT: 1,000
SALES (est): 35.71MM **Privately Held**
Web: www.isbh.org
SIC: 8322 8399 8331 Individual and family services; Health systems agency; Job training and related services

(G-11549)
LEHIGH OUTFITTERS LLC (HQ)
Also Called: Slipgrips
39 E Canal St (45764-1247)
PHONE.................................740 753-1951
Joseph J Sebes, *Pr*

Nelsonville - Athens County (G-11550)

GEOGRAPHIC SECTION

Richard Simms, *Managing Member**
Joe Hanning, *
◆ **EMP:** 200 **EST:** 1921
SQ FT: 24,000
SALES (est): 165.11MM
SALES (corp-wide): 461.83MM **Publicly Held**
Web: www.customfit.me
SIC: 5661 5139 Men's shoes; Shoes
PA: Rocky Brands, Inc.
39 E Canal St
Nelsonville OH 45764
740 753-9100

(G-11550)
US FOOTWEAR HOLDINGS LLC
39 E Canal St (45764-1247)
PHONE...................................740 753-9100
Jason S Brooks, *Managing Member*
EMP: 121 **EST:** 2020
SALES (est): 47.44MM
SALES (corp-wide): 461.83MM **Publicly Held**
SIC: 5139 3021 Footwear; Rubber and plastics footwear
PA: Rocky Brands, Inc.
39 E Canal St
Nelsonville OH 45764
740 753-9100

New Albany
Franklin County

(G-11551)
ABERCROMBIE & FITCH TRADING CO (DH)
Also Called: Abercrombie & Fitch
6301 Fitch Path (43054)
PHONE...................................614 283-6500
Fran Horowitz, *CEO*
Scott Lipesky, *Ex VP*
◆ **EMP:** 60 **EST:** 1892
SALES (est): 139.78MM
SALES (corp-wide): 4.28B **Publicly Held**
SIC: 5136 5137 5641 5621 Men's and boy's clothing; Women's and children's clothing; Children's and infants' wear stores; Women's clothing stores
HQ: J.M.H. Trademark, Inc.
6301 Fitch Path
New Albany OH 43054

(G-11552)
ACCEL INC
9000 Smiths Mill Rd (43054-6647)
PHONE...................................614 656-1100
Tara Abraham, *CEO*
David Abraham, *
▲ **EMP:** 200 **EST:** 1995
SQ FT: 305,000
SALES (est): 18.94MM **Privately Held**
Web: www.accel-inc.com
SIC: 7389 Packaging and labeling services

(G-11553)
ACTALENT SERVICES LLC
8100 Walton Pkwy (43054-7564)
PHONE...................................614 328-4900
EMP: 215
SALES (corp-wide): 15.88B **Privately Held**
Web: www.actalentservices.com
SIC: 8711 Engineering services
HQ: Actalent Services, Llc
7301 Parkway Dr
Hanover MD 21076
410 579-6456

(G-11554)
AIMHI INC
10299 Johnstown Rd (43054-9751)
PHONE...................................614 939-0112
EMP: 27 **EST:** 1997
SQ FT: 9,960
SALES (est): 533.52K **Privately Held**
Web: www.goaimhi.com
SIC: 7999 7699 Shooting range operation; Gun services

(G-11555)
ALENE CANDLES LLC
8860 Smiths Mill Rd Ste 100 (43054-6654)
PHONE...................................614 933-4005
EMP: 159
Web: www.alene.com
SIC: 5199 Candles
PA: Alene Candles, Llc
51 Scarborough Ln
Milford NH 03055

(G-11556)
ALLSTARS TRAVEL GROUP INC
Also Called: Troilo & Associates
7775 Walton Pkwy Ste 100 (43054-8202)
PHONE...................................614 901-4100
EMP: 120 **EST:** 1998
SALES (est): 22.96MM **Privately Held**
Web: www.atgglobaltravel.com
SIC: 4724 Tourist agency arranging transport, lodging and car rental

(G-11557)
BRODHEAD VILLAGE LTD (PA)
Also Called: Wallick Company, The
160 W Main St (43054-1188)
PHONE...................................614 863-4640
Thomas A Feusse, *Pt*
EMP: 60 **EST:** 1982
SQ FT: 13,000
SALES (est): 9.34MM **Privately Held**
Web: www.wallick.com
SIC: 6513 Apartment building operators

(G-11558)
CAPITAL CITY ELECTRIC INC
9798 Karmar Ct Ste B (43054)
PHONE...................................614 933-8700
Danita Kessler, *Prin*
Eric Baker, *Acctg Mgr*
Thomas Kessler, *Prin*
L Dale Smith, *Prin*
Mike Priestas, *Prin*
EMP: 45 **EST:** 2005
SQ FT: 4,500
SALES (est): 9.3MM **Privately Held**
Web: www.capcityelectric.com
SIC: 1731 General electrical contractor

(G-11559)
COLUMBUS CTR FOR HUMN SVCS INC
6227 Harlem Rd (43054-9707)
PHONE...................................614 245-8180
Rebecca Sharp, *CEO*
EMP: 73
SALES (corp-wide): 21.85MM **Privately Held**
Web: www.opendoorcolumbus.org
SIC: 8059 Home for the mentally retarded, ex. skilled or intermediate
PA: Columbus Center For Human Services, Inc.
540 Industrial Mile Rd
Columbus OH 43228
614 641-2904

(G-11560)
COMMUNICATION OPTIONS INC
4689 Reynoldsburg New Albany Rd (43054-9585)
PHONE...................................614 901-7095
EMP: 28
SIC: 4813 Local and long distance telephone communications

(G-11561)
DFS CORPORATE SERVICES LLC
Also Called: Discover Financial Services
6500 New Albany Rd E (43054-8730)
PHONE...................................614 283-2499
Don Probst, *Mgr*
EMP: 400
SALES (corp-wide): 20.61B **Publicly Held**
Web: www.discoverglobalnetwork.com
SIC: 7389 Credit card service
HQ: Dfs Corporate Services Llc
2500 Lake Cook Rd 2
Riverwoods IL 60015
224 405-0900

(G-11562)
E2 INFOSYSTEMS LTD
7775 Walton Pkwy (43054-8202)
PHONE...................................833 832-4637
EMP: 32 **EST:** 2010
SALES (est): 2.07MM **Privately Held**
Web: www.e2infosystems.com
SIC: 7371 Computer software development

(G-11563)
EVANS MCHWART HMBLTON TLTON IN (PA)
Also Called: E M H & T
5500 New Albany Rd Ste 100 (43054-8703)
PHONE...................................614 775-4500
Sandra C Doyle-ahern, *Pr*
Douglas E Romer, *
EMP: 285 **EST:** 1925
SQ FT: 13,200
SALES (est): 37.37MM
SALES (corp-wide): 37.37MM **Privately Held**
Web: www.emht.com
SIC: 8713 8711 Surveying services; Consulting engineer

(G-11564)
EXHIBITPRO INC
8900 Smiths Mill Rd (43054-6705)
P.O. Box 537 (43054-0537)
PHONE...................................614 885-9541
Lori Miller, *CEO*
Lori J Miller, *
Edward Miller, *
Greg Lindsey, *
EMP: 30 **EST:** 1991
SQ FT: 15,000
SALES (est): 4.49MM **Privately Held**
Web: www.exhibitpro.net
SIC: 7336 7389 Commercial art and graphic design; Trade show arrangement

(G-11565)
FEAZEL ROOFING LLC
7895 Walton Pkwy (43054-8482)
PHONE...................................614 898-7663
Leo Ruberto, *Managing Member*
Todd Feazel, *
EMP: 46 **EST:** 1987
SQ FT: 9,000
SALES (est): 127.28MM **Privately Held**
Web: www.feazelinc.com
SIC: 1761 Roofing contractor

(G-11566)
FRANKLIN CMPT SVCS GROUP INC
6650 Walnut St (43054-9138)
PHONE...................................614 431-3327
EMP: 45 **EST:** 1989
SALES (est): 7.02MM **Privately Held**
Web: www.fcsg.com
SIC: 7379 Computer related consulting services

(G-11567)
GOLF CLUB CO
4522 Kitzmiller Rd (43054-9565)
P.O. Box 369 (43054-0369)
PHONE...................................614 855-7326
C T Rice, *Pr*
George Mcelroy, *Ch Bd*
Grant Marrow, *
EMP: 55 **EST:** 1967
SQ FT: 5,000
SALES (est): 4.39MM **Privately Held**
Web: www.thegolfclub.cc
SIC: 7997 Country club, membership

(G-11568)
HOMESIDE FINANCIAL LLC
7775 Walton Pkwy Ste 400 (43054-8203)
PHONE...................................614 907-7696
Dan Snyder, *Prin*
EMP: 38 **EST:** 2015
SALES (est): 9.65MM **Privately Held**
Web: www.gohomeside.com
SIC: 6282 Investment advice

(G-11569)
INSURNCE OFFICE CENTL OHIO INC
165 W Main St (43054-9227)
P.O. Box 780 (43054-0780)
PHONE...................................614 939-5471
Herbert P Wolman, *Pr*
Brian Laverty, *VP*
Don Lambie, *VP*
EMP: 41 **EST:** 1927
SQ FT: 3,000
SALES (est): 7.29MM **Privately Held**
Web: www.ioco-columbus.com
SIC: 6411 Insurance agents, nec

(G-11570)
JOINT IMPLANT SURGEONS INC
Also Called: Ortholink Physicians
7727 Smiths Mill Rd 200 (43054-7568)
PHONE...................................614 221-6331
Adolph V Lombardi Junior Md, *
Thomas H Mallory Md, *Pr*
Rebecca Dunaway, *
EMP: 35 **EST:** 1967
SQ FT: 2,500
SALES (est): 3.6MM **Privately Held**
Web: www.jisortho.com
SIC: 8011 Orthopedic physician

(G-11571)
JORDAN HOSPITALITY GROUP LLC
6891 Jersey Dr (43054-1124)
PHONE...................................614 406-5139
EMP: 40 **EST:** 2018
SALES (est): 1.82MM **Privately Held**
SIC: 8741 Restaurant management

(G-11572)
LEO YSSNOFF JWISH CMNTY CTR GR
Also Called: New Albany Pre-School
150 E Dublin Granville Rd (43054-8593)
PHONE...................................614 775-0312
Sherrie Borneberg, *Brnch Mgr*
EMP: 161
SALES (corp-wide): 12.7MM **Privately Held**

GEOGRAPHIC SECTION   New Boston - Scioto County (G-11594)

Web: www.columbusjcc.org
SIC: 8641 8211 Social club, membership; Preparatory school
PA: The Jewish Community Center Of Greater Columbus
1125 College Ave
Columbus OH 43209
614 231-2731

(G-11573)
LLC A HAYSTACK MSSION ESSNTIAL
Also Called: Mission Essential Group Co
6525 W Campus Oval (43054-8830)
PHONE..............................614 750-1908
David Slovina, *Pr*
Corbin Ricker, *
EMP: 75 EST: 2018
SALES (est): 3.23MM **Privately Held**
Web: www.missionessential.com
SIC: 8742 Management consulting services

(G-11574)
MISSION ESSENTIAL GROUP LLC (PA)
6525 W Campus Oval Ste 101 (43054-8830)
PHONE..............................614 416-2345
Jon Ricker, *CEO*
Al Pisani, *
Greg Miller, *
Leonard Hicks, *
EMP: 70 EST: 2004
SQ FT: 8,000
SALES (est): 72.14MM
SALES (corp-wide): 72.14MM **Privately Held**
Web: www.missionessential.com
SIC: 7389 8748 Translation services; Safety training service

(G-11575)
MOUNT CARMEL HEALTH
55 N High St Ste A (43054-7098)
PHONE..............................614 855-4878
Diane Beggs, *Brnch Mgr*
EMP: 119
SALES (corp-wide): 2.49B **Privately Held**
Web: www.mountcarmelhealth.com
SIC: 8062 General medical and surgical hospitals
HQ: Mount Carmel Health
5300 N Meadows Dr
Grove City OH 43123
614 234-5000

(G-11576)
MOUNT CARMEL HEALTH SYSTEM
7333 Smiths Mill Rd (43054-9291)
PHONE..............................614 775-6600
EMP: 775
SALES (corp-wide): 2.49B **Privately Held**
Web: www.mountcarmelhealth.com
SIC: 8062 General medical and surgical hospitals
HQ: Mount Carmel Health System
1039 Kingsmill Pkwy
Columbus OH 43229
614 234-6000

(G-11577)
NEESAI CAD DESIGNS LLC
68 N High St Bldg A (43054-8915)
PHONE..............................614 822-7701
Sophie Khay, *CEO*
Sophie Khay, *Prin*
Sara Thach, *
EMP: 32 EST: 2010
SALES (est): 954.7K **Privately Held**
SIC: 8711 1731 Engineering services; Fiber optic cable installation

(G-11578)
NEW ALBANY CNTRY CLB CMNTY ASS
1 Club Ln (43054-9377)
PHONE..............................614 939-8500
Brent Bradbury, *Pr*
Bob Wesselman, *
Ted B Hipsher, *
EMP: 150 EST: 1990
SQ FT: 55,000
SALES (est): 13.15MM **Privately Held**
Web: www.nacc.com
SIC: 7997 Country club, membership

(G-11579)
NEW ALBANY COUNTRY CLUB LLC
1 Club Ln (43054-9377)
PHONE..............................614 939-8500
EMP: 156 EST: 2018
SALES (est): 10.02MM **Privately Held**
Web: www.nacc.com
SIC: 7997 7371 Country club, membership; Computer software development and applications

(G-11580)
NEW ALBANY LINKS DEV CO LTD
7100 New Albany Links Dr (43054-8194)
PHONE..............................614 939-5914
T Bruce Oldendick, *Pr*
Thomas Bruce Oldendick, *
EMP: 41 EST: 2000
SQ FT: 1,932
SALES (est): 1.28MM **Privately Held**
Web: www.newalbanylinks.com
SIC: 7992 Public golf courses

(G-11581)
NEW ALBANY SURGERY CENTER LLC
5040 Forest Dr Ste 100 (43054-9187)
PHONE..............................614 775-1616
Jacqueline A Primeau, *Prin*
EMP: 175 EST: 2001
SQ FT: 95,000
SALES (est): 37.42MM
SALES (corp-wide): 2.49B **Privately Held**
Web: www.newalbanysurgerycenter.com
SIC: 8062 General medical and surgical hospitals
HQ: Mount Carmel Health
5300 N Meadows Dr
Grove City OH 43123
614 234-5000

(G-11582)
NIAGARA HEALTH CORPORATION
Also Called: New Albany Family Health
55 N High St Ste A (43054-7098)
PHONE..............................614 855-4878
Dianne Beggs, *Mgr*
EMP: 3001
SALES (corp-wide): 2.49B **Privately Held**
SIC: 8741 8011 Hospital management; Offices and clinics of medical doctors
HQ: Niagara Health Corporation
6150 E Broad St
Columbus OH 43213

(G-11583)
QWAIDE ENTERPRISES LLC
Also Called: Gng Music Instruction
6044 Phar Lap Dr (43054-8106)
PHONE..............................614 209-0551
Gregory N Gould, *Owner*
EMP: 30 EST: 2008
SALES (est): 2.18MM **Privately Held**
Web: www.gngmusicinstruction.com
SIC: 8748 Business consulting, nec

(G-11584)
RED ROOF INNS INC (HQ)
Also Called: Red Roof Inn
7815 Walton Pkwy (43054-8482)
PHONE..............................614 744-2600
Andrew Alexander, *CEO*
Joe Merz, *
Marina Macdonald, *CMO*
Brendan P Foley, *
EMP: 525 EST: 1998
SALES (est): 473.2MM **Privately Held**
Web: www.redrooffranchising.com
SIC: 7011 6794 Hotels and motels; Franchises, selling or licensing
PA: Wrrh Investments Lp
5747 San Felipe St # 4650
Houston TX 77057

(G-11585)
RHYME SOFTWARE CORPORATION
102 W Main St (43054-7500)
PHONE..............................888 213-3728
Joe Anstine, *CEO*
Mike Blackwell, *
EMP: 65 EST: 2016
SALES (est): 5.33MM **Privately Held**
Web: www.priorauthnow.com
SIC: 7371 Software programming applications

(G-11586)
RYDER LAST MILE INC (HQ)
Also Called: Mxd Group
7795 Walton Pkwy (43054-0001)
PHONE..............................866 711-3129
Terry Solvedt, *CEO*
Eva M Kalawski, *
Marie Graul, *
◆ EMP: 70 EST: 1974
SALES (est): 151.68MM
SALES (corp-wide): 11.78B **Publicly Held**
Web: www.mxdgroup.com
SIC: 4213 7389 Trucking, except local; Financial services
PA: Ryder System, Inc.
2333 Pnce De Leon Blvd St
Coral Gables FL 33134
305 500-3726

(G-11587)
SHREMSHOCK ARCHITECTS INC (PA)
Also Called: S A I
7775 Walton Pkwy Ste 250 (43054-8207)
PHONE..............................614 545-4550
EMP: 100 EST: 1980
SALES (est): 14.85MM **Privately Held**
Web: www.shremshock.com
SIC: 8712 Architectural engineering

(G-11588)
THIRTY-ONE GIFTS LLC (PA)
Also Called: Thirty One Gifts
8131 Smiths Mill Rd (43054-1183)
P.O. Box 789 (43086-0789)
PHONE..............................614 414-4300
Cynthia M Monroe, *CEO*
EMP: 225 EST: 2009
SQ FT: 1,000,000
SALES (est): 239.55MM
SALES (corp-wide): 239.55MM **Privately Held**
Web: www.mythirtyone.com
SIC: 5947 4226 Gift shop; Textile warehousing

(G-11589)
VELA INVESTMENT MANAGEMENT LLC
220 Market St Ste 208 (43054)
PHONE..............................614 653-8352
EMP: 28 EST: 2019
SALES (est): 4.62MM **Privately Held**
Web: www.vela-im.com
SIC: 6282 Investment advisory service

(G-11590)
WALLICK CONSTRUCTION LLC
160 W Main St Ste 200 (43054-1189)
PHONE..............................614 863-4640
John Leonard, *Managing Member*
EMP: 40 EST: 2006
SQ FT: 32,000
SALES (est): 10.01MM **Privately Held**
Web: www.wallick.com
SIC: 1542 Commercial and office building, new construction

(G-11591)
WALLICK PROPERTIES MIDWEST LLC (PA)
160 W Main St # 200 (43054-1189)
PHONE..............................419 381-7477
Howard Wallick, *Managing Member*
Troi Rambo, *
Julie Wallick, *
Tom Feusse, *
Dave Hendy, *
EMP: 650 EST: 1966
SQ FT: 32,000
SALES (est): 49.7MM
SALES (corp-wide): 49.7MM **Privately Held**
Web: www.wallick.com
SIC: 6531 Real estate managers

(G-11592)
WHITE FNCE SURGICAL SUITES LLC
7277 Smiths Mill Rd Ste 300 (43054)
PHONE..............................614 289-6282
Keith Berend, *Mng Pt*
EMP: 44 EST: 2012
SQ FT: 93,000
SALES (est): 7.52MM
SALES (corp-wide): 20.55B **Publicly Held**
Web: www.whitefencesurg.com
SIC: 8011 Ambulatory surgical center
PA: Tenet Healthcare Corporation
14201 Dallas Pkwy
Dallas TX 75254
469 893-2200

New Boston
Scioto County

(G-11593)
HERITAGE LEGACY HLTH SVCS LLC
Also Called: Heritage Pinte Assisted Living
3304 Rhodes Ave (45662-4914)
PHONE..............................740 456-8245
Deborah Voiers-akers, *Prin*
Steven Akers, *
EMP: 28 EST: 2019
SALES (est): 885.14K **Privately Held**
SIC: 8361 Residential care

(G-11594)
HERITAGE PROFESSIONAL SERVICES
Also Called: Heritage Square New Boston
3304 Rhodes Ave (45662-4914)
PHONE..............................740 456-8245
Gilbert E Lawson, *Pr*
Irene Leadingham, *Sec*
EMP: 34 EST: 1985
SALES (est): 2.41MM **Privately Held**
Web: www.heritagesquareonline.com
SIC: 8052 Personal care facility

(PA)=Parent Co (HQ)=Headquarters
✪ = New Business established in last 2 years

New Boston - Scioto County (G-11595) — GEOGRAPHIC SECTION

(G-11595)
SOUTH CENTRAL OHIO EDUCTL CTR (PA)
522 Glenwood Ave (45662-5505)
PHONE...........................740 456-0517
Darren Jenkins, *Superintnt*
Tom Hoggard, *
Andrew Riehl, *
EMP: 79 **EST:** 1931
SALES (est): 9.32MM
SALES (corp-wide): 9.32MM Privately Held
Web: www.scoesc.org
SIC: 8299 8748 Arts and crafts schools; Testing services

New Bremen
Auglaize County

(G-11596)
COUNTY OF AUGLAIZE
Also Called: Auglaize County Board of Mr/Dd
20 E 1st St (45869-1165)
PHONE...........................419 629-2419
Alvin Willis, *Superintnt*
EMP: 54
SALES (corp-wide): 45.72MM Privately Held
Web: www.auglaizedd.org
SIC: 8361 9111 Mentally handicapped home; County supervisors' and executives' office
PA: County Of Auglaize
  209 S Blackhoof St # 201
  Wapakoneta OH 45895
  419 739-6710

(G-11597)
CROWN ASSOCIATES LLC
Also Called: Crown Associates of Ohio
40 S Washington St (45869-1288)
P.O. Box 97 (45869-0097)
PHONE...........................419 629-2220
Brad Smith, *Sec*
EMP: 73 **EST:** 1996
SALES (est): 9.78MM Privately Held
SIC: 8742 Management consulting services

(G-11598)
KINNINGER PROD WLDG CO INC
710 Kuenzel Dr (45869-9699)
P.O. Box 33 (45869-0033)
PHONE...........................419 629-3491
Kevin Thobe, *Pr*
Cheryl Thobe, *
Donna Thobe, *
EMP: 53 **EST:** 1966
SQ FT: 54,000
SALES (est): 2.9MM Privately Held
Web: www.kinningerwelding.com
SIC: 7692 Welding repair

(G-11599)
MARKETING ESSENTIALS LLC
14 N Washington St (45869-1150)
P.O. Box 114 (45869-0114)
PHONE...........................419 629-0080
EMP: 41 **EST:** 2009
SALES (est): 893.65K Privately Held
Web: www.mktgessentials.com
SIC: 8743 2741 2721 2711 Public relations and publicity; Internet publishing and broadcasting; Magazines: publishing only, not printed on site; Newspapers: publishing only, not printed on site

New Carlisle
Clark County

(G-11600)
BLS TRUCKING INC
1730 Dalton Dr (45344-2307)
P.O. Box 696 (45377-0696)
PHONE...........................937 224-0494
EMP: 260 **EST:** 1980
SALES (est): 33.44MM Privately Held
Web: www.blstrucking.com
SIC: 4214 Local trucking with storage

(G-11601)
HEALTH PARTNERS WESTERN OHIO
Also Called: New Carlisle Cmnty Hlth Ctr
106 N Main St (45344-1835)
PHONE...........................937 667-1122
EMP: 27
SALES (corp-wide): 70.67MM Privately Held
Web: www.hpwohio.org
SIC: 8099 Blood related health services
PA: Health Partners Of Western Ohio
  329 N West St
  Lima OH 45801
  419 221-3072

(G-11602)
KAFFENBARGER TRUCK EQP CO (PA)
10100 Ballentine Pike (45344-9534)
PHONE...........................937 845-3804
Larry Kaffenbarger, *Pr*
Edward W Dunn, *
Everett L Kaffenbarger, *
◆ **EMP:** 110 **EST:** 1961
SQ FT: 30,000
SALES (est): 22.65MM
SALES (corp-wide): 22.65MM Privately Held
Web: www.knapheide.com
SIC: 3713 5013 Truck bodies (motor vehicles); Truck parts and accessories

(G-11603)
LIFEWAY FOR YOUTH (PA)
127 Quick Rd (45344-9253)
PHONE...........................937 845-3625
Michael Berner, *Pr*
EMP: 41 **EST:** 1994
SQ FT: 1,736
SALES (est): 1.01MM
SALES (corp-wide): 1.01MM Privately Held
Web: www.benchmarkfamilyservices.org
SIC: 8322 Individual and family services

(G-11604)
LOUDERBACK FMLY INVSTMENTS INC
Also Called: Professional Property Maint
3545 Dayton Lakeview Rd (45344-2345)
P.O. Box 24383 (45424-0383)
PHONE...........................937 845-1762
EMP: 31 **EST:** 1970
SQ FT: 6,000
SALES (est): 943.71K Privately Held
Web: www.professionalpropertymaintenance.com
SIC: 7349 0781 Building maintenance, except repairs; Landscape services

(G-11605)
SECURITY NATIONAL BANK & TR CO
201 N Main St (45344-1851)
PHONE...........................937 845-3811
Jeffrey Williams, *Mgr*
EMP: 50
SALES (corp-wide): 564.3MM Publicly Held
Web: www.parknationalbank.com
SIC: 6021 National trust companies with deposits, commercial
HQ: The Security National Bank And Trust Co
  50 N 3rd St
  Newark OH 43055
  740 426-6384

(G-11606)
SITE GROUP INC
2484 Addison New Carlisle Rd (45344-7528)
PHONE...........................937 845-7305
EMP: 34 **EST:** 1995
SQ FT: 2,920
SALES (est): 1.05MM Privately Held
Web: www.sitegrouplandscaping.com
SIC: 0781 Landscape services

(G-11607)
STUDEBAKER NURSERIES INC
Also Called: Studebaker Wholesale Nurseries
11140 Milton Carlisle Rd (45344-9235)
PHONE...........................800 845-0584
William Studebaker, *Pr*
Dan W Studebaker, *
EMP: 46 **EST:** 1956
SQ FT: 2,500
SALES (est): 4.55MM Privately Held
Web: www.studebakernurseries.com
SIC: 0181 Nursery stock, growing of

(G-11608)
TEXAS MIGRANT COUNCIL INC
476 N Dayton Lakeview Rd (45344-2109)
PHONE...........................937 846-0699
Beverly Quinn, *Dir*
EMP: 45
SALES (corp-wide): 27.86MM Privately Held
Web: mail.tmccentral.org
SIC: 8351 Child day care services
PA: Texas Migrant Council, Inc.
  712 W Colorado St
  Pearsall TX 78061
  956 722-5174

New Concord
Muskingum County

(G-11609)
CERNER CORPORATION
Also Called: Resource Systems
140 S Friendship Dr (43762-9453)
PHONE...........................740 826-7678
EMP: 76
SALES (corp-wide): 49.95B Publicly Held
Web: www.oracle.com
SIC: 7372 7371 Home entertainment computer software; Custom computer programming services
HQ: Cerner Corporation
  8779 Hillcrest Rd
  Kansas City MO 64138
  816 221-1024

(G-11610)
FREEDOM CONSTRUCTION ENTPS INC
60500 Patch Rd (43762-9553)
PHONE...........................740 255-5818
Roy Heskett, *Pr*
Nathan Worthington, *
EMP: 42 **EST:** 2016
SQ FT: 25,000
SALES (est): 5.18MM Privately Held
SIC: 1611 General contractor, highway and street construction

(G-11611)
GUERNSY-MUSKINGUM ELC COOP INC (PA)
Also Called: GUERNSEY-MUSKINGUM ELECTRIC CO
17 S Liberty St (43762-1230)
PHONE...........................740 826-7661
Shirley Stutz, *Pr*
Brian Hill, *Pr*
John Enos, *Sec*
EMP: 42 **EST:** 1938
SQ FT: 15,000
SALES (est): 40.64MM
SALES (corp-wide): 40.64MM Privately Held
Web: www.gmenergy.com
SIC: 4911 Distribution, electric power

(G-11612)
TK GAS SERVICES INC
2303 John Glenn Hwy (43762-9310)
PHONE...........................740 826-0303
Ted Korte, *Pr*
Jill Pattison, *
EMP: 50 **EST:** 1991
SQ FT: 4,000
SALES (est): 5.17MM Privately Held
Web: www.tkgasservices.com
SIC: 1389 4212 4213 Oil field services, nec; Local trucking, without storage; Trucking, except local

(G-11613)
ZANDEX HEALTH CARE CORPORATION
Also Called: Beckett House At New Concord
1280 Friendship Dr (43762-1024)
PHONE...........................740 454-1400
EMP: 184
Web: www.cedarhillcare.org
SIC: 8052 8051 8361 Intermediate care facilities; Skilled nursing care facilities; Residential care
PA: Zandex Health Care Corporation
  1122 Taylor St
  Zanesville OH 43701

New Franklin
Summit County

(G-11614)
CLINTON ALUMINUM ACQUISITION LLC
Also Called: Clinton Alum & Stainless Stl
6270 Van Buren Rd (44216-9743)
PHONE...........................330 882-6743
EMP: 300
Web: www.clintonaluminum.com
SIC: 5051 Metals service centers and offices

(G-11615)
EAST OHIO GAS COMPANY
Also Called: Dominion Energy Ohio
6500 Hampsher Rd (44216-8905)
PHONE...........................330 266-2169
Greg Theril, *Mgr*
EMP: 65
SALES (corp-wide): 39.69B Privately Held
Web: www.dominiongaschoice.com
SIC: 4924 Natural gas distribution
HQ: The East Ohio Gas Company
  1201 E 55th St
  Cleveland OH 44103
  800 362-7557

(G-11616)
ST LUKE LUTHERAN COMMUNITY
615 Latham Ln (44319-4338)
PHONE................................330 644-3914
Reverend L W Lautenschlager, *Brnch Mgr*
EMP: 27
SQ FT: 19,346
SALES (corp-wide): 3.06MM **Privately Held**
Web: www.stllc.org
SIC: 8052 Personal care facility
PA: St. Luke Lutheran Community
  220 Applegrove St Ne
  Canton OH
  330 499-8341

New Knoxville
Auglaize County

(G-11617)
HOGE LUMBER COMPANY (PA)
Also Called: Hoge Brush
701 S Main St State (45871)
PHONE................................419 753-2263
John H Hoge, *Pr*
Bruce L Hoge, *
Clark T Froning, *
Jack R Hoge, *
▲ **EMP:** 34 **EST:** 1904
SQ FT: 400,000
SALES (est): 4.71MM
SALES (corp-wide): 4.71MM **Privately Held**
Web: www.hoge.com
SIC: 3448 1521 2521 Prefabricated metal buildings and components; New construction, single-family houses; Cabinets, office: wood

(G-11618)
NK TELCO INC
301 W South St (45871-9127)
PHONE................................419 753-5000
Preston Meyer, *Prin*
EMP: 38 **EST:** 1999
SALES (est): 4.51MM **Privately Held**
Web: www.nktelco.com
SIC: 4812 Radiotelephone communication

New Lebanon
Montgomery County

(G-11619)
HARBORSIDE DAYTON LTD PARTNR
Also Called: New Lebanon Center
101 Mills Pl (45345-1430)
PHONE................................937 687-1311
Jesse Ray, *Mgr*
EMP: 955
SALES (corp-wide): 5.86B **Publicly Held**
Web: www.newlebanonhc.com
SIC: 8051 Convalescent home with continuous nursing care
HQ: Harborside Of Dayton Limited Partnership
  155 Federal St Ste 1100
  Boston MA

(G-11620)
RITE AID OF OHIO INC
Also Called: Rite Aid
590 W Main St (45345-9172)
PHONE................................937 687-3456
James Hipple, *Mgr*
EMP: 47
SALES (corp-wide): 24.09B **Publicly Held**
Web: www.riteaid.com
SIC: 5912 7384 Drug stores; Photofinishing laboratory
HQ: Rite Aid Of Ohio, Inc.
  1200 Intrepid Ave Ste 2
  Philadelphia PA 19112

New Lexington
Perry County

(G-11621)
COUNTY OF PERRY
Also Called: Perry County Home
5550 State Route 37 E (43764-3701)
PHONE................................740 342-1213
Tara Layne, *Dir*
EMP: 28
Web: www.perrycountyohio.net
SIC: 8322 Senior citizens' center or association
PA: County Of Perry
  128 S Main St
  New Lexington OH 43764
  740 342-2045

(G-11622)
COUNTY OF PERRY
Also Called: Perry County Senior Center
520 1st St (43764-1416)
PHONE................................740 342-4264
Sandra Abram, *Dir*
EMP: 28
Web: www.perrycountyohio.net
SIC: 8322 Senior citizens' center or association
PA: County Of Perry
  128 S Main St
  New Lexington OH 43764
  740 342-2045

(G-11623)
COUNTY OF PERRY
Also Called: Perry County Engineer
2645 Old Somerset Rd (43764-9547)
PHONE................................740 342-2191
Kenton C Cannon, *Dir*
EMP: 28
Web: www.perrycountyohio.net
SIC: 8711 Engineering services
PA: County Of Perry
  128 S Main St
  New Lexington OH 43764
  740 342-2045

(G-11624)
COUNTY OF PERRY
601 Senior Dr (43764-1575)
PHONE................................740 342-0416
Robin Demattia, *Brnch Mgr*
EMP: 28
Web: www.perrycountyohio.net
SIC: 9199 8051 7997 General government administration, County government; Mental retardation hospital; Country club, membership
PA: County Of Perry
  128 S Main St
  New Lexington OH 43764
  740 342-2045

(G-11625)
HOCKINGTHENSPERRY CMNTY ACTION
Also Called: New Lexington Head Start
228 W Jefferson St (43764-1014)
PHONE................................740 342-1333
Donna Mccord, *Dir*
EMP: 51
SALES (corp-wide): 30.74MM **Privately Held**
Web: www.hapcap.org
SIC: 8351 Head Start center, except in conjunction with school
PA: Hocking.Athens.Perry Community Action
  3 Cardaras Dr
  Glouster OH 45732
  740 767-4500

(G-11626)
HOPEWELL HEALTH CENTERS INC
Also Called: Primary Health Care Clinic
2541 Panther Dr Ne (43764-9081)
P.O. Box 149 (43764-0149)
PHONE................................740 342-4192
Rachel Barnett, *Mgr*
EMP: 35
SALES (corp-wide): 66.73MM **Privately Held**
Web: www.hopewellhealth.org
SIC: 8011 Clinic, operated by physicians
PA: Hopewell Health Centers, Inc.
  1049 Western Ave
  Chillicothe OH 45601
  740 773-1006

(G-11627)
INTERIM HLTH CARE OF NRTHWSTER
445 W Broadway St (43764-1097)
PHONE................................740 343-4112
EMP: 98
SALES (corp-wide): 52.16MM **Privately Held**
Web: www.interimhealthcare.com
SIC: 8082 Home health care services
HQ: Interim Health Care Of Northwestern Ohio, Inc
  3100 W Central Ave # 250
  Toledo OH 43606

(G-11628)
LORI HOLDING CO (PA)
Also Called: Siemer Distributing
1400 Commerce Dr (43764-9500)
PHONE................................740 342-3230
Joseph A Siemer Iii, *Pr*
EMP: 30 **EST:** 1980
SALES (est): 4.77MM
SALES (corp-wide): 4.77MM **Privately Held**
Web: www.siemermeats.com
SIC: 5147 5143 5199 5142 Meats, fresh; Cheese; Ice, manufactured or natural; Packaged frozen goods

(G-11629)
MOUNT ALOYSIUS CORP
5375 Tile Plant Rd Se (43764-9801)
P.O. Box 598 (43764-0598)
PHONE................................740 342-3343
Jean Ann Arbaugh, *Pr*
William Shimp, *
George Fisher, *
EMP: 78 **EST:** 1969
SALES (est): 11.18MM **Privately Held**
Web: www.mountaloysius.org
SIC: 8361 8052 Retarded home; Intermediate care facilities

(G-11630)
PEOPLES NAT BNK OF NEW LXNGTON (HQ)
Also Called: Peoples National Bank
110 N Main St (43764-1261)
P.O. Box 111 (43764-0111)
PHONE................................740 342-5111
G Courtney Haning, *CEO*
Brenda Wright, *
Tony L Davis, *
EMP: 40 **EST:** 1932
SALES (est): 6.67MM
SALES (corp-wide): 6.67MM **Privately Held**
Web: www.psbohio.com
SIC: 6022 State commercial banks
PA: Peoples National Bancshares, Inc.
  110 N Main St
  New Lexington OH 43764
  740 342-5111

(G-11631)
PERRY COUNTY FMLY PRACTICE INC
Also Called: Genesis Hospital
1625 Airport Rd (43764-9749)
P.O. Box 596 (43764-0596)
PHONE................................740 342-3435
Steven Ulrich, *Pr*
EMP: 63 **EST:** 1981
SQ FT: 2,640
SALES (est): 9.73MM **Privately Held**
Web: www.genesishcs.org
SIC: 8011 8071 Clinic, operated by physicians; Medical laboratories

New London
Huron County

(G-11632)
204 W MAIN STREET OPER CO LLC
Also Called: Rehab Nursing Ctr At Firelands
204 W Main St (44851-1070)
PHONE................................419 929-1563
Amy Donaldson, *Admn*
EMP: 48 **EST:** 1978
SALES (est): 2.49MM **Privately Held**
Web: www.cienahealthcare.com
SIC: 8051 Convalescent home with continuous nursing care

(G-11633)
PRIMETALS TECHNOLOGIES USA LLC
81 E Washburn St (44851-1247)
PHONE................................419 929-1554
John Bailey, *Mgr*
EMP: 50
Web: www.primetals.com
SIC: 7699 5084 Industrial equipment services; Industrial machinery and equipment
HQ: Primetals Technologies Usa Llc
  5895 Windward Pkwy Fl 2
  Alpharetta GA 30005
  770 740-3800

New Madison
Darke County

(G-11634)
LUDY GREENHOUSE MFG CORP (PA)
122 Railroad St (45346-5016)
P.O. Box 141 (45346-0141)
PHONE................................800 255-5839
Stephan A Scantland, *Pr*
Deborah Scantland, *
EMP: 58 **EST:** 1957
SQ FT: 2,500
SALES (est): 10.14MM
SALES (corp-wide): 10.14MM **Privately Held**
Web: www.ludy.com
SIC: 1542 3448 Greenhouse construction; Greenhouses, prefabricated metal

New Middletown
Mahoning County

(G-11635)
CONTROL SYSTEM MFG INC
10725 Struthers Rd (44442-9704)
PHONE.................................330 542-0000
Rex Cyrus, *Owner*
EMP: 50 **EST:** 2003
SQ FT: 7,500
SALES (est): 9.32MM **Privately Held**
Web: www.controlsystemmfg.com
SIC: 5063 Electrical supplies, nec

(G-11636)
RAPPS ENTERPRISES INC
Also Called: Dairy Queen
10201 Main St (44442-9717)
P.O. Box 286 (44442-0286)
PHONE.................................330 542-2362
Randy Rapp, *Pr*
Elaine Rapp, *Sec*
EMP: 47 **EST:** 1973
SALES (est): 231.06K **Privately Held**
Web: www.dairyqueen.com
SIC: 5812 7542 Ice cream stands or dairy bars; Carwashes

New Paris
Preble County

(G-11637)
AATISH HOSPITALITY LLC
Also Called: Fairfield Inn
9797 Us Route 40 W (45347-1521)
PHONE.................................937 437-8009
EMP: 31 **EST:** 2003
SQ FT: 53,273
SALES (est): 960.96K **Privately Held**
Web: fairfield.marriott.com
SIC: 7011 Hotels and motels

New Philadelphia
Tuscarawas County

(G-11638)
ALL ABOUT CHILDREN INC
217 Commercial Ave Se (44663-2338)
PHONE.................................330 339-9519
Nancy Reed, *Dir*
EMP: 111
SALES (corp-wide): 994.78K **Privately Held**
Web: www.allaboutchildren.net
SIC: 8351 Group day care center
PA: All About Children, Inc.
217 Commercial Ave Sw
New Philadelphia OH 44663
330 874-3484

(G-11639)
ALLSTATE TRCK SLS ESTRN OHIO L
Also Called: Alstate-Peterbilt-Trucks
327 Stonecreek Rd Nw (44663-6902)
PHONE.................................330 339-5555
Jesse Smitley, *Mgr*
EMP: 33
SALES (corp-wide): 8.8MM **Privately Held**
Web: www.peterbilt.com
SIC: 5511 5531 7538 Automobiles, new and used; Auto and truck equipment and parts; General truck repair
PA: Allstate Truck Sales Of Eastern Ohio, Llc
10700 Lyndale Ave S
Minneapolis MN 55420
952 703-3444

(G-11640)
AMERIDIAL INC
521 W High Ave (44663-2053)
PHONE.................................330 339-7222
EMP: 139
SALES (corp-wide): 224.77MM **Privately Held**
Web: www.fusioncx.com
SIC: 7389 Telemarketing services
HQ: Ameridial, Inc.
4877 Higbee Ave Nw Fl 2
Canton OH 44718
234 542-5036

(G-11641)
BAIR GOODIE AND ASSOC INC
153 N Broadway St Ste 5 (44663-2660)
PHONE.................................330 343-3499
Frank Bair, *Pr*
Charles R Goodie, *
EMP: 40 **EST:** 1977
SALES (est): 2.67MM **Privately Held**
Web: www.bairgoodie.com
SIC: 8711 8713 Civil engineering; Surveying services

(G-11642)
CHILDRENS HOSP MED CTR AKRON
1045 W High Ave (44663-2071)
PHONE.................................330 308-5432
Susan Karitides, *Brnch Mgr*
EMP: 54
SALES (corp-wide): 1.4B **Privately Held**
Web: www.akronchildrens.org
SIC: 8069 8062 Childrens' hospital; General medical and surgical hospitals
PA: Childrens Hospital Medical Center Of Akron
1 Perkins Sq
Akron OH 44308
330 543-1000

(G-11643)
COPLEY OHIO NEWSPAPERS INC
Also Called: Times Reporter/Midwest Offset
629 Wabash Ave Nw (44663-4145)
P.O. Box 9901 (44711-0901)
PHONE.................................330 364-5577
Kevin Kampman, *Publisher*
EMP: 177
SALES (corp-wide): 2.66B **Publicly Held**
Web: www.cantonrep.com
SIC: 2711 2752 7313 2791 Commercial printing and newspaper publishing combined; Offset printing; Newspaper advertising representative; Typesetting
HQ: Copley Ohio Newspapers Inc
500 Market Ave S
Canton OH 44702
585 598-0030

(G-11644)
CORNERSTONE SUPPORT SERVICES (PA)
Also Called: Southeast
344 W High Ave (44663-2152)
PHONE.................................330 339-7850
Sandra Stevenson, *Dir*
Carrie Baker, *
Joe Wilson, *
EMP: 75 **EST:** 1989
SQ FT: 2,856
SALES (est): 4.78MM **Privately Held**
Web: www.southeasthc.org
SIC: 8093 Mental health clinic, outpatient

(G-11645)
CORPORATION FOR OH APPALACHIAN
1260 Monroe St Nw Ste 39s (44663-4147)
PHONE.................................330 364-8882
Sherri Guthrie, *Brnch Mgr*
EMP: 32
SALES (corp-wide): 25.67MM **Privately Held**
Web: www.coadinc.org
SIC: 8351 Head Start center, except in conjunction with school
PA: Corporation For Ohio Appalachian Development
1 Pinchot Pl
Athens OH 45701
740 594-8499

(G-11646)
COUNTY OF TUSCARAWAS
Also Called: Tuscarawas Cnty Job Fmly Svcs
389 16th St Sw (44663-6401)
PHONE.................................330 339-7791
Lynn Angellzzi, *Mgr*
EMP: 53
Web: www.tcjfs.org
SIC: 8322 9199 Probation office; General government administration, County government
PA: County Of Tuscarawas
125 E High Ave
New Philadelphia OH 44663
330 364-8811

(G-11647)
CRANE CARRIER COMPANY LLC (HQ)
1951 Reiser Ave Se (44663-3348)
PHONE.................................918 286-2889
Randy Rollins, *Pr*
EMP: 145 **EST:** 1973
SALES (est): 47.9MM
SALES (corp-wide): 50.87MM **Privately Held**
Web: www.cranecarrier.com
SIC: 5013 3713 Truck parts and accessories; Truck bodies and parts
PA: Battle Motors, Inc.
612 Hampton Dr Ste B
Venice CA 90291
562 536-3614

(G-11648)
CRANE CARRIER HOLDINGS LLC
1951 Reiser Ave Se (44663-3348)
PHONE.................................918 286-2889
EMP: 150 **EST:** 2018
Web: www.cranecarrier.com
SIC: 6719 5013 3713 Investment holding companies, except banks; Truck parts and accessories; Truck bodies and parts

(G-11649)
DEARTH MANAGEMENT COMPANY
Also Called: Moring View Care Center
2594 E High Ave (44663-6737)
PHONE.................................330 339-3595
Loraine Lady, *Dir*
EMP: 92
SALES (corp-wide): 24.94MM **Privately Held**
SIC: 8052 8051 Personal care facility; Skilled nursing care facilities
PA: Dearth Management Company
134 Northwoods Blvd Ste C
Columbus OH
614 847-1070

(G-11650)
ENERGY POWER SERVICES INC
3251 Brightwood Rd Se (44663-7410)
PHONE.................................330 343-2312
Allen M Milarcik, *Pr*
EMP: 30 **EST:** 2010
SALES (est): 1.02MM **Privately Held**
Web: www.energypowerservices.com
SIC: 4212 Local trucking, without storage

(G-11651)
FENTON BROS ELECTRIC CO
Also Called: Fenton's Festival of Lights
235 Ray Ave Ne (44663-2813)
P.O. Box 996 (44663-0996)
PHONE.................................330 343-0093
Tom Fenton, *Pr*
Dennis Fenton, *
Chris Fenton, *
Brian Fenton, *
Harold E Fenton, *Stockholder**
EMP: 30 **EST:** 1947
SQ FT: 37,000
SALES (est): 12.09MM **Privately Held**
SIC: 5063 7694 Electrical supplies, nec; Electric motor repair

(G-11652)
HARCATUS TR-CNTY CMNTY ACTION
504 Bowers Ave Nw (44663-4107)
PHONE.................................330 602-5442
EMP: 57
SALES (corp-wide): 10.01MM **Privately Held**
Web: www.harcatus.org
SIC: 8351 Head Start center, except in conjunction with school
PA: Harcatus Tri-County Community Action Organization
821 Anola St
Dover OH 44622
740 922-0933

(G-11653)
HICKS ROOFING INC
Also Called: Hicks Industrial Roofing
2162 Pleasant Valley Rd Ne (44663-8079)
PHONE.................................330 364-7737
Michael Hicks, *Pr*
Beth Hicks, *
EMP: 40 **EST:** 1948
SQ FT: 14,600
SALES (est): 4.92MM **Privately Held**
Web: www.hicksroofing.com
SIC: 1761 Roofing contractor

(G-11654)
HOSPICE TUSCARAWAS COUNTY INC (PA)
Also Called: COMMUNITY HOSPICE
716 Commercial Ave Sw (44663-9367)
PHONE.................................330 343-7605
Norman Mast, *Pr*
Nicholas Reynolds, *
EMP: 100 **EST:** 1986
SQ FT: 22,500
SALES (est): 15.17MM **Privately Held**
Web: www.ohioshospice.org
SIC: 8052 Personal care facility

(G-11655)
HUNTINGTON NATIONAL BANK
205 N Broadway St (44663-2611)
PHONE.................................330 343-2527
Sue Klann, *Mgr*
EMP: 36
SALES (corp-wide): 10.84B **Publicly Held**
Web: www.huntington.com

GEOGRAPHIC SECTION

New Richmond - Clermont County (G-11676)

SIC: 6029 6021 Commercial banks, nec; National commercial banks
HQ: The Huntington National Bank
41 S High St
Columbus OH 43215
614 480-4293

(G-11656)
HYDRAULIC PARTS STORE INC
145 1st Dr Ne (44663-2857)
P.O. Box 808 (44663-0808)
PHONE.................................330 364-6667
Robert M Henning Senior, *Pr*
EMP: 42 EST: 1983
SQ FT: 25,000
SALES (est): 1.66MM **Privately Held**
SIC: 5084 3594 3593 3492 Hydraulic systems equipment and supplies; Fluid power pumps and motors; Fluid power cylinders and actuators; Fluid power valves and hose fittings

(G-11657)
LOWES HOME CENTERS LLC
Also Called: Lowe's
495 Mill Ave Se (44663)
PHONE.................................330 339-1936
Ken Kaiser, *Brnch Mgr*
EMP: 91
SALES (corp-wide): 86.38B **Publicly Held**
Web: www.lowes.com
SIC: 5211 5031 5722 5064 Home centers; Building materials, exterior; Household appliance stores; Electrical appliances, television and radio
HQ: Lowe's Home Centers, Llc
1000 Lowes Blvd
Mooresville NC 28117
336 658-4000

(G-11658)
MULTI-CNTY JVNILE ATTNTION SYS
Multi County Juvenile ATT Ctr
241 University Dr Ne (44663-9451)
PHONE.................................330 339-7775
Pamela Maybaugh, *Dir*
EMP: 52
SQ FT: 3,016
SALES (corp-wide): 8.57MM **Privately Held**
Web: www.mcjas.org
SIC: 8322 Individual and family services
PA: Multi-County Juvenile Attention System
815 Faircrest St Sw
Canton OH 44706
330 484-6471

(G-11659)
MUSKINGUM WTRSHED CNSRVNCY DST (PA)
1319 3rd St Nw (44663-1305)
P.O. Box 349 (44663-0349)
PHONE.................................330 343-6647
Craig Butler, *Ex Dir*
John M Hoopingarner, *
James Cugliari, *
EMP: 75 EST: 1933
SQ FT: 9,000
SALES (est): 78.16K
SALES (corp-wide): 78.16K **Privately Held**
Web: www.mwcd.org
SIC: 7033 Campgrounds

(G-11660)
N P MOTEL SYSTEM INC
Also Called: Holiday Inn
145 Bluebell Dr Sw (44663-9660)
PHONE.................................330 339-7731
EMP: 33 EST: 1995
SALES (est): 371.89K **Privately Held**
Web: www.holidayinn.com

SIC: 7011 Hotels and motels

(G-11661)
PERSONAL FMLY CNSLING SVCS OF
Also Called: Personal & Family Counseling
1433 5th St Nw (44663-1223)
PHONE.................................330 343-8171
EMP: 38 EST: 1972
SALES (est): 818.84K **Privately Held**
Web: www.thementaldesk.com
SIC: 8322 Social service center

(G-11662)
REA & ASSOCIATES INC (PA)
419 W High Ave (44663-3621)
P.O. Box 1020 (44663-5120)
PHONE.................................330 339-6651
Leman G Beall, *Pr*
Debi Gellenbeck, *
Jeremiah Senften, *
EMP: 58 EST: 1938
SQ FT: 680
SALES (est): 41.3MM
SALES (corp-wide): 41.3MM **Privately Held**
Web: www.reacpa.com
SIC: 8721 Certified public accountant

(G-11663)
RIVERFRONT ANTIQUE MALL INC
1203 Front Ave Sw (44663-2066)
PHONE.................................330 339-4448
Mark Natoli, *Pr*
EMP: 30 EST: 1992
SQ FT: 84,000
SALES (est): 1.83MM **Privately Held**
SIC: 6512 5932 Property operation, retail establishment; Antiques

(G-11664)
RIVERVIEW HOSPITALITY CORP
Also Called: Hampton Inn
1299 W High Ave (44663-6943)
PHONE.................................330 339-7000
James L Saltzgiver Senior, *CEO*
EMP: 52 EST: 1998
SALES (est): 1.02MM **Privately Held**
Web: www.hilton.com
SIC: 7011 Hotels and motels

(G-11665)
RK FAMILY INC
1203 Front Ave Sw (44663-2066)
PHONE.................................330 308-5075
EMP: 195
SALES (corp-wide): 1.22B **Privately Held**
Web: www.ruralking.com
SIC: 5191 Farm supplies
PA: Rk Family, Inc.
4216 Dewitt Ave
Mattoon IL 61938
217 235-7102

(G-11666)
SCHOENBRUNN HEALTHCARE
2594 E High Ave (44663-6737)
PHONE.................................330 339-3595
Shaul Flank, *Owner*
EMP: 909 EST: 2008
SALES (est): 6.07MM
SALES (corp-wide): 35.53MM **Privately Held**
Web: www.schoenbrunnhealthcare.com
SIC: 8059 8051 8011 Nursing home, except skilled and intermediate care facility; Skilled nursing care facilities; Clinic, operated by physicians
PA: Progressive Quality Care, Inc.
5553 Broadview Rd
Parma OH 44134
216 661-6800

(G-11667)
SOUTH BRDWAY HLTHCARE GROUP IN
Also Called: Amberwood Manor
245 S Broadway St # 251 (44663-3842)
PHONE.................................330 339-2151
George S Repchick, *Pr*
William I Weisberg, *VP*
EMP: 253 EST: 2002
SALES (est): 3.35MM
SALES (corp-wide): 655.44MM **Privately Held**
Web: www.saberhealth.com
SIC: 8051 Convalescent home with continuous nursing care
PA: Saber Healthcare Group, L.L.C.
23700 Commerce Park
Beachwood OH 44122
216 292-5706

(G-11668)
STARLIGHT ENTERPRISES INC
Also Called: S.E.I.
400 E High Ave (44663-2549)
P.O. Box 1054 (44663-5154)
PHONE.................................330 339-2020
Cassie Elvin, *Dir*
Eleanor Scott, *
EMP: 175 EST: 1967
SQ FT: 27,300
SALES (est): 1.86MM **Privately Held**
Web: www.thinksei.org
SIC: 8331 7349 Sheltered workshop; Janitorial service, contract basis

(G-11669)
TUCSON INC
3497 University Dr Ne (44663-6711)
PHONE.................................330 339-4935
James R Demuth, *Pr*
EMP: 41 EST: 2001
SQ FT: 2,250
SALES (est): 8.16MM **Privately Held**
Web: www.tucsonohio.com
SIC: 1611 General contractor, highway and street construction

(G-11670)
TUSCARWAS ORAL MXLLFCIAL SRGER
Also Called: Doan, Randall
1456 Kaderly St Nw (44663-1243)
PHONE.................................330 364-8665
C Randall Doan D.d.s., *Pr*
EMP: 27 EST: 1983
SALES (est): 456.22K **Privately Held**
SIC: 8021 Maxillofacial specialist

(G-11671)
UNITED PARCEL SERVICE INC
Also Called: UPS
241 8th Street Ext Sw (44663-2027)
PHONE.................................330 339-6281
Matt Walker, *Mgr*
EMP: 41
SALES (corp-wide): 90.96B **Publicly Held**
Web: www.ups.com
SIC: 4215 4513 Parcel delivery, vehicular; Air courier services
HQ: United Parcel Service, Inc.
55 Glenlake Pkwy
Atlanta GA 30328
404 828-6000

(G-11672)
VEOLIA WTS USA INC
Also Called: GE Water & Process Tech
2118 Reiser Ave Se (44663-3332)
PHONE.................................330 339-2292
Tom Johnston, *Brnch Mgr*

EMP: 32
Web: www.watertechnologies.com
SIC: 5169 Chemicals and allied products, nec
HQ: Veolia Wts Usa, Inc.
3600 Horizon Blvd
Trevose PA 19053
866 439-2837

(G-11673)
WOOD ELECTRIC INC
210 11th St Nw (44663-1510)
PHONE.................................330 339-7002
Larry Wood, *Pr*
Lisa Wood, *
EMP: 42 EST: 1988
SQ FT: 8,000
SALES (est): 2.26MM **Privately Held**
Web: www.woodelectric.net
SIC: 1731 General electrical contractor

(G-11674)
YOUR HOME COURT ADVANTAGE LLC
122 W High Ave (44663-3802)
PHONE.................................330 364-6602
EMP: 40
SALES (corp-wide): 4.36MM **Privately Held**
Web: www.yourhomecourtadvantage.com
SIC: 6531 Real estate agents and managers
PA: Your Home Court Advantage, Llc
7953 Pittsburg Ave Nw
North Canton OH 44720
330 587-5587

New Plymouth
Vinton County

(G-11675)
HUNTLEY TRUCKING CO
23525 Pumpkin Ridge Rd (45654-8964)
P.O. Box 6 (45654-0006)
PHONE.................................740 385-7615
Lee Huntley, *Sec*
Steven Huntley, *
Kent Maxwell, *
EMP: 35 EST: 1957
SALES (est): 1.07MM **Privately Held**
SIC: 4212 4213 Lumber and timber trucking; Trucking, except local

New Richmond
Clermont County

(G-11676)
DUKE ENERGY OHIO INC
Also Called: Beckjord Power Station
757 Us Highway 52 (45157-9709)
PHONE.................................513 467-5000
Jim Cumbow, *Mgr*
EMP: 1189
SALES (corp-wide): 29.06B **Publicly Held**
Web: www.duke-energy.com
SIC: 4911 Distribution, electric power
HQ: Duke Energy Ohio, Inc.
139 E 4th St
Cincinnati OH 45202
704 382-3853

New Riegel
Seneca County

(G-11677)
B M MACHINE
27 S Perry St (44853-9778)
PHONE..................419 595-2898
Robert Mathias, *Pr*
EMP: 41
SALES (corp-wide): 904.52K **Privately Held**
Web: www.bmmachine.com
SIC: 7699 3499 4213 Industrial machinery and equipment repair; Aerosol valves, metal ; Heavy machinery transport
PA: B M Machine
11722 W County Road 6
Alvada OH 44802
419 595-2898

(G-11678)
CLOUSE CONSTRUCTION CORP (PA)
4382 Township Road 90 (44853-9762)
PHONE..................419 448-1365
EMP: 43 **EST:** 1975
SALES (est): 15.21MM
SALES (corp-wide): 15.21MM **Privately Held**
Web: www.clouseconstruction.com
SIC: 1541 Steel building construction

New Springfield
Mahoning County

(G-11679)
SNYDERS ANTIQUE AUTO PARTS INC
12925 Woodworth Rd (44443-8722)
PHONE..................330 549-5313
Donald Snyder Iii, *Pr*
Donald Snyder Junior, *VP*
▲ **EMP:** 30 **EST:** 1960
SALES (est): 3.83MM **Privately Held**
Web: www.snydersantiqueauto.com
SIC: 5531 5013 Automotive parts; Automotive supplies and parts

New Vienna
Clinton County

(G-11680)
HUHTAMAKI INC
Also Called: Huhtamaki Plastics
5566 New Vienna Rd (45159-9533)
P.O. Box 326 (45159-0326)
PHONE..................937 987-3078
Howard Liming, *Brnch Mgr*
EMP: 201
SALES (corp-wide): 4.53B **Privately Held**
Web: www.huhtamaki.com
SIC: 5199 Packaging materials
HQ: Huhtamaki, Inc.
9201 Packaging Dr
De Soto KS 66018
913 583-3025

New Washington
Crawford County

(G-11681)
BUCYRUS COMMUNITY PHYSICIANS
120 W Main St (44854-9431)
PHONE..................419 492-2200
Tom Klitzka, *Prin*
EMP: 128 **EST:** 2010
SALES (est): 71.14K
SALES (corp-wide): 444.64K **Privately Held**
Web: www.avitahealth.org
SIC: 8011 Internal medicine, physician/surgeon
PA: Avita Health System
269 Portland Way S
Galion OH 44833
419 468-4841

(G-11682)
CREST BENDING INC
108 John St (44854-9702)
P.O. Box 458 (44854-0458)
PHONE..................419 492-2108
Robert E Studer, *Pr*
EMP: 45 **EST:** 1966
SQ FT: 50,000
SALES (est): 4.59MM **Privately Held**
Web: www.crestbending.com
SIC: 3312 7692 3498 3317 Tubes, steel and iron; Welding repair; Fabricated pipe and fittings; Steel pipe and tubes

(G-11683)
STUDER-OBRINGER INC
525 S Kibler St (44854-9524)
P.O. Box 278 (44854-0278)
PHONE..................419 492-2121
Kenneth Falter, *Pr*
John Cronau, *
Jim Alt, *
Steve Obringer, *
Andy Studer, *
EMP: 46 **EST:** 1967
SQ FT: 1,500
SALES (est): 7.43MM **Privately Held**
Web: www.lrbcg.com
SIC: 1542 1541 Commercial and office building, new construction; Industrial buildings and warehouses

New Waterford
Columbiana County

(G-11684)
SUSTAIN LLC
4547 Bentwood Rd (44445-8733)
PHONE..................888 525-0029
Marc Brenner, *CEO*
Daniel Croghan, *
Samuel Ward, *
EMP: 33 **EST:** 2016
SALES (est): 17.69MM **Privately Held**
Web: www.sustainenvironmental.com
SIC: 4212 4953 Hazardous waste transport; Hazardous waste collection and disposal

New Weston
Darke County

(G-11685)
ELDORA SPEEDWAY INC
13929 State Route 118 (45348-9799)
PHONE..................317 299-6066
Jared Frood, *Pr*
EMP: 40 **EST:** 2005
SALES (est): 582.92K **Privately Held**
Web: www.eldoraspeedway.com
SIC: 7948 Auto race track operation

Newark
Licking County

(G-11686)
AMERICAN HLTH NETWRK OHIO LLC
Also Called: Pediatric Physicians of Newark
1920 Tamarack Rd (43055-2303)
PHONE..................740 344-5437
Lynn Kraner, *Mgr*
EMP: 30
SALES (corp-wide): 371.62B **Publicly Held**
Web: www.ahni.com
SIC: 8011 Pediatrician
HQ: American Health Network Of Ohio, Llc
5900 Parkwood Pl
Dublin OH 43016
614 794-4500

(G-11687)
AMERICAN NATIONAL RED CROSS
Also Called: American Red Cross
1272 W Main St Ste 505 (43055-2053)
PHONE..................740 344-2510
EMP: 31
SALES (corp-wide): 3.18B **Privately Held**
Web: www.redcross.org
SIC: 8322 Social service center
PA: The American National Red Cross
431 18th St Nw
Washington DC 20006
202 737-8300

(G-11688)
ARLINGTON CARE CTR
Also Called: Arlington Nursing Home
98 S 30th St (43055-1940)
PHONE..................740 344-0303
Edward L Byington Senior, *Pr*
EMP: 363 **EST:** 1962
SQ FT: 50,000
SALES (est): 9.96MM
SALES (corp-wide): 58.43MM **Privately Held**
Web: www.arlington-care.net
SIC: 8051 8052 Convalescent home with continuous nursing care; Intermediate care facilities
PA: Carington Health Systems
8200 Beckett Park Dr
Hamilton OH 45011
513 682-2700

(G-11689)
ARMSTRONG STEEL ERECTORS INC
50 S 4th St (43055-5436)
P.O. Box 577 (43058-0577)
PHONE..................740 345-4503
Diane M Reed, *Pr*
Roy Mc Intosh, *
Michael Rath Stkldr, *Prin*
EMP: 50 **EST:** 1954
SQ FT: 20,000
SALES (est): 8.54MM **Privately Held**
Web: www.armstrongsteelerectors.com
SIC: 1622 Bridge construction

(G-11690)
BEHAVRAL HLTHCARE PRTNERS CNTL (PA)
65 Messimer Dr Unit 2 (43055-1899)
P.O. Box 4670 (43058-4670)
PHONE..................740 522-8477
Kathryn E Saylor, *CEO*
EMP: 130 **EST:** 1955
SALES (est): 10.91MM
SALES (corp-wide): 10.91MM **Privately Held**
Web: www.bhcpartners.org
SIC: 8093 Mental health clinic, outpatient

(G-11691)
CHERRY JACK LTD PARTNERSHIP
Also Called: Cherry Valley Lodge
2299 Cherry Valley Rd Se (43055-9393)
PHONE..................740 788-1200
Carol Thress, *Genl Mgr*
EMP: 200 **EST:** 1992
SALES (est): 4.59MM **Privately Held**
Web: www.cherryvalleyhotel.com
SIC: 7011 5812 Motels; Eating places

(G-11692)
CHERRY VALLEY LODGE
Also Called: Cherry Valley Lodge and Coco
2299 Cherry Valley Rd Se (43055-9393)
P.O. Box 771207 (77215-1207)
PHONE..................740 788-1200
Steve Hsu, *Pr*
Larry Murphy, *Genl Mgr*
EMP: 33 **EST:** 2005
SALES (est): 2.11MM **Privately Held**
Web: www.cherryvalleyinn.com
SIC: 7011 5812 5091 Hotels; Restaurant, family: independent; Water slides (recreation park)

(G-11693)
COMMUNITY ACTION PRGRAM COMM O
Also Called: Leads Eastland Center
986 E Main St (43055-6940)
PHONE..................740 345-8750
EMP: 67
SALES (corp-wide): 14.41MM **Privately Held**
Web: www.faircaa.org
SIC: 8322 Social service center
PA: Community Action Program Commission Of The Lancaster Fairfield County Area
1743 E Main St
Lancaster OH 43130
740 653-1711

(G-11694)
CONSUMER SUPPORT SERVICES INC
640 Industrial Pkwy (43056-1528)
PHONE..................740 522-5464
EMP: 83
SALES (corp-wide): 29.01MM **Privately Held**
Web: www.cssohio.org
SIC: 8322 Social service center
PA: Consumer Support Services Inc
2040 Cherry Valley Rd # 1
Newark OH 43055
740 788-8257

(G-11695)
CONSUMER SUPPORT SERVICES INC
100 James St (43055-3931)
PHONE..................740 344-3600
EMP: 56
SALES (corp-wide): 29.01MM **Privately Held**
Web: www.cssohio.org
SIC: 8322 Social service center
PA: Consumer Support Services Inc
2040 Cherry Valley Rd # 1
Newark OH 43055
740 788-8257

(G-11696)
COUGHLIN CHEVROLET TOYOTA INC

GEOGRAPHIC SECTION
Newark - Licking County (G-11718)

Also Called: Coughlin Automotive
1850 N 21st St (43055-3186)
P.O. Box 749 (43062-0749)
PHONE.................................740 366-1381
Al Coughlin, *Pr*
Al Coughlin Junior, *Sec*
Bill Vina, *
Max Forster, *
EMP: 90 **EST:** 1955
SQ FT: 50,000
SALES (est): 25.98MM
SALES (corp-wide): 75.69MM **Privately Held**
Web: www.coughlincars.com
SIC: 5511 7532 5531 5521 Automobiles, new and used; Top and body repair and paint shops; Auto and home supply stores; Used car dealers
PA: Coughlin Chevrolet, Inc.
    9000 Broad St Sw
    Pataskala OH 43062
    740 964-9191

(G-11697)
COURTESY AMBULANCE INC
1890 W Main St (43055-1134)
PHONE.................................740 522-8588
Lois Griggs, *Pr*
Clair Griggs, *
EMP: 74 **EST:** 1972
SQ FT: 1,000
SALES (est): 2.79MM **Privately Held**
Web: www.courtesyambulance.com
SIC: 4119 Ambulance service

(G-11698)
COURTYARD BY MARRIOTT
Also Called: Courtyard By Marriott
500 Highland Blvd (43055-2112)
PHONE.................................740 344-1800
Quinn Miller, *Prin*
EMP: 34 **EST:** 2007
SALES (est): 1.02MM **Privately Held**
Web: www.marriott.com
SIC: 7011 Hotels and motels

(G-11699)
ENERGY COOPERATIVE INC (HQ)
1500 Granville Rd (43055-1536)
P.O. Box 4970 (43058-4970)
PHONE.................................740 348-1206
Dave Potter, *Pr*
Charles Manning, *
David L Hite, *
EMP: 49 **EST:** 1998
SALES (est): 61.79MM
SALES (corp-wide): 130.87MM **Privately Held**
Web: www.myenergycoop.com
SIC: 8611 5983 4924 4911 Public utility association; Fuel oil dealers; Natural gas distribution; Electric services
PA: Licking Rural Electrification, Inc.
    11339 Mount Vernon Rd
    Utica OH 43080
    740 892-2071

(G-11700)
FIRST FDRAL SAV LN ASSN NEWARK (PA)
Also Called: FIRST FEDERAL SAVINGS
2 N 2nd St (43055-5610)
P.O. Box 4460 (43058-4460)
PHONE.................................740 345-3494
Paul M Thompson, *Pr*
Sarah R Wallace, *
Michael S Young, *
Glen L Griebel, *
EMP: 33 **EST:** 1934
SQ FT: 5,000
SALES (est): 9.96MM
SALES (corp-wide): 9.96MM **Privately Held**
Web: www.firstfedohio.com
SIC: 6035 Federal savings and loan associations

(G-11701)
GENERTION HLTH RHBLTTION CTR L
Also Called: Flint Ridge Nursing & Rehab
1450 W Main St (43055-1825)
PHONE.................................740 348-1300
EMP: 92 **EST:** 1997
SALES (est): 5.99MM **Privately Held**
Web: www.flintridgehc.com
SIC: 8052 8051 Intermediate care facilities; Skilled nursing care facilities

(G-11702)
GOLF GALAXY GOLFWORKS INC
Also Called: Golfworks, The
4820 Jacksontown Rd (43056-9377)
P.O. Box 3008 (43058-3008)
PHONE.................................740 328-4193
Mark Mccormick, *CEO*
Jerry Datz, *
Mark Wilson, *
Richard C Nordvoid, *
▲ **EMP:** 150 **EST:** 1974
SQ FT: 80,000
SALES (est): 20.39MM
SALES (corp-wide): 12.98B **Publicly Held**
Web: www.golfworks.com
SIC: 5091 2731 3949 5941 Golf equipment; Books, publishing only; Golf equipment; Golf, tennis, and ski shops
HQ: Golf Galaxy, Llc
    345 Ct St
    Coraopolis PA 15108

(G-11703)
GW BUSINESS SOLUTIONS LLC
65 S 5th St (43055-5404)
PHONE.................................740 345-9861
Timothy Young, *Pr*
EMP: 148 **EST:** 2013
SQ FT: 9,000
SALES (est): 7.39MM **Privately Held**
SIC: 8331 5932 Community service employment training program; Used merchandise stores

(G-11704)
HEATH NURSING CARE CENTER
717 S 30th St (43056-1294)
PHONE.................................740 522-1171
Robert Lehman, *Pr*
Luke Sutherland, *
EMP: 51
SALES (est): 9.73MM **Privately Held**
Web: www.cienahealthcare.com
SIC: 8051 8059 Skilled nursing care facilities; Convalescent home

(G-11705)
HOLLOWAY VENTURES LLC
76 Fairfield Dr (43055-9704)
PHONE.................................740 641-3592
Brian Holloway, *Pr*
Brian Holloway, *Managing Member*
EMP: 28 **EST:** 2019
SALES (est): 930.28K **Privately Held**
Web: www.hollowaybuildingservices.com
SIC: 7389 Business Activities at Non-Commercial Site

(G-11706)
HOPE TIMBER PALLET RECYCL LLC
Also Called: Hope Timber
141 Union St (43055-3976)
P.O. Box 502 (43023-0502)
PHONE.................................740 344-1788
▼ **EMP:** 36 **EST:** 2005
SALES (est): 2.72MM **Privately Held**
Web: www.hopetimbermulch.com
SIC: 2448 4953 Pallets, wood; Recycling, waste materials

(G-11707)
HOSPICE OF CENTRAL OHIO (PA)
Also Called: PALLIATIVE CARE OF OHIO
2269 Cherry Valley Rd Se (43055-9323)
PHONE.................................740 344-0311
TOLL FREE: 800
Kerry Hamilton, *CEO*
Michele Mcmahon, *Ex Dir*
Calvin Robinson, *
EMP: 90 **EST:** 1982
SALES (est): 27.18MM **Privately Held**
Web: www.hospiceofcentralohio.org
SIC: 8052 Personal care facility

(G-11708)
HOUSTON DICK PLBG & HTG INC
Also Called: Houston Plumbing & Heating
724 Montgomery Rd Ne (43055-9461)
PHONE.................................740 763-3961
Richard F Houston, *Pr*
Patricia Houston, *
Beverly Dodson, *
Beth L Cramer, *
EMP: 40 **EST:** 1963
SQ FT: 8,000
SALES (est): 5.39MM **Privately Held**
Web: www.houstonplumbingheating.com
SIC: 1711 Plumbing contractors

(G-11709)
INDUS NEWARK HOTEL LLC
Also Called: Newark Metropolitan Hotel
50 N 2nd St (43055-5622)
PHONE.................................740 322-6455
Martin Schrader, *Brnch Mgr*
EMP: 35
SALES (corp-wide): 1.46MM **Privately Held**
Web: www.newarkmetrohotel.com
SIC: 7011 Hotel, franchised
PA: Indus Newark Hotel Llc
    4265 Sawyer Rd
    Columbus OH 43219
    740 322-6455

(G-11710)
JAY GANESH LLC
1219 W Church St (43055-2101)
PHONE.................................740 344-2136
Babulal N Patel, *Prin*
EMP: 29 **EST:** 2009
SALES (est): 267.28K **Privately Held**
SIC: 7011 Hotels and motels

(G-11711)
KRIBHA LLC
Also Called: Hampton Inn-Newark/Heath
1008 Hebron Rd (43056-1121)
PHONE.................................740 788-8991
Ashok Patel, *Managing Member*
EMP: 31 **EST:** 2003
SALES (est): 990.57K **Privately Held**
Web: www.hilton.com
SIC: 7011 Hotels and motels

(G-11712)
LAYTON INC (PA)
169 Dayton Rd Ne (43055-8879)
PHONE.................................740 349-7101
Gerard Layton, *Pr*
Steve Carson, *
EMP: 36 **EST:** 1986
SQ FT: 9,200
SALES (est): 5.62MM
SALES (corp-wide): 5.62MM **Privately Held**
Web: www.laytoninc.net
SIC: 1794 Excavation work

(G-11713)
LICKING AREA COMPUTER ASSN
150 S Quentin Rd 3rd Fl (43055-4670)
PHONE.................................740 345-3400
Jon Bowers, *Ex Dir*
EMP: 77 **EST:** 2014
SALES (est): 2.43MM **Privately Held**
Web: www.laca.org
SIC: 8641 Civic and social associations

(G-11714)
LICKING COUNTY ADULT CRT SVCS
Also Called: Probation Department
1 Courthouse Sq (43055-5516)
PHONE.................................740 670-5734
Kelly Miller, *Chief*
EMP: 36 **EST:** 2009
SALES (est): 156.37K **Privately Held**
Web: www.lickingcounty.gov
SIC: 8322 Probation office

(G-11715)
LICKING COUNTY AGING PROGRAM
1058 E Main St (43055-6940)
PHONE.................................740 345-0821
David Bibler, *Dir*
EMP: 85 **EST:** 1972
SQ FT: 11,930
SALES (est): 5.38MM **Privately Held**
Web: www.lcap.org
SIC: 8322 8399 Meal delivery program; Health systems agency

(G-11716)
LICKING COUNTY BOARD OF MRDD
Also Called: Community Employment Services
116 N 22nd St (43055-2755)
P.O. Box 4910 (43058-4910)
PHONE.................................740 349-6588
Nancy Neely, *Superintnt*
EMP: 182 **EST:** 1968
SALES (est): 2.2MM
SALES (corp-wide): 170.07MM **Privately Held**
Web: www.lcountydd.org
SIC: 8322 Social services for the handicapped
PA: County Of Licking
    20 S 2nd St
    Newark OH 43055
    740 670-5040

(G-11717)
LICKING MEMORIAL HLTH SYSTEMS (PA)
1320 W Main St (43055-1822)
PHONE.................................220 564-4000
Robert Montagnese, *Pr*
Sallie Arnett, *
Rob Montagnese, *
Kim D Fleming, *
EMP: 990 **EST:** 1984
SALES (est): 332.47MM **Privately Held**
Web: www.lmhealth.org
SIC: 8741 6411 Hospital management; Insurance agents, brokers, and service

(G-11718)
LICKING MEMORIAL HOSPITAL
Also Called: Simon, Richard E MD
1320 W Main St (43055-3699)
PHONE.................................740 348-1750
Richard E Simon, *Prin*
EMP: 347

Web: www.lmhealth.org
SIC: 8011 8062 Internal medicine, physician/surgeon; General medical and surgical hospitals
HQ: Licking Memorial Hospital
1320 W Main St
Newark OH 43055
740 348-4137

(G-11719)
LICKING MEMORIAL HOSPITAL
Also Called: Lincoln Memorial Behavioral
200 Messimer Dr (43055-3627)
PHONE..................740 348-4870
Ann Reho, *Dir*
EMP: 347
Web: www.lmhealth.org
SIC: 8062 General medical and surgical hospitals
HQ: Licking Memorial Hospital
1320 W Main St
Newark OH 43055
740 348-4137

(G-11720)
LICKING MEMORIAL HOSPITAL (HQ)
Also Called: Licking Memorial Health Systems
1320 W Main St (43055-3699)
PHONE..................740 348-4137
Robert A Montagnese, *Pr*
Cynthia L Webster, *INTERIM VICE PRESIDENT FINANCIAL SERVICES*
Sallie Arnett, *
Craig Cairns, *
Veronica Link, *
EMP: 41 EST: 1898
SQ FT: 394,784
SALES (est): 331.97MM **Privately Held**
Web: www.lmhealth.org
SIC: 8062 General medical and surgical hospitals
PA: Licking Memorial Health Systems
1320 W Main St
Newark OH 43055

(G-11721)
LICKING-KNOX GOODWILL INDS INC (PA)
65 S 5th St (43055-5404)
P.O. Box 828 (43058-0828)
PHONE..................740 345-9861
Timothy J Young, *CEO*
Vicki M Osborn, *
EMP: 60 EST: 1977
SQ FT: 17,000
SALES (est): 11.26MM
SALES (corp-wide): 11.26MM **Privately Held**
Web: www.goodwillnewark.com
SIC: 8331 8741 5932 Community service employment training program; Management services; Used merchandise stores

(G-11722)
LINCARE INC
1961 Tamarack Rd (43055-1300)
PHONE..................740 349-8236
Jill Mcritchie, *Brnch Mgr*
EMP: 29
Web: www.lincare.com
SIC: 7352 Medical equipment rental
HQ: Lincare Inc.
19387 Us Highway 19 N
Clearwater FL 33764
727 530-7700

(G-11723)
LOWES HOME CENTERS LLC
Also Called: Lowe's
888 Hebron Rd (43056-1399)
PHONE..................740 522-0003
John Armstrong, *Mgr*
EMP: 134
SALES (corp-wide): 86.38B **Publicly Held**
Web: www.lowes.com
SIC: 5211 5031 5722 5064 Home centers; Building materials, exterior; Household appliance stores; Electrical appliances, television and radio
HQ: Lowe's Home Centers, Llc
1000 Lowes Blvd
Mooresville NC 28117
336 658-4000

(G-11724)
MATESICH DISTRIBUTING CO
1190 E Main St (43055-8803)
PHONE..................740 349-8686
TOLL FREE: 800
John C Matesich Iii, *CEO*
James M Matesich, *
▲ EMP: 91 EST: 1928
SQ FT: 103,000
SALES (est): 23.1MM **Privately Held**
Web: www.matesichbeer.com
SIC: 5181 Beer and other fermented malt liquors

(G-11725)
MC MAHON REALESTATE CO (PA)
Also Called: Coldwell Banker
591 Country Club Dr (43055-2102)
PHONE..................740 344-2250
Joseph Mc Mahon, *Owner*
EMP: 28 EST: 1975
SALES (est): 1.71MM
SALES (corp-wide): 1.71MM **Privately Held**
Web: www.allaboutlickingcounty.com
SIC: 6531 Real estate agent, residential

(G-11726)
MCN HEALTH LLC
2000 Tamarack Rd (43055-1183)
P.O. Box 1008 (43216-1008)
PHONE..................740 788-6000
EMP: 160
SIC: 8062 General medical and surgical hospitals

(G-11727)
MEDICAL AND SURGICAL ASSOC
Also Called: MSA Family Medicine
1930 Tamarack Rd (43055-2303)
PHONE..................740 522-7600
Michael Campolo, *Pr*
EMP: 50 EST: 1994
SALES (est): 5.79MM **Privately Held**
Web: www.msaprimarycare.com
SIC: 8011 General and family practice, physician/surgeon

(G-11728)
MEDICAL BENEFITS MUTL LF INSUR (PA)
Also Called: Medben Companies
1975 Tamarack Rd (43055-1300)
P.O. Box 1009 (43058-1009)
PHONE..................740 522-8425
Douglas Freeman, *Pr*
C Arthur Morrow, *
Kurt Harden, *
Thomas Hoffman, *
EMP: 150 EST: 1938
SQ FT: 32,000
SALES (est): 67.07MM
SALES (corp-wide): 67.07MM **Privately Held**
Web: www.medben.com
SIC: 6321 Health insurance carriers

(G-11729)
MGJ ENTERPRISES INC
963 N 21st St (43055-2921)
PHONE..................740 364-1360
EMP: 29
SALES (corp-wide): 969.44MM **Privately Held**
Web: www.vectorsecurity.com
SIC: 4813 Internet connectivity services
HQ: Mgj Enterprises, Inc.
2000 Ericsson Dr
Warrendale PA 15086
866 525-8529

(G-11730)
MILESTONE VENTURES LLC
1776 Tamarack Rd (43055-1359)
PHONE..................317 908-2093
Dittmar Schaefer, *Brnch Mgr*
EMP: 27
SIC: 5031 Veneer
PA: Milestone Ventures, Llc
2924 Hallie Ln
Granville OH 43023

(G-11731)
MODERN WELDING CO OHIO INC
1 Modern Way (43055-3921)
P.O. Box 4430 (43058-4430)
PHONE..................740 344-9425
TOLL FREE: 800
John W Jones, *Pr*
Doug Rothert, *VP*
Jerry Waller, *VP*
James M Ruth, *Ex VP*
EMP: 30 EST: 1932
SQ FT: 52,000
SALES (est): 9.06MM
SALES (corp-wide): 130.45MM **Privately Held**
Web: www.modweldco.com
SIC: 3443 5051 Tanks, lined: metal plate; Metals service centers and offices
PA: Modern Welding Company, Inc.
2880 New Hartford Rd
Owensboro KY 42303
270 685-4400

(G-11732)
MOUNDBUILDERS COUNTRY CLUB CO
125 N 33rd St (43055-2014)
PHONE..................740 344-4500
EMP: 58 EST: 1950
SQ FT: 50,000
SALES (est): 2.15MM **Privately Held**
Web: www.moundbuilderscc.com
SIC: 7997 5812 7992 5941 Country club, membership; Restaurant, family: independent; Public golf courses; Sporting goods and bicycle shops

(G-11733)
NATIONAL GAS & OIL CORPORATION (DH)
Also Called: Permian Oil & Gas Division
1500 Granville Rd (43055-1500)
P.O. Box 4970 (43058-4970)
PHONE..................740 344-2102
William Sullivan Junior, *Ch Bd*
Patrick J Mc Gonagle, *Pr*
Todd P Ware, *VP*
Gordon M King, *VP*
EMP: 36 EST: 1941
SQ FT: 10,000
SALES (est): 53.77MM
SALES (corp-wide): 130.87MM **Privately Held**
Web: www.theenergycoop.com

SIC: 4922 4924 4932 4911 Natural gas transmission; Natural gas distribution; Gas and other services combined; Electric services
HQ: National Gas & Oil Company Inc
1500 Granville Rd
Newark OH 43055
740 344-2102

(G-11734)
NATIONWIDE CHILDRENS HOSPITAL
75 S Terrace Ave (43055-1355)
PHONE..................740 522-3221
EMP: 101
SALES (corp-wide): 3.6B **Privately Held**
Web: www.nationwidechildrens.org
SIC: 8082 8011 Home health care services; Medical centers
PA: Nationwide Children's Hospital
700 Childrens Dr
Columbus OH 43205
614 722-2000

(G-11735)
NEWARK FAMILY PHYSICIANS INC
Also Called: American Health Network
1272 W Main St (43055-2053)
PHONE..................740 348-1788
Carl Waggoner Md, *Pr*
G Frank Gabe Md, *Sec*
Craig B Cairns Md, *Treas*
EMP: 42 EST: 1965
SALES (est): 491.38K **Privately Held**
Web: www.lmhealth.org
SIC: 8062 General medical and surgical hospitals

(G-11736)
NEWARK LEASING LLC
Also Called: NEWARK CARE AND REHABILITATION
75 Mcmillen Dr (43055-1808)
PHONE..................740 344-0357
EMP: 175 EST: 2017
SALES (est): 12.31MM **Privately Held**
SIC: 8051 Convalescent home with continuous nursing care

(G-11737)
OHIO HEART GROUP INC
1311 W Main St (43055-1821)
PHONE..................740 348-0012
Rhonda Cowdery, *Brnch Mgr*
EMP: 42
SALES (corp-wide): 5.39MM **Privately Held**
Web: www.ohioheartgroup.com
SIC: 8031 8011 Offices and clinics of osteopathic physicians; Offices and clinics of medical doctors
PA: Ohio Heart Group, Inc.
800 E Broad St
Columbus OH 43205
614 252-8300

(G-11738)
PARK NATIONAL BANK (HQ)
50 N 3rd St (43055)
P.O. Box 3500 (43058)
PHONE..................740 349-8451
Dan Delawder, *Ch*
David Trautman, *
Cheryl Snyder, *
Thomas J Button, *
John W Kozak, *
EMP: 150 EST: 1909
SALES (est): 487.39MM
SALES (corp-wide): 564.3MM **Publicly Held**
Web: www.parknationalbank.com

GEOGRAPHIC SECTION

Newbury - Geauga County (G-11760)

SIC: 6021 National commercial banks
PA: Park National Corporation
50 N 3rd St
Newark OH 43055
740 349-8451

(G-11739)
PARK NATIONAL CORPORATION (PA)
Also Called: Park National Bank
50 N 3rd St (43055)
P.O. Box 3500 (43058)
PHONE..................740 349-8451
David L Trautman, CEO
Matthew R Miller, Pr
Brady T Burt, CFO
EMP: 156 EST: 1992
SALES (est): 564.3MM
SALES (corp-wide): 564.3MM Publicly Held
Web: investor.parknationalcorp.com
SIC: 6021 National commercial banks

(G-11740)
PATHWAYS OF CENTRAL OHIO
1627 Bryn Mawr Dr (43055-1505)
PHONE..................740 345-6166
Kristin Mccloud, Ex Dir
EMP: 30 EST: 1970
SQ FT: 7,000
SALES (est): 1.56MM Privately Held
Web: www.pathwaysofcentralohio.com
SIC: 8322 Social service center

(G-11741)
PHOENIX MASONRY LTD
645 W Church St (43055-4223)
P.O. Box 814 (43058-0814)
PHONE..................740 344-5787
Steven Stone, Pr
EMP: 60 EST: 1977
SALES (est): 4.7MM Privately Held
SIC: 1741 Masonry and other stonework

(G-11742)
PREMIER HOME HEALTH LLC
35 S Park Pl Ste 350 (43055-5565)
PHONE..................740 403-6806
EMP: 34 EST: 2017
SALES (est): 1.8MM Privately Held
Web: www.ohiopremierhomehealth.com
SIC: 8099 Health and allied services, nec

(G-11743)
PRIORITY EQUIPMENT RENTAL LTD
581 Country Club Dr Ste D (43055)
PHONE..................724 227-3070
Larry Kirkpatrick, Pr
EMP: 37 EST: 2013
SALES (est): 865.19K Privately Held
Web: www.equipmentrentalimperialpa.com
SIC: 7359 Equipment rental and leasing, nec

(G-11744)
R & R PIPELINE INC (PA)
155 Dayton Rd Ne (43055-8879)
P.O. Box 37 (43058-0037)
PHONE..................740 345-3692
Rick Reed, Pr
Jeff Emery, *
EMP: 35 EST: 1984
SQ FT: 7,400
SALES (est): 9.75MM
SALES (corp-wide): 9.75MM Privately Held
Web: www.rrpipelineinc.com
SIC: 1623 Pipeline construction, nsk

(G-11745)
REESE PYLE DRAKE & MEYER (PA)
36 N 2nd St (43055-5610)
P.O. Box 919 (43058-0919)
PHONE..................740 345-3431
Robert N Drake, Managing Member
Ann Munro Kennedy, Pt
David W Wenger, Pt
William Douglas Lowe, Pt
EMP: 42 EST: 1904
SQ FT: 12,000
SALES (est): 4.31MM
SALES (corp-wide): 4.31MM Privately Held
Web: www.reesepyle.com
SIC: 8111 General practice attorney, lawyer

(G-11746)
RICHARDSON GLASS SERVICE INC (PA)
Also Called: RICHARDSON GLASS SERVICE INC DBA LEE'S GLASS SERVICE
1165 Mount Vernon Rd (43055)
PHONE..................740 366-5090
TOLL FREE: 888
Mark W Mcpeek, Pr
Laura Mcpeek, VP
EMP: 52 EST: 1941
SQ FT: 21,480
SALES (est): 15.31MM
SALES (corp-wide): 15.31MM Privately Held
Web: www.richardsonglass.com
SIC: 1793 Glass and glazing work

(G-11747)
SECURITY NATIONAL BANK & TR CO (HQ)
Also Called: Security National Bank
50 N 3rd St (43055-5523)
P.O. Box 1726 (45501-1726)
PHONE..................740 426-6384
H Scott Cunningham, Ch Bd
William C Fralick, Pr
J William Stapleton, Ex VP
Daniel M O'keefe, VP
EMP: 120 EST: 1903
SQ FT: 40,000
SALES (est): 10.79MM
SALES (corp-wide): 564.3MM Publicly Held
Web: www.parknationalbank.com
SIC: 6021 National trust companies with deposits, commercial
PA: Park National Corporation
50 N 3rd St
Newark OH 43055
740 349-8451

(G-11748)
SPENCER HALF-WAY HOUSE INC
Also Called: Spencer Halfway Hse
69 Granville St (43055-4983)
PHONE..................740 345-5074
Patrick Evan, Dir
EMP: 27 EST: 1970
SALES (est): 433.64K Privately Held
Web: www.bhcpartners.org
SIC: 8361 Halfway group home, persons with social or personal problems

(G-11749)
ST FRANCIS DE SALES CHURCH
Also Called: Roman Catholic Church
40 Granville St (43055-5084)
PHONE..................740 345-9874
Pastor David Sizemore, Prin
Pastor Dean Mathewson, Prin
Pastor William Hritsko, Prin
R Penhallurick, Pastor
Maggie Wright, Dir
EMP: 95 EST: 1883
SALES (est): 1.18MM Privately Held
Web: www.stfrancisparish.net
SIC: 8661 8211 8351 Catholic Church; Kindergarten; Preschool center

(G-11750)
STATE FARM GENERAL INSUR CO
Also Called: State Farm Insurance
1440 Granville Rd (43055-1538)
P.O. Box 8903 (61702-8903)
PHONE..................740 364-5000
Lee Baumann, VP
EMP: 90
SALES (corp-wide): 27.88B Privately Held
Web: www.statefarm.com
SIC: 6411 Insurance agents and brokers
HQ: State Farm General Insurance Co Inc
1 State Farm Plz
Bloomington IL 61701
309 766-2311

(G-11751)
TRUE CORE FEDERAL CREDIT UNION
215 Deo Dr (43055-3051)
PHONE..................740 345-6608
Fred Longstreth, Pr
Dorothy Ridenbaugh, *
EMP: 45 EST: 1940
SALES (est): 10.06MM Privately Held
Web: www.truecore.org
SIC: 6061 Federal credit unions

(G-11752)
WASTE MANAGEMENT OHIO INC
Also Called: Waste Management
100 Ecology Row (43055-8894)
PHONE..................740 345-1212
EMP: 100
SALES (corp-wide): 14.91B Publicly Held
SIC: 4953 Refuse systems
HQ: Waste Management Of Ohio, Inc.
1700 N Broad St
Fairborn OH 45324

(G-11753)
WASTE-AWAY SYSTEMS LLC
995 Keller Dr (43056-9635)
PHONE..................740 349-2783
Seth E Ellington, Managing Member
EMP: 30 EST: 2014
SALES (est): 2.12MM Privately Held
Web: www.wasteawaysystems.com
SIC: 4953 Refuse collection and disposal services

(G-11754)
WILSON SHANNON & SNOW INC
10 W Locust St Uppr (43055-5508)
PHONE..................740 345-6611
Philip Z Shannon, Pr
Noble B Snow Iii, Sec
William W Weidaw, VP
EMP: 35 EST: 1954
SQ FT: 4,500
SALES (est): 4.93MM Privately Held
Web: www.wssinc.net
SIC: 8721 Certified public accountant

(G-11755)
WILSONS HILLVIEW FARM INC
Also Called: Wilson's Garden Center
10923 Lambs Ln (43055-8897)
PHONE..................740 763-2873
Ned Wilson, Pr
Harry Wilson, *
Mitzie Wilson, *
EMP: 35 EST: 1965
SQ FT: 80,000
SALES (est): 519.18K Privately Held
Web: www.gardencenterohio.com
SIC: 0181 5992 Shrubberies, grown under cover (e.g. greenhouse production); Florists

(G-11756)
YEATER ALENE K MD
Also Called: Govana Hospital
15 Messimer Dr (43055-1841)
PHONE..................740 348-4694
Alene Yeater, Owner
EMP: 40 EST: 2015
SALES (est): 1.01MM Privately Held
SIC: 8011 Offices and clinics of medical doctors

Newburgh Heights
Cuyahoga County

(G-11757)
CITY OF CLEVELAND
4600 Harvard Ave (44105-3224)
PHONE..................216 348-7277
Dwight Wilson, Pr
EMP: 28
SALES (corp-wide): 972.69MM Privately Held
Web: www.clevelandohio.gov
SIC: 4941 Water supply
PA: City Of Cleveland
601 Lakeside Ave E Rm 210
Cleveland OH 44114
216 664-2000

(G-11758)
OHIO BULK TRANSFER COMPANY INC
3203 Harvard Ave (44105-3065)
PHONE..................216 883-7200
James A Palladino, Pr
Carmen Palladino, *
EMP: 97 EST: 1964
SQ FT: 5,777
SALES (est): 2.25MM
SALES (corp-wide): 29.28MM Privately Held
Web: www.ohiobulk.com
SIC: 4212 Local trucking, without storage
HQ: J A P Holding Company Ii Inc
3203 Harvard Ave
Newburgh Heights OH 44105
216 883-7200

Newbury
Geauga County

(G-11759)
CAMP HO MITA KODA FOUNDATION
14040 Auburn Rd (44065-9703)
PHONE..................440 739-4095
Theodore Rusinoff, Bd of Dir
EMP: 50 EST: 2017
SQ FT: 1,894
SALES (est): 950.4K Privately Held
Web: www.camphomitakoda.org
SIC: 7032 Sporting and recreational camps

(G-11760)
FAIRMOUNT NURSING HOME INC
Also Called: Holly Hill Nursing Home
10190 Fairmount Rd (44065-9531)
P.O. Box 337 (44065-0337)
PHONE..................440 338-8220
George Ohman, Pr
EMP: 95 EST: 1959
SQ FT: 28,000
SALES (est): 8.63MM Privately Held
Web: www.ohmanfamilyliving.com

SIC: 8052 8051 Intermediate care facilities; Skilled nursing care facilities

(G-11761)
KINETICO INCORPORATED (HQ)
10845 Kinsman Rd (44065-8702)
PHONE..............................440 564-9111
◆ EMP: 287 EST: 1970
SALES (est): 91.57MM
SALES (corp-wide): 635.39MM Privately Held
Web: www.kinetico.com
SIC: 3589 5074 6799 Water treatment equipment, industrial; Water heaters and purification equipment; Investors, nec
PA: Axel Johnson Inc.
155 Spring St Fl 6
New York NY 10012
646 291-2445

(G-11762)
KUHNLE BROTHERS INC
Also Called: Kuhnle Bros Trucking
14905 Cross Creek Pkwy (44065-9788)
P.O. Box 375 (44065-0375)
PHONE..............................440 564-7168
Kim Thomas Kuhnle, CEO
Kim Taylor Kuhnle, CEO
Kim Thomas Kuhnle, Pr
Robert Russell, *
Thomas Kuhnle, *
EMP: 150 EST: 1963
SQ FT: 20,000
SALES (est): 20.65MM Privately Held
Web: www.kuhnlebrothers.com
SIC: 4213 4212 Trucking, except local; Local trucking, without storage

(G-11763)
PRECIOUS CARGO TRNSP INC
15050 Cross Creek Pkwy (44065)
P.O. Box 23617 (44023)
PHONE..............................440 543-9272
Richard Wervey, Pr
EMP: 30 EST: 1993
SQ FT: 10,000
SALES (est): 1.94MM Privately Held
Web: www.pctbus.com
SIC: 4141 4119 4131 Local bus charter service; Limousine rental, with driver; Intercity and rural bus transportation

(G-11764)
SCOT BURTON CONTRACTORS LLC
11330 Kinsman Rd (44065-9666)
PHONE..............................440 564-1011
Scot Paulitsch, *
EMP: 40 EST: 2000
SQ FT: 6,000
SALES (est): 9.98MM Privately Held
Web: www.burtonscot.com
SIC: 1611 Highway and street paving contractor

(G-11765)
US HOTEL OSP VENTURES LLC
Also Called: Punderson Mnor Ldge Cnfrnce Ct
11755 Kinsman Rd (44065-9691)
PHONE..............................440 564-9144
EMP: 29
SALES (corp-wide): 5.81MM Privately Held
Web: www.pundersonmanor.com
SIC: 7011 Resort hotel
PA: U.S. Hotel Osp Ventures, Llc
3200 W Maple St Ste 2001
Sioux Falls SD 57107
605 334-2371

Newcomerstown
Tuscarawas County

(G-11766)
CFS FAMILY HOLDINGS INC
500 Enterprise Dr (43832-9241)
PHONE..............................740 492-0595
EMP: 50
SALES (corp-wide): 9.73B Publicly Held
Web: www.caitofoods.com
SIC: 4225 General warehousing and storage
HQ: Cfs Family Holdings, Inc.
8735 E 33rd St
Indianapolis IN 46226
800 652-8165

(G-11767)
EAGLE HARDWOODS INC
6138 Stonecreek Rd (43832-9162)
P.O. Box 96 (43840-0096)
PHONE..............................330 339-8838
Ronald D Furbay, Pr
Loy E Wiggins Junior, VP
▼ EMP: 40 EST: 1992
SQ FT: 1,344
SALES (est): 7.03MM Privately Held
Web: www.eaglehardwoods.com
SIC: 5031 Lumber: rough, dressed, and finished

(G-11768)
H3D TOOL CORPORATION
Also Called: High Definition Tooling
295 Enterprise Dr (43832-8954)
P.O. Box 314 (43832-0314)
PHONE..............................740 498-5181
EMP: 48 EST: 1994
SQ FT: 20,000
SALES (est): 7.12MM Privately Held
Web: www.h3dtool.com
SIC: 3545 5085 Diamond cutting tools for turning, boring, burnishing, etc.; Industrial supplies

(G-11769)
HUNTINGTON NATIONAL BANK
100 W Main St (43832-1041)
PHONE..............................740 498-8376
Bob Ervin, Mgr
EMP: 31
SQ FT: 1,404
SALES (corp-wide): 10.84B Publicly Held
Web: www.huntington.com
SIC: 6029 6021 Commercial banks, nec; National commercial banks
HQ: The Huntington National Bank
41 S High St
Columbus OH 43215
614 480-4293

(G-11770)
MSI EXPRESS INC
301 Enterprise Dr (43832-9240)
PHONE..............................740 498-4700
EMP: 84
SALES (corp-wide): 179.67MM Privately Held
Web: www.msiexpress.com
SIC: 7389 Packaging and labeling services
PA: Msi Express, Inc.
5900 Carlson Ave
Portage IN 46368
219 762-4855

(G-11771)
NEWCOMERSTOWN DEVELOPMENT INC
Also Called: RIVERSIDE MANOR NURSING & REHA
1100 E State Rd (43832-9446)
PHONE..............................740 498-5165
Dwayne Shepherd, Admn
EMP: 41 EST: 1977
SQ FT: 40,000
SALES (est): 6.02MM Privately Held
Web: www.riversidemanor.com
SIC: 8051 Skilled nursing care facilities

(G-11772)
NEWCOMERSTOWN PROGRESS CORP
Also Called: Riverside Manor
1100 E State Rd (43832-9446)
PHONE..............................740 498-5165
Dwayne Shepherd, Admn
Terry Overholser, *
Wayne Mortine, *
Roger Bambeck, *
EMP: 130 EST: 1973
SQ FT: 35,000
SALES (est): 6.99MM Privately Held
Web: www.riversidemanor.com
SIC: 8051 8049 Convalescent home with continuous nursing care; Physical therapist

(G-11773)
NORTH AMERICAN DENTAL MGT LLC
Also Called: Complete Dntl Care Nwcmerstown
110 S River St (43832-1118)
PHONE..............................740 498-5155
EMP: 1061
SALES (corp-wide): 62.77MM Privately Held
Web: www.nadentalgroup.com
SIC: 8021 Dental clinic
PA: North American Dental Management, Llc
125 Enterprise Dr Ste 200
Pittsburgh PA 15275
724 698-2500

Newton Falls
Trumbull County

(G-11774)
DENTAL ASSOC NEWTON FLS INC
2000 Milton Blvd (44444-8703)
PHONE..............................330 872-5737
Charles R Verbanic D.d.s., Pr
Scott Warner, VP
EMP: 28 EST: 1975
SALES (est): 802.73K Privately Held
Web: www.dentalassociatesofnewtonfalls.com
SIC: 8021 Dentists' office

(G-11775)
HOOBERRY & ASSOCIATES INC
Also Called: Laurie Ann Nursing Home
2200 Milton Blvd (44444-8746)
PHONE..............................330 872-1991
Doris Hooberry, Pr
Sharon Jones, *
EMP: 37 EST: 1985
SQ FT: 15,415
SALES (est): 5.44MM Privately Held
SIC: 8051 Convalescent home with continuous nursing care

(G-11776)
HUNTINGTON NATIONAL BANK
215 E Broad St (44444-1710)
PHONE..............................330 841-0142
Dean Evans, Mgr
EMP: 36
SALES (corp-wide): 10.84B Publicly Held
Web: www.huntington.com
SIC: 6029 6022 Commercial banks, nec; State commercial banks
HQ: The Huntington National Bank
41 S High St
Columbus OH 43215
614 480-4293

(G-11777)
LIBERTY ASHTABULA HOLDINGS
Also Called: Holiday Inn
4185 State Route 5 (44444-9566)
PHONE..............................330 872-6000
Ketki Shah, Pr
Raxit Shah, Sec
EMP: 35 EST: 1998
SALES (est): 488.95K Privately Held
Web: www.hiexpress.com
SIC: 7011 Hotels and motels

(G-11778)
THE CADLE COMPANY (PA)
Also Called: Cadle Company, The
100 N Center St (44444-1380)
PHONE..............................330 872-0918
Daniel Cadle, Pr
Ruth Cadle, *
EMP: 125 EST: 1987
SQ FT: 25,000
SALES (est): 35.24MM
SALES (corp-wide): 35.24MM Privately Held
Web: www.cadleco.com
SIC: 6211 6282 Mortgages, buying and selling; Investment advice

Niles
Trumbull County

(G-11779)
AAA EAST CENTRAL
Also Called: AAA
937 Youngstown Warren Rd (44446-4625)
PHONE..............................330 652-6466
Dru Winings, Mgr
EMP: 32
SQ FT: 15,000
SALES (corp-wide): 1.08B Privately Held
Web: www.aaa.com
SIC: 8699 4724 Automobile owners' association; Travel agencies
HQ: Aaa East Central
5900 Baum Blvd Ste 2
Pittsburgh PA 15206
412 363-5100

(G-11780)
AARIS THERAPY GROUP INC
950 Youngstown Warren Rd (44446-4626)
PHONE..............................330 505-1606
Tiffany Hurlbut, Pr
EMP: 40 EST: 2003
SALES (est): 812.31K Privately Held
Web: www.aaristherapy.com
SIC: 8049 Physical therapist

(G-11781)
AUTUMN HILLS CARE CENTER INC
2565 Niles Vienna Rd (44446-4400)
PHONE..............................330 652-2053
Michael J Coats, Pr
Doctor Carl R Gillette, VP
EMP: 51 EST: 1986
SQ FT: 37,000
SALES (est): 10.35MM Privately Held
Web: www.continuinghc.com
SIC: 8051 Convalescent home with continuous nursing care

GEOGRAPHIC SECTION

North Bend - Hamilton County (G-11804)

(G-11782)
CADENCE CARE NETWORK
165 E Park Ave (44446-2352)
P.O. Box 683 (44446-0683)
PHONE...................................330 544-8005
Matt Kresic, *CEO*
EMP: 50 **EST:** 1990
SALES (est): 8.09MM **Privately Held**
Web: www.cadencecare.org
SIC: 8322 Childrens' aid society

(G-11783)
CAFARO COMPANY (PA)
Also Called: Cafaro
5577 Youngstown Warren Rd (44446-4803)
PHONE...................................330 747-2661
Anthony M Cafaro Senior, *Pr*
John Cafaro, *
EMP: 200 **EST:** 1972
SQ FT: 1,100,000
SALES (est): 26.23MM
SALES (corp-wide): 26.23MM **Privately Held**
Web: www.cafarocompany.com
SIC: 6512 Property operation, retail establishment

(G-11784)
CARARO CO INC
Also Called: Eastwood Mall
492 Wood Ave (44446)
PHONE...................................330 652-6980
Ken Kollar, *Pr*
William M Cafaro, *
Anthony M Cafaro, *
Joseph Nohra, *
EMP: 42 **EST:** 1965
SALES (est): 2.62MM **Privately Held**
SIC: 6512 Commercial and industrial building operation

(G-11785)
COATES CAR CARE INC
59 Youngstown Warren Rd (44446-4592)
PHONE...................................330 652-4180
James M Coates Senior, *Pr*
James M Coates Junior, *VP*
Jamie Williams, *
EMP: 38 **EST:** 1959
SQ FT: 38,000
SALES (est): 1.26MM **Privately Held**
Web: www.coatescarcare.com
SIC: 7539 7542 7549 Automotive repair shops, nec; Carwash, self-service; Lubrication service, automotive

(G-11786)
CONSUMER SUPPORT SERVICES INC
1254 Youngstown Warren Rd Ste B (44446)
PHONE...................................330 652-8800
Patty Beckley, *Ex Dir*
EMP: 100
SALES (corp-wide): 29.01MM **Privately Held**
Web: www.cssohio.org
SIC: 8082 Home health care services
PA: Consumer Support Services Inc
2040 Cherry Valley Rd # 1
Newark OH 43055
740 788-8257

(G-11787)
DANESSA CONSTRUCTION LLC
Also Called: Construction
620 Sophia Ct (44446-3827)
PHONE...................................330 219-1312
Vincent Gatta, *Managing Member*
EMP: 70 **EST:** 2014
SALES (est): 7.82MM **Privately Held**
SIC: 1521 1742 1751 Single-family housing construction; Drywall; Lightweight steel framing (metal stud) installation

(G-11788)
DSV BUILDERS INC
1544 N Main St (44446-1246)
PHONE...................................330 652-3784
EMP: 85
SIC: 1542 Commercial and office building, new construction

(G-11789)
FAIRHAVEN INDUSTRIES
45 North Rd (44446-1918)
PHONE...................................330 652-6168
Douglas Markorwit, *Genl Mgr*
EMP: 36 **EST:** 2007
SALES (est): 529.53K **Privately Held**
Web: www.fairhavenind.com
SIC: 8361 Mentally handicapped home

(G-11790)
FAIRHAVEN INDUSTRIES INC (PA)
45 North Rd (44446-1918)
PHONE...................................330 505-3644
Douglas Burkhardt, *Prin*
EMP: 205 **EST:** 1963
SALES (est): 19.44MM
SALES (corp-wide): 19.44MM **Privately Held**
SIC: 8331 Sheltered workshop

(G-11791)
FAIRHAVEN SHELTERED WORKSHOP
Also Called: FAIRHAVEN SHELTERED WORKSHOP INC
6000 Youngstown Warren Rd (44446-4624)
PHONE...................................330 652-1116
Rocco Maiorca, *Brnch Mgr*
EMP: 147
SALES (corp-wide): 19.44MM **Privately Held**
SIC: 8331 Sheltered workshop
PA: Fairhaven Industries, Inc.
45 North Rd
Niles OH 44446
330 505-3644

(G-11792)
KALOGEROU ENTERPRISES INC
430 Youngstown Warren Rd (44446-4354)
PHONE...................................330 544-9696
John Kalogerou, *Dir*
EMP: 68 **EST:** 2014
SALES (est): 1.5MM **Privately Held**
SIC: 8748 Business consulting, nec

(G-11793)
MIKE COATES CNSTR CO INC
800 Summit Ave (44446-3695)
PHONE...................................330 652-0190
Michael J Coates Junior, *Pr*
Michael J Coates Senior, *Pr*
Michael J Coates Junior, *VP*
Joanne Coates, *
EMP: 150 **EST:** 1958
SQ FT: 15,000
SALES (est): 35.46MM **Privately Held**
Web: www.mikecoatesconstruction.com
SIC: 1542 1541 Institutional building construction; Industrial buildings and warehouses

(G-11794)
NILES RESIDENTIAL CARE LLC
Also Called: Manor At Autumn Hills
2567 Niles Vienna Rd (44446-5401)
PHONE...................................216 727-3996
Brian Haylor, *Prin*
Mark Sprenger, *Prin*
Benjamin Parsons, *Prin*
Scott Sprenger, *Prin*
Jeff Bunner, *Prin*
EMP: 65 **EST:** 2016
SALES (est): 2.3MM **Privately Held**
SIC: 8059 Nursing and personal care, nec

(G-11795)
PALISDES BSBAL A CAL LTD PRTNR
Also Called: Mahoning Valley Scrappers
111 Eastwood Mall Blvd (44446-4841)
PHONE...................................330 505-0000
Alan Levin, *Pt*
EMP: 29 **EST:** 1994
SALES (est): 2.93MM **Privately Held**
Web: www.mlbdraftleague.com
SIC: 7997 Baseball club, except professional and semi-professional

(G-11796)
SELECT STEEL INC
1825 Hunter Ave (44446-1672)
PHONE...................................330 652-1756
Jeffrey A Gotthardt, *Pr*
Glenn E Gotthardt, *
EMP: 40 **EST:** 1992
SQ FT: 76,000
SALES (est): 9.36MM **Privately Held**
Web: www.selectstl.com
SIC: 5051 Steel

(G-11797)
TIMKEN COMPANY
1819 N Main St (44446-1251)
P.O. Box 458036 (44145-8036)
PHONE...................................234 262-3000
Richard Hill, *Mgr*
EMP: 43
SALES (corp-wide): 4.77B **Publicly Held**
Web: www.timken.com
SIC: 5085 Bearings
PA: The Timken Company
4500 Mount Pleasant St Nw
North Canton OH 44720
234 262-3000

(G-11798)
WESTERN RESERVE MECHANICAL INC
3041 S Main St (44446-1313)
PHONE...................................330 652-3888
Linda Leger, *Pr*
Larry Moore, *
Mark Leger, *
EMP: 50 **EST:** 1988
SALES (est): 9.48MM **Privately Held**
Web: www.wrmech.com
SIC: 1711 Mechanical contractor

(G-11799)
WHEATLAND TUBE LLC
Also Called: Wheatland Tube Company
1800 Hunter Ave (44446-1671)
PHONE...................................724 342-6851
Mark Bahrey, *Brnch Mgr*
EMP: 133
Web: www.wheatland.com
SIC: 3317 3312 5051 Steel pipe and tubes; Blast furnaces and steel mills; Iron and steel (ferrous) products
HQ: Wheatland Tube, Llc
1 Council Ave
Wheatland PA 16161
800 257-8182

North Baltimore
Wood County

(G-11800)
GRIFFIN INDUSTRIES LLC
Also Called: Darling International
12850 Quarry Rd (45872-9627)
PHONE...................................419 257-3560
Doug Buckner, *Brnch Mgr*
EMP: 44
SALES (corp-wide): 6.53B **Publicly Held**
Web: www.griffinind.com
SIC: 5191 5149 Animal feeds; Bakery products
HQ: Griffin Industries Llc
4221 Alexandria Pike
Cold Spring KY 41076
859 781-2010

(G-11801)
HANCOCK-WOOD ELECTRIC COOP INC (PA)
1399 Business Park Dr S (45872)
P.O. Box 190 (45872)
PHONE...................................419 257-3241
George Walton, *Pr*
EMP: 35 **EST:** 1938
SALES (est): 51.06MM
SALES (corp-wide): 51.06MM **Privately Held**
Web: www.hwe.coop
SIC: 4911 Distribution, electric power

(G-11802)
THE D S BROWN COMPANY (HQ)
300 E Cherry St (45872-1227)
P.O. Box 158 (45872-0158)
PHONE...................................419 257-3561
◆ **EMP:** 220 **EST:** 1992
SALES (est): 49.1MM
SALES (corp-wide): 1.38B **Publicly Held**
Web: www.dsbrown.com
SIC: 3061 3441 5032 Mechanical rubber goods; Fabricated structural metal for bridges; Paving materials
PA: Gibraltar Industries, Inc.
3556 Lake Shore Rd # 100
Buffalo NY 14219
716 826-6500

North Bend
Hamilton County

(G-11803)
DOLLRIES GROUP LLC
3284 Cherryridge Dr (45052-9520)
PHONE...................................513 834-6105
Chris Dollries, *Prin*
EMP: 27
SALES (corp-wide): 1.95MM **Privately Held**
Web: www.thedollriesgroup.com
SIC: 7389 Design services
PA: The Dollries Group Llc
7361 E Kemper Rd Ste D
Cincinnati OH 45249
513 834-6105

(G-11804)
VISTRA ENERGY CORP
Also Called: Miami Fort Power Station
11021 Brower Rd (45052-9755)
PHONE...................................513 467-4900
Tim Thiemann, *Mgr*
EMP: 205
SALES (corp-wide): 14.78B **Publicly Held**
Web: www.vistracorp.com

North Benton - Portage County (G-11805)

SIC: 4911 Fossil fuel electric power generation
PA: Vistra Corp.
6555 Sierra Dr
Irving TX 75039
214 812-4600

North Benton
Portage County

(G-11805)
FOUNDERS SERVICE & MFG INC
10535 12th St (44449-9608)
PHONE...................330 584-7759
EMP: 98
SALES (corp-wide): 2.32MM **Privately Held**
SIC: 5051 Foundry products
PA: Founders Service & Manufacturing, Inc.
879 State Route 14
Deerfield OH 44411
330 584-7759

North Canton
Stark County

(G-11806)
8001 RED BUCKEYE LANDLORD LLC
Also Called: Danbury Huber Heights
8230 Pittsburg Ave Nw (44720-5619)
PHONE...................937 506-4733
EMP: 67 **EST:** 2017
SALES (est): 729.45MM
SALES (corp-wide): 5.86B **Publicly Held**
Web: www.storypoint.com
SIC: 8059 Domiciliary care
HQ: Welltower Op Llc
4500 Dorr St
Toledo OH 43615
419 247-2800

(G-11807)
ADVANTAGE HOME HEALTH SVCS INC
7951 Pittsburg Ave Nw (44720-5669)
PHONE...................330 491-8161
Kun Woo Nam, *Pr*
Maria N Swisher, *
EMP: 36 **EST:** 2008
SALES (est): 7MM **Privately Held**
Web: www.advantagehomehealthservices.com
SIC: 8082 Home health care services

(G-11808)
ADVANTAGE TANK LINES INC (HQ)
4366 Mount Pleasant St Nw (44720-5446)
PHONE...................330 491-0474
Dennis Nash, *Pr*
Carl H Young, *CFO*
Bill Downey, *Ex VP*
Robert Schurer, *Ex VP*
EMP: 35 **EST:** 2005
SALES (est): 28.79MM
SALES (corp-wide): 1.55B **Privately Held**
Web: www.thekag.com
SIC: 4213 Trucking, except local
PA: The Kenan Advantage Group Inc
4366 Mt Pleasant St Nw
North Canton OH 44720
800 969-5419

(G-11809)
AKRON-CANTON REGIONAL AIRPORT
Also Called: Akron Canton Airport
5400 Lauby Rd Ste 9 (44720)
PHONE...................330 499-4059
Renato Camacho, *Prin*
Renato Camacho, *CEO*
Kristie Vanauken, *
EMP: 50 **EST:** 1946
SQ FT: 150,000
SALES (est): 20.68MM **Privately Held**
Web: www.akroncantonairport.com
SIC: 4581 8721 Airport; Accounting, auditing, and bookkeeping

(G-11810)
ALIGNEMENT ENGINE INC
8050 Freedom Ave Nw (44720-6912)
PHONE...................330 401-8251
Sam Cassatt, *CEO*
EMP: 30 **EST:** 2021
SALES (est): 3MM **Privately Held**
SIC: 5045 Computer peripheral equipment

(G-11811)
ALL AMRCAN GTTER PROTECTION LL
800 N Main St (44720-2011)
PHONE...................330 470-4100
EMP: 43 **EST:** 2017
SALES (est): 4.14MM **Privately Held**
Web: www.allamericangutterprotection.com
SIC: 1761 Gutter and downspout contractor

(G-11812)
ARTHUR MDDLTON CPITL HLDNGS IN (PA)
8000 Freedom Ave Nw (44720-6912)
PHONE...................330 966-9000
Rodney L Napier, *Ch Bd*
EMP: 99 **EST:** 2007
SALES (est): 37.5MM **Privately Held**
Web: www.amch.com
SIC: 8111 8721 8741 Legal services; Accounting, auditing, and bookkeeping; Administrative management

(G-11813)
AWP INC (PA)
Also Called: Area Wide Protective
4244 Mount Pleasant St Nw Ste 100 (44720-5469)
PHONE...................330 677-7401
Rob Sehnert, *Pr*
Jack Peak, *
Don Weidig, *
Dan Gillen, *Chief Human Resources Officer**
George Bullock Lll, *
EMP: 600 **EST:** 1981
SQ FT: 5,500
SALES (est): 539.72MM
SALES (corp-wide): 539.72MM **Privately Held**
Web: www.awpsafety.com
SIC: 8711 Electrical or electronic engineering

(G-11814)
CANTON-STARK CNTY SWER CLG INC
Also Called: Roto-Rooter
7300 Freedom Ave Nw (44720-7126)
PHONE...................330 456-7890
Mark Stepoway, *Pr*
Tami Lupe, *
EMP: 107 **EST:** 1932
SALES (est): 3.85MM **Privately Held**
Web: www.rotorooter.com
SIC: 7699 Sewer cleaning and rodding

(G-11815)
CAVENEY INC
Also Called: SERVPRO
7801 Cleveland Ave Nw (44720-5657)
PHONE...................330 497-4600
John Caveney, *Pr*
Linda L Caveney, *
EMP: 50 **EST:** 1975
SQ FT: 5,200
SALES (est): 2.05MM **Privately Held**
Web: www.servpronorthweststarkcounty.com
SIC: 7349 Building maintenance services, nec

(G-11816)
CHO BEDFORD INC
Also Called: Commercial Fluid Power
320 Witwer St Ne (44720-2538)
PHONE...................330 433-2270
Melvin White, *Mgr*
▲ **EMP:** 27
SALES (corp-wide): 9.77MM **Privately Held**
Web: www.commercialfluidpower.com
SIC: 5084 Industrial machinery and equipment
PA: Cho Bedford, Inc.
2997 Progress St
Dover OH 44622
330 343-8896

(G-11817)
CKP HEATING AND COOLING LLC
Also Called: Honeywell Authorized Dealer
555 N Main St Ste 5 (44720)
PHONE...................330 791-3029
Ty Price, *Managing Member*
EMP: 32 **EST:** 2006
SALES (est): 6MM **Privately Held**
Web: www.ckphvac.com
SIC: 1711 Warm air heating and air conditioning contractor

(G-11818)
COMDOC INC (DH)
Also Called: Comdoc
8247 Pittsburg Ave Nw (44720-5677)
PHONE...................330 896-2346
Riley Lochridge, *Ch Bd*
Gordy Opitz, *
Larry Frank, *
Steven T Owen, *
EMP: 125 **EST:** 1955
SALES (est): 47.03MM
SALES (corp-wide): 6.89B **Publicly Held**
Web: www.comdoc.com
SIC: 7699 5044 7359 Photocopy machine repair; Office equipment; Business machine and electronic equipment rental services
HQ: Xerox Business Solutions Inc
8701 Florida Mining Blvd
Tampa FL 33624

(G-11819)
CPX CANTON AIRPORT LLC
Also Called: Embassy Stes Akrn-Canton Arprt
7883 Freedom Ave Nw (44720-6907)
PHONE...................330 305-0500
Gordon Snyder, *Pr*
EMP: 49 **EST:** 2015
SQ FT: 129,291
SALES (est): 3.33MM **Privately Held**
Web: www.hilton.com
SIC: 7011 Hotels and motels

(G-11820)
DELTA MEDIA GROUP INC
7015 Sunset Strip Ave Nw (44720-7078)
PHONE...................330 493-0350
Noel England, *Pr*
EMP: 65 **EST:** 2000
SALES (est): 3.88MM **Privately Held**
Web: www.deltagroup.com
SIC: 7372 Application computer software

(G-11821)
DESIGN RSTRTION RCNSTRCTION IN
4305 Mount Pleasant St Nw Ste 103 (44720-5429)
PHONE...................330 563-0010
Ray Santiago, *Pr*
Greg Campbell, *
Mike Rankin, *
Don Schultz, *Stockholder**
EMP: 38 **EST:** 1994
SQ FT: 9,000
SALES (est): 8.11MM **Privately Held**
Web: www.designrestoration.net
SIC: 1799 Post disaster renovations

(G-11822)
DIEBOLD GLOBAL FINANCE CORP
350 Orchard Ave Ne (44720)
PHONE...................330 490-6900
Jonathan B Leiken, *Pr*
Greg Geswein, *Pr*
Wally Odell, *Ch Bd*
Robert J Warren, *VP*
Charee Francis-vogelsang, *VP*
EMP: 57 **EST:** 1983
SALES (est): 6.8MM
SALES (corp-wide): 1.63B **Publicly Held**
Web: www.dieboldnixdorf.com
SIC: 6141 Personal credit institutions
PA: Diebold Nixdorf, Incorporated
350 Orchard Ave Ne
North Canton OH 44720
330 490-4000

(G-11823)
DIEBOLD NIXDORF INCORPORATED
5995 Mayfair Rd (44720-1511)
PHONE...................330 899-1300
Mark Blotna, *Mgr*
EMP: 70
SALES (corp-wide): 1.63B **Publicly Held**
Web: www.dieboldnixdorf.com
SIC: 7699 Automated teller machine (ATM) repair
PA: Diebold Nixdorf, Incorporated
350 Orchard Ave Ne
North Canton OH 44720
330 490-4000

(G-11824)
DIEBOLD NIXDORF INCORPORATED
Also Called: Diebold Direct
5995 Mayfair Rd (44720-1511)
PHONE...................330 899-2510
David Newvine, *Brnch Mgr*
EMP: 91
SALES (corp-wide): 1.63B **Publicly Held**
Web: shop.dieboldnixdorf.com
SIC: 5044 Bank automatic teller machines
PA: Diebold Nixdorf, Incorporated
350 Orchard Ave Ne
North Canton OH 44720
330 490-4000

(G-11825)
DISTTECH INC
Also Called: Disttech
4366 Mount Pleasant St Nw (44720-5446)
PHONE...................800 969-5419
EMP: 675
Web: www.thekag.com
SIC: 4213 Liquid petroleum transport, non-local

(G-11826)
DONOR CARE CENTER INC
4535 Strausser St Nw (44720-6979)
PHONE...................330 497-4888

GEOGRAPHIC SECTION
North Canton - Stark County (G-11847)

Yvonne Hutchins, *Prin*
EMP: 29 **EST:** 2019
SALES (est): 242.79K **Privately Held**
SIC: 8099 Health and allied services, nec

(G-11827)
ELIXIR PHARMACY LLC
Also Called: Envision Rx Options
7835 Freedom Ave Nw (44720-6907)
PHONE.................................330 491-4200
Bruce Scott, *Pr*
John Baker Senior, *VP*
Eugene Samuels, *
EMP: 112 **EST:** 2008
SALES (est): 27.09MM
SALES (corp-wide): 24.09B **Publicly Held**
Web: www.elixirsolutions.com
SIC: 5122 Pharmaceuticals
PA: Rite Aid Corporation
1200 Intrepid Ave Ste 2
Philadelphia PA 19112
717 761-2633

(G-11828)
ENVIROSERVE INC (HQ)
Also Called: Enviroserve
7640 Whipple Ave Nw (44720-6924)
PHONE.................................330 361-7764
Nathan Savage, *CEO*
James Kozak, *
Kenneth Kozak, *
EMP: 130 **EST:** 1990
SQ FT: 7,200
SALES (est): 53.26MM **Privately Held**
Web: www.enviroserve.com
SIC: 8744 4953 Environmental remediation; Hazardous waste collection and disposal
PA: One Rock Capital Partners, Llc
45 Rockefeller Plz Fl 39
New York NY

(G-11829)
EVANS CONSTRUCTION
4585 Aultman Ave Nw (44720-8235)
PHONE.................................330 305-9355
Dean Evans, *Prin*
Dave Evans, *
Craig Evans, *
EMP: 40 **EST:** 1968
SALES (est): 2.4MM **Privately Held**
SIC: 1521 Single-family housing construction

(G-11830)
FISHER FOODS MARKETING INC (PA)
4855 Frank Ave Nw (44720-7425)
PHONE.................................330 497-3000
Jeffrey A Fisher, *Pr*
Jack B Fisher, *
EMP: 200 **EST:** 1930
SQ FT: 100,000
SALES (est): 47.02MM
SALES (corp-wide): 47.02MM **Privately Held**
Web: www.fishersfoods.com
SIC: 5411 8741 Supermarkets, independent; Management services

(G-11831)
FLOWER FACTORY INC
Also Called: Flower Factory Super Store
5655 Whipple Ave Nw (44720-7720)
PHONE.................................330 494-7978
◆ **EMP:** 360
SIC: 5199 Gifts and novelties

(G-11832)
FRED OLIVIERI CONSTRUCTION CO (PA)
Also Called: Fred Olivieri Construction Co
6315 Promway Ave Nw (44720-7695)
PHONE.................................330 494-1007
Alfred A Olivieri, *CEO*
Dean L Olivieri, *
Virginia C Olivieri, *
Timothy L Feller, *
▲ **EMP:** 153 **EST:** 1959
SQ FT: 12,600
SALES (est): 48.19MM
SALES (corp-wide): 48.19MM **Privately Held**
Web: www.fredolivieri.com
SIC: 1542 Commercial and office building, new construction

(G-11833)
GBS CORP (PA)
Also Called: GBS Filing Solutions
7233 Freedom Ave Nw (44720-7123)
P.O. Box 2340 (44720-0340)
PHONE.................................330 494-5330
Eugene Calabria, *CEO*
Eugene Calabria, *Pr*
Laurence Merriman, *
Michele Benson, *
Michael Merriman, *
▲ **EMP:** 150 **EST:** 1971
SQ FT: 115,000
SALES (est): 190.76MM
SALES (corp-wide): 190.76MM **Privately Held**
Web: www.gbscorp.com
SIC: 2675 2672 2761 2759 Folders, filing, die-cut: made from purchased materials; Labels (unprinted), gummed: made from purchased materials; Manifold business forms; Commercial printing, nec

(G-11834)
GEI WIDE FORMAT SOLUTIONS
3874 Highland Park Nw (44720-4538)
PHONE.................................330 494-8189
EMP: 30 **EST:** 2019
SALES (est): 268.32K **Privately Held**
Web: www.visualedgeit.com
SIC: 5084 Industrial machinery and equipment

(G-11835)
GRAPHIC ENTERPRISES INC
3874 Highland Park Nw (44720-4538)
PHONE.................................800 553-6616
Brian Frank, *Pr*
Yvonne Brown, *
▲ **EMP:** 54 **EST:** 2003
SQ FT: 10,000
SALES (est): 20.78MM
SALES (corp-wide): 270MM **Privately Held**
Web: www.visualedgeit.com
SIC: 5044 Photocopy machines
PA: Visual Edge Technology, Inc.
3874 Highland Park Nw
Canton OH 44720
330 494-9694

(G-11836)
GRAPHIC ENTPS OFF SLUTIONS INC
Also Called: Graphic Enterprises
3874 Highland Park Nw (44720-4538)
PHONE.................................800 553-6616
Austin Vanchieri, *CEO*
Brian Frank, *
Yvonne Brown, *
EMP: 120 **EST:** 2005
SALES (est): 19.14MM **Privately Held**
Web: www.visualedgeit.com
SIC: 5044 Copying equipment

(G-11837)
GRAYBAR ELECTRIC COMPANY INC
3805 Highland Park Nw (44720-4537)
PHONE.................................330 526-2800
James Lostoski, *Brnch Mgr*
EMP: 35
SQ FT: 40,000
SALES (corp-wide): 11.04B **Privately Held**
Web: www.graybar.com
SIC: 5063 Electrical supplies, nec
PA: Graybar Electric Company, Inc.
34 N Meramec Ave
Saint Louis MO 63105
314 573-9200

(G-11838)
HARRIS DAY ARCHITECTS INC
6677 Frank Ave Nw (44720-7259)
PHONE.................................330 493-3722
R Jeffrey Day, *Pr*
Elaine Harris, *Sec*
EMP: 39 **EST:** 1969
SQ FT: 3,000
SALES (est): 4.7MM **Privately Held**
Web: www.solharrisday.com
SIC: 8712 Architectural engineering

(G-11839)
HAYMAKER TREE & LAWN INC
Also Called: Haymaker Tree and Lawn
6854 Wales Ave Nw (44720-6331)
PHONE.................................330 499-5037
Mark Haymaker, *Pr*
John Haymaker, *
Allison Haymaker, *
EMP: 35 **EST:** 1968
SALES (est): 1.55MM **Privately Held**
Web: www.haymakertreeandlawn.com
SIC: 0783 Planting, pruning, and trimming services

(G-11840)
HUNTINGTON NATIONAL BANK
Also Called: Home Mortgage
4879 Portage St Nw (44720-8422)
PHONE.................................330 966-5353
EMP: 31
SALES (corp-wide): 10.84B **Publicly Held**
Web: www.huntington.com
SIC: 6029 Commercial banks, nec
HQ: The Huntington National Bank
41 S High St
Columbus OH 43215
614 480-4293

(G-11841)
KAG SPECIALTY PRODUCTS GROUP LLC (HQ)
4366 Mount Pleasant St Nw (44720-5446)
PHONE.................................330 409-1124
EMP: 40 **EST:** 1946
SALES (est): 47.94MM
SALES (corp-wide): 1.55B **Privately Held**
Web: www.thekag.com
SIC: 4213 4731 Contract haulers; Truck transportation brokers
PA: The Kenan Advantage Group Inc
4366 Mt Pleasant St Nw
North Canton OH 44720
800 969-5419

(G-11842)
KAISER FOUNDATION HOSPITALS
Also Called: North Canton Medical Offices
4914 Portage St Nw (44720)
PHONE.................................800 524-7377
EMP: 29
SALES (corp-wide): 70.8B **Privately Held**
Web: www.kaisercenter.com

SIC: 8011 Offices and clinics of medical doctors
HQ: Kaiser Foundation Hospitals Inc
1 Kaiser Plz
Oakland CA 94612
510 271-6611

(G-11843)
KARCHER GROUP INC
5590 Lauby Rd Ste 8 (44720-1500)
PHONE.................................330 493-6141
Geoff Karcher, *Pr*
EMP: 42 **EST:** 2000
SALES (est): 7.91MM **Privately Held**
Web: www.tkg.com
SIC: 7374 Computer graphics service

(G-11844)
KENAN ADVANTAGE GROUP INC (PA)
Also Called: Transport Service Co.
4366 Mount Pleasant St Nw (44720)
PHONE.................................800 969-5419
Charlie Delacey, *CEO*
Grant Mitchell, *
Ralph Lee, *
EMP: 114 **EST:** 1982
SQ FT: 86,500
SALES (est): 1.55B
SALES (corp-wide): 1.55B **Privately Held**
Web: www.thekag.com
SIC: 4212 4213 Local trucking, without storage; Liquid petroleum transport, non-local

(G-11845)
KEYBANK NATIONAL ASSOCIATION
Also Called: Keybank
932 N Main St (44720-1920)
PHONE.................................330 499-2566
Joel Martineau Mgr, *Mgr*
EMP: 32
SALES (corp-wide): 10.4B **Publicly Held**
Web: www.key.com
SIC: 6021 National commercial banks
HQ: Keybank National Association
127 Public Sq Ste 5600
Cleveland OH 44114
800 539-2968

(G-11846)
KIRK KEY INTERLOCK COMPANY LLC
9048 Meridian Cir Nw (44720-8387)
PHONE.................................330 833-8223
James G Owens, *Managing Member*
▼ **EMP:** 47 **EST:** 1932
SQ FT: 26,000
SALES (est): 12.16MM
SALES (corp-wide): 2.23B **Privately Held**
Web: www.sentricsafetygroup.com
SIC: 3429 5063 Keys, locks, and related hardware; Electrical apparatus and equipment
PA: Halma Public Limited Company
Misbourne Court Rectory Way
Amersham BUCKS HP7 0
149 472-1111

(G-11847)
MEDICAL TRANSPORT SYSTEMS INC
Also Called: Stark Summit Ambulance
909 Las Olas Blvd Nw (44720-6130)
PHONE.................................330 837-9818
Ronald Cordray, *Pr*
Karla Mcclaskey, *VP*
Jeffrey Finkelstein, *
Arthur Leb, *
EMP: 41 **EST:** 1978
SALES (est): 1.88MM **Privately Held**

North Canton - Stark County (G-11848)

Web: www.starksummit.com
SIC: 4119 Ambulance service

(G-11848)
MICROPLEX INC
7568 Whipple Ave Nw (44720-6921)
PHONE.................................330 498-0600
Valerie Walters, *Pr*
John Walters, *
Jon Harst, *
Susan Harst, *
EMP: 30 EST: 1985
SQ FT: 12,000
SALES (est): 5.29MM **Privately Held**
Web: www.microplex-inc.com
SIC: 3496 3679 5045 Cable, uninsulated wire: made from purchased wire; Harness assemblies, for electronic use: wire or cable; Computer peripheral equipment

(G-11849)
MIDWEST DIGITAL INC
4721 Eagle St Nw (44720-7083)
PHONE.................................330 966-4744
Brian Stimer, *Pr*
▲ EMP: 65 EST: 1990
SALES (est): 7.47MM **Privately Held**
Web: www.imperium.net
SIC: 5065 Communication equipment

(G-11850)
MYERS CONTROLLED POWER LLC (HQ)
219 E Maple St Ste 100-200 (44720-2586)
PHONE.................................330 834-3200
James Owens, *Pr*
▲ EMP: 119 EST: 2005
SALES (est): 52.84MM
SALES (corp-wide): 172.09MM **Privately Held**
Web: www.myerspower.com
SIC: 5063 Electrical apparatus and equipment
PA: Myers Power Products, Inc.
     219 E Maple Ste 100/200e
     North Canton OH 44720
     330 834-3200

(G-11851)
PIEDMONT AIRLINES INC
Also Called: American Airlines/Eagle
5400 Lauby Rd (44720-1598)
PHONE.................................330 499-3260
Jill Walthers, *Mgr*
EMP: 105
SALES (corp-wide): 52.79B **Publicly Held**
Web: www.piedmont-airlines.com
SIC: 4512 Air passenger carrier, scheduled
HQ: Piedmont Airlines, Inc.
     5443 Airport Terminal Rd
     Salisbury MD 21804
     410 572-5100

(G-11852)
POLYMER PACKAGING INC (PA)
7755 Freedom Ave Nw (44720-6905)
PHONE.................................330 832-2000
Larry L Lanham, *CEO*
Chris Thomazin, *
William D Lanham, *
Jeffrey S Davis, *
◆ EMP: 86 EST: 1986
SALES (est): 48.95MM
SALES (corp-wide): 48.95MM **Privately Held**
Web: www.polymerpkg.com
SIC: 5113 5162 2621 2821 Paper, wrapping or coarse, and products; Plastics products, nec; Wrapping and packaging papers; Plastics materials and resins

(G-11853)
POWELL ELECTRICAL SYSTEMS INC
Also Called: Pemco North Canton Division
8967 Pleasantwood Ave Nw (44720-4761)
PHONE.................................330 966-1750
Bob Gens, *Brnch Mgr*
EMP: 92
SQ FT: 41,600
SALES (corp-wide): 699.31MM **Publicly Held**
Web: www.powellind.com
SIC: 3678 5063 3699 Electronic connectors; Electrical apparatus and equipment; Electrical equipment and supplies, nec
HQ: Powell Electrical Systems, Inc.
     8550 Mosley Rd
     Houston TX 77075
     713 944-6900

(G-11854)
PROVANTAGE LLC
7576 Freedom Ave Nw (44720-6902)
PHONE.................................330 494-3781
Arno Zirngibl, *CEO*
Scott Dibattista, *
▼ EMP: 60 EST: 1984
SQ FT: 30,000
SALES (est): 37.95MM **Privately Held**
Web: www.provantage.com
SIC: 5961 5719 5734 5045 Computer software, mail order; Housewares, nec; Computer software and accessories; Computers, peripherals, and software

(G-11855)
PSA AIRLINES INC
5430 N Hangar Ln Bldg 3 (44720-1509)
PHONE.................................330 490-2939
EMP: 59
SALES (corp-wide): 52.79B **Publicly Held**
Web: www.psaairlines.com
SIC: 4512 Air passenger carrier, scheduled
HQ: Psa Airlines, Inc.
     3400 Terminal Rd
     Vandalia OH 45377
     937 454-1116

(G-11856)
PURPLE LAND MANAGEMENT LLC
5590 Lauby Rd Ste 5 (44720-1500)
PHONE.................................740 238-4259
Rick Bell, *Genl Mgr*
EMP: 79
SALES (corp-wide): 12.46MM **Privately Held**
Web: www.purplelandmgmt.com
SIC: 8741 Management services
PA: Purple Land Management, Llc
     210 E 8th St
     Fort Worth TX 76102
     817 717-3835

(G-11857)
QUESTAR SOLUTIONS LLC
7948 Freedom Ave Nw (44720-6910)
PHONE.................................330 966-2070
Charles Ostrout Junior, *Mgr*
▼ EMP: 50 EST: 1989
SQ FT: 20,000
SALES (est): 20.51MM **Privately Held**
Web: www.questarsolutions.com
SIC: 5199 Packaging materials
PA: Mauser Packaging Solutions Intermediate Company, Inc.
     1515 W 22nd St Ste 1100
     Oak Brook IL 60523

(G-11858)
REPUBLIC TELCOM WORLDWIDE LLC
8000 Freedom Ave Nw (44720-6912)
PHONE.................................330 244-8285
Monica Wallace, *Brnch Mgr*
EMP: 52
SIC: 7389 Telephone services
HQ: Republic Telcom Worldwide, Llc
     3939 Everhard Rd Nw
     Canton OH 44709

(G-11859)
ROCK HOMES INC
Also Called: Fox Enterprise Services
7630 Freedom Ave Nw (44720-6904)
PHONE.................................330 497-5200
Delilah Volpe, *CEO*
Anthony Volpe, *
Delilah Volpe, *VP*
EMP: 45 EST: 1999
SALES (est): 9.09MM **Privately Held**
Web: www.foxenterpriseservices.com
SIC: 1761 1751 Roofing, siding, and sheetmetal work; Carpentry work

(G-11860)
SANCTARY GRNDE SNIOR LVING LLC
Also Called: Danbury Sanctuary Grande
(Even Range 850 - 898) Applegrove St Nw (44720)
PHONE.................................330 470-4411
William J Lemmon, *Prin*
EMP: 70 EST: 2015
SALES (est): 1.22MM **Privately Held**
Web: www.storypoint.com
SIC: 6513 Retirement hotel operation

(G-11861)
SCHROER PROPERTIES NAVARRE INC (PA)
Also Called: Altercare of Navarre
339 E Maple St (44720-2506)
P.O. Box 497 (44232-0497)
PHONE.................................330 498-8200
Gerald F Schroer, *Pr*
Suzanne F Schroer, *
EMP: 76 EST: 1986
SQ FT: 30,000
SALES (est): 30.14MM **Privately Held**
Web: www.abshealth.com
SIC: 8082 Home health care services

(G-11862)
SPECTRUM ORTHPEDICS INC CANTON
7442 Frank Ave Nw (44720-7018)
PHONE.................................330 455-5367
Mark Shepard, *Pr*
P W Welch, *
Doctor Robert Manns, *Sec*
EMP: 60 EST: 1969
SQ FT: 6,000
SALES (est): 1.41MM **Privately Held**
Web: www.orthounitedohio.com
SIC: 8011 Orthopedic physician

(G-11863)
STOLLE MACHINERY COMPANY LLC
Also Called: Stolle Canton
4337 Excel St (44720-6995)
PHONE.................................330 494-6382
EMP: 51
SALES (corp-wide): 492.99MM **Privately Held**
Web: www.stollemachinery.com
SIC: 5084 Industrial machinery and equipment
PA: Stolle Machinery Company, Llc
     6949 S Potomac St
     Centennial CO 80112
     303 708-9044

(G-11864)
TIGER 2010 LLC (PA)
6929 Portage St Nw (44720-6535)
PHONE.................................330 236-5100
EMP: 30 EST: 2010
SQ FT: 2,400
SALES (est): 1.6MM
SALES (corp-wide): 1.6MM **Privately Held**
Web: www.akroncantonhomesonline.com
SIC: 6531 Real estate agent, residential

(G-11865)
TIMKEN COMPANY (PA)
Also Called: TIMKEN
4500 Mount Pleasant St Nw (44720-5450)
P.O. Box 6929 (44706-0929)
PHONE.................................234 262-3000
Richard G Kyle, *Pr*
John M Timken Junior, *Ch Bd*
Philip D Fracassa, *Ex VP*
Christopher A Coughlin, *Group President*
Hansal N Patel, *VP*
◆ EMP: 1335 EST: 1899
SALES (est): 4.77B
SALES (corp-wide): 4.77B **Publicly Held**
Web: www.timken.com
SIC: 3562 5085 Ball and roller bearings; Bearings, bushings, wheels, and gears

(G-11866)
TIMKEN CORPORATION (DH)
4500 Mount Pleasant St Nw (44720-5450)
PHONE.................................330 471-3378
Richard G Kyle, *CEO*
William R Burkhart, *
Christopher A Coughlin, *
Ronald J Myers, *
◆ EMP: 50 EST: 1957
SALES (est): 98.63MM
SALES (corp-wide): 4.77B **Publicly Held**
Web: www.timken.com
SIC: 5085 5051 Bearings; Aluminum bars, rods, ingots, sheets, pipes, plates, etc.
HQ: Timken Us Llc
     336 Mechanic St
     Lebanon NH 03766
     603 448-3000

(G-11867)
TRADEFULL LLC
2100 International Pkwy (44720-1373)
PHONE.................................888 203-0826
Ronald K Starkey, *Prin*
EMP: 66 EST: 2018
SALES (est): 5.3MM **Privately Held**
Web: www.tradefull.com
SIC: 4731 Freight transportation arrangement

(G-11868)
UNITED ARCHITECTURAL MTLS INC
7830 Cleveland Ave Nw (44720-5658)
PHONE.................................330 433-9220
Shelly Nesbitt, *Pr*
Robert W Eckinger, *
EMP: 36 EST: 2005
SALES (est): 11.45MM **Privately Held**
Web: www.unitedarchitectural.com
SIC: 8712 Architectural services

(G-11869)
UNITED GL & PANL SYSTEMS INC
8040 Whipple Ave Nw (44720-6932)
PHONE.................................330 244-9745
EMP: 42 EST: 1996
SQ FT: 36,000
SALES (est): 4.25MM **Privately Held**
Web: www.ugps.com
SIC: 1793 1761 Glass and glazing work; Roofing, siding, and sheetmetal work

(G-11870)
VISUAL EDGE IT INC (PA)
Also Called: Counsel
3874 Highland Park Nw (44720-4538)
PHONE..................................800 828-4801
Austin Vanchieri, *CEO*
Melissa Mann, *
Michael Mills, *
John Bingle, *
EMP: 1007 **EST:** 2018
SALES (est): 219.98MM
SALES (corp-wide): 219.98MM **Privately Held**
Web: www.visualedgeit.com
SIC: 5044 Office equipment

North Jackson
Mahoning County

(G-11871)
ANTONINE SSTERS ADULT DAY CARE
2675 N Lipkey Rd (44451-9649)
PHONE..................................330 538-9822
Madeleine Iskandar, *Dir*
EMP: 41 **EST:** 1994
SQ FT: 3,211
SALES (est): 441.09K **Privately Held**
Web: www.antoninevillage.org
SIC: 8322 Adult day care center

(G-11872)
HILLTRUX TANK LINES INC
200 Rosemont Rd (44451-9631)
P.O. Box 696 (44451-0696)
PHONE..................................330 538-3700
EMP: 50 **EST:** 2007
SALES (est): 2.66MM **Privately Held**
Web: www.hilltrux.com
SIC: 4213 Contract haulers

(G-11873)
LIBERTY STEEL PRODUCTS INC (PA)
11650 Mahoning Ave (44451-9688)
P.O. Box 175 (44451-0175)
PHONE..................................330 538-2236
James M Grasso, *Prin*
James T Weller Senior, *Ch Bd*
Andrew J Weller Junior, *V Ch Bd*
James M Grasso, *CFO*
Matt Frisby, *Prin*
◆ **EMP:** 40 **EST:** 1965
SQ FT: 110,000
SALES (est): 42.59MM
SALES (corp-wide): 42.59MM **Privately Held**
Web: www.libertysteelproducts.com
SIC: 5051 Steel

(G-11874)
NORTH JCKSON SPECIALTY STL LLC
Also Called: Universal Stainless
2058 S Bailey Rd (44451-9639)
PHONE..................................330 538-9621
EMP: 33
Web: www.univstainless.com
SIC: 5051 Steel
HQ: North Jackson Specialty Steel, Llc
600 Mayer St
Bridgeville PA 15017
412 257-7600

(G-11875)
OHIO UTILITIES PROTECTION SVC
12467 Mahoning Ave (44451-9617)
P.O. Box 729 (44451-0729)
PHONE..................................800 311-3692
Roger L Lipscomb Junior, *Pr*
EMP: 51 **EST:** 1972
SQ FT: 2,000
SALES (est): 8.33MM **Privately Held**
Web: www.oups.org
SIC: 8611 8748 1623 Public utility association; Business consulting, nec; Underground utilities contractor

(G-11876)
PMC SYSTEMS LIMITED
12155 Commissioner Dr (44451-9640)
P.O. Box 486 (44451-0486)
PHONE..................................330 538-2268
John Frano, *Pr*
Paul Graff, *
EMP: 30 **EST:** 1983
SQ FT: 3,000
SALES (est): 4.55MM **Privately Held**
Web: www.pmcsystems.com
SIC: 3625 8711 Electric controls and control accessories, industrial; Electrical or electronic engineering

(G-11877)
RAILWORKS TRACK SERVICES LLC
Also Called: Railworks Track Services, Inc.
1550 N Bailey Rd (44451-8612)
P.O. Box 555 (08080-0555)
PHONE..................................330 538-2261
Roger K Boggess, *Pr*
Gene Cellini, *
Benjamin D Levy, *
Teresa Roundtree, *
EMP: 300 **EST:** 1962
SQ FT: 3,000
SALES (est): 38.15MM
SALES (corp-wide): 1.16B **Privately Held**
Web: www.railworks.com
SIC: 1629 Railroad and railway roadbed construction
PA: Railworks Corporation
5 Penn Plz Fl 15
New York NY 10001
212 502-7900

(G-11878)
TRI COUNTY TOWER LLC
8900 Mahoning Ave (44451-9750)
P.O. Box 4206 (44515-0206)
PHONE..................................330 538-9874
Chris Thomas, *CEO*
▼ **EMP:** 28 **EST:** 1982
SALES (est): 4.97MM **Privately Held**
Web: www.tricountytower.com
SIC: 1623 7389 Transmitting tower (telecommunication) construction; Business services, nec

(G-11879)
US LUMBER GROUP LLC
489 Rosemont Rd (44451-9717)
PHONE..................................330 538-3386
Scott Honthy, *Brnch Mgr*
EMP: 27
SALES (corp-wide): 790.63MM **Privately Held**
Web: portal.uslumber.com
SIC: 5031 Lumber: rough, dressed, and finished
HQ: U.S. Lumber Group, Llc
2160 Satellite Blvd # 450
Duluth GA 30097
678 474-4577

North Lawrence
Stark County

(G-11880)
US TUBULAR PRODUCTS INC
Also Called: Benmit Division
14852 Lincoln Way W (44666)
PHONE..................................330 832-1734
Jeffrey J Cunningham, *Pr*
Brian Cunningham, *
Connye Cunningham, *
EMP: 60 **EST:** 1973
SQ FT: 100,000
SALES (est): 4.83MM **Privately Held**
Web: www.benmit.com
SIC: 8734 3498 Hydrostatic testing laboratory ; Tube fabricating (contract bending and shaping)

North Lima
Mahoning County

(G-11881)
ARMSTRONG UTILITIES INC
Also Called: Armstrong Cable Services
9328 Woodworth Rd (44452-9712)
PHONE..................................330 758-6411
EMP: 58
Web: www.agoc.com
SIC: 4841 Cable television services
HQ: Armstrong Utilities, Inc.
1 Armstrong Pl
Butler PA 16001
724 283-0925

(G-11882)
ASSUMPTION VILLAGE
Also Called: Marian Living Center
9800 Market St (44452-9560)
PHONE..................................330 549-2434
Admiral Mary Luke, *Prin*
EMP: 200 **EST:** 1974
SQ FT: 7,440
SALES (est): 13.04MM **Privately Held**
Web: www.villageenterprises.org
SIC: 8051 Convalescent home with continuous nursing care

(G-11883)
B & T EXPRESS INC (PA)
400 Miley Rd (44452-8545)
P.O. Box 468 (44452-0468)
PHONE..................................330 549-0000
Breen O'malley, *Pr*
Tom Cook, *VP*
Bill Rypcinski, *VP Opers*
EMP: 398 **EST:** 1986
SQ FT: 25,000
SALES (est): 50MM
SALES (corp-wide): 50MM **Privately Held**
Web: www.btxpinc.com
SIC: 4213 Heavy hauling, nec

(G-11884)
BG TRUCKING & CNSTR INC
11330 Market St (44452-9720)
P.O. Box 308 (44452-0308)
PHONE..................................234 759-3440
Bernard Lewis, *Pr*
Alicia Lewis, *
Geneva Lewis, *
EMP: 50 **EST:** 1984
SALES (est): 2.53MM **Privately Held**
SIC: 1771 5211 Blacktop (asphalt) work; Masonry materials and supplies

(G-11885)
CAPRICE HEALTH CARE INC
Also Called: CAPRICE HEALTH CARE CENTER
9184 Market St (44452-9558)
PHONE..................................330 965-9200
Jeniffer See, *Admn*
Celeste Hawkins, *
EMP: 46 **EST:** 1998
SALES (est): 8.41MM **Privately Held**
Web: www.inspirahealthgroup.com
SIC: 8051 8093 8082 8052 Convalescent home with continuous nursing care; Specialty outpatient clinics, nec; Home health care services; Intermediate care facilities

(G-11886)
CHRISTOPHER BURKEY
Also Called: Christopher Burkey Plumbing
1185 W Pine Lake Rd (44452-9783)
PHONE..................................330 770-9607
Christopher Burkey, *Owner*
EMP: 30 **EST:** 2008
SALES (est): 1.45MM **Privately Held**
SIC: 1711 Plumbing contractors

(G-11887)
COGUN INC
11369 Market St (44452-9782)
P.O. Box 704 (44452-0704)
PHONE..................................330 549-5321
EMP: 48
Web: www.cogun.com
SIC: 1542 Religious building construction

(G-11888)
GUARDIAN HLTHCARE HM OFF I LLC
Also Called: Rolling Acres Care Center
9625 Market St (44452-8564)
PHONE..................................330 549-0898
Laurie Ference, *Brnch Mgr*
EMP: 394
SIC: 8051 Convalescent home with continuous nursing care
PA: Guardian Healthcare Home Office I, Llc
8796 Route 219
Brockway PA 15824

(G-11889)
JOE DICKEY ELECTRIC INC
180 W South Range Rd (44452-9578)
P.O. Box 158 (44452-0158)
PHONE..................................330 549-3976
Joseph Dickey Junior, *CEO*
Joseph Dickey Junior, *Ch Bd*
David A Dickey, *
Joseph Dickey Iii, *VP*
Eric Carlson, *
EMP: 80 **EST:** 1957
SALES (est): 17.37MM **Privately Held**
Web: www.dickeyelectric.com
SIC: 1731 General electrical contractor

(G-11890)
LAKESIDE MANOR INC
Also Called: Glenellen
9661 Market St (44452-8564)
PHONE..................................330 549-2545
James E Mcmurray, *Pr*
Roger F Herrmann, *
EMP: 30 **EST:** 1997
SALES (est): 3.19MM **Privately Held**
Web: www.briarfield.net
SIC: 8361 8052 Aged home; Intermediate care facilities

(G-11891)
LIBERTY MAHONING LLC
Also Called: Holiday Inn

North Lima - Mahoning County (G-11892)

10111 Market St (44452-9556)
PHONE................330 549-0070
EMP: 33 EST: 2000
SALES (est): 627.37K Privately Held
Web: www.holidayinn.com
SIC: 7011 Hotels and motels

(G-11892)
LIFEFLEET LLC
11000 Market St Ste 4 (44452-9801)
P.O. Box 239 (44445-0239)
PHONE................330 549-9716
EMP: 42
SALES (corp-wide): 473.33K Privately Held
SIC: 4119 Ambulance service
PA: Lifefleet Llc
11365 Western Reserve Rd
Salem OH 44460
330 518-5253

North Olmsted
Cuyahoga County

(G-11893)
CARGILL INCORPORATED
Also Called: Cargill
24950 Country Club Blvd Ste 450 (44070-5333)
PHONE................440 716-4664
Dale Sehrenbach, Mgr
EMP: 28
SALES (corp-wide): 176.74B Privately Held
Web: www.cargill.com
SIC: 5169 Industrial salts and polishes
PA: Cargill, Incorporated
15407 Mcginty Rd W
Wayzata MN 55391
800 227-4455

(G-11894)
CITY OF NORTH OLMSTED
Also Called: Commission On Partransit
5200 Dover Center Rd (44070-3129)
PHONE................440 777-8000
A E Boessneck, Brnch Mgr
EMP: 47
SALES (corp-wide): 42.41MM Privately Held
Web: www.north-olmsted.com
SIC: 4111 Local and suburban transit
PA: City Of North Olmsted
5200 Dover Ctr Rd
North Olmsted OH 44070
440 716-4171

(G-11895)
CITY OF NORTH OLMSTED
Also Called: Springvale Golf Crse Ballroom
5873 Canterbury Rd (44070-4522)
PHONE................440 777-0678
Marty Young, Brnch Mgr
EMP: 35
SALES (corp-wide): 42.41MM Privately Held
Web: www.springvalegolfcourseandballroom.com
SIC: 7389 Convention and show services
PA: City Of North Olmsted
5200 Dover Ctr Rd
North Olmsted OH 44070
440 716-4171

(G-11896)
CITY OF NORTH OLMSTED
Also Called: Olmsted Parks and Recreation
26000 Lorain Rd (44070-2738)
PHONE................440 734-8200
Ted Disaldo, Commsnr
EMP: 59
SALES (corp-wide): 42.41MM Privately Held
Web: www.north-olmsted.com
SIC: 7999 Recreation center
PA: City Of North Olmsted
5200 Dover Ctr Rd
North Olmsted OH 44070
440 716-4171

(G-11897)
CLEVELAND CLINIC FOUNDATION
Also Called: Cleveland Clinic Foundation
24700 Lorain Rd Ste 207 (44070-2068)
PHONE................440 250-5737
Roger Mansnerus, Prin
EMP: 66
SALES (corp-wide): 14.48B Privately Held
Web: www.clevelandclinic.org
SIC: 8062 General medical and surgical hospitals
PA: The Cleveland Clinic Foundation
9500 Euclid Ave
Cleveland OH 44195
216 636-8335

(G-11898)
CLEVELAND CLNIC HLTH SYSTM-WST
Also Called: Justin Center
24700 Lorain Rd Ste 100 (44070-2068)
PHONE................440 716-9810
Nancy Axton, Mgr
EMP: 68
SQ FT: 11,027
SALES (corp-wide): 14.48B Privately Held
Web: my.clevelandclinic.org
SIC: 8748 8741 8071 Testing services; Hospital management; Medical laboratories
HQ: Cleveland Clinic Health System-Western Region
18101 Lorain Ave
Cleveland OH 44111
216 476-7000

(G-11899)
COMMUTEAIR LLC (PA)
Also Called: Commutair
24950 Country Club Blvd Ste 200 (44070-5342)
PHONE................440 779-4588
John Sullivan, Ch Bd
Sean Frick, *
EMP: 200 EST: 1989
SQ FT: 41,000
SALES (est): 121.75MM Privately Held
Web: www.commuteair.com
SIC: 4512 Air passenger carrier, scheduled

(G-11900)
DAY STAR STAFFING LLC
26697 Brookpark Road Ext (44070-3137)
PHONE................440 481-1060
EMP: 38 EST: 2017
SALES (est): 977K Privately Held
Web: www.thejobsquad.com
SIC: 7361 Employment agencies

(G-11901)
FORTNEY & WEYGANDT INC
31269 Bradley Rd (44070-3875)
PHONE................440 716-4000
Mitchell Lapin, Pr
Greg Freeh, *
Kristen Martin, *
EMP: 50 EST: 1978
SQ FT: 21,000
SALES (est): 66.73MM
SALES (corp-wide): 77.24MM Privately Held
Web: www.fortneyweygandt.com
SIC: 1541 1542 Industrial buildings, new construction, nec; Commercial and office building, new construction
PA: R. L. Fortney Management, Inc.
31269 Bradley Rd
North Olmsted OH 44070
440 716-4000

(G-11902)
FORTUNE BRNDS WTR INNVTONS LLC
25300 Al Moen Dr (44070-5619)
PHONE................440 962-2782
EMP: 76 EST: 2018
SALES (est): 477.48K Privately Held
SIC: 8742 Management consulting services

(G-11903)
GRAND HERITAGE HOTEL PORTLAND
Also Called: Hampton Inn Cleveland
25105 Country Club Blvd (44070-5312)
PHONE................440 734-4477
Meghan Carruthers, Genl Mgr
EMP: 797
SALES (corp-wide): 11.25MM Privately Held
Web: www.hilton.com
SIC: 7011 Hotels
PA: Grand Heritage Hotel Portland
39 Bay Dr
Annapolis MD 21403
410 280-9800

(G-11904)
GUARDIAN ENVIRONMENTAL INC
29510 Lorain Rd (44070-3909)
PHONE................304 224-2011
James Colavita, CEO
EMP: 45 EST: 2001
SALES (est): 2.51MM Privately Held
Web: www.guardianenvironmental.com
SIC: 8748 Environmental consultant

(G-11905)
HIGH-TECH POOLS INC
31330 Industrial Pkwy (44070-4787)
PHONE................440 979-5070
Jeff Hammerschmidt, Pr
▲ EMP: 30 EST: 1989
SQ FT: 7,800
SALES (est): 5.88MM Privately Held
Web: www.hightechpools.com
SIC: 1799 Swimming pool construction

(G-11906)
HORIZON EDUCATION CENTERS
4001 David Dr (44070-2903)
PHONE................440 779-6536
Mary Molnar, Mgr
EMP: 27
SQ FT: 12,483
SALES (corp-wide): 19.97MM Privately Held
Web: www.horizoneducationcenters.org
SIC: 8322 Geriatric social service
PA: Horizon Education Centers
25300 Lorain Rd Fl 2
North Olmsted OH 44070
440 779-1930

(G-11907)
JOHNSON ROSE LLC
27997 Terrace Dr (44070-4963)
PHONE................440 785-9892
Jeffrey Johnson, Prin
EMP: 30
SALES (corp-wide): 984.9K Privately Held
Web: www.arthursshoetree.com
SIC: 6531 Real estate agents and managers
PA: Johnson Rose Llc
27235 Wolf Rd
Bay Village OH 44140
440 871-2340

(G-11908)
KEYBANK NATIONAL ASSOCIATION
26380 Brookpark Road (44070-3375)
PHONE................440 734-7700
Lois Cerny, Brnch Mgr
EMP: 32
SALES (corp-wide): 10.4B Publicly Held
Web: www.key.com
SIC: 6021 National commercial banks
HQ: Keybank National Association
127 Public Sq Ste 5600
Cleveland OH 44114
800 539-2968

(G-11909)
OHIO AUTO LOAN SERVICES INC
27600 Lorain Rd (44070-4040)
PHONE................440 716-1710
EMP: 37
Web: www.autocashusa.com
SIC: 6141 Automobile loans, including insurance
HQ: Ohio Auto Loan Services, Inc.
8601 Dunwoody Pl Ste 406
Atlanta GA 30350
770 552-9840

(G-11910)
OLMSTED MANOR LTD
Also Called: Joshua Tree Care Center
27500 Mill Rd (44070-3115)
PHONE................440 777-8444
EMP: 73
SALES (corp-wide): 721.53K Privately Held
Web: www.olmstedmanor.org
SIC: 8051 Skilled nursing care facilities
PA: Olmsted Manor, Ltd.
16210 Lorain Ave
Cleveland OH

(G-11911)
PROFESSIONAL TRAVEL INC (PA)
25000 Country Club Blvd Ste 170 (44070-5338)
PHONE................440 734-8800
Bob Sturm, CEO
Rob Turk, *
Todd Stoneman, *
EMP: 75 EST: 1963
SQ FT: 6,000
SALES (est): 24.68MM
SALES (corp-wide): 24.68MM Privately Held
Web: www.dt.com
SIC: 4724 Tourist agency arranging transport, lodging and car rental

(G-11912)
R L FORTNEY MANAGEMENT INC (PA)
Also Called: Fortney & Weygandt
31269 Bradley Rd (44070-3875)
PHONE................440 716-4000
Mitchell Lapin, Pr
Greg Freeh, *
Kristen Martin, *
EMP: 60 EST: 1978
SALES (est): 77.24MM
SALES (corp-wide): 77.24MM Privately Held
Web: www.fortneyweygandt.com
SIC: 1542 Commercial and office building, new construction

GEOGRAPHIC SECTION
North Ridgeville - Lorain County (G-11934)

(G-11913)
RELATIONAL SOLUTIONS INC
Also Called: R.S.i
25050 Country Club Blvd Ste 105 (44070-5356)
PHONE....................................440 899-3296
Rob York, Pr
EMP: 36 **EST:** 1996
SQ FT: 2,700
SALES (est): 3.72MM **Privately Held**
Web: www.relationalsolutions.com
SIC: 7375 7374 Data base information retrieval; Data processing service
PA: Larsen And Toubro Limited
L&T House, Ballard Estate,
Mumbai MH 40000

(G-11914)
SCHIRMER CONSTRUCTION CO
31350 Industrial Pkwy (44070-4787)
PHONE....................................440 716-4900
Fred Schirmer, CEO
James A Yungman, CEO
Frederick Schirmer, *
John M Roche, VP
Nick Iafigliola, Pr
EMP: 45 **EST:** 1980
SQ FT: 38,500
SALES (est): 10.32MM **Privately Held**
Web: www.schirmerco.com
SIC: 1541 1542 Industrial buildings, new construction, nec; Commercial and office building, new construction

(G-11915)
SLEEPMED INCORPORATED
Also Called: Sleepmed
25000 Country Club Blvd Ste 120 (44070-5344)
PHONE....................................440 716-8139
Tom Rosenbalm, Mgr
EMP: 36
Web: www.sleepmedinc.com
SIC: 8011 8069 Specialized medical practitioners, except internal; Specialty hospitals, except psychiatric
HQ: Sleepmed Incorporated
3330 Cumberland Blvd Se # 800
Atlanta GA 30339

(G-11916)
SUBURBAN COLLISION CENTERS
26618 Brookpark Road Ext (44070-3136)
PHONE....................................440 777-1717
Angelo Papotto, Pr
EMP: 39 **EST:** 1960
SQ FT: 8,000
SALES (est): 3.53MM **Privately Held**
Web: www.suburbancollision.com
SIC: 7532 Body shop, automotive

(G-11917)
SUNNYSIDE CARS INC
27000 Lorain Rd (44070-3212)
PHONE....................................440 777-9911
TOLL FREE: 800
Kirt Frye, Pr
EMP: 44 **EST:** 1988
SALES (est): 22.74MM **Privately Held**
Web: www.sunnysidetoyota.com
SIC: 5511 7538 7532 7515 Automobiles, new and used; General automotive repair shops; Top and body repair and paint shops ; Passenger car leasing

(G-11918)
W B MASON CO INC
31387 Industrial Pkwy (44070-4764)
PHONE....................................216 267-5000
Richard C Voigt, Brnch Mgr
EMP: 47
SALES (corp-wide): 1.01B **Privately Held**
Web: www.wbmason.com
SIC: 5112 5044 5021 Stationery and office supplies; Office equipment; Office furniture, nec
PA: W. B. Mason Co., Inc.
59 Centre St
Brockton MA 02301
508 586-3434

(G-11919)
WELCOME HOUSE INC
Also Called: West Haven IV
29756 Lorain Rd (44070-3914)
PHONE....................................440 471-7601
EMP: 56
SQ FT: 3,132
SALES (corp-wide): 16.35MM **Privately Held**
Web: www.welcomehouseinc.org
SIC: 8361 Mentally handicapped home
PA: Welcome House, Inc.
802 Sharon Dr Ste A
Westlake OH 44145
440 356-2330

(G-11920)
WELLINGTON PLACE LLC
Also Called: O'NEIL HEALTHCARE - NORTH OLMS
4800 Clague Rd Apt 108 (44070-6209)
PHONE....................................440 734-9933
EMP: 55 **EST:** 1997
SALES (est): 8.86MM **Privately Held**
Web: www.oneilhc.com
SIC: 8051 Skilled nursing care facilities

North Ridgeville
Lorain County

(G-11921)
ALL AMERICAN SPORTS CORP (HQ)
Also Called: Riddell All American Sport
7501 Performance Ln (44039-2765)
PHONE....................................440 366-8225
Don Gleisner, Pr
▲ **EMP:** 27 **EST:** 2004
SALES (est): 51.98MM **Privately Held**
Web: www.shopallamericansports.com
SIC: 7699 Recreational sporting equipment repair services
PA: Rbg Holdings Corp.
7855 Haskell Ave 350
Van Nuys CA 91406

(G-11922)
ALTERCARE INC (PA)
Also Called: Northridge Health Center
35990 Westminister Ave (44039-1399)
PHONE....................................440 327-5285
Robert A Wickes, Pr
EMP: 37 **EST:** 1983
SQ FT: 30,000
SALES (est): 6.9MM
SALES (corp-wide): 6.9MM **Privately Held**
Web: www.embassyhealthcare.net
SIC: 8051 Convalescent home with continuous nursing care

(G-11923)
AMARA HOMECARE BEDFORD TEL NO
35136 Center Ridge Rd (44039-6004)
PHONE....................................440 353-0600
Radu Dumitrescu, Brnch Mgr
EMP: 55
Web: www.amarahomecare.biz
SIC: 8082 8059 Home health care services; Personal care home, with health care
PA: Amara Homecare (Bedford Tel No)
5285 Northfield Rd
Bedford Heights OH 44146

(G-11924)
CENTER RIDGE NURSING HOME INC
Also Called: Oneill Hlthcare - N Ridgeville
38600 Center Ridge Rd (44039-2837)
PHONE....................................440 808-5500
John T O'neill, Pr
EMP: 200 **EST:** 1991
SQ FT: 45,000
SALES (est): 11.61MM **Privately Held**
Web: www.oneillhc.com
SIC: 8059 8052 8051 Nursing home, except skilled and intermediate care facility; Intermediate care facilities; Skilled nursing care facilities

(G-11925)
CLEVELAND CLINIC FOUNDATION
Also Called: Cleveland Clinic Health System
35105 Center Ridge (44039-3081)
PHONE....................................440 327-1050
EMP: 33
SALES (corp-wide): 14.48B **Privately Held**
Web: www.clevelandclinic.org
SIC: 8062 General medical and surgical hospitals
PA: The Cleveland Clinic Foundation
9500 Euclid Ave
Cleveland OH 44195
216 636-8335

(G-11926)
CUYAHOGA VENDING CO INC
Also Called: Cuyahoga Group, The
39405 Taylor Pkwy (44035-6264)
PHONE....................................440 353-9595
TOLL FREE: 800
EMP: 128
SALES (corp-wide): 22.36MM **Privately Held**
Web: www.cuyahogagroup.com
SIC: 7359 2099 Vending machine rental; Food preparations, nec
PA: Cuyahoga Vending Co., Inc.
14250 Industrial Ave S # 104
Maple Heights OH 44137
216 663-1457

(G-11927)
FIRST SOURCE TITLE AGENCY INC
7717 Victory Ln Ste B (44039-3472)
PHONE....................................216 986-0970
Michael R Mcnamara, Pr
EMP: 34 **EST:** 2004
SALES (est): 5.83MM **Privately Held**
Web: www.firstsourcetitle.com
SIC: 6211 Mortgages, buying and selling

(G-11928)
FOREVERGREEN LAWN CARE
38601 Sugar Ridge Rd (44039-3526)
PHONE....................................440 327-8987
Michael J Babet, Pr
Debbie M Babet, *
Pam Karkoff, *
EMP: 35 **EST:** 1993
SALES (est): 957.75K **Privately Held**
Web: www.4evergreenlawn.com
SIC: 0782 0783 Lawn care services; Planting, pruning, and trimming services

(G-11929)
HUNTINGTON NATIONAL BANK
35621 Center Ridge Rd (44039-3062)
PHONE....................................440 327-7054
Robert Bunsey, Brnch Mgr
EMP: 31
SALES (corp-wide): 10.84B **Publicly Held**
Web: www.huntington.com
SIC: 6029 Commercial banks, nec
HQ: The Huntington National Bank
41 S High St
Columbus OH 43215
614 480-4293

(G-11930)
JIMS ELECTRIC INC
39221 Center Ridge Rd (44039-2747)
PHONE....................................440 327-8800
James Tweardy, Pr
Kim Tweardy, *
EMP: 40 **EST:** 1980
SQ FT: 14,000
SALES (est): 5.28MM **Privately Held**
Web: www.jimselectric.net
SIC: 1731 General electrical contractor

(G-11931)
LORAIN COUNTY SENIOR CARE INC
Also Called: Home Instead Senior Care
35590 Center Ridge Rd Ste 101 (44039-3057)
PHONE....................................440 353-3080
Karin Wolff, Pr
EMP: 32 **EST:** 2008
SALES (est): 1.01MM **Privately Held**
Web: www.loraincountyseniornetwork.org
SIC: 8082 Home health care services

(G-11932)
MOORES RV INC
35999 Lorain Rd (44039-4470)
PHONE....................................800 523-1904
TOLL FREE: 800
Robert S Moore, Ch Bd
Julia Moore, Sec
Diane Moore, Stockholder
EMP: 32 **EST:** 1961
SQ FT: 19,000
SALES (est): 2.1MM **Privately Held**
Web: www.mooresrv.com
SIC: 5561 7538 Travel trailers: automobile, new and used; Recreational vehicle repairs

(G-11933)
PETRO-COM CORP (PA)
32523 Lorain Rd (44039-3423)
PHONE....................................440 327-6900
Manny Sclimenti Senior, Pr
Sharon Sclimenti, *
EMP: 29 **EST:** 1987
SQ FT: 10,000
SALES (est): 3.28MM
SALES (corp-wide): 3.28MM **Privately Held**
Web: www.petrocomcorp.com
SIC: 7699 Service station equipment repair

(G-11934)
RHENIUM ALLOYS INC (PA)
Also Called: Rhenium Alloys
38683 Taylor Pkwy (44035-6200)
PHONE....................................440 365-7388
Mike Prokop, Pr
▲ **EMP:** 41 **EST:** 1994
SQ FT: 35,500
SALES (est): 11.75MM
SALES (corp-wide): 11.75MM **Privately Held**
Web: www.rhenium.com
SIC: 3313 3356 3498 3339 Electrometallurgical products; Tungsten, basic shapes; Fabricated pipe and fittings; Primary nonferrous metals, nec

North Ridgeville - Lorain County (G-11935)

GEOGRAPHIC SECTION

(G-11935)
RUDOLPH LIBBE INC
4937 Mills Industrial Pkwy (44039-1953)
PHONE.................216 369-0198
EMP: 157
SALES (corp-wide): 512.7MM **Privately Held**
Web: www.rlgbuilds.com
SIC: 1541 Industrial buildings and warehouses
HQ: Rudolph Libbe Inc.
6494 Latcha Rd
Walbridge OH 43465
419 241-5000

(G-11936)
SCHILL LDSCPG LAWN CARE SVCS L (PA)
Also Called: Schill Grounds Management
5000 Mills Industrial Pkwy (44039-1971)
PHONE.................440 327-3030
Joseph H Schill, *Pr*
Gerald J Schill Junior, *VP*
James Schill, *
EMP: 63 **EST:** 1993
SQ FT: 10,000
SALES (est): 10.27MM **Privately Held**
Web: www.schilllandscaping.com
SIC: 0781 0782 4959 Landscape architects; Lawn services; Snowplowing

North Royalton
Cuyahoga County

(G-11937)
2IMMERSIVE4U CORPORATION ◊
3661 Wallings Rd (44133-3101)
PHONE.................440 570-4055
Dusan Simic, *CEO*
EMP: 49 **EST:** 2022
SALES (est): 1.51MM **Privately Held**
Web: www.2immersive4u.com
SIC: 7371 Computer software development and applications

(G-11938)
BLOSSOM HILL INC (PA)
Also Called: HAVEN HILL HOME
10983 Abbey Rd (44133-2537)
PHONE.................440 652-6749
Halle Weber, *Dir*
EMP: 47 **EST:** 1968
SQ FT: 9,000
SALES (est): 110.89K
SALES (corp-wide): 110.89K **Privately Held**
Web: www.blossom-hill.org
SIC: 8052 Personal care facility

(G-11939)
DIGIOIA-SUBURBAN EXCVTG LLC
11293 Royalton Rd (44133-4409)
PHONE.................440 237-1978
Terry Monnolly, *
EMP: 85 **EST:** 1976
SQ FT: 23,000
SALES (est): 20.34MM **Privately Held**
Web: www.digioiasuburban.com
SIC: 1623 1794 Water main construction; Excavation work

(G-11940)
FMS CONSTRUCTION COMPANY
13821 Progress Pkwy (44133-4303)
PHONE.................330 225-9320
David C Fox, *Brnch Mgr*
EMP: 35
SALES (corp-wide): 17.53MM **Privately Held**
Web: www.fmsconstruction.net
SIC: 1521 Single-family housing construction
PA: Fms Construction Company
300 S Main St
Sharpsburg PA 15215
412 782-1170

(G-11941)
G & P CONSTRUCTION LLC
10139 Royalton Rd Ste D (44133-4473)
PHONE.................855 494-4830
Nicholas Gorey, *Managing Member*
EMP: 50 **EST:** 2019
SALES (est): 4.97MM **Privately Held**
SIC: 5046 5084 1791 2542 Shelving, commercial and industrial; Industrial machinery and equipment; Structural steel erection; Shelving angles or slotted bars, except wood

(G-11942)
H & D STEEL SERVICE INC
Also Called: H & D Steel Service Center
9960 York Alpha Dr (44133-3588)
PHONE.................800 666-3390
Raymond Gary Schreiber, *Ch Bd*
Joseph Bubba, *Pr*
James P Schreiber, *VP Opers*
Joseph A Cachat, *Prin*
R G Schreiber, *Prin*
▲ **EMP:** 50 **EST:** 1972
SQ FT: 125,000
SALES (est): 24.75MM **Privately Held**
Web: www.hdsteel.com
SIC: 5051 3541 5085 Iron or steel flat products; Home workshop machine tools, metalworking; Industrial tools

(G-11943)
LARGE & LOVING CARDS INC
13676 York Rd # 1 (44133-3640)
PHONE.................440 877-0261
James Hall, *Prin*
EMP: 33
Web: www.largeandlovingcards.com
SIC: 5947 5112 Greeting cards; Greeting cards
PA: Large & Loving Cards, Inc.
3581 Mark Dr
Broadview Heights OH 44147

(G-11944)
LUNAR TOOL & MOLD INC
9860 York Alpha Dr (44133-3586)
PHONE.................440 237-2141
Friedrich Hoffman Junior, *Pr*
EMP: 28 **EST:** 1965
SQ FT: 20,000
SALES (est): 906.38K **Privately Held**
Web: www.lunarmold.com
SIC: 3544 7692 Special dies and tools; Welding repair

(G-11945)
NCC HARVEST INC
13405 York Rd (44133-3632)
P.O. Box 33399 (44133-0399)
PHONE.................440 582-3300
Milo Abercrombie, *Prin*
EMP: 53 **EST:** 2005
SALES (est): 20.47MM **Privately Held**
Web: www.necare.org
SIC: 8322 Individual and family services

(G-11946)
NORTHEAST CARE CENTER INC
Also Called: Northeast Care Ctr Sprague
7001 W Sprague Rd (44133-1800)
PHONE.................440 888-9320
EMP: 74
SALES (corp-wide): 79.39K **Privately Held**
Web: www.necare.org
SIC: 8361 8052 Mentally handicapped home ; Intermediate care facilities
PA: Northeast Care Center, Inc.
13405 York Rd
Cleveland OH
440 582-3300

(G-11947)
ONLINE LIQUIDATION AUCTION LLC
8748 Ridge Rd (44133-1862)
PHONE.................440 596-8733
Andrew Levandovski, *
Nikolay Gatalyak, *
EMP: 45 **EST:** 2015
SALES (est): 2.42MM **Privately Held**
Web: www.olabid.com
SIC: 7389 Auctioneers, fee basis

(G-11948)
PRUSAKS PRECISION CNSTR INC
10701 Royalton Rd Ste A (44133-4471)
PHONE.................440 655-8564
Tom Prusak, *CFO*
Renee Prusak, *
EMP: 33 **EST:** 1999
SALES (est): 2.2MM **Privately Held**
Web: www.prusaks.com
SIC: 1751 Cabinet and finish carpentry

(G-11949)
ROYAL RDMER LTHRAN CH N RYLTN
Also Called: Royal Rdeemer Lutheran Ch Schl
11680 Royalton Rd (44133-4461)
PHONE.................440 237-7958
James Martin, *
Gary Likowski, *
EMP: 40 **EST:** 1958
SQ FT: 69,342
SALES (est): 2.52MM **Privately Held**
Web: www.rrls.org
SIC: 8661 8351 8211 8322 Lutheran Church; Preschool center; Kindergarten; Social service center

(G-11950)
SUBURBAN MAINT & CNSTR INC
16330 York Rd Ste 2 (44133-5551)
P.O. Box 33009 (44133-0009)
PHONE.................440 237-7765
Brian Stucky, *
EMP: 35 **EST:** 1992
SQ FT: 12,000
SALES (est): 2.98MM **Privately Held**
Web: www.smciconstruction.com
SIC: 1799 1771 Waterproofing; Concrete repair

Northfield
Summit County

(G-11951)
ADESA OHIO LLC
Also Called: Adesa Cleveland
210 E Twinsburg Rd (44067-2848)
PHONE.................330 467-8280
Jim Hellet, *Ch Bd*
William Stackhouse, *
Harold E Varvel Junior, *Sec*
Don Harris, *
EMP: 40 **EST:** 1989
SQ FT: 150,000
SALES (est): 6.19MM **Publicly Held**
Web: www.adesa.com
SIC: 5012 Automobile auction
HQ: Adesa Corporation, Llc
11299 Illinois St
Carmel IN 46032

(G-11952)
BALANCED CARE CORPORATION
Also Called: Outlook Pointe
997 W Aurora Rd (44067-1605)
PHONE.................330 908-1166
Toni Montgomery, *Dir*
EMP: 35
SIC: 8741 8051 8621 Nursing and personal care facility management; Skilled nursing care facilities; Professional organizations
PA: Balanced Care Corporation
5000 Ritter Rd Ste 202
Mechanicsburg PA 17055

(G-11953)
BRENTWOOD LIFE CARE COMPANY
Also Called: Brentwood Health Care Center
907 W Aurora Rd (44067-1605)
PHONE.................330 468-2273
Brent Classen, *Owner*
EMP: 135 **EST:** 1989
SQ FT: 38,700
SALES (est): 12.86MM **Privately Held**
Web: www.brentwoodhcc.com
SIC: 8051 Convalescent home with continuous nursing care

(G-11954)
CLEVELAND CLNIC HLTH SYSTM-AST
Also Called: Sagamore Hills Medical Center
863 W Aurora Rd (44067-1603)
PHONE.................330 468-0190
Jennifer Simmons, *Brnch Mgr*
EMP: 42
SALES (corp-wide): 14.48B **Privately Held**
Web: www.clevelandclinic.org
SIC: 8062 8093 General medical and surgical hospitals; Specialty outpatient clinics, nec
HQ: Cleveland Clinic Health System-East Region
6803 Mayfield Rd Ste 500
Cleveland OH 44124
440 312-6010

(G-11955)
FERFOLIA FUNERAL HOMES INC
356 W Aurora Rd (44067-2104)
PHONE.................216 663-4222
Donald Berfolia, *Pr*
Donald L Berfolia, *
Alice Ferfolia, *
Theresa Ferfolia, *
EMP: 36 **EST:** 1927
SQ FT: 15,000
SALES (est): 2.31MM **Privately Held**
Web: www.ferfoliafuneralhomes.com
SIC: 7261 Funeral home

(G-11956)
HELP FOUNDATION INC
10333 Northfield Rd Ste 20b (44067)
PHONE.................216 432-4810
EMP: 31
Web: www.helpfoundationinc.org
SIC: 8733 8322 Noncommercial social research organization; Individual and family services
PA: Help Foundation, Inc.
26900 Euclid Ave
Euclid OH 44132

(G-11957)
HUNTINGTON NATIONAL BANK
8300 Golden Link Blvd (44067-2070)
PHONE.................330 467-7127
Carlie Newton, *Mgr*
EMP: 36

GEOGRAPHIC SECTION
Northwood - Wood County (G-11977)

SALES (corp-wide): 10.84B **Publicly Held**
Web: www.huntington.com
SIC: 6029 Commercial banks, nec
HQ: The Huntington National Bank
41 S High St
Columbus OH 43215
614 480-4293

(G-11958)
INNOVATIVE LOGISTICS SVCS INC
201 E Twinsburg Rd (44067)
P.O. Box 560206 (44056)
PHONE..................................330 468-6422
EMP: 55 EST: 1994
SQ FT: 8,000
SALES (est): 9.75MM **Privately Held**
Web: srose5150.wixsite.com
SIC: 4731 Freight forwarding

(G-11959)
JACKSON COMFORT SYSTEMS INC
Also Called: Jackson Comfort Htg Coolg Sys
499 E Twinsburg Rd (44067-2851)
PHONE..................................330 468-3111
Paul Jackson, *Pr*
Mark Jackson, *
Donna Jackson, *
Gary Jackson, *
EMP: 30 EST: 1976
SQ FT: 13,000
SALES (est): 5.43MM **Privately Held**
Web: www.jacksoncomfort.com
SIC: 1711 Warm air heating and air conditioning contractor

(G-11960)
LOWES HOME CENTERS LLC
Also Called: Lowe's
8224 Golden Link Blvd (44067-2067)
PHONE..................................330 908-2750
Dave Rhodes, *Mgr*
EMP: 86
SALES (corp-wide): 86.38B **Publicly Held**
Web: www.lowes.com
SIC: 5211 5031 5722 5064 Home centers; Building materials, exterior; Household appliance stores; Electrical appliances, television and radio
HQ: Lowe's Home Centers, Llc
1000 Lowes Blvd
Mooresville NC 28117
336 658-4000

(G-11961)
NORTHFIELD PARK ASSOCIATES LLC
Also Called: MGM Northfield Park
10777 Northfield Rd (44067-1236)
PHONE..................................330 908-7625
EMP: 133
SALES (corp-wide): 16.16B **Publicly Held**
Web: mgmnorthfieldpark.mgmresorts.com
SIC: 7011 Casino hotel
HQ: Park Northfield Associates Llc
10705 Northfield Rd
Northfield OH 44067
330 467-4101

(G-11962)
OHIO DEPT MNTAL HLTH ADDCTION
Also Called: Northcast Bhvral Hlthcare Sys
1756 Sagamore Rd (44067-1086)
PHONE..................................330 467-7131
Douglas Kern, *CEO*
EMP: 173
Web: mha.ohio.gov
SIC: 8063 9431 Psychiatric hospitals; Mental health agency administration, government

HQ: Ohio Department Of Mental Health And Addiction Services
30 E Broad St Fl 36
Columbus OH 43215

(G-11963)
P DAKOTA INC (PA)
Also Called: Dak P Kids
154 E Aurora Rd (44067-2053)
PHONE..................................833 325-6827
Arline Burks, *CEO*
Pearline Gant, *
Dakota Gant, *
Jamie Johnstone, *
EMP: 288 EST: 1994
SALES (est): 3.35MM
SALES (corp-wide): 3.35MM **Privately Held**
SIC: 7812 7819 Commercials, television: tape or film; Wardrobe rental for motion picture film production

(G-11964)
PARK NORTHFIELD ASSOCIATES LLC (HQ)
Also Called: Northfield Park Racetrack
10705 Northfield Rd (44067-1236)
P.O. Box 374 (44067)
PHONE..................................330 467-4101
EMP: 142 EST: 2004
SALES (est): 22.99MM
SALES (corp-wide): 16.16B **Publicly Held**
Web: mgmnorthfieldpark.mgmresorts.com
SIC: 7948 Harness horse racing
PA: Mgm Resorts International
3600 Las Vegas Blvd S
Las Vegas NV 89109
702 693-7120

(G-11965)
REVILLE TIRE CO (PA)
Also Called: Reville Wholesale Distributing
8044 Olde 8 Rd (44067-2830)
PHONE..................................330 468-1900
Robert J Reville, *Pr*
Richard H Reville, *
Raymond L Reville Iii, *VP*
Michael Reville, *
Robert Seman, *
EMP: 65 EST: 1970
SQ FT: 30,000
SALES (est): 9.79MM
SALES (corp-wide): 9.79MM **Privately Held**
SIC: 5014 Automobile tires and tubes

(G-11966)
SPITZER CHEVROLET INC
333 E Aurora Rd (44067)
PHONE..................................330 467-4141
Alan Spitzer, *Ch Bd*
Janet May, *
Gary Blanchard, *
EMP: 29 EST: 1980
SQ FT: 45,000
SALES (est): 5.46MM **Privately Held**
Web: www.chevrolet.com
SIC: 5511 7539 7538 5521 Automobiles, new and used; Automotive repair shops, nec; General automotive repair shops; Used car dealers

(G-11967)
UHC UNITED HEATING & COOLG LLC
Also Called: Uhc Construction Services
41 Leonard Ave (44067-1913)
PHONE..................................866 931-0118
Cindy Hamad, *Managing Member*
Bryon Hamad, *Managing Member*

Cindy Hamad, *CFO*
EMP: 30 EST: 2006
SQ FT: 4,000
SALES (est): 14.76MM **Privately Held**
Web: www.uhccorp.com
SIC: 1542 8742 Nonresidential construction, nec; Construction project management consultant

---

Northwood
Wood County

(G-11968)
A E D INC
Also Called: Interstate Coml GL & Door
2845 Crane Way (43619-1098)
PHONE..................................419 661-9999
Daniel Erickson, *Pr*
Walter Erickson, *
Pamela Erickson, *
EMP: 33 EST: 1988
SQ FT: 11,500
SALES (est): 2.56MM **Privately Held**
SIC: 1793 Glass and glazing work

(G-11969)
BLOCK COMMUNICATIONS INC
Also Called: Buckeye Broadband
2700 Oregon Rd (43619-1057)
PHONE..................................419 724-2539
Walter H Carstensen, *Pr*
EMP: 91
SALES (corp-wide): 910.95MM **Privately Held**
Web: www.blockcommunications.com
SIC: 4841 4813 Cable television services; Local and long distance telephone communications
PA: Block Communications, Inc.
405 Madison Ave Ste 2100
Toledo OH 43604
419 724-6212

(G-11970)
BUCKEYE TELESYSTEM INC (HQ)
2700 Oregon Rd (43619-1057)
P.O. Box 1116 (43528-1116)
PHONE..................................419 724-9898
Thomas K Dawson, *VP*
John E Martin, *
Thomas Dawson, *
Fritz Byers, *
Brian Rex, *
EMP: 60 EST: 1997
SALES (est): 97.7MM
SALES (corp-wide): 910.95MM **Privately Held**
Web: www.trusttelesystem.com
SIC: 4813 Internet connectivity services
PA: Block Communications, Inc.
405 Madison Ave Ste 2100
Toledo OH 43604
419 724-6212

(G-11971)
CAMPBELL INC (PA)
Also Called: Total Solutions
2875 Crane Way (43619-1098)
PHONE..................................419 476-4444
K Keith Campbell, *Pr*
Peter J Vavrinek, *
Robert A Eaton, *
EMP: 47 EST: 1968
SQ FT: 14,650
SALES (est): 15.44MM
SALES (corp-wide): 15.44MM **Privately Held**
Web: www.campbellinc.com
SIC: 1711 Warm air heating and air conditioning contractor

(G-11972)
CLINLOGIX LLC (HQ)
6750 Wales Rd (43619-1012)
PHONE..................................215 855-9054
Jean Marie Markham, *
EMP: 48 EST: 1998
SALES (est): 9.32MM
SALES (corp-wide): 101.29MM **Privately Held**
Web: www.namsa.com
SIC: 8742 Hospital and health services consultant
PA: North American Science Associates, Llc
6750 Wales Rd
Northwood OH 43619
419 666-9455

(G-11973)
EMI ENTERPRISES INC
Also Called: Envelope Mart
2639 Tracy Rd (43619-1006)
P.O. Box 307 (43697-0307)
PHONE..................................419 666-0012
Norman Shapiro, *Pr*
Myron Shapiro, *
Gregory Shapiro, *
EMP: 45 EST: 1974
SQ FT: 15,000
SALES (est): 22.87MM **Privately Held**
Web: www.envelopemart.com
SIC: 5112 Envelopes

(G-11974)
FLOWERS BAKING CO OHIO LLC
8071 Wales Rd (43619-1033)
PHONE..................................419 661-2586
Donna Hardesty, *Prin*
EMP: 47
SALES (corp-wide): 5.09B **Publicly Held**
SIC: 5193 5149 Flowers, fresh; Bakery products
HQ: Flowers Baking Co. Of Ohio, Llc
325 W Alexis Rd Ste 1
Toledo OH 43612
419 269-9202

(G-11975)
FUTURE LODGING NORTHWOOD LLC
Also Called: Comfort Inn
2426 Oregon Rd (43619-1123)
PHONE..................................419 666-2600
Akram G Namou, *Pr*
Malik Aboolnour, *
Amer Hannosh, *
EMP: 30 EST: 1995
SALES (est): 1.38MM **Privately Held**
Web: www.choicehotels.com
SIC: 7011 Hotels and motels

(G-11976)
KANTAR MEDIA RESEARCH INC
2700 Oregon Rd (43619-1057)
PHONE..................................419 666-8800
Michael Harding, *Prin*
EMP: 85
SALES (corp-wide): 18.5B **Privately Held**
Web: www.kantar.com
SIC: 8732 Market analysis or research
HQ: Kantar Media Research Inc.
114 5th Ave Fl 9
New York NY 10011
212 991-6000

(G-11977)
LIGHTSPEED LLC
2700 Oregon Rd (43619-1057)
PHONE..................................419 666-8800
Dan Boehm, *Brnch Mgr*
EMP: 76

Northwood - Wood County (G-11978)

SALES (corp-wide): 484.05MM **Privately Held**
Web: www.techlss.com
SIC: 8732 Market analysis or research
HQ: Lightspeed Llc
  175 Greenwich St Fl 35
  New York NY 10007

(G-11978)
MOTOR CARRIER SERVICE INC
815 Lemoyne Rd (43619-1815)
PHONE.................................419 693-6207
Keith A Tuttle, Pr
EMP: 110 EST: 1979
SQ FT: 10,000
SALES (est): 8.9MM **Privately Held**
Web: www.mcstrucks.com
SIC: 4213 Contract haulers

(G-11979)
NORTH AMERCN SCIENCE ASSOC LLC (PA)
Also Called: Namsa
6750 Wales Rd (43619-1012)
PHONE.................................419 666-9455
John J Gorski, Pr
Jane A Kervin, *
Joel R Gorski, *
Gina Skolmowski, *
Mike Brookman, *
EMP: 250 EST: 1967
SQ FT: 135,000
SALES (est): 101.29MM
SALES (corp-wide): 101.29MM **Privately Held**
Web: www.namsa.com
SIC: 8731 8734 Medical research, commercial; Testing laboratories

(G-11980)
NWO BEVERAGE INC
Also Called: N W O
6700 Wales Rd (43619-1012)
PHONE.................................419 725-2162
Pj Sullivan, VP
Joe Schetz, *
Tim Sullivan, *
EMP: 48 EST: 2008
SALES (est): 13.35MM **Privately Held**
Web: www.nwobeverage.com
SIC: 5181 Beer and other fermented malt liquors

(G-11981)
OBR COOLING TOWERS INC
2845 Crane Way (43619-1098)
PHONE.................................419 243-3443
Peter Poll, Pr
John Hall, *
Philip Poll, *
Debra Haas, *
EMP: 45 EST: 1984
SALES (est): 10.62MM **Privately Held**
Web: www.obrcoolingtowers.com
SIC: 7699 3444 Industrial equipment services ; Cooling towers, sheet metal

(G-11982)
PRESCRIPTION SUPPLY INC
2233 Tracy Rd (43619-1302)
PHONE.................................419 661-6600
Thomas Schoen, Pr
Jacquelyn J Harbauer, *
EMP: 75 EST: 1955
SQ FT: 30,000
SALES (est): 64.72MM **Privately Held**
Web: www.prescriptionsupply.com
SIC: 5122 Pharmaceuticals

(G-11983)
R L BONDY INSULATION LLC
2830 Crane Way (43619-1095)
PHONE.................................419 843-6283
Paul Justen, Brnch Mgr
EMP: 37
SALES (corp-wide): 202.99MM **Privately Held**
Web: www.macombgroup.com
SIC: 1742 Insulation, buildings
HQ: R. L. Bondy Insulation Llc
  6600 E15 Mile Rd
  Sterling Heights MI 48312

(G-11984)
THYSSENKRUPP LOGISTICS INC (DH)
Also Called: Copper and Brass Sales Div
8001 Thyssenkrupp Pkwy (43619-2082)
PHONE.................................419 662-1800
Joachim Limberg, Ch
Christian Dohr, Prin
James Baber, *
Werner Adamofsky, Prin
Brian Diephuis, Prin
▲ EMP: 35 EST: 1998
SALES (est): 30.15MM
SALES (corp-wide): 40.78B **Privately Held**
Web: www.thyssenkrupp.com
SIC: 4213 Trucking, except local
HQ: Thyssenkrupp Materials Na, Inc.
  22355 W 11 Mile Rd
  Southfield MI 48033
  248 233-5600

(G-11985)
TOWLIFT INC
2860 Crane Way (43619-1095)
PHONE.................................419 666-1333
Brent Cannon, Mgr
EMP: 35
SALES (corp-wide): 246.16MM **Privately Held**
Web: www.towlift.com
SIC: 5084 7353 7699 Materials handling machinery; Heavy construction equipment rental; Industrial equipment services
HQ: Towlift, Inc.
  1395 Valley Belt Rd
  Brooklyn Heights OH 44131
  216 749-6800

(G-11986)
TREU HOUSE OF MUNCH INC
8000 Arbor Dr (43619-7505)
PHONE.................................419 666-7770
Richard G Esser, Pr
Rick Niehaus, *
Todd Esser, *
James Layman, *
EMP: 100 EST: 1875
SQ FT: 120,000
SALES (est): 18.01MM **Privately Held**
Web: www.treuhouse.com
SIC: 5181 Beer and other fermented malt liquors

(G-11987)
WOJOS HEATING & AC INC
5523 Woodville Rd (43619-2209)
PHONE.................................419 693-3220
Thomas Wojo Ciehowfki, Pr
EMP: 50 EST: 1970
SALES (est): 3.21MM **Privately Held**
Web: www.wojosheating.com
SIC: 1711 Warm air heating and air conditioning contractor

(G-11988)
YANFENG US AUTO INTR SYSTEMS I
Also Called: Johnson Contrls Authorized Dlr
7560 Arbor Dr (43619-7500)
PHONE.................................419 662-4905
Keith Wandell, Pr
EMP: 46
Web: www.johnsoncontrols.com
SIC: 2531 5075 Public building and related furniture; Warm air heating and air conditioning
HQ: Yanfeng International Automotive Technology Us I Llc
  41935 W 12 Mile Rd
  Novi MI 48377
  248 319-7333

Norton
Summit County

(G-11989)
AMERICAN ROADWAY LOGISTICS INC
2661 Barber Rd (44203-1056)
PHONE.................................330 659-2003
Heidi Claxton, Pr
Jonathon Claxton, *
Harold Schaffer, *
EMP: 30 EST: 2006
SALES (est): 4.96MM **Privately Held**
Web: www.arlinc.us
SIC: 7359 Work zone traffic equipment (flags, cones, barrels, etc.)

(G-11990)
BARBERTON TREE SERVICE INC
Also Called: Barberton Tree
3307 Clark Mill Rd (44203-1027)
PHONE.................................330 848-2344
Keith Luck, Pr
EMP: 50 EST: 1978
SQ FT: 5,000
SALES (est): 2.08MM **Privately Held**
Web: www.barbertontree.com
SIC: 0783 Pruning services, ornamental tree

(G-11991)
CAPITAL LAND SERVICES INC
Also Called: Cls Group
3665 Brookside Dr (44203-5503)
PHONE.................................330 338-4709
Shawn Sincavaig, Brnch Mgr
EMP: 34
SALES (corp-wide): 674.34MM **Privately Held**
Web: www.telamon.com
SIC: 1542 Commercial and office building contractors
HQ: Capital Land Services, Inc.
  1000 E 116th St
  Carmel IN 46032
  405 348-5460

(G-11992)
CLINTON ALUMINUM DIST INC (PA)
Also Called: Clinton Aluminum
2811 Eastern Rd (44203)
PHONE.................................330 882-6743
Timothy Logan, Pr
▲ EMP: 63 EST: 2010
SALES (est): 78.78MM
SALES (corp-wide): 78.78MM **Privately Held**
Web: www.clintonaluminum.com
SIC: 5051 Steel

(G-11993)
COMPASS SYSTEMS & SALES LLC
Also Called: Compass S&S
5185 New Haven Cir (44203-4672)
PHONE.................................330 733-2111
Robert S Sherrod, Pr
Mark Rubin, *
Phil Hart, *
Brenda Pavlantos, *
▼ EMP: 56 EST: 2014
SQ FT: 43,500
SALES (est): 11.48MM **Privately Held**
Web: www.compasssystems.com
SIC: 3542 0724 Mechanical (pneumatic or hydraulic) metal forming machines; Cotton ginning

(G-11994)
DRIVERS ON CALL LLC
1263 Norton Ave (44203-6528)
PHONE.................................330 867-5193
Andrew W Mcpherson, Pr
EMP: 129 EST: 2011
SQ FT: 2,200
SALES (est): 4.12MM **Privately Held**
Web: www.driversoncall.us
SIC: 4212 Moving services

(G-11995)
NARAGON COMPANIES INC
2197 Wadsworth Rd (44203-5328)
PHONE.................................330 745-7700
Michael Naragon, Pr
Jeff Naragon, *
EMP: 30 EST: 1984
SQ FT: 1,780
SALES (est): 2.25MM **Privately Held**
Web: www.naragoncompanies.com
SIC: 1711 5261 Irrigation sprinkler system installation; Hydroponic equipment and supplies

(G-11996)
NELSEN CORPORATION (PA)
3250 Barber Rd (44203-1012)
P.O. Box 1028 (44203-9428)
PHONE.................................330 745-6000
Ronald E Nelsen, CEO
David Nelsen, *
Kim Bell, *
Jeanette Nelsen, *
◆ EMP: 39 EST: 1954
SQ FT: 33,000
SALES (est): 24.96MM
SALES (corp-wide): 24.96MM **Privately Held**
Web: www.nelsencorp.com
SIC: 5084 Pumps and pumping equipment, nec

(G-11997)
PERFECT POWER WASH
3443 Summit Rd (44203-5342)
PHONE.................................330 697-0131
Michael Palubiak, Prin
EMP: 58 EST: 2013
SALES (est): 16.6MM **Privately Held**
Web: www.perfectpowerwash.com
SIC: 7542 Carwashes

Norwalk
Huron County

(G-11998)
ABS COMMUNICATION LLC
51 E Main St Ste B (44857-1514)
PHONE.................................419 293-5026
EMP: 50 EST: 2016
SALES (est): 3.48MM **Privately Held**
SIC: 4813 Telephone communication, except radio

GEOGRAPHIC SECTION
Norwalk - Huron County (G-12021)

(G-11999)
ADVANCED CMPT CONNECTIONS LLC
Also Called: Wireless Connections
166 Milan Ave (44857-1146)
PHONE..............................419 668-4080
Michael Cowan, *Pr*
Suzanne Cowan, *
EMP: 32 **EST:** 1991
SQ FT: 28,000
SALES (est): 9.57MM **Privately Held**
Web: www.wirelessconnections.net
SIC: 5045 4813 Computer peripheral equipment; Internet host services

(G-12000)
AMERICAN EXCELSIOR COMPANY
180 Cleveland Rd (44857-9021)
PHONE..............................419 663-3241
Terry A Sadowski, *Mgr*
EMP: 51
SALES (corp-wide): 121.68MM **Privately Held**
Web: www.americanexcelsior.com
SIC: 4226 Special warehousing and storage, nec
HQ: American Excelsior Company Inc
    850 Avenue H E
    Arlington TX 76011
    817 385-3500

(G-12001)
ARMETON US CO
205 Republic St (44857-1157)
P.O. Box 234 (44857-0234)
PHONE..............................419 660-9296
Arion Habestor, *CEO*
Tiara Habestor, *
EMP: 30 **EST:** 2015
SALES (est): 2.67MM **Privately Held**
Web: www.armeton.si
SIC: 1791 Concrete reinforcement, placing of

(G-12002)
BORGERS OHIO INC
400 Industrial Pkwy (44857-3102)
PHONE..............................419 663-3700
Harpak Mozaffari, *Pr*
◆ **EMP:** 318 **EST:** 2014
SALES (est): 93.91MM **Privately Held**
Web: www.autoneum.com
SIC: 5013 Automotive supplies and parts
PA: Autoneum Holding Ag
    Schlosstalstrasse 43
    Winterthur ZH 8406

(G-12003)
BUCKEYE EXCAVATING & CNSTR INC
191 State Route 61 (44857-9703)
PHONE..............................419 663-3113
David Nickoli, *Pr*
Jeffrey Nickoli, *Treas*
Keith Moffit, *Sec*
EMP: 37 **EST:** 1998
SQ FT: 7,000
SALES (est): 2.43MM **Privately Held**
SIC: 1623 1794 Underground utilities contractor; Excavation work

(G-12004)
CAROL RUTA
Also Called: Best Western
351 Milan Ave (44857-1159)
PHONE..............................419 663-3501
George Ruta, *Pr*
EMP: 51 **EST:** 1997
SALES (est): 266.15K **Privately Held**
Web: www.bestwestern.com
SIC: 7011 Hotels and motels

(G-12005)
CLE TRANSPORTATION COMPANY
203 Republic St (44857-1157)
PHONE..............................567 805-4008
Igor Stankic, *Pr*
Daniela Stankic, *
EMP: 62 **EST:** 2016
SALES (est): 4.4MM **Privately Held**
Web: www.cletransportation.com
SIC: 4213 Trucking, except local

(G-12006)
CLEVELAND CLINIC FOUNDATION
Also Called: Cleveland Clinic
272 Benedict Ave (44857-2374)
PHONE..............................419 660-6946
EMP: 33
SALES (corp-wide): 14.48B **Privately Held**
Web: www.clevelandclinic.org
SIC: 8062 8049 8031 General medical and surgical hospitals; Acupuncturist; Offices and clinics of osteopathic physicians
PA: The Cleveland Clinic Foundation
    9500 Euclid Ave
    Cleveland OH 44195
    216 636-8335

(G-12007)
CLI INCORPORATED
306 S Norwalk Rd W (44857)
PHONE..............................419 668-8840
John Schwartz, *Pr*
EMP: 50 **EST:** 1976
SQ FT: 20,000
SALES (est): 1.46MM **Privately Held**
Web: www.clisupports.com
SIC: 8331 Sheltered workshop

(G-12008)
DURABLE CORPORATION
75 N Pleasant St (44857-1218)
P.O. Box 290 (44857-0290)
PHONE..............................800 537-1603
Jon M Anderson, *CEO*
Tom Secor, *
Marcia Norris, *
▲ **EMP:** 60 **EST:** 1923
SQ FT: 3,000
SALES (est): 9.9MM **Privately Held**
Web: www.durablecorp.com
SIC: 3069 2273 5013 Mats or matting, rubber, nec; Mats and matting; Bumpers

(G-12009)
ENTERPRISE HILL FARM INC
5264 Huber Rd (44857-9610)
PHONE..............................419 668-0242
Eric Heyman, *Pr*
Adam Heyman, *VP*
Jane Tinker, *Sec*
Kurt Heyman, *Treas*
Chase R Heyman, *Dir*
EMP: 30 **EST:** 1951
SALES (est): 837.8K **Privately Held**
SIC: 0191 4213 General farms, primarily crop ; Trucking, except local

(G-12010)
FISHER - TITUS HEALTH (PA)
272 Benedict Ave (44857)
PHONE..............................419 668-8101
Patrick J Martin, *Pr*
EMP: 800 **EST:** 1985
SQ FT: 200,000
SALES (est): 41.4MM
SALES (corp-wide): 41.4MM **Privately Held**
SIC: 8062 8051 General medical and surgical hospitals; Skilled nursing care facilities

(G-12011)
FISHER-TITUS MEDICAL CENTER
368 Milan Ave Ste D (44857-3106)
PHONE..............................419 663-6464
Deborah Keith, *Pr*
EMP: 84
SALES (corp-wide): 158.84MM **Privately Held**
Web: www.fishertitus.org
SIC: 8062 General medical and surgical hospitals
PA: Fisher-Titus Medical Center
    272 Benedict Ave
    Norwalk OH 44857
    419 668-8101

(G-12012)
FISHER-TITUS MEDICAL CENTER
Also Called: Carriage House
175 Shady Lane Dr Ofc (44857-2387)
PHONE..............................419 668-4228
Terri William, *Admn*
EMP: 83
SALES (corp-wide): 158.84MM **Privately Held**
Web: www.fishertitus.org
SIC: 8052 Intermediate care facilities
PA: Fisher-Titus Medical Center
    272 Benedict Ave
    Norwalk OH 44857
    419 668-8101

(G-12013)
FISHER-TITUS MEDICAL CENTER (PA)
272 Benedict Ave (44857-2374)
PHONE..............................419 668-8101
TOLL FREE: 800
Brent Burkey, *Pr*
Miriam Batke, *Chief Human Resources Officer*
Katie Chieda, *
Scott Endsley, *
Suzanne Farmer, *
▲ **EMP:** 600 **EST:** 1911
SQ FT: 83,000
SALES (est): 158.84MM
SALES (corp-wide): 158.84MM **Privately Held**
Web: www.fishertitus.org
SIC: 8052 8062 Intermediate care facilities; General medical and surgical hospitals

(G-12014)
GAYMONT LEASING LLC
Also Called: Gaymont Care & Rehabilitation
66 Norwood Ave (44857-2337)
PHONE..............................419 668-8258
EMP: 36 **EST:** 2018
SALES (est): 5.99MM **Privately Held**
Web: www.gaymontcare.com
SIC: 8051 Convalescent home with continuous nursing care

(G-12015)
LAKE ERIE CONSTRUCTION CO
25 S Norwalk Rd E (44857-9259)
P.O. Box 777 (44857-0777)
PHONE..............................419 668-3302
David P Bleile, *Pr*
Raymond Chapin, *
Kenneth Bleile, *
Michael Bleile, *
EMP: 200 **EST:** 1977
SQ FT: 6,000
SALES (est): 24.38MM **Privately Held**
Web: www.lakeerieconstruction.com
SIC: 1611 Guardrail construction, highways

(G-12016)
MAPLE CITY ICE COMPANY (PA)
371 Cleveland Rd (44857-9027)
PHONE..............................419 668-2531
Patricia Hipp, *Pr*
John Hipp, *
Gerard Hipp, *
Jeff Hipp, *
EMP: 41 **EST:** 1917
SQ FT: 57,000
SALES (est): 16.72MM
SALES (corp-wide): 16.72MM **Privately Held**
Web: www.maplecityice.net
SIC: 5181 Beer and other fermented malt liquors

(G-12017)
MARK SCHAFFER EXCVTG TRCKG INC
1623 Old State Rd N (44857-9377)
PHONE..............................419 668-5990
Mark Schaffer, *Pr*
Mary Jo Moyer, *
Diane Schaffer, *
EMP: 55 **EST:** 1977
SQ FT: 100,000
SALES (est): 10.83MM **Privately Held**
Web: www.markschaffer-excavating.com
SIC: 1794 1623 1795 Excavation and grading, building construction; Water, sewer, and utility lines; Wrecking and demolition work

(G-12018)
NORWALK CUSTODIAL SERVICE
33 E Water St (44857-2152)
PHONE..............................419 668-1517
Scott D Gardner, *Pr*
EMP: 89 **EST:** 1973
SALES (est): 1.13MM **Privately Held**
SIC: 7349 5084 Janitorial service, contract basis; Cleaning equipment, high pressure, sand or steam

(G-12019)
NORWALK GOLF PROPERTIES INC
Also Called: Eagle Creek Golf Club
2406 New State Rd (44857-7100)
PHONE..............................419 668-8535
Robert Bleile, *Pr*
Marc Schaffer, *
Ken Bleile, *
Gary Wilkins, *
EMP: 46 **EST:** 1994
SQ FT: 100
SALES (est): 1.55MM **Privately Held**
SIC: 7992 6514 Public golf courses; Dwelling operators, except apartments

(G-12020)
PALAZZO BROTHERS ELECTRIC INC
2811 State Route 18 (44857-8829)
PHONE..............................419 668-1100
Joseph M Palazzo, *Pr*
EMP: 32 **EST:** 1990
SQ FT: 2,674
SALES (est): 4.3MM **Privately Held**
Web: www.palazzoelectric.com
SIC: 1731 1799 General electrical contractor ; Sign installation and maintenance

(G-12021)
PLOGER TRANSPORTATION LLC (PA)
300 Cleveland Rd (44857)
PHONE..............................419 465-2100
EMP: 41 **EST:** 2000

Norwalk - Huron County (G-12022)

SQ FT: 2,000
SALES (est): 15MM
SALES (corp-wide): 15MM **Privately Held**
Web: www.plogertrans.com
SIC: 4213 Trucking, except local

(G-12022)
R & L TRANSFER INC
Also Called: R & L Carriers
1403 State Route 18 (44857-9519)
PHONE..............................216 531-3324
Chris Viock, *Brnch Mgr*
EMP: 398
SIC: 4213 4212 Trucking, except local; Local trucking, without storage
HQ: R & L Transfer, Inc.
  600 Gilliam Rd
  Wilmington OH 45177
  937 382-1494

(G-12023)
RENAISSANCE HOUSE INC
48 Executive Dr Ste 1 (44857-2492)
PHONE..............................419 663-1316
Joan Tommas, *Mgr*
EMP: 35
SALES (corp-wide): 3.75MM **Privately Held**
Web: www.renaissancehouseinc.org
SIC: 8361 Retarded home
PA: Renaissance House, Inc.
  103 N Washington St
  Tiffin OH 44883
  419 447-7901

(G-12024)
RK FAMILY INC
1600 Us Highway 20 W (44857-9549)
PHONE..............................419 660-0363
EMP: 195
SALES (corp-wide): 1.22B **Privately Held**
Web: www.ruralking.com
SIC: 5191 Farm supplies
PA: Rk Family, Inc.
  4216 Dewitt Ave
  Mattoon IL 61938
  217 235-7102

(G-12025)
ROBINS & MORTON CORPORATION
285 Benedict Ave (44857-2347)
PHONE..............................419 660-2980
Bill Stevens, *Mgr*
EMP: 32
SALES (corp-wide): 543.64MM **Privately Held**
Web: www.robinsmorton.com
SIC: 1542 Commercial and office building, new construction
HQ: Robins & Morton Corporation
  400 Shades Creek Pkwy # 200
  Birmingham AL 35209

(G-12026)
SAND ROAD ENTERPRISES INC
Also Called: Miller Landscape & Gardens
4352 Sand Rd (44857-9706)
PHONE..............................419 668-3670
William Miller, *Pr*
Steven Miller, *Sec*
EMP: 28 EST: 1983
SALES (est): 469.11K **Privately Held**
Web: www.millerlandscapeandgardens.com
SIC: 0782 5261 4959 Landscape contractors ; Retail nurseries and garden stores; Snowplowing

(G-12027)
SC STRATEGIC SOLUTIONS LLC
600 Industrial Pkwy (44857-3103)
PHONE..............................567 424-6054
Chad Stein, *Managing Member*
EMP: 151 EST: 2007
SALES (est): 12.5MM **Privately Held**
Web: www.scstrategicsolutions.com
SIC: 7372 7374 Application computer software; Data processing and preparation

(G-12028)
STV HOLDINGS INC
Also Called: Sirna & Sons Produce
650 Us Highway 20 E (44857-9502)
PHONE..............................419 668-4857
James Soisson, *Brnch Mgr*
EMP: 150
SALES (corp-wide): 27.82MM **Privately Held**
Web: www.sirnaandsonsproduce.com
SIC: 5148 Fruits, fresh
PA: Stv Holdings, Inc.
  7176 State Route 88
  Ravenna OH 44266
  800 824-1868

(G-12029)
TWILIGHT GRDNS HLTHCARE GROUP
Also Called: Twilight Gardens Home
196 W Main St (44857-1915)
PHONE..............................419 668-2086
George S Repchick, *Pr*
William I Weisberg, *
EMP: 40 EST: 1960
SQ FT: 5,500
SALES (est): 4.53MM
SALES (corp-wide): 655.44MM **Privately Held**
Web: www.twilighthc.com
SIC: 8051 8052 Convalescent home with continuous nursing care; Intermediate care facilities
PA: Saber Healthcare Group, L.L.C.
  23700 Commerce Park
  Beachwood OH 44122
  216 292-5706

(G-12030)
WASINIAK CONSTRUCTION INC
2519 State Route 61 (44857-9181)
PHONE..............................419 668-8624
John Wasiniak, *Pr*
James Wasiniak, *
EMP: 60 EST: 1968
SQ FT: 1,000
SALES (est): 7.9MM **Privately Held**
Web: www.wasiniak.com
SIC: 1741 1771 Masonry and other stonework; Concrete work

(G-12031)
ZEITER TRUCKING INC
Also Called: Zeiter Leasing
2590 State Route 18 (44857-8831)
PHONE..............................419 668-2229
Richard D Zeiter, *Pr*
Mark Zeiter, *
Steven Zeiter, *
Kim Zieter, *
EMP: 45 EST: 1963
SALES (est): 2.42MM **Privately Held**
Web: www.zeitertrucking.com
SIC: 4212 Dump truck haulage

Norwood
Hamilton County

(G-12032)
EMD MILLIPORE CORPORATION
2909 Highland Ave (45212-2411)
PHONE..............................513 631-0445
Michael Mulligan, *VP*
EMP: 150
SQ FT: 100,000
SALES (corp-wide): 22.82B **Privately Held**
Web: www.emdmillipore.com
SIC: 8731 3295 2899 2842 Biotechnical research, commercial; Minerals, ground or treated; Chemical preparations, nec; Polishes and sanitation goods
HQ: Emd Millipore Corporation
  400 Summit Dr
  Burlington MA 01803
  800 645-5476

(G-12033)
FRESENIUS VASCULAR CARE INC
4600 Smith Rd (45212-2793)
PHONE..............................513 351-2494
Jeffrey Snodgrass, *Brnch Mgr*
EMP: 50
SALES (corp-wide): 21.15B **Privately Held**
Web: www.azuravascularcare.com
SIC: 8011 Cardiologist and cardio-vascular specialist
HQ: Fresenius Vascular Care, Inc.
  52 E Swdesford Rd Ste 110
  Berwyn PA 19312
  610 644-8900

(G-12034)
NORWOOD TOWERS HEALTHCARE LLC
Also Called: Norwood Towers Post Acute
1500 Sherman Ave (45212-2510)
PHONE..............................513 631-6800
Jason Murray, *Prin*
Mark Hancock, *
EMP: 97 EST: 2019
SALES (est): 6.95MM
SALES (corp-wide): 1.64B **Privately Held**
SIC: 8051 Skilled nursing care facilities
PA: Providence Group, Inc.
  262 N University Ave
  Farmington UT 84025
  801 447-9829

(G-12035)
UBER GREENLIGHT HUB
4803 Montgomery Rd Bldg D (45212-1152)
PHONE..............................800 593-7069
EMP: 33 EST: 2019
SALES (est): 87.61K **Privately Held**
Web: www.howiuber.com
SIC: 6512 Commercial and industrial building operation

Novelty
Geauga County

(G-12036)
ALT MEDIA STUDIOS LLC
13572 Chillicothe Rd (44072-9537)
P.O. Box 23483 (44023-0483)
PHONE..............................440 777-6666
Steve Difranco, *Pr*
Steven Difranco, *
EMP: 30 EST: 2002
SALES (est): 956.79K **Privately Held**
Web: www.amst.com
SIC: 7374 8742 Computer graphics service; Marketing consulting services

(G-12037)
ASM INTERNATIONAL
9639 Kinsman Rd (44073-0002)
PHONE..............................440 338-5151
Thomas Dudley, *CEO*
▲ EMP: 80 EST: 1913
SQ FT: 55,000
SALES (est): 7.42MM **Privately Held**
Web: www.asminternational.org
SIC: 2731 2721 7389 7999 Books, publishing only; Periodicals, publishing only ; Advertising, promotional, and trade show services; Exhibition operation

(G-12038)
GEAUGA COUNTY HUMANE SOC INC
Also Called: HUMANE SOCIETY SHELTER GEAUGA
15463 Chillicothe Rd (44072-9646)
P.O. Box 116 (44072-0116)
PHONE..............................440 338-4819
Sharon Harvey, *Dir*
Bruce Wain, *Pr*
Brian Greene, *Treas*
Peter Shelton, *Sec*
EMP: 33 EST: 1974
SQ FT: 1,400
SALES (est): 2.39MM **Privately Held**
Web: www.rescuevillage.org
SIC: 8699 Animal humane society

(G-12039)
INTERSERVICE CORPORATION
7301 Wharton Rd (44072-9754)
PHONE..............................216 272-3519
Charles J O'toole, *Pr*
EMP: 130 EST: 1962
SALES (est): 2.82MM **Privately Held**
SIC: 8741 Management services

(G-12040)
O C I CONSTRUCTION CO INC
8560 Pekin Rd (44072-9717)
PHONE..............................440 338-3166
Robert Wantz, *Pr*
Daniel Wantz, *
EMP: 38 EST: 1980
SQ FT: 3,000
SALES (est): 2.07MM **Privately Held**
Web: www.ociconstruction.com
SIC: 1521 Single-family housing construction

(G-12041)
PATTIE GROUP INC (PA)
Also Called: Pattie's Landscaping
15533 Chillicothe Rd (44072-9646)
PHONE..............................440 338-1288
Steve Pattie, *Pr*
William Pattie, *
EMP: 85 EST: 1968
SQ FT: 2,000
SALES (est): 11.62MM
SALES (corp-wide): 11.62MM **Privately Held**
Web: www.pattiegroup.com
SIC: 0781 Landscape services

(G-12042)
PATTON PEST CONTROL CO
15526 Chillicothe Rd (44072-9646)
PHONE..............................440 338-3101
John S Patton, *Pr*
Patty Patton, *VP*
Molly Patton, *CEO*
EMP: 29 EST: 1964
SQ FT: 1,000
SALES (est): 696.18K **Privately Held**
Web: www.pattonpest.com
SIC: 7342 Pest control in structures

GEOGRAPHIC SECTION

(G-12043)
SECURESTATE LLC
9330 Fairmount Rd (44072-9766)
PHONE.................216 927-0115
Ken Stasiak, *Managing Member*
Stephen Marchewitz, *
Sue Satink, *
EMP: 45 **EST:** 2001
SALES (est): 6.19MM **Privately Held**
Web: www.securestate.com
SIC: 7382 Security systems services

Oak Harbor
Ottawa County

(G-12044)
COUNTY OF OTTAWA
Also Called: Ottawa Cnty Rvrview Hlthcare C
8180 W State Route 163 (43449-8855)
PHONE..................567 262-3600
John Ambrosecchia, *Admn*
EMP: 200
SQ FT: 20,000
SALES (corp-wide): 53.18MM **Privately Held**
Web: co.ottawa.oh.us
SIC: 8051 9111 8111 Convalescent home with continuous nursing care; County supervisors' and executives' office; General practice attorney, lawyer
PA: County Of Ottawa
 315 Madison St Ste 201
 Port Clinton OH 43452
 419 734-6700

(G-12045)
H B MAGRUDER MEMORIAL HOSP
Also Called: Oak Harbor Medical Center
11697 W State Route 163 (43449-9113)
PHONE..................419 734-3131
Kim Bright, *Genl Mgr*
EMP: 155
SALES (corp-wide): 59.68MM **Privately Held**
Web: www.magruderhospital.com
SIC: 8062 8011 General medical and surgical hospitals; Offices and clinics of medical doctors
PA: H. B. Magruder Memorial Hospital
 615 Fulton St
 Port Clinton OH 43452
 419 734-3131

(G-12046)
OAK HARBOR LIONS CLUB INC
101 S Brookside Dr (43449-1276)
P.O. Box 144 (43449-0144)
PHONE..................419 898-3828
EMP: 34 **EST:** 2010
SALES (est): 17.11K **Privately Held**
Web: www.ohlions.org
SIC: 8611 Community affairs and services

(G-12047)
RIVERVIEW INDUSTRIES INC
8380 W State Route 163 (43449-8859)
PHONE..................419 898-5250
Brenda Smith, *Ex Dir*
EMP: 51 **EST:** 1973
SALES (est): 3.73MM **Privately Held**
Web: www.rviinc.org
SIC: 8331 Manpower training

Oakwood
Montgomery County

(G-12048)
KUNESH EYE CENTER INC
Also Called: Oakwood Optical
2601 Far Hills Ave Ste 2 (45419-1634)
PHONE..................937 298-1703
Kristine Kunesh Part Md, *Pr*
Kristine Kunesh-part Md, *Pr*
Michael T Kunesh, *
John Kunesh, *
Lucy Helmers, *
EMP: 28 **EST:** 1973
SALES (est): 5.12MM **Privately Held**
Web: www.kunesh.com
SIC: 8011 Opthalmologist

(G-12049)
LENDLY LLC
105 Sugar Camp Cir (45409-1977)
PHONE..................844 453-6359
Douglas Dotson, *Mgr*
EMP: 32 **EST:** 2021
SALES (est): 328.48K **Privately Held**
Web: www.lendly.com
SIC: 7389 Financial services

(G-12050)
LUXE OMNI INC
2331 Far Hills Ave Ste 100 (45419-1538)
PHONE..................937 929-0511
Christina Gentry, *Pr*
EMP: 28 **EST:** 2021
SALES (est): 1.35MM **Privately Held**
Web: www.luxeomni.com
SIC: 6531 Real estate brokers and agents

(G-12051)
NCP HOLDINGS LP (PA)
205 Sugar Camp Cir (45409-1970)
PHONE..................937 228-5600
Therese Mcnea-wiley, *Pt*
EMP: 39 **EST:** 2012
SALES (est): 19.36MM
SALES (corp-wide): 19.36MM **Privately Held**
SIC: 7389 Financial services

(G-12052)
TOTAL LOAN SERVICES LLC
205 Sugar Camp Cir (45409-1970)
PHONE..................937 228-5600
EMP: 75 **EST:** 2018
SALES (est): 14.21MM
SALES (corp-wide): 19.36MM **Privately Held**
Web: www.gettotal.com
SIC: 6163 Loan agents
PA: Ncp Holdings, L.P.
 205 Sugar Camp Cir
 Dayton OH 45409
 937 228-5600

Oakwood
Paulding County

(G-12053)
COOPER HATCHERY INC (PA)
Also Called: Cooper Farms
22348 Rd 140 (45873-9303)
PHONE..................419 594-3325
James R Cooper, *CEO*
Gary A Cooper, *
Dianne Cooper, *
Anada E Cooper, *
Janice Fiely, *
EMP: 225 **EST:** 1934
SQ FT: 47,000
SALES (est): 93.22MM
SALES (corp-wide): 93.22MM **Privately Held**
SIC: 0254 0253 2015 5153 Poultry hatcheries; Turkey farm; Turkey, processed, nsk; Grains

(G-12054)
STONECO INC
13762 Road 179 (45873-9012)
PHONE..................419 393-2555
Rick Welch, *Superintnt*
EMP: 45
SALES (corp-wide): 32.72B **Privately Held**
Web: www.shellyco.com
SIC: 1422 2951 Crushed and broken limestone; Asphalt paving mixtures and blocks
HQ: Stoneco, Inc.
 1700 Fostoria Ave Ste 200
 Findlay OH 45840
 419 422-8854

Oakwood Village
Cuyahoga County

(G-12055)
BUILDING INTEGRATED SVCS LLC
7777 First Pl (44146-6733)
PHONE..................330 733-9191
EMP: 60 **EST:** 2015
SALES (est): 9.57MM **Privately Held**
Web: www.bisedge.com
SIC: 1711 Plumbing, heating, air-conditioning

(G-12056)
RGT SERVICES LLC
Also Called: Fowler Company, The
26185 Broadway Ave (44146-6512)
PHONE..................440 786-9777
EMP: 50
SQ FT: 14,000
SALES (est): 24MM **Privately Held**
SIC: 1711 1731 Mechanical contractor; General electrical contractor

(G-12057)
ROCK HOUSE ENTRMT GROUP INC
7809 First Pl (44146-6707)
PHONE..................440 232-7625
Matt Radicelli, *Pr*
▲ **EMP:** 120 **EST:** 1996
SALES (est): 11.02MM **Privately Held**
Web: www.rthgroup.com
SIC: 7929 Disc jockey service

(G-12058)
SWIFT FILTERS INC (PA)
24040 Forbes Rd (44146-5650)
PHONE..................440 735-0995
Edwin C Swift Junior, *Pr*
Charles C Swift, *
EMP: 37 **EST:** 1995
SQ FT: 6,000
SALES (est): 6.21MM
SALES (corp-wide): 6.21MM **Privately Held**
Web: www.swiftfilters.com
SIC: 3569 5075 Filters; Air filters

(G-12059)
THERMO FISHER SCIENTIFIC INC
Also Called: Remel Products
1 Thermo Fisher Way (44146-6536)
PHONE..................800 871-8909
EMP: 27
SALES (corp-wide): 44.91B **Publicly Held**
Web: www.thermofisher.com
SIC: 5047 2835 3841 Diagnostic equipment, medical; Diagnostic substances; Surgical and medical instruments
PA: Thermo Fisher Scientific Inc.
 168 3rd Ave
 Waltham MA 02451
 781 622-1000

(G-12060)
VIEWRAY INC (PA)
2 Thermo Fisher Way (44146-6536)
PHONE..................440 703-3210
Paul Ziegler, *CEO*
Daniel Moore, *Ch Bd*
Cassie Mahar, *Interim Chief Financial Officer*
Martin Fuzz, *CMO*
James F Dempsey, *CSO*
▲ **EMP:** 52 **EST:** 2004
SALES (est): 102.21MM
SALES (corp-wide): 102.21MM **Publicly Held**
Web: www.viewray.com
SIC: 3845 5047 Electromedical equipment; Therapy equipment

(G-12061)
VIEWRAY SYSTEMS INC ✪
2 Thermo Fisher Way (44146-6536)
PHONE..................303 339-0500
Brad Nelson, *Pr*
EMP: 42 **EST:** 2023
SALES (est): 1.66MM **Privately Held**
SIC: 5047 Medical and hospital equipment

Oberlin
Lorain County

(G-12062)
AGRINOMIX LLC
300 Creekside Dr (44074-1272)
PHONE..................440 774-2981
Robert Lando, *CEO*
Charles Kirschner, *
▲ **EMP:** 64 **EST:** 1993
SQ FT: 74,800
SALES (est): 24.76MM **Privately Held**
Web: www.agrinomix.com
SIC: 5083 5084 Planting machinery and equipment; Materials handling machinery

(G-12063)
ARRC ONE LLC
55 S Main St Pmb 107 (44074-1626)
PHONE..................440 754-0855
Antwon Mccray, *Pr*
EMP: 50 **EST:** 2018
SALES (est): 2.12MM **Privately Held**
SIC: 7389 7361 Business Activities at Non-Commercial Site; Employment agencies

(G-12064)
BON SECOURS MERCY HEALTH INC
Also Called: Mercy Allen Hospital
200 W Lorain St (44074-1026)
PHONE..................440 774-6800
EMP: 59
SALES (corp-wide): 6.92B **Privately Held**
Web: www.bonsecours.com
SIC: 8062 General medical and surgical hospitals
PA: Bon Secours Mercy Health, Inc.
 1701 Mercy Health Pl
 Cincinnati OH 45237
 513 956-3729

(G-12065)
CITY OF OBERLIN (PA)
Also Called: Oberlin Municpl Light Pwr Sys

Oberlin - Lorain County

85 S Main St (44074-1603)
PHONE..................................440 775-1531
Ron Rimbert, *Pr*
Rob Disperdo, *
Sharon Soucy, *
Eric Norenberg, *
Beth Krosse, *
EMP: 47 **EST:** 1833
SQ FT: 10,000
SALES (est): 13.58MM
SALES (corp-wide): 13.58MM **Privately Held**
Web: www.cityofoberlin.com
SIC: 9111 8611 City and town managers' office; Business associations

(G-12066)
CUSTOM CLEANING SVCS BY HORTON
305 Artino St Unit A (44074-1276)
PHONE..................................440 774-1222
Todd Zack, *Pr*
EMP: 40 **EST:** 2021
SALES (est): 571.5K **Privately Held**
Web: www.ccsoberlin.com
SIC: 7349 Janitorial service, contract basis

(G-12067)
CUSTOM CLG SVCS DISASTER LLC ◆
305 Artino St Unit A (44074-0147)
P.O. Box 147
PHONE..................................440 774-1222
EMP: 30 **EST:** 2022
SALES (est): 559.91K **Privately Held**
Web: www.ccsoberlin.com
SIC: 8322 Disaster service

(G-12068)
EXPRESS SEED COMPANY
Also Called: Express Seed
51051 Us Highway 20 (44074-1253)
PHONE..................................440 774-2259
Scott Valentine, *CEO*
John Van Wingerden, *
Dawn Van Wingerden, *
▲ **EMP:** 60 **EST:** 1982
SQ FT: 30,000
SALES (est): 20.53MM **Privately Held**
Web: www.expressseed.com
SIC: 5193 5191 Plants, potted; Flower and field bulbs

(G-12069)
GREEN CIRCLE GROWERS INC (PA)
51051 Us Highway 20 (44074-9637)
PHONE..................................440 775-1411
John Van Wingerden, *Pr*
John Van Wingerden, *Pr*
Dawn Van Wingerden, *
Norman Daxter, *
◆ **EMP:** 184 **EST:** 1972
SQ FT: 2,500
SALES (est): 47.14MM
SALES (corp-wide): 47.14MM **Privately Held**
Web: www.greencirclegrowers.com
SIC: 0181 Flowers: grown under cover (e.g., greenhouse production)

(G-12070)
GREEN CIRCLE GROWERS INC
15650 State Route 511 (44074-9699)
PHONE..................................440 775-1411
Van Wingerden John, *Brnch Mgr*
EMP: 416
SALES (corp-wide): 47.14MM **Privately Held**
Web: www.greencirclegrowers.com
SIC: 0181 Flowers: grown under cover (e.g., greenhouse production)

PA: Green Circle Growers, Inc.
51051 Us Highway 20
Oberlin OH 44074
440 775-1411

(G-12071)
KENDAL AT OBERLIN
600 Kendal Dr (44074)
PHONE..................................440 775-0094
EMP: 222 **EST:** 1987
SALES (est): 21.21MM **Privately Held**
Web: kao.kendal.org
SIC: 8051 8052 Skilled nursing care facilities ; Intermediate care facilities
PA: The Kendal Corporation
591 Collaboration Way # 603
Newark DE 19713

(G-12072)
MCCONNELL EXCAVATING LTD
15804 State Route 58 (44074-9580)
PHONE..................................440 774-4578
Eric Mcconnell, *Genl Pt*
EMP: 47 **EST:** 1993
SALES (est): 10.15MM **Privately Held**
Web: www.earthmovin.com
SIC: 1794 7389 Excavation and grading, building construction; Business services, nec

(G-12073)
NATIONAL ASSN CLLEGE STRES INC (PA)
Also Called: N A C S
500 E Lorain St (44074-1238)
PHONE..................................440 775-7777
Ed Schlichenmayer, *CEO*
Jane Nizza, *
Hugh Keogh, *
EMP: 75 **EST:** 1923
SQ FT: 27,000
SALES (est): 5.95MM
SALES (corp-wide): 5.95MM **Privately Held**
Web: www.nacs.org
SIC: 8611 Trade associations

(G-12074)
OBERLIN COLLEGE
Also Called: Allen Memorial Art Museum
87 N Main St (44074-1151)
PHONE..................................440 775-8665
Katherine Solender, *Dir*
EMP: 28
SALES (corp-wide): 221.17MM **Privately Held**
Web: www.oberlin.edu
SIC: 8221 8412 College, except junior; Museum
PA: Oberlin College
173 W Lorain St
Oberlin OH 44074
440 775-8121

(G-12075)
PARTNERSHIP LLC
Also Called: Partnership
528 E Lorain St (44074-1238)
PHONE..................................440 471-8310
John J Finucane Junior, *Pr*
Brian Ferancy, *BSNS Development*
Paul Freeman, *BSNS SYS*
EMP: 45 **EST:** 2002
SALES (est): 378.7K
SALES (corp-wide): 5.95MM **Privately Held**
Web: www.partnership.com
SIC: 4213 Less-than-truckload (LTL)
PA: National Association Of College Stores, Inc.
500 E Lorain St

Oberlin OH 44074
440 775-7777

(G-12076)
STINER AND SONS CNSTR INC
13728 Hale Rd (44074-9783)
PHONE..................................440 775-2345
Timothy M Stiner, *Pr*
Ken Stiner, *
Ronald Stiner, *
Dennis Steiner, *
EMP: 30 **EST:** 1988
SQ FT: 1,000
SALES (est): 3.3MM **Privately Held**
SIC: 1521 Single-family housing construction

(G-12077)
WESSELL GENERATIONS INC
Also Called: WELCOME NURSING HOME
417 S Main St (44074-1749)
PHONE..................................440 775-1491
Jill Herron, *Adm/Dir*
Heidi Freas, *
Kelly Wessell, *
Meghan Wessell, *
EMP: 96 **EST:** 1945
SQ FT: 40,766
SALES (est): 7.36MM **Privately Held**
Web: www.welcomenursinghome.com
SIC: 8051 Convalescent home with continuous nursing care

Obetz
Franklin County

(G-12078)
AAJ ENTERPRISES INC
Also Called: Wednesday Auto Auction
4700 Groveport Rd (43207-5217)
PHONE..................................614 497-2000
Cam Hitchcock, *CEO*
EMP: 1240 **EST:** 1958
SQ FT: 60,000
SALES (est): 221.89MM
SALES (corp-wide): 387.35MM **Privately Held**
Web: www.americasaa.com
SIC: 5012 5521 Automobile auction; Used car dealers
PA: American Auto Auction Group Llc
10333 N Meridian St # 200
Carmel IN 46290
843 579-2886

(G-12079)
CARDINAL HEALTH INC
2320 Mcgaw Rd (43207-4805)
PHONE..................................614 497-9552
Kelly Byrd, *Brnch Mgr*
EMP: 43
SALES (corp-wide): 205.01B **Publicly Held**
Web: www.cardinalhealth.com
SIC: 5122 5047 8741 Pharmaceuticals; Surgical equipment and supplies; Management services
PA: Cardinal Health, Inc.
7000 Cardinal Pl
Dublin OH 43017
614 757-5000

(G-12080)
HOGAN TRUCK LEASING INC
2499 Mcgaw Rd (43207-4513)
PHONE..................................314 802-5995
EMP: 28
SALES (corp-wide): 127.28MM **Privately Held**
Web: www.hogan1.com

SIC: 7359 Equipment rental and leasing, nec
PA: Hogan Truck Leasing, Inc.
2150 Schuetz Rd Ste 210
Saint Louis MO 63146
314 421-6000

(G-12081)
LEMON GROUP LLC
Also Called: Mid-America Store Fixtures
2195 Broehm Rd (43207-5206)
PHONE..................................614 409-9850
EMP: 32 **EST:** 2011
SALES (est): 5.52MM **Privately Held**
Web: www.midasf.com
SIC: 6153 2541 Factoring services; Wood partitions and fixtures

(G-12082)
PAR INTERNATIONAL INC
2160 Mcgaw Rd (43207-4801)
PHONE..................................614 529-1300
Eli Goldach, *Pr*
Dan Goldach, *
Dan Stergiou, *
Marjorie Goldach Shipping, *Coordtr*
◆ **EMP:** 30 **EST:** 1990
SQ FT: 300,000
SALES (est): 6.12MM **Privately Held**
Web: www.parglobaldistribution.com
SIC: 5013 5199 Automotive supplies and parts; Gifts and novelties

(G-12083)
SQUEAKY BANANA INC
4852 Frusta Dr Ste D (43207-4581)
PHONE..................................614 492-1208
Salvador Condemi, *Brnch Mgr*
EMP: 69
SALES (corp-wide): 2.57MM **Privately Held**
SIC: 4789 Cargo loading and unloading services
PA: Squeaky Banana, Inc.
2380 S Halsted St
Chicago IL 60608
815 423-7000

(G-12084)
SYNERGY HOTELS LLC
Also Called: Holiday Inn
4870 Old Rathmell Ct (43207-4580)
P.O. Box 773 (43054-0773)
PHONE..................................614 492-9000
Stephen Berger, *Mgr*
Mike Duncan, *
EMP: 30 **EST:** 1997
SALES (est): 2.37MM **Privately Held**
Web: www.choicehotels.com
SIC: 7011 7991 Hotels; Physical fitness facilities

(G-12085)
UNITED PARCEL SERVICE INC
Also Called: UPS
2450 Rathmell Rd (43207-4591)
P.O. Box 557 (43528-0557)
PHONE..................................614 272-8500
EMP: 588
SALES (corp-wide): 90.96B **Publicly Held**
Web: www.ups.com
SIC: 4215 Parcel delivery, vehicular
HQ: United Parcel Service, Inc.
55 Glenlake Pkwy
Atlanta GA 30328
404 828-6000

GEOGRAPHIC SECTION
Ontario - Richland County (G-12107)

Okeana
Butler County

(G-12086)
KISSEL ENTERTAINMENT LLC
Also Called: Kissel Rides & Shows
3748 State Line Rd (45053-9506)
P.O. Box 2340 (35046-2340)
PHONE.................................513 266-4505
EMP: 45 **EST:** 2005
SALES (est): 858.03K **Privately Held**
Web: www.kisselentertainment.com
SIC: 7999 Carnival operation

Old Washington
Guernsey County

(G-12087)
SOUTHSTERN OHIO CNSLING CTR LL
239a Old National Rd (43768-5000)
P.O. Box 94 (43768-0094)
PHONE.................................740 260-9440
Amanda Mcglumphy, CEO
Amanda L Mcglumphy, Prin
EMP: 32 **EST:** 2012
SALES (est): 511.72K **Privately Held**
Web: www.southeasternohiocounseling.com
SIC: 8322 General counseling services

Olmsted Falls
Cuyahoga County

(G-12088)
OHIOGUIDESTONE
24567 West Rd (44138-2344)
PHONE.................................440 235-0918
EMP: 132
SALES (corp-wide): 86.77MM **Privately Held**
Web: www.ohioguidestone.org
SIC: 8361 Residential care
PA: Ohioguidestone
434 Eastland Rd
Berea OH 44017
440 234-2006

Olmsted Twp
Cuyahoga County

(G-12089)
ELIZA JENNINGS INC
26376 John Rd Ofc (44138-1283)
PHONE.................................216 226-5000
Deborah Lewis Hiller, Prin
EMP: 102 **EST:** 1985
SALES (est): 3.4MM **Privately Held**
Web: www.elizajennings.org
SIC: 6411 Pension and retirement plan consultants

(G-12090)
ELIZA JNNNGS SNIOR CARE NETWRK (PA)
26376 John Rd Ofc C (44138-1283)
PHONE.................................216 226-5000
Deborah Hiller, CEO
Jim Rogerson, *
EMP: 210 **EST:** 1987
SALES (est): 4.45MM **Privately Held**
Web: www.elizajennings.org
SIC: 8051 Skilled nursing care facilities

(G-12091)
LENAU PARK
Also Called: DONAUSCHWABEN'S GERMANAMERICAN
7370 Columbia Rd (44138-1502)
P.O. Box 38160 (44138-0160)
PHONE.................................440 235-2646
EMP: 40 **EST:** 1952
SQ FT: 32,075
SALES (est): 628.49K **Privately Held**
Web: www.donauschwabencleveland.com
SIC: 7997 8641 Country club, membership; Civic and social associations

(G-12092)
OLMSTED FALLS CITY BD EDUCATN
Also Called: Olmsted Falls Cty SC Bus Gar
26894 Schady Rd (44138-1708)
PHONE.................................440 427-6350
Al Cantrell, Mgr
EMP: 59
SQ FT: 12,352
SALES (corp-wide): 57.5MM **Privately Held**
Web: www.ofcs.net
SIC: 4151 School buses
PA: Olmsted Falls Board Of Education
26937 Bagley Rd
Olmsted Twp OH 44138
440 427-6000

(G-12093)
OLMSTED RESIDENCE CORPORATION
Also Called: Renaissance, The
26376 John Rd Ofc (44138-1283)
PHONE.................................440 235-7100
Deborah Hiller, CEO
EMP: 180 **EST:** 1985
SQ FT: 256,000
SALES (est): 9.79MM **Privately Held**
SIC: 8322 6531 Senior citizens' center or association; Real estate managers
PA: Eliza Jennings Senior Care Network
26376 John Rd Ofc C
Olmsted Twp OH 44138

(G-12094)
STRIKE ZONE INC
Also Called: Swings N Things Family Fun Pk
8501 Stearns Rd (44138-1738)
PHONE.................................440 235-4420
Tim Sorge, Pr
EMP: 85 **EST:** 1982
SQ FT: 24,000
SALES (est): 5.08MM **Privately Held**
Web: www.sntfun.com
SIC: 7999 7993 5812 Recreation services; Video game arcade; Ice cream stands or dairy bars

Ontario
Richland County

(G-12095)
3RD STREET COMMUNITY CLINIC
Also Called: 3RD STREET FAMILY HEALTH SERVI
1404 Park Ave W (44906-2719)
PHONE.................................419 522-6191
Gerad Pollick, Pr
Robert A Bowers, *
EMP: 57 **EST:** 1994
SALES (est): 20.77MM **Privately Held**
Web: www.thirdstreetfamily.org
SIC: 8011 Clinic, operated by physicians

(G-12096)
ADENA CORPORATION
Also Called: Adena Corp Mansfield Ohio
1310 W 4th St (44906-1828)
PHONE.................................419 529-4456
Randy A Payne, Pr
Dwight Farmer, *
Brad Geissman, *
Tom Blunk, *
David M Bush, *
EMP: 160 **EST:** 1982
SQ FT: 7,000
SALES (est): 119.31MM **Privately Held**
Web: www.adenacorporation.com
SIC: 1541 1542 Industrial buildings, new construction, nec; Nonresidential construction, nec

(G-12097)
ADVANCED EYE CARE CENTER INC
Also Called: Advanced Eye Care Csmtc Lser C
1991 Park Ave W (44906-2233)
PHONE.................................419 521-3937
Harold Ballitch, Pr
EMP: 37 **EST:** 1997
SQ FT: 1,500
SALES (est): 2.84MM **Privately Held**
Web: www.drballitch.com
SIC: 8011 Opthalmologist

(G-12098)
ADVANTAGE CREDIT UNION INC (PA)
700 Stumbo Rd (44906-1279)
P.O. Box 2674 (44906-0674)
PHONE.................................419 529-5603
Wesley P Volz, Pr
Charles Skara, *
EMP: 28 **EST:** 1961
SALES (est): 1.8MM
SALES (corp-wide): 1.8MM **Privately Held**
Web: www.advantage4.org
SIC: 6061 Federal credit unions

(G-12099)
ALL AMERICAN TRNSP SVCS LLC
575 Beer Rd (44906-1214)
PHONE.................................419 589-7433
James Blevins, Managing Member
EMP: 35 **EST:** 2015
SALES (est): 2.42MM **Privately Held**
SIC: 4789 Cargo loading and unloading services

(G-12100)
CENTRAL STAR
Also Called: Central Star Home Health Svcs
2003 W 4th St Ste 116 (44906-1865)
PHONE.................................419 756-9449
Steve Sternbock, CEO
Julie Charlton, *
EMP: 358 **EST:** 1983
SALES (est): 2.05MM
SALES (corp-wide): 24.46MM **Privately Held**
Web: www.centralstarhomehealth.com
SIC: 8082 Home health care services
PA: Star Multi Care Services, Inc.
115 Broadhollow Rd # 275
Melville NY 11747
631 423-6689

(G-12101)
CFC MANSFIELD LLC
Also Called: TGI Friday's
900 N Lexington Springmill Rd (44906-1119)
PHONE.................................216 328-1121
EMP: 27 **EST:** 2016
SALES (est): 936.64K **Privately Held**
Web: www.tgifridays.com
SIC: 8741 Management services

(G-12102)
CHILDRENS HOSP MED CTR AKRON
2003 W 4th St (44906-1865)
PHONE.................................419 529-6285
EMP: 54
SALES (corp-wide): 1.4B **Privately Held**
Web: www.akronchildrens.org
SIC: 8062 8011 General medical and surgical hospitals; Pediatrician
PA: Childrens Hospital Medical Center Of Akron
1 Perkins Sq
Akron OH 44308
330 543-1000

(G-12103)
DTA INC
Also Called: Arnold's Landscaping
3180 Park Ave W (44906-1059)
PHONE.................................419 529-2920
Darrell Arnold, Pr
EMP: 50 **EST:** 2000
SALES (est): 2.14MM **Privately Held**
Web: www.arnoldslandscaping3128.com
SIC: 0782 Landscape contractors

(G-12104)
EXECUTIVE MANAGEMENT SERVICES
1225 Home Rd N (44906-1407)
PHONE.................................419 529-8800
Lawrence Grin, Pr
EMP: 941 **EST:** 1999
SALES (est): 235.57K **Privately Held**
SIC: 7349 Janitorial service, contract basis
PA: Executive Management Services, Inc.
4177 N Ems Blvd
Indianapolis IN 46250

(G-12105)
GRAHAM CHEVROLET-CADILLAC CO
Also Called: Ford
1515 W 4th St (44906-1857)
P.O. Box 340 (43702-0340)
PHONE.................................419 989-4012
James Graham, Pr
Ken Williams, *
Clay Graham, *
Brian Graham, *
EMP: 147 **EST:** 1957
SQ FT: 44,000
SALES (est): 37.96MM **Privately Held**
Web: www.grahamchevycadillac.com
SIC: 5511 7515 7513 5521 Automobiles, new and used; Passenger car leasing; Truck rental and leasing, no drivers; Used car dealers

(G-12106)
HANDS ENTERPRISES LTD
575 Urwin Pkwy (44906-3352)
PHONE.................................419 528-1389
Carson T Smart, Prin
EMP: 40 **EST:** 2017
SALES (est): 987.17K **Privately Held**
SIC: 7389 Business services, nec

(G-12107)
HUNTINGTON NATIONAL BANK
2313 Village Park Ct (44906-1167)
PHONE.................................419 747-2265
EMP: 31
SALES (corp-wide): 10.84B **Publicly Held**
Web: www.huntington.com
SIC: 6029 6021 Commercial banks, nec; National commercial banks

Ontario - Richland County (G-12108)

GEOGRAPHIC SECTION

HQ: The Huntington National Bank
41 S High St
Columbus OH 43215
614 480-4293

(G-12108)
JACKSON CORPORATION
Also Called: Worner Roofing
4135 Park Ave W (44903-8611)
P.O. Box 183 (44862-0183)
PHONE.............................419 525-0170
Rick Worner, *Pr*
EMP: 31 EST: 1987
SALES (est): 1.05MM **Privately Held**
Web: www.wornerroofing.com
SIC: 1761 Roofing contractor

(G-12109)
JOHNNY APPLESEED BRDCSTG CO
Also Called: Wvno-FM
2900 Park Ave W (44906-1062)
PHONE.............................419 529-5900
Gunther S Meisse, *CEO*
EMP: 42
SQ FT: 17,000
SALES (est): 5.38MM **Privately Held**
Web: www.wmfd.com
SIC: 4832 4833 Radio broadcasting stations; Television broadcasting stations

(G-12110)
JOYCE BUICK INC
Also Called: Joyce Buick GMC of Mansfield
1400 Park Ave W (44906-2799)
PHONE.............................419 529-3211
William F Joyce, *Pr*
Brian M Joyce, *
EMP: 37 EST: 1957
SQ FT: 32,000
SALES (est): 9.81MM **Privately Held**
Web: www.mansfieldbuickgmc.com
SIC: 5511 7532 Automobiles, new and used; Body shop, automotive

(G-12111)
LAKE ERIE ELECTRIC INC
Also Called: Charnan Div
539 Home Rd N (44906-2325)
P.O. Box 2539 (44906-0539)
PHONE.............................419 529-4611
Larry Mooney, *Mgr*
EMP: 107
SALES (corp-wide): 111.7MM **Privately Held**
Web: www.lakeerieelectric.com
SIC: 1731 General electrical contractor
PA: Lake Erie Electric, Inc.
25730 1st St
Westlake OH 44145
440 835-5565

(G-12112)
LIFETOUCH NAT SCHL STUDIOS INC
Also Called: Lifetouch
2291 W 4th St (44906-1261)
PHONE.............................423 892-3817
David Crum, *Brnch Mgr*
EMP: 37
SALES (corp-wide): 2.47B **Privately Held**
Web: www.lifetouch.com
SIC: 7221 Photographer, still or video
HQ: Lifetouch National School Studios Inc.
11000 Viking Dr Ste 300
Eden Prairie MN 55344
952 826-4000

(G-12113)
LOWES HOME CENTERS LLC
Also Called: Lowe's
940 N Lexington Springmill Rd (44906-1119)
PHONE.............................419 747-1920
Dan Messord, *Mgr*
EMP: 143
SALES (corp-wide): 86.38B **Publicly Held**
Web: www.lowes.com
SIC: 5211 5031 5722 5064 Home centers; Building materials, exterior; Household appliance stores; Electrical appliances, television and radio
HQ: Lowe's Home Centers, Llc
1000 Lowes Blvd
Mooresville NC 28117
336 658-4000

(G-12114)
MANSFIELD WHSNG & DIST INC (HQ)
Also Called: Mansfield Express
222 Tappan Dr N (44906-1333)
P.O. Box 2685 (44906-0685)
PHONE.............................419 522-3510
Stuart Lichter, *Ch Bd*
Brian Glowaski, *
EMP: 130 EST: 1992
SQ FT: 1,500,000
SALES (est): 11.72MM
SALES (corp-wide): 24.64MM **Privately Held**
Web: www.mwdlogistics.com
SIC: 4225 4213 General warehousing; Trucking, except local
PA: Mwd Logistics, Inc.
222 Tappan Dr N
Ontario OH 44906
419 522-3510

(G-12115)
MARCO PHOTO SERVICE INC
1655 Nussbaum Pkwy (44906-2300)
PHONE.............................419 529-9010
Rick Casey, *Pr*
EMP: 75 EST: 1965
SQ FT: 45,000
SALES (est): 9.25MM **Privately Held**
Web: www.marcophotoservice.com
SIC: 7384 Photofinishing laboratory

(G-12116)
MAXIM HEALTHCARE SERVICES INC
Also Called: Mansfield Homecare & Staffing
2293 Village Park Ct (44906-1167)
PHONE.............................419 747-8040
Scott Thompson, *Brnch Mgr*
EMP: 153
Web: www.maximhealthcare.com
SIC: 8082 Home health care services
PA: Maxim Healthcare Services, Inc.
7227 Lee Deforest Dr
Columbia MD 21046

(G-12117)
MEDCENTRAL HEALTH SYSTEM
Also Called: Medcentral Hlth Sys Spt Mdcine
1750 W 4th St Ste 1 (44906-1796)
PHONE.............................419 526-8900
Brian Brickner, *Dir*
EMP: 258
SALES (corp-wide): 4.29B **Privately Held**
Web: www.medcentral.org
SIC: 8062 8011 General medical and surgical hospitals; Occupational and industrial specialist, physician/surgeon
HQ: Medcentral Health System
335 Glessner Ave
Mansfield OH 44903
419 526-8000

(G-12118)
OHIO AUTO LOAN SERVICES INC
Also Called: Ohio Auto Loan Services
695 N Lexington Springmill Rd (44906-1224)
PHONE.............................419 982-8013
EMP: 37
SIC: 6141 Automobile loans, including insurance
HQ: Ohio Auto Loan Services, Inc.
8601 Dunwoody Pl Ste 406
Atlanta GA 30350
770 552-9840

(G-12119)
OHIO DST 5 AREA AGCY ON AGING
2131 Park Ave W (44906-1226)
PHONE.............................419 522-5612
James Hairston, *COO*
Duana Patton, *CEO*
EMP: 123 EST: 1989
SALES (est): 37.93MM **Privately Held**
Web: www.aaa5ohio.org
SIC: 8322 Senior citizens' center or association

(G-12120)
ONTARIO LOCAL SCHOOL DISTRICT
Also Called: Transportation Department
3644 Pearl St (44906-1066)
PHONE.............................419 529-3814
Pat Duffner, *Dir*
EMP: 33
Web: www.ontarioschools.org
SIC: 4151 School buses
PA: Ontario Local School District
457 Shelby Ontario Rd
Ontario OH 44906

(G-12121)
ONTARIO MECHANICAL LLC
2880 Park Ave W (44906-1026)
PHONE.............................419 529-2578
EMP: 30 EST: 2012
SALES (est): 4.2MM **Privately Held**
Web: www.ontariomechanical.com
SIC: 1761 1791 1711 Sheet metal work, nec; Structural steel erection; Mechanical contractor

(G-12122)
P R MACHINE WORKS INC
1825 Nussbaum Pkwy (44906-2360)
PHONE.............................419 529-5748
Mark Romanchuk, *Pr*
Mark J Romanchuk, *
▲ **EMP:** 75 EST: 1964
SQ FT: 14,100
SALES (est): 9.18MM **Privately Held**
Web: www.prmachineworks.com
SIC: 3599 1531 Machine shop, jobbing and repair

(G-12123)
PREMIER HOTELS INC
Also Called: Country Suites By Carlson
2069 Walker Lake Rd (44906-1423)
PHONE.............................419 747-2227
Karen Alworth, *Prin*
EMP: 30 EST: 2008
SALES (est): 435.39K **Privately Held**
Web: www.radissonhotels.com
SIC: 7011 Hotels and motels

(G-12124)
SOUTHERN CARE INC
2291 W 4th St Ste G (44906-1261)
PHONE.............................419 774-0555
Michael Pardy, *Brnch Mgr*
EMP: 62
Web: www.gentivahs.com
SIC: 8052 Personal care facility
PA: Southern Care, Inc
1000 Urban Center Dr # 115
Vestavia AL 35242

(G-12125)
STARTEK INC
850 W 4th St (44906-2534)
PHONE.............................419 528-7801
Brenda Young, *Brnch Mgr*
EMP: 66
SALES (corp-wide): 385.07MM **Privately Held**
Web: www.startek.com
SIC: 7389 Telemarketing services
HQ: Startek, Inc.
6200 S Syracuse Way # 485
Greenwood Village CO 80111
303 262-4500

(G-12126)
UNIVERSAL ENTERPRISES INC (PA)
Also Called: Universal Refrigeration Div
545 Beer Rd (44906-1214)
PHONE.............................419 529-3500
George Reece, *Pr*
Ralph Ridenour, *
Linda Ritchie, *
Rob Ridenour, *
Todd Kiger, *
EMP: 180 EST: 1952
SALES (est): 25.25MM
SALES (corp-wide): 25.25MM **Privately Held**
Web: www.ueinc.us
SIC: 1711 7374 Warm air heating and air conditioning contractor; Computer graphics service

(G-12127)
ZARA CONSTRUCTION INC
3240 Park Ave W (44906-1052)
PHONE.............................419 525-3613
Joseph Zara, *Pr*
EMP: 28 EST: 1993
SALES (est): 4.92MM **Privately Held**
Web: www.zaraconstructioninc.com
SIC: 1522 Remodeling, multi-family dwellings

Oregon
Lucas County

(G-12128)
BAY AREA CREDIT UNION INC
4202 Navarre Ave (43616-3585)
PHONE.............................419 698-2962
Jennifer Ferguson, *Pr*
Anna Balmert, *VP*
EMP: 48 EST: 1934
SALES (est): 3.65MM **Privately Held**
Web: www.bayareacu.com
SIC: 6061 Federal credit unions

(G-12129)
BAY PARK COMMUNITY HOSPITAL
Also Called: Promedica Bay Park Hospital
2801 Bay Park Dr (43616-4920)
PHONE.............................419 690-7900
Arturo Polizzi, *Genl Mgr*
EMP: 48
SALES (corp-wide): 187.07MM **Privately Held**
Web: www.promedica.org
SIC: 8062 General medical and surgical hospitals
HQ: Bay Park Community Hospital
100 Madison Ave
Toledo OH 43604
567 585-9600

(G-12130)
BUCKEYE PIPE LINE SERVICES CO
3321 York St (43616-1215)
P.O. Box 167567 (43616-7567)

PHONE.....................419 698-8770
Bob Mcdowel, *Mgr*
EMP: 392
SALES (corp-wide): 4.9B **Privately Held**
Web: www.buckeye.com
SIC: 4612 Crude petroleum pipelines
HQ: Buckeye Pipe Line Services Company
  6161 Hamilton Blvd
  Allentown PA 18106
  484 232-4000

(G-12131)
C & W TANK CLEANING COMPANY
50 N Lallendorf Rd (43616-1847)
PHONE.....................419 691-1995
James C Parker, *Pr*
EMP: 65 **EST:** 1979
SQ FT: 6,000
SALES (est): 5.17MM **Privately Held**
Web: www.cwtank.com
SIC: 8748 Environmental consultant

(G-12132)
DESOTO DIALYSIS LLC
Also Called: Lucas County Home Training
2702 Navarre Ave Ste 203 (43616-3224)
PHONE.....................419 691-1514
EMP: 27 **EST:** 2007
SALES (est): 4.63MM **Publicly Held**
SIC: 8092 Kidney dialysis centers
PA: Davita Inc.
  2000 16th St
  Denver CO 80202

(G-12133)
ESWAGNER COMPANY INC
Also Called: Esw
840 Patchen Rd (43616-3132)
PHONE.....................419 691-8651
Lewis John Wagner, *CEO*
Phyllis J Wagner, *
John C Wagner, *
EMP: 60 **EST:** 1949
SQ FT: 8,500
SALES (est): 28.21MM **Privately Held**
Web: www.eswagner.com
SIC: 1794 1622 1611 1623 Excavation and grading, building construction; Bridge construction; Concrete construction: roads, highways, sidewalks, etc.; Sewer line construction

(G-12134)
GREAT EASTERN THEATRE COMPANY
4500 Navarre Ave (43616-3520)
PHONE.....................419 691-9668
Kevin Christy, *Brnch Mgr*
EMP: 73
SALES (corp-wide): 3.04MM **Privately Held**
Web: www.paramountcinemafremont.com
SIC: 7832 Motion picture theaters, except drive-in
PA: Great Eastern Theatre Company
  3361 Executive Pkwy # 300
  Toledo OH 43606
  419 537-9682

(G-12135)
LITTLE SSTERS OF POOR BLTMORE
Also Called: Scared Heart Nursing Home
860 Ansonia St Ste 13d (43616-3100)
PHONE.....................419 698-4331
Mother Contance, *Admn*
EMP: 92
SALES (corp-wide): 3.97MM **Privately Held**
Web: www.littlesistersofthepoorbaltimore.org

SIC: 8051 Skilled nursing care facilities
PA: Little Sisters Of The Poor, Baltimore, Inc.
  601 Maiden Choice Ln
  Baltimore MD 21228
  410 744-9367

(G-12136)
MERCY HLTH - ST CHRLES HOSP LL
2600 Navarre Ave (43616-3207)
PHONE.....................419 696-7200
Jeffrey Dempseyn, *CEO*
Jacalyn Liebowitz, *
F J Gallagher, *
Joseph W Rossler, *
Rolf H Scheidel, *
EMP: 1200 **EST:** 1953
SQ FT: 515,000
SALES (est): 133.54MM
SALES (corp-wide): 6.92B **Privately Held**
Web: www.mercy.com
SIC: 8062 General medical and surgical hospitals
PA: Bon Secours Mercy Health, Inc.
  1701 Mercy Health Pl
  Cincinnati OH 45237
  513 956-3729

(G-12137)
NORTHTOWNE SQUARE LTD PARTNR
Also Called: Comfort Inn
2930 Navarre Ave (43616-3373)
PHONE.....................419 691-8911
Karen Magnone, *Mgr*
Darrell Ducat, *Genl Pt*
EMP: 35 **EST:** 1983
SQ FT: 36,000
SALES (est): 794.39K **Privately Held**
Web: www.choicehotels.com
SIC: 7011 Hotels and motels

(G-12138)
OPTIVUE INC
Also Called: Ohio Vision of Toledo Inc Opt
2740 Narvar Ave (43616-3216)
PHONE.....................419 891-1391
William Martin, *Prin*
Mary Martin, *Pr*
Connie Richards, *Sec*
EMP: 38 **EST:** 2002
SALES (est): 6.82MM **Privately Held**
Web: www.midwesteyeconsultants.com
SIC: 8011 8042 Opthalmologist; Specialized optometrists

(G-12139)
ORCHARD VILLA INC
2841 Munding Dr (43616-3290)
PHONE.....................419 697-4100
EMP: 82 **EST:** 1996
SALES (est): 10.54MM **Privately Held**
Web: www.lhshealth.com
SIC: 8059 8052 8051 Nursing home, except skilled and intermediate care facility; Intermediate care facilities; Skilled nursing care facilities

(G-12140)
OREGON CLINIC INC
3841 Navarre Ave (43616-3472)
PHONE.....................419 691-8132
Riaz N Chaudhary Md, *Pr*
EMP: 66 **EST:** 1974
SQ FT: 16,000
SALES (est): 2.28MM **Privately Held**
Web: www.oregonclinic.com
SIC: 8011 General and family practice, physician/surgeon

(G-12141)
OTTIVUE (PA)
Also Called: Optio-Vision By Kahn & Diehl
2740 Navarre Ave (43616-3216)
PHONE.....................419 693-4444
Connie Richards, *CEO*
EMP: 70 **EST:** 1955
SALES (est): 4.99MM
SALES (corp-wide): 4.99MM **Privately Held**
SIC: 8042 Specialized optometrists

(G-12142)
PROMEDICA HEALTH SYSTEMS INC
Also Called: PROMEDICA HEALTH SYSTEMS, INC.
2801 Bay Park Dr (43616-4920)
PHONE.....................419 690-7700
EMP: 94
SALES (corp-wide): 187.07MM **Privately Held**
Web: www.promedica.org
SIC: 8062 General medical and surgical hospitals
PA: Promedica Health System, Inc.
  100 Madison Ave
  Toledo OH 43604
  567 585-9600

(G-12143)
TOLEDO CLINIC CANCER CENTERS
2751 Bay Park Dr Ste 206 (43616-4922)
PHONE.....................419 691-4235
EMP: 63
SALES (corp-wide): 278.69K **Privately Held**
Web: www.toledoclinic.com
SIC: 8099 Childbirth preparation clinic
PA: Toledo Clinic Cancer Centers
  4126 N Hlland Sylvania Rd
  Toledo OH 43623
  419 479-5605

(G-12144)
TOLEDO REFINING COMPANY LLC (DH)
1819 Woodville Rd (43616-3159)
PHONE.....................419 698-6600
EMP: 27 **EST:** 2010
SALES (est): 178.36MM
SALES (corp-wide): 38.32B **Publicly Held**
Web: www.pbfenergy.com
SIC: 1629 Oil refinery construction
HQ: Pbf Holding Company Llc
  1 Sylvan Way Ste 2
  Parsippany NJ 07054

(G-12145)
TOWNEPLACE MANAGEMENT LLC
Also Called: Marriott
2851 Navarre Ave (43616-3303)
PHONE.....................419 724-0044
EMP: 58
SALES (corp-wide): 23.71B **Publicly Held**
Web: www.marriott.com
SIC: 7011 Hotels and motels
HQ: Towneplace Management, Llc
  10400 Fernwood Rd
  Bethesda MD 20817

(G-12146)
US HOTEL OSP VENTURES LLC
Also Called: Maumee Bay Ldge Conference Ctr
1750 State Park Rd Ste 2 (43616-5800)
PHONE.....................419 836-9009
EMP: 29
SALES (corp-wide): 5.81MM **Privately Held**
SIC: 7011 Resort hotel
PA: U.S. Hotel Osp Ventures, Llc

3200 W Maple St Ste 2001
Sioux Falls SD 57107
605 334-2371

(G-12147)
WALLEYE POWER LLC
4701 Bay Shore Rd (43616-1038)
PHONE.....................567 298-7400
Joanne Piasecki, *
EMP: 62 **EST:** 2017
SALES (est): 49MM **Privately Held**
SIC: 4911 Fossil fuel electric power generation

(G-12148)
YOUNG MNS CHRSTN ASSN OF GRTER
Also Called: Eastern Community YMCA
2960 Pickle Rd (43616-4051)
PHONE.....................419 691-3523
EMP: 231
SALES (corp-wide): 29.37MM **Privately Held**
Web: www.ymcatoledo.org
SIC: 8641 7991 8351 7032 Youth organizations; Physical fitness facilities; Child day care services; Youth camps
PA: The Young Men's Christian Association Of Greater Toledo
  6465 Sylvania Ave
  Sylvania OH 43560
  419 729-8135

Oregonia
Warren County

(G-12149)
BUTTERFIELD RECOVERY GROUP LLC
Also Called: Cedar Oaks Wellness Center
5778 State Route 350 (45054-9760)
PHONE.....................513 932-4673
Ted Paarlberg, *Managing Member*
EMP: 30 **EST:** 2019
SALES (est): 1.5MM **Privately Held**
Web: www.cedaroakswellness.com
SIC: 8361 Rehabilitation center, residential: health care incidental

(G-12150)
YOUNG MNS CHRSTN ASSN GRTER DY
Also Called: Dayton YMCA Camp Kern
5291 State Route 350 (45054-9746)
PHONE.....................513 932-3756
C Addison, *Ex Dir*
EMP: 211
SALES (corp-wide): 36.75MM **Privately Held**
Web: www.campkern.org
SIC: 8641 7032 Youth organizations; Summer camp, except day and sports instructional
PA: Young Men's Christian Association Of Greater Dayton
  118 W 1st St Ste 300
  Dayton OH 45402
  937 223-5201

Orient
Pickaway County

(G-12151)
EITEL TOWING SERVICE INC
Also Called: Eitels Amrcas Towing Trnsp Svc
7111 Stahl Rd (43146-9601)
PHONE.....................614 877-4139

Stacy L Wills, *Pr*
EMP: 30 **EST:** 1961
SQ FT: 10,000
SALES (est): 4.64MM **Privately Held**
Web: www.eitelstowing.com
SIC: 7549 Towing service, automotive

(G-12152)
OHIO DEPARTMENT REHABILITAT
11271 State Route 762 (43146-9005)
PHONE.................................614 877-4516
Steve Bowers, *Mgr*
EMP: 50 **EST:** 2012
SALES (est): 5.65MM **Privately Held**
Web: www.ohio.gov
SIC: 8322 Rehabilitation services

(G-12153)
PEAK PERFORMANCE SOLUTIONS INC
10639 Welch Rd (43146-9050)
PHONE.................................614 344-4640
Steve R Isaac, *CEO*
EMP: 31 **EST:** 2005
SQ FT: 8,000
SALES (est): 4.27MM **Privately Held**
Web: www.ebix.com
SIC: 6311 Life insurance

(G-12154)
PICKAWAY GROWERS LLC
Also Called: Green Legacy
12061 Federal Rd (43146-9052)
PHONE.................................614 344-4956
Daniel Vanwingerden, *CEO*
EMP: 35 **EST:** 2020
SALES (est): 3.69MM **Privately Held**
SIC: 5193 5992 Flowers and florists supplies; Flowers, fresh

Orrville
Wayne County

(G-12155)
ANIMAL SUPPLY COMPANY LLC
Also Called: ASC- Orrville
1630 Commerce Dr (44667-2509)
PHONE.................................330 642-6037
Maryann Toney, *Mgr*
EMP: 37
SALES (corp-wide): 397.81MM **Privately Held**
Web: www.animalsupply.com
SIC: 5099 Firearms and ammunition, except sporting
PA: Animal Supply Company, Llc
2403 E Interstate Hwy 30
Grand Prairie TX 75050
972 616-9600

(G-12156)
ASPIRE ENERGY OF OHIO LLC (HQ)
300 Tracy Bridge Rd (44667-9384)
PHONE.................................330 682-7726
Tony Kovacevich, *Pr*
Ralph Knoll, *
EMP: 39 **EST:** 1997
SQ FT: 11,446
SALES (est): 19.99MM
SALES (corp-wide): 670.6MM **Publicly Held**
Web: www.aspireenergyco.com
SIC: 4923 Gas transmission and distribution
PA: Chesapeake Utilities Corporation
500 Energy Ln
Dover DE 19901
302 734-6799

(G-12157)
AULTMAN HEALTH FOUNDATION
832 S Main St (44667-2208)
PHONE.................................330 682-3010
EMP: 1772
SALES (corp-wide): 77.49MM **Privately Held**
Web: www.aultman.org
SIC: 8062 General medical and surgical hospitals
PA: Aultman Health Foundation
2600 6th St Sw
Canton OH 44710
330 452-9911

(G-12158)
CHEMSPEC USA INC
9287 Smucker Rd (44667-9795)
PHONE.................................330 669-8512
▲ **EMP:** 54 **EST:** 1975
SALES (est): 27.83MM
SALES (corp-wide): 5.18B **Publicly Held**
SIC: 2819 2851 2891 5013 Catalysts, chemical; Lacquer: bases, dopes, thinner; Adhesives; Motor vehicle supplies and new parts
PA: Axalta Coating Systems Ltd.
50 Applied Bnk Blvd Ste 3
Glen Mills PA 19342
855 547-1461

(G-12159)
CULINARY METZ MANAGEMENT LLC
1 Strawberry Ln (44667-1241)
PHONE.................................330 684-3368
A J Lafland, *Bmch Mgr*
EMP: 136
Web: www.metzculinary.com
SIC: 7389 Brokers' services
PA: Culinary Metz Management Llc
2 Woodland Dr
Dallas PA 18612

(G-12160)
D + S DISTRIBUTION INC
425 Collins Blvd (44667-9752)
PHONE.................................330 804-5590
EMP: 88
SALES (corp-wide): 24.36MM **Privately Held**
Web: www.dsdistribution.com
SIC: 7538 General automotive repair shops
PA: D + S Distribution, Inc.
3500 Old Airport Rd
Wooster OH 44691
800 752-5993

(G-12161)
D + S DISTRIBUTION INC
Also Called: D S Dstrbution Inc Smith Foods
175 Allen Ave (44667-9021)
PHONE.................................800 752-5993
EMP: 88
SALES (corp-wide): 24.36MM **Privately Held**
Web: www.dsdistribution.com
SIC: 4225 General warehousing and storage
PA: D + S Distribution, Inc.
3500 Old Airport Rd
Wooster OH 44691
800 752-5993

(G-12162)
DECO-CRETE SUPPLY INC
133 N Kohler Rd (44667-9632)
PHONE.................................330 682-5678
Jason Geiser, *Prin*
EMP: 50 **EST:** 2009
SALES (est): 5.8MM **Privately Held**
Web: www.deco-cretesupply.com
SIC: 1771 Concrete work

(G-12163)
DUNLAP FMLY PHYSCANS INC PROF (PA)
830 S Main St Ste Rear (44667-2218)
PHONE.................................330 684-2015
Larry Sander, *Pr*
EMP: 31 **EST:** 1980
SALES (est): 2.43MM
SALES (corp-wide): 2.43MM **Privately Held**
Web: www.aultmandocs.com
SIC: 8011 General and family practice, physician/surgeon

(G-12164)
E&H HARDWARE GROUP LLC
Also Called: Ace Hardware
1400 W High St (44667-1444)
PHONE.................................330 683-2060
EMP: 250
SALES (corp-wide): 22.61MM **Privately Held**
Web: www.acehardware.com
SIC: 5072 5251 Hardware; Hardware stores
PA: E&H Hardware Group, Llc
115 S Market St
Wooster OH 44691
330 465-0017

(G-12165)
GG OHIO INC
Also Called: Amtrac Railroad Contrs Ohio
11842 Lincoln Way E (44667-9597)
PHONE.................................330 683-7206
Rickey J Geib, *Pr*
Lynn Lawson, *
Brian L Lawson, *
Mary A Shank, *
EMP: 55 **EST:** 1969
SQ FT: 10,000
SALES (est): 10.99MM **Privately Held**
Web: www.amtracohio.com
SIC: 1629 Railroad and railway roadbed construction

(G-12166)
IMHOFF CONSTRUCTION SVCS INC
Also Called: Imhoff Construction
315 E Market St (44667-1805)
PHONE.................................330 683-4498
Scott Imhoff, *Pr*
Lisle Liston, *
Tom Miller, *Stockholder**
EMP: 40 **EST:** 1985
SQ FT: 9,000
SALES (est): 6.83MM **Privately Held**
Web: www.imhoffinc.com
SIC: 1542 1541 Institutional building construction; Industrial buildings, new construction, nec

(G-12167)
JARRETT COMPANIES INC
Also Called: Jarrett Warehousing
1781 N Main St (44667-9172)
PHONE.................................330 682-0099
Mike Jarrett, *CEO*
EMP: 50 **EST:** 2004
SALES (est): 1.71MM **Privately Held**
Web: www.jarrettcareers.com
SIC: 7361 Employment agencies

(G-12168)
JARRETT LOGISTICS SYSTEMS INC
1347 N Main St (44667-9761)
PHONE.................................330 682-0099
Michael Jarrett, *Pr*
Matt Angell, *
EMP: 150 **EST:** 2004
SQ FT: 73,000
SALES (est): 47.69MM **Privately Held**
Web: www.gojarrett.com
SIC: 8742 4731 Transportation consultant; Freight transportation arrangement

(G-12169)
JM SMUCKER LLC (HQ)
1 Strawberry Ln (44667-1298)
PHONE.................................330 682-3000
Mark T Smucker, *CEO*
EMP: 51 **EST:** 2002
SALES (est): 753.48MM
SALES (corp-wide): 8.53B **Publicly Held**
Web: www.smuckers.com
SIC: 5149 2047 Specialty food items; Dog food
PA: The J M Smucker Company
1 Strawberry Ln
Orrville OH 44667
330 682-3000

(G-12170)
MENNONITE MUTUAL INSURANCE CO
1000 S Main St (44667-2254)
P.O. Box 300 (44667-0300)
PHONE.................................330 682-2986
David L Lehman, *Pr*
EMP: 70 **EST:** 1895
SQ FT: 6,400
SALES (est): 5MM **Privately Held**
Web: www.mennonitemutual.com
SIC: 6411 Insurance agents, nec

(G-12171)
NATIONAL BANCSHARES CORPORATION
112 W Market St (44667-1847)
PHONE.................................330 682-1010
EMP: 113
Web: www.farmersbankgroup.com
SIC: 6021 National commercial banks

(G-12172)
ORRVILLE TRUCKING & GRADING CO (PA)
475 Orr St (44667-9764)
P.O. Box 220 (44667-0220)
PHONE.................................330 682-4010
Auvil Richmond, *Pr*
John H Wilson, *
EMP: 50 **EST:** 1953
SQ FT: 15,000
SALES (est): 7.15MM
SALES (corp-wide): 7.15MM **Privately Held**
Web: www.orrvilletrucking.com
SIC: 3273 3272 5031 Ready-mixed concrete; Concrete products, nec; Building materials, exterior

(G-12173)
SOUTHWOOD PALLET LLC ◆
8849 Lincoln Way E (44667-9335)
PHONE.................................330 682-3747
EMP: 65 **EST:** 2022
SALES (est): 2.79MM **Privately Held**
SIC: 2448 7389 Wood pallets and skids; Log and lumber broker

(G-12174)
VENTRAC
500 Venture Dr (44667-2508)
P.O. Box 148 (44667-0148)
PHONE.................................330 682-0159
EMP: 80 **EST:** 2015
SALES (est): 6.84MM **Privately Held**
Web: www.ventrac.com
SIC: 5046 Commercial equipment, nec

GEOGRAPHIC SECTION
Ottawa - Putnam County (G-12194)

(G-12175)
WHOLESOME PET CO INC
1630 Commerce Dr (44667-2509)
PHONE...............................877 345-7297
Allan Bauman, *Pr*
Rose Bauman, *
EMP: 67 **EST:** 1999
SALES (est): 2.3MM
SALES (corp-wide): 397.81MM **Privately Held**
SIC: 5199 Pet supplies
PA: Animal Supply Company, Llc
2403 E Interstate Hwy 30
Grand Prairie TX 75050
972 616-9600

(G-12176)
WILL-BURT COMPANY (PA)
401 Collins Blvd (44667-9752)
P.O. Box 900 (44667-0900)
PHONE...............................330 682-7015
Richard Lewin, *CEO*
Jeffrey Evans, *
Bruce Inzetta, *
Dan Plumly, *
▲ **EMP:** 105 **EST:** 1918
SALES (est): 62.58MM
SALES (corp-wide): 62.58MM **Privately Held**
Web: www.willburt.com
SIC: 3599 5039 3443 3449 Machine shop, jobbing and repair; Prefabricated structures; Fabricated plate work (boiler shop); Miscellaneous metalwork

Orwell
Ashtabula County

(G-12177)
COUNTRY NEIGHBOR PROGRAM INC (PA)
39 S Maple St (44076-9501)
P.O. Box 212 (44076-0212)
PHONE...............................440 437-6311
Barbara Klingensmith, *Ex Dir*
Lester Marrison, *Pr*
William Enstrom, *Bd of Dir*
Carl Plickert, *Sec*
Kasey Obrien, *Pr*
EMP: 38 **EST:** 1981
SQ FT: 8,000
SALES (est): 3.02MM
SALES (corp-wide): 3.02MM **Privately Held**
Web: www.countryneighbor.org
SIC: 8322 Referral service for personal and social problems

(G-12178)
EAGLE POINTE SKILLED REHAB LLC
87 Staley Rd (44076-8377)
PHONE...............................440 437-7171
Paula Bohlen, *Managing Member*
EMP: 50 **EST:** 2020
SALES (est): 1.61MM **Privately Held**
Web: www.eaglepointerehab.com
SIC: 8051 Convalescent home with continuous nursing care

(G-12179)
ORWELL TIRE SERVICE INC
Also Called: Kauffman Tire Co
431 E Main St (44076-9506)
PHONE...............................440 437-6515
Mark Kauffman, *Pr*
EMP: 72 **EST:** 1992
SQ FT: 20,000
SALES (est): 473.17K

SALES (corp-wide): 1.56B **Privately Held**
SIC: 5531 7538 Automotive tires; General automotive repair shops
HQ: Treadmaxx Tire Distributors, Llc
2832 Anvil Block Rd
Ellenwood GA 30294
404 762-4944

Osgood
Darke County

(G-12180)
DYNAMIC WELD CORPORATION
Also Called: Dynamic Weld
242 N St (45351)
P.O. Box 127 (45351)
PHONE...............................419 582-2900
Harry Heitkamp, *Pr*
Gene Niekamp, *Prin*
Ernie Davenport, *Prin*
Steve Wilker, *Prin*
Sue Heitkamp, *Prin*
EMP: 44 **EST:** 1981
SQ FT: 35,000
SALES (est): 5.97MM **Privately Held**
Web: www.dynamicweld.com
SIC: 3444 7692 Sheet metalwork; Welding repair

(G-12181)
OSGOOD STATE BANK INC (HQ)
275 W Main St (45351-1022)
P.O. Box 69 (45351-0069)
PHONE...............................419 582-2681
Jon Alexander, *Ch*
EMP: 31 **EST:** 1915
SQ FT: 4,500
SALES (est): 17.34MM **Privately Held**
Web: www.osgoodbank.com
SIC: 6022 6163 State trust companies accepting deposits, commercial; Loan brokers
PA: Osb Bancorp, Inc.
275 W Main St
Osgood OH 45351

Ostrander
Delaware County

(G-12182)
MILL CREEK GOLF COURSE CORP
Also Called: Mill Creek Golf Club
7259 Penn Rd (43061-9430)
PHONE...............................740 666-7711
TOLL FREE: 800
Jeanne Bash, *Pr*
Janice E Curtis, *Treas*
Nancy Plant, *Sec*
EMP: 28 **EST:** 1972
SQ FT: 1,700
SALES (est): 433.26K **Privately Held**
Web: www.millcreekgolfclub.com
SIC: 7992 7997 Public golf courses; Golf club, membership

(G-12183)
MILLCREEK GARDENS LLC
15088 Smart Cole Rd (43061-9319)
P.O. Box 130 (43061-0130)
PHONE...............................740 666-7125
Megan Armstrong, *
EMP: 36 **EST:** 1978
SQ FT: 100,000
SALES (est): 11.31MM **Privately Held**
Web: www.millcreekplants.com
SIC: 5193 Nursery stock

(G-12184)
SHELLY MATERIALS INC
8328 Watkins Rd (43061-9311)
PHONE...............................740 666-5841
Keith Siler, *VP*
EMP: 43
SALES (corp-wide): 32.72B **Privately Held**
Web: www.shellyco.com
SIC: 2951 1611 3274 1422 Asphalt and asphaltic paving mixtures (not from refineries); Surfacing and paving; Lime; Crushed and broken limestone
HQ: Shelly Materials, Inc.
80 Park Dr
Thornville OH 43076
740 246-6315

Ottawa
Putnam County

(G-12185)
AUTUMN COURT OPERATING CO LLC
Also Called: AUTUMN COURT
1925 E 4th St (45875-1577)
PHONE...............................419 523-4370
Joseph Hazelbaker, *Prin*
Brian Hazelbaker, *
Ralph Hazelbaker, *
EMP: 51 **EST:** 2020
SALES (est): 2.82MM **Privately Held**
Web: www.autumncourtottawa.com
SIC: 8051 Skilled nursing care facilities

(G-12186)
HUNTINGTON NATIONAL BANK
332 E Main St (45875-1946)
PHONE...............................419 523-6880
Angela Verhoff, *Mgr*
EMP: 36
SALES (corp-wide): 10.84B **Publicly Held**
Web: www.huntington.com
SIC: 6029 6022 Commercial banks, nec; State commercial banks
HQ: The Huntington National Bank
41 S High St
Columbus OH 43215
614 480-4293

(G-12187)
INDUSTRIAL MILLWRIGHT SVCS LLC
1024 Heritage Trl (45875-8521)
PHONE...............................419 523-9147
Duane Greear, *Managing Member*
Lisa Greear, *
EMP: 28 **EST:** 2003
SALES (est): 1.73MM **Privately Held**
Web: www.industrialmillwrightservices.com
SIC: 1796 3449 Millwright; Bars, concrete reinforcing: fabricated steel

(G-12188)
LOVING CARE DAY CARE OTTAWA LL
Also Called: Loving Care Learning Center
360 N Locust St Ste A (45875-1473)
PHONE...............................419 523-3133
EMP: 34 **EST:** 1989
SQ FT: 5,500
SALES (est): 948.14K **Privately Held**
Web: www.lovingcarelearningcenter.com
SIC: 8351 Group day care center

(G-12189)
NELSON MANUFACTURING COMPANY
6448 State Route 224 (45875-9789)
PHONE...............................419 523-5321

Anthony Niese, *Pr*
Chad Stall, *
Amy Niese, *
▼ **EMP:** 80 **EST:** 1947
SQ FT: 46,000
SALES (est): 15MM **Privately Held**
Web: www.nelsontrailers.com
SIC: 3715 7539 Semitrailers for truck tractors; Trailer repair

(G-12190)
NIESE LEASING INC
12465 Road J (45875-9436)
P.O. Box 226 (45875-0226)
PHONE...............................419 523-4400
Kevin J Niese, *Pr*
Gerald Niese, *
EMP: 30 **EST:** 1967
SALES (est): 997.18K **Privately Held**
SIC: 4213 Trucking, except local

(G-12191)
PANDORA MANUFACTURING LLC (PA)
157 W Main St (45875-1721)
PHONE...............................419 384-3241
Dave Roper, *Managing Member*
EMP: 51 **EST:** 1975
SQ FT: 113,000
SALES (est): 2.49MM
SALES (corp-wide): 2.49MM **Privately Held**
Web: www.pandoramanufacturing.com
SIC: 7389 Packaging and labeling services

(G-12192)
PUTNAM CNTY COMMISSIONERS OFF
Also Called: County Garage
304 E 2nd St (45875-1922)
PHONE...............................419 523-6832
Randy Brinkman, *Superintnt*
EMP: 38
Web: co.putnam.oh.us
SIC: 9621 7538 Regulation, administration of transportation, County government; General automotive repair shops
PA: Putnam County Commissioners Office
245 E Main St Ste 101
Ottawa OH 45875
419 523-8700

(G-12193)
PUTNAM CNTY HOMECARE & HOSPICE
575 Ottawa Glandorf Rd Ste 3 (45875)
P.O. Box 312 (45875-0312)
PHONE...............................419 523-4449
Pamela Sager, *Ex Dir*
Jodie Lammers, *
EMP: 63 **EST:** 1966
SALES (est): 1.36MM **Privately Held**
Web: www.pchh.net
SIC: 8082 Home health care services

(G-12194)
PUTNAM COUNTY PUBLIC HLTH DEPT
256 E Williamstown Rd (45875-1870)
PHONE...............................419 523-5608
Kim Rieman, *Health Commissioner*
EMP: 27 **EST:** 2001
SQ FT: 4,000
SALES (est): 442K **Privately Held**
Web: www.putnamhealth.com
SIC: 8099 Physical examination and testing services

(G-12195)
R K INDUSTRIES INC
725 N Locust St (45875-1466)
P.O. Box 306 (45875-0306)
PHONE.................................419 523-5001
Ann Woodyard, *Pr*
Barry Woodyard, *
Joe Maag, *
Kimberly French, *
▲ **EMP:** 85 **EST:** 1983
SQ FT: 45,000
SALES (est): 15.37MM **Privately Held**
Web: www.rkindustries.org
SIC: 7692 3465 Automotive welding; Automotive stampings

(G-12196)
YOUNG MNS CHRSTN ASSN OF AKRON
Also Called: Putnam County Y M C A
101 Putnam Pkwy (45875-8657)
PHONE.................................419 523-5233
Lynn Watchnan, *Mgr*
EMP: 51
SALES (corp-wide): 21.21MM **Privately Held**
Web: www.akronymca.org
SIC: 8641 8351 Recreation association; Child day care services
PA: The Young Men's Christian Association Of Akron Ohio
50 S Mn St Ste Ll100
Akron OH 44308
330 376-1335

Ottawa Hills
Lucas County

(G-12197)
ABDOUNI ENTERPRISES LLC
3945 Hillandale Rd Apt W (43606-7714)
PHONE.................................419 345-6773
EMP: 31
SIC: 8748 Business consulting, nec
PA: Abdouni Enterprises Llc
5153 Main St
Sylvania OH

Ottoville
Putnam County

(G-12198)
MILLER CONTRACTING GROUP INC
Also Called: Miller Construction
17359 State Route 66 (45876)
P.O. Box 162 (45876-0162)
PHONE.................................419 453-3825
Alan J Miller, *Pr*
Patrick Miller, *
EMP: 44 **EST:** 1973
SALES (est): 12.54MM **Privately Held**
Web: www.millercontractinggroup.com
SIC: 1542 1521 Commercial and office building, new construction; Single-family housing construction

Owensville
Clermont County

(G-12199)
CLERMONT CNTY BD DVLPMNTAL DSB
Also Called: Thomas A Wildey School
204 State Rte Hwy 50 Benton Rd (45160)
P.O. Box 8 (45160-0008)
PHONE.................................513 732-7015
Jay Williams, *Prin*
EMP: 47
SALES (corp-wide): 2.02MM **Privately Held**
Web: www.clermontdd.org
SIC: 8322 Individual and family services
PA: Clermont County Board Of Developmental Disabilities
2040 Us Highway 50
Batavia OH 45103
513 732-7000

Oxford
Butler County

(G-12200)
AMOXFORD INC
Also Called: Baymont Inn & Suites
5190 College Corner Pike (45056-1004)
PHONE.................................513 523-2722
Steven Lee, *Pr*
Unhyang Lee, *Treas*
EMP: 64 **EST:** 1997
SALES (est): 512.86K **Privately Held**
Web: www.wyndhamhotels.com
SIC: 7011 Bed and breakfast inn

(G-12201)
BETA THETA PI FRATERNITY (PA)
5134 Bonham Rd (45056-1429)
P.O. Box 6277 (45056-6067)
PHONE.................................513 523-7591
Stephen B Becker, *
EMP: 30 **EST:** 1839
SQ FT: 18,000
SALES (est): 8.94MM
SALES (corp-wide): 8.94MM **Privately Held**
Web: www.beta.org
SIC: 8641 University club

(G-12202)
BUTLER COUNTY OF OHIO
Also Called: Reily Township
6093 Reily Millville Rd (45056-9507)
PHONE.................................513 757-4683
Sue Breen, *Mgr*
EMP: 35
Web: www.bcohio.gov
SIC: 9224 8099 Fire department, volunteer; Medical rescue squad
PA: Butler, County Of Ohio
315 High St Fl 6
Hamilton OH 45011
513 887-3278

(G-12203)
BUTLER RURAL ELECTRIC COOP
3888 Stillwell Beckett Rd (45056-9115)
PHONE.................................513 867-4400
Michael Sims, *Genl Mgr*
Thomas Mc Quiston, *Pr*
Sam Woodruff, *VP*
Mary Beth Dorrel, *Sec*
Michael L Sims, *Prin*
EMP: 38 **EST:** 1936
SQ FT: 27,000
SALES (est): 37.25MM **Privately Held**
Web: www.butlerrural.coop
SIC: 4911 Distribution, electric power

(G-12204)
CAPITOL VARSITY SPORTS INC
6723 Ringwood Rd (45056)
P.O. Box 669 (45056)
PHONE.................................513 523-4126
Bob Fawley, *Pr*
EMP: 37 **EST:** 1954
SQ FT: 22,000
SALES (est): 8.15MM **Privately Held**
Web: www.capitolvarsity.com
SIC: 5941 7699 Specialty sport supplies, nec ; Recreational sporting equipment repair services

(G-12205)
CASH FLOW SOLUTIONS INC
Also Called: Ribbit
5166 College Corner Pike (45056-1004)
PHONE.................................513 524-2320
Kasey Princell, *Ch Bd*
Kasey Princell, *CEO*
Di Princell, *Pr*
EMP: 51 **EST:** 1998
SQ FT: 6,000
SALES (est): 9.37MM **Privately Held**
Web: www.validifi.com
SIC: 8748 7374 Business consulting, nec; Computer processing services

(G-12206)
CVS REVCO DS INC
Also Called: CVS
123 W Spring St (45056-1768)
PHONE.................................513 523-6378
EMP: 75
SALES (corp-wide): 357.78B **Publicly Held**
Web: www.cvs.com
SIC: 5912 7384 Drug stores; Photofinishing laboratory
HQ: Cvs Revco D.S., Inc.
1 Cvs Dr
Woonsocket RI 02895
401 765-1500

(G-12207)
DANIEL COHEN ENTERPRISES INC
152 Stone Creek Dr (45056-9758)
PHONE.................................513 896-4547
Jack Cohen, *Pr*
EMP: 133 **EST:** 1970
SQ FT: 40,000
SALES (est): 393.18K
SALES (corp-wide): 138.63MM **Privately Held**
SIC: 5093 Ferrous metal scrap and waste
PA: Cohen Brothers, Inc.
1520 14th Ave
Middletown OH 45044
513 422-3696

(G-12208)
FIRST TRANSIT INC
203 S Locust St (45056-1759)
PHONE.................................513 524-2877
Carolyn Kelley, *Brnch Mgr*
EMP: 54
SALES (corp-wide): 4.23MM **Privately Held**
Web: www.transdevna.com
SIC: 4111 Local and suburban transit
HQ: First Transit, Inc.
600 Vine St Ste 1400
Cincinnati OH 45202
513 241-2200

(G-12209)
MAPLE KNOLL COMMUNITIES INC
6727 Contreras Rd (45056-8769)
PHONE.................................513 524-7990
Lina Mares, *Ex Dir*
EMP: 189
SALES (corp-wide): 46.12MM **Privately Held**
Web: www.mkcommunities.org
SIC: 8051 8361 Convalescent home with continuous nursing care; Residential care
PA: Knoll Maple Communities Inc
11100 Springfield Pike
Cincinnati OH 45246
513 782-2400

(G-12210)
MCCULLOUGH-HYDE MEM HOSP INC (PA)
110 N Poplar St (45056-1204)
PHONE.................................513 523-2111
Richard Norman, *Ch*
Bryan D Hehemann, *
Chris Lauer, *
Alan D Oak, *
EMP: 446 **EST:** 1957
SQ FT: 115,000
SALES (est): 52.1MM
SALES (corp-wide): 52.1MM **Privately Held**
Web: www.trihealth.com
SIC: 8062 General medical and surgical hospitals

(G-12211)
MIAMI UNIVERSITY
Also Called: Marcum Conference Center
Fisher Dr (45056)
PHONE.................................513 529-6911
Cornch Waite, *Mgr*
EMP: 107
SALES (corp-wide): 394.64MM **Privately Held**
Web: www.miamioh.edu
SIC: 8221 7389 University; Convention and show services
PA: Miami University
501 E High St
Oxford OH 45056
513 529-1809

(G-12212)
MIAMI UNIVERSITY
Also Called: Office of Divisional Support
725 E Chestnut St (45056-3450)
PHONE.................................513 529-1230
EMP: 56
SQ FT: 2,001
SALES (corp-wide): 394.64MM **Privately Held**
Web: www.miamioh.edu
SIC: 7389 8221 Fund raising organizations; University
PA: Miami University
501 E High St
Oxford OH 45056
513 529-1809

(G-12213)
MINI UNIVERSITY INC
401 Western College Dr (45056-1902)
PHONE.................................513 275-5184
Ruth Williamson, *Dir*
EMP: 70
SALES (corp-wide): 5.16MM **Privately Held**
Web: www.miniuniversity.net
SIC: 8351 Preschool center
PA: Mini University, Inc.
115 Harbert Dr Ste A
Dayton OH 45440
937 426-1414

(G-12214)
OXFORD HOSPITALITY GROUP INC
Also Called: Comfort Inn
5056 College Corner Pike (45056-1103)
PHONE.................................513 524-0114
Dennis Day, *Pr*
EMP: 47 **EST:** 1996
SALES (est): 550.17K **Privately Held**
Web: www.choicehotels.com
SIC: 7011 Hotels and motels

GEOGRAPHIC SECTION

Painesville - Lake County (G-12235)

(G-12215)
OXFORD MOTEL & LP
Also Called: Best Western Sycamore Inn
6 E Sycamore St (45056-1212)
PHONE.................513 523-0000
James Wespiser, *Pt*
Joseph Wespiser, *Admn*
Richard Wespiser, *Admn*
EMP: 34 **EST:** 1991
SALES (est): 486.32K **Privately Held**
Web: www.bestwestern.com
SIC: 7011 Hotel, franchised

(G-12216)
RDI CORPORATION
110 S Locust St Ste A (45056-1751)
PHONE.................513 524-3320
George Trebbi, *Pr*
EMP: 74
SALES (corp-wide): 52.44MM **Privately Held**
Web: www.rdi-connect.com
SIC: 7389 Telemarketing services
PA: The Rdi Corporation
4350 Glndale Mlford Rd St
Cincinnati OH 45242
513 984-5927

(G-12217)
SCHNEIDER ELECTRIC USA INC
Also Called: Schneider Electric
5735 College Corner Pike (45056-9715)
PHONE.................513 523-4171
Thomsa Mcdonald, *Brnch Mgr*
EMP: 500
SALES (corp-wide): 82.05K **Privately Held**
Web: www.se.com
SIC: 3699 3677 3612 3357 Electrical equipment and supplies, nec; Electronic coils and transformers; Transformers, except electric; Nonferrous wiredrawing and insulating
HQ: Schneider Electric Usa, Inc.
One Boston Pl Ste 2700
Boston MA 02108
978 975-9600

(G-12218)
TALAWANDA CITY SCHOOL DISTRICT
Also Called: Talawanda H S
5301 University Park Blvd (45056)
PHONE.................513 273-3200
Kelly Spivey, *Superintnt*
EMP: 53
SALES (corp-wide): 48.64MM **Privately Held**
Web: www.talawanda.org
SIC: 8211 8741 Public elementary and secondary schools; Management services
PA: Talawanda City School District
131 W Chestnut St
Oxford OH 45056
513 273-3100

Painesville
Lake County

(G-12219)
ABB ENTERPRISE SOFTWARE INC
Also Called: ABB ENTERPRISE SOFTWARE INC.
29801 Eucland Ave (44077)
PHONE.................440 585-6716
EMP: 41
Web: www.abb.com
SIC: 7389 Contractors' disbursement control
HQ: Abb Inc.
305 Gregson Dr
Cary NC 27511

(G-12220)
ACTIVE PLUMBING SUPPLY CO (PA)
216 Richmond St (44077-3227)
PHONE.................440 352-4411
Chuck Rathburn, *Pr*
EMP: 62 **EST:** 1956
SQ FT: 50,000
SALES (est): 30.57MM
SALES (corp-wide): 30.57MM **Privately Held**
Web: www.activeplumbing.com
SIC: 5074 Plumbing fittings and supplies

(G-12221)
AUTOZONE INC
Also Called: Autozone
1487 Mentor Ave (44077-1801)
PHONE.................440 639-2247
EMP: 28
SALES (corp-wide): 17.46B **Publicly Held**
Web: www.autozonepro.com
SIC: 5531 5045 5734 Automotive parts; Computer software; Software, business and non-game
PA: Autozone, Inc.
123 S Front St
Memphis TN 38103
901 495-6500

(G-12222)
CLASSIC BICK OLDSMBILE CDLIAC
Also Called: Classic Oldsmobile
1700 Mentor Ave (44077-1438)
PHONE.................440 639-4500
Ralph W Wilson, *Pr*
EMP: 46 **EST:** 1987
SQ FT: 35,000
SALES (est): 4.53MM **Privately Held**
Web: www.buick.com
SIC: 5511 7515 Automobiles, new and used; Passenger car leasing

(G-12223)
CONSUMER SUPPORT SERVICES INC
368 Blackbrook Rd Ste 100 (44077-1286)
PHONE.................440 354-7082
EMP: 65
SALES (corp-wide): 29.01MM **Privately Held**
Web: www.cssohio.org
SIC: 8322 Social service center
PA: Consumer Support Services Inc
2040 Cherry Valley Rd # 1
Newark OH 43055
740 788-8257

(G-12224)
COUNTY OF LAKE
Also Called: Lake County Crime Laboratory
235 Fairgrounds Rd (44077-1904)
PHONE.................440 350-2793
Charles Colson, *Admn*
EMP: 29
SALES (corp-wide): 219.71MM **Privately Held**
Web: www.lakecountyohio.gov
SIC: 8734 8071 Forensic laboratory; Medical laboratories
PA: County Of Lake
8 N State St Ste 215
Painesville OH 44077
440 350-2500

(G-12225)
CROSSCOUNTRY MORTGAGE LLC
2709 N Ridge Rd (44077-4805)
PHONE.................440 354-5206
EMP: 56
SALES (corp-wide): 803.24MM **Privately Held**
Web: www.crosscountrymortgage.com
SIC: 6162 Mortgage bankers and loan correspondents
PA: Crosscountry Mortgage, Llc
6850 Miller Rd
Brecksville OH 44141
440 845-3700

(G-12226)
CROSSROAD HEALTH
Also Called: Cross Roads Head Start
1083 Mentor Ave (44077-1829)
PHONE.................440 358-7370
Susan Walsh, *Mgr*
EMP: 150
SALES (corp-wide): 8.28MM **Privately Held**
Web: www.crossroadshealth.org
SIC: 8351 Head Start center, except in conjunction with school
PA: Crossroads Health
8445 Munson Rd
Mentor OH 44060
440 255-1700

(G-12227)
DIZER CORP
1912 Mentor Ave (44077-1325)
PHONE.................440 368-0201
Jagdish Medarametla, *CEO*
EMP: 170 **EST:** 1999
SQ FT: 2,300
SALES (corp-wide): 10.42MM **Privately Held**
Web: www.dizercorp.com
SIC: 7371 8711 Computer software development; Engineering services

(G-12228)
ECUMENCAL SHLTER NTWRK LK CNTY
Also Called: PROJECT HOPE
25 Freedom Rd (44077-1232)
P.O. Box 2035 (44077-7035)
PHONE.................440 354-6417
Judy Hamlett, *Dir*
EMP: 27 **EST:** 1993
SQ FT: 3,050
SALES (est): 1.22MM **Privately Held**
Web: www.projecthopeforthehomeless.org
SIC: 8082 Home health care services

(G-12229)
HOMESTEAD I HLTHCARE GROUP LLC
Also Called: Grand River Health & Rehab Ctr
1515 Brookstone Blvd (44077-3393)
PHONE.................440 226-8869
George S Repchick, *Pr*
William I Weisberg, *
EMP: 126 **EST:** 2012
SALES (est): 5.79MM
SALES (corp-wide): 655.44MM **Privately Held**
Web: www.saberhealth.com
SIC: 8051 Convalescent home with continuous nursing care
PA: Saber Healthcare Group, L.L.C.
23700 Commerce Park
Beachwood OH 44122
216 292-5706

(G-12230)
HOMESTEAD II HLTHCARE GROUP LL
Also Called: Homestead II
60 Wood St (44077-3396)
PHONE.................440 352-0788
George S Repchick, *Pr*
William I Weisberg, *VP*
EMP: 89 **EST:** 2012
SALES (est): 3.5MM
SALES (corp-wide): 655.44MM **Privately Held**
Web: www.saberhealth.com
SIC: 8051 Convalescent home with continuous nursing care
PA: Saber Healthcare Group, L.L.C.
23700 Commerce Park
Beachwood OH 44122
216 292-5706

(G-12231)
LAKE CNTY YUNG MNS CHRSTN ASSN (PA)
933 Mentor Ave Fl 2 (44077-2519)
PHONE.................440 352-3303
Richard Bennett, *CEO*
EMP: 150 **EST:** 1867
SQ FT: 80,000
SALES (est): 13.16MM
SALES (corp-wide): 13.16MM **Privately Held**
Web: www.lakecountyymca.org
SIC: 8641 7991 8351 7032 Youth organizations; Physical fitness facilities; Child day care services; Youth camps

(G-12232)
LAKE HOSPITAL SYS HM HLTH SVCS
9485 (44077)
PHONE.................440 639-0900
Martha Haluszka, *Dir*
EMP: 50 **EST:** 1994
SALES (est): 999.35K **Privately Held**
Web: www.uhhospitals.org
SIC: 8082 Home health care services

(G-12233)
LAKE METROPARKS (PA)
11211 Spear Rd (44077)
P.O. Box 1140 (43215)
PHONE.................440 639-7275
Paul Palagyi, *Ex Dir*
Dennis Eckert, *
Frank Polisga Comsnr, *Prin*
Gretchen Disanto Comsnr, *Prin*
EMP: 223 **EST:** 1958
SQ FT: 25,000
SALES (est): 23.35MM
SALES (corp-wide): 23.35MM **Privately Held**
Web: www.lakemetroparks.com
SIC: 7999 Recreation services

(G-12234)
LAKE-GEAUGA RECOVERY CTRS INC
796 Oak St (44077-4335)
PHONE.................440 354-2848
EMP: 30
SALES (corp-wide): 6.55MM **Privately Held**
Web: www.lgrc.us
SIC: 8093 Substance abuse clinics (outpatient)
PA: Lake-Geauga Recovery Centers, Inc.
9083 Mentor Ave
Mentor OH 44060
440 255-0678

(G-12235)
LAKETRAN
555 Lakeshore Blvd (44077-1121)
P.O. Box 158 (44045-0158)
PHONE.................440 350-1000
Ray Jurkowski, *CEO*
Andrew Alpenweg, *
EMP: 63 **EST:** 1975
SQ FT: 150,000

Painesville - Lake County (G-12236)

SALES (est): 10.03MM **Privately Held**
Web: www.laketran.com
SIC: **4111** Subway operation

(G-12236)
MCNEIL INDUSTRIES INC
835 Richmond Rd Ste 2 (44077-1143)
PHONE..................................440 951-7756
Randall J Mcneil, *Pr*
▲ **EMP: 30 EST:** 1986
SQ FT: 18,000
SALES (est): 5.02MM **Privately Held**
Web: www.mcneilindustries.com
SIC: **3366** 5085 Bushings and bearings; Seals, industrial

(G-12237)
MORTON SALT INC
570 Headlands Rd (44077-1145)
P.O. Box 428 (44045-0428)
PHONE..................................440 354-9901
Paul Shank, *Brnch Mgr*
EMP: 108
SALES (corp-wide): 1.22B **Privately Held**
Web: www.mortonsalt.com
SIC: **5169** Chemicals and allied products, nec
HQ: Morton Salt, Inc.
444 W Lake St Ste 3000
Chicago IL 60606

(G-12238)
MULTI-CARE INC
Also Called: Homestead II
60 Wood St (44077-3332)
PHONE..................................440 352-0788
Morton J Weisburg, *Mgr*
EMP: 175
SALES (corp-wide): 11.18MM **Privately Held**
Web: www.saberhealth.com
SIC: **8051** Convalescent home with continuous nursing care
PA: Multi-Care, Inc.
23700 Commerce Park
Beachwood OH 44122
216 292-5706

(G-12239)
MULTI-CARE INC
Also Called: Homestead 1
1515 Brookstone Blvd (44077-8210)
PHONE..................................440 357-6181
Amy Sanfilippo, *Admn*
EMP: 60
SALES (corp-wide): 11.18MM **Privately Held**
Web: www.saberhealth.com
SIC: **8051** 8059 Skilled nursing care facilities; Nursing home, except skilled and intermediate care facility
PA: Multi-Care, Inc.
23700 Commerce Park
Beachwood OH 44122
216 292-5706

(G-12240)
OMEGASEA LTD LIABILITY CO
Also Called: Omegasea
1000 Bacon Rd (44077-4637)
PHONE..................................440 639-2372
EMP: 50
SIC: **5146** Fish and seafoods

(G-12241)
PERSONACARE OF OHIO INC
Also Called: Kindred Trnstnal Care Rhbltio
70 Normandy Dr (44077-1616)
PHONE..................................440 357-1311
EMP: 150
SALES (corp-wide): 13.68B **Privately Held**
SIC: **8051** Skilled nursing care facilities
HQ: Personacare Of Ohio Inc
1801 Macy Dr
Roswell GA 30076

(G-12242)
R W SIDLEY INCORPORATED (PA)
Also Called: R. W. Sidley
436 Casement Ave (44077-3817)
P.O. Box 150 (44077-0150)
PHONE..................................440 352-9343
Robert C Sidley, *Ch Bd*
Robert J Buescher, *
Dan Kennedy, *
Kevin Campany, *
Iola Black, *
▲ **EMP: 30 EST:** 1933
SQ FT: 10,000
SALES (est): 83.57MM
SALES (corp-wide): 83.57MM **Privately Held**
Web: www.rwsidley.com
SIC: **1771** 3299 Concrete work; Blocks and brick, sand lime

(G-12243)
STAFAST PRODUCTS INC (PA)
Also Called: Stafast West
505 Lakeshore Blvd (44077-1197)
PHONE..................................440 357-5546
Donald S Selle, *Pr*
Joan Selle, *
Stephen Selle, *
Christian Selle, *
Daniel Selle, *
◆ **EMP: 40 EST:** 1958
SQ FT: 20,600
SALES (est): 24.8MM
SALES (corp-wide): 24.8MM **Privately Held**
Web: shop.stafast.com
SIC: **5085** 3452 Fasteners, industrial: nuts, bolts, screws, etc.; Bolts, nuts, rivets, and washers

(G-12244)
YARDMASTER INC (PA)
1447 N Ridge Rd (44077-4494)
PHONE..................................440 357-8400
Kurt Kluznik, *CEO*
Rick Colwell, *
Ed Gallagher, *
EMP: 100 EST: 1978
SQ FT: 6,000
SALES (est): 16.61MM
SALES (corp-wide): 16.61MM **Privately Held**
Web: www.yardmaster.com
SIC: **0782** Landscape contractors

Pandora
Putnam County

(G-12245)
FIRST NATIONAL BANK OF PANDORA (DH)
Also Called: First National Bank
102 E Main St (45877-8706)
P.O. Box 329 (45877-0329)
PHONE..................................419 384-3221
Todd Monson, *Pr*
Jim Downhower, *
EMP: 28 EST: 1919
SQ FT: 10,000
SALES (est): 10.46MM
SALES (corp-wide): 10.46MM **Privately Held**
Web: www.e-fnb.com
SIC: **6021** National commercial banks
HQ: Pandora Bancshares, Incorporated
102 E Main St
Pandora OH 45877
419 384-3221

(G-12246)
HILTY MEMORIAL HOME INC
304 Hilty Dr (45877-9476)
P.O. Box 359 (45877-0359)
PHONE..................................419 384-3218
Laura Both, *CEO*
Jason Cox, *
EMP: 45 EST: 1979
SQ FT: 25,707
SALES (est): 5.43MM **Privately Held**
Web: www.mhcoliving.org
SIC: **8051** 8322 8049 Convalescent home with continuous nursing care; Old age assistance; Physical therapist

Paris
Stark County

(G-12247)
STALLION OILFIELD CNSTR LLC
3361 Baird Ave Se (44669-9769)
PHONE..................................330 868-2083
Chrysta Dansby, *Brnch Mgr*
EMP: 54
Web: www.stallionis.com
SIC: **1389** Oil field services, nec
PA: Stallion Oilfield Construction, Llc
950 Corbindale Rd Ste 400
Houston TX 77024

Parma
Cuyahoga County

(G-12248)
ALL IN STAFFING
5561 Ridge Rd (44129-2372)
PHONE..................................330 315-1530
Matthew Ridler, *Ofcr*
EMP: 40 EST: 2020
SALES (est): 224.28K **Privately Held**
Web: www.all-instaffing.com
SIC: **8742** Management consulting services

(G-12249)
AMERICAN NATIONAL RED CROSS
Also Called: American Nat Red Cross - Blood
5585 Pearl Rd (44129-2544)
PHONE..................................216 303-5476
EMP: 31
SALES (corp-wide): 3.18B **Privately Held**
Web: www.redcross.org
SIC: **8322** Social service center
PA: The American National Red Cross
431 18th St Nw
Washington DC 20006
202 737-8300

(G-12250)
BROADVIEW NURSING HOME INC
Also Called: BROADVIEW MULTI-CARE CENTER
5520 Broadview Rd (44134-1699)
PHONE..................................216 661-5084
Harold Shachter, *Pr*
Mike Flank, *
Erna Laufer, *
EMP: 84 EST: 1964
SQ FT: 68,000
SALES (est): 15.75MM **Privately Held**
Web: www.lhshealth.com
SIC: **8051** Convalescent home with continuous nursing care

(G-12251)
CELLCO PARTNERSHIP
Also Called: Verizon Wireless
7779 Day Dr (44129-5604)
PHONE..................................440 886-5461
Michael Haney, *Brnch Mgr*
EMP: 71
SALES (corp-wide): 133.97B **Publicly Held**
Web: www.verizon.com
SIC: **4812** Cellular telephone services
HQ: Cellco Partnership
1 Verizon Way
Basking Ridge NJ 07920

(G-12252)
CONTINUUM CARE HOME HEALTH LLC
12380 Plaza Dr Ste 103 (44130-1043)
PHONE..................................216 898-8399
Anna Wildner, *Prin*
EMP: 30 EST: 2011
SALES (est): 2.21MM **Privately Held**
Web: www.continuumcarehomehealth.com
SIC: **8052** Personal care facility

(G-12253)
CUYAHOGA COUNTY OF BOARD HLTH
5550 Venture Dr (44130-9315)
PHONE..................................216 201-2000
Terrence Allen, *Commsnr*
Terrence Allen, *Commsnr*
EMP: 142 EST: 2011
SALES (est): 28.34MM **Privately Held**
Web: www.ccbh.net
SIC: **8099** Health and allied services, nec

(G-12254)
GES GRAPHITE INC (PA)
Also Called: G E S
12300 Snow Rd (44130-1001)
PHONE..................................216 658-6660
Keith Kearney, *CEO*
Baker Kearney, *
Hunter Kearney, *
◆ **EMP: 31 EST:** 1985
SQ FT: 100,000
SALES (est): 10.16MM **Privately Held**
Web: www.ges-agm.com
SIC: **5085** 3624 Industrial supplies; Carbon and graphite products

(G-12255)
HUNTINGTON NATIONAL BANK
6690 Ridge Rd (44129-5707)
PHONE..................................440 886-1959
Robert Camp, *Brnch Mgr*
EMP: 31
SALES (corp-wide): 10.84B **Publicly Held**
Web: www.huntington.com
SIC: **6029** Commercial banks, nec
HQ: The Huntington National Bank
41 S High St
Columbus OH 43215
614 480-4293

(G-12256)
METROHEALTH SYSTEM
Also Called: Parma Medical Center
12301 Snow Rd (44130-1002)
PHONE..................................216 524-7377
Akram Boutros, *Prin*
EMP: 142
SALES (corp-wide): 620.72MM **Privately Held**
Web: www.metrohealth.org
SIC: **8011** Medical centers
PA: The Metrohealth System
2500 Metrohealth Dr

GEOGRAPHIC SECTION

Cleveland OH 44109
216 778-7800

(G-12257)
METROPOLITAN POOL SERVICE CO
Also Called: Metropolitan Pools
3427 Brookpark Rd (44134-1298)
PHONE..................................216 741-9451
Todd Whitlock, Pr
Robert Matney, *
EMP: 40 **EST:** 1961
SQ FT: 6,000
SALES (est): 4.31MM **Privately Held**
Web: www.metropools.com
SIC: 1799 5999 5091 7389 Swimming pool construction; Swimming pool chemicals, equipment, and supplies; Swimming pools, equipment and supplies; Swimming pool and hot tub service and maintenance

(G-12258)
NATIONWIDE HEALTH MGT LLC
5700 Chevrolet Blvd (44130-1412)
PHONE..................................440 888-8888
EMP: 75 **EST:** 2005
SALES (est): 2.03MM **Privately Held**
SIC: 8082 Home health care services

(G-12259)
OWNERS MANAGEMENT COMPANY
5555 Powers Blvd (44129-5462)
PHONE..................................440 439-3800
Fred Rzepka, *
Paul T Wilms, *
EMP: 40 **EST:** 1965
SALES (est): 2.54MM **Privately Held**
Web: www.ownerslive.com
SIC: 6513 6531 Apartment building operators ; Real estate agents and managers

(G-12260)
PARMA COMMUNITY GENERAL HOSP (PA)
7007 Powers Blvd (44129-5437)
P.O. Box 73270n (44193-0001)
PHONE..................................440 743-3000
Patricia A Ruflin, Pr
Barry Franklin, *
Susan Laskin, *
EMP: 1667 **EST:** 1956
SQ FT: 415,000
SALES (est): 100.97MM
SALES (corp-wide): 100.97MM **Privately Held**
Web: www.uhhospitals.org
SIC: 8062 General medical and surgical hospitals

(G-12261)
PEARL LEASING CO LLC
Also Called: Greenbrier Healthcare Center
6455 Pearl Rd (44130-2984)
PHONE..................................513 530-1600
Richard Odenthal, CEO
EMP: 50 **EST:** 2004
SALES (est): 2.41MM **Privately Held**
Web: www.communicarehealth.com
SIC: 8051 Skilled nursing care facilities

(G-12262)
PRIDE DLVRY & INSTALLATION LLC
8730 Brookpark Rd (44129-6810)
PHONE..................................216 749-7481
EMP: 60 **EST:** 2019
SALES (est): 4.71MM **Privately Held**
Web: www.pridedandi.com
SIC: 4212 Delivery service, vehicular

(G-12263)
PROGRESSIVE QUALITY CARE INC (PA)
5553 Broadview Rd (44134-1604)
PHONE..................................216 661-6800
Mike Flank, Pr
EMP: 51 **EST:** 2001
SQ FT: 500,000
SALES (est): 35.53MM
SALES (corp-wide): 35.53MM **Privately Held**
Web: www.progressivequalitycare.com
SIC: 7389 Personal service agents, brokers, and bureaus

(G-12264)
RYCON CONSTRUCTION INC
7661 W Ridgewood Dr (44129-5537)
PHONE..................................440 481-3770
EMP: 109
Web: www.ryconinc.com
SIC: 1542 Commercial and office building, new construction
PA: Rycon Construction, Inc.
2501 Smallman St Ste 100
Pittsburgh PA 15222

(G-12265)
ST AUGUSTINE MANOR
Also Called: Holy Family Home and Hospice
6707 State Rd (44134-4517)
PHONE..................................440 888-7722
Kristin Graham, Dir
EMP: 189
SALES (corp-wide): 6.57MM **Privately Held**
Web: www.staugministries.org
SIC: 8082 Home health care services
PA: St Augustine Manor
7801 Detroit Ave
Cleveland OH
216 634-7400

(G-12266)
TRADESOURCE INC
5504 State Rd (44134-2250)
PHONE..................................216 801-4944
EMP: 57
Web: www.tradesource.com
SIC: 7361 Employment agencies
PA: Tradesource, Inc.
205 Hallene Rd Ste 211
Warwick RI 02886

(G-12267)
XPO LOGISTICS FREIGHT INC
12901 Snow Rd (44130-1004)
PHONE..................................216 433-1000
Gene Carson, Brnch Mgr
EMP: 88
SALES (corp-wide): 7.74B **Publicly Held**
Web: www.xpo.com
SIC: 4213 4212 Contract haulers; Local trucking, without storage
HQ: Xpo Logistics Freight, Inc.
2211 Old Erhart Rd Ste 10
Ann Arbor MI 48105
800 755-2728

(G-12268)
Y & E ENTERTAINMENT GROUP LLC
Also Called: Make Believe
8303 Day Dr (44129-5610)
PHONE..................................440 385-5500
Yuri Abramovich, Managing Member
Elena Abramovich, *
EMP: 47 **EST:** 2016
SQ FT: 23,000
SALES (est): 1.06MM **Privately Held**
Web: www.makebelieveparma.com

SIC: 7929 Entertainment service

Pataskala
Licking County

(G-12269)
ALLEN REFRACTORIES COMPANY
131 Shackelford Rd (43062-9106)
PHONE..................................740 927-8000
James A Shackelford, CEO
James A Shackelford, Pr
Margaret O'connor Shackelford, Ex VP
James Gibson, *
EMP: 245 **EST:** 1970
SQ FT: 32,000
SALES (est): 38.36MM **Privately Held**
Web: www.allenrefractories.com
SIC: 1741 5085 Refractory or acid brick masonry; Refractory material

(G-12270)
CONTRACT LUMBER INC (PA)
3245 Hazelton Etna Rd Sw (43062-8532)
PHONE..................................740 964-3147
Harold T Bieser, Ch
Richard Hiegel, *
James Holloway, *
EMP: 150 **EST:** 1989
SQ FT: 35,000
SALES (est): 72.48MM
SALES (corp-wide): 72.48MM **Privately Held**
Web: www.contractlumber.com
SIC: 1761 5211 1751 Roofing contractor; Lumber and other building materials; Framing contractor

(G-12271)
COUGHLIN CHEVROLET INC (PA)
Also Called: Coughlin Automotive Group
9000 Broad St Sw (43062-7879)
P.O. Box 1480 (43062-1480)
PHONE..................................740 964-9191
Al Coughlin, Pr
Michael Coughlin, *
Frederick J Simon, *
EMP: 100 **EST:** 1980
SALES (est): 75.69MM
SALES (corp-wide): 75.69MM **Privately Held**
Web: www.coughlinpataskala.com
SIC: 5511 5012 7538 7532 Automobiles, new and used; Automobiles and other motor vehicles; General automotive repair shops; Top and body repair and paint shops

(G-12272)
CRAWFORD MECHANICAL SVCS INC
Also Called: Plumbing Mechanical
9464 Jersey Mill Rd Nw (43062-9749)
PHONE..................................614 478-9424
William T Crawford, Pr
Suzette Crawford, *
EMP: 70 **EST:** 1994
SALES (est): 13.38MM **Privately Held**
Web: www.crawfordmech.com
SIC: 1711 Plumbing contractors

(G-12273)
DYNAMIC CONSTRUCTION INC
Also Called: Dynamic Construction
172 Coors Blvd (43062-7313)
PHONE..................................740 927-8898
Mark S Gray, Pr
EMP: 60 **EST:** 1997
SQ FT: 1,200
SALES (est): 23.07MM **Privately Held**
Web: www.dynamicconstruction.net

SIC: 1542 Commercial and office building, new construction

(G-12274)
ENERGY TRUCKING LLC (PA)
Also Called: Energy Trucking
24 Front St Ste 210 (43062-8357)
PHONE..................................740 240-2204
Akmal Ismailov, CEO
Julia Gracheva, COO
EMP: 70 **EST:** 2015
SALES (est): 30MM
SALES (corp-wide): 30MM **Privately Held**
Web: www.energytrucking.com
SIC: 4213 Heavy hauling, nec

(G-12275)
ILLUMINATE USA LLC ✪
3600 Etna Pkwy (43062)
PHONE..................................614 598-9742
EMP: 585 **EST:** 2023
SALES (est): 10.48MM **Privately Held**
SIC: 7389 Personal service agents, brokers, and bureaus

(G-12276)
SALO INC
350 S Main St # B (43062-9626)
PHONE..................................740 964-2904
EMP: 187
SALES (corp-wide): 52.16MM **Privately Held**
Web: www.interim-health.com
SIC: 8082 Home health care services
PA: Salo, Inc.
300 W Wlson Brdge Rd Ste
Columbus OH 43085
614 436-9404

(G-12277)
SOUTHWEST LCKING KNDRGRTEN CTR
927 South St Unit B (43062-6014)
P.O. Box 120 (43018-0120)
PHONE..................................740 927-1130
EMP: 28 **EST:** 1995
SALES (est): 817.45K **Privately Held**
Web: www.swl.k12.oh.us
SIC: 8351 Nursery school

(G-12278)
THAYER PWR COMM LINE CNSTR LLC (HQ)
Also Called: Thayer Power & Comm Line
12345 Worthington Rd Nw (43062)
PHONE..................................740 927-0021
Rudy Esteves, CEO
Kevin Liederbach, CFO
EMP: 29 **EST:** 2009
SQ FT: 16,000
SALES (est): 108.6MM
SALES (corp-wide): 200.7MM **Privately Held**
Web: www.thayerpc.com
SIC: 1623 Communication line and transmission tower construction
PA: Calera Capital Management, Inc.
580 Clifornia St Ste 2200
San Francisco CA 94104
415 632-5200

(G-12279)
VISION HOME HEALTH CARE LLC
14057 Broad St Sw (43062-8266)
PHONE..................................614 338-8100
Haftu Asamerew, Pr
EMP: 36 **EST:** 2013
SALES (est): 3.76MM **Privately Held**
Web: www.visionhhc.com

SIC: 8082 Home health care services

Patriot
Gallia County

(G-12280)
BUCKEYE RURAL ELC COOP INC
4848 State Route 325 (45658-8960)
P.O. Box 200 (45674-0200)
PHONE..............................740 379-2025
TOLL FREE: 800
David Lester, *Ch Bd*
Tedd Mollohon, *
Tonda Meadows, *
Maggie M Rucker, *
EMP: 45 EST: 1938
SALES (est): 45MM **Privately Held**
Web: www.buckeyerec.coop
SIC: 4911 Distribution, electric power

Paulding
Paulding County

(G-12281)
COMMUNITY HLTH PRFSSIONALS INC
Also Called: Paulding Area Visiting Nurses
250 Dooley Dr Ste A (45879-8846)
PHONE..............................419 399-4708
Peggy Carnhan, *Mgr*
EMP: 39
SALES (corp-wide): 12.27MM **Privately Held**
Web: www.comhealthpro.org
SIC: 8082 Visiting nurse service
PA: Community Health Professionals, Inc.
1159 Westwood Dr
Van Wert OH 45891
419 238-9223

(G-12282)
COUNTY OF CUYAHOGA
112 N Williams St (45879-1281)
PHONE..............................419 399-8260
Anna Campbell, *Brnch Mgr*
EMP: 45
Web: www.cuyahogabdd.org
SIC: 8322 Probation office
PA: County Of Cuyahoga
1215 W 3rd St
Cleveland OH 44113
216 443-7022

(G-12283)
GARDENS AT PAULDING OPER LLC
199 Road 103 (45879-8776)
PHONE..............................419 399-4940
Joseph Hazelbaker, *Prin*
Brian Hazelbaker, *Prin*
Ralph Hazelbaker, *Prin*
EMP: 68 EST: 2020
SALES (est): 941.58K **Privately Held**
SIC: 8059 Nursing and personal care, nec

(G-12284)
HERBERT E ORR COMPANY INC
335 W Wall St (45879-1163)
P.O. Box 209 (45879-0209)
PHONE..............................419 399-4866
Greg Johnson, *Pr*
Donna J Garman, *Treas*
Ken Metzger, *
EMP: 125 EST: 1952
SQ FT: 48,000
SALES (est): 17.41MM **Privately Held**
Web: www.heorr.com
SIC: 5013 3479 Wheels, motor vehicle; Painting of metal products

(G-12285)
PAULDING COUNTY HOSPITAL
Also Called: Paulding County Hospital
1035 W Wayne St (45879)
PHONE..............................419 399-4080
Gary Adkins, *CEO*
Randy Ruge, *
Tom Litzenberg, *
Michael Winans, *
Ron Etzler, *
EMP: 213 EST: 1928
SQ FT: 36,000
SALES (est): 26.33MM **Privately Held**
Web: www.pauldingcountyhospital.com
SIC: 8062 Hospital, affiliated with AMA residency

(G-12286)
PAULDING EXEMPTED VLG SCHL DST (PA)
405 N Water St (45879-1251)
PHONE..............................419 594-3309
John Baysinger, *Superintnt*
Greg Reinhart, *
EMP: 30 EST: 1884
SALES (est): 20.51MM
SALES (corp-wide): 20.51MM **Privately Held**
Web: www.pauldingschools.org
SIC: 8351 8211 Preschool center; Elementary and secondary schools

(G-12287)
PAULDING-PUTNAM ELECTRIC COOP (PA)
Also Called: PAULDING PUTNAM ELECTRIC COOPE
401 Mc Donald Pike (45879-9270)
PHONE..............................419 399-5015
George Carter, *Pr*
EMP: 30 EST: 1935
SALES (est): 47.97MM
SALES (corp-wide): 47.97MM **Privately Held**
Web: www.ppec.coop
SIC: 4911 Distribution, electric power

Peebles
Adams County

(G-12288)
GENERAL ELECTRIC COMPANY
Also Called: GE
1200 Jaybird Rd (45660-9550)
PHONE..............................937 587-2631
Dean Schultz, *Mgr*
EMP: 200
SALES (corp-wide): 67.95B **Publicly Held**
Web: www.ge.com
SIC: 8734 Testing laboratories
PA: General Electric Company
1 Aviation Way
Cincinnati OH 45215
617 443-3000

Pemberville
Wood County

(G-12289)
HIRZEL TRANSFER CO
115 Columbus St (43450-7029)
P.O. Box A (43450-0428)
PHONE..............................419 287-3288
Joseph Hirzel, *Pr*
Karl Hirzel Junior, *Sec*
William Hirzel, *
EMP: 42 EST: 1984
SALES (est): 494.04K

SALES (corp-wide): 60.4MM **Privately Held**
SIC: 4212 Truck rental with drivers
PA: Hirzel Canning Company
411 Lemoyne Rd
Northwood OH 43619
419 693-0531

(G-12290)
NORTH BRANCH NURSERY INC
3359 Kesson Rd (43450-9204)
P.O. Box 353 (43450-0353)
PHONE..............................419 287-4679
Thomas Oberhouse, *Pr*
Lynnette Oberhouse, *
EMP: 50 EST: 1982
SQ FT: 3,200
SALES (est): 4.84MM **Privately Held**
Web: www.northbranchnursery.com
SIC: 0782 5261 5193 1521 Landscape contractors; Retail nurseries and garden stores; Flowers and florists supplies; Patio and deck construction and repair

(G-12291)
OTTERBEIN PORTAGE VALLEY INC
Also Called: Otterbein Prtage Vly Rtrment C
20311 Pemberville Rd Ofc (43450-9411)
PHONE..............................888 749-4950
TOLL FREE: 888
Thomas Keith, *Dir*
EMP: 150 EST: 1975
SQ FT: 96,000
SALES (est): 5.25MM
SALES (corp-wide): 74.71MM **Privately Held**
Web: www.otterbein.org
SIC: 8051 8052 6513 Skilled nursing care facilities; Intermediate care facilities; Apartment building operators
PA: Otterbein Homes
3855 Lower Market St # 300
Lebanon OH 45036
513 933-5400

(G-12292)
OTTERBEIN SNIOR LFSTYLE CHICES
Also Called: OTTERBEIN SENIOR LIFESTYLE CHOICES
20311 Pemberville Rd (43450-9413)
PHONE..............................419 833-7000
EMP: 37
SALES (corp-wide): 74.71MM **Privately Held**
Web: www.otterbein.org
SIC: 8361 Aged home
PA: Otterbein Homes
3855 Lower Market St # 300
Lebanon OH 45036
513 933-5400

Peninsula
Summit County

(G-12293)
CONSERVNCY FOR CYHOGA VLY NAT
Also Called: CVNPA
1403 W Hines Hill Rd (44264-9646)
PHONE..............................330 657-2909
Deb Yandala, *CEO*
Sheryl Hoffman, *CDO*
EMP: 55 EST: 2004
SALES (est): 8.38MM **Privately Held**
Web: www.conservancyforcvnp.org
SIC: 8699 Charitable organization

(G-12294)
SUNCREST GARDENS INC
5157 Akron Cleveland Rd (44264-9515)
PHONE..............................330 650-4969
Richard Haury, *Pr*
EMP: 125 EST: 1976
SQ FT: 1,000
SALES (est): 19.95MM **Privately Held**
Web: www.suncrestgardens.com
SIC: 0781 0782 Landscape services; Lawn and garden services

(G-12295)
WAYSIDE FARM INC
Also Called: Wayside Frms Nrsing Rhblttion
4557 Quick Rd (44264-9708)
PHONE..............................330 666-7716
Rebecca K Pool, *Pr*
Doctor Loren Pool, *VP*
EMP: 93 EST: 1962
SQ FT: 14,000
SALES (est): 7.57MM **Privately Held**
Web: www.waysidefarmnh.com
SIC: 8051 Skilled nursing care facilities

(G-12296)
WHOLECYCLE INC
Also Called: State 8 Motorcycle & Atv
100 Cuyahoga Falls Industrial Pkwy (44264-9569)
PHONE..............................330 929-8123
◆ EMP: 40 EST: 1990
SQ FT: 25,000
SALES (est): 7.78MM **Privately Held**
Web: www.state8.com
SIC: 5012 5571 3799 Motorcycles; Motorcycles; All terrain vehicles (ATV)

Pepper Pike
Cuyahoga County

(G-12297)
APM MANAGEMENT LLC
30195 Chagrin Blvd Ste 320n (44124-5758)
PHONE..............................216 468-0050
Tom Lang, *CFO*
EMP: 28 EST: 2012
SALES (est): 900.36K **Privately Held**
SIC: 7299 Apartment locating service

(G-12298)
CITY OF PEPPER PIKE (PA)
28000 Shaker Blvd (44124-5049)
PHONE..............................216 831-9604
Richard Bain, *Mayor*
Bruce H Akers, *
EMP: 40 EST: 1924
SQ FT: 10,000
SALES (est): 18.55MM
SALES (corp-wide): 18.55MM **Privately Held**
Web: www.pepperpike.org
SIC: 8111 Legal services

(G-12299)
FRANK SANTO LLC
Also Called: Santo Salon & Spa
31100 Pinetree Rd Ste 100 (44124-5963)
PHONE..............................216 831-9374
EMP: 29 EST: 1998
SALES (est): 967.32K **Privately Held**
Web: www.santosalon.com
SIC: 7231 Hairdressers

(G-12300)
JEWISH DAY SCHL ASSN GRTER CLV (PA)
Also Called: Schechter, Gross Day School
27601 Fairmount Blvd (44124)

PHONE................216 763-1400
Rabbi Jim Rogozen, *Headmaster*
EMP: 52 **EST**: 1979
SQ FT: 59,000
SALES (est): 6.35MM
SALES (corp-wide): 6.35MM **Privately Held**
Web: www.grossschechter.org
SIC: 8211 8351 Private elementary and secondary schools; Group day care center

(G-12301)
MILL STEEL CO
Cleveland Metal Exchange
3550 Lander Rd Ste 200 (44124-5727)
PHONE................216 464-4480
Randy Horvat, *Brnch Mgr*
EMP: 35
SALES (corp-wide): 175.49MM **Privately Held**
Web: www.millsteel.com
SIC: 5051 Steel
PA: The Mill Steel Co
2905 Lucerne Dr Se
Grand Rapids MI 49546
800 247-6455

(G-12302)
Q MEDICAL LLC
Also Called: Quadra Tooling and Automation
30100 Chagrin Blvd Ste 201 (44124-5722)
PHONE................440 903-1827
Mauricio Arellano, *CEO*
Roy Showman, *
EMP: 420 **EST**: 2019
SALES (est): 16.44MM
SALES (corp-wide): 5.69B **Privately Held**
Web: www.qco.net
SIC: 8071 Testing laboratories
HQ: Q Holding Company
1700 Highland Rd
Twinsburg OH 44087
440 903-1827

Perry
Lake County

(G-12303)
ADDUS HOMECARE CORPORATION
3721 N Ridge Rd (44081-9579)
PHONE................440 219-0245
EMP: 115
Web: www.addus.com
SIC: 8082 Home health care services
PA: Addus Homecare Corporation
6303 Cowboys Way Ste 600
Frisco TX 75034

(G-12304)
CAR PARTS WAREHOUSE INC
Also Called: CPW-32
3382 N Ridge Rd (44081-9530)
PHONE................216 496-6540
Tony Difiore, *Pr*
EMP: 40
SALES (corp-wide): 48.99MM **Privately Held**
Web: www.cartpartswarehouse.net
SIC: 5013 Automotive supplies and parts
PA: Car Parts Warehouse, Inc.
5200 W 130th St
Brookpark OH 44142
216 281-4500

(G-12305)
COTTAGE GARDENS INC
Also Called: Classic Growers Co
4992 Middle Ridge Rd (44081-8700)
PHONE................440 259-2900

Thomas Varcak, *Brnch Mgr*
EMP: 90
SQ FT: 3,640
SALES (corp-wide): 25.26MM **Privately Held**
Web: www.cottagegardensinc.com
SIC: 0181 5193 Nursery stock, growing of; Flowers and florists supplies
PA: The Cottage Gardens Inc
2611 S Waverly Hwy
Lansing MI 48911
517 882-5728

(G-12306)
LAKE COUNTY PARTS WAREHOUSE INC
3382 N Ridge Rd (44081-9530)
PHONE................440 259-2991
▲ **EMP**: 40
SIC: 5013 Automotive supplies and parts

(G-12307)
LAKE COUNTY YMCA
Also Called: Outdoor Family Center
4540 River Rd (44081-8613)
PHONE................440 259-2724
Richard Bennett, *Dir*
EMP: 129
SALES (corp-wide): 13.16MM **Privately Held**
Web: www.lakecountyymca.org
SIC: 8641 7991 8351 7032 Youth organizations; Physical fitness facilities; Child day care services; Youth camps
PA: Lake County Young Men's Christian Association
933 Mentor Ave Fl 2
Painesville OH 44077
440 352-3303

(G-12308)
LAKE HOSPITAL SYSTEM INC
Also Called: Primehealth Perry Hlth & Welln
2 Success Blvd (44081-9404)
PHONE................440 375-8590
EMP: 107
SALES (corp-wide): 878.24MM **Privately Held**
Web: www.uhhospitals.org
SIC: 8322 Community center
HQ: Lake Hospital System, Inc.
7590 Auburn Rd
Concord Township OH 44077
440 375-8100

(G-12309)
MID-WEST MATERIALS INC
3687 Shepard Rd (44081-9694)
P.O. Box 345 (44081-0345)
PHONE................440 259-5200
Brian D Robbins, *Prin*
Noreen Goldstein, *
Sharon Koppelman, *
Michael Alley, *
EMP: 49 **EST**: 1952
SQ FT: 220,000
SALES (est): 46.75MM **Privately Held**
Web: www.midwestmaterials.com
SIC: 5051 Steel

(G-12310)
NEW AVNUES TO INDEPENDENCE INC
5051 S Rdg Rd (44081)
P.O. Box 312 (44081-0312)
PHONE................440 259-4300
Pat Hartman, *Mgr*
EMP: 97
SALES (corp-wide): 15.06MM **Privately Held**
Web: www.newavenues.net

SIC: 8361 Retarded home
PA: New Avenues To Independence, Inc.
3615 Superior Ave E 4404a
Cleveland OH 44114
216 481-1907

(G-12311)
PERRY FITNESS CENTER
1 Success Blvd (44081-9404)
PHONE................440 259-9499
William Laine, *Dir*
EMP: 34 **EST**: 2002
SALES (est): 146.47K **Privately Held**
Web: www.perry-lake.org
SIC: 7991 Physical fitness facilities

(G-12312)
WILLOWBEND NURSERIES LLC
4654 Davis Rd (44081-9667)
PHONE................440 259-3121
Brent Cherkala, *
▲ **EMP**: 40 **EST**: 2007
SALES (est): 2MM **Privately Held**
SIC: 0181 Nursery stock, growing of

Perrysburg
Wood County

(G-12313)
AUTO MALL RENTAL & LEASING LLC
26875 Dixie Hwy (43551-1716)
PHONE................419 874-4331
EMP: 62 **EST**: 2019
SALES (est): 1.13MM **Privately Held**
Web: www.perrysburgautomall.com
SIC: 7359 Equipment rental and leasing, nec

(G-12314)
AUTOMATION & CONTROL TECH LTD
28210 Cedar Park Blvd (43551-4865)
PHONE................419 661-6400
▲ **EMP**: 27 **EST**: 2006
SQ FT: 8,500
SALES (est): 5.83MM **Privately Held**
Web: www.act-repair.com
SIC: 7629 Electronic equipment repair

(G-12315)
AUTOZONE INC
Also Called: Autozone
650 E South Boundary St (43551-2507)
PHONE................419 872-2813
EMP: 27
SALES (corp-wide): 17.46B **Publicly Held**
Web: www.autozonepro.com
SIC: 5531 5045 5734 Automotive parts; Computer software; Software, business and non-game
PA: Autozone, Inc.
123 S Front St
Memphis TN 38103
901 495-6500

(G-12316)
BELMONT COUNTRY CLUB
29601 Bates Rd (43551-3899)
PHONE................419 666-1472
Bill Ammann, *Pr*
Gary Kovach, *
EMP: 51 **EST**: 1967
SALES (est): 1.67MM **Privately Held**
Web: www.thebelmontcountryclub.com
SIC: 7997 Country club, membership

(G-12317)
BLANCHARD VALLEY WNS CARE LLC
1103 Village Square Dr (43551-1783)
PHONE................419 420-0904
Lorie A Thomas, *Prin*
EMP: 28 **EST**: 2011
SALES (est): 432.64K **Privately Held**
SIC: 8011 Gynecologist

(G-12318)
BOTTOMLINE INK CORPORATION
Also Called: Blink Marketing Logistics
7829 Ponderosa Rd (43551-4854)
PHONE................419 897-8000
Nicholas J Cron, *Prin*
Mike Davison, *
▲ **EMP**: 29 **EST**: 1991
SQ FT: 58,000
SALES (est): 8.37MM **Privately Held**
Web: www.alwaysblink.com
SIC: 2759 5199 Advertising literature: printing, nsk; Advertising specialties

(G-12319)
BROWN & BROWN OF OHIO LLC (HQ)
Also Called: Nationwide
360 3 Meadows Dr (43551-3197)
P.O. Box 428 (43552-0428)
PHONE................419 874-1974
James K Mc Whinnie, *CEO*
Daniel E Dumbauld, *
Jack N Conley, *
EMP: 45 **EST**: 1975
SQ FT: 20,000
SALES (est): 24.09MM
SALES (corp-wide): 3.57B **Publicly Held**
Web: www.bbrown.com
SIC: 6411 Insurance agents, nec
PA: Brown & Brown, Inc.
300 N Beach St
Daytona Beach FL 32114
386 252-9601

(G-12320)
BUCKINGHAM MANAGEMENT LLC
1000 Hollister Ln (43551-6950)
PHONE................844 361-5559
EMP: 48
Web: www.buckingham.com
SIC: 6513 Apartment building operators
PA: Buckingham Management, L.L.C.
941 N Meridian St
Indianapolis IN 46204

(G-12321)
BURKETT AND SONS INC
Also Called: Burkett Restaurant Equipment
28740 Glenwood Rd (43551-3014)
P.O. Box 984 (43697-0984)
PHONE................419 242-7377
Jameel Burkett, *Pr*
▼ **EMP**: 50 **EST**: 1977
SQ FT: 95,000
SALES (est): 24.58MM **Privately Held**
Web: www.burkett.com
SIC: 5046 Restaurant equipment and supplies, nec

(G-12322)
CARGOTEC SERVICES USA INC
12233 Williams Rd (43551-6802)
PHONE................419 482-6000
EMP: 47 **EST**: 2006
SALES (est): 2.53MM **Privately Held**
Web: www.hiab.com
SIC: 8741 Management services
PA: Cargotec Oyj
Porkkalankatu 5

Perrysburg - Wood County (G-12323) — GEOGRAPHIC SECTION

(G-12323)
CAVINS TRUCKING & GARAGE LLC (PA)
100 J St # C (43551-4418)
PHONE...............................419 661-9947
EMP: 30 **EST:** 1987
SALES (est): 2.05MM **Privately Held**
SIC: 4213 Contract haulers

(G-12324)
CITY OF PERRYSBURG
Also Called: Bureau of Sanitation
11980 Route Roached Rd (43551)
PHONE...............................419 872-8020
EMP: 32
SQ FT: 1,664
SALES (corp-wide): 36.17MM **Privately Held**
Web: ci.perrysburg.oh.us
SIC: 4953 9111 Refuse systems; Mayors' office
PA: City Of Perrysburg
26100 Fort Meigs Rd
Perrysburg OH 43551
419 872-8018

(G-12325)
COMMERCIAL COMFORT SYSTEMS INC
26610 Eckel Rd Ste 3a (43551-1254)
P.O. Box 8792 (43537-8792)
PHONE...............................419 481-4444
Francis Lanciaux, *Pr*
Laurel Lanzio, *
EMP: 34 **EST:** 1998
SQ FT: 25,300
SALES (est): 4.8MM **Privately Held**
Web: www.commercialcomfort.com
SIC: 1711 Warm air heating and air conditioning contractor

(G-12326)
CRITICAL BUSINESS ANALYSIS INC
Also Called: CBA
133 W 2nd St Ste 1 (43551-1479)
PHONE...............................419 874-0800
John Gordon, *CEO*
Donald Monteleone, *
EMP: 48 **EST:** 1984
SQ FT: 5,000
SALES (est): 4.66MM **Privately Held**
Web: www.cbainc.com
SIC: 8243 7371 8742 8741 Software training, computer; Custom computer programming services; Construction project management consultant; Financial management for business

(G-12327)
CRONIN AUTO INC
26875 Dixie Hwy (43551-1716)
PHONE...............................419 874-4371
Thomas G Schmidt, *Pr*
EMP: 250 **EST:** 1938
SQ FT: 55,000
SALES (est): 52.07MM **Privately Held**
Web: www.perrysburgautomall.com
SIC: 5511 5521 5012 7538 Automobiles, new and used; Used car dealers; Automobiles and other motor vehicles; General automotive repair shops

(G-12328)
CUTTING EDGE COUNTERTOPS INC
1300 Flagship Dr (43551-1375)
PHONE...............................419 873-9500
Doug Heerdegen, *Pr*
Jeff Erickson, *
Jon Cousino, *
Rob Loughridge, *
◆ **EMP:** 32 **EST:** 2004
SQ FT: 24,000
SALES (est): 6.17MM **Privately Held**
Web: www.cectops.com
SIC: 3281 1743 Granite, cut and shaped; Marble installation, interior

(G-12329)
DAYTON FREIGHT LINES INC
28240 Oregon Rd (43551-4739)
PHONE...............................419 661-8600
Bill Nieset, *Mgr*
EMP: 151
SALES (corp-wide): 6.59B **Privately Held**
Web: www.daytonfreight.com
SIC: 4213 Trucking, except local
PA: Dayton Freight Lines, Inc.
6450 Poe Ave
Dayton OH 45414
937 264-4060

(G-12330)
DAYTON HEIDELBERG DISTRG CO
Heidelberg Distributing Co
912 3rd St (43551-4356)
PHONE...............................419 666-9783
Tom Mchugh, *Mgr*
EMP: 161
SALES (corp-wide): 2.07B **Privately Held**
Web: www.heidelbergdistributing.com
SIC: 5181 Beer and other fermented malt liquors
HQ: Dayton Heidelberg Distributing Co., Llc
3601 Dryden Rd
Moraine OH 45439
937 222-8692

(G-12331)
DCO LLC (DH)
900 E Boundary St Ste 8a (43551-2406)
PHONE...............................419 931-9086
Joe Stancati, *Managing Member*
Bricy Stringham, *
◆ **EMP:** 31 **EST:** 1904
SALES (est): 45.51MM **Privately Held**
SIC: 3751 8741 Motor scooters and parts; Financial management for business
HQ: Enstar Holdings (Us) Llc
150 2nd Ave N Fl 3
Saint Petersburg FL 33701
727 217-2900

(G-12332)
DEPOT DIRECT INC
Also Called: Kenakore Solutions
487 J St (43551-4303)
PHONE...............................419 661-1233
▲ **EMP:** 42
Web: www.kenakoresolutions.com
SIC: 5084 7389 2741 Hydraulic systems equipment and supplies; Printing broker; Miscellaneous publishing

(G-12333)
DILLIN ENGINEERED SYSTEMS CORP
8030 Broadstone Rd (43551-4856)
PHONE...............................419 666-6789
David A Smith, *Pr*
EMP: 50 **EST:** 2000
SQ FT: 40,000
SALES (est): 8.98MM **Privately Held**
Web: www.dillin.net
SIC: 8711 3535 Mechanical engineering; Conveyors and conveying equipment

(G-12334)
DOLD HOMES INC (PA)
26610 Eckel Rd (43551-1247)
PHONE...............................419 874-2535
William H Dold, *Pr*
Mary Lou Dold, *
EMP: 45 **EST:** 1976
SQ FT: 16,000
SALES (est): 9.45MM
SALES (corp-wide): 9.45MM **Privately Held**
SIC: 1521 1531 New construction, single-family houses; Speculative builder, single-family houses

(G-12335)
ENVIROCARE LAWN & LDSCP LLC
24112 Lime City Rd (43551-9043)
PHONE...............................419 874-6779
Jeff Eberly, *Prin*
Bob Welch, *
EMP: 40 **EST:** 1999
SALES (est): 2.84MM **Privately Held**
Web: www.envirocarelawnandlandscape.com
SIC: 0782 Lawn care services

(G-12336)
GENESIS HEALTHCARE LLC
28546 Starbright Blvd (43551-4686)
PHONE...............................419 666-0935
EMP: 461
Web: www.genesishcc.com
SIC: 8051 8052 Convalescent home with continuous nursing care; Intermediate care facilities
HQ: Genesis Healthcare Llc
101 E State St
Kennett Square PA 19348

(G-12337)
GENOX TRANSPORTATION INC
25750 Oregon Rd (43551-9778)
PHONE...............................419 837-2023
Kevin Matthews, *Pr*
Lisa Mathews, *CFO*
EMP: 50 **EST:** 2013
SALES (est): 2.27MM **Privately Held**
Web: www.genoxtransportation.com
SIC: 4789 Transportation services, nec

(G-12338)
GIVENS LIFTING SYSTEMS INC
26437 Southpoint Rd (43551-1371)
PHONE...............................419 724-9001
Ray Givens, *Pr*
EMP: 50 **EST:** 2015
SALES (est): 11.95MM
SALES (corp-wide): 11.54MM **Privately Held**
Web: www.givensliftingsystems.com
SIC: 5084 Materials handling machinery
PA: Givens Engineering Inc
327 Sovereign Rd
London ON N6M 1
519 453-9008

(G-12339)
GLOW INDUSTRIES INC
12962 Eckel Junction Rd (43551-1309)
PHONE...............................419 872-4772
◆ **EMP:** 58
SIC: 5199 5331 Variety store merchandise; Variety stores

(G-12340)
HCF OF PERRYSBURG INC
Also Called: Manor At Perrysburg, The
250 Manor Dr (43551-3118)
PHONE...............................419 874-0306
Kenneth Zeilinski, *Mgr*
EMP: 99 **EST:** 2002
SALES (est): 9.51MM
SALES (corp-wide): 305.93MM **Privately Held**
Web: www.manoratperrysburg.com
SIC: 8051 Convalescent home with continuous nursing care
PA: Hcf Management, Inc.
1100 Shawnee Rd
Lima OH 45805
419 999-2010

(G-12341)
HEARTLAND PERRYSBURG OH LLC
Also Called: Promedica Sklled Nrsing Rhbltt
10540 Fremont Pike (43551-3356)
PHONE...............................419 874-3578
Sara Louk, *Prin*
EMP: 42 **EST:** 2007
SALES (est): 4.57MM **Privately Held**
SIC: 8051 Convalescent home with continuous nursing care

(G-12342)
HERB THYME FARMS INC
8600 S Wilkinson Way Ste G (43551-2598)
PHONE...............................866 386-0854
EMP: 500
Web: www.herbthyme.com
SIC: 0191 General farms, primarily crop

(G-12343)
HIAB USA INC (HQ)
12233 Williams Rd (43551-6802)
PHONE...............................419 482-6000
Roland Sunden, *Pr*
Lennart Brelin, *
Doug Heerdegen, *
◆ **EMP:** 70 **EST:** 1962
SQ FT: 56,000
SALES (est): 138.21MM **Privately Held**
Web: www.hiab.com
SIC: 5084 3536 Cranes, industrial; Cranes, industrial plant
PA: Cargotec Oyj
Porkkalankatu 5
Helsinki 00180

(G-12344)
HOSPICE OF NORTHWEST OHIO (PA)
30000 E River Rd (43551-3429)
PHONE...............................419 661-4001
Judy Seibenick, *Ex Dir*
Thomas Myers, *
EMP: 300 **EST:** 1978
SQ FT: 48,000
SALES (est): 21.62MM **Privately Held**
Web: www.hospicenwo.org
SIC: 8052 Personal care facility

(G-12345)
HOSTER HOTELS LLC
Also Called: Home2 Suites, The
5995 Levis Commons Blvd (43551-7112)
PHONE...............................419 931-8900
Robert Volker, *Managing Member*
EMP: 30 **EST:** 2018
SALES (est): 1.03MM **Privately Held**
SIC: 7011 Hotels

(G-12346)
IMCO CARBIDE TOOL INC
Also Called: Toledo Cutting Tools
28170 Cedar Park Blvd (43551-4872)
PHONE...............................419 661-6313
Perry L Osburn, *Ch Bd*
Matthew S Osburn, *
Julie Whitlow, *
EMP: 90 **EST:** 1977
SQ FT: 25,000

SALES (est): 22.45MM **Privately Held**
Web: www.imcousa.com
SIC: 5084 3545 Machine tools and accessories; Tools and accessories for machine tools

(G-12347)
INGRAM ENTERTAINMENT HOLDINGS
Also Called: Ingram Entertainment
668 1st St (43551-4480)
PHONE.................................419 662-3132
EMP: 153
SALES (corp-wide): 400MM **Privately Held**
Web: www.ingramentertainment.com
SIC: 7929 Entertainers and entertainment groups
PA: Ingram Entertainment Holdings Inc
2 Ingram Blvd
La Vergne TN 37089
615 287-4000

(G-12348)
JERL MACHINE INC
11140 Avenue Rd (43551-2825)
PHONE.................................419 873-0270
Carol Coe, *CEO*
Linda Hetrick, *
Kristi Coe, *
Jayson Coy, *
EMP: 61 **EST:** 1974
SQ FT: 76,000
SALES (est): 10.96MM **Privately Held**
Web: www.jerl.com
SIC: 7692 3599 Welding repair; Machine shop, jobbing and repair

(G-12349)
KIEMLE-HANKINS COMPANY (PA)
Also Called: Kiemle-Hankins
94 H St (43551-4497)
P.O. Box 507 (43697-0507)
PHONE.................................419 661-2430
Stephen Martindale, *Ch*
Tim Martindale, *
Jeffrey Lee, *
EMP: 50 **EST:** 1928
SQ FT: 50,000
SALES (est): 14.06MM
SALES (corp-wide): 14.06MM **Privately Held**
Web: www.kiemlehankins.com
SIC: 7694 7629 3699 Electric motor repair; Electrical equipment repair services; Electrical equipment and supplies, nec

(G-12350)
KINGSTON RSDNCE PERRYSBURG LLC
333 E Boundary St (43551-2861)
PHONE.................................419 872-6200
EMP: 168 **EST:** 1996
SALES (est): 17.47MM **Privately Held**
Web: www.kingstonhealthcare.com
SIC: 8361 8051 Aged home; Skilled nursing care facilities
PA: Kingston Healthcare Company
1 Seagate Ste 1960
Toledo OH 43604

(G-12351)
LAKESIDE INTERIOR CONTRACTORS INC
26970 Eckel Rd (43551-1214)
PHONE.................................419 867-1300
EMP: 175 **EST:** 1989
SALES (est): 20.56MM **Privately Held**
Web: www.lakesideinterior.com

SIC: 1742 1791 1751 1752 Plastering, plain or ornamental; Structural steel erection; Carpentry work; Floor laying and floor work, nec

(G-12352)
LAKEWOOD GREENHOUSE INC
29800 Sussex Rd (43551-3465)
PHONE.................................419 691-3541
Walter F Krueger Junior, *Pr*
Mary M Krueger, *
▲ **EMP:** 45 **EST:** 1900
SALES (est): 1.02MM **Privately Held**
Web: lakewoodgreenhouse.square.site
SIC: 0181 Flowers: grown under cover (e.g., greenhouse production)

(G-12353)
LEVIS COMMONS HOTEL LLC
Also Called: Hilton Garden Inn Perrysburg
6165 Levis Commons Blvd (43551-7269)
PHONE.................................419 873-3573
Izzet Sueri, *Mgr*
EMP: 98 **EST:** 2006
SALES (est): 7.31MM
SALES (corp-wide): 8.68MM **Privately Held**
Web: toledoperrysburg.hgi.com
SIC: 7011 Hotels
PA: Gateway Hospitality Group Inc
8921 Canyon Falls Blvd # 140
Twinsburg OH 44087
330 405-9800

(G-12354)
LOWER GREAT LAKES KENWORTH INC
Also Called: Whiteford Kenworth
12650 Eckel Junction Rd (43551-1303)
P.O. Box 387 (43552-0387)
PHONE.................................419 874-3511
Roger Euler, *Mgr*
EMP: 39
SQ FT: 10,000
SALES (corp-wide): 49.97MM **Privately Held**
Web: www.whitefordkenworth.com
SIC: 5012 7538 5013 Trucks, commercial; General automotive repair shops; Motor vehicle supplies and new parts
PA: Lower Great Lakes Kenworth, Inc.
4625 W Western Ave
South Bend IN 46619
574 234-9007

(G-12355)
LOWES HOME CENTERS LLC
Also Called: Lowe's
10295 Fremont Pike (43551-3334)
PHONE.................................419 874-6758
Darcy Mueller, *Brnch Mgr*
EMP: 148
SALES (corp-wide): 86.38B **Publicly Held**
Web: www.lowes.com
SIC: 5211 5031 5722 5064 Home centers; Building materials, exterior; Household appliance stores; Electrical appliances, television and radio
HQ: Lowe's Home Centers, Llc
1000 Lowes Blvd
Mooresville NC 28117
336 658-4000

(G-12356)
MERCY HEALTH (DH)
Also Called: Bon Secure Mercy Health
12621 Eckel Junction Rd (43551-1304)
PHONE.................................513 639-2800
John M Starcher Junior, *Pr*
EMP: 461 **EST:** 1985
SALES (est): 275.27MM

SALES (corp-wide): 6.92B **Privately Held**
Web: www.mercy.com
SIC: 8062 General medical and surgical hospitals
HQ: Community Mercy Health System
100 Medical Center Dr
Springfield OH 45504

(G-12357)
MIDWEST ENVIRONMENTAL INC
28757 Glenwood Rd (43551-3015)
PHONE.................................419 382-9200
Dale Bruhl, *Pr*
EMP: 30 **EST:** 2014
SALES (est): 2.45MM **Privately Held**
Web: www.midwestenvironmental.com
SIC: 8744 Environmental remediation

(G-12358)
NORPLAS INDUSTRIES INC
232 J St (43551-4416)
PHONE.................................419 666-6119
Joe Leonard, *Brnch Mgr*
EMP: 274
SALES (corp-wide): 37.84B **Privately Held**
Web: www.norplas.com
SIC: 4225 General warehousing and storage
HQ: Norplas Industries Inc.
7825 Caple Blvd
Northwood OH 43619
419 662-3200

(G-12359)
OHIO MACHINERY CO
Also Called: Caterpillar Authorized Dealer
25970 Dixie Hwy (43551-1701)
PHONE.................................419 874-7975
Randy Mccabe, *Mgr*
EMP: 90
SQ FT: 19,000
SALES (corp-wide): 185.86MM **Privately Held**
Web: www.ohiocat.com
SIC: 5082 7359 General construction machinery and equipment; Equipment rental and leasing, nec
PA: Ohio Machinery Co.
3993 E Royalton Rd
Broadview Heights OH 44147
440 526-6200

(G-12360)
OHIOANS HOME HEALTHCARE INC
28315 Kensington Ln (43551-4164)
PHONE.................................419 843-4422
EMP: 95 **EST:** 2007
SQ FT: 3,500
SALES (est): 26.35MM **Privately Held**
Web: www.ohioanshhc.com
SIC: 8082 Visiting nurse service

(G-12361)
ONPOINT GROUP LLC (PA)
3235 Levis Commons Blvd (43551-7145)
PHONE.................................567 336-9764
Tom Cox, *CEO*
Chris Davanzo, *
Kirk Yosick, *
Kevin Snyder, *CIO*
EMP: 500 **EST:** 2012
SALES (est): 596.1MM
SALES (corp-wide): 596.1MM **Privately Held**
Web: www.onpointgroup.com
SIC: 5084 Materials handling machinery

(G-12362)
PERRYSBURG BOARD OF EDUCATION
Also Called: Perrysburg Bus Garage
25715 Fort Meigs Rd (43551-1138)

PHONE.................................419 874-3127
Michael Cline, *Mgr*
EMP: 411
SALES (corp-wide): 18.93MM **Privately Held**
Web: www.perrysburgschools.net
SIC: 4151 School buses
PA: Perrysburg Board Of Education Inc
140 E Indiana Ave
Perrysburg OH 43551
419 874-9131

(G-12363)
PERSON CENTERED SERVICES INC
741 Commerce Dr (43551-5274)
PHONE.................................419 874-4900
EMP: 37
Web: www.activeday.com
SIC: 8322 Adult day care center
PA: Person Centered Services, Inc.
1421 N Court St
Circleville OH 43113

(G-12364)
PRECISION STRIP INC
7401 Ponderosa Rd (43551-4858)
PHONE.................................419 661-1100
Greg Bergman, *Mgr*
EMP: 87
SALES (corp-wide): 14.81B **Publicly Held**
Web: www.precision-strip.com
SIC: 5051 Steel
HQ: Precision Strip Inc.
86 S Ohio St
Minster OH 45865
419 628-2343

(G-12365)
PROHEALTH PARTNERS INC
12661 Eckil Junction (43551-1304)
PHONE.................................419 491-7150
Rich Adam, *Pr*
EMP: 59 **EST:** 2009
SALES (est): 4.02MM **Privately Held**
Web: www.prohealthpartners.org
SIC: 8049 Physical therapist

(G-12366)
RAINSTAR CAPITAL GROUP
7630 Reitz Rd Lot 138 (43551-9194)
PHONE.................................419 801-4113
EMP: 41 **EST:** 2017
SALES (est): 131.45K **Privately Held**
Web: www.rainstarcapitalgroup.com
SIC: 6799 Investors, nec

(G-12367)
ROADLINK USA MIDWEST LLC (DH)
29180 Glenwood Rd (43551-3021)
PHONE.................................419 686-2113
EMP: 45 **EST:** 1981
SQ FT: 56,000
SALES (est): 3.76MM **Privately Held**
SIC: 4213 4214 Trucking, except local; Local trucking with storage
HQ: Roadlink Usa, Inc.
1 Kellaway Dr
Randolph MA 02368
888 622-6076

(G-12368)
SCHROEDER COMPANY (PA)
27024 W River Rd (43551-1019)
PHONE.................................419 473-3139
Edward J Schroeder Junior, *Pr*
◆ **EMP:** 40 **EST:** 1977
SALES (est): 4.35MM
SALES (corp-wide): 4.35MM **Privately Held**
Web: www.schroederpropertymanagement.com

Perrysburg - Wood County (G-12369)

SIC: **1522** 6531 Apartment building construction; Real estate managers

(G-12369)
SIGMA TECHNOLOGIES LTD
27096 Oakmead Dr (43551-2657)
PHONE.................................419 874-9262
EMP: 45 **EST**: 1998
SALES (est): 12.19MM **Privately Held**
Web: www.teamsigma.com
SIC: **8711** Consulting engineer

(G-12370)
SKYWORKS LLC
26501 Baker Dr (43551-8848)
PHONE.................................419 662-8630
Bill Hartman, Mgr
EMP: 43
SALES (corp-wide): 104.12MM **Privately Held**
Web: www.skyworksllc.com
SIC: **7353** Cranes and aerial lift equipment, rental or leasing
PA: Skyworks, L.L.C.
100 Theilman Dr
Buffalo NY 14206
716 822-5438

(G-12371)
ST CLARE COMMONS
12469 Five Point Rd (43551-9615)
PHONE.................................419 931-0050
EMP: 39 **EST**: 2008
SALES (est): 9.41MM **Privately Held**
Web: www.chilivingcommunities.org
SIC: **8051** Skilled nursing care facilities

(G-12372)
SUNRISE HOSPITALITY INC
Also Called: Holiday Inn Stes Tledo Sthwst-
27355 Carronade Dr (43551-3369)
PHONE.................................567 331-8900
Natalie Kniss, Prin
EMP: 50
Web: www.holidayinn.com
SIC: **7011** Hotels
PA: Sunrise Hospitality, Inc.
27355 Carronade Dr
Perrysburg OH 43551

(G-12373)
SUNRISE HOSPITALITY INC
Also Called: Ground Round Grill Bar Prrysbur
27355 Carronade Dr (43551-3369)
PHONE.................................567 331-8613
Natalie Kniss, Prin
EMP: 50
Web: www.sunrisehospitality.com
SIC: **7011** Hotels
PA: Sunrise Hospitality, Inc.
27355 Carronade Dr
Perrysburg OH 43551

(G-12374)
T I G FLEET SERVICE INC
7401 Fremont Pike (43551-9432)
PHONE.................................419 250-6333
Thomas Kepler, CEO
EMP: 29 **EST**: 2012
SALES (est): 2.74MM **Privately Held**
Web: www.tigfleet.com
SIC: **7538** General automotive repair shops

(G-12375)
TFS LTD (HQ)
Also Called: Tfs
3235 Levis Commons Blvd (43551-7145)
PHONE.................................419 868-8853
Tom Cox, CEO
Michael Quimby, *
Chris Davanzo, *
EMP: 78 **EST**: 2004
SALES (est): 82.11MM
SALES (corp-wide): 596.1MM **Privately Held**
Web: www.tfsglobal.com
SIC: **5084** Materials handling machinery
PA: Onpoint Group, Llc
3235 Levis Commons Blvd
Perrysburg OH 43551
567 336-9764

(G-12376)
THRIVE MINISTRIES INC
Also Called: Thrive Childcare
1134 Professional Dr (43551-2579)
PHONE.................................419 873-0870
EMP: 47
SALES (corp-wide): 2.34MM **Privately Held**
Web: www.thrivechildcare.org
SIC: **8351** Preschool center
PA: Thrive Ministries, Inc.
3530 Seaman Rd
Oregon OH 43616
419 691-6313

(G-12377)
TL INDUSTRIES INC (PA)
28271 Cedar Park Blvd Ste 8 (43551-4883)
PHONE.................................419 666-8144
Joseph Young, Pr
Joseph Young, VP
Theodore Stetschulte, *
EMP: 105 **EST**: 1970
SALES (est): 24.11MM
SALES (corp-wide): 24.11MM **Privately Held**
Web: www.tlindustries.com
SIC: **8711** 3444 3629 3679 Electrical or electronic engineering; Sheet metalwork; Battery chargers, rectifying or nonrotating; Loads, electronic

(G-12378)
TMT WAREHOUSING LLC
655 D St (43551-4908)
PHONE.................................419 662-3146
EMP: 160 **EST**: 2000
SALES (est): 3.67MM **Privately Held**
Web: www.tmtcompanies.net
SIC: **4225** General warehousing and storage

(G-12379)
TORRENCE SOUND EQUIPMENT COMPANY
29050 Glenwood Rd (43551-3094)
PHONE.................................419 661-0678
EMP: 32 **EST**: 1955
SALES (est): 4.89MM **Privately Held**
Web: www.torrencesound.com
SIC: **1731** Electrical work

(G-12380)
TRT MANAGEMENT CORPORATION (PA)
Also Called: Kenakore Solutions
487 J St (43551-4303)
PHONE.................................419 661-1233
Bruce Gonring, CEO
Chris Huver, *
EMP: 35 **EST**: 2015
SQ FT: 128,000
SALES (est): 4.52MM
SALES (corp-wide): 4.52MM **Privately Held**
Web: www.kenakoresolutions.com
SIC: **4225** General warehousing

(G-12381)
TRZ HOLDINGS INC
28350 Kensington Ln (43551-4173)
P.O. Box 231 (43430-0231)
PHONE.................................419 931-0072
Toby Miller, Pr
Deborah M Gordon, VP
EMP: 32 **EST**: 2001
SQ FT: 4,500
SALES (est): 2.23MM **Privately Held**
Web: www.tranztec.com
SIC: **7371** Computer software development

(G-12382)
UNITED PARCEL SERVICE INC
Also Called: UPS
12171 Eckel Rd (43551-1241)
PHONE.................................419 872-0211
EMP: 72
SALES (corp-wide): 90.96B **Publicly Held**
Web: www.ups.com
SIC: **4215** 7538 Parcel delivery, vehicular; General automotive repair shops
HQ: United Parcel Service, Inc.
55 Glenlake Pkwy
Atlanta GA 30328
404 828-6000

(G-12383)
UNITED RENTALS NORTH AMER INC
Also Called: United Rentals
620 Eckel Rd (43551-1202)
P.O. Box 240 (43552-0240)
PHONE.................................800 877-3687
Mike Lowell, Brnch Mgr
EMP: 43
SALES (corp-wide): 14.33B **Publicly Held**
Web: www.unitedrentals.com
SIC: **7353** 7359 Cranes and aerial lift equipment, rental or leasing; Equipment rental and leasing, nec
HQ: United Rentals (North America), Inc.
100 Frst Stmford Pl Ste 7
Stamford CT 06902
203 622-3131

(G-12384)
US UTILITY ELECTRICAL SVCS
3592 Genoa Rd (43551-9702)
PHONE.................................419 837-9753
Gerald Heminger, Pr
Kathryn Chlebowski, *
Jinnefer Marquartz, *
EMP: 40 **EST**: 1998
SQ FT: 2,400
SALES (est): 2.78MM **Privately Held**
Web: www.usutilitycontractors.com
SIC: **1731** General electrical contractor

(G-12385)
WADSWORTH-SLAWSON INC
Also Called: Wadsworth Solutions Northeast
1500 Michael Owens Way (43551-2975)
PHONE.................................216 391-7263
Brit R Wadsworth, CEO
Thomas H Mcclave, Pr
Gary L Mcclave, VP
David Sommer, *
EMP: 32 **EST**: 1999
SALES (est): 6.6MM **Privately Held**
Web: www.wadsworthsolutions.com
SIC: **5075** Warm air heating and air conditioning

(G-12386)
WELDED CONSTRUCTION LP
26933 Eckel Rd (43551-1215)
P.O. Box 470 (43552-0470)
PHONE.................................419 874-3548
Donald W Thorn, Pt
Craig Bodette, Pt
Alex Epstein, Pt
Jim Hurley, Pt
EMP: 40 **EST**: 1946
SQ FT: 30,000
SALES (est): 25.2MM
SALES (corp-wide): 5.07B **Privately Held**
SIC: **1623** Oil and gas pipeline construction
HQ: Bechtel Corporation
12011 Sunset Hills Rd # 110
Reston VA 20190
571 392-6300

(G-12387)
WHELCO INDUSTRIAL LTD
28210 Cedar Park Blvd (43551-4865)
PHONE.................................419 385-4627
EMP: 51 **EST**: 1992
SQ FT: 12,000
SALES (est): 7.31MM **Privately Held**
Web: www.whelco.com
SIC: **7694** Electric motor repair

(G-12388)
WILLARD KELSEY SOLAR GROUP LLC
1775 Progress Dr (43551-2014)
PHONE.................................419 931-2001
Michael Cicak Managing, CEO
▼ **EMP**: 45 **EST**: 2007
SALES (est): 4.64MM **Privately Held**
Web: www.wksolargroup.com
SIC: **1711** Solar energy contractor

(G-12389)
XPO LOGISTICS FREIGHT INC
28291 Glenwood Rd (43551-4809)
PHONE.................................419 666-3022
Robert Bull, Mgr
EMP: 85
SALES (corp-wide): 7.74B **Publicly Held**
Web: www.xpo.com
SIC: **4731** Freight transportation arrangement
HQ: Xpo Logistics Freight, Inc.
2211 Old Erhart Rd Ste 10
Ann Arbor MI 48105
800 755-2728

(G-12390)
YOUNG MNS CHRSTN ASSN OF GRTER
Also Called: YMCA of Greater Toledo
13415 Eckel Junction Rd (43551-1320)
PHONE.................................419 251-9622
Joe Hillrich, Prin
EMP: 84
SALES (corp-wide): 29.37MM **Privately Held**
Web: www.ymcatoledo.org
SIC: **8641** Youth organizations
PA: The Young Men's Christian Association Of Greater Toledo
6465 Sylvania Ave
Sylvania OH 43560
419 729-8135

Perrysville
Ashland County

(G-12391)
COWEN TRUCK LINE INC
2697 State Rte 39 (44864-9535)
P.O. Box 480 (44864-0480)
PHONE.................................419 938-3401
Tim Cowen, Pr
Wayne Heller, Prin
Steve Bryan, Prin
Harold Long, Prin
Keith Mccoy, Prin
EMP: 85 **EST**: 1972

GEOGRAPHIC SECTION

SQ FT: 20,000
SALES (est): 18.72MM **Privately Held**
Web: www.cowentruckline.com
SIC: 4213 4212 Contract haulers; Local trucking, without storage

(G-12392)
MANSFIELD PLUMBING PDTS LLC (HQ)
150 E 1st St (44864-9421)
P.O. Box 334 (44805-0334)
PHONE.................419 938-5211
Jim Morando, *Pr*
◆ EMP: 600 EST: 1929
SQ FT: 700,000
SALES (est): 97.96MM **Privately Held**
Web: www.mansfieldplumbing.com
SIC: 3261 3463 3088 3431 Vitreous plumbing fixtures; Plumbing fixture forgings, nonferrous; Plastics plumbing fixtures; Bathtubs: enameled iron, cast iron, or pressed metal
PA: Organizacion Corona S A
    Calle 100 8 A 55 Torre C Piso 9
    Bogota

(G-12393)
S & S AGGREGATES INC
Also Called: Shelly & Sands Zanesville OH
4540 State Route 39 (44864-9600)
PHONE.................419 938-5604
EMP: 288
SALES (corp-wide): 433.35MM **Privately Held**
Web: www.shellyandsands.com
SIC: 1442 Construction sand mining
HQ: S & S Aggregates, Inc
    3570 S River Rd
    Zanesville OH 43701
    740 453-0721

Petersburg
Mahoning County

(G-12394)
DAVE SUGAR EXCAVATING LLC
11640 S State Line Rd (44454-9705)
P.O. Box 459 (44442-0459)
PHONE.................330 542-1100
EMP: 35 EST: 2002
SALES (est): 2.4MM **Privately Held**
SIC: 1794 1795 1623 Excavation work; Wrecking and demolition work; Water, sewer, and utility lines

(G-12395)
SUBTROPOLIS MINING CO
Also Called: Subtropolis Mine
5455 E Garfield Rd (44454)
PHONE.................330 549-2165
EMP: 48
SALES (corp-wide): 2.38MM **Privately Held**
Web: www.efccfamily.com
SIC: 1221 Bituminous coal and lignite-surface mining
PA: Subtropolis Mining Co.
    10900 South Ave
    North Lima OH 44452
    330 549-2165

Pickerington
Fairfield County

(G-12396)
ACCESS URGENT MEDICAL CARE PIC
1797 Hill Rd N (43147-7997)
P.O. Box 110 (43054-0110)
PHONE.................614 306-0116
Nino Diiullo, *Owner*
EMP: 27 EST: 2015
SALES (est): 272.05K **Privately Held**
Web: www.accessurgentmedicalcare.com
SIC: 8011 Clinic, operated by physicians

(G-12397)
AMERICAN MOTORCYCLE ASSN (PA)
Also Called: American Motorcyclist Assn
13515 Yarmouth Dr (43147)
PHONE.................614 856-1900
Robert Dingman, *Pr*
Robert M Dingman, *
Jeff Wolens, *
▲ EMP: 51 EST: 1924
SQ FT: 30,000
SALES (est): 13.43MM
SALES (corp-wide): 13.43MM **Privately Held**
Web: www.americanmotorcyclist.com
SIC: 8699 Automobile owners' association

(G-12398)
ANTIOCH CNNCTION CANTON MI LLC
799 Windmiller Dr (43147-8199)
PHONE.................614 531-9285
Gary Smelser, *Managing Member*
EMP: 50 EST: 2013
SQ FT: 86,000
SALES (est): 5.58MM **Privately Held**
SIC: 8059 Nursing home, except skilled and intermediate care facility

(G-12399)
ANTIOCH SALEM FIELDS FREDERICK
799 Windmiller Dr (43147-8199)
PHONE.................614 531-9285
Gary Smelser, *Managing Member*
EMP: 50 EST: 2014
SQ FT: 90,000
SALES (est): 986.86K **Privately Held**
SIC: 8059 Nursing home, except skilled and intermediate care facility

(G-12400)
BUCKEYE COMMERCIAL CLG INC
12936 Stonecreek Dr Ste F (43147-8846)
PHONE.................614 866-4700
David Myers, *Pr*
EMP: 95 EST: 2002
SALES (est): 1.14MM **Privately Held**
Web: www.buckeyecommercialcleaning.com
SIC: 7349 Janitorial service, contract basis

(G-12401)
E-MERGE REAL ESTATE
12910 Stonecreek Dr (43147-8919)
PHONE.................614 804-5600
Mickey Dipiero Dipiero, *Prin*
EMP: 73 EST: 2017
SALES (est): 2.24MM **Privately Held**
Web: loreerupe.e-merge.com
SIC: 6531 Real estate brokers and agents

(G-12402)
HAMPTON INN COLUMBUS EAST
Also Called: Hampton Inn
1890 Winderly Ln (43147-8636)
PHONE.................614 864-8383
Kantu Patel, *Pr*
Urmila K Patel, *
EMP: 67 EST: 1994
SQ FT: 75,000
SALES (est): 808.05K **Privately Held**
Web: www.hilton.com
SIC: 7011 Hotels and motels

(G-12403)
HOME ECHO CLUB INC
Also Called: Echo Mnor Nrsing Rhbltion Ctr
10270 Blacklick Eastern Rd (43147-9225)
PHONE.................614 864-1718
William T Johnson, *Pr*
EMP: 52 EST: 1929
SQ FT: 66,000
SALES (est): 5.86MM **Privately Held**
SIC: 8052 8051 Intermediate care facilities; Skilled nursing care facilities

(G-12404)
J CLARKE SANDERS DDS INC
Also Called: Stonecreek Dental
11295 Stonecreek Dr Ste C (43147-9138)
PHONE.................614 864-3196
EMP: 49 EST: 1985
SALES (est): 4.25MM **Privately Held**
Web: www.helpmysmile.com
SIC: 8021 Dentists' office

(G-12405)
KINDRED NURSING CENTERS E LLC
Also Called: Kindred Trnstnal Care Rhbltion
1300 Hill Rd N (43147-8986)
PHONE.................314 631-3000
Brian Newman, *Brnch Mgr*
EMP: 91
SALES (corp-wide): 13.68B **Privately Held**
Web: www.kindredhospitals.com
SIC: 8051 Convalescent home with continuous nursing care
HQ: Kindred Nursing Centers East, L.L.C.
    680 S 4th St
    Louisville KY 40202
    502 596-7300

(G-12406)
NATIONWIDE CHILDRENS HOSPITAL
1310 Hill Rd N (43147-7814)
PHONE.................614 864-9216
EMP: 127
SALES (corp-wide): 3.6B **Privately Held**
Web: www.nationwidechildrens.org
SIC: 8069 Childrens' hospital
PA: Nationwide Children's Hospital
    700 Childrens Dr
    Columbus OH 43205
    614 722-2000

(G-12407)
ORUM STAIR RSDNTL BRKG OH
1217 Hill Rd N (43147-8888)
PHONE.................614 920-8100
EMP: 50 EST: 2002
SALES (est): 2.1MM **Privately Held**
SIC: 6531 Real estate agents and managers

(G-12408)
R G BARRY CORPORATION (HQ)
Also Called: RG Barry Brands
13405 Yarmouth Dr (43147-8493)
PHONE.................614 864-6400
Bob Mullaney, *CEO*
Elizabeth Ambargis, *
▲ EMP: 516 EST: 1947
SQ FT: 55,000
SALES (est): 192.68MM
SALES (corp-wide): 192.68MM **Privately Held**
Web: www.rgbarry.com
SIC: 5136 5137 5139 Men's and boys' furnishings; Handbags; Slippers, house
PA: Mrgb Hold Co.
    382 Greenwich Ave Apt 1
    Greenwich CT 06830
    203 987-3500

(G-12409)
RAINBOW STATION DAY CARE INC
Also Called: Rainbow Station
1829 Winderly Ln (43147-8637)
PHONE.................614 759-8667
Tracy Tasch, *Dir*
EMP: 27
SALES (corp-wide): 1.01MM **Privately Held**
Web: www.registrar-transfers.com
SIC: 8351 8748 Group day care center; Educational consultant
PA: Rainbow Station Day Care Inc
    226 Durand St
    Pickerington OH 43147
    614 759-8667

(G-12410)
RAINBOW STATION DAY CARE INC (PA)
Also Called: Rainbow Child - Officeview
226 Durand St (43147-7941)
PHONE.................614 759-8667
Bonnie Gibbs, *Pr*
EMP: 36 EST: 1984
SQ FT: 7,000
SALES (est): 1.01MM
SALES (corp-wide): 1.01MM **Privately Held**
Web: www.rainbowstation.com
SIC: 8351 Group day care center

(G-12411)
RE/MAX
Also Called: Re/Max
1131 Hill Rd N (43147-8887)
PHONE.................614 694-0255
EMP: 89 EST: 2018
SALES (est): 693.03K **Privately Held**
Web: www.sellingcentralohiohomes.com
SIC: 6531 Real estate agent, residential

(G-12412)
SHRI MAHALAXMI INC
1899 Winderly Ln (43147-8637)
PHONE.................614 860-9804
Kantu R Patel, *Pr*
Urmila K Patel, *VP*
EMP: 31 EST: 2001
SQ FT: 61,000
SALES (est): 457.01K **Privately Held**
SIC: 7011 Hotels

(G-12413)
VOLUNTEER ENERGY SERVICES INC (PA)
Also Called: Volunteer Energy
790 Windmiller Dr Ste A (43147)
PHONE.................614 856-3128
David Warner, *CFO*
Richard Curnutte Senior, *Pr*
Richard Curnutte Junior, *Sec*
Marc Runck, *
EMP: 50 EST: 2001
SQ FT: 8,000
SALES (est): 19.45MM
SALES (corp-wide): 19.45MM **Privately Held**
Web: www.volunteerenergy.com
SIC: 4924 Natural gas distribution

Piketon
Pike County

(G-12414)
ACT FOR HEALTH INC
1862 Shyville Rd (45661-9749)

Piketon - Pike County

PHONE................740 443-5000
EMP: 273
SALES (corp-wide): 41.86MM **Privately Held**
Web: www.procasemanagement.com
SIC: 8741 Business management
PA: Act For Health, Inc.
500 E 8th Ave
Denver CO 80203
303 253-7470

(G-12415)
BECHTEL JACOBS COMPANY LLC
3930 Us Highway 23 Anx (45661-9113)
PHONE................740 897-2700
John Meersman, *Mgr*
EMP: 111
SALES (corp-wide): 5.07B **Privately Held**
Web: www.bechtel.com
SIC: 1731 General electrical contractor
HQ: Bechtel Jacobs Company Llc
12011 Sunset Hills Rd # 1
Reston VA 20190
865 241-1151

(G-12416)
COMMUNITY ACTION CMMTTEE PIKE (PA)
941 Market St (45661-9757)
P.O. Box 799 (45661-0799)
PHONE................740 289-2371
Gary Roberts, *Ex Dir*
Rebecca Adkins, *
EMP: 115 **EST**: 1965
SQ FT: 21,360
SALES (est): 28MM
SALES (corp-wide): 28MM **Privately Held**
Web: www.pikecac.org
SIC: 8322 Family service agency

(G-12417)
DIAZ CONSTRUCTION INC
535 Seif Rd (45661-9523)
P.O. Box 699 (45661-0699)
PHONE................740 289-4898
Felix P Diaz, *Pr*
EMP: 27 **EST**: 1986
SALES (est): 1.88MM **Privately Held**
Web: www.diazconstruction.net
SIC: 1541 Industrial buildings, new construction, nec

(G-12418)
DKM CONSTRUCTION INC
W Perimeter Rd (45661)
PHONE................740 289-3006
Dennis Martin, *Pr*
William Martin, *
Debbie Martin, *
EMP: 40 **EST**: 1992
SQ FT: 2,400
SALES (est): 3.94MM **Privately Held**
SIC: 1541 1542 Industrial buildings and warehouses; Commercial and office building, new construction

(G-12419)
FLUOR-BWXT PORTSMOUTH LLC
3930 Us Highway 23 Anx (45661-9113)
P.O. Box 548 (45661-0548)
PHONE................866 706-6992
Mark Ashby, *Managing Member*
Tracy Heidelberg, *CFO*
EMP: 1200 **EST**: 2009
SALES (est): 149.65MM
SALES (corp-wide): 15.47B **Publicly Held**
Web: www.fbportsmouth.com
SIC: 1795 Wrecking and demolition work
PA: Fluor Corporation
6700 Las Colinas Blvd
Irving TX 75039

469 398-7000

(G-12420)
GLOCKNER OIL COMPANY INC
4407 Us Highway 23 (45661-9703)
P.O. Box 428 (45661-0428)
PHONE................740 289-2979
EMP: 44 **EST**: 1975
SALES (est): 26.27MM
SALES (corp-wide): 27.25MM **Privately Held**
Web: www.glockneroil.com
SIC: 5172 Petroleum brokers
PA: The Glockner Chevrolet Company
4368 Us Route 23
Portsmouth OH 45662
740 353-2161

(G-12421)
H C F INC
Also Called: Pleasant Hl Otptent Thrapy Ctr
7143 Us Hwy 23 (45661)
PHONE................740 289-2528
Jim Unverferth, *Pr*
EMP: 30 **EST**: 1968
SALES (est): 1.62MM **Privately Held**
SIC: 8059 Nursing home, except skilled and intermediate care facility

(G-12422)
HCF MANAGEMENT INC
7143 Us Highway 23 (45661-9527)
PHONE................740 289-2394
Amy Clemons, *Admn*
EMP: 29
SALES (corp-wide): 305.93MM **Privately Held**
Web: www.hcfinc.com
SIC: 8051 8322 Skilled nursing care facilities; Rehabilitation services
PA: Hcf Management, Inc.
1100 Shawnee Rd
Lima OH 45805
419 999-2010

(G-12423)
INNOVTIVE SLTONS UNLIMITED LLC
7040 Us 23 (45661)
PHONE................740 289-3282
Richard Warner, *Mgr*
EMP: 121
SQ FT: 5,000
Web: www.insolves.com
SIC: 8711 7363 Consulting engineer; Help supply services
PA: Innovative Solutions Unlimited, Llc
1862 Shyville Rd
Piketon OH 45661

(G-12424)
INNOVTIVE SLTONS UNLIMITED LLC (PA)
1862 Shyville Rd (45661-9749)
PHONE................740 289-3282
Jennifer Barbarits, *CEO*
Jennifer Barbarits, *Managing Member*
Frank Barbarits, *
EMP: 53 **EST**: 2002
SQ FT: 3,000
SALES (est): 24.79MM **Privately Held**
Web: www.insolves.com
SIC: 7363 8711 Employee leasing service; Consulting engineer

(G-12425)
OHIO VALLEY ELECTRIC CORP (HQ)
Also Called: Ovec
3932 Us Rte 23 (45661)
P.O. Box 468 (45661-0468)
PHONE................740 289-7200
Nicholas Akins, *Pr*

Mark Piefer, *
John Brodt, *
Freeman T Eagleson, *
Thomas Denney, *
EMP: 93 **EST**: 1952
SQ FT: 100,000
SALES (est): 761.5MM
SALES (corp-wide): 18.98B **Privately Held**
Web: www.ovec.com
SIC: 4911 Generation, electric power
PA: American Electric Power Company, Inc.
1 Riverside Plz Fl 1 # 1
Columbus OH 43215
614 716-1000

(G-12426)
PAVILION AT PKTON FOR NRSING R
Also Called: PAVILION AT PIKETON, THE
7143 Us Highway 23 (45661-9527)
PHONE................740 289-2394
EMP: 99 **EST**: 2018
SALES (est): 10.76MM **Privately Held**
Web: www.pavilionoh.com
SIC: 8399 Advocacy group

(G-12427)
PIKETON NURSING CENTER INC
Also Called: EDGEWOOD MANOR OF WESTERVILLE
300 Overlook Dr (45661-9760)
PHONE................740 289-4074
James Renacci, *Pr*
EMP: 581 **EST**: 1988
SALES (est): 3.44MM
SALES (corp-wide): 491MM **Privately Held**
Web: www.piketonnursingcenter.com
SIC: 8051 Convalescent home with continuous nursing care
HQ: Consulate Management Company, Llc
800 Concourse Pkwy S # 200
Maitland FL 32751
407 571-1550

(G-12428)
PLEASANT HILL LEASING LLC
Also Called: Pleasant Hill Manor
7143 Us Rte 23 S (45661)
PHONE................740 289-2394
Jody Kupchak, *
EMP: 130 **EST**: 2016
SALES (est): 3.76MM **Privately Held**
SIC: 8051 Mental retardation hospital

(G-12429)
RITCHIES FOOD DISTRIBUTORS INC
527 S West St (45661-8042)
PHONE................740 443-6303
James P Ritchie, *Pr*
Nancy Ritchie, *
Twyla Suter, *
Joyce Lightle, *
EMP: 31 **EST**: 1958
SALES (est): 8.73MM **Privately Held**
Web: www.ritchiefoods.com
SIC: 5146 5147 5142 5149 Seafoods; Meats, fresh; Packaged frozen goods; Canned goods: fruit, vegetables, seafood, meats, etc.

(G-12430)
URANIUM DISPOSITION SVCS LLC
3930 Us Highway 23 Anx (45661-9113)
PHONE................740 289-3620
Paul Kreitz, *Brnch Mgr*
EMP: 103
SALES (corp-wide): 33.78MM **Privately Held**
Web: www.uds-llc.com
SIC: 1629 Waste disposal plant construction
PA: Uranium Disposition Services, Llc

1020 Monarch St Ste 100
Lexington KY 40513
859 296-0023

(G-12431)
VNS FEDERAL SERVICES LLC (PA)
Also Called: Veolia Nuclear Solutions
1571 Shyville Rd (45661-9201)
PHONE................740 443-7005
Billy Morrison, *CEO*
Steve Moore, *
Jim Gardner, *
Keith Tucker, *
Thomas Kaupas, *
EMP: 30 **EST**: 1992
SALES (est): 144.88MM **Privately Held**
Web: www.vnsfederalservices.com
SIC: 4959 8744 8711 Sanitary services, nec; Facilities support services; Engineering services

(G-12432)
WASTREN - ENRGX MSSION SPPORT
Also Called: Wems
1571 Shyville Rd (45661-9201)
P.O. Box 307 (45661-0307)
PHONE................740 897-3724
Jim Gardner, *
Glenn Henderson, *
Keith Tucker, *
EMP: 170 **EST**: 2009
SALES (est): 26.64MM **Privately Held**
Web: www.wems-llc.com
SIC: 8744 Facilities support services
PA: Vns Federal Services, Llc
1571 Shyville Rd
Piketon OH 45661

Pioneer
Williams County

(G-12433)
MAASS - MIDWEST MFG INC
Also Called: Menards Holiday City Dist Ctr
14502 County Road 15 (43554-8705)
PHONE................419 485-6905
Carl Carlburg, *CEO*
EMP: 834 **EST**: 2008
SALES (est): 8.32MM
SALES (corp-wide): 1.7B **Privately Held**
SIC: 7349 Building maintenance, except repairs
PA: Menard, Inc.
5101 Menard Dr
Eau Claire WI 54703
715 876-2000

Piqua
Miami County

(G-12434)
A M LEONARD INC
Also Called: Gardeners Edge
241 Fox Dr (45356-9265)
P.O. Box 816 (45356-0816)
PHONE................937 773-2694
Betty L Ziegler, *Pr*
◆ **EMP**: 90 **EST**: 1885
SQ FT: 120,000
SALES (est): 46.85MM **Privately Held**
Web: www.amleo.com
SIC: 5072 5191 Garden tools, hand; Farm supplies

GEOGRAPHIC SECTION

Piqua - Miami County (G-12456)

(G-12435)
B D TRANSPORTATION INC
9590 Looney Rd (45356-2584)
P.O. Box 813 (45356-0813)
PHONE....................................937 773-9280
John Douglas, *Pr*
Teresa Douglas, *
EMP: 30 **EST:** 2000
SQ FT: 1,000
SALES (est): 3.69MM **Privately Held**
SIC: 4213 4212 Contract haulers; Local trucking, without storage

(G-12436)
BUCKEYE STATE MUTUAL INSUR CO (PA)
Also Called: Buckeye Insurance Group
1 Heritage Pl (45356-4148)
PHONE....................................937 778-5000
R Douglas Haines, *Pr*
Rob Bornhorst, *
EMP: 60 **EST:** 1897
SQ FT: 17,000
SALES (est): 23.34MM
SALES (corp-wide): 23.34MM **Privately Held**
Web: www.buckeye-ins.com
SIC: 6311 Life insurance

(G-12437)
COILPLUS INC
Also Called: Coilplus Berwick
100 Steelway Dr (45356-7530)
PHONE....................................937 778-8884
Terry Harold, *Mgr*
EMP: 83
Web: www.coilplus.com
SIC: 5051 Steel
HQ: Coilplus, Inc.
6250 N River Rd Ste 6050
Rosemont IL 60018

(G-12438)
COUNCIL ON RUR SVC PRGRAMS INC (PA)
201 Robert M Davis Pkwy Ste B (45356-8342)
PHONE....................................937 778-5220
Daniel Schwanitz, *Ex Dir*
EMP: 40 **EST:** 1972
SALES (est): 19.72MM
SALES (corp-wide): 19.72MM **Privately Held**
Web: www.councilonruralservices.org
SIC: 8399 Community action agency

(G-12439)
COUNCIL ON RUR SVC PRGRAMS INC
Also Called: Beary Land
285 Robert M Davis Pkwy (45356-8342)
PHONE....................................937 773-0773
Shirley Hathaway, *Dir*
EMP: 89
SALES (corp-wide): 19.72MM **Privately Held**
Web: www.councilonruralservices.org
SIC: 8399 8351 8322 Community action agency; Child day care services; Individual and family services
PA: Council On Rural Service Programs, Inc.
201 Robert M Davis Pkwy B
Piqua OH 45356
937 778-5220

(G-12440)
CRANE PUMPS & SYSTEMS INC
Also Called: Pacific Valve
420 3rd St (45356-3918)
PHONE....................................937 773-2442
Allan Oak, *Brnch Mgr*
EMP: 175
SALES (corp-wide): 2.09B **Publicly Held**
Web: www.cranepumps.com
SIC: 5085 3494 Valves and fittings; Valves and pipe fittings, nec
HQ: Crane Pumps & Systems, Inc.
420 3rd St
Piqua OH 45356
937 773-2442

(G-12441)
EPSILYTE HOLDINGS LLC
Also Called: Compounded Eps
555 E Statler Rd (45356-9227)
PHONE....................................937 778-9500
Matt Cox, *Brnch Mgr*
EMP: 75
SALES (corp-wide): 9.52MM **Privately Held**
Web: www.epsilyte.com
SIC: 2821 5162 Polystyrene resins; Resins
PA: Epsilyte Holdings Llc
1330 Lake Robbins Dr # 310
The Woodlands TX 77380
815 224-1525

(G-12442)
FRANCIS C SKINNER PAINTING SVC
Also Called: F C Skinner Painting Service
4633 W State Route 36 (45356)
P.O. Box 1441 (45356-1041)
PHONE....................................937 773-3858
Dave Middleton, *Pr*
EMP: 29 **EST:** 1944
SALES (est): 1.01MM **Privately Held**
Web: www.skinnerpainting.com
SIC: 1721 Exterior commercial painting contractor

(G-12443)
HARTZELL HARDWOODS INC (PA)
1025 S Roosevelt Ave (45356)
P.O. Box 919 (45356)
PHONE....................................937 773-7054
James Robert Hartzell, *Ch Bd*
Jeffery Bannister, *
Kelly Hostetter, *
Jane Osborn, *
▼ **EMP:** 65 **EST:** 1928
SQ FT: 275,000
SALES (est): 20.89MM
SALES (corp-wide): 20.89MM **Privately Held**
Web: www.hartzellhardwoods.com
SIC: 5031 2421 2426 Lumber: rough, dressed, and finished; Sawmills and planing mills, general; Hardwood dimension and flooring mills

(G-12444)
HCF OF PIQUA INC
Also Called: HEALTH CARE FACILITIES
1840 W High St (45356-9399)
PHONE....................................937 773-0040
James Unberferth, *Pr*
EMP: 163 **EST:** 2008
SQ FT: 41,920
SALES (est): 9.97MM
SALES (corp-wide): 305.93MM **Privately Held**
Web: www.piquamanor.com
SIC: 8051 Convalescent home with continuous nursing care
PA: Hcf Management, Inc.
1100 Shawnee Rd
Lima OH 45805
419 999-2010

(G-12445)
INDUSTRY PRODUCTS CO (PA)
500 W Statler Rd (45356-8281)
PHONE....................................937 778-0585
Linda Cleveland, *Pr*
▲ **EMP:** 366 **EST:** 1966
SQ FT: 335,000
SALES (est): 44.52MM
SALES (corp-wide): 44.52MM **Privately Held**
Web: www.industryproductsco.com
SIC: 7692 3053 3714 3544 Automotive welding; Gaskets, all materials; Motor vehicle parts and accessories; Special dies, tools, jigs, and fixtures

(G-12446)
M&C HOTEL INTERESTS INC
987 E Ash St Ste 171 (45356-4198)
PHONE....................................937 778-8100
Larry Chester, *Mgr*
EMP: 227
Web: www.richfield.com
SIC: 7011 Hotels
HQ: M&C Hotel Interests, Inc.
6560 Greenwood Plaza Blvd
Greenwood Village CO 80111

(G-12447)
MERCER HOSPITALITY INC
Also Called: La Quinta Inn
950 E Ash St (45356-4104)
PHONE....................................937 615-0140
EMP: 29 **EST:** 2009
SALES (est): 114.54K **Privately Held**
Web: www.lq.com
SIC: 7011 Hotels and motels

(G-12448)
MIAMI CO YMCA CHILD CARE
Also Called: YMCA
325 W Ash St (45356-2203)
PHONE....................................937 778-5241
James Mcmaken, *Ex Dir*
EMP: 30 **EST:** 2010
SALES (est): 192.45K **Privately Held**
Web: www.miamicountyymca.net
SIC: 8641 Youth organizations

(G-12449)
MIAMI VALLEY STEEL SERVICE INC
201 Fox Dr (45356-9265)
PHONE....................................937 773-7127
Louis Moran, *CEO*
Jill Kindell, *
▼ **EMP:** 140 **EST:** 1982
SQ FT: 320,000
SALES (est): 48.04MM **Privately Held**
Web: www.miamivalleysteel.com
SIC: 5051 Steel

(G-12450)
MONARCH DENTAL CORP
Also Called: Dental Care One
987 E Ash St Ste 154 (45356-4198)
PHONE....................................937 778-0150
Rena Vennemeyer, *Mgr*
EMP: 34
SALES (corp-wide): 303.67MM **Privately Held**
Web: www.monarchdental.com
SIC: 8021 Dental clinic
HQ: Monarch Dental Corp
7989 Belt Line Rd Ste 90
Dallas TX 75248

(G-12451)
PIONEER RURAL ELECTRIC COOP (PA)
344 W Us Route 36 (45356-9255)
PHONE....................................800 762-0997
TOLL FREE: 800
Ronald Salyer, *Pr*
EMP: 48 **EST:** 1936
SQ FT: 32,000
SALES (est): 75.42MM
SALES (corp-wide): 75.42MM **Privately Held**
Web: www.pioneerec.com
SIC: 4911 Distribution, electric power

(G-12452)
PIQUA COUNTRY CLUB HOLDING CO
Also Called: Piqua Country Club Pool
9812 Country Club Rd (45356-9594)
PHONE....................................937 773-7744
Don Goettpmoeller, *Treas*
Don Grieshop, *
EMP: 50 **EST:** 1928
SQ FT: 9,000
SALES (est): 999.08K **Privately Held**
Web: www.piquacountryclub.com
SIC: 7997 5812 7911 Country club, membership; Eating places; Dance hall or ballroom operation

(G-12453)
PIQUA MATERIALS INC
Also Called: Piqua Mineral Division
1750 W Statler Rd (45356-9264)
PHONE....................................937 773-4824
John Harris, *Brnch Mgr*
EMP: 79
SQ FT: 16,808
Web: www.piquamaterials.com
SIC: 1422 3274 Limestones, ground; Lime
PA: Piqua Materials, Inc.
11641 Mosteller Rd Ste 1
Cincinnati OH 45241

(G-12454)
PIQUA STEEL CO (PA)
Also Called: PSC Crane & Rigging
4243 W Us Route 36 (45356-9334)
PHONE....................................937 773-3632
James R Sever, *Pr*
Earl F Sever Iii, *Ch*
Randy Sever, *Business Development*
Nancy J Sever, *Sec*
EMP: 73 **EST:** 1933
SQ FT: 30,000
SALES (est): 34.9MM
SALES (corp-wide): 34.9MM **Privately Held**
Web: www.pscind.com
SIC: 4225 7353 1796 7359 General warehousing; Cranes and aerial lift equipment, rental or leasing; Machine moving and rigging; Equipment rental and leasing, nec

(G-12455)
PIQUA TRANSFER & STORAGE CO
9782 Looney Rd (45356-2587)
P.O. Box 823 (45356-0823)
PHONE....................................937 773-3743
John D Laughman, *Pr*
H L Lane, *
Damita Hoblit, *
EMP: 86 **EST:** 1904
SQ FT: 24,000
SALES (est): 8.76MM **Privately Held**
Web: www.piquatransfer.com
SIC: 4213 4214 Contract haulers; Local trucking with storage

(G-12456)
PLASTIC RECYCLING TECH INC (PA)
Also Called: Prt
9054 N County Road 25a (45356-7522)

Piqua - Miami County (G-12457)

PHONE.....................937 615-9286
Matthew Kreigel, *Pr*
Mark Miller, *
Stacy Jent, *
Stephen Larger, *
EMP: 30 **EST:** 1988
SALES (est): 23.08MM **Privately Held**
Web: www.plasticrecyclingtech.com
SIC: 4953 Recycling, waste materials

(G-12457)
R C HEMM GLASS SHOPS INC (PA)
Also Called: Hemm Glass
514 S Main St (45356-3942)
PHONE.....................937 773-5591
Jeff Hemm, *Pr*
EMP: 32 **EST:** 1948
SQ FT: 20,000
SALES (est): 10.58MM
SALES (corp-wide): 10.58MM **Privately Held**
Web: www.hemmglass.com
SIC: 1793 5231 Glass and glazing work; Glass

(G-12458)
SCOTT STEEL LLC
125 Clark Ave Ste A (45356-3807)
PHONE.....................937 552-9670
EMP: 30 **EST:** 2008
SALES (est): 17.02MM **Privately Held**
Web: www.scottsteelllc.com
SIC: 5051 Steel

(G-12459)
TRUPOINTE COOPERATIVE INC
215 Looney Rd (45356-4147)
P.O. Box 870 (43420-0870)
PHONE.....................937 575-6780
EMP: 450
Web: www.sunriseco-op.com
SIC: 5153 5191 Grains; Farm supplies

(G-12460)
UNITY NATIONAL BANK (HQ)
Also Called: Third Savings
215 N Wayne St (45356-2227)
P.O. Box 913 (45356-0913)
PHONE.....................937 773-0752
Scott Rasor, *Pr*
Scott Gabriel, *
EMP: 42 **EST:** 1884
SQ FT: 6,000
SALES (est): 2.76MM
SALES (corp-wide): 564.3MM **Publicly Held**
Web: www.parknationalbank.com
SIC: 6021 National commercial banks
PA: Park National Corporation
50 N 3rd St
Newark OH 43055
740 349-8451

(G-12461)
VALVOLINE INSTANT OIL CHNGE FR
Also Called: Valvoline Instant Oil Change
1275 E Ash St (45356-4107)
PHONE.....................937 773-0112
EMP: 37
Web: www.valvoline.com
SIC: 7549 Automotive maintenance services
HQ: Valvoline Instant Oil Change Franchising, Inc.
100 Valvoline Way
Lexington KY 40509

(G-12462)
VETERANS OF FOREIGN WARS OF US
Also Called: Veterans of Foreign Wars
8756 N County Road 25a (45356-9512)

P.O. Box 4874 (45356)
PHONE.....................937 773-9122
EMP: 62
SALES (corp-wide): 105.25MM **Privately Held**
SIC: 8641 Veterans' organization
PA: Veterans Of Foreign Wars Of The United States
406 W 34th St Fl 11
Kansas City MO 64111
816 756-3390

Plain City
Madison County

(G-12463)
A-1 ADVANCED PLUMBING INC
Also Called: Advanced Plumbing
8299 Memorial Dr (43064-8623)
PHONE.....................614 873-0548
Wesley Zimmer, *Pr*
Eearl Sagraves, *
EMP: 30 **EST:** 1981
SQ FT: 4,500
SALES (est): 2.3MM **Privately Held**
Web: www.advancedplumbinginc.com
SIC: 1711 Plumbing contractors

(G-12464)
A2Z FIELD SERVICES LLC
7450 Industrial Pkwy Ste 105 (43064-9292)
P.O. Box 3215 (43016-0100)
PHONE.....................614 873-0211
William Mcmullen, *Managing Member*
Amie Sparks, *
Jennifer Sells, *
EMP: 130 **EST:** 2001
SQ FT: 6,000
SALES (est): 19.48MM **Privately Held**
Web: www.a2zfieldservices.com
SIC: 7389 Building inspection service

(G-12465)
ABBRUZZESE BROTHERS INC (PA)
7775 Smith Calhoun Rd (43064-9192)
P.O. Box 215 (43026-0215)
PHONE.....................614 873-1550
Jim Abbruzzese, *Pr*
John Abbruzzese, *
Joe Abbruzzese, *
EMP: 31 **EST:** 1985
SQ FT: 7,200
SALES (est): 2.27MM **Privately Held**
Web: www.abbzinc.com
SIC: 0782 Lawn care services

(G-12466)
AMERICAN COATINGS CORPORATION
Also Called: Americoat
7510 Montgomery Rd (43064-8611)
PHONE.....................614 335-1000
Philip Freedman, *Pr*
EMP: 30 **EST:** 1997
SALES (est): 4.36MM **Privately Held**
SIC: 1611 Surfacing and paving

(G-12467)
AMERICAN PAVEMENTS INC
7475 Montgomery Rd (43064-8612)
PHONE.....................614 873-2191
EMP: 45 **EST:** 2017
SQ FT: 5,000
SALES (est): 5.4MM **Privately Held**
Web: www.americanpavements.com
SIC: 1611 Highway and street paving contractor

(G-12468)
ASI COMMERCIAL ROOFG MAINT INC
Also Called: A S I
8633 Memorial Dr (43064-8608)
PHONE.....................614 873-2057
David Phillips, *Pr*
EMP: 55 **EST:** 2002
SQ FT: 6,000
SALES (est): 17.96MM **Privately Held**
Web: www.asirfg.com
SIC: 1761 Roofing contractor

(G-12469)
BENCHMARK LANDSCAPE CNSTR INC
9600 Industrial Pkwy (43064-9426)
PHONE.....................614 873-8080
Roy Ed Veley, *Pr*
Mark Chamberlain, *
Devon Stanley, *Managing Member*
Doug Heindel, *Managing Member*
Matt Hecht, *Managing Member*
EMP: 38 **EST:** 1996
SQ FT: 1,900
SALES (est): 2.63MM **Privately Held**
Web: www.benchmarkohio.com
SIC: 0782 Landscape contractors

(G-12470)
BINDERY & SPC PRESSWORKS INC
Also Called: Pressworks
351 W Bigelow Ave (43064-1152)
PHONE.....................614 873-4623
Dick Izzard, *Pr*
Betty Izzard, *
Mark Izzard, *
Doug Izzard, *
Tami Roberts, *
EMP: 74 **EST:** 1978
SQ FT: 42,000
SALES (est): 18.97MM **Privately Held**
Web: www.pressworks.us
SIC: 2791 7331 2759 2789 Typesetting; Mailing service; Commercial printing, nec; Bookbinding and related work

(G-12471)
BULK TRANSIT CORPORATION (PA)
7177 Indl Pkwy (43064)
PHONE.....................614 873-4632
Ronald De Wolf, *Pr*
Paul F Beery, *
Gloria De Wolf, *
EMP: 40 **EST:** 1986
SQ FT: 5,000
SALES (est): 28.24MM
SALES (corp-wide): 28.24MM **Privately Held**
Web: www.bulktransit.com
SIC: 4213 Contract haulers

(G-12472)
CSI COMPLETE INC
8080 Corporate Blvd (43064-9220)
PHONE.....................800 343-0641
Doug Webb, *CEO*
EMP: 36 **EST:** 2013
SALES (est): 224.28K **Privately Held**
Web: www.tenpointcomplete.com
SIC: 7374 Data processing service
PA: Douglas Webb & Associates, Inc.
8080 Corporate Blvd
Plain City OH 43064

(G-12473)
DKMP CONSULTING INC
8000 Corporate Blvd (43064-9220)
PHONE.....................614 733-0979
Mark Patel, *Pr*

Matthew S Patel, *
EMP: 105 **EST:** 1996
SQ FT: 33,000
SALES (est): 16.93MM
SALES (corp-wide): 1.04B **Privately Held**
Web: www.otcindustrial.com
SIC: 5063 Electrical apparatus and equipment
PA: Ohio Transmission Llc
1900 Jetway Blvd
Columbus OH 43219
614 342-6247

(G-12474)
DUTCHMAN HOSPITALITY GROUP INC
Also Called: Der Dutchman's Restaurant
445 S Jefferson Ave (43064-1166)
PHONE.....................614 873-3414
Dan Yoder, *Brnch Mgr*
EMP: 101
SALES (corp-wide): 25.45MM **Privately Held**
Web: www.dhgroup.com
SIC: 5812 5947 5149 Italian restaurant; Gift shop; Bakery products
PA: Dutchman Hospitality Group, Inc.
4985 Walnut St
Walnut Creek OH 44687
330 893-2926

(G-12475)
EMSI INC (PA)
8220 Industrial Pkwy (43064-9371)
P.O. Box 175 (43017-0175)
PHONE.....................614 876-9988
Mark Wehinger, *Pr*
Gregory C Farell, *
EMP: 39 **EST:** 1994
SALES (est): 23.76K
SALES (corp-wide): 23.76K **Privately Held**
Web: www.landscapepros.com
SIC: 0782 Landscape contractors

(G-12476)
ENVIROCORE INC
Also Called: Envirocore
8250 Estates Pkwy (43064-8410)
PHONE.....................614 263-6554
Chris Rismiller, *CEO*
Joe Fleck, *
EMP: 35 **EST:** 2002
SALES (est): 406.61K **Privately Held**
Web: www.envirocore.com
SIC: 8641 Environmental protection organization

(G-12477)
FAIRFIELD HOMES INC
Also Called: Madison Square Apartments
445 Fairfield Dr Ofc (43064-1274)
PHONE.....................614 873-3533
Leonard F Gorsuch, *Brnch Mgr*
EMP: 121
SALES (corp-wide): 25.24MM **Privately Held**
Web: www.fairfieldhomesohio.com
SIC: 6513 1522 6531 1542 Apartment building operators; Residential construction, nec; Real estate agents and managers; Nonresidential construction, nec
PA: Fairfield Homes Inc.
603 W Wheeling St
Lancaster OH 43130
740 653-3583

(G-12478)
GK PACKAGING INC (PA)
Also Called: Plain City Molding
7680 Commerce Pl (43064-9222)
PHONE.....................614 873-3900

GEOGRAPHIC SECTION

Plymouth - Huron County (G-12501)

Gene J Kuzma, *Pr*
Jeff Kuzma, *
Betty Jo Jerome, *
▲ **EMP:** 94 **EST:** 1983
SQ FT: 70,000
SALES (est): 23.81MM
SALES (corp-wide): 23.81MM **Privately Held**
Web: www.gkpackaging.com
SIC: 5199 Packaging materials

(G-12479)
HEIL AND HORNIK LLC
Also Called: Elysium Tennis
7637c Commerce Pl (43064-9223)
PHONE..................614 873-8749
EMP: 27 **EST:** 2009
SALES (est): 899.92K **Privately Held**
Web: www.elysiumtennis.com
SIC: 7997 Tennis club, membership

(G-12480)
HERITAGE EQUIPMENT COMPANY
9000 Heritage Dr (43064-8744)
PHONE..................614 873-3941
Louis Cascelli, *CEO*
Eric J Zwirner, *
▲ **EMP:** 30 **EST:** 1982
SQ FT: 10,000
SALES (est): 8.31MM **Privately Held**
Web: www.heritage-equipment.com
SIC: 5084 Dairy products manufacturing machinery, nec

(G-12481)
HIYES LOGISTICS
8400 Industrial Pkwy Ste C (43064-9231)
PHONE..................614 558-0198
Lina Cio, *Owner*
EMP: 50 **EST:** 2017
SALES (est): 1.91MM **Privately Held**
SIC: 4731 Freight consolidation

(G-12482)
HOSTETLER TRUCKING INC
6495 Converse Huff Rd (43064-9185)
PHONE..................614 873-8885
Edna Hostetler, *Pr*
Nelson Hostetler, *VP*
EMP: 32 **EST:** 1972
SALES (est): 1.07MM **Privately Held**
SIC: 4212 Dump truck haulage

(G-12483)
K AMALIA ENTERPRISES INC
Also Called: Mjr Sales
8025 Corporate Blvd (43064-9208)
PHONE..................614 733-3800
Jeff Bradshaw, *Pr*
Mark Lauferswieler, *
Michael Cacchio, *
▲ **EMP:** 46 **EST:** 1992
SQ FT: 53,000
SALES (est): 2.72MM **Privately Held**
Web: www.dfwh.com
SIC: 5699 5136 Designers, apparel; Men's and boy's clothing

(G-12484)
MADE FROM SCRATCH INC
Also Called: Celebrations
7500 Montgomery Rd (43064-8611)
PHONE..................614 873-3344
Larry G Clark, *Pr*
EMP: 40 **EST:** 1977
SQ FT: 12,000
SALES (est): 4.78MM **Privately Held**
Web: www.pinkfloyd-guitar.com
SIC: 7359 5812 5149 5992 Party supplies rental services; Caterers; Bakery products; Florists

(G-12485)
MARTIN CONTROL SYSTEMS INC
Also Called: Martincsi
8460 Estates Ct (43064-8015)
PHONE..................614 761-5600
EMP: 28 **EST:** 1988
SQ FT: 12,000
SALES (est): 5.3MM **Privately Held**
Web: www.martincsi.com
SIC: 8711 Consulting engineer

(G-12486)
MAZA INC
7635 Commerce Pl (43064-9223)
PHONE..................614 760-0003
Chris Watson, *Pr*
▲ **EMP:** 65 **EST:** 1991
SQ FT: 15,400
SALES (est): 10.65MM
SALES (corp-wide): 86.38B **Publicly Held**
SIC: 5211 5999 5032 Masonry materials and supplies; Monuments and tombstones; Marble building stone
PA: Lowe's Companies, Inc.
1000 Lowes Blvd
Mooresville NC 28117
704 758-1000

(G-12487)
MEDIA SOURCE INC (PA)
7858 Industrial Pkwy (43064-9468)
PHONE..................614 873-7635
Randall J Asmo, *Pr*
Steve Zales, *
Jill Dorne, *
Dave Myers, *
Victor F Ganzi, *
EMP: 60 **EST:** 1980
SQ FT: 4,800
SALES (est): 24.72MM
SALES (corp-wide): 24.72MM **Privately Held**
Web: www.mediasourceinc.com
SIC: 5192 Books

(G-12488)
PAINTING COMPANY
6969 Industrial Pkwy (43064-8799)
PHONE..................614 873-1334
Jeffery D Sammons Incorp, *Prin*
David Asman, *
Terry Asman, *
EMP: 105 **EST:** 1979
SALES (est): 16.23MM **Privately Held**
Web: www.thepaintingcompany.com
SIC: 1721 Commercial painting

(G-12489)
PATTERSON POOLS LLC
Also Called: Patterson Pools
8155 Memorial Dr (43064-7586)
PHONE..................614 334-2629
Philip F Patterson, *Prin*
EMP: 37 **EST:** 1946
SQ FT: 18,000
SALES (est): 4.01MM **Privately Held**
Web: www.pattersonpools.com
SIC: 1799 Swimming pool construction

(G-12490)
PRECISION TOOLS SERVICE INC
8205 Estates Pkwy Ste I (43064-8018)
PHONE..................614 873-8000
EMP: 89 **EST:** 1998
SALES (est): 4.74MM **Privately Held**
Web: www.ptservice.com
SIC: 5084 Industrial machinery and equipment

(G-12491)
R & S HALLEY AND COMPANY INC
Also Called: Darby Creek Nursery
9050 Amity Pike (43064-9314)
PHONE..................614 771-0388
Jeffrey Turnbull, *Pr*
Lucinda Turnbull, *
EMP: 35 **EST:** 1993
SALES (est): 2.49MM **Privately Held**
Web: www.darbycreeknursery.net
SIC: 0181 0782 Nursery stock, growing of; Landscape contractors

(G-12492)
REGAL-ELITE INC
Also Called: Paul G. Toys
8140 Business Way (43064-9209)
PHONE..................614 873-3800
Paul G Hartman, *CEO*
▲ **EMP:** 57 **EST:** 1973
SQ FT: 7,000
SALES (est): 5.05MM **Privately Held**
SIC: 5199 Gifts and novelties

(G-12493)
SCHEIDERER TRANSPORT INC
8520 State Route 161 E (43064-9101)
PHONE..................614 873-5103
Roger C Scheiderer, *Pr*
EMP: 55 **EST:** 1950
SQ FT: 10,000
SALES (est): 2.62MM **Privately Held**
Web: www.scheiderertransport.com
SIC: 4213 Contract haulers

(G-12494)
SELECT SIRES INC (PA)
11740 Us Highway 42 N (43064)
PHONE..................614 873-4683
EMP: 140 **EST:** 1965
SALES (est): 20.68MM
SALES (corp-wide): 20.68MM **Privately Held**
Web: www.selectsires.com
SIC: 0751 Artificial insemination services, livestock

(G-12495)
TRADESMEN GROUP INC (PA)
8465 Rausch Dr (43064-8064)
PHONE..................614 799-0889
Melissa West, *Pr*
EMP: 37 **EST:** 1997
SQ FT: 12,000
SALES (est): 15.5MM
SALES (corp-wide): 15.5MM **Privately Held**
Web: www.tradesmengroup.com
SIC: 1541 Renovation, remodeling and repairs: industrial buildings

(G-12496)
TRIO ORTHODONTICS
7420 State Route 161 E (43064-7565)
PHONE..................614 889-7613
Jared Zwick, *Prin*
EMP: 25 **EST:** 2015
SALES (est): 945.27K **Privately Held**
Web: www.smiledoctors.com
SIC: 8021 Orthodontist

(G-12497)
VELOCYS INC
8520 Warner Rd (43064-3561)
PHONE..................614 733-3300
David Pummell, *CEO*
Susan Robertson, *
Doctor Paul F Schubert, *COO*
EMP: 60 **EST:** 2000
SALES (est): 16.38MM
SALES (corp-wide): 290.16K **Privately Held**
Web: www.velocys.com
SIC: 8731 3559 Commercial physical research; Sewing machines and hat and zipper making machinery
PA: Velocys Plc
Robert Robinson Avenue The Oxford Science Park
Oxford OXON
186 580-0821

(G-12498)
YASKAWA AMERICA INC
8628 Industrial Pkwy Ste A (43064-8069)
PHONE..................614 733-3200
Jill Hoff, *Brnch Mgr*
EMP: 50
Web: www.yaskawa.com
SIC: 5084 Industrial machinery and equipment
HQ: Yaskawa America, Inc.
2121 S Norman Dr
Waukegan IL 60085
847 887-7000

Pleasant Plain
Warren County

(G-12499)
MID-WESTERN CHILDRENS HOME
Also Called: VILLAGE CHRISTIAN SCHOOLS
4585 Long Spurling Rd (45162-9790)
P.O. Box 48 (45162-0048)
PHONE..................513 877-2141
James Frampton, *Pr*
Cotton Blakely, *
Ron Hartman, *
Barry Boverie, *
EMP: 32 **EST:** 1967
SQ FT: 68,283
SALES (est): 1.34MM **Privately Held**
Web: www.mid-western.org
SIC: 8361 Children's home

(G-12500)
MILLER INDUSTRIAL SVC TEAM INC
8485 State Route 132 (45162-9226)
P.O. Box 188 (45152-0188)
PHONE..................513 877-2708
Debbie Miller, *Pr*
EMP: 100 **EST:** 2003
SQ FT: 11,590
SALES (est): 10.02MM **Privately Held**
Web: www.mistinc.com
SIC: 1542 Commercial and office building, new construction

Plymouth
Huron County

(G-12501)
BESTWAY TRANSPORT CO (PA)
2040 Sandusky St Rt 61n (44865-9412)
PHONE..................419 687-2000
Rich M Myers, *Pr*
Beverly Tuttle, *
EMP: 30 **EST:** 1980
SQ FT: 5,300
SALES (est): 2.45MM
SALES (corp-wide): 2.45MM **Privately Held**
SIC: 4213 Trucking, except local

Poland - Mahoning County (G-12502) GEOGRAPHIC SECTION

Poland
Mahoning County

(G-12502)
CENTER FOR RHBLTTION AT HMPTON
1517 E Western Reserve Rd (44514-3254)
PHONE..................................330 792-7681
Kathy Prasad, *Prin*
EMP: 30 **EST:** 2013
SALES (est): 3.08MM **Privately Held**
Web: www.woodlandsllc.com
SIC: 8052 Intermediate care facilities

(G-12503)
COLDWELL BANKER FIRST PLACE RE
Also Called: Coldwell Banker
1275 Boardman Poland Rd Ste 1 (44514-3911)
PHONE..................................330 726-8161
EMP: 36 **EST:** 1987
SALES (est): 1.4MM **Privately Held**
Web: www.coldwellbanker.com
SIC: 6531 Real estate agent, residential

(G-12504)
HUNTINGTON NATIONAL BANK
2 S Main St (44514-1914)
PHONE..................................330 314-1395
EMP: 31
SALES (corp-wide): 10.84B **Publicly Held**
Web: www.huntington.com
SIC: 6029 Commercial banks, nec
HQ: The Huntington National Bank
   41 S High St
   Columbus OH 43215
   614 480-4293

(G-12505)
LAKE CLUB
1140 Paulin Rd (44514-3239)
PHONE..................................330 549-3996
EMP: 200 **EST:** 2010
SALES (est): 10.32MM **Privately Held**
Web: www.thelakeclubohio.com
SIC: 7997 Golf club, membership

(G-12506)
PHARMACY DATA MANAGEMENT
8530 Crossroad Dr (44514-4381)
PHONE..................................330 757-0724
EMP: 61 **EST:** 2020
SALES (est): 4.48MM **Privately Held**
Web: www.pdmi.com
SIC: 8741 Management services

(G-12507)
RED ROOF INNS INC
Also Called: Red Roof Inn
1051 Tiffany S (44514-1977)
PHONE..................................330 758-1999
EMP: 40
Web: www.redroof.com
SIC: 7011 Hotels and motels
HQ: Red Roof Inns, Inc.
   7815 Walton Pkwy
   New Albany OH 43054
   614 744-2600

(G-12508)
RESERVE RUN GOLF CLUB LLC
Also Called: Quarry Pines
625 E Western Reserve Rd (44514-3356)
P.O. Box 14189 (44514-7189)
PHONE..................................330 758-1017
EMP: 80 **EST:** 1999
SALES (est): 2.38MM **Privately Held**
Web: www.ohiogolf.net

SIC: 7992 Public golf courses

(G-12509)
SHEPHERD OF VLY LTHRAN RTRMENT
Also Called: Shepards Meadows
301 W Western Reserve Rd (44514-3527)
PHONE..................................330 726-7110
EMP: 37
SALES (corp-wide): 42.58MM **Privately Held**
Web: www.shepherdofthevalley.com
SIC: 8361 Aged home
PA: Shepherd Of The Valley Lutheran
   Retirement Services, Inc.
   5525 Silica Rd
   Youngstown OH 44515
   330 530-4038

(G-12510)
SUNRISE SENIOR LIVING LLC
Also Called: Sunrise of Poland
335 W Mckinley Way (44514-1681)
PHONE..................................330 707-1313
Nicole Lagata, *Brnch Mgr*
EMP: 50
SALES (corp-wide): 2.92B **Privately Held**
Web: www.sunriseseniorliving.com
SIC: 8051 Skilled nursing care facilities
HQ: Sunrise Senior Living, Llc
   7902 Westpark Dr
   Mc Lean VA 22102

(G-12511)
VANTAGE SOLUTIONS INC
Also Called: Reach24
207 S Main St (44514-2070)
PHONE..................................330 757-4864
Paul Burgoyne, *CEO*
EMP: 64 **EST:** 2013
SALES (est): 2.4MM **Privately Held**
SIC: 7371 Computer software development and applications

Polk
Ashland County

(G-12512)
FALLING STAR FARM LTD
Also Called: Dairy Farm
626 State Route 89 (44866-9712)
PHONE..................................419 945-2651
EMP: 31 **EST:** 1986
SALES (est): 4.99MM **Privately Held**
Web: www.meyerhatchery.com
SIC: 0254 Chicken hatchery

Pomeroy
Meigs County

(G-12513)
COUNTY OF MEIGS
Also Called: Meigs County Emrgncy Med Svcs
Mulburry Heights Stn 11 (45769)
P.O. Box 748 (45769-0748)
PHONE..................................740 992-6617
Patsy Warner, *Dir*
EMP: 32
SQ FT: 2,000
Web: www.meigscountyclerkofcourts.com
SIC: 4119 Ambulance service
PA: County Of Meigs
   100 E 2nd St Rm 201
   Pomeroy OH 45769
   740 992-5290

(G-12514)
PDK CONSTRUCTION INC
34070 Crew Rd (45769-9715)
P.O. Box 683 (45769-0683)
PHONE..................................740 992-6451
Phillip R Harrison, *Pr*
Donald Roush, *
EMP: 27 **EST:** 1985
SQ FT: 4,080
SALES (est): 1.26MM **Privately Held**
SIC: 1611 Guardrail construction, highways

(G-12515)
POMEROY OPCO LLC
36759 Rocksprings Rd (45769-9730)
PHONE..................................740 992-6606
EMP: 84 **EST:** 2014
SALES (est): 2.68MM **Privately Held**
SIC: 8051 Skilled nursing care facilities

Port Clinton
Ottawa County

(G-12516)
A T EMMETT LLC
2028 E State Rd (43452-2525)
P.O. Box 516 (43452-0516)
PHONE..................................419 734-2520
EMP: 27
SQ FT: 6,000
SALES (est): 784.4K **Privately Held**
Web: www.at-emmett.com
SIC: 1731 General electrical contractor

(G-12517)
ANIMAL MGT SVCS OHIO INC
Also Called: African Safari Wildlife Park
267 S Lightner Rd (43452-3851)
PHONE..................................248 398-6533
Jon Mikosz, *Prin*
EMP: 35
Web: www.africansafariwildlifepark.com
SIC: 8422 Zoological garden, noncommercial
PA: Animal Management Services Of Ohio Inc.
   25600 Woodward Ave Ste 11
   Royal Oak MI 48067

(G-12518)
CATAWBA-CLEVELAND DEV CORP (PA)
Also Called: Catawba Island Marina
4235 E Beachclub Rd (43452)
PHONE..................................419 797-4424
James V Stouffer, *CEO*
EMP: 99 **EST:** 1971
SQ FT: 4,500
SALES (est): 17.62MM
SALES (corp-wide): 17.62MM **Privately Held**
Web: www.cicclub.com
SIC: 7997 4493 6519 Country club, membership; Marinas; Real property lessors, nec

(G-12519)
CHOICES BEHAVIORAL HEALTH CARE
201 Madison St (43452-1168)
PHONE..................................419 960-4009
Luther Jones, *CEO*
EMP: 29
SALES (corp-wide): 3.36MM **Privately Held**
Web: www.choicesbhc.com
SIC: 8093 Mental health clinic, outpatient
PA: Choices Behavioral Health Care
   5151 Monroe St Ste 204
   Toledo OH 43623

   419 865-5690

(G-12520)
COMMODORE PRRY INNS SUITES LLC
255 W Lakeshore Dr (43452-9477)
PHONE..................................419 732-2645
EMP: 33 **EST:** 2002
SALES (est): 485.41K **Privately Held**
Web: www.commodoreperry.com
SIC: 7011 5812 Hotels; Eating places

(G-12521)
COVENANT CARE OHIO INC
Also Called: Edgewood Manor Nursing Center
1330 Fulton St (43452-9297)
PHONE..................................419 898-5506
Denise Day, *Brnch Mgr*
EMP: 94
SIC: 8051 Convalescent home with continuous nursing care
HQ: Covenant Care Ohio, Inc.
   120 Vantis Dr Ste 200
   Aliso Viejo CA 92656
   949 349-1200

(G-12522)
D & G FOCHT CONSTRUCTION CO
2040 E State Rd (43452-2525)
P.O. Box 446 (43452-0446)
PHONE..................................419 732-2412
Douglas Focht, *Pr*
Jeanette Focht, *
EMP: 35 **EST:** 1975
SQ FT: 5,000
SALES (est): 4.72MM **Privately Held**
Web: www.fochtconstruction.com
SIC: 1541 1542 Industrial buildings, new construction, nec; Commercial and office building, new construction

(G-12523)
EAGLES CLB AT QAIL HLLOW CNDO
219 Madison St (43452-1142)
PHONE..................................419 734-1000
David Leonard, *CEO*
EMP: 50 **EST:** 1974
SALES (est): 576.43K **Privately Held**
SIC: 8641 Social club, membership

(G-12524)
EDGEWOOD MNOR RHBLTTION HLTHCA
1330 Fulton St (43452-9297)
PHONE..................................732 730-7360
Yisrael Friedman, *Prin*
EMP: 84 **EST:** 2018
SALES (est): 1.25MM **Privately Held**
Web: www.edgewoodmanorhc.com
SIC: 8051 Skilled nursing care facilities

(G-12525)
FELLHAUER MECHANICAL SYSTEMS
Also Called: Fellhauer In-Focus
2435 E Gill Rd (43452-2555)
PHONE..................................419 734-3674
John Fellhauer, *Pr*
EMP: 40 **EST:** 2003
SALES (est): 4MM **Privately Held**
SIC: 1711 7382 3651 Mechanical contractor; Security systems services; Household audio and video equipment

(G-12526)
GIVING TREE INC
Also Called: Giving Tre, The
335 Buckeye Blvd (43452-1423)
PHONE..................................419 734-2942
Mariann David, *Prin*

GEOGRAPHIC SECTION

Portsmouth - Scioto County (G-12547)

EMP: 30
SALES (corp-wide): 302.1MM **Privately Held**
SIC: 8093 Mental health clinic, outpatient
HQ: The Giving Tree Inc
   11969 W State Route 105
   Oak Harbor OH 43449
   419 898-0077

(G-12527)
GOODNIGHT INN INC
Also Called: Best Western
1734 E Perry St (43452-1426)
PHONE...............................419 734-2274
Jane Schawb, *Mgr*
EMP: 29
SALES (corp-wide): 2.97MM **Privately Held**
Web: www.bestwestern.com
SIC: 7011 Hotels and motels
PA: Goodnight Inn, Inc.
   11313 Us Highway 250 N
   Milan OH 44846
   419 626-3610

(G-12528)
GOOFY GOLF II INC
Also Called: Monsoon Lagoon Water Park
1530 S Danbury North Rd (43452-3920)
PHONE...............................419 732-6671
John Heilman, *Pr*
Patricia Heilman, *Sec*
EMP: 29 EST: 1988
SQ FT: 5,000
SALES (est): 851.14K **Privately Held**
Web: www.wateringholeatmonsoon.com
SIC: 7999 Miniature golf course operation

(G-12529)
GREAT LKES CMNTY ACTION PARTNR
Also Called: Child Development
1854 E Perry St Ste 500 (43452-1582)
PHONE...............................419 732-7007
Brenda Barton, *Dir*
EMP: 32
SALES (corp-wide): 53.21MM **Privately Held**
Web: www.glcap.org
SIC: 8351 8331 Preschool center; Job training services
PA: Great Lakes Community Action Partnership
   127 S Front St
   Fremont OH 43420
   419 333-6068

(G-12530)
GRIFFINGS FLYING SERVICE INC
Also Called: Griffing's Airport
3255 E State Rd (43452-2542)
PHONE...............................419 734-5400
H Thomas Griffing Junior, *Pr*
H Thomas Griffing Iii, *VP*
EMP: 39 EST: 1937
SQ FT: 4,500
SALES (est): 4.62MM **Privately Held**
Web: www.flygriffing.com
SIC: 4581 4522 8249 Airport; Flying charter service; Aviation school

(G-12531)
GUNDLACH SHEET METAL WORKS INC
Also Called: Shilling AC Heating & Plumbing
2439 E Gill Rd (43452-2555)
PHONE...............................419 734-7351
EMP: 43
SALES (corp-wide): 17.84MM **Privately Held**
Web: www.gundlachsheetmetal.com

SIC: 1711 Warm air heating and air conditioning contractor
PA: Gundlach Sheet Metal Works, Inc.
   910 Columbus Ave
   Sandusky OH 44870
   419 626-4525

(G-12532)
H B MAGRUDER MEMORIAL HOSP
Also Called: James Mc Lean MD
621 Fulton St (43452-2034)
PHONE...............................419 732-6520
Doctor James Mc Lean, *Prin*
EMP: 154
SALES (corp-wide): 59.68MM **Privately Held**
Web: www.magruderhospital.com
SIC: 8062 8011 General medical and surgical hospitals; Offices and clinics of medical doctors
PA: H. B. Magruder Memorial Hospital
   615 Fulton St
   Port Clinton OH 43452
   419 734-3131

(G-12533)
H B MAGRUDER MEMORIAL HOSP
611 Fulton St (43452-2008)
PHONE...............................419 734-4539
EMP: 155
SALES (corp-wide): 59.68MM **Privately Held**
Web: www.magruderhospital.com
SIC: 8062 General medical and surgical hospitals
PA: H. B. Magruder Memorial Hospital
   615 Fulton St
   Port Clinton OH 43452
   419 734-3131

(G-12534)
HUNTINGTON NATIONAL BANK
Also Called: Home Mortgage
120 Madison St (43452-1165)
PHONE...............................419 734-2157
Sandra Bogard, *Mgr*
EMP: 31
SALES (corp-wide): 10.84B **Publicly Held**
Web: www.huntington.com
SIC: 6029 6162 6021 Commercial banks, nec; Mortgage bankers; National commercial banks
HQ: The Huntington National Bank
   41 S High St
   Columbus OH 43215
   614 480-4293

(G-12535)
HUNTINGTON NATIONAL BANK
123 Monroe St (43452-1029)
PHONE...............................419 734-2157
EMP: 31
SALES (corp-wide): 10.84B **Publicly Held**
Web: www.huntington.com
SIC: 6029 Commercial banks, nec
HQ: The Huntington National Bank
   41 S High St
   Columbus OH 43215
   614 480-4293

(G-12536)
LAKELAND MOTEL INC
Also Called: Lakeland Motel & Charter Svc
121 E Perry St (43452-1105)
PHONE...............................419 734-2101
Don Clemons, *Pr*
Donald Clemons, *Pr*
EMP: 34
SQ FT: 11,000
SALES (est): 567.25K **Privately Held**
SIC: 7011 Motels

(G-12537)
LAKESIDE MARINE INC (PA)
Also Called: Lakeside Marine Boat Sales
650 Se Catawba Rd (43452-2643)
PHONE...............................419 732-7160
Lowell E Joy, *Pr*
Elaine Joy, *
EMP: 35 EST: 1968
SQ FT: 200,000
SALES (est): 5.57MM
SALES (corp-wide): 5.57MM **Privately Held**
SIC: 5551 4493 Motor boat dealers; Marine basins

(G-12538)
MJS SNOW & LANDSCAPE LLC
6660 W Fritchie Rd (43452-8408)
PHONE...............................419 656-6724
EMP: 71 EST: 2003
SALES (est): 2.51MM **Privately Held**
SIC: 0781 1771 1611 4213 Landscape services; Concrete repair; Surfacing and paving; Contract haulers

(G-12539)
RJ RUNGE COMPANY INC
3539 Ne Catawba Rd (43452-9609)
P.O. Box 977 (43452-0977)
PHONE...............................419 740-5781
Richard J Runge, *CEO*
Amy Runge, *
EMP: 30 EST: 2004
SQ FT: 3,000
SALES (est): 4.85MM **Privately Held**
Web: www.rjrunge.com
SIC: 1731 8748 8741 Electrical work; Business consulting, nec; Construction management

(G-12540)
RL TRUCKING INC
58 Grande Lake Dr (43452-2476)
P.O. Box 458 (43452-0458)
PHONE...............................419 732-4177
Linda Burke, *CEO*
Roland Burke, *
EMP: 145 EST: 1987
SQ FT: 1,000
SALES (est): 10.54MM **Privately Held**
SIC: 4213 Trucking, except local

Port Washington
Tuscarawas County

(G-12541)
BATES METAL PRODUCTS INC
403 E Mn St (43837)
P.O. Box 68 (43837-0068)
PHONE...............................740 498-8371
James A Bates, *Pr*
Terry L Bates, *
Betty Bates, *
EMP: 60 EST: 1956
SQ FT: 106,500
SALES (est): 11.93MM **Privately Held**
Web: www.batesmetal.com
SIC: 4783 2542 3993 3469 Packing and crating; Racks, merchandise display or storage: except wood; Signs and advertising specialties; Metal stampings, nec

Portland
Meigs County

(G-12542)
CECIL T BRINAGER (PA)
Also Called: Brinager, Tye & Sons Produce
53640 Portland Rd (45770-9705)
PHONE...............................740 843-5280
Cecil Brinager, *Owner*
EMP: 55 EST: 1989
SALES (est): 3.83MM **Privately Held**
SIC: 5148 Fruits

Portsmouth
Scioto County

(G-12543)
ADVANTAGE SKILLED CARE LLC
1656 Coles Blvd (45662-2632)
PHONE...............................740 353-9200
Kathy Pierron, *Managing Member*
EMP: 28 EST: 2003
SALES (est): 91.37K **Privately Held**
Web: www.yourchoicehealthcare.net
SIC: 8082 Visiting nurse service

(G-12544)
AMERICAN AMBULETTE & AMBULANCE SERVICE INC
Also Called: Medcorp
729 6th St (45662-4030)
PHONE...............................937 237-1105
EMP: 650
SIC: 4119 Ambulance service

(G-12545)
B B & E INC
1630 Kendall Ave (45662-4844)
P.O. Box 1488 (45662-1488)
PHONE...............................740 354-5469
Bobby L Evans, *Pr*
Ronald J Evans, *VP*
EMP: 35 EST: 1978
SQ FT: 3,000
SALES (est): 1.14MM **Privately Held**
SIC: 1711 Plumbing contractors

(G-12546)
BIG SANDY FURNITURE INC
Also Called: Big Sandy Furniture Store 5
730 10th St (45662-4033)
PHONE...............................740 354-3193
Tyler Conley, *Brnch Mgr*
EMP: 68
Web: www.bigsandysuperstore.com
SIC: 4225 5722 5712 General warehousing and storage; Gas household appliances; Furniture stores
HQ: Big Sandy Furniture, Inc.
   8375 Gallia Pike
   Franklin Furnace OH 45629
   740 574-2113

(G-12547)
BUCKEYE FREST RSMOUNT PAVILION ✪
20 Easter Dr (45662-8659)
PHONE...............................740 354-4505
Jonathan Harrison, *Admn*
EMP: 120 EST: 2022
SALES (est): 3.51MM **Privately Held**
Web: www.buckeyeforestrosemountpavilion.com
SIC: 8051 Skilled nursing care facilities

Portsmouth - Scioto County (G-12548)

(G-12548)
COMMUNITY ACTION ORGNZTION SCO (PA)
433 3rd St (45662-3811)
P.O. Box 1525 (45662-1525)
PHONE.................................740 354-7541
Steve Sturgill, *Ex Dir*
EMP: 194 **EST:** 1965
SQ FT: 6,000
SALES (est): 21.41MM
SALES (corp-wide): 21.41MM **Privately Held**
Web: www.caosciotocounty.org
SIC: 8322 8331 Social service center; Community service employment training program

(G-12549)
COMPASS COMMUNITY HEALTH
Also Called: Health Mart
1634 11th St (45662-4526)
PHONE.................................740 355-7102
Ed Hughes, *CEO*
Lora Gampp, *
EMP: 40 **EST:** 2012
SALES (est): 6.11MM **Privately Held**
Web: www.compasscommunityhealth.org
SIC: 8011 8093 5912 Offices and clinics of medical doctors; Mental health clinic, outpatient; Drug stores

(G-12550)
DESCO FEDERAL CREDIT UNION (PA)
401 Chillicothe St (45662-4013)
P.O. Box 1546 (45662-1546)
PHONE.................................740 354-7791
Richard Powell, *CEO*
Richard Powell, *Pr*
Lou Bennett, *
Joyce Myers, *
EMP: 43 **EST:** 1963
SQ FT: 10,000
SALES (est): 19.92MM
SALES (corp-wide): 19.92MM **Privately Held**
Web: www.descofcu.org
SIC: 6061 Federal credit unions

(G-12551)
DIALYSIS CLINIC INC
1207 17th St (45662-3573)
PHONE.................................740 351-0596
Andrew Mazon, *Mgr*
EMP: 31
SALES (corp-wide): 1.99MM **Privately Held**
Web: www.dciinc.org
SIC: 8092 Kidney dialysis centers
PA: Dialysis Clinic, Inc.
1633 Church St Ste 500
Nashville TN 37203
615 327-3061

(G-12552)
GRACIE PLUM INVESTMENTS INC
Also Called: Gracie Plum Investments
609 2nd St Unit 2 (45662-3974)
PHONE.................................740 355-9029
Francesca G Hartop, *CEO*
▼ **EMP:** 27 **EST:** 1999
SQ FT: 3,150
SALES (est): 4.67MM **Privately Held**
Web: www.atp4health.com
SIC: 7372 7374 7371 Application computer software; Data processing and preparation; Custom computer programming services

(G-12553)
HEMPSTEAD MANOR
727 8th St (45662-4020)
PHONE.................................740 354-8150
Linda Purek, *Pr*
EMP: 45 **EST:** 1974
SQ FT: 80,000
SALES (est): 2.35MM **Privately Held**
Web: www.hempsteadmanor.com
SIC: 8051 8052 Convalescent home with continuous nursing care; Intermediate care facilities

(G-12554)
HILL VIEW RETIREMENT CENTER
1610 28th St (45662-2641)
PHONE.................................740 354-3135
John Prose, *Pr*
EMP: 174 **EST:** 1983
SQ FT: 14,500
SALES (est): 12.15MM **Privately Held**
Web: www.hillviewretirement.org
SIC: 8361 Aged home

(G-12555)
HOME CARE NETWORK INC
1716 11th St (45662-4528)
PHONE.................................740 353-2329
EMP: 144
Web: www.hcnmidwest.net
SIC: 8082 Home health care services
PA: Home Care Network, Inc.
1191 Lyons Rd
Dayton OH 45458

(G-12556)
INFRA-METALS CO
1 Sturgill Way (45662-5179)
PHONE.................................740 353-1350
Oak Williams, *Brnch Mgr*
EMP: 57
SALES (corp-wide): 14.81B **Publicly Held**
Web: www.infra-metals.com
SIC: 5051 Steel
HQ: Infra-Metals Co.
6 Penns Trl Ste 201
Newtown PA 18940
215 741-1000

(G-12557)
INTERIM HEALTHCARE (PA)
4130 Gallia St (45662-5511)
PHONE.................................740 354-5550
Donna Southworth, *Pr*
EMP: 82 **EST:** 1994
SALES (est): 4.31MM **Privately Held**
Web: www.interimhealthcare.com
SIC: 8082 Home health care services

(G-12558)
J&H RNFRCING STRL ERECTORS INC
Also Called: J & H Erectors
55 River Ave (45662-4712)
P.O. Box 60 (45662-0060)
PHONE.................................740 355-0141
Donald Hadsell, *Pr*
Lisa Hadsell, *
EMP: 150 **EST:** 1980
SQ FT: 30,000
SALES (est): 29.67MM **Privately Held**
SIC: 1542 1791 Commercial and office building contractors; Iron work, structural

(G-12559)
JAY HASH LLC
Also Called: Hopesource
800 Gallia St Ste 600 (45662-4097)
PHONE.................................740 353-4673
Kevin Blevins, *
EMP: 65 **EST:** 2015
SALES (est): 1.39MM **Privately Held**
Web: www.hopesourcetreatment.com
SIC: 8322 Individual and family services

(G-12560)
KENTUCKY HEART INSTITUTE INC
2001 Scioto Trl Ste 200 (45662-2845)
PHONE.................................740 353-8100
Debbie Bell, *Prin*
EMP: 191
SALES (corp-wide): 822.62K **Privately Held**
Web: www.kingsdaughtershealth.com
SIC: 8011 Cardiologist and cardio-vascular specialist
PA: Kentucky Heart Institute, Inc
613 23rd St
Ashland KY 41101
606 329-1997

(G-12561)
LEGAL AID SOUTHEAST CENTL OHIO
Also Called: South Eastern Ohio Legal Svcs
800 Gallia St Ste 700 (45662-4035)
PHONE.................................740 354-7563
TOLL FREE: 800
EMP: 51
SALES (corp-wide): 10.47MM **Privately Held**
Web: www.seols.org
SIC: 8111 Legal aid service
PA: Legal Aid Of Southeast And Central Ohio
1108 City Park Ave # 200
Columbus OH 43206
614 221-7201

(G-12562)
LIFE AMBULANCE SERVICE INC
729 6th St (45662-4030)
PHONE.................................740 354-6169
EMP: 833
Web: www.lifeambulance.com
SIC: 4119 Ambulance service

(G-12563)
MECHANICAL CONSTRUCTION CO
Also Called: McCo
2302 8th St (45662-4798)
PHONE.................................740 353-5668
Darrell Stapleton, *Pr*
W Michael Stapleton, *
Jackie Enz, *
EMP: 50 **EST:** 1957
SQ FT: 10,000
SALES (est): 13.33K **Privately Held**
Web: www.mechanicalconstruction.us
SIC: 1711 1761 Plumbing contractors; Sheet metal work, nec

(G-12564)
PEOPLES BANK
503 Chillicothe St (45662-4015)
PHONE.................................740 354-3177
EMP: 52
SALES (corp-wide): 526.82MM **Publicly Held**
Web: www.peoplesbancorp.com
SIC: 6022 State trust companies accepting deposits, commercial
HQ: Peoples Bank
138 Putnam St
Marietta OH 45750
740 373-3155

(G-12565)
PORTSMOUTH HOSPITAL CORP
Also Called: KING'S DAUGHTERS' MEDICAL CENT
1901 Argonne Rd (45662-2827)
P.O. Box 151 (41105-0151)
PHONE.................................740 991-4000
David Jones, *Ch*
Alex Krivchenia Md, *Dir*
Charlie Borders, *
Dan Cassidy, *
Fred Jackson, *
EMP: 549 **EST:** 2010
SALES (est): 23.37MM
SALES (corp-wide): 538.89MM **Privately Held**
Web: www.portsmouthhospital.com
SIC: 8011 Medical centers
HQ: Ashland Hospital Corporation
2201 Lexington Ave
Ashland KY 41101
606 408-4000

(G-12566)
REYNOLDS & CO INC
Also Called: Reynolds & Company Cpa's
839 Gallia St (45662-4137)
P.O. Box 1364 (45662-1364)
PHONE.................................740 353-1040
Greg Brown, *Prin*
Ronald F Champan, *
William H Tacket, *Stockholder**
Gregory C Brown, *Stockholder**
Roger D Conley, *Stockholder**
EMP: 47 **EST:** 1967
SQ FT: 6,000
SALES (est): 394.54K **Privately Held**
Web: www.reynolds-cpa.com
SIC: 8721 Certified public accountant

(G-12567)
SCIOTO CNTY COUNSELING CTR INC (PA)
Also Called: COUNSELING CENTER, THE
411 Court St (45662-3932)
PHONE.................................740 354-6685
Ed Hughes, *Ex Dir*
Rick Calvin, *
Melanie Colmer, *
EMP: 127 **EST:** 1978
SALES (est): 41.34MM **Privately Held**
Web: www.thecounselingcenter.org
SIC: 8322 Alcoholism counseling, nontreatment

(G-12568)
SCIOTO RESIDENTIAL SERVICES
2333 Vinton Ave (45662-3741)
PHONE.................................740 353-0288
Lisa Francis, *Prin*
EMP: 27
SALES (corp-wide): 5.3MM **Privately Held**
Web: www.srs-scioto.org
SIC: 8361 Retarded home
PA: Scioto Residential Services, Inc
9 Plaza Dr
Portsmouth OH 45662
740 354-7958

(G-12569)
SOUTHERN OHIO MEDICAL CENTER
Also Called: Somc
1805 27th St (45662-2640)
PHONE.................................740 354-5000
Elizabeth Blevins, *Dir*
EMP: 987
SALES (corp-wide): 546.1MM **Privately Held**
Web: www.somc.org
SIC: 8062 General medical and surgical hospitals
PA: Southern Ohio Medical Center
1805 27th St
Portsmouth OH 45662
740 354-5000

GEOGRAPHIC SECTION

Powell - Delaware County (G-12590)

(G-12570)
SOUTHERN OHIO MEDICAL CENTER
1025 Robinson Ave (45662-3586)
PHONE.................................740 356-8171
Greg Gilliland, *Brnch Mgr*
EMP: 90
SALES (corp-wide): 546.1MM **Privately Held**
Web: www.somc.org
SIC: 8062 General medical and surgical hospitals
PA: Southern Ohio Medical Center
1805 27th St
Portsmouth OH 45662
740 354-5000

(G-12571)
SOUTHERN OHIO MEDICAL CENTER (PA)
Also Called: Scioto Memorial Hosp Campus
1805 27th St (45662-2640)
PHONE.................................740 354-5000
Randal M Arnett, *Pr*
Robert E Dever, *
Kendall Stewart Md, *Dir*
Claudia Burchett, *Client Service Vice President**
Cindy Brown, *
▲ EMP: 200 EST: 1954
SALES (est): 546.1MM
SALES (corp-wide): 546.1MM **Privately Held**
Web: www.somc.org
SIC: 8062 General medical and surgical hospitals

(G-12572)
SOUTHERN OHIO MEDICAL CENTER
724 8th St (45662-4021)
PHONE.................................740 356-5600
Randal Arnett, *Pr*
EMP: 90
SALES (corp-wide): 546.1MM **Privately Held**
Web: www.somc.org
SIC: 8062 General medical and surgical hospitals
PA: Southern Ohio Medical Center
1805 27th St
Portsmouth OH 45662
740 354-5000

(G-12573)
SOUTHERN OHIO MEDICAL CENTER
Also Called: Somc Urgent Care Ctr Prtsmouth
1248 Kinneys Ln (45662-2927)
PHONE.................................740 356-5000
Greg Gilliland, *Dir*
EMP: 30
SALES (corp-wide): 546.1MM **Privately Held**
Web: www.somc.org
SIC: 8062 General medical and surgical hospitals
PA: Southern Ohio Medical Center
1805 27th St
Portsmouth OH 45662
740 354-5000

(G-12574)
SOUTHERN OHIO MEDICAL CENTER
1202 18th St Ste 4 (45662-2922)
PHONE.................................740 356-6160
Emily Carson, *Mgr*
EMP: 90
SALES (corp-wide): 546.1MM **Privately Held**
Web: www.somc.org
SIC: 7991 Physical fitness facilities
PA: Southern Ohio Medical Center
1805 27th St

Portsmouth OH 45662
740 354-5000

(G-12575)
STAR INC
2625 Gallia St (45662-4805)
PHONE.................................740 354-1517
John Kantz, *Pr*
Kelly Hunter, *
John Burke, *
EMP: 150 EST: 1972
SQ FT: 32,000
SALES (est): 3.12MM **Privately Held**
Web: www.star.de
SIC: 8331 7349 Job training services; Building maintenance services, nec

(G-12576)
THE GLOCKNER CHEVROLET COMPANY (PA)
Also Called: Glockner Chvrlet Oldsmbile Cdl
4368 Us Highway 23 (45662)
P.O. Box 1308 (45662-1308)
PHONE.................................740 353-2161
EMP: 110 EST: 1927
SALES (est): 27.25MM
SALES (corp-wide): 27.25MM **Privately Held**
Web: www.glocknerchevy.com
SIC: 5013 5172 5511 Automotive supplies and parts; Diesel fuel; Automobiles, new and used

(G-12577)
TRACTOR SUPPLY COMPANY
Also Called: Tractor Supply Co.
4000 Rhodes Ave Ste A (45662-5573)
PHONE.................................740 456-0000
EMP: 38
SALES (corp-wide): 14.56B **Publicly Held**
Web: www.tractorsupply.com
SIC: 5191 Farm supplies
PA: Tractor Supply Company
5401 Virginia Way
Brentwood TN 37027
615 440-4000

(G-12578)
UNITED PARCEL SERVICE INC
Also Called: UPS
21 Gingersnap Rd (45662-8825)
PHONE.................................740 962-7971
EMP: 31
SALES (corp-wide): 90.96B **Publicly Held**
Web: www.ups.com
SIC: 4215 Parcel delivery, vehicular
HQ: United Parcel Service, Inc.
55 Glenlake Pkwy
Atlanta GA 30328
404 828-6000

(G-12579)
UNITED SCOTO SENIOR ACTIVITIES (PA)
Also Called: SENIOR CITIZENS CENTER
117 Market St 119 (45662)
P.O. Box 597 (45662-0597)
PHONE.................................740 354-6672
Renee Ellis, *Dir*
Chester Neff, *
Laurna Garlinger, *
EMP: 32
SALES (est): 635.19K
SALES (corp-wide): 635.19K **Privately Held**
Web: www.sciotogives.org
SIC: 8322 8111 7349 5812 Senior citizens' center or association; Legal services; Building maintenance services, nec; Eating places

(G-12580)
UNITY I HOME HEALTHCARE LLC
221 Market St (45662-3831)
PHONE.................................740 351-0500
EMP: 30 EST: 2004
SQ FT: 1,926
SALES (est): 2.45MM **Privately Held**
Web: www.unity1homehealthcare.com
SIC: 8082 Home health care services

(G-12581)
VALLEY WHOLESALE FOODS INC (PA)
Also Called: Vf Valley
415 Market St (45662-3834)
P.O. Box 1281 (45662-1281)
PHONE.................................740 354-5216
Ernest J Vastine Senior, *Pr*
Peggy Vastine, *VP*
Margaret Jo Vastine, *Sec*
Jim Vastine, *Prin*
Jay Vastine, *Prin*
EMP: 32 EST: 1973
SQ FT: 40,000
SALES (est): 9.6MM
SALES (corp-wide): 9.6MM **Privately Held**
Web: www.vwfoods.com
SIC: 5141 Food brokers

Powell
Delaware County

(G-12582)
A GRADE AHEAD INC
10202 Sawmill Pkwy (43065-9189)
PHONE.................................614 389-3830
EMP: 70 EST: 2017
SALES (est): 642.96K **Privately Held**
Web: www.agradeahead.com
SIC: 7999 Instruction schools, camps, and services

(G-12583)
AIR TAHOMA INC (PA)
2615 Carriage Rd (43065-9703)
PHONE.................................614 774-0728
Noel Rude, *Pr*
EMP: 82 EST: 1996
SALES (est): 1.82MM
SALES (corp-wide): 1.82MM **Privately Held**
SIC: 4522 Air cargo carriers, nonscheduled

(G-12584)
APEX SOFTWARE TECHNOLOGIES INC
Also Called: Apex Payroll
445 Village Park Dr (43065-6666)
PHONE.................................614 932-2167
EMP: 29
SALES (corp-wide): 392.74MM **Privately Held**
Web: www.apexhcm.com
SIC: 8731 5045 Commercial physical research; Computers, peripherals, and software
HQ: Apex Software Technologies, Inc.
44 Milton Ave
Alpharetta GA 30009

(G-12585)
ARMADA LTD
23 Clairedan Dr (43065-8064)
PHONE.................................614 505-7256
Thomas Foos, *Pr*
Jeff Podracky, *
EMP: 70 EST: 2005
SALES (est): 5.6MM **Privately Held**
Web: www.armadausa.com

SIC: 8742 Management consulting services

(G-12586)
BEST FRNDS VETERINARY HOSP INC
275 W Olentangy St (43065-8719)
PHONE.................................614 889-7387
Thomas Ritchie, *Prin*
Rex Riggs, *Prin*
EMP: 46 EST: 2008
SALES (est): 2.54MM **Privately Held**
Web: www.bestfriendsvethospital.com
SIC: 0742 Animal hospital services, pets and other animal specialties

(G-12587)
BUCKEYE STATE BANCSHARES INC
9494 Wedgewood Blvd (43065-9496)
PHONE.................................614 796-4747
Shawn Keller, *Pr*
EMP: 36 EST: 2018
SALES (est): 935.8K
SALES (corp-wide): 5.23MM **Privately Held**
Web: www.joinbsb.com
SIC: 6021 National commercial banks
PA: Buckeye State Bank
9494 Wedgewood Blvd
Powell OH 43065
614 796-4747

(G-12588)
CLICK4CARE INC
50 S Liberty St Ste 200 (43065-4006)
PHONE.................................614 431-3700
Rob Gillette, *CEO*
EMP: 40 EST: 2006
SQ FT: 10,000
SALES (est): 4.57MM
SALES (corp-wide): 8.02B **Publicly Held**
Web: www.click4care.com
SIC: 7371 Computer software systems analysis and design, custom
HQ: Healthedge Software, Inc.
30 Corporate Dr Ste 150
Burlington MA 01803
781 285-1300

(G-12589)
COLUMBUS ZOOLOGICAL PARK ASSN (PA)
Also Called: Columbus Zoo and Aquarium
4850 Powell Rd (43065)
P.O. Box 400 (43065)
PHONE.................................614 645-3400
TOLL FREE: 800
Tom Stalf, *Pr*
Greg Bell, *
Lewis Greene, *
John Gannon, *
Terri Kepes, *
EMP: 200 EST: 1930
SQ FT: 25,000
SALES (est): 89.9MM **Privately Held**
Web: www.columbuszoo.org
SIC: 8422 5947 7992 Zoological garden, noncommercial; Gift shop; Public golf courses

(G-12590)
CTV MEDIA INC (PA)
1490 Manning Pkwy (43065-9171)
PHONE.................................614 848-5800
Kathryn C Dixon, *Pr*
EMP: 30 EST: 1980
SQ FT: 20,000
SALES (est): 9.23MM
SALES (corp-wide): 9.23MM **Privately Held**
Web: www.ctvmedia.com

Powell - Delaware County (G-12591)

SIC: **7313** 7319 Electronic media advertising representatives; Media buying service

(G-12591)
FUNDABLE LLC
1322 Manning Pkwy Unit A (43065-1111)
PHONE..................614 364-4523
Wil Schroter, *Prin*
EMP: 31 **EST:** 2012
SALES (est): 333.49K **Privately Held**
Web: www.fundable.com
SIC: **7371** Computer software development and applications

(G-12592)
GANZHORN SUITES INC
1322 Manning Pkwy Unit B (43065-1111)
PHONE..................614 356-9810
Eleanor Alvarez, *Pr*
EMP: 65 **EST:** 2015
SALES (est): 4.37MM **Privately Held**
Web: www.ganzhorn.com
SIC: **8322** Old age assistance

(G-12593)
JBENTLEY STUDIO & SPA LLC
8882 Moreland St (43065-6678)
PHONE..................614 790-8828
EMP: 55 **EST:** 2006
SQ FT: 7,500
SALES (est): 974.49K **Privately Held**
Web: www.jbentley.com
SIC: **7231** 7991 Unisex hair salons; Spas

(G-12594)
KAISER CONSULTING LLC
818 Riverbend Ave (43065-7067)
PHONE..................614 378-5361
Lori Kaiser, *Managing Member*
EMP: 93 **EST:** 2004
SALES (est): 1.04MM **Privately Held**
Web: www.kaiserconsulting.com
SIC: **8721** 8742 Accounting, auditing, and bookkeeping; Financial consultant

(G-12595)
KAISER TECHNOLOGY LLC
34 Grace Dr (43065-8466)
PHONE..................614 300-1088
EMP: 84 **EST:** 2017
SALES (est): 477.93K **Privately Held**
Web: www.kaiserconsulting.com
SIC: **8721** Accounting services, except auditing

(G-12596)
KELLER MORTGAGE LLC
Also Called: Smarter Mortgages
9482 Wedgewood Blvd Ste 200 (43065-7261)
PHONE..................614 310-3100
John Fearon, *Brnch Mgr*
EMP: 61
SALES (corp-wide): 5.66B **Privately Held**
Web: www.kwlends.com
SIC: **6162** Mortgage bankers
HQ: Keller Mortgage, Llc
4725 Lakehurst Ct Ste 400
Dublin OH 43016

(G-12597)
KINSALE GOLF & FITNES CLB LLC
3737 Village Club Dr (43065-8196)
PHONE..................740 881-6500
Donald Kenny, *Managing Member*
EMP: 189 **EST:** 2003
SQ FT: 1,537
SALES (est): 12.19MM **Privately Held**
Web: www.golfkinsale.com

SIC: **7992** 7991 Public golf courses; Health club

(G-12598)
MANGOS PLACE
3967 Presidential Pkwy Ste I (43065-7367)
PHONE..................614 499-1611
Mary Curtis, *Prin*
William Scott Curtis, *
EMP: 60 **EST:** 2018
SALES (est): 1MM **Privately Held**
Web: www.mangosplace.com
SIC: **8351** Group day care center

(G-12599)
MKC ASSOCIATES INC
90 Hidden Ravines Dr (43065-8736)
PHONE..................740 657-3202
Patrick Carroll, *Brnch Mgr*
EMP: 43
SALES (corp-wide): 6.05MM **Privately Held**
Web: www.mkcinc.com
SIC: **8712** 8711 Architectural engineering; Engineering services
PA: Mkc Associates, Inc.
161 N 4th St Ste 200
Columbus OH
740 657-3202

(G-12600)
MORESTEAMCOM LLC (PA)
9961 Brewster Ln (43065-7571)
PHONE..................614 602-8190
William Hathaway, *CEO*
Bill Hathaway, *Pr*
EMP: 33 **EST:** 2000
SALES (est): 69.87K
SALES (corp-wide): 69.87K **Privately Held**
Web: www.moresteam.com
SIC: **8331** Job training and related services

(G-12601)
NATIONAL CARE ADVISORS LLC
3982 Powell Rd Ste 231 (43065-7662)
PHONE..................937 748-9412
Ann Koerner, *CEO*
EMP: 43 **EST:** 2008
SALES (est): 6.14MM **Privately Held**
Web: www.nationalcareadvisors.com
SIC: **6282** Investment advice

(G-12602)
OPTIMUM TECHNOLOGY INC (PA)
Also Called: Oti
9922 Brewster Ln (43065-7571)
PHONE..................614 785-1110
Jagdish M Davda, *Pr*
Frank Xavier, *
EMP: 28 **EST:** 1984
SALES (est): 6.91MM
SALES (corp-wide): 6.91MM **Privately Held**
Web: www.otech.com
SIC: **7379** Online services technology consultants

(G-12603)
PRIMROSE SCHOOL LEWIS CENTE
Also Called: Primrose School
8273 Owenfield Dr (43065-9752)
PHONE..................740 548-5808
Lisa Swainey, *Prin*
EMP: 43 **EST:** 2008
SALES (est): 2.01MM **Privately Held**
Web: www.primroselewiscenter.com
SIC: **8351** Preschool center

(G-12604)
SCIOTO RESERVE INC (PA)
Also Called: Scioto Reserve Golf & Athc CLB
7383 Scioto Pkwy (43065-7956)
PHONE..................740 881-9082
Regan Koivesto, *Prin*
Joe Bush, *
Andy Montgomery, *
Scott Schraer, *
Jeff Olson, *
EMP: 53 **EST:** 1990
SALES (est): 9.15MM
SALES (corp-wide): 9.15MM **Privately Held**
Web: www.sciotoreserve.com
SIC: **7992** 7997 7991 Public golf courses; Membership sports and recreation clubs; Physical fitness facilities

(G-12605)
SCIOTO RESERVE INC
Also Called: Scioto Reserve Country Club
3982 Powell Rd Ste 332 (43065-7662)
PHONE..................740 881-6500
EMP: 41
SALES (corp-wide): 9.15MM **Privately Held**
Web: www.sciotoreserve.com
SIC: **7992** Public golf courses
PA: Scioto Reserve, Inc.
7383 Scioto Pkwy
Powell OH 43065
740 881-9082

(G-12606)
SCIOTO RESERVE INC
7743 Riverside Dr (43065-7815)
PHONE..................740 881-3903
Scott Schraer, *Brnch Mgr*
EMP: 62
SALES (corp-wide): 9.15MM **Privately Held**
Web: www.sciotoreserve.com
SIC: **7997** Country club, membership
PA: Scioto Reserve, Inc.
7383 Scioto Pkwy
Powell OH 43065
740 881-9082

(G-12607)
SEI ENGINEERS INC
65 Hidden Ravines Dr Ste 200 (43065-5179)
PHONE..................740 657-1860
Frank Mamone, *Pr*
Joseph M Dreher, *VP*
Alan Mccomas, *VP*
EMP: 36 **EST:** 1984
SQ FT: 5,300
SALES (est): 1.49MM **Privately Held**
Web: www.seiengineers.com
SIC: **8711** 8741 Consulting engineer; Construction management

(G-12608)
W R SHEPHERD INC (PA)
390 W Olentangy St (43065-9858)
PHONE..................614 889-2896
William Bill R Shepherd, *Pr*
Sharon Shepherd, *Sec*
Brad Shepperd, *VP*
EMP: 30 **EST:** 1975
SQ FT: 4,000
SALES (est): 2.98MM
SALES (corp-wide): 2.98MM **Privately Held**
SIC: **1752** Floor laying and floor work, nec

(G-12609)
WEDGEWOOD GOLF & COUNTRY CLUB
9600 Wedgewood Blvd (43065-8788)
PHONE..................614 793-9600
James Simonton, *Pr*
Pat Dugan, *
Steve Jackson, *
Robert Baker, *
Nancy Kelly, *
EMP: 140 **EST:** 1988
SQ FT: 43,500
SALES (est): 10.71MM **Privately Held**
Web: www.wedgewoodgolfcc.com
SIC: **7997** Country club, membership

Powhatan Point
Belmont County

(G-12610)
COAL SERVICES INC
Also Called: Coal Services Group
155 Highway 7 S (43942-1033)
PHONE..................740 795-5220
Don Gentry, *Pr*
Robert Moore, *
Michael O Mckown, *Prin*
EMP: 471 **EST:** 1999
SALES (est): 3.24MM
SALES (corp-wide): 4.34B **Privately Held**
SIC: **8741** 8711 1231 1222 Management services; Engineering services; Anthracite mining; Bituminous coal-underground mining
HQ: The American Coal Company
9085 Highway 34 N
Galatia IL 62935
618 268-6311

(G-12611)
UTAHAMERICAN ENERGY INC
153 Highway 7 S (43942-1033)
P.O. Box 910 (84520-0910)
PHONE..................435 888-4000
David Hibbs, *Brnch Mgr*
EMP: 138
SALES (corp-wide): 4.34B **Privately Held**
SIC: **1222** Bituminous coal-underground mining
HQ: Utahamerican Energy, Inc.
45 W Sego Lily Dr Ste 401
Sandy UT 84070
435 888-4000

Proctorville
Lawrence County

(G-12612)
HOLZER CLINIC LLC
Also Called: Holzer Clinic Lawrence County
98 State St (45669-8163)
P.O. Box 646 (45669-0646)
PHONE..................740 886-9403
Nathan Miller, *Mgr*
EMP: 33
SALES (corp-wide): 337.52MM **Privately Held**
Web: www.holzerclinic.com
SIC: **8011** 8049 General and family practice, physician/surgeon; Physical therapist
HQ: Holzer Clinic Llc
90 Jackson Pike
Gallipolis OH 45631
740 446-5411

GEOGRAPHIC SECTION
Ravenna - Portage County (G-12634)

(G-12613)
SUPERIOR MARINE WAYS INC
5852 County Rd 1 Suoth Pt (45669)
P.O. Box 519 (45669-0519)
PHONE.....................740 894-6224
Dale Manns, *Mgr*
EMP: 130
SALES (corp-wide): 21.4MM **Privately Held**
Web: www.superiormarineinc.com
SIC: 3731 7699 Barges, building and repairing; Boat repair
PA: Superior Marine Ways, Inc.
5852 County Road 1
South Point OH 45680
740 894-6224

(G-12614)
THERMAL SOLUTIONS INC (PA)
9329 County Road 107 (45669)
P.O. Box 661 (45669)
PHONE.....................740 886-2861
John Stevens, *Pr*
Mark Artrip, *COO*
John Browning, *CFO*
EMP: 39 **EST:** 2000
SQ FT: 1,200
SALES (est): 14.37MM
SALES (corp-wide): 14.37MM **Privately Held**
Web: www.thermalsolutionsinc.com
SIC: 1742 1799 Insulation, buildings; Fireproofing buildings

(G-12615)
THREE GABLES SURGERY CTR LLC
5897 County Road 107 (45669-8852)
PHONE.....................740 886-9911
EMP: 129 **EST:** 2000
SALES (est): 15.59MM
SALES (corp-wide): 61.87MM **Privately Held**
Web: www.threegablessurgery.com
SIC: 8011 Ambulatory surgical center
PA: Nueterra Dc Holdings, Llc
11221 Roe Ave Ste 1a
Leawood KS 66211
913 387-0689

Prospect
Marion County

(G-12616)
CUMMINS FACILITY SERVICES LLC
5202 Marion Waldo Rd (43342-9758)
P.O. Box 350 (43356-0350)
PHONE.....................740 726-9800
EMP: 350 **EST:** 2010
SALES (est): 23.61MM **Privately Held**
Web: www.cumminsfs.com
SIC: 7349 Janitorial service, contract basis

Put In Bay
Ottawa County

(G-12617)
ISLAND SERVICE COMPANY
Also Called: Middle Bass Ferry Company, The
341 Bayview Ave (43456)
P.O. Box 360 (43456)
PHONE.....................419 285-3695
Marvin Booker, *CEO*
Eric Booker, *Pr*
Pat Thwaite, *
EMP: 40 **EST:** 1975
SQ FT: 250,000
SALES (est): 892.43K **Privately Held**
Web: www.the-boardwalk.com

SIC: 5812 5541 7997 4493 Eating places; Marine service station; Boating club, membership; Marinas

Randolph
Portage County

(G-12618)
EAST MANUFACTURING CORPORATION (PA)
1871 State Rte 44 (44265)
P.O. Box 277 (44265-0277)
PHONE.....................330 325-9921
Howard D Booher, *CEO*
David De Poincy, *Pr*
Robert J Bruce, *VP*
Donald C Pecano, *CFO*
Mark T Tate, *Sec*
▼ **EMP:** 266 **EST:** 1968
SQ FT: 350,000
SALES (est): 83.89MM
SALES (corp-wide): 83.89MM **Privately Held**
Web: www.eastmfg.com
SIC: 3715 5013 7539 Trailer bodies; Truck parts and accessories; Automotive repair shops, nec

Ravenna
Portage County

(G-12619)
BALANCED CARE CORPORATION
141 Chestnut Hill Dr Apt 213 (44266-3916)
PHONE.....................330 296-4545
Joanne Maytasy, *Dir*
EMP: 55
SIC: 8741 Nursing and personal care facility management
PA: Balanced Care Corporation
5000 Ritter Rd Ste 202
Mechanicsburg PA 17055

(G-12620)
BUCKEYE RSDNTIAL SOLUTIONS LLC
320 E Main St Ste 301 (44266-3102)
PHONE.....................330 235-9183
Matthew Ferrell, *CFO*
Chad Konkle, *
EMP: 75 **EST:** 2012
SQ FT: 12,000
SALES (est): 4.44MM **Privately Held**
Web: www.buckeyeresidential.com
SIC: 8082 Home health care services

(G-12621)
CHILDRENS ADVANTAGE
771 N Freedom St (44266-2470)
PHONE.....................330 296-5552
Dee Keller, *Off Mgr*
EMP: 47 **EST:** 2012
SALES (est): 3.59MM **Privately Held**
Web: www.childrensadvantage.org
SIC: 8093 Mental health clinic, outpatient

(G-12622)
CHRISTMAS HOME HEALTH LLC
4300 Lynn Rd Ste 203b (44266-7840)
PHONE.....................440 708-6442
Barbara A Simpson, *CEO*
EMP: 50 **EST:** 2012
SALES (est): 706.17K **Privately Held**
SIC: 8099 Health and allied services, nec

(G-12623)
COMPETITIVE INTERIORS INC
625 Enterprise Pkwy (44266-8058)
PHONE.....................330 297-1281
Paul Cunningham, *Pr*
Nancy Cunningham, *
EMP: 120 **EST:** 1989
SQ FT: 5,104
SALES (est): 10.63MM **Privately Held**
Web: www.competitiveinteriors.com
SIC: 1751 1742 Carpentry work; Drywall

(G-12624)
COUNTY OF PORTAGE
Portage County Commissioners
8116 Infirmary Rd (44266-8047)
PHONE.....................330 297-3670
Gene Roberts, *Dir*
EMP: 65
Web: www.portagecountyauditor.org
SIC: 4941 Water supply
PA: County Of Portage
449 S Meridian St 7th Flr
Ravenna OH 44266
330 297-3561

(G-12625)
COUNTY OF PORTAGE
Prosecuting Attorney's Office
466 S Chestnut St (44266-3006)
PHONE.....................330 297-3850
EMP: 30
Web: www.portagecountyauditor.org
SIC: 9222 8111 Public prosecutors' office; Legal services
PA: County Of Portage
449 S Meridian St 7th Flr
Ravenna OH 44266
330 297-3561

(G-12626)
FRESHEDGE LLC
Also Called: Sirna & Sons Produce
7176 State Route 88 (44266-9189)
PHONE.....................330 298-2222
Thomas Serna, *Genl Mgr*
EMP: 190
SALES (corp-wide): 3.63B **Privately Held**
Web: www.freshedgefoods.com
SIC: 5148 Fruits, fresh
HQ: Freshedge, Llc
4501 Massachusetts Ave
Indianapolis IN 46218
317 981-3599

(G-12627)
HAASZ AUTOMALL LLC (PA)
Also Called: Haasz Automall
4886 State Route 59 (44266-8838)
PHONE.....................330 296-2866
Kevin Haasz, *Pr*
EMP: 38 **EST:** 2003
SALES (est): 8.53MM **Privately Held**
Web: www.haaszautomall.net
SIC: 5531 7539 Automotive parts; Automotive repair shops, nec

(G-12628)
HUMMEL CONSTRUCTION COMPANY
127 E Main St (44266-3103)
PHONE.....................330 274-8584
Eric W Hummel, *Pr*
Marty Snode, *
EMP: 40 **EST:** 1971
SQ FT: 5,000
SALES (est): 10.95MM **Privately Held**
Web: www.hummelconstruction.com
SIC: 1542 Commercial and office building, new construction

(G-12629)
HUNTINGTON NATIONAL BANK
230 Cedar Ave (44266)
PHONE.....................330 296-2214
Donna Kovelyan, *Brnch Mgr*
EMP: 31
SALES (corp-wide): 10.84B **Publicly Held**
Web: www.huntington.com
SIC: 6029 6021 Commercial banks, nec; National commercial banks
HQ: The Huntington National Bank
41 S High St
Columbus OH 43215
614 480-4293

(G-12630)
INDEPENDENCE FOUNDATION INC
575 E Lake St (44266-3429)
PHONE.....................330 296-2851
EMP: 160 **EST:** 2010
SALES (est): 165.7K
SALES (corp-wide): 5.02MM **Privately Held**
Web: www.indport2.org
SIC: 8641 Civic and social associations
PA: Independence Of Portage County, Inc.
161 E Main St
Ravenna OH 44266
330 296-2851

(G-12631)
KENMORE RESEARCH COMPANY
935 N Freedom St (44266-2496)
PHONE.....................330 297-1407
Gave Moorehouse, *Brnch Mgr*
EMP: 98
SALES (corp-wide): 881.02MM **Privately Held**
Web: www.swagelok.com
SIC: 8731 8734 Commercial physical research; Testing laboratories
HQ: Kenmore Research Company
29500 Solon Rd
Cleveland OH 44139
440 248-4600

(G-12632)
LONGMEADOW CARE CENTER INC
565 Bryn Mawr St (44266-9696)
PHONE.....................330 297-5781
Dave Cruser, *Prin*
EMP: 36 **EST:** 1975
SALES (est): 6.39MM **Privately Held**
SIC: 8051 Skilled nursing care facilities

(G-12633)
NBD INTERNATIONAL INC
100 Romito St Ste E (44266-2883)
P.O. Box 1003 (44266-1003)
PHONE.....................330 296-0221
Jack Schwartz, *Pr*
Michaeline Bodi, *
EMP: 45 **EST:** 1993
SQ FT: 6,500
SALES (est): 4.97MM **Privately Held**
Web: www.nbdint.com
SIC: 8742 7929 Business planning and organizing services; Entertainment service

(G-12634)
PARKER-HANNIFIN CORPORATION
Parflex Div
1300 N Freedom St (44266-8405)
PHONE.....................330 296-2871
John Fox, *Brnch Mgr*
EMP: 250
SALES (corp-wide): 19.07B **Publicly Held**
Web: www.parker.com
SIC: 5084 Hydraulic systems equipment and supplies
PA: Parker-Hannifin Corporation

Ravenna - Portage County (G-12635)

6035 Parkland Blvd
Cleveland OH 44124
216 896-3000

(G-12635)
PINNACLE TRTMNT CTRS OH-I LLC
Also Called: Recovery Works Portage
6847 N Chestnut St (44266-3929)
PHONE...................................330 577-5881
EMP: 35 **EST:** 2015
SALES (est): 1.07MM **Privately Held**
Web: www.pinnacletreatment.com
SIC: 8093 Substance abuse clinics (outpatient)

(G-12636)
PORTAGE CNTY BD DVLPMNTAL DSBL
Also Called: Happy Day School
2500 Brady Lake Rd (44266-1610)
PHONE...................................330 678-2400
Gail Mcalister, *Prin*
EMP: 151
SALES (corp-wide): 4.87MM **Privately Held**
Web: www.portagedd.org
SIC: 8322 Social services for the handicapped
PA: Portage County Board Of Developmental Disabilities
2606 Brady Lake Rd
Ravenna OH 44266
330 297-6209

(G-12637)
PORTAGE COMMUNITY BANK (HQ)
Also Called: PORTAGE COMMUNITY BANK
1311 E Main St (44266-3329)
PHONE...................................330 296-8090
Richard Coe, *Pr*
John Forberg, *
Donald Herman, *
Robert S Standardi, *Chief Risk Officer*
EMP: 35 **EST:** 1997
SALES (est): 17.77MM
SALES (corp-wide): 17.77MM **Privately Held**
Web: www.pcbbank.com
SIC: 6022 State trust companies accepting deposits, commercial
PA: Portage Bancshares Inc.
1311 E Main St
Ravenna OH 44266
330 296-8090

(G-12638)
PORTAGE COUNTY BOARD (PA)
2606 Brady Lake Rd (44266-1604)
PHONE...................................330 297-6209
Patrick Macke, *Superintnt*
Diane Cotton, *
EMP: 34 **EST:** 1967
SALES (est): 4.87MM
SALES (corp-wide): 4.87MM **Privately Held**
Web: www.portagedd.org
SIC: 8361 Mentally handicapped home

(G-12639)
PORTAGE PRVATE INDUST CNCIL IN
Also Called: PORTAGE LEARNING CENTERS
145 N Chestnut St Lowr (44266)
PHONE...................................330 297-7795
Karen Johnson, *Dir*
James Tinnin, *
Rebecca Gorczyca, *
Suzanne Livinggood, *
EMP: 70 **EST:** 1974
SALES (est): 4.79MM **Privately Held**
Web: www.portagelearningcenters.com
SIC: 8351 8331 Head Start center, except in conjunction with school; Job training services

(G-12640)
RAVENNA SCHOOL DISTRICT
Also Called: Ravenna City Schools Warehouse
315 N Walnut St (44266-2325)
PHONE...................................330 297-4138
William Wisniewski, *Dir*
EMP: 29
SALES (corp-wide): 35.38MM **Privately Held**
Web: www.ravennaschools.us
SIC: 4225 General warehousing and storage
PA: Ravenna School District
507 E Main St
Ravenna OH 44266
330 296-9679

(G-12641)
REHAB CENTER
Also Called: Rehabcenter
6847 N Chestnut St (44266-3929)
P.O. Box 1204 (44266-1204)
PHONE...................................330 297-2770
Stephen Colecchi, *CEO*
Richard E Clough, *
David Baldwin, *
Linda Breedlove, *
EMP: 158 **EST:** 1998
SALES (est): 2.43MM **Privately Held**
SIC: 8049 8093 Physical therapist; Rehabilitation center, outpatient treatment

(G-12642)
ROBINSON HEALTH SYSTEM INC
Also Called: Sportclinic
6847 N Chestnut St Ste 100 (44266-3929)
P.O. Box 1204 (44266-1204)
PHONE...................................330 297-8844
Stephen Colecchi, *Pr*
EMP: 3542
SALES (corp-wide): 878.24MM **Privately Held**
Web: www.uhhospitals.org
SIC: 8062 8049 General medical and surgical hospitals; Physical therapist
HQ: Robinson Health System, Inc.
6847 N Chestnut St
Ravenna OH 44266
330 297-0811

(G-12643)
ROBINSON HEALTH SYSTEM INC (HQ)
Also Called: University Hosp Prtage Med Ctr
6847 N Chestnut St (44266)
P.O. Box 1204 (44266)
PHONE...................................330 297-0811
Stephen Colecchi, *Pr*
Linda Breedlove, *
Neil Everett, *
Bradley Raum, *
EMP: 1200 **EST:** 1905
SQ FT: 307,000
SALES (est): 184.83MM
SALES (corp-wide): 878.24MM **Privately Held**
Web: www.robinsonmemorial.org
SIC: 8062 8011 General medical and surgical hospitals; Offices and clinics of medical doctors
PA: University Hospitals Health System, Inc.
3605 Warrensville Ctr Rd
Shaker Heights OH 44122
216 767-8900

(G-12644)
SMITHERS MSE INC
1150 N Freedom St (44266-2457)
PHONE...................................330 297-1495
James Topio, *Brnch Mgr*
EMP: 50
SQ FT: 30,000
SALES (corp-wide): 115.78MM **Privately Held**
Web: www.smithers.com
SIC: 8734 Product testing laboratories
HQ: Smithers Mse Inc
425 W Market St
Akron OH 44303
330 762-7441

(G-12645)
TSK ASSISTED LIVING SVCS INC
Also Called: Visiting Angels
240 W Riddle Ave (44266-2949)
PHONE...................................330 297-2000
Scott Ball, *Pr*
Steven W Kastenhuber, *
EMP: 60 **EST:** 2012
SALES (est): 1.81MM **Privately Held**
Web: www.visitingangels.com
SIC: 8082 Home health care services

(G-12646)
WOODLANDS HEALTHCARE GROUP LLC
Also Called: WoodInds Hlth Rhbilitation Ctr
6831 N Chestnut St (44266-3929)
PHONE...................................330 297-4564
EMP: 45
SALES (corp-wide): 5.9MM **Privately Held**
Web: www.saberhealth.com
SIC: 8051 Convalescent home with continuous nursing care
PA: Woodlands Healthcare Group, Llc
6831 N Chestnut St
Ravenna OH 44266
330 297-4564

Rayland
Jefferson County

(G-12647)
HEAVENLY HOME HEALTH LLC
1800 Old State Route 7 (43943-7962)
PHONE...................................740 859-4735
EMP: 30 **EST:** 2011
SALES (est): 843.78K **Privately Held**
SIC: 8082 Home health care services

(G-12648)
VALLEY HOSPICE INC (PA)
10686 State Route 150 (43943-7847)
PHONE...................................740 859-5041
Karen Nicols, *Pr*
EMP: 30 **EST:** 1985
SALES (est): 7.66MM **Privately Held**
Web: www.valleyhospice.org
SIC: 8052 Personal care facility

Reynoldsburg
Franklin County

(G-12649)
ABACUS CORPORATION
1676 Brice Rd (43068-2704)
PHONE...................................614 367-7000
April Calausi, *Brnch Mgr*
EMP: 448
SALES (corp-wide): 100.7MM **Privately Held**
Web: www.abacuscorporation.com
SIC: 7361 Executive placement
PA: Abacus Corporation
610 Gusryan St
Baltimore MD 21224
410 633-1900

(G-12650)
ACCURATE ELECTRIC CNSTR INC
6901 Americana Pkwy (43068-4116)
PHONE...................................614 863-1844
Robert S Beal, *Pr*
Ralph Stout, *
EMP: 160 **EST:** 1983
SQ FT: 10,000
SALES (est): 28.31MM **Privately Held**
Web: www.aecohio.com
SIC: 1731 General electrical contractor

(G-12651)
AMERICAN CRANE INC
Also Called: American Crane & Lift Trck Svc
7791 Taylor Rd Sw Ste A (43068-9632)
PHONE...................................614 496-2268
Richard W Palmer Junior, *Pr*
Scott Hughes, *
EMP: 34 **EST:** 1994
SQ FT: 25,000
SALES (est): 2.65MM **Privately Held**
Web: www.americancraneinc.com
SIC: 7389 7353 5082 Crane and aerial lift service; Cranes and aerial lift equipment, rental or leasing; Cranes, construction

(G-12652)
AMERICAN JERSEY CATTLE ASSN (PA)
6486 E Main St (43068-2493)
PHONE...................................614 861-3636
Neal Smith, *CEO*
Vickie White, *
EMP: 35 **EST:** 1868
SQ FT: 9,000
SALES (est): 3.36MM
SALES (corp-wide): 3.36MM **Privately Held**
Web: www.usjersey.com
SIC: 8611 Trade associations

(G-12653)
AMERICAN KENDA RBR INDUS LTD (HQ)
Also Called: Kenda USA
7095 Americana Pkwy (43068-4118)
PHONE...................................866 536-3287
Chi-jen Yang, *Pr*
Ching-huey Yang, *Treas*
▲ **EMP:** 42 **EST:** 1978
SQ FT: 100,000
SALES (est): 54.49MM **Privately Held**
Web: www.kendatire.com
SIC: 5014 Automobile tires and tubes
PA: Kenda Rubber Ind. Co., Ltd.
No.146,Sec.1, Chung Shan Road,
Yuanlin City CHA 51003

(G-12654)
BEAUTYAVENUES LLC (HQ)
Also Called: Bath and Body Works
7 Limited Pkwy E (43068-5300)
PHONE...................................614 856-6000
Charles Mcguigan, *CEO*
◆ **EMP:** 147 **EST:** 2005
SALES (est): 95.74MM
SALES (corp-wide): 7.43B **Publicly Held**
SIC: 5999 5122 2844 Toiletries, cosmetics, and perfumes; Perfumes; Face creams or lotions
PA: Bath & Body Works, Inc.
3 Limited Pkwy
Columbus OH 43230
614 415-7000

GEOGRAPHIC SECTION

Reynoldsburg - Franklin County (G-12677)

(G-12655)
BREAD FINANCIAL HOLDINGS INC
6939 Americana Pkwy (43068-4171)
PHONE................................614 729-5800
EMP: 58
Web: www.alliancedata.com
SIC: 7389 Credit card service
PA: Bread Financial Holdings, Inc.
    3095 Loyalty Cir
    Columbus OH 43219

(G-12656)
BUSINESS ADMNSTRATORS CONS INC (PA)
6331 E Livingston Ave (43068-2756)
P.O. Box 107 (43068-0107)
PHONE................................614 863-8780
Richard Raup, *Pr*
EMP: 47 **EST:** 1980
SQ FT: 4,600
SALES (est): 5.14MM
SALES (corp-wide): 5.14MM **Privately Held**
Web: www.bactpa.com
SIC: 6411 Insurance information and consulting services

(G-12657)
CENTRAL OHIO PRIMARY CARE
6488 E Main St Ste C (43068-7310)
PHONE................................614 552-2300
EMP: 108
Web: www.copcp.com
SIC: 8011 General and family practice, physician/surgeon
PA: Central Ohio Primary Care Physicians, Inc.
    655 Africa Rd
    Westerville OH 43082

(G-12658)
CHARDON LABORATORIES INC
7300 Tussing Rd (43068-4111)
PHONE................................614 860-1000
Robert S Butt, *CEO*
Mark Davenport, *
EMP: 50 **EST:** 1966
SQ FT: 10,000
SALES (est): 9.14MM **Privately Held**
Web: www.chardonlabs.com
SIC: 7389 Water softener service

(G-12659)
COLUMBUS FRNKLIN CNTY MTRO PK
Also Called: Blacklick Woods Metro Park
6975 E Livingston Ave (43068-3015)
PHONE................................614 891-0700
Ken Rich, *Mgr*
EMP: 33
SALES (corp-wide): 18.39MM **Privately Held**
Web: www.metroparks.net
SIC: 7999 Recreation services
PA: Columbus & Franklin County Metropolitan Park District
    1069 W Main St Unit B
    Westerville OH 43081
    614 891-0700

(G-12660)
DIMENSIONAL METALS INC (PA)
Also Called: D M I
58 Klema Dr N (43068-9691)
PHONE................................740 927-3633
Stephen C Wissman, *CEO*
Phillip Gastaldo, *
Steven Gastaldo, *
EMP: 43 **EST:** 1988
SQ FT: 34,000
SALES (est): 15.64MM **Privately Held**
Web: www.dmimetals.com
SIC: 1761 3444 3531 Sheet metal work, nec; Sheet metalwork; Roofing equipment

(G-12661)
DREIER & MALLER INC (PA)
6508 Taylor Rd Sw (43068-9633)
PHONE................................614 575-0065
Stewart Dreier, *Pr*
Steve Maller, *
EMP: 28 **EST:** 1989
SALES (est): 2.16MM **Privately Held**
Web: www.dreierandmaller.com
SIC: 7389 7699 5084 Pipeline and power line inspection service; Sewer cleaning and rodding; Measuring and testing equipment, electrical

(G-12662)
ECHO 24 INC (PA)
167 Cypress St Sw Ste A (43068-9692)
PHONE................................740 964-7081
Anthony J Gunter, *Pr*
Lisa L Gunter C.p.a., *Prin*
EMP: 40 **EST:** 2001
SQ FT: 2,000
SALES (est): 9.57MM
SALES (corp-wide): 9.57MM **Privately Held**
Web: www.echo24.com
SIC: 4813 Telephone communication, except radio

(G-12663)
FIRST HOSPITALITY COMPANY LLC
Also Called: Fairfield Inn
2826 Taylor Road Ext (43068-9555)
PHONE................................614 864-4555
Amar Pandey, *Pt*
EMP: 54 **EST:** 1999
SALES (est): 2.7MM **Privately Held**
Web: fairfield.marriott.com
SIC: 7011 Hotels and motels

(G-12664)
GPAX INC
555 Lancaster Ave (43068-1128)
PHONE................................614 501-7622
Gary James, *Pt*
EMP: 32 **EST:** 2002
SALES (est): 2.25MM
SALES (corp-wide): 53.76MM **Privately Held**
Web: www.gpax.com
SIC: 5199 Packaging materials
PA: Dynalab, Inc.
    555 Lancaster Ave
    Reynoldsburg OH 43068
    614 866-9999

(G-12665)
GREEN KING COMPANY INC
9562 Taylor Rd Sw (43068-3228)
PHONE................................614 861-4132
Adam T High, *Pr*
Erik High, *
EMP: 30 **EST:** 1965
SQ FT: 4,000
SALES (est): 1.02MM **Privately Held**
SIC: 0782 Landscape contractors

(G-12666)
HOME DEPOT USA INC
Also Called: Home Depot, The
2480 Brice Rd (43068)
PHONE................................614 577-1601
Mark Smith, *Brnch Mgr*
EMP: 110
SALES (corp-wide): 152.67B **Publicly Held**
Web: www.homedepot.com
SIC: 5211 7359 Home centers; Tool rental
HQ: Home Depot U.S.A., Inc.
    2445 Springfield Ave
    Vauxhall NJ 07088

(G-12667)
LBS INTERNATIONAL INC
Also Called: Friendly Care Agency
6501 E Livingston Ave Ste 4 (43068-3561)
PHONE................................614 866-3688
Sam I Lantsman, *Pr*
Larisa B Lantsman, *
EMP: 37 **EST:** 1994
SALES (est): 1.89MM **Privately Held**
Web: www.lbsinternational.com
SIC: 8082 Visiting nurse service

(G-12668)
LOWES HOME CENTERS LLC
Also Called: Lowe's
8231 E Broad St (43068-9732)
PHONE................................614 769-9940
Jeff Fetters, *Brnch Mgr*
EMP: 86
SALES (corp-wide): 86.38B **Publicly Held**
Web: www.lowes.com
SIC: 5211 5031 5722 5064 Home centers; Building materials, exterior; Household appliance stores; Electrical appliances, television and radio
HQ: Lowe's Home Centers, Llc
    1000 Lowes Blvd
    Mooresville NC 28117
    336 658-4000

(G-12669)
METROPOLITIAN FAMILY CARE INC
Also Called: Metropolitan Family Care
7094 E Main St (43068-2010)
PHONE................................614 237-1067
Andrew J Pultz Md, *Pr*
Diana Max, *Mgr*
EMP: 37 **EST:** 1940
SALES (est): 3.2MM **Privately Held**
Web: www.metropolitanfc.com
SIC: 8011 General and family practice, physician/surgeon

(G-12670)
MII BRAND IMPORT LLC (HQ)
Also Called: L Brands
4 Limited Pkwy E (43068-5300)
PHONE................................614 256-7267
Leslie H Wexner, *CEO*
James M Schwartz, *
Stuart Burgdoerfer, *
◆ **EMP:** 125 **EST:** 1992
SALES (est): 379.76MM
SALES (corp-wide): 6.18B **Publicly Held**
SIC: 5137 5136 Women's and children's clothing; Men's and boy's clothing
PA: Victoria's Secret & Co.
    4 Limited Pkwy E
    Reynoldsburg OH 43068
    614 577-7000

(G-12671)
OAKWOOD MANAGEMENT COMPANY (PA)
6950 Americana Pkwy Ste A (43068-4126)
PHONE................................614 866-8702
John D Wymer, *Pr*
Donald W Kelley, *
Tim M Kelley, *
Patrick J Kelley, *
Dana L Moore, *
EMP: 45 **EST:** 1970
SQ FT: 10,000
SALES (est): 34.62MM
SALES (corp-wide): 34.62MM **Privately Held**
Web: www.liveoakwood.com
SIC: 6531 Real estate managers

(G-12672)
PREMIER BROADCASTING CO INC
Also Called: Massey's Pizza
177 Cypress St Sw (43068-9692)
PHONE................................614 866-0700
David Pallone, *Pr*
James Pallone, *
EMP: 49 **EST:** 1992
SALES (est): 908.24K **Privately Held**
Web: www.masseyspizza.com
SIC: 5812 6794 Pizza restaurants; Franchises, selling or licensing

(G-12673)
PXP OHIO
6800 Tussing Rd (43068-7044)
PHONE................................614 575-4242
Greg Scott, *Owner*
EMP: 28 **EST:** 2001
SQ FT: 15,688
SALES (est): 2.7MM **Privately Held**
Web: www.pxpohio.com
SIC: 7389 Printing broker

(G-12674)
RAINBOW STATION DAY CARE INC
Also Called: Rainbow Child - Reynoldsburg
8315 Taylor Rd Sw (43068-9628)
PHONE................................614 575-5040
Loretta Taylor, *Dir*
EMP: 27
SALES (corp-wide): 1.01MM **Privately Held**
Web: www.registrar-transfers.com
SIC: 8351 8748 Group day care center; Educational consultant
PA: Rainbow Station Day Care Inc
    226 Durand St
    Pickerington OH 43147
    614 759-8667

(G-12675)
REM-OHIO INC
Also Called: REM Ohio Waivered Services
6402 E Main St Ste 103 (43068-2356)
PHONE................................614 367-1370
EMP: 38
SALES (corp-wide): 19.17MM **Privately Held**
Web: www.rem-oh.com
SIC: 8361 Retarded home
PA: Rem-Ohio, Inc
    6921 York Ave S
    Minneapolis MN 55435
    952 925-5067

(G-12676)
RENASCENCE OTTAWA LLC
6880 Tussing Rd (43068-4101)
PHONE................................614 863-4640
EMP: 60 **EST:** 2001
SALES (est): 3.9MM **Privately Held**
SIC: 1522 Multi-family dwelling construction, nec

(G-12677)
ROSE TRANSPORT INC
6747 Taylor Rd Sw (43068-9674)
PHONE................................614 864-4004
John W Spencer, *Pr*
Ralph Spencer, *
EMP: 71 **EST:** 1990
SQ FT: 14,000
SALES (est): 2MM
SALES (corp-wide): 59.21MM **Privately Held**
SIC: 4212 Local trucking, without storage
HQ: Mulch Manufacturing, Inc.

Reynoldsburg - Franklin County (G-12678)   GEOGRAPHIC SECTION

6747 Taylor Rd Sw
Reynoldsburg OH 43068
614 864-4004

(G-12678)
TS TECH AMERICAS INC (HQ)
8458 E Broad St (43068-9749)
PHONE..............................614 575-4100
Minoru Maeda, *Pr*
Jason J Ma, *Ex VP*
Takayuki Taniuchi, *
Hiroshi Suzuki, *
▲ **EMP**: 350 **EST**: 2013
SALES (est): 915.06MM **Privately Held**
Web: www.tstech.com
SIC: 5099 2396 Child restraint seats, automotive; Automotive trimmings, fabric
PA: Ts Tech Co., Ltd.
    3-7-27, Sakaecho
    Asaka STM 351-0

(G-12679)
VALVOLINE INSTANT OIL CHNGE FR
Also Called: Valvoline Instant Oil Change
8217 E Broad St (43068-9732)
PHONE..............................614 452-4682
Craig Moughler, *Pr*
EMP: 52
Web: www.valvoline.com
SIC: 7549 Automotive maintenance services
HQ: Valvoline Instant Oil Change
    Franchising, Inc.
    100 Valvoline Way
    Lexington KY 40509

(G-12680)
WALLICK CONSTRUCTION CO (PA)
Also Called: Wallick
6880 Tussing Rd (43068-4128)
P.O. Box 1023 (43216-1023)
PHONE..............................614 863-4640
EMP: 50 **EST**: 1966
SALES (est): 16.34MM
SALES (corp-wide): 16.34MM **Privately Held**
Web: www.wallick.com
SIC: 1542 1522 Commercial and office building, new construction; Multi-family dwellings, new construction

(G-12681)
WESLEY RIDGE INC
Also Called: METHODIST ELDER CARE SERVICES
2225 Taylor Park Dr (43068-8053)
PHONE..............................614 759-0023
Robert L Rouse, *CEO*
EMP: 44 **EST**: 1996
SALES (est): 3.94MM **Privately Held**
Web: www.lec.org
SIC: 8059 8052 Personal care home, with health care; Intermediate care facilities

(G-12682)
WHITESTONE GROUP INC
6422 E Main St Ste 101 (43068-2358)
PHONE..............................614 501-7007
John Clark, *Pr*
R Gene Hart, *
Bill Smith, *
EMP: 300 **EST**: 2000
SQ FT: 2,500
SALES (est): 28.91MM **Privately Held**
Web: www.whitestonegroup.us
SIC: 7381 Security guard service

(G-12683)
WOODWARD EXCAVATING CO
7340 Tussing Rd (43068-4111)
PHONE..............................614 866-4384
John Woodward, *Pr*

Brad Woodward, *
Clay Woodward, *
EMP: 27 **EST**: 1960
SQ FT: 7,200
SALES (est): 1.84MM **Privately Held**
Web: www.golfcomplex.com
SIC: 1623 Underground utilities contractor

Richfield
Summit County

(G-12684)
5145 CORPORATION
Also Called: Hampton Inn
4860 Brecksville Rd (44286-9621)
PHONE..............................330 659-6662
Minesh Shah, *Pr*
EMP: 54 **EST**: 1993
SQ FT: 38,000
SALES (est): 887.29K **Privately Held**
Web: www.hilton.com
SIC: 7011 Hotels and motels

(G-12685)
AMERICAN ENVMTL GROUP LTD
Also Called: Tetra Tech
3600 Brecksville Rd Ste 100 (44286-9668)
PHONE..............................330 659-5930
Carl Apicella, *Managing Member*
Peter Augustin, *
Mike Maurer, *
Ernest Vallorz, *
▲ **EMP**: 450 **EST**: 2002
SALES (est): 39.96MM
SALES (corp-wide): 4.52B **Publicly Held**
SIC: 8748 Environmental consultant
PA: Tetra Tech, Inc.
    3475 E Foothill Blvd
    Pasadena CA 91107
    626 351-4664

(G-12686)
AMERICAN HIGHWAYS INSUR AGCY
3250 Interstate Dr (44286-9000)
PHONE..............................330 659-8900
Alan Spachman, *Prin*
EMP: 30 **EST**: 2008
SALES (est): 4.82MM **Publicly Held**
Web: www.highwaysinsurance.com
SIC: 6411 Insurance agents, nec
HQ: National Interstate Corporation
    3250 Interstate Dr
    Richfield OH 44286

(G-12687)
ANTHONY ALLEGA CEM CONTR INC
5146 Allega Way (44286-9817)
PHONE..............................216 447-0814
John Allega, *Pr*
Joseph Allega, *
James Allega, *
Jeffrey F Wallis, *
EMP: 50 **EST**: 1946
SALES (est): 16.25MM **Privately Held**
Web: www.allega.com
SIC: 1771 Concrete work

(G-12688)
BLUE STREAM LLC (PA)
4360 Brecksville Rd (44286-9457)
PHONE..............................330 659-6166
Pradip Kamat, *Managing Member*
EMP: 55 **EST**: 2005
SALES (est): 4.6MM **Privately Held**
Web: www.bluestreamrehab.com
SIC: 8361 Rehabilitation center, residential; health care incidental

(G-12689)
BRECKSVILLE LEASING CO LLC
Also Called: Pine Valley Care Center
4360 Brecksville Rd (44286-9457)
PHONE..............................330 659-6166
EMP: 48 **EST**: 2007
SALES (est): 6.09MM **Privately Held**
SIC: 8051 Convalescent home with continuous nursing care

(G-12690)
CARRARA COMPANIES INC (PA)
2406 Farmstead Rd (44286-9375)
PHONE..............................330 659-2800
TOLL FREE: 888
Justin Sucato, *Pr*
Julie Sucato, *
EMP: 28 **EST**: 1996
SALES (est): 18.58MM
SALES (corp-wide): 18.58MM **Privately Held**
Web: www.carraracompanies.com
SIC: 1541 Renovation, remodeling and repairs: industrial buildings

(G-12691)
CHARLES SCHWAB & CO INC
Also Called: Charles Schwab
4150 Kinross Lakes Pkwy (44286-9369)
P.O. Box 5050 (44286-5050)
PHONE..............................330 908-4478
EMP: 36
SALES (corp-wide): 18.84B **Publicly Held**
Web: www.schwab.com
SIC: 6211 Brokers, security
HQ: Charles Schwab & Co., Inc.
    3000 Schwab Way
    Westlake TX 76262
    415 636-7000

(G-12692)
COMMUNICARE HEALTH SVCS INC
Also Called: Pine Valley Care Center
4360 Brecksville Rd (44286-9457)
PHONE..............................330 659-6166
EMP: 115
SALES (corp-wide): 392.92MM **Privately Held**
Web: www.communicarehealth.com
SIC: 8051 Convalescent home with continuous nursing care
PA: Communicare Health Services, Inc.
    10123 Alliance Rd
    Blue Ash OH 45242
    513 530-1654

(G-12693)
DAWSON COMPANIES
3900 Kinross Lakes Pkwy (44286-9445)
PHONE..............................440 333-9000
Rob Odney, *Prin*
EMP: 90 **EST**: 2013
SALES (est): 3.02MM **Privately Held**
Web: www.assuredpartners.com
SIC: 6411 Insurance brokers, nec

(G-12694)
DENTAL CERAMICS INC
3404 Brecksville Rd (44286-9662)
PHONE..............................330 523-5240
John Lavicka, *Pr*
EMP: 27 **EST**: 1963
SALES (est): 5.43MM **Privately Held**
Web: www.dentalceramicsusa.com
SIC: 8072 3843 Crown and bridge production; Dental equipment and supplies

(G-12695)
EMPACO EQUIPMENT CORPORATION (PA)

Also Called: Emil Pawuk & Associates
2958 Brecksville Rd (44286-9747)
P.O. Box 535 (44286-0535)
PHONE..............................330 659-9393
Emil M Pawuk Senior, *Pr*
Emil M Pawuk Junior, *VP*
C B Wheeler, *
L R Gaiduk, *
EMP: 40 **EST**: 1970
SQ FT: 11,280
SALES (est): 15.19MM
SALES (corp-wide): 15.19MM **Privately Held**
Web: www.empacoequipment.com
SIC: 1799 Service station equipment

(G-12696)
ESTES EXPRESS LINES
2755 Brecksville Rd (44286-9735)
PHONE..............................330 659-9750
EMP: 37
SALES (corp-wide): 3.56B **Privately Held**
Web: www.estes-express.com
SIC: 4731 Freight transportation arrangement
PA: Estes Express Lines
    3901 W Broad St
    Richmond VA 23230
    804 353-1900

(G-12697)
EXPLORER RV INSURANCE AGCY INC
Also Called: GMAC Insurance
3250 Interstate Dr (44286-9000)
P.O. Box 568 (44286-0568)
PHONE..............................330 659-8900
Alan R Spachman, *Prin*
EMP: 34 **EST**: 2004
SALES (est): 4.23MM **Publicly Held**
Web: www.natl.com
SIC: 6411 Insurance agents, nec
HQ: National Interstate Corporation
    3250 Interstate Dr
    Richfield OH 44286

(G-12698)
FEDEX CUSTOM CRITICAL INC (HQ)
Also Called: Fedex
4205 Highlander Pkwy (44286-9077)
P.O. Box 5000 (44232-5000)
PHONE..............................234 310-4090
Ramona Hood, *CEO*
Alan B Graf Junior, *Ch Bd*
EMP: 500 **EST**: 1967
SQ FT: 103,000
SALES (est): 443.67MM
SALES (corp-wide): 90.16B **Publicly Held**
Web: www.fedex.com
SIC: 4731 Freight forwarding
PA: Fedex Corporation
    942 Shady Grove Rd S
    Memphis TN 38120
    901 818-7500

(G-12699)
IRG REALTY ADVISORS LLC (PA)
4020 Kinross Lakes Pkwy Ste 200 (44286-9084)
PHONE..............................330 659-4060
Tracy C Green, *Managing Member*
Becky Smith, *
EMP: 30 **EST**: 2001
SQ FT: 1,200
SALES (est): 25.51MM
SALES (corp-wide): 25.51MM **Privately Held**
Web: www.irgra.com
SIC: 6531 Real estate managers

GEOGRAPHIC SECTION

Richmond Heights - Cuyahoga County (G-12721)

(G-12700)
KINGS MEDICAL COMPANY
4125 Highlander Pkwy Ste 150 (44286-9085)
PHONE.................330 653-3968
Clark Labaski, *Contrlr*
EMP: 197 **EST:** 1981
SALES (est): 4.17MM
SALES (corp-wide): 46.07MM **Privately Held**
Web: www.kingsmedical.com
SIC: 8742 Banking and finance consultant
PA: King's Medical Group, Inc.
4125 Highlander Pkwy # 15
Richfield OH 44286
330 528-1765

(G-12701)
NATIONAL INTERSTATE CORP (HQ)
3250 Interstate Dr (44286-9000)
PHONE.................330 659-8900
Anthony J Mercurio, *Pr*
Arthur J Gonzales, *
Terry E Phillips, *
Julie A Mcgraw, *CFO*
Gary N Monda, *CIO*
EMP: 336 **EST:** 1989
SQ FT: 143,000
SALES (est): 548.76MM **Publicly Held**
Web: www.natl.com
SIC: 6331 6411 Fire, marine, and casualty insurance; Property and casualty insurance agent
PA: American Financial Group, Inc.
301 E 4th St
Cincinnati OH 45202

(G-12702)
NATIONAL INTERSTATE INSUR CO (DH)
3250 Interstate Dr (44286-9000)
PHONE.................330 659-8900
Tony Mercurio, *CEO*
Alan R Spachman, *
Shawn Los, *
Arthur M Kraus, *
George Skuggen, *
EMP: 200 **EST:** 1989
SQ FT: 22,000
SALES (est): 231.68MM **Publicly Held**
Web: www.natl.com
SIC: 6331 Fire, marine, and casualty insurance
HQ: National Interstate Corporation
3250 Interstate Dr
Richfield OH 44286

(G-12703)
NAVIGATE360 LLC (PA)
Also Called: Navigate360
3900 Kinross Lakes Pkwy Ste 200 (44286-9445)
PHONE.................330 661-0106
Julia Goebel, *CMO*
EMP: 150 **EST:** 2013
SQ FT: 4,000
SALES (est): 23.68MM
SALES (corp-wide): 23.68MM **Privately Held**
Web: www.navigate360.com
SIC: 8748 Safety training service

(G-12704)
NEWARK CORPORATION
Newark Electronics Div
4180 Highlander Pkwy (44286-9352)
PHONE.................330 523-4457
Michelle Evans, *Mgr*
EMP: 300
SALES (corp-wide): 26.54B **Publicly Held**
Web: www.newark.com
SIC: 5065 Electronic parts
HQ: Newark Corporation
300 S Riverside Plz # 2200
Chicago IL 60606
773 784-5100

(G-12705)
OHIO TPK & INFRASTRUCTURE COMM
Also Called: Boston Maintenance Bldg
3245 Boston Mills Rd (44286-9455)
PHONE.................440 234-2081
Lynn Parker, *Mgr*
EMP: 48
SQ FT: 24,800
Web: www.ohioturnpike.org
SIC: 1611 0782 9621 Highway and street maintenance; Highway lawn and garden maintenance services; Regulation, administration of transportation
HQ: Ohio Turnpike And Infrastructure Commission
682 Prospect St
Berea OH 44017
440 234-2081

(G-12706)
PLATINUM COURIERS INC
4615 W Streetsboro Rd (44286-9227)
PHONE.................216 370-8972
Sheranda Johnson, *Managing Member*
EMP: 50 **EST:** 2019
SALES (est): 1.6MM **Privately Held**
SIC: 4215 Package delivery, vehicular

(G-12707)
REGIONAL EXPRESS INC
4615 W Streetsboro Rd Ste 203 (44286-9227)
PHONE.................516 458-3514
Salvatore Caiazzo Junior, *Pr*
EMP: 54 **EST:** 2017
SALES (est): 3.59MM **Privately Held**
SIC: 4731 Freight transportation arrangement

(G-12708)
RICHFELD BNQUET CNFRNCE CTR LL
Also Called: Quality Inn
4742 Brecksville Rd (44286-9619)
PHONE.................330 659-6151
EMP: 38 **EST:** 2004
SALES (est): 1.13MM **Privately Held**
Web: www.choicehotels.com
SIC: 7011 Hotels and motels

(G-12709)
SAIA MOTOR FREIGHT LINE LLC
2920 Brecksville Rd Ste B (44286-9265)
PHONE.................330 659-4277
M Pawuk, *Brnch Mgr*
EMP: 51
SALES (corp-wide): 2.88B **Publicly Held**
SIC: 4213 Contract haulers
HQ: Saia Motor Freight Line, Llc
11465 Johns Creek Pkwy # 400
Duluth GA 30097
770 232-5067

(G-12710)
SNAP-ON BUSINESS SOLUTIONS INC (HQ)
4025 Kinross Lakes Pkwy (44286-9371)
PHONE.................330 659-1600
Timothy Chambers, *Pr*
Jarry Baracz, *
Michael Maddison, *
EMP: 300 **EST:** 1987
SQ FT: 88,000
SALES (est): 126.89MM
SALES (corp-wide): 4.73B **Publicly Held**
Web: sbs.snapon.com
SIC: 7372 Business oriented computer software
PA: Snap-On Incorporated
2801 80th St
Kenosha WI 53143
262 656-5200

(G-12711)
TFORCE FREIGHT INC
3495 Brecksville Rd (44286-9663)
PHONE.................330 659-6693
Jerry Ruediger, *Mgr*
EMP: 36
SQ FT: 3,500
SALES (corp-wide): 8.81B **Privately Held**
Web: www.tforcefreight.com
SIC: 4213 4212 Contract haulers; Local trucking, without storage
HQ: Tforce Freight, Inc.
1000 Semmes Ave
Richmond VA 23224
800 333-7400

(G-12712)
THORSON BAKER & ASSOCIATES INC (PA)
3030 W Streetsboro Rd (44286-9632)
PHONE.................330 659-6688
EMP: 56 **EST:** 1997
SQ FT: 48,000
SALES (est): 25.6MM **Privately Held**
Web: www.thorsonbaker.com
SIC: 8711 Consulting engineer

(G-12713)
WHITEYS RESTAURANT INC
Also Called: Whitey's Booze & Burgers
3600 Brecksville Rd Frnt Frnt (44286-9668)
PHONE.................330 659-3600
Jonathan Bigadza, *Pr*
EMP: 27 **EST:** 1954
SQ FT: 10,000
SALES (est): 441.65K **Privately Held**
Web: www.whiteyschili.com
SIC: 5812 5813 7033 American restaurant; Tavern (drinking places); Trailer park

(G-12714)
WMK LLC (PA)
Also Called: Mobilityworks
4199 Kinross Lakes Pkwy Ste 300 (44286)
PHONE.................234 312-2000
▲ **EMP:** 35 **EST:** 1986
SALES (est): 218.57MM
SALES (corp-wide): 218.57MM **Privately Held**
Web: www.mobilityworks.com
SIC: 5511 7532 Automobiles, new and used; Customizing services, nonfactory basis

Richmond Heights
Cuyahoga County

(G-12715)
ASSOCIATED ESTATES REALTY CORPORATION
1 Integrity Pkwy (44143-1500)
PHONE.................216 261-5000
EMP: 400
SIC: 6798 1531 Real estate investment trusts; Speculative builder, multi-family dwellings

(G-12716)
CCP INDUSTRIES INC
Also Called: Ccp Industries
26301 Curtiss Wright Pkwy Ste 200 (44143-1454)
P.O. Box 6500 (44101-1500)
PHONE.................216 535-4227
▼ **EMP:** 400
SIC: 5169 2392 2297 2273 Specialty cleaning and sanitation preparations; Household furnishings, nec; Nonwoven fabrics; Carpets and rugs

(G-12717)
CSG CLEVELAND ENTERPRISES INC (PA)
Also Called: Cynergies Solutions Group
26301 Curtiss Wright Pkwy Ste 115 (44143-4413)
PHONE.................440 918-9341
Debbie Holy, *Pr*
Eleanor Chalko, *
EMP: 38 **EST:** 1998
SQ FT: 3,000
SALES (est): 7.13MM
SALES (corp-wide): 7.13MM **Privately Held**
SIC: 7371 Custom computer programming services

(G-12718)
FLEXJET INC
355 Richmond Rd (44143-4405)
PHONE.................866 309-2214
EMP: 36
SALES (corp-wide): 160.16MM **Privately Held**
Web: www.flexjet.com
SIC: 4581 Airports, flying fields, and services
HQ: Flexjet, Inc.
26180 Curtiss Wright Pkwy
Cleveland OH 44143
216 261-3880

(G-12719)
FLIGHT OPTIONS INC (PA)
26180 Curtiss Wright Pkwy (44143)
PHONE.................216 261-3880
Kenneth Ricci, *Ch*
Robert Pinkas, *
Travis Metz, *
Michael J Silvestro, *
J Chris Herzberg, *
EMP: 500 **EST:** 1998
SQ FT: 30,000
SALES (est): 160.16MM
SALES (corp-wide): 160.16MM **Privately Held**
Web: www.flightoptions.com
SIC: 7359 Aircraft rental

(G-12720)
FLIGHT OPTIONS INTL INC (HQ)
355 Richmond Rd (44143-4405)
PHONE.................216 261-3500
Ed Mc Donald, *Pr*
EMP: 33 **EST:** 1979
SQ FT: 15,000
SALES (est): 24.2MM
SALES (corp-wide): 160.16MM **Privately Held**
SIC: 7359 Aircraft rental
PA: Flight Options, Inc.
26180 Curtis Wright Pkwy
Richmond Heights OH 44143
216 261-3880

(G-12721)
PLEZALL WIPERS INC
26301 Curtiss Wright Pkwy Ste 200 (44143-4413)
PHONE.................216 535-4300
Ken Vuylsteke, *Pr*
Tom Friedl, *CFO*
▼ **EMP:** 39 **EST:** 1954
SQ FT: 12,500

Richmond Heights - Cuyahoga County (G-12722)

SALES (est): 2.36MM **Privately Held**
SIC: **5093** Waste rags

(G-12722)
RICHMOND MEDICAL CENTER (PA)
27100 Chardon Rd (44143-1116)
PHONE.................................440 585-6500
Laurie Delgado, *Pr*
EMP: 398 EST: 1996
SALES (est): 9.77MM
SALES (corp-wide): 9.77MM **Privately Held**
SIC: **8062** 8011 General medical and surgical hospitals; Medical centers

(G-12723)
UH REGIONAL HOSPITALS (HQ)
Also Called: UNIVERSITY HOSPITALS
27100 Chardon Rd (44143-1116)
PHONE.................................440 585-6439
EMP: 51 EST: 2000
SALES (est): 125.58MM
SALES (corp-wide): 878.24MM **Privately Held**
Web: www.uhhospitals.org
SIC: **8062** General medical and surgical hospitals
PA: University Hospitals Health System, Inc.
3605 Warrensville Ctr Rd
Shaker Heights OH 44122
216 767-8900

Richwood
Union County

(G-12724)
RICHWOOD BANKING COMPANY (HQ)
28 N Franklin St (43344-1027)
P.O. Box 148 (43344-0148)
PHONE.................................740 943-2317
Nancy K Hoffman, *Pr*
Chad Hoffman, *VP*
EMP: 27 EST: 1867
SALES (est): 45.49MM **Privately Held**
Web: www.richwoodbank.com
SIC: **6022** State trust companies accepting deposits, commercial
PA: Richwood Bancshares, Inc.
28 N Franklin St
Richwood OH 43344

Ridgeville Corners
Henry County

(G-12725)
APA SOLAR LLC
Also Called: Ap-Alternatives
20 345 County Road X (43555)
PHONE.................................419 267-5280
David Von Deylen, *Ch Bd*
Kristi Von Deylen, *
Joshua Von Deylen, *
EMP: 100 EST: 2008
SQ FT: 5,000
SALES (est): 25.79MM **Privately Held**
Web: www.apasolar.com
SIC: **1791** Iron work, structural

Rio Grande
Gallia County

(G-12726)
AREA AGENCY ON AGING DST 7 INC (PA)
160 Dorsey Dr (45674-7517)
P.O. Box 154 (45674-0154)
PHONE.................................800 582-7277
Melissa Dever, *Ex Dir*
Pamela Matura, *
EMP: 43 EST: 1979
SALES (est): 63.29MM
SALES (corp-wide): 63.29MM **Privately Held**
Web: www.aaa7.org
SIC: **8322** Senior citizens' center or association

Ripley
Brown County

(G-12727)
OHIO VALLEY MANOR INC
5280 Us Highway 62 And 68 (45167-8650)
PHONE.................................937 392-4318
Dave Seesholtz, *Ch*
George Balz, *
Dale G Wilson, *
Evelyn Seesholtz, *
Gary Seesholtz, *
EMP: 101 EST: 1968
SQ FT: 72,000
SALES (est): 15.85MM **Privately Held**
Web: www.ohiovalleymanor.com
SIC: **8059** 8052 8051 Convalescent home; Intermediate care facilities; Skilled nursing care facilities

(G-12728)
OVM INVESTMENT GROUP LLC
5280 Us Highway 62 And 68 (45167-8650)
PHONE.................................937 392-0145
Allan Acheson, *CFO*
Steven Boymel, *
EMP: 220 EST: 2017
SQ FT: 150,000
SALES (est): 5.41MM **Privately Held**
SIC: **8051** Skilled nursing care facilities

Rittman
Wayne County

(G-12729)
APOSTOLIC CHRISTIAN HOME INC
10680 Steiner Rd (44270-9518)
PHONE.................................330 927-1010
Dave Maletich, *Admn*
EMP: 90 EST: 1974
SQ FT: 23,000
SALES (est): 9.74MM **Privately Held**
Web: www.apostolichome.org
SIC: **8059** 8052 8051 Nursing home, except skilled and intermediate care facility; Intermediate care facilities; Skilled nursing care facilities

(G-12730)
LARIA CHEVROLET-BUICK INC
112 E Ohio Ave (44270-1537)
PHONE.................................330 925-2015
TOLL FREE: 866
John W Laria, *Pr*
EMP: 40 EST: 1934
SALES (est): 9.14MM **Privately Held**
Web: www.lariachevybuick.com
SIC: **5511** 5521 5012 Automobiles, new and used; Used car dealers; Automobiles and other motor vehicles

(G-12731)
MORTON SALT INC
151 Industrial Ave (44270-1593)
PHONE.................................330 925-3015
Mark Wallace, *Brnch Mgr*
EMP: 150
SALES (corp-wide): 1.22B **Privately Held**
Web: www.mortonsalt.com
SIC: **5149** 2899 Salt, edible; Chemical preparations, nec
HQ: Morton Salt, Inc.
444 W Lake St Ste 3000
Chicago IL 60606

(G-12732)
RITTMAN INC
Also Called: Mull Iron
10 Mull Dr (44270-9777)
PHONE.................................330 927-6855
Chester Mull Junior, *Pr*
William Mull, *
Beth Mull, *
Richard J Wendelken, *
Robert A O'neil, *Prin*
EMP: 60 EST: 1983
SQ FT: 34,000
SALES (est): 9.33MM **Privately Held**
Web: www.mulliron.net
SIC: **3441** 1791 Fabricated structural metal; Structural steel erection

Rock Creek
Ashtabula County

(G-12733)
GLENBEIGH (PA)
Also Called: Rock Creek Medical Center
2863 State Route 45 N (44084-9352)
P.O. Box 298 (44084-0298)
PHONE.................................440 563-3400
Pat Weston-hall, *CEO*
Joseph Vendel, *
Richard Trice, *
Charlene Wise, *Adm/Asst*
EMP: 42 EST: 1981
SALES (est): 15.18MM
SALES (corp-wide): 15.18MM **Privately Held**
Web: www.glenbeigh.com
SIC: **8093** Substance abuse clinics (outpatient)

(G-12734)
GLENBEIGH HEALTH SOURCES INC (PA)
2863 State Route 45 N (44084-9352)
P.O. Box 298 (44084-0298)
PHONE.................................440 951-7000
EMP: 140 EST: 1995
SALES (est): 26.26MM **Privately Held**
Web: www.glenbeigh.com
SIC: **8069** Drug addiction rehabilitation hospital

Rockbridge
Hocking County

(G-12735)
GLENLAUREL INC
Also Called: Glenlurel-A Scottish Cntry Inn
14940 Mount Olive Rd (43149-9736)
P.O. Box 684 (43085-0684)
PHONE.................................740 385-4070
EMP: 41 EST: 1976
SQ FT: 20,000
SALES (est): 2.39MM **Privately Held**
Web: www.glenlaurel.com
SIC: **5812** 7011 Eating places; Inns

(G-12736)
TANSKY MOTORS INC (PA)
Also Called: Toyota of Logan
11973 Dalton Rd (43149-9777)
PHONE.................................650 322-7069
John Tansky, *Pr*
Marian Tansky, *
EMP: 28 EST: 1947
SALES (est): 5.5MM
SALES (corp-wide): 5.5MM **Privately Held**
Web: www.tanskymotorinc.com
SIC: **5511** 7538 7532 7515 Automobiles, new and used; General automotive repair shops; Top and body repair and paint shops; Passenger car leasing

Rockford
Mercer County

(G-12737)
TSM LOGISTICS LLC
4567 Old Town Run Rd (45882-9331)
PHONE.................................419 234-6074
Steve Marks, *Brnch Mgr*
EMP: 45
SIC: **4212** Local trucking, without storage
PA: Tsm Logistics, Llc
2421 S Nappanee St
Elkhart IN 46517

Rocky River
Cuyahoga County

(G-12738)
A W S INC
Also Called: S A W - Rcky Rver Adult Trning
20120 Detroit Rd (44116-2421)
PHONE.................................440 333-1791
Katherine L Johnson, *Brnch Mgr*
EMP: 663
SALES (corp-wide): 3.95MM **Privately Held**
Web: www.sawinc.org
SIC: **8331** 7331 Vocational training agency; Direct mail advertising services
PA: A W S Inc
14775 Broadway Ave
Maple Heights OH 44137
216 861-0250

(G-12739)
AMERICAN MULTI-CINEMA INC
Also Called: AMC
21653 Center Ridge Rd (44116-3917)
PHONE.................................440 331-2826
Eric Supple, *Mgr*
EMP: 28
Web: www.amctheatres.com
SIC: **7832** Motion picture theaters, except drive-in
HQ: American Multi-Cinema, Inc.
11500 Ash St
Leawood KS 66211
913 213-2000

(G-12740)
EARNEST MACHINE PRODUCTS CO (PA)
Also Called: Earnest Machine
1250 Linda St Ste 301 (44116-1854)
PHONE.................................440 895-8400
Kirk Zehnder, *Pr*
Brian Mamich, *
♦ EMP: 50 EST: 1951
SQ FT: 68,000
SALES (est): 22.56MM
SALES (corp-wide): 22.56MM **Privately Held**

GEOGRAPHIC SECTION

Rootstown - Portage County (G-12762)

Web: www.earnestmachine.com
SIC: **5085** Fasteners, industrial: nuts, bolts, screws, etc.

(G-12741)
FITWORKS HOLDING LLC
20001 Center Ridge Rd (44116-3659)
PHONE..............................440 333-4141
Max Stillwagon, *Mgr*
EMP: 47
Web: www.fitworks.com
SIC: **7991** **7997** Health club; Membership sports and recreation clubs
PA: Fitworks Holding, Llc
   849 Brainard Rd
   Cleveland OH 44143

(G-12742)
HUNTINGTON NATIONAL BANK
19975 Center Ridge Rd (44116-3640)
PHONE..............................216 515-0022
EMP: 31
SALES (corp-wide): 10.84B **Publicly Held**
Web: www.huntington.com
SIC: **6029** Commercial banks, nec
HQ: The Huntington National Bank
   41 S High St
   Columbus OH 43215
   614 480-4293

(G-12743)
HUNTINGTON NATIONAL BANK
19880 Detroit Rd (44116-1851)
PHONE..............................216 515-0022
EMP: 31
SALES (corp-wide): 10.84B **Publicly Held**
Web: www.huntington.com
SIC: **6029** Commercial banks, nec
HQ: The Huntington National Bank
   41 S High St
   Columbus OH 43215
   614 480-4293

(G-12744)
JAG HEALTHCARE INC
220 Buckingham Rd (44116-1623)
PHONE..............................440 385-4370
James Griffiths, *Pr*
David Cooley, *
Richard Gebhard, *
Miriam Walters, *
EMP: 650 EST: 2005
SALES (est): 22.84MM **Privately Held**
Web: www.jaghealthcare.com
SIC: **8082** Home health care services

(G-12745)
JP RECOVERY SERVICES INC
Also Called: Patient Financial Services
20220 Center Ridge Rd Ste 200 (44116-3501)
PHONE..............................440 331-2200
John Beirne, *Pr*
John Murray, *
EMP: 150 EST: 1998
SQ FT: 23,500
SALES (est): 10.69MM **Privately Held**
Web: www.jprmp.com
SIC: **7322** Collection agency, except real estate

(G-12746)
KENSINGTON INTRMDIATE SCHL PTA
20140 Lake Rd (44116-1515)
PHONE..............................440 356-6770
EMP: 32 EST: 2010
SALES (est): 308.83K **Privately Held**
Web: www.rrcs.org
SIC: **8641** Parent-teachers' association

(G-12747)
KEYBANK NATIONAL ASSOCIATION
19234 Detroit Rd (44116-1706)
PHONE..............................216 502-3260
EMP: 32
SALES (corp-wide): 10.4B **Publicly Held**
Web: www.key.com
SIC: **6021** National commercial banks
HQ: Keybank National Association
   127 Public Sq Ste 5600
   Cleveland OH 44114
   800 539-2968

(G-12748)
LOWES HOME CENTERS LLC
Also Called: Lowe's
20639 Center Ridge Rd (44116-3449)
PHONE..............................440 331-1027
Lorie Thomas, *Brnch Mgr*
EMP: 167
SALES (corp-wide): 86.38B **Publicly Held**
Web: www.lowes.com
SIC: **5211** 5031 5722 5064 Home centers; Building materials, exterior; Household appliance stores; Electrical appliances, television and radio
HQ: Lowe's Home Centers, Llc
   1000 Lowes Blvd
   Mooresville NC 28117
   336 658-4000

(G-12749)
NIEDERST MANAGEMENT LTD
P.O. Box 16685 (44116-0685)
PHONE..............................440 331-8800
Michael Niederst, *Brnch Mgr*
EMP: 151
SALES (corp-wide): 13.66MM **Privately Held**
Web: www.nmresidential.com
SIC: **8741** Business management
PA: Niederst Management, Ltd
   22730 Frview Ctr Dr Ste 1
   Cleveland OH 44126
   440 331-8800

(G-12750)
NORMANDY II LTD PARTNERSHIP
Also Called: Normandy Care Center, The
22709 Lake Rd (44116-1021)
PHONE..............................440 333-5401
David Orlean, *Pt*
Debra Sue Orlean, *Pt*
Susan Orlean, *Pt*
EMP: 150 EST: 1988
SALES (est): 8.39MM **Privately Held**
Web: www.thenormandy.com
SIC: **8051** Convalescent home with continuous nursing care

(G-12751)
PAMEE LLC
18500 Lake Rd (44116-1744)
PHONE..............................216 232-9255
EMP: 50 EST: 2020
SALES (est): 2.07MM **Privately Held**
Web: www.pamee.com
SIC: **7372** Prepackaged software

(G-12752)
RIVER OAKS RCQUET CLB ASSOC IN
21220 Center Ridge Rd Ste B (44116-3289)
PHONE..............................440 331-4980
John Leech, *Pr*
Charles T Simon, *
EMP: 50 EST: 1974
SQ FT: 130,000
SALES (est): 1.09MM **Privately Held**
SIC: **7997** Membership sports and recreation clubs

(G-12753)
SUNRISE SENIOR LIVING LLC
Also Called: Sunrise of Rocky River
21600 Detroit Rd (44116-2218)
PHONE..............................440 895-2383
Natalie Antosh, *Mgr*
EMP: 46
SALES (corp-wide): 2.92B **Privately Held**
Web: www.sunriseseniorliving.com
SIC: **8051** 8361 Skilled nursing care facilities; Aged home
HQ: Sunrise Senior Living, Llc
   7902 Westpark Dr
   Mc Lean VA 22102

(G-12754)
UBS AMERICAS INC
Also Called: UBS Financial Services
18500 Lake Rd Ste 400 (44116-1744)
PHONE..............................440 356-5237
Kevin Ryan, *Mgr*
EMP: 99
Web: www.ubs.com
SIC: **6282** Investment advisory service
HQ: Ubs Americas Inc.
   600 Washington Blvd
   Stamford CT 06901
   203 719-3000

(G-12755)
VER-A-FAST CORP
20545 Center Ridge Rd Ste 300 (44116-3423)
PHONE..............................440 331-0250
Robert Bensman, *Pr*
Cathleen Soprano, *
Steve Lucek, *
EMP: 49 EST: 1976
SQ FT: 13,000
SALES (est): 4.99MM **Privately Held**
Web: www.verafast.com
SIC: **8743** Public relations and publicity

(G-12756)
WESTWOOD COUNTRY CLUB COMPANY
22625 Detroit Rd (44116-2024)
P.O. Box 16459 (44116-0459)
PHONE..............................440 331-3016
Richard Mcclure, *Pr*
Thomas M Cawley, *
Alice R Alexander, *
Robert J Koepke, *
EMP: 75 EST: 1913
SQ FT: 53,000
SALES (est): 8.09MM **Privately Held**
Web: www.westwoodcountryclub.org
SIC: **7997** Country club, membership

(G-12757)
WOMENS WELSH CLUBS OF AMERICA
Also Called: WELSH HOME FOR THE AGED
22199 Center Ridge Rd (44116-3925)
PHONE..............................440 331-0420
Sarah Cook, *Admn*
EMP: 100 EST: 1921
SQ FT: 31,206
SALES (est): 10.74MM **Privately Held**
Web: www.welshhome.com
SIC: **8361** 8051 Aged home; Convalescent home with continuous nursing care

(G-12758)
ZULLIX LLC
18500 Lake Rd (44116-1744)
PHONE..............................440 536-9300
EMP: 30 EST: 2021
SALES (est): 2.68MM **Privately Held**
SIC: **7372** Application computer software

Rootstown
Portage County

(G-12759)
INFORMTION APPLIED LRNG EVLTIO
Also Called: Alec
4332 Tallmadge Rd (44272-9213)
PHONE..............................214 329-9100
Konstantine Onapolous, *CEO*
Kenneth Onapolous, *
Melody Onapolous, *
EMP: 151 EST: 1993
SQ FT: 3,000
SALES (est): 7.07MM **Privately Held**
Web: www.aleconline.org
SIC: **8748** Business consulting, nec

(G-12760)
JET RUBBER COMPANY
4457 Tallmadge Rd (44272-9610)
PHONE..............................330 325-1821
Franklin R Brubaker, *Prin*
Karen Crooks, *
EMP: 43 EST: 1954
SQ FT: 20,000
SALES (est): 5.46MM **Privately Held**
Web: www.jetrubber.com
SIC: **3069** 3053 3533 5085 Molded rubber products; Gaskets; packing and sealing devices; Gas field machinery and equipment; Rubber goods, mechanical

(G-12761)
LEEDA SERVICES INC
4123 Tallmadge Rd (44272-9657)
PHONE..............................330 325-1560
EMP: 118
SALES (corp-wide): 8.03MM **Privately Held**
Web: www.leedanortheast.com
SIC: **8322** Social service center
PA: Leeda Services Inc
   1441 Parkman Rd Nw
   Warren OH 44485
   330 392-6006

(G-12762)
MILLER TRANSFER AND RIGGING CO (HQ)
Also Called: Miller Transfer
3833 State Route 183 (44272-9799)
P.O. Box 453 (44272-0453)
PHONE..............................330 325-2521
Mitchell J Unger, *Pr*
David Cochran, *
Kenneth H Rusinoff, *
Patrick A Archer, *
EMP: 50 EST: 1968
SQ FT: 10,000
SALES (est): 40.34MM
SALES (corp-wide): 50.33MM **Privately Held**
SIC: **4213** Heavy machinery transport
PA: United Transport Industries, Inc
   1310 N King St
   Wilmington DE 19801
   330 325-2521

Roseville
Muskingum County

(G-12763)
CLAY BURLEY PRODUCTS CO (PA)
455 Gordon St (43777-1110)
P.O. Box 35 (43777-0035)
PHONE..................................740 452-3633
Peter Petratsas, *Pr*
▲ **EMP:** 50 **EST:** 1922
SQ FT: 180,000
SALES (est): 4.82MM
SALES (corp-wide): 4.82MM **Privately Held**
Web: www.burleyclay.com
SIC: 3269 5032 Stoneware pottery products; Ceramic wall and floor tile, nec

Rossburg
Darke County

(G-12764)
CAL-MAINE FOODS INC
3078 Washington Rd (45362-9500)
PHONE..................................937 337-9576
EMP: 61
SALES (corp-wide): 3.15B **Publicly Held**
Web: www.calmainefoods.com
SIC: 0252 2015 Chicken eggs; Poultry slaughtering and processing
PA: Cal-Maine Foods, Inc.
1052 Hghland Clny Pkwy St
Ridgeland MS 39157
601 948-6813

Rossford
Wood County

(G-12765)
CAPITAL TIRE INC (PA)
Also Called: Pro Tire
7001 Integrity Dr (43460)
PHONE..................................419 241-5111
Thomas B Geiger Junior, *Pr*
Thomas B Geiger, *
Carl J Eby, *VP*
Robert J Scheick, *
Brian Haas, *
▲ **EMP:** 40 **EST:** 1919
SQ FT: 100,000
SALES (est): 79.32MM
SALES (corp-wide): 79.32MM **Privately Held**
Web: www.capitaltire.com
SIC: 5014 Automobile tires and tubes

(G-12766)
COURTYARD BY MARRIOTT ROSSFORD
Also Called: Courtyard By Marriott
9789 Clark Dr (43460-1700)
PHONE..................................419 872-5630
Arne Sorenson's, *Pr*
EMP: 51 **EST:** 1997
SALES (est): 1.58MM **Privately Held**
Web: courtyard.marriott.com
SIC: 7011 Hotels and motels

(G-12767)
INDUSTRIAL POWER SYSTEMS INC
Also Called: I P S
146 Dixie Hwy (43460-1215)
PHONE..................................419 531-3121
Kevin Gray, *CEO*
Kevin D Gray, *
Jeremiah Johnson, *
Tim Grosteffon, *
Mike Williams, *
EMP: 300 **EST:** 1985
SQ FT: 20,000
SALES (est): 60.52MM **Privately Held**
Web: www.ipscontractor.com
SIC: 1711 3498 1731 1796 Mechanical contractor; Coils, pipe: fabricated from purchased pipe; General electrical contractor; Millwright

(G-12768)
MEDICAL MUTUAL OF OHIO
9848 Olde Us 20 (43460-1722)
P.O. Box 943 (43697-0943)
PHONE..................................419 473-7100
Joel Mercer, *Prin*
EMP: 152
SALES (corp-wide): 2.75B **Privately Held**
Web: www.medmutual.com
SIC: 6411 Insurance agents, nec
PA: Medical Mutual Of Ohio
2060 E 9th St
Cleveland OH 44115
216 687-7000

(G-12769)
MURPHY TRACTOR & EQP CO INC
9400 Bass Pro Blvd (43460-1734)
PHONE..................................316 633-7215
Rod Young, *CFO*
EMP: 50
Web: www.murphytractor.com
SIC: 5082 General construction machinery and equipment
HQ: Murphy Tractor & Equipment Co., Inc.
5375 N Deere Rd
Park City KS 67219
855 246-9124

Russia
Shelby County

(G-12770)
FRANCIS-SCHULZE CO
3880 Rangeline Rd (45363-9711)
P.O. Box 245 (45363-0245)
PHONE..................................937 295-3941
Ralph Schulze, *Pr*
Rita Schulze, *
EMP: 29 **EST:** 1943
SQ FT: 50,000
SALES (est): 5.15MM **Privately Held**
Web: www.francisschulze.com
SIC: 3442 5031 Metal doors; Building materials, exterior

Sabina
Clinton County

(G-12771)
EARLEY & ROSS LTD
Also Called: Autumn Years Nursing Center
580 E Washington St (45169-1253)
PHONE..................................740 634-3301
Tim Ross, *Pt*
EMP: 51 **EST:** 1973
SALES (est): 2.86MM **Privately Held**
Web: earley-ross-ltd.sbcontract.com
SIC: 8052 Intermediate care facilities

Saint Clairsville
Belmont County

(G-12772)
ACNR RIVER TOWING INC
46226 National Rd (43950-8742)
PHONE..................................740 338-3100
James Turner, *Pr*
Anthony Vcelka Ii, *Treas*
EMP: 60 **EST:** 2020
SALES (est): 1.91MM **Privately Held**
SIC: 4449 Log rafting and towing

(G-12773)
ALTERNATIVE RESIDENCES TWO INC (PA)
Also Called: Wiley Avenue Group Home
100 W Main St Lowr (43950-1269)
PHONE..................................740 526-0514
Shirley M Johnson, *Ch*
Lavelle Lloyd, *
EMP: 150 **EST:** 1979
SALES (est): 2.27MM
SALES (corp-wide): 2.27MM **Privately Held**
SIC: 8361 8052 Mentally handicapped home ; Intermediate care facilities

(G-12774)
BELCO WORKS INC
Also Called: BELCO WORKS
68425 Hammond Rd (43950-8783)
PHONE..................................740 695-0500
Anne Haning, *CEO*
EMP: 94 **EST:** 1966
SQ FT: 5,000
SALES (est): 4.19MM **Privately Held**
Web: www.belcoworks.com
SIC: 8331 3993 3931 2448 Sheltered workshop; Signs and advertising specialties ; Musical instruments; Wood pallets and skids

(G-12775)
BELMONT COUNTY HOME
Also Called: Park Health Center
100 Pine Ave (43950-9738)
PHONE..................................740 695-4925
Mike Maistros, *Dir*
Mark Thomas, *
Gordy Longshaw, *
Chuck Probst, *
EMP: 100 **EST:** 1920
SALES (est): 8.91MM **Privately Held**
Web: www.park-health.net
SIC: 8051 Skilled nursing care facilities
PA: Belmont County Of Ohio
101 W Main St
Saint Clairsville OH 43950
740 695-2121

(G-12776)
BELMONT COUNTY OF OHIO
Also Called: Animal Shelter Blemont CN
45244 National Rd (43950-8707)
PHONE..................................740 695-4708
Verna Painter, *Brnch Mgr*
EMP: 29
SQ FT: 2,532
Web: www.visitbelmontcounty.com
SIC: 8699 Animal humane society
PA: Belmont County Of Ohio
101 W Main St
Saint Clairsville OH 43950
740 695-2121

(G-12777)
BELMONT COUNTY OF OHIO
Also Called: Belmont County Engineering
101 W Main St (43950)
PHONE..................................740 695-1580
Dave Sloan, *Superintnt*
EMP: 60
Web: www.belmontcountycoc.org
SIC: 1611 Highway and street maintenance
PA: Belmont County Of Ohio
101 W Main St
Saint Clairsville OH 43950
740 695-2121

(G-12778)
BELMONT COUNTY OF OHIO
Also Called: Belmont County Sani Sewer Dst
67711 Oak View Rd (43950-7719)
P.O. Box 457 (43950-0457)
PHONE..................................740 695-3144
Mark Esposito, *Dir*
EMP: 40
Web: www.belmontsheriff.com
SIC: 4941 4952 Water supply; Sewerage systems
PA: Belmont County Of Ohio
101 W Main St
Saint Clairsville OH 43950
740 695-2121

(G-12779)
BELMONT HILLS COUNTRY CLUB
47080 National Rd (43950-8711)
P.O. Box 219 (43950-0219)
PHONE..................................740 695-2181
Thomas Dowler, *Pr*
EMP: 75 **EST:** 1938
SQ FT: 30,000
SALES (est): 1.46MM **Privately Held**
Web: www.belmonthillscc.net
SIC: 7997 Country club, membership

(G-12780)
BELMONT MANOR INC
51999 Guirino Dr (43950-8314)
PHONE..................................740 695-4404
Giuseppe G Lancia, *Prin*
Giuseppe Lancia, *
Guirino Lancia, *
Janet Nolan, *
EMP: 50 **EST:** 1992
SALES (est): 3.65MM **Privately Held**
Web: www.lanciahealthcare.com
SIC: 8071 Medical laboratories

(G-12781)
BHC FOX RUN HOSPITAL INC
Also Called: Fox Run Ctr For Chldren Adlscn
67670 Traco Dr (43950-9375)
PHONE..................................740 695-2131
TOLL FREE: 800
Joe Smith, *CFO*
William Hale, *
Karen Maxwell, *
EMP: 50 **EST:** 1988
SQ FT: 8,200
SALES (est): 6.35MM **Privately Held**
Web: www.foxruncenter.com
SIC: 8063 8093 Psychiatric hospitals; Mental health clinic, outpatient

(G-12782)
BORDAS & BORDAS PLLC
106 E Main St (43950-1526)
PHONE..................................740 695-8141
EMP: 52 **EST:** 1977
SALES (est): 196.08K
SALES (corp-wide): 9.3MM **Privately Held**
Web: www.bordaslaw.com
SIC: 8111 General practice attorney, lawyer
PA: Bordas & Bordas Pllc
1358 National Rd
Wheeling WV 26003
304 242-8410

GEOGRAPHIC SECTION   Saint Clairsville - Belmont County (G-12804)

(G-12783)
CARMIKE CINEMAS LLC
Also Called: Carmike Cinemas
700 Banfield Rd (43950)
PHONE................740 695-3919
Kory Long, *Mgr*
EMP: 62
Web: www.amctheatres.com
SIC: 7832 Exhibitors, itinerant: motion picture
HQ: Carmike Cinemas, Llc
11500 Ash St
Leawood KS 66211
913 213-2000

(G-12784)
CATHOLIC CHRTIES STHSTERN OHIO
Also Called: St Mary's Central
226 W Main St (43950-1156)
PHONE................740 695-3189
Nannette Kennedy, *Prin*
EMP: 130
SALES (corp-wide): 25.04MM **Privately Held**
Web: www.diosteub.org
SIC: 8322 8211 Individual and family services; Catholic elementary school
PA: Catholic Charities Of Southeastern Ohio
422 Washington St Ste 1
Steubenville OH 43952
740 282-3631

(G-12785)
COAL RESOURCES INC (PA)
46226 National Rd (43950-8742)
PHONE................216 765-1240
EMP: 37 **EST:** 1988
SALES (est): 95.36MM **Privately Held**
SIC: 1221 Bituminous coal and lignite-surface mining

(G-12786)
COMMUNITY ACTION COMM BLMONT C (PA)
Also Called: COMMUNITY ACTION COMMISSION OF
153 1/2 W Main St (43950-1224)
PHONE................740 695-0293
Gary Obloy, *Ex Dir*
Shirley Mallory, *
EMP: 30 **EST:** 1965
SQ FT: 3,600
SALES (est): 5.58MM
SALES (corp-wide): 5.58MM **Privately Held**
Web: www.cacbelmont.org
SIC: 8322 8351 1742 Social service center; Head Start center, except in conjunction with school; Insulation, buildings

(G-12787)
COMMUNITY MENTAL HEALTH SVC (PA)
Also Called: Community Mental Health Svcs
68353 Bannock Rd (43950-9736)
PHONE................740 695-9344
Mary Denoble, *Ex Dir*
Jack Stephens, *
Katherine Whinnery, *
EMP: 61 **EST:** 1970
SQ FT: 6,000
SALES (est): 4.97MM
SALES (corp-wide): 4.97MM **Privately Held**
Web: www.southeasthc.org
SIC: 8011 8093 Clinic, operated by physicians; Specialty outpatient clinics, nec

(G-12788)
CORPORATE AVIATION SVCS INC
46226 National Rd (43950-8742)
PHONE................740 338-3100
Robert Murray, *Pr*
EMP: 96 **EST:** 1998
SALES (est): 4.95MM **Privately Held**
SIC: 7363 Pilot service, aviation
HQ: American Coal Sales Company
46226 National Rd
Saint Clairsville OH 43950
740 338-3100

(G-12789)
DAYS INN
Also Called: Days Inn Saint Clairsville
52601 Holiday Dr (43950-9313)
PHONE................740 695-0100
Rajendra Patel, *Pr*
Debbie Britton, *Genl Mgr*
EMP: 88 **EST:** 1986
SQ FT: 5,000
SALES (est): 898.46K **Privately Held**
Web: www.wyndhamhotels.com
SIC: 7011 Hotels and motels

(G-12790)
DORO INC
Also Called: Super 8 Motel
68400 Matthews Dr (43950-1733)
PHONE................740 695-1994
Dorothy Drzyzostaniak, *Pr*
EMP: 28 **EST:** 1988
SALES (est): 245.23K **Privately Held**
Web: www.wyndhamhotels.com
SIC: 7011 Hotels and motels

(G-12791)
EAST OHIO HOSPITAL LLC
106 Plaza Dr (43950-8736)
PHONE................740 695-5955
Joan Busby, *Brnch Mgr*
EMP: 131
SALES (corp-wide): 50.49MM **Privately Held**
Web: www.eohospital.com
SIC: 8062 General medical and surgical hospitals
PA: East Ohio Hospital, Llc
90 N 4th St
Martins Ferry OH 43935
740 633-1100

(G-12792)
FORTIS ENERGY SERVICES INC
66999 Executive Dr (43950-7402)
PHONE................248 283-7100
EMP: 51
SALES (corp-wide): 41.09MM **Privately Held**
Web: www.fortisenergyservices.com
SIC: 1381 Drilling oil and gas wells
PA: Fortis Energy Services, Inc.
2844 Livernois Rd
Troy MI 48099
248 283-7100

(G-12793)
FRANKLIN COUNTY COAL COMPANY
46226 National Rd (43950-8742)
PHONE................740 338-3100
Robert E Murray, *CEO*
EMP: 301 **EST:** 2019
SALES (est): 12.22MM
SALES (corp-wide): 4.34B **Privately Held**
SIC: 1221 Bituminous coal and lignite-surface mining
HQ: Murray American Energy, Inc.
46226 National Rd
Saint Clairsville OH 43950
740 338-3100

(G-12794)
HUNTINGTON NATIONAL BANK
154 W Main St (43950-1225)
P.O. Box 249 (43950-0249)
PHONE................740 695-3323
Carol Debonis, *Brnch Mgr*
EMP: 41
SALES (corp-wide): 10.84B **Publicly Held**
Web: www.huntington.com
SIC: 6029 6022 Commercial banks, nec; State commercial banks
HQ: The Huntington National Bank
41 S High St
Columbus OH 43215
614 480-4293

(G-12795)
KELCHNER INC
47443 National Rd (43950-8814)
PHONE................330 476-9737
EMP: 65
SALES (corp-wide): 5.9B **Privately Held**
Web: www.kelchner.com
SIC: 1794 Excavation work
HQ: Kelchner, Inc.
50 Advanced Dr
Springboro OH 45066
937 704-9890

(G-12796)
KENAMERICAN RESOURCES INC
46226 National Rd (43950-8742)
PHONE................740 338-3100
Bob Sandidge, *Pr*
Robert E Murray, *Dir*
Randy L Wiles, *VP*
James R Turner, *Treas*
Michael O Mckown, *Sec*
EMP: 165 **EST:** 1994
SALES (est): 46.9MM **Privately Held**
SIC: 1222 Bituminous coal-underground mining
HQ: Mill Creek Mining Company
46226 National Rd
Saint Clairsville OH 43950

(G-12797)
LM CONSTRCTION TRRY LVRINI INC
67682 Clark Rd (43950-9257)
P.O. Box 339 (43950-0339)
PHONE................740 695-9604
Terry Lavorini, *Pr*
Mickey Mickler, *
Lisa Lavorini, *
EMP: 50 **EST:** 1997
SQ FT: 10,000
SALES (est): 5MM **Privately Held**
Web: www.lmconstructionincorporated.com
SIC: 1542 1742 1541 Commercial and office building, new construction; Plastering, plain or ornamental; Industrial buildings and warehouses

(G-12798)
LODGING ASSOC ST CLRSVILLE INC
Also Called: Americas Best Value Inn
51260 National Rd (43950-8513)
PHONE................740 695-5038
Bill Goff, *Prin*
Daniel A Fouss, *Prin*
EMP: 36 **EST:** 1993
SALES (est): 386.9K **Privately Held**
Web: www.sonesta.com
SIC: 7011 Inns

(G-12799)
LOWES HOME CENTERS LLC
Also Called: Lowe's
50421 Valley Plaza Dr (43950-1749)
PHONE................740 699-3000
Cary Johnson, *Mgr*
EMP: 95
SALES (corp-wide): 86.38B **Publicly Held**
Web: www.lowes.com
SIC: 5211 5031 5722 5064 Home centers; Building materials, exterior; Household appliance stores; Electrical appliances, television and radio
HQ: Lowe's Home Centers, Llc
1000 Lowes Blvd
Mooresville NC 28117
336 658-4000

(G-12800)
MARIETTA COAL CO (PA)
67705 Friends Church Rd (43950-9500)
P.O. Box 2 (43950-0002)
PHONE................740 695-2197
George Nicolozakes, *Ch*
Paul Gill, *
John Nicolozakes, *
EMP: 50 **EST:** 1946
SQ FT: 4,300
SALES (est): 9.66MM
SALES (corp-wide): 9.66MM **Privately Held**
SIC: 1221 Surface mining, bituminous, nec

(G-12801)
MARSHALL COUNTY COAL COMPANY
46226 National Rd (43950-8742)
PHONE................740 338-3100
Robert E Murray, *CEO*
EMP: 473 **EST:** 2013
SALES (est): 84.81MM
SALES (corp-wide): 4.34B **Privately Held**
SIC: 5052 Coal
HQ: Murray American Energy, Inc.
46226 National Rd
Saint Clairsville OH 43950
740 338-3100

(G-12802)
MCKEEN SECURITY INC (PA)
69100 Bayberry Dr Ste 200 (43950-9194)
P.O. Box 740 (43950-0740)
PHONE................740 699-1301
EMP: 98 **EST:** 1995
SALES (est): 1.93MM **Privately Held**
Web: www.themckeengroup.com
SIC: 7381 Security guard service

(G-12803)
MEIGS COUNTY COAL COMPANY
46226 National Rd (43950-8742)
PHONE................740 338-3100
Robert E Murray, *CEO*
EMP: 358 **EST:** 2013
SALES (est): 9.18MM
SALES (corp-wide): 4.34B **Privately Held**
SIC: 1221 Bituminous coal and lignite-surface mining
HQ: Murray American Energy, Inc.
46226 National Rd
Saint Clairsville OH 43950
740 338-3100

(G-12804)
MON RIVER TOWING INC
46226 National Rd (43950-8742)
PHONE................740 338-3100
James L Guttman, *Pr*
Alan C Guttman, *VP*
Ivan Melnick, *VP Fin*
Richard Guttman, *VP*
EMP: 451 **EST:** 1960
SQ FT: 2,050
SALES (est): 1.8MM
SALES (corp-wide): 4.34B **Privately Held**

Saint Clairsville - Belmont County (G-12805)

SIC: **4449** River transportation, except on the St. Lawrence Seaway
HQ: Consolidation Coal Company Inc
1000 Horizon Vue Dr
Canonsburg PA 15317
740 338-3100

(G-12805)
MOUNTAIN SUPPLY AND SVC LLC
66895 Executive Dr (43950-8468)
PHONE..............................304 547-1119
Henry Mclaughlin, Mgr
EMP: 30
Web: www.mountainoilfield.com
SIC: **5082** Oil field equipment
PA: Mountain Supply And Service, Llc
1127 Judson Rd Ste 249
Longview TX 75601

(G-12806)
MUHLENBERG COUNTY COAL CO LLC
46226 National Rd (43950-8742)
PHONE..............................740 338-3100
Robert E Murray, CEO
EMP: 55 EST: 2018
SALES (est): 22.49MM
SALES (corp-wide): 4.34B **Privately Held**
SIC: **1221** Bituminous coal and lignite-surface mining
HQ: Western Kentucky Consolidated Resources, Llc
46226 National Rd
Saint Clairsville OH 43950
740 338-3100

(G-12807)
MURRAY AMERICAN ENERGY INC (DH)
46226 National Rd (43950)
PHONE..............................740 338-3100
Robert E Murray, Pr
Robert D Moore, VP
Jason D Witt, Sec
Michael D Loiacono, Treas
EMP: 129 EST: 2013
SALES (est): 799.53MM
SALES (corp-wide): 4.34B **Privately Held**
SIC: **1221** Bituminous coal surface mining
HQ: Ohio Valley Resources, Inc.
29325 Chgrin Blvd Ste 300
Beachwood OH 44122
216 765-1240

(G-12808)
NOMAC DRILLING LLC
67090 Executive Dr (43950-8473)
PHONE..............................724 324-2205
EMP: 139
SALES (corp-wide): 4.15B **Publicly Held**
Web: www.patenergy.com
SIC: **1381** Drilling oil and gas wells
HQ: Nomac Drilling, L.L.C.
3400 S Radio Rd
El Reno OK 73036
405 422-2754

(G-12809)
OHIO COUNTY COAL COMPANY
46226 National Rd (43950-8742)
PHONE..............................740 338-3100
Robert Moore, CEO
EMP: 58 EST: 2013
SALES (est): 23.63MM
SALES (corp-wide): 140.95MM **Privately Held**
SIC: **5052** Coal
PA: American Consolidated Natural Resources, Inc.
46226 National Rd
Saint Clairsville OH 43950

740 338-3100

(G-12810)
OHIO VALLEY COAL COMPANY
46226 National Rd (43950-8742)
PHONE..............................740 926-1351
Robert E Murray, CEO
Robert D Moore, *
Michael O Mckown, Sr VP
John R Forrelli, *
Ryan M Murray C, Pr
EMP: 400 EST: 1969
SQ FT: 40,380
SALES (est): 95.82MM
SALES (corp-wide): 4.34B **Privately Held**
SIC: **1241** Coal mining services
HQ: Ohio Valley Resources, Inc.
29325 Chgrin Blvd Ste 300
Beachwood OH 44122
216 765-1240

(G-12811)
PARAMUNT SPPORT SVC OF ST CLRS
252 W Main St Ste H (43950-1065)
P.O. Box 543 (43950-0543)
PHONE..............................740 526-0540
Brent Kovalski, Pr
EMP: 30 EST: 2005
SALES (est): 1.58MM **Privately Held**
Web: www.paramountsupportservices.com
SIC: **8082** Home health care services

(G-12812)
RED ROOF INNS INC
Also Called: Red Roof Inn
68301 Red Roof Ln (43950-1706)
PHONE..............................740 695-4057
EMP: 37
Web: www.redroof.com
SIC: **7011** Hotels and motels
HQ: Red Roof Inns, Inc.
7815 Walton Pkwy
New Albany OH 43054
614 744-2600

(G-12813)
RES-CARE INC
66387 Airport Rd (43950-9421)
PHONE..............................740 526-0285
Tonya Bartyzel, Brnch Mgr
EMP: 75
SALES (corp-wide): 8.83B **Publicly Held**
Web: www.rescare.com
SIC: **8082** Home health care services
HQ: Res-Care, Inc.
805 N Whittington Pkwy
Louisville KY 40222
502 394-2100

(G-12814)
RES-CARE INC
67051 Executive Dr (43950-9421)
PHONE..............................740 695-4931
Tonya Mangerie, Mgr
EMP: 123
SALES (corp-wide): 8.83B **Publicly Held**
Web: www.rescare.com
SIC: **8082** Home health care services
HQ: Res-Care, Inc.
805 N Whittington Pkwy
Louisville KY 40222
502 394-2100

(G-12815)
SOMNUS CORPORATION
Also Called: Hampton Inn
51130 National Rd (43950-9118)
PHONE..............................740 695-3961
Edward Hitchman, Pr

EMP: 47 EST: 1992
SALES (est): 335.02K **Privately Held**
Web: www.stclairsvillehotel.com
SIC: **7011** Hotels and motels

(G-12816)
TRI-COUNTY HELP CENTER INC (PA)
104 1/2 N Marietta St (43950)
P.O. Box 494 (43950)
PHONE..............................740 695-5441
Karen Scott, Ex Dir
EMP: 32 EST: 1980
SQ FT: 2,021
SALES (est): 1.07MM
SALES (corp-wide): 1.07MM **Privately Held**
Web: www.tricountyhelp.org
SIC: **8322** Emergency shelters

(G-12817)
TRINITY RHABILITATION SVCS LLC
72640 Fairpoint New Athens Rd (43950)
PHONE..............................740 695-0069
Sue Lewis, CEO
EMP: 67 EST: 2009
SALES (est): 3.05MM **Privately Held**
Web: www.trinityrehabservices.com
SIC: **8093** Rehabilitation center, outpatient treatment

(G-12818)
UNITED PARCEL SERVICE INC
Also Called: UPS
44191 Lafferty Rd (43950-9743)
PHONE..............................740 968-3508
James Stickradt, Mgr
EMP: 31
SALES (corp-wide): 90.96B **Publicly Held**
Web: www.ups.com
SIC: **4215** Parcel delivery, vehicular
HQ: United Parcel Service, Inc.
55 Glenlake Pkwy
Atlanta GA 30328
404 828-6000

(G-12819)
WASHINGTON COUNTY COAL COMPANY
46226 National Rd (43950-8742)
PHONE..............................740 338-3100
Robert D Moore, CEO
EMP: 330 EST: 2013
SALES (est): 13.36MM
SALES (corp-wide): 4.34B **Privately Held**
SIC: **1221** Bituminous coal surface mining
HQ: Murray American Energy, Inc.
46226 National Rd
Saint Clairsville OH 43950
740 338-3100

(G-12820)
WESTERN BRANCH DIESEL LLC
Also Called: John Deere Authorized Dealer
67755 Friends Church Rd (43950-9500)
PHONE..............................740 695-6301
Rich Mcclelland, Brnch Mgr
EMP: 29
SALES (corp-wide): 192.64MM **Privately Held**
Web: www.westernbranchdiesel.com
SIC: **5084** Engines and parts, diesel
HQ: Western Branch Diesel, Llc
3504 Shipwright St
Portsmouth VA 23703
757 673-7000

(G-12821)
WESTERN KENTUCKY COAL CO LLC
46226 National Rd (43950-8742)

PHONE..............................740 338-3334
EMP: 50 EST: 2018
SALES (est): 4.92MM
SALES (corp-wide): 4.34B **Privately Held**
SIC: **1081** Metal mining services
HQ: Western Kentucky Consolidated Resources, Llc
46226 National Rd
Saint Clairsville OH 43950
740 338-3100

(G-12822)
WESTERN KY COAL RESOURCES LLC (DH)
46226 National Rd (43950)
PHONE..............................740 338-3100
EMP: 40 EST: 2018
SALES (est): 209.36MM
SALES (corp-wide): 4.34B **Privately Held**
SIC: **1222** Bituminous coal-underground mining
HQ: Murray Kentucky Energy, Inc.
46226 National Rd W
Saint Clairsville OH 43950
740 338-3100

(G-12823)
ZANDEX HEALTH CARE CORPORATION
Also Called: Forest Hill Retirement Cmnty
100 Reservoir Rd (43950-1064)
PHONE..............................740 695-7233
Heather Borkoski, Mgr
EMP: 170
SQ FT: 1,920
Web: www.cedarhillcare.org
SIC: **8052** 8051 8059 Personal care facility; Skilled nursing care facilities; Nursing home, except skilled and intermediate care facility
PA: Zandex Health Care Corporation
1122 Taylor St
Zanesville OH 43701

Saint Henry
Mercer County

(G-12824)
BRUNS BUILDING & DEV CORP INC
Also Called: Ohio and Indiana Roofing Co
1429 Cranberry Rd (45883-9749)
PHONE..............................419 925-4095
Robert E Bruns, CEO
Mike Bruns, Pr
Dave Bruns, Ex VP
Dan Bruns, VP
Gerald Bruns, Sec
▲ EMP: 86 EST: 1951
SQ FT: 10,000
SALES (est): 22.46MM **Privately Held**
Web: www.bruns1951.com
SIC: **1761** Roofing contractor

(G-12825)
GARDENS AT ST HENRY OPER LLC
Also Called: GARDENS AT ST. HENRY, THE
522 Western Ave (45883-9777)
PHONE..............................419 678-9800
Joseph Hazelbaker, Prin
Brian Hazlbaker, VP
Ralph Hazelbaker, Treas
EMP: 68 EST: 2020
SALES (est): 1.97MM **Privately Held**
SIC: **8059** Nursing and personal care, nec

GEOGRAPHIC SECTION

Salem - Columbiana County (G-12845)

Saint Louisville
Licking County

(G-12826)
HOUSE OF NEW HOPE
8135 Mount Vernon Rd (43071-9670)
PHONE..................................740 345-5437
EMP: 49 **EST:** 1992
SQ FT: 18,000
SALES (est): 3.56MM **Privately Held**
Web: www.houseofnewhope.org
SIC: 8322 Individual and family services

Saint Marys
Auglaize County

(G-12827)
JC PENNEY CORPORATION INC
Also Called: JC Penney
1170 Indiana Ave (45885-1307)
PHONE..................................419 394-7610
FAX: 419 394-6355
EMP: 70
SALES (corp-wide): 12.55B **Publicly Held**
SIC: 5311 7231 Department stores, non-discount; Hairdressers
HQ: J.C. Penney Corporation, Inc.
  6501 Legacy Dr
  Plano TX 75024
  972 431-1000

(G-12828)
JOINT TOWNSHIP DST MEM HOSP
Also Called: Grand Lake Health System
200 Saint Clair Ave (45885-2494)
PHONE..................................419 394-3335
Kevin Harlan, *Dir*
EMP: 36
SALES (corp-wide): 100.28MM **Privately Held**
Web: www.grandlakehealth.org
SIC: 8062 8082 General medical and surgical hospitals; Home health care services
PA: Joint Township District Memorial Hospital
  200 Saint Clair Ave
  Saint Marys OH 45885
  419 394-3335

(G-12829)
JOINT TOWNSHIP DST MEM HOSP (PA)
Also Called: GRAND LAKE HEALTH SYSTEM
200 Saint Clair Ave (45885-2494)
PHONE..................................419 394-3335
Kevin W Harlan, *CEO*
Jeff Vossler, *Treasurer Finance*
Jill Dickman, *Sec*
EMP: 400 **EST:** 1989
SQ FT: 170,000
SALES (est): 100.28MM
SALES (corp-wide): 100.28MM **Privately Held**
Web: www.grandlakehealth.org
SIC: 8062 8051 General medical and surgical hospitals; Skilled nursing care facilities

(G-12830)
JOINT TOWNSHIP DST MEM HOSP
Also Called: Grand Lake Primary Care
1140 S Knoxville Ave # A (45885-2609)
PHONE..................................419 394-9959
Jeffrey W Vossler, *VP*
EMP: 39
SALES (corp-wide): 100.28MM **Privately Held**

Web: www.grandlakehealth.org
SIC: 8062 General medical and surgical hospitals
PA: Joint Township District Memorial Hospital
  200 Saint Clair Ave
  Saint Marys OH 45885
  419 394-3335

(G-12831)
JOINT TOWNSHIP HOME HEALTH
1122 E Spring St (45885-2402)
PHONE..................................419 394-3335
Linda Haines, *Prin*
EMP: 63 **EST:** 1988
SALES (est): 844.15K
SALES (corp-wide): 100.28MM **Privately Held**
Web: www.grandlakehealth.org
SIC: 8062 General medical and surgical hospitals
PA: Joint Township District Memorial Hospital
  200 Saint Clair Ave
  Saint Marys OH 45885
  419 394-3335

(G-12832)
JTD HEALTH SYSTEMS INC
Also Called: Speech Center
200 Saint Clair Ave (45885-2400)
PHONE..................................419 394-3335
Kevin W Harlan, *Admn*
Jill Dickman, *
Jeff Vossler, *
EMP: 84 **EST:** 1953
SQ FT: 150,000
SALES (est): 1.86MM **Privately Held**
SIC: 8062 General medical and surgical hospitals

(G-12833)
OTTERBEIN HOMES
11300 Yost Cir (45885-9585)
PHONE..................................419 394-1622
EMP: 28
SALES (corp-wide): 74.71MM **Privately Held**
Web: www.otterbein.org
SIC: 8051 Skilled nursing care facilities
PA: Otterbein Homes
  3855 Lower Market St # 300
  Lebanon OH 45036
  513 933-5400

(G-12834)
OTTERBEIN HOMES
Also Called: Otterbein St Mrys Rtrment Cmnt
11230 State Route 364 (45885-9534)
PHONE..................................419 394-2366
Fred Wiswell, *Mgr*
EMP: 37
SALES (corp-wide): 74.71MM **Privately Held**
Web: www.otterbein.org
SIC: 8322 8361 8051 Senior citizens' center or association; Residential care; Skilled nursing care facilities
PA: Otterbein Homes
  3855 Lower Market St # 300
  Lebanon OH 45036
  513 933-5400

(G-12835)
PRO-PET LLC
1601 Mckinley Rd (45885-1864)
P.O. Box 369 (45885-0369)
PHONE..................................419 394-3374
◆ **EMP:** 93 **EST:** 1996
SQ FT: 5,000
SALES (est): 106.04K

SALES (corp-wide): 176.74B **Privately Held**
SIC: 2047 2048 4212 7389 Cat food; Prepared feeds, nec; Animal and farm product transportation services; Packaging and labeling services
PA: Cargill, Incorporated
  15407 Mcginty Rd W
  Wayzata MN 55391
  800 227-4455

(G-12836)
ST MARYS CITY BOARD EDUCATION
Also Called: East Elementary School
650 Armstrong St (45885-1840)
PHONE..................................419 394-2616
Susan Sherman, *Prin*
EMP: 103
SALES (corp-wide): 8MM **Privately Held**
Web: www.smriders.net
SIC: 8211 8351 Public elementary and secondary schools; Child day care services
PA: St Marys City Board Of Education
  2250 State Route 66
  Saint Marys OH 45885
  419 394-4312

Saint Paris
Champaign County

(G-12837)
AGRI BUSINESS FINANCE INC
11921 Wick Ct (43072-9486)
PHONE..................................937 663-0186
Bradley Reed, *Pr*
EMP: 45
SALES (corp-wide): 892.15K **Privately Held**
Web: www.agribusinessfinance.net
SIC: 8742 6159 Financial consultant; Agricultural credit institutions
PA: Agri Business Finance, Inc.
  1330 N Anderson St
  Greensburg IN

(G-12838)
NEW NGHBORS RSDENTIAL SVCS INC
444 E Main St (43072-9365)
PHONE..................................937 717-5731
Brenda Mcalexander, *CEO*
EMP: 35 **EST:** 2004
SALES (est): 680.93K **Privately Held**
Web: www.nn-rs.com
SIC: 8361 Mentally handicapped home

Salem
Columbiana County

(G-12839)
BENTLEY LEASING CO LLC
Also Called: SALEM WEST HEALTHCARE CENTER
2511 Bentley Dr (44460-2503)
PHONE..................................330 337-9503
Charles Stoltz, *CEO*
Isaac Rosedale, *CFO*
Steve Rosedale, *COO*
EMP: 3830 **EST:** 2018
SALES (est): 6.01MM **Privately Held**
Web: www.communicarehealth.com
SIC: 8051 Skilled nursing care facilities

(G-12840)
CTM INTEGRATION INCORPORATED
1318 Quaker Cir (44460-1051)
P.O. Box 589 (44460-0589)
PHONE..................................330 332-1800

Thomas C Rumsey, *Pr*
Dan Mc Laughlin, *
EMP: 36 **EST:** 1980
SQ FT: 30,000
SALES (est): 4.91MM **Privately Held**
Web: www.ctmlabelingsystems.com
SIC: 3565 5084 3549 Packaging machinery; Industrial machinery and equipment; Metalworking machinery, nec

(G-12841)
EASTERN OHIO CONSERVATION CLUB
10366 W Calla Rd (44460-9633)
PHONE..................................330 799-7393
Leonard Stafforey, *Pr*
EMP: 90 **EST:** 1948
SALES (est): 46.76K **Privately Held**
Web: www.easternohiocc.com
SIC: 7997 Membership sports and recreation clubs

(G-12842)
GORDON BROTHERS INC (PA)
Also Called: Gordon Bros Water
776 N Ellsworth Ave (44460-1600)
P.O. Box 358 (44460-0358)
PHONE..................................800 331-7611
TOLL FREE: 800
Bruce Gordon, *Ch Bd*
Ned Jones, *
EMP: 39 **EST:** 1945
SQ FT: 4,500
SALES (est): 4.77MM
SALES (corp-wide): 4.77MM **Privately Held**
Web: www.gordonbroswater.com
SIC: 7359 5999 5078 5074 Equipment rental and leasing, nec; Water purification equipment; Refrigeration equipment and supplies; Plumbing and hydronic heating supplies

(G-12843)
HICKEY METAL FABRICATION ROOFG
Also Called: Hickey Metal Fabrication
873 Georgetown Rd (44460-9710)
PHONE..................................330 337-9329
Bob Hickey, *Pr*
Robert R Hickey, *
Leo Hickey, *
Robert Peters, *
Lois Peters, *
▲ **EMP:** 30 **EST:** 1990
SALES (est): 10.56MM **Privately Held**
Web: www.hickeymetal.com
SIC: 1761 Sheet metal work, nec

(G-12844)
INTEGRATED PRJ RESOURCES LLC
542 E State St (44460)
P.O. Box 2120 (44601-0120)
PHONE..................................330 272-0998
Tina Hertzel, *Managing Member*
Emma Wetzl, *
Aaron Cosma, *
Michael Canterino, *
EMP: 45 **EST:** 2003
SQ FT: 2,500
SALES (est): 5.07MM **Privately Held**
Web: www.integratedprojectresources.com
SIC: 8742 Business planning and organizing services

(G-12845)
L B BRUNK & SONS INC
Also Called: Brunk's Stoves
10460 Salem Warren Rd (44460-9666)
PHONE..................................330 332-0359

Salem - Columbiana County (G-12846)

Lawrence B Brunk, *Pr*
Joseph Brunk, *
EMP: 35 **EST:** 1977
SQ FT: 2,000
SALES (est): 2.21MM **Privately Held**
Web: www.brunksfireplace.com
SIC: 5074 5561 Fireplaces, prefabricated; Recreational vehicle dealers

(G-12846)
MAC MANUFACTURING INC
1453 Allen Rd (44460-1004)
PHONE..............................330 829-1680
Cora Mcdonald, *Brnch Mgr*
EMP: 104
Web: www.mactrailer.com
SIC: 3715 5012 Truck trailers; Trailers for trucks, new and used
HQ: Mac Manufacturing, Inc.
14599 Commerce St
Alliance OH 44601

(G-12847)
POLLOCK RESEARCH & DESIGN INC
Simmers Crane Design & Svc Co
1134 Salem Pkwy (44460-1063)
PHONE..............................330 332-3300
Randy L Stull, *Mgr*
EMP: 45
SALES (corp-wide): 49.18MM **Privately Held**
Web: www.readingcrane.com
SIC: 8711 7389 7353 3537 Civil engineering; Crane and aerial lift service; Heavy construction equipment rental; Industrial trucks and tractors
PA: Pollock Research & Design, Inc.
11 Vanguard Dr
Reading PA 19606
610 582-7203

(G-12848)
PVE SHEFFLER LLC
Also Called: PVE SHEFFLER, LLC
1156 E State St (44460-2230)
PHONE..............................330 332-5200
EMP: 69
SALES (corp-wide): 17.3MM **Privately Held**
Web: www.pve-llc.com
SIC: 8713 Surveying services
PA: Pve, Llc
2000 Georgetown Dr # 101
Sewickley PA 15143
724 444-1100

(G-12849)
QUALITY FABRICATED METALS INC
14000 W Middletown Rd (44460-9184)
PHONE..............................330 332-7008
EMP: 38 **EST:** 1987
SQ FT: 42,000
SALES (est): 863K **Privately Held**
Web: www.fabricatedmetals.com
SIC: 3469 1799 Stamping metal for the trade; Welding on site

(G-12850)
QUICK MED URGENT CARE LLC
120 N Lincoln Ave (44460-2904)
PHONE..............................234 320-7770
EMP: 103
SALES (corp-wide): 11.05MM **Privately Held**
SIC: 8011 Freestanding emergency medical center
PA: Quick Med Urgent Care, Llc
3499 Belmont Ave
Youngstown OH 44505
330 476-2260

(G-12851)
SALEM CITY SCHOOLS
1150 Pennsylvania Ave (44460-2784)
PHONE..............................330 332-2321
Thomas Nather, *Dir*
EMP: 35
SALES (corp-wide): 29.3MM **Privately Held**
Web: www.salemquakers.k12.oh.us
SIC: 7538 General automotive repair shops
PA: Salem City Schools
1226 E State St
Salem OH 44460
330 332-0316

(G-12852)
SALEM COMMUNITY CENTER INC
1098 N Ellsworth Ave (44460-1536)
PHONE..............................330 332-5885
Heather Young, *Dir*
EMP: 75 **EST:** 2000
SALES (est): 2.47MM **Privately Held**
Web: www.salemcommunitycenter.com
SIC: 8322 Community center

(G-12853)
SALEM COMMUNITY HOSPITAL
Also Called: Salem Home Health Care Center
2235 E Pershing St Ste G (44460-3470)
PHONE..............................330 337-9922
Jeff Turney, *Mgr*
EMP: 44
SALES (corp-wide): 130.12MM **Privately Held**
Web: www.salemhomemedical.com
SIC: 8062 General medical and surgical hospitals
PA: Salem Community Hospital
1995 E State St
Salem OH 44460
330 332-1551

(G-12854)
SALEM COMMUNITY HOSPITAL (PA)
Also Called: SALEM REGIONAL MEDICAL CENTER
1995 E State St (44460-2400)
PHONE..............................330 332-1551
Anita Hackstedde Md, *CEO*
Michael Giangardella, *
EMP: 760 **EST:** 1969
SQ FT: 300,000
SALES (est): 130.12MM
SALES (corp-wide): 130.12MM **Privately Held**
Web: www.salemregional.com
SIC: 8062 8051 General medical and surgical hospitals; Skilled nursing care facilities

(G-12855)
SALEM HEALTHCARE MGT LLC
1985 E Pershing St (44460-3411)
PHONE..............................330 332-1588
Alan Schwartz, *Managing Member*
EMP: 33 **EST:** 2009
SALES (est): 2.24MM **Privately Held**
Web: www.salemcircleofcare.com
SIC: 8051 Skilled nursing care facilities

(G-12856)
VENTRA SALEM LLC (HQ)
800 Pennsylvania Ave (44460-2783)
PHONE..............................330 337-8002
▲ **EMP:** 725 **EST:** 2008
SQ FT: 400,000
SALES (est): 215.45MM
SALES (corp-wide): 1.56B **Privately Held**
SIC: 5013 Automotive supplies and parts
PA: Flex-N-Gate Llc
1306 E University Ave
Urbana IL 61802
217 384-6600

(G-12857)
WEST BRANCH NURSING HOME LTD
Also Called: Pleasant View N Retirement Ctr
451 Valley Rd (44460-9725)
PHONE..............................330 537-4621
Tim Chesney, *Pr*
EMP: 62 **EST:** 1998
SALES (est): 3.99MM **Privately Held**
SIC: 8082 Home health care services

(G-12858)
WITMERS INC
39821 Salem Unity Rd (44460-9696)
P.O. Box 368 (44408-0368)
PHONE..............................330 427-2147
Ralph Witmer, *CEO*
Nelson Witmer, *
Grace Styer, *
EMP: 30 **EST:** 1937
SQ FT: 20,000
SALES (est): 5.2MM **Privately Held**
Web: www.witmersconstruction.com
SIC: 5999 1542 7699 Farm equipment and supplies; Agricultural building contractors; Farm machinery repair

Salineville
Columbiana County

(G-12859)
CIRCLE J HOME HEALTH CARE INC (PA)
412 State Route 164 (43945-7701)
PHONE..............................330 482-0877
Betty Johnson, *Pr*
EMP: 67 **EST:** 1989
SALES (est): 5.31MM
SALES (corp-wide): 5.31MM **Privately Held**
SIC: 8082 Home health care services

(G-12860)
M3 MIDSTREAM LLC
Also Called: Salineville Office
10 E Main St (43945-1134)
PHONE..............................330 679-5580
EMP: 34
SALES (corp-wide): 57MM **Privately Held**
Web: www.momentummidstream.com
SIC: 1382 Oil and gas exploration services
PA: M3 Midstream Llc
600 Travis St Ste 5600
Houston TX 77002
713 783-3000

Sandusky
Erie County

(G-12861)
ABILITY WORKS INC
Also Called: MRDD
3920 Columbus Ave (44870-5791)
PHONE..............................419 626-1048
Allison Young, *Dir*
EMP: 125 **EST:** 1973
SALES (est): 2.27MM **Privately Held**
Web: www.ability-works.com
SIC: 8331 8322 7389 Sheltered workshop; Individual and family services; Business Activities at Non-Commercial Site

(G-12862)
ALL PHASE POWER AND LTG INC
Also Called: Insight Technical Services
3501 Cleveland Rd (44870-4421)
P.O. Box 2515 (44871-2515)
PHONE..............................419 624-9640
William Tunnell, *Pr*
William Tunnell, *CEO*
Frank Kath, *
Janice Tunnell, *
Jude Poggiali, *
EMP: 35 **EST:** 1989
SALES (est): 4.76MM **Privately Held**
Web: www.allphasepl.com
SIC: 1731 General electrical contractor

(G-12863)
AUGUST CORSO SONS INC
Also Called: Corso's Flower & Garden Center
3404 Milan Rd (44870-5678)
P.O. Box 1575 (44871-1575)
PHONE..............................419 626-0765
Chad Corso, *Pr*
August J Corso, *
John Corso, *
Chad Corso, *VP*
Fritz Mueller, *
▲ **EMP:** 120 **EST:** 1941
SQ FT: 8,000
SALES (est): 23.92MM **Privately Held**
Web: www.corsos.com
SIC: 5193 5261 Flowers and nursery stock; Retail nurseries and garden stores

(G-12864)
BAYSHORE COUNSELING SVCS INC (PA)
1634 Sycamore Line (44870-4132)
PHONE..............................419 626-9156
Tim Naughton, *Ex Dir*
EMP: 35 **EST:** 1981
SQ FT: 3,700
SALES (est): 2.18MM **Privately Held**
Web: www.bayshorecs.com
SIC: 8093 Mental health clinic, outpatient

(G-12865)
BROHL & APPELL INC
140 Lane St (44870-3565)
P.O. Box 1419 (44871-1419)
PHONE..............................419 625-6761
EMP: 32
SIC: 5063 5074 Electrical apparatus and equipment; Plumbing and hydronic heating supplies

(G-12866)
BROOK PLUM COUNTRY CLUB
3712 Galloway Rd (44870-6021)
PHONE..............................419 625-5394
Dan Moncher, *Pr*
Craig Wood, *
EMP: 100 **EST:** 1915
SQ FT: 33,469
SALES (est): 2.8MM **Privately Held**
Web: www.plumbrookcountryclub.com
SIC: 7997 Country club, membership

(G-12867)
CAFARO NORTHWEST PARTNERSHIP
Also Called: Sandusky Mall
4314 Milan Rd (44870-5897)
PHONE..............................419 626-8575
Neil Grey, *Mgr*
EMP: 27
Web: www.sandusky-mall.com
SIC: 6512 Shopping center, property operation only
PA: Cafaro Northwest Partnership

GEOGRAPHIC SECTION

Sandusky - Erie County (G-12889)

2445 Belmont Ave
Youngstown OH 44505

(G-12868)
CAI HOLDINGS LLC
1707 George St (44870-1736)
PHONE..............................419 656-3568
Christopher Andrews, *Managing Member*
EMP: 55 **EST:** 2018
SALES (est): 16K **Privately Held**
SIC: 6719 Investment holding companies, except banks

(G-12869)
CAPITAL SECURITIES OF AMERICA
233 E Water St (44870-2527)
PHONE..............................419 609-9489
Tony Kromer, *Mgr*
EMP: 38
SIC: 6211 Security brokers and dealers
HQ: Capital Securities Of America Inc
1011 Edison St Nw
Hartville OH 44632

(G-12870)
CASTAWAY BAY RESORT
2001 Cleveland Rd (44870-4403)
PHONE..............................419 627-2500
Brian Piesser, *Prin*
EMP: 29 **EST:** 2007
SALES (est): 477.76K **Privately Held**
Web: www.castawaybay.com
SIC: 7011 7299 Resort hotel; Banquet hall facilities

(G-12871)
CEDAR FAIR LP (PA)
Also Called: AUNTIE ANNE'S
1 Cedar Point Dr (44870)
PHONE..............................419 627-2344
Richard A Zimmerman, *Pr*
Tim V Fisher, *COO*
Monica Sauls, *Chief Human Resource Officer*
Robert White, *CCO*
Christian Dieckmann, *CSO*
▲ **EMP:** 600 **EST:** 1987
SALES (est): 1.8B
SALES (corp-wide): 1.8B **Publicly Held**
Web: www.cedarfair.com
SIC: 7996 5461 5812 Theme park, amusement; Pretzels; Restaurant, family: chain

(G-12872)
CEDAR FAIR SOUTHWEST INC (HQ)
1 Cedar Point Dr (44870-5259)
PHONE..............................419 626-0830
Matthew A Ouimet, *CEO*
▲ **EMP:** 28 **EST:** 2014
SALES (est): 5.22MM
SALES (corp-wide): 1.8B **Publicly Held**
Web: www.cedarfair.com
SIC: 7832 Motion picture theaters, except drive-in
PA: Cedar Fair, L.P.
1 Cedar Point Dr
Sandusky OH 44870
419 627-2344

(G-12873)
CEDAR POINT PARK LLC (HQ)
1 Cedar Point Dr (44870-5259)
PHONE..............................419 626-0830
Matthew A Ouimet, *CEO*
Carrie Boldman, *VP*
EMP: 51 **EST:** 2014
SALES (est): 49.23MM
SALES (corp-wide): 1.8B **Publicly Held**
Web: www.cedarpoint.com
SIC: 7996 7011 Amusement parks; Resort hotel
PA: Cedar Fair, L.P.
1 Cedar Point Dr
Sandusky OH 44870
419 627-2344

(G-12874)
CEDAR POINT PARK LLC
Cedar Point Soak City
1 Cedar Point Dr (44870-5259)
PHONE..............................419 627-2350
Jason Mcclure, *Genl Mgr*
EMP: 41
SALES (corp-wide): 1.8B **Publicly Held**
Web: www.cedarpoint.com
SIC: 7996 7999 Theme park, amusement; Waterslide operation
HQ: Cedar Point Park Llc
1 Cedar Point Dr
Sandusky OH 44870
419 626-0830

(G-12875)
CEDAR POINT PARK LLC
Also Called: Castaway Bay
2001 Cleveland Rd (44870-4403)
PHONE..............................419 627-2500
Robert Gigliotti, *Mgr*
EMP: 63
SALES (corp-wide): 1.8B **Publicly Held**
Web: www.cedarpoint.com
SIC: 7996 7011 Theme park, amusement; Resort hotel
HQ: Cedar Point Park Llc
1 Cedar Point Dr
Sandusky OH 44870
419 626-0830

(G-12876)
CEDAR POINT PARK LLC
Also Called: Hotel Breakers
1 Cedar Point Dr (44870-5259)
PHONE..............................419 627-2106
Travis Mincey, *Mgr*
EMP: 68
SALES (corp-wide): 1.8B **Publicly Held**
Web: www.cedarpoint.com
SIC: 7011 Resort hotel
HQ: Cedar Point Park Llc
1 Cedar Point Dr
Sandusky OH 44870
419 626-0830

(G-12877)
CEDAR POINT PARK LLC
Also Called: Breakers Express Hotel
1201 Cedar Point Dr (44870-5201)
PHONE..............................888 950-5062
EMP: 35
SALES (corp-wide): 1.8B **Publicly Held**
Web: www.cedarpoint.com
SIC: 7011 Resort hotel
HQ: Cedar Point Park Llc
1 Cedar Point Dr
Sandusky OH 44870
419 626-0830

(G-12878)
CEDAR POINT PARK LLC
Also Called: Lighthouse Point
1201 Cedar Point Dr (44870-5201)
PHONE..............................419 627-2106
EMP: 41
SALES (corp-wide): 1.8B **Publicly Held**
Web: www.cedarpoint.com
SIC: 7011 7033 Tourist camps, cabins, cottages, and courts; Recreational vehicle parks
HQ: Cedar Point Park Llc
1 Cedar Point Dr

Sandusky OH 44870
419 626-0830

(G-12879)
CHI LIVING COMMUNITIES
2025 Hayes Ave (44870-4739)
PHONE..............................419 627-2273
EMP: 117
SALES (corp-wide): 69.78MM **Privately Held**
Web: www.chilivingcommunities.org
SIC: 8051 Skilled nursing care facilities
PA: Chi Living Communities
930 S Wynn Rd
Oregon OH 43616
567 455-0414

(G-12880)
CIVISTA BANCSHARES INC (PA)
100 E Water St (44870-2524)
P.O. Box 5016 (44871-5016)
PHONE..............................419 625-4121
Dennis G Shaffer, *Pr*
James O Miller, *Ch Bd*
Richard J Dutton, *Sr VP*
Todd A Michel, *Sr VP*
Lance A Morrison, *Sr VP*
EMP: 48 **EST:** 1987
SALES (est): 219.9MM **Publicly Held**
Web: www.fcza.com
SIC: 6022 State commercial banks

(G-12881)
CIVISTA BANK (HQ)
100 E Water St (44870)
P.O. Box 5016 (44871)
PHONE..............................419 625-4121
John O Bacon, *Pr*
David A Voight, *
James O Miller, *
Donna J Dalferro, *
Charles C Riesterer, *
EMP: 100 **EST:** 1898
SQ FT: 23,000
SALES (est): 150.5MM **Publicly Held**
Web: www.civista.bank
SIC: 6022 State trust companies accepting deposits, commercial
PA: Civista Bancshares, Inc.
100 E Water St
Sandusky OH 44870

(G-12882)
CLEVELAND CLINIC FOUNDATION
Also Called: North Coast Cancer Campus
417 Quarry Lakes Dr (44870-8635)
PHONE..............................419 609-2812
EMP: 66
SALES (corp-wide): 14.48B **Privately Held**
Web: www.clevelandclinic.org
SIC: 8062 8011 8741 General medical and surgical hospitals; Medical centers; Management services
PA: The Cleveland Clinic Foundation
9500 Euclid Ave
Cleveland OH 44195
216 636-8335

(G-12883)
CLP GW SANDUSKY TENANT LP
Also Called: Great Wolf Lodge
4600 Milan Rd (44870-5840)
PHONE..............................419 609-6000
EMP: 354
Web: www.greatwolf.com
SIC: 7011 Resort hotel

(G-12884)
COMMUNITY ACTION COMM ERIE HRO (PA)
908 Seavers Way (44870-4659)

P.O. Box 2500 (44871-2500)
PHONE..............................419 626-6540
Janice W Warner, *Ex Dir*
Emma Moore, *
Pervis D Brown, *
EMP: 40 **EST:** 1965
SQ FT: 10,934
SALES (est): 10.74MM
SALES (corp-wide): 10.74MM **Privately Held**
Web: www.cacehr.org
SIC: 8399 Community action agency

(G-12885)
CONCORD HEALTH CARE INC
Also Called: Briarfield of Sandusky
620 W Strub Rd (44870-5779)
PHONE..............................419 626-5373
EMP: 50
SIC: 8051 Convalescent home with continuous nursing care
PA: Concord Health Care Inc
202 Churchill Hubbard Rd
Youngstown OH 44505

(G-12886)
COUNTY OF ERIE
Also Called: Erie County Hwy Dept
2700 Columbus Ave (44870-5551)
PHONE..............................419 627-7710
John Farschman, *Prin*
EMP: 36
SALES (corp-wide): 77.73MM **Privately Held**
Web: eriecounty.oh.gov
SIC: 8711 9111 Engineering services; County supervisors' and executives' office
PA: County Of Erie
2900 Columbus Ave
Sandusky OH 44870
419 627-7682

(G-12887)
DECORATE WITH STYLE INC
Also Called: By Design
2419 E Perkins Ave Ste E (44870-7998)
PHONE..............................419 621-5577
EMP: 27 **EST:** 1994
SQ FT: 6,000
SALES (est): 1.9MM **Privately Held**
Web: www.decorateinstyle.com
SIC: 7389 5231 5023 Interior decorating; Wallpaper; Decorative home furnishings and supplies

(G-12888)
ECONO LODGE
1904 Cleveland Rd (44870-4307)
PHONE..............................419 627-8000
George Spadaro, *Pr*
EMP: 44 **EST:** 1973
SALES (est): 257.66K **Privately Held**
Web: www.choicehotels.com
SIC: 7011 Hotels and motels

(G-12889)
ERIE BLACKTOP INC
4507 Tiffin Ave (44870-9646)
P.O. Box 2308 (44871-2308)
PHONE..............................419 625-7374
Dean Wikel, *Pr*
Chris Schaeffer, *
James Kromer, *
EMP: 30 **EST:** 1992
SQ FT: 560
SALES (est): 7.19MM
SALES (corp-wide): 22.53MM **Privately Held**
Web: www.erieblacktop.com
SIC: 1611 Highway and street paving contractor

Sandusky - Erie County (G-12890)

PA: Erie Materials, Inc.
4507 Tiffin Ave
Sandusky OH 44870
419 625-7374

(G-12890)
ERIE CONSTRUCTION GROUP INC
4507 Tiffin Ave (44870-9646)
P.O. Box 2308 (44871-2308)
PHONE..............................419 625-7374
Dean Wikel, *Pr*
Chris Schaffer, *
Chris Walters, *
EMP: 51 **EST:** 1978
SALES (est): 2.31MM
SALES (corp-wide): 22.53MM **Privately Held**
Web: www.erieblacktop.com
SIC: 1611 General contractor, highway and street construction
PA: Erie Materials, Inc.
4507 Tiffin Ave
Sandusky OH 44870
419 625-7374

(G-12891)
ERIE COUNTY CABLEVISION INC
Also Called: Cable System, The
409 E Market St (44870-2814)
PHONE..............................419 627-0800
David Huey, *Pr*
Patrick L Deville, *
EMP: 188 **EST:** 1970
SQ FT: 8,600
SALES (est): 7.39MM
SALES (corp-wide): 910.95MM **Privately Held**
Web: www.buckeyebroadband.com
SIC: 4841 Cable television services
PA: Block Communications, Inc.
405 Madison Ave Ste 2100
Toledo OH 43604
419 724-6212

(G-12892)
ERIE TRUCKING INC
Also Called: Erie Blacktop
4507 Tiffin Ave (44870-9646)
P.O. Box 2308 (44871-2308)
PHONE..............................419 625-7374
Dean Wikel, *Pr*
Chris Schaeffer, *
Chris Walters, *
EMP: 44 **EST:** 1927
SQ FT: 1,000
SALES (est): 2.65MM
SALES (corp-wide): 22.53MM **Privately Held**
Web: www.erieblacktop.com
SIC: 4213 Contract haulers
PA: Erie Materials, Inc.
4507 Tiffin Ave
Sandusky OH 44870
419 625-7374

(G-12893)
FEICK CONTRACTORS INC
224 E Water St (44870-2545)
PHONE..............................419 625-3241
John A Feick, *Pr*
Carl M Feick, *VP*
EMP: 29 **EST:** 1852
SQ FT: 4,000
SALES (est): 2.37MM **Privately Held**
Web: www.feickcontractors.com
SIC: 1542 Commercial and office building, new construction

(G-12894)
FIRELANDS REGIONAL HEALTH SYS
Also Called: Pain Management
703 Tyler St Ste 352 (44870-3391)
PHONE..............................419 557-6161
Linda Ricci, *Prin*
EMP: 36
SALES (corp-wide): 302.1MM **Privately Held**
Web: www.bellevuehospital.com
SIC: 8062 General medical and surgical hospitals
PA: Firelands Regional Health System
1111 Hayes Ave
Sandusky OH 44870
419 557-7485

(G-12895)
FIRELANDS REGIONAL HEALTH SYS
Also Called: Firelnds Rgnal Med Ctr S Cmpus
1912 Hayes Ave (44870-4736)
PHONE..............................419 557-7455
Doug Talkington, *Dir Opers*
EMP: 52
SALES (corp-wide): 302.1MM **Privately Held**
Web: www.bellevuehospital.com
SIC: 8062 General medical and surgical hospitals
PA: Firelands Regional Health System
1111 Hayes Ave
Sandusky OH 44870
419 557-7485

(G-12896)
FIRELANDS REGIONAL HEALTH SYS (PA)
Also Called: Firelands Regional Medical Ctr
1111 Hayes Ave (44870-3323)
PHONE..............................419 557-7485
TOLL FREE: 800
Martin E Tursky, *CEO*
Daniel Moncher, *
EMP: 1300 **EST:** 1982
SQ FT: 320,000
SALES (est): 302.1MM
SALES (corp-wide): 302.1MM **Privately Held**
Web: www.bellevuehospital.com
SIC: 8062 General medical and surgical hospitals

(G-12897)
FIRELANDS REGIONAL HEALTH SYS
Also Called: Firelnds Cnsling Recovery Svcs
1925 Hayes Ave (44870-4737)
P.O. Box 5005 (44871-5005)
PHONE..............................419 557-5177
TOLL FREE: 800
Marsha Mruk, *Dir*
EMP: 31
SALES (corp-wide): 302.1MM **Privately Held**
Web: www.bellevuehospital.com
SIC: 8093 Mental health clinic, outpatient
PA: Firelands Regional Health System
1111 Hayes Ave
Sandusky OH 44870
419 557-7485

(G-12898)
FIRELANDS REGIONAL HEALTH SYS
Also Called: Out Patient
1101 Decatur St (44870-3364)
PHONE..............................419 626-7400
EMP: 36
SALES (corp-wide): 302.1MM **Privately Held**
Web: www.bellevuehospital.com
SIC: 6324 Hospital and medical service plans
PA: Firelands Regional Health System
1111 Hayes Ave
Sandusky OH 44870
419 557-7485

(G-12899)
FIRST CHICE MED STFFING OHIO I
1164 Cleveland Rd (44870-4036)
PHONE..............................419 626-9740
Charles Slone, *Pr*
EMP: 27
SALES (corp-wide): 6.66MM **Privately Held**
Web: www.firstchoiceohio.com
SIC: 8742 Hospital and health services consultant
PA: First Choice Medical Staffing Of Ohio, Inc.
1457 W 117th St
Cleveland OH 44107
216 521-2222

(G-12900)
GOODWILL INDS ERIE HRON OTTAWA (PA)
Also Called: GOODWILL INDUSTRIES OF ERIE, H
419 W Market St (44870-2411)
PHONE..............................419 625-4744
Robert Talcott, *Pr*
Eric Kochendoerfer, *
EMP: 50 **EST:** 1973
SQ FT: 30,000
SALES (est): 11.58MM
SALES (corp-wide): 11.58MM **Privately Held**
Web: www.goodwillsandusky.org
SIC: 8322 5932 Individual and family services; Clothing, secondhand

(G-12901)
GREAT BEAR LODGE SANDUSKY LLC
Also Called: Great Wolf Lodge
4600 Milan Rd (44870-5840)
PHONE..............................419 609-6000
John Emery, *CEO*
Elan Blutinger, *
Randy Churchey, *
Michael M Knetter, *
Jim Calder, *
EMP: 300 **EST:** 2000
SALES (est): 11.69MM **Privately Held**
Web: www.greatwolf.com
SIC: 7011 Resort hotel

(G-12902)
GUNDLACH SHEET METAL WORKS INC (PA)
Also Called: Honeywell Authorized Dealer
910 Columbus Ave (44870-3594)
PHONE..............................419 626-4525
Terry W Gundlach, *Ch*
Roger M Gundlach, *
Terry Kette, *
Andrew Gundluch, *
EMP: 33 **EST:** 1889
SQ FT: 17,000
SALES (est): 17.84MM
SALES (corp-wide): 17.84MM **Privately Held**
Web: www.gundlachsheetmetal.com
SIC: 1711 3444 Warm air heating and air conditioning contractor; Sheet metalwork

(G-12903)
HOME DEPOT USA INC
Also Called: Home Depot, The
715 Crossings Rd (44870)
PHONE..............................419 626-6493
James Mieden, *Mgr*
EMP: 133
SALES (corp-wide): 152.67B **Publicly Held**
Web: www.homedepot.com
SIC: 5211 7359 Home centers; Tool rental
HQ: Home Depot U.S.A., Inc.
2445 Springfield Ave
Vauxhall NJ 07088

(G-12904)
HOTY ENTERPRISES INC (PA)
5003 Milan Rd (44870-5845)
PHONE..............................419 609-7000
John M Hoty, *Pr*
Angelo Hoty, *
Zack Hoty, *
Todd Hart, *
Kula Hoty Lynch, *
EMP: 28 **EST:** 1976
SQ FT: 6,000
SALES (est): 4.09MM
SALES (corp-wide): 4.09MM **Privately Held**
Web: www.hoty.com
SIC: 6512 Commercial and industrial building operation

(G-12905)
ISAAC FOSTER MACK CO (PA)
Also Called: Sandusky Newspaper Group
314 W Market St (44870-2410)
PHONE..............................419 625-5500
Dudley A White Junior, *Ch Bd*
David A Rau, *
Susan E White, *
EMP: 140 **EST:** 1822
SQ FT: 45,000
SALES (est): 92.2MM
SALES (corp-wide): 92.2MM **Privately Held**
Web: www.sanduskyregister.com
SIC: 4832 2711 2752 Radio broadcasting stations; Newspapers; Commercial printing, lithographic

(G-12906)
JO-ANN STORES LLC
Also Called: Joann Stores
756 Crossings Rd (44870-8902)
PHONE..............................419 621-8101
EMP: 27
SALES (corp-wide): 2.22B **Privately Held**
Web: www.joann.com
SIC: 8299 5999 5149 Educational services; Art and architectural supplies; Pet foods
HQ: Jo-Ann Stores, Llc
5555 Darrow Rd
Hudson OH 44236
330 656-2600

(G-12907)
K & K INTERIORS INC (PA)
2230 Superior St (44870-1843)
PHONE..............................419 627-0039
Kyle R Camp, *Pr*
Mark Wall, *
◆ **EMP:** 40 **EST:** 1996
SQ FT: 125,000
SALES (est): 22.3MM
SALES (corp-wide): 22.3MM **Privately Held**
Web: www.kkinteriors.com
SIC: 5023 Homefurnishings

(G-12908)
KINGS DOMINION LLC (HQ)
1 Cedar Point Dr (44870-5259)
PHONE..............................419 626-0830
Matthew A Ouimet, *Managing Member*
▲ **EMP:** 38 **EST:** 2014
SALES (est): 2.48MM
SALES (corp-wide): 1.8B **Publicly Held**
Web: www.kingsdominion.com
SIC: 7996 Theme park, amusement
PA: Cedar Fair, L.P.

GEOGRAPHIC SECTION

Sandusky - Erie County (G-12931)

1 Cedar Point Dr
Sandusky OH 44870
419 627-2344

(G-12909)
KINGS ISLAND PARK LLC (HQ)
1 Cedar Point Dr (44870-5259)
PHONE..................419 626-0830
EMP: 27 **EST:** 2014
SALES (est): 10.08MM
SALES (corp-wide): 1.8B **Publicly Held**
Web: www.visitkingsisland.com
SIC: 7996 Theme park, amusement
PA: Cedar Fair, L.P.
  1 Cedar Point Dr
  Sandusky OH 44870
  419 627-2344

(G-12910)
LMN DEVELOPMENT LLC (PA)
Also Called: Kalahari Resort
7000 Kalahari Dr (44870-8628)
PHONE..................419 433-7200
Todd Nelson, *Pr*
Mary Bonte-stath, *CFO*
EMP: 119 **EST:** 2003
SALES (est): 47.16MM
SALES (corp-wide): 47.16MM **Privately Held**
Web: www.kalahariresorts.com
SIC: 7011 7996 5091 Resort hotel; Amusement parks; Water slides (recreation park)

(G-12911)
LODGING INDUSTRY INC
Also Called: Super 8 Motel
5410 Milan Rd (44870-5846)
PHONE..................419 625-7070
Tammi Holmer, *Mgr*
EMP: 31
SALES (corp-wide): 10.63MM **Privately Held**
Web: www.wyndhamhotels.com
SIC: 7011 Hotels and motels
PA: Lodging Industry, Inc.
  910 Lorain Blvd Ste N
  Elyria OH
  440 323-9820

(G-12912)
LOWES HOME CENTERS LLC
Also Called: Lowe's
5500 Milan Rd Ste 304 (44870-7805)
PHONE..................419 624-6000
EMP: 153
SALES (corp-wide): 86.38B **Publicly Held**
Web: www.lowes.com
SIC: 5211 5031 5722 5064 Home centers; Building materials, exterior; Household appliance stores; Electrical appliances, television and radio
HQ: Lowe's Home Centers, Llc
  1000 Lowes Blvd
  Mooresville NC 28117
  336 658-4000

(G-12913)
MAGNUM MANAGEMENT CORPORATION
1 Cedar Point Dr (44870-5259)
PHONE..................419 627-2344
Richard L Kinzel, *CEO*
▲ **EMP:** 243 **EST:** 1983
SQ FT: 6,000
SALES (est): 8.48MM
SALES (corp-wide): 1.8B **Publicly Held**
Web: www.cedarpoint.com
SIC: 4785 6552 7996 Toll bridge operation; Subdividers and developers, nec; Amusement parks

PA: Cedar Fair, L.P.
  1 Cedar Point Dr
  Sandusky OH 44870
  419 627-2344

(G-12914)
MATHEWS FORD SANDUSKY INC
Also Called: Quick Lane
610 E Perkins Ave (44870-4912)
PHONE..................419 626-4721
TOLL FREE: 800
Thurman Mathews Junior, *Pr*
Tim Mathews, *
Bob Mathews, *
EMP: 46 **EST:** 1935
SQ FT: 15,000
SALES (est): 7.95MM **Privately Held**
Web: www.mathewsford.com
SIC: 5511 7538 Automobiles, new and used; General automotive repair shops

(G-12915)
MILLENNIUM OPERATIONS LLC (HQ)
1 Cedar Point Dr (44870-5259)
PHONE..................419 626-0830
EMP: 50 **EST:** 2015
SALES (est): 2.54MM
SALES (corp-wide): 1.8B **Publicly Held**
Web: www.cedarpoint.com
SIC: 7996 Theme park, amusement
PA: Cedar Fair, L.P.
  1 Cedar Point Dr
  Sandusky OH 44870
  419 627-2344

(G-12916)
MURRAY & MURRAY CO LPA (PA)
111 E Shoreline Dr Ste 1 (44870-2579)
PHONE..................419 624-3000
John Murray, *Pr*
Dennis E Murray Senior, *Pr*
Patrick T Murray, *
John T Murray, *Pr*
Dennis E Murray Junior, *Pr*
EMP: 31 **EST:** 1931
SQ FT: 33,000
SALES (est): 4.66MM
SALES (corp-wide): 4.66MM **Privately Held**
Web: www.murrayandmurray.com
SIC: 8111 General practice attorney, lawyer

(G-12917)
MV TRANSPORTATION INC
1230 N Depot St (44870-3165)
PHONE..................419 627-0740
Peter Carey, *Brnch Mgr*
EMP: 209
SALES (corp-wide): 1.31B **Privately Held**
Web: www.mvtransit.com
SIC: 4111 Local and suburban transit
PA: Mv Transportation, Inc.
  2711 N Hskell Ave Ste 150
  Dallas TX 75204
  972 391-4600

(G-12918)
NASA/GLENN RESEARCH CENTER
Also Called: NASA
6100 Columbus Ave (44870-9660)
PHONE..................419 625-1123
Richard Kunath, *Brnch Mgr*
EMP: 840
Web: www.nasa.gov
SIC: 8733 Scientific research agency
HQ: Nasa Glenn Research Center
  21000 Brookpark Rd
  Cleveland OH 44135
  216 433-4000

(G-12919)
NOMS INTERNAL MEDICINE
2500 W Strub Rd Ste 230 (44870-5390)
PHONE..................419 626-6891
Jeffery A Garman, *Pr*
Robert J Vaschack, *VP*
EMP: 56 **EST:** 1994
SALES (est): 2.04MM **Privately Held**
Web: www.nomshealthcare.com
SIC: 8011 General and family practice, physician/surgeon

(G-12920)
NORTH COAST PROF CO LLC
Also Called: Firelands Physicians Group
1912 Hayes Ave # 1 (44870-4736)
PHONE..................419 557-5541
Martin Tursky, *CEO*
EMP: 46 **EST:** 1989
SALES (est): 7.29MM **Privately Held**
SIC: 8011 Primary care medical clinic

(G-12921)
O E MEYER CO (PA)
3303 Tiffin Ave (44870-9784)
P.O. Box 479 (44871-0479)
PHONE..................419 625-1256
Rodney S Belden, *CEO*
David Belden, *MED*
Craig A Wood, *INDUS*
▲ **EMP:** 95 **EST:** 1918
SQ FT: 46,000
SALES (est): 47.42MM **Privately Held**
Web: www.oemeyer.com
SIC: 5084 5047 Welding machinery and equipment; Medical and hospital equipment

(G-12922)
OHIO DEPT JOB & FMLY SVCS
221 W Parish St (44870-4877)
PHONE..................419 626-6781
EMP: 30
Web: jfs.ohio.gov
SIC: 8322 Individual and family services
HQ: Ohio Department Of Job And Family Services
  30 E Broad St Fl 32
  Columbus OH 43215

(G-12923)
OHIO TRUCK SALES LLC
1801 George St (44870-1738)
PHONE..................419 582-8087
EMP: 59 **EST:** 2013
SALES (est): 12.27MM **Privately Held**
Web: www.ohiotrucks.com
SIC: 5012 Trucks, commercial

(G-12924)
PROVIDENCE CARE CENTER
2025 Hayes Ave (44870)
PHONE..................419 627-2273
Denice Day, *Admn*
Stacy Lemco, *
EMP: 160 **EST:** 1989
SALES (est): 12.35MM **Privately Held**
Web: www.chilivingcommunities.org
SIC: 8062 Hospital, affiliated with AMA residency

(G-12925)
RED BARN GROUP INC
2110 Caldwell St (44870)
PHONE..................419 625-7838
Rebekah Weston, *CEO*
EMP: 35 **EST:** 2016
SALES (est): 2.22MM **Privately Held**
Web: www.redbarn-engineering.com
SIC: 8711 Civil engineering

(G-12926)
RENAISSANCE HOUSE INC
158 E Market St Ste 805 (44870-2556)
PHONE..................419 626-1110
Robert Weinhardt, *Dir*
EMP: 28
SALES (corp-wide): 3.75MM **Privately Held**
Web: www.renaissancehouseinc.org
SIC: 8741 8052 Hospital management; Intermediate care facilities
PA: Renaissance House, Inc.
  103 N Washington St
  Tiffin OH 44883
  419 447-7901

(G-12927)
REXEL USA INC
Also Called: Brohl & Appell
140 Lane St (44870-3560)
PHONE..................419 625-6761
Mary Ebert, *Rgnl Mgr*
EMP: 29
SALES (corp-wide): 2.67MM **Privately Held**
Web: www.rexelusa.com
SIC: 5063 5074 Electrical supplies, nec; Plumbing and hydronic heating supplies
HQ: Rexel Usa, Inc.
  5429 Lyndon B Jhnson Fwy
  Dallas TX 75240

(G-12928)
S & S REALTY LTD
Also Called: Rodeway Inn Nort
1021 Cleveland Rd (44870-4035)
PHONE..................419 625-0362
George Sortino, *Pr*
James Sortino, *
EMP: 50 **EST:** 1956
SQ FT: 4,000
SALES (est): 1.69MM **Privately Held**
Web: www.choicehotels.com
SIC: 7011 5812 Hotels and motels; Eating places

(G-12929)
SANDUSKY ORTHOPEDIC SURGEONS
1401 Bone Creek Dr (44870-7267)
PHONE..................419 625-4900
Kam M Wong Md, *Pr*
Michael J Felter Md, *Sec*
James R Berry Md, *VP*
EMP: 33 **EST:** 1982
SQ FT: 4,000
SALES (est): 2.18MM **Privately Held**
SIC: 8011 Orthopedic physician

(G-12930)
SANDUSKY YACHT CLUB INC
529 E Water St (44870-2875)
PHONE..................419 625-6567
Mike Thuemmler, *Genl Mgr*
EMP: 47 **EST:** 1894
SQ FT: 25,000
SALES (est): 2.71MM **Privately Held**
Web: www.sanduskyyachtclub.com
SIC: 7997 Yacht club, membership

(G-12931)
SHIVELY BROTHERS INC
2509 Hayes Ave (44870-5359)
PHONE..................419 626-5091
EMP: 32
SALES (corp-wide): 76.29MM **Privately Held**
Web: www.shivelybros.com
SIC: 8711 Machine tool design
PA: Shively Brothers, Inc.
  2919 S Grand Traverse St

Flint MI 48507
810 232-7401

(G-12932)
SI-MO REMODELING INC
Also Called: Simo Creations Unlimited
1802 Knupke St (44870-4393)
PHONE..................................419 609-9036
Leroy E Sizemore, *Pr*
EMP: 30 **EST:** 1996
SALES (est): 1.7MM **Privately Held**
SIC: 1521 General remodeling, single-family houses

(G-12933)
SORTINO MANAGEMENT & DEV CO
Also Called: Days Inn
4315 Milan Rd (44870-5384)
PHONE..................................419 627-8884
Pat Ward, *Mgr*
EMP: 27
SALES (corp-wide): 2.08MM **Privately Held**
Web: www.sortino.biz
SIC: 7011 Hotels and motels
PA: Sortino Management & Development Co
1210 Sycamore Line
Sandusky OH 44870
419 625-0362

(G-12934)
STEIN HOSPICE SERVICE INC (PA)
1200 Sycamore Line (44870-4029)
PHONE..................................800 625-5269
TOLL FREE: 800
Jan Bucholz, *CEO*
▲ **EMP:** 50 **EST:** 1982
SALES (est): 12.45MM
SALES (corp-wide): 12.45MM **Privately Held**
Web: www.steinhospice.org
SIC: 8052 Personal care facility

(G-12935)
STEIN HOSPICE SERVICES INC
Also Called: STEIN HOSPICE SERVICES, INC.
126 Columbus Ave (44870-2502)
PHONE..................................419 502-0019
Gail Shatzer, *Brnch Mgr*
EMP: 106
SALES (corp-wide): 12.45MM **Privately Held**
Web: www.steinhospice.org
SIC: 8069 Specialty hospitals, except psychiatric
PA: Stein Hospice Service, Inc.
1200 Sycamore Line
Sandusky OH 44870
800 625-5269

(G-12936)
THORSPORT INC
2520 Campbell St (44870-5309)
P.O. Box 2277 (44871-2277)
PHONE..................................419 621-8800
David Thorson, *Prin*
EMP: 31 **EST:** 2005
SALES (est): 1.03MM **Privately Held**
Web: www.thorsport.com
SIC: 7948 Motor vehicle racing and drivers

(G-12937)
TRIPLE CROWN SERVICES COMPANY
3811 Old Railroad Rd (44870-9638)
PHONE..................................419 625-0372
EMP: 48
SALES (corp-wide): 12.16B **Publicly Held**
Web: www.triplecrownsvc.com

SIC: 4213 Trucking, except local
HQ: Triple Crown Services Company
512 E Twnship Line Rd Ste
Blue Bell PA 19422

(G-12938)
UNITED CHURCH HOMES INC
Also Called: Parkview Health Care
3800 Boardwalk Blvd (44870-7044)
PHONE..................................419 621-1900
Ken Keller, *Admn*
EMP: 69
SALES (corp-wide): 115.52MM **Privately Held**
Web: www.unitedchurchhomes.org
SIC: 8361 Aged home
PA: United Church Homes, Inc.
170 E Center St
Marion OH 43302
800 837-2211

(G-12939)
US TSUBAKI POWER TRANSM LLC
Also Called: Engineering Chain Div
1010 Edgewater Ave (44870-1601)
PHONE..................................419 626-4560
Myron Timmer, *VP*
EMP: 180
Web: www.ustsubaki.com
SIC: 5049 3568 3714 3462 Engineers' equipment and supplies, nec; Chain, power transmission; Motor vehicle parts and accessories; Iron and steel forgings
HQ: U.S. Tsubaki Power Transmission Llc
301 E Marquardt Dr
Wheeling IL 60090
847 459-9500

(G-12940)
VISTEON CORPORATION
Also Called: Flex-N-Gate
3020 Tiffin Ave (44870-5352)
PHONE..................................419 627-3600
Peter Sherry Junior, *Prin*
EMP: 31 **EST:** 2000
SALES (est): 1.79MM **Privately Held**
Web: www.visteon.com
SIC: 8742 Business management consultant

Sardinia
Brown County

(G-12941)
TRACTOR SUPPLY COMPANY
7110 Bachman Rd (45171-9456)
PHONE..................................937 446-9425
EMP: 31
SALES (corp-wide): 14.56B **Publicly Held**
Web: www.tractorsupply.com
SIC: 5191 Farm supplies
PA: Tractor Supply Company
5401 Virginia Way
Brentwood TN 37027
615 440-4000

Scio
Harrison County

(G-12942)
M3 MIDSTREAM LLC
Also Called: Harrison Hub
37950 Crimm Rd (43988-8761)
PHONE..................................740 945-1170
EMP: 34
SALES (corp-wide): 57MM **Privately Held**
Web: www.momentummidstream.com
SIC: 1382 Oil and gas exploration services
PA: M3 Midstream Llc

600 Travis St Ste 5600
Houston TX 77002
713 783-3000

(G-12943)
TAPPAN LAKE MARINA INC
Also Called: Tappan Marina
33315 Cadiz Dennison Rd (43988-9724)
PHONE..................................740 269-2031
Dick Henry, *Pr*
Cathrine Cramblett, *
Sandra Henry, *
EMP: 27 **EST:** 1943
SALES (est): 430.75K **Privately Held**
Web: www.mwcd.org
SIC: 5812 4493 Ethnic food restaurants; Marinas

Seaman
Adams County

(G-12944)
HEALTHSOURCE OF OHIO INC
Also Called: Southern Ohio Women's Health
218 Stern Rd (45679-9607)
PHONE..................................937 386-0049
Marry Hetzel, *Opers Mgr*
EMP: 28
SALES (corp-wide): 67.96MM **Privately Held**
Web: www.healthsourceofohio.org
SIC: 8093 8021 8031 8011 Specialty outpatient clinics, nec; Offices and clinics of dentists; Offices and clinics of osteopathic physicians; Offices and clinics of medical doctors
PA: Healthsource Of Ohio, Inc.
424 Wards Corner Rd # 200
Loveland OH 45140
513 576-7700

Sebring
Mahoning County

(G-12945)
APEX CONTROL SYSTEMS INC
751 N Johnson Rd (44672-1011)
P.O. Box 66 (44672-0066)
PHONE..................................330 938-2588
EMP: 65 **EST:** 1992
SALES (est): 12MM **Privately Held**
Web: www.apexcontrol.com
SIC: 3625 8748 3676 3643 Electric controls and control accessories, industrial; Business consulting, nec; Electronic resistors; Current-carrying wiring services

(G-12946)
COPELAND OAKS
715 S Johnson Rd (44672-1709)
PHONE..................................330 938-1050
David Mannigan, *Admn*
EMP: 401
SALES (corp-wide): 14.39MM **Privately Held**
Web: www.copelandoaks.com
SIC: 6513 Retirement hotel operation
PA: Copeland Oaks
800 S 15th St
Sebring OH 44672
330 938-6126

(G-12947)
COPELAND OAKS (PA)
800 S 15th St (44672)
PHONE..................................330 938-6126
TOLL FREE: 800
Dave Mannion, *Contrlr*

Phillip Braisted, *
Dave Mannion, *CFO*
EMP: 99 **EST:** 1963
SQ FT: 383,672
SALES (est): 14.39MM
SALES (corp-wide): 14.39MM **Privately Held**
Web: www.copelandoaks.com
SIC: 6513 Retirement hotel operation

(G-12948)
CRANDALL MEDICAL CENTER
800 S 15th St Ste A (44672-2048)
PHONE..................................330 938-6126
David M Mannion, *CEO*
Audrey Fox, *
EMP: 49 **EST:** 1979
SQ FT: 77,300
SALES (est): 13.8MM **Privately Held**
Web: www.crandallmedicalcenter.com
SIC: 8051 Convalescent home with continuous nursing care

(G-12949)
GENERAL COMMERCIAL CORPORATION (PA)
Also Called: Keller Marketing
110 S 15th St (44672-2002)
PHONE..................................330 938-1000
EMP: 28 **EST:** 1946
SALES (est): 9.68MM
SALES (corp-wide): 9.68MM **Privately Held**
Web: www.gcc-usa.com
SIC: 5199 Advertising specialties

Senecaville
Guernsey County

(G-12950)
MUSKINGUM WTRSHED CNSRVNCY DST
Also Called: Seneca Lake Park
22172 Park Rd (43780-9613)
PHONE..................................740 685-6013
Gary Perrish, *Superintnt*
EMP: 142
SALES (corp-wide): 78.16K **Privately Held**
Web: www.mwcd.org
SIC: 7033 Campgrounds
PA: Muskingum Watershed Conservancy District
1319 3rd St Nw
New Philadelphia OH 44663
330 343-6647

Seven Hills
Cuyahoga County

(G-12951)
BLUE CHIP CONSULTING GROUP LLC
6000 Lombardo Ctr Ste 650 (44131-6916)
PHONE..................................216 503-6001
James Filicko, *Managing Member*
EMP: 28 **EST:** 2004
SQ FT: 14,000
SALES (est): 10.41MM **Privately Held**
Web: www.corebts.com
SIC: 7379 Online services technology consultants
HQ: Core Bts, Inc.
5875 Castle Creek Parkway
Indianapolis IN 46250
317 566-6200

GEOGRAPHIC SECTION
Shaker Heights - Cuyahoga County (G-12972)

(G-12952)
CITY OF SEVEN HILLS
7777 Summitview Dr (44131-4441)
PHONE..................216 524-6262
Jennifer Burger, *Chief*
EMP: 58
SALES (corp-wide): 18.55MM **Privately Held**
Web: www.sevenhillsohio.org
SIC: 7999 Recreation center
PA: City Of Seven Hills
  7325 Summitview Dr
  Seven Hills OH 44131
  216 524-4421

(G-12953)
COMPASSUS
6000 Lombardo Ctr Ste 140 (44131-6906)
PHONE..................440 249-6036
Sharon Essi, *Ex Dir*
EMP: 73 EST: 2016
SALES (est): 488.55K **Privately Held**
Web: www.compassus.com
SIC: 8052 Personal care facility

(G-12954)
COMPMANAGEMENT INC
5700 Lombardo Ctr Ste 150 (44131-6922)
PHONE..................440 546-7100
Todd Keserich Mgr`, *Mgr*
EMP: 40
Web: www.compmgt.com
SIC: 8748 Business consulting, nec
HQ: Compmanagement, Inc.
  6377 Emerald Pkwy
  Dublin OH 43016
  614 376-5300

(G-12955)
NELSON
Also Called: Ka Architecture
6000 Lombardo Ctr Ste 500 (44131-6910)
PHONE..................216 781-9144
James B Heller, *Pr*
Thomas M Milanich, *
Alan W Siliko, *
EMP: 108 EST: 1960
SQ FT: 30,000
SALES (est): 10.47MM **Privately Held**
Web: www.nelsonworldwide.com
SIC: 8712 Architectural engineering

(G-12956)
OHIO EDUCATIONAL CREDIT UN INC (PA)
4141 Rockside Rd Ste 400 (44131-2537)
P.O. Box 93079 (44101-5079)
PHONE..................216 621-6296
Jerome R Valco, *CEO*
Richard Gore, *
Tony H Smith Senior, *Sec*
Art Boehm, *
EMP: 38 EST: 1933
SQ FT: 27,000
SALES (est): 7.23MM
SALES (corp-wide): 7.23MM **Privately Held**
Web: www.ohecu.com
SIC: 6061 Federal credit unions

(G-12957)
PALADINA HEALTH LLC
Also Called: PALADINA HEALTH, LLC
5700 Lombardo Ctr (44131-2540)
PHONE..................440 368-0930
Angelia White, *Brnch Mgr*
EMP: 30
SALES (corp-wide): 478.59MM **Privately Held**
Web: www.eversidehealth.com

SIC: 8099 Blood related health services
HQ: Everside Health, Llc
  1400 Wewatta St Ste 350
  Denver CO 80202
  866 808-6005

(G-12958)
SCA OF CA LLC (DH)
4141 Rockside Rd Ste 100 (44131-2537)
PHONE..................216 777-2750
Christopher Valerian, *Managing Member*
EMP: 42 EST: 2021
SALES (est): 2.02K
SALES (corp-wide): 536.39MM **Privately Held**
SIC: 4959 Sweeping service: road, airport, parking lot, etc.
HQ: Sca Acquisitions, Llc
  4141 Rockside Rd Ste 100
  Seven Hills OH 44131
  216 777-2750

(G-12959)
SCA OF MI LLC (DH)
4141 Rockside Rd Ste 100 (44131-2537)
PHONE..................216 777-2750
Christopher Valerian, *Managing Member*
John Landefeld, *CFO*
Daniel Nauert, *VP*
EMP: 39 EST: 2020
SALES (est): 10.93MM
SALES (corp-wide): 536.39MM **Privately Held**
SIC: 4959 Sweeping service: road, airport, parking lot, etc.
HQ: Sca Acquisitions, Llc
  4141 Rockside Rd Ste 100
  Seven Hills OH 44131
  216 777-2750

(G-12960)
SCA OF SC LLC
4141 Rockside Rd Ste 100 (44131-2537)
PHONE..................216 777-2750
Christopher Valerian, *Pr*
John Landefeld, *
EMP: 41 EST: 2020
SALES (est): 9.99MM
SALES (corp-wide): 536.39MM **Privately Held**
Web: www.sweepingcorp.com
SIC: 4959 Sweeping service: road, airport, parking lot, etc.
HQ: Sca Acquisitions, Llc
  4141 Rockside Rd Ste 100
  Seven Hills OH 44131
  216 777-2750

(G-12961)
SELF-FUNDED PLANS INC (PA)
6000 Lombardo Ctr (44131-2579)
PHONE..................216 566-1455
Donna B Luby, *Pr*
Marsha A Phillips, *Client Services Vice President*
Donald Messinger, *
John Haines, *
EMP: 45 EST: 1980
SALES (est): 6.08MM
SALES (corp-wide): 6.08MM **Privately Held**
Web: www.sfpi.com
SIC: 6411 Insurance agents, nec

Seven Mile
Butler County

(G-12962)
ENCORE PRECAST LLC
416 W Ritter (45062)
P.O. Box 380 (45062-0380)
PHONE..................513 726-5678
Charles Ehlers, *Prin*
EMP: 35 EST: 2001
SALES (est): 11.23MM **Privately Held**
Web: www.encoreprecastllc.com
SIC: 3272 5032 5211 Septic tanks, concrete; Concrete and cinder building products; Concrete and cinder block

Seville
Medina County

(G-12963)
BENCHMARK CRAFTSMAN INC
Also Called: Benchmark Craftsmen
4700 Greenwich Rd (44273-8848)
PHONE..................866 313-4700
Nathan Sublett, *Pr*
EMP: 30 EST: 2002
SALES (est): 4.49MM **Privately Held**
Web: benchmark.us.com
SIC: 7389 3993 Exhibit construction by industrial contractors; Displays and cutouts, window and lobby

(G-12964)
RAWIGA COUNTRY CLUB INC
10353 Rawiga Rd (44273-9700)
PHONE..................330 336-2220
Jeanne Pritchard, *Prin*
EMP: 46 EST: 1958
SQ FT: 19,000
SALES (est): 392.69K **Privately Held**
Web: www.rawigacc.com
SIC: 7997 Country club, membership

(G-12965)
SOCIETY FOR HNDCPPED CTZENS OF (PA)
Also Called: Ark of Medina County, The
4283 Paradise Rd (44273-9353)
PHONE..................330 722-1900
Janine Dalton, *Dir*
EMP: 35 EST: 1953
SQ FT: 4,800
SALES (est): 9.62MM
SALES (corp-wide): 9.62MM **Privately Held**
Web: www.thesocietylink.org
SIC: 8361 8052 Mentally handicapped home ; Intermediate care facilities

(G-12966)
STELLAR SRKG ACQUISITION LLC
Also Called: Stellar Automotive Group
4935 Enterprise Pkwy (44273-8930)
PHONE..................330 769-8484
◆ EMP: 33 EST: 1990
SQ FT: 40,000
SALES (est): 5.47MM **Privately Held**
Web: www.stellargroupinc.com
SIC: 5013 Truck parts and accessories

(G-12967)
WHOLESALE DECOR LLC (PA)
Also Called: Timeless By Design
286 W Greenwich Rd (44273-8881)
PHONE..................877 745-5050
◆ EMP: 48 EST: 1974
SALES (est): 9.33MM

SALES (corp-wide): 9.33MM **Privately Held**
Web: www.ohiowholesale.com
SIC: 5023 Decorative home furnishings and supplies

(G-12968)
WORLD TRCK TOWING RECOVERY INC
4970 Park Ave W (44273-9376)
PHONE..................330 723-1116
Michael Schoen, *CEO*
Mike Schoen, *
EMP: 29 EST: 2001
SALES (est): 4.93MM **Privately Held**
Web: www.a1worldtruck.com
SIC: 7549 4789 5521 Towing service, automotive; Cargo loading and unloading services; Trucks, tractors, and trailers: used

Shadyside
Belmont County

(G-12969)
DJD EXPRESS INC
56461 Ferry Landing Rd (43947-9705)
P.O. Box 124 (43942-0124)
PHONE..................740 676-7464
Nancy Lucas, *Off Mgr*
EMP: 55 EST: 2004
SALES (est): 1.96MM **Privately Held**
SIC: 8742 Management consulting services

(G-12970)
OHIO EDISON COMPANY
Also Called: Burger Plant
57246 Ferry Landing Rd (43947-9701)
P.O. Box 8 (43947-0008)
PHONE..................740 671-2900
Peter Robinson, *Mgr*
EMP: 36
Web: www.firstenergycorp.com
SIC: 4911 4939 Generation, electric power; Combination utilities, nec
HQ: Ohio Edison Company
  76 S Main St Bsmt
  Akron OH 44308
  800 736-3402

(G-12971)
VIRGINIA OHIO-WEST EXCVTG CO
Also Called: Owv Exc
56461 Ferry Landing Rd (43947-9705)
P.O. Box 128 (43942-0128)
PHONE..................740 676-7464
Dennis Hendershot, *CEO*
Roger Lewis, *
Brian Hendershot, *
Kevin Winkler, *
Daniel Boltz, *Prin*
EMP: 120 EST: 1984
SQ FT: 2,800
SALES (est): 19.49MM **Privately Held**
Web: www.owvexcavating.com
SIC: 1794 Excavation work

Shaker Heights
Cuyahoga County

(G-12972)
ABA INSURANCE SERVICES INC
3401 Tuttle Rd Ste 300 (44122)
PHONE..................800 274-5222
John N Wells, *CEO*
EMP: 56 EST: 2009
SALES (est): 13.97MM **Publicly Held**
Web: www.abais.com

Shaker Heights - Cuyahoga County (G-12973)

SIC: 6411 Insurance agents, nec
PA: American Financial Group, Inc.
301 E 4th St
Cincinnati OH 45202

(G-12973)
ALTERNTIVE RSRCES HOMECARE INC
3445 Menlo Rd (44120-4245)
PHONE..................................216 256-3049
Christina Doss, *CEO*
EMP: 75 **EST:** 2021
SALES (est): 1.09MM **Privately Held**
SIC: 8322 7389 Substance abuse counseling ; Business Activities at Non-Commercial Site

(G-12974)
BELLEFAIRE JEWISH CHLD BUR (PA)
Also Called: Bellefaire Jewish Chld Bur
22001 Fairmount Blvd (44118)
PHONE..................................216 932-2800
Adam G Jacobs, *Ex Dir*
Leigh Johnson, *
EMP: 375 **EST:** 1868
SQ FT: 102,000
SALES (est): 41.81MM
SALES (corp-wide): 41.81MM **Privately Held**
Web: www.bellefairejcb.org
SIC: 8361 8322 Emotionally disturbed home; Individual and family services

(G-12975)
CELLULAR TECHNOLOGY LIMITED
Also Called: Ctl Analyzers
20521 Chagrin Blvd Ste 200 (44122-5350)
PHONE..................................216 791-5084
EMP: 40 **EST:** 1998
SQ FT: 30,000
SALES (est): 8.75MM **Privately Held**
Web: www.immunospot.com
SIC: 8071 3821 Medical laboratories; Clinical laboratory instruments, except medical and dental

(G-12976)
EQUITY ENGINEERING GROUP INC (PA)
20600 Chagrin Blvd Ste 1200 (44122-5342)
PHONE..................................216 283-9519
David A Osage, *Pr*
Joel Andreani, *
Joseph Simari, *
EMP: 60 **EST:** 2001
SQ FT: 27,000
SALES (est): 24.38MM
SALES (corp-wide): 24.38MM **Privately Held**
Web: www.e2g.com
SIC: 8711 Consulting engineer

(G-12977)
HARBOR RETIREMENT ASSOC LLC
Also Called: Harborchase of Shaker Heights
17000 Van Aken Blvd (44120-3613)
PHONE..................................216 925-4898
Terry Hornikel, *Ex Dir*
EMP: 54
SALES (corp-wide): 51.17MM **Privately Held**
Web: www.hraseniorliving.com
SIC: 8361 Aged home
PA: Harbor Retirement Associates, Llc
958 20th Pl
Vero Beach FL 32960
772 492-5002

(G-12978)
HOLISTIC HLPERS HM HLTH CARE L
3570 Warrensville Center Rd Ste 210 (44122-5288)
PHONE..................................216 331-5014
EMP: 60 **EST:** 2017
SALES (est): 200K **Privately Held**
SIC: 8082 Home health care services

(G-12979)
JCHERIE LLC
3645 Norwood Rd (44122-4911)
PHONE..................................216 453-1051
Cherie Mcelroy-burch, *Genl Mgr*
EMP: 30 **EST:** 2014
SALES (est): 617.45K **Privately Held**
SIC: 5621 7389 Women's clothing stores; Business services, nec

(G-12980)
LAUREL SCHOOL (PA)
1 Lyman Cir (44120)
PHONE..................................216 464-1441
Heather Ettinger, *Pr*
Ann Klotz, *
EMP: 161 **EST:** 1926
SQ FT: 70,000
SALES (est): 34.77MM
SALES (corp-wide): 34.77MM **Privately Held**
Web: www.laurelschool.org
SIC: 8211 8351 Private combined elementary and secondary school; Preschool center

(G-12981)
MCGLINCHEY STAFFORD PLLC
3401 Tuttle Rd Ste 200 (44122-6357)
PHONE..................................216 378-9905
Mark S Edelman, *Mgr*
EMP: 32
SALES (corp-wide): 48.61MM **Privately Held**
Web: www.mcglinchey.com
SIC: 8111 General practice attorney, lawyer
PA: Mcglinchey Stafford, Pllc
601 Poydras St Ste 1200
New Orleans LA 70130
504 586-1200

(G-12982)
MFF SOMERSET LLC
Also Called: Shaker Grdns Nursing Rehab Ctr
3550 Northfield Rd (44122-5253)
PHONE..................................216 752-5600
EMP: 32 **EST:** 2011
SALES (est): 11.7MM **Privately Held**
Web: www.shakergardens.com
SIC: 8051 Convalescent home with continuous nursing care

(G-12983)
SHAKER HEIGHTS COUNTRY CLUB CO
3300 Courtland Blvd (44122)
PHONE..................................216 991-3660
Phil Boova, *CEO*
Gerald Breen, *
Allen Waddle, *
Michael Abdalian, *
Charles O Toole, *
EMP: 225 **EST:** 1913
SQ FT: 62,000
SALES (est): 6.09MM **Privately Held**
Web: www.shakerheightscc.org
SIC: 7997 Country club, membership

(G-12984)
SHAKER HTS HIGH SCHL CREW PRNT
15911 Aldersyde Dr (44120-2598)
PHONE..................................216 991-6138
EMP: 72 **EST:** 2011
SALES (est): 68.04K **Privately Held**
Web: www.shaker.org
SIC: 6513 Apartment building operators

(G-12985)
SPECIALIZED ALTERNATIVES FOR F
Also Called: Safy of Cleveland
20600 Chagrin Blvd Ste 900 (44122-5327)
PHONE..................................216 295-7239
Dru Whitaker, *Prin*
EMP: 159
SALES (corp-wide): 22.34MM **Privately Held**
Web: www.safy.org
SIC: 8322 Child related social services
PA: Specialized Alternatives For Families And Youth Of Ohio, Inc.
10100 Elida Rd
Delphos OH 45833
419 695-8010

(G-12986)
UNIVERSITY HSPTALS CLVLAND MED
3605 Warrensville Center Rd (44122-9100)
PHONE..................................216 844-3323
Janet Miller, *Brnch Mgr*
EMP: 1542
SALES (corp-wide): 878.24MM **Privately Held**
Web: www.uhhospitals.org
SIC: 8062 General medical and surgical hospitals
HQ: University Hospitals Cleveland Medical Center
11100 Euclid Ave
Cleveland OH 44106

(G-12987)
UNIVERSITY HSPTALS HLTH SYS IN (PA)
Also Called: University Hospitals
3605 Warrensville Center Rd (44122-9100)
PHONE..................................216 767-8900
Thomas S Zenty, *CEO*
Janet L Miller, *
Bradley Bond, *
Kim Monaco, *
Eric Beck, *
▲ **EMP:** 950 **EST:** 1863
SALES (est): 878.24MM
SALES (corp-wide): 878.24MM **Privately Held**
Web: www.uhhospitals.org
SIC: 8062 Hospital, medical school affiliation

(G-12988)
VIGILANT GLOBAL TRADE SVCS LLC (PA)
3140 Courtland Blvd Ste 3400 (44122-2808)
PHONE..................................260 417-1825
Derek Abramovitch, *
EMP: 48 **EST:** 2007
SALES (est): 4.9MM **Privately Held**
Web: www.vigilantgts.com
SIC: 8611 7389 Trade associations; Business Activities at Non-Commercial Site

Sharon Center
Medina County

(G-12989)
RUHLIN COMPANY (PA)
6931 Ridge Rd (44274)
PHONE..................................330 239-2800
James L Ruhlin, *Pr*
Michael Deiwert, *VP*
Sean Demlow, *CFO*
EMP: 228 **EST:** 1915
SQ FT: 16,500
SALES (est): 121.99MM
SALES (corp-wide): 121.99MM **Privately Held**
Web: www.ruhlin.com
SIC: 1542 1541 1622 1611 Commercial and office building, new construction; Industrial buildings, new construction, nec; Bridge construction; General contractor, highway and street construction

(G-12990)
SOUTHEAST SECURITY CORPORATION
1385 Wolf Creek Trail (44274)
P.O. Box 326 (44274-0326)
PHONE..................................330 239-4600
Matt Lentine, *Pr*
Denise Lentine, *
EMP: 40 **EST:** 1986
SQ FT: 8,000
SALES (est): 8.68MM **Privately Held**
Web: www.southeastsecurity.com
SIC: 1731 Fire detection and burglar alarm systems specialization

(G-12991)
VELOTTA COMPANY
6740 Ridge Road (44274)
P.O. Box 267 (44274)
PHONE..................................330 239-1211
Robert P Velotta, *Pr*
Michael Velotta, *
Carolann V Stercula, *
Thomas F Velotta, *
EMP: 47 **EST:** 1976
SQ FT: 4,500
SALES (est): 6.08MM **Privately Held**
Web: www.velottacompany.com
SIC: 1611 1622 General contractor, highway and street construction; Bridge construction

Sharonville
Hamilton County

(G-12992)
CAMBRIDGE TRS INC
Also Called: Sonesta Es Cincinnati
2670 E Kemper Rd (45241-1816)
PHONE..................................617 231-3176
EMP: 40
SALES (corp-wide): 28.33MM **Privately Held**
Web: www.sonesta.com
SIC: 7011 Hotels
PA: Cambridge Trs, Inc.
255 Washington St Ste 100
Newton MA

(G-12993)
DUBOIS CHEMICALS INC (HQ)
3630 E Kemper Rd (45241-2011)
PHONE..................................800 438-2647
Jeff Welsh, *CEO*
Chris Heinold, *
▼ **EMP:** 37 **EST:** 2008
SALES (est): 533.59MM
SALES (corp-wide): 5.31MM **Privately Held**
Web: www.duboischemicals.com
SIC: 5169 Chemicals and allied products, nec
PA: Altas Partners Lp
79 Wellington St W Suite 3500
Toronto ON M5K 1
416 306-9800

GEOGRAPHIC SECTION   Shiloh - Richland County (G-13014)

(G-12994)
GATEWAY HOTEL LTD
Also Called: Hilton
11149 Dowlin Dr (45241-1835)
PHONE.................................513 772-2837
EMP: 43 EST: 2000
SALES (est): 518.09K **Privately Held**
Web: www.hilton.com
SIC: 7011 Hotels and motels

(G-12995)
MANAV ENTERPRISES INC
11018 Reading Rd (45241-1929)
PHONE.................................513 563-4606
EMP: 28
SALES (corp-wide): 340.09K **Privately Held**
SIC: 7389 Personal service agents, brokers, and bureaus
PA: Manav Enterprises, Inc.
    6379 Mueller Lakes Ln
    Loveland OH 45140
    513 831-5687

Sheffield Lake
Lorain County

(G-12996)
LANCE GLOBAL LOGISTICS LLC
3825 E Lake Rd (44054-1007)
PHONE.................................440 522-3822
Keith Belanger, *Managing Member*
EMP: 60 EST: 2020
SALES (est): 1.67MM **Privately Held**
SIC: 4215 Package delivery, vehicular

Sheffield Village
Lorain County

(G-12997)
ADVANCED DESIGN INDUSTRIES INC
Also Called: ADI
4686 French Creek Rd (44054-2716)
PHONE.................................440 277-4141
Jerome Winiasz, *Pr*
Thomas Winiasz, *
Edward J Winiasz, *
R G Brooks Junior, *Prin*
▲ EMP: 38 EST: 1955
SQ FT: 27,000
SALES (est): 2.41MM **Privately Held**
Web: www.advanceddesignindustries.com
SIC: 3569 3599 8711 Robots, assembly line; industrial and commercial; Machine shop, jobbing and repair; Designing: ship, boat, machine, and product

(G-12998)
GREEN IMPRESSIONS LLC
842 Abbe Rd (44054-2302)
PHONE.................................440 240-8508
Joseph Schill, *Prin*
Joseph Schill, *Pr*
James P Louth, *
EMP: 62 EST: 2011
SALES (est): 6.46MM **Privately Held**
Web: www.mygreenimpressions.com
SIC: 7349 0782 0781 4959 Building maintenance services, nec; Lawn and garden services; Landscape services; Snowplowing

(G-12999)
ILER NETWORKING & CMPT LTD
5061 N Abbe Rd Ste 3 (44035-1496)
PHONE.................................440 748-8083
Kent P Iler, *Prin*
EMP: 28 EST: 2002
SALES (est): 4.64MM **Privately Held**
Web: www.iler.com
SIC: 7379 Computer related consulting services

(G-13000)
JACK COOPER TRANSPORT CO INC
Also Called: Jack Cooper Transport Company, Inc.
5211 Oster Rd (44054-1568)
PHONE.................................440 949-2044
Larry Suscha, *Brnch Mgr*
EMP: 53
SALES (corp-wide): 510.05MM **Privately Held**
Web: www.jackcooper.com
SIC: 4213 Automobiles, transport and delivery
HQ: Jack Cooper Transport Company, Llc
    2345 Grand Blvd Ste 2400
    Kansas City MO 64108
    816 983-4000

(G-13001)
LUXURY HEATING COMPANY
Also Called: L & H Wholesale & Supply
5327 Ford Rd (44035-1349)
PHONE.................................440 366-0971
William Samek, *Pr*
Michael Samek, *
EMP: 65 EST: 1947
SALES (est): 5.38MM **Privately Held**
Web: www.luxuryheatingco.com
SIC: 1711 5075 Warm air heating and air conditioning contractor; Warm air heating and air conditioning

(G-13002)
MIKE FORD BASS INC
Also Called: Bass Truck Center
5050 Detroit Rd (44035-1464)
PHONE.................................440 934-3673
James B Bass, *Pr*
Mike Bass, *
Barbara Bass, *
EMP: 100 EST: 1977
SQ FT: 29,000
SALES (est): 31.85MM **Privately Held**
Web: www.mikebassford.net
SIC: 5511 7538 Automobiles, new and used; General automotive repair shops

(G-13003)
OTOOLE MCLGHLIN DLEY PCORA LP
Also Called: Omdp Attorneys & Counselors
5455 Detroit Rd (44054-2933)
PHONE.................................440 930-4001
Dennis O'toole, *Pt*
Russell Mclaughlin, *Pt*
John D Latchney, *
EMP: 30 EST: 1951
SALES (est): 4.16MM **Privately Held**
Web: www.dooleygembala.com
SIC: 8111 General practice law office

Shelby
Richland County

(G-13004)
ABRAXAS CORNELL GROUP LLC
Also Called: Abraxas Foundation of Ohio
2775 State Route 39 (44875-9466)
PHONE.................................419 747-3322
Erich Dumbeck, *Admn*
EMP: 110
SALES (corp-wide): 75.66MM **Privately Held**
SIC: 8069 8361 Alcoholism rehabilitation hospital; Residential care
HQ: Cornell Abraxas Group, Llc
    2840 Liberty Ave Ste 300
    Pittsburgh PA 15222
    800 227-2927

(G-13005)
CENTRAL OHIO ASSOCIATES LTD
18 Allison Dr (44875)
P.O. Box 646 (44875-0646)
PHONE.................................419 342-2045
Stephen Rosen, *Pt*
Benjamin Rosen, *Pt*
Uehuda Mendelson, *Pt*
EMP: 33 EST: 1965
SQ FT: 2,500,000
SALES (est): 1.99MM **Privately Held**
Web: www.centralohiowarehouse.com
SIC: 6512 Nonresidential building operators

(G-13006)
COOPER ENTERPRISES INC
89 Curtis Dr (44875-8400)
P.O. Box 50 (44875-0050)
PHONE.................................419 347-5232
EMP: 70 EST: 1965
SALES (est): 23.45MM **Privately Held**
Web: www.cooperenterprises.com
SIC: 5087 2452 Service establishment equipment; Prefabricated wood buildings

(G-13007)
MEDCENTRAL HEALTH SYSTEM
199 W Main St (44875-1490)
PHONE.................................419 342-5015
EMP: 215
SALES (corp-wide): 4.29B **Privately Held**
Web: www.medcentral.org
SIC: 8062 8049 General medical and surgical hospitals; Physical therapist
HQ: Medcentral Health System
    335 Glessner Ave
    Mansfield OH 44903
    419 526-8000

(G-13008)
PHILLIPS MFG AND TOWER CO (PA)
Also Called: Shelby Welded Tube Div
5578 State Route 61 N (44875)
P.O. Box 125 (44875)
PHONE.................................419 347-1720
Angela Phillip, *CEO*
Theresa Wallace, *
EMP: 85 EST: 1970
SQ FT: 90,000
SALES (est): 37.42MM
SALES (corp-wide): 37.42MM **Privately Held**
Web: www.phillipstube.com
SIC: 3312 3498 3317 7692 Tubes, steel and iron; Fabricated pipe and fittings; Steel pipe and tubes; Welding repair

(G-13009)
R & J TRUCKING INC
147 Curtis Dr (44875-9501)
PHONE.................................330 758-0841
EMP: 33
Web: www.americanbulkcommodities.com
SIC: 4212 Dump truck haulage
HQ: R & J Trucking, Inc.
    8063 Southern Blvd
    Youngstown OH 44512
    800 262-9365

(G-13010)
R S HANLINE AND CO INC (PA)
Also Called: Hanline Fresh
17 Republic Ave (44875-2142)
P.O. Box 494 (44875-0494)
PHONE.................................419 347-8077
▲ EMP: 115 EST: 1986
SALES (est): 41.64MM
SALES (corp-wide): 41.64MM **Privately Held**
Web: www.rshanline.com
SIC: 5141 2099 Groceries, general line; Food preparations, nec

(G-13011)
SHELBY HEALTH & WELLNESS CTR
31 E Main St (44875-1262)
PHONE.................................419 525-6795
EMP: 31 EST: 2019
SALES (est): 144.59K **Privately Held**
Web: www.thirdstreetfamily.org
SIC: 8099 Health and allied services, nec

Sherrodsville
Carroll County

(G-13012)
REGARD RECOVERY FLORIDA LLC
Also Called: The Bluff
2650 Lodge Rd Sw (44675-9718)
PHONE.................................330 866-0900
Brett Mcgennis, *Brnch Mgr*
EMP: 100
SALES (corp-wide): 2.93MM **Privately Held**
SIC: 8093 8361 Substance abuse clinics (outpatient); Mentally handicapped home
PA: Regard Recovery Of Florida Llc
    6460 Nw 5th Way
    Fort Lauderdale FL

Sherwood
Defiance County

(G-13013)
VETERANS OF FOREIGN WARS OF US
115 Cedar St (43556)
P.O. Box 4587 (43556-0587)
PHONE.................................419 899-2775
EMP: 62
SALES (corp-wide): 105.25MM **Privately Held**
SIC: 8641 Veterans' organization
PA: Veterans Of Foreign Wars Of The United States
    406 W 34th St Fl 11
    Kansas City MO 64111
    816 756-3390

Shiloh
Richland County

(G-13014)
RUMPKE WASTE INC
170 Noble Rd E (44878-9723)
PHONE.................................419 895-0058
Richard Kostelnick, *Mgr*
EMP: 166
Web: www.rumpke.com
SIC: 4953 Recycling, waste materials
HQ: Rumpke Waste, Inc.
    10795 Hughes Rd
    Cincinnati OH 45251
    513 851-0122

Shreve
Wayne County

(G-13015)
AGRI-SLUDGE INC
8047 State Route 754 (44676-9409)
PHONE.................................330 567-2500
Thomas Abraham, *Pr*
Linda Young, *Sec*
EMP: 28 **EST:** 1977
SALES (est): 2.92MM **Privately Held**
Web: www.agrisludge.com
SIC: 4953 Sludge disposal sites

(G-13016)
CRW INC
3716 S Elyria Rd (44676-9529)
PHONE.................................330 264-3785
TOLL FREE: 800
Chris Wood, *Pr*
Charles R Wood, *
▲ **EMP:** 43 **EST:** 1988
SQ FT: 9,800
SALES (est): 2.43MM **Privately Held**
Web: www.crwfreightmgmt.com
SIC: 4213 Contract haulers

Sidney
Shelby County

(G-13017)
AG TRUCKING INC
798 S Vandemark Rd (45365-8139)
PHONE.................................937 497-7770
Katie Stamp, *Mgr*
EMP: 31
SALES (corp-wide): 23.74MM **Privately Held**
Web: www.agtrucking.com
SIC: 4213 4212 Contract haulers; Local trucking, without storage
PA: Ag Trucking Inc
  2430 Lincolnway E
  Goshen IN 46526
  574 642-3351

(G-13018)
AMOS MEDIA COMPANY (PA)
Also Called: Coin World
1660 Campbell Rd Ste A (45365)
P.O. Box 4129 (45365)
PHONE.................................937 638-0967
Bruce Boyd, *Pr*
John O Amos, *
▲ **EMP:** 200 **EST:** 1876
SQ FT: 90,000
SALES (est): 37.68MM
SALES (corp-wide): 37.68MM **Privately Held**
Web: www.coinworld.com
SIC: 2721 2711 2796 7389 Magazines: publishing only, not printed on site; Newspapers, publishing and printing; Platemaking services; Appraisers, except real estate

(G-13019)
AREA ENERGY & ELECTRIC INC (PA)
Also Called: Honeywell Authorized Dealer
2001 Commerce Dr (45365-9393)
PHONE.................................937 498-4784
Kenneth Schlater, *Prin*
Todd Weigandt, *Prin*
Joe Lachey, *
Mike Marshall, *Prin*
Brian Moloney, *
EMP: 219 **EST:** 1983
SQ FT: 20,000
SALES (est): 50.99MM
SALES (corp-wide): 50.99MM **Privately Held**
Web: www.areaelectric.com
SIC: 1731 1711 General electrical contractor; Heating and air conditioning contractors

(G-13020)
BAUMFOLDER CORPORATION (DH)
1660 Campbell Rd (45365-2480)
PHONE.................................937 492-1281
Janice Benanzer, *Pr*
◆ **EMP:** 44 **EST:** 1917
SQ FT: 125,000
SALES (est): 10MM
SALES (corp-wide): 2.58B **Privately Held**
Web: www.baumfolder.com
SIC: 3579 7389 3554 Binding machines, plastic and adhesive; Packaging and labeling services; Folding machines, paper
HQ: Heidelberg Americas Inc
  1000 Gutenberg Dr Nw
  Kennesaw GA 30144

(G-13021)
BELTING COMPANY OF CINCINNATI
Also Called: Cbt Company
301 Stolle Ave (45365-7807)
PHONE.................................937 498-2104
James E Stahl Junior, *Pr*
EMP: 59
SALES (corp-wide): 264.36MM **Privately Held**
Web: www.cbtcompany.com
SIC: 5063 Electrical apparatus and equipment
PA: The Belting Company Of Cincinnati
  5500 Ridge Ave
  Cincinnati OH 45213
  513 621-9050

(G-13022)
BELTING COMPANY OF CINCINNATI
Also Called: Cbt Company
2450 Ross St (45365-8834)
PHONE.................................937 498-2104
EMP: 59
SALES (corp-wide): 264.36MM **Privately Held**
Web: www.cbtcompany.com
SIC: 5085 5063 Bearings; Power transmission equipment, electric
PA: The Belting Company Of Cincinnati
  5500 Ridge Ave
  Cincinnati OH 45213
  513 621-9050

(G-13023)
CLEAN ALL SERVICES INC
Also Called: Clean All Services
324 Adams St Bldg 1 (45365-2328)
P.O. Box 4127 (45365-4127)
PHONE.................................937 498-4146
Steve Shuchat, *Pr*
Rebecca Fair, *
Gary Shuchat, *
Derek O'leary, *Mgr*
EMP: 203 **EST:** 1982
SQ FT: 6,000
SALES (est): 5.68MM **Privately Held**
Web: www.cleanall.com
SIC: 7349 Janitorial service, contract basis

(G-13024)
CONTINENTAL EXPRESS INC
10450 State Route 47 W (45365-9009)
PHONE.................................937 497-2100
Russell L Gottemoeller, *CEO*
Russell L Gottemoeller, *Pr*
Rene Gottemoeller, *
Kiera Sullivan, *
David Treadway, *Prin*
EMP: 550 **EST:** 1984
SQ FT: 31,000
SALES (est): 95.97MM **Privately Held**
Web: www.continentalexpressinc.com
SIC: 4213 4212 Refrigerated products transport; Local trucking, without storage

(G-13025)
COUNCIL ON RUR SVC PRGRAMS INC
Also Called: Shelby County Child Care
1502 N Main Ave (45365-1761)
PHONE.................................937 492-8787
Brenda Lillicrap, *Mgr*
EMP: 66
SALES (corp-wide): 19.72MM **Privately Held**
Web: www.councilonruralservices.org
SIC: 8399 8351 Community action agency; Head Start center, except in conjunction with school
PA: Council On Rural Service Programs, Inc.
  201 Robert M Davis Pkwy B
  Piqua OH 45356
  937 778-5220

(G-13026)
COUNTY OF SHELBY
Also Called: Shelby County Highway Dept
500 Gearhart Rd (45365-9404)
PHONE.................................937 498-7244
Robert Geuy, *Mgr*
EMP: 65
SQ FT: 3,200
SALES (corp-wide): 53.29MM **Privately Held**
Web: co.shelby.oh.us
SIC: 1611 Highway and street construction
PA: County Of Shelby
  129 E Court St
  Sidney OH 45365
  937 498-7226

(G-13027)
COUNTY OF SHELBY
Also Called: Fair Haven Shelby County Home
2901 Fair Rd (45365-9534)
PHONE.................................937 492-6900
EMP: 71
SALES (corp-wide): 53.29MM **Privately Held**
Web: co.shelby.oh.us
SIC: 8059 8052 8051 Nursing home, except skilled and intermediate care facility; Intermediate care facilities; Skilled nursing care facilities
PA: County Of Shelby
  129 E Court St
  Sidney OH 45365
  937 498-7226

(G-13028)
COVER CROP SHOP LLC
Also Called: Center Seeds
739 S Vandemark Rd (45365-8959)
PHONE.................................937 417-3972
Eric L Belcher, *Managing Member*
EMP: 78
SALES (corp-wide): 2.9MM **Privately Held**
Web: www.sustain.farm
SIC: 5191 Seeds: field, garden, and flower
PA: Cover Crop Shop, Llc
  40 W 4th St
  Minster OH 45865
  937 417-3972

(G-13029)
DICKMAN SUPPLY INC (PA)
1991 St Marys Ave (45365)
P.O. Box 569 (45365-0569)
PHONE.................................937 492-6166
TOLL FREE: 800
Tim Geise, *Pr*
Timothy Geise, *
Marla Geise, *
Chris Geise, *Operations*
Luke Allen, *
EMP: 78 **EST:** 1953
SQ FT: 28,000
SALES (est): 105.18MM
SALES (corp-wide): 105.18MM **Privately Held**
Web: www.dickmansupply.com
SIC: 5063 5084 Electrical apparatus and equipment; Drilling bits

(G-13030)
EAGLE BRIDGE CO
800 S Vandemark Rd (45365-8139)
P.O. Box 59 (45365-0059)
PHONE.................................937 492-5654
Richard Franz, *Pr*
Thomas Frantz, *
EMP: 80 **EST:** 2001
SALES (est): 18.98MM **Privately Held**
Web: www.eaglebridge.net
SIC: 1622 Bridge construction

(G-13031)
FDL AUTOMATION AND SUPPLY CO
301 Stolle Ave (45365-7807)
PHONE.................................937 498-2104
EMP: 28
Web: www.heitmeyerconsultinginc.com
SIC: 5063 Electrical apparatus and equipment

(G-13032)
FERGUSON CONSTRUCTION COMPANY (PA)
400 Canal St (45365-2312)
P.O. Box 726 (45365-0726)
PHONE.................................937 498-2381
Martin Given, *Pr*
EMP: 150 **EST:** 1920
SQ FT: 40,000
SALES (est): 73.11MM
SALES (corp-wide): 73.11MM **Privately Held**
Web: www.ferguson-construction.com
SIC: 1541 1542 Industrial buildings, new construction, nec; Commercial and office building, new construction

(G-13033)
FRESH TRANSPORTATION CO LTD
2695 Hidden Ridge Dr (45365-8493)
PHONE.................................937 492-9876
Gilardi Frank, *CEO*
Philip Gilardi, *
EMP: 68 **EST:** 2000
SALES (est): 877.48K **Publicly Held**
SIC: 4731 Freight transportation arrangement
PA: Us Foods Holding Corp.
  9399 W Higgins Rd Ste 100
  Rosemont IL 60018

(G-13034)
FRESHWAY FOODS COMPANY INC (DH)
Also Called: Fresh and Limited
601 Stolle Ave (45365-8895)
PHONE.................................937 498-4664
Frank Gilardi Junior, *Ch Bd*
Phil Gilardi, *Pr*
Devon Beer, *CFO*

GEOGRAPHIC SECTION

Sidney - Shelby County (G-13055)

EMP: 100 EST: 1988
SQ FT: 90,000
SALES (est): 81.59MM **Publicly Held**
Web: www.freshwayfoods.com
SIC: 5148 2099 Vegetables, fresh; Food preparations, nec
HQ: Us Foods, Inc.
9399 W Higgins Rd Ste 500
Rosemont IL 60018

(G-13035)
GERMAIN OF SIDNEY III LLC ✪
Also Called: Germain Ford of Sidney
2343 Michigan St (45365-9079)
PHONE.................937 498-4014
EMP: 32 EST: 2023
SALES (est): 8.51MM **Privately Held**
Web: www.buckeyefordsidney.com
SIC: 5511 7538 Automobiles, new and used; General automotive repair shops

(G-13036)
KIRK NATIONALEASE CO (PA)
3885 Michigan St (45365-8623)
P.O. Box 4369 (45365-4369)
PHONE.................937 498-1151
Jeff Phlitot, *Pr*
Tom Menker, *
Deb Hovestreybt, *
James R Harvey, *
Martha Kirk, *Prin*
EMP: 40 EST: 1920
SQ FT: 20,000
SALES (est): 24.65MM
SALES (corp-wide): 24.65MM **Privately Held**
Web: www.knl.cc
SIC: 7513 7538 Truck leasing, without drivers ; Truck engine repair, except industrial

(G-13037)
LOCHARD INC
Also Called: Do It Best
903 Wapakoneta Ave (45365-1409)
P.O. Box 260 (45365-0260)
PHONE.................937 492-8811
Michael Lochard, *Pr*
Donald W Lochard, *
EMP: 75 EST: 1945
SQ FT: 44,500
SALES (est): 8.72MM **Privately Held**
Web: www.lochardplumbingheatingandcooling.com
SIC: 1711 5251 3599 Mechanical contractor; Hardware stores; Machine and other job shop work

(G-13038)
LOWELL MACKENZIE
1610 Wapakoneta Ave (45365-1434)
PHONE.................614 451-6669
EMP: 32
SALES (corp-wide): 399.8K **Privately Held**
Web: mackenziejohns.mypixieset.com
SIC: 7389 Financial services
PA: Lowell Mackenzie
1001 Lakeside Ave E
Cleveland OH 44114
216 621-7715

(G-13039)
LOWES HOME CENTERS LLC
Also Called: Lowe's
2700 Michigan St (45365-9007)
PHONE.................937 498-8400
Mike Herrera, *Mgr*
EMP: 138
SALES (corp-wide): 86.38B **Publicly Held**
Web: www.lowes.com
SIC: 5211 5031 5722 5064 Home centers; Building materials, exterior; Household appliance stores; Electrical appliances, television and radio
HQ: Lowe's Home Centers, Llc
1000 Lowes Blvd
Mooresville NC 28117
336 658-4000

(G-13040)
MASTIC HOME EXTERIORS INC
Ply Gem Siding Group
2405 Campbell Rd (45365-9529)
PHONE.................937 497-7008
Bob Parker, *Brnch Mgr*
EMP: 250
SALES (corp-wide): 5.58B **Privately Held**
Web: www.plygem.com
SIC: 5031 Windows
HQ: Mastic Home Exteriors, Inc.
2600 Grand Blvd Ste 900
Kansas City MO 64108
816 426-8200

(G-13041)
NK PARTS INDUSTRIES INC (HQ)
777 S Kuther Rd (45365-8861)
PHONE.................937 498-4651
◆ EMP: 150 EST: 1987
SALES (est): 104.94MM **Privately Held**
Web: www.nkparts.com
SIC: 5013 1796 4731 Motor vehicle supplies and new parts; Machine moving and rigging ; Freight transportation arrangement
PA: Nikkon Holdings Co., Ltd.
6-17, Akashicho
Chuo-Ku TKY 104-0

(G-13042)
OCCUPATIONAL HEALTH SERVICES
Also Called: Wilson Mem Hosp Occptnal Clnic
915 Michigan St (45365-2401)
PHONE.................937 492-7296
Cindy Bay, *Mgr*
EMP: 47 EST: 1999
SALES (est): 1.39MM **Privately Held**
Web: www.wilsonhealth.org
SIC: 8011 8748 8049 Internal medicine, physician/surgeon; Business consulting, nec ; Offices of health practitioner

(G-13043)
OHIO LIVING
Also Called: Ohio Living Dorothy Love
3003 Cisco Rd (45365-9343)
PHONE.................937 498-2391
Anne Roller, *Prin*
EMP: 330
Web: www.ohioliving.org
SIC: 8059 8051 8052 Rest home, with health care; Skilled nursing care facilities; Intermediate care facilities
PA: Ohio Living
9200 Worthington Rd # 300
Westerville OH 43082

(G-13044)
OHIO LIVING HOLDINGS
Also Called: Ohio Lving HM Hlth Grter Dyton
3003 Cisco Rd (45365-9343)
PHONE.................937 415-5666
Laurence C Gumina, *Prin*
Kevin Futryk, *
Paul Flannery, *
Barbara Sears, *
Raafat Zaki, *
EMP: 65 EST: 2010
SALES (est): 1.05MM **Privately Held**
Web: www.ohioliving.org
SIC: 8051 Skilled nursing care facilities

(G-13045)
OHIO VLY INTEGRATION SVCS INC
2005 Commerce Dr (45365-9393)
PHONE.................937 492-0008
John M Garmhausen, *Pr*
EMP: 35 EST: 1998
SALES (est): 4.53MM
SALES (corp-wide): 50.99MM **Privately Held**
Web: www.ovis.cc
SIC: 7382 Burglar alarm maintenance and monitoring
PA: Area Energy & Electric, Inc.
2001 Commerce Dr
Sidney OH 45365
937 498-4784

(G-13046)
REGAL PLUMBING & HEATING CO
9303 State Route 29 W (45365)
PHONE.................937 492-2894
Gary Thoma, *Pr*
Sandy Bruns, *
Phil Wyen, *Stockholder*
EMP: 45 EST: 1978
SQ FT: 21,000
SALES (est): 12.66MM **Privately Held**
Web: www.regalmechanical.com
SIC: 1711 Mechanical contractor

(G-13047)
SHELBY COUNTY MEM HOSP ASSN
Also Called: The Pavilion
705 Fulton St (45365-3203)
PHONE.................937 492-9591
Marianne Wildermuth, *Mgr*
EMP: 48
SALES (corp-wide): 108.88MM **Privately Held**
Web: www.shelbysnf.com
SIC: 8051 8062 Skilled nursing care facilities ; General medical and surgical hospitals
PA: Shelby County Memorial Hospital Association
915 Michigan St
Sidney OH 45365
937 498-2311

(G-13048)
SHELBY COUNTY MEM HOSP ASSN (PA)
Also Called: WILSON HEALTH
915 Michigan St (45365-2401)
PHONE.................937 498-2311
TOLL FREE: 800
Mark Dooley, *Pr*
Craig Lannoye, *
Jean Eckert, *
Julie Covault, *
EMP: 679 EST: 1930
SQ FT: 116,000
SALES (est): 108.88MM
SALES (corp-wide): 108.88MM **Privately Held**
Web: www.wilsonhealth.org
SIC: 8062 General medical and surgical hospitals

(G-13049)
SHELBY GOLF COURSE INC
Also Called: Shelby Oaks Golf Course
9900 Sidney Freyburg Rd (45365-7257)
P.O. Box 4639 (45365-4639)
PHONE.................937 492-2883
Rob Fridley, *Pr*
EMP: 30 EST: 1965
SQ FT: 2,500
SALES (est): 227.83K **Privately Held**
Web: www.shelbyoaks.com
SIC: 7997 5812 Golf club, membership; American restaurant

(G-13050)
SIDNEY ELECTRIC COMPANY (PA)
Also Called: Sidney Electric
840 S Vandemark Rd (45365-8139)
PHONE.................419 222-1109
John S Frantz, *Pr*
Mike Ellett, *
EMP: 59 EST: 1957
SQ FT: 20,000
SALES (est): 27.07MM
SALES (corp-wide): 27.07MM **Privately Held**
Web: www.sidneyelectric.com
SIC: 1731 General electrical contractor

(G-13051)
SIDNEY HOST LLC
Also Called: Hampton Inn
1600 Hampton Ct (45365-7540)
PHONE.................937 498-8888
Jim Lucas, *Managing Member*
EMP: 50 EST: 1996
SALES (est): 919.73K **Privately Held**
Web: www.hilton.com
SIC: 7011 Hotels and motels

(G-13052)
SIDNEY LODGES
Also Called: Comfort Inn
1959 Michigan St (45365-9073)
PHONE.................937 492-3001
Sidney Lodges, *Pr*
Sydney Lodges, *Pr*
Mary Ann Sisco, *Genl Mgr*
EMP: 30 EST: 1989
SALES (est): 200.96K **Privately Held**
Web: www.sidneymoose.com
SIC: 7011 Motels

(G-13053)
SIDNEY-SHELBY COUNTY YMCA (PA)
Also Called: YOUNG MEN'S CHRISTIAN ASSOCIAT
300 E Parkwood St (45365-1642)
PHONE.................937 492-9134
Ed Thomas, *CEO*
Dennis Ruble, *
EMP: 35 EST: 1968
SALES (est): 126.24K
SALES (corp-wide): 126.24K **Privately Held**
Web: www.sidney-ymca.org
SIC: 8641 8661 8322 Youth organizations; Religious organizations; Individual and family services

(G-13054)
SLAGLE MECHANICAL CONTRACTORS
877 W Russell Rd (45365-8633)
P.O. Box 823 (45365-0823)
PHONE.................937 492-4151
Jerry Kingseed, *Pr*
Gary Smith, *
Bob Snarr, *
Richard Wallace, *
Dale Brockman, *
EMP: 45 EST: 1948
SQ FT: 32,000
SALES (est): 14.56MM **Privately Held**
Web: www.slaglemech.com
SIC: 1711 1761 Plumbing contractors; Sheet metal work, nec

(G-13055)
SOLLMANN ELECTRIC CO
310 E Russell Rd (45365-1765)
PHONE.................937 492-0346
EMP: 33 EST: 1973
SALES (est): 4.77MM **Privately Held**
Web: www.sollmannelectric.com

Sidney - Shelby County (G-13056)

SIC: **1731** General electrical contractor

(G-13056)
SUNRISE HOSPITALITY INC
Also Called: Holiday Inn Express & Suites
450 Folkerth Ave (45365-9002)
PHONE..................................937 492-6010
Tom Schumaker, *Pr*
Doug Steimke, *Sec*
EMP: **50** EST: 1996
SALES (est): 451.47K **Privately Held**
Web: www.sunrisehospitality.com
SIC: **7011** Hotels and motels

(G-13057)
WAPPOO WOOD PRODUCTS INC
Also Called: Interntnal Pckg Pallets Crates
12877 Kirkwood Rd (45365-8102)
PHONE..................................937 492-1166
Thomas G Baker, *Ch Bd*
T Adam Baker, *
Gary O'connor, *Prin*
Matthew Baker, *
EMP: **40** EST: 1980
SQ FT: 21,800
SALES (est): 12.6MM **Privately Held**
Web: www.wappoowood.com
SIC: **5031** 2435 2436 2421 Lumber: rough, dressed, and finished; Hardwood veneer and plywood; Softwood veneer and plywood; Sawmills and planing mills, general

(G-13058)
WESTERN OHIO MORTGAGE CORP
733 Fair Rd (45365-2946)
PHONE..................................937 497-9662
Teresa Rose, *Pr*
Bruce Rose, *VP*
Kim Mishwitz, *Sec*
EMP: **42** EST: 1999
SALES (est): 10.02MM **Privately Held**
Web: www.westernohiomortgage.com
SIC: **6162** Mortgage bankers and loan correspondents

(G-13059)
XPO LOGISTICS FREIGHT INC
2021 Campbell Rd (45365-2474)
PHONE..................................937 492-3899
EMP: **59**
SALES (corp-wide): 7.74B **Publicly Held**
Web: www.xpo.com
SIC: **4213** Contract haulers
HQ: Xpo Logistics Freight, Inc.
 2211 Old Erhart Rd Ste 10
 Ann Arbor MI 48105
 800 755-2728

Silver Lake
Summit County

(G-13060)
SILVER LAKE COUNTRY CLUB
1325 Graham Rd (44224-2999)
PHONE..................................330 688-6066
Doug Koepnick, *Ch*
Mike Stevens, *
Bob Dedman Junior, *Ch Bd*
EMP: **34** EST: 1957
SQ FT: 15,000
SALES (est): 586.23K **Privately Held**
Web: www.invitedclubs.com
SIC: **7997** 7992 5941 5812 Country club, membership; Public golf courses; Sporting goods and bicycle shops; Eating places

Solon
Cuyahoga County

(G-13061)
ACLARA TECHNOLOGIES LLC
30400 Solon Rd (44139-3416)
PHONE..................................440 528-7200
Gary Moore, *Brnch Mgr*
EMP: **104**
SALES (corp-wide): 5.37B **Publicly Held**
Web: www.hubbell.com
SIC: **3824** 3825 3829 7371 Mechanical and electromechanical counters and devices; Instruments to measure electricity; Measuring and controlling devices, nec; Custom computer programming services
HQ: Aclara Technologies Llc
 77 W Port Plz Dr Ste 500
 Saint Louis MO 63146
 314 895-6400

(G-13062)
ADVANCEMENT LLC
Also Called: Ppi Technical Communications
32200 Solon Rd (44139-3540)
PHONE..................................440 248-8550
EMP: **200**
Web: www.ppitechcom.com
SIC: **8711** 7361 Consulting engineer; Employment agencies

(G-13063)
AIR VENTURI LTD
Also Called: Air Venturi
5135 Naiman Pkwy (44139-1003)
PHONE..................................216 292-2570
Valentin Gamerman, *Pr*
EMP: **54** EST: 2010
SQ FT: 70,000
SALES (est): 5.02MM **Privately Held**
Web: www.airventuri.com
SIC: **5091** Sporting and recreation goods
PA: Pyramyd Air Ltd.
 5135 Naiman Pkwy
 Solon OH 44139

(G-13064)
AIRBORNE ACQUISITION INC (HQ)
30500 Aurora Rd Ste 100 (44139)
PHONE..................................216 438-6111
Elek Puskas, *CEO*
EMP: **35** EST: 2009
SALES (est): 2.53MM
SALES (corp-wide): 6.58B **Publicly Held**
SIC: **6726** Investment offices, nec
PA: Transdigm Group Incorporated
 1301 E 9th St Ste 3000
 Cleveland OH 44114
 216 706-2960

(G-13065)
AMERICAN RING
30450 Bruce Industrial Pkwy (44139-3940)
PHONE..................................414 355-9206
EMP: **36** EST: 2018
SALES (est): 1.48MM **Privately Held**
Web: www.americanring.com
SIC: **5085** Industrial supplies

(G-13066)
APPLE HOSPITALITY FIVE INC
Also Called: Homewood Suites
6085 Enterprise Pkwy (44139-2754)
PHONE..................................440 519-9500
Perfetto Robyn, *Mgr*
EMP: **38** EST: 1999
SALES (est): 470.27K **Privately Held**
Web: homewoodsuites3.hilton.com
SIC: **7011** Hotels and motels

(G-13067)
ARCO HEATING & AC CO (PA)
5325 Naiman Pkwy Ste J (44139-1019)
PHONE..................................216 663-3211
Brian Friedman, *Pr*
EMP: **45** EST: 1922
SQ FT: 50,000
SALES (est): 4.89MM
SALES (corp-wide): 4.89MM **Privately Held**
Web: www.goarco.com
SIC: **1711** Warm air heating and air conditioning contractor

(G-13068)
ARROW ELECTRONICS INC
Power & Signal Group
5440 Naiman Pkwy (44139-1010)
PHONE..................................440 349-1300
EMP: **87**
SALES (corp-wide): 34.48B **Publicly Held**
SIC: **5065** Electronic parts
PA: Arrow Electronics, Inc.
 9201 E Dry Creek Rd
 Centennial CO 80112
 303 824-4000

(G-13069)
AURORA WHOLESALERS LLC (PA)
Also Called: Mazel Company, The
31000 Aurora Rd (44139)
PHONE..................................440 248-5200
Reuven Dessler, *Managing Member*
Jacob Koval, *
◆ EMP: **80** EST: 1975
SQ FT: 1,000,000
SALES (est): 33.99MM
SALES (corp-wide): 33.99MM **Privately Held**
Web: www.themazelcompany.com
SIC: **5199** General merchandise, non-durable

(G-13070)
B D G WRAP-TITE INC (PA)
Also Called: Wrap-Tite
6200 Cochran Rd (44139-3308)
PHONE..................................440 349-5400
Suresh Bafna, *CEO*
Sunil Daga, *
◆ EMP: **40** EST: 2004
SQ FT: 89,000
SALES (est): 23.04MM
SALES (corp-wide): 23.04MM **Privately Held**
Web: www.wraptite.com
SIC: **3069** 5199 Film, rubber; Leather goods, except footwear, gloves, luggage, belting

(G-13071)
C & S CLEANING SERVICES INC
Also Called: Solon Janitorial Services
31200 Solon Rd Ste 10 (44139-3583)
P.O. Box 39100 (44139-0100)
PHONE..................................440 349-5907
Christine Hayes, *Pr*
Scott Hayes, *
EMP: **60** EST: 2009
SALES (est): 966.12K **Privately Held**
Web: www.solonjanitorial.com
SIC: **7349** Janitorial service, contract basis

(G-13072)
CARNEGIE COMPANIES INC
6190 Cochran Rd Ste A (44139-3323)
PHONE..................................440 232-2300
Paul Pesses, *Pr*
Peter Meisel, *
EMP: **50** EST: 1991
SQ FT: 20,000
SALES (est): 8.96MM **Privately Held**
Web: www.carnegiecos.com
SIC: **6531** Real estate agent, commercial

(G-13073)
CARTEMP USA INC (PA)
29100 Aurora Rd (44139-1855)
PHONE..................................440 715-1000
EMP: **250** EST: 1995
SALES (est): 22.88MM **Privately Held**
Web: www.alamo.com
SIC: **7514** Rent-a-car service

(G-13074)
CBG BIOTECH LTD CO
30175 Solon Industrial Pkwy (44139-4321)
PHONE..................................800 941-9484
Gerald W Camiener, *Prin*
EMP: **52**
Web: www.cbgbiotech.com
SIC: **8732** 5084 Research services, except laboratory; Industrial machinery and equipment
PA: Cbg Biotech, Ltd. Co.
 100 Glenview Pl Apt 1003
 Naples FL 34108

(G-13075)
CHANNEL PRODUCTS INC (PA)
30700 Solon Industrial Pkwy (44139-4333)
PHONE..................................440 423-0113
Teresa Hack, *Pr*
Wayne Monaco, *
James Becker, *Prin*
Suzanne French, *Prin*
Steve Marrero, *Prin*
▲ EMP: **70** EST: 1972
SQ FT: 50,000
SALES (est): 11.37MM
SALES (corp-wide): 11.37MM **Privately Held**
Web: www.channelproducts.com
SIC: **7363** 3679 3643 3625 Manpower pools; Electronic circuits; Current-carrying wiring services; Relays and industrial controls

(G-13076)
CLEVELAND CLINIC FOUNDATION
Also Called: Cleveland Clinic Pain MGT Dept
33001 Solon Rd Ste 112 (44139-2864)
PHONE..................................216 444-2200
Jim Mccallick, *Prin*
EMP: **74**
SALES (corp-wide): 14.48B **Privately Held**
Web: my.clevelandclinic.org
SIC: **8062** General medical and surgical hospitals
PA: The Cleveland Clinic Foundation
 9500 Euclid Ave
 Cleveland OH 44195
 216 636-8335

(G-13077)
CORE-MARK HOLDING COMPANY INC
30300 Emerald Valley Pkwy (44139-4394)
PHONE..................................650 589-9445
Tom Perkins, *Brnch Mgr*
EMP: **150**
SALES (corp-wide): 57.25B **Publicly Held**
Web: www.core-mark.com
SIC: **5194** Cigarettes
HQ: Core-Mark Holding Company, Inc.
 1500 Solana Blvd Ste 3200
 Westlake TX 76262
 940 293-8600

(G-13078)
CORPORATE PLANS INC
Also Called: CPI-Hr
6830 Cochran Rd (44139-3966)

GEOGRAPHIC SECTION
Solon - Cuyahoga County (G-13099)

PHONE..............................440 542-7800
James Hopkins, *CEO*
Brian Meharry, *
Tom Wirbel, *
EMP: 45 **EST:** 1977
SQ FT: 3,000
SALES (est): 2.1MM **Privately Held**
Web: cpihr.aleragroup.com
SIC: 8742 6411 Compensation and benefits planning consultant; Insurance agents, brokers, and service

(G-13079)
CREATIVE PLAYROOM
Also Called: Solon Creative Playroom Center
32750 Solon Rd Ste 3 (44139-2865)
PHONE..............................440 248-3100
Joan Wenk, *Owner*
EMP: 40
SALES (corp-wide): 1.65MM **Privately Held**
Web: www.creativeplayrooms.com
SIC: 8351 Montessori child development center
PA: Creative Playroom
16574 Broadway Ave
Cleveland OH 44137
216 475-6464

(G-13080)
CUSTOM PRODUCTS CORPORATION (PA)
7100 Cochran Rd (44139-4306)
PHONE..............................440 528-7100
Timothy Stepanek, *Pr*
John Stepanek, *
William Stepanek Junior, *VP*
▲ **EMP:** 77 **EST:** 1974
SQ FT: 82,000
SALES (est): 11.43MM
SALES (corp-wide): 11.43MM **Privately Held**
Web: www.customproducts.net
SIC: 7389 5131 5199 2761 Packaging and labeling services; Labels; Packaging materials; Manifold business forms

(G-13081)
DELTA DIVERSIFIED INC
30625 Solon Rd Ste F (44139-3473)
PHONE..............................440 914-9400
Jim Hyde, *Pr*
EMP: 34 **EST:** 1979
SALES (est): 1.99MM **Privately Held**
Web: www.deltadiversified.net
SIC: 7361 Executive placement

(G-13082)
EFFICIENT COLLABORATIVE RETAIL (PA)
Also Called: Ecrm
27070 Miles Rd Ste A (44139-1162)
PHONE..............................440 498-0500
Greg Farrar, *CEO*
Brian Nelson, *CFO*
EMP: 66 **EST:** 1994
SQ FT: 6,000
SALES (est): 25.25MM **Privately Held**
Web: ecrm.marketgate.com
SIC: 8742 Marketing consulting services

(G-13083)
EMERGNCY RSPNSE TRNING SLTONS
6001 Cochran Rd Ste 300 (44139-3302)
PHONE..............................440 349-2700
Clay Richter, *Prin*
EMP: 33
SALES (corp-wide): 450.37MM **Privately Held**
Web: www.ertsonline.com
SIC: 8748 Environmental consultant
HQ: Emergency Response And Training Solutions, Incorporated
11231 Phlips Indus Blvd E
Jacksonville FL 32256

(G-13084)
EPICOR EDI SOURCE INC
Also Called: 1 Edi Source
31875 Solon Rd (44139-3553)
PHONE..............................440 519-7800
Vince Lowder, *Pr*
Vanessa Bustamante, *CFO*
EMP: 80 **EST:** 1989
SQ FT: 30,000
SALES (est): 16.19MM **Privately Held**
Web: www.1edisource.com
SIC: 7379 7371 Computer related consulting services; Software programming applications
PA: Epicor Software Corporation
807 Las Cimas Pkwy # 400
Austin TX 78746

(G-13085)
FAK GROUP INC
Also Called: Raf Automation
6750 Arnold Miller Pkwy (44139-4363)
PHONE..............................440 498-8465
Thomas J Koly, *Pr*
Willard E Frissell, *Sec*
EMP: 28 **EST:** 1953
SQ FT: 22,000
SALES (est): 4.72MM
SALES (corp-wide): 92.94MM **Privately Held**
Web: www.rafautomation.com
SIC: 7629 Electrical equipment repair services
PA: Electro-Matic Ventures, Inc.
23409 Industrial Park Ct
Farmington Hills MI 48335
248 478-1182

(G-13086)
FASTENER TOOL & SUPPLY INC (PA)
42500 Victory Pkwy (44139-3928)
PHONE..............................440 248-2710
▲ **EMP:** 64 **EST:** 1977
SALES (est): 20.21MM
SALES (corp-wide): 20.21MM **Privately Held**
Web: www.fastenertool.com
SIC: 5072 Miscellaneous fasteners

(G-13087)
FEDMET INTERNATIONAL CORP
Also Called: Baldwin International
30403 Bruce Industrial Pkwy (44139-3941)
PHONE..............................440 248-9500
Edward Siegle, *Pr*
Marion Britton, *VP Fin*
Edward Weber, *COO*
EMP: 55 **EST:** 1988
SQ FT: 44,500
SALES (est): 4.64MM
SALES (corp-wide): 3.28B **Privately Held**
Web: www.russelmetals.com
SIC: 5051 Steel
PA: Russel Metals Inc
6600 Financial Dr
Mississauga ON L5N 7
905 819-7777

(G-13088)
FENETECH LLC
32125 Solon Rd Ste 100 (44139-3535)
PHONE..............................330 995-2830
Ron Crowl, *Pr*
EMP: 150 **EST:** 1997
SALES (est): 15.96MM
SALES (corp-wide): 16.68MM **Privately Held**
Web: www.fenetech.com
SIC: 7371 Computer software development
PA: Cyncly
2020-400 Boul Armand-Frappier
Laval QC H7V 4
514 332-4110

(G-13089)
FINDAWAY WORLD LLC (PA)
31999 Aurora Rd (44139)
PHONE..............................440 893-0808
Mitch Kroll, *CEO*
▲ **EMP:** 50 **EST:** 2004
SALES (est): 23.3MM **Privately Held**
Web: www.playaway.com
SIC: 5999 8331 3669 5192 Audio-visual equipment and supplies; Job training and related services; Visual communication systems; Periodicals

(G-13090)
FMI MEDICAL SYSTEMS INC
29001 Solon Rd Unit A (44139-3469)
PHONE..............................440 600-5952
Harry Jang, *Pr*
William K Mccroskey, *Prin*
EMP: 40 **EST:** 2011
SALES (est): 10.7MM **Privately Held**
Web: www.fmimedical.com
SIC: 8071 X-ray laboratory, including dental
PA: Minfound Medical Syetems Co., Ltd.
Floor 1-2, Building 5, No.129, Yifeng Road, Economic Technology
Hangzhou ZJ 31001

(G-13091)
GARDINER SERVICE COMPANY LLC (PA)
Also Called: Gardiner
31200 Bainbridge Rd Ste 1 (44139-2298)
P.O. Box 39280 (44139-0280)
PHONE..............................440 248-3400
William Gardiner, *Ch Bd*
Todd Barnhart, *
Gary Gardiner, *Stockholder**
Todd Gardiner, *Stockholder**
Rob Mackinlay, *
EMP: 132 **EST:** 1957
SQ FT: 64,000
SALES (est): 68.27MM
SALES (corp-wide): 68.27MM **Privately Held**
Web: www.whgardiner.com
SIC: 5075 1711 7623 Air conditioning and ventilation equipment and supplies; Plumbing, heating, air-conditioning; Refrigeration service and repair

(G-13092)
GLENRIDGE MACHINE CO
37435 Fawn Path Dr (44139-2507)
PHONE..............................440 975-1055
▲ **EMP:** 33
Web: www.glenridgemachine.com
SIC: 3599 7692 Machine shop, jobbing and repair; Welding repair

(G-13093)
GOSIGER HOLDINGS INC
Also Called: Gosiger Machine Tools
30600 Solon Industrial Pkwy (44139-4332)
PHONE..............................734 582-2100
Brad Gecowets, *Mgr*
EMP: 34
SQ FT: 11,794
SALES (corp-wide): 142.92MM **Privately Held**
Web: www.gosiger.com
SIC: 5084 Machine tools and accessories
PA: Gosiger Holdings, Inc.
108 Mcdonough St
Dayton OH 45402
937 228-5174

(G-13094)
HD SUPPLY FACILITIES MAINT LTD
30311 Emerald Valley Pkwy (44139-4339)
PHONE..............................440 542-9188
Steve Yaney, *Mgr*
EMP: 70
SALES (corp-wide): 152.67B **Publicly Held**
Web: www.hdsupplysolutions.com
SIC: 5087 5072 5085 Cleaning and maintenance equipment and supplies; Hardware; Industrial supplies
HQ: Hd Supply Facilities Maintenance, Ltd.
3400 Cumberland Blvd Se
Atlanta GA 30339
770 852-9000

(G-13095)
HDT GLOBAL INC
30500 Aurora Rd Ste 100 (44139-2776)
PHONE..............................216 438-6111
EMP: 650
SIC: 8711 Engineering services

(G-13096)
HUNTER DEFENSE TECH INC (PA)
Also Called: Hdt Global
30500 Aurora Rd Ste 100 (44139-2776)
PHONE..............................216 438-6111
Vincent Buffa, *Pr*
Greg Miller, *
Carl Pates, *
Barry Sullivan, *
▼ **EMP:** 50 **EST:** 2000
SQ FT: 26,000
SALES (est): 416.26MM **Privately Held**
Web: www.hdtglobal.com
SIC: 3433 3569 3822 8331 Room and wall heaters, including radiators; Filters; Environmental controls; Sheltered workshop

(G-13097)
HUNTINGTON NATIONAL BANK
33175 Aurora Rd (44139-3613)
PHONE..............................216 515-0024
EMP: 31
SALES (corp-wide): 10.84B **Publicly Held**
Web: www.huntington.com
SIC: 6029 Commercial banks, nec
HQ: The Huntington National Bank
41 S High St
Columbus OH 43215
614 480-4293

(G-13098)
IMPERIAL HEATING AND COOLG INC (PA)
30685 Solon Industrial Pkwy Ste A (44139-4388)
PHONE..............................440 498-1788
Todd Rickard Ozanich, *Pr*
EMP: 47 **EST:** 1988
SQ FT: 19,000
SALES (est): 11.44MM
SALES (corp-wide): 11.44MM **Privately Held**
Web: www.lionssharecompany.com
SIC: 1711 Warm air heating and air conditioning contractor

(G-13099)
INDUSTRIAL COML PRPTS LLC
6675 Parkland Blvd Ste 100 (44139-4345)
PHONE..............................440 539-1046
Christopher Semarjian, *Prin*

Solon - Cuyahoga County (G-13100)

EMP: 70 **EST:** 2014
SALES (est): 2.67MM **Privately Held**
Web: www.icpllc.com
SIC: 6531 6512 Real estate agents and managers; Nonresidential building operators

(G-13100)
INSURANCECOM INC (PA)
Also Called: Comparisonmarket Insur Agcy
30775 Bainbridge Rd Ste 210 (44139)
PHONE.................................440 498-0001
Robert Klapper, *CEO*
David L Roush, *Ch Bd*
EMP: 58 **EST:** 2000
SQ FT: 41,000
SALES (est): 55.97MM **Privately Held**
Web: www.insurance.com
SIC: 6411 Insurance agents, nec

(G-13101)
INTERDESIGN INC (PA)
Also Called: Swiss Tech Products
30725 Solon Industrial Pkwy (44139)
P.O. Box 39606 (44139)
PHONE.................................440 248-0178
Chris Quinn, *CEO*
Robert Immerman, *
Robert Woolnough, *
◆ **EMP:** 236 **EST:** 1974
SQ FT: 178,096
SALES (est): 101.36MM
SALES (corp-wide): 101.36MM **Privately Held**
Web: www.idesignlivesimply.com
SIC: 5023 Homefurnishings

(G-13102)
JET EAST INC
Also Called: Das Aviation
32405 Aurora Rd (44139-2818)
PHONE.................................215 937-9020
EMP: 202 **EST:** 2011
SALES (est): 1.03MM
SALES (corp-wide): 310.92MM **Privately Held**
SIC: 4581 Aircraft maintenance and repair services
PA: West Star Aviation, Llc
796 Heritage Way
Grand Junction CO 81506
970 243-7500

(G-13103)
KEITHLEY INSTRUMENTS LLC (DH)
28775 Aurora Rd (44139-1891)
PHONE.................................440 248-0400
Joseph P Keithley, *Pr*
Linda C Rae, *
Mark J Plush, *
Daniel A Faia, *SUPPORT**
Larry L Pendergrass, *New Product Development Vice President**
▲ **EMP:** 102 **EST:** 1946
SQ FT: 125,000
SALES (est): 94.04MM
SALES (corp-wide): 6.07B **Publicly Held**
Web: www.tek.com
SIC: 3823 7371 3825 Computer interface equipment, for industrial process control; Computer software development; Test equipment for electronic and electric measurement
HQ: Tektronix, Inc.
14150 Sw Karl Braun Dr
Beaverton OR 97077
800 833-9200

(G-13104)
KNOCH CORPORATION
30505 Bainbridge Rd (44139-2287)
PHONE.................................330 244-1440
James B Fenske, *Pr*
David J Walker, *
Annette Destefano, *
Mike Jirele, *
David Archer, *General**
EMP: 53 **EST:** 1983
SALES (est): 22.5MM **Privately Held**
Web: www.knochcorp.com
SIC: 1542 1541 Commercial and office building, new construction; Industrial buildings, new construction, nec

(G-13105)
LOCUS AG SOLUTIONS LLC
30600 Aurora Rd Ste 180 (44139-2761)
PHONE.................................440 248-8787
EMP: 41 **EST:** 2019
SALES (est): 3.26MM **Privately Held**
Web: www.locusag.com
SIC: 0711 Soil preparation services

(G-13106)
LOCUS MANAGEMENT LLC
Also Called: Locus Performance Ingredients
30600 Aurora Rd Ste 180 (44139)
PHONE.................................888 510-0004
Donald Sweeney, *
Sean Farmer, *
Karthik Karathur, *
Kenneth Alibek, *
EMP: 70 **EST:** 2017
SALES (est): 6.07MM **Privately Held**
Web: www.locusingredients.com
SIC: 8741 Management services

(G-13107)
LORD CORPORATION
Also Called: Stellar Technology
33585 Bainbridge Rd (44139-2958)
PHONE.................................440 542-0012
Darren Mccully, *Brnch Mgr*
EMP: 40
SALES (corp-wide): 19.07B **Publicly Held**
Web: www.lord.com
SIC: 5084 Instruments and control equipment
HQ: Lord Corporation
111 Lord Dr
Cary NC 27511
919 468-5979

(G-13108)
LP INSURANCE SERVICES LLC
Also Called: Loan Protector Insurance Svcs
6000 Cochran Rd (44139-3318)
PHONE.................................877 369-5721
Dennis Swit, *CEO*
Mike Dimas, *VP*
Serf Hernandez, *COO*
EMP: 200 **EST:** 2018
SQ FT: 21,000
SALES (est): 19.16MM **Privately Held**
SIC: 6411 Insurance agents and brokers

(G-13109)
LUTHERAN MEDICAL CENTER INC (HQ)
33001 Solon Rd Ste 112 (44139-2864)
PHONE.................................440 519-6800
David Pesre, *CEO*
Christopher Winters, *
EMP: 320 **EST:** 1895
SQ FT: 350,000
SALES (est): 111.07MM
SALES (corp-wide): 14.48B **Privately Held**
Web: www.lutheranhospital.org
SIC: 8062 8011 8069 General medical and surgical hospitals; Offices and clinics of medical doctors; Specialty hospitals, except psychiatric
PA: The Cleveland Clinic Foundation
9500 Euclid Ave
Cleveland OH 44195
216 636-8335

(G-13110)
M & A DISTRIBUTING CO INC (PA)
Also Called: M & A Distribution
31031 Diamond Pkwy (44139-5463)
PHONE.................................440 703-4580
John M Antonucci, *Pr*
EMP: 41 **EST:** 1981
SQ FT: 12,000
SALES (est): 22.18MM
SALES (corp-wide): 22.18MM **Privately Held**
SIC: 5182 5181 Wine and distilled beverages; Beer and other fermented malt liquors

(G-13111)
MILES FARMERS MARKET INC
28560 Miles Rd (44139-1184)
PHONE.................................440 248-5222
Frank Cangemi, *Pr*
Dave Rondini, *
Joseph Degaetano, *
EMP: 150 **EST:** 1972
SQ FT: 50,000
SALES (est): 21.34MM **Privately Held**
Web: www.milesfarmersmarket.com
SIC: 5431 5148 Fruit stands or markets; Fruits, fresh

(G-13112)
MONT GRANITE INC (PA)
6130 Cochran Rd (44139-3306)
PHONE.................................440 287-0101
Dinesh Bafna, *Pr*
▲ **EMP:** 32 **EST:** 1989
SQ FT: 80,000
SALES (est): 20.23MM **Privately Held**
Web: www.montsurfaces.com
SIC: 5032 Granite building stone

(G-13113)
MP BIOMEDICALS LLC
29525 Fountain Pkwy (44139-4351)
PHONE.................................440 337-1200
Dragon Kraojovic, *Brnch Mgr*
EMP: 130
SALES (corp-wide): 601.99MM **Privately Held**
Web: www.mpbio.com
SIC: 8731 2869 2834 8071 Biological research; Enzymes; Pharmaceutical preparations; Medical laboratories
HQ: Mp Biomedicals, Llc
6 Thomas
Irvine CA 92618
949 833-2500

(G-13114)
MRI SOFTWARE LLC (PA)
28925 Fountain Pkwy (44139-4356)
PHONE.................................800 321-8770
EMP: 280 **EST:** 1971
SALES (est): 20.23K
SALES (corp-wide): 20.23K **Privately Held**
Web: www.mrisoftware.com
SIC: 7374 7371 6531 Data processing and preparation; Computer software development; Real estate agents and managers

(G-13115)
MUSTARD SEED HEALTH FD MKT INC
6025 Kruse Dr Ste 100 (44139-2378)
PHONE.................................440 519-3663
Margaret Kanfer-nabors, *Ch Bd*
EMP: 35
SALES (corp-wide): 27.81MM **Privately Held**
Web: www.mustardseedmarket.com
SIC: 5499 7299 5812 2051 Gourmet food stores; Banquet hall facilities; Caterers; Bread, cake, and related products
PA: Mustard Seed Health Food Market, Inc.
3885 Medina Rd
Akron OH 44333
330 666-7333

(G-13116)
NATIONAL ENTP SYSTEMS INC (PA)
Also Called: Nes
29125 Solon Rd (44139)
PHONE.................................440 542-1360
Ernest Pollak, *Pr*
Ellen Pollak, *
EMP: 119 **EST:** 1987
SQ FT: 48,000
SALES (est): 36.37MM
SALES (corp-wide): 36.37MM **Privately Held**
Web: www.nes1.com
SIC: 7322 Collection agency, except real estate

(G-13117)
NESTLE USA INC
30500 Bainbridge Rd (44139-2216)
PHONE.................................440 349-5757
EMP: 41
Web: www.nestleusa.com
SIC: 6733 Trusts, nec
HQ: Nestle Usa, Inc.
1812 N Moore St
Arlington VA 22209
703 682-4600

(G-13118)
NESTLE USA INC
Nestle Pizza Division
30003 Bainbridge Rd (44139-2290)
PHONE.................................440 349-5757
Tom Carrico, *Brnch Mgr*
EMP: 185
Web: www.nestleusa.com
SIC: 7389 5812 Personal service agents, brokers, and bureaus; Pizza restaurants
HQ: Nestle Usa, Inc.
1812 N Moore St
Arlington VA 22209
703 682-4600

(G-13119)
NOCO COMPANY (PA)
Also Called: Noco
30339 Diamond Pkwy Ste 102 (44139-5473)
PHONE.................................216 464-8131
William Nook Senior, *CEO*
◆ **EMP:** 100 **EST:** 1914
SQ FT: 100,000
SALES (est): 31.92MM
SALES (corp-wide): 31.92MM **Privately Held**
Web: www.no.co
SIC: 2899 5063 5072 3714 Chemical preparations, nec; Wire and cable; Power tools and accessories; Booster (jump-start) cables, automotive

(G-13120)
OLR AMERICA INC
31300 Solon Rd (44139-3570)
PHONE.................................612 436-4970
EMP: 45 **EST:** 2002
SALES (est): 3.33MM **Privately Held**
Web: www.olrretail.com
SIC: 7379 Online services technology consultants

GEOGRAPHIC SECTION
Solon - Cuyahoga County (G-13146)

(G-13121)
OMNI PROPERTY COMPANIES LLC
33095 Bainbridge Rd (44139-2834)
PHONE..................216 514-1950
Patrick T Finley, *Mgr*
EMP: 50 **EST:** 2007
SALES (est): 2.48MM **Privately Held**
Web: www.omnismartliving.com
SIC: 8742 Business management consultant

(G-13122)
OPTIMAS OE SOLUTIONS LLC
6565 Davis Industrial Pkwy (44139-3559)
PHONE..................440 546-4400
EMP: 34
SALES (corp-wide): 673.07MM **Privately Held**
Web: www.optimas.com
SIC: 5063 Electrical apparatus and equipment
HQ: Optimas Oe Solutions, Llc
1441 N Wood Dale Rd
Wood Dale IL 60191
224 999-1000

(G-13123)
P K WADSWORTH HEATING & COOLG
34280 Solon Rd Frnt (44139-2668)
PHONE..................440 248-4821
Paul K Wadsworth Junior, *Pr*
EMP: 45 **EST:** 1945
SQ FT: 6,000
SALES (est): 11.27MM **Privately Held**
Web: www.pkwadsworth.com
SIC: 1711 Warm air heating and air conditioning contractor

(G-13124)
PARK VIEW FEDERAL SAVINGS BANK
30000 Aurora Rd (44139-2728)
PHONE..................440 248-7171
EMP: 181
SIC: 6035 Federal savings banks

(G-13125)
PAUL MOSS LLC
Also Called: Moss Affiliate Marketing
5895 Harper Rd (44139-1832)
PHONE..................216 765-1580
EMP: 35 **EST:** 2009
SALES (est): 5.01MM **Privately Held**
Web: www.mossaffiliatemarketing.com
SIC: 6411 Insurance information and consulting services

(G-13126)
PICASSO FOR NAIL LLC
35494 Spatterdock Ln (44139-5094)
PHONE..................440 308-4470
EMP: 30 **EST:** 2007
SALES (est): 553.56K **Privately Held**
SIC: 7231 Manicurist, pedicurist

(G-13127)
PLANET AID INC
30901c Carter St (44139-3519)
PHONE..................440 542-1171
Keld Duss, *Mgr*
EMP: 34
SALES (corp-wide): 35.67MM **Privately Held**
Web: www.planetaid.org
SIC: 5932 8399 Clothing, secondhand; Fund raising organization, non-fee basis
PA: Planet Aid, Inc.
47 Sumner St Ste C
Milford MA 01757
508 893-0644

(G-13128)
PLAYAWAY PRODUCTS LLC ✪
31999 Aurora Rd Ste 1 (44139-2854)
PHONE..................440 893-0808
Gene Lamarca, *CEO*
EMP: 75 **EST:** 2023
SALES (est): 6.02MM
SALES (corp-wide): 54.57MM **Privately Held**
SIC: 7371 Software programming applications
HQ: Penguin Random House Llc
1745 Broadway
New York NY 10019
212 782-9000

(G-13129)
PRECISION ENGRG & CONTG INC
31340 Solon Rd Ste 25 (44139-3574)
PHONE..................440 349-1204
Chandrasekhar Narendrula, *Pr*
Prem Latha Narendrula, *
EMP: 65 **EST:** 2001
SQ FT: 5,460
SALES (est): 23MM **Privately Held**
Web: www.precisioneng.us
SIC: 8711 1623 Construction and civil engineering; Underground utilities contractor

(G-13130)
PRESSCO TECHNOLOGY INC
29200 Aurora Rd (44139-1847)
PHONE..................440 715-2559
EMP: 27 **EST:** 2019
SALES (est): 9.02MM **Privately Held**
SIC: 7379 Computer related consulting services

(G-13131)
PRESTAN PRODUCTS LLC
5101 Naiman Pkwy (44139-1017)
P.O. Box 24219 (44124-0219)
PHONE..................440 229-5100
Dan Moon, *CEO*
Christopher Bryniarski, *
◆ **EMP:** 42 **EST:** 2004
SALES (est): 8.95MM **Privately Held**
Web: www.prestanproducts.com
SIC: 5047 Medical and hospital equipment

(G-13132)
PTMJ ENTERPRISES INC
32000 Aurora Rd (44139-2875)
P.O. Box 391437 (44139-8437)
PHONE..................440 543-8000
Peter Joyce, *Pr*
▲ **EMP:** 64 **EST:** 1980
SALES (est): 3.95MM **Privately Held**
Web: www.signumdisplays.com
SIC: 2541 1799 Display fixtures, wood; Closet organizers, installation and design

(G-13133)
PVF CAPITAL CORP
30000 Aurora Rd (44139-2728)
PHONE..................440 248-7171
EMP: 199
Web: www.parkviewfederal.com
SIC: 6035 Federal savings institutions

(G-13134)
R & D NESTLE CENTER INC
29300 Cannon Rd (44139-1561)
PHONE..................440 264-2200
EMP: 89
Web: www.nestle.com
SIC: 8731 Food research
HQ: R & D Nestle Center Inc
809 Collins Ave
Marysville OH 43040
937 642-7015

(G-13135)
R L MORRISSEY & ASSOC INC (PA)
Also Called: American Ring & Tool Co
30450 Bruce Industrial Pkwy (44139-3940)
PHONE..................440 498-3730
James N Morrissey, *Pr*
Jack Morrissey, *
Robert H Morrissey, *
William F Chinnock, *
▲ **EMP:** 40 **EST:** 1958
SQ FT: 28,000
SALES (est): 21.13MM
SALES (corp-wide): 21.13MM **Privately Held**
Web: www.americanring.com
SIC: 5085 5051 5013 Fasteners, industrial: nuts, bolts, screws, etc.; Stampings, metal; Automotive supplies and parts

(G-13136)
RADIX WIRE CO (PA)
Also Called: Radix Wire Company, The
30333 Emerald Valley Pkwy (44139-4394)
PHONE..................216 731-9191
Keith D Nootbaar, *Pr*
Marylou Vermerris, *
Jim Schaefer, *
Brain Bukovec, *
EMP: 60 **EST:** 1944
SALES (est): 20.56MM
SALES (corp-wide): 20.56MM **Privately Held**
Web: www.radix-wire.com
SIC: 3357 5051 Nonferrous wiredrawing and insulating; Cable, wire

(G-13137)
RELAM INC (PA)
Also Called: Railway Equipment Lsg & Maint
7695 Bond St (44139-5350)
PHONE..................440 232-3354
Carl Eberhardt, *Pr*
Linda Ertel, *Sec*
David Horth, *Stockholder*
Craig Phelon, *CFO*
EMP: 35 **EST:** 1992
SQ FT: 4,800
SALES (est): 26.6MM **Privately Held**
Web: www.relaminc.com
SIC: 7353 Heavy construction equipment rental

(G-13138)
RIZE HOME LLC (PA)
Also Called: Mantua Bed Frames
31050 Diamond Pkwy (44139-5478)
PHONE..................800 333-8333
David Jaffe, *CEO*
Edward Weintraub, *
Jeff Weekly, *CFO*
Marc Spector, *
◆ **EMP:** 75 **EST:** 1954
SQ FT: 67,500
SALES (est): 38.73MM
SALES (corp-wide): 38.73MM **Privately Held**
Web: www.rizehome.com
SIC: 5021 2514 Bedsprings; Frames for box springs or bedsprings: metal

(G-13139)
ROLLHOUSE ENTERTAINMENT S
33185 Bainbridge Rd (44139-2835)
PHONE..................440 248-4080
EMP: 73 **EST:** 2018
SALES (est): 2.51MM **Privately Held**
Web: www.therollhouse.com
SIC: 7929 Entertainers and entertainment groups

(G-13140)
RSR PARTNERS LLC
Also Called: Regency Technologies
6111 Cochran Rd (44139-3305)
PHONE..................440 248-3991
Jim Levine, *CEO*
EMP: 219
SALES (corp-wide): 27.64MM **Privately Held**
Web: www.regencytechnologies.com
SIC: 4953 Recycling, waste materials
PA: Rsr Partners Llc
4550 Darrow Rd
Stow OH 44224
440 519-1768

(G-13141)
SERVICELINK FIELD SERVICES LLC
30825 Aurora Rd Ste 140 (44139-2733)
PHONE..................440 424-0058
Robert J Caruso, *Pr*
EMP: 2531 **EST:** 1998
SALES (est): 1.58MM
SALES (corp-wide): 7.99B **Publicly Held**
SIC: 7389 Inspection and testing services
HQ: Black Knight Infoserv, Llc
601 Riverside Ave
Jacksonville FL 32204

(G-13142)
SIGNUM LLC (PA)
32000 Aurora Rd Ste C (44139-2849)
PHONE..................440 248-2233
Todd Mccuaig, *Managing Member*
EMP: 100 **EST:** 2016
SALES (est): 20.73MM
SALES (corp-wide): 20.73MM **Privately Held**
Web: www.signumdisplays.com
SIC: 7319 Sample distribution

(G-13143)
SNF WADSWORTH LLC
Also Called: Golden Leaf
5625 Emerald Ridge Pkwy (44139-1860)
PHONE..................330 336-3472
Melissa Nelson, *Managing Member*
EMP: 31 **EST:** 2002
SALES (est): 520.31K **Privately Held**
SIC: 8051 Skilled nursing care facilities

(G-13144)
SOLON LODGING ASSOCIATES LLC
Also Called: Springhill Suites
30100 Aurora Rd (44139-2730)
PHONE..................440 248-9600
EMP: 118 **EST:** 2004
SALES (est): 4.63MM
SALES (corp-wide): 23.71B **Publicly Held**
Web: www.springhillsolon.com
SIC: 7011 Hotels and motels
PA: Marriott International, Inc.
7750 Wisconsin Ave
Bethesda MD 20814
301 380-3000

(G-13145)
SOLON PNTE AT EMRALD RIDGE LLC
5625 Emerald Ridge Pkwy (44139-1860)
PHONE..................440 498-3000
EMP: 48 **EST:** 2007
SALES (est): 7.07MM **Privately Held**
SIC: 8051 Convalescent home with continuous nursing care

(G-13146)
SOURCE DIAGNOSTICS LLC (PA)
5275 Naiman Pkwy Ste E (44139-1033)
PHONE..................440 542-9481

Solon - Cuyahoga County (G-13147)

Keith Marchand, *Managing Member*
EMP: 37 **EST:** 2004
SALES (est): 4.42MM **Privately Held**
Web: www.sourcediagnostics.com
SIC: 8082 Home health care services

(G-13147)
SOUTHERN GLZERS DSTRS OHIO LLC
7800 Cochran Rd (44139-4342)
PHONE..................................440 542-7000
EMP: 67
SALES (corp-wide): 7.27B **Privately Held**
SIC: 5181 5182 Beer and ale; Wine and distilled beverages
HQ: Southern Glazer's Distributors Of Ohio, Llc
4800 Poth Rd
Columbus OH 43213

(G-13148)
SPI LLC
Also Called: Glt Products
6810 Cochran Rd (44139-3908)
PHONE..................................440 914-1122
Jon Perry, *CEO*
EMP: 37
SALES (corp-wide): 5.19B **Publicly Held**
Web: www.gltproducts.com
SIC: 5031 Building materials, interior
HQ: Spi Llc
2101 Rexford Rd Ste 300e
Charlotte NC 28211
704 336-9555

(G-13149)
STOCK FAIRFIELD CORPORATION
Also Called: Stock Equipment Company
30825 Aurora Rd # 150 (44139-2733)
PHONE..................................440 543-6000
Robert Ciavarella, *Pr*
EMP: 170 **EST:** 2007
SALES (est): 34.35MM
SALES (corp-wide): 2.67MM **Privately Held**
Web: www.schenckprocess.com
SIC: 5063 8711 3535 3823 Power transmission equipment, electric; Electrical or electronic engineering; Conveyors and conveying equipment; Process control instruments
HQ: Schenck Process Llc
7901 Nw 107th Ter
Kansas City MO 64153
816 891-9300

(G-13150)
STRATFORD COMMONS INC
7000 Cochran Rd (44139-4304)
PHONE..................................440 914-0900
Maureen Moffatte, *Pr*
Prentice Lipsey, *
EMP: 78 **EST:** 2001
SALES (est): 10.65MM **Privately Held**
Web: www.stratfordcommons.com
SIC: 8059 8052 Nursing home, except skilled and intermediate care facility; Intermediate care facilities

(G-13151)
SUPPLY TECHNOLOGIES LLC
Also Called: I L S
5370 Naiman Pkwy (44139-1024)
P.O. Box 39636 (44139-0636)
PHONE..................................440 248-8170
John Ham, *Brnch Mgr*
EMP: 30
SALES (corp-wide): 1.66B **Publicly Held**
Web: www.supplytechnologies.com
SIC: 5085 Fasteners and fastening equipment
HQ: Supply Technologies Llc
6065 Parkland Blvd
Cleveland OH 44124
440 947-2100

(G-13152)
SWAGELOK COMPANY
Also Called: Training Services Group
29495 F A Lennon Dr (44139-2764)
PHONE..................................440 349-5962
Joseph Sarakaitis, *Mgr*
EMP: 73
SALES (corp-wide): 881.02MM **Privately Held**
Web: www.aldvalve.com
SIC: 5085 Valves and fittings
PA: Swagelok Company
29500 Solon Rd
Solon OH 44139
440 248-4600

(G-13153)
SWAGELOK COMPANY
32550 Old South Miles Rd (44139-2829)
PHONE..................................440 542-1250
EMP: 35
SALES (corp-wide): 952.18MM **Privately Held**
SIC: 5085 Valves and fittings
PA: Swagelok Company
29500 Solon Rd
Solon OH 44139
440 248-4600

(G-13154)
SWAGELOK COMPANY
29495 F A Lennon Dr (44139-2764)
PHONE..................................440 349-5934
Nick Lubar, *Mgr*
EMP: 100
SALES (corp-wide): 881.02MM **Privately Held**
Web: www.aldvalve.com
SIC: 5051 3593 3498 3494 Tubing, metal; Fluid power cylinders and actuators; Fabricated pipe and fittings; Valves and pipe fittings, nec
PA: Swagelok Company
29500 Solon Rd
Solon OH 44139
440 248-4600

(G-13155)
TAMERAN GRAPHIC SYSTEMS INC
Also Called: Tameran
30300 Solon Industrial Pkwy Ste F (44139-4382)
PHONE..................................440 349-7100
Mark A Wise, *CEO*
▲ **EMP:** 50 **EST:** 2000
SQ FT: 40,000
SALES (est): 5.3MM **Privately Held**
Web: www.tameran.com
SIC: 5044 Office equipment

(G-13156)
THERMEDX LLC
31200 Solon Rd Ste 1 (44139-3583)
PHONE..................................440 542-0883
Douglas L Carr, *CEO*
▲ **EMP:** 27 **EST:** 2007
SALES (est): 11.58MM
SALES (corp-wide): 20.5B **Publicly Held**
Web: www.thermedx.com
SIC: 5047 Medical equipment and supplies
PA: Stryker Corporation
1941 Stryker Way
Portage MI 49002
269 385-2600

(G-13157)
UNFORS RAYSAFE INC
6045 Cochran Rd (44139-3303)
PHONE..................................508 435-5600
EMP: 45
SALES (corp-wide): 6.07B **Publicly Held**
Web: www.raysafe.com
SIC: 5047 Medical equipment and supplies
HQ: Unfors Raysafe, Inc.
6920 Seaway Blvd
Everett WA 98203
508 435-5600

(G-13158)
VAN DYNE-CROTTY CO
Also Called: Spirit Services
30400 Bruce Industrial Pkwy (44139-3929)
PHONE..................................440 248-6935
Jeff Brewer, *Mgr*
EMP: 69
SQ FT: 41,454
SALES (corp-wide): 16MM **Privately Held**
Web: www.getspirit.com
SIC: 7218 7213 Industrial uniform supply; Linen supply
PA: Van Dyne-Crotty Co.
2150 Fairwood Ave
Columbus OH 43207
614 684-0048

(G-13159)
VENTURE LIGHTING INTL INC (HQ)
7905 Cochran Rd Ste 300 (44139-5471)
PHONE..................................800 451-2606
Sabu Krishnan, *CEO*
Shawn Toney, *
Wayne Vespoli, *
Amy Patrick, *
◆ **EMP:** 68 **EST:** 1981
SALES (est): 51.44MM **Privately Held**
Web: www.venturelighting.com
SIC: 5063 Lighting fixtures
PA: Advanced Lighting Technologies, Llc
6675 Parkland Blvd
Solon OH 44139

(G-13160)
VETERANS OF FOREIGN WARS OF US
Also Called: Solon VFW Post 1863
6340 Melbury Ave (44139-3615)
PHONE..................................440 349-1863
EMP: 64
SALES (corp-wide): 105.25MM **Privately Held**
SIC: 8641 Veterans' organization
PA: Veterans Of Foreign Wars Of The United States
406 W 34th St Fl 11
Kansas City MO 64111
816 756-3390

(G-13161)
VINCENT LIGHTING SYSTEMS CO (PA)
6161 Cochran Rd Ste D (44139-3324)
PHONE..................................216 475-7600
TOLL FREE: 800
Paul Vincent, *CEO*
Bill Groener, *
Joni Roecker, *
Walter Weber, *
Christopher Shick, *SRVCS**
EMP: 29 **EST:** 1978
SALES (est): 24.72MM
SALES (corp-wide): 24.72MM **Privately Held**
Web: www.vls.com
SIC: 5063 7359 5999 Lighting fixtures; Equipment rental and leasing, nec; Theatrical equipment and supplies

(G-13162)
VINTAGE WINE DISTRIBUTOR INC (PA)
6555 Davis Industrial Pkwy (44139-3549)
PHONE..................................440 248-1750
▲ **EMP:** 40 **EST:** 1972
SALES (est): 9.67MM
SALES (corp-wide): 9.67MM **Privately Held**
Web: www.vintwine.com
SIC: 5182 Wine

(G-13163)
WEYMOUTH VALLEY INC
Also Called: Signature Solon Golf Course
39000 Signature Dr (44139-5266)
PHONE..................................440 498-8888
Gary Cramer, *CEO*
EMP: 60 **EST:** 2000
SQ FT: 5,734
SALES (est): 3.74MM **Privately Held**
Web: www.signatureofsoloncc.com
SIC: 7997 5813 5812 Country club, membership; Drinking places; Eating places

(G-13164)
WIDEWATERS EDR SOLON HT CO LLC
6035 Enterprise Pkwy (44139-2754)
PHONE..................................440 542-0400
EMP: 50 **EST:** 2006
SALES (est): 1.3MM **Privately Held**
SIC: 7011 Hotels and motels

(G-13165)
WINNCOM TECHNOLOGIES CORP
28900 Fountain Pkwy Unit B (44139)
PHONE..................................440 498-9510
Gregory Raskin, *Pr*
◆ **EMP:** 120 **EST:** 1996
SQ FT: 16,000
SALES (est): 25MM **Privately Held**
Web: www.winncom.com
SIC: 5065 8711 Communication equipment; Engineering services
HQ: Winncom Technologies Holding Limited
Suite 144 The Capel Building
Dublin 7

(G-13166)
WINSTON PRODUCTS LLC
30339 Diamond Pkwy Ste 105 (44139-5472)
PHONE..................................440 945-6912
Winston Breeden Iii, *CEO*
Scott Jared, *
▲ **EMP:** 100 **EST:** 2004
SQ FT: 115,000
SALES (est): 37.45MM **Privately Held**
Web: www.winstonproducts.us
SIC: 5199 Architects' supplies (non-durable)

Somerville
Butler County

(G-13167)
WOODLAND COUNTRY MANOR INC
4166 Somerville Rd (45064-9707)
PHONE..................................513 523-4449
Ealeta Dingeldine, *Pr*
EMP: 58 **EST:** 1970
SQ FT: 1,401
SALES (est): 7.42MM **Privately Held**
Web: www.woodlandcountrymanor.net
SIC: 8051 Convalescent home with continuous nursing care

GEOGRAPHIC SECTION   Spencerville - Allen County (G-13187)

South Amherst
Lorain County

(G-13168)
ECHOING HILLS VILLAGE INC
Also Called: Echoing Lake/Renouard Home
235 W Main St (44001-2925)
PHONE..................440 986-3085
EMP: 39
SQ FT: 3,682
SALES (corp-wide): 39.8MM **Privately Held**
Web: www.ehvi.org
SIC: 7032 8059 Sporting and recreational camps; Home for the mentally retarded, ex. skilled or intermediate
PA: Echoing Hills Village, Inc.
36272 County Road 79
Warsaw OH 43844
740 327-2311

(G-13169)
ELECTRICAL ACCENTS LLC
104 N Lake St Ste C (44001-2877)
PHONE..................440 988-2852
Daryl Wolfram, *Managing Member*
EMP: 47 **EST:** 2003
SALES (est): 4.93MM **Privately Held**
Web: www.electricalaccentsllc.com
SIC: 1731 General electrical contractor

South Euclid
Cuyahoga County

(G-13170)
AEROCONTROLEX GROUP INC
Also Called: Aerocontrolex
4223 Monticello Blvd (44121-2814)
PHONE..................216 291-6025
Chris Swartz, *Pr*
EMP: 99 **EST:** 1954
SQ FT: 55,000
SALES (est): 40.89MM
SALES (corp-wide): 6.58B **Publicly Held**
Web: www.aerocontrolex.com
SIC: 3492 5084 3594 Valves, hydraulic, aircraft; Industrial machinery and equipment ; Fluid power pumps and motors
HQ: Transdigm, Inc.
1350 Euclid Ave
Cleveland OH 44115

(G-13171)
LADNEIR HEALTHCARE SERVICE LLC
4225 Mayfield Rd Ste 201 (44121-3037)
PHONE..................216 744-7296
EMP: 36 **EST:** 2015
SALES (est): 2.02MM **Privately Held**
Web: www.ladneirhomeservice.care
SIC: 8082 Home health care services

South Lebanon
Warren County

(G-13172)
LOWES HOME CENTERS LLC
Also Called: Lowe's
575 Corwin Nixon Blvd (45065-1199)
PHONE..................513 445-1000
Bill Goodlick, *Brnch Mgr*
EMP: 143
SALES (corp-wide): 86.38B **Publicly Held**
Web: www.lowes.com
SIC: 5211 5031 5722 5064 Home centers; Building materials, exterior; Household appliance stores; Electrical appliances, television and radio
HQ: Lowe's Home Centers, Llc
1000 Lowes Blvd
Mooresville NC 28117
336 658-4000

South Point
Lawrence County

(G-13173)
ASHLAND HOSPITAL CORPORATION
Also Called: King Daughters Family Care Ctr
384 County Road 120 S (45680-7807)
PHONE..................740 894-2080
Shelly Mcgraw, *Mgr*
EMP: 74
SALES (corp-wide): 538.89MM **Privately Held**
Web: www.kdmc.com
SIC: 8011 8062 Medical centers; General medical and surgical hospitals
HQ: Ashland Hospital Corporation
2201 Lexington Ave
Ashland KY 41101
606 408-4000

(G-13174)
DBI SERVICES LLC
2393 County Road 1 (45680-8462)
PHONE..................410 590-4181
Paul D Deangelo, *Managing Member*
EMP: 30
Web: www.dbiservices.com
SIC: 0783 Ornamental shrub and tree services
HQ: Dbi Services, Llc
100 N Conahan Dr
Hazleton PA 18201

(G-13175)
GRANDVIEW INN INC
Also Called: Grandview Inn
154 County Road 450 (45680-8853)
PHONE..................740 377-4388
Victor Hardan, *Pr*
EMP: 50 **EST:** 1965
SALES (est): 457.26K **Privately Held**
Web: www.grandviewinnohio.com
SIC: 7011 Motels

(G-13176)
LAWRENCE CNTY BD DEV DSBLITIES
Also Called: Lawrence Cnty Erly Chldhood Ct
1749 County Road 1 (45680-8850)
PHONE..................740 377-2356
EMP: 46
Web: www.lawrencedd.org
SIC: 8322 8351 Child related social services; Child day care services
PA: Lawrence County Board Of Dev Disabilities
604 Carlton Davidson Ln
Coal Grove OH 45638
740 532-7401

(G-13177)
LOWES HOME CENTERS LLC
Also Called: Lowe's
294 County Road 120 S (45680-7553)
PHONE..................740 894-7120
EMP: 190
SALES (corp-wide): 86.38B **Publicly Held**
Web: www.lowes.com
SIC: 5211 5031 5722 5064 Home centers; Building materials, exterior; Household appliance stores; Electrical appliances, television and radio
HQ: Lowe's Home Centers, Llc
1000 Lowes Blvd
Mooresville NC 28117
336 658-4000

(G-13178)
MCGINNIS INC (HQ)
502 2nd St E (45680-9446)
P.O. Box 534 (45680-0534)
PHONE..................740 377-4391
Rickey Lee Griffith, *Pr*
Bruce D Mcginnis, *CEO*
Bill Jessie, *
D Dwaine Stephens, *
EMP: 193 **EST:** 1971
SQ FT: 5,000
SALES (est): 22.72MM **Privately Held**
Web: www.mcnational.com
SIC: 4491 3731 Marine cargo handling; Barges, building and repairing
PA: Mcnational, Inc.
502 2nd St E
South Point OH 45680

(G-13179)
MCNATIONAL INC (PA)
502 2nd St E (45680-9446)
P.O. Box 534 (45680-0534)
PHONE..................740 377-4391
Rick Griffith, *Pr*
C Clayton Johnson, *
C Barry Gipson, *
Bruce D Mcginnis, *CEO*
EMP: 97 **EST:** 1988
SQ FT: 5,000
SALES (est): 130.89MM **Privately Held**
Web: www.mcnational.com
SIC: 3731 7699 4491 Barges, building and repairing; Aircraft and heavy equipment repair services; Marine cargo handling

(G-13180)
MERCIERS INCORPORATED
Also Called: Mercier's Tree Experts
2393 County Road 1 (45680-8462)
PHONE..................410 590-4181
Craig Mercier, *Pr*
EMP: 110 **EST:** 1978
SQ FT: 2,500
SALES (est): 4.97MM **Privately Held**
Web: www.merciers.com
SIC: 0783 Ornamental shrub and tree services

(G-13181)
MIKE ENYART & SONS INC
Also Called: Mesi
77 Private Drive 615 (45680-1259)
P.O. Box 9 (45680-0009)
PHONE..................740 523-0235
Michael Enyart, *Pr*
Tommy Enyart, *
EMP: 85 **EST:** 2006
SALES (est): 11.69MM **Privately Held**
Web: www.mesi-ohio.com
SIC: 1623 1794 Sewer line construction; Excavation work

(G-13182)
QUALITY CARE NURSING SVC INC
Also Called: Ultimate Health Care
501 Washington St Ste 13 (45680-9606)
PHONE..................740 377-9095
Douglas Freeman, *CEO*
James Carver, *
Douglas Freeman, *Prin*
EMP: 200 **EST:** 1995
SQ FT: 5,500
SALES (est): 9.86MM **Privately Held**
Web: www.qcnservices.net
SIC: 8082 8051 Home health care services; Skilled nursing care facilities

(G-13183)
RIVERS BEND HEALTH CARE LLC
335 Township Road 1026 (45680-7842)
PHONE..................740 894-3476
EMP: 100 **EST:** 2003
SQ FT: 27,341
SALES (est): 8.99MM **Privately Held**
Web: www.rbhcohio.com
SIC: 8051 8052 Convalescent home with continuous nursing care; Intermediate care facilities

(G-13184)
XPO LOGISTICS FREIGHT INC
Also Called: Xpo Logistics
96 Private Drive 339 (45680-8919)
PHONE..................740 894-3859
Andrew Sikes, *Mgr*
EMP: 48
SALES (corp-wide): 7.74B **Publicly Held**
Web: www.xpo.com
SIC: 4213 Contract haulers
HQ: Xpo Logistics Freight, Inc.
2211 Old Erhart Rd Ste 10
Ann Arbor MI 48105
800 755-2728

South Webster
Scioto County

(G-13185)
ALLARD EXCAVATION LLC
8336 Bennett School House Rd (45682-9029)
PHONE..................740 778-2242
Margaret Allard, *Managing Member*
Mark Allard, *
EMP: 85 **EST:** 2010
SALES (est): 5.2MM **Privately Held**
Web: www.allardexcavation.com
SIC: 1794 Excavation work

South Zanesville
Muskingum County

(G-13186)
BACO LLC
Also Called: Bright Bginnings Childcare Ctr
3921 Northpointe Dr (43701-7361)
PHONE..................740 454-4840
Melissa Berga, *Owner*
Fran Defrofiers, *Owner*
EMP: 50 **EST:** 2009
SALES (est): 470.16K **Privately Held**
SIC: 8351 Group day care center

Spencerville
Allen County

(G-13187)
CHARLES RIVER LABORATORIES INC
Also Called: Pre-Clinical Services
640 N Elizabeth St (45887-1064)
PHONE..................419 647-4196
Malcolm Blair Ph.d., *Mgr*
EMP: 47
SALES (corp-wide): 4.13B **Publicly Held**
Web: www.criver.com

Spencerville - Allen County (G-13188) GEOGRAPHIC SECTION

SIC: 8731 Biotechnical research, commercial
HQ: Charles River Laboratories, Inc.
251 Ballardvale St
Wilmington MA 01887
781 222-6000

(G-13188)
HCF OF ROSELAWN INC
420 E 4th St (45887-1235)
PHONE....................................419 647-4115
David Walsh, VP
EMP: 160 EST: 2015
SALES (est): 38.06MM
SALES (corp-wide): 305.93MM **Privately Held**
Web: www.roselawnmanor.com
SIC: 8051 8322 8093 Convalescent home with continuous nursing care; Rehabilitation services; Rehabilitation center, outpatient treatment
PA: Hcf Management, Inc.
1100 Shawnee Rd
Lima OH 45805
419 999-2010

(G-13189)
INVINCIBLE FIRE CO INC
Also Called: SPENCERVILLE FIRE DEPARTMENT
204 S Canal St (45887-1124)
PHONE....................................419 647-4615
Dave Holtzhauer, Pr
Jim Agil, *
Richard Wilson, *
EMP: 29 EST: 1900
SQ FT: 836
SALES (est): 159.58K **Privately Held**
SIC: 7389 Personal service agents, brokers, and bureaus

(G-13190)
PFP HOLDINGS LLC
220 S Elizabeth St (45887-1315)
P.O. Box 126 (45887-0126)
PHONE....................................419 647-4191
◆ EMP: 750
SIC: 3069 5199 Foam rubber; Foam rubber

Springboro
Warren County

(G-13191)
ADVANCED ENGRG SOLUTIONS INC
Also Called: Aesi
250 Advanced Dr (45066-1802)
PHONE....................................937 743-6900
Khang D.o.s., Pr
Thomas J Harrington, *
▲ EMP: 70 EST: 1995
SQ FT: 44,000
SALES (est): 9.83MM **Privately Held**
Web: www.advancedinternational.com
SIC: 8711 3544 Consulting engineer; Special dies, tools, jigs, and fixtures

(G-13192)
ALFONS HAAR INC
150 Advanced Dr (45066)
PHONE....................................937 560-2031
◆ EMP: 31 EST: 1993
SQ FT: 5,000
SALES (est): 8.91MM
SALES (corp-wide): 63.34MM **Privately Held**
Web: www.alfons-haar.us
SIC: 5084 3599 8711 Packaging machinery and equipment; Custom machinery; Engineering services

PA: Alfons Haar Maschinenbau Gmbh & Co. Kg
Fangdieckstr. 67
Hamburg HH 22547
40833910

(G-13193)
ASSOCIATED PROF ENGRG CONS LLC
Also Called: Apec
204 Hiawatha Trl (45066-3010)
PHONE....................................937 746-4600
Kenneth Meine, Mng Pt
EMP: 28 EST: 1985
SQ FT: 9,000
SALES (est): 2.56MM **Privately Held**
Web: www.apec.com
SIC: 8711 Consulting engineer

(G-13194)
BROTHERS TRADING CO INC (PA)
Also Called: Victory Wholesale Group
400 Victory Ln (45066-3046)
P.O. Box 216 (45066-0216)
PHONE....................................937 746-1010
David Kantor, Pr
Richard Kantor, *
Scott Mattis, *
◆ EMP: 150 EST: 1985
SQ FT: 25,000
SALES (est): 243.01MM
SALES (corp-wide): 243.01MM **Privately Held**
Web: www.vwg.com
SIC: 5141 5122 5149 Food brokers; Drugs, proprietaries, and sundries; Groceries and related products, nec

(G-13195)
BROTHERS TRADING CO INC
Also Called: Victory Wholesale Groceries
425 Victory Ln (45066-3047)
PHONE....................................937 746-1010
Scott Mattis, Mgr
EMP: 44
SALES (corp-wide): 243.01MM **Privately Held**
Web: www.vwg.com
SIC: 5141 Food brokers
PA: Brothers Trading Co., Inc.
400 Victory Ln
Springboro OH 45066
937 746-1010

(G-13196)
CHILDVINE INC
Also Called: Kids 'r' Kids 3 OH
790 N Main St (45066-8944)
PHONE....................................937 748-1260
Edward Doczy, Pr
Bonnie Doczy, *
EMP: 34 EST: 2002
SQ FT: 15,000
SALES (est): 409.75K **Privately Held**
Web: www.kidsrkids.com
SIC: 8351 Preschool center

(G-13197)
COLDWELL BNKR HRITG RLTORS LLC
Also Called: Coldwell Banker
20 S Main St (45066-2302)
PHONE....................................937 435-7759
Jenny Knott, Off Mgr
EMP: 28
SALES (corp-wide): 8.98MM **Privately Held**
Web: www.coldwellbankerishome.com
SIC: 6531 Real estate agent, residential
PA: Coldwell Banker Heritage Realtors Llc
4486 Indian Ripple Rd
Dayton OH 45440
937 434-7600

(G-13198)
FAIRWAY INDEPENDENT MRTG CORP
40 Remick Blvd (45066-9168)
PHONE....................................937 304-1443
EMP: 44
Web: www.fairwayindependentmc.com
SIC: 6162 Mortgage bankers
PA: Fairway Independent Mortgage Corporation
4750 S Biltmore Ln
Madison WI 53718

(G-13199)
GRAPHIC SYSTEMS SERVICES INC
Also Called: G S S
400 S Pioneer Blvd (45066-3001)
PHONE....................................937 746-0708
EMP: 41 EST: 1995
SQ FT: 100,000
SALES (est): 7.63MM
SALES (corp-wide): 573MM **Publicly Held**
Web: www.didde.com
SIC: 7699 3555 Industrial equipment services ; Printing presses
PA: Eastman Kodak Company
343 State St
Rochester NY 14650
585 724-4000

(G-13200)
HARDY DIAGNOSTICS
Also Called: Quickslide
429 S Pioneer Blvd (45066-3002)
PHONE....................................937 550-2768
Shelly Austin, Mgr
EMP: 75
SALES (corp-wide): 95.87MM **Privately Held**
Web: www.hardydiagnostics.com
SIC: 5047 Medical equipment and supplies
PA: Hardy Diagnostics Inc.
1430 W Mccoy Ln
Santa Maria CA 93455
805 346-2766

(G-13201)
HILLSPRING HEALTH CARE CENTER
Also Called: CARESPRING
325 E Central Ave (45066-8553)
PHONE....................................937 748-1100
Greg Weaver, Brnch Mgr
Barry Dortz, CEO
EMP: 58 EST: 1997
SQ FT: 55,611
SALES (est): 14.27MM
SALES (corp-wide): 84.56MM **Privately Held**
Web: www.carespring.com
SIC: 8051 Convalescent home with continuous nursing care
PA: Carespring Health Care Management, Llc
390 Wards Corner Rd
Loveland OH 45140
513 943-4000

(G-13202)
KELCHNER INC (DH)
50 Advanced Dr (45066-1805)
PHONE....................................937 704-9890
Todd Kelchner, CEO
Troy Norvell, *
EMP: 114 EST: 1948
SQ FT: 8,600
SALES (est): 75.76MM
SALES (corp-wide): 5.9B **Privately Held**
Web: www.kelchner.com

SIC: 1794 1389 Excavation work; Mud service, oil field drilling
HQ: Wood Group Uk Limited
Sir Ian Wood House
Aberdeen AB12
122 450-0400

(G-13203)
MOUND TECHNOLOGIES INC
25 Mound Park Dr (45066-2402)
PHONE....................................937 748-2937
Thomas Miller, Pr
John Barger, *
Shelia A Campbell, *
EMP: 45 EST: 2003
SQ FT: 40,000
SALES (est): 17.81MM
SALES (corp-wide): 48.46MM **Privately Held**
Web: www.moundtechnologies.com
SIC: 3441 1791 3446 Building components, structural steel; Structural steel erection; Gates, ornamental metal
PA: Heartland, Inc.
1005 N 19th St
Middlesboro KY 40965
606 248-7323

(G-13204)
NATIONS ROOF OF OHIO LLC
Also Called: Affilate Ntons Roof LLC Lthia
275 S Pioneer Blvd (45066-1180)
PHONE....................................937 439-4160
Chuck Painter, Pr
Andrew Strauser, VP
EMP: 50 EST: 2006
SALES (est): 10.06MM **Privately Held**
Web: www.nationsroofohio.com
SIC: 1761 Roofing contractor
PA: Nations Roof, Llc
851 E I65 Svc Rd S # 300
Mobile AL 36606

(G-13205)
PARTS EXPRESS INTERNATIONAL INC (PA)
Also Called: Dayton Loudspeaker Co.
725 Pleasant Valley Dr (45066-1158)
PHONE....................................800 338-0531
◆ EMP: 59 EST: 1986
SALES (est): 24.85MM
SALES (corp-wide): 24.85MM **Privately Held**
Web: www.parts-express.com
SIC: 5065 5999 Electronic parts; Electronic parts and equipment

(G-13206)
PDI COMMUNICATION SYSTEMS INC (PA)
Also Called: P D I
40 Greenwood Ln (45066-3033)
PHONE....................................937 743-6010
Louis Vilardo, Pr
Kent Carver, *
Cindy Doxrud, *
◆ EMP: 60 EST: 1976
SQ FT: 78,000
SALES (est): 23.91MM
SALES (corp-wide): 23.91MM **Privately Held**
Web: www.pdiarm.com
SIC: 5047 Medical equipment and supplies

(G-13207)
SPRINGBORO FAMILY HEALTH CARE
Also Called: Springboro Family Medicine
630 N Main St Ste 210 (45066-7519)
PHONE....................................937 748-4211
Susan Grau, CEO

GEOGRAPHIC SECTION — Springfield - Clark County (G-13229)

EMP: 49 **EST:** 1995
SALES (est): 529.18K **Privately Held**
Web: www.springboro.org
SIC: 8062 General medical and surgical hospitals

(G-13208)
SYCAMORE CREEK COUNTRY CLUB
8300 Country Club Ln (45066-8436)
PHONE..................937 748-0791
David Gagner, *Pr*
Bradley Pollak, *
EMP: 120 **EST:** 1959
SALES (est): 4.43MM **Privately Held**
Web: www.sycamorecreekcc.org
SIC: 7997 Country club, membership

(G-13209)
WOODHULL LLC (PA)
125 Commercial Way (45066-3079)
PHONE..................937 294-5311
Susan S Woodhull, *Owner*
EMP: 39 **EST:** 2000
SQ FT: 6,500
SALES (est): 10.5MM **Privately Held**
Web: www.woodhullusa.com
SIC: 5999 7699 Photocopy machines; Photocopy machine repair

(G-13210)
YOUNG MNS CHRSTN ASSN GRTER DY
Also Called: Coffman Branch
88 Remick Blvd (45066-9168)
PHONE..................937 223-5201
Dale Brunner, *Dir*
EMP: 175
SQ FT: 2,512
SALES (corp-wide): 36.75MM **Privately Held**
Web: www.daytonymca.org
SIC: 8641 8351 7997 7991 Youth organizations; Child day care services; Membership sports and recreation clubs; Physical fitness facilities
PA: Young Men's Christian Association Of Greater Dayton
118 W 1st St Ste 300
Dayton OH 45402
937 223-5201

(G-13211)
YOUR AGENCY INC
Also Called: Allstate
664 N Main St (45066-9553)
PHONE..................937 550-9596
Michael T Steinke, *Prin*
EMP: 40 **EST:** 2011
SALES (est): 762.63K **Privately Held**
Web: www.youragencyinc.com
SIC: 6411 Insurance agents, nec

Springfield
Clark County

(G-13212)
A & K ISHVAR INC
Also Called: Comfort Suites
121 Raydo Cir (45506-3556)
PHONE..................937 322-0707
Hemantkumar Patel, *Pr*
Smita Ben Patel, *VP*
EMP: 57 **EST:** 2004
SQ FT: 40,000
SALES (est): 861.54K **Privately Held**
Web: www.choicehotels.com
SIC: 7011 Hotel, franchised

(G-13213)
ABILITIES CONNECTION
2160 Old Selma Rd (45505-4600)
PHONE..................937 525-7400
EMP: 40 **EST:** 2018
SALES (est): 212.33K **Privately Held**
Web: www.tacind.com
SIC: 8322 Social services for the handicapped

(G-13214)
AETNA BUILDING MAINTENANCE INC
Also Called: Aetna Integrated Services
525 N Yellow Springs St (45504-2462)
PHONE..................937 324-5711
Paul Greenland, *CEO*
EMP: 111
SALES (corp-wide): 5.16MM **Privately Held**
Web: www.gdi.com
SIC: 7349 5113 8744 Janitorial service, contract basis; Industrial and personal service paper; Facilities support services
HQ: Atalian Us Ohio Valley, Inc.
646 Parsons Ave
Columbus OH 43206
614 476-1818

(G-13215)
AKD CLEANING SERVICE OF TEXAS
100 W Main St (45502-1312)
P.O. Box 741392 (75374-1392)
PHONE..................937 521-3900
Steve Eisentrager, *Prin*
EMP: 98 **EST:** 2014
SALES (est): 9.87MM **Privately Held**
Web: www.ovsurgical.com
SIC: 7699 Cleaning services

(G-13216)
AMERICAN SECURITY INSURANCE CO
1 Assurant Way (45505-4717)
PHONE..................937 327-7700
Michael Lawson, *Prin*
EMP: 168
SALES (corp-wide): 11.13B **Publicly Held**
Web: www.assurant.com
SIC: 6311 Life insurance
HQ: American Security Insurance Company
260 Interstate N Cir Se
Atlanta GA 30339
770 763-1000

(G-13217)
ANDRITZ INC
Also Called: Andritz Sprout Bauer
3200 Upper Valley Pike (45504-4520)
PHONE..................937 390-3400
Mark Sabourin, *Mgr*
EMP: 128
SALES (corp-wide): 7.83B **Privately Held**
Web: www.andritz.com
SIC: 8734 Testing laboratories
HQ: Andritz Inc.
5405 Windward Pkwy 100w
Alpharetta GA 30004
770 640-2500

(G-13218)
ARCHDIOCESE OF CINCINNATI
Also Called: Catholic Scial Svcs Sprngfied
701 E Columbia St (45503-4404)
PHONE..................937 325-8715
Keith Williamsom, *Dir*
EMP: 40
SALES (corp-wide): 222.98MM **Privately Held**
Web: www.catholiccharitiesusa.org

SIC: 8322 Individual and family services
PA: Archdiocese Of Cincinnati
100 E 8th St Fl 8
Cincinnati OH 45202
513 421-3131

(G-13219)
ARCTECH FABRICATING INC (PA)
1317 Lagonda Ave (45503-4001)
P.O. Box 1447 (45501-1447)
PHONE..................937 525-9353
James C Roberts Ii, *Pr*
Tina Roberts, *
Leonard Mcconnaghey, *CEO*
EMP: 29 **EST:** 1992
SQ FT: 13,200
SALES (est): 6.23MM **Privately Held**
Web: www.arctechfabricating.com
SIC: 7692 3441 Welding repair; Fabricated structural metal

(G-13220)
AVENTURA AT OAKWOOD VLG LLC ✪
1500 Villa Rd (45503-1656)
PHONE..................937 390-9000
Audrey Berg, *Managing Member*
EMP: 200 **EST:** 2022
SALES (est): 7.95MM **Privately Held**
Web: www.aventurehg.com
SIC: 8051 Convalescent home with continuous nursing care

(G-13221)
BENJAMIN STEEL COMPANY INC (PA)
Also Called: Benjamin Steel
777 Benjamin Dr (45502-8846)
PHONE..................937 322-8600
▲ **EMP:** 99 **EST:** 1935
SALES (est): 99.72MM
SALES (corp-wide): 99.72MM **Privately Held**
Web: www.benjaminsteel.com
SIC: 5051 Structural shapes, iron or steel

(G-13222)
BOARD OF DIRS OF WTTNBERG CLLE
Also Called: Wittenberg University
225 N Fountain Ave (45504-2534)
P.O. Box 720 (45501-0720)
PHONE..................937 327-6310
Mary Jo Darr, *Brnch Mgr*
EMP: 64
SALES (corp-wide): 89.9MM **Privately Held**
Web: www.wittenberg.edu
SIC: 8221 6163 University; Loan brokers
PA: The Board Of Directors Of Wittenberg College
200 W Ward St
Springfield OH 45504
937 327-6231

(G-13223)
BONBRIGHT DISTRIBUTORS INC
2024 Selma Rd (45505-4238)
PHONE..................937 222-1001
EMP: 41
SALES (corp-wide): 21.41MM **Privately Held**
Web: www.bonbright.com
SIC: 5181 Beer and other fermented malt liquors
PA: Bonbright Distributors, Inc.
1 Arena Park Dr
Dayton OH 45417
937 222-1001

(G-13224)
CATHOLIC CHARITIES OF SOUTHWST
Also Called: Catholic Charities
701 E Columbia St (45503-4404)
PHONE..................937 325-8715
EMP: 99 **EST:** 2011
SALES (est): 655.27K **Privately Held**
Web: www.ccswoh.org
SIC: 8322 Social service center

(G-13225)
CENTRAL FIRE PROTECTION CO INC
583 Selma Rd (45505)
P.O. Box 1448 (45501)
PHONE..................937 322-0713
Gary Adkins, *Pr*
Gary Adkins, *VP*
Helen Gifford, *
EMP: 34 **EST:** 1983
SALES (est): 5.5MM **Privately Held**
SIC: 1799 Coating, caulking, and weather, water, and fireproofing

(G-13226)
CHOICES IN COMMUNITY LIVING
2100 E High St Ste 113 (45505-1388)
PHONE..................937 325-0344
Kesha Tuttle, *Mgr*
EMP: 66
SALES (corp-wide): 14.1MM **Privately Held**
Web: www.partnersohio.com
SIC: 8361 8322 Retarded home; Individual and family services
PA: Choices In Community Living Inc
1651 Needmore Rd Ste B
Dayton OH 45414
937 898-3655

(G-13227)
CITY OF SPRINGFIELD
Also Called: SPRINGFIELD, CITY OF (INC)
50 E Columbia St (45502-1133)
PHONE..................937 328-3701
Roger Tacket, *Brnch Mgr*
EMP: 27
SALES (corp-wide): 83.3MM **Privately Held**
Web: www.springfieldohio.gov
SIC: 9199 7521 General government administration, Local government; Automobile parking
PA: City Of Springfield
76 E High St
Springfield OH 45502
937 324-7357

(G-13228)
CITY OF SPRINGFIELD
Also Called: Reed Park Golf Course
1325 S Bird Rd (45505-3503)
PHONE..................937 324-7725
Brad Reid, *Mgr*
EMP: 35
SALES (corp-wide): 83.3MM **Privately Held**
Web: www.golfreidpark.com
SIC: 7992 Public golf courses
PA: City Of Springfield
76 E High St
Springfield OH 45502
937 324-7357

(G-13229)
CLARK SCHAEFER HACKETT & CO
14 E Main St Ste 500 (45502-1364)
PHONE..................937 399-2000
John Mckinnon, *Prin*
EMP: 40
SALES (corp-wide): 26.49MM **Privately Held**

(PA)=Parent Co (HQ)=Headquarters
✪ = New Business established in last 2 years

Springfield - Clark County (G-13230) — GEOGRAPHIC SECTION

Web: www.cshco.com
SIC: 8721 Certified public accountant
PA: Clark, Schaefer, Hackett & Co.
10100 Innovation Dr # 400
Miamisburg OH 45342
937 226-0070

(G-13230)
CLARK CNTY BD DVLPMNTAL DSBLTI
110 W Leffel Ln (45506-3522)
PHONE.................................937 328-5200
Mary Brandstetter, *Dir*
EMP: 49
SALES (corp-wide): 21.21MM **Privately Held**
Web: www.clarkdd.org
SIC: 8361 Retarded home
PA: Clark County Board Of Developmental Disabilities
2527 Kenton St
Springfield OH 45505
937 328-2675

(G-13231)
CLARK CNTY BD DVLPMNTAL DSBLTI
Also Called: Clark County Mrdd Trnsp
50 W Leffel Ln (45506-3520)
PHONE.................................937 328-5240
Elmer M Beard, *Dir*
EMP: 78
SQ FT: 1,270
SALES (corp-wide): 21.21MM **Privately Held**
Web: www.clarkdd.org
SIC: 8322 Social service center
PA: Clark County Board Of Developmental Disabilities
2527 Kenton St
Springfield OH 45505
937 328-2675

(G-13232)
CLARK COUNTY BOARD OF DEVELOPM (PA)
Also Called: Town & Country School
2527 Kenton St (45505-3352)
PHONE.................................937 328-2675
Jennifer Rousculp-miller, *Superintnt*
Robert Bender, *
Ravi Shankar, *
EMP: 28 EST: 1952
SQ FT: 15,000
SALES (est): 21.21MM
SALES (corp-wide): 21.21MM **Privately Held**
Web: www.clarkdd.org
SIC: 8322 Rehabilitation services

(G-13233)
CLARK COUNTY COMBINED HLTH DST (PA)
529 E Home Rd (45503-2710)
PHONE.................................937 390-5600
EMP: 62 EST: 1920
SALES (est): 4.19MM **Privately Held**
Web: www.ccchd.com
SIC: 8621 Health association

(G-13234)
CLARK MEMORIAL HOME ASSN
106 Kewbury Rd (45504-1199)
PHONE.................................937 399-4262
Sylvia Rosenlieb, *Dir*
EMP: 27 EST: 1899
SALES (est): 641.81K **Privately Held**
Web: www.clarkmemorialhome.com
SIC: 8361 Aged home

(G-13235)
CLARK STATE COMMUNITY COLLEGE
Also Called: CLARK STATE COMMUNITY COLLEGE
300 S Fountain Ave (45506)
P.O. Box 570 (45501-0570)
PHONE.................................937 328-3841
EMP: 30
SALES (corp-wide): 12.28MM **Privately Held**
Web: www.clarkstate.edu
SIC: 7389 8699 Convention and show services; Reading rooms and other cultural organizations
PA: Clark State College
570 E Leffel Ln
Springfield OH 45505
937 325-0691

(G-13236)
COILPLUS INC
Coilplus Berwick
4801 Gateway Blvd (45502-8866)
PHONE.................................614 866-1338
R Terry Harrold, *Div Pres*
EMP: 51
Web: www.coilplus.com
SIC: 5051 Steel
HQ: Coilplus, Inc.
6250 N River Rd Ste 6050
Rosemont IL 60018

(G-13237)
COILPLUS INC
Coilplus Ohio
4801 Gateway Blvd (45502-8866)
PHONE.................................937 322-4455
Pat Weeks, *Div Pres*
EMP: 42
Web: www.coilplus.com
SIC: 5051 Steel
HQ: Coilplus, Inc.
6250 N River Rd Ste 6050
Rosemont IL 60018

(G-13238)
COMMUNITY MERCY HEALTH SYSTEM (HQ)
Also Called: Mercy Hlth Fndtion Springfield
100 Medical Center Dr (45504-2687)
PHONE.................................937 523-5500
EMP: 75 EST: 2004
SALES (est): 651.43MM
SALES (corp-wide): 6.92B **Privately Held**
Web: www.mercy.com
SIC: 8062 General medical and surgical hospitals
PA: Bon Secours Mercy Health, Inc.
1701 Mercy Health Pl
Cincinnati OH 45237
513 956-3729

(G-13239)
COMMUNITY MERCY HLTH PARTNERS (DH)
Also Called: MERCY HEALTH FOUNDATION, SPRIN
100 Medical Center Dr (45504-2687)
PHONE.................................937 523-6670
Paul Hiltz, *CEO*
John Dempsey, *VP*
Marianne Potina, *VP*
Sherry Nelson, *VP*
Gary A Hagens, *COO*
EMP: 192 EST: 1969
SALES (est): 376.16MM
SALES (corp-wide): 6.92B **Privately Held**
Web: www.mercy.com
SIC: 8062 General medical and surgical hospitals
HQ: Community Mercy Health System
100 Medical Center Dr
Springfield OH 45504

(G-13240)
COMPUNET CLINICAL LABS LLC
2100 Emmanuel Way (45502-7218)
PHONE.................................937 342-0015
Melissa Williams, *Brnch Mgr*
EMP: 48
SALES (corp-wide): 2.41MM **Privately Held**
Web: www.compunetlab.com
SIC: 8071 Medical laboratories
HQ: Compunet Clinical Laboratories, Llc
2308 Sandridge Dr
Moraine OH 45439
937 296-0844

(G-13241)
CONTINENTAL HOME HEALTH CARE
2100 E High St Ste 112 (45505-1388)
PHONE.................................937 323-4499
EMP: 50
Web: www.continentalhhc.net
SIC: 8082 Home health care services
PA: Continental Home Health Care Inc
5898 Cleveland Ave # 100
Columbus OH 43231

(G-13242)
CORROTEC INC
1125 W North St (45504-2713)
PHONE.................................937 325-3585
David A Stratton, *CEO*
Aristides G Gianakopoulos, *
John C Stratton, *
Walter A Wildman, *
EMP: 37 EST: 1981
SQ FT: 28,500
SALES (est): 12.96MM **Privately Held**
Web: www.corrotec.com
SIC: 3559 7699 3479 3625 Electroplating machinery and equipment; Tank repair; Coating of metals with plastic or resins; Electric controls and control accessories, industrial

(G-13243)
COUNTY OF CLARK
Also Called: Environmental Health Dept
529 E Home Rd (45503-2710)
PHONE.................................937 390-5600
Charles Patterson, *Commsnr*
EMP: 28
SALES (corp-wide): 126.96MM **Privately Held**
Web: www.clarkcountyohio.gov
SIC: 8099 Health screening service
PA: County Of Clark
50 E Columbia St Fl 5
Springfield OH 45502
937 521-2005

(G-13244)
COVENANT CARE OHIO INC
Also Called: Villa Springfield
701 Villa Rd (45503-1330)
PHONE.................................937 399-5551
Rhonda Nissley, *Brnch Mgr*
EMP: 90
Web: www.villaspringfield.com
SIC: 8051 Convalescent home with continuous nursing care
HQ: Covenant Care Ohio, Inc.
120 Vantis Dr Ste 200
Aliso Viejo CA 92656
949 349-1200

(G-13245)
CREFIII WRMAUG SPRNGFELD LSSEE
Also Called: Courtyard Springfield Downtown
100 S Fountain Ave (45502-1208)
PHONE.................................937 322-3600
Becky Krieger, *Genl Mgr*
Craig Nussbaum, *
EMP: 31 EST: 2015
SALES (est): 971.87K **Privately Held**
SIC: 5812 7011 American restaurant; Resort hotel

(G-13246)
DAYTON CHILDRENS HOSPITAL
Also Called: Ohio Pediatric Care Alliance
1644 N Limestone St (45503-2652)
PHONE.................................937 398-5464
Deborah A Feldman, *Pr*
EMP: 79
SALES (corp-wide): 639.25MM **Privately Held**
Web: www.childrensdayton.org
SIC: 8011 Pediatrician
PA: Dayton Children's Hospital
1 Childrens Plz
Dayton OH 45404
937 641-3000

(G-13247)
DIXIE DISTRIBUTING COMPANY
200 W High St (45506-1630)
P.O. Box 141130 (43214-6130)
PHONE.................................937 322-0033
FAX: 859 322-0034
▲ EMP: 33 EST: 1939
SALES (est): 5.39MM **Privately Held**
SIC: 5013 Motorcycle parts

(G-13248)
DOLE FRESH VEGETABLES INC
Also Called: Dole
600 Benjamin Dr (45502-8860)
PHONE.................................937 525-4300
Lenny Pelifian, *Brnch Mgr*
EMP: 190
SALES (corp-wide): 3.64B **Privately Held**
SIC: 5148 2099 Fruits, fresh; Food preparations, nec
HQ: Dole Fresh Vegetables, Inc.
2959 Salinas Hwy
Monterey CA 93940

(G-13249)
E HOME BEHAVIORAL LLC
Also Called: Ethan Crossing Recovery Center
2317 E Home Rd (45503-2520)
PHONE.................................513 530-1600
Richard Odenthal, *Prin*
Sandra Smiddy, *
EMP: 50 EST: 2019
SALES (est): 2.56MM **Privately Held**
Web: www.ethancrossingspringfield.com
SIC: 8093 Mental health clinic, outpatient

(G-13250)
EAGLEWOOD CARE CENTER
2000 Villa Rd (45503-1761)
PHONE.................................937 399-7195
Babur Khaan, *Admn*
EMP: 160 EST: 1986
SQ FT: 29,000
SALES (est): 9.01MM **Privately Held**
SIC: 8051 6513 Convalescent home with continuous nursing care; Apartment building operators

(G-13251)
FAMILY PRCTICE ASSOC SPRNGFELD

GEOGRAPHIC SECTION
Springfield - Clark County (G-13273)

2701 Moorefield Rd (45502-8207)
PHONE..................937 399-6650
Sally Abbott Md, *Pt*
Richard Gordon Md, *Pt*
EMP: 28 EST: 1970
SALES (est): 2.09MM **Privately Held**
Web:
www.familypracticeassociatesmd.com
SIC: 8011 General and family practice, physician/surgeon

(G-13252)
FIRST DVRSITY STFFING GROUP IN
560 E High St (45505-1010)
PHONE..................937 323-4114
George Ten, *Pr*
EMP: 47 EST: 2008
SQ FT: 6,000
SALES (est): 4.77MM **Privately Held**
Web: www.firstdiversity.com
SIC: 7361 Executive placement

(G-13253)
GOOD SHEPHERD VILLAGE LLC
Also Called: Good Shepard Village
422 N Burnett Rd (45503-4821)
PHONE..................937 322-1911
EMP: 76 EST: 1965
SALES (est): 10.54MM **Privately Held**
Web: www.goodshepherdvillage.org
SIC: 8051 Convalescent home with continuous nursing care

(G-13254)
HOMETOWN URGENT CARE
Also Called: HOMETOWN URGENT CARE
1200 Vester Ave (45503-1304)
PHONE..................937 342-9520
Toni Rogers, *Brnch Mgr*
EMP: 55
SALES (corp-wide): 23.51MM **Privately Held**
Web: www.hometownurgentcare.com
SIC: 8062 8049 8011 General medical and surgical hospitals; Occupational therapist; Medical centers
PA: Urgent Care Specialists Llc
2400 Corp Exch Dr Ste 102
Columbus OH 43231
614 505-7633

(G-13255)
HUNTINGTON NATIONAL BANK
5 W North St (45504-2544)
PHONE..................937 390-1779
Adora Mertens, *Mgr*
EMP: 36
SALES (corp-wide): 10.84B **Publicly Held**
Web: www.huntington.com
SIC: 6029 6021 Commercial banks, nec; National commercial banks
HQ: The Huntington National Bank
41 S High St
Columbus OH 43215
614 480-4293

(G-13256)
IH CREDIT UNION INC (PA)
5000 Urbana Rd (45502-9539)
PHONE..................937 390-1800
Robb White, *Pr*
James E Kitchen, *Bd of Dir*
EMP: 43 EST: 1934
SALES (est): 15.79MM
SALES (corp-wide): 15.79MM **Privately Held**
Web: www.ihcreditunion.com
SIC: 6061 Federal credit unions

(G-13257)
IMPERIAL EXPRESS INC
202 N Limestone St Ste 300 (45503-4246)
P.O. Box 1767 (45501-1767)
PHONE..................937 399-9400
Charles Crabill, *Pr*
Dale Briggs, *
James Valentine, *
EMP: 44 EST: 1993
SQ FT: 4,000
SALES (est): 4.72MM **Privately Held**
Web: www.imperialexpress.net
SIC: 4213 Trucking, except local

(G-13258)
INDIANA HOSPITALITY GROUP
Also Called: Holiday Inn Ex Stes Sprngfeld
204 Raydo Cir (45506-3557)
PHONE..................937 505-1670
EMP: 78
SALES (corp-wide): 635.77K **Privately Held**
Web: www.hiexpress.com
SIC: 7011 Hotels and motels
PA: Indiana Hospitality Group
51038 Shamrock Hills Ct
Granger IN 46530
574 931-2860

(G-13259)
INSIDE OUT (PA)
Also Called: INSIDE OUT CHILD CARE
501 S Wittenberg Ave (45506-2101)
PHONE..................937 525-7880
William R Stout, *Pr*
EMP: 40 EST: 1998
SQ FT: 60,000
SALES (est): 2.46MM
SALES (corp-wide): 2.46MM **Privately Held**
Web: www.ioyouth.org
SIC: 8322 Social service center

(G-13260)
INTERNATIONAL TRUCK & ENG CORP
6125 Urbana Rd (45502-9279)
PHONE..................937 390-4045
Bob Baker, *Prin*
Mister Daniel Ustian, *Ch Bd*
Robert A Boardman, *
John R Horne, *
Robert C Lannert, *
EMP: 1500 EST: 1999
SALES (est): 48.61MM **Privately Held**
Web: www.navistar.com
SIC: 4212 Local trucking, without storage

(G-13261)
JKL DEVELOPMENT COMPANY (PA)
Also Called: Splish Splash Auto Bath
2101 E Home Rd (45503-2516)
PHONE..................937 390-0358
Jack Sayers, *Pr*
EMP: 30 EST: 1988
SALES (est): 2.19MM **Privately Held**
SIC: 7542 Carwash, automatic

(G-13262)
KAPP CONSTRUCTION INC
Also Called: Kapp Construction
329 Mount Vernon Ave (45503-4143)
P.O. Box 629 (45501-0629)
PHONE..................937 324-0134
Randy Kapp, *Pr*
EMP: 45 EST: 1985
SALES (est): 14.41MM **Privately Held**
Web: www.kappconstruction.com

SIC: 1542 1541 Commercial and office building, new construction; Industrial buildings and warehouses

(G-13263)
LOBBY SHOPPES INC
Also Called: Lobby Shoppes Inc-Springfield
200 N Murray St (45503-4297)
P.O. Box 1200 (45501-1200)
PHONE..................937 324-0002
Michael H Chakeres, *Pr*
EMP: 222 EST: 1946
SQ FT: 15,000
SALES (est): 4.43MM **Privately Held**
Web: www.lobbyshoppes.com
SIC: 5812 5145 Concessionaire; Confectionery

(G-13264)
LOWES HOME CENTERS LLC
Also Called: Lowe's
1601 N Bechtle Ave (45504-1576)
PHONE..................937 327-6000
Mark Sprague, *Mgr*
EMP: 153
SALES (corp-wide): 86.38B **Publicly Held**
Web: www.lowes.com
SIC: 5211 5031 5722 5064 Home centers; Building materials, exterior; Household appliance stores; Electrical appliances, television and radio
HQ: Lowe's Home Centers, Llc
1000 Lowes Blvd
Mooresville NC 28117
336 658-4000

(G-13265)
MCGREGOR MTAL LEFFEL WORKS LLC
900 W Leffel Ln (45506-3538)
P.O. Box 1103 (45501-1103)
PHONE..................937 325-5561
Daniel Mcgregor, *Pr*
Dane A Belden, *
Hugh Barnett, *
▲ EMP: 60 EST: 1991
SQ FT: 44,000
SALES (est): 12.16MM
SALES (corp-wide): 105.36MM **Privately Held**
Web: www.rosecitymfg.com
SIC: 7692 Automotive welding
PA: Mcgregor Metal Yellow Springs Works Llc
2100 S Yellow Springs St
Springfield OH 45506
937 325-5561

(G-13266)
MCKINLEY HALL INC
2624 Lexington Ave (45505)
PHONE..................937 328-5300
Wendy Doolittle, *CEO*
EMP: 50 EST: 1986
SQ FT: 31,770
SALES (est): 4.54MM **Privately Held**
Web: www.mckinleyhall.org
SIC: 8069 8093 8051 Alcoholism rehabilitation hospital; Specialty outpatient clinics, nec; Skilled nursing care facilities

(G-13267)
MED-TRANS INC (PA)
714 W Columbia St (45504-2734)
P.O. Box 1048 (45501-1048)
PHONE..................937 325-4926
TOLL FREE: 800
Luanne George, *Pr*
William George, *
Edward G Bailey, *
EMP: 100 EST: 1988

SQ FT: 7,600
SALES (est): 5.06MM
SALES (corp-wide): 5.06MM **Privately Held**
Web: www.med-trans.com
SIC: 4119 Ambulance service

(G-13268)
MENTAL HEALTH SERVICE
474 N Yellow Springs St (45504-2463)
PHONE..................937 399-9500
Curt Gillespie, *CEO*
EMP: 48 EST: 2014
SALES (est): 2.15MM **Privately Held**
Web: www.mhscc.org
SIC: 8093 Mental health clinic, outpatient

(G-13269)
MENTAL HLTH SVCS FOR CLARK CNT (PA)
474 N Yellow Springs St (45504-2463)
PHONE..................937 399-9500
Kelly Rigger, *CEO*
Marybeth Taylor, *CFO*
EMP: 150 EST: 1969
SQ FT: 30,000
SALES (est): 13.56MM
SALES (corp-wide): 13.56MM **Privately Held**
Web: www.mhscc.org
SIC: 8063 Mental hospital, except for the mentally retarded

(G-13270)
MERCY HEALTH FOUNDATION
100 W Mccreight Ave Ste 200 (45504-1885)
PHONE..................937 523-6670
Kristy Kohl Mccready, *Pr*
EMP: 365 EST: 2018
SALES (est): 236.73K
SALES (corp-wide): 6.92B **Privately Held**
SIC: 6732 Charitable trust management
HQ: Community Mercy Health Partners
100 Medical Center Dr
Springfield OH 45504

(G-13271)
MERCY HEALTH YOUNGSTOWN LLC
362 S Burnett Rd (45505-2604)
PHONE..................440 960-4389
EMP: 100
SALES (corp-wide): 6.92B **Privately Held**
Web: www.mercy.com
SIC: 8062 8071 Hospital, affiliated with AMA residency; Ultrasound laboratory
HQ: Mercy Health Youngstown Llc
1044 Belmont Ave
Youngstown OH 44504

(G-13272)
MERCY HLTH - SPRNGFLD CNCER C
148 W North St (45504-2547)
PHONE..................937 323-5001
Paul Hiltz, *CEO*
Chris Howe, *COO*
EMP: 1023 EST: 2011
SALES (est): 7.98MM
SALES (corp-wide): 6.92B **Privately Held**
Web: www.mercy.com
SIC: 8062 General medical and surgical hospitals
HQ: Community Mercy Health Partners
100 Medical Center Dr
Springfield OH 45504

(G-13273)
MIAMI VALLEY INTL TRCKS INC
121 S Spring St (45502-1247)

Springfield - Clark County (G-13274)

PHONE..................937 324-5526
EMP: 34
SALES (corp-wide): 23.45MM Privately Held
Web: www.mvigroup.net
SIC: 5511 7513 5531 New and used car dealers; Truck rental and leasing, no drivers; Truck equipment and parts
PA: Miami Valley International Trucks, Inc.
7655 Poe Ave
Dayton OH 45414
937 898-3660

(G-13274)
MIAMI VLY CHILD DEV CTRS INC
Also Called: Clark County Office
1450 S Yellow Springs St (45506-2545)
PHONE..................937 325-2559
Diane Johnson, Mgr
EMP: 38
SALES (corp-wide): 43.26MM Privately Held
Web: www.mvcdc.org
SIC: 8351 Head Start center, except in conjunction with school
PA: Miami Valley Child Development Centers, Inc.
215 Horace St
Dayton OH 45402
937 226-5664

(G-13275)
MOYNO INC
Also Called: Nov Process & Flow Tech
1895 W Jefferson St (45506-1115)
P.O. Box 1343 (45401-1343)
PHONE..................937 327-3111
▲ EMP: 200
Web: www.moyno.com
SIC: 7699 Industrial equipment services

(G-13276)
NEW METHOD PACKAGING LLC
1805 Commerce Rd (45504-2019)
PHONE..................937 324-3838
Neil Miller, Managing Member
Kevin Miller, *
EMP: 44 EST: 1982
SQ FT: 79,000
SALES (est): 9.59MM Privately Held
Web: www.newmethodpackaging.com
SIC: 5199 Packaging materials

(G-13277)
NIGHTINGALE MONTESSORI INC
Also Called: NIGHTINGALE MONTESSORI SCHOOL
2525 N Limestone St (45503-1195)
PHONE..................937 324-0336
Nancy Schwab, Admn
Admiral Nancy Schwab, Prin
Sheila Brown, Sec
Maria Taylor, Pr
Guyia Wilson, Dir
EMP: 38 EST: 1978
SALES (est): 2.36MM Privately Held
Web: www.nightingalemontessori.org
SIC: 8211 8351 Private elementary and secondary schools; Montessori child development center

(G-13278)
OESTERLEN - SVCS FOR YOUTH INC
Also Called: SOCIAL MINISTRY ORGANIZATION
1918 Mechanicsburg Rd (45503-3147)
PHONE..................937 399-6101
Donald Warner, Ex Dir
EMP: 95 EST: 1903
SQ FT: 10,204
SALES (est): 5.85MM Privately Held

Web: www.oesterlen.org
SIC: 8211 8661 8361 Private special education school; Community Church; Residential care

(G-13279)
OHIO VALLEY MEDICAL CENTER LLC
100 E Main St (45502-1308)
PHONE..................937 521-3900
Steve Eisentrager, Pr
James Cromwell, *
Ajay Mangal, *
Ronny Shumaker, *
EMP: 99 EST: 2009
SALES (est): 49.62MM Privately Held
Web: www.ovsurgical.com
SIC: 8062 General medical and surgical hospitals

(G-13280)
OPPORTNTIES FOR INDVDUAL CHNGE
Also Called: OIC
920 W Main St (45504-2754)
PHONE..................937 323-6461
Michael Calabrese, Ex Dir
William Ray Board, Ch
EMP: 44 EST: 1971
SALES (est): 4.34MM Privately Held
Web: www.oicofclarkco.org
SIC: 8331 Manpower training

(G-13281)
PENTAFLEX INC
4981 Gateway Blvd (45502-8867)
PHONE..................937 325-5551
Dave Arndt, Pr
Julie Mcgregor, Treas
Walter Wildman, *
◆ EMP: 110 EST: 1972
SQ FT: 146,000
SALES (est): 21.51MM Privately Held
Web: www.pentaflex.com
SIC: 3469 7692 Stamping metal for the trade; Welding repair

(G-13282)
PHYSICANS SRGONS FOR WOMEN INC
1821 E High St (45505-1225)
PHONE..................937 323-7340
David R Billing Md, Pt
EMP: 32 EST: 1975
SQ FT: 6,000
SALES (est): 2.06MM Privately Held
Web: www.physurg.net
SIC: 8011 Gynecologist

(G-13283)
R&M MATERIALS HANDLING INC
Also Called: R & M
4400 Gateway Blvd (45502-9337)
PHONE..................937 328-5100
Jim Vandegrift, Pr
Guy Shumaker, *
Steve Mayes, *
Todd Robenson, *
◆ EMP: 41 EST: 1920
SALES (est): 17.02MM Privately Held
Web: www.rmhoist.com
SIC: 5084 Materials handling machinery
HQ: Kci Holding Usa Inc.
4401 Gateway Blvd
Springfield OH 45502

(G-13284)
REMINGTON STEEL INC
1120 S Burnett Rd (45505-3408)
P.O. Box 1491 (45501-1491)

PHONE..................937 322-2414
▲ EMP: 59
SIC: 5051 3714 Steel; Clutches, motor vehicle

(G-13285)
RICHWOOD BANKING COMPANY
2454 N Limestone St (45503-1110)
PHONE..................937 390-0470
EMP: 30
Web: www.richwoodbank.com
SIC: 6022 State trust companies accepting deposits, commercial
HQ: The Richwood Banking Company
28 N Franklin St
Richwood OH 43344
740 943-2317

(G-13286)
ROBINSON INSULATION CO INC
Also Called: Ohio Gypsum Supply
4715 Urbana Rd (45502-9503)
PHONE..................937 323-9599
Garth S Robinson, Pr
Ryan J Robinson, *
Jennifer Robinson, *
EMP: 35 EST: 1975
SQ FT: 8,000
SALES (est): 2.56MM Privately Held
Web: www.robinsoninsulation.com
SIC: 1742 5032 Insulation, buildings; Drywall materials

(G-13287)
ROGER STORER & SON INC
315 S Center St Ste 1 (45506-1662)
P.O. Box 869 (45501-0869)
PHONE..................937 325-9873
Roger D Storer, Pr
Jeff G Storer, VP
Carol Storer, Sec
EMP: 27 EST: 1967
SQ FT: 14,000
SALES (est): 561.64K Privately Held
Web: www.rogerstorer-son.com
SIC: 1711 Plumbing contractors

(G-13288)
ROLLINS MOVING AND STORAGE INC
1050 Wheel St (45503-3545)
PHONE..................937 525-4013
Clyde Depuy, Brnch Mgr
EMP: 123
SALES (corp-wide): 11.14MM Privately Held
Web: www.rollinsmoving.com
SIC: 4214 4213 Household goods moving and storage, local; Household goods transport
PA: Rollins Moving And Storage, Inc.
1900 E Leffel Ln
Springfield OH 45505
937 325-2484

(G-13289)
SDX HOME CARE OPERATIONS LLC
Also Called: Comfort Keepers
101 N Fountain Ave (45502-1118)
PHONE..................937 322-6288
EMP: 99 EST: 2010
SALES (est): 10.81MM Privately Held
Web: www.comfortkeepers.com
SIC: 8082 Home health care services

(G-13290)
SECURITY NATIONAL BANK & TR CO
2730 E Main St (45503-5117)
PHONE..................937 325-0351
Jenny Reed, Brnch Mgr
EMP: 44

SALES (corp-wide): 564.3MM Publicly Held
Web: www.parknationalbank.com
SIC: 6021 National commercial banks
HQ: The Security National Bank And Trust Co
50 N 3rd St
Newark OH 43055
740 426-6384

(G-13291)
SELF RELIANCE INC
3674 E National Rd Ste 3 (45505-1545)
PHONE..................937 525-0809
William Smith, Pr
Jay Crawford, *
EMP: 32 EST: 1996
SALES (est): 730.77K Privately Held
Web: www.self-relianceinc.com
SIC: 8322 Social services for the handicapped

(G-13292)
SPRINGFELD CTR FOR FMLY MDCINE
3250 Middle Urbana Rd (45502-9285)
PHONE..................937 399-7777
Mark S Roberto, Owner
EMP: 32 EST: 1987
SALES (est): 2.33MM Privately Held
SIC: 8011 General and family practice, physician/surgeon

(G-13293)
SPRINGFIELD HALTHCARE GROUP INC
Also Called: Springfield Nursing And Rehabilitation Center
404 E Mccreight Ave (45503-3653)
PHONE..................937 399-8311
George S Repchick, Pr
William I Weisberg, *
EMP: 185 EST: 2009
SALES (est): 6.14MM
SALES (corp-wide): 655.44MM Privately Held
Web: www.saberhealth.com
SIC: 8051 Skilled nursing care facilities
PA: Saber Healthcare Group, L.L.C.
23700 Commerce Park
Beachwood OH 44122
216 292-5706

(G-13294)
SPRINGFIELD BUSINESS EQP CO (PA)
Also Called: Business Equipment Co
3783 W National Rd (45504-3516)
PHONE..................937 322-3828
TOLL FREE: 800
J D Lindeman, Pr
Lisa Lindeman, *
EMP: 31 EST: 1970
SALES (est): 10.38MM
SALES (corp-wide): 10.38MM Privately Held
Web: www.becosolutions.com
SIC: 5044 5021 Office equipment; Office furniture, nec

(G-13295)
SPRINGFIELD MASONIC COMMUNITY
2655 W National Rd (45504-3617)
PHONE..................937 325-1531
Tom J Stofac, Admn
EMP: 43 EST: 2015
SALES (est): 10.46MM Privately Held
Web: www.omcoh.org

GEOGRAPHIC SECTION

Steubenville - Jefferson County (G-13318)

SIC: 8399 Community development groups

(G-13296)
STORRIE DIALYSIS LLC
Also Called: Midwest Springfield Dialysis
2200 N Limestone St Ste 104 (45503-2665)
PHONE.................................937 390-3125
EMP: 50
SIC: 8092 Kidney dialysis centers
HQ: Storrie Dialysis, Llc
2200 N Limestone St # 104
Springfield OH 45503

(G-13297)
SURGICAL ASSOC SPRINGFIELD INC
30 Warder St Ste 220 (45504-2581)
PHONE.................................937 521-1111
Marios P Panayides Md, *CEO*
Peter W Wagner Md, *VP*
Joseph G Demeter Md, *Sec*
Richard Medelman Md, *Treas*
Jennifer Daniels, *Pt*
EMP: 32 **EST:** 1965
SALES (est): 1.91MM **Privately Held**
Web: www.sassurgeryandvein.com
SIC: 8011 Surgeon

(G-13298)
TAC INDUSTRIES INC
Also Called: Town & Country Adult Services
2160 Old Selma Rd (45505-4600)
PHONE.................................937 328-5200
EMP: 60
SALES (corp-wide): 10.48MM **Privately Held**
Web: www.tacind.com
SIC: 8331 Job training and related services
PA: Tac Industries, Inc.
2160 Old Selma Rd
Springfield OH 45505
937 328-5200

(G-13299)
TAC INDUSTRIES INC (PA)
2160 Old Selma Rd (45505-4600)
PHONE.................................937 328-5200
James Zahora, *CEO*
Michael Ahern, *
EMP: 280 **EST:** 1960
SQ FT: 52,800
SALES (est): 10.48MM
SALES (corp-wide): 10.48MM **Privately Held**
Web: www.tacind.com
SIC: 8741 2399 8331 Management services; Nets, launderers and dyers; Work experience center

(G-13300)
THE COMMUNITY HOSPITAL OF SPRINGFIELD AND CLARK COUNTY
Also Called: Community Hosp Schl Nursing
100 Medical Center Dr (45504-2687)
PHONE.................................937 325-0531
EMP: 1300
SIC: 8062 8051 General medical and surgical hospitals; Skilled nursing care facilities

(G-13301)
THE COMMUNITY MERCY FOUNDATION
1 S Limestone St Ste 700 (45502-1249)
P.O. Box 688 (45501-0688)
PHONE.................................937 328-7000
EMP: 2270
SIC: 8641 Civic and social associations

(G-13302)
TOPRE AMERICA CORPORATION
1100 Reaper Ave (45503-3588)
PHONE.................................256 339-8407
EMP: 117
Web: www.topre.co.jp
SIC: 8742 Management consulting services
HQ: Topre America Corporation
1580 County Rd Ste 222
Cullman AL 35057
256 735-2600

(G-13303)
TRI-STATE FOREST LOGISTICS LLC
Also Called: Rhl Logistics
2105 Sheridan Ave (45505-2419)
PHONE.................................937 323-6325
Thomas Latham, *CEO*
Robert Latham, *
Tom Berghouse, *
EMP: 50 **EST:** 2019
SALES (est): 2.22MM **Privately Held**
SIC: 4212 Local trucking, without storage

(G-13304)
TRI-STATE FOREST PRODUCTS INC (PA)
2105 Sheridan Ave (45505-2419)
PHONE.................................937 323-6325
▲ **EMP:** 44 **EST:** 1991
SQ FT: 68,000
SALES (est): 94.38MM **Privately Held**
Web: www.tsfpi.com
SIC: 5031 Lumber: rough, dressed, and finished

(G-13305)
TRIEC ELECTRICAL SERVICES INC
1630 Progress Rd (45505-4467)
PHONE.................................937 323-3721
Kenneth Stagner, *Pr*
Scott Yeazell, *
Michael Cain, *
Mike Cain, *
EMP: 35 **EST:** 1952
SQ FT: 10,500
SALES (est): 5.33MM **Privately Held**
Web: www.triec.com
SIC: 1731 General electrical contractor

(G-13306)
U S XPRESS INC
825 W Leffel Ln (45506-3535)
PHONE.................................937 328-4100
Richard Schaefer, *Brnch Mgr*
EMP: 583
Web: www.usxpress.com
SIC: 4213 Contract haulers
HQ: U. S. Xpress, Inc.
4080 Jenkins Rd
Chattanooga TN 37421
866 266-7270

(G-13307)
UNTD ELDERLY CLARK C SPRNGFELD (PA)
Also Called: UNITED SENIOR SERVICES
125 W Main St (45502-1311)
PHONE.................................937 323-4948
Maureen Fagans, *Ex Dir*
Randy Yontz, *
Joyce Ware, *
EMP: 99 **EST:** 1968
SQ FT: 24,000
SALES (est): 5.55MM
SALES (corp-wide): 5.55MM **Privately Held**
Web: www.ussohio.org
SIC: 8322 Senior citizens' center or association

(G-13308)
URGENT CARE SPECIALISTS LLC
1301 W 1st St (45504-1920)
PHONE.................................937 322-6222
EMP: 55
SALES (corp-wide): 23.51MM **Privately Held**
Web: www.wellnow.com
SIC: 8011 Freestanding emergency medical center
PA: Urgent Care Specialists Llc
2400 Corp Exch Dr Ste 102
Columbus OH 43231
614 505-7633

(G-13309)
WALLICK CONSTRUCTION CO
Also Called: Eaglewood Villa
3001 Middle Urbana Rd (45502-9284)
PHONE.................................937 399-7009
Kay Dotson, *Mgr*
EMP: 83
SALES (corp-wide): 16.34MM **Privately Held**
Web: www.wallick.com
SIC: 6513 8361 Retirement hotel operation; Residential care
PA: Wallick Construction Co.
6880 Tussing Rd
Reynoldsburg OH 43068
614 863-4640

(G-13310)
WALMART INC
Also Called: Walmart
2100 N Bechtle Ave (45504-1575)
PHONE.................................937 399-0370
Heather Price, *Mgr*
EMP: 200
SQ FT: 206,588
SALES (corp-wide): 648.13B **Publicly Held**
Web: corporate.walmart.com
SIC: 5311 5411 7231 Department stores, discount; Supermarkets, greater than 100,000 square feet (hypermarket); Manicurist, pedicurist
PA: Walmart Inc.
702 Sw 8th St
Bentonville AR 72716
479 273-4000

(G-13311)
WELCOME HOSPITALITY CORP
Also Called: Red Roof Inn
155 W Leffel Ln (45506-3521)
PHONE.................................937 325-5356
Ajay Patel, *CEO*
Dipak Patel, *Pr*
EMP: 43 **EST:** 1998
SALES (est): 965.43K **Privately Held**
Web: www.redroof.com
SIC: 7011 Hotels and motels

(G-13312)
WESTFIELD STEEL INC
Also Called: Remington Steel
1120 S Burnett Rd (45505-3408)
PHONE.................................937 322-2414
Frank Bair, *Brnch Mgr*
EMP: 60
SALES (corp-wide): 86.07MM **Privately Held**
Web: www.westfieldsteel.com
SIC: 5051 3714 Steel; Clutches, motor vehicle
PA: Westfield Steel Inc
530 W State Road 32
Westfield IN 46074
317 896-5587

(G-13313)
WOODROW MANUFACTURING CO
4300 River Rd (45502-7517)
P.O. Box 1567 (45501-1567)
PHONE.................................937 399-9333
John K Woodrow, *Pr*
Patrick T Mcatee, *VP*
EMP: 28 **EST:** 1964
SQ FT: 26,000
SALES (est): 1.13MM **Privately Held**
Web: www.woodrowcorp.com
SIC: 7336 3479 2752 2396 Silk screen design; Etching on metals; Commercial printing, lithographic; Automotive and apparel trimmings

(G-13314)
WOODRUFF ENTERPRISES INC
4951 Gateway Blvd (45502-8867)
PHONE.................................937 399-9300
Todd Woodruff, *Pr*
EMP: 43 **EST:** 2001
SALES (est): 7.45MM **Privately Held**
Web: www.woodruffenterprises.com
SIC: 4222 4789 Refrigerated warehousing and storage; Pipeline terminal facilities, independently operated

Steubenville
Jefferson County

(G-13315)
ADDUS HEALTHCARE INC
1406 Cadiz Rd (43953-9058)
PHONE.................................630 296-3400
Diane Kumarich, *Brnch Mgr*
EMP: 85
Web: www.addus.com
SIC: 8082 Home health care services
HQ: Addus Healthcare, Inc.
2300 Warrenville Rd
Downers Grove IL 60515
630 296-3400

(G-13316)
ASSOCIATED HOME HEALTH INC
Also Called: Carter Heath Care
2199 Ste B (43952)
PHONE.................................740 264-6311
Kelly Brylie, *Brnch Mgr*
EMP: 33
Web: www.carterhealthcare.com
SIC: 8082 Visiting nurse service
PA: Associated Home Health Inc
3300 Ne 58th St
Fort Lauderdale FL 33308

(G-13317)
BARIUM HOLDINGS COMPANY INC
515 Kingsdale Rd (43952-4321)
PHONE.................................740 282-9776
Deborah A Venci, *Pr*
EMP: 30 **EST:** 2010
SALES (est): 1.19MM **Privately Held**
Web: www.bariumchemicals.com
SIC: 8742 Management consulting services

(G-13318)
CARRIAGE INN OF STEUBENVILLE
3102 Saint Charles Dr (43952-3556)
PHONE.................................740 264-7161
Brad Conto, *Admn*
EMP: 233
SALES (corp-wide): 10.05MM **Privately Held**
Web: www.carriageinnofsteubenville.com
SIC: 8051 Skilled nursing care facilities
PA: Carriage Inn Of Steubenville, Inc

Steubenville - Jefferson County (G-13319)

3015 Newmark Dr
Miamisburg OH 45342
740 264-7161

(G-13319)
CATHOLIC CHRTIES STHSTERN OHIO
Also Called: St John Central High School
422 Washington St # 1 (43952-2159)
PHONE.................................740 676-4932
Sheila Blackmore, *Prin*
EMP: 259
SALES (corp-wide): 25.04MM **Privately Held**
Web: www.diosteub.org
SIC: 8211 8322 Elementary and secondary schools; Individual and family services
PA: Catholic Charities Of Southeastern Ohio
422 Washington St Ste 1
Steubenville OH 43952
740 282-3631

(G-13320)
COLUMBIA GAS OF OHIO INC
Also Called: Columbia
300 Luray Dr (43953-3901)
P.O. Box 2160 (43953-0160)
PHONE.................................740 264-5577
Clair M Colburn Junior, *Brnch Mgr*
EMP: 90
SALES (corp-wide): 5.51B **Publicly Held**
Web: www.columbiagasohio.com
SIC: 4924 Natural gas distribution
HQ: Columbia Gas Of Ohio, Inc.
290 W Nationwide Blvd # 1
Columbus OH 43215
614 460-6000

(G-13321)
DLC TRANSPORT INC
320 N 5th St (43952-2016)
PHONE.................................740 282-1763
Donna Colalella, *Pr*
EMP: 40 **EST:** 1990
SQ FT: 43,000
SALES (est): 1.62MM **Privately Held**
SIC: 4213 Contract haulers

(G-13322)
DQR 4 TED
Also Called: DQR 4 TED
108 S Hollywood Blvd (43952-2421)
PHONE.................................740 264-4323
EMP: 29
SALES (corp-wide): 181.45K **Privately Held**
SIC: 7389 Personal service agents, brokers, and bureaus
PA: Dqr4ted, Llc
41 11th St
Wheeling WV 26003
740 623-2056

(G-13323)
FAMOUS DISTRIBUTION INC
Also Called: Johnson Contrls Authorized Dlr
934 Adams St (43952-2709)
PHONE.................................740 282-0951
EMP: 28
Web: www.famous-supply.com
SIC: 5075 5033 5031 Furnaces, heating: electric; Asphalt felts and coating; Kitchen cabinets
HQ: Famous Distribution Inc
2620 Ridgewood Rd
Akron OH 44313
330 762-9621

(G-13324)
FAYETTE PARTS SERVICE INC
Also Called: NAPA
1512 Sunset Blvd (43952-1303)
PHONE.................................740 282-4547
EMP: 31
SALES (corp-wide): 45.91MM **Privately Held**
Web: www.fayettepartsservice.com
SIC: 5013 Automotive supplies and parts
PA: Fayette Parts Service, Inc.
325 E Main St
Uniontown PA
724 785-2506

(G-13325)
FIRST CHICE AMER CMNTY FDRAL C
762 Canton Rd Ste 3 (43954-4149)
PHONE.................................800 427-4835
EMP: 27
SALES (corp-wide): 15.56MM **Privately Held**
Web: www.firstchoiceamericacu.org
SIC: 6061 Federal credit unions
PA: First Choice America Community Federal Credit Union
3501 Main St
Weirton WV 26062
304 748-8600

(G-13326)
FLEETPRIDE INC
620 South St (43952-2802)
PHONE.................................740 282-2711
Larry Remp, *Brnch Mgr*
EMP: 34
Web: www.fleetpride.com
SIC: 7538 5511 7692 Truck engine repair, except industrial; Trucks, tractors, and trailers: new and used; Welding repair
HQ: Fleetpride, Inc.
600 Las Colinas Blvd E # 400
Irving TX 75039
469 249-7500

(G-13327)
GOOD VENTURE ENTERPRISES LLC
Also Called: Holiday Inn
1235 University Blvd (43952-1792)
PHONE.................................740 282-0901
EMP: 34 **EST:** 1999
SALES (est): 459.73K **Privately Held**
Web: www.holidayinn.com
SIC: 7011 Hotels and motels

(G-13328)
GRAE-CON CONSTRUCTION INC (PA)
Also Called: Grae-Con Contructions
880 Kingsdale Rd (43952-4361)
P.O. Box 1778 (43952-7778)
PHONE.................................740 282-6830
Robert A Gribben Junior, *Pr*
Robert A Gribben Iii, *VP*
Shirley Gribben, *
John A Humpe Iii, *Ex VP*
EMP: 43 **EST:** 1987
SQ FT: 23,000
SALES (est): 25.46MM
SALES (corp-wide): 25.46MM **Privately Held**
Web: www.graecon.com
SIC: 1542 Commercial and office building, new construction

(G-13329)
HAMPTON INN
820 University Blvd (43952-1704)
PHONE.................................740 282-9800
Prem Patel, *Prin*
EMP: 29 **EST:** 2008
SALES (est): 507.35K **Privately Held**
Web: www.hilton.com
SIC: 7011 Hotels and motels

(G-13330)
HEADWINDS LP
1294 Bantam Ridge Rd (43953-4279)
PHONE.................................724 209-5543
Keith Ryals, *Pr*
Mike Koziara, *Treas*
Christopher Mcmahon, *Pt*
EMP: 35 **EST:** 2013
SALES (est): 1.89MM **Privately Held**
SIC: 8734 Testing laboratories

(G-13331)
HOFRICHTER BROTHERS INC
680 Lovers Ln (43953-3314)
PHONE.................................740 314-5669
Jeff S Pavkovich, *Brnch Mgr*
EMP: 35
SALES (corp-wide): 4.69MM **Privately Held**
SIC: 7336 Graphic arts and related design
PA: Hofrichter Brothers, Inc.
2388 La Mirada Dr
Vista CA 92081
760 727-9533

(G-13332)
JEFFERSON CNTY CMNTY ACTION CN (PA)
114 N 4th St (43952-2132)
PHONE.................................740 282-0971
Barbara West, *Ex Dir*
EMP: 126 **EST:** 1965
SALES (est): 4.77MM
SALES (corp-wide): 4.77MM **Privately Held**
Web: www.jeffersoncountyac.org
SIC: 8399 9111 Community action agency; County supervisors' and executives' office

(G-13333)
KATMAI GOVERNMENT SERVICES LLC
100 Welday Ave Ste D (43953-3779)
PHONE.................................740 314-5432
David R Stephens, *Brnch Mgr*
EMP: 270
SALES (corp-wide): 101.95MM **Privately Held**
Web: www.katmaicorp.com
SIC: 8744 Facilities support services
HQ: Katmai Government Services, Llc
11001 Omlley Cntre Dr Ste
Anchorage AK 99515

(G-13334)
LANCIA NURSING HOMES INC
Also Called: Lancia Villa Royal
1852 Sinclair Ave (43953-3328)
PHONE.................................740 264-7101
Joseph Lancia, *Pr*
Linda Lancia, *
EMP: 125 **EST:** 1950
SQ FT: 5,000
SALES (est): 3.7MM **Privately Held**
Web: www.lanciahealthcare.com
SIC: 8051 Convalescent home with continuous nursing care

(G-13335)
LAUREL HEALTH CARE COMPANY
Also Called: Laurels of Steubenville, The
500 Stanton Blvd (43952-3706)
PHONE.................................740 264-5042
Steve Welhorsky, *Brnch Mgr*
EMP: 100
Web: www.cienahealthcare.com
SIC: 8051 Skilled nursing care facilities
HQ: Laurel Health Care Company
8181 Worthington Rd Uppr
Westerville OH 43082

(G-13336)
LOWES HOME CENTERS LLC
Also Called: Lowe's
4115 Mall Dr (43952-3007)
PHONE.................................740 266-3500
EMP: 138
SALES (corp-wide): 86.38B **Publicly Held**
Web: www.lowes.com
SIC: 5211 5031 5722 5064 Home centers; Building materials, exterior; Household appliance stores; Electrical appliances, television and radio
HQ: Lowe's Home Centers, Llc
1000 Lowes Blvd
Mooresville NC 28117
336 658-4000

(G-13337)
LTAC INVESTORS LLC
Also Called: Lifeline Hospital
200 School St (43953-9610)
PHONE.................................740 346-2600
EMP: 150
SIC: 8062 General medical and surgical hospitals

(G-13338)
MEDI HOME HEALTH AGENCY INC (HQ)
Also Called: Medi-Home Care
105 Main St (43953-3733)
PHONE.................................740 266-3977
Ronnie L Young, *Pr*
James Hardman, *
John Keim, *
Mary Craver, *
Gregory Varner, *
EMP: 50 **EST:** 1995
SALES (est): 146.97K
SALES (corp-wide): 14.21MM **Privately Held**
SIC: 8082 7361 5169 Home health care services; Nurses' registry; Oxygen
PA: Medical Services Of America, Inc.
171 Monroe Ln
Lexington SC 29072
803 957-0500

(G-13339)
MEDICAL GROUP ASSOCIATES INC
114 Brady Cir E (43952-1478)
P.O. Box 492 (43952-5492)
PHONE.................................740 283-4773
Stephen G Kuruc, *Pr*
EMP: 32 **EST:** 1979
SQ FT: 16,400
SALES (est): 1.96MM **Privately Held**
SIC: 8011 Physicians' office, including specialists

(G-13340)
MOUGIANIS INDUSTRIES INC
Also Called: Alexander Great Distributing
1626 Cadiz Rd (43953-7630)
P.O. Box 2100 (43953-0100)
PHONE.................................740 264-6372
Anthony N Mougianis, *Pr*
EMP: 60 **EST:** 1987
SQ FT: 8,000
SALES (est): 2.12MM **Privately Held**
Web: www.apolloprocleaning.com
SIC: 7349 5087 Janitorial service, contract basis; Cleaning and maintenance equipment and supplies

GEOGRAPHIC SECTION   Stow - Summit County (G-13363)

(G-13341)
OTIS ELEVATOR COMPANY
1 Farm Spring (43953)
PHONE.....................740 282-1461
EMP: 29
SALES (corp-wide): 14.21B **Publicly Held**
Web: www.otis.com
SIC: 5084 Elevators
HQ: Otis Elevator Company
    1 Carrier Pl
    Farmington CT 06032
    860 674-3000

(G-13342)
SACHS MANAGEMENT CORP
Also Called: Holiday Inn
1401 University Blvd (43952-1781)
PHONE.....................740 282-0901
Don Richardson, *Mgr*
EMP: 90
SALES (corp-wide): 443.8K **Privately Held**
Web: www.holidayinn.com
SIC: 7011 5812 Hotels and motels; Eating places
PA: Sachs Management Corp.
    3131 S Dixie Dr Ste 421
    Moraine OH
    937 299-1209

(G-13343)
STEUBENVILLE COUNTRY CLUB INC
413 Lovers Ln (43953-3309)
PHONE.....................740 264-0521
Robert Chapman, *Pr*
Anthony Sheposh, *
EMP: 46 **EST:** 1908
SQ FT: 5,000
SALES (est): 1.24MM **Privately Held**
Web: www.steubenvillecc.com
SIC: 7997 Country club, membership

(G-13344)
STEUBNVLLE CNTRY CLB MANOR INC
575 Lovers Ln (43953-3311)
PHONE.....................740 266-6118
James Bolger, *Pr*
Rena Bolger, *
Stephen Bolger, *
Denise Boyle, *
EMP: 46 **EST:** 1994
SALES (est): 4.22MM **Privately Held**
Web: www.bolgerhealthcare.com
SIC: 8051 Convalescent home with continuous nursing care

(G-13345)
THE VOTO MANUFACTURERS SALES COMPANY (PA)
Also Called: Voto Sales
500 N 3rd St (43952-1958)
P.O. Box 1299 (43952-6299)
PHONE.....................740 282-3621
▲ **EMP:** 40 **EST:** 1938
SALES (est): 16.72MM
SALES (corp-wide): 16.72MM **Privately Held**
Web: www.votosales.com
SIC: 5085 Industrial supplies

(G-13346)
TRINITY HEALTH SYSTEM (DH)
Also Called: Trinity Medical Center East
380 Summit Ave (43952-2667)
PHONE.....................740 283-7000
EMP: 300 **EST:** 1995
SQ FT: 1,004,854
SALES (est): 277.07MM **Privately Held**
Web: www.trinityhealth.com
SIC: 8062 8011 General medical and surgical hospitals; Offices and clinics of medical doctors
HQ: Sylvania Franciscan Health
    1715 Indian Wood Cir # 200
    Maumee OH

(G-13347)
TRINITY HOSPITAL HOLDING CO (DH)
Also Called: Trinity Medical Center East
380 Summit Ave (43952-2667)
PHONE.....................740 264-8000
Fred B Bower, *Pr*
Albert Pavlik, *
Clyde Metzger Md, *Ch Bd*
EMP: 600 **EST:** 1996
SALES (est): 207.57MM **Privately Held**
Web: www.trinityhealth.com
SIC: 8062 8741 General medical and surgical hospitals; Management services
HQ: Trinity Health System
    380 Summit Ave
    Steubenville OH 43952

(G-13348)
TRINITY SCHOOL OF NURSING
380 Summit Ave (43952-2667)
PHONE.....................740 283-7525
Patricia Gerlando, *Pr*
Melissa Hassan, *Dir*
EMP: 43 **EST:** 1920
SALES (est): 614.46K **Privately Held**
Web: www.trinityson.com
SIC: 8062 Hospital, professional nursing school

(G-13349)
TRINITY WEST
4000 Johnson Rd (43952-2300)
PHONE.....................740 264-8000
Fred B Brower, *Pr*
EMP: 1640 **EST:** 1913
SQ FT: 600,000
SALES (est): 139.77MM **Privately Held**
Web: www.trinityhealth.com
SIC: 8062 General medical and surgical hospitals
HQ: Trinity Hospital Holding Company
    380 Summit Ave
    Steubenville OH 43952
    740 264-8000

(G-13350)
VILLA VISTA ROYALE LLC
1800 Sinclair Ave (43953-3328)
PHONE.....................740 264-7301
Guirino Lancia, *
EMP: 50 **EST:** 2019
SALES (est): 4.13MM **Privately Held**
SIC: 8052 Intermediate care facilities

(G-13351)
W TOV TV9
9 Red Donley Plz (43952-3278)
PHONE.....................740 282-9999
EMP: 27 **EST:** 2019
SALES (est): 1.23MM **Privately Held**
Web: www.wtov9.com
SIC: 4833 Television broadcasting stations

Stow
Summit County

(G-13352)
ACRT INC (PA)
4500 Courthouse Blvd Ste 150 (44224-6837)
PHONE.....................800 622-2562
Michael Weidner, *CEO*
Todd Jones, *
EMP: 35 **EST:** 1985
SALES (est): 68.06MM
SALES (corp-wide): 68.06MM **Privately Held**
Web: www.acrt.com
SIC: 8748 8731 Environmental consultant; Environmental research

(G-13353)
AKRON GENERAL HEALTH SYSTEM
4300 Allen Rd (44224-1032)
PHONE.....................330 945-9300
EMP: 705
SALES (corp-wide): 14.48B **Privately Held**
Web: www.akrongeneral.org
SIC: 8099 Childbirth preparation clinic
HQ: Akron General Health System
    1 Akron General Ave
    Akron OH 44307
    330 344-6000

(G-13354)
AKRON METROPOLITAN HSING AUTH
500 Hardman Dr (44224-4883)
PHONE.....................330 920-1652
EMP: 62
SALES (corp-wide): 78.34MM **Privately Held**
Web: www.akronhousing.org
SIC: 9531 8211 7299 6513 Housing authority, nonoperating: government; Kindergarten; Apartment locating service; Apartment building operators
PA: Akron Metropolitan Housing Authority
    100 W Cedar St Ste 100 # 100
    Akron OH 44307
    330 762-9631

(G-13355)
BERMEX INC
4500 Courthouse Blvd Ste 150 (44224-6835)
PHONE.....................330 945-7500
Todd Jones, *Pr*
Linda Zaremski, *
David Mack, *
EMP: 271 **EST:** 1997
SALES (est): 23.99MM
SALES (corp-wide): 68.06MM **Privately Held**
Web: bermex.acrt.com
SIC: 7389 Meter readers, remote
PA: Acrt, Inc.
    4500 Courthouse Blvd # 150
    Stow OH 44224
    800 622-2562

(G-13356)
BRIARWOOD INC
Also Called: BRIARWOOD HEALTHCARE CENTER, T
3700 Englewood Dr (44224-3223)
PHONE.....................330 688-1828
Jonathan B Trimble, *Pr*
EMP: 100 **EST:** 1990
SQ FT: 37,000
SALES (est): 4.29MM **Privately Held**
Web: www.thebriarwood.com
SIC: 8059 8051 Rest home, with health care; Convalescent home with continuous nursing care

(G-13357)
CENTIMARK CORPORATION
Also Called: Questmark
700 Alpha Pkwy (44224-1078)
PHONE.....................330 920-3560
EMP: 120
SALES (corp-wide): 783.89MM **Privately Held**
Web: www.centimark.com
SIC: 1761 1752 Roofing, siding, and sheetmetal work; Floor laying and floor work, nec
PA: Centimark Corporation
    12 Grandview Cir
    Canonsburg PA 15317
    724 514-8700

(G-13358)
CHEMIMAGE FILTER TECH LLC
1100 Campus Dr Ste 500 (44224-1767)
PHONE.....................330 686-2726
George Ventouris, *Prin*
EMP: 47
Web: www.chemimage.com
SIC: 8731 Commercial physical research
PA: Chemimage Filter Technologies, Llc
    7301 Penn Ave
    Pittsburgh PA 15208

(G-13359)
CLEANPRO JANITORIAL SVC LLC
5026 Hudson Dr (44224-7100)
P.O. Box 483 (44236-0483)
PHONE.....................330 592-9860
EMP: 32
SALES (est): 905.81K **Privately Held**
Web: www.cleanpro-janitorial.com
SIC: 7349 Janitorial service, contract basis

(G-13360)
CROSSCOUNTRY MORTGAGE LLC
4704 Darrow Rd Ste 1 (44224-1438)
PHONE.....................330 655-5626
EMP: 56
SALES (corp-wide): 803.24MM **Privately Held**
Web: www.crosscountrymortgage.com
SIC: 6162 Mortgage bankers and loan correspondents
PA: Crosscountry Mortgage, Llc
    6850 Miller Rd
    Brecksville OH 44141
    440 845-3700

(G-13361)
CROSSCOUNTRY MORTGAGE LLC
3226 Kent Rd Ste 105 (44224-4466)
PHONE.....................330 715-4878
EMP: 56
SALES (corp-wide): 803.24MM **Privately Held**
Web: www.crosscountrymortgage.com
SIC: 6162 Mortgage bankers and loan correspondents
PA: Crosscountry Mortgage, Llc
    6850 Miller Rd
    Brecksville OH 44141
    440 845-3700

(G-13362)
CUSTOM MOVERS SERVICES INC
Also Called: CMS
3290 Kent Rd (44224-4512)
PHONE.....................330 564-0507
Dean Barker, *Pr*
EMP: 41 **EST:** 1995
SALES (est): 6.77MM **Privately Held**
Web: www.custommoversservices.com
SIC: 4212 Moving services

(G-13363)
DENTALONE PARTNERS INC
4176 Kent Rd (44224-4344)
PHONE.....................844 214-4179
EMP: 107
SALES (corp-wide): 85.13MM **Privately Held**

Stow - Summit County (G-13364)

Web: www.dentalworks.com
SIC: 8021 Dental clinic
PA: Dentalone Partners, Inc.
6700 Pinecrest Dr Ste 150
Plano TX 75024
972 755-0800

(G-13364)
DORTRNIC SERVICE-TALLMADGE INC
Also Called: Action Door of Stow
3878 Hudson Dr (44224-2913)
PHONE.................................330 928-2727
Michelle Mastantuono, Pr
EMP: 29 EST: 1991
SALES (est): 4.58MM
SALES (corp-wide): 17.91MM Privately Held
SIC: 1751 7699 5031 Garage door, installation or erection; Door and window repair; Doors, nec
PA: Dortronic Service Inc.
201 E Granger Rd
Cleveland OH 44131
216 739-3667

(G-13365)
EMERITUS CORPORATION
Also Called: Emeritus At Stow
5511 Fishcreek Rd (44224-1435)
PHONE.................................330 342-0934
Kelli Phillips, Brnch Mgr
EMP: 92
SALES (corp-wide): 2.83B Publicly Held
Web: www.emeritus.org
SIC: 8051 Skilled nursing care facilities
HQ: Emeritus Corporation
6737 W Wa St Ste 2300
Milwaukee WI 53214

(G-13366)
ENVIROSCIENCE INC (PA)
5070 Stow Rd (44224-1530)
PHONE.................................330 688-0111
Daniel G Dunstan, Dir
Martin A Hilovsky, *
James Krejsa, *
Michael O'brien, Dir
H F Burkhardt, Dir
EMP: 76 EST: 1989
SQ FT: 24,000
SALES (est): 22.83MM Privately Held
Web: www.enviroscienceinc.com
SIC: 8734 8748 Water testing laboratory; Business consulting, nec

(G-13367)
EVANT (PA)
1221 Commerce Dr (44224-1744)
PHONE.................................330 920-1517
Sherry D Gedeon, Ex Dir
EMP: 36 EST: 1975
SALES (est): 4.97MM
SALES (corp-wide): 4.97MM Privately Held
Web: www.evantinc.org
SIC: 8361 Mentally handicapped home

(G-13368)
FITWORKS HOLDING LLC
4301 Kent Rd Ste 26 (44224-4364)
PHONE.................................330 688-2329
Chuck Ortiz, Mgr
EMP: 48
Web: www.fitworks.com
SIC: 7991 Health club
PA: Fitworks Holding, Llc
849 Brainard Rd
Cleveland OH 44143

(G-13369)
GEEP USA INC
Also Called: Geep
4550 Darrow Rd (44224-1804)
PHONE.................................919 544-1443
Jeff Jermyn, Pr
Lew Coffin, *
◆ EMP: 50 EST: 2002
SALES (est): 10MM Privately Held
SIC: 5093 5065 Metal scrap and waste materials; Electronic parts and equipment, nec

(G-13370)
GENEVA CHERVENIC REALTY INC
3589 Darrow Rd (44224-4000)
PHONE.................................330 686-8400
David Chervenic, Pr
EMP: 37 EST: 1973
SQ FT: 2,500
SALES (est): 1.05MM Privately Held
Web: kwchervenic.yourkwoffice.com
SIC: 6531 Real estate agent, residential

(G-13371)
GLOBAL MAIL INC
Also Called: Dhl Ecommerce
542 Seasons Rd (44224-1022)
PHONE.................................330 849-3248
EMP: 39
SALES (corp-wide): 88.87B Privately Held
SIC: 4513 Air courier services
HQ: Global Mail, Inc.
2700 S Comm Pkwy Ste 300
Weston FL 33331
800 805-9306

(G-13372)
HAMPTON INN STOW
Also Called: Hampton By Hilton
4331 Lakepointe Corporate Dr (44224-6806)
PHONE.................................330 945-4160
Lisa Zifer, Prin
EMP: 27 EST: 2007
SALES (est): 444.5K Privately Held
Web: www.hilton.com
SIC: 7011 Hotels and motels

(G-13373)
HOBBY LOBBY STORES INC
Also Called: Hobby Lobby
4332 Kent Rd Ste 3 (44224-4391)
PHONE.................................330 686-1508
EMP: 27
SALES (corp-wide): 1.92B Privately Held
Web: www.hobbylobby.com
SIC: 5945 5023 Arts and crafts supplies; Frames and framing, picture and mirror
PA: Hobby Lobby Stores, Inc.
7707 Sw 44th St
Oklahoma City OK 73179
405 745-1100

(G-13374)
HOPE HOMES INC
2044 Bryn Mawr Dr (44224-2616)
PHONE.................................330 688-4935
Dayna Worthy, Brnch Mgr
EMP: 29
SALES (corp-wide): 4.64MM Privately Held
Web: www.hopehomes.org
SIC: 8082 Home health care services
PA: Hope Homes, Inc.
2300 Call Rd
Stow OH 44224
330 686-5342

(G-13375)
HOTEL STOW LP
Also Called: Courtyard By Marriott
4047 Bridgewater Pkwy (44224-6306)
PHONE.................................330 945-9722
Jason Jackson, Genl Mgr
EMP: 40 EST: 2008
SALES (est): 508.27K Privately Held
Web: courtyard.marriott.com
SIC: 7011 Hotels and motels

(G-13376)
HYDRAULIC MANIFOLDS USA LLC
Also Called: Selling Precision
4540 Boyce Pkwy (44224-1769)
PHONE.................................973 728-1214
Nimit Patel, Managing Member
EMP: 30 EST: 2017
SALES (est): 5.02MM Privately Held
Web: www.hydraulicmanifoldsusa.com
SIC: 5084 5085 3492 Hydraulic systems equipment and supplies; Hydraulic and pneumatic pistons and valves; Valves, hydraulic, aircraft

(G-13377)
INSTANTWHIP-AKRON INC
Also Called: Instantwhip
4870 Hudson Dr (44224-1708)
PHONE.................................614 488-2536
Fred Smith, Pr
G Frederick Smith, *
Thomas Michaelides, *
Kevin Sheaffer, *
EMP: 40 EST: 1936
SALES (est): 9.15MM Privately Held
Web: www.instantwhip.com
SIC: 5143 Milk and cream, fluid

(G-13378)
INTERCHEZ LGISTICS SYSTEMS INC
600 Alpha Pkwy (44224-1065)
P.O. Box 2115 (44224-0115)
PHONE.................................330 923-5080
Sharlene Chesnes, Pr
Cassie Mcclellan, COO
EMP: 36 EST: 2002
SQ FT: 10,000
SALES (est): 6.4MM Privately Held
Web: www.interchez.com
SIC: 8742 Transportation consultant

(G-13379)
KIDS-PLAY INC
4530 Kent Rd (44224-4329)
PHONE.................................330 678-5554
EMP: 29
SALES (corp-wide): 990.2K Privately Held
SIC: 8351 Preschool center
PA: Kids-Play, Inc.
195 S Main St Ste 202b
Akron OH 44308
234 571-5505

(G-13380)
LOWES HOME CENTERS LLC
Also Called: Lowe's
3570 Hudson Dr (44224-2907)
PHONE.................................330 920-9280
EMP: 143
SQ FT: 134,995
SALES (corp-wide): 86.38B Publicly Held
Web: www.lowes.com
SIC: 5211 5031 5722 5064 Home centers; Building materials, exterior; Household appliance stores; Electrical appliances, television and radio
HQ: Lowe's Home Centers, Llc
1000 Lowes Blvd
Mooresville NC 28117
336 658-4000

(G-13381)
MARHOFER DEVELOPMENT CO LLC
1585 Commerce Dr (44224-1711)
PHONE.................................330 686-2262
Gene Kapity, Mgr
EMP: 40
SALES (corp-wide): 28.19MM Privately Held
Web: www.marhofer.com
SIC: 7532 Exterior repair services
PA: Marhofer Development Co., Llc
3423 Darrow Rd
Stow OH 44224
330 688-6644

(G-13382)
MATCO TOOLS CORPORATION (HQ)
Also Called: Matco Tools
4403 Allen Rd (44224)
P.O. Box 1429 (44224)
PHONE.................................330 929-4949
Mike Dwyer, Pr
Raymond Michaud, Finance Treasurer*
▲ EMP: 400 EST: 1953
SALES (est): 134.73MM
SALES (corp-wide): 3.1B Publicly Held
Web: www.matcotools.com
SIC: 5013 5072 3469 3423 Tools and equipment, automotive; Hardware; Metal stampings, nec; Hand and edge tools, nec
PA: Vontier Corporation
5438 Wade Park Blvd # 601
Raleigh NC 27607
984 275-6000

(G-13383)
OPERATING TAX SYSTEMS LLC
3924 Clock Pointe Trl Ste 105 (44224)
PHONE.................................330 940-3967
EMP: 7467 EST: 1998
SQ FT: 3,500
SALES (est): 444.13K
SALES (corp-wide): 1.29B Privately Held
SIC: 7371 Computer software development
PA: Riverside Partners L.L.C.
45 Rockefeller Plz # 400
New York NY 10111
212 265-6575

(G-13384)
OSMANS PIES INC
3678 Elm Rd (44224-3954)
PHONE.................................330 607-9083
Ethel Osman, Pr
Terry Osman, *
Cheryl Osman Crowe, *
EMP: 30 EST: 1949
SQ FT: 3,500
SALES (est): 600K Privately Held
SIC: 5461 5149 2052 2051 Retail bakeries; Bakery products; Cookies and crackers; Bread, cake, and related products

(G-13385)
PLASTICS FAMILY HOLDINGS INC
Also Called: PLASTICS FAMILY HOLDINGS INC
4700 Hudson Dr (44224-1706)
PHONE.................................330 733-9595
TOLL FREE: 800
Mike Selton, Mgr
EMP: 36
SQ FT: 17,000
Web: www.lairdplastics.com
SIC: 5162 Plastics products, nec
HQ: Plastics Family Holdings, Inc.
5800 Cmpus Circ Dr E Ste
Irving TX 75063
469 299-7000

GEOGRAPHIC SECTION

Stratton - Jefferson County (G-13407)

(G-13386)
PRECISION ENDOSCOPY AMER INC (PA)
4575 Hudson Dr (44224-1725)
PHONE..............................410 527-9598
John Thormann, *CEO*
Christian Mills, *
Ted Honeywell, *
EMP: 30 **EST:** 1991
SQ FT: 13,000
SALES (est): 1.87MM **Privately Held**
SIC: 7699 Medical equipment repair, non-electric

(G-13387)
RB WATKINS INC
Also Called: RB Watkins An Alstom Company
778 Mccauley Rd Unit 140 (44224-1067)
PHONE..............................330 688-4061
EMP: 30
SIC: 4931 Electric and other services combined

(G-13388)
REIDY MEDICAL SUPPLY INC
1397 Commerce Dr (44224-1736)
PHONE..............................800 398-2723
Ted Stitzel, *Pr*
Rita Stitzel, *
EMP: 30 **EST:** 1992
SQ FT: 8,000
SALES (est): 10.14MM **Privately Held**
Web: www.reidymed.com
SIC: 5047 Medical equipment and supplies

(G-13389)
RSR PARTNERS LLC (PA)
Also Called: Regency Technologies
4550 Darrow Rd (44224-1804)
PHONE..............................440 519-1768
Steven Joseph, *Managing Member*
▼ **EMP:** 81 **EST:** 2006
SALES (est): 27.64MM
SALES (corp-wide): 27.64MM **Privately Held**
Web: www.regencytechnologies.com
SIC: 5084 Recycling machinery and equipment

(G-13390)
SPECTRUM SURGICAL INSTRUMENTS CORP
4575 Hudson Dr (44224-1725)
P.O. Box 2725 (31902-2725)
PHONE..............................800 783-9251
EMP: 200
SIC: 7699 5047 Caliper, gauge, and other machinists' instrument repair; Instruments, surgical and medical

(G-13391)
STAYBRIDGE SUITES
4351 Steels Pointe (44224-6819)
PHONE..............................330 945-4180
Megan Lali, *Genl Mgr*
EMP: 27 **EST:** 2008
SALES (est): 542.86K **Privately Held**
Web: www.staybridgesuites.com
SIC: 7011 Hotels and motels

(G-13392)
STOUFFER REALTY INC
4936 Darrow Rd (44224-1406)
PHONE..............................330 564-0711
Gary Stouffer, *Owner*
EMP: 38
SALES (corp-wide): 9.74MM **Privately Held**
Web: www.stoufferrealty.com
SIC: 6531 Real estate agent, residential
PA: Stouffer Realty, Inc.
130 N Miller Rd Ste A
Fairlawn OH 44333
330 835-4900

(G-13393)
STOW DENTAL GROUP INC
Also Called: Schlosser, David W DDS
3506 Darrow Rd (44224-4098)
PHONE..............................330 688-6456
David Wiedie D.d.s., *Pr*
Doctor Eric Schikowski, *VP*
Doctor Mark Iati, *VP*
Doctor Kenneth Sladky, *Sec*
Doctor David Scholsser, *Treas*
EMP: 39 **EST:** 1966
SQ FT: 3,500
SALES (est): 4.19MM **Privately Held**
Web: www.stowdental.com
SIC: 8021 Dentists' office

(G-13394)
STOW OPCO LLC
Also Called: Arbors At Stow
2910 Lermitage Pl (44224-5219)
PHONE..............................502 429-8062
Robert Norcross, *CEO*
EMP: 99 **EST:** 2014
SQ FT: 60,000
SALES (est): 8.76MM **Privately Held**
Web: www.arborsatstow.com
SIC: 8051 Convalescent home with continuous nursing care

(G-13395)
STRUKTOL COMPANY AMERICA LLC (DH)
Also Called: Struktol
201 E Steels Corners Rd (44224-4921)
P.O. Box 1649 (44224-0649)
PHONE..............................330 928-5188
Mark Skakun Iii, *Pr*
Mark Skakun Iii, *Pr*
Paul A Danilowicz, *Dir*
◆ **EMP:** 43 **EST:** 1977
SQ FT: 60,000
SALES (est): 56.68MM
SALES (corp-wide): 355.83K **Privately Held**
Web: www.struktol.com
SIC: 5169 Chemicals and allied products, nec
HQ: Schill + Seilacher "struktol" Gmbh
Moorfleeter Str. 28
Hamburg HH 22113
40733620

(G-13396)
SUMMA HEALTH
Also Called: Lab Care
3869 Darrow Rd Ste 208 (44224-2677)
PHONE..............................330 688-4531
Carla Davenport, *Brnch Mgr*
EMP: 59
SALES (corp-wide): 1.78B **Privately Held**
Web: www.summahealth.org
SIC: 8062 8071 General medical and surgical hospitals; Medical laboratories
PA: Summa Health System
1077 Gorge Blvd
Akron OH 44310
330 375-3000

(G-13397)
SWRH PHYSICIANS INC
3913 Darrow Rd (44224-2621)
PHONE..............................330 923-5899
EMP: 74
SALES (corp-wide): 965.86K **Privately Held**
Web: www.wrhpi.org
SIC: 8011 General and family practice, physician/surgeon
PA: Swrh Physicians, Inc.
3033 State Rd
Cuyahoga Falls OH 44223
330 923-5899

(G-13398)
TRAXIUM LLC
Also Called: Printing Concepts
4246 Hudson Dr (44224-2251)
PHONE..............................330 572-8200
Frank Tuzzio, *
Devin Gilespie, *
Tiffani Gerber, *
EMP: 49 **EST:** 1977
SQ FT: 45,000
SALES (est): 9.88MM **Privately Held**
Web: www.printingconcepts.com
SIC: 7331 2789 2752 2759 Direct mail advertising services; Bookbinding and related work; Offset printing; Letterpress printing

(G-13399)
TWIN SISTERS PRODUCTIONS LLC
4710 Hudson Dr (44224-1706)
PHONE..............................330 631-0361
▲ **EMP:** 40
Web: www.twinsisters.com
SIC: 3999 5092 5961 7389 Education aids, devices and supplies; Toys and hobby goods and supplies; Educational supplies and equipment, mail order; Music recording producer

(G-13400)
VERITIV PUBG & PRINT MGT INC (DH)
Also Called: Graphic Communications
4852 Gray Ln (44224-1061)
PHONE..............................614 288-0911
Matt Dawley, *Pr*
David Earney, *CFO*
Allan Dragone, *CEO*
Bill King, *Sr VP*
John Patneau, *Sr VP*
◆ **EMP:** 31 **EST:** 1979
SALES (est): 50.52MM
SALES (corp-wide): 14.52B **Privately Held**
Web: www.bulkleydunton.com
SIC: 5111 7389 Fine paper; Printing broker
HQ: Veritiv Corporation
1000 Abrnthy Rd Ne Bldg 4
Atlanta GA 30328
770 391-8200

(G-13401)
VOOKS INC
4584 Bunker Ln (44224-5158)
PHONE..............................503 694-9217
Marshall L Bex Iv, *CEO*
EMP: 80 **EST:** 2021
SALES (est): 2.65MM **Privately Held**
Web: www.vooks.com
SIC: 7822 7371 Motion picture and tape distribution; Computer software development and applications

(G-13402)
WINDSTREAM SERVICES LLC
Also Called: WINDSTREAM SERVICES, LLC
4574 Chatwood Dr (44224-1956)
PHONE..............................330 650-7044
EMP: 29
SALES (corp-wide): 6.77B **Privately Held**
Web: www.windstreamenterprise.com
SIC: 4813 Telephone communication, except radio
HQ: Windstream Services Pe, Llc
4001 N Rodney Parham Rd
Little Rock AR 72212
501 748-7000

Strasburg
Tuscarawas County

(G-13403)
CITIZENS STATE BNK OF STRSBURG
Also Called: Citizens Bank
202 N Wooster Ave (44680-1046)
P.O. Box 165 (44680-0165)
PHONE..............................330 878-5551
Ed Allensworth, *VP*
Scott Everson, *Pr*
EMP: 27 **EST:** 1924
SQ FT: 3,000
SALES (est): 1.87MM
SALES (corp-wide): 40.9MM **Publicly Held**
SIC: 6021 National commercial banks
PA: United Bancorp, Inc.
201 S 4th St
Martins Ferry OH 43935
740 633-0445

(G-13404)
OXFORD MINING COMPANY INC
7551 Reed Rd Nw (44680-8902)
P.O. Box 135 (44680-0135)
PHONE..............................330 878-5120
Chuck Ungurean, *Owner*
EMP: 138
SALES (corp-wide): 814.89MM **Privately Held**
SIC: 5052 Coal
HQ: Oxford Mining Company, Inc.
544 Chestnut St
Coshocton OH 43812
740 622-6302

(G-13405)
PRIME NDT SERVICES INC
10119 Oh-21 (44680)
PHONE..............................330 878-4202
EMP: 80 **EST:** 1996
SALES (est): 20MM **Privately Held**
Web: www.rae.com
SIC: 8734 Testing laboratories

(G-13406)
SSB COMMUNITY BANK
152 N Wooster Ave (44680-1136)
P.O. Box 107 (44680-0107)
PHONE..............................330 878-5555
Doug Hensel, *Pr*
Gene Hensel, *Ch*
Larry Kaser, *VP*
EMP: 27 **EST:** 1924
SALES (est): 9.26MM **Privately Held**
Web: www.ssbonline.com
SIC: 6022 State commercial banks
PA: Strasburg Bancorp, Inc.
224 N Bodmer Ave
Strasburg OH

Stratton
Jefferson County

(G-13407)
JERSEY CENTRAL PWR & LIGHT CO
Also Called: Firstenergy
29503 State Route 7 (43961-7216)
PHONE..............................740 537-6391
John Kreptowski, *Mgr*
EMP: 200
Web: www.firstenergycorp.com
SIC: 4911 Electric services

Streetsboro - Portage County (G-13408)

HQ: Jersey Central Power & Light Company
76 S Main St
Akron OH 44308
800 736-3402

Streetsboro
Portage County

(G-13408)
A DUIE PYLE INC
10225 Philipp Pkwy (44241-4040)
PHONE..................................330 342-7750
Rich Gadus, *Brnch Mgr*
EMP: 66
SALES (corp-wide): 494.71MM **Privately Held**
Web: www.aduiepyle.com
SIC: 4225 7519 General warehousing; Trailer rental
PA: A. Duie Pyle Inc.
650 Westtown Rd
West Chester PA 19382
610 696-5800

(G-13409)
AGRATRONIX LLC
1790 Miller Pkwy (44241-4633)
PHONE..................................330 562-2222
Gerald Stephens, *Managing Member*
▲ **EMP:** 30 **EST:** 2007
SALES (est): 10.95MM **Privately Held**
Web: www.agratronix.com
SIC: 5039 3699 3446 Wire fence, gates, and accessories; Electric fence chargers; Fences, gates, posts, and flagpoles

(G-13410)
BOULDER CREEK GOLF CLUB
9700 Page Rd (44241-5014)
PHONE..................................330 626-2828
Ken Haniford, *Mgr*
EMP: 31 **EST:** 2015
SALES (est): 1.07MM **Privately Held**
Web: www.bouldercreekohio.com
SIC: 7992 Public golf courses

(G-13411)
CER HOTELS LLC
Also Called: TownePlace Suites By Marriott
795 Mondial Pkwy (44241-4574)
PHONE..................................330 422-1855
Maninder S Chhabra, *Managing Member*
EMP: 50 **EST:** 2007
SALES (est): 2.29MM **Privately Held**
Web: www.marriott.com
SIC: 7011 Hotel, franchised

(G-13412)
GARDENS WESTERN RESERVE INC (PA)
9975 Greentree Pkwy (44241-4328)
PHONE..................................330 342-9100
Richard Piekarski, *Prin*
EMP: 42 **EST:** 2000
SALES (est): 7.41MM
SALES (corp-wide): 7.41MM **Privately Held**
Web: www.gardensofwesternreserve.com
SIC: 8059 8322 Rest home, with health care; Adult day care center

(G-13413)
GEIS COMPANIES LLC
10020 Aurora Hudson Rd (44241-1621)
PHONE..................................330 528-3500
Greg Geis, *Managing Member*
EMP: 146 **EST:** 1967
SALES (est): 8.85MM **Privately Held**
Web: www.geiscompanies.com
SIC: 1542 Commercial and office building, new construction

(G-13414)
GORELL ENTERPRISES INC (DH)
Also Called: Gorell Windows & Doors
10250 Philipp Pkwy (44241-4765)
PHONE..................................724 465-1800
Wayne C Gorell, *Ch Bd*
Brian Zimmerman, *
Michael A Rempel, *
Arnold S Levitt, *
EMP: 360 **EST:** 1993
SQ FT: 240,000
SALES (est): 83.37MM
SALES (corp-wide): 1.2B **Privately Held**
SIC: 3089 5031 Plastics hardware and building products; Doors and windows
HQ: Soft-Lite L.L.C.
10250 Philipp Pkwy
Streetsboro OH 44241
330 528-3400

(G-13415)
HIGHLAND SOM DEVELOPMENT (PA)
Also Called: GEIS COMPANY
10020 Aurora Hudson Rd (44241-1621)
PHONE..................................330 528-3500
Erwin Geis, *Pt*
EMP: 32 **EST:** 1979
SALES (est): 257.73K
SALES (corp-wide): 257.73K **Privately Held**
Web: www.geiscompanies.com
SIC: 6552 Land subdividers and developers, commercial

(G-13416)
HUNTINGTON NATIONAL BANK
9240 Market Square Dr (44241-5207)
PHONE..................................330 626-3426
Mary Stegenga, *Mgr*
EMP: 31
SALES (corp-wide): 10.84B **Publicly Held**
Web: www.huntington.com
SIC: 6029 6021 Commercial banks, nec; National commercial banks
HQ: The Huntington National Bank
41 S High St
Columbus OH 43215
614 480-4293

(G-13417)
HUNTINGTON NATIONAL BANK
9717 State Route 14 (44241-5219)
PHONE..................................330 626-3431
Shawn Scalia, *Mgr*
EMP: 36
SALES (corp-wide): 10.84B **Publicly Held**
Web: www.huntington.com
SIC: 6029 Commercial banks, nec
HQ: The Huntington National Bank
41 S High St
Columbus OH 43215
614 480-4293

(G-13418)
IS ACQUISITION INC (HQ)
Also Called: Integrity Stainless
3000 Crane Centre Dr (44241-5035)
PHONE..................................440 287-0150
Andy Markowitz, *VP*
Jerry Gideon, *Prin*
▲ **EMP:** 45 **EST:** 2005
SALES (est): 33.05MM
SALES (corp-wide): 2.16B **Publicly Held**
Web: www.integritystainless.com
SIC: 5051 Steel
PA: Olympic Steel, Inc.
22901 Millcreek Blvd Ste 6
Cleveland OH 44122
216 292-3800

(G-13419)
JOSEPH INDUSTRIES INC
Also Called: BUCKEYE FASTENERS COMPANY
10039 Aurora Hudson Rd (44241-1600)
PHONE..................................330 528-0091
Clyde Faust, *Pr*
Linda Kerekes, *
▲ **EMP:** 52 **EST:** 1969
SQ FT: 76,260
SALES (est): 7.05MM
SALES (corp-wide): 46.16MM **Privately Held**
Web: www.joseph.com
SIC: 3714 5084 3713 3566 Motor vehicle parts and accessories; Lift trucks and parts; Truck and bus bodies; Speed changers, drives, and gears
PA: Fastener Industries, Inc.
1 Berea Cmns Ste 209
Berea OH 44017
440 243-0034

(G-13420)
LOWES HOME CENTERS LLC
Also Called: Lowe's
1210 State Route 303 (44241-4591)
PHONE..................................330 626-2980
Tim Mercer, *Brnch Mgr*
EMP: 143
SALES (corp-wide): 86.38B **Publicly Held**
Web: www.lowes.com
SIC: 5211 5031 5722 5064 Home centers; Building materials, exterior; Household appliance stores; Electrical appliances, television and radio
HQ: Lowe's Home Centers, Llc
1000 Lowes Blvd
Mooresville NC 28117
336 658-4000

(G-13421)
MARK DURA INC
72 Emerald Ave (44241-4114)
P.O. Box 868 (44202-0868)
PHONE..................................330 995-0883
Curtis Britton, *CEO*
Frank Gibson, *
EMP: 30 **EST:** 2002
SQ FT: 13,000
SALES (est): 2.25MM **Privately Held**
Web: www.duramarkinc.com
SIC: 1721 Pavement marking contractor

(G-13422)
MEANDER HSPTALITY GROUP II LLC
Also Called: Hampton Inn
800 Mondial Pkwy (44241-4540)
PHONE..................................330 422-0500
EMP: 36 **EST:** 1999
SQ FT: 1,232
SALES (est): 813.81K **Privately Held**
Web: www.hilton.com
SIC: 7011 Hotels and motels

(G-13423)
MONDELEZ GLOBAL LLC
Also Called: Nabisco
545 Mondial Pkwy (44241-4510)
P.O. Box 340 (15347-0340)
PHONE..................................330 626-6500
Doug Evans, *Brnch Mgr*
EMP: 28
Web: www.mondelezinternational.com
SIC: 5149 Crackers, cookies, and bakery products
HQ: Mondelez Global Llc
905 W Fulton Market # 200
Chicago IL 60607
847 943-4000

(G-13424)
ONEX CONSTRUCTION INC
1430 Miller Pkwy (44241-4640)
PHONE..................................330 995-9015
Ken Finnerty, *Pr*
Paul Marshal, *Stockholder**
▲ **EMP:** 40 **EST:** 1996
SQ FT: 20,000
SALES (est): 11.23MM **Privately Held**
Web: www.onexconstruction.com
SIC: 1741 Refractory or acid brick masonry

(G-13425)
R & H SERVICE INC
Also Called: Americas Best Value Inn
9420 State Route 14 (44241-5226)
PHONE..................................330 626-2888
Rajni S Patel, *Pr*
Hema R Patel, *Mgr*
EMP: 34 **EST:** 1986
SALES (est): 213.78K **Privately Held**
Web: www.sonesta.com
SIC: 7011 Inns

(G-13426)
ROBINSON HEALTH SYSTEM INC
Also Called: Robinson Hlth Affl Med Ctr One
9424 State Route 14 (44241-5226)
PHONE..................................330 626-3455
EMP: 3542
SALES (corp-wide): 878.24MM **Privately Held**
Web: www.robinsonmemorial.org
SIC: 8062 8011 General medical and surgical hospitals; Primary care medical clinic
HQ: Robinson Health System, Inc.
6847 N Chestnut St
Ravenna OH 44266
330 297-0811

(G-13427)
SINGER STEEL COMPANY
Also Called: Ryerson
10100 Singer Dr (44241-4639)
P.O. Box 2279 (44241-0279)
PHONE..................................330 562-7200
EMP: 30 **EST:** 1923
SALES (est): 9.55MM **Publicly Held**
SIC: 5051 Steel
HQ: Joseph T. Ryerson & Son, Inc.
227 W Monroe St Fl 27
Chicago IL 60606
312 292-5000

(G-13428)
SOFT-LITE LLC (HQ)
Also Called: Soft-Lite Windows
10250 Philipp Pkwy (44241-4765)
PHONE..................................330 528-3400
Roy Anderson, *Pr*
Kyle Pozek, *
EMP: 160 **EST:** 1937
SQ FT: 200,000
SALES (est): 93.85MM
SALES (corp-wide): 1.2B **Privately Held**
Web: www.soft-lite.com
SIC: 5031 Windows
PA: Harvey Industries, Llc
1400 Main St Fl 3 Ste 3
Waltham MA 02451
800 598-5400

(G-13429)
STREETSBORO BOARD EDUCATION
Also Called: Streetsboro Bus Garage
1901 Annalane Dr (44241-1730)
PHONE..................................330 626-4909

GEOGRAPHIC SECTION Strongsville - Cuyahoga County (G-13449)

Sharon Deyoung, *Dir*
EMP: 56
SALES (corp-wide): 1.69MM **Privately Held**
Web: www.scsrockets.org
SIC: 4151 School buses
PA: Streetsboro Board Of Education
9000 Kirby Ln
Streetsboro OH 44241
330 626-4900

(G-13430)
STREETSBORO OPCO LLC
Also Called: Arbors At Streetsboro
1645 Maplewood Dr (44241-5662)
PHONE..................................502 429-8062
Robert Norcross, *CEO*
EMP: 27 **EST:** 2014
SALES (est): 5.35MM **Privately Held**
Web: www.arborsatstreetsboro.com
SIC: 8051 Convalescent home with continuous nursing care

(G-13431)
TALIS CLINICAL LLC
650 Mondial Pkwy (44241)
PHONE..................................234 284-2399
Roger Hungerford, *CEO*
Gary Colister, *
Karen Alexander, *
EMP: 59 **EST:** 2012
SQ FT: 9,500
SALES (est): 10.43MM
SALES (corp-wide): 7.13B **Privately Held**
Web: www.talisclinical.com
SIC: 7371 Computer software development
HQ: Getinge Ab (Publ)
Lindholmspiren 7a
GOteborg 417 5
103350000

(G-13432)
THE ANDREWS MOVING AND STORAGE COMPANY (PA)
Also Called: United Van Lines
10235 Philipp Pkwy (44241-4040)
PHONE..................................330 656-8700
▲ **EMP:** 40 **EST:** 1908
SALES (est): 10.48MM
SALES (corp-wide): 10.48MM **Privately Held**
Web: www.andrewsmoving.com
SIC: 4213 4212 4214 Household goods transport; Local trucking, without storage; Household goods moving and storage, local

(G-13433)
UNITED TECHNICAL SUPPORT SVCS
10325 State Route 43 Ste F (44241-4945)
PHONE..................................330 562-3330
Ronal Duffy, *CEO*
James F Cecil, *COO*
Larry Cornell, *Sec*
EMP: 125 **EST:** 2000
SQ FT: 5,000
SALES (est): 19.97MM **Privately Held**
Web: www.utss.net
SIC: 7373 1796 Local area network (LAN) systems integrator; Machinery installation

(G-13434)
UNITY HEALTH NETWORK LLC
9330 Market Square Dr Ste 100 (44241-3958)
PHONE..................................330 626-0549
Terry Kingery, *Brnch Mgr*
EMP: 27
SALES (corp-wide): 51.74MM **Privately Held**
Web: www.unityhealthnetwork.com

SIC: 8043 8011 5999 Offices and clinics of podiatrists; Orthopedic physician; Orthopedic and prosthesis applications
PA: Unity Health Network, Llc
2750 Front St
Cuyahoga Falls OH 44221
330 923-5899

(G-13435)
WESTERN RSRVE RACQUET CLB CORP
11013 Aurora Hudson Rd (44241-1630)
PHONE..................................330 653-3103
Terry Travies, *Genl Mgr*
EMP: 49 **EST:** 1970
SQ FT: 80,000
SALES (est): 830.18K **Privately Held**
Web: www.wrrfc.com
SIC: 7991 Health club

(G-13436)
WINGATE INN
9705 State Route 14 (44241-5219)
PHONE..................................330 422-9900
Niranjan Patel, *Pr*
EMP: 71 **EST:** 2000
SALES (est): 432.9K **Privately Held**
Web: www.wyndhamhotels.com
SIC: 7011 Hotels and motels

Strongsville
Cuyahoga County

(G-13437)
A-ROO COMPANY LLC (HQ)
22360 Royalton Rd (44149-3826)
P.O. Box 360050 (44136-0001)
PHONE..................................440 238-8850
Sharon Gilbert, *
▲ **EMP:** 55 **EST:** 2004
SQ FT: 50,000
SALES (est): 22.73MM
SALES (corp-wide): 22.73MM **Privately Held**
Web: www.a-roo.com
SIC: 5199 Packaging materials
PA: Professional Packaging Company Inc
22360 Royalton Rd
Strongsville OH 44149
440 238-8850

(G-13438)
ACCESS CATALOG COMPANY LLC
21848 Commerce Pkwy Ste 100 (44149-5559)
PHONE..................................440 572-5377
Jim Vangieson, *Mgr*
EMP: 113
SALES (corp-wide): 1.31B **Privately Held**
SIC: 5065 5046 Electronic parts and equipment, nec; Coffee brewing equipment and supplies
HQ: Access Catalog Company, L.L.C.
10880 Linpage Pl
Saint Louis MO 63132
314 301-3300

(G-13439)
ACUATIVE CORPORATION
8237 Dow Cir (44136-1761)
PHONE..................................440 202-4500
EMP: 60
SALES (corp-wide): 98.17MM **Privately Held**
Web: www.acuative.com
SIC: 5065 Telephone and telegraphic equipment
PA: Acuative Corporation
695 Us Highway 46 Ste 305
Fairfield NJ 07004
862 926-5600

(G-13440)
ALL FOILS INC
16100 Imperial Pkwy (44149-0600)
PHONE..................................440 572-3645
Kevin C Foos, *Pr*
V Erik Konsen, *
Robert F Gesing, *
Karen Mittman Ctrl, *Prin*
Thomas L Johnston, *
◆ **EMP:** 75 **EST:** 1980
SQ FT: 140,000
SALES (est): 23.11MM
SALES (corp-wide): 35.45MM **Privately Held**
Web: www.allfoils.com
SIC: 5051 Steel
PA: R B Technologies, Inc.
16100 Imperial Pkwy
Strongsville OH 44149
440 572-3645

(G-13441)
ALTENHEIM FOUNDATION INC
Also Called: Altenheim Foundation
18627 Shurmer Rd (44136-6150)
PHONE..................................440 238-3361
Greg Mcdaniels, *Pr*
EMP: 47 **EST:** 1990
SALES (est): 2.58MM **Privately Held**
Web: www.altenheim.com
SIC: 8051 Convalescent home with continuous nursing care

(G-13442)
APPH WICHITA INC
Also Called: Apph
15900 Foltz Pkwy (44149-5531)
PHONE..................................316 943-5752
Mike Meshey, *Pr*
Jon Sharrock, *
▲ **EMP:** 50 **EST:** 1959
SALES (est): 3.72MM
SALES (corp-wide): 400.71MM **Privately Held**
SIC: 7699 3594 3728 Aircraft and heavy equipment repair services; Fluid power pumps and motors; Aircraft parts and equipment, nec
PA: Heroux-Devtek Inc
1111 Rue Saint-Charles O Bureau 600
Longueuil QC J4K 5
450 679-5450

(G-13443)
APPLIED MINT SUPS SLUTIONS LLC (HQ)
14790 Foltz Pkwy (44149-4723)
PHONE..................................216 456-3600
EMP: 36 **EST:** 1982
SQ FT: 102,850
SALES (est): 50.13MM
SALES (corp-wide): 4.41B **Publicly Held**
Web: www.appliedmss.com
SIC: 5085 Industrial supplies
PA: Applied Industrial Technologies, Inc.
1 Applied Plz
Cleveland OH 44115
216 426-4000

(G-13444)
ARCHWAY MARKETING SERVICES INC
20770 Westwood Dr (44149-3907)
P.O. Box 360450 (44136-0041)
PHONE..................................440 572-0725
EMP: 70
Web: www.archway.com

SIC: 8742 Marketing consulting services
HQ: Archway Marketing Services, Inc.
8775 Zachary Ln N
Maple Grove MN 55369

(G-13445)
BEARING & DRIVE SYSTEMS INC
Also Called: Inc, Stearns-Stafford
15157 Foltz Pkwy (44149-4730)
PHONE..................................440 846-4272
EMP: 74
SALES (corp-wide): 24.83MM **Privately Held**
Web: www.bdsbearing.com
SIC: 5085 Bearings
PA: Bearing & Drive Systems, Inc.
14888 Foltz Pkwy
Strongsville OH 44149
440 846-9700

(G-13446)
BROOKER INSURANCE AGENCY INC
Also Called: Nationwide
10749 Pearl Rd Ste 1a (44136-3347)
PHONE..................................440 238-5454
Malcolm Brooker Junior, *Pr*
EMP: 44 **EST:** 1920
SQ FT: 9,000
SALES (est): 7.31MM **Privately Held**
Web: www.brooker-ins.com
SIC: 6411 Insurance agents, nec

(G-13447)
CATENSYS US INC
21487 Royalton Rd (44149-3809)
PHONE..................................330 273-4383
Marc Mcgrath, *Brnch Mgr*
EMP: 342
SALES (corp-wide): 66.25B **Privately Held**
Web: www.schaeffler.us
SIC: 5085 Bearings
HQ: Schaeffler Group Usa Inc.
308 Springhill Farm Rd
Fort Mill SC 29715
803 548-8500

(G-13448)
CLERAC LLC (DH)
Also Called: National Car Rental
8249 Mohawk Dr (44136-1795)
PHONE..................................440 345-3999
EMP: 50 **EST:** 1991
SQ FT: 11,894
SALES (est): 50.15MM
SALES (corp-wide): 7.04B **Privately Held**
Web: www.nationalcar.com
SIC: 7515 7514 Passenger car leasing; Rent-a-car service
HQ: Enterprise Mobility
600 Corporate Park Dr
Saint Louis MO 63105
314 512-5000

(G-13449)
CLEVELAND CLINIC FOUNDATION
Also Called: Cleveland Clinic
16761 Southpark Ctr (44136-9302)
PHONE..................................440 878-2500
Rachel R Heers, *Prin*
EMP: 1794 **EST:** 1982
SALES (est): 55.99MM
SALES (corp-wide): 14.48B **Privately Held**
Web: my.clevelandclinic.org
SIC: 8062 General medical and surgical hospitals
PA: The Cleveland Clinic Foundation
9500 Euclid Ave
Cleveland OH 44195
216 636-8335

Strongsville - Cuyahoga County (G-13450)

(G-13450)
CROSSROADS REO INC
17075 Pearl Rd Ste 1 (44136-6009)
PHONE..................................440 846-0077
Daniel Keltner, *Prin*
EMP: 39 **EST:** 2010
SALES (est): 215.47K **Privately Held**
Web: www.crossroads-reo.com
SIC: 6531 Real estate agent, residential

(G-13451)
D&J QUALITY CARE ENTPS INC
Also Called: Comforcare Home Care
13315 Prospect Rd (44149-3853)
PHONE..................................440 638-7001
Deborah Vermillion, *Prin*
Johnny Vermillion, *
EMP: 99 **EST:** 2020
SALES (est): 2.06MM **Privately Held**
Web: www.comforcare.com
SIC: 8082 Home health care services

(G-13452)
DENTALONE PARTNERS INC
13339 Pearl Rd (44136-3403)
PHONE..................................440 238-1591
EMP: 107
SALES (corp-wide): 85.13MM **Privately Held**
Web: www.dentalworks.com
SIC: 8021 Dental clinic
PA: Dentalone Partners, Inc.
  6700 Pinecrest Dr Ste 150
  Plano TX 75024
  972 755-0800

(G-13453)
EUROFINS TESTOIL INC
Also Called: Testoil, Inc.
20338 Progress Dr (44149-3220)
PHONE..................................216 251-2510
Mary Messuti, *Pr*
EMP: 100 **EST:** 1988
SQ FT: 2,000
SALES (est): 843.88K
SALES (corp-wide): 220.81K **Privately Held**
Web: www.testoil.com
SIC: 8734 Testing laboratories
HQ: Eurofins Environment Testing America
  Holdings, Inc.
  343 W Main St
  Leola PA

(G-13454)
EUTHENICS INC (PA)
8235 Mohawk Dr (44136-1795)
PHONE..................................440 260-1555
Ron Bender, *Pr*
Richard S Wasosky, *
EMP: 33 **EST:** 1972
SQ FT: 8,000
SALES (est): 2.8MM
SALES (corp-wide): 2.8MM **Privately Held**
Web: www.euthenics-inc.com
SIC: 8711 Civil engineering

(G-13455)
FALLING LEASING CO LLC
Also Called: FALLING WATER HEALTHCARE CENTE
18840 Falling Water Rd (44136-4200)
PHONE..................................440 238-1100
EMP: 49 **EST:** 1996
SQ FT: 60,000
SALES (est): 10.62MM **Privately Held**
Web: www.communicarehealth.com
SIC: 8051 Convalescent home with continuous nursing care

(G-13456)
FERRY CAP & SET SCREW COMPANY
12200 Alameda Dr (44149-3050)
PHONE..................................440 783-3126
EMP: 88
SALES (corp-wide): 15.78B **Publicly Held**
SIC: 5085 Fasteners, industrial: nuts, bolts, screws, etc.
HQ: Ferry Cap & Set Screw Company
  13300 Bramley Ave
  Lakewood OH 44107
  216 649-7400

(G-13457)
FOUNDATION SOFTWARE LLC (PA)
17999 Foltz Pkwy (44149-5565)
PHONE..................................330 220-8383
Fred Ode, *CEO*
Kathleen Ode, *Sec*
Paul Noonan, *CGO*
EMP: 479 **EST:** 1985
SQ FT: 16,000
SALES (est): 147.47MM
SALES (corp-wide): 147.47MM **Privately Held**
Web: www.foundationsoft.com
SIC: 7372 7371 Prepackaged software; Software programming applications

(G-13458)
GREENHUSE SLTONS ACQSITION LLC
Also Called: Llk Greenhouse Solutions
14800 Foltz Pkwy (44149-4725)
PHONE..................................440 236-8332
EMP: 33 **EST:** 2020
SALES (est): 2.38MM **Privately Held**
Web: www.llk-solutions.com
SIC: 6799 Investors, nec

(G-13459)
HDI LANDING GEAR USA INC
15900 Foltz Pkwy (44149-5531)
PHONE..................................440 783-5255
EMP: 200
SALES (corp-wide): 400.71MM **Privately Held**
Web: www.herouxdevtek.com
SIC: 7389 Automobile recovery service
HQ: Hdi Landing Gear Usa Inc.
  663 Montgomery Ave
  Springfield OH 45506

(G-13460)
HERITAGE POOL SUPPLY GROUP INC
Also Called: Emsco Distributors
22350 Royalton Rd (44149-3826)
P.O. Box 360660 (44136-0011)
PHONE..................................440 238-2100
Mark Stoyanoff, *Brnch Mgr*
EMP: 80
SALES (corp-wide): 152.67B **Publicly Held**
Web: www.heritagepoolsupplygroup.com
SIC: 5091 Swimming pools, equipment and supplies
HQ: Heritage Pool Supply Group, Inc.
  7440 State Highway 121
  Mckinney TX 75070
  214 491-4149

(G-13461)
HEWLETTCO INC
Also Called: Goddard School
13590 Falling Water Rd (44136-4319)
PHONE..................................440 238-4600
Robyn T Hewlett, *Pr*
Tracy Swanson, *Prin*
Craig Bach, *Prin*
L Dale Todd, *VP*
Maragaret Todd, *Sec*
EMP: 37 **EST:** 2006
SQ FT: 10,000
SALES (est): 488.9K **Privately Held**
Web: www.goddardschool.com
SIC: 8351 Preschool center

(G-13462)
HOME DEPOT USA INC
Also Called: Home Depot, The
8199 Pearl Rd (44136)
PHONE..................................440 826-9092
Ron Salizar, *Mgr*
EMP: 100
SALES (corp-wide): 152.67B **Publicly Held**
Web: www.homedepot.com
SIC: 5211 7359 Home centers; Tool rental
HQ: Home Depot U.S.A., Inc.
  2445 Springfield Ave
  Vauxhall NJ 07088

(G-13463)
HUGHES CORPORATION (PA)
Also Called: Weschler Instruments
16900 Foltz Pkwy (44149)
PHONE..................................440 238-2550
Paul Layne, *CEO*
David E Hughes, *
Douglas Hughes, *
Michael F Dorman, *
Esther Carpenter, *
EMP: 30 **EST:** 1941
SQ FT: 11,500
SALES (est): 26.85MM
SALES (corp-wide): 26.85MM **Privately Held**
Web: www.weschler.com
SIC: 5063 3825 Electrical apparatus and equipment; Instruments to measure electricity

(G-13464)
IMARC RESEARCH INC
22560 Lunn Rd (44149-4895)
PHONE..................................440 801-1540
Sandra Maddock, *CEO*
Brandy Chittester, *
EMP: 60 **EST:** 1999
SALES (est): 9.92MM **Privately Held**
Web: www.imarcuniversity.com
SIC: 8742 8731 Hospital and health services consultant; Commercial physical research
HQ: Avania, Llc
  100 Crowley Dr Ste 216
  Marlborough MA 01752
  508 351-8632

(G-13465)
IMPAC HOTEL GROUP LLC
Also Called: Holiday Inn Slect Strongsville
15471 Royalton Rd (44136-5441)
PHONE..................................440 238-8800
Ryan Mccarbery, *Mgr*
EMP: 38 **EST:** 1997
SALES (est): 3.36MM **Privately Held**
Web: www.holidayinn.com
SIC: 7011 Hotels and motels
HQ: Lodgian, Llc
  2711 N Haskell Ave # 170
  Dallas TX 75204
  214 754-8300

(G-13466)
INTRALOT INC
13500 Darice Pkwy Ste C (44149-3840)
PHONE..................................440 268-2900
EMP: 41
Web: www.intralot.com
SIC: 7379 Online services technology consultants
HQ: Intralot, Inc.
  11360 Technology Cir
  Duluth GA 30097
  678 473-7200

(G-13467)
KAISER FOUNDATION HOSPITALS
Also Called: Strongsville Medical Offices
17406 Royalton Rd (44136-5144)
PHONE..................................216 524-7377
EMP: 29
SALES (corp-wide): 70.8B **Privately Held**
Web: www.kaisercenter.com
SIC: 8011 Medical centers
HQ: Kaiser Foundation Hospitals Inc
  1 Kaiser Plz
  Oakland CA 94612
  510 271-6611

(G-13468)
KEMPER COMPANY
Also Called: Kemper House of Strongsville
10890 Prospect Rd (44149-2256)
PHONE..................................440 846-1100
John Kemper, *Brnch Mgr*
EMP: 63
SALES (corp-wide): 23.1MM **Privately Held**
Web: www.kemperhouse.com
SIC: 8748 Business consulting, nec
PA: The Kemper Company
  21851 Center Ridge Rd # 408
  Cleveland OH 44116
  216 472-4200

(G-13469)
KRAFT FLUID SYSTEMS INC
14300 Foltz Pkwy (44149-4798)
P.O. Box 637448 (45263-7448)
PHONE..................................440 238-5545
▲ **EMP:** 44 **EST:** 1972
SALES (est): 10.34MM **Privately Held**
Web: www.kraftelectricdrives.com
SIC: 5084 Industrial machinery and equipment

(G-13470)
LINCOLN MOVING & STORAGE CO
20036 Progress Dr (44149-3214)
PHONE..................................216 741-5500
TOLL FREE: 888
Eugene Dietrich, *VP*
Lawrence H Roush, *
Sharon Dietrich, *
Edith Roush, *
EMP: 70 **EST:** 1976
SALES (est): 4.7MM **Privately Held**
Web: www.movingclevelandoh.com
SIC: 1799 4213 4214 Office furniture installation; Trucking, except local; Local trucking with storage

(G-13471)
LITEHOUSE PRODUCTS LLC (PA)
Also Called: Litehouse Pools & Spas
10883 Pearl Rd Ste 301 (44136-3359)
PHONE..................................440 638-2350
▲ **EMP:** 50 **EST:** 2004
SALES (est): 38.85MM
SALES (corp-wide): 38.85MM **Privately Held**
Web: www.litehouse.com
SIC: 5091 3949 5999 5712 Swimming pools, equipment and supplies; Water sports equipment; Swimming pools, above ground ; Outdoor and garden furniture

GEOGRAPHIC SECTION
Strongsville - Cuyahoga County (G-13494)

(G-13472)
LONG BUSINESS SYSTEMS INC
Also Called: Lbs
10749 Pearl Rd Ste 2a (44136-3347)
P.O. Box 3598 (75019-5546)
PHONE..................440 846-8500
Scott Long, *Pr*
EMP: 28 **EST:** 1989
SQ FT: 6,000
SALES (est): 1.61MM **Privately Held**
Web: www.lbsi.com
SIC: 8748 Business consulting, nec

(G-13473)
LOWES HOME CENTERS LLC
Also Called: Lowe's
9149 Pearl Rd (44136-1414)
PHONE..................440 239-2630
John Lerch, *Mgr*
EMP: 143
SALES (corp-wide): 86.38B **Publicly Held**
Web: www.lowes.com
SIC: 5211 5031 5722 5064 Home centers; Building materials, exterior; Household appliance stores; Electrical appliances, television and radio
HQ: Lowe's Home Centers, Llc
1000 Lowes Blvd
Mooresville NC 28117
336 658-4000

(G-13474)
MARIA GARDENS LLC (PA)
20465 Royalton Rd (44149-4967)
P.O. Box 360256 (44136-0005)
PHONE..................440 238-7637
David Stopper, *Pr*
Rosemary Stopper, *
Dave Stopper Senior, *Prin*
EMP: 44 **EST:** 1993
SQ FT: 85,000
SALES (est): 4.9MM
SALES (corp-wide): 4.9MM **Privately Held**
Web: www.mariagardens.net
SIC: 0181 5193 5992 Flowers: grown under cover (e.g., greenhouse production); Plants, potted; Plants, potted

(G-13475)
MEDICAL MUTUAL SERVICES LLC (HQ)
Also Called: Antares Management Solutions
17800 Royalton Rd (44136-5149)
PHONE..................440 878-4800
Rick Chiricosta, *Pr*
Ray Mueller, *Ex VP*
EMP: 250 **EST:** 1997
SQ FT: 15,000
SALES (est): 99.02MM
SALES (corp-wide): 2.75B **Privately Held**
SIC: 7374 7375 Data processing and preparation; Information retrieval services
PA: Medical Mutual Of Ohio
2060 E 9th St
Cleveland OH 44115
216 687-7000

(G-13476)
MKE HOLDINGS INC (PA)
22350 Royalton Rd (44149)
P.O. Box 360660 (44136)
PHONE..................440 238-2100
Mark Stoyanoff, *Pr*
Richard Laneve, *
EMP: 28 **EST:** 1974
SQ FT: 100,000
SALES (est): 41MM
SALES (corp-wide): 41MM **Privately Held**
Web: www.opaquatics.com
SIC: 5091 Swimming pools, equipment and supplies

(G-13477)
MUELLER ART COVER & BINDING CO
12005 Alameda Dr (44149-3016)
PHONE..................440 238-3303
TOLL FREE: 888
Edmond Mueller, *Pr*
EMP: 45 **EST:** 1932
SQ FT: 38,000
SALES (est): 2.7MM **Privately Held**
Web: www.muellerartcover.com
SIC: 2782 7336 Looseleaf binders and devices; Graphic arts and related design

(G-13478)
NATIONAL AUTO EXPERTS LLC
8370 Dow Cir Ste 100 (44136-1797)
PHONE..................440 274-5114
EMP: 107 **EST:** 2006
SALES (est): 22.74MM
SALES (corp-wide): 23.51MM **Privately Held**
Web: us.portfolioco.com
SIC: 7538 General automotive repair shops
PA: Portfolio Holding, Inc.
25541 Commercentre Dr
Lake Forest CA 92630
877 705-4001

(G-13479)
OHIO CLLBRTIVE LRNG SLTONS INC (PA)
Also Called: Smart Solutions
17171 Golden Star Dr (44136)
PHONE..................216 595-5289
Anand Julka, *Pr*
▲ **EMP:** 50 **EST:** 1983
SALES (est): 9.5MM
SALES (corp-wide): 9.5MM **Privately Held**
SIC: 7372 8741 Business oriented computer software; Business management

(G-13480)
PSE CREDIT UNION INC
12700 Prospect Rd (44149-2972)
PHONE..................440 572-3830
EMP: 27
SQ FT: 3,574
SALES (corp-wide): 9.02MM **Privately Held**
Web: www.psecreditunion.org
SIC: 6061 Federal credit unions
PA: Pse Credit Union, Inc.
5255 Regency Dr
Cleveland OH 44129
440 843-8300

(G-13481)
RADEBAUGH-FETZER COMPANY
Also Called: Gill Podiatry Supply Co
22400 Ascoa Ct (44149-4766)
PHONE..................440 878-4700
Eric Boggs, *Pr*
Judith Boggs, *
EMP: 30 **EST:** 1911
SQ FT: 42,000
SALES (est): 9.3MM **Privately Held**
SIC: 5047 Physician equipment and supplies

(G-13482)
SHIPPING PILOT LLC
13000 Darice Pkwy (44149-3800)
PHONE..................505 744-7669
Greg Airel, *Pr*
EMP: 47 **EST:** 2020
SALES (est): 3.94MM **Privately Held**
Web: www.shippingpilot.co
SIC: 4731 Freight transportation arrangement

(G-13483)
SHORELINE TRANSPORTATION INC
Also Called: Shoreline Company
20137 Progress Dr (44149-3215)
PHONE..................440 878-2000
Janeen Mazzeo-sparks, *Pr*
Donald Sparks, *
EMP: 240 **EST:** 1996
SQ FT: 35,000
SALES (est): 10.79MM **Privately Held**
Web: www.shorelineexpressinc.com
SIC: 4212 4213 4731 Local trucking, without storage; Trucking, except local; Transportation agents and brokers

(G-13484)
SHURMER PLACE AT ALTENHEIM
18821 Shurmer Rd (44136-6100)
PHONE..................440 238-9001
Paul Pasota, *Ex Dir*
Paul Pasotam, *
EMP: 51 **EST:** 2000
SALES (est): 8.67MM **Privately Held**
Web: www.altenheim.com
SIC: 8361 Aged home

(G-13485)
SOLUTION INDUSTRIES INC
21555 Drake Rd (44149-6616)
PHONE..................440 816-9500
John Radel, *Pr*
▲ **EMP:** 59 **EST:** 2003
SALES (est): 10.82MM **Privately Held**
Web: www.solutionind.com
SIC: 5085 Fasteners, industrial: nuts, bolts, screws, etc.

(G-13486)
SROKA INC
21265 Westwood Dr (44149-2905)
PHONE..................440 572-2811
▲ **EMP:** 35 **EST:** 1984
SALES (est): 4.23MM **Privately Held**
Web: www.srokausa.com
SIC: 5084 Materials handling machinery

(G-13487)
STATE FARM GENERAL INSUR CO
Also Called: State Farm Insurance
11220 Pearl Rd (44136-3312)
PHONE..................440 268-0600
Dane A Donaldson, *Brnch Mgr*
EMP: 54
SALES (corp-wide): 27.88B **Privately Held**
Web: www.statefarm.com
SIC: 6411 Insurance agents and brokers
HQ: State Farm General Insurance Co Inc
1 State Farm Plz
Bloomington IL 61701
309 766-2311

(G-13488)
STRONGSVLLE LDGING ASSOC I LTD
Also Called: Holiday Inn
15471 Royalton Rd (44136-5441)
PHONE..................440 238-8800
EMP: 100 **EST:** 1987
SQ FT: 65,414
SALES (est): 946.2K **Privately Held**
Web: www.holidayinn.com
SIC: 7011 Hotels and motels

(G-13489)
STRONGVILLE RECREATION COMPLEX
18688 Royalton Rd (44136-5127)
PHONE..................440 580-3230
Colleen Grady, *Brnch Mgr*
EMP: 189
SALES (corp-wide): 72.16K **Privately Held**
Web: www.strongsville.org
SIC: 7996 Theme park, amusement
PA: Strongville Recreation Complex
18100 Royalton Rd
Cleveland OH 44136
440 878-6000

(G-13490)
STUD WELDING ASSOCIATES INC
Also Called: Stud Welding
12200 Alameda Dr (44149-3021)
PHONE..................440 783-3160
▼ **EMP:** 70
SIC: 5085 3496 1799 Fasteners, industrial: nuts, bolts, screws, etc.; Clips and fasteners, made from purchased wire; Welding on site

(G-13491)
TELETRONICS SERVICES INC (PA)
Also Called: Teletronics Communications
22550 Ascoa Ct (44149-4700)
PHONE..................216 778-6500
Gale Kenney, *CEO*
Thomas Ursem; *
Gary Reffert, *
EMP: 33 **EST:** 1980
SQ FT: 12,000
SALES (est): 9.52MM
SALES (corp-wide): 9.52MM **Privately Held**
Web: www.teletronics-inc.com
SIC: 5065 Telephone equipment

(G-13492)
TTX
22550 Ascoa Ct (44149-4700)
PHONE..................216 778-6500
Margi Casebolt, *Asstg*
EMP: 49 **EST:** 2019
SALES (est): 1.39MM **Privately Held**
Web: www.ttx-inc.com
SIC: 4741 Rental of railroad cars

(G-13493)
UNION HOME MORTGAGE CORP (PA)
Also Called: Vloan
8241 Dow Cir (44136-1761)
PHONE..................800 767-4684
Bill Cosgrove, *CEO*
C William Cosgrove, *Pr*
Michael Zuren, *VP*
Jim R Wickham, *VP*
Mick Szoka, *VP*
EMP: 35 **EST:** 1970
SQ FT: 15,000
SALES (est): 306.62MM
SALES (corp-wide): 306.62MM **Privately Held**
Web: www.uhm.com
SIC: 6162 Mortgage bankers

(G-13494)
US TANK ALLIANCE INC
19511 Progress Dr Ste 3 (44149-3262)
PHONE..................440 238-7705
Kathy Pasternak, *Brnch Mgr*
EMP: 74
SALES (corp-wide): 15.7MM **Privately Held**
Web: www.ustankweb.com
SIC: 1623 Oil and gas pipeline construction
PA: Us Tank Alliance, Inc.
7400 Skyline Dr E Ste A
Columbus OH 43235
614 923-0154

Strongsville - Cuyahoga County (G-13495)

(G-13495)
VIO MED SPA STRONGSVILLE LLC
16738 Pearl Rd (44136-6049)
PHONE..................................440 268-6100
EMP: 57 **EST:** 2019
SALES (est): 546.79K **Privately Held**
Web: www.viomedspa.com
SIC: 7991 Spas

(G-13496)
VOLPINI LAW LLC
15300 Pearl Rd Ste 201 (44136-5036)
PHONE..................................216 956-4133
EMP: 28 **EST:** 2018
SALES (est): 874.07K **Privately Held**
Web: www.volpinilaw.com
SIC: 8111 General practice law office

(G-13497)
WALLOVER ENTERPRISES INC (DH)
21845 Drake Rd (44149-6610)
PHONE..................................440 238-9250
George M Marquis, *Pr*
William C Cutri, *
EMP: 30 **EST:** 1863
SQ FT: 28,000
SALES (est): 39.25MM
SALES (corp-wide): 1.95B **Publicly Held**
SIC: 2992 8734 Oils and greases, blending and compounding; Product testing laboratories
HQ: Quaker Houghton Pa, Inc.
901 E Hector St
Conshohocken PA 19428
610 832-4000

(G-13498)
WDHT ENTERPRISES INC
14675 Foltz Pkwy (44149-4720)
PHONE..................................440 846-0200
Donald Mills Ii, *Pr*
Robert Mills, *
EMP: 110 **EST:** 1983
SQ FT: 160,000
SALES (est): 22.98MM **Privately Held**
Web: www.millsvanlines.com
SIC: 4212 Moving services

Struthers
Mahoning County

(G-13499)
CRED-KAP INC
Also Called: Maplecrest Nursing HM For Aged
400 Sexton St (44471-1141)
P.O. Box 5185 (44514-0185)
PHONE..................................330 755-1466
Christopher Daprile, *Pr*
Lisa Daprile, *VP*
EMP: 60 **EST:** 1960
SALES (est): 5.68MM **Privately Held**
Web: www.maplecrestnursing.com
SIC: 8051 Convalescent home with continuous nursing care

(G-13500)
INDUSTRIAL PPING SPCALISTS INC
100 S Bridge St Ste 3 (44471-1973)
PHONE..................................330 750-2800
EMP: 38
SALES (corp-wide): 111.16MM **Privately Held**
Web: www.ipipes.com
SIC: 5051 Pipe and tubing, steel
PA: Industrial Piping Specialists, Inc.
606 N 145th East Ave
Tulsa OK 74116
918 437-9100

(G-13501)
JS BOVA EXCAVATING LLC
235 State St (44471-1958)
P.O. Box 296 (44471-0296)
PHONE..................................234 254-4040
Louis Joseph Bova, *Managing Member*
Sherri Bova, *
EMP: 36 **EST:** 2013
SQ FT: 2,100
SALES (est): 7.62MM **Privately Held**
Web: www.jsbova.com
SIC: 1794 1623 Excavation work; Underground utilities contractor

(G-13502)
PSYCARE INC
Also Called: Psycare Struthers
520 Youngstown Poland Rd (44471-1103)
PHONE..................................330 318-3078
EMP: 87
Web: www.psycare.com
SIC: 8093 Mental health clinic, outpatient
PA: Psycare Inc
2980 Belmont Ave
Youngstown OH 44505

(G-13503)
RUDZIK EXCAVATING INC
401 Lowellville Rd (44471-2076)
PHONE..................................330 755-1540
Bonnie L Rudzik, *Sec*
Jeffrey A Rudzik, *
EMP: 45 **EST:** 1998
SQ FT: 3,000
SALES (est): 11.24MM **Privately Held**
Web: www.rudzikexcavating.com
SIC: 1794 1799 Excavation and grading, building construction; Building site preparation

Stryker
Williams County

(G-13504)
CORRECTION COMMISSION NW OHIO
3151 County Road 2425 (43557-9418)
PHONE..................................419 428-3800
Jim Dennis, *Ex Dir*
EMP: 187 **EST:** 1983
SQ FT: 189,000
SALES (est): 8.18MM **Privately Held**
Web: www.ccnoregionaljail.org
SIC: 8744 Correctional facility

(G-13505)
QUADCO REHABILITATION CTR INC (PA)
Also Called: NORTHWEST PRODUCTS
427 N Defiance St (43557-9472)
PHONE..................................419 682-1011
Bruce Abell, *Ex Dir*
EMP: 287 **EST:** 1967
SQ FT: 24,000
SALES (est): 1.38MM
SALES (corp-wide): 1.38MM **Privately Held**
Web: www.quadcorehab.org
SIC: 8331 2448 2441 Vocational rehabilitation agency; Wood pallets and skids; Nailed wood boxes and shook

(G-13506)
WOOLACE ELECTRIC CORP
1978 County Road 22a (43557-9778)
PHONE..................................419 428-3161
William D Woolace, *Pr*
Benjamin Woolace, *
Tyler Woolace, *Stockholder*

Eric Woolave, *Stockholder*
EMP: 35 **EST:** 1963
SQ FT: 2,600
SALES (est): 5.15MM **Privately Held**
Web: www.woolace.com
SIC: 1731 General electrical contractor

Sugar Grove
Fairfield County

(G-13507)
COLUMBIA GULF TRANSMISSION LLC
Also Called: Columbia Energy
6175 Old Logan Rd (43155-9795)
PHONE..................................740 746-9105
EMP: 73
SALES (corp-wide): 11.6B **Privately Held**
SIC: 4924 Natural gas distribution
HQ: Columbia Gulf Transmission, Llc
700 Louisiana St
Houston TX 77002
877 287-1782

Sugarcreek
Tuscarawas County

(G-13508)
D YODER HARDWOODS LLC
Also Called: Homestead Finishing
2131 County Road 70 (44681-9669)
PHONE..................................330 852-8105
EMP: 65 **EST:** 2004
SALES (est): 5.43MM **Privately Held**
SIC: 5021 Furniture

(G-13509)
DUTCH CREEK FOODS INC
1411 Old Route 39 Ne (44681-7400)
PHONE..................................330 852-2631
Mike Palmer, *Pr*
EMP: 27 **EST:** 1988
SQ FT: 25,000
SALES (est): 10.42MM
SALES (corp-wide): 25.45MM **Privately Held**
Web: www.dutchcreekfoods.com
SIC: 5147 Meats, fresh
PA: Dutchman Hospitality Group, Inc.
4985 Walnut St
Walnut Creek OH 44687
330 893-2926

(G-13510)
DUTCHMAN HOSPITALITY GROUP INC
1357 Old Route 39 Ne (44681-7666)
P.O. Box 525 (44681-0525)
PHONE..................................330 852-2586
Jennifer Sigman, *Brnch Mgr*
EMP: 58
SALES (corp-wide): 25.45MM **Privately Held**
Web: www.dhgroup.com
SIC: 7011 Bed and breakfast inn
PA: Dutchman Hospitality Group, Inc.
4985 Walnut St
Walnut Creek OH 44687
330 893-2926

(G-13511)
KAUFMAN REALTY & AUCTIONS LLC
1047 W Main St (44681-9318)
P.O. Box 422 (44681-0422)
PHONE..................................330 852-4111
Jr Miller, *Mgr*
EMP: 32 **EST:** 2011
SALES (est): 222.09K **Privately Held**

Web: www.kaufmanrealty.com
SIC: 7389 Auctioneers, fee basis

(G-13512)
PROVIA HOLDINGS INC (PA)
Also Called: Provia - Heritage Stone
2150 State Route 39 (44681-9201)
PHONE..................................330 852-4711
Bill Mullet, *Prin*
Brian Miller, *
Larry Troyer, *
Willis Schlabach, *
Phil Wengerd, *
EMP: 180 **EST:** 1972
SQ FT: 280,000
SALES (est): 140.5MM
SALES (corp-wide): 140.5MM **Privately Held**
Web: www.provia.com
SIC: 3442 5031 Metal doors; Door frames, all materials

(G-13513)
PROVIA LLC (HQ)
2150 State Route 39 (44681-9201)
PHONE..................................330 852-4711
Brian Miller, *Pr*
Larry Troyer, *
William Mullet, *
EMP: 30 **EST:** 2017
SQ FT: 10,000
SALES (est): 87.99MM
SALES (corp-wide): 140.5MM **Privately Held**
Web: www.provia.com
SIC: 5031 Windows
PA: Provia Holdings, Inc.
2150 State Route 39
Sugarcreek OH 44681
330 852-4711

Sunbury
Delaware County

(G-13514)
AD FARROW LLC
7754 E State Route 37 (43074-9636)
PHONE..................................740 965-9900
Robert B Althoff, *Brnch Mgr*
EMP: 28
SALES (corp-wide): 4.71MM **Privately Held**
Web: www.farrowhd.com
SIC: 5571 7699 Motorcycles; Motorcycle repair service
PA: A.D. Farrow Llc
491 W Broad St
Columbus OH 43215
614 228-6353

(G-13515)
AIRRIVA LLC
970 Joe Walker Rd (43074-9200)
PHONE..................................614 345-3996
Josiah Myers, *CEO*
EMP: 35 **EST:** 2019
SALES (est): 2.6MM **Privately Held**
Web: www.airriva.com
SIC: 6512 Nonresidential building operators

(G-13516)
AMERICAN SHOWA INC
677 W Cherry St (43074-9803)
PHONE..................................740 965-4040
EMP: 30
SIC: 8731 Commercial research laboratory
HQ: American Showa, Inc.
707 W Cherry St
Sunbury OH 43074
740 965-1133

GEOGRAPHIC SECTION

Sylvania - Lucas County (G-13538)

(G-13517)
ARBYS
7259 E State Route 37 (43074-8957)
PHONE.................................740 369-0317
EMP: 31 **EST:** 1996
SALES (est): 151.89K **Privately Held**
Web: www.arbys.com
SIC: 5812 7011 Fast-food restaurant, chain; Hotels and motels

(G-13518)
CHAMPIONSHIP MANAGEMENT CO INC
Also Called: North Star Golf Club
1150 Wilson Rd (43074-9633)
PHONE.................................740 524-4653
Robert Weiler, *Pr*
EMP: 47 **EST:** 1981
SALES (est): 3.57MM **Privately Held**
Web: www.thenorthstargolfclub.com
SIC: 7992 Public golf courses

(G-13519)
DBP ENTERPRISES LLC
Also Called: Holiday Inn
7301 E State Route 37 (43074-9210)
PHONE.................................740 513-2399
Daxa Patel, *Managing Member*
EMP: 51 **EST:** 2000
SALES (est): 428K **Privately Held**
Web: www.holidayinn.com
SIC: 7011 Hotels and motels

(G-13520)
DIAMONDBACK GOLF LLC
Also Called: Rattlesnake Ridge Golf Club
1 Rattlesnake Dr (43074-8018)
PHONE.................................614 410-1313
Max Brown, *Pr*
J Randall Beyer, *CFO*
EMP: 51 **EST:** 2003
SALES (est): 2.85MM **Privately Held**
Web: www.rrgolfclub.com
SIC: 7992 Public golf courses

(G-13521)
FIRE GUARD LLC
35 E Granville St (43074-9130)
P.O. Box 730 (43011-0730)
PHONE.................................740 625-5181
Nick Mcgovern, *Pr*
EMP: 50 **EST:** 1999
SALES (est): 2.51MM **Privately Held**
Web: www.fireguardllc.net
SIC: 1711 Fire sprinkler system installation

(G-13522)
MORNING VIEW DELAWARE INC
Also Called: Country View of Sunbury
14961 N Old 3c Rd (43074-9716)
PHONE.................................740 965-3984
Brian Colleran, *Pr*
Daniel Parker, *VP*
Ryan Kray, *Sec*
John Krystowski, *Treas*
EMP: 150 **EST:** 2003
SALES (est): 9.24MM **Privately Held**
Web: www.countryview-sunbury.net
SIC: 8059 Nursing home, except skilled and intermediate care facility

(G-13523)
OHASHI TECHNICA USA INC (HQ)
111 Burrer Dr (43074-9233)
PHONE.................................740 965-5115
Mamoru Shibasaki, *Prin*
Hikaru Tateiwa, *
▲ **EMP:** 50 **EST:** 1987
SQ FT: 110,000
SALES (est): 26.4MM **Privately Held**

Web: www.ohashiusa.com
SIC: 5013 5072 3452 Automotive supplies and parts; Hardware; Bolts, nuts, rivets, and washers
PA: Ohashi Technica Inc.
4-3-13, Toranomon
Minato-Ku TKY 105-0

(G-13524)
RESTAURANT SPECIALTIES INC
Also Called: RSI Construction
801 W Cherry St Ste 200 (43074-8598)
PHONE.................................614 885-9707
Paul Tanzillo, *Pr*
Gregory Hunt, *
Mark Petry, *
EMP: 32 **EST:** 1981
SQ FT: 4,000
SALES (est): 8.66MM **Privately Held**
Web: www.rsibuilds.com
SIC: 1542 Commercial and office building, new construction

Swanton
Fulton County

(G-13525)
FOUNDATION STEEL LLC
Also Called: Foundation Steel
12525 Airport Hwy (43558-9613)
P.O. Box 210 (43558-0210)
PHONE.................................419 402-4241
EMP: 182 **EST:** 2008
SALES (est): 18.84MM **Privately Held**
Web: www.foundationsteel.com
SIC: 1791 1622 Iron work, structural; Bridge, tunnel, and elevated highway construction

(G-13526)
HARBORSIDE HEALTHCARE LLC
Also Called: Swanton Vly Care Rhblttion Ctr
401 W Airport Hwy (43558-1447)
PHONE.................................419 825-1111
EMP: 125
SALES (corp-wide): 5.86B **Publicly Held**
Web: www.genesishcc.com
SIC: 8051 Convalescent home with continuous nursing care
HQ: Harborside Healthcare, Llc
5100 Sun Ave Ne
Albuquerque NM 87109

(G-13527)
NATIONAL FLIGHT SERVICES INC
10971 E Airport Service Rd (43558)
PHONE.................................419 865-2311
Tom Wiles, *Pr*
John Crummey, *
Larry Lowry, *
EMP: 105 **EST:** 1992
SQ FT: 49,000
SALES (est): 26.75MM **Privately Held**
Web: www.nationalflight.com
SIC: 4581 Aircraft servicing and repairing
PA: Nfs Holdings, Inc.
10971 E Airport Svc Rd
Swanton OH 43558

(G-13528)
RWAM BROS INC
420 N Hallett Avenue (43558-1144)
PHONE.................................419 826-3671
Lawrence Schmidt, *Pr*
Robert V Schmidt, *
William J Schmidt, *
Allen J Schmidt, *
Michael P Schmidt, *
▲ **EMP:** 30 **EST:** 1991
SQ FT: 610,000

SALES (est): 3.69MM
SALES (corp-wide): 3.69MM **Privately Held**
Web: www.schmidtbrosinc.com
SIC: 0181 5193 Bedding plants, growing of; Flowers and florists supplies
PA: Mapleview Farms, Inc
2425 S Fulton Lucas Rd
Swanton OH 43558
419 826-3671

(G-13529)
SWANTON HLTH CARE RTRMENT CTR
214 S Munson Rd (43558-1210)
PHONE.................................419 825-1145
Lisa Mitchell, *Pr*
Scott Mitchell, *
EMP: 74 **EST:** 1985
SQ FT: 19,000
SALES (est): 15.04MM **Privately Held**
SIC: 8051 8052 Convalescent home with continuous nursing care; Intermediate care facilities

(G-13530)
TOLEDO-LUCAS COUNTY PORT AUTH
Also Called: Toledo Express Airport
11013 Airport Hwy Ste 11 (43558-9403)
PHONE.................................419 865-2351
Paul L Toht Junior, *Dir*
EMP: 80
SALES (corp-wide): 24.13MM **Privately Held**
Web: www.toledoexpress.com
SIC: 4581 Airport
PA: Toledo-Lucas County Port Authority
1 Maritime Plz Ste 701
Toledo OH 43604
419 243-8251

(G-13531)
VALLEYWOOD GOLF CLUB INC
13501 Airport Hwy (43558-8550)
PHONE.................................419 826-3991
Ron Dickson, *Pr*
Louie Carson, *
Neil Toeppe, *
EMP: 37 **EST:** 1929
SQ FT: 6,500
SALES (est): 820.39K **Privately Held**
Web: www.valleywoodgc.com
SIC: 7992 Public golf courses

Sycamore
Wyandot County

(G-13532)
MILKY ACRES LLC
6348 Parks Rd (44882-9689)
PHONE.................................419 561-1364
Gregory Hartschuh, *Brnch Mgr*
EMP: 29
SALES (corp-wide): 191.97K **Privately Held**
SIC: 5153 0115 0241 Soybeans; Corn; Dairy farms
PA: Milky Acres, Llc
1401 New Washington Rd
Bloomville OH 44818
419 284-3721

(G-13533)
VILLAGE OF SYCAMORE
Also Called: Village of Sycamore
132 North Sycamore Avenue (44882-7521)
P.O. Box 317 (44882-0317)
PHONE.................................419 927-4262

Charles Clark, *Brnch Mgr*
EMP: 68
SIC: 4911 Electric services
PA: Village Of Sycamore
134 N Sycamore Ave
Sycamore OH 44882
419 927-5412

(G-13534)
VILLAGE OF SYCAMORE
P.O. Box 83 (44882-0083)
PHONE.................................419 927-2357
Bob Stover, *Mgr*
EMP: 68
SIC: 9511 7999 Water control and quality agency, government; Recreation services
PA: Village Of Sycamore
134 N Sycamore Ave
Sycamore OH 44882
419 927-5412

Sylvania
Lucas County

(G-13535)
ABILITY CTR OF GREATER TOLEDO (PA)
5605 Monroe St (43560)
PHONE.................................419 517-7123
Timothy Harrington, *Pr*
Richard Gunden, *
Susan Golden, *
Charles G Oswald, *1st**
Judge Charles D Abood Ii, *Vice Chairman*
EMP: 39 **EST:** 1920
SQ FT: 13,000
SALES (est): 5.54MM
SALES (corp-wide): 5.54MM **Privately Held**
Web: www.abilitycenter.org
SIC: 8361 Residential care for the handicapped

(G-13536)
BRECKSVLL-BRDVIEW HTS CY SCHL
7240 Erie St (43560-1136)
PHONE.................................419 885-8103
EMP: 45
SALES (corp-wide): 65.27MM **Privately Held**
Web: www.bbhcsd.org
SIC: 8351 Preschool center
PA: Brecksville-Broadview Heights City School District
6638 Mill Rd
Brecksville OH 44141
440 740-4000

(G-13537)
BRINT ELECTRIC INC
Also Called: Gusco Energy
7825 W Central Ave (43560)
PHONE.................................419 841-3326
EMP: 65 **EST:** 1970
SALES (est): 10.04MM **Privately Held**
Web: www.brintelectric.com
SIC: 1731 Electrical work

(G-13538)
CAVALEAR CORPORATION
6444 Monroe St (43560-1454)
PHONE.................................419 882-7125
David P Miller, *Ch Bd*
Richard J Smith, *Sec*
EMP: 33 **EST:** 1952
SQ FT: 9,900
SALES (est): 3.14MM **Privately Held**

Sylvania - Lucas County (G-13539)   GEOGRAPHIC SECTION

SIC: **6552** 1521 6531 Subdividers and developers, nec; New construction, single-family houses; Real estate agents and managers

(G-13539)
CITY OF SYLVANIA
Also Called: Tam-O-Shanter Sports Complex
7060 Sylvania Ave (43560-3680)
PHONE..................................419 885-1167
Tom Cline, *Mgr*
EMP: 38
SQ FT: 3,775
SALES (corp-wide): 21.7MM **Privately Held**
Web: www.cityofsylvania.com
SIC: **7999** 7997 Ice skating rink operation; Membership sports and recreation clubs
PA: City Of Sylvania
  6730 Monroe St Ste 201
  Sylvania OH 43560
  419 885-8930

(G-13540)
DENTAL HEALTH ASSOC
3924 Sylvan Lakes Blvd (43560-8701)
PHONE..................................419 882-4510
William Huntzinger, *Prin*
EMP: 30 **EST:** 2009
SALES (est): 1.53MM **Privately Held**
Web: www.itneverhurtstosmile.com
SIC: **8021** Dentists' office

(G-13541)
DIRECTIONS CREDIT UNION INC (PA)
5121 Whiteford Rd (43560-2904)
PHONE..................................419 720-4769
Barry Shaner, *Pr*
Julie B Linch, *Member Services Vice President*
Frederick Comes, *
EMP: 57 **EST:** 1953
SQ FT: 15,000
SALES (est): 51.32MM
SALES (corp-wide): 51.32MM **Privately Held**
Web: www.directionscu.org
SIC: **6061** Federal credit unions

(G-13542)
EBONY CONSTRUCTION CO
3510 Centennial Rd (43560-9739)
PHONE..................................419 841-3455
Amy Hall, *Pr*
Michael Bass, *
EMP: 35 **EST:** 1986
SQ FT: 2,200
SALES (est): 9.15MM **Privately Held**
Web: www.ebonyco.com
SIC: **1611** 5082 Highway and street paving contractor; Construction and mining machinery

(G-13543)
ENDEVIS LLC
9313 Bowman Farms Ln (43560-7207)
PHONE..................................419 482-4848
EMP: 32
SALES (corp-wide): 43.76MM **Privately Held**
Web: www.endevis.com
SIC: **7361** Executive placement
HQ: Endevis, L.L.C.
  7643 Kings Pointe Rd # 100
  Toledo OH 43617
  419 482-4848

(G-13544)
FLOWER HOSPITAL (HQ)
5200 Harroun Rd (43560-2196)
PHONE..................................419 824-1444
Kevin Webb, *Pr*
EMP: 889 **EST:** 1910
SALES (est): 144.57MM
SALES (corp-wide): 187.07MM **Privately Held**
Web: www.promedica.org
SIC: **8062** General medical and surgical hospitals
PA: Promedica Health System, Inc.
  100 Madison Ave
  Toledo OH 43604
  567 585-9600

(G-13545)
FLOWER HOSPITAL
Also Called: Lake Park At Flower Hospital
5100 Harroun Rd (43560-2110)
PHONE..................................419 824-1000
Mark Mullahy, *Mgr*
EMP: 437
SALES (corp-wide): 187.07MM **Privately Held**
Web: www.promedica.org
SIC: **8051** 8052 Extended care facility; Intermediate care facilities
HQ: Flower Hospital
  5200 Harroun Rd
  Sylvania OH 43560
  419 824-1444

(G-13546)
GBQ PARTNERS LLC
5580 Monroe St Ste 210 (43560-2561)
PHONE..................................419 885-8338
Bret Clark, *Brnch Mgr*
EMP: 45
SALES (corp-wide): 14.27MM **Privately Held**
Web: www.gbq.com
SIC: **8721** 7291 Certified public accountant; Tax return preparation services
PA: Gbq Partners Llc
  230 W St Ste 700
  Columbus OH 43215
  614 221-1120

(G-13547)
GUARDIAN ANGELS HM HLTH CARE I
Also Called: Guardian Angels Senior HM Svc
8553 Sylvania Metamora Rd (43560-9629)
PHONE..................................419 517-7797
Sharee Youssef, *Pr*
EMP: 70 **EST:** 2005
SQ FT: 2,000
SALES (est): 888.17K **Privately Held**
Web: www.ga-shs.com
SIC: **8082** Home health care services

(G-13548)
HARBORSIDE SYLVANIA LLC
Also Called: Sylvania Center
5757 Whiteford Rd (43560-1632)
PHONE..................................419 882-1875
Stephen Guillard, *Ch Bd*
EMP: 70 **EST:** 1959
SQ FT: 5,000
SALES (est): 11.17MM
SALES (corp-wide): 5.86B **Publicly Held**
Web: www.sylvaniastem.org
SIC: **8052** 8051 Intermediate care facilities; Skilled nursing care facilities
HQ: Genesis Hc Llc
  101 E State St
  Kennett Square PA 19348
  610 444-6350

(G-13549)
HCRMC-PROMEDICA LLC
Also Called: Promedica Sklled Nrsing Rhbltt
5360 Harroun Rd (43560-2114)
PHONE..................................419 540-6000
EMP: 754 **EST:** 2012
SALES (est): 1.14MM
SALES (corp-wide): 187.07MM **Privately Held**
SIC: **8052** Intermediate care facilities
PA: Promedica Health System, Inc.
  100 Madison Ave
  Toledo OH 43604
  567 585-9600

(G-13550)
HIGHLAND MEADOWS GOLF CLUB (PA)
7455 Erie St (43560-1183)
PHONE..................................419 882-7153
Andy Masten, *Mgr*
EMP: 44 **EST:** 1925
SQ FT: 15,000
SALES (est): 3.62MM
SALES (corp-wide): 3.62MM **Privately Held**
Web: www.hmgolfclub.org
SIC: **7997** Country club, membership

(G-13551)
INFUSION PARTNERS INC
Also Called: CHS
3315 Centennial Rd Ste Aa (43560-9419)
PHONE..................................419 843-2100
Linda Smith, *Mgr*
EMP: 32
SALES (corp-wide): 19.28MM **Privately Held**
Web: www.optioncarehealth.com
SIC: **8082** Home health care services
HQ: Infusion Partners, Inc.
  4623 Wesley Ave Ste H
  Cincinnati OH 45212

(G-13552)
INTEGRATED RESOURCES INC
7901 Sylvania Ave (43560-9732)
PHONE..................................419 885-7122
Scott Stansley, *Pr*
Richard Stansley Junior, *Sec*
EMP: 40 **EST:** 1989
SQ FT: 10,000
SALES (est): 3.25MM **Privately Held**
SIC: **3273** 8741 Ready-mixed concrete; Management services

(G-13553)
JDRM ENGINEERING INC
5604 Main St Ste 200 (43560-1950)
PHONE..................................419 824-2400
EMP: 44 **EST:** 1995
SQ FT: 8,500
SALES (est): 8.74MM **Privately Held**
Web: www.jdrm.com
SIC: **8711** Mechanical engineering

(G-13554)
JEWISH CMNTY CTR OF TOLEDO
Also Called: JCC
6465 Sylvania Ave (43560-3916)
PHONE..................................419 885-4485
Eric Goldstein, *Ex Dir*
EMP: 44 **EST:** 1905
SQ FT: 50,000
SALES (est): 94.56K **Privately Held**
Web: www.jewishtoledo.org
SIC: **8322** Community center

(G-13555)
KINSTON CARE CENTER SYLVANI
4121 King Rd (43560-4438)
PHONE..................................419 517-8200
Denise Mcgee, *Prin*
EMP: 37 **EST:** 2005
SALES (est): 16.29MM **Privately Held**
Web: www.kingstonhealthcare.com
SIC: **8051** Convalescent home with continuous nursing care

(G-13556)
MOUNTAIN CREST OH OPCO LLC
Also Called: Divine Rhblttion Nrsing At Syl
5757 Whiteford Rd (43560-1632)
PHONE..................................419 882-1875
Isaak Markovits, *Prin*
EMP: 80 **EST:** 2019
SALES (est): 3.12MM **Privately Held**
Web: www.divinesylvania.com
SIC: **8051** Skilled nursing care facilities

(G-13557)
NORTHERN OHIO INVESTMENT CO
Also Called: Noic
6444 Monroe St Ste 6 (43560-1455)
P.O. Box 787 (43560-0787)
PHONE..................................419 885-8300
Ralph D Vinciguerra, *Pr*
Mark Vinciguerra, *
Pauline Schnell, *
Marty Vihn, *
EMP: 53 **EST:** 1926
SQ FT: 5,000
SALES (est): 9.46MM **Privately Held**
Web: www.uhm.com
SIC: **6162** Mortgage bankers

(G-13558)
NORTHWEST ELECTRICAL CONTG INC
3149 Centennial Rd (43560-9689)
PHONE..................................419 865-4757
Jody Mc Collum, *Pr*
Kathy Mc Collum, *
▲ **EMP:** 30 **EST:** 1985
SQ FT: 8,800
SALES (est): 4.41MM **Privately Held**
Web: www.nwelect.com
SIC: **1731** General electrical contractor

(G-13559)
OHIO CON SAWING & DRLG INC (PA)
8534 Central Ave (43560-9748)
PHONE..................................419 841-1330
James R Aston, *Pr*
Thomas A Lenix, *
EMP: 29 **EST:** 1981
SALES (est): 13.75MM
SALES (corp-wide): 13.75MM **Privately Held**
Web: www.ohioconcrete.com
SIC: **1771** Concrete repair

(G-13560)
PROFESSNL GLFERS ASSN OF AMER
5201 Corey Rd (43560-2202)
PHONE..................................419 882-3197
Jason Stuller, *Prin*
EMP: 30 **EST:** 2010
SALES (est): 479.49K
SALES (corp-wide): 487.89K **Privately Held**
SIC: **8699** Athletic organizations
PA: Jason Stuller Pro Shop, Llc
  5201 Corey Rd
  Sylvania OH 43560
  419 882-3197

GEOGRAPHIC SECTION   Symmes Township - Hamilton County (G-13581)

(G-13561)
PROMEDICA CNTNING CARE SVCS CO
Also Called: PROMEDICA
5855 Monroe St Ste 200 (43560-2270)
PHONE....................419 885-1715
EMP: 5154 EST: 2002
SALES (est): 10.56MM
SALES (corp-wide): 187.07MM **Privately Held**
SIC: 8062 General medical and surgical hospitals
PA: Promedica Health System, Inc.
     100 Madison Ave
     Toledo OH 43604
     567 585-9600

(G-13562)
PROMEDICA HEALTH SYSTEM INC
Also Called: Woodley Park Internal Med
5700 Monroe St Unit 209 (43560-2735)
PHONE....................419 291-6720
EMP: 283
SALES (corp-wide): 187.07MM **Privately Held**
Web: www.promedica.org
SIC: 8062 General medical and surgical hospitals
PA: Promedica Health System, Inc.
     100 Madison Ave
     Toledo OH 43604
     567 585-9600

(G-13563)
PROMEDICA HEALTH SYSTEMS INC
Also Called: Promedica Health Care
5200 Harroun Rd (43560-2168)
PHONE....................419 824-1444
EMP: 1666
SALES (corp-wide): 187.07MM **Privately Held**
Web: www.promedica.org
SIC: 8062 General medical and surgical hospitals
PA: Promedica Health System, Inc.
     100 Madison Ave
     Toledo OH 43604
     567 585-9600

(G-13564)
PROMEDICA OF SYLVANIA OH LLC
Also Called: Promedica Grlich Mmory Care Ct
5320 Harroun Rd (43560-2114)
PHONE....................844 247-5337
EMP: 1069 EST: 2017
SALES (est): 2.33MM
SALES (corp-wide): 187.07MM **Privately Held**
SIC: 8062 General medical and surgical hospitals
PA: Promedica Health System, Inc.
     100 Madison Ave
     Toledo OH 43604
     567 585-9600

(G-13565)
PROMEDICA PHYSCN CNTINUUM SVCS
Also Called: PROMEDICA
5855 Monroe St Fl 1 (43560-2270)
PHONE....................419 824-7200
Lee Hammerling Md, *Pr*
EMP: 101 EST: 1994
SALES (est): 66.63MM
SALES (corp-wide): 187.07MM **Privately Held**
SIC: 8741 7361 8721 Management services; Employment agencies; Accounting, auditing, and bookkeeping
PA: Promedica Health System, Inc.
     100 Madison Ave
     Toledo OH 43604
     567 585-9600

(G-13566)
PROMEDICA TOLEDO HOSPITAL
Caring Services
5520 Monroe St (43560-2538)
PHONE....................419 291-2273
Carrol Scholtz, *Dir*
EMP: 82
SALES (corp-wide): 187.07MM **Privately Held**
Web: www.promedica.org
SIC: 8361 8082 Rehabilitation center, residential; health care incidental; Home health care services
HQ: Toledo Promedica Hospital
     2142 N Cove Blvd
     Toledo OH 43606
     419 291-4000

(G-13567)
RECYCLE WASTE SERVICES INC
3793 Silica Rd # B (43560-9814)
PHONE....................419 517-1323
Ryan Stansley, *Pr*
Jeffrey Stansley, *
EMP: 55 EST: 2009
SALES (est): 8.24MM **Privately Held**
Web: www.recyclewasteservices.com
SIC: 4953 Recycling, waste materials

(G-13568)
REGENCY HOSPITAL TOLEDO LLC
Also Called: SELECT PHYSICAL THEREPAHY AND
5220 Alexis Rd (43560-2504)
P.O. Box 2034 (17055-0793)
PHONE....................419 318-5700
Rod Laughlin, *Managing Member*
EMP: 30 EST: 2005
SALES (est): 28.46MM
SALES (corp-wide): 6.2B **Publicly Held**
Web: www.regencyhospital.com
SIC: 8062 Hospital, med school affiliated with nursing and residency
HQ: Select Medical Corporation
     4714 Gettysburg Rd
     Mechanicsburg PA 17055
     717 972-1100

(G-13569)
REVE SALON AND SPA INC
5633 Main St (43560-1929)
PHONE....................419 885-1140
Carmen Gauer-wigma, *Owner*
EMP: 55 EST: 1987
SQ FT: 1,200
SALES (est): 2.11MM **Privately Held**
Web: www.revesalonandspa.com
SIC: 7231 Hairdressers

(G-13570)
RIVER CENTRE CLINIC
Also Called: Toledo Cntre For Eting Dsrders
5465 Main St (43560-2155)
PHONE....................419 885-8800
Michael Anderson, *Dir*
EMP: 27 EST: 1996
SALES (est): 933.28K **Privately Held**
Web: www.toledocenter.com
SIC: 8093 Mental health clinic, outpatient

(G-13571)
ROOT LLC (DH)
5470 Main St Ste 100 (43560)
PHONE....................419 874-0077
Rich Berens, *CEO*
EMP: 58 EST: 1985
SQ FT: 17,000
SALES (est): 45.26MM **Privately Held**
Web: www.rootinc.com
SIC: 8742 Business management consultant
HQ: Accenture Inc.
     161 N Clark St Ste 1100
     Chicago IL 60601
     312 693-0161

(G-13572)
SMITH TRUCKING INC
3775 Centennial Rd (43560-9734)
P.O. Box 9 (49228-0009)
PHONE....................419 841-8676
Henry Smith, *Pr*
EMP: 35 EST: 2005
SALES (est): 1.12MM **Privately Held**
SIC: 4213 Trucking, except local

(G-13573)
STANSLEY MINERAL RESOURCES INC (PA)
3793 Silica Rd # B (43560-9814)
PHONE....................419 843-2813
Rick Stansley, *CEO*
Jeff Stansley, *
Richard Stansley Junior, *Sec*
Mandy Billau, *
EMP: 35 EST: 1978
SQ FT: 10,000
SALES (est): 4.76MM
SALES (corp-wide): 4.76MM **Privately Held**
SIC: 1442 Gravel mining

(G-13574)
SYLVANIA CMNTY SVCS CTR INC
4747 N Holland Sylvania Rd (43560)
PHONE....................419 885-2451
Claire A Proctor, *Ex Dir*
EMP: 40 EST: 1977
SALES (est): 2.84MM **Privately Held**
Web: www.sylvaniacommunityservices.org
SIC: 8322 8351 Child related social services; Child day care services

(G-13575)
SYLVANIA COUNTRY CLUB
5201 Corey Rd (43560-2202)
PHONE....................419 392-0530
Shawne Lnd, *Pr*
EMP: 99 EST: 1916
SALES (est): 4.23MM **Privately Held**
Web: www.sylvaniacc.org
SIC: 7997 Country club, membership

(G-13576)
SYLVANIA VETERINARY HOSPITAL (PA)
4801 N Holland Sylvania Rd (43560)
PHONE....................419 885-4421
Robert B Esplin, *Pr*
Carol Esplin, *
EMP: 43 EST: 1974
SQ FT: 2,250
SALES (est): 2.51MM
SALES (corp-wide): 2.51MM **Privately Held**
Web: www.sylvaniavet.com
SIC: 0742 Animal hospital services, pets and other animal specialties

(G-13577)
THERMODYN CORPORATION (PA)
Also Called: Sealing Resource Div
3550 Silica Rd (43560-9731)
PHONE....................419 841-7782
▲ EMP: 33 EST: 1979
SALES (est): 11.53MM
SALES (corp-wide): 11.53MM **Privately Held**
Web: www.thermodyn.com
SIC: 5085 Gaskets

(G-13578)
VIN DEVERS INC (PA)
5570 Monroe St (43560-2560)
PHONE....................888 847-9535
Jason Perry, *Prin*
Mikel Maras Senior, *Finance*
Duane Anderson, *Prin*
Keith Solomon, *Prin*
Heather Russell, *TO Finance*
EMP: 110 EST: 1956
SQ FT: 40,000
SALES (est): 47.88MM
SALES (corp-wide): 47.88MM **Privately Held**
Web: www.vindevers.com
SIC: 5511 5521 7538 7515 Automobiles, new and used; Used car dealers; General automotive repair shops; Passenger car leasing

(G-13579)
YOUNG MNS CHRSTN ASSN OF GRTER (PA)
Also Called: YMCA of Greater Toledo
6465 Sylvania Ave (43560-3916)
PHONE....................419 729-8135
Todd Tibbits, *Pr*
Stephanie Dames, *
Brian Keel, *
EMP: 50 EST: 1865
SALES (est): 29.37MM
SALES (corp-wide): 29.37MM **Privately Held**
Web: www.ymcatoledo.org
SIC: 8641 7991 8351 7032 Youth organizations; Physical fitness facilities; Child day care services; Youth camps

Symmes Township
Hamilton County

(G-13580)
PAYRIX SOLUTIONS LLC (HQ)
Also Called: Flush Payment
8500 Governors Hill Dr (45249)
PHONE....................718 506-9250
Boruh Greenberg, *Managing Member*
EMP: 28 EST: 2009
SALES (est): 10.08MM
SALES (corp-wide): 9.82B **Publicly Held**
Web: www.benchmarkmerchantsolutions.com
SIC: 7389 Credit card service
PA: Fidelity National Information Services, Inc.
     347 Riverside Ave
     Jacksonville FL 32202
     904 438-6000

(G-13581)
WORLDPAY INC (PA)
8500 Governors Hill Dr (45249)
PHONE....................866 622-2390
Charles D Drucker, *Pr*
EMP: 548 EST: 2009
SALES (est): 516.57MM
SALES (corp-wide): 516.57MM **Privately Held**
Web: www.worldpay.com
SIC: 7389 Credit card service

Symmes Twp
Hamilton County

(G-13582)
BEST PAYMENT SOLUTIONS INC (HQ)
8500 Governors Hill Dr (45249-1384)
PHONE...............................630 321-0117
Jared Warner, *Pr*
EMP: 35 **EST:** 2000
SALES (est): 24.76MM
SALES (corp-wide): 516.57MM **Privately Held**
Web: www.best-payment.com
SIC: 7389 Credit card service
PA: Worldpay, Inc.
   8500 Governors Hill Dr
   Symmes Township OH 45249
   866 622-2390

(G-13583)
WORLDPAY LLC (DH)
8500 Governors Hill Dr (45249-1384)
EMP: 350 **EST:** 2009
SALES (est): 101.93MM
SALES (corp-wide): 516.57MM **Privately Held**
Web: www.fisglobal.com
SIC: 7374 Data processing service
HQ: Worldpay Holding, Llc
   8500 Governors Hill Dr
   Symmes Twp OH 45249
   513 358-6192

(G-13584)
WORLDPAY HOLDING LLC (HQ)
8500 Governors Hill Dr (45249-1384)
PHONE...............................513 358-6192
Charles Drucker, *Pr*
Mark Heimbouch, *CFO*
Bob Bartlett, *CIO*
Carlos Lima, *COO*
EMP: 160 **EST:** 2008
SALES (est): 101.93MM
SALES (corp-wide): 516.57MM **Privately Held**
Web: www.worldpay.com
SIC: 7389 Credit card service
PA: Worldpay, Inc.
   8500 Governors Hill Dr
   Symmes Township OH 45249
   866 622-2390

(G-13585)
WORLDPAY ISO INC (HQ)
Also Called: Government Payment Solutions
8500 Governors Hill Dr (45249-1384)
PHONE...............................502 961-5200
Charles D Drucker, *CEO*
George Willett, *Treas*
Mark Schatz, *Sec*
EMP: 114 **EST:** 1993
SALES (est): 43.96MM
SALES (corp-wide): 516.57MM **Privately Held**
SIC: 7389 Credit card service
PA: Worldpay, Inc.
   8500 Governors Hill Dr
   Symmes Township OH 45249
   866 622-2390

Tallmadge
Summit County

(G-13586)
AUTOSALES INCORPORATED
Also Called: Atech Motorsports
1234 Southeast Ave (44278-3161)
PHONE...............................330 630-0888
EMP: 38
SALES (corp-wide): 105.55MM **Privately Held**
Web: www.summitracing.com
SIC: 5013 Automotive supplies and parts
PA: Autosales, Incorporated
   1200 Southeast Ave
   Tallmadge OH 44278
   800 230-3030

(G-13587)
CHILDRENS HOSP MED CTR AKRON
Also Called: Family Child Learning Center
143 Northwest Ave Bldg A (44278-1806)
PHONE...............................330 633-2055
Marilyn Espesherwindt, *Dir*
EMP: 54
SALES (corp-wide): 1.4B **Privately Held**
Web: www.akronchildrens.org
SIC: 8733 8322 Medical research; Child related social services
PA: Childrens Hospital Medical Center Of Akron
   1 Perkins Sq
   Akron OH 44308
   330 543-1000

(G-13588)
CITY OF TALLMADGE
Also Called: Tallmadge Reacreation Center
46 N Munroe Rd (44278-2055)
PHONE...............................330 634-2349
Thomas Headrick, *Brnch Mgr*
EMP: 31
SALES (corp-wide): 25.92MM **Privately Held**
Web: www.tallmadge-ohio.org
SIC: 7997 Membership sports and recreation clubs
PA: City Of Tallmadge
   46 North Ave
   Tallmadge OH 44278
   330 633-0857

(G-13589)
COLON LEASING CO LLC
Also Called: Colony Healthcare Center, The
563 Colony Park Dr (44278-2859)
PHONE...............................513 530-1600
Richard Odenthal, *Prin*
Sandra Smiddy, *
EMP: 50 **EST:** 2018
SALES (est): 8.48MM **Privately Held**
Web: www.communicarehealth.com
SIC: 8051 Convalescent home with continuous nursing care

(G-13590)
COUNTY OF SUMMIT
Also Called: Summit County Developmental
89 E Howe Rd (44278-1003)
PHONE...............................330 634-8000
Thomas Armstrong, *Mgr*
EMP: 700
SALES (corp-wide): 494.44MM **Privately Held**
Web: www.summitdd.org
SIC: 9431 8322 Administration of public health programs, County government; Individual and family services
PA: Summit County
   650 Dan St
   Akron OH 44310
   330 643-2500

(G-13591)
DERMAMED COATINGS COMPANY LLC
381 Geneva Ave (44278)
PHONE...............................330 634-9449
▲ **EMP:** 40 **EST:** 1997
SQ FT: 10,000
SALES (est): 10.93MM **Privately Held**
Web: www.dermamed.net
SIC: 5047 Medical and hospital equipment

(G-13592)
GIONINOS PIZZERIA INC
676 Eastwood Ave (44278-3139)
PHONE...............................330 630-2010
Samuel A Owen, *Pr*
Charles Owen, *VP*
EMP: 31 **EST:** 1976
SQ FT: 1,600
SALES (est): 664.24K **Privately Held**
Web: www.gioninos.com
SIC: 5812 6794 Pizza restaurants; Franchises, selling or licensing

(G-13593)
HANGER PRSTHTICS ORTHTICS E IN (HQ)
33 North Ave Ste 101 (44278-1900)
PHONE...............................330 633-9807
Vinit K Asar, *CEO*
Samuel M Liang, *
EMP: 34 **EST:** 1990
SALES (est): 48.15MM
SALES (corp-wide): 1.12B **Privately Held**
SIC: 5999 8741 Orthopedic and prosthesis applications; Management services
PA: Hanger, Inc.
   10910 Domain Dr Ste 300
   Austin TX 78758
   512 777-3800

(G-13594)
HEATHER KNOLL RTREMENT VLG INC
Also Called: HEATHER KNOLL NURSING CENTER
1134 North Ave (44278-1065)
PHONE...............................330 688-8600
Lisa Slomovitz, *Pr*
Nicole Sprenger, *
EMP: 99 **EST:** 1992
SALES (est): 9.33MM **Privately Held**
SIC: 8051 Convalescent home with continuous nursing care

(G-13595)
HUNTINGTON NATIONAL BANK
27 Northwest Ave (44278-1805)
PHONE...............................330 634-0841
David Johnson, *Mgr*
EMP: 36
SALES (corp-wide): 10.84B **Publicly Held**
Web: www.huntington.com
SIC: 6029 Commercial banks, nec
HQ: The Huntington National Bank
   41 S High St
   Columbus OH 43215
   614 480-4293

(G-13596)
J D WILLIAMSON CNSTR CO INC
441 Geneva Ave (44278-2704)
P.O. Box 113 (44278-0113)
PHONE...............................330 633-1258
Joel D Williamson, *Pr*
Veronica Williamson, *
John Englehart, *
EMP: 99 **EST:** 1969
SQ FT: 3,000
SALES (est): 26.25MM **Privately Held**
Web: www.jdwilliamsonconstruction.com
SIC: 1542 Commercial and office building, new construction

(G-13597)
KANDEL COLD STORAGE INC
365 Munroe Falls Rd (44278-3337)
PHONE...............................330 798-4111
Jeffrey T Witschey, *Prin*
EMP: 65 **EST:** 2003
SALES (est): 4.26MM
SALES (corp-wide): 14.66B **Publicly Held**
Web: www.kandel.com
SIC: 4225 General warehousing and storage
HQ: Total Distribution Services, Inc.
   301 W Bay St Ste 9
   Jacksonville FL 32202
   904 633-5817

(G-13598)
KEYBANK NATIONAL ASSOCIATION
76 Tallmadge Cir (44278-2307)
PHONE...............................330 633-5335
Donna Brown, *Mgr*
EMP: 32
SALES (corp-wide): 10.4B **Publicly Held**
Web: www.key.com
SIC: 6021 National commercial banks
HQ: Keybank National Association
   127 Public Sq Ste 5600
   Cleveland OH 44114
   800 539-2968

(G-13599)
LEPPO INC (PA)
Also Called: Leppo Rents
176 West Ave (44278-2145)
P.O. Box 154 (44278-0154)
PHONE...............................330 633-3999
Dale Leppo, *CEO*
Glenn Leppo, *Pr*
Joanne Sweeney, *Treas*
EMP: 33 **EST:** 1945
SQ FT: 44,000
SALES (est): 163.76MM
SALES (corp-wide): 163.76MM **Privately Held**
Web: www.lepporents.com
SIC: 5082 7353 7629 General construction machinery and equipment; Heavy construction equipment rental; Business machine repair, electric

(G-13600)
LIVING ASSISTANCE SERVICES INC
Also Called: Visiting Angels
22 Northwest Ave (44278-1808)
PHONE...............................330 733-1532
Jodi Wood, *Pr*
EMP: 35 **EST:** 2000
SALES (est): 3.48MM **Privately Held**
Web: www.visitingangels.com
SIC: 8082 Home health care services

(G-13601)
NOVUS CLINIC
518 West Ave (44278-2117)
PHONE...............................330 630-9699
Donald C Stephens Md, *Prin*
EMP: 57 **EST:** 2005
SALES (est): 12.75MM **Privately Held**
Web: www.novusclinic.com
SIC: 8011 Opthalmologist

(G-13602)
S D MYERS INC
180 South Ave (44278-2864)
PHONE...............................330 630-7000
Scott Myers, *Ch Bd*
Dale Bissonette, *
Allan Ross, *
David Myers, *
EMP: 230 **EST:** 1965
SQ FT: 220,000
SALES (est): 26.15MM **Privately Held**

Web: www.sdmyers.com
SIC: 8734 7629 Testing laboratories;
   Electrical equipment repair services

(G-13603)
SD MYERS LLC
180 South Ave (44278-2864)
PHONE.................................330 630-7000
Scott Myers, *CEO*
Dale Bissonette, *
Beth Raies, *
Sindi Harrison Attorney, *Prin*
Ed Muckley, *
EMP: 200 EST: 2016
SQ FT: 200,000
SALES (est): 26.52MM **Privately Held**
Web: www.sdmyers.com
SIC: 8734 Testing laboratories

(G-13604)
SPEELMAN ELECTRIC INC
235 Northeast Ave (44278-1401)
PHONE.................................330 633-1410
Christeen Parsons, *CEO*
Richard Speelman, *
Christeen Parsons, *CFO*
EMP: 115 EST: 1987
SQ FT: 7,000
SALES (est): 31.72MM **Privately Held**
Web: www.speelmanelectric.com
SIC: 1731 General electrical contractor

(G-13605)
SUMMA WESTERN RESERVE HOSP LLC
Also Called: Wrhpi Cardiovascular Tstg Ctr
116 East Ave Ste 3 (44278-2300)
PHONE.................................330 633-7782
EMP: 31
SALES (corp-wide): 155.93MM **Privately Held**
Web: www.westernreservehospital.org
SIC: 8062 Hospital, AMA approved residency
HQ: Western Reserve Hospital, Llc
   1900 23rd St
   Cuyahoga Falls OH 44223

(G-13606)
SUMMIT FACILITY OPERATIONS LLC
Also Called: EDGEWOOD MANOR OF WESTERVILLE
330 Southwest Ave (44278-2235)
PHONE.................................330 633-0555
James Renacci, *Pr*
C Douglas Warner, *VP*
Ann J Warner, *Treas*
Christy Yoho, *Dir*
EMP: 777 EST: 1940
SALES (est): 7.01MM
SALES (corp-wide): 491MM **Privately Held**
SIC: 8052 8051 Intermediate care facilities;
   Skilled nursing care facilities
HQ: Consulate Management Company, Llc
   800 Concourse Pkwy S # 200
   Maitland FL 32751
   407 571-1550

(G-13607)
SYSTEM OPTICS CSMT SRGCAL ARTS
Also Called: Novus Clinic
518 West Ave (44278-2117)
PHONE.................................330 630-9699
Todd L Beyer D.o.s., *Pr*
EMP: 38 EST: 1987
SQ FT: 11,378
SALES (est): 2.17MM **Privately Held**
Web: www.novusclinic.com
SIC: 8011 Opthalmologist

(G-13608)
TALLMADGE COLLISION CENTER (PA)
195 Northeast Ave (44278-1450)
P.O. Box 458 (44278-0458)
PHONE.................................330 630-2188
Robert Black Iii, *Pr*
Kenneth Dixon, *
EMP: 33 EST: 1987
SQ FT: 11,000
SALES (est): 2.63MM **Privately Held**
Web: www.tcccollision.com
SIC: 7532 Body shop, automotive

(G-13609)
UNITED DENTAL LABORATORIES (PA)
261 South Ave (44278-2819)
P.O. Box 418 (44278-0418)
PHONE.................................330 253-1810
Richard Delapa Junior, *Pr*
EMP: 35 EST: 1923
SQ FT: 15,000
SALES (est): 2.54MM
SALES (corp-wide): 2.54MM **Privately Held**
Web: www.uniteddentallabs.com
SIC: 8072 3843 Denture production; Dental equipment and supplies

(G-13610)
UNITY HEALTH NETWORK LLC
Also Called: Unity Health Network
116 East Ave (44278-2300)
PHONE.................................330 633-7782
Robert A Kent, *Admn*
EMP: 27
SALES (corp-wide): 51.74MM **Privately Held**
Web: www.unityhealthnetwork.org
SIC: 8099 Blood related health services
PA: Unity Health Network, Llc
   2750 Front St
   Cuyahoga Falls OH 44221
   330 923-5899

(G-13611)
WARDJET LLC
180 South Ave (44278-2813)
PHONE.................................330 677-9100
Rich Ward, *Pr*
Jennifer Nelson, *
✦ EMP: 91 EST: 1999
SQ FT: 12,000
SALES (est): 28.54MM
SALES (corp-wide): 16.65MM **Privately Held**
Web: www.wardjet.com
SIC: 5084 Industrial machinery and equipment
PA: Axyz International Inc
   5 Medicorum Place
   Waterdown ON L8B 0
   905 634-4940

(G-13612)
WEAVER INDUSTRIES INC
66 Osceola Ave (44278-2742)
PHONE.................................330 379-3660
Paul Habeck, *Prin*
EMP: 65
SALES (corp-wide): 7.88MM **Privately Held**
Web: www.weaverindustries.org
SIC: 7389 Packaging and labeling services
PA: Weaver Industries, Inc.
   520 S Main St Ste 2441
   Akron OH 44311
   330 379-3660

Terrace Park
Hamilton County

(G-13613)
BROWN & BROWN OF OHIO LLC
Also Called: Berry Insurance Group
706 Indian Hill Rd (45174-1017)
PHONE.................................513 831-2200
James Whinnie, *Brnch Mgr*
EMP: 57
SALES (corp-wide): 3.57B **Publicly Held**
Web: www.bbinsurance.com
SIC: 6411 Insurance agents and brokers
HQ: Brown & Brown Of Ohio, Llc
   360 3 Meadows Dr
   Perrysburg OH 43551
   419 874-1974

(G-13614)
ST THOMAS EPISCOPAL CHURCH
Also Called: St Thomas Nursery School
100 Miami Ave (45174-1175)
PHONE.................................513 831-6908
EMP: 33 EST: 1800
SQ FT: 7,360
SALES (est): 2.32MM **Privately Held**
Web: www.stthomasepiscopal.org
SIC: 8661 8351 Episcopal Church; Child day care services

The Plains
Athens County

(G-13615)
BUCKEYE COMMUNITY SERVICES INC
Also Called: Harmon Road Group Home
33 Hartman Rd (45780)
PHONE.................................740 797-4166
Kim Mcvey, *Prin*
EMP: 98
SALES (corp-wide): 15.43MM **Privately Held**
Web: www.buckeyecommunityservices.org
SIC: 8361 Retarded home
PA: Buckeye Community Services, Incorporated
   220 Morton St
   Jackson OH 45640
   740 286-5039

(G-13616)
RESIDNTIAL HM FOR DVLPMNTLLY D
49 Connett Rd (45780-1407)
PHONE.................................740 677-0500
EMP: 31
SALES (corp-wide): 9.71MM **Privately Held**
Web: www.rhdd.org
SIC: 8361 Mentally handicapped home
PA: Residential Home For The Developmentally Disabled Incorporated
   925 Chestnut St
   Coshocton OH 43812
   740 622-9778

Thompson
Geauga County

(G-13617)
HEMLY TOOL SUPPLY INC
16600 Thompson Rd (44086-8744)
P.O. Box 395 (44064-0395)
PHONE.................................800 445-1068
EMP: 28 EST: 1982
SALES (est): 6.88MM **Privately Held**
Web: www.hemlytool.com
SIC: 5084 Metalworking machinery

(G-13618)
R W SIDLEY INCORPORATED
Sidley Contracting
6900 Madison Rd (44086-9774)
P.O. Box 70 (44086-0070)
PHONE.................................440 298-3232
Ray Kennedy, *Mgr*
EMP: 104
SQ FT: 3,000
SALES (corp-wide): 83.57MM **Privately Held**
Web: www.rwsidley.com
SIC: 1799 5032 3272 Erection and dismantling of forms for poured concrete; Limestone; Concrete products, nec
PA: R. W. Sidley Incorporated
   436 Casement Ave
   Painesville OH 44077
   440 352-9343

Thornville
Perry County

(G-13619)
BTMC CORPORATION
15056 Harbor Point Dr W (43076-8063)
PHONE.................................614 891-1454
Ronald Groves, *Pr*
Albert Witpkopp, *COO*
EMP: 44 EST: 1978
SQ FT: 43,000
SALES (est): 3.39MM **Privately Held**
SIC: 5013 Truck parts and accessories

(G-13620)
FAIRFELD GRDNS RHBLTTION CARE
Also Called: Country Ln Grdns Rhblttion Nrs
7820 Pleasantville Rd Ne (43076-8704)
PHONE.................................740 536-7381
Mordy Lahasky, *Managing Member*
EMP: 27 EST: 2015
SALES (est): 19.43MM **Privately Held**
Web: www.countrylaneghc.com
SIC: 8051 Convalescent home with continuous nursing care

(G-13621)
SHELLY COMPANY (DH)
Also Called: Shelly Materials
80 Park Dr (43076-9397)
P.O. Box 266 (43076-0266)
PHONE.................................740 246-6315
EMP: 75 EST: 1989
SALES (est): 595.35MM
SALES (corp-wide): 32.72B **Privately Held**
Web: www.shellyco.com
SIC: 1611 Surfacing and paving
HQ: Crh Americas Materials, Inc.
   900 Ashwood Pkwy Ste 700
   Atlanta GA 30338

(G-13622)
SHELLY MATERIALS INC (DH)
Also Called: Shelly Company, The
80 Park Dr (43076-9397)
P.O. Box 266 (43076-0266)
PHONE.................................740 246-6315
John Power, *Pr*
Ted Lemon, *
Doug Radabaugh N, *Sec*
EMP: 100 EST: 1938
SALES (est): 461.47MM
SALES (corp-wide): 32.72B **Privately Held**
Web: www.shellyco.com

SIC: **1422** 1442 2951 4492 Crushed and broken limestone; Construction sand and gravel; Concrete, asphaltic (not from refineries); Tugboat service
HQ: Shelly Company
80 Park Dr
Thornville OH 43076
740 246-6315

(G-13623)
THORNVILLE FAMILY MED CTR INC
41 Foster Dr (43076-8010)
P.O. Box 281 (43076-0281)
PHONE.................................740 246-6361
Larry Cowan D.o.s., *Owner*
EMP: **36** EST: 1982
SALES (est): 1.97MM **Privately Held**
Web: www.genesishcs.org
SIC: **8062** General medical and surgical hospitals

Tiffin
Seneca County

(G-13624)
BALLREICH BROS INC
Also Called: Ballreichs Potato Chips Snacks
186 Ohio Ave (44883-1746)
PHONE.................................419 447-1814
EMP: **105**
Web: www.ballreich.com
SIC: **2096** 2099 4226 Potato chips and other potato-based snacks; Food preparations, nec; Special warehousing and storage, nec

(G-13625)
CONCORDNCE HLTHCARE SLTONS LLC (PA)
Also Called: Seneca Medical
85 Shaffer Park Dr (44883-9290)
PHONE.................................419 447-0222
Lisa Hohman, *CEO*
Jaysen Stevenson, *
Todd Howell, *
EMP: **90** EST: 2015
SALES (est): 446.66MM
SALES (corp-wide): 446.66MM **Privately Held**
Web: www.concordancehealthcare.com
SIC: **5047** Medical and hospital equipment

(G-13626)
CSJI-TIFFIN INC
Also Called: ST FRANCIS SENIOR MINISTRIES
182 Saint Francis Ave (44883)
PHONE.................................419 447-2723
Gabriel Stoll, *Ex Dir*
EMP: **99** EST: 2018
SALES (est): 11.28MM **Privately Held**
Web: www.csjinitiatives.org
SIC: **8051** Skilled nursing care facilities

(G-13627)
DEPARTMENT OF HEALTH OHIO
Also Called: Tiffin Developmental Center
600 N River Rd (44883-1173)
PHONE.................................419 447-1450
Peggy S Bockey, *Mgr*
EMP: **48**
Web: odh.ohio.gov
SIC: **8361** 9431 Mentally handicapped home ; Administration of public health programs, State government
HQ: Department Of Health Ohio
246 N High St
Columbus OH 43215

(G-13628)
ICP INC (PA)
Also Called: Institutional Care Pharmacy
1815 W County Road 54 (44883-7723)
PHONE.................................419 447-6216
James W Unverferth, *Pr*
EMP: **71** EST: 1985
SQ FT: 22,000
SALES (est): 27.69MM
SALES (corp-wide): 27.69MM **Privately Held**
Web: www.icppharm.com
SIC: **5122** 5047 5912 Patent medicines; Medical and hospital equipment; Drug stores and proprietary stores

(G-13629)
J B & COMPANY INCORPORATED
1480 S County Road 594 (44883-2677)
P.O. Box 520 (44883-0520)
PHONE.................................419 447-1716
TOLL FREE: 800
EMP: **60**
Web: www.tectaamerica.com
SIC: **1761** Roofing contractor

(G-13630)
JB ROOFING A TECTA AMER CO LLC
1480 S County Road 594 (44883-2677)
PHONE.................................419 447-1716
EMP: **35** EST: 2021
SALES (est): 285.65K **Privately Held**
Web: www.tectaamerica.com
SIC: **1761** Roofing contractor

(G-13631)
M G Q INC
Also Called: Maple Grove Companies
1525 W County Road 42 (44883-8457)
P.O. Box 130 (44861-0130)
PHONE.................................419 992-4236
Lynn Radabaugh, *Pr*
Tim Bell, *
Lynn Radabaugh, *VP*
Bob Chesebro, *
Bruce Chubb, *
▲ EMP: **42** EST: 1999
SALES (est): 8.94MM **Privately Held**
Web: www.mgqinc.com
SIC: **4214** 1481 Local trucking with storage; Mine and quarry services, nonmetallic minerals

(G-13632)
MERCY HEALTH - TIFFIN HOSP LLC
45 St Lawrence Dr (44883-8310)
PHONE.................................419 455-7000
Lynn Detterman, *Pr*
Andrew Morgan, *
EMP: **430** EST: 1970
SQ FT: 241,000
SALES (est): 102.78MM
SALES (corp-wide): 6.92B **Privately Held**
Web: www.mercy.com
SIC: **8062** General medical and surgical hospitals
PA: Bon Secours Mercy Health, Inc.
1701 Mercy Health Pl
Cincinnati OH 45237
513 956-3729

(G-13633)
MERKLEY PROFESSIONALS INC
19 W Market St Ste A (44883-2772)
PHONE.................................419 447-9541
Leigh Beidelschies, *Prin*
EMP: **27** EST: 2019
SALES (est): 553.17K **Privately Held**
SIC: **8021** Offices and clinics of dentists

(G-13634)
MOHAWK GOLF CLUB
4399 S State Route 231 (44883-9308)
P.O. Box 506 (44883-0506)
PHONE.................................419 447-5876
Robert Durbin, *Pr*
Robert Sankey, *
EMP: **27** EST: 1924
SALES (est): 611.15K **Privately Held**
Web: www.mohawkgolf.com
SIC: **7997** 5812 5813 Golf club, membership ; Eating places; Bar (drinking places)

(G-13635)
NORTH CENTRAL AREA TRANSIT (PA)
Also Called: S C A T
3446 S Township Road 151 (44883-9499)
P.O. Box 922 (44883-0922)
PHONE.................................419 937-2428
Mary Habig, *CEO*
EMP: **35** EST: 1993
SALES (est): 2.14MM
SALES (corp-wide): 2.14MM **Privately Held**
Web: www.senecascat.org
SIC: **4119** Vanpool operation

(G-13636)
OHIO DEPT RHBILITATION CORECTN
Also Called: Adult Parole Authority
111 N Washington St (44883-1522)
PHONE.................................419 448-0004
Dave Miller, *Mgr*
EMP: **69**
SIC: **8322** 9223 Parole office; Correctional institutions
HQ: Ohio Department Of Rehabilitation And Correction
4545 Fisher Rd Ste D
Columbus OH 43228

(G-13637)
ORIANA HOUSE INC
3055 S State Route 100 (44883-8868)
PHONE.................................419 447-1444
Jason Varney, *Brnch Mgr*
EMP: **147**
SALES (corp-wide): 68.05MM **Privately Held**
Web: www.orianahouse.org
SIC: **7322** Collection agency, except real estate
PA: Oriana House, Inc.
885 E Buchtel Ave
Akron OH 44305
330 535-8116

(G-13638)
P T SVCS REHABILITATION INC
Also Called: Optima Rehabilitation Services
27 S Lawrence Dr Ste 104 (44883-8313)
P.O. Box 833 (44883-0833)
PHONE.................................419 455-8600
Michael Herbert, *Brnch Mgr*
EMP: **273**
SALES (corp-wide): 9.98MM **Privately Held**
Web: www.ptsrehab.com
SIC: **8093** Rehabilitation center, outpatient treatment
PA: P. T. Services Rehabilitation, Inc.
2550 S State Route 100
Tiffin OH 44883
419 447-7203

(G-13639)
QUICK TAB II INC (PA)
241 Heritage Dr (44883-9504)
P.O. Box 723 (44883-0723)
PHONE.................................419 448-6622
Chuck Daughenbaugh, *CEO*
Charles Eingle, *
Mike Daughenbaugh, *
▼ EMP: **64** EST: 1992
SQ FT: 30,000
SALES (est): 11.59MM **Privately Held**
Web: www.qt2.com
SIC: **2752** 5112 2791 2789 Forms, business; lithographed; Stationery and office supplies; Typesetting; Bookbinding and related work

(G-13640)
RK FAMILY INC
2300 W Market St (44883-8877)
PHONE.................................419 443-1663
Tim F Lode, *Prin*
EMP: **268**
SALES (corp-wide): 1.22B **Privately Held**
Web: www.ruralking.com
SIC: **5191** Farm supplies
PA: Rk Family, Inc.
4216 Dewitt Ave
Mattoon IL 61938
217 235-7102

(G-13641)
SALVATION ARMY
Also Called: Salvation Army
505 E Market St (44883-1767)
P.O. Box 341 (44883-0341)
PHONE.................................419 447-2252
George Polariek, *Brnch Mgr*
EMP: **27**
SQ FT: 86,946
SALES (corp-wide): 2.41B **Privately Held**
Web: www.saconnects.org
SIC: **5932** 8741 8641 Used merchandise stores; Management services; Civic and social associations
HQ: The Salvation Army
440 W Nyack Rd Ofc
West Nyack NY 10994
845 620-7200

(G-13642)
SENECA COUNTY
Also Called: Seneca County Human Services
3362 S Township Rd (44883)
PHONE.................................419 447-5011
Kathy Oliver, *Mgr*
EMP: **64**
SALES (corp-wide): 61.95MM **Privately Held**
Web: www.sencoeng.com
SIC: **6371** Welfare pensions
PA: Seneca County
111 Madison St
Tiffin OH 44883
419 447-4550

(G-13643)
SENECA COUNTY BOARD MR/DD -
780 E County Road 20 (44883-9351)
PHONE.................................419 447-7521
Lewis Hurst, *Prin*
EMP: **44** EST: 2004
SALES (est): 2.12MM **Privately Held**
Web: www.senecadd.org
SIC: **8322** Social services for the handicapped

(G-13644)
SENECA MEDICAL LLC (HQ)
85 Shaffer Park Dr (44883-9290)
P.O. Box 399 (44883-0399)
PHONE.................................800 447-0225
Roger Benz, *CEO*
Buddy Wert, *
Lisa Hohman, *CSO*
Todd Howell, *
Dave Myers, *CCO*

▲ **EMP:** 235 **EST:** 1989
SALES (est): 84.62MM
SALES (corp-wide): 446.66MM **Privately Held**
SIC: 5047 Medical equipment and supplies
PA: Concordance Healthcare Solutions Llc
   85 Shaffer Park Dr
   Tiffin OH 44883
   419 447-0222

(G-13645)
TIFFIN CMNTY YMCA RCRATION CTR (PA)
Also Called: YMCA
180 Summit St (44883-3168)
PHONE.................419 447-8711
Kathy Jentgen, *Pr*
EMP: 74 **EST:** 1974
SQ FT: 70,000
SALES (est): 2.18MM
SALES (corp-wide): 2.18MM **Privately Held**
Web: www.bucyrustiffinymca.org
SIC: 7997 8641 Membership sports and recreation clubs; Community membership club

(G-13646)
TIFFIN LOADER CRANE COMPANY
4151 W State Route 18 (44883-8997)
PHONE.................419 448-8156
Mark Woody, *Pr*
Anthony J Reser, *
EMP: 55 **EST:** 1985
SQ FT: 60,000
SALES (est): 20.68MM
SALES (corp-wide): 242.12K **Privately Held**
Web: www.palfingerusa.com
SIC: 5084 Cranes, industrial
HQ: Palfinger Ag
   LamprechtshausenerBundesstraBe 8
   Bergheim 5101
   66222810

(G-13647)
TIFFIN PAPER COMPANY (PA)
Also Called: TPC Food Service
401 Wall St (44883-1351)
P.O. Box 129 (44883-0129)
PHONE.................419 447-2121
Thomas M Maiberger, *Pr*
Tony Paulus, *
Kevin Maiberger, *
EMP: 40 **EST:** 1963
SQ FT: 40,000
SALES (est): 29.72MM
SALES (corp-wide): 29.72MM **Privately Held**
Web: www.tpcfoodservice.com
SIC: 5149 2064 Groceries and related products, nec; Candy and other confectionery products

(G-13648)
VOA REHABILITATION CENTERS INC
48 St Lawrence Dr (44883-8310)
PHONE.................419 447-7151
EMP: 28
SALES (corp-wide): 1.91MM **Privately Held**
Web: www.voans.org
SIC: 8051 Skilled nursing care facilities
PA: Voa Rehabilitation Centers, Inc.
   50 St Lawrence Dr
   Tiffin OH 44883
   567 207-2230

(G-13649)
VOLUNTERS AMER CARE FACILITIES
Also Called: Volunteer Amer Atmwood Care Ct
670 E State Route 18 (44883-1856)
PHONE.................419 447-7151
Sally Turner, *Brnch Mgr*
EMP: 145
SALES (corp-wide): 56.23MM **Privately Held**
SIC: 8051 Convalescent home with continuous nursing care
PA: Volunteers Of America Care Facilities
   7530 Market Place Dr
   Eden Prairie MN 55344
   952 941-0305

Tipp City
Miami County

(G-13650)
11TH HOUR STAFFING INC
5108 Summerset Dr (45371-8142)
P.O. Box 24649 (45424-0649)
PHONE.................937 405-1900
Carrie Brunello, *Pr*
EMP: 75 **EST:** 2008
SALES (est): 5.05MM **Privately Held**
Web: www.11thhourstaffing.com
SIC: 7361 Employment agencies

(G-13651)
AFTER HOURS FAMILY CARE INC
Also Called: UPPER VALLEY MEDICAL CENTER
450 N Hyatt St Ste 204 (45371-1488)
PHONE.................937 667-2614
Shirley Warren, *Mgr*
EMP: 38 **EST:** 1981
SALES (est): 167.71MM **Privately Held**
Web: www.premierhealth.com
SIC: 8062 General medical and surgical hospitals

(G-13652)
AILERON
8860 Wildcat Rd (45371-9135)
PHONE.................937 669-6500
EMP: 43 **EST:** 1998
SQ FT: 71,000
SALES (est): 7.3MM **Privately Held**
Web: www.aileron.org
SIC: 8742 Business management consultant

(G-13653)
BRUNS CONSTRUCTION ENTERPRISES INC
Also Called: Springfield Home and Hardware
3050 S Tipp Cowlesville Rd (45371-3020)
PHONE.................937 339-2300
EMP: 45 **EST:** 1982
SALES (est): 11.65MM **Privately Held**
Web: www.brunsgc.com
SIC: 1542 1541 Commercial and office building, new construction; Industrial buildings, new construction, nec

(G-13654)
CALVARY CONTRACTING INC
4125 Gibson Dr (45371-9064)
PHONE.................937 754-0300
John C Moon, *Pr*
Denise Moon, *
EMP: 27 **EST:** 1990
SQ FT: 3,600
SALES (est): 3.94MM **Privately Held**
Web: www.calvarycontracting.com

SIC: 1542 Commercial and office building, new construction

(G-13655)
CHILD ADLSCENT SPCLTY CARE DYT
1483 W Main St (45371-2803)
PHONE.................937 667-7711
Kevin Horvath Md, *Pr*
EMP: 30 **EST:** 1985
SALES (est): 2.06MM **Privately Held**
Web: www.childandadolescentcare.com
SIC: 8011 Pediatrician

(G-13656)
DAIHEN INC (HQ)
Also Called: Advanced Welding Division
1400 Blauser Dr (45371-2471)
PHONE.................937 667-0800
Masaaki Nakaoka, *Pr*
▲ **EMP:** 38 **EST:** 1979
SQ FT: 45,000
SALES (est): 34.33MM **Privately Held**
Web: www.daihen-usa.com
SIC: 5084 Welding machinery and equipment
PA: Daihen Corp.
   2-1-11, Tagawa, Yodogawa-Ku
   Osaka OSK 532-0

(G-13657)
DAN & MARIA DAVIS INC
Also Called: Hickory Rver Smkehouse Tipp Cy
135 S Garber Dr (45371-1147)
PHONE.................937 669-2271
Daniel Davis Ii, *Pr*
Maria Davis, *VP*
EMP: 32 **EST:** 2010
SALES (est): 1.01MM **Privately Held**
SIC: 7389 Business Activities at Non-Commercial Site

(G-13658)
ENVIRONMENT CTRL OF MIAMI CNTY
Also Called: Environment Control
7939 S County Road 25a Ste A (45371-9107)
P.O. Box 877 (45371-0877)
PHONE.................937 669-9900
Ted Pauling, *Pr*
Sheryl Pauling, *
William Schneider, *Stockholder*
EMP: 65 **EST:** 1982
SQ FT: 3,000
SALES (est): 1.91MM **Privately Held**
Web: www.environmentcontrol.com
SIC: 7349 Janitorial service, contract basis

(G-13659)
HIGH-TEC INDUSTRIAL SERVICES ✪
15 Industry Park Ct (45371-3060)
PHONE.................937 667-1772
Christopher Griffin, *Pr*
Daniel Whitlock, *VP*
Kyle Packer, *Sec*
EMP: 60 **EST:** 2023
SQ FT: 11,000
SALES (est): 2.6MM **Privately Held**
SIC: 1799 7349 3589 Construction site cleanup; Building and office cleaning services; Commercial cleaning equipment

(G-13660)
HOSS II INC
Also Called: Voss Honda
155 S Garber Dr (45371-1147)
PHONE.................937 669-4300
John Voss, *Pr*
John E Voss, *

EMP: 40 **EST:** 1991
SALES (est): 8.31MM **Privately Held**
Web: www.vosshonda.com
SIC: 5511 7539 Automobiles, new and used; Automotive repair shops, nec

(G-13661)
KETTERING ADVENTIST HEALTHCARE
Also Called: Kettering Health Network
70 Weller Dr (45371-3306)
PHONE.................937 506-3112
EMP: 70
SALES (corp-wide): 1.58B **Privately Held**
SIC: 8049 Acupuncturist
PA: Kettering Adventist Healthcare
   3535 Southern Blvd
   Dayton OH 45429
   937 298-4331

(G-13662)
MEIJER DIST DC 804 CORP
4240 S County Rd 25a (45371-2950)
PHONE.................616 791-5821
Richard Keyes, *Pr*
EMP: 400 **EST:** 1934
SALES (est): 8.59MM **Privately Held**
SIC: 6512 Property operation, retail establishment

(G-13663)
MILLER PIPELINE LLC
11990 Peters Pike (45371-9669)
PHONE.................937 506-8837
Jim Wilson, *Mgr*
EMP: 400
SALES (corp-wide): 2.13B **Privately Held**
Web: www.millerpipeline.com
SIC: 1623 Pipeline construction, nsk
HQ: Miller Pipeline, Llc
   8850 Crawfordsville Rd
   Indianapolis IN 46234
   317 293-0278

(G-13664)
PRECISION STRIP INC
315 Park Ave (45371-1887)
PHONE.................937 667-6255
Jerry Huber, *Mgr*
EMP: 74
SQ FT: 3,080
SALES (corp-wide): 14.81B **Publicly Held**
Web: www.precision-strip.com
SIC: 4225 3312 General warehousing and storage; Blast furnaces and steel mills
HQ: Precision Strip Inc.
   86 S Ohio St
   Minster OH 45865
   419 628-2343

(G-13665)
TIPP CITY VETERINARY HOSP INC
4900 S County Road 25a (45371-2912)
PHONE.................937 667-8489
James Mathias, *Pr*
Ben Spinks, *
EMP: 61 **EST:** 1995
SALES (est): 3.17MM **Privately Held**
Web: www.tippvet.com
SIC: 0742 Animal hospital services, pets and other animal specialties

(G-13666)
TOOL TESTING LAB INC
11601 N Dixie Dr (45371-9108)
PHONE.................937 898-5696
Ted Bowden, *Pr*
EMP: 35
Web: www.ttlcal.com

SIC: 8734 5251 Product certification, safety or performance; Tools
PA: Tool Testing Lab, Inc.
  11601 N Dixie Dr
  Tipp City OH 45371

(G-13667)
TRANSFREIGHT LLC
1351 Blauser Dr (45371-2474)
PHONE..................................937 576-2800
Darrell Dewberry, *Mgr*
EMP: 274
SALES (corp-wide): 2.11B **Privately Held**
SIC: 4731 Freight forwarding
HQ: Transfreight, Llc
  3940 Olympic Blvd Ste 500
  Erlanger KY 41018
  859 372-5930

(G-13668)
UVMC NURSING CARE INC
Also Called: Springmeade
4375 S County Road 25a (45371-2956)
PHONE..................................937 667-7500
Tom Nick, *Admn*
EMP: 126
Web: www.premierhealth.com
SIC: 8361 8051 Aged home; Skilled nursing care facilities
PA: Uvmc Nursing Care, Inc.
  3130 N County Road 25a
  Troy OH 45373

(G-13669)
WESTAR CONSTRUCTION INC
4225 Gibson Dr (45371-9452)
PHONE..................................937 667-8402
Jonathan H Springer, *Pr*
Catherine Springer, *
EMP: 35 **EST:** 1999
SQ FT: 6,000
SALES (est): 6.2MM **Privately Held**
SIC: 1541 Industrial buildings and warehouses

Toledo
Lucas County

(G-13670)
21ST CENTURY HEALTH SPA INC (PA)
343 New Towne Square Dr (43612-4626)
PHONE..................................419 476-5585
Ronald R Hemelgarn, *Owner*
EMP: 30 **EST:** 1972
SQ FT: 10,000
SALES (est): 2.52MM
SALES (corp-wide): 2.52MM **Privately Held**
SIC: 5091 Fitness equipment and supplies

(G-13671)
AAA CLUB ALLIANCE INC (PA)
Also Called: AAA Mid-Atlantic
3201 Meijer Dr (43617)
PHONE..................................419 843-1200
Karl Halbedl, *Pr*
EMP: 83 **EST:** 1910
SQ FT: 24,000
SALES (est): 8.93MM
SALES (corp-wide): 8.93MM **Privately Held**
Web: cluballiance.aaa.com
SIC: 8699 Automobile owners' association

(G-13672)
AAA STANDARD SERVICES INC
4117 South Ave (43615-6231)
PHONE..................................419 535-0274
Steven Johnson, *Pr*
Dale Johnson Senior, *Prin*
EMP: 49 **EST:** 1971
SQ FT: 24,500
SALES (est): 2.78MM **Privately Held**
Web: www.aaastandardservices.com
SIC: 7349 1521 Janitorial service, contract basis; Repairing fire damage, single-family houses

(G-13673)
ABBOTT TOOL INC
Also Called: ATI
405 Dura Ave (43612-2619)
PHONE..................................419 476-6742
Arthur Stange, *VP*
Leonard Livecchi, *
Karle Stange, *
EMP: 33 **EST:** 1973
SQ FT: 12,000
SALES (est): 3.06MM **Privately Held**
Web: www.abbotttool.com
SIC: 3469 7692 Machine parts, stamped or pressed metal; Welding repair

(G-13674)
ACME DYNAMITE
Also Called: Hc Solutions Management
3816 Hoiles Ave (43612-1256)
P.O. Box 232 (48117-0232)
PHONE..................................313 867-5309
Jill Johnson, *Managing Member*
Jill Calkins, *
EMP: 40 **EST:** 2020
SALES (est): 2MM **Privately Held**
SIC: 8741 Management services

(G-13675)
ADVOCTES FOR BSIC LGAL EQLITY (PA)
Also Called: Able
525 Jefferson Ave (43604-1094)
PHONE..................................419 255-0814
Joseph Tafelski, *Dir*
EMP: 50 **EST:** 1969
SALES (est): 10.89MM
SALES (corp-wide): 10.89MM **Privately Held**
Web: www.ablelaw.org
SIC: 8111 Legal aid service

(G-13676)
AIDE FOR YOU LLC
3131 Executive Pkwy Ste 220 (43606-1327)
PHONE..................................419 214-0111
EMP: 37 **EST:** 2019
SALES (est): 280K **Privately Held**
Web: www.aideforu.com
SIC: 8082 Home health care services

(G-13677)
AL PEAKE & SONS INC
4949 Stickney Ave (43612-3716)
PHONE..................................419 243-9284
Philip Peake, *Pr*
EMP: 30 **EST:** 1974
SQ FT: 57,408
SALES (est): 10.99MM **Privately Held**
Web: www.alpeake.com
SIC: 5148 Fruits, fresh

(G-13678)
ALLEN COUNTY PROPERTY LLC
Also Called: Windgate Inn, The
457 S Reynolds Rd (43615-5953)
PHONE..................................419 534-4234
EMP: 29 **EST:** 1999
SALES (est): 551.59K **Privately Held**
Web: www.wyndhamhotels.com
SIC: 7011 Hotels

(G-13679)
ALRO STEEL CORPORATION
3003 Airport Hwy (43609-1405)
P.O. Box 964 (43697-0964)
PHONE..................................419 720-5300
Keith Daly, *Mgr*
EMP: 57
SALES (corp-wide): 3.43B **Privately Held**
Web: www.alro.com
SIC: 5051 5085 5162 3444 Steel; Industrial supplies; Plastics materials, nec; Sheet metalwork
PA: Alro Steel Corporation
  3100 E High St
  Jackson MI 49203
  517 787-5500

(G-13680)
AMBULATORY CARE PHARMACY
Also Called: ST VINCENT MEDICAL CENTER
2213 Cherry St (43608-2603)
PHONE..................................419 251-2545
Phillip Nelson, *Owner*
EMP: 72 **EST:** 2000
SALES (est): 591.39MM **Privately Held**
SIC: 8062 General medical and surgical hospitals

(G-13681)
AMCS GROUP INC
2942 Centennial Rd (43617-1833)
PHONE..................................419 891-1100
Michael Winton, *Brnch Mgr*
EMP: 77
Web: www.amcsgroup.com
SIC: 7371 Computer software development and applications
HQ: Amcs Group Inc.
  119 S 5th St
  Oxford PA 19363

(G-13682)
AMERICAN GOLF CORPORATION
Also Called: Detwiler Park Golf Course
4001 N Summit St (43611-3067)
PHONE..................................419 726-9353
Lynne Murnan, *Mgr*
EMP: 28
Web: www.toledocitygolf.com
SIC: 7992 Public golf courses
HQ: American Golf Corporation
  909 N Pacific Coast Hwy # 650
  El Segundo CA 90245
  310 664-4000

(G-13683)
AMERICAN INTERIORS INC (PA)
302 S Byrne Rd Bldg 100 (43615-6208)
PHONE..................................419 535-1808
Steve Essig, *Pr*
Rick Essig, *
◆ **EMP:** 50 **EST:** 1993
SQ FT: 140,000
SALES (est): 52.02MM **Privately Held**
Web: www.aminteriors.com
SIC: 5021 Office furniture, nec

(G-13684)
AMERICAN NATIONAL RED CROSS
Also Called: American Nat Red Cross - Blood
1111 Research Dr (43614-2798)
PHONE..................................419 382-2707
Mary Rietzke, *Mgr*
EMP: 165
SALES (corp-wide): 3.18B **Privately Held**
Web: www.redcross.org
SIC: 8322 Social service center
PA: The American National Red Cross
  431 18th St Nw
  Washington DC 20006
  202 737-8300

(G-13685)
AMERICAN NATIONAL RED CROSS
Also Called: American Nat Red Cross - Blood
3510 Executive Pkwy (43606-1319)
PHONE..................................800 733-2767
Donald Baker, *CEO*
EMP: 31
SQ FT: 9,481
SALES (corp-wide): 3.18B **Privately Held**
Web: www.redcross.org
SIC: 8322 Social service center
PA: The American National Red Cross
  431 18th St Nw
  Washington DC 20006
  202 737-8300

(G-13686)
AMERICAN NATIONAL RED CROSS
Also Called: Red Cross
3100 W Central Ave Ste 200 (43606-2914)
PHONE..................................419 329-2900
Tim Yenrick, *Ex Dir*
EMP: 52
SALES (corp-wide): 3.18B **Privately Held**
Web: www.redcross.org
SIC: 8322 Social service center
PA: The American National Red Cross
  431 18th St Nw
  Washington DC 20006
  202 737-8300

(G-13687)
AMERICAN POSTS LLC (PA)
810 Chicago St (43611-3609)
PHONE..................................419 720-0652
David Feniger, *Managing Member*
EMP: 30 **EST:** 2005
SALES (est): 10.73MM
SALES (corp-wide): 10.73MM **Privately Held**
Web: www.americanposts.com
SIC: 3312 5051 Rods, iron and steel: made in steel mills; Steel

(G-13688)
ANDERS DERMATOLOGY INC
Also Called: Anders Medical
4126 N Holland Sylvania Rd Ste 200 (43623)
PHONE..................................419 473-3257
EMP: 32 **EST:** 1969
SALES (est): 6.02MM **Privately Held**
Web: www.andersderm.com
SIC: 8011 Dermatologist

(G-13689)
ANSPACH MEEKS ELLENBERGER LLP (PA)
25 S Huron St (43604-8705)
PHONE..................................419 447-6181
Robert M Anspach, *Pt*
Mark D Meeks, *Pt*
Richard F Ellenberg, *Pt*
▲ **EMP:** 36 **EST:** 1986
SALES (est): 9.72MM
SALES (corp-wide): 9.72MM **Privately Held**
Web: www.anspachlaw.com
SIC: 8111 General practice attorney, lawyer

(G-13690)
ANTONIO SOFO SON IMPORTING CO (PA)
Also Called: Sofo Importing Company
253 Waggoner Blvd (43612-1952)
PHONE..................................419 476-4211
Mike Sofo, *Pr*
Joseph J Sofo Junior, *Prin*

GEOGRAPHIC SECTION
Toledo - Lucas County (G-13711)

Paul Peer, *
Wilma Jean Sofo, *
Antonio J Sofo, *
▲ **EMP:** 206 **EST:** 1940
SQ FT: 180,000
SALES (est): 91.08MM
SALES (corp-wide): 91.08MM Privately Held
Web: www.sofofoods.com
SIC: 5499 5149 Gourmet food stores; Specialty food items

(G-13691)
APPLIED TECHNOLOGY INTEGRATION (PA)
Also Called: ATI
3130 Executive Pkwy Fl 5 (43606-5532)
PHONE..............................419 537-9052
D Craig Winn, *CEO*
Michael Ankney, *Dir*
Matt George, *Dir*
EMP: 43 **EST:** 1986
SALES (est): 6.57MM Privately Held
Web: www.atiintegration.com
SIC: 8711 Consulting engineer

(G-13692)
APS MEDICAL BILLING
Also Called: A P S Medical Billing
5620 Southwyck Blvd (43614-1501)
PHONE..............................419 866-1804
Harold S Rickard, *Prin*
Nancy Condon, *
Margaret Rickard, *
Judy Udell, *
EMP: 65 **EST:** 1965
SALES (est): 14.99MM
SALES (corp-wide): 62.18MM Privately Held
Web: www.apsmedbill.com
SIC: 8721 Billing and bookkeeping service
PA: United Collection Bureau, Inc.
5620 Southwyck Blvd
Toledo OH 43614
419 866-6227

(G-13693)
AREA OFFICE ON AGING NRTHWSTER
2155 Arlington Ave (43609-1997)
PHONE..............................419 382-0624
Billie Johnson, *Ex Dir*
EMP: 96 **EST:** 1980
SALES (est): 34.87MM Privately Held
Web: www.areaofficeonaging.com
SIC: 8322 8082 Senior citizens' center or association; Home health care services

(G-13694)
ATTARI DELIVERY LLC
5533 Southwyck Blvd Ste 101 (43614)
PHONE..............................443 251-8172
Muhammad Bilal, *CEO*
EMP: 85 **EST:** 2021
SALES (est): 4.95MM Privately Held
SIC: 4731 Freight transportation arrangement

(G-13695)
AUTO-WARES INC
Also Called: Maxi Automotive Toledo
3404 N Holland Sylvania Rd (43615)
PHONE..............................419 867-1927
EMP: 87
SALES (corp-wide): 584.44MM Privately Held
Web: www.autowares.com
SIC: 5013 Automotive supplies and parts
HQ: Auto-Wares, Inc.
440 Kirtland St Sw
Grand Rapids MI 49507
616 243-2125

(G-13696)
AUTOWAY INVESTORS LTD
6800 W Central Ave (43617-1135)
PHONE..............................419 841-6691
EMP: 40 **EST:** 1996
SALES (est): 1.67MM Privately Held
SIC: 7371 Computer software systems analysis and design, custom

(G-13697)
B B I T INC
1946 N 13th St Ste 101 (43604-7257)
PHONE..............................419 259-3600
Bill Bollin, *CEO*
Ellaine Canning, *
Bob Sands, *
EMP: 150 **EST:** 1984
SALES (est): 46.44MM
SALES (corp-wide): 146.57MM Privately Held
SIC: 5072 Hardware
PA: Bostwick-Braun Company
7349 Crossleigh Ct
Toledo OH 43617
419 259-3600

(G-13698)
BAGEL PLACE INC (PA)
Also Called: Barry Bagels
3444 Secor Rd (43606-1546)
PHONE..............................419 537-9377
Mark Greenblatt, *Pr*
Judie A Greenblatt, *
EMP: 50 **EST:** 1972
SALES (est): 18.55MM
SALES (corp-wide): 18.55MM Privately Held
Web: www.barrybagels.com
SIC: 5461 5411 5812 5149 Bagels; Delicatessen stores; Caterers; Bakery products

(G-13699)
BARRINGTON TOLEDO LLC
Also Called: W N W O
300 S Byrne Rd (43615-6217)
PHONE..............................419 535-0024
Chris Popf, *Genl Mgr*
Victoria Scott, *Mgr*
EMP: 44 **EST:** 2006
SALES (est): 2.26MM
SALES (corp-wide): 156.16MM Privately Held
SIC: 4833 Television broadcasting stations
HQ: Barrington Broadcasting Group Llc
1270 Ave Of The Amrcas Fl
New York NY 10020
847 884-1877

(G-13700)
BAY PARK COMMUNITY HOSPITAL
2142 N Cove Blvd (43606-3895)
PHONE..............................419 690-8725
Katherine Szilagyi, *Admn*
EMP: 48
SALES (corp-wide): 187.07MM Privately Held
Web: www.promedica.org
SIC: 8062 General medical and surgical hospitals
HQ: Bay Park Community Hospital
100 Madison Ave
Toledo OH 43604
567 585-9600

(G-13701)
BAY PARK COMMUNITY HOSPITAL (HQ)
Also Called: Promedica
100 Madison Ave (43604-1516)
PHONE..............................567 585-9600
Randy Oostra, *Pr*
Michael Browning, *
EMP: 391 **EST:** 1986
SQ FT: 270,000
SALES (est): 102.06MM
SALES (corp-wide): 187.07MM Privately Held
Web: www.promedica.org
SIC: 8062 General medical and surgical hospitals
PA: Promedica Health System, Inc.
100 Madison Ave
Toledo OH 43604
567 585-9600

(G-13702)
BCI MISSISSIPPI BROADBAND LLC
Also Called: Maxx South Broadband
5552 Southwyck Blvd (43614-1536)
PHONE..............................419 724-7295
EMP: 30
SALES (corp-wide): 910.95MM Privately Held
SIC: 8721 Accounting, auditing, and bookkeeping
HQ: Bci Mississippi Broadband, Llc
105 Allison Cv
Oxford MS 38655
662 259-3211

(G-13703)
BELLAS LAWN & LANDSCAPE LLC
3017 Hill Ave Ste A (43607-2957)
PHONE..............................419 536-9003
Mike Bella, *Owner*
EMP: 50 **EST:** 2005
SALES (est): 2.39MM Privately Held
Web: www.bellaslawnandlandscape.com
SIC: 0782 0781 5083 Lawn care services; Landscape services; Irrigation equipment

(G-13704)
BELLE TIRE DISTRIBUTORS INC
Also Called: Andersons Tireman Auto Centers
750 S Reynolds Rd (43615-6316)
PHONE..............................419 535-3033
Chad Faber, *Brnch Mgr*
EMP: 35
SALES (corp-wide): 569.43MM Privately Held
Web: www.thetireman.com
SIC: 5531 7538 Automotive tires; General automotive repair shops
PA: Belle Tire Distributors, Inc.
1000 Enterprise Dr
Allen Park MI 48101
888 462-3553

(G-13705)
BIOLIFE PLASMA SERVICES LP
4711 Talmadge Rd (43623-3008)
PHONE..............................419 313-3406
Curtis Brown, *Center Manager*
EMP: 50
SIC: 8099 Blood donor station
HQ: Biolife Plasma Services L.P.
1200 Lakeside Dr
Bannockburn IL 60015
224 940-2000

(G-13706)
BIONIX DEVELOPMENT CORPORATION
5154 Enterprise Blvd (43612-3807)
PHONE..............................800 551-7096
EMP: 28 **EST:** 1991
SALES (est): 821.84K Privately Held
Web: www.bionix.com
SIC: 8741 Management services

(G-13707)
BMWC CONSTRUCTORS INC
913 Madison Ave (43604-5533)
PHONE..............................419 490-2000
Nick Randles, *Brnch Mgr*
EMP: 106
SALES (corp-wide): 565.29MM Privately Held
Web: www.bmwc.com
SIC: 1711 Mechanical contractor
HQ: Bmwc Constructors, Inc.
4488 Nw Yeon Ave
Portland OR 97210
317 267-0400

(G-13708)
BOHL CRANE INC
1104 Custer Dr (43612-3011)
PHONE..............................419 214-3940
EMP: 60
SALES (corp-wide): 27.59MM Privately Held
Web: www.bohlco.com
SIC: 5084 Industrial machinery and equipment
PA: Bohl Crane, Inc.
534 W Laskey Rd
Toledo OH 43612
419 476-7525

(G-13709)
BOHL EQUIPMENT COMPANY (PA)
534 W Laskey Rd (43612-3299)
PHONE..............................800 962-4802
Robert D Bohl, *Pr*
Douglas E Bohl, *
Steven Bohl, *
A M Frease, *
H A Bohl, *
▲ **EMP:** 62 **EST:** 1954
SQ FT: 11,300
SALES (est): 25.4MM
SALES (corp-wide): 25.4MM Privately Held
Web: www.bohlco.com
SIC: 5084 Materials handling machinery

(G-13710)
BOLLIN & SONS INC
Also Called: Bollin Label Systems
6001 Brent Dr (43611-1090)
PHONE..............................419 693-6573
Mark D Bollin, *Pr*
Chris Younkman, *
EMP: 40 **EST:** 1969
SQ FT: 21,000
SALES (est): 14.54MM Privately Held
Web: www.bollin.com
SIC: 5084 7389 2851 2759 Packaging machinery and equipment; Design services; Paints and allied products; Commercial printing, nec

(G-13711)
BOLT EXPRESS LLC (PA)
Also Called: Strike Logistics
7255 Crossleigh Ct Ste 108 (43617-1556)
P.O. Box 759 (43697-0759)
PHONE..............................419 729-6698
Guy Sanderson, *CEO*
Chuck King, *
EMP: 98 **EST:** 2001
SQ FT: 5,000
SALES (est): 92.69MM
SALES (corp-wide): 92.69MM Privately Held
Web: www.bolt-express.com
SIC: 4731 Freight forwarding

Toledo - Lucas County (G-13712) — GEOGRAPHIC SECTION

(G-13712)
BON SECOURS MERCY HEALTH INC
2213 Cherry St (43608-2603)
PHONE.................419 251-2659
EMP: 30
SALES (corp-wide): 6.92B Privately Held
Web: www.bonsecours.com
SIC: 8062 General medical and surgical hospitals
PA: Bon Secours Mercy Health, Inc.
1701 Mercy Health Pl
Cincinnati OH 45237
513 956-3729

(G-13713)
BOSTWICK-BRAUN COMPANY (PA)
7349 Crossleigh Ct (43617)
PHONE.................419 259-3600
Chris Beach, Prin
Chris Beach, CEO
Elaine Canning, Prin
▲ EMP: 55 EST: 1855
SQ FT: 23,000
SALES (est): 146.57MM
SALES (corp-wide): 146.57MM Privately Held
Web: www.bostwick-braun.com
SIC: 5072 5084 5063 5083 Builders' hardware, nec; Industrial machinery and equipment; Electrical apparatus and equipment; Lawn and garden machinery and equipment

(G-13714)
BOWSER-MORNER INC
Also Called: Bowser Morner and Associates
1419 Miami St (43605-3314)
P.O. Box 838 (43697-0838)
PHONE.................419 691-4800
EMP: 29
SALES (corp-wide): 17.99MM Privately Held
Web: www.bowser-morner.com
SIC: 8734 Metallurgical testing laboratory
PA: Bowser-Morner, Inc.
4518 Taylorsville Rd
Dayton OH 45424
937 236-8805

(G-13715)
BOYS & GIRLS CLUB OF TOLEDO (PA)
Also Called: BOYS CLUB CAMP ASSOCIATION
2250 N Detroit Ave (43606-4690)
PHONE.................419 241-4258
Dave Wehrmeister, Ex Dir
EMP: 32 EST: 1892
SQ FT: 35,000
SALES (est): 804.18K
SALES (corp-wide): 804.18K Privately Held
Web: www.bgctoledo.org
SIC: 8641 Boy Scout organization

(G-13716)
BRENT INDUSTRIES INC
2922 South Ave (43609-1328)
PHONE.................419 382-8693
Royse Willie, Brnch Mgr
EMP: 30
SQ FT: 42,000
SALES (corp-wide): 5.7MM Privately Held
Web: www.brentindustries.com
SIC: 7218 Safety glove supply
PA: Brent Industries, Inc.
289 Cooper Ave
Brent AL 35034
205 926-4801

(G-13717)
BREWER HOLDCO INC
4500 Dorr St (43615-4040)
PHONE.................419 247-2800
George L Chapman, CEO
EMP: 476 EST: 2012
SALES (est): 5.18B
SALES (corp-wide): 5.86B Publicly Held
SIC: 6513 Apartment building operators
HQ: Welltower Op Llc
4500 Dorr St
Toledo OH 43615
419 247-2800

(G-13718)
BROADBAND EXPRESS LLC
1915 Nebraska Ave (43607-3800)
PHONE.................419 536-9127
EMP: 55
SALES (corp-wide): 4.18B Publicly Held
Web: recruiting.ultipro.com
SIC: 1731 1623 Cable television installation; Communication line and transmission tower construction
HQ: Broadband Express, Llc
374 Westdale Ave Ste B
Westerville OH 43082
614 823-6464

(G-13719)
BRONDES FORD (PA)
Also Called: Brondes Ford Toledo
5545 Secor Rd (43623-1998)
PHONE.................419 473-1411
Phillip Brondes Junior, Pr
John Stedcke, *
Phillip Brondes Senior, VP
Drew Conkle, *
▼ EMP: 39 EST: 1958
SALES (est): 23.61MM
SALES (corp-wide): 23.61MM Privately Held
Web: www.brondesfordtoledo.com
SIC: 5511 7538 7532 Automobiles, new and used; General automotive repair shops; Top and body repair and paint shops

(G-13720)
BROWN MOTOR SALES CO (PA)
Also Called: Brown Motors
5625 W Central Ave (43615-1505)
PHONE.................419 531-0151
Rob Brown Junior, Pr
Robert W Brown Junior, Ex VP
EMP: 39 EST: 1914
SQ FT: 46,000
SALES (est): 8.19MM
SALES (corp-wide): 8.19MM Privately Held
SIC: 7538 7532 7515 5531 General automotive repair shops; Top and body repair and paint shops; Passenger car leasing; Auto and home supply stores

(G-13721)
BRYANS TREATMENT CENTER
1701 W Sylvania Ave (43613-4635)
P.O. Box 665 (43528-0665)
PHONE.................216 208-0634
Teresa Dennis, CEO
EMP: 30 EST: 2018
SALES (est): 1.03MM Privately Held
Web: www.bryanstreatmentcenter.net
SIC: 8093 Substance abuse clinics (outpatient)

(G-13722)
BUCKEYE CHECK CASHING INC
1221 S Reynolds Rd (43615-6909)
PHONE.................419 382-5385
EMP: 35
Web: www.ccfi.com
SIC: 6099 Check cashing agencies
HQ: Buckeye Check Cashing, Inc.
5165 Emerald Pkwy Ste 100
Dublin OH 43017
614 798-5900

(G-13723)
BURBANK INC
Also Called: Seagate Roofg & Waterproofing
623 Burbank Dr (43607-3234)
PHONE.................419 698-3434
Thomas K Elder, Pr
EMP: 40 EST: 1988
SQ FT: 10,000
SALES (est): 4.67MM Privately Held
Web: www.seagateforyourhome.com
SIC: 1761 1799 1751 Roofing contractor; Waterproofing; Window and door (prefabricated) installation

(G-13724)
CANAAN COMPANIES INC
328 21st St (43604-5037)
PHONE.................419 842-8373
James House, Pr
EMP: 42 EST: 2001
SQ FT: 12,000
SALES (est): 5.4MM Privately Held
Web: www.canaancompanies.com
SIC: 1542 1799 1741 1541 Commercial and office building, new construction; Coating, caulking, and weather, water, and fireproofing; Masonry and other stonework; Industrial buildings, new construction, nec

(G-13725)
CAUFFIEL INDUSTRIES CORP
Also Called: Caufiel Technology
3171 N Republic Blvd Ste 102 (43615-1515)
EMP: 30 EST: 1953
SIC: 6719 Investment holding companies, except banks

(G-13726)
CAUFFIEL TECHNOLOGIES CORPORATION
3171 N Republic Blvd Ste 207 (43615)
PHONE.................419 843-7262
▼ EMP: 50
SIC: 4225 General warehousing

(G-13727)
CENTRAL COCA-COLA BTLG CO INC
Also Called: Coca-Cola
3970 Catawba St (43612-1404)
PHONE.................419 476-6622
Paul Kenny, Mgr
EMP: 140
SALES (corp-wide): 45.75B Publicly Held
Web: www.coca-cola.com
SIC: 2086 2087 5149 Bottled and canned soft drinks; Syrups, drink; Groceries and related products, nec
HQ: Central Coca-Cola Bottling Company, Inc.
555 Taxter Rd Ste 550
Elmsford NY 10523
914 789-1100

(G-13728)
CENTURY EQUIPMENT INC (PA)
5959 Angola Rd (43615-6332)
P.O. Box 352889 (43635-2889)
PHONE.................419 865-7400
Martin O'brien, Pr
Robert E O'brien, Ch Bd
Rick Puffenberger, *
EMP: 35 EST: 1950
SQ FT: 42,000
SALES (est): 24.57MM
SALES (corp-wide): 24.57MM Privately Held
Web: www.centuryequip.com
SIC: 5083 5088 Mowers, power; Golf carts

(G-13729)
CHAMBERS LEASING SYSTEMS CORP (PA)
3100 N Summit St (43611)
P.O. Box 5337 (43611)
PHONE.................419 726-9747
James Chambers, Pr
Edman Lee, VP
EMP: 38 EST: 1980
SQ FT: 6,200
SALES (est): 2.29MM Privately Held
Web: www.ventureexpress.com
SIC: 4213 Trucking, except local

(G-13730)
CHAS F MANN PAINTING CO
Also Called: Spray Repair Services Div
3638 Marine Rd (43609-1020)
PHONE.................419 385-7151
Charles F Mann Iv, Pr
Richard T Mann, *
EMP: 43 EST: 1923
SQ FT: 26,000
SALES (est): 3.17MM Privately Held
SIC: 1721 Commercial painting

(G-13731)
CHERRY ST MISSION MINISTRIES (PA)
1501 Monroe St (43604-5760)
PHONE.................419 242-5141
Ann Ebbert, Pr
EMP: 43 EST: 1947
SQ FT: 120,000
SALES (est): 8.16MM
SALES (corp-wide): 8.16MM Privately Held
Web: www.cherrystreetmission.org
SIC: 8361 Rehabilitation center, residential: health care incidental

(G-13732)
CHIEF DELIVERY LLC
7620 W Bancroft St (43617-1604)
P.O. Box 351793 (43635-1793)
PHONE.................419 277-6190
Keith Clonch, Pr
EMP: 90 EST: 2020
SALES (est): 2.37MM Privately Held
SIC: 4215 7389 Package delivery, vehicular; Business Activities at Non-Commercial Site

(G-13733)
CHRISTEN & SONS COMPANY (PA)
Also Called: Christen Detroit
714 George St (43608-2914)
P.O. Box 547 (43697-0547)
PHONE.................419 243-4161
Frederick R Christen, Pr
Marlene Christen, *
EMP: 50 EST: 1897
SQ FT: 60,000
SALES (est): 4.3MM
SALES (corp-wide): 4.3MM Privately Held
Web: www.cdetroit.com
SIC: 1761 Roofing, siding, and sheetmetal work

(G-13734)
CHRISTIAN HOME CARE LLC
5555 Airport Hwy Ste 200 (43615-7320)
PHONE.................419 254-2840
Jonette T Crabtree, Prin
EMP: 31 EST: 2009

GEOGRAPHIC SECTION

Toledo - Lucas County (G-13756)

SALES (est): 2.08MM **Privately Held**
Web: www.christianhomecare.com
SIC: 8082 Home health care services

(G-13735)
CIRALSKY & ASSOCIATES INC
Also Called: Ciralsky Steel
1604 Prosperity Rd (43612-2918)
PHONE..................................419 470-1328
William Ciralsky, *Pr*
EMP: 48 EST: 1972
SQ FT: 100,000
SALES (est): 1.71MM **Privately Held**
Web: www.coilsteelprocessing.com
SIC: 5051 Steel

(G-13736)
CITIZENS BANK NATIONAL ASSN
3410 Secor Rd Ste 510 (43606-1548)
PHONE..................................419 720-0009
EMP: 31
SALES (corp-wide): 12.19B **Publicly Held**
Web: www.citizensbank.com
SIC: 6021 National commercial banks
HQ: Citizens Bank, National Association
    1 Citizens Plz
    Providence RI 02903
    401 456-7096

(G-13737)
CITY OF TOLEDO
Also Called: Fleet Operations
555 N Expressway Dr (43608-1512)
PHONE..................................419 936-2507
Ken Naeidert, *Mgr*
EMP: 51
SALES (corp-wide): 383.27MM **Privately Held**
Web: toledo.oh.gov
SIC: 7538 General truck repair
PA: City Of Toledo
    1 Government Ctr Ste 2050
    Toledo OH 43604
    419 245-1050

(G-13738)
CITY OF TOLEDO
Also Called: Toledo City Parks
2201 Ottawa Dr (43606-4338)
PHONE..................................419 936-2875
Tom Crothers, *Brnch Mgr*
EMP: 64
SALES (corp-wide): 383.27MM **Privately Held**
Web: toledo.oh.gov
SIC: 8999 9221 Natural resource preservation service; Police protection
PA: City Of Toledo
    1 Government Ctr Ste 2050
    Toledo OH 43604
    419 245-1050

(G-13739)
CITY OF TOLEDO
Also Called: Dept of Neighborhoods
1 Government Ctr Ste 1800 (43604-2275)
PHONE..................................419 245-1400
Tom Carouthers, *Brnch Mgr*
EMP: 38
SALES (corp-wide): 383.27MM **Privately Held**
Web: toledo.oh.gov
SIC: 9531 8611 Housing programs, planning and development: government; Business associations
PA: City Of Toledo
    1 Government Ctr Ste 2050
    Toledo OH 43604
    419 245-1050

(G-13740)
CITY OF TOLEDO
600 Jefferson Ave Ste 300 (43604-1012)
PHONE..................................419 936-2275
Warian E Henry, *Commsnr*
EMP: 64
SALES (corp-wide): 383.27MM **Privately Held**
Web: toledo.oh.gov
SIC: 8711 Engineering services
PA: City Of Toledo
    1 Government Ctr Ste 2050
    Toledo OH 43604
    419 245-1050

(G-13741)
CITY OF TOLEDO
Also Called: Municipal Government
1 Government Ctr Ste 2200 (43604-2295)
PHONE..................................419 245-1001
Jesse Torrence, *Ex Dir*
EMP: 38
SALES (corp-wide): 383.27MM **Privately Held**
Web: toledo.oh.gov
SIC: 8611 9111 Business associations; Mayors' office
PA: City Of Toledo
    1 Government Ctr Ste 2050
    Toledo OH 43604
    419 245-1050

(G-13742)
CITY OF TOLEDO
Also Called: Toledo Police Dept
525 N Erie St Ste 2 (43604-3345)
PHONE..................................419 245-3209
Tom Davis, *Brnch Mgr*
EMP: 78
SALES (corp-wide): 383.27MM **Privately Held**
Web: toledo.oh.gov
SIC: 5049 Law enforcement equipment and supplies
PA: City Of Toledo
    1 Government Ctr Ste 2050
    Toledo OH 43604
    419 245-1050

(G-13743)
CITY OF TOLEDO
Also Called: Utilities Department
420 Madison Ave Ste 100 (43604-1219)
PHONE..................................419 245-1800
Robert C Stevenson, *Prin*
EMP: 89
SALES (corp-wide): 383.27MM **Privately Held**
Web: toledo.oh.gov
SIC: 4941 9111 4952 4924 Water supply; Mayors' office; Sewerage systems; Natural gas distribution
PA: City Of Toledo
    1 Government Ctr Ste 2050
    Toledo OH 43604
    419 245-1050

(G-13744)
CITY OF TOLEDO
Also Called: Sewer & Drainage Services
4032 Creekside Ave (43612-1478)
PHONE..................................419 936-2924
Kelly O'brien, *Mgr*
EMP: 77
SQ FT: 102,840
SALES (corp-wide): 383.27MM **Privately Held**
Web: toledo.oh.gov
SIC: 4952 9111 4959 Sewerage systems; Mayors' office; Sanitary services, nec
PA: City Of Toledo
    1 Government Ctr Ste 2050
    Toledo OH 43604
    419 245-1050

(G-13745)
CJ LOGISTICS AMERICA LLC
1260 W Laskey Rd (43612-2909)
PHONE..................................847 390-6800
Dean Whitacre, *Mgr*
EMP: 97
Web: america.cjlogistics.com
SIC: 4225 General warehousing and storage
HQ: Cj Logistics America, Llc
    1750 S Wolf Rd
    Des Plaines IL 60018

(G-13746)
CLEAN TEAM INC
419 N Westwood Ave (43607-3347)
P.O. Box 140923 (43614-0923)
PHONE..................................419 537-8770
EMP: 32 EST: 2007
SALES (est): 2.49MM **Privately Held**
Web: www.cleanteamclean.com
SIC: 7699 Cleaning services

(G-13747)
COACT ASSOCIATES LTD
2748 Centennial Rd (43617-1829)
PHONE..................................866 646-4400
Mark Frasco, *Pr*
EMP: 30 EST: 2003
SQ FT: 10,000
SALES (est): 4.78MM **Privately Held**
Web: www.teamcoact.com
SIC: 8748 Environmental consultant

(G-13748)
COLLABORATIVE INC
1 Seagate Ste 118 (43604)
PHONE..................................419 242-7405
Frank G Beans, *CFO*
Frank G Beans, *Pr*
Paul Hollenbeck, *
Dan J Tabor, *
Michael Dinardo, *
EMP: 50 EST: 1973
SQ FT: 12,000
SALES (est): 9.86MM **Privately Held**
Web: www.tc.design
SIC: 8712 0781 7389 5021 Architectural engineering; Landscape architects; Interior designer; Office and public building furniture

(G-13749)
COLUMBIA GAS OF OHIO INC
Also Called: Columbia
2901 E Manhattan Blvd (43611-1713)
PHONE..................................419 539-6046
Jack Klein, *Brnch Mgr*
EMP: 94
SQ FT: 80,340
SALES (corp-wide): 5.51B **Publicly Held**
Web: www.columbiagasohio.com
SIC: 4924 Natural gas distribution
HQ: Columbia Gas Of Ohio, Inc.
    290 W Nationwide Blvd # 1
    Columbus OH 43215
    614 460-6000

(G-13750)
COMMERCE PAPER COMPANY
Also Called: Commerce Paper
302 S Byrne Rd Bldg 200 (43615-6208)
P.O. Box 140395 (43614-0395)
PHONE..................................419 241-9101
Craig D Roberts, *Pr*
Jeffrey M Roberts, *
George E Kirk, *
Morgan Levi, *
EMP: 45 EST: 1917
SQ FT: 100,000
SALES (est): 6.81MM **Privately Held**
Web: www.commercepaper.com
SIC: 5113 Industrial and personal service paper

(G-13751)
COMMUNI CARE INC
Also Called: Advanced Health Care Center
955 Garden Lake Pkwy (43614-2777)
PHONE..................................419 382-2200
Ramzieh Shousher, *Ex Dir*
EMP: 50 EST: 2010
SALES (est): 1.74MM **Privately Held**
Web: www.communicarehealth.com
SIC: 8051 Convalescent home with continuous nursing care

(G-13752)
COMMUNITY ISP INC
3035 Moffat Rd (43615-1836)
PHONE..................................419 867-6060
Jeffrey Klingshirn, *CEO*
Dustin Wade, *
EMP: 39 EST: 1998
SQ FT: 42,000
SALES (est): 5.25MM **Privately Held**
Web: www.cisp.com
SIC: 4813 7375 Internet connectivity services ; Information retrieval services

(G-13753)
COMPASS CORP FOR RECOVERY SVCS
Also Called: Sasi
2005 Ashland Ave (43620-1163)
PHONE..................................419 241-8827
EMP: 100
SALES (est): 3.72MM **Privately Held**
SIC: 8069 Drug addiction rehabilitation hospital

(G-13754)
COMPASSION HEALTH TOLEDO
1638n Broadway St (43609-3240)
PHONE..................................419 537-9185
Janet Robinson, *Prin*
Anne Ruch, *Ex Dir*
EMP: 32 EST: 2015
SALES (est): 1.35MM **Privately Held**
Web: www.compassionhealthtoledo.org
SIC: 8099 Health and allied services, nec

(G-13755)
COMPRHNSIVE ADDCTION SVC SYSTE
Also Called: Compass
2005 Ashland Ave (43620-1703)
PHONE..................................419 241-8827
Ross Chaban, *Ex Dir*
EMP: 52 EST: 1969
SQ FT: 68,000
SALES (est): 3.17MM **Privately Held**
Web: www.zepfcenter.org
SIC: 8361 8093 Rehabilitation center, residential: health care incidental; Specialty outpatient clinics, nec

(G-13756)
CONCEPT REHAB INC (PA)
6591 W Central Ave (43617-1087)
PHONE..................................419 843-6002
Joan E Bayer, *CEO*
Martha Shaker, *
Marianne Hassen, *Marketing*
EMP: 77 EST: 1984
SALES (est): 23.1MM **Privately Held**
Web: www.conceptrehab.com
SIC: 8093 Rehabilitation center, outpatient treatment

Toledo - Lucas County (G-13757)   GEOGRAPHIC SECTION

(G-13757)
CONCORD CARE CENTER OF TOLEDO
Also Called: Briarfield At Glanzman Road
3121 Glanzman Rd (43614-3802)
PHONE..................................419 385-6616
Debra A Ifft, *CEO*
Gail Fischer, *
EMP: 90 **EST:** 1999
SALES (est): 5.39MM **Privately Held**
Web:
www.concordcarecenteroftoledo.com
SIC: 8051 Convalescent home with continuous nursing care

(G-13758)
CONNECTING KIDS TO MEALS INC
1501 Monroe St (43604-5760)
P.O. Box 9363 (43697-9363)
PHONE..................................419 720-1106
Wendi R Huntley, *Pr*
Tony Siebeneck, *
EMP: 65 **EST:** 2001
SQ FT: 3,852
SALES (est): 1.72MM **Privately Held**
Web: www.feedlucaschildren.org
SIC: 8322 Childrens' aid society

(G-13759)
CONSULTANTS LABORATORY MEDICI
2130 W Central Ave Ste 300 (43606-3818)
PHONE..................................419 535-9629
F Michael Walsh, *Prin*
EMP: 40 **EST:** 1989
SALES (est): 939.85K **Privately Held**
SIC: 8071 Pathological laboratory
HQ: Aurora Diagnostics, Llc
    1355 River Bend Dr
    Dallas TX 75247

(G-13760)
CONTAINER GRAPHICS CORP
305 Ryder Rd (43607-3105)
PHONE..................................419 531-5133
Bill Beaker, *Brnch Mgr*
EMP: 31
SQ FT: 24,200
SALES (corp-wide): 4MM **Privately Held**
Web: www.containergraphics.com
SIC: 7336 3545 3944 Graphic arts and related design; Cutting tools for machine tools; Dice and dice cups
PA: Container Graphics Corp.
    114 Ednbrgh S Dr Ste 104
    Cary NC 27511
    919 481-4200

(G-13761)
COOPER-SMITH ADVERTISING LLC
3500 Granite Cir (43617-1172)
PHONE..................................419 470-5900
Kimberly Cooper, *Pr*
Brad Rieger, *
Jeri Fasig, *
Michele Hall, *
EMP: 60 **EST:** 1963
SQ FT: 11,000
SALES (est): 100MM **Privately Held**
Web: www.cooper-smith.com
SIC: 7311 Advertising consultant

(G-13762)
COUNTY OF LUCAS
Also Called: Board Lucas Cnty Commissioners
1 Government Ctr Ste 800 (43604-2259)
PHONE..................................419 213-4500
Michael Beazley, *Admn*
EMP: 68
SALES (corp-wide): 569.39MM **Privately Held**

Web: co.lucas.oh.us
SIC: 9121 8721 Legislative bodies, County government; Accounting, auditing, and bookkeeping
PA: County Of Lucas
    1 Government Ctr Ste 600
    Toledo OH 43604
    419 213-4406

(G-13763)
COUNTY OF LUCAS
Also Called: Child Support Enforcement Agcy
701 Adams St (43604-6623)
P.O. Box 10018 (43699-0018)
PHONE..................................419 213-3000
Mary Carol Torsok, *Dir*
EMP: 60
SALES (corp-wide): 569.39MM **Privately Held**
Web: co.lucas.oh.us
SIC: 8322 9111 Individual and family services ; County supervisors' and executives' office
PA: County Of Lucas
    1 Government Ctr Ste 600
    Toledo OH 43604
    419 213-4406

(G-13764)
COUNTY OF LUCAS
Also Called: Lucas County Prosecutors Off
700 Adams St Ste 250 (43604-5659)
PHONE..................................419 213-4700
Angela Barchick, *Off Mgr*
EMP: 95
SALES (corp-wide): 569.39MM **Privately Held**
Web: co.lucas.oh.us
SIC: 8111 9111 Specialized law offices, attorneys; County supervisors' and executives' office
PA: County Of Lucas
    1 Government Ctr Ste 600
    Toledo OH 43604
    419 213-4406

(G-13765)
COUNTY OF LUCAS
Also Called: Lucas Cnty Brd of Mntl Rtrdtn
2001 Collingwood Blvd (43620-1649)
PHONE..................................419 248-3585
John Trunk, *Superintnt*
EMP: 126
SALES (corp-wide): 569.39MM **Privately Held**
Web: co.lucas.oh.us
SIC: 8211 9111 8741 8011 School for retarded, nec; County supervisors' and executives' office; Management services; Offices and clinics of medical doctors
PA: County Of Lucas
    1 Government Ctr Ste 600
    Toledo OH 43604
    419 213-4406

(G-13766)
COUNTY OF LUCAS
Also Called: Lucas County Regional Hlth Dst
635 N Erie St (43604-5317)
PHONE..................................419 213-4018
David L Grossman Md, *Brnch Mgr*
EMP: 384
SALES (corp-wide): 569.39MM **Privately Held**
Web: co.lucas.oh.us
SIC: 8011 Health maintenance organization
PA: County Of Lucas
    1 Government Ctr Ste 600
    Toledo OH 43604
    419 213-4406

(G-13767)
COUNTY OF LUCAS
Also Called: Lucas County Coroners Office
2595 Arlington Ave (43614-2673)
PHONE..................................419 213-3903
Jame Patrick Md, *Prin*
EMP: 162
SALES (corp-wide): 569.39MM **Privately Held**
Web: co.lucas.oh.us
SIC: 8011 9111 Pathologist; County supervisors' and executives' office
PA: County Of Lucas
    1 Government Ctr Ste 600
    Toledo OH 43604
    419 213-4406

(G-13768)
COUSINS WASTE CONTROL LLC (HQ)
1701 E Matzinger Rd (43612-3841)
PHONE..................................419 726-1500
Brian Recatto, *Managing Member*
▲ **EMP:** 64 **EST:** 1967
SQ FT: 4,000
SALES (est): 4.44MM
SALES (corp-wide): 5.41B **Publicly Held**
SIC: 4212 4959 Hazardous waste transport; Oil spill cleanup
PA: Clean Harbors, Inc.
    42 Longwater Dr
    Norwell MA 02061
    781 792-5000

(G-13769)
COVENANT CARE OHIO INC
Also Called: Fairview Sklled Nrsing Rhbltti
4420 South Ave (43615-6417)
PHONE..................................419 531-4201
Jim Framsted, *Mgr*
EMP: 398
SIC: 8051 Convalescent home with continuous nursing care
HQ: Covenant Care Ohio, Inc.
    120 Vantis Dr Ste 200
    Aliso Viejo CA 92656
    949 349-1200

(G-13770)
CRIMINAL JSTICE CRDNTING CNCIL
1 Government Ctr Ste 1720 (43604-2230)
PHONE..................................567 200-6850
Holly Mathews, *Ex Dir*
EMP: 42
SALES (est): 2.32MM **Privately Held**
Web: www.lucascountycjcc.org
SIC: 8111 Legal services

(G-13771)
CUMULUS MEDIA INC
Also Called: Wxkr
3225 Arlington Ave (43614-2427)
PHONE..................................419 725-5700
Andy Stuart, *Mgr*
EMP: 62
SALES (corp-wide): 844.55MM **Publicly Held**
Web: www.cumulusmedia.com
SIC: 4832 Radio broadcasting stations
PA: Cumulus Media Inc.
    780 Johnson Fy Rd Ne # 500
    Atlanta GA 30342
    404 949-0700

(G-13772)
DEALER SUPPLY AND EQP LTD
1549 Campbell St (43607-4321)
PHONE..................................419 724-8473
Thomas W Heintschel, *Pr*
EMP: 30 **EST:** 2015
SALES (est): 500.72K **Privately Held**

SIC: 7549 Automotive maintenance services

(G-13773)
DECAHEALTH INC
5151 Monroe St Ste 104 (43623-3456)
PHONE..................................866 908-3514
Michael S Mcgowan, *Pr*
William James, *
Chad Graham, *
EMP: 80 **EST:** 2000
SALES (est): 9.81MM **Privately Held**
Web: www.decahealth.com
SIC: 8082 Home health care services

(G-13774)
DEFIANCE HOSPITAL INC
Also Called: Defiance Regional Medical Ctr
300 N Summit St (43604-1513)
PHONE..................................419 783-6955
Carl A Sixeas, *Prin*
Tim Jakacki, *
Bernie Nawrocki, *
EMP: 359 **EST:** 1949
SALES (est): 81.61MM
SALES (corp-wide): 187.07MM **Privately Held**
Web: www.promedica.org
SIC: 8062 General medical and surgical hospitals
PA: Promedica Health System, Inc.
    100 Madison Ave
    Toledo OH 43604
    567 585-9600

(G-13775)
DENNIS TOP SOIL & LDSCPG INC
Also Called: Gardenland
6340 Dorr St (43615-4310)
P.O. Box 10 (49228-0010)
PHONE..................................419 865-5656
Robert T Dennis, *Pr*
EMP: 28 **EST:** 1960
SQ FT: 7,270
SALES (est): 343.68K **Privately Held**
SIC: 0782 5193 5261 Landscape contractors ; Nursery stock; Nursery stock, seeds and bulbs

(G-13776)
DENTAL CENTER NORTHWEST OHIO
2138 Madison Ave (43604-5131)
PHONE..................................419 241-6215
Melinda Cree, *Dir*
EMP: 50 **EST:** 1920
SALES (est): 4.69MM **Privately Held**
Web: 486.cf2.myftpupload.com
SIC: 8021 Dental clinic

(G-13777)
DENTALONE PARTNERS INC
3504 Secor Rd Ste 330 (43606-1544)
PHONE..................................419 534-3005
EMP: 107
SALES (corp-wide): 85.13MM **Privately Held**
Web: www.dentalworks.com
SIC: 8021 Dental clinic
PA: Dentalone Partners, Inc.
    6700 Pinecrest Dr Ste 150
    Plano TX 75024
    972 755-0800

(G-13778)
DI SALLE REAL ESTATE CO
405 Madison Ave (43604-1211)
PHONE..................................419 255-6909
Daniel J Disalle, *Admn*
EMP: 27
SALES (corp-wide): 6.88MM **Privately Held**
Web: www.disallerealestate.com

GEOGRAPHIC SECTION
Toledo - Lucas County (G-13799)

SIC: 6531 Real estate agent, residential
PA: Di Salle Real Estate Co.
1909 River Rd
Maumee OH 43537
419 893-0751

(G-13779)
DIGESTIVE HLTH CRE CNSLTNTS OF
Also Called: Mount Carmel St Anns Hospital
3439 Granite Cir (43617-1161)
PHONE..................419 843-7996
EMP: 30
SQ FT: 8,000
SALES (est): 4.07MM **Privately Held**
Web: www.digestivenwo.com
SIC: 8011 Gastronomist

(G-13780)
DIMECH SERVICES INC
5505 Enterprise Blvd (43612)
PHONE..................419 727-0111
Janice Sheahan, *Pr*
James E Sheahan, *
Ronald Sheahan, *
Josh Quinlivan, *
Roger Sheahan, *
EMP: 30 **EST:** 1980
SQ FT: 12,700
SALES (est): 7.33MM **Privately Held**
Web: www.dimech.com
SIC: 1711 Mechanical contractor

(G-13781)
DIOCESE TLEDO PREST RETIREMENT
1933 Spielbusch Ave (43604-5360)
PHONE..................419 244-6711
EMP: 47 **EST:** 2014
SALES (est): 1.19MM
SALES (corp-wide): 56.4MM **Privately Held**
Web: www.toledodiocese.org
SIC: 6371 Pension funds
PA: The Roman Catholic Diocese Of Toledo In America
1933 Spielbusch Ave
Toledo OH 43604
419 244-6711

(G-13782)
DMC TECHNOLOGY GROUP INC
Also Called: DMC Consulting
7657 Kings Pointe Rd (43617-1514)
PHONE..................419 535-2900
J Patrick Sheehan, *Pr*
EMP: 30 **EST:** 1993
SQ FT: 13,000
SALES (est): 8.36MM **Privately Held**
Web: www.dmctechgroup.com
SIC: 7379 7371 5045 7378 Computer related consulting services; Custom computer programming services; Computers, peripherals, and software; Computer maintenance and repair

(G-13783)
DOUBLE A SOLUTIONS LLC
Also Called: Janitorial Manager
3139 N Republic Blvd (43615-1507)
PHONE..................256 489-6458
Archie Hinel, *Managing Member*
EMP: 54 **EST:** 2003
SALES (est): 760.53K **Privately Held**
Web: www.doubleasolutions.net
SIC: 7371 Computer software development

(G-13784)
DUNBAR MECHANICAL INC (PA)
2806 N Reynolds Rd (43615-2034)
PHONE..................419 537-1900
Stephen E Dunbar, *Pr*
EMP: 65 **EST:** 1956
SQ FT: 115,000
SALES (est): 51.9MM
SALES (corp-wide): 51.9MM **Privately Held**
Web: www.dunbarinc.com
SIC: 1711 Mechanical contractor

(G-13785)
EASTMAN & SMITH LTD
1 Seagate Ste 2400 (43604-1576)
P.O. Box 10032 (43699-0032)
PHONE..................419 241-6000
Patrick J Johnson, *Cncil Mbr*
David F Cooper, *Cncil Mbr*
Rudolph A Peckinpaugh, *Cncil Mbr*
James F Nooney, *Cncil Mbr*
John T Landwehr, *Cncil Mbr*
EMP: 150 **EST:** 1844
SQ FT: 48,000
SALES (est): 7.81K **Privately Held**
Web: www.eastmansmith.com
SIC: 8111 General practice attorney, lawyer

(G-13786)
ELECTRO PRIME GROUP LLC (PA)
Also Called: Electro Prime
4510 Lint Ave Ste B (43612-2658)
PHONE..................419 476-0100
John L Lauffer, *Managing Member*
Kevin Meade, *
▲ **EMP:** 70 **EST:** 2005
SQ FT: 20,100
SALES (est): 75.67MM **Privately Held**
Web: www.electroprime.com
SIC: 3471 5169 Plating and polishing; Anti-corrosion products

(G-13787)
ELITE SALON DISTRIBUTORS LLC
1038 N Holland Sylvania Rd (43615)
PHONE..................419 902-0545
Jerel Hess, *Brnch Mgr*
EMP: 40
SALES (corp-wide): 243.55K **Privately Held**
Web: www.elitesalondistributor.com
SIC: 7231 Hairdressers
PA: Elite Salon Distributors, Llc
8200 W Central Ave
Toledo OH
419 882-4749

(G-13788)
ELKAY OHIO PLUMBING PDTS CO (DH)
Also Called: Mr Direct
7634 New West Rd (43617-4201)
PHONE..................419 841-1820
Timothy J Jahnke, *CEO*
Ronald C Katz, *
John E Graves, *
◆ **EMP:** 254 **EST:** 1979
SQ FT: 90,000
SALES (est): 217.68MM **Publicly Held**
Web: www.elkay.com
SIC: 5074 Plumbing fittings and supplies
HQ: Elkay Manufacturing Company Inc
1333 Butterfield Rd # 200
Downers Grove IL 60515
630 574-8484

(G-13789)
EMERGENCY PHYSICIANS OF NORTHW
2142 N Cove Blvd (43606-3895)
PHONE..................419 291-4101
Robert Wood, *Prin*
EMP: 112
SALES (corp-wide): 509.7K **Privately Held**
Web: www.epnotoledo.com
SIC: 8011 General and family practice, physician/surgeon
PA: Emergency Physicians Of Northwest Ohio-Toledo, Llc
5923 Renaissance Pl
Toledo OH 43623
419 291-3627

(G-13790)
EMERITUS CORPORATION
Also Called: Emeritus Parklane
142 23rd St Ofc (43604-6507)
PHONE..................419 255-4455
Mary Sweeny, *Dir*
EMP: 51
SALES (corp-wide): 2.83B **Publicly Held**
Web: www.emeritus.org
SIC: 6513 Retirement hotel operation
HQ: Emeritus Corporation
6737 W Wa St Ste 2300
Milwaukee WI 53214

(G-13791)
EMPRISE TECHNOLOGIES LLC
5693 Swan Creek Dr (43614-1102)
PHONE..................419 720-6982
Kim Edwards, *Pr*
Marc Savage, *
EMP: 30 **EST:** 1999
SALES (est): 3.65MM **Privately Held**
Web: www.emprise1.com
SIC: 7371 8748 8742 Computer software development; Business consulting, nec; Management information systems consultant

(G-13792)
EMSSONS FAURECIA CTRL SYSTEMS (DH)
543 Matzinger Rd (43612-2638)
PHONE..................812 341-2000
David Degraaf, *Pr*
Mark Stidham, *
Christophe Schmidt, *
▲ **EMP:** 130 **EST:** 1988
SQ FT: 40,000
SALES (est): 1.39B
SALES (corp-wide): 100.93MM **Privately Held**
SIC: 3714 5013 Mufflers (exhaust), motor vehicle; Motor vehicle supplies and new parts
HQ: Faurecia Emissions Control Technologies Usa, Llc
2800 High Meadow Cir
Auburn Hills MI 48326

(G-13793)
END-USER COMPUTING INC
Also Called: Toast.net Internet Service
4841 Monroe St Ste 307 (43623-5320)
PHONE..................419 292-2200
Kevin David, *Pr*
Karen David, *VP*
EMP: 96 **EST:** 1989
SQ FT: 4,000
SALES (est): 6.02MM **Privately Held**
Web: www.toast.net
SIC: 4813 7375 Proprietary online service networks; Information retrieval services

(G-13794)
ERIE CONSTRUCTION MID-WEST INC
Also Called: Erie Construction Mid-west, Inc.
4271 Monroe St (43606-1943)
P.O. Box 2698 (43606-0698)
PHONE..................419 472-4200
Patrick Trompeter, *Pr*
EMP: 87
SALES (corp-wide): 139.2MM **Privately Held**
Web: www.eriehome.com
SIC: 5211 1761 Siding; Siding contractor
PA: Erie Construction Mid-West, Llc
3516 Granite Cir
Toledo OH 43617
567 408-2145

(G-13795)
ERIE CONSTRUCTION MID-WEST INC
Also Called: Erie Construction
3516 Granite Cir (43617-1172)
PHONE..................419 472-4200
Jeremy Fritz, *Mgr*
EMP: 495
SALES (corp-wide): 139.2MM **Privately Held**
Web: www.eriehome.com
SIC: 1521 1761 5211 General remodeling, single-family houses; Siding contractor; Door and window products
PA: Erie Construction Mid-West, Llc
3516 Granite Cir
Toledo OH 43617
567 408-2145

(G-13796)
ERIE CONSTRUCTION MID-WEST LLC (PA)
3516 Granite Cir (43617-1172)
P.O. Box 2698 (43606-0698)
PHONE..................567 408-2145
Patrick J Trompeter, *CEO*
Philip C Davis, *
EMP: 129 **EST:** 1982
SALES (est): 139.2MM
SALES (corp-wide): 139.2MM **Privately Held**
Web: www.eriehome.com
SIC: 1521 General remodeling, single-family houses

(G-13797)
ERIE SHRES CNCIL INC BOY SCUTS
Also Called: Boy Scouts Of America
5600 W Sylvania Ave (43623-3307)
P.O. Box 152079 (75015-2079)
PHONE..................419 241-7293
Ed Bobwell, *Ex Dir*
EMP: 686 **EST:** 1910
SQ FT: 2,000
SALES (est): 507.04K
SALES (corp-wide): 238.8MM **Privately Held**
Web: www.erieshorescouncil.org
SIC: 8641 Boy Scout organization
PA: Boy Scouts Of America
1325 W Walnut Hill Ln
Irving TX 75038
972 580-2000

(G-13798)
ERNST & YOUNG LLP
Also Called: Ey
1 Seagate Ste 2510 (43604-1522)
PHONE..................419 244-8000
Christine L Mabrey, *Mgr*
EMP: 40
Web: www.ey.com
SIC: 8721 Certified public accountant
HQ: Ernst & Young Llp
1 Manhattan W Fl 6
New York NY 10001
703 747-0049

(G-13799)
ESTES EXPRESS LINES
Also Called: Estes Express Lines 92
5330 Angola Rd Ste B (43615-6379)
PHONE..................419 531-1500
Bruce Roberts, *Mgr*

Toledo - Lucas County (G-13800)

EMP: 50
SALES (corp-wide): 3.56B **Privately Held**
Web: www.estes-express.com
SIC: 4213 Contract haulers
PA: Estes Express Lines
3901 W Broad St
Richmond VA 23230
804 353-1900

(G-13800)
EXPEDITUS TRANSPORT LLC
Also Called: Expeditus
7644 Kings Pointe Rd (43617-1500)
PHONE..............................419 464-9450
EMP: 38 **EST:** 2012
SALES (est): 7.1MM **Privately Held**
Web: www.etships.com
SIC: 4212 Truck rental with drivers

(G-13801)
EXPRESSO CAR WASH SYSTEMS INC
Also Called: Expresso Car Wash 5
1750 S Reynolds Rd (43614-1404)
PHONE..............................419 866-7099
EMP: 35
SALES (corp-wide): 2.75MM **Privately Held**
SIC: 7542 Carwash, automatic
PA: Expresso Car Wash Systems Inc
201 Illinois Ave
Maumee OH 43537
419 893-1406

(G-13802)
FAMILY CHILD ABUSE PRVNTION CT (PA)
2460 Cherry St (43608-2667)
PHONE..............................419 244-3053
Christie Jenkins, *CEO*
Fionne Wright, *Off Mgr*
EMP: 33 **EST:** 1974
SQ FT: 3,000
SALES (est): 3.17MM
SALES (corp-wide): 3.17MM **Privately Held**
Web: www.fcapc.org
SIC: 8322 Child related social services

(G-13803)
FAMILY SERVICE OF NW OHIO (PA)
701 Jefferson Ave Ste 301 (43604-6957)
P.O. Box 1010 (43697-1010)
PHONE..............................419 321-6455
Tim Yennick, *Pr*
Linda Condit, *
EMP: 83 **EST:** 1904
SQ FT: 12,000
SALES (est): 3.64MM
SALES (corp-wide): 3.64MM **Privately Held**
Web: www.fsno.org
SIC: 8322 8082 Social service center; Home health care services

(G-13804)
FCA US LLC
Also Called: Toledo North Assembly Plant
4400 Chrysler Dr (43608-4000)
PHONE..............................419 727-7285
Robert Seabolt, *Prin*
EMP: 28
Web: www.stellantis.com
SIC: 7538 General automotive repair shops
HQ: Fca Us Llc
1000 Chrysler Dr
Auburn Hills MI 48326

(G-13805)
FIFTH THIRD BNK NRTHWSTERN OHI
Also Called: Fifth Third Bank
1 Seagate Ste 2200 (43604-1525)
P.O. Box 1868 (43603-1868)
PHONE..............................419 259-7820
Robert Laclair, *Pr*
EMP: 83 **EST:** 1989
SALES (est): 8.12MM
SALES (corp-wide): 12.64B **Publicly Held**
SIC: 6022 State trust companies accepting deposits, commercial
PA: Fifth Third Bancorp
38 Fountain Square Plz
Cincinnati OH 45263
800 972-3030

(G-13806)
FINDLEY INC (PA)
200 N Saint Clair St (43604-1541)
PHONE..............................419 255-1360
John M Weber, *Pr*
Robert J Rogers, *
Marc Stockwell, *
Kyle Pifher, *
EMP: 75 **EST:** 1969
SALES (est): 21.05MM
SALES (corp-wide): 21.05MM **Privately Held**
Web: www.usicg.com
SIC: 8742 Compensation and benefits planning consultant

(G-13807)
FIRST CHOICE MEDICAL STAFFING
5445 Southwyck Blvd Ste 208 (43614)
PHONE..............................419 861-2722
Christopher Sterben, *Brnch Mgr*
EMP: 79
SALES (corp-wide): 6.66MM **Privately Held**
Web: www.firstchoiceohio.com
SIC: 8082 Home health care services
PA: First Choice Medical Staffing Of Ohio, Inc.
1457 W 117th St
Cleveland OH 44107
216 521-2222

(G-13808)
FIRST STUDENT INC
419 N Westwood (43607-3347)
PHONE..............................419 382-9915
Inez Evans, *Mgr*
EMP: 78
Web: www.firststudentinc.com
SIC: 4151 School buses
PA: First Student, Inc.
191 Rosa Parks St Ste 800
Cincinnati OH 45202

(G-13809)
FIRST TDT LLC
Also Called: Renaissance Toledo
444 N Summit St (43604-1514)
PHONE..............................419 244-2444
Stephen L Schwartz, *Managing Member*
EMP: 99 **EST:** 2015
SALES (est): 2.44MM **Privately Held**
SIC: 7011 Hotels and motels

(G-13810)
FOUNTAINS AT CANTERBURY
Also Called: Canterbury Retirement Cmnty
4500 Dorr St (43615-4040)
PHONE..............................405 751-3600
Danny Eischen, *Ex Dir*
EMP: 44 **EST:** 1995
SALES (est): 9.67MM **Privately Held**
Web: canterbury.watermarkcommunities.com
SIC: 8051 8361 8052 Skilled nursing care facilities; Geriatric residential care; Intermediate care facilities

(G-13811)
FRANCISCAN CARE CTR SYLVANIA
4111 N Holland Sylvania Rd (43623)
PHONE..............................419 882-2087
Shawn T Litton, *CEO*
EMP: 2205 **EST:** 2000
SQ FT: 25,712
SALES (est): 7.87MM **Privately Held**
Web: www.chilivingcommunities.org
SIC: 8051 Convalescent home with continuous nursing care
HQ: Sylvania Franciscan Health
1715 Indian Wood Cir # 200
Maumee OH

(G-13812)
FRANKEL DENTAL
Also Called: John Frankel DDS
5012 Talmadge Rd Ste 100 (43623-2168)
PHONE..............................419 474-9611
Jonathan Frankel, *Pt*
EMP: 32 **EST:** 1943
SALES (est): 3.57MM **Privately Held**
Web: www.jonfrankeldentistry.com
SIC: 8021 Dentists' office

(G-13813)
FRED CHRISTEN & SONS COMPANY (PA)
Also Called: Christndtroit Div of Fred Chrs
714 George St (43608-2914)
P.O. Box 547 (43697-0547)
PHONE..............................419 243-4161
Fredrick R Christen, *
Fredrick R Christen, *
Marlene P Christen, *
EMP: 60 **EST:** 1929
SQ FT: 32,000
SALES (est): 26.75MM
SALES (corp-wide): 26.75MM **Privately Held**
Web: www.cdetroit.com
SIC: 1761 Roofing contractor

(G-13814)
FRUCHTMAN ADVERTISING INC
Also Called: Fruchtman Marketing
6800 W Central Ave Ste F3 (43617-1164)
PHONE..............................419 539-2770
Michael Fruchtman, *CEO*
Ellen Fruchtman, *Pr*
EMP: 28 **EST:** 1981
SQ FT: 4,500
SALES (est): 1.02MM **Privately Held**
Web: www.fruchtman.com
SIC: 7311 Advertising consultant

(G-13815)
G G MARCK & ASSOCIATES INC (PA)
Also Called: Marck & Associates
300 Phillips Ave (43612-1470)
PHONE..............................419 478-0900
Gary Marck, *Pr*
Christopher Miller, *
◆ **EMP:** 40 **EST:** 1986
SQ FT: 300,000
SALES (est): 15.12MM
SALES (corp-wide): 15.12MM **Privately Held**
Web: www.itinow.com
SIC: 5023 Kitchenware

(G-13816)
GA BUSINESS PURCHASER LLC
Also Called: Guardian Alarm
3222 W Central Ave (43606-2929)
PHONE..............................419 255-8400
Cris Zielinski, *Brnch Mgr*
EMP: 46
SALES (corp-wide): 40.77MM **Privately Held**
Web: www.guardianalarm.com
SIC: 1731 5063 7382 Fire detection and burglar alarm systems specialization; Burglar alarm systems; Security systems services
PA: Ga Business Purchaser Llc
26711 Northwestern Hwy
Southfield MI 48033
248 423-1000

(G-13817)
GARDEN II LEASING CO LLC
Also Called: COMMUNICARE HEALTH SERVICES
1015 Garden Lake Pkwy (43614-2779)
PHONE..............................419 381-0037
Robert Desotelle, *CEO*
EMP: 100 **EST:** 2007
SALES (est): 11.44MM
SALES (corp-wide): 392.92MM **Privately Held**
Web: www.communicarehealth.com
SIC: 8062 General medical and surgical hospitals
PA: Communicare Health Services, Inc.
10123 Alliance Rd
Blue Ash OH 45242
513 530-1654

(G-13818)
GARDNER CEMENT CONTRACTORS
Also Called: Gardner
821 Warehouse Rd (43615-6472)
PHONE..............................419 389-0768
Robert W Gardner, *Pr*
Lynn A Gardner, *
EMP: 75 **EST:** 1980
SQ FT: 6,200
SALES (est): 4.76MM **Privately Held**
Web: www.gardnercorp.com
SIC: 1771 Concrete work

(G-13819)
GEO GRADEL CO
3135 Front St (43605-1009)
P.O. Box 8337 (43605-0337)
PHONE..............................419 691-7123
John F Gradel, *Pr*
Frederick T Sander, *
Alan Raven, *
Frank Justen, *
EMP: 65 **EST:** 1903
SQ FT: 12,200
SALES (est): 23.92MM **Privately Held**
Web: www.geogradelco.com
SIC: 1794 Excavation and grading, building construction

(G-13820)
GEORGE P BALLAS BUICK GMC TRCK (PA)
Also Called: Budget Rent-A-Car
5715 W Central Ave (43615-1401)
P.O. Box 352470 (43635-2470)
PHONE..............................419 535-1000
George P Ballas, *Pr*
Robert Fowler, *
Richard Farrar, *
EMP: 40 **EST:** 1968
SQ FT: 55,000
SALES (est): 12.55MM
SALES (corp-wide): 12.55MM **Privately Held**

GEOGRAPHIC SECTION
Toledo - Lucas County (G-13840)

Web: www.ballasbuickgmc.com
SIC: 5511 7514 7532 5521 Automobiles, new and used; Rent-a-car service; Top and body repair and paint shops; Used car dealers

(G-13821)
GIANT INDUSTRIES INC
900 N Westwood Ave (43607-3261)
PHONE.................................419 531-4600
Raymond Simon, *CEO*
Edward Simon, *
Wolfgang Drescher, *
▲ **EMP:** 40 **EST:** 1990
SQ FT: 83,000
SALES (est): 13.28MM **Publicly Held**
Web: www.giantpumps.com
SIC: 3581 3589 5084 3594 Automatic vending machines; Car washing machinery; Pumps and pumping equipment, nec; Fluid power pumps and motors
PA: Marathon Petroleum Corporation
539 S Main St
Findlay OH 45840

(G-13822)
GOODWILL INDS NW OHIO INC (PA)
1120 Madison Ave (43604-7538)
P.O. Box 336 (43697-0336)
PHONE.................................419 255-0070
Robert Huber, *Pr*
Raymond W Byers, *
Amy Wachob, *
EMP: 100 **EST:** 1933
SQ FT: 66,000
SALES (est): 19.69MM
SALES (corp-wide): 19.69MM **Privately Held**
Web: www.goodwillnwohio.com
SIC: 5932 8331 Clothing, secondhand; Vocational rehabilitation agency

(G-13823)
GRAMMER INDUSTRIES LLC (DH)
1429 Coining Dr (43612-2932)
PHONE.................................864 284-9616
Richard Westwood, *VP*
▲ **EMP:** 73 **EST:** 1999
SALES (est): 22.11MM **Privately Held**
Web: www.grammer.com
SIC: 5013 Seat covers
HQ: Grammer Ag
Grammer Allee 2
Ursensollen BY 92289
9621660

(G-13824)
GRAY MEDIA GROUP INC
Also Called: Wtvg-TV
4247 Dorr St (43607-2134)
PHONE.................................419 534-3886
Peter Veto, *VP*
EMP: 68
SALES (corp-wide): 3.28B **Publicly Held**
Web: www.wlbt.com
SIC: 4833 Television translator station
HQ: Gray Media Group, Inc.
201 Monroe St Fl 20
Montgomery AL 36104

(G-13825)
GRAYBAR ELECTRIC COMPANY INC
1333 E Manhattan Blvd (43608-1523)
PHONE.................................419 729-1641
Don Morris, *Brnch Mgr*
EMP: 34
SQ FT: 31,570
SALES (corp-wide): 11.04B **Privately Held**
Web: www.graybar.com
SIC: 5063 5065 Electrical supplies, nec; Electronic parts and equipment, nec

PA: Graybar Electric Company, Inc.
34 N Meramec Ave
Saint Louis MO 63105
314 573-9200

(G-13826)
GREAT LAKES INDUS CONTG LTD
Also Called: Glic Electrical
3060 South Ave (43609-1334)
PHONE.................................419 945-4542
Scott Horner, *Mgr*
EMP: 41
SALES (corp-wide): 3.99MM **Privately Held**
Web: www.glicelectrical.com
SIC: 1731 General electrical contractor
PA: Great Lakes Industrial Contracting, Ltd.
580 Longbow Dr
Maumee OH 43537
419 945-4542

(G-13827)
GREAT LAKES MKTG ASSOC INC
Also Called: Great Lakes Marketing
3361 Executive Pkwy Ste 201 (43606-1337)
PHONE.................................419 534-4700
Lori Dixon, *Pr*
EMP: 35 **EST:** 1964
SQ FT: 5,151
SALES (est): 2.41MM **Privately Held**
Web: www.glm.com
SIC: 8732 Market analysis or research

(G-13828)
GREAT LKES CMNTY ACTION PARTNR
1500 N Superior St Ste 303 (43604-2157)
PHONE.................................419 729-8035
EMP: 31
SALES (corp-wide): 53.21MM **Privately Held**
Web: www.glcap.org
SIC: 8322 Social service center
PA: Great Lakes Community Action Partnership
127 S Front St
Fremont OH 43420
419 333-6068

(G-13829)
GREENFIELD HEALTH SYSTEMS CORP (PA)
Also Called: Dialysis Partners of NW Ohio
3401 Glendale Ave Ste 110 (43614-2490)
PHONE.................................419 389-9681
Deanna Shaffer, *Pr*
Eva Costilla, *
Deanna Shaffer, *Admn*
EMP: 48 **EST:** 1982
SQ FT: 10,000
SALES (est): 2.53MM
SALES (corp-wide): 2.53MM **Privately Held**
SIC: 8092 Kidney dialysis centers

(G-13830)
GROGANS TOWNE CHRYSLER INC (PA)
6100 Telegraph Rd (43612)
PHONE.................................419 476-0761
Mark Floyd, *Pr*
Ed J Lishewski, *
Denny Amrhiem, *
▼ **EMP:** 100 **EST:** 1959
SQ FT: 50,000
SALES (est): 38.79MM
SALES (corp-wide): 38.79MM **Privately Held**

Web: www.groganstownechryslerdodge.com
SIC: 5511 7515 7513 7538 Automobiles, new and used; Passenger car leasing; Truck leasing, without drivers; General automotive repair shops

(G-13831)
GROSS ELECTRIC INC (PA)
2807 N Reynolds Rd (43615)
P.O. Box 352377 (43635)
PHONE.................................419 537-1818
Richard J Gross, *Ch Bd*
Laurie Gross, *
Joseph Gross, *
H C Reinhard, *
EMP: 35 **EST:** 1910
SQ FT: 36,000
SALES (est): 37.18MM
SALES (corp-wide): 37.18MM **Privately Held**
Web: www.grosselectric.com
SIC: 5063 5719 Electrical supplies, nec; Lighting fixtures

(G-13832)
HANKS PLUMBING & HEATING CO
Also Called: H P H Plumbing
2000 The Blfs (43615-3084)
PHONE.................................419 843-2222
EMP: 30 **EST:** 1964
SALES (est): 4.16MM **Privately Held**
SIC: 1711 Plumbing, heating, air-conditioning

(G-13833)
HANSON PRODUCTIONS INC
200 N Saint Clair St Ste 100 (43604-1524)
PHONE.................................419 327-6100
Steven Hanson, *Pr*
Jennifer Samson, *
EMP: 50 **EST:** 1991
SQ FT: 8,000
SALES (est): 5.24MM **Privately Held**
Web: www.hansoninc.com
SIC: 7922 Television program, including commercial producers

(G-13834)
HARBOR (PA)
3909 Woodley Rd (43606)
P.O. Box 8970 (43623)
PHONE.................................419 479-3233
Dale Shreve, *CEO*
EMP: 90 **EST:** 1941
SALES (est): 46.84MM
SALES (corp-wide): 46.84MM **Privately Held**
Web: www.harbor.org
SIC: 8093 Mental health clinic, outpatient

(G-13835)
HARBORSIDE POINTE PLACE LLC
Also Called: Point Place
6101 N Summit St (43611-1242)
PHONE.................................419 727-7870
George V Hager Junior, *Prin*
Mark Grieselding, *
EMP: 101 **EST:** 1991
SALES (est): 5.25MM **Privately Held**
SIC: 8051 Convalescent home with continuous nursing care

(G-13836)
HART ASSOCIATES INC
Also Called: Hart
811 Madison Ave (43604-5626)
PHONE.................................419 893-9600
Michael K Hart, *Pr*
EMP: 55 **EST:** 1965
SQ FT: 20,000
SALES (est): 11.9MM **Privately Held**

Web: www.hartinc.com
SIC: 7311 Advertising consultant

(G-13837)
HAYNES REAL ESTATE INC
Also Called: Coldwell Banker
4349 Talmadge Rd Ste 4 (43623-3527)
PHONE.................................419 475-8383
Robert Harwaldt, *Brnch Mgr*
EMP: 29
SALES (corp-wide): 4.44MM **Privately Held**
Web: www.coldwellbanker.com
SIC: 6531 Real estate agent, residential
PA: Haynes Real Estate, Inc.
15489 S Telg Rd Ste A
Monroe MI 48161
734 242-0275

(G-13838)
HCR MANORCARE INC (HQ)
Also Called: Promedica Senior Care
333 N Summit (43604-1531)
P.O. Box 10086 (43699-0086)
PHONE.................................419 252-5500
Angela Brandt, *Pr*
Steve Cavanaugh, *
Julie Beckert, *Marketing**
EMP: 301 **EST:** 2005
SALES (est): 752.53MM
SALES (corp-wide): 187.07MM **Privately Held**
Web: www.promedicaseniorcare.org
SIC: 8051 Convalescent home with continuous nursing care
PA: Promedica Health System, Inc.
100 Madison Ave
Toledo OH 43604
567 585-9600

(G-13839)
HCR MANORCARE MED SVCS FLA LLC (PA)
Also Called: Manorcare Health Services
333 N Summit St Ste 100 (43604-2617)
P.O. Box 10086 (43699-0086)
PHONE.................................419 252-5500
Paul Ormond, *Pr*
R Jeffrey Bixler, *
Douglas G Haag, *
Keith Weikel, *
Steve Cavannough, *
EMP: 200 **EST:** 2007
SQ FT: 210,000
SALES (est): 389.07MM
SALES (corp-wide): 389.07MM **Privately Held**
Web: www.promedicaseniorcare.org
SIC: 8051 Convalescent home with continuous nursing care

(G-13840)
HEALTH CARE RTREMENT CORP AMER (DH)
333 N Summit St Ste 103 (43604-2617)
P.O. Box 10086 (43699-0086)
PHONE.................................419 252-5500
Paul A Ormond, *Ch Bd*
Spence C Moler, *
Stephen Guillard, *
Steven Cavanaugh, *
Richard Parr, *
EMP: 243 **EST:** 1944
SALES (est): 28.67MM
SALES (corp-wide): 187.07MM **Privately Held**
Web: www.promedicaseniorcare.org
SIC: 8051 Convalescent home with continuous nursing care
HQ: Manor Care, Inc.
333 N Summit St

Toledo - Lucas County (G-13841)　　　　GEOGRAPHIC SECTION

Toledo OH 43604

(G-13841)
HEALTH CARE RTRMENT CORP AMER
Also Called: Heartland of Charleston 4109
333 N Summit St (43604-1531)
PHONE..............................304 925-4771
EMP: 180 **EST:** 2007
SALES (est): 10.39MM
SALES (corp-wide): 187.07MM **Privately Held**
SIC: 8082 Home health care services
HQ: Manor Care, Inc.
　333 N Summit St
　Toledo OH 43604

(G-13842)
HEARTLAND HEALTHCARE SVCS LLC (PA)
Also Called: Sun Pharmacy
4755 South Ave (43615-6422)
PHONE..............................419 535-8435
Jeffrey Cremean, *CFO*
Dorothy Kuhl, *
EMP: 130 **EST:** 1994
SQ FT: 72,000
SALES (est): 46.64MM **Privately Held**
Web: www.heartlandhealthcareservices.com
SIC: 5122 Pharmaceuticals

(G-13843)
HEARTLAND RHBLITATION SVCS INC (DH)
3425 Executive Pkwy Ste 128 (43606-1326)
PHONE..............................419 537-0764
Pat Smith, *Prin*
EMP: 75 **EST:** 1981
SALES (est): 7.65MM
SALES (corp-wide): 187.07MM **Privately Held**
SIC: 8093 Rehabilitation center, outpatient treatment
HQ: Manor Care, Inc.
　333 N Summit St
　Toledo OH 43604

(G-13844)
HEATHER DOWNS CNTRY CLB ASSOC
3910 Heatherdowns Blvd (43614-3245)
PHONE..............................419 385-0248
Joseph Breaker, *Pr*
Roger Coe, *VP*
Garth Tabay, *Treas*
EMP: 46 **EST:** 1926
SQ FT: 30,000
SALES (est): 668.47K **Privately Held**
Web: www.heatherdowns.com
SIC: 7992 Public golf courses

(G-13845)
HEATHERDOWNS OPERATING CO LLC
Also Called: Heathrdwns Rhblttion Rsdntial
2401 Cass Rd (43614-3119)
PHONE..............................419 382-5050
Joseph Hazelbaker, *Prin*
Brian Hazelbaker, *
Ralph Hazelbaker, *
EMP: 90 **EST:** 2020
SALES (est): 5.91MM **Privately Held**
SIC: 8051 Skilled nursing care facilities

(G-13846)
HENRY GURTZWEILER INC
921 Galena St (43611-3717)
PHONE..............................419 729-3955

William H Myers, *Pr*
Greg Myers, *
Robert Thomason, *
EMP: 75 **EST:** 1946
SQ FT: 15,000
SALES (est): 24.01MM **Privately Held**
Web: www.ohiosteelerectors.com
SIC: 1791 Precast concrete structural framing or panels, placing of

(G-13847)
HOLLYWOOD CASINO TOLEDO
1968 Miami St (43605-3359)
PHONE..............................419 661-5200
Chris Wilson, *Prin*
EMP: 242 **EST:** 2011
SALES (est): 15.6MM **Privately Held**
Web: www.hollywoodcasinotoledo.com
SIC: 7011 Casino hotel

(G-13848)
HOME DEPOT USA INC
Also Called: Home Depot, The
1035 W Alexis Rd (43612)
PHONE..............................419 476-4573
Darcy Miller, *Mgr*
EMP: 165
SQ FT: 9,900
SALES (corp-wide): 152.67B **Publicly Held**
Web: www.homedepot.com
SIC: 5211 7359 Home centers; Tool rental
HQ: Home Depot U.S.A., Inc.
　2445 Springfield Ave
　Vauxhall NJ 07088

(G-13849)
HOME DEPOT USA INC
Also Called: Home Depot, The
3200 Secor Rd (43606)
PHONE..............................419 537-1920
Don Mandabille, *Mgr*
EMP: 125
SALES (corp-wide): 152.67B **Publicly Held**
Web: www.homedepot.com
SIC: 5211 7359 Home centers; Tool rental
HQ: Home Depot U.S.A., Inc.
　2445 Springfield Ave
　Vauxhall NJ 07088

(G-13850)
HOOVER & WELLS INC
Also Called: Rez Stone
2011 Seaman St (43605-1908)
PHONE..............................419 691-9220
Margaret Hoover, *Ch Bd*
John Corsini, *
James Mc Collum, *
Barbara Corsini, *
Lisa Pudlicki, *
EMP: 120 **EST:** 1978
SQ FT: 23,448
SALES (est): 32.54MM **Privately Held**
Web: www.hooverwells.com
SIC: 1752 2891 2851 Wood floor installation and refinishing; Adhesives and sealants; Paints and allied products

(G-13851)
HOSPICE OF NORTHWEST OHIO
800 S Detroit Ave (43609-1910)
PHONE..............................419 661-4001
Judy Seibenick, *Brnch Mgr*
EMP: 75
Web: www.hospicenwo.org
SIC: 8052 Personal care facility
PA: Hospice Of Northwest Ohio
　30000 E River Rd
　Perrysburg OH 43551

(G-13852)
HOSPITAL COUNCIL OF NW OHIO
3231 Central Park W Ste 200 (43617-3009)
PHONE..............................419 842-0800
W Scott Fry, *CEO*
Kim Temple, *Contrlr*
EMP: 31 **EST:** 1972
SQ FT: 3,000
SALES (est): 7.64MM **Privately Held**
Web: www.hcno.org
SIC: 8611 Trade associations

(G-13853)
HUNTINGTON NATIONAL BANK
800 Madison Ave (43604-5612)
PHONE..............................419 249-7877
Rosa Duran, *Prin*
EMP: 36
SALES (corp-wide): 10.84B **Publicly Held**
Web: www.huntington.com
SIC: 6029 Commercial banks, nec
HQ: The Huntington National Bank
　41 S High St
　Columbus OH 43215
　614 480-4293

(G-13854)
HUNTINGTON NATIONAL BANK
4773 Glendale Ave (43614-1913)
PHONE..............................419 254-7016
Jean Baker, *Brnch Mgr*
EMP: 41
SALES (corp-wide): 10.84B **Publicly Held**
Web: www.huntington.com
SIC: 6029 6022 Commercial banks, nec; State commercial banks
HQ: The Huntington National Bank
　41 S High St
　Columbus OH 43215
　614 480-4293

(G-13855)
HUNTINGTON NATIONAL BANK
4105 Talmadge Rd (43623-3503)
PHONE..............................419 254-7052
Jeff Apardian, *Mgr*
EMP: 41
SALES (corp-wide): 10.84B **Publicly Held**
Web: www.huntington.com
SIC: 6029 6022 Commercial banks, nec; State commercial banks
HQ: The Huntington National Bank
　41 S High St
　Columbus OH 43215
　614 480-4293

(G-13856)
HUNTINGTON NATIONAL BANK
Also Called: Home Mortgage
519 Madison Ave (43604-1580)
PHONE..............................419 249-3340
Nicole Woodard, *Prin*
EMP: 46
SALES (corp-wide): 10.84B **Publicly Held**
Web: www.huntington.com
SIC: 6029 6162 6022 Commercial banks, nec; Mortgage bankers; State commercial banks
HQ: The Huntington National Bank
　41 S High St
　Columbus OH 43215
　614 480-4293

(G-13857)
HYLANT ADMINISTRATIVE SERVICES (PA)
811 Madison Ave Fl 11 (43604-5626)
P.O. Box 2083 (43603-2083)
PHONE..............................419 255-1020
Joe Seay, *Pr*
Michael Ugljesa, *

Dennis Michel, *
Bill Petro, *
EMP: 31 **EST:** 1994
SALES (est): 2.79MM
SALES (corp-wide): 2.79MM **Privately Held**
Web: www.ohioplan.com
SIC: 6411 Insurance agents, nec

(G-13858)
HYLANT GROUP INC (PA)
Also Called: Nationwide
811 Madison Ave (43604-5684)
P.O. Box 1687 (43603-1687)
PHONE..............................419 255-1020
Bubba Berenzweig, *CEO*
Joe Herman, *
Andy Dale, *
EMP: 73 **EST:** 1935
SQ FT: 80,000
SALES (est): 100.85MM
SALES (corp-wide): 100.85MM **Privately Held**
Web: www.hylant.com
SIC: 6411 Insurance agents, nec

(G-13859)
IET INC
3539 Glendale Ave Ste C (43614-3457)
PHONE..............................419 385-1233
Timothy C Stansfield, *Pr*
Ronda Massey, *
Theresa Smith, *
EMP: 40 **EST:** 1989
SQ FT: 14,000
SALES (est): 6.51MM **Privately Held**
Web: www.ieteng.com
SIC: 8711 Consulting engineer

(G-13860)
IMPACT PRODUCTS LLC (HQ)
2840 Centennial Rd (43617-1898)
PHONE..............................419 841-2891
Laura Marcero, *
Terry Neal, *Pr*
◆ **EMP:** 76 **EST:** 2001
SQ FT: 155,000
SALES (est): 70.26MM
SALES (corp-wide): 104.62MM **Privately Held**
Web: www.impact-products.com
SIC: 5087 5084 2392 3089 Janitors' supplies ; Safety equipment; Mops, floor and dust; Buckets, plastics
PA: Supply Source Enterprises, Inc.
　150 4th Ave N Ste 1810
　Nashville TN 37219
　919 387-1059

(G-13861)
IMPACT SALES SOLUTIONS INC
5241 Southwyck Blvd Ste 104 (43614)
PHONE..............................419 466-0131
John Fortner, *Pr*
Kary William, *
Leu Douglas, *
John Fortner, *Treas*
EMP: 40 **EST:** 2006
SALES (est): 2.47MM **Privately Held**
Web: www.impactretention.com
SIC: 8748 8732 Business consulting, nec; Commercial nonphysical research

(G-13862)
IN HOME HEALTH INC (PA)
Also Called: Home Health Plus
333 N Summit St (43604-1531)
P.O. Box 10086 (43699-0086)
PHONE..............................419 252-5500
C Michael Ford, *Ch Bd*
Bruce Schroeder, *Interim Chief Financial Officer*

GEOGRAPHIC SECTION
Toledo - Lucas County (G-13883)

EMP: 119 EST: 2005
SQ FT: 20,900
SALES (est): 51.51MM
SALES (corp-wide): 51.51MM **Privately Held**
SIC: 8082 Home health care services

(G-13863)
INNOVATIVE CONTROLS CORP
1354 E Bdwy St (43605-3667)
PHONE..................419 691-6684
Louis M Soltis, *Pr*
Anson F Schultz, *
EMP: 37 EST: 1974
SQ FT: 20,000
SALES (est): 8.69MM **Privately Held**
Web: www.innovativecontrolscorp.com
SIC: 3613 3535 8711 3823 Control panels, electric; Conveyors and conveying equipment; Engineering services; Process control instruments

(G-13864)
INVERNESS CLUB
4601 Dorr St (43615-4038)
PHONE..................419 578-9000
E C Benington, *Pr*
EMP: 66 EST: 2013
SALES (est): 10.73MM **Privately Held**
Web: www.invernessclub.com
SIC: 7997 Country club, membership

(G-13865)
J & S INDUSTRIAL MCH PDTS INC
123 Oakdale Ave (43605-3322)
PHONE..................419 691-1380
Nancy Colyer, *Prin*
Donald R Colyer, *
Elton E Bowland, *
John Sehr, *
George Bowland, *
EMP: 85 EST: 1946
SQ FT: 32,000
SALES (est): 3.82MM **Privately Held**
Web: www.jsindustrialmachine.com
SIC: 3559 7692 Glass making machinery: blowing, molding, forming, etc.; Welding repair

(G-13866)
JENNITE CO
4694 W Bancroft St (43615-3946)
PHONE..................419 531-1791
Robert Wheeler Junior, *Pr*
Thomas Wheeler, *
EMP: 29 EST: 1946
SQ FT: 2,800
SALES (est): 2.2MM **Privately Held**
Web: www.jennite.com
SIC: 1771 Blacktop (asphalt) work

(G-13867)
JK SERVICES
7868 W Central Ave (43617-1530)
PHONE..................419 843-2608
Tyler Kahn, *Owner*
EMP: 38 EST: 2001
SALES (est): 270.74K **Privately Held**
SIC: 4119 Automobile rental, with driver

(G-13868)
JOB1USA INC (HQ)
701 Jefferson Ave Ste 202 (43604-6957)
P.O. Box 1480 (43603-1480)
PHONE..................419 255-5005
Bruce F Rumpf, *CEO*
Eloise Huston, *
Don Reynolds, *
Sue Daniels, *
EMP: 149 EST: 1951
SQ FT: 35,000
SALES (est): 46.73MM
SALES (corp-wide): 50.52MM **Privately Held**
Web: www.job1usa.com
SIC: 7381 7363 7361 Security guard service; Temporary help service; Employment agencies
PA: The Rumpf Corporation
701 Jefferson Ave
Toledo OH 43604
419 255-5005

(G-13869)
JOHN E BRUNNER MD
Also Called: Endocrine & Diabetes Care Ctr
3140 W Central Ave (43606-2920)
PHONE..................419 537-5111
EMP: 30 EST: 2002
SALES (est): 4.39MM **Privately Held**
Web: www.edcc.net
SIC: 8011 General and family practice, physician/surgeon

(G-13870)
JONES & HENRY ENGINEERS LTD (PA)
3103 Executive Pkwy Ste 300 (43606-1372)
PHONE..................419 473-9611
Bradley F Lowery, *Pr*
Gregg J Simon S, *VP*
Theodore A Bennett, *Asst VP*
Peter A Latta, *Sec*
EMP: 50 EST: 1926
SALES (est): 12.82MM
SALES (corp-wide): 12.82MM **Privately Held**
Web: www.jheng.com
SIC: 8711 Civil engineering

(G-13871)
JOSINA LOTT FOUNDATION
Also Called: JOSINA LOTT RESIDENTIAL HOME
120 S Holland Sylvania Rd (43615-5622)
PHONE..................419 866-9013
Michael Malone, *Dir*
EMP: 28 EST: 1973
SQ FT: 23,600
SALES (est): 23.6K **Privately Held**
Web: www.josinalott.org
SIC: 8361 Mentally handicapped home

(G-13872)
K A BERGQUIST INC (PA)
Also Called: Bergquist
1100 King Rd (43617-2002)
PHONE..................419 865-4196
Robert Barry, *Pr*
Larry Hinkley, *
Charles E Ide Junior, *Prin*
Hilda C Bergquist, *
Karl Bergquist, *
▼ EMP: 30 EST: 1963
SQ FT: 30,000
SALES (est): 34.78MM
SALES (corp-wide): 34.78MM **Privately Held**
Web: www.bergquistinc.com
SIC: 5084 1711 Propane conversion equipment; Plumbing, heating, air-conditioning

(G-13873)
K KERN PAINTING LLC
211 N Reynolds Rd Ste A (43615-5200)
PHONE..................419 966-0812
EMP: 32 EST: 2016
SALES (est): 942.66K **Privately Held**
Web: www.kkernpainting.com
SIC: 1721 Residential painting

(G-13874)
K-LIMITED CARRIER LTD (HQ)
131 Matzinger Rd (43612-2623)
PHONE..................419 269-0002
Dean Kaplan, *CEO*
Kim Kaplan, *
John Spurling, *
Dennis Perna, *
Melanie Feeley, *
EMP: 65 EST: 1997
SQ FT: 8,200
SALES (est): 23.26MM
SALES (corp-wide): 1.55B **Privately Held**
Web: www.k-ltd.com
SIC: 4213 Contract haulers
PA: The Kenan Advantage Group Inc
4366 Mt Pleasant St Nw
North Canton OH 44720
800 969-5419

(G-13875)
KAY SURATI
Also Called: Hampton Inn
5865 Hagman Rd (43612-3877)
PHONE..................419 727-8725
Kay Surati, *Owner*
Kay Surhei, *Genl Mgr*
EMP: 43 EST: 2000
SQ FT: 49,943
SALES (est): 648.69K **Privately Held**
Web: www.hilton.com
SIC: 7011 Hotels and motels

(G-13876)
KEYBANK NATIONAL ASSOCIATION
5037 Suder Ave (43611-1429)
PHONE..................419 727-6280
Fran Ticherne, *Sec*
EMP: 38
SALES (corp-wide): 10.4B **Publicly Held**
Web: www.key.com
SIC: 6021 National commercial banks
HQ: Keybank National Association
127 Public Sq Ste 5600
Cleveland OH 44114
800 539-2968

(G-13877)
KEYBANK NATIONAL ASSOCIATION
4106 Talmadge Rd (43623-3504)
PHONE..................419 473-2088
Vivian Lewis, *Prin*
EMP: 38
SALES (corp-wide): 10.4B **Publicly Held**
Web: www.key.com
SIC: 6021 National commercial banks
HQ: Keybank National Association
127 Public Sq Ste 5600
Cleveland OH 44114
800 539-2968

(G-13878)
KEYBANK NATIONAL ASSOCIATION
Also Called: Key Bank
7350 W Central Ave (43617-1121)
PHONE..................567 455-4022
Diane Pokrywka, *Mgr*
EMP: 44
SALES (corp-wide): 10.4B **Publicly Held**
Web: www.key.com
SIC: 6021 National commercial banks
HQ: Keybank National Association
127 Public Sq Ste 5600
Cleveland OH 44114
800 539-2968

(G-13879)
KINGSTON HEALTHCARE COMPANY (PA)
Also Called: Kingston Residence
1 Seagate Ste 1960 (43604-1592)
PHONE..................419 247-2880
M George Rumman, *Pr*
Kent Libbe, *
F D Wolfe, *
Larry A Nirschl, *
EMP: 50 EST: 1989
SQ FT: 3,000
SALES (est): 97.91MM **Privately Held**
Web: www.kingstonhealthcare.com
SIC: 8059 8741 Nursing home, except skilled and intermediate care facility; Nursing and personal care facility management

(G-13880)
KNIGHT INSURANCE AGENCY INC
Also Called: Nationwide
22 N Erie St (43604-6943)
PHONE..................419 241-5133
Kenneth Knight, *Ch Bd*
Boyd Bonner, *
Diane Hipp, *
EMP: 38 EST: 1859
SQ FT: 2,000
SALES (est): 11.29MM **Privately Held**
Web: www.knightinsurance.com
SIC: 6411 Insurance agents, nec

(G-13881)
LABOR READY MIDWEST INC
Also Called: Labor Ready
3606 W Sylvania Ave Ste 8 (43623-4455)
PHONE..................419 382-6565
William Harris, *Mgr*
EMP: 60
SALES (corp-wide): 1.91B **Publicly Held**
Web: www.peopleready.com
SIC: 7363 Temporary help service
HQ: Labor Ready Midwest, Inc
1015 A St Unit A
Tacoma WA 98402
253 383-9101

(G-13882)
LATHROP COMPANY INC (DH)
28 N Saint Clair St (43604-1001)
PHONE..................419 893-7000
Steven M Johnson, *Pr*
Joseph R Kovaleski, *VP*
Douglas F Martin, *VP*
Mark T Kusner, *Treas*
EMP: 50 EST: 1895
SQ FT: 20,000
SALES (est): 41.61MM **Privately Held**
Web: www.turnerconstruction.com
SIC: 1542 8741 1541 Commercial and office building, new construction; Construction management; Industrial buildings and warehouses
HQ: Turner Construction Company Inc
66 Hudson Blvd E
New York NY 10001
212 229-6000

(G-13883)
LEADING FAMILIES HOME
2283 Ashland Ave (43620-1205)
PHONE..................419 244-2175
EMP: 34 EST: 2019
SALES (est): 1.35MM **Privately Held**
Web: www.lfhtoledo.org
SIC: 7359 Equipment rental and leasing, nec

Toledo - Lucas County (G-13884) — GEOGRAPHIC SECTION

(G-13884)
LEGAL AID WESTERN OHIO INC
Also Called: Lawo
525 Jefferson Ave # 400 (43604-1094)
PHONE..............................419 724-0030
Kevin Mulder, *Dir*
EMP: 49 **EST:** 1999
SALES (est): 3.57MM **Privately Held**
Web: www.lawolaw.org
SIC: 8111 Legal aid service

(G-13885)
LEVITAN ENTERPRISE LLC
6020 W Bancroft St Unit 350061
(43635-8137)
PHONE..............................628 208-7016
EMP: 60 **EST:** 2005
SALES (est): 1.2MM **Privately Held**
SIC: 8742 Management consulting services

(G-13886)
LEXAMED LTD
705 Front St (43605-2107)
PHONE..............................419 693-5307
Rocile Parton, *Mgr*
EMP: 40 **EST:** 2006
SALES (est): 5.7MM **Privately Held**
Web: www.lexamed.com
SIC: 8734 Testing laboratories

(G-13887)
LIBBEY INC
Also Called: Cordelia Mrtin Hlth Ctr At Lbb
1250 Western Ave (43609-2208)
PHONE..............................419 671-6000
Joy Gregory, *Brnch Mgr*
EMP: 116
Web: www.libbey.com
SIC: 8011 Offices and clinics of medical doctors
PA: Libbey Inc.
300 Madison Ave
Toledo OH 43604

(G-13888)
LIBERTY PROVIDER LLC
Also Called: Visiting Angels Toledo
7110 W Central Ave Ste A (43617-3118)
PHONE..............................419 517-7000
William Bruck, *Prin*
EMP: 99 **EST:** 2018
SALES (est): 2.28MM **Privately Held**
SIC: 8082 Home health care services

(G-13889)
LIFESTAR AMBULANCE INC
2200 Jefferson Ave Fl 5 (43604-7102)
PHONE..............................419 245-6210
William Sutton, *Pr*
EMP: 35 **EST:** 2004
SALES (est): 1.01MM **Privately Held**
SIC: 4119 Ambulance service

(G-13890)
LMSI LLC
Also Called: Lighthouse Lab Services
2710 Centennial Rd (43617-1829)
PHONE..............................800 838-0602
Christine Williams, *Prin*
EMP: 47
SALES (corp-wide): 20.64MM **Privately Held**
Web: www.lighthouselabservices.com
SIC: 8734 Testing laboratories
PA: Lmsi, Llc
1337 Hndred Oaks Dr Ste A
Charlotte NC 28217
980 209-0349

(G-13891)
LOGISTICS INC
6010 Skyview Dr (43612-4715)
PHONE..............................419 478-1514
Aaron Alberts, *Brnch Mgr*
EMP: 45
SALES (corp-wide): 26.1MM **Privately Held**
Web: www.reliabledelivery.com
SIC: 7389 Courier or messenger service
PA: Logistics Inc.
21450 Trolley Indus Dr
Taylor MI 48180
734 641-1600

(G-13892)
LOUISVLLE TITLE AGCY FOR NW OH (PA)
Also Called: Louisville Title Agency
626 Madison Ave Ste 100 (43604-1106)
PHONE..............................419 248-4611
John W Martin, *Pr*
EMP: 80 **EST:** 1948
SQ FT: 20,000
SALES (est): 5.59MM
SALES (corp-wide): 5.59MM **Privately Held**
Web: www.louisvilletitle.com
SIC: 6541 Title and trust companies

(G-13893)
LOVING FAMILY HOME CARE INC
2600 N Reynolds Rd Ste 101a (43615-2084)
PHONE..............................888 469-2178
Solarix Fireheart, *CEO*
EMP: 60 **EST:** 2009
SQ FT: 1,400
SALES (est): 2.59MM **Privately Held**
Web: www.lovingfamilyhomecare.com
SIC: 8082 Visiting nurse service

(G-13894)
LOWES HOME CENTERS LLC
Also Called: Lowe's
7000 W Central Ave (43617-1115)
PHONE..............................419 843-9758
Jim Weirick, *Mgr*
EMP: 148
SALES (corp-wide): 86.38B **Publicly Held**
Web: www.lowes.com
SIC: 5211 5031 5722 5064 Home centers; Building materials, exterior; Household appliance stores; Electrical appliances, television and radio
HQ: Lowe's Home Centers, Llc
1000 Lowes Blvd
Mooresville NC 28117
336 658-4000

(G-13895)
LUCAS CNTY BD DVLPMNTAL DSBLTI
1154 Larc Ln (43614-2768)
PHONE..............................419 380-4000
Deb Yenrick, *Superintnt*
EMP: 122 **EST:** 2010
SALES (est): 1.13MM **Privately Held**
Web: www.lucasdd.org
SIC: 8322 Individual and family services

(G-13896)
LUCAS COUNTY OHIO
1 Government Ctr Ste 600 (43604-2255)
PHONE..............................419 213-4808
EMP: 98 **EST:** 2007
SALES (est): 2.67MM **Privately Held**
Web: www.lucascountydogs.com
SIC: 8611 Business associations

(G-13897)
LUCAS COUNTY CHILDREN SERVICES
705 Adams St (43604-3419)
PHONE..............................419 213-3247
EMP: 350 **EST:** 2019
SALES (est): 2.39MM
SALES (corp-wide): 569.39MM **Privately Held**
Web: co.lucas.oh.us
SIC: 8322 Child related social services
PA: County Of Lucas
1 Government Ctr Ste 600
Toledo OH 43604
419 213-4406

(G-13898)
LUTHERAN HOME
131 N Wheeling St Ofc (43605-1545)
PHONE..............................419 724-1414
EMP: 64
SQ FT: 2,979
SALES (est): 9.39MM **Privately Held**
SIC: 8361 Aged home

(G-13899)
LUTHERAN HOMES SOCIETY INC (PA)
Also Called: Genacross Lutheran Services
2021 N Mccord Rd (43615-3030)
PHONE..............................419 861-4990
W Richard Marshall, *Pr*
EMP: 35 **EST:** 1860
SALES (est): 54.58MM
SALES (corp-wide): 54.58MM **Privately Held**
Web: www.genacrosslutheranservices.org
SIC: 8361 Aged home

(G-13900)
LUTHERAN MEMORIAL HOME INC
2021 N Mccord Rd (43615-3030)
PHONE..............................419 502-5700
Jason Bennett, *Ex Dir*
EMP: 82 **EST:** 1974
SQ FT: 44,000
SALES (est): 6.14MM **Privately Held**
Web: www.genacrosslutheranservices.org
SIC: 8052 8059 Personal care facility; Rest home, with health care

(G-13901)
LYMAN W LGGINS URBAN AFFIRS CT
Also Called: Nutrition Program
2155 Arlington Ave (43609-1903)
PHONE..............................419 385-2532
Lisa Hughley, *Dir*
EMP: 38 **EST:** 1970
SALES (est): 806.82K **Privately Held**
Web: www.areaofficeonaging.com
SIC: 8322 Senior citizens' center or association

(G-13902)
M3 CLEANING SERVICES INC
511 Phillips Ave (43612-1328)
PHONE..............................419 725-2100
Meredith Miller, *Pr*
Matt Miller, *
EMP: 200 **EST:** 2021
SALES (est): 5.08MM **Privately Held**
SIC: 7349 Janitorial service, contract basis

(G-13903)
MADISON AVENUE MKTG GROUP INC
1600 Madison Ave (43604-5464)
PHONE..............................419 473-9000
Gerald R Brown Junior, *Pr*
EMP: 48 **EST:** 1989
SQ FT: 7,000
SALES (est): 7.14MM **Privately Held**
Web: www.madavegroup.com
SIC: 7313 8999 7311 7812 Electronic media advertising representatives; Advertising copy writing; Advertising agencies; Video production

(G-13904)
MANAGED CARE ADVISORY GROUP
3434 Granite Cir # 1 (43617-1160)
PHONE..............................800 355-0466
Tim Schmidt, *CEO*
EMP: 30 **EST:** 2004
SALES (est): 4.1MM **Privately Held**
Web: www.mcaginc.com
SIC: 8742 Financial consultant

(G-13905)
MANOR CARE INC (HQ)
333 N Summit St (43604-1531)
P.O. Box 10086 (43699-0086)
PHONE..............................419 252-5500
Paul A Ormond, *Pr*
Stephen L Guillard, *
Steven M Cavanaugh, *
Richard A Parr Ii, *General Vice President*
Spencer C Moler, *
EMP: 66 **EST:** 1991
SALES (est): 6.25MM
SALES (corp-wide): 187.07MM **Privately Held**
Web: www.promedicaseniorcare.org
SIC: 8051 8082 8062 Extended care facility; Home health care services; General medical and surgical hospitals
PA: Promedica Health System, Inc.
100 Madison Ave
Toledo OH 43604
567 585-9600

(G-13906)
MANOR CARE WILMINGTON DE LLC
Also Called: Promedica Sklled Nrsing Rhbltt
100 Madison Ave (43604-1516)
PHONE..............................567 585-9600
EMP: 1886 **EST:** 2007
SALES (est): 5.79MM
SALES (corp-wide): 187.07MM **Privately Held**
Web: www.promedica.org
SIC: 8051 Convalescent home with continuous nursing care
PA: Promedica Health System, Inc.
100 Madison Ave
Toledo OH 43604
567 585-9600

(G-13907)
MANOR CR-PIKE CREEK WLMNGTON D
Also Called: Promedica Sklled Nrsing Rhbltt
100 Madison Ave (43604-1516)
PHONE..............................567 585-9600
EMP: 132 **EST:** 2007
SALES (est): 15.48MM
SALES (corp-wide): 187.07MM **Privately Held**
SIC: 8051 Convalescent home with continuous nursing care
PA: Promedica Health System, Inc.
100 Madison Ave
Toledo OH 43604
567 585-9600

GEOGRAPHIC SECTION
Toledo - Lucas County (G-13928)

(G-13908)
MANORCARE HEALTH SERVICES LLC (DH)
Also Called: Manorcare Hlth Srvcs-Tica Rdge
333 N Summit St Ste 100 (43604-2617)
PHONE..............................419 252-5500
Barry A Lazarus, *Prin*
EMP: 27 **EST:** 2009
SALES (est): 106.61MM
SALES (corp-wide): 187.07MM **Privately Held**
Web: www.promedicaseniorcare.org
SIC: 8051 Convalescent home with continuous nursing care
HQ: Manor Care, Inc.
333 N Summit St
Toledo OH 43604

(G-13909)
MANORCARE HEALTH SVCS VA INC
333 N Summit St Ste 100 (43604-2617)
P.O. Box 10086 (43699-0086)
PHONE..............................419 252-5500
Paul Ormond, *CEO*
Steve Cavanaugh, *
EMP: 100 **EST:** 1997
SALES (est): 10.79MM
SALES (corp-wide): 389.07MM **Privately Held**
Web: www.promedicaseniorcare.org
SIC: 8051 Convalescent home with continuous nursing care
PA: Hcr Manorcare Medical Services Of Florida, Llc
333 N Summit St Ste 100
Toledo OH 43604
419 252-5500

(G-13910)
MARCOS INC
Also Called: Marco's Pizza
5252 Monroe St (43623-3140)
PHONE..............................419 885-4844
Pasquale Giammarco, *Pr*
Anne Giammarco, *
EMP: 98 **EST:** 1978
SQ FT: 1,000
SALES (est): 767.94K **Privately Held**
Web: www.marcos.com
SIC: 5812 6794 Pizzeria, chain; Franchises, selling or licensing

(G-13911)
MARSHALL & MELHORN LLC
4 Seagate Ste 800 (43604-1599)
PHONE..............................419 249-7100
Justice G Johnson Junior, *Pt*
Thomas W Palmer, *Pt*
Phillip S Oberlin, *Pt*
Michael S Scalzo, *Pt*
Marshall A Bennett Junior, *Pt*
EMP: 90 **EST:** 1896
SQ FT: 21,270
SALES (est): 7.95MM **Privately Held**
Web: www.marshall-melhorn.com
SIC: 8111 General practice attorney, lawyer

(G-13912)
MARTIN + WD APPRISAL GROUP LTD
43 S Saint Clair St (43604-8735)
PHONE..............................419 241-4998
EMP: 30 **EST:** 2000
SQ FT: 3,000
SALES (est): 1.71MM **Privately Held**
Web: www.martin-woodappraisal.com
SIC: 6531 Appraiser, real estate

(G-13913)
MEDICAL CLLEGE OHIO PHYSCANS L
Also Called: UNIVERSITY OF TOLEDO PHYSICIAN
3355 Glendale Ave Fl 3 (43614-2426)
PHONE..............................419 383-7100
EMP: 67 **EST:** 2004
SALES (est): 114.99MM **Privately Held**
Web: utmc.utoledo.edu
SIC: 8011 Physical medicine, physician/surgeon

(G-13914)
MEDVET ASSOCIATES LLC
Also Called: Medvet Toledo
2921 Douglas Rd (43606-3502)
PHONE..............................419 473-0328
Jeanna Beck, *Brnch Mgr*
EMP: 68
Web: www.medvet.com
SIC: 0742 Animal hospital services, pets and other animal specialties
PA: Medvet Associates, Llc
350 E Wilson Bridge Rd
Worthington OH 43085

(G-13915)
MERCY HEALTH DERMATOLOGY
3425 Executive Pkwy (43606-1333)
PHONE..............................567 225-3407
EMP: 50 **EST:** 2020
SALES (est): 565.86K **Privately Held**
Web: www.mercy.com
SIC: 8062 General medical and surgical hospitals

(G-13916)
MERCY HEALTH NORTH LLC
2200 Jefferson Ave (43604-7101)
PHONE..............................419 251-1359
EMP: 7200 **EST:** 1981
SQ FT: 4,000
SALES (est): 169.03MM
SALES (corp-wide): 6.92B **Privately Held**
Web: www.mercy.com
SIC: 8062 General medical and surgical hospitals
PA: Bon Secours Mercy Health, Inc.
1701 Mercy Health Pl
Cincinnati OH 45237
513 956-3729

(G-13917)
MERCY HLTH - ST ANNE HOSP LLC
3404 W Sylvania Ave (43623-4467)
PHONE..............................419 407-2663
EMP: 62 **EST:** 1997
SALES (est): 10.86MM **Privately Held**
Web: www.mercy.com
SIC: 8062 General medical and surgical hospitals

(G-13918)
MERCY HLTH - ST VNCENT MED CTR
Also Called: Mercy Clinic
2200 Jefferson Ave (43604-7101)
PHONE..............................419 251-0580
Steven L Mickus, *Prin*
EMP: 547
SALES (corp-wide): 478.77MM **Privately Held**
Web: www.mercy.com
SIC: 8062 General medical and surgical hospitals
PA: Mercy Health - St. Vincent Medical Center Llc
2213 Cherry St
Toledo OH 43608
419 251-3232

(G-13919)
MERCY HLTH - ST VNCENT MED CTR (PA)
Also Called: St. Vncent Hosp Mdial Ctr Tled
2213 Cherry St (43608)
PHONE..............................419 251-3232
Steven Mickus, *Pr*
Beverly J Mcbride, *Ch Bd*
Julie Higgins, *
Robert A Sullivan, *
Samantha Platzke, *CFO*
EMP: 3600 **EST:** 1875
SQ FT: 634,165
SALES (est): 478.77MM
SALES (corp-wide): 478.77MM **Privately Held**
Web: www.mercy.com
SIC: 8062 General medical and surgical hospitals

(G-13920)
MERCY HLTH - ST VNCENT MED CTR
Also Called: Franklin Park Pediatrics
2000 Regency Ct Ste 103 (43623-3075)
PHONE..............................419 475-5433
Marybeth Waterfield, *Mgr*
EMP: 704
SALES (corp-wide): 478.77MM **Privately Held**
Web: www.franklinparkpediatrics.com
SIC: 8011 Pediatrician
PA: Mercy Health - St. Vincent Medical Center Llc
2213 Cherry St
Toledo OH 43608
419 251-3232

(G-13921)
MERIT HOUSE LLC
4645 Lewis Ave (43612-2336)
PHONE..............................419 478-5131
John Stone, *Pr*
EMP: 150 **EST:** 2013
SALES (est): 4.32MM **Privately Held**
Web: www.merithousetoledo.com
SIC: 8051 Skilled nursing care facilities

(G-13922)
METRO FIBER & CABLE CNSTR
5566 Southwyck Blvd (43614-1536)
PHONE..............................419 724-9802
EMP: 200
SALES (est): 6.25MM
SALES (corp-wide): 1.11B **Privately Held**
SIC: 1731 Sound equipment specialization
HQ: Buckeye Cablevision, Inc.
2700 Oregon Rd
Northwood OH 43619
419 724-9802

(G-13923)
MIDAS AUTO SYSTEMS EXPERTS
1101 Monroe St (43604-5811)
PHONE..............................419 243-7281
Randolph Katz, *Prin*
EMP: 663 **EST:** 1990
SALES (est): 19.04MM **Privately Held**
SIC: 7533 Muffler shop, sale or repair and installation

(G-13924)
MIDWEST TRMNALS TLEDO INTL INC
Also Called: Facility 1
3518 Saint Lawrence Dr (43605-1079)
PHONE..............................419 897-6868
Brad Hendricks, *Mgr*
EMP: 35
SALES (corp-wide): 23.97MM **Privately Held**
Web: www.midwestterminals.com
SIC: 4225 4491 General warehousing; Stevedoring
HQ: Midwest Terminals Of Toledo, International, Inc.
383 W Dussel Dr
Maumee OH 43537
419 897-6868

(G-13925)
MIZAR MOTORS INC (HQ)
Also Called: Great Lakes Western Star
6003 Benore Rd (43612-3905)
PHONE..............................419 729-2400
Rudy Vogel, *Pr*
John C Bates, *Ch*
Simon Les, *Ch*
Mark Ridenour, *Sec*
Linda K Shinkle, *Prin*
EMP: 60 **EST:** 1986
SQ FT: 60,000
SALES (est): 10.66MM
SALES (corp-wide): 230.06MM **Privately Held**
Web: www.toledofreightliner.com
SIC: 4213 7538 5511 Heavy hauling, nec; Truck engine repair, except industrial; Trucks, tractors, and trailers: new and used
PA: Centaur, Inc.
2401 Front St
Toledo OH 43605
419 469-8000

(G-13926)
MODERN BUILDERS SUPPLY INC (PA)
Also Called: Polaris Technologies
3500 Phillips Ave (43608-1070)
P.O. Box 80025 (43608-0025)
PHONE..............................419 241-3961
Kevin Leggett, *CEO*
Larry Leggett, *
G Taylor Evans Iii, *Treas*
Eric Leggett, *
Jack Marstellar, *
EMP: 200 **EST:** 1944
SQ FT: 40,000
SALES (est): 346.23MM
SALES (corp-wide): 346.23MM **Privately Held**
Web: www.modernbuilderssupply.com
SIC: 3089 5032 3446 3442 Windows, plastics ; Brick, stone, and related material; Architectural metalwork; Metal doors, sash, and trim

(G-13927)
MONDELEZ GLOBAL LLC
Also Called: Kraft Foods
2221 Front St (43605-1231)
P.O. Box 2208 (43603-2208)
PHONE..............................419 691-5200
William Epperson, *Brnch Mgr*
EMP: 100
Web: www.mondelezinternational.com
SIC: 5149 Groceries and related products, nec
HQ: Mondelez Global Llc
905 W Fulton Market # 200
Chicago IL 60607
847 943-4000

(G-13928)
MORGAN SERVICES INC
34 10th St (43604-6912)
PHONE..............................419 243-2214
Pat Wheeler, *Brnch Mgr*
EMP: 79
SALES (corp-wide): 72.96MM **Privately Held**
Web: www.morganservices.com

Toledo - Lucas County (G-13929)   GEOGRAPHIC SECTION

SIC: **7213** 7218 Linen supply; Industrial launderers
PA: Morgan Services, Inc.
3647 N Michigan Ave
Chicago IL 60601
312 346-3181

(G-13929)
MUD MADE LOGISTICS CORPORATION
3647 Douglas Rd (43613-4832)
PHONE..................................614 284-2772
Derrell Barton, *Pr*
EMP: 31 EST: 2021
SALES (est): 2.1MM **Privately Held**
SIC: **4731** Freight transportation arrangement

(G-13930)
NATIONAL EXCH CLB FNDTION FOR
Also Called: NATIONAL SERVICE CLUB
3050 W Central Ave (43606-1757)
PHONE..................................419 535-3232
Chris Rice, *Ex VP*
EMP: 29 EST: 1911
SQ FT: 22,500
SALES (est): 1.75MM **Privately Held**
Web: www.nationalexchangeclub.org
SIC: **8322** Child related social services

(G-13931)
NEIGHBORHOOD PROPERTIES INC
2753 W Central Ave (43606-3439)
PHONE..................................419 473-2604
John Hoover, *Pr*
Lori Tyler, *
EMP: 50 EST: 1988
SALES (est): 9.77MM **Privately Held**
Web: www.neighborhoodproperties.org
SIC: **6513** 6531 Retirement hotel operation; Real estate agents and managers

(G-13932)
NEIGHBRHOOD HLTH ASSN TLEDO IN (PA)
Also Called: Toledo Family Health Center
313 Jefferson Ave (43604-1004)
PHONE..................................419 720-7883
Doni Miller, *CEO*
Larry Leyland, *
EMP: 35 EST: 1969
SQ FT: 9,000
SALES (est): 8.98MM
SALES (corp-wide): 8.98MM **Privately Held**
Web: www.nhainc.org
SIC: **8093** Specialty outpatient clinics, nec

(G-13933)
NESCO INC
5425 Monroe St (43623-2876)
PHONE..................................419 794-7452
EMP: 162
SALES (corp-wide): 514.23MM **Privately Held**
Web: www.nescoresource.com
SIC: **8742** Business planning and organizing services
PA: Nesco, Inc.
6140 Parkland Blvd # 110
Cleveland OH 44124
440 461-6000

(G-13934)
NEW CINGULAR WIRELESS SVCS INC
Also Called: AT&T
4906 Monroe St (43623-3650)
PHONE..................................419 473-9756
Sherri Lazette, *Brnch Mgr*
EMP: 33

SALES (corp-wide): 122.43B **Publicly Held**
SIC: **4812** Cellular telephone services
HQ: New Cingular Wireless Services, Inc.
7277 164th Ave Ne
Redmond WA 98052
425 827-4500

(G-13935)
NONEMAN REAL ESTATE COMPANY
3519 Secor Rd (43606-1504)
PHONE..................................419 531-4020
Dennis J Noneman, *Pr*
EMP: 30 EST: 1979
SQ FT: 3,200
SALES (est): 2.34MM **Privately Held**
Web: www.noneman.com
SIC: **6531** Real estate brokers and agents

(G-13936)
NORON INC
Also Called: Honeywell Authorized Dealer
5465 Enterprise Blvd (43612-3812)
PHONE..................................419 726-2677
Kevin Boeke, *Pr*
EMP: 35 EST: 1996
SQ FT: 15,000
SALES (est): 5.61MM **Privately Held**
Web: www.noroninc.com
SIC: **1711** Warm air heating and air conditioning contractor

(G-13937)
NORTH SOUTH DELIVERY LLC
5272 Tractor Rd Ste H (43612-3424)
PHONE..................................419 478-7400
EMP: 27 EST: 2017
SALES (est): 220.06K **Privately Held**
SIC: **4731** Freight forwarding
PA: Freight Rite, Inc.
4352 W Sylvania Ave
Toledo OH 43623

(G-13938)
NORTHWEST OHIO CARDIOLOGY CONS (PA)
2121 Hughes Dr Ste 850 (43606-3845)
PHONE..................................419 842-3000
Everett M Bush Md, *Pr*
Daryl Moreau, *
James Bingle, *
EMP: 70 EST: 1960
SQ FT: 5,000
SALES (est): 10.35MM
SALES (corp-wide): 10.35MM **Privately Held**
SIC: **8011** Cardiologist and cardio-vascular specialist

(G-13939)
NORTHWEST OHIO GSTRNTRLGSTS AS
4841 Monroe St Ste 111 (43623-4390)
PHONE..................................419 471-1350
EMP: 46 EST: 1995
SALES (est): 1.56MM **Privately Held**
Web: www.nwogastro.com
SIC: **8011** Gastronomist

(G-13940)
NORTHWESTERN HOLDING LLC
805 Chicago St (43611-3626)
PHONE..................................419 726-0850
David Feniger, *Managing Member*
Todd Mccain, *COO*
EMP: 70 EST: 2018
SALES (est): 11.11MM **Privately Held**
SIC: **5051** Metals service centers and offices

(G-13941)
NOVA PASSPORT HOME CARE LLC
Also Called: Beacon of Light Health Agency
242 S Reynolds Rd Ste A (43615-6164)
PHONE..................................419 531-9060
Shirley Foster, *Managing Member*
EMP: 37 EST: 2007
SQ FT: 4,500
SALES (est): 2.42MM **Privately Held**
Web: www.beaconoflightltd.com
SIC: **8051** 8742 Convalescent home with continuous nursing care; Hospital and health services consultant

(G-13942)
NUCENTURY TEXTILE SERVICES LLC (PA)
Also Called: Nucentury Textiles Linen Svcs
1 Southard Ave (43604)
P.O. Box 20130 (43610)
PHONE..................................419 241-2267
Jim Pacitti, *Managing Member*
EMP: 76 EST: 1998
SQ FT: 1,000
SALES (est): 4.58MM
SALES (corp-wide): 4.58MM **Privately Held**
Web: www.nucentex.com
SIC: **7213** Linen supply

(G-13943)
NZR RETAIL OF TOLEDO INC
4820 Monroe St (43606)
P.O. Box 8523 (43623)
PHONE..................................419 724-0005
Nick Hasan, *CEO*
Yazeed Qaimari, *
EMP: 85 EST: 1999
SQ FT: 2,000,000
SALES (est): 22.1MM **Privately Held**
Web: www.expiredwixdomain.com
SIC: **5172** Gasoline

(G-13944)
OHIO DEPT DVLPMNTAL DSBILITIES
Also Called: Northwest Ohio Dvlopmental Ctr
1101 S Detroit Ave (43614-2704)
PHONE..................................419 385-0231
Dan Housepian, *Mgr*
EMP: 247
SIC: **8361** 9431 Retarded home; Administration of public health programs, State government
HQ: Ohio Department Of Developmental Disabilities
30 E Broad St Fl 13
Columbus OH 43215

(G-13945)
OHIO DEPT MNTAL HLTH ADDCTION
Also Called: Northcoast Behavior Healthcare
930 S Detroit Ave (43614-2701)
PHONE..................................419 381-1881
Joe Reichert, *Pr*
EMP: 133
Web: mha.ohio.gov
SIC: **8063** 9431 Psychiatric hospitals; Mental health agency administration, government
HQ: Ohio Department Of Mental Health And Addiction Services
30 E Broad St Fl 36
Columbus OH 43215

(G-13946)
OHIO LIVING
Also Called: Swan Creek Retirement Village
5916 Cresthaven Ln Ste 110 (43614-1292)
PHONE..................................419 865-4445
Ane Roller, *Mgr*
EMP: 305
Web: www.ohioliving.org

SIC: **8361** Aged home
PA: Ohio Living
9200 Worthington Rd # 300
Westerville OH 43082

(G-13947)
OHIO LIVING HOLDINGS
Also Called: Ohio Lving HM Hlth Grter Tledo
1730 S Reynolds Rd (43616-1402)
PHONE..................................419 865-1499
Laurence C Gumina, *CEO*
Kevin Futryk, *
Paul Flannery, *
Barbara Sears, *
Raafat Zaki, *
EMP: 65 EST: 2010
SALES (est): 951.69K **Privately Held**
Web: www.ohioliving.org
SIC: **8051** Skilled nursing care facilities

(G-13948)
OHIO SKATE INC (PA)
5735 Opportunity Dr (43612-2902)
P.O. Box 6777 (43612-0777)
PHONE..................................419 476-2808
Joseph Yambor, *Pr*
EMP: 50 EST: 1971
SQ FT: 24,000
SALES (est): 810.86K
SALES (corp-wide): 810.86K **Privately Held**
Web: www.ohioskate.com
SIC: **7999** 5941 Roller skating rink operation; Skating equipment

(G-13949)
OHLMAN FARM & GREENHOUSE INC
3901 Hill Ave (43607-2636)
PHONE..................................419 535-5586
Lawrence J Ohlman, *Pr*
▲ EMP: 35 EST: 1882
SALES (est): 846.63K **Privately Held**
Web: www.ohlmangreenhouse.com
SIC: **0181** Flowers: grown under cover (e.g., greenhouse production)

(G-13950)
OMNISOURCE LLC
2453 Hill Ave (43607-3610)
PHONE..................................419 537-1631
Jon Kinsman, *Brnch Mgr*
EMP: 68
Web: www.omnisource.com
SIC: **5093** Ferrous metal scrap and waste
HQ: Omnisource, Llc
7575 W Jefferson Blvd
Fort Wayne IN 46804
260 422-5541

(G-13951)
OVERHEAD INC (PA)
Also Called: Overhead Door Co of Toledo
340 New Towne Square Dr (43612-4606)
PHONE..................................419 476-7811
TOLL FREE: 800
Michael Huss, *Pr*
Lee J Huss, *
Diane Huss, *
EMP: 40 EST: 1932
SQ FT: 27,000
SALES (est): 9.59MM
SALES (corp-wide): 9.59MM **Privately Held**
Web: www.overheadinc.com
SIC: **1751** 5211 5719 Garage door, installation or erection; Garage doors, sale and installation; Fireplaces and wood burning stoves

GEOGRAPHIC SECTION
Toledo - Lucas County (G-13973)

(G-13952)
OWENS CORNING SALES LLC (HQ)
1 Owens Corning Pkwy (43659-0001)
P.O. Box 13950 (27709-3950)
PHONE..................................419 248-8000
Brian Chambers, *Pr*
Stephen K Krull, *VP*
David L Johns, *VP*
◆ **EMP:** 1000 **EST:** 2006
SQ FT: 400,000
SALES (est): 1.9B **Publicly Held**
SIC: 3296 2952 3229 3089 Fiberglass insulation; Asphalt felts and coatings; Glass fibers, textile; Windows, plastics
PA: Owens Corning
   1 Owens Corning Pkwy
   Toledo OH 43659

(G-13953)
OWENS CRNING INSLTING SYSTM (HQ)
1 Owens Corning Pkwy (43659-1000)
PHONE..................................419 248-8000
EMP: 58 **EST:** 2006
SALES (est): 78.49MM **Publicly Held**
SIC: 5033 Roofing, siding, and insulation
PA: Owens Corning
   1 Owens Corning Pkwy
   Toledo OH 43659

(G-13954)
OWENS-CORNING FIBERGLAS CORP (HQ)
1 Owens Corning Pkwy (43659-0001)
PHONE..................................419 248-8000
Glen Hiner, *Pr*
Charles H Dana, *VP*
C Michael Gegenheimer, *Sec*
EMP: 27 **EST:** 1938
SALES (est): 13.47MM **Publicly Held**
SIC: 5033 Insulation materials
PA: Owens Corning
   1 Owens Corning Pkwy
   Toledo OH 43659

(G-13955)
PACE PLUS CORP
Also Called: Arista Home Care Solutions
7850 W Central Ave (43617-1530)
PHONE..................................419 754-1897
Clayton Birney, *Pr*
Carri Brown, *
EMP: 77 **EST:** 2014
SALES (est): 2.8MM **Privately Held**
Web: www.aristahc.com
SIC: 8082 Home health care services

(G-13956)
PARK INN
Also Called: Park Inn
101 N Summit St (43604-1033)
PHONE..................................419 241-3000
Michael Sapara, *Prin*
EMP: 97 **EST:** 1995
SALES (est): 2.12MM **Privately Held**
Web: www.radissonhotels.com
SIC: 7011 Hotels and motels

(G-13957)
PARKVIEW MANOR INC
Also Called: Liberty West Nursing Center
2051 Collingwood Blvd (43620-1649)
PHONE..................................419 243-5191
Amanda Gibson, *Mgr*
EMP: 160
SALES (corp-wide): 7.11MM **Privately Held**
SIC: 8051 Convalescent home with continuous nursing care
PA: Park View Manor, Inc.

425 Lauricella Ct
Englewood OH 45322
937 296-1550

(G-13958)
PARKWAY OPERATING CO LLC
Also Called: Advanced Healthcare
955 Garden Lake Pkwy (43614-2777)
PHONE..................................513 530-1600
Richard Odenthal, *Prin*
Sandra Smiddy, *
EMP: 50 **EST:** 2018
SIC: 6719 Holding companies, nec

(G-13959)
PARKWAY SURGERY CENTER INC
2120 W Central Ave (43606-3834)
EMP: 55 **EST:** 1998
SALES (est): 4.75MM **Privately Held**
SIC: 8011 Urologist

(G-13960)
PATHOLOGY LABORATORIES INC (DH)
Also Called: Pathlabs
1946 N 13th St Ste 301 (43604-7264)
PHONE..................................419 255-4600
TOLL FREE: 800
Marian C Mcvicker, *Pr*
Vicki L Hite, *Prin*
EMP: 160 **EST:** 1946
SQ FT: 18,000
SALES (est): 44.87MM **Privately Held**
Web: www.pathlabs.org
SIC: 8071 Pathological laboratory
HQ: Clinical Pathology Laboratories, Inc.
   9200 Wall St
   Austin TX 78754

(G-13961)
PATHWAY INC
Also Called: Pathway
505 Hamilton St (43604-8520)
PHONE..................................419 242-7304
Cheryl Grice, *CEO*
Robert Jordan, *
Jason Mueller, *
EMP: 30 **EST:** 1964
SQ FT: 13,000
SALES (est): 9.39MM **Privately Held**
Web: www.pathwaytoledo.org
SIC: 8322 7361 Social service center; Employment agencies

(G-13962)
PENN NATIONAL HOLDING COMPANY
Also Called: PENN NATIONAL HOLDING COMPANY
1968 Miami St (43605-3359)
PHONE..................................419 661-5200
Jacques Arragon, *Brnch Mgr*
EMP: 217
SALES (corp-wide): 6.36B **Publicly Held**
Web: www.pngaming.com
SIC: 7011 Casino hotel
HQ: Penn National Holdings, Llc
   825 Berkshire Blvd # 203
   Wyomissing PA 19610
   610 373-2400

(G-13963)
PHILIO INC
Also Called: New Concepts
111 S Byrne Rd (43615-6212)
P.O. Box 20068 (43610-0068)
PHONE..................................419 531-5544
Janice Edwards, *Ex Dir*
EMP: 35 **EST:** 2004
SALES (est): 3.07MM **Privately Held**

Web: www.newconceptsiop.org
SIC: 8093 Substance abuse clinics (outpatient)

(G-13964)
PITT-OHIO EXPRESS LLC
5200 Stickney Ave (43612-3723)
PHONE..................................419 726-6523
EMP: 270
SALES (corp-wide): 508.23MM **Privately Held**
Web: www.pittohioexpress.com
SIC: 4213 Contract haulers
PA: Pitt-Ohio Express, Llc
   15 27th St
   Pittsburgh PA 15222
   412 232-3015

(G-13965)
PORT LAWRENCE TITLE AND TR CO (DH)
4 Seagate Ste 101 (43604-1520)
PHONE..................................419 244-4605
Marggretta Laskey, *Pr*
Gerald Stewart, *
Victor Crouch, *
Steve Sczesny, *
EMP: 40 **EST:** 1931
SQ FT: 16,200
SALES (est): 44.82MM **Publicly Held**
Web: local.firstam.com
SIC: 6361 6531 Real estate title insurance; Real estate agents and managers
HQ: First American Title Insurance Company
   1 First American Way
   Santa Ana CA 92707
   800 854-3643

(G-13966)
PRESIDIO INFRSTRCTURE SLTONS L
20 N Saint Clair St (43604-1074)
PHONE..................................419 241-8303
Kirsten Smith, *Brnch Mgr*
EMP: 50
SALES (corp-wide): 3.03B **Privately Held**
Web: www.presidio.com
SIC: 7373 Office computer automation systems integration
HQ: Presidio Infrastructure Solutions Llc
   6355 E Paris Ave Se
   Caledonia MI 49316
   616 871-1500

(G-13967)
PROFESSIONAL ELECTRIC PDTS CO
Also Called: Pepco
501 Phillips Ave (43612-1328)
P.O. Box 12020 (43612-0020)
PHONE..................................419 269-3790
Jim Deraedt, *Brnch Mgr*
EMP: 31
SQ FT: 24,394
SALES (corp-wide): 12.53MM **Privately Held**
Web: www.pepconet.com
SIC: 5063 Electrical supplies, nec
HQ: Professional Electric Products Co Inc
   33210 Lakeland Blvd
   Eastlake OH 44095
   800 872-7000

(G-13968)
PROMEDICA EMPLOYMENT SVCS LLC
Also Called: Heartland Employment Svcs LLC
100 Madison Ave (43604-1516)
P.O. Box 10086 (43699-0086)
PHONE..................................419 824-7529
EMP: 715 **EST:** 2004
SALES (est): 37.08MM

SALES (corp-wide): 187.07MM **Privately Held**
SIC: 7363 Medical help service
HQ: Manor Care, Inc.
   333 N Summit St
   Toledo OH 43604

(G-13969)
PROMEDICA GNT-URINARY SURGEONS (PA)
2100 W Central Ave (43606-3800)
PHONE..................................419 531-8558
Gregor K Emmert Md, *Pr*
Richard I Tapper Md, *Treas*
Mayer Waynestein Md, *VP*
Daniel S Murtagh Md, *Sec*
EMP: 30 **EST:** 1970
SQ FT: 7,000
SALES (est): 4.94MM
SALES (corp-wide): 4.94MM **Privately Held**
Web: www.promedica.org
SIC: 8062 General medical and surgical hospitals

(G-13970)
PROMEDICA HEALTH SYSTEM INC
3922 Woodley Rd Ste 100 (43606-1134)
PHONE..................................419 291-2121
EMP: 157
SALES (corp-wide): 187.07MM **Privately Held**
Web: www.promedica.org
SIC: 8062 General medical and surgical hospitals
PA: Promedica Health System, Inc.
   100 Madison Ave
   Toledo OH 43604
   567 585-9600

(G-13971)
PROMEDICA HEALTH SYSTEM INC
Also Called: Consultants In Lab Medicine
3170 W Central Ave Ste C (43606-2945)
PHONE..................................419 534-6600
Karen Varwig, *Mgr*
EMP: 346
SALES (corp-wide): 187.07MM **Privately Held**
Web: www.promedica.org
SIC: 8742 8011 Business management consultant; Offices and clinics of medical doctors
PA: Promedica Health System, Inc.
   100 Madison Ave
   Toledo OH 43604
   567 585-9600

(G-13972)
PROMEDICA HEALTH SYSTEM INC (PA)
Also Called: Promedica
100 Madison Ave (43604-1516)
PHONE..................................567 585-9600
Arturo Polizzi, *CEO*
Terry Metzger, *
Donna Zuk, *Chief Accounting Officer*
EMP: 4500 **EST:** 1986
SALES (est): 187.07MM
SALES (corp-wide): 187.07MM **Privately Held**
Web: www.promedica.org
SIC: 6324 5912 8351 8741 Health Maintenance Organization (HMO), insurance only; Drug stores; Child day care services; Management services

(G-13973)
PROMEDICA HEALTH SYSTEMS INC
Also Called: Wildwood Family Practice
2865 N Reynolds Rd Ste 130 (43615-2100)

Toledo - Lucas County (G-13974)

GEOGRAPHIC SECTION

PHONE..................419 578-7036
Cathy Cantor, *Prin*
EMP: 283
SALES (corp-wide): 187.07MM **Privately Held**
Web: www.promedica.org
SIC: 8062 General medical and surgical hospitals
PA: Promedica Health System, Inc.
100 Madison Ave
Toledo OH 43604
567 585-9600

(G-13974)
PROMEDICA HEALTH SYSTEMS INC
Also Called: PROMEDICA HEALTH SYSTEMS, INC.
2142 N Cove Blvd (43606-3895)
PHONE..................419 291-4000
Tina Johnson, *Brnch Mgr*
EMP: 1917
SALES (corp-wide): 187.07MM **Privately Held**
Web: www.promedica.org
SIC: 8062 General medical and surgical hospitals
PA: Promedica Health System, Inc.
100 Madison Ave
Toledo OH 43604
567 585-9600

(G-13975)
PROMEDICA HEALTH SYSTEMS INC
Also Called: Billing Department
300 N Summit St Ste 100 (43604-1515)
PHONE..................800 477-4035
EMP: 251
SALES (corp-wide): 187.07MM **Privately Held**
Web: www.promedica.org
SIC: 8721 Billing and bookkeeping service
PA: Promedica Health System, Inc.
100 Madison Ave
Toledo OH 43604
567 585-9600

(G-13976)
PROMEDICA TOLEDO HOSPITAL (HQ)
Also Called: PROMEDICA
2142 N Cove Blvd (43606-3895)
PHONE..................419 291-4000
Alan Brass, *CEO*
Barbara Steele, *
Cathy Hanley, *
Kevin Webb, *
EMP: 4900 **EST:** 1876
SALES (est): 1.28B
SALES (corp-wide): 187.07MM **Privately Held**
Web: www.promedica.org
SIC: 8011 8062 Medical centers; Hospital, professional nursing school with AMA residency
PA: Promedica Health System, Inc.
100 Madison Ave
Toledo OH 43604
567 585-9600

(G-13977)
PROMEDICA TOLEDO HOSPITAL
Also Called: Family Medicine Residency
2051 W Central Ave (43606-3948)
PHONE..................419 291-2051
Luoito Edje, *Prin*
EMP: 70
SALES (corp-wide): 187.07MM **Privately Held**
Web: www.promedica.org
SIC: 8062 General medical and surgical hospitals
HQ: Toledo Promedica Hospital
2142 N Cove Blvd
Toledo OH 43606
419 291-4000

(G-13978)
PROMEDICA TOLEDO HOSPITAL
Also Called: Promedica
2150 W Central Ave Ste A (43606-3859)
PHONE..................419 291-8701
Kathy Jaworski, *Mgr*
EMP: 50
SALES (corp-wide): 187.07MM **Privately Held**
Web: www.promedica.org
SIC: 8062 General medical and surgical hospitals
HQ: Toledo Promedica Hospital
2142 N Cove Blvd
Toledo OH 43606
419 291-4000

(G-13979)
PROMEDICA WLDWOOD ORTHPDIC SPI
2901 N Reynolds Rd (43615-2035)
PHONE..................419 578-7107
Kadra Ganim, *Prin*
EMP: 111 **EST:** 2011
SALES (est): 35.45MM
SALES (corp-wide): 187.07MM **Privately Held**
Web: www.promedica.org
SIC: 8062 General medical and surgical hospitals
HQ: Toledo Promedica Hospital
2142 N Cove Blvd
Toledo OH 43606
419 291-4000

(G-13980)
PUBLIC BRDCSTG FNDTION OF NW O (PA)
Also Called: Wgte-Tv-Fm
1270 S Detroit Ave (43614)
PHONE..................419 380-4600
Marlon P Kiser, *Pr*
EMP: 60 **EST:** 1953
SQ FT: 45,000
SALES (est): 4.2MM
SALES (corp-wide): 4.2MM **Privately Held**
Web: www.wgte.org
SIC: 4833 4832 Television broadcasting stations; Radio broadcasting stations

(G-13981)
RANKIN WIESENBURGER AND OTTO
Also Called: Dental Group West
5532 W Central Ave Ste 101 (43615-0713)
PHONE..................419 539-2160
Richard Thomas, *Pr*
R Weisenburger, *VP*
EMP: 51 **EST:** 1969
SALES (est): 1.49MM **Privately Held**
Web: www.dentalgroupwest.com
SIC: 8021 Dentists' office

(G-13982)
REAL ESTATE VLTION PRTNERS LLC
Also Called: Valuation Partners
300 Madison Ave Ste 900 (43604-1595)
PHONE..................281 313-1571
William Fall, *CEO*
Janice Buchele, *
Joseph Zavac, *
EMP: 50 **EST:** 2012
SALES (est): 1.24MM **Privately Held**
Web: www.opteonsolutions.com
SIC: 7389 Appraisers, except real estate

(G-13983)
RED ROOF INNS INC
Also Called: Red Roof Inn
3530 Executive Pkwy (43606-1319)
PHONE..................419 536-0118
Yolanda Dennison, *Genl Mgr*
EMP: 40
Web: www.redroof.com
SIC: 7011 Hotels and motels
HQ: Red Roof Inns, Inc.
7815 Walton Pkwy
New Albany OH 43054
614 744-2600

(G-13984)
REGENCY PARK SURGERY CTR LLC
2000 Regency Ct Ste 101 (43623-3075)
PHONE..................419 882-0003
EMP: 29 **EST:** 1997
SALES (est): 9.37MM **Privately Held**
Web: www.rpasc.com
SIC: 8011 Surgeon

(G-13985)
REGENT ELECTRIC INC
Also Called: Regent
5235 Tractor Rd (43612-3439)
PHONE..................419 476-8333
Kevin Mc Carthy, *Pr*
Brian Mc Carthy, *
Chas Slates, *
James Tice, *
Gail Taylor, *
EMP: 75 **EST:** 1957
SQ FT: 10,000
SALES (est): 5.7MM **Privately Held**
Web: www.regentelectric.com
SIC: 1731 General electrical contractor

(G-13986)
REICHLE KLEIN GROUP INC
Also Called: CB Richard Ellis
1 Seagate Fl 26 (43604-1527)
PHONE..................419 861-1100
Daniel M Klein, *Pr*
Harlan E Reichle, *VP*
EMP: 49 **EST:** 1993
SQ FT: 6,000
SALES (est): 9.4MM **Privately Held**
Web: www.rkgcommercial.com
SIC: 6531 Real estate agent, commercial

(G-13987)
REMAX PREFERRED ASSOCIATES LLC
3306 Executive Pkwy Ste 101 (43606-1335)
PHONE..................419 720-5600
EMP: 127 **EST:** 2001
SALES (est): 4.93MM **Privately Held**
Web: www.metrotoledorealestate.com
SIC: 6531 Real estate agent, residential

(G-13988)
RESCUE INCORPORATED
Also Called: RESCUE MENTAL HEALTH & ADDICTI
3350 Collingwood Blvd Ste 2 (43610-1173)
P.O. Box 80309 (43608-0309)
PHONE..................419 255-9585
John Debruyne, *CEO*
EMP: 125 **EST:** 1974
SQ FT: 13,500
SALES (est): 7.48MM **Privately Held**
Web: www.rescuemhs.com
SIC: 8063 8361 8093 Mental hospital, except for the mentally retarded; Residential care; Specialty outpatient clinics, nec

(G-13989)
REUBEN CO (PA)
24 S Huron St (43604-8706)
PHONE..................419 241-3400
George S Wade Junior, *Pr*
George S Wade Senior, *Ch Bd*
EMP: 42 **EST:** 1942
SQ FT: 1,000
SALES: 1.94MM
SALES (corp-wide): 1.94MM **Privately Held**
Web: www.reubenco.com
SIC: 6531 Real estate managers

(G-13990)
REYNOLDS ROAD SURGICAL CTR LLC
Also Called: Wildwood Surgical Center
2865 N Reynolds Rd Ste 190 (43615)
PHONE..................419 578-7500
Jackie Durkin, *Mgr*
Casey Johnson, *Mgr*
EMP: 48 **EST:** 1997
SALES (est): 6.46MM **Privately Held**
Web: www.wildwoodsurgical.com
SIC: 8011 Ambulatory surgical center

(G-13991)
RICHARD HEALTH SYSTEMS LLC
5237 Renwyck Dr Ste A (43615-5963)
PHONE..................419 534-2371
EMP: 200 **EST:** 2005
SALES (est): 10.59MM **Privately Held**
Web: www.richardhealthsystems.com
SIC: 8082 Visiting nurse service

(G-13992)
RMF NOOTER LLC
915 Matzinger Rd (43612-3820)
PHONE..................419 727-1970
Don Majchrowski, *Pr*
Jimmy Nelson, *
Mike Pollans, *
EMP: 100 **EST:** 2003
SALES (est): 57.71MM
SALES (corp-wide): 515.59MM **Privately Held**
Web: www.cicgroup.com
SIC: 1711 1731 7699 1796 Mechanical contractor; Electrical work; Boiler and heating repair services; Installing building equipment
HQ: Nooter Construction Company
1500 S 2nd St
Saint Louis MO 63104

(G-13993)
ROBERT F LINDSAY CO (PA)
4268 Rose Garden Dr (43623-3457)
PHONE..................419 476-6221
Thomas Lindsay, *Pr*
Marge Czarnecki, *
Margaret M Lindsay, *
Timothy O'leary, *VP*
Ann Veasey, *
EMP: 60 **EST:** 1951
SQ FT: 2,500
SALES (est): 1.46MM
SALES (corp-wide): 1.46MM **Privately Held**
SIC: 6531 Real estate agent, commercial

(G-13994)
ROHRBCHERS LIGHT CRONE TRIMBLE
405 Madison Ave Fl 8 (43604-1207)
PHONE..................419 471-1160
Mark Trimble, *Pr*
David J Rohrbacher, *Mgr*
Matthew Rohrbacher, *VP*

GEOGRAPHIC SECTION — Toledo - Lucas County

Diane Fockler, *Mgr*
C Randolph Light, *VP*
EMP: 42 **EST:** 1950
SALES (est): 1.64MM **Privately Held**
SIC: 8111 General practice attorney, lawyer

(G-13995)
ROMAN CATHOLIC DIOCESE TOLEDO
Also Called: Catholic Club
1601 Jefferson Ave (43604-5724)
PHONE..............................419 243-7255
Hope Bland, *Dir*
EMP: 60
SALES (corp-wide): 56.4MM **Privately Held**
Web: www.catholiccharitiesnwo.org
SIC: 8351 Child day care services
PA: The Roman Catholic Diocese Of Toledo In America
  1933 Spielbusch Ave
  Toledo OH 43604
  419 244-6711

(G-13996)
ROMAN CATHOLIC DIOCESE TOLEDO
Also Called: Diocese Tld/Catholic Cmtry Off
5725 Hill Ave (43615-5852)
PHONE..............................419 531-5747
Jack Hoeflinger, *Mgr*
EMP: 48
SALES (corp-wide): 56.4MM **Privately Held**
Web: www.toledodiocese.org
SIC: 6531 Cemetery management service
PA: The Roman Catholic Diocese Of Toledo In America
  1933 Spielbusch Ave
  Toledo OH 43604
  419 244-6711

(G-13997)
ROMANOFF ELECTRIC CO LLC
5570 Enterprise Blvd (43612-3860)
PHONE..............................937 640-7925
Dennis Quebe, *CEO*
Dana Hostdelar, *Pr*
Roger Van Der Horst, *VP Fin*
EMP: 396 **EST:** 1927
SQ FT: 21,000
SALES (est): 44.29MM
SALES (corp-wide): 12.58B **Publicly Held**
Web: www.quebeholdingsinc.com
SIC: 1731 General electrical contractor
HQ: Quebe Holdings, Inc.
  1985 Founders Dr
  Dayton OH 45420
  937 222-2290

(G-13998)
RONALD MCDONALD HSE CHRTIES NW
3883 Monroe St (43606-3930)
PHONE..............................419 471-4663
Lynda Ackerman, *Ex Dir*
EMP: 36 **EST:** 1982
SALES (est): 1.67MM **Privately Held**
Web: www.rmhctoledo.org
SIC: 8322 Social service center

(G-13999)
RUMPF CORPORATION (PA)
Also Called: Job1usa
701 Jefferson Ave (43604-6955)
P.O. Box 1480 (43603-1480)
PHONE..............................419 255-5005
Bruce F Rumpf, *CEO*
Elizabeth B Rumpf, *
EMP: 40 **EST:** 1951
SALES (est): 50.52MM

SALES (corp-wide): 50.52MM **Privately Held**
Web: www.job1usa.com
SIC: 7361 7363 7381 Employment agencies; Temporary help service; Security guard service

(G-14000)
RUSK INDUSTRIES INC
Also Called: Everdry Waterproofing Toledo
2930 Centennial Rd (43617-1833)
PHONE..............................419 841-6055
Kenneth Rusk, *Pr*
Dawn Curtis, *
EMP: 60 **EST:** 1986
SQ FT: 9,000
SALES (est): 14.13MM **Privately Held**
Web: www.everdrytoledo.com
SIC: 1799 Waterproofing

(G-14001)
RYAN SENIOR CARE LLC
Also Called: Glendale Assisted Living, The
5020 Ryan Rd (43614-2065)
PHONE..............................419 389-0800
Linda Johnson, *Ex Dir*
EMP: 100 **EST:** 2015
SALES (est): 2.61MM **Privately Held**
SIC: 6513 Retirement hotel operation

(G-14002)
SABCO INDUSTRIES INC
5242 Angola Rd Ste 150 (43615-6334)
PHONE..............................419 531-5347
Robert Sulier, *Pr*
John Pershing, *
▲ **EMP:** 28 **EST:** 1961
SALES (est): 893.85K **Privately Held**
SIC: 7699 5085 3993 3412 Tank repair and cleaning services; Barrels, new or reconditioned; Signs and advertising specialties; Metal barrels, drums, and pails

(G-14003)
SAIA MOTOR FREIGHT LINE LLC
1919 E Manhattan Blvd (43608-1534)
PHONE..............................419 726-9761
Jim Bryan, *Brnch Mgr*
EMP: 51
SALES (corp-wide): 2.88B **Publicly Held**
SIC: 4213 Contract haulers
HQ: Saia Motor Freight Line, Llc
  11465 Johns Creek Pkwy # 400
  Duluth GA 30097
  770 232-5067

(G-14004)
SAMUEL SON & CO (USA) INC
Samuel Automotive N.a
1500 Coining Dr (43612-2905)
PHONE..............................419 470-7070
EMP: 75
SALES (corp-wide): 504.18MM **Privately Held**
Web: www.samuel.com
SIC: 5051 Steel
PA: Samuel, Son & Co. (Usa) Inc.
  1401 Davey Rd Ste 300
  Woodridge IL 60517
  800 323-4424

(G-14005)
SAR ENTERPRISES LLC
Also Called: Home Instead Senior Care
2631 W Central Ave (43606-3548)
PHONE..............................419 472-8181
Lisa Rozanski, *
EMP: 46 **EST:** 2000
SALES (est): 3.02MM **Privately Held**
Web: www.homeinstead.com

SIC: 8082 Home health care services

(G-14006)
SCAR HOLDINGS LLC
505 E Alexis Rd (43612-3728)
PHONE..............................419 214-0890
Carlos Espinosa, *Pt*
EMP: 50 **EST:** 2017
SIC: 6719 Holding companies, nec

(G-14007)
SEAWAY SPONGE & CHAMOIS CO (PA)
Also Called: Seaway Building Services
458 2nd St (43605-2006)
P.O. Box 8037 (43605-0037)
PHONE..............................419 691-4694
Terry Vandervlucht, *Pr*
EMP: 45 **EST:** 1960
SALES (est): 1.04MM
SALES (corp-wide): 1.04MM **Privately Held**
SIC: 7349 5087 Janitorial service, contract basis; Janitors' supplies

(G-14008)
SENTINEL FLUID CONTROLS LLC (DH)
5702 Opportunity Dr (43612-2903)
PHONE..............................419 478-9086
Larry Peterson, *Managing Member*
Terry Moore, *
EMP: 50 **EST:** 2002
SALES (est): 13.13MM
SALES (corp-wide): 4.41B **Publicly Held**
Web: www.sentinelfluidcontrols.com
SIC: 5084 Hydraulic systems equipment and supplies
HQ: Applied Fluid Power Holdings, Llc
  330 Garnet Way Ste 1212
  Pittsburgh PA

(G-14009)
SFN GROUP INC
Also Called: Spherion Outsourcing Group
1212 E Alexis Rd (43612-3974)
PHONE..............................419 727-4104
Peter Rogowski, *Mgr*
EMP: 717
SALES (corp-wide): 28.63B **Privately Held**
Web: www.spherion.com
SIC: 7363 Temporary help service
HQ: Sfn Group, Inc.
  2050 Spectrum Blvd
  Fort Lauderdale FL 33309
  954 308-7600

(G-14010)
SHINING STAR RSDNTIAL SVCS LLC
360 S Reynolds Rd Ste A (43615-5976)
P.O. Box 146 (43528-0146)
PHONE..............................419 318-0932
EMP: 55 **EST:** 2010
SQ FT: 3,000
SALES (est): 2.08MM **Privately Held**
Web: www.thephoenixresidential.com
SIC: 8361 Rehabilitation center, residential: health care incidental

(G-14011)
SHORT FREIGHT LINES INC
6180 Benore Rd (43612-4801)
PHONE..............................419 729-1691
Dee Palmerton, *Mgr*
EMP: 38
SALES (corp-wide): 2.22MM **Privately Held**
Web: www.shortfreightlines.com
SIC: 4213 4231 Contract haulers; Trucking terminal facilities

PA: Short Freight Lines, Inc.
  459 S River Rd
  Bay City MI
  989 893-3505

(G-14012)
SHRADER TIRE & OIL INC (PA)
2045 W Sylvania Ave Ste 51 (43613-4588)
PHONE..............................419 472-2128
James W Shrader Junior, *Ch Bd*
Joseph W Schrader, *Pr*
John Shrader, *VP*
Mark Meyer, *Sec*
▲ **EMP:** 35 **EST:** 1948
SQ FT: 33,000
SALES (est): 97.58MM
SALES (corp-wide): 97.58MM **Privately Held**
Web: www.shradertireandoil.com
SIC: 5014 5172 5013 Tires and tubes; Petroleum products, nec; Motor vehicle supplies and new parts

(G-14013)
SHUMAKER LOOP & KENDRICK LLP (PA)
1000 Jackson St (43604-5573)
PHONE..............................419 241-9000
David F Waterman, *Mng Pt*
Paul Favorite, *COO*
Susan Kowlaski, *CFO*
Kenneth Crooks, *COO*
EMP: 210 **EST:** 1925
SQ FT: 110,000
SALES (est): 68.51MM
SALES (corp-wide): 68.51MM **Privately Held**
Web: www.shumaker.com
SIC: 8111 General practice attorney, lawyer

(G-14014)
SKYLIGHT FINANCIAL GROUP LLC
1 Maritime Plz Fl 4 (43604-1853)
PHONE..............................419 885-0011
Rick Rudnicki, *Pr*
EMP: 99
SALES (corp-wide): 11.05MM **Privately Held**
Web: www.skylightfinancialgroup.com
SIC: 8742 Financial consultant
PA: Skylight Financial Group, Llc
  2012 W 25th St Ste 900
  Cleveland OH 44113
  216 621-5680

(G-14015)
SLEEP NETWORK INC (PA)
3450 W Central Ave Ste 118 (43606-1418)
PHONE..............................419 535-9282
EMP: 46 **EST:** 1990
SQ FT: 3,000
SALES (est): 4.66MM **Privately Held**
SIC: 8741 Management services

(G-14016)
SLIDDY ENT LLC
Also Called: Sliddy Entertainment
417 Bronson Ave (43608-1938)
PHONE..............................419 376-1797
Charles Lee, *Prin*
Troy Reed, *
Michelle Lee, *
EMP: 50 **EST:** 2016
SALES (est): 157.21K **Privately Held**
SIC: 7929 Entertainers and entertainment groups

(G-14017)
SMB CONSTRUCTION CO INC (PA)
5120 Jackman Rd (43613-2923)
PHONE..............................419 269-1473

Toledo - Lucas County (G-14018) — GEOGRAPHIC SECTION

TOLL FREE: 800
Jim Mossing, *Pr*
Rob Keel, *
Jeff Mossing, *
EMP: 49 **EST:** 1979
SQ FT: 33,000
SALES (est): 8.46MM
SALES (corp-wide): 8.46MM **Privately Held**
Web: www.smbconstruction.com
SIC: 1521 6513 1542 Repairing fire damage, single-family houses; Apartment building operators; Commercial and office buildings, renovation and repair

(G-14018)
SOLOMON LEI & ASSOCIATES INC
Also Called: Solomon, Lei & Associates
947 Belmont Ave (43607-4244)
PHONE.................................419 246-6931
Floyd Abercrombie, *CEO*
EMP: 27 **EST:** 2016
SALES (est): 1MM **Privately Held**
SIC: 7389

(G-14019)
SPA FITNESS CENTERS INC (PA)
Also Called: Utah Spas
343 New Towne Square Dr (43612-4626)
PHONE.................................419 476-6018
Robert Rice, *Pr*
Kenneth Melby, *
EMP: 50 **EST:** 1975
SQ FT: 1,200
SALES (est): 3.46MM
SALES (corp-wide): 3.46MM **Privately Held**
Web: www.superfitnesstoledo.com
SIC: 7991 Spas

(G-14020)
SPENGLER NATHANSON PLL
4 Seagate Ste 400 (43604-2622)
PHONE.................................419 241-2201
Richard Wolff, *Mng Pt*
Truman A Greenwood, *Pt*
James R Jeffery, *Pt*
David G Wise, *Pt*
Theodore M Rowen, *Pt*
EMP: 47 **EST:** 1941
SQ FT: 26,000
SALES (est): 3.79MM **Privately Held**
Web: www.snlaw.com
SIC: 8111 General practice attorney, lawyer

(G-14021)
SPRINGLEAF FINCL HOLDINGS LLC
Also Called: Springleaf Financial Svc.
5950 Airport Hwy Ste 1 (43615-7362)
PHONE.................................419 841-0785
Gerald Oslakodic, *Brnch Mgr*
EMP: 375
SALES (corp-wide): 1.89B **Privately Held**
Web: www.onemainfinancial.com
SIC: 7389 6021 Finishing services; National commercial banks
PA: Springleaf Financial Holdings, Llc
  601 Nw 2nd St Ste 300
  Evansville IN 47708
  800 961-5577

(G-14022)
SPRINT COMMUNICATIONS CO LP
1708 W Alexis Rd (43613-2349)
PHONE.................................419 725-2444
EMP: 158
SALES (corp-wide): 78.56B **Publicly Held**
SIC: 4812 Cellular telephone services
HQ: Sprint Communications Company L.P.
  6391 Sprint Pkwy
  Overland Park KS 66251
  800 829-0965

(G-14023)
SSOE INC (PA)
Also Called: Ssoe Group
1001 Madison Ave (43604)
PHONE.................................419 255-3830
EMP: 388 **EST:** 1948
SALES (est): 154.41MM
SALES (corp-wide): 154.41MM **Privately Held**
Web: www.ssoe.com
SIC: 8711 8712 8742 1541 Structural engineering; Architectural engineering; Management consulting services; Industrial buildings and warehouses

(G-14024)
SSOE SYSTEMS INC
Also Called: Ssoe Group
1001 Madison Ave (43604-5585)
PHONE.................................419 255-3830
David F Sipes, *Pr*
James Jaros, *Sec*
Harold R Howell, *VP*
EMP: 100 **EST:** 1980
SQ FT: 25,000
SALES (est): 10.17MM
SALES (corp-wide): 154.41MM **Privately Held**
Web: www.ssoe.com
SIC: 1541 1542 Industrial buildings, new construction, nec; Nonresidential construction, nec
PA: Ssoe, Inc.
  1001 Madison Ave
  Toledo OH 43604
  419 255-3830

(G-14025)
ST ANNE MERCY HOSPITAL
Also Called: MERCY
3404 W Sylvania Ave (43623-4480)
PHONE.................................419 407-2663
Richard Evans, *CEO*
Doctor Mahjabeen M Islam Md, *Prin*
Doctor Agha Shahid Md, *Prin*
EMP: 103 **EST:** 2011
SALES (est): 144.65MM **Privately Held**
Web: www.mercy.com
SIC: 8062 General medical and surgical hospitals

(G-14026)
ST PAULS COMMUNITY CENTER
230 13th St (43604-5443)
P.O. Box 9564 (43697-9564)
PHONE.................................419 255-5520
Ruth Arden, *Ex Dir*
EMP: 34 **EST:** 1976
SQ FT: 9,464
SALES (est): 1.79MM **Privately Held**
Web: www.spcctoledo.org
SIC: 8322 Community center

(G-14027)
ST PERFORMING ARTS LLC
Also Called: Stranahan Theater & Great Hall
4645 Heatherdowns Blvd (43614-3154)
PHONE.................................419 381-8851
Laura M Contos, *Admn*
Laura M Contos, *Prin*
Stephen Hymans, *
Cheryl Byrne, *
Sarah Beavers, *
EMP: 28 **EST:** 1969
SALES (est): 2.47MM **Privately Held**
Web: www.stranahantheater.com
SIC: 6512 Nonresidential building operators

(G-14028)
STAFFWORKS GROUP 2 INC
1244 Broadway St Ste 8 (43609-2895)
PHONE.................................419 515-0655
EMP: 35
SALES (corp-wide): 14.77MM **Privately Held**
Web: www.staffworksgroup.com
SIC: 8748 Business consulting, nec
PA: Staffworks Group 2, Inc.
  42855 Garfield Rd Ste 117
  Clinton Township MI 48038
  248 416-1090

(G-14029)
SUNSET HOUSE INC
Also Called: Woodlands At Sunset House
4020 Indian Rd (43606-2292)
PHONE.................................419 536-4645
Vickie Bartlett, *CEO*
EMP: 89 **EST:** 1873
SQ FT: 1,800
SALES (est): 9.89MM **Privately Held**
Web: www.otterbein.org
SIC: 8361 8052 Aged home; Intermediate care facilities

(G-14030)
SURGICAL PARTNERS INC
Also Called: Allan Miller Do
4235 Secor Rd (43623-4231)
PHONE.................................419 841-6600
Jonathan Wright, *Prin*
Allan Miller D.o.s., *Prin*
EMP: 28 **EST:** 1990
SALES (est): 958.53K **Privately Held**
Web: www.toledoclinic.com
SIC: 8011 General and family practice, physician/surgeon

(G-14031)
SYLVANIA FRANCISCAN HEALTH
5942 Renaissance Pl Ste A (43623-4708)
PHONE.................................419 824-3674
Deb Nolan, *Prin*
EMP: 484
Web: www.sylvaniafranciscanhealth.org
SIC: 8361 Aged home
HQ: Sylvania Franciscan Health
  1715 Indian Wood Cir # 200
  Maumee OH

(G-14032)
SYNCREON AMERICA INC
Also Called: SYNCREON AMERICA INC.
1515 Matzinger Rd (43612-3828)
PHONE.................................419 727-4593
EMP: 79
Web: www.syncreon.com
SIC: 4731 Freight transportation arrangement
HQ: Syncreon America Inc
  2851 High Meadow Cir # 25
  Auburn Hills MI 48326
  248 377-4700

(G-14033)
TAS INC
433 Dearborn Ave (43605-1709)
PHONE.................................419 693-3353
Sandra Susor, *Pr*
EMP: 44 **EST:** 1992
SQ FT: 500
SALES (est): 1.08MM **Privately Held**
Web: www.tasinc.net
SIC: 1731 General electrical contractor

(G-14034)
TECOGLAS INC
3400 Executive Pkwy Ste 4 (43606-1338)
P.O. Box 2927 (43606-0927)
PHONE.................................419 537-9750
John Polcyn, *Prin*
Darrel G Howard, *
Scott Slater, *
EMP: 55 **EST:** 1976
SQ FT: 1,000
SALES (est): 496.42K
SALES (corp-wide): 43.55MM **Privately Held**
Web: www.teco.com
SIC: 8711 Engineering services
PA: Toledo Engineering Co., Inc.
  3400 Executive Pkwy Ste 4
  Toledo OH 43606
  419 537-9711

(G-14035)
TEGNA INC
Also Called: Wtol
730 N Summit St (43604-1808)
PHONE.................................419 248-1111
EMP: 120
SALES (corp-wide): 2.91B **Publicly Held**
Web: www.tegna.com
SIC: 4833 Television broadcasting stations
PA: Tegna Inc.
  8350 Broad St Ste 2000
  Tysons VA 22102
  703 873-6600

(G-14036)
TELEDYNE BROWN ENGINEERING INC
Teledyne Turbine Engines
1330 W Laskey Rd (43612-2911)
P.O. Box 12268 (43612-0268)
PHONE.................................419 470-3000
Joe Poddany, *Brnch Mgr*
EMP: 100
SALES (corp-wide): 5.64B **Publicly Held**
Web: www.tbe.com
SIC: 8734 Testing laboratories
HQ: Teledyne Brown Engineering, Inc.
  300 Sparkman Dr Nw
  Huntsville AL 35805
  256 726-1000

(G-14037)
TEMBEC BTLSR INC
2112 Sylvan Ave (43606-4767)
P.O. Box 2570 (43606-0570)
PHONE.................................419 244-5856
James M Lopez, *Pr*
Lawrence Rowley, *
Dan Wozniak, *
◆ **EMP:** 32 **EST:** 1902
SQ FT: 84,000
SALES (est): 9.65MM
SALES (corp-wide): 1.64B **Publicly Held**
Web: www.lrbgchemicals.com
SIC: 2821 5169 Plastics materials and resins; Industrial chemicals
HQ: Tembec Inc.
  100-4 Place Ville-Marie
  Montreal QC H3B 2
  514 871-0137

(G-14038)
TFORCE FREIGHT INC
3235 Nebraska Ave (43607-2817)
PHONE.................................419 537-1445
Michael Cook, *Prin*
EMP: 51
SQ FT: 66,785
SALES (corp-wide): 8.81B **Privately Held**
Web: www.tforcefreight.com
SIC: 4213 Contract haulers
HQ: Tforce Freight, Inc.
  1000 Semmes Ave
  Richmond VA 23224
  800 333-7400

GEOGRAPHIC SECTION

Toledo - Lucas County (G-14061)

(G-14039)
TG OF TOLEDO LLC (PA)
Also Called: Toledo Mirror & Glass
103 Avondale Ave (43604-8207)
PHONE.................................419 241-3151
James P Nicholson, *Managing Member*
EMP: 32 **EST:** 1918
SQ FT: 40,000
SALES (est): 2.97MM
SALES (corp-wide): 2.97MM **Privately Held**
Web: www.toledomirror.com
SIC: 1793 Glass and glazing work

(G-14040)
THE EAST TOLEDO FAMILY CTR INC (PA)
1020 Varland Ave (43605-3299)
PHONE.................................419 691-1429
Kim Partin, *Dir*
Kim Partin, *Ex Dir*
EMP: 70 **EST:** 1900
SQ FT: 23,755
SALES (est): 3.01MM
SALES (corp-wide): 3.01MM **Privately Held**
Web: www.etfc.org
SIC: 8322 Social service center

(G-14041)
THREAD INFORMATION DESIGN INC
Also Called: Thread Marketing Group
4635 W Alexis Rd (43623-1005)
PHONE.................................419 887-6801
Judy Mcfarland, *CEO*
Joe Sharp, *
EMP: 35 **EST:** 1986
SQ FT: 11,000
SALES (est): 5.62MM **Privately Held**
Web: www.threadgroup.com
SIC: 7311 Advertising agencies

(G-14042)
THYSSENKRUPP MATERIALS NA INC
1212 E Alexis Rd (43612-3974)
PHONE.................................419 662-1845
EMP: 36
SALES (corp-wide): 40.78B **Privately Held**
Web: www.thyssenkrupp-materials-na.com
SIC: 5051 Steel
HQ: Thyssenkrupp Materials Na, Inc.
22355 W 11 Mile Rd
Southfield MI 48033
248 233-5600

(G-14043)
TJ METZGERS INC
Also Called: Metzgers
207 Arco Dr (43607-2906)
PHONE.................................419 861-8611
EMP: 72 **EST:** 1976
SQ FT: 63,146
SALES (est): 13.39MM **Privately Held**
Web: www.metzgers.com
SIC: 2789 2791 7335 2752 Bookbinding and related work; Photocomposition, for the printing trade; Color separation, photographic and movie film; Offset printing

(G-14044)
TK HOMECARE LLC
Also Called: Visiting Angels
7110 W Central Ave Ste A (43617-3118)
PHONE.................................419 517-7000
Tamera Riggs, *Pr*
EMP: 132 **EST:** 2007
SALES (est): 4.14MM **Privately Held**
Web: www.visitingangels.com
SIC: 8082 Home health care services

(G-14045)
TKY ASSOCIATES LLC
Also Called: Comfort Keepers
2451 N Reynolds Rd (43615-2840)
PHONE.................................419 535-7777
Todd A Kuney, *Managing Member*
Julie Kuney, *Genl Mgr*
EMP: 30 **EST:** 2011
SQ FT: 1,600
SALES (est): 2.21MM **Privately Held**
Web: www.comfortkeepers.com
SIC: 8082 8049 Home health care services; Nurses and other medical assistants

(G-14046)
TLEVAY INC
Also Called: Foundation Pk Alzheimers Care
1621 S Byrne Rd (43614-3456)
PHONE.................................419 385-3958
EMP: 248 **EST:** 2009
SALES (est): 34.19K
SALES (corp-wide): 16.25MM **Privately Held**
Web: www.foundationpark.com
SIC: 8051 Skilled nursing care facilities
PA: Nursing Care Management Of America, Inc.
7265 Kenwood Rd Ste 300
Cincinnati OH 45236
513 793-8804

(G-14047)
TM FINAL LTD
1549 Campbell St (43607-4321)
P.O. Box 3456 (43607-0456)
PHONE.................................419 724-8473
Randy Jones, *Pt*
Bradley Cox, *Pt*
EMP: 265 **EST:** 1981
SQ FT: 40,000
SALES (est): 24.27MM **Privately Held**
Web: www.thetireman.com
SIC: 5531 7538 Automotive tires; General automotive repair shops

(G-14048)
TOLCO CORPORATION (PA)
Also Called: Tolco
1920 Linwood Ave (43604-5293)
PHONE.................................419 241-1113
George L Notarianni, *Pr*
◆ **EMP:** 72 **EST:** 1961
SQ FT: 30,000
SALES (est): 21.61MM
SALES (corp-wide): 21.61MM **Privately Held**
Web: www.tolcocorp.com
SIC: 5085 3563 3586 3561 Bottler supplies; Spraying outfits: metals, paints, and chemicals (compressor); Measuring and dispensing pumps; Pumps and pumping equipment

(G-14049)
TOLEDO AREA INSULATOR WKRS JAC
Also Called: Heat and Frost Insulators Jatc
4535 Hill Ave (43615-5301)
PHONE.................................419 531-5911
EMP: 85
SALES (est): 1.66MM **Privately Held**
SIC: 1799 Special trade contractors, nec

(G-14050)
TOLEDO AREA RGIONAL TRNST AUTH (PA)
Also Called: Tarta
1127 W Central Ave (43610-1062)
P.O. Box 792 (43697-0792)
PHONE.................................419 243-7433
James K Gee, *Genl Mgr*
EMP: 319 **EST:** 1971
SQ FT: 8,000
SALES (est): 50.15MM
SALES (corp-wide): 50.15MM **Privately Held**
Web: www.tarta.com
SIC: 4111 Bus line operations

(G-14051)
TOLEDO BAR ASSOCIATION INC
311 N Superior St (43604-1421)
PHONE.................................419 242-9363
Trish Branam, *Dir*
The Honourable Marsh Manaham, *Pr*
EMP: 50 **EST:** 1878
SALES (est): 1.02MM **Privately Held**
Web: www.toledobar.org
SIC: 8621 8111 Bar association; Legal services

(G-14052)
TOLEDO BUILDING SERVICES CO
2121 Adams St (43604-5088)
P.O. Box 2223 (43603-2223)
PHONE.................................419 241-3101
Joel B Friedman, *Ch Bd*
Judith Friedman, *
Ward Whiting, *
Lawrence M Friedman, *
EMP: 940 **EST:** 1909
SQ FT: 20,000
SALES (est): 14.6MM **Privately Held**
Web: www.toledobuildingservices.com
SIC: 7349 Janitorial service, contract basis

(G-14053)
TOLEDO CARDIOLOGY CONS INC (PA)
2409 Cherry St Ste 100 (43608-2670)
PHONE.................................419 251-6183
Thomas G Welch Md, *Pr*
Ameer Kabour Md, *VP*
EMP: 40 **EST:** 1973
SQ FT: 8,000
SALES (est): 6.25MM **Privately Held**
Web: www.toledocardiology.com
SIC: 8011 Cardiologist and cardio-vascular specialist

(G-14054)
TOLEDO CLINIC INC (PA)
4235 Secor Rd (43623-4299)
PHONE.................................419 473-3561
Ian S Elliot, *Pr*
Wiliam Sternfeld, *
Sanjiv Bais, *
Timothy Husted, *
E L Doermann, *
▲ **EMP:** 500 **EST:** 1962
SQ FT: 14,600
SALES (est): 119.13MM
SALES (corp-wide): 119.13MM **Privately Held**
Web: www.toledoclinic.com
SIC: 8011 Physicians' office, including specialists

(G-14055)
TOLEDO CLINIC INC
3909 Woodley Rd Ste 800 (43606-1169)
PHONE.................................419 841-1600
EMP: 83
SALES (corp-wide): 119.13MM **Privately Held**
Web: www.toledoclinic.com
SIC: 8011 Physicians' office, including specialists
PA: Toledo Clinic, Inc.
4235 Secor Rd
Toledo OH 43623
419 473-3561

(G-14056)
TOLEDO CLINIC INC
1414 S Byrne Rd (43614-2363)
PHONE.................................419 381-9977
EMP: 83
SALES (corp-wide): 119.13MM **Privately Held**
Web: www.toledoclinic.com
SIC: 8043 Offices and clinics of podiatrists
PA: Toledo Clinic, Inc.
4235 Secor Rd
Toledo OH 43623
419 473-3561

(G-14057)
TOLEDO CLINIC INC
Also Called: Toledo Clinic Physical Therapy
4235 Secor Rd (43623-4299)
PHONE.................................419 479-5960
Tom Schlembach, *Mgr*
EMP: 84
SALES (corp-wide): 119.13MM **Privately Held**
Web: www.toledoclinic.com
SIC: 8049 Physical therapist
PA: Toledo Clinic, Inc.
4235 Secor Rd
Toledo OH 43623
419 473-3561

(G-14058)
TOLEDO CLUB
709 Madison Ave Ste 305 (43604-5475)
PHONE.................................419 243-2200
Ronald Paerson, *Pr*
EMP: 78 **EST:** 1889
SALES (est): 6.56MM **Privately Held**
Web: www.toledoclub.org
SIC: 7997 8641 Country club, membership; Social club, membership

(G-14059)
TOLEDO INN NORTH LLC
Also Called: Comfort Inn
445 E Alexis Rd (43612-3708)
PHONE.................................419 476-0170
Mary Mpehrson, *Prin*
EMP: 50 **EST:** 1998
SQ FT: 36,226
SALES (est): 495.8K **Privately Held**
Web: www.choicehotels.com
SIC: 7011 Hotels and motels

(G-14060)
TOLEDO INNVTION CTR LNDLORD LL
100 Madison Ave (43604-1516)
PHONE.................................419 585-3684
EMP: 157 **EST:** 2021
SALES (est): 509.38K
SALES (corp-wide): 187.07MM **Privately Held**
SIC: 8741 Management services
PA: Promedica Health System, Inc.
100 Madison Ave
Toledo OH 43604
567 585-9600

(G-14061)
TOLEDO MTRO AREA CNCIL GVRNMNT
300 Martin Luther King Jr Dr Ste 300 (43604-8815)
P.O. Box 9508 (43697-9508)
PHONE.................................419 241-9155
Anthony L Reams, *Pr*
Mark Stahl, *
EMP: 27 **EST:** 1968

Toledo - Lucas County (G-14062)

SQ FT: 12,200
SALES (est): 4.23MM **Privately Held**
Web: www.tmacog.org
SIC: **8748** City planning

(G-14062)
TOLEDO MUD HENS BASBAL CLB INC
Also Called: Toledo Mud Hens
406 Washington St Fl 5 (43604)
PHONE.................................419 725-4367
Michael Miller, *Owner*
Joe Napoli, *
Charles Bracken, *
EMP: 85 EST: 1964
SALES (est): 10.81MM **Privately Held**
Web: www.mudhens.com
SIC: **7997** Baseball club, except professional and semi-professional

(G-14063)
TOLEDO MUSEUM OF ART
2445 Monroe St (43620-1500)
P.O. Box 1013 (43697-1013)
PHONE.................................419 255-8000
Brian Kennedy, *Pr*
Carol Bintz, *
Mary K Siefke, *
Todd Ahrens, *
Kathy Danko-mcghee, *Dir*
▲ EMP: 225 EST: 1901
SQ FT: 200,000
SALES (est): 28.97MM **Privately Held**
Web: www.toledomuseum.org
SIC: **8412** Museum

(G-14064)
TOLEDO RGONAL CHAMBER COMMERCE
300 Madison Ave Ste 200 (43604-1568)
PHONE.................................419 243-8191
Wendy Gramza, *Pr*
EMP: 58 EST: 1894
SALES (est): 3.35MM **Privately Held**
Web: www.toledochamber.com
SIC: **8611** 8742 Chamber of Commerce; Financial consultant

(G-14065)
TOLEDO SCIENCE CENTER
Also Called: IMAGINATION STATION
1 Discovery Way (43604-1579)
PHONE.................................419 244-2674
Lori Hauser, *Ex Dir*
Chip Hambro, *
Daniel Frick, *
EMP: 50 EST: 1996
SQ FT: 100,000
SALES (est): 5.09MM **Privately Held**
Web: www.imaginationstationtoledo.org
SIC: **8412** Museum

(G-14066)
TOLEDO SOCIETY FOR THE BLIND
Also Called: SIGHT CENTER OF NORTHWEST OHIO
1002 Garden Lake Pkwy (43614-2780)
PHONE.................................419 720-3937
Stacey Butts, *Dir*
EMP: 44 EST: 1923
SQ FT: 32,000
SALES (est): 1.45MM **Privately Held**
Web: www.sightcentertoledo.org
SIC: **8082** 8042 Home health care services; Low vision specialist optometrist

(G-14067)
TOLEDO WALLEYE PROF HOCKEY CLB
Also Called: Toledo Walleye Hockey
500 Jefferson Ave (43604-1010)
PHONE.................................419 725-4350
Joe Napoli, *Pr*
EMP: 71 EST: 2013
SALES (est): 436.95K **Privately Held**
Web: www.toledowalleye.com
SIC: **7997** Membership sports and recreation clubs

(G-14068)
TOLEDO ZOO
2700 Broadway St (43609-3100)
P.O. Box 140130 (43614-0130)
PHONE.................................419 385-5721
Lorie Wittler, *Dir*
Jeff Sailer, *Dir*
EMP: 42
SALES (est): 7.96MM **Privately Held**
Web: www.toledozoo.org
SIC: **8422** Animal and reptile exhibit

(G-14069)
TOLEDO ZOOLOGICAL SOCIETY (PA)
2 Hippo Way (43609-4100)
P.O. Box 140130 (43614-0130)
PHONE.................................419 385-4040
Lamont Thurston, *Pr*
Anne Baker, *
EMP: 183 EST: 1900
SALES (est): 6.26MM
SALES (corp-wide): 6.26MM **Privately Held**
Web: www.toledozoo.org
SIC: **8422** Zoological garden, noncommercial

(G-14070)
TOLEDO ZOOLOGICAL SOCIETY
749 Spencer St (43609-2929)
PHONE.................................419 385-4040
EMP: 267
SALES (corp-wide): 6.26MM **Privately Held**
Web: www.toledozoo.org
SIC: **8422** Zoological garden, noncommercial
PA: The Toledo Zoological Society
     2 Hippo Way
     Toledo OH 43609
     419 385-4040

(G-14071)
TOTAL WIRELESS
2005 Glendale Ave (43614-2802)
PHONE.................................419 724-2363
EMP: 63 EST: 2018
SALES (est): 594.07K **Privately Held**
SIC: **4812** Cellular telephone services

(G-14072)
TOWLIFT INC
Also Called: Forklift of Toledo
140 N Byrne Rd (43607-2603)
PHONE.................................419 531-6110
James Schuller, *Brnch Mgr*
EMP: 35
SQ FT: 14,408
SALES (corp-wide): 246.16MM **Privately Held**
Web: www.forkliftsoftoledo.com
SIC: **5084** Materials handling machinery
HQ: Towlift, Inc.
     1395 Valley Belt Rd
     Brooklyn Heights OH 44131
     216 749-6800

(G-14073)
TRANSTAR ELECTRIC INC
Also Called: Transtar Electric SEC & Tech
767 Warehouse Rd (43615-6491)
PHONE.................................419 385-7573
Daniel L Bollin, *Pr*
Scott Bollin, *
Becky Bollin, *
EMP: 60 EST: 1978
SQ FT: 7,000
SALES (est): 13.03MM **Privately Held**
Web: www.transtarcorp.com
SIC: **1731** General electrical contractor

(G-14074)
TRIANGLE LEASING CORP
6041 Benore Rd (43612-3964)
P.O. Box 6996 (43612-0996)
PHONE.................................419 729-3868
Richard Clair, *Pr*
James Clair, *VP*
EMP: 30 EST: 1984
SQ FT: 3,600
SALES (est): 897.15K **Privately Held**
Web: www.nsttransport.com
SIC: **7513** 4212 4213 Truck rental and leasing, no drivers; Local trucking, without storage; Trucking, except local

(G-14075)
TSL LTD (PA)
5217 Monroe St Ste A1 (43623-4604)
P.O. Box 23100 (43623-0100)
PHONE.................................419 843-3200
Donald J Finnegan, *Pr*
Anne Marlow, *
EMP: 2495 EST: 1986
SQ FT: 3,600
SALES (est): 27.54MM
SALES (corp-wide): 27.54MM **Privately Held**
Web: www.tsl1.com
SIC: **7363** Truck driver services

(G-14076)
TTL ASSOCIATES INC (HQ)
1915 N 12th St (43604-5305)
PHONE.................................419 241-4556
Thomas Uhler, *CEO*
Robert Ruse, *
Jeffrey Elliot, *
Curtis Roupe, *
EMP: 70 EST: 2003
SQ FT: 40,000
SALES (est): 24.69MM
SALES (corp-wide): 34.37MM **Privately Held**
Web: www.ctconsultants.com
SIC: **8711** 8748 8741 Consulting engineer; Environmental consultant; Construction management
PA: C.T. Consultants, Inc.
     8150 Sterling Ct
     Mentor OH 44060
     440 951-9000

(G-14077)
TUFFY ASSOCIATES CORP (PA)
Also Called: Tuffy Auto Service Centers
7150 Granite Cir Ste 100 (43617-3114)
PHONE.................................419 865-6900
Adina Harel, *Ch Bd*
Roger Hill, *
Yoav Navon, *
Albert Nissim, *
Karen Velliquette, *
EMP: 50 EST: 1970
SQ FT: 5,000
SALES (est): 104.71MM
SALES (corp-wide): 104.71MM **Privately Held**
Web: www.tuffy.com
SIC: **6794** 7533 7539 Franchises, selling or licensing; Muffler shop, sale or repair and installation; Brake repair, automotive

(G-14078)
U HAUL CO OF NORTHWESTERN OHIO (DH)
Also Called: U-Haul
50 W Alexis Rd (43612-3692)
PHONE.................................419 478-1101
Lonnie Enderle, *Pr*
Christopher Johnson, *
Pamela D Davis, *
Ali Gillentine, *
EMP: 40 EST: 2000
SQ FT: 14,000
SALES (est): 10.33MM
SALES (corp-wide): 5.86B **Publicly Held**
Web: offline.uhaul.com
SIC: **7513** 7519 7359 Truck rental and leasing, no drivers; Trailer rental; Equipment rental and leasing, nec
HQ: U-Haul International, Inc.
     2727 N Central Ave
     Phoenix AZ 85004
     602 263-6011

(G-14079)
U S RAIL CORPORATION OF OHIO
Also Called: U S Rail Holdings
7846 W Central Ave (43617-1530)
PHONE.................................419 720-7588
Gabriel D Hall, *Pr*
Danielle Hall, *VP*
EMP: 43 EST: 2004
SQ FT: 4,000
SALES (est): 2.2MM **Privately Held**
Web: www.usrailcorp.com
SIC: **4011** Railroads, line-haul operating

(G-14080)
U S XPRESS INC
401 Adams St (43604-1401)
PHONE.................................419 244-6384
EMP: 416
Web: www.usxpress.com
SIC: **4213** Trucking, except local
HQ: U. S. Xpress, Inc.
     4080 Jenkins Rd
     Chattanooga TN 37421
     866 266-7270

(G-14081)
UNISON BHVIORAL HLTH GROUP INC (PA)
1425 Starr Ave (43605-2456)
P.O. Box 10015 (43699-0015)
PHONE.................................419 214-4673
Jeff De Lay, *Pr*
Stacey Bock, *
Deborah Krohn, *
Lee Vivod, *
Melissa Studer, *
EMP: 75 EST: 1972
SQ FT: 17,100
SALES (est): 23.67MM
SALES (corp-wide): 23.67MM **Privately Held**
Web: www.unisonhealth.org
SIC: **8093** Mental health clinic, outpatient

(G-14082)
UNITED COLLECTION BUREAU INC (PA)
Also Called: Ucb
5620 Southwyck Blvd (43614-1501)
PHONE.................................419 866-6227
Harold Sam Rickard, *Ch Bd*
Sanju Sharma, *
Harold S Rickard Iii, *Pr*
Margaret Rickard, *
Joan Overcashier, *
EMP: 165 EST: 1959
SQ FT: 3,500
SALES (est): 62.18MM

GEOGRAPHIC SECTION
Toledo - Lucas County (G-14104)

SALES (corp-wide): 62.18MM **Privately Held**
Web: www.ucbinc.com
SIC: 7322 Collection agency, except real estate

(G-14083)
UNITED PARCEL SERVICE INC
Also Called: UPS
1212 E Alexis Rd (43612-3974)
PHONE..............................419 891-6841
EMP: 31
SALES (corp-wide): 90.96B **Publicly Held**
Web: www.ups.com
SIC: 4215 Package delivery, vehicular
HQ: United Parcel Service, Inc.
55 Glenlake Pkwy
Atlanta GA 30328
404 828-6000

(G-14084)
UNITED WAY OF GREATER TOLEDO (PA)
Also Called: UNITED WAY
1001 Madison Ave # 100 (43604-5535)
PHONE..............................419 254-4742
Bill Kitson, CEO
Jane Moore, VP
Kim Sidwell, VP
Kathleen Doty, VP
EMP: 35 EST: 1918
SALES (est): 7.87MM
SALES (corp-wide): 7.87MM **Privately Held**
Web: www.unitedwaytoledo.org
SIC: 8322 Social service center

(G-14085)
UNIVERSAL MARKETING GROUP LLC
5454 Airport Hwy (43615-7302)
PHONE..............................419 720-6581
Jason Birch, CFO
Steven Horst, *
EMP: 99 EST: 2003
SALES (est): 10.33MM **Privately Held**
Web: www.umg1.com
SIC: 8742 5963 Marketing consulting services; Direct sales, telemarketing

(G-14086)
UNIVERSITY OF TOLEDO
Also Called: University of Toledo Med Ctr
3000 Arlington Ave (43614-2598)
PHONE..............................419 383-4000
EMP: 3200
SALES (corp-wide): 864.43MM **Privately Held**
Web: www.utoledo.edu
SIC: 8062 8221 Hospital, affiliated with AMA residency; College, except junior
PA: The University Of Toledo
2801 W Bancroft St
Toledo OH 43606
419 530-4636

(G-14087)
UNIVERSITY OF TOLEDO
Also Called: Health Science Campus
3000 Arlington Ave (43614-2598)
PHONE..............................419 383-5322
Jeffrey Gold, Pr
EMP: 29
SALES (corp-wide): 864.43MM **Privately Held**
Web: www.utoledo.edu
SIC: 8011 8221 Radiologist; University
PA: The University Of Toledo
2801 W Bancroft St
Toledo OH 43606
419 530-4636

(G-14088)
UNIVERSITY TLEDO PHYSICIANS LLC
4510 Dorr St (43615-4040)
PHONE..............................419 931-0030
Christopher Cooper Md, Ch Bd
EMP: 50 EST: 2004
SALES (est): 7.75MM **Privately Held**
Web: www.utoledophysicians.com
SIC: 8099 Medical services organization

(G-14089)
VALUCENTRIC LLC
300 Madison Ave (43604-1595)
PHONE..............................410 912-2085
Maria Jock, Prin
EMP: 33 EST: 2016
SALES (est): 2.02MM **Privately Held**
Web: www.valucentric.com
SIC: 6531 Appraiser, real estate

(G-14090)
VAN DYK MORTGAGE CORPORATION
111 N Reynolds Rd (43615-5257)
PHONE..............................419 720-4384
EMP: 27
SALES (corp-wide): 108.25MM **Privately Held**
Web: www.vandykmortgage.com
SIC: 6211 6162 Mortgages, buying and selling; Mortgage bankers and loan correspondents
PA: Van Dyk Mortgage Corporation
2449 Camelot Ct Se
Grand Rapids MI 49546
616 940-3000

(G-14091)
VCA ANIMAL HOSPITALS INC
Also Called: VCA Holly Farms
6705 W Bancroft St (43615-3002)
PHONE..............................419 841-3323
EMP: 42
SQ FT: 3,227
SALES (corp-wide): 42.84B **Privately Held**
Web: www.vcahospitals.com
SIC: 0742 Animal hospital services, pets and other animal specialties
HQ: Vca Animal Hospitals, Inc.
12401 W Olympic Blvd
Los Angeles CA 90064

(G-14092)
VESTIS CORPORATION
Also Called: Aramark
5120 Advantage Dr (43612-3876)
PHONE..............................419 729-5454
Tom Schrishuhn, Mgr
EMP: 150
SQ FT: 17,920
SALES (corp-wide): 2.83B **Publicly Held**
Web: www.vestis.com
SIC: 7218 7213 Industrial uniform supply; Uniform supply
PA: Vestis Corporation
500 Colonial Center Pkwy # 1
Roswell GA 30076
470 226-3655

(G-14093)
VISION ASSOCIATES INC (PA)
Also Called: Ofori, Jason MD
2865 N Reynolds Rd Ste 170 (43615-2076)
PHONE..............................419 578-7598
Rodney Mccarthy, Prin
EMP: 48 EST: 1997
SALES (est): 11.84MM
SALES (corp-wide): 11.84MM **Privately Held**
Web: www.promedica.org
SIC: 8011 Opthalmologist

(G-14094)
VISTULA MANAGEMENT COMPANY
1931 Scottwood Ave Ste 700 (43620-1614)
P.O. Box 4719 (43610-0719)
PHONE..............................419 242-2300
John Kiely, CEO
Kathleen Crowley, *
Douglas Wilkins, *
EMP: 70 EST: 1980
SALES (est): 1.93MM **Privately Held**
Web: www.vmc.org
SIC: 6531 Real estate managers

(G-14095)
W GTE TV 30 FM 91 PUB BRDCSTG
1270 S Detroit Ave (43614-2794)
P.O. Box 30 (43614-0030)
PHONE..............................419 380-4600
Marlon Kiser, Prin
EMP: 61 EST: 1953
SALES (est): 401.93K **Privately Held**
Web: www.wgte.org
SIC: 4833 Television broadcasting stations

(G-14096)
WABE MAQUAW HOLDINGS INC
17 Corey Creek Rd (43623-1183)
PHONE..............................419 243-1191
Dennis G Johnson, Pr
Paul E Johnson, *
Kevin Brennan, *
Ben Brown, *
Paul Johnson, *
EMP: 90 EST: 1922
SQ FT: 20,000
SALES (est): 14.26MM **Privately Held**
SIC: 6411 Insurance agents, nec

(G-14097)
WASHINGTON LOCAL SCHOOLS
Also Called: Bus Garage & Maintenance Dept
5201 Douglas Rd (43613-2640)
PHONE..............................419 473-8356
John Bettis, Mgr
EMP: 37
SALES (corp-wide): 116.11MM **Privately Held**
Web: www.wls4kids.org
SIC: 4173 4151 Maintenance facilities for motor vehicle passenger transport; School buses
PA: Washington Local Schools
3505 W Lincolnshire Blvd Of
Toledo OH 43606
419 473-8224

(G-14098)
WATERMARK RTRMENT CMMNTIES INC
Also Called: Fountains At Canterbury
4500 Dorr St (43615-4040)
PHONE..............................405 751-3600
Danny Eischen, Mgr
EMP: 70
Web: www.watermarkcommunities.com
SIC: 8361 8051 Residential care; Skilled nursing care facilities
HQ: Watermark Retirement Communities, Inc.
2020 W Rudasill Rd
Tucson AZ 85704

(G-14099)
WEBMD HEALTH CORP
100 N Byrne Rd (43607-2603)
P.O. Box 3494 (43607-0494)
PHONE..............................419 324-8000
Carol Demario, Prin
EMP: 48 EST: 2010
SALES (est): 1.33MM **Privately Held**

SIC: 8099 Health and allied services, nec

(G-14100)
WELCH PACKAGING GROUP INC
Also Called: Welch Packaging
1240 Matzinger Rd (43612-3849)
PHONE..............................419 726-3491
Robert Dorst, Prin
EMP: 150
SALES (corp-wide): 457.79MM **Privately Held**
Web: www.welchpkg.com
SIC: 5199 Packaging materials
PA: Welch Packaging Group, Inc.
1020 Herman St
Elkhart IN 46516
574 295-2460

(G-14101)
WELLES-BOWEN REALTY INC
2460 N Reynolds Rd (43615-2884)
PHONE..............................419 535-0011
David Browning, Pr
Kevin Smith, *
EMP: 174 EST: 1988
SALES (est): 2.8MM **Privately Held**
Web: www.wellesbowen.com
SIC: 6531 6163 Real estate agent, residential ; Mortgage brokers arranging for loans, using money of others

(G-14102)
WELLTOWER INC (PA)
4500 Dorr St (43615-4040)
PHONE..............................419 247-2800
Shankh Mitra, CEO
Kenneth J Bacon, Ch Bd
John F Burkart, Ex VP
Timothy G Mchugh, Ex VP
Matthew G Mcqueen, Corporate Secretary
EMP: 78 EST: 1970
SALES (est): 5.86B
SALES (corp-wide): 5.86B **Publicly Held**
Web: www.welltower.com
SIC: 6798 Real estate investment trusts

(G-14103)
WELLTOWER OP LLC (HQ)
Also Called: Welltower Inc.
4500 Dorr St (43615-4040)
PHONE..............................419 247-2800
Shankh Mitra, CIO
Kenneth J Bacon, *
Joshua T Fieweger, CAO
Timothy G Mchugh, Sr VP
Matthew G Mcqueen, Corporate Secretary
▲ EMP: 100 EST: 1970
SALES (est): 4.61B
SALES (corp-wide): 5.86B **Publicly Held**
Web: www.welltower.com
SIC: 6513 6798 Apartment building operators ; Real estate investment trusts
PA: Welltower Inc.
4500 Dorr St
Toledo OH 43615
419 247-2800

(G-14104)
WEST SIDE MONTESSORI
7115 W Bancroft St (43615)
PHONE..............................419 866-1931
Lynn Fisher, Pr
EMP: 85 EST: 1975
SQ FT: 22,700
SALES (est): 8.14MM **Privately Held**
Web: www.montessoritoledo.org
SIC: 8211 8351 Private elementary school; Montessori child development center

Toledo - Lucas County (G-14105) — GEOGRAPHIC SECTION

(G-14105)
WEST TOLEDO ANIMAL HOSP LTD
Also Called: Hoffman, Debbie
4404 Secor Rd (43623-4236)
PHONE...............................419 475-1527
James R Galvin D.v.m., *Owner*
EMP: 28 **EST:** 1948
SQ FT: 3,790
SALES (est): 4.98MM **Privately Held**
Web: www.westtoledoanimalhospital.com
SIC: 0742 Animal hospital services, pets and other animal specialties

(G-14106)
WESTROCK COMMERCIAL LLC
1635 Coining Dr (43612-2906)
PHONE...............................419 476-9101
EMP: 53
SALES (corp-wide): 20.31B **Publicly Held**
SIC: 5112 2752 Stationery and office supplies; Commercial printing, lithographic
HQ: Westrock Commercial, Llc
501 S 5th St
Richmond VA 23219
804 444-1000

(G-14107)
WICHMAN CO
Also Called: Arlington Commercial Supply
7 N Westwood Ave (43607-3339)
PHONE...............................419 385-6438
Edwin A Wichman, *CEO*
Paul B Bires, *Pr*
EMP: 31 **EST:** 1969
SQ FT: 5,500
SALES (est): 1.6MM **Privately Held**
Web: www.arlingtonsupply.com
SIC: 1711 Warm air heating and air conditioning contractor

(G-14108)
WILLIAMFALL GROUP INC
300 Madison Ave (43604-1561)
PHONE...............................419 418-5252
William Schlosser, *Admn*
EMP: 32 **EST:** 2019
SALES (est): 215.49K **Privately Held**
Web: www.williamfallgroup.com
SIC: 6531 Appraiser, real estate

(G-14109)
WTVG INC
Also Called: Wtvg 13 ABC
4247 Dorr St (43607-2134)
PHONE...............................419 531-1313
EMP: 100
SIC: 4833 Television broadcasting stations

(G-14110)
WURTEC INCORPORATED (PA)
6200 Brent Dr (43611-1081)
PHONE...............................419 726-1066
Steven P Wurth, *Pr*
Jane A Wurth, *
◆ **EMP:** 62 **EST:** 1985
SQ FT: 43,000
SALES (est): 27.61MM
SALES (corp-wide): 27.61MM **Privately Held**
Web: www.wurtec.com
SIC: 5065 5084 Telephone and telegraphic equipment; Elevators

(G-14111)
YARK AUTOMOTIVE GROUP INC (PA)
Also Called: Yark Subaru
3335 Meijer Dr Ste 400 (43617-3105)
PHONE...............................419 841-7771
Douglas Kearns, *CEO*
John W Yark, *
Max Forster, *
Dj Yark, *
EMP: 300 **EST:** 1971
SALES (est): 155.32MM
SALES (corp-wide): 155.32MM **Privately Held**
Web: www.yarkauto.com
SIC: 5511 7515 7521 Automobiles, new and used; Passenger car leasing; Indoor parking services

(G-14112)
YOUNG MNS CHRSTN ASSN OF GRTER
Also Called: YMCA
1500 N Superior St Fl 2 (43604-2149)
PHONE...............................419 474-3995
Regina Carter, *Prin*
EMP: 63
SALES (corp-wide): 29.37MM **Privately Held**
Web: www.ymcatoledo.org
SIC: 8641 7991 8351 7032 Youth organizations; Physical fitness facilities; Child day care services; Youth camps
PA: The Young Men's Christian Association Of Greater Toledo
6465 Sylvania Ave
Sylvania OH 43560
419 729-8135

(G-14113)
YOUNG MNS CHRSTN ASSN OF GRTER
Also Called: YMCA
2110 Tremainsville Rd (43613-3409)
PHONE...............................419 475-3496
Jason Trame, *Ex Dir*
EMP: 84
SALES (corp-wide): 29.37MM **Privately Held**
Web: www.ymcatoledo.org
SIC: 8641 Youth organizations
PA: The Young Men's Christian Association Of Greater Toledo
6465 Sylvania Ave
Sylvania OH 43560
419 729-8135

(G-14114)
YOUNG MNS CHRSTN ASSN OF GRTER
5025 Glendale Ave (43614-1855)
PHONE...............................419 381-7980
Sherry Shaffer, *Prin*
EMP: 64
SALES (corp-wide): 29.37MM **Privately Held**
Web: www.ymcatoledo.org
SIC: 8641 Youth organizations
PA: The Young Men's Christian Association Of Greater Toledo
6465 Sylvania Ave
Sylvania OH 43560
419 729-8135

(G-14115)
YOUNG MNS CHRSTN ASSN OF GRTER
Also Called: Y. M. C. A.
2053 N 14th St (43620-1912)
PHONE...............................419 241-7218
Michael Ashford, *Prin*
EMP: 84
SALES (corp-wide): 29.37MM **Privately Held**
Web: www.ymcatoledo.org

SIC: 8641 7991 8351 7032 Youth organizations; Physical fitness facilities; Child day care services; Youth camps
PA: The Young Men's Christian Association Of Greater Toledo
6465 Sylvania Ave
Sylvania OH 43560
419 729-8135

(G-14116)
YOUNG WNS CHRSTN ASSN OF LIMA
Also Called: YWCA
1018 Jefferson Ave (43604-5941)
PHONE...............................419 241-3230
Jennifer Lawson, *Dir*
Carol Simons, *
EMP: 49 **EST:** 1919
SQ FT: 5,156
SALES (est): 478.09K **Privately Held**
Web: www.ywcanwo.org
SIC: 8641 Youth organizations

(G-14117)
YWCA OF NORTHWEST OHIO
Also Called: YWCA
1018 Jefferson Ave (43604-5944)
PHONE...............................419 241-3235
Lisa Mcduffie, *Ex Dir*
Shelly Ulrich, *
Taryn Payne, *
Teri Sass, *
EMP: 78 **EST:** 1891
SQ FT: 82,470
SALES (est): 8.55MM **Privately Held**
Web: www.ywcanwo.org
SIC: 8351 7032 8322 Child day care services; Youth camps; Emergency shelters

(G-14118)
ZEIGLER HABILITATION HOMES INC
540 Independence Rd (43607-2650)
PHONE...............................419 973-7629
Michael Zeigler, *Prin*
EMP: 40 **EST:** 2004
SALES (est): 2.15MM **Privately Held**
SIC: 1521 Single-family housing construction

(G-14119)
ZEPF CENTER (PA)
6605 W Central Ave Ste 100 (43617)
PHONE...............................419 841-7701
Adam Nutt, *Admn*
Adam Nutt, *CFO*
EMP: 70 **EST:** 1974
SQ FT: 25,000
SALES (est): 39.28MM
SALES (corp-wide): 39.28MM **Privately Held**
Web: www.zepfcenter.org
SIC: 8069 8093 Drug addiction rehabilitation hospital; Mental health clinic, outpatient

(G-14120)
ZEPF HOUSING CORP ONE INC
Also Called: Ottawa House
5310 Hill Ave (43615)
PHONE...............................419 531-0019
Kendell Alexander, *Ex Dir*
EMP: 283 **EST:** 1985
SALES (est): 89.37K
SALES (corp-wide): 39.28MM **Privately Held**
Web: www.zepfcenter.org
SIC: 6513 Apartment building operators
PA: Zepf Center
6605 W Central Ave
Toledo OH 43617
419 841-7701

Toronto
Jefferson County

(G-14121)
BUCKEYE MECHANICAL CONTG INC
2325 Township Rd 370 (43964-7992)
PHONE...............................740 282-0089
Robert Hickle, *Pr*
Dennis Hickle, *
Earla Hickle, *Corporate Secretary**
Aimee Glenn, *
EMP: 46 **EST:** 1984
SALES (est): 4.74MM **Privately Held**
Web: www.buckeyemechanicalcontracting.com
SIC: 1711 7389 Mechanical contractor; Business Activities at Non-Commercial Site

(G-14122)
CATTRELL COMPANIES INC
906 Franklin St (43964-1152)
P.O. Box 367 (43964-0367)
PHONE...............................740 537-2481
Christine Hargrave, *Pr*
Thomas L Wilson, *
George R Cattrell, *
EMP: 52 **EST:** 1939
SQ FT: 4,000
SALES (est): 24.03MM **Privately Held**
Web: www.cattrell.com
SIC: 1711 1731 1542 Mechanical contractor; General electrical contractor; Commercial and office building contractors

Trenton
Butler County

(G-14123)
JEWISH HOSPITAL LLC
841 W State St (45067-9777)
PHONE...............................513 988-6067
Susan Smith, *Brnch Mgr*
EMP: 372
SALES (corp-wide): 88.72MM **Privately Held**
Web: www.mercy.com
SIC: 8062 General medical and surgical hospitals
PA: Jewish Hospital, Llc
4777 E Galbraith Rd
Cincinnati OH 45236
513 686-3000

(G-14124)
PRIMARY CARE NTWRK PRMIER HLTH
Also Called: Glickfield, W Scott MD
3590 Busenbark Rd Ste 400 (45067-9602)
PHONE...............................513 988-6369
Kenneth Prunier, *CEO*
EMP: 41
SALES (corp-wide): 25.36MM **Privately Held**
Web: www.premierhealth.com
SIC: 8011 General and family practice, physician/surgeon
PA: Primary Care Network Of Premier Health Partners
110 N Main St Ste 350
Dayton OH 45402
937 226-7085

(G-14125)
US RADIUS SERVICES INC
5498 Alan B Shepherd St (45067-9577)
PHONE...............................929 505-1063
Luiz Durao, *CEO*
EMP: 49 **EST:** 2019

GEOGRAPHIC SECTION

Troy - Miami County (G-14147)

SALES (est): 4.62MM **Privately Held**
Web: www.usradius.com
SIC: 1623 Underground utilities contractor

(G-14126)
UTILITIES SERVICES RADIUS LLC ✪
Also Called: Usradius
5498 Alan B Shepherd St (45067-9577)
PHONE...................................800 515-7650
Luiz Carlos Melo Durao, *Managing Member*
EMP: 144 EST: 2023
SALES (est): 11.23MM **Privately Held**
SIC: 1623 Electric power line construction

Trotwood
Montgomery County

(G-14127)
E T FINANCIAL SERVICE INC
Also Called: Jackson Hewitt Tax Service
4550 Salem Ave (45416-1700)
PHONE...................................937 716-1726
Emmanuel Umoren, *Pr*
Theo Adegdoruwa, *
EMP: 40 EST: 1995
SQ FT: 1,800
SALES (est): 871.48K **Privately Held**
Web: www.jacksonhewitt.com
SIC: 7291 8721 7389 Tax return preparation services; Billing and bookkeeping service; Financial services

(G-14128)
STARS YUTH ENRCHMENT PRGRAM IN
4972 Maplecreek Dr (45426-1604)
PHONE...................................513 978-7735
Tyree Fields, *Pr*
EMP: 50 EST: 2019
SALES (est): 424.03K **Privately Held**
Web: www.starsyep.org
SIC: 7032 Sporting camps

Troy
Miami County

(G-14129)
ARETT SALES CORP
Also Called: ARETT SALES CORP
1261 Brukner Dr (45373-3843)
PHONE...................................937 552-2005
David Mccarthy, *Brnch Mgr*
EMP: 45
SALES (corp-wide): 78.15MM **Privately Held**
Web: www.arett.com
SIC: 4225 General warehousing
PA: Arett Sales Corporation
    9285 Commerce Hwy
    Pennsauken NJ 08110
    856 751-1224

(G-14130)
BROCK AIR PRODUCTS INC (PA)
Also Called: 1hvac
2331 W State Route 55 (45373-9234)
PHONE...................................937 335-2626
Kevin Brock, *CEO*
▲ EMP: 51 EST: 2002
SQ FT: 6,000
SALES (est): 40.48MM
SALES (corp-wide): 40.48MM **Privately Held**
Web: www.1hvac.com
SIC: 5075 Air conditioning and ventilation equipment and supplies

(G-14131)
CLOPAY TRANSPORTATION COMPANY
1400 W Market St (45373-3889)
PHONE...................................937 440-6790
◆ EMP: 100 EST: 1940
SALES (est): 20.59MM
SALES (corp-wide): 2.69B **Publicly Held**
SIC: 4213 Trucking, except local
HQ: Clopay Corporation
    8585 Duke Blvd
    Mason OH 45040
    800 282-2260

(G-14132)
COUNTY OF MIAMI
Also Called: Miami Co Highway Dept
2100 N County Road 25a (45373-1333)
PHONE...................................937 335-1314
Jerry Jackson, *Mgr*
EMP: 48
Web: co.miami.oh.us
SIC: 8744 Base maintenance (providing personnel on continuing basis)
PA: County Of Miami
    201 W Main St
    Troy OH 45373
    937 440-5900

(G-14133)
DAYTON PHYSICIANS LLC
3130 N County Road 25a (45373-1337)
PHONE...................................937 440-4210
EMP: 78
SALES (corp-wide): 22.86MM **Privately Held**
Web: www.daytonphysicians.com
SIC: 8011 Oncologist
PA: Dayton Physicians, Llc
    6680 Poe Ave Ste 200
    Dayton OH 45414
    937 280-8400

(G-14134)
DUNGAN & LEFEVRE CO LPA (PA)
210 W Main St (45373-3240)
PHONE...................................937 339-0511
William J Mc Graw Iii, *Pr*
EMP: 27 EST: 1973
SQ FT: 4,200
SALES (est): 2.15MM
SALES (corp-wide): 2.15MM **Privately Held**
Web: www.duganattorney.com
SIC: 8111 General practice attorney, lawyer

(G-14135)
FAUST HRRLSON FLKER MCCRTHY SC
12 S Cherry St (45373-3206)
P.O. Box 8 (45373-0008)
PHONE...................................937 335-8324
John Fulkner, *Pt*
William Fulker, *Pt*
Robert A Mc Carthy, *Pt*
Robert Harrelson, *Pt*
Robert Schlemner, *Pt*
EMP: 28 EST: 1900
SALES (est): 776.89K **Privately Held**
Web: www.fhfmslaw.com
SIC: 8111 General practice attorney, lawyer

(G-14136)
GENESIS HEALTHCARE
Also Called: Troy Center
2 Crescent Dr (45373-2714)
PHONE...................................937 875-4604
EMP: 509 EST: 2014
SALES (est): 10.79MM
SALES (corp-wide): 5.86B **Publicly Held**
Web: www.genesishcc.com
SIC: 8051 Convalescent home with continuous nursing care
HQ: Toledo Harborside Limited Partnership
    101 Sun Ave Ne
    Albuquerque NM 87109

(G-14137)
HARBORSIDE HEALTHCARE LLC
512 Crescent Dr (45373-2718)
PHONE...................................937 335-7161
Jason Coe, *Brnch Mgr*
EMP: 35
SALES (corp-wide): 5.86B **Publicly Held**
Web: www.genesishcc.com
SIC: 8051 Convalescent home with continuous nursing care
HQ: Harborside Healthcare, Llc
    5100 Sun Ave Ne
    Albuquerque NM 87109

(G-14138)
HOBART INTERNATIONAL HOLDINGS
701 S Ridge Ave (45373-3000)
PHONE...................................937 332-3000
Thomas H Rodgers, *VP*
Richard Gleitsmann, *
EMP: 250 EST: 1913
SQ FT: 500,000
SALES (est): 98.6MM
SALES (corp-wide): 16.11B **Publicly Held**
Web: www.hobartcorp.com
SIC: 5046 Restaurant equipment and supplies, nec
PA: Illinois Tool Works Inc.
    155 Harlem Ave
    Glenview IL 60025
    847 724-7500

(G-14139)
HOSPICE OF MIAMI COUNTY INC
3230 N County Road 25a (45373-1338)
P.O. Box 502 (45373-0502)
PHONE...................................937 335-5191
Carey Short, *Ex Dir*
EMP: 50 EST: 1982
SALES (est): 11.46MM **Privately Held**
Web: www.hospiceofmiamicounty.org
SIC: 8052 Personal care facility

(G-14140)
IMAGINE NETWORKS LLC
1100 Wayne St (45373-3048)
PHONE...................................937 552-2340
Josh Luthman, *Pr*
Paul Deitz, *
EMP: 34 EST: 2006
SQ FT: 1,000
SALES (est): 2.59MM **Privately Held**
Web: www.imaginenetworksllc.com
SIC: 4813 Internet connectivity services

(G-14141)
ITW FOOD EQUIPMENT GROUP LLC (HQ)
Also Called: Hobart
701 S Ridge Ave (45374-0001)
PHONE...................................937 332-2396
Harold B Smith, *CEO*
Tom Szafranski, *
Chris O Herlihy, *
Axel Beck, *
◆ EMP: 1100 EST: 2002
SALES (est): 1.58B
SALES (corp-wide): 16.11B **Publicly Held**
Web: www.itwfoodequipment.com
SIC: 5046 3556 Restaurant equipment and supplies, nec; Food products machinery
PA: Illinois Tool Works Inc.
    155 Harlem Ave
    Glenview IL 60025
    847 724-7500

(G-14142)
KNAPKE CABINETS INC
2 E Main St (45373-3202)
PHONE...................................937 335-8383
Bernie Knapke, *Pr*
EMP: 35 EST: 2001
SALES (est): 1.62MM **Privately Held**
Web: www.knapkecabinets.com
SIC: 2434 1521 Wood kitchen cabinets; General remodeling, single-family houses

(G-14143)
KOMYO AMERICA CO INC
Also Called: North America Hub-East
151 Commerce Center Blvd (45373-9039)
PHONE...................................937 339-0157
Gregory Huey, *Mgr*
EMP: 44
Web: www.komyologistics.com
SIC: 4731 Freight forwarding
HQ: Komyo America Co., Inc.
    11590 Township Rd 298
    East Liberty OH 43319

(G-14144)
KREGEL PROPERTIES LLC
66 Industry Ct (45373-2497)
PHONE...................................937 885-3250
EMP: 50 EST: 2010
SALES (est): 1.65MM **Privately Held**
SIC: 6512 Nonresidential building operators

(G-14145)
LOWES HOME CENTERS LLC
Also Called: Lowe's
2000 W Main St (45373-1019)
PHONE...................................937 339-2544
Jerry Breger, *Mgr*
EMP: 148
SALES (corp-wide): 86.38B **Publicly Held**
Web: www.lowes.com
SIC: 5211 5031 5722 5064 Home centers; Building materials, exterior; Household appliance stores; Electrical appliances, television and radio
HQ: Lowe's Home Centers, Llc
    1000 Lowes Blvd
    Mooresville NC 28117
    336 658-4000

(G-14146)
MIAMI CNTY CMNTY ACTION CUNCIL
Also Called: Miami Metropolitan Hsing Auth
1695 Troy Sidney Rd (45373-9794)
PHONE...................................937 335-7921
Jack Baird, *Dir*
EMP: 35 EST: 1966
SQ FT: 11,000
SALES (est): 739.47K **Privately Held**
Web: www.miamicac.org
SIC: 8399 6513 Community action agency; Apartment building operators

(G-14147)
MIGHTY MAC INVESTMENTS INC (PA)
1494 Lytle Rd (45373-9401)
P.O. Box 39 (45373-0039)
PHONE...................................937 335-2928
Jeffrey W Earhart, *Pr*
Scott W Earhart, *
Michael W Earhart, *
EMP: 40 EST: 1971
SQ FT: 21,000
SALES (est): 25.29MM
SALES (corp-wide): 25.29MM **Privately Held**
Web: www.superiorpluspropane.com

(G-14148)
NATIONWIDE TRUCK BROKERS INC
3355 S County Road 25a (45373-9384)
PHONE.................................937 335-9229
EMP: 192
SALES (corp-wide): 7.23MM **Privately Held**
Web: www.ntbtrk.com
SIC: 4213 Contract haulers
HQ: Nationwide Truck Brokers, Inc.
    4203 Rger B Chffee Mem Dr
    Wyoming MI 49548
    616 878-5554

(G-14149)
OHIO MACHINERY CO
Also Called: Ohio Cat
1281 Brukner Dr (45373-3843)
PHONE.................................937 335-7660
TOLL FREE: 888
Greg Hallaway, *Mgr*
EMP: 65
SALES (corp-wide): 185.86MM **Privately Held**
Web: www.ohiocat.com
SIC: 5082 General construction machinery and equipment
PA: Ohio Machinery Co.
    3993 E Royalton Rd
    Broadview Heights OH 44147
    440 526-6200

(G-14150)
OMNI WELLNESS GROUP LLC
1149 Experiment Farm Rd (45373-1071)
PHONE.................................937 540-9920
Bruce A Clapp, *Brnch Mgr*
EMP: 42
SALES (corp-wide): 266.64K **Privately Held**
Web: www.omni-wellness-group.com
SIC: 8099 Childbirth preparation clinic
PA: Omni Wellness Group Llc
    35 Rockridge Rd Ste A
    Englewood OH 45322
    937 540-9920

(G-14151)
OVERFELD ERLY CHLDHOOD PROGRAM
172 S Ridge Ave (45373-2704)
PHONE.................................937 339-5111
Karen Mccoy, *Ex Dir*
Lorna Dawes, *Dir*
EMP: 31 **EST:** 1960
SQ FT: 8,460
SALES (est): 763.44K **Privately Held**
Web: www.overfield.org
SIC: 8351 Preschool center

(G-14152)
PRECISION DUCT SYSTEMS LLC
2331 W State Route 55 (45373-9234)
PHONE.................................937 335-2626
Kevin Brock, *CEO*
EMP: 116 **EST:** 2019
SALES (est): 11.96MM
SALES (corp-wide): 40.48MM **Privately Held**
Web: www.1hvac.com
SIC: 1711 Mechanical contractor
PA: Brock Air Products, Inc.
    2331 W State Route 55
    Troy OH 45373
    937 335-2626

(G-14153)
R P L CORPORATION
Also Called: Motel 6
1375 W Market St (45373-3858)
PHONE.................................937 335-0021
William A Roll Md, *Pr*
Juan M Palomar Md, *Treas*
Frank Scott, *
▲ **EMP:** 49 **EST:** 1986
SQ FT: 200,000
SALES (est): 249.43K **Privately Held**
Web: www.motel6.com
SIC: 7011 5812 5813 Hotels and motels; Family restaurants; Cocktail lounge

(G-14154)
REM-OHIO INC
721 Lincoln Ave (45373-3176)
PHONE.................................937 335-8267
EMP: 32
SALES (corp-wide): 19.17MM **Privately Held**
Web: www.rem-oh.com
SIC: 8361 Retarded home
PA: Rem-Ohio, Inc
    6921 York Ave S
    Minneapolis MN 55435
    952 925-5067

(G-14155)
REMEDI SENIORCARE OF OHIO LLC (DH)
962 S Dorset Rd (45373-4705)
PHONE.................................800 232-4239
Rene Deller, *Genl Mgr*
John Jay Meyer, *
EMP: 27 **EST:** 1938
SQ FT: 20,000
SALES (est): 96.04MM
SALES (corp-wide): 342.05MM **Privately Held**
Web: www.remedirx.com
SIC: 5122 Pharmaceuticals
HQ: Remedi Seniorcare Holding Corporation
    1 Olympic Pl Ste 600
    Towson MD 21204

(G-14156)
ROBERT KELLY & BUCIO LLP
10 N Market St (45373-3281)
PHONE.................................937 332-9300
EMP: 35
Web: www.rkblawyers.com
SIC: 8111 General practice attorney, lawyer
PA: Robert, Kelly & Bucio Llp
    118 N Main Ave
    Sidney OH 45365

(G-14157)
RT INDUSTRIES INC
Also Called: Riverside of Miami County
1625 Troy Sidney Rd (45373-9794)
PHONE.................................937 339-8313
Karen Mayer, *Brnch Mgr*
EMP: 140
SALES (corp-wide): 3.05MM **Privately Held**
Web: www.rtindustries.org
SIC: 8331 9111 Sheltered workshop; County supervisors' and executives' office
PA: R.T. Industries, Inc.
    110 Foss Way
    Troy OH 45373
    937 335-5784

(G-14158)
S&S MANAGEMENT
Also Called: Holiday Inn
60 Troy Town Dr (45373-2328)
PHONE.................................937 332-1700
EMP: 30 **EST:** 1998
SALES (est): 329.89K **Privately Held**
Web: www.holidayinn.com
SIC: 7011 Hotels and motels

(G-14159)
SCHAEFER & COMPANY
3205 S County Road 25a (45373-9384)
PHONE.................................937 339-2638
Greg Oldiges, *Pr*
R K Pfeiffenberger, *Sec*
T S Williams, *Treas*
Martin Williams, *VP*
Pete Wehner, *Genl Mgr*
EMP: 29 **EST:** 1947
SQ FT: 6,000
SALES (est): 928.26K **Privately Held**
Web: www.schaeferandcompany.com
SIC: 1761 1751 1799 Roofing contractor; Window and door (prefabricated) installation ; Home/office interiors finishing, furnishing and remodeling

(G-14160)
SPS INC
Also Called: Hampton Inn
45 Troy Town Dr (45373-2327)
PHONE.................................937 339-7801
EMP: 48 **EST:** 1994
SALES (est): 444.56K **Privately Held**
Web: www.hilton.com
SIC: 7011 7991 5813 Hotels and motels; Physical fitness facilities; Drinking places

(G-14161)
TROY CHRISTIAN SCHOOLS INC
1586 Mckaig Rd (45373-2670)
PHONE.................................937 339-5692
Gary Wilber, *Superintnt*
EMP: 34 **EST:** 1980
SQ FT: 32,000
SALES (est): 6.99MM **Privately Held**
Web: www.troychristianschools.org
SIC: 8211 8351 Catholic combined elementary and secondary school; Child day care services

(G-14162)
TROY CITY SCHOOL DISTRICT
Also Called: Troy Hayner Cultural Center
301 W Main St (45373-3241)
PHONE.................................937 339-0457
Linda Lee Jolly, *Mgr*
EMP: 39
SALES (corp-wide): 63.79MM **Privately Held**
Web: www.troyhayner.org
SIC: 7999 Recreation center
PA: Troy City School District
    500 N Market St
    Troy OH 45373
    937 332-6700

(G-14163)
TROY COUNTRY CLUB
1830 Peters Rd (45373-3868)
P.O. Box 459 (45373-0459)
PHONE.................................937 335-5691
Philip Zwierzchowski, *Mgr*
EMP: 50 **EST:** 1922
SQ FT: 5,000
SALES (est): 2.54MM **Privately Held**
Web: www.troycountryclub.net
SIC: 7997 Country club, membership

(G-14164)
TROY HOTEL II LLC
Also Called: Fairfield Inn & Suites Troy
83 Troy Town Dr (45373-2327)
PHONE.................................937 332-1446
Julie Isley, *Genl Mgr*
EMP: 34 **EST:** 1998
SALES (est): 522.16K **Privately Held**
Web: fairfield.marriott.com
SIC: 7011 7991 Hotels and motels; Physical fitness facilities

(G-14165)
TROY RHBLTTION HLTHCARE CTR LL
Also Called: Troy Nursing & Rehab
512 Crescent Dr (45373-2718)
PHONE.................................937 335-7161
Moshe Weintraub, *Prin*
Fraida S Oratz, *
EMP: 90 **EST:** 2019
SALES (est): 5.53MM **Privately Held**
Web: www.troycarecenter.com
SIC: 8051 Skilled nursing care facilities

(G-14166)
UPPER VALLEY MEDICAL CENTER (HQ)
3130 N County Road 25a (45373-1337)
PHONE.................................937 440-4000
EMP: 1120 **EST:** 1926
SALES (est): 164.65MM
SALES (corp-wide): 2.41MM **Privately Held**
Web: www.premierhealth.com
SIC: 8011 8062 Offices and clinics of medical doctors; General medical and surgical hospitals
PA: Premier Health Partners
    110 N Main St Ste 450
    Dayton OH 45402
    937 499-9596

(G-14167)
UPPER VALLEY MEDICAL CENTER
3130 N County Road 25a (45373-1337)
PHONE.................................937 440-4820
Jane Heath, *Mgr*
EMP: 246
SALES (corp-wide): 2.41MM **Privately Held**
Web: www.premierhealth.com
SIC: 8299 8093 Meditation therapy; Respiratory therapy clinic
HQ: Upper Valley Medical Center
    3130 N County Road 25a
    Troy OH 45373

(G-14168)
UPPERVALLEY PROFESSIONAL CORP
3130 N County Road 25a (45373-1337)
PHONE.................................937 440-4000
Michael Maiberger, *Pr*
EMP: 34 **EST:** 1974
SQ FT: 169,000
SALES (est): 916.27K **Privately Held**
Web: www.premierhealth.com
SIC: 8011 General and family practice, physician/surgeon

(G-14169)
UVMC MANAGEMENT CORPORATION (HQ)
Also Called: MIAMI VALLEY
3130 N County Road 25a (45373-1309)
PHONE.................................937 440-4000
Michael Maiberger, *Pr*
EMP: 103 **EST:** 1985
SQ FT: 169,000
SALES (est): 1.44MM
SALES (corp-wide): 2.41MM **Privately Held**
Web: www.premierhealth.com

SIC: 5172 5541 5983 Fuel oil; Filling stations, gasoline; Fuel oil dealers

SIC: 8051 8062 Skilled nursing care facilities; General medical and surgical hospitals
PA: Premier Health Partners
  110 N Main St Ste 450
  Dayton OH 45402
  937 499-9596

(G-14170)
UVMC NURSING CARE INC
Also Called: Koester Pavilion Nursing Home
3232 N County Road 25a (45373-1338)
PHONE..................937 440-7663
Pat Meyer, *Mgr*
EMP: 147
SQ FT: 57,216
Web: www.premierhealth.com
SIC: 8051 Convalescent home with continuous nursing care
PA: Uvmc Nursing Care, Inc.
  3130 N County Road 25a
  Troy OH 45373

Twinsburg
Summit County

(G-14171)
ASSURAMED INC (HQ)
Also Called: Assuramed
1810 Summit Commerce Park (44087-2300)
PHONE..................330 963-6998
Michael B Petras Junior, *CEO*
Chris Lindroth, *
Mark Wells, *
Kurt Packer, *
EMP: 185 **EST:** 2012
SALES (est): 187.16MM
SALES (corp-wide): 205.01B **Publicly Held**
SIC: 5047 Medical and hospital equipment
PA: Cardinal Health, Inc.
  7000 Cardinal Pl
  Dublin OH 43017
  614 757-5000

(G-14172)
ATLAS STEEL PRODUCTS CO (PA)
Also Called: AB Tube Company
7990 Bavaria Rd (44087-2252)
PHONE..................330 425-1600
John Adams, *Pr*
Fred Barrera, *
▲ **EMP:** 147 **EST:** 1957
SQ FT: 120,000
SALES (est): 94.36MM
SALES (corp-wide): 94.36MM **Privately Held**
Web: www.atlassteel.com
SIC: 5051 Steel

(G-14173)
AVID TECHNOLOGIES INC
2112 Case Pkwy Ste 1 (44087-2378)
P.O. Box 468 (44087-0468)
PHONE..................330 487-0770
David Shen, *CEO*
David Shen, *CEO*
Arnie Grever, *
Joseph R Daprile, *
Paul M Barlak, *
EMP: 45 **EST:** 2014
SQ FT: 12,000
SALES (est): 7.62MM
SALES (corp-wide): 26.54B **Publicly Held**
Web: www.avnet.com
SIC: 8711 5045 Consulting engineer; Computer software
HQ: Premier Farnell Corp.
  4180 Highlander Pkwy
  Richfield OH 44286
  330 659-0459

(G-14174)
BALANCED LOGISTICS BRKG LLC
3601 Shady Timber Dr (44087-4945)
PHONE..................216 296-4817
Ebony Jackson, *Prin*
EMP: 84 **EST:** 2021
SALES (est): 2.45MM **Privately Held**
Web: www.balancedlogisticsllc.com
SIC: 4213 Trucking, except local

(G-14175)
CEM-BASE INC
8530 N Boyle Pkwy (44087-2267)
PHONE..................330 405-4105
John R Morris Iii, *CEO*
EMP: 40 **EST:** 1995
SALES (est): 17MM
SALES (corp-wide): 29.9MM **Privately Held**
Web: www.cembase.com
SIC: 1771 Concrete work
PA: Tri-Mor, Corp.
  8530 N Boyle Pkwy
  Twinsburg OH 44087
  330 963-3101

(G-14176)
CHILDRENS HOSP MED CTR AKRON
8054 Darrow Rd (44087-2381)
PHONE..................330 425-3344
Jeanne Fenton, *Brnch Mgr*
EMP: 55
SALES (corp-wide): 1.4B **Privately Held**
Web: www.akronchildrens.org
SIC: 8062 General medical and surgical hospitals
PA: Childrens Hospital Medical Center Of Akron
  1 Perkins Sq
  Akron OH 44308
  330 543-1000

(G-14177)
CLEVELAND ELECTRIC LABS CO (PA)
Also Called: Cleveland Electric Labs
1776 Enterprise Pkwy (44087-2246)
PHONE..................800 447-2207
Jack Allan Lieske, *Pr*
Val Jean Lieske, *
Rebecca Lieske, *
C M Lemmon, *
EMP: 42 **EST:** 1920
SQ FT: 30,000
SALES (est): 10.84MM
SALES (corp-wide): 10.84MM **Privately Held**
Web: www.clevelandelectriclabs.com
SIC: 3823 7699 Thermocouples, industrial process type; Professional instrument repair services

(G-14178)
CONTRACTORS STEEL COMPANY
8383 Boyle Pkwy (44087-2236)
PHONE..................330 425-3050
Mitch Kubasek, *Mgr*
EMP: 59
SQ FT: 58,000
SALES (corp-wide): 582.71MM **Privately Held**
Web: www.upgllc.com
SIC: 5051 3498 3312 Steel; Fabricated pipe and fittings; Blast furnaces and steel mills
HQ: Contractors Steel Company
  48649 Schooner St
  Van Buren Twp MI 48111
  734 464-4000

(G-14179)
CTEK INC
9347 Ravenna Rd Ste B (44087-2463)
PHONE..................330 963-0981
EMP: 113
SALES (corp-wide): 90.57MM **Privately Held**
Web: www.smartercharger.com
SIC: 5013 Motor vehicle supplies and new parts
HQ: Ctek, Inc.
  5521 N Cumberland Ave # 1104
  Chicago IL 60656

(G-14180)
DCTECH LTD
2241 Pinnacle Pkwy (44087-5300)
P.O. Box 366 (44272-0366)
PHONE..................330 687-3977
Jeff Sadar, *Prin*
EMP: 50 **EST:** 2008
SALES (est): 2.38MM **Privately Held**
Web: www.dctechusa.com
SIC: 8711 Engineering services

(G-14181)
DF SUPPLY INC
Also Called: Df Supply
8500 Hadden Rd (44087-2114)
PHONE..................330 650-9226
◆ **EMP:** 38 **EST:** 1982
SQ FT: 10,000
SALES (est): 32MM **Privately Held**
Web: www.dfsupplyinc.com
SIC: 5031 5211 3499 1731 Fencing, wood; Fencing; Barricades, metal; Access control systems specialization

(G-14182)
DMD MANAGEMENT INC
Also Called: Legacy Place
2463 Sussex Blvd (44087-2442)
PHONE..................330 405-6040
Amy Kraynak, *Brnch Mgr*
EMP: 239
SQ FT: 41,918
Web: www.lhshealth.com
SIC: 8051 Convalescent home with continuous nursing care
PA: Dmd Management, Inc.
  12380 Plaza Dr
  Cleveland OH 44130

(G-14183)
EARLE M JORGENSEN COMPANY
Also Called: EMJ Cleveland Plate
2060 Enterprise Pkwy (44087-2210)
PHONE..................330 425-1500
Barbara Nemeth, *Brnch Mgr*
EMP: 75
SALES (corp-wide): 14.81B **Publicly Held**
Web: www.emjmetals.com
SIC: 5051 Steel
HQ: Earle M. Jorgensen Company
  10650 Alameda St
  Lynwood CA 90262
  323 567-1122

(G-14184)
EARLE M JORGENSEN COMPANY
Also Called: EMJ Cleveland
2060 Enterprise Pkwy (44087-2210)
PHONE..................330 425-1500
Ed King, *Brnch Mgr*
EMP: 100
SQ FT: 75,000
SALES (corp-wide): 14.81B **Publicly Held**
Web: www.emjmetals.com
SIC: 5051 Steel
HQ: Earle M. Jorgensen Company
  10650 Alameda St
  Lynwood CA 90262
  323 567-1122

(G-14185)
ELIXIR RX OPTIONS LLC (DH)
Also Called: Envision Pharmaceutical Svcs
2181 E Aurora Rd Ste 101 (44087-1962)
PHONE..................330 405-8080
Barry Katz, *Pr*
Catherine Stroutman, *
William M Toomajian, *
EMP: 75 **EST:** 2000
SQ FT: 2,500
SALES (est): 48.25MM
SALES (corp-wide): 24.09B **Publicly Held**
Web: www.elixirsolutions.com
SIC: 8742 Compensation and benefits planning consultant
HQ: Envision Pharmaceutical Holdings Llc
  2181 E Aurora Rd Ste 201
  Twinsburg OH 44087
  800 361-4542

(G-14186)
EMERALD TRANSFORMER PPM LLC
1672 Highland Rd (44087-2219)
PHONE..................330 425-3825
EMP: 352
SALES (corp-wide): 492.09MM **Privately Held**
Web: www.emeraldtransformer.com
SIC: 8641 Environmental protection organization
HQ: Emerald Transformer Ppm Llc
  9820 Westpoint Dr Ste 300
  Indianapolis IN 46256

(G-14187)
ENVIRONMENT CTRL BEACHWOOD INC
Also Called: Environment Control
1897 E Aurora Rd (44087-1917)
PHONE..................330 405-6201
James Hennessy, *Pr*
EMP: 33 **EST:** 1994
SQ FT: 4,000
SALES (est): 603.58K **Privately Held**
Web: www.environmentcontrol.com
SIC: 7349 Janitorial service, contract basis

(G-14188)
ESSENDANT CO
2100 Highland Rd (44087-2229)
PHONE..................800 733-4091
Dave Martin, *Mgr*
EMP: 169
Web: www.essendant.com
SIC: 5112 5044 Office supplies, nec; Office equipment
HQ: Essendant Co.
  1 Pkwy N Blvd Ste 100
  Deerfield IL 60015
  847 627-7000

(G-14189)
ESSENDANT CO
2477 Edison Blvd (44087-2340)
PHONE..................330 425-7343
Dan Elko, *Mgr*
EMP: 29
Web: www.essendant.com
SIC: 5112 Office supplies, nec
HQ: Essendant Co.
  1 Pkwy N Blvd Ste 100
  Deerfield IL 60015
  847 627-7000

(G-14190)
FACIL NORTH AMERICA INC (HQ)
Also Called: Streetsboro Operations
2242 Pinnacle Pkwy Ste 100 (44087-5301)

Twinsburg - Summit County (G-14191)

PHONE...................................330 487-2500
Rene Achten, *CEO*
Daniel Michiels, *CFO*
◆ **EMP**: 210 **EST**: 1967
SQ FT: 150,000
SALES (est): 162.26MM
SALES (corp-wide): 8.12MM **Privately Held**
Web: www.facil.be
SIC: **5072** 3452 5085 Nuts (hardware); Nuts, metal; Fasteners, industrial: nuts, bolts, screws, etc.
PA: Facil Corporate
Geleenlaan 20
Genk 3600
89410450

(G-14191)
FASTENERS FOR RETAIL INC (PA)
Also Called: Siffron
8181 Darrow Rd (44087-2303)
P.O. Box 932397 (45263-0001)
PHONE...................................330 998-7800
◆ **EMP**: 310 **EST**: 1961
SALES (est): 115.08MM
SALES (corp-wide): 115.08MM **Privately Held**
Web: www.siffron.com
SIC: **5046** Store fixtures and display equipment

(G-14192)
FREEDOM USA INC
Also Called: Avadirect.com
2045 Midway Dr (44087-1933)
PHONE...................................216 503-6374
Alex Sonis, *CEO*
EMP: 35 **EST**: 2000
SQ FT: 8,000
SALES (est): 9.39MM **Privately Held**
Web: www.avadirect.com
SIC: **3572** 7373 7379 3575 Computer storage devices; Systems engineering, computer related; Computer related maintenance services; Computer terminals

(G-14193)
FRENCH COMPANY LLC
Also Called: Facility Connect
8289 Darrow Rd (44087-2307)
PHONE...................................330 963-4344
Scott Dahl, *CEO*
John Durkey, *
Christine Callahan, *OF STRATEGIC Development*
David Mechenbier, *
EMP: 75 **EST**: 1980
SALES (est): 10.71MM
SALES (corp-wide): 983.85MM **Privately Held**
Web: www.technibilt.com
SIC: **7699** 8741 Cleaning services; Management services
HQ: Technibilt, Ltd.
700 Technibilt Dr
Newton NC 28658

(G-14194)
FUJIFILM HLTHCARE AMRICAS CORP (DH)
1959 Summit Commerce Park (44087-2371)
PHONE...................................330 425-1313
Jun Higuchi, *Pr*
Richard Kurz, *
Richard Katz, *Legal Counsel*
Robert Mccarthy, *Technology Vice President*
Henry Izawa, *OF BUS INTEGRATION*
▲ **EMP**: 436 **EST**: 1989
SQ FT: 54,000
SALES (est): 108.63MM **Privately Held**
Web: healthcaresolutions-us.fujifilm.com
SIC: **5047** Diagnostic equipment, medical
HQ: Fujifilm Healthcare Corporation
9-7-3, Akasaka
Minato-Ku TKY 107-0

(G-14195)
GREAT LAKES FASTENERS INC (PA)
Also Called: Great Lakes Fasteners & Sup Co
2204 E Enterprise Pkwy (44087)
PHONE...................................330 425-4488
Kevin Weidinger, *Pr*
Kevin Weidinger, *Pr*
Tim Umberger, *VP*
▲ **EMP**: 65 **EST**: 2010
SALES (est): 12.54MM
SALES (corp-wide): 12.54MM **Privately Held**
Web: www.glfus.com
SIC: **5085** 3452 Fasteners, industrial: nuts, bolts, screws, etc.; Bolts, nuts, rivets, and washers

(G-14196)
ICM DISTRIBUTING COMPANY INC
Also Called: Inventory Controlled Mdsg
1755 Enterprise Pkwy Ste 200 (44087)
PHONE...................................234 212-3030
Harry Singer, *Pr*
Phillip B Singer, *
▼ **EMP**: 35 **EST**: 2006
SQ FT: 80,000
SALES (est): 21.99MM
SALES (corp-wide): 24.01MM **Privately Held**
Web: www.icmint.com
SIC: **5049** 5092 5199 5122 School supplies; Toys, nec; General merchandise, non-durable; Hair preparations
PA: Sandusco, Inc.
1755 Entp Pkwy Ste 200
Twinsburg OH 44087
440 357-5964

(G-14197)
J T EATON & CO INC
1393 Highland Rd (44087-2213)
PHONE...................................330 425-7801
Bart Baker, *Ex VP*
Benjamin Baker, *
Jack A Polenick, *
Paul Millet, *
Stanley Baker, *
◆ **EMP**: 30 **EST**: 1932
SQ FT: 45,000
SALES (est): 4.59MM **Privately Held**
Web: www.jteaton.com
SIC: **7342** Pest control services

(G-14198)
KAISER FOUNDATION HOSPITALS
Also Called: Twinsburg Medical Offices
8920 Canyon Falls Blvd (44087-1990)
PHONE...................................330 486-2800
EMP: 29
SALES (corp-wide): 70.8B **Privately Held**
Web: www.kaisercenter.com
SIC: **8011** Medical centers
HQ: Kaiser Foundation Hospitals Inc
1 Kaiser Plz
Oakland CA 94612
510 271-6611

(G-14199)
KEYBANK NATIONAL ASSOCIATION
2566 E Aurora Rd (44087-2148)
PHONE...................................330 425-4434
Trudy Shertinger, *Mgr*
EMP: 32
SALES (corp-wide): 10.4B **Publicly Held**
Web: www.key.com
SIC: **6021** National commercial banks
HQ: Keybank National Association
127 Public Sq Ste 5600
Cleveland OH 44114
800 539-2968

(G-14200)
KIMBLE RECYCL & DISPOSAL INC
8500 Chamberlin Rd (44087-2096)
PHONE...................................330 963-5493
Peter Gutwein, *Brnch Mgr*
EMP: 32
Web: www.kimblecompanies.com
SIC: **4953** Recycling, waste materials
PA: Kimble Recycling & Disposal, Inc.
3596 State Route 39 Nw
Dover OH 44622

(G-14201)
LIGHTING SERVICES INC
Also Called: Kda Lighting Services
9001 Dutton Dr (44087-1930)
PHONE...................................330 405-4879
EMP: 57 **EST**: 1998
SQ FT: 5,000
SALES (est): 16.27MM **Privately Held**
Web: www.lighting-servicesinc.com
SIC: **5063** Lighting fixtures

(G-14202)
LOU RITENOUR DECORATORS INC
Also Called: Ritenour Industrial
2066 Case Pkwy S (44087-2360)
PHONE...................................330 425-3232
Michael Ritenour, *Pr*
Karen Ritenour, *
EMP: 100 **EST**: 1960
SQ FT: 8,000
SALES (est): 19.99MM **Privately Held**
Web: www.louritenour.com
SIC: **1721** Interior commercial painting contractor

(G-14203)
MAVAL INDUSTRIES LLC (PA)
Also Called: Maval Manufacturing
1555 Enterprise Pkwy (44087-2239)
PHONE...................................330 405-1600
John Dougherty, *Pr*
Dale Lumby, *
◆ **EMP**: 137 **EST**: 1986
SQ FT: 88,000
SALES (est): 24.57MM
SALES (corp-wide): 24.57MM **Privately Held**
Web: www.mavalgear.com
SIC: **3714** 8711 Power steering equipment, motor vehicle; Consulting engineer

(G-14204)
MEDIA COLLECTIONS INC
Also Called: Joseph, Mann & Creed
8948 Canyon Falls Blvd Ste 200 (44087-1900)
PHONE...................................216 831-5626
Perry Creed, *Pr*
Bill Mann, *
EMP: 63 **EST**: 2000
SQ FT: 10,000
SALES (est): 9.97MM **Privately Held**
Web: www.jmcbiz.com
SIC: **7322** Collection agency, except real estate

(G-14205)
MERC ACQUISITIONS INC
Also Called: Electric Sweeper Service Co
1933 Highland Rd (44087-2224)
PHONE...................................216 524-4141
Robert Merckle, *Pr*
Gale Merckle, *
▲ **EMP**: 104 **EST**: 1924
SQ FT: 27,000
SALES (est): 24.87MM **Privately Held**
Web: www.essco.net
SIC: **5064** Appliance parts, household

(G-14206)
MIRKA USA INC
2375 Edison Blvd (44087-2376)
PHONE...................................330 963-6421
Garrett Hedges, *Pr*
Mark Kush, *
◆ **EMP**: 72 **EST**: 1985
SQ FT: 24,000
SALES (est): 30.56MM
SALES (corp-wide): 642.86MM **Privately Held**
Web: www.mirkacollision.us
SIC: **5085** Abrasives
HQ: Mirka Oy
Pensalantie 210
Jepua 66850

(G-14207)
NATIONAL DCP LLC
8794 Independence Pkwy Ste 100 (44087-1965)
PHONE...................................216 410-3215
EMP: 99
Web: www.nationaldcp.com
SIC: **8741** Management services
PA: National Dcp, Llc
3805 Crestwood Pkwy Nw # 40
Duluth GA 30096

(G-14208)
NORTH COAST COMMERCIAL ROOFING SYSTEMS INC
2440 Edison Blvd (44087-2340)
PHONE...................................330 425-3359
EMP: 200
SIC: **5033** Roofing and siding materials

(G-14209)
OLIVER STEEL PLATE CO
7851 Bavaria Rd (44087-2263)
PHONE...................................330 425-7000
▲ **EMP**: 65
SIC: **5051** 3444 3443 3398 Metals service centers and offices; Sheet metalwork; Fabricated plate work (boiler shop); Metal heat treating

(G-14210)
PEPPERL + FUCHS INC (DH)
1600 Enterprise Pkwy (44087-2245)
PHONE...................................330 425-3555
Wolfgang Mueller, *Pr*
▲ **EMP**: 130 **EST**: 1983
SQ FT: 55,050
SALES (est): 99.67MM
SALES (corp-wide): 1.05B **Privately Held**
Web: www.pepperl-fuchs.com
SIC: **5065** 3625 3822 3674 Electronic parts and equipment, nec; Relays and industrial controls; Environmental controls; Semiconductors and related devices
HQ: Pepperl + Fuchs Enterprises, Inc.
1600 Enterprise Pkwy
Twinsburg OH 44087
330 425-3555

(G-14211)
PEPPERL+FUCHS AMERICAS INC
1600 Enterprise Pkwy (44087-2245)
PHONE...................................330 425-3555
Alexander Gress, *Pr*
EMP: 80 **EST**: 2017
SALES (est): 13.19MM
SALES (corp-wide): 1.05B **Privately Held**

GEOGRAPHIC SECTION
Twinsburg - Summit County (G-14232)

SIC: 5065 Electronic parts
HQ: Pepperl + Fuchs Enterprises, Inc.
1600 Enterprise Pkwy
Twinsburg OH 44087
330 425-3555

(G-14212)
PEPPERL+FUCHS MFG INC
1600 Enterprise Pkwy (44087-2245)
PHONE...................330 425-3555
Alexander Gress, *Pr*
EMP: 110 **EST:** 2017
SALES (est): 24.83MM
SALES (corp-wide): 1.05B **Privately Held**
SIC: 5065 Electronic parts and equipment, nec
HQ: Pepperl + Fuchs Enterprises, Inc.
1600 Enterprise Pkwy
Twinsburg OH 44087
330 425-3555

(G-14213)
PEPSI-COLA METRO BTLG CO INC
Also Called: Pepsi-Cola
1999 Enterprise Pkwy (44087-2253)
PHONE...................330 425-8236
Charlie Powers, *Mgr*
EMP: 107
SALES (corp-wide): 86.39B **Publicly Held**
Web: www.pepsico.com
SIC: 2086 5149 Bottled and canned soft drinks; Groceries and related products, nec
HQ: Pepsi-Cola Metropolitan Bottling Company, Inc.
700 Anderson Hill Rd
Purchase NY 10577
914 767-6000

(G-14214)
PSI ASSOCIATES LLC
Also Called: PSI
2112 Case Pkwy Ste 10 (44087-2378)
P.O. Box 468 (44087-0468)
PHONE...................330 425-8474
Steve Rosenberg, *Pr*
Doctor Colleen Lorberl, *COO*
EMP: 163 **EST:** 1977
SQ FT: 1,500
SALES (est): 8.41MM **Privately Held**
Web: www.psi-solutions.org
SIC: 7361 8049 Employment agencies; Clinical psychologist

(G-14215)
RELINK MEDICAL LLC (PA)
1755 Enterprise Pkwy Ste 400 (44087)
PHONE...................330 954-1199
Scott Campbell, *CAO*
EMP: 39 **EST:** 2015
SALES (est): 16.61MM
SALES (corp-wide): 16.61MM **Privately Held**
Web: www.relinkmedical.com
SIC: 5047 Medical equipment and supplies

(G-14216)
RGH ENTERPRISES LLC (HQ)
Also Called: Cardinal Health At Home
1810 Summit Commerce Park (44087-2300)
PHONE...................330 963-6996
▲ **EMP:** 700 **EST:** 1990
SALES (est): 188.52MM
SALES (corp-wide): 205.01B **Publicly Held**
Web: www.edgepark.com
SIC: 8011 5999 5047 Medical centers; Medical apparatus and supplies; Surgical equipment and supplies
PA: Cardinal Health, Inc.
7000 Cardinal Pl
Dublin OH 43017
614 757-5000

(G-14217)
RICHTER & ASSOCIATES INC
8948 Canyon Falls Blvd Ste 400 (44087-1900)
PHONE...................216 593-7140
Jennifer Richter, *Pr*
EMP: 78 **EST:** 2001
SALES (est): 8.9MM **Privately Held**
Web: www.richterhc.com
SIC: 8741 Financial management for business

(G-14218)
SAFRAN POWER USA LLC (DH)
Also Called: Safran
8380 Darrow Rd (44087-2329)
PHONE...................330 487-2000
EMP: 77 **EST:** 2013
SALES (est): 74.04MM
SALES (corp-wide): 781.02MM **Privately Held**
Web: www.safran-group.com
SIC: 8711 8741 Engineering services; Business management
HQ: Safran Usa, Inc.
700 S Washington St # 320
Alexandria VA 22314
703 351-9898

(G-14219)
SPENCER PRODUCTS CO (HQ)
1859 Summit Commerce Park (44087-2370)
PHONE...................330 487-5200
◆ **EMP:** 30 **EST:** 1954
SALES (est): 21.26MM
SALES (corp-wide): 21.26MM **Privately Held**
Web: www.spencerprodco.com
SIC: 5085 Fasteners, industrial: nuts, bolts, screws, etc.
PA: The Tuttle Group Inc
1859 Summit Commerce Park
Twinsburg OH
330 487-5200

(G-14220)
SSP FITTINGS CORP (PA)
Also Called: SSP
8250 Boyle Pkwy (44087-2200)
PHONE...................330 425-4250
Jeffrey E King, *CEO*
Betsy S King, *
David B King, *
O F Douglas, *
F B Douglas, *
▲ **EMP:** 100 **EST:** 1926
SQ FT: 165,000
SALES (est): 30.98MM
SALES (corp-wide): 30.98MM **Privately Held**
Web: www.myssp.com
SIC: 3494 5085 3498 3492 Pipe fittings; Industrial supplies; Fabricated pipe and fittings; Fluid power valves and hose fittings

(G-14221)
STUERTZ MACHINERY INC
Also Called: Sturtz Machinery
1624 Highland Rd (44087-2219)
PHONE...................330 405-0444
▲ **EMP:** 32 **EST:** 1997
SALES (est): 13.3MM
SALES (corp-wide): 2.67MM **Privately Held**
Web: www.stuertz.com
SIC: 5084 Industrial machinery and equipment
HQ: Sturtz Maschinenbau Gmbh
Linzer Str. 24
Neustadt (Wied) RP 53577
26833090

(G-14222)
THIRD FDRAL SAV LN ASSN CLVLAN
Also Called: Third Federal Savings
9057 Darrow Rd (44087-2138)
PHONE...................330 963-3130
Jennifer Ardelian, *Mgr*
EMP: 28
SALES (corp-wide): 1.05B **Publicly Held**
Web: www.thirdfederal.com
SIC: 6035 Federal savings and loan associations
HQ: Third Federal Savings And Loan Association Of Cleveland
7007 Broadway Ave
Cleveland OH 44105
800 844-7333

(G-14223)
TRI-MOR CORP (PA)
Also Called: Trimor
8530 N Boyle Pkwy (44087-2267)
PHONE...................330 963-3101
John R Morris Iii, *CEO*
Rich Desgee, *
Eryn Atrip, *
EMP: 80 **EST:** 1981
SALES (est): 29.9MM
SALES (corp-wide): 29.9MM **Privately Held**
Web: www.trimor.com
SIC: 1771 Blacktop (asphalt) work

(G-14224)
TURFSCAPE LLC
8490 Tower Dr (44087-2000)
PHONE...................330 405-7979
George M Hohman Junior, *Pr*
Marysue Hohman, *
EMP: 110 **EST:** 1988
SALES (est): 9.56MM **Privately Held**
Web: www.turfscapeohio.com
SIC: 0782 Landscape contractors

(G-14225)
UNIVERSITY HOSPITAL
8819 Commons Blvd (44087-4101)
PHONE...................330 486-9610
Larry Mcelroy, *Brnch Mgr*
EMP: 84
SALES (corp-wide): 25.52MM **Privately Held**
Web: www.uhhospitals.org
SIC: 8062 8221 Hospital, medical school affiliation; University
PA: University Hospital
3315 N Ridge Rd E Ste 100
Ashtabula OH 44004
440 964-8387

(G-14226)
US ADVANCED SYSTEMS LLC
1900 Case Pkwy S (44087-2358)
PHONE...................330 425-0020
Don Stetner, *Pr*
EMP: 42 **EST:** 2019
SALES (est): 5.33MM **Privately Held**
Web: www.usadsy.com
SIC: 5084 Industrial machinery and equipment

(G-14227)
US FOODS INC
8000 Bavaria Rd (44087-2262)
PHONE...................330 963-6789
Steve Preston, *Brnch Mgr*
EMP: 37
Web: www.usfoods.com
SIC: 5141 5149 Food brokers; Groceries and related products, nec
HQ: Us Foods, Inc.
9399 W Higgins Rd Ste 500
Rosemont IL 60018

(G-14228)
VERIZON WIRELESS
2000 Highland Rd (44087-2227)
PHONE...................330 963-1300
Jeffrey Gardner, *CFO*
EMP: 197
SALES (corp-wide): 100MM **Privately Held**
Web: www.verizonwireless.com
SIC: 4812 Cellular telephone services
PA: Verizon Wireless
15505 Sand Canyon Ave
Irvine CA 92618
949 286-7000

(G-14229)
VERSAPAY CORPORATION
1900 Enterprise Pkwy Ste A (44087)
PHONE...................216 535-9016
Craig O'neill, *Brnch Mgr*
EMP: 97
SALES (corp-wide): 3.59MM **Privately Held**
Web: www.versapay.com
SIC: 7389 Credit card service
PA: Versapay Corporation
18 King Street E 18th Fl
Toronto ON M5C 1
647 258-9380

(G-14230)
VMI GROUP INC
8413 Tower Dr (44087-2000)
PHONE...................330 405-4146
Neille Vitale, *Pr*
EMP: 90 **EST:** 2012
SQ FT: 800
SALES (est): 10.17MM **Privately Held**
Web: www.thevmigroup.com
SIC: 1771 1721 1791 Concrete work; Pavement marking contractor; Precast concrete structural framing or panels, placing of

(G-14231)
WORTHNGTON SMUEL COIL PROC LLC (HQ)
Also Called: Samuel Steel Pickling Company
1400 Enterprise Pkwy (44087-2242)
PHONE...................330 963-3777
Rick Snyder, *Prin*
EMP: 45 **EST:** 1989
SQ FT: 115,000
SALES (est): 20.65MM
SALES (corp-wide): 4.92B **Publicly Held**
Web: www.samuelsteelpickling.com
SIC: 7389 5051 3471 3398 Metal slitting and shearing; Metals service centers and offices ; Plating and polishing; Metal heat treating
PA: Worthington Enterprises, Inc.
200 W Old Wlson Bridge Rd
Worthington OH 43085
614 438-3210

(G-14232)
YOUNG CHEMICAL CO LLC (HQ)
1755 Enterprise Pkwy Ste 400 (44087)
PHONE...................330 486-4210
Mike Leighty, *CFO*
EMP: 32 **EST:** 2008
SALES (est): 10.75MM
SALES (corp-wide): 10.75MM **Privately Held**
Web: www.pvschemicals.com

SIC: 5169 Industrial chemicals
PA: Paro Services Co.
1755 Entp Pkwy Ste 100
Twinsburg OH 44087
330 467-1300

Uhrichsville
Tuscarawas County

(G-14233)
EMBER COMPLETE CARE
Also Called: EMBER COMPLETE CARE
730 N Water St (44683-1456)
PHONE.................................740 922-6968
Dennis Grandison, *Brnch Mgr*
EMP: 54
Web: www.embercomplete.com
SIC: 8082 Home health care services
PA: Ember Complete Care, Inc.
1800 N Water Street Ext
Uhrichsville OH 44683

(G-14234)
EMBER COMPLETE CARE INC (PA)
1800 N Water Street Ext (44683-1044)
P.O. Box 369 (44683-0369)
PHONE.................................740 922-6888
EMP: 42 EST: 1997
SALES (est): 9.39MM **Privately Held**
Web: www.embercomplete.com
SIC: 8082 Visiting nurse service

(G-14235)
NORTH STAR METALS MFG CO
6850 Edwards Ridge Rd Se (44683-5602)
P.O. Box 309 (44629-0309)
PHONE.................................740 254-4567
Darren Galbraith, *Pr*
EMP: 32 EST: 1997
SQ FT: 40,000
SALES (est): 23.08MM **Privately Held**
Web: www.northstarmetals.com
SIC: 1542 Nonresidential construction, nec

(G-14236)
NOVELIS ALR RECYCLING OHIO LLC
Also Called: Imco Recycling
7335 Newport Rd Se (44683-6368)
PHONE.................................740 922-2373
Sean M Stack, *CEO*
Robert R Holian, *
▲ EMP: 164 EST: 1992
SALES (est): 47.61MM **Privately Held**
Web: www.novelis.com
SIC: 3341 4953 Aluminum smelting and refining (secondary); Recycling, waste materials
PA: Hindalco Industries Limited
Plot-612/613, Tower 4,
Mumbai MH 40001

(G-14237)
UHRICHSVILLE HLTH CARE CTR INC
Also Called: Beacon Point Rehab
5166 Spanson Dr Se (44683-1346)
PHONE.................................740 922-2208
Brian Colleran, *Pr*
EMP: 44 EST: 1981
SQ FT: 25,000
SALES (est): 2.38MM **Privately Held**
Web: www.claymont-health.net
SIC: 8051 Convalescent home with continuous nursing care

(G-14238)
XPO LOGISTICS FREIGHT INC
2401 N Water Street Ext (44683-2400)
PHONE.................................740 922-5614
Larry Mccraken, *Brnch Mgr*
EMP: 51
SALES (corp-wide): 7.74B **Publicly Held**
Web: www.xpo.com
SIC: 4213 Contract haulers
HQ: Xpo Logistics Freight, Inc.
2211 Old Erhart Rd Ste 10
Ann Arbor MI 48105
800 755-2728

Union City
Darke County

(G-14239)
CROTINGER NURSING HOME INC
Also Called: Center of Hope
907 E Central St (45390-1605)
PHONE.................................937 968-5284
Meta Sue Livingston, *Pr*
Jamie Livingston, *
Phil Crawford, *
Eric Hiatt, *
EMP: 49 EST: 1961
SQ FT: 16,000
SALES (est): 2.22MM **Privately Held**
SIC: 8051 Convalescent home with continuous nursing care

Uniontown
Stark County

(G-14240)
AKRON GENERAL HEALTH SYSTEM
1940 Town Park Blvd (44685-7855)
PHONE.................................330 896-5070
EMP: 1587
SALES (corp-wide): 14.48B **Privately Held**
Web: www.akrongeneral.org
SIC: 8062 General medical and surgical hospitals
HQ: Akron General Health System
1 Akron General Ave
Akron OH 44307
330 344-6000

(G-14241)
AMERATHON LLC
3575 Forest Lake Dr Ste 500 (44685-8142)
PHONE.................................216 409-7201
Joe Martin, *Opers Mgr*
EMP: 50
SIC: 8071 Testing laboratories
HQ: Amerathon, Llc
671 Ohio Pike Ste K
Cincinnati OH 45245
513 752-7300

(G-14242)
BONTRAGER EXCAVATING CO INC
11087 Cleveland Ave Nw (44685-8677)
PHONE.................................330 499-8775
Brian Bontrager, *Pr*
Helen Bontrager, *
Eric Bontrager, *
EMP: 27 EST: 1972
SALES (est): 1.29MM **Privately Held**
SIC: 1794 Excavation work

(G-14243)
CAHILL CORPORATION
3951 Creek Wood Ln (44685-7786)
PHONE.................................330 724-1224
Edwin A Huth Junior, *Pr*
Lori Martin, *
EMP: 35 EST: 1907
SQ FT: 5,000
SALES (est): 1.31MM **Privately Held**
Web: www.cahillcorp.com

SIC: 1711 Mechanical contractor

(G-14244)
CAMBRIA GREEN MANAGEMENT LLC
Also Called: Cambria Stes Akrn-Canton Arprt
1787 Thorn Dr (44685-9573)
PHONE.................................330 899-1263
Chris Bitikofer, *Genl Mgr*
EMP: 28 EST: 2006
SALES (est): 715.55K **Privately Held**
Web: www.choicehotels.com
SIC: 7011 Hotels and motels

(G-14245)
CHESTERFIELD SERVICES INC
Also Called: Chesterfield Claims Services
3520 Forest Lake Dr (44685-8105)
PHONE.................................330 896-9777
EMP: 48 EST: 1991
SALES (est): 6.9MM **Privately Held**
Web: www.chesterfieldhealth.com
SIC: 8082 7371 Home health care services; Computer software development and applications

(G-14246)
CONSTRUCTION LABOR CONTRS LLC
3755 Boettler Oaks Dr Ste F (44685-9597)
PHONE.................................330 724-1906
Mike Temesi, *Brnch Mgr*
EMP: 244
Web: www.powerlaborusa.com
SIC: 7361 Labor contractors (employment agency)
HQ: Construction Labor Contractors, Llc
9760 Shepard Rd
Macedonia OH 44056
330 247-1080

(G-14247)
D & A PLUMBING & HEATING INC
11197 Cleveland Ave Nw (44685-9401)
P.O. Box 1017 (44685-1017)
PHONE.................................330 499-8733
Eric Seifert, *Pr*
Eugene Seifert, *Pr*
EMP: 36 EST: 1960
SQ FT: 3,200
SALES (est): 2.45MM **Privately Held**
Web: www.crowngroupohio.com
SIC: 1711 Warm air heating and air conditioning contractor

(G-14248)
DIEBOLD NIXDORF INCORPORATED
Also Called: North Amer Sls & Svc Ret Div
3800 Tabs Dr (44685-9564)
PHONE.................................330 899-0097
John Tyler, *Brnch Mgr*
EMP: 59
SALES (corp-wide): 1.63B **Publicly Held**
Web: www.dieboldnixdorf.com
SIC: 5049 Bank equipment and supplies
PA: Diebold Nixdorf, Incorporated
350 Orchard Ave Ne
North Canton OH 44720
330 490-4000

(G-14249)
DIRECTION HM AKRON CNTON AREA (PA)
1550 Corporate Woods Pkwy (44685-8730)
PHONE.................................330 896-9172
Barbara Kallenbach, *CFO*
Gary Cook, *
EMP: 135 EST: 1980
SQ FT: 19,502
SALES (est): 61.45MM

SALES (corp-wide): 61.45MM **Privately Held**
Web: www.dhad.org
SIC: 8322 Senior citizens' center or association

(G-14250)
FAIRWAY INDEPENDENT MRTG CORP
1840 Town Park Blvd Ste D (44685-7799)
PHONE.................................330 587-9152
Jason Kruger, *Brnch Mgr*
EMP: 45
Web: www.fairwayindependentmc.com
SIC: 6162 Mortgage bankers
PA: Fairway Independent Mortgage Corporation
4750 S Biltmore Ln
Madison WI 53718

(G-14251)
FE MORAN SEC SOLUTIONS LLC (DH)
Also Called: Honeywell Authorized Dealer
3800 Tabs Dr (44685-9564)
PHONE.................................217 403-6444
Tony Byerly, *Pr*
Stephen Filbert, *CFO*
Joe Jordan, *CSO*
EMP: 31 EST: 2015
SALES (est): 39.53MM
SALES (corp-wide): 12.7B **Privately Held**
Web: www.securitastechnology.com
SIC: 7382 Security systems services
HQ: Securitas Technology Corporation
3800 Tabs Dr
Uniontown OH 44685
800 548-4478

(G-14252)
FEDEX TRUCKLOAD BROKERAGE INC
1475 Boettler Rd (44685-9584)
P.O. Box 5000 (44232-5000)
PHONE.................................800 463-3339
Virginia Albanese, *Pr*
EMP: 123 EST: 2006
SALES (est): 37.25MM
SALES (corp-wide): 90.16B **Publicly Held**
Web: truckload.fedex.com
SIC: 4731 Freight transportation arrangement
HQ: Fedex Custom Critical, Inc.
4205 Highlander Pkwy
Richfield OH 44286
234 310-4090

(G-14253)
GARDINER SERVICE COMPANY LLC
Also Called: Trane, The
1530 Corporate Woods Pkwy Ste 200 (44685-7852)
PHONE.................................330 896-9358
William Gardiner, *Brnch Mgr*
EMP: 69
SALES (corp-wide): 68.27MM **Privately Held**
Web: www.whgardiner.com
SIC: 1711 Mechanical contractor
PA: Gardiner Service Company Llc
31200 Bainbridge Rd Ste 1
Solon OH 44139
440 248-3400

(G-14254)
HAMMOND CONSTRUCTION INC
1550 Corporate Woods Pkwy (44685-8730)
PHONE.................................330 455-7039
William A Schurman, *Pr*
Victor Gramoy Junior, *Sec*
John Kirkpatrick, *
EMP: 80 EST: 1973

GEOGRAPHIC SECTION

Upper Arlington - Franklin County (G-14277)

SALES (est): 46.46MM **Privately Held**
Web: www.hammondconstruction.com
SIC: 1542 1541 8741 Commercial and office building contractors; Industrial buildings and warehouses; Construction management

(G-14255)
HANKOOK TIRE AMERICA CORP
Also Called: Hankook Tire Akron Office
3535 Forest Lake Dr (44685-8105)
PHONE..................330 896-6199
Raymond Labuda, Mgr
EMP: 40
Web: www.hankook-atc.com
SIC: 5014 5013 Automobile tires and tubes; Automotive batteries
HQ: Hankook Tire America Corporation
333 Commerce St Ste 600
Nashville TN 37201
615 432-0700

(G-14256)
HATTIE LRLHAM CTR FOR CHLDREN
1402 Boettler Rd, Ste B (44685-9219)
PHONE..................330 274-2272
EMP: 41
SALES (corp-wide): 61.41MM **Privately Held**
Web: www.hattielarlham.org
SIC: 8361 Mentally handicapped home
PA: Hattie Larlham Center For Children With Disabilities
9772 Diagonal Rd
Mantua OH 44255
330 274-2272

(G-14257)
HEREFORD SECURITY GROUP
Also Called: Hereford Group
3280 Parfoure Blvd (44685-7832)
PHONE..................330 644-1371
Brian Mcpeters, Pr
Brian M Mcpeters, Pr
EMP: 99 EST: 2001
SALES (est): 1.1MM **Privately Held**
SIC: 7381 Detective and armored car services

(G-14258)
MAYFAIR COUNTRY CLUB INC
Also Called: Mayfair Country Club
2229 Raber Rd (44685-8844)
PHONE..................330 699-2209
David Springer, Pr
Jeannie Springer, *
EMP: 57
SQ FT: 15,582
SALES (est): 1.09MM **Privately Held**
Web: www.mayfaircountryclub.com
SIC: 7992 Public golf courses

(G-14259)
MILLMAN SURVEYING INC
3475 Forest Lake Dr Ste 175 (44685)
PHONE..................330 342-0723
Deron Millman, Brnch Mgr
EMP: 31
Web: www.millmanland.com
SIC: 8713 Surveying services
HQ: Millman Surveying, Inc.
950 Main Ave
Cleveland OH 44113

(G-14260)
NEW INNOVATIONS INC
3540 Forest Lake Dr (44685-8105)
PHONE..................330 899-9954
Stephen C Reed, CEO
Denise M Reed, *
EMP: 31 EST: 1991
SQ FT: 7,500
SALES (est): 4.7MM **Privately Held**
Web: www.new-innov.com
SIC: 7371 Computer software development

(G-14261)
OAK CLINIC
3838 Massillon Rd Ste 360 (44685-7965)
PHONE..................330 896-9625
Timothy Carrabine, CEO
EMP: 36 EST: 2000
SALES (est): 56.71MM **Privately Held**
Web: www.oakclinic.com
SIC: 8093 Specialty outpatient clinics, nec

(G-14262)
RAINTREE COUNTRY CLUB INC
4350 Mayfair Rd (44685-8137)
PHONE..................330 699-3232
John Rainieri Senior, Pr
John Rainieri Junior, VP
Melinda Haynes, Sec
EMP: 27 EST: 1993
SQ FT: 10,000
SALES (est): 604.86K **Privately Held**
Web: www.golfraintree.com
SIC: 7997 Country club, membership

(G-14263)
SCHEESER BUCKLEY MAYFIELD LLC
1540 Corporate Woods Pkwy (44685-8730)
PHONE..................330 896-4664
EMP: 43 EST: 2006
SALES (est): 5.31MM **Privately Held**
Web: www.sbmce.com
SIC: 8711 Consulting engineer

(G-14264)
SECURITAS TECHNOLOGY CORP
Also Called: Securitas Electronic
3800 Tabs Dr (44685-9564)
PHONE..................800 548-4478
Kevin Engelhardt, Pr
EMP: 56
SALES (corp-wide): 12.7B **Privately Held**
Web: www.securitastechnology.com
SIC: 7382 Protective devices, security
HQ: Securitas Technology Corporation
3800 Tabs Dr
Uniontown OH 44685
800 548-4478

(G-14265)
SUMMA HEALTH
Also Called: SUMMA HEALTH
3838 Massillon Rd Ste 320 (44685-7965)
PHONE..................330 899-5599
Karl Tan, Mgr
EMP: 75
SALES (corp-wide): 1.78B **Privately Held**
Web: www.summahealth.org
SIC: 8062 General medical and surgical hospitals
PA: Summa Health System
1077 Gorge Blvd
Akron OH 44310
330 375-3000

(G-14266)
SUMMIT OPHTHALMOLOGY INC
3838 Massillon Rd Ste 370 (44685-6215)
PHONE..................330 899-9641
EMP: 89
SALES (corp-wide): 2.38MM **Privately Held**
Web: www.summiteyemd.com
SIC: 8011 Opthalmologist
PA: Summit Ophthalmology Inc
1 Park West Blvd Ste 150
Akron OH 44320
330 864-8060

(G-14267)
SURGERE LLC
3500 Massillon Rd Ste 100 (44685)
PHONE..................330 966-3746
William J Wappler, CEO
EMP: 65 EST: 2005
SALES (est): 9.64MM **Privately Held**
Web: www.surgere.com
SIC: 8742 Business management consultant

(G-14268)
TOTAL LOOP INC
1790 Town Park Blvd Ste A (44685-7972)
PHONE..................888 614-5667
Vincenzo Rubino, Pr
EMP: 100 EST: 2012
SALES (est): 9.75MM **Privately Held**
Web: www.totalloop.com
SIC: 5045 Computer software

(G-14269)
UNDERGROUND SERVICES INC
3223 Rockingham St Nw (44685-6831)
P.O. Box 190 (44685-0190)
PHONE..................330 323-0166
Robert S Fisher, Pr
EMP: 48
SIC: 8711 Engineering services
PA: Underground Services, Inc.
703 Werstler Ave Nw
Canton OH 44720

(G-14270)
WH MIDWEST LLC (PA)
Also Called: Wayne Homes
3777 Boettler Oaks Dr (44685-7733)
PHONE..................330 896-7611
David E Logsdon, Managing Member
William A Post, *
EMP: 60 EST: 2010
SQ FT: 16,000
SALES (est): 38.16MM
SALES (corp-wide): 38.16MM **Privately Held**
SIC: 1521 New construction, single-family houses

(G-14271)
XPO LOGISTICS FREIGHT INC
3733 Massillon Rd (44685-7730)
PHONE..................330 896-7300
EMP: 51
SALES (corp-wide): 7.74B **Publicly Held**
Web: www.xpo.com
SIC: 4213 4231 4212 Contract haulers; Trucking terminal facilities; Local trucking, without storage
HQ: Xpo Logistics Freight, Inc.
2211 Old Erhart Rd Ste 10
Ann Arbor MI 48105
800 755-2728

(G-14272)
YOUNG MNS CHRSTN ASSN OF AKRON
Also Called: YMCA
3800 Massillon Rd (44685-8725)
PHONE..................330 899-9622
Lorie Lautphenglager, Dir
EMP: 38
SALES (corp-wide): 21.21MM **Privately Held**
Web: www.akronymca.org
SIC: 8641 8351 Recreation association; Child day care services
PA: The Young Men's Christian Association Of Akron Ohio
50 S Mn St Ste Ll100
Akron OH 44308
330 376-1335

(G-14273)
YP LLC
Also Called: AT&T
1530 Corporate Woods Pkwy Ste 100 (44685-6707)
P.O. Box 665 (44232-0665)
PHONE..................330 896-6000
EMP: 178
SALES (corp-wide): 916.96MM **Publicly Held**
Web: www.adt.com
SIC: 7382 Security systems services
HQ: Yp Llc
2247 Northlake Pkwy Fl 4
Tucker GA 30084
866 570-8863

University Heights
Cuyahoga County

(G-14274)
121ECOMMERCE LLC
2447 Bromley Rd (44118-3961)
PHONE..................216 586-6656
Benjamin Chafetz, CEO
Smadar Chafetz, *
Benjamin Chafetz, Genl Mgr
EMP: 50 EST: 2014
SALES (est): 3.48MM **Privately Held**
Web: www.121ecommerce.com
SIC: 7371 Computer software development

Upper Arlington
Franklin County

(G-14275)
AMERICAS URGENT CARE
Also Called: AMERICA'S URGENT CARE
4661 Sawmill Rd Ste 101 (43220-6123)
PHONE..................614 929-2721
EMP: 108
Web: www.uaurgentcare.com
SIC: 8011 Freestanding emergency medical center
PA: Americas Urgent Care Of Hunters Creek Llc
6525 W Campus Oval # 150
New Albany OH 43054

(G-14276)
ARLINGTON CRT NRSING HM SVC IN (PA)
Also Called: Arlington Crt Sklled Nrsing Rh
1605 Nw Professional Plz (43220-3866)
PHONE..................614 545-5502
Allan Vrable, Pr
Linda Vrable, *
James Merrill, *
EMP: 63 EST: 1970
SQ FT: 50,000
SALES (est): 5.21MM
SALES (corp-wide): 5.21MM **Privately Held**
Web: www.optalishealthcare.com
SIC: 8052 8051 Intermediate care facilities; Extended care facility

(G-14277)
DELTA GAMMA FRATERNITY (PA)
Also Called: ANCHOR TRADER
3250 Riverside Dr (43221-1725)
P.O. Box 21397 (43221-0397)
PHONE..................614 481-8169
Betsy Fouss, Ex Dir
Heather Daverio, *
EMP: 45 EST: 1873
SQ FT: 22,000
SALES (est): 9.85MM

Upper Arlington - Franklin County (G-14278)

SALES (corp-wide): 9.85MM **Privately Held**
Web: www.deltagamma.org
SIC: 8641 Fraternal associations

(G-14278)
FIRST MERCHANTS BANK
2130 Tremont Ctr (43221-3110)
PHONE...................614 486-9000
Paul Demas, *Brnch Mgr*
EMP: 30
SALES (corp-wide): 999.49MM **Publicly Held**
Web: www.firstmerchants.com
SIC: 6029 6163 Commercial banks, nec; Loan brokers
HQ: First Merchants Bank
9301 S Innovation Dr
Daleville IN 47334
800 205-3464

(G-14279)
LANE AVENUE HOTEL HOLDINGS LLC
Also Called: TownePlace Suites Columbus N
1640 W Lane Ave (43221-3925)
PHONE...................614 486-5433
Brent Crawford, *Prin*
Allison Srail, *Prin*
EMP: 40 EST: 2018
SALES (est): 1.1MM **Privately Held**
Web: www.marriott.com
SIC: 7011 Hotels and motels

(G-14280)
MANIFEST SOLUTIONS CORP
Also Called: Manifest Software
2035 Riverside Dr (43221-4012)
PHONE...................614 930-2800
EMP: 65 EST: 1994
SALES (est): 10.34MM **Privately Held**
Web: www.manifestcorp.com
SIC: 7371 7373 Computer software systems analysis and design, custom; Local area network (LAN) systems integrator

(G-14281)
ORTHOPAEDIC & TRAUMA SURGEONS INC
Also Called: Ohio Orthopedic Ctr Excellence
4605 Sawmill Rd (43220-2246)
PHONE...................614 827-8700
EMP: 90
SIC: 8011 Orthopedic physician

(G-14282)
SUNRISE SENIOR LIVING LLC
Also Called: Sunrise On The Scioto
3500 Riverside Dr (43221-1753)
PHONE...................614 457-3500
Suzanne Johns, *Mgr*
EMP: 49
SALES (corp-wide): 2.92B **Privately Held**
Web: www.sunriseseniorliving.com
SIC: 8059 8051 Rest home, with health care; Skilled nursing care facilities
HQ: Sunrise Senior Living, Llc
7902 Westpark Dr
Mc Lean VA 22102

(G-14283)
VISION DEVELOPMENT INC
3300 Riverside Dr Ste 100 (43221-1766)
PHONE...................614 487-1804
P Brent Wrightsel, *Pr*
EMP: 40 EST: 1994
SQ FT: 2,300
SALES (est): 5.32MM **Privately Held**
Web: www.visiondevinc.com

SIC: 6552 Subdividers and developers, nec

Upper Sandusky
Wyandot County

(G-14284)
ANGELINE INDUSTRIES INC
210 N Sandusky Ave (43351-1234)
PHONE...................419 294-4488
Todd Dilley, *Dir*
EMP: 45 EST: 1975
SALES (est): 1.07MM **Privately Held**
Web: www.wycbdd.org
SIC: 8331 Sheltered workshop

(G-14285)
COMMERCIAL BANCSHARES INC
118 S Sandusky Ave (43351-1424)
P.O. Box 90 (43351-0090)
PHONE...................419 294-5781
EMP: 98
Web: www.csbanking.com
SIC: 6022 State commercial banks

(G-14286)
COUNTY OF WYANDOT
Also Called: Wyandot County Home
7830 State Highway 199 (43351-9333)
PHONE...................419 294-1714
David Oucid, *Owner*
EMP: 53
SALES (corp-wide): 28.39MM **Privately Held**
Web: www.wyandotchamber.com
SIC: 8059 Nursing home, except skilled and intermediate care facility
PA: County Of Wyandot
109 S Sandusky Ave Rm 10
Upper Sandusky OH 43351
419 294-6436

(G-14287)
CUSTOM AGRI SYSTEMS INC
1289 N Warpole St (43351-9381)
PHONE...................419 209-0940
Rick Storch, *Pr*
EMP: 30
SALES (corp-wide): 35.63MM **Privately Held**
Web: www.casindustries.com
SIC: 0723 Grain drying services
PA: Custom Agri Systems, Inc.
255 County Road R
Napoleon OH 43545
419 599-5180

(G-14288)
FAIRBORN EQUIPMENT COMPANY INC (PA)
225 Tarhe Trl (43351-8700)
P.O. Box 123 (43351-0123)
PHONE...................419 209-0760
Mark Dillon, *Pr*
John H Elgin, *
EMP: 39 EST: 1991
SQ FT: 55,000
SALES (est): 24.46MM
SALES (corp-wide): 24.46MM **Privately Held**
Web: www.fairbornequipment.com
SIC: 5084 Materials handling machinery

(G-14289)
FIRST CTZENS NAT BNK OF UPPER (PA)
100 N Sandusky Ave (43351-1254)
P.O. Box 299 (43351-0299)
PHONE...................419 294-2351
Mark Johnson, *Pr*

Brant Zucker, *
Jevon Reile, *CIO**
Jenny Romich, *CLO**
Pam Baker, *
EMP: 40 EST: 1860
SALES (est): 11.04MM
SALES (corp-wide): 11.04MM **Privately Held**
Web: www.firstcitizensnational.com
SIC: 6021 National commercial banks

(G-14290)
KIMMEL CORPORATION (PA)
225 N Sandusky Ave (43351-1233)
P.O. Box 98 (43351-0098)
PHONE...................419 294-1959
TOLL FREE: 800
Kurt Kimmel, *Pr*
Mark Kimmel, *
Debbie Amos, *
EMP: 58 EST: 1931
SQ FT: 30,000
SALES (est): 4.17MM
SALES (corp-wide): 4.17MM **Privately Held**
Web: www.kimmeluniform.com
SIC: 7216 7218 7213 Drycleaning plants, except rugs; Laundered mat and rug supply ; Towel supply

(G-14291)
LUCAS FUNERAL HOMES INC (PA)
Also Called: Lucas-Batton Funeral Homes
476 S Sandusky Ave (43351-1597)
PHONE...................419 294-1985
Daniel P Lucas, *Pr*
EMP: 33 EST: 1913
SQ FT: 3,000
SALES (est): 1.05MM
SALES (corp-wide): 1.05MM **Privately Held**
Web: www.lucasfuneralhomes.com
SIC: 7261 5999 Funeral home; Alarm and safety equipment stores

(G-14292)
SCHMIDT MACHINE COMPANY
Also Called: S M C
7013 State Highway 199 (43351-9347)
PHONE...................419 294-3814
TOLL FREE: 800
Bill Junior, *Pr*
Randy F Schmidt, *
Kevin Schmidt, *
Darlene Mooney, *
Dorothy M Schmidt, *
EMP: 50 EST: 1935
SQ FT: 2,500
SALES (est): 9.62MM **Privately Held**
Web: www.schmidtmachine.com
SIC: 3599 7692 5083 Machine shop, jobbing and repair; Welding repair; Farm equipment parts and supplies

(G-14293)
SK HOSPITALITY LLC
Also Called: Quality Inn
105 Comfort Dr (43351-9623)
PHONE...................419 294-3891
EMP: 116
SALES (corp-wide): 665.33K **Privately Held**
Web: www.choicehotels.com
SIC: 7011 Hotels and motels
PA: Sk Hospitality, Llc
24 N Bridge St
Chillicothe OH 45601
740 603-4910

(G-14294)
UNITED CHURCH HOMES INC
Also Called: Fairhaven Community
850 Marseilles Ave (43351-1648)
PHONE...................419 294-4973
Daniel Miller, *Dir*
EMP: 43
SALES (corp-wide): 115.52MM **Privately Held**
Web: www.unitedchurchhomes.org
SIC: 8059 8661 8052 Personal care home, with health care; Religious organizations; Intermediate care facilities
PA: United Church Homes, Inc.
170 E Center St
Marion OH 43302
800 837-2211

(G-14295)
WYANDOT CNTY CNCIL ON AGING IN
127 S Sandusky Ave (43351-1451)
PHONE...................419 294-5733
Sherri Wagner, *Ex Dir*
Virginia Blankenship, *
EMP: 35 EST: 1974
SQ FT: 4,000
SALES (est): 963.02K **Privately Held**
Web: www.wyandotseniors.com
SIC: 8322 Senior citizens' center or association

(G-14296)
XPO LOGISTICS FREIGHT INC
1850 E Wyandot Ave (43351-9652)
PHONE...................419 294-5728
Paul Masano, *Mgr*
EMP: 31
SALES (corp-wide): 7.74B **Publicly Held**
Web: www.xpo.com
SIC: 4213 Contract haulers
HQ: Xpo Logistics Freight, Inc.
2211 Old Erhart Rd Ste 10
Ann Arbor MI 48105
800 755-2728

Urbana
Champaign County

(G-14297)
BEYOND HOMECARE LLC
31 1/2 Monument Sq (43078-2059)
PHONE...................937 704-4002
Jessica Thomas, *Prin*
Shawana Bonner, *Prin*
EMP: 40 EST: 2017
SALES (est): 996.61K **Privately Held**
Web: www.beyond-homecare.com
SIC: 8082 Home health care services

(G-14298)
BOSTON COMPANY INC
Also Called: The Boston Company Inc.
121 N Main St (43078-1601)
PHONE...................937 652-0410
EMP: 1068
SALES (corp-wide): 17.5B **Publicly Held**
Web: www.boston.gov
SIC: 5149 Coffee and tea
HQ: The Boston Company Inc
1 Boston Pl Ste 2100
Boston MA 02108
617 722-7000

(G-14299)
CARDILGIST OF CLARK CHMPIGN CN
900 E Court St (43078-1887)
PHONE...................937 653-8897
Akber Mohammed, *Pr*

EMP: 105
SIC: 8011 Cardiologist and cardio-vascular specialist
PA: Cardiologist Of Clark & Champaign Counties Inc
100 W Mccreight Ave # 150
Springfield OH 45504

(G-14300)
CHAMPAIGN CNTY BOARD OF DD
Also Called: Champaign County Board of Mrdd
1250 E Us Highway 36 (43078-8002)
P.O. Box 829 (43078-0829)
PHONE................................937 653-5217
Jeanne Bowman, *Pr*
Max Coates, *
Bill Kremer, *
EMP: 295 **EST:** 2011
SALES (est): 2.15MM
SALES (corp-wide): 31.76MM **Privately Held**
Web: www.champaigncbdd.org
SIC: 8322 9431 Individual and family services; Child health program administration, government
PA: County Of Champaign
1250 E State Rt 29 Ste 3
Urbana OH 43078
937 653-5217

(G-14301)
CHAMPAIGN RESIDENTIAL SVCS INC (PA)
1150 Scioto St Ste 201 (43078-2292)
P.O. Box 29 (43078-0029)
PHONE................................937 653-1320
Than Johnson, *CEO*
Ed Corwin, *
Jeff Mcculla, *Treas*
Mary Ann Metherd, *
EMP: 70 **EST:** 1976
SQ FT: 40,000
SALES (est): 40.28MM
SALES (corp-wide): 40.28MM **Privately Held**
Web: www.crsi-oh.com
SIC: 8361 Retarded home

(G-14302)
CHAMPAIGN TRANSIT SYSTEM
1512 S Us Highway 68 Ste K100 (43078-9198)
PHONE................................937 653-8777
Gary Ledford, *Dir*
Glenda Harper, *Dir*
EMP: 103 **EST:** 1988
SQ FT: 1,100
SALES (est): 477.29K
SALES (corp-wide): 31.76MM **Privately Held**
Web: co.champaign.oh.us
SIC: 4111 Local and suburban transit
PA: County Of Champaign
1250 E State Rt 29 Ste 3
Urbana OH 43078
937 653-5217

(G-14303)
CITIZENS NAT BNK URBANA OHIO
1 Monument Sq (43078-9918)
PHONE................................937 653-1200
James Wilson, *Pr*
Timothy Bunnell, *
EMP: 56 **EST:** 1865
SQ FT: 8,000
SALES (est): 2.42MM
SALES (corp-wide): 564.3MM **Publicly Held**
SIC: 6021 National commercial banks
PA: Park National Corporation

50 N 3rd St
Newark OH 43055
740 349-8451

(G-14304)
CMBB LLC
Also Called: Bundy Baking Solutions
417 E Water St (43078-2367)
P.O. Box 150 (43078-0150)
PHONE................................937 652-2151
Russell T Bundy, *Managing Member*
Elizabeth A Bundy, *Sec*
William Mccoy, *Prin*
EMP: 170 **EST:** 2006
SQ FT: 55,800
SALES (est): 15.81MM **Privately Held**
Web: www.bundybakingsolutions.com
SIC: 5046 7699 Bakery equipment and supplies; Baking pan glazing and cleaning

(G-14305)
COUNTY OF CHAMPAIGN
Also Called: Champaign County Engineer
428 Beech St (43078-1920)
P.O. Box 669 (43078-0669)
PHONE................................937 653-4848
EMP: 64
SALES (corp-wide): 31.76MM **Privately Held**
Web: engineer.co.champaign.oh.us
SIC: 8711 Consulting engineer
PA: County Of Champaign
1250 E State Rt 29 Ste 3
Urbana OH 43078
937 653-5217

(G-14306)
COUNTY OF CHAMPAIGN
Also Called: Champaign County Auditor
1512 S Us Highway 68 Ste B300 (43078-9198)
PHONE................................937 653-2711
Bonnie Warman, *Mgr*
EMP: 39
SALES (corp-wide): 31.76MM **Privately Held**
Web: www.champaigndjfs.org
SIC: 8721 Accounting, auditing, and bookkeeping
PA: County Of Champaign
1250 E State Rt 29 Ste 3
Urbana OH 43078
937 653-5217

(G-14307)
FIRST TRANSIT INC
2200 S Us Highway 68 (43078-9470)
PHONE................................937 652-4175
Pam Hoffner, *Brnch Mgr*
EMP: 76
SALES (est): 4.23MM **Privately Held**
Web: www.transdevna.com
SIC: 4111 Bus transportation
HQ: First Transit, Inc.
600 Vine St Ste 1400
Cincinnati OH 45202
513 241-2200

(G-14308)
GRIMES AEROSPACE COMPANY
Also Called: Honeywell
550 State Route 55 (43078-9482)
PHONE................................937 484-2001
Bruce Blagg, *Brnch Mgr*
EMP: 66
SALES (corp-wide): 36.66B **Publicly Held**

SIC: 5088 7699 3812 3769 Aircraft and parts, nec; Aircraft and heavy equipment repair services; Search and navigation equipment; Space vehicle equipment, nec
HQ: Grimes Aerospace Company
550 State Route 55
Urbana OH 43078
937 484-2000

(G-14309)
J & J SCHLAEGEL INC
1250 E Us Highway 36 (43078-8002)
PHONE................................937 652-2045
Jerry Schlaegel, *Pr*
Jeff Schlaegel, *
EMP: 36 **EST:** 1987
SQ FT: 625
SALES (est): 4.03MM **Privately Held**
SIC: 1622 Bridge construction

(G-14310)
RITTAL CORPORATION
1000 S Edgewood Ave (43078-9694)
PHONE................................937 399-0500
◆ **EMP:** 43 **EST:** 2014
SALES (est): 4.39MM **Privately Held**
Web: www.rittal.com
SIC: 7389 Automobile recovery service

(G-14311)
RITTAL NORTH AMERICA LLC
1 Rittal Pl (43078-5003)
PHONE................................937 399-0500
Gregg Holst, *Brnch Mgr*
EMP: 209
SALES (corp-wide): 167.14K **Privately Held**
Web: www.rittal.com
SIC: 1731 Energy management controls
HQ: Rittal North America Llc
425 N Martingale Rd # 1540
Schaumburg IL 60173
847 240-4600

(G-14312)
RUSSELL T BUNDY ASSOCIATES INC (PA)
Also Called: Bundy Baking Solutions
417 E Water St (43078-2154)
P.O. Box 150 (43078-0150)
PHONE................................937 652-2151
Gilbert Bundy, *CEO*
Elizabeth A Bundy, *Sec*
◆ **EMP:** 55 **EST:** 1964
SQ FT: 55,800
SALES (est): 50.03MM
SALES (corp-wide): 50.03MM **Privately Held**
Web: www.bundybakingsolutions.com
SIC: 5046 7699 Bakery equipment and supplies; Baking pan glazing and cleaning

(G-14313)
SHIPPERS AUTOMOTIVE GROUP LLC
1155 Phoenix Dr (43078-8203)
PHONE................................937 484-7780
Chris Watkins, *Prin*
EMP: 150 **EST:** 1991
SALES (est): 4.93MM **Privately Held**
Web: www.shippersautomotive.com
SIC: 4225 General warehousing and storage

(G-14314)
URBANA COUNTRY CLUB
4761 E Us Highway 36 (43078-9596)
P.O. Box 835 (43078-0835)
PHONE................................937 653-1690
William White, *Pr*
EMP: 31 **EST:** 1923

SALES (est): 1.84MM **Privately Held**
Web: www.urbana.club
SIC: 7997 Country club, membership

(G-14315)
URBANA HEALTHCARE GROUP LLC
Also Called: Urbana Health & Rehab Center
741 E Water St (43078-2156)
PHONE................................937 652-1381
EMP: 240 **EST:** 2007
SALES (est): 4.25MM
SALES (corp-wide): 655.44MM **Privately Held**
Web: www.saberhealth.com
SIC: 8051 8093 Convalescent home with continuous nursing care; Rehabilitation center, outpatient treatment
PA: Saber Healthcare Group, L.L.C.
23700 Commerce Park
Beachwood OH 44122
216 292-5706

(G-14316)
VERNON FUNERAL HOMES INC
235 Miami St (43078-2024)
PHONE................................937 653-8888
Dave Vernon, *Brnch Mgr*
EMP: 46
Web: www.vernonfh.com
SIC: 7261 Funeral home
PA: Vernon Funeral Homes, Inc.
257 W Main St
Mechanicsburg OH 43044

(G-14317)
WHITES SERVICE CENTER INC
Also Called: White'S Ford
1246 N Main St (43078)
P.O. Box 38129 (43078)
PHONE................................937 653-5279
Jeffrey White, *Pr*
James Donahue, *
James White, *
EMP: 32 **EST:** 1948
SQ FT: 18,000
SALES (est): 5.17MM **Privately Held**
Web: www.whitesautogroup.com
SIC: 5511 5013 5012 Automobiles, new and used; Automotive supplies and parts; Trucks, commercial

Urbancrest
Franklin County

(G-14318)
AASHNA CORPORATION
Also Called: Knights Inn
3131 Broadway (43123-1400)
PHONE................................614 871-0065
Premal Patel, *Prin*
EMP: 37 **EST:** 1998
SQ FT: 4,355
SALES (est): 463.41K **Privately Held**
Web: www.sonesta.com
SIC: 7011 Hotels and motels

(G-14319)
BESTDRIVE LLC
Also Called: Bestdrive
3315 Urbancrest Industrial Dr (43123-1783)
PHONE................................614 284-7549
EMP: 539
SALES (corp-wide): 45.02B **Privately Held**
Web: www.bestdrivetire.com
SIC: 5014 Tires and tubes
HQ: Bestdrive, Llc
854 Paragon Way
Rock Hill SC 29730
800 450-3187

Urbancrest - Franklin County (G-14320)

(G-14320)
HAYDEN VALLEY FOODS INC (PA)
Also Called: Tropical Nut & Fruit
3150 Urbancrest Industrial Dr (43123-1767)
PHONE..................................614 539-7233
▲ EMP: 72 EST: 1984
SALES (est): 32.98MM Privately Held
Web: www.haydenvalleyfoods.com
SIC: 5149 2068 2064 2034 Fruits, dried; Salted and roasted nuts and seeds; Candy and other confectionery products; Dried and dehydrated fruits, vegetables and soup mixes

(G-14321)
MCKESSON MEDICAL-SURGIAL INC
Also Called: McKesson
3500 Centerpoint Dr Ste A (43123-1495)
PHONE..................................614 539-2600
EMP: 200
SALES (corp-wide): 308.95B Publicly Held
Web: www.mckesson.com
SIC: 5122 Pharmaceuticals
HQ: Mckesson Medical-Surgical Inc.
9954 Mayland Dr Ste 4000
Richmond VA 23233
855 571-2100

(G-14322)
PALMER-DONAVIN MFG CO (PA)
3210 Centerpoint Dr (43123-1464)
P.O. Box 2109 (43216-2109)
PHONE..................................800 652-1234
Robert J Woodward Junior, Ch Bd
Ronald Calhoun, *
Robert J Mccollow, VP Opers
David Zimmerman, *
Eric Belke, Marine Division Vice President*
▲ EMP: 57 EST: 1907
SQ FT: 73,000
SALES (est): 292.82MM
SALES (corp-wide): 292.82MM Privately Held
Web: www.palmerdonavin.com
SIC: 5033 Roofing and siding materials

(G-14323)
SYSCO GUEST SUPPLY LLC
Also Called: Guest Supply Services
3330 Urbancrest Industrial Dr (43123-1769)
PHONE..................................614 539-9348
Kenneth Bliss, Brnch Mgr
EMP: 40
SALES (corp-wide): 76.32B Publicly Held
Web: www.guestsupply.com
SIC: 5122 Toilet soap
HQ: Sysco Guest Supply, Llc
300 Davidson Ave
Somerset NJ 08873
732 537-2297

(G-14324)
TERRAFIRM CONSTRUCTION LLC
3458 Lewis Centre Way (43123-6502)
PHONE..................................913 433-2998
Michael Coccia, Treas
EMP: 48 EST: 2014
SALES (est): 1.17MM
SALES (corp-wide): 43.17MM Privately Held
Web: www.terrafirmconstruction.com
SIC: 1799 Caulking (construction)
PA: C.J. Mahan Construction Company, Llc
3458 Lewis Centre Way
Grove City OH 43123
614 277-4545

(G-14325)
UNITED PARCEL SERVICE INC
Also Called: UPS
3500 Centerpoint Dr (43123-1495)
PHONE..................................614 277-3300
EMP: 93
SALES (corp-wide): 90.96B Publicly Held
Web: www.ups.com
SIC: 4215 Parcel delivery, vehicular
HQ: United Parcel Service, Inc.
55 Glenlake Pkwy
Atlanta GA 30328
404 828-6000

(G-14326)
WATKINS AND SHEPARD TRCKG INC
3430 Urbancrest Industrial Dr (43123-1726)
PHONE..................................614 832-0440
EMP: 93
SALES (corp-wide): 5.5B Publicly Held
Web: www.wksh.com
SIC: 4213 Trucking, except local
HQ: Watkins And Shepard Trucking, Inc.
3101 Packerland Dr
Green Bay WI 54313
406 532-6121

(G-14327)
WESTPATRICK CORP
3458 Lewis Centre Way (43123-6502)
PHONE..................................614 875-8200
Charles Jeffrey Mahan, Pr
Douglas R Mccrae, Mng Pt
Gary D Yancer, Mng Pt
EMP: 40 EST: 1975
SALES (est): 8.45MM Privately Held
SIC: 1622 1611 Bridge construction; General contractor, highway and street construction

Utica
Licking County

(G-14328)
LICKING RUR ELCTRIFICATION INC (PA)
11339 Mount Vernon Rd (43080-7703)
P.O. Box 455 (43080-0455)
PHONE..................................740 892-2071
Charles Manning, Pr
Charles Manning, CEO
Dave Mussard, Ch
Neil Buxton, VP
Arland K Rogers, *
EMP: 58 EST: 1936
SQ FT: 20,000
SALES (est): 130.87MM
SALES (corp-wide): 130.87MM Privately Held
Web: www.theenergycoop.com
SIC: 4911 Distribution, electric power

(G-14329)
LIVING CARE ALTRNTVES OF UTICA
Also Called: Utica Nursing Home
233 N Main St (43080-7705)
P.O. Box 2126 (43056-0126)
PHONE..................................740 892-3414
Thomas J Rosser, Pr
EMP: 47 EST: 1960
SQ FT: 7,500
SALES (est): 2.54MM Privately Held
Web: www.uticaanimalcarecenter.com
SIC: 8052 Personal care facility

(G-14330)
VELVET ICE CREAM COMPANY (PA)
Also Called: Ye Olde Mille Shoppe
11324 Mount Vernon Rd (43080-7703)
P.O. Box 588 (43080-0588)
PHONE..................................740 892-3921
EMP: 60 EST: 1960
SALES (est): 21.87MM
SALES (corp-wide): 21.87MM Privately Held
Web: www.velveticecream.com
SIC: 2024 8412 5812 5947 Ice cream, bulk; Museum; American restaurant; Gift shop

Valley City
Medina County

(G-14331)
ARNOLD CORPORATION
Also Called: Arnold Company
5965 Grafton Rd (44280-9329)
P.O. Box 368022 (44136-9722)
PHONE..................................330 225-2600
◆ EMP: 107
SIC: 5083 3524 Lawn and garden machinery and equipment; Lawn and garden mowers and accessories

(G-14332)
CHGC INC
Also Called: Cherokee Hills Golf Club
5740 Center Rd (44280-9746)
PHONE..................................330 225-6122
Ed Haddad, Pr
Marcia Haddad, *
Mark Haddad, *
EMP: 49 EST: 1984
SQ FT: 20,000
SALES (est): 987.64K Privately Held
Web: www.coppertopgolf.com
SIC: 7992 5812 Public golf courses; Eating places

(G-14333)
DUNLOP AND JOHNSTON INC
5498 Innovation Dr (44280-9352)
PHONE..................................330 220-2700
William H Spencer, CEO
Randolph B Spencer, *
EMP: 30 EST: 1910
SQ FT: 15,000
SALES (est): 10.36MM Privately Held
Web: www.dunlopandjohnston.com
SIC: 1542 1541 Commercial and office building, new construction; Industrial buildings and warehouses

(G-14334)
LIFE CARE CENTERS AMERICA INC
Also Called: Life Care Centers of Medina
2400 Columbia Rd (44280)
PHONE..................................330 483-3131
Steve Wolf, Mgr
EMP: 51
SALES (corp-wide): 139.21MM Privately Held
Web: www.lcca.com
SIC: 8051 8052 Convalescent home with continuous nursing care; Intermediate care facilities
PA: Life Care Centers Of America, Inc.
3570 Keith St Nw
Cleveland TN 37312
423 472-9585

(G-14335)
LUK-AFTERMARKET SERVICE INC
Also Called: As Automotive Systems
5370 Wegman Dr (44280-9700)
PHONE..................................330 273-4383
◆ EMP: 65
Web: www.repxpert.us
SIC: 5013 Motor vehicle supplies and new parts

(G-14336)
MTD HOLDINGS INC (HQ)
5965 Grafton Rd (44280)
P.O. Box 368022 (44136)
PHONE..................................330 225-2600
Curtis E Moll, CEO
Jeff Deuch, *
◆ EMP: 500 EST: 1946
SALES (est): 1.84B
SALES (corp-wide): 15.78B Publicly Held
Web: www.mtdparts.com
SIC: 3544 6141 3469 3524 Special dies and tools; Financing: automobiles, furniture, etc., not a deposit bank; Metal stampings, nec; Lawn and garden equipment
PA: Stanley Black & Decker, Inc.
1000 Stanley Dr
New Britain CT 06053
860 225-5111

(G-14337)
THREE D METALS INC (PA)
Also Called: Three D Metals
5462 Innovation Dr (44280-9352)
PHONE..................................330 220-0451
Chris Berry, Pr
Steve Switaj, *
David Chudzinski, *
▲ EMP: 72 EST: 1983
SQ FT: 146,000
SALES (est): 121.54MM
SALES (corp-wide): 121.54MM Privately Held
Web: www.threedmetals.com
SIC: 5051 Steel

Van Buren
Hancock County

(G-14338)
HOME DEPOT USA INC
Also Called: Home Depot, The
1989 Allen Township 142 (45889)
PHONE..................................419 299-2000
EMP: 71
SALES (corp-wide): 152.67B Publicly Held
Web: www.homedepot.com
SIC: 4225 General warehousing and storage
HQ: Home Depot U.S.A., Inc.
2445 Springfield Ave
Vauxhall NJ 07088

Van Wert
Van Wert County

(G-14339)
ALEXANDER AND BEBOUT INC
10098 Lincoln Hwy (45891-9351)
PHONE..................................419 238-9567
Thomas Alexander, Pr
T J Staude, *
Lori Dasher, *
Sylvia Alexander, *
EMP: 62 EST: 1965
SQ FT: 9,500
SALES (est): 17.02MM Privately Held
Web: www.alexanderbebout.com
SIC: 1521 New construction, single-family houses

(G-14340)
ALL AMERICA INSURANCE COMPANY (HQ)
800 S Washington St (45891-2357)
PHONE..................................419 238-1010
Francis W Purmort Iii, Pr
Thad Eikenbary, *

GEOGRAPHIC SECTION

Van Wert - Van Wert County (G-14362)

Edward R Buhl, *
Paul C Woirol, *
Jeffrey L Hanson, *
EMP: 350 **EST:** 1961
SQ FT: 200,000
SALES (est): 115.31MM
SALES (corp-wide): 605.39MM **Privately Held**
Web: www.central-insurance.com
SIC: 6411 Insurance agents, nec
PA: Central Mutual Insurance Company
800 S Washington St
Van Wert OH 45891
419 238-1010

(G-14341)
CENTRAL MUTUAL INSURANCE CO (PA)
Also Called: Central Insurance Companies
800 S Washington St (45891-2357)
PHONE...............................419 238-1010
Francis W Purmort Iii, *Ch Bd*
Edward Buhl, *Sec*
Jeff Hanson, *VP*
Thad Eikenbary, *Asst VP*
Jessica Seymour, *CFO*
EMP: 385 **EST:** 1876
SQ FT: 200,000
SALES (est): 605.39MM
SALES (corp-wide): 605.39MM **Privately Held**
Web: www.central-insurance.com
SIC: 6331 Property damage insurance

(G-14342)
COMMUNITY HLTH PRFSSIONALS INC (PA)
Also Called: Celina Area Vsting Nurses Assn
1159 Westwood Dr (45891-2464)
PHONE...............................419 238-9223
Brent Tow, *Pr*
EMP: 140 **EST:** 1974
SQ FT: 13,500
SALES (est): 12.27MM
SALES (corp-wide): 12.27MM **Privately Held**
Web: www.comhealthpro.org
SIC: 8082 7361 Visiting nurse service; Nurses' registry

(G-14343)
ENT REALTY CORP
140 Fox Rd (45891-2475)
PHONE...............................888 881-4368
William M Culp, *Brnch Mgr*
EMP: 139
Web: www.entfortwayne.com
SIC: 8011 Ears, nose, and throat specialist; physician/surgeon
PA: Ent Realty Corp.
10021 Dupont Circle Ct
Fort Wayne IN 46825

(G-14344)
FAMILY HLTH CARE NW OHIO INC
1191 Westwood Dr (45891-2464)
PHONE...............................419 238-6747
Jennifer Smith, *Ex Dir*
EMP: 29 **EST:** 2004
SALES (est): 4.42MM **Privately Held**
Web: www.familyhealthnwo.org
SIC: 8011 Clinic, operated by physicians

(G-14345)
GLM TRANSPORT INC (PA)
1300 Production Dr (45891-2143)
PHONE...............................419 363-2041
Daniel Ruhe, *Pr*
Edward Ruhe, *
Tyson Bailey, *
Ty Conrad, *
EMP: 30 **EST:** 1990
SALES (est): 11.47MM **Privately Held**
Web: www.glmtransport.com
SIC: 4212 4213 Local trucking, without storage; Trucking, except local

(G-14346)
HCF OF VAN WERT INC
Also Called: HEALTH CARE FACILITIES
160 Fox Rd (45891-2440)
PHONE...............................419 999-2010
James Unberferth, *Pr*
EMP: 197 **EST:** 2008
SALES (est): 5.76MM
SALES (corp-wide): 305.93MM **Privately Held**
Web: www.vanwertmanor.com
SIC: 8051 Convalescent home with continuous nursing care
PA: Hcf Management, Inc.
1100 Shawnee Rd
Lima OH 45805
419 999-2010

(G-14347)
KMC HOLDINGS LLC
Also Called: Kennedy Manufacturing
1260 Industrial Dr (45891-2433)
PHONE...............................419 238-2442
▲ **EMP:** 130
Web: www.buykennedy.com
SIC: 3841 3469 5021 Surgical and medical instruments; Boxes: tool, lunch, mail, etc.: stamped metal; Racks

(G-14348)
LINCOLNVIEW LOCAL SCHOOLS (PA)
15945 Middle Point Rd (45891-9769)
PHONE...............................419 968-2226
Doug Fries, *Superintnt*
Troy Bowersock, *
EMP: 120 **EST:** 1960
SALES (est): 4.97MM
SALES (corp-wide): 4.97MM **Privately Held**
Web: www.lincolnview.k12.oh.us
SIC: 8211 8741 Public elementary school; Management services

(G-14349)
PLASTIC RECYCLING TECH INC
7600 Us Route 127 (45891-9363)
PHONE...............................419 238-9395
Matt Kreigel, *Brnch Mgr*
EMP: 33
Web: www.plasticrecyclingtech.com
SIC: 4953 Recycling, waste materials
PA: Plastic Recycling Technology, Inc.
9054 N County Road 25a
Piqua OH 45356

(G-14350)
PRIVATE DUTY SERVICES INC
1157 Westwood Dr (45891-2464)
PHONE...............................419 238-3714
Brent Tow, *Pr*
EMP: 200 **EST:** 1994
SQ FT: 5,000
SALES (est): 1.59MM **Privately Held**
Web: www.allaboutfamilyprivateduty.net
SIC: 8082 8322 Visiting nurse service; Individual and family services

(G-14351)
STORE & HAUL INC
Also Called: Store & Haul Trucking
1001 Vision Dr (45891-9385)
PHONE...............................419 238-4284
Curt Rager, *Pr*
Jerry Rager, *
EMP: 38 **EST:** 1991
SALES (est): 5.14MM **Privately Held**
Web: www.storeandhaul.com
SIC: 4213 Trucking, except local

(G-14352)
THOMAS EDSON ERLY CHLDHOOD CTR
813 N Franklin St (45891-1303)
P.O. Box 604 (45891-0604)
PHONE...............................419 238-1514
James Stripe, *Superintnt*
EMP: 52 **EST:** 1971
SQ FT: 5,000
SALES (est): 1.08MM **Privately Held**
Web: www.vanwertdd.org
SIC: 8211 8361 School for retarded, nec; Mentally handicapped home

(G-14353)
TRUCENT RENEWABLE CHEM LLC
1202 Industrial Dr (45891-2483)
PHONE...............................877 280-7212
EMP: 94
SALES (corp-wide): 2.08MM **Privately Held**
Web: www.trucent.com
SIC: 8731 Chemical laboratory, except testing
PA: Trucent Renewable Chemicals Llc
7400 Newman Blvd
Dexter MI 48130
877 280-7212

(G-14354)
VALAM HOSPITALITY INC
Also Called: Holiday Inn
840 N Washington St (45891-1269)
PHONE...............................419 232-6040
N B Patel, *Pr*
EMP: 37 **EST:** 1996
SQ FT: 30,000
SALES (est): 487.18K **Privately Held**
Web: www.holidayinn.com
SIC: 7011 Hotels and motels

(G-14355)
VAN RUE INCORPORATED
Also Called: VANCREST HEALTH CARE CENTER
10357 Van Wert Decatur Rd (45891-8425)
PHONE...............................419 238-0715
Mark A White, *Pr*
Steve White, *
Carol White, *Stockholder**
EMP: 51 **EST:** 1960
SQ FT: 90,000
SALES (est): 6.71MM **Privately Held**
Web: www.vancrest.com
SIC: 8051 Convalescent home with continuous nursing care

(G-14356)
VAN WERT CNTY DAY CARE CTR INC
Also Called: WEE CARE LEARNING CENTER
10485 Van Wert Decatur Rd (45891-9209)
P.O. Box 107 (45891-0107)
PHONE...............................419 238-9918
Faith Fadian, *Dir*
EMP: 39 **EST:** 1979
SALES (est): 1.29MM **Privately Held**
Web: www.vwdaycare.com
SIC: 8351 Group day care center

(G-14357)
VAN WERT COUNTY HOSPITAL ASSN (PA)
Also Called: VAN WERT HEALTH
1250 S Washington St (45891-2551)
PHONE...............................419 238-2390
Jon Bagley, *Ch*
Mark Minick, *
Gary Clay, *
Angela Snyder, *
Edgar Silalahi, *
EMP: 338 **EST:** 1905
SQ FT: 80,000
SALES (est): 68.59MM
SALES (corp-wide): 68.59MM **Privately Held**
Web: www.vanwerthospital.org
SIC: 8062 General medical and surgical hospitals

(G-14358)
VAN WERT FAMILY PHYSICIANS LLC
1178 Professional Dr (45891-2461)
PHONE...............................419 238-6251
Jayne Smith, *Prin*
EMP: 27 **EST:** 2005
SALES (est): 3.34MM **Privately Held**
Web: www.vanwertfamilyphysicians.com
SIC: 8011 General and family practice, physician/surgeon

(G-14359)
VAN WERT FEDERAL SAV BNK INC
976 S Shannon St (45891-2243)
P.O. Box 575 (45891-0575)
PHONE...............................419 238-9662
Gary L Clay, *Pr*
EMP: 46 **EST:** 1889
SQ FT: 5,000
SALES (est): 3.35MM **Privately Held**
Web: www.vanwertfederal.com
SIC: 6035 Federal savings and loan associations

(G-14360)
VAN WERT MEDICAL SERVICES LTD
140 Fox Rd Ste 105 (45891-2490)
PHONE...............................419 238-7727
Mark Minick, *Pr*
EMP: 124 **EST:** 2017
SALES (est): 2.68MM
SALES (corp-wide): 68.59MM **Privately Held**
Web: www.vanwerthospital.org
SIC: 8062 General medical and surgical hospitals
PA: The Van Wert County Hospital Association
1250 S Washington St
Van Wert OH 45891
419 238-2390

(G-14361)
VANCREST MANAGEMENT CORP
120 W Main St Ste 200 (45891-1761)
PHONE...............................419 238-0715
Mark Mccleery, *CEO*
Mark White, *Pr*
Jon Bagley, *VP Opers*
EMP: 52 **EST:** 2003
SALES (est): 3.15MM **Privately Held**
Web: www.vancrest.com
SIC: 8051 Skilled nursing care facilities

(G-14362)
YOUNG MNS CHRSTN ASSN OF VAN W
Also Called: YMCA
241 W Main St (45891-1673)
PHONE...............................419 238-0443
Brad Perrot, *Dir*
EMP: 32 **EST:** 1914
SALES (est): 1.03MM **Privately Held**
Web: www.vwymca.org

Vandalia
Montgomery County

(G-14363)
AMERICAN AIRLINES INC
3600 Terminal Rd (45377-1079)
PHONE.................................937 890-6668
Cyrus Spaulding, *Genl Mgr*
EMP: 40
SALES (corp-wide): 52.79B **Publicly Held**
Web: www.psaairlines.com
SIC: 4512 Air passenger carrier, scheduled
HQ: American Airlines, Inc.
   1 Skyview Dr
   Fort Worth TX 76155
   682 278-9000

(G-14364)
AVIS ADMINISTRATION
3300 Valet Dr (45377-1000)
PHONE.................................937 898-2581
Robert Salerno, *Pr*
Cindy Rose, *
EMP: 67 **EST:** 2003
SALES (est): 354.13K **Privately Held**
Web: www.avis.com
SIC: 7514 Rent-a-car service

(G-14365)
BALANCING COMPANY INC (PA)
898 Center Dr (45377-3130)
P.O. Box 490 (45377-0490)
PHONE.................................937 898-9111
Michael Belcher, *CEO*
Michael W Belcher, *
Jack Boeke, *
EMP: 28 **EST:** 1967
SQ FT: 53,000
SALES (est): 4.76MM
SALES (corp-wide): 4.76MM **Privately Held**
Web: www.balco.com
SIC: 3599 8734 3544 Machine shop, jobbing and repair; Testing laboratories; Special dies, tools, jigs, and fixtures

(G-14366)
BASIC DRUGS INC
Also Called: Basic Vitamins
300 Corporate Center Dr (45377-1162)
P.O. Box 412 (45377-0412)
PHONE.................................937 898-4010
Nancy Green, *Pr*
Doris Fischer Lamb, *
Robert F Fischer Junior, *Sec*
Sharon Erbaugh, *
John Fischer, *
EMP: 36 **EST:** 1970
SQ FT: 12,200
SALES (est): 8.21MM **Privately Held**
Web: www.basicvitamins.com
SIC: 5122 Vitamins and minerals

(G-14367)
BND RENTALS INC
Also Called: Vandalia Rental
950 Engle Rd (45377-9690)
P.O. Box 160 (45377-0160)
PHONE.................................937 898-5061
Randy Barney, *Pr*
Kathy Barney, *
Carl B Nickel, *
Jack W Barney, *
EMP: 32 **EST:** 1961
SQ FT: 25,000
SALES (est): 11.58MM **Privately Held**
Web: www.vandaliarental.com
SIC: 7359 Tool rental

(G-14368)
CAREY ELECTRIC CO
3925 Vanco Ln (45377-9743)
PHONE.................................937 669-3399
Gerald Harter, *Pr*
Rick O'cull, *Pr*
Anita Bernard, *
EMP: 75 **EST:** 1973
SQ FT: 3,500
SALES (est): 16.87MM **Privately Held**
Web: www.careyelectric.com
SIC: 1731 General electrical contractor

(G-14369)
CHEWY INC
3280 Lightner Rd (45377-9673)
PHONE.................................937 669-4839
EMP: 271
SALES (corp-wide): 11.15B **Publicly Held**
Web: www.chewy.com
SIC: 4225 General warehousing and storage
PA: Chewy, Inc.
   7700 W Sunrise Blvd
   Plantation FL 33322
   786 320-7111

(G-14370)
CINTAS CORPORATION NO 2
Also Called: Cintas
850 Center Dr (45377-3151)
PHONE.............................800 444-2687
James Lillies, *Mgr*
EMP: 100
SALES (corp-wide): 8.82B **Publicly Held**
Web: www.cintas.com
SIC: 5137 7213 Uniforms, women's and children's; Uniform supply
HQ: Cintas Corporation No. 2
   6800 Cintas Blvd
   Mason OH 45040

(G-14371)
CITY OF DAYTON
Also Called: Aviation, Department of
3600 Terminal Rd Ste 300 (45377-3313)
PHONE.................................937 454-8200
Terrence Slaybaugh, *Dir*
EMP: 135
SQ FT: 672
SALES (corp-wide): 283.1MM **Privately Held**
Web: www.daytonohio.gov
SIC: 4581 4512 Airport; Air transportation, scheduled
PA: City Of Dayton
   101 W 3rd St
   Dayton OH 45402
   937 333-3333

(G-14372)
CROWN SOLUTIONS CO LLC
Also Called: Crown Solutions
913 Industrial Park Dr (45377-3115)
PHONE.................................937 890-4075
EMP: 200
SIC: 8711 3589 Consulting engineer; Water treatment equipment, industrial

(G-14373)
DATWYLER SLING SLTIONS USA INC
Also Called: Columbia
875 Center Dr (45377-3129)
PHONE.................................937 387-2800
Brian Bueltel, *Sls Dir*
Mark Bueltel, *Site Accounts Manager*
◆ **EMP:** 67 **EST:** 1985
SQ FT: 100,000
SALES (est): 21.46MM **Privately Held**
Web: usa.datwyler.com
SIC: 5085 3069 3061 Seals, industrial; Molded rubber products; Mechanical rubber goods
HQ: Keystone Holdings, Inc.
   875 Center Dr
   Vandalia OH 45377

(G-14374)
DAYTON OSTEOPATHIC HOSPITAL
Also Called: Dayton Medical Imaging
113 W National Rd (45377-1934)
PHONE.................................937 898-9729
EMP: 27
SALES (corp-wide): 2.46B **Privately Held**
Web: www.ketteringhealth.org
SIC: 8062 General medical and surgical hospitals
HQ: Dayton Osteopathic Hospital
   405 W Grand Ave
   Dayton OH 45405
   937 762-1629

(G-14375)
EDORA LOGISTICS INC
212 W National Rd (45377-1937)
PHONE.................................937 573-9090
David Looper, *Pr*
EMP: 40 **EST:** 2019
SALES (est): 1.3MM **Privately Held**
SIC: 4212 Local trucking, without storage

(G-14376)
EXHIBIT CONCEPTS INC (PA)
700 Crossroads Ct (45377-9675)
PHONE.................................937 890-7000
▼ **EMP:** 90 **EST:** 1978
SALES (est): 10.31MM
SALES (corp-wide): 10.31MM **Privately Held**
Web: www.exhibitconcepts.com
SIC: 7389 5032 2435 Exhibit construction by industrial contractors; Brick, stone, and related material; Hardwood veneer and plywood

(G-14377)
FAR OAKS ORTHOPEDISTS INC
55 Elva Ct Ste 100 (45377-1875)
PHONE.................................937 298-0452
Dan Morris, *Mgr*
EMP: 32
SALES (corp-wide): 3.2MM **Privately Held**
Web: www.faroaksorthopedists.com
SIC: 8011 Offices and clinics of medical doctors
PA: Far Oaks Orthopedists, Inc.
   6438 Wilmington Pike # 220
   Dayton OH 45459
   937 433-5309

(G-14378)
FEDERAL EXPRESS CORPORATION
Also Called: Fedex
3605 Concorde Dr (45377-3310)
PHONE.............................800 463-3339
EMP: 28
SALES (corp-wide): 90.16B **Publicly Held**
Web: www.fedex.com
SIC: 4513 Letter delivery, private air
HQ: Federal Express Corporation
   3610 Hacks Cross Rd
   Memphis TN 38125
   901 369-3600

(G-14379)
GREEN AGAIN TURF INC
109 Helke Rd (45377-1307)
PHONE.................................937 203-0693
Dustin Jennings, *Prin*
EMP: 50 **EST:** 2020
SALES (est): 575.43K **Privately Held**
SIC: 0782 Turf installation services, except artificial

(G-14380)
HERAEUS EPURIO LLC
Also Called: Heraeus Prceous Mtls N Amer Dyc
970 Industrial Park Dr (45377-3116)
PHONE.................................937 264-1000
Jrgen Heraeus, *Ch*
Robert Housman, *
Ram B Sharma, *
Santosh K Gupta, *
▲ **EMP:** 31 **EST:** 2012
SQ FT: 28,000
SALES (est): 23.63MM
SALES (corp-wide): 2.67MM **Privately Held**
Web: www.heraeus-group.com
SIC: 2869 2819 8731 Industrial organic chemicals, nec; Chemicals, high purity: refined from technical grade; Chemical laboratory, except testing
HQ: Heraeus Holding Gesellschaft Mit Beschrankter Haftung
   Heraeusstr. 12-14
   Hanau HE 63450
   6181350

(G-14381)
HORIZON HOME HEALTH CARE LLC
410 Corporate Center Dr (45377-1164)
PHONE.................................937 410-3838
EMP: 122 **EST:** 2003
SALES (est): 6.76MM **Privately Held**
Web: www.hhhcohio.com
SIC: 8082 Home health care services

(G-14382)
LINCOTEK MEDICAL LLC
Coorstek Medical Logan
811 Northwoods Blvd (45377-9468)
PHONE.................................435 753-7675
Kim Baugh, *Brnch Mgr*
EMP: 127
SALES (corp-wide): 60.11MM **Privately Held**
Web: www.lincotek.com
SIC: 5047 Medical equipment and supplies
PA: Lincotek Medical Llc
   3110 Stage Post Dr # 101
   Bartlett TN 38133
   877 583-0677

(G-14383)
MEDICAL MANAGEMENT INTL INC
Also Called: Banfield Pet Hospital 1299
361 E National Rd (45377-2305)
P.O. Box 87586 (98687-7586)
PHONE.................................937 325-4509
Kenith Burnett, *Brnch Mgr*
EMP: 34
SALES (corp-wide): 42.84B **Privately Held**
Web: www.banfield.com
SIC: 0742 Animal hospital services, pets and other animal specialties
HQ: Medical Management International, Inc.
   18101 Se 6th Way
   Vancouver WA 98683

(G-14384)
MIAMI VALLEY HOSPITAL
211 Kenbrook Dr (45377-2400)
PHONE.................................937 208-7065
Bill Quilter, *Mgr*
EMP: 493
SALES (corp-wide): 1.48B **Privately Held**
Web: www.premierhealth.com

At top of page (continued entry):
SIC: 8641 7991 8351 7032 Youth organizations; Physical fitness facilities; Child day care services; Youth camps

GEOGRAPHIC SECTION

Vermilion - Erie County (G-14407)

SIC: 8062 General medical and surgical hospitals
HQ: Miami Valley Hospital
1 Wyoming St
Dayton OH 45409
937 208-8000

(G-14385)
NATIONAL ALLIANCE SEC AGCY INC (PA)
303 Corporate Center Dr Ste 322 (45377-1171)
PHONE..............................866 636-3098
Deborah Young, *Pr*
Terry Young, *COO*
EMP: 27 EST: 2005
SALES (est): 1.98MM **Privately Held**
Web: www.nationalalliancesecurity.com
SIC: 7381 Security guard service

(G-14386)
NIMERS & WOODY II INC (PA)
Also Called: M A C
1625 Fieldstone Way (45377-9317)
PHONE..............................937 454-0722
▲ EMP: 173 EST: 1976
SALES (est): 24.85MM
SALES (corp-wide): 24.85MM **Privately Held**
Web: www.mac-cable.com
SIC: 3699 5051 3679 Electrical equipment and supplies, nec; Cable, wire; Harness assemblies, for electronic use: wire or cable

(G-14387)
PRIMARY CARE NTWRK PRMIER HLTH
Also Called: Needmore Road Primary Care
600 Aviator Ct (45377-9473)
PHONE..............................937 278-5854
Kenneth Prunier, *CEO*
EMP: 31
SALES (corp-wide): 25.36MM **Privately Held**
Web: www.premierhealth.com
SIC: 8011 General and family practice, physician/surgeon
PA: Primary Care Network Of Premier Health Partners
110 N Main St Ste 350
Dayton OH 45402
937 226-7085

(G-14388)
PRIMARY CR NTWRK PRMR HLTH PRT
900 S Dixie Dr Ste 40 (45377-2656)
PHONE..............................937 890-6644
EMP: 31
SALES (corp-wide): 25.36MM **Privately Held**
Web: www.premierhealth.com
SIC: 8011 Physical medicine, physician/surgeon
PA: Primary Care Network Of Premier Health Partners
110 N Main St Ste 350
Dayton OH 45402
937 226-7085

(G-14389)
PSA AIRLINES INC (HQ)
Also Called: US Airways Express
3400 Terminal Rd (45377-1041)
PHONE..............................937 454-1116
Keith D Houk, *Pr*
Timothy Keuscher, *
James Schear, *
EMP: 250 EST: 1980
SQ FT: 18,600
SALES (est): 30.28K

SALES (corp-wide): 52.79B **Publicly Held**
Web: www.psaairlines.com
SIC: 4512 Air passenger carrier, scheduled
PA: American Airlines Group Inc.
1 Skyview Dr
Fort Worth TX 76155
682 278-9000

(G-14390)
R B JERGENS CONTRACTORS INC
11418 N Dixie Dr (45377-9736)
PHONE..............................937 669-9799
William Jergens, *Pr*
Rhonda Rhoades, *MNG*
EMP: 99 EST: 1961
SALES (est): 30.86MM **Privately Held**
Web: www.rbjergens.com
SIC: 1611 General contractor, highway and street construction

(G-14391)
R D JERGENS CONTRACTORS INC (PA)
11418 N Dixie Dr (45377-9736)
P.O. Box 309 (45377-0309)
PHONE..............................937 669-9799
William Jergens, *Pr*
Dave Tennery, *
Kevin Harshberger, *
Ruth Jergens, *
EMP: 100 EST: 1987
SQ FT: 14,000
SALES (est): 22.63MM **Privately Held**
Web: www.rbjergens.com
SIC: 1611 1623 Highway and street construction; Underground utilities contractor

(G-14392)
SKATEWORLD INC
Also Called: Skateworld of Vandalia
333 S Brown School Rd (45377-3105)
P.O. Box 501 (45377-0501)
PHONE..............................937 890-6550
Charlie Clark, *Mgr*
EMP: 35
SALES (corp-wide): 996.41K **Privately Held**
Web: www.skateworldofvandalia.com
SIC: 7999 Roller skating rink operation
PA: Skateworld, Inc.
1601 E David Rd
Dayton OH 45429
937 294-4032

(G-14393)
STEVENS AROSPC DEF SYSTEMS LLC
3500 Hangar Dr (45377-1055)
PHONE..............................937 454-3400
EMP: 63
SALES (corp-wide): 96.07MM **Privately Held**
Web: www.stevensaerospace.com
SIC: 4581 Aircraft servicing and repairing
HQ: Stevens Aerospace And Defense Systems Llc
600 Delaware St
Greenville SC 29605
864 678-6000

(G-14394)
THE EXPEDITING CO (PA)
1295 S Brown School Rd (45377-9469)
PHONE..............................937 890-1524
EMP: 80 EST: 1989
SALES (est): 22.79MM
SALES (corp-wide): 22.79MM **Privately Held**
Web: www.expco.com

SIC: 4213 Trucking, except local

(G-14395)
TRIAD TECHNOLOGIES LLC (PA)
985 Falls Creek Dr (45377-9686)
PHONE..............................937 832-2861
EMP: 29 EST: 1981
SALES (est): 54.72MM
SALES (corp-wide): 54.72MM **Privately Held**
Web: www.triadtechnologies.com
SIC: 5084 Hydraulic systems equipment and supplies

(G-14396)
UNIBILT INDS HLTH & WELFARE TR
4671 Poplar Creek Rd (45377-9681)
P.O. Box 373 (45377-0373)
PHONE..............................937 890-7570
EMP: 80 EST: 2011
SALES (est): 1.63MM **Privately Held**
Web: www.unibiltcustomhomes.com
SIC: 6733 Trusts, nec

(G-14397)
UNITED AIRLINES INC
Also Called: Continental Airlines
3600 Terminal Rd (45377-1093)
PHONE..............................937 454-2009
Robert Hall, *Mgr*
EMP: 27
SALES (corp-wide): 53.72B **Publicly Held**
Web: www.united.com
SIC: 4512 Air passenger carrier, scheduled
HQ: United Airlines, Inc.
233 S Wacker Dr Ste 710
Chicago IL 60606
872 825-4000

(G-14398)
UNIVERSAL SERVICES AMERICA LP
Also Called: Allied Universal
407 Corporate Center Dr Ste D (45377-1176)
PHONE..............................937 454-9035
EMP: 5058
SALES (corp-wide): 12.86B **Privately Held**
Web: www.aus.com
SIC: 7381 7349 Detective and armored car services; Building maintenance services, nec
HQ: Universal Services Of America, Lp
450 Exchange
Irvine CA 92602
866 877-1965

(G-14399)
US EXPEDITING LOGISTICS LLC
4311 Old Springfield Rd (45377-9576)
PHONE..............................937 235-1014
EMP: 32 EST: 2004
SALES (est): 5MM **Privately Held**
Web: www.usexpediting.com
SIC: 4731 Freight forwarding

(G-14400)
US SECURITY ASSOCIATES INC
69 N Dixie Dr Ste F (45377-2060)
PHONE..............................937 454-9035
Greg Reynolds, *Mgr*
EMP: 1145
SALES (corp-wide): 946.48MM **Privately Held**
Web: www.ussecurityassociates.com
SIC: 7381 Security guard service
HQ: U.S. Security Associates, Inc.
200 Mansell Ct E Fl 5
Roswell GA 30076

(G-14401)
VANCARE INC
Also Called: Vandalia Park
208 N Cassel Rd (45377-2926)
PHONE..............................937 898-4202
Mark Schertzinger, *Admn*
EMP: 65 EST: 1996
SQ FT: 10,000
SALES (est): 2.29MM **Privately Held**
SIC: 8051 8052 Skilled nursing care facilities ; Intermediate care facilities

(G-14402)
VANDALIA BUTLER EMRGNCY FD CTR
208 N Cassel Rd (45377-2926)
P.O. Box 141 (45377-0141)
PHONE..............................937 898-4202
EMP: 54 EST: 2010
SALES (est): 200.1K **Privately Held**
SIC: 8082 Home health care services

(G-14403)
WAIBEL ENERGY SYSTEMS INC
Also Called: Buildinglogix
815 Falls Creek Dr (45377-9695)
P.O. Box 670 (45377-0670)
PHONE..............................937 264-4343
EMP: 67 EST: 1959
SALES (est): 22.09MM **Privately Held**
Web: www.gowaibel.com
SIC: 1711 5075 Heating and air conditioning contractors; Warm air heating and air conditioning

Vermilion
Erie County

(G-14404)
ADULT COMFORT CARE INC
5710 Lake St (44089-1013)
P.O. Box 647 (44089-0647)
PHONE..............................440 320-3335
Melva Sherwood, *Prin*
EMP: 31 EST: 2012
SALES (est): 268.53K **Privately Held**
Web: www.accadulthomecare.com
SIC: 8082 Home health care services

(G-14405)
IRG OPERATING LLC
Also Called: Cleveland Quarries
850 W River Rd (44089-1530)
PHONE..............................440 963-4008
EMP: 36 EST: 2007
SALES (est): 4.92MM **Privately Held**
Web: www.clevelandquarries.com
SIC: 1411 Sandstone, dimension-quarrying

(G-14406)
KADEMNOS WSHART HNES DLYK ZHER
1513 State Rd (44089-9604)
PHONE..............................440 967-6136
Duffield E Milkie, *Mng Pt*
Maurice L Mcdermond, *Sec*
John Frankel, *
EMP: 32 EST: 1973
SALES (est): 2.34MM **Privately Held**
Web: www.ohattorneys.com
SIC: 8111 General practice attorney, lawyer

(G-14407)
KINGSTON HEALTHCARE COMPANY
Also Called: Kingston of Vermilion
4210 Telegraph Ln (44089-3748)
PHONE..............................440 967-1800
Heather Shirley, *Brnch Mgr*
EMP: 32

Vermilion - Erie County (G-14408)

Web: www.kingstonhealthcare.com
SIC: 8051 8059 Skilled nursing care facilities; Home for the mentally retarded, ex. skilled or intermediate
PA: Kingston Healthcare Company
1 Seagate Ste 1960
Toledo OH 43604

(G-14408)
SHARPNACK CHEVROLET CO (PA)
5401 Portage Dr (44089-1432)
PHONE.................................800 752-7513
Joseph Sharpnack Junior, *Pr*
Thomas C Sharpnack, *
Janet S Sharpnack, *
EMP: 35 **EST:** 1949
SQ FT: 20,800
SALES (est): 7.15MM
SALES (corp-wide): 7.15MM **Privately Held**
Web: www.sharpnackdirect.com
SIC: 5511 7538 7532 7515 Automobiles, new and used; General automotive repair shops; Top and body repair and paint shops; Passenger car leasing

(G-14409)
SIX SIGMA LOGISTICS INC
6745 Cliffside Dr (44089)
PHONE.................................440 666-6026
Ron O'connell, *Pr*
EMP: 50 **EST:** 2018
SALES (est): 985.9K **Privately Held**
SIC: 7389 Courier or messenger service

(G-14410)
VERMILION FAMILY YMCA
1230 Beechview Dr (44089-1604)
PHONE.................................440 967-4208
W Robert Johnston Ii, *Dir*
Jim Turton, *
Anne Stock, *
Jo Brown, *
Don Lebeau, *
EMP: 49 **EST:** 1965
SALES (est): 438.59K **Privately Held**
Web: www.clevelandymca.org
SIC: 8351 8641 7991 7997 Child day care services; Youth organizations; Physical fitness facilities; Membership sports and recreation clubs

(G-14411)
VERMILION LOCAL SCHOOLS
Also Called: Vermilion School Bus Garage
1065 Decatur St (44089-1167)
PHONE.................................440 204-1700
Linda Griffin, *Brnch Mgr*
EMP: 59
SALES (corp-wide): 26.16MM **Privately Held**
Web: www.vermilionschools.org
SIC: 4151 School buses
PA: Vermilion Local Schools
1250 Sanford St Ste A
Vermilion OH 44089
440 204-1700

Versailles
Darke County

(G-14412)
A L SMITH TRUCKING INC
8984 Murphy Rd (45380-9752)
PHONE.................................937 526-3651
Dave Fullenkamp, *Pr*
EMP: 38 **EST:** 1956
SQ FT: 9,600
SALES (est): 4.54MM **Privately Held**

Web: www.alsmithtrucking.com
SIC: 4213 4212 Contract haulers; Local trucking, without storage

(G-14413)
BNSF LOGISTICS LLC
Also Called: T E S - East
611 Marker Rd (45380-9334)
P.O. Box 176 (45380-0176)
PHONE.................................937 526-3141
Chuck Borchers, *Brnch Mgr*
EMP: 40
SALES (corp-wide): 364.48B **Publicly Held**
Web: www.bnsflogistics.com
SIC: 4731 Truck transportation brokers
HQ: Bnsf Logistics, Llc
3200 Olympus Blvd Ste 200
Coppell TX 75019
800 275-8521

(G-14414)
CLASSIC CARRIERS INC (PA)
Also Called: Classic Carriers
151 Industrial Pkwy (45380-9756)
P.O. Box 295 (45380-0295)
PHONE.................................937 604-8118
Jim Subler, *Pr*
Ed Ruhe, *Prin*
Jerold Richards, *Prin*
Tim Subler, *Prin*
Kelly Luthman, *Prin*
EMP: 47 **EST:** 1985
SALES (est): 14.04MM
SALES (corp-wide): 14.04MM **Privately Held**
Web: www.classiccarriers.com
SIC: 4213 Contract haulers

(G-14415)
COVENANT CARE OHIO INC
Also Called: Versailles Health Care Center
200 Marker Rd (45380-9494)
PHONE.................................937 526-5570
Marilyn Barga, *Brnch Mgr*
EMP: 502
Web: www.versaillesrehab.com
SIC: 8051 8011 Convalescent home with continuous nursing care; Offices and clinics of medical doctors
HQ: Covenant Care Ohio, Inc.
120 Vantis Dr Ste 200
Aliso Viejo CA 92656
949 349-1200

(G-14416)
POHL TRANSPORTATION INC
9297 Mcgreevey Rd (45380-9771)
P.O. Box 334 (45380-0334)
PHONE.................................800 837-2122
EMP: 80 **EST:** 1991
SALES (est): 10.14MM **Privately Held**
Web: www.pohltransportation.com
SIC: 4213 Trucking, except local

(G-14417)
WEAVER BROS INC (PA)
Also Called: Tri County Eggs
895 E Main St (45380-1533)
P.O. Box 333 (45380-0333)
PHONE.................................937 526-3907
Timothy John Weaver, *Pr*
Kreg Kohli, *
Audrey Weaver, *
Geo L Weaver, *
John D Weaver, *
▲ **EMP:** 60 **EST:** 1931
SQ FT: 20,000
SALES (est): 24.19MM
SALES (corp-wide): 24.19MM **Privately Held**

Web: www.weavereggs.com
SIC: 0252 5143 2015 Chicken eggs; Dairy products, except dried or canned; Poultry slaughtering and processing

Vickery
Sandusky County

(G-14418)
AT&T CORP
Also Called: AT&T
1591 County Road 260 (43464)
PHONE.................................419 547-0578
EMP: 69
SALES (corp-wide): 122.43B **Publicly Held**
Web: www.att.com
SIC: 4813 Local and long distance telephone communications
HQ: At&t Enterprises, Llc
208 S Akard St
Dallas TX 75202
800 403-3302

Vienna
Trumbull County

(G-14419)
EAST INC
3976 King Graves Rd (44473-6900)
PHONE.................................330 609-1339
Duane Hambrick, *Prin*
EMP: 35 **EST:** 2007
SALES (est): 511.7K **Privately Held**
SIC: 4119 Ambulance service

(G-14420)
LATROBE SPCIALTY MTLS DIST INC (HQ)
1551 Vienna Pkwy (44473-8703)
PHONE.................................330 609-5137
Gregory A Pratt, *Ch Bd*
Timothy R Armstrong, *
Thomas F Cramsey, *
James D Dee, *
Matthew S Enoch, *
◆ **EMP:** 80 **EST:** 1996
SQ FT: 189,000
SALES (est): 22.1MM
SALES (corp-wide): 2.55B **Publicly Held**
SIC: 3312 5051 Stainless steel; Steel
PA: Carpenter Technology Corporation
1735 Market St Fl 15
Philadelphia PA 19103
610 208-2000

(G-14421)
LITCO INTERNATIONAL INC (PA)
1 Litco Dr (44473-9600)
P.O. Box 150 (44473-0150)
PHONE.................................330 539-5433
Lionel Trebilcock, *CEO*
Gary Trebilcock, *
Gary Sharon, *
◆ **EMP:** 88 **EST:** 1962
SQ FT: 13,000
SALES (est): 22.35MM
SALES (corp-wide): 22.35MM **Privately Held**
Web: www.litco.com
SIC: 2448 5031 Pallets, wood; Particleboard

(G-14422)
MILLWOOD INC (PA)
Also Called: Millwood
3708 International Blvd (44473-9796)
PHONE.................................330 393-4400
▲ **EMP:** 30 **EST:** 1992

SQ FT: 20,000
SALES (est): 327.83MM **Privately Held**
Web: www.millwoodinc.com
SIC: 4225 4731 General warehousing and storage; Freight transportation arrangement

(G-14423)
MILLWOOD NATURAL LLC
3708 International Blvd (44473-9796)
PHONE.................................330 393-4400
Lionel Trebilcock, *Pt*
EMP: 30 **EST:** 2013
SALES (est): 2.2MM **Privately Held**
Web: www.millwoodinc.com
SIC: 3565 4731 Packaging machinery; Freight transportation arrangement
PA: Millwood, Inc.
3708 International Blvd
Vienna OH 44473

(G-14424)
WINNER AVIATION CORPORATION
1453 Youngstown Kingsville Rd Ne (44473-9790)
PHONE.................................330 856-5000
EMP: 156 **EST:** 1995
SQ FT: 5,000
SALES (est): 22.18MM **Privately Held**
Web: www.winner-aviation.com
SIC: 7629 4581 Aircraft electrical equipment repair; Aircraft maintenance and repair services

Vinton
Gallia County

(G-14425)
STEELIAL WLDG MET FBRCTION INC
Also Called: Steelial Cnstr Met Fabrication
70764 State Route 124 (45686-8545)
PHONE.................................740 669-5300
Larry Allen Hedrick Junior, *Pr*
Krista Lynnete Hedrick, *
EMP: 32 **EST:** 1998
SQ FT: 40,000
SALES (est): 7.66MM **Privately Held**
Web: www.steelial.com
SIC: 1623 3441 3444 Pipe laying construction; Fabricated structural metal; Sheet metalwork

Wadsworth
Medina County

(G-14426)
AKRON INN LIMITED PARTNERSHIP
Also Called: Ramada Inn
5 Park Centre Dr (44281-9431)
PHONE.................................330 336-7692
Shawn Leattherman, *Owner*
Rosemary Knepp, *Mgr*
Kim Outritch, *Prin*
EMP: 60 **EST:** 1988
SALES (est): 397.18K **Privately Held**
Web: www.wyndhamhotels.com
SIC: 7011 Hotels and motels

(G-14427)
ALTERCARE INC
Also Called: Altercare of Wadsworth
147 Garfield St (44281-1431)
PHONE.................................330 335-2555
Diana Jackson, *Mgr*
EMP: 27
SALES (corp-wide): 6.9MM **Privately Held**
Web: www.altercareonline.com

GEOGRAPHIC SECTION

Wadsworth - Medina County (G-14448)

SIC: 8051 8052 Convalescent home with continuous nursing care; Intermediate care facilities
PA: Altercare, Inc.
35990 Westminister Ave
North Ridgeville OH 44039
440 327-5285

(G-14428)
AMERICAN HOSPITALITY GROUP INC (HQ)
Also Called: A H G
200 Smokerise Dr (44281-9499)
P.O. Box 438 (44282-0438)
PHONE..................................330 336-6684
Robert Leatherman Junior, *Pr*
Robert Leatherman Senior, *Ch Bd*
Neil Winger, *
Robin Winger, *
Phyllis Leatherman, *
EMP: 384 EST: 1972
SQ FT: 20,000
SALES (est): 43.29MM
SALES (corp-wide): 43.29MM **Privately Held**
Web: www.americanhg.com
SIC: 8741 Hotel or motel management
PA: Leatherman Nursing Centers Corporation
200 Smokerise Dr Ste 300
Wadsworth OH 44281
330 336-6684

(G-14429)
BEAVER DAM HEALTH CARE CENTER
Also Called: Beverly
365 Johnson Rd (44281-8609)
PHONE..................................330 335-1558
Rick Michell, *Genl Mgr*
EMP: 27
SQ FT: 28,324
SALES (corp-wide): 825.65MM **Privately Held**
Web: www.beaverdamhcc.com
SIC: 8059 8052 8051 Convalescent home; Intermediate care facilities; Skilled nursing care facilities
PA: Golden Living Llc
5220 Tennyson Pkwy # 400
Plano TX 75024
972 372-6300

(G-14430)
CITY OF WADSWORTH
Also Called: Electrical Service Dept
365 College St (44281-1147)
PHONE..................................330 334-1581
Peter A Giacomo, *Superintnt*
EMP: 49
SALES (corp-wide): 25.47MM **Privately Held**
Web: www.wadsworthcity.com
SIC: 7629 9111 Electrical repair shops; Mayors' office
PA: City Of Wadsworth
120 Maple St Uppr
Wadsworth OH 44281
330 335-1521

(G-14431)
CITY OF WADSWORTH
Also Called: Dog Warden
311 Broad St (44281)
PHONE..................................330 334-1581
EMP: 37
SALES (corp-wide): 25.47MM **Privately Held**
Web: www.wadsworthcity.com
SIC: 0752 Animal boarding services
PA: City Of Wadsworth
120 Maple St Uppr
Wadsworth OH 44281
330 335-1521

(G-14432)
CLEVELAND CLINIC FOUNDATION
1 Park Centre Dr (44281-7100)
PHONE..................................330 334-4620
EMP: 33
SALES (corp-wide): 14.48B **Privately Held**
Web: www.clevelandclinic.org
SIC: 8062 General medical and surgical hospitals
PA: The Cleveland Clinic Foundation
9500 Euclid Ave
Cleveland OH 44195
216 636-8335

(G-14433)
COMMUNITY CAREGIVERS
230 Quadral Dr Ste D (44281-8375)
PHONE..................................330 725-9800
Michael T Nemeth, *Brnch Mgr*
EMP: 51
SALES (corp-wide): 5.13MM **Privately Held**
Web: www.commcareinc.org
SIC: 8082 Home health care services
PA: Community Caregivers
66 S Miller Rd Ste 200
Fairlawn OH 44333
330 836-8585

(G-14434)
CORNWELL QUALITY TOOLS COMPANY
Also Called: Distribution Service Company
635 Seville Rd (44281-1077)
PHONE..................................330 335-2933
Dal Ringler, *Mgr*
EMP: 50
SALES (corp-wide): 55.65MM **Privately Held**
Web: www.cornwelltools.com
SIC: 5013 5085 Tools and equipment, automotive; Industrial supplies
PA: The Cornwell Quality Tools Company
667 Seville Rd
Wadsworth OH 44281
330 336-3506

(G-14435)
HOME INSTEAD SENIOR CARE
1 Park Centre Dr Ste 15 (44281-9452)
PHONE..................................330 334-4664
Pam Myers, *Pr*
EMP: 49 EST: 1970
SALES (est): 669.78K **Privately Held**
Web: www.homeinstead.com
SIC: 8082 8322 Home health care services; Individual and family services

(G-14436)
HUBBELL POWER SYSTEMS INC
Ohio Brass
8711 Wadsworth Rd (44281-8438)
PHONE..................................330 335-2361
Chris Davis, *Brnch Mgr*
EMP: 111
SALES (corp-wide): 5.37B **Publicly Held**
Web: www.hubbell.com
SIC: 5063 Electrical apparatus and equipment
HQ: Hubbell Power Systems, Inc.
200 Center Point Cir # 200
Columbia SC 29210
803 216-2600

(G-14437)
HUNTINGTON NATIONAL BANK
1081 Williams Reserve Blvd (44281-9316)
PHONE..................................330 334-1091
Ron Caydo, *Brnch Mgr*
EMP: 31
SALES (corp-wide): 10.84B **Publicly Held**
Web: www.huntington.com
SIC: 6029 Commercial banks, nec
HQ: The Huntington National Bank
41 S High St
Columbus OH 43215
614 480-4293

(G-14438)
HUNTINGTON NATIONAL BANK
129 High St (44281-1857)
PHONE..................................330 334-1591
Dwight Weaver, *Mgr*
EMP: 31
SALES (corp-wide): 10.84B **Publicly Held**
Web: www.huntington.com
SIC: 6029 6021 Commercial banks, nec; National commercial banks
HQ: The Huntington National Bank
41 S High St
Columbus OH 43215
614 480-4293

(G-14439)
LEATHERMAN NURSING CTRS CORP (PA)
200 Smokerise Dr Ste 300 (44281-9499)
PHONE..................................330 336-6684
Robert Leatherman, *Pr*
Phyllis Leatherman, *
EMP: 384 EST: 1973
SQ FT: 20,000
SALES (est): 43.29MM
SALES (corp-wide): 43.29MM **Privately Held**
SIC: 8741 Management services

(G-14440)
LIFECARE HOSPICE
Also Called: Lifecare Palliative Medicine
102 Main St (44281-1453)
PHONE..................................330 336-6595
EMP: 90
SIC: 8322 Individual and family services
PA: Lifecare Hospice
1900 Akron Rd
Wooster OH 44691

(G-14441)
LOUIS PERRY & ASSOCIATES INC
165 Smokerise Dr (44281-8702)
PHONE..................................330 334-1585
Louis B Perry, *Pr*
EMP: 135 EST: 1985
SQ FT: 31,000
SALES (est): 18.78MM
SALES (corp-wide): 1.42B **Privately Held**
Web: www.cdmsmith.com
SIC: 8711 8712 Consulting engineer; Architectural services
PA: Cdm Smith Inc
75 State St Ste 701
Boston MA 02109
617 452-6000

(G-14442)
LOWES HOME CENTERS LLC
Also Called: Lowe's
1065 Williams Reserve Blvd (44281-9316)
PHONE..................................330 335-1900
Dave Labuda, *Mgr*
EMP: 138
SQ FT: 137,480
SALES (corp-wide): 86.38B **Publicly Held**
Web: www.lowes.com
SIC: 5211 5031 5722 5064 Home centers; Building materials, exterior; Household appliance stores; Electrical appliances, television and radio
HQ: Lowe's Home Centers, Llc
1000 Lowes Blvd
Mooresville NC 28117
336 658-4000

(G-14443)
MEDINA CNTY SHELTERED INDS INC
Also Called: WINDFALL INDUSTRIES
150 Quadral Dr Ste D (44281-8352)
PHONE..................................330 334-4491
Jim Brown, *Ex Dir*
EMP: 47 EST: 1963
SQ FT: 40,000
SALES (est): 2.38MM **Privately Held**
Web: www.windfallindustries.org
SIC: 8331 Sheltered workshop

(G-14444)
MONITORING CTRL COMPLIANCE INC
Also Called: M C C
150 Smokerise Dr (44281-8701)
PHONE..................................330 725-7766
Charles Elkins, *Pr*
Tara Elkins, *
EMP: 52 EST: 2005
SALES (est): 8.43MM **Privately Held**
Web: www.landfillgasom.com
SIC: 1731 Environmental system control installation

(G-14445)
OHIO EDISON COMPANY
9681 Silvercreek Rd (44281-9008)
PHONE..................................330 336-9880
Bruce J Busse, *Brnch Mgr*
EMP: 36
Web: www.firstenergycorp.com
SIC: 4911 Electric services
HQ: Ohio Edison Company
76 S Main St Bsmt
Akron OH 44308
800 736-3402

(G-14446)
ONEILL INSURANCE AGENCY INC
Also Called: O'Neill Group The
111 High St (44281-1857)
P.O. Box 440 (44282-0440)
PHONE..................................330 334-1561
EMP: 40 EST: 1996
SQ FT: 14,091
SALES (est): 9.45MM **Privately Held**
Web: www.oneillinsurance.com
SIC: 6411 Insurance agents, nec

(G-14447)
PERRAM ELECTRIC INC
6882 Ridge Rd (44281-9706)
PHONE..................................330 239-2661
Zoltan J Kovacs, *Pr*
Lori A Stanley, *
James Strausbaugh, *
Dave Powell, *
John Lavis, *
EMP: 40 EST: 1986
SQ FT: 2,500
SALES (est): 13.65MM **Privately Held**
Web: www.perramelectric.com
SIC: 1731 General electrical contractor

(G-14448)
PLASTICS R UNIQUE INC
330 Grandview Ave (44281-1161)
PHONE..................................330 334-4820
Kenneth R Boersma, *Pr*
EMP: 30 EST: 1988

Wadsworth - Medina County

SQ FT: 12,300
SALES (est): 5MM **Privately Held**
Web: www.plasticsrunique.com
SIC: 3089 5162 Plastics containers, except foam; Plastics materials, nec

(G-14449)
RETAIL RENOVATIONS INC (PA)
7530 State Rd (44281-9794)
PHONE..................................330 334-4501
Gary Williams, *CEO*
Frank Northcutt, *
Rhonda Williams, *
Lisa Williams, *
EMP: 29 EST: 1989
SALES (est): 3.44MM **Privately Held**
Web: www.retailrenovations.com
SIC: 1521 Single-family housing construction

(G-14450)
REVOLUTION TRUCKING LLC
257 Main St Ste 103 (44281-1447)
PHONE..................................330 975-4145
James Adams, *Managing Member*
EMP: 28 EST: 2019
SALES (est): 8.78MM **Privately Held**
Web: www.revolutiontrucking.com
SIC: 4212 Local trucking, without storage

(G-14451)
SECOND WIND VITAMINS INC (PA)
Also Called: Celebrate Vitamins
516 Corporate Pkwy (44281-8398)
PHONE..................................330 336-9260
Victor Giaconia, *CEO*
EMP: 32 EST: 2008
SQ FT: 6,000
SALES (est): 5.92MM
SALES (corp-wide): 5.92MM **Privately Held**
Web: www.celebratevitamins.com
SIC: 5122 5499 Vitamins and minerals; Vitamin food stores

(G-14452)
STABLE STEP LLC
Also Called: Powersteps
961 Seville Rd (44281-8316)
PHONE..................................800 491-1571
EMP: 150 EST: 2015
SALES (est): 5.06MM **Privately Held**
SIC: 3842 5047 5999 Foot appliances, orthopedic; Orthopedic equipment and supplies; Orthopedic and prosthesis applications

(G-14453)
SUMMA HEALTH SYSTEM
195 Wadsworth Rd (44281-9537)
PHONE..................................330 334-1504
EMP: 520
SALES (corp-wide): 1.78B **Privately Held**
Web: www.summahealth.org
SIC: 8062 General medical and surgical hospitals
PA: Summa Health System
1077 Gorge Blvd
Akron OH 44310
330 375-3000

(G-14454)
TAPCO TUBE CO INC
6600 Ridge Rd (44281-9743)
PHONE..................................330 576-1750
EMP: 75 EST: 2010
SALES (est): 7MM **Privately Held**
SIC: 5051 Steel

(G-14455)
THE CORNWELL QUALITY TOOLS COMPANY (PA)
Also Called: Cornwell Quality Tools
667 Seville Rd (44281-1077)
PHONE..................................330 336-3506
▲ EMP: 80 EST: 1919
SALES (est): 55.65MM
SALES (corp-wide): 55.65MM **Privately Held**
Web: www.cornwelltools.com
SIC: 5085 3423 6794 Industrial supplies; Mechanics' hand tools; Franchises, selling or licensing

(G-14456)
THE WADSWORTH-RITTMAN AREA HOSPITAL ASSOCIATION
Also Called: Wadsworth-Rittman Hospital
195 Wadsworth Rd (44281-9537)
P.O. Box 18 (44282-0018)
PHONE..................................330 334-1504
TOLL FREE: 800
EMP: 520
Web: www.wrhhs.org
SIC: 8062 General medical and surgical hospitals

(G-14457)
WADSWORTH HIE MANAGEMENT INC
Also Called: Holiday Inn
231 Park Centre Dr (44281-7106)
PHONE..................................330 334-7666
Louie Lemaster, *Genl Mgr*
Robert Leatherman, *Pr*
EMP: 61 EST: 1999
SALES (est): 1.08MM **Privately Held**
Web: www.hiexpress.com
SIC: 7011 Hotels and motels

Wakeman
Huron County

(G-14458)
CONCAST BIRMINGHAM LLC
Also Called: Concast Birmingham, Inc.
14315 State Route 113 (44889-8320)
PHONE..................................440 965-4455
▲ EMP: 80 EST: 1995
SALES (est): 25.47MM
SALES (corp-wide): 30.83MM **Privately Held**
Web: www.concast.com
SIC: 5051 Metals service centers and offices
PA: A Cubed, Llc
131 Myoma Rd
Mars PA 16046
724 538-4000

(G-14459)
FISHER-TITUS MEDICAL CENTER
24 Hyde St (44889-9301)
PHONE..................................440 839-2226
EMP: 83
SALES (corp-wide): 158.84MM **Privately Held**
Web: www.fishertitus.org
SIC: 8011 General and family practice, physician/surgeon
PA: Fisher-Titus Medical Center
272 Benedict Ave
Norwalk OH 44857
419 668-8101

Walbridge
Wood County

(G-14460)
BHP ENERGY LLC
Also Called: GEM ENERGY
6842 Commodore Dr (43465-9765)
PHONE..................................866 720-2700
EMP: 268 EST: 2008
SALES (est): 17.18MM **Privately Held**
Web: www.rlgbuilds.com
SIC: 8748 Energy conservation consultant

(G-14461)
GEM INDUSTRIAL INC (HQ)
6842 Commodore Dr (43465-9793)
P.O. Box 716 (43697-0716)
PHONE..................................419 666-6554
Bill Rudolph, *Ch*
Steve Johnson, *Pr*
Douglas R Heyman, *Sr VP*
Scott Kepp, *Technical Vice President*
EMP: 88 EST: 1982
SQ FT: 33,000
SALES (est): 47.16MM
SALES (corp-wide): 512.7MM **Privately Held**
Web: www.rlgbuilds.com
SIC: 1711 1731 1796 Mechanical contractor; General electrical contractor; Machinery installation
PA: The Rudolph/Libbe Companies Inc
6494 Latcha Rd
Walbridge OH 43465
419 241-5000

(G-14462)
NAGLE LOGISTICS GROUP COMPANY
4520 Moline Martin Rd (43465-9786)
PHONE..................................419 661-2500
Patrick Nagle, *Pr*
EMP: 72 EST: 2021
SALES (est): 4.78MM **Privately Held**
Web: www.naglecompanies.com
SIC: 4731 Transportation agents and brokers

(G-14463)
PROFESSIONAL TRANSPORTATION
Also Called: P T I
30801 Drouillard Rd (43465-1037)
PHONE..................................419 661-0576
Justin Purkey, *Brnch Mgr*
EMP: 500
SALES (corp-wide): 116.28MM **Privately Held**
Web: www.professionaltransportationinc.com
SIC: 4119 7363 Local passenger transportation, nec; Help supply services
HQ: Professional Transportation Inc
3700 E Morgan Ave
Evansville IN 47715

(G-14464)
RUDOLPH LIBBE INC (HQ)
6494 Latcha Rd (43465-9788)
PHONE..................................419 241-5000
Timothy Alter, *Pr*
Philip J Rudolph, *
William Rudolph, *
Jeff Schaller, *
EMP: 186 EST: 1955
SQ FT: 50,000
SALES (est): 308.63MM
SALES (corp-wide): 512.7MM **Privately Held**
Web: www.rlgbuilds.com

SIC: 1541 1542 Industrial buildings, new construction, nec; Nonresidential construction, nec
PA: The Rudolph/Libbe Companies Inc
6494 Latcha Rd
Walbridge OH 43465
419 241-5000

(G-14465)
RUDOLPH/LIBBE COMPANIES INC (PA)
Also Called: Rudolph/Libbe
6494 Latcha Rd (43465-9788)
PHONE..................................419 241-5000
Bill Rudolph, *Ch*
Allan J Libbe, *
John A Libbe, *
Robert Pruger, *
Frederick W Rudolph, *
EMP: 52 EST: 1986
SQ FT: 40,000
SALES (est): 512.7MM
SALES (corp-wide): 512.7MM **Privately Held**
Web: www.rlgbuilds.com
SIC: 1541 1542 Industrial buildings and warehouses; Commercial and office building contractors

(G-14466)
SCHWERMAN TRUCKING CO
6626 State Route 795 (43465-9448)
PHONE..................................419 666-0818
Gary Richardson, *Brnch Mgr*
EMP: 54
SALES (corp-wide): 140.73MM **Privately Held**
Web: www.tankstar.com
SIC: 4213 Contract haulers
HQ: Schwerman Trucking Co.
611 S 28th St
Milwaukee WI 53215
414 671-1600

(G-14467)
TOLEDO NAGLE INC
Also Called: Nagle Line
4520 Moline Martin Rd (43465-9786)
P.O. Box 76717 (44101)
PHONE..................................419 661-2500
EMP: 65 EST: 1989
SALES (est): 20MM **Privately Held**
Web: www.naglecompanies.com
SIC: 4213 Trucking, except local

(G-14468)
WESTERN STATES ENVELOPE CO
Also Called: Western States Envelope Label
6859 Commodore Dr (43465-9765)
PHONE..................................419 666-7480
Shelly Hinkle, *Mgr*
EMP: 41
SALES (corp-wide): 106.57MM **Privately Held**
Web: www.wsel.com
SIC: 5112 2677 Envelopes; Envelopes
PA: Western States Envelope Company
4480 N 132nd St
Butler WI 53007
262 781-5540

(G-14469)
WOLFES ROOFING INC
6568 State Route 795 (43465-9760)
PHONE..................................419 666-6233
David A Wolfe, *Pr*
Florine Wolfe, *VP*
EMP: 40 EST: 1974
SALES (est): 4.44MM **Privately Held**
Web: www.wolfesroofing.com

GEOGRAPHIC SECTION

Wapakoneta - Auglaize County (G-14488)

SIC: **1761** Roofing contractor

Waldo
Marion County

(G-14470)
COLUMBUS DISTRIBUTING COMPANY
Delmar Distributing
6829 Waldo Delaware Rd (43356-9115)
PHONE..................740 726-2211
Tom Wallsmith, *Mgr*
EMP: 65
SALES (corp-wide): 48.9MM **Privately Held**
Web: www.columbusdistributing.com
SIC: 5181 Beer and other fermented malt liquors
PA: The Columbus Distributing Company
4949 Freeway Dr E
Columbus OH 43229
614 846-1000

Walnut Creek
Holmes County

(G-14471)
DUTCHMAN HOSPITALITY GROUP INC
4949 State Rte 515 (44687)
P.O. Box 177 (44687-0177)
PHONE..................330 893-3636
Mike Palmer, *Brnch Mgr*
EMP: 58
SALES (corp-wide): 25.45MM **Privately Held**
Web: www.dhgroup.com
SIC: 7011 Hotels
PA: Dutchman Hospitality Group, Inc.
4985 Walnut St
Walnut Creek OH 44687
330 893-2926

(G-14472)
WALNUT HILLS INC
4748 Olde Pump St (44687)
P.O. Box 127 (44687-0127)
PHONE..................330 852-2457
Levi Troyer, *CEO*
David Miller, *
Lillis Troyer, *
EMP: 46 **EST:** 1961
SQ FT: 36,000
SALES (est): 2.52MM **Privately Held**
Web: www.greencroft.org
SIC: 8052 8051 Intermediate care facilities; Skilled nursing care facilities

(G-14473)
WALNUT HLLS RTRMENT CMMNTIES I
4748 Olde Pump St (44687)
P.O. Box 127 (44687-0127)
PHONE..................330 893-3200
Rob Aneshansel, *Pr*
Scott Martin, *Treas*
Dale Shenk, *Asst Tr*
Rydell Bontrager, *Sec*
Garrett Roach, *Ch*
EMP: 115 **EST:** 1974
SALES (est): 10.53MM **Privately Held**
Web: www.greencroft.org
SIC: 8361 Aged home

Walnut Hills
Hamilton County

(G-14474)
GREATER CNCNNATI BHVRAL HLTH S (PA)
1501 Madison Rd Fl 2 (45206-1706)
PHONE..................513 354-7000
Jeff O'neil, *CEO*
Patricia Hassel, *
EMP: 220 **EST:** 1971
SQ FT: 25,000
SALES (est): 38.31MM
SALES (corp-wide): 38.31MM **Privately Held**
Web: www.gcbhs.com
SIC: 8093 Mental health clinic, outpatient

(G-14475)
NEW LIFE PROPERTIES INC
1501 Madison Rd Ste 2 (45206-1706)
PHONE..................513 221-3350
Robert C Mecum, *Ex Dir*
EMP: 82 **EST:** 1978
SQ FT: 13,700
SALES (est): 229.2K
SALES (corp-wide): 30.45MM **Privately Held**
SIC: 6514 Residential building, four or fewer units: operation
PA: Lighthouse Youth Services, Inc.
401 E Mcmillan St
Cincinnati OH 45206
513 221-3350

Walton Hills
Cuyahoga County

(G-14476)
MASON STRUCTURAL STEEL LLC
7500 Northfield Rd (44146-6187)
PHONE..................440 439-1040
Scott Berlin, *Pr*
Scott Polster, *VP*
Doug Shymske, *COO*
EMP: 28 **EST:** 2017
SALES (est): 2.83MM **Privately Held**
Web: www.masonsteel.com
SIC: 3441 5031 5074 Fabricated structural metal; Doors and windows; Fireplaces, prefabricated

(G-14477)
MSSI GROUP INC
Also Called: Mason Steel
7500 Northfield Rd (44146-6110)
PHONE..................440 439-1040
Leonard N Polster, *CEO*
Keith Polster, *
J Moldaver, *
Joseph Patchan, *
Sol W Wyman, *
EMP: 100 **EST:** 1958
SQ FT: 75,000
SALES (est): 17.39MM **Privately Held**
Web: www.masonsteel.com
SIC: 3441 5031 5074 Fabricated structural metal; Doors and windows; Fireplaces, prefabricated

(G-14478)
PREMISE SOLUTIONS LLC
7105 Krick Rd (44146-4417)
PHONE..................440 703-8200
Christopher Dombroski, *Prin*
EMP: 42 **EST:** 2016
SALES (est): 7.4MM **Privately Held**
Web: www.premisesolutions.com

SIC: **8748** Systems analysis and engineering consulting services

(G-14479)
RUSH TRUCK LEASING INC
Also Called: Cleveland Idealease East
7307 Young Dr Ste E (44146-5385)
PHONE..................330 798-0600
EMP: 32
SALES (corp-wide): 7.93B **Publicly Held**
Web: www.rushenterprises.com
SIC: 5012 7538 5531 5014 Automobiles and other motor vehicles; General automotive repair shops; Auto and home supply stores; Tires and tubes
HQ: Rush Truck Leasing, Inc.
11777 Highway Dr
Cincinnati OH 45241
513 733-8510

(G-14480)
SMITH & OBY COMPANY
7676 Northfield Rd (44146-5519)
PHONE..................440 735-5333
Gary Y Klie, *Ch*
Michael A Brandt, *
Ronald Vranich, *
Bryan Rogan, *
Jeff H Klie, *
EMP: 80 **EST:** 1898
SQ FT: 6,500
SALES (est): 20.5MM **Privately Held**
Web: www.smithandoby.com
SIC: 1711 Warm air heating and air conditioning contractor

Wapakoneta
Auglaize County

(G-14481)
COM NET INC
1720 Willipie St (45895)
PHONE..................419 739-3100
EMP: 60 **EST:** 1993
SALES (est): 13.02MM **Privately Held**
Web: www.cniteam.com
SIC: 4813 7375 Internet connectivity services ; Information retrieval services

(G-14482)
COUNTY OF AUGLAIZE
Auglaize Acres Nursing Home
13093 Infirmary Rd (45895-9325)
P.O. Box 328 (45895-0328)
PHONE..................419 738-3816
Bob Coverstone, *Mgr*
EMP: 83
SALES (corp-wide): 45.72MM **Privately Held**
Web: www.auglaizecounty.org
SIC: 8059 9121 Nursing home, except skilled and intermediate care facility; Legislative bodies
PA: County Of Auglaize
209 S Blackhoof St # 201
Wapakoneta OH 45895
419 739-6710

(G-14483)
FROST ROOFING INC
2 Broadway St (45895-2056)
P.O. Box 1959 (45895-0959)
PHONE..................419 739-2701
Jj Smithey, *Pr*
EMP: 65 **EST:** 2002
SQ FT: 200,000
SALES (est): 9.76MM **Privately Held**
Web: www.frost-roofing.com

SIC: **1761** Roofing contractor

(G-14484)
GARDENS WAPAKONETA OPER CO LLC
Also Called: Gardens At Wapskoneta, The
505 Walnut St (45895-1868)
PHONE..................419 738-0725
Joseph Hazelbaker, *Pr*
Brian Hazelbaker, *
Joseph Hazelbaker, *Treas*
EMP: 28 **EST:** 1999
SALES (est): 2.35MM **Privately Held**
Web: www.wapakoneta.com
SIC: 8051 Convalescent home with continuous nursing care

(G-14485)
HCF OF WAPAKONETA INC
Also Called: Wapakoneta Manor
1010 Lincoln Hwy (45895-9347)
PHONE..................419 738-3711
Josiah Meyer, *Mgr*
EMP: 43 **EST:** 1970
SALES (est): 8.01MM **Privately Held**
Web: www.wapakonetamanor.com
SIC: 8051 Convalescent home with continuous nursing care

(G-14486)
KYOCERA PRECISION TOOLS INC
321 Commerce Rd (45895-8373)
PHONE..................419 738-6652
Donna Deters, *Brnch Mgr*
EMP: 70
Web: global.kyocera.com
SIC: 5065 5013 Electronic parts and equipment, nec; Motor vehicle supplies and new parts
HQ: Kyocera Precision Tools, Inc.
102 Industrial Park Rd
Hendersonville NC 28792
800 823-7284

(G-14487)
LIMA MEMORIAL HOSPITAL LA
1251 Lincoln Hwy (45895-7356)
PHONE..................419 738-5151
Joy Brown, *Brnch Mgr*
EMP: 415 **EST:** 2007
SALES (est): 1.65MM
SALES (corp-wide): 240.6MM **Privately Held**
SIC: 8062 General medical and surgical hospitals
HQ: Lima Memorial Hospital
1001 Bellefontaine Ave
Lima OH 45804
419 228-3335

(G-14488)
LOWES HOME CENTERS LLC
Also Called: Lowe's
1340 Bellefontaine St (45895-9776)
PHONE..................419 739-1300
Rich Phillips, *Brnch Mgr*
EMP: 143
SALES (corp-wide): 86.38B **Publicly Held**
Web: www.lowes.com
SIC: 5211 5031 5722 5064 Home centers; Building materials, exterior; Household appliance stores; Electrical appliances, television and radio
HQ: Lowe's Home Centers, Llc
1000 Lowes Blvd
Mooresville NC 28117
336 658-4000

Wapakoneta - Auglaize County (G-14489) GEOGRAPHIC SECTION

(G-14489)
PETERSON CONSTRUCTION COMPANY
18817 State Route 501 (45895-9392)
P.O. Box 2058 (45895-0558)
PHONE.................419 941-2233
Donald J Bergfeld, *Pr*
Douglas J Crusey, *
EMP: 150 **EST:** 1949
SQ FT: 5,000
SALES (est): 58.02MM **Privately Held**
Web: www.petersonconstructionco.com
SIC: 1542 1629 Commercial and office building, new construction; Waste water and sewage treatment plant construction

(G-14490)
PRATT PAPER (OH) LLC
602 Leon Pratt Dr (45895-9548)
PHONE.................567 320-3353
Anthony Pratt, *Ch*
Brian Mcpheely, *CEO*
EMP: 32 **EST:** 2018
SALES (est): 97.48MM **Privately Held**
SIC: 2621 4953 Paper mills; Recycling, waste materials

(G-14491)
S & S MANAGEMENT INC
Also Called: Holiday Inn
1510 Saturn Dr (45895-9782)
PHONE.................567 356-4151
EMP: 53
SALES (corp-wide): 9.26MM **Privately Held**
Web: www.holidayinn.com
SIC: 7011 5812 7999 Hotels and motels; Eating places; Pool parlor
PA: S & S Management Inc
   550 Folkerth Ave 100
   Sidney OH 45365
   937 498-9645

(G-14492)
TSC COMMUNICATIONS INC
Also Called: Telephone Service Company
2 Willipie St (45895-1969)
P.O. Box 408 (45895-0408)
PHONE.................419 739-2200
EMP: 52 **EST:** 1894
SQ FT: 40,000
SALES (est): 820.22K
SALES (corp-wide): 15.5MM **Privately Held**
Web: www.telserco.com
SIC: 4813 4812 7375 Internet connectivity services; Paging services; Information retrieval services
PA: Telephone Service Company
   2 Willipie St
   Wapakoneta OH 45895
   419 739-2200

(G-14493)
WAPAKNETA FMLY YUNG MNS CHRSTN
Also Called: YMCA
1100 Defiance St (45895-1022)
PHONE.................419 739-9622
Joshua Little, *CEO*
Lisa Atkins, *
EMP: 55 **EST:** 1997
SALES (est): 2.73MM **Privately Held**
Web: www.wapakymca.org
SIC: 8641 8661 8699 Youth organizations; Religious organizations; Charitable organization

Warren
Trumbull County

(G-14494)
ADEL YOUSSEF MD
Also Called: Gastoenterology Clinic
1622 E Market St (44483-6613)
PHONE.................330 399-7215
Adel Youssef Md, *Owner*
EMP: 38 **EST:** 1965
SQ FT: 3,000
SALES (est): 2.73MM **Privately Held**
Web: www.northeastohiogastro.com
SIC: 8011 Gastronomist

(G-14495)
AIR MANAGEMENT GROUP LLC
Also Called: Avalon Inn and Resort
1 American Way Ne # 20 (44484-5531)
PHONE.................330 856-1900
Merry H Pieper, *Prin*
John Kouvas, *Prin*
EMP: 45 **EST:** 2003
SALES (est): 685.23K **Privately Held**
Web: www.avalongcc.com
SIC: 7011 Hotels

(G-14496)
AJAX TOCCO MAGNETHERMIC CORP (HQ)
1745 Overland Ave Ne (44483)
PHONE.................800 547-1527
Thomas Illencik, *Pr*
Steven White, *
◆ **EMP:** 200 **EST:** 2002
SQ FT: 200,000
SALES (est): 13.99MM
SALES (corp-wide): 1.66B **Publicly Held**
Web: www.ajaxtocco.com
SIC: 3567 7699 3612 Metal melting furnaces, industrial: electric; Industrial machinery and equipment repair; Electric furnace transformers
PA: Park-Ohio Holdings Corp.
   6065 Parkland Blvd Ste 1
   Cleveland OH 44124
   440 947-2000

(G-14497)
AMERICAN CEMETERY SERVICES LLP
4049 Youngstown Rd Se (44484-3345)
PHONE.................330 345-8379
Jeff Roberts, *Brnch Mgr*
EMP: 53
SALES (corp-wide): 114.95K **Privately Held**
Web: www.robertsfuneralhome.com
SIC: 6553 Cemetery subdividers and developers
PA: American Cemetery Services, Llp
   7129 Cleveland Rd
   Wooster OH 44691
   330 345-5665

(G-14498)
AMERICAN NATIONAL RED CROSS
Also Called: American Red Cross Med Educa
126 Valley Cir Ne (44484-1090)
PHONE.................330 469-6403
EMP: 31
SALES (corp-wide): 3.18B **Privately Held**
Web: www.redcross.org
SIC: 8322 Social service center
PA: The American National Red Cross
   431 18th St Nw
   Washington DC 20006
   202 737-8300

(G-14499)
ANDERSON AND DUBOSE INC
Also Called: Anderson-Dubose Co, The
5300 Tod Ave Sw (44481-9767)
PHONE.................440 248-8800
Warren Anderson, *Pr*
EMP: 100 **EST:** 1991
SQ FT: 210,497
SALES (est): 799.15MM **Privately Held**
Web: www.a-d.us
SIC: 5142 5141 Packaged frozen goods; Groceries, general line

(G-14500)
AVALON GOLF AND CNTRY CLB INC
1 American Way Ne (44484-5531)
PHONE.................330 856-8898
Ronald E Klingle, *Prin*
EMP: 104 **EST:** 2008
SALES (est): 2.13MM
SALES (corp-wide): 80.52MM **Publicly Held**
Web: www.avalongcc.com
SIC: 7997 Country club, membership
PA: Avalon Holdings Corporation
   1 American Way Ne
   Warren OH 44484
   330 856-8800

(G-14501)
AVALON HOLDINGS CORPORATION (PA)
Also Called: Avalon
1 American Way Ne (44484-5531)
PHONE.................330 856-8800
Ronald E Klingle, *Ch Bd*
Frances R Klingle, *Chief*
Stefanie Villella, *Interim Chief Financial Officer*
EMP: 52 **EST:** 1998
SQ FT: 37,000
SALES (est): 80.52MM
SALES (corp-wide): 80.52MM **Publicly Held**
Web: www.avalonholdings.com
SIC: 4953 7999 7991 4724 Hazardous waste collection and disposal; Golf services and professionals; Physical fitness facilities; Travel agencies

(G-14502)
AVALON INN SERVICES INC
Also Called: Avalon Inn
9519 E Market St (44484-5599)
PHONE.................330 856-1900
Thomas Keegan, *Pr*
John Kouvas, *
EMP: 77 **EST:** 1968
SALES (est): 683.91K **Privately Held**
Web: www.avalongcc.com
SIC: 7011 5813 Hotel, franchised; Cocktail lounge

(G-14503)
AVALON LAKES GOLF INC (HQ)
Also Called: Avalon Lakes Pro Shop
1 American Way Ne (44484-5531)
PHONE.................330 856-8898
Jeff Shaffer, *Pr*
EMP: 36 **EST:** 1970
SALES (est): 4.74MM
SALES (corp-wide): 80.52MM **Publicly Held**
Web: www.avalongcc.com
SIC: 7992 Public golf courses
PA: Avalon Holdings Corporation
   1 American Way Ne
   Warren OH 44484
   330 856-8800

(G-14504)
AVALON RESORT AND SPA LLC
9519 E Market St (44484-5511)
PHONE.................330 856-1900
Bryan Saksa, *CFO*
Bunny Bronson, *
EMP: 120 **EST:** 2014
SQ FT: 50,000
SALES (est): 971.62K
SALES (corp-wide): 80.52MM **Publicly Held**
Web: www.avalongcc.com
SIC: 7011 Hotels and motels
PA: Avalon Holdings Corporation
   1 American Way Ne
   Warren OH 44484
   330 856-8800

(G-14505)
AVI FOOD SYSTEMS INC (PA)
2590 Elm Rd Ne (44483)
PHONE.................330 372-6000
John Payiavlas, *Ch Bd*
Anthony J Payiavlas, *
Patrice Kouvas, *
EMP: 284 **EST:** 1960
SQ FT: 11,000
SALES (est): 432.96MM
SALES (corp-wide): 432.96MM **Privately Held**
Web: www.avifoodsystems.com
SIC: 5962 5812 8742 Merchandising machine operators; Caterers; Food and beverage consultant

(G-14506)
BERK ENTERPRISES INC (PA)
Also Called: Berk Paper & Supply
1554 Thomas Rd Ne (44484)
P.O. Box 2187 (44484)
PHONE.................330 369-1192
Robert Berk, *Pr*
Franks Valley, *
▲ **EMP:** 82 **EST:** 1976
SQ FT: 240,000
SALES (est): 48.14MM
SALES (corp-wide): 48.14MM **Privately Held**
Web: www.berkbrands.com
SIC: 5113 Bags, paper and disposable plastic

(G-14507)
BIG BLUE TRUCKING INC
518 Perkins Jones Rd Ne (44483-1849)
PHONE.................330 372-1421
Sandra N Clark, *Pr*
EMP: 47 **EST:** 2004
SALES (est): 4.51MM **Privately Held**
Web: www.bigbluetrucking.com
SIC: 4212 Local trucking, without storage

(G-14508)
BROTHERS AUTO TRANSPORT LLC
2188 Lyntz Townline Rd Sw (44481-8702)
PHONE.................330 824-0082
Dan Carney, *CEO*
EMP: 50
Web: www.brothersautotransport.com
SIC: 4789 Pipeline terminal facilities, independently operated
PA: Brothers Auto Transport, Llc
   593 Male Rd
   Wind Gap PA 18091

(G-14509)
COLE VALLEY MOTOR COMPANY LTD (PA)
4111 Elm Rd Ne (44483)
P.O. Box 1500 (44482)
PHONE.................330 372-1665
David Cole, *Pt*

GEOGRAPHIC SECTION

Warren - Trumbull County (G-14533)

Tom Cole, *Pt*
EMP: 62 **EST:** 1992
SQ FT: 25,000
SALES (est): 21.82MM
SALES (corp-wide): 21.82MM **Privately Held**
Web: www.colevalleycadillac.com
SIC: 5511 5531 7538 Automobiles, new and used; Automotive parts; General automotive repair shops

(G-14510)
COMMUNITY DIALYSIS CENTER
Also Called: Cdc of Warren
1950 Niles Cortland Rd Ne Ste 12 (44484)
PHONE..............................330 609-0370
Mike Brajer, *Mgr*
EMP: 106
Web: www.cdcare.org
SIC: 8092 Kidney dialysis centers
PA: Community Dialysis Center
18720 Chagrin Blvd
Shaker Heights OH 44122

(G-14511)
COMMUNITY HEALTH SYSTEMS INC
Also Called: Valley Care Health System
1350 E Market St (44483-6608)
PHONE..............................330 841-9011
Cindy Burns, *Prin*
EMP: 54 **EST:** 2010
SALES (est): 24.84MM **Privately Held**
Web: www.steward.org
SIC: 8062 General medical and surgical hospitals

(G-14512)
COMMUNITY SKLLED HLTH CARE CNT
1320 Mahoning Ave Nw (44483-2002)
PHONE..............................330 373-1160
Robert Annaess, *Admn*
EMP: 200 **EST:** 1946
SQ FT: 42,000
SALES (est): 9.64MM **Privately Held**
Web: www.communityskilled.com
SIC: 8051 Convalescent home with continuous nursing care

(G-14513)
CONLEY GROUP INC
Also Called: Concord Steel of Ohio
197 W Market St Ste 202 (44481-1024)
PHONE..............................330 372-2030
Paul Vessey, *Brnch Mgr*
EMP: 30
Web: www.conplastics.com
SIC: 5051 3471 Steel; Plating and polishing
PA: Conley Group, Inc.
21 Powder Hill Rd
Lincoln RI 02865

(G-14514)
COUNTY OF TRUMBULL
Also Called: Trumbull County Engineers
650 N River Rd Nw (44483-2255)
PHONE..............................330 675-2640
John Latell, *Dir*
EMP: 29
Web: clerk.co.trumbull.oh.us
SIC: 1611 9111 Highway and street maintenance; County supervisors' and executives' office
PA: County Of Trumbull
160 High St Nw
Warren OH 44481
330 675-2420

(G-14515)
COV-RO INC
3900 E Market St Ste 1 (44484-4708)
PHONE..............................330 856-3176
Albert Covelli, *Pr*
Michael Marando, *
EMP: 40 **EST:** 1964
SQ FT: 16,000
SALES (est): 1.01MM **Privately Held**
SIC: 7699 7623 5661 Restaurant equipment repair; Air conditioning repair; Men's shoes

(G-14516)
CREATIVE LEARNING WORKSHOP LLC (PA)
1268 N River Rd Ne Ste 1 (44483-2371)
PHONE..............................330 393-5929
EMP: 36 **EST:** 2007
SALES (est): 5.96MM
SALES (corp-wide): 5.96MM **Privately Held**
Web: www.theclw.com
SIC: 8331 Vocational rehabilitation agency

(G-14517)
DIAMOND ROOFING SYSTEMS LLP
Also Called: Diamond Roofing Systems
8600 E Market St Ste 4 (44484-2375)
PHONE..............................330 856-2500
John Pilch, *Prin*
Rusty Myers, *Prin*
EMP: 50 **EST:** 2013
SALES (est): 4.75MM **Privately Held**
Web: www.diamondroofingsystems.com
SIC: 1761 Roofing contractor

(G-14518)
DIANE SAUER CHEVROLET INC
700 Niles Rd Se (44483-5951)
PHONE..............................330 373-1600
Diane Sauer, *Pr*
EMP: 46 **EST:** 1964
SALES (est): 29.95MM **Privately Held**
Web: www.dianesauerchevy.com
SIC: 5511 7513 7359 Automobiles, new and used; Truck leasing, without drivers; Business machine and electronic equipment rental services

(G-14519)
FIRST PLACE BANK
185 E Market St (44481-1118)
P.O. Box 551 (44482-0551)
PHONE..............................330 726-3396
EMP: 874
SIC: 6035 Federal savings and loan associations

(G-14520)
FIRST STEP RECOVERY LLC
2737 Youngstown Rd Se (44484-5002)
PHONE..............................330 369-8022
Cindy Woodford, *CEO*
EMP: 34 **EST:** 2015
SALES (est): 5.48MM **Privately Held**
Web: www.wecaremoreohio.com
SIC: 8093 Substance abuse clinics (outpatient)

(G-14521)
FORUM HEALTH
1350 E Market St 302 (44483-6608)
PHONE..............................330 841-9011
EMP: 5000
SIC: 8741 8011 Hospital management; Internal medicine, physician/surgeon

(G-14522)
G H A T INC
Also Called: Thompson Heating & Cooling Co
219 N River Rd Nw (44483-2246)
PHONE..............................330 392-8838
William J Wiery Junior, *CEO*
EMP: 28 **EST:** 1952
SQ FT: 2,000
SALES (est): 560.74K **Privately Held**
Web: www.trustthompson.com
SIC: 1711 Mechanical contractor

(G-14523)
GILLETTE ASSOCIATES LP
3310 Elm Rd Ne (44483-2614)
PHONE..............................330 372-1960
Charles E Stein, *Genl Pt*
Nadile Stein, *Pt*
EMP: 49 **EST:** 1991
SQ FT: 27,947
SALES (est): 829.6K **Privately Held**
SIC: 8059 Nursing home, except skilled and intermediate care facility

(G-14524)
GILLETTE NURSING HOME INC
3310 Elm Rd Ne (44483-2662)
PHONE..............................330 372-1960
Charles E Stein, *Adm/Dir*
Janet L Stein, *
EMP: 81 **EST:** 1936
SQ FT: 42,000
SALES (est): 8.34MM **Privately Held**
Web: www.gillettenursing-home.com
SIC: 8052 8051 Intermediate care facilities; Skilled nursing care facilities

(G-14525)
HARBOR OPERATOR LLC
Also Called: Washington Square Nursing Ctr
202 Washington St Nw (44483-4735)
PHONE..............................330 399-8997
Sam Sherman, *Managing Member*
Jeff Goldstein, *Managing Member*
EMP: 30 **EST:** 2013
SALES (est): 17.89MM **Privately Held**
Web: www.washingtonsquarehealthcare.com
SIC: 8051 Convalescent home with continuous nursing care

(G-14526)
HOWLAND CRNERS TWNE CNTRY VTRN
Also Called: Towne & Country Vet Clinic
8000 E Market St (44484-2228)
PHONE..............................330 856-1862
Rufus Sparks, *Pr*
Charles Moxley, *
EMP: 30 **EST:** 1975
SALES (est): 1.7MM **Privately Held**
Web: www.tc-vet.com
SIC: 0742 0741 Veterinarian, animal specialties; Animal hospital services, livestock

(G-14527)
HUNTINGTON NATIONAL BANK
8202 E Market St (44484-2337)
PHONE..............................330 609-5029
Nancy Jurkovic, *Mgr*
EMP: 31
SALES (corp-wide): 10.84B **Publicly Held**
Web: www.huntington.com
SIC: 6029 Commercial banks, nec
HQ: The Huntington National Bank
41 S High St
Columbus OH 43215
614 480-4293

(G-14528)
HUNTINGTON NATIONAL BANK
525 Niles Cortland Rd (44484)
PHONE..............................330 841-0197
Sharon Carlson, *Mgr*
EMP: 31
SQ FT: 898
SALES (corp-wide): 10.84B **Publicly Held**
Web: www.huntington.com
SIC: 6029 6022 Commercial banks, nec; State commercial banks
HQ: The Huntington National Bank
41 S High St
Columbus OH 43215
614 480-4293

(G-14529)
HUNTINGTON NATIONAL BANK
108 Main Ave Sw Lbby (44481-1010)
PHONE..............................330 841-0205
Rick Blossom, *CEO*
EMP: 36
SALES (corp-wide): 10.84B **Publicly Held**
Web: www.huntington.com
SIC: 6021 6022 6029 National commercial banks; State commercial banks; Commercial banks, nec
HQ: The Huntington National Bank
41 S High St
Columbus OH 43215
614 480-4293

(G-14530)
JACK GIBSON CONSTRUCTION CO
2460 Parkman Rd Nw (44485-1757)
P.O. Box 2056 (44484-0056)
PHONE..............................330 394-5280
John C Gibson Junior, *CEO*
John C Gibson Senior, *Ch*
E James Breese, *
Marilyn E Hughes, *
Craig Fauvie, *
EMP: 100 **EST:** 1982
SQ FT: 27,000
SALES (est): 21.81MM **Privately Held**
Web: www.jackgibsonconstruction.com
SIC: 1542 1629 8741 1541 School building construction; Industrial plant construction; Construction management; Industrial buildings and warehouses

(G-14531)
JARO TRANSPORTATION SVCS INC (PA)
975 Post Rd Nw (44483-2083)
P.O. Box 1890 (44482-1890)
PHONE..............................330 393-5659
James N Sti Ffy, *CEO*
Rick Pompeo, *
Terry Fiorina, *
EMP: 136 **EST:** 1979
SQ FT: 5,000
SALES (est): 50.55MM
SALES (corp-wide): 50.55MM **Privately Held**
Web: www.jarotrans.com
SIC: 4213 Trucking, except local

(G-14532)
KENILWORTH STEEL CO
8700 E Market St Ste 11 (44484-2340)
PHONE..............................330 373-1885
▲ **EMP:** 28
Web: www.plate.com
SIC: 5051 Steel

(G-14533)
KIDDIE DAY CARE OF CHAMPION
5033 Mahoning Ave Nw (44483-1407)
PHONE..............................330 847-9393
Steve Callahan, *Dir*

Bonnie Callahan, *Owner*
EMP: 28 **EST:** 2001
SALES (est): 236.02K **Privately Held**
Web: www.thekiddieddaycare.com
SIC: 8351 Preschool center

(G-14534)
LEEDA SERVICES INC (PA)
1441 Parkman Rd Nw (44485-2156)
PHONE..................................330 392-6006
Winifred Hosking, *Pr*
EMP: 30 **EST:** 2000
SALES (est): 8.03MM
SALES (corp-wide): 8.03MM **Privately Held**
Web: www.leedanortheast.com
SIC: 8052 Home for the mentally retarded, with health care

(G-14535)
LIBERTY STEEL INDUSTRIES INC (PA)
2207 Larchmont Ave Ne (44483-2834)
PHONE..................................330 372-6363
James T Weller, *Pr*
Phil Lapmardo, *CFO*
EMP: 104 **EST:** 2015
SQ FT: 145,000
SALES (est): 25.59MM
SALES (corp-wide): 25.59MM **Privately Held**
Web: www.libertysteelind.com
SIC: 5051 Steel

(G-14536)
LOWES HOME CENTERS LLC
Also Called: Lowe's
940 Niles Cortland Rd Se (44484-2537)
PHONE..................................330 609-8000
EMP: 115
SQ FT: 1,315
SALES (corp-wide): 86.38B **Publicly Held**
Web: www.lowes.com
SIC: 5211 5031 5722 5064 Home centers; Building materials, exterior; Household appliance stores; Electrical appliances, television and radio
HQ: Lowe's Home Centers, Llc
1000 Lowes Blvd
Mooresville NC 28117
336 658-4000

(G-14537)
MAIN LITE ELECTRIC CO INC
Also Called: Electrical Contractor
3000 Sferra Ave Nw (44483-2266)
P.O. Box 828 (44482-0828)
PHONE..................................330 369-8333
Toni Harnar, *Pr*
Toni M Harnar, *
Colleen Beil, *
Kevin D Beil, *
John H Harnar, *
EMP: 43 **EST:** 1988
SQ FT: 13,000
SALES (est): 5.32MM **Privately Held**
Web: www.mainliteelectric.com
SIC: 1731 1623 General electrical contractor ; Electric power line construction

(G-14538)
MATTHEW T HOVANIC INC
Also Called: Homac Auto & Van Wash
579 Washington St Ne (44483-4932)
PHONE..................................330 898-3387
Matthew T Hovanic, *Pr*
Deana Hovanic, *
EMP: 30 **EST:** 1994
SALES (est): 501.27K **Privately Held**
SIC: 7542 Washing and polishing, automotive

(G-14539)
MERCY HEALTH YOUNGSTOWN LLC
Also Called: Mercy Hlth-St Jseph Wrren Hosp
667 Eastland Ave Se (44484-4503)
PHONE..................................330 841-4000
EMP: 100
SALES (corp-wide): 6.92B **Privately Held**
Web: www.bonsecours.com
SIC: 8062 Hospital, affiliated with AMA residency
HQ: Mercy Health Youngstown Llc
1044 Belmont Ave
Youngstown OH 44504

(G-14540)
MOCHA HOUSE INC (PA)
467 High St Ne (44481-1226)
PHONE..................................330 392-3020
George N Liakaris, *Pr*
Nick G Liakaris, *
Bill M Axiotis, *
EMP: 33 **EST:** 1992
SQ FT: 10,000
SALES (est): 2.5MM **Privately Held**
Web: www.mochahouse.com
SIC: 5812 5461 7299 Coffee shop; Retail bakeries; Banquet hall facilities

(G-14541)
MSSL CONSOLIDATED INC
8640 E Market St (44484-2346)
PHONE..................................330 766-5510
V C Sehgal, *Ch*
Laksh V Sehgal, *Vice Chairman*
Sukant Gupta, *
EMP: 409 **EST:** 2014
SIC: 6719 Investment holding companies, except banks
PA: Samvardhana Motherson International Limited
Corporate Tower, 11th Floor, Plot No. 1, Noida UP 20180

(G-14542)
NATIONAL MENTOR HOLDINGS INC
4451 Mahoning Ave Nw (44483-1977)
PHONE..................................234 806-5361
EMP: 323
SALES (corp-wide): 1.64B **Privately Held**
Web: www.sevitahealth.com
SIC: 8082 Home health care services
HQ: National Mentor Holdings, Inc.
313 Congress St Fl 5
Boston MA 02210
617 790-4800

(G-14543)
NEOCAP/CBCF
Also Called: Northeast Ohio Community Alter
411 Pine Ave Se (44483-5706)
PHONE..................................330 675-2669
James Corfman, *Ex Dir*
EMP: 35 **EST:** 1998
SALES (est): 2.39MM **Privately Held**
Web: www.neocap.org
SIC: 8744 Correctional facility

(G-14544)
NORTH WOOD REALTY
Also Called: Century 21
1985 Niles Cortland Rd Se (44484-3037)
PHONE..................................330 856-3915
EMP: 85
SALES (corp-wide): 1.87MM **Privately Held**
Web: www.thepreferredrealty.com
SIC: 6531 Real estate agent, residential
PA: North Wood Realty
1315 Boardman Poland Rd # 7
Youngstown OH 44514
330 423-0837

(G-14545)
PARKMAN AUTOMOTIVE LLC
2625 Parkman Rd Nw (44485-1762)
PHONE..................................234 223-2806
EMP: 27
SALES (corp-wide): 395.77K **Privately Held**
Web: www.parkmanautomotive.com
SIC: 7538 General automotive repair shops
PA: Parkman Automotive Llc
262 Youngs Run Dr Nw
Warren OH 44483
330 847-2250

(G-14546)
PERISHABLE SHIPG SOLUTIONS LLC
1701 Henn Pkwy Sw (44481-8656)
PHONE..................................724 944-9024
Stephanie Riffell, *Brnch Mgr*
EMP: 30
SIC: 4222 5961 Warehousing, cold storage or refrigerated; Electronic shopping
HQ: Perishable Shipping Solutions, Llc
46500 Humboldt Dr
Novi MI

(G-14547)
PHILLIPS HTHCARE LLC DBA CRING
1577 Woodland St Ne (44483-5301)
PHONE..................................330 531-6110
EMP: 50 **EST:** 2012
SALES (est): 560.43K **Privately Held**
SIC: 8322 8361 8082 8059 Geriatric social service; Geriatric residential care; Home health care services; Nursing and personal care, nec

(G-14548)
POLIVKA INTERNATIONAL CO INC
8256 E Market St Ste 114 (44484-2300)
PHONE..................................704 321-0802
EMP: 45
Web: www.polivkaintl.com
SIC: 1611 Concrete construction: roads, highways, sidewalks, etc.
PA: Polivka International Company, Inc.
13700 Prvdence Rd Ste 200
Matthews NC 28104

(G-14549)
PSYCARE INC
8577 E Market St (44484-2390)
PHONE..................................330 856-6663
Terrence Heltzel, *Dir*
Douglas Darnall, *
EMP: 37 **EST:** 1985
SALES (est): 894.95K **Privately Held**
Web: www.psycare.com
SIC: 8093 8011 Mental health clinic, outpatient; Psychiatric clinic

(G-14550)
SANESE SERVICES INC
Also Called: Sanese Services
2590 Elm Rd Ne (44483-2904)
P.O. Box 110 (44482-0110)
PHONE..................................614 436-1234
TOLL FREE: 800
EMP: 850
Web: www.avifoodsystems.com
SIC: 5962 5812 7389 Food vending machines; Eating places; Coffee service

(G-14551)
SANFREY FREIGHT SERVICES INC
695 Summit St Nw Ste 1 (44485-2800)
P.O. Box 1770 (44482-1770)
PHONE..................................330 372-1883
EMP: 31

SALES (corp-wide): 2.55M **Privately Held**
Web: www.sanfrey.com
SIC: 4212 4213 Local trucking, without storage; Contract haulers
PA: Sanfrey Freight Services Inc
1256 Elm Rd Ne
Warren OH 44483
330 372-1883

(G-14552)
SEVEN SEVENTEEN CREDIT UN INC (PA)
3181 Larchmont Ave Ne (44483-2498)
PHONE..................................330 372-8100
Gary L Soukenik, *CEO*
Jerome J Mcgee, *CFO*
EMP: 173 **EST:** 1957
SQ FT: 40,000
SALES (est): 78.13MM
SALES (corp-wide): 78.13MM **Privately Held**
Web: www.717cu.com
SIC: 6061 Federal credit unions

(G-14553)
SHEPHERD OF VLY LTHRAN RTRMENT
4100 N River Rd Ne (44484-1041)
PHONE..................................330 856-9232
Donald Kacmar, *Ex Dir*
EMP: 31
SALES (corp-wide): 42.58MM **Privately Held**
Web: www.shepherdofthevalley.com
SIC: 8361 Aged home
PA: Shepherd Of The Valley Lutheran Retirement Services, Inc.
5525 Silica Rd
Youngstown OH 44515
330 530-4038

(G-14554)
SIMS BUICK-GMC TRUCK INC
Also Called: Sims GMC Trucks
3100 Elm Rd Ne (44483-2698)
PHONE..................................330 372-3500
William Sims, *Pr*
Kenneth Sims, *
EMP: 50 **EST:** 1969
SQ FT: 36,000
SALES (est): 21.23MM **Privately Held**
Web: www.simsbuickgmc.com
SIC: 5511 5012 Automobiles, new and used; Automobiles and other motor vehicles

(G-14555)
ST JOSEPH RIVERSIDE HOSPITAL
667 Eastland Ave Se (44484-4503)
PHONE..................................330 841-4000
EMP: 1100
SIC: 8062 General medical and surgical hospitals

(G-14556)
STARR CONSTRUCTION & DEMO LLC
2887 N Salem Warren Rd (44481-9508)
PHONE..................................330 538-7214
EMP: 35 **EST:** 2014
SALES (est): 3MM **Privately Held**
SIC: 1794 Excavation work

(G-14557)
STEIN STEEL MILL SERVICES LLC
4000 Mahoning Ave Nw (44483-1924)
PHONE..................................440 526-9301
John Desmond, *Pr*
EMP: 99 **EST:** 1980
SALES (est): 14.56MM **Privately Held**

GEOGRAPHIC SECTION — Warren - Trumbull County (G-14578)

Web: www.steininc.com
SIC: 5051 Steel
HQ: Stein, Llc
3 Summit Park Dr Ste 425
Independence OH 44131
440 526-9301

(G-14558)
STEMCOR USA INC
Kenilworth Steel
8700 E Market St Ste 11 (44484-2340)
PHONE..................................330 373-1885
Shawn Gill, *CEO*
EMP: 28
Web: www.stemcor.com
SIC: 5051 Steel
HQ: Stemcor Usa Inc.
1 Financial Plz Ste 2020
Fort Lauderdale FL 33394
212 563-0262

(G-14559)
STEWARD HLLSIDE RHBLTTION HOSP
Also Called: Elm Road Rhblttion Svcs A Svc
8747 Squires Ln Ne (44484)
PHONE..................................330 841-3700
Ralph De La Torre, *Pr*
EMP: 53 **EST:** 2010
SALES (est): 24.92MM **Privately Held**
Web: www.hillsiderehabhospital.org
SIC: 8062 General medical and surgical hospitals
HQ: Steward Health Care System Llc
1900 N Pearl St Ste 2400
Dallas TX 75201

(G-14560)
STEWARD NORTHSIDE MED CTR INC
Also Called: Northside Medical Center
1350 E Market St (44483)
PHONE..................................330 884-1000
Ralph De La Torre, *Prin*
EMP: 182 **EST:** 2010
SALES (est): 164.6MM **Privately Held**
Web: www.northsidemedicalcenter.net
SIC: 8062 General medical and surgical hospitals
HQ: Steward Health Care System Llc
1900 N Pearl St Ste 2400
Dallas TX 75201

(G-14561)
STEWARD TRUMBULL MEM HOSP INC
Also Called: Trumbull Memorial Hospital
1350 E Market St (44482)
P.O. Box 1269 (44482)
PHONE..................................330 841-9011
TOLL FREE: 800
Ronald Bierman, *Pr*
Shawn Dilmore, *COO*
Steven Snyder, *CFO*
Cindy Russo, *Pr*
John R Castellano, *CRO*
EMP: 1000 **EST:** 1984
SQ FT: 600,000
SALES (est): 141.95MM **Privately Held**
Web: www.trumbullregional.org
SIC: 8062 8049 General medical and surgical hospitals; Physical therapist
HQ: Steward Health Care System Llc
1900 N Pearl St Ste 2400
Dallas TX 75201

(G-14562)
SUPERIOR WALLS OF OHIO INC
1401 Pine Ave Se (44483)
PHONE..................................330 393-4101
George Schuler, *Pr*

▼ **EMP:** 60 **EST:** 1997
SQ FT: 60,000
SALES (est): 4.69MM **Privately Held**
SIC: 1791 Precast concrete structural framing or panels, placing of

(G-14563)
TAYLOR STEEL INC
Also Called: Taylor Coil Processing
2260 Industrial Trce Sw (44481-9264)
PHONE..................................330 824-8600
EMP: 90 **EST:** 1979
SALES (est): 13.52MM
SALES (corp-wide): 298.73MM **Privately Held**
Web: www.taylorsteel.com
SIC: 7389 5051 Metal slitting and shearing; Steel
PA: Taylor Steel Inc
477 Arvin Ave
Stoney Creek ON L8E 2
905 662-4925

(G-14564)
TRUMBULL CMNTY ACTION PROGRAM (PA)
1230 Palmyra Rd Sw (44485-3730)
PHONE..................................330 393-2507
Ms. Mamie C Hunt, *Bd of Dir*
Henry Angelo, *
Doctor Kraig Markland, *Bd of Dir*
Phyllis Cayson, *
B J Pollard, *
EMP: 65 **EST:** 1987
SALES (est): 7.59MM
SALES (corp-wide): 7.59MM **Privately Held**
Web: www.tcaphelps.org
SIC: 8399 Community action agency

(G-14565)
TRUMBULL COUNTY ENGINEERING (PA)
650 N River Rd Nw (44483-2255)
PHONE..................................330 675-2640
EMP: 59 **EST:** 1984
SALES (est): 2.61MM **Privately Held**
Web: engineer.co.trumbull.oh.us
SIC: 8711 Engineering services

(G-14566)
TRUMBULL INDUSTRIES INC (PA)
Also Called: Trumbull Industries
400 Dietz Rd Ne (44483-2708)
P.O. Box 30 (44482-0030)
PHONE..................................800 477-1799
▲ **EMP:** 100 **EST:** 1922
SALES (est): 162.11MM
SALES (corp-wide): 162.11MM **Privately Held**
Web: www.trumbull.com
SIC: 5074 5085 5064 Plumbing and hydronic heating supplies; Industrial supplies; Appliance parts, household

(G-14567)
TRUMBULL MEM HOSP FOUNDATION
Also Called: MAHONING VALLEY HEMATOLOGY ONC
1350 E Market St (44483-6608)
PHONE..................................330 841-9376
Henry Sebold, *CFO*
Charles Johns, *Pr*
EMP: 58 **EST:** 1890
SALES (est): 576.05K **Privately Held**
Web: www.trumbullregional.org
SIC: 8062 General medical and surgical hospitals

(G-14568)
TURN AROUND GROUP INC
Also Called: Sunrise Industries Harps Jantr
1512 Phoenix Rd Ne (44483-2855)
PHONE..................................330 372-0064
EMP: 80 **EST:** 1999
SALES (est): 2.41MM **Privately Held**
Web: www.tagdn.com
SIC: 7349 Janitorial service, contract basis

(G-14569)
URGENT CARE SPECIALISTS LLC
1997 Niles Cortland Rd Se (44484-3037)
PHONE..................................330 505-9400
Tammy Russell, *Pr*
EMP: 55
SALES (corp-wide): 23.51MM **Privately Held**
Web: www.wellnow.com
SIC: 8011 Freestanding emergency medical center
PA: Urgent Care Specialists Llc
2400 Corp Exch Dr Ste 102
Columbus OH 43231
614 505-7633

(G-14570)
US SAFETYGEAR INC (PA)
Also Called: US Safetygear
5001 Enterprise Dr Nw (44481-8713)
P.O. Box 309 (44430-0309)
PHONE..................................330 898-1344
Tarry A Alberini, *CEO*
Tarry A Alberini, *Prin*
John C Conley, *
EMP: 40 **EST:** 1989
SQ FT: 102,000
SALES (est): 27.07MM
SALES (corp-wide): 27.07MM **Privately Held**
Web: www.ussafetygear.com
SIC: 5084 5999 Safety equipment; Safety supplies and equipment

(G-14571)
VALVOLINE INSTANT OIL CHNGE FR
Also Called: Valvoline Instant Oil Change
2769 Elm Rd Ne (44483-2601)
PHONE..................................330 372-4416
EMP: 37
Web: www.valvoline.com
SIC: 7549 Lubrication service, automotive
HQ: Valvoline Instant Oil Change Franchising, Inc.
100 Valvoline Way
Lexington KY 40509

(G-14572)
VISITING NRSE ASSN HSPICE NRTH
Also Called: Forum Health At Home-Hospice
8747 Squires Ln Ne (44484-1649)
PHONE..................................330 841-5440
Walter J Pishkur, *Pr*
Mike Sellman, *
EMP: 55 **EST:** 1933
SALES (est): 1.8MM **Privately Held**
SIC: 8082 Home health care services

(G-14573)
VWC LIQUIDATION COMPANY LLC
1701 Henn Pkwy Sw (44481-8656)
PHONE..................................330 372-6776
James E Collins Senior, *Managing Member*
EMP: 130 **EST:** 2001
SQ FT: 50,000
SALES (est): 17.63MM **Privately Held**
SIC: 1799 5031 Window treatment installation; Lumber, plywood, and millwork

(G-14574)
WARREN CITY BOARD EDUCATION
Also Called: Transportation Center
600 Roanoke Ave Sw (44483-6473)
PHONE..................................330 841-2265
Phyllis Linderman, *Prin*
EMP: 37
SALES (corp-wide): 88.83MM **Privately Held**
Web: www.warrencityschools.org
SIC: 4226 Special warehousing and storage, nec
PA: Warren City Board Of Education
105 High St Ne
Warren OH 44481
330 841-2321

(G-14575)
WARREN DIALYSIS CENTER LLC
Also Called: AMERICAN RENAL
8720 E Market St Ste 1a (44484-2364)
PHONE..................................330 609-5502
Marlys Brajer, *Managing Member*
EMP: 41 **EST:** 2009
SALES (est): 2.85MM
SALES (corp-wide): 822.52MM **Privately Held**
Web: www.warren.health
SIC: 8092 Kidney dialysis centers
HQ: American Renal Associates Holdings, Inc.
500 Cummings Ctr Ste 6550
Beverly MA 01915

(G-14576)
WJ SERVICE CO INC (PA)
Also Called: W J Alarm Service
2592 Elm Rd Ne (44483-2904)
PHONE..................................330 372-5040
James Paylavlas, *Pr*
Nicholas Paylavlas, *
Tony Paylavlas, *
EMP: 45 **EST:** 1979
SQ FT: 29,704
SALES (est): 2.48MM
SALES (corp-wide): 2.48MM **Privately Held**
Web: www.wjalarm.com
SIC: 7349 7382 Janitorial service, contract basis; Security systems services

(G-14577)
WSB REHABILITATION SVCS INC
4329 Mahoning Ave Nw Ste B (44483-1910)
PHONE..................................330 847-7819
Kelly Jenkins, *Brnch Mgr*
EMP: 524
SALES (corp-wide): 23MM **Privately Held**
Web: www.blueskytherapy.net
SIC: 8093 Rehabilitation center, outpatient treatment
PA: Wsb Rehabilitation Services, Inc.
510 W Main St
Canfield OH 44406
330 533-1338

(G-14578)
XPO LOGISTICS FREIGHT INC
6700 Muth Rd Sw (44481-9276)
PHONE..................................330 824-2242
Farris Scott, *Mgr*
EMP: 79
SALES (corp-wide): 7.74B **Publicly Held**
Web: www.xpo.com
SIC: 4213 Contract haulers
HQ: Xpo Logistics Freight, Inc.
2211 Old Erhart Rd Ste 10
Ann Arbor MI 48105
800 755-2728

Warrensville Heights
Cuyahoga County

(G-14579)
CLEVELAND CLNIC HLTH SYSTM-WST
Also Called: South Pointe Hospital
20000 Harvard Ave (44122-6805)
PHONE..................216 491-6000
Doctor Brian Heart, *Pr*
EMP: 232
SQ FT: 1,644
SALES (corp-wide): 14.48B **Privately Held**
Web: my.clevelandclinic.org
SIC: 8741 8062 Hospital management; General medical and surgical hospitals
HQ: Cleveland Clinic Health System- Western Region
18101 Lorain Ave
Cleveland OH 44111
216 476-7000

(G-14580)
DIGITAL FORENSICS CORP LLC
4400 Renaissance Pkwy (44128-5794)
PHONE..................888 210-1296
EMP: 27 **EST:** 2016
SALES (est): 724.31K **Privately Held**
Web: www.digitalforensics.com
SIC: 7371 Computer software development and applications

(G-14581)
GRACE HOSPITAL
20000 Harvard Ave (44122-6805)
PHONE..................216 687-1500
EMP: 32
SALES (corp-wide): 9.47MM **Privately Held**
Web: www.gracehospital.org
SIC: 8062 Hospital, affiliated with AMA residency
PA: Grace Hospital
2307 W 14th St
Cleveland OH 44113
216 687-1500

(G-14582)
INTEGRATED HEALTH SERVICES INC
19201 Cranwood Pkwy (44128-4043)
PHONE..................440 856-5475
Dan Green, *Managing Member*
EMP: 30
SALES (est): 578.78K **Privately Held**
SIC: 8099 Health and allied services, nec

(G-14583)
LAZURITE INC
4760 Richmond Rd Ste 400 (44128-5979)
PHONE..................216 334-3127
Eugene Malinskiy, *CEO*
Leah Brownlee, *
EMP: 27 **EST:** 2015
SALES (est): 3.7MM **Privately Held**
Web: www.lazurite.co
SIC: 8731 8733 Medical research, commercial; Medical research

(G-14584)
LITTLE SSTERS OF POOR BLTMORE
Also Called: St Mary & Joseph Home
4291 Richmond Rd (44122-6103)
P.O. Box 221277 (44122-0996)
PHONE..................216 464-1222
Anne Donnelly, *Pr*
EMP: 91
SALES (corp-wide): 3.97MM **Privately Held**
Web: www.littlesistersofthepoorbaltimore.org
SIC: 8051 8052 Skilled nursing care facilities; Intermediate care facilities
PA: Little Sisters Of The Poor, Baltimore, Inc.
601 Maiden Choice Ln
Baltimore MD 21228
410 744-9367

(G-14585)
PARIS HOME HEALTH CARE LLC
4630 Richmond Rd Ste 270c (44128-5954)
PHONE..................888 416-9889
Paris Parker, *CEO*
Paris Ariane Parker, *Managing Member*
EMP: 35 **EST:** 2019
SALES (est): 1.47MM **Privately Held**
Web: www.parishomehealth.com
SIC: 8082 Home health care services

(G-14586)
PROFESSIONAL BLDG MAINT INC
26851 Miles Rd Ste 206 (44128-5991)
PHONE..................440 666-8509
Joseph Mcabier, *Pr*
EMP: 70 **EST:** 1986
SALES (est): 1.1MM **Privately Held**
Web: www.probuildmaint.com
SIC: 7349 Cleaning service, industrial or commercial

(G-14587)
REGENCY HOSPITAL COMPANY LLC
Also Called: Regency Hospital - Cleveland E
4200 Interchange Corporate Center Rd (44128-5631)
PHONE..................216 910-3800
EMP: 226
SALES (corp-wide): 6.2B **Publicly Held**
Web: www.regencyhospital.com
SIC: 8062 General medical and surgical hospitals
HQ: Regency Hospital Company, L.L.C.
4714 Gettysburg Rd
Mechanicsburg PA 17055
419 318-5700

(G-14588)
SPECIAL METALS CORPORATION (DH)
Also Called: PCC Metals Group
4832 Richmond Rd Ste 100 (44128-5993)
PHONE..................216 755-3030
Ken Buck, *Pr*
Joseph Snowden, *VP*
◆ **EMP:** 461 **EST:** 1964
SQ FT: 14,000
SALES (est): 527.09MM
SALES (corp-wide): 364.48B **Publicly Held**
Web: www.specialmetals.com
SIC: 5051 Steel
HQ: Precision Castparts Corp.
5885 Meadows Rd Ste 620
Lake Oswego OR 97035
503 946-4800

(G-14589)
TITANIUM METALS CORPORATION (DH)
Also Called: Timet
4832 Richmond Rd Ste 100 (44128-5993)
PHONE..................740 537-5600
James W Brown, *VP*
Robert D Graham, *
Andrew B Nace, *
Scott E Sullivan, *
Harold C Simmons, *
◆ **EMP:** 30 **EST:** 1955
SALES (est): 830.91MM
SALES (corp-wide): 364.48B **Publicly Held**
Web: www.timet.com
SIC: 5051 Metal wires, ties, cables, and screening
HQ: Precision Castparts Corp.
5885 Meadows Rd Ste 620
Lake Oswego OR 97035
503 946-4800

(G-14590)
WF HANN & SONS LLC (PA)
Also Called: W.F. Hann & Sons
26401 Miles Rd (44128-5930)
PHONE..................216 831-4200
Karen Johnson, *Pr*
Carl Grassi, *Stockholder*
Fred Disanto, *Stockholder*
EMP: 40 **EST:** 1907
SQ FT: 12,500
SALES (est): 11.71MM
SALES (corp-wide): 11.71MM **Privately Held**
Web: www.wfhann.com
SIC: 1711 Plumbing contractors

Warsaw
Coshocton County

(G-14591)
ECHOING HILLS VILLAGE INC (PA)
Also Called: Echoing Ridge Residential Ctr
36272 County Road 79 (43844-9770)
PHONE..................740 327-2311
Harry C Busch, *Pr*
Buddy Busch, *
John Swanson, *
EMP: 110 **EST:** 1966
SQ FT: 2,500
SALES (est): 39.8MM
SALES (corp-wide): 39.8MM **Privately Held**
Web: www.ehvi.org
SIC: 7032 8051 8361 8322 Sporting and recreational camps; Mental retardation hospital; Residential care; Individual and family services

Waterford
Washington County

(G-14592)
LANG MASONRY CONTRACTORS INC
405 Watertown Rd (45786-5248)
PHONE..................740 749-3512
Damian Lang, *Pr*
Doug Taylor, *
EMP: 70 **EST:** 1984
SALES (est): 29.06MM **Privately Held**
Web: www.langmasonry.com
SIC: 1741 Stone masonry

Waterville
Lucas County

(G-14593)
BROWNING MESONIC COMMUNITY (PA)
8883 Browning Dr (43566-9757)
PHONE..................419 878-4055
Dave Subleski, *Dir*
EMP: 35 **EST:** 1981
SQ FT: 350,000
SALES (est): 9.1MM
SALES (corp-wide): 9.1MM **Privately Held**
Web: www.omcoh.org
SIC: 8361 Aged home

(G-14594)
SOMETHING SPECIAL LRNG CTR INC (PA)
8251 Waterville Swanton Rd (43566-9725)
PHONE..................419 878-4190
Mary Wolfe, *Pr*
EMP: 28 **EST:** 1983
SQ FT: 5,000
SALES (est): 2.41MM **Privately Held**
Web: www.somethingspecial.us
SIC: 8351 Group day care center

(G-14595)
ST LUKES HOSPITAL
Also Called: St Lukes Wtrvlle Physcl Thrapy
900 Waterville Monclova Rd (43566-1168)
PHONE..................419 441-1002
Scott Giest, *Brnch Mgr*
EMP: 1217
SALES (corp-wide): 6.92B **Privately Held**
Web: www.mclaren.org
SIC: 8049 8071 Physical therapist; Medical laboratories
HQ: St. Luke's Hospital
5901 Monclova Rd
Maumee OH 43537
419 893-5911

(G-14596)
WATERVILLE FMLY PHYSICIANS INC
Also Called: Bruss, Mark R MD
900 Waterville Monclova Rd Ste A (43566)
PHONE..................419 878-2026
Robert L Sido Md, *Pr*
Mark Bruss Md, *VP*
EMP: 36 **EST:** 1963
SALES (est): 2.14MM **Privately Held**
Web: www.watervillegas.com
SIC: 8011 General and family practice, physician/surgeon

Wauseon
Fulton County

(G-14597)
ALL HEART HOME CARE LLC
132 S Fulton St (43567)
P.O. Box 896 (43517)
PHONE..................419 298-0034
Kelly Wilhelm, *Mgr*
EMP: 44 **EST:** 2012
SALES (est): 720.56K **Privately Held**
SIC: 8082 Home health care services

(G-14598)
CORNERSTONE WAUSEON INC
Also Called: Wauseon Machine & Mfg Inc
995 Enterprise Ave (43567-9333)
PHONE..................419 337-0940
Ryan Anair, *CEO*
Peter Paras Junior, *VP*
Matthew Bombick, *
Ellen Hadymon, *
EMP: 190 **EST:** 2013
SALES (est): 20.24MM **Privately Held**
SIC: 3441 3559 7629 3547 Fabricated structural metal; Automotive related machinery; Electrical repair shops; Rolling mill machinery

(G-14599)
DONS AUTOMOTIVE GROUP LLC
720 N Shoop Ave (43567-1838)
P.O. Box 208 (43567-0208)
PHONE..................419 337-3010
TOLL FREE: 800

GEOGRAPHIC SECTION

EMP: 35 EST: 1999
SALES (est): 10.89MM **Privately Held**
Web: www.donsautogroup.com
SIC: **5511** 5521 5012 Automobiles, new and used; Used car dealers; Automobiles and other motor vehicles

(G-14600)
FULTON COUNTY HEALTH CENTER
138 E Elm St (43567-1457)
PHONE..................................419 335-1919
EMP: 55
SALES (corp-wide): 102.48MM **Privately Held**
Web: www.fultoncountyhealthcenter.org
SIC: **8049** Physical therapist
PA: Fulton County Health Center
725 S Shoop Ave
Wauseon OH 43567
419 335-2015

(G-14601)
FULTON COUNTY HEALTH CENTER
Also Called: Fulton Manor Nursing Home
725 S Shoop Ave (43567-1701)
PHONE..................................419 335-2017
Patricia Finn, *CEO*
EMP: 136
SALES (corp-wide): 102.48MM **Privately Held**
Web: www.fultoncountyhealthcenter.org
SIC: **8062** 8051 General medical and surgical hospitals; Skilled nursing care facilities
PA: Fulton County Health Center
725 S Shoop Ave
Wauseon OH 43567
419 335-2015

(G-14602)
FULTON COUNTY HEALTH CENTER (PA)
725 S Shoop Ave (43567-1701)
PHONE..................................419 335-2015
Carl Hill, *Pr*
Sandra K Barber, *
Janice Fitzenreiter, *
Patti Finn, *
Mark Hagans, *
EMP: 451 EST: 1927
SQ FT: 164,276
SALES (est): 102.48MM
SALES (corp-wide): 102.48MM **Privately Held**
Web: www.fultoncountyhealthcenter.org
SIC: **8062** General medical and surgical hospitals

(G-14603)
FULTON COUNTY HEALTH DEPT
606 S Shoop Ave (43567-1712)
PHONE..................................419 337-0915
EMP: 50 EST: 1950
SALES (est): 3.47MM **Privately Held**
Web: www.fultoncountyhealthdept.com
SIC: **8093** Family planning clinic

(G-14604)
GRIESER LOGISTICS LLC
19230 County Road F (43567-9481)
PHONE..................................419 445-9256
Dave Grieser, *Pt*
EMP: 35 EST: 2001
SALES (est): 1.63MM **Privately Held**
Web: www.griesertransportation.com
SIC: **4789** Transportation services, nec

(G-14605)
IAC WAUSEON LLC
555 W Linfoot St (43567-9558)
PHONE..................................419 335-1000
Mike Biglin, *Managing Member*
▲ EMP: 48 EST: 2007
SALES (est): 2.76MM **Privately Held**
SIC: **5599** 7538 Aircraft dealers; General automotive repair shops

(G-14606)
MRS DENNIS POTATO FARM INC
15370 County Road K (43567-8891)
PHONE..................................419 335-2778
Suzanne Dennis, *Pr*
Timothy Dennis, *
EMP: 30 EST: 1987
SQ FT: 27,000
SALES (est): 4.74MM **Privately Held**
Web: www.apartmentsdelta.com
SIC: **0134** Irish potatoes

(G-14607)
NOFZIGER DOOR SALES INC (PA)
Also Called: Haas Doors
320 Sycamore St (43567-1100)
PHONE..................................419 337-9900
Edward L Nofziger, *Pr*
Carol Nofziger, *
▼ EMP: 173 EST: 1938
SQ FT: 200,000
SALES (est): 39.6MM
SALES (corp-wide): 39.6MM **Privately Held**
Web: www.archboldohiogaragedoors.com
SIC: **3442** 1751 5211 Metal doors; Garage door, installation or erection; Doors, wood or metal, except storm

(G-14608)
SARAS GARDEN
620 W Leggett St (43567-1348)
P.O. Box 150 (43567-0150)
PHONE..................................419 335-7272
William Frank, *Prin*
Matthew Rychener, *
Bill Frank, *
David Burkholder, *
Julian Giovarelli, *
EMP: 66 EST: 2004
SALES (est): 3.19MM **Privately Held**
Web: www.sarasgarden.org
SIC: **8011** Medical centers

(G-14609)
TOLEDO CLINIC INC
1080 N Shoop Ave (43567-1821)
PHONE..................................419 330-5288
EMP: 83
SALES (corp-wide): 119.13MM **Privately Held**
Web: www.toledoclinic.com
SIC: **8011** Physicians' office, including specialists
PA: Toledo Clinic, Inc.
4235 Secor Rd
Toledo OH 43623
419 473-3561

Waverly
Pike County

(G-14610)
ADENA HEALTH SYSTEM
Also Called: Adena Pike Medical Center
100 Dawn Ln (45690-9138)
PHONE..................................740 947-2186
EMP: 30
SALES (corp-wide): 678.56MM **Privately Held**
Web: www.adena.org
SIC: **8062** General medical and surgical hospitals
PA: Adena Health System
272 Hospital Rd
Chillicothe OH 45601
740 779-7500

(G-14611)
BUCKEYE COMMUNITY SERVICES INC
Also Called: Grandview Avenue Home
207 Remy Ct (45690-2000)
PHONE..................................740 941-1639
EMP: 113
SALES (corp-wide): 15.43MM **Privately Held**
Web: www.buckeyecommunityservices.org
SIC: **8059** Home for the mentally retarded, ex. skilled or intermediate
PA: Buckeye Community Services, Incorporated
220 Morton St
Jackson OH 45640
740 286-5039

(G-14612)
FIRST NATIONAL BANK OF WAVERLY (PA)
Also Called: First National Bank
107 N Market St (45690)
P.O. Box 147 (45690)
PHONE..................................740 947-2136
Robert E Foster, *Pr*
Dwight A Massie, *
EMP: 50 EST: 1901
SQ FT: 17,000
SALES (est): 6.08MM
SALES (corp-wide): 6.08MM **Privately Held**
Web: www.thefirstnational.com
SIC: **6021** National commercial banks

(G-14613)
FOILL INC
201 E North St (45690-1149)
PHONE..................................740 947-1117
Margaret D Foill, *Pr*
Chip Foill, *VP*
Rick Foill, *VP*
EMP: 31 EST: 1991
SQ FT: 2,000
SALES (est): 2.57MM **Privately Held**
SIC: **1623** 1541 Water and sewer line construction; Industrial buildings and warehouses

(G-14614)
OHIO DEPT MNTAL HLTH ADDCTION
Also Called: Recovery Council, The
111 N High St (45690-1343)
PHONE..................................740 947-7581
Tom Johnson, *Dir*
EMP: 106
Web: www.therecovercouncil.org
SIC: **8093** 9431 Rehabilitation center, outpatient treatment; Administration of public health programs, State government
HQ: Ohio Department Of Mental Health And Addiction Services
30 E Broad St Fl 36
Columbus OH 43215

(G-14615)
PIKE COUNTY
Also Called: Engineering Office
502 Pike St (45690-9685)
PHONE..................................740 947-9339
Denny Salisbury, *Engr*
EMP: 30
Web: www.pikecountycourt.org

SIC: **8711** 9111 1611 Engineering services; County supervisors' and executives' office; Highway and street construction
PA: Pike County
230 Waverly Plz Ste 200
Waverly OH 45690
740 947-4125

(G-14616)
PIKE COUNTY RECOVERY COUNCIL (PA)
218 E North St (45690-1148)
P.O. Box 226 (45690-0226)
PHONE..................................740 835-8437
EMP: 76 EST: 2001
SALES (est): 14.01MM **Privately Held**
Web: www.therecoverycouncil.org
SIC: **8069** Drug addiction rehabilitation hospital

(G-14617)
RES-CARE INC
Also Called: RES Care
212 Saint Anns Ln (45690-1039)
PHONE..................................740 941-1178
EMP: 61
SALES (corp-wide): 8.83B **Publicly Held**
Web: www.rescare.com
SIC: **8052** Home for the mentally retarded, with health care
HQ: Res-Care, Inc.
805 N Whittington Pkwy
Louisville KY 40222
502 394-2100

(G-14618)
RUMPKE OF OHIO INC
11775 State Route 220 (45690-9714)
PHONE..................................740 947-7082
EMP: 220
Web: www.rumpke.com
SIC: **4953** 4212 Refuse collection and disposal services; Garbage collection and transport, no disposal
HQ: Rumpke Of Ohio, Inc
3800 Struble Rd
Cincinnati OH 45251
888 582-3107

(G-14619)
SOUTHERN OHIO MEDICAL CENTER
300 E 2nd St (45690-1323)
PHONE..................................740 947-7662
EMP: 66
SALES (corp-wide): 546.1MM **Privately Held**
Web: www.somc.org
SIC: **8031** 8011 Offices and clinics of osteopathic physicians; Offices and clinics of medical doctors
PA: Southern Ohio Medical Center
1805 27th St
Portsmouth OH 45662
740 354-5000

Wayne
Wood County

(G-14620)
C & G TRANSPORTATION INC
11100 Wayne Rd (43466-9846)
PHONE..................................419 288-2653
Gary Harrison, *Pr*
Cathy Harrison, *
EMP: 50 EST: 1997
SALES (est): 4.42MM **Privately Held**
Web: www.cgtransport.com
SIC: **4212** Local trucking, without storage

Waynesburg
Stark County

(G-14621)
AMERICAN LANDFILL INC
Also Called: Waste Management
7916 Chapel St Se (44688-9700)
PHONE.................................330 866-3265
A Maurice Myers, *Ch Bd*
EMP: 61 **EST:** 1982
SQ FT: 26,000
SALES (est): 10MM
SALES (corp-wide): 20.43B **Publicly Held**
Web: americanlandfill.wm.com
SIC: 4953 Recycling, waste materials
HQ: Waste Management Holdings Inc
  800 Capitol St Ste 3000
  Houston TX 77002
  713 512-6200

Waynesville
Warren County

(G-14622)
FIELDS FAMILY ENTERPRISES INC
Also Called: Waynesville Pharmacy
415 S Main St (45068-9553)
PHONE.................................513 897-1000
James E Fields, *Pr*
Ellen Fields, *VP*
EMP: 30 **EST:** 1980
SQ FT: 6,000
SALES (est): 1.77MM **Privately Held**
Web: www.waynesvillepharmacy.com
SIC: 5912 7011 Drug stores; Motels

(G-14623)
GRANDMAS GARDENS INC
8107 State Route 48 (45068-8732)
PHONE.................................937 885-2973
Douglas B Rhinehart, *Pr*
James B Rhinehart, *
Pat Rhinehart, *
Paulette Rhinehart Stlk Hldr, *Prin*
EMP: 40 **EST:** 1977
SQ FT: 2,500
SALES (est): 2.36MM **Privately Held**
Web: www.grandmasgardens.net
SIC: 5261 0782 Nursery stock, seeds and bulbs; Landscape contractors

(G-14624)
HOME THE FRIENDS INC
Also Called: FRIENDS BOARDING HOME
514 High St (45068-9784)
P.O. Box 677 (45068-0677)
PHONE.................................513 897-6050
Admiral Wendy Waters, *Prin*
Admiral Wendy Waters-connell, *Prin*
EMP: 52 **EST:** 1904
SQ FT: 35,000
SALES (est): 61.07K **Privately Held**
SIC: 8051 Skilled nursing care facilities

(G-14625)
MBI TREE SERVICE LLC
9447 Cold Springs Ln (45068-9019)
PHONE.................................513 926-9857
Luis Paez, *
EMP: 29 **EST:** 2017
SALES (est): 1.13MM **Privately Held**
Web: www.mbitreeservice.com
SIC: 0783 Planting, pruning, and trimming services

(G-14626)
OHIO LIVING QUAKER HEIGHTS
514 High St (45068-9784)
PHONE.................................937 897-6050
Laurence C Gumina, *Prin*
Donald Edwards, *
Sandra Adam, *
James Joyce, *
Terry White, *
EMP: 34 **EST:** 1904
SALES (est): 7.2MM **Privately Held**
Web: www.ohioliving.org
SIC: 6513 Retirement hotel operation

(G-14627)
PROVIDENCE MEDICAL GROUP LLC
4353 E State Route 73 (45068-8812)
PHONE.................................513 897-0085
EMP: 34
Web: www.provmed.com
SIC: 8099 Blood related health services
PA: Providence Medical Group, Llc
  2723 S 7th St Ste A
  Terre Haute IN 47802

(G-14628)
VERIZON BUS NETWRK SVCS LLC
Also Called: Verizon Business
9073 Lytle Ferry Rd (45068-9494)
PHONE.................................513 897-1501
David Estell, *Mgr*
EMP: 175
SQ FT: 81,086
SALES (corp-wide): 133.97B **Publicly Held**
Web: www.verizonwireless.com
SIC: 4812 Cellular telephone services
HQ: Verizon Business Network Services Llc
  1 Verizon Way
  Basking Ridge NJ 07920
  908 559-2000

Wellington
Lorain County

(G-14629)
CLEVELAND CLINIC FOUNDATION
805 Patriot Dr Ste E (44090-8951)
PHONE.................................440 647-0004
Michael P Harrington, *Bmch Mgr*
EMP: 33
SALES (corp-wide): 14.48B **Privately Held**
Web: www.clevelandclinic.org
SIC: 8062 General medical and surgical hospitals
PA: The Cleveland Clinic Foundation
  9500 Euclid Ave
  Cleveland OH 44195
  216 636-8335

(G-14630)
COUNTY OF LORAIN
Also Called: South Lrrain Cnty Amblance Dst
179 E Herrick Ave (44090-1302)
PHONE.................................440 647-5803
Pat Wilkinson, *Mgr*
EMP: 33
SALES (corp-wide): 253.29MM **Privately Held**
Web: www.loraincounty.us
SIC: 4119 Ambulance service
PA: County Of Lorain
  226 Middle Ave
  Elyria OH 44035
  440 329-5201

(G-14631)
ELMS RETIREMENT VILLAGE INC
136 S Main St Rear (44090-3301)
P.O. Box 88126 (60188-0126)
PHONE.................................440 647-2414
Anthony Sprenger, *Pr*
Donel Sprenger, *
Mark Sprenger, *
EMP: 284 **EST:** 1968
SQ FT: 21,000
SALES (est): 4.64MM **Privately Held**
Web: www.sprengerhealthcare.com
SIC: 8052 8059 8051 Intermediate care facilities; Convalescent home; Skilled nursing care facilities
PA: Sprenger Enterprises, Inc.
  3905 Oberlin Ave Ste 1
  Lorain OH 44053

(G-14632)
EXPERT CRANE INC
Also Called: Expert Crane
720 Shiloh Ave (44090-1190)
PHONE.................................216 451-9900
James C Doty, *Pr*
Rebecca Doty, *
EMP: 47 **EST:** 1977
SALES (est): 11MM **Privately Held**
Web: www.expertcrane.com
SIC: 3536 7699 1796 5084 Hoists, cranes, and monorails; Industrial machinery and equipment repair; Machinery installation; Cranes, industrial

(G-14633)
HUNTINGTON NATIONAL BANK
Also Called: First Wellington Bank Branch
817 N Main St (44090-1057)
PHONE.................................440 647-4533
James Branch, *Brnch Mgr*
EMP: 31
SALES (corp-wide): 10.84B **Publicly Held**
Web: www.huntington.com
SIC: 6029 Commercial banks, nec
HQ: The Huntington National Bank
  41 S High St
  Columbus OH 43215
  614 480-4293

(G-14634)
MODERN POURED WALLS INC
41807 State Route 18 (44090-9677)
P.O. Box 598 (44050-0598)
PHONE.................................440 647-6661
W S Smith, *Pr*
EMP: 49 **EST:** 1976
SQ FT: 2,500
SALES (est): 8.84MM **Privately Held**
Web: www.mpwcs.com
SIC: 1771 1794 Foundation and footing contractor; Excavation work

(G-14635)
WHITNEY HOME CARE LLC
508 Dickson St Ste 3 (44090-1300)
PHONE.................................440 647-2200
Susan Lucio, *Managing Member*
EMP: 43 **EST:** 2018
SALES (est): 700K **Privately Held**
Web: www.whitneyhomecare.com
SIC: 8082 Home health care services

Wellston
Jackson County

(G-14636)
CITY OF WELLSTON
Also Called: Wellston Auditor's Office
203 E Broadway St (45692-1521)
PHONE.................................740 384-2428
Gary L Crabtree, *Auditor*
EMP: 60
Web: www.cityofwellston.org
SIC: 9111 8721 City and town managers' office; Auditing services
PA: City Of Wellston
  203 E Broadway St
  Wellston OH 45692
  740 384-2720

(G-14637)
EDGEWOOD MANOR OF WELLSTON
Also Called: CONSULATE HEALTHCARE
405 N Park Ave (45692-1111)
PHONE.................................740 384-5611
Jeff Jellerson, *Pr*
EMP: 53 **EST:** 1966
SALES (est): 3.97MM **Privately Held**
Web: www.edgewoodmanorofwellston.com
SIC: 8052 Intermediate care facilities

(G-14638)
JACKSN-VINTON CMNTY ACTION INC (PA)
Also Called: JACKSON VINTON COMMUNITY ACTIO
118 S New York Ave (45692-1540)
PHONE.................................740 384-3722
Megan Sowers, *Ex Dir*
Michelle Green, *
EMP: 30 **EST:** 1965
SQ FT: 12,000
SALES (est): 6.23MM
SALES (corp-wide): 6.23MM **Privately Held**
Web: www.jvcai.org
SIC: 8399 9111 Community action agency; County supervisors' and executives' office

(G-14639)
JACKSON CNTY HLTH FCLITIES INC
Also Called: JENKINS MEMORIAL HEALTH FACILI
142 Jenkins Memorial Rd (45692-9561)
PHONE.................................740 384-0722
Theresa Womeldorf, *Admn*
David Nichols, *
EMP: 97 **EST:** 1971
SALES (est): 7.24MM **Privately Held**
Web: www.jenkinscare.org
SIC: 8051 Skilled nursing care facilities

(G-14640)
LANDMARK PROPERTIES GROUP LLC
23 S Ohio Ave (45692-1239)
PHONE.................................740 701-7511
EMP: 36
SALES (corp-wide): 771.77K **Privately Held**
Web: www.landmarkprop.com
SIC: 6512 Nonresidential building operators
PA: Landmark Properties Group, Llc
  50 W Main St
  Chillicothe OH 45601
  740 701-7511

(G-14641)
RUMPKE WASTE INC
28 A W Long Rd (45692-9799)
PHONE.................................740 384-4400
Kevin W Luther, *Dir*
EMP: 206
Web: www.rumpke.com
SIC: 4953 Recycling, waste materials
HQ: Rumpke Waste, Inc.
  10795 Hughes Rd
  Cincinnati OH 45251
  513 851-0122

GEOGRAPHIC SECTION
West Chester - Butler County (G-14661)

Wellsville
Columbiana County

(G-14642)
VETERANS OF FOREIGN WARS OF US
359 Main St (43968-1669)
PHONE...................330 532-1423
EMP: 65
SALES (corp-wide): 105.25MM Privately Held
SIC: 8641 Veterans' organization
PA: Veterans Of Foreign Wars Of The United States
406 W 34th St Fl 11
Kansas City MO 64111
816 756-3390

West Alexandria
Preble County

(G-14643)
COUNTY OF PREBLE
1251 State Route 503 N (45381-9733)
PHONE...................937 839-5845
EMP: 37
SALES (corp-wide): 35.63MM Privately Held
Web: www.prebco.org
SIC: 6733 Trusts, nec
PA: County Of Preble
101 E Main St
Eaton OH 45320
937 456-8143

West Carrollton
Montgomery County

(G-14644)
BOUNDLESS CMNTY PATHWAYS INC (PA)
700 Liberty Ln (45449-2135)
PHONE...................937 461-0034
Phil Hartje, Genl Mgr
Elvia Thomas, Adult Service Director*
EMP: 700 EST: 1970
SQ FT: 50,000
SALES (est): 2.9MM
SALES (corp-wide): 2.9MM Privately Held
Web: www.moncoent.org
SIC: 8331 2789 Sheltered workshop; Bookbinding and related work

(G-14645)
DAYTON CLASSICS BASBAL CLB INC
165 S Alex Rd (45449-1909)
PHONE...................937 974-6722
EMP: 36
SALES (corp-wide): 247.34K Privately Held
SIC: 7997 Membership sports and recreation clubs
PA: Dayton Classics Baseball Club, Inc.
3578 Kettering Blvd
Moraine OH 45439
937 297-0763

West Chester
Butler County

(G-14646)
ACUREN INSPECTION INC
4692 Brate Dr # 200 (45011-3558)
PHONE...................513 671-7073
Jim Bailey, Pr
EMP: 120
SALES (corp-wide): 1.5B Privately Held
Web: www.acuren.com
SIC: 7389 Inspection and testing services
HQ: Acuren Inspection, Inc.
30 Main St Ste 402
Danbury CT 06810
203 702-8740

(G-14647)
ADVANTAGE RN LLC (PA)
Also Called: Advantage Local
9021 Meridian Way (45069-6539)
PHONE...................866 301-4045
EMP: 100 EST: 2003
SQ FT: 8,400
SALES (est): 48.02MM
SALES (corp-wide): 48.02MM Privately Held
Web: www.advantagern.com
SIC: 7361 Nurses' registry

(G-14648)
AERO FULFILLMENT SERVICES CORP
Also Called: Aero Fulfillment
6023 Union Centre Blvd Steb (45069)
PHONE...................513 874-4112
EMP: 75
SQ FT: 264,000
SALES (corp-wide): 47.77MM Privately Held
Web: www.aerofulfillment.com
SIC: 4225 General warehousing
PA: Aero Fulfillment Services Corporation
3900 Aero Dr
Mason OH 45040
800 225-7145

(G-14649)
AFC INDUSTRIES INC (HQ)
Also Called: Advanced Fastener
9030 Port Union Rialto Rd (45069-2937)
PHONE...................513 874-7456
Kevin Godin, CEO
Robert T Tomlinson, *
Steve Sullivan, *
▲ EMP: 28 EST: 1987
SALES (est): 177.78MM Privately Held
Web: www.afcind.com
SIC: 5085 Fasteners, industrial: nuts, bolts, screws, etc.
PA: Bertram Capital Management, Llc
950 Tower Ln Ste 1000
Foster City CA 94404

(G-14650)
AMERIMED LLC
Also Called: Amerimed, Inc.
9961 Cincinnati Dayton Rd (45069-3823)
PHONE...................513 942-3670
Dan Deitz, CEO
Dan Dietz, *
EMP: 574 EST: 1985
SQ FT: 6,300
SALES (est): 11.78MM Privately Held
Web: www.chihealthathome.com
SIC: 5999 7363 5047 Medical apparatus and supplies; Help supply services; Medical and hospital equipment
HQ: American Nursing Care, Inc.
6281 Tri Ridge Blvd # 300
Loveland OH 45140
513 576-0262

(G-14651)
BGR INC (PA)
Also Called: Triangle Label
6392 Gano Rd (45069-4869)
PHONE...................800 628-9195
TOLL FREE: 800
Roger Neiheisel, Pr
Allen Backscheider, *
Dean Backscheider, *
▲ EMP: 75 EST: 1973
SQ FT: 225,000
SALES (est): 81.48MM
SALES (corp-wide): 81.48MM Privately Held
Web: www.packbgr.com
SIC: 5199 7389 Packaging materials; Packaging and labeling services

(G-14652)
BOBCAT ENTERPRISES INC (PA)
Also Called: Bobcat Enterprises
9605 Princeton Glendale Rd (45011-8802)
P.O. Box 46345 (45246-0345)
PHONE...................513 874-8945
TOLL FREE: 800
Thomas L Trapp, CEO
Lois Trapp, *
▲ EMP: 85 EST: 1975
SQ FT: 15,000
SALES (est): 50.82MM
SALES (corp-wide): 50.82MM Privately Held
Web: www.bobcat-ent.com
SIC: 5082 7353 Contractor's materials; Heavy construction equipment rental

(G-14653)
BP 10 INC
Also Called: Bagpack
9486 Sutton Pl (45011-9698)
PHONE...................513 346-3900
Steven Dreyer, Pr
Ronald C Dreyer, *
EMP: 30 EST: 1988
SQ FT: 40,000
SALES (est): 9.93MM Privately Held
Web: www.flex-pack.com
SIC: 5199 2752 Packaging materials; Commercial printing, lithographic

(G-14654)
BRANDS INSURANCE AGENCY INC
6449 Allen Rd Ste 1 (45069-3803)
P.O. Box 62267 (45262-0267)
PHONE...................513 777-7775
Alfred T Brands, Pr
Allison Brands, *
Mat Brands, *
EMP: 42 EST: 1967
SQ FT: 4,400
SALES (est): 7.96MM Privately Held
Web: www.brandsinsurance.com
SIC: 6411 Insurance agents, nec

(G-14655)
BREHOB CORPORATION
Also Called: Brehob Crane and Hoist Div
9790 Windisch Rd (45069-3808)
PHONE...................513 755-1300
TOLL FREE: 800
Al Bunker, Brnch Mgr
EMP: 27
SALES (corp-wide): 63.31MM Privately Held
Web: www.brehob.com
SIC: 5063 7629 1731 Motors, electric; Electrical repair shops; Electrical work
PA: Brehob Corporation
1334 S Meridian St
Indianapolis IN 46225
317 231-8080

(G-14656)
BURRILLA LLC ✪
7969 Cincinnati Dayton Rd Ste F (45069-6633)
PHONE...................513 615-9350
EMP: 30 EST: 2022
SALES (est): 1.42MM Privately Held
SIC: 8742 7389 Sales (including sales management) consultant; Business Activities at Non-Commercial Site

(G-14657)
CAMBRIDGE EYE ASSOCIATES INC
Also Called: Cambridge Eye Doctors
8100 Beckett Center Dr (45069-5015)
PHONE...................513 527-9700
William Sullivan, Pr
EMP: 175 EST: 1975
SQ FT: 20,000
SALES (est): 742.19K Privately Held
SIC: 8042 5995 Offices and clinics of optometrists; Contact lenses, prescription

(G-14658)
CAMEO SOLUTIONS INC
Also Called: Bcbd
9078 Union Centre Blvd Ste 200 (45069)
PHONE...................513 645-4220
EMP: 40 EST: 2004
SQ FT: 6,800
SALES (est): 8.46MM
SALES (corp-wide): 103.15MM Privately Held
Web: www.neweratech.com
SIC: 7373 Value-added resellers, computer systems
PA: New Era Technology, Inc.
1325 Ave Of The Amrcas 27
New York NY 10019
973 253-7600

(G-14659)
CARROLLS LLC
Also Called: National Tire Wholesale
2939 Crescentville Rd (45069-3883)
PHONE...................513 733-5559
Bill Snider, Mgr
EMP: 30
Web: www.carrollorg.com
SIC: 5014 Automobile tires and tubes
HQ: Carroll's, Llc
4281 Old Dixie Hwy
Atlanta GA 30354
404 366-5476

(G-14660)
CBN WESTSIDE TECHNOLOGIES INC
Also Called: TSS Technologies
8800 Global Way (45069-7070)
PHONE...................513 772-7000
Brent Nichols, Pr
Charles B Nichols Junior, VP
Mark Nichols, *
Scott Nichols, *
Leila B Nichols, *
▲ EMP: 400 EST: 1948
SQ FT: 75,000
SALES (est): 25.68MM Privately Held
SIC: 3599 8711 Machine shop, jobbing and repair; Mechanical engineering

(G-14661)
CECO CONCRETE CONSTRUCTION LLC
Also Called: Ceco Concrete Construction
4535 Port Union Rd (45011-9766)
PHONE...................513 874-6953
Rick Cevasco, Mgr
EMP: 124
Web: www.cecoconcrete.com
SIC: 1799 1771 Erection and dismantling of forms for poured concrete; Concrete work
HQ: Ceco Concrete Construction, L.L.C.
10100 N Ambassador Dr # 400
Kansas City MO 64153

West Chester - Butler County (G-14662) — GEOGRAPHIC SECTION

(G-14662)
CEDAR ELEC HOLDINGS CORP
5440 W Chester Rd (45069-2950)
PHONE..............................773 804-6288
Dave Smidebush, *Brnch Mgr*
EMP: 70
SALES (corp-wide): 142.84MM **Privately Held**
Web: www.cedarelectronics.com
SIC: 3812 5013 5015 Navigational systems and instruments; Tools and equipment, automotive; Automotive supplies, used: wholesale and retail
PA: Cedar Electronics Holdings Corp.
    1701 Golf Rd Ste 3-900
    Rolling Meadows IL 60008
    800 964-3138

(G-14663)
CHESTER WEST MEDICAL CENTER
Also Called: West Chester Hospital
7700 University Dr (45069-2505)
PHONE..............................513 298-3000
EMP: 1200 **EST:** 2009
SALES (est): 100.59MM **Privately Held**
Web: www.uchealth.com
SIC: 8062 General medical and surgical hospitals
PA: Uc Health, Llc.
    3200 Burnet Ave
    Cincinnati OH 45229

(G-14664)
CHI NATIONAL HOME CARE
9031 Meridian Way (45069-6539)
PHONE..............................513 942-3670
Bernie Tarvin, *Brnch Mgr*
EMP: 93
Web: www.chihealthathome.com
SIC: 5047 Medical equipment and supplies
HQ: Chi National Home Care
    6281 Tri Ridge Blvd # 300
    Loveland OH 45140
    513 576-0262

(G-14665)
CHRIST HOSPITAL
7589 Tylers Place Blvd (45069-6308)
PHONE..............................513 755-4700
EMP: 57
SALES (corp-wide): 1.3B **Privately Held**
Web: www.thechristhospital.com
SIC: 8062 General medical and surgical hospitals
PA: The Christ Hospital
    2139 Auburn Ave
    Cincinnati OH 45219
    513 585-2000

(G-14666)
CIP INTERNATIONAL INC
Also Called: Commercial Interior Products
9575 Le Saint Dr (45014-5447)
PHONE..............................513 874-9925
Thomas Huff, *CEO*
Thomas Huff, *Ch Bd*
Kathleen Huff, *
Mark Elmlinger, *
Jay Voss, *
◆ **EMP:** 83 **EST:** 1975
SQ FT: 140,000
SALES (est): 17.37MM **Privately Held**
Web: www.cipretail.com
SIC: 7389 2541 Interior designer; Store fixtures, wood

(G-14667)
CL ZIMMERMAN DELAWARE LLC
Also Called: G M Z
5115 Excello Ct (45069-3091)
PHONE..............................513 860-9300
Tom Wells, *Pr*
▲ **EMP:** 30 **EST:** 1999
SQ FT: 70,000
SALES (est): 23.74MM **Privately Held**
Web: shop.collectorz.com
SIC: 5169 Industrial chemicals
HQ: Azelis Americas, Llc
    33 Riverside Ave Ste 507
    Westport CT 06880
    203 274-8691

(G-14668)
CLARITY RETAIL SERVICES LLC
Also Called: Jkrg Construction Services
5115 Excello Ct (45069-3091)
PHONE..............................513 800-9369
James R Gavigan, *Pr*
Lance H Madden, *
EMP: 75 **EST:** 2015
SQ FT: 3,200
SALES (est): 5.31MM **Privately Held**
Web: www.clarity-retail.com
SIC: 7389 8742 3999 3577 Interior designer; Sales (including sales management) consultant; Barber and beauty shop equipment; Graphic displays, except graphic terminals

(G-14669)
CLARK THEDERS INSURANCE AGENCY
9938 Crescent Park Dr (45069-3895)
PHONE..............................513 779-2800
Jonathan Theders, *Pr*
Richard R Theders, *
Jason M Randolph, *
EMP: 47 **EST:** 1954
SQ FT: 6,000
SALES (est): 8.28MM **Privately Held**
Web: www.risksource.com
SIC: 6411 Insurance agents, nec

(G-14670)
CLARKDIETRICH ENGRG SVCS LLC
Also Called: Clarkwstern Dtrich Bldg System
9050 Centre Pointe Dr Ste 400 (45069)
PHONE..............................513 870-1100
William Courtney, *CEO*
Greg Ralph, *Ex VP*
Keith Harr, *Sec*
EMP: 523 **EST:** 2011
SALES (est): 1.51MM
SALES (corp-wide): 4.92B **Publicly Held**
Web: www.clarkdietrich.com
SIC: 8711 Consulting engineer
HQ: Clarkwestern Dietrich Building Systems Llc
    9050 Cntre Pnte Dr Ste 40
    West Chester OH 45069

(G-14671)
CLARKWSTERN DTRICH BLDG SYSTEM (HQ)
Also Called: Clarkdietrich
9050 Centre Pointe Dr Ste 400 (45069)
PHONE..............................513 870-1100
▼ **EMP:** 110 **EST:** 2011
SQ FT: 80,000
SALES (est): 282.46MM
SALES (corp-wide): 4.92B **Publicly Held**
Web: www.clarkdietrich.com
SIC: 3444 8711 3081 Studs and joists, sheet metal; Engineering services; Vinyl film and sheet
PA: Worthington Enterprises, Inc.
    200 W Old Wlson Bridge Rd
    Worthington OH 43085
    614 438-3210

(G-14672)
COLDWELL BANKER WEST SHELL
Also Called: Coldwell Banker
7311 Tylers Corner Dr (45069-6344)
PHONE..............................513 777-7900
Larry Thimmes, *Mgr*
EMP: 45
SALES (corp-wide): 25.71MM **Privately Held**
Web: www.coldwellbanker.com
SIC: 6531 Real estate agent, residential
PA: Coldwell Banker West Shell
    9321 Montgomery Rd Ste C
    Montgomery OH 45242
    513 794-9494

(G-14673)
CONTECH TRCKG & LOGISTICS LLC
9025 Centre Pointe Dr Ste 400 (45069)
PHONE..............................513 645-7000
Rick Gaynorr, *Managing Member*
Steve Kerls, *
EMP: 74 **EST:** 2004
SALES (est): 12.46MM **Privately Held**
SIC: 4731 Freight forwarding
HQ: Contech Engineered Solutions Llc
    9025 Centre Pointe Dr # 400
    West Chester OH 45069
    513 645-7000

(G-14674)
CONTINGENT NETWORK SERVICES LLC
4400 Port Union Rd (45011-9714)
PHONE..............................513 616-5773
EMP: 228
SIC: 7379 7373 Computer related maintenance services; Computer systems analysis and design

(G-14675)
CONTRACT SWEEPERS & EQP CO
10136 Mosteller Ln (45069-3872)
P.O. Box Osteller L (45069)
PHONE..............................513 577-7900
TOLL FREE: 800
EMP: 35
SALES (corp-wide): 22.72MM **Privately Held**
Web: www.sweepers.com
SIC: 4959 5084 Snowplowing; Cleaning equipment, high pressure, sand or steam
PA: Contract Sweepers & Equipment Company
    2137 Parkwood Ave
    Columbus OH 43219
    614 221-7441

(G-14676)
CORNERSTONE BRANDS INC (DH)
Also Called: Cornerstone
5568 W Chester Rd (45069-2914)
P.O. Box 1308 (45071-1308)
PHONE..............................513 603-1000
Judy A Schmeling, *Pr*
Patrick Vonderhaar, *
Paul Tarvin, *
◆ **EMP:** 1000 **EST:** 1998
SQ FT: 55,000
SALES (est): 1.27B **Publicly Held**
Web: www.cornerstonefitnessohio.com
SIC: 5021 Furniture
HQ: Hsn, Inc.
    1 Hsn Dr
    Saint Petersburg FL 33729

(G-14677)
CORNERSTONE BRANDS GROUP INC
5568 W Chester Rd (45069-2914)
PHONE..............................513 603-1000
Judy A Schmeling, *Pr*
▼ **EMP:** 918 **EST:** 1995
SQ FT: 1,000,000
SALES (est): 22.14MM **Publicly Held**
SIC: 5961 8742 Catalog and mail-order houses; Marketing consulting services
HQ: Cornerstone Brands, Inc.
    5568 W Chester Rd
    West Chester OH 45069
    513 603-1000

(G-14678)
CORNERSTONE CONSOLIDATED SERVICES GROUP INC
Also Called: Cornerstone Brnds Group
5568 W Chester Rd (45069-2914)
PHONE..............................513 603-1100
▲ **EMP:** 910
SIC: 5961 4226 Catalog and mail-order houses; Special warehousing and storage, nec

(G-14679)
CRESCENT PARK CORPORATION (PA)
9817 Crescent Park Dr (45069-3867)
PHONE..............................513 759-7000
Chris Taylor, *CEO*
David E Taylor Senior, *Ch Bd*
Tom Schwallie, *
David Combs, *
EMP: 160 **EST:** 1986
SQ FT: 700,000
SALES (est): 138.12MM **Privately Held**
Web: www.crescentpark.com
SIC: 4225 4222 7389 8741 General warehousing; Refrigerated warehousing and storage; Packaging and labeling services; Management services

(G-14680)
CRISTO HOMES
7594 Tylers Place Blvd Ste A (45069-6313)
PHONE..............................513 755-0570
Adam Cristo, *Owner*
EMP: 27 **EST:** 2011
SALES (est): 2.35MM **Privately Held**
Web: www.cristohomes.com
SIC: 1522 1521 Residential construction, nec ; Mobile home repair, on site

(G-14681)
CUMMINS INC
5400 Rialto Rd (45069-3092)
PHONE..............................513 563-6670
Robert Fontilla, *Brnch Mgr*
EMP: 40
SALES (corp-wide): 34.06B **Publicly Held**
Web: www.cummins.com
SIC: 5084 Engines and parts, diesel
PA: Cummins Inc.
    500 Jackson St
    Columbus IN 47201
    812 377-5000

(G-14682)
DATATECH DEPOT (EAST) INC
4750 Ashley Dr (45011-9704)
PHONE..............................513 860-5651
Tom Le, *Pr*
EMP: 39 **EST:** 1998
SALES (est): 2.83MM
SALES (corp-wide): 3.45MM **Privately Held**
Web: www.dtdi.com
SIC: 7378 Computer and data processing equipment repair/maintenance
PA: Datatech Depot, Inc.
    249 E Emerson Ave Ste G
    Orange CA 92865

GEOGRAPHIC SECTION

West Chester - Butler County (G-14705)

909 430-0930

(G-14683)
DAWSON LOGISTICS LLC
Also Called: Cincinnati Port Union Facility
4350 Port Union Rd Ste B (45011-9801)
PHONE...................................217 689-2610
Don Garza, *Brnch Mgr*
EMP: 35
SALES (corp-wide): 5.47MM **Privately Held**
Web: www.dawsonlogistics.com
SIC: 4214 Local trucking with storage
PA: Dawson Logistics, Llc
122 Eastgate Dr
Danville IL 61834
217 903-5400

(G-14684)
DEANHOUSTON CREATIVE GROUP INC
Also Called: Warehouse Facility
9393 Princeton Glendale Rd (45011-9707)
PHONE...................................513 659-5051
EMP: 30
SALES (corp-wide): 12.57MM **Privately Held**
Web: www.deanhouston.com
SIC: 7311 Advertising agencies
PA: Deanhouston Creative Group, Inc.
525 Scott St
Covington KY 41011
513 421-6622

(G-14685)
DILLON HOLDINGS LLC
Also Called: Visiting Angels Lving Assstnce
8050 Beckett Center Dr Ste 103 (45069-5017)
PHONE...................................513 942-5600
EMP: 105 **EST:** 2006
SQ FT: 1,200
SALES (est): 4.96MM **Privately Held**
Web: www.visitingangels.com
SIC: 8082 Home health care services

(G-14686)
E-TECHNOLOGIES GROUP LLC (HQ)
Also Called: E Technologies Group
8614 Jacquemin Dr (45069)
PHONE...................................513 771-7271
EMP: 100 **EST:** 1993
SALES (est): 101.57MM
SALES (corp-wide): 106.23MM **Privately Held**
Web: www.etechgroup.com
SIC: 8711 Consulting engineer
PA: E-Technologies Group, Inc.
8614 Jacquemin Dr
West Chester OH 45069
513 771-7271

(G-14687)
ENTERTRAINMENT INC
Also Called: Entertrainment Junction
7379 Squire Ct (45069-2314)
PHONE...................................513 898-8000
EMP: 30 **EST:** 2006
SALES (est): 2.17MM **Privately Held**
Web: www.entertrainmentjunction.com
SIC: 8412 Museum

(G-14688)
ESTES EXPRESS LINES
6459 Allen Rd (45069-3848)
PHONE...................................513 779-9581
John Flynn, *Brnch Mgr*
EMP: 50
SALES (corp-wide): 3.56B **Privately Held**
Web: www.estes-express.com
SIC: 4213 Contract haulers

PA: Estes Express Lines
3901 W Broad St
Richmond VA 23230
804 353-1900

(G-14689)
FAMECCANICA NORTH AMERICA INC
Also Called: Fameccanica North America
8511 Trade Center Dr Bldg 4 (45011)
PHONE...................................513 645-0629
Nicola Zampognaro, *CEO*
Eugenio Venturato, *
EMP: 60 **EST:** 2009
SALES (est): 28.77MM **Privately Held**
Web: www.fameccanica.com
SIC: 5084 Textile machinery and equipment
HQ: Fameccanica.Data Spa
Via Aterno 136
San Giovanni Teatino CH 66020
08545531

(G-14690)
FASTEMS LLC
9850 Windisch Rd (45069-3806)
PHONE...................................513 779-4614
▲ **EMP:** 42 **EST:** 2006
SALES (est): 7.14MM **Privately Held**
Web: www.fastems.com
SIC: 7371 Computer software development

(G-14691)
FERGUSON ENTERPRISES LLC
Also Called: Ferguson Integrated Services
2945 Crescentville Rd (45069-3883)
P.O. Box 2940 (23609-0940)
PHONE...................................513 771-6566
Andy Norkey, *Brnch Mgr*
EMP: 50
SALES (corp-wide): 29.73B **Privately Held**
Web: www.ferguson.com
SIC: 5074 Plumbing fittings and supplies
HQ: Ferguson Enterprises, Llc
751 Lakefront Cmns
Newport News VA 23606
757 969-4011

(G-14692)
FLYING PIG LOGISTICS INC
9047 Sutton Pl (45011-9316)
PHONE...................................513 300-9331
Michael Eltonhead, *CEO*
EMP: 50
SALES (est): 1.28MM **Privately Held**
SIC: 4215 7389 Courier services, except by air; Business Activities at Non-Commercial Site

(G-14693)
FOCUS ON YOUTH INC
8904 Brookside Ave (45069-3139)
PHONE...................................513 644-1030
Bryan Forney, *Ex Dir*
Christina Kappn, *
Tracy Saber, *
Penny Dugan, *
EMP: 30 **EST:** 1992
SQ FT: 6,200
SALES (est): 4.08MM **Privately Held**
Web: www.focusonyouth.com
SIC: 8322 Youth center

(G-14694)
FRANKLIN EQUIPMENT LLC
4764 Ashley Dr (45011-9704)
PHONE...................................513 893-9105
EMP: 48
SALES (corp-wide): 14.33B **Publicly Held**
Web: www.unitedrentals.com

SIC: 7359 Equipment rental and leasing, nec
HQ: Franklin Equipment, Llc
4141 Hamilton Square Blvd
Groveport OH 43125

(G-14695)
FREDRICS CORPORATION (PA)
7664 Voice Of America Centre Dr (45069-2794)
PHONE...................................513 874-2226
Frederic Holzberger, *Pr*
Frederic Holzberger, *Pr*
Gary J Trame, *
▲ **EMP:** 140 **EST:** 1983
SQ FT: 35,000
SALES (est): 10.12MM
SALES (corp-wide): 10.12MM **Privately Held**
Web: www.avedafi.edu
SIC: 5122 7231 Drugs, proprietaries, and sundries; Beauty schools

(G-14696)
FRENCHIES OF IG LLC
8730 Cincinnati Dayton Rd Apt 1001 (45069-9100)
PHONE...................................513 445-2841
EMP: 33
SALES (corp-wide): 67.03K **Privately Held**
SIC: 0751 Artificial insemination services, livestock
PA: Frenchies Of Ig Llc
3759 Westmont Dr
Cincinnati OH 45205
513 445-2841

(G-14697)
GLOBAL WORKPLACE SOLUTIONS LLC (PA)
Also Called: G W S
9823 Cincinnati Dayton Rd (45069-3825)
PHONE...................................513 759-6000
Lynn Sabatalo, *
Mark Shafor, *
Stephen Sabatalo, *
Robert Faillo, *
EMP: 39 **EST:** 2005
SALES (est): 31.73MM **Privately Held**
Web: www.gwspartners.com
SIC: 4213 Trucking, except local

(G-14698)
GOLDEN RESOURCES INCORPORATED
Also Called: Golden Technology
7681 Tylers Place Blvd (45069-6392)
PHONE...................................513 342-6290
Brian Marcum, *CEO*
Chris Guin, *Finance & Operations*
EMP: 32 **EST:** 2010
SALES (est): 2.85MM **Privately Held**
Web: www.goldenitinc.com
SIC: 7379 Computer related consulting services

(G-14699)
GRAND ENCORE CINCINNATI LLC
Also Called: Encore Label & Packaging
9230 Port Union Rialto Rd (45069-2907)
PHONE...................................513 482-7500
Rick Wills, *Genl Mgr*
Melissa Hafley, *
EMP: 50 **EST:** 2019
SALES (est): 2.14MM **Privately Held**
Web: www.encorelp.com
SIC: 7389 Packaging and labeling services

(G-14700)
GRAPHEL CORPORATION
Also Called: Carbon Products

6115 Centre Park Dr (45069-3869)
PHONE...................................513 779-6166
David Trinkley, *Pr*
Mark Grammer, *
EMP: 140 **EST:** 1965
SQ FT: 35,000
SALES (est): 23.29MM **Privately Held**
Web: www.graphel.com
SIC: 5052 3599 3624 Coal and other minerals and ores; Machine shop, jobbing and repair; Electrodes, thermal and electrolytic uses: carbon, graphite

(G-14701)
GROUNDSPRO LLC
9405 Sutton Pl (45011)
PHONE...................................513 242-1700
Anthony Wilson, *Managing Member*
EMP: 130 **EST:** 2012
SALES (est): 16.06MM
SALES (corp-wide): 16.06MM **Privately Held**
Web: www.groundspro.com
SIC: 0782 Highway lawn and garden maintenance services
PA: Cl Services Acquisition Llc
2389 Hamilton Cleves Rd
Hamilton OH

(G-14702)
GUARDIAN SAVINGS BANK (PA)
Also Called: FEDERAL SAVINGS BANK
6100 W Chester Rd (45069-2943)
PHONE...................................513 942-3535
Louis Beck, *Ch Bd*
Don Bailey, *
Paul Warner, *
Kevin Motley, *
Yvonne Rich, *
EMP: 45 **EST:** 1895
SQ FT: 4,000
SALES (est): 43.29MM
SALES (corp-wide): 43.29MM **Privately Held**
Web: www.guardiansavingsbank.com
SIC: 6163 6035 Loan brokers; Federal savings banks

(G-14703)
GWS FF&E LLC
9823 Cincinnati Dayton Rd (45069-3825)
PHONE...................................513 759-6000
John Planes, *Prin*
EMP: 30 **EST:** 2012
SALES (est): 948.16K **Privately Held**
SIC: 7389 4214 Styling of fashions, apparel, furniture, textiles, etc.; Furniture moving and storage, local
PA: Global Workplace Solutions Llc
9823 Cincinnati Dayton Rd
West Chester OH 45069

(G-14704)
HARMON INC
4290 Port Union Rd (45011-9713)
PHONE...................................513 645-1550
Roger Matthews, *Branch*
EMP: 61
SALES (corp-wide): 1.42B **Publicly Held**
Web: www.harmoninc.com
SIC: 5039 Glass construction materials
HQ: Harmon, Inc.
1650 W 82nd St Ste 1100
Minneapolis MN 55431
952 944-5700

(G-14705)
HARMON INC
9111 Meridian Way (45069-6534)
PHONE...................................513 645-1550
John Burger, *Mgr*

West Chester - Butler County (G-14706) — GEOGRAPHIC SECTION

EMP: 35
SALES (corp-wide): 1.42B **Publicly Held**
Web: www.harmoninc.com
SIC: 5039 Glass construction materials
HQ: Harmon, Inc.
 1650 W 82nd St Ste 1100
 Minneapolis MN 55431
 952 944-5700

(G-14706)
HEALTH WITH HART SNIOR SVCS LL
7368 Kingsgate Way Unit A (45069-3367)
PHONE..................513 229-8888
Richard Maniscalco, *Managing Member*
EMP: 42 **EST:** 2015
SALES (est): 1.53MM **Privately Held**
Web: www.healthwithheart.com
SIC: 8082 Home health care services

(G-14707)
HEARINGLIFE USA INC
7735 Tylers Place Blvd (45069-4684)
PHONE..................513 759-2999
EMP: 73
SALES (corp-wide): 2.67MM **Privately Held**
Web: www.hearinglife.com
SIC: 8049 8011 5999 Audiologist; Offices and clinics of medical doctors; Hearing aids
HQ: Hearinglife Usa, Inc.
 2501 Cttontail Ln Ste 101
 Somerset NJ 08873
 732 529-7120

(G-14708)
HILLANDALE HEALTH CARE INC
Also Called: Chesterwood Village
8073 Tylersville Rd Ofc (45069-2591)
PHONE..................513 777-1400
James E Dixon, *Ex Dir*
Greg Dixon, *Pr*
Pamela Martin Covic, *Sec*
Steve Dixon, *Treas*
Don Dixon, *VP*
EMP: 30 **EST:** 1964
SQ FT: 12,000
SALES (est): 14.67MM
SALES (corp-wide): 32.83MM **Privately Held**
Web: www.hillandale.com
SIC: 8051 Skilled nursing care facilities
PA: Hillandale Communities, Inc.
 4166 Tonya Trl
 Hamilton OH 45011
 513 342-4476

(G-14709)
IMPERIAL DADE INTRMDATE HLDNGS
Mailender
9500 Glades Dr (45011-9400)
PHONE..................800 998-5453
Chris Ward, *Brnch Mgr*
EMP: 45
SALES (corp-wide): 2.09MM **Privately Held**
SIC: 5087 Janitors' supplies
PA: Imperial Dade Intermediate Holdings, Llc
 255 Route 1 And 9
 Jersey City NJ 07306
 201 437-7440

(G-14710)
IMPROVEIT HOME REMODELING INC
Also Called: Improveit HM Rmdlg An Ohio Enr
8930 Global Way (45069-7071)
PHONE..................937 514-7546
EMP: 29
Web: www.improveitusa.com
SIC: 1521 General remodeling, single-family houses
PA: Improveit Home Remodeling, Inc.
 4580 Bridgeway Ave Ste B
 Columbus OH 43219

(G-14711)
INDUSTRIAL SORTING SERVICES
9220 Glades Dr (45011-8821)
PHONE..................513 772-6501
Joe Walden, *Pr*
EMP: 35 **EST:** 1999
SALES (est): 4.42MM **Privately Held**
Web: www.industrialsorting.com
SIC: 7549 Automotive maintenance services

(G-14712)
INDUSTRIAL TUBE AND STEEL CORP
9206 Port Union Rialto Rd (45069-2907)
PHONE..................513 777-5512
Mark Armstrong, *Mgr*
EMP: 44
SALES (corp-wide): 48.35MM **Privately Held**
Web: www.industrialtube.com
SIC: 5051 Steel
PA: Industrial Tube And Steel Corporation
 4658 Crystal Pkwy
 Kent OH 44240
 330 474-5530

(G-14713)
INNOMARK COMMUNICATIONS LLC
8531 Trade Ctr Dr (45011-9355)
PHONE..................513 379-7800
EMP: 83
SALES (corp-wide): 96.09MM **Privately Held**
Web: www.innomarkcom.com
SIC: 7319 Display advertising service
PA: Innomark Communications Llc
 420 Distribution Cir
 Fairfield OH 45014
 888 466-6627

(G-14714)
J&B STEEL ERECTORS INC
Also Called: J&B Steel Contractors
9430 Sutton Pl (45011-9698)
PHONE..................513 874-1722
Toya Estes, *Pr*
EMP: 42 **EST:** 1998
SQ FT: 32,000
SALES (est): 6.85MM **Privately Held**
Web: www.jbsteel.com
SIC: 1611 General contractor, highway and street construction

(G-14715)
JP FLOORING SYSTEMS INC
9097 Union Centre Blvd (45069-4861)
PHONE..................513 346-4300
Phil Shrimper, *Pr*
EMP: 50 **EST:** 1988
SQ FT: 100,000
SALES (est): 23.75MM **Privately Held**
Web: www.americasfloorsource.com
SIC: 5023 5713 Wood flooring; Floor tile
PA: America's Floor Source, Llc
 3442 Millennium Ct
 Columbus OH 43219

(G-14716)
KABLE NEWS COMPANY INC (HQ)
4275 Thunderbird Ln (45014-5483)
PHONE..................815 734-4151
Michael P Duloc, *Pr*
Bruce Obendorf, *
Myra Santos, *
▲ **EMP:** 243 **EST:** 1932
SALES (est): 23.52MM
SALES (corp-wide): 23.52MM **Privately Held**
Web: www.kablefulfillment.com
SIC: 5192 7389 Magazines; Subscription fulfillment services: magazine, newspaper, etc.
PA: Kable Product Services, Inc.
 4275 Thunderbird Ln
 West Chester OH 45014
 513 671-2800

(G-14717)
KC ROBOTICS INC
9000 Le Saint Dr (45014-2241)
PHONE..................513 860-4442
Paul Carrier, *Pr*
Kenneth P Carrier Junior, *Pr*
Constance M Carrier, *
◆ **EMP:** 43 **EST:** 1989
SQ FT: 18,000
SALES (est): 10.18MM **Privately Held**
Web: www.kcrobotics.com
SIC: 3569 7373 Robots, assembly line: industrial and commercial; Systems integration services

(G-14718)
KEMBA CREDIT UNION INC (PA)
5600 Chappell Crossing Blvd (45069)
PHONE..................513 762-5070
Dan Sutton, *Pr*
Dan Schroer, *CFO*
EMP: 75 **EST:** 1934
SALES (est): 66.36MM
SALES (corp-wide): 66.36MM **Privately Held**
Web: www.kemba.com
SIC: 6061 Federal credit unions

(G-14719)
KLEINGERS GROUP INC (PA)
Also Called: Kleingers Group
6219 Centre Park Dr (45069-3866)
PHONE..................513 779-7851
Jim Kleingers Pe Ps, *CEO*
Steve Korte Pe, *
Karen Brock, *
Dave Cox Ps, *Dir*
Jay Stewart Aicp Esq, *Dir*
EMP: 77 **EST:** 1993
SQ FT: 25,000
SALES (est): 29.13MM **Privately Held**
Web: www.kleingers.com
SIC: 8711 8713 0781 Consulting engineer; Surveying services; Landscape architects

(G-14720)
KONE INC
6323 Centre Park Dr (45069-3863)
PHONE..................513 755-6195
Wayne Dowty, *Mgr*
EMP: 30
Web: www.kone.us
SIC: 7699 Elevators: inspection, service, and repair
HQ: Kone Inc.
 3333 Warrenville Rd # 700
 Lisle IL 60532
 630 577-1650

(G-14721)
KOPCO GRAPHICS INC (PA)
9750 Crescent Prk Dr (45069-3894)
PHONE..................513 874-7230
EMP: 30 **EST:** 1989
SALES (est): 24.44MM **Privately Held**
Web: www.fortissolutionsgroup.com
SIC: 5199 2759 Packaging materials; Flexographic printing

(G-14722)
LESAINT LOGISTICS INC
4487 Le Saint Ct (45014-2229)
PHONE..................513 874-3900
Jeff Pennington, *Pr*
▲ **EMP:** 232 **EST:** 1983
SQ FT: 900,000
SALES (est): 31.41MM
SALES (corp-wide): 4.2B **Publicly Held**
SIC: 4225 4212 General warehousing and storage; Local trucking, without storage
HQ: Lesaint Logistics, Llc
 868 W Crossroads Pkwy
 Romeoville IL 60446
 630 243-5950

(G-14723)
LIFETOUCH NAT SCHL STUDIOS INC
Also Called: Lifetouch
9782 Windisch Rd (45069-3808)
PHONE..................513 772-2110
Jody Mello, *Mgr*
EMP: 35
SALES (corp-wide): 2.47B **Privately Held**
Web: www.lifetouch.com
SIC: 7221 Photographer, still or video
HQ: Lifetouch National School Studios Inc.
 11000 Viking Dr Ste 300
 Eden Prairie MN 55344
 952 826-4000

(G-14724)
LITHKO CONTRACTING LLC (PA)
Also Called: Lithko
2958 Crescentville Rd (45069-4827)
PHONE..................513 564-2000
Robert Strobel, *Pr*
Perry Hausfeld, *
Ben Cutting, *
Brian Cullen, *
EMP: 150 **EST:** 1994
SQ FT: 10,000
SALES (est): 140.5MM
SALES (corp-wide): 140.5MM **Privately Held**
Web: www.lithko.com
SIC: 1771 Concrete work

(G-14725)
LONG-STANTON MFG COMPANY
9388 Sutton Pl (45011-9702)
PHONE..................513 874-8020
Daniel B Cunningham, *Pr*
Tom Kachovec, *
Tim Hershey, *
▲ **EMP:** 50 **EST:** 1862
SQ FT: 66,000
SALES (est): 9.5MM **Privately Held**
Web: www.longstanton.com
SIC: 3444 7692 3469 3544 Sheet metalwork; Welding repair; Metal stampings, nec; Special dies, tools, jigs, and fixtures

(G-14726)
LOWES HOME CENTERS LLC
Also Called: Lowe's
7975 Tylersville Square Dr (45069-4691)
PHONE..................513 755-4300
EMP: 138
SALES (corp-wide): 86.38B **Publicly Held**
Web: www.lowes.com
SIC: 5211 5031 5722 5064 Home centers; Building materials, exterior; Household appliance stores; Electrical appliances, television and radio
HQ: Lowe's Home Centers, Llc
 1000 Lowes Blvd
 Mooresville NC 28117
 336 658-4000

GEOGRAPHIC SECTION
West Chester - Butler County (G-14749)

(G-14727)
LUMIERE DETOX CENTER
7593 Tylers Place Blvd (45069-6308)
PHONE.................513 644-2275
EMP: 48 **EST:** 2016
SALES (est): 5.44MM **Privately Held**
Web: www.lumierehealingcenters.com
SIC: 8093 Substance abuse clinics (outpatient)

(G-14728)
MAILENDER INC
9500 Glades Dr (45011-9400)
PHONE.................513 942-5453
Robert Tillis, *CEO*
▲ **EMP:** 62 **EST:** 1936
SQ FT: 65,000
SALES (est): 46.22MM
SALES (corp-wide): 1.65B **Privately Held**
Web: www.mailender.com
SIC: 5113 Paper, wrapping or coarse, and products
 PA: Imperial Bag & Paper Co. Llc
   255 Route 1 And 9
   Jersey City NJ 07306
   201 437-7440

(G-14729)
MARTIN-BROWER COMPANY LLC
Also Called: Distribution Center
4260 Port Union Rd (45011-9768)
PHONE.................513 773-2301
Ryan Rozen, *Genl Mgr*
EMP: 163
Web: www.martinbrower.com
SIC: 2013 2015 5087 Frozen meats, from purchased meat; Poultry, processed: frozen ; Restaurant supplies
 HQ: The Martin-Brower Company L L C
   6250 N River Rd Ste 9000
   Rosemont IL 60018
   847 227-6500

(G-14730)
MILLWOOD INC
4438 Muhlhauser Rd Ste 100 (45011-9776)
PHONE.................513 860-4567
Antonio Delgado, *Brnch Mgr*
EMP: 39
Web: www.millwoodinc.com
SIC: 3565 5084 Packaging machinery; Packaging machinery and equipment
 PA: Millwood, Inc.
   3708 International Blvd
   Vienna OH 44473

(G-14731)
MISA METALS INC
Also Called: J R Metals
9050 Centre Pointe Dr (45069-4874)
PHONE.................212 660-6000
▲ **EMP:** 400
SIC: 5051 Steel

(G-14732)
MITCHELLS SALON & DAY SPA
Also Called: MITCHELL'S SALON & DAY SPA INC
7795 University Ct Ste A (45069)
PHONE.................513 793-0900
Sherry Williams, *Brnch Mgr*
EMP: 195
SALES (corp-wide): 13.49MM **Privately Held**
Web: www.mitchellssalon.com
SIC: 7231 Hairdressers
 PA: Mitchell's Salon & Day Spa, Inc.
   5901 E Galbraith Rd # 230
   Cincinnati OH 45236
   513 793-0900

(G-14733)
MKJB INC
Also Called: Meadows Healthcare
4515 Guildford Dr (45069-8571)
PHONE.................513 851-8400
Karen Jamison, *CEO*
EMP: 90
SALES (corp-wide): 4.88MM **Privately Held**
Web: www.gardenparkhc.com
SIC: 8059 8051 Nursing home, except skilled and intermediate care facility; Skilled nursing care facilities
 PA: Mkjb Inc
   3536 Washington Ave
   Cincinnati OH 45229
   513 751-4900

(G-14734)
MONDELEZ GLOBAL LLC
Also Called: Nabisco
8900 Global Way (45069-7071)
PHONE.................513 714-0308
Gary Carroll, *Mgr*
EMP: 47
Web: www.mondelezinternational.com
SIC: 5149 5141 Crackers, cookies, and bakery products; Groceries, general line
 HQ: Mondelez Global Llc
   905 W Fulton Market # 200
   Chicago IL 60607
   847 943-4000

(G-14735)
MVAH MANAGEMENT LLC
Also Called: Pivotal HP Management
9100 Centre Pointe Dr (45069-4846)
PHONE.................513 964-1140
EMP: 46 **EST:** 2017
SALES (est): 1.1MM **Privately Held**
Web: www.pivotal-hp.com
SIC: 8741 Management services

(G-14736)
OGARA GROUP INC
4350 Port Union Rd (45011-9797)
PHONE.................513 275-8456
EMP: 1271
SALES (corp-wide): 52.21MM **Privately Held**
Web: www.ogaragroup.com
SIC: 8111 General practice attorney, lawyer
 PA: The O'gara Group Inc.
   7870 E Kemper Rd Ste 460
   Cincinnati OH 45249
   513 881-9800

(G-14737)
OPTIMAS OE SOLUTIONS LLC
4440 Mulhauser Road (45011-9767)
PHONE.................513 881-4600
EMP: 34
SALES (corp-wide): 673.07MM **Privately Held**
Web: www.optimas.com
SIC: 5063 Electrical apparatus and equipment
 HQ: Optimas Oe Solutions, Llc
   1441 N Wood Dale Rd
   Wood Dale IL 60191
   224 999-1000

(G-14738)
ORTHOPEDIC CONS CINCINNATI (PA)
Also Called: Wellington Orthpd Spt Medicine
7798 Discovery Dr Ste A (45069-7747)
PHONE.................513 733-8894
Edward Miller, *Ch*
Robert S Heidt Md Senior, *Pr*
Robert S Heidt Junior, *VP*
Michael Welch, *
Warren G Harding, *
▲ **EMP:** 45 **EST:** 1968
SALES (est): 20.42MM
SALES (corp-wide): 20.42MM **Privately Held**
Web: www.orthocincy.com
SIC: 8011 Orthopedic physician

(G-14739)
OVERHEAD DOOR CO- CINCINNATI
Also Called: Overhead Doors
9345 Princeton Glendale Rd (45011-9707)
P.O. Box 8187 (45069-8187)
PHONE.................513 346-4000
EMP: 145
SQ FT: 70,000
SALES (est): 9.4MM
SALES (corp-wide): 17.08MM **Privately Held**
Web: www.overheaddoorcincy.com
SIC: 5211 1761 1751 1742 Garage doors, sale and installation; Roofing, siding, and sheetmetal work; Carpentry work; Plastering, drywall, and insulation
 PA: Garage Door Systems, Llc
   8811 Bash St
   Indianapolis IN 46256
   317 343-4580

(G-14740)
PACIFIC LIFE INSURANCE COMPANY
9078 Union Centre Blvd (45069-4992)
PHONE.................513 241-5000
Bob Ditommaso, *Genl Mgr*
EMP: 30
SALES (corp-wide): 12.84B **Privately Held**
Web: www.pacificlife.com
SIC: 6311 Life insurance carriers
 HQ: Pacific Life Insurance Company
   700 Newport Center Dr
   Newport Beach CA 92660
   949 219-3011

(G-14741)
PEOPLES COMMUNITY BANCORP INC (PA)
6100 W Chester Rd (45069-2943)
PHONE.................513 870-3530
Jerry D Williams, *Pr*
Thomas J Noe, *Ex VP*
Fred L Darlington, *Corporate Secretary*
Jerry L Gore, *RETAIL BANKING*
Lori M Henn, *Sr VP*
EMP: 78 **EST:** 1999
SALES (est): 20.05MM
SALES (corp-wide): 20.05MM **Privately Held**
SIC: 6021 National commercial banks

(G-14742)
PIPE PRODUCTS INC
5122 Rialto Rd (45069-2923)
P.O. Box 2778 (23609-0778)
PHONE.................513 587-7532
▲ **EMP:** 150
SIC: 5051 3498 5085 Pipe and tubing, steel; Pipe fittings, fabricated from purchased pipe ; Valves and fittings

(G-14743)
PLANES MOVING & STORAGE INC (PA)
Also Called: Planes Companies
9823 Cincinnati Dayton Rd (45069-3825)
PHONE.................513 759-6000
John J Planes, *CEO*
John Sabatalo, *
Jeffrey Ankenbauer, *
Raymond Gundrum, *
Robert Faillo, *
▲ **EMP:** 200 **EST:** 1928
SQ FT: 250,000
SALES (est): 95.96MM
SALES (corp-wide): 95.96MM **Privately Held**
Web: www.teamplanes.com
SIC: 4214 4213 Household goods moving and storage, local; Trucking, except local

(G-14744)
POPE & ASSOCIATES INC
Also Called: Pope Consulting
9277 Centre Pointe Dr Ste 150 (45069)
PHONE.................513 671-1277
Patricia Pope, *Pr*
EMP: 46 **EST:** 1979
SQ FT: 1,650
SALES (est): 2.43MM **Privately Held**
Web: www.popeconsulting.com
SIC: 8742 Training and development consultant

(G-14745)
PREMIERE SERVICE MORTGAGE CORP (PA)
6266 Centre Park Dr (45069-3865)
PHONE.................513 546-9895
EMP: 40 **EST:** 1994
SALES (est): 5.03MM **Privately Held**
SIC: 6163 Mortgage brokers arranging for loans, using money of others

(G-14746)
PRESTIGE TECHNICAL SVCS INC (PA)
7908 Cincinnati Dayton Rd Ste T (45069-3382)
PHONE.................513 779-6800
Joan Mears, *Pr*
EMP: 94 **EST:** 1988
SQ FT: 2,700
SALES (est): 4.23MM
SALES (corp-wide): 4.23MM **Privately Held**
Web: www.prestigetechnical.com
SIC: 7363 Engineering help service

(G-14747)
PRIME VALET CLEANERS INC
8204 Princeton Glendale Rd (45069-1675)
PHONE.................513 860-9595
Twila Hopkins, *Mgr*
EMP: 38
SIC: 7216 Drycleaning plants, except rugs
 PA: Prime Valet Cleaners, Inc.
   5647 Union Centre Dr
   West Chester OH

(G-14748)
PRINT MANAGEMENT PARTNERS INC
Go2 Partners
6285 Schumacher Park Dr (45069-4806)
PHONE.................513 942-9202
James O'brien, *Brnch Mgr*
EMP: 36
Web: www.go2partners.com
SIC: 8742 Marketing consulting services
 PA: Print Management Partners, Inc.
   701 Lee St Ste 1050
   Des Plaines IL 60016

(G-14749)
PROVISION LIVING LLC
Also Called: Premier Senior Living
5531 Chappell Crossing Blvd (45069)
PHONE.................513 847-9050
EMP: 52
Web: www.provisionliving.com
SIC: 8361 Aged home

West Chester - Butler County (G-14750)

PA: Provision Living, Llc
9450 Manchester Rd # 207
Saint Louis MO 63119

(G-14750)
QUALITY CONSTRUCTION MGT INC
Also Called: Q C M
7395 Kingsgate Way (45069-2453)
PHONE..................513 779-8425
Barbara Jennings, *Pr*
Tim Sheperd, *
Barbra Jennings, *
Debbey Sheperd, *
EMP: 100 **EST:** 1999
SQ FT: 1,300
SALES (est): 4.07MM **Privately Held**
Web: www.qcm-inc.net
SIC: 8731 8741 Commercial physical research; Construction management

(G-14751)
QUASONIX INC (PA)
Also Called: Quasonix
6025 Schumacher Park Dr (45069-4812)
PHONE..................513 942-1287
Terrance Hill, *Pr*
Pamela S Hill, *
EMP: 37 **EST:** 2002
SQ FT: 15,000
SALES (est): 24.46MM
SALES (corp-wide): 24.46MM **Privately Held**
Web: www.quasonix.com
SIC: 5065 3663 3812 3669 Communication equipment; Airborne radio communications equipment; Antennas, radar or communications; Intercommunication systems, electric

(G-14752)
QUEEN CITY POLYMERS INC (PA)
6101 Schumacher Park Dr (45069-3818)
PHONE..................513 779-0990
James M Powers, *Pr*
James L Powers, *
EMP: 40 **EST:** 1982
SQ FT: 33,000
SALES (est): 8.75MM
SALES (corp-wide): 8.75MM **Privately Held**
Web: www.qcpinc.net
SIC: 3089 5162 Injection molding of plastics; Plastics products, nec

(G-14753)
R3 SAFETY LLC (DH)
Also Called: United American Sales
6021 Union Centre Blvd (45014-2290)
PHONE..................800 421-7081
Michael Hernandez, *
EMP: 42 **EST:** 1972
SQ FT: 45,000
SALES (est): 17.27MM
SALES (corp-wide): 14.5B **Privately Held**
Web: www.r3safety.net
SIC: 5084 Welding machinery and equipment
HQ: Bunzl Usa, Inc.
1 Cityplace Dr Ste 200
Saint Louis MO 63141
314 997-5959

(G-14754)
RAM CNSTRCTION SVCS CNCNNATI L
Also Called: Ram Construction Services
4710 Ashley Dr (45011-3594)
PHONE..................513 297-1857
Bob Mazur, *Pr*
Kevin Houle, *CFO*
John Mazur, *VP*
EMP: 42 **EST:** 2005
SALES (est): 2.56MM
SALES (corp-wide): 87.39MM **Privately Held**
SIC: 1799 1541 1542 Waterproofing; Renovation, remodeling and repairs: industrial buildings; Commercial and office buildings, renovation and repair
PA: Ram Construction Services Of Michigan, Inc.
13800 Eckles Rd
Livonia MI 48150
734 464-3800

(G-14755)
RES-CARE INC
7908 Cincinnati Dayton Rd (45069-6608)
PHONE..................513 858-4550
Angie Mick, *Pr*
EMP: 55
SALES (corp-wide): 8.83B **Publicly Held**
Web: www.rescare.com
SIC: 8082 Home health care services
HQ: Res-Care, Inc.
805 N Whittington Pkwy
Louisville KY 40222
502 394-2100

(G-14756)
RIVER CITY FURNITURE LLC (PA)
Also Called: Rcf Group, The
6454 Centre Park Dr (45069-4800)
PHONE..................513 612-7303
Scott Robertson, *
Bryan Lindholz, *
EMP: 32 **EST:** 2003
SQ FT: 7,500
SALES (est): 25.61MM
SALES (corp-wide): 25.61MM **Privately Held**
Web: www.thercfgroup.com
SIC: 7389 5712 1752 0782 Interior design services; Office furniture; Resilient floor laying; Mowing services, lawn

(G-14757)
RIVERFRONT DIVERSIFIED INC
Also Called: Ever Dry of Cincinnati
9814 Harwood Ct (45014-7589)
PHONE..................513 874-7200
James Giclty, *Pr*
EMP: 70 **EST:** 1985
SQ FT: 12,000
SALES (est): 10.61MM **Privately Held**
Web: www.everdrycincy.com
SIC: 1799 Waterproofing

(G-14758)
RRR EXPRESS LLC
Also Called: Rrr Logistics
6432 Centre Park Dr (45069-4800)
PHONE..................800 723-3424
Steven D Hall, *Managing Member*
Lee Scheven, *
EMP: 44 **EST:** 2001
SQ FT: 31,000
SALES (est): 1.33MM **Privately Held**
SIC: 4213 Trucking, except local

(G-14759)
RYANS ALL-GLASS INCORPORATED (PA)
9401 Le Saint Dr (45014-5447)
PHONE..................513 771-4440
Bruce Ryan, *Pr*
Ken Ryan, *
EMP: 30 **EST:** 1982
SALES (est): 6.58MM
SALES (corp-wide): 6.58MM **Privately Held**
Web: www.ryansallglass.com
SIC: 1793 7536 1751 Glass and glazing work; Automotive glass replacement shops; Window and door (prefabricated) installation

(G-14760)
SABIN ROBBINS LLC
9365 Allen Rd (45069-3846)
PHONE..................513 874-5270
▲ **EMP:** 140
Web: www.sabinrobbins.com
SIC: 5111 Fine paper

(G-14761)
SCHNEIDER ELECTRIC USA INC
Also Called: Schneider Electric
9870 Crescent Park Dr (45069-3800)
PHONE..................513 777-4445
Jim Newcomb, *Mgr*
EMP: 75
SALES (corp-wide): 82.05K **Privately Held**
Web: www.se.com
SIC: 3613 3643 3612 3823 Switchgear and switchboard apparatus; Bus bars (electrical conductors); Power transformers, electric; Controllers, for process variables, all types
HQ: Schneider Electric Usa, Inc.
One Boston Pl Ste 2700
Boston MA 02108
978 975-9600

(G-14762)
SCHUMACHER DEVELOPMENT INC
6355 Centre Park Dr (45069-3863)
P.O. Box 626 (45071-0626)
PHONE..................513 777-9800
Larry Schumacher, *Pr*
Mark Schumacher, *VP*
Mike Schumacher, *VP*
EMP: 57 **EST:** 1964
SQ FT: 14,000
SALES (est): 2.27MM **Privately Held**
Web: www.schumacher-dugan.com
SIC: 1542 Commercial and office building, new construction

(G-14763)
SHETLER MOVING & STOR OF OHIO
Also Called: Shelter Moving & Storage
9917 Charter Park Dr (45069-3890)
PHONE..................513 755-0700
Thomas J Shelter Senior, *Pr*
Robert O Shetler, *
Thomas J Shetler Junior, *Sec*
Thomas J Shetler Senior, *Pr*
EMP: 27 **EST:** 1985
SQ FT: 25,000
SALES (est): 810.55K **Privately Held**
Web: www.shetlermoving.com
SIC: 4213 4214 Household goods transport; Furniture moving and storage, local

(G-14764)
SIBCY CLINE INC
Also Called: Sibcy Cline Realtors
7677 Voice Of America Centre Dr (45069-2795)
PHONE..................513 777-8100
Patty Letzler, *Mgr*
EMP: 120
SALES (corp-wide): 98.72MM **Privately Held**
Web: www.sibcycline.com
SIC: 6531 6162 Real estate agent, residential; Mortgage bankers
PA: Sibcy Cline, Inc.
8044 Montgomery Rd # 300
Cincinnati OH 45236
513 984-4100

(G-14765)
SIBCY CLINE INC
Also Called: Sibcy Cline Realtors
7677 Voice Of America Centre Dr (45069-2795)
PHONE..................513 677-1830
Madeline Hoge, *Genl Mgr*
EMP: 120
SALES (corp-wide): 98.72MM **Privately Held**
Web: www.sibcycline.com
SIC: 6531 Real estate agent, residential
PA: Sibcy Cline, Inc.
8044 Montgomery Rd # 300
Cincinnati OH 45236
513 984-4100

(G-14766)
SKIDMORE SALES & DISTRG CO INC (PA)
Also Called: Skidmore Sales
9889 Cincinnati Dayton Rd (45069-3825)
PHONE..................513 755-4200
Gerald Skidmore, *Ch*
Douglas S Skidmore, *
Jim Mccarthy, *Pr*
Mark Overbeck, *
Steve Jackson, *
◆ **EMP:** 36 **EST:** 1963
SQ FT: 150,000
SALES (est): 145.72MM
SALES (corp-wide): 145.72MM **Privately Held**
Web: www.skidmoresales.com
SIC: 5149 5169 Groceries and related products, nec; Chemicals and allied products, nec

(G-14767)
SOGETI USA LLC
9050 Centre Pointe Dr (45069-4874)
PHONE..................937 291-8142
EMP: 68
SALES (corp-wide): 415.14MM **Privately Held**
Web: us.sogeti.com
SIC: 7379 Online services technology consultants
HQ: Sogeti Usa Llc
10100 Innovation Dr # 200
Miamisburg OH 45342
937 291-8100

(G-14768)
SPRANDEL ENTERPRISES INC
Also Called: Quality Towing
6467 Gano Rd (45069-4830)
P.O. Box 1873 (45071-1873)
PHONE..................513 777-6622
Michael Sprandel, *Pr*
EMP: 27 **EST:** 1989
SALES (est): 1.92MM **Privately Held**
Web: www.quality-towing.com
SIC: 7549 Towing service, automotive

(G-14769)
STATE FARM GENERAL INSUR CO
Also Called: State Farm Insurance
4837 Realtor Road Ste B (45069)
PHONE..................513 870-0285
Steve Saunders, *Owner*
EMP: 54
SALES (corp-wide): 27.88B **Privately Held**
Web: www.stevesaunders.net
SIC: 6411 Insurance agents and brokers
HQ: State Farm General Insurance Co Inc
1 State Farm Plz
Bloomington IL 61701
309 766-2311

GEOGRAPHIC SECTION
West Chester - Butler County (G-14793)

(G-14770)
SUNESIS CONSTRUCTION CO
2610 Crescentville Rd (45069-3819)
PHONE..................513 326-6000
Rick Jones, *Pr*
Steve Abernathy, *
Bill Huber, *
Albert C Eiselein Junior, *Prin*
Richard Jones, *
EMP: 125 **EST:** 1991
SQ FT: 3,000
SALES (est): 51.94MM **Privately Held**
Web: www.sunesisconstruction.com
SIC: 1623 1622 1611 Water, sewer, and utility lines; Bridge construction; General contractor, highway and street construction

(G-14771)
T-MOBILE CENTRAL LLC
8234 Princeton Glendale Rd (45069-1675)
PHONE..................513 855-3170
EMP: 99
SALES (corp-wide): 78.56B **Publicly Held**
Web: www.t-mobile.com
SIC: 4812 Cellular telephone services
HQ: T-Mobile Central Llc
  6270 E Broad St
  Columbus OH 43213

(G-14772)
TAYLOR WAREHOUSE CORPORATION
Also Called: Taylor Warehouse Corporation
9287 Meridian Way (45069)
PHONE..................513 771-1850
Grant Taylor, *Brnch Mgr*
EMP: 43
SALES (corp-wide): 2.12MM **Privately Held**
SIC: 4225 General warehousing and storage
PA: Taylor Warehouse Corporation
  9756 International Blvd
  West Chester OH 45246
  513 771-1850

(G-14773)
THREEBOND INTERNATIONAL
6184 Schumacher Park Dr (45069-4802)
PHONE..................513 759-8771
EMP: 75 **EST:** 2018
SALES (est): 7.15MM **Privately Held**
Web: www.threebond.com
SIC: 6512 Commercial and industrial building operation

(G-14774)
TOTAL QUALITY LOGISTICS LLC
8488 Shepherd Farm Dr (45069-5933)
PHONE..................800 580-3101
Larry Shepherd, *Brnch Mgr*
EMP: 71
SALES (corp-wide): 8.85B **Privately Held**
Web: www.tql.com
SIC: 4731 Truck transportation brokers
HQ: Total Quality Logistics, Llc
  4289 Ivy Pointe Blvd
  Cincinnati OH 45245

(G-14775)
TRADEGLOBAL LLC
Also Called: Tradeglobal
9271 Meridian Way (45069-6523)
PHONE..................866 345-5835
Dave Cook, *CEO*
Dave Eckley, *
EMP: 117 **EST:** 2011
SALES (est): 10.61MM **Privately Held**
SIC: 7371 Computer software development
PA: Singapore Post Limited
  10 Eunos Road 8
  Singapore 40860

(G-14776)
TRADES CNSTR STAFFING INC
9604 Lackawana Ct (45069-4356)
PHONE..................833 668-0444
Larry Bailey, *Pr*
Larry Bailey, *Prin*
EMP: 200 **EST:** 2020
SALES (est): 5MM **Privately Held**
SIC: 7361 Employment agencies

(G-14777)
TRAILINES INCORPORATED
10045 Windisch Rd (45069-3801)
PHONE..................513 755-7900
EMP: 36 **EST:** 1981
SALES (est): 5.63MM **Privately Held**
Web: www.trailines.com
SIC: 5013 7539 Trailer parts and accessories; Trailer repair

(G-14778)
TRIHEALTH INC
Also Called: Trihelth Orthpaedic Spine Inst
4900 Wunnenberg Way (45069-4985)
PHONE..................513 860-6820
EMP: 163
Web: www.trihealth.com
SIC: 8733 Noncommercial research organizations
HQ: Trihealth, Inc.
  625 Eden Park Dr
  Cincinnati OH 45202
  513 569-5400

(G-14779)
TUTOR TIME LEARNING CTRS LLC
7218 Liberty Way (45069-1519)
PHONE..................513 755-6690
Jean Scott, *Dir*
EMP: 176
Web: www.tutortime.com
SIC: 8351 Preschool center
HQ: Tutor Time Learning Centers, Llc
  21333 Haggerty Rd Ste 300
  Novi MI 48375
  248 697-9000

(G-14780)
UC HEALTH LLC
7759 University Dr (45069-6578)
PHONE..................513 475-8282
EMP: 51
Web: www.uchealth.com
SIC: 8099 Childbirth preparation clinic
PA: Uc Health, Llc.
  3200 Burnet Ave
  Cincinnati OH 45229

(G-14781)
UC HEALTH LLC
7710 University Ct (45069)
PHONE..................513 475-7777
EMP: 51
Web: www.uchealth.com
SIC: 8011 Medical centers
PA: Uc Health, Llc.
  3200 Burnet Ave
  Cincinnati OH 45229

(G-14782)
UC HEALTH LLC
Also Called: Uc Helth W Chster Surgical Ctr
7750 Discovery Dr (45069-2598)
PHONE..................513 475-8300
EMP: 86
Web: www.uchealth.com
SIC: 8062 General medical and surgical hospitals
PA: Uc Health, Llc.
  3200 Burnet Ave
  Cincinnati OH 45229

(G-14783)
UC HEALTH LLC
7700 University Ct Ste 1800 (45069-2524)
PHONE..................513 475-7458
EMP: 222
Web: www.uchealth.com
SIC: 8062 General medical and surgical hospitals
PA: Uc Health, Llc.
  3200 Burnet Ave
  Cincinnati OH 45229

(G-14784)
UC HEALTH LLC
Also Called: U C Health Dermatology
7690 Discovery Dr Unit 3100 (45069-6542)
PHONE..................513 475-7630
EMP: 35
Web: www.uchealth.com
SIC: 8748 Business consulting, nec
PA: Uc Health, Llc.
  3200 Burnet Ave
  Cincinnati OH 45229

(G-14785)
UC HEALTH LLC
7798 Discovery Dr Ste F (45069-7747)
PHONE..................513 298-3000
EMP: 34
Web: www.uchealth.com
SIC: 8741 Hospital management
PA: Uc Health, Llc.
  3200 Burnet Ave
  Cincinnati OH 45229

(G-14786)
UNION CENTRE HOTEL LLC
Also Called: MARRIOTT HOTELS
6189 Muhlhauser Rd (45069-4842)
PHONE..................513 874-7335
Brian Perkins, *Genl Mgr*
EMP: 167 **EST:** 2012
SALES (est): 54.92K **Privately Held**
Web: www.marriott.com
SIC: 7011 Hotels and motels

(G-14787)
UNIVERSITY CNCNNATI MED CTR LL
7690 Discovery Dr Unit 3000 (45069-6542)
PHONE..................513 475-8300
John Tew Junior, *Brnch Mgr*
EMP: 2372
Web: www.uchealth.com
SIC: 8062 General medical and surgical hospitals
HQ: University Of Cincinnati Medical Center, Llc
  3199 Highland Ave
  Cincinnati OH 45219
  513 584-1000

(G-14788)
UNIVERSITY OF CINCINNATI PHYS
Also Called: Uc Physicians At Univ Pointe
7700 University Ct Ste 1800 (45069-2524)
PHONE..................513 475-8000
Dan Gahl, *Admn*
EMP: 95
Web: www.uchealth.com
SIC: 8011 Offices and clinics of medical doctors
HQ: University Of Cincinnati Physicians, Inc.
  222 Piedmont Ave Ste 2200
  Cincinnati OH 45219

(G-14789)
VARO ENGINEERS INC
9078 Union Centre Blvd Ste 350 (45069)
PHONE..................513 729-9313
Tim Burnham, *CEO*
EMP: 48
SALES (corp-wide): 110.61MM **Privately Held**
Web: www.salasobrien.com
SIC: 8711 Consulting engineer
HQ: Varo Engineers, Inc.
  2751 Tuller Pkwy
  Dublin OH 43017
  614 459-0424

(G-14790)
VENDORS SUPPLY INC
Also Called: Vendor Supply of Ohio
6448 Gano Rd (45069-4829)
P.O. Box 62883 (45262-0883)
PHONE..................513 755-2111
Ken Morgan, *Mgr*
EMP: 30
SALES (corp-wide): 49.66MM **Privately Held**
Web: www.vendorssupply.com
SIC: 5141 Food brokers
PA: Vendors Supply, Inc.
  201 Saluda River Rd
  Columbia SC 29210
  803 772-6390

(G-14791)
VISIBLE SUPPLY CHAIN MGT LLC
Also Called: Visible Logistics
9271 Meridian Way (45069-6523)
PHONE..................801 859-3082
Raven Montoya, *Mgr*
EMP: 29
SALES (corp-wide): 2.41MM **Privately Held**
Web: www.maersk.com
SIC: 4731 Freight transportation arrangement
HQ: Visible Supply Chain Management, Llc
  5160 W Wiley Post Way
  Salt Lake City UT 84116
  877 728-5328

(G-14792)
VITRAN EXPRESS INC
2789 Crescentville Rd (45069-3816)
PHONE..................513 771-4894
EMP: 33
Web: www.vitran.com
SIC: 4213 Less-than-truckload (LTL)
PA: Vitran Express, Inc.
  12225 Stephens Rd
  Warren MI 48089

(G-14793)
WARSTEINER IMPORTERS AGENCY
Also Called: Warsteiner USA
9359 Allen Rd (45069-3846)
PHONE..................513 942-9872
Geoffery Westaphar, *Pr*
James L Webster, *
▲ **EMP:** 50 **EST:** 1989
SQ FT: 10,000
SALES (est): 21.48MM
SALES (corp-wide): 144.21K **Privately Held**
Web: www.warsteiner.us
SIC: 5181 Beer and other fermented malt liquors
PA: Warsteiner International Kg
  Domring 4-10
  Warstein NW
  2902880

West Chester - Butler County

(G-14794)
WETHERNGTON GOLF CNTRY CLB INC (PA)
7337 Country Club Ln (45069-1598)
PHONE................513 755-2582
Michael Purich, *Prin*
EMP: 42 EST: 1990
SALES (est): 2.66MM **Privately Held**
Web: www.wetheringtongcc.com
SIC: 7997 Country club, membership

(G-14795)
WINELCO INC
6141 Centre Park Dr (45069-3869)
PHONE................513 755-8050
Michael Ullman, *Pr*
EMP: 40 EST: 1958
SQ FT: 17,000
SALES (est): 5.22MM **Privately Held**
Web: www.winelco.com
SIC: 7699 5084 Industrial equipment services; Industrial machinery and equipment

(G-14796)
WOLSELEY INDUSTRIAL GROUP
5122 Rialto Rd (45069-2923)
PHONE................513 587-7532
EMP: 27 EST: 2013
SALES (est): 5.46MM
SALES (corp-wide): 20.83B **Privately Held**
SIC: 7389 Business Activities at Non-Commercial Site
HQ: Ferguson Enterprises, Inc.
12500 Jefferson Ave
Newport News VA 23606
757 874-7795

West Chester
Hamilton County

(G-14797)
ABB INC
4828 Business Center Way (45246-1318)
PHONE................513 860-1749
Jerry Pike, *Brnch Mgr*
EMP: 41
Web: www.abb.com
SIC: 5063 Switchgear
HQ: Abb Inc.
305 Gregson Dr
Cary NC 27511

(G-14798)
AMERICAN BUSINESS FORMS INC
Also Called: American Solutions For Bus
10000 International Blvd (45246-4839)
PHONE................513 312-2522
EMP: 30
SALES (corp-wide): 380.8MM **Privately Held**
Web: home.americanbus.com
SIC: 5112 5199 2759 Business forms; Advertising specialties; Promotional printing
PA: American Business Forms, Inc.
31 E Minnesota Ave
Glenwood MN 56334
320 634-5471

(G-14799)
ATMOS360 INC
Also Called: Atmos 360 A Systems Solutions
4690 Interstate Dr Ste A (45246-1142)
PHONE................513 772-4777
EMP: 45 EST: 1989
SALES (est): 9MM **Privately Held**
Web: www.atmos360.com
SIC: 8711 3565 3564 Consulting engineer; Packaging machinery; Blowers and fans

(G-14800)
BEIERSDORF INC
5232 E Provident Dr (45246-1040)
PHONE................513 682-7300
Jim Kenton, *Brnch Mgr*
EMP: 168
SALES (corp-wide): 12.51B **Privately Held**
Web: www.beiersdorfusa.com
SIC: 2844 5122 3842 2841 Face creams or lotions; Antiseptics; Bandages and dressings; Soap: granulated, liquid, cake, flaked, or chip
HQ: Beiersdorf, Inc.
301 Tresser Blvd Ste 1500
Stamford CT 06901
203 563-5800

(G-14801)
BRIDGE LOGISTICS INC
5 Circle Freeway Dr (45246-1201)
PHONE................513 874-7444
James Campbell, *CEO*
William P Lanham, *
EMP: 50 EST: 2003
SQ FT: 10,000
SALES (est): 22.47MM **Privately Held**
Web: www.bridgelogisticsinc.com
SIC: 4213 Trucking, except local

(G-14802)
CARDINAL HEALTH SYSTEMS INC
Also Called: Cardinal Health
5532 Spellmire Dr (45246-4856)
PHONE................513 874-5940
Jason Sasser, *Mgr*
EMP: 1567
SQ FT: 16,600
SALES (corp-wide): 205.01B **Publicly Held**
SIC: 5122 Pharmaceuticals
HQ: Cardinal Health Systems, Inc.
14 Schoolhouse Rd
Somerset NJ 08873
732 537-6544

(G-14803)
CHASE INDUSTRIES INC (DH)
Also Called: Chase Doors
10021 Commerce Park Dr (45246-1333)
PHONE................513 860-5565
Bill German, *Pr*
Todd Ray, *
Alan D Baker, *
Drew Bachman, *
◆ EMP: 80 EST: 1996
SQ FT: 280,000
SALES (est): 50.36MM
SALES (corp-wide): 448.01MM **Privately Held**
Web: www.chasedoors.com
SIC: 1751 Garage door, installation or erection
HQ: Senneca Holdings, Inc.
11502 Century Blvd
Cincinnati OH 45246
800 543-4455

(G-14804)
CINCINNATI CONTAINER COMPANY (PA)
5060 Duff Dr (45246-1309)
P.O. Box 825 (45036-0825)
PHONE................513 874-6724
◆ EMP: 40 EST: 1932
SALES (est): 23MM
SALES (corp-wide): 23MM **Privately Held**
Web: www.cincinnaticontainer.com
SIC: 5085 Glass bottles

(G-14805)
CINCINNATI PRCISION INSTRS INC
Also Called: C. P. I.
253 Circle Freeway Dr (45246-1205)
PHONE................513 874-2122
TOLL FREE: 800
Steve Plymire, *Pr*
Dan Bollmer, *
Ed Testerman, *
EMP: 50 EST: 1962
SQ FT: 12,800
SALES (est): 9.5MM **Privately Held**
Web: www.trescal.com
SIC: 8734 Calibration and certification

(G-14806)
CORECREW LLC
4670 Dues Dr (45246-1009)
PHONE................855 692-6733
EMP: 30 EST: 2019
SALES (est): 243.19K **Privately Held**
Web: www.corecrew.com
SIC: 7361 Employment agencies

(G-14807)
DEANHOUSTON INC
Also Called: Dean Houston
4612 Interstate Dr (45246-1110)
PHONE................740 646-2914
EMP: 33 EST: 2018
SALES (est): 822.53K **Privately Held**
Web: www.deanhouston.com
SIC: 4731 Freight transportation arrangement

(G-14808)
E S I INC (DH)
Also Called: Wagner Industrial Electric
4696 Devitt Dr (45246-1104)
PHONE................513 454-3741
Tom Schrout, *Pr*
Douglas Hurley, *
Cahrley Hartshorn, *
Gary Laidman, *
Vernon A Raile, *
EMP: 100 EST: 1966
SQ FT: 9,000
SALES (est): 63.69MM
SALES (corp-wide): 4.66B **Publicly Held**
Web: www.esielectrical.com
SIC: 1731 General electrical contractor
HQ: Mdu Construction Services Group, Inc.
1150 W Century Ave
Bismarck ND 58503
701 530-1000

(G-14809)
EMPIRE PACKING COMPANY LP
Also Called: Cincinnatti Processing
113 Circle Freeway Dr (45246-1203)
PHONE................513 942-5400
Dennis Hioghmas, *Genl Mgr*
· EMP: 60
SALES (corp-wide): 138.53MM **Privately Held**
Web: www.ledbetterfoods.com
SIC: 5147 2013 2011 Meats, fresh; Sausages and other prepared meats; Meat packing plants
PA: Empire Packing Company, L.P.
1837 Harbor Ave
Memphis TN 38113
901 948-4788

(G-14810)
ESSENDANT CO
9775 International Blvd (45246-4855)
PHONE................513 942-1354
Glynn Magness, *Brnch Mgr*
EMP: 59
Web: www.essendant.com
SIC: 5112 Office supplies, nec
HQ: Essendant Co.
1 Pkwy N Blvd Ste 100
Deerfield IL 60015
847 627-7000

(G-14811)
FILTERFRESH COFFEE SERVICE INC
Also Called: Filterfresh
4890 Duff Dr Ste D (45246-1100)
PHONE................513 681-8911
Yasna Hood, *Mgr*
EMP: 53
Web: www.gcd.com
SIC: 7389 Coffee service
HQ: Filterfresh Coffee Service Inc.
1101 Market St Fl 7
Philadelphia PA 19107

(G-14812)
FISHEL COMPANY
Also Called: Team Special
4740 Interstate Dr Ste R (45246-1146)
PHONE................513 956-5210
Bob Dinuocio, *Genl Mgr*
EMP: 28
SALES (corp-wide): 758.31MM **Privately Held**
Web: www.teamfishel.com
SIC: 4822 Teletypewriter services
PA: The Fishel Company
1366 Dublin Rd
Columbus OH 43215
614 274-8100

(G-14813)
GATEWAY TIRE OF TEXAS INC
Also Called: Dunlap & Kyle
4 W Crescentville Rd (45246-1215)
PHONE................513 874-2500
William A Patton, *Mgr*
EMP: 35
SALES (corp-wide): 114.34MM **Privately Held**
SIC: 5014 Tires and tubes
HQ: Gateway Tire Of Texas, Inc.
1525 W Belt Line Rd
Carrollton TX 75006
972 446-6500

(G-14814)
GSF USA INC
9850 Princeton Glendale Rd Ste B (45246-1034)
PHONE................513 733-1451
Tim Rupard, *Brnch Mgr*
EMP: 175
SALES (corp-wide): 56.52MM **Privately Held**
Web: www.gsf-usa.com
SIC: 7349 Janitorial service, contract basis
HQ: Gsf Usa, Inc.
1030 E Washington St
Indianapolis IN 46202

(G-14815)
HANSEN ADKINS AUTO TRNSPT INC
200 W Crescentville Rd (45246-1217)
PHONE................562 430-4100
Robert C Roehrig, *Brnch Mgr*
EMP: 31
Web: www.hansenadkins.com
SIC: 4789 Pipeline terminal facilities, independently operated
PA: Hansen & Adkins Auto Transport, Inc.
3552 Green Ave
Los Alamitos CA 90720

GEOGRAPHIC SECTION — West Chester - Hamilton County (G-14839)

(G-14816)
HELPING HANDS HEALTHCARE INC
9692 Cincinnati Columbus Rd (45241-1071)
P.O. Box 979 (45071-0979)
PHONE................513 755-4181
Chris Ellis, *CEO*
EMP: 236 **EST:** 1999
SALES (est): 4.55MM **Privately Held**
Web: www.hhhcare.com
SIC: 8082 Home health care services

(G-14817)
HILLMAN GROUP INC
Sealtight
9950 Princeton Glendale Rd (45246-1116)
PHONE................513 874-5905
David Quehl, *Mgr*
EMP: 33
SALES (corp-wide): 1.48B **Publicly Held**
Web: www.hillmangroup.com
SIC: 7319 Aerial advertising services
HQ: The Hillman Group Inc
   1280 Kemper Meadow Dr
   Cincinnati OH 45240
   513 851-4900

(G-14818)
HWZ DISTRIBUTION GROUP LLC
40 W Crescentville Rd (45246-1238)
PHONE................513 618-0300
EMP: 135
SIC: 5032 Drywall materials

(G-14819)
HYDROTECH INC (PA)
Also Called: Enpro
10052 Commerce Park Dr (45246-1338)
PHONE................888 651-5712
◆ **EMP:** 51 **EST:** 1967
SALES (est): 25.63MM
SALES (corp-wide): 25.63MM **Privately Held**
Web: www.hydrotech.com
SIC: 5084 3492 Industrial machinery and equipment; Control valves, fluid power: hydraulic and pneumatic

(G-14820)
INTELLIGRATED INC
10045 International Blvd (45246-4845)
PHONE................513 874-0788
EMP: 2457
SALES (corp-wide): 36.66B **Publicly Held**
Web: sps.honeywell.com
SIC: 3535 5084 7371 Conveyors and conveying equipment; Industrial machinery and equipment; Custom computer programming services
HQ: Intelligrated, Inc.
   7901 Innovation Way
   Mason OH 45040
   866 936-7300

(G-14821)
JELD-WEN INC
400 Circle Freeway Dr (45246-1214)
PHONE................513 874-6771
Rick Carlson, *Brnch Mgr*
EMP: 102
Web: www.mmidoor.com
SIC: 5031 Millwork
HQ: Jeld-Wen, Inc.
   2645 Silver Crescent Dr
   Charlotte NC 28273
   800 535-3936

(G-14822)
JMS EXPRESS INC
5055 Duff Dr # 2 (45246-1308)
PHONE................855 267-4242
Jamol Djalilov, *Prin*
EMP: 30 **EST:** 2020
SALES (est): 2.78MM **Privately Held**
SIC: 4789 Transportation services, nec

(G-14823)
MARKET DAY LLC
Also Called: Market Day Distribution
5581 Spellmire Dr Bldg 6 (45246-4841)
PHONE................513 860-1370
Brian Lynch, *Mgr*
EMP: 338
SALES (corp-wide): 5.88B **Privately Held**
Web: www.marketdaylocal.com
SIC: 7389 Fund raising organizations
HQ: Market Day, Llc.
   1300 Gezon Pkwy Sw
   Wyoming MI 49509
   630 285-1470

(G-14824)
MCNERNEY & ASSOCIATES LLC
Also Called: P J McNerney & Associates
5443 Duff Dr (45246-1323)
PHONE................513 241-9951
Patrick Mcnerney, *Mgr*
Patrick J Mcnerney, *Pr*
Jan Mcnerney, *VP*
◆ **EMP:** 42 **EST:** 1983
SALES (est): 4.5MM **Privately Held**
Web: www.pjmcnerney.com
SIC: 2752 4783 Offset printing; Packing goods for shipping

(G-14825)
MH LOGISTICS CORP
Also Called: Mh Equipment
106 Circle Freeway Dr (45246-1204)
PHONE................513 681-2200
Paul Hagedorn, *Mgr*
EMP: 90
SALES (corp-wide): 309.83MM **Privately Held**
Web: www.mhequipment.com
SIC: 5084 Materials handling machinery
PA: M.H. Logistics Corp.
   8901 N Industrial Rd
   Peoria IL 61615
   309 579-8020

(G-14826)
O K I SUPPLY CO
Also Called: O K I Bering
9901 Princeton Glendale Rd Ste A (45246-1115)
PHONE................513 341-4002
◆ **EMP:** 200
SIC: 5085 Industrial supplies

(G-14827)
OKI BERING MANAGEMENT CO
Also Called: Oki Bering
9901 Princeton Glendale Rd Ste A (45246-1115)
PHONE................513 341-4002
◆ **EMP:** 60
SIC: 8741 Management services

(G-14828)
PITT-OHIO EXPRESS LLC
5000 Duff Dr (45246-1309)
PHONE................513 860-3424
Brant Actin, *Mgr*
EMP: 270
SALES (corp-wide): 508.23MM **Privately Held**
Web: www.pittohioexpress.com
SIC: 4213 4212 Contract haulers; Local trucking, without storage
PA: Pitt-Ohio Express, Llc
   15 27th St
   Pittsburgh PA 15222
   412 232-3015

(G-14829)
QUALITY ASSOCIATES INC
9842 International Blvd (45246-4852)
PHONE................513 242-4477
▲ **EMP:** 300
SIC: 7389 7361 Packaging and labeling services; Employment agencies

(G-14830)
RECKER AND BOERGER INC
Also Called: Recker & Boerger Appliances
10115 Transportation Way (45246-1317)
PHONE................513 942-9663
Allen Boerger, *CEO*
Steven A Boerger, *
Jim Recker, *
▲ **EMP:** 100 **EST:** 1962
SALES (est): 24.63MM **Privately Held**
Web: www.reckerandboergerhomeappliance.com
SIC: 5722 1711 Electric household appliances, major; Warm air heating and air conditioning contractor

(G-14831)
RESOLUTE INDUSTRIAL LLC
Also Called: Mobile Air and Power Rentals
9950 Commerce Park Dr (45246-1332)
PHONE................513 779-7909
Chad Swain, *Mgr*
EMP: 39
SALES (corp-wide): 2.14B **Privately Held**
Web: www.mobileair.com
SIC: 7359 5075 Equipment rental and leasing, nec; Warm air heating equipment and supplies
HQ: Resolute Industrial, Llc
   298 Messner Dr
   Wheeling IL 60090
   800 537-9675

(G-14832)
SEXTON INDUSTRIAL INC
366 Circle Freeway Dr (45246-1208)
PHONE................513 530-5555
Abbe Sexton, *Pr*
Ron Sexton, *
Dan Towne, *
EMP: 150 **EST:** 1998
SQ FT: 85,000
SALES (est): 20.08MM **Privately Held**
Web: www.artisanmechanical.com
SIC: 1711 3443 Mechanical contractor; Industrial vessels, tanks, and containers

(G-14833)
STAR DISTRIBUTION AND MFG LLC
Also Called: Star Manufacturring
10179 Commerce Park Dr (45246-1335)
PHONE................513 860-3573
Mario Listo, *Pr*
Bob Hinkle, *
EMP: 48 **EST:** 2009
SALES (est): 8.33MM **Privately Held**
Web: www.starmanufacture.com
SIC: 3613 8711 8742 Control panels, electric ; Engineering services; Management engineering

(G-14834)
STOROPACK INC (DH)
Also Called: Foam Pac Materials Company
4758 Devitt Dr (45246-1106)
PHONE................513 874-0314
Hans Reichenecker, *Ch Bd*
Daniel Wachter, *
Gregg Battaglia, *
Joe Lagrasta, *
Lester Whisnant, *
▲ **EMP:** 50 **EST:** 1978
SQ FT: 35,000
SALES (est): 152.02MM
SALES (corp-wide): 635.28MM **Privately Held**
Web: www.storopack.us
SIC: 5199 3086 2671 Packaging materials; Packaging and shipping materials, foamed plastics; Paper; coated and laminated packaging
HQ: Storopack Hans Reichenecker Gmbh
   Untere Rietstr. 30
   Metzingen BW 72555
   71231640

(G-14835)
SUPERIOR ENVMTL SLTONS SES INC
Also Called: S E S
9976 Joseph James Dr (45246-1340)
PHONE................513 874-6910
Chester Yeager, *Brnch Mgr*
EMP: 143
SALES (corp-wide): 108.19MM **Privately Held**
Web: www.sesinc.com
SIC: 8999 Earth science services
PA: Superior Environmental Solutions Llc
   9996 Joseph James Dr
   West Chester OH 45246
   513 874-8355

(G-14836)
SUPERIOR ENVMTL SOLUTIONS LLC (PA)
Also Called: SES
9996 Joseph James Dr (45246-1340)
PHONE................513 874-8355
Dean Wallace, *Pr*
Chester Yeager, *
EMP: 95 **EST:** 1998
SQ FT: 10,000
SALES (est): 108.19MM
SALES (corp-wide): 108.19MM **Privately Held**
Web: www.sesinc.com
SIC: 4959 Environmental cleanup services

(G-14837)
T&T ENTERPRISES OF OHIO INC
5100 Duff Dr (45246-1311)
PHONE................513 942-1141
Eric Trautman Senior, *CEO*
Eric O Trautman Senior, *CEO*
EMP: 42 **EST:** 1996
SQ FT: 8,500
SALES (est): 26.24MM **Privately Held**
Web: www.ttohio.com
SIC: 4212 Mail carriers, contract

(G-14838)
TAYLOR DISTRIBUTING COMPANY
9756 International Blvd (45246-4854)
PHONE................513 771-1850
Rex Taylor, *Pr*
John A Taylor, *
James B Taylor, *
Drew Taylor, *
▲ **EMP:** 80 **EST:** 1850
SALES (est): 17.45MM **Privately Held**
Web: www.taylordistributing.com
SIC: 4213 Trucking, except local

(G-14839)
TAYLOR LOGISTICS INC (PA)
9756 International Blvd (45246-4854)
PHONE................513 771-1850
John Taylor, *Pr*
Rex C Taylor, *Pr*

West Chester - Hamilton County (G-14840)   GEOGRAPHIC SECTION

John A Taylor, *Prin*
EMP: 67 **EST:** 2002
SQ FT: 192,000
SALES (est): 61.55MM **Privately Held**
Web: www.taylorlogistics.com
SIC: 4731 Transportation agents and brokers

(G-14840)
TAYLOR WAREHOUSE CORPORATION (PA)
9756 International Blvd (45246)
PHONE.................513 771-1850
John A Taylor, *CEO*
John A Taylor, *Pr*
Grant Taylor, *
Noelle Taylor, *
EMP: 32 **EST:** 1972
SQ FT: 192,000
SALES (est): 2.12MM
SALES (corp-wide): 2.12MM **Privately Held**
Web: www.taylorlogistics.com
SIC: 4225 General warehousing

(G-14841)
TCCC INC (PA)
Also Called: Unique Lawn Care
9624 Cincinnati Columbus Rd (45241-4123)
PHONE.................513 779-1111
Tim Neichter, *Pr*
EMP: 32 **EST:** 2003
SALES (est): 2.37MM **Privately Held**
Web: www.unique-lawncare.com
SIC: 0782 Lawn care services

(G-14842)
UNITED GROUP SERVICES INC (PA)
9740 Near Dr (45246-1013)
PHONE.................800 633-9690
Mark Mosley, *Stockholder*
Daniel Freese, *
Kevin Sell, *
Don Mattingly, *
EMP: 200 **EST:** 1982
SQ FT: 45,500
SALES (est): 39.18MM
SALES (corp-wide): 39.18MM **Privately Held**
Web: www.united-gs.com
SIC: 3498 1711 Fabricated pipe and fittings; Process piping contractor

(G-14843)
US FOODS INC
5445 Spellmire Dr (45246-4842)
PHONE.................614 539-7993
Ron Jordon, *Mgr*
EMP: 36
Web: www.usfoods.com
SIC: 5141 5149 5148 5143 Food brokers; Groceries and related products, nec; Fresh fruits and vegetables; Dairy products, except dried or canned
HQ: Us Foods, Inc.
9399 W Higgins Rd Ste 500
Rosemont IL 60018

(G-14844)
VERST GROUP LOGISTICS INC
9696 International Blvd (45246-4859)
PHONE.................859 379-1230
Jeff Antrobus, *Brnch Mgr*
EMP: 55
SALES (corp-wide): 183.56MM **Privately Held**
Web: www.verstlogistics.com
SIC: 4225 4731 8741 General warehousing; Freight transportation arrangement; Management services
PA: Verst Group Logistics, Inc.

300 Shorland Dr
Walton KY 41094
859 485-1212

(G-14845)
VOLPENHEIN BROTHERS ELECTRIC INC
474 W Crescentville Rd (45246-1221)
PHONE.................513 385-9355
EMP: 75 **EST:** 1987
SALES (est): 14.43MM **Privately Held**
Web: www.vbe.cc
SIC: 1731 General electrical contractor

(G-14846)
XPO LOGISTICS FREIGHT INC
5289 Duff Dr (45246-1330)
PHONE.................513 870-0044
Donald Gallam, *Mgr*
EMP: 96
SALES (corp-wide): 7.74B **Publicly Held**
Web: www.xpo.com
SIC: 4213 4212 Contract haulers; Local trucking, without storage
HQ: Xpo Logistics Freight, Inc.
2211 Old Erhart Rd Ste 10
Ann Arbor MI 48105
800 755-2728

West Jefferson
Madison County

(G-14847)
AMPLIFYBIO LLC (PA)
1425 Plain-City Georgesville Rd (43162)
PHONE.................833 641-2006
J Kelly Ganjei, *Pr*
Harry Ledebur, *VP*
Roy Barnewall, *Dir*
EMP: 67 **EST:** 2021
SALES (est): 43.81MM
SALES (corp-wide): 43.81MM **Privately Held**
Web: www.amplify-bio.com
SIC: 8731 Biotechnological research, commercial

(G-14848)
ARBORS WEST LLC
Also Called: ARBORS WEST SUBACUTE & REHABIL
375 W Main St (43162-1298)
PHONE.................614 879-7661
Alison Morris, *Admn*
EMP: 40 **EST:** 1968
SQ FT: 50,000
SALES (est): 6.36MM **Privately Held**
Web: www.arborswest.com
SIC: 8059 8051 Nursing home, except skilled and intermediate care facility; Skilled nursing care facilities

(G-14849)
CJ LOGSTICS HOLDINGS AMER CORP
Also Called: CJ LOGISTICS HOLDINGS AMERICA CORPORATION
125 Enterprise Pkwy (43162-9414)
PHONE.................614 879-9659
Rick Emerson, *Brnch Mgr*
EMP: 55
Web: america.cjlogistics.com
SIC: 4225 4213 4212 4731 General warehousing and storage; Trucking, except local; Local trucking, without storage; Freight consolidation
HQ: Cj Logistics America, Llc
1750 S Wolf Rd
Des Plaines IL 60018

(G-14850)
FC COMPASSUS LLC
Also Called: Compassus- W Jefferson Hospice
487 W Main St Ste B (43162-1178)
PHONE.................380 207-1526
EMP: 49
SALES (corp-wide): 47.41MM **Privately Held**
Web: www.compassus.com
SIC: 8052 Personal care facility
PA: Fc Compassus, Llc
10 Cadillac Dr Ste 400
Brentwood TN 37027
615 224-8028

(G-14851)
FISHER CAST STEEL PRODUCTS INC (PA)
6 W Town St (43162-1293)
P.O. Box 1368 (43015-8368)
PHONE.................614 879-8325
John Harmeyer, *Pr*
Vira Maruli, *
Max Robbins, *
Richard Metcalf, *
▲ **EMP:** 42 **EST:** 1956
SQ FT: 800
SALES (est): 13.91MM
SALES (corp-wide): 13.91MM **Privately Held**
Web: www.fishercaststeel.com
SIC: 5051 Steel

(G-14852)
FORREST TRUCKING COMPANY
540 Taylor Blair Rd (43162-9718)
PHONE.................614 879-8642
Ace Forrest, *Brnch Mgr*
EMP: 41
SALES (corp-wide): 3.77MM **Privately Held**
Web: www.forresttrucking.com
SIC: 4212 Dump truck haulage
PA: Forrest Trucking Company
7 E 1st St
London OH 43140
614 879-7347

(G-14853)
TOAGOSEI AMERICA INC
Also Called: Krazy Glue
1450 W Main St (43162-9730)
PHONE.................614 718-3855
Tatsuo Mishio, *Pr*
Toshio Nakao, *
▲ **EMP:** 100 **EST:** 1989
SQ FT: 64,000
SALES (est): 37.06MM **Privately Held**
Web: www.aronalpha.net
SIC: 5169 2891 Chemicals and allied products, nec; Adhesives
PA: Toagosei Co., Ltd.
1-14-1, Nishishimbashi
Minato-Ku TKY 105-0

(G-14854)
UTI CORP
Also Called: Utility Technologies Intl
2685 Plain City Georgesville Rd Ne (43162)
PHONE.................614 879-7316
Richard Dickerson, *CEO*
◆ **EMP:** 80 **EST:** 1999
SALES (est): 2.02MM **Privately Held**
Web: www.uti-corp.com
SIC: 8711 Consulting engineer

West Lafayette
Coshocton County

(G-14855)
BRASSBOYS ENTERPRISES INC
Also Called: Hickory Flat Golf Course
54188 Township Road 155 (43845-9501)
PHONE.................740 545-7796
Ed Berkshire, *Mgr*
EMP: 29
SQ FT: 20,000
SALES (corp-wide): 2.07MM **Privately Held**
SIC: 7992 Public golf courses
PA: Brassboys Enterprises, Inc.
98 Elizabeth St
Newcomerstown OH 43832
740 498-7202

(G-14856)
GENTLEBROOK INC
21990 Orchard St (43845-9613)
PHONE.................740 545-7487
Mike Sleutz, *Brnch Mgr*
EMP: 138
SALES (corp-wide): 21.11MM **Privately Held**
Web: www.gentlebrook.org
SIC: 1521 Single-family housing construction
PA: Gentlebrook, Inc.
880 Sunnyside St Sw
Hartville OH 44632
330 877-3694

(G-14857)
JONES METAL PRODUCTS COMPANY
Jones-Zylon Company
305 N Center St (43845-1001)
PHONE.................740 545-6341
EMP: 40
SALES (corp-wide): 11MM **Privately Held**
SIC: 5047 3842 Hospital equipment and supplies, nec; Surgical appliances and supplies
PA: Jones Metal Products Company Llc
200 N Center St
West Lafayette OH 43845
740 545-6381

(G-14858)
RIDGEWOOD GOVERNMENT SVCS LLC
21190 County Road 151 (43845-9739)
PHONE.................740 294-7261
EMP: 49 **EST:** 2011
SALES (est): 1.21MM **Privately Held**
SIC: 8741 Management services

West Liberty
Logan County

(G-14859)
ADRIEL SCHOOL INC (PA)
Also Called: ADRIEL
414 N Detroit St (43357-9690)
P.O. Box 188 (43357-0188)
PHONE.................937 465-0010
Michael Mullins, *CEO*
EMP: 100 **EST:** 1896
SQ FT: 60,000
SALES (est): 529.65K
SALES (corp-wide): 529.65K **Privately Held**
Web: www.adriel.org

SIC: 8361 8063 8211 Emotionally disturbed home; Mental hospital, except for the mentally retarded; Private special education school

(G-14860)
MARY RUTAN HOSPITAL
Also Called: Mad River Family Practice
381 Township Road 191 (43357-9534)
PHONE..................................937 599-1411
Harry L Graber, *Brnch Mgr*
EMP: 42
SALES (corp-wide): 329.98K Privately Held
Web: www.maryrutan.org
SIC: 8062 General medical and surgical hospitals
HQ: Mary Rutan Hospital
205 E Palmer Rd
Bellefontaine OH 43311
937 592-4015

(G-14861)
OHIO CAVERNS INC
Also Called: Ohio Caverns
2210 State Route 245 E (43357-9779)
PHONE..................................937 465-4017
Eric Evans, *Pr*
EMP: 28 EST: 1963
SQ FT: 3,600
SALES (est): 876.14K Privately Held
Web: www.ohiocaverns.com
SIC: 7999 Cave operation

West Mansfield
Logan County

(G-14862)
DAYLAY EGG FARM INC
11177 Township Road 133 (43358-9709)
PHONE..................................937 355-6531
Kurt Lausecker, *Pr*
▲ EMP: 135 EST: 1978
SQ FT: 3,200
SALES (est): 4.93MM Privately Held
SIC: 0252 2015 Chicken eggs; Poultry slaughtering and processing

West Salem
Wayne County

(G-14863)
JOHNSON BROS RUBBER CO (PA)
42 W Buckeye St (44287-9747)
P.O. Box 812 (44287-0812)
PHONE..................................419 853-4122
Lawrence G Cooke, *Pr*
Eric Vail, *
◆ EMP: 100 EST: 1947
SQ FT: 70,000
SALES (est): 21.76MM
SALES (corp-wide): 21.76MM Privately Held
Web: www.johnsonbrosrubbercompany.com
SIC: 5199 3061 Foams and rubber; Mechanical rubber goods

West Union
Adams County

(G-14864)
ADAMS - BROWN COUNTIES
Also Called: Adams - Brown Counties Economic Opportunities, Inc
95 Trefz Rd (45693-9613)
PHONE..................................937 544-2650
Dan Wickerham, *Brnch Mgr*
EMP: 37
SALES (corp-wide): 19.1MM Privately Held
Web: www.abcap.net
SIC: 4953 Recycling, waste materials
PA: Adams & Brown Counties Economic Opportunities, Inc.
406 W Plum St
Georgetown OH 45121
937 378-6041

(G-14865)
ADAMS COUNTY REGIONAL MED CTR
11110 State Rte 41 (45693-8806)
PHONE..................................937 900-2316
Bill May, *CEO*
EMP: 250 EST: 1951
SQ FT: 94,600
SALES (est): 41.13MM Privately Held
Web: www.acrmc.com
SIC: 8062 General medical and surgical hospitals

(G-14866)
AREA AGENCY ON AGING DST 7 INC
123 W Main St (45693-1303)
PHONE..................................740 245-5306
Barbara Bond, *Prin*
EMP: 73
SALES (corp-wide): 63.29MM Privately Held
Web: www.aaa7.org
SIC: 8322 Senior citizens' center or association
PA: Area Agency On Aging District 7, Inc.
160 Dorsey Dr
Rio Grande OH 45674
800 582-7277

(G-14867)
CLAYTON RAILROAD CNSTR LLC
500 Lane Rd (45693-9440)
PHONE..................................937 549-2952
Jim Mcadams, *Pr*
Jim Mcadams Junior, *Superintnt*
Bob Staun, *
EMP: 40 EST: 2008
SQ FT: 1,000
SALES (est): 7.79MM Privately Held
Web: www.claytonrailroad.com
SIC: 1622 Bridge construction

(G-14868)
COUNTY OF ADAMS
Also Called: Children Services
300 N Wilson Dr (45693-1157)
PHONE..................................937 544-5067
Jill Wright, *Dir*
EMP: 36
SALES (corp-wide): 42.54MM Privately Held
Web: www.adamscountyoh.gov
SIC: 8322 Child related social services
PA: County Of Adams
11260 State Route 41
West Union OH 45693
937 544-3286

(G-14869)
EAGLE CREEK HLTHCARE GROUP INC
Also Called: Eagle Creek Nursing Center
141 Spruce Ln (45693-8807)
PHONE..................................937 544-5631
George S Repchick, *Pr*
William I Weisberg, *
EMP: 394 EST: 1982
SQ FT: 15,551
SALES (est): 6.03MM
SALES (corp-wide): 655.44MM Privately Held
Web: www.saberhealth.com
SIC: 8051 8052 Skilled nursing care facilities ; Intermediate care facilities
PA: Saber Healthcare Group, L.L.C.
23700 Commerce Park
Beachwood OH 44122
216 292-5706

(G-14870)
H & G NURSING HOMES INC
Also Called: Adams County Manor
10856 State Route 41 (45693-9671)
PHONE..................................937 544-2205
John Houser, *Pr*
Ben Houser, *VP*
EMP: 72 EST: 1953
SQ FT: 6,700
SALES (est): 4.99MM Privately Held
Web: www.hg-nh.com
SIC: 8052 8051 Personal care facility; Skilled nursing care facilities

(G-14871)
OAKDALE ESTATES II INV LLC
310 Rice Dr (45693-9545)
PHONE..................................216 520-1250
EMP: 99 EST: 2016
SALES (est): 2.36MM Privately Held
Web: www.oakdalesenior.com
SIC: 6799 Investors, nec

(G-14872)
SHAWNEE MENTAL HEALTH CTR INC
192 Chestnut Ridge Rd (45693-9584)
PHONE..................................937 544-5581
Gerorg Staker, *Dir*
EMP: 34
SALES (corp-wide): 15.31MM Privately Held
Web: www.shawneefamilyhealthcenter.com
SIC: 8093 8399 Mental health clinic, outpatient; Health systems agency
PA: Shawnee Mental Health Center, Inc.
901 Washington St
Portsmouth OH
740 354-7702

(G-14873)
SOUTHERN OHIO MEDICAL CENTER
90 Cic Blvd (45693-8024)
PHONE..................................937 544-8989
EMP: 112
SALES (corp-wide): 546.1MM Privately Held
Web: www.somc.org
SIC: 8062 General medical and surgical hospitals
PA: Southern Ohio Medical Center
1805 27th St
Portsmouth OH 45662
740 354-5000

West Unity
Williams County

(G-14874)
CONVERSION TECH INTL INC
700 Oak St (43570-9457)
PHONE..................................419 924-5566
Chester Cromwell, *Pr*
Jason Cromwell, *
▲ EMP: 33 EST: 1999
SQ FT: 130,000
SALES (est): 5.3MM Privately Held
Web: www.conversiontechnologies.com
SIC: 2891 7389 Adhesives; Laminating service

(G-14875)
THREE-D TRANSPORT INC
14237 Us Highway 127 (43570-9799)
PHONE..................................419 924-5368
Daniel Meyers, *Pr*
Debra Meyers, *
EMP: 40 EST: 1995
SQ FT: 15,200
SALES (est): 2.52MM Privately Held
SIC: 4213 Trucking, except local

Westerville
Delaware County

(G-14876)
ABB INC
Also Called: ABB Industrial Systems
579 Executive Campus Dr Frnt (43082-9801)
PHONE..................................614 818-6300
Roger Billy, *Brnch Mgr*
EMP: 122
Web: www.abb.com
SIC: 5063 Power transmission equipment, electric
HQ: Abb Inc.
305 Gregson Dr
Cary NC 27511

(G-14877)
AMERICAN CERAMIC SOCIETY (PA)
550 Polaris Pkwy Ste 510 (43082-7132)
PHONE..................................614 890-4700
Mark Mecklenborg, *Ex Dir*
Michael Johnson, *
EMP: 35 EST: 1900
SQ FT: 10,126
SALES (est): 9.32MM
SALES (corp-wide): 9.32MM Privately Held
Web: www.ceramics.org
SIC: 2721 8621 Periodicals, publishing and printing; Scientific membership association

(G-14878)
BANC AMER PRCTICE SLUTIONS INC
600 N Cleveland Ave Ste 300 (43082-6920)
PHONE..................................614 794-8247
EMP: 98 EST: 1996
SQ FT: 115,000
SALES (est): 3.52MM
SALES (corp-wide): 171.91B Publicly Held
SIC: 6021 National commercial banks
PA: Bank Of America Corporation
100 N Tryon St
Charlotte NC 28202
704 386-5681

(G-14879)
CENTER FOR SRGCAL DRMTLOGY INC
Also Called: Center For Srgcal Drmtlogy Drm
428 County Line Rd W (43082-7294)
PHONE..................................614 847-4100
Ronald J Siegle, *Pr*
Peter C Seline, *
Brian P Biernat, *
EMP: 43 EST: 2001
SQ FT: 19,200
SALES (est): 6.03MM Privately Held
Web: www.centerforsurgicaldermatology.com
SIC: 8011 Dermatologist

Westerville - Delaware County (G-14880) — GEOGRAPHIC SECTION

(G-14880)
CENTRAL OHIO PRMRY CARE PHYSCA
Also Called: Northside Internal Medicine
400 Altair Pkwy (43082-7652)
PHONE.................................614 882-0708
EMP: 65
Web: www.copcp.com
SIC: 8011 8999 Internal medicine practitioners; Physics consultant
PA: Central Ohio Primary Care Physicians, Inc.
655 Africa Rd
Westerville OH 43082

(G-14881)
CENTRAL OHIO PRMRY CARE PHYSCA
507 Executive Campus Dr Ste 160 (43082-9838)
PHONE.................................614 891-9505
Katrina Tansky, Brnch Mgr
EMP: 36
Web: www.copcp.com
SIC: 8011 General and family practice, physician/surgeon
PA: Central Ohio Primary Care Physicians, Inc.
655 Africa Rd
Westerville OH 43082

(G-14882)
CENTRAL OHIO PRMRY CARE PHYSCA (PA)
Also Called: Central Ohio Primary Care
655 Africa Rd (43082-9808)
PHONE.................................614 326-2672
EMP: 60 EST: 1994
SALES (est): 106.55MM Privately Held
Web: www.copcp.com
SIC: 8011 General and family practice, physician/surgeon

(G-14883)
COMPRHNSIVE EYCARE CNTL OHIO I
Also Called: Landis, Gregory C Od
450 Alkyre Run Ste 100 (43082-6910)
PHONE.................................614 890-5692
George Chioran Md, Pr
Steve Suh Md, VP
EMP: 38 EST: 1975
SQ FT: 2,000
SALES (est): 5.23MM Privately Held
Web: www.compeyecare.com
SIC: 8011 Opthalmologist

(G-14884)
COPCP
570 Polaris Pkwy Ste 200 (43082-7901)
PHONE.................................614 865-6570
J William Wulf, Prin
EMP: 37 EST: 2010
SALES (est): 978.95K Privately Held
Web: www.copcp.com
SIC: 8011 General and family practice, physician/surgeon

(G-14885)
COTTER HOUSE WORTHINGTON LLC
470 Olde Worthington Rd Ste 100 (43082-8985)
PHONE.................................614 540-2414
Donald R Kenney Junior, Mgr
EMP: 56 EST: 2018
SALES (est): 5.51MM Privately Held
Web: www.cotterhouseworthington.com
SIC: 8059 Nursing home, except skilled and intermediate care facility

(G-14886)
CSC INSURANCE AGENCY INC
Also Called: Pro Century
550 Polaris Pkwy Ste 300 (43082-7113)
P.O. Box 163340 (43216-3340)
PHONE.................................614 895-2000
Chrisopher J Timm, CEO
EMP: 101 EST: 1984
SQ FT: 16,000
SALES (est): 2.09MM
SALES (corp-wide): 439.84K Privately Held
Web: www.centurysurety.com
SIC: 6411 Insurance brokers, nec
HQ: Century Surety Company
465 N Cleveland Ave
Westerville OH 43082
614 895-2000

(G-14887)
D L RYAN COMPANIES LLC
Also Called: Ryan Partnership
440 Polaris Pkwy Ste 350 (43082-6999)
PHONE.................................614 436-6558
Peter Tamapoll, Prin
EMP: 68
SIC: 8743 8742 Sales promotion; Marketing consulting services
HQ: D. L. Ryan Companies, Llc
10 Westport Rd Unit 10 # 10
Wilton CT 06897
203 210-3000

(G-14888)
DEVCARE SOLUTIONS LTD
579 Executive Campus Dr Ste 370 (43082-9847)
PHONE.................................614 221-2277
Janaki Thiru, Pr
Ramkumar Regupathy, *
EMP: 47 EST: 2005
SQ FT: 600
SALES (est): 7.32MM Privately Held
Web: www.devcare.com
SIC: 8748 7371 7373 Systems engineering consultant, ex. computer or professional; Custom computer programming services; Systems engineering, computer related

(G-14889)
DHL EXPRESS (USA) INC
570 Polaris Pkwy Ste 110 (43082-7902)
PHONE.................................614 865-8325
Nick Kaufman, Brnch Mgr
EMP: 42
SALES (corp-wide): 88.87B Privately Held
SIC: 4731 Freight forwarding
HQ: Dhl Express (Usa), Inc.
16592 Collections Ctr Dr
Chicago IL 60693
954 888-7000

(G-14890)
DHL INFRMTION SVCS AMRICAS INC (HQ)
550 Polaris Pkwy (43082-7045)
PHONE.................................614 865-5993
Frank Appel, CEO
EMP: 27 EST: 2007
SALES (est): 3.55MM
SALES (corp-wide): 88.87B Privately Held
SIC: 7371 Custom computer programming services
PA: Deutsche Post Ag
Charles-De-Gaulle-Str. 20
Bonn NW 53113
2281820

(G-14891)
DONALD R KENNEY & CO RLTY LLC (PA)
Also Called: Triangle Commercial Properties
470 Olde Worthington Rd Ste 101 (43082-8986)
PHONE.................................614 540-2404
Donald R Kenney, Owner
Andy Diblasi, Prin
EMP: 50 EST: 1968
SQ FT: 5,000
SALES (est): 21.74MM
SALES (corp-wide): 21.74MM Privately Held
Web: www.drk-realty.com
SIC: 1522 Apartment building construction

(G-14892)
EXEL HOLDINGS (USA) INC (DH)
570 Polaris Pkwy Ste 110 (43082-7902)
PHONE.................................614 865-8500
Scott Sureddin, CEO
Jose Fernando Nava, *
Tim Sprosty, *
Lynn Anderson, *
Scot Hofacker, *
◆ EMP: 200 EST: 1984
SALES (est): 1.32B
SALES (corp-wide): 88.87B Privately Held
Web: www.exel.com
SIC: 4226 4213 Special warehousing and storage, nec; Household goods transport
HQ: Exel Limited
Solstice House
Milton Keynes BUCKS MK9 1
134 430-2000

(G-14893)
EXEL INC (DH)
Also Called: Dhl Supply Chain USA
360 Westar Blvd 4th Fl (43082-7627)
PHONE.................................614 865-5819
Scott Sureddin, CEO
Scot Hofacker, *
Tim Sprosty, *
Scott Cubbler, OF LIFE SCIENCES & HEALTHCARE*
Luis Eraa, OF THE Technology Business UNIT*
◆ EMP: 500 EST: 1983
SALES (est): 1.32B
SALES (corp-wide): 88.87B Privately Held
Web: www.onestoporderform.com
SIC: 4213 4225 4581 Trucking, except local; General warehousing; Air freight handling at airports
HQ: Exel Holdings (Usa) Inc.
570 Polaris Pkwy Ste 110
Westerville OH 43082
614 865-8500

(G-14894)
EXEL INC
Also Called: Genesis Logistics
570 Polaris Pkwy Ste 110 (43082-7902)
PHONE.................................614 865-8294
Brian Locasto, Brnch Mgr
EMP: 30
SALES (corp-wide): 88.87B Privately Held
Web: www.onestoporderform.com
SIC: 4731 Freight forwarding
HQ: Exel Inc.
360 Westar Blvd Fl 4
Westerville OH 43082
614 865-5819

(G-14895)
FERIDEAN COMMONS LLC
6885 Freeman Rd (43082-9113)
PHONE.................................614 898-7488
Fred H Powrie Iii, Managing Member
EMP: 45 EST: 1998
SQ FT: 1,748
SALES (est): 4.93MM Privately Held
Web: www.feridean.com
SIC: 8361 Aged home

(G-14896)
GERBIG SNELL/WEISHEIMER ADVERTISING LLC
Also Called: Gsw Worldwide
500 Olde Worthington Rd (43082-8913)
PHONE.................................614 848-4848
EMP: 290 EST: 2001
SALES (est): 51.25MM
SALES (corp-wide): 5.39B Privately Held
Web: www.gsw-w.com
SIC: 7311 Advertising agencies
HQ: Syneos Health Communications, Inc.
500 Olde Worthington Rd
Westerville OH 43082
614 543-6650

(G-14897)
GRACE BRTHREN CH COLUMBUS OHIO (PA)
Also Called: Grace Polaris Church
8724 Olde Worthington Rd (43082-8840)
P.O. Box 1650 (43086-1650)
PHONE.................................614 888-7733
Michael L Yoder, Lead Pastor
James Augspurger, Executive Pastor*
James S Kanzeg, *
EMP: 27 EST: 1964
SALES (est): 9.05MM
SALES (corp-wide): 9.05MM Privately Held
Web: www.gracepolaris.org
SIC: 8661 8351 Brethren Church; Child day care services

(G-14898)
HAWA INCORPORATED (PA)
570 Polaris Pkwy (43082-7900)
PHONE.................................614 451-1711
Douglas S Coffey, Pr
Chris A Pore, *
Neb Heminger, *
EMP: 29 EST: 1954
SALES (est): 5.23MM
SALES (corp-wide): 5.23MM Privately Held
Web: www.hawainc.com
SIC: 8711 Consulting engineer

(G-14899)
HOWARD WERSHBALE & CO
460 Polaris Pkwy # 310 (43082-8212)
PHONE.................................614 794-8710
John Vidmar, Prin
EMP: 37
Web: www.hwco.cpa
SIC: 8721 Certified public accountant
PA: Howard, Wershbale & Co.
28601 Chagrin Blvd # 210
Woodmere OH 44122

(G-14900)
INTEGRATED WHSE SOLUTIONS INC
Also Called: Columbus Foam Products
700 Northfield Rd (43082-9394)
PHONE.................................614 899-5080
EMP: 45
SALES (corp-wide): 11.51B Privately Held
Web: www.bluffmanufacturing.com
SIC: 7641 Reupholstery
HQ: Integrated Warehouse Solutions, Inc.
651 N Burleson Blvd
Burleson TX 76028
817 293-3018

Westerville - Delaware County

(G-14901)
JUDGE GROUP INC
440 Polaris Pkwy Ste 290 (43082-7987)
PHONE..............................614 891-8337
EMP: 59
SALES (corp-wide): 684.46MM **Privately Held**
Web: www.judge.com
SIC: 7361 Executive placement
PA: The Judge Group Inc
151 S Warner Rd Ste 100
Wayne PA 19087
610 667-7700

(G-14902)
JULIAN & GRUBE INC
Also Called: Trimble & Julian
333 County Line Rd W Ste A (43082-6908)
PHONE..............................614 846-1899
EMP: 50 **EST:** 1995
SQ FT: 4,000
SALES (est): 4.17MM **Privately Held**
Web: www.jginc.biz
SIC: 8721 Certified public accountant

(G-14903)
KLEINGERS GROUP INC
350 Worthington Rd (43082-8327)
PHONE..............................614 882-4311
Steven R Korte, *Mgr*
EMP: 53
Web: www.kleingers.com
SIC: 8711 Civil engineering
PA: The Kleingers Group Inc
6219 Centre Park Dr
West Chester OH 45069

(G-14904)
LAKES GOLF & COUNTRY CLUB INC
6740 Worthington Rd (43082-9491)
PHONE..............................614 882-2582
Tod Ortlip, *Pr*
Jay Ortlip, *
Leigh Allen, *
Jim Spragg, *
EMP: 50 **EST:** 1990
SQ FT: 40,000
SALES (est): 9.29MM **Privately Held**
Web: www.lakesclub.com
SIC: 7997 Country club, membership

(G-14905)
LAUREL HEALTH CARE COMPANY (HQ)
8181 Worthington Rd Uppr (43082-8071)
PHONE..............................614 794-8800
Bradford Payne, *Pr*
Jack Alcott, *
Timothy Patton, *
Barbara Lombardi, *
Carol Bailey, *
EMP: 67 **EST:** 1992
SALES (est): 271.43MM **Privately Held**
Web: www.cienahealthcare.com
SIC: 8051 Skilled nursing care facilities
PA: Laurel Health Care Company Of North Worthing
8181 Worthington Rd
Westerville OH 43082

(G-14906)
LAUREL HLTH CARE BATTLE CREEK (HQ)
Also Called: Laurels of Bedford, The
8181 Worthington Rd (43082-8067)
PHONE..............................614 794-8800
Thomas Franke, *Owner*
Dennis Sherman, *
Kevin Belew, *
James Franke, *
Jack Alcott, *VP Opers*
EMP: 40 **EST:** 1973
SALES (est): 24.13MM **Privately Held**
Web: www.cienahealthcare.com
SIC: 8051 Skilled nursing care facilities
PA: Laurel Health Care Company Of North Worthing
8181 Worthington Rd
Westerville OH 43082

(G-14907)
LAUREL HLTH CARE OF MT PLASANT (HQ)
Also Called: Laurels of Mt Pleasant
8181 Worthington Rd Lower 2 (43082-8067)
PHONE..............................614 794-8800
Thomas Franke, *Ch*
Dennis Sherman, *
Kevin Belew, *
James Franke, *
Jack Alcott, *VP Opers*
EMP: 63 **EST:** 1962
SALES (est): 25.71MM **Privately Held**
Web: www.cienahealthcare.com
SIC: 8051 Convalescent home with continuous nursing care
PA: Laurel Health Care Company Of North Worthing
8181 Worthington Rd
Westerville OH 43082

(G-14908)
MARZETTI MANUFACTURING COMPANY (DH)
380 Polaris Pkwy Ste 400 (43082-8069)
PHONE..............................856 205-1485
Lenny Amorso Junior, *Pr*
EMP: 115 **EST:** 2018
SALES (est): 133.47MM
SALES (corp-wide): 1.82B **Publicly Held**
Web: www.marzetti.com
SIC: 5149 Bakery products
HQ: T.Marzetti Company
380 Polaris Pkwy Ste 400
Westerville OH 43082
614 846-2232

(G-14909)
MEDALLION CLUB (PA)
5000 Club Dr (43082-9551)
PHONE..............................614 794-6999
Tateo Tanigawa, *Pr*
EMP: 120 **EST:** 1991
SQ FT: 57,000
SALES (est): 11.37MM
SALES (corp-wide): 11.37MM **Privately Held**
Web: www.medallionclub.com
SIC: 7997 7991 5941 5813 Country club, membership; Physical fitness facilities; Sporting goods and bicycle shops; Drinking places

(G-14910)
MODERN MEDICAL INC
250 Progressive Way (43082-9615)
P.O. Box 549 (43035-0549)
PHONE..............................800 547-3330
Joseph G Favazzo, *Pr*
Raymond Black, *
EMP: 130 **EST:** 1986
SQ FT: 40,000
SALES (est): 21.87MM
SALES (corp-wide): 371.62B **Publicly Held**
Web: workcompauto.optum.com
SIC: 5999 5912 5047 Medical apparatus and supplies; Drug stores and proprietary stores; Medical and hospital equipment
HQ: Healthcare Solutions, Inc.
175 Kelsey Ln
Tampa FL 33619

(G-14911)
MON HEALTH CARE INC (HQ)
Also Called: Mon Healthcare
375 N West St (43082-1400)
PHONE..............................304 285-2700
Darryl Duncan, *Pr*
Darryl Duncan, *Pr*
Nicholas Grubbs, *CFO*
Mike Deprospero, *Sec*
EMP: 30 **EST:** 1985
SALES (est): 13.14MM
SALES (corp-wide): 19.41MM **Privately Held**
Web: www.monhealth.com
SIC: 8051 Skilled nursing care facilities
PA: Grafton City Hospital Inc.
1 Hospital Plz
Grafton WV 26354
304 265-0400

(G-14912)
MOUNT CARMEL HEALTH
444 N Cleveland Ave Ste 220 (43082-8387)
PHONE..............................614 234-4060
EMP: 119
SALES (corp-wide): 2.49B **Privately Held**
Web: www.mountcarmelhealth.com
SIC: 8322 8049 8011 Rehabilitation services; Physical therapist; Sports medicine specialist, physician
HQ: Mount Carmel Health
5300 N Meadows Dr
Grove City OH 43123
614 234-5000

(G-14913)
MPOWER INC
548 Chestnut Ave (43082-6050)
PHONE..............................614 783-0478
Dejuante Mckee, *Pr*
EMP: 30 **EST:** 2005
SALES (est): 3.15MM **Privately Held**
SIC: 1542 Nonresidential construction, nec

(G-14914)
NATIONAL AUTO CARE CORPORATION (HQ)
440 Polaris Pkwy Ste 250 (43082-6082)
PHONE..............................800 548-1875
Christina Schrank, *Pr*
Paul Leary, *Ex VP*
Steven Juresich, *Sr VP*
Laura Clark, *CFO*
EMP: 31 **EST:** 1984
SQ FT: 15,000
SALES (est): 37.04MM
SALES (corp-wide): 221.62MM **Privately Held**
Web: www.nationalautocare.com
SIC: 6411 Insurance agents, nec
PA: Apco Holdings, Llc
6010 Atlantic Blvd
Norcross GA 30071
678 225-1000

(G-14915)
NATIONWIDE CHILDRENS HOSPITAL
Also Called: Close To Home Health Care Ctr
433 N Cleveland Ave (43082-8095)
PHONE..............................614 355-8300
Larry Long, *Dir*
EMP: 152
SALES (corp-wide): 3.6B **Privately Held**
Web: www.nationwidechildrens.org
SIC: 8069 8082 Childrens' hospital; Home health care services
PA: Nationwide Children's Hospital
700 Childrens Dr
Columbus OH 43205
614 722-2000

(G-14916)
NATIONWIDE CHILDRENS HOSPITAL
455 Executive Campus Dr (43082-8870)
PHONE..............................614 355-6100
EMP: 101
SALES (corp-wide): 3.6B **Privately Held**
Web: www.nationwidechildrens.org
SIC: 8062 General medical and surgical hospitals
PA: Nationwide Children's Hospital
700 Childrens Dr
Columbus OH 43205
614 722-2000

(G-14917)
NVR INC
6407 Tournament Dr (43082-8379)
PHONE..............................740 548-0136
EMP: 33
SIC: 1521 New construction, single-family houses
PA: Nvr, Inc.
11700 Plaza America Dr # 500
Reston VA 20190

(G-14918)
OAK HLTH CARE INVSTORS DFNCE I (HQ)
Also Called: Laurels of Defiance, The
8181 Worthington Rd (43082-8067)
PHONE..............................614 794-8800
EMP: 30 **EST:** 1995
SALES (est): 26.55MM **Privately Held**
Web: www.cienahealthcare.com
SIC: 8051 Skilled nursing care facilities
PA: Laurel Health Care Company Of North Worthing
8181 Worthington Rd
Westerville OH 43082

(G-14919)
OAK HLTH CARE INVSTORS MSSLLON (DH)
8181 Worthington Rd (43082-8067)
PHONE..............................614 794-8800
EMP: 49 **EST:** 1994
SALES (est): 23.13MM **Privately Held**
SIC: 6512 Nonresidential building operators
HQ: Laurel Health Care Company
8181 Worthington Rd Uppr
Westerville OH 43082

(G-14920)
OHIO CVIL SVC EMPLYEES ASSN AF
Also Called: O.C.S.E.A
390 Worthington Rd Ste A (43082-8329)
PHONE..............................614 865-4700
Ron Alexander, *Pr*
Eddie L Parks, *
Kathleen M Stewart, *
EMP: 92 **EST:** 1948
SQ FT: 40,000
SALES (est): 32.52MM **Privately Held**
Web: www.ocsea.org
SIC: 8631 8611 Labor union; Business associations

(G-14921)
OHIO LIVING (PA)
9200 Worthington Rd Ste 300 (43082-7634)
PHONE..............................614 888-7800
Laurence Gumina, *
Robert Stillman, *
EMP: 50 **EST:** 1922
SALES (est): 205.62MM **Privately Held**
Web: www.ohioliving.org

Westerville - Delaware County (G-14922)

GEOGRAPHIC SECTION

SIC: 8361 Rest home, with health care incidental

(G-14922)
OHIO PRSBT RTRMENT SVCS DEV CO
Also Called: Ohio Living
9200 Worthington Rd Ste 300 (43082-7634)
PHONE..................614 888-7800
Laurence C Gumina, CEO
EMP: 30 EST: 2016
SALES (est): 842.79K Privately Held
Web: www.ohioliving.org
SIC: 8322 Senior citizens' center or association

(G-14923)
OHIO PRSBT RTRMENT SVCS FNDTIO
Also Called: OPRS FOUNDATION
9200 Worthington Rd Ste 300 (43082-7634)
PHONE..................614 888-7800
EMP: 49 EST: 1986
SALES (est): 151.36MM Privately Held
Web: www.ohioliving.org
SIC: 7389 Fund raising organizations

(G-14924)
OPTUMRX INC
250 Progressive Way (43082-9615)
PHONE..................614 794-3300
EMP: 530
SALES (corp-wide): 371.62B Publicly Held
Web: www.optumrx.com
SIC: 6411 Medical insurance claim processing, contract or fee basis
HQ: Optumrx, Inc.
11000 Optum Cir
Eden Prairie MN 55344

(G-14925)
ORTHOPEDIC ONE INC
340 Polaris Pkwy (43082-7971)
PHONE..................614 839-2300
EMP: 38
Web: www.orthopedicone.com
SIC: 8011 Orthopedic physician
PA: Orthopedic One, Inc.
170 Taylor Station Rd # 260
Columbus OH 43213

(G-14926)
ORTON EDWARD JR CRMIC FNDATION
6991 S Old 3c Hwy (43082-9026)
P.O. Box 2760 (43086-2760)
PHONE..................614 895-2663
Jonathan Hinton, Ch Bd
Richard R Stedman Attorney, Prin
J Gary Childress, Secretary General*
Doctor James Williams, Trst
Doctor Stephen Freiman, Trst
▼ EMP: 31 EST: 1896
SQ FT: 34,260
SALES (est): 7.13MM Privately Held
Web: www.ortonceramic.com
SIC: 3269 3826 3825 8748 Cones, pyrometric: earthenware; Analytical instruments; Instruments to measure electricity; Testing services

(G-14927)
OTTO INSURANCE GROUP LLC
5855 Chandler Ct (43082-9050)
PHONE..................740 278-7888
Mark Otto, Managing Member
EMP: 45 EST: 2012
SALES (est): 2.58MM Privately Held
Web: www.otto-ins.com
SIC: 6411 Insurance agents, nec

(G-14928)
POLARIS INNKEEPERS LLC
Also Called: Fairfield Inn
9000 Worthington Rd (43082-8851)
PHONE..................614 568-0770
Kezia Cromer, Mgr
EMP: 48 EST: 2005
SALES (est): 1.7MM Privately Held
Web: fairfield.marriott.com
SIC: 7011 Hotels and motels

(G-14929)
POLARIS PKWY INTRNAL MDCINE PD
110 Polaris Pkwy Ste 230 (43082-8026)
PHONE..................614 865-4800
EMP: 31 EST: 2002
SALES (est): 2.28MM Privately Held
Web: www.copcp.com
SIC: 8011 General and family practice, physician/surgeon

(G-14930)
POWELL ENTERPRISES INC
Also Called: Goddard School, The
8750 Olde Worthington Rd (43082-8853)
PHONE..................614 882-0111
Steve Powell, Pr
Marykay Weite, *
EMP: 41 EST: 1999
SALES (est): 941.18K Privately Held
Web: www.goddardschool.com
SIC: 8351 Preschool center

(G-14931)
PROGRESSIVE MEDICAL LLC
Also Called: Helios
250 Progressive Way (43082-9615)
PHONE..................614 794-3300
EMP: 530
SIC: 6411 Medical insurance claim processing, contract or fee basis

(G-14932)
RE/MAX AFFILIATES INC
Also Called: Re/Max
570 N State St Ste 110 (43082-8075)
PHONE..................614 891-1661
Jeff Gongwer, Pr
EMP: 89 EST: 2004
SALES (est): 642.72K Privately Held
Web: www.reaffiliates.com
SIC: 6531 Real estate agent, residential

(G-14933)
REFLEXIS SYSTEMS INC
579 Executive Campus Dr Ste 310 (43082-9847)
PHONE..................614 948-1931
EMP: 194
SALES (corp-wide): 4.58B Publicly Held
Web: www.zebra.com
SIC: 7371 Computer software development
HQ: Reflexis Systems, Inc.
3 Allied Dr Ste 400
Dedham MA 02026
781 493-3400

(G-14934)
RENAISSANCE HOTEL MGT CO LLC
Also Called: Marriott
409 Altair Pkwy (43082-7573)
PHONE..................614 882-6800
EMP: 59
SALES (corp-wide): 23.71B Publicly Held
Web: www.marriott.com
SIC: 7011 Hotels and motels
HQ: Renaissance Hotel Operating Company
10400 Fernwood Rd
Bethesda MD 20817

(G-14935)
REVOLUTION GROUP INC
670 Meridian Way (43082-7648)
PHONE..................614 212-1111
EMP: 80 EST: 1995
SALES (est): 23.8MM Privately Held
Web: www.revolutiongroup.com
SIC: 7379 7372 4813 8741 Computer related consulting services; Prepackaged software; Internet connectivity services; Management services

(G-14936)
SALESFUEL INC
600 N Cleveland Ave Ste 260 (43082-6920)
PHONE..................614 794-0500
EMP: 54 EST: 2019
SALES (est): 4.52MM Privately Held
Web: www.salesfuel.com
SIC: 8742 Management consulting services

(G-14937)
SEQUENT INC (PA)
Also Called: Sequent Information Solutions
570 Polaris Pkwy Ste 125 (43082-7924)
PHONE..................614 436-5880
Joan Ziegler, CEO
Joseph W Cole, *
EMP: 85 EST: 1995
SALES (est): 12.07MM Privately Held
Web: www.sequent.biz
SIC: 7363 8748 Employee leasing service; Employee programs administration

(G-14938)
STATUS SOLUTIONS LLC
Also Called: Status Solutions
999 County Line Rd W # A (43082-7237)
PHONE..................434 296-1789
EMP: 80 EST: 2001
SALES (est): 14.37MM Privately Held
Web: www.statussolutions.com
SIC: 3669 5063 Emergency alarms; Alarm systems, nec

(G-14939)
SYNEOS HEALTH COMMUNICATIONS INC (DH)
500 Olde Worthington Rd (43082-8913)
PHONE..................614 543-6650
EMP: 76 EST: 1935
SALES (est): 80.68MM
SALES (corp-wide): 5.39B Privately Held
Web: www.syneoshealth.com
SIC: 7311 Advertising consultant
HQ: Inventiv Health, Inc.
1030 Sync St
Morrisville NC 27560
800 416-0555

(G-14940)
SYNERFAC INC
440 Polaris Pkwy Ste 130 (43082-6999)
PHONE..................614 416-6010
Paul Dutwin, Brnch Mgr
EMP: 50
SALES (corp-wide): 23.12MM Privately Held
Web: www.synerfac.com
SIC: 7361 Employment agencies
PA: Synerfac, Inc.
100 W Cmmons Blvd Ste 100
New Castle DE 19720
302 324-9400

(G-14941)
T2 FINANCIAL LLC
Also Called: Revolution Mortgage
579 Executive Campus Dr (43082-9801)
PHONE..................614 697-2021
EMP: 253 EST: 2017
SALES (est): 4.92MM Privately Held
Web: www.revolutionmortgage.com
SIC: 7389 Financial services

(G-14942)
TITLE FIRST AGENCY INC (HQ)
495 Executive Campus Dr Ste 110 (43082-8870)
PHONE..................614 347-8383
Sean Stoner, Pr
Tony Nauta, *
Paul Thompson, *
Tammy Leach, *
Darrel Slater, *
EMP: 30 EST: 1956
SALES (est): 33.85MM
SALES (corp-wide): 2.26B Publicly Held
Web: www.titlefirst.com
SIC: 6361 7375 Real estate title insurance; Data base information retrieval
PA: Stewart Information Services Corporation
1360 Post Oak Blvd Ste 10
Houston TX 77056
713 625-8100

(G-14943)
TPC AND THOMAS LLC
Also Called: Change 4 Growth
371 County Line Rd W Ste 100b (43082-7149)
PHONE..................614 354-0717
Beth Thomas, CEO
EMP: 52 EST: 2017
SALES (est): 512.13K Publicly Held
SIC: 8742 Management consulting services
PA: Information Services Group, Inc.
2187 Atlantic St
Stamford CT 06902

(G-14944)
TRANSTECH CONSULTING INC
600 N Cleveland Ave Ste 190 (43082-6920)
PHONE..................614 751-0575
David Wolfe, Pr
Jeffrey B Cook, *
Edward C Williams, *
EMP: 177 EST: 1991
SQ FT: 15,000
SALES (est): 660.64K Privately Held
Web: www.transtechconsulting.com
SIC: 8742 Business management consultant
HQ: Blue Horseshoe Solutions, Llc
11939 N Meridian St # 300
Carmel IN 46032
317 573-2583

(G-14945)
TRG MAINTENANCE LLC
514 N State St Ste B (43082-9073)
PHONE..................614 891-4850
Kristy Mcgrath, Prin
EMP: 920 EST: 2011
SALES (est): 1.25MM Privately Held
SIC: 7349 Building maintenance services, nec
PA: Titan Restaurant Group, Llc
514 N State St Ste B
Westerville OH 43082

(G-14946)
TRI ADVERTISING INC
Also Called: Triad Marketing & Media
371 County Line Rd W Ste 150 (43082-7150)

GEOGRAPHIC SECTION
Westerville - Franklin County (G-14969)

PHONE.....................614 548-0913
Dave Keller, *CEO*
EMP: 28 **EST:** 1972
SQ FT: 6,300
SALES (est): 6.64MM **Privately Held**
Web: www.triad-inc.com
SIC: 7311 Advertising consultant

(G-14947)
TRIDIA HOSPICE CARE INC
Also Called: TRIDIA HOSPICE & PALLIATIVE CA
110 Polaris Pkwy Ste 302 (43082-7054)
PHONE.....................614 915-8882
Daniel Parker, *Prin*
EMP: 81 **EST:** 2009
SALES (est): 38.41MM **Privately Held**
Web: www.bellacarehospice.net
SIC: 8052 Personal care facility

(G-14948)
VERTIV CORPORATION
610 Executive Campus Dr (43082-8870)
PHONE.....................614 841-6400
EMP: 250
SALES (corp-wide): 6.86B **Publicly Held**
Web: www.vertiv.com
SIC: 7378 Computer maintenance and repair
HQ: Vertiv Corporation
  505 N Cleveland Ave
  Westerville OH 43082
  614 888-0246

(G-14949)
VERTIV CORPORATION (DH)
Also Called: Geist
505 N Cleveland Ave (43082-7130)
P.O. Box 29186 (43229-0186)
PHONE.....................614 888-0246
Giordano Albertazzi, *CEO*
David Fallon, *CFO*
Jason Forcier, *Ex VP*
◆ **EMP:** 1300 **EST:** 1965
SQ FT: 330,000
SALES (est): 1.3B
SALES (corp-wide): 6.86B **Publicly Held**
Web: www.vertiv.com
SIC: 3585 3613 7629 Air conditioning equipment, complete; Regulators, power; Electronic equipment repair
HQ: Vertiv Group Corporation
  505 N Cleveland Ave
  Westerville OH 43082
  614 888-0246

(G-14950)
VERTIV SERVICES INC
Also Called: Vertiv
610 Executive Campus Dr (43082-8870)
P.O. Box 8539 (63126-0539)
PHONE.....................614 841-6400
EMP: 592
SIC: 7378 Computer maintenance and repair

(G-14951)
VILLAGE COMMUNITIES LLC
470 Olde Worthington Rd Ste 100 (43082-8986)
PHONE.....................614 540-2400
Tre Giller, *Prin*
Nancy Inman, *Prin*
EMP: 113 **EST:** 2004
SALES (est): 23.02MM **Privately Held**
Web: www.villagecommunities.com
SIC: 6531 Rental agent, real estate

(G-14952)
WESTERVILLE FAMILY PHYSICIANS
Also Called: Jeannie Hughes
400 Altair Pkwy (43082-7653)
PHONE.....................614 899-2700
EMP: 39 **EST:** 1992
SALES (est): 1.78MM **Privately Held**
Web: www.copcp.com
SIC: 8011 General and family practice, physician/surgeon

(G-14953)
WESTERVILLE INTERNAL MEDICINE
484 County Line Rd W Ste 200 (43082-7080)
PHONE.....................614 891-8080
John Hanyak Md, *Pr*
EMP: 35 **EST:** 1980
SALES (est): 420.88K **Privately Held**
Web: www.copcp.com
SIC: 8011 General and family practice, physician/surgeon

(G-14954)
WESTERVILLE SENIOR DEV LTD
Also Called: Parkside Village
730 N Spring Rd (43082-1803)
PHONE.....................614 794-9300
William J Lemmon, *Managing Member*
EMP: 99 **EST:** 2011
SALES (est): 2.84MM **Privately Held**
Web: www.westerville.org
SIC: 6513 Retirement hotel operation

Westerville
Franklin County

(G-14955)
ACCESS DRYWALL SUPPLY CO INC
297 Old County Line Rd (43081-1602)
P.O. Box 550 (43086-0550)
PHONE.....................614 890-2111
Robert C Porter Senior, *Pr*
Robert Porter Junior, *VP*
EMP: 27 **EST:** 1969
SQ FT: 10,000
SALES (est): 6.98MM **Privately Held**
SIC: 5032 5084 Drywall materials; Industrial machinery and equipment

(G-14956)
AFFINION GROUP LLC
300 W Schrock Rd (43081-1189)
PHONE.....................614 895-1803
Peg Ayers, *Brnch Mgr*
EMP: 1952
Web: www.tenerity.com
SIC: 8699 Personal interest organization
HQ: Affinion Group, Llc
  6 High Ridge Park Bldg A
  Stamford CT 06905

(G-14957)
AIMS SUPPORTED LIVING LLC
948 Cross Country Dr W (43081-3580)
PHONE.....................614 805-1507
Awal Inusa, *CEO*
EMP: 35 **EST:** 2017
SALES (est): 1.05MM **Privately Held**
Web: www.aimssupportedliving.com
SIC: 8082 Home health care services

(G-14958)
AMERICAN BUSINESS FORMS INC
Also Called: American Solutions For Bus
178 Granby Pl W (43081-6209)
PHONE.....................614 664-0202
EMP: 29
SALES (corp-wide): 380.8MM **Privately Held**
Web: home.americanbus.com
SIC: 5112 Business forms
PA: American Business Forms, Inc.
  31 E Minnesota Ave
  Glenwood MN 56334
  320 634-5471

(G-14959)
ANNEHURST VETERINARY HOSPITAL
25 Collegeview Rd (43081-1463)
PHONE.....................614 818-4221
Mark Harris, *Owner*
EMP: 39 **EST:** 1969
SQ FT: 2,000
SALES (est): 3.56MM **Privately Held**
Web: www.theanimalcareclinics.com
SIC: 0742 0752 Animal hospital services, pets and other animal specialties; Animal boarding services

(G-14960)
ASH BROTHERS HOME HEALTH CARE
635 Park Meadow Rd Ste 115 (43081)
PHONE.....................614 882-3600
EMP: 40 **EST:** 2009
SALES (est): 837.9K **Privately Held**
Web: www.ashhomecare.com
SIC: 8082 Home health care services

(G-14961)
ASSOCTION FOR DVLPMNTLLY DSBLE (PA)
Also Called: A D D
769 Brooksedge Blvd (43081-2821)
PHONE.....................614 486-4361
Robert L Archer, *CEO*
J Clifford Wilcox, *
Rebecca Baird, *
John Poston, *
Shirley Constantino-russell, *Sec*
EMP: 38 **EST:** 1971
SQ FT: 10,000
SALES (est): 16.46MM
SALES (corp-wide): 16.46MM **Privately Held**
Web: www.hattielarlham.org
SIC: 8361 8322 Mentally handicapped home ; Individual and family services

(G-14962)
BON APPETIT MANAGEMENT CO
100 W Home St (43081-1408)
PHONE.....................614 823-1880
Bill Taylor, *Genl Mgr*
EMP: 207
SALES (corp-wide): 39.16B **Privately Held**
Web: www.bamco.com
SIC: 8741 Restaurant management
HQ: Bon Appetit Management Co.
  201 Rdwood Shres Pkwy Ste
  Redwood City CA 94065
  650 798-8000

(G-14963)
BREAD FINANCIAL HOLDINGS INC
220 W Schrock Rd (43081-2873)
PHONE.....................614 729-5000
John Cowan, *Mgr*
EMP: 150
Web: www.alliancedata.com
SIC: 7389 Credit card service
PA: Bread Financial Holdings, Inc.
  3095 Loyalty Cir
  Columbus OH 43219

(G-14964)
CARLETON REALTY INC (PA)
580 W Schrock Rd (43081-8996)
PHONE.....................614 431-5700
Robert Kutschbach, *Pr*
Diana Kutschbach, *VP*
EMP: 27 **EST:** 1990
SALES (est): 8.16MM
SALES (corp-wide): 8.16MM **Privately Held**
Web: www.carletonrealty.com
SIC: 6531 Real estate agent, residential

(G-14965)
CEIBA ENTERPRISES INCORPORATED
Also Called: Gracor Language Services
159 Baranof W (43081-6205)
PHONE.....................614 818-3220
Rosario Hubbard, *Pr*
Thomas Hubbard Junior, *VP*
EMP: 102 **EST:** 1994
SALES (est): 3.52MM **Privately Held**
SIC: 7389 Translation services

(G-14966)
CHUTE GERDEMAN INC
501 W Schrock Rd Ste 201 (43081-8029)
PHONE.....................614 469-1001
Brian Shafley, *CEO*
Elle C Gerdeman, *
Wendy Johnson, *
George Nauman, *
Jay Highland, *
EMP: 64 **EST:** 1989
SALES (est): 10.29MM
SALES (corp-wide): 10.29MM **Privately Held**
Web: www.chutegerdeman.com
SIC: 7389 8712 Interior designer; Architectural services
PA: Foote, Cone & Belding, Inc.
  875 N Michigan Ave # 1850
  Chicago IL 60611
  312 425-5626

(G-14967)
CK CONSTRUCTION GROUP INC
Also Called: Corna Kokosing
6245 Westerville Rd (43081-4041)
PHONE.....................614 901-8844
Lori M Gillett, *CEO*
James P Negron, *
Matt Wushinske, *
Mitch Vincent, *
James E Graves, *
▲ **EMP:** 265 **EST:** 1995
SQ FT: 23,000
SALES (est): 323.65MM **Privately Held**
Web: www.ckbuilds.com
SIC: 1541 1542 8741 1791 Industrial buildings and warehouses; Nonresidential construction, nec; Construction management; Structural steel erection

(G-14968)
CLOSEOUT DISTRIBUTION LLC (HQ)
Also Called: Big Lots
4900 E Dublin Granville Rd (43081)
PHONE.....................614 278-6800
Michael J Potter, *CEO*
▲ **EMP:** 600 **EST:** 1999
SALES (est): 179.43MM
SALES (corp-wide): 4.72B **Publicly Held**
SIC: 5092 Toys and games
PA: Big Lots, Inc.
  4900 E Dblin Granville Rd
  Columbus OH 43081
  614 278-6800

(G-14969)
COLUMBUS CLNY FOR ELDRLY CARE
Also Called: COLUMBUS COLONY ELDERLY CARE
1150 Colony Dr (43081-3624)
PHONE.....................614 891-5055
Richard Huebner, *Pr*

Westerville - Franklin County (G-14970)

Howard Snyder, *
EMP: 180 **EST:** 1977
SQ FT: 50,000
SALES (est): 8.2MM **Privately Held**
Web: www.columbuscolonyelderlycare.org
SIC: 8051 Convalescent home with continuous nursing care

(G-14970)
COLUMBUS FRKLN CNTY PK (PA)
Also Called: Metro Parks
1069 W Main St Unit B (43081-1186)
PHONE.................................614 891-0700
Tim Moloney, *Dir*
John O'meara, *Dir*
EMP: 50 **EST:** 1945
SALES (est): 18.39MM
SALES (corp-wide): 18.39MM **Privately Held**
Web: www.metroparks.net
SIC: 7999 Recreation services

(G-14971)
COLUMBUS FRNKLIN CNTY MTRO PK
Also Called: Blendonwoods Metro Park
4265 E Dublin Granville Rd (43081-4478)
PHONE.................................614 895-6219
Dan Bissonette, *Genl Mgr*
EMP: 49
SALES (corp-wide): 18.39MM **Privately Held**
Web: www.metroparks.net
SIC: 7999 Recreation services
PA: Columbus & Franklin County Metropolitan Park District
1069 W Main St Unit B
Westerville OH 43081
614 891-0700

(G-14972)
COLUMBUS PRESCR PHRMS INC
975 Eastwind Dr Ste 155 (43081-3344)
P.O. Box 12550 (43212-0550)
PHONE.................................614 294-1600
Mark A Witchey, *Pr*
Jack A Witchey, *
Nick T Kalogeras, *
EMP: 32 **EST:** 1976
SQ FT: 15,000
SALES (est): 5.39MM **Privately Held**
SIC: 5047 5912 Surgical equipment and supplies; Drug stores

(G-14973)
COMMUNICATIONS III INC (PA)
921 Eastwind Dr Ste 104 (43081-5316)
P.O. Box 178 (43054-0178)
PHONE.................................614 901-7720
Scott Halliday, *Pr*
Hugh Cathey, *
Steve Vogelmeier, *
Peter Halliday, *Stockholder**
EMP: 27 **EST:** 1984
SQ FT: 12,000
SALES (est): 3.27MM
SALES (corp-wide): 3.27MM **Privately Held**
SIC: 5065 8748 Communication equipment; Telecommunications consultant

(G-14974)
CONCORD COUNSELING SERVICES
700 Brooksedge Blvd (43081-3394)
PHONE.................................614 882-9338
Mary Sommer, *Ex Dir*
Neil Edgar, *
EMP: 50 **EST:** 1972
SQ FT: 4,300
SALES (est): 7.04MM **Privately Held**
Web: www.concordcounseling.org
SIC: 8399 8322 Health and welfare council; Individual and family services

(G-14975)
DANIEL N RIZEK
93 E Broadway Ave (43081-1505)
PHONE.................................614 895-0006
Daniel N Rizek, *Prin*
EMP: 96 **EST:** 2010
SALES (est): 453.62K **Privately Held**
Web: notes.udayton.edu
SIC: 0742 Veterinary services, specialties

(G-14976)
DIVERSIFIED SYSTEMS INC
100 Dorchester Sq N Ste 103 (43081-7305)
PHONE.................................614 476-9939
Archie D Williamson Junior, *CEO*
EMP: 35 **EST:** 1990
SQ FT: 3,000
SALES (est): 5.23MM **Privately Held**
Web: www.diversifiedsystems.com
SIC: 7379 8742 7371 Data processing consultant; Management consulting services; Computer software systems analysis and design, custom

(G-14977)
EDGEWOOD MANOR WESTERVILLE LLC
Also Called: BUCKEYE TERRACE REHABILITATION
140 N State St (43081-1426)
PHONE.................................614 882-4055
EMP: 34 **EST:** 2017
SALES (est): 6.45MM **Privately Held**
Web: www.buckeyenwh.com
SIC: 8051 Convalescent home with continuous nursing care

(G-14978)
EXEL N AMERCN LOGISTICS INC (DH)
570 Players Pkwy (43081)
PHONE.................................800 272-1052
Randy Briggs, *Pr*
Hugh Evans, *VP*
◆ **EMP:** 125 **EST:** 1990
SQ FT: 100,000
SALES (est): 197.55MM
SALES (corp-wide): 88.87B **Privately Held**
SIC: 4731 Freight forwarding
HQ: Dhl Global Forwarding (Uk) Limited
Eastworth House
Chertsey KT16
247 693-7770

(G-14979)
FOCUSCFO LLC
575 Charring Cross Dr Ste 102 (43081-4958)
PHONE.................................614 944-5760
Brad A Martyn, *Owner*
EMP: 123 **EST:** 2010
SALES (est): 5.54MM **Privately Held**
Web: www.focuscfo.com
SIC: 7361 Employment agencies

(G-14980)
FRANKLIN EQUIPMENT LLC
5755 Westerville Rd (43081-9366)
PHONE.................................614 948-3409
EMP: 48
SALES (corp-wide): 14.33B **Publicly Held**
Web: www.unitedrentals.com
SIC: 7359 Equipment rental and leasing, nec
HQ: Franklin Equipment, Llc
4141 Hamilton Square Blvd
Groveport OH 43125

(G-14981)
GODDARD SCHOOL
Also Called: Goddard School, The
1260 County Line Rd (43081-6000)
PHONE.................................614 865-2100
Raymond Murray, *Pr*
EMP: 29 **EST:** 2009
SALES (est): 529.51K **Privately Held**
Web: www.goddardschool.com
SIC: 8351 Preschool center

(G-14982)
GRAVES CARE SERVICES LLC
Also Called: Visiting Angels
100 Dorchester Sq N Ste 101 (43081-7304)
PHONE.................................614 392-2820
Paul Graves, *CEO*
Paul Graves, *Sole Member*
EMP: 32 **EST:** 2012
SALES (est): 1.25MM **Privately Held**
Web: www.visitingangels.com
SIC: 8082 Home health care services

(G-14983)
HEARTLAND VLG WSTRVLLE OH RC L
Also Called: Promedica Sklled Nrsing Rhbltt
1060 Eastwind Dr (43081-3331)
PHONE.................................614 895-1038
Melissa Berger, *Mgr*
EMP: 1509 **EST:** 2015
SALES (est): 42.77MM
SALES (corp-wide): 187.07MM **Privately Held**
Web: www.westerville.org
SIC: 8051 Convalescent home with continuous nursing care
PA: Promedica Health System, Inc.
100 Madison Ave
Toledo OH 43604
567 585-9600

(G-14984)
HEITMEYER GROUP LLC
501 W Schrock Rd Ste 410 (43081-8035)
PHONE.................................614 699-5770
EMP: 117 **EST:** 1999
SALES (est): 11.77MM **Privately Held**
Web: www.heitmeyerconsulting.com
SIC: 7361 Executive placement

(G-14985)
HOLDCO LLC
Also Called: Road Runner Holdco
4151 Executive Pkwy Ste 150 (43081-3867)
PHONE.................................614 255-7285
Kurtis Rose, *Mgr*
EMP: 27
SALES (corp-wide): 54.61B **Publicly Held**
SIC: 4813 Online service providers
HQ: Holdco, Llc
13820 Sunrise Valley Dr
Herndon VA 20171
703 345-2400

(G-14986)
HOPEBRIDGE LLC
773 Brooksedge Blvd (43081-2821)
PHONE.................................855 324-0885
Angie Graff, *Brnch Mgr*
EMP: 37
SALES (corp-wide): 598.8MM **Privately Held**
Web: www.hopebridge.com
SIC: 8093 Mental health clinic, outpatient
HQ: Hopebridge, Llc
3500 Depauw Blvd Ste 3070
Indianapolis IN 46268

(G-14987)
HUNTINGTON NATIONAL BANK
Also Called: Huntington
630 S State St (43081-3317)
PHONE.................................614 480-0016
Andy Bailey, *Mgr*
EMP: 36
SALES (corp-wide): 10.84B **Publicly Held**
Web: www.huntington.com
SIC: 6029 6021 Commercial banks, nec; National commercial banks
HQ: The Huntington National Bank
41 S High St
Columbus OH 43215
614 480-4293

(G-14988)
IFS FINANCIAL SERVICES INC (DH)
370 S Cleveland Ave (43081-8917)
PHONE.................................513 362-8000
Jill T Mcgruder, *Pr*
EMP: 35 **EST:** 1991
SQ FT: 2,000
SALES (est): 26.35MM **Privately Held**
SIC: 6211 6282 Security brokers and dealers; Investment advice
HQ: The Western & Southern Life Insurance Company
400 Broadway Mail Stop G
Cincinnati OH 45202
513 629-1800

(G-14989)
IMMEDIATE HEALTH ASSOCIATES
Also Called: Wedgewood Urgent Care
575 Copeland Mill Rd Ste 1d (43081)
PHONE.................................614 794-0481
Frank Orth D.o.s., *Pr*
Edward Boudreau D.o.s., *VP*
Patricia Robitaille, *
EMP: 30 **EST:** 1987
SALES (est): 4.35MM **Privately Held**
Web: www.ihainc.org
SIC: 8011 Freestanding emergency medical center

(G-14990)
ITS TECHNOLOGIES INC
4111 Executive Pkwy Ste 201 (43081-3869)
PHONE.................................614 901-2265
Roger Radeloff, *Brnch Mgr*
EMP: 75
SALES (corp-wide): 13.77MM **Privately Held**
Web: www.wehirepeople.com
SIC: 7361 Executive placement
PA: Its Technologies, Inc.
7060 Spring Mdws Dr W D
Holland OH 43528
419 842-2100

(G-14991)
KINDERCARE LEARNING CTRS LLC
Also Called: Kindercare
1255 County Line Rd (43081-6001)
PHONE.................................614 901-4000
Amy Seivert, *Mgr*
EMP: 32
SALES (corp-wide): 967.64MM **Privately Held**
Web: www.kindercare.com
SIC: 8351 Group day care center
HQ: Kindercare Learning Centers, Llc
650 Ne Holladay St # 1400
Portland OR 97232

(G-14992)
KOKOSING INC (PA)
6235 Westerville Rd Ste 200 (43081)
PHONE.................................614 212-5700
William Burgett, *CEO*

GEOGRAPHIC SECTION
Westerville - Franklin County (G-15013)

Dan Compston, *
Marsha Rianhart, *
Dan Walker, *
Tom Muraski, *
EMP: 100 **EST:** 2015
SALES (est): 1.17B
SALES (corp-wide): 1.17B **Privately Held**
Web: www.kokosing.biz
SIC: 1611 General contractor, highway and street construction

(G-14993)
KOKOSING CONSTRUCTION CO INC (HQ)
6235 Westerville Rd (43081-4041)
P.O. Box 226 (43019-0226)
PHONE..................614 228-1029
Wm Bryce Burgett, CEO
W Brian Burgett, *
W Barth Burgett, EQUIP
Daniel Walker, *
Daniel J Compston, *
▲ **EMP:** 200 **EST:** 1981
SALES (est): 519.15MM
SALES (corp-wide): 1.17B **Privately Held**
Web: www.kokosing.biz
SIC: 1611 1622 1629 1542 General contractor, highway and street construction; Bridge construction; Waste water and sewage treatment plant construction; Commercial and office building, new construction
PA: Kokosing, Inc.
6235 Wstrville Rd Ste 200
Westerville OH 43081
614 212-5700

(G-14994)
KOKOSING CONSTRUCTION CO INC
6235 Westerville Rd (43081-4041)
PHONE..................614 228-1029
Mike Helbing, Mgr
EMP: 170
SQ FT: 2,527
SALES (corp-wide): 1.17B **Privately Held**
Web: www.kokosing.biz
SIC: 1611 1622 General contractor, highway and street construction; Bridge, tunnel, and elevated highway construction
HQ: Kokosing Construction Company, Inc.
6235 Westerville Rd
Westerville OH 43081
614 228-1029

(G-14995)
KOKOSING INDUSTRIAL INC (HQ)
Also Called: Kokosing Solar
6235 Westerville Rd (43081-4041)
P.O. Box 226 (43019-0226)
PHONE..................614 212-5700
W Brian Burgett, CEO
EMP: 80 **EST:** 2015
SALES (est): 129.79MM
SALES (corp-wide): 1.17B **Privately Held**
Web: www.kokosing.biz
SIC: 1629 Dams, waterways, docks, and other marine construction
PA: Kokosing, Inc.
6235 Wstrville Rd Ste 200
Westerville OH 43081
614 212-5700

(G-14996)
KOKOSING MOSSER JOINT VENTURE ✪
6235 Westerville Rd (43081-4041)
PHONE..................740 848-4955
Tom Muraski, Prin
EMP: 130 **EST:** 2022
SALES (est): 2.65MM
SALES (corp-wide): 1.17B **Privately Held**
Web: www.kokosing.biz
SIC: 1542 Commercial and office building, new construction
HQ: Kokosing Industrial, Inc.
6235 Westerville Rd
Westerville OH 43081
614 212-5700

(G-14997)
M RETAIL ENGINEERING INC
750 Brooksedge Blvd (43081-2820)
PHONE..................614 818-2323
Dan Gilmore, Pr
Shigeyoshi A Mori, *
David Gonzalez, *
Ron Koons, *
George Schmidt, *
EMP: 45 **EST:** 1997
SQ FT: 10,000
SALES (est): 4.2MM **Privately Held**
Web: mengineering.us.com
SIC: 8711 Consulting engineer

(G-14998)
MES PAINTING AND GRAPHICS LTD
8298 Harlem Rd (43081-9565)
PHONE..................614 496-1696
Michael Scherl, CEO
EMP: 42 **EST:** 1994
SALES (est): 2.56MM **Privately Held**
Web: www.mespaintingandgraphics.com
SIC: 1721 3993 Commercial painting; Signs and advertising specialties

(G-14999)
MICRO INDUSTRIES CORPORATION (PA)
8399 Green Meadows Dr N (43081)
PHONE..................740 548-7878
Michael Curran, Pr
John Curran, *
William Jackson, *
Amanda Curran, *
EMP: 67 **EST:** 1979
SQ FT: 52,000
SALES (est): 9.8MM
SALES (corp-wide): 9.8MM **Privately Held**
Web: www.microindustries.com
SIC: 8711 3674 Engineering services; Semiconductor circuit networks

(G-15000)
MODERN OFFICE METHODS INC
929 Eastwind Dr Ste 220 (43081-3362)
PHONE..................614 891-3693
Dan Vail, VP
EMP: 34
SALES (corp-wide): 45.16MM **Privately Held**
Web: www.momnet.com
SIC: 5999 7629 Business machines and equipment; Business machine repair, electric
PA: Modern Office Methods, Inc.
4747 Lake Forest Dr
Cincinnati OH 45242
513 791-0909

(G-15001)
MOUNT CARMEL HEALTH
955 Eastwind Dr (43081-3376)
PHONE..................614 776-5164
EMP: 85
SALES (corp-wide): 2.49B **Privately Held**
Web: www.mountcarmelhealth.com
SIC: 8099 Childbirth preparation clinic
HQ: Mount Carmel Health
5300 N Meadows Dr
Grove City OH 43123
614 234-5000

(G-15002)
MOUNT CARMEL HEALTH
Also Called: Mount Carmel Home Care
501 W Schrock Rd Ste 350 (43081-7155)
PHONE..................614 234-0100
Cindy Salvator, Dir
EMP: 187
SALES (corp-wide): 2.49B **Privately Held**
Web: www.mountcarmelhealth.com
SIC: 8062 General medical and surgical hospitals
HQ: Mount Carmel Health
5300 N Meadows Dr
Grove City OH 43123
614 234-5000

(G-15003)
MOUNT CRMEL CNTL OHIO NRLGCAL
955 Eastwind Dr Ste B (43081-3376)
PHONE..................614 268-9561
David Yashon Md, Pr
Doctor Mullin, Prin
EMP: 33 **EST:** 1960
SALES (est): 1.1MM **Privately Held**
Web: www.mountcarmelhealth.com
SIC: 8011 Surgeon

(G-15004)
NATIONAL GROUND WATER ASSN INC
Also Called: NGWA
601 Dempsey Rd (43081-8978)
PHONE..................614 898-7791
Richard Thron, Pr
Kevin B Mccray, CEO
Paul Humes, *
Jeffrey Williams, *
EMP: 34 **EST:** 1946
SQ FT: 13,600
SALES (est): 6.04MM **Privately Held**
Web: www.ngwa.org
SIC: 8611 Trade associations

(G-15005)
NATIONWIDE CHILDRENS HOSPITAL
187 W Schrock Rd (43081-2890)
PHONE..................614 866-3473
EMP: 431
SALES (corp-wide): 3.6B **Privately Held**
Web: www.nationwidechildrens.org
SIC: 8062 General medical and surgical hospitals
PA: Nationwide Children's Hospital
700 Childrens Dr
Columbus OH 43205
614 722-2000

(G-15006)
NATIONWIDE CHILDRENS HOSPITAL
275 W Schrock Rd (43081-2874)
PHONE..................614 355-8315
Steve Allen, CEO
EMP: 72 **EST:** 2011
SALES (est): 815.43K **Privately Held**
Web: www.nationwidechildrens.org
SIC: 8062 General medical and surgical hospitals

(G-15007)
NEW RIVER ELECTRICAL CORP
Also Called: New River Electric
6005 Westerville Rd (43081-4055)
PHONE..................614 891-1142
Tom Wolden, Mgr
EMP: 840
SALES (corp-wide): 584.2MM **Privately Held**
Web: www.newriverelectrical.com
SIC: 1731 General electrical contractor
PA: New River Electrical Corporation
15 Cloverdale Pl
Cloverdale VA 24077
540 966-1650

(G-15008)
OLLOM DENTAL GROUP LLC
1245 S Sunbury Rd Ste 201 (43081-9444)
PHONE..................614 392-8090
Chad Ollom, Brnch Mgr
EMP: 114
SALES (corp-wide): 1.01MM **Privately Held**
SIC: 8021 Dentists' office
PA: Ollom Dental Group Llc
7477 Ratchford Ct
New Albany OH 43054
614 572-5600

(G-15009)
OPTIMUM SYSTEM PRODUCTS INC (PA)
Also Called: Optimum Graphics
921 Eastwind Dr Ste 133 (43081-3363)
PHONE..................614 885-4464
John Martin, CEO
Dorothy Martin, *
EMP: 40 **EST:** 1985
SQ FT: 75,000
SALES (est): 3.75MM
SALES (corp-wide): 3.75MM **Privately Held**
Web: www.optimumcompanies.com
SIC: 2752 5112 Business form and card printing, lithographic; Business forms

(G-15010)
ORTHONEURO (PA)
Also Called: Ortho Neuro
70 S Cleveland Ave (43081-1398)
PHONE..................614 890-6555
Francis O Donnell, Pr
Brian Hart, *
Jacqueline Petty, CAO*
EMP: 30 **EST:** 1973
SQ FT: 20,000
SALES (est): 25.52MM
SALES (corp-wide): 25.52MM **Privately Held**
Web: www.orthoneuro.com
SIC: 8011 Orthopedic physician

(G-15011)
PATROL URBAN SERVICES LLC
4563 E Walnut St (43081-9693)
PHONE..................614 620-4672
Robert S Urban, Pr
EMP: 35 **EST:** 2011
SALES (est): 1MM **Privately Held**
SIC: 7381 Security guard service

(G-15012)
PRECISION BRDBAND INSTLLTONS I
7642 Red Bank Rd (43081)
PHONE..................614 523-2917
Frederick P Steininger, CEO
Chris Steininger, *
EMP: 140 **EST:** 2008
SALES (est): 7.7MM **Privately Held**
Web: www.precision-broadband.com
SIC: 1731 Cable television installation

(G-15013)
ROMANELLI & HUGHES BUILDING CO
Also Called: Romanelli & Hughes Contractors
148 W Schrock Rd (43081-4915)
PHONE..................614 891-2042
David Hughes, Pr

Westerville - Franklin County (G-15014)

Vincent Romanelli, *
Darrel R Miller, *
EMP: 42 **EST:** 1970
SQ FT: 5,000
SALES (est): 24.87MM **Privately Held**
Web: www.rh-homes.com
SIC: 1521 1542 New construction, single-family houses; Commercial and office building, new construction

(G-15014)
ROUSH EQUIPMENT INC (PA)
Also Called: Roush Honda
100 W Schrock Rd (43081-2832)
PHONE...............................614 882-1535
Jeffrey A Brindley, *Pr*
EMP: 129 **EST:** 1965
SQ FT: 16,000
SALES (est): 46.94MM
SALES (corp-wide): 46.94MM **Privately Held**
Web: www.roushhonda.com
SIC: 5511 7538 7532 7515 Automobiles, new and used; General automotive repair shops; Top and body repair and paint shops; Passenger car leasing

(G-15015)
SOGETI USA LLC
Also Called: Sogeti
240 S State St (43081-2233)
PHONE...............................614 847-4477
Kevin Cheesman, *Mgr*
EMP: 110
SALES (corp-wide): 415.14MM **Privately Held**
Web: us.sogeti.com
SIC: 7379 7373 Online services technology consultants; Computer integrated systems design
HQ: Sogeti Usa Llc
10100 Innovation Dr # 200
Miamisburg OH 45342
937 291-8100

(G-15016)
SURVEYING AND MAPPING LLC
929 Eastwind Dr Ste 201 (43081-3362)
PHONE...............................512 447-0575
EMP: 76
SALES (corp-wide): 140.24MM **Privately Held**
Web: www.sam.biz
SIC: 8713 Surveying services
HQ: Surveying And Mapping, Llc
4801 Sw Pkwy Ste 2-1
Austin TX 78735

(G-15017)
TK ELEVATOR CORPORATION
929 Eastwind Dr Ste 218 (43081-3362)
PHONE...............................614 895-8370
EMP: 81
SALES (corp-wide): 2.67MM **Privately Held**
Web: www.tkelevator.com
SIC: 1796 7699 5084 Elevator installation and conversion; Elevators: inspection, service, and repair; Elevators
HQ: Tk Elevator Corporation
788 Cir 75 Pkwy Se # 500
Atlanta GA 30339
678 319-3240

(G-15018)
TRILEGIANT CORPORATION
300 W Schrock Rd (43081-2893)
PHONE...............................614 823-5215
EMP: 288
Web: www.trilegiant.com

SIC: 8641 Community membership club
HQ: Trilegiant Corporation
6 High Ridge Park Bldg A
Stamford CT 06905
203 416-2000

(G-15019)
TURTLE GOLF MANAGEMENT LTD (HQ)
Also Called: Little Turtle Golf Club
5400 Little Turtle Way W (43081-7821)
PHONE...............................614 882-5920
EMP: 56 **EST:** 1988
SQ FT: 23,000
SALES (est): 2.08MM **Privately Held**
Web: www.littleturtlegolf.com
SIC: 8742 7997 General management consultant; Country club, membership
PA: Turtle Golf Property, Ltd.
5400 Little Turtle Way W
Westerville OH 43081

(G-15020)
UNITED STATES TROTTING ASSN (PA)
6130 S Sunbury Rd (43081-9309)
PHONE...............................614 224-2291
Michael Panner, *CEO*
EMP: 60 **EST:** 1938
SQ FT: 20,000
SALES (est): 9.83MM
SALES (corp-wide): 9.83MM **Privately Held**
Web: www.ustrotting.com
SIC: 8611 Trade associations

(G-15021)
WHITE OAK PARTNERS INC
5150 E Dublin Granville Rd Ste 130 (43081-8701)
PHONE...............................614 855-1155
EMP: 67
SALES (est): 24.28MM **Privately Held**
Web: www.whiteoakpartners.com
SIC: 6799 Investors, nec

(G-15022)
WL ELECTRIC INC
6155 Westerville Rd (43081-4057)
PHONE...............................614 882-2160
Walid Latif, *Pr*
EMP: 30 **EST:** 1985
SQ FT: 2,400
SALES (est): 2.12MM **Privately Held**
SIC: 1731 General electrical contractor

Westfield Center
Medina County

(G-15023)
1848 VENTURES LLC
1 Park Cir (44251-9700)
PHONE...............................330 887-0187
EMP: 228 **EST:** 2019
SALES (est): 3.64MM
SALES (corp-wide): 1.68B **Privately Held**
Web: www.1848ventures.com
SIC: 7371 7389 Computer software development and applications; Business services, nec
HQ: Westfield Insurance Company
1 Park Cir
Westfield Center OH 44251
800 243-0210

(G-15024)
AMERICAN SELECT INSURANCE CO
1 Park Cir (44251)
P.O. Box 5001 (44251)

PHONE...............................330 887-0101
Robert Kiraty, *Treas*
EMP: 93 **EST:** 1850
SQ FT: 100,000
SALES (est): 10.47MM
SALES (corp-wide): 1.68B **Privately Held**
Web: www.westfieldinsurance.com
SIC: 6331 Fire, marine, and casualty insurance
PA: Ohio Farmers Insurance Company
1 Park Cir
Westfield Center OH 44251
800 243-0210

(G-15025)
OHIO FARMERS INSURANCE COMPANY (PA)
Also Called: Westfield Group
1 Park Cir (44251-9700)
P.O. Box 5001 (44251-5001)
PHONE...............................800 243-0210
Edward J Largent Iii, *CEO*
Ed Largent, *Pr*
Frank A Carrino, *Corporate Secretary*
Joe Kohmann, *CFO*
EMP: 1753 **EST:** 1848
SQ FT: 200,000
SALES (est): 1.68B
SALES (corp-wide): 1.68B **Privately Held**
Web: www.westfieldinsurance.com
SIC: 6411 6331 Property and casualty insurance agent; Fire, marine, and casualty insurance

(G-15026)
WESTFIELD BANK FSB (DH)
Also Called: Westfield Bank
2 Park Cir (44251-9744)
P.O. Box 5002 (44251-5002)
PHONE...............................800 368-8930
Michael Toth, *Pr*
Timothy E Phillips, *
EMP: 39 **EST:** 2002
SALES (est): 77.91MM
SALES (corp-wide): 1.68B **Privately Held**
Web: www.westfield-bank.com
SIC: 6022 State commercial banks
HQ: Westfield Bancorp, Inc.
2 Park Cir
Westfield Center OH 44251

(G-15027)
WESTFIELD INSURANCE COMPANY (HQ)
1 Park Cir (44251-9700)
P.O. Box 5001 (44251-5001)
PHONE...............................800 243-0210
James R Clay, *CEO*
Roger Mc Manus, *
Robert Krisowaty, *
George Wiswesser, *CIO*
Joe Kohmann, *
EMP: 123 **EST:** 1929
SQ FT: 500,000
SALES (est): 279.66MM
SALES (corp-wide): 1.68B **Privately Held**
Web: www.westfieldinsurance.com
SIC: 6411 6331 Property and casualty insurance agent; Fire, marine, and casualty insurance
PA: Ohio Farmers Insurance Company
1 Park Cir
Westfield Center OH 44251
800 243-0210

(G-15028)
WESTFIELD NATIONAL INSUR CO (HQ)
1 Park Cir (44251)
P.O. Box 5001 (44251)
PHONE...............................330 887-0101

R Cary Blair, *Pr*
Otto Bosshard, *Sr VP*
EMP: 55 **EST:** 1968
SQ FT: 100,000
SALES (est): 147.98MM
SALES (corp-wide): 1.68B **Privately Held**
Web: www.westfieldinsurance.com
SIC: 6331 6411 Property damage insurance; Property and casualty insurance agent
PA: Ohio Farmers Insurance Company
1 Park Cir
Westfield Center OH 44251
800 243-0210

Westlake
Cuyahoga County

(G-15029)
ACHIEVEMENT CTRS FOR CHILDREN
24211 Center Ridge Rd (44145-4211)
PHONE...............................440 250-2520
Scott Peplin, *Mgr*
EMP: 66
SALES (corp-wide): 11.08MM **Privately Held**
Web: www.achievementcenters.org
SIC: 8322 Social service center
PA: Achievement Centers For Children
4255 Northfield Rd
Cleveland OH 44128
216 292-9700

(G-15030)
ALL PRO FREIGHT SYSTEMS INC (PA)
1006 Crocker Rd (44145-1031)
PHONE...............................440 934-2222
Chris Haas, *Pr*
Diana L Cisar, *
▲ **EMP:** 80 **EST:** 1990
SQ FT: 109,000
SALES (est): 25.41MM **Privately Held**
Web: www.allprofreight.com
SIC: 4213 4214 4225 Trucking, except local; Local trucking with storage; General warehousing

(G-15031)
ALTA PARTNERS LLC
902 Westpoint Pkwy Ste 320 (44145-1534)
PHONE...............................440 808-3654
EMP: 30 **EST:** 1990
SALES (est): 3.01MM **Privately Held**
Web: www.altapartnersllc.com
SIC: 8011 General and family practice, physician/surgeon

(G-15032)
ALUMINUM LINE PRODUCTS COMPANY (PA)
Also Called: Alpco
24460 Sperry Cir (44145-1591)
PHONE...............................440 835-8880
Richard A Daniel, *Pr*
James E Guerin, *
Gregory P Thompson, *
Ray Avramovich, *
David Lyster, *
◆ **EMP:** 100 **EST:** 1960
SQ FT: 100,000
SALES (est): 36.55MM
SALES (corp-wide): 36.55MM **Privately Held**
Web: www.aluminumline.com
SIC: 5051 3365 3999 Steel; Aluminum foundries; Barber and beauty shop equipment

GEOGRAPHIC SECTION

Westlake - Cuyahoga County (G-15056)

(G-15033)
AMARK LOGISTICS INC
28915 Clemens Rd (44145-1122)
PHONE.....................440 892-4500
EMP: 28
SALES (corp-wide): 1.95MM **Privately Held**
Web: www.amarklogistics.com
SIC: **4789** Cargo loading and unloading services
PA: Amark Logistics, Inc.
4644 W Gandy Blvd 4-202
Tampa FL 33611
813 421-3900

(G-15034)
ARDMORE POWER LOGISTICS LLC
Also Called: Ardmore Logistics
24610 Detroit Rd Ste 1200 (44145-2561)
PHONE.....................216 502-0640
David Cottenden, *Managing Member*
EMP: 29 EST: 2000
SQ FT: 6,000
SALES (est): 12.52MM **Privately Held**
Web: www.ardmorelogistics.com
SIC: **8742 4731** Transportation consultant; Domestic freight forwarding

(G-15035)
ASSOCIATES IN DERMATOLOGY INC (PA)
2205 Crocker Rd (44145-6710)
PHONE.....................440 249-0274
Paul G Hazen, *Pr*
Conley W Engstrom, *
John Jay Stewart, *
Karen Turgeon, *
EMP: 32 EST: 1950
SALES (est): 4.48MM
SALES (corp-wide): 4.48MM **Privately Held**
Web: www.healthyskinmd.com
SIC: **8011** Dermatologist

(G-15036)
BAPTIST HEALTH
P.O. Box 458032 (44145-8032)
PHONE.....................502 253-4700
EMP: 59 EST: 2019
SALES (est): 9.82MM **Privately Held**
SIC: **8099** Health and allied services, nec

(G-15037)
BAY FURNACE SHEET METAL CO
Also Called: Bay Heating & Air Conditioning
24530 Sperry Dr (44145-1578)
PHONE.....................440 871-3777
Lynn Robinson, *Pr*
Billie Robinson, *
Kori Robinson, *
EMP: 30 EST: 1944
SQ FT: 4,800
SALES (est): 4.78MM **Privately Held**
Web: www.bayfurnace.com
SIC: **1711** Warm air heating and air conditioning contractor

(G-15038)
BELLA CAPELLI INC
Also Called: Bella Capelli Salon
24350 Center Ridge Rd (44145-4212)
PHONE.....................440 899-1225
Sandra Borrelli, *Pr*
Serina Peck, *
EMP: 76 EST: 1997
SALES (est): 4.28MM **Privately Held**
Web: www.bellacapelli.com
SIC: **7231** Hairdressers

(G-15039)
BLOSSOM HILL INC
Also Called: Center Ridge House
28700 Center Ridge Rd (44145-5213)
PHONE.....................440 250-9182
Lynne Urbanski, *Dir*
EMP: 43
SALES (corp-wide): 110.89K **Privately Held**
Web: www.blossom-hill.org
SIC: **8322** Individual and family services
PA: Blossom Hill, Inc.
10983 Abbey Rd
North Royalton OH 44133
440 652-6749

(G-15040)
BORCHERS AMERICAS INC (HQ)
Also Called: Om Group
811 Sharon Dr (44145-1522)
PHONE.....................440 899-2950
Devlin Riley, *CEO*
◆ EMP: 60 EST: 1946
SQ FT: 30,000
SALES (est): 45.3MM
SALES (corp-wide): 1.69B **Privately Held**
Web: www.borchers.com
SIC: **8731 2819 2899 2992** Commercial physical research; Industrial inorganic chemicals, nec; Chemical preparations, nec; Lubricating oils and greases
PA: Milliken & Company
920 Milliken Rd
Spartanburg SC 29303
864 503-2020

(G-15041)
BUDGET DUMPSTER LLC (PA)
Also Called: Budget Dumpster Rental
830 Canterbury Rd (44145-1403)
PHONE.....................866 284-6164
EMP: 31 EST: 2009
SALES (est): 4.63MM
SALES (corp-wide): 4.63MM **Privately Held**
Web: www.budgetdumpster.com
SIC: **7359** Equipment rental and leasing, nec

(G-15042)
CAFF LLC
Also Called: Alego Health
24651 Center Ridge Rd Ste 400 (44145-5635)
P.O. Box 450679 (44145-0613)
PHONE.....................440 918-4570
Jacqueline Forestall, *Managing Member*
EMP: 34 EST: 2004
SQ FT: 9,000
SALES (est): 1.26MM **Privately Held**
SIC: **8742** Hospital and health services consultant

(G-15043)
CALYX LLC
Also Called: Managed Cloud Service Provider
909 Canterbury Rd Ste O (44145-7212)
PHONE.....................216 916-0639
Jason Fordu, *CEO*
William Bryson, *
Brian Caine, *
EMP: 30 EST: 2005
SALES (est): 4.93MM **Privately Held**
Web: www.calyxit.com
SIC: **7379 8742** Computer related consulting services; Management information systems consultant

(G-15044)
CAMBRIDGE TRS INC
Also Called: Sonesta Es Stes Clvland Wstlak
30100 Clemens Rd (44145-1013)
PHONE.....................617 231-3176
EMP: 27 EST: 2012
SALES (est): 258.92K **Privately Held**
Web: www.sonesta.com
SIC: **7011** Hotels

(G-15045)
CAREER CNNCTONS STFFING SVCS I
Also Called: Go2it Group
26260 Center Ridge Rd (44145-4016)
PHONE.....................440 471-8210
Beverly Sandvick, *Asst Sec*
Beverly Sandvick, *Pr*
EMP: 50 EST: 1997
SQ FT: 1,500
SALES (est): 8.84MM **Privately Held**
Web: www.go2itgroup.com
SIC: **7373 7376 7378 7379** Computer systems analysis and design; Computer facilities management; Computer maintenance and repair; Computer related maintenance services

(G-15046)
CARNEGIE MANAGEMENT & DEV CORP
27500 Detroit Rd Ste 300 (44145-5913)
PHONE.....................440 892-6800
Rustom R Khouri, *CEO*
Mary Khouri, *CAO*
Steven M Edelman, *
James Mckinney, *VP*
EMP: 30 EST: 1985
SQ FT: 17,000
SALES (est): 5.76MM **Privately Held**
Web: www.carnegiecorp.com
SIC: **6512 6552** Commercial and industrial building operation; Subdividers and developers, nec

(G-15047)
CD BLOCK K HOTEL LLC
Also Called: Hyatt Place
2020 Crocker Rd (44145-1963)
PHONE.....................440 871-3100
Todd Lentz, *Genl Mgr*
EMP: 34 EST: 2016
SALES (est): 2.48MM **Privately Held**
Web: clevelandwestlake.place.hyatt.com
SIC: **7011** Hotels

(G-15048)
CHOICELOCAL LLC
24960 Center Ridge Rd (44145-5640)
PHONE.....................855 867-5622
EMP: 87 EST: 2016
SALES (est): 4.45MM **Privately Held**
Web: www.choicelocal.com
SIC: **8742** Marketing consulting services

(G-15049)
CITY OF WESTLAKE
Also Called: Meadowood Golf Course
29800 Center Ridge Rd (44145-5121)
PHONE.....................440 835-6442
EMP: 28
SALES (corp-wide): 63.98MM **Privately Held**
Web: www.cityofwestlake.org
SIC: **7992** Public golf courses
PA: City Of Westlake
27700 Hilliard Blvd
Westlake OH 44145
440 871-3300

(G-15050)
CITY OF WESTLAKE
Also Called: Recreation Center
28955 Hilliard Blvd (44145-2938)
PHONE.....................440 808-5700
Colleen Rump, *Brnch Mgr*
EMP: 57
SALES (corp-wide): 63.98MM **Privately Held**
Web: www.cityofwestlake.org
SIC: **7999 8322 7991** Recreation center; Individual and family services; Physical fitness facilities
PA: City Of Westlake
27700 Hilliard Blvd
Westlake OH 44145
440 871-3300

(G-15051)
CLEVELAND ARPRT HSPITALITY LLC
1100 Crocker Rd (44145-1033)
PHONE.....................440 871-6000
Steve Burroughs, *Genl Mgr*
Tom Hipman, *
EMP: 96 EST: 1988
SALES (est): 9.07MM **Publicly Held**
SIC: **7011 5813 5812** Hotels; Drinking places; Eating places
PA: Travel + Leisure Co.
6277 Sea Harbor Dr
Orlando FL 32821

(G-15052)
COMPEL FITNESS LLC
25935 Detroit Rd (44145-2452)
PHONE.....................216 965-5694
EMP: 98 EST: 2020
SALES (est): 876.34K **Privately Held**
Web: www.compelfitness.com
SIC: **7991** Physical fitness facilities

(G-15053)
CONCORD RESERVE
2116 Dover Center Rd (44145-3154)
PHONE.....................440 871-0090
Charles Rinne, *CEO*
EMP: 50 EST: 2015
SALES (est): 19.02MM **Privately Held**
Web: www.lec.org
SIC: **8361** Aged home

(G-15054)
CONVEYER & CASTER CORP (PA)
Also Called: Conveyer Cstr-Qpment For Indus
29570 Clemens Rd (44145-1007)
P.O. Box 901802 (44190-1802)
PHONE.....................877 598-8534
▲ EMP: 30 EST: 1961
SALES (est): 26MM
SALES (corp-wide): 26MM **Privately Held**
Web: www.casterspecialists.com
SIC: **5084** Materials handling machinery

(G-15055)
CORNERSTONE MANAGED PRPTS LLC
25255 Center Ridge Rd (44145)
PHONE.....................440 263-7708
James E Dixon Junior, *Managing Member*
EMP: 30 EST: 2007
SALES (est): 2.75MM **Privately Held**
Web: www.cmpliving.com
SIC: **6512** Nonresidential building operators

(G-15056)
DCT TELECOM GROUP LLC
Also Called: Momentum Telecom
27877 Clemens Rd (44145-1167)
PHONE.....................440 892-0300
Anthony S Romano, *CEO*
Anthony Rehak, *
EMP: 35 EST: 1993
SALES (est): 4.83MM

Westlake - Cuyahoga County (G-15057) GEOGRAPHIC SECTION

SALES (corp-wide): 167.8MM **Privately Held**
Web: www.gomomentum.com
SIC: 4813 Internet connectivity services
HQ: Momentum Telecom, Inc.
    1 Concourse Pkwy Ste 600
    Atlanta GA 30328

(G-15057)
EQUITY TRUST COMPANY
1 Equity Way (44145)
P.O. Box 451339 (44145)
PHONE..................440 323-5491
Michael Dea, *Pr*
Mike Smyth, *
Amy Hall, *PEOPLE**
John Kish, *CIO**
EMP: 312 **EST:** 2002
SQ FT: 1,000
SALES (est): 77.97MM **Privately Held**
Web: www.trustetc.com
SIC: 6733 Personal investment trust management

(G-15058)
EZ SALES TEAMKELLER WILLI
2001 Crocker Rd (44145-6966)
PHONE..................216 916-7778
EMP: 51 **EST:** 2018
SALES (est): 617.13K **Privately Held**
Web: www.ezsalesteam.com
SIC: 6531 Real estate agent, residential

(G-15059)
FACTS MANAGEMENT COMPANY
Also Called: Private School Aid Service
28446 W Preston Pl (44145-6782)
PHONE..................440 892-4272
David J Byrnes, *Brnch Mgr*
EMP: 68
SALES (corp-wide): 2.06B **Publicly Held**
Web: www.factsmgt.com
SIC: 7389 Financial services
HQ: Facts Management Company
    121 S 13th St Ste 201
    Lincoln NE 68508

(G-15060)
FAR WEST CENTER (PA)
29133 Health Campus Dr (44145-5256)
PHONE..................440 835-6212
Kelly Dylag, *Dir*
EMP: 35 **EST:** 1974
SQ FT: 10,000
SALES (est): 1.13MM
SALES (corp-wide): 1.13MM **Privately Held**
Web: www.farwestcenter.com
SIC: 8322 8399 Family counseling services; Health systems agency

(G-15061)
GLOBAL TCHNICAL RECRUITERS INC
27887 Clemens Rd Ste 1 (44145-1181)
PHONE..................440 365-1670
EMP: 55
SALES (corp-wide): 8.59MM **Privately Held**
Web: www.gtrjobs.com
SIC: 7361 Executive placement
PA: Global Technical Recruiters Inc.
    27887 Clemens Rd Ste 1
    Westlake OH 44145
    216 251-9560

(G-15062)
GROUND EFFECTS LLC
31000 Viking Pkwy (44145-1001)
PHONE..................440 565-5925
Jim Scott, *Pr*
EMP: 50
Web: www.gfxltd.com
SIC: 7549 Automotive customizing services, nonfactory basis
HQ: Ground Effects Llc
    3435 Van Slyke Rd
    Flint MI 48507
    810 250-5560

(G-15063)
HARBORSIDE CLVELAND LTD PARTNR
Also Called: West Bay Center
27601 Westchester Pkwy (44145-1251)
PHONE..................440 871-5900
Nadine Kodysz, *Dir*
EMP: 125
SALES (corp-wide): 5.86B **Publicly Held**
SIC: 8051 Convalescent home with continuous nursing care
HQ: Harborside Of Cleveland Limited Partnership
    101 Sun Ave Ne
    Albuquerque NM 87109
    505 821-3355

(G-15064)
HARBORSIDE CLVELAND LTD PARTNR
Also Called: West Bay Care Rhbilitation Ctr
27601 Westchester Pkwy (44145-1251)
PHONE..................440 871-5900
Nadine Kodysz, *Dir*
EMP: 85
SALES (corp-wide): 5.86B **Publicly Held**
SIC: 8051 Skilled nursing care facilities
HQ: Harborside Of Cleveland Limited Partnership
    101 Sun Ave Ne
    Albuquerque NM 87109
    505 821-3355

(G-15065)
HEAD MERCANTILE CO INC
Also Called: SOS Group, The
29065 Clemens Rd Ste 200 (44145-1179)
PHONE..................440 847-2700
TOLL FREE: 800
James Scharfeld, *Pr*
Steven Scharfeld, *
EMP: 80 **EST:** 1975
SQ FT: 12,000
SALES (est): 2.31MM **Privately Held**
SIC: 7322 Adjustment and collection services

(G-15066)
HOSPICE OF THE WESTERN RESERVE
Also Called: HOSPICE OF THE WESTERN RESERVE, INC
30080 Hospice Way (44145-1077)
PHONE..................440 414-7349
EMP: 38
SALES (corp-wide): 76.67MM **Privately Held**
Web: www.hospicewr.org
SIC: 8052 Personal care facility
PA: Hospice Of The Western Reserve, Inc.
    17876 Saint Clair Ave
    Cleveland OH 44110
    216 383-2222

(G-15067)
HURST CONSTRUCTION INC
26185 Center Ridge Rd (44145-4015)
PHONE..................440 234-5656
Daniel J Hurst, *Pr*
Patrick G Hurst, *
EMP: 47 **EST:** 1998
SQ FT: 12,000
SALES (est): 12.16MM **Privately Held**
Web: www.hurstremodel.com
SIC: 1521 General remodeling, single-family houses

(G-15068)
HYLAND SOFTWARE INC (HQ)
Also Called: Onbase
28105 Clemens Rd (44145-1100)
PHONE..................440 788-5000
Bill Priemer, *CEO*
Nancy Person, *
Ed Mcquiston, *CCO*
John Phelan, *CPO**
Noreen Kilbane, *CAO**
EMP: 1800 **EST:** 1991
SQ FT: 150,000
SALES (est): 827.71MM
SALES (corp-wide): 1.2B **Privately Held**
Web: www.hyland.com
SIC: 7372 Application computer software
PA: Thoma Cressey Bravo, Inc.
    300 N La Slle Dr Ste 4350
    Chicago IL 60654
    312 254-3300

(G-15069)
IMCD US LLC (HQ)
Also Called: Hs Services
2 Equity Way Ste 210 (44145-1050)
PHONE..................216 228-8900
Jean-paul Scheepens, *Pr*
John L Mastrantoni, *
Thomas V Valkenburg, *
Bruce D Jarosz, *
Vlad Miller, *
▲ **EMP:** 46 **EST:** 1978
SALES (est): 227.45MM **Privately Held**
Web: www.imcdus.com
SIC: 2834 5169 5191 Pharmaceutical preparations; Chemicals and allied products, nec; Chemicals, agricultural
PA: Imcd N.V.
    Wilhelminaplein 32
    Rotterdam ZH

(G-15070)
INFINITY HEALTH SERVICES INC (PA)
Also Called: American Home Health Services,
975 Crocker Rd # A (44145-1030)
PHONE..................440 614-0145
Norma Goodman, *Pr*
EMP: 68 **EST:** 1997
SQ FT: 2,700
SALES (est): 4.55MM
SALES (corp-wide): 4.55MM **Privately Held**
SIC: 8082 Home health care services

(G-15071)
ITS TRAFFIC SYSTEMS INC
28915 Clemens Rd Ste 200 (44145-1177)
PHONE..................440 892-4500
Randall Houlas, *Pr*
Robert Houlas, *
▲ **EMP:** 57 **EST:** 1962
SQ FT: 10,000
SALES (est): 12.07MM **Privately Held**
Web: www.itstraffic.com
SIC: 8748 Traffic consultant

(G-15072)
J BECKER SOLUTIONS INC
1762 Mendelssohn Dr (44145-2351)
PHONE..................888 421-1155
Jon Steinman, *CFO*
EMP: 99
SALES (corp-wide): 8.22MM **Privately Held**
Web: www.jbs.dev
SIC: 7371 Computer software development
PA: J. Becker Solutions, Inc.
    610 Chadds Ford Dr Ste 23
    Chadds Ford PA 19317
    888 421-1155

(G-15073)
J P FARLEY CORPORATION (PA)
29055 Clemens Rd (44145-1135)
P.O. Box 458022 (44145-8022)
PHONE..................440 250-4300
James P Farley, *Pr*
Patricia Hannigan, *
EMP: 50 **EST:** 1979
SQ FT: 15,000
SALES (est): 28.76MM
SALES (corp-wide): 28.76MM **Privately Held**
Web: www.jpfarley.com
SIC: 6311 6321 6324 Life insurance; Accident and health insurance; Hospital and medical service plans

(G-15074)
LAKE ERIE ELECTRIC INC (PA)
25730 1st St (44145-1432)
P.O. Box 450859 (44145-0619)
PHONE..................440 835-5565
Peter J Corogin, *Pr*
Dennis Tarnay, *Prin*
Armando Francisco, *
EMP: 65 **EST:** 1952
SQ FT: 15,000
SALES (est): 111.7MM
SALES (corp-wide): 111.7MM **Privately Held**
Web: www.lakeerieelectric.com
SIC: 1731 General electrical contractor

(G-15075)
LIFE CARE CENTERS AMERICA INC
Also Called: Life Care Center of Cleveland
26520 Center Ridge Rd (44145-4033)
PHONE..................440 871-3030
Mary Ann Dubyoski, *Admn*
EMP: 179
SALES (corp-wide): 139.21MM **Privately Held**
Web: www.lcca.com
SIC: 8051 Convalescent home with continuous nursing care
PA: Life Care Centers Of America, Inc.
    3570 Keith St Nw
    Cleveland TN 37312
    423 472-9585

(G-15076)
LOGOS COMMUNICATIONS SYSTEMS INC
26100 1st St (44145-1478)
PHONE..................440 871-0777
EMP: 54
SIC: 7373 4899 Computer integrated systems design; Communication signal enhancement network services

(G-15077)
LORAD LLC (PA)
Also Called: Diversified Fall Protection
24400 Sperry Dr. (44145)
PHONE..................800 504-4016
Ken Paliwoda, *Managing Member*
EMP: 30 **EST:** 2000
SALES (est): 45.1MM
SALES (corp-wide): 45.1MM **Privately Held**
Web: www.fallprotect.com
SIC: 5084 Safety equipment

(G-15078)
LULULEMON USA INC
201 Market St (44145-6996)
PHONE..................440 250-0415

GEOGRAPHIC SECTION
Westlake - Cuyahoga County (G-15100)

EMP: 30
SIC: 5137 5331 Women's and children's sportswear and swimsuits; Variety stores
HQ: Lululemon Usa Inc.
2201 140th Ave E
Sumner WA 98390
604 732-6124

(G-15079)
MARITAIN HEALTH (PA)
24651 Center Ridge Rd Ste 200 (44145-5635)
PHONE.............................440 249-5750
Donald T Baker, *Pr*
Alex Hahn, *Ch Bd*
EMP: 80 **EST:** 1993
SQ FT: 21,000
SALES (est): 2.17MM **Privately Held**
SIC: 8742 Compensation and benefits planning consultant

(G-15080)
MOMENTUM FLEET MGT GROUP INC
24481 Detroit Rd (44145-1580)
PHONE.............................440 759-2219
Jack Pyros, *Pr*
EMP: 56 **EST:** 2005
SALES (est): 2.11MM **Privately Held**
Web: www.momentumgroups.com
SIC: 8741 6159 3699 Management services; Automobile finance leasing; Electrical equipment and supplies, nec

(G-15081)
NATIONAL AT/TRCKSTOPS HLDNGS C (DH)
Also Called: 76 Auto
24601 Center Ridge Rd Ste 200 (44145-5634)
PHONE.............................440 808-9100
Jonathan Pertchik, *CEO*
Edwin P Kuhn, *Ch*
Timothy Doane, *Ch Bd*
Michael H Hinderliter, *Sr VP*
EMP: 700 **EST:** 1993
SQ FT: 60,000
SALES (est): 400.94MM
SALES (corp-wide): 171.22B **Privately Held**
Web: www.ta-petro.com
SIC: 5541 7538 5812 5411 Filling stations, gasoline; General truck repair; Eating places; Convenience stores
HQ: Travelcenters Of America Inc.
24601 Center Ridge Rd # 200
Westlake OH 44145

(G-15082)
NATIONS LENDING CORPORATION
30700 Center Ridge Rd Ste 3 (44145-5197)
PHONE.............................440 842-4817
EMP: 70
SALES (corp-wide): 164.99MM **Privately Held**
Web: www.nationslending.com
SIC: 6162 Mortgage bankers and loan correspondents
PA: Nations Lending Corporation
4 Summit Park Dr Ste 200
Independence OH 44131
216 363-6901

(G-15083)
NEWPORT TANK CNTRS USA LLC (PA)
Also Called: Newport
2055 Crocker Rd Ste 300 (44145-1993)
PHONE.............................440 356-8866
◆ **EMP:** 274 **EST:** 1995
SALES (est): 43.88MM **Privately Held**
Web: www.newporttank.com

SIC: 4783 Containerization of goods for shipping

(G-15084)
NICK MAYER LINCOLN-MERCURY INC
Also Called: Quick Lane
24400 Center Ridge Rd (44145-4213)
PHONE.............................877 836-5314
Patricia Mayer, *Pr*
Jack Gannon, *
EMP: 74 **EST:** 1966
SALES (est): 22.52MM **Privately Held**
Web: www.nickmayer.com
SIC: 5511 7538 7515 Automobiles, new and used; General automotive repair shops; Passenger car leasing

(G-15085)
NORTH BAY CONSTRUCTION INC
Also Called: Pe
25800 1st St Ste 1 (44145-1481)
PHONE.............................440 835-1898
James J Manns, *CEO*
Michael S Kovatch, *
Evan Mullaney, *
EMP: 31 **EST:** 1983
SQ FT: 12,000
SALES (est): 5.31MM **Privately Held**
Web: www.northbayconstruction.com
SIC: 1799 7389 1796 1711 Hydraulic equipment, installation and service; Design, commercial and industrial; Installing building equipment; Plumbing, heating, air-conditioning

(G-15086)
NORTH EAST MECHANICAL INC
Also Called: Westland Heating & AC
26200 1st St (44145-1460)
PHONE.............................440 871-7525
Zachary Mitchell, *Pr*
EMP: 50 **EST:** 1985
SQ FT: 6,000
SALES (est): 10.5MM **Privately Held**
Web: www.westlandhvac.com
SIC: 1711 Refrigeration contractor

(G-15087)
NORTH SHORE GASTROENTEROLOGY
850 Columbia Rd Ste 200 (44145-7215)
PHONE.............................216 663-7064
EMP: 32
SALES (est): 2.53MM **Privately Held**
Web: www.northshoregastro.org
SIC: 8011 Gastronomist

(G-15088)
NORTH SHORE GSTRENTEROLOGY INC
Also Called: North Shore Gstrntrlogy Endsco
850 Columbia Rd Ste 200 (44145-7215)
PHONE.............................440 808-1212
Tabbaa Mousab Md, *Pr*
EMP: 48 **EST:** 1993
SALES (est): 9.84MM **Privately Held**
Web: www.northshoregastro.org
SIC: 8011 Gastronomist

(G-15089)
NORTHERN TIER HOSPITALITY LLC
Also Called: Best Western Grnd Victoria Inn
1100 Crocker Rd (44145-1033)
PHONE.............................570 888-7711
EMP: 44 **EST:** 1998
SALES (est): 1.09MM **Privately Held**
Web: www.twintierhospitality.com
SIC: 7011 Hotels and motels

(G-15090)
OH-16 CLVLAND WSTLAKE PRPRTYS
Also Called: TownePlace Stes Clvlnd Wstlak
25052 Sperry Dr (44145-1535)
PHONE.............................440 892-4275
Mona Rigdon, *Brnch Mgr*
EMP: 30
SALES (corp-wide): 676.82K **Privately Held**
Web: www.marriott.com
SIC: 7011 Hotel, franchised
PA: Oh-16 Cleveland Westlake Property Sub Llc
25050 Sperry Dr
Westlake OH 44145
440 871-3756

(G-15091)
OHIO MEDICAL GROUP (PA)
29325 Health Campus Dr Ste 3 (44145-8201)
PHONE.............................440 414-9400
Othma Shemisa Md, *Pr*
EMP: 50 **EST:** 1984
SALES (est): 4.16MM
SALES (corp-wide): 4.16MM **Privately Held**
Web: www.uhhospitals.org
SIC: 8062 General medical and surgical hospitals

(G-15092)
ORTHOPAEDIC ASSOCIATES INC
24723 Detroit Rd (44145-2526)
PHONE.............................440 892-1440
Manuel Martinez, *Prin*
EMP: 40 **EST:** 1970
SALES (est): 7.18MM **Privately Held**
Web: www.oaidocs.com
SIC: 8011 Orthopedic physician

(G-15093)
OUR HOUSE INC
27633 Bassett Rd (44145-3093)
PHONE.............................440 835-2110
Marguerite Vanderwyst, *Pr*
EMP: 35 **EST:** 1975
SQ FT: 44,000
SALES (est): 984.33K **Privately Held**
Web: www.ourhouseinc.com
SIC: 6514 Dwelling operators, except apartments

(G-15094)
PALMER HOLLAND INC
191 American Blvd Ste 300 (44145-8102)
P.O. Box 78000 (48278-0001)
PHONE.............................440 686-2300
Vince Misiti, *CEO*
Bradley Steven, *
Bert Bradley, *
Dorothy Waldern, *
Fred Palmer Iii, *Prin*
▲ **EMP:** 200 **EST:** 1925
SALES (est): 103.73MM **Privately Held**
Web: www.palmerholland.com
SIC: 5169 Industrial chemicals

(G-15095)
PAPYRUS-RECYCLED GREETINGS INC
1 American Blvd (44145)
PHONE.............................773 348-6410
Leonard Levine, *CFO*
Philip Friedmann, *VP*
Michael Keiser, *VP*
▲ **EMP:** 100 **EST:** 1972
SALES (est): 11.2MM
SALES (corp-wide): 14.52B **Privately Held**

Web: aggreetingsgateway.amgreetings.com
SIC: 2771 5199 Greeting cards; Gifts and novelties
HQ: American Greetings Corporation
1 American Blvd
Cleveland OH 44145
216 252-7300

(G-15096)
PAVEMENT TECHNOLOGY INC
Also Called: Resources Technology
24144 Detroit Rd (44145-1515)
PHONE.............................440 892-1895
Colin M Durante, *Pr*
John Schlegel, *
Eileen Durante, *
EMP: 48 **EST:** 1972
SQ FT: 13,000
SALES (est): 10.95MM **Privately Held**
Web: www.pavetechinc.com
SIC: 1611 Surfacing and paving

(G-15097)
PHARMED CORPORATION
Also Called: Pharmed Institutional Pharmacy
24340 Sperry Dr (44145-1565)
PHONE.............................440 250-5400
Elias J Coury, *Pr*
Norman Fox, *
Steve Demeter, *
Charles Freireich, *
Nancy Thorne, *
EMP: 70 **EST:** 1971
SQ FT: 36,000
SALES (est): 18.08MM **Privately Held**
Web: www.pharmedcorp.com
SIC: 5047 5122 Medical and hospital equipment; Drugs and drug proprietaries

(G-15098)
PINES MANUFACTURING INC (PA)
Also Called: Pines Technology
29100 Lakeland Blvd (44145)
PHONE.............................440 835-5553
Ian Williamson, *Pr*
Donald Rebar, *Ch Bd*
▲ **EMP:** 45 **EST:** 1993
SQ FT: 48,000
SALES (est): 9.54MM **Privately Held**
Web: www.pines-eng.com
SIC: 5084 3542 3549 3547 Industrial machinery and equipment; Bending machines; Metalworking machinery, nec; Rolling mill machinery

(G-15099)
PLANET HEALTHCARE LLC
24651 Center Ridge Rd Ste 475 (44145-5635)
PHONE.............................888 845-2539
Michael Stomberg, *CEO*
Tim Bauwens, *
Carolyn Durham, *
Jim Patton, *
EMP: 100 **EST:** 2014
SQ FT: 100,000
SALES (est): 8.82MM
SALES (corp-wide): 188.16MM **Privately Held**
Web: www.planet-healthcare.com
SIC: 7363 7389 Temporary help service; Drafting service, except temporary help
HQ: Propharma Group, Llc
107 W Hargett St
Raleigh NC 27601
888 242-0559

(G-15100)
PROGRAM TRANSPORTATION INC
815 Crocker Rd Ste 6 (44145-1072)

Westlake - Cuyahoga County (G-15101)

PHONE....................440 772-4134
Kelley Stewart, *Pr*
EMP: 32 **EST**: 2007
SALES (est): 1.74MM **Privately Held**
SIC: 4789 Transportation services, nec

(G-15101)
R AND J CORPORATION
Also Called: Haynes Manufacturing Company
24142 Detroit Rd (44145-1515)
PHONE....................440 871-6009
Beth Kloos, *Pr*
Timothy Kloos, *VP*
EMP: 42 **EST**: 1902
SQ FT: 23,000
SALES (est): 9.04MM **Privately Held**
Web: www.haynesmfg.com
SIC: 3556 5084 7389 3053 Food products machinery; Food industry machinery; Design, commercial and industrial; Gaskets; packing and sealing devices

(G-15102)
R E WARNER & ASSOCIATES INC
25777 Detroit Rd Ste 200 (44145-2484)
PHONE....................440 835-9400
Theodore Beltavski, *Pr*
Frank Johnson, *
EMP: 92 **EST**: 1951
SQ FT: 23,473
SALES (est): 17.67MM **Privately Held**
Web: www.rewarner.com
SIC: 8713 8712 8711 Surveying services; Architectural engineering; Mechanical engineering

(G-15103)
RADIOMETER AMERICA INC
810 Sharon Dr (44145-1598)
PHONE....................440 871-8900
Richard Keller, *Brnch Mgr*
EMP: 27
SALES (corp-wide): 23.89B **Publicly Held**
Web: www.radiometeramerica.com
SIC: 5047 Medical equipment and supplies
HQ: Radiometer America Inc.
250 S Krmer Blvd Ms B1 Sw
Brea CA 92821
800 736-0600

(G-15104)
RMS OF OHIO INC
Also Called: RMS Management
24651 Center Ridge Rd Ste 300 (44145-5635)
PHONE....................440 617-6605
EMP: 127
SALES (corp-wide): 9.41MM **Privately Held**
Web: www.teamrms.com
SIC: 8742 8741 Management consulting services; Business management
PA: Rms Of Ohio, Inc.
733 E Dblin Grnvlle Rd St
Columbus OH 43229
614 844-6767

(G-15105)
SCOTT FETZER COMPANY (PA)
Also Called: Kirby Vacuum Cleaner
28800 Clemens Rd (44145)
PHONE....................440 892-3000
Kenneth J Semelsberger, *Ch Bd*
Bob Mcbride, *Pr*
John Grepta, *
Vince Nardy, *MERGER & ACQUISITIONS**
◆ **EMP**: 40 **EST**: 1986
SQ FT: 80,000
SALES (est): 226
SALES (corp-wide): 226 **Privately Held**
Web: www.scottfetzer.com

SIC: 7699 Industrial equipment services

(G-15106)
SEELEY SVDGE EBERT GOURASH LPA
Also Called: SSE&g
26600 Detroit Rd (44145-2395)
PHONE....................216 566-8200
Gregory Seeley, *Mng Pt*
Glenn J Seeley, *Prin*
EMP: 29 **EST**: 1979
SQ FT: 15,108
SALES (est): 5.33MM **Privately Held**
Web: www.sseg-law.com
SIC: 8111 General practice attorney, lawyer

(G-15107)
SGT CLANS WSTLAKE HOLDINGS LLC
25247 Detroit Rd (44145-2536)
PHONE....................440 653-5146
Andrew Bendik, *Prin*
EMP: 27 **EST**: 2017
SALES (est): 579.91K **Privately Held**
SIC: 6531 Real estate brokers and agents

(G-15108)
SHAMROCK COMPANIES INC (PA)
Also Called: Shamrock Acquisition Company
24090 Detroit Rd (44145-1513)
P.O. Box 450980 (44145-0623)
PHONE....................440 899-9510
Tim Connor, *CEO*
Gary A Lesjak, *CFO*
Dave Fechter, *COO*
▲ **EMP**: 65 **EST**: 1982
SQ FT: 42,500
SALES (est): 87.67MM **Privately Held**
Web: www.shamrockcompanies.net
SIC: 5112 5199 7336 7389 Business forms; Advertising specialties; Art design services; Brokers' services

(G-15109)
SIMPLIFIED LOGISTICS LLC
28915 Clemens Rd Ste 220 (44145-1177)
PHONE....................440 250-8912
David Klugman, *Managing Member*
Robert H Maisch Junior, *Managing Member*
Samuel Avampato, *Managing Member*
Sheila Taylor, *CFO*
EMP: 27 **EST**: 2003
SALES (est): 7.81MM **Privately Held**
Web: www.simplifiedlogistics.com
SIC: 7375 On-line data base information retrieval

(G-15110)
SPECTRUM RTRMENT CMMNITIES LLC
27569 Detroit Rd Apt 251 (44145-5917)
PHONE....................440 892-9777
EMP: 52
SALES (corp-wide): 108.41MM **Privately Held**
Web: www.spectrumretirement.com
SIC: 6513 Retirement hotel operation
PA: Spectrum Retirement Communities, Llc
4600 S Syracuse St # 110
Denver CO 80237
800 686-8465

(G-15111)
ST JOHNS WEST SHORE HOSP PHRM
29000 Center Ridge Rd (44145-5219)
PHONE....................440 835-8000
Fred M De Grandis, *Pr*
EMP: 29 **EST**: 2011
SALES (est): 5.37MM **Privately Held**

Web: www.uhhospitals.org
SIC: 8062 General medical and surgical hospitals

(G-15112)
SUNRISE SENIOR LIVING LLC
Also Called: Brighton Gardens of Westlake
27819 Center Ridge Rd Ofc (44145-3920)
PHONE....................440 808-0074
Michael Beard, *Prin*
EMP: 47
SALES (corp-wide): 2.92B **Privately Held**
Web: www.sunriseseniorliving.com
SIC: 8051 Skilled nursing care facilities
HQ: Sunrise Senior Living, Llc
7902 Westpark Dr
Mc Lean VA 22102

(G-15113)
TA OPERATING LLC (DH)
Also Called: Open Road Distributing
24601 Center Ridge Rd Ste 200 (44145-5677)
PHONE....................440 808-9100
Thomas O Brien, *CEO*
Andrew J Rebholz, *Ex VP*
Ara Bagdasarian, *Ex VP*
Barry Richards, *Ex VP*
EMP: 300 **EST**: 1993
SQ FT: 60,000
SALES (est): 1.27B
SALES (corp-wide): 171.22B **Privately Held**
Web: www.ta-petro.com
SIC: 5541 7538 5812 5411 Filling stations, gasoline; General truck repair; Eating places; Convenience stores
HQ: Travelcenters Of America Inc.
24601 Center Ridge Rd # 200
Westlake OH 44145

(G-15114)
TECHNOLOGY RECOVERY GROUP LTD (PA)
Also Called: Trg Repair
31390 Viking Pkwy (44145-1063)
PHONE....................440 250-9970
Sean Kennedy, *Pr*
Chris Free, *CFO*
EMP: 68 **EST**: 1999
SQ FT: 20,000
SALES (est): 82.52MM **Privately Held**
Web: www.trgsolutions.com
SIC: 7379 8734 Computer related consulting services; Testing laboratories

(G-15115)
THUNDERYARD SOLUTIONS LLC
1382 W Melrose Dr (44145-2838)
PHONE....................281 222-3644
Laurence Van Der Oord, *Managing Member*
EMP: 30 **EST**: 2018
SALES (est): 1.16MM **Privately Held**
SIC: 7379 Computer related maintenance services

(G-15116)
TOWNEPLACE SUITES BY MARRIOTT
Also Called: TownePlace Suites By Marriott
25052 Sperry Dr (44145-1535)
PHONE....................440 871-3756
EMP: 29 **EST**: 2007
SALES (est): 716.23K **Privately Held**
Web: www.marriott.com
SIC: 7011 Hotel, franchised

(G-15117)
TRAVELCENTERS OF AMERICA INC (DH)

24601 Center Ridge Rd Ste 200 (44145-5677)
P.O. Box 451100 (44145-0627)
PHONE....................440 808-9100
Debi Boffa, *CEO*
Gregory Franks, *Pr*
Babu Rajalingam, *CFO*
Michael J Barton, *CAO*
EMP: 944 **EST**: 1992
SALES (est): 10.84B
SALES (corp-wide): 171.22B **Privately Held**
Web: www.tatravelcenters.com
SIC: 5541 7538 5812 Gasoline service stations; General truck repair; Eating places
HQ: Bp Products North America Inc.
501 Westlake Park Blvd
Houston TX 77079
281 366-2000

(G-15118)
UHHS WESTLAKE MEDICAL CENTER
960 Clague Rd Ste 3201 (44145-1588)
PHONE....................440 250-2070
Anna Kessler, *Admn*
EMP: 36 **EST**: 1999
SALES (est): 9.91MM **Privately Held**
Web: www.uhhospitals.org
SIC: 8062 General medical and surgical hospitals

(G-15119)
UNITED CRBRAL PLSY ASSN GRTER
28687 Center Ridge Rd (44145-3810)
PHONE....................440 835-5511
Trish Otter, *Mgr*
EMP: 45
SALES (corp-wide): 15.74MM **Privately Held**
Web: www.ucpcleveland.org
SIC: 8361 Mentally handicapped home
PA: United Cerebral Palsy Association Of Greater Cleveland, Inc.
10011 Euclid Ave
Cleveland OH 44106
216 791-8363

(G-15120)
UNIVERSITY HOSPITAL
Also Called: St. John's Medical Center
29101 Health Campus Dr Ste 200 (44145-5270)
PHONE....................440 835-8922
Delia Di, *Brnch Mgr*
EMP: 84
SALES (corp-wide): 25.52MM **Privately Held**
Web: www.uhhospitals.org
SIC: 8221 8062 Colleges and universities; General medical and surgical hospitals
PA: University Hospital
3315 N Ridge Rd E Ste 100
Ashtabula OH 44004
440 964-8387

(G-15121)
UNIVERSITY HSPTALS ST JOHN MED
Also Called: Westshore Prmry Care Assoc Inc
29000 Center Ridge Rd (44145-5219)
PHONE....................440 835-8000
EMP: 1200 **EST**: 1981
SALES (est): 188.09MM
SALES (corp-wide): 878.24MM **Privately Held**
Web: www.uhhospitals.org
SIC: 8062 General medical and surgical hospitals
PA: University Hospitals Health System, Inc.
3605 Warrensville Ctr Rd
Shaker Heights OH 44122

GEOGRAPHIC SECTION
Whitehouse - Lucas County (G-15142)

216 767-8900

(G-15122)
UNIVERSITY PRMRY CARE PRCTICES
Also Called: University Primary Care Practices
26908 Detroit Rd Ste 201 (44145-2399)
PHONE..................440 808-1283
EMP: 35
SALES (corp-wide): 878.24MM Privately Held
SIC: 8011 General and family practice, physician/surgeon
HQ: University Primary Care Practices, Inc.
4212 State Route 306 # 304
Willoughby OH 44094
440 946-7391

(G-15123)
WELLINGTON TECHNOLOGIES INC
802 Sharon Dr (44145-1539)
PHONE..................440 238-4377
EMP: 32 EST: 1996
SQ FT: 13,000
SALES (est): 1.02MM Privately Held
Web: www.audaxsolutions.com
SIC: 7378 Computer maintenance and repair

(G-15124)
WESTLAKE TEN INC
25777 Detroit Rd (44145-2450)
PHONE..................440 250-9804
Bradley W Clark, CEO
Edward M Deangelo, VP
EMP: 29 EST: 2002
SALES (est): 6.42MM Privately Held
Web: www.spyglass.net
SIC: 8741 8748 Financial management for business; Telecommunications consultant

(G-15125)
WLKOP LLC
Also Called: ORCHARDS OF WESTLAKE LIVING &
4000 Crocker Rd (44145-6312)
PHONE..................440 892-2100
EMP: 140 EST: 2002
SALES (est): 9.83MM Privately Held
SIC: 8011 8051 Clinic, operated by physicians; Skilled nursing care facilities

(G-15126)
YOUNG MNS CHRSTN ASSN GRTER CL
Also Called: Westshore Ymca/Westlake Chrn
1575 Columbia Rd (44145-2404)
PHONE..................440 808-8150
Laurie Wise, Brnch Mgr
EMP: 45
SALES (corp-wide): 25.51MM Privately Held
Web: www.clevelandymca.org
SIC: 8641 8661 8322 7991 Youth organizations; Religious organizations; Individual and family services; Physical fitness facilities
PA: Young Men's Christian Association Of Greater Cleveland
1301 E 9th St Fl 9
Cleveland OH 44114
216 781-1337

Wheelersburg
Scioto County

(G-15127)
BEST CARE NRSING RHBLTTION CTR
2159 Dogwood Ridge Rd (45694-9044)
PHONE..................740 574-2558
Wanda Meade, VP
EMP: 1639 EST: 1964
SQ FT: 40,000
SALES (est): 51.7MM
SALES (corp-wide): 1.03B Privately Held
Web: www.bestcarenursingandrehab.com
SIC: 8051 8093 Convalescent home with continuous nursing care; Specialty outpatient clinics, nec
HQ: Diversicare Management Services Lp
1621 Galleria Blvd
Brentwood TN 37027

(G-15128)
COLLINS ASSOC TCHNCAL SVCS INC
7991 Ohio River Rd (45694-1620)
P.O. Box 263 (45694-0263)
PHONE..................740 574-2320
James L Collins, Pr
EMP: 125 EST: 1980
SQ FT: 8,000
SALES (est): 1.84MM Privately Held
SIC: 8741 Construction management

(G-15129)
KIDS WORLD DAYCARE
191 Hansgen Morgan Rd (45694-8841)
PHONE..................740 776-4548
Tammy Skeens, Owner
EMP: 27 EST: 1995
SALES (est): 228.96K Privately Held
SIC: 8351 Group day care center

(G-15130)
LOWES HOME CENTERS LLC
Also Called: Lowe's
7915 Ohio River Rd (45694-1618)
PHONE..................740 574-6200
Brian Clifford, Mgr
EMP: 143
SALES (corp-wide): 86.38B Publicly Held
Web: www.lowes.com
SIC: 5211 5031 5722 5064 Home centers; Building materials, exterior; Household appliance stores; Electrical appliances, television and radio
HQ: Lowe's Home Centers, Llc
1000 Lowes Blvd
Mooresville NC 28117
336 658-4000

(G-15131)
MEDCOR SAFETY LLC
Also Called: Worldwide Sfety Prfssonals LLC
9076 Ohio River Rd (45694-1924)
P.O. Box 64 (45694-0064)
PHONE..................740 876-4003
EMP: 35 EST: 1984
SALES (est): 3.05MM
SALES (corp-wide): 107.8MM Privately Held
Web: www.medcor.com
SIC: 8742 Business management consultant
PA: Medcor, Inc.
4805 Prime Pkwy
Mchenry IL 60050
815 363-9500

(G-15132)
SOUTHERN OHIO MEDICAL CENTER
Also Called: S O M C Urgent Care
8770 Ohio River Rd (45694-1918)
PHONE..................740 574-9090
EMP: 112
SALES (corp-wide): 546.1MM Privately Held
Web: www.somc.org
SIC: 8062 General medical and surgical hospitals
PA: Southern Ohio Medical Center
1805 27th St
Portsmouth OH 45662
740 354-5000

(G-15133)
SOUTHERN OHIO MEDICAL CENTER
8430 Hayport Rd (45694-1831)
PHONE..................740 574-4022
Gary Coovert, Brnch Mgr
EMP: 112
SALES (corp-wide): 546.1MM Privately Held
Web: www.somc.org
SIC: 8062 General medical and surgical hospitals
PA: Southern Ohio Medical Center
1805 27th St
Portsmouth OH 45662
740 354-5000

(G-15134)
TRI-AMERICA CONTRACTORS INC (PA)
1664 State Route 522 (45694-7828)
PHONE..................740 574-0148
Scott Taylor, Pr
Teresa Smith, *
EMP: 37 EST: 1997
SQ FT: 34,000
SALES (est): 9.42MM
SALES (corp-wide): 9.42MM Privately Held
Web: www.triaminc.com
SIC: 3498 3441 1629 Fabricated pipe and fittings; Fabricated structural metal; Industrial plant construction

Whitehall
Franklin County

(G-15135)
BUCKEYE CHECK CASHING INC
Also Called: Checksmart
4100 E Broad St (43213-1214)
PHONE..................614 863-2522
EMP: 35
Web: www.ccfi.com
SIC: 6099 Check cashing agencies
HQ: Buckeye Check Cashing, Inc.
5165 Emerald Pkwy Ste 100
Dublin OH 43017
614 798-5900

(G-15136)
CERELIA USA BAKERY INC
430 N Yearling Rd (43213-1070)
PHONE..................614 471-9994
EMP: 39 EST: 2020
SALES (est): 10.55MM Privately Held
Web: www.cerelia.com
SIC: 5149 Crackers, cookies, and bakery products

Whitehouse
Lucas County

(G-15137)
ANTHONY WAYNE LOCAL SCHOOLS
Also Called: Anthony Wayne Trnsp Dept
6320 Industrial Pkwy (43571-9792)
P.O. Box 2487 (43571-0487)
PHONE..................419 877-0451
Randy Hardy, Superintnt
EMP: 48
SQ FT: 5,580
SALES (corp-wide): 60.17MM Privately Held
Web: www.anthonywayneschools.org
SIC: 4151 4111 School buses; Local and suburban transit
PA: Anthony Wayne Local Schools
9565 Bucher Rd
Whitehouse OH 43571
419 877-0466

(G-15138)
BITTERSWEET INC (PA)
Also Called: BITTERSWEET FARMS
12660 Archbold Whitehouse Rd (43571-9566)
PHONE..................419 875-6986
Vicki Obee-hilty, Ex Dir
EMP: 70 EST: 1977
SQ FT: 20,000
SALES (est): 7.08MM
SALES (corp-wide): 7.08MM Privately Held
Web: www.bittersweetfarms.org
SIC: 8361 2032 8052 Mentally handicapped home; Canned specialties; Intermediate care facilities

(G-15139)
BLUE CREEK HEALTHCARE LLC
11239 Waterville St (43571-9813)
PHONE..................419 877-5338
EMP: 95 EST: 2017
SALES (est): 6.41MM Privately Held
Web: www.bluecreekhc.com
SIC: 8051 Skilled nursing care facilities

(G-15140)
DEWESOFT LLC
Also Called: Dewesoft
10730 Logan St (43571-9697)
PHONE..................855 339-3669
Andrew Nowicki, CEO
EMP: 60 EST: 2012
SALES (est): 5.08MM Privately Held
Web: www.dewesoft.com
SIC: 7373 3825 Systems software development services; Instruments to measure electricity
HQ: Dewesoft D.O.O.
Gabrsko 11a
Trbovlje 1420

(G-15141)
DOYLE JA CORPORATION
Also Called: Homes By Josh Doyle
10075 Waterville St (43571-9409)
P.O. Box 161 (43542-0161)
PHONE..................419 705-1091
Joshua Doyle, Pr
EMP: 31 EST: 2007
SALES (est): 3.45MM Privately Held
Web: www.homesbyjoshdoyle.com
SIC: 1521 New construction, single-family houses

(G-15142)
FROG AND TOAD INC
Also Called: Whitehouse Inn
10835 Waterville St (43571-9181)
P.O. Box 2506 (43571-0506)
PHONE..................419 877-1180
John Fronk, Pr
Anthony Fronk, *
EMP: 46 EST: 1996
SALES (est): 1.09MM Privately Held
Web: www.thewhitehouseinn.net
SIC: 7011 Inns

Whitehouse - Lucas County (G-15143)

(G-15143)
LEADERSHIP CIRCLE LLC
10918 Springbrook Ct (43571-9674)
PHONE.....................................801 518-2980
Robert J Anderson Junior, *CDO*
Betsy Leatherman, *
Nathan Delahunty, *
▲ **EMP:** 30 **EST:** 1986
SALES (est): 2.47MM **Privately Held**
Web: www.leadershipcircle.com
SIC: 7379 Online services technology consultants

(G-15144)
WHITEHOUSE OPERATOR LLC
Also Called: Whitehouse Country Manor
11239 Waterville St (43571-9813)
PHONE.....................................419 877-5338
EMP: 60 **EST:** 2002
SQ FT: 27,015
SALES (est): 4MM **Privately Held**
Web: www.whitehousehc.com
SIC: 8051 Skilled nursing care facilities

Wickliffe
Lake County

(G-15145)
ANDY RUSSO JR INC
29200 Anderson Rd (44092-2312)
PHONE.....................................440 585-1456
Andy Russo Junior, *Pr*
EMP: 61
Web: www.arjinc.net
SIC: 1761 Ceilings, metal: erection and repair
PA: Andy Russo Jr. Inc.
3555 W Oquendo Rd Ste C
Las Vegas NV 89118

(G-15146)
BERTIN STEEL PROCESSING INC
1271 E 289th St Ste 1 (44092-2358)
P.O. Box 350 (44092-0350)
PHONE.....................................440 943-0094
Bernard D'ambrosi, *Pr*
Denny Perrino, *
▲ **EMP:** 47 **EST:** 1988
SQ FT: 300,000
SALES (est): 6.78MM **Privately Held**
Web: www.bertinsteel.com
SIC: 5051 Steel

(G-15147)
DMD MANAGEMENT INC
Also Called: Legacy Health Services
1919 Bishop Rd (44092-2518)
PHONE.....................................440 944-9400
EMP: 238
Web: www.lhshealth.com
SIC: 8741 Nursing and personal care facility management
PA: Dmd Management, Inc.
12380 Plaza Dr
Cleveland OH 44130

(G-15148)
EAST OHIO GAS COMPANY
Also Called: Dominion Energy Ohio
29555 Clayton Ave (44092-1924)
PHONE.....................................216 736-6917
EMP: 46
SALES (corp-wide): 39.69B **Privately Held**
Web: www.dominiongaschoice.com
SIC: 4924 Natural gas distribution
HQ: The East Ohio Gas Company
1201 E 55th St
Cleveland OH 44103
800 362-7557

(G-15149)
FOTI CONTRACTING LLC
1164 Lloyd Rd (44092-2314)
PHONE.....................................330 656-3454
EMP: 250 **EST:** 2002
SALES (est): 23.76MM **Privately Held**
Web: www.foticontracting.com
SIC: 1542 Nonresidential construction, nec

(G-15150)
GREAT LAKES CRUSHING LTD
30831 Euclid Ave (44092-1042)
PHONE.....................................440 944-5500
Mark M Belich, *Managing Member*
Mark M Belich, *Genl Pt*
EMP: 60 **EST:** 1996
SQ FT: 10,000
SALES (est): 8.85MM **Privately Held**
Web: www.glcrushing.com
SIC: 7359 1623 1629 1611 Equipment rental and leasing, nec; Underground utilities contractor; Land clearing contractor; Grading

(G-15151)
GTM SERVICE INC (PA)
Also Called: Parts Pro Automotive Warehouse
1366 Rockefeller Rd (44092-1973)
PHONE.....................................440 944-5099
Michael Mcphee, *Pr*
Laura Mcphee, *Prin*
EMP: 40 **EST:** 1981
SQ FT: 12,000
SALES (est): 24.38MM
SALES (corp-wide): 24.38MM **Privately Held**
Web: www.partsproautomotive.com
SIC: 5013 Truck parts and accessories

(G-15152)
HORIZON PERSONNEL RESOURCES (PA)
1516 Lincoln Rd (44092-2411)
PHONE.....................................440 585-0031
Daniel L Schivitz, *Pr*
Stephen Majercik, *VP*
EMP: 51 **EST:** 1989
SQ FT: 2,200
SALES (est): 9.09MM **Privately Held**
Web: www.horizonpersonnel.com
SIC: 7363 7361 Temporary help service; Employment agencies

(G-15153)
IMMACULATE LANDSCAPERS LLC ✪
1221 E 305th St (44092-1522)
PHONE.....................................440 724-1024
James Barnes, *Managing Member*
EMP: 30 **EST:** 2022
SALES (est): 691.37K **Privately Held**
SIC: 0781 Landscape services

(G-15154)
INN AT WICKLIFFE LLC
Also Called: Ramada Inn
28600 Ridgehills Dr (44092-2788)
PHONE.....................................440 585-0600
Ghanshyam Patel, *Managing Member*
EMP: 42 **EST:** 2008
SALES (est): 365.46K **Privately Held**
Web: www.wyndhamhotels.com
SIC: 7011 Hotels and motels

(G-15155)
JJO CONSTRUCTION INC
30047 Regent Rd (44092)
P.O. Box 713 (44061)
PHONE.....................................216 347-7802
Joseph J Orel, *Pr*
EMP: 40 **EST:** 1993
SQ FT: 7,500
SALES (est): 24.98MM **Privately Held**
Web: www.jjoconstruction.com
SIC: 1542 Commercial and office building, new construction

(G-15156)
LAZAR BROTHERS INC
Also Called: Stanley Steemer
30030 Lakeland Blvd (44092-1745)
PHONE.....................................440 585-9333
Terrance Lazar, *Pr*
Dennis E Lazar, *Sec*
Donald Lazar, *VP*
EMP: 31 **EST:** 1979
SQ FT: 8,100
SALES (est): 851.51K **Privately Held**
Web: www.stanleysteemer.com
SIC: 7217 Carpet and furniture cleaning on location

(G-15157)
MCSTEEN & ASSOCIATES INC
1415 E 286th St (44092-2506)
PHONE.....................................440 585-9800
Kevin Woeste, *CEO*
Molly Woeste, *
Maureen Feller, *
Debbie Feller, *BRD*
Terry Feller, *BRD*
EMP: 60 **EST:** 1968
SQ FT: 6,200
SALES (est): 5MM **Privately Held**
Web: www.mcsteen.com
SIC: 8713 Surveying services

(G-15158)
NORTHCOAST MOVING ENTPS INC
Also Called: Two Men and A Truck/Cleveland
1420 Lloyd Rd (44092-2320)
PHONE.....................................440 943-3900
Lynn Meilander, *Pr*
EMP: 60 **EST:** 1992
SQ FT: 27,000
SALES (est): 4.97MM **Privately Held**
Web: www.twomenandatruck.com
SIC: 4212 Moving services

(G-15159)
PARKER-HANNIFIN CORPORATION
Also Called: Precision Rebuilding Division
30242 Lakeland Blvd (44092-1747)
PHONE.....................................610 926-1115
Mark Kritz, *Mgr*
EMP: 27
SALES (corp-wide): 19.07B **Publicly Held**
Web: www.parker.com
SIC: 5084 Hydraulic systems equipment and supplies
PA: Parker-Hannifin Corporation
6035 Parkland Blvd
Cleveland OH 44124
216 896-3000

(G-15160)
PCC AIRFOILS LLC
Also Called: PCC Air Fils Llc-Cramics Group
1470 E 289th St (44092-2306)
PHONE.....................................440 944-1880
Angela Dukes, *Brnch Mgr*
EMP: 422
SALES (corp-wide): 364.48B **Publicly Held**
Web: www.pccairfoils.com
SIC: 5088 Aircraft equipment and supplies, nec
HQ: Pcc Airfoils, Llc
3401 Entp Pkwy Ste 200
Cleveland OH 44122
216 831-3590

(G-15161)
PERFECT CUT-OFF INC
29201 Anderson Rd (44092-2337)
PHONE.....................................440 943-0000
Michael V Picciano, *Pr*
Valerie Picciano, *
▲ **EMP:** 35 **EST:** 1973
SALES (est): 2.8MM **Privately Held**
Web: www.perfectcutoff.com
SIC: 7389 Metal cutting services

(G-15162)
RIDGEHILLS HOTEL LTD PARTNR
Also Called: Holiday Inn
28600 Ridgehills Dr (44092-2788)
PHONE.....................................440 585-0600
Patti Martin, *Mgr*
EMP: 55
SQ FT: 53,998
SALES (corp-wide): 1.77MM **Privately Held**
Web: www.holidayinn.com
SIC: 7011 5813 5812 Hotels and motels; Drinking places; Eating places
PA: Ridgehills Hotel Limited Partnership
1350 W 3rd St
Cleveland OH 44113
216 464-2860

(G-15163)
STG INTERMODAL INC
29115 Anderson Rd (44092-2357)
PHONE.....................................440 833-0924
Steve Brown, *Brnch Mgr*
EMP: 30
SALES (corp-wide): 3.63B **Privately Held**
Web: www.stgusa.com
SIC: 4731 Freight forwarding
HQ: Stg Intermodal, Inc.
5165 Emerald Pkwy Ste 300
Dublin OH 43017
614 923-1400

(G-15164)
THERMAL TREATMENT CENTER INC (HQ)
Also Called: Nettleton Steel Treating Div
28910 Lakeland Blvd (44092-2321)
PHONE.....................................216 881-8100
Carmen Paponitti, *Pr*
Jack Luck, *
Louise Profughi, *
EMP: 35 **EST:** 1945
SALES (est): 7.97MM
SALES (corp-wide): 9.44MM **Privately Held**
Web: www.htgmetals.com
SIC: 3398 8711 Metal heat treating; Engineering services
PA: Hi Tecmetal Group, Inc.
28910 Lakeland Blvd
Wickliffe OH 44092
216 881-8100

(G-15165)
WICKLIFFE COUNTRY PLACE LTD
Also Called: LEGACY HEALTH SERVICES
1919 Bishop Rd (44092-2518)
PHONE.....................................440 944-9400
Bruce Daskal, *Pr*
EMP: 152 **EST:** 1978
SALES (est): 13.34MM **Privately Held**
Web: www.lhshealth.com
SIC: 8051 Convalescent home with continuous nursing care
PA: Dmd Management, Inc.
12380 Plaza Dr
Cleveland OH 44130

Willard
Huron County

(G-15166)
COMMUNITY ACTION COMM ERIE HRO
Also Called: Willard Head Start Center
1530 S Conwell Ave (44890-9448)
PHONE...............................419 935-6481
Rosemary O'dell, *Admn*
EMP: 38
SALES (corp-wide): 10.74MM **Privately Held**
Web: www.cacehr.org
SIC: **8322** 8351 Family service agency; Child day care services
PA: Community Action Commission Of Erie, Huron & Richland Counties, Inc.
908 Seavers Way
Sandusky OH 44870
419 626-6540

(G-15167)
DUTCH MAID LOGISTICS INC
3377 State Rte 224 E (44890)
P.O. Box 365 (44890-0365)
PHONE...............................419 935-0136
EMP: 220 EST: 1977
SALES (est): 28.36MM **Privately Held**
Web: www.dutchmaid.com
SIC: **4213** 4212 Trucking, except local; Local trucking, without storage

(G-15168)
HOLTHOUSE FARMS OF OHIO INC (PA)
Also Called: Life Brand
4373 State Route 103 S (44890-9219)
PHONE...............................419 935-0151
Stanton Holthouse, *Prin*
Jordon Holthouse, *
Connie Holthouse, *
Carol Holthouse, *
EMP: 125 EST: 1930
SQ FT: 20,000
SALES (est): 9.33MM
SALES (corp-wide): 9.33MM **Privately Held**
Web: www.holthousefarms.com
SIC: **0161** 0191 Vegetables and melons; General farms, primarily crop

(G-15169)
LANDMARK RECOVERY OHIO LLC
725 Wessor Ave (44890-9417)
PHONE...............................855 950-5035
EMP: 272
SALES (corp-wide): 14.71MM **Privately Held**
Web: www.landmarkrecovery.com
SIC: **8322** Rehabilitation services
PA: Landmark Recovery Of Ohio, Llc
720 Cool Springs Blvd # 500
Franklin TN 37067
888 448-0302

(G-15170)
LIBERTY NURSING OF WILLARD
Also Called: Hillside Acres Nursing Home
370 E Howard St (44890-1656)
PHONE...............................419 935-0148
Linda Blackurek, *Pr*
EMP: 83 EST: 1964
SQ FT: 58,000
SALES (est): 3.43MM **Privately Held**
SIC: **8051** 8052 Convalescent home with continuous nursing care; Intermediate care facilities
PA: Lbk Health Care, Inc.

4336 W Franklin St Ste A
Bellbrook OH 45305

(G-15171)
MERCY HLTH - WILLARD HOSP LLC
Also Called: Mercy Hospital of Willard
1100 Neal Zick Rd (44890-9287)
PHONE...............................419 964-5000
Lynn Detterman, *
Ronald E Heinlen, *
Andrew Morgan, *
EMP: 225 EST: 1929
SQ FT: 70,000
SALES (est): 24.53MM
SALES (corp-wide): 6.92B **Privately Held**
Web: www.mercy.com
SIC: **8062** General medical and surgical hospitals
HQ: Mercy Health Cincinnati Llc
1701 Mercy Health Pl
Cincinnati OH 45237
513 952-5000

(G-15172)
PAM TRANSPORTATION SVCS INC
2501 Miller Rd (44890-9562)
P.O. Box 383 (44890-0383)
PHONE...............................419 935-9501
Fred Blank, *Mgr*
EMP: 44
SALES (corp-wide): 810.81MM **Publicly Held**
Web: www.pamtransport.com
SIC: **4213** 4231 Trucking, except local; Trucking terminal facilities
PA: P.A.M. Transportation Services, Inc.
297 W Henri De Tonti Blvd
Tontitown AR 72762
479 361-9111

(G-15173)
PRISTINE SENIOR LIVING OF
Also Called: Pristine Senior Living and
370 E Howard St (44890-1656)
PHONE...............................419 935-0148
Brian Femia, *Managing Member*
EMP: 60 EST: 2015
SALES (est): 645.4K **Privately Held**
Web: www.pristinesrwillard.com
SIC: **8059** Nursing and personal care, nec

(G-15174)
TRILOGY HEALTH SERVICES LLC
Also Called: Willows At Willard, The
1050 Neal Zick Rd (44890-9288)
PHONE...............................419 935-6511
Leigh Ann Barney, *Pr*
EMP: 100
SQ FT: 28,442
SALES (corp-wide): 779.79MM **Privately Held**
Web: www.trilogyjobs.com
SIC: **8051** 8361 Skilled nursing care facilities ; Residential care
HQ: Trilogy Health Services, Llc
303 N Hurstbourne Pkwy # 200
Louisville KY 40222

(G-15175)
WIERS FARM INCORPORATED (PA)
4465 State Route 103 S (44890-9220)
P.O. Box 385 (44890-0385)
PHONE...............................419 935-0131
EMP: 49 EST: 1896
SALES (est): 25.09MM
SALES (corp-wide): 25.09MM **Privately Held**
Web: www.wiersfarm.com
SIC: **0161** Vegetables and melons

Williamsburg
Clermont County

(G-15176)
APPALACHIAN INC
2280 Hales Way (45176-7504)
PHONE...............................937 444-3043
EMP: 36 EST: 1996
SALES (est): 2.9MM **Privately Held**
Web: www.appalachian.org
SIC: **1522** Apartment building construction

(G-15177)
B DRY SYSTEM INC
Also Called: B-Dry System
3481 Concord Hennings Mill Rd (45176-9148)
P.O. Box 311 (45040-0311)
PHONE...............................513 724-3444
David Barno, *Mgr*
EMP: 31
SALES (corp-wide): 2.62MM **Privately Held**
Web: www.bdry.com
SIC: **1799** Waterproofing
PA: B Dry System Inc
1341 Copley Rd
Akron OH 44320
888 779-2379

(G-15178)
CECOS INTERNATIONAL INC
Also Called: Site K62
5092 Aber Rd (45176-9532)
PHONE...............................513 724-6114
Connie Dall, *Mgr*
EMP: 33
SALES (corp-wide): 14.96B **Publicly Held**
SIC: **4953** Refuse collection and disposal services
HQ: Cecos International, Inc.
5600 Niagara Falls Blvd
Niagara Falls NY 14304
716 282-2676

(G-15179)
DUALITE SALES & SERVICE INC (PA)
Also Called: Dualite
1 Dualite Ln (45176-1121)
PHONE...............................513 724-7100
Gregory Schube, *CEO*
Kevin Syberg, *
E Lynn Webb, *
Paula Mueller, *
Kenneth Syberg, *
◆ EMP: 150 EST: 1991
SQ FT: 214,500
SALES (est): 32.02MM **Privately Held**
Web: www.dualite.com
SIC: **5099** Signs, except electric

(G-15180)
LOCUST RIDGE NURSING HOME INC
12745 Elm Corner Rd (45176-9621)
PHONE...............................937 444-2920
Howard L Meeker, *Pr*
Steven L Meeker, *
EMP: 125 EST: 1967
SQ FT: 20,000
SALES (est): 9.15MM **Privately Held**
Web: www.locustridgehc.com
SIC: **8051** Convalescent home with continuous nursing care

(G-15181)
REPUBLIC SERVICES KENTUCKY LLC
Also Called: Republic Services

5092 Aber Rd (45176-9532)
P.O. Box 117 (41097-0117)
PHONE...............................859 824-5466
Jim Hext, *Mgr*
EMP: 171
SALES (corp-wide): 14.96B **Publicly Held**
SIC: **4953** Refuse collection and disposal services
HQ: Republic Services Of Kentucky, Llc
2408 Sir Barton Way # 27
Lexington KY 40509
859 967-0591

Willoughby
Lake County

(G-15182)
A J GOULDER ELECTRIC CO
4307 Hamann Pkwy (44094-5625)
PHONE...............................440 942-4026
Keith Eldridge, *Pr*
Connie Eldridge, *
Bret Thomas, *
Amy Gallo, *
EMP: 44 EST: 1955
SQ FT: 4,500
SALES (est): 4.83MM **Privately Held**
Web: www.ajgoulderelectric.com
SIC: **1731** General electrical contractor

(G-15183)
ALL LIFT SERVICE COMPANY INC
Also Called: All Industrial Engine Service
4607 Hamann Pkwy (44094-5631)
PHONE...............................440 585-1542
John L Gelsimino, *Pr*
John P Gelsimino, *
EMP: 47 EST: 1972
SQ FT: 38,000
SALES (est): 8.73MM **Privately Held**
Web: www.alllift.com
SIC: **7699** 5013 7359 5084 Industrial truck repair; Truck parts and accessories; Industrial truck rental; Trucks, industrial

(G-15184)
ALPHA IMAGING INC
4455 Glenbrook Rd (44094-8219)
PHONE...............................440 953-3800
Albert D Perrico, *Prin*
EMP: 71 EST: 1986
SALES (est): 2.85MM **Privately Held**
Web: www.alpha-imaging.com
SIC: **5047** Medical equipment and supplies

(G-15185)
ALPHA IMAGING LLC (PA)
4455 Glenbrook Rd (44094-8219)
PHONE...............................440 953-3800
Albert D Perrico, *Pr*
Michael Perrico, *
Gia Perrico Stcklder, *Prin*
Pete Davis, *
Scott Macgregor, *
EMP: 70 EST: 1986
SQ FT: 7,500
SALES (est): 22.55MM
SALES (corp-wide): 22.55MM **Privately Held**
Web: www.alpha-imaging.com
SIC: **5047** 7699 X-ray machines and tubes; X-ray equipment repair

(G-15186)
ANDREWS APARTMENTS LTD
4420 Sherwin Rd (44094-7994)
PHONE...............................440 946-3600
Douglas Price, *Prin*
EMP: 153 EST: 2008

Willoughby - Lake County (G-15187)

SALES (est): 1.74MM
SALES (corp-wide): 47.06MM **Privately Held**
SIC: 6513 Apartment building operators
PA: The K&D Group Inc
4420 Sherwin Rd Ste 1
Willoughby OH 44094
440 946-3600

(G-15187)
BEAVER DAM HEALTH CARE CENTER
Also Called: Beverly
9679 Chillicothe Rd (44094-8503)
PHONE..............................440 256-8100
Jim Homa, *Ex Dir*
EMP: 32
SALES (corp-wide): 825.65MM **Privately Held**
Web: www.beaverdamhcc.com
SIC: 8059 Convalescent home
PA: Golden Living Llc
5220 Tennyson Pkwy # 400
Plano TX 75024
972 372-6300

(G-15188)
CONTEMPORARY ELECTRIC INC
38150 Strumbly Pl (44094-6590)
PHONE..............................440 975-9965
Russ Miozzi, *Prin*
EMP: 30
SALES (corp-wide): 2.27MM **Privately Held**
SIC: 1731 General electrical contractor
PA: Contemporary Electric, Inc.
5947 Graydon Dr
Seven Hills OH
216 398-6725

(G-15189)
DMS INC
37121 Euclid Ave Ste 1 (44094-5671)
PHONE..............................440 951-9838
Ben Ulrich, *Pr*
Al Pasquale, *VP*
◆ EMP: 105 EST: 1976
SQ FT: 1,200
SALES (est): 4.21MM **Privately Held**
SIC: 8742 8711 3316 Management consulting services; Engineering services; Cold finishing of steel shapes

(G-15190)
EAST END RO BURTON INC
Also Called: Riders Inn
792 Mentor Ave (44094)
PHONE..............................440 942-2742
Elaine R Crane, *Pr*
EMP: 41 EST: 1948
SQ FT: 7,801
SALES (est): 418.92K **Privately Held**
Web: www.ridersinn.com
SIC: 7011 Motels

(G-15191)
EMERITUS CORPORATION
Also Called: Eden Vista of Willoughby
35300 Kaiser Ct (44094-6633)
PHONE..............................440 269-8600
Laurie Bonarrigo, *Brnch Mgr*
EMP: 154
SALES (corp-wide): 2.83B **Publicly Held**
Web: www.emeritus.com
SIC: 8051 Skilled nursing care facilities
HQ: Emeritus Corporation
6737 W Wa St Ste 2300
Milwaukee WI 53214

(G-15192)
EXODUS INTEGRITY SERVICES INC
Also Called: Eis
37111 Euclid Ave Ste F (44094-5659)
PHONE..............................440 918-0140
Jim Ciricola, *Pr*
Pete Mc Millan, *
EMP: 44 EST: 1997
SQ FT: 2,000
SALES (est): 2.18MM **Privately Held**
Web: www.gotoeisinc.com
SIC: 7371 7361 Custom computer programming services; Employment agencies

(G-15193)
FLUID LINE PRODUCTS INC
38273 Western Pkwy (44094-7591)
P.O. Box 1000 (44096-1000)
PHONE..............................440 946-9470
John Skalicki, *Ch Bd*
John J Hetzer, *
Zelko Skalicki, *
Stella Ann Hetzer, *
EMP: 128 EST: 1974
SQ FT: 62,000
SALES (est): 23.26MM **Privately Held**
Web: www.fluidlineproducts.com
SIC: 5084 Hydraulic systems equipment and supplies

(G-15194)
HOLDEN ARBORETUM
9500 Sperry Rd (44094-5172)
PHONE..............................440 946-4400
Clem Hamilton, *Pr*
Jim Ansberry, *
EMP: 62 EST: 1932
SQ FT: 80,000
SALES (est): 11.55MM **Privately Held**
Web: www.holdenfg.org
SIC: 8412 Museum

(G-15195)
K&D MANAGEMENT LLC (PA)
4420 Sherwin Rd Ste 1 (44094-7995)
PHONE..............................440 946-3600
Douglas E Price, *Managing Member*
EMP: 343 EST: 2011
SALES (est): 11.53MM
SALES (corp-wide): 11.53MM **Privately Held**
SIC: 6513 Apartment building operators

(G-15196)
KIRTLAND COUNTRY CLUB COMPANY
39438 Kirtland Rd (44094-9201)
PHONE..............................440 942-4400
Brian Bollar, *Pr*
Roy Johnson, *
Mark T Petzinc, *
EMP: 100 EST: 1920
SQ FT: 15,000
SALES (est): 6.99MM **Privately Held**
Web: www.kirtlandcc.org
SIC: 7997 Country club, membership

(G-15197)
KUCERA INTERNATIONAL INC (PA)
Also Called: Kucera South
38133 Western Pkwy (44094-7589)
PHONE..............................440 975-4230
John W Antalovich Senior, *Ch Bd*
John W Antalovich Junior, *Pr*
Scott Antalovich, *VP*
Jack Kurant, *Sec*
EMP: 65 EST: 1948
SQ FT: 20,000
SALES (est): 9.75MM
SALES (corp-wide): 9.75MM **Privately Held**
Web: www.kucerainternational.com
SIC: 7335 8713 7389 8711 Aerial photography, except mapmaking; Surveying services; Photogrammatic mapping; Mining engineer

(G-15198)
LAKE COUNTY YMCA
Also Called: West End Branch
37100 Euclid Ave (44094-5612)
PHONE..............................440 946-1160
Robert Hoffman, *Brnch Mgr*
EMP: 144
SALES (corp-wide): 13.16MM **Privately Held**
Web: www.lakecountyymca.org
SIC: 8641 7991 8351 7032 Youth organizations; Physical fitness facilities; Child day care services; Youth camps
PA: Lake County Young Men's Christian Association
933 Mentor Ave Fl 2
Painesville OH 44077
440 352-3303

(G-15199)
LAKE HOSPITAL SYSTEM INC
Also Called: Lake-West Hospital
36000 Euclid Ave (44094-4625)
PHONE..............................440 953-9600
Cynthia Moore Hardy, *Prin*
EMP: 107
SALES (corp-wide): 878.24MM **Privately Held**
Web: www.uhhospitals.org
SIC: 8062 General medical and surgical hospitals
HQ: Lake Hospital System, Inc.
7590 Auburn Rd
Concord Township OH 44077
440 375-8100

(G-15200)
LAKE HOSPITAL SYSTEM INC
Also Called: Willoughby Physical Therapy
34881 Euclid Ave (44094-4503)
PHONE..............................440 975-0027
Janene Yokoyama, *Brnch Mgr*
EMP: 107
SALES (corp-wide): 878.24MM **Privately Held**
Web: www.uhhospitals.org
SIC: 8062 General medical and surgical hospitals
HQ: Lake Hospital System, Inc.
7590 Auburn Rd
Concord Township OH 44077
440 375-8100

(G-15201)
LAKE HOSPITAL SYSTEM INC
36060 Euclid Ave Ste 202 (44094-4661)
PHONE..............................440 942-4226
EMP: 107
SALES (corp-wide): 878.24MM **Privately Held**
Web: www.uhhospitals.org
SIC: 8062 General medical and surgical hospitals
HQ: Lake Hospital System, Inc.
7590 Auburn Rd
Concord Township OH 44077
440 375-8100

(G-15202)
LAKELAND FOUNDATION
7700 Clocktower Dr C2089 (44094-5198)
PHONE..............................440 525-7094
Bob Cahen, *Ex Dir*
EMP: 48 EST: 1981
SALES (est): 2.06MM **Privately Held**

Web: www.lakelandcc.edu
SIC: 8299 7371 Educational services; Computer software development and applications

(G-15203)
LAURELWOOD HOSPITAL (PA)
Also Called: Laurelwood Ctr For Bhvral Hlth
35900 Euclid Ave (44094-4648)
PHONE..............................440 953-3000
TOLL FREE: 800
Richard Warden, *Pr*
EMP: 225 EST: 1930
SQ FT: 160,000
SALES (est): 29.94MM
SALES (corp-wide): 29.94MM **Privately Held**
SIC: 8063 8069 Psychiatric hospitals; Substance abuse hospitals

(G-15204)
LEIKIN MOTOR COMPANIES INC
38750 Mentor Ave (44094-7929)
PHONE..............................440 946-6900
Ronald Leikin, *Pr*
EMP: 62 EST: 1968
SQ FT: 40,000
SALES (est): 22.06MM **Privately Held**
Web: www.leikinmotor.com
SIC: 5511 7532 7514 5531 Automobiles, new and used; Top and body repair and paint shops; Passenger car rental; Auto and home supply stores

(G-15205)
LIFE SAFETY ENTERPRISES INC
4699 Hamann Pkwy (44094-5631)
PHONE..............................440 918-1641
EMP: 46 EST: 1995
SALES (est): 1.5MM **Privately Held**
Web: www.lifesafetyenterprises.com
SIC: 8748 Safety training service

(G-15206)
LITTLE SCHOLARS INC
37912 3rd St (44094-6137)
PHONE..............................440 951-3596
Michelle Lewis, *Pr*
Moreen Mott, *VP*
EMP: 28 EST: 1978
SALES (est): 533.79K **Privately Held**
Web: www.littlescholars.net
SIC: 8351 Preschool center

(G-15207)
LOWES HOME CENTERS LLC
Also Called: Lowe's
36300 Euclid Ave (44094-4415)
PHONE..............................440 942-2759
Richard Brown, *Brnch Mgr*
EMP: 157
SALES (corp-wide): 86.38B **Publicly Held**
Web: www.lowes.com
SIC: 5211 5031 5722 5064 Home centers; Building materials, exterior; Household appliance stores; Electrical appliances, television and radio
HQ: Lowe's Home Centers, Llc
1000 Lowes Blvd
Mooresville NC 28117
336 658-4000

(G-15208)
LUCID INVESTMENTS INC
4034 Skiff St (44094-6217)
PHONE..............................216 972-0058
Derek Jones, *Pr*
Derek M Jones, *
EMP: 70 EST: 2009
SALES (est): 2.36MM **Privately Held**

GEOGRAPHIC SECTION
Willoughby Hills - Lake County (G-15232)

SIC: **6799** 5812 Investors, nec; Pizza restaurants

(G-15209)
MAIN SEQUENCE TECHNOLOGY INC
Also Called: PC Recorder
4420 Sherwin Rd Ste 3 (44094-7995)
PHONE..............................440 946-5214
Grachian Kubicek, *Mgr*
EMP: 35
SALES (corp-wide): 6.58MM **Privately Held**
Web: www.pcrecruiter.net
SIC: **7371** Computer software development
PA: Main Sequence Technology, Inc.
5370 Pinehill Dr
Mentor On The Lake OH 44060
440 946-5214

(G-15210)
MAK BURTNETT INC
9183 Chillicothe Rd Ste A (44094-9263)
PHONE..............................440 256-8080
EMP: 28
SALES (corp-wide): 114.3K **Privately Held**
SIC: **7389** Personal service agents, brokers, and bureaus
PA: Mak Burtnett Inc.
5229 Maple Springs Dr
Chagrin Falls OH

(G-15211)
MAROUS BROTHERS CNSTR INC
36933 Vine St (44094-6340)
PHONE..............................440 951-3904
Adelbert Marous, *Pr*
Scott Marous, *
Kenneth Marous, *
EMP: 300 EST: 1980
SALES (est): 120.01K **Privately Held**
Web: www.marousbrothers.com
SIC: **1521** 1751 New construction, single-family houses; Carpentry work

(G-15212)
MOVING AHEAD SERVICES LLC
35160 Topps Industrial Pkwy Ste 5 (44094-4675)
PHONE..............................440 256-2224
Jeffrey L Collins, *Prin*
EMP: 40 EST: 2010
SQ FT: 15,000
SALES (est): 5.73MM **Privately Held**
Web: www.movingaheadservices.com
SIC: **4212** Moving services

(G-15213)
NEUNDORFER INC
Also Called: Neundorfer Engineering Service
4590 Hamann Pkwy (44094-5691)
PHONE..............................440 942-8990
Michael Neundorfer, *CEO*
EMP: 50 EST: 1958
SQ FT: 38,000
SALES (est): 8.16MM **Privately Held**
Web: www.neundorfer.com
SIC: **8711** 3564 Pollution control engineering; Precipitators, electrostatic

(G-15214)
OHIO BROACH & MACHINE COMPANY
35264 Topps Industrial Pkwy (44094-4684)
PHONE..............................440 946-1040
Charles P Van De, *Mother*
Christopher C Van De, *Mother*
Richard Van De, *Mother*
Neil Van De, *Mother*
James L Lutz, *

▼ EMP: 34 EST: 1956
SQ FT: 52,000
SALES (est): 4.35MM **Privately Held**
Web: www.ohiobroach.com
SIC: **3541** 7699 3545 3599 Broaching machines; Knife, saw and tool sharpening and repair; Machine tool accessories; Machine shop, jobbing and repair

(G-15215)
OHIO LIVING
Also Called: Breckenridge Village
36855 Ridge Rd (44094-4128)
PHONE..............................440 942-4342
Jeannie Zuydhoek, *Brnch Mgr*
EMP: 508
Web: www.ohioliving.org
SIC: **8361** Aged home
PA: Ohio Living
9200 Worthington Rd # 300
Westerville OH 43082

(G-15216)
OHIO LIVING HOLDINGS
Also Called: Ohio Lving HM Hlth Grter Clvla
36500 Euclid Ave Apt 152 (44094-7993)
PHONE..............................440 953-1256
Laurence C Gumina, *CEO*
Kevin Futryk, *
Paul Flannery, *
Barbara Sears, *
Raafat Zaki, *
EMP: 65 EST: 2010
SALES (est): 585.02K **Privately Held**
Web: www.ohioliving.org
SIC: **8099** Health and allied services, nec

(G-15217)
PACE DRIVERS INC
35104 Euclid Ave Ste 101 (44094-4565)
PHONE..............................216 377-6831
Jason Peterson, *CEO*
EMP: 70 EST: 2014
SALES (est): 1.35MM **Privately Held**
Web: www.pacepersonnel.com
SIC: **4119** Automobile rental, with driver

(G-15218)
PAULO PRODUCTS COMPANY
Also Called: American Brzing Div Paulo Pdts
4428 Hamann Pkwy (44094-5628)
PHONE..............................440 942-0153
Bob Muto, *Brnch Mgr*
EMP: 38
SALES (corp-wide): 98.96MM **Privately Held**
Web: www.paulo.com
SIC: **7692** 1799 Brazing; Coating of concrete structures with plastic
PA: Paulo Products Company
5711 W Park Ave
Saint Louis MO 63110
314 647-7500

(G-15219)
Q4-2 INC
9250 Amber Wood Dr (44094-9351)
PHONE..............................440 256-3870
Brian J Scotese, *Pr*
EMP: 50 EST: 1983
SALES (est): 5MM **Privately Held**
Web: www.q4-2.com
SIC: **8748** 7371 Business consulting, nec; Custom computer programming services

(G-15220)
RED ROOF INNS INC
Also Called: Red Roof Inn
4166 State Route 306 (44094-9203)
PHONE..............................440 946-9872
Crista Shiel, *CEO*

EMP: 40
Web: www.redroof.com
SIC: **7011** Hotels and motels
HQ: Red Roof Inns, Inc.
7815 Walton Pkwy
New Albany OH 43054
614 744-2600

(G-15221)
SIGNATURE HEALTH INC
Also Called: NORTH COAST CENTER
38882 Mentor Ave (44094-7875)
PHONE..............................440 953-9999
EMP: 800 EST: 1993
SALES (est): 92.34MM **Privately Held**
Web: www.signaturehealthinc.org
SIC: **8093** Mental health clinic, outpatient

(G-15222)
TECHNICAL ASSURANCE INC
38112 2nd St (44094-6107)
PHONE..............................440 953-3147
EMP: 50 EST: 1993
SQ FT: 6,500
SALES (est): 5.01MM **Privately Held**
Web: www.technicalassurance.com
SIC: **7389** 8711 8744 1541 Building inspection service; Engineering services; Facilities support services; Industrial buildings and warehouses

(G-15223)
THE FINE ARTS ASSOCIATION
Also Called: SCHOOL OF FINE ARTS, THE
38660 Mentor Ave (44094)
PHONE..............................440 951-7500
Linda Wise, *CEO*
EMP: 39 EST: 1957
SQ FT: 30,000
SALES (est): 2.49MM **Privately Held**
Web: www.fineartsassociation.org
SIC: **7911** Dance studio and school

(G-15224)
U S MOLDING MACHINERY CO INC
38294 Pelton Rd (44094-7765)
PHONE..............................440 918-1701
Zac Cohen, *Pr*
Jerry Harper, *
Robert Luck, *
Bill Sprowls, *
EMP: 28 EST: 1980
SQ FT: 12,500
SALES (est): 4.92MM **Privately Held**
Web: www.usmolding.com
SIC: **3089** 7699 Injection molding of plastics; Industrial equipment services

(G-15225)
VECTOR TECHNICAL INC (PA)
4860 Robinhood Dr (44094)
PHONE..............................440 946-8800
Tim Bleich, *Pr*
EMP: 159 EST: 1992
SQ FT: 2,000
SALES (est): 8MM **Privately Held**
Web: www.vectortechnicalinc.com
SIC: **7361** Executive placement

(G-15226)
WILLO PUTT-PUTT COURSE INC
38886 Mentor Ave (44094-7875)
P.O. Box 566 (44096-0566)
PHONE..............................440 951-7888
Charlotte Hagerty, *Pr*
EMP: 30 EST: 1970
SALES (est): 218.25K **Privately Held**
SIC: **7999** 7996 Recreation center; Amusement parks

(G-15227)
WILLOUGHBY IR & WASTE MTLS LLC
3884 Church St (44094-6202)
PHONE..............................440 946-8990
EMP: 404 EST: 1926
SQ FT: 10,000
SALES (est): 1.23MM
SALES (corp-wide): 45.95MM **Privately Held**
Web: www.fptscrap.com
SIC: **5093** Ferrous metal scrap and waste
PA: Soave Enterprises L.L.C.
3400 E Lafayette St
Detroit MI 48207
313 567-7000

(G-15228)
WILLOUGHBY SERVICES INC (PA)
38230 Glenn Ave (44094-7808)
PHONE..............................440 953-9191
Raymond D Disanto, *Pr*
EMP: 55 EST: 1994
SQ FT: 1,200
SALES (est): 7.28MM
SALES (corp-wide): 7.28MM **Privately Held**
Web: www.roycesecurity.com
SIC: **7381** Security guard service

(G-15229)
WOODHILL SUPPLY INC (PA)
4665 Beidler Rd (44094-4645)
PHONE..............................440 269-1100
Arnold Kaufman, *Pr*
Rosalyn Kaufman, *
Bruce Shaw, *
EMP: 38 EST: 1958
SQ FT: 150,000
SALES (est): 17.06MM
SALES (corp-wide): 17.06MM **Privately Held**
Web: www.woodhillsupply.com
SIC: **5074** Plumbing fittings and supplies

Willoughby Hills
Lake County

(G-15230)
ANIMAL HOSPITAL INC
2735 Som Center Rd (44094-9121)
PHONE..............................440 946-2800
Deborah Dennis, *Pr*
Doctor J S Murray, *Pr*
EMP: 37 EST: 1960
SALES (est): 2.51MM **Privately Held**
Web: www.ahicares.com
SIC: **0742** Animal hospital services, pets and other animal specialties

(G-15231)
CLEVELAND CLINIC FOUNDATION
2570 Som Center Rd (44094-9607)
PHONE..............................440 516-8896
EMP: 41
SALES (corp-wide): 14.48B **Privately Held**
Web: www.clevelandclinic.org
SIC: **8062** General medical and surgical hospitals
PA: The Cleveland Clinic Foundation
9500 Euclid Ave
Cleveland OH 44195
216 636-8335

(G-15232)
CLEVELAND CLNIC RHBLTION PHYSC
29017 Chardon Rd (44092-1475)
PHONE..............................440 516-5400

Garry Calabres, *Dir*
EMP: 156 **EST:** 2004
SALES (est): 1.5MM
SALES (corp-wide): 14.48B **Privately Held**
Web: my.clevelandclinic.org
SIC: 8093 Rehabilitation center, outpatient treatment
PA: The Cleveland Clinic Foundation
9500 Euclid Ave
Cleveland OH 44195
216 636-8335

(G-15233)
MICRO PRODUCTS CO INC
26653 Curtiss Wright Pkwy (44092-2832)
PHONE..................................440 943-0258
Arthur Anton, *Pr*
Frank Roddy, *
Ernie Mansour, *
EMP: 48 **EST:** 1981
SQ FT: 10,000
SALES (est): 814.99K
SALES (corp-wide): 881.02MM **Privately Held**
SIC: 3471 7389 Plating of metals or formed products; Grinding, precision: commercial or industrial
PA: Swagelok Company
29500 Solon Rd
Solon OH 44139
440 248-4600

(G-15234)
PRODUCE PACKAGING INC
27853 Chardon Rd (44092-2703)
PHONE..................................216 391-6129
EMP: 150 **EST:** 1994
SALES (est): 43.25MM
SALES (corp-wide): 43.25MM **Privately Held**
Web: www.ppifresh.net
SIC: 2099 5148 4222 Food preparations, nec ; Fresh fruits and vegetables; Refrigerated warehousing and storage
PA: Great Lakes Packers, Inc.
400 Great Lakes Pkwy
Bellevue OH 44811
419 483-2956

Willowick
Lake County

(G-15235)
CITY OF WILLOWICK
Also Called: Manary Pool
30100 Arnold Rd (44095-4961)
PHONE..................................440 516-3011
Martin Gusauskas, *Mgr*
EMP: 35
Web: www.cityofwillowick.com
SIC: 7999 Swimming pool, non-membership
PA: City Of Willowick
30435 Lake Shore Blvd
Willowick OH 44095
440 585-1234

(G-15236)
LAKE HOSPITAL SYSTEM INC
29804 Lake Shore Blvd (44095-4611)
PHONE..................................440 833-2095
EMP: 107
SALES (corp-wide): 878.24MM **Privately Held**
Web: www.uhhospitals.org
SIC: 8062 General medical and surgical hospitals
HQ: Lake Hospital System, Inc.
7590 Auburn Rd
Concord Township OH 44077
440 375-8100

Wilmington
Clinton County

(G-15237)
ABX AIR INC (HQ)
145 Hunter Dr (45177-9550)
PHONE..................................937 382-5591
John Starkovich, *Pr*
W Joseph Payne, *VP*
Joe Hete, *CEO*
Patrick Fluegeman, *COO*
James H Carey, *Prin*
▲ **EMP:** 500 **EST:** 1980
SQ FT: 37,000
SALES (est): 152.8MM **Publicly Held**
Web: www.abxair.com
SIC: 4513 5088 4581 8299 Letter delivery, private air; Aircraft and parts, nec; Aircraft servicing and repairing; Flying instruction
PA: Air Transport Services Group, Inc.
145 Hunter Dr
Wilmington OH 45177

(G-15238)
AG-PRO OHIO LLC
Also Called: John Deere Authorized Dealer
7550 N Us Highway 68 (45177-9517)
PHONE..................................937 486-5211
Kent Beam, *Mgr*
EMP: 44
SALES (corp-wide): 204.78MM **Privately Held**
Web: www.agprocompanies.com
SIC: 5083 7699 5261 Agricultural machinery and equipment; Antique repair and restoration, except furniture, autos; Lawnmowers and tractors
HQ: Ag-Pro Ohio, Llc
19595 Us Highway 84 E
Boston GA 31626
229 498-8833

(G-15239)
AIR TRANSPORT INTL INC
145 Hunter Dr Ste 2 (45177-9551)
PHONE..................................937 382-5591
Dennis Manibusan, *Prin*
EMP: 231 **EST:** 2014
SALES (est): 54.04MM **Publicly Held**
Web: www.airtransport.cc
SIC: 4789 Pipeline terminal facilities, independently operated
PA: Air Transport Services Group, Inc.
145 Hunter Dr
Wilmington OH 45177

(G-15240)
AIR TRANSPORT SVCS GROUP INC (PA)
Also Called: ATSG
145 Hunter Dr Ste 2 (45177)
P.O. Box 966 (45177)
PHONE..................................937 382-5591
Joseph C Hete, *Ch Bd*
Michael L Berger, *Pr*
Quint O Turner, *CFO*
Edward J Koharik, *COO*
W Joseph Payne, *CLO*
EMP: 202 **EST:** 1980
SQ FT: 310,000
SALES (est): 2.07B **Publicly Held**
Web: www.atsginc.com
SIC: 4513 Air courier services

(G-15241)
AIRBORNE GLOBAL SOLUTIONS INC
145 Hunter Dr (45177-9550)
PHONE..................................937 382-5591
Ricardo Corrado, *Pr*
Scott Glasser, *
EMP: 75 **EST:** 2011
SALES (est): 4.55MM **Publicly Held**
Web: www.airborneglobal.com
SIC: 4513 Air courier services
PA: Air Transport Services Group, Inc.
145 Hunter Dr
Wilmington OH 45177

(G-15242)
AIRBORNE MAINT ENGRG SVCS INC
Also Called: Airborne
1111 Airport Rd (45177-8904)
PHONE..................................937 366-2559
Brady Price, *Brnch Mgr*
EMP: 156
Web: www.airbornemx.com
SIC: 7699 5088 Aircraft and heavy equipment repair services; Aircraft and parts, nec
HQ: Airborne Maintenance And Engineering Services, Inc.
145 Hunter Dr
Wilmington OH 45177

(G-15243)
AIRBORNE MAINT ENGRG SVCS INC (HQ)
145 Hunter Dr (45177-9550)
PHONE..................................937 382-5591
Todd France, *Pr*
Mark Price, *
EMP: 190 **EST:** 2009
SALES (est): 133.54MM **Publicly Held**
Web: www.airbornemx.com
SIC: 7699 5088 Aircraft and heavy equipment repair services; Aircraft and parts, nec
PA: Air Transport Services Group, Inc.
145 Hunter Dr
Wilmington OH 45177

(G-15244)
AMES MATERIAL SERVICES INC
145 Hunter Dr (45177-9550)
P.O. Box 966 (45177-0966)
PHONE..................................937 382-5591
Joseph Hete, *Pr*
John Graver, *
EMP: 190 **EST:** 1982
SALES (est): 5.72MM **Publicly Held**
Web: www.atsginc.com
SIC: 4513 Air courier services
PA: Air Transport Services Group, Inc.
145 Hunter Dr
Wilmington OH 45177

(G-15245)
ARENA HORSE SHOWS LLC (PA)
Also Called: World Equestrian Center, The
4095 State Route 730 (45177-8473)
PHONE..................................937 382-0985
EMP: 39 **EST:** 2016
SALES (est): 8.6MM
SALES (corp-wide): 8.6MM **Privately Held**
Web: www.worldequestriancenter.com
SIC: 7999 Riding and rodeo services

(G-15246)
ARENA HORSE SHOWS OCALA LLC
Also Called: World Equestrian Center
600 Gilliam Rd (45177-9089)
PHONE..................................239 275-2314
Roby Roberts, *Pr*
Jeff Haungs, *
EMP: 100 **EST:** 2019
SALES (est): 5.16MM
SALES (corp-wide): 8.6MM **Privately Held**
Web: www.worldequestriancenter.com
SIC: 7941 Stadium event operator services
PA: Arena Horse Shows, L.L.C.
4095 State Route 730
Wilmington OH 45177
937 382-0985

(G-15247)
BRIMSTONE & FIRE LLC
Also Called: Ohio Renaissance Festival
317 Brimstone Rd (45177-8531)
PHONE..................................937 776-5182
David E Ashcraft, *Prin*
Charles Biehn, *
EMP: 50 **EST:** 2014
SALES (est): 2.35MM **Privately Held**
SIC: 7941 Sports clubs, managers, and promoters

(G-15248)
CLINTON CNTY CMNTY ACTION PRGR (PA)
789 N Nelson Ave (45177-8348)
P.O. Box 32 (45177-0032)
PHONE..................................937 382-8365
Dean Knapp, *Dir*
EMP: 65 **EST:** 1965
SQ FT: 11,782
SALES (est): 8.35MM
SALES (corp-wide): 8.35MM **Privately Held**
Web: www.clintoncap.org
SIC: 8399 Community action agency

(G-15249)
CLINTON MEMORIAL HOSPITAL (PA)
610 W Main St (45177-2125)
P.O. Box 600 (45177-0600)
PHONE..................................937 382-6611
TOLL FREE: 800
Mark Dooley, *Pr*
Bradley Boggus, *
Bradley Mabry, *
EMP: 475 **EST:** 1951
SQ FT: 200,000
SALES (est): 89.21MM
SALES (corp-wide): 89.21MM **Privately Held**
Web: www.cmhregional.com
SIC: 8062 General medical and surgical hospitals

(G-15250)
EQUIPMENT MGT SVC & REPR INC
Also Called: Emsar
270 Davids Dr (45177-2491)
PHONE..................................937 383-1052
▲ **EMP:** 27 **EST:** 1993
SQ FT: 10,000
SALES (est): 16.62MM
SALES (corp-wide): 44.26MM **Privately Held**
Web: www.emsar.com
SIC: 7699 Medical equipment repair, non-electric
PA: Csa Service Solutions, Llc
9208 Wtrford Cntre Blvd S
Austin TX 78758
877 487-5360

(G-15251)
FERNO GROUP INC (PA)
Also Called: Ferno Washington
Weil Way 70 (45177-9371)
PHONE..................................937 382-1451
Joe Bourgraf, *Pr*
EMP: 115 **EST:** 2010
SALES (est): 14.96MM
SALES (corp-wide): 14.96MM **Privately Held**
Web: www.ferno.com
SIC: 6111 Export/Import Bank

GEOGRAPHIC SECTION
Wilmington - Clinton County (G-15273)

(G-15252)
FERNO-WASHINGTON INC (PA)
Also Called: Ferno
70 Weil Way (45177-9300)
PHONE.................877 733-0911
Joseph Bourgraf, *Pr*
Elroy Bourgraf, *
◆ **EMP:** 243 **EST:** 1955
SQ FT: 212,000
SALES (est): 90.87MM
SALES (corp-wide): 90.87MM **Privately Held**
Web: www.ferno.com
SIC: 5047 3842 Medical equipment and supplies; Splints, pneumatic and wood

(G-15253)
FIFTH THIRD BNK OF STHERN OH I
Also Called: Fifth Third Bank
995 Rombach Ave Frnt Frnt (45177-1957)
PHONE.................937 382-2620
Jana Wells, *Mgr*
EMP: 44
SALES (corp-wide): 12.64B **Publicly Held**
SIC: 6022 State trust companies accepting deposits, commercial
HQ: The Fifth Third Bank Of Southern Oh Inc
511 N High St
Hillsboro OH 45133
937 840-5353

(G-15254)
FRESENIUS MED CARE WLMNGTON HM
Also Called: Fresenius Kdney Care Wlmngton
164 Holiday Dr (45177-8731)
PHONE.................937 382-3379
Bryant Garrett, *Brnch Mgr*
EMP: 36
SALES (corp-wide): 236.36K **Privately Held**
Web: www.kidneycareohio.com
SIC: 8092 Kidney dialysis centers
PA: Fresenius Medical Care Wilmington Home, Llc
920 Winter St
Waltham MA 02451
781 699-9000

(G-15255)
GREENWOOD MOTOR LINES INC (HQ)
Also Called: R & L Carriers
600 Gilliam Rd (45177-9089)
P.O. Box 271 (45177-0271)
PHONE.................800 543-5589
EMP: 300 **EST:** 1973
SALES (est): 78.32MM **Privately Held**
Web: www.rlcarriers.com
SIC: 4213 4212 Trucking, except local; Local trucking, without storage
PA: R & L Carriers, Inc.
600 Gilliam Rd
Wilmington OH 45177

(G-15256)
LAW OFFCES RBERT A SCHRGER LPA
Also Called: Schuerger Law Group
1113 Airport Rd (45177-8904)
PHONE.................614 824-5731
EMP: 30 **EST:** 2009
SQ FT: 15,000
SALES (est): 4.7MM **Privately Held**
Web: www.schuergerlaw.com
SIC: 8111 General practice attorney, lawyer

(G-15257)
LGSTX SERVICES INC (HQ)
145 Hunter Dr (45177)
PHONE.................866 931-2337
Gary Stover, *Pr*
Todd Reed, *OF Business Development**
EMP: 28 **EST:** 2010
SALES (est): 30.68MM **Publicly Held**
Web: www.lgstx.com
SIC: 4513 Air courier services
PA: Air Transport Services Group, Inc.
145 Hunter Dr
Wilmington OH 45177

(G-15258)
LIBERTY CAPITAL INC (PA)
3435 Airborne Rd Ste B (45177-8951)
P.O. Box 1000 (45177-1000)
PHONE.................937 382-1000
James R Powell, *Pr*
John H Powell, *
Kent Powell, *Stockholder**
EMP: 71 **EST:** 1985
SALES (est): 43.19MM
SALES (corp-wide): 43.19MM **Privately Held**
Web: www.libertycapitalpartners.com
SIC: 6022 State commercial banks

(G-15259)
LIBERTY SAVINGS BANK FSB (HQ)
2251 Rombach Ave (45177-1995)
P.O. Box 1000 (45177-1000)
PHONE.................937 382-1000
James R Powell, *CEO*
John H Powell, *V Ch Bd*
Robert E Reed, *Pr*
Bruce Clapp, *VP*
Timothy Fiedler, *VP*
EMP: 113 **EST:** 1889
SQ FT: 50,000
SALES (est): 43.19MM
SALES (corp-wide): 43.19MM **Privately Held**
Web: www.libertysavingsbank.com
SIC: 6022 State commercial banks
PA: Liberty Capital, Inc.
3435 Airborne Rd Ste B
Wilmington OH 45177
937 382-1000

(G-15260)
LOWES HOME CENTERS LLC
Also Called: Lowe's
1175 Rombach Ave (45177-1940)
PHONE.................937 383-7000
EMP: 143
SALES (corp-wide): 86.38B **Publicly Held**
Web: www.lowes.com
SIC: 5211 5031 5722 5064 Home centers; Building materials, exterior; Household appliance stores; Electrical appliances, television and radio
HQ: Lowe's Home Centers, Llc
1000 Lowes Blvd
Mooresville NC 28117
336 658-4000

(G-15261)
NB&T FINANCIAL GROUP INC
48 N South St (45177-2212)
PHONE.................937 382-1441
EMP: 392
SIC: 6021 National commercial banks

(G-15262)
OHIO AUTO LOAN SERVICES INC
2855 Progress Way Ste 300 (45177-7607)
PHONE.................937 556-4687
EMP: 37
SIC: 6141 Automobile loans, including insurance
HQ: Ohio Auto Loan Services, Inc.
8601 Dunwoody Pl Ste 406
Atlanta GA 30350
770 552-9840

(G-15263)
PC CONNECTION INC
Also Called: Connection
3336 Progress Way Bldg 11 (45177-8928)
PHONE.................937 382-4800
John Moran, *Mgr*
EMP: 175
SALES (corp-wide): 2.85B **Publicly Held**
Web: www.connection.com
SIC: 4226 5045 Special warehousing and storage, nec; Computers, peripherals, and software
PA: Pc Connection, Inc.
730 Milford Rd
Merrimack NH 03054
603 683-2000

(G-15264)
PC CONNECTION SALES CORP
2870 Old State Route 73 Ste 1 (45177-9383)
PHONE.................937 382-4800
John Moran, *Mgr*
EMP: 70
SALES (corp-wide): 2.85B **Publicly Held**
SIC: 4225 5961 General warehousing and storage; Computers and peripheral equipment, mail order
HQ: Pc Connection Sales Corp
730 Milford Rd
Merrimack NH 03054
603 423-2000

(G-15265)
R & L CARRIERS INC (PA)
Also Called: Rl Carriers
600 Gilliam Rd (45177-9089)
P.O. Box 271 (45177-0271)
PHONE.................800 543-5589
EMP: 1500 **EST:** 1965
SALES (est): 1.28B **Privately Held**
Web: www.rlcarriers.com
SIC: 4213 Trucking, except local

(G-15266)
R & L TRANSFER INC
1221 Warren Dr (45177-2546)
PHONE.................937 305-9287
EMP: 383
SIC: 4213 Trucking, except local
HQ: R & L Transfer, Inc.
600 Gilliam Rd
Wilmington OH 45177
937 382-1494

(G-15267)
R & L TRANSFER INC
2483 W Us Highway 22 3 (45177-7693)
PHONE.................614 871-3813
Joseph W Plye, *Brnch Mgr*
EMP: 444
SIC: 4213 Trucking, except local
HQ: R & L Transfer, Inc.
600 Gilliam Rd
Wilmington OH 45177
937 382-1494

(G-15268)
R & L TRANSFER INC (HQ)
600 Gilliam Rd (45177-9089)
P.O. Box 10020 (45164-2000)
PHONE.................937 382-1494
EMP: 1000 **EST:** 1967
SALES (est): 244.87MM **Privately Held**

SIC: 4213 Less-than-truckload (LTL)
PA: R & L Carriers, Inc.
600 Gilliam Rd
Wilmington OH 45177

(G-15269)
R & M LEASING INC
Also Called: Roberts Truck Parts
600 Gilliam Rd (45177-9089)
P.O. Box 271 (45177-0271)
PHONE.................937 382-6800
EMP: 150 **EST:** 1977
SALES (est): 53.97MM **Privately Held**
Web: www.robertstrucksales.com
SIC: 5531 7538 Truck equipment and parts; General truck repair
PA: R & L Carriers, Inc.
600 Gilliam Rd
Wilmington OH 45177

(G-15270)
RLR INVESTMENTS LLC
Also Called: Castaways On The River, The
600 Gilliam Rd (45177-9089)
PHONE.................937 382-1494
EMP: 100 **EST:** 2007
SALES (est): 13.57MM **Privately Held**
Web: www.rlcarriers.com
SIC: 4222 Warehousing, cold storage or refrigerated

(G-15271)
ROSE & DOBYNS AN OHIO PARTNR (PA)
Also Called: Rose & Dobyns
97 N South St (45177-1644)
PHONE.................937 382-2838
Gordon Rose, *Pt*
J Michael Dobyns, *Pt*
Richard Federle Junior, *Pt*
John Porter, *Pt*
Michael Campbell, *Pt*
EMP: 38 **EST:** 1983
SALES (est): 2.32MM **Privately Held**
Web: www.rosedobyns.com
SIC: 8111 General practice attorney, lawyer

(G-15272)
S & S MANAGEMENT INC
Also Called: Holiday Inn
155 Holiday Dr (45177-8763)
PHONE.................937 382-5858
Bryan Powell, *Genl Mgr*
EMP: 54
SALES (corp-wide): 9.26MM **Privately Held**
Web: www.ssmngtinc.com
SIC: 7011 Hotels and motels
PA: S & S Management Inc
550 Folkerth Ave 100
Sidney OH 45365
937 498-9645

(G-15273)
SEWELL LEASING CORPORATION
Also Called: Sewell Motor Express
370 Davids Dr (45177-2424)
PHONE.................937 382-3847
Janet Sewell, *CEO*
Jay Sewell, *
Leslie Williams, *
▲ **EMP:** 70 **EST:** 1921
SQ FT: 90,000
SALES (est): 11.45MM **Privately Held**
Web: www.go-sewell.com
SIC: 4213 4212 Contract haulers; Local trucking, without storage

Wilmington - Clinton County (G-15274)

(G-15274)
STORES CONSULTING GROUP LLC
783 Mitchell Rd (45177-8522)
PHONE..................................717 309-5302
EMP: 29 **EST:** 2010
SALES (est): 491.18K **Privately Held**
Web: www.storesconsulting.com
SIC: 8748 Business consulting, nec

(G-15275)
TRACTOR SUPPLY COMPANY
Also Called: Tractor Supply
1627 Rombach Ave Ste B (45177-1965)
P.O. Box 608 (45177-0608)
PHONE..................................937 382-2595
Mike Camp, *Mgr*
EMP: 31
SALES (corp-wide): 14.56B **Publicly Held**
Web: www.tractorsupply.com
SIC: 5999 5261 5531 5251 Feed and farm supply; Lawn and garden equipment; Truck equipment and parts; Tools
PA: Tractor Supply Company
5401 Virginia Way
Brentwood TN 37027
615 440-4000

(G-15276)
UNITED PARCEL SERVICE INC
Also Called: UPS
2500 S Us Highway 68 (45177-8698)
PHONE..................................937 382-0658
EMP: 41
SALES (corp-wide): 90.96B **Publicly Held**
Web: www.ups.com
SIC: 4215 Package delivery, vehicular
HQ: United Parcel Service, Inc.
55 Glenlake Pkwy
Atlanta GA 30328
404 828-6000

(G-15277)
VINTEK INC
Also Called: Vintek
3268 Progress Way (45177-7700)
PHONE..................................937 382-8986
Lawrence Highbloom, *Prin*
Troy L Moore, *
Eileen Chu Hing, *
EMP: 83 **EST:** 1990
SQ FT: 2,500
SALES (est): 7.51MM
SALES (corp-wide): 16.61B **Privately Held**
SIC: 8742 7373 Industry specialist consultants; Value-added resellers, computer systems
HQ: Dealertrack Technologies, Inc.
3400 New Hyde Park Rd
New Hyde Park NY 11042
516 734-3600

(G-15278)
WILMINGTON HALTHCARE GROUP INC
Also Called: WILMINGTON NURSING & REHABILIT
75 Hale St (45177-2104)
PHONE..................................937 382-1621
George S Repchick, *Pr*
William I Weisberg, *
EMP: 56 **EST:** 1969
SQ FT: 15,000
SALES (est): 5.88MM **Privately Held**
Web: www.saberhealth.com
SIC: 8051 Convalescent home with continuous nursing care

(G-15279)
WILMINGTON MEDICAL ASSOCIATES
1184 W Locust St (45177-2009)
PHONE..................................937 382-1616
Thomas Neville Md, *Pr*
Tracy Coomer, *
EMP: 65 **EST:** 1975
SQ FT: 10,000
SALES (est): 4.98MM **Privately Held**
Web: www.wilmingtonmedical.com
SIC: 8062 General medical and surgical hospitals

(G-15280)
WILMINGTON SAVINGS BANK
184 N South St (45177-1659)
PHONE..................................937 382-1659
John P Chambers, *Pr*
Robert Wagenseller, *Ch Bd*
Mark A Williams, *Corporate Vice President*
Ronald A Shidaker, *VP*
Kevin Motley, *CFO*
EMP: 31 **EST:** 1890
SQ FT: 6,000
SALES (est): 6.52MM **Privately Held**
Web: www.wilmingtonsavings.com
SIC: 6022 State commercial banks

Wilmot
Stark County

(G-15281)
AMISH DOOR INC (PA)
Also Called: Amish Door Restaurant
1210 Winesburg St (44689)
P.O. Box 215 (44689-0215)
PHONE..................................330 359-5464
Milo Miller, *Pr*
Yvonne Torrence, *
Katherine Miller, *Stockholder*
Eric Gerber, *
EMP: 155 **EST:** 1957
SQ FT: 7,500
SALES (est): 9.67MM
SALES (corp-wide): 9.67MM **Privately Held**
Web: www.amishdoor.com
SIC: 5947 5812 7011 2051 Gift shop; Restaurant, family: independent; Hotels and motels; Bread, cake, and related products

(G-15282)
TRADEMARK EXTERIORS LLC
1504 Us Route 62 (44689-9605)
PHONE..................................330 893-0000
Steve Lapp, *CEO*
EMP: 53 **EST:** 2008
SALES (est): 4.42MM **Privately Held**
Web: www.trademarkexteriors.com
SIC: 1761 Siding contractor

Winchester
Adams County

(G-15283)
1ST STOP INC (PA)
Also Called: Cantrell's Motel
18856 State Route 136 (45697-9793)
P.O. Box 175 (45697-0175)
PHONE..................................937 695-0318
Robert Cantrell, *Pr*
Linda Cantrell, *
EMP: 30 **EST:** 1982
SQ FT: 12,000
SALES (est): 49.58MM
SALES (corp-wide): 49.58MM **Privately Held**
Web: www.1ststopinc.com

SIC: 5541 7011 Filling stations, gasoline; Motels

(G-15284)
ADAMS & BROWN COUNTIES ECONOMI
19221 State Route 136 (45697-0135)
P.O. Box 188 (45697-0188)
PHONE..................................937 695-0316
EMP: 37
SALES (corp-wide): 19.1MM **Privately Held**
Web: www.abcap.net
SIC: 8399 Community action agency
PA: Adams & Brown Counties Economic Opportunities, Inc.
406 W Plum St
Georgetown OH 45121
937 378-6041

(G-15285)
ADAMS BROWN CNTIES ECNMIC OPPR
Also Called: Adams Brown Wthrzation Program
19211 Main St (45697)
P.O. Box 188 (45697-0188)
PHONE..................................937 695-0316
Gary Tabor, *Dir*
EMP: 60
SALES (corp-wide): 19.1MM **Privately Held**
Web: www.abcap.net
SIC: 8399 Community action agency
PA: Adams & Brown Counties Economic Opportunities, Inc.
406 W Plum St
Georgetown OH 45121
937 378-6041

(G-15286)
CANTRELL OIL COMPANY
Also Called: Winchester Wholesale
18856 State Route 136 (45697-9793)
P.O. Box 175 (45697-0175)
PHONE..................................937 695-8003
EMP: 46 **EST:** 1974
SQ FT: 4,800
SALES (est): 12.66MM **Privately Held**
SIC: 5141 5169 Food brokers; Essential oils

(G-15287)
FIRST STATE BANK (PA)
Also Called: FIRST STATE BANK
19230 State Route 136 (45697-9571)
PHONE..................................937 695-0331
Chris Baxla, *Ch*
Michael Pell, *
David Richey, *
EMP: 30 **EST:** 1884
SQ FT: 9,363
SALES (est): 35.1MM
SALES (corp-wide): 35.1MM **Privately Held**
Web: www.fsb4me.com
SIC: 6022 State commercial banks

Windham
Portage County

(G-15288)
OHIO TPK & INFRASTRUCTURE COMM
Also Called: Hiram Maintenance Bldg
9196 State Route 700 (44288-9744)
PHONE..................................330 527-2169
R Underwood, *Superintnt*
EMP: 87
Web: www.ohioturnpike.org

SIC: 1611 0782 9621 Highway and street maintenance; Highway lawn and garden maintenance services; Regulation, administration of transportation
HQ: Ohio Turnpike And Infrastructure Commission
682 Prospect St
Berea OH 44017
440 234-2081

(G-15289)
OLD FORGE SERVICES INC
1490 Shanksdown Rd (44288-9606)
P.O. Box 67 (44260-0067)
PHONE..................................330 733-5531
EMP: 28 **EST:** 1987
SALES (est): 3.2MM **Privately Held**
Web: www.oldforgeservices.com
SIC: 5199 4212 Packaging materials; Local trucking, without storage

Winesburg
Holmes County

(G-15290)
R W SAUDER INC
Also Called: Sauder's Quality Eggs
2648 Us Rt 62 (44690)
PHONE..................................330 359-5440
Wayne Troyer, *Mgr*
EMP: 75
SALES (corp-wide): 44.78MM **Privately Held**
Web: www.saudereggs.com
SIC: 5144 Eggs
PA: R. W. Sauder, Inc.
570 Furnace Hills Pike
Lititz PA 17543
717 626-2074

Wintersville
Jefferson County

(G-15291)
ADDUS HOMECARE CORPORATION
Also Called: Addus Home Care
1406 Cadiz Rd (43953-9058)
PHONE..................................866 684-0385
EMP: 144
Web: www.addus.com
SIC: 8082 Home health care services
PA: Addus Homecare Corporation
6303 Cowboys Way Ste 600
Frisco TX 75034

(G-15292)
BATES BROS AMUSEMENT CO
1506 Fernwood Rd (43953-7640)
PHONE..................................740 266-2950
Eric Bates, *Pr*
Dolores Bates, *
EMP: 42 **EST:** 1965
SALES (est): 1.52MM **Privately Held**
Web: www.batesbros.com
SIC: 7999 Amusement ride

(G-15293)
EASTERN OHIO CORRECTION CENTER
470 State Rte 43 (43953)
P.O. Box 2400 (43953-0400)
PHONE..................................740 765-4324
Kayleen Murray, *Prin*
EMP: 35 **EST:** 1990
SALES (est): 4.34MM **Privately Held**
Web: www.eocc41.org
SIC: 8322 Rehabilitation services

GEOGRAPHIC SECTION

Wooster - Wayne County (G-15313)

(G-15294)
FAYETTE PARTS SERVICE INC
Also Called: NAPA
618 Canton Rd (43953-4118)
PHONE.............................724 880-3616
Carl Dellapenna, *Brnch Mgr*
EMP: 31
SALES (corp-wide): 45.91MM **Privately Held**
Web: www.fayettepartsservice.com
SIC: 7549 5531 Automotive maintenance services; Automotive parts
PA: Fayette Parts Service, Inc.
325 E Main St
Uniontown PA
724 785-2506

(G-15295)
HOME IS WHERE HART IS HM CARE
Also Called: Hiwthi Home Care LLC
105 N Avalon Dr (43953-3717)
PHONE.............................740 457-5240
Roger Isla, *Managing Member*
EMP: 27 EST: 2013
SALES (est): 1.08MM **Privately Held**
SIC: 8082 Home health care services

(G-15296)
REICHART LEASING CO LLC
Also Called: Dixon Healthcare Center
135 Reichart Ave (43953-4050)
PHONE.............................513 530-1600
Richard Odenthal, *Prin*
Sandra Smiddy, *
EMP: 50 EST: 2018
SALES (est): 5.68MM **Privately Held**
Web: www.communicarehealth.com
SIC: 8051 Convalescent home with continuous nursing care

(G-15297)
WALMART INC
Also Called: Walmart
843 State Route 43 (43952-7099)
PHONE.............................740 765-5700
Doug Corbolotti, *Brnch Mgr*
EMP: 119
SALES (corp-wide): 648.13B **Publicly Held**
Web: corporate.walmart.com
SIC: 4225 General warehousing and storage
PA: Walmart Inc.
702 Sw 8th St
Bentonville AR 72716
479 273-4000

Woodmere
Cuyahoga County

(G-15298)
EDUCARE MEDICAL STAFFING LLP
27600 Chagrin Blvd Ste 240 (44122-4498)
PHONE.............................216 938-9374
Naushay Adams, *Pt*
Naushay Adams, *Genl Pt*
Karrema Breazeale, *Genl Pt*
Chanel Stabler, *Genl Pt*
EMP: 50 EST: 2018
SALES (est): 1.31MM **Privately Held**
Web: www.educaremedicalstaffing.com
SIC: 7361 Employment agencies

(G-15299)
HOWARD WERSHBALE & CO (PA)
28601 Chagrin Blvd Ste 210 (44122-4546)
P.O. Box 22985 (44122-0985)
PHONE.............................216 831-1200
Harvey Wershbale, *CEO*
Stanley J Olejarski, *Pr*
John Fleischer, *Stockholder*
Mel Howard, *Stockholder*
William Kutschbach, *Stockholder*
EMP: 51 EST: 1990
SQ FT: 3,374
SALES (est): 12.73MM **Privately Held**
Web: www.hwco.cpa
SIC: 8721 Certified public accountant

Woodsfield
Monroe County

(G-15300)
CITIZENS NAT BNK OF WDSFELD TH (HQ)
143 S Main St (43793-1022)
P.O. Box 230 (43793-0230)
PHONE.............................740 472-1696
Stanley Heft, *Ch Bd*
Carey Bott, *
Bruce Climber, *
EMP: 30 EST: 1933
SQ FT: 3,500
SALES (est): 3.42MM **Privately Held**
Web: www.cnbwoodsfield.com
SIC: 6021 National commercial banks
PA: Cnb Bancorp, Inc.
143 S Main St
Woodsfield OH 43793

(G-15301)
COUNTY OF MONROE
Also Called: Monroe County Care Center
47045 Moore Ridge Rd (43793-9484)
P.O. Box 352 (43793-0352)
PHONE.............................740 472-0144
Marilyn Stepp, *Mgr*
EMP: 78
Web: www.monroecountyohio.net
SIC: 8051 Skilled nursing care facilities
PA: County Of Monroe
101 N Main St Rm 34
Woodsfield OH 43793
740 472-1341

(G-15302)
SAFE AUTO INSURANCE COMPANY
47060 Black Walnut Pkwy (43793-9521)
PHONE.............................740 472-1900
Jon P Diamond, *Brnch Mgr*
EMP: 261
Web: www.safeauto.com
SIC: 6411 Insurance agents, nec
HQ: Safe Auto Insurance Company
4 Easton Oval
Columbus OH 43219

(G-15303)
VETERANS OF FOREIGN WARS OF US
112 N Sycamore St (43793-1032)
PHONE.............................740 472-1199
FAX: 740 472-1199
EMP: 62
SALES (corp-wide): 105.25MM **Privately Held**
SIC: 8641 Veterans' organization
PA: Veterans Of Foreign Wars Of The United States
406 W 34th St Fl 11
Kansas City MO 64111
816 756-3390

(G-15304)
WOODSFIELD OPCO LLC
Also Called: Arbors At Woodsfield
37930 Airport Rd (43793-9247)
PHONE.............................740 472-1678
EMP: 56 EST: 2014
SQ FT: 60,000
SALES (est): 4.34MM **Privately Held**
Web: www.arborsatwoodsfield.com
SIC: 8051 Convalescent home with continuous nursing care

Woodstock
Champaign County

(G-15305)
WOODSTOCK HEALTHCARE GROUP INC
Also Called: SPRING MEADOWS CARE CENTER
1649 Park Rd (43084-9713)
PHONE.............................937 826-3351
George S Repchick, *Pr*
William I Weisberg, *
EMP: 27 EST: 1992
SQ FT: 20,000
SALES (est): 2.9MM **Privately Held**
SIC: 8051 Convalescent home with continuous nursing care

Woodville
Sandusky County

(G-15306)
ROUEN CHRYSLER PLYMOUTH DODGE
Also Called: Rouen Dodge
1091 Fremont Pike (43469-9606)
P.O. Box 185 (43469-0185)
PHONE.............................419 837-6228
Michael J Rouen, *Pr*
EMP: 34 EST: 1948
SQ FT: 20,000
SALES (est): 10.92MM **Privately Held**
Web: www.rouenchryslerdodgejeep.com
SIC: 5511 7515 7513 5521 Automobiles, new and used; Passenger car leasing; Truck rental and leasing, no drivers; Used car dealers

Wooster
Wayne County

(G-15307)
AKRON BRASS HOLDING CORP (HQ)
343 Venture Blvd (44691-7564)
PHONE.............................330 264-5678
Sean Tillinghast, *Pr*
EMP: 39 EST: 2009
SALES (est): 89.76MM
SALES (corp-wide): 3.27B **Publicly Held**
Web: www.akronbrass.com
SIC: 3647 3699 6719 Vehicular lighting equipment; Electrical equipment and supplies, nec; Investment holding companies, except banks
PA: Idex Corporation
3100 Sanders Rd Ste 301
Northbrook IL 60062
847 498-7070

(G-15308)
ALAN MANUFACTURING INC
3927 E Lincoln Way (44691-8997)
P.O. Box 24875 (44124-0875)
PHONE.............................330 262-1555
Richard Bluestone, *Pr*
▲ EMP: 36 EST: 1993
SQ FT: 110,000
SALES (est): 2.49MM **Privately Held**
Web: www.alanmfg.com
SIC: 3444 3822 1711 1761 Sheet metalwork; Environmental controls; Plumbing, heating, air-conditioning; Roofing, siding, and sheetmetal work

(G-15309)
ALBRIGHT WELDING SUPPLY CO INC (PA)
3132 E Lincoln Way (44691-3757)
P.O. Box 35 (44691-0035)
PHONE.............................330 264-2021
TOLL FREE: 800
James E Horst, *Pr*
Robert V Horst Junior, *VP*
Rebecca Horst, *
EMP: 31 EST: 1928
SQ FT: 14,500
SALES (est): 9.71MM
SALES (corp-wide): 9.71MM **Privately Held**
Web: www.albrightwelding.com
SIC: 5084 5085 5999 Welding machinery and equipment; Welding supplies; Welding supplies

(G-15310)
BAUER CORPORATION (PA)
Also Called: Bauer Ladder
2540 Progress Dr (44691-7970)
PHONE.............................800 321-4760
Mark Mcconnell, *Pr*
Ward Mcconnel, *Ch*
Norman Miller Stkldr, *Prin*
John Vasichko, *
EMP: 30 EST: 1916
SQ FT: 71,500
SALES (est): 5.15MM **Privately Held**
Web: www.bauerladder.com
SIC: 5082 3499 3446 3441 Ladders; Metal ladders; Architectural metalwork; Fabricated structural metal

(G-15311)
BEST WOOSTER INC
Also Called: Best Western Wooster Plaza
243 E Liberty St Ste 11 (44691-4366)
PHONE.............................330 264-7750
Stephen Sun, *Pr*
EMP: 40 EST: 1971
SQ FT: 97,000
SALES (est): 958.74K **Privately Held**
SIC: 7011 Hotels

(G-15312)
BOGNER CONSTRUCTION COMPANY
305 Mulberry St (44691-4735)
P.O. Box 887 (44691-0887)
PHONE.............................330 262-6730
Theodore R Bogner, *Pr*
Robert E Bogner, *
J C Johnston Iii, *Prin*
EMP: 75 EST: 1979
SQ FT: 5,000
SALES (est): 30.44MM **Privately Held**
Web: www.bognergroup.com
SIC: 1542 Commercial and office building, new construction

(G-15313)
BOGNER CORPORATION
427 S Grant St (44691-4711)
P.O. Box 216 (44691-0216)
PHONE.............................330 262-6393
Brian Bogner, *Pr*
EMP: 100 EST: 2008
SALES (est): 10.05MM **Privately Held**
Web: www.bognergroup.com
SIC: 1542 Commercial and office building, new construction

Wooster - Wayne County (G-15314)

(G-15314)
BOYS AND GIRLS CLB WOOSTER INC
124 N Walnut St (44691-4808)
P.O. Box 149 (44691-0149)
PHONE...............................330 988-1616
Christine Lindeman, *Prin*
EMP: 56 **EST:** 2013
SALES (est): 647.72K **Privately Held**
Web: www.bgcwooster.org
SIC: 7997 Membership sports and recreation clubs

(G-15315)
BUCKEYE PIPELINE CNSTR INC
7835 Millersburg Rd (44691-9472)
PHONE...............................330 804-0101
Brian C, *Pr*
EMP: 30 **EST:** 1997
SALES (est): 1.09MM **Privately Held**
SIC: 1623 Oil and gas pipeline construction

(G-15316)
CAMPBELL CONSTRUCTION INC (PA)
1159 Blachleyville Rd (44691-9750)
PHONE...............................330 262-5186
John Campbell, *Pr*
Richard Hauenstein, *
Mary Louise Campbell, *
Nancy J Campbell, *
Robert B Campbell, *
EMP: 68 **EST:** 1953
SQ FT: 12,000
SALES (est): 15.48MM
SALES (corp-wide): 15.48MM **Privately Held**
Web: www.campbell-construction.com
SIC: 1542 Commercial and office building, new construction

(G-15317)
CATHOLIC CHARITIES CORPORATION
Also Called: Catholic Charities
521 Beall Ave (44691-3589)
PHONE...............................330 262-7836
Robert Durdle, *Dir*
EMP: 78
Web: www.catholiccharitiesusa.org
SIC: 8399 8322 Fund raising organization, non-fee basis; Individual and family services
PA: Catholic Charities Corporation
7911 Detroit Ave
Cleveland OH 44102

(G-15318)
CERTIFIED ANGUS BEEF LLC (HQ)
206 Riffel Rd (44691-8588)
PHONE...............................330 345-2333
Brent Eichar, *
EMP: 90 **EST:** 2000
SQ FT: 42,000
SALES (est): 21.8MM
SALES (corp-wide): 46.66MM **Privately Held**
Web: www.certifiedangusbeef.com
SIC: 8611 Business associations
PA: American Angus Association Inc
3201 Frederick Ave
Saint Joseph MO 64506
816 383-5100

(G-15319)
CHILDRENS HOSP MED CTR AKRON
128 E Milltown Rd (44691-6109)
PHONE...............................330 345-1100
EMP: 54
SALES (corp-wide): 1.4B **Privately Held**
Web: www.akronchildrens.org
SIC: 8011 8069 Psychiatrist; Childrens' hospital
PA: Childrens Hospital Medical Center Of Akron
1 Perkins Sq
Akron OH 44308
330 543-1000

(G-15320)
CHRISTIAN CHLD HM OHIO INC
2685 Armstrong Rd (44691)
P.O. Box 765 (44691)
PHONE...............................330 345-7949
Steve Porter, *Pr*
Kevin R Hewitt, *
EMP: 100 **EST:** 1969
SQ FT: 12,000
SALES (est): 14.89MM **Privately Held**
Web: www.ccho.org
SIC: 8361 8093 8322 Children's home; Substance abuse clinics (outpatient); Individual and family services

(G-15321)
CITY OF WOOSTER
Also Called: Wooster Community Hospital
1761 Beall Ave (44691-2342)
PHONE...............................330 263-8100
William Sheron, *CEO*
EMP: 854
SALES (corp-wide): 34.82MM **Privately Held**
Web: www.woosteroh.com
SIC: 8062 5912 General medical and surgical hospitals; Drug stores
PA: City Of Wooster
538 N Market St
Wooster OH 44691
330 263-5200

(G-15322)
CLEVELAND CLINIC FOUNDATION
Also Called: Cleveland Clinic Wooster
1740 Cleveland Rd (44691-2204)
PHONE...............................330 287-4500
Tom Kelly, *Mgr*
EMP: 254
SALES (corp-wide): 14.48B **Privately Held**
Web: www.clevelandclinic.org
SIC: 8062 General medical and surgical hospitals
PA: The Cleveland Clinic Foundation
9500 Euclid Ave
Cleveland OH 44195
216 636-8335

(G-15323)
CLEVELAND CLINIC FOUNDATION
Also Called: Womans Health Center
1739 Cleveland Rd (44691-2203)
PHONE...............................330 287-4930
Cathy Fischer, *Mgr*
EMP: 33
SALES (corp-wide): 14.48B **Privately Held**
Web: www.clevelandclinic.org
SIC: 8011 8062 Physicians' office, including specialists; General medical and surgical hospitals
PA: The Cleveland Clinic Foundation
9500 Euclid Ave
Cleveland OH 44195
216 636-8335

(G-15324)
CLEVELAND CLNIC HLTH SYSTM-AST
Also Called: Cleveland Clinic Wooster
721 E Milltown Rd (44691-1331)
PHONE...............................330 287-4830
Wendy Simmons, *Prin*
EMP: 62
SALES (corp-wide): 14.48B **Privately Held**
Web: my.clevelandclinic.org
SIC: 8062 8093 General medical and surgical hospitals; Specialty outpatient clinics, nec
HQ: Cleveland Clinic Health System-East Region
6803 Mayfield Rd Ste 500
Cleveland OH 44124
440 312-6010

(G-15325)
COMMUNITY ACTION - WYNE/MEDINA (PA)
905 Pittsburgh Ave (44691-4296)
PHONE...............................330 264-8677
Donald Ackerman, *CFO*
EMP: 80 **EST:** 1964
SQ FT: 1,700
SALES (est): 12.75MM
SALES (corp-wide): 12.75MM **Privately Held**
Web: www.cawm.org
SIC: 8322 Social service center

(G-15326)
COMPAK INC
1130 Riffel Rd (44691-8502)
PHONE...............................330 345-5666
Jerry Baker, *Pr*
EMP: 35 **EST:** 2012
SALES (est): 2.1MM **Privately Held**
SIC: 4225 General warehousing and storage

(G-15327)
COUNSLING CTR OF WYNE HLMES CN (PA)
2285 Benden Dr (44691-2568)
PHONE...............................330 264-9029
Susan Buchwalter, *CEO*
EMP: 100 **EST:** 1953
SALES (est): 6.86MM
SALES (corp-wide): 6.86MM **Privately Held**
Web: www.ccwhc.org
SIC: 8322 General counseling services

(G-15328)
COUNTY OF WAYNE
Wayne County Care Center
876 S Geyers Chapel Rd (44691-3908)
PHONE...............................330 262-1786
Carol Van Pelt, *Admn*
EMP: 91
SALES (corp-wide): 110.86MM **Privately Held**
Web: www.wayneohio.org
SIC: 8059 9111 Personal care home, with health care; County supervisors' and executives' office
PA: County Of Wayne
428 W Liberty St
Wooster OH 44691
330 287-5400

(G-15329)
COUNTY OF WAYNE
Also Called: Wayne County Childrens Svcs
2534 Burbank Rd (44691-1675)
PHONE...............................330 345-5340
Thomas Roelant, *Dir*
EMP: 85
SALES (corp-wide): 110.86MM **Privately Held**
Web: www.wayneohio.org
SIC: 8361 9111 Children's home; County supervisors' and executives' office
PA: County Of Wayne
428 W Liberty St
Wooster OH 44691
330 287-5400

(G-15330)
COUNTY OF WAYNE
Also Called: Wayne County Engineers
Wooster
3151 W Old Lincoln Way (44691-3262)
PHONE...............................330 287-5500
Roger K Terrell, *Brnch Mgr*
EMP: 85
SALES (corp-wide): 110.86MM **Privately Held**
Web: www.wayneohio.org
SIC: 8711 Heating and ventilation engineering
PA: County Of Wayne
428 W Liberty St
Wooster OH 44691
330 287-5400

(G-15331)
COUNTY OF WAYNE
128 E Milltown Rd Ste 105 (44691-1276)
PHONE...............................330 345-5891
Joanna Farrager, *Brnch Mgr*
EMP: 28
SALES (corp-wide): 110.86MM **Privately Held**
Web: www.visitwaynecountyohio.com
SIC: 8011 8049 9199 General and family practice, physician/surgeon; Coroner; General government administration, County government
PA: County Of Wayne
428 W Liberty St
Wooster OH 44691
330 287-5400

(G-15332)
CRITCHFELD CRTCHFELD JHNSTON L (PA)
Also Called: Ccj
225 N Market St (44691-3511)
P.O. Box 599 (44691-0599)
PHONE...............................330 264-4444
J Douglas Drushal, *Pt*
Daniel H Plumly, *Pt*
John C Johnston Iii, *Pt*
Peggy Schmitz, *Pt*
EMP: 50 **EST:** 1941
SALES (est): 11.51MM
SALES (corp-wide): 11.51MM **Privately Held**
Web: www.ccj.com
SIC: 8111 General practice law office

(G-15333)
DANBURY WODS AT GRNFELD CRSSIN
Also Called: Danbury Wooster
939 Portage Rd (44691-2039)
PHONE...............................330 264-0355
William J Lemmons, *Managing Member*
EMP: 57 **EST:** 2013
SALES (est): 1.67MM **Privately Held**
Web: www.storypoint.com
SIC: 6531 Real estate agents and managers

(G-15334)
DAYS INNS OF AMERICA
789 E Milltown Rd (44691-1255)
PHONE...............................330 345-1500
Donna Selby, *Prin*
EMP: 30 **EST:** 2010
SALES (est): 452.46K **Privately Held**
Web: www.wyndhamhotels.com
SIC: 7011 Hotels and motels

(G-15335)
EAST OHIO GAS COMPANY
Also Called: Dominion Energy Ohio
1049 Heyl Rd (44691-9786)

GEOGRAPHIC SECTION
Wooster - Wayne County (G-15357)

PHONE.................................330 478-3114
Tina Navarro, *Mgr*
EMP: 74
SALES (corp-wide): 39.69B **Privately Held**
Web: www.dominiongaschoice.com
SIC: 4924 Natural gas distribution
HQ: The East Ohio Gas Company
1201 E 55th St
Cleveland OH 44103
800 362-7557

(G-15336)
ECONO LODGE WOOSTER INC
Also Called: Econo Lodge
2137 E Lincoln Way (44691-3817)
PHONE.................................330 264-8883
Stephen Sun, *Pr*
Susan Sun, *VP*
EMP: 39 **EST:** 1985
SQ FT: 11,436
SALES (est): 485.99K **Privately Held**
Web: www.choicehotels.com
SIC: 7011 5813 Motels; Cocktail lounge

(G-15337)
ENGINEERING ASSOCIATES INC
1935 Eagle Pass (44691-5316)
PHONE.................................330 345-6556
Kent Baker, *Pr*
Gary Daugherty, *Treas*
Frederick A Seling, *VP*
Ronny Portz, *Sec*
EMP: 54 **EST:** 1957
SQ FT: 9,000
SALES (est): 3.69MM **Privately Held**
Web: www.eaohio.com
SIC: 8711 Civil engineering

(G-15338)
FRIENDLY WHOLESALE CO
655 Cushman St (44691-3677)
P.O. Box 659 (44691-0659)
PHONE.................................724 224-6580
TOLL FREE: 800
Matthew Plocki, *Pr*
Mark Davidson, *VP*
EMP: 28 **EST:** 1950
SQ FT: 22,000
SALES (est): 1.96MM
SALES (corp-wide): 11.24MM **Privately Held**
Web: www.fwholesale.net
SIC: 5113 5145 5087 5194 Industrial and personal service paper; Confectionery; Janitors' supplies; Tobacco and tobacco products
PA: Pitt Specialty Supply, Inc.
405 Allegheny St
Tarentum PA 15084
724 224-6580

(G-15339)
FRIENDS IN DEED INC
365 Riffel Rd Ste E (44691-8592)
PHONE.................................330 345-9222
Carolyn Smith, *Pr*
EMP: 30 **EST:** 1992
SALES (est): 810K **Privately Held**
SIC: 8082 Home health care services

(G-15340)
GLENDORA HEALTH CARE CENTER
1552 N Honeytown Rd (44691-9511)
PHONE.................................330 264-0912
Shaw Flank, *Pr*
Terry J Ferguson, *
Linda Ferguson, *
EMP: 40 **EST:** 1990
SQ FT: 11,000
SALES (est): 2.45MM **Privately Held**
Web: www.glendoracarecenter.com
SIC: 8051 Convalescent home with continuous nursing care

(G-15341)
GOODWILL INDS WYNE HLMES CNTIE (PA)
1034 Nold Ave (44691-3642)
P.O. Box 1188 (44691-7083)
PHONE.................................330 264-1300
Judy Delaney, *Pr*
EMP: 30 **EST:** 1979
SQ FT: 21,000
SALES (est): 8.33MM
SALES (corp-wide): 8.33MM **Privately Held**
Web: www.goodwillconnect.org
SIC: 8331 5932 Sheltered workshop; Used merchandise stores

(G-15342)
HAMPTON INN WOOSTER
Also Called: Hampton Inn
4253 Burbank Rd (44691-9077)
PHONE.................................330 345-4424
Abbas K Shikary, *Pr*
EMP: 59 **EST:** 1992
SALES (est): 515.67K **Privately Held**
Web: www.hilton.com
SIC: 7011 Hotels and motels

(G-15343)
HEALTHCARE 2000 CMNTY CLNIC IN
Also Called: VIOLA STARTZMAN CLINIC
1874 Cleveland Rd (44691-2263)
PHONE.................................330 262-2500
John Moritz, *Ex Dir*
EMP: 30 **EST:** 1995
SALES (est): 1.26MM **Privately Held**
Web: www.startzmanclinic.org
SIC: 8011 Clinic, operated by physicians

(G-15344)
HERMAN BAIR ENTERPRISE
Also Called: Ej Therapy
2714 Akron Rd (44691-7933)
PHONE.................................330 262-4449
Eunice Herman, *Pr*
EMP: 38 **EST:** 2000
SALES (est): 459.02K **Privately Held**
Web: www.ejtherapy.com
SIC: 8049 Nutrition specialist

(G-15345)
HOMETOWN URGENT CARE
Also Called: HOMETOWN URGENT CARE
4164 Burbank Rd (44691-9077)
PHONE.................................937 252-2000
EMP: 37
SALES (corp-wide): 23.51MM **Privately Held**
Web: www.hometownurgentcare.com
SIC: 8049 8011 7291 Occupational therapist; Medical centers; Tax return preparation services
PA: Urgent Care Specialists Llc
2400 Corp Exch Dr Ste 102
Columbus OH 43231
614 505-7633

(G-15346)
HORIZONS TUSCARAWAS/CARROLL
Also Called: HORIZONS OF TUSCARAWAS/CARROLL
527 N Market St (44691-3495)
PHONE.................................330 262-4183
Jack Robinson, *Mgr*
EMP: 158
Web: www.laughlinufomegaconference.com
SIC: 8361 Mentally handicapped home

PA: Horizons Of Tuscarawas & Carroll Counties Inc
220 W 4th St
Dover OH 44622

(G-15347)
HUNTINGTON NATIONAL BANK
135 E Liberty St (44691-4345)
P.O. Box 37 (44691-0037)
PHONE.................................330 263-2751
Erica Piatt, *Mgr*
EMP: 31
SALES (corp-wide): 10.84B **Publicly Held**
Web: www.huntington.com
SIC: 6029 Commercial banks, nec
HQ: The Huntington National Bank
41 S High St
Columbus OH 43215
614 480-4293

(G-15348)
KEN MILLER SUPPLY INC
1537 Blachleyville Rd (44691-9752)
P.O. Box 1086 (44691-7081)
PHONE.................................330 264-9146
Kirk Miller, *CEO*
Lindy Chandler, *
Brandon Grosjean, *Prin*
Cole Miller, *Prin*
◆ **EMP:** 70 **EST:** 1959
SQ FT: 5,000
SALES (est): 22.67MM **Privately Held**
Web: www.kenmillersupply.com
SIC: 5084 Oil well machinery, equipment, and supplies

(G-15349)
KMB MANAGEMENT SERVICES CORP
Also Called: Wooster Inn, The
801 E Wayne Ave (44691-2388)
PHONE.................................330 263-2660
Ken Bogucki, *Pr*
Kenneth J Bogucki, *
EMP: 30 **EST:** 2009
SALES (est): 951.12K **Privately Held**
Web: www.thewoosterinn.com
SIC: 7011 Hotels

(G-15350)
KOKOSING CONSTRUCTION INC
1516 Timken Rd (44691-9401)
PHONE.................................330 263-4168
Brian Burgett, *Pr*
▲ **EMP:** 78 **EST:** 1923
SQ FT: 20,000
SALES (est): 3.85MM **Privately Held**
Web: www.kokosing.biz
SIC: 1611 General contractor, highway and street construction

(G-15351)
LIFECARE HOSPICE (PA)
Also Called: LIFECARE PALLIVATIVE MEDICINE
1900 Akron Rd (44691-2518)
PHONE.................................330 264-4899
Kurt Holmes, *CEO*
Tim Pettorini, *
EMP: 30 **EST:** 1982
SQ FT: 8,006
SALES (est): 20.9MM **Privately Held**
Web: www.ohioshospicelifecare.org
SIC: 8052 Personal care facility

(G-15352)
LOWES HOME CENTERS LLC
Also Called: Lowe's
3788 Burbank Rd (44691-9076)
PHONE.................................330 287-2261
EMP: 143

SALES (corp-wide): 86.38B **Publicly Held**
Web: www.lowes.com
SIC: 5211 5031 5722 5064 Home centers; Building materials, exterior; Household appliance stores; Electrical appliances, television and radio
HQ: Lowe's Home Centers, Llc
1000 Lowes Blvd
Mooresville NC 28117
336 658-4000

(G-15353)
MANCAN INC
435 Beall Ave (44691-3521)
PHONE.................................330 264-5375
EMP: 2097
SALES (corp-wide): 44.4MM **Privately Held**
Web: www.mancan.com
SIC: 7361 Placement agencies
PA: Mancan, Inc.
48 1st St Nw
Massillon OH 44647
330 832-4595

(G-15354)
MCCLINTOCK ELECTRIC INC
402 E Henry St (44691-4393)
PHONE.................................330 264-6380
Michael J Mcclintock, *Pr*
Ralph D Mcclintock, *VP*
EMP: 35 **EST:** 1963
SQ FT: 2,400
SALES (est): 8.22MM **Privately Held**
Web: www.mcclintockelectric.com
SIC: 1731 General electrical contractor

(G-15355)
METALS USA CRBN FLAT RLLED INC (DH)
Also Called: Metals USA
1070 W Liberty St (44691-3308)
P.O. Box 999 (44691-0999)
PHONE.................................330 264-8416
James C Hernoon, *Pr*
▲ **EMP:** 96 **EST:** 1921
SQ FT: 140,000
SALES (est): 102.17MM
SALES (corp-wide): 14.81B **Publicly Held**
Web: www.metalsusa.com
SIC: 5051 Steel
HQ: Metals Usa, Inc.
800 W Cypress Creed Rd St
Fort Lauderdale FL 33309
215 673-3595

(G-15356)
MIDLAND COUNCIL GOVERNMENTS
Also Called: Tri-County Computer Svcs Assn
2125 Eagle Pass (44691-5320)
PHONE.................................330 264-6047
EMP: 35 **EST:** 1981
SQ FT: 10,000
SALES (est): 2.2MM **Privately Held**
Web: www.tccsa.net
SIC: 7374 8211 Data processing and preparation; Elementary and secondary schools

(G-15357)
MILLER SUPPLY OF WVA INC (PA)
1537 Blachleyville Rd (44691-9752)
P.O. Box 1086 (44691-7081)
PHONE.................................330 264-9146
Jack K Miller, *Pr*
Max A Miller, *
Kenneth R Miller, *
▲ **EMP:** 50 **EST:** 1964
SALES (est): 8.32MM
SALES (corp-wide): 8.32MM **Privately Held**

Wooster - Wayne County (G-15358) — GEOGRAPHIC SECTION

Web: www.kenmillersupply.com
SIC: 5084 Oil well machinery, equipment, and supplies

(G-15358)
MILLTOWN FAMILY PHYSICIANS
128 E Milltown Rd Ste 105 (44691-1276)
PHONE..................................330 345-8060
EMP: 38 EST: 1996
SALES (est): 5.58MM **Privately Held**
Web: www.milltownfamily.com
SIC: 8011 General and family practice, physician/surgeon

(G-15359)
NICK AMSTER INC (PA)
1700b Old Mansfield Rd (44691-7212)
PHONE..................................330 264-9667
Rich Patterson, CEO
EMP: 46 EST: 1965
SQ FT: 18,000
SALES (est): 2.87MM
SALES (corp-wide): 2.87MM **Privately Held**
Web: www.nickamster.com
SIC: 8331 Sheltered workshop

(G-15360)
NICK AMSTER INC
326 N Hillcrest Dr Ste C (44691-3745)
PHONE..................................330 264-9667
EMP: 74
SALES (corp-wide): 2.87MM **Privately Held**
Web: www.nickamster.com
SIC: 8322 Social service center
PA: Nick Amster, Inc.
    1700b Old Mansfield Rd
    Wooster OH 44691
    330 264-9667

(G-15361)
NOBLETEK LLC ◆
1909 Old Mansfield Rd Ste B (44691-9474)
PHONE..................................330 287-1500
Nick Westover, Managing Member
EMP: 35 EST: 2022
SALES (est): 2.58MM
SALES (corp-wide): 13.8MM **Privately Held**
Web: www.nobletek.com
SIC: 7363 Engineering help service
PA: Inceptra Llc
    1900 N Commerce Pkwy
    Weston FL 33326
    954 442-5400

(G-15362)
OCCUPTNAL MDCINE ASSOC WYNE CN
Also Called: Center For Occptional Medicine
2201 Benden Dr Ste 100 (44691-5355)
PHONE..................................330 263-7270
Jeff Vandorsten, Pr
EMP: 91 EST: 1997
SALES (est): 2.81MM **Privately Held**
Web: www.themedprogroup.com
SIC: 8011 Clinic, operated by physicians

(G-15363)
OHIO STATE UNIVERSITY
Also Called: O A R D C
1680 Madison Ave (44691-4114)
PHONE..................................330 263-3700
Steven A Slack, Dir
EMP: 53
SALES (corp-wide): 8.24B **Privately Held**
Web: www.osu.edu
SIC: 8731 8221 Agricultural research; University
PA: The Ohio State University
    281 W Ln Ave
    Columbus OH 43210
    614 292-6446

(G-15364)
ONEEIGHTY INC
Also Called: Steps At Liberty Center
104 Spink St (44691)
PHONE..................................330 263-6021
Bobbi Douglas, CEO
Bobbi Douglas, Ex Dir
Thomas Fenzl, *
EMP: 75 EST: 1979
SQ FT: 25,000
SALES (est): 10.24MM **Privately Held**
Web: www.one-eighty.org
SIC: 8322 General counseling services

(G-15365)
PALLOTTA FORD INC
Also Called: Pallotta Ford Lincoln Mercury
4141 Cleveland Rd (44691-1227)
PHONE..................................330 345-5051
Mike Pallotta, Pr
EMP: 54 EST: 1961
SALES (est): 18.49MM **Privately Held**
Web: www.pallottaford.com
SIC: 5511 7538 Automobiles, new and used; General automotive repair shops

(G-15366)
PERSONAL TOUCH HM CARE IPA INC
543 Riffel Rd Ste F (44691-8591)
PHONE..................................330 263-1112
Norene Scheck, Brnch Mgr
EMP: 165
SALES (corp-wide): 251.89MM **Privately Held**
Web: www.pthomecare.com
SIC: 8082 Home health care services
PA: Personal Touch Home Care Ipa, Inc.
    1985 Marcus Ave Ste 202
    New Hyde Park NY 11042
    718 468-4747

(G-15367)
PORTS PETROLEUM COMPANY INC (PA)
Also Called: Fuel Mart
1337 Blachleyville Rd (44691-9705)
P.O. Box 1046 (44691-7046)
PHONE..................................330 264-1885
EMP: 50 EST: 1948
SALES (est): 101.22MM
SALES (corp-wide): 101.22MM **Privately Held**
Web: www.portspetroleum.com
SIC: 5172 5983 5541 Gasoline; Fuel oil dealers; Filling stations, gasoline

(G-15368)
RED ROVER LLC (DH)
Also Called: Santmyer Coml Fling Netwrk LLC
3000 Old Airport Rd (44691-9520)
PHONE..................................330 262-6501
Zach Santmyer, Pr
Terry Santmyer, Ch Bd
Nate Santmyer Commercial, Field Director
Terry Lacy, CFO
Dave First, Contrlr
EMP: 36 EST: 2004
SALES (est): 5.66MM
SALES (corp-wide): 26.83MM **Privately Held**
Web: www.santmyer.com
SIC: 5983 5171 5169 5541 Fuel oil dealers; Petroleum bulk stations and terminals; Chemicals and allied products, nec; Gasoline Stations with convenience stores
HQ: Santmyer Holdings, Inc.
    3000 Old Airport Rd
    Wooster OH 44691
    330 262-6501

(G-15369)
RK FAMILY INC
3541 E Lincoln Way (44691-3716)
PHONE..................................330 264-5475
Tom Waites, Prin
EMP: 170
SALES (corp-wide): 1.22B **Privately Held**
Web: www.ruralking.com
SIC: 5191 Farm supplies
PA: Rk Family, Inc.
    4216 Dewitt Ave
    Mattoon IL 61938
    217 235-7102

(G-15370)
ROD LIGHTNING MUTUAL INSUR CO (PA)
2845 Benden Dr (44691-2596)
P.O. Box 36 (44691-0036)
PHONE..................................330 262-9060
John P Murphy, Pr
F Emerson Logee, *
Kenneth B Stockman, *
EMP: 265 EST: 1906
SALES (est): 43.68MM
SALES (corp-wide): 43.68MM **Privately Held**
Web: www.wrg-ins.com
SIC: 6411 6331 Property and casualty insurance agent; Automobile insurance

(G-15371)
SANTMYER LOGISTICS INC
Also Called: Santmyer Transportation, Inc.
3000 Old Airport Rd (44691-9520)
PHONE..................................330 262-6501
Zach Santmyer, Pr
Terry Santmyer, *
Nate Santmyer Commercial, Field Director
Terry Lacy, *
David First, *
EMP: 80 EST: 2002
SALES (est): 4.96MM
SALES (corp-wide): 26.83MM **Privately Held**
Web: www.santmyer.com
SIC: 5983 5171 5169 5541 Fuel oil dealers; Petroleum bulk stations and terminals; Chemicals and allied products, nec; Filling stations, gasoline
HQ: Santmyer Holdings, Inc.
    3000 Old Airport Rd
    Wooster OH 44691
    330 262-6501

(G-15372)
SCHAEFFLER GROUP USA INC
Also Called: Schaeffler Group US
3401 Old Airport Rd (44691-9581)
PHONE..................................330 202-6215
EMP: 1633
SALES (corp-wide): 66.25B **Privately Held**
Web: www.schaeffler.us
SIC: 6411 Insurance agents, brokers, and service
HQ: Schaeffler Group Usa Inc.
    308 Springhill Farm Rd
    Fort Mill SC 29715
    803 548-8500

(G-15373)
SCHMID MECHANICAL INC
207 N Hillcrest Dr (44691-3720)
PHONE..................................330 264-3633
Timothy Schmid, Pr
EMP: 34 EST: 1961
SQ FT: 2,400
SALES (est): 811.88K **Privately Held**
Web: www.schmid-net.com
SIC: 1711 Mechanical contractor

(G-15374)
SCHMIDS SERVICE NOW INC
Also Called: Snyder's Service Now
258 S Columbus Ave (44691)
PHONE..................................330 499-0157
TOLL FREE: 888
EMP: 45 EST: 1993
SALES (est): 4.68MM **Privately Held**
SIC: 1711 5722 Warm air heating and air conditioning contractor; Electric household appliances

(G-15375)
SCOT INDUSTRIES INC
6578 Ashland Rd (44691-9233)
P.O. Box 1106 (44691-7081)
PHONE..................................330 262-7585
Robert G Gralinski, Mgr
EMP: 99
SQ FT: 2,018
SALES (corp-wide): 98.03MM **Privately Held**
Web: www.scotindustries.com
SIC: 5051 7389 3498 3471 Steel; Metal cutting services; Fabricated pipe and fittings; Plating and polishing
PA: Scot Industries, Inc.
    3756 F M 250 N
    Lone Star TX 75668
    903 639-2551

(G-15376)
SHEARER FARM INC
Also Called: John Deere Authorized Dealer
7762 Cleveland Rd (44691-7700)
PHONE..................................330 345-9023
EMP: 140
Web: www.agprocompanies.com
SIC: 3523 5082 Fertilizing machinery, farm; Construction and mining machinery

(G-15377)
SIYA MOTEL LLC
969 Timken Rd (44691-4181)
PHONE..................................330 264-6211
Victor V Natwarlal, Prin
EMP: 27 EST: 2005
SALES (est): 302.88K **Privately Held**
SIC: 7011 Motels

(G-15378)
STYX ACQUISITION LLC
3540 Burbank Rd (44691-8539)
PHONE..................................330 264-9900
Daniel Shanahan, Pr
EMP: 2076
SALES (corp-wide): 87.84MM **Privately Held**
Web: www.buehlers.com
SIC: 6799 Investors, nec
PA: Styx Acquisition, Llc
    1401 Old Mansfield Rd
    Wooster OH 44691
    330 264-4355

(G-15379)
TREADMAXX TIRE DISTRS INC
Also Called: Mister Tire
519 Madison Ave (44691-4705)
PHONE..................................404 762-4944
Chad Ackerman, Brnch Mgr
EMP: 72
SQ FT: 15,000
SALES (corp-wide): 1.56B **Privately Held**
Web: locations.mrtire.com
SIC: 5531 5014 Automotive tires; Tires and tubes

GEOGRAPHIC SECTION

Wooster - Wayne County (G-15400)

HQ: Treadmaxx Tire Distributors, Llc
2832 Anvil Block Rd
Ellenwood GA 30294
404 762-4944

(G-15380)
TRICOR INDUSTRIAL INC (PA)
Also Called: Tricor Metals
3225 W Old Lincoln Way (44691-3258)
P.O. Box 752 (44691-0752)
PHONE..................330 264-3299
Nancy A Stitzlein, *CEO*
Michael D Stitzlein, *
◆ **EMP:** 77 **EST:** 1977
SQ FT: 140,000
SALES (est): 90.27MM
SALES (corp-wide): 90.27MM **Privately Held**
Web: www.tricormetals.com
SIC: 5085 5169 3444 5051 Fasteners, industrial: nuts, bolts, screws, etc.; Chemicals and allied products, nec; Sheet metalwork; Metals service centers and offices

(G-15381)
VILLAGE NETWORK (PA)
2000 Noble Dr (44691-5353)
PHONE..................330 264-3232
James T Miller, *CEO*
Richard W Rodman, *Ex VP*
Bel Klockenga, *CFO*
EMP: 216 **EST:** 1945
SQ FT: 16,816
SALES (est): 52.33MM
SALES (corp-wide): 52.33MM **Privately Held**
Web: www.thevillagenetwork.org
SIC: 8361 Boys' towns

(G-15382)
WAYNE MANOR II INC
4138 Swanson Blvd (44691-9653)
PHONE..................330 345-2835
Nicole Sprenger, *Prin*
EMP: 31 **EST:** 2001
SALES (est): 1.05MM **Privately Held**
SIC: 6513 Retirement hotel operation

(G-15383)
WAYNE SAVINGS BANCSHARES INC (PA)
151 N Market St (44691-4809)
PHONE..................330 264-5767
EMP: 114 **EST:** 2001
SALES (est): 48.68MM **Publicly Held**
Web: www.waynesavings.com
SIC: 6022 State commercial banks

(G-15384)
WAYNE SAVINGS COMMUNITY BANK (HQ)
151 N Market St (44691-4809)
P.O. Box 858 (44691-0858)
PHONE..................330 264-5767
James R Vansickle Ii, *Pr*
EMP: 66 **EST:** 1899
SQ FT: 12,500
SALES (est): 28.55MM **Publicly Held**
Web: www.waynesavings.com
SIC: 6022 State commercial banks
PA: Wayne Savings Bancshares, Inc.
151 N Market St
Wooster OH 44691

(G-15385)
WEAVER CUSTOM HOMES INC
124 E Liberty St Ste A (44691-4421)
PHONE..................330 264-5444
Merle Stutzman, *Pr*
Ron Wenger, *
Diann Miller, *
EMP: 40 **EST:** 1953
SQ FT: 2,300
SALES (est): 7.81MM **Privately Held**
Web: www.weavercustomhomes.com
SIC: 1531 1521 1542 Speculative builder, single-family houses; New construction, single-family houses; Commercial and office building, new construction

(G-15386)
WEST VIEW MANOR INC
Also Called: WEST VIEW MANOR RETIREMENT CEN
1715 Mechanicsburg Rd (44691-2640)
PHONE..................330 264-8640
Robert Wetter, *CFO*
Robert Griggs, *
Carole Van Pelt, *
Mike Jackson, *
EMP: 225 **EST:** 1956
SQ FT: 126,000
SALES (est): 13.19MM **Privately Held**
Web: www.vvhl.healthcare
SIC: 8051 8361 Convalescent home with continuous nursing care; Geriatric residential care

(G-15387)
WESTERN RESERVE GROUP (PA) ✪
2865 Benden Dr (44691)
P.O. Box 36 (44691)
PHONE..................330 262-9060
Kevin Day, *Pr*
EMP: 255 **EST:** 2022
SALES (est): 189.05MM
SALES (corp-wide): 189.05MM **Privately Held**
Web: www.wrg-ins.com
SIC: 6331 Fire, marine, and casualty insurance: mutual

(G-15388)
WHITAKER-MYERS INSUR AGCY INC
Also Called: Aten & Mennetti Insurance Agcy
3524 Commerce Pkwy (44691)
PHONE..................330 345-5000
Scott D Allen, *Pr*
John W Mccord, *Ch*
EMP: 48 **EST:** 1869
SQ FT: 7,500
SALES (est): 8.4MM **Privately Held**
Web: www.whitakerwealth.com
SIC: 6411 Insurance agents, nec

(G-15389)
WOOSTER AMBLTORY SRGERY CTR LL
3373 Commerce Pkwy Ste 1 (44691-7130)
PHONE..................330 804-2000
Tori L Caillat, *Prin*
EMP: 36 **EST:** 2006
SALES (est): 5.49MM **Privately Held**
Web: www.woostersurgerycenter.com
SIC: 8011 Surgeon

(G-15390)
WOOSTER CHRISTIAN SCHOOL INC
4599 Burbank Rd Ste B (44691-9099)
PHONE..................330 345-6436
Randy Claes, *Prin*
EMP: 43 **EST:** 2007
SALES (est): 1.4MM **Privately Held**
Web: www.woosterchristianschool.org
SIC: 8211 8351 Private elementary and secondary schools; Preschool center

(G-15391)
WOOSTER CITY SCHOOLS
Also Called: Wooster Cy Schls Mntnace Cmpl
318 Branstetter St (44691-3366)
PHONE..................330 262-9616
Bob Henry, *Mgr*
EMP: 63
SQ FT: 960
SALES (corp-wide): 54.92MM **Privately Held**
Web: www.woostercityschools.org
SIC: 4225 General warehousing
PA: Wooster City Schools
144 N Market St
Wooster OH 44691
330 988-1111

(G-15392)
WOOSTER CMNTY HOSP BLMNGTON ME
Also Called: Wooster Community Hospital
1761 Beall Ave (44691-2342)
PHONE..................330 263-8100
EMP: 56 **EST:** 2018
SALES (est): 9.99MM **Privately Held**
Web: www.woosterhospital.org
SIC: 8049 8011 Nurses, registered and practical; Offices and clinics of medical doctors

(G-15393)
WOOSTER COMMUNITY HOSP AUX INC (PA)
1761 Beall Ave (44691-2342)
PHONE..................330 263-8389
I L Neyhar, *Dir*
J Soliday, *Dir*
R Horn, *Dir*
EMP: 98 **EST:** 1977
SALES (est): 361.75K
SALES (corp-wide): 361.75K **Privately Held**
Web: www.woosterhospital.org
SIC: 8011 Offices and clinics of medical doctors

(G-15394)
WOOSTER ENT ASSOCIATES INC
1749 Cleveland Rd (44691-2203)
PHONE..................330 264-9699
Arun K Mathur Md, *Pr*
EMP: 45 **EST:** 1973
SALES (est): 2.16MM **Privately Held**
Web: www.woosterent.com
SIC: 8011 Ears, nose, and throat specialist: physician/surgeon

(G-15395)
WOOSTER HYDROSTATICS INC
4570 W Old Lincoln Way (44691-3234)
PHONE..................330 263-6555
Steve Matthew, *CEO*
Clay Matthew Ctrl, *Prin*
▲ **EMP:** 45 **EST:** 1990
SQ FT: 41,500
SALES (est): 23.5MM **Privately Held**
Web: www.woosterhydrostatics.com
SIC: 7699 5084 Pumps and pumping equipment repair; Pumps and pumping equipment, nec

(G-15396)
WOOSTER MOTOR WAYS INC (PA)
3501 W Old Lincoln Way (44691-3253)
P.O. Box 19 (44691-0019)
PHONE..................330 264-9557
Paul M Williams, *Pr*
Jack Simmons, *
Janine Kiser, *
David W Hochstetler, *
Marsha Williams-glawitch, *Stockholder*
EMP: 140 **EST:** 1963
SQ FT: 40,000
SALES (est): 25.43MM
SALES (corp-wide): 25.43MM **Privately Held**
Web: www.woostermotorways.com
SIC: 4214 4226 4212 Local trucking with storage; Special warehousing and storage, nec; Local trucking, without storage

(G-15397)
WOOSTER OPHTHALMOLOGISTS INC
Also Called: Eye Surgery Center of Wooster
3519 Friendsville Rd (44691-1241)
PHONE..................330 345-7800
Harry A Zink, *Pr*
John W Thomas, *
Thomas C Fenzl, *
Jeffrey W Perkins, *
EMP: 45 **EST:** 1981
SQ FT: 20,000
SALES (est): 4.85MM **Privately Held**
Web: www.woostereyecenter.com
SIC: 8011 Opthalmologist

(G-15398)
WOOSTER ORTHPDICS SPRTSMDCINE
Also Called: Practice Bldrs Wster Orthpdic
3373 Commerce Pkwy Ste 2 (44691-7130)
PHONE..................330 804-9712
James W Gesler, *Prin*
EMP: 50 **EST:** 1984
SALES (est): 5.12MM **Privately Held**
Web: www.woosterortho.com
SIC: 8011 Orthopedic physician

(G-15399)
WQKT 1045 FM
Also Called: Wooster Radio
186 S Hillcrest Dr (44691-3727)
PHONE..................330 264-5122
Ken Nemeth, *Mgr*
Craig Walton, *
Timothy V Dix, *
Ken Nemeth, *Genl Mgr*
EMP: 341 **EST:** 1977
SQ FT: 2,600
SALES (est): 987.3K
SALES (corp-wide): 467.21MM **Privately Held**
Web: www.wqkt.com
SIC: 4832 7929 Radio broadcasting stations; Entertainers and entertainment groups
PA: Dix 1898, Inc.
212 E Liberty St
Wooster OH
330 264-3511

(G-15400)
WWST CORPORATION LLC
Also Called: Wqkt/Wkvx
186 S Hillcrest Dr (44691-3727)
PHONE..................330 264-5122
Craig Walton, *Genl Mgr*
EMP: 297 **EST:** 1996
SALES (est): 2.28MM
SALES (corp-wide): 467.21MM **Privately Held**
Web: www.wqkt.com
SIC: 4832 Radio broadcasting stations
PA: Dix 1898, Inc.
212 E Liberty St
Wooster OH
330 264-3511

Wooster - Wayne County (G-15401)

GEOGRAPHIC SECTION

(G-15401)
XCESS LIMITED
1605 Sylvan Rd (44691-3841)
PHONE..............................330 347-4901
EMP: 27
SALES (corp-wide): 6.66MM **Privately Held**
Web: www.xcesslimited.com
SIC: 7389 Personal service agents, brokers, and bureaus
PA: Xcess Limited
    789 Industrial Blvd
    Wooster OH 44691
    330 601-0800

(G-15402)
YOUNG MNS CHRSTN ASSN WSTER OH
Also Called: YMCA OF THE USA
680 Woodland Ave (44691-2743)
PHONE..............................330 264-3131
W Robert Johnston, *Dir*
Jeff Vincent, *
EMP: 37 **EST:** 1939
SQ FT: 30,000
SALES (est): 4.06MM **Privately Held**
SIC: 7999 8641 7997 7991 Recreation center ; Youth organizations; Membership sports and recreation clubs; Physical fitness facilities

---

Worthington
Franklin County

(G-15403)
AAA OHIO AUTO CLUB
90 E Wilson Bridge Rd (43085-2325)
PHONE..............................614 431-7800
Ronald Carr, *Pr*
EMP: 60 **EST:** 1978
SALES (est): 10.49MM **Privately Held**
Web: cluballiance.aaa.com
SIC: 7549 Automotive maintenance services

(G-15404)
ANDREWS ARCHITECTS INC
Also Called: Andrews William Architct/ Bldg
130 E Wilson Bridge Rd Ste 50 (43085-2327)
PHONE..............................614 766-1117
William Andrews, *Pr*
EMP: 38 **EST:** 1978
SALES (est): 4.65MM **Privately Held**
Web: www.andrewsarchitects.com
SIC: 8712 Architectural engineering

(G-15405)
ARC HEALTHCARE LLC
6877 N High St Ste 100 (43085-2579)
PHONE..............................888 552-0677
Amanda Ratliff, *CEO*
EMP: 45 **EST:** 2012
SALES (est): 101.81MM **Privately Held**
Web: www.myarchealthcare.com
SIC: 8742 4226 6411 8721 Management consulting services; Special warehousing and storage, nec; Insurance adjusters; Accounting, auditing, and bookkeeping

(G-15406)
BOUNDLESS STRGC RESOURCES INC
445 E Dublin Granville Rd Ste H (43085-3192)
PHONE..............................614 844-3800
Michele Lamarche, *Ex Dir*
Kristen Wilcock, *Dir*
Ardena Underwood, *Dir*
EMP: 37 **EST:** 2002
SALES (est): 19.46MM **Privately Held**
Web: www.stepbystepacademy.org
SIC: 8748 Business consulting, nec

(G-15407)
CF BANKSHARES INC (PA)
7000 N High St (43085-2500)
PHONE..............................614 334-7979
Timothy T O'dell, *Pr*
Robert E Hoeweler, *Ch Bd*
Kevin J Beerman Senior, *Finance Officer*
EMP: 73 **EST:** 1998
SALES (est): 112.31MM
SALES (corp-wide): 112.31MM **Publicly Held**
SIC: 6021 National commercial banks

(G-15408)
CHILLER LLC
401 E Wilson Bridge Rd (43085-2320)
PHONE..............................614 433-9600
EMP: 39
SALES (corp-wide): 4.89MM **Privately Held**
Web: www.thechiller.com
SIC: 7999 Ice skating rink operation
PA: Chiller Llc
    7001 Dublin Park Dr
    Dublin OH 43016
    614 764-1000

(G-15409)
CIVIL & ENVIRONMENTAL CONS INC
250 W Old Wilson Bridge Rd Ste 260 (43085-2285)
PHONE..............................614 540-6633
John Dinunzio, *Mgr*
EMP: 56
SALES (corp-wide): 179.1MM **Privately Held**
Web: www.cecinc.com
SIC: 8711 Consulting engineer
PA: Civil & Environmental Consultants, Inc.
    700 Cherrington Pkwy
    Moon Twp PA 15108
    412 429-2324

(G-15410)
CREATIVE FINCL STAFFING LLC
Also Called: CFS Services
150 E Wilson Bridge Rd Ste 340 (43085-6311)
PHONE..............................614 343-7800
EMP: 28
Web: www.cfstaffing.com
SIC: 7363 7361 Temporary help service; Employment agencies
PA: Creative Financial Staffing, Llc
    21 Custom House St # 210
    Boston MA 02110

(G-15411)
CSI INTERNATIONAL INC
690 Lakeview Plaza Blvd Ste C (43085)
PHONE..............................614 781-1571
J Espinosa, *Pr*
EMP: 941
Web: www.csiinternational.com
SIC: 7349 Janitorial service, contract basis
PA: Csi International, Inc.
    217 N Howard Ave
    Tampa FL 33606

(G-15412)
DATAFIELD INC
Also Called: A P T
25 W New England Ave (43085-3582)
PHONE..............................614 847-9600
EMP: 126 **EST:** 1990
SQ FT: 8,000
SALES (est): 12.36MM **Privately Held**
Web: www.datafieldusa.com
SIC: 7379 Computer related consulting services

(G-15413)
ELITE EXPEDITING CORP (PA)
450 W Wilson Bridge Rd Ste 345 (43085-5226)
PHONE..............................614 279-1181
D Jay Floyd, *Pr*
EMP: 34 **EST:** 2000
SALES (est): 4.66MM
SALES (corp-wide): 4.66MM **Privately Held**
Web: www.eliteexp.com
SIC: 4215 Package delivery, vehicular

(G-15414)
EPIQURIAN INNS
Also Called: Worthington Inn, The
649 High St (43085-4105)
PHONE..............................614 885-2600
Burke Showe, *Owner*
Hugh Showe Ii, *Mgr*
EMP: 71 **EST:** 1830
SQ FT: 28,000
SALES (est): 1.97MM **Privately Held**
Web: www.worthingtoninn.com
SIC: 7011 5812 5813 Hotels; American restaurant; Drinking places

(G-15415)
FAIRBORN EQUIPMENT CO OHIO INC
670 Lakeview Plaza Blvd (43085-4783)
PHONE..............................614 384-5466
William Mcbrayer, *Brnch Mgr*
EMP: 39
SALES (corp-wide): 6.5MM **Privately Held**
Web: www.fairbornequipment.com
SIC: 5084 Materials handling machinery
PA: Fairborn Equipment Company Of Ohio, Inc.
    3816 Welden Dr Ste A
    Lebanon OH 45036
    513 492-9422

(G-15416)
FARRIS ENTERPRISES INC (PA)
Also Called: Mammoth Restoration and Clg
7465 Worthington Galena Rd Ste A (43085-6714)
PHONE..............................614 367-9611
Matthew Farris, *Pr*
EMP: 36 **EST:** 2006
SQ FT: 2,700
SALES (est): 5.54MM **Privately Held**
Web: columbus.pauldavis.com
SIC: 1521 Repairing fire damage, single-family houses

(G-15417)
GO SUSTAINABLE ENERGY LLC
5701 N High St Ste 112 (43085-3960)
PHONE..............................614 268-4263
John Seryak, *CEO*
EMP: 27 **EST:** 2006
SALES (est): 2.99MM **Privately Held**
Web: www.gosustainableenergy.com
SIC: 8748 Energy conservation consultant

(G-15418)
HAZAMA ANDO CORPORATION
500 W Wilson Bridge Rd Ste 130 (43085-2238)
PHONE..............................614 985-4906
Kenji Hosaka, *Brnch Mgr*
EMP: 28
SQ FT: 2,000
Web: www.ad-hzm.co.jp
SIC: 1611 General contractor, highway and street construction
PA: Hazama Ando Corporation
    1-9-1, Higashishimbashi
    Minato-Ku TKY 105-0

(G-15419)
HE HARI INC
Also Called: Holiday Inn
7007 N High St (43085-2329)
PHONE..............................614 436-0700
Vijay Phapha, *Brnch Mgr*
EMP: 89
SALES (corp-wide): 2.09MM **Privately Held**
Web: www.holidayinn.com
SIC: 7011 Hotels and motels
PA: He Hari, Inc.
    9388 Wilbrook Dr
    Powell OH 43065
    614 846-6600

(G-15420)
HECO OPERATIONS INC
Also Called: SERVPRO
7440 Pingue Dr (43085-1741)
PHONE..............................614 888-5700
Patricia Heid, *Owner*
Robert Heid, *
Richard Cottrill, *
EMP: 160 **EST:** 1977
SQ FT: 19,150
SALES (est): 6.97MM **Privately Held**
Web: www.servpronortheastcolumbus.com
SIC: 7349 Building maintenance services, nec

(G-15421)
I AM BOUNDLESS INC
445 E Dublin Granville Rd Ste G (43085-3183)
PHONE..............................614 844-3800
Ed Harper, *Dir*
EMP: 285 **EST:** 1980
SALES (est): 48.7MM **Privately Held**
Web: www.iamboundless.org
SIC: 8361 Mentally handicapped home

(G-15422)
IHS SERVICES INC
667 Lakeview Plaza Blvd Ste D (43085)
PHONE..............................614 396-9980
EMP: 51
Web: www.ihsservices.info
SIC: 7231 Beauty shops
PA: Ihs Services, Inc.
    5888 Cleveland Ave # 201
    Columbus OH

(G-15423)
INTERIM HLTHCARE CAMBRIDGE INC (PA)
Also Called: Interim Services
300 W Wilson Bridge Rd Ste 250 (43085-2271)
PHONE..............................740 432-2966
EMP: 36 **EST:** 1986
SQ FT: 7,500
SALES (est): 5.07MM **Privately Held**
Web: www.interimhealthcare.com
SIC: 8082 7363 Home health care services; Help supply services

(G-15424)
JUICE TECHNOLOGIES INC
Also Called: Plug Smart
640 Lakeview Plaza Blvd Ste J (43085)
PHONE..............................800 518-5576
Richard Housh, *CEO*
Dave Zehala, *

GEOGRAPHIC SECTION — Worthington - Franklin County (G-15448)

Tom Martin, *
EMP: 27 EST: 2008
SALES (est): 8.19MM **Privately Held**
Web: www.plugsmart.com
SIC: **8748** 7389 8734 8741 Business consulting, nec; Product certification, safety or performance; Management services

(G-15425)
KELLER WILLIAMS RLTY SUPPLIERS
100 E Wilson Bridge Rd Ste 100 (43085-2326)
PHONE.................................614 403-2411
Sharon Brooks, *Prin*
EMP: 28 EST: 2011
SALES (est): 744.29K **Privately Held**
Web: keller-williams-capital-partners-realty.kw.com
SIC: **6531** Real estate agent, residential

(G-15426)
KHD COMPANY LLC
5878 N High St Fl 2 (43085)
PHONE.................................614 935-9939
Kevin Kim, *CEO*
EMP: 45 EST: 2020
SALES (est): 5.83MM **Privately Held**
SIC: **1541** 1531 1629 8741 Industrial buildings and warehouses; Industrial plant construction; Construction management

(G-15427)
KLINGBEIL CAPITAL MGT LTD (PA)
500 W Wilson Bridge Rd Ste 145 (43085-2272)
P.O. Box 1474 (20122-8474)
PHONE.................................415 398-0106
EMP: 55 EST: 2000
SALES (est): 117.5MM **Privately Held**
Web: www.kcm.com
SIC: **6799** 8741 Real estate investors, except property operators; Management services

(G-15428)
KUDU DYNAMICS LLC
500 W Wilson Bridge Rd Ste 316 (43085-2238)
PHONE.................................973 209-0305
Mike Frantzen, *Managing Member*
EMP: 78 EST: 2015
SALES (est): 1.15MM **Privately Held**
Web: www.kududyn.com
SIC: **8711** Engineering services

(G-15429)
L JC HOME CARE LLC
Also Called: Firstlght HM Care Dblin Hliard
130 E Wilson Bridge Rd Ste 300 (43085-2327)
PHONE.................................614 495-0276
Marianne E Christman, *Managing Member*
Lyndon Christman, *
EMP: 95 EST: 2015
SALES (est): 2.09MM **Privately Held**
SIC: **8082** Home health care services

(G-15430)
LAURELS OF WORTHINGTON
1030 High St (43085-4090)
PHONE.................................614 885-0408
Kristine Trovan, *Admn*
EMP: 52 EST: 2002
SALES (est): 9.12MM **Privately Held**
Web: www.cienahealthcare.com
SIC: **8051** Convalescent home with continuous nursing care

(G-15431)
LEADERS MOVING COMPANY
Also Called: Leaders Moving & Storage Co
7455 Alta View Blvd (43085-5891)
PHONE.................................614 785-9595
EMP: 50 EST: 1994
SQ FT: 30,000
SALES (est): 9.06MM **Privately Held**
Web: www.leadersmoving.com
SIC: **4212** 4214 Moving services; Furniture moving and storage, local

(G-15432)
LEI CBUS LLC
7492 Sancus Blvd (43085-4923)
PHONE.................................614 302-8830
EMP: 50 EST: 2014
SALES (est): 1.97MM **Privately Held**
SIC: **1521** Single-family housing construction

(G-15433)
LONG & WILCOX LLC
250 W Old Wilson Bridge Rd Ste 140 (43085-2215)
PHONE.................................614 273-3100
EMP: 37 EST: 2001
SQ FT: 2,590
SALES (est): 2.12MM **Privately Held**
Web: www.longandwilcox.com
SIC: **1522** 1542 Residential construction, nec; Commercial and office building, new construction

(G-15434)
LUTHERAN SCIAL SVCS CENTL OHIO (PA)
500 W Wilson Bridge Rd Ste 245 (43085-2238)
PHONE.................................419 289-3523
Larry Crowell, *Pr*
Rose Craig, *
Rick Davis, *
Philip D Helser, *
Heather Mccracken, *VP*
EMP: 40 EST: 1914
SQ FT: 9,000
SALES (est): 24.05MM
SALES (corp-wide): 24.05MM **Privately Held**
Web: www.lssnetworkofhope.org
SIC: **8322** Social service center

(G-15435)
MEDVET ASSOCIATES LLC
Also Called: Medvet Columbus
300 E Wilson Bridge Rd Ste 100 (43085-2300)
PHONE.................................614 486-5800
Galie Bowersmith, *Brnch Mgr*
EMP: 323
Web: www.medvet.com
SIC: **0742** Animal hospital services, pets and other animal specialties
PA: Medvet Associates, Llc
350 E Wilson Bridge Rd
Worthington OH 43085

(G-15436)
MEDVET ASSOCIATES LLC (PA)
Also Called: Med Vet Associates
350 E Wilson Bridge Rd (43085-2321)
PHONE.................................614 846-5800
Linda Lehmkuhl, *CEO*
Eric Schertel, *
Stephen Ley, *
EMP: 295 EST: 2009
SALES (est): 235.54MM **Privately Held**
Web: www.medvet.com
SIC: **0742** Animal hospital services, pets and other animal specialties

(G-15437)
MEDVET CALIFORNIA INC (HQ)
350 E Wilson Bridge Rd (43085-2321)
PHONE.................................614 846-5800
EMP: 58 EST: 2019
SALES (est): 2.57MM **Privately Held**
SIC: **0742** Animal hospital services, pets and other animal specialties
PA: Medvet Associates, Llc
350 E Wilson Bridge Rd
Worthington OH 43085

(G-15438)
MEDVET LOUISIANA LLC (HQ)
Also Called: Louisana Vtrnary Rfrrral Ctr LL
300 E Wilson Bridge Rd (43085-2300)
PHONE.................................614 846-5800
Debra Mauterer, *
EMP: 62 EST: 1999
SALES (est): 1.44MM **Privately Held**
Web: www.medvet.com
SIC: **0742** Animal hospital services, pets and other animal specialties
PA: Medvet Associates, Llc
350 E Wilson Bridge Rd
Worthington OH 43085

(G-15439)
MEDVET TEXAS LLC (HQ)
350 E Wilson Bridge Rd (43085)
PHONE.................................682 223-9770
EMP: 78 EST: 2016
SALES (est): 2.08MM **Privately Held**
SIC: **0742** Animal hospital services, pets and other animal specialties
PA: Medvet Associates, Llc
350 E Wilson Bridge Rd
Worthington OH 43085

(G-15440)
MILE INC (PA)
Also Called: Lion's Den
110 E Wilson Bridge Rd Ste 100 (43085-2317)
PHONE.................................614 794-2203
Michael R Moran, *Pr*
EMP: 61 EST: 1978
SALES (est): 11.33MM **Privately Held**
Web: www.lionsden.com
SIC: **7841** 5942 Video tape rental; Book stores

(G-15441)
MOUNT CARMEL HEALTH
81 E Wilson Bridge Rd (43085-2301)
PHONE.................................614 234-9889
Connie Shook, *Pr*
EMP: 102
SALES (corp-wide): 2.49B **Privately Held**
Web: www.mountcarmelhealth.com
SIC: **8062** General medical and surgical hospitals
HQ: Mount Carmel Health
5300 N Meadows Dr
Grove City OH 43123
614 234-5000

(G-15442)
MOUNT CARMEL HEALTH SYSTEM
81 E Wilson Bridge Rd (43085-2301)
PHONE.................................614 234-9889
EMP: 533
SALES (corp-wide): 2.49B **Privately Held**
Web: www.mountcarmelhealth.com
SIC: **8062** General medical and surgical hospitals
HQ: Mount Carmel Health System
1039 Kingsmill Pkwy
Columbus OH 43229
614 234-6000

(G-15443)
OHIO ASSN CNTY BRDS SRVING PPL
Also Called: OACB
73 E Wilson Bridge Rd Ste B1 (43085-2359)
PHONE.................................614 431-0616
Dan Ohler, *Ex Dir*
EMP: 40 EST: 1983
SALES (est): 6.57MM **Privately Held**
Web: www.oacbdd.org
SIC: **8322** Social service center

(G-15444)
OHIO AUTOMOBILE CLUB (PA)
Also Called: AAA
90 E Wilson Bridge Rd Fl 1 (43085-2387)
PHONE.................................614 431-7901
Mark Shaw, *Pr*
Tom Keyes, *
EMP: 200 EST: 1913
SQ FT: 1,172
SALES (est): 74.32MM
SALES (corp-wide): 74.32MM **Privately Held**
Web: www.aaaohio.com
SIC: **8699** Automobile owners' association

(G-15445)
OPOCUS
300 W Wilson Bridge Rd Ste 300 (43085-2299)
PHONE.................................800 724-8802
Edward Da Sommer, *Admn*
EMP: 140 EST: 2010
SALES (est): 9.76MM **Privately Held**
Web: www.opoc.us
SIC: **8748** Business consulting, nec

(G-15446)
PHIL GIESSLER
Also Called: Camtaylor Co Realtors
882 High St Ste A (43085-4159)
PHONE.................................614 888-0307
Phil Giessler, *Owner*
EMP: 31 EST: 1968
SALES (est): 307.13K **Privately Held**
Web: www.camtaylor.com
SIC: **6531** 6512 Real estate brokers and agents; Nonresidential building operators

(G-15447)
PINNACLE REALTY MANAGEMENT CO
402 E Wilson Bridge Rd (43085-2366)
PHONE.................................614 430-3678
EMP: 51
SALES (corp-wide): 146.69MM **Privately Held**
SIC: **6531** Real estate brokers and agents
HQ: Pinnacle Realty Management Company
11235 Se 6th St Ste 200
Bellevue WA 98004

(G-15448)
PRIORITY MORTGAGE CORP
150 E Wilson Bridge Rd Ste 350 (43085-6302)
PHONE.................................614 431-1141
Samuel J Hill, *CEO*
Gary W Erler, *
David Mckee, *VP*
Marianne Viola, *
Lisa Kendle, *
EMP: 28 EST: 1983
SQ FT: 6,000
SALES (est): 4.56MM **Privately Held**
Web: www.prioritymortgage.com

Worthington - Franklin County (G-15449) — GEOGRAPHIC SECTION

SIC: **6162** Mortgage bankers and loan correspondents

(G-15449)
PSP OPERATIONS INC
Also Called: SERVPRO of Northeast Columbus
7440 Pingue Dr (43085-1741)
PHONE..............................614 888-5700
Kenneth Parker, *Prin*
EMP: 27 **EST:** 2014
SALES (est): 1.56MM **Privately Held**
Web:
www.servpronortheastcolumbus.com
SIC: **7349** Building maintenance services, nec

(G-15450)
RADIAN GUARANTY INC
250 E Wilson Bridge Rd Ste 175 (43085-2323)
PHONE..............................614 847-8300
Cindy Brandt, *Brnch Mgr*
EMP: 78
Web: www.radian.com
SIC: **6351** Mortgage guarantee insurance
HQ: Radian Guaranty Inc.
    550 E Swdsford Rd Ste 350
    Wayne PA 19087
    215 564-6600

(G-15451)
RESIDENTIAL MGT SYSTEMS INC (PA)
250 E Wilson Bridge Rd Ste 205 (43085-2323)
PHONE..............................614 880-6009
Joseph Cozzolino, *Pr*
Dixon Buehler, *
EMP: 41 **EST:** 1983
SQ FT: 8,325
SALES (est): 7.1MM
SALES (corp-wide): 7.1MM **Privately Held**
Web: www.teamrms.com
SIC: **8361** Mentally handicapped home

(G-15452)
RESOURCE ONE CMPT SYSTEMS INC
651 Lakeview Plaza Blvd Ste E (43085)
PHONE..............................614 485-4800
Stampp W Corbin, *Pr*
EMP: 43 **EST:** 1994
SALES (est): 3.86MM **Privately Held**
Web: www.rocs.com
SIC: **5734 7378** Computer and software stores; Computer maintenance and repair

(G-15453)
RESOURCE ONE SOLUTIONS LLC
651 Lakeview Plaza Blvd Ste E (43085)
P.O. Box 1565 (43017-6565)
PHONE..............................614 485-8500
EMP: 49 **EST:** 2008
SALES (est): 547.01K **Privately Held**
SIC: **7379** Online services technology consultants

(G-15454)
SAAMA TECHNOLOGIES INC
100 W Old Wilson Bridge Rd Ste 201 (43085-2255)
PHONE..............................614 652-6100
EMP: 57
SALES (corp-wide): 57.6MM **Privately Held**
Web: www.saama.com
SIC: **7371** Computer software development
PA: Saama Technologies, Inc.
    900 E Hamilton Ave # 200
    Campbell CA 95008
    408 371-1900

(G-15455)
SAFELITE GLASS CORP
Guardian Auto Glass
600 Lakeview Plaza Blvd Ste A (43085)
P.O. Box 29167 (43229-0167)
PHONE..............................614 431-4936
Paul Janisse, *Dir*
EMP: 40
SALES (corp-wide): 3.16B **Privately Held**
Web: www.safelite.com
SIC: **7536** Automotive glass replacement shops
HQ: Safelite Glass Corp.
    7400 Safelite Way
    Columbus OH 43235
    614 210-9000

(G-15456)
SHIRK ODNVAN CNSLTING ENGINEERS
370 E Wilson Bridge Rd (43085-2321)
PHONE..............................614 436-6465
EMP: 31 **EST:** 1990
SALES (est): 1.95MM **Privately Held**
Web: www.shirkodonovan.com
SIC: **8711** Consulting engineer

(G-15457)
SPECILZED MED BLLING RVNUE RCV (PA)
Also Called: Specialized Medical Billing
330 E Wilson Bridge Rd Ste 100 (43085-6309)
PHONE..............................614 461-8154
Adrianne Nittala, *CEO*
EMP: 27 **EST:** 2021
SQ FT: 6,800
SALES (est): 2.92MM
SALES (corp-wide): 2.92MM **Privately Held**
Web: www.specializedmedbilling.com
SIC: **8721** Billing and bookkeeping service

(G-15458)
SPECILZED MED BLLING RVNUE RCV
330 E Wilson Bridge Rd Ste 100 (43085-6309)
PHONE..............................614 461-8154
Adrianne Nittala, *CEO*
EMP: 32
SALES (corp-wide): 2.92MM **Privately Held**
Web: www.specializedmedbilling.com
SIC: **8721** Billing and bookkeeping service
PA: Specialized Medical Billing & Revenue Recovery Services Llc
    330 E Wilson Bridge Rd # 100
    Worthington OH 43085
    614 461-8154

(G-15459)
ST MORITZ SECURITY SVCS INC
705 Lakeview Plaza Blvd Ste G (43085)
PHONE..............................614 351-8798
Gary Harney, *Brnch Mgr*
EMP: 54
SALES (corp-wide): 27.97MM **Privately Held**
Web: www.smssi.com
SIC: **7381** Security guard service
PA: St. Moritz Security Services, Inc.
    4600 Clairton Blvd
    Pittsburgh PA 15236
    412 885-3144

(G-15460)
SWIMINC INCORPORATED
Also Called: WORTHINGTON SWIMMING POOL
400 W Dublin Granville Rd (43085-3590)
PHONE..............................614 885-1619
Tom Bubenik, *Pr*
Ron Lemerech, *
Chris Hadden, *
EMP: 29 **EST:** 1953
SALES (est): 1.83MM **Privately Held**
Web: www.worthingtonpools.com
SIC: **7997 5812 7991** Swimming club, membership; Concessionaire; Physical fitness facilities

(G-15461)
THERAPY ADVANTAGE GROUP LLC
965 High St (43085-4057)
PHONE..............................614 784-0400
Mindy M Griffin, *Prin*
EMP: 67 **EST:** 2014
SALES (est): 1.69MM **Privately Held**
Web: www.therapyadvantageinc.com
SIC: **8093** Rehabilitation center, outpatient treatment

(G-15462)
THOMAS GLASS COMPANY INC (PA)
400 E Wilson Bridge Rd Ste A (43085-2363)
PHONE..............................614 268-8611
Andrew T Gum, *Pr*
EMP: 35 **EST:** 1973
SQ FT: 4,000
SALES (est): 4.45MM
SALES (corp-wide): 4.45MM **Privately Held**
SIC: **1793** Glass and glazing work

(G-15463)
TRANSINTERNATIONAL SYSTEM INC (DH)
130 E Wilson Bridge Rd Ste 150 (43085-2327)
P.O. Box 109 (43085-0109)
PHONE..............................614 891-4942
Mark Stewart, *Pr*
John S Stewart, *
EMP: 45 **EST:** 1967
SQ FT: 4,000
SALES (est): 34.07MM
SALES (corp-wide): 805.41MM **Privately Held**
Web: www.imcc.com
SIC: **4731 8741** Foreign freight forwarding; Management services
HQ: Imc Companies, Llc
    1305 Schilling Blvd W
    Collierville TN 38017

(G-15464)
ULTIMATE HOME SERVICES LLC
7340 Sancus Blvd (43085-1512)
PHONE..............................614 888-8698
Rick Weber, *Owner*
Mathew Hwang, *
EMP: 41 **EST:** 2008
SALES (est): 5.16MM **Privately Held**
Web: www.ultimatehhcs.com
SIC: **8082** Home health care services

(G-15465)
VALASSIS DIRECT MAIL INC
100 W Old Wilson Bridge Rd Ste 106 (43085-2255)
PHONE..............................614 987-2200
Jim Clancy, *Mgr*
EMP: 38
Web: www.vericast.com
SIC: **7331** Mailing service
HQ: Valassis Direct Mail, Inc.
    15955 La Cantera Pkwy
    San Antonio TX 78256
    800 437-0479

(G-15466)
VETRAD LLC
Also Called: Vetrad
300 E Wilson Bridge Rd (43085-2300)
PHONE..............................888 483-8723
EMP: 32 **EST:** 2019
SALES (est): 1.89MM **Privately Held**
Web: www.vet-rad.com
SIC: **0742** Animal hospital services, pets and other animal specialties
PA: Medvet Associates, Llc
    350 E Wilson Bridge Rd
    Worthington OH 43085

(G-15467)
WENTZ HC HOLDINGS INC
Also Called: Honeywell Authorized Dealer
6969 Worthington Galena Rd Ste A (43085-2322)
PHONE..............................614 294-4966
Brad Wentz, *Pr*
Gary Eleks, *Sec*
EMP: 35 **EST:** 1948
SQ FT: 6,200
SALES (est): 8.58MM
SALES (corp-wide): 215.03MM **Privately Held**
Web: www.buckeyeheat.com
SIC: **1711** Warm air heating and air conditioning contractor
PA: Wrench Group Llc
    1819 Main St Ste 1300
    Sarasota FL 34236
    941 477-3771

(G-15468)
WEST OHIO CNFRNCE OF UNTD MTHD (PA)
Also Called: United Methodist Camps
32 Wesley Blvd (43085-3585)
PHONE..............................614 844-6200
Bishop Bruce R Ouch, *Prin*
R Stanley Sutton, *
Gregory V Palmer, *
Barb Sholis, *
Marcus Atha Suprtnd, *Prin*
EMP: 39 **EST:** 1928
SQ FT: 16,587
SALES (est): 7.65MM
SALES (corp-wide): 7.65MM **Privately Held**
Web: www.westohioumc.org
SIC: **7032 8661** Recreational camps; Methodist Church

(G-15469)
WHALEN AND COMPANY CPAS INC
Also Called: Whalen & Co CPA
250 W Old Wilson Bridge Rd (43085-2285)
PHONE..............................614 396-4200
Richard D Crabtree, *Pt*
Laura B Wojciechowski, *
Lisa G Shuneson, *
Linda Hickey, *
EMP: 92 **EST:** 1945
SQ FT: 7,500
SALES (est): 4.44MM **Privately Held**
Web: www.whalencpa.com
SIC: **8721** Certified public accountant

(G-15470)
WILLIAM O CLEVERLEY & ASSOC
438 E Wilson Bridge Rd Ste 200 (43085-2382)
PHONE..............................614 543-7777
William O Cleverley, *CEO*

William O Cleverley, *Pr*
Linda S Cleverley, *
EMP: 38 **EST:** 2000
SQ FT: 5,000
SALES (est): 8.5MM **Privately Held**
Web: www.cleverleyassociates.com
SIC: 8742 Financial consultant

(G-15471)
WORTHINGTON INDUSTRIES INC
200 W Old Wilson Bridge Rd (43085-2247)
PHONE.................................909 594-7777
John P Mcconnell, *CEO*
Mark Russell, *Pr*
Andy Rose, *CFO*
EMP: 47 **EST:** 1986
SALES (est): 1.73MM **Privately Held**
Web: www.worthingtonenterprises.com
SIC: 1541 Industrial buildings and warehouses

(G-15472)
WORTHINGTON PUBLIC LIBRARY
820 High St (43085-3182)
PHONE.................................614 807-2626
Meribah H Mansfield, *Dir*
EMP: 130 **EST:** 1804
SALES (est): 2.31MM **Privately Held**
Web: www.worthingtonlibraries.org
SIC: 8231 8742 Public library; Management consulting services

Wright Patterson Afb
Greene County

(G-15473)
88TH MDSS/SGSM MM-HT1135 ✪
4881 Sugar Maple Dr (45433-5529)
PHONE.................................937 257-8935
Jessica L Probst Flight, *Chief*
EMP: 2500 **EST:** 2023
SALES (est): 11.35MM **Privately Held**
SIC: 8011 Group health association

(G-15474)
AIR FORCE RESEARCH LABORATORY
Also Called: Afrl/Rx
2977 Hobson Way Bldg 653 (45433)
PHONE.................................937 255-9209
EMP: 99 **EST:** 1917
SALES (est): 10.53MM **Privately Held**
Web: www.afresearchlab.com
SIC: 8733 Physical research, noncommercial

(G-15475)
WPAFB MEDICAL CENTER
4881 Sugar Maple Dr (45433-5529)
PHONE.................................937 522-2778
EMP: 30 **EST:** 2014
SALES (est): 234.01K **Privately Held**
Web: wpafb.af.mil
SIC: 8011 Medical centers

Wshngtn Ct Hs
Fayette County

(G-15476)
ADENA HEALTH SYSTEM
308 Highland Ave Unit C (43160-1993)
PHONE.................................740 779-7500
Adedoyin Adetoro, *Prin*
EMP: 35
SALES (corp-wide): 678.56MM **Privately Held**
Web: www.adena.org
SIC: 8062 General medical and surgical hospitals
PA: Adena Health System
272 Hospital Rd
Chillicothe OH 45601
740 779-7500

(G-15477)
CARLTON MANOR NURSING AND REHABILITATION CENTER INC
Also Called: Carlton Manor
726 Rawlings St (43160-1518)
PHONE.................................740 335-7143
EMP: 155
SIC: 8052 8051 8361 Intermediate care facilities; Convalescent home with continuous nursing care; Residential care

(G-15478)
COMMUNITY ACTION COMM FYTTE CN (PA)
1400 Us Highway 22 Nw (43160-8604)
PHONE.................................740 335-7282
Lucinda Baughn, *Ex Dir*
EMP: 80 **EST:** 1964
SQ FT: 2,000
SALES (est): 9.69MM
SALES (corp-wide): 9.69MM **Privately Held**
Web: www.cacfayettecounty.org
SIC: 8322 Social service center

(G-15479)
FAMILY LIQUIDATION COMPANY INC
2754 Us Highway 22 Nw (43160-9510)
PHONE.................................937 780-3075
Fred B Cox Junior, *Pr*
Fred B Cox Iii, *VP*
Gregory R Cox, *
Cindy Cox, *
EMP: 93 **EST:** 1993
SALES (est): 4.34MM **Privately Held**
Web: www.jrjnet.com
SIC: 1794 7631 1771 Excavation and grading, building construction; Watch repair ; Driveway contractor

(G-15480)
FARM CREDIT SVCS MID-AMERICA (PA)
1540 Us Highway 62 Sw (43160-8849)
PHONE.................................740 335-3306
Wendy Osborne, *VP*
EMP: 33 **EST:** 1981
SALES (est): 26MM
SALES (corp-wide): 26MM **Privately Held**
Web: www.fcma.com
SIC: 6141 Consumer finance companies

(G-15481)
FAYETTE CNTY FMLY YUNG MNS CHR
Also Called: FAYETTE COUNTY FAMILY YMCA
100 Civic Dr (43160-9186)
P.O. Box 1021 (43160-8021)
PHONE.................................740 335-0477
Douglas Saunders, *CEO*
EMP: 85 **EST:** 2000
SQ FT: 35,000
SALES (est): 1.3MM **Privately Held**
Web: www.faycoymca.org
SIC: 8641 Youth organizations

(G-15482)
FAYETTE COUNTY MEMORIAL HOSP (PA)
1430 Columbus Ave (43160-1791)
PHONE.................................740 335-1210
Jane Bissel, *CFO*
Tammie Wilson, *
EMP: 224 **EST:** 1950
SALES (est): 90K
SALES (corp-wide): 90K **Privately Held**
Web: www.adena.org
SIC: 8062 General medical and surgical hospitals

(G-15483)
FAYETTE HOSPICE COUNTY INC
222 N Oakland Ave (43160-1234)
P.O. Box 849 (43160-0849)
PHONE.................................740 335-0149
Milissa J Knisley, *Ex Dir*
EMP: 37 **EST:** 1987
SQ FT: 2,176
SALES (est): 6.12MM **Privately Held**
Web: www.hospiceoffayettecounty.org
SIC: 8052 Personal care facility

(G-15484)
FAYETTE MEDICAL CENTER
1430 Columbus Ave (43160-1703)
PHONE.................................740 335-1210
Vickie Davidson, *Prin*
EMP: 28 **EST:** 2016
SALES (est): 2.46MM **Privately Held**
Web: www.adena.org
SIC: 8011 Medical centers

(G-15485)
FAYETTE PROGRESSIVE INDS INC
Also Called: FAYETTE COUNTY MRDD
1330 Robinson Rd Se (43160-9201)
PHONE.................................740 335-7453
Mark Schwartz, *Dir*
Steve Hilgeman, *
EMP: 42 **EST:** 1976
SALES (est): 759.31K **Privately Held**
Web: www.fayettedd.com
SIC: 8322 Individual and family services

(G-15486)
FOUR SEASONS WASHINGTON LLC
201 Courthouse Pkwy (43160-6001)
PHONE.................................740 895-6101
Tim A Ross, *Managing Member*
Tracy Ross, *
EMP: 80 **EST:** 2014
SALES (est): 4.2MM **Privately Held**
Web: www.fourseasonsofwashington.com
SIC: 8051 Convalescent home with continuous nursing care

(G-15487)
HCF OF COURT HOUSE INC
Also Called: HEALTH CARE FACILITIES
555 N Glenn Ave (43160-2711)
PHONE.................................740 335-9290
India Williamson, *Admn*
EMP: 120 **EST:** 2006
SALES (est): 8.3MM
SALES (corp-wide): 305.93MM **Privately Held**
Web: www.courthousemanor.com
SIC: 8051 Convalescent home with continuous nursing care
PA: Hcf Management, Inc.
1100 Shawnee Rd
Lima OH 45805
419 999-2010

(G-15488)
HCF OF WASHINGTON INC
Also Called: St. Cthrnes Manor Wash Crt Hse
555 N Glenn Ave (43160-2711)
PHONE.................................419 999-2010
Barbara Masella, *VP*
EMP: 31
Web: www.stcatherinescourthouse.com
SIC: 8059 Nursing home, except skilled and intermediate care facility
PA: Hcf Of Washington, Inc.
250 S Glenn Ave
Wshngtn Ct Hs OH 43160

(G-15489)
LOWES HOME CENTERS LLC
Also Called: Lowe's
1895 Lowes Blvd (43160-8611)
PHONE.................................740 636-2100
EMP: 81
SALES (corp-wide): 86.38B **Publicly Held**
Web: www.lowes.com
SIC: 4225 General warehousing and storage
HQ: Lowe's Home Centers, Llc
1000 Lowes Blvd
Mooresville NC 28117
336 658-4000

(G-15490)
MCKESSON CORPORATION
3000 Kenskill Ave (43160-8615)
PHONE.................................740 636-3500
Robert Kearney, *Dir*
EMP: 48
SALES (corp-wide): 308.95B **Publicly Held**
Web: www.mckesson.com
SIC: 5122 Pharmaceuticals
PA: Mckesson Corporation
6555 State Highway 161
Irving TX 75039
972 446-4800

(G-15491)
MID ATLANTIC STOR SYSTEMS INC
1551 Robinson Rd Se (43160-9201)
PHONE.................................740 335-2019
Jerry Morris, *Pr*
Jeanette Morris, *
John Fox, *
EMP: 75 **EST:** 1984
SQ FT: 25,000
SALES (est): 21.59MM **Privately Held**
Web: www.midatlanticstorage.com
SIC: 1791 Storage tanks, metal: erection

(G-15492)
ROSE & DOBYNS AN OHIO PARTNR
298 N Fayette St (43160-1306)
PHONE.................................740 335-4700
EMP: 30
Web: www.rosedobyns.com
SIC: 8111 General practice attorney, lawyer
PA: Rose & Dobyns An Ohio Partnership
97 N South St
Wilmington OH 45177

(G-15493)
SCIOTO PNT VLY MENTAL HLTH CTR
Also Called: Scioto Pnt Vly Mental Hlth Ctr
1300 E Paint St (43160-1676)
PHONE.................................740 335-6935
Ed Sipe, *Mgr*
EMP: 119
SALES (corp-wide): 14.09MM **Privately Held**
Web: www.spvmhc.org
SIC: 8093 8322 8069 Mental health clinic, outpatient; Crisis intervention center; Drug addiction rehabilitation hospital
PA: Scioto-Paint Valley Mental Health Center
4449 State Route 159
Chillicothe OH 45601
740 775-1260

(G-15494)
SEED CONSULTANTS INC (DH)
648 Miami Trace Rd Sw (43160-9661)
P.O. Box 370 (43160-0370)
PHONE..................................740 333-8644
Chris Jeffries, *Genl Mgr*
EMP: 50 **EST:** 1987
SQ FT: 32,500
SALES (est): 9.14MM
SALES (corp-wide): 17.23B **Publicly Held**
Web: www.seedconsultants.com
SIC: 5261 5191 Nursery stock, seeds and bulbs; Seeds: field, garden, and flower
HQ: Pioneer Hi-Bred International, Inc.
  7100 Nw 62nd Ave
  Johnston IA 50131
  515 535-3200

(G-15495)
VERMEER HEARTLAND INC (PA)
2574 Us Highway 22 Nw (43160-8751)
PHONE..................................740 335-8571
EMP: 28 **EST:** 1981
SALES (est): 20.04MM
SALES (corp-wide): 20.04MM **Privately Held**
Web: www.vermeerhl.com
SIC: 5082 General construction machinery and equipment

Wyoming
Hamilton County

(G-15496)
LACLEDE DEVELOPMENT COMPANY
220 Elm Ave (45215-4328)
PHONE..................................513 702-4391
David Birvsall, *Brnch Mgr*
EMP: 30
SALES (corp-wide): 2.67B **Publicly Held**
SIC: 6531 Broker of manufactured homes, on site
HQ: Laclede Development Company
  700 Market St Fl 6
  Saint Louis MO 63101
  314 241-5668

Xenia
Greene County

(G-15497)
4 PAWS FOR ABILITY INC
Also Called: 4 PAWS FOR ABILITY INC
207 Dayton Ave (45385-2831)
PHONE..................................937 374-0385
EMP: 52
SALES (corp-wide): 5.45MM **Privately Held**
Web: www.4pawsforability.org
SIC: 0752 Training services, pet and animal specialties (not horses)
PA: 4 Paws For Ability, Inc.
  253 Dayton Ave
  Xenia OH 45385
  937 374-0385

(G-15498)
AK GROUP HOTELS INC
Also Called: Ramada Xenia
300 Xenia Towne Sq (45385-2949)
PHONE..................................937 372-9921
Rajesh Agrawala, *Pr*
Ketan Kadkia, *VP*
EMP: 92 **EST:** 2003
SQ FT: 40,000
SALES (est): 517.4K **Privately Held**
Web: www.wyndhamhotels.com
SIC: 7011 5812 Hotels; Restaurant, family: independent

(G-15499)
ATHLETES IN ACTION SPT CMPLEX (HQ)
Also Called: Athletes In Action
651 Taylor Dr (45385-7246)
PHONE..................................937 352-1000
Mark Householder, *Pr*
EMP: 100 **EST:** 1976
SQ FT: 5,227,200
SALES (est): 17.65MM
SALES (corp-wide): 423.98MM **Privately Held**
Web: www.athletesinaction.org
SIC: 8699 Athletic organizations
PA: Campus Crusade For Christ Inc
  100 Lake Hart Dr
  Orlando FL 32832
  407 826-2000

(G-15500)
CITY OF XENIA
Sanitation Division
966 Towler Rd (45385-2412)
PHONE..................................937 376-7260
Jim Jones, *Dir*
EMP: 37
SQ FT: 730
SALES (corp-wide): 9.23MM **Privately Held**
Web: ci.xenia.oh.us
SIC: 8744 Base maintenance (providing personnel on continuing basis)
PA: City Of Xenia
  107 E Main St
  Xenia OH 45385
  937 376-7232

(G-15501)
CITY OF XENIA
Also Called: Xenia Waster Water
779 Ford Rd (45385-9538)
PHONE..................................937 376-7271
Chris Burger, *Prin*
EMP: 37
SALES (corp-wide): 9.23MM **Privately Held**
Web: ci.xenia.oh.us
SIC: 4953 Sewage treatment facility
PA: City Of Xenia
  107 E Main St
  Xenia OH 45385
  937 376-7232

(G-15502)
COMPUNET CLINICAL LABS LLC
1214 N Monroe Dr (45385-1622)
PHONE..................................937 372-9681
EMP: 48
SALES (corp-wide): 2.41MM **Privately Held**
Web: www.compunetlab.com
SIC: 8071 Medical laboratories
HQ: Compunet Clinical Laboratories, Llc
  2308 Sandridge Dr
  Moraine OH 45439
  937 296-0844

(G-15503)
DETROIT TIRE & AUTO SUPPLY INC
Also Called: Detroit Tire
968 W 2nd St (45385-3620)
PHONE..................................937 426-0949
Steve Whitehead, *Pr*
John Marshall, *Sec*
Charles Marshall Ii, *Treas*
▲ **EMP:** 47 **EST:** 1948
SQ FT: 24,265
SALES (est): 4.9MM **Privately Held**
Web: www.detroittiresales.com
SIC: 5531 7538 Automotive tires; General automotive repair shops

(G-15504)
ESCALANTE - CNTRY CLB OF N LLC
Also Called: Country Club of The North
1 Club North Dr (45385-9399)
PHONE..................................937 374-5000
Michael A Mess, *Pr*
EMP: 28 **EST:** 1991
SALES (est): 1.08MM **Privately Held**
Web: www.countryclubofthenorth.com
SIC: 7997 Country club, membership

(G-15505)
EVANHOE & ASSOCIATES INC
492 W 2nd St Ste 208 (45385-3765)
PHONE..................................937 235-2995
EMP: 50 **EST:** 1996
SALES (est): 9.92MM **Privately Held**
Web: www.evanhoe.com
SIC: 7373 7371 7376 7379 Value-added resellers, computer systems; Custom computer programming services; Computer facilities management; Diskette duplicating service

(G-15506)
FAMILY VLNCE PRVNTION CTR GREN
Also Called: FAMILY VIOLENCE PREVENTION CEN
380 Bellbrook Ave (45385-3638)
PHONE..................................937 372-4552
Connie Fisher, *Ex Dir*
EMP: 27 **EST:** 1978
SQ FT: 1,104
SALES (est): 1.38MM **Privately Held**
Web: www.violencefreefutures.org
SIC: 8322 Social service center

(G-15507)
FIRST TRANSIT INC
1180 S Patton St (45385-5670)
PHONE..................................937 374-6402
Dennis Green, *Mgr*
EMP: 137
SALES (corp-wide): 4.23MM **Privately Held**
Web: www.transdevna.com
SIC: 4111 Local and suburban transit
HQ: First Transit, Inc.
  600 Vine St Ste 1400
  Cincinnati OH 45202
  513 241-2200

(G-15508)
FIRSTGROUP AMERICA INC
921 Yellowstone Rd (45385-1531)
PHONE..................................937 372-3876
EMP: 312
SALES (corp-wide): 5.71B **Privately Held**
Web: www.firststudentinc.com
SIC: 4111 4151 Bus transportation; School buses
HQ: Firstgroup America, Inc.
  191 Rosa Parks St
  Cincinnati OH 45202
  513 241-2200

(G-15509)
GOLDEN AGE SENIOR CITIZENS
338 S Progress Dr (45385-2796)
PHONE..................................937 376-4353
Naomi Trout, *Dir*
EMP: 49 **EST:** 1968
SALES (est): 1.61MM **Privately Held**
Web: www.xarsc-seniorcenter.org
SIC: 8322 Senior citizens' center or association

(G-15510)
GREENE INC
Also Called: DOCUMENT SOLUTIONS
121 Fairground Rd (45385-9543)
PHONE..................................937 562-4200
Dennis Rhodes, *Dir*
Mary Nissen, *
EMP: 100 **EST:** 1971
SQ FT: 2,086
SALES (est): 1.97MM **Privately Held**
Web: www.greeneinc.org
SIC: 8331 Sheltered workshop

(G-15511)
GREENE COUNTY
Also Called: Adult Probation
45 N Detroit St Rm 7 (45385-2998)
PHONE..................................937 562-5266
Kathryn Wilson, *Dir*
EMP: 36
SALES (corp-wide): 140.65MM **Privately Held**
Web: co.greene.oh.us
SIC: 8322 9223 Probation office; Correctional institutions
PA: Greene County
  35 Greene St
  Xenia OH 45385
  937 562-5006

(G-15512)
GREENE COUNTY
Also Called: Human Services
541 Ledbetter Rd (45385-5334)
PHONE..................................937 562-6000
Philip Mastn, *Dir*
EMP: 32
SALES (corp-wide): 140.65MM **Privately Held**
Web: co.greene.oh.us
SIC: 8322 Public welfare center
PA: Greene County
  35 Greene St
  Xenia OH 45385
  937 562-5006

(G-15513)
GREENE COUNTY
Also Called: Greene County Services
641 Dayton Xenia Rd (45385-2605)
PHONE..................................937 562-7800
Carl Geisler, *Dir*
EMP: 32
SALES (corp-wide): 140.65MM **Privately Held**
Web: co.greene.oh.us
SIC: 8744 Base maintenance (providing personnel on continuing basis)
PA: Greene County
  35 Greene St
  Xenia OH 45385
  937 562-5006

(G-15514)
GREENE COUNTY
Also Called: Green County Engineer
615 Dayton Xenia Rd (45385-2605)
PHONE..................................937 562-7500
Robert Geyer, *Brnch Mgr*
EMP: 64
SALES (corp-wide): 140.65MM **Privately Held**
Web: co.greene.oh.us
SIC: 8711 9221 Engineering services; State highway patrol
PA: Greene County
  35 Greene St
  Xenia OH 45385

GEOGRAPHIC SECTION
Yellow Springs - Greene County (G-15537)

937 562-5006

(G-15515)
GREENE COUNTY BOARD OF DD
245 N Valley Rd (45385-9301)
PHONE..................................937 562-6500
EMP: 29 EST: 2001
SALES (est): 563.88K Privately Held
Web: www.greenedd.org
SIC: 8322 Social services for the handicapped

(G-15516)
GREENE COUNTY COUNCIL ON AGING
Also Called: GREENE COUNTY PUBLIC HEALTH
360 Wilson Dr (45385-1870)
PHONE..................................937 374-5600
Melissa Branum, CEO
EMP: 50 EST: 1981
SQ FT: 13,000
SALES (est): 6.53MM Privately Held
Web: www.gcph.info
SIC: 8322 Social service center

(G-15517)
GREENE MEMORIAL HOSPITAL INC (DH)
1141 N Monroe Dr (45385-1600)
PHONE..................................937 352-2000
Michael R Stephens, CEO
Timothy Pollard, *
EMP: 600 EST: 1951
SALES (est): 33.25MM
SALES (corp-wide): 2.46B Privately Held
Web: www.ketteringhealth.org
SIC: 8062 Hospital, affiliated with AMA residency
HQ: Greene Health Partners
   1141 N Monroe Dr
   Xenia OH 45385
   937 352-2000

(G-15518)
GREENE OAKS
Also Called: Greene Oaks Health Center
164 Office Park Dr (45385-1647)
PHONE..................................937 352-2800
John Flannigan, Ex Dir
EMP: 59 EST: 1980
SQ FT: 18,000
SALES (est): 3.52MM
SALES (corp-wide): 2.46B Privately Held
SIC: 8062 General medical and surgical hospitals
HQ: Kettering Affiliated Health Services, Inc
   3535 Southern Blvd
   Dayton OH 45429
   937 298-4331

(G-15519)
GREENVILLE NURSING SERVICES
1142 N Monroe Dr (45385-1620)
PHONE..................................937 736-2272
Christian Owusu, Prin
Millicent Mensah Owusu, *
EMP: 30 EST: 2016
SALES (est): 1.21MM Privately Held
SIC: 8082 Home health care services

(G-15520)
HOME RUN INC (PA)
1299 Lavelle Dr (45385-7402)
PHONE..................................800 543-9198
Gary Harlow, Pr
Dennis Harlow, *
Thomas Baker, *
EMP: 35 EST: 1966
SQ FT: 12,800
SALES (est): 10.3MM
SALES (corp-wide): 10.3MM Privately Held
Web: www.homeruninc.com
SIC: 4213 4212 Building materials transport; Local trucking, without storage

(G-15521)
HOMETOWN URGENT CARE
Also Called: HOMETOWN URGENT CARE
101 S Orange St (45385-3603)
PHONE..................................937 372-6012
Ritu Singla, Prin
EMP: 55
SALES (corp-wide): 23.51MM Privately Held
Web: www.wellnow.com
SIC: 8031 8011 Offices and clinics of osteopathic physicians; Clinic, operated by physicians
PA: Urgent Care Specialists Llc
   2400 Corp Exch Dr Ste 102
   Columbus OH 43231
   614 505-7633

(G-15522)
INFINITY LABS LLC
171 E Krepps Rd (45385-9778)
P.O. Box 341072 (45434-1072)
PHONE..................................937 317-0030
Kenneth Edge, CEO
EMP: 45 EST: 2020
SALES (est): 2.83MM Privately Held
Web: www.i-labs.tech
SIC: 8731 Biological research

(G-15523)
LIBERTY NURSING HOME INC
Also Called: Heathergreene Nursing Homes
126 Wilson Dr (45385-1899)
PHONE..................................937 376-2121
Linda Black-kurek, Pr
Maryann La Vigne, *
EMP: 45 EST: 1967
SALES (est): 6.54MM Privately Held
Web: www.libertynursingcenters.com
SIC: 8051 Extended care facility

(G-15524)
LOWES HOME CENTERS LLC
Also Called: Lowe's
126 Hospitality Dr (45385-2777)
PHONE..................................937 347-4000
Jeremy Austin, Mgr
EMP: 119
SALES (corp-wide): 86.38B Publicly Held
Web: www.lowes.com
SIC: 5211 5031 5722 5064 Home centers; Building materials, exterior; Household appliance stores; Electrical appliances, television and radio
HQ: Lowe's Home Centers, Llc
   1000 Lowes Blvd
   Mooresville NC 28117
   336 658-4000

(G-15525)
MACAIR AVIATION LLC
Also Called: Macair
140 N Valley Rd (45385-9301)
PHONE..................................937 347-1302
EMP: 32 EST: 2012
SALES (est): 952.65K Privately Held
Web: www.macair.us
SIC: 8299 7363 7997 4581 Airline training; Pilot service, aviation; Flying field, maintained by aviation clubs; Airports and flying fields

(G-15526)
MEDICAL URGENCY PREP SVCS INC
Also Called: Medx
36 N Detroit St Ste 102 (45385-2963)
PHONE..................................937 374-2420
Tobey Mckee, Ch Bd
EMP: 30
SALES (est): 553.04K Privately Held
SIC: 8099 Health and allied services, nec

(G-15527)
MIAMI VLY JVNILE RHBLTTION CTR
2100 Greene Way Blvd (45385-2677)
PHONE..................................937 562-4000
Gary Neidenthal, Dir
EMP: 28 EST: 2001
SALES (est): 1.03MM Privately Held
Web: www.greenecountyohio.gov
SIC: 8322 Rehabilitation services

(G-15528)
MRL MATERIALS RESOURCES LLC
Also Called: Mrl
123 Fairground Rd (45385-9543)
P.O. Box 341091 (45434-1091)
PHONE..................................937 531-6657
EMP: 40 EST: 2009
SALES (est): 4.12MM Privately Held
Web: www.icmrl.net
SIC: 8999 8734 3812 8711 Scientific consulting; Metallurgical testing laboratory; Defense systems and equipment; Engineering services

(G-15529)
NATIONWIDE BIWEEKLY ADM INC
Also Called: Nba
855 Lower Bellbrook Rd (45385-7306)
PHONE..................................937 376-5800
Daniel Lipsky, Pr
John S Gregory, Prin
EMP: 105 EST: 2002
SQ FT: 25,000
SALES (est): 17.34MM Privately Held
Web: www.nbabiweekly.com
SIC: 6099 Clearinghouse associations, bank or check

(G-15530)
REDDY ELECTRIC CO
1145 Bellbrook Ave (45385-4061)
PHONE..................................937 372-8205
Robert J Lafreniere, Pr
Steve Stanek, *
Jeff Eldridge, *
EMP: 140 EST: 1966
SQ FT: 7,000
SALES (est): 24.14MM Privately Held
Web: www.reddyelectric.com
SIC: 1731 General electrical contractor

(G-15531)
SUGAR VALLEY COUNTRY CLUB
1250 Mead Rd (45385)
PHONE..................................937 372-4820
James Keyes, Pt
Steve Foreman, Pt
EMP: 30 EST: 1979
SALES (est): 237.68K Privately Held
SIC: 7997 7992 5812 Membership sports and recreation clubs; Public golf courses; Eating places

(G-15532)
TCN BEHAVIORAL HEALTH SVCS INC (PA)
Also Called: COMMUNITY NETWORK THE
452 W Market St (45385)
PHONE..................................937 376-8700
Lynn West, CEO
EMP: 180 EST: 1990
SALES (est): 19.01MM
SALES (corp-wide): 19.01MM Privately Held
Web: www.tcn.org
SIC: 8322 8093 General counseling services; Specialty outpatient clinics, nec

(G-15533)
TEAM GREEN LAWN LLC
1070 Union Rd (45385-7216)
PHONE..................................937 673-4315
Josh Anderson, Managing Member
EMP: 40 EST: 2009
SALES (est): 564.17K Privately Held
SIC: 0782 Lawn care services

Yellow Springs
Greene County

(G-15534)
ANTIOCH UNIVERSITY
1 Morgan Pl (45387-1683)
PHONE..................................937 769-1366
Joan Straumanis, Prin
EMP: 112
SALES (corp-wide): 83.35MM Privately Held
Web: www.antioch.edu
SIC: 8731 8221 Commercial physical research; Colleges and universities
PA: Antioch University
   900 Dayton St
   Yellow Springs OH 45387
   937 769-1370

(G-15535)
FRIENDS HEALTH CARE ASSN (PA)
Also Called: FRIENDS CARE CENTER
150 E Herman St (45387-1601)
PHONE..................................937 767-7363
Karl Zalar, Dir
EMP: 105 EST: 1980
SQ FT: 25,000
SALES (est): 6.57MM
SALES (corp-wide): 6.57MM Privately Held
Web: www.friendshealthcare.org
SIC: 8051 Skilled nursing care facilities

(G-15536)
YELLOW SPRINGS PRIMARY CARE
888 Dayton St Unit 102 (45387-1778)
PHONE..................................937 767-1088
Donald Gronbeck, Prin
EMP: 29 EST: 2013
SALES (est): 1.85MM Privately Held
SIC: 8011 Primary care medical clinic

(G-15537)
YOUNGS JERSEY DAIRY INC
Also Called: Golden Jersey Inn
6880 Springfield Xenia Rd (45387-9610)
PHONE..................................937 325-0629
C Daniel Young, CEO
C Robert Young, *
William H Young, *
Debra Whittaker, *
EMP: 300 EST: 1964
SQ FT: 35,000
SALES (est): 10.58MM Privately Held
Web: www.youngsdairy.com
SIC: 5812 5451 5947 7999 Ice cream stands or dairy bars; Dairy products stores; Gift shop; Golf driving range

Yorkshire
Darke County

(G-15538)
WINNER CORPORATION (PA)
Also Called: Winner's Meat Service
8544 State Route 705 (45388-9784)
P.O. Box 39 (45351-0039)
PHONE.................................419 582-4321
Brian K Winner, *Pr*
Alan Winner, *
Terrance Winner, *
Ted Winner, *
Jay Winner, *
EMP: 40 **EST:** 1928
SQ FT: 6,500
SALES (est): 33.94MM
SALES (corp-wide): 33.94MM **Privately Held**
Web: www.winnersmeats.com
SIC: 0213 0751 5154 5147 Hog feedlot; Slaughtering: custom livestock services; Hogs; Meats and meat products

Youngstown
Mahoning County

(G-15539)
A P OHORO COMPANY
3130 Belmont Ave (44505-1802)
P.O. Box 2228 (44504-0228)
PHONE.................................330 759-9317
Daniel J O Horo, *Ch*
Daniel P O Horo, *
Duane C Thompson, *
Thomas P Metzinger, *
Fred Leunis, *
EMP: 90 **EST:** 1948
SQ FT: 6,000
SALES (est): 20.42MM **Privately Held**
Web: www.apohoro.com
SIC: 1629 1622 1623 1611 Waste water and sewage treatment plant construction; Bridge construction; Sewer line construction ; Highway and street construction

(G-15540)
A1 INDUSTRIAL PAINTING INC
894 Coitsville Hubbard Rd (44505)
P.O. Box 509 (44405)
PHONE.................................330 750-9441
EMP: 50 **EST:** 2008
SALES (est): 5.62MM **Privately Held**
Web: www.a1industrialpainting.com
SIC: 1721 1389 Industrial painting; Construction, repair, and dismantling services

(G-15541)
ADVANCED DRMTLOGY SKIN CNCER C
987 Boardman Canfield Rd (44512-4222)
PHONE.................................330 965-8760
Tonia Alsano, *Managing Member*
EMP: 30 **EST:** 2005
SALES (est): 6.14MM **Privately Held**
Web: www.advancedderm.net
SIC: 8011 Dermatologist

(G-15542)
ADVANCED UROLOGY INC (PA)
904 Sahara Trl Ste 1 (44514-3695)
PHONE.................................330 758-9787
Richard D Nord Md, *Pr*
EMP: 27 **EST:** 1966
SQ FT: 10,000
SALES (est): 2.19MM
SALES (corp-wide): 2.19MM **Privately Held**
Web: www.advanceduro.com
SIC: 8011 Urologist

(G-15543)
AEY ELECTRIC INC
801 N Meridian Rd (44509-1008)
PHONE.................................330 792-5745
Robert Aey, *Pr*
Richard J Aey, *Sec*
EMP: 27 **EST:** 1964
SQ FT: 10,000
SALES (est): 1MM **Privately Held**
Web: www.aeyelectric.com
SIC: 1731 General electrical contractor

(G-15544)
AI-MEDIA INC
241 W Federal St (44503-1207)
PHONE.................................213 337-8552
EMP: 29 **EST:** 2016
SALES (est): 1.92MM **Privately Held**
Web: www.ai-media.tv
SIC: 4833 7389 Television broadcasting stations; Radio transcription service
PA: Ai-Media Technologies Limited
L 1 103 Miller St
North Sydney NSW 2060

(G-15545)
AI-MEDIA TECHNOLOGIES LLC
Also Called: Educaption
241 W Federal St Ste 201-B (44503-1207)
P.O. Box 278 (60148-0278)
PHONE.................................800 335-0911
Philip Hyssong, *Managing Member*
Julie Stone, *Contrlr*
EMP: 33 **EST:** 2007
SALES (est): 15MM **Privately Held**
Web: www.ai-media.tv
SIC: 7819 7389 Film processing, editing, and titling: motion picture; Translation services
PA: Ai-Media Technologies Limited
L 1 103 Miller St
North Sydney NSW 2060

(G-15546)
ALTA BEHAVIORAL HEALTHCARE
711 Belmont Ave (44502-1039)
PHONE.................................330 793-2487
Joseph Shorokey, *CEO*
EMP: 54 **EST:** 2016
SALES (est): 792.38K **Privately Held**
Web: www.altabehavioralhealthcare.org
SIC: 8099 Health and allied services, nec

(G-15547)
ALTA CARE GROUP INC
711 Belmont Ave (44502-1039)
PHONE.................................330 793-2487
Joseph Shorokey, *Ex Dir*
EMP: 50 **EST:** 1970
SQ FT: 7,428
SALES (est): 16.37MM **Privately Held**
Web: www.altabehavioralhealthcare.org
SIC: 8093 Mental health clinic, outpatient

(G-15548)
AMERICAN BEAUTY LANDSCAPING
5415 South Ave (44512-2453)
PHONE.................................330 788-1501
Roger Myers, *Pr*
EMP: 34 **EST:** 1979
SALES (est): 453.76K **Privately Held**
Web: www.growinggood.com
SIC: 0782 4959 Landscape contractors; Sanitary services, nec

(G-15549)
AMERICAN BULK COMMODITIES INC (PA)
Also Called: R & J Trucking
8063 Southern Blvd (44512-6306)
P.O. Box 9454 (44513-0454)
PHONE.................................330 758-0841
Ronald Carrocce, *Pr*
Mark Carrocce, *
Troy Carrocce, *
Gary Carrocce, *
EMP: 200 **EST:** 1992
SQ FT: 50,000
SALES (est): 78.79MM **Privately Held**
Web: www.americanbulkcommodities.com
SIC: 7532 6531 7363 4212 Paint shop, automotive; Real estate managers; Truck driver services; Dump truck haulage

(G-15550)
AMERICAN NATIONAL RED CROSS
Also Called: THE AMERICAN NATIONAL RED CROSS
8392 Tod Ave (44512-6300)
PHONE.................................330 726-6063
EMP: 41
SALES (corp-wide): 3.18B **Privately Held**
Web: www.redcross.org
SIC: 8322 Social service center
PA: The American National Red Cross
431 18th St Nw
Washington DC 20006
202 737-8300

(G-15551)
AMERICAN PAPER GROUP INC
Also Called: American Paper Products Co Div
8401 Southern Blvd (44512-6709)
P.O. Box 3120 (44513-3120)
PHONE.................................330 758-4545
Thomas W Pietrocini, *Ch Bd*
Don Allevach, *
EMP: 400 **EST:** 1915
SQ FT: 95,000
SALES (est): 27.71MM **Privately Held**
SIC: 2677 7331 Envelopes; Mailing service

(G-15552)
ASSOCIATES IN NEPHROLOGY LTD
7153 Tiffany Blvd (44514-1965)
PHONE.................................330 729-1355
Gayle Masbercilla, *Brnch Mgr*
EMP: 30 **EST:** 2011
SALES (est): 815.69K **Privately Held**
SIC: 8011 Nephrologist

(G-15553)
AUSTINTOWN DAIRY INC
780 Bev Rd (44512-6424)
P.O. Box 9484 (44513-0484)
PHONE.................................330 629-6170
Joseph Creighton, *Pr*
Thomas Creighton, *
EMP: 40 **EST:** 1963
SALES (est): 5.99MM **Privately Held**
Web: www.austintowndairy.com
SIC: 5143 5451 Milk; Ice cream (packaged)

(G-15554)
B & B CONTRS & DEVELOPERS INC
4531 Belmont Ave Ste A (44505-1041)
PHONE.................................330 270-5020
Geno Leshnack, *Pr*
James Cononico, *
Donald D'andrea, *Ex VP*
Brenda Leshnack, *
Samuel J Decaria, *
EMP: 80 **EST:** 1987
SQ FT: 12,000
SALES (est): 10.6MM **Privately Held**

Web: www.bbcdonline.com
SIC: 1542 1541 Commercial and office building, new construction; Industrial buildings, new construction, nec

(G-15555)
BANNER SUPPLY COMPANY INC (PA)
103 E Indianola Ave (44507-1597)
PHONE.................................330 782-1171
EMP: 30 **EST:** 1974
SALES (est): 26.53MM
SALES (corp-wide): 26.53MM **Privately Held**
Web: www.bannersupplyinc.com
SIC: 5033 5074 Roofing, siding, and insulation; Heating equipment (hydronic)

(G-15556)
BEECHER CARLSON INSUR SVCS LLC
7600 Market St (44512-6078)
PHONE.................................330 726-8177
EMP: 75
SALES (corp-wide): 3.57B **Publicly Held**
Web: www.bbrown.com
SIC: 6411 Insurance agents, nec
HQ: Beecher Carlson Insurance Services, Llc
6 Concourse Pkwy Ste 2300
Atlanta GA 30328
404 460-1426

(G-15557)
BEL-PARK ANESTHESIA
1044 Belmont Ave (44504-1006)
P.O. Box 460 (44406-0460)
PHONE.................................330 480-3658
Steve Scharf, *Prin*
EMP: 32 **EST:** 2005
SALES (est): 4.87MM **Privately Held**
Web: www.belpark.net
SIC: 8011 Anesthesiologist

(G-15558)
BELMONT BHC PINES HOSPITAL INC
615 Churchill Hubbard Rd (44505-1332)
PHONE.................................330 759-2700
TOLL FREE: 800
George Perry, *Pr*
EMP: 89 **EST:** 1991
SQ FT: 32,000
SALES (est): 21.06MM **Privately Held**
Web: www.belmontpines.com
SIC: 8063 8011 8093 8062 Psychiatric hospitals; Offices and clinics of medical doctors; Mental health clinic, outpatient; General medical and surgical hospitals

(G-15559)
BOAK & SONS INC
75 Victoria Rd (44515-2023)
PHONE.................................330 793-5646
Samuel G Boak, *Pr*
EMP: 200 **EST:** 1974
SQ FT: 38,000
SALES (est): 24.12MM **Privately Held**
Web: www.boakandsons.com
SIC: 1761 1742 1542 1541 Roofing contractor; Insulation, buildings; Nonresidential construction, nec; Industrial buildings and warehouses

(G-15560)
BOARDMAN LOCAL SCHOOLS
Also Called: Boardman School Bus Garage
7777 Glenwood Ave (44512-5824)
PHONE.................................330 726-3409
Ryan Dunn, *Supervisor*
EMP: 60

GEOGRAPHIC SECTION
Youngstown - Mahoning County (G-15581)

SALES (corp-wide): 48MM **Privately Held**
Web: www.boardman.k12.oh.us
SIC: 4151 8211 School buses; Public elementary and secondary schools
PA: Boardman Local Schools
7777 Glenwood Ave
Youngstown OH 44512
330 726-3400

(G-15561)
BOLT CONSTRUCTION INC
Also Called: Bolt Construction Co
10422 South Ave (44514-3459)
P.O. Box 5470 (44514-0470)
PHONE..................330 549-0349
John Miller, *Pr*
Melinda Miletta-miller, *VP*
Shirley Miletta, *
Bruno Miletta, *Corporate Secretary**
EMP: 90 **EST:** 1981
SQ FT: 15,000
SALES (est): 13.4MM **Privately Held**
Web: www.boltconstruction.com
SIC: 1623 Pipeline construction, nsk

(G-15562)
BON SECOURS MERCY HEALTH INC
Also Called: St. Elizabeth Youngstown Hosp
1044 Belmont Ave (44504-1006)
PHONE..................330 746-7211
EMP: 50
SALES (corp-wide): 6.92B **Privately Held**
Web: www.bonsecours.com
SIC: 8062 General medical and surgical hospitals
PA: Bon Secours Mercy Health, Inc.
1701 Mercy Health Pl
Cincinnati OH 45237
513 956-3729

(G-15563)
BON SECOURS MERCY HEALTH INC
Also Called: St Elizabeth Boardman Hospital
8401 Market St (44512-6725)
PHONE..................330 729-1420
Margaret Baker, *Mgr*
EMP: 121
SALES (corp-wide): 6.92B **Privately Held**
Web: www.bonsecours.com
SIC: 8011 8071 Freestanding emergency medical center; Medical laboratories
PA: Bon Secours Mercy Health, Inc.
1701 Mercy Health Pl
Cincinnati OH 45237
513 956-3729

(G-15564)
BOSTON RETAIL PRODUCTS INC
Boston Group
225 Hubbard Rd (44505-3120)
PHONE..................330 744-8100
Sandford Kessler, *Mgr*
EMP: 42
SALES (corp-wide): 24.26MM **Privately Held**
Web: www.boston-group.com
SIC: 5051 Metals service centers and offices
PA: Boston Retail Products, Inc.
3 Highwood Dr Ste 100w
Tewksbury MA 01876
781 395-7417

(G-15565)
BRIARFIELD MANOR LLC
461 S Canfield Niles Rd (44515-4089)
PHONE..................330 270-3468
EMP: 150 **EST:** 2000
SQ FT: 1,330
SALES (est): 9.88MM **Privately Held**
Web: www.briarfield.net
SIC: 8051 Skilled nursing care facilities

(G-15566)
BRIARFIELD OF BOARDMAN LLC
830 Boardman Canfield Rd (44512-4213)
PHONE..................330 259-9393
Diane Reese, *Prin*
EMP: 31 **EST:** 2011
SALES (est): 473.58K **Privately Held**
Web: www.briarfield.net
SIC: 8082 Home health care services

(G-15567)
BUCKEYE LEASING INC
8063 Southern Blvd (44512-6306)
PHONE..................330 758-0841
Ronald Carrocce, *Pr*
Gary Carrocce, *Sec*
Mark Carrocce, *VP*
EMP: 53 **EST:** 1988
SQ FT: 50,000
SALES (est): 979.09K **Privately Held**
SIC: 7363 Truck driver services
PA: American Bulk Commodities Inc
8063 Southern Blvd
Youngstown OH 44512

(G-15568)
BUTLER INSTITUTE AMERICAN ART (PA)
524 Wick Ave (44502-1213)
PHONE..................330 743-1711
Louis A Zona, *Ex Dir*
EMP: 28 **EST:** 1919
SQ FT: 80,000
SALES (est): 2MM
SALES (corp-wide): 2MM **Privately Held**
Web: www.butlerart.com
SIC: 8412 Museum

(G-15569)
CALLOS RESOURCE LLC (PA)
Also Called: Callos Prof Employment II
755 Boardman Canfield Rd Ste N2-Up (44512-4300)
PHONE..................330 788-3033
John Callos, *Ch*
Thomas Walsh, *
Eric Sutton, *
EMP: 30 **EST:** 1965
SQ FT: 8,200
SALES (est): 21.07MM
SALES (corp-wide): 21.07MM **Privately Held**
Web: www.nescoresource.com
SIC: 7363 Temporary help service

(G-15570)
CANFIELD LEASING CO LLC
Also Called: Canfield Healthcare Center
2958 Canfield Rd (44511-2805)
PHONE..................513 530-1600
Richard Odenthal, *Prin*
Sandra Smiddy, *
EMP: 71 **EST:** 2018
SALES (est): 927.47K **Privately Held**
Web: www.communicarehealth.com
SIC: 8099 Health and allied services, nec

(G-15571)
CARDIOVASCULAR ASSOCIATES INC
Also Called: Ohio Heart Instit
1001 Belmont Ave (44504-1003)
PHONE..................330 747-6446
Sadiq Husain Md, *Pr*
Shawki Habib Md, *VP*
Paul Wright, *Sec*
Ates Labib Md, *Treas*
EMP: 29 **EST:** 1973
SQ FT: 23,000
SALES (est): 374.75K **Privately Held**
SIC: 8011 Cardiologist and cardio-vascular specialist

(G-15572)
CATHOLIC CHRTIES REGIONAL AGCY
Also Called: Catholic Charities
319 W Rayen Ave (44502-1119)
PHONE..................330 744-3320
Nancy Voitus, *Ex Dir*
John Edwards, *
EMP: 29 **EST:** 1946
SALES (est): 2.22MM **Privately Held**
Web: www.ccdoy.org
SIC: 8322 Social service center

(G-15573)
CAVALIER MOBILE X-RAY CO
590 E Western Reserve Rd Bldg 10d (44514)
P.O. Box 3371 (44513)
PHONE..................330 726-0202
John Cavalier, *Pr*
Christine A Cavalier, *Sec*
Thomas J Cavalier, *Stockholder*
John D Cavalier, *Stockholder*
EMP: 37 **EST:** 1990
SALES (est): 5.69MM **Privately Held**
Web: www.cmxray.com
SIC: 8071 X-ray laboratory, including dental

(G-15574)
CERNI LEASING LLC
5751 Cerni Pl (44515-1174)
PHONE..................515 967-3300
James Ohalloran, *Pr*
EMP: 375 **EST:** 2009
SALES (est): 50.31MM
SALES (corp-wide): 357.54MM **Privately Held**
SIC: 5012 Automobiles and other motor vehicles
PA: Trivista Companies, Inc.
3311 Adventureland Dr
Altoona IA 50009
515 967-3300

(G-15575)
CERNI MOTOR SALES INC (HQ)
5751 Cerni Pl (44515-1174)
P.O. Box 4176 (44515-0176)
PHONE..................330 652-9917
John P Cerni, *Pr*
Joe Notarianni, *
Charles Cerni, *
EMP: 82 **EST:** 1961
SQ FT: 37,000
SALES (est): 50.83MM
SALES (corp-wide): 357.54MM **Privately Held**
Web: www.cernimotors.com
SIC: 5012 Trucks, commercial
PA: Trivista Companies, Inc.
3311 Adventureland Dr
Altoona IA 50009
515 967-3300

(G-15576)
CHILDRENS HOSP MED CTR AKRON
8423 Market St Ste 300 (44512-6778)
PHONE..................330 629-6085
Patrick J Doherty, *Brnch Mgr*
EMP: 54
SALES (corp-wide): 1.4B **Privately Held**
Web: www.akronchildrens.org
SIC: 8069 Childrens' hospital
PA: Childrens Hospital Medical Center Of Akron
1 Perkins Sq
Akron OH 44308
330 543-1000

(G-15577)
CHRISTUS HLTH SOUTHEAST TEXAS
Also Called: Hmhp Sleep Lab
7000 South Ave Ste 4 (44512-3644)
PHONE..................330 726-0771
Angela Duncan, *Brnch Mgr*
EMP: 112
SALES (corp-wide): 3.91B **Privately Held**
Web: www.christushealth.org
SIC: 8062 General medical and surgical hospitals
HQ: Christus Health Southeast Texas
2830 Calder St
Beaumont TX 77702
409 892-7171

(G-15578)
CITY OF YOUNGSTOWN (PA)
26 S Phelps St Bsmt (44503)
PHONE..................330 742-8700
Jamael Tito Brown, *Mayor*
EMP: 300 **EST:** 1797
SQ FT: 45,000
SALES (est): 78.32MM
SALES (corp-wide): 78.32MM **Privately Held**
Web: www.blackstonetheseries.com
SIC: 8741 Administrative management

(G-15579)
CLIMATE PROS LLC
52 E Myrtle Ave (44507-1268)
PHONE..................330 744-2732
Roy Guerrieri, *Brnch Mgr*
EMP: 88
Web: www.hattenbach.com
SIC: 5078 1711 2434 2541 Commercial refrigeration equipment; Refrigeration contractor; Wood kitchen cabinets; Cabinets, except refrigerated: show, display, etc.: wood
PA: Climate Pros, Llc
2190 Gladstone Ct Ste E
Glendale Heights IL 60139

(G-15580)
COCCA DEVELOPMENT LTD
100 Debartolo Pl Ste 400 (44512-6099)
PHONE..................330 729-1010
Anthony L Cocca, *CEO*
Jim Shipley, *VP*
Marc Barca, *VP*
Lynn E Davenport, *CFO*
Kelly Cocca, *Prin*
EMP: 70 **EST:** 1982
SQ FT: 20,000
SALES (est): 26.62MM **Privately Held**
Web: www.coccadevelopment.com
SIC: 1542 Nonresidential construction, nec

(G-15581)
COHEN & COMPANY LTD
201 E Commerce St Ste 400 (44503-1690)
PHONE..................330 743-1040
Frank J Dixon, *Mgr*
EMP: 102
SALES (corp-wide): 36MM **Privately Held**
Web: www.cohencpa.com
SIC: 8721 Certified public accountant
PA: Cohen & Company, Ltd.
1350 Euclid Ave Ste 800
Cleveland OH 44115
216 579-1040

Youngstown - Mahoning County (G-15582)

(G-15582)
COMPASS FAMILY AND CMNTY SVCS
246 Broadway Ave (44504-1752)
PHONE...............................330 782-5664
EMP: 48
SALES (corp-wide): 11.89MM **Privately Held**
Web: www.compassfamily.org
SIC: 8361 Rehabilitation center, residential: health care incidental
PA: Compass Family And Community Services
535 Marmion Ave
Youngstown OH 44502
330 782-5664

(G-15583)
COMPASS FAMILY AND CMNTY SVCS
284 Broadway Ave (44504-1752)
PHONE...............................330 743-9275
Joseph F Caruso, *Brnch Mgr*
EMP: 48
SALES (corp-wide): 11.89MM **Privately Held**
Web: www.compassfamily.org
SIC: 8322 Social service center
PA: Compass Family And Community Services
535 Marmion Ave
Youngstown OH 44502
330 782-5664

(G-15584)
COMPASS FAMILY AND CMNTY SVCS (PA)
Also Called: Family Service Agency
535 Marmion Ave (44502-2323)
PHONE...............................330 782-5664
Joseph F Caruso, *CEO*
Mark Wingert, *
David Arnold, *
EMP: 34 **EST:** 1917
SQ FT: 9,600
SALES (est): 11.89MM
SALES (corp-wide): 11.89MM **Privately Held**
Web: www.compassfamily.org
SIC: 8322 8093 8361 Emergency shelters; Drug clinic, outpatient; Residential care

(G-15585)
COMPCO LAND COMPANY (PA)
85 E Hylda Ave (44507-1762)
PHONE...............................330 482-0200
Clarence R Smith Junior, *Ch*
Gregory B Smith Senior, *Pr*
Douglas A Hagy, *
EMP: 60 **EST:** 1970
SQ FT: 42,000
SALES (est): 6.37MM
SALES (corp-wide): 6.37MM **Privately Held**
SIC: 6512 Commercial and industrial building operation

(G-15586)
COMPMANAGEMENT INC
4706 Brookwood Rd (44512-1427)
PHONE...............................330 782-0363
John Wagner, *Brnch Mgr*
EMP: 33
Web: www.compmgt.com
SIC: 6331 Workers' compensation insurance
HQ: Compmanagement, Inc.
6377 Emerald Pkwy
Dublin OH 43016
614 376-5300

(G-15587)
COMPREHENSIVE LOGISTICS CO INC
4944 Belmont Ave Ste 201 (44505-1055)
P.O. Box 247 (44473-0247)
PHONE...............................563 445-6001
Chadd Webster, *Mgr*
EMP: 55
Web: www.complog.com
SIC: 4225 General warehousing
PA: Comprehensive Logistics, Co., Inc.
8200 Hlth Ctr Blvd Ste 10
Bonita Springs FL 34135

(G-15588)
CONCORD HEALTH CARE INC (PA)
202 Churchill Hubbard Rd (44505-1325)
PHONE...............................330 759-2357
EMP: 50 **EST:** 1994
SALES (est): 4.86MM **Privately Held**
SIC: 8051 8052 Convalescent home with continuous nursing care; Intermediate care facilities

(G-15589)
CORECIVIC INC
Also Called: Northast Ohio Crrctnal Fclty 1
2240 Hubbard Rd (44505-3157)
P.O. Box 1857 (44501-1857)
PHONE...............................330 746-3777
D Bryan Gardner, *Prin*
EMP: 70
SALES (corp-wide): 1.9B **Publicly Held**
Web: www.cca.com
SIC: 8744 Correctional facility
PA: Corecivic, Inc.
5501 Virginia Way Ste 110
Brentwood TN 37027
615 263-3000

(G-15590)
CROSSRADS SLEEP DSRDERS CTR LL
721 Boardman Poland Rd Ste 204 (44512-5107)
PHONE...............................330 965-0220
EMP: 29 **EST:** 2004
SALES (est): 2.2MM **Privately Held**
Web: www.sleepandsnoringspecialist.com
SIC: 8052 Personal care facility

(G-15591)
DANIEL A TERRERI & SONS INC
1091 N Meridian Rd (44509-1016)
PHONE...............................330 538-2950
Daniel Terreri, *Pr*
Karen Augustine, *
Thomas Corroto, *
EMP: 27 **EST:** 1950
SQ FT: 5,000
SALES (est): 1.05MM **Privately Held**
SIC: 1791 1795 1799 Storage tanks, metal; erection; Demolition, buildings and other structures; Asbestos removal and encapsulation

(G-15592)
DANRIDGE NURSING HOME INC
31 Maranatha Ct (44505-4970)
PHONE...............................330 746-5157
Joanne Blunt, *Admn*
Julius Blunt, *
Leigh Greene, *
EMP: 37 **EST:** 1959
SQ FT: 29,000
SALES (est): 1.75MM **Privately Held**
SIC: 8051 Convalescent home with continuous nursing care

(G-15593)
DATA RECOVERY SERVICES LLC
Also Called: D R S
1343 Belmont Ave (44504-1117)
PHONE...............................330 397-0100
EMP: 70
SIC: 7379 Computer related consulting services

(G-15594)
DE-CAL INC
8392 Tod Ave Ste 1 (44512-6300)
PHONE...............................330 272-0021
EMP: 156
Web: www.de-cal.com
SIC: 1711 Mechanical contractor
PA: De-Cal, Inc.
24659 Schoenherr Rd
Warren MI 48089

(G-15595)
DEARING COMPRESSOR AND PUMP COMPANY (PA)
3974 Simon Rd (44512-1318)
P.O. Box 6044 (44501-6044)
PHONE...............................330 783-2258
EMP: 32 **EST:** 1945
SALES (est): 19.44MM
SALES (corp-wide): 19.44MM **Privately Held**
Web: www.dearingcomp.com
SIC: 7699 7359 5084 5085 Compressor repair; Equipment rental and leasing, nec; Compressors, except air conditioning; Industrial supplies

(G-15596)
DIAMOND STEEL CONSTRUCTION
8270 Raupp Ave (44512-6301)
P.O. Box 3107 (44513-3107)
PHONE...............................330 549-5500
Clarence R Smith Junior, *Ch Bd*
David Collins, *
Robert Smith, *
Gregory B Smith, *
EMP: 40 **EST:** 1928
SQ FT: 9,000
SALES (est): 2.72MM **Privately Held**
Web: www.diamondsteel.com
SIC: 1791 Structural steel erection

(G-15597)
DIRECTION HOME EASTRN OHIO INC
1030 N Meridian Rd (44509-4017)
PHONE...............................330 505-2355
Joseph Rossi, *CEO*
Don Dockry, *
EMP: 140 **EST:** 2009
SALES (est): 9.7MM **Privately Held**
Web: www.dheo.org
SIC: 8322 Senior citizens' center or association

(G-15598)
DISTRICT BOARD HEALTH MAHONING
50 Westchester Dr (44515-3991)
PHONE...............................330 270-2855
Matthew A Stefanak, *
Edward J Janik, *
EMP: 32 **EST:** 2010
SALES (est): 1.09MM **Privately Held**
Web: www.mahoninghealth.org
SIC: 8099 Health and allied services, nec

(G-15599)
DOCTORS PAIN CENTER LLC
Also Called: Doctor's Pain Clinic
1011 Boardman Canfield Rd (44512-4226)
PHONE...............................330 629-2888
Tracy Neuendorf, *Managing Member*
EMP: 38 **EST:** 1991
SALES (est): 3.39MM **Privately Held**
Web: www.doctorspainclinic.com
SIC: 8031 Offices and clinics of osteopathic physicians

(G-15600)
DON WALTER KITCHEN DISTRS INC (PA)
260 Victoria Rd (44515-2024)
PHONE...............................330 793-9338
Gary Walter, *Pr*
Randy Walter, *
EMP: 30 **EST:** 1973
SQ FT: 60,000
SALES (est): 9.65MM
SALES (corp-wide): 9.65MM **Privately Held**
Web: www.donwalterkitchen.com
SIC: 5064 5031 Electrical appliances, major; Kitchen cabinets

(G-15601)
DONALD P PIPINO COMPANY LTD
Also Called: Pipino
7600 Market St (44512-6078)
PHONE...............................330 726-8177
EMP: 75
Web: www.dpipino.com
SIC: 6411 Insurance agents, nec

(G-15602)
DOUBLETREE BY HILTON
44 E Federal St (44503-1853)
PHONE...............................330 333-8284
EMP: 27 **EST:** 2017
SALES (est): 858.01K **Privately Held**
Web: www.hilton.com
SIC: 7011 Hotels and motels

(G-15603)
EASTER SEAL SOCIETY OF (PA)
Also Called: EASTER SEALS
299 Edwards St (44502-1599)
PHONE...............................330 743-1168
Kenan Sklenar, *CEO*
Diane Hardenbrook, *
EMP: 75 **EST:** 1951
SQ FT: 26,265
SALES (est): 3.88MM
SALES (corp-wide): 3.88MM **Privately Held**
Web: www.easterseals.com
SIC: 8322 8093 Individual and family services; Rehabilitation center, outpatient treatment

(G-15604)
EASTERN OHIO PLMONARY CONS INC
960 Windham Ct Ste 1 (44512)
PHONE...............................330 726-3357
John Politis, *Pt*
Rebecca Bailey, *Prin*
Selin Abo Jonadi, *Prin*
Ritha Kartan, *Pt*
Lawrence Goldstein, *Pt*
EMP: 32 **EST:** 1988
SALES (est): 2.15MM **Privately Held**
Web: www.easternohiopulmonary.com
SIC: 8011 Pulmonary specialist, physician/surgeon

(G-15605)
EASTGATE RGNAL CNCIL GVRNMENTS
100 E Federal St Ste 1000 (44503-1809)
PHONE...............................330 779-3800

GEOGRAPHIC SECTION

Youngstown - Mahoning County (G-15628)

John Getchey, *Ex Dir*
John Smith, *Ch*
EMP: 30 **EST:** 1972
SALES (est): 829.37K **Privately Held**
Web: www.eastgatecog.org
SIC: 8399 Regional planning organization

(G-15606)
ECHO 360 INC (PA)
6000 Mahoning Ave (44515-2225)
PHONE..................877 324-6360
Frederick Singer, *CEO*
Anthony Abate, *
Chris Huff, *
EMP: 80 **EST:** 2007
SALES (est): 31MM **Privately Held**
Web: www.echo360.com
SIC: 7371 Computer software development

(G-15607)
EDM MANAGEMENT INC
1419 Boardman Canfield Rd Ste 500 (44512-8071)
PHONE..................330 726-5790
Edward Reese, *CEO*
Diane Reese, *
Rob Rupeka, *
EMP: 50 **EST:** 2003
SQ FT: 5,000
SALES (est): 4.99MM **Privately Held**
Web: www.edmmgt.com
SIC: 8741 Business management

(G-15608)
EYE CARE ASSOCIATES INC (PA)
10 Dutton Dr (44502-1899)
PHONE..................330 746-7691
Robert J Gerberry, *VP*
Robert J Gerberry Md, *VP*
H S Wang Md, *President Ophthalmology*
Keith Wilson Md, *Ophthalmology Vice President*
Sergul Erzurum Md, *VP*
EMP: 55 **EST:** 1955
SQ FT: 10,000
SALES (est): 10.91MM
SALES (corp-wide): 10.91MM **Privately Held**
Web: www.eyecareassociates.com
SIC: 8011 Opthalmologist

(G-15609)
FALCON TRANSPORT CO
4944 Belmont Ave (44505-1055)
P.O. Box 6147 (44501-6147)
PHONE..................330 793-1345
EMP: 1490
SIC: 4213 Heavy hauling, nec

(G-15610)
FARMERS TRUST COMPANY
City Ctr One Bldg Ste 700 (44501)
PHONE..................330 744-4351
Thomas J Cavalier, *Pr*
EMP: 50 **EST:** 1997
SQ FT: 9,500
SALES (est): 6.73MM
SALES (corp-wide): 255.2MM **Publicly Held**
Web: www.farmerstrustco.com
SIC: 6211 Stock brokers and dealers
PA: Farmers National Banc Corp.
20 S Broad St
Canfield OH 44406
330 533-3341

(G-15611)
FERSENIUS MEDICAL CENTER
Also Called: Physicans Dlysis Cntr-Yngstown
1340 Belmont Ave (44504-1125)
PHONE..................330 746-2860
EMP: 180
SALES (corp-wide): 9.77MM **Privately Held**
Web: www.kidneygroup.com
SIC: 8011 Nephrologist
PA: Fersenius Medical Center
2425 Garden Way Ste 102
Hermitage PA 16148
724 347-0700

(G-15612)
FIRST CHOICE COMMUNICATIONS
648 Marshall St (44502-1419)
PHONE..................330 439-5440
EMP: 28 **EST:** 2018
SALES (est): 375.45K **Privately Held**
Web: www.fccinstalls.com
SIC: 4899 Communication services, nec

(G-15613)
FORGE INDUSTRIES INC (PA)
4450 Market St (44512-1512)
PHONE..................330 960-2468
William T James Ii, *Ch Bd*
W Thomas James Iii, *VP*
Carl G James, *
Dan Maisonville, *
Gary Davis, *
▲ **EMP:** 1250 **EST:** 1900
SQ FT: 1,500
SALES (est): 1.51B
SALES (corp-wide): 1.51B **Privately Held**
SIC: 5085 3566 3599 3531 Bearings; Gears, power transmission, except auto; Machine shop, jobbing and repair; Road construction and maintenance machinery

(G-15614)
FSCREATIONS CORPORATION (HQ)
Also Called: Einstruction Corporation
255 W Federal St (44503-1207)
PHONE..................330 746-3015
Rich Fennessy, *CEO*
Tim Torno, *
▲ **EMP:** 100 **EST:** 1982
SQ FT: 8,000
SALES (est): 35.81MM
SALES (corp-wide): 91.49MM **Privately Held**
Web: www.echo360.com
SIC: 7371 7379 5045 7372 Computer software development; Computer related consulting services; Computers, peripherals, and software; Prepackaged software
PA: Turning Technologies, Llc
6000 Mahoning Ave Ste 254
Youngstown OH 44501
330 746-3015

(G-15615)
FYDA FRGHTLINER YOUNGSTOWN INC
Also Called: Fyda Truck & Equipment
5260 76 Dr (44515-1148)
PHONE..................330 797-0224
Walter R Fyda, *Pr*
Elizabeth Fyda, *
EMP: 70 **EST:** 1954
SQ FT: 60,000
SALES (est): 18.05MM **Privately Held**
Web: www.fydafreightliner.com
SIC: 5012 7538 Trucks, commercial; General truck repair

(G-15616)
GALAXIE INDUSTRIAL SVCS LLC
837 E Western Reserve Rd (44514-3360)
P.O. Box 11140 (44511-0140)
PHONE..................330 503-2334
EMP: 34 **EST:** 2010
SQ FT: 20,000
SALES (est): 2.48MM **Privately Held**
Web: www.galaxieis.com
SIC: 7349 Cleaning service, industrial or commercial

(G-15617)
GASSER CHAIR CO INC
2547 Logan Ave (44505)
PHONE..................330 742-2234
EMP: 52
SALES (corp-wide): 24.66MM **Privately Held**
Web: www.gasserchair.com
SIC: 5021 Chairs
PA: Gasser Chair Co., Inc.
4136 Logan Way
Youngstown OH 44505
330 534-2234

(G-15618)
GATEWAYS TO BETTER LIVING INC (PA)
6000 Mahoning Ave Ste 234 (44515-2225)
PHONE..................330 792-2854
Gail Riess, *Ex Dir*
EMP: 30 **EST:** 1972
SQ FT: 3,000
SALES (est): 21.74MM
SALES (corp-wide): 21.74MM **Privately Held**
Web: www.gatewaystbl.com
SIC: 8361 Retarded home

(G-15619)
GENERTONS BHVRAL HLTH - YNGSTO
196 Colonial Dr (44505-2139)
PHONE..................234 855-0523
Tyson Bartosh, *CFO*
EMP: 43 **EST:** 2016
SALES (est): 17.65MM **Privately Held**
Web: www.generationsbehavioralhealth.com
SIC: 8063 Psychiatric hospitals

(G-15620)
GENEVA LIBERTY STEEL LTD (PA)
Also Called: Genmak Geneva Liberty
947 Martin Luther King Jr Blvd (44502)
P.O. Box 6124 (44501)
PHONE..................330 740-0103
EMP: 40 **EST:** 2002
SQ FT: 85,000
SALES (est): 49.39MM
SALES (corp-wide): 49.39MM **Privately Held**
Web: www.genevaliberty.com
SIC: 3316 7389 Strip, steel, flat bright, cold-rolled: purchased hot-rolled; Scrap steel cutting

(G-15621)
GIFFIN MANAGEMENT GROUP INC
Also Called: Chelsea Court Apartments
6300 South Ave Apt 1200 (44512-3639)
PHONE..................330 758-4695
Dale Giffin, *Pr*
EMP: 49
Web: www.wyndhamhotels.com
SIC: 6513 Apartment building operators
PA: Giffin Management Group Inc
2725 Airview Blvd Ste 204
Portage MI 49002

(G-15622)
GREAT LAKES TELCOM LTD (PA)
Also Called: BROADBAND HOSPITALITY
590 E Western Reserve Rd Bldg 9c (44514)
PHONE..................330 629-8848
Vincent Lucci Junior, *CEO*
EMP: 30 **EST:** 1998
SQ FT: 9,200
SALES (est): 28.97MM **Privately Held**
SIC: 3663 4813 1623 1731 Satellites, communications; Internet connectivity services; Telephone and communication line construction; Telephone and telephone equipment installation

(G-15623)
GREENHEART COMPANIES LLC
6001 Southern Blvd Ste 105 (44512)
PHONE..................330 259-3070
EMP: 47 **EST:** 2011
SALES (est): 5.81MM **Privately Held**
Web: www.greenheartcompanies.com
SIC: 7389 Exhibit construction by industrial contractors

(G-15624)
GREENWOOD CHEVROLET INC
4695 Mahoning Ave (44515)
PHONE..................330 270-1299
Gregory Greenwood, *Pr*
Wayne Bud C Greenwood Junior, *VP*
EMP: 146 **EST:** 1960
SQ FT: 50,000
SALES (est): 22.58MM **Privately Held**
Web: www.greenwoodchevrolet.com
SIC: 5511 7538 5521 Automobiles, new and used; General automotive repair shops; Used car dealers

(G-15625)
GROUND TECH INC
Also Called: Safe Dig
240 Sinter Ct (44510-1076)
PHONE..................330 270-0700
Mathew Frontino, *Pr*
Mathew Frontino, *Pr*
Joseph Bianco, *
EMP: 30 **EST:** 2002
SQ FT: 40,000
SALES (est): 2.22MM **Privately Held**
Web: www.groundtech-inc.com
SIC: 1794 Excavation work

(G-15626)
HD DAVIS CPAS LLC
4308 Belmont Ave Ste 1 (44505-1071)
PHONE..................330 759-8522
EMP: 52 **EST:** 2011
SALES (est): 2.51MM **Privately Held**
Web: www.hdgrowthpartners.com
SIC: 7389 Financial services

(G-15627)
HEALTH CARE SOLUTIONS INC
Also Called: HEALTH CARE SOLUTIONS, INC
6961 Southern Blvd Ste B (44512-4653)
PHONE..................330 729-9491
Tim Pattons, *COO*
EMP: 211
Web: www.nyuhealthcaresolutions.com
SIC: 8059 Personal care home, with health care
PA: Healthcare Solutions, Inc.
3741 Plaza Dr Ste 1a
Ann Arbor MI 48108

(G-15628)
HEART CENTER OF N EASTRN OHIO (PA)
Also Called: Heart Center Northeastern Ohio
250 Debartolo Pl Ste 2750 (44512-6026)
PHONE..................330 758-7703
Paula Peterson, *Admn*
EMP: 47 **EST:** 1974
SALES (est): 2.85MM

Youngstown - Mahoning County (G-15629)

SALES (corp-wide): 2.85MM **Privately Held**
SIC: 8011 Cardiologist and cardio-vascular specialist

(G-15629)
HENRY H STMBUGH ADITORIUM ASSN
Also Called: HH STAMBAUGH
1000 5th Ave Frnt (44504)
PHONE.................................330 747-5175
Matthew Pagac, *CEO*
Anna Jean Cushwa, *
Barbara Armstrong, *
M Lucille Johns, *
Paul Fryman, *
EMP: 27 **EST:** 1926
SQ FT: 10,000
SALES (est): 1.94MM **Privately Held**
Web: www.stambaughauditorium.com
SIC: 6512 Auditorium and hall operation

(G-15630)
HOLLYWOOD GMING AT MHNING VLY
655 N Canfield Niles Rd (44515-1102)
PHONE.................................330 505-8700
EMP: 99 **EST:** 2014
SALES (est): 5.21MM **Privately Held**
Web: www.hollywoodmahoningvalley.com
SIC: 7011 Casino hotel

(G-15631)
HOME SAVINGS LOAN COMPANY
275 W Federal St (44503-1200)
PHONE.................................304 594-0013
EMP: 29 **EST:** 2017
SALES (est): 1.54MM **Privately Held**
SIC: 6035 Federal savings banks

(G-15632)
HOMECARE WITH HEART LLC
821 Kentwood Dr Ste B (44512-5061)
PHONE.................................330 726-0700
Stephen Jones, *
EMP: 125 **EST:** 2005
SALES (est): 5.01MM **Privately Held**
Web: www.homecarewithheart.com
SIC: 5047 8049 8082 Medical equipment and supplies; Nurses and other medical assistants; Home health care services

(G-15633)
HOMETOWN URGENT CARE
Also Called: HOMETOWN URGENT CARE
1305 Boardman Poland Rd (44514-1935)
PHONE.................................330 629-2300
Tammy Russell, *Brnch Mgr*
EMP: 37
SALES (corp-wide): 23.51MM **Privately Held**
Web: www.hometownurgentcare.com
SIC: 8049 8011 7291 Occupational therapist; Medical centers; Tax return preparation services
PA: Urgent Care Specialists Llc
2400 Corp Exch Dr Ste 102
Columbus OH 43231
614 505-7633

(G-15634)
HUMILITY HOUSE
Also Called: Humility House Assisted Living
755 Ohltown Rd (44515-1075)
PHONE.................................330 505-0144
Roco Parrell, *Dir*
EMP: 100 **EST:** 1999
SALES (est): 5.49MM **Privately Held**
SIC: 8051 8052 Skilled nursing care facilities; Intermediate care facilities

(G-15635)
HUNTINGTON NATIONAL BANK
4682 Belmont Ave (44505-1012)
PHONE.................................330 314-1410
EMP: 31
SALES (corp-wide): 10.84B **Publicly Held**
Web: www.huntington.com
SIC: 6029 Commercial banks, nec
HQ: The Huntington National Bank
41 S High St
Columbus OH 43215
614 480-4293

(G-15636)
HUNTINGTON NATIONAL BANK
3939 Market St (44512-1112)
PHONE.................................330 314-1380
EMP: 36
SALES (corp-wide): 10.84B **Publicly Held**
Web: www.huntington.com
SIC: 6029 Commercial banks, nec
HQ: The Huntington National Bank
41 S High St
Columbus OH 43215
614 480-4293

(G-15637)
IN YOUNGSTOWN AREA GDWILL INDS (PA)
2747 Belmont Ave (44505-1819)
PHONE.................................330 759-7921
Shelley Murray, *Interim Chief Executive Officer*
Toby Mirto, *
EMP: 180 **EST:** 1892
SQ FT: 84,000
SALES (est): 10.57MM
SALES (corp-wide): 10.57MM **Privately Held**
Web: www.goodwillyoungstown.org
SIC: 8331 5932 Vocational rehabilitation agency; Clothing and shoes, secondhand

(G-15638)
INDUSTRIAL WASTE CONTROL INC
240 Sinter Ct (44510-1076)
PHONE.................................330 270-9900
EMP: 75 **EST:** 1994
SQ FT: 40,000
SALES (est): 8.91MM **Privately Held**
Web: www.iwc-inc.com
SIC: 1799 4953 Exterior cleaning, including sandblasting; Refuse collection and disposal services

(G-15639)
INFOCISION MANAGEMENT CORP
6951 Southern Blvd Ste E (44512-4655)
PHONE.................................330 726-0872
Carl Albright, *Mgr*
EMP: 171
SALES (corp-wide): 115.4MM **Privately Held**
Web: www.infocision.com
SIC: 7389 Telemarketing services
PA: Infocision Management Corporation
325 Springside Dr
Akron OH 44333
330 668-1411

(G-15640)
INFOCISION MANAGEMENT CORP
5740 Patriot Blvd (44515-1170)
PHONE.................................330 544-1400
EMP: 170
SALES (corp-wide): 115.4MM **Privately Held**
Web: www.infocision.com
SIC: 7389 8732 Telemarketing services; Commercial nonphysical research
PA: Infocision Management Corporation
325 Springside Dr
Akron OH 44333
330 668-1411

(G-15641)
INTERNTIONAL TOWERS I OHIO LTD
25 Market St (44503-1731)
PHONE.................................216 520-1250
Frank Sinito, *Genl Pt*
EMP: 99 **EST:** 2015
SALES (est): 1.93MM **Privately Held**
SIC: 6513 Apartment building operators

(G-15642)
JOHN ZIDIAN CO INC (HQ)
574 Mcclurg Rd (44512-6405)
PHONE.................................330 743-6050
Harry Shood, *CFO*
♦ **EMP:** 50 **EST:** 1983
SQ FT: 29,000
SALES (est): 25.94MM
SALES (corp-wide): 91.82MM **Privately Held**
Web: www.giarussa.com
SIC: 5141 Groceries, general line
PA: Zidian Management Corp.
574 Mcclurg Rd
Boardman OH 44512
330 743-6050

(G-15643)
JS PARIS EXCAVATING INC
185 Industrial Rd (44509-2914)
P.O. Box 2448 (44509-0448)
PHONE.................................330 538-9876
James S Paris Junior, *Pr*
Jason A Paris, *
EMP: 50 **EST:** 1990
SALES (est): 19.65MM **Privately Held**
Web: www.jspexcavating.com
SIC: 1794 1795 Excavation and grading, building construction; Demolition, buildings and other structures

(G-15644)
KALEEL BROS INC
Also Called: Kaleel Brothers
761 Bev Rd (44512-6423)
P.O. Box 538 (44501-0538)
PHONE.................................330 758-0861
EMP: 75 **EST:** 1933
SALES (est): 48.2MM **Privately Held**
Web: www.kaleelbrothers.com
SIC: 5148 5142 5149 5113 Fresh fruits and vegetables; Packaged frozen goods; Canned goods: fruit, vegetables, seafood, meats, etc.; Industrial and personal service paper

(G-15645)
KELNA INC
Also Called: Lads N' Lasses
8388 Tod Ave (44512-6366)
PHONE.................................330 729-0167
Alison Carrocce, *Dir*
Maryann Durcan, *Dir*
Donna Mcgrath, *Pr*
Nancy Jacubec, *VP Opers*
EMP: 33 **EST:** 1983
SALES (est): 229.77K **Privately Held**
Web: www.weecareohio.com
SIC: 8351 8211 Preschool center; Kindergarten

(G-15646)
KIDNEY GROUP INC
1340 Belmont Ave Ste 2300 (44504-1129)
PHONE.................................330 746-1488
Nathaniel Doe, *Pr*
Ramish Soundararajan, *
Kathlyn Padgitt, *
Anup Bains, *
Nathaniel Dowe, *
EMP: 50 **EST:** 1982
SALES (est): 2.62MM **Privately Held**
Web: www.kidneygroup.com
SIC: 8011 8092 Nephrologist; Kidney dialysis centers

(G-15647)
KNAPP CTR FOR CHLDHOOD DEV LLC
1051 Tiffany S (44514-1977)
PHONE.................................330 629-2955
Julie Knapp, *Prin*
EMP: 30 **EST:** 2014
SALES (est): 11.97MM **Privately Held**
Web: www.knappcenter.org
SIC: 8049 Clinical psychologist

(G-15648)
LENCYK MASONRY CO INC
7671 South Ave (44512-5724)
PHONE.................................330 729-9780
Lawrence Lencyk, *Pr*
Jacquelyn Lencyk, *
EMP: 30 **EST:** 1984
SALES (est): 4.97MM **Privately Held**
Web: www.lencykmasonry.com
SIC: 1741 Tuckpointing or restoration

(G-15649)
LIBERTY HOSPITALITY INC
Also Called: Comfort Inn
4055 Belmont Ave (44505-1035)
PHONE.................................330 759-3180
Raxit Shah, *Pr*
Ketki Shah, *Pr*
EMP: 40 **EST:** 1984
SQ FT: 86,000
SALES (est): 482.16K **Privately Held**
Web: www.choicehotels.com
SIC: 7011 Hotels and motels

(G-15650)
LIBERTY MAINTENANCE INC
777 N Meridian Rd (44509-1006)
P.O. Box 631 (44405-0631)
PHONE.................................330 755-7711
Emanouel Frangos, *Pr*
Nikolaos Frangos, *
Themelina Frangos, *Corporate Secretary**
Christine Kalikatzaros, *Corporate Secretary**
EMP: 70 **EST:** 1986
SQ FT: 7,900
SALES (est): 11.14MM **Privately Held**
Web: www.libertymaintenanceinc.com
SIC: 1622 Bridge, tunnel, and elevated highway construction

(G-15651)
LIBERTY-SPS JV LTD PARTNERSHIP ✪
777 N Meridian Rd (44509-1006)
PHONE.................................330 755-7711
Themelina Frangos, *Sec*
EMP: 70 **EST:** 2023
SALES (est): 2.53MM **Privately Held**
SIC: 1721 Bridge painting

(G-15652)
LINEAGE LOGISTICS LLC
1130 Performance Pl (44502-4003)
PHONE.................................330 559-4860
Mark Nelson, *CEO*
Stephanie Riffell, *COO*
EMP: 40 **EST:** 2016
SALES (est): 24.49MM **Privately Held**
Web: www.onelineage.com

GEOGRAPHIC SECTION

Youngstown - Mahoning County (G-15673)

SIC: 5199 Packaging materials

(G-15653)
LOWES HOME CENTERS LLC
Also Called: Lowe's
1100 Doral Dr (44514-1904)
PHONE..................330 965-4500
EMP: 143
SALES (corp-wide): 86.38B **Publicly Held**
Web: www.lowes.com
SIC: **5211** 5031 5722 5064 Home centers; Building materials, exterior; Household appliance stores; Electrical appliances, television and radio
HQ: Lowe's Home Centers, Llc
1000 Lowes Blvd
Mooresville NC 28117
336 658-4000

(G-15654)
LYDEN OIL COMPANY
3711 Leharps Dr (44515-1457)
PHONE..................330 792-1100
EMP: 38
Web: www.lydenoil.com
SIC: **5172** Crude oil
PA: Lyden Oil Company
30692 Tracy Rd
Walbridge OH 43465

(G-15655)
MAHONING COUNTY
Also Called: Mahoning County Engineers
940 Bears Den Rd (44511-1218)
PHONE..................330 799-1581
Richard Marsico, *Prin*
EMP: 48
SALES (corp-wide): 233.47MM **Privately Held**
Web: www.youngstownlive.com
SIC: **8711** 4959 Engineering services; Road, airport, and parking lot maintenance services
PA: The Mahoning County
21 W Boardman St Ste 200
Youngstown OH 44503
330 740-2130

(G-15656)
MAHONING COUNTY
Sanitary Engineering Dept
761 Industrial Rd (44509-2921)
PHONE..................330 793-5514
Joseph Warinf, *Mgr*
EMP: 40
SALES (corp-wide): 233.47MM **Privately Held**
Web: www.youngstownlive.com
SIC: **9511** 4953 Sanitary engineering agency, government; Garbage: collecting, destroying, and processing
PA: The Mahoning County
21 W Boardman St Ste 200
Youngstown OH 44503
330 740-2130

(G-15657)
MAHONING COUNTY
130 Javit Ct (44515-2409)
PHONE..................330 797-2925
Jim Groner, *Ex Dir*
EMP: 34
SALES (corp-wide): 233.47MM **Privately Held**
Web: www.mahoningdd.org
SIC: **8059** Home for the mentally retarded, ex. skilled or intermediate
PA: The Mahoning County
21 W Boardman St Ste 200
Youngstown OH 44503
330 740-2130

(G-15658)
MAHONING COUNTY CHILDRENS SVCS
222 W Federal St Fl 4 (44503-1222)
PHONE..................330 941-8888
Denise Stewart, *Dir*
EMP: 44 EST: 2006
SALES (est): 3.35MM **Privately Held**
Web: www.mahoningkids.com
SIC: **8322** Adoption services

(G-15659)
MAHONING VLY HMTLOGY ONCLOGY A
Also Called: Cancer Care Center
500 Gypsy Ln (44504-1316)
P.O. Box 240 (44501-0240)
PHONE..................330 318-1100
Kathy Clark, *Mgr*
EMP: 30 EST: 1978
SALES (est): 867.86K **Privately Held**
SIC: **8011** 8093 Hematologist; Specialty outpatient clinics, nec

(G-15660)
MAHONING VLY INFUSIONCARE INC (PA)
Also Called: Mvi Home Care
4891 Belmont Ave (44505-1015)
PHONE..................330 759-9487
EMP: 120 EST: 1995
SQ FT: 16,200
SALES (est): 6.26MM **Privately Held**
Web: www.thrivemv.org
SIC: **8059** 8082 Personal care home, with health care; Home health care services

(G-15661)
MAHONING YNGSTOWN CMNTY ACTION (PA)
Also Called: Mycap
1325 5th Ave (44504-1702)
PHONE..................330 747-7921
Richard A Roller Ii, *Ex Dir*
Anthony B Flask, *
Harry Meshel, *
J Ronald Pittman, *
EMP: 51 EST: 1965
SALES (est): 3.73MM
SALES (corp-wide): 3.73MM **Privately Held**
Web: www.mycaphelp.com
SIC: **8732** 8399 8322 Economic research; Advocacy group; Community center

(G-15662)
MAHONING YOUNGSTOWN COMMUNITY
Also Called: Head Start Program
1988 Mccartney Rd (44505-5033)
PHONE..................330 747-0236
FAX: 330 747-0240
EMP: 45
SALES (corp-wide): 3.29MM **Privately Held**
SIC: **8732** 8351 Economic research; Child day care services
PA: Mahoning Youngstown Community Action Partnership
1325 5th Ave
Youngstown OH 44504
330 747-7921

(G-15663)
MAHONING YOUNGSTOWN COMMUNITY
1350 5th Ave (44504-1728)
PHONE..................330 747-7921
EMP: 30
SALES (corp-wide): 3.73MM **Privately Held**
Web: www.mycaphelp.com
SIC: **6021** National commercial banks
PA: Mahoning Youngstown Community Action Partnership
1325 5th Ave
Youngstown OH 44504
330 747-7921

(G-15664)
MEADOWBROOK MALL COMPANY (PA)
2445 Belmont Ave (44505-2405)
P.O. Box 2186 (44504-0186)
PHONE..................330 747-2661
Anthony M Cafaro, *Pt*
EMP: 45 EST: 1980
SQ FT: 12,000
SALES (est): 2.45MM
SALES (corp-wide): 2.45MM **Privately Held**
Web: www.cafarocompany.com
SIC: **6512** 6531 Commercial and industrial building operation; Real estate agents and managers

(G-15665)
MERCY HEALTH YOUNGSTOWN LLC (HQ)
Also Called: St Elizabeth Health Center
1044 Belmont Ave (44504-1006)
P.O. Box 1790 (44501-1790)
PHONE..................330 746-7211
EMP: 2500 EST: 1996
SALES (est): 463.32MM
SALES (corp-wide): 6.92B **Privately Held**
Web: www.mercy.com
SIC: **8062** 8071 Hospital, affiliated with AMA residency; Ultrasound laboratory
PA: Bon Secours Mercy Health, Inc.
1701 Mercy Health Pl
Cincinnati OH 45237
513 956-3729

(G-15666)
MERIDIAN HEALTHCARE (PA)
527 N Meridian Rd (44509)
PHONE..................330 797-0070
EMP: 60 EST: 1974
SALES (est): 19.22MM **Privately Held**
Web: www.meridianhealthcare.net
SIC: **8093** Substance abuse clinics (outpatient)

(G-15667)
MILL CREEK METROPOLITAN PARK
Also Called: Mill Creek Golf Course
Boardman Canfield Rd (44502)
P.O. Box 596 (44406-0596)
PHONE..................330 740-7112
Dennis Miller, *Dir*
EMP: 30
SALES (corp-wide): 9.92MM **Privately Held**
Web: www.millcreekmetroparks.org
SIC: **7992** Public golf courses
PA: Mill Creek Metropolitan Park
1 W Golf Dr
Youngstown OH 44512
330 702-3000

(G-15668)
MILL CREEK METROPOLITAN PARK
Also Called: Fellows Riverside Gardens
123 Mckinley Ave (44509-2859)
PHONE..................330 740-7116
Keith Kaiser, *Dir*
EMP: 30
SALES (corp-wide): 9.92MM **Privately Held**
Web: www.millcreekmetroparks.org
SIC: **7999** Recreation services
PA: Mill Creek Metropolitan Park
1 W Golf Dr
Youngstown OH 44512
330 702-3000

(G-15669)
MS CONSULTANTS INC (PA)
333 E Federal St (44503-1821)
PHONE..................330 744-5321
Thomas E Mosure, *Pr*
Raymond J Briya, *
Michael D Kratofil, *
EMP: 105 EST: 1965
SQ FT: 20,000
SALES (est): 53.77MM
SALES (corp-wide): 53.77MM **Privately Held**
Web: www.msconsultants.com
SIC: **8711** 8712 Consulting engineer; Architectural services

(G-15670)
MURANSKY COMPANIES LLC
7629 Market St Ste 200 (44512-6082)
PHONE..................330 729-7400
Ed W Muransky, *Ch*
Eliot N Meyers, *Prin*
EMP: 31 EST: 2005
SALES (est): 1.2MM **Privately Held**
Web: www.muransky.com
SIC: **8742** Real estate consultant

(G-15671)
MURPHY CONTRACTING CO
285 Andrews Ave (44505-3059)
P.O. Box 1833 (44501-1833)
PHONE..................330 743-8915
Donald Gubany, *Pr*
Len Summers, *
Michael Gentile, *
EMP: 30 EST: 1942
SQ FT: 7,000
SALES (est): 11.06MM **Privately Held**
Web: www.murphycontracting.com
SIC: **1542** 1541 Commercial and office building, new construction; Industrial buildings, new construction, nec

(G-15672)
NANNICOLA WHOLESALE CO
Also Called: Bingo Division
2750 Salt Springs Rd (44509-1034)
PHONE..................330 799-0888
Charles Nannicola, *Mgr*
EMP: 70
SALES (corp-wide): 15.94MM **Privately Held**
Web: www.nannicola.com
SIC: **5092** 5199 Bingo games and supplies; Gifts and novelties
PA: Nannicola Wholesale Co.
3650 Connecticut Ave
Youngstown OH 44515
330 799-0888

(G-15673)
NATIONAL HEAT EXCH CLG CORP
8397 Southern Blvd (44512-6319)
PHONE..................330 482-0893
EMP: 40 EST: 1995
SQ FT: 52,000
SALES (est): 8.96MM
SALES (corp-wide): 35 **Privately Held**
Web: www.nationalheatexchange.com
SIC: **7699** Industrial equipment cleaning
PA: Conco Services Llc
530 Jones St
Verona PA 15147
412 828-1166

Youngstown - Mahoning County (G-15674)

(G-15674)
NATIONAL HERITG ACADEMIES INC
Also Called: Stambaugh Charter Academy
2420 Donald Ave (44509-1306)
PHONE.................................330 792-4806
EMP: 45
Web: www.nhaschools.com
SIC: 8741 Management services
PA: National Heritage Academies, Inc.
3850 Broadmoor Ave Se # 201
Grand Rapids MI 49512

(G-15675)
NATIONAL MENTOR HOLDINGS INC
100 Debartolo Pl Ste 330 (44512-7011)
PHONE.................................330 491-4331
EMP: 485
SALES (corp-wide): 1.64B Privately Held
Web: www.sevitahealth.com
SIC: 8093 Mental health clinic, outpatient
HQ: National Mentor Holdings, Inc.
313 Congress St Fl 5
Boston MA 02210
617 790-4800

(G-15676)
NICHALEX INC
Also Called: Wee Care Day Care Lrng Centre
801 Kentwood Dr (44512-5004)
PHONE.................................330 726-1422
Donna Mcgrath, Pr
EMP: 27 EST: 1994
SALES (est): 444.14K Privately Held
Web: www.weecareohio.com
SIC: 8351 Group day care center

(G-15677)
NICHOLAS CARNEY-MC INC
Also Called: Carney McNicholas
100 Victoria Rd (44515-2037)
P.O. Box 4717 (44515-0717)
PHONE.................................330 792-5460
EMP: 71
SIC: 4214 4212 4213 Furniture moving and storage, local; Local trucking, without storage; Household goods transport

(G-15678)
NORTH STAR PAINTING CO INC
Also Called: K&K Painting Company, Inc.
3526 Mccartney Rd (44505-5006)
PHONE.................................330 743-2333
Irene Kalouris, Pr
Nick Kalouris, *
EMP: 50 EST: 1987
SALES (est): 3.69MM Privately Held
Web: www.northstarpaintingco.com
SIC: 1721 Bridge painting

(G-15679)
OHIO AUTO LOAN SERVICES INC
226 Boardman Canfield Rd (44512-4805)
PHONE.................................330 272-9488
EMP: 37
SIC: 6141 Automobile loans, including insurance
HQ: Ohio Auto Loan Services, Inc.
8601 Dunwoody Pl Ste 406
Atlanta GA 30350
770 552-9840

(G-15680)
OHIO EDISON COMPANY
730 South Ave (44502-2011)
PHONE.................................330 740-7754
Jeff Elser, Brnch Mgr
EMP: 109
Web: www.firstenergycorp.com
SIC: 4911 Distribution, electric power
HQ: Ohio Edison Company
76 S Main St Bsmt
Akron OH 44308
800 736-3402

(G-15681)
OHIO HEART INSTITUTE INC (PA)
1001 Belmont Ave (44504-1088)
PHONE.................................330 747-6446
Wahoub Hout, Pr
EMP: 27 EST: 1985
SQ FT: 23,000
SALES (est): 2.24MM
SALES (corp-wide): 2.24MM Privately Held
Web: www.ohioheartinstitute.com
SIC: 8093 Specialty outpatient clinics, nec

(G-15682)
OHIO LIVING
Also Called: Park Vista Retirement Cmnty
1216 5th Ave (44504-1605)
PHONE.................................330 746-2944
Mary L Cochran, Brnch Mgr
EMP: 355
Web: www.ohioliving.org
SIC: 8051 8052 6513 Skilled nursing care facilities; Intermediate care facilities; Apartment building operators
PA: Ohio Living
9200 Worthington Rd # 300
Westerville OH 43082

(G-15683)
OHIO NORTH E HLTH SYSTEMS INC (PA)
Also Called: ONE HEALTH OHIO AT YOUNGSTOWN
726 Wick Ave (44505-2827)
PHONE.................................330 747-9551
Ronald Dwinnells, CEO
Maxine Speer, *
William Addington, *
EMP: 32 EST: 1989
SALES (est): 25.71MM Privately Held
Web: www.onehealthohio.org
SIC: 8099 8082 Physical examination and testing services; Home health care services

(G-15684)
OHIO VALLEY MALL COMPANY
2445 Belmont Ave (44505-2405)
PHONE.................................330 747-2661
William A Cafaro, Pr
EMP: 30 EST: 1976
SALES (est): 1.5MM Privately Held
Web: www.ohiovalleymall.net
SIC: 6512 Shopping center, property operation only

(G-15685)
OMNI MANOR INC
Also Called: Omni Nursing Home
3245 Vestal Rd (44509-1069)
PHONE.................................330 793-5648
Paul Fabian, Mgr
EMP: 1000
SALES (corp-wide): 23.03MM Privately Held
Web: www.windsorhouseinc.com
SIC: 8051 Convalescent home with continuous nursing care
PA: Omni Manor, Inc.
101 W Liberty St
Girard OH 44420
330 545-1550

(G-15686)
ORTHOPAEDIC SURGERY CENTE
8551 Crossroad Dr (44514-4382)
PHONE.................................330 758-1065
EMP: 32 EST: 2020
SALES (est): 5.26MM Privately Held
Web: www.theorthosurgerycenter.com
SIC: 8011 Orthopedic physician

(G-15687)
P & S BAKERY INC
2720 Intertech Dr (44509)
PHONE.................................330 707-4141
David George, Pr
Bonnie George, *
EMP: 50 EST: 1973
SQ FT: 20,000
SALES (est): 13.21MM Privately Held
Web: www.psbakeryinc.com
SIC: 5149 Bakery products

(G-15688)
PANELMATIC INC
Also Called: Panelmatic Youngstown
1125 Meadowbrook Ave (44512-1884)
PHONE.................................330 782-8007
Gary M Urso, Brnch Mgr
EMP: 29
SALES (corp-wide): 56.9MM Privately Held
Web: www.panelmatic.com
SIC: 3613 8711 Control panels, electric; Designing: ship, boat, machine, and product
PA: Panelmatic, Inc.
6806 Willow Brook Park
Houston TX 77066
888 757-1957

(G-15689)
PATEL LLC
4055 Belmont Ave (44505-1035)
PHONE.................................330 759-3180
Ashok Patel, Genl Mgr
EMP: 41 EST: 2002
SQ FT: 11,992
SALES (est): 298.88K Privately Held
SIC: 7011 Hotels and motels

(G-15690)
PDMI
8530 Crossroad Dr (44514-4381)
PHONE.................................330 757-0724
EMP: 78 EST: 2020
SALES (est): 754.95K Privately Held
Web: www.pdmi.com
SIC: 8748 Business consulting, nec

(G-15691)
PEDIATRIC ASSOC YOUNGSTOWN
Also Called: Pediatric Associates
4308 Belmont Ave Ste 1 (44505-1071)
PHONE.................................330 965-7454
Kahlid Iqbal, Pt
Iriffat Iqbal Md, Pt
Omar S Sheaikh Md, Pt
Betty J Klahr Md, Pt
EMP: 30 EST: 1994
SALES (est): 338.81K Privately Held
Web: www.youngstownpeds.com
SIC: 8011 Pediatrician

(G-15692)
PENNSYLVANIA TL SLS & SVC INC (PA)
Also Called: Penn Tool
625 Bev Rd (44512-6421)
P.O. Box 5557 (44514-0557)
PHONE.................................330 758-0845
Robert Baxter, Pr
▲ EMP: 93 EST: 1978
SQ FT: 100,000
SALES (est): 45.51MM
SALES (corp-wide): 45.51MM Privately Held
Web: www.penntoolsalesandservice.com

SIC: 7699 5085 5084 Tool repair services; Industrial tools; Hoists

(G-15693)
PHANTOM FIREWORKS INC
555 Mrtin Lther King Blvd (44502-1102)
PHONE.................................330 746-1064
◆ EMP: 450
SIC: 5092 Fireworks

(G-15694)
PHARMACY DATA MANAGEMENT INC
Also Called: Pharmacy Benefit Direct
1170 E Western Reserve Rd (44514-3201)
P.O. Box 5300 (44514-0300)
PHONE.................................330 757-1500
Douglas Wittenauer, Pr
EMP: 54 EST: 1983
SQ FT: 14,000
SALES (est): 27.86MM Privately Held
Web: www.pdmi.com
SIC: 6371 Pension, health, and welfare funds

(G-15695)
PLEVNIAK CONSTRUCTION INC
Also Called: Plevniak Construction
1235 Townsend Ave (44505-1293)
PHONE.................................330 718-1600
Christopher Plevniak, CEO
EMP: 31
SALES (est): 3.03MM Privately Held
SIC: 1542 Commercial and office buildings, renovation and repair

(G-15696)
POTENTIAL DEVELOPMENT PROGRAM
2405 Market St (44507-1432)
PHONE.................................330 746-7641
Paul Garchar, CEO
EMP: 120 EST: 1953
SQ FT: 7,800
SALES (est): 5.3MM Privately Held
Web: www.potentialdevelopment.org
SIC: 8399 8351 Health systems agency; Preschool center

(G-15697)
PREMIER BANK (HQ)
275 W Federal St (44503)
P.O. Box 248 (43512)
PHONE.................................330 742-0500
William J Small, Ch Bd
James L Rohrs, *
Gregory R Allen, Chief Lending Officer*
Jeffrey D Vereecke, Operations*
John Boesling, *
EMP: 50 EST: 1900
SQ FT: 10,000
SALES (est): 323.18MM Publicly Held
Web: www.yourpremierbank.com
SIC: 6022 State commercial banks
PA: Premier Financial Corp.
601 Clinton St
Defiance OH 43512

(G-15698)
PRODIGAL MEDIA COMPANY INC
42 Mcclurg Rd (44512-6700)
PHONE.................................330 707-2088
EMP: 30 EST: 1994
SALES (est): 5.94MM Privately Held
Web: www.prodigalcompany.com
SIC: 7311 Advertising agencies

(G-15699)
PROUT BOILER HTG & WLDG INC
3124 Temple St (44510-1048)
PHONE.................................330 744-0293

Wes Prout, *Pr*
Richard Dalleske, *
Donald Raybuck, *
Linda Prout, *Stockholder*
EMP: 50 **EST:** 1945
SQ FT: 3,000
SALES (est): 10.17MM **Privately Held**
Web: www.proutboiler.com
SIC: 1711 7692 3443 Boiler maintenance contractor; Welding repair; Fabricated plate work (boiler shop)

(G-15700)
PSYCARE INC (PA)
2980 Belmont Ave (44505-1834)
PHONE..................................330 759-2310
Douglas Darnall, *CEO*
EMP: 63 **EST:** 1985
SALES (est): 9.64MM **Privately Held**
Web: www.psycare.com
SIC: 8093 Mental health clinic, outpatient

(G-15701)
PULMONARY REHABILITATION
925 Trailwood Dr (44512-5008)
P.O. Box 14130 (44514-7130)
PHONE..................................330 758-7575
Sam Birnbaum, *Ex Dir*
EMP: 32 **EST:** 1980
SQ FT: 7,700
SALES (est): 2.42MM **Privately Held**
Web: www.pulmonarymedicineconsult.com
SIC: 8011 Pulmonary specialist, physician/surgeon

(G-15702)
QUADAX INC
17 Colonial Dr Ste 101 (44505-2163)
PHONE..................................330 759-4600
Sharon Lloyd, *Brnch Mgr*
EMP: 239
SALES (corp-wide): 40.39MM **Privately Held**
Web: www.quadax.com
SIC: 8721 7389 7363 Billing and bookkeeping service; Automobile recovery service; Medical help service
PA: Quadax, Inc.
    7500 Old Oak Blvd
    Middleburg Heights OH 44130
    440 777-6300

(G-15703)
R & J TRUCKING INC (HQ)
8063 Southern Blvd (44512-6306)
P.O. Box 9454 (44513-0454)
PHONE..................................800 262-9365
Ronald Carrocce, *Pr*
Ron Carrocce, *
Gary Carrocce, *
Mark Carrocce, *
Rob Reed, *
EMP: 40 **EST:** 1981
SQ FT: 7,800
SALES (est): 74.19MM **Privately Held**
Web: www.americanbulkcommodities.com
SIC: 4212 Dump truck haulage
PA: American Bulk Commodities Inc
    8063 Southern Blvd
    Youngstown OH 44512

(G-15704)
R & L TRANSFER INC
5550 Dunlap Rd (44515-2042)
PHONE..................................330 743-3609
Jim Laronde, *Mgr*
EMP: 260
Web: www.rlcarriers.com

SIC: 4213 Automobiles, transport and delivery
HQ: R & L Transfer, Inc.
    600 Gilliam Rd
    Wilmington OH 45177
    937 382-1494

(G-15705)
R & R INC (PA)
Also Called: R & R Cleveland Mack Sales
44 Victoria Rd (44515-2022)
PHONE..................................330 799-1536
Daniel Ralich, *Pr*
Evelyn Savich, *
David Hutter, *
EMP: 29 **EST:** 1965
SQ FT: 24,000
SALES (est): 25.62MM
SALES (corp-wide): 25.62MM **Privately Held**
Web: www.rrtrucks.com
SIC: 5511 5012 7538 5013 Trucks, tractors, and trailers: new and used; Trucks, commercial; General truck repair; Truck parts and accessories

(G-15706)
REACH LIVERY TAXI LLC
814 Marshall St (44502-1421)
P.O. Box 90151 (44509-0151)
PHONE..................................330 278-8080
Amy Raburn, *Managing Member*
EMP: 30 **EST:** 2018
SALES (est): 686.48K **Privately Held**
SIC: 4119 Local passenger transportation, nec

(G-15707)
RECMV2 INC ✪
Also Called: 1 Cochran Buick GMC
7997 Market St (44512-5932)
PHONE..................................330 367-5461
EMP: 66 **EST:** 2022
SALES (est): 1.84MM **Privately Held**
Web: www.gm.com
SIC: 5012 Automobiles and other motor vehicles

(G-15708)
RICHARD LAWRENCE TEABERRY INC (PA)
1900 Hubbard Rd (44505-3128)
P.O. Box 6014 (44501-6014)
EMP: 35 **EST:** 1947
SQ FT: 50,000
SALES (est): 26.3MM
SALES (corp-wide): 26.3MM **Privately Held**
Web: www.rexelusa.com
SIC: 5063 Electrical supplies, nec

(G-15709)
RNW HOLDINGS INC
200 Division Street Ext (44510-1000)
P.O. Box 478 (44501-0478)
PHONE..................................330 792-0600
Major Hammond, *Brnch Mgr*
EMP: 42
SIC: 5093 1795 3341 Scrap and waste materials; Wrecking and demolition work; Secondary nonferrous metals
HQ: Rnw Holdings, Inc.
    26949 Chagrin Blvd # 305
    Cleveland OH 44122
    216 831-0510

(G-15710)
ROMAN CTHLIC DOCESE YOUNGSTOWN
Also Called: Calvary Cemetery

248 S Belle Vista Ave (44509-2252)
PHONE..................................330 792-4721
Don Goncy, *Superintnt*
EMP: 39
SALES (corp-wide): 54.72MM **Privately Held**
Web: www.warrenjfk.com
SIC: 6553 Cemeteries, real estate operation
PA: Roman Catholic Diocese Of Youngstown
    144 W Wood St
    Youngstown OH 44503
    330 744-8451

(G-15711)
RON CARROCCE TRUCKING CO INC
8063 Southern Blvd (44512-6306)
P.O. Box 9454 (44513-0454)
PHONE..................................330 758-0841
Ronald Carrocce, *Pr*
Gary Carrocce, *
Mark Carrocce, *
EMP: 50 **EST:** 1956
SQ FT: 50,000
SALES (est): 3.63MM **Privately Held**
Web: www.americanbulkcommodities.com
SIC: 4212 Dump truck haulage
PA: American Bulk Commodities Inc
    8063 Southern Blvd
    Youngstown OH 44512

(G-15712)
RON-JOY NURSING HOME INC
7246 Ronjoy Pl (44512-4299)
PHONE..................................330 286-9122
Felix S Savon, *Pr*
EMP: 125 **EST:** 1956
SQ FT: 26,000
SALES (est): 2.32MM **Privately Held**
Web: www.ronjoynursinghome.com
SIC: 6512 Commercial and industrial building operation

(G-15713)
ROTH BROS INC (DH)
3847 Crum Rd (44515-1414)
P.O. Box 4209 (44515-0209)
PHONE..................................330 793-5571
Rich Thomas, *Pr*
Michael A Wardle, *
Thomas E Froelich, *
Richard M Wardle, *
Stephen P Koneval, *
EMP: 240 **EST:** 1923
SQ FT: 120,000
SALES (est): 91.07MM
SALES (corp-wide): 246.43MM **Privately Held**
Web: www.sodexoroth.com
SIC: 1711 1761 Warm air heating and air conditioning contractor; Roofing contractor
HQ: Sodexo, Inc.
    915 Meeting St Fl 15
    North Bethesda MD 20852
    301 987-4000

(G-15714)
ROTH ROOFING PRODUCTS LLC
Also Called: Sodexo Roth
3847 Crum Rd (44515-1414)
PHONE..................................800 872-7684
EMP: 57 **EST:** 2010
SALES (est): 9.96MM
SALES (corp-wide): 246.43MM **Privately Held**
Web: www.sodexoroth.com
SIC: 8741 Business management
HQ: Sodexo, Inc.
    915 Meeting St Fl 15
    North Bethesda MD 20852
    301 987-4000

(G-15715)
S MERIDIAN LEASING CO LLC
Also Called: Austintown Healthcare Center
650 S Meridian Rd (44509-2932)
PHONE..................................513 530-1600
Richard Odenthal, *Prin*
Sandra Smiddy, *
EMP: 50 **EST:** 2018
SALES (est): 7.57MM **Privately Held**
Web: www.communicarehealth.com
SIC: 8051 Convalescent home with continuous nursing care

(G-15716)
SANTON ELECTRIC INC
Also Called: Santon Electric Company
7870 Southern Blvd (44512-6022)
PHONE..................................330 758-0082
▼ **EMP:** 95 **EST:** 1975
SALES (est): 9.39MM **Privately Held**
Web: www.santonelectric.com
SIC: 1731 General electrical contractor

(G-15717)
SATERI HOME INC (PA)
7246 Ronjoy Pl (44512-4357)
PHONE..................................330 758-8106
Felix S Savon, *Pr*
EMP: 100 **EST:** 1977
SQ FT: 26,000
SALES (est): 25.53MM
SALES (corp-wide): 25.53MM **Privately Held**
SIC: 6513 8051 5999 7352 Apartment building operators; Skilled nursing care facilities; Medical apparatus and supplies; Medical equipment rental

(G-15718)
SECOND HRVEST FDBANK OF MHNING
2805 Salt Springs Rd (44509-1037)
PHONE..................................330 792-5522
Michael Iberis, *Ex Dir*
EMP: 34 **EST:** 1982
SQ FT: 20,000
SALES (est): 20.04MM **Privately Held**
Web: www.mahoningvalleysecondharvest.org
SIC: 8322 Social service center

(G-15719)
SELECT SPCALTY HOSP - BOARDMAN
8401 Market St Fl 7 (44512-6725)
PHONE..................................330 729-1750
EMP: 41
SALES (est): 13.7MM
SALES (corp-wide): 6.2B **Publicly Held**
Web: www.selectspecialtyhospitals.com
SIC: 8062 General medical and surgical hospitals
PA: Select Medical Holdings Corporation
    4714 Gettysburg Rd
    Mechanicsburg PA 17055
    717 972-1100

(G-15720)
SELECT SPCLTY HOSP - YNGSTOWN
1044 Belmont Ave Fl 4 (44504-1006)
PHONE..................................330 480-3488
Jeanne Barkanko, *Mgr*
Brian Davis, *
EMP: 141 **EST:** 1998
SALES (est): 9.3MM
SALES (corp-wide): 6.2B **Publicly Held**
Web: www.selectspecialtyhospitals.com

Youngstown - Mahoning County (G-15721) — GEOGRAPHIC SECTION

SIC: 8093 8051 8069 Rehabilitation center, outpatient treatment; Skilled nursing care facilities; Specialty hospitals, except psychiatric
HQ: Select Medical Corporation
4714 Gettysburg Rd
Mechanicsburg PA 17055
717 972-1100

(G-15721)
SEREX CORPORATION (PA)
55 Victoria Rd (44515-2023)
P.O. Box 9022 (44513-0022)
PHONE.................................330 726-6062
Leonard Morris, *VP*
Gregory Pastore, *VP Sls*
Russel Hodge, *Pr*
EMP: 34 **EST:** 1971
SQ FT: 14,900
SALES (est): 2.24MM
SALES (corp-wide): 2.24MM **Privately Held**
Web: www.serex.ca
SIC: 7699 Vending machine repair

(G-15722)
SHEPHERD OF VLY LTHRAN RTRMENT (PA)
Also Called: SHEPHERDS WOODS
5525 Silica Rd (44515-1002)
PHONE.................................330 530-4038
Donald Kacmar, *Ex Dir*
Lynn Miller Corporate, *Mktg Dir*
Victoria Brown, *
EMP: 42 **EST:** 1972
SALES (est): 42.58MM
SALES (corp-wide): 42.58MM **Privately Held**
Web: www.shepherdofthevalley.com
SIC: 8361 Aged home

(G-15723)
SHEPHERD OF VLY LTHRAN RTRMENT
Also Called: Shepards Wood Nursing
7148 West Blvd (44512-4336)
PHONE.................................330 726-9061
Richard Limongi, *Mgr*
EMP: 37
SALES (corp-wide): 42.58MM **Privately Held**
Web: www.shepherdofthevalley.com
SIC: 8051 Skilled nursing care facilities
PA: Shepherd Of The Valley Lutheran Retirement Services, Inc.
5525 Silica Rd
Youngstown OH 44515
330 530-4038

(G-15724)
SIFFRIN RESIDENTIAL ASSN
Also Called: Bridge The
136 Westchester Dr Ste 1 (44515-3965)
PHONE.................................330 799-8932
EMP: 165
SALES (corp-wide): 11.03MM **Privately Held**
Web: www.siffrin.org
SIC: 8322 8051 7361 5047 Social services for the handicapped; Mental retardation hospital; Placement agencies; Technical aids for the handicapped
PA: Siffrin Inc.
3688 Dressler Rd Nw
Canton OH 44718
330 478-0263

(G-15725)
SIMON ROOFING AND SHTMTL CORP (PA)
Also Called: Simon Roofing
70 Karago Ave (44512-5949)
P.O. Box 951109 (44193-0005)
PHONE.................................330 629-7392
Stephen Manser, *Pr*
Rocco Augustine, *VP*
Alex J Simon Junior, *CFO*
EMP: 105 **EST:** 1900
SQ FT: 30,000
SALES (est): 86.22MM
SALES (corp-wide): 86.22MM **Privately Held**
Web: www.simonroofing.com
SIC: 1761 2952 Roofing contractor; Asphalt felts and coatings

(G-15726)
SOLAR FLEXRACK LLC
3207 Innovation Pl (44509-4025)
PHONE.................................888 380-8138
Tom Jensen, *Prin*
EMP: 27 **EST:** 2014
SALES (est): 747.53K **Privately Held**
Web: www.flexrack.com
SIC: 1711 Solar energy contractor

(G-15727)
SOUTHERN CARE INC
970 Windham Ct Ste 9 (44512-5082)
PHONE.................................330 797-8940
Janet Johnson, *Brnch Mgr*
EMP: 53
Web: www.gentivahs.com
SIC: 8082 Home health care services
PA: Southern Care, Inc
1000 Urban Center Dr # 115
Vestavia AL 35242

(G-15728)
SPECILZED HM CARE PRVIDERS LLC
Also Called: Specialized Senior Care
6006 Market St (44512-2918)
PHONE.................................330 758-8740
Michael Creatore, *Prin*
EMP: 49 **EST:** 2014
SALES (est): 1.5MM **Privately Held**
Web: www.specializedseniorcare.com
SIC: 8082 Home health care services

(G-15729)
ST MORITZ SECURITY SVCS INC
Also Called: Saint Moritz Security Services
32 N Four Mile Run Rd (44515-3003)
PHONE.................................330 270-5922
Joe Bonacci, *Ofcr*
EMP: 54
SQ FT: 741
SALES (corp-wide): 27.97MM **Privately Held**
Web: www.smssi.com
SIC: 7381 Security guard service
PA: St. Moritz Security Services, Inc.
4600 Clairton Blvd
Pittsburgh PA 15236
412 885-3144

(G-15730)
STATE ALARM INC (PA)
Also Called: State Alarm Systems
5956 Market St (44512-2916)
PHONE.................................888 726-8111
Donald P Shury, *Pr*
Brenda Dull, *
EMP: 35 **EST:** 1953
SQ FT: 2,300
SALES (est): 9.32MM
SALES (corp-wide): 9.32MM **Privately Held**
Web: www.gillmoresecurity.com
SIC: 5999 5063 7382 1731 Alarm signal systems; Burglar alarm systems; Burglar alarm maintenance and monitoring; Fire detection and burglar alarm systems specialization

(G-15731)
STROLLO ARCHITECTS INC
201 W Federal St (44503-1203)
PHONE.................................330 743-1177
Gregg Strollo, *Pr*
Joseph Yank, *
Terry Mccoy, *Sec*
Rodney Lamberson, *
Robert Hanahan, *
EMP: 39 **EST:** 1956
SALES (est): 9.55MM **Privately Held**
Web: www.strolloarchitects.com
SIC: 8712 Architectural engineering

(G-15732)
SURGERY CTR AT SOUTHWOODS LLC
Also Called: Surgical Hosp At Southwoods
7630 Southern Blvd (44512-5633)
PHONE.................................330 729-8000
Edward Muransky, *CEO*
EMP: 115 **EST:** 2010
SALES (est): 47.35MM **Privately Held**
Web: www.southwoodshealth.com
SIC: 8011 Surgeon

(G-15733)
TELE-SOLUTIONS INC (PA)
6001 Southern Blvd Ste 102 (44512)
PHONE.................................330 782-2888
Deane Wurst, *Pr*
John Antonucci, *Stockholder**
EMP: 27 **EST:** 1985
SQ FT: 4,200
SALES (est): 4.77MM
SALES (corp-wide): 4.77MM **Privately Held**
Web: www.tsi-networks.com
SIC: 5065 1731 Telephone equipment; Telephone and telephone equipment installation

(G-15734)
THE HOME SAVINGS AND LOAN COMPANY OF YOUNGSTOWN OHIO
275 W Federal St (44503-1200)
P.O. Box 1111 (44501-1111)
PHONE.................................330 742-0500
EMP: 228
SIC: 6036 6163 Savings and loan associations, not federally chartered; Loan brokers

(G-15735)
TOWN & COUNTRY PLBG & HTG INC
6400 Southern Blvd (44512-3429)
PHONE.................................330 726-5755
Ken Pavlik, *Pr*
Carol Pavlik, *VP*
EMP: 30 **EST:** 1976
SQ FT: 1,600
SALES (est): 484.82K **Privately Held**
SIC: 1711 Heating and air conditioning contractors

(G-15736)
TRI AREA ELECTRIC CO INC
Also Called: Tri Area Electric
37 Wayne Ave (44502-1900)
PHONE.................................330 744-0151
EMP: 50 **EST:** 1976
SALES (est): 3.86MM **Privately Held**
Web: www.tri-area.net
SIC: 1731 General electrical contractor

(G-15737)
TRUMBULL INDUSTRIES INC
1040 N Meridian Rd (44509-1090)
PHONE.................................330 270-7800
Sam H Miller, *Brnch Mgr*
EMP: 65
SALES (corp-wide): 162.11MM **Privately Held**
Web: www.trumbull.com
SIC: 5074 Plumbing fittings and supplies
PA: Trumbull Industries, Inc.
400 Dietz Rd Ne
Warren OH 44483
330 372-0201

(G-15738)
TURNING POINT RESIDENTIAL INC
357 E Midlothian Blvd (44507-1978)
PHONE.................................330 788-0669
Kathy Phillips, *CEO*
Mary Tusinac, *
EMP: 33 **EST:** 2001
SQ FT: 666
SALES (est): 977.37K **Privately Held**
Web: www.turningpointresidential.org
SIC: 8082 Home health care services

(G-15739)
TURNING PT COUNSELING SVCS INC (PA)
611 Belmont Ave (44502-1037)
PHONE.................................330 744-2991
Joseph Sylvester, *Ex Dir*
Amanda French, *Dir*
B P Massman, *Prin*
S M Berkowitz, *Prin*
EMP: 78 **EST:** 2003
SALES (est): 2.4MM
SALES (corp-wide): 2.4MM **Privately Held**
SIC: 8322 General counseling services

(G-15740)
TURNING TECHNOLOGIES LLC (PA)
6000 Mahoning Ave (44515-2225)
PHONE.................................330 746-3015
Mike Broderick, *Managing Member*
Dave Kauer, *
Doctor Tina Rooks, *Sr VP*
Kevin Owens, *
Sheila Hura, *
◆ **EMP:** 152 **EST:** 2002
SALES (est): 91.49MM
SALES (corp-wide): 91.49MM **Privately Held**
Web: www.echo360.com
SIC: 7372 Business oriented computer software

(G-15741)
U S WEATHERFORD L P
1100 Performance Pl (44502-4001)
PHONE.................................330 746-2502
EMP: 172
Web: www.weatherford.com
SIC: 1389 Oil field services, nec
HQ: U S Weatherford L P
179 Weatherford Dr
Schriever LA 70395
985 493-6100

(G-15742)
UNITED COMMUNITY FINANCIAL CORP
Also Called: United Community
275 W Federal St (44503-1200)
PHONE.................................330 742-0500
EMP: 503
Web: www.ucfconline.com

GEOGRAPHIC SECTION

Zanesfield - Logan County (G-15764)

SIC: **6036** State savings banks, not federally chartered

(G-15743)
UNITED PARCEL SERVICE INC
Also Called: UPS
95 Karago Ave Ste 4 (44512-5951)
PHONE..................................800 742-5877
EMP: 52
SALES (corp-wide): 90.96B **Publicly Held**
Web: www.ups.com
SIC: 4215 Package delivery, vehicular
HQ: United Parcel Service, Inc.
 55 Glenlake Pkwy
 Atlanta GA 30328
 404 828-6000

(G-15744)
UNITED WAY OF YNGSTOWN THE MHN
Also Called: UNITED-WAY
255 Watt St (44505-3049)
PHONE..................................330 746-8494
Robert P Hannon, *Pr*
EMP: 37 **EST:** 1919
SQ FT: 2,800
SALES (est): 3.58MM **Privately Held**
Web: www.ymvunitedway.org
SIC: 8322 Social service center

(G-15745)
V AND V APPLIANCE PARTS INC (PA)
27 W Myrtle Ave (44507-1193)
PHONE..................................330 743-5144
Bruce Lazar, *Pr*
Victor Lazar, *
Judy Lazar, *
Albert E Brennan, *
Vincent Rypien, *
EMP: 40 **EST:** 1959
SQ FT: 16,000
SALES (est): 24.74MM
SALES (corp-wide): 24.74MM **Privately Held**
Web: www.vvapplianceparts.com
SIC: 5064 Appliance parts, household

(G-15746)
VALLEY INDUSTRIAL TRUCKS INC (PA)
1152 Meadowbrook Ave (44512-1887)
PHONE..................................330 788-4081
James E Hammond, *Pr*
✦ **EMP:** 32 **EST:** 1956
SQ FT: 45,000
SALES (est): 10.7MM
SALES (corp-wide): 10.7MM **Privately Held**
Web: www.valleyindustrialtrucks.com
SIC: 7359 5084 Equipment rental and leasing, nec; Materials handling machinery

(G-15747)
VALVOLINE INSTANT OIL CHNGE FR
Also Called: Valvoline Instant Oil Change
7210 South Ave (44512-3637)
PHONE..................................330 726-5676
EMP: 45
Web: www.valvoline.com
SIC: 7549 Automotive maintenance services
HQ: Valvoline Instant Oil Change Franchising, Inc.
 100 Valvoline Way
 Lexington KY 40509

(G-15748)
VIBRA HOSP MAHONING VLY LLC
Also Called: Mahoning Valley Hospital
8049 South Ave (44512-6154)
PHONE..................................330 726-5000
Mary Jane Larmon, *Managing Member*
EMP: 96 **EST:** 1999
SALES (est): 18.9MM
SALES (corp-wide): 690.44MM **Privately Held**
Web: www.vibrahealthcare.com
SIC: 8062 General medical and surgical hospitals
PA: Vibra Healthcare, Llc
 4600 Lena Dr
 Mechanicsburg PA 17055
 717 591-5700

(G-15749)
W H O T INC (PA)
4040 Simon Rd Ste 1 (44512-1362)
PHONE..................................330 783-1000
Brad Marshall, *Pr*
EMP: 70 **EST:** 1956
SQ FT: 4,000
SALES (est): 2.58MM
SALES (corp-wide): 2.58MM **Privately Held**
SIC: 4832 Radio broadcasting stations, music format

(G-15750)
W T LEONES TRI-AREA ELC INC
Also Called: Tri Area Electric
37 Wayne Ave (44502-1937)
PHONE..................................330 744-0151
W T Leone, *CEO*
W T Leone, *Prin*
W T Leone Ii, *Prin*
Matthew Leone, *Prin*
Hennie Suter, *Prin*
EMP: 45 **EST:** 1979
SALES (est): 9.75MM **Privately Held**
SIC: 4911 Electric services

(G-15751)
WALDON MANAGEMENT CORP (PA)
111 Westchester Dr (44515-3964)
PHONE..................................330 792-7688
Walter Terlecky, *Pr*
EMP: 30 **EST:** 1972
SALES (est): 1.53MM
SALES (corp-wide): 1.53MM **Privately Held**
Web: www.waldonmanagement.com
SIC: 6531 6512 Cooperative apartment manager; Commercial and industrial building operation

(G-15752)
WESTERN RESERVE TRANSIT AUTH (PA)
604 Mahoning Ave (44502-1491)
PHONE..................................330 744-8431
Jim Ferraro, *Dir*
EMP: 82
SALES (est): 8.56MM
SALES (corp-wide): 8.56MM **Privately Held**
Web: www.wrtaonline.com
SIC: 4111 Bus line operations

(G-15753)
WFMJ TELEVISION INC
101 W Boardman St (44503-1305)
P.O. Box 689 (44501-0689)
PHONE..................................330 744-8611
Betty Brown, *Pr*
Mark Brown, *
John Grdic, *
EMP: 105 **EST:** 1953
SALES (est): 8.3MM **Privately Held**
SIC: 4833 Television broadcasting stations

(G-15754)
YOUNG MENS CHRISTIAN ASSN
Also Called: Youngstown YMCA Association
45 Mcclurg Rd (44512-6737)
PHONE..................................330 480-5656
Ken Rudge, *CEO*
EMP: 80
SALES (corp-wide): 10.38MM **Privately Held**
Web: www.ymcayo.org
SIC: 8641 7991 8351 7032 Youth organizations; Physical fitness facilities; Child day care services; Youth camps
PA: Young Men's Christian Association Of Youngstown Ohio
 17 N Champion St
 Youngstown OH 44503
 330 744-8411

(G-15755)
YOUNG MNS CHRSTN ASSN YNGSTOWN (PA)
Also Called: YMCA OF YOUNGSTOWN
17 N Champion St (44503-1602)
P.O. Box 1287 (44501-1287)
PHONE..................................330 744-8411
Kenneth Rudge, *CEO*
Tom Lodge, *
EMP: 80 **EST:** 1884
SALES (est): 10.38MM
SALES (corp-wide): 10.38MM **Privately Held**
Web: www.ymcayo.org
SIC: 8641 8322 7997 Youth organizations; Youth center; Membership sports and recreation clubs

(G-15756)
YOUNGSTOWN AREA JWISH FDRATION (PA)
Also Called: Heritage Mnor Jwish HM For Age
505 Gypsy Ln (44504-1314)
PHONE..................................330 746-3251
Andrew Lipkin, *CEO*
Andrew Lipkin, *Ex Dir*
David Stauffer, *
EMP: 120 **EST:** 1935
SQ FT: 100,000
SALES (est): 20.51MM
SALES (corp-wide): 20.51MM **Privately Held**
Web: www.jewishyoungstown.org
SIC: 8699 8322 8059 7991 Charitable organization; Social service center; Nursing home, except skilled and intermediate care facility; Physical fitness facilities

(G-15757)
YOUNGSTOWN COUNTRY CLUB
1402 Country Club Dr (44505-2299)
PHONE..................................330 759-1040
Jim Dibacco, *Pr*
Karl Schroedel, *
EMP: 90 **EST:** 1898
SALES (est): 2.23MM **Privately Held**
Web: www.youngstowncountryclub.com
SIC: 7997 5941 5812 Country club, membership; Sporting goods and bicycle shops; Eating places

(G-15758)
YOUNGSTOWN HOSPITALITY LLC
Also Called: Hampton Inn
4400 Belmont Ave (44505-1008)
PHONE..................................330 759-9555
Shirish N Shah, *Pr*
Majula S Shah, *VP*
EMP: 36 **EST:** 2001
SQ FT: 40,000
SALES (est): 2.76MM **Privately Held**
Web: www.hilton.com

SIC: 7011 Hotels and motels

(G-15759)
YOUNGSTOWN NGHBORHOOD DEV CORP
Also Called: YNDC
820 Canfield Rd (44511-2345)
PHONE..................................330 480-0423
Ian Beniston, *Ex Dir*
EMP: 30 **EST:** 2008
SQ FT: 1,200
SALES (est): 5.99MM **Privately Held**
Web: www.yndc.org
SIC: 8322 8699 Social service center; Charitable organization

(G-15760)
YOUNGSTOWN PIPE & STEEL LLC
4111 Simon Rd (44512-1323)
PHONE..................................330 783-2700
David Cornelius, *Admn*
EMP: 50
Web: www.yopipe.com
SIC: 5051 Pipe and tubing, steel
HQ: Youngstown Pipe & Steel, Llc
 45 S Montgomery Ave
 Youngstown OH 44506
 330 783-2700

(G-15761)
YOUTH INTENSIVE SERVICES INC
238 S Meridian Rd (44509-2925)
PHONE..................................330 318-3436
Dewayne Thompson, *Prin*
EMP: 27 **EST:** 2014
SALES (est): 5.65MM **Privately Held**
Web: www.youthintensiveservices.com
SIC: 7363 Help supply services

(G-15762)
YWCA MAHONING VALLEY
Also Called: YWCA
25 W Rayen Ave (44503-1000)
PHONE..................................330 746-6361
Connie Schaffer, *Dir*
EMP: 45 **EST:** 1904
SALES (est): 2.08MM **Privately Held**
Web: www.ywcamahoningvalley.org
SIC: 8641 7991 8351 7032 Youth organizations; Physical fitness facilities; Child day care services; Youth camps

(G-15763)
ZINZ CNSTR & RESTORATION INC
6487 Mahoning Ave (44515-2025)
P.O. Box 477 (44460-0477)
PHONE..................................330 332-7939
Bruce L Zinz, *Pr*
EMP: 30 **EST:** 2002
SALES (est): 4.77MM **Privately Held**
Web: www.zinzconstruction.com
SIC: 1521 General remodeling, single-family houses

Zanesfield
Logan County

(G-15764)
MAD RIVER MOUNTAIN RESORT
Also Called: Mad River
1000 Snow Valley Rd (43360-9774)
P.O. Box 22 (43311-0022)
PHONE..................................937 303-3646
Bruce Mowrey, *Owner*
EMP: 43 **EST:** 2002
SALES (est): 5.51MM **Privately Held**
Web: www.skimadriver.com
SIC: 7011 Resort hotel

Zanesville
Muskingum County

(G-15765)
AG-PRO OHIO LLC
Also Called: John Deere Authorized Dealer
4394 Northpointe Dr (43701-5968)
PHONE..................740 450-7446
EMP: 36
SALES (corp-wide): 204.78MM **Privately Held**
Web: www.agprocompanies.com
SIC: **5999** 5082 Farm equipment and supplies; Construction and mining machinery
HQ: Ag-Pro Ohio, Llc
19595 Us Highway 84 E
Boston GA 31626
229 498-8833

(G-15766)
ALTERNACARE
2951 Maple Ave (43701-1406)
PHONE..................740 454-4248
Sue Hoover, *Ex Dir*
EMP: 328 EST: 1996
SALES (est): 458.85K
SALES (corp-wide): 513.77MM **Privately Held**
Web: www.alternacareinc.com
SIC: **8699** Charitable organization
HQ: Bethesda Care System
2951 Maple Ave
Zanesville OH 43701

(G-15767)
AMERICAN NURSING CARE INC
Also Called: American Nursing Care
1206 Brandywine Blvd Ste A (43701-1755)
PHONE..................614 847-0555
Diana Phelps, *Mgr*
EMP: 260
Web: www.americannursingcare.com
SIC: **8051** 8361 Skilled nursing care facilities; Residential care
HQ: American Nursing Care, Inc.
6281 Tri Ridge Blvd # 300
Loveland OH 45140
513 576-0262

(G-15768)
AVI FOOD SYSTEMS INC
333 Richards Rd (43701-4643)
PHONE..................740 452-9363
Donald Hormann, *Mgr*
EMP: 31
SALES (corp-wide): 432.96MM **Privately Held**
Web: www.avifoodsystems.com
SIC: **5962** 5812 5046 Merchandising machine operators; Eating places; Commercial equipment, nec
PA: Avi Food Systems, Inc.
2590 Elm Rd Ne
Warren OH 44483
330 372-6000

(G-15769)
BALLAS EGG PRODUCTS CORP
40 N 2nd St (43701-3402)
P.O. Box 2217 (43702-2217)
PHONE..................614 453-0386
Leonard Ballas, *Pr*
Joseph G Saliba, *VP*
Craig Ballas, *
▼ EMP: 100 EST: 1961
SQ FT: 200,000
SALES (est): 8.48MM **Privately Held**
Web: www.wabashvalleyeggs.com
SIC: **2015** 5144 Egg processing; Eggs

(G-15770)
BETHESDA HOSPITAL ASSOCIATION
2951 Maple Ave (43701-1465)
PHONE..................740 454-4000
Thomas Sieber, *Pr*
Charles Hunter, *
Paul Masterson, *
EMP: 336 EST: 1888
SQ FT: 400,000
SALES (est): 2.45MM
SALES (corp-wide): 513.77MM **Privately Held**
Web: www.genesishcs.org
SIC: **8062** 8063 8082 General medical and surgical hospitals; Psychiatric hospitals; Home health care services
PA: Genesis Healthcare System
2951 Maple Ave
Zanesville OH 43701
740 454-5000

(G-15771)
BLOOMER CANDY CO
3610 National Rd (43701-8812)
P.O. Box 3450 (43702-3450)
PHONE..................740 452-7501
William S Barry, *Pr*
Teresa Young-barry, *Sec*
Tom Barry, *
Pat Barry, *
Robert Barry, *
EMP: 130 EST: 1893
SQ FT: 150,000
SALES (est): 5.47MM **Privately Held**
Web: www.bloomercandy.com
SIC: **5145** 2064 Confectionery; Candy and other confectionery products

(G-15772)
BUCKEYE COMPANIES (PA)
999 Zane St (43701-3863)
P.O. Box 1480 (43702-1480)
PHONE..................740 452-3641
C E Straker, *Pr*
M Dean Cole, *
Stephen R Straker, *
EMP: 31 EST: 1982
SALES (est): 10.11MM
SALES (corp-wide): 10.11MM **Privately Held**
Web: www.thebuckeyecompanies.com
SIC: **3533** 5083 Drill rigs; Agricultural machinery and equipment

(G-15773)
BUCKEYE SUPPLY COMPANY (HQ)
999 Zane St Ste A (43701-3863)
P.O. Box 1480 (43702-1480)
PHONE..................740 452-3641
C E Straker, *CEO*
Stephen R Straker, *
George French, *
Larry Messner, *
EMP: 30 EST: 1929
SQ FT: 50,000
SALES (est): 9.17MM
SALES (corp-wide): 10.11MM **Privately Held**
Web: www.buckeyedrill.com
SIC: **5083** 5084 Lawn and garden machinery and equipment; Pumps and pumping equipment, nec
PA: Buckeye Companies
999 Zane St
Zanesville OH 43701
740 452-3641

(G-15774)
BUCKINGHAM COAL COMPANY LLC
11 N 4th St (43701-3409)
P.O. Box 340 (43702-0340)
EMP: 80 EST: 1994
SALES (est): 25MM
SALES (corp-wide): 814.89MM **Privately Held**
SIC: **1221** Bituminous coal and lignite-surface mining
HQ: Wcc Land Holding Company, Inc.
9540 Maroon Cir Unit 300
Englewood CO 80112
855 922-6463

(G-15775)
CAMBRIDGE COUNSELING CENTER
Also Called: Zanesville
326 Main St (43701-3426)
PHONE..................740 450-7790
Susan Lynch, *Owner*
EMP: 150
SALES (corp-wide): 2.45MM **Privately Held**
Web: www.cambridgecounselingcenter.org
SIC: **8322** General counseling services
PA: Cambridge Counseling Center, Inc.
317 Highland Ave
Cambridge OH 43725
740 435-9766

(G-15776)
CARESERVE (HQ)
Also Called: Sunny View Nursing Home
2991 Maple Ave (43701-1499)
PHONE..................740 454-4000
Thomas Sieber, *Pr*
Paul Masterson, *
Shelly Fuller, *
EMP: 151 EST: 1974
SQ FT: 25,000
SALES (est): 26.98MM
SALES (corp-wide): 513.77MM **Privately Held**
SIC: **8051** Convalescent home with continuous nursing care
PA: Genesis Healthcare System
2951 Maple Ave
Zanesville OH 43701
740 454-5000

(G-15777)
CEDAR HILL OPCO LLC
Also Called: Cedar Hlls Hlthcare Rhbltition
1136 Adair Ave (43701-2804)
PHONE..................740 454-6823
EMP: 69 EST: 2018
SALES (est): 3.1MM **Privately Held**
Web: www.continuinghc.com
SIC: **8051** Skilled nursing care facilities

(G-15778)
CEDAR RIDGE BEHAVIORAL HE
56 N 5th St (43701-3504)
PHONE..................740 801-0655
EMP: 40 EST: 2018
SALES (est): 385.52K **Privately Held**
Web: www.crbhs.org
SIC: **8093** Mental health clinic, outpatient

(G-15779)
CENTERY NATIONAL BANK
14 S 5th St (43701-3517)
PHONE..................740 454-2521
Thomas M Lyall, *Pr*
William Phillips, *Ch*
Barbara A Gibbs, *Sr VP*
Maryann Thornton, *Sec*
EMP: 44 EST: 1887
SQ FT: 10,000
SALES (est): 681.04K **Privately Held**
Web: www.parknationalbank.com
SIC: **6035** Federal savings and loan associations

(G-15780)
CENTURY NATIONAL BANK (HQ)
14 S 5th St (43701-3526)
PHONE..................740 454-2521
Tom Lyall, *CEO*
William A Phillips, *Ch Bd*
Mary Ann Thornton, *Treas*
Ray Omen, *Sr VP*
Barbara Gibbs, *Sr VP*
EMP: 39 EST: 1886
SQ FT: 25,000
SALES (est): 7.17MM
SALES (corp-wide): 564.3MM **Publicly Held**
Web: www.parknationalbank.com
SIC: **6021** National commercial banks
PA: Park National Corporation
50 N 3rd St
Newark OH 43055
740 349-8451

(G-15781)
CITY OF ZANESVILLE
Also Called: Waste Water Treatment Plant
401 Market St Rm 1 (43701-3520)
PHONE..................740 455-0641
Dan Smith, *Superintnt*
EMP: 37
Web: www.coz.org
SIC: **4952** Sewerage systems
PA: City Of Zanesville
401 Market St Rm 1
Zanesville OH 43701
740 455-0601

(G-15782)
COLUMBIA GAS OF OHIO INC
2429 Linden Ave (43701-1998)
PHONE..................740 450-1215
Steve Jablonski, *Brnch Mgr*
EMP: 81
SALES (corp-wide): 5.51B **Publicly Held**
Web: www.columbiagasohio.com
SIC: **4924** Natural gas distribution
HQ: Columbia Gas Of Ohio, Inc.
290 W Nationwide Blvd # 1
Columbus OH 43215
614 460-6000

(G-15783)
COMFORT INN
Also Called: Comfort Inn
500 Monroe St (43701-3884)
P.O. Box 160 (43702-0160)
PHONE..................740 454-4144
Timothy Longstreth, *Pr*
Larry L Wade, *VP*
EMP: 54 EST: 1985
SALES (est): 948.9K **Privately Held**
Web: www.choicehotels.com
SIC: **7011** 8661 Hotels and motels; Religious organizations

(G-15784)
COMMUNITY AMBULANCE SERVICE
Also Called: BETHESDA CARE
952 Linden Ave (43701-3062)
PHONE..................740 454-6800
EMP: 124 EST: 1994
SQ FT: 8,000
SALES (est): 6.87MM
SALES (corp-wide): 513.77MM **Privately Held**
Web: www.genesishcs.org
SIC: **4119** 8661 Ambulance service; Religious organizations

GEOGRAPHIC SECTION

Zanesville - Muskingum County (G-15804)

PA: Genesis Healthcare System
2951 Maple Ave
Zanesville OH 43701
740 454-5000

(G-15785)
DEV INVESTMENTS OF OHIO INC
Also Called: Amerihost Inn
320 Scenic Crest Dr (43701)
PHONE..................................740 454-9332
Sanjay Amin, *Pr*
Tameeka Cochran, *Genl Mgr*
Wesley Shook, *Mgr*
EMP: 31 **EST:** 2003
SALES (est): 329.5K **Privately Held**
SIC: 7011 Hotel, franchised

(G-15786)
DUTRO FORD LINCOLN-MERCURY INC (PA)
Also Called: Dutro Lincoln Mercury
132 S 5th St (43701-3513)
P.O. Box 1265 (43702-1265)
PHONE..................................740 452-6334
James F Graham, *Pr*
Kenneth D Williams, *General Vice President*
Bryan Graham, *
EMP: 75 **EST:** 1940
SQ FT: 30,000
SALES (est): 10.32MM
SALES (corp-wide): 10.32MM **Privately Held**
Web: www.dutros.com
SIC: 5511 5012 7538 5531 Automobiles, new and used; Automobiles and other motor vehicles; General automotive repair shops; Auto and truck equipment and parts

(G-15787)
ECLIPSE RESOURCES - OHIO LLC
4900 Boggs Rd (43701-9491)
P.O. Box 910 (43702-0910)
PHONE..................................740 452-4503
Benjamin W Hulburt, *Managing Member*
Christopher K Hulburt, *
Thomas S Liberatore, *
Brian Panetta, *
Bryan M Moody, *
EMP: 113 **EST:** 2013
SALES (est): 1.95MM
SALES (corp-wide): 6.52B **Publicly Held**
SIC: 1381 Drilling oil and gas wells
HQ: Eclipse Resources I, Lp
122 W John Crptr Fwy Ste
Irving TX 75039
814 308-9754

(G-15788)
G & J PEPSI-COLA BOTTLERS INC
Also Called: Pepsico
336 N Sixth St (43701)
PHONE..................................740 354-9191
TOLL FREE: 800
Rick Stone, *Brnch Mgr*
EMP: 35
SALES (corp-wide): 404.54MM **Privately Held**
Web: www.gjpepsi.com
SIC: 2086 5149 Carbonated soft drinks, bottled and canned; Groceries and related products, nec
PA: G & J Pepsi-Cola Bottlers Inc
9435 Waterstone Blvd # 390
Cincinnati OH 45249
513 785-6160

(G-15789)
GENESIS
Also Called: Genesis
3287 Maple Ave (43701-1312)
PHONE..................................740 453-3122
EMP: 46 **EST:** 2018
SALES (est): 335.76K **Privately Held**
Web: www.genesishcs.org
SIC: 8741 Management services

(G-15790)
GENESIS HEALTHCARE SYSTEM
Also Called: Genesis Police Department
800 Forest Ave (43701-2821)
PHONE..................................740 454-5922
EMP: 71
SALES (corp-wide): 513.77MM **Privately Held**
Web: www.genesishcs.org
SIC: 8062 General medical and surgical hospitals
PA: Genesis Healthcare System
2951 Maple Ave
Zanesville OH 43701
740 454-5000

(G-15791)
GENESIS HEALTHCARE SYSTEM (PA)
Also Called: BETHESDA CARE
2951 Maple Ave (43701-1406)
PHONE..................................740 454-5000
Matthew Perry, *Pr*
Paul Masterson, *
Al Burns, *
EMP: 1500 **EST:** 1996
SALES (est): 513.77MM
SALES (corp-wide): 513.77MM **Privately Held**
Web: www.genesishcs.org
SIC: 8062 General medical and surgical hospitals

(G-15792)
GENESIS HEALTHCARE SYSTEM
2529 Maple Ave (43701-1833)
PHONE..................................740 454-5913
EMP: 73
SALES (corp-wide): 513.77MM **Privately Held**
Web: www.genesishcs.org
SIC: 8062 General medical and surgical hospitals
PA: Genesis Healthcare System
2951 Maple Ave
Zanesville OH 43701
740 454-5000

(G-15793)
GENESIS HEALTHCARE SYSTEM
2800 Maple Ave (43701-1716)
PHONE..................................740 454-4585
EMP: 55
SALES (corp-wide): 513.77MM **Privately Held**
Web: www.genesishcs.org
SIC: 8062 General medical and surgical hospitals
PA: Genesis Healthcare System
2951 Maple Ave
Zanesville OH 43701
740 454-5000

(G-15794)
GENESIS HEALTHCARE SYSTEM
2800 Maple Ave Ste A (43701-1750)
PHONE..................................740 586-6732
Cindy Gaylord, *Mgr*
EMP: 36
SALES (corp-wide): 513.77MM **Privately Held**
Web: www.genesishcs.org
SIC: 8062 General medical and surgical hospitals
PA: Genesis Healthcare System
2951 Maple Ave
Zanesville OH 43701
740 454-5000

(G-15795)
GENESIS HEALTHCARE SYSTEM
Also Called: Hospice Care of Bethesda
2951 Maple Ave (43701-1406)
P.O. Box 3028 (43702-3028)
PHONE..................................740 454-4566
EMP: 34
SALES (corp-wide): 513.77MM **Privately Held**
Web: www.genesishcs.org
SIC: 8062 General medical and surgical hospitals
PA: Genesis Healthcare System
2951 Maple Ave
Zanesville OH 43701
740 454-5000

(G-15796)
GOSS SUPPLY COMPANY (PA)
620 Marietta St (43701)
P.O. Box 2580 (43702)
PHONE..................................740 454-2571
TOLL FREE: 800
Terry L Goss, *Pr*
Andy Goss, *
Clarence A Goss, *
Don J Hollingsworth, *
Pasquale Gallina, *
EMP: 47 **EST:** 1954
SQ FT: 40,000
SALES (est): 20.18MM
SALES (corp-wide): 20.18MM **Privately Held**
Web: www.goss-supply.com
SIC: 5085 Hose, belting, and packing

(G-15797)
GOTTLIEB JHNSON BEAM DAL PNTE
320 Main St (43701-3426)
P.O. Box 190 (43702-0190)
PHONE..................................740 452-7555
TOLL FREE: 888
Cole Gerzner, *Mng Pt*
Miles D Fries, *Pt*
James R Krischak, *Pt*
Jeff R Beam, *Pt*
Don Dal Ponte, *Pt*
EMP: 32 **EST:** 1965
SQ FT: 3,500
SALES (est): 861.46K **Privately Held**
Web: www.zanesvillelaw.com
SIC: 8111 General practice attorney, lawyer

(G-15798)
HARTLEY COMPANY
Also Called: Fleming Heating S/M & Roofing
1950 East Pike (43701-4620)
PHONE..................................740 439-6668
Gary Stiers, *Mgr*
EMP: 28
SALES (corp-wide): 26.35MM **Privately Held**
Web: www.bellstores.com
SIC: 1711 1761 Ventilation and duct work contractor; Roofing contractor
PA: The Hartley Company
319 Wheeling Ave
Cambridge OH 43725
740 432-2328

(G-15799)
HEALTH CARE SPECIALISTS
945 Bethesda Dr Ste 300 (43701-1880)
PHONE..................................740 454-4530
Myron Knell, *Pr*
EMP: 27 **EST:** 1998
SALES (est): 945.93K **Privately Held**

SIC: 8062 General medical and surgical hospitals

(G-15800)
HELEN PURCELL HOME
1854 Norwood Blvd (43701-2337)
PHONE..................................740 453-1745
R Moehrman Junior, *Admn*
Robert Moehrman Junior, *Pr*
Gina Dilly, *
EMP: 50 **EST:** 1885
SQ FT: 55,000
SALES (est): 2.52MM **Privately Held**
Web: www.helenpurcell.org
SIC: 8361 Aged home

(G-15801)
HOSPICE OF GENESIS HEALTH
Also Called: Genesis Hspces Pallitaive Care
713 Forest Ave (43701-2819)
PHONE..................................740 454-5381
TOLL FREE: 800
Sally Scheffler, *Dir*
Renee Sparks, *
EMP: 40 **EST:** 1998
SALES (est): 2.82MM **Privately Held**
Web: www.genesishcs.org
SIC: 8062 8082 8051 General medical and surgical hospitals; Home health care services; Skilled nursing care facilities

(G-15802)
HUNTINGTON NATIONAL BANK
428 Main St (43701-3515)
P.O. Box 4658 (43702)
PHONE..................................740 452-8444
Mark Carpenter, *Mgr*
EMP: 41
SALES (corp-wide): 10.84B **Publicly Held**
Web: www.huntington.com
SIC: 6029 6021 Commercial banks, nec; National commercial banks
HQ: The Huntington National Bank
41 S High St
Columbus OH 43215
614 480-4293

(G-15803)
HUNTINGTON NATIONAL BANK
Also Called: Huntington
2801 Maple Ave (43701-1715)
P.O. Box 4658 (43702)
PHONE..................................740 455-7048
Danny Mizer, *Mgr*
EMP: 36
SALES (corp-wide): 10.84B **Publicly Held**
Web: www.huntington.com
SIC: 6029 6021 Commercial banks, nec; National commercial banks
HQ: The Huntington National Bank
41 S High St
Columbus OH 43215
614 480-4293

(G-15804)
INTERIM HLTH CARE OF NRTHWSTER
Also Called: Interim Healthcare
2809 Bell St Ste D (43701-1741)
PHONE..................................740 453-5130
Deb Studer, *Mgr*
EMP: 98
SALES (corp-wide): 52.16MM **Privately Held**
Web: www.interimhealthcare.com
SIC: 8082 Home health care services
HQ: Interim Health Care Of Northwestern Ohio, Inc
3100 W Central Ave # 250
Toledo OH 43606

Zanesville - Muskingum County (G-15805) — GEOGRAPHIC SECTION

(G-15805)
KESSLER SIGN COMPANY (PA)
Also Called: Kessler Outdoor Advertising
2669 National Rd (43701-8257)
P.O. Box 785 (43702-0785)
PHONE................................740 453-0668
TOLL FREE: 800
Robert Kessler, *CEO*
Adam Kessler, *
Rodger Kessler, *
David Kessler, *
Elaine Kessler-kuntz, *Treas*
EMP: 50 EST: 1971
SQ FT: 25,000
SALES (est): 9.7MM
SALES (corp-wide): 9.7MM **Privately Held**
Web: www.kesslersignco.com
SIC: 3993 7312 Signs, not made in custom sign painting shops; Outdoor advertising services

(G-15806)
LEPI ENTERPRISES INC
630 Gw Morse St (43701-3304)
P.O. Box 457 (43702-0457)
PHONE................................740 453-2980
TOLL FREE: 800
James Lepi, *Ch*
Michael Lepi, *
Jeff Lepi, *
Cathy L George, *
Kenneth M Mortimer, *
EMP: 100 EST: 1953
SQ FT: 20,000
SALES (est): 9.96MM **Privately Held**
Web: www.lepienterprises.com
SIC: 1799 1541 Asbestos removal and encapsulation; Industrial buildings and warehouses

(G-15807)
LOWES HOME CENTERS LLC
Also Called: Lowe's
3755 Frazeysburg Rd (43701-1015)
PHONE................................740 450-5500
Chapman Joe, *Mgr*
EMP: 157
SALES (corp-wide): 86.38B **Publicly Held**
Web: www.lowes.com
SIC: 5211 5031 5722 5064 Home centers; Building materials, exterior; Household appliance stores; Electrical appliances, television and radio
HQ: Lowe's Home Centers, Llc
1000 Lowes Blvd
Mooresville NC 28117
336 658-4000

(G-15808)
LUBURGH INC (PA)
4174 East Pike (43701-8425)
PHONE................................740 452-3668
Otto Luburgh, *Pr*
Henry Luburgh, *
Andrew Luburgh, *
EMP: 29 EST: 1985
SALES (est): 9.55MM **Privately Held**
Web: www.msmisp.com
SIC: 1794 Excavation work

(G-15809)
M A M INC
Also Called: Media & Marketing Associates
1926 Norwood Blvd (43701-2145)
P.O. Box 2451 (43702-2451)
PHONE................................740 588-9882
Mark Kelly, *Mgr*
EMP: 29
SALES (corp-wide): 290.27K **Privately Held**
Web: www.mmainc.com
SIC: 7311 Advertising agencies
PA: M A M Inc
4250 Tavener Rd
Newark OH 43056
740 763-2931

(G-15810)
MARQUEE BROADCASTING OHIO INC ✪
Also Called: Whiz - TV & Radio
629 Downard Rd (43701-5108)
PHONE................................740 452-5431
EMP: 43 EST: 2022
SALES (est): 331.53K **Privately Held**
SIC: 4832 4833 Radio broadcasting stations; Television broadcasting stations

(G-15811)
MATTINGLY FOODS INC
Also Called: Mattingly Foods
302 State St (43701-3200)
P.O. Box 760 (43702-0760)
PHONE................................740 454-0136
Rick Barnes, *CEO*
Barbara Callahan, *
Andrew Hess, *
Benjamin Hess, *
Brandon Hess, *
EMP: 240 EST: 1946
SQ FT: 225,000
SALES (est): 33.55MM **Privately Held**
Web: www.mattinglycold.com
SIC: 5149 5142 5141 Canned goods: fruit, vegetables, seafood, meats, etc.; Fruit juices, frozen; Groceries, general line

(G-15812)
MEDICAL ASSOC OF ZANESVILLE
Also Called: Prime Care
1210 Ashland Ave (43701-2806)
PHONE................................740 454-8551
Daniel Cheerer, *Pr*
Donald Merz, *Sec*
EMP: 63 EST: 1959
SQ FT: 1,500
SALES (est): 3.23MM **Privately Held**
Web: www.genesishcs.org
SIC: 8062 General medical and surgical hospitals

(G-15813)
MUSKINGUM CNTY DRG ALCHOL SBST
Also Called: Muskingum Behavioral Health
1127 W Main St (43701-3147)
PHONE................................740 454-1266
Yolanda Taylor, *CEO*
Steven Carrel, *
Yolanda Taylor, *COO*
EMP: 40 EST: 1980
SALES (est): 2.38MM **Privately Held**
Web: www.muskingumbehavioralhealth.com
SIC: 8322 8093 8069 Individual and family services; Alcohol clinic, outpatient; Drug addiction rehabilitation hospital

(G-15814)
MUSKINGUM COUNTY OHIO
Also Called: Muskingum County Engineers Off
109 Graham St (43701-3103)
PHONE................................740 453-0381
Dug Davis, *Mgr*
EMP: 30
SALES (corp-wide): 92.26MM **Privately Held**
Web: www.ohiomuskingumsheriff.org
SIC: 8711 Engineering services
PA: Muskingum County, Ohio
401 Main St
Zanesville OH 43701
740 455-7100

(G-15815)
MUSKINGUM IRON & METAL CO
345 Arthur St (43701-5850)
P.O. Box 815 (43702-0815)
PHONE................................740 452-9351
TOLL FREE: 800
Jack Joseph, *Pr*
Robert Joseph, *
Joshua Joseph, *
Arthur L Joseph, *
Shirley L Joseph, *
EMP: 36 EST: 1929
SQ FT: 30,000
SALES (est): 16.95MM **Privately Held**
Web: www.muskingumiron.com
SIC: 4953 Recycling, waste materials

(G-15816)
MUSKINGUM STARLIGHT INDUSTRIES (PA)
1304 Newark Rd (43701-2621)
PHONE................................740 453-4622
Mary Thompson Sufferd, *Dir*
Larry Wheeler, *
EMP: 75 EST: 1959
SQ FT: 11,500
SALES (est): 2.37MM
SALES (corp-wide): 2.37MM **Privately Held**
Web: www.muskingumdd.org
SIC: 8331 Sheltered workshop

(G-15817)
MUSKINGUM STARLIGHT INDUSTRIES
Also Called: Starlight Special School
1330 Newark Rd (43701-2623)
PHONE................................740 453-4622
Larry Wheeler, *Genl Mgr*
EMP: 100
SALES (corp-wide): 2.37MM **Privately Held**
Web: www.muskingumdd.org
SIC: 8731 8211 Commercial physical research; Private special education school
PA: Muskingum Starlight Industries Inc
1304 Newark Rd
Zanesville OH 43701
740 453-4622

(G-15818)
NATIONAL GAS & OIL CORPORATION
1423 Lake Dr (43701-5922)
PHONE................................740 454-7252
Dan Price, *Mgr*
EMP: 35
SALES (corp-wide): 130.87MM **Privately Held**
Web: www.myenergycoop.com
SIC: 4923 4924 4922 Gas transmission and distribution; Natural gas distribution; Natural gas transmission
HQ: The National Gas & Oil Corporation
1500 Granville Rd
Newark OH 43055
740 344-2102

(G-15819)
NATIONWIDE CHILDRENS HOSPITAL
1166 Military Rd (43701-1562)
PHONE................................740 588-0237
Heather Lawrence, *Brnch Mgr*
EMP: 101
SALES (corp-wide): 3.6B **Privately Held**
Web: www.nationwidechildrens.org
SIC: 8062 General medical and surgical hospitals
PA: Nationwide Children's Hospital
700 Childrens Dr
Columbus OH 43205
614 722-2000

(G-15820)
NEIGHBORHOOD HOSPITALITY INC
Also Called: Plebees
3181 Maple Ave (43701-1460)
PHONE................................740 588-9244
EMP: 46
SALES (corp-wide): 162.89K **Privately Held**
SIC: 7011 Hotels and motels
PA: Neighborhood Hospitality Inc
4610 Gallia St
Portsmouth OH

(G-15821)
OHIO AUTO LOAN SERVICES INC
Also Called: Ohio Auto Loan Services
1834 Maple Ave (43701-2236)
PHONE................................740 624-8547
Douglas Edgell, *Brnch Mgr*
EMP: 37
SIC: 6141 Automobile loans, including insurance
HQ: Ohio Auto Loan Services, Inc.
8601 Dunwoody Pl Ste 406
Atlanta GA 30350
770 552-9840

(G-15822)
OHIO MACHINERY CO
Also Called: Caterpillar Authorized Dealer
3415 East Pike (43701-8419)
PHONE................................740 453-0563
Rick Hensel, *Mgr*
EMP: 65
SQ FT: 18,000
SALES (corp-wide): 185.86MM **Privately Held**
Web: www.ohiocat.com
SIC: 5082 7629 General construction machinery and equipment; Electrical repair shops
PA: Ohio Machinery Co.
3993 E Royalton Rd
Broadview Heights OH 44147
440 526-6200

(G-15823)
ORTHOPDIC ASSOC ZANESVILLE INC
2854 Bell St (43701-1721)
PHONE................................740 454-3273
Karl C Saunders, *Pr*
EMP: 56 EST: 1969
SALES (est): 11.51MM **Privately Held**
Web: www.orthozane.com
SIC: 8011 Orthopedic physician

(G-15824)
OXFORD MINING COMPANY INC
1855 Kemper Ct (43701-4634)
PHONE................................740 588-0190
Joe Douglas, *Brnch Mgr*
EMP: 121
SALES (corp-wide): 814.89MM **Privately Held**
SIC: 1221 Bituminous coal and lignite-surface mining
HQ: Oxford Mining Company, Inc.
544 Chestnut St
Coshocton OH 43812
740 622-6302

(G-15825)
P & D TRANSPORTATION INC (PA)
Also Called: Putnam Truck Load Direct
1705 Moxahala Ave (43701-5952)
P.O. Box 2909 (43702-2909)

GEOGRAPHIC SECTION
Zanesville - Muskingum County (G-15844)

PHONE.................................740 454-1221
Patrick L Hennessey, *Pr*
Ronald J Kunkel, *
Dan Hennessey, *
EMP: 40 **EST:** 1985
SALES (est): 10.32MM
SALES (corp-wide): 10.32MM **Privately Held**
SIC: 4213 Contract haulers

(G-15826)
PEABODY COAL COMPANY
2810 East Pike Apt 3 (43701-9197)
PHONE.................................740 450-2420
J T Kneen, *Prin*
EMP: 28
SALES (corp-wide): 4.95B **Publicly Held**
SIC: 1241 Coal mining services
HQ: Peabody Coal Company
    701 Market St
    Saint Louis MO 63101
    314 342-3400

(G-15827)
PHILO BAND BOOSTERS
1359 Wheeling Ave (43701-4538)
PHONE.................................740 221-3023
Chad Stemm, *Finance*
EMP: 30 **EST:** 2017
SALES (est): 96.31K **Privately Held**
SIC: 7929 Entertainers and entertainment groups

(G-15828)
PRODUCERS SERVICE LLC
109 Graham St (43701-3103)
P.O. Box 2277 (43702-2277)
PHONE.................................740 454-6253
EMP: 39 **EST:** 2005
SALES (est): 4.75MM **Privately Held**
SIC: 6799 Real estate investors, except property operators
PA: Psc Holdings, Inc.
    109 Graham St
    Zanesville OH 43701

(G-15829)
PRODUCERS SERVICE CORPORATION
109 Graham St (43701-3103)
P.O. Box 2277 (43702-2277)
PHONE.................................740 454-6253
EMP: 98 **EST:** 1981
SALES (est): 49.65MM **Privately Held**
SIC: 1389 Hydraulic fracturing wells
PA: Psc Holdings, Inc.
    109 Graham St
    Zanesville OH 43701

(G-15830)
PROFESSIONAL PLUMBING SVCS INC
3570 Old Wheeling Rd (43701-9684)
PHONE.................................740 454-1066
Michael L Burkhart, *Pr*
Catherine Nash Burkhart, *
EMP: 28 **EST:** 1983
SQ FT: 5,200
SALES (est): 1.73MM **Privately Held**
Web: www.professionalplumbingservicesinc.com
SIC: 1711 Plumbing contractors

(G-15831)
SURGICAL ASSOCIATES INC
Also Called: Surgical Assocs of Zanesville
2916 Vangader Dr (43701-1744)
PHONE.................................740 453-0661
Debra Williams, *Prin*
EMP: 94 **EST:** 1940
SALES (est): 1.38MM **Privately Held**
SIC: 8062 General medical and surgical hospitals

(G-15832)
TRAVELODGE ZANESVILLE
Also Called: Travelodge
58 N 6th St (43701-3602)
PHONE.................................740 453-0611
Zeny Patel, *Prin*
EMP: 31 **EST:** 2003
SALES (est): 518.21K **Privately Held**
Web: travel-inn-zanesville.booked.net
SIC: 7011 Hotels and motels

(G-15833)
TRILOGY REHAB SERVICES LLC
Also Called: Trilogy
2991 Maple Ave (43701-1499)
PHONE.................................740 452-3000
EMP: 128
SALES (corp-wide): 146.9MM **Privately Held**
Web: www.trilogyhs.com
SIC: 8051 Skilled nursing care facilities
PA: Trilogy Rehab Services, Llc
    303 N Hurstbourne Pkwy # 200
    Louisville KY 40222
    800 335-1060

(G-15834)
TSMM MANAGEMENT LLC
Also Called: Primrose Rtrment Cmnty Znsvlle
4212 Northpointe Dr (43701-5970)
PHONE.................................740 450-1100
James L Thares, *Managing Member*
EMP: 46 **EST:** 2011
SALES (est): 1.46MM **Privately Held**
Web: www.primroseretirement.com
SIC: 6513 Retirement hotel operation

(G-15835)
U S XPRESS INC
2705 E Pointe Dr (43701-7294)
PHONE.................................740 452-4153
Duane Stare, *Mgr*
EMP: 483
Web: www.usxpress.com
SIC: 4213 Contract haulers
HQ: U. S. Xpress, Inc.
    4080 Jenkins Rd
    Chattanooga TN 37421
    866 266-7270

(G-15836)
UNITED PARCEL SERVICE INC
Also Called: UPS
1507 Augusta St (43701-4155)
PHONE.................................800 742-5877
EMP: 41
SALES (corp-wide): 90.96B **Publicly Held**
Web: www.ups.com
SIC: 4215 Package delivery, vehicular
HQ: United Parcel Service, Inc.
    55 Glenlake Pkwy
    Atlanta GA 30328
    404 828-6000

(G-15837)
ZANDEX HEALTH CARE CORPORATION
Also Called: Willow Haven Nursing Home
1020 Taylor St (43701-2656)
P.O. Box 2038 (43702-2038)
PHONE.................................740 454-9747
Mark Richard, *Mgr*
EMP: 194
Web: www.cedarhillcare.org
SIC: 8051 8052 8059 Convalescent home with continuous nursing care; Intermediate care facilities; Rest home, with health care
PA: Zandex Health Care Corporation
    1122 Taylor St
    Zanesville OH 43701

(G-15838)
ZANDEX HEALTH CARE CORPORATION
Also Called: Ceder Hill
1136 Adair Ave (43701-2804)
PHONE.................................740 452-4636
Rich Stephens, *Mgr*
EMP: 185
Web: www.cedarhillcare.org
SIC: 8052 8051 Intermediate care facilities; Skilled nursing care facilities
PA: Zandex Health Care Corporation
    1122 Taylor St
    Zanesville OH 43701

(G-15839)
ZANDEX HEALTH CARE CORPORATION
Also Called: Adams Lane Care Center
1856 Adams Ln (43701-2612)
P.O. Box 638 (43702-0638)
PHONE.................................740 454-9769
Cathy Kocher, *Admn*
EMP: 175
SQ FT: 20,000
Web: www.cedarhillcare.org
SIC: 8052 8051 Intermediate care facilities; Skilled nursing care facilities
PA: Zandex Health Care Corporation
    1122 Taylor St
    Zanesville OH 43701

(G-15840)
ZANESVILLE COUNTRY CLUB
1300 Country Club Dr (43701-1464)
P.O. Box 2490 (43702-2490)
PHONE.................................740 452-2726
Michael Micheli, *Pr*
Ken Corbin, *
Michael Barron, *
EMP: 78 **EST:** 1931
SQ FT: 15,000
SALES (est): 3.15MM **Privately Held**
Web: www.zanesvillecc.com
SIC: 7997 Country club, membership

(G-15841)
ZANESVILLE METRO HSING AUTH
407 Pershing Rd (43701-6871)
PHONE.................................740 454-9714
Steven G Randles, *Ex Dir*
EMP: 60 **EST:** 1938
SALES (est): 1.96MM **Privately Held**
Web: www.zanesvillehousing.org
SIC: 6513 Apartment building operators

(G-15842)
ZANESVILLE SURGERY CENTER LLC
2907 Bell St (43701-1720)
PHONE.................................740 453-5713
Glenda Rogers, *Admn*
EMP: 39 **EST:** 1999
SALES (est): 1.98MM **Privately Held**
Web: www.zanesvillesc.com
SIC: 8011 Surgeon

(G-15843)
ZANESVLLE WLFARE ORGNZTION GDW (PA)
Also Called: GOODWILL RETAIL STORE
3610 West Pike (43701-9335)
PHONE.................................740 450-6060
Louis Cvetnic, *CEO*
EMP: 30 **EST:** 1914
SQ FT: 40,000
SALES (est): 13.48MM
SALES (corp-wide): 13.48MM **Privately Held**
Web: www.ohwvagoodwill.org
SIC: 8331 5932 Sheltered workshop; Used merchandise stores

(G-15844)
ZEMBA BROS INC
3401 East Pike (43701-8419)
P.O. Box 1270 (43702-1270)
PHONE.................................740 452-1880
EMP: 47 **EST:** 1989
SQ FT: 36,000
SALES (est): 12.18MM **Privately Held**
Web: www.zembacompanies.com
SIC: 1794 1711 1623 4212 Excavation and grading, building construction; Septic system construction; Sewer line construction; Local trucking, without storage

SIC INDEX

Standard Industrial Classification Alphabetical Index

SIC NO	PRODUCT

A

3291 Abrasive products
6321 Accident and health insurance
8721 Accounting, auditing, and bookkeeping
2891 Adhesives and sealants
7322 Adjustment and collection services
9611 Administration of general economic programs
9431 Administration of public health programs
9441 Administration of social and manpower programs
9451 Administration of veterans' affairs
7311 Advertising agencies
7319 Advertising, nec
2879 Agricultural chemicals, nec
3563 Air and gas compressors
4513 Air courier services
4522 Air transportation, nonscheduled
4512 Air transportation, scheduled
9511 Air, water, and solid waste management
3724 Aircraft engines and engine parts
3728 Aircraft parts and equipment, nec
4581 Airports, flying fields, and services
2812 Alkalies and chlorine
3363 Aluminum die-castings
3365 Aluminum foundries
3353 Aluminum sheet, plate, and foil
7999 Amusement and recreation, nec
7996 Amusement parks
3826 Analytical instruments
0752 Animal specialty services
1231 Anthracite mining
6513 Apartment building operators
2389 Apparel and accessories, nec
3446 Architectural metalwork
8712 Architectural services
7694 Armature rewinding shops
2952 Asphalt felts and coatings
2951 Asphalt paving mixtures and blocks
5531 Auto and home supply stores
7533 Auto exhaust system repair shops
3581 Automatic vending machines
7521 Automobile parking
5012 Automobiles and other motor vehicles
2396 Automotive and apparel trimmings
5599 Automotive dealers, nec
7536 Automotive glass replacement shops
7539 Automotive repair shops, nec
7549 Automotive services, nec
3465 Automotive stampings
7537 Automotive transmission repair shops

B

2673 Bags: plastic, laminated, and coated
2674 Bags: uncoated paper and multiwall
3562 Ball and roller bearings
6712 Bank holding companies
7241 Barber shops
7231 Beauty shops
5181 Beer and ale
2836 Biological products, except diagnostic
1221 Bituminous coal and lignite-surface mining
1222 Bituminous coal-underground mining
2782 Blankbooks and looseleaf binders
3312 Blast furnaces and steel mills
3564 Blowers and fans
5551 Boat dealers
3732 Boatbuilding and repairing
3452 Bolts, nuts, rivets, and washers
2732 Book printing
2731 Book publishing
5942 Book stores
2789 Bookbinding and related work
5192 Books, periodicals, and newspapers
8422 Botanical and zoological gardens
2086 Bottled and canned soft drinks
7933 Bowling centers
2051 Bread, cake, and related products
5032 Brick, stone, and related material
1622 Bridge, tunnel, and elevated highway
2211 Broadwoven fabric mills, cotton
2221 Broadwoven fabric mills, manmade
3991 Brooms and brushes
7349 Building maintenance services, nec
4142 Bus charter service, except local
4173 Bus terminal and service facilities
8611 Business associations
8748 Business consulting, nec
7389 Business services, nec

C

4841 Cable and other pay television services
5946 Camera and photographic supply stores
2064 Candy and other confectionery products
5441 Candy, nut, and confectionery stores
2033 Canned fruits and specialties
2032 Canned specialties
2394 Canvas and related products
3624 Carbon and graphite products
3955 Carbon paper and inked ribbons
1751 Carpentry work
7217 Carpet and upholstery cleaning
2273 Carpets and rugs
7542 Carwashes
0119 Cash grains, nec
5961 Catalog and mail-order houses
2823 Cellulosic manmade fibers
3241 Cement, hydraulic
6553 Cemetery subdividers and developers
2022 Cheese; natural and processed
2899 Chemical preparations, nec
5169 Chemicals and allied products, nec
2131 Chewing and smoking tobacco
0252 Chicken eggs
8351 Child day care services
5641 Children's and infants' wear stores
2066 Chocolate and cocoa products
8641 Civic and social associations
1459 Clay and related minerals, nec
5052 Coal and other minerals and ores
1241 Coal mining services
2295 Coated fabrics, not rubberized
7993 Coin-operated amusement devices
7215 Coin-operated laundries and cleaning
3316 Cold finishing of steel shapes
8221 Colleges and universities
4939 Combination utilities, nec
7336 Commercial art and graphic design
6029 Commercial banks, nec
5046 Commercial equipment, nec
3646 Commercial lighting fixtures
8732 Commercial nonphysical research
7335 Commercial photography
8731 Commercial physical research
2754 Commercial printing, gravure
2752 Commercial printing, lithographic
2759 Commercial printing, nec
6221 Commodity contracts brokers, dealers
4899 Communication services, nec
3669 Communications equipment, nec
5734 Computer and software stores
7376 Computer facilities management
7373 Computer integrated systems design
7378 Computer maintenance and repair
3577 Computer peripheral equipment, nec
7379 Computer related services, nec
7377 Computer rental and leasing
3572 Computer storage devices
3575 Computer terminals
5045 Computers, peripherals, and software
3271 Concrete block and brick
3272 Concrete products, nec
1771 Concrete work
5145 Confectionery
5082 Construction and mining machinery
3531 Construction machinery
5039 Construction materials, nec
1442 Construction sand and gravel
2679 Converted paper products, nec
3535 Conveyors and conveying equipment
2052 Cookies and crackers
3366 Copper foundries
2298 Cordage and twine
0115 Corn
9223 Correctional institutions
2653 Corrugated and solid fiber boxes
0724 Cotton ginning
4215 Courier services, except by air
9211 Courts
7323 Credit reporting services
0721 Crop planting and protection
0723 Crop preparation services for market
1311 Crude petroleum and natural gas
4612 Crude petroleum pipelines
1423 Crushed and broken granite
1422 Crushed and broken limestone
1429 Crushed and broken stone, nec
3643 Current-carrying wiring devices
2391 Curtains and draperies
3087 Custom compound purchased resins
7371 Custom computer programming services
3281 Cut stone and stone products
3421 Cutlery
2865 Cyclic crudes and intermediates

D

0241 Dairy farms
5451 Dairy products stores
5143 Dairy products, except dried or canned
7911 Dance studios, schools, and halls
7374 Data processing and preparation
8243 Data processing schools
0175 Deciduous tree fruits
4412 Deep sea foreign transportation of freight
2034 Dehydrated fruits, vegetables, soups
3843 Dental equipment and supplies
8072 Dental laboratories
5311 Department stores
7381 Detective and armored car services
2835 Diagnostic substances
2675 Die-cut paper and board
1411 Dimension stone
7331 Direct mail advertising services
5963 Direct selling establishments
7342 Disinfecting and pest control services
2085 Distilled and blended liquors
2047 Dog and cat food
5714 Drapery and upholstery stores
2591 Drapery hardware and blinds and shades
1381 Drilling oil and gas wells
5813 Drinking places
5912 Drug stores and proprietary stores
5122 Drugs, proprietaries, and sundries
2023 Dry, condensed, evaporated products
7216 Drycleaning plants, except rugs
5099 Durable goods, nec
6514 Dwelling operators, except apartments

E

5812 Eating places
4931 Electric and other services combined
3634 Electric housewares and fans
4911 Electric services
5063 Electrical apparatus and equipment
5064 Electrical appliances, television and radio
3699 Electrical equipment and supplies, nec
3629 Electrical industrial apparatus
7629 Electrical repair shops
1731 Electrical work
3845 Electromedical equipment

SIC INDEX

SIC NO	PRODUCT
3313	Electrometallurgical products
3677	Electronic coils and transformers
3679	Electronic components, nec
3571	Electronic computers
3678	Electronic connectors
5065	Electronic parts and equipment, nec
3676	Electronic resistors
8211	Elementary and secondary schools
3534	Elevators and moving stairways
7361	Employment agencies
3694	Engine electrical equipment
8711	Engineering services
7929	Entertainers and entertainment groups
2677	Envelopes
3822	Environmental controls
7359	Equipment rental and leasing, nec
1794	Excavation work
9111	Executive offices

F

SIC NO	PRODUCT
2381	Fabric dress and work gloves
3499	Fabricated metal products, nec
3498	Fabricated pipe and fittings
3443	Fabricated plate work (boiler shop)
3069	Fabricated rubber products, nec
3441	Fabricated structural metal
2399	Fabricated textile products, nec
8744	Facilities support services
5083	Farm and garden machinery
3523	Farm machinery and equipment
4221	Farm product warehousing and storage
5191	Farm supplies
3965	Fasteners, buttons, needles, and pins
6111	Federal and federally sponsored credit
6061	Federal credit unions
6035	Federal savings institutions
1061	Ferroalloy ores, except vanadium
2875	Fertilizers, mixing only
2655	Fiber cans, drums, and similar products
9311	Finance, taxation, and monetary policy
9224	Fire protection
6331	Fire, marine, and casualty insurance
5146	Fish and seafoods
3211	Flat glass
2087	Flavoring extracts and syrups, nec
5713	Floor covering stores
1752	Floor laying and floor work, nec
5992	Florists
2041	Flour and other grain mill products
5193	Flowers and florists supplies
3824	Fluid meters and counting devices
2026	Fluid milk
3593	Fluid power cylinders and actuators
3594	Fluid power pumps and motors
3492	Fluid power valves and hose fittings
2657	Folding paperboard boxes
0182	Food crops grown under cover
2099	Food preparations, nec
3556	Food products machinery
5139	Footwear
0851	Forestry services
4731	Freight transportation arrangement
4432	Freight transportation on the great lakes
5148	Fresh fruits and vegetables
2038	Frozen specialties, nec
5431	Fruit and vegetable markets
5989	Fuel dealers, nec
5983	Fuel oil dealers
6099	Functions related to depository banking
7261	Funeral service and crematories
5021	Furniture
5712	Furniture stores

G

SIC NO	PRODUCT
3944	Games, toys, and children's vehicles
7212	Garment pressing and cleaners' agents
4932	Gas and other services combined
4925	Gas production and/or distribution
4923	Gas transmission and distribution
3053	Gaskets; packing and sealing devices
5541	Gasoline service stations
7538	General automotive repair shops
0291	General farms, primarily animals
0191	General farms, primarily crop
9199	General government, nec
3569	General industrial machinery,
0219	General livestock, nec
8062	General medical and surgical hospitals
4225	General warehousing and storage
5947	Gift, novelty, and souvenir shop
1793	Glass and glazing work
5153	Grain and field beans
0172	Grapes
3321	Gray and ductile iron foundries
2771	Greeting cards
5149	Groceries and related products, nec
5141	Groceries, general line
5411	Grocery stores
3761	Guided missiles and space vehicles

H

SIC NO	PRODUCT
3423	Hand and edge tools, nec
5072	Hardware
5251	Hardware stores
3429	Hardware, nec
2426	Hardwood dimension and flooring mills
2435	Hardwood veneer and plywood
2353	Hats, caps, and millinery
8099	Health and allied services, nec
3433	Heating equipment, except electric
7353	Heavy construction equipment rental
1629	Heavy construction, nec
7363	Help supply services
1611	Highway and street construction
5945	Hobby, toy, and game shops
0213	Hogs
3536	Hoists, cranes, and monorails
6719	Holding companies, nec
8082	Home health care services
5023	Homefurnishings
6324	Hospital and medical service plans
7011	Hotels and motels
5722	Household appliance stores
3639	Household appliances, nec
3651	Household audio and video equipment
3631	Household cooking equipment
2392	Household furnishings, nec
3633	Household laundry equipment
3632	Household refrigerators and freezers
3635	Household vacuum cleaners
9531	Housing programs
0971	Hunting, trapping, game propagation

I

SIC NO	PRODUCT
2024	Ice cream and frozen deserts
8322	Individual and family services
5113	Industrial and personal service paper
1541	Industrial buildings and warehouses
3567	Industrial furnaces and ovens
2813	Industrial gases
2819	Industrial inorganic chemicals, nec
7218	Industrial launderers
5084	Industrial machinery and equipment
3599	Industrial machinery, nec
2869	Industrial organic chemicals, nec
3543	Industrial patterns
1446	Industrial sand
5085	Industrial supplies
3537	Industrial trucks and tractors
3491	Industrial valves
7375	Information retrieval services
4785	Inspection and fixed facilities
1796	Installing building equipment
3825	Instruments to measure electricity
6411	Insurance agents, brokers, and service
6399	Insurance carriers, nec
4131	Intercity and rural bus transportation
8052	Intermediate care facilities
3519	Internal combustion engines, nec
6282	Investment advice
6726	Investment offices, nec
6799	Investors, nec
0134	Irish potatoes
3462	Iron and steel forgings
1011	Iron ores
4971	Irrigation systems

J

SIC NO	PRODUCT
5094	Jewelry and precious stones
5944	Jewelry stores
3911	Jewelry, precious metal
8331	Job training and related services
8222	Junior colleges

K

SIC NO	PRODUCT
8092	Kidney dialysis centers
2253	Knit outerwear mills

L

SIC NO	PRODUCT
8631	Labor organizations
3821	Laboratory apparatus and furniture
3083	Laminated plastics plate and sheet
9512	Land, mineral, and wildlife conservation
0781	Landscape counseling and planning
7219	Laundry and garment services, nec
3524	Lawn and garden equipment
0782	Lawn and garden services
3199	Leather goods, nec
9222	Legal counsel and prosecution
8111	Legal services
9121	Legislative bodies
8231	Libraries
6311	Life insurance
3648	Lighting equipment, nec
3274	Lime
7213	Linen supply
5984	Liquefied petroleum gas dealers
5921	Liquor stores
5154	Livestock
0751	Livestock services, except veterinary
6163	Loan brokers
4111	Local and suburban transit
4141	Local bus charter service
4119	Local passenger transportation, nec
4214	Local trucking with storage
4212	Local trucking, without storage
2992	Lubricating oils and greases
3161	Luggage
5211	Lumber and other building materials
5031	Lumber, plywood, and millwork

M

SIC NO	PRODUCT
3545	Machine tool accessories
3541	Machine tools, metal cutting type
3542	Machine tools, metal forming type
8742	Management consulting services
6722	Management investment, open-ended
8741	Management services
2761	Manifold business forms
2097	Manufactured ice
3999	Manufacturing industries, nec
4493	Marinas
4491	Marine cargo handling
3953	Marking devices
1741	Masonry and other stonework
2515	Mattresses and bedsprings
3829	Measuring and controlling devices, nec
3586	Measuring and dispensing pumps
5421	Meat and fish markets
2011	Meat packing plants
5147	Meats and meat products
3061	Mechanical rubber goods
5047	Medical and hospital equipment
7352	Medical equipment rental
8071	Medical laboratories
8699	Membership organizations, nec
7997	Membership sports and recreation clubs
7041	Membership-basis organization hotels
5136	Men's and boy's clothing
2311	Men's and boy's suits and coats
2326	Men's and boy's work clothing
5611	Men's and boys' clothing stores
3143	Men's footwear, except athletic
5962	Merchandising machine operators
3412	Metal barrels, drums, and pails
3411	Metal cans

SIC INDEX

SIC NO	PRODUCT
3479	Metal coating and allied services
3442	Metal doors, sash, and trim
3497	Metal foil and leaf
3398	Metal heat treating
2514	Metal household furniture
1081	Metal mining services
3431	Metal sanitary ware
3469	Metal stampings, nec
5051	Metals service centers and offices
3549	Metalworking machinery, nec
2431	Millwork
3296	Mineral wool
3295	Minerals, ground or treated
3532	Mining machinery
5699	Miscellaneous apparel and accessories
6159	Miscellaneous business credit
3496	Miscellaneous fabricated wire products
5499	Miscellaneous food stores
5399	Miscellaneous general merchandise
5719	Miscellaneous homefurnishings
3449	Miscellaneous metalwork
1499	Miscellaneous nonmetallic mining
7299	Miscellaneous personal services
2741	Miscellaneous publishing
5999	Miscellaneous retail stores, nec
6162	Mortgage bankers and correspondents
7822	Motion picture and tape distribution
7812	Motion picture and video production
7832	Motion picture theaters, except drive-in
3714	Motor vehicle parts and accessories
5015	Motor vehicle parts, used
5013	Motor vehicle supplies and new parts
3711	Motor vehicles and car bodies
5571	Motorcycle dealers
3751	Motorcycles, bicycles, and parts
3621	Motors and generators
8412	Museums and art galleries
5736	Musical instrument stores
3931	Musical instruments

N

SIC NO	PRODUCT
2441	Nailed wood boxes and shook
2241	Narrow fabric mills
6021	National commercial banks
9711	National security
4924	Natural gas distribution
1321	Natural gas liquids
4922	Natural gas transmission
5511	New and used car dealers
5994	News dealers and newsstands
2711	Newspapers
2873	Nitrogenous fertilizers
8733	Noncommercial research organizations
3644	Noncurrent-carrying wiring devices
5199	Nondurable goods, nec
3364	Nonferrous die-castings except aluminum
3463	Nonferrous forgings
3369	Nonferrous foundries, nec
3356	Nonferrous rolling and drawing, nec
3357	Nonferrous wiredrawing and insulating
3299	Nonmetallic mineral products,
1481	Nonmetallic mineral services
6512	Nonresidential building operators
1542	Nonresidential construction, nec
2297	Nonwoven fabrics
8059	Nursing and personal care, nec

O

SIC NO	PRODUCT
5044	Office equipment
2522	Office furniture, except wood
3579	Office machines, nec
8041	Offices and clinics of chiropractors
8021	Offices and clinics of dentists
8011	Offices and clinics of medical doctors
8042	Offices and clinics of optometrists
8031	Offices and clinics of osteopathic physicians
8043	Offices and clinics of podiatrists
8049	Offices of health practitioner
1382	Oil and gas exploration services
3533	Oil and gas field machinery
1389	Oil and gas field services, nec
1531	Operative builders

SIC NO	PRODUCT
3851	Ophthalmic goods
5048	Ophthalmic goods
5995	Optical goods stores
3827	Optical instruments and lenses
0181	Ornamental nursery products
0783	Ornamental shrub and tree services
7312	Outdoor advertising services

P

SIC NO	PRODUCT
5142	Packaged frozen goods
3565	Packaging machinery
4783	Packing and crating
5231	Paint, glass, and wallpaper stores
1721	Painting and paper hanging
2851	Paints and allied products
5198	Paints, varnishes, and supplies
3554	Paper industries machinery
2621	Paper mills
2671	Paper; coated and laminated packaging
2672	Paper; coated and laminated, nec
2631	Paperboard mills
2542	Partitions and fixtures, except wood
7515	Passenger car leasing
7514	Passenger car rental
4729	Passenger transportation arrangement
6794	Patent owners and lessors
6371	Pension, health, and welfare funds
2721	Periodicals
6141	Personal credit institutions
3172	Personal leather goods, nec
2999	Petroleum and coal products, nec
5171	Petroleum bulk stations and terminals
5172	Petroleum products, nec
2911	Petroleum refining
2834	Pharmaceutical preparations
2874	Phosphatic fertilizers
7334	Photocopying and duplicating services
7384	Photofinish laboratories
3861	Photographic equipment and supplies
5043	Photographic equipment and supplies
7221	Photographic studios, portrait
7991	Physical fitness facilities
2035	Pickles, sauces, and salad dressings
5131	Piece goods and notions
1742	Plastering, drywall, and insulation
3085	Plastics bottles
3086	Plastics foam products
5162	Plastics materials and basic shapes
2821	Plastics materials and resins
3088	Plastics plumbing fixtures
3089	Plastics products, nec
2796	Platemaking services
3471	Plating and polishing
2395	Pleating and stitching
5074	Plumbing and hydronic heating supplies
3432	Plumbing fixture fittings and trim
1711	Plumbing, heating, air-conditioning
9221	Police protection
2842	Polishes and sanitation goods
8651	Political organizations
3264	Porcelain electrical supplies
2096	Potato chips and similar snacks
3269	Pottery products, nec
5144	Poultry and poultry products
0254	Poultry hatcheries
2015	Poultry slaughtering and processing
7211	Power laundries, family and commercial
3568	Power transmission equipment, nec
3546	Power-driven handtools
3448	Prefabricated metal buildings
2452	Prefabricated wood buildings
7372	Prepackaged software
2048	Prepared feeds, nec
2045	Prepared flour mixes and doughs
3229	Pressed and blown glass, nec
3399	Primary metal products
3339	Primary nonferrous metals, nec
3672	Printed circuit boards
5111	Printing and writing paper
3555	Printing trades machinery
3823	Process control instruments
3231	Products of purchased glass

SIC NO	PRODUCT
5049	Professional equipment, nec
8621	Professional organizations
8063	Psychiatric hospitals
2531	Public building and related furniture
7992	Public golf courses
9229	Public order and safety, nec
8743	Public relations services
2611	Pulp mills
3561	Pumps and pumping equipment

R

SIC NO	PRODUCT
7948	Racing, including track operation
3663	Radio and t.v. communications equipment
7622	Radio and television repair
4832	Radio broadcasting stations
5731	Radio, television, and electronic stores
7313	Radio, television, publisher representatives
4812	Radiotelephone communication
3743	Railroad equipment
4011	Railroads, line-haul operating
3273	Ready-mixed concrete
6531	Real estate agents and managers
6798	Real estate investment trusts
6519	Real property lessors, nec
2493	Reconstituted wood products
5561	Recreational vehicle dealers
4613	Refined petroleum pipelines
4222	Refrigerated warehousing and storage
3585	Refrigeration and heating equipment
5078	Refrigeration equipment and supplies
7623	Refrigeration service and repair
4953	Refuse systems
9621	Regulation, administration of transportation
3625	Relays and industrial controls
8661	Religious organizations
4741	Rental of railroad cars
7699	Repair services, nec
8361	Residential care
1522	Residential construction, nec
5461	Retail bakeries
5261	Retail nurseries and garden stores
7641	Reupholstery and furniture repair
3547	Rolling mill machinery
5033	Roofing, siding, and insulation
1761	Roofing, siding, and sheetmetal work
7021	Rooming and boarding houses
3021	Rubber and plastics footwear
3052	Rubber and plastics hose and beltings

S

SIC NO	PRODUCT
2068	Salted and roasted nuts and seeds
2656	Sanitary food containers
2676	Sanitary paper products
4959	Sanitary services, nec
2013	Sausages and other prepared meats
6036	Savings institutions, except federal
2421	Sawmills and planing mills, general
3596	Scales and balances, except laboratory
4151	School buses
8299	Schools and educational services
5093	Scrap and waste materials
3451	Screw machine products
3812	Search and navigation equipment
3341	Secondary nonferrous metals
7338	Secretarial and court reporting
6231	Security and commodity exchanges
6211	Security brokers and dealers
7382	Security systems services
3674	Semiconductors and related devices
5087	Service establishment equipment
3589	Service industry machinery, nec
7819	Services allied to motion pictures
8999	Services, nec
2652	Setup paperboard boxes
4952	Sewerage systems
5949	Sewing, needlework, and piece goods
3444	Sheet metalwork
3731	Shipbuilding and repairing
5661	Shoe stores
6153	Short-term business credit
3993	Signs and advertising specialties
1521	Single-family housing construction

SIC INDEX

SIC NO	PRODUCT
8051	Skilled nursing care facilities
2841	Soap and other detergents
8399	Social services, nec
2436	Softwood veneer and plywood
0711	Soil preparation services
3769	Space vehicle equipment, nec
3544	Special dies, tools, jigs, and fixtures
3559	Special industry machinery, nec
1799	Special trade contractors, nec
4226	Special warehousing and storage, nec
8069	Specialty hospitals, except psychiatric
8093	Specialty outpatient clinics, nec
3566	Speed changers, drives, and gears
3949	Sporting and athletic goods, nec
5091	Sporting and recreation goods
7032	Sporting and recreational camps
5941	Sporting goods and bicycle shops
7941	Sports clubs, managers, and promoters
6022	State commercial banks
6062	State credit unions
5112	Stationery and office supplies
5943	Stationery stores
4961	Steam and air-conditioning supply
3325	Steel foundries, nec
3324	Steel investment foundries
3317	Steel pipe and tubes
3493	Steel springs, except wire
3315	Steel wire and related products
1791	Structural steel erection
2439	Structural wood members, nec
6552	Subdividers and developers, nec
6351	Surety insurance
3841	Surgical and medical instruments
3842	Surgical appliances and supplies
8713	Surveying services
3613	Switchgear and switchboard apparatus
4013	Switching and terminal services
2822	Synthetic rubber

T

SIC NO	PRODUCT
3795	Tanks and tank components
7291	Tax return preparation services
4121	Taxicabs
4822	Telegraph and other communications
3661	Telephone and telegraph apparatus
4813	Telephone communication, except radio
4833	Television broadcasting stations
1743	Terrazzo, tile, marble, mosaic work
8734	Testing laboratories
2299	Textile goods, nec
3552	Textile machinery
7922	Theatrical producers and services
0811	Timber tracts
2296	Tire cord and fabrics
7534	Tire retreading and repair shops
3011	Tires and inner tubes
5014	Tires and tubes
6541	Title abstract offices
6361	Title insurance
5194	Tobacco and tobacco products
5993	Tobacco stores and stands
2844	Toilet preparations
7532	Top and body repair and paint shops
4492	Towing and tugboat service
5092	Toys and hobby goods and supplies
7033	Trailer parks and campsites
3612	Transformers, except electric
5088	Transportation equipment and supplies
3799	Transportation equipment, nec
4789	Transportation services, nec
4724	Travel agencies
3792	Travel trailers and campers
3713	Truck and bus bodies
7513	Truck rental and leasing, without drivers
3715	Truck trailers
4231	Trucking terminal facilities
4213	Trucking, except local
6733	Trusts, nec
6732	Trusts: educational, religious, etc.
3511	Turbines and turbine generator sets
0253	Turkeys and turkey eggs
2791	Typesetting

U

SIC NO	PRODUCT
3081	Unsupported plastics film and sheet
3082	Unsupported plastics profile shapes
2512	Upholstered household furniture
9532	Urban and community development
5521	Used car dealers
5932	Used merchandise stores
7519	Utility trailer rental

V

SIC NO	PRODUCT
3494	Valves and pipe fittings, nec
5331	Variety stores
0161	Vegetables and melons
3647	Vehicular lighting equipment
0741	Veterinary services for livestock
0742	Veterinary services, specialties
7841	Video tape rental
3261	Vitreous plumbing fixtures
8249	Vocational schools, nec

W

SIC NO	PRODUCT
5075	Warm air heating and air conditioning
7631	Watch, clock, and jewelry repair
3873	Watches, clocks, watchcases, and parts
4941	Water supply
4449	Water transportation of freight
4499	Water transportation services, nec
1781	Water well drilling
1623	Water, sewer, and utility lines
7692	Welding repair
5182	Wine and distilled beverages
2084	Wines, brandy, and brandy spirits
3495	Wire springs
5632	Women's accessory and specialty stores
5137	Women's and children's clothing
2337	Women's and misses' suits and coats
5621	Women's clothing stores
3144	Women's footwear, except athletic
2449	Wood containers, nec
2511	Wood household furniture
2434	Wood kitchen cabinets
2521	Wood office furniture
2448	Wood pallets and skids
2541	Wood partitions and fixtures
2491	Wood preserving
2499	Wood products, nec
2517	Wood television and radio cabinets
3553	Woodworking machinery
1795	Wrecking and demolition work

X

SIC NO	PRODUCT
3844	X-ray apparatus and tubes

SIC INDEX

Standard Industrial Classification Numerical Index

| SIC NO | PRODUCT |

01 agricultural production - crops
0115 Corn
0119 Cash grains, nec
0134 Irish potatoes
0161 Vegetables and melons
0172 Grapes
0175 Deciduous tree fruits
0181 Ornamental nursery products
0182 Food crops grown under cover
0191 General farms, primarily crop

02 agricultural production - livestock and animal specialties
0213 Hogs
0219 General livestock, nec
0241 Dairy farms
0252 Chicken eggs
0253 Turkeys and turkey eggs
0254 Poultry hatcheries
0291 General farms, primarily animals

07 agricultural services
0711 Soil preparation services
0721 Crop planting and protection
0723 Crop preparation services for market
0724 Cotton ginning
0741 Veterinary services for livestock
0742 Veterinary services, specialties
0751 Livestock services, except veterinary
0752 Animal specialty services
0781 Landscape counseling and planning
0782 Lawn and garden services
0783 Ornamental shrub and tree services

08 forestry
0811 Timber tracts
0851 Forestry services

09 fishing, hunting and trapping
0971 Hunting, trapping, game propagation

10 metal mining
1011 Iron ores
1061 Ferroalloy ores, except vanadium
1081 Metal mining services

12 coal mining
1221 Bituminous coal and lignite-surface mining
1222 Bituminous coal-underground mining
1231 Anthracite mining
1241 Coal mining services

13 oil and gas extraction
1311 Crude petroleum and natural gas
1321 Natural gas liquids
1381 Drilling oil and gas wells
1382 Oil and gas exploration services
1389 Oil and gas field services, nec

14 mining and quarrying of nonmetallic minerals, except fuels
1411 Dimension stone
1422 Crushed and broken limestone
1423 Crushed and broken granite
1429 Crushed and broken stone, nec
1442 Construction sand and gravel
1446 Industrial sand
1459 Clay and related minerals, nec
1481 Nonmetallic mineral services
1499 Miscellaneous nonmetallic mining

15 construction - general contractors & operative builders
1521 Single-family housing construction
1522 Residential construction, nec
1531 Operative builders
1541 Industrial buildings and warehouses
1542 Nonresidential construction, nec

16 heamy construction, except building construction, contractor
1611 Highway and street construction
1622 Bridge, tunnel, and elevated highway
1623 Water, sewer, and utility lines
1629 Heavy construction, nec

17 construction - special trade contractors
1711 Plumbing, heating, air-conditioning
1721 Painting and paper hanging
1731 Electrical work
1741 Masonry and other stonework
1742 Plastering, drywall, and insulation
1743 Terrazzo, tile, marble, mosaic work
1751 Carpentry work
1752 Floor laying and floor work, nec
1761 Roofing, siding, and sheetmetal work
1771 Concrete work
1781 Water well drilling
1791 Structural steel erection
1793 Glass and glazing work
1794 Excavation work
1795 Wrecking and demolition work
1796 Installing building equipment
1799 Special trade contractors, nec

20 food and kindred products
2011 Meat packing plants
2013 Sausages and other prepared meats
2015 Poultry slaughtering and processing
2022 Cheese; natural and processed
2023 Dry, condensed, evaporated products
2024 Ice cream and frozen deserts
2026 Fluid milk
2032 Canned specialties
2033 Canned fruits and specialties
2034 Dehydrated fruits, vegetables, soups
2035 Pickles, sauces, and salad dressings
2038 Frozen specialties, nec
2041 Flour and other grain mill products
2045 Prepared flour mixes and doughs
2047 Dog and cat food
2048 Prepared feeds, nec
2051 Bread, cake, and related products
2052 Cookies and crackers
2064 Candy and other confectionery products
2066 Chocolate and cocoa products
2068 Salted and roasted nuts and seeds
2084 Wines, brandy, and brandy spirits
2085 Distilled and blended liquors
2086 Bottled and canned soft drinks
2087 Flavoring extracts and syrups, nec
2096 Potato chips and similar snacks
2097 Manufactured ice
2099 Food preparations, nec

21 tobacco products
2131 Chewing and smoking tobacco

22 textile mill products
2211 Broadwoven fabric mills, cotton
2221 Broadwoven fabric mills, manmade
2241 Narrow fabric mills
2253 Knit outerwear mills
2273 Carpets and rugs
2295 Coated fabrics, not rubberized
2296 Tire cord and fabrics
2297 Nonwoven fabrics
2298 Cordage and twine
2299 Textile goods, nec

23 apparel, finished products from fabrics & similar materials
2311 Men's and boy's suits and coats
2326 Men's and boy's work clothing
2337 Women's and misses' suits and coats
2353 Hats, caps, and millinery
2381 Fabric dress and work gloves
2389 Apparel and accessories, nec
2391 Curtains and draperies
2392 Household furnishings, nec
2394 Canvas and related products
2395 Pleating and stitching
2396 Automotive and apparel trimmings
2399 Fabricated textile products, nec

24 lumber and wood products, except furniture
2421 Sawmills and planing mills, general
2426 Hardwood dimension and flooring mills
2431 Millwork
2434 Wood kitchen cabinets
2435 Hardwood veneer and plywood
2436 Softwood veneer and plywood
2439 Structural wood members, nec
2441 Nailed wood boxes and shook
2448 Wood pallets and skids
2449 Wood containers, nec
2452 Prefabricated wood buildings
2491 Wood preserving
2493 Reconstituted wood products
2499 Wood products, nec

25 furniture and fixtures
2511 Wood household furniture
2512 Upholstered household furniture
2514 Metal household furniture
2515 Mattresses and bedsprings
2517 Wood television and radio cabinets
2521 Wood office furniture
2522 Office furniture, except wood
2531 Public building and related furniture
2541 Wood partitions and fixtures
2542 Partitions and fixtures, except wood
2591 Drapery hardware and blinds and shades

26 paper and allied products
2611 Pulp mills
2621 Paper mills
2631 Paperboard mills
2652 Setup paperboard boxes
2653 Corrugated and solid fiber boxes
2655 Fiber cans, drums, and similar products
2656 Sanitary food containers
2657 Folding paperboard boxes
2671 Paper; coated and laminated packaging
2672 Paper; coated and laminated, nec
2673 Bags: plastic, laminated, and coated
2674 Bags: uncoated paper and multiwall
2675 Die-cut paper and board
2676 Sanitary paper products
2677 Envelopes
2679 Converted paper products, nec

27 printing, publishing and allied industries
2711 Newspapers
2721 Periodicals
2731 Book publishing
2732 Book printing
2741 Miscellaneous publishing
2752 Commercial printing, lithographic
2754 Commercial printing, gravure
2759 Commercial printing, nec
2761 Manifold business forms
2771 Greeting cards
2782 Blankbooks and looseleaf binders
2789 Bookbinding and related work

SIC INDEX

SIC NO	PRODUCT
2791	Typesetting
2796	Platemaking services

28 chemicals and allied products

2812 Alkalies and chlorine
2813 Industrial gases
2819 Industrial inorganic chemicals, nec
2821 Plastics materials and resins
2822 Synthetic rubber
2823 Cellulosic manmade fibers
2834 Pharmaceutical preparations
2835 Diagnostic substances
2836 Biological products, except diagnostic
2841 Soap and other detergents
2842 Polishes and sanitation goods
2844 Toilet preparations
2851 Paints and allied products
2865 Cyclic crudes and intermediates
2869 Industrial organic chemicals, nec
2873 Nitrogenous fertilizers
2874 Phosphatic fertilizers
2875 Fertilizers, mixing only
2879 Agricultural chemicals, nec
2891 Adhesives and sealants
2899 Chemical preparations, nec

29 petroleum refining and related industries

2911 Petroleum refining
2951 Asphalt paving mixtures and blocks
2952 Asphalt felts and coatings
2992 Lubricating oils and greases
2999 Petroleum and coal products, nec

30 rubber and miscellaneous plastic products

3011 Tires and inner tubes
3021 Rubber and plastics footwear
3052 Rubber and plastics hose and beltings
3053 Gaskets; packing and sealing devices
3061 Mechanical rubber goods
3069 Fabricated rubber products, nec
3081 Unsupported plastics film and sheet
3082 Unsupported plastics profile shapes
3083 Laminated plastics plate and sheet
3085 Plastics bottles
3086 Plastics foam products
3087 Custom compound purchased resins
3088 Plastics plumbing fixtures
3089 Plastics products, nec

31 leather and leather products

3143 Men's footwear, except athletic
3144 Women's footwear, except athletic
3161 Luggage
3172 Personal leather goods, nec
3199 Leather goods, nec

32 stone, clay, glass, and concrete products

3211 Flat glass
3229 Pressed and blown glass, nec
3231 Products of purchased glass
3241 Cement, hydraulic
3261 Vitreous plumbing fixtures
3264 Porcelain electrical supplies
3269 Pottery products, nec
3271 Concrete block and brick
3272 Concrete products, nec
3273 Ready-mixed concrete
3274 Lime
3281 Cut stone and stone products
3291 Abrasive products
3295 Minerals, ground or treated
3296 Mineral wool
3299 Nonmetallic mineral products,

33 primary metal industries

3312 Blast furnaces and steel mills
3313 Electrometallurgical products
3315 Steel wire and related products
3316 Cold finishing of steel shapes
3317 Steel pipe and tubes
3321 Gray and ductile iron foundries
3324 Steel investment foundries

SIC NO	PRODUCT
3325	Steel foundries, nec
3339	Primary nonferrous metals, nec
3341	Secondary nonferrous metals
3353	Aluminum sheet, plate, and foil
3356	Nonferrous rolling and drawing, nec
3357	Nonferrous wiredrawing and insulating
3363	Aluminum die-castings
3364	Nonferrous die-castings except aluminum
3365	Aluminum foundries
3366	Copper foundries
3369	Nonferrous foundries, nec
3398	Metal heat treating
3399	Primary metal products

34 fabricated metal products

3411 Metal cans
3412 Metal barrels, drums, and pails
3421 Cutlery
3423 Hand and edge tools, nec
3429 Hardware, nec
3431 Metal sanitary ware
3432 Plumbing fixture fittings and trim
3433 Heating equipment, except electric
3441 Fabricated structural metal
3442 Metal doors, sash, and trim
3443 Fabricated plate work (boiler shop)
3444 Sheet metalwork
3446 Architectural metalwork
3448 Prefabricated metal buildings
3449 Miscellaneous metalwork
3451 Screw machine products
3452 Bolts, nuts, rivets, and washers
3462 Iron and steel forgings
3463 Nonferrous forgings
3465 Automotive stampings
3469 Metal stampings, nec
3471 Plating and polishing
3479 Metal coating and allied services
3491 Industrial valves
3492 Fluid power valves and hose fittings
3493 Steel springs, except wire
3494 Valves and pipe fittings, nec
3495 Wire springs
3496 Miscellaneous fabricated wire products
3497 Metal foil and leaf
3498 Fabricated pipe and fittings
3499 Fabricated metal products, nec

35 industrial and commercial machinery and computer equipment

3511 Turbines and turbine generator sets
3519 Internal combustion engines, nec
3523 Farm machinery and equipment
3524 Lawn and garden equipment
3531 Construction machinery
3532 Mining machinery
3533 Oil and gas field machinery
3534 Elevators and moving stairways
3535 Conveyors and conveying equipment
3536 Hoists, cranes, and monorails
3537 Industrial trucks and tractors
3541 Machine tools, metal cutting type
3542 Machine tools, metal forming type
3543 Industrial patterns
3544 Special dies, tools, jigs, and fixtures
3545 Machine tool accessories
3546 Power-driven handtools
3547 Rolling mill machinery
3549 Metalworking machinery, nec
3552 Textile machinery
3553 Woodworking machinery
3554 Paper industries machinery
3555 Printing trades machinery
3556 Food products machinery
3559 Special industry machinery, nec
3561 Pumps and pumping equipment
3562 Ball and roller bearings
3563 Air and gas compressors
3564 Blowers and fans
3565 Packaging machinery
3566 Speed changers, drives, and gears
3567 Industrial furnaces and ovens

SIC NO	PRODUCT
3568	Power transmission equipment, nec
3569	General industrial machinery,
3571	Electronic computers
3572	Computer storage devices
3575	Computer terminals
3577	Computer peripheral equipment, nec
3579	Office machines, nec
3581	Automatic vending machines
3585	Refrigeration and heating equipment
3586	Measuring and dispensing pumps
3589	Service industry machinery, nec
3593	Fluid power cylinders and actuators
3594	Fluid power pumps and motors
3596	Scales and balances, except laboratory
3599	Industrial machinery, nec

36 electronic & other electrical equipment & components

3612 Transformers, except electric
3613 Switchgear and switchboard apparatus
3621 Motors and generators
3624 Carbon and graphite products
3625 Relays and industrial controls
3629 Electrical industrial apparatus
3631 Household cooking equipment
3632 Household refrigerators and freezers
3633 Household laundry equipment
3634 Electric housewares and fans
3635 Household vacuum cleaners
3639 Household appliances, nec
3643 Current-carrying wiring devices
3644 Noncurrent-carrying wiring devices
3646 Commercial lighting fixtures
3647 Vehicular lighting equipment
3648 Lighting equipment, nec
3651 Household audio and video equipment
3661 Telephone and telegraph apparatus
3663 Radio and t.v. communications equipment
3669 Communications equipment, nec
3672 Printed circuit boards
3674 Semiconductors and related devices
3676 Electronic resistors
3677 Electronic coils and transformers
3678 Electronic connectors
3679 Electronic components, nec
3694 Engine electrical equipment
3699 Electrical equipment and supplies, nec

37 transportation equipment

3711 Motor vehicles and car bodies
3713 Truck and bus bodies
3714 Motor vehicle parts and accessories
3715 Truck trailers
3724 Aircraft engines and engine parts
3728 Aircraft parts and equipment, nec
3731 Shipbuilding and repairing
3732 Boatbuilding and repairing
3743 Railroad equipment
3751 Motorcycles, bicycles, and parts
3761 Guided missiles and space vehicles
3769 Space vehicle equipment, nec
3792 Travel trailers and campers
3795 Tanks and tank components
3799 Transportation equipment, nec

38 measuring, photographic, medical, & optical goods, & clocks

3812 Search and navigation equipment
3821 Laboratory apparatus and furniture
3822 Environmental controls
3823 Process control instruments
3824 Fluid meters and counting devices
3825 Instruments to measure electricity
3826 Analytical instruments
3827 Optical instruments and lenses
3829 Measuring and controlling devices, nec
3841 Surgical and medical instruments
3842 Surgical appliances and supplies
3843 Dental equipment and supplies
3844 X-ray apparatus and tubes
3845 Electromedical equipment
3851 Ophthalmic goods
3861 Photographic equipment and supplies

SIC INDEX

SIC NO	PRODUCT
3873	Watches, clocks, watchcases, and parts

39 miscellaneous manufacturing industries

- 3911 Jewelry, precious metal
- 3931 Musical instruments
- 3944 Games, toys, and children's vehicles
- 3949 Sporting and athletic goods, nec
- 3953 Marking devices
- 3955 Carbon paper and inked ribbons
- 3965 Fasteners, buttons, needles, and pins
- 3991 Brooms and brushes
- 3993 Signs and advertising specialties
- 3999 Manufacturing industries, nec

40 railroad transportation

- 4011 Railroads, line-haul operating
- 4013 Switching and terminal services

41 local & suburban transit & interurban highway transportation

- 4111 Local and suburban transit
- 4119 Local passenger transportation, nec
- 4121 Taxicabs
- 4131 Intercity and rural bus transportation
- 4141 Local bus charter service
- 4142 Bus charter service, except local
- 4151 School buses
- 4173 Bus terminal and service facilities

42 motor freight transportation

- 4212 Local trucking, without storage
- 4213 Trucking, except local
- 4214 Local trucking with storage
- 4215 Courier services, except by air
- 4221 Farm product warehousing and storage
- 4222 Refrigerated warehousing and storage
- 4225 General warehousing and storage
- 4226 Special warehousing and storage, nec
- 4231 Trucking terminal facilities

44 water transportation

- 4412 Deep sea foreign transportation of freight
- 4432 Freight transportation on the great lakes
- 4449 Water transportation of freight
- 4491 Marine cargo handling
- 4492 Towing and tugboat service
- 4493 Marinas
- 4499 Water transportation services, nec

45 transportation by air

- 4512 Air transportation, scheduled
- 4513 Air courier services
- 4522 Air transportation, nonscheduled
- 4581 Airports, flying fields, and services

46 pipelines, except natural gas

- 4612 Crude petroleum pipelines
- 4613 Refined petroleum pipelines

47 transportation services

- 4724 Travel agencies
- 4729 Passenger transportation arrangement
- 4731 Freight transportation arrangement
- 4741 Rental of railroad cars
- 4783 Packing and crating
- 4785 Inspection and fixed facilities
- 4789 Transportation services, nec

48 communications

- 4812 Radiotelephone communication
- 4813 Telephone communication, except radio
- 4822 Telegraph and other communications
- 4832 Radio broadcasting stations
- 4833 Television broadcasting stations
- 4841 Cable and other pay television services
- 4899 Communication services, nec

49 electric, gas and sanitary services

- 4911 Electric services
- 4922 Natural gas transmission
- 4923 Gas transmission and distribution
- 4924 Natural gas distribution
- 4925 Gas production and/or distribution
- 4931 Electric and other services combined
- 4932 Gas and other services combined
- 4939 Combination utilities, nec
- 4941 Water supply
- 4952 Sewerage systems
- 4953 Refuse systems
- 4959 Sanitary services, nec
- 4961 Steam and air-conditioning supply
- 4971 Irrigation systems

50 wholesale trade - durable goods

- 5012 Automobiles and other motor vehicles
- 5013 Motor vehicle supplies and new parts
- 5014 Tires and tubes
- 5015 Motor vehicle parts, used
- 5021 Furniture
- 5023 Homefurnishings
- 5031 Lumber, plywood, and millwork
- 5032 Brick, stone, and related material
- 5033 Roofing, siding, and insulation
- 5039 Construction materials, nec
- 5043 Photographic equipment and supplies
- 5044 Office equipment
- 5045 Computers, peripherals, and software
- 5046 Commercial equipment, nec
- 5047 Medical and hospital equipment
- 5048 Ophthalmic goods
- 5049 Professional equipment, nec
- 5051 Metals service centers and offices
- 5052 Coal and other minerals and ores
- 5063 Electrical apparatus and equipment
- 5064 Electrical appliances, television and radio
- 5065 Electronic parts and equipment, nec
- 5072 Hardware
- 5074 Plumbing and hydronic heating supplies
- 5075 Warm air heating and air conditioning
- 5078 Refrigeration equipment and supplies
- 5082 Construction and mining machinery
- 5083 Farm and garden machinery
- 5084 Industrial machinery and equipment
- 5085 Industrial supplies
- 5087 Service establishment equipment
- 5088 Transportation equipment and supplies
- 5091 Sporting and recreation goods
- 5092 Toys and hobby goods and supplies
- 5093 Scrap and waste materials
- 5094 Jewelry and precious stones
- 5099 Durable goods, nec

51 wholesale trade - nondurable goods

- 5111 Printing and writing paper
- 5112 Stationery and office supplies
- 5113 Industrial and personal service paper
- 5122 Drugs, proprietaries, and sundries
- 5131 Piece goods and notions
- 5136 Men's and boy's clothing
- 5137 Women's and children's clothing
- 5139 Footwear
- 5141 Groceries, general line
- 5142 Packaged frozen goods
- 5143 Dairy products, except dried or canned
- 5144 Poultry and poultry products
- 5145 Confectionery
- 5146 Fish and seafoods
- 5147 Meats and meat products
- 5148 Fresh fruits and vegetables
- 5149 Groceries and related products, nec
- 5153 Grain and field beans
- 5154 Livestock
- 5162 Plastics materials and basic shapes
- 5169 Chemicals and allied products, nec
- 5171 Petroleum bulk stations and terminals
- 5172 Petroleum products, nec
- 5181 Beer and ale
- 5182 Wine and distilled beverages
- 5191 Farm supplies
- 5192 Books, periodicals, and newspapers
- 5193 Flowers and florists supplies
- 5194 Tobacco and tobacco products
- 5198 Paints, varnishes, and supplies
- 5199 Nondurable goods, nec

52 building materials, hardware, garden supplies & mobile homes

- 5211 Lumber and other building materials
- 5231 Paint, glass, and wallpaper stores
- 5251 Hardware stores
- 5261 Retail nurseries and garden stores

53 general merchandise stores

- 5311 Department stores
- 5331 Variety stores
- 5399 Miscellaneous general merchandise

54 food stores

- 5411 Grocery stores
- 5421 Meat and fish markets
- 5431 Fruit and vegetable markets
- 5441 Candy, nut, and confectionery stores
- 5451 Dairy products stores
- 5461 Retail bakeries
- 5499 Miscellaneous food stores

55 automotive dealers and gasoline service stations

- 5511 New and used car dealers
- 5521 Used car dealers
- 5531 Auto and home supply stores
- 5541 Gasoline service stations
- 5551 Boat dealers
- 5561 Recreational vehicle dealers
- 5571 Motorcycle dealers
- 5599 Automotive dealers, nec

56 apparel and accessory stores

- 5611 Men's and boys' clothing stores
- 5621 Women's clothing stores
- 5632 Women's accessory and specialty stores
- 5641 Children's and infants' wear stores
- 5661 Shoe stores
- 5699 Miscellaneous apparel and accessories

57 home furniture, furnishings and equipment stores

- 5712 Furniture stores
- 5713 Floor covering stores
- 5714 Drapery and upholstery stores
- 5719 Miscellaneous homefurnishings
- 5722 Household appliance stores
- 5731 Radio, television, and electronic stores
- 5734 Computer and software stores
- 5736 Musical instrument stores

58 eating and drinking places

- 5812 Eating places
- 5813 Drinking places

59 miscellaneous retail

- 5912 Drug stores and proprietary stores
- 5921 Liquor stores
- 5932 Used merchandise stores
- 5941 Sporting goods and bicycle shops
- 5942 Book stores
- 5943 Stationery stores
- 5944 Jewelry stores
- 5945 Hobby, toy, and game shops
- 5946 Camera and photographic supply stores
- 5947 Gift, novelty, and souvenir shop
- 5949 Sewing, needlework, and piece goods
- 5961 Catalog and mail-order houses
- 5962 Merchandising machine operators
- 5963 Direct selling establishments
- 5983 Fuel oil dealers
- 5984 Liquefied petroleum gas dealers
- 5989 Fuel dealers, nec
- 5992 Florists
- 5993 Tobacco stores and stands
- 5994 News dealers and newsstands
- 5995 Optical goods stores
- 5999 Miscellaneous retail stores, nec

60 depository institutions

- 6021 National commercial banks
- 6022 State commercial banks
- 6029 Commercial banks, nec
- 6035 Federal savings institutions

SIC INDEX

SIC NO	PRODUCT
6036	Savings institutions, except federal
6061	Federal credit unions
6062	State credit unions
6099	Functions related to depository banking

61 nondepository credit institutions

6111	Federal and federally sponsored credit
6141	Personal credit institutions
6153	Short-term business credit
6159	Miscellaneous business credit
6162	Mortgage bankers and correspondents
6163	Loan brokers

62 security & commodity brokers, dealers, exchanges & services

6211	Security brokers and dealers
6221	Commodity contracts brokers, dealers
6231	Security and commodity exchanges
6282	Investment advice

63 insurance carriers

6311	Life insurance
6321	Accident and health insurance
6324	Hospital and medical service plans
6331	Fire, marine, and casualty insurance
6351	Surety insurance
6361	Title insurance
6371	Pension, health, and welfare funds
6399	Insurance carriers, nec

64 insurance agents, brokers and service

6411	Insurance agents, brokers, and service

65 real estate

6512	Nonresidential building operators
6513	Apartment building operators
6514	Dwelling operators, except apartments
6519	Real property lessors, nec
6531	Real estate agents and managers
6541	Title abstract offices
6552	Subdividers and developers, nec
6553	Cemetery subdividers and developers

67 holding and other investment offices

6712	Bank holding companies
6719	Holding companies, nec
6722	Management investment, open-ended
6726	Investment offices, nec
6732	Trusts: educational, religious, etc.
6733	Trusts, nec
6794	Patent owners and lessors
6798	Real estate investment trusts
6799	Investors, nec

70 hotels, rooming houses, camps, and other lodging places

7011	Hotels and motels
7021	Rooming and boarding houses
7032	Sporting and recreational camps
7033	Trailer parks and campsites
7041	Membership-basis organization hotels

72 personal services

7211	Power laundries, family and commercial
7212	Garment pressing and cleaners' agents
7213	Linen supply
7215	Coin-operated laundries and cleaning
7216	Drycleaning plants, except rugs
7217	Carpet and upholstery cleaning
7218	Industrial launderers
7219	Laundry and garment services, nec
7221	Photographic studios, portrait
7231	Beauty shops
7241	Barber shops
7261	Funeral service and crematories
7291	Tax return preparation services
7299	Miscellaneous personal services

73 business services

7311	Advertising agencies
7312	Outdoor advertising services
7313	Radio, television, publisher representatives
7319	Advertising, nec
7322	Adjustment and collection services
7323	Credit reporting services
7331	Direct mail advertising services
7334	Photocopying and duplicating services
7335	Commercial photography
7336	Commercial art and graphic design
7338	Secretarial and court reporting
7342	Disinfecting and pest control services
7349	Building maintenance services, nec
7352	Medical equipment rental
7353	Heavy construction equipment rental
7359	Equipment rental and leasing, nec
7361	Employment agencies
7363	Help supply services
7371	Custom computer programming services
7372	Prepackaged software
7373	Computer integrated systems design
7374	Data processing and preparation
7375	Information retrieval services
7376	Computer facilities management
7377	Computer rental and leasing
7378	Computer maintenance and repair
7379	Computer related services, nec
7381	Detective and armored car services
7382	Security systems services
7384	Photofinish laboratories
7389	Business services, nec

75 automotive repair, services and parking

7513	Truck rental and leasing, without drivers
7514	Passenger car rental
7515	Passenger car leasing
7519	Utility trailer rental
7521	Automobile parking
7532	Top and body repair and paint shops
7533	Auto exhaust system repair shops
7534	Tire retreading and repair shops
7536	Automotive glass replacement shops
7537	Automotive transmission repair shops
7538	General automotive repair shops
7539	Automotive repair shops, nec
7542	Carwashes
7549	Automotive services, nec

76 miscellaneous repair services

7622	Radio and television repair
7623	Refrigeration service and repair
7629	Electrical repair shops
7631	Watch, clock, and jewelry repair
7641	Reupholstery and furniture repair
7692	Welding repair
7694	Armature rewinding shops
7699	Repair services, nec

78 motion pictures

7812	Motion picture and video production
7819	Services allied to motion pictures
7822	Motion picture and tape distribution
7832	Motion picture theaters, except drive-in
7841	Video tape rental

79 amusement and recreation services

7911	Dance studios, schools, and halls
7922	Theatrical producers and services
7929	Entertainers and entertainment groups
7933	Bowling centers
7941	Sports clubs, managers, and promoters
7948	Racing, including track operation
7991	Physical fitness facilities
7992	Public golf courses
7993	Coin-operated amusement devices
7996	Amusement parks
7997	Membership sports and recreation clubs
7999	Amusement and recreation, nec

80 health services

8011	Offices and clinics of medical doctors
8021	Offices and clinics of dentists
8031	Offices and clinics of osteopathic physicians
8041	Offices and clinics of chiropractors
8042	Offices and clinics of optometrists
8043	Offices and clinics of podiatrists
8049	Offices of health practitioner
8051	Skilled nursing care facilities
8052	Intermediate care facilities
8059	Nursing and personal care, nec
8062	General medical and surgical hospitals
8063	Psychiatric hospitals
8069	Specialty hospitals, except psychiatric
8071	Medical laboratories
8072	Dental laboratories
8082	Home health care services
8092	Kidney dialysis centers
8093	Specialty outpatient clinics, nec
8099	Health and allied services, nec

81 legal services

8111	Legal services

82 educational services

8211	Elementary and secondary schools
8221	Colleges and universities
8222	Junior colleges
8231	Libraries
8243	Data processing schools
8249	Vocational schools, nec
8299	Schools and educational services

83 social services

8322	Individual and family services
8331	Job training and related services
8351	Child day care services
8361	Residential care
8399	Social services, nec

84 museums, art galleries and botanical and zoological gardens

8412	Museums and art galleries
8422	Botanical and zoological gardens

86 membership organizations

8611	Business associations
8621	Professional organizations
8631	Labor organizations
8641	Civic and social associations
8651	Political organizations
8661	Religious organizations
8699	Membership organizations, nec

87 engineering, accounting, research, and management services

8711	Engineering services
8712	Architectural services
8713	Surveying services
8721	Accounting, auditing, and bookkeeping
8731	Commercial physical research
8732	Commercial nonphysical research
8733	Noncommercial research organizations
8734	Testing laboratories
8741	Management services
8742	Management consulting services
8743	Public relations services
8744	Facilities support services
8748	Business consulting, nec

89 services, not elsewhere classified

8999	Services, nec

91 executive, legislative & general government, except finance

9111	Executive offices
9121	Legislative bodies
9199	General government, nec

92 justice, public order and safety

9211	Courts
9221	Police protection
9222	Legal counsel and prosecution
9223	Correctional institutions
9224	Fire protection
9229	Public order and safety, nec

93 public finance, taxation and monetary policy

SIC INDEX

SIC NO	PRODUCT

9311 Finance, taxation, and monetary policy

94 administration of human resource programs
9431 Administration of public health programs
9441 Administration of social and manpower programs
9451 Administration of veterans' affairs

95 administration of environmental quality and housing programs
9511 Air, water, and solid waste management
9512 Land, mineral, and wildlife conservation
9531 Housing programs
9532 Urban and community development

96 administration of economic programs
9611 Administration of general economic programs
9621 Regulation, administration of transportation

97 national security and international affairs
9711 National security

SIC SECTION

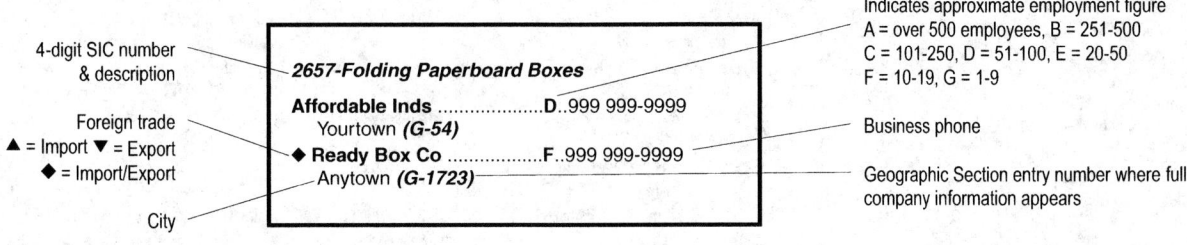

- The SIC codes in this section are from the latest Standard Industrial Classification manual published by the U.S. Government's Office of Management and Budget. For more information regarding SICs, see the Explanatory Notes.
- Companies may be listed under multiple classifications.

01 AGRICULTURAL PRODUCTION - CROPS

0115 Corn

Milky Acres LLC .... E 419 561-1364
  Sycamore *(G-13532)*

0119 Cash grains, nec

Hertzfeld Poultry Farms Inc .... D 419 832-2070
  Grand Rapids *(G-8845)*
McMaster Farms LLC .... D 330 482-2913
  Columbiana *(G-5237)*

0134 Irish potatoes

McMaster Farms LLC .... D 330 482-2913
  Columbiana *(G-5237)*
Mrs Dennis Potato Farm Inc .... E 419 335-2778
  Wauseon *(G-14606)*

0161 Vegetables and melons

Chefs Garden Inc .... C 419 433-4947
  Huron *(G-9385)*
Holthouse Farms of Ohio Inc .... C 419 935-0151
  Willard *(G-15168)*
Kingsway Farm & Storage Inc .... E 330 877-6241
  Hartville *(G-9128)*
McMaster Farms LLC .... D 330 482-2913
  Columbiana *(G-5237)*
Wiers Farm Incorporated .... E 419 935-0131
  Willard *(G-15175)*

0172 Grapes

Mapleside Valley LLC .... D 330 225-5576
  Brunswick *(G-1462)*

0175 Deciduous tree fruits

Irons Fruit Farm .... E 513 932-2853
  Lebanon *(G-9769)*
Mapleside Valley LLC .... D 330 225-5576
  Brunswick *(G-1462)*

0181 Ornamental nursery products

A Brown and Sons Nursery Inc .... D 937 836-5826
  Brookville *(G-1444)*
▲ Aris Horticulture Inc .... D 330 745-2143
  Barberton *(G-693)*
Barnes Nursery Inc .... E 800 421-8722
  Huron *(G-9384)*
Cottage Gardens Inc .... D 440 259-2900
  Perry *(G-12305)*
▲ Cuthbert Greenhouse Inc .... E 614 836-3866
  Groveport *(G-8981)*
Davey Tree Expert Company .... C 330 673-9511
  Kent *(G-9570)*
Deans Greenhouse Inc .... E 440 871-2050
  Cleveland *(G-4158)*
Deckers Nursery Inc .... E 614 836-2130
  Groveport *(G-8982)*
▲ Dummen Na Inc .... E 614 850-9551
  Columbus *(G-5789)*
Green Circle Growers Inc .... B 440 775-1411
  Oberlin *(G-12070)*
◆ Green Circle Growers Inc .... C 440 775-1411
  Oberlin *(G-12069)*
Henderson Turf Farm Inc .... E 937 748-1559
  Franklin *(G-8640)*
HJ Benken Flor & Greenhouses .... E 513 891-1040
  Cincinnati *(G-2830)*
▲ Lakewood Greenhouse Inc .... E 419 691-3541
  Perrysburg *(G-12352)*
Lowes Investments Inc .... E 440 543-5123
  Chagrin Falls *(G-1984)*
Maria Gardens LLC .... E 440 238-7637
  Strongsville *(G-13474)*
Mike Ward Landscaping LLC .... E 513 683-6436
  Maineville *(G-10228)*
North Branch Nursery Inc .... E 419 287-4679
  Pemberville *(G-12290)*
▲ Ohlman Farm & Greenhouse Inc .... E 419 535-5586
  Toledo *(G-13949)*
R & S Halley and Company Inc .... E 614 771-0388
  Plain City *(G-12491)*
▲ Rwam Bros Inc .... E 419 826-3671
  Swanton *(G-13528)*
Sln Nursery LLC .... E 937 845-3130
  Franklin *(G-8650)*
Studebaker Nurseries Inc .... E 800 845-0584
  New Carlisle *(G-11607)*
▲ Thorsens Greenhouse LLC .... E 740 363-5069
  Delaware *(G-7830)*
Timbuk Farms Inc .... D 740 587-2178
  Granville *(G-8855)*
▲ Willoway Nurseries Inc .... C 440 934-4435
  Avon *(G-669)*
▲ Willowbend Nurseries LLC .... E 440 259-3121
  Perry *(G-12312)*
Wilsons Hillview Farm Inc .... E 740 763-2873
  Newark *(G-11755)*

0182 Food crops grown under cover

80 Acres Urban Agriculture Inc .... D 888 547-1569
  Hamilton *(G-9015)*

0191 General farms, primarily crop

Clovervale Farms LLC .... D 440 960-0146
  Amherst *(G-426)*
Deerfield Farms .... E 330 584-4715
  Deerfield *(G-7740)*
Enterprise Hill Farm Inc .... E 419 668-0242
  Norwalk *(G-12009)*
Family Farm & Home Inc .... E 419 783-1702
  Defiance *(G-7745)*
Hannah Farm LLC .... E 419 295-3929
  Bloomville *(G-1118)*
Hasselkus Farms Inc .... E 419 862-3735
  Elmore *(G-8230)*
Heimerl Farms Ltd .... E 740 967-0063
  Johnstown *(G-9546)*
Henderson Turf Farm Inc .... E 937 748-1559
  Franklin *(G-8640)*
Herb Thyme Farms Inc .... B 866 386-0854
  Perrysburg *(G-12342)*
Hertzfeld Poultry Farms Inc .... D 419 832-2070
  Grand Rapids *(G-8845)*
Holthouse Farms of Ohio Inc .... C 419 935-0151
  Willard *(G-15168)*
I-O Properties LLC .... C 419 852-7836
  Coldwater *(G-5214)*
Nature Fresh Farms Usa Inc .... E 419 330-5080
  Delta *(G-7853)*
Ohio Ecological Fd & Frm Assn .... E 614 421-2022
  Columbus *(G-6415)*
Rhoads Farm Inc .... D 740 404-5696
  Circleville *(G-3720)*
Rohrs Farms .... E 419 757-0110
  Mc Guffey *(G-10802)*
Sugar Creek Vly Frm & Game CLB .... E 330 492-3071
  Canton *(G-1863)*

02 AGRICULTURAL PRODUCTION - LIVESTOCK AND ANIMAL SPECIALTIES

0213 Hogs

Shur-Green Farms LLC .... D 937 547-9633
  Ansonia *(G-446)*
Winner Corporation .... E 419 582-4321
  Yorkshire *(G-15538)*

0219 General livestock, nec

Pork Champ LLC .... E 740 493-2164
  Lucasville *(G-10179)*

02 AGRICULTURAL PRODUCTION - LIVESTOCK AND ANIMAL SPECIALTIES

0241 Dairy farms

▲ Miceli Dairy Products Co................... D 216 791-6222
   Cleveland *(G-4572)*

Milky Acres LLC................................. E 419 561-1364
   Sycamore *(G-13532)*

Youngs Jersey Dairy Inc...................... B 937 325-0629
   Yellow Springs *(G-15537)*

0252 Chicken eggs

Cal-Maine Foods Inc............................ D 937 337-9576
   Rossburg *(G-12764)*

▲ Daylay Egg Farm Inc............................ C 937 355-6531
   West Mansfield *(G-14862)*

▲ Weaver Bros Inc................................. D 937 526-3907
   Versailles *(G-14417)*

0253 Turkeys and turkey eggs

Cooper Hatchery Inc............................ C 419 594-3325
   Oakwood *(G-12053)*

V H Cooper & Co Inc........................... C 419 375-4116
   Fort Recovery *(G-8611)*

0254 Poultry hatcheries

Cooper Hatchery Inc............................ C 419 594-3325
   Oakwood *(G-12053)*

Falling Star Farm Ltd........................... E 419 945-2651
   Polk *(G-12512)*

0291 General farms, primarily animals

Pork Champ LLC................................. E 740 493-2164
   Lucasville *(G-10179)*

07 AGRICULTURAL SERVICES

0711 Soil preparation services

Henderson Turf Farm Inc...................... E 937 748-1559
   Franklin *(G-8640)*

Locus AG Solutions LLC....................... E 440 248-8787
   Solon *(G-13105)*

0721 Crop planting and protection

Rentokil North America Inc................... E 440 964-5641
   Ashtabula *(G-547)*

0723 Crop preparation services for market

Andersons Inc..................................... C 419 893-5050
   Maumee *(G-10692)*

Custom Agri Systems Inc...................... E 419 209-0940
   Upper Sandusky *(G-14287)*

F L Emmert Company........................... E 513 721-5808
   Cincinnati *(G-2645)*

Freshealth LLC.................................... D 614 231-3601
   Columbus *(G-5895)*

Great Lakes Packers Inc....................... E 419 483-2956
   Bellevue *(G-1045)*

0724 Cotton ginning

▼ Compass Systems & Sales LLC........ D 330 733-2111
   Norton *(G-11993)*

0741 Veterinary services for livestock

Howland Crners Twne Cntry Vtrn........... E 330 856-1862
   Warren *(G-14526)*

Tri County Veterinary Service................. E 937 693-2131
   Anna *(G-444)*

0742 Veterinary services, specialties

Animal Care Unlimited Inc..................... E 614 766-2317
   Columbus *(G-5370)*

Animal Hospital Inc............................. E 440 946-2800
   Willoughby Hills *(G-15230)*

Annehurst Veterinary Hospital................ E 614 818-4221
   Westerville *(G-14959)*

Avon Lake Vet Holdings Inc................... E 440 933-5297
   Avon Lake *(G-674)*

Beechwold Veterinary Hospital............... E 614 268-8666
   Columbus *(G-5430)*

Best Frnds Veterinary Hosp Inc.............. E 614 889-7387
   Powell *(G-12586)*

Bigger Road Veterinary Clinic................. E 937 435-3262
   Dayton *(G-7194)*

Cincinnati Anmal Rfrral Emrgnc.............. D 513 530-0911
   Cincinnati *(G-2393)*

Colerain Animal Clinic Inc..................... E 513 923-4400
   Cincinnati *(G-2475)*

Daniel N Rizek.................................... D 614 895-0006
   Westerville *(G-14975)*

Howland Crners Twne Cntry Vtrn........... E 330 856-1862
   Warren *(G-14526)*

Keith E Huston DVM Llc..................... E 440 461-2226
   Cleveland *(G-4453)*

Kings Veterinary Hospital...................... E 513 697-0400
   Loveland *(G-10145)*

Knapp Veterinary Hospital Inc................ E 614 267-3124
   Columbus *(G-6123)*

Madeira Veterinary Hospital................... E 513 561-7467
   Cincinnati *(G-3001)*

Medical Management Intl Inc................. E 937 325-4509
   Vandalia *(G-14383)*

Medvet Associates Inc......................... D 937 293-2714
   Moraine *(G-11423)*

Medvet Associates LLC........................ D 614 829-5070
   Canal Winchester *(G-1612)*

Medvet Associates LLC........................ C 513 561-0069
   Cincinnati *(G-3034)*

Medvet Associates LLC........................ C 216 362-6000
   Cleveland *(G-4548)*

Medvet Associates LLC........................ D 614 870-0480
   Columbus *(G-6224)*

Medvet Associates LLC........................ C 330 665-4996
   Copley *(G-6961)*

Medvet Associates LLC........................ E 330 530-8387
   Girard *(G-8820)*

Medvet Associates LLC........................ C 937 293-2714
   Moraine *(G-11424)*

Medvet Associates LLC........................ D 419 473-0328
   Toledo *(G-13914)*

Medvet Associates LLC........................ B 614 486-5800
   Worthington *(G-15435)*

Medvet Associates LLC........................ B 614 846-5800
   Worthington *(G-15436)*

Medvet California LLC.......................... D 614 846-5800
   Worthington *(G-15437)*

Medvet Louisiana LLC.......................... D 614 846-5800
   Worthington *(G-15438)*

Medvet Texas LLC.............................. D 682 223-9770
   Worthington *(G-15439)*

Northern Ohio Animal Healthcar............. E 419 499-4949
   Milan *(G-11209)*

Northstar Animal Care.......................... D 614 846-5800
   Columbus *(G-6370)*

Obetz Animal Hospital......................... E 614 491-5676
   Columbus *(G-6381)*

Ohio State University........................... E 614 292-6661
   Columbus *(G-6455)*

Petsmart LLC..................................... E 614 418-9389
   Columbus *(G-6518)*

Robert C Barney Dvm Inc..................... E 216 221-5380
   Lakewood *(G-9682)*

Stow-Kent Animal Hospital Inc............... E 330 673-1002
   Kent *(G-9599)*

Stow-Kent Animal Hospital Inc............... E 330 673-0049
   Kent *(G-9598)*

Suburban Veterinarian Clinic.................. E 937 433-2160
   Dayton *(G-7649)*

Sylvania Veterinary Hospital.................. E 419 885-4421
   Sylvania *(G-13576)*

Tipp City Veterinary Hosp Inc................. D 937 667-8489
   Tipp City *(G-13665)*

Tri County Veterinary Service................. E 937 693-2131
   Anna *(G-444)*

Tri Zob Inc.. E 216 252-4500
   Cleveland *(G-5036)*

VCA Animal Hospitals Inc..................... E 419 423-7232
   Findlay *(G-8596)*

VCA Animal Hospitals Inc..................... E 419 841-3323
   Toledo *(G-14091)*

Vetrad LLC.. E 888 483-8723
   Worthington *(G-15466)*

Village Veterinary Clinic........................ E 440 461-2226
   Cleveland *(G-5107)*

West Toledo Animal Hosp Ltd................ E 419 475-1527
   Toledo *(G-14105)*

0751 Livestock services, except veterinary

Frenchies of Ig LLC............................. E 513 445-2841
   West Chester *(G-14696)*

Hertzfeld Poultry Farms Inc................... D 419 832-2070
   Grand Rapids *(G-8845)*

Landes Fresh Meats Inc....................... E 937 836-3613
   Clayton *(G-3734)*

Select Sires Inc.................................. C 614 873-4683
   Plain City *(G-12494)*

Winner Corporation............................. E 419 582-4321
   Yorkshire *(G-15538)*

0752 Animal specialty services

4 Paws For Ability Inc.......................... D 937 374-0385
   Xenia *(G-15497)*

Animal Care Unlimited Inc..................... E 614 766-2317
   Columbus *(G-5370)*

Annehurst Veterinary Hospital................ E 614 818-4221
   Westerville *(G-14959)*

Avon Lake Vet Holdings Inc................... E 440 933-5297
   Avon Lake *(G-674)*

City of Wadsworth............................... E 330 334-1581
   Wadsworth *(G-14431)*

Coba/Select Sires Inc.......................... D 614 878-5333
   Columbus *(G-5590)*

Csa Animal Nutrition LLC..................... E 866 615-8084
   Dayton *(G-7264)*

◆ Heading4ward Investment Co........... D 937 293-9994
   Moraine *(G-11416)*

Petsmart Inc..................................... E 513 336-0365
   Mason *(G-10591)*

Petsmart LLC..................................... E 614 418-9389
   Columbus *(G-6518)*

Wolf and Woof LLC............................. E 614 527-2267
   Hilliard *(G-9246)*

0781 Landscape counseling and planning

▲ Acro Tool & Die Company................. E 330 773-5173
   Akron *(G-14)*

All Ohio Landscaping Inc...................... D 330 650-2226
   Hudson *(G-9329)*

Bellas Lawn & Landscape LLC............... E 419 536-9003
   Toledo *(G-13703)*

Blendon Gardens Inc........................... E 614 840-0500
   Lewis Center *(G-9811)*

Bremec Group Inc............................... E 440 951-0770
   Chesterland *(G-2032)*

Brightview Landscape Svcs Inc............... C 614 478-2085
   Columbus *(G-5466)*

Burgess & Niple Inc............................. D 703 631-6041
   Columbus *(G-5486)*

07 AGRICULTURAL SERVICES

Civil & Environmental Cons Inc............ E 513 985-0226
  Blue Ash *(G-1150)*
Collaborative Inc.................................... E 419 242-7405
  Toledo *(G-13748)*
Evans Landscaping Inc........................... E 513 271-1119
  Cincinnati *(G-2639)*
Five Seasons Landscape MGT Inc......... D 740 964-2915
  Etna *(G-8329)*
Garmann/Miller & Assoc Inc.................. E 419 628-4240
  Minster *(G-11316)*
Green Impressions LLC......................... D 440 240-8508
  Sheffield Village *(G-12998)*
Greenscapes Landscape Co Inc.............. D 614 837-1869
  Columbus *(G-5955)*
Hemlock Landscapes Inc........................ E 440 247-3631
  Chagrin Falls *(G-1978)*
HWH Archtcts-Ngnrs-Plnners Inc........... D 216 875-4000
  Cleveland *(G-4394)*
Immaculate Landscapers LLC................ E 440 724-1024
  Wickliffe *(G-15153)*
Impullitti Landscaping LLC................... D 440 834-1866
  Burton *(G-1530)*
Ironsite Inc... E 740 965-4616
  Galena *(G-8736)*
Joes Ldscpg Beavercreek Inc.................. E 937 427-1133
  Beavercreek Township *(G-942)*
Klamfoth Inc... E 614 833-5007
  Canal Winchester *(G-1611)*
Kleingers Group Inc................................ D 513 779-7851
  West Chester *(G-14719)*
Lewis Landscaping & Nurs Inc............... E 330 666-2655
  Copley *(G-6959)*
Louderback Fmly Invstments Inc........... E 937 845-1762
  New Carlisle *(G-11604)*
Maslyk Landscaping Inc......................... E 440 748-3635
  Columbia Station *(G-5229)*
McGill Smith Punshon Inc..................... E 513 759-0004
  Cincinnati *(G-3023)*
Meyers Ldscp Svcs & Nurs Inc.............. E 614 210-1194
  Lewis Center *(G-9828)*
Mjs Snow & Landscape LLC.................. D 419 656-6724
  Port Clinton *(G-12538)*
Mksk Inc... D 614 621-2796
  Columbus *(G-6254)*
Mksk Inc... E 614 621-2796
  Columbus *(G-6253)*
Myers/Schmalenberger Inc..................... E 614 621-2796
  Columbus *(G-6285)*
▲ Oakland Nursery Inc............................ E 614 268-3834
  Columbus *(G-6380)*
Oaoc Enterprise Inc................................ E 216 584-8677
  Cleveland *(G-4678)*
Pattie Group Inc..................................... D 440 338-1288
  Novelty *(G-12041)*
Peabody Landscape Cnstr Inc................ D 614 488-2877
  Columbus *(G-6506)*
Professional Pavement Svcs LLC........... E 740 726-2222
  Delaware *(G-7821)*
Rentokil North America Inc................... E 614 837-0099
  Groveport *(G-8999)*
Royal Landscape Gardening Inc............. E 216 883-7000
  Cleveland *(G-4858)*
Sajovie Brothers Ldscpg Inc................... E 216 662-4983
  Maple Heights *(G-10345)*
Schill Ldscpg Lawn Care Svcs L............ D 513 271-5296
  Blue Ash *(G-1243)*
Schill Ldscpg Lawn Care Svcs L............ D 440 327-3030
  North Ridgeville *(G-11936)*
Seilers Landscaping Inc......................... E 513 791-2824
  Cincinnati *(G-3355)*
Site Group Inc....................................... E 937 845-7305
  New Carlisle *(G-11606)*
Suncrest Gardens Inc............................. C 330 650-4969
  Peninsula *(G-12294)*
Tucker Landscaping Inc......................... D 440 786-9840
  Bedford *(G-990)*
Yardmaster of Columbus Inc.................. E 614 863-4510
  Blacklick *(G-1115)*

0782 Lawn and garden services

4859 Hills & Dales Inc........................... D 330 479-9175
  Canton *(G-1649)*
Abbruzzese Brothers Inc........................ E 614 873-1550
  Plain City *(G-12465)*
American Beauty Landscaping............... E 330 788-1501
  Youngstown *(G-15548)*
Ameriscape Inc....................................... E 614 863-5400
  Blacklick *(G-1109)*
Archdiocese of Cincinnati...................... C 513 489-0300
  Cincinnati *(G-2213)*
Barnes Nursery Inc................................ E 800 421-8722
  Huron *(G-9384)*
Bellas Lawn & Landscape LLC.............. E 419 536-9003
  Toledo *(G-13703)*
Benchmark Landscape Cnstr Inc........... E 614 873-8080
  Plain City *(G-12469)*
Big Grens Lawn Svc Snow Plwing........ E 937 539-8163
  Bellefontaine *(G-1022)*
Bremec Group Inc.................................. E 440 951-0770
  Chesterland *(G-2032)*
Buck and Sons Ldscp Svc Inc............... E 614 876-5359
  Hilliard *(G-9186)*
Buckeye Ecocare..................................... E 937 435-4727
  Miamisburg *(G-11028)*
Centerville Landscaping Inc.................. E 937 433-5395
  Dayton *(G-7219)*
Chores Unlimited Inc............................ D 440 439-5455
  Cleveland *(G-3971)*
Davey Tree Expert Company................. C 330 673-9511
  Kent *(G-9570)*
▲ De Haven Home and Garden.............. E 419 227-7003
  Lima *(G-9883)*
Dell Willo Nursery Inc........................... E 419 289-0606
  Ashland *(G-496)*
Dennis Top Soil & Ldscpg Inc................ E 419 865-5656
  Toledo *(G-13775)*
Di Santo Companies Inc........................ E 216 292-7772
  Cleveland *(G-4164)*
Dta Inc.. E 419 529-2920
  Ontario *(G-12103)*
Edko LLC.. E 614 863-5946
  Columbus *(G-5808)*
Emsi Inc.. E 614 876-9988
  Plain City *(G-12475)*
Envirocare Lawn & Ldscp LLC............. E 419 874-6779
  Perrysburg *(G-12335)*
Forevergreen Lawn Care........................ E 440 327-8987
  North Ridgeville *(G-11928)*
Forevergreen Lawn Care Inc.................. E 440 376-7515
  Elyria *(G-8252)*
Germann Bros LLC................................. E 614 905-7314
  Lewis Center *(G-9822)*
Gonda Lawn Care LLC.......................... E 330 701-7232
  Masury *(G-10678)*
Grandmas Gardens Inc........................... E 937 885-2973
  Waynesville *(G-14623)*
Green Again Turf Inc............................. E 937 203-0693
  Vandalia *(G-14379)*
Green Impressions LLC......................... D 440 240-8508
  Sheffield Village *(G-12998)*
Green King Company Inc...................... E 614 861-4132
  Reynoldsburg *(G-12665)*
Greenscapes Landscape Co Inc.............. D 614 837-1869
  Columbus *(G-5955)*
Grizzly Golf Center Inc.......................... B 513 398-5200
  Mason *(G-10557)*
Groundspro LLC..................................... C 513 242-1700
  West Chester *(G-14701)*
Groundsystems Inc................................. E 937 903-5325
  Moraine *(G-11415)*
Groundsystems LLC............................... E 800 570-0213
  Blue Ash *(G-1180)*
Hemlock Landscapes Inc........................ E 440 247-3631
  Chagrin Falls *(G-1978)*
Henderson Turf Farm Inc....................... E 937 748-1559
  Franklin *(G-8640)*
Hyde Park Ldscp & Tree Svc Inc.......... E 513 731-1334
  Cincinnati *(G-2860)*
Keller Group Limited............................. E 614 866-9551
  Columbus *(G-6108)*
Klamfoth Inc... E 614 833-5007
  Canal Winchester *(G-1611)*
Kurtz Bros Central Ohio LLC................ E 614 873-2000
  Dublin *(G-8051)*
Miami Valley Memory Grdns Assn........ E 937 885-7779
  Dayton *(G-7497)*
Mike Ward Landscaping LLC................ E 513 683-6436
  Maineville *(G-10228)*
▲ Motz Group Inc................................... E 513 533-6452
  Cincinnati *(G-3081)*
North Branch Nursery Inc...................... E 419 287-4679
  Pemberville *(G-12290)*
Ohio Tpk & Infrastructure Comm.......... D 440 234-2081
  Berea *(G-1077)*
Ohio Tpk & Infrastructure Comm.......... D 440 234-2081
  Richfield *(G-12705)*
Ohio Tpk & Infrastructure Comm.......... D 330 527-2169
  Windham *(G-15288)*
Paramount Lawn Service Inc................. E 513 984-5200
  Loveland *(G-10157)*
Peter A Wimberly Company Inc............ E 513 271-2332
  Milford *(G-11248)*
R & S Halley and Company Inc............ E 614 771-0388
  Plain City *(G-12491)*
Richland Newhope Inds Inc................... C 419 774-4400
  Mansfield *(G-10313)*
River City Furniture LLC....................... E 513 612-7303
  West Chester *(G-14756)*
Rob Richter Landscaping Inc................. E 513 539-0300
  Monroe *(G-11350)*
Robiden Inc... E 513 421-0000
  Fairfield Township *(G-8464)*
Royal Landscape Gardening Inc............. E 216 883-7000
  Cleveland *(G-4858)*
Sand Road Enterprises Inc.................... E 419 668-3670
  Norwalk *(G-12026)*
Scherzinger Corporation......................... D 513 531-7848
  Cincinnati *(G-3347)*
Schill Ldscpg Lawn Care Svcs L............ D 440 327-3030
  North Ridgeville *(G-11936)*
♦ Scotts Company LLC.......................... C 937 644-0011
  Marysville *(G-10508)*
Siebenthaler Company............................ D 937 274-1154
  Beavercreek *(G-905)*
Suncrest Gardens Inc............................. C 330 650-4969
  Peninsula *(G-12294)*
Tccc Inc.. E 513 779-1111
  West Chester *(G-14841)*
Team Green Lawn LLC.......................... E 937 673-4315
  Xenia *(G-15533)*
TLC Landscaping LLC........................... E 440 248-4852
  Cleveland *(G-5021)*
Todds Enviroscapes Inc......................... C 330 875-0768
  Louisville *(G-10123)*
Turf Care Supply Corp........................... D 740 633-8247
  Martins Ferry *(G-10471)*

Employee Codes: A=Over 500 employees, B=251-500
C=101-250, D=51-100, E=20-50, F=10-19, G=1-9

2024 Harris Ohio
Services Directory

07 AGRICULTURAL SERVICES

Turfscape LLC .... C 330 405-7979
 Twinsburg (G-14224)
Universal Lawncare LLC .... E 513 289-9391
 Cincinnati (G-3562)
University of Cincinnati .... D 513 556-6381
 Cincinnati (G-3590)
Warstler Bros Landscaping Inc .... E 330 492-9500
 Canton (G-1883)
Wilson Enterprises Inc .... E 614 444-8873
 Columbus (G-6896)
Winn-Scapes Inc .... E 614 866-9466
 Gahanna (G-8734)
Wright Mulch Inc .... E 419 228-1173
 Lima (G-9988)
Yardmaster Inc .... D 440 357-8400
 Painesville (G-12244)
Ziehler Landscaping .... E 937 312-9575
 Dayton (G-7736)

0783 Ornamental shrub and tree services

Asplundh Tree Expert LLC .... E 740 467-1028
 Millersport (G-11297)
Barberton Tree Service Inc .... E 330 848-2344
 Norton (G-11990)
Davey Resource Group Inc .... E 859 630-9879
 Cincinnati (G-2541)
Davey Resource Group Inc .... E 330 673-5685
 Kent (G-9568)
Davey Tree Expert Company .... D 330 673-9511
 Columbus (G-5741)
Davey Tree Expert Company .... D 330 678-5818
 Kent (G-9569)
Davey Tree Expert Company .... C 330 673-9511
 Kent (G-9570)
Dbi Services LLC .... E 410 590-4181
 South Point (G-13174)
Edwards Land Clearing Inc .... E 440 988-4477
 Amherst (G-428)
Forevergreen Lawn Care .... E 440 327-8987
 North Ridgeville (G-11928)
Haymaker Tree & Lawn Inc .... E 330 499-5037
 North Canton (G-11839)
Hyde Park Ldscp & Tree Svc Inc ..... E 513 731-1334
 Cincinnati (G-2860)
Lefke Tree Experts LLC .... E 513 325-1783
 Loveland (G-10146)
Madison Tree Care & Ldscpg Inc ..... E 513 576-6391
 Milford (G-11241)
MBI Tree Service LLC .... E 513 926-9857
 Waynesville (G-14625)
Merciers Incorporated .... C 410 590-4181
 South Point (G-13180)
Metrohealth System .... B 216 957-2100
 Cleveland (G-4563)
Nelson Tree Service Inc .... E 937 294-1313
 Dayton (G-7529)

08 FORESTRY

0811 Timber tracts

▲ Acro Tool & Die Company .... E 330 773-5173
 Akron (G-14)
Davey Tree Expert Company .... C 330 673-9511
 Kent (G-9570)
Timbuk Farms Inc .... D 740 587-2178
 Granville (G-8855)

0851 Forestry services

Odnr .... E 614 338-4742
 Columbus (G-6383)

09 FISHING, HUNTING AND TRAPPING

0971 Hunting, trapping, game propagation

Miami Valley Gaming & Racg LLC ... C 513 934-7070
 Lebanon (G-9778)

10 METAL MINING

1011 Iron ores

Cleveland-Cliffs Intl Holdg Co .... D 216 694-5700
 Cleveland (G-4075)
Cliffs Mining Services Company ...... C 218 262-5913
 Cleveland (G-4078)
Cliffs Natural Resources Explo .... C 216 694-5700
 Cleveland (G-4079)
The Cleveland-Cliffs Iron Co .... C 216 694-5700
 Cleveland (G-4997)
Tilden Mining Company LC .... A 216 694-5700
 Cleveland (G-5020)
Wabush Mnes Clffs Min Mnging A ... B 216 694-5700
 Cleveland (G-5118)

1061 Ferroalloy ores, except vanadium

▲ Rhenium Alloys Inc .... E 440 365-7388
 North Ridgeville (G-11934)

1081 Metal mining services

Cliffs UTAC Holding LLC .... D 216 694-5700
 Cleveland (G-4081)
Western Kentucky Coal Co LLC ...... E 740 338-3334
 Saint Clairsville (G-12821)

12 COAL MINING

1221 Bituminous coal and lignite-surface mining

B&N Coal Inc .... E 740 783-3575
 Dexter City (G-7867)
Buckingham Coal Company LLC .... D
 Zanesville (G-15774)
▼ Cliffs Logan County Coal LLC ...... C 216 694-5700
 Cleveland (G-4077)
Coal Resources Inc .... E 216 765-1240
 Saint Clairsville (G-12785)
Coal Services Inc .... B 740 795-5220
 Powhatan Point (G-12610)
Franklin County Coal Company ...... B 740 338-3100
 Saint Clairsville (G-12793)
Kimble Company .... C 330 343-1226
 Dover (G-7891)
Marietta Coal Co .... E 740 695-2197
 Saint Clairsville (G-12800)
Meigs County Coal Company .... B 740 338-3100
 Saint Clairsville (G-12803)
Muhlenberg County Coal Co LLC .... D 740 338-3100
 Saint Clairsville (G-12806)
Murray American Energy Inc .... C 740 338-3100
 Saint Clairsville (G-12807)
Nacco Industries Inc .... E 440 229-5151
 Cleveland (G-4616)
Oxford Mining Company Inc .... C 740 588-0190
 Zanesville (G-15824)
Oxford Mining Company - KY LLC ... E 740 622-6302
 Coshocton (G-6996)
Rosebud Mining Company .... D 740 768-2275
 Bergholz (G-1088)
Subtropolis Mining Co .... E 330 549-2165
 Petersburg (G-12395)

Valley Mining Inc .... C 740 922-3942
 Dennison (G-7862)
Washington County Coal Company .. B 740 338-3100
 Saint Clairsville (G-12819)
Waterloo Coal Company Inc .... D 740 286-0004
 Jackson (G-9529)
Westmoreland Resources Gp LLC ... D 740 622-6302
 Coshocton (G-7004)

1222 Bituminous coal-underground mining

Coal Services Inc .... B 740 795-5220
 Powhatan Point (G-12610)
Kenamerican Resources Inc .... C 740 338-3100
 Saint Clairsville (G-12796)
Rosebud Mining Company .... D 740 768-2275
 Bergholz (G-1088)
Utahamerican Energy Inc .... C 435 888-4000
 Powhatan Point (G-12611)
Western KY Coal Resources LLC .... E 740 338-3100
 Saint Clairsville (G-12822)

1231 Anthracite mining

Coal Services Inc .... B 740 795-5220
 Powhatan Point (G-12610)

1241 Coal mining services

Appalachian Fuels LLC .... C 606 928-0460
 Dublin (G-7939)
Coal Services Inc .... B 740 795-5220
 Powhatan Point (G-12610)
Ohio Valley Coal Company .... B 740 926-1351
 Saint Clairsville (G-12810)
Peabody Coal Company .... E 740 450-2420
 Zanesville (G-15826)
Rosebud Mining Company .... D 740 658-4217
 Freeport (G-8663)
Suncoke Energy Inc .... E 513 727-5571
 Middletown (G-11188)

13 OIL AND GAS EXTRACTION

1311 Crude petroleum and natural gas

Bijoe Development Inc .... E 330 674-5981
 Millersburg (G-11274)
City of Lancaster .... E 740 687-6670
 Lancaster (G-9701)
D & L Energy Inc .... E 330 270-1201
 Canton (G-1730)
Interstate Gas Supply LLC .... B 877 995-4447
 Dublin (G-8041)
◆ Knight Material Tech LLC .... D 330 488-1651
 East Canton (G-8169)

1321 Natural gas liquids

Husky Marketing and Supply Co ..... E 614 210-2300
 Dublin (G-8033)
Markwest Utica Emg LLC .... C 740 942-4810
 Jewett (G-9543)

1381 Drilling oil and gas wells

Eclipse Resources - Ohio LLC .... C 740 452-4503
 Zanesville (G-15787)
Fortis Energy Services Inc .... D 248 283-7100
 Saint Clairsville (G-12792)
Kilbarger Construction Inc .... C 740 385-6019
 Logan (G-10031)
Nomac Drilling LLC .... C 330 476-7040
 Carrollton (G-1910)
Nomac Drilling LLC .... C 724 324-2205
 Saint Clairsville (G-12808)
Warren Drilling Co Inc .... C 740 783-2775
 Dexter City (G-7868)

SIC SECTION
15 CONSTRUCTION - GENERAL CONTRACTORS & OPERATIVE BUILDERS

1382 Oil and gas exploration services

Antero Resources Corporation............... E 303 357-7310
  Caldwell *(G-1545)*
Antero Resources Corporation............... D 740 760-1000
  Marietta *(G-10356)*
BD Oil Gathering Corp.......................... E 740 374-9355
  Marietta *(G-10357)*
Blue Racer Midstream LLC..................... D 740 630-7556
  Cambridge *(G-1556)*
Diversified Production LLC.................... C 740 373-8771
  Marietta *(G-10366)*
Dlz Ohio Inc.. C 614 888-0040
  Columbus *(G-5778)*
Husky Marketing and Supply Co............ E 614 210-2300
  Dublin *(G-8033)*
M3 Midstream LLC................................ E 330 223-2220
  Kensington *(G-9554)*
M3 Midstream LLC................................ E 330 679-5580
  Salineville *(G-12860)*
M3 Midstream LLC................................ E 740 945-1170
  Scio *(G-12942)*
Ngo Development Corporation............... B 740 622-9560
  Coshocton *(G-6993)*
Precision Geophysical Inc...................... E 330 674-2198
  Millersburg *(G-11290)*
Utica East Ohio Midstream LLC.............. B 740 431-4168
  Dennison *(G-7861)*

1389 Oil and gas field services, nec

A1 Industrial Painting Inc...................... E 330 750-9441
  Youngstown *(G-15540)*
Bijoe Development Inc.......................... E 330 674-5981
  Millersburg *(G-11274)*
CDK Perforating LLC............................ D 817 862-9834
  Marietta *(G-10361)*
EP Ferris & Associates Inc..................... E 614 299-2999
  Columbus *(G-5823)*
Global Energy Partners LLC.................. E 419 756-8027
  Mansfield *(G-10267)*
Ingle-Barr Inc...................................... D 740 702-6117
  Chillicothe *(G-2072)*
Kelchner Inc.. C 937 704-9890
  Springboro *(G-13202)*
Klx Energy Services LLC....................... E 740 922-1155
  Midvale *(G-11204)*
Performance Technologies LLC............... D 330 875-1216
  Louisville *(G-10119)*
Producers Service Corporation............... D 740 454-6253
  Zanesville *(G-15829)*
Recon... D 740 609-3050
  Bridgeport *(G-1377)*
Siler Excavation Services...................... E 513 400-8628
  Milford *(G-11257)*
Stallion Oilfield Cnstr LLC..................... D 330 868-2083
  Paris *(G-12247)*
▲ Stingray Pressure Pumping LLC........ D 405 648-4177
  Belmont *(G-1055)*
Tk Gas Services Inc............................. E 740 826-0303
  New Concord *(G-11612)*
U S Weatherford L P............................. C 330 746-2502
  Youngstown *(G-15741)*
Universal Well Services Inc................... D 814 333-2656
  Millersburg *(G-11294)*
◆ Westerman Inc................................. C 800 338-8265
  Bremen *(G-1372)*
Wyoming Casing Service Inc................. D 330 479-8785
  Canton *(G-1888)*

14 MINING AND QUARRYING OF NONMETALLIC MINERALS, EXCEPT FUELS

1411 Dimension stone

Irg Operating LLC................................ E 440 963-4008
  Vermilion *(G-14405)*
National Lime and Stone Co.................. E 419 562-0771
  Bucyrus *(G-1513)*
Stoneco Inc... E 419 422-8854
  Findlay *(G-8588)*
Waterloo Coal Company Inc................... D 740 286-0004
  Jackson *(G-9529)*

1422 Crushed and broken limestone

Beazer East Inc................................... E 937 364-2311
  Hillsboro *(G-9249)*
Bluffton Stone Co................................. E 419 358-6941
  Bluffton *(G-1279)*
Carmeuse Lime Inc.............................. E 419 986-5200
  Bettsville *(G-1098)*
Custar Stone Co................................... E 419 669-4327
  Napoleon *(G-11520)*
Kellstone Inc....................................... E 419 746-2396
  Kelleys Island *(G-9553)*
▲ Lang Stone Company Inc................. E 614 235-4099
  Columbus *(G-6139)*
National Lime and Stone Co.................. E 419 562-0771
  Bucyrus *(G-1513)*
National Lime and Stone Co.................. E 419 396-7671
  Carey *(G-1894)*
National Lime and Stone Co.................. E 740 548-4206
  Delaware *(G-7819)*
National Lime and Stone Co.................. E 419 228-3434
  Lima *(G-9937)*
National Lime and Stone Co.................. E 740 387-3485
  Marion *(G-10446)*
Oglebay Norton Mar Svcs Co LLC......... A 216 861-3300
  Cleveland *(G-4680)*
◆ Omya Industries Inc........................ D 513 387-4600
  Mason *(G-10586)*
Piqua Materials Inc.............................. D 937 773-4824
  Piqua *(G-12453)*
Shelly Materials Inc............................. E 740 666-5841
  Ostrander *(G-12184)*
Shelly Materials Inc............................. D 740 246-6315
  Thornville *(G-13622)*
Stoneco Inc... E 419 893-7645
  Maumee *(G-10771)*
Stoneco Inc... E 419 393-2555
  Oakwood *(G-12054)*
The National Lime and Stone Company. E 419 422-4341
  Findlay *(G-8593)*

1423 Crushed and broken granite

The National Lime and Stone Company. E 419 422-4341
  Findlay *(G-8593)*

1429 Crushed and broken stone, nec

Great Lakes Crushing Ltd...................... D 440 944-5500
  Wickliffe *(G-15150)*
Medina Supply Company....................... E 330 364-4411
  Medina *(G-10864)*

1442 Construction sand and gravel

Central Allied Enterprises Inc................. E 330 477-6751
  Canton *(G-1706)*
Central Ready Mix LLC......................... E 513 402-5001
  Cincinnati *(G-2337)*
Hilltop Basic Resources Inc................... D 513 621-1500
  Cincinnati *(G-2826)*
▲ John R Jurgensen Co....................... B 513 771-0820
  Cincinnati *(G-2913)*
Kenmore Construction Co Inc................ D 330 832-8888
  Massillon *(G-10649)*
National Lime and Stone Co.................. E 419 396-7671
  Carey *(G-1894)*
S & S Aggregates Inc........................... B 419 938-5604
  Perrysville *(G-12393)*
Shelly Materials Inc............................. D 740 246-6315
  Thornville *(G-13622)*
Smith Concrete Co................................ E 740 373-7441
  Dover *(G-7901)*
Stansley Mineral Resources Inc.............. E 419 843-2813
  Sylvania *(G-13573)*
The National Lime and Stone Company. E 419 422-4341
  Findlay *(G-8593)*
The Olen Corporation............................ D 614 491-1515
  Columbus *(G-6761)*
Watson Gravel Inc................................ E 513 863-0070
  Hamilton *(G-9091)*
Welch Holdings Inc.............................. E 513 353-3220
  Cincinnati *(G-3647)*

1446 Industrial sand

◆ Covia Holdings LLC.......................... D 800 255-7263
  Independence *(G-9426)*
Wedron Silica LLC................................ E 815 433-2449
  Independence *(G-9498)*

1459 Clay and related minerals, nec

Waterloo Coal Company Inc................... D 740 286-0004
  Jackson *(G-9529)*

1481 Nonmetallic mineral services

Barr Engineering Incorporated............... E 614 714-0299
  Columbus *(G-5420)*
▲ M G Q Inc....................................... E 419 992-4236
  Tiffin *(G-13631)*

1499 Miscellaneous nonmetallic mining

Graftech Holdings Inc........................... D 216 676-2000
  Independence *(G-9434)*
The National Lime and Stone Company. E 419 422-4341
  Findlay *(G-8593)*

15 CONSTRUCTION - GENERAL CONTRACTORS & OPERATIVE BUILDERS

1521 Single-family housing construction

3d Building Systems LLC...................... E 614 351-9695
  Columbus *(G-5287)*
50 X 20 Holding Company Inc............... E 330 865-4663
  Akron *(G-7)*
50 X 20 Holding Company Inc............... E 740 238-4262
  Belmont *(G-1053)*
50 X 20 Holding Company Inc............... D 330 478-4500
  Canton *(G-1650)*
A1 Complete Inc.................................. E 216 691-0363
  Cleveland *(G-3754)*
AAA Emergency Service........................ E 513 554-6473
  Loveland *(G-10125)*
AAA Standard Services Inc................... E 419 535-0274
  Toledo *(G-13672)*
Ackermann Enterprises Inc.................... D 513 842-3100
  Cincinnati *(G-2141)*
Alexander and Bebout Inc..................... D 419 238-9567
  Van Wert *(G-14339)*

15 CONSTRUCTION - GENERAL CONTRACTORS & OPERATIVE BUILDERS

American Suncraft Co Inc............................ E 937 849-9475
  Medway *(G-10907)*

Apco Industries Inc..................................... D 614 224-2345
  Columbus *(G-5371)*

Apex Restoration Contrs Ltd....................... E 513 489-1795
  Cincinnati *(G-2209)*

Bruns Construction Entps LLC................... E 419 586-9367
  Celina *(G-1917)*

Buckeye Cmnty Hope Foundation.............. D 614 942-2014
  Columbus *(G-5474)*

C V Perry & Co.. E 614 221-4131
  Columbus *(G-5490)*

Cahill Cnstr Inc Cahill Cnstr........................ E 614 442-8570
  Columbus *(G-5492)*

Cardinal Builders Inc................................... E 614 237-1000
  Columbus *(G-5507)*

Cavalear Corporation.................................. E 419 882-7125
  Sylvania *(G-13538)*

Cbtk Group Inc.. E 330 359-9111
  Dundee *(G-8168)*

Cleary Company.. E 614 459-4000
  Columbus *(G-5582)*

Cleveland Construction Inc......................... C 440 255-8000
  Mason *(G-10539)*

Combs Interior Specialties Inc.................... D 937 879-2047
  Fairborn *(G-8369)*

Construction Mechanics Inc........................ C 330 630-9239
  Akron *(G-122)*

Construction One Inc.................................. E 614 235-0057
  Columbus *(G-5685)*

Continental Bldg Systems LLC................... E 614 221-1818
  Columbus *(G-5690)*

Cricket Construction Ltd............................. E 330 536-8773
  Lowellville *(G-10167)*

Cristo Homes.. E 513 755-0570
  West Chester *(G-14680)*

Dan Marchetta Cnstr Co Inc........................ E 330 668-4800
  Akron *(G-131)*

Danessa Construction Llc.......................... D 330 219-1212
  Niles *(G-11787)*

David W Milliken... E 740 998-5023
  Frankfort *(G-8629)*

Deerfield Farms... E 330 584-4715
  Deerfield *(G-7740)*

Design Homes & Development Co............. E 937 438-3667
  Dayton *(G-7311)*

Dold Homes Inc... E 419 874-2535
  Perrysburg *(G-12334)*

Double Z Construction Company................ D 614 274-9334
  Columbus *(G-5783)*

Doyle Ja Corporation.................................. E 419 705-1091
  Whitehouse *(G-15141)*

Dublin Building Systems Co........................ E 614 760-5831
  Dublin *(G-7989)*

Dun Rite Home Improvement Inc................ E 330 650-5322
  Macedonia *(G-10191)*

Dutch Valley Home Inc................................ C 330 273-8322
  Hinckley *(G-9269)*

Einheit Electric Co...................................... E 216 661-6000
  Independence *(G-9429)*

Elite Southern Cnstr LLC........................... D 614 441-1285
  Marysville *(G-10484)*

Erie Construction Mid-West Inc.................. D 937 898-4688
  Dayton *(G-7339)*

Erie Construction Mid-West Inc.................. B 419 472-4200
  Toledo *(G-13795)*

Erie Construction Mid-West LLC................ C 567 408-2145
  Toledo *(G-13796)*

Evans Construction..................................... E 330 305-9355
  North Canton *(G-11829)*

Farris Enterprises Inc................................. E 614 367-9611
  Worthington *(G-15416)*

Ferguson Construction Company................ E 614 876-8496
  Columbus *(G-5855)*

Fms Construction Company........................ E 330 225-9320
  North Royalton *(G-11940)*

G & G Concrete Cnstr LLC......................... E 614 475-4151
  Columbus *(G-5903)*

GCI Construction LLC................................ E 216 831-6100
  Beachwood *(G-794)*

Gentlebrook Inc... C 740 545-7487
  West Lafayette *(G-14856)*

Goettle Co... D 513 825-8100
  Cincinnati *(G-2737)*

Great Lakes Companies Inc........................ D 513 554-0720
  Cincinnati *(G-2762)*

Greater Dayton Cnstr Ltd............................ D 937 426-3577
  Beavercreek *(G-923)*

H & H Custom Homes LLC........................ E 419 994-4070
  Loudonville *(G-10109)*

▲ Hoge Lumber Company.......................... E 419 753-2263
  New Knoxville *(G-11617)*

Home Green Home Inc................................ E 513 900-1702
  Cincinnati *(G-2838)*

Homes America Inc..................................... E 614 848-8551
  Columbus *(G-6004)*

Homewood Corporation.............................. C 614 898-7200
  Columbus *(G-6007)*

Hoppes Construction LLC.......................... D 580 310-0090
  Malvern *(G-10234)*

Hughes Kitchens and Bath LLC.................. E 330 455-5269
  Canton *(G-1777)*

Hurst Construction Inc................................ E 440 234-5656
  Westlake *(G-15067)*

Improveit Home Remodeling Inc................. E 937 204-1551
  Dayton *(G-7420)*

Improveit Home Remodeling Inc................. E 937 514-7546
  West Chester *(G-14710)*

Improveit Home Remodeling Inc................. D 614 297-5121
  Columbus *(G-6044)*

Ingle-Barr Inc... E 614 421-0201
  Columbus *(G-6052)*

Ingle-Barr Inc... D 740 702-6117
  Chillicothe *(G-2072)*

J & D Home Improvement Inc..................... D 800 288-0831
  Columbus *(G-6076)*

J & W Enterprises Inc................................. E 740 774-4500
  Chillicothe *(G-2074)*

Jack Gray.. D 216 688-0466
  Cincinnati *(G-2892)*

Jtf Construction Inc..................................... D 513 860-9835
  Fairfield *(G-8423)*

Justin Doyle Homes.................................... E 513 623-1418
  Mason *(G-10570)*

K Hovnanian Summit Homes LLC.............. E 330 454-4048
  Canton *(G-1788)*

Knapke Cabinets Inc................................... E 937 335-8383
  Troy *(G-14142)*

Knose Concrete Constructn Inc.................. E 513 738-8200
  Hamilton *(G-9058)*

Kopf Construction Corporation................... D 440 933-6908
  Avon Lake *(G-680)*

Lei Cbus LLC.. E 614 302-8830
  Worthington *(G-15432)*

Level Up Custom Cnstr Inc......................... E 888 505-9676
  Cleveland *(G-4491)*

M M Construction.. E 513 553-0106
  Bethel *(G-1093)*

M/I Financial Corp....................................... E 614 418-8700
  Columbus *(G-6185)*

M/I Homes Central Ohio LLC..................... E 614 418-8000
  Columbus *(G-6187)*

M/I Homes Service LLC............................. E 614 418-8300
  Columbus *(G-6188)*

Mab Home Remodeling LLC....................... E 216 761-1360
  Cleveland *(G-4512)*

Marous Brothers Cnstr Inc......................... B 440 951-3904
  Willoughby *(G-15211)*

Menard Inc... D 513 737-2204
  Fairfield Township *(G-8463)*

Menard Inc... D 937 630-3550
  Miamisburg *(G-11072)*

Miller Contracting Group Inc...................... E 419 453-3825
  Ottoville *(G-12198)*

Moyer Industries Inc................................... D 937 832-7283
  Clayton *(G-3736)*

Neals Construction Company..................... E 513 489-7700
  Cincinnati *(G-3102)*

Nicholson Builders Inc............................... E 614 846-7388
  Columbus *(G-6358)*

North Bay Construction Inc........................ E 440 835-1898
  Westlake *(G-15085)*

North Branch Nursery Inc........................... E 419 287-4679
  Pemberville *(G-12290)*

Nvr Inc... E 440 232-5534
  Bedford *(G-977)*

Nvr Inc... E 740 548-0136
  Westerville *(G-14917)*

O C I Construction Co Inc.......................... E 440 338-3166
  Novelty *(G-12040)*

Oberer Development Co.............................. E 937 910-0851
  Miamisburg *(G-11077)*

Oberer Residential Cnstr Ltd...................... D 937 278-0851
  Miamisburg *(G-11078)*

On Deck Services Inc................................. E 513 759-2854
  Liberty Township *(G-9855)*

Oster Services LLC.................................... E 440 596-8489
  Lakewood *(G-9680)*

Pirhl Contractors LLC................................. E 216 378-9690
  Cleveland *(G-4751)*

Premier Groupe LLC................................... E 937 272-1520
  Miamisburg *(G-11087)*

Ram Restoration LLC.................................. E 937 347-7418
  Dayton *(G-7580)*

Registered Contractors Inc........................ E 440 205-0873
  Mentor *(G-10990)*

Retail Renovations Inc................................ E 330 334-4501
  Wadsworth *(G-14449)*

Robert Lucke Homes Inc............................ E 513 683-3300
  Cincinnati *(G-3313)*

Rockford Homes Inc................................... D 614 785-0015
  Columbus *(G-5281)*

Romanelli & Hughes Building Co................ E 614 891-2042
  Westerville *(G-15013)*

Runyon & Sons Roofing Inc....................... D 440 974-6810
  Mentor *(G-10993)*

Schmidt Builders Inc................................... E 513 779-9300
  Cincinnati *(G-3348)*

Shoemaker Masonry Cnstr LLC.................. E 989 948-2377
  Cleves *(G-5195)*

Si-MO Remodeling Inc................................ E 419 609-9036
  Sandusky *(G-12932)*

Simple Bath Ltd... E 614 888-2284
  Hilliard *(G-9232)*

Skilkengold Development LLC.................... E 614 418-3100
  Columbus *(G-6685)*

Smb Construction Co Inc........................... E 419 269-1473
  Toledo *(G-14017)*

Snavely Building Company......................... E 440 585-9091
  Chagrin Falls *(G-1966)*

Snavely Development Company.................. E 440 585-9091
  Chagrin Falls *(G-1967)*

Society Handicapped Citz Medin................ C 330 722-1710
  Medina *(G-10891)*

Stiner and Sons Cnstr Inc.......................... E 440 775-2345
  Oberlin *(G-12076)*

15 CONSTRUCTION - GENERAL CONTRACTORS & OPERATIVE BUILDERS

Strawser Construction Inc .... C 513 874-6192
  Hamilton *(G-9083)*

Sure Home Improvements LLC .... E 614 975-7727
  Columbus *(G-6734)*

The Galehouse Companies Inc .... E 330 658-2023
  Doylestown *(G-7916)*

Timeline Construction LLC .... E 330 595-4462
  Akron *(G-334)*

Towne Development Group Ltd .... E 513 381-8696
  Cincinnati *(G-3489)*

Trimat Construction Inc .... E 740 388-9515
  Bidwell *(G-1106)*

Trinity Home Builders LLC .... E 614 898-7200
  Etna *(G-8331)*

Tusing Builders Ltd .... E 419 465-3100
  Monroeville *(G-11359)*

Vibo Construction Inc .... E 614 210-6780
  Dublin *(G-8155)*

Weaver Custom Homes Inc .... E 330 264-5444
  Wooster *(G-15385)*

Wegman Company .... D 513 381-1111
  Cincinnati *(G-3645)*

Wh Midwest LLC .... D 330 896-7611
  Uniontown *(G-14270)*

Wingler Construction Corp .... E 614 626-8546
  Columbus *(G-6898)*

Woda Construction Inc .... E 614 396-3200
  Columbus *(G-6900)*

Zeigler Habilitation Homes Inc .... E 419 973-7629
  Toledo *(G-14118)*

Zinz Cnstr & Restoration Inc .... E 330 332-7939
  Youngstown *(G-15763)*

1522 Residential construction, nec

Ackermann Enterprises Inc .... D 513 842-3100
  Cincinnati *(G-2141)*

Appalachian Inc .... E 937 444-3043
  Williamsburg *(G-15176)*

Cardinal Builders Inc .... E 614 237-1000
  Columbus *(G-5507)*

Cathedral Holdings Inc .... D 513 271-6400
  Cincinnati *(G-2322)*

Cbtk Group Inc .... E 330 359-9111
  Dundee *(G-8168)*

Central Ohio Contractors Inc .... D 740 369-7700
  Delaware *(G-7784)*

Cristo Homes .... E 513 755-0570
  West Chester *(G-14680)*

Danis Industrial Cnstr Co .... D 937 228-1225
  Miamisburg *(G-11044)*

Donald R Kenney & Co Rlty LLC .... E 614 540-2404
  Westerville *(G-14891)*

Fabrizi Trucking & Pav Co Inc .... D 440 277-0127
  Lorain *(G-10074)*

Fairfield Homes Inc .... C 614 873-3533
  Plain City *(G-12477)*

Fairfield Homes Inc .... E 740 653-3583
  Lancaster *(G-9714)*

Forest City Residential Dev .... E 440 888-8664
  Cleveland *(G-4274)*

Forest City Residential Dev .... E 216 621-6060
  Cleveland *(G-4275)*

G J Goudreau & Co .... E 216 351-5233
  Cleveland *(G-4297)*

Garland Group Inc .... E 614 294-4411
  Columbus *(G-5916)*

GCI Construction LLC .... E 216 831-6100
  Beachwood *(G-794)*

Greater Dayton Cnstr Ltd .... D 937 426-3577
  Beavercreek *(G-923)*

I & M J Gross Company .... E 440 237-1681
  Cleveland *(G-4397)*

Installed Building Pdts Inc .... C 614 221-3399
  Columbus *(G-6057)*

Joint Development & Hsing Corp .... D 513 381-8696
  Cincinnati *(G-2919)*

Kaiyuh Services LLC .... D 907 569-9599
  Dayton *(G-7432)*

Klingbeil Management Group Co .... E 614 220-8900
  Columbus *(G-6120)*

Kopf Construction Corporation .... D 440 933-6908
  Avon Lake *(G-680)*

L R G Inc .... D 937 890-0510
  Dayton *(G-7447)*

Lifestyle Communities Ltd .... E 614 918-2000
  Columbus *(G-6162)*

Long & Wilcox LLC .... E 614 273-3100
  Worthington *(G-15433)*

Messer Construction Co .... D 513 242-1541
  Cincinnati *(G-3050)*

Miller Yount Paving Inc .... E 561 951-7416
  Cortland *(G-6973)*

Mv Residential Cnstr LLC .... A 513 588-1000
  Cincinnati *(G-3093)*

National Housing Corporation .... E 614 481-8106
  Columbus *(G-6299)*

Oberer Development Co .... E 937 910-0851
  Miamisburg *(G-11077)*

Oberer Residential Cnstr Ltd .... E 937 278-0851
  Miamisburg *(G-11078)*

Otterbein Homes .... B 513 933-5400
  Lebanon *(G-9781)*

◆ Pivotek LLC .... E 513 372-6205
  Milford *(G-11250)*

Ram Restoration LLC .... E 937 347-7418
  Dayton *(G-7580)*

Renascence Ottawa LLC .... D 614 863-4640
  Reynoldsburg *(G-12676)*

Rockford Homes Inc .... E 614 785-0015
  Columbus *(G-5281)*

Runyon & Sons Roofing Inc .... D 440 974-6810
  Mentor *(G-10993)*

S & G 3 LLC .... E 937 988-0050
  Dayton *(G-7600)*

Safeguard Properties MGT LLC .... A 216 739-2900
  Cleveland *(G-4870)*

Schnippel Construction Inc .... E 937 693-3831
  Botkins *(G-1300)*

◆ Schroeder Company .... E 419 473-3139
  Perrysburg *(G-12368)*

Snavely Building Company .... E 440 585-9091
  Chagrin Falls *(G-1966)*

Snavely Development Company .... E 440 585-9091
  Chagrin Falls *(G-1967)*

T O J Inc .... E 440 352-1900
  Mentor *(G-11002)*

Taylor Companies Ohio Inc .... E 330 677-8380
  Kent *(G-9602)*

Titan Reinforcing LLC .... E 513 539-4000
  Monroe *(G-11352)*

Towne Building Group Inc .... D 513 381-8696
  Cincinnati *(G-3488)*

Transcon Builders Inc .... E 440 439-3400
  Cleveland *(G-5030)*

Turnbull-Wahlert Construction Inc .... D 513 731-7300
  Cincinnati *(G-3535)*

Turner Construction Company .... C 513 721-4224
  Cincinnati *(G-3536)*

Urban Five Construction .... E 614 241-2070
  Columbus *(G-6830)*

Wallick Construction Co .... E 614 863-4640
  Reynoldsburg *(G-12680)*

Welty Building Company Ltd .... E 330 867-2400
  Fairlawn *(G-8503)*

Woda Construction Inc .... E 614 396-3200
  Columbus *(G-6900)*

Zara Construction Inc .... E 419 525-3613
  Ontario *(G-12127)*

1531 Operative builders

Associated Estates Realty Corporation . B 216 261-5000
  Richmond Heights *(G-12715)*

Dold Homes Inc .... E 419 874-2535
  Perrysburg *(G-12334)*

Epcon Cmmnties Franchising Inc .... D 614 761-1010
  Dublin *(G-8005)*

Glencoe Restoration Group LLC .... E 330 752-1244
  Akron *(G-177)*

KHD Company LLC .... E 614 935-9939
  Worthington *(G-15426)*

M/I Homes Inc .... B 614 418-8000
  Columbus *(G-6186)*

Mainthia Technologies Inc .... D 216 433-2198
  Cleveland *(G-4516)*

Nrp Holdings LLC .... C 216 475-8900
  Cleveland *(G-4669)*

▲ P R Machine Works Inc .... D 419 529-5748
  Ontario *(G-12122)*

Resource International Inc .... C 614 823-4949
  Columbus *(G-6587)*

Samuel Joseph Corp .... E 330 983-6557
  Akron *(G-294)*

Schmidt Builders Inc .... E 513 779-9300
  Cincinnati *(G-3348)*

The Galehouse Companies Inc .... E 330 658-2023
  Doylestown *(G-7916)*

Weaver Custom Homes Inc .... E 330 264-5444
  Wooster *(G-15385)*

1541 Industrial buildings and warehouses

Adena Corporation .... C 419 529-4456
  Ontario *(G-12096)*

Aecom Energy & Cnstr Inc .... E 216 622-2300
  Cleveland *(G-3771)*

Akron Board of Education .... E 330 761-1660
  Akron *(G-22)*

Allen-Keith Construction Co .... D 330 266-2220
  Canton *(G-1659)*

Austin Building and Design Inc .... E 440 544-2600
  Cleveland *(G-3839)*

Ayrshire Inc .... E 440 286-9507
  Chardon *(G-1994)*

B & B Contrs & Developers Inc .... D 330 270-5020
  Youngstown *(G-15554)*

Beem Construction Inc .... E 937 693-3176
  Botkins *(G-1298)*

Boak & Sons Inc .... C 330 793-5646
  Youngstown *(G-15559)*

Bruns Construction Enterprises Inc ...... E 937 339-2300
  Tipp City *(G-13653)*

Burkshire Construction Company .... E 440 885-9700
  Cleveland *(G-3911)*

Butt Construction Company Inc .... E 937 426-1313
  Dayton *(G-7127)*

Canaan Companies Inc .... E 419 842-8373
  Toledo *(G-13724)*

Cardinal Group Inc .... C 330 252-1047
  Akron *(G-80)*

Carrara Companies Inc .... E 330 659-2800
  Richfield *(G-12690)*

Cathedral Holdings Inc .... D 513 271-6400
  Cincinnati *(G-2322)*

Cavanaugh Building Corporation .... D 330 753-6658
  Akron *(G-83)*

Central Ohio Building Co Inc .... E 614 475-6392
  Columbus *(G-5536)*

Employee Codes: A=Over 500 employees, B=251-500
C=101-250, D=51-100, E=20-50, F=10-19, G=1-9

15 CONSTRUCTION - GENERAL CONTRACTORS & OPERATIVE BUILDERS

▲ CK Construction Group Inc............... B 614 901-8844
   Westerville *(G-14967)*

Clouse Construction Corp..................... E 419 448-1365
   New Riegel *(G-11678)*

Continental Building Company............... D 614 221-1800
   Columbus *(G-5692)*

Continental RE Companies..................... C 614 221-1800
   Columbus *(G-5695)*

D & G Focht Construction Co................. E 419 732-2412
   Port Clinton *(G-12522)*

DAG Construction Co Inc....................... E 513 542-8597
   Cincinnati *(G-2534)*

Danis Building Construction Co.............. E 513 984-9696
   Cincinnati *(G-2537)*

Danis Building Construction Co.............. C 614 761-8385
   Columbus *(G-5739)*

Danis Building Construction Co.............. E 937 228-1225
   Miamisburg *(G-11042)*

Davis Construction Management............ E 440 248-7770
   Cleveland *(G-4151)*

Ddw Consulting Inc................................. D 937 299-9920
   Moraine *(G-11403)*

Delventhal Company............................... E 419 244-5570
   Millbury *(G-11267)*

Desalvo Construction Company............. E 330 759-8145
   Hubbard *(G-9321)*

Diaz Construction Inc............................. E 740 289-4898
   Piketon *(G-12417)*

DKM Construction Inc............................ E 740 289-3006
   Piketon *(G-12418)*

Drake Construction Company................ E 216 664-6500
   Cleveland *(G-4183)*

Dugan & Meyers Cnstr Svcs Ltd............. E 614 257-7430
   Columbus *(G-5258)*

Dugan & Meyers LLC............................. D 513 891-4300
   Blue Ash *(G-1164)*

Dunlop and Johnston Inc........................ E 330 220-2700
   Valley City *(G-14333)*

Elford Inc... C 614 488-4000
   Columbus *(G-5811)*

◆ Enerfab LLC....................................... B 513 641-0500
   Cincinnati *(G-2620)*

Equity Cnstr Solutions LLC..................... E 614 802-2900
   Hilliard *(G-9195)*

Equity LLC.. D 614 802-2900
   Hilliard *(G-9196)*

Exxcel Project Management LLC............ E 614 621-4500
   Columbus *(G-5840)*

F & M Mafco Inc..................................... E 513 367-2151
   Harrison *(G-9105)*

Ferguson Construction Company............ E 937 274-1173
   Dayton *(G-7350)*

Ferguson Construction Company............ C 937 498-2381
   Sidney *(G-13032)*

Ferrous Metal Transfer Co..................... E 216 671-8500
   Brooklyn *(G-1409)*

Foill Inc... E 740 947-1117
   Waverly *(G-14613)*

Fortney & Weygandt Inc......................... E 440 716-4000
   North Olmsted *(G-11901)*

Fryman-Kuck General Contrs Inc............ E 937 274-2892
   Dayton *(G-7371)*

Geiger Brothers Inc................................ B 740 286-0800
   Jackson *(G-9518)*

H A Dorsten Inc..................................... E 419 628-2327
   Minster *(G-11317)*

Hammond Construction Inc.................... D 330 455-7039
   Uniontown *(G-14254)*

Head Inc... E 614 338-8501
   Columbus *(G-5975)*

Helm and Associates Inc........................ E 419 893-1480
   Maumee *(G-10731)*

Hume Supply Inc.................................... E 419 991-5751
   Lima *(G-9992)*

Ic Holding Company............................... C 440 746-9200
   Brecksville *(G-1355)*

Imhoff Construction Svcs Inc.................. E 330 683-4498
   Orrville *(G-12166)*

Ingle-Barr Inc... E 614 421-0201
   Columbus *(G-6052)*

Ingle-Barr Inc... D 740 702-6117
   Chillicothe *(G-2072)*

J & F Construction and Dev Inc.............. E 419 562-6662
   Bucyrus *(G-1510)*

J & J General Maintenance Inc............... D 740 533-9729
   Ironton *(G-9509)*

Jack Gibson Construction Co................. D 330 394-5280
   Warren *(G-14530)*

Jance & Company Incorporated............. E 440 255-5800
   Mentor *(G-10954)*

Kapp Construction Inc........................... E 937 324-0134
   Springfield *(G-13262)*

KHD Company LLC................................. E 614 935-9939
   Worthington *(G-15426)*

Knoch Corporation................................. D 330 244-1440
   Solon *(G-13104)*

▲ Kokosing Construction Co Inc............. C 614 228-1029
   Westerville *(G-14993)*

Koroseal Interior Products LLC............... C 855 753-5474
   Marietta *(G-10379)*

Kramer & Feldman Inc........................... E 513 821-7444
   Cincinnati *(G-2950)*

Lathrop Company Inc............................. E 419 893-7000
   Toledo *(G-13882)*

Lepi Enterprises Inc............................... D 740 453-2980
   Zanesville *(G-15806)*

Liebel-Flarsheim Company LLC.............. C 513 761-2700
   Cincinnati *(G-2975)*

Link Construction Group Inc.................. E 937 292-7774
   Bellefontaine *(G-1030)*

Lm Constrction Trry Lvrini Inc................. E 740 695-9604
   Saint Clairsville *(G-12797)*

M & W Construction Entps LLC............... E 419 227-2000
   Lima *(G-9932)*

McGraw/Kokosing Inc............................. B 614 212-5700
   Monroe *(G-11344)*

McKnight Development Corp.................. E 614 875-1689
   Grove City *(G-8933)*

Mel Lanzer Co.. E 419 592-2801
   Napoleon *(G-11528)*

Messer Construction Co......................... D 513 242-1541
   Cincinnati *(G-3050)*

Mike Coates Cnstr Co Inc....................... C 330 652-0190
   Niles *(G-11793)*

Miles-Mcclellan Cnstr Co Inc.................. E 614 487-7744
   Columbus *(G-6248)*

Monarch Construction Company............ C 513 351-6900
   Cincinnati *(G-3077)*

Mosser Construction Inc........................ E 419 861-5100
   Maumee *(G-10749)*

Mosser Construction Inc........................ C 419 334-3801
   Fremont *(G-8694)*

Murphy Contracting Co........................... E 330 743-8915
   Youngstown *(G-15671)*

Mv Commercial Construction LLC........... E 513 774-8400
   Cincinnati *(G-3092)*

Nicolozakes Trckg & Cnstr Inc................ E 740 432-5648
   Cambridge *(G-1577)*

Norris Brothers Co Inc........................... C 216 771-2233
   Cleveland *(G-4647)*

Nyman Construction Co......................... E 216 475-7800
   Cleveland *(G-4675)*

Protective Coatings Inc.......................... E 937 275-7711
   Dayton *(G-7572)*

R G Smith Company............................... D 330 456-3415
   Canton *(G-1839)*

R L Fender Construction Co................... E 937 258-9604
   Dayton *(G-7576)*

Ram Cnstrction Svcs Cncnnati L............. E 513 297-1857
   West Chester *(G-14754)*

Refrigeration Systems Company............ D 614 263-0913
   Columbus *(G-6571)*

Registered Contractors Inc.................... E 440 205-0873
   Mentor *(G-10990)*

Rudolph Libbe Inc.................................. C 216 369-0198
   North Ridgeville *(G-11935)*

Rudolph Libbe Inc.................................. C 419 241-5000
   Walbridge *(G-14464)*

Rudolph/Libbe Companies Inc............... D 419 241-5000
   Walbridge *(G-14465)*

Ruhlin Company..................................... C 330 239-2800
   Sharon Center *(G-12989)*

Ruscilli Construction Co Inc................... D 614 876-9484
   Dublin *(G-8111)*

Schirmer Construction Co...................... E 440 716-4900
   North Olmsted *(G-11914)*

Schnippel Construction Inc.................... E 937 693-3831
   Botkins *(G-1300)*

Setterlin Building Company................... D 614 459-7077
   Columbus *(G-6666)*

Shook National Corporation.................. C 937 276-6666
   Dayton *(G-7617)*

Simmons Brothers Corporation.............. E 330 722-1415
   Medina *(G-10889)*

Skanska USA Building Inc...................... D 513 421-0082
   Cincinnati *(G-3383)*

Ssoe Inc... B 419 255-3830
   Toledo *(G-14023)*

Ssoe Systems Inc................................... D 419 255-3830
   Toledo *(G-14024)*

Standard Contg & Engrg Inc.................. E 440 243-1001
   Brookpark *(G-1440)*

Star Builders Inc.................................... E 440 986-5951
   Amherst *(G-434)*

Studer-Obringer Inc............................... E 419 492-2121
   New Washington *(G-11683)*

Symba & Snap Gourmet Foods Inc......... E 407 252-9581
   Cleveland *(G-4972)*

Technical Assurance Inc......................... E 440 953-3147
   Willoughby *(G-15222)*

Testa Enterprises Inc............................. E 330 926-9060
   Cuyahoga Falls *(G-7105)*

The Apostolos Group Inc....................... C 330 670-9900
   Copley *(G-6966)*

The Hc Companies Inc........................... D 440 313-4712
   Elyria *(G-8297)*

Tradesmen Group Inc............................ E 614 799-0889
   Plain City *(G-12495)*

Trisco Systems Incorporated................. C 419 339-3906
   Lima *(G-9973)*

Turner Construction Company............... C 513 721-4224
   Cincinnati *(G-3536)*

Tuttle Construction Inc.......................... C 419 228-6262
   Lima *(G-9974)*

Universal Contracting Corp.................... E 513 482-2700
   Cincinnati *(G-3561)*

Westar Construction Inc........................ E 937 667-8402
   Tipp City *(G-13669)*

Whiting-Turner Contracting Co.............. B 440 449-9200
   Cleveland *(G-5145)*

Williams Bros Builders Inc..................... E 440 365-3261
   Elyria *(G-8301)*

Wmog Inc... E 419 334-3801
   Fremont *(G-8709)*

Worthington Industries Inc.................... E 909 594-7777
   Worthington *(G-15471)*

15 CONSTRUCTION - GENERAL CONTRACTORS & OPERATIVE BUILDERS

York Street Fresh Foods LLC............... E 201 868-9088
Cincinnati *(G-3685)*

1542 Nonresidential construction, nec

3d Building Systems LLC....................... E 614 351-9695
Columbus *(G-5287)*

A P & P Dev & Cnstr Co............................ E 330 833-8886
Massillon *(G-10628)*

Adams-Robinson Enterprises Inc............ E 937 274-5318
Dayton *(G-7155)*

Adena Corporation.................................. C 419 529-4456
Ontario *(G-12096)*

Aecom Energy & Cnstr Inc........................ E 216 622-2300
Cleveland *(G-3771)*

Alvada Const Inc..................................... C 419 595-4224
Findlay *(G-8508)*

American Prservation Bldrs LLC............. D 216 236-2007
Cleveland *(G-3806)*

Apex Restoration Contrs Ltd..................... E 513 489-1795
Cincinnati *(G-2209)*

Arbor Construction Co Inc...................... E 216 360-8989
Cleveland *(G-3829)*

Armcorp Construction Inc......................... E 419 778-7024
Celina *(G-1916)*

Austin Building and Design Inc................ C 440 544-2600
Cleveland *(G-3839)*

B & B Contrs & Developers Inc................. D 330 270-5020
Youngstown *(G-15554)*

Beck Suppliers Inc.................................... E 419 426-3051
Attica *(G-598)*

Boak & Sons Inc....................................... C 330 793-5646
Youngstown *(G-15559)*

Bogner Construction Company............... D 330 262-6730
Wooster *(G-15312)*

Bogner Corporation................................. D 330 262-6393
Wooster *(G-15313)*

Bostleman Corp....................................... E
Holland *(G-9281)*

Boyas Enterprises I Inc............................ E 216 524-3620
Cleveland *(G-3886)*

Brackett Builders Inc................................ E 937 339-7505
Dayton *(G-7200)*

Brenmar Construction Inc....................... D 740 286-2151
Jackson *(G-9516)*

Brexton Construction LLC....................... E 614 441-4110
Columbus *(G-5464)*

▲ Brumbaugh Construction Inc............... E 937 692-5107
Arcanum *(G-453)*

Bruns Construction Enterprises Inc........ E 937 339-2300
Tipp City *(G-13653)*

Burkshire Construction Company........... E 440 885-9700
Cleveland *(G-3911)*

Butt Construction Company Inc.............. E 937 426-1313
Dayton *(G-7127)*

Calvary Contracting Inc........................... E 937 754-0300
Tipp City *(G-13654)*

Campbell Construction Inc..................... D 330 262-5186
Wooster *(G-15316)*

Canaan Companies Inc........................... E 419 842-8373
Toledo *(G-13724)*

Canton Floors Inc.................................... E 330 492-1121
Canton *(G-1701)*

Capital Land Services Inc....................... E 330 338-4709
Norton *(G-11991)*

Cathedral Holdings Inc........................... D 513 271-6400
Cincinnati *(G-2322)*

Cattrell Companies Inc............................ D 740 537-2481
Toronto *(G-14122)*

Cavanaugh Building Corporation............ D 330 753-6658
Akron *(G-83)*

Central Ohio Building Co Inc.................. E 614 475-6392
Columbus *(G-5536)*

Chaney Roofing Maintenance Inc........... E 419 639-2761
Clyde *(G-5199)*

Cintech Construction Inc......................... E 513 563-1991
Cincinnati *(G-2447)*

▲ CK Construction Group Inc.................. B 614 901-8844
Westerville *(G-14967)*

Cleveland Construction Inc..................... C 440 255-8000
Mason *(G-10539)*

▲ Cleveland Construction Inc.................. C 440 255-8000
Mentor *(G-10923)*

Cocca Development Ltd......................... D 330 729-1010
Youngstown *(G-15580)*

Cogun Inc.. E 330 549-5321
North Lima *(G-11887)*

Colaianni Construction Inc..................... E 740 769-2362
Dillonvale *(G-7869)*

Combs Interior Specialties Inc................ D 937 879-2047
Fairborn *(G-8369)*

Conger Construction Group Inc.............. E 513 932-1206
Lebanon *(G-9760)*

Corporate Cleaning Inc........................... E 614 203-6051
Columbus *(G-5702)*

D & G Focht Construction Co................. E 419 732-2412
Port Clinton *(G-12522)*

DAG Construction Co Inc....................... E 513 542-8597
Cincinnati *(G-2534)*

Dan Marchetta Cnstr Co Inc.................... E 330 668-4800
Akron *(G-131)*

Danis Building Construction Co............. E 513 984-9696
Cincinnati *(G-2537)*

Danis Building Construction Co............. E 614 761-8385
Columbus *(G-5739)*

Danis Building Construction Co............. E 937 228-1225
Miamisburg *(G-11042)*

Davis Construction Management............ E 440 248-7770
Cleveland *(G-4151)*

Ddw Consulting Inc................................. D 937 299-9920
Moraine *(G-11403)*

Delventhal Company............................... E 419 244-5570
Millbury *(G-11267)*

Desalvo Construction Company.............. E 330 759-8145
Hubbard *(G-9321)*

Design Homes & Development Co......... E 937 438-3667
Dayton *(G-7311)*

DKM Construction Inc............................. E 740 289-3006
Piketon *(G-12418)*

Donleys Inc.. D 216 524-6800
Cleveland *(G-4178)*

Drake Construction Company................. E 216 664-6500
Cleveland *(G-4183)*

DSV Builders Inc..................................... D 330 652-3784
Niles *(G-11788)*

Dugan & Meyers Cnstr Svcs Ltd.............. E 614 257-7430
Columbus *(G-5258)*

Dugan & Meyers Industrial LLC.............. D 513 539-4000
Monroe *(G-11338)*

Dugan & Meyers LLC............................... C 513 891-4300
Monroe *(G-11339)*

Duncan Oil Co... E 937 426-5945
Dayton *(G-7131)*

Dunlop and Johnston Inc........................ E 330 220-2700
Valley City *(G-14333)*

Dynamic Construction Inc....................... D 740 927-8898
Pataskala *(G-12273)*

Eckinger Construction Company............. E 330 453-2566
Canton *(G-1744)*

Elford Inc... C 614 488-4000
Columbus *(G-5811)*

Enerfab Process Solutions LLC.............. D 513 641-0500
Cincinnati *(G-2622)*

Equity Cnstr Solutions LLC..................... E 614 802-2900
Hilliard *(G-9195)*

Equity LLC... D 614 802-2900
Hilliard *(G-9196)*

Exxcel Project Management LLC............ E 614 621-4500
Columbus *(G-5840)*

Fairfield Homes Inc................................ C 614 873-3533
Plain City *(G-12477)*

Feick Contractors Inc............................. E 419 625-3241
Sandusky *(G-12893)*

Ferguson Construction Company........... E 937 274-1173
Dayton *(G-7350)*

Ferguson Construction Company........... C 937 498-2381
Sidney *(G-13032)*

Fiorilli Construction Co Inc..................... E 216 696-5845
Medina *(G-10836)*

Ford Development Corp......................... D 513 772-1521
Cincinnati *(G-2693)*

Forest City Residential Dev.................... E 216 621-6060
Cleveland *(G-4275)*

Fortney & Weygandt Inc......................... E 440 716-4000
North Olmsted *(G-11901)*

Foti Contracting LLC.............................. C 330 656-3454
Wickliffe *(G-15149)*

▲ Fred Olivieri Construction Co.............. C 330 494-1007
North Canton *(G-11832)*

Fryman-Kuck General Contrs Inc........... E 937 274-2892
Dayton *(G-7371)*

G J Goudreau & Co................................. E 216 351-5233
Cleveland *(G-4297)*

Geis Companies LLC.............................. C 330 528-3500
Streetsboro *(G-13413)*

Gilbane Building Company.................... E 614 948-4000
Columbus *(G-5934)*

Grae-Con Construction Inc.................... E 740 282-6830
Steubenville *(G-13328)*

Greater Dayton Cnstr Ltd....................... D 937 426-3577
Beavercreek *(G-923)*

Gutknecht Construction Company......... E 614 532-5410
Columbus *(G-5962)*

H A Dorsten Inc...................................... E 419 628-2327
Minster *(G-11317)*

Hammond Construction Inc................... D 330 455-7039
Uniontown *(G-14254)*

Hanlin-Rainaldi Construction................. E 614 436-4204
Columbus *(G-5970)*

Head Inc.. E 614 338-8501
Columbus *(G-5975)*

Hi-Five Development Svcs Inc................ E 513 336-9280
Mason *(G-10561)*

Hummel Construction Company............. E 330 274-8584
Ravenna *(G-12628)*

Ideal Company Inc.................................. E 937 836-8683
Clayton *(G-3733)*

Imhoff Construction Svcs Inc................. E 330 683-4498
Orrville *(G-12166)*

Ingle-Barr Inc.. D 740 702-6117
Chillicothe *(G-2072)*

J & F Construction and Dev Inc.............. E 419 562-6662
Bucyrus *(G-1510)*

J D Williamson Cnstr Co Inc................... D 330 633-1258
Tallmadge *(G-13596)*

J&H Rnfrcing Strl Erectors Inc............... C 740 355-0141
Portsmouth *(G-12558)*

Jack Gibson Construction Co................. D 330 394-5280
Warren *(G-14530)*

James Hunt Construction Co Inc............ E 513 721-0559
Cincinnati *(G-2898)*

Jance & Company Incorporated............. E 440 255-5800
Mentor *(G-10954)*

Jhi Group Inc... C 419 465-4611
Monroeville *(G-11356)*

JJO Construction Inc.............................. E 216 347-7802
Wickliffe *(G-15155)*

Employee Codes: A=Over 500 employees, B=251-500
C=101-250, D=51-100, E=20-50, F=10-19, G=1-9

15 CONSTRUCTION - GENERAL CONTRACTORS & OPERATIVE BUILDERS

JLJI Enterprises Inc .... C 216 481-2175
   Euclid *(G-8351)*

John G Johnson Construction Co .... D 216 938-5050
   Cleveland *(G-4440)*

Kapp Construction Inc .... E 937 324-0134
   Springfield *(G-13262)*

Knoch Corporation .... D 330 244-1440
   Solon *(G-13104)*

▲ Kokosing Construction Co Inc .... C 614 228-1029
   Westerville *(G-14993)*

Kokosing Mosser Joint Venture .... C 740 848-4955
   Westerville *(G-14996)*

Kramer & Feldman Inc .... E 513 821-7444
   Cincinnati *(G-2950)*

Krumroy-Cozad Cnstr Corp .... E 330 376-4136
   Akron *(G-217)*

▲ L Brands Store Dsign Cnstr Inc .... C 614 415-7000
   Columbus *(G-6131)*

L R G Inc .... D 937 890-0510
   Dayton *(G-7447)*

Lathrop Company Inc .... E 419 893-7000
   Toledo *(G-13882)*

Lincoln Construction Inc .... E 614 457-6015
   Columbus *(G-6166)*

Link Construction Group Inc .... E 937 292-7774
   Bellefontaine *(G-1030)*

Lm Constrction Trry Lvrini Inc .... E 740 695-9604
   Saint Clairsville *(G-12797)*

Long & Wilcox LLC .... E 614 273-3100
   Worthington *(G-15433)*

◆ Ltccorp Government Services-Oh Inc B 419 794-3500
   Maumee *(G-10742)*

Ludy Greenhouse Mfg Corp .... D 800 255-5839
   New Madison *(G-11634)*

M & W Construction Entps LLC .... E 419 227-2000
   Lima *(G-9932)*

Marietta Silos LLC .... E 740 373-2822
   Marietta *(G-10386)*

Mark-L Inc .... E 614 863-8832
   Gahanna *(G-8722)*

McKnight Development Corp .... E 614 875-1689
   Grove City *(G-8933)*

MCR Services Inc .... E 614 421-0860
   Columbus *(G-6219)*

Megen Construction Company Inc .... E 513 742-9191
   Cincinnati *(G-3036)*

Mel Lanzer Co .... E 419 592-2801
   Napoleon *(G-11528)*

Messer Construction Co .... C 513 672-5000
   Cincinnati *(G-3049)*

Messer Construction Co .... E 614 275-0141
   Columbus *(G-6228)*

Messer Construction Co .... E 937 291-1300
   Dayton *(G-7482)*

Messer Construction Co .... D 513 242-1541
   Cincinnati *(G-3050)*

Metis Construction Svcs LLC .... D 330 677-7333
   Kent *(G-9587)*

MI - De - Con Inc .... D 740 532-2277
   Ironton *(G-9512)*

Midwest Contracting Inc .... E 419 866-4560
   Holland *(G-9297)*

Mike Coates Cnstr Co Inc .... C 330 652-0190
   Niles *(G-11793)*

Miles-Mcclellan Cnstr Co Inc .... E 614 487-7744
   Columbus *(G-6248)*

Miller Contracting Group Inc .... E 419 453-3825
   Ottoville *(G-12198)*

Miller Industrial Svc Team Inc .... E 513 877-2708
   Pleasant Plain *(G-12500)*

Monarch Construction Company .... C 513 351-6900
   Cincinnati *(G-3077)*

Mosser Construction Inc .... E 419 861-5100
   Maumee *(G-10749)*

Mosser Construction Inc .... C 419 334-3801
   Fremont *(G-8694)*

Mpower Inc .... E 614 783-0478
   Westerville *(G-14913)*

Muha Construction Inc .... E 937 435-0678
   Dayton *(G-7517)*

Multicon Builders Inc .... E 614 463-1142
   Columbus *(G-6283)*

Murphy Contracting Co .... E 330 743-8915
   Youngstown *(G-15671)*

National Housing Corporation .... E 614 481-8106
   Columbus *(G-6299)*

North Star Metals Mfg Co .... E 740 254-4567
   Uhrichsville *(G-14235)*

Nyman Construction Co .... E 216 475-7800
   Cleveland *(G-4675)*

Oberer Development Co .... E 937 910-0851
   Miamisburg *(G-11077)*

Ohio Diversified Services Inc .... E 440 356-7000
   Cleveland *(G-4687)*

Ohio Maint & Renovation Inc .... E 330 315-3101
   Akron *(G-254)*

Ozanne Construction Co Inc .... E 216 696-2876
   Cleveland *(G-4712)*

Panzica Construction Co .... C 440 442-4300
   Cleveland *(G-4715)*

Pepper Cnstr Co Ohio LLC .... E 513 563-7700
   Blue Ash *(G-1221)*

Peterson Construction Company .... C 419 941-2233
   Wapakoneta *(G-14489)*

◆ Pivotek LLC .... E 513 372-6205
   Milford *(G-11250)*

Pleasant Valley Cnstr Co .... D 330 239-0176
   Medina *(G-10877)*

Plevniak Construction Inc .... E 330 718-1600
   Youngstown *(G-15695)*

Procon Prof Cnstr Svcs Inc .... E 740 474-5455
   Circleville *(G-3719)*

R L Fender Construction Co .... E 937 258-9604
   Dayton *(G-7576)*

R L Fortney Management Inc .... D 440 716-4000
   North Olmsted *(G-11912)*

Ram Cnstrction Svcs Cncnnati L .... E 513 297-1857
   West Chester *(G-14754)*

Reece-Campbell Inc .... D 513 542-4600
   Cincinnati *(G-3279)*

Registered Contractors Inc .... E 440 205-0873
   Mentor *(G-10990)*

Renier Construction Corp .... E 614 866-4580
   Columbus *(G-6578)*

Restaurant Specialties Inc .... E 614 885-9707
   Sunbury *(G-13524)*

Righter Co Inc .... E 614 272-9700
   Columbus *(G-6588)*

Robertson Cnstr Svcs Inc .... D 740 929-1000
   Heath *(G-9137)*

Robins & Morton Corporation .... E 419 660-2980
   Norwalk *(G-12025)*

Romanelli & Hughes Building Co .... E 614 891-2042
   Westerville *(G-15013)*

◆ Rough Brothers Mfg Inc .... D 513 242-0310
   Cincinnati *(G-3325)*

Rudolph Libbe Inc .... C 419 241-5000
   Walbridge *(G-14464)*

Rudolph/Libbe Companies Inc .... D 419 241-5000
   Walbridge *(G-14465)*

Ruhlin Company .... C 330 239-2800
   Sharon Center *(G-12989)*

Runyon & Sons Roofing Inc .... D 440 974-6810
   Mentor *(G-10993)*

Ruscilli Construction Co Inc .... D 614 876-9484
   Dublin *(G-8111)*

Rycon Construction Inc .... C 440 481-3770
   Parma *(G-12264)*

Schirmer Construction Co .... E 440 716-4900
   North Olmsted *(G-11914)*

Schmidt Builders Inc .... E 513 779-9300
   Cincinnati *(G-3348)*

Schnippel Construction Inc .... E 937 693-3831
   Botkins *(G-1300)*

Schumacher Development Inc .... D 513 777-9800
   West Chester *(G-14762)*

Setterlin Building Company .... D 614 459-7077
   Columbus *(G-6666)*

Shook Construction Co .... E 937 276-6666
   Moraine *(G-11438)*

Shook National Corporation .... C 937 276-6666
   Dayton *(G-7617)*

Singleton Construction LLC .... D 740 756-7331
   Lancaster *(G-9741)*

Site Worx LLC .... E 513 229-0295
   Lebanon *(G-9789)*

Skanska USA Building Inc .... D 513 421-0082
   Cincinnati *(G-3383)*

Smb Construction Co Inc .... E 419 269-1473
   Toledo *(G-14017)*

Smoot Construction Co Ohio .... E 614 253-9000
   Columbus *(G-6691)*

Snavely Building Company .... E 440 585-9091
   Chagrin Falls *(G-1966)*

Ssoe Systems Inc .... D 419 255-3830
   Toledo *(G-14024)*

Star Builders Inc .... E 440 986-5951
   Amherst *(G-434)*

Stockmeister Enterprises Inc .... E 740 286-1619
   Jackson *(G-9525)*

Studer-Obringer Inc .... E 419 492-2121
   New Washington *(G-11683)*

T O J Inc .... E 440 352-1900
   Mentor *(G-11002)*

Tab Construction Company Inc .... E 330 454-5228
   Canton *(G-1868)*

The Apostolos Group Inc .... C 330 670-9900
   Copley *(G-6966)*

The Galehouse Companies Inc .... E 330 658-2023
   Doylestown *(G-7916)*

Transamerica Building Co .... E 614 457-8322
   Columbus *(G-6783)*

Tri-C Construction Company Inc .... E 330 836-2722
   Akron *(G-337)*

Trisco Systems Incorporated .... C 419 339-3906
   Lima *(G-9973)*

Turnbull-Wahlert Construction Inc .... D 513 731-7300
   Cincinnati *(G-3535)*

Turner Construction Company .... C 513 721-4224
   Cincinnati *(G-3536)*

Turner Construction Company .... E 216 522-1180
   Cleveland *(G-5041)*

Turner Construction Company .... D 614 984-3000
   Columbus *(G-6794)*

Tusing Builders Ltd .... E 419 465-3100
   Monroeville *(G-11359)*

Tuttle Construction Inc .... C 419 228-6262
   Lima *(G-9974)*

Uhc United Heating & Coolg LLC .... E 866 931-0118
   Northfield *(G-11967)*

Ulliman Schutte Cnstr LLC .... E 937 247-0375
   Miamisburg *(G-11099)*

Universal Contracting Corp .... E 513 482-2700
   Cincinnati *(G-3561)*

Universal Development MGT Inc .... E 330 759-7017
   Girard *(G-8829)*

16 HEAMY CONSTRUCTION, EXCEPT BUILDING CONSTRUCTION, CONTRACTOR

Valicor Federal Services LLC .... E 313 724-8600
  Blue Ash *(G-1267)*
Wallick Construction Co .... E 614 863-4640
  Reynoldsburg *(G-12680)*
Wallick Construction LLC .... E 614 863-4640
  New Albany *(G-11590)*
Weaver Custom Homes Inc .... E 330 264-5444
  Wooster *(G-15385)*
Welty Building Company Ltd .... E 330 867-2400
  Fairlawn *(G-8503)*
▲ West Roofing Systems Inc .... E 800 356-5748
  Lagrange *(G-9652)*
Whiting-Turner Contracting Co .... B 440 449-9200
  Cleveland *(G-5145)*
Whiting-Turner Contracting Co .... E 614 459-6515
  Columbus *(G-6888)*
Williams Bros Builders Inc .... E 440 365-3261
  Elyria *(G-8301)*
Wingler Construction Corp .... E 614 626-8546
  Columbus *(G-6898)*
Winsupply Inc .... D 937 294-5331
  Moraine *(G-11450)*
Witmers Inc .... E 330 427-2147
  Salem *(G-12858)*

16 HEAMY CONSTRUCTION, EXCEPT BUILDING CONSTRUCTION, CONTRACTOR

1611 Highway and street construction

A & A Safety Inc .... E 513 943-6100
  Amelia *(G-409)*
A P OHoro Company .... D 330 759-9317
  Youngstown *(G-15539)*
Aecom Energy & Cnstr Inc .... E 216 622-2300
  Cleveland *(G-3771)*
Altruism Society Inc .... E 877 283-4001
  Beachwood *(G-765)*
Ambrose Asphalt Inc .... E 419 774-1780
  Mansfield *(G-10243)*
American Coatings Corporation .... E 614 335-1000
  Plain City *(G-12466)*
American Pavements Inc .... E 614 873-2191
  Plain City *(G-12467)*
American Precast Refractories .... E 614 876-8416
  Columbus *(G-5359)*
Barbicas Construction Co .... E 330 733-9101
  Akron *(G-61)*
Belmont County of Ohio .... D 740 695-1580
  Saint Clairsville *(G-12777)*
Brock & Sons Inc .... E 513 874-4555
  Fairfield *(G-8395)*
Carter Site Development LLC .... E 513 831-8843
  Miamiville *(G-11109)*
Central Allied Enterprises Inc .... E 330 477-6751
  Canton *(G-1706)*
Cincinnati Asphalt Corporation .... D 513 367-0250
  Harrison *(G-9098)*
City of Aurora .... E 330 562-8662
  Aurora *(G-611)*
City of Brecksville .... C 440 526-1384
  Brecksville *(G-1350)*
City of Cuyahoga Falls .... E 330 971-8030
  Cuyahoga Falls *(G-7060)*
Colas Construction USA Inc .... C 513 272-5648
  Cincinnati *(G-2471)*
Colas Solutions LLC .... B 513 272-5648
  Cincinnati *(G-2472)*
Columbus Asphalt Paving Inc .... E 614 759-9800
  Columbus *(G-5611)*

Cook Paving and Cnstr Co .... E 216 267-7705
  Independence *(G-9424)*
County of Ashtabula .... C 440 576-2816
  Jefferson *(G-9538)*
County of Delaware .... C 740 833-2400
  Delaware *(G-7788)*
County of Shelby .... D 937 498-7244
  Sidney *(G-13026)*
County of Trumbull .... E 330 675-2640
  Warren *(G-14514)*
Crp Contracting .... D 614 338-8501
  Columbus *(G-5732)*
Eaton Construction Co Inc .... D 740 474-3414
  Circleville *(G-3707)*
Ebony Construction Co .... E 419 841-3455
  Sylvania *(G-13542)*
Erie Blacktop Inc .... E 419 625-7374
  Sandusky *(G-12889)*
Erie Construction Group Inc .... D 419 625-7374
  Sandusky *(G-12890)*
ESwagner Company Inc .... D 419 691-8651
  Oregon *(G-12133)*
Fabrizi Trucking & Pav Co Inc .... D 440 234-1284
  Cleveland *(G-4233)*
Fabrizi Trucking & Pav Co Inc .... D 440 277-0127
  Lorain *(G-10074)*
Ferrous Metal Transfer Co .... E 216 671-8500
  Brooklyn *(G-1409)*
Fox Services Inc .... E 513 858-2022
  Fairfield *(G-8414)*
Fred A Nemann Co .... E 513 467-9400
  Cincinnati *(G-2702)*
Freedom Construction Entps Inc .... E 740 255-5818
  New Concord *(G-11610)*
Fryman-Kuck General Contrs Inc .... E 937 274-2892
  Dayton *(G-7371)*
Gerken Materials Inc .... E 419 533-2421
  Napoleon *(G-11524)*
Great Lakes Crushing Ltd .... D 440 944-5500
  Wickliffe *(G-15150)*
Hazama Ando Corporation .... E 614 985-4906
  Worthington *(G-15418)*
Hi-Way Paving Inc .... D 614 876-1700
  Hilliard *(G-9198)*
Hicon Inc .... E 513 242-3612
  Cincinnati *(G-2819)*
Houck Asphalt Maintenance LLC .... E 513 734-4500
  Bethel *(G-1092)*
▲ Independence Excavating Inc .... E 216 524-1700
  Independence *(G-9437)*
J Kuhn Enterprises Inc .... C 614 481-8838
  Columbus *(G-6078)*
J&B Steel Erectors Inc .... E 513 874-1722
  West Chester *(G-14714)*
Jamison Cnstr Solutions Inc .... E 513 377-0705
  Fairfield *(G-8422)*
▲ John R Jurgensen Co .... B 513 771-0820
  Cincinnati *(G-2913)*
K & M Construction Company .... D 330 723-3681
  Medina *(G-10849)*
Kelly Paving Inc .... E 740 373-6495
  Marietta *(G-10377)*
Kenmore Construction Co Inc .... D 330 832-8888
  Massillon *(G-10649)*
▲ Kenmore Construction Co Inc .... C 330 762-8936
  Akron *(G-215)*
Kokosing Construction Inc .... D 614 212-5700
  Westerville *(G-14992)*
▲ Kokosing Construction Inc .... D 330 263-4168
  Wooster *(G-15350)*
Kokosing Construction Co Inc .... D 740 694-6315
  Fredericktown *(G-8662)*

Kokosing Construction Co Inc .... C 419 524-5656
  Mansfield *(G-10279)*
Kokosing Construction Co Inc .... C 614 228-1029
  Westerville *(G-14994)*
▲ Kokosing Construction Co Inc .... C 614 228-1029
  Westerville *(G-14993)*
Lake Erie Construction Co .... C 419 668-3302
  Norwalk *(G-12015)*
M P Dory Co .... D 614 444-2138
  Columbus *(G-6183)*
MBC Holdings Inc .... E 419 445-1015
  Archbold *(G-462)*
McDaniels Cnstr Corp Inc .... D 614 252-5852
  Columbus *(G-6213)*
Miller Bros Const Inc .... A 419 445-1015
  Archbold *(G-463)*
Mjs Snow & Landscape LLC .... D 419 656-6724
  Port Clinton *(G-12538)*
Moyer Industries Inc .... D 937 832-7283
  Clayton *(G-3736)*
Nas Ventures .... E 614 338-8501
  Columbus *(G-6287)*
Nerone & Sons Inc .... E 216 662-2235
  Cleveland *(G-4635)*
Nickolas M Savko & Sons Inc .... C 614 451-2242
  Columbus *(G-6359)*
Ohio Tpk & Infrastructure Comm .... D 440 234-2081
  Berea *(G-1077)*
Ohio Tpk & Infrastructure Comm .... E 440 234-2081
  Richfield *(G-12705)*
Ohio Tpk & Infrastructure Comm .... D 330 527-2169
  Windham *(G-15288)*
Pavement Protectors Inc .... E 614 875-9989
  Grove City *(G-8944)*
Pavement Prtners Cncinnati LLC .... E 513 367-0250
  Harrison *(G-9113)*
Pavement Technology Inc .... E 440 892-1895
  Westlake *(G-15096)*
Pdk Construction Inc .... D 740 992-6451
  Pomeroy *(G-12514)*
Perk Company Inc .... E 216 391-1444
  Cleveland *(G-4741)*
Pike County .... E 740 947-9339
  Waverly *(G-14615)*
Pinnacle Paving & Sealing LLC .... E 513 474-4900
  Milford *(G-11249)*
Polivka International Co Inc .... E 704 321-0802
  Warren *(G-14548)*
Precision Paving Inc .... E 419 499-7283
  Milan *(G-11211)*
R B Jergens Contractors Inc .... D 937 669-9799
  Vandalia *(G-14390)*
R D Jergens Contractors Inc .... D 937 669-9799
  Vandalia *(G-14391)*
Ronyak Paving Inc .... E 440 279-0616
  Chardon *(G-2018)*
Ruhlin Company .... C 330 239-2800
  Sharon Center *(G-12989)*
Scot Burton Contractors LLC .... E 440 564-1011
  Newbury *(G-11764)*
Security Fence Group Inc .... E 513 681-3700
  Cincinnati *(G-3353)*
Sheedy Paving Inc .... E 614 252-2111
  Columbus *(G-6670)*
Shelly Company .... D 740 246-6315
  Thornville *(G-13621)*
Shelly Materials Inc .... E 740 666-5841
  Ostrander *(G-12184)*
Stonegate Construction Inc .... E 740 423-9170
  Belpre *(G-1060)*
Sunesis Construction Co .... C 513 326-6000
  West Chester *(G-14770)*

16 HEAMY CONSTRUCTION, EXCEPT BUILDING CONSTRUCTION, CONTRACTOR

Superior Paving & Materials................ E 330 499-5849
  Canton *(G-1866)*

Tab Construction Company Inc................ E 330 454-5228
  Canton *(G-1868)*

▲ Terminal Ready-Mix Inc................ E 440 288-0181
  Lorain *(G-10103)*

The Beaver Excavating Co................ A 330 478-2151
  Canton *(G-1871)*

The Great Lakes Construction Co........ C 330 220-3900
  Hinckley *(G-9272)*

Township of Copley................ E 330 666-1853
  Copley *(G-6967)*

Trafftech Inc................ E 216 361-8808
  Cleveland *(G-5029)*

Trucco Construction Co Inc................ C 740 417-9010
  Delaware *(G-7831)*

Tucson Inc................ E 330 339-4935
  New Philadelphia *(G-11669)*

Unique Paving Materials Corp................ E 216 341-7711
  Cleveland *(G-5051)*

Vandalia Blcktop Slcoating Inc................ E 937 454-0571
  Dayton *(G-7700)*

Velotta Company................ E 330 239-1211
  Sharon Center *(G-12991)*

Westpatrick Corp................ E 614 875-8200
  Urbancrest *(G-14327)*

Wmog Inc................ E 419 334-3801
  Fremont *(G-8709)*

Xtreme Elements LLC................ C 330 612-0075
  Akron *(G-367)*

1622 Bridge, tunnel, and elevated highway

A P OHoro Company................ D 330 759-9317
  Youngstown *(G-15539)*

Aecom Energy & Cnstr Inc................ E 216 622-2300
  Cleveland *(G-3771)*

Armstrong Steel Erectors Inc................ E 740 345-4503
  Newark *(G-11689)*

▲ Brumbaugh Construction Inc................ E 937 692-5107
  Arcanum *(G-453)*

CJ Mahan Construction Co LLC................ D 614 277-4545
  Grove City *(G-8909)*

Clayton Railroad Cnstr LLC................ E 937 549-2952
  West Union *(G-14867)*

Colas Construction USA Inc................ C 513 272-5648
  Cincinnati *(G-2471)*

Colas Solutions LLC................ B 513 272-5648
  Cincinnati *(G-2472)*

Complete General Cnstr Co................ C 614 258-9515
  Columbus *(G-5677)*

Eagle Bridge Co................ D 937 492-5654
  Sidney *(G-13030)*

ESwagner Company Inc................ D 419 691-8651
  Oregon *(G-12133)*

▲ Fenton Rigging & Contg Inc................ C 513 631-5500
  Cincinnati *(G-2657)*

Foundation Steel LLC................ C 419 402-4241
  Swanton *(G-13525)*

Fryman-Kuck General Contrs Inc................ E 937 274-2892
  Dayton *(G-7371)*

J & J Schlaegel Inc................ E 937 652-2045
  Urbana *(G-14309)*

Kokosing Construction Co Inc................ D 740 694-6315
  Fredericktown *(G-8662)*

Kokosing Construction Co Inc................ C 614 228-1029
  Westerville *(G-14994)*

▲ Kokosing Construction Co Inc................ C 614 228-1029
  Westerville *(G-14993)*

Liberty Maintenance Inc................ D 330 755-7711
  Youngstown *(G-15650)*

MBC Holdings Inc................ E 419 445-1015
  Archbold *(G-462)*

National Engrg & Contg Co................ E 440 238-3331
  Cleveland *(G-4625)*

▼ Ohio Bridge Corporation................ C 740 432-6334
  Cambridge *(G-1578)*

Prus Construction Company................ C 513 321-7774
  Cincinnati *(G-3256)*

Righter Co Inc................ E 614 272-9700
  Columbus *(G-6588)*

Ruhlin Company................ C 330 239-2800
  Sharon Center *(G-12989)*

Salini Impregilo/Healy................ C 216 539-2050
  Cleveland *(G-4871)*

Sunesis Construction Co................ C 513 326-6000
  West Chester *(G-14770)*

Velotta Company................ E 330 239-1211
  Sharon Center *(G-12991)*

Vernon Nagel Inc................ D 419 592-3861
  Napoleon *(G-11534)*

Westpatrick Corp................ E 614 875-8200
  Urbancrest *(G-14327)*

1623 Water, sewer, and utility lines

A Crano Excavating Inc................ E 330 630-1061
  Akron *(G-8)*

A P OHoro Company................ D 330 759-9317
  Youngstown *(G-15539)*

AAA Flexible Pipe Clg Corp................ E 216 341-2900
  Cleveland *(G-3755)*

Adleta Inc................ E 513 554-1469
  Cincinnati *(G-2145)*

Advanced Rhbilitation Tech Ltd................ E 419 636-2684
  Bryan *(G-1477)*

Aecom Energy & Cnstr Inc................ E 216 622-2300
  Cleveland *(G-3771)*

Aero Communications Inc................ A 734 467-8121
  Beachwood *(G-763)*

American Power Tower LLC................ E 440 261-2245
  Jefferson *(G-9537)*

Anderzack-Pitzen Cnstr Inc................ D 419 644-2111
  Metamora *(G-11016)*

Bi-Con Services Inc................ B 740 685-2542
  Derwent *(G-7864)*

Bill Hawk Inc................ D 330 833-5558
  Massillon *(G-10632)*

Bmu77 LLC................ E 740 652-1679
  Lancaster *(G-9696)*

Bolt Construction Inc................ D 330 549-0349
  Youngstown *(G-15561)*

Broadband Express LLC................ D 419 536-9127
  Toledo *(G-13718)*

Brock & Sons Inc................ E 513 874-4555
  Fairfield *(G-8395)*

Buckeye Excavating & Cnstr Inc................ E 419 663-3113
  Norwalk *(G-12003)*

Buckeye Pipeline Cnstr Inc................ E 330 804-0101
  Wooster *(G-15315)*

Capitol Tunneling Inc................ E 614 444-0255
  Columbus *(G-5505)*

Charles H Hamilton Co................ D 513 683-2442
  Maineville *(G-10226)*

City of Dayton................ E 937 333-3725
  Dayton *(G-7232)*

Cook Paving and Cnstr Co................ E 216 267-7705
  Independence *(G-9424)*

County of Clermont................ E 513 732-7970
  Batavia *(G-738)*

County of Delaware................ E 740 833-2240
  Delaware *(G-7787)*

CST Utilities L L C................ D 614 801-9600
  Grove City *(G-8913)*

Custom Cable Construction Inc................ D 330 351-1207
  Canton *(G-1729)*

Darby Creek Excavating Inc................ D 740 477-8600
  Circleville *(G-3706)*

Dave Sugar Excavating LLC................ E 330 542-1100
  Petersburg *(G-12394)*

Degen Excavating Inc................ D 419 225-6871
  Lima *(G-9884)*

Digioia-Suburban Excvtg LLC................ D 440 237-1978
  North Royalton *(G-11939)*

Don Wartko Construction Co................ D 330 673-5252
  Kent *(G-9572)*

Edgar Trent Cnstr Co LLC................ D 419 683-4939
  Crestline *(G-7022)*

ESwagner Company Inc................ D 419 691-8651
  Oregon *(G-12133)*

Ewers Utility Service LLC................ E 740 326-4451
  Mount Vernon *(G-11487)*

Fields Excavating Inc................ D 740 532-1780
  Kitts Hill *(G-9647)*

Fishel Company................ C 614 850-4400
  Columbus *(G-5867)*

Fishel Company................ D 614 921-8504
  Columbus *(G-5868)*

Fishel Company................ E 937 233-2268
  Dayton *(G-7355)*

Fishel Company................ D 614 274-8100
  Columbus *(G-5869)*

Foill Inc................ E 740 947-1117
  Waverly *(G-14613)*

Ford Development Corp................ D 513 772-1521
  Cincinnati *(G-2693)*

Fred A Nemann Co................ E 513 467-9400
  Cincinnati *(G-2702)*

George J Igel & Co Inc................ A 614 445-8421
  Columbus *(G-5928)*

Geotex Construction Svcs Inc................ E 614 444-5690
  Columbus *(G-5929)*

Gleason Construction Co Inc................ E 419 865-7480
  Holland *(G-9285)*

Global Energy Partners LLC................ E 419 756-8027
  Mansfield *(G-10267)*

Great Lakes Crushing Ltd................ D 440 944-5500
  Wickliffe *(G-15150)*

Great Lakes Telcom Ltd................ E 330 629-8848
  Youngstown *(G-15622)*

Greater Cincinnati Water Works................ C 513 591-7700
  Cincinnati *(G-2770)*

Gudenkauf LLC................ C 614 488-1776
  Columbus *(G-5961)*

H M Miller Construction Co................ D 330 628-4811
  Mogadore *(G-11327)*

Integrity Pipeline Services LLC................ D 419 886-9907
  Bellville *(G-1051)*

J & J General Maintenance Inc................ D 740 533-9729
  Ironton *(G-9509)*

J B Express Inc................ D 740 702-9830
  Chillicothe *(G-2075)*

J Daniel & Company Inc................ D 513 575-3100
  Loveland *(G-10143)*

Jack Conie & Sons Corp................ E 614 291-5931
  Columbus *(G-6080)*

JS Bova Excavating LLC................ E 234 254-4040
  Struthers *(G-13501)*

Kenneth G Myers Cnstr Co Inc................ D 419 639-2051
  Green Springs *(G-8860)*

Kirk Williams Piping & Plbg Co................ E 614 875-9023
  Grove City *(G-8932)*

▲ Kokosing Construction Co Inc................ C 614 228-1029
  Westerville *(G-14993)*

KS Energy Services LLC................ C 513 271-0276
  Cincinnati *(G-2955)*

Main Lite Electric Co Inc................ E 330 369-8333
  Warren *(G-14537)*

17 CONSTRUCTION - SPECIAL TRADE CONTRACTORS

Mark Schaffer Excvtg Trckg Inc .... D 419 668-5990
  Norwalk (G-12017)
Mid-Ohio Contracting Inc .... E 330 343-2925
  Dover (G-7893)
Mid-Ohio Pipeline Company Inc .... E 419 884-3772
  Mansfield (G-10298)
Mike Enyart & Sons Inc .... D 740 523-0235
  South Point (G-13181)
Miller Pipeline LLC .... B 937 506-8837
  Tipp City (G-13663)
Minnesota Limited LLC .... C 330 343-4612
  Dover (G-7894)
Miracle Plumbing & Heating Co .... E 330 477-2402
  Canton (G-1809)
National Engrg & Contg Co .... E 440 238-3331
  Cleveland (G-4625)
Nelson Stark Company .... C 513 489-0866
  Cincinnati (G-3105)
Nerone & Sons Inc .... E 216 662-2235
  Cleveland (G-4635)
Nickolas M Savko & Sons Inc .... E 614 451-2242
  Columbus (G-6359)
North Bay Construction Inc .... E 440 835-1898
  Westlake (G-15085)
Ohio Utilities Protection Svc .... D 800 311-3692
  North Jackson (G-11875)
Parallel Technologies Inc .... D 614 798-9700
  Dublin (G-8087)
Precision Engrg & Contg Inc .... D 440 349-1204
  Solon (G-13129)
Premium Utility Contractor Inc .... E 951 313-0808
  East Palestine (G-8198)
Quality Lines Inc .... C 740 815-1165
  Findlay (G-8580)
R & R Pipeline Inc .... E 740 345-3692
  Newark (G-11744)
R D Jergens Contractors Inc .... D 937 669-9799
  Vandalia (G-14391)
R L A Utilities .... E 513 554-1453
  Cincinnati (G-3272)
Rla Utilities LLC .... E 513 554-1470
  Cincinnati (G-3308)
Sky Climber Twr Solutions LLC .... E 740 203-3900
  Delaware (G-7826)
South Shore Cable Cnstr Inc .... D 440 816-0033
  Cleveland (G-4921)
Steelial Wldg Met Fbrction Inc .... E 740 669-5300
  Vinton (G-14425)
Sunesis Construction Co .... C 513 326-6000
  West Chester (G-14770)
Sunesis Environmental LLC .... E 513 326-6000
  Fairfield (G-8444)
Sws Environmental Service Inc .... E 513 793-7417
  Cincinnati (G-3429)
Terrace Construction Co Inc .... D 216 739-3170
  Cleveland (G-4986)
Thayer Pwr Comm Line Cnstr LLC .... D 330 922-4950
  Cuyahoga Falls (G-7106)
Thayer Pwr Comm Line Cnstr LLC .... D 740 927-0021
  Pataskala (G-12278)
The Beaver Excavating Co .... A 330 478-2151
  Canton (G-1871)
▼ Tri County Tower LLC .... E 330 538-9874
  North Jackson (G-11878)
Trucco Construction Co Inc .... C 740 417-9010
  Delaware (G-7831)
Underground Utilities Inc .... D 419 465-2587
  Monroeville (G-11360)
Universal Recovery Systems Inc .... D 614 299-0184
  Columbus (G-6821)
US Radius Services Inc .... E 929 505-1063
  Trenton (G-14125)

US Tank Alliance Inc .... D 440 238-7705
  Strongsville (G-13494)
Usic Locating Services LLC .... E 513 554-0456
  Cincinnati (G-3611)
Utilicon Corporation .... E 216 391-8500
  Cleveland (G-5095)
Utilities Services Radius LLC .... C 800 515-7650
  Trenton (G-14126)
Vallejo Company .... E 216 741-3933
  Cleveland (G-5096)
Vernon Nagel Inc .... D 419 592-3861
  Napoleon (G-11534)
Welded Construction LP .... E 419 874-3548
  Perrysburg (G-12386)
Wenger Excavating Inc .... E 330 837-4767
  Dalton (G-7122)
Woodward Excavating Co .... E 614 866-4384
  Reynoldsburg (G-12683)
Zemba Bros Inc .... E 740 452-1880
  Zanesville (G-15844)

1629 Heavy construction, nec

A P OHoro Company .... D 330 759-9317
  Youngstown (G-15539)
Aecom Energy & Cnstr Inc .... E 216 622-2300
  Cleveland (G-3771)
Apex Environmental LLC .... E 740 543-4389
  Amsterdam (G-435)
Babcock & Wilcox Cnstr Co LLC .... D 330 753-9750
  Akron (G-58)
◆ Babcock & Wilcox Company .... A 330 753-4511
  Akron (G-59)
Brunk Excavating Inc .... E 513 360-0308
  Monroe (G-11335)
Danis Companies .... B 937 228-1225
  Miamisburg (G-11043)
▲ Delta Railroad Cnstr Inc .... D 440 992-2997
  Ashtabula (G-532)
Edwards Land Clearing Inc .... E 440 988-4477
  Amherst (G-428)
◆ Enerfab LLC .... B 513 641-0500
  Cincinnati (G-2620)
ESwagner Company Inc .... D 419 691-8651
  Oregon (G-12133)
Fritz-Rumer-Cooke Co Inc .... E 614 444-8844
  Columbus (G-5900)
Fryman-Kuck General Contrs Inc .... E 937 274-2892
  Dayton (G-7371)
Gg Ohio Inc .... D 330 683-7206
  Orrville (G-12165)
▲ Goettle Holding Company Inc .... C 513 825-8100
  Cincinnati (G-2738)
Great Lakes Crushing Ltd .... D 440 944-5500
  Wickliffe (G-15150)
▲ Independence Excavating Inc .... E 216 524-1700
  Independence (G-9437)
ISI Systems Inc .... E 740 942-0050
  Cadiz (G-1541)
Jack Conie & Sons Corp .... E 614 291-5931
  Columbus (G-6080)
Jack Gibson Construction Co .... D 330 394-5280
  Warren (G-14530)
KHD Company LLC .... E 614 935-9939
  Worthington (G-15426)
▲ Kokosing Construction Co Inc .... C 614 228-1029
  Westerville (G-14993)
Kokosing Industrial Inc .... D 614 212-5700
  Westerville (G-14995)
M T Golf Course Managment Inc .... E 513 923-1188
  Cincinnati (G-2998)
Metropolitan Envmtl Svcs Inc .... D 614 771-1881
  Hilliard (G-9213)

Pae & Associates Inc .... D 937 833-0013
  Dayton (G-7544)
Peterson Construction Company .... C 419 941-2233
  Wapakoneta (G-14489)
Petro Environmental Tech .... E 513 489-6789
  Cincinnati (G-3202)
Platinum Restoration Inc .... E 440 327-0699
  Elyria (G-8286)
Railworks Track Services Llc .... B 330 538-2261
  North Jackson (G-11877)
Royal Landscape Gardening Inc .... E 216 883-7000
  Cleveland (G-4858)
Scg Fields LLC .... E 440 546-1200
  Brecksville (G-1366)
Shook Construction Co .... D 937 276-6666
  Moraine (G-11438)
Shook National Corporation .... C 937 276-6666
  Dayton (G-7617)
Siemens Energy Inc .... E 740 393-8897
  Mount Vernon (G-11508)
Sports Surfaces Cnstr LLC .... E 440 546-1200
  Brecksville (G-1368)
Sunesis Environmental LLC .... D 513 326-6000
  Fairfield (G-8444)
The Great Lakes Construction Co .... C 330 220-3900
  Hinckley (G-9272)
Toledo Refining Company LLC .... E 419 698-6600
  Oregon (G-12144)
Tri-America Contractors Inc .... E 740 574-0148
  Wheelersburg (G-15134)
Uranium Disposition Svcs LLC .... C 740 289-3620
  Piketon (G-12430)
Valley Mining Inc .... C 740 922-3942
  Dennison (G-7862)
Whiting-Turner Contracting Co .... B 440 449-9200
  Cleveland (G-5145)

17 CONSTRUCTION - SPECIAL TRADE CONTRACTORS

1711 Plumbing, heating, air-conditioning

1 Tom Plumber LLC .... E 866 758-6237
  Milford (G-11214)
A Bee C Service Inc .... E 440 735-1505
  Cleveland (G-3747)
A J Stockmeister Inc .... E 740 286-2106
  Jackson (G-9515)
A-1 Advanced Plumbing Inc .... E 614 873-0548
  Plain City (G-12463)
AAA Pipe Cleaning Corporation .... C 216 341-2900
  Cleveland (G-3756)
Accurate Mechanical Inc .... D 740 681-1332
  Lancaster (G-9690)
▲ Advanced Mechanical Svcs Inc .... E 937 879-7426
  Fairborn (G-8366)
Aggressive Mechanical Inc .... E 614 443-3280
  Columbus (G-5329)
Air Force One Inc .... D 614 889-0121
  Dublin (G-7926)
Air-Temp Climate Control Inc .... E 216 579-1552
  Cleveland (G-3779)
Airtron Inc .... D 614 274-2345
  Columbus (G-5333)
Airtron Inc .... E 859 371-7780
  Miamisburg (G-11022)
▲ Alan Manufacturing Inc .... E 330 262-1555
  Wooster (G-15308)
All Temp Refrigeration Inc .... E 419 692-5016
  Delphos (G-7836)
Allegiant Plumbing LLC .... E 614 824-5002
  Columbus (G-5335)

Employee Codes: A=Over 500 employees, B=251-500
C=101-250, D=51-100, E=20-50, F=10-19, G=1-9

17 CONSTRUCTION - SPECIAL TRADE CONTRACTORS — SIC SECTION

American Air Furnace Company .... D 614 876-1702
   Grove City *(G-8895)*

American Dream Solar & Win Inc .... D 513 543-5645
   Amelia *(G-410)*

American Mechanical Group Inc .... E 614 575-3720
   Columbus *(G-5353)*

American Plumbing .... E 440 871-8293
   Bay Village *(G-757)*

Anderson Autmtc Htg & AC Inc .... E 512 574-0005
   Cleves *(G-5186)*

Apollo Heating & AC Inc .... E 513 271-3600
   Cincinnati *(G-2210)*

Applied Mechanical Systems Inc .... C 937 854-3073
   Dayton *(G-7176)*

Arco Heating & AC Co .... E 216 663-3211
   Solon *(G-13067)*

Area Energy & Electric Inc .... C 937 498-4784
   Sidney *(G-13019)*

Arise Incorporated .... E 440 746-8860
   Brecksville *(G-1344)*

Atalian US Ohio Valley Inc .... B 614 476-1818
   Columbus *(G-5400)*

Atlas Capital Services Inc .... D 614 294-7373
   Columbus *(G-5401)*

B B & E Inc .... E 740 354-5469
   Portsmouth *(G-12545)*

◆ Babcock & Wilcox Company .... A 330 753-4511
   Akron *(G-59)*

Bachmans Inc .... E 513 943-5300
   Batavia *(G-726)*

Bay Furnace Sheet Metal Co .... E 440 871-3777
   Westlake *(G-15037)*

Bay Mechanical & Elec Corp .... D 440 282-6816
   Lorain *(G-10058)*

Bell & Blaire LLC .... E 330 794-5647
   Munroe Falls *(G-11513)*

Blind & Son LLC .... D 330 753-7711
   Barberton *(G-695)*

Bmwc Constructors Inc .... C 419 490-2000
   Toledo *(G-13707)*

Brewer-Garrett Company .... C 440 243-3535
   Middleburg Heights *(G-11113)*

Bruner Corporation .... C 614 334-9000
   Hilliard *(G-9185)*

Buck and Sons Ldscp Svc Inc .... E 614 876-5359
   Hilliard *(G-9186)*

Buckeye Mechanical Contg Inc .... E 740 282-0089
   Toronto *(G-14121)*

Building Integrated Svcs LLC .... D 330 733-9191
   Oakwood Village *(G-12055)*

Butler Heating Company .... E 937 253-8871
   Dayton *(G-7208)*

Cac Group LLC .... E 740 369-4328
   Delaware *(G-7782)*

Cahill Corporation .... E 330 724-1224
   Uniontown *(G-14243)*

Campbell Inc .... E 419 476-4444
   Northwood *(G-11971)*

Care Heating and Cooling Inc .... E 614 841-1555
   Lewis Center *(G-9812)*

Cattrell Companies Inc .... D 740 537-2481
   Toronto *(G-14122)*

Cbkb Inc .... E 440 946-6019
   Mentor *(G-10919)*

Centerville Landscaping Inc .... E 937 433-5495
   Dayton *(G-7219)*

Chemed Corporation .... C 513 762-6690
   Cincinnati *(G-2352)*

◆ Chick Master Incubator Company .... D 330 722-5591
   Medina *(G-10819)*

Christopher Burkey .... E 330 770-9607
   North Lima *(G-11886)*

Cincinnati Air Conditioning Co .... D 513 721-5622
   Cincinnati *(G-2392)*

Ckp Heating and Cooling LLC .... E 330 791-3029
   North Canton *(G-11817)*

Climate Pros LLC .... D 216 881-5200
   Cleveland *(G-4083)*

Climate Pros LLC .... D 330 744-2732
   Youngstown *(G-15579)*

Coleman Spohn Corporation .... E 216 431-8070
   Cleveland *(G-4086)*

Columbs/Worthington Htg AC Inc .... E 614 771-5381
   Columbus *(G-5605)*

Columbus Heating & Vent Co .... C 614 274-1177
   Columbus *(G-5635)*

Comfort Express Inc .... E 740 389-4400
   Delaware *(G-7786)*

Comfort Systems USA Ohio Inc .... E 440 703-1600
   Bedford *(G-957)*

Commercial Comfort Systems Inc .... E 419 481-4444
   Perrysburg *(G-12325)*

Complete Mechanical Svcs LLC .... D 513 489-3080
   Blue Ash *(G-1158)*

Crawford Mechanical Svcs Inc .... D 614 478-9424
   Pataskala *(G-12272)*

Custom AC & Htg Co .... D 614 552-4822
   Gahanna *(G-8714)*

D & A Plumbing & Heating Inc .... E 330 499-8733
   Uniontown *(G-14247)*

David R White Services Inc .... E 740 594-8381
   Athens *(G-564)*

De-Cal Inc .... C 330 272-0021
   Youngstown *(G-15594)*

Debra-Kuempel Inc .... D 513 271-6500
   Cincinnati *(G-2552)*

Dimech Services Inc .... E 419 727-0111
   Toledo *(G-13780)*

Dovetail Construction Co Inc .... E 740 592-1800
   Cleveland *(G-4181)*

Dunbar Mechanical Inc .... E 440 220-2000
   Eastlake *(G-8201)*

Dunbar Mechanical Inc .... D 419 537-1900
   Toledo *(G-13784)*

Echols Heating and AC Inc .... E 330 773-3500
   Coventry Township *(G-7007)*

Ecohouse LLC .... E 614 456-7641
   Columbus *(G-5805)*

Ecoplumbers LLC .... E 614 299-9903
   Hilliard *(G-9194)*

◆ Enerfab LLC .... B 513 641-0500
   Cincinnati *(G-2620)*

Enerfab Power & Industrial Inc .... A 513 470-5526
   Cincinnati *(G-2621)*

Energy MGT Specialists Inc .... E 216 676-9045
   Cleveland *(G-4215)*

Enervise LLC .... E 614 885-9800
   Columbus *(G-5817)*

Enervise Incorporated .... D 513 761-6000
   Blue Ash *(G-1167)*

Enginring Exclince Nat Accnts .... D 844 969-3923
   Blue Ash *(G-1168)*

Envirnmental Engrg Systems Inc .... E 937 228-6492
   Dayton *(G-7336)*

Envirocontrol Systems Inc .... E 937 275-4718
   Dayton *(G-7337)*

Falls Heating & Cooling Inc .... E 330 929-8777
   Cuyahoga Falls *(G-7073)*

▲ Farber Corporation .... E 614 294-1626
   Columbus *(G-5850)*

Favret Company .... D 614 488-5211
   Columbus *(G-5852)*

Fellhauer Mechanical Systems .... E 419 734-3674
   Port Clinton *(G-12525)*

Fire Guard LLC .... E 740 625-5181
   Sunbury *(G-13521)*

Fitzenrider Inc .... E 419 784-0828
   Defiance *(G-7747)*

Fowler Electric Co .... E 440 735-2385
   Bedford *(G-960)*

Franck and Fric Incorporated .... D 216 524-4451
   Cleveland *(G-4284)*

Freeland Contracting Co .... E 614 443-2718
   Columbus *(G-5894)*

Frye Mechanical Inc .... D 937 222-8750
   Dayton *(G-7370)*

G H A T Inc .... E 330 392-8838
   Warren *(G-14522)*

G Mechanical Inc .... E 614 844-6750
   Columbus *(G-5905)*

Gardiner Service Company LLC .... D 330 896-9358
   Uniontown *(G-14253)*

Gardiner Service Company LLC .... C 440 248-3400
   Solon *(G-13091)*

Geauga Mechanical Company .... D 440 285-2000
   Chardon *(G-2000)*

Geiger Brothers Inc .... B 740 286-0800
   Jackson *(G-9518)*

Gem Industrial Inc .... D 419 666-6554
   Walbridge *(G-14461)*

Gemini Solar LLC .... E 833 339-2097
   Groveport *(G-8991)*

General Temperature Ctrl Inc .... E 614 837-3888
   Canal Winchester *(G-1607)*

Genes Rfrgn Htg & AC Inc .... E 330 723-4104
   Medina *(G-10838)*

GM Mechanical Inc .... D 937 473-3006
   Covington *(G-7018)*

Grabill Plumbing & Heating .... E 330 756-2075
   Beach City *(G-761)*

Gross Plumbing Incorporated .... E 440 324-9999
   Elyria *(G-8253)*

Guenther Mechanical Inc .... C 419 289-6900
   Ashland *(G-500)*

Gundlach Sheet Metal Works Inc .... E 419 734-7351
   Port Clinton *(G-12531)*

Gundlach Sheet Metal Works Inc .... E 419 626-4525
   Sandusky *(G-12902)*

Hank Bloom Services Inc .... E 440 946-7823
   Mentor *(G-10945)*

Hanks Plumbing & Heating Co .... E 419 843-2222
   Toledo *(G-13832)*

Hartley Company .... E 740 439-6668
   Zanesville *(G-15798)*

Haslett Heating & Cooling Inc .... E 614 299-2133
   Dublin *(G-8027)*

Helm and Associates Inc .... E 419 893-1480
   Maumee *(G-10731)*

Houston Dick Plbg & Htg Inc .... E 740 763-3961
   Newark *(G-11708)*

Igs Solar LLC .... D 844 447-7652
   Dublin *(G-8034)*

Imperial Heating and Coolg Inc .... E 440 498-1788
   Solon *(G-13098)*

Industrial Power Systems Inc .... B 419 531-3121
   Rossford *(G-12767)*

Inloes Mechanical Inc .... E 513 896-9499
   Hamilton *(G-9054)*

Integra Svcs Intermediate LLC .... B 317 409-2130
   Mentor *(G-10952)*

J & D Home Improvement Inc .... D 800 288-0831
   Columbus *(G-6076)*

J & J General Maintenance Inc .... D 740 533-9729
   Ironton *(G-9509)*

J W Geopfert Co Inc .... E 330 762-2293
   Akron *(G-208)*

17 CONSTRUCTION - SPECIAL TRADE CONTRACTORS

Jackson Comfort Systems Inc .... E 330 468-3111
　Northfield *(G-11959)*
Jacobs Mechanical Co .... C 513 681-6800
　Cincinnati *(G-2895)*
Jennings Heating Company Inc .... E 330 784-1286
　Akron *(G-210)*
Jfdb Ltd .... C 513 870-0601
　Cincinnati *(G-2912)*
John F Gallagher Plumbing Co .... D 440 946-4256
　Eastlake *(G-8204)*
Jonle Co Inc .... E 513 662-2282
　Cincinnati *(G-2920)*
Julian Speer Co .... D 614 261-6331
　Columbus *(G-6100)*
▼ K A Bergquist Inc .... E 419 865-4196
　Toledo *(G-13872)*
K Company Incorporated .... C 330 773-5125
　Coventry Township *(G-7012)*
Ke Gutridge LLC .... D 614 299-2133
　Dublin *(G-8047)*
Ken Neyer Plumbing Inc .... E 513 353-3311
　Cleves *(G-5190)*
Kidron Electric Inc .... E 330 857-2871
　Kidron *(G-9637)*
◆ Kinetics Noise Control Inc .... C 614 889-0480
　Dublin *(G-8049)*
Kinn Bros Plbg Htg & AC Inc .... E 419 562-1484
　Bucyrus *(G-1511)*
Kirk Williams Company Inc .... D 614 875-9023
　Grove City *(G-8931)*
Kirk Williams Piping & Plbg Co .... D 614 875-9023
　Grove City *(G-8932)*
Kuempel Service Inc .... E 513 271-6500
　Cincinnati *(G-2956)*
▲ Langdon Inc .... E 513 733-5955
　Cincinnati *(G-2965)*
Limbach Company LLC .... B 614 299-2175
　Columbus *(G-6164)*
Limbach Company LLC .... C 614 299-2175
　Columbus *(G-6165)*
Lippincott Plmbng-Hting AC Inc .... E 419 222-0856
　Lima *(G-9928)*
Lochard Inc .... D 937 492-8811
　Sidney *(G-13037)*
Lucas Plumbing & Heating Inc .... E 440 282-4567
　Lorain *(G-10091)*
Luxury Heating Company .... D 440 366-0971
　Sheffield Village *(G-13001)*
Marvin W Mielke Inc .... D 330 725-8845
　Medina *(G-10853)*
McAfee Heating & AC Co Inc .... E 937 438-1976
　Dayton *(G-7472)*
McPhillips Plbg Htg & AC Co .... E 216 481-1400
　Cleveland *(G-4542)*
Mechancal Optmzers Cncnnati Ht .... E 513 467-1444
　Cincinnati *(G-3024)*
Mechancal/Industrial Contg Inc .... E 513 489-8282
　Cincinnati *(G-3025)*
Mechanical Cnstr Managers LLC .... C 937 274-1987
　Dayton *(G-7474)*
Mechanical Construction Co .... E 740 353-5668
　Portsmouth *(G-12563)*
Mechanical Systems Dayton Inc .... D 937 254-3235
　Dayton *(G-7136)*
Metro Heating and AC Co .... E 614 777-1237
　Hilliard *(G-9212)*
Mid-Ohio Air Conditioning Corp .... E 614 291-4664
　Columbus *(G-6236)*
Midwestern Plumbing Svc Inc .... E 513 753-0050
　Cincinnati *(G-3060)*
Mielke Holdings LLC .... D 330 725-8845
　Medina *(G-10866)*

Miracle Plumbing & Heating Co .... E 330 477-2402
　Canton *(G-1809)*
Mj Baumann Co Inc .... D 614 759-7100
　Columbus *(G-6252)*
Monroe Plumbing Inc .... D 440 708-0006
　Burton *(G-1531)*
Morrison Inc .... E 740 373-5869
　Marietta *(G-10392)*
Muetzel Plumbing & Heating Co .... D 614 299-7700
　Columbus *(G-6282)*
Naragon Companies Inc .... E 330 745-7700
　Norton *(G-11995)*
National Heating and AC Co .... E 513 621-4620
　Blue Ash *(G-1214)*
National Tab LLC .... E 513 860-2050
　Cincinnati *(G-3097)*
Nbw Inc .... E 216 377-1700
　Cleveland *(G-4629)*
Nelson Stark Company .... C 513 489-0866
　Cincinnati *(G-3105)*
Neptune Plumbing & Heating Co .... E 216 475-9100
　Cleveland *(G-4634)*
Nieman Plumbing Inc .... D 513 851-5588
　Cincinnati *(G-3117)*
Noll Fisher Incorporated .... E 937 394-4181
　Anna *(G-443)*
Noron Inc .... E 419 726-2677
　Toledo *(G-13936)*
North Amrcn Utlity Sltions LLC .... E 513 313-2323
　Cleves *(G-5191)*
North Bay Construction Inc .... E 440 835-1898
　Westlake *(G-15085)*
North East Mechanical Inc .... E 440 871-7525
　Westlake *(G-15086)*
Northern Plumbing Systems .... E 513 831-5111
　Goshen *(G-8837)*
Ohio Fabricators Inc .... D 330 745-4406
　Akron *(G-250)*
Ontario Mechanical LLC .... E 419 529-2578
　Ontario *(G-12121)*
Osterwisch Company Inc .... D 513 791-3282
　Cincinnati *(G-3174)*
P K Wadsworth Heating & Coolg .... E 440 248-4821
　Solon *(G-13123)*
Peck-Hannaford Briggs Svc Corp .... D 513 681-1200
　Cincinnati *(G-3193)*
Perfection Group Inc .... C 513 772-7545
　Cincinnati *(G-3196)*
Perfection Services Inc .... C 513 772-7545
　Cincinnati *(G-3197)*
▲ Pioneer Pipe Inc .... A 740 376-2400
　Marietta *(G-10399)*
Pleasant Valley Corporation .... D 330 239-0176
　Medina *(G-10878)*
Pre-Fore Inc .... E 740 467-2206
　Millersport *(G-11298)*
Precision Duct Systems LLC .... C 937 335-2626
　Troy *(G-14152)*
Process Construction Inc .... E 513 251-2211
　Cincinnati *(G-3237)*
Process Construction Inc .... D 513 251-2211
　Cincinnati *(G-3238)*
Professional Plumbing Svcs Inc .... E 740 454-1066
　Zanesville *(G-15830)*
Prout Boiler Htg & Wldg Inc .... E 330 744-0293
　Youngstown *(G-15699)*
Queen City Mechanicals Inc .... E 513 353-1430
　Cincinnati *(G-3262)*
Reader Tinning & Roofing Co .... E 216 451-1355
　Cleveland *(G-4810)*
▲ Recker and Boerger Inc .... D 513 942-9663
　West Chester *(G-14830)*

Regal Plumbing & Heating Co .... E 937 492-2894
　Sidney *(G-13046)*
Reliant Mechanical Inc .... D 937 644-0074
　East Liberty *(G-8175)*
Relmec Mechanical LLC .... C 216 391-1030
　Cleveland *(G-4823)*
Reupert Heating and AC Co Inc .... E 513 922-5050
　Cincinnati *(G-3293)*
Rgt Services LLC .... E 440 786-9777
　Oakwood Village *(G-12056)*
Rmf Nooter LLC .... D 419 727-1970
　Toledo *(G-13992)*
Robertson Plumbing & Heating .... E 330 863-0611
　Malvern *(G-10235)*
Robinson Htg Air-Conditioning .... E 513 422-6812
　Middletown *(G-11184)*
Roger Storer & Son Inc .... E 937 325-9873
　Springfield *(G-13287)*
Romanoff Group LLC .... E 614 755-4500
　Gahanna *(G-8730)*
Roth Bros Inc .... C 330 793-5571
　Youngstown *(G-15713)*
Roto-Rooter Development Co .... D 513 762-6690
　Cincinnati *(G-3322)*
Roto-Rooter Services Company .... D 513 762-6690
　Cincinnati *(G-3324)*
RPC Mechanical Services .... E 513 733-1641
　Cincinnati *(G-3327)*
S A Comunale Co Inc .... D 419 334-3841
　Fremont *(G-8700)*
S A Comunale Co Inc .... D 440 684-9325
　Highland Heights *(G-9171)*
S A Comunale Co Inc .... C 330 706-3040
　Barberton *(G-708)*
S-T Acquisition Company LLC .... E 440 735-1505
　Cleveland *(G-4868)*
S&D/Osterfeld Mech Contrs Inc .... D 937 277-1700
　Dayton *(G-7602)*
Sauer Construction LLC .... D 614 853-2500
　Columbus *(G-6644)*
Sauer Group LLC .... C 614 853-2500
　Columbus *(G-6645)*
Schmid Mechanical Inc .... E 330 264-3633
　Wooster *(G-15373)*
Schmids Service Now Inc .... E 330 499-0157
　Wooster *(G-15374)*
Schweizer Dipple Inc .... D 440 786-8090
　Cleveland *(G-4884)*
Scioto LLC .... B 937 644-0888
　Marysville *(G-10507)*
Sexton Industrial Inc .... C 513 530-5555
　West Chester *(G-14832)*
Sisler Heating & Cooling Inc .... E 330 722-7101
　Medina *(G-10890)*
Slagle Mechanical Contractors .... E 937 492-4151
　Sidney *(G-13054)*
Smith & Oby Company .... D 440 735-5333
　Walton Hills *(G-14480)*
Smith & Oby Service Co .... E 440 735-5322
　Bedford *(G-985)*
Smith-Boughan Inc .... D 419 991-8040
　Lima *(G-9961)*
Smylie One Heating & Cooling .... E 440 449-4328
　Bedford *(G-986)*
Solar Flexrack LLC .... E 888 380-8138
　Youngstown *(G-15726)*
Speer Industries Incorporated .... E 614 261-6331
　Columbus *(G-6704)*
Stack Heating and Cooling LLC .... D 440 937-9134
　Avon *(G-665)*
Standard Plumbing & Heating Co .... D 330 453-5150
　Canton *(G-1856)*

Employee Codes: A=Over 500 employees, B=251-500
C=101-250, D=51-100, E=20-50, F=10-19, G=1-9

17 CONSTRUCTION - SPECIAL TRADE CONTRACTORS

Steingass Mechanical Contg LLC .... E 330 725-6090
  Medina *(G-10893)*
Sutton & Associates Inc .... E 614 487-9096
  Columbus *(G-6737)*
Swingle J and P Plumbing & Htg .... E 330 723-4840
  Medina *(G-10896)*
Tanner Heating & AC Inc .... E 937 299-2500
  Moraine *(G-11442)*
TH Martin Inc .... D 216 741-2020
  Cleveland *(G-4990)*
The Geiler Company .... C 513 574-1200
  Cincinnati *(G-3466)*
The Hattenbach Company .... D 216 881-5200
  Cleveland *(G-5001)*
The Peck-Hannaford Briggs Co .... E 513 681-4600
  Cincinnati *(G-3468)*
Thomas J Dyer Company .... C 513 321-8100
  Cincinnati *(G-3474)*
Titan Mechanical Solutions LLC .... E 513 738-5800
  Harrison *(G-9117)*
Town & Country Plbg & Htg Inc .... E 330 726-5755
  Youngstown *(G-15735)*
TP Mechanical Contractors LLC .... C 513 851-8881
  Cincinnati *(G-3498)*
TP Mechanical Contractors Inc .... D 614 253-8556
  Columbus *(G-6777)*
▲ Trades Equipment LLC .... E 419 625-4444
  Independence *(G-9491)*
Trep Ltd .... E 419 717-5624
  Napoleon *(G-11533)*
United Group Services Inc .... C 800 633-9690
  West Chester *(G-14842)*
Universal Enterprises Inc .... C 419 529-3500
  Ontario *(G-12126)*
Vaughn Industries LLC .... D 740 548-7100
  Lewis Center *(G-9840)*
▲ Vaughn Industries LLC .... B 419 396-3900
  Carey *(G-1895)*
Vulcan Enterprises Inc .... E 419 396-3535
  Carey *(G-1896)*
Wadsworth Service Inc .... E 419 861-8181
  Middleburg Heights *(G-11134)*
Waibel Energy Systems Inc .... D 937 264-4343
  Vandalia *(G-14403)*
Warner Mechanical Corporation .... E 419 332-7116
  Fremont *(G-8708)*
Waterworks LLC .... C 614 253-7246
  Columbus *(G-6870)*
Wca Group LLC .... C 513 540-2761
  Fairfield *(G-8453)*
Wells Brothers Inc .... D 937 394-7559
  Anna *(G-445)*
Wentz Hc Holdings Inc .... E 614 294-4966
  Worthington *(G-15467)*
Western Reserve Mechanical Inc .... D 330 652-3888
  Niles *(G-11798)*
WF Hann & Sons LLC .... E 216 831-4200
  Warrensville Heights *(G-14590)*
Whisler Plumbing & Heating Inc .... D 330 833-2875
  Massillon *(G-10673)*
Wichman Co .... E 419 385-6438
  Toledo *(G-14107)*
▼ Willard Kelsey Solar Group LLC .... E 419 931-2001
  Perrysburg *(G-12388)*
Wojos Heating & AC Inc .... E 419 693-3220
  Northwood *(G-11987)*
Zemba Bros Inc .... E 740 452-1880
  Zanesville *(G-15844)*

1721 Painting and paper hanging

A & A Safety Inc .... E 513 943-6100
  Amelia *(G-409)*
A1 Industrial Painting Inc .... E 330 750-9441
  Youngstown *(G-15540)*
Apbn Inc .... E 724 964-8252
  Campbell *(G-1591)*
August Groh & Sons Inc .... E 513 821-0090
  Cincinnati *(G-2229)*
Cartruck Packaging Inc .... E 216 631-7225
  Cleveland *(G-3931)*
Chas F Mann Painting Co .... E 419 385-7151
  Toledo *(G-13730)*
Cleveland Construction Inc .... C 440 255-8000
  Mason *(G-10539)*
Dean Contracting Inc .... E 440 260-7590
  Cleveland *(G-4157)*
Dependable Painting Co .... E 216 431-4470
  Cleveland *(G-4162)*
E B Miller Contracting Inc .... E 513 531-7030
  Cincinnati *(G-2592)*
Eagle Industrial Painting LLC .... E 330 866-5965
  Canton *(G-1739)*
F C Franchising Systems Inc .... E 513 563-8339
  Montgomery *(G-11368)*
Flamos Enterprises Inc .... E 330 478-0009
  Canton *(G-1755)*
Francis C Skinner Painting Svc .... E 937 773-3858
  Piqua *(G-12442)*
Frank Novak & Sons Inc .... D 216 475-2495
  Cleveland *(G-4285)*
Houck Asphalt Maintenance LLC .... E 513 734-4500
  Bethel *(G-1092)*
Howard Painting Inc .... E 419 782-7786
  Defiance *(G-7749)*
Johnson & Fischer Incorporated .... E 614 276-8868
  Columbus *(G-6094)*
K Kern Painting LLC .... E 419 966-0812
  Toledo *(G-13873)*
Lakeside Interior Contractors Inc .... C 419 867-1300
  Perrysburg *(G-12351)*
Liberty-Sps JV Ltd Partnership .... D 330 755-7711
  Youngstown *(G-15651)*
Lou Ritenour Decorators Inc .... D 330 425-3232
  Twinsburg *(G-14202)*
Mark Dura Inc .... E 330 995-0883
  Streetsboro *(G-13421)*
Mes Painting and Graphics Ltd .... E 614 496-1696
  Westerville *(G-14998)*
Muha Construction Inc .... E 937 435-0678
  Dayton *(G-7517)*
Napoleon Machine LLC .... E 419 591-7010
  Napoleon *(G-11530)*
North Star Painting Co Inc .... E 330 743-2333
  Youngstown *(G-15678)*
Painting Company .... C 614 873-1334
  Plain City *(G-12488)*
Perry Interiors Inc .... E 513 761-9333
  Batavia *(G-745)*
Preferred Acquisition Co LLC .... D 216 587-0957
  Cleveland *(G-4767)*
Protective Coatings Inc .... E 937 275-7711
  Dayton *(G-7572)*
Reilly Painting & Contg Inc .... E 216 371-8160
  Cleveland Heights *(G-5183)*
Salix Ltd .... D 513 381-2679
  Cincinnati *(G-3344)*
The Apostolos Group Inc .... C 330 670-9900
  Copley *(G-6966)*
Vmi Group Inc .... D 330 405-4146
  Twinsburg *(G-14230)*

1731 Electrical work

A J Goulder Electric Co .... E 440 942-4026
  Willoughby *(G-15182)*
A T Emmett LLC .... E 419 734-2520
  Port Clinton *(G-12516)*
Abbott Electric Inc .... D 330 343-8941
  Dover *(G-7871)*
Abbott Electric Inc .... D 330 452-6601
  Canton *(G-1652)*
Accurate Electric Cnstr Inc .... C 614 863-1844
  Reynoldsburg *(G-12650)*
Acpi Systems Inc .... E 513 738-3840
  Hamilton *(G-9016)*
Acree-Daily Corporation .... E 614 452-7300
  Columbus *(G-5308)*
Active Electric Incorporated .... D 937 299-1885
  Dayton *(G-7154)*
Advanced Elec Specialists Inc .... D 330 237-9930
  Brunswick *(G-1449)*
Aey Electric Inc .... E 330 792-5745
  Youngstown *(G-15543)*
All Phase Power and Ltg Inc .... E 419 624-9640
  Sandusky *(G-12862)*
AMS Construction Inc .... D 513 398-6689
  Maineville *(G-10224)*
AMS Construction Inc .... D 513 794-0410
  Loveland *(G-10127)*
ANR Electric LLC .... D 330 644-4454
  Coventry Township *(G-7006)*
Apollo Heating & AC Inc .... E 513 271-3600
  Cincinnati *(G-2210)*
Archiable Electric Company .... D 513 621-1307
  Cincinnati *(G-2214)*
Area Energy & Electric Inc .... C 937 498-4784
  Sidney *(G-13019)*
Armstrong Utilities Inc .... D 330 723-3536
  Medina *(G-10808)*
Atalian US Ohio Valley Inc .... B 614 476-1818
  Columbus *(G-5400)*
Atkins & Stang Inc .... D 513 242-8300
  Cincinnati *(G-2226)*
Atlas Industrial Contrs LLC .... B 614 841-4500
  Columbus *(G-5403)*
Automation Zone Inc .... E 419 684-8050
  Castalia *(G-1914)*
B & J Electrical Company Inc .... E 513 351-7100
  Cincinnati *(G-2234)*
Bansal Construction Inc .... E 513 874-5410
  Fairfield *(G-8392)*
Banta Electrical Contrs Inc .... E 513 353-4446
  Cleves *(G-5187)*
Bay Mechanical & Elec Corp .... D 440 282-6816
  Lorain *(G-10058)*
BCU Electric Inc .... D 419 281-8944
  Ashland *(G-480)*
Beacon Electric Company .... D 513 851-0711
  Cincinnati *(G-2242)*
Bechtel Jacobs Company LLC .... C 740 897-2700
  Piketon *(G-12415)*
Biz Com Electric LLC .... E 513 961-7200
  Cincinnati *(G-2263)*
Bodie Electric Inc .... E 419 435-3672
  Fostoria *(G-8613)*
Brehob Corporation .... E 513 755-1300
  West Chester *(G-14655)*
Brint Electric Inc .... D 419 841-3326
  Sylvania *(G-13537)*
Broadband Express LLC .... D 513 834-8085
  Cincinnati *(G-2282)*
Broadband Express LLC .... D 216 712-7505
  Cleveland *(G-3898)*
Broadband Express LLC .... D 419 536-9127
  Toledo *(G-13718)*
Calvin Electric LLC .... E 937 670-2558
  Clayton *(G-3731)*

17 CONSTRUCTION - SPECIAL TRADE CONTRACTORS

Capital City Electric Inc ..... E 614 933-8700	Frey Electric Inc ..... D 513 385-0700	Lake Erie Electric Inc ..... C 330 724-1241
New Albany *(G-11558)*	Cincinnati *(G-2708)*	Akron *(G-218)*
Carey Electric Co ..... D 937 669-3399	GA Business Purchaser LLC ..... E 419 255-8400	Lake Erie Electric Inc ..... C 937 743-1220
Vandalia *(G-14368)*	Toledo *(G-13816)*	Franklin *(G-8644)*
Cattrell Companies Inc ..... D 740 537-2481	Garber Electrical Contrs Inc ..... D 937 771-5202	Lake Erie Electric Inc ..... C 419 529-4611
Toronto *(G-14122)*	Englewood *(G-8306)*	Ontario *(G-12111)*
Chapel Electric Co LLC ..... B 937 222-2290	▲ Gatesair Inc ..... D 513 459-3400	LAKE ERIE ELECTRIC INC ..... D 440 835-5565
Dayton *(G-7221)*	Mason *(G-10553)*	Westlake *(G-15074)*
Claypool Electric Inc ..... C 740 653-5683	Gateway Electric LLC ..... C 216 518-5500	Lake Horry Electric ..... D 440 808-8791
Lancaster *(G-9702)*	Cleveland *(G-4304)*	Chagrin Falls *(G-1961)*
Cls Facilities MGT Svcs Inc ..... E 440 602-4600	Geiger Brothers Inc ..... B 740 286-0800	Legrand North America LLC ..... B 937 224-0639
Mentor *(G-10924)*	Jackson *(G-9518)*	Dayton *(G-7451)*
Combined Technologies Inc ..... E 513 595-5900	Gem Electric ..... E 440 286-6200	Lippincott Plmbng-Hting AC Inc ..... E 419 222-0856
Cincinnati *(G-2478)*	Chardon *(G-2003)*	Lima *(G-9928)*
Contemporary Electric Inc ..... E 440 975-9965	Gem Industrial Inc ..... D 419 666-6554	Live Technologies LLC ..... E 614 278-7777
Willoughby *(G-15188)*	Walbridge *(G-14461)*	Columbus *(G-6171)*
Converse Electric Inc ..... D 614 808-4377	General Electric Company ..... C 513 583-3500	M-Pact Corporation ..... E 513 679-2023
Grove City *(G-8912)*	Cincinnati *(G-2724)*	Cincinnati *(G-2999)*
County of Montgomery ..... E 937 225-6294	Generator One LLC ..... E 440 942-8449	Main Lite Electric Co Inc ..... E 330 369-8333
Dayton *(G-7251)*	Mentor *(G-10941)*	Warren *(G-14537)*
▲ Craftsman Electric Inc ..... E 513 891-4426	Genric Inc ..... B 937 553-9250	Maxwell Lightning Protection ..... E 937 228-7250
Cincinnati *(G-2514)*	Marysville *(G-10486)*	Dayton *(G-7469)*
CTS Construction Inc ..... D 513 489-8290	Gillmore Security Systems Inc ..... E 440 232-1000	▲ Mayers Electric Co Inc ..... C 513 272-2900
Cincinnati *(G-2521)*	Cleveland *(G-4313)*	Cincinnati *(G-3019)*
D E Williams Electric Inc ..... E 440 543-1222	Great Lakes Indus Contg Ltd ..... E 419 945-4542	McClintock Electric Inc ..... E 330 264-6380
Chagrin Falls *(G-1957)*	Toledo *(G-13826)*	Wooster *(G-15354)*
▲ Darana Hybrid Inc ..... D 513 860-4490	Great Lakes Telcom Ltd ..... E 330 629-8848	McKeever & Niekamp Electric ..... E 937 431-9363
Hamilton *(G-9036)*	Youngstown *(G-15622)*	Beavercreek *(G-890)*
Davis H Elliot Cnstr Co Inc ..... D 937 847-8025	Guardian Protection Svcs Inc ..... E 330 797-1570	McPhillips Plbg Htg & AC Co ..... C 216 481-1400
Miamisburg *(G-11045)*	Bedford *(G-962)*	Cleveland *(G-4542)*
Davis Pickering & Company Inc ..... D 740 373-5896	Harrington Electric Company ..... D 216 361-5101	Metro Fiber & Cable Cnstr ..... C 419 724-9802
Marietta *(G-10365)*	Cleveland *(G-4351)*	Toledo *(G-13922)*
◆ Daymark Safety Systems ..... D 419 353-2458	Hatzel and Buehler Inc ..... E 216 777-6000	Miller Cable Company ..... D 419 639-2091
Bowling Green *(G-1316)*	Cleveland *(G-4352)*	Green Springs *(G-8861)*
Delta Electrical Contrs Ltd ..... E 513 421-7744	Helm and Associates Inc ..... E 419 893-1480	Monitoring Ctrl Compliance Inc ..... D 330 725-7766
Cincinnati *(G-2557)*	Maumee *(G-10731)*	Wadsworth *(G-14444)*
Denier Electric Co Inc ..... E 614 338-4664	Herbst Electric LLC ..... D 216 621-5890	Mutual Electric Company ..... E 937 254-6211
Grove City *(G-8915)*	Cleveland *(G-4359)*	Dayton *(G-7519)*
Denier Electric Co Inc ..... C 513 738-2641	Hilscher-Clarke Electric Co ..... C 740 622-5557	Nationwide Energy Partners LLC ..... E 614 918-2031
Harrison *(G-9101)*	Coshocton *(G-6986)*	Columbus *(G-6328)*
◆ Df Supply Inc ..... E 330 650-9226	Hilscher-Clarke Electric Co ..... E 330 452-9806	Neesai Cad Designs LLC ..... E 614 822-7701
Twinsburg *(G-14181)*	Canton *(G-1772)*	New Albany *(G-11577)*
Dovetail Construction Co Inc ..... E 740 592-1800	Industrial Comm & Sound Inc ..... E 614 276-8123	New River Electrical Corp ..... A 614 891-1142
Cleveland *(G-4181)*	Cincinnati *(G-2868)*	Westerville *(G-15007)*
E S I Inc ..... C 937 298-7481	Industrial Power Systems Inc ..... B 419 531-3121	Newcome Corp ..... E 614 848-5688
Moraine *(G-11405)*	Rossford *(G-12767)*	Columbus *(G-5273)*
E S I Inc ..... D 513 454-3741	Info-Hold Inc ..... E 513 248-5600	Noll Fisher Incorporated ..... E 937 394-4181
West Chester *(G-14808)*	Cincinnati *(G-2870)*	Anna *(G-443)*
Eco Engineering Inc ..... D 513 985-8300	▲ Instrmntation Ctrl Systems Inc ..... E 513 662-2600	▼ Northeast Ohio Electric LLC ..... B 216 587-9512
Cincinnati *(G-2604)*	Cincinnati *(G-2873)*	Cleveland *(G-4662)*
▲ Eighth Day Sound Systems Inc ..... E 440 995-2647	J & J General Maintenance Inc ..... D 740 533-9729	▲ Northwest Electrical Contg Inc ..... E 419 865-4757
Highland Heights *(G-9165)*	Ironton *(G-9509)*	Sylvania *(G-13558)*
Electric Connection Inc ..... D 614 436-1121	J W Didado Electric Inc ..... C 330 374-0070	Northwestern Ohio SEC Systems ..... E 419 227-1655
Columbus *(G-5810)*	Akron *(G-207)*	Lima *(G-9942)*
Electrical Accents LLC ..... E 440 988-2852	Jess Howard Electric Company ..... C 614 864-2167	Ohio Valley Elec Svcs LLC ..... D 513 771-2410
South Amherst *(G-13169)*	Blacklick *(G-1113)*	Blue Ash *(G-1217)*
Electrical Corp America Inc ..... C 440 245-3007	Jims Electric Inc ..... E 440 327-8800	Osterwisch Company Inc ..... D 513 791-3282
Lorain *(G-10072)*	North Ridgeville *(G-11930)*	Cincinnati *(G-3174)*
Emcor Facilities Services Inc ..... D 513 948-8469	Joe Dickey Electric Inc ..... D 330 549-3976	Palazzo Brothers Electric Inc ..... E 419 668-1100
Cincinnati *(G-2612)*	North Lima *(G-11889)*	Norwalk *(G-12020)*
▲ Enertech Electrical Inc ..... E 330 536-2131	JW Didado Electric LLC ..... D 330 374-0070	Penn-Ohio Electrical Company ..... E 330 448-1234
Lowellville *(G-10168)*	Akron *(G-213)*	Masury *(G-10680)*
Erb Electric Co ..... C 740 633-5055	Kastle Electric Company ..... C 937 254-2681	Perram Electric Inc ..... E 330 239-2661
Bridgeport *(G-1376)*	Moraine *(G-11419)*	Wadsworth *(G-14447)*
Ferenc/Lakeside Electric Inc ..... D 216 426-1880	Kathman Electric Co Inc ..... E 513 353-3365	Pleasant Valley Corporation ..... D 330 239-0176
Cleveland *(G-4248)*	Cleves *(G-5189)*	Medina *(G-10878)*
Fishel Company ..... C 614 850-4400	Kidron Electric Inc ..... E 330 857-2871	Pomeroy It Solutions Sls Inc ..... E 440 717-1364
Columbus *(G-5867)*	Kidron *(G-9637)*	Brecksville *(G-1363)*
Fishel Company ..... D 614 274-8100	Kraft Electrical Contg Inc ..... E 513 467-0500	Pomeroy It Solutions Sls Inc ..... D 614 876-6521
Columbus *(G-5869)*	Cincinnati *(G-2949)*	Columbus *(G-6536)*
Fowler Electric Co ..... E 440 735-2385	Kween Industries Inc ..... D 513 932-2293	Precision Brdband Instltons I ..... C 614 523-2917
Bedford *(G-960)*	Lebanon *(G-9772)*	Westerville *(G-15012)*

Employee Codes: A=Over 500 employees, B=251-500
C=101-250, D=51-100, E=20-50, F=10-19, G=1-9

17 CONSTRUCTION - SPECIAL TRADE CONTRACTORS — SIC SECTION

Precision Electrical Svcs Inc............................ E 740 474-4490
   Circleville *(G-3718)*

Primetech Communications Inc...................... D 513 942-6000
   Hamilton *(G-9074)*

Professnal Cbling Slutions LLC...................... D 513 733-9473
   Cincinnati *(G-3246)*

Quebe Holdings Inc.. D 937 222-2290
   Dayton *(G-7575)*

Reddy Electric Co... C 937 372-8205
   Xenia *(G-15530)*

Regent Electric Inc... D 419 476-8333
   Toledo *(G-13985)*

Reliable Contractors Inc................................. D 937 433-0262
   Dayton *(G-7583)*

Rgt Services LLC... E 440 786-9777
   Oakwood Village *(G-12056)*

Rittal North America LLC............................... C 937 399-0500
   Urbana *(G-14311)*

RJ Runge Company Inc.................................. E 419 740-5781
   Port Clinton *(G-12539)*

Rmf Nooter LLC.. D 419 727-1970
   Toledo *(G-13992)*

Robinson Htg Air-Conditioning....................... E 513 422-6812
   Middletown *(G-11184)*

Roehrenbeck Electric Inc............................... E 614 443-9709
   Columbus *(G-6607)*

Romanoff Elc Residential LLC....................... D 614 755-4500
   Gahanna *(G-8728)*

Romanoff Electric Inc..................................... C 614 755-4500
   Gahanna *(G-8729)*

Romanoff Electric Co LLC.............................. B 937 640-7925
   Toledo *(G-13997)*

Romanoff Group LLC...................................... E 614 755-4500
   Gahanna *(G-8730)*

Royal Electric Cnstr Corp............................... E 614 253-6600
   Columbus *(G-6614)*

▼ Santon Electric Inc....................................... D 330 758-0082
   Youngstown *(G-15716)*

Saturn Electric Inc.. E 937 278-2580
   Dayton *(G-7611)*

Security Fence Group Inc............................... E 513 681-3700
   Cincinnati *(G-3353)*

Servall Electric Company Inc......................... E 513 771-5584
   Cincinnati *(G-3361)*

Settle Muter Electric Ltd................................. C 614 866-7554
   Columbus *(G-6667)*

Shannon Electric LLC..................................... E 216 378-3620
   Cleveland *(G-4899)*

Shawntech Communications Inc.................... E 937 898-4900
   Miamisburg *(G-11093)*

Sidney Electric Company................................ D 419 222-1109
   Sidney *(G-13050)*

Siemens Energy Inc.. E 740 393-8897
   Mount Vernon *(G-11508)*

Sievers Security Inc.. E 216 291-2222
   Cleveland *(G-4905)*

Sollmann Electric Co....................................... E 937 492-0346
   Sidney *(G-13055)*

South Shore Electric Inc................................. E 440 366-6289
   Elyria *(G-8296)*

Southeast Security Corporation..................... E 330 239-4600
   Sharon Center *(G-12990)*

Speelman Electric Inc..................................... C 330 633-1410
   Tallmadge *(G-13604)*

State Alarm Inc.. E 888 726-8111
   Youngstown *(G-15730)*

Studebaker Electric Company........................ D 937 890-9510
   Dayton *(G-7648)*

Target Systems Inc... E 440 239-1600
   Cleveland *(G-4977)*

TAS Inc.. E 419 693-3453
   Toledo *(G-14033)*

Taylor CJ Development Inc............................. D 330 628-5501
   Mogadore *(G-11332)*

Tele-Solutions Inc... E 330 782-2888
   Youngstown *(G-15733)*

The Wagner-Smith Company.......................... B 866 338-0398
   Moraine *(G-11444)*

Thompson Electric Inc.................................... C 330 686-2300
   Munroe Falls *(G-11514)*

TMI Electrical Contractors Inc........................ E 513 821-9900
   Cincinnati *(G-3482)*

Torrence Sound Equipment Company............. E 419 661-0678
   Perrysburg *(G-12379)*

Transtar Electric Inc....................................... D 419 385-7573
   Toledo *(G-14073)*

Tri Area Electric Co Inc.................................. E 330 744-0151
   Youngstown *(G-15736)*

Triec Electrical Services Inc........................... E 937 323-3721
   Springfield *(G-13305)*

Turnkey Technology LLC................................ E 513 725-2177
   Cincinnati *(G-3537)*

TWC Entrprises Elec Contrs LLC.................... E 740 467-9004
   Millersport *(G-11299)*

Ullman Electric & Technol.............................. C 216 432-5777
   Cleveland *(G-5048)*

Universal Recovery Systems Inc.................... D 614 299-0184
   Columbus *(G-6821)*

US Communications and Elc Inc.................... D 440 519-0880
   Cleveland *(G-5091)*

US Utility Electrical Svcs............................... E 419 837-9753
   Perrysburg *(G-12384)*

Vaughn Industries LLC................................... D 419 396-3900
   Fostoria *(G-8627)*

Vaughn Industries LLC................................... D 740 548-7100
   Lewis Center *(G-9840)*

▲ Vaughn Industries LLC................................. B 419 396-3900
   Carey *(G-1895)*

Vec Inc.. D 330 539-4044
   Girard *(G-8830)*

Volpenhein Brothers Electric Inc.................... D 513 385-9355
   West Chester *(G-14845)*

Wells Brothers Inc.. D 937 394-7559
   Anna *(G-445)*

Westfield Electric Inc..................................... E 419 862-0078
   Gibsonburg *(G-8807)*

▲ Wireless Environment LLC.......................... E 216 455-0192
   Mayfield Village *(G-10797)*

WI Electric Inc.. E 614 882-2160
   Westerville *(G-15022)*

Wood Electric Inc... E 330 339-7002
   New Philadelphia *(G-11673)*

Woolace Electric Corp.................................... E 419 428-3161
   Stryker *(G-13506)*

X F Construction Svcs Inc.............................. E 614 575-2700
   Columbus *(G-6911)*

Zenith Systems LLC....................................... B 216 406-7916
   Atwater *(G-602)*

Zenith Systems LLC....................................... C 216 587-9510
   Cleveland *(G-5174)*

1741 Masonry and other stonework

Able Roofing LLC... D 614 444-2253
   Columbus *(G-5296)*

Allen Refractories Company.......................... C 740 927-8000
   Pataskala *(G-12269)*

Appelgren Ltd... E 330 945-6402
   Cuyahoga Falls *(G-7040)*

Canaan Companies Inc.................................. E 419 842-8373
   Toledo *(G-13724)*

Carlisle Msnry/Cnstruction Inc...................... E 740 966-5045
   Johnstown *(G-9545)*

▲ Cleveland Marble Mosaic Co....................... C 216 749-2840
   Cleveland *(G-4054)*

Design Built Construction Inc........................ E 419 563-0185
   Bucyrus *(G-1507)*

Giambrone Masonry Inc................................. E
   Hudson *(G-9354)*

Harold K Phllips Rstration Inc....................... E 614 443-5699
   Columbus *(G-5972)*

Hicon Inc... E 513 242-3612
   Cincinnati *(G-2819)*

Industrial First Inc.. C 216 991-8605
   Bedford *(G-966)*

International Masonry Inc.............................. E 614 469-8338
   Columbus *(G-6069)*

J & D Home Improvement Inc....................... D 800 288-0831
   Columbus *(G-6076)*

Jess Hauer Masonry Inc................................ E 513 521-2178
   Cincinnati *(G-2903)*

Lang Masonry Contractors Inc...................... D 740 749-3512
   Waterford *(G-14592)*

Lencyk Masonry Co Inc................................. E 330 729-9780
   Youngstown *(G-15648)*

Medhurst Mason Contractors Inc.................. C 440 543-8885
   Chagrin Falls *(G-1986)*

Miter Masonry Contractors............................ E 513 821-3334
   Arlington Heights *(G-470)*

North Central Insulation Inc.......................... D 330 262-1998
   Apple Creek *(G-451)*

Nr Lee Restoration Ltd................................... E 419 692-2233
   Delphos *(G-7842)*

Ohio State Home Services Inc....................... D 614 850-5600
   Hilliard *(G-9223)*

▲ Onex Construction Inc................................. E 330 995-9015
   Streetsboro *(G-13424)*

Phoenix Masonry Ltd..................................... D 740 344-5787
   Newark *(G-11741)*

Pioneer Cldding Glzing Systems.................... E 216 816-4242
   Cleveland *(G-4749)*

Platinum Restoration Inc............................... E 440 327-0699
   Elyria *(G-8286)*

Protective Coatings Inc................................. E 937 275-7711
   Dayton *(G-7572)*

Ray St Clair Roofing Inc................................ E 513 874-1234
   Fairfield *(G-8436)*

▲ The Schaefer Group Inc............................... E 937 253-3342
   Beavercreek *(G-932)*

Wasiniak Construction Inc............................ D 419 668-8624
   Norwalk *(G-12030)*

Zavarella Brothers Cnstr Co........................... E 440 232-2243
   Cleveland *(G-5173)*

1742 Plastering, drywall, and insulation

A & A Wall Systems Inc................................. E 513 489-0086
   Cincinnati *(G-2128)*

ABS Coastal Insulating LLC.......................... E 843 360-1045
   Columbus *(G-5297)*

All Construction Services Inc........................ B 330 225-1653
   Brunswick *(G-1450)*

Architctral Intr Rstrtions Inc......................... E 216 241-2255
   Cleveland *(G-3831)*

Boak & Sons Inc... C 330 793-5646
   Youngstown *(G-15559)*

Brocon Construction Inc................................ E 614 871-7300
   Grove City *(G-8900)*

Builder Services Group Inc........................... E 614 263-9378
   Columbus *(G-5483)*

Builder Services Group Inc........................... E 513 942-2204
   Hamilton *(G-9019)*

Central Insulation Systems Inc..................... E 513 242-0600
   Cincinnati *(G-2336)*

Cleveland Construction Inc........................... C 440 255-8000
   Mason *(G-10539)*

▲ Cleveland Construction Inc......................... E 440 255-8000
   Mentor *(G-10923)*

17 CONSTRUCTION - SPECIAL TRADE CONTRACTORS

Community Action Comm Blmont C......... E 740 695-0293
  Saint Clairsville *(G-12786)*
Compass Construction Inc.................... D 614 761-7800
  Dublin *(G-7969)*
Competitive Interiors Inc..................... C 330 297-1281
  Ravenna *(G-12623)*
Construction Systems Inc.................... D 614 252-0708
  Columbus *(G-5686)*
Danessa Construction Llc.................... D 330 219-1212
  Niles *(G-11787)*
Dayton Walls & Ceilings Inc................. D 937 277-0531
  Dayton *(G-7305)*
Edwards Mooney & Moses................... C 614 351-1439
  Columbus *(G-5809)*
Fairfield Insul & Drywall LLC................ E 740 654-8811
  Lancaster *(G-9715)*
Frank Novak & Sons Inc..................... D 216 475-2495
  Cleveland *(G-4285)*
Global Insulation Inc........................... E 330 479-3100
  Canton *(G-1763)*
IBP Corporation Holdings Inc............... A 614 692-6360
  Columbus *(G-6038)*
Industrial Insul Coatings LLC............... E 800 506-1399
  Girard *(G-8816)*
Installed Building Pdts II LLC............... E 626 812-6070
  Columbus *(G-6056)*
Installed Building Pdts LLC.................. D 330 798-9640
  Akron *(G-202)*
Installed Building Pdts LLC.................. E 419 884-0676
  Mansfield *(G-10272)*
Installed Building Products LLC............ C 614 221-3399
  Columbus *(G-6059)*
J & B Acoustical Inc........................... D 419 884-1155
  Mansfield *(G-10273)*
Lakeside Interior Contractors Inc.......... C 419 867-1300
  Perrysburg *(G-12351)*
Liberty Insulation Co Inc..................... D 513 621-0108
  Milford *(G-11236)*
Lm Constrction Trry Lvrini Inc............... E 740 695-9604
  Saint Clairsville *(G-12797)*
North Central Insulation Inc................. D 330 262-1998
  Apple Creek *(G-451)*
North Central Insulation Inc................. D 740 548-8125
  Lewis Center *(G-9832)*
OK Interiors Corp.............................. C 513 742-3278
  Cincinnati *(G-3153)*
Overhead Door Co- Cincinnati.............. C 513 346-4000
  West Chester *(G-14739)*
Pedersen Insulation Company............. E 614 471-3788
  Columbus *(G-6508)*
R E Kramig & Co Inc.......................... E 513 761-4010
  Cincinnati *(G-3270)*
R L Bondy Insulation LLC.................... E 419 843-6283
  Northwood *(G-11983)*
Robinson Insulation Co Inc................. E 937 323-9599
  Springfield *(G-13286)*
T and D Interiors Incorporated............. E 419 331-4372
  Lima *(G-9969)*
Thermal Solutions Inc........................ D 513 742-2836
  Fairfield *(G-8447)*
Thermal Solutions Inc........................ E 740 886-2861
  Proctorville *(G-12614)*
Valley Interior Systems Inc................. D 614 351-8440
  Columbus *(G-6840)*
Valley Interior Systems Inc................. D 937 890-7319
  Dayton *(G-7699)*
Valley Interior Systems Inc................. B 513 961-0400
  Cincinnati *(G-3613)*
Western Reserve Interiors Inc............. E 216 447-1081
  Cleveland *(G-5137)*
Wilson Insulation Company LLC........... D 626 812-6070
  Columbus *(G-6897)*

1743 Terrazzo, tile, marble, mosaic work

▲ Cleveland Marble Mosaic Co............. C 216 749-2840
  Cleveland *(G-4054)*
◆ Cutting Edge Countertops Inc........... E 419 873-9500
  Perrysburg *(G-12328)*
▲ Ironrock Capital Incorporated............ D 330 484-4887
  Canton *(G-1782)*
Legacy Ntral Stone Srfaces LLC........... E 419 420-7440
  Findlay *(G-8558)*
Southwestern Tile and MBL Co............. E 614 464-1257
  Columbus *(G-6700)*
Tile Shop LLC.................................. E 513 554-4435
  Cincinnati *(G-3480)*
Weiffenbach Marble & Tile Co.............. E 937 832-7055
  Englewood *(G-8326)*

1751 Carpentry work

A-E Door Sales and Service Inc............ E 513 742-1984
  Cincinnati *(G-2132)*
Alside Inc....................................... D 419 865-0934
  Maumee *(G-10687)*
Burbank Inc.................................... E 419 698-3434
  Toledo *(G-13723)*
Cabinet Restylers Inc........................ D 419 281-8449
  Ashland *(G-486)*
◆ Chase Industries Inc....................... D 513 860-5565
  West Chester *(G-14803)*
Combs Interior Specialties Inc.............. D 937 879-2047
  Fairborn *(G-8369)*
Command Roofing Co........................ C 937 298-1155
  Moraine *(G-11398)*
Competitive Interiors Inc..................... C 330 297-1281
  Ravenna *(G-12623)*
Contract Lumber Inc.......................... C 740 964-3147
  Pataskala *(G-12270)*
Danessa Construction Llc.................... D 330 219-1212
  Niles *(G-11787)*
Dayton Door Sales Inc....................... D 937 253-9181
  Dayton *(G-7280)*
Dortrnic Service-Tallmadge Inc............. D 330 928-2727
  Stow *(G-13364)*
Dortronic Service Inc......................... E 216 739-3667
  Cleveland *(G-4180)*
Fairfield Insul & Drywall LLC................ E 740 654-8811
  Lancaster *(G-9715)*
Finelli Ornamental Iron Co.................. E 440 248-0050
  Cleveland *(G-4251)*
▲ Fortune Brands Windows Inc............ C 614 532-3500
  Columbus *(G-5879)*
▲ Forum Manufacturing Inc................. E 937 349-8685
  Milford Center *(G-11265)*
GMI Holdings Inc.............................. C 330 897-4424
  Baltic *(G-689)*
Hgc Construction Co......................... D 513 861-8866
  Cincinnati *(G-2818)*
J & R Door LLC................................ E 740 623-2782
  Coshocton *(G-6989)*
Lakeside Interior Contractors Inc.......... C 419 867-1300
  Perrysburg *(G-12351)*
Marous Brothers Cnstr Inc.................. B 440 951-3904
  Willoughby *(G-15211)*
Metal Framing Enterprises LLC............ E 216 433-7080
  Cleveland *(G-4558)*
Midwest Curtainwalls Inc.................... D 216 641-7900
  Cleveland *(G-4580)*
Mill Tech LLC................................... E 614 496-9778
  Canal Winchester *(G-1613)*
▼ Nofziger Door Sales Inc................... C 419 337-9900
  Wauseon *(G-14607)*
OK Interiors Corp.............................. C 513 742-3278
  Cincinnati *(G-3153)*

Overhead Door Co- Cincinnati.............. C 513 346-4000
  West Chester *(G-14739)*
Overhead Door Corporation................ D 330 674-7015
  Mount Hope *(G-11468)*
Overhead Door................................. E 419 476-7811
  Toledo *(G-13951)*
Prusaks Precision Cnstr Inc................. E 440 655-8564
  North Royalton *(G-11948)*
Ray St Clair Roofing Inc..................... E 513 874-1234
  Fairfield *(G-8436)*
Riverside Cnstr Svcs Inc..................... E 513 723-0900
  Cincinnati *(G-3307)*
Rock Homes Inc................................ E 330 497-5200
  North Canton *(G-11859)*
Rwlp Company.................................. E 216 883-2424
  Cleveland *(G-4866)*
Ryans All-Glass Incorporated............... E 513 771-4440
  West Chester *(G-14759)*
Schaefer & Company......................... E 937 339-2638
  Troy *(G-14159)*
Schlabach Wood Design Inc................ E 330 897-2600
  Baltic *(G-691)*
T Allen Inc...................................... C 440 234-2366
  Berea *(G-1084)*
Wayne Gar Door Sls & Svc Inc............ E 330 343-6679
  Dover *(G-7909)*

1752 Floor laying and floor work, nec

Centimark Corporation....................... C 330 920-3560
  Stow *(G-13357)*
Clays Heritage Carpet Inc................... E 330 497-1280
  Canton *(G-1711)*
▲ Cleveland Construction Inc.............. E 440 255-8000
  Mentor *(G-10923)*
Frank Novak & Sons Inc..................... D 216 475-2495
  Cleveland *(G-4285)*
Hoover & Wells Inc............................ C 419 691-9220
  Toledo *(G-13850)*
J L G Co Inc.................................... E 513 248-1755
  Loveland *(G-10144)*
Jackson Bluford and Son Inc............... D 513 831-6231
  Milford *(G-11234)*
JD Music Tile Co............................... E 740 420-9611
  Circleville *(G-3711)*
Lakeside Interior Contractors Inc.......... C 419 867-1300
  Perrysburg *(G-12351)*
Messina Floor Covering LLC................ D 216 595-0100
  Cleveland *(G-4557)*
OK Interiors Corp.............................. C 513 742-3278
  Cincinnati *(G-3153)*
Preferred Acquisition Co LLC............... D 216 587-0957
  Cleveland *(G-4767)*
Progressive Flooring Svcs Inc.............. E 614 868-9005
  Etna *(G-8334)*
Protective Coatings Inc...................... E 937 275-7711
  Dayton *(G-7572)*
River City Furniture LLC..................... E 513 612-7303
  West Chester *(G-14756)*
Schoch Tile & Carpet Inc.................... E 513 922-3466
  Cincinnati *(G-3350)*
Spectra Holdings Inc......................... E 614 921-8493
  Columbus *(G-6702)*
T and D Interiors Incorporated............. E 419 331-4372
  Lima *(G-9969)*
◆ Tremco Incorporated....................... B
  Beachwood *(G-847)*
W R Shepherd Inc............................. E 614 889-2896
  Powell *(G-12608)*

1761 Roofing, siding, and sheetmetal work

1st Choice Roofing Company............... E 216 227-7755
  Cleveland *(G-3743)*

17 CONSTRUCTION - SPECIAL TRADE CONTRACTORS

A W Farrell & Son Inc .... E 513 334-0715
  Milford *(G-11215)*

Able Roofing LLC .... D 614 444-2253
  Columbus *(G-5296)*

Advanced Cnstr Group Inc .... E 419 891-1505
  Maumee *(G-10685)*

Advanced Industrial Roofg Inc .... D 330 837-1999
  Massillon *(G-10629)*

▲ Alan Manufacturing Inc .... E 330 262-1555
  Wooster *(G-15308)*

All Amrcan Gtter Protection LL .... E 330 470-4100
  North Canton *(G-11811)*

All-Type Welding & Fabrication .... E 440 439-3990
  Cleveland *(G-3792)*

Anchor Metal Processing Inc .... E 216 362-1850
  Cleveland *(G-3814)*

Andy Russo Jr Inc .... D 440 585-1456
  Wickliffe *(G-15145)*

Apco Industries Inc .... D 614 224-2345
  Columbus *(G-5371)*

Asi Commercial Roofg Maint Inc .... D 614 873-2057
  Plain City *(G-12468)*

Avon Lake Sheet Metal Co .... E 440 933-3505
  Avon Lake *(G-673)*

Beck Company .... E 216 883-0909
  Cleveland *(G-3861)*

Boak & Sons Inc .... C 330 793-5646
  Youngstown *(G-15559)*

▲ Bruns Building & Dev Corp Inc .... D 419 925-4095
  Saint Henry *(G-12824)*

Burbank Inc .... E 419 698-3434
  Toledo *(G-13723)*

Cabinet Restylers Inc .... D 419 281-8449
  Ashland *(G-486)*

Cardinal Builders Inc .... E 614 237-1000
  Columbus *(G-5507)*

Cardinal Group Inc .... C 330 252-1047
  Akron *(G-80)*

Centimark Corporation .... C 330 920-3560
  Stow *(G-13357)*

▲ Champion Opco LLC .... B 513 327-7338
  Cincinnati *(G-2345)*

Chaney Roofing Maintenance Inc .... E 419 639-2761
  Clyde *(G-5199)*

Christen & Sons Company .... E 419 243-4161
  Toledo *(G-13733)*

Command Roofing Co .... C 937 298-1155
  Moraine *(G-11398)*

Contract Lumber Inc .... C 740 964-3147
  Pataskala *(G-12270)*

Damschroder Roofing Inc .... E 419 332-5000
  Fremont *(G-8674)*

Deer Park Roofing Inc .... E 513 891-9151
  Cincinnati *(G-2553)*

Defabco Inc .... D 614 231-2700
  Columbus *(G-5749)*

Diamond Roofing Systems LLP .... E 330 856-2500
  Warren *(G-14517)*

Dimensional Metals Inc .... E 740 927-3633
  Reynoldsburg *(G-12660)*

DJ Roofing & Imprvs LLC .... E 419 307-5712
  Fremont *(G-8675)*

Dun Rite Home Improvement Inc .... E 330 650-5322
  Macedonia *(G-10191)*

▲ Durable Slate Co .... D 614 299-5522
  Columbus *(G-5794)*

Eckstein Roofing Company .... E 513 941-1511
  Cincinnati *(G-2603)*

Erie Construction Mid-West Inc .... D 937 898-4688
  Dayton *(G-7339)*

Erie Construction Mid-West Inc .... D 419 472-4200
  Toledo *(G-13794)*

Erie Construction Mid-West Inc .... B 419 472-4200
  Toledo *(G-13795)*

Feazel Roofing LLC .... E 614 898-7663
  New Albany *(G-11565)*

Franck and Fric Incorporated .... D 216 524-4451
  Cleveland *(G-4284)*

Fred Christen & Sons Company .... D 419 243-4161
  Toledo *(G-13813)*

Frost Roofing Inc .... D 419 739-2701
  Wapakoneta *(G-14483)*

Geauga Mechanical Company .... D 440 285-2000
  Chardon *(G-2000)*

Global Insulation Inc .... E 330 479-3100
  Canton *(G-1763)*

Harold J Becker Company Inc .... E 614 279-1414
  Dayton *(G-7398)*

Hartley Company .... E 740 439-6668
  Zanesville *(G-15798)*

Henderson Roofing & Cnstr Inc .... E 330 323-1500
  Middlebranch *(G-11112)*

▲ Hickey Metal Fabrication Roofg .... E 330 337-9329
  Salem *(G-12843)*

Hicks Roofing Inc .... E 330 364-7737
  New Philadelphia *(G-11653)*

Hinson Roofing & Shtmtl Inc .... E 513 367-4477
  Harrison *(G-9109)*

Holmes Siding Contractors Ltd .... E 330 674-3382
  Millersburg *(G-11280)*

Industrial First Inc .... C 216 991-8605
  Bedford *(G-966)*

Installed Building Products LLC .... C 614 221-3399
  Columbus *(G-6059)*

J B & Company Incorporated .... D 419 447-1716
  Tiffin *(G-13629)*

Jackson Corporation .... E 419 525-0170
  Ontario *(G-12108)*

JB Roofing A Tecta Amer Co LLC .... E 419 447-1716
  Tiffin *(G-13630)*

Kelley Brothers Roofing Inc .... D 513 829-7717
  Fairfield *(G-8425)*

Kerkan Roofing Inc .... D 513 821-0556
  Cincinnati *(G-2938)*

◆ Kirk & Blum Manufacturing Co .... C 513 458-2600
  Cincinnati *(G-2942)*

Legacy Roofing Services LLC .... D 330 645-6000
  Coventry Township *(G-7013)*

M & W Construction Entps LLC .... E 419 227-2000
  Lima *(G-9932)*

Meade Construction Inc .... E 740 694-5525
  Lexington *(G-9844)*

Mechanical Cnstr Managers LLC .... C 937 274-1987
  Dayton *(G-7474)*

Mechanical Construction Co .... E 740 353-5668
  Portsmouth *(G-12563)*

Molloy Roofing Company .... E 513 791-7400
  Blue Ash *(G-1212)*

N F Mansuetto & Sons Inc .... E 740 633-7320
  Martins Ferry *(G-10469)*

Nations Roof of Ohio LLC .... E 937 439-4160
  Springboro *(G-13204)*

Northern Ohio Roofg Shtmtl Inc .... E 440 322-8262
  Elyria *(G-8282)*

Nr Lee Restoration Ltd .... E 419 692-2233
  Delphos *(G-7842)*

Ohio Fabricators Inc .... D 330 745-4406
  Akron *(G-250)*

Ontario Mechanical LLC .... E 419 529-2578
  Ontario *(G-12121)*

Overhead Door Co- Cincinnati .... C 513 346-4000
  West Chester *(G-14739)*

◆ Owens Corning Sales LLC .... A 419 248-8000
  Toledo *(G-13952)*

▼ Phinney Industrial Roofing .... D 614 308-9000
  Columbus *(G-6522)*

Precision Impacts LLC .... D 937 530-8254
  Miamisburg *(G-11086)*

Protective Coatings Inc .... E 937 275-7711
  Dayton *(G-7572)*

R G Smith Company .... D 330 456-3415
  Canton *(G-1839)*

Ray St Clair Roofing Inc .... E 513 874-1234
  Fairfield *(G-8436)*

Reader Tinning & Roofing Co .... E 216 451-1355
  Cleveland *(G-4810)*

Reilly Painting & Contg Inc .... E 216 371-8160
  Cleveland Heights *(G-5183)*

Richland Co & Associates Inc .... E 419 782-0141
  Defiance *(G-7766)*

Rmt Acquisition Inc .... E 513 241-5566
  Cincinnati *(G-3311)*

Rock Homes Inc .... E 330 497-5200
  North Canton *(G-11859)*

Roofsmith Restoration Inc .... D 330 812-4245
  Akron *(G-287)*

Roth Bros Inc .... C 330 793-5571
  Youngstown *(G-15713)*

Schaefer & Company .... E 937 339-2638
  Troy *(G-14159)*

Sibley Inc .... E 440 233-5836
  Elyria *(G-8295)*

Simon Roofing and Shtmtl Corp .... C 330 629-7392
  Youngstown *(G-15725)*

Slagle Mechanical Contractors .... E 937 492-4151
  Sidney *(G-13054)*

Summit Enterprises Contg Corp .... E 513 426-1623
  Lebanon *(G-9791)*

T & F Systems Inc .... D
  Cleveland *(G-4974)*

Technique Roofing Systems LLC .... E 419 680-2025
  Helena *(G-9157)*

Tecta America Zero Company LLC .... D 513 541-1848
  Cincinnati *(G-3450)*

Terik Roofing Inc .... E 330 785-0060
  Coventry Township *(G-7016)*

Tops Roofing Inc .... E 937 228-6074
  Dayton *(G-7673)*

Trademark Exteriors LLC .... D 330 893-0000
  Wilmot *(G-15282)*

◆ Tremco Incorporated .... B
  Beachwood *(G-847)*

Trucraft Roofing LLC .... E 513 965-9200
  Milford *(G-11263)*

United GL & Panl Systems Inc .... E 330 244-9745
  North Canton *(G-11869)*

United Roofing & Sheet Metal .... E 419 865-5576
  Holland *(G-9310)*

Universal Windows Direct Inc .... D 614 418-5232
  Columbus *(G-6822)*

Wagner Metals LLC .... E 419 594-7445
  Defiance *(G-7774)*

▲ West Roofing Systems Inc .... E 800 356-5748
  Lagrange *(G-9652)*

Wm Kramer and Son Inc .... D 513 353-1142
  Cleves *(G-5196)*

Wolfes Roofing Inc .... E 419 666-6233
  Walbridge *(G-14469)*

1771 Concrete work

21st Century Con Cnstr Inc .... E 216 362-0900
  Cleveland *(G-3744)*

Adleta Inc .... E 513 554-1469
  Cincinnati *(G-2145)*

Anthony Allega Cem Contr Inc .... E 216 447-0814
  Richfield *(G-12687)*

SIC SECTION

17 CONSTRUCTION - SPECIAL TRADE CONTRACTORS

Arledge Construction Inc....................... E 614 732-4258
  Columbus *(G-5385)*

Atlas Construction Company................... D 614 475-2282
  Columbus *(G-5402)*

Baker Equipment and Mtls Ltd................. E 513 422-6697
  Monroe *(G-11333)*

Barbicas Construction Co........................ E 330 733-9101
  Akron *(G-61)*

BG Trucking & Cnstr Inc.......................... E 234 759-3440
  North Lima *(G-11884)*

Briskey Concrete Inc............................... E 517 403-9869
  Galena *(G-8735)*

Ceco Concrete Construction LLC............. C 513 874-6953
  West Chester *(G-14661)*

Cem-Base Inc... E 330 405-4105
  Twinsburg *(G-14175)*

Charles H Hamilton Co............................ D 513 683-2442
  Maineville *(G-10226)*

Cincinnati Asphalt Corporation................ D 513 367-0250
  Harrison *(G-9098)*

▲ CK Construction Group Inc.................. B 614 901-8844
  Westerville *(G-14967)*

Cleveland Concrete Cnstr Inc.................. D 216 741-3954
  Brooklyn Heights *(G-1415)*

Cook Paving and Cnstr Co....................... E 216 267-7705
  Independence *(G-9424)*

Cross-Roads Asphalt Recycling Inc......... E 440 236-5066
  Columbia Station *(G-5226)*

Deco-Crete Supply Inc............................ E 330 682-5678
  Orrville *(G-12162)*

DOT Diamond Core Drilling Inc................ E 440 322-6466
  Elyria *(G-8242)*

Elastizell Systems Inc............................. E 937 298-1313
  Moraine *(G-11406)*

Eldorado Stone LLC................................ E 330 698-3931
  Apple Creek *(G-449)*

Engineered Con Structures Corp............. E
  Cleveland *(G-4216)*

Family Liquidation Company Inc............. D 937 780-3075
  Wshngtn Ct Hs *(G-15479)*

Foor Concrete Co Inc.............................. E 740 513-4346
  Delaware *(G-7798)*

Gardner Cement Contractors.................. D 419 389-0768
  Toledo *(G-13818)*

Gateway Con Forming Svcs Inc............... D 513 353-2000
  Miamitown *(G-11106)*

▲ Goettle Holding Company Inc.............. C 513 825-8100
  Cincinnati *(G-2738)*

Houck Asphalt Maintenance LLC............ E 513 734-4500
  Bethel *(G-1092)*

Incredible Products LLC.......................... E 567 297-3700
  Lima *(G-9910)*

▲ Independence Excavating Inc............. E 216 524-1700
  Independence *(G-9437)*

J & D Home Improvement Inc................. D 800 288-0831
  Columbus *(G-6076)*

J Kuhn Enterprises Inc............................ C 614 481-8838
  Columbus *(G-6078)*

Jamison Cnstr Solutions Inc.................... E 513 377-0705
  Fairfield *(G-8422)*

Jennite Co.. E 419 531-1791
  Toledo *(G-13866)*

Jostin Construction Inc........................... E 513 559-9390
  Cincinnati *(G-2921)*

K & M Construction Company................. D 330 723-3681
  Medina *(G-10849)*

Latorre Concrete Cnstr Inc...................... E 614 257-1401
  Columbus *(G-6144)*

Lithko Contracting LLC........................... C 513 564-2000
  West Chester *(G-14724)*

Lithko Restoration Tech LLC................... E 513 863-5500
  Monroe *(G-11343)*

Mansfield Cement Flooring Inc............... E 419 884-3733
  Mansfield *(G-10286)*

Metcon Ltd.. E 937 447-9200
  Dayton *(G-7483)*

Miller Yount Paving Inc........................... E 561 951-7416
  Cortland *(G-6973)*

Mjs Snow & Landscape LLC.................... D 419 656-6724
  Port Clinton *(G-12538)*

Modern Day Concrete Cnstr Inc.............. E 513 738-1026
  Harrison *(G-9112)*

Modern Poured Walls Inc........................ E 440 647-6661
  Wellington *(G-14634)*

Norris Brothers Co Inc............................ C 216 771-2233
  Cleveland *(G-4647)*

North Coast Concrete Inc....................... E 216 642-1114
  Cleveland *(G-4648)*

Ohio Con Sawing & Drlg Inc.................... E 419 841-1330
  Sylvania *(G-13559)*

Perrin Asphalt Co Inc.............................. D 330 253-1020
  Akron *(G-265)*

Platform Cement Inc............................... E 440 602-9750
  Mentor *(G-10984)*

Poured LLC... E 614 432-0804
  Columbus *(G-6538)*

Professional Pavement Svcs LLC............ E 740 726-2222
  Delaware *(G-7821)*

Prus Construction Company................... C 513 321-7774
  Cincinnati *(G-3256)*

▲ R W Sidley Incorporated..................... E 440 352-9343
  Painesville *(G-12242)*

Reitter Stucco Inc.................................. E 614 291-2212
  Columbus *(G-6575)*

Safety Grooving & Grinding LP................ E
  Napoleon *(G-11532)*

Scioto Darby Concrete Inc..................... D 614 876-3114
  Hilliard *(G-9229)*

Shepherd Excavating Inc........................ E 614 889-1115
  Dublin *(G-8118)*

Sika Mbcc US LLC................................... A 216 839-7500
  Beachwood *(G-838)*

Standard Contg & Engrg Inc.................... D 440 243-1001
  Brookpark *(G-1440)*

Suburban Maint & Cnstr Inc.................... E 440 237-7765
  North Royalton *(G-11950)*

Tallmadge Asphalt and Pav..................... D 330 677-0000
  Kent *(G-9601)*

The Beaver Excavating Co...................... A 330 478-2151
  Canton *(G-1871)*

Towne Construction Svcs LLC................ C 513 561-3700
  Batavia *(G-749)*

◆ Trewbric III Inc................................... E 614 444-2184
  Columbus *(G-6785)*

Tri-Mor Corp... D 330 963-3101
  Twinsburg *(G-14223)*

Triple Q Foundations Co Inc.................... E 513 932-3121
  Lebanon *(G-9795)*

Trucco Construction Co Inc.................... C 740 417-9010
  Delaware *(G-7831)*

USA Precast Concrete Limited................ D 330 854-9600
  Canal Fulton *(G-1595)*

Vmi Group Inc... D 330 405-4146
  Twinsburg *(G-14230)*

Wasiniak Construction Inc...................... D 419 668-8624
  Norwalk *(G-12030)*

Williams Concrete Cnstr Co Inc.............. E 330 745-6388
  Akron *(G-361)*

1781 Water well drilling

Collector Wells Intl Inc........................... D 614 888-6263
  Columbus *(G-5596)*

Moodys of Dayton Inc............................. E 614 443-3898
  Miamisburg *(G-11074)*

1791 Structural steel erection

APA Solar LLC.. D 419 267-5280
  Ridgeville Corners *(G-12725)*

Armeton US Co.. E 419 660-9296
  Norwalk *(G-12001)*

Black Swamp Steel Inc........................... E 419 867-8050
  Holland *(G-9280)*

◆ Cbc Global... E 330 482-3373
  Columbiana *(G-5232)*

Chc Fabricating Corp.............................. D 513 821-7757
  Cincinnati *(G-2348)*

▲ CK Construction Group Inc.................. B 614 901-8844
  Westerville *(G-14967)*

Daniel A Terreri & Sons Inc.................... E 330 538-2950
  Youngstown *(G-15591)*

Diamond Steel Construction................... E 330 549-5500
  Youngstown *(G-15596)*

Dublin Building Systems Co.................... E 614 760-5831
  Dublin *(G-7989)*

Foundation Steel LLC............................. C 419 402-4241
  Swanton *(G-13525)*

Frederick Steel Company LLC................ D 513 821-6400
  Cincinnati *(G-2703)*

G & P Construction LLC.......................... E 855 494-4830
  North Royalton *(G-11941)*

Henry Gurtzweiler Inc............................ D 419 729-3955
  Toledo *(G-13846)*

Industrial First Inc................................. C 216 991-8605
  Bedford *(G-966)*

J&H Rnfrcing Strl Erectors Inc................ C 740 355-0141
  Portsmouth *(G-12558)*

Kelley Steel Erectors Inc....................... D 440 232-1573
  Cleveland *(G-4455)*

Lakeside Interior Contractors Inc........... C 419 867-1300
  Perrysburg *(G-12351)*

Marysville Steel Inc............................... E 937 642-5971
  Marysville *(G-10494)*

Mid Atlantic Stor Systems Inc................ D 740 335-2019
  Wshngtn Ct Hs *(G-15491)*

Mound Technologies Inc......................... E 937 748-2937
  Springboro *(G-13203)*

▲ Northbend Archtctural Pdts Inc.......... E 513 577-7988
  Cincinnati *(G-3121)*

Ontario Mechanical LLC......................... E 419 529-2578
  Ontario *(G-12121)*

Orbit Movers & Erectors Inc................... E 937 277-8080
  Dayton *(G-7540)*

Rittman Inc... D 330 927-6855
  Rittman *(G-12732)*

Sofco Erectors Inc................................. C 513 771-1600
  Cincinnati *(G-3392)*

▼ Superior Walls of Ohio Inc.................. D 330 393-4101
  Warren *(G-14562)*

Vmi Group Inc... D 330 405-4146
  Twinsburg *(G-14230)*

1793 Glass and glazing work

A E D Inc... E 419 661-9999
  Northwood *(G-11968)*

▲ Advanced Auto Glass Inc................... E 412 373-6675
  Akron *(G-17)*

▲ Afg Industries Inc.............................. D 614 322-4580
  Grove City *(G-8893)*

Anderson Aluminum Corporation............ D 614 476-4877
  Columbus *(G-5368)*

Diers2018co Inc..................................... E 513 242-9250
  Cincinnati *(G-2563)*

Fuyao Glass America Inc........................ A 937 951-9263
  Moraine *(G-11412)*

JMd Architectural Pdts Inc..................... E 614 527-0306
  Hilliard *(G-9206)*

Employee Codes: A=Over 500 employees, B=251-500
C=101-250, D=51-100, E=20-50, F=10-19, G=1-9

2024 Harris Ohio
Services Directory

17 CONSTRUCTION - SPECIAL TRADE CONTRACTORS

Lakeland Glass Co. .... E 440 277-4527
   Lorain *(G-10082)*

Pioneer Cldding Glzing Systems............ E 216 816-4242
   Cleveland *(G-4749)*

▲ Pioneer Cldding Glzing Systems........ D 513 583-5925
   Mason *(G-10593)*

R C Hemm Glass Shops Inc .... E 937 773-5591
   Piqua *(G-12457)*

Richardson Glass Service Inc .... D 740 366-5090
   Newark *(G-11746)*

Ryans All-Glass Incorporated .... E 513 771-4440
   West Chester *(G-14759)*

Tg of Toledo LLC .... E 419 241-3151
   Toledo *(G-14039)*

Thomas Glass Company Inc .... E 614 268-8611
   Worthington *(G-15462)*

United GL & Panl Systems Inc................ E 330 244-9745
   North Canton *(G-11869)*

Wiechart Enterprises Inc .... E 419 227-0027
   Lima *(G-9987)*

1794 Excavation work

A Crano Excavating Inc .... E 330 630-1061
   Akron *(G-8)*

Allard Excavation LLC .... D 740 778-2242
   South Webster *(G-13185)*

Alliance Crane & Rigging Inc .... E 330 823-8823
   Louisville *(G-10111)*

Anderzack-Pitzen Cnstr Inc .... D 419 644-2111
   Metamora *(G-11016)*

B & B Wrecking & Excvtg Inc .... E 216 429-1700
   Cleveland *(G-3846)*

Bansal Construction Inc .... E 513 874-5410
   Fairfield *(G-8392)*

Best Communications Inc .... E 440 758-5854
   Conneaut *(G-6941)*

Bontrager Excavating Co Inc .... E 330 499-8775
   Uniontown *(G-14242)*

Boyas Enterprises I Inc .... E 216 524-3620
   Cleveland *(G-3886)*

Brunk Excavating Inc .... E 513 360-0308
   Monroe *(G-11335)*

Buckeye Excavating & Cnstr Inc .... E 419 663-3113
   Norwalk *(G-12003)*

Charles H Hamilton Co............................ D 513 683-2442
   Maineville *(G-10226)*

Chieftain Trucking & Excav Inc .... E 216 485-8034
   Cleveland *(G-3968)*

Cincinnati Asphalt Corporation .... D 513 367-0250
   Harrison *(G-9098)*

Darby Creek Excavating Inc.................... E 740 477-8600
   Circleville *(G-3706)*

Dave Sugar Excavating LLC.................... E 330 542-1100
   Petersburg *(G-12394)*

Degen Excavating Inc.............................. D 419 225-6871
   Lima *(G-9884)*

Digioia-Suburban Excvtg LLC................ D 440 237-1978
   North Royalton *(G-11939)*

Don Wartko Construction Co .... D 330 673-5252
   Kent *(G-9572)*

Elect General Contractors Inc................ E 740 420-3437
   Circleville *(G-3708)*

Elite Excavating Company Inc................ E 419 683-4200
   Mansfield *(G-10261)*

Eslich Wrecking Company...................... E 330 488-8300
   Louisville *(G-10116)*

ESwagner Company Inc.......................... D 419 691-8651
   Oregon *(G-12133)*

Evans Landscaping Inc............................ E 513 271-1119
   Cincinnati *(G-2639)*

Family Liquidation Company Inc............ D 937 780-3075
   Wshngtn Ct Hs *(G-15479)*

Fechko Excavating Inc .... D 330 722-2890
   Medina *(G-10834)*

Fechko Excavating LLC............................ D 330 722-2890
   Medina *(G-10835)*

Fishel Company.. E 937 233-2268
   Dayton *(G-7355)*

Ford Development Corp.......................... E 513 772-1521
   Cincinnati *(G-2693)*

Fortuna Construction Co Inc.................. E 440 892-3834
   Cleveland *(G-4278)*

Fox Services Inc...................................... E 513 858-2022
   Fairfield *(G-8414)*

◆ Gayston Corporation.............................. C 937 743-6050
   Miamisburg *(G-11057)*

Geo Gradel Co .... D 419 691-7123
   Toledo *(G-13819)*

George J Igel & Co Inc .... A 614 445-8421
   Columbus *(G-5928)*

Geotex Construction Svcs Inc................ E 614 444-5690
   Columbus *(G-5929)*

GM Mechanical Inc.................................. D 937 473-3006
   Covington *(G-7018)*

▲ Goettle Holding Company Inc............ C 513 825-8100
   Cincinnati *(G-2738)*

Ground Tech Inc...................................... E 330 270-0700
   Youngstown *(G-15625)*

Harris & Heavener Excvtg Inc................ E 740 927-1423
   Etna *(G-8330)*

Henry Jergens Contractor Inc................ E 937 233-1830
   Dayton *(G-7405)*

▲ Independence Excavating Inc............ E 216 524-1700
   Independence *(G-9437)*

J & J General Maintenance Inc.............. D 740 533-9729
   Ironton *(G-9509)*

Jamison Cnstr Solutions Inc.................. E 513 377-0705
   Fairfield *(G-8422)*

John Eramo & Sons Inc .... D 614 777-0020
   Hilliard *(G-9207)*

John F Gallagher Plumbing Co.............. D 440 946-4256
   Eastlake *(G-8204)*

JS Bova Excavating LLC.......................... E 234 254-4040
   Struthers *(G-13501)*

JS Paris Excavating Inc........................... E 330 538-9876
   Youngstown *(G-15643)*

Junction Tavern Inc................................ D 330 477-4694
   Canton *(G-1787)*

Kelchner Inc.. D 330 476-9737
   Saint Clairsville *(G-12795)*

Kelchner Inc.. C 937 704-9890
   Springboro *(G-13202)*

Kirila Contractors Inc.............................. E 330 448-4055
   Brookfield *(G-1406)*

Klumm Bros .... E 419 829-3166
   Holland *(G-9292)*

KMu Trucking & Excvtg LLC.................... E 440 934-1008
   Avon *(G-659)*

Larry Lang Excavating Inc...................... E 740 984-4750
   Beverly *(G-1101)*

Layton Inc.. E 740 349-7101
   Newark *(G-11712)*

Loveland Excavating Inc........................ E 513 965-6600
   Fairfield *(G-8427)*

Luburgh Inc.. E 740 452-3668
   Zanesville *(G-15808)*

Mark Schaffer Excvtg Trckg Inc.............. D 419 668-5990
   Norwalk *(G-12017)*

Martin Greg Excavating Inc.................... E 513 727-9300
   Middletown *(G-11171)*

McConnell Excavating Ltd...................... E 440 774-4578
   Oberlin *(G-12072)*

Metropolitan Envmtl Svcs Inc................ D 614 771-1881
   Hilliard *(G-9213)*

Mike Enyart & Sons Inc.......................... D 740 523-0235
   South Point *(G-13181)*

Mike Pusateri Excavating Inc................ E 330 385-5221
   East Liverpool *(G-8186)*

Miller Yount Paving Inc.......................... E 561 951-7416
   Cortland *(G-6973)*

Modern Poured Walls Inc...................... E 440 647-6661
   Wellington *(G-14634)*

Mr Excavator Inc...................................... D 440 256-2008
   Kirtland *(G-9646)*

Nelson Stark Company............................ C 513 489-0866
   Cincinnati *(G-3105)*

Nickolas M Savko & Sons Inc................ C 614 451-2242
   Columbus *(G-6359)*

Nicolozakes Trckg & Cnstr Inc................ E 740 432-5648
   Cambridge *(G-1577)*

Northast Ohio Trnching Svc Inc............ E 216 663-6006
   Cleveland *(G-4661)*

Ohio State Home Services Inc.............. D 614 850-5600
   Hilliard *(G-9223)*

Performance Site Company.................... C 614 445-7161
   Columbus *(G-6516)*

R D Jones Excavating Inc...................... E 419 648-5870
   Harrod *(G-9122)*

Rack & Ballauer Excvtg Co Inc.............. E 513 738-7000
   Hamilton *(G-9077)*

Rudzik Excavating Inc............................ E 330 755-1540
   Struthers *(G-13503)*

S E T Inc.. E 330 536-6724
   Lowellville *(G-10171)*

Seals Construction Inc............................ E 614 836-7200
   Canal Winchester *(G-1616)*

Sehlhorst Equipment Svcs Inc................ E 513 353-9300
   Cleves *(G-5193)*

Sehlhorst Equipment Svcs LLC.............. E 513 353-9300
   Cleves *(G-5194)*

▲ Sheckler Excavating Inc.................... D 330 866-1999
   Malvern *(G-10237)*

Siler Excavation Services........................ E 513 400-8628
   Milford *(G-11257)*

Sisler Heating & Cooling Inc.................. E 330 722-7101
   Medina *(G-10890)*

Smith & Associates Excavating.............. E 740 362-3355
   Columbus *(G-6690)*

Standard Contg & Engrg Inc.................. D 440 243-1001
   Brookpark *(G-1440)*

Starr Construction & Demo LLC............ E 330 538-7214
   Warren *(G-14556)*

Steingass Mechanical Contg LLC.......... E 330 725-6090
   Medina *(G-10893)*

Stonegate Construction Inc.................... E 740 423-9170
   Belpre *(G-1060)*

The Beaver Excavating Co...................... A 330 478-2151
   Canton *(G-1871)*

Trimat Construction Inc.......................... E 740 388-9515
   Bidwell *(G-1106)*

Trucco Construction Co Inc.................... C 740 417-9010
   Delaware *(G-7831)*

Utter Construction Inc............................ C 513 876-2246
   Bethel *(G-1096)*

Vandalia Blcktop Slcoating Inc.............. E 937 454-0571
   Dayton *(G-7700)*

Virginia Ohio-West Excvtg Co................ C 740 676-7464
   Shadyside *(G-12971)*

Wenger Excavating Inc............................ E 330 837-4767
   Dalton *(G-7122)*

Zemba Bros Inc.. E 740 452-1880
   Zanesville *(G-15844)*

1795 Wrecking and demolition work

Affordable Dem & Hlg Inc...................... E 216 429-1874
   Cleveland *(G-3772)*

17 CONSTRUCTION - SPECIAL TRADE CONTRACTORS

Aztec Services Group Inc .... D 513 541-2002
  Cincinnati (G-2233)
B & B Wrecking & Excvtg Inc .... E 216 429-1700
  Cleveland (G-3846)
Boyas Enterprises I Inc .... E 216 524-3620
  Cleveland (G-3886)
Brunk Excavating Inc .... E 513 360-0308
  Monroe (G-11335)
Cook Paving and Cnstr Co .... E 216 267-7705
  Independence (G-9424)
Daniel A Terreri & Sons Inc .... E 330 538-2950
  Youngstown (G-15591)
Dave Sugar Excavating LLC .... E 330 542-1100
  Petersburg (G-12394)
Eslich Wrecking Company .... E 330 488-8300
  Louisville (G-10116)
Fluor-Bwxt Portsmouth LLC .... A 866 706-6992
  Piketon (G-12419)
Fortuna Construction Co Inc .... E 440 892-3834
  Cleveland (G-4278)
Fox Services Inc .... E 513 858-2022
  Fairfield (G-8414)
▲ Independence Excavating Inc .... E 216 524-1700
  Independence (G-9437)
JS Paris Excavating Inc .... E 330 538-9876
  Youngstown (G-15643)
Mark Schaffer Excvtg Trckg Inc .... D 419 668-5990
  Norwalk (G-12017)
Mz-Russell Inc .... E 216 675-2727
  Cleveland (G-4615)
ORourke Wrecking Company .... D 513 871-1400
  Cincinnati (G-3169)
Rnw Holdings Inc .... E 330 792-0600
  Youngstown (G-15709)
Sunesis Environmental LLC .... D 513 326-6000
  Fairfield (G-8444)
SW Griffin Co LLC .... E 513 601-3894
  Blue Ash (G-1248)
SW Griffin Co Llc .... E 513 678-4741
  Blue Ash (G-1249)

1796 Installing building equipment

Atlas Industrial Contrs LLC .... B 614 841-4500
  Columbus (G-5403)
▲ Canton Erectors Inc .... E 330 453-7363
  Massillon (G-10634)
◆ Clopay Corporation .... C 800 282-2260
  Mason (G-10540)
CTS Construction Inc .... D 513 489-8290
  Cincinnati (G-2521)
Expert Crane Inc .... E 216 451-9900
  Wellington (G-14632)
▲ Fenton Rigging & Contg Inc .... E 513 631-5500
  Cincinnati (G-2657)
Gem Industrial Inc .... D 419 666-6554
  Walbridge (G-14461)
Hensley Industries Inc .... E 513 769-6666
  Cincinnati (G-2817)
Hgc Construction Co .... E 513 861-8866
  Cincinnati (G-2818)
◆ Hy-Tek Material Handling LLC .... D 614 497-2500
  Columbus (G-6030)
Industrial Millwright Svcs LLC .... E 419 523-9147
  Ottawa (G-12187)
Industrial Power Systems Inc .... B 419 531-3121
  Rossford (G-12767)
K F T Inc .... E 513 241-5910
  Cincinnati (G-2925)
◆ McGill Airclean LLC .... D 614 829-1200
  Columbus (G-6215)
Myers Machinery Movers Inc .... E 614 871-5052
  Grove City (G-8938)

Nbw Inc .... E 216 377-1700
  Cleveland (G-4629)
◆ Nk Parts Industries Inc .... C 937 498-4651
  Sidney (G-13041)
Norris Brothers Co Inc .... C 216 771-2233
  Cleveland (G-4647)
North Bay Construction Inc .... E 440 835-1898
  Westlake (G-15085)
Orbit Movers & Erectors Inc .... E 937 277-8080
  Dayton (G-7540)
Otis Elevator Company .... E 216 573-2333
  Cleveland (G-4709)
Piqua Steel Co .... D 937 773-3632
  Piqua (G-12454)
Rmf Nooter LLC .... D 419 727-1970
  Toledo (G-13992)
S Gary Shmker Rgging Trnspt L .... E 330 899-9090
  Akron (G-292)
▲ Spallinger Millwright Svc Co .... E 419 225-5830
  Lima (G-9962)
Standard Contg & Engrg Inc .... D 440 243-1001
  Brookpark (G-1440)
Tesar Industrial Contrs Inc .... D 216 741-8008
  Cleveland (G-4987)
Tk Elevator Corporation .... C 513 241-6000
  Cincinnati (G-3481)
Tk Elevator Corporation .... D 614 895-8930
  Westerville (G-15017)
United Technical Support Svcs .... C 330 562-3330
  Streetsboro (G-13433)

1799 Special trade contractors, nec

AAA Emergency Service .... E 513 554-6473
  Loveland (G-10125)
Aerco Sandblasting Company .... E 419 224-2464
  Lima (G-9860)
▲ Afg Industries Inc .... D 614 322-4580
  Grove City (G-8893)
Aka Team Inc .... E 216 751-2000
  Cleveland (G-3781)
Allied Builders Inc .... E 937 226-0311
  Dayton (G-7163)
Allied Environmental Svcs Inc .... E 419 227-4004
  Lima (G-9864)
Archer Corporation .... E 330 455-9995
  Canton (G-1670)
ARS Aleut Construction LLC .... E 225 381-2991
  Columbus (G-5387)
Associated Materials Fin Inc .... D 330 922-7624
  Cuyahoga Falls (G-7042)
B Dry System Inc .... E 513 724-3444
  Williamsburg (G-15177)
Barr Engineering Incorporated .... E 614 714-0299
  Columbus (G-5420)
Basement Dctor HM Imprv Ctr CP .... D 800 880-8324
  Etna (G-8328)
Blue Chip Pavement Maintenance Inc .... D 513 321-9595
  Cincinnati (G-2268)
Bogie Industries Inc Ltd .... E 330 745-3105
  Akron (G-72)
Boyas Enterprises I Inc .... E 216 524-3620
  Cleveland (G-3886)
Brilliant Electric Sign Co Ltd .... E 216 741-3800
  Brooklyn Heights (G-1413)
Buckeye Pools Inc .... E 937 434-7916
  Dayton (G-7203)
Burbank Inc .... E 419 698-3434
  Toledo (G-13723)
Burnett Pools Inc .... E 330 372-1725
  Cortland (G-6968)
Cabinet Restylers Inc .... D 419 281-8449
  Ashland (G-486)

Canaan Companies Inc .... E 419 842-8373
  Toledo (G-13724)
Capital Fire Protection Co .... E 614 279-9448
  Columbus (G-5500)
Cardinal Builders Inc .... E 614 237-1000
  Columbus (G-5507)
Carpe Diem Industries LLC .... D 419 358-0129
  Bluffton (G-1280)
Carpe Diem Industries LLC .... D 419 659-5639
  Columbus Grove (G-6921)
Ceco Concrete Construction LLC .... C 513 874-6953
  West Chester (G-14661)
Central Fire Protection Co Inc .... E 937 322-0713
  Springfield (G-13225)
Central Insulation Systems Inc .... E 513 242-0600
  Cincinnati (G-2336)
▲ Cleveland Granite & Marble LLC .... E 216 291-7637
  Cleveland (G-4047)
Closets By Design .... E 513 469-6130
  Blue Ash (G-1152)
Columbus Dnv Inc .... C 614 761-1214
  Dublin (G-7966)
Coon Caulking & Sealants Inc .... D 330 875-2100
  Louisville (G-10115)
Daniel A Terreri & Sons Inc .... E 330 538-2950
  Youngstown (G-15591)
Danite Holdings Ltd .... E 614 444-3333
  Columbus (G-5740)
Deerfield Farms .... E 330 584-4715
  Deerfield (G-7740)
Design Rstrtion Rcnstrction In .... D 330 563-0010
  North Canton (G-11821)
Empaco Equipment Corporation .... D 330 659-9393
  Richfield (G-12695)
Environmental Quality MGT .... D 513 825-7500
  Cincinnati (G-2628)
Erie Construction Mid-West Inc .... D 937 898-4688
  Dayton (G-7339)
Feecorp Corporation .... E 614 837-3010
  Canal Winchester (G-1606)
Fire-Seal LLC .... E 614 454-4440
  Columbus (G-5859)
Flamos Enterprises Inc .... E 330 478-0009
  Canton (G-1755)
Fortuna Construction Co Inc .... E 440 892-3834
  Cleveland (G-4278)
▲ Goettle Holding Company Inc .... C 513 825-8100
  Cincinnati (G-2738)
Gus Holthaus Signs Inc .... E 513 861-0060
  Cincinnati (G-2783)
Harold J Becker Company Inc .... E 614 279-1414
  Dayton (G-7398)
High-TEC Industrial Services .... D 937 667-1772
  Tipp City (G-13659)
▲ High-Tech Pools Inc .... E 440 979-5070
  North Olmsted (G-11905)
Identitek Systems Inc .... D 330 832-9844
  Massillon (G-10648)
Industrial Fiberglass Spc Inc .... E 937 222-9000
  Dayton (G-7421)
Industrial Waste Control Inc .... D 330 270-9900
  Youngstown (G-15638)
J & D Home Improvement Inc .... D 800 288-0831
  Columbus (G-6076)
Jaco Waterproofing LLC .... E 513 738-0084
  Fairfield (G-8421)
Janson Industries .... D 330 455-7029
  Canton (G-1783)
Johnson Restoration LLC .... E 937 907-5056
  Dayton (G-7430)
Jtc Contracting Inc .... E 216 635-0745
  Cleveland (G-4443)

Employee Codes: A=Over 500 employees, B=251-500
C=101-250, D=51-100, E=20-50, F=10-19, G=1-9

17 CONSTRUCTION - SPECIAL TRADE CONTRACTORS

▲ Konkus Marble & Granite Inc............ C 614 876-4000
  Columbus (G-6125)
Leaf Home LLC................................... E 800 290-6106
  Hudson (G-9362)
▲ Lefeld Welding & Stl Sups Inc .... E 419 678-2397
  Coldwater (G-5216)
Lepi Enterprises Inc............................. D 740 453-2980
  Zanesville (G-15806)
Lincoln Moving & Storage Co.............. D 216 741-5500
  Strongsville (G-13470)
M T Golf Course Managment Inc......... E 513 923-1188
  Cincinnati (G-2998)
◆ Master Builders LLC .... E 800 228-3318
  Beachwood (G-811)
Metropolitan Pool Service Co............... E 216 741-9451
  Parma (G-12257)
▲ Mills Fence Co LLC.......................... E 513 631-0333
  Cincinnati (G-3066)
▲ Motz Group Inc................................. E 513 533-6452
  Cincinnati (G-3081)
Nanogate North America LLC.............. C 419 524-3778
  Mansfield (G-10302)
National Cnstr Rentals Inc................... E 614 308-1100
  Columbus (G-6294)
▲ National Electro-Coatings Inc........... D 216 898-0080
  Cleveland (G-4624)
▲ Nestaway LLC................................... D 216 587-1500
  Cleveland (G-4636)
North Bay Construction Inc.................. E 440 835-1898
  Westlake (G-15085)
Northpointe Property MGT LLC........... C 614 579-9712
  Columbus (G-6369)
▲ Ohio Pools & Spas Inc..................... E 330 494-7755
  Canton (G-1823)
Ohio State Home Services Inc............. D 614 850-5600
  Hilliard (G-9223)
Ohio State Home Services Inc............. C 330 467-1055
  Macedonia (G-10201)
◆ Organized Living Inc........................ E 513 489-9300
  Cincinnati (G-3167)
Palazzo Brothers Electric Inc............... E 419 668-1100
  Norwalk (G-12020)
Patterson Pools LLC............................ E 614 334-2629
  Plain City (G-12489)
Paulo Products Company..................... E 440 942-0153
  Willoughby (G-15218)
Pedersen Insulation Company.............. E 614 471-3788
  Columbus (G-6508)
Precision Environmental Co................. B 216 642-6040
  Independence (G-9470)
Priority III Contracting Inc.................... E 513 922-0203
  Cincinnati (G-3230)
▲ Ptmj Enterprises Inc......................... D 440 543-8000
  Solon (G-13132)
Quality Control Services LLC............... E 216 862-9264
  Cleveland (G-4800)
Quality Fabricated Metals Inc.............. E 330 332-7008
  Salem (G-12849)
R E Kramig & Co Inc........................... C 513 761-4010
  Cincinnati (G-3270)
R W Sidley Incorporated...................... C 440 298-3232
  Thompson (G-13618)
Ram Cnstrction Svcs Cncnnati L......... E 513 297-1857
  West Chester (G-14754)
Ram Restoration LLC........................... E 937 347-7418
  Dayton (G-7580)
Riverfront Diversified Inc..................... C 513 874-7200
  West Chester (G-14757)
Rudzik Excavating Inc.......................... E 330 755-1540
  Struthers (G-13503)
Rusk Industries Inc.............................. D 419 841-6055
  Toledo (G-14000)

Salvanalle Inc....................................... E 419 529-4700
  Mansfield (G-10315)
Schaefer & Company........................... E 937 339-2638
  Troy (G-14159)
Security Fence Group Inc.................... E 513 681-3700
  Cincinnati (G-3353)
Signature Control Systems LLC........... E 614 864-2222
  Columbus (G-6679)
Sika Mbcc US LLC............................... A 216 839-7500
  Beachwood (G-838)
▼ Stud Welding Associates Inc............ D 440 783-3160
  Strongsville (G-13490)
Style-Line Incorporated........................ E 614 291-0600
  Columbus (G-6725)
Suburban Maint & Cnstr Inc................ E 440 237-7765
  North Royalton (G-11950)
Terrafirm Construction LLC................. E 913 433-2998
  Urbancrest (G-14324)
Thermal Solutions Inc.......................... E 740 886-2861
  Proctorville (G-12614)
Toledo Area Insulator Wkrs Jac........... D 419 531-5911
  Toledo (G-14049)
United - Maier Signs Inc...................... D 513 681-6600
  Cincinnati (G-3551)
Vertneys LLC....................................... E 937 272-0585
  Dayton (G-7702)
Vwc Liquidation Company LLC........... C 330 372-6776
  Warren (G-14573)
Waco Scaffolding & Equipment Inc..... A 216 749-8900
  Cleveland (G-5119)
We Fresh N Refresh LLC..................... E 216 937-9798
  Cleveland (G-5123)
Wegman Construction Company.......... E 513 381-1111
  Cincinnati (G-3646)
Welty Building Company Ltd............... D 216 931-2400
  Cleveland (G-5130)
Wmk LLC.. E 440 951-4335
  Bedford (G-993)
X F Construction Svcs Inc.................... E 614 575-2700
  Columbus (G-6911)
Ziebart of Ohio Inc............................... E 440 845-6031
  Cleveland (G-5175)

20 FOOD AND KINDRED PRODUCTS

2011 Meat packing plants

Comber Holdings Inc........................... E 216 961-8600
  Cleveland (G-4090)
Empire Packing Company LP.............. D 513 942-5400
  West Chester (G-14809)
◆ Fresh Mark Inc................................. B 330 832-7491
  Massillon (G-10641)
King Kold Inc....................................... E 937 836-2731
  Englewood (G-8311)
The Ellenbee-Leggett Company Inc..... C 513 874-3200
  Fairfield (G-8446)
V H Cooper & Co Inc........................... C 419 375-4116
  Fort Recovery (G-8611)
Winner Corporation.............................. E 419 582-4321
  Yorkshire (G-15538)

2013 Sausages and other prepared meats

A To Z Portion Ctrl Meats Inc.............. E 419 358-2926
  Bluffton (G-1276)
Empire Packing Company LP.............. D 513 942-5400
  West Chester (G-14809)
◆ Fresh Mark Inc................................. B 330 832-7491
  Massillon (G-10641)
King Kold Inc....................................... E 937 836-2731
  Englewood (G-8311)

Lipari Foods Operating Co LLC........... E 330 893-2479
  Millersburg (G-11284)
Martin-Brower Company LLC.............. C 513 773-2301
  West Chester (G-14729)
The Ellenbee-Leggett Company Inc..... C 513 874-3200
  Fairfield (G-8446)
◆ White Castle System Inc.................. B 614 228-5781
  Columbus (G-6883)
Winner Corporation.............................. E 419 582-4321
  Yorkshire (G-15538)

2015 Poultry slaughtering and processing

▼ Ballas Egg Products Corp................ D 614 453-0386
  Zanesville (G-15769)
Cal-Maine Foods Inc............................ D 937 337-9576
  Rossburg (G-12764)
Cooper Hatchery Inc............................ C 419 594-3325
  Oakwood (G-12053)
▲ Daylay Egg Farm Inc........................ C 937 355-6531
  West Mansfield (G-14862)
Fort Recovery Equity Inc..................... E 419 375-4119
  Fort Recovery (G-8609)
Martin-Brower Company LLC.............. C 513 773-2301
  West Chester (G-14729)
The Ellenbee-Leggett Company Inc..... C 513 874-3200
  Fairfield (G-8446)
V H Cooper & Co Inc........................... C 419 375-4116
  Fort Recovery (G-8611)
▲ Weaver Bros Inc............................... D 937 526-3907
  Versailles (G-14417)

2022 Cheese; natural and processed

◆ Great Lakes Cheese Co Inc.............. B 440 834-2500
  Hiram (G-9274)
▲ Hans Rothenbuhler & Son Inc......... E 440 632-6000
  Middlefield (G-11140)
Lipari Foods Operating Co LLC........... E 330 893-2479
  Millersburg (G-11284)
▲ Miceli Dairy Products Co................. D 216 791-6222
  Cleveland (G-4572)

2023 Dry, condensed, evaporated products

▲ Hans Rothenbuhler & Son Inc......... E 440 632-6000
  Middlefield (G-11140)
Instantwhip-Columbus Inc................... E 614 871-9447
  Grove City (G-8928)

2024 Ice cream and frozen deserts

Johnsons Real Ice Cream LLC............ C 614 231-0014
  Columbus (G-6095)
United Dairy Farmers Inc..................... C 513 396-8700
  Cincinnati (G-3553)
Velvet Ice Cream Company................. D 740 892-3921
  Utica (G-14330)
Youngs Jersey Dairy Inc...................... B 937 325-0629
  Yellow Springs (G-15537)

2026 Fluid milk

Borden Dairy Co Cincinnati LLC.......... E 513 948-8811
  Cleveland (G-3881)
Instantwhip-Columbus Inc................... E 614 871-9447
  Grove City (G-8928)
United Dairy Farmers Inc..................... C 513 396-8700
  Cincinnati (G-3553)

2032 Canned specialties

Bittersweet Inc..................................... D 419 875-6725
  Whitehouse (G-15138)
Cheese Holdings Inc............................ E 330 893-2479
  Millersburg (G-11275)
Clovervale Farms LLC......................... D 440 960-0146
  Amherst (G-426)

SIC SECTION

▲ Hayden Valley Foods Inc.................... D..... 614 539-7233
   Urbancrest *(G-14320)*
▲ More Than Gourmet Holdings Inc..... E..... 330 762-6652
   Akron *(G-237)*
▲ Skyline Cem Holdings LLC................ C..... 513 874-1188
   Fairfield *(G-8441)*

2033 Canned fruits and specialties

Clovervale Farms LLC......................... D..... 440 960-0146
   Amherst *(G-426)*

2034 Dehydrated fruits, vegetables, soups

▲ Hayden Valley Foods Inc.................... D..... 614 539-7233
   Urbancrest *(G-14320)*

2035 Pickles, sauces, and salad dressings

▲ National Foods Packaging Inc............ E..... 216 622-2740
   Cleveland *(G-4626)*

2038 Frozen specialties, nec

Clovervale Farms LLC......................... D..... 440 960-0146
   Amherst *(G-426)*
King Kold Inc.. E..... 937 836-2731
   Englewood *(G-8311)*
▲ Skyline Cem Holdings LLC................ C..... 513 874-1188
   Fairfield *(G-8441)*

2041 Flour and other grain mill products

Keynes Bros Inc.................................. D..... 740 385-6824
   Logan *(G-10030)*
Mennel Milling Company..................... E..... 740 385-6824
   Logan *(G-10034)*
Minster Farmers Coop Exch................. D..... 419 628-4705
   Minster *(G-11319)*

2045 Prepared flour mixes and doughs

Busken Bakery Inc.............................. D..... 513 871-2114
   Cincinnati *(G-2294)*
Cassanos Inc...................................... E..... 937 294-8400
   Dayton *(G-7215)*
▲ National Foods Packaging Inc............ E..... 216 622-2740
   Cleveland *(G-4626)*

2047 Dog and cat food

JM Smucker LLC................................ D..... 330 682-3000
   Orrville *(G-12169)*
◆ Pro-Pet LLC......................................D..... 419 394-3374
   Saint Marys *(G-12835)*

2048 Prepared feeds, nec

Centerra Co-Op................................... E..... 419 281-2153
   Ashland *(G-490)*
Cooper Farms Inc............................... D..... 419 375-4116
   Fort Recovery *(G-8606)*
Cooper Hatchery Inc........................... C..... 419 594-3325
   Oakwood *(G-12053)*
Hanby Farms Inc................................ E..... 740 763-3554
   Nashport *(G-11535)*
◆ Pro-Pet LLC......................................D..... 419 394-3374
   Saint Marys *(G-12835)*
▲ Provimi North America Inc................. B..... 937 770-2400
   Lewisburg *(G-9842)*

2051 Bread, cake, and related products

Amish Door Inc................................... C..... 330 359-5464
   Wilmot *(G-15281)*
Buns of Delaware Inc.......................... E..... 740 363-2867
   Delaware *(G-7781)*
Klosterman Baking Co LLC................. D..... 513 242-5667
   Cincinnati *(G-2944)*
Mustard Seed Health Fd Mkt Inc.......... D..... 440 519-3663
   Solon *(G-13115)*

Osmans Pies Inc................................. E..... 330 607-9083
   Stow *(G-13384)*
◆ White Castle System Inc................... B..... 614 228-5781
   Columbus *(G-6883)*

2052 Cookies and crackers

Ditsch Usa LLC................................... E..... 513 782-8888
   Cincinnati *(G-2568)*
Osmans Pies Inc................................. E..... 330 607-9083
   Stow *(G-13384)*

2064 Candy and other confectionery products

▲ Amerisource Health Svcs LLC............ D..... 614 492-8177
   Columbus *(G-5364)*
Bloomer Candy Co.............................. C..... 740 452-7501
   Zanesville *(G-15771)*
▲ Hayden Valley Foods Inc.................... D..... 614 539-7233
   Urbancrest *(G-14320)*
◆ Jml Holdings Inc...............................E..... 419 866-7500
   Holland *(G-9291)*
Tiffin Paper Company.......................... E..... 419 447-2121
   Tiffin *(G-13647)*

2066 Chocolate and cocoa products

Gorant Chocolatier LLC....................... C..... 330 726-8821
   Boardman *(G-1288)*

2068 Salted and roasted nuts and seeds

▲ Hayden Valley Foods Inc.................... D..... 614 539-7233
   Urbancrest *(G-14320)*

2084 Wines, brandy, and brandy spirits

▲ Paramount Distillers Inc..................... B..... 216 671-6300
   Cleveland *(G-4718)*

2085 Distilled and blended liquors

▲ Paramount Distillers Inc..................... B..... 216 671-6300
   Cleveland *(G-4718)*
Watershed Distillery LLC..................... E..... 614 357-1936
   Columbus *(G-6869)*

2086 Bottled and canned soft drinks

American Bottling Company................ C..... 614 237-4201
   Columbus *(G-5346)*
Borden Dairy Co Cincinnati LLC.......... E..... 513 948-8811
   Cleveland *(G-3881)*
Central Coca-Cola Btlg Co Inc............. E..... 330 875-1487
   Akron *(G-86)*
Central Coca-Cola Btlg Co Inc............. E..... 740 474-2180
   Circleville *(G-3705)*
Central Coca-Cola Btlg Co Inc............. E..... 419 476-6622
   Toledo *(G-13727)*
G & J Pepsi-Cola Bottlers Inc.............. E..... 740 593-3366
   Athens *(G-568)*
G & J Pepsi-Cola Bottlers Inc.............. B..... 740 354-9191
   Franklin Furnace *(G-8654)*
G & J Pepsi-Cola Bottlers Inc.............. E..... 740 354-9191
   Zanesville *(G-15788)*
Pepsi-Cola Metro Btlg Co Inc.............. E..... 937 461-4664
   Dayton *(G-7549)*
Pepsi-Cola Metro Btlg Co Inc.............. C..... 330 425-8236
   Twinsburg *(G-14213)*

2087 Flavoring extracts and syrups, nec

Agrana Fruit Us Inc............................. C..... 937 693-3821
   Anna *(G-442)*
Central Coca-Cola Btlg Co Inc............. E..... 419 476-6622
   Toledo *(G-13727)*
▲ Wiley Companies................................ C..... 740 622-0755
   Coshocton *(G-7005)*

2096 Potato chips and similar snacks

Ballreich Bros Inc................................ C..... 419 447-1814
   Tiffin *(G-13624)*
Jones Potato Chip Co.......................... E..... 419 529-9424
   Mansfield *(G-10276)*
Mike-Sells Potato Chip Co................... E..... 937 228-9400
   Dayton *(G-7504)*
Mike-Sells West Virginia Inc................ D..... 937 228-9400
   Dayton *(G-7505)*
◆ Shearers Foods LLC..........................A..... 800 428-6843
   Massillon *(G-10669)*

2097 Manufactured ice

Lori Holding Co.................................... E..... 740 342-3230
   New Lexington *(G-11628)*
Velvet Ice Cream Company................. E..... 419 562-2009
   Bucyrus *(G-1519)*

2099 Food preparations, nec

Agrana Fruit Us Inc............................. C..... 937 693-3821
   Anna *(G-442)*
Ballreich Bros Inc................................ C..... 419 447-1814
   Tiffin *(G-13624)*
Bfc Inc.. E..... 330 364-6645
   Dover *(G-7873)*
Chefs Garden Inc................................ C..... 419 433-4947
   Huron *(G-9385)*
Cuyahoga Vending Co Inc................... C..... 440 353-9595
   North Ridgeville *(G-11926)*
Dno Inc... D..... 614 231-3601
   Columbus *(G-5779)*
Dole Fresh Vegetables Inc.................. C..... 937 525-4300
   Springfield *(G-13248)*
Domino Foods Inc................................ C..... 216 432-3222
   Cleveland *(G-4175)*
Freshway Foods Company Inc............. D..... 937 498-4664
   Sidney *(G-13034)*
Gold Star Chili Inc............................... E..... 513 231-4541
   Cincinnati *(G-2740)*
Lipari Foods Operating Co LLC........... E..... 330 893-2479
   Millersburg *(G-11284)*
▲ National Foods Packaging Inc............ E..... 216 622-2740
   Cleveland *(G-4626)*
Ohio Hckry Hrvest Brnd Pdts In.......... E..... 330 644-6266
   Coventry Township *(G-7014)*
Produce Packaging Inc........................ C..... 216 391-6129
   Willoughby Hills *(G-15234)*
▲ R S Hanline and Co Inc..................... C..... 419 347-8077
   Shelby *(G-13010)*
Tarrier Foods Corp.............................. E..... 614 876-8594
   Columbus *(G-6749)*

21 TOBACCO PRODUCTS

2131 Chewing and smoking tobacco

◆ Scandinavian Tob Group Ln Ltd.........C..... 770 934-4594
   Akron *(G-295)*

22 TEXTILE MILL PRODUCTS

2211 Broadwoven fabric mills, cotton

▼ Ccp Industries Inc.............................. B..... 216 535-4227
   Richmond Heights *(G-12716)*
▲ Inside Outfitters Inc............................ E..... 614 798-3500
   Lewis Center *(G-9824)*
Lumenomics Inc.................................. E..... 614 798-3500
   Lewis Center *(G-9827)*

2221 Broadwoven fabric mills, manmade

▲ Inside Outfitters Inc............................ E..... 614 798-3500
   Lewis Center *(G-9824)*

Employee Codes: A=Over 500 employees, B=251-500
C=101-250, D=51-100, E=20-50, F=10-19, G=1-9

22 TEXTILE MILL PRODUCTS

Lumenomics Inc................................. E 614 798-3500
  Lewis Center *(G-9827)*
▲ Weaver Leather LLC......................... D 330 674-7548
  Millersburg *(G-11296)*

2241 Narrow fabric mills

Crane Consumables Inc....................... E 513 539-9980
  Middletown *(G-11160)*
◆ Keuchel & Associates Inc.................E 330 945-9455
  Cuyahoga Falls *(G-7085)*
▲ Samsel Rope & Marine Supply Co..... E 216 241-0333
  Cleveland *(G-4875)*

2253 Knit outerwear mills

E Retailing Associates LLC.................... D 614 300-5785
  Columbus *(G-5798)*

2273 Carpets and rugs

▼ Ccp Industries Inc............................. B 216 535-4227
  Richmond Heights *(G-12716)*
▲ Durable Corporation......................... D 800 537-1603
  Norwalk *(G-12008)*

2295 Coated fabrics, not rubberized

Laserflex Corporation........................... D 614 850-9500
  Hilliard *(G-9209)*

2296 Tire cord and fabrics

Mfh Partners Inc.................................. B 440 461-4100
  Cleveland *(G-4571)*

2297 Nonwoven fabrics

▼ Ccp Industries Inc............................. B 216 535-4227
  Richmond Heights *(G-12716)*

2298 Cordage and twine

▲ Atwood Rope Manufacturing Inc....... E 614 920-0534
  Canal Winchester *(G-1598)*

2299 Textile goods, nec

◆ Standard Textile Co Inc....................B 513 761-9255
  Cincinnati *(G-3409)*

23 APPAREL, FINISHED PRODUCTS FROM FABRICS & SIMILAR MATERIALS

2311 Men's and boy's suits and coats

Lion First Responder Ppe Inc................ D 937 898-1949
  Dayton *(G-7456)*
Lion Group Inc.................................... D 937 898-1949
  Dayton *(G-7457)*
Vgs Inc... C 216 431-7800
  Cleveland *(G-5102)*

2326 Men's and boy's work clothing

Cintas Corporation............................... D 513 631-5750
  Cincinnati *(G-2443)*
◆ Cintas Corporation...........................A 513 459-1200
  Cincinnati *(G-2442)*
Cintas Corporation No 2....................... D 330 966-7800
  Canton *(G-1709)*
Cintas Sales Corporation...................... B 513 459-1200
  Cincinnati *(G-2445)*
Vgs Inc... C 216 431-7800
  Cleveland *(G-5102)*

2337 Women's and misses' suits and coats

Cintas Corporation............................... D 513 631-5750
  Cincinnati *(G-2443)*

◆ Cintas Corporation...........................A 513 459-1200
  Cincinnati *(G-2442)*
Cintas Corporation No 2....................... D 330 966-7800
  Canton *(G-1709)*

2353 Hats, caps, and millinery

▲ Barbs Graffiti Inc............................. E 216 881-5550
  Cleveland *(G-3849)*

2381 Fabric dress and work gloves

▲ Wcm Holdings Inc........................... C 513 705-2100
  Cincinnati *(G-3643)*
▲ West Chester Holdings LLC............. C 513 705-2100
  Cincinnati *(G-3655)*

2389 Apparel and accessories, nec

Costume Specialists Inc....................... E 614 464-2115
  Columbus *(G-5706)*
Walter F Stephens Jr Inc...................... E 937 746-0521
  Franklin *(G-8652)*

2391 Curtains and draperies

Accent Drapery Co Inc........................ E 614 488-0741
  Columbus *(G-5300)*
Janson Industries................................ D 330 455-7029
  Canton *(G-1783)*
Style-Line Incorporated........................ E 614 291-0600
  Columbus *(G-6725)*
Vocational Services Inc....................... E 216 431-8085
  Cleveland *(G-5113)*

2392 Household furnishings, nec

▲ Casco Mfg Solutions Inc.................. D 513 681-0003
  Cincinnati *(G-2318)*
▼ Ccp Industries Inc............................. B 216 535-4227
  Richmond Heights *(G-12716)*
Ekco Cleaning Inc............................... C 513 733-8882
  Cincinnati *(G-2608)*
◆ Impact Products LLC.......................D 419 841-2891
  Toledo *(G-13860)*
▲ Nestaway LLC................................. D 216 587-1500
  Cleveland *(G-4636)*

2394 Canvas and related products

▲ Inside Outfitters Inc......................... E 614 798-3500
  Lewis Center *(G-9824)*
Lumenomics Inc................................. E 614 798-3500
  Lewis Center *(G-9827)*
▲ Samsel Rope & Marine Supply Co..... E 216 241-0333
  Cleveland *(G-4875)*

2395 Pleating and stitching

▲ Barbs Graffiti Inc............................. E 216 881-5550
  Cleveland *(G-3849)*
▲ Shamrock Companies Inc................ D 440 899-9510
  Westlake *(G-15108)*

2396 Automotive and apparel trimmings

◆ Associated Premium Corporation......E 513 679-4444
  Cincinnati *(G-2219)*
Bates Metal Products Inc..................... D 740 498-8371
  Port Washington *(G-12541)*
Brown Cnty Bd Mntal Rtardation........... E 937 378-4891
  Georgetown *(G-8798)*
▲ General Theming Contrs LLC........... C 614 252-6342
  Columbus *(G-5925)*
Screen Works Inc............................... E 937 264-9111
  Dayton *(G-7613)*
▲ TS Tech Americas Inc...................... B 614 575-4100
  Reynoldsburg *(G-12678)*
Woodrow Manufacturing Co................. E 937 399-9333
  Springfield *(G-13313)*

2399 Fabricated textile products, nec

TAC Industries Inc............................... B 937 328-5200
  Springfield *(G-13299)*

24 LUMBER AND WOOD PRODUCTS, EXCEPT FURNITURE

2421 Sawmills and planing mills, general

Baillie Lumber Co LP............................ E 419 462-2000
  Galion *(G-8745)*
▲ Combs Manufacturing Inc................ D 330 784-3151
  Akron *(G-114)*
▼ Hartzell Hardwoods Inc.................... D 937 773-7054
  Piqua *(G-12443)*
Sawmill Road Management Co LLC...... E 937 342-9071
  Columbus *(G-6646)*
▲ Stephen M Trudick........................... E 440 834-1891
  Burton *(G-1533)*
The F A Requarth Company................. E 937 224-1141
  Dayton *(G-7665)*
Wappoo Wood Products Inc................. E 937 492-1166
  Sidney *(G-13057)*

2426 Hardwood dimension and flooring mills

Baillie Lumber Co LP............................ E 419 462-2000
  Galion *(G-8745)*
▼ Hartzell Hardwoods Inc.................... D 937 773-7054
  Piqua *(G-12443)*
Holmes Lumber & Bldg Ctr Inc.............. E 330 479-8314
  Canton *(G-1775)*
Holmes Lumber & Bldg Ctr Inc.............. C 330 674-9060
  Millersburg *(G-11279)*
▲ Stephen M Trudick........................... E 440 834-1891
  Burton *(G-1533)*
Wappoo Wood Products Inc................. E 937 492-1166
  Sidney *(G-13057)*

2431 Millwork

◆ Clopay Corporation..........................C 800 282-2260
  Mason *(G-10540)*
Holmes Lumber & Bldg Ctr Inc.............. E 330 479-8314
  Canton *(G-1775)*
Holmes Lumber & Bldg Ctr Inc.............. C 330 674-9060
  Millersburg *(G-11279)*
Khempco Bldg Sup Co Ltd Partnr......... D 740 549-0465
  Delaware *(G-7811)*
▲ L E Smith Company......................... D 419 636-4555
  Bryan *(G-1486)*
Riverside Cnstr Svcs Inc...................... E 513 723-0900
  Cincinnati *(G-3307)*
Rockwood Products Ltd...................... E 330 893-2392
  Millersburg *(G-11291)*
S R Door Inc....................................... D 740 927-3558
  Hebron *(G-9153)*
▲ Stephen M Trudick........................... E 440 834-1891
  Burton *(G-1533)*
The F A Requarth Company................. E 937 224-1141
  Dayton *(G-7665)*
The Galehouse Companies Inc............. E 330 658-2023
  Doylestown *(G-7916)*

2434 Wood kitchen cabinets

Climate Pros LLC................................ D 216 881-5200
  Cleveland *(G-4083)*
Climate Pros LLC................................ D 330 744-2732
  Youngstown *(G-15579)*
Holmes Lumber & Bldg Ctr Inc.............. E 330 479-8314
  Canton *(G-1775)*
Holmes Lumber & Bldg Ctr Inc.............. C 330 674-9060
  Millersburg *(G-11279)*

SIC SECTION

Knapke Cabinets Inc............................. E 937 335-8383
 Troy *(G-14142)*
▲ Masterbrand Cabinets LLC.................. B 812 482-2527
 Beachwood *(G-812)*
Riverside Cnstr Svcs Inc......................... E 513 723-0900
 Cincinnati *(G-3307)*
The Hattenbach Company....................... D 216 881-5200
 Cleveland *(G-5001)*

2435 Hardwood veneer and plywood

▼ Exhibit Concepts Inc............................ D 937 890-7000
 Vandalia *(G-14376)*
▲ Sims-Lohman Inc................................. E 513 651-3510
 Cincinnati *(G-3379)*
Wappoo Wood Products Inc.................... E 937 492-1166
 Sidney *(G-13057)*

2436 Softwood veneer and plywood

Wappoo Wood Products Inc.................... E 937 492-1166
 Sidney *(G-13057)*

2439 Structural wood members, nec

Buckeye Components LLC...................... E 330 482-5163
 Columbiana *(G-5231)*
Holmes Lumber & Bldg Ctr Inc................ E 330 479-8314
 Canton *(G-1775)*
Holmes Lumber & Bldg Ctr Inc................ C 330 674-9060
 Millersburg *(G-11279)*
Khempco Bldg Sup Co Ltd Partnr............. D 740 549-0465
 Delaware *(G-7811)*
▲ Thomas Do-It Center Inc...................... E 740 446-2002
 Gallipolis *(G-8769)*

2441 Nailed wood boxes and shook

Lalac One LLC..................................... E 216 432-4422
 Cleveland *(G-4482)*
Quadco Rehabilitation Ctr Inc.................. B 419 682-1011
 Stryker *(G-13505)*

2448 Wood pallets and skids

Belco Works Inc.................................... D 740 695-0500
 Saint Clairsville *(G-12774)*
▼ Hope Timber Pallet Recycl LLC.............. E 740 344-1788
 Newark *(G-11706)*
◆ Litco International Inc............................D 330 539-5433
 Vienna *(G-14421)*
Quadco Rehabilitation Ctr Inc.................. E 419 445-1950
 Archbold *(G-466)*
Quadco Rehabilitation Ctr Inc.................. B 419 682-1011
 Stryker *(G-13505)*
Richland Newhope Inds Inc..................... C 419 774-4400
 Mansfield *(G-10313)*
Southwood Pallet LLC............................ D 330 682-3747
 Orrville *(G-12173)*
Universal Pallets Inc............................... E 614 444-1095
 Columbus *(G-6820)*

2449 Wood containers, nec

Brimar Packaging Inc.............................. E 440 934-3080
 Avon *(G-641)*

2452 Prefabricated wood buildings

Carter-Jones Lumber Company................ E 440 834-8164
 Middlefield *(G-11139)*
Cooper Enterprises Inc........................... D 419 347-5232
 Shelby *(G-13006)*
Vinyl Design Corporation........................ E 419 283-4009
 Holland *(G-9313)*

2491 Wood preserving

Flagship Trading Corporation................... E
 Cleveland *(G-4263)*

The F A Requarth Company..................... E 937 224-1141
 Dayton *(G-7665)*

2493 Reconstituted wood products

Mpc Inc... E 440 835-1405
 Cleveland *(G-4605)*

2499 Wood products, nec

◆ Gayston Corporation............................C 937 743-6050
 Miamisburg *(G-11057)*
H Hafner & Sons Inc............................. E 513 321-1895
 Cincinnati *(G-2786)*
◆ Scotts Company LLC...........................C 937 644-0011
 Marysville *(G-10508)*

25 FURNITURE AND FIXTURES

2511 Wood household furniture

Gencraft Designs LLC............................ E 330 359-6251
 Navarre *(G-11537)*
Vocational Services Inc........................... E 216 431-8085
 Cleveland *(G-5113)*
Western & Southern Lf Insur Co............... A 513 629-1800
 Cincinnati *(G-3659)*

2512 Upholstered household furniture

◆ Sauder Woodworking Co......................A 419 446-2711
 Archbold *(G-467)*

2514 Metal household furniture

◆ Rize Home LLC..................................D 800 333-8333
 Solon *(G-13138)*

2515 Mattresses and bedsprings

▲ Casco Mfg Solutions Inc....................... D 513 681-0003
 Cincinnati *(G-2318)*
Walter F Stephens Jr Inc......................... E 937 746-0521
 Franklin *(G-8652)*

2517 Wood television and radio cabinets

Kraftmaid Trucking Inc........................... D 440 632-2531
 Middlefield *(G-11142)*

2521 Wood office furniture

▲ Hoge Lumber Company........................ E 419 753-2263
 New Knoxville *(G-11617)*

2522 Office furniture, except wood

▲ Casco Mfg Solutions Inc....................... D 513 681-0003
 Cincinnati *(G-2318)*
Jsc Employee Leasing Corp..................... D 330 773-8971
 Akron *(G-212)*
▲ National Electro-Coatings Inc................. D 216 898-0080
 Cleveland *(G-4624)*

2531 Public building and related furniture

Bell Vault and Monu Works Inc................ E 937 866-2444
 Miamisburg *(G-11025)*
◆ Evenflo Company Inc...........................E 937 415-3300
 Miamisburg *(G-11053)*
Soft Touch Wood LLC............................ E 330 545-4204
 Girard *(G-8826)*
Yanfeng US Auto Intr Systems I............... E 419 662-4905
 Northwood *(G-11988)*

2541 Wood partitions and fixtures

Cabinet Restylers Inc............................. D 419 281-8449
 Ashland *(G-486)*
◆ CIP International Inc............................D 513 874-9925
 West Chester *(G-14666)*
Climate Pros LLC.................................. D 216 881-5200
 Cleveland *(G-4083)*

26 PAPER AND ALLIED PRODUCTS

Climate Pros LLC.................................. D 330 744-2732
 Youngstown *(G-15579)*
Ingle-Barr Inc....................................... D 740 702-6117
 Chillicothe *(G-2072)*
▲ L E Smith Company............................. D 419 636-4555
 Bryan *(G-1486)*
Lemon Group LLC................................. E 614 409-9850
 Obetz *(G-12081)*
Partitions Plus Incorporated.................... E 419 422-2600
 Findlay *(G-8575)*
▲ Ptmj Enterprises Inc............................ D 440 543-8000
 Solon *(G-13132)*
The Hattenbach Company....................... D 216 881-5200
 Cleveland *(G-5001)*

2542 Partitions and fixtures, except wood

Bates Metal Products Inc........................ D 740 498-8371
 Port Washington *(G-12541)*
G & P Construction LLC......................... E 855 494-4830
 North Royalton *(G-11941)*
HP Manufacturing Company Inc............... D 216 361-6500
 Cleveland *(G-4386)*
◆ Organized Living Inc............................ E 513 489-9300
 Cincinnati *(G-3167)*
◆ Panacea Products Corporation...............E 614 850-7000
 Columbus *(G-6497)*

2591 Drapery hardware and blinds and shades

Golden Drapery Supply Inc...................... E 216 351-3283
 Cleveland *(G-4318)*
▲ Inside Outfitters Inc............................. E 614 798-3500
 Lewis Center *(G-9824)*
Lumenomics Inc.................................... E 614 798-3500
 Lewis Center *(G-9827)*

26 PAPER AND ALLIED PRODUCTS

2611 Pulp mills

Rumpke Transportation Co LLC............... B 513 242-4600
 Cincinnati *(G-3331)*

2621 Paper mills

Eclipse 3d/Pi LLC................................. E 614 626-8536
 Columbus *(G-5804)*
◆ Polymer Packaging Inc.........................D 330 832-2000
 North Canton *(G-11852)*
Pratt Paper (oh) LLC.............................. E 567 320-3353
 Wapakoneta *(G-14490)*
Welch Packaging Group Inc.................... C 614 870-2000
 Columbus *(G-6874)*

2631 Paperboard mills

Norse Dairy Systems Inc........................ C 614 294-4931
 Columbus *(G-6363)*
Pactiv LLC... D 614 771-5400
 Columbus *(G-6496)*

2652 Setup paperboard boxes

Brimar Packaging Inc.............................. E 440 934-3080
 Avon *(G-641)*

2653 Corrugated and solid fiber boxes

Adapt-A-Pak Inc................................... E 937 845-0386
 Fairborn *(G-8365)*
Brimar Packaging Inc.............................. E 440 934-3080
 Avon *(G-641)*
Cambridge Packaging Inc........................ E 740 432-3351
 Cambridge *(G-1560)*

26 PAPER AND ALLIED PRODUCTS

◆ Cleveland Supplyone Inc .... E 216 514-7000
Cleveland (G-4068)

Protective Packg Solutions LLC .... E 513 769-5777
Cincinnati (G-3255)

Skybox Packaging LLC .... C 419 525-7209
Mansfield (G-10317)

Systems Pack Inc .... E 330 467-5729
Macedonia (G-10207)

2655 Fiber cans, drums, and similar products

Sonoco Products Company .... D 937 429-0040
Beavercreek Township (G-949)

2656 Sanitary food containers

Clovernook Ctr For Blind Vslly .... C 513 522-3860
Cincinnati (G-2464)

Kerry Inc .... E 760 685-2548
Byesville (G-1535)

Ricking Holding Co .... E 513 825-3551
Cleveland (G-4839)

2657 Folding paperboard boxes

Brimar Packaging Inc .... E 440 934-3080
Avon (G-641)

2671 Paper; coated and laminated packaging

Bollin & Sons Inc .... E 419 693-6573
Toledo (G-13710)

▲ Custom Products Corporation .... D 440 528-7100
Solon (G-13080)

Norse Dairy Systems Inc .... C 614 294-4931
Columbus (G-6363)

Springdot Inc .... D 513 542-4000
Cincinnati (G-3401)

▲ Storopack Inc .... E 513 874-0314
West Chester (G-14834)

Universal Packg Systems Inc .... C 513 732-2000
Batavia (G-751)

Universal Packg Systems Inc .... C 513 735-4777
Batavia (G-752)

Universal Packg Systems Inc .... C 513 674-9400
Cincinnati (G-3563)

Versa-Pak Ltd .... E 419 586-5466
Celina (G-1931)

2672 Paper; coated and laminated, nec

Beiersdorf Inc .... C 513 682-7300
West Chester (G-14800)

Bollin & Sons Inc .... E 419 693-6573
Toledo (G-13710)

▲ GBS Corp .... C 330 494-5330
North Canton (G-11833)

◆ Kent Adhesive Products Co .... D 330 678-1626
Kent (G-9583)

Novagard Solutions Inc .... C 216 881-8111
Cleveland (G-4668)

Tekni-Plex Inc .... E 419 491-2399
Holland (G-9307)

2673 Bags: plastic, laminated, and coated

◆ Ampac Holdings LLC .... A 513 671-1777
Cincinnati (G-2194)

▲ Dazpak Flexible Packaging Corp .... D 614 252-2121
Columbus (G-5746)

2674 Bags: uncoated paper and multiwall

◆ Ampac Holdings LLC .... A 513 671-1777
Cincinnati (G-2194)

2675 Die-cut paper and board

▲ GBS Corp .... C 330 494-5330
North Canton (G-11833)

◆ Kent Adhesive Products Co .... D 330 678-1626
Kent (G-9583)

Springdot Inc .... D 513 542-4000
Cincinnati (G-3401)

2676 Sanitary paper products

▲ Giant Industries Inc .... E 419 531-4600
Toledo (G-13821)

2677 Envelopes

American Paper Group Inc .... B 330 758-4545
Youngstown (G-15551)

◆ Ampac Holdings LLC .... A 513 671-1777
Cincinnati (G-2194)

▲ Jbm Packaging Company .... C 513 933-8333
Lebanon (G-9770)

Pac Worldwide Corporation .... E 800 535-0039
Monroe (G-11347)

Western States Envelope Co .... E 419 666-7480
Walbridge (G-14468)

2679 Converted paper products, nec

▼ Buckeye Paper Co Inc .... E 330 477-5925
Canton (G-1692)

◆ General Data Company Inc .... B 513 752-7978
Cincinnati (G-2105)

◆ Kent Adhesive Products Co .... D 330 678-1626
Kent (G-9583)

▲ Millcraft Group LLC .... D 216 441-5500
Independence (G-9452)

Tekni-Plex Inc .... E 419 491-2399
Holland (G-9307)

◆ The Blonder Company .... C 216 431-3560
Cleveland (G-4992)

27 PRINTING, PUBLISHING AND ALLIED INDUSTRIES

2711 Newspapers

American City Bus Journals Inc .... B 937 528-4400
Dayton (G-7170)

▲ Amos Media Company .... C 937 638-0967
Sidney (G-13018)

Copley Ohio Newspapers Inc .... C 330 364-5577
New Philadelphia (G-11643)

Crain Communications Inc .... E 330 836-9180
Cuyahoga Falls (G-7065)

Franklin Communications Inc .... E 614 459-9769
Columbus (G-5886)

Gazette Publishing Company .... D 419 335-2010
Napoleon (G-11523)

Isaac Foster Mack Co .... C 419 625-5500
Sandusky (G-12905)

Marketing Essentials LLC .... E 419 629-0080
New Bremen (G-11599)

2721 Periodicals

AGS Custom Graphics Inc .... D 330 963-7770
Macedonia (G-10188)

American Ceramic Society .... E 614 890-4700
Westerville (G-14877)

▲ Amos Media Company .... C 937 638-0967
Sidney (G-13018)

▲ Asm International .... D 440 338-5151
Novelty (G-12037)

C & S Associates Inc .... E 440 461-9661
Highland Heights (G-9163)

CFM Religion Pubg Group LLC .... D 513 931-4050
Cincinnati (G-2339)

Crain Communications Inc .... E 330 836-9180
Cuyahoga Falls (G-7065)

▲ F+w Media Inc .... A 513 531-2690
Blue Ash (G-1171)

Family Motor Coach Assn Inc .... E 513 474-3622
Cincinnati (G-2647)

Great Lakes Publishing Company .... D 216 771-2833
Cleveland (G-4330)

▲ Lorenz Corporation .... D 937 228-6118
Dayton (G-7459)

Marketing Essentials LLC .... E 419 629-0080
New Bremen (G-11599)

Schaeffers Investment Research Inc .... D 513 589-3800
Blue Ash (G-1242)

2731 Book publishing

▲ Asm International .... D 440 338-5151
Novelty (G-12037)

▲ Bendon Inc .... D 419 207-3600
Ashland (G-482)

◆ Bookmasters Inc .... C 419 281-1802
Ashland (G-483)

▲ F+w Media Inc .... A 513 531-2690
Blue Ash (G-1171)

▲ Golf Galaxy Golfworks Inc .... C 740 328-4193
Newark (G-11702)

Hubbard Company .... E 419 784-4455
Defiance (G-7750)

McGraw-Hill Schl Edcatn Hldngs .... A 419 207-7400
Ashland (G-507)

▲ Precision Metalforming Assn .... E 216 901-8800
Independence (G-9471)

Tgs International Inc .... E 330 893-4828
Millersburg (G-11293)

Wolters Kluwer Clinical D .... D 330 650-6506
Hudson (G-9378)

World Harvest Church Inc .... C 614 837-1990
Canal Winchester (G-1620)

▲ Zaner-Bloser Inc .... C 614 486-0221
Columbus (G-6918)

2732 Book printing

Hubbard Company .... E 419 784-4455
Defiance (G-7750)

2741 Miscellaneous publishing

▲ Amos Media Company .... C 937 638-0967
Sidney (G-13018)

AT&T Corp .... E 614 223-8236
Columbus (G-5399)

Cerkl Incorporated .... D 513 813-8425
Blue Ash (G-1147)

Deemsys Inc .... D 614 322-9928
Gahanna (G-8715)

▲ Depot Direct Inc .... E 419 661-1233
Perrysburg (G-12332)

ITM Marketing Inc .... C 740 295-3575
Coshocton (G-6988)

▲ Lexisnexis Group .... C 937 865-6800
Miamisburg (G-11069)

▲ Lorenz Corporation .... D 937 228-6118
Dayton (G-7459)

Marketing Essentials LLC .... E 419 629-0080
New Bremen (G-11599)

ONeil & Associates Inc .... C 937 865-0800
Miamisburg (G-11079)

Quality Solutions Inc .... E 440 933-9946
Cleveland (G-4801)

Schaeffers Investment Research Inc .... D 513 589-3800
Blue Ash (G-1242)

2752 Commercial printing, lithographic

A-A Blueprint Co Inc .... E 330 794-8803
Akron (G-11)

SIC SECTION

28 CHEMICALS AND ALLIED PRODUCTS

AGS Custom Graphics Inc..................D 330 963-7770
Macedonia *(G-10188)*

Amsive OH LLC..................................D 937 885-8000
Miamisburg *(G-11024)*

Angstrom Graphics Inc Midwest........C 216 271-5300
Cleveland *(G-3817)*

Baesman Group Inc...........................D 614 771-2300
Hilliard *(G-9181)*

Bindery & Spc Pressworks Inc...........D 614 873-4623
Plain City *(G-12470)*

Black River Group Inc........................E 419 524-6699
Mansfield *(G-10245)*

◆ Bookmasters Inc..............................C 419 281-1802
Ashland *(G-483)*

BP 10 Inc..E 513 346-3900
West Chester *(G-14653)*

▲ Consolidated Graphics Group Inc......C 216 881-9191
Cleveland *(G-4104)*

Copley Ohio Newspapers Inc.............C 330 364-5577
New Philadelphia *(G-11643)*

Coyne Graphic Finishing Inc..............E 740 397-6232
Mount Vernon *(G-11481)*

▲ Fine Line Graphics Corp...................C 614 486-0276
Columbus *(G-5857)*

Friends Service Co Inc......................D 419 427-1704
Findlay *(G-8534)*

Highland Computer Forms Inc...........D 937 393-4215
Hillsboro *(G-9257)*

Hkm Drect Mkt Cmmnications Inc.....D 800 860-4456
Cleveland *(G-4367)*

Hubbard Company.............................E 419 784-4455
Defiance *(G-7750)*

▼ ICM Distributing Company Inc..........E 234 212-3030
Twinsburg *(G-14196)*

Isaac Foster Mack Co........................D 419 625-5500
Sandusky *(G-12905)*

◆ McNerney & Associates LLC............E 513 241-9951
West Chester *(G-14824)*

◆ Novelty Advertising Co Inc................E 740 622-3113
Coshocton *(G-6994)*

Optimum System Products Inc...........E 614 885-4464
Westerville *(G-15009)*

Printers Devil Inc................................E 330 650-1218
Hudson *(G-9369)*

Queen City Reprographics..................C 513 326-2300
Cincinnati *(G-3265)*

▼ Quick Tab II Inc.................................D 419 448-6622
Tiffin *(G-13639)*

▲ Richardson Printing Corp..................D 800 848-9752
Marietta *(G-10404)*

Springdot Inc......................................D 513 542-4000
Cincinnati *(G-3401)*

Tj Metzgers Inc..................................D 419 861-8611
Toledo *(G-14043)*

Traxium LLC.......................................E 330 572-8200
Stow *(G-13398)*

◆ Vectra Inc..C 614 351-6868
Columbus *(G-6843)*

Westrock Commercial LLC.................D 419 476-9101
Toledo *(G-14106)*

Woodrow Manufacturing Co...............E 937 399-9333
Springfield *(G-13313)*

◆ Workflowone LLC..............................A 877 735-4966
Dayton *(G-7726)*

2754 Commercial printing, gravure

▲ Shamrock Companies Inc..................D 440 899-9510
Westlake *(G-15108)*

The Photo-Type Engraving Company...D 513 281-0999
Cincinnati *(G-3469)*

◆ Workflowone LLC..............................A 877 735-4966
Dayton *(G-7726)*

2759 Commercial printing, nec

A-A Blueprint Co Inc..........................E 330 794-8803
Akron *(G-11)*

▲ Aero Fulfillment Services Corp..........D 800 225-7145
Mason *(G-10517)*

AGS Custom Graphics Inc.................D 330 963-7770
Macedonia *(G-10188)*

American Business Forms Inc...........E 513 312-2522
West Chester *(G-14798)*

Bindery & Spc Pressworks Inc...........D 614 873-4623
Plain City *(G-12470)*

Bollin & Sons Inc...............................E 419 693-6573
Toledo *(G-13710)*

▲ Bottomline Ink Corporation...............E 419 897-8000
Perrysburg *(G-12318)*

▲ CMC Group Inc.................................D 419 354-2591
Bowling Green *(G-1313)*

▲ Consolidated Graphics Group Inc......C 216 881-9191
Cleveland *(G-4104)*

▲ Custom Products Corporation............D 440 528-7100
Solon *(G-13080)*

Eci Macola/Max LLC.........................C 978 539-6186
Dublin *(G-8000)*

◆ GBS Corp..C 330 494-5330
North Canton *(G-11833)*

◆ General Data Company Inc...............B 513 752-7978
Cincinnati *(G-2105)*

▲ General Theming Contrs LLC............C 614 252-6342
Columbus *(G-5925)*

Hkm Drect Mkt Cmmnications Inc.....D 800 860-4456
Cleveland *(G-4367)*

◆ Kaufman Container Company............C 216 898-2000
Cleveland *(G-4450)*

Kopco Graphics Inc............................E 513 874-7230
West Chester *(G-14721)*

▲ Lorenz Corporation............................D 937 228-6118
Dayton *(G-7459)*

Samuels Products Inc........................E 513 891-4456
Blue Ash *(G-1239)*

Springdot Inc......................................D 513 542-4000
Cincinnati *(G-3401)*

Tj Metzgers Inc..................................D 419 861-8611
Toledo *(G-14043)*

Traxium LLC.......................................E 330 572-8200
Stow *(G-13398)*

◆ Workflowone LLC..............................A 877 735-4966
Dayton *(G-7726)*

2761 Manifold business forms

▲ Custom Products Corporation............D 440 528-7100
Solon *(G-13080)*

▲ Eleet Cryogenics Inc.........................E 330 874-4009
Bolivar *(G-1294)*

◆ GBS Corp..C 330 494-5330
North Canton *(G-11833)*

2771 Greeting cards

▲ Papyrus-Recycled Greetings Inc.......D 773 348-6410
Westlake *(G-15095)*

2782 Blankbooks and looseleaf binders

Mueller Art Cover & Binding Co.........E 440 238-3303
Strongsville *(G-13477)*

2789 Bookbinding and related work

A-A Blueprint Co Inc..........................E 330 794-8803
Akron *(G-11)*

AGS Custom Graphics Inc.................D 330 963-7770
Macedonia *(G-10188)*

Baesman Group Inc...........................D 614 771-2300
Hilliard *(G-9181)*

Bindery & Spc Pressworks Inc...........D 614 873-4623
Plain City *(G-12470)*

Black River Group Inc........................E 419 524-6699
Mansfield *(G-10245)*

Boundless Cmnty Pathways Inc........A 937 461-0034
West Carrollton *(G-14644)*

▲ Consolidated Graphics Group Inc......C 216 881-9191
Cleveland *(G-4104)*

Copley Ohio Newspapers Inc.............C 330 364-5577
New Philadelphia *(G-11643)*

Cott Systems Inc...............................D 614 847-4405
Columbus *(G-5707)*

▼ Quick Tab II Inc.................................D 419 448-6622
Tiffin *(G-13639)*

Tj Metzgers Inc..................................D 419 861-8611
Toledo *(G-14043)*

Traxium LLC.......................................E 330 572-8200
Stow *(G-13398)*

2791 Typesetting

A-A Blueprint Co Inc..........................E 330 794-8803
Akron *(G-11)*

AGS Custom Graphics Inc.................D 330 963-7770
Macedonia *(G-10188)*

Baesman Group Inc...........................D 614 771-2300
Hilliard *(G-9181)*

Bindery & Spc Pressworks Inc...........D 614 873-4623
Plain City *(G-12470)*

Black River Group Inc........................E 419 524-6699
Mansfield *(G-10245)*

◆ Bookmasters Inc..............................C 419 281-1802
Ashland *(G-483)*

▲ Consolidated Graphics Group Inc......C 216 881-9191
Cleveland *(G-4104)*

Copley Ohio Newspapers Inc.............C 330 364-5577
New Philadelphia *(G-11643)*

Hkm Drect Mkt Cmmnications Inc.....D 800 860-4456
Cleveland *(G-4367)*

▼ Quick Tab II Inc.................................D 419 448-6622
Tiffin *(G-13639)*

The Photo-Type Engraving Company...D 513 281-0999
Cincinnati *(G-3469)*

Tj Metzgers Inc..................................D 419 861-8611
Toledo *(G-14043)*

Wolters Kluwer Clinical D...................D 330 650-6506
Hudson *(G-9378)*

◆ Workflowone LLC..............................A 877 735-4966
Dayton *(G-7726)*

2796 Platemaking services

▲ Amos Media Company......................C 937 638-0967
Sidney *(G-13018)*

Anderson & Vreeland Inc...................D 419 636-5002
Bryan *(G-1479)*

The Photo-Type Engraving Company...D 513 281-0999
Cincinnati *(G-3469)*

◆ Wood Graphics Inc............................E 513 771-6300
Cincinnati *(G-3680)*

28 CHEMICALS AND ALLIED PRODUCTS

2812 Alkalies and chlorine

National Lime and Stone Co..............E 419 396-7671
Carey *(G-1894)*

2813 Industrial gases

Delille Oxygen Company....................E 614 444-1177
Columbus *(G-5752)*

National Gas & Oil Corporation.........E 740 344-2102
Newark *(G-11733)*

28 CHEMICALS AND ALLIED PRODUCTS

2819 Industrial inorganic chemicals, nec

Aldrich Chemical................................D..... 937 859-1808
   Miamisburg *(G-11023)*

BASF Catalysts LLC..............................C..... 216 360-5005
   Cleveland *(G-3853)*

◆ Borchers Americas Inc.....................D..... 440 899-2950
   Westlake *(G-15040)*

▲ Calvary Industries Inc......................E..... 513 874-1113
   Fairfield *(G-8398)*

▲ Chemspec Usa Inc..........................D..... 330 669-8512
   Orrville *(G-12158)*

▲ Cirba Solutions Us Inc......................E..... 740 653-6290
   Lancaster *(G-9700)*

◆ Dover Chemical Corporation..............C..... 330 343-7711
   Dover *(G-7880)*

Flexsys Inc..B..... 212 605-6000
   Akron *(G-165)*

◆ Gayston Corporation.........................C..... 937 743-6050
   Miamisburg *(G-11057)*

▲ Heraeus Epurio LLC.........................E..... 937 264-1000
   Vandalia *(G-14380)*

◆ Malco Products Inc...........................C..... 330 753-0361
   Barberton *(G-700)*

2821 Plastics materials and resins

Amros Industries Inc............................E..... 216 433-0010
   Cleveland *(G-3812)*

◆ Avient Corporation............................D..... 440 930-1000
   Avon Lake *(G-672)*

Epsilyte Holdings LLC..........................D..... 937 778-9500
   Piqua *(G-12441)*

Flex Technologies Inc..........................D..... 330 897-6311
   Baltic *(G-688)*

◆ Flexsys America LP..........................D..... 330 666-4111
   Akron *(G-164)*

Freeman Manufacturing & Sup Co.......E..... 440 934-1902
   Avon *(G-651)*

Genius Solutions Engrg Co..................E..... 419 794-9914
   Maumee *(G-10727)*

Hexion Inc...C..... 888 443-9466
   Columbus *(G-5989)*

▼ Hexion Topco LLC...........................D..... 614 225-4000
   Columbus *(G-5990)*

◆ Ineos ABS (usa) LLC........................C..... 513 467-2400
   Addyston *(G-4)*

Kraton Polymers US LLC.....................B..... 740 423-7571
   Belpre *(G-1056)*

◆ Network Polymers Inc......................E..... 330 773-2700
   Akron *(G-241)*

◆ Polymer Packaging Inc....................D..... 330 832-2000
   North Canton *(G-11852)*

◆ Tembec Btlsr Inc..............................E..... 419 244-5856
   Toledo *(G-14037)*

2822 Synthetic rubber

◆ Flexsys America LP..........................D..... 330 666-4111
   Akron *(G-164)*

Kraton Polymers US LLC.....................B..... 740 423-7571
   Belpre *(G-1056)*

Lyondell Chemical Company................C..... 513 530-4000
   Cincinnati *(G-2996)*

Mondo Polymer Technologies Inc........E..... 740 376-9396
   Marietta *(G-10391)*

Novagard Solutions Inc.......................C..... 216 881-8111
   Cleveland *(G-4668)*

◆ Shin-Etsu Silicones of America Inc...C..... 330 630-9460
   Akron *(G-299)*

2823 Cellulosic manmade fibers

◆ Flexsys America LP..........................D..... 330 666-4111
   Akron *(G-164)*

2834 Pharmaceutical preparations

Abbott Laboratories.............................D..... 847 937-6100
   Columbus *(G-5294)*

American Regent Inc...........................D..... 614 436-2222
   Hilliard *(G-9178)*

▲ Cardinal Health 414 LLC..................C..... 614 757-5000
   Dublin *(G-7956)*

▲ Imcd Us LLC....................................E..... 216 228-8900
   Westlake *(G-15069)*

Medpace Holdings Inc.........................C..... 513 579-9911
   Cincinnati *(G-3033)*

Mp Biomedicals LLC............................C..... 440 337-1200
   Solon *(G-13113)*

Omnicare Phrm of Midwest LLC..........D..... 513 719-2600
   Cincinnati *(G-3160)*

Optum Infusion Svcs 550 LLC.............D..... 866 442-4679
   Cincinnati *(G-3166)*

Standard Wellness Company LLC.......C..... 330 931-1037
   Cleveland *(G-4941)*

Teva Womens Health LLC...................C..... 513 731-9900
   Cincinnati *(G-3460)*

2835 Diagnostic substances

▲ Cardinal Health 414 LLC..................C..... 614 757-5000
   Dublin *(G-7956)*

Revvity Health Sciences Inc................E..... 330 825-4525
   Akron *(G-281)*

Thermo Fisher Scientific Inc.................E..... 800 871-8909
   Oakwood Village *(G-12059)*

2836 Biological products, except diagnostic

Bio-Blood Components Inc..................C..... 614 294-3183
   Columbus *(G-5441)*

EMD Millipore Corporation...................C..... 513 631-0445
   Norwood *(G-12032)*

Revvity Health Sciences Inc................E..... 330 825-4525
   Akron *(G-281)*

2841 Soap and other detergents

Beiersdorf Inc......................................C..... 513 682-7300
   West Chester *(G-14800)*

Chemstation International Inc..............E..... 937 294-8265
   Moraine *(G-11397)*

Cincinnati - Vulcan Company...............D..... 513 242-5300
   Cincinnati *(G-2391)*

◆ Malco Products Inc...........................C..... 330 753-0361
   Barberton *(G-700)*

▲ Pioneer Manufacturing Inc...............D..... 216 671-5500
   Cleveland *(G-4750)*

State Industrial Products Corp..............D..... 740 929-6370
   Hebron *(G-9154)*

◆ State Industrial Products Corp..........B..... 877 747-6986
   Cleveland *(G-4944)*

▼ Washing Systems LLC.....................C..... 800 272-1974
   Loveland *(G-10166)*

2842 Polishes and sanitation goods

▲ Alco-Chem Inc..................................E..... 330 253-3535
   Akron *(G-43)*

Chemstation International Inc..............E..... 937 294-8265
   Moraine *(G-11397)*

Cincinnati - Vulcan Company...............D..... 513 242-5300
   Cincinnati *(G-2391)*

Consolidated Coatings Corp.................A..... 216 514-7596
   Cleveland *(G-4106)*

EMD Millipore Corporation...................C..... 513 631-0445
   Norwood *(G-12032)*

◆ Malco Products Inc...........................C..... 330 753-0361
   Barberton *(G-700)*

▲ Pioneer Manufacturing Inc...............D..... 216 671-5500
   Cleveland *(G-4750)*

◆ State Industrial Products Corp..........B..... 877 747-6986
   Cleveland *(G-4944)*

◆ Tolco Corporation.............................D..... 419 241-1113
   Toledo *(G-14048)*

◆ Tremco Incorporated........................B
   Beachwood *(G-847)*

2844 Toilet preparations

◆ Beautyavenues LLC.........................C..... 614 856-6000
   Reynoldsburg *(G-12654)*

Beiersdorf Inc......................................C..... 513 682-7300
   West Chester *(G-14800)*

Luminex HM Dcor Frgrnce Hldg C......B..... 513 563-1113
   Blue Ash *(G-1204)*

▲ Nehemiah Manufacturing Co LLC....D..... 513 351-5700
   Cincinnati *(G-3103)*

Universal Packg Systems Inc..............C..... 513 732-2000
   Batavia *(G-751)*

Universal Packg Systems Inc..............C..... 513 735-4777
   Batavia *(G-752)*

Universal Packg Systems Inc..............C..... 513 674-9400
   Cincinnati *(G-3563)*

2851 Paints and allied products

◆ Akrochem Corporation......................D..... 330 535-2100
   Akron *(G-19)*

Bollin & Sons Inc.................................E..... 419 693-6573
   Toledo *(G-13710)*

▲ Chemspec Usa Inc..........................D..... 330 669-8512
   Orrville *(G-12158)*

◆ Comex North America Inc................D..... 303 307-2100
   Cleveland *(G-4092)*

Consolidated Coatings Corp.................A..... 216 514-7596
   Cleveland *(G-4106)*

Hexpol Compounding LLC....................C..... 440 834-4644
   Burton *(G-1528)*

Hoover & Wells Inc..............................E..... 419 691-9220
   Toledo *(G-13850)*

◆ Master Builders LLC.........................E..... 800 228-3318
   Beachwood *(G-811)*

Matrix Sys Auto Finishes LLC...............B..... 248 668-8135
   Massillon *(G-10654)*

▲ Teknol Inc...D..... 937 264-0190
   Dayton *(G-7661)*

◆ Tremco Incorporated........................B
   Beachwood *(G-847)*

2865 Cyclic crudes and intermediates

Hexpol Compounding LLC....................C..... 440 834-4644
   Burton *(G-1528)*

2869 Industrial organic chemicals, nec

▲ Alco-Chem Inc..................................E..... 330 253-3535
   Akron *(G-43)*

Aldrich Chemical.................................D..... 937 859-1808
   Miamisburg *(G-11023)*

◆ Borchers Americas Inc.....................D..... 440 899-2950
   Westlake *(G-15040)*

◆ Dover Chemical Corporation............C..... 330 343-7711
   Dover *(G-7880)*

▲ Heraeus Epurio LLC.........................E..... 937 264-1000
   Vandalia *(G-14380)*

▼ Hexion Topco LLC...........................D..... 614 225-4000
   Columbus *(G-5990)*

Lyondell Chemical Company................C..... 513 530-4000
   Cincinnati *(G-2996)*

Mp Biomedicals LLC............................C..... 440 337-1200
   Solon *(G-13113)*

Novagard Solutions Inc.......................C..... 216 881-8111
   Cleveland *(G-4668)*

◆ Shin-Etsu Silicones of America Inc...C..... 330 630-9460
   Akron *(G-299)*

SIC SECTION

▲ Wiley Companies... C 740 622-0755
Coshocton *(G-7005)*

2873 Nitrogenous fertilizers

◆ Scotts Company LLC............................C 937 644-0011
Marysville *(G-10508)*

▲ Scotts Miracle-Gro Company............. B 937 644-0011
Marysville *(G-10509)*

2874 Phosphatic fertilizers

Andersons Inc.. C 419 893-5050
Maumee *(G-10692)*

◆ Scotts Company LLC............................C 937 644-0011
Marysville *(G-10508)*

2875 Fertilizers, mixing only

Werlor Inc.. E 419 784-4285
Defiance *(G-7775)*

2879 Agricultural chemicals, nec

Abbott Laboratories................................ D 847 937-6100
Columbus *(G-5294)*

◆ Scotts Company LLC............................C 937 644-0011
Marysville *(G-10508)*

▲ Scotts Miracle-Gro Company............. B 937 644-0011
Marysville *(G-10509)*

2891 Adhesives and sealants

▲ Chemspec Usa Inc............................. D 330 669-8512
Orrville *(G-12158)*

▲ Cincinnati Assn For The Blind............ C 513 221-8558
Cincinnati *(G-2395)*

Consolidated Coatings Corp.................. A 216 514-7596
Cleveland *(G-4106)*

▲ Conversion Tech Intl Inc..................... E 419 924-5566
West Unity *(G-14874)*

Evans Adhesive Corporation................. E 614 451-2665
Columbus *(G-5833)*

Hexpol Compounding LLC..................... C 440 834-4644
Burton *(G-1528)*

Hoover & Wells Inc................................ E 419 691-9220
Toledo *(G-13850)*

Sika Mbcc US LLC................................ A 216 839-7500
Beachwood *(G-838)*

Sonoco Products Company................... D 937 429-0040
Beavercreek Township *(G-949)*

◆ Technical Rubber Company Inc.........C 740 967-9015
Johnstown *(G-9549)*

▲ Teknol Inc.. D 937 264-0190
Dayton *(G-7661)*

▲ Toagosei America Inc......................... D 614 718-3855
West Jefferson *(G-14853)*

◆ Tremco Incorporated........................... B
Beachwood *(G-847)*

▲ United McGill Corporation................... E 614 829-1200
Groveport *(G-9007)*

2899 Chemical preparations, nec

Aldrich Chemical.................................... D 937 859-1808
Miamisburg *(G-11023)*

◆ Applied Specialties Inc........................ E 440 933-9442
Avon Lake *(G-671)*

Ashland Chemco Inc............................. C 614 790-3333
Columbus *(G-5394)*

◆ Borchers Americas Inc....................... D 440 899-2950
Westlake *(G-15040)*

Chemstation International Inc................ E 937 294-8265
Moraine *(G-11397)*

Cincinnati - Vulcan Company................. D 513 242-5300
Cincinnati *(G-2391)*

Distillata Company................................. D 216 771-2900
Cleveland *(G-4167)*

◆ Dover Chemical Corporation...............C 330 343-7711
Dover *(G-7880)*

EMD Millipore Corporation..................... C 513 631-0445
Norwood *(G-12032)*

◆ Flexsys America LP............................ D 330 666-4111
Akron *(G-164)*

Formlabs Ohio Inc................................. E 419 837-9783
Millbury *(G-11268)*

Hexpol Compounding LLC..................... C 440 834-4644
Burton *(G-1528)*

Luxfer Magtech Inc................................ E 513 772-3066
Cincinnati *(G-2995)*

◆ Malco Products Inc.............................C 330 753-0361
Barberton *(G-700)*

◆ Master Builders LLC........................... E 800 228-3318
Beachwood *(G-811)*

Morton Salt Inc...................................... C 330 925-3015
Rittman *(G-12731)*

◆ Noco Company................................... D 216 464-8131
Solon *(G-13119)*

Polymer Additives Holdings Inc............. E 216 875-7200
Independence *(G-9469)*

▲ Rhenium Alloys Inc............................. E 440 365-7388
North Ridgeville *(G-11934)*

Sigma-Aldrich Corporation..................... D 216 206-5424
Cleveland *(G-4907)*

◆ State Industrial Products Corp............B 877 747-6986
Cleveland *(G-4944)*

▲ Teknol Inc.. D 937 264-0190
Dayton *(G-7661)*

29 PETROLEUM REFINING AND RELATED INDUSTRIES

2911 Petroleum refining

Gfl Environmental Svcs USA Inc............ E 614 441-4001
Columbus *(G-5932)*

◆ Knight Material Tech LLC................... D 330 488-1651
East Canton *(G-8169)*

▲ Marathon Petroleum Corporation....... A 419 422-2121
Findlay *(G-8561)*

2951 Asphalt paving mixtures and blocks

Bluffton Stone Co.................................. E 419 358-6941
Bluffton *(G-1279)*

Central Allied Enterprises Inc................ E 330 477-6751
Canton *(G-1706)*

Gerken Materials Inc............................. E 419 533-2421
Napoleon *(G-11524)*

Hy-Grade Corporation............................ E 216 341-7711
Cleveland *(G-4395)*

Mplx Terminals LLC............................... D 330 479-5539
Canton *(G-1811)*

Shelly Materials Inc............................... E 740 666-5841
Ostrander *(G-12184)*

Shelly Materials Inc............................... D 740 246-6315
Thornville *(G-13622)*

Stoneco Inc.. E 419 393-2555
Oakwood *(G-12054)*

Stoneco Inc.. E 419 422-8854
Findlay *(G-8588)*

2952 Asphalt felts and coatings

Consolidated Coatings Corp.................. A 216 514-7596
Cleveland *(G-4106)*

Garland/Dbs Inc..................................... C 216 641-7500
Cleveland *(G-4302)*

Hy-Grade Corporation............................ E 216 341-7711
Cleveland *(G-4395)*

◆ Owens Corning Sales LLC................. A 419 248-8000
Toledo *(G-13952)*

▲ Pioneer Manufacturing Inc.................. D 216 671-5500
Cleveland *(G-4750)*

Simon Roofing and Shtmtl Corp............ C 330 629-7392
Youngstown *(G-15725)*

◆ State Industrial Products Corp............B 877 747-6986
Cleveland *(G-4944)*

◆ Tremco Incorporated........................... B
Beachwood *(G-847)*

2992 Lubricating oils and greases

◆ Borchers Americas Inc....................... D 440 899-2950
Westlake *(G-15040)*

◆ Chemical Solvents Inc........................ E 216 741-9310
Cleveland *(G-3965)*

Cincinnati - Vulcan Company................. D 513 242-5300
Cincinnati *(G-2391)*

R and J Corporation............................... E 440 871-6009
Westlake *(G-15101)*

◆ State Industrial Products Corp............B 877 747-6986
Cleveland *(G-4944)*

Universal Oil Inc..................................... E 216 771-4300
Cleveland *(G-5068)*

Wallover Enterprises Inc........................ E 440 238-9250
Strongsville *(G-13497)*

2999 Petroleum and coal products, nec

◆ The Kindt-Collins Company LLC........ D 216 252-4122
Cleveland *(G-5003)*

30 RUBBER AND MISCELLANEOUS PLASTIC PRODUCTS

3011 Tires and inner tubes

◆ Goodyear Tire & Rubber Company..... A 330 796-2121
Akron *(G-179)*

◆ Technical Rubber Company Inc.........C 740 967-9015
Johnstown *(G-9549)*

3021 Rubber and plastics footwear

Georgia-Boot Inc.................................... D 740 753-1951
Nelsonville *(G-11545)*

US Footwear Holdings LLC.................... C 740 753-9100
Nelsonville *(G-11550)*

3052 Rubber and plastics hose and beltings

Allied Fabricating & Wldg Co.................. E 614 751-6664
Columbus *(G-5338)*

Myers Industries Inc.............................. E 330 253-5592
Akron *(G-238)*

Polychem LLC.. D 419 547-1400
Clyde *(G-5207)*

◆ Watteredge LLC.................................. D 440 933-6110
Avon Lake *(G-684)*

3053 Gaskets; packing and sealing devices

◆ Accel Performance Group LLC...........C 216 658-6413
Independence *(G-9394)*

▲ Industry Products Co.......................... B 937 778-0585
Piqua *(G-12445)*

Jet Rubber Company............................. E 330 325-1821
Rootstown *(G-12760)*

Johnson Bros Rubber Co Inc................ E 419 752-4814
Greenwich *(G-8892)*

◆ Ohio Gasket and Shim Co Inc............ E 330 630-0626
Akron *(G-251)*

R and J Corporation............................... E 440 871-6009
Westlake *(G-15101)*

3061 Mechanical rubber goods

◆ Datwyler Sling Sltions USA Inc........... D 937 387-2800
Vandalia *(G-14373)*

30 RUBBER AND MISCELLANEOUS PLASTIC PRODUCTS

◆ Johnson Bros Rubber Co..............D..... 419 853-4122
West Salem *(G-14863)*

◆ The D S Brown Company..............C..... 419 257-3561
North Baltimore *(G-11802)*

3069 Fabricated rubber products, nec

◆ B D G Wrap-Tite Inc.................E..... 440 349-5400
Solon *(G-13070)*

◆ Datwyler Sling Sltions USA Inc........D..... 937 387-2800
Vandalia *(G-14373)*

▲ Durable Corporation..................D..... 800 537-1603
Norwalk *(G-12008)*

◆ Flexsys America LP...................D..... 330 666-4111
Akron *(G-164)*

Jet Rubber Company....................E..... 330 325-1821
Rootstown *(G-12760)*

Myers Industries Inc..................E..... 330 253-5592
Akron *(G-238)*

◆ Pfp Holdings LLC.....................A..... 419 647-4191
Spencerville *(G-13190)*

◆ Rhein Chemie Corporation.............C..... 440 279-2367
Chardon *(G-2017)*

Tahoma Enterprises Inc................D..... 330 745-9016
Barberton *(G-714)*

▼ Tahoma Rubber & Plastics Inc.........D..... 330 745-9016
Barberton *(G-715)*

◆ Trico Products Corporation...........C..... 248 371-1700
Cleveland *(G-5038)*

▲ Westlake Dimex LLC...................C..... 740 374-3100
Marietta *(G-10414)*

3081 Unsupported plastics film and sheet

◆ Ampac Holdings LLC...................A..... 513 671-1777
Cincinnati *(G-2194)*

◆ Avient Corporation...................D..... 440 930-1000
Avon Lake *(G-672)*

▼ Clarkwstern Dtrich Bldg System.......C..... 513 870-1100
West Chester *(G-14671)*

◆ Clopay Corporation...................C..... 800 282-2260
Mason *(G-10540)*

◆ General Data Company Inc.............B..... 513 752-7978
Cincinnati *(G-2105)*

▲ Industry Products Co.................B..... 937 778-0585
Piqua *(G-12445)*

Toga-Pak Inc..........................E..... 937 294-7311
Dayton *(G-7672)*

3082 Unsupported plastics profile shapes

▲ Alkon Corporation....................D..... 419 355-9111
Fremont *(G-8665)*

HP Manufacturing Company Inc..........D..... 216 361-6500
Cleveland *(G-4386)*

◆ Trico Products Corporation...........C..... 248 371-1700
Cleveland *(G-5038)*

3083 Laminated plastics plate and sheet

Applied Medical Technology Inc........E..... 440 717-4000
Brecksville *(G-1343)*

◆ Organized Living Inc.................E..... 513 489-9300
Cincinnati *(G-3167)*

▲ TS Trim Industries Inc...............B..... 614 837-4114
Canal Winchester *(G-1618)*

3085 Plastics bottles

▲ Phoenix Technologies Intl LLC........E..... 419 353-7738
Bowling Green *(G-1330)*

3086 Plastics foam products

▲ Acor Orthopaedic LLC.................E..... 216 662-4500
Cleveland *(G-3764)*

◆ Ampac Packaging LLC..................C..... 513 671-1777
Cincinnati *(G-2195)*

▼ Armaly LLC...........................E..... 740 852-3621
London *(G-10037)*

Myers Industries Inc..................E..... 330 253-5592
Akron *(G-238)*

◆ Skybox Packaging LLC.................C..... 419 525-7209
Mansfield *(G-10317)*

◆ Storopack Inc........................E..... 513 874-0314
West Chester *(G-14834)*

3087 Custom compound purchased resins

◆ Avient Corporation...................D..... 440 930-1000
Avon Lake *(G-672)*

Flex Technologies Inc.................D..... 330 897-6311
Baltic *(G-688)*

Freeman Manufacturing & Sup Co........E..... 440 934-1902
Avon *(G-651)*

Hexpol Compounding LLC................C..... 440 834-4644
Burton *(G-1528)*

3088 Plastics plumbing fixtures

◆ Mansfield Plumbing Pdts LLC..........A..... 419 938-5211
Perrysville *(G-12392)*

3089 Plastics products, nec

Alside Inc............................D..... 419 865-0934
Maumee *(G-10687)*

▼ Armaly LLC...........................E..... 740 852-3621
London *(G-10037)*

▲ Associated Materials LLC.............A..... 330 929-1811
Cuyahoga Falls *(G-7041)*

Associated Materials Group Inc........C..... 330 929-1811
Cuyahoga Falls *(G-7043)*

▲ Champion Opco LLC....................B..... 513 327-7338
Cincinnati *(G-2345)*

Cpp Group Holdings LLC................E..... 216 453-4800
Cleveland *(G-4134)*

▲ First Choice Packaging Inc...........C..... 419 333-4100
Fremont *(G-8676)*

Gorell Enterprises Inc................B..... 724 465-1800
Streetsboro *(G-13414)*

Hendrickson International Corp........D..... 740 929-5600
Hebron *(G-9143)*

HP Manufacturing Company Inc..........D..... 216 361-6500
Cleveland *(G-4386)*

◆ Impact Products LLC..................D..... 419 841-2891
Toledo *(G-13860)*

Indelco Custom Products Inc...........E..... 216 797-7300
Euclid *(G-8349)*

▼ Japo Inc.............................E..... 614 263-2850
Columbus *(G-6084)*

▲ Lenz Inc.............................E..... 937 277-9364
Dayton *(G-7452)*

Modern Builders Supply Inc............C..... 419 241-3961
Toledo *(G-13926)*

Myers Industries Inc..................E..... 330 253-5592
Akron *(G-238)*

◆ Owens Corning Sales LLC..............A..... 419 248-8000
Toledo *(G-13952)*

Plastics R Unique Inc.................E..... 330 334-4820
Wadsworth *(G-14448)*

Queen City Polymers Inc...............E..... 513 779-0990
West Chester *(G-14752)*

▲ S&V Industries Inc...................E..... 330 666-1986
Medina *(G-10886)*

Samuel Son & Co (usa) Inc.............D..... 740 522-2500
Heath *(G-9138)*

Style Crest Enterprises Inc...........D..... 419 355-8586
Fremont *(G-8705)*

Tahoma Enterprises Inc................D..... 330 745-9016
Barberton *(G-714)*

▼ Tahoma Rubber & Plastics Inc.........D..... 330 745-9016
Barberton *(G-715)*

U S Development Corp..................D..... 330 673-6900
Kent *(G-9604)*

U S Molding Machinery Co Inc..........E..... 440 918-1701
Willoughby *(G-15224)*

United States Plastic Corp............D..... 419 228-2242
Lima *(G-9976)*

Vinyl Design Corporation..............E..... 419 283-4009
Holland *(G-9313)*

▲ Westlake Dimex LLC...................C..... 740 374-3100
Marietta *(G-10414)*

◆ Xaloy LLC............................C..... 330 726-4000
Austintown *(G-637)*

31 LEATHER AND LEATHER PRODUCTS

3143 Men's footwear, except athletic

▲ Acor Orthopaedic LLC.................E..... 216 662-4500
Cleveland *(G-3764)*

Georgia-Boot Inc......................D..... 740 753-1951
Nelsonville *(G-11545)*

3144 Women's footwear, except athletic

▲ Acor Orthopaedic LLC.................E..... 216 662-4500
Cleveland *(G-3764)*

Georgia-Boot Inc......................D..... 740 753-1951
Nelsonville *(G-11545)*

3161 Luggage

▲ Weaver Leather LLC...................D..... 330 674-7548
Millersburg *(G-11296)*

3172 Personal leather goods, nec

▲ Hamilton Manufacturing Corp..........E..... 419 867-4858
Holland *(G-9287)*

▲ Weaver Leather LLC...................D..... 330 674-7548
Millersburg *(G-11296)*

3199 Leather goods, nec

▲ Weaver Leather LLC...................D..... 330 674-7548
Millersburg *(G-11296)*

32 STONE, CLAY, GLASS, AND CONCRETE PRODUCTS

3211 Flat glass

S R Door Inc..........................D..... 740 927-3558
Hebron *(G-9153)*

Trulite GL Alum Solutions LLC.........D..... 740 929-2443
Hebron *(G-9156)*

3229 Pressed and blown glass, nec

◆ American De Rosa Lamparts LLC........D
Cuyahoga Falls *(G-7038)*

Industrial Fiberglass Spc Inc.........E..... 937 222-9000
Dayton *(G-7421)*

Integris Composites Inc...............D..... 740 928-0326
Hebron *(G-9144)*

▲ Mosser Glass Inc.....................E..... 740 439-1827
Cambridge *(G-1576)*

◆ Owens Corning Sales LLC..............A..... 419 248-8000
Toledo *(G-13952)*

3231 Products of purchased glass

▲ Afg Industries Inc...................D..... 614 322-4580
Grove City *(G-8893)*

▲ Enclosure Suppliers LLC..............E..... 513 782-3900
Cincinnati *(G-2619)*

Rumpke Transportation Co LLC..........B..... 513 242-4600
Cincinnati *(G-3331)*

SIC SECTION

◆ Safelite Group Inc..................................A 614 210-9000
Columbus *(G-6632)*

▲ Sims Bros Inc.. D 740 387-9041
Marion *(G-10454)*

Trulite GL Alum Solutions LLC................. D 740 929-2443
Hebron *(G-9156)*

3241 Cement, hydraulic

Huron Cement Products Company.......... E 419 433-4161
Huron *(G-9390)*

3261 Vitreous plumbing fixtures

◆ Mansfield Plumbing Pdts LLC..............A 419 938-5211
Perrysville *(G-12392)*

3264 Porcelain electrical supplies

▲ Channel Products Inc........................... D 440 423-0113
Solon *(G-13075)*

Weldco Inc... E 513 744-9353
Cincinnati *(G-3649)*

3269 Pottery products, nec

▲ Clay Burley Products Co....................... E 740 452-3633
Roseville *(G-12763)*

▼ Orton Edward Jr Crmic Fndation........... E 614 895-2663
Westerville *(G-14926)*

3271 Concrete block and brick

Green Impressions LLC............................ D 440 240-8508
Sheffield Village *(G-12998)*

Quality Block & Supply Inc....................... E 330 364-4411
Mount Eaton *(G-11458)*

3272 Concrete products, nec

Bell Vault and Monu Works Inc................ E 937 866-2444
Miamisburg *(G-11025)*

Eldorado Stone LLC................................. E 330 698-3931
Apple Creek *(G-449)*

Encore Precast LLC................................. E 513 726-5678
Seven Mile *(G-12962)*

Hilltop Basic Resources Inc..................... D 513 621-1500
Cincinnati *(G-2826)*

Huron Cement Products Company.......... E 419 433-4161
Huron *(G-9390)*

▲ Lang Stone Company Inc..................... E 614 235-4099
Columbus *(G-6139)*

Orrville Trucking & Grading Co................ E 330 682-4010
Orrville *(G-12172)*

R W Sidley Incorporated.......................... C 440 298-3232
Thompson *(G-13618)*

Smith Concrete Co................................... E 740 373-7441
Dover *(G-7901)*

3273 Ready-mixed concrete

Beazer East Inc....................................... E 937 364-2311
Hillsboro *(G-9249)*

Central Ready Mix LLC........................... E 513 402-5001
Cincinnati *(G-2337)*

Collinwood Shale Brick Sup Co................ E 216 587-2700
Cleveland *(G-4088)*

D W Dickey and Son Inc.......................... D 330 424-1441
Lisbon *(G-10001)*

Grafton Ready Mix Concret Inc................ C 440 926-2911
Grafton *(G-8839)*

Hilltop Basic Resources Inc..................... D 513 621-1500
Cincinnati *(G-2826)*

Huron Cement Products Company.......... E 419 433-4161
Huron *(G-9390)*

Integrated Resources Inc......................... E 419 885-6122
Sylvania *(G-13552)*

▲ Kuhlman Corporation............................ E 419 897-6000
Maumee *(G-10737)*

Orrville Trucking & Grading Co................ E 330 682-4010
Orrville *(G-12172)*

Quality Block & Supply Inc....................... E 330 364-4411
Mount Eaton *(G-11458)*

Sakrete Inc... E 513 242-3644
Cincinnati *(G-3343)*

Smith Concrete Co................................... E 740 373-7441
Dover *(G-7901)*

Smyrna Ready Mix Concrete LLC............ E 937 855-0410
Germantown *(G-8805)*

▲ Terminal Ready-Mix Inc....................... E 440 288-0181
Lorain *(G-10103)*

The National Lime and Stone Company.. E 419 422-4341
Findlay *(G-8593)*

3274 Lime

Bluffton Stone Co..................................... E 419 358-6941
Bluffton *(G-1279)*

National Lime and Stone Co..................... E 419 396-7671
Carey *(G-1894)*

Piqua Materials Inc.................................. D 937 773-4824
Piqua *(G-12453)*

Shelly Materials Inc................................. E 740 666-5841
Ostrander *(G-12184)*

3281 Cut stone and stone products

Beazer East Inc....................................... E 937 364-2311
Hillsboro *(G-9249)*

Bell Vault and Monu Works Inc................ E 937 866-2444
Miamisburg *(G-11025)*

◆ Cutting Edge Countertops Inc..............E 419 873-9500
Perrysburg *(G-12328)*

Kellstone Inc... E 419 746-2396
Kelleys Island *(G-9553)*

▲ Lang Stone Company Inc..................... E 614 235-4099
Columbus *(G-6139)*

National Lime and Stone Co..................... E 419 562-0771
Bucyrus *(G-1513)*

National Lime and Stone Co..................... E 419 396-7671
Carey *(G-1894)*

3291 Abrasive products

▲ Cleveland Granite & Marble LLC......... E 216 291-7637
Cleveland *(G-4047)*

◆ Lawrence Industries Inc.......................E 216 518-7000
Cleveland *(G-4483)*

▲ Mill-Rose Company............................. C 440 255-9171
Mentor *(G-10975)*

National Lime and Stone Co..................... E 419 396-7671
Carey *(G-1894)*

3295 Minerals, ground or treated

EMD Millipore Corporation....................... C 513 631-0445
Norwood *(G-12032)*

3296 Mineral wool

◆ Kinetics Noise Control Inc....................C 614 889-0480
Dublin *(G-8049)*

Mpc Inc.. E 440 835-1405
Cleveland *(G-4605)*

◆ Owens Corning Sales LLC...................A 419 248-8000
Toledo *(G-13952)*

3299 Nonmetallic mineral products,

▲ R W Sidley Incorporated....................... E 440 352-9343
Painesville *(G-12242)*

33 PRIMARY METAL INDUSTRIES

3312 Blast furnaces and steel mills

▲ Adams Elevator Equipment Co............ D 847 581-2900
Holland *(G-9276)*

Alba Manufacturing Inc............................ D 513 874-0551
Fairfield *(G-8388)*

▲ All Ohio Threaded Rod Co Inc............. E 216 426-1800
Cleveland *(G-3791)*

Alro Steel Corporation.............................. E 937 253-6121
Dayton *(G-7167)*

American Posts LLC................................ E 419 720-0652
Toledo *(G-13687)*

Brenmar Construction Inc........................ D 740 286-2151
Jackson *(G-9516)*

C & R Inc... E 614 497-1130
Groveport *(G-8975)*

Cohen Brothers Inc.................................. E 513 422-3696
Middletown *(G-11158)*

Contractors Steel Company..................... D 330 425-3050
Twinsburg *(G-14178)*

Crest Bending Inc.................................... E 419 492-2108
New Washington *(G-11682)*

▲ Franklin Iron & Metal Corp................... C 937 253-8184
Dayton *(G-7367)*

◆ Garden Street Iron & Metal Inc............ E 513 721-4660
Cincinnati *(G-2715)*

JSW Steel USA Ohio Inc.......................... B 740 535-8172
Mingo Junction *(G-11314)*

◆ Kirtland Capital Partners LP.................E 216 593-0100
Beachwood *(G-806)*

Lapham-Hickey Steel Corp....................... E 614 443-4881
Columbus *(G-6140)*

▲ Latrobe Spcialty Mtls Dist Inc...............D 330 609-5137
Vienna *(G-14420)*

Major Metals Company............................ E 419 886-4600
Mansfield *(G-10285)*

McWane Inc... B 740 622-6651
Coshocton *(G-6992)*

Mid-America Steel Corp........................... E 800 282-3466
Cleveland *(G-4575)*

◆ Nucor Steel Marion Inc........................B 740 383-4011
Marion *(G-10448)*

Ohio Steel Sheet and Plate Inc................ E 800 827-2401
Hubbard *(G-9322)*

Phillips Mfg and Tower Co....................... D 419 347-1720
Shelby *(G-13008)*

▲ Pioneer Pipe Inc.................................. A 740 376-2400
Marietta *(G-10399)*

Precision Strip Inc................................... D 937 667-6255
Tipp City *(G-13664)*

▲ S&V Industries Inc............................... E 330 666-1986
Medina *(G-10886)*

Shaq Inc.. D 770 427-0402
Beachwood *(G-836)*

Wheatland Tube LLC............................... C 724 342-6851
Niles *(G-11799)*

Worthington Enterprises Inc.................... D 513 539-9291
Monroe *(G-11355)*

Worthngton Smuel Coil Proc LLC............ E 330 963-3777
Twinsburg *(G-14231)*

Zekelman Industries Inc........................... C 740 432-2146
Cambridge *(G-1588)*

3313 Electrometallurgical products

Morris Technologies Inc........................... E 513 733-1611
Cincinnati *(G-3080)*

▲ Rhenium Alloys Inc.............................. E 440 365-7388
North Ridgeville *(G-11934)*

3315 Steel wire and related products

Bayloff Stmped Pdts Knsman Inc............. D 330 876-4511
Kinsman *(G-9644)*

▲ Richards Whl Fence Co Inc................. E 330 773-0423
Akron *(G-282)*

3316 Cold finishing of steel shapes

33 PRIMARY METAL INDUSTRIES

▲ All Ohio Threaded Rod Co Inc .... E 216 426-1800
  Cleveland *(G-3791)*

Alro Steel Corporation .... E 937 253-6121
  Dayton *(G-7167)*

◆ Dms Inc .... C 440 951-9838
  Willoughby *(G-15189)*

Geneva Liberty Steel Ltd .... E 330 740-0103
  Youngstown *(G-15620)*

Mid-America Steel Corp .... E 800 282-3466
  Cleveland *(G-4575)*

◆ Nucor Steel Marion Inc .... B 740 383-4011
  Marion *(G-10448)*

3317 Steel pipe and tubes

Alro Steel Corporation .... E 937 253-6121
  Dayton *(G-7167)*

Crest Bending Inc .... E 419 492-2108
  New Washington *(G-11682)*

◆ Kirtland Capital Partners LP .... E 216 593-0100
  Beachwood *(G-806)*

Major Metals Company .... E 419 886-4600
  Mansfield *(G-10285)*

Phillips Mfg and Tower Co .... D 419 347-1720
  Shelby *(G-13008)*

Unison Industries LLC .... B 904 667-9904
  Dayton *(G-7143)*

Wheatland Tube LLC .... C 724 342-6851
  Niles *(G-11799)*

Zekelman Industries Inc .... C 740 432-2146
  Cambridge *(G-1588)*

3321 Gray and ductile iron foundries

Amsted Industries Incorporated .... D 614 836-2323
  Groveport *(G-8969)*

McWane Inc .... B 740 622-6651
  Coshocton *(G-6992)*

3324 Steel investment foundries

B W Grinding Co .... E 419 923-1376
  Lyons *(G-10187)*

3325 Steel foundries, nec

▲ Jmac Inc .... E 614 436-2418
  Columbus *(G-6092)*

Worthington Enterprises Inc .... D 513 539-9291
  Monroe *(G-11355)*

Worthngton Stelpac Systems LLC .... C 614 438-3205
  Columbus *(G-6908)*

3339 Primary nonferrous metals, nec

◆ Aci Industries Ltd .... E 740 368-4160
  Delaware *(G-7776)*

▲ Rhenium Alloys Inc .... E 440 365-7388
  North Ridgeville *(G-11934)*

3341 Secondary nonferrous metals

◆ Aci Industries Ltd .... E 740 368-4160
  Delaware *(G-7776)*

▲ Cirba Solutions Us Inc .... E 740 653-6290
  Lancaster *(G-9700)*

Cohen Brothers Inc .... E 513 422-3696
  Middletown *(G-11158)*

▲ Fpt Cleveland LLC .... C 216 441-3800
  Cleveland *(G-4282)*

▲ Franklin Iron & Metal Corp .... E 937 253-8184
  Dayton *(G-7367)*

▲ Garden Street Iron & Metal Inc .... E 513 721-4660
  Cincinnati *(G-2715)*

Mw Metals Group LLC .... D 937 222-5992
  Dayton *(G-7522)*

▲ National Bronze Mtls Ohio Inc .... E 440 277-1226
  Lorain *(G-10094)*

▲ Novelis Alr Recycling Ohio LLC .... C 740 922-2373
  Uhrichsville *(G-14236)*

Precision Strip Inc .... D 419 674-4186
  Kenton *(G-9622)*

Rm Advisory Group Inc .... E 513 242-2100
  Cincinnati *(G-3309)*

Rnw Holdings Inc .... E 330 792-0600
  Youngstown *(G-15709)*

Rumpke Transportation Co LLC .... B 513 242-4600
  Cincinnati *(G-3331)*

▲ Sims Bros Inc .... D 740 387-9041
  Marion *(G-10454)*

Thyssenkrupp Materials NA Inc .... D 216 883-8100
  Independence *(G-9490)*

▲ Wieland Metal Svcs Foils LLC .... D 330 823-1700
  Alliance *(G-405)*

3353 Aluminum sheet, plate, and foil

▲ Monarch Steel Company Inc .... E 216 587-8000
  Cleveland *(G-4598)*

▲ Wieland Metal Svcs Foils LLC .... D 330 823-1700
  Alliance *(G-405)*

3356 Nonferrous rolling and drawing, nec

▲ Rhenium Alloys Inc .... E 440 365-7388
  North Ridgeville *(G-11934)*

▲ Victory White Metal Company .... D 216 271-1400
  Cleveland *(G-5104)*

3357 Nonferrous wiredrawing and insulating

Cbst Acquisition LLC .... D 513 361-9600
  Cincinnati *(G-2326)*

Legrand North America LLC .... B 937 224-0639
  Dayton *(G-7451)*

Projects Unlimited Inc .... C 937 918-2200
  Dayton *(G-7571)*

Radix Wire Co .... D 216 731-9191
  Solon *(G-13136)*

Schneider Electric Usa Inc .... B 513 523-4171
  Oxford *(G-12217)*

Scott Fetzer Company .... C 216 267-9000
  Cleveland *(G-4885)*

3363 Aluminum die-castings

Akron Foundry Co .... C 330 745-3101
  Akron *(G-28)*

Seilkop Industries Inc .... E 513 761-1035
  Cincinnati *(G-3356)*

◆ The Kindt-Collins Company LLC .... D 216 252-4122
  Cleveland *(G-5003)*

Yoder Industries Inc .... C 937 278-5769
  Dayton *(G-7731)*

3364 Nonferrous die-castings except aluminum

◆ American De Rosa Lamparts LLC .... D
  Cuyahoga Falls *(G-7038)*

◆ The Kindt-Collins Company LLC .... D 216 252-4122
  Cleveland *(G-5003)*

Yoder Industries Inc .... C 937 278-5769
  Dayton *(G-7731)*

3365 Aluminum foundries

Akron Foundry Co .... C 330 745-3101
  Akron *(G-28)*

◆ Aluminum Line Products Company .... D 440 835-8880
  Westlake *(G-15032)*

▲ Miba Bearings US LLC .... B 740 962-4242
  Mcconnelsville *(G-10803)*

Yoder Industries Inc .... C 937 278-5769
  Dayton *(G-7731)*

3366 Copper foundries

▲ McNeil Industries Inc .... E 440 951-7756
  Painesville *(G-12236)*

▲ National Bronze Mtls Ohio Inc .... E 440 277-1226
  Lorain *(G-10094)*

3369 Nonferrous foundries, nec

Akron Foundry Co .... C 330 745-3101
  Akron *(G-28)*

Yoder Industries Inc .... C 937 278-5769
  Dayton *(G-7731)*

3398 Metal heat treating

Carpe Diem Industries LLC .... D 419 358-0129
  Bluffton *(G-1280)*

Carpe Diem Industries LLC .... D 419 659-5639
  Columbus Grove *(G-6921)*

◆ Clifton Steel Company .... D 216 662-6111
  Maple Heights *(G-10336)*

Gerdau McSteel Atmsphere Annli .... E 330 478-0314
  Canton *(G-1761)*

Lapham-Hickey Steel Corp .... E 614 443-4881
  Columbus *(G-6140)*

McOn Inds Inc .... E 937 294-2681
  Moraine *(G-11422)*

▲ Oliver Steel Plate Co .... D 330 425-7000
  Twinsburg *(G-14209)*

Thermal Treatment Center Inc .... E 216 881-8100
  Wickliffe *(G-15164)*

Worthngton Smuel Coil Proc LLC .... E 330 963-3777
  Twinsburg *(G-14231)*

3399 Primary metal products

Bogie Industries Inc Ltd .... E 330 745-3105
  Akron *(G-72)*

Contitech Usa Inc .... D 937 644-8900
  Marysville *(G-10481)*

▲ Midwest Motor Supply Co .... C 800 233-1294
  Columbus *(G-6244)*

34 FABRICATED METAL PRODUCTS

3411 Metal cans

◆ G & S Metal Products Co Inc .... C 216 441-0700
  Cleveland *(G-4295)*

◆ Organized Living Inc .... E 513 489-9300
  Cincinnati *(G-3167)*

3412 Metal barrels, drums, and pails

▲ Sabco Industries Inc .... E 419 531-5347
  Toledo *(G-14002)*

Williams Scotsman Inc .... D 614 449-8675
  Columbus *(G-6894)*

3421 Cutlery

◆ G & S Metal Products Co Inc .... C 216 441-0700
  Cleveland *(G-4295)*

◆ Npk Construction Equipment Inc .... D 440 232-7900
  Bedford *(G-976)*

3423 Hand and edge tools, nec

▲ C B Mfg & Sls Co Inc .... D 937 866-5986
  Miamisburg *(G-11030)*

Cornwell Quality Tools Company .... D 330 628-2627
  Mogadore *(G-11325)*

▲ Matco Tools Corporation .... B 330 929-4949
  Stow *(G-13382)*

Sewer Rodding Equipment Co .... C 419 991-2065
  Lima *(G-9959)*

34 FABRICATED METAL PRODUCTS

▲ The Cornwell Quality Tool............... D 330 336-3506
Wadsworth *(G-14455)*

3429 Hardware, nec

▲ Action Coupling & Eqp Inc................ D 330 279-4242
Holmesville *(G-9316)*

Gateway Con Forming Svcs Inc........... D 513 353-2000
Miamitown *(G-11106)*

▼ Kirk Key Interlock Company LLC...... E 330 833-8223
North Canton *(G-11846)*

Qualitor Subsidiary H Inc.................... C 419 562-7987
Bucyrus *(G-1517)*

▲ Samsel Rope & Marine Supply Co..... E 216 241-0333
Cleveland *(G-4875)*

3431 Metal sanitary ware

◆ Lvd Acquisition LLC..........................D 614 861-1350
Columbus *(G-6181)*

◆ Mansfield Plumbing Pdts LLC............A 419 938-5211
Perrysville *(G-12392)*

3432 Plumbing fixture fittings and trim

◆ Mansfield Plumbing Pdts LLC............A 419 938-5211
Perrysville *(G-12392)*

◆ Merit Brass Co...................................... C 216 261-9800
Cleveland *(G-4554)*

◆ Waxman Industries Inc.......................C 440 439-1830
Bedford Heights *(G-1005)*

Zekelman Industries Inc......................C 740 432-2146
Cambridge *(G-1588)*

3433 Heating equipment, except electric

▼ Hunter Defense Tech Inc..................... E 216 438-6111
Solon *(G-13096)*

3441 Fabricated structural metal

▲ A & G Manufacturing Co Inc............... E 419 468-7433
Galion *(G-8740)*

Allied Fabricating & Wldg Co............... E 614 751-6664
Columbus *(G-5338)*

Alro Steel Corporation.......................... E 937 253-6121
Dayton *(G-7167)*

Arctech Fabricating Inc........................ E 937 525-9353
Springfield *(G-13219)*

Armor Consolidated Inc........................A 513 923-5260
Mason *(G-10520)*

Bauer Corporation................................ E 800 321-4760
Wooster *(G-15310)*

Blackburns Fabrication Inc................... E 614 875-0784
Columbus *(G-5444)*

Breitinger Company.............................. C 419 526-4255
Mansfield *(G-10248)*

◆ Buck Equipment Inc.............................E 614 539-3039
Grove City *(G-8901)*

C-N-D Industries Inc............................. E 330 478-8811
Massillon *(G-10633)*

Chc Fabricating Corp............................ D 513 821-7757
Cincinnati *(G-2348)*

◆ Clifton Steel Company..........................D 216 662-6111
Maple Heights *(G-10336)*

Cohen Brothers Inc............................... E 513 422-3696
Middletown *(G-11158)*

Cornerstone Wauseon Inc.................... C 419 337-0940
Wauseon *(G-14598)*

Dearing Compressor and Pu................ E 330 783-2258
Youngstown *(G-15595)*

Debra-Kuempel Inc............................... D 513 271-6500
Cincinnati *(G-2552)*

Defabco Inc... D 614 231-2700
Columbus *(G-5749)*

Franck and Fric Incorporated............... D 216 524-4451
Cleveland *(G-4284)*

Frederick Steel Company LLC............. D 513 821-6400
Cincinnati *(G-2703)*

George Steel Fabricating Inc................ E 513 932-2887
Lebanon *(G-9766)*

JJ&pl Services-Consulting LLC........... D 330 923-5783
Cuyahoga Falls *(G-7082)*

▲ Langdon Inc.. E 513 733-5955
Cincinnati *(G-2965)*

Lapham-Hickey Steel Corp.................. E 614 443-4881
Columbus *(G-6140)*

Laserflex Corporation........................... D 614 850-9600
Hilliard *(G-9209)*

◆ Lefeld Welding & Stl Sups Inc............. E 419 678-2397
Coldwater *(G-5216)*

Lyco Corporation.................................. E 412 973-9176
Lowellville *(G-10169)*

Marysville Steel Inc.............................. E 937 642-5971
Marysville *(G-10494)*

Mason Structural Steel LLC................. E 440 439-1040
Walton Hills *(G-14476)*

McWane Inc.. B 740 622-6651
Coshocton *(G-6992)*

Mound Technologies Inc...................... E 937 748-2937
Springboro *(G-13203)*

Mssi Group Inc..................................... D 440 439-1040
Walton Hills *(G-14477)*

◆ Nucor Steel Marion Inc........................B 740 383-4011
Marion *(G-10448)*

▲ Pioneer Pipe Inc................................... A 740 376-2400
Marietta *(G-10399)*

Precision Welding Corporation............. E 216 524-6110
Cleveland *(G-4765)*

R G Smith Company............................. D 330 456-3415
Canton *(G-1839)*

Rittman Inc.. D 330 927-6855
Rittman *(G-12732)*

Rmt Acquisition Inc.............................. E 513 241-5566
Cincinnati *(G-3311)*

St Lawrence Holdings LLC.................. E 330 562-9000
Maple Heights *(G-10347)*

◆ St Lawrence Steel Corporation............E 330 562-9000
Maple Heights *(G-10348)*

▲ Steel Eqp Specialists Inc.................... D 330 823-8260
Alliance *(G-401)*

Steelial Wldg Met Fbrction Inc............. E 740 669-5300
Vinton *(G-14425)*

◆ The D S Brown Company......................C 419 257-3561
North Baltimore *(G-11802)*

Tri-America Contractors Inc................. E 740 574-0148
Wheelersburg *(G-15134)*

Triangle Precision Industries................ D 937 299-6776
Dayton *(G-7678)*

Turn-Key Industrial Svcs LLC.............. D 614 274-1128
Grove City *(G-8960)*

Werks Kraft Engineering LLC.............. E 330 721-7374
Medina *(G-10902)*

Williams Scotsman Inc......................... D 614 449-8675
Columbus *(G-6894)*

Worthington Enterprises Inc................. D 513 539-9291
Monroe *(G-11355)*

3442 Metal doors, sash, and trim

▲ Associated Materials LLC................... A 330 929-1811
Cuyahoga Falls *(G-7041)*

Associated Materials Group Inc........... C 330 929-1811
Cuyahoga Falls *(G-7043)*

Associated Mtls Holdings LLC............. A 330 929-1811
Cuyahoga Falls *(G-7044)*

▲ Champion Opco LLC.......................... B 513 327-7338
Cincinnati *(G-2345)*

◆ Clopay Corporation..............................C 800 282-2260
Mason *(G-10540)*

Francis-Schulze Co............................... E 937 295-3941
Russia *(G-12770)*

Midwest Curtainwalls Inc..................... D 216 641-7900
Cleveland *(G-4580)*

Modern Builders Supply Inc................ C 419 241-3961
Toledo *(G-13926)*

▼ Nofziger Door Sales Inc...................... C 419 337-9900
Wauseon *(G-14607)*

Provia Holdings Inc.............................. C 330 852-4711
Sugarcreek *(G-13512)*

S R Door Inc... D 740 927-3558
Hebron *(G-9153)*

▲ Stephen M Trudick............................... E 440 834-1891
Burton *(G-1533)*

3443 Fabricated plate work (boiler shop)

▲ A & G Manufacturing Co Inc............... E 419 468-7433
Galion *(G-8740)*

▲ American Tank & Fabricating Co......... D 216 252-1500
Cleveland *(G-3808)*

▲ Amko Service Company...................... C 330 364-8857
Midvale *(G-11203)*

Armor Consolidated Inc........................A 513 923-5260
Mason *(G-10520)*

◆ Babcock & Wilcox Company............... A 330 753-4511
Akron *(G-59)*

Bi-Con Services Inc.............................. B 740 685-2542
Derwent *(G-7864)*

▲ Bico Akron Inc..................................... D 330 794-1716
Mogadore *(G-11324)*

Breitinger Company.............................. C 419 526-4255
Mansfield *(G-10248)*

C & R Inc.. E 614 497-1130
Groveport *(G-8975)*

◆ Cbc Global..E 330 482-3373
Columbiana *(G-5232)*

◆ Clifton Steel Company..........................D 216 662-6111
Maple Heights *(G-10336)*

Complete Mechanical Svcs LLC.......... D 513 489-3080
Blue Ash *(G-1158)*

Curtiss-Wright Flow Ctrl Corp.............. D 513 528-7900
Cincinnati *(G-2101)*

Debra-Kuempel Inc............................... D 513 271-6500
Cincinnati *(G-2552)*

Defabco Inc... D 614 231-2700
Columbus *(G-5749)*

▲ Eleet Cryogenics Inc............................ E 330 874-4009
Bolivar *(G-1294)*

◆ Enerfab LLC..B 513 641-0500
Cincinnati *(G-2620)*

Gaspar Inc.. D 330 477-2222
Canton *(G-1759)*

◆ Gayston Corporation.............................C 937 743-6050
Miamisburg *(G-11057)*

▲ General Tool Company........................ C 513 733-5500
Cincinnati *(G-2728)*

▲ Industrial Repair and Mfg.................... E 419 822-4232
Delta *(G-7851)*

▲ Jergens Inc... C 216 486-5540
Cleveland *(G-4437)*

JMw Welding and Mfg Inc.................... E 330 484-2428
Canton *(G-1785)*

◆ Kirk & Blum Manufacturing Co............C 513 458-2600
Cincinnati *(G-2942)*

▲ Langdon Inc.. E 513 733-5955
Cincinnati *(G-2965)*

Lapham-Hickey Steel Corp.................. E 614 443-4881
Columbus *(G-6140)*

▲ Long-Stanton Mfg Company................ E 513 874-8020
West Chester *(G-14725)*

◆ Loveman Steel Corporation..................D 440 232-6200
Bedford *(G-969)*

34 FABRICATED METAL PRODUCTS

Modern Welding Co Ohio Inc................. E 740 344-9425
  Newark *(G-11731)*
Nbw Inc... E 216 377-1700
  Cleveland *(G-4629)*
▲ Oliver Steel Plate Co........................ D 330 425-7000
  Twinsburg *(G-14209)*
▲ Pioneer Pipe Inc............................... A 740 376-2400
  Marietta *(G-10399)*
Prout Boiler Htg & Wldg Inc................. E 330 744-0293
  Youngstown *(G-15699)*
Quintus Technologies LLC................. E 614 891-2732
  Lewis Center *(G-9834)*
R G Smith Company............................ D 330 456-3415
  Canton *(G-1839)*
Rmt Acquisition Inc............................. E 513 241-5566
  Cincinnati *(G-3311)*
S-P Company Inc................................. D 330 782-5651
  Columbiana *(G-5240)*
Schweizer Dipple Inc........................... D 440 786-8090
  Cleveland *(G-4884)*
Sexton Industrial Inc........................... C 513 530-5555
  West Chester *(G-14832)*
St Lawrence Holdings LLC................. E 330 562-9000
  Maple Heights *(G-10347)*
◆ St Lawrence Steel Corporation........ E 330 562-9000
  Maple Heights *(G-10348)*
Stanwade Metal Products Inc............. E 330 772-2421
  Hartford *(G-9123)*
Swagelok Company.............................. D 440 349-5934
  Solon *(G-13154)*
Triangle Precision Industries.............. D 937 299-6776
  Dayton *(G-7678)*
▲ Will-Burt Company............................ C 330 682-7015
  Orrville *(G-12176)*

3444 Sheet metalwork

▲ A & G Manufacturing Co Inc............ E 419 468-7433
  Galion *(G-8740)*
▲ Acro Tool & Die Company................ E 330 773-5173
  Akron *(G-14)*
▲ Alan Manufacturing Inc................... E 330 262-1555
  Wooster *(G-15308)*
Allied Fabricating & Wldg Co.............. E 614 751-6664
  Columbus *(G-5338)*
Alro Steel Corporation......................... E 614 878-7271
  Columbus *(G-5340)*
Alro Steel Corporation......................... D 419 720-5300
  Toledo *(G-13679)*
▲ American Frame Corporation........... D 419 893-5595
  Maumee *(G-10690)*
Anchor Metal Processing Inc.............. E 216 362-1850
  Cleveland *(G-3814)*
Avon Lake Sheet Metal Co................... E 440 933-3505
  Avon Lake *(G-673)*
Bayloff Stmped Pdts Knsman Inc........ D 330 876-4511
  Kinsman *(G-9644)*
Bogie Industries Inc Ltd..................... E 330 745-3105
  Akron *(G-72)*
Breitinger Company............................. C 419 526-4255
  Mansfield *(G-10248)*
C & R Inc.. E 614 497-1130
  Groveport *(G-8975)*
C-N-D Industries Inc........................... E 330 478-8811
  Massillon *(G-10633)*
▼ Clarkwstern Dtrich Bldg System...... C 513 870-1100
  West Chester *(G-14671)*
▲ Darana Hybrid Inc............................ D 513 860-4490
  Hamilton *(G-9036)*
Defabco Inc.. D 614 231-2700
  Columbus *(G-5749)*
Dimensional Metals Inc....................... E 740 927-3633
  Reynoldsburg *(G-12660)*

Dynamic Weld Corporation.................. E 419 582-2900
  Osgood *(G-12180)*
Famous Industries Inc......................... E 330 535-1811
  Akron *(G-157)*
Franck and Fric Incorporated............. D 216 524-4451
  Cleveland *(G-4284)*
Gaspar Inc.. D 330 477-2222
  Canton *(G-1759)*
▲ General Tool Company..................... C 513 733-5500
  Cincinnati *(G-2728)*
GM Mechanical Inc.............................. D 937 473-3006
  Covington *(G-7018)*
Gundlach Sheet Metal Works Inc....... E 419 626-4525
  Sandusky *(G-12902)*
Interstate Contractors LLC................. E 513 372-5393
  Mason *(G-10568)*
Jacobs Mechanical Co......................... C 513 681-6800
  Cincinnati *(G-2895)*
◆ Kirk & Blum Manufacturing Co........ C 513 458-2600
  Cincinnati *(G-2942)*
Kirk Williams Company Inc................. E 614 875-9023
  Grove City *(G-8931)*
◆ Langdon Inc...................................... E 513 733-5955
  Cincinnati *(G-2965)*
Lima Sheet Metal Machine & Mfg........ E 419 229-1161
  Lima *(G-9927)*
▲ Long-Stanton Mfg Company............ E 513 874-8020
  West Chester *(G-14725)*
McWane Inc.. B 740 622-6651
  Coshocton *(G-6992)*
◆ N Wasserstrom & Sons Inc.............. C 614 228-5550
  Columbus *(G-6286)*
◆ Oatey Supply Chain Svcs Inc.......... C 216 267-7100
  Cleveland *(G-4679)*
Obr Cooling Towers Inc...................... E 419 243-3443
  Northwood *(G-11981)*
Ohio Blow Pipe Company.................... E 216 681-7379
  Cleveland *(G-4682)*
Ohio Steel Sheet and Plate Inc........... E 800 827-2401
  Hubbard *(G-9322)*
▲ Oliver Steel Plate Co....................... D 330 425-7000
  Twinsburg *(G-14209)*
Precision Mtal Fabrication Inc............ D 937 235-9261
  Dayton *(G-7559)*
Precision Welding Corporation........... E 216 524-6110
  Cleveland *(G-4765)*
R G Smith Company............................ D 330 456-3415
  Canton *(G-1839)*
Rmt Acquisition Inc............................. E 513 241-5566
  Cincinnati *(G-3311)*
Schweizer Dipple Inc........................... D 440 786-8090
  Cleveland *(G-4884)*
Scott Fetzer Company.......................... C 216 267-9000
  Cleveland *(G-4885)*
Steelial Wldg Met Fbrction Inc............. E 740 669-5300
  Vinton *(G-14425)*
TL Industries Inc................................. C 419 666-8144
  Perrysburg *(G-12377)*
Triangle Precision Industries.............. D 937 299-6776
  Dayton *(G-7678)*
◆ Tricor Industrial Inc......................... D 330 264-3299
  Wooster *(G-15380)*
▲ United McGill Corporation............... E 614 829-1200
  Groveport *(G-9007)*
▲ Universal Steel Company................ D 216 883-4972
  Cleveland *(G-5069)*
◆ Will-Burt Company............................ C 330 682-7015
  Orrville *(G-12176)*

3446 Architectural metalwork

▲ A & G Manufacturing Co Inc............ E 419 468-7433
  Galion *(G-8740)*

▲ Agratronix LLC................................. E 330 562-2222
  Streetsboro *(G-13409)*
Armor Consolidated Inc...................... A 513 923-5260
  Mason *(G-10520)*
Bauer Corporation............................... E 800 321-4760
  Wooster *(G-15310)*
Chc Fabricating Corp.......................... D 513 821-7757
  Cincinnati *(G-2348)*
Debra-Kuempel Inc.............................. D 513 271-6500
  Cincinnati *(G-2552)*
Finelli Ornamental Iron Co.................. E 440 248-0050
  Cleveland *(G-4251)*
◆ Kinetics Noise Control Inc............... C 614 889-0480
  Dublin *(G-8049)*
▲ Langdon Inc...................................... E 513 733-5955
  Cincinnati *(G-2965)*
Modern Builders Supply Inc............... C 419 241-3961
  Toledo *(G-13926)*
Mound Technologies Inc..................... E 937 748-2937
  Springboro *(G-13203)*
▲ Spallinger Millwright Svc Co........... E 419 225-5830
  Lima *(G-9962)*
Stephens Pipe & Steel LLC................. C 740 869-2257
  Mount Sterling *(G-11475)*
◆ Trewbric III Inc................................. E 614 444-2184
  Columbus *(G-6785)*
Triangle Precision Industries.............. D 937 299-6776
  Dayton *(G-7678)*
Waco Scaffolding & Equipment Inc.... A 216 749-8900
  Cleveland *(G-5119)*

3448 Prefabricated metal buildings

▲ Enclosure Suppliers LLC................. E 513 782-3900
  Cincinnati *(G-2619)*
▲ Hoge Lumber Company.................... E 419 753-2263
  New Knoxville *(G-11617)*
Ludy Greenhouse Mfg Corp................ D 800 255-5839
  New Madison *(G-11634)*
Pioneer Cldding Glzing Systems........ E 216 816-4242
  Cleveland *(G-4749)*
◆ Rough Brothers Mfg Inc................... D 513 242-0310
  Cincinnati *(G-3325)*
Williams Scotsman Inc....................... D 614 449-8675
  Columbus *(G-6894)*

3449 Miscellaneous metalwork

Gateway Con Forming Svcs Inc.......... D 513 353-2000
  Miamitown *(G-11106)*
Industrial Millwright Svcs LLC........... E 419 523-9147
  Ottawa *(G-12187)*
Midwest Curtainwalls Inc................... C 216 641-7900
  Cleveland *(G-4580)*
▼ Ohio Bridge Corporation.................. C 740 432-6334
  Cambridge *(G-1578)*
Precision Impacts LLC....................... D 937 530-8254
  Miamisburg *(G-11086)*
◆ Watteredge LLC................................ D 440 933-6110
  Avon Lake *(G-684)*
▲ Will-Burt Company............................ C 330 682-7015
  Orrville *(G-12176)*

3451 Screw machine products

◆ NSK Industries Inc............................ D 330 923-4112
  Cuyahoga Falls *(G-7091)*
Qualitor Subsidiary H Inc................... C 419 562-7987
  Bucyrus *(G-1517)*

3452 Bolts, nuts, rivets, and washers

▲ Atlas Bolt & Screw Company LLC.... C 419 289-6171
  Ashland *(G-478)*
◆ Facil North America Inc................... C 330 487-2500
  Twinsburg *(G-14190)*

SIC SECTION

34 FABRICATED METAL PRODUCTS

Fastener Industries Inc .... E 440 891-2031
  Berea *(G-1069)*

▲ Great Lakes Fasteners Inc .... D 330 425-4488
  Twinsburg *(G-14195)*

▲ Jergens Inc .... C 216 486-5540
  Cleveland *(G-4437)*

▲ Ohashi Technica USA Inc .... E 740 965-5115
  Sunbury *(G-13523)*

Simpson Strong-Tie Company Inc .... C 614 876-8060
  Columbus *(G-6683)*

◆ Stafast Products Inc .... E 440 357-5546
  Painesville *(G-12243)*

◆ Supply Technologies LLC .... C 440 947-2100
  Cleveland *(G-4966)*

3462 Iron and steel forgings

▲ Anchor Flange Company .... D 513 527-3512
  Cincinnati *(G-2196)*

Rudd Equipment Company Inc .... D 513 321-7833
  Cincinnati *(G-3329)*

US Tsubaki Power Transm LLC .... C 419 626-4560
  Sandusky *(G-12939)*

3463 Nonferrous forgings

◆ Mansfield Plumbing Pdts LLC .... A 419 938-5211
  Perrysville *(G-12392)*

3465 Automotive stampings

Falls Stamping & Welding Co .... C 330 928-1191
  Cuyahoga Falls *(G-7075)*

Honda Dev & Mfg Amer LLC .... C 937 644-0724
  Marysville *(G-10488)*

▲ R K Industries Inc .... D 419 523-5001
  Ottawa *(G-12195)*

▲ TS Trim Industries Inc .... B 614 837-4114
  Canal Winchester *(G-1618)*

3469 Metal stampings, nec

Abbott Tool Inc .... E 419 476-6742
  Toledo *(G-13673)*

▲ Acro Tool & Die Company .... E 330 773-5173
  Akron *(G-14)*

Bates Metal Products Inc .... D 740 498-8371
  Port Washington *(G-12541)*

Bayloff Stmped Pdts Knsman Inc .... D 330 876-4511
  Kinsman *(G-9644)*

Breitinger Company .... C 419 526-4255
  Mansfield *(G-10248)*

Falls Stamping & Welding Co .... C 330 928-1191
  Cuyahoga Falls *(G-7075)*

◆ G & S Metal Products Co Inc .... C 216 441-0700
  Cleveland *(G-4295)*

▲ KMC Holdings LLC .... C 419 238-2442
  Van Wert *(G-14347)*

▲ Long-Stanton Mfg Company .... E 513 874-8020
  West Chester *(G-14725)*

▲ Matco Tools Corporation .... B 330 929-4949
  Stow *(G-13382)*

Mid-America Steel Corp .... E 800 282-3466
  Cleveland *(G-4575)*

◆ Mtd Holdings Inc .... B 330 225-2600
  Valley City *(G-14336)*

◆ Ohio Gasket and Shim Co Inc .... E 330 630-0626
  Akron *(G-251)*

◆ Pentaflex Inc .... C 937 325-5551
  Springfield *(G-13281)*

Quality Fabricated Metals Inc .... E 330 332-7008
  Salem *(G-12849)*

S-P Company Inc .... D 330 782-5651
  Columbiana *(G-5240)*

Scott Fetzer Company .... C 216 267-9000
  Cleveland *(G-4885)*

Seilkop Industries Inc .... E 513 761-1035
  Cincinnati *(G-3356)*

◆ Supply Technologies LLC .... C 440 947-2100
  Cleveland *(G-4966)*

3471 Plating and polishing

Carpe Diem Industries LLC .... D 419 358-0129
  Bluffton *(G-1280)*

Carpe Diem Industries LLC .... D 419 659-5639
  Columbus Grove *(G-6921)*

▲ Chemical Solvents Inc .... E 216 741-9310
  Cleveland *(G-3965)*

Conley Group Inc .... E 330 372-2030
  Warren *(G-14513)*

▲ Electro Prime Group LLC .... D 419 476-0100
  Toledo *(G-13786)*

▲ Miba Bearings US LLC .... B 740 962-4242
  Mcconnelsville *(G-10803)*

Micro Products Co Inc .... E 440 943-0258
  Willoughby Hills *(G-15233)*

Scot Industries Inc .... D 330 262-7585
  Wooster *(G-15375)*

▲ Wieland Metal Svcs Foils LLC .... D 330 823-1700
  Alliance *(G-405)*

Worthington Enterprises Inc .... D 513 539-9291
  Monroe *(G-11355)*

Worthngton Smuel Coil Proc LLC .... E 330 963-3777
  Twinsburg *(G-14231)*

Yoder Industries Inc .... C 937 278-5769
  Dayton *(G-7731)*

3479 Metal coating and allied services

Canfield Metal Coating Corp .... D 330 702-3876
  Canfield *(G-1623)*

Carpe Diem Industries LLC .... D 419 358-0129
  Bluffton *(G-1280)*

Carpe Diem Industries LLC .... D 419 659-5639
  Columbus Grove *(G-6921)*

Corrotec Inc .... E 937 325-3585
  Springfield *(G-13242)*

◆ Enerfab LLC .... B 513 641-0500
  Cincinnati *(G-2620)*

▲ Godfrey & Wing Inc .... E 330 562-1440
  Aurora *(G-615)*

Herbert E Orr Company Inc .... E 419 399-4866
  Paulding *(G-12284)*

◆ NSK Industries Inc .... D 330 923-4112
  Cuyahoga Falls *(G-7091)*

SH Bell Company .... E 412 963-9910
  East Liverpool *(G-8193)*

Woodrow Manufacturing Co .... E 937 399-9333
  Springfield *(G-13313)*

3491 Industrial valves

▲ Alkon Corporation .... D 419 355-9111
  Fremont *(G-8665)*

◆ Kaplan Industries Inc .... D 856 779-8181
  Harrison *(G-9111)*

◆ Waxman Industries Inc .... C 440 439-1830
  Bedford Heights *(G-1005)*

3492 Fluid power valves and hose fittings

Aerocontrolex Group Inc .... D 216 291-6025
  South Euclid *(G-13170)*

▲ Alkon Corporation .... D 419 355-9111
  Fremont *(G-8665)*

Hydraulic Manifolds USA LLC .... E 973 728-1214
  Stow *(G-13376)*

Hydraulic Parts Store Inc .... E 330 364-6667
  New Philadelphia *(G-11656)*

◆ Hydrotech Inc .... D 888 651-5712
  West Chester *(G-14819)*

◆ Kirtland Capital Partners LP .... E 216 593-0100
  Beachwood *(G-806)*

▲ Mid-State Sales Inc .... D 614 864-1811
  Columbus *(G-6241)*

Parker-Hannifin Corporation .... D 937 456-5571
  Eaton *(G-8219)*

◆ Pressure Connections Corp .... D 614 863-6930
  Columbus *(G-6543)*

▲ SSP Fittings Corp .... D 330 425-4250
  Twinsburg *(G-14220)*

Superior Holding LLC .... E 216 651-9400
  Cleveland *(G-4964)*

Superior Products LLC .... D 216 651-9400
  Cleveland *(G-4965)*

3493 Steel springs, except wire

Hendrickson International Corp .... D 740 929-5600
  Hebron *(G-9143)*

3494 Valves and pipe fittings, nec

▲ Anchor Flange Company .... D 513 527-3512
  Cincinnati *(G-2196)*

Crane Pumps & Systems Inc .... C 937 773-2442
  Piqua *(G-12440)*

▲ Fcx Performance Inc .... E 614 253-1996
  Columbus *(G-5853)*

◆ Kirtland Capital Partners LP .... E 216 593-0100
  Beachwood *(G-806)*

▲ Mid-State Sales Inc .... D 614 864-1811
  Columbus *(G-6241)*

Parker-Hannifin Corporation .... C 614 279-7070
  Columbus *(G-6500)*

Parker-Hannifin Corporation .... D 937 456-5571
  Eaton *(G-8219)*

◆ Pressure Connections Corp .... D 614 863-6930
  Columbus *(G-6543)*

▲ Robeck Fluid Power Co .... D 330 562-1140
  Aurora *(G-624)*

▲ SSP Fittings Corp .... D 330 425-4250
  Twinsburg *(G-14220)*

Stephens Pipe & Steel LLC .... C 740 869-2257
  Mount Sterling *(G-11475)*

Superior Holding LLC .... E 216 651-9400
  Cleveland *(G-4964)*

Superior Products LLC .... D 216 651-9400
  Cleveland *(G-4965)*

Swagelok Company .... D 440 349-5934
  Solon *(G-13154)*

◆ Waxman Industries Inc .... C 440 439-1830
  Bedford Heights *(G-1005)*

3495 Wire springs

Barnes Group Inc .... C 419 891-9292
  Maumee *(G-10698)*

3496 Miscellaneous fabricated wire products

A K Athletic Equipment Inc .... E 614 920-3069
  Canal Winchester *(G-1597)*

Contitech Usa Inc .... D 937 644-8900
  Marysville *(G-10481)*

Gateway Con Forming Svcs Inc .... D 513 353-2000
  Miamitown *(G-11106)*

Microplex Inc .... E 330 498-0600
  North Canton *(G-11848)*

◆ Panacea Products Corporation .... E 614 850-7000
  Columbus *(G-6497)*

R G Smith Company .... D 330 456-3415
  Canton *(G-1839)*

Schweizer Dipple Inc .... D 440 786-8090
  Cleveland *(G-4884)*

Stephens Pipe & Steel LLC .... C 740 869-2257
  Mount Sterling *(G-11475)*

34 FABRICATED METAL PRODUCTS

▼ Stud Welding Associates Inc............ D 440 783-3160
Strongsville *(G-13490)*

3497 Metal foil and leaf

▲ Wieland Metal Svcs Foils LLC........... D 330 823-1700
Alliance *(G-405)*

3498 Fabricated pipe and fittings

Atlas Industrial Contrs LLC................. B 614 841-4500
Columbus *(G-5403)*

Bi-Con Services Inc............................... B 740 685-2542
Derwent *(G-7864)*

Contractors Steel Company................. D 330 425-3050
Twinsburg *(G-14178)*

Crest Bending Inc................................ E 419 492-2108
New Washington *(G-11682)*

Elliott Tool Technologies Ltd................. D 937 253-6133
Dayton *(G-7333)*

GM Mechanical Inc.............................. D 937 473-3006
Covington *(G-7018)*

Indelco Custom Products Inc.............. E 216 797-7300
Euclid *(G-8349)*

Industrial Power Systems Inc............. B 419 531-3121
Rossford *(G-12767)*

◆ Kirtland Capital Partners LP................ E 216 593-0100
Beachwood *(G-806)*

Parker-Hannifin Corporation................. D 937 456-5571
Eaton *(G-8219)*

Phillips Mfg and Tower Co................... D 419 347-1720
Shelby *(G-13008)*

▲ Pioneer Pipe Inc.................................. A 740 376-2400
Marietta *(G-10399)*

▲ Pipe Products Inc................................. C 513 587-7532
West Chester *(G-14742)*

◆ Pressure Connections Corp................ D 614 863-6930
Columbus *(G-6543)*

▲ Rhenium Alloys Inc............................. E 440 365-7388
North Ridgeville *(G-11934)*

S-P Company Inc................................. D 330 782-5651
Columbiana *(G-5240)*

Scot Industries Inc.............................. D 330 262-7585
Wooster *(G-15375)*

▲ SSP Fittings Corp............................... D 330 425-4250
Twinsburg *(G-14220)*

Swagelok Company............................... D 440 349-5934
Solon *(G-13154)*

Tri-America Contractors Inc................. E 740 574-0148
Wheelersburg *(G-15134)*

Unison Industries LLC......................... B 904 667-9904
Dayton *(G-7143)*

United Group Services Inc................... C 800 633-9690
West Chester *(G-14842)*

US Tubular Products Inc..................... D 330 832-1734
North Lawrence *(G-11880)*

Zekelman Industries Inc...................... C 740 432-2146
Cambridge *(G-1588)*

3499 Fabricated metal products, nec

Accurate Mechanical Inc..................... D 740 681-1332
Lancaster *(G-9690)*

B M Machine....................................... E 419 595-2898
New Riegel *(G-11677)*

Bauer Corporation............................... E 800 321-4760
Wooster *(G-15310)*

◆ Df Supply Inc..................................... E 330 650-9226
Twinsburg *(G-14181)*

EZ Grout Corporation Inc..................... E 740 962-2024
Malta *(G-10232)*

Jfdb Ltd.. C 513 870-0501
Cincinnati *(G-2912)*

◆ Ohio Gasket and Shim Co Inc............. E 330 630-0626
Akron *(G-251)*

◆ Walker National Inc............................. E 614 492-1614
Columbus *(G-6864)*

▲ Winkle Industries Inc.......................... D 330 823-9730
Alliance *(G-407)*

35 INDUSTRIAL AND COMMERCIAL MACHINERY AND COMPUTER EQUIPMENT

3511 Turbines and turbine generator sets

Babcock & Wilcox Holdings Inc............ A 704 625-4900
Akron *(G-60)*

Eaton Leasing Corporation................... B 216 382-2292
Beachwood *(G-788)*

▲ Miba Bearings US LLC........................ B 740 962-4242
Mcconnelsville *(G-10803)*

Onpower Inc.. E 513 228-2100
Lebanon *(G-9779)*

◆ Rolls-Royce Energy Systems Inc......... A 703 834-1700
Mount Vernon *(G-11506)*

Siemens Energy Inc............................. E 740 393-8897
Mount Vernon *(G-11508)*

Steam Trbine Altrntive Rsrces.............. E 740 387-5535
Marion *(G-10455)*

3519 Internal combustion engines, nec

General Electric Company.................... A 617 443-3000
Cincinnati *(G-2725)*

▲ Miba Bearings US LLC........................ B 740 962-4242
Mcconnelsville *(G-10803)*

▲ Miscor Group Ltd................................ B 330 830-3500
Massillon *(G-10658)*

3523 Farm machinery and equipment

◆ Chick Master Incubator Company........ D 330 722-5591
Medina *(G-10819)*

Gerald Grain Center Inc....................... E 419 445-2451
Archbold *(G-459)*

◆ Ohio Machinery Co.............................. C 440 526-6200
Broadview Heights *(G-1394)*

Shearer Farm Inc................................ C 330 345-9023
Wooster *(G-15376)*

Stephens Pipe & Steel LLC.................. C 740 869-2257
Mount Sterling *(G-11475)*

3524 Lawn and garden equipment

◆ Arnold Corporation.............................. C 330 225-2600
Valley City *(G-14331)*

Franklin Equipment LLC...................... D 614 228-2014
Groveport *(G-8990)*

◆ Mtd Holdings Inc................................. B 330 225-2600
Valley City *(G-14336)*

▲ Power Distributors LLC....................... D 614 876-3533
Columbus *(G-6539)*

◆ Scotts Company LLC........................... C 937 644-0011
Marysville *(G-10508)*

3531 Construction machinery

◆ Buck Equipment Inc............................ E 614 539-3039
Grove City *(G-8901)*

◆ Chemineer Inc.................................... C 937 454-3200
Dayton *(G-7222)*

Dimensional Metals Inc....................... E 740 927-3633
Reynoldsburg *(G-12660)*

▲ Forge Industries Inc........................... A 330 960-2468
Youngstown *(G-15613)*

Lake Township Trustees...................... E 419 836-1143
Millbury *(G-11270)*

◆ Mesa Industries Inc............................. E 513 321-2950
Cincinnati *(G-3048)*

◆ Npk Construction Equipment Inc......... D 440 232-7900
Bedford *(G-976)*

◆ Pubco Corporation............................... D 216 881-5300
Cleveland *(G-4797)*

The Wagner-Smith Company................ B 866 338-0398
Moraine *(G-11444)*

3532 Mining machinery

Maag Automatik Inc............................. E 330 677-2225
Kent *(G-9586)*

◆ Npk Construction Equipment Inc......... D 440 232-7900
Bedford *(G-976)*

◆ Reduction Engineering Inc................... E 330 677-2225
Kent *(G-9593)*

3533 Oil and gas field machinery

Buckeye Companies.............................. E 740 452-3641
Zanesville *(G-15772)*

Jet Rubber Company............................ E 330 325-1821
Rootstown *(G-12760)*

◆ Multi Products Company...................... E 330 674-5981
Millersburg *(G-11287)*

3534 Elevators and moving stairways

▲ Adams Elevator Equipment Co............ D 847 581-2900
Holland *(G-9276)*

Otis Elevator Company........................ E 216 573-2333
Cleveland *(G-4709)*

3535 Conveyors and conveying equipment

◆ Air Technical Industries Inc................. E 440 951-5191
Mentor *(G-10909)*

Alba Manufacturing Inc........................ D 513 874-0551
Fairfield *(G-8388)*

Allied Fabricating & Wldg Co............... E 614 751-6664
Columbus *(G-5338)*

Defabco Inc.. D 614 231-2700
Columbus *(G-5749)*

Dillin Engineered Systems Corp........... E 419 666-6789
Perrysburg *(G-12333)*

◆ Grob Systems Inc............................... A 419 358-9015
Bluffton *(G-1281)*

Innovative Controls Corp..................... E 419 691-6684
Toledo *(G-13863)*

Intelligrated Inc................................... A 513 874-0788
West Chester *(G-14820)*

▲ Intelligrated Systems Inc.................... A 866 936-7300
Mason *(G-10565)*

Intelligrated Systems LLC.................... A 513 701-7300
Mason *(G-10566)*

◆ Intelligrated Systems Ohio LLC........... A 513 701-7300
Mason *(G-10567)*

K F T Inc.. D 513 241-5910
Cincinnati *(G-2925)*

Mfh Partners Inc................................. B 440 461-4100
Cleveland *(G-4571)*

Stock Fairfield Corporation.................. C 440 543-6000
Solon *(G-13149)*

Werks Kraft Engineering LLC............... E 330 721-7374
Medina *(G-10902)*

3536 Hoists, cranes, and monorails

◆ Air Technical Industries Inc................. E 440 951-5191
Mentor *(G-10909)*

Expert Crane Inc................................. E 216 451-9900
Wellington *(G-14632)*

◆ Hiab USA Inc..................................... D 419 482-6000
Perrysburg *(G-12343)*

Trane Technologies Company LLC....... E 419 633-6800
Bryan *(G-1494)*

3537 Industrial trucks and tractors

SIC SECTION

35 INDUSTRIAL AND COMMERCIAL MACHINERY AND COMPUTER EQUIPMENT

Forte Industrial Equipmen............... E 513 398-2800
 Mason *(G-10550)*
General Electric Company............... E 513 977-1500
 Cincinnati *(G-2723)*
◆ Intelligrated Systems Ohio LLC........... A 513 701-7300
 Mason *(G-10567)*
Pollock Research & Design Inc............. E 330 332-3300
 Salem *(G-12847)*
Stock Fairfield Corporation............. C 440 543-6000
 Solon *(G-13149)*

3541 Machine tools, metal cutting type

▲ Acro Tool & Die Company............... E 330 773-5173
 Akron *(G-14)*
Cardinal Builders Inc............... E 614 237-1000
 Columbus *(G-5507)*
▲ Channel Products Inc............... D 440 423-0113
 Solon *(G-13075)*
Elliott Tool Technologies Ltd............. E 937 253-6133
 Dayton *(G-7333)*
▲ H & D Steel Service Inc............. E 800 666-3390
 North Royalton *(G-11942)*
◆ Lawrence Industries Inc............. E 216 518-7000
 Cleveland *(G-4483)*
▼ Ohio Broach & Machine Company............. E 440 946-1040
 Willoughby *(G-15214)*

3542 Machine tools, metal forming type

▲ Addition Manufacturing Te............... C 513 228-7000
 Lebanon *(G-9752)*
Anderson & Vreeland Inc............... D 419 636-5002
 Bryan *(G-1479)*
▼ Compass Systems & Sales LLC............ D 330 733-2111
 Norton *(G-11993)*
Elliott Tool Technologies Ltd............. E 937 253-6133
 Dayton *(G-7333)*
Monode Marking Products Inc............. E 440 975-8802
 Mentor *(G-10976)*
▲ Pines Manufacturing Inc............. E 440 835-5553
 Westlake *(G-15098)*

3543 Industrial patterns

Freeman Manufacturing & Sup Co......... E 440 934-1902
 Avon *(G-651)*

3544 Special dies, tools, jigs, and fixtures

5me LLC............... E 513 719-1600
 Cincinnati *(G-2095)*
▲ Acro Tool & Die Company............... E 330 773-5173
 Akron *(G-14)*
▲ Addition Manufacturing Te............... C 513 228-7000
 Lebanon *(G-9752)*
▲ Advanced Engrg Solutions Inc............. D 937 743-6900
 Springboro *(G-13191)*
Athens Mold and Machine Inc............. D 740 593-6613
 Athens *(G-559)*
Balancing Company Inc............. E 937 898-9111
 Vandalia *(G-14365)*
Cornerstone Wauseon Inc............. C 419 337-0940
 Wauseon *(G-14598)*
▲ EMI Corp............... D 937 596-5511
 Jackson Center *(G-9531)*
Falls Stamping & Welding Co............. C 330 928-1191
 Cuyahoga Falls *(G-7075)*
▲ General Tool Company............. E 513 733-5500
 Cincinnati *(G-2728)*
▲ Hi-Tek Manufacturing Inc............. C 513 459-1094
 Mason *(G-10562)*
▲ Industry Products Co............. B 937 778-0585
 Piqua *(G-12445)*
▲ Jergens Inc............. C 216 486-5540
 Cleveland *(G-4437)*

Koebbe Products Inc............. D 513 753-4200
 Amelia *(G-417)*
Lincoln Electric Automtn Inc............. B 937 295-2120
 Fort Loramie *(G-8605)*
▲ Long-Stanton Mfg Company............. E 513 874-8020
 West Chester *(G-14725)*
Lunar Tool & Mold Inc............. E 440 237-2141
 North Royalton *(G-11944)*
◆ Mtd Holdings Inc............. B 330 225-2600
 Valley City *(G-14336)*
Seilkop Industries Inc............. E 513 761-1035
 Cincinnati *(G-3356)*
Stan-Kell LLC............. E 440 998-1116
 Ashtabula *(G-550)*
Straight 72 Inc............. D 740 943-5730
 Marysville *(G-10511)*
Tipp Machine & Tool Inc............. C 937 890-8428
 Dayton *(G-7669)*
Worthington Industries Inc............. E 614 438-3028
 Columbus *(G-6906)*

3545 Machine tool accessories

Chardon Tool & Supply Co Inc............. E 440 286-6440
 Chardon *(G-1997)*
Container Graphics Corp............. E 419 531-5133
 Toledo *(G-13760)*
H3d Tool Corporation............. D 740 498-5181
 Newcomerstown *(G-11768)*
Imco Carbide Tool Inc............. D 419 661-6313
 Perrysburg *(G-12346)*
▲ Jergens Inc............. C 216 486-5540
 Cleveland *(G-4437)*
Johnson Bros Rubber Co Inc............. E 419 752-4814
 Greenwich *(G-8892)*
▲ Kyocera SGS Precision Tls Inc............. C 330 688-6667
 Cuyahoga Falls *(G-7086)*
▼ Ohio Broach & Machine Company............. E 440 946-1040
 Willoughby *(G-15214)*

3546 Power-driven handtools

◆ F & M Mafco Inc............. C 513 367-2151
 Harrison *(G-9104)*
Huron Cement Products Company............. E 419 433-4161
 Huron *(G-9390)*
▲ Kyocera Senco Indus Tls Inc............. D 513 388-2000
 Cincinnati *(G-2958)*
▲ Npk Construction Equipment Inc............. D 440 232-7900
 Bedford *(G-976)*
Sewer Rodding Equipment Co............. C 419 991-2065
 Lima *(G-9959)*
Trane Technologies Company LLC............. E 419 633-6800
 Bryan *(G-1494)*
Wolf Machine Company............. E 513 791-5194
 Blue Ash *(G-1274)*

3547 Rolling mill machinery

▲ Addition Manufacturing Te............... C 513 228-7000
 Lebanon *(G-9752)*
Cornerstone Wauseon Inc............. C 419 337-0940
 Wauseon *(G-14598)*
▲ Park Corporation............. B 216 267-4870
 Medina *(G-10874)*
▲ Pines Manufacturing Inc............. E 440 835-5553
 Westlake *(G-15098)*
▲ Steel Eqp Specialists Inc............. D 330 823-8260
 Alliance *(G-401)*

3549 Metalworking machinery, nec

▲ Addition Manufacturing Te............... C 513 228-7000
 Lebanon *(G-9752)*
Ctm Integration Incorporated............. E 330 332-1800
 Salem *(G-12840)*

EZ Grout Corporation Inc............. E 740 962-2024
 Malta *(G-10232)*
▼ Hunter Defense Tech Inc............. E 216 438-6111
 Solon *(G-13096)*
▲ Pines Manufacturing Inc............. E 440 835-5553
 Westlake *(G-15098)*
South Shore Controls Inc............. E 440 259-2500
 Mentor *(G-10998)*

3552 Textile machinery

Wolf Machine Company............. E 513 791-5194
 Blue Ash *(G-1274)*

3553 Woodworking machinery

Seilkop Industries Inc............. E 513 761-1035
 Cincinnati *(G-3356)*

3554 Paper industries machinery

◆ Baumfolder Corporation............. E 937 492-1281
 Sidney *(G-13020)*
◆ Chemineer Inc............. C 937 454-3200
 Dayton *(G-7222)*

3555 Printing trades machinery

Anderson & Vreeland Inc............. D 419 636-5002
 Bryan *(G-1479)*
Graphic Systems Services Inc............. E 937 746-0708
 Springboro *(G-13199)*
◆ Wood Graphics Inc............. E 513 771-6300
 Cincinnati *(G-3680)*

3556 Food products machinery

◆ Chemineer Inc............. C 937 454-3200
 Dayton *(G-7222)*
Frost Engineering Inc............. E 513 541-6330
 Cincinnati *(G-2710)*
◆ G & S Metal Products Co Inc............. C 216 441-0700
 Cleveland *(G-4295)*
◆ Gold Medal Products Co............. B 513 769-7676
 Cincinnati *(G-2739)*
◆ Harry C Lobalzo & Sons Inc............. E 330 666-6758
 Akron *(G-184)*
Innovative Controls Corp............. E 419 691-6684
 Toledo *(G-13863)*
◆ ITW Food Equipment Group LLC............. A 937 332-2396
 Troy *(G-14141)*
Lima Sheet Metal Machine & Mfg............. E 419 229-1161
 Lima *(G-9927)*
◆ N Wasserstrom & Sons Inc............. C 614 228-5550
 Columbus *(G-6286)*
Norse Dairy Systems Inc............. C 614 294-4931
 Columbus *(G-6363)*
R and J Corporation............. E 440 871-6009
 Westlake *(G-15101)*
Wolf Machine Company............. E 513 791-5194
 Blue Ash *(G-1274)*

3559 Special industry machinery, nec

◆ Chemineer Inc............. C 937 454-3200
 Dayton *(G-7222)*
Cornerstone Wauseon Inc............. C 419 337-0940
 Wauseon *(G-14598)*
Corrotec Inc............. E 937 325-3585
 Springfield *(G-13242)*
▲ Equipment Mfrs Intl Inc............. E 216 651-6700
 Cleveland *(G-4217)*
▲ Guild Associates Inc............. D 614 798-8215
 Dublin *(G-8023)*
J & S Industrial Mch Pdts Inc............. D 419 691-1380
 Toledo *(G-13865)*
◆ Knight Material Tech LLC............. D 330 488-1651
 East Canton *(G-8169)*

Employee Codes: A=Over 500 employees, B=251-500
C=101-250, D=51-100, E=20-50, F=10-19, G=1-9

35 INDUSTRIAL AND COMMERCIAL MACHINERY AND COMPUTER EQUIPMENT — SIC SECTION

Linden-Two Inc .... E 330 928-4064
  Cuyahoga Falls *(G-7087)*

▲ Rubber City Machinery Corp .... E 330 434-3500
  Akron *(G-288)*

Velocys Inc .... D 614 733-3300
  Plain City *(G-12497)*

3561 Pumps and pumping equipment

◆ Dreison International Inc .... C 216 362-0755
  Cleveland *(G-4184)*

General Electric Company .... E 216 883-1000
  Cleveland *(G-4310)*

▲ Giant Industries Inc .... E 419 531-4600
  Toledo *(G-13821)*

Indelco Custom Products Inc .... E 216 797-7300
  Euclid *(G-8349)*

◆ Tolco Corporation .... D 419 241-1113
  Toledo *(G-14048)*

Trane Technologies Company LLC .... E 419 633-6800
  Bryan *(G-1494)*

▲ Wayne/Scott Fetzer Company .... C 800 237-0987
  Harrison *(G-9119)*

3562 Ball and roller bearings

◆ Timken Company .... A 234 262-3000
  North Canton *(G-11865)*

3563 Air and gas compressors

Autobody Supply Company Inc .... D 614 228-4328
  Columbus *(G-5407)*

◆ Tolco Corporation .... D 419 241-1113
  Toledo *(G-14048)*

3564 Blowers and fans

Atmos360 Inc .... E 513 772-4777
  West Chester *(G-14799)*

◆ Dreison International Inc .... C 216 362-0755
  Cleveland *(G-4184)*

Kirk Williams Company Inc .... D 614 875-9023
  Grove City *(G-8931)*

▲ Langdon Inc .... E 513 733-5955
  Cincinnati *(G-2965)*

◆ McGill Airclean LLC .... D 614 829-1200
  Columbus *(G-6215)*

Neundorfer Inc .... E 440 942-8990
  Willoughby *(G-15213)*

Ohio Blow Pipe Company .... E 216 681-7379
  Cleveland *(G-4682)*

Rmt Acquisition Inc .... E 513 241-5566
  Cincinnati *(G-3311)*

◆ Tosoh America Inc .... B 614 539-8622
  Grove City *(G-8959)*

▲ United McGill Corporation .... E 614 829-1200
  Groveport *(G-9007)*

▼ Verantis Corporation .... E 440 243-0700
  Middleburg Heights *(G-11133)*

3565 Packaging machinery

▲ Advanced Poly-Packaging Inc .... C 330 785-4000
  Akron *(G-18)*

Atmos360 Inc .... E 513 772-4777
  West Chester *(G-14799)*

Ctm Integration Incorporated .... E 330 332-1800
  Salem *(G-12840)*

G and J Automatic Systems Inc .... E 216 741-6070
  Cleveland *(G-4296)*

Millwood Inc .... E 513 860-4567
  West Chester *(G-14730)*

Millwood Natural LLC .... E 330 393-4400
  Vienna *(G-14423)*

Norse Dairy Systems Inc .... C 614 294-4931
  Columbus *(G-6363)*

◆ OKL Can Line Inc .... E
  Cincinnati *(G-3155)*

Universal Packg Systems Inc .... C 513 732-2000
  Batavia *(G-751)*

Universal Packg Systems Inc .... C 513 735-4777
  Batavia *(G-752)*

Universal Packg Systems Inc .... C 513 674-9400
  Cincinnati *(G-3563)*

3566 Speed changers, drives, and gears

Ametek Tchnical Indus Pdts Inc .... D 330 673-3451
  Kent *(G-9559)*

Eaton Leasing Corporation .... B 216 382-2292
  Beachwood *(G-788)*

◆ Forge Industries Inc .... A 330 960-2468
  Youngstown *(G-15613)*

▲ Great Lakes Power Products Inc ..... D 440 951-5111
  Mentor *(G-10943)*

▲ Joseph Industries Inc .... D 330 528-0091
  Streetsboro *(G-13419)*

▼ Matlock Electric Co Inc .... E 513 731-9600
  Cincinnati *(G-3015)*

◆ Wasserstrom Company .... B 614 228-6525
  Columbus *(G-6867)*

Werks Kraft Engineering LLC .... E 330 721-7374
  Medina *(G-10902)*

3567 Industrial furnaces and ovens

◆ Ajax Tocco Magnethermic Corp .... C 800 547-1527
  Warren *(G-14496)*

Hannon Company .... D 330 456-4728
  Canton *(G-1770)*

Novagard Solutions Inc .... C 216 881-8111
  Cleveland *(G-4668)*

Resilience Fund III LP .... E 216 292-0200
  Cleveland *(G-4830)*

▲ The Schaefer Group Inc .... E 937 253-3342
  Beavercreek *(G-932)*

▲ United McGill Corporation .... E 614 829-1200
  Groveport *(G-9007)*

3568 Power transmission equipment, nec

General Electric Company .... E 216 883-1000
  Cleveland *(G-4310)*

▲ Logan Clutch Corporation .... E 440 808-4258
  Cleveland *(G-4504)*

Mfh Partners Inc .... B 440 461-4100
  Cleveland *(G-4571)*

US Tsubaki Power Transm LLC .... C 419 626-4560
  Sandusky *(G-12939)*

3569 General industrial machinery,

A-1 Sprinkler Company Inc .... D 937 859-6198
  Miamisburg *(G-11019)*

▲ Action Coupling & Eqp Inc .... D 330 279-4242
  Holmesville *(G-9316)*

▲ Advanced Design Industries Inc ...... E 440 277-4141
  Sheffield Village *(G-12997)*

◆ Air Technical Industries Inc .... E 440 951-5191
  Mentor *(G-10909)*

▲ Ats Systems Oregon Inc .... C 541 738-0932
  Lewis Center *(G-9808)*

Cascade Corporation .... E 419 425-3675
  Findlay *(G-8521)*

Fire Foe Corp .... E 330 759-9834
  Girard *(G-8811)*

▼ Hunter Defense Tech Inc .... E 216 438-6111
  Solon *(G-13096)*

◆ Kc Robotics Inc .... E 513 860-4442
  West Chester *(G-14717)*

Remtec Engineering .... E 513 860-4299
  Mason *(G-10601)*

Sentient Studios Ltd .... E 330 204-8636
  Fairlawn *(G-8499)*

Swift Filters Inc .... E 440 735-0995
  Oakwood Village *(G-12058)*

3571 Electronic computers

Park Place Technologies LLC .... C 877 778-8707
  Cleveland *(G-4724)*

▲ Systemax Manufacturing Inc .... D 937 368-2300
  Dayton *(G-7658)*

3572 Computer storage devices

Freedom Usa Inc .... E 216 503-6374
  Twinsburg *(G-14192)*

Park Place Technologies LLC .... C 877 778-8707
  Cleveland *(G-4724)*

▲ Pinnacle Data Systems Inc .... C 614 748-1150
  Groveport *(G-8995)*

3575 Computer terminals

Freedom Usa Inc .... E 216 503-6374
  Twinsburg *(G-14192)*

▲ Pinnacle Data Systems Inc .... C 614 748-1150
  Groveport *(G-8995)*

3577 Computer peripheral equipment, nec

Clarity Retail Services LLC .... D 513 800-9369
  West Chester *(G-14668)*

▼ Data Processing Sciences .... D 513 791-7100
  Cincinnati *(G-2539)*

Government Acquisitions Inc .... E 513 721-8700
  Cincinnati *(G-2744)*

Sierra Nevada Corporation .... C 937 431-2800
  Beavercreek *(G-906)*

▲ Systemax Manufacturing Inc .... D 937 368-2300
  Dayton *(G-7658)*

▲ Vmetro Inc .... D 281 584-0728
  Fairborn *(G-8386)*

3579 Office machines, nec

◆ Baumfolder Corporation .... E 937 492-1281
  Sidney *(G-13020)*

3581 Automatic vending machines

▲ Giant Industries Inc .... E 419 531-4600
  Toledo *(G-13821)*

◆ Gold Medal Products Co .... B 513 769-7676
  Cincinnati *(G-2739)*

3585 Refrigeration and heating equipment

Columbus Heating & Vent Co .... C 614 274-1177
  Columbus *(G-5635)*

▲ Hydro-Dyne Inc .... E 330 832-5076
  Massillon *(G-10647)*

◆ Lvd Acquisition LLC .... D 614 861-1350
  Columbus *(G-6181)*

◆ Vertiv Corporation .... A 614 888-0246
  Westerville *(G-14949)*

Vertiv JV Holdings LLC .... A 614 888-0246
  Columbus *(G-6846)*

3586 Measuring and dispensing pumps

◆ Tolco Corporation .... D 419 241-1113
  Toledo *(G-14048)*

3589 Service industry machinery, nec

City of Middletown .... D 513 425-7781
  Middletown *(G-11157)*

Crown Solutions Co LLC .... C 937 890-4075
  Vandalia *(G-14372)*

◆ De Nora Tech LLC .... D 440 710-5334
  Concord Township *(G-6924)*

SIC SECTION
36 ELECTRONIC & OTHER ELECTRICAL EQUIPMENT & COMPONENTS

▲ Enting Water Conditioning Inc........... E 937 294-5100
 Moraine *(G-11407)*
▲ Giant Industries Inc........................... E 419 531-4600
 Toledo *(G-13821)*
◆ Gold Medal Products Co................... B 513 769-7676
 Cincinnati *(G-2739)*
High-TEC Industrial Services............... D 937 667-1772
 Tipp City *(G-13659)*
◆ Kinetico Incorporated........................ B 440 564-9111
 Newbury *(G-11761)*
Lima Sheet Metal Machine & Mfg........ E 419 229-1161
 Lima *(G-9927)*
MPW Industrial Svcs Group Inc........... B 740 927-8790
 Hebron *(G-9150)*
◆ William R Hague Inc......................... D 614 836-2115
 Groveport *(G-9014)*

3593 Fluid power cylinders and actuators

▲ American Hydraulic Svcs Inc............ E 606 739-8680
 Ironton *(G-9502)*
Eaton Leasing Corporation................... B 216 382-2292
 Beachwood *(G-788)*
Hydraulic Parts Store Inc.................... E 330 364-6667
 New Philadelphia *(G-11656)*
▲ Robeck Fluid Power Co.................... D 330 562-1140
 Aurora *(G-624)*
▲ Steel Eqp Specialists Inc.................. D 330 823-8260
 Alliance *(G-401)*
Swagelok Company............................. D 440 349-5934
 Solon *(G-13154)*

3594 Fluid power pumps and motors

Aerocontrolex Group Inc..................... D 216 291-6025
 South Euclid *(G-13170)*
▲ Anchor Flange Company.................. D 513 527-3512
 Cincinnati *(G-2196)*
▲ Apph Wichita Inc.............................. E 316 943-5752
 Strongsville *(G-13442)*
Eaton Leasing Corporation................... B 216 382-2292
 Beachwood *(G-788)*
▲ Giant Industries Inc.......................... E 419 531-4600
 Toledo *(G-13821)*
Hydraulic Parts Store Inc.................... E 330 364-6667
 New Philadelphia *(G-11656)*
▲ Robeck Fluid Power Co.................... D 330 562-1140
 Aurora *(G-624)*
Trane Technologies Company LLC...... E 419 633-6800
 Bryan *(G-1494)*

3596 Scales and balances, except laboratory

◆ Mettler-Toledo LLC........................... A 614 438-4511
 Columbus *(G-5270)*

3599 Industrial machinery, nec

▲ A & G Manufacturing Co Inc............ E 419 468-7433
 Galion *(G-8740)*
▲ Addition Manufacturing Te................ C 513 228-7000
 Lebanon *(G-9752)*
▲ Advanced Design Industries Inc....... E 440 277-4141
 Sheffield Village *(G-12997)*
◆ Alfons Haar Inc................................. E 937 560-2031
 Springboro *(G-13192)*
All-Type Welding & Fabrication............ E 440 439-3990
 Cleveland *(G-3792)*
Anchor Metal Processing Inc............... E 216 362-1850
 Cleveland *(G-3814)*
Athens Mold and Machine Inc............. D 740 593-6613
 Athens *(G-559)*
Atlas Machine and Supply Inc............. E 502 584-7262
 Hamilton *(G-9017)*
Balancing Company Inc....................... E 937 898-9111
 Vandalia *(G-14365)*

C-N-D Industries Inc........................... E 330 478-8811
 Massillon *(G-10633)*
▲ Cbn Westside Technologies Inc....... B 513 772-7000
 West Chester *(G-14660)*
▲ Combs Manufacturing Inc................ D 330 784-3151
 Akron *(G-114)*
Cornerstone Wauseon Inc................... C 419 337-0940
 Wauseon *(G-14598)*
Drt Holdings Inc................................... D 937 298-7391
 Dayton *(G-7317)*
▲ East End Welding LLC..................... C 330 677-6000
 Kent *(G-9573)*
▲ Forge Industries Inc......................... A 330 960-2468
 Youngstown *(G-15613)*
▲ General Tool Company..................... C 513 733-5500
 Cincinnati *(G-2728)*
George Steel Fabricating Inc............... E 513 932-2887
 Lebanon *(G-9766)*
▲ Glenridge Machine Co..................... E 440 975-1055
 Solon *(G-13092)*
Graphel Corporation............................. E 513 779-6166
 West Chester *(G-14700)*
Hahn Automation Group Us Inc........... D 937 886-3232
 Miamisburg *(G-11058)*
▲ Hi-Tek Manufacturing Inc................. C 513 459-1094
 Mason *(G-10562)*
Indelco Custom Products Inc.............. E 216 797-7300
 Euclid *(G-8349)*
◆ Interscope Manufacturing Inc........... E 513 423-8866
 Middletown *(G-11166)*
Jerl Machine Inc.................................. D 419 873-0270
 Perrysburg *(G-12348)*
Laserflex Corporation.......................... D 614 850-9600
 Hilliard *(G-9209)*
▲ Lawrence Industries Inc................... E 216 518-7000
 Cleveland *(G-4483)*
Lima Sheet Metal Machine & Mfg........ E 419 229-1161
 Lima *(G-9927)*
Lincoln Electric Automtn Inc................ B 937 295-2120
 Fort Loramie *(G-8605)*
Lochard Inc.. D 937 492-8811
 Sidney *(G-13037)*
Meta Manufacturing Corporation......... E 513 793-6382
 Blue Ash *(G-1210)*
Metcut Research Associates Inc......... D 513 271-5100
 Cincinnati *(G-3052)*
Metro Design Inc.................................. E 440 458-4200
 Elyria *(G-8274)*
Minerva Welding and Fabg Inc............ E 330 868-7731
 Minerva *(G-11310)*
Morris Technologies Inc....................... E 513 733-1611
 Cincinnati *(G-3080)*
Napoleon Machine LLC........................ E 419 591-7010
 Napoleon *(G-11530)*
Narrow Way Custom Tech Inc.............. E 937 743-1611
 Carlisle *(G-1898)*
◆ Npk Construction Equipment Inc...... D 440 232-7900
 Bedford *(G-976)*
▼ Ohio Broach & Machine Company.... E 440 946-1040
 Willoughby *(G-15214)*
◆ Ohio Gasket and Shim Co Inc.......... E 330 630-0626
 Akron *(G-251)*
▲ P R Machine Works Inc................... D 419 529-5748
 Ontario *(G-12122)*
◆ Princeton Tool Inc............................. C 440 290-8666
 Mentor *(G-10985)*
◆ RL Best Company............................. E 330 758-8601
 Boardman *(G-1290)*
S-P Company Inc................................. D 330 782-5651
 Columbiana *(G-5240)*
Sample Machining Inc......................... E 937 258-3338
 Dayton *(G-7609)*

Schmidt Machine Company................. E 419 294-3814
 Upper Sandusky *(G-14292)*
Sponseller Group Inc........................... E 419 861-3000
 Holland *(G-9304)*
Stan-Kell LLC....................................... E 440 998-1116
 Ashtabula *(G-550)*
Starwin Industries LLC........................ E 937 293-8568
 Dayton *(G-7639)*
▲ Steel Eqp Specialists Inc.................. D 330 823-8260
 Alliance *(G-401)*
Tipp Machine & Tool Inc...................... C 937 890-8428
 Dayton *(G-7669)*
Triangle Precision Industries............... D 937 299-6776
 Dayton *(G-7678)*
▲ Ultra Tech Machinery Inc................. E 330 929-5544
 Cuyahoga Falls *(G-7113)*
Valley Machine Tool Inc....................... E 513 899-2737
 Morrow *(G-11456)*
▲ Will-Burt Company............................ C 330 682-7015
 Orrville *(G-12176)*
Wm Plotz Machine and Forge Co........ E 216 861-0441
 Cleveland *(G-5156)*
Wulco Inc... D 513 379-6115
 Hamilton *(G-9093)*
▲ Wulco Inc... D 513 679-2600
 Cincinnati *(G-3682)*

36 ELECTRONIC & OTHER ELECTRICAL EQUIPMENT & COMPONENTS

3612 Transformers, except electric

◆ Ajax Tocco Magnethermic Corp......... C 800 547-1527
 Warren *(G-14496)*
Eaton Leasing Corporation................... B 216 382-2292
 Beachwood *(G-788)*
Fishel Company................................... C 614 850-4400
 Columbus *(G-5867)*
General Electric Company................... E 216 883-1000
 Cleveland *(G-4310)*
Hannon Company................................ D 330 456-4728
 Canton *(G-1770)*
▼ Matlock Electric Co Inc.................... E 513 731-9600
 Cincinnati *(G-3015)*
Schneider Electric Usa Inc.................. B 513 523-4171
 Oxford *(G-12217)*
Schneider Electric Usa Inc.................. D 513 777-4445
 West Chester *(G-14761)*

3613 Switchgear and switchboard apparatus

General Electric Company................... E 216 883-1000
 Cleveland *(G-4310)*
Innovative Controls Corp..................... E 419 691-6684
 Toledo *(G-13863)*
▲ Instrmntation Ctrl Systems Inc.......... E 513 662-2600
 Cincinnati *(G-2873)*
Panelmatic Inc..................................... E 330 782-8007
 Youngstown *(G-15688)*
Schneider Electric Usa Inc.................. D 513 777-4445
 West Chester *(G-14761)*
Scott Fetzer Company.......................... C 216 267-9000
 Cleveland *(G-4885)*
Star Distribution and Mfg LLC............. E 513 860-3573
 West Chester *(G-14833)*
◆ Vertiv Corporation............................. A 614 888-0246
 Westerville *(G-14949)*

3621 Motors and generators

Ametek Tchnical Indus Pdts Inc.......... D 330 673-3451
 Kent *(G-9559)*
◆ Dreison International Inc................... C 216 362-0755
 Cleveland *(G-4184)*

Employee Codes: A=Over 500 employees, B=251-500
C=101-250, D=51-100, E=20-50, F=10-19, G=1-9

36 ELECTRONIC & OTHER ELECTRICAL EQUIPMENT & COMPONENTS

Electric Service Co Inc .... E 513 271-6387
   Cincinnati *(G-2610)*
General Electric Company .... E 216 883-1000
   Cleveland *(G-4310)*
Hannon Company .... D 330 456-4728
   Canton *(G-1770)*

3624 Carbon and graphite products

◆ De Nora Tech LLC .... D 440 710-5334
   Concord Township *(G-6924)*
◆ Ges Graphite Inc .... E 216 658-6660
   Parma *(G-12254)*
Graftech Holdings Inc .... D 216 676-2000
   Independence *(G-9434)*
Graphel Corporation .... C 513 779-6166
   West Chester *(G-14700)*
▲ Mill-Rose Company .... C 440 255-9171
   Mentor *(G-10975)*

3625 Relays and industrial controls

Apex Control Systems Inc .... D 330 938-2588
   Sebring *(G-12945)*
▲ Chandler Systems Incorporated .... D 888 363-9434
   Ashland *(G-491)*
▲ Channel Products Inc .... D 440 423-0113
   Solon *(G-13075)*
Command Alkon Incorporated .... E 614 799-0600
   Dublin *(G-7967)*
Corrotec Inc .... E 937 325-3585
   Springfield *(G-13242)*
Curtiss-Wright Controls .... E 937 252-5601
   Fairborn *(G-8371)*
Innovative Controls Corp .... E 419 691-6684
   Toledo *(G-13863)*
◆ Kinetics Noise Control Inc .... C 614 889-0480
   Dublin *(G-8049)*
Machine Drive Company .... D 513 793-7077
   Cincinnati *(G-3000)*
▲ Pepperl + Fuchs Inc .... C 330 425-3555
   Twinsburg *(G-14210)*
PMC Systems Limited .... E 330 538-2268
   North Jackson *(G-11876)*
Projects Unlimited Inc .... C 937 918-2200
   Dayton *(G-7571)*
Schneider Electric Usa Inc .... D 513 777-4445
   West Chester *(G-14761)*
▲ Standex Electronics Inc .... D 513 871-3777
   Fairfield *(G-8443)*
Stock Fairfield Corporation .... C 440 543-6000
   Solon *(G-13149)*

3629 Electrical industrial apparatus

◆ Noco Company .... D 216 464-8131
   Solon *(G-13119)*
TL Industries Inc .... C 419 666-8144
   Perrysburg *(G-12377)*

3631 Household cooking equipment

Nacco Industries Inc .... E 440 229-5151
   Cleveland *(G-4616)*

3632 Household refrigerators and freezers

Whirlpool Corporation .... E 740 383-7122
   Marion *(G-10464)*

3633 Household laundry equipment

Whirlpool Corporation .... E 740 383-7122
   Marion *(G-10464)*

3634 Electric housewares and fans

Johnson Bros Rubber Co Inc .... E 419 752-4814
   Greenwich *(G-8892)*

Nacco Industries Inc .... E 440 229-5151
   Cleveland *(G-4616)*

3635 Household vacuum cleaners

▲ Stanley Steemer Intl Inc .... C 614 764-2007
   Dublin *(G-8124)*

3639 Household appliances, nec

Sandco Industries .... E 419 547-3273
   Clyde *(G-5209)*

3643 Current-carrying wiring devices

Apex Control Systems Inc .... D 330 938-2588
   Sebring *(G-12945)*
▲ Channel Products Inc .... D 440 423-0113
   Solon *(G-13075)*
◆ Dreison International Inc .... C 216 362-0755
   Cleveland *(G-4184)*
Legrand North America LLC .... B 937 224-0639
   Dayton *(G-7451)*
Projects Unlimited Inc .... C 937 918-2200
   Dayton *(G-7571)*
Schneider Electric Usa Inc .... D 513 777-4445
   West Chester *(G-14761)*
Simpson Strong-Tie Company Inc .... C 614 876-8060
   Columbus *(G-6683)*
◆ Watteredge LLC .... D 440 933-6110
   Avon Lake *(G-684)*

3644 Noncurrent-carrying wiring devices

Koebbe Products Inc .... D 513 753-4200
   Amelia *(G-417)*
◆ Vertiv Energy Systems Inc .... A 440 288-1122
   Lorain *(G-10107)*
Zekelman Industries Inc .... C 740 432-2146
   Cambridge *(G-1588)*

3646 Commercial lighting fixtures

◆ Best Lighting Products Inc .... D 740 964-1198
   Etna *(G-8332)*
LSI Industries Inc .... C 913 281-1100
   Blue Ash *(G-1202)*
▲ LSI Lightron Inc .... A 845 562-5500
   Blue Ash *(G-1203)*

3647 Vehicular lighting equipment

Akron Brass Holding Corp .... E 330 264-5678
   Wooster *(G-15307)*
Grimes Aerospace Company .... D 937 484-2001
   Urbana *(G-14308)*

3648 Lighting equipment, nec

▲ Will-Burt Company .... C 330 682-7015
   Orrville *(G-12176)*

3651 Household audio and video equipment

Fellhauer Mechanical Systems .... E 419 734-3674
   Port Clinton *(G-12525)*
▲ Floyd Bell Inc .... D 614 294-4000
   Columbus *(G-5874)*
◆ Pioneer Automotive Tech Inc .... C 937 746-2293
   Miamisburg *(G-11084)*

3661 Telephone and telegraph apparatus

Commercial Electric Pdts Corp .... E 216 241-2886
   Cleveland *(G-4094)*
DTE Inc .... E 419 522-3428
   Mansfield *(G-10259)*
▲ Floyd Bell Inc .... D 614 294-4000
   Columbus *(G-5874)*
◆ Vertiv Energy Systems Inc .... A 440 288-1122
   Lorain *(G-10107)*

3663 Radio and t.v. communications equipment

Circle Prime Manufacturing .... E 330 923-0019
   Cuyahoga Falls *(G-7054)*
▲ Gatesair Inc .... D 513 459-3400
   Mason *(G-10553)*
Great Lakes Telcom Ltd .... E 330 629-8848
   Youngstown *(G-15622)*
L-3 Cmmncations Nova Engrg Inc .... C 877 282-1168
   Mason *(G-10571)*
Quasonix Inc .... E 513 942-1287
   West Chester *(G-14751)*
Starwin Industries LLC .... E 937 293-8568
   Dayton *(G-7639)*

3669 Communications equipment, nec

▼ Data Processing Sciences .... D 513 791-7100
   Cincinnati *(G-2539)*
▲ Findaway World LLC .... E 440 893-0808
   Solon *(G-13089)*
▲ Floyd Bell Inc .... D 614 294-4000
   Columbus *(G-5874)*
Quasonix Inc .... E 513 942-1287
   West Chester *(G-14751)*
Security Fence Group Inc .... E 513 681-3700
   Cincinnati *(G-3353)*
Status Solutions LLC .... D 434 296-1789
   Westerville *(G-14938)*

3672 Printed circuit boards

Circle Prime Manufacturing .... E 330 923-0019
   Cuyahoga Falls *(G-7054)*
Metzenbaum Sheltered Inds Inc .... D 440 729-1919
   Chesterland *(G-2041)*
Projects Unlimited Inc .... C 937 918-2200
   Dayton *(G-7571)*
▲ Vmetro Inc .... D 281 584-0728
   Fairborn *(G-8386)*
Wurth Electronics Ics Inc .... E 937 415-7700
   Miamisburg *(G-11104)*

3674 Semiconductors and related devices

Ceso Inc .... E 937 435-8584
   Miamisburg *(G-11035)*
Leidos Inc .... D 937 656-8433
   Beavercreek *(G-886)*
Micro Industries Corporation .... D 740 548-7878
   Westerville *(G-14999)*
▲ Pepperl + Fuchs Inc .... C 330 425-3555
   Twinsburg *(G-14210)*

3676 Electronic resistors

Apex Control Systems Inc .... D 330 938-2588
   Sebring *(G-12945)*

3677 Electronic coils and transformers

Electric Service Co Inc .... E 513 271-6387
   Cincinnati *(G-2610)*
Schneider Electric Usa Inc .... B 513 523-4171
   Oxford *(G-12217)*

3678 Electronic connectors

Powell Electrical Systems Inc .... D 330 966-1750
   North Canton *(G-11853)*

3679 Electronic components, nec

Aeroseal LLC .... E 937 428-9300
   Dayton *(G-7158)*
▲ Aeroseal LLC .... E 937 428-9300
   Miamisburg *(G-11021)*

SIC SECTION

37 TRANSPORTATION EQUIPMENT

▲ Channel Products Inc .... D 440 423-0113
Solon *(G-13075)*

Leidos Inc .... D 937 656-8433
Beavercreek *(G-886)*

Microplex Inc .... E 330 498-0600
North Canton *(G-11848)*

Mjo Industries Inc .... D 800 590-4055
Huber Heights *(G-9325)*

▲ Nimers & Woody II Inc .... C 937 454-0722
Vandalia *(G-14386)*

Projects Unlimited Inc .... C 937 918-2200
Dayton *(G-7571)*

Ra Consultants LLC .... E 513 469-6600
Blue Ash *(G-1229)*

TL Industries Inc .... C 419 666-8144
Perrysburg *(G-12377)*

Vertiv JV Holdings LLC .... A 614 888-0246
Columbus *(G-6846)*

3694 Engine electrical equipment

Electra Sound Inc .... D 216 433-9600
Avon Lake *(G-678)*

Power Acquisition LLC .... D 614 228-5000
Dublin *(G-8093)*

▲ Tri-W Group Inc .... A 614 228-5000
Columbus *(G-6786)*

W W Williams Company LLC .... D 614 228-5000
Dublin *(G-8158)*

3699 Electrical equipment and supplies, nec

▲ Agratronix LLC .... E 330 562-2222
Streetsboro *(G-13409)*

Akron Brass Holding Corp .... E 330 264-5678
Wooster *(G-15307)*

Allen Fields Assoc Inc .... E 513 228-1010
Lebanon *(G-9753)*

Ci Disposition Co .... D 216 587-5200
Brooklyn Heights *(G-1414)*

Circle Prime Manufacturing .... E 330 923-0019
Cuyahoga Falls *(G-7054)*

Commercial Electric Pdts Corp ...... E 216 241-2886
Cleveland *(G-4094)*

◆ GMI Holdings Inc .... B 800 354-3643
Mount Hope *(G-11466)*

Hannon Company .... D 330 456-4728
Canton *(G-1770)*

Kiemle-Hankins Company .... E 419 661-2430
Perrysburg *(G-12349)*

▼ Matlock Electric Co Inc .... E 513 731-9600
Cincinnati *(G-3015)*

Momentum Fleet MGT Group Inc .. D 440 759-2219
Westlake *(G-15080)*

▲ Nimers & Woody II Inc .... C 937 454-0722
Vandalia *(G-14386)*

◆ Philips Med Systems Clvland In .... B 440 483-3000
Cleveland *(G-4746)*

Powell Electrical Systems Inc .... D 330 966-1750
North Canton *(G-11853)*

▼ Riverside Drives Inc .... E 216 362-1211
Cleveland *(G-4844)*

Schneider Electric Usa Inc .... B 513 523-4171
Oxford *(G-12217)*

37 TRANSPORTATION EQUIPMENT

3711 Motor vehicles and car bodies

Falls Stamping & Welding Co .... C 330 928-1191
Cuyahoga Falls *(G-7075)*

Honda Dev & Mfg Amer LLC .... C 937 644-0724
Marysville *(G-10488)*

▼ Sutphen Corporation .... C 800 726-7030
Dublin *(G-8136)*

3713 Truck and bus bodies

ARE Inc .... A 330 830-7800
Massillon *(G-10631)*

Brown Industrial Inc .... E 937 693-3838
Botkins *(G-1299)*

Cipted Corp .... D 412 829-2120
Monroe *(G-11336)*

Crane Carrier Company LLC .... C 918 286-2889
New Philadelphia *(G-11647)*

Crane Carrier Holdings LLC .... C 918 286-2889
New Philadelphia *(G-11648)*

Hendrickson International Corp ..... D 740 929-5600
Hebron *(G-9143)*

▲ Joseph Industries Inc .... D 330 528-0091
Streetsboro *(G-13419)*

◆ Kaffenbarger Truck Eqp Co .... C 937 845-3804
New Carlisle *(G-11602)*

▼ QT Equipment Company .... E 330 724-3055
Akron *(G-275)*

Sutphen Towers Inc .... D 614 876-1262
Hilliard *(G-9234)*

◆ Venco Venturo Industries LLC ..... E 513 772-8448
Cincinnati *(G-3619)*

3714 Motor vehicle parts and accessories

◆ Accel Performance Group LLC ..... C 216 658-6413
Independence *(G-9394)*

◆ Adelmans Truck Parts Corp .... E 330 456-0206
Canton *(G-1655)*

Amsted Industries Incorporated ..... D 614 836-2323
Groveport *(G-8969)*

ARE Inc .... A 330 830-7800
Massillon *(G-10631)*

◆ Bendix Coml Vhcl Systems LLC ... B 440 329-9000
Avon *(G-640)*

◆ Buyers Products Company .... C 440 974-8888
Mentor *(G-10915)*

Doran Mfg LLC .... D 866 816-7233
Blue Ash *(G-1163)*

◆ Emssons Faurecia Ctrl Systems ... C 812 341-2000
Toledo *(G-13792)*

Falls Stamping & Welding Co .... C 330 928-1191
Cuyahoga Falls *(G-7075)*

Hendrickson International Corp ..... D 740 929-5600
Hebron *(G-9143)*

Hi-Tek Manufacturing Inc .... C 513 459-1094
Mason *(G-10562)*

◆ Industry Products Co .... B 937 778-0585
Piqua *(G-12445)*

◆ Interstate Diesel Service Inc .... C 216 881-0015
Cleveland *(G-4420)*

▲ Joseph Industries Inc .... D 330 528-0091
Streetsboro *(G-13419)*

Keystone Auto Glass Inc .... D 419 509-0497
Maumee *(G-10736)*

▲ Leadec Corp .... E 513 731-3590
Blue Ash *(G-1200)*

Lucas Sumitomo Brakes Inc .... E 513 934-0024
Lebanon *(G-9776)*

◆ Mahle Behr Mt Sterling Inc .... B 740 869-3333
Mount Sterling *(G-11474)*

◆ Maval Industries LLC .... C 330 405-1600
Twinsburg *(G-14203)*

◆ Noco Company .... D 216 464-8131
Solon *(G-13119)*

◆ Pioneer Automotive Tech Inc .... C 937 746-2293
Miamisburg *(G-11084)*

Qualitor Subsidiary H Inc .... C 419 562-7987
Bucyrus *(G-1517)*

▲ Remington Steel Inc .... D 937 322-2414
Springfield *(G-13284)*

▲ Thyssenkrupp Bilstein Amer Inc ... C 513 881-7600
Hamilton *(G-9086)*

Toledo Molding & Die LLC .... D 419 692-6022
Delphos *(G-7846)*

◆ Trico Products Corporation .... C 248 371-1700
Cleveland *(G-5038)*

▲ TS Trim Industries Inc .... B 614 837-4114
Canal Winchester *(G-1618)*

Unison Industries LLC .... B 904 667-9904
Dayton *(G-7143)*

US Tsubaki Power Transm LLC ..... C 419 626-4560
Sandusky *(G-12939)*

▲ Venco Venturo Industries LLC ..... E 513 772-8448
Cincinnati *(G-3619)*

Westfield Steel Inc .... D 937 322-2414
Springfield *(G-13312)*

3715 Truck trailers

▼ East Manufacturing Corporation .... B 330 325-9921
Randolph *(G-12618)*

Mac Manufacturing Inc .... C 330 829-1680
Salem *(G-12846)*

▲ Mac Manufacturing Inc .... A 330 823-9900
Alliance *(G-390)*

◆ Mac Trailer Manufacturing Inc ..... A 800 795-8454
Alliance *(G-391)*

▼ Nelson Manufacturing Company ... D 419 523-5321
Ottawa *(G-12189)*

3724 Aircraft engines and engine parts

At Holdings Corporation .... A 216 692-6000
Cleveland *(G-3837)*

◆ Dreison International Inc .... C 216 362-0755
Cleveland *(G-4184)*

▲ Hi-Tek Manufacturing Inc .... C 513 459-1094
Mason *(G-10562)*

▲ Miba Bearings US LLC .... B 740 962-4242
Mcconnelsville *(G-10803)*

Pas Technologies Inc .... D 937 840-1053
Hillsboro *(G-9266)*

3728 Aircraft parts and equipment, nec

▲ Apph Wichita Inc .... E 316 943-5752
Strongsville *(G-13442)*

Arctos Mission Solutions LLC .... E 813 609-5591
Beavercreek *(G-858)*

At Holdings Corporation .... A 216 692-6000
Cleveland *(G-3837)*

Drt Holdings Inc .... D 937 298-7391
Dayton *(G-7317)*

Eaton Industrial Corporation .... C 216 692-5456
Cleveland *(G-4204)*

General Electric Company .... E 513 977-1500
Cincinnati *(G-2723)*

Lincoln Electric Automtn Inc .... B 937 295-2120
Fort Loramie *(G-8605)*

Starwin Industries LLC .... E 937 293-8568
Dayton *(G-7639)*

Transdigm Group Incorporated ...... B 216 706-2960
Cleveland *(G-5031)*

Unison Industries LLC .... B 904 667-9904
Dayton *(G-7143)*

3731 Shipbuilding and repairing

Great Lakes Group .... C 216 621-4854
Cleveland *(G-4329)*

McGinnis Inc .... C 740 377-4391
South Point *(G-13178)*

McNational Inc .... D 740 377-4391
South Point *(G-13179)*

37 TRANSPORTATION EQUIPMENT

◆ Pinney Dock & Transport LLC..............D 440 964-7186
   Ashtabula *(G-546)*

Superior Marine Ways Inc........................C 740 894-6224
   Proctorville *(G-12613)*

The Great Lakes Towing Company........D 216 621-4854
   Cleveland *(G-5000)*

3732 Boatbuilding and repairing

Don Wartko Construction Co...................D 330 673-5252
   Kent *(G-9572)*

3743 Railroad equipment

Amsted Industries Incorporated..............D 614 836-2323
   Groveport *(G-8969)*

◆ Buck Equipment Inc..............................E 614 539-3039
   Grove City *(G-8901)*

▼ Jk-Co LLC..E 419 422-5240
   Findlay *(G-8552)*

Johnson Bros Rubber Co Inc..................E 419 752-4814
   Greenwich *(G-8892)*

3751 Motorcycles, bicycles, and parts

◆ Dco LLC..E 419 931-9086
   Perrysburg *(G-12331)*

▲ Ktm North America Inc........................D 855 215-6360
   Amherst *(G-430)*

3761 Guided missiles and space vehicles

Starwin Industries LLC............................E 937 293-8568
   Dayton *(G-7639)*

3769 Space vehicle equipment, nec

Curtiss-Wright Controls...........................E 937 252-5001
   Fairborn *(G-8371)*

General Electric Company.......................E 513 977-1500
   Cincinnati *(G-2723)*

Grimes Aerospace Company..................D 937 484-2001
   Urbana *(G-14308)*

Sunpower Inc...D 740 594-2221
   Athens *(G-592)*

3792 Travel trailers and campers

ARE Inc..A 330 830-7800
   Massillon *(G-10631)*

3795 Tanks and tank components

Integris Composites Inc..........................D 740 928-0326
   Hebron *(G-9144)*

3799 Transportation equipment, nec

◆ Wholecycle Inc......................................E 330 929-8123
   Peninsula *(G-12296)*

38 MEASURING, PHOTOGRAPHIC, MEDICAL, & OPTICAL GOODS, & CLOCKS

3812 Search and navigation equipment

Cedar Elec Holdings Corp.......................D 773 804-6288
   West Chester *(G-14662)*

Circle Prime Manufacturing....................E 330 923-0019
   Cuyahoga Falls *(G-7054)*

General Electric Company......................A 617 443-3000
   Cincinnati *(G-2725)*

Genpact LLC...E 513 763-7660
   Cincinnati *(G-2729)*

Grimes Aerospace Company..................D 937 484-2001
   Urbana *(G-14308)*

Mrl Materials Resources LLC..................E 937 531-6657
   Xenia *(G-15528)*

Northrop Grmman Tchncal Svcs I..........D 937 320-3100
   Beavercreek Township *(G-945)*

Quasonix Inc..E 513 942-1287
   West Chester *(G-14751)*

3821 Laboratory apparatus and furniture

Cellular Technology Limited....................E 216 791-5084
   Shaker Heights *(G-12975)*

Dentronix Inc...D 330 916-7300
   Cuyahoga Falls *(G-7070)*

▲ Gilson Company Inc............................E 740 548-7298
   Lewis Center *(G-9823)*

Health Aid of Ohio Inc............................E 216 252-3900
   Cleveland *(G-4353)*

Ies Systems Inc.......................................E 330 533-6683
   Canfield *(G-1632)*

◆ Mettler-Toledo LLC...............................A 614 438-4511
   Columbus *(G-5270)*

◆ Philips Med Systems Clvland In..........B 440 483-3000
   Cleveland *(G-4746)*

Teledyne Instruments Inc.......................E 513 229-7000
   Mason *(G-10614)*

3822 Environmental controls

▲ Alan Manufacturing Inc.......................E 330 262-1555
   Wooster *(G-15308)*

◆ Babcock & Wilcox Company................A 330 753-4511
   Akron *(G-59)*

Cincinnati Air Conditioning Co................D 513 721-5622
   Cincinnati *(G-2392)*

Evokes LLC...E 513 947-8433
   Mason *(G-10545)*

▼ Hunter Defense Tech Inc.....................E 216 438-6111
   Solon *(G-13096)*

Melink Corporation..................................D 513 685-0958
   Milford *(G-11242)*

▲ Pepperl + Fuchs Inc............................C 330 425-3555
   Twinsburg *(G-14210)*

3823 Process control instruments

▲ Airmate Co Inc.....................................D 419 636-3184
   Bryan *(G-1478)*

◆ Alpha Technologies Svcs LLC.............D 330 745-1641
   Hudson *(G-9331)*

Cleveland Electric Labs Co.....................E 800 447-2207
   Twinsburg *(G-14177)*

Command Alkon Incorporated................E 614 799-0600
   Dublin *(G-7967)*

Innovative Controls Corp........................E 419 691-6684
   Toledo *(G-13863)*

▲ Keithley Instruments LLC...................C 440 248-0400
   Solon *(G-13103)*

◆ Mettler-Toledo LLC..............................A 614 438-4511
   Columbus *(G-5270)*

Schneider Electric Usa Inc......................D 513 777-4445
   West Chester *(G-14761)*

Stock Fairfield Corporation.....................C 440 543-6000
   Solon *(G-13149)*

Trane Technologies Company LLC........E 419 633-6800
   Bryan *(G-1494)*

3824 Fluid meters and counting devices

Aclara Technologies LLC........................C 440 528-7200
   Solon *(G-13061)*

Commercial Electric Pdts Corp...............E 216 241-2886
   Cleveland *(G-4094)*

3825 Instruments to measure electricity

Aclara Technologies LLC........................C 440 528-7200
   Solon *(G-13061)*

▲ Adams Elevator Equipment Co...........D 847 581-2900
   Holland *(G-9276)*

Bionix Safety Technologies Ltd...............E 419 727-0552
   Maumee *(G-10702)*

Dewesoft LLC..D 855 339-3669
   Whitehouse *(G-15140)*

Drs Signal Technologies Inc...................E 937 429-7470
   Beavercreek *(G-878)*

Hannon Company....................................D 330 456-4728
   Canton *(G-1770)*

Hughes Corporation................................E 440 238-2550
   Strongsville *(G-13463)*

▲ Keithley Instruments LLC...................C 440 248-0400
   Solon *(G-13103)*

Nu-Di Products Co Inc............................D 216 251-9070
   Cleveland *(G-4672)*

▼ Orton Edward Jr Crmic Fndation.........E 614 895-2663
   Westerville *(G-14926)*

Resonant Sciences LLC..........................E 937 431-8180
   Beavercreek *(G-929)*

▲ Vmetro Inc..D 281 584-0728
   Fairborn *(G-8386)*

◆ Westerman Inc......................................C 800 338-8265
   Bremen *(G-1372)*

3826 Analytical instruments

Bionix Safety Technologies Ltd...............E 419 727-0552
   Maumee *(G-10702)*

Dentronix Inc...D 330 916-7300
   Cuyahoga Falls *(G-7070)*

◆ Mettler-Toledo LLC..............................A 614 438-4511
   Columbus *(G-5270)*

▼ Orton Edward Jr Crmic Fndation.........E 614 895-2663
   Westerville *(G-14926)*

Teledyne Instruments Inc.......................E 513 229-7000
   Mason *(G-10614)*

3827 Optical instruments and lenses

▲ Volk Optical Inc....................................D 440 942-6161
   Mentor *(G-11010)*

3829 Measuring and controlling devices, nec

Aclara Technologies LLC........................C 440 528-7200
   Solon *(G-13061)*

Bionix Safety Technologies Ltd...............E 419 727-0552
   Maumee *(G-10702)*

▲ Gilson Company Inc............................E 740 548-7298
   Lewis Center *(G-9823)*

◆ Kinetics Noise Control Inc...................C 614 889-0480
   Dublin *(G-8049)*

Matrix Research Inc................................D 937 427-8433
   Beavercreek *(G-927)*

◆ Multilink Inc..C 440 366-6966
   Elyria *(G-8276)*

Smithers Group Inc.................................D 330 833-8548
   Massillon *(G-10671)*

Super Systems Inc..................................E 513 772-0060
   Cincinnati *(G-3428)*

Tegam Inc..E 440 466-6100
   Geneva *(G-8789)*

Teledyne Instruments Inc.......................E 513 229-7000
   Mason *(G-10614)*

3841 Surgical and medical instruments

Abbott Laboratories.................................D 847 937-6100
   Columbus *(G-5294)*

Applied Medical Technology Inc.............E 440 717-4000
   Brecksville *(G-1343)*

Beam Technologies Inc..........................B 800 648-1179
   Columbus *(G-5428)*

▲ Casco Mfg Solutions Inc.....................D 513 681-0003
   Cincinnati *(G-2318)*

Dentronix Inc...D 330 916-7300
   Cuyahoga Falls *(G-7070)*

SIC SECTION — 40 RAILROAD TRANSPORTATION

▲ Ethicon Endo-Surgery Inc.................. A 513 337-7000
   Blue Ash *(G-1170)*
◆ General Data Company Inc.................. B 513 752-7978
   Cincinnati *(G-2105)*
▲ Haag-Streit Usa Inc.......................... D 513 398-3937
   Mason *(G-10559)*
▲ KMC Holdings LLC............................. C 419 238-2442
   Van Wert *(G-14347)*
▲ Mill-Rose Company............................ C 440 255-9171
   Mentor *(G-10975)*
Morris Technologies Inc........................ E 513 733-1611
   Cincinnati *(G-3080)*
Nelson Labs Fairfield Inc...................... E 973 227-6882
   Broadview Heights *(G-1393)*
Thermo Fisher Scientific Inc................. E 800 871-8909
   Oakwood Village *(G-12059)*

3842 Surgical appliances and supplies

▲ Acor Orthopaedic LLC........................ E 216 662-4500
   Cleveland *(G-3764)*
Beiersdorf Inc...................................... C 513 682-7300
   West Chester *(G-14800)*
◆ Cardinal Health Inc........................... A 614 757-5000
   Dublin *(G-7950)*
Dentronix Inc...................................... D 330 916-7300
   Cuyahoga Falls *(G-7070)*
◆ Ferno-Washington Inc...................... C 877 733-0911
   Wilmington *(G-15252)*
Jones Metal Products Company........... E 740 545-6341
   West Lafayette *(G-14857)*
▲ Julius Zorn Inc.................................. D 330 923-4999
   Cuyahoga Falls *(G-7083)*
Lion First Responder Ppe Inc............... D 937 898-1949
   Dayton *(G-7456)*
Novagard Solutions Inc....................... C 216 881-8111
   Cleveland *(G-4668)*
◆ Philips Med Systems Clvland In......... B 440 483-3000
   Cleveland *(G-4746)*
Stable Step LLC.................................. C 800 491-1571
   Wadsworth *(G-14452)*
▲ Wcm Holdings Inc............................. C 513 705-2100
   Cincinnati *(G-3643)*
▲ West Chester Holdings LLC.............. C 513 705-2100
   Cincinnati *(G-3655)*

3843 Dental equipment and supplies

◆ Boxout LLC.. C 833 462-7746
   Hudson *(G-9334)*
Dental Ceramics Inc............................ E 330 523-5240
   Richfield *(G-12694)*
Dentronix Inc...................................... D 330 916-7300
   Cuyahoga Falls *(G-7070)*
United Dental Laboratories................. E 330 253-1810
   Tallmadge *(G-13609)*

3844 X-ray apparatus and tubes

Metro Design Inc................................. E 440 458-4200
   Elyria *(G-8274)*
◆ Philips Med Systems Clvland In......... B 440 483-3000
   Cleveland *(G-4746)*

3845 Electromedical equipment

▲ Viewray Inc....................................... D 440 703-3210
   Oakwood Village *(G-12060)*

3851 Ophthalmic goods

Diversified Ophthalmics Inc................. E 803 783-3454
   Cincinnati *(G-2570)*
Essilor Laboratories Amer Inc............. E 614 274-0840
   Columbus *(G-5831)*
Steiner Eoptics Inc............................. D 937 426-2341
   Miamisburg *(G-11095)*

▲ Volk Optical Inc................................. D 440 942-6161
   Mentor *(G-11010)*

3861 Photographic equipment and supplies

▲ American Frame Corporation............. D 419 893-5595
   Maumee *(G-10690)*

3873 Watches, clocks, watchcases, and parts

Sgi Matrix LLC.................................... D 937 438-9033
   Miamisburg *(G-11092)*

39 MISCELLANEOUS MANUFACTURING INDUSTRIES

3911 Jewelry, precious metal

◆ Associated Premium Corporation....... E 513 679-4444
   Cincinnati *(G-2219)*
Marfo Company................................... D 614 276-3352
   Columbus *(G-6197)*

3931 Musical instruments

Belco Works Inc.................................. D 740 695-0500
   Saint Clairsville *(G-12774)*
▲ Jatiga Inc.. D 859 817-7100
   Blue Ash *(G-1191)*

3944 Games, toys, and children's vehicles

▲ AW Faber-Castell Usa Inc................. D 216 643-4660
   Independence *(G-9408)*
Container Graphics Corp..................... E 419 531-5133
   Toledo *(G-13760)*

3949 Sporting and athletic goods, nec

▲ Golf Galaxy Golfworks Inc.................. C 740 328-4193
   Newark *(G-11702)*
▲ Litehouse Products LLC.................... E 440 638-2350
   Strongsville *(G-13471)*
▲ Zebec of North America Inc.............. E 513 829-5533
   Fairfield *(G-8455)*

3953 Marking devices

System Seals Inc................................ E 216 220-1800
   Brecksville *(G-1369)*

3955 Carbon paper and inked ribbons

◆ Pubco Corporation............................. E 216 881-5300
   Cleveland *(G-4797)*

3965 Fasteners, buttons, needles, and pins

▲ Midwest Motor Supply Co.................. C 800 233-1294
   Columbus *(G-6244)*

3991 Brooms and brushes

Ekco Cleaning Inc............................... C 513 733-8882
   Cincinnati *(G-2608)*
▲ Mill Rose Laboratories Inc................. E 440 974-6730
   Mentor *(G-10974)*
▲ Mill-Rose Company............................ C 440 255-9171
   Mentor *(G-10975)*
▲ Stephen M Trudick............................ E 440 834-1891
   Burton *(G-1533)*

3993 Signs and advertising specialties

A & A Safety Inc................................. E 513 943-6100
   Amelia *(G-409)*
Archer Corporation............................. D 330 455-9995
   Canton *(G-1670)*
◆ Associated Premium Corporation....... E 513 679-4444
   Cincinnati *(G-2219)*
Bates Metal Products Inc................... D 740 498-8371
   Port Washington *(G-12541)*

Belco Works Inc.................................. D 740 695-0500
   Saint Clairsville *(G-12774)*
Benchmark Craftsman Inc................... E 866 313-4700
   Seville *(G-12963)*
Brilliant Electric Sign Co Ltd................ D 216 741-3800
   Brooklyn Heights *(G-1413)*
Brown Cnty Bd Mntal Rtardation........ E 937 378-4891
   Georgetown *(G-8798)*
Danite Holdings Ltd............................ E 614 444-3333
   Columbus *(G-5740)*
Gus Holthaus Signs Inc...................... E 513 861-0060
   Cincinnati *(G-2783)*
HP Manufacturing Company Inc.......... D 216 361-6500
   Cleveland *(G-4386)*
Identitek Systems Inc......................... D 330 832-9844
   Massillon *(G-10648)*
Kessler Sign Company........................ E 740 453-0668
   Zanesville *(G-15805)*
Mes Painting and Graphics Ltd........... E 614 496-1696
   Westerville *(G-14998)*
Orange Barrel Media LLC.................... E 614 294-4898
   Columbus *(G-6477)*
Paul Peterson Safety Div Inc.............. E 614 486-4375
   Columbus *(G-6505)*
▲ Sabco Industries Inc......................... E 419 531-5347
   Toledo *(G-14002)*
Screen Works Inc............................... E 937 264-9111
   Dayton *(G-7613)*
United - Maier Signs Inc..................... D 513 681-6600
   Cincinnati *(G-3551)*

3999 Manufacturing industries, nec

◆ Aluminum Line Products Company..... D 440 835-8880
   Westlake *(G-15032)*
Automtve Rfnish Clor Sltons I............. E 330 461-6067
   Medina *(G-10810)*
Clarity Retail Services LLC................. D 513 800-9369
   West Chester *(G-14668)*
◆ Downing Enterprises Inc.................... D 330 666-3888
   Copley *(G-6956)*
◆ Gayston Corporation......................... C 937 743-6050
   Miamisburg *(G-11057)*
Gorant Chocolatier LLC....................... C 330 726-8821
   Boardman *(G-1288)*
◆ Heading4ward Investment Co............ D 937 293-9994
   Moraine *(G-11416)*
Janson Industries............................... D 330 455-7029
   Canton *(G-1783)*
◆ Mace Personal Def & SEC Inc............ E 440 424-5321
   Cleveland *(G-4514)*
Morris Technologies Inc...................... E 513 733-1611
   Cincinnati *(G-3080)*
RB Sigma LLC..................................... D 440 290-0577
   Mentor *(G-10988)*
▲ Twin Sisters Productions LLC............ E 330 631-0361
   Stow *(G-13399)*

40 RAILROAD TRANSPORTATION

4011 Railroads, line-haul operating

Cliffs Resources Inc............................ C 216 694-5700
   Cleveland *(G-4080)*
Columbus & Ohio River RR Co............. E 740 622-8092
   Coshocton *(G-6979)*
CSX Transportation Inc...................... D 740 362-7924
   Delaware *(G-7792)*
CSX Transportation Inc...................... C 440 245-3930
   Lorain *(G-10070)*
Indiana & Ohio Rail Corp.................... E 513 860-1000
   Cincinnati *(G-2867)*
Nimishillen & Tuscarawas LLC............ D 330 438-5821
   Canton *(G-1820)*

40 RAILROAD TRANSPORTATION

Norfolk Southern Corporation............ D 440 992-2238
  Ashtabula *(G-542)*
Norfolk Southern Corporation............ E 937 472-0067
  Eaton *(G-8217)*
Norfolk Southern Railway Co............. D 440 439-1827
  Bedford *(G-975)*
Norfolk Southern Railway Co............. C 614 771-2183
  Columbus *(G-6362)*
Republic N&T Railroad Inc................. E 330 438-5826
  Canton *(G-1844)*
U S Rail Corporation of Ohio.............. E 419 720-7588
  Toledo *(G-14079)*
Wheeling & Lake Erie Rlwy Co........... B 330 767-3401
  Brewster *(G-1374)*

4013 Switching and terminal services

Road & Rail Services Inc................... D 502 365-5361
  Fostoria *(G-8624)*

41 LOCAL & SUBURBAN TRANSIT & INTERURBAN HIGHWAY TRANSPORTATION

4111 Local and suburban transit

Anthony Wayne Local Schools........... E 419 877-0451
  Whitehouse *(G-15137)*
Butler Cnty Rgional Trnst Auth........... C 513 785-5237
  Hamilton *(G-9024)*
Central Ohio Transit Authority............ E 614 275-5800
  Columbus *(G-5545)*
Central Ohio Transit Authority............ E 614 228-1776
  Columbus *(G-5547)*
Central Ohio Transit Authority............ E 614 275-5800
  Columbus *(G-5548)*
Central Ohio Transit Authority............ A 614 275-5800
  Columbus *(G-5546)*
Champaign Transit System................ C 937 653-8777
  Urbana *(G-14302)*
City of North Olmsted......................... E 440 777-8000
  North Olmsted *(G-11894)*
Columbus City School District............ E 614 365-6542
  Columbus *(G-5623)*
Creekside Cargo Inc.......................... E 216 688-1770
  Cleveland *(G-4137)*
First Group Investment Partnr............ D 513 241-2200
  Cincinnati *(G-2674)*
First Transit Inc................................... D 440 834-1020
  Burton *(G-1527)*
First Transit Inc................................... D 440 365-0224
  Elyria *(G-8251)*
First Transit Inc................................... D 513 524-2877
  Oxford *(G-12208)*
First Transit Inc................................... D 937 652-4175
  Urbana *(G-14307)*
First Transit Inc................................... C 937 374-6402
  Xenia *(G-15507)*
Firstgroup America Inc....................... A 513 241-2200
  Cincinnati *(G-2686)*
Firstgroup America Inc....................... B 937 372-3876
  Xenia *(G-15508)*
Firstgroup America Inc....................... D 513 241-2200
  Cincinnati *(G-2684)*
Firstgroup Usa Inc.............................. B 513 241-2200
  Cincinnati *(G-2687)*
Greater Cleveland Regional............... A 216 575-3932
  Cleveland *(G-4333)*
Greater Cleveland Regiona................ B 216 566-5100
  Cleveland *(G-4334)*
Greater Clvland Rgnal Trnst Au.......... A 216 781-1110
  Cleveland *(G-4335)*

Greater Clvland Rgnal Trnst Au.......... A 216 566-5107
  Cleveland *(G-4336)*
Greater Dyton Rgnal Trnst Auth......... A 937 425-8400
  Dayton *(G-7387)*
Greater Dyton Rgnal Trnst Auth......... D 937 425-8310
  Dayton *(G-7386)*
Ironton Lwrnce Cnty Area Cmnty....... B 740 532-3534
  Ironton *(G-9508)*
Laidlaw Transit Services Inc............... E 513 241-2200
  Cincinnati *(G-2964)*
Laketran... D 440 350-1000
  Painesville *(G-12235)*
Metro Regional Transit Auth............... C 330 762-0341
  Akron *(G-230)*
Metro Regional Transit Auth............... C 330 762-0341
  Akron *(G-229)*
Mv Transportation Inc......................... B 740 681-5086
  Cincinnati *(G-3094)*
Mv Transportation Inc......................... C 419 627-0740
  Sandusky *(G-12917)*
Norfolk Southern Railway Co............. C 855 667-3655
  East Palestine *(G-8197)*
Pickaway Cnty Cmnty Action Org...... E 740 477-1655
  Circleville *(G-3716)*
Portage Area Rgonal Trnsp Auth....... D 330 678-1287
  Kent *(G-9591)*
Rapid Transit Line............................... E 216 621-9500
  Cleveland *(G-4808)*
Southwest Ohio Rgnal Trnst Aut........ A 513 632-7511
  Cincinnati *(G-3394)*
Southwest Ohio Rgnal Trnst Aut........ D 513 621-4455
  Cincinnati *(G-3393)*
Stark Area Regional Trnst Auth.......... C 330 477-2782
  Canton *(G-1857)*
Toledo Area Rgional Trnst Auth......... B 419 243-7433
  Toledo *(G-14050)*
United Scoto Senior Activities............ E 740 354-6672
  Portsmouth *(G-12579)*
Universal Transportation Syste.......... C 513 829-1287
  Fairfield *(G-8450)*
Western Reserve Transit Auth........... D 330 744-8431
  Youngstown *(G-15752)*

4119 Local passenger transportation, nec

A Blessed Path Inc............................. D 330 244-0657
  Canton *(G-1651)*
Allure Scents LLC.............................. E 330 312-2019
  Canton *(G-1661)*
American Ambulette & Ambu............. A 937 237-1105
  Portsmouth *(G-12544)*
American Livery Service Inc............... E 216 221-9330
  Cleveland *(G-3802)*
Apex Transit Solutions LLC............... E 216 938-5606
  Cleveland *(G-3819)*
Bkp Ambulance District...................... E 419 674-4574
  Kenton *(G-9610)*
Bradford Fire Rescue Svcs Inc........... E 937 448-2686
  Bradford *(G-1340)*
Capital Transportation Inc.................. C 614 258-0400
  Columbus *(G-5501)*
Catholic Chrties of Sthwstern............. D 513 241-7745
  Cincinnati *(G-2323)*
Cems of Ohio Inc................................ B 614 751-6651
  Columbus *(G-5526)*
City of Cleveland................................. E 216 664-2555
  Cleveland *(G-3981)*
City of Cleveland................................. E 216 664-2555
  Cleveland *(G-3982)*
Cloverleaf Transport Co..................... D 419 599-5015
  Napoleon *(G-11519)*
Coloma Emergency Ambulance Inc.. D 269 343-2224
  Huntsville *(G-9383)*

SIC SECTION

Community Ambulance Service......... C 740 454-6800
  Zanesville *(G-15784)*
Community Care Amblance Netwrk... D 440 992-1401
  Ashtabula *(G-527)*
Connect Trnsp Svcs LLC................... E 740 656-5042
  Chillicothe *(G-2061)*
Coshocton Cnty Emrgncy Med Svc.. C 740 622-4294
  Coshocton *(G-6980)*
County of Carroll................................. E 330 627-1900
  Carrollton *(G-1905)*
County of Lorain.................................. E 440 647-5803
  Wellington *(G-14630)*
County of Meigs.................................. E 740 992-6617
  Pomeroy *(G-12513)*
Courtesy Ambulance Inc.................... D 740 522-8588
  Newark *(G-11697)*
Direct Expediting Llc.......................... E 877 880-3400
  Mason *(G-10544)*
Donald Mrtens Sons Amblnce Svc.... D 216 265-4211
  Cleveland *(G-4176)*
East Inc... E 330 609-1339
  Vienna *(G-14419)*
Ems Team LLC.................................. E 800 735-8190
  Dayton *(G-7335)*
Eric Boeppler Fmly Ltd Partnr............ D 513 860-3324
  Fairfield *(G-8412)*
Fairborn City School District............... E 937 878-1772
  Fairborn *(G-8375)*
First Care Ohio LLC........................... D 513 563-8811
  Cincinnati *(G-2670)*
Firstgroup America Inc....................... A 513 241-2200
  Cincinnati *(G-2686)*
Firstgroup America Inc....................... D 513 241-2200
  Cincinnati *(G-2684)*
Fisher - Titus Affiliated Svcs............... B 419 663-1367
  Milan *(G-11205)*
Guernsey Health Systems.................. A 740 439-3561
  Cambridge *(G-1573)*
Hanco Ambulance Inc........................ E 419 423-2912
  Findlay *(G-8540)*
Henderson Rd Rest Systems Inc....... E 614 442-3310
  Columbus *(G-5984)*
Hopkins Airport Limousine Svc.......... C 216 267-8810
  Cleveland *(G-4376)*
Jk Services... E 419 843-2608
  Toledo *(G-13867)*
Lakefront Lines Inc............................. C 216 267-8810
  Brookpark *(G-1436)*
Life Ambulance Service Inc................ A 740 354-6169
  Portsmouth *(G-12562)*
Lifecare Ambulance Inc..................... E 440 323-2527
  Elyria *(G-8269)*
Lifefleet LLC....................................... E 330 549-9716
  North Lima *(G-11892)*
Lifestar Ambulance Inc...................... E 419 245-6210
  Toledo *(G-13889)*
Lynx Ems LLC.................................... E 513 530-1600
  Blue Ash *(G-1205)*
Med-Trans Inc..................................... D 937 325-4926
  Springfield *(G-13267)*
Meda-Care Transportation Inc........... E 513 521-4799
  Cincinnati *(G-3026)*
Medcorp Inc.. C 419 425-9700
  Findlay *(G-8566)*
Medic Rspnse Ambulance Svc Inc.... E 419 522-1998
  Mansfield *(G-10295)*
Medical Transport Systems Inc.......... E 330 837-9818
  North Canton *(G-11847)*
Medpro LLC.. D 937 336-5586
  Eaton *(G-8215)*
Metrohealth System............................ B 216 957-4000
  Cleveland *(G-4561)*

SIC SECTION

42 MOTOR FREIGHT TRANSPORTATION

Metrohealth System............................... C 216 778-3867
   Cleveland *(G-4567)*

Mt Orab Fire Department Inc................. E 937 444-3945
   Mount Orab *(G-11472)*

North Central Area Transit..................... E 419 937-2428
   Tiffin *(G-13635)*

North Star Critical Care LLC................... E 330 386-9110
   East Liverpool *(G-8188)*

Ohio Medical Trnsp Inc.......................... D 614 791-4400
   Columbus *(G-6437)*

Pace Drivers Inc..................................... D 216 377-6831
   Willoughby *(G-15217)*

Partners In Prime................................... E 513 867-1998
   Hamilton *(G-9071)*

Petermann Ltd.. C 740 967-7533
   Johnstown *(G-9548)*

Petermann Ltd.. E 513 351-7383
   Cincinnati *(G-3200)*

Physicians Ambulance Svc Inc.............. E 216 454-4911
   Brecksville *(G-1362)*

Pickaway Cnty Cmnty Action Org........... E 740 477-1655
   Circleville *(G-3716)*

Portage Path Behavorial Health............. E 330 762-6110
   Akron *(G-270)*

Precious Cargo Trnsp Inc....................... E 440 543-9272
   Newbury *(G-11763)*

Professional Transportation................... B 419 661-0576
   Walbridge *(G-14463)*

Reach Livery Taxi LLC........................... E 330 278-8080
   Youngstown *(G-15706)*

Rob Lynn Inc... E 330 773-6470
   Akron *(G-284)*

Smith Ambulance Service Inc................ E 330 825-0205
   Barberton *(G-709)*

Smith Ambulance Service Inc................ E 330 602-0050
   Dover *(G-7900)*

Spirit Medical Transport LLC................. D 937 548-2800
   Greenville *(G-8886)*

Stofcheck Ambulance Svc Inc............... E 740 499-2200
   La Rue *(G-9649)*

Superior Ar-Grund Amblnce Svc............ C 630 832-2000
   Grove City *(G-8958)*

Tri-County Ambulance Svc Inc............... E 440 951-4600
   Mentor *(G-11005)*

United Amblnce Svc of Cmbridge.......... E 740 685-2277
   Byesville *(G-1537)*

United Scoto Senior Activities................ E 740 354-6672
   Portsmouth *(G-12579)*

4121 Taxicabs

Ace Taxi Service Inc.............................. D 216 361-4700
   Cleveland *(G-3762)*

Columbus Green Cabs Inc..................... E 614 783-3663
   Columbus *(G-5634)*

Pickaway Cnty Cmnty Action Org........... E 740 477-1655
   Circleville *(G-3716)*

4131 Intercity and rural bus transportation

Firstgroup America Inc.......................... D 513 241-2200
   Cincinnati *(G-2684)*

Greyhound Lines Inc.............................. E 513 721-4450
   Cincinnati *(G-2776)*

Greyhound Lines Inc.............................. E 513 421-7442
   Cincinnati *(G-2777)*

Greyhound Lines Inc.............................. E 614 221-0577
   Columbus *(G-5956)*

Precious Cargo Trnsp Inc....................... E 440 543-9272
   Newbury *(G-11763)*

4141 Local bus charter service

A T V Inc.. C 614 252-5060
   Columbus *(G-5292)*

Accel Schools Ohio LLC......................... C 330 535-7728
   Akron *(G-12)*

First Student Inc.................................... E 513 241-2200
   Cincinnati *(G-2681)*

Firstgroup America Inc.......................... D 513 241-2200
   Cincinnati *(G-2684)*

Lakefront Lines Inc................................ C 216 267-8810
   Brookpark *(G-1436)*

Petermann Ltd.. E 513 351-7383
   Cincinnati *(G-3200)*

Precious Cargo Trnsp Inc....................... E 440 543-9272
   Newbury *(G-11763)*

Queen City Transportation LLC............. B 513 941-8700
   Cincinnati *(G-3268)*

S B S Transit Inc................................... E 440 288-2222
   Elyria *(G-8292)*

4142 Bus charter service, except local

Buckeye Charter Service Inc................. E 937 879-3000
   Dayton *(G-7202)*

Buckeye Charter Service Inc................. E 419 222-2455
   Lima *(G-9871)*

Croswell of Williamsburg LLC................ D 800 782-8747
   Dayton *(G-7262)*

Greyhound Lines Inc.............................. E 614 221-0577
   Columbus *(G-5956)*

Hat White Management LLC.................. C 800 525-7967
   Akron *(G-188)*

Lakefront Lines Inc................................ C 216 267-8810
   Brookpark *(G-1436)*

Pioneer Trails Inc.................................. E 330 674-1234
   Millersburg *(G-11288)*

Queen City Transportation LLC............. B 513 941-8700
   Cincinnati *(G-3268)*

S B S Transit Inc................................... E 440 288-2222
   Elyria *(G-8292)*

Starforce National Corporation.............. C 513 979-3600
   Cincinnati *(G-3412)*

Supreme Ventures LLC.......................... E 614 372-0355
   Columbus *(G-6733)*

4151 School buses

Anthony Wayne Local Schools.............. E 419 877-0451
   Whitehouse *(G-15137)*

Beachwood City Schools....................... D 216 464-6609
   Cleveland *(G-3859)*

Boardman Local Schools....................... D 330 726-3409
   Youngstown *(G-15560)*

Canton City School District.................... D 330 456-6710
   Canton *(G-1699)*

Cleveland Municipal School Dst............ D 216 634-7005
   Cleveland *(G-4062)*

Dublin City Schools............................... D 614 764-5926
   Dublin *(G-7990)*

First Group Investment Partnr............... D 513 241-2200
   Cincinnati *(G-2674)*

First Student Inc.................................... D 513 531-6888
   Cincinnati *(G-2677)*

First Student Inc.................................... E 513 761-6100
   Cincinnati *(G-2678)*

First Student Inc.................................... D 513 554-0105
   Cincinnati *(G-2679)*

First Student Inc.................................... E 513 761-5136
   Cincinnati *(G-2680)*

First Student Inc.................................... B 937 645-0201
   Dayton *(G-7354)*

First Student Inc.................................... C 440 284-8030
   Elyria *(G-8250)*

First Student Inc.................................... D 216 767-7600
   Euclid *(G-8343)*

First Student Inc.................................... D 419 382-9915
   Toledo *(G-13808)*

First Student Inc.................................... E 513 241-2200
   Cincinnati *(G-2681)*

Firstgroup America Inc.......................... A 513 419-8611
   Cincinnati *(G-2685)*

Firstgroup America Inc.......................... A 513 241-2200
   Cincinnati *(G-2686)*

Firstgroup America Inc.......................... B 937 372-3876
   Xenia *(G-15508)*

Firstgroup America Inc.......................... D 513 241-2200
   Cincinnati *(G-2684)*

Firstgroup Usa Inc................................. B 513 241-2200
   Cincinnati *(G-2687)*

Fremont City Schools............................ D 419 332-6454
   Fremont *(G-8679)*

Girard City School District..................... E 330 545-6407
   Girard *(G-8813)*

Lakota Local School District.................. E 513 777-2150
   Liberty Township *(G-9853)*

Lima City School District........................ E 419 996-3400
   Lima *(G-9919)*

Mad River Local School Dst................... E 937 237-4275
   Dayton *(G-7464)*

Mentor Exempted Vlg Schl Dst.............. D 440 974-5260
   Mentor *(G-10968)*

Miller Trnsp Bus Svc Inc........................ D 614 915-7211
   Columbus *(G-6250)*

Olmsted Falls City Bd Educatn.............. D 440 427-6350
   Olmsted Twp *(G-12092)*

Ontario Local School District................. E 419 529-3814
   Ontario *(G-12120)*

Perrysburg Board of Education.............. B 419 874-3127
   Perrysburg *(G-12362)*

Petermann Ltd.. C 330 773-4222
   Akron *(G-266)*

Petermann Ltd.. C 513 539-0324
   Monroe *(G-11349)*

Petermann Ltd.. E 513 351-7383
   Cincinnati *(G-3200)*

Petermann Northeast LLC..................... C 513 351-7383
   Cincinnati *(G-3201)*

Queen City Transportation LLC............. B 513 941-8700
   Cincinnati *(G-3268)*

S B S Transit Inc................................... E 440 288-2222
   Elyria *(G-8292)*

Streetsboro Board Education................ D 330 626-4909
   Streetsboro *(G-13429)*

Vermilion Local Schools........................ D 440 204-1700
   Vermilion *(G-14411)*

Washington Local Schools.................... E 419 473-8356
   Toledo *(G-14097)*

4173 Bus terminal and service facilities

Hans Truck and Trlr Repr Inc................ D 216 581-0046
   Cleveland *(G-4349)*

Lakota Local School District.................. E 513 777-2150
   Liberty Township *(G-9853)*

Washington Local Schools.................... E 419 473-8356
   Toledo *(G-14097)*

42 MOTOR FREIGHT TRANSPORTATION

4212 Local trucking, without storage

1st Carrier Corp..................................... E 740 477-2587
   Circleville *(G-3701)*

937 Delivers Cooperative...................... E 937 802-0709
   Dayton *(G-7148)*

A L Smith Trucking Inc.......................... E 937 526-3651
   Versailles *(G-14412)*

AG Trucking Inc..................................... E 937 497-7770
   Sidney *(G-13017)*

42 MOTOR FREIGHT TRANSPORTATION

Aim Integrated Logistics Inc .... B 330 759-0438
   Girard *(G-8808)*

Aim Leasing Company .... D 330 759-0438
   Girard *(G-8809)*

All My Sons Mvg Stor Cncnnati .... D 513 440-5924
   Cincinnati *(G-2161)*

All Trucks Inc .... E 614 800-4595
   Hilliard *(G-9176)*

American Bulk Commodities Inc .... C 330 758-0841
   Youngstown *(G-15549)*

B D Transportation Inc .... E 937 773-9280
   Piqua *(G-12435)*

Berner Trucking Inc .... C 330 343-5812
   Dover *(G-7872)*

Big Blue Trucking Inc .... E 330 372-1421
   Warren *(G-14507)*

Bob Miller Rigging Inc .... E 419 422-7477
   Findlay *(G-8518)*

Botha Trucking LLC .... D 330 695-2296
   Fredericksburg *(G-8658)*

Bowling Transportation Inc .... E 419 436-9590
   Fostoria *(G-8614)*

Brookside Holdings LLC .... E 419 925-4457
   Maria Stein *(G-10353)*

Bryan Truck Line Inc .... D 419 485-8373
   Montpelier *(G-11382)*

C & G Transportation Inc .... E 419 288-2653
   Wayne *(G-14620)*

Capitol Express Entps Inc .... D 614 279-2819
   Columbus *(G-5504)*

City Dash LLC .... C 513 562-2000
   Cincinnati *(G-2450)*

City of Akron .... E 330 375-2650
   Akron *(G-101)*

City of Dayton .... D 937 333-4860
   Dayton *(G-7230)*

CJ Logstics Holdings Amer Corp .... D 614 879-9659
   West Jefferson *(G-14849)*

Constrction Wste Hlg Prtners L .... E 614 683-0001
   Columbus *(G-5683)*

Containerport Group Inc .... E 440 333-1330
   Columbus *(G-5689)*

Continental Express Inc .... A 937 497-2100
   Sidney *(G-13024)*

Corrigan Moving Systems .... E 440 243-5860
   Cleveland *(G-4118)*

Cotter Moving & Storage Co .... E 330 535-5115
   Akron *(G-125)*

▲ Cousins Waste Control LLC .... D 419 726-1500
   Toledo *(G-13768)*

Cowen Truck Line Inc .... D 419 938-3401
   Perrysville *(G-12391)*

Cs Trucking LLC .... C 330 878-1990
   Dover *(G-7878)*

Custom Movers Services Inc .... E 330 564-0507
   Stow *(G-13362)*

D & V Trucking Inc .... E 330 482-9440
   Columbiana *(G-5233)*

◆ Daystar Transportation LLC .... E 740 852-9202
   London *(G-10041)*

Dayton Freight Lines Inc .... C 937 264-4060
   Dayton *(G-7284)*

Dayton Synchrnous Spport Ctr I .... E 937 226-1559
   Dayton *(G-7302)*

Dedicated Transport LLC .... C 216 641-2500
   Brooklyn Heights *(G-1416)*

Dill-Elam Inc .... E 513 575-0017
   Loveland *(G-10135)*

Dr Transportation Inc .... E 216 588-6110
   Cleveland *(G-4182)*

Drivers On Call LLC .... C 330 867-5193
   Norton *(G-11994)*

Dutch Maid Logistics Inc .... C 419 935-0136
   Willard *(G-15167)*

Dyno Nobel Transportation .... D 740 439-5050
   Cambridge *(G-1569)*

E & V Ventures Inc .... E 330 794-6683
   Akron *(G-143)*

Early Express Services Inc .... E 937 223-5801
   Dayton *(G-7322)*

Edora Logistics Inc .... E 937 573-9090
   Vandalia *(G-14375)*

Energy Power Services Inc .... E 330 343-2312
   New Philadelphia *(G-11650)*

Environmental Enterprises Inc .... C 513 772-2818
   Cincinnati *(G-2627)*

Expeditus Transport LLC .... E 419 464-9450
   Toledo *(G-13800)*

Fabrizi Trucking & Pav Co Inc .... D 440 234-1284
   Cleveland *(G-4233)*

Fedex Ground Package Sys Inc .... D 800 463-3339
   Grove City *(G-8919)*

Ferrous Metal Transfer Co .... E 216 671-8500
   Brooklyn *(G-1409)*

Findlay Truck Line Inc .... D 419 422-1945
   Findlay *(G-8531)*

First Group Investment Partnr .... D 513 241-2200
   Cincinnati *(G-2674)*

Firstgroup Usa Inc .... B 513 241-2200
   Cincinnati *(G-2687)*

Forrest Trucking Company .... E 614 879-8642
   West Jefferson *(G-14852)*

Fraley & Schilling Inc .... E 740 598-4118
   Brilliant *(G-1380)*

Fst Brokerage Services Inc .... D 614 529-7900
   Dublin *(G-8017)*

Fultz & Son Inc .... E 419 547-9365
   Clyde *(G-5201)*

Garner Trucking Inc .... D 419 422-5742
   Findlay *(G-8536)*

Gateway Distribution LLC .... D 888 806-8206
   Cincinnati *(G-2717)*

Glm Transport Inc .... E 419 363-2041
   Van Wert *(G-14345)*

Golden Hawk Inc .... D 419 683-3304
   Crestline *(G-7023)*

Greenwood Motor Lines Inc .... B 800 543-5589
   Wilmington *(G-15255)*

H Hafner & Sons Inc .... E 513 321-1895
   Cincinnati *(G-2786)*

Hc Transport Inc .... E 513 574-1800
   Cincinnati *(G-2807)*

Henderson Turf Farm Inc .... E 937 748-1559
   Franklin *(G-8640)*

Hirzel Transfer Co .... E 419 287-3288
   Pemberville *(G-12289)*

Home Run Inc .... E 800 543-9198
   Xenia *(G-15520)*

Hostetler Trucking Inc .... E 614 873-8885
   Plain City *(G-12482)*

Howland Logistics LLC .... E 513 469-5263
   Cincinnati *(G-2851)*

Huntley Trucking Co .... E 740 385-7615
   New Plymouth *(G-11675)*

Hyway Trucking Company .... D 419 423-7145
   Findlay *(G-8548)*

Iddings Trucking Inc .... C 740 568-1780
   Marietta *(G-10372)*

International Truck & Eng Corp .... A 937 390-4045
   Springfield *(G-13260)*

J P Jenks Inc .... D 440 428-4500
   Madison *(G-10218)*

J P Transportation Co Inc .... E 513 424-6978
   Middletown *(G-11167)*

J V Enviroserve Limited Partnership ..... E 216 642-1311
   Cleveland *(G-4427)*

J-Trac Inc .... E 419 524-3456
   Mansfield *(G-10274)*

Jackson Bluford and Son Inc .... D 513 831-6231
   Milford *(G-11234)*

Jmt Cartage Inc .... E 330 478-2430
   Canton *(G-1784)*

K R Drenth Trucking Inc .... D 708 983-6340
   Cincinnati *(G-2926)*

Kenan Advantage Group Inc .... C 800 969-5419
   North Canton *(G-11844)*

Keroam Transportation Inc .... C 937 274-7033
   Dayton *(G-7434)*

Klingshirn & Sons Trucking .... E 937 338-5000
   Burkettsville *(G-1524)*

KMu Trucking & Excvtg LLC .... E 440 934-1008
   Avon *(G-659)*

Kuhnle Brothers Inc .... C 440 564-7168
   Newbury *(G-11762)*

Kuntzman Trucking Inc .... E 330 821-9160
   Alliance *(G-387)*

L V Trucking Inc .... E 614 275-4994
   Columbus *(G-6132)*

Leaders Moving Company .... E 614 785-9595
   Worthington *(G-15431)*

▲ Lesaint Logistics Inc .... C 513 874-3900
   West Chester *(G-14722)*

LT Harnett Trucking Inc .... E 440 997-5528
   Ashtabula *(G-541)*

Mail Contractors America Inc .... D 513 769-5967
   Cincinnati *(G-3003)*

McK Trucking Inc .... E 419 622-1111
   Haviland *(G-9132)*

Mid-East Truck & Tractor Service Inc .... D 330 488-0398
   East Canton *(G-8170)*

Midwest Logistics Systems Ltd .... D 419 584-1414
   Celina *(G-1928)*

Mikes Trucking Ltd .... E 614 879-8808
   Galloway *(G-8773)*

Moeller Trucking Inc .... D 419 925-4799
   Maria Stein *(G-10354)*

Monesi Trucking & Eqp Repr Inc .... E 614 921-9183
   Columbus *(G-6258)*

Move Ez Inc .... D 844 466-8339
   Columbus *(G-6280)*

Moving Ahead Services LLC .... E 440 256-2224
   Willoughby *(G-15212)*

Myers Machinery Movers Inc .... E 614 871-5052
   Grove City *(G-8938)*

▲ Neighborhood Logistics Co Inc .... E 440 466-0020
   Geneva *(G-8787)*

Nest Tenders Limited .... D 614 901-1570
   Columbus *(G-6345)*

Nicholas Carney-Mc Inc .... D 330 792-5460
   Youngstown *(G-15677)*

Nicolozakes Trckg & Cnstr Inc .... E 740 432-5648
   Cambridge *(G-1577)*

Northcoast Moving Entps Inc .... E 440 943-3900
   Wickliffe *(G-15158)*

Ohio Bulk Transfer Company Inc .... D 216 883-7200
   Newburgh Heights *(G-11758)*

Old Forge Services Inc .... E 330 733-5531
   Windham *(G-15289)*

One Way Express Incorporated .... E 440 439-9182
   Cleveland *(G-4699)*

P I & I Motor Express Inc .... C 330 448-4035
   Masury *(G-10679)*

Panther II Transportation Inc .... C 800 685-0657
   Medina *(G-10872)*

Panther Premium Logistics Inc .... B 800 685-0657
   Medina *(G-10873)*

SIC SECTION   42 MOTOR FREIGHT TRANSPORTATION

Payne Trucking Co .... E 440 998-5538
　Ashtabula *(G-545)*
Pitt-Ohio Express LLC .... C 216 433-9000
　Cleveland *(G-4752)*
Pitt-Ohio Express LLC .... B 513 860-3424
　West Chester *(G-14828)*
Precision Strip Transport Inc .... E 419 628-2343
　Minster *(G-11321)*
Pride Dlvry & Installation LLC .... D 216 749-7481
　Parma *(G-12262)*
Priority Dispatch Inc .... E 513 791-3900
　Blue Ash *(G-1222)*
◆ Pro-Pet LLC .... D 419 394-3374
　Saint Marys *(G-12835)*
Quick Delivery Service Inc .... E 330 453-3709
　Canton *(G-1838)*
R & J Trucking Inc .... E 440 960-1508
　Lorain *(G-10099)*
R & J Trucking Inc .... E 740 374-3050
　Marietta *(G-10402)*
R & J Trucking Inc .... E 330 758-0841
　Shelby *(G-13009)*
R & J Trucking Inc .... E 800 262-9365
　Youngstown *(G-15703)*
R & L Transfer Inc .... B 330 482-5800
　Columbiana *(G-5239)*
R & L Transfer Inc .... B 216 531-3324
　Norwalk *(G-12022)*
Ray Hamilton Companies .... E 513 641-5400
　Cincinnati *(G-3274)*
Red Rover LLC .... E 330 262-6501
　Wooster *(G-15368)*
Reis Trucking Inc .... E 513 353-1960
　Cleves *(G-5192)*
Reliable Appl Installation Inc .... E 614 246-6840
　Columbus *(G-6576)*
Republic Services Ohio Hlg LLC .... E 513 771-4200
　Cincinnati *(G-3289)*
Revolution Trucking LLC .... E 330 975-4145
　Wadsworth *(G-14450)*
Rising Sun Express LLC .... D 937 596-6167
　Jackson Center *(G-9533)*
River City Furniture Inc .... E 513 612-7303
　West Chester *(G-14756)*
Robert M Neff Inc .... E 614 444-1562
　Columbus *(G-6604)*
Ron Carrocce Trucking Co Inc .... E 330 758-0841
　Youngstown *(G-15711)*
Rood Trucking Company Inc .... C 330 652-3519
　Mineral Ridge *(G-11304)*
Rose Transport Inc .... D 614 864-4004
　Reynoldsburg *(G-12677)*
Ross Consolidated Corp .... E 440 748-5800
　Grafton *(G-8841)*
Rt80 Express Inc .... E 330 706-0900
　Barberton *(G-707)*
Rumpke of Ohio Inc .... C 740 947-7082
　Waverly *(G-14618)*
Rumpke Waste Inc .... C 513 242-4401
　Cincinnati *(G-3333)*
Rumpke Waste Inc .... C 937 378-4126
　Georgetown *(G-8801)*
Rumpke Waste Inc .... C 937 548-1939
　Greenville *(G-8883)*
Rush Package Delivery Inc .... D 937 297-6182
　Columbus *(G-6621)*
S & T Truck and Auto Svc Inc .... E 614 272-8163
　Columbus *(G-6624)*
S B Morabito Trucking Inc .... D 216 441-3070
　Bedford *(G-984)*
Sanfrey Freight Services Inc .... E 330 372-1883
　Warren *(G-14551)*

Santmyer Logistics Inc .... D 330 262-6501
　Wooster *(G-15371)*
Savage Companies .... E 216 642-1311
　Cleveland *(G-4877)*
Savage Services Corporation .... E 216 268-7290
　Cleveland *(G-4878)*
Schindewolf Express Inc .... D 937 585-5919
　De Graff *(G-7739)*
Sebastiani Trucking Inc .... D 330 286-0059
　Canfield *(G-1641)*
▲ Sewell Leasing Corporation .... D 937 382-3847
　Wilmington *(G-15273)*
Shoreline Transportation Inc .... C 440 878-2000
　Strongsville *(G-13483)*
Spears Transfer & Expediting .... D 937 275-2443
　Dayton *(G-7633)*
Special Service Transportation Inc .... E 330 273-0755
　Brunswick *(G-1470)*
Spring Grove Rsrce Rcovery Inc .... E 513 681-6242
　Cincinnati *(G-3398)*
Springfield Cartage LLC .... E 937 222-2120
　Dayton *(G-7635)*
Steve Crawford Trucking Inc .... E 866 748-9505
　Byesville *(G-1536)*
Summit NW Corporation .... D 503 255-3826
　Dublin *(G-8134)*
Sustain LLC .... E 888 525-0029
　New Waterford *(G-11684)*
T&T Enterprises of Ohio Inc .... E 513 942-1141
　West Chester *(G-14837)*
Tesar Industrial Contrs Inc .... D 216 741-8008
　Cleveland *(G-4987)*
Tforce Freight Inc .... E 937 236-4700
　Dayton *(G-7664)*
Tforce Freight Inc .... E 330 659-6693
　Richfield *(G-12711)*
Tforce Logistics East LLC .... E 614 276-6000
　Columbus *(G-6757)*
▲ The Andrews Moving and St .... E 330 656-8700
　Streetsboro *(G-13432)*
Tk Gas Services Inc .... E 740 826-0303
　New Concord *(G-11612)*
Trans-States Express Inc .... D 513 679-7100
　Cincinnati *(G-3501)*
Transportation Unlimited Inc .... A 216 426-0088
　Cleveland *(G-5033)*
Tri-State Forest Logistics LLC .... E 937 323-6325
　Springfield *(G-13303)*
Triangle Leasing Corp .... E 419 729-3868
　Toledo *(G-14074)*
Tricont Trucking Company .... C 614 527-7398
　Columbus *(G-6789)*
Trio Trucking Inc .... D 513 679-7100
　Cincinnati *(G-3527)*
Tsm Logistics LLC .... E 419 234-6074
　Rockford *(G-12737)*
Universal Disposal Inc .... E 440 286-3153
　Chardon *(G-2023)*
Vallejo Company .... E 216 741-3933
　Cleveland *(G-5096)*
Valley Transportation Inc .... E 419 289-6200
　Ashland *(G-514)*
Varney Dispatch Inc .... E 513 682-4200
　Cincinnati *(G-3616)*
Vin Devers Inc .... C 888 847-9535
　Sylvania *(G-13578)*
W L Logan Trucking Company .... C 330 478-1404
　Canton *(G-1882)*
Waterworks LLC .... C 614 253-7246
　Columbus *(G-6870)*
Wdht Enterprises Inc .... C 440 846-0200
　Strongsville *(G-13498)*

Werlor Inc .... E 419 784-4285
　Defiance *(G-7775)*
White Swan Inc .... E 707 615-5005
　Columbus *(G-6886)*
Wil-Sites Truck Lines LLC .... E 614 444-8873
　Columbus *(G-6891)*
Wnb Group LLC .... E 513 641-5400
　Cincinnati *(G-3677)*
Wooster Motor Ways Inc .... C 330 264-9557
　Wooster *(G-15396)*
Xpo Logistics Freight Inc .... C 614 876-7100
　Columbus *(G-6912)*
Xpo Logistics Freight Inc .... D 216 433-1000
　Parma *(G-12267)*
Xpo Logistics Freight Inc .... D 330 896-7300
　Uniontown *(G-14271)*
Xpo Logistics Freight Inc .... D 513 870-0044
　West Chester *(G-14846)*
Zeiter Trucking Inc .... E 419 668-2229
　Norwalk *(G-12031)*
Zemba Bros Inc .... E 740 452-1880
　Zanesville *(G-15844)*

4213 Trucking, except local

1st Carrier Corp .... E 740 477-2587
　Circleville *(G-3701)*
A L Smith Trucking Inc .... E 937 526-3651
　Versailles *(G-11412)*
Ace Doran Hauling & Rigging Co ...... D 513 681-7900
　Cincinnati *(G-2140)*
Advance Trnsp Systems Inc .... D 513 818-4311
　Cincinnati *(G-2147)*
Advantage Tank Lines Inc .... E 330 491-0474
　North Canton *(G-11808)*
AG Container Transport LLC .... D 740 862-8866
　Lockbourne *(G-10009)*
AG Trucking Inc .... E 937 497-7770
　Sidney *(G-13017)*
▲ All Pro Freight Systems Inc .... D 440 934-2222
　Westlake *(G-15030)*
Ameri-Line Inc .... E 440 316-4500
　Columbia Station *(G-5223)*
Arctic Express Inc .... C 614 876-4008
　Hilliard *(G-9180)*
Arms Trucking Co Inc .... E 800 362-1343
　Huntsburg *(G-9380)*
▲ Artemis Fine Arts Inc .... E 214 357-2577
　Akron *(G-56)*
◆ As Logistics Inc .... D 513 863-4627
　Liberty Township *(G-9847)*
Atlas Transportation LLC .... E 202 963-4241
　Medina *(G-10809)*
Awl Transport Inc .... D 330 899-3444
　Mantua *(G-10328)*
B & L Transport Inc .... E 866 848-2888
　Millersburg *(G-11272)*
B & T Express Inc .... B 330 549-0000
　North Lima *(G-11883)*
B D Transportation Inc .... E 937 773-9280
　Piqua *(G-12435)*
B M Machine .... E 419 595-2898
　New Riegel *(G-11677)*
Badilad LLC .... E 330 805-3173
　Cuyahoga Falls *(G-7046)*
Balanced Logistics Brkg LLC .... D 216 296-4817
　Twinsburg *(G-14174)*
Berlin Transportation LLC .... E 330 674-3395
　Millersburg *(G-11273)*
Bestway Transport Co .... E 419 687-2000
　Plymouth *(G-12501)*
Black Horse Brothers Inc .... E 267 265-0013
　Cuyahoga Falls *(G-7050)*

Employee Codes: A=Over 500 employees, B=251-500
C=101-250, D=51-100, E=20-50, F=10-19, G=1-9

42 MOTOR FREIGHT TRANSPORTATION

Bowling Transportation Inc .... D 419 436-9590
  Fostoria *(G-8614)*

Brendamour Moving & Stor Inc .... D 800 354-9715
  Cincinnati *(G-2279)*

Bridge Logistics Inc .... E 513 874-7444
  West Chester *(G-14801)*

Brookside Holdings LLC .... E 419 925-4457
  Maria Stein *(G-10353)*

Brown Logistics Solutions Inc .... E 614 866-9111
  Columbus *(G-5471)*

Bryan Truck Line Inc .... D 419 485-8373
  Montpelier *(G-11382)*

Bulk Transit Corporation .... E 614 873-4632
  Plain City *(G-12471)*

Burd Brothers Inc .... E 513 708-7787
  Dayton *(G-7206)*

Burd Brothers Inc .... E 800 538-2873
  Batavia *(G-729)*

BWC Trucking Company Inc .... E 740 532-5188
  Ironton *(G-9505)*

By-Line Transit Inc .... E 937 642-2500
  Marysville *(G-10477)*

Cargo Solution Express Inc .... E 614 980-0351
  Columbus *(G-5511)*

Cavins Trucking & Garage LLC .... E 419 661-9947
  Perrysburg *(G-12323)*

Chambers Leasing Systems Corp .... E 937 547-9777
  Greenville *(G-8867)*

Chambers Leasing Systems Corp .... E 937 642-4260
  Marysville *(G-10479)*

Chambers Leasing Systems Corp .... E 419 726-9747
  Toledo *(G-13729)*

Cimarron Express Inc .... D 419 855-7713
  Genoa *(G-8793)*

City Dash LLC .... C 513 562-2000
  Cincinnati *(G-2450)*

CJ Logstics Holdings Amer Corp .... D 614 879-9659
  West Jefferson *(G-14849)*

▲ Clark Trucking Inc .... C 937 642-0335
  East Liberty *(G-8171)*

Classic Carriers Inc .... E 937 604-8118
  Versailles *(G-14414)*

Cle Transportation Company .... D 567 805-4008
  Norwalk *(G-12005)*

Cliff Viessman Inc .... D 937 454-6490
  Dayton *(G-7236)*

◆ Clopay Transportation Company .... D 937 440-6790
  Troy *(G-14131)*

Containerport Group Inc .... E 440 333-1330
  Columbus *(G-5689)*

Continental Express Inc .... A 937 497-2100
  Sidney *(G-13024)*

Cotter Moving & Storage Co .... E 330 535-5115
  Akron *(G-125)*

Covenant Transport Inc .... A 423 821-1212
  Columbus *(G-5715)*

Cowen Truck Line Inc .... D 419 938-3401
  Perrysville *(G-12391)*

Coy Bros Inc .... E 330 533-6864
  Canfield *(G-1627)*

Craig Transportation Co .... E 419 874-7981
  Maumee *(G-10714)*

Crete Carrier Corporation .... C 614 853-4500
  Columbus *(G-5726)*

▲ Crw Inc .... E 330 264-3785
  Shreve *(G-13016)*

Dayton Freight Lines Inc .... C 614 860-1080
  Columbus *(G-5744)*

Dayton Freight Lines Inc .... B 937 236-4880
  Dayton *(G-7283)*

Dayton Freight Lines Inc .... D 330 346-0750
  Kent *(G-9571)*

Dayton Freight Lines Inc .... D 419 589-0350
  Mansfield *(G-10257)*

Dayton Freight Lines Inc .... C 419 661-8600
  Perrysburg *(G-12329)*

Dayton Freight Lines Inc .... C 937 264-4060
  Dayton *(G-7284)*

Dedicated Transport LLC .... C 216 641-2500
  Brooklyn Heights *(G-1416)*

Diamond Logistics Inc .... C 614 274-9750
  Columbus *(G-5763)*

Dill-Elam Inc .... E 513 575-0017
  Loveland *(G-10135)*

▲ Dist-Trans Inc .... C 614 497-1660
  Columbus *(G-5773)*

Disttech Inc .... A 800 969-5419
  North Canton *(G-11825)*

DLC Transport Inc .... E 740 282-1763
  Steubenville *(G-13321)*

Drew Ag-Transport Inc .... D 937 548-3200
  Greenville *(G-8872)*

Dutch Maid Logistics Inc .... C 419 935-0136
  Willard *(G-15167)*

Dworkin Inc .... E 216 271-5318
  Cleveland *(G-4192)*

Eastern Express Inc .... C 513 267-1212
  Middletown *(G-11161)*

Eastern Express Logistics Inc .... E 800 348-6514
  Cleveland *(G-4199)*

Energy Trucking LLC .... D 740 240-2204
  Pataskala *(G-12274)*

Enterprise Hill Farm Inc .... E 419 668-0242
  Norwalk *(G-12009)*

Erie Trucking Inc .... E 419 625-7374
  Sandusky *(G-12892)*

Estes Express Lines .... D 614 275-6000
  Columbus *(G-5832)*

Estes Express Lines .... E 419 531-1500
  Toledo *(G-13799)*

Estes Express Lines .... E 513 779-9581
  West Chester *(G-14688)*

◆ Exel Holdings (usa) Inc .... C 614 865-8500
  Westerville *(G-14892)*

◆ Exel Inc .... B 614 865-5819
  Westerville *(G-14893)*

Fabrizi Trucking & Pav Co Inc .... D 440 277-0127
  Lorain *(G-10074)*

Falcon Transport Co .... A 330 793-1345
  Youngstown *(G-15609)*

FANTON Logistics Inc .... D 216 341-2400
  Cleveland *(G-4241)*

Fedex Ground Package Sys Inc .... D 800 463-3339
  Grove City *(G-8919)*

▲ Fedex Supplychain Systems Inc .... A
  Hudson *(G-9348)*

Ferrous Metal Transfer Co .... E 216 671-8500
  Brooklyn *(G-1409)*

Fetter Son Farms Ltd Lblty Co .... E 740 465-2961
  Morral *(G-11453)*

First Group Investment Partnr .... E 513 241-2200
  Cincinnati *(G-2674)*

Firstenterprises Inc .... B 740 369-5100
  Delaware *(G-7797)*

Firstgroup Usa Inc .... B 513 241-2200
  Cincinnati *(G-2687)*

Fleetmaster Express Inc .... E 419 420-1835
  Findlay *(G-8533)*

Foodliner Inc .... E 937 898-0075
  Dayton *(G-7361)*

Fraley & Schilling Inc .... E 740 598-4118
  Brilliant *(G-1380)*

Garner Trnsp Group Inc .... C 419 422-5742
  Findlay *(G-8535)*

Garner Trucking Inc .... D 419 422-5742
  Findlay *(G-8536)*

General Transport & Cons Inc .... E 330 645-6055
  Akron *(G-173)*

General Transport Incorporated .... E 330 786-3400
  Akron *(G-174)*

Gillson Solutions Inc .... E 937 751-0119
  Dayton *(G-7375)*

Glm Transport Inc .... E 419 363-2041
  Van Wert *(G-14345)*

Global Workplace Solutions LLC .... E 513 759-6000
  West Chester *(G-14697)*

Golden Hawk Transportation Co .... D 419 683-3304
  Crestline *(G-7024)*

Green Lines Transportation Inc .... E 330 863-2111
  Malvern *(G-10233)*

Greenwood Motor Lines Inc .... B 800 543-5589
  Wilmington *(G-15255)*

Harris Distributing Co .... E 513 541-4222
  Cincinnati *(G-2801)*

Hillsboro Transportation Co .... E 513 772-9223
  Cincinnati *(G-2825)*

Hilltrux Tank Lines Inc .... E 330 538-3700
  North Jackson *(G-11872)*

Hodges Trucking Company LLC .... E 405 947-7764
  Navarre *(G-11538)*

Home Run Inc .... E 800 543-9198
  Xenia *(G-15520)*

Horizon Freight System Inc .... E 216 341-7410
  Cleveland *(G-4378)*

Horizon Mid Atlantic Inc .... D 800 480-6829
  Cleveland *(G-4379)*

Huntley Trucking Co .... E 740 385-7615
  New Plymouth *(G-11675)*

Hyway Trucking Company .... D 419 423-7145
  Findlay *(G-8548)*

Iddings Trucking Inc .... C 740 568-1780
  Marietta *(G-10372)*

Imperial Express Inc .... E 937 399-9400
  Springfield *(G-13257)*

Integres Global Logistics Inc .... D 866 347-2101
  Medina *(G-10847)*

J B Hunt Transport Inc .... D 419 547-2777
  Clyde *(G-5204)*

J P Jenks Inc .... D 440 428-4500
  Madison *(G-10218)*

J P Transportation Co Inc .... E 513 424-6978
  Middletown *(G-11167)*

J Rayl Transport Inc .... D 330 784-1134
  Akron *(G-206)*

J-Trac Inc .... E 419 524-3456
  Mansfield *(G-10274)*

Jack Cooper Transport Co Inc .... D 440 949-2044
  Sheffield Village *(G-13000)*

Jaro Transportation Svcs Inc .... C 330 393-5659
  Warren *(G-14531)*

Jmt Cartage Inc .... E 330 478-2430
  Canton *(G-1784)*

K-Limited Carrier Ltd .... D 419 269-0002
  Toledo *(G-13874)*

Kag Specialty Products Group LLC .... E 330 409-1124
  North Canton *(G-11841)*

Kaplan Trucking Company .... D 216 341-3322
  Cleveland *(G-4448)*

Kenan Advantage Group Inc .... C 800 969-5419
  North Canton *(G-11844)*

Keroam Transportation Inc .... D 937 274-7033
  Dayton *(G-7434)*

Klingshirn & Sons Trucking .... E 937 338-5000
  Burkettsville *(G-1524)*

Kroger Dedicated Logistics Co .... E 309 691-9670
  Cincinnati *(G-2954)*

42 MOTOR FREIGHT TRANSPORTATION

Kuhnle Brothers Inc .... C 440 564-7168
  Newbury *(G-11762)*
Kuntzman Trucking Inc .... E 330 821-9160
  Alliance *(G-387)*
L V Trucking Inc .... E 614 275-4994
  Columbus *(G-6132)*
Landstar Global Logistics Inc .... D 740 575-4700
  Coshocton *(G-6990)*
◆ Lewis & Michael Inc .... E 937 252-6683
  Dayton *(G-7453)*
Lh Trucking Inc .... E 513 398-1682
  Mason *(G-10573)*
Lincoln Moving & Storage Co .... D 216 741-5500
  Strongsville *(G-13470)*
LT Harnett Trucking Inc .... E 440 997-5528
  Ashtabula *(G-541)*
Luckey Transfer LLC .... D 800 435-4371
  Lima *(G-9931)*
Lykins Companies Inc .... E 513 831-8820
  Milford *(G-11238)*
Lykins Transportation Inc .... E 513 831-8820
  Milford *(G-11240)*
Mansfield Whsng & Dist Inc .... C 419 522-3510
  Ontario *(G-12114)*
Mark D Sandridge Inc .... E 330 764-6106
  Medina *(G-10852)*
Mast Trucking Inc .... D 330 674-8913
  Millersburg *(G-11285)*
Miller Transfer and Rigging Co .... E 330 325-2521
  Rootstown *(G-12762)*
Mizar Motors Inc .... D 419 729-2400
  Toledo *(G-13925)*
Mjs Snow & Landscape LLC .... D 419 656-6724
  Port Clinton *(G-12538)*
Moeller Trucking Inc .... E 419 925-4799
  Maria Stein *(G-10354)*
Motor Carrier Service Inc .... C 419 693-6207
  Northwood *(G-11978)*
Myers Machinery Movers Inc .... E 614 871-5052
  Grove City *(G-8938)*
Nationwide Truck Brokers Inc .... C 937 335-9229
  Troy *(G-14148)*
Nicholas Carney-Mc Inc .... D 330 792-5460
  Youngstown *(G-15677)*
Nick Strimbu Inc .... C 330 448-4046
  Dover *(G-7896)*
Nicolozakes Trckg & Cnstr Inc .... E 740 432-5648
  Cambridge *(G-1577)*
Niese Leasing Inc .... E 419 523-4400
  Ottawa *(G-12190)*
One Way Express Incorporated .... E 440 439-9182
  Cleveland *(G-4699)*
Osborne Trucking Company .... E 513 874-2090
  Fairfield *(G-8435)*
P & D Transportation Inc .... E 740 454-1221
  Zanesville *(G-15825)*
P I & I Motor Express Inc .... C 330 448-4035
  Masury *(G-10679)*
Pacer Transport Inc .... D 614 923-1400
  Dublin *(G-8085)*
PAm Transportation Svcs Inc .... E 419 935-9501
  Willard *(G-15172)*
Panther II Transportation Inc .... C 800 685-0657
  Medina *(G-10872)*
Panther Premium Logistics Inc .... B 800 685-0657
  Medina *(G-10873)*
Partnership LLC .... E 440 471-8310
  Oberlin *(G-12075)*
Phoenix Cargo LLC .... C 614 407-3322
  Grove City *(G-8945)*
Piqua Transfer & Storage Co .... D 937 773-3743
  Piqua *(G-12455)*

Pitt-Ohio Express LLC .... C 216 433-9000
  Cleveland *(G-4752)*
Pitt-Ohio Express LLC .... C 614 801-1064
  Grove City *(G-8946)*
Pitt-Ohio Express LLC .... B 419 726-6523
  Toledo *(G-13964)*
Pitt-Ohio Express LLC .... B 513 860-3424
  West Chester *(G-14828)*
▲ Planes Moving & Storage Inc .... C 513 759-6000
  West Chester *(G-14743)*
Planes Mvg & Stor Co Columbus .... D 614 777-9090
  Columbus *(G-6528)*
Platinum Carriers LLC .... D 877 318-9607
  Garfield Heights *(G-8778)*
Platinum Express LLC .... E 937 235-9540
  Dayton *(G-7557)*
Ploger Transportation LLC .... E 419 465-2100
  Norwalk *(G-12021)*
Pohl Transportation Inc .... D 800 837-2122
  Versailles *(G-14416)*
Predator Trucking Company .... E 330 530-0712
  Mc Donald *(G-10801)*
Pros Freight Corporation .... E 440 543-7555
  Chagrin Falls *(G-1987)*
R & J Trucking Inc .... E 740 374-3050
  Marietta *(G-10402)*
R & L Carriers Inc .... A 800 543-5589
  Wilmington *(G-15265)*
R & L Transfer Inc .... B 330 482-5800
  Columbiana *(G-5239)*
R & L Transfer Inc .... B 216 531-3324
  Norwalk *(G-12022)*
R & L Transfer Inc .... B 937 305-9287
  Wilmington *(G-15266)*
R & L Transfer Inc .... B 614 871-3813
  Wilmington *(G-15267)*
R & L Transfer Inc .... B 330 743-3609
  Youngstown *(G-15704)*
R & L Transfer Inc .... A 937 382-1494
  Wilmington *(G-15268)*
Rands Trucking Inc .... E 740 397-1144
  Mount Vernon *(G-11504)*
▲ RDF Logistics Inc .... C 440 282-9060
  Lorain *(G-10100)*
RDF Trucking Corporation .... D 440 282-9060
  Lorain *(G-10101)*
Richard Wolfe Trucking Inc .... E 740 392-2445
  Mount Vernon *(G-11505)*
Rising Sun Express LLC .... D 937 596-6167
  Jackson Center *(G-9533)*
RL Trucking Inc .... C 419 732-4177
  Port Clinton *(G-12540)*
Roadlink USA Midwest LLC .... E 419 686-2113
  Perrysburg *(G-12367)*
Robert G Owen Trucking Inc .... E 330 756-1013
  Navarre *(G-11539)*
Robert M Neff Inc .... E 614 444-1562
  Columbus *(G-6604)*
Roeder Cartage Company Inc .... D 419 221-1600
  Lima *(G-9954)*
Roger Bettis Trucking Inc .... E 330 863-2111
  Malvern *(G-10236)*
Rollins Moving and Storage Inc .... C 937 525-4013
  Springfield *(G-13288)*
Ron Burge Trucking Inc .... E 330 624-5373
  Burbank *(G-1522)*
Rood Trucking Company Inc .... C 330 652-3519
  Mineral Ridge *(G-11304)*
Ross Transportation Svcs Inc .... C 440 748-5900
  Grafton *(G-8843)*
Rrr Express LLC .... E 800 723-3424
  West Chester *(G-14758)*

Rt80 Express Inc .... E 330 706-0900
  Barberton *(G-707)*
Ruan Transport Corporation .... E 330 484-1450
  Canton *(G-1847)*
◆ Ryder Last Mile Inc .... D 866 711-3129
  New Albany *(G-11586)*
Saia Motor Freight Line LLC .... D 614 870-8778
  Columbus *(G-6636)*
Saia Motor Freight Line LLC .... D 937 237-0140
  Dayton *(G-7604)*
Saia Motor Freight Line LLC .... D 330 659-4277
  Richfield *(G-12709)*
Saia Motor Freight Line LLC .... D 419 726-9761
  Toledo *(G-14003)*
Sanfrey Freight Services Inc .... E 330 372-1883
  Warren *(G-14551)*
Scheiderer Transport Inc .... D 614 873-5103
  Plain City *(G-12493)*
Schindewolf Express Inc .... D 937 585-5919
  De Graff *(G-7739)*
Schneider Nat Carriers Inc .... A 740 362-6910
  Delaware *(G-7825)*
Schroeder Associates Inc .... E 419 258-5075
  Antwerp *(G-448)*
Schwerman Trucking Co .... D 419 666-0818
  Walbridge *(G-14466)*
▲ Sewell Leasing Corporation .... D 937 382-3847
  Wilmington *(G-15273)*
Shama Express LLC .... D 216 925-6530
  Grafton *(G-8844)*
Shetler Moving & Stor of Ohio .... E 513 755-0700
  West Chester *(G-14763)*
Shoreline Transportation Inc .... C 440 878-2000
  Strongsville *(G-13483)*
Short Freight Lines Inc .... E 419 729-1691
  Toledo *(G-14011)*
Smith Trucking Inc .... E 419 841-8676
  Sylvania *(G-13572)*
Spader Freight Services Inc .... D 419 547-1117
  Clyde *(G-5210)*
Special Service Transportation Inc .... E 330 273-0755
  Brunswick *(G-1470)*
Store & Haul Inc .... E 419 238-4284
  Van Wert *(G-14351)*
Swx Enterprises Inc .... E 216 676-4600
  Brookpark *(G-1441)*
▲ Taylor Distributing Company .... D 513 771-1850
  West Chester *(G-14838)*
Tennfreight Inc .... E 615 977-2125
  Cincinnati *(G-3456)*
Tesar Industrial Contrs Inc .... D 216 741-8008
  Cleveland *(G-4987)*
Tforce Freight Inc .... E 513 771-7555
  Cincinnati *(G-3461)*
Tforce Freight Inc .... D 614 238-2355
  Columbus *(G-6756)*
Tforce Freight Inc .... E 937 236-4700
  Dayton *(G-7664)*
Tforce Freight Inc .... E 330 448-0440
  Masury *(G-10681)*
Tforce Freight Inc .... E 330 659-6693
  Richfield *(G-12711)*
Tforce Freight Inc .... D 419 537-1445
  Toledo *(G-14038)*
▲ The Andrews Moving and St .... E 330 656-8700
  Streetsboro *(G-13432)*
The Expediting Co .... D 937 890-1524
  Vandalia *(G-14394)*
Thomas E Keller Trucking Inc .... B 419 784-4805
  Defiance *(G-7772)*
Thomas Trucking Inc .... E 513 731-8411
  Cincinnati *(G-3475)*

Employee Codes: A=Over 500 employees, B=251-500
C=101-250, D=51-100, E=20-50, F=10-19, G=1-9

42 MOTOR FREIGHT TRANSPORTATION

Three-D Transport Inc .... E 419 924-5368
  West Unity *(G-14875)*
▲ Thyssenkrupp Logistics Inc .... E 419 662-1800
  Northwood *(G-11984)*
Tk Gas Services Inc .... E 740 826-0303
  New Concord *(G-11612)*
Toledo Nagle Inc .... D 419 661-2500
  Walbridge *(G-14467)*
Top Line Express Inc .... E 419 221-1705
  Lima *(G-9972)*
Top Notch Truckers Inc .... D 540 787-7777
  Cuyahoga Falls *(G-7108)*
Trans-Continental Systems Inc .... E 513 769-4774
  Cincinnati *(G-3500)*
Trans-States Express Inc .... D 513 679-7100
  Cincinnati *(G-3501)*
Transportation Unlimited Inc .... A 216 426-0088
  Cleveland *(G-5033)*
Triad Transport Inc .... E 614 491-9497
  Columbus *(G-6788)*
Triangle Leasing Corp .... E 419 729-3868
  Toledo *(G-14074)*
Trio Trucking Inc .... D 513 679-7100
  Cincinnati *(G-3527)*
Triple Crown Services Company .... E 419 625-0672
  Sandusky *(G-12937)*
Triple T Transport Inc .... C 740 657-3244
  Lewis Center *(G-9839)*
Trowbridge Storage Company .... E 614 766-0116
  Groveport *(G-9006)*
U S Xpress Inc .... B 440 743-7177
  Cleveland *(G-5045)*
U S Xpress Inc .... B 740 363-0700
  Delaware *(G-7832)*
U S Xpress Inc .... A 937 328-4100
  Springfield *(G-13306)*
U S Xpress Inc .... B 419 244-6384
  Toledo *(G-14080)*
U S Xpress Inc .... B 740 452-4153
  Zanesville *(G-15835)*
Usher Transport Inc .... D 614 875-0528
  Grove City *(G-8962)*
Van Mayberrys & Storage Inc .... E 937 298-8800
  Moraine *(G-11445)*
Velvet Blue Transport Co Inc .... E 330 478-1426
  Canton *(G-1880)*
Vitran Express Inc .... D 216 426-8584
  Cleveland *(G-5111)*
Vitran Express Inc .... E 614 870-2255
  Columbus *(G-6852)*
Vitran Express Inc .... E 513 771-4894
  West Chester *(G-14792)*
W L Logan Trucking Company .... C 330 478-1404
  Canton *(G-1882)*
Wannemacher Enterprises Inc .... E 419 225-9060
  Lima *(G-9979)*
Watkins and Shepard Trckg Inc .... D 614 832-0440
  Urbancrest *(G-14326)*
World Shipping Inc .... E 440 356-7676
  Cleveland *(G-5159)*
Xpo Logistics Freight Inc .... C 614 876-7100
  Columbus *(G-6912)*
Xpo Logistics Freight Inc .... D 937 898-9808
  Dayton *(G-7730)*
Xpo Logistics Freight Inc .... E 937 364-2361
  Hillsboro *(G-9268)*
Xpo Logistics Freight Inc .... E 216 433-1000
  Parma *(G-12267)*
Xpo Logistics Freight Inc .... D 937 492-3899
  Sidney *(G-13059)*
Xpo Logistics Freight Inc .... E 740 894-3859
  South Point *(G-13184)*

Xpo Logistics Freight Inc .... D 740 922-5614
  Uhrichsville *(G-14238)*
Xpo Logistics Freight Inc .... D 330 896-7300
  Uniontown *(G-14271)*
Xpo Logistics Freight Inc .... E 419 294-5728
  Upper Sandusky *(G-14296)*
Xpo Logistics Freight Inc .... D 330 824-2242
  Warren *(G-14578)*
Xpo Logistics Freight Inc .... D 513 870-0044
  West Chester *(G-14846)*
Yowell Transportation Svc Inc .... D 937 294-5933
  Moraine *(G-11451)*
Zartran LLC .... D 513 870-4800
  Hamilton *(G-9094)*
Zipline Logistics LLC .... E 888 469-4754
  Columbus *(G-6920)*
Zumstein Inc .... D 419 375-4132
  Fort Recovery *(G-8612)*

4214 Local trucking with storage

▲ All Pro Freight Systems Inc .... D 440 934-2222
  Westlake *(G-15030)*
Arms Trucking Co Inc .... E 800 362-1343
  Huntsburg *(G-9380)*
Aviation Auto Trnsp Spclsts In .... E 502 785-4657
  Fort Loramie *(G-8603)*
Bls Trucking Inc .... B 937 224-0494
  New Carlisle *(G-11600)*
Brendamour Moving & Stor Inc .... D 800 354-9715
  Cincinnati *(G-2279)*
▲ Clark Trucking Inc .... C 937 642-0335
  East Liberty *(G-8171)*
Commercial Works Inc .... D 614 870-2342
  Columbus *(G-5667)*
Cordell Transportation Co LLC .... C 937 277-7271
  Dayton *(G-7249)*
Dawson Logistics LLC .... D 217 689-2610
  West Chester *(G-14683)*
Getgo Transportation Co LLC .... E 419 666-6850
  Millbury *(G-11269)*
Gws FF&e LLC .... E 513 759-6000
  West Chester *(G-14703)*
J-Trac Inc .... E 419 524-3456
  Mansfield *(G-10274)*
King Tut Logistics LLC .... E 614 538-0509
  Columbus *(G-6117)*
Landstar Global Logistics Inc .... D 740 575-4700
  Coshocton *(G-6990)*
Leaders Moving Company .... E 614 785-9595
  Worthington *(G-15431)*
◆ Lewis & Michael Inc .... E 937 252-6683
  Dayton *(G-7453)*
Lincoln Moving & Storage Co .... D 216 741-5500
  Strongsville *(G-13470)*
▲ M G Q Inc .... E 419 992-4236
  Tiffin *(G-13631)*
▲ Moving Solutions Inc .... D 440 946-9300
  Mentor *(G-10977)*
National Shunt Service LLC .... B 978 637-2293
  Dublin *(G-8068)*
▲ Neighborhood Logistics Co Inc .... E 440 466-0020
  Geneva *(G-8787)*
Nicholas Carney-Mc Inc .... D 330 792-5460
  Youngstown *(G-15677)*
Piqua Transfer & Storage Co .... D 937 773-3743
  Piqua *(G-12455)*
▲ Planes Moving & Storage Inc .... C 513 759-6000
  West Chester *(G-14743)*
Planes Mvg & Stor Co Columbus .... D 614 777-9090
  Columbus *(G-6528)*
Ray Hamilton Companies .... E 513 641-5400
  Cincinnati *(G-3274)*

River City Furniture LLC .... E 513 612-7303
  West Chester *(G-14756)*
Roadlink USA Midwest LLC .... E 419 686-2113
  Perrysburg *(G-12367)*
Rollins Moving and Storage Inc .... C 937 525-4013
  Springfield *(G-13288)*
Royalty Trucking Inc .... C 513 771-1860
  Mason *(G-10603)*
Shetler Moving & Stor of Ohio .... E 513 755-0700
  West Chester *(G-14763)*
Spears Transfer & Expediting .... D 937 275-2443
  Dayton *(G-7633)*
▲ The Andrews Moving and St .... E 330 656-8700
  Streetsboro *(G-13432)*
Trowbridge Storage Company .... E 614 766-0116
  Groveport *(G-9006)*
Van Mayberrys & Storage Inc .... E 937 298-8800
  Moraine *(G-11445)*
Wnb Group LLC .... E 513 641-5400
  Cincinnati *(G-3677)*
Wooster Motor Ways Inc .... C 330 264-9557
  Wooster *(G-15396)*
Yowell Transportation Svc Inc .... D 937 294-5933
  Moraine *(G-11451)*

4215 Courier services, except by air

Barberton Laundry and Clg Inc .... D 330 825-6911
  Barberton *(G-694)*
Centaur Mail Inc .... E 419 887-5857
  Maumee *(G-10708)*
Chief Delivery LLC .... D 419 277-6190
  Toledo *(G-13732)*
City Dash LLC .... C 513 562-2000
  Cincinnati *(G-2450)*
Elite Expediting Corp .... E 614 279-1181
  Worthington *(G-15413)*
Flying Pig Logistics Inc .... E 513 300-9331
  West Chester *(G-14692)*
Lance Global Logistics LLC .... D 440 522-3822
  Sheffield Lake *(G-12996)*
Light Speed Lgistics Ltd Lblty .... C 330 412-0567
  Canton *(G-1796)*
LMI Transports Inc .... E 513 921-4564
  Cincinnati *(G-2984)*
Platinum Couriers Inc .... E 216 370-8972
  Richfield *(G-12706)*
Robert M Neff Inc .... E 614 444-1562
  Columbus *(G-6604)*
Tforce Logistics East LLC .... E 614 276-6000
  Columbus *(G-6757)*
United Parcel Service Inc .... D 740 592-4570
  Athens *(G-596)*
United Parcel Service Inc .... E 440 275-3301
  Austinburg *(G-634)*
United Parcel Service Inc .... E 740 598-4293
  Brilliant *(G-1381)*
United Parcel Service Inc .... E 419 586-8556
  Celina *(G-1930)*
United Parcel Service Inc .... A 513 852-6135
  Cincinnati *(G-3555)*
United Parcel Service Inc .... C 513 241-5289
  Cincinnati *(G-3556)*
United Parcel Service Inc .... C 513 782-4000
  Cincinnati *(G-3557)*
United Parcel Service Inc .... B 800 742-5877
  Cleveland *(G-5063)*
United Parcel Service Inc .... E 216 676-4560
  Cleveland *(G-5064)*
United Parcel Service Inc .... E 440 826-2591
  Cleveland *(G-5065)*
United Parcel Service Inc .... D 614 841-7159
  Columbus *(G-6809)*

SIC SECTION

42 MOTOR FREIGHT TRANSPORTATION

United Parcel Service Inc.............................. B 614 870-4111
   Columbus *(G-6810)*

United Parcel Service Inc.............................. E 419 782-3552
   Defiance *(G-7773)*

United Parcel Service Inc.............................. E 419 424-9494
   Findlay *(G-8595)*

United Parcel Service Inc.............................. D 330 545-0177
   Girard *(G-8828)*

United Parcel Service Inc.............................. E 513 863-1681
   Hamilton *(G-9089)*

United Parcel Service Inc.............................. E 419 222-7399
   Lima *(G-9975)*

United Parcel Service Inc.............................. E 419 747-3080
   Mansfield *(G-10320)*

United Parcel Service Inc.............................. E 740 373-0772
   Marietta *(G-10407)*

United Parcel Service Inc.............................. E 614 383-4580
   Marion *(G-10463)*

United Parcel Service Inc.............................. A 419 891-6776
   Maumee *(G-10777)*

United Parcel Service Inc.............................. E 330 339-6281
   New Philadelphia *(G-11671)*

United Parcel Service Inc.............................. A 614 272-8500
   Obetz *(G-12085)*

United Parcel Service Inc.............................. D 419 872-0211
   Perrysburg *(G-12382)*

United Parcel Service Inc.............................. E 740 962-7971
   Portsmouth *(G-12578)*

United Parcel Service Inc.............................. E 740 968-3508
   Saint Clairsville *(G-12818)*

United Parcel Service Inc.............................. E 419 891-6841
   Toledo *(G-14083)*

United Parcel Service Inc.............................. D 614 277-3300
   Urbancrest *(G-14325)*

United Parcel Service Inc.............................. E 937 382-0658
   Wilmington *(G-15276)*

United Parcel Service Inc.............................. D 800 742-5877
   Youngstown *(G-15743)*

United Parcel Service Inc.............................. D 800 742-5877
   Zanesville *(G-15836)*

4221 Farm product warehousing and storage

Consolidated Grain & Barge Co................... E 513 244-7400
   Cincinnati *(G-2495)*

Deerfield AG Services Inc............................ E 330 584-4715
   Massillon *(G-10637)*

Deerfield Farms Service Inc.......................... D 330 584-4715
   Deerfield *(G-7741)*

Luckey Farmers Inc....................................... E 419 665-2322
   Lindsey *(G-9995)*

4222 Refrigerated warehousing and storage

Americold Logistics LLC............................... D 419 599-5015
   Napoleon *(G-11515)*

Americold Logistics LLC............................... E 419 599-5015
   Napoleon *(G-11516)*

Crescent Park Corporation............................ C 513 759-7000
   West Chester *(G-14679)*

Fresh Mark Inc.. B 330 833-9870
   Massillon *(G-10640)*

Perishable Shipg Solutions LLC.................... E 724 944-9024
   Warren *(G-14546)*

Produce Packaging Inc................................. C 216 391-6129
   Willoughby Hills *(G-15234)*

RLR Investments LLC................................... D 937 382-1494
   Wilmington *(G-15270)*

Woodruff Enterprises Inc............................... E 937 399-9300
   Springfield *(G-13314)*

4225 General warehousing and storage

151 W 4th Cincinnati LLC.............................. D 312 283-3683
   Cincinnati *(G-2119)*

A Duie Pyle Inc... D 330 342-7750
   Streetsboro *(G-13408)*

Aero Fulfillment Services Corp..................... D 513 874-4112
   West Chester *(G-14648)*

▲ Aero Fulfillment Services Corp................. D 800 225-7145
   Mason *(G-10517)*

Aldelano Corporation..................................... E 909 861-3970
   Lima *(G-9861)*

▲ All Pro Freight Systems Inc...................... D 440 934-2222
   Westlake *(G-15030)*

Allegion S&S Holding Co Inc........................ C 513 766-4300
   Blue Ash *(G-1127)*

AM Industrial Group LLC.............................. E 216 267-6783
   Cleveland *(G-3798)*

Amazon.. E 951 733-5325
   Columbus *(G-5342)*

Andersons Inc... E 419 891-6479
   Maumee *(G-10693)*

Arett Sales Corp... E 937 552-2005
   Troy *(G-14129)*

Asw Global LLC.. E 330 899-1003
   Canton *(G-1672)*

Asw Global LLC.. D 330 798-5184
   Mogadore *(G-11323)*

▲ Asw Global LLC.. D 330 733-6291
   Mogadore *(G-11322)*

Aviation Auto Trnsp Spclsts In..................... E 502 785-4657
   Fort Loramie *(G-8603)*

B D S Inc.. E 513 921-8441
   Cincinnati *(G-2235)*

Backyard Storage Solutions LLC.................. D 330 723-4412
   Medina *(G-10813)*

Basista Furniture Inc...................................... E 216 398-5900
   Cleveland *(G-3854)*

Bendon Inc... D 419 903-0403
   Ashland *(G-481)*

Big Lots Stores Inc... E 614 278-6800
   Columbus *(G-5438)*

Big Sandy Furniture Inc................................. D 740 894-4242
   Chesapeake *(G-2028)*

Big Sandy Furniture Inc................................. D 740 775-4244
   Chillicothe *(G-2052)*

Big Sandy Furniture Inc................................. D 740 354-3193
   Portsmouth *(G-12546)*

▲ Big Sandy Furniture Inc........................... D 740 574-2113
   Franklin Furnace *(G-8653)*

Burd Brothers Inc... E 800 538-2873
   Batavia *(G-729)*

Cartcom Inc... D 740 644-0912
   Hebron *(G-9141)*

▲ Caruso Inc... E 513 860-9200
   Cincinnati *(G-2316)*

▼ Cauffiel Technologies Corporation........... E 419 843-7262
   Toledo *(G-13726)*

Central Whse Operations Inc........................ D 330 453-3709
   Canton *(G-1707)*

CFS Family Holdings Inc.............................. E 740 492-0595
   Newcomerstown *(G-11766)*

Chewy Inc... B 937 669-4839
   Vandalia *(G-14369)*

Childrens Hospital Medical Ctr.................... A 513 636-4200
   Cincinnati *(G-2370)*

CJ Logistics America LLC............................ D 847 390-6800
   Toledo *(G-13745)*

CJ Logstics Holdings Amer Corp................ D 614 879-9659
   West Jefferson *(G-14849)*

Commercial Warehouse & Cartage............. D 614 409-3901
   Groveport *(G-8978)*

▲ Commonwealth Warehouse Inc............... E 513 791-1966
   Cincinnati *(G-2482)*

Compak Inc... E 330 345-5666
   Wooster *(G-15326)*

Comprehensive Logistics Co Inc................. D 563 445-6001
   Youngstown *(G-15587)*

▲ Contanda Terminals LLC.......................... E 513 921-8441
   Cincinnati *(G-2500)*

Cotter Mdse Stor of Ohio............................. E 330 773-9177
   Akron *(G-124)*

Cotter Moving & Storage Co........................ E 330 535-5115
   Akron *(G-125)*

Crescent Park Corporation............................ C 513 759-7000
   West Chester *(G-14679)*

D + S Distribution Inc.................................... D 800 752-5993
   Orrville *(G-12161)*

Durant Dc LLC.. B 614 278-6800
   Columbus *(G-5795)*

Eddie Bauer LLC.. E 614 497-8200
   Groveport *(G-8983)*

▼ Eddie Buer Flfillment Svcs Inc................. A 614 497-8200
   Groveport *(G-8984)*

Elyria Foundry Company LLC...................... D 440 322-4657
   Elyria *(G-8246)*

Essilor of America Inc................................... E 614 492-0888
   Groveport *(G-8986)*

◆ Exel Inc.. B 614 865-5819
   Westerville *(G-14893)*

Fabrizi Trucking & Pav Co Inc..................... D 440 234-1284
   Cleveland *(G-4233)*

▲ Faro Services Inc...................................... C 614 497-1700
   Groveport *(G-8988)*

Ferry Cap & Set Screw Company............... D 440 315-9291
   Lakewood *(G-9665)*

First Group Investment Partnr..................... D 513 241-2200
   Cincinnati *(G-2674)*

Firstgroup Usa Inc... B 513 241-2200
   Cincinnati *(G-2687)*

Fremont Logistics LLC................................... E 419 333-0669
   Fremont *(G-8680)*

G & S Metal Products Co Inc...................... D 216 831-2388
   Cleveland *(G-4294)*

Getgo Transportation Co LLC..................... E 419 666-6850
   Millbury *(G-11269)*

Goodwill Ester Seals Miami Vly.................. B 937 461-4800
   Dayton *(G-7380)*

Graham Investment Co.................................. D 740 382-0902
   Marion *(G-10429)*

Home Depot USA Inc.................................... D 419 299-2000
   Van Buren *(G-14338)*

▲ Hyperlogistics Group Inc........................... E 614 497-0800
   Columbus *(G-6035)*

Ieh Auto Parts LLC.. E 216 351-2560
   Cleveland *(G-4403)*

Imcd Us LLC... C 216 228-8900
   Akron *(G-200)*

Impact Fulfillment Svcs LLC........................ C 614 262-8911
   Columbus *(G-6043)*

J B Express Inc... D 740 702-9830
   Chillicothe *(G-2075)*

J-Trac Inc... E 419 524-3456
   Mansfield *(G-10274)*

Kandel Cold Storage Inc.............................. D 330 798-4111
   Tallmadge *(G-13597)*

Keller Logistics Group Inc........................... E 866 276-9486
   Defiance *(G-7751)*

King Tut Logistics LLC................................. E 614 538-0509
   Columbus *(G-6117)*

Kohls Department Stores Inc...................... E 419 421-5301
   Findlay *(G-8554)*

Kroger Co... A 859 630-6959
   Delaware *(G-7812)*

Kroger Co... D 859 630-6959
   Milford *(G-11235)*

▲ Kroger Company.. A 740 657-2124
   Delaware *(G-7813)*

42 MOTOR FREIGHT TRANSPORTATION

Lakota Local School District................ E 513 777-2150
   Liberty Township *(G-9853)*
▲ Lesaint Logistics Inc........................ C 513 874-3900
   West Chester *(G-14722)*
◆ Lewis & Michael Inc......................... E 937 252-6683
   Dayton *(G-7453)*
Lowes Home Centers LLC................ D 740 636-2100
   Wshngtn Ct Hs *(G-15489)*
M A Folkes Company Inc................... E 513 785-4200
   Hamilton *(G-9062)*
Mansfield Whsng & Dist Inc............... C 419 522-3510
   Ontario *(G-12114)*
Micro Electronics Inc.......................... B 614 334-1430
   Columbus *(G-6233)*
Mid State Systems Inc....................... E 740 928-1115
   Hebron *(G-9148)*
Midwest Trmnals Tledo Intl Inc........... E 419 897-6868
   Toledo *(G-13924)*
▲ Millwood Inc.................................... E 330 393-4400
   Vienna *(G-14422)*
Mwd Logistics Inc............................... E 440 266-2500
   Mentor *(G-10978)*
▲ National Distribution Centers.......... C 419 422-3432
   Columbus *(G-6295)*
▲ Neighborhood Logistics Co Inc....... E 440 466-0020
   Geneva *(G-8787)*
Networking Partners Inc.................... C 727 417-7447
   Cincinnati *(G-3107)*
Norplas Industries Inc........................ B 419 666-6119
   Perrysburg *(G-12358)*
▲ North Coast Logistics Inc............... E 216 362-7159
   Brookpark *(G-1438)*
Odw Logistics Inc.............................. E 614 549-5000
   Lockbourne *(G-10013)*
Ohio Desk Company......................... E 216 623-0600
   Brooklyn Heights *(G-1426)*
PC Connection Sales Corp................ D 937 382-4800
   Wilmington *(G-15264)*
Penney Opco LLC.............................. B 614 863-7043
   Columbus *(G-6513)*
Peoples Cartage Inc........................... E 330 833-8571
   Massillon *(G-10661)*
Piqua Steel Co................................... D 937 773-3632
   Piqua *(G-12454)*
Precision Strip Inc.............................. D 419 674-4186
   Kenton *(G-9622)*
Precision Strip Inc.............................. D 937 667-6255
   Tipp City *(G-13664)*
Quaker Sales & Dist Inc..................... A 914 767-7010
   Lockbourne *(G-10014)*
R R Donnelley & Sons Company....... E 614 539-5527
   Grove City *(G-8947)*
Ravenna School District..................... E 330 297-4138
   Ravenna *(G-12640)*
◆ Redhawk Global LLC...................... E 614 487-8505
   Columbus *(G-6569)*
Reliable Rnners Curier Svc Inc........... E 440 578-1011
   Mentor *(G-10991)*
Revitalize Industries LLC.................... E 440 570-3473
   Cleveland *(G-4834)*
Revitalize Industries LLC.................... E 440 570-3473
   Maple Heights *(G-10344)*
SH Bell Company............................... E 412 963-9910
   East Liverpool *(G-8193)*
Shippers Automotive Group LLC....... C 937 484-7780
   Urbana *(G-14313)*
▲ Spartan Whse & Dist Co Inc........... D 614 497-1777
   Columbus *(G-6701)*
▲ Specialty Chemical Sales Inc......... E 216 267-4248
   Cleveland *(G-4928)*
Springs Window Fashions LLC......... E 614 492-6770
   Groveport *(G-9002)*

Stationers Inc..................................... E 740 423-1400
   Belpre *(G-1059)*
Summit NW Corporation.................... D 503 255-3826
   Dublin *(G-8134)*
Taylor Warehouse Corporation........... E 513 771-1850
   West Chester *(G-14772)*
Taylor Warehouse Corporation........... E 513 771-1850
   West Chester *(G-14840)*
▲ Terminal Warehouse Inc................. C 330 773-2056
   Canton *(G-1870)*
Tmt Warehousing LLC........................ C 419 662-3146
   Perrysburg *(G-12378)*
Trane Technologies Company LLC.... E 419 633-6800
   Bryan *(G-1494)*
TRT Management Corporation........... E 419 661-1233
   Perrysburg *(G-12380)*
Utility Trailer Mfg Co.......................... B 513 436-2600
   Batavia *(G-753)*
Van Boxel Stor Solutions LLC............ E 440 721-1504
   Chardon *(G-2025)*
◆ Vectra Inc....................................... E 614 351-6868
   Columbus *(G-6843)*
Verst Group Logistics Inc................... E 513 772-2494
   Cincinnati *(G-3621)*
Verst Group Logistics Inc................... C 859 379-1207
   Cincinnati *(G-3622)*
Verst Group Logistics Inc................... C 513 782-1725
   Cincinnati *(G-3623)*
Verst Group Logistics Inc................... D 859 379-1230
   West Chester *(G-14844)*
W W Grainger Inc............................... E 330 425-8388
   Macedonia *(G-10209)*
Wad Investments Oh Inc................... E 513 891-4477
   Cincinnati *(G-3637)*
Walmart Inc.. E 614 409-5500
   Lockbourne *(G-10017)*
Walmart Inc.. C 740 765-5700
   Wintersville *(G-15297)*
Wannemacher Enterprises Inc........... E 419 225-9060
   Lima *(G-9979)*
Warehouse Svcs Group Ltd Lblty...... E 419 868-6400
   Holland *(G-9314)*
Williams Scotsman Inc....................... E 978 228-0305
   Fairfield *(G-8454)*
Wooster City Schools......................... D 330 262-9616
   Wooster *(G-15391)*
◆ Workflowone LLC........................... A 877 735-4966
   Dayton *(G-7726)*
Xtreme Express LLC.......................... C 614 735-0291
   Columbus *(G-6914)*
Ysi Management LLC........................ E 440 891-4100
   Cleveland *(G-5170)*

4226 Special warehousing and storage, nec

Abbott Laboratories........................... D 847 937-6100
   Columbus *(G-5294)*
Access Info Holdings LLC.................. A 614 777-1701
   Columbus *(G-5302)*
Access Information MGT Corp........... A 614 777-1701
   Columbus *(G-5303)*
American Excelsior Company............ D 419 663-3241
   Norwalk *(G-12000)*
ARC Healthcare LLC......................... E 888 552-0677
   Worthington *(G-15405)*
B D S Inc.. E 513 921-8441
   Cincinnati *(G-2235)*
Ballreich Bros Inc............................... C 419 447-1814
   Tiffin *(G-13624)*
Briar-Gate Realty Inc.......................... D 614 299-2121
   Grove City *(G-8899)*
▲ Cornerstone Consolidated.............. A 513 603-1100
   West Chester *(G-14678)*

◆ Exel Holdings (usa) Inc................... C 614 865-8500
   Westerville *(G-14892)*
Fox... E 419 352-1673
   Bowling Green *(G-1320)*
High Line Corporation........................ E 330 848-8800
   Akron *(G-192)*
Honda Logistics North Amer Inc........ A 937 642-0335
   East Liberty *(G-8172)*
▲ Kuhlman Corporation...................... E 419 897-6000
   Maumee *(G-10737)*
Lalac One LLC................................... E 216 432-4422
   Cleveland *(G-4482)*
▲ Midwest Express Inc...................... A 937 642-0335
   East Liberty *(G-8173)*
Nx Autmotive Logistics USA Inc........ C 937 642-8333
   East Liberty *(G-8174)*
PC Connection Inc............................. C 937 382-4800
   Wilmington *(G-15263)*
Radial South LP................................. B 678 584-4047
   Groveport *(G-8997)*
Ray Hamilton Companies................... E 513 641-5400
   Cincinnati *(G-3274)*
SH Bell Company............................... E 412 963-9910
   East Liverpool *(G-8193)*
Thirty-One Gifts LLC.......................... C 614 414-4300
   New Albany *(G-11588)*
Vrc Companies LLC........................... D 614 299-2122
   Grove City *(G-8964)*
Vrc Companies LLC........................... E 419 381-7762
   Maumee *(G-10778)*
Warren City Board Education............. E 330 841-2265
   Warren *(G-14574)*
Wooster Motor Ways Inc.................... C 330 264-9557
   Wooster *(G-15396)*

4231 Trucking terminal facilities

Chieftain Trucking & Excav Inc........... E 216 485-8034
   Cleveland *(G-3968)*
Dayton Freight Lines Inc.................... B 937 236-4880
   Dayton *(G-7283)*
Delta Shipping Inc.............................. E 619 261-7456
   Grove City *(G-8914)*
J Rayl Transport Inc........................... D 330 784-1134
   Akron *(G-206)*
PAm Transportation Svcs Inc............. E 419 935-9501
   Willard *(G-15172)*
Pitt-Ohio Express LLC....................... C 216 433-9000
   Cleveland *(G-4752)*
Red Rover LLC................................... E 330 262-6501
   Wooster *(G-15368)*
Santmyer Logistics Inc....................... D 330 262-6501
   Wooster *(G-15371)*
Short Freight Lines Inc....................... E 419 729-1691
   Toledo *(G-14011)*
Tek Logistics LLC............................... E 614 260-9250
   Columbus *(G-6753)*
Tforce Freight Inc............................... E 513 771-7555
   Cincinnati *(G-3461)*
Xpo Logistics Freight Inc.................... C 614 876-7100
   Columbus *(G-6912)*
Xpo Logistics Freight Inc.................... D 330 896-7300
   Uniontown *(G-14271)*

44 WATER TRANSPORTATION

4412 Deep sea foreign transportation of freight

◆ Midwest Transatlantic Lines Inc....... E 440 243-1993
   Berea *(G-1074)*

4432 Freight transportation on the great lakes

The Interlake Steamship Co................. B 440 260-6900
  Middleburg Heights *(G-11131)*

4449 Water transportation of freight

Acnr River Towing Inc........................ D 740 338-3100
  Saint Clairsville *(G-12772)*
Midland Company............................... A 513 947-5503
  Amelia *(G-418)*
Mon River Towing Inc......................... B 740 338-3100
  Saint Clairsville *(G-12804)*

4491 Marine cargo handling

Cincinnati Bulk Terminals LLC............. E 513 621-4800
  Cincinnati *(G-2402)*
McGinnis Inc..................................... C 740 377-4391
  South Point *(G-13178)*
McNational Inc.................................. D 740 377-4391
  South Point *(G-13179)*
Midwest Trmnals Tledo Intl Inc............ E 419 897-6868
  Toledo *(G-13924)*
◆ Pinney Dock & Transport LLC........... D 440 964-7186
  Ashtabula *(G-546)*
River Services Inc.............................. C 612 588-8141
  Cincinnati *(G-3300)*

4492 Towing and tugboat service

A M & O Towing Inc........................... E 330 385-0639
  Negley *(G-11540)*
Bellaire Harbor Service LLC................ E 740 676-4305
  Bellaire *(G-1006)*
Great Lakes Group............................. C 216 621-4854
  Cleveland *(G-4329)*
Shelly Materials Inc........................... D 740 246-6315
  Thornville *(G-13622)*
The Great Lakes Towing Company....... D 216 621-4854
  Cleveland *(G-5000)*

4493 Marinas

Beaver Park Marina Inc...................... E 440 282-6308
  Lorain *(G-10059)*
Catawba-Cleveland Dev Corp.............. D 419 797-4424
  Port Clinton *(G-12518)*
Island Service Company..................... E 419 285-3695
  Put In Bay *(G-12617)*
Lakeside Marine Inc........................... E 419 732-7160
  Port Clinton *(G-12537)*
S B S Transit Inc............................... E 440 288-2222
  Elyria *(G-8292)*
Saw Mill Creek Ltd............................. E 419 433-3800
  Huron *(G-9392)*
Tappan Lake Marina Inc..................... E 740 269-2031
  Scio *(G-12943)*

4499 Water transportation services, nec

MPW Industrial Water Svcs Inc........... C 800 827-8790
  Hebron *(G-9151)*

45 TRANSPORTATION BY AIR

4512 Air transportation, scheduled

American Airlines Inc......................... E 937 890-6668
  Vandalia *(G-14363)*
City of Dayton................................... C 937 454-8200
  Vandalia *(G-14371)*
Commuteair LLC................................ C 440 779-4588
  North Olmsted *(G-11899)*
Executive Jet Management Inc........... B 513 979-6600
  Cincinnati *(G-2644)*
Flight Express Inc.............................. D 305 379-8686
  Columbus *(G-5873)*
Lane Aviation Corporation................... C 614 237-3747
  Columbus *(G-6138)*
Piedmont Airlines Inc......................... C 330 499-3260
  North Canton *(G-11851)*
Psa Airlines Inc................................. D 330 490-2939
  North Canton *(G-11855)*
Psa Airlines Inc................................. C 937 454-1116
  Vandalia *(G-14389)*
United Airlines Inc............................. C 216 501-4700
  Cleveland *(G-5053)*
United Airlines Inc............................. E 216 501-5644
  Cleveland *(G-5054)*
United Airlines Inc............................. E 216 501-5169
  Cleveland *(G-5055)*
United Airlines Inc............................. E 937 454-2009
  Vandalia *(G-14397)*
United Parcel Service Inc................... D 614 237-9171
  Columbus *(G-6811)*
United Parcel Service Inc................... E 216 676-1570
  Middleburg Heights *(G-11132)*

4513 Air courier services

▲ Abx Air Inc.................................... B 937 382-5591
  Wilmington *(G-15237)*
Air Transport Svcs Group Inc.............. C 937 382-5591
  Wilmington *(G-15240)*
Airborne Global Solutions Inc.............. D 937 382-5591
  Wilmington *(G-15241)*
Ames Material Services Inc................ E 937 382-5591
  Wilmington *(G-15244)*
Federal Express Corporation............... E 800 463-3339
  Vandalia *(G-14378)*
Global Mail Inc.................................. E 330 849-3248
  Stow *(G-13371)*
Lgstx Services Inc............................. E 866 931-2337
  Wilmington *(G-15257)*
United Parcel Service Inc................... D 440 826-2508
  Cleveland *(G-5066)*
United Parcel Service Inc................... D 614 385-9100
  Columbus *(G-6812)*
United Parcel Service Inc................... E 419 782-3552
  Defiance *(G-7773)*
United Parcel Service Inc................... E 419 222-7399
  Lima *(G-9975)*
United Parcel Service Inc................... E 330 339-6281
  New Philadelphia *(G-11671)*

4522 Air transportation, nonscheduled

Aerodynmics Inc Ardynamics Inc......... E 404 596-8751
  Beachwood *(G-764)*
Air Evac Ems Inc............................... C 417 274-6754
  Lancaster *(G-9692)*
Air Tahoma Inc.................................. D 614 774-0728
  Powell *(G-12583)*
Airnet Systems Inc............................ E 614 409-4900
  Columbus *(G-5331)*
Executive Jet Management Inc........... B 513 979-6600
  Cincinnati *(G-2644)*
Griffings Flying Service Inc................. E 419 734-5400
  Port Clinton *(G-12530)*
Jetselect LLC.................................... E 954 648-0998
  Columbus *(G-6087)*
◆ Jilco Industries Inc......................... E 330 698-0280
  Kidron *(G-9636)*
Lane Aviation Corporation................... C 614 237-3747
  Columbus *(G-6138)*
McKinley Air Transport Inc................. E 330 497-6956
  Canton *(G-1802)*
Netjets Aviation Inc........................... E 614 239-5500
  Columbus *(G-6348)*
Netjets International Inc..................... A 614 239-5500
  Columbus *(G-6349)*
Netjets Sales Inc............................... C 614 239-5500
  Columbus *(G-6350)*
Ohio Medical Trnsp Inc...................... D 614 791-4400
  Columbus *(G-6437)*
Options Flight Support Inc.................. A 216 261-3500
  Cleveland *(G-4705)*
Panther II Transportation Inc.............. C 800 685-0657
  Medina *(G-10872)*

4581 Airports, flying fields, and services

▲ Abx Air Inc.................................... B 937 382-5591
  Wilmington *(G-15237)*
Aero Propulsion Support Inc............... E 513 367-9452
  Harrison *(G-9096)*
Air General Inc.................................. E 216 501-5643
  Cleveland *(G-3778)*
Akron-Canton Regional Airport............ E 330 499-4059
  North Canton *(G-11809)*
Capital City Aviation Inc..................... E 614 459-2541
  Columbus *(G-5497)*
City of Cleveland............................... A 216 265-6000
  Cleveland *(G-3980)*
City of Dayton................................... C 937 454-8200
  Vandalia *(G-14371)*
Cleveland Hopkins Intl Arprt............... E 216 265-6000
  Cleveland *(G-4051)*
Columbus Regional Airport Auth.......... B 614 239-4000
  Columbus *(G-5652)*
Constant Aviation LLC........................ C 800 440-9004
  Cleveland *(G-4108)*
Corporate Wngs - Cleveland LLC......... D 216 261-9000
  Cleveland *(G-4117)*
Executive Jet Management Inc........... B 513 979-6600
  Cincinnati *(G-2644)*
◆ Exel Inc.. B 614 865-5819
  Westerville *(G-14893)*
Flexjet Inc.. E 866 309-2214
  Richmond Heights *(G-12718)*
Foxtrot Aviation Services LLC............. E 330 806-7477
  Canton *(G-1757)*
General Electric Company................... A 617 443-3000
  Cincinnati *(G-2725)*
Griffings Flying Service Inc................. E 419 734-5400
  Port Clinton *(G-12530)*
Hhd Aviation LLC............................... D 513 426-8378
  Hamilton *(G-9052)*
Jet East Inc...................................... C 215 937-9020
  Solon *(G-13102)*
Lane Aviation Corporation................... C 614 237-3747
  Columbus *(G-6138)*
Macair Aviation LLC........................... E 937 347-1302
  Xenia *(G-15525)*
McKinley Air Transport Inc................. E 330 497-6956
  Canton *(G-1802)*
Menzies Aviation (texas) Inc............... D 216 265-3777
  Cleveland *(G-4553)*
National Flight Services Inc................ C 419 865-2311
  Swanton *(G-13527)*
Plane Detail LLC................................ E 614 734-1201
  Galena *(G-8739)*
Safegate Airport Systems Inc............. E 763 535-9299
  Columbus *(G-6628)*
Servisair LLC.................................... C 216 267-9910
  Cleveland *(G-4897)*
Sky Quest LLC.................................. D 216 362-9904
  Cleveland *(G-4912)*
Stevens Arospc Def Systems LLC........ D 937 454-3400
  Vandalia *(G-14393)*
TAS Aviation Defiance Inc.................. E 419 658-4444
  Defiance *(G-7771)*
Toledo-Lucas County Port Auth........... D 419 865-2351
  Swanton *(G-13530)*

45 TRANSPORTATION BY AIR

True Wing Aviation LLC .... E 937 657-3990
  Lebanon *(G-9796)*
Unison Industries LLC .... B 904 667-9904
  Dayton *(G-7143)*
Winner Aviation Corporation .... C 330 856-5000
  Vienna *(G-14424)*

46 PIPELINES, EXCEPT NATURAL GAS

4612 Crude petroleum pipelines

BP Oil Pipeline Company .... A 216 398-8685
  Cleveland *(G-3887)*
Buckeye Pipe Line Services Co .... B 419 698-8770
  Oregon *(G-12130)*
Hardin Street Marine LLC .... D 419 672-6500
  Findlay *(G-8544)*
▲ Marathon Pipe Line LLC .... C 419 422-2121
  Findlay *(G-8563)*
Mplx LP .... E 419 421-2121
  Findlay *(G-8571)*

4613 Refined petroleum pipelines

Integrity Kksing Ppline Svcs L .... C 740 694-6315
  Fredericktown *(G-8660)*
▲ Marathon Pipe Line LLC .... C 419 422-2121
  Findlay *(G-8563)*
Mplx LP .... E 419 421-2121
  Findlay *(G-8571)*

47 TRANSPORTATION SERVICES

4724 Travel agencies

AAA Club Alliance Inc .... E 513 984-3553
  Cincinnati *(G-2133)*
AAA Club Alliance Inc .... A 513 762-3301
  Cincinnati *(G-2134)*
AAA East Central .... E 330 652-6466
  Niles *(G-11779)*
AAA Miami Valley .... D 937 224-2896
  Dayton *(G-7150)*
Allstars Travel Group Inc .... C 614 901-4100
  New Albany *(G-11556)*
American Ex Trvl Rlted Svcs In .... E 330 922-5700
  Cuyahoga Falls *(G-7039)*
Avalon Holdings Corporation .... D 330 856-8800
  Warren *(G-14501)*
Chima Travel Bureau Inc .... E 330 867-4770
  Fairlawn *(G-8470)*
Khm Consulting Inc .... E 330 460-5635
  Brunswick *(G-1461)*
Medus Travelers .... D 513 678-2179
  Blue Ash *(G-1208)*
Professional Travel Inc .... D 440 734-8800
  North Olmsted *(G-11911)*
West Enterprises Inc .... E 614 237-4488
  Columbus *(G-6879)*

4729 Passenger transportation arrangement

Rush Expediting Inc .... E 937 885-0894
  Dayton *(G-7598)*

4731 Freight transportation arrangement

A Plus Expediting & Logistics .... E 937 424-0220
  Dayton *(G-7149)*
Aim Leasing Company .... D 330 759-0438
  Girard *(G-8809)*
Air Transport Intl Ltd Lblty .... A 501 615-3500
  Holland *(G-9277)*
Airnet Systems Inc .... E 614 409-4900
  Columbus *(G-5331)*
Alliance Customs Clearance .... E 513 794-9400
  Cincinnati *(G-2162)*
Ameri-Line Inc .... E 440 316-4500
  Columbia Station *(G-5223)*
American Marine Express Inc .... E 216 268-3005
  Cleveland *(G-3803)*
Ardmore Power Logistics LLC .... E 216 502-0640
  Westlake *(G-15034)*
Ascent Global Logistics LLC .... C 330 342-8700
  Hudson *(G-9332)*
Ascent Globl Lgstics Hldngs In .... E 603 881-3350
  Hudson *(G-9333)*
Attari Delivery LLC .... D 443 251-8172
  Toledo *(G-13694)*
Bbi Logistics LLC .... C 800 809-2172
  Columbus *(G-5425)*
Berkshire Local School Dst .... E 440 834-4123
  Burton *(G-1525)*
Bleckmann USA LLC .... E 740 809-2645
  Columbus *(G-5446)*
Blue Flag Logistics LLC .... D 502 975-8473
  Columbus *(G-5449)*
Bnsf Logistics LLC .... E 937 526-3141
  Versailles *(G-14413)*
Bolt Express LLC .... D 419 729-6698
  Toledo *(G-13711)*
Buckeye Transfer LLC .... D 330 719-0375
  Lisbon *(G-9997)*
Ceva Logistics LLC .... C 614 482-5000
  Groveport *(G-8977)*
CJ Logstics Holdings Amer Corp .... D 614 879-9659
  West Jefferson *(G-14849)*
Claust LLC .... E 440 783-2847
  Columbia Station *(G-5224)*
Cleveland Motor Carrier Inc .... D 440 901-9192
  Madison *(G-10213)*
Complete Care Providers Inc .... E 937 825-4698
  Cincinnati *(G-2487)*
Con-Way Multimodal Inc .... D 614 923-1400
  Dublin *(G-7971)*
◆ Concord Express Inc .... E 718 656-7821
  Groveport *(G-8979)*
▲ Containerport Group Inc .... D 440 333-1330
  Cleveland *(G-4112)*
Contech Trckg & Logistics LLC .... D 513 645-7000
  West Chester *(G-14673)*
Craig Transportation Co .... E 419 874-7981
  Maumee *(G-10714)*
DATA Den Inc .... E 216 622-0900
  Cleveland *(G-4149)*
Dayton Freight Lines Inc .... B 937 236-4880
  Dayton *(G-7283)*
Dayton Synchrnous Spport Ctr I .... E 937 226-1559
  Dayton *(G-7302)*
Deanhouston Inc .... E 740 646-2914
  West Chester *(G-14807)*
Dhl Express (usa) Inc .... E 614 865-8325
  Westerville *(G-14889)*
Diamond W LLC .... D 970 434-9435
  Clarington *(G-3729)*
Distribution Data Incorporated .... D 216 362-3009
  Brookpark *(G-1433)*
DSV Solutions LLC .... C 740 989-1200
  Little Hocking *(G-10008)*
Ease Logistics Services LLC .... C 614 553-7007
  Dublin *(G-7999)*
Esj Carrier Corporation .... E 513 728-7388
  Fairfield *(G-8413)*
Estes Express Lines .... E 330 659-9750
  Richfield *(G-12696)*
Exel Global Logistics Inc .... C 440 243-5900
  Cleveland *(G-4231)*
Exel Global Logistics Inc .... C 614 409-4500
  Columbus *(G-5838)*
Exel Inc .... D 614 836-1265
  Groveport *(G-8987)*
Exel Inc .... E 614 865-8294
  Westerville *(G-14894)*
◆ Exel N Amercn Logistics Inc .... C 800 272-1052
  Westerville *(G-14978)*
Expeditors Intl Wash Inc .... D 440 243-9900
  Cleveland *(G-4232)*
▲ Faro Services Inc .... C 614 497-1700
  Groveport *(G-8988)*
Fedex Custom Critical Inc .... B 234 310-4090
  Richfield *(G-12698)*
▲ Fedex Supplychain Systems Inc .... A
  Hudson *(G-9348)*
Fedex Truckload Brokerage Inc .... C 800 463-3339
  Uniontown *(G-14252)*
First Star Logistics LLC .... E 812 637-3251
  Cincinnati *(G-2676)*
Fresh Transportation Co Ltd .... D 937 492-9876
  Sidney *(G-13033)*
Garner Trucking Inc .... E 419 422-5742
  Findlay *(G-8536)*
Gateway Freight Forwarding Inc .... D 513 248-1514
  Cincinnati *(G-2718)*
Geist Logistics LLC .... E 954 463-6910
  Columbus *(G-5923)*
Gozal Incorporated .... E 833 603-0303
  Hooven *(G-9317)*
Grays Trnsp & Logistics LLC .... E 614 656-3460
  Columbus *(G-5949)*
Gxo Logistics Supply Chain Inc .... E 614 305-1705
  Grove City *(G-8923)*
Hiyes Logistics .... E 614 558-0198
  Plain City *(G-12481)*
IHS Enterprise LLC .... C 216 588-9078
  Independence *(G-9436)*
Innovative Logistics Svcs Inc .... D 330 468-6422
  Northfield *(G-11958)*
Integrity Ex Logistics LLC .... B 888 374-5138
  Cincinnati *(G-2877)*
J B Express Inc .... D 740 702-9830
  Chillicothe *(G-2075)*
J Rayl Transport Inc .... D 330 784-1134
  Akron *(G-206)*
Jarrett Logistics Systems Inc .... C 330 682-0099
  Orrville *(G-12168)*
Kag Specialty Products Group LLC .... E 330 409-1124
  North Canton *(G-11841)*
Keller Logistics Group Inc .... E 866 276-9486
  Defiance *(G-7751)*
Kgbo Holdings Inc .... D 513 831-2600
  Cincinnati *(G-2107)*
Komyo America Co Inc .... E 937 339-0157
  Troy *(G-14143)*
Kuehne + Nagel Inc .... C 440 243-6070
  Berea *(G-1072)*
Kw International Inc .... E 513 942-8999
  Cincinnati *(G-2957)*
Landstar Global Logistics Inc .... D 740 575-4700
  Coshocton *(G-6990)*
Lesaint Logistics Trnsp Inc .... E 513 942-3056
  Fairfield *(G-8426)*
Logistics Legacy LLC .... E 513 244-3026
  Cincinnati *(G-2985)*
Martin Logistics Incorporated .... D 330 456-8000
  Canton *(G-1800)*
Mid Ohio Vly Bulk Trnspt Inc .... E 740 373-2481
  Marietta *(G-10390)*
◆ Midwest Transatlantic Lines Inc .... E 440 243-1993
  Berea *(G-1074)*

▲ Millwood Inc .... E 330 393-4400
  Vienna (G-14422)
Millwood Natural LLC .... E 330 393-4400
  Vienna (G-14423)
▲ Moving Solutions Inc .... D 440 946-9300
  Mentor (G-10977)
Mud Made Logistics Corporation .... E 614 284-2772
  Toledo (G-13929)
Nagle Logistics Group Company .... D 419 661-2500
  Walbridge (G-14462)
National Freight Inc .... E 614 575-8490
  Columbus (G-6298)
Nations Express Inc .... E 440 234-4330
  Brunswick (G-1465)
Newark Parcel Service Company .... E 614 253-3777
  Columbus (G-6353)
Nfi Industries Inc .... E 740 527-9060
  Hebron (G-9152)
Nippon Express USA Inc .... E 614 295-0030
  Grove City (G-8941)
Nissin Intl Trnspt USA Inc .... D 937 644-2644
  Marysville (G-10500)
◆ Nk Parts Industries Inc .... C 937 498-4651
  Sidney (G-13041)
North South Delivery LLC .... E 419 478-7400
  Toledo (G-13937)
Nutrition Trnsp Svcs LLC .... D 937 962-2661
  Lewisburg (G-9841)
Odw Logistics Inc .... D 513 785-4980
  Hamilton (G-9069)
◆ Odw Logistics Inc .... B 614 549-5000
  Columbus (G-6384)
Odw Lts LLC .... C 800 978-3168
  Hamilton (G-9070)
Overland Xpress LLC .... E 513 528-1158
  Cincinnati (G-3177)
Owens Intermodal LLC .... E 419 365-2704
  Maumee (G-10753)
Pacer Transport Inc .... D 614 923-1400
  Dublin (G-8085)
Ploger Transportation LLC .... E 419 465-2100
  Monroeville (G-11358)
Ptc Transintemational System Ltd .... E 513 738-0900
  Hamilton (G-9075)
R&L Hero Delivery LLC .... D 937 824-0291
  Dayton (G-7140)
Ray Hamilton Companies .... E 513 641-5400
  Cincinnati (G-3274)
◆ Redhawk Global LLC .... E 614 487-8505
  Columbus (G-6569)
Regional Express Inc .... E 516 458-3514
  Richfield (G-12707)
Rondy Fleet Services Inc .... E 330 745-9016
  Barberton (G-706)
Ryan Logistics Inc .... D 937 642-4158
  Marysville (G-10506)
Ryder Integrated Logistics Inc .... E 614 801-0224
  Grove City (G-8949)
Savino Del Bene USA Inc .... C 347 960-5568
  Middleburg Heights (G-11127)
Schneider Nat Carriers Inc .... A 740 362-6910
  Delaware (G-7825)
Shipping Pilot LLC .... E 505 744-7669
  Strongsville (G-13482)
Shoreline Transportation Inc .... C 440 878-2000
  Strongsville (G-13483)
Stg Cartage LLC .... A 614 923-1400
  Dublin (G-8127)
Stg Cartage LLC .... E 614 923-1400
  Dublin (G-8128)
Stg Intermodal Inc .... E 440 833-0924
  Wickliffe (G-15163)

◆ Stg Intermodal Inc .... D 614 923-1400
  Dublin (G-8129)
◆ STG Intermodal Solutions Inc .... C 614 923-1400
  Dublin (G-8130)
◆ Stg Stacktrain LLC .... C 614 923-1400
  Dublin (G-8131)
Stridas LLC .... E 513 725-4626
  Cincinnati (G-3423)
Summit NW Corporation .... D 503 255-3826
  Dublin (G-8134)
Supreme Xpress Trnsp Inc .... D 234 738-4047
  Akron (G-327)
Syncreon America Inc .... D 419 727-4593
  Toledo (G-14032)
T S Expediting Services Inc .... D 419 837-2401
  Millbury (G-11271)
Taylor Logistics Inc .... D 513 771-1850
  West Chester (G-14839)
▲ Tazmanian Freight Fwdg Inc .... E 216 265-7881
  Middleburg Heights (G-11130)
Tforce Freight Inc .... E 216 676-4560
  Cleveland (G-4988)
Tgs International Inc .... E 330 893-4828
  Millersburg (G-11293)
Tjm Express Inc .... E 216 385-4164
  Berea (G-1085)
Total Quality Logistics LLC .... D 513 831-2600
  Akron (G-336)
Total Quality Logistics LLC .... C 800 580-3101
  Centerville (G-1952)
Total Quality Logistics LLC .... D 513 831-2600
  Cincinnati (G-2116)
Total Quality Logistics LLC .... D 513 831-2600
  Cincinnati (G-3485)
Total Quality Logistics LLC .... E 513 831-2600
  Milford (G-11261)
Total Quality Logistics LLC .... D 800 580-3101
  West Chester (G-14774)
Tradefull LLC .... D 888 203-0826
  North Canton (G-11867)
Transfreight LLC .... B 937 576-2800
  Tipp City (G-13667)
Transinternational System Inc .... E 614 891-4942
  Worthington (G-15463)
TV Minority Company Inc .... E 937 832-9350
  Englewood (G-8324)
UPS Supply Chain Solutions Inc .... E 360 332-5222
  Cleveland (G-5088)
UPS Supply Chain Solutions Inc .... E 614 208-0396
  Columbus (G-6829)
US Expediting Logistics LLC .... E 937 235-1014
  Vandalia (G-14399)
Verst Group Logistics Inc .... E 513 772-2494
  Cincinnati (G-3621)
Verst Group Logistics Inc .... D 859 379-1230
  West Chester (G-14844)
Vinebrook Homes LLC .... B 855 513-5678
  Dayton (G-7707)
Visible Supply Chain MGT LLC .... E 801 859-3082
  West Chester (G-14791)
Wnb Group LLC .... E 513 641-5400
  Cincinnati (G-3677)
◆ Workflowone LLC .... A 877 735-4966
  Dayton (G-7726)
◆ World Ex Shipg Trnsp Fwdg Svcs ...... E 440 826-5055
  Middleburg Heights (G-11135)
World Shipping Inc .... E 440 356-7676
  Cleveland (G-5159)
Xpo Cartage Inc .... E 614 766-6891
  Dublin (G-8166)
Xpo Logistics Freight Inc .... E 419 499-8888
  Milan (G-11213)

Xpo Logistics Freight Inc .... D 419 666-3022
  Perrysburg (G-12389)
Xtreme Express LLC .... C 614 735-0291
  Columbus (G-6914)

4741 Rental of railroad cars

Andersons Inc .... C 419 893-5050
  Maumee (G-10692)
◆ Djj Holding Corporation .... C 513 419-6200
  Cincinnati (G-2572)
Ttx .... E 216 778-6500
  Strongsville (G-13492)

4783 Packing and crating

▲ Amerisource Health Svcs LLC .... D 614 492-8177
  Columbus (G-5364)
Bates Metal Products Inc .... D 740 498-8371
  Port Washington (G-12541)
Containerport Group Inc .... E 440 333-1330
  Columbus (G-5689)
Crescent Park Corporation .... C 513 759-7000
  West Chester (G-14679)
▲ Dysart Corporation .... E 614 837-1201
  Canal Winchester (G-1604)
Flick Lumber Co Inc .... E 419 468-6278
  Galion (G-8748)
Impact Fulfillment Svcs LLC .... C 614 262-8911
  Columbus (G-6043)
Inquiry Systems Inc .... E 614 464-3800
  Columbus (G-6055)
Lalac One LLC .... E 216 432-4422
  Cleveland (G-4482)
◆ McNerney & Associates LLC .... E 513 241-9951
  West Chester (G-14824)
Morral Companies LLC .... E 740 465-3251
  Morral (G-11454)
◆ Newport Tank Cntrs USA LLC .... B 440 356-8866
  Westlake (G-15083)
Star Packaging Inc .... E 614 564-9936
  Columbus (G-6711)
T L C Packaging Inc .... E 330 722-7622
  Medina (G-10897)

4785 Inspection and fixed facilities

▲ Magnum Management Corporation .... C 419 627-2334
  Sandusky (G-12913)
Municipal Building Inspection .... C 440 399-0850
  Bedford Heights (G-999)
Ohio Tpk & Infrastructure Comm .... C 440 234-2081
  Berea (G-1076)

4789 Transportation services, nec

A-1 Qlity Lgstcal Slutions LLC .... E 513 353-0173
  Cincinnati (G-2131)
Air Transport Intl Inc .... C 937 382-5591
  Wilmington (G-15239)
All American Trnsp Svcs LLC .... E 419 589-7433
  Ontario (G-12099)
Allens Ronnell Trnsp LLC .... E 440 453-2273
  Cleveland (G-3794)
Amark Logistics Inc .... E 440 892-4500
  Westlake (G-15033)
Andersons Inc .... C 419 893-5050
  Maumee (G-10692)
Brothers Auto Transport LLC .... E 330 824-0082
  Warren (G-14508)
Bushra Transportation LLC .... E 614 745-1584
  Columbus (G-5488)
Cathcart Rail LLC .... E 380 390-2058
  Columbus (G-5249)
Cathcart Repair Facilities LLC .... E
  Columbus (G-5250)

47 TRANSPORTATION SERVICES

Centran Logistics Inc .... E 216 271-7100
  Cleveland (G-3955)
Cincinnati & Ohio Rlwy Svc LLC .... E 513 371-3277
  Hamilton (G-9027)
Coldliner Express Inc .... D 614 570-0836
  Columbus (G-5592)
Contrlled Chaos Enrgy Svcs LLC .... E 740 257-0724
  Belmont (G-1054)
County of Montgomery .... D 937 225-6140
  Dayton (G-7250)
Creekside Cargo Inc .... E 216 688-1770
  Cleveland (G-4137)
CRST International Inc .... E 513 552-1935
  Cincinnati (G-2518)
CT Logistics Inc .... C 216 267-1636
  Cleveland (G-4143)
D&A Transport LLC .... E 513 570-7153
  Cincinnati (G-2531)
Dayton Synchrnous Spport Ctr I .... E 937 226-1559
  Dayton (G-7302)
Genox Transportation Inc .... E 419 837-2023
  Perrysburg (G-12337)
Goldway Trans LLC .... D 330 828-0008
  Cincinnati (G-2741)
Grieser Logistics LLC .... E 419 445-9256
  Wauseon (G-14604)
Haggerty Logistics Inc .... D 734 713-9800
  Cincinnati (G-2792)
Hansen Adkins Auto Trnspt Inc .... E 562 430-4100
  West Chester (G-14815)
Health Care Logistics Inc .... D 800 848-1633
  Galloway (G-8771)
Hogan Services Inc .... E 614 491-8402
  Columbus (G-5997)
▼ Jk-Co LLC .... E 419 422-5240
  Findlay (G-8552)
JMS Express Inc .... E 855 267-4242
  West Chester (G-14822)
Jumbo Logistics LLC .... E 216 662-5420
  Macedonia (G-10195)
Kettering City School District .... E 937 499-1770
  Dayton (G-7437)
Odw Logistics Inc .... E 937 770-5602
  Brookville (G-1447)
Odw Logistics Inc .... E 614 549-5000
  Englewood (G-8316)
Program Transportation Inc .... E 440 772-4134
  Westlake (G-15100)
Road & Rail Services Inc .... D 502 365-5361
  Fostoria (G-8624)
Road & Rail Services Inc .... D 937 578-0089
  Marysville (G-10505)
School Transportation .... E 937 855-3897
  Germantown (G-8804)
Schroeder Associates Inc .... E 419 258-5075
  Antwerp (G-448)
Senior Touch Solution .... E 216 862-4841
  Cleveland (G-4895)
Skyways Logistics LLC .... D 614 333-0333
  Columbus (G-6687)
Snow Transport & Brokerage .... E 937 474-8058
  Dayton (G-7623)
Squeaky Banana Inc .... D 614 492-1208
  Obetz (G-12083)
Tforce Freight Inc .... E 216 676-4560
  Cleveland (G-4988)
Titan Logistics Ltd .... E 614 901-4212
  Columbus (G-6770)
Transfreight LLC .... B 937 865-9270
  Dayton (G-7676)
United Parcel Service Inc .... E 800 742-5877
  Groveport (G-9008)

Williams Last Mile HM Lgstics .... E 937 313-9096
  Dayton (G-7724)
Wings of Love Services LLC .... E 937 789-8192
  Dayton (G-7144)
Woodruff Enterprises Inc .... E 937 399-9300
  Springfield (G-13314)
World Trck Towing Recovery Inc .... E 330 723-1116
  Seville (G-12968)

48 COMMUNICATIONS

4812 Radiotelephone communication

AT&T Corp .... E 614 223-8236
  Columbus (G-5399)
Axiom Wireless Llc .... E 330 863-4410
  Magnolia (G-10223)
Cellco Partnership .... D 419 281-1714
  Ashland (G-489)
Cellco Partnership .... D 440 893-6100
  Chagrin Falls (G-1954)
Cellco Partnership .... D 330 697-2211
  Fairlawn (G-8469)
Cellco Partnership .... D 330 764-7380
  Medina (G-10818)
Cellco Partnership .... D 440 886-5461
  Parma (G-12251)
Cincinnati Bell Wireless Company .... C 513 397-9548
  Cincinnati (G-2400)
Cleveland Unlimited Inc .... B
  Independence (G-9422)
Horizon Pcs Inc .... C 740 772-8200
  Chillicothe (G-2071)
New Cingular Wireless Svcs Inc .... E 614 847-5880
  Columbus (G-5272)
New Cingular Wireless Svcs Inc .... E 440 324-7200
  Elyria (G-8280)
New Cingular Wireless Svcs Inc .... E 216 901-1296
  Independence (G-9458)
New Cingular Wireless Svcs Inc .... E 440 975-8304
  Mentor (G-10979)
New Cingular Wireless Svcs Inc .... E 419 473-9756
  Toledo (G-13934)
Nextlink Wireless LLC .... A 216 619-3200
  Independence (G-9459)
Nk Telco Inc .... E 419 753-5000
  New Knoxville (G-11618)
Page Plus Cellular .... D 800 550-2436
  Holland (G-9299)
Sprint Communications Co LP .... C 419 725-2444
  Toledo (G-14022)
Sprint Corporation .... C 216 661-2977
  Cleveland (G-4937)
T-Mobile .... E 740 500-4250
  Circleville (G-3726)
T-Mobile Central LLC .... D 513 855-3170
  West Chester (G-14771)
Total Wireless .... D 419 724-2363
  Toledo (G-14071)
TSC Communications Inc .... D 419 739-2200
  Wapakoneta (G-14492)
Verizon Bus Netwrk Svcs LLC .... C 513 897-1501
  Waynesville (G-14628)
Verizon New York Inc .... A 614 301-2498
  Hilliard (G-9240)
Verizon Wireless .... C 330 963-1300
  Twinsburg (G-14228)
Verizon Wireless Inc .... E 937 434-2355
  Dayton (G-7701)
Wireless Center Inc .... D 216 503-3777
  Cleveland (G-5152)
Wireless Partners LLC .... C 614 850-0040
  Hilliard (G-9245)

4813 Telephone communication, except radio

ABS Communication LLC .... E 419 293-5026
  Norwalk (G-11998)
Advanced Cmpt Connections LLC .... E 419 668-4080
  Norwalk (G-11999)
Altoria Solutions LLC .... E 513 612-2007
  Cincinnati (G-2174)
AT&T Corp .... D 513 407-4446
  Cincinnati (G-2224)
AT&T Corp .... E 614 223-8236
  Columbus (G-5399)
AT&T Corp .... D 419 547-0578
  Vickery (G-14418)
AT&T Teleholdings Inc .... C 330 385-9967
  East Liverpool (G-8178)
Best Communications Inc .... E 440 758-5854
  Conneaut (G-6941)
Block Communications Inc .... D 419 724-2539
  Northwood (G-11969)
Bluespring Software Inc .... E 513 794-1764
  Blue Ash (G-1138)
Brcom Inc .... D 513 397-9900
  Cincinnati (G-2278)
Buckeye Telesystem Inc .... D 419 724-9898
  Northwood (G-11970)
Cardinal Commercecom Inc .... E 440 352-8444
  Mentor (G-10917)
Cass Information Systems Inc .... E 614 839-4503
  Columbus (G-5517)
Cavalier Tele Mid-Atlantic LLC .... A 614 884-0000
  Columbus (G-5521)
Century Tel of Odon Inc .... C 440 244-8544
  Lorain (G-10062)
Chillicothe Telephone Company .... C 740 772-8200
  Chillicothe (G-2060)
◆ Cincinnati Bell Inc .... B 513 397-9900
  Cincinnati (G-2398)
Cincinnati Bell Tele Co LLC .... B 513 397-9900
  Cincinnati (G-2399)
Cincinnati Bell Wireless Company .... C 513 397-9548
  Cincinnati (G-2400)
Com Net Inc .... D 419 739-3100
  Wapakoneta (G-14481)
Communication Options Inc .... E 614 901-7095
  New Albany (G-11560)
Community Isp Inc .... E 419 867-6060
  Toledo (G-13752)
Conneaut Telephone Company .... E 440 593-7140
  Conneaut (G-6942)
County of Lorain .... D 440 324-5777
  Elyria (G-8239)
▼ Data Processing Sciences .... D 513 791-7100
  Cincinnati (G-2539)
Dct Telecom Group LLC .... E 440 892-0300
  Westlake (G-15056)
Doylestown Telephone Company .... E 330 658-2121
  Doylestown (G-7915)
Echo 24 Inc .... E 740 964-7081
  Reynoldsburg (G-12662)
End-User Computing Inc .... D 419 292-2200
  Toledo (G-13793)
▲ F+w Media Inc .... A 513 531-2690
  Blue Ash (G-1171)
Great Lakes Telcom Ltd .... E 330 629-8848
  Youngstown (G-15622)
Holdco LLC .... E 614 255-7285
  Westerville (G-14985)
Imagine Networks LLC .... E 937 552-2340
  Troy (G-14140)
Intellinet Corporation .... D 216 289-4100
  Chardon (G-2008)

SIC SECTION

48 COMMUNICATIONS

Kraftmaid Trucking Inc .... D 440 632-2531
   Middlefield *(G-11142)*
Massillon Cable TV Inc .... D 330 833-4134
   Massillon *(G-10652)*
McCracken Group Inc .... E 513 697-2000
   Cincinnati *(G-3022)*
MCI Communications Svcs LLC .... D 440 635-0418
   Chardon *(G-2012)*
MCI Communications Svcs LLC .... E 216 265-9953
   Cleveland *(G-4541)*
Medina Fiber LLC .... E 330 366-2008
   Medina *(G-10859)*
Mgj Enterprises Inc .... E 740 364-1360
   Newark *(G-11729)*
Midwest Communications LLC .... E 419 420-8000
   Findlay *(G-8569)*
Morelia Group LLC .... E 513 469-1500
   Cincinnati *(G-3079)*
Mvd Communications LLC .... D 513 683-4711
   Mason *(G-10582)*
Myteam1 LLC .... E 877 698-3262
   Dayton *(G-7523)*
Ohio Bell Telephone Company .... A 614 224-7424
   Columbus *(G-6395)*
Ohio Bell Telephone Company .... A 216 822-9700
   Brecksville *(G-1360)*
Oxcyon Inc .... E 440 239-3345
   Akron *(G-259)*
Pantek Incorporated .... E 216 344-1614
   Independence *(G-9465)*
Pearl Interactive Network Inc .... B 614 556-4470
   Columbus *(G-6507)*
Png Telecommunications Inc .... D 513 942-7900
   Cincinnati *(G-3218)*
Qwest Corporation .... D 614 793-9258
   Dublin *(G-8104)*
Revolution Group Inc .... D 614 212-1111
   Westerville *(G-14935)*
Round Room LLC .... E 937 429-2230
   Beavercreek *(G-902)*
Round Room LLC .... E 330 880-0660
   Massillon *(G-10666)*
Roundtable Learning LLC .... E 440 220-5252
   Chagrin Falls *(G-1988)*
Rxp Ohio LLC .... D 614 937-2844
   Columbus *(G-6623)*
Server Suites Llc .... C 513 831-5528
   Loveland *(G-10158)*
Southerntier Telecom Inc .... E 330 550-2733
   Girard *(G-8827)*
Southstern Ohio Vlntary Edcatn .... E 740 594-7663
   Athens *(G-591)*
TSC Communications Inc .... D 419 739-2200
   Wapakoneta *(G-14492)*
United Telephone Company Ohio .... C 419 227-1660
   Lima *(G-9977)*
Windstream Services LLC .... E 216 394-0065
   Cleveland *(G-5149)*
Windstream Services LLC .... E 216 242-6315
   Euclid *(G-8364)*
Windstream Services LLC .... E 330 650-7044
   Stow *(G-13402)*
Yp LLC .... C 216 642-4000
   Cleveland *(G-5169)*

4822 Telegraph and other communications

Fishel Company .... E 513 956-5210
   West Chester *(G-14812)*
▲ Stratacache Inc .... C 937 224-0485
   Dayton *(G-7646)*

4832 Radio broadcasting stations

Alpha Media LLC .... E 330 456-7166
   Canton *(G-1662)*
Alpha Media LLC .... E 937 294-5858
   Dayton *(G-7166)*
Bucyrus Radio Group .... E 614 451-2191
   Columbus *(G-5480)*
Cincinnati Public Radio Inc .... E 513 352-9185
   Cincinnati *(G-2419)*
Cumulus Media Inc .... E 513 241-9898
   Cincinnati *(G-2523)*
Cumulus Media Inc .... D 419 725-5700
   Toledo *(G-13771)*
Elyria-Lorain Broadcasting Co .... E 440 322-3761
   Elyria *(G-8248)*
Franklin Communications Inc .... E 614 459-9769
   Columbus *(G-5886)*
Hubbard Radio Cincinnati LLC .... D 513 699-5100
   Cincinnati *(G-2854)*
▲ Ideastream .... C 216 916-6100
   Cleveland *(G-4401)*
Isaac Foster Mack Co .... E 419 625-5500
   Sandusky *(G-12905)*
Johnny Appleseed Brdcstg Co .... E 419 529-5900
   Ontario *(G-12109)*
Lakewood Rngers Edcatn Fndtion .... E 216 521-2100
   Lakewood *(G-9676)*
Marquee Broadcasting Ohio Inc .... E 740 452-5431
   Zanesville *(G-15810)*
North American Broadcasting .... D 614 481-7800
   Columbus *(G-6364)*
Ohio State University .... D 614 292-9678
   Columbus *(G-6454)*
Pillar of Fire .... E 513 542-1212
   Cincinnati *(G-3211)*
Public Brdcstg Fndtion of NW O .... D 419 380-4600
   Toledo *(G-13980)*
Rubber City Radio Group Inc .... D 330 869-9800
   Akron *(G-289)*
TCI .... E 513 557-3200
   Cincinnati *(G-3444)*
W H O T Inc .... D 330 783-1000
   Youngstown *(G-15749)*
Wkhr Radio Inc .... E 440 708-0915
   Bainbridge *(G-687)*
Wqkt 1045 FM .... B 330 264-5122
   Wooster *(G-15399)*
Wwcd Ltd .... E 614 221-9923
   Columbus *(G-6910)*
Wwst Corporation LLC .... B 330 264-5122
   Wooster *(G-15400)*
Xavier University .... E 513 745-3335
   Cincinnati *(G-3683)*

4833 Television broadcasting stations

Ai-Media Inc .... E 213 337-8552
   Youngstown *(G-15544)*
Barrington Toledo LLC .... E 419 535-0024
   Toledo *(G-13699)*
Fox Sports Net Ohio LLC .... D 216 415-3300
   Cleveland *(G-4280)*
Fox Television Stations Inc .... C 216 431-8888
   Cleveland *(G-4281)*
Gray Media Group Inc .... D 513 421-1919
   Cincinnati *(G-2752)*
Gray Media Group Inc .... D 216 367-7300
   Cleveland *(G-4327)*
Gray Media Group Inc .... D 419 534-3886
   Toledo *(G-13824)*
Greater Cncnnati TV Edctl Fndt .... D 513 381-4033
   Cincinnati *(G-2773)*
Greater Dayton Public TV Inc .... D 937 220-1600
   Dayton *(G-7384)*

Ion Media Stations Inc .... B 561 659-4122
   Cincinnati *(G-2886)*
Johnny Appleseed Brdcstg Co .... E 419 529-5900
   Ontario *(G-12109)*
Lima Communications Corp .... D 419 228-8835
   Lima *(G-9921)*
Marquee Broadcasting Ohio Inc .... E 740 452-5431
   Zanesville *(G-15810)*
Miami Valley Broadcasting Corp .... C 937 259-2111
   Dayton *(G-7486)*
New World Communications .... C 216 432-4041
   Cleveland *(G-4639)*
Nexstar Broadcasting Inc .... C 614 263-4444
   Columbus *(G-6354)*
Northastern Eductl TV Ohio Inc .... C 330 677-4549
   Kent *(G-9589)*
Ohio State University .... D 614 292-9678
   Columbus *(G-6454)*
Ohio/Oklahoma Hearst TV Inc .... D 513 412-5000
   Cincinnati *(G-3152)*
Outlet Broadcasting Inc .... C 614 263-4444
   Columbus *(G-6493)*
Public Brdcstg Fndtion of NW O .... D 419 380-4600
   Toledo *(G-13980)*
Scripps Media Inc .... D 513 977-3000
   Cincinnati *(G-3351)*
Sinclair Media II Inc .... C 614 481-6666
   Columbus *(G-6684)*
Tegna Inc .... C 419 248-1111
   Toledo *(G-14035)*
W GTE TV 30 FM 91 Pub Brdcstg .... D 419 380-4600
   Toledo *(G-14095)*
W Tov Tv9 .... E 740 282-9999
   Steubenville *(G-13351)*
Wbns TV Inc .... C 614 460-3700
   Columbus *(G-6872)*
Wfmj Television Inc .... C 330 744-8611
   Youngstown *(G-15753)*
Wfts .... D 513 721-9900
   Cincinnati *(G-3667)*
Wfts .... D 216 431-5555
   Cleveland *(G-5144)*
Winston Brdcstg Netwrk Inc .... C 330 928-5711
   Cuyahoga Falls *(G-7118)*
Wkyc-Tv Inc .... C 216 344-3300
   Cleveland *(G-5155)*
Wtvg Inc .... D 419 531-1313
   Toledo *(G-14109)*

4841 Cable and other pay television services

Armstrong Utilities Inc .... D 330 723-3536
   Medina *(G-10808)*
Armstrong Utilities Inc .... D 330 758-6411
   North Lima *(G-11881)*
ASC of Cincinnati Inc .... E 513 886-7100
   Lebanon *(G-9755)*
Block Communications Inc .... D 419 724-2539
   Northwood *(G-11969)*
Charter Communications .... E 614 588-5036
   Columbus *(G-5551)*
Chillicothe Telephone Company .... C 740 772-8200
   Chillicothe *(G-2060)*
Coaxial Cmmnctons of Sthern OH .... D 513 797-4400
   Columbus *(G-5589)*
Erie County Cablevision Inc .... C 419 627-0800
   Sandusky *(G-12891)*
Massillon Cable TV Inc .... D 330 833-4134
   Massillon *(G-10652)*
McTv Inc .... D 330 833-4134
   Massillon *(G-10655)*
Spectrum MGT Holdg Co LLC .... E 614 344-4159
   Columbus *(G-6703)*

48 COMMUNICATIONS

State Alarm Inc .... E 888 726-8111
  Youngstown *(G-15730)*
Sun Yer Bunz LLC .... D 937 222-3474
  Dayton *(G-7652)*
Time Warner Cable Entps LLC .... E 513 489-5000
  Blue Ash *(G-1255)*
Time Warner Cable Entps LLC .... E 614 255-6289
  Columbus *(G-6768)*
Time Warner Cable Entps LLC .... E 614 481-5072
  Columbus *(G-6769)*

4899 Communication services, nec

A M Communications Ltd .... D 419 528-3051
  Galion *(G-8741)*
Advance Ohio Media LLC .... D 216 999-3900
  Cleveland *(G-3770)*
Allied Communications Corp .... E 614 588-3370
  Dublin *(G-7931)*
◆ Calvert Wire & Cable Corp .... E 216 433-7600
  Cleveland *(G-3919)*
First Choice Communications .... E 330 439-5440
  Youngstown *(G-15612)*
Geben Communications LLC .... D 614 327-2102
  Columbus *(G-5922)*
Logos Communications Systems Inc .... D 440 871-0777
  Westlake *(G-15076)*
Oovoo LLC .... D 917 515-2074
  Kettering *(G-9631)*
SImg Brand LLC .... E 216 333-6468
  Cleveland *(G-4914)*
Springdot Inc .... D 513 542-4000
  Cincinnati *(G-3401)*
Telcom Construction Svcs Inc .... D 330 239-6900
  Medina *(G-10899)*
Twenty First Century Comm .... D 614 442-1215
  Columbus *(G-6795)*
Velocity A Managed Svcs Co Inc .... C 419 868-9983
  Holland *(G-9311)*
Wireless Master LLC .... D 877 995-5888
  Hilliard *(G-9244)*

49 ELECTRIC, GAS AND SANITARY SERVICES

4911 Electric services

AEP Energy Partners Inc .... C 614 716-1000
  Columbus *(G-5321)*
AEP Generating Company .... A 614 223-1000
  Columbus *(G-5322)*
AEP Investments Holding Co Inc .... B 614 583-2900
  Columbus *(G-5323)*
AEP Power Marketing Inc .... A 614 716-1000
  Columbus *(G-5324)*
AEP Texas Central Company .... A 614 716-1000
  Columbus *(G-5325)*
AEP Texas Inc .... D 614 716-1000
  Columbus *(G-5326)*
AEP Texas North Company .... B 614 716-1000
  Columbus *(G-5327)*
American Electric Pwr Svc Corp .... D 614 582-1742
  Columbus *(G-5349)*
▲ American Electric Pwr Svc Corp ...... B 614 716-1000
  Columbus *(G-5348)*
◆ American Municipal Power Inc .... C 614 540-1111
  Columbus *(G-5354)*
Andrew Casey Electric LLC .... E 937 765-4210
  Dayton *(G-7174)*
Appalachian Power Company .... C 330 438-7102
  Canton *(G-1669)*
▲ Appalachian Power Company .... C 614 716-1000
  Columbus *(G-5374)*

Buckeye Power Inc .... C 740 598-6534
  Brilliant *(G-1378)*
Buckeye Power Inc .... E 614 781-0573
  Columbus *(G-5477)*
Buckeye Rural Elc Coop Inc .... E 740 379-2025
  Patriot *(G-12280)*
Butler Rural Electric Coop .... E 513 867-4400
  Oxford *(G-12203)*
Cardinal Operating Company .... B 740 598-4164
  Brilliant *(G-1379)*
Carroll Electric Coop Inc .... E 330 627-2116
  Carrollton *(G-1903)*
▲ Cinergy Corp .... A 513 421-9500
  Cincinnati *(G-2440)*
City of Cleveland .... D 216 664-4277
  Cleveland *(G-3983)*
City of Cuyahoga Falls .... E 330 971-8000
  Cuyahoga Falls *(G-7055)*
City of Dublin .... D 614 410-4750
  Dublin *(G-7964)*
City of Lebanon .... E 513 228-3200
  Lebanon *(G-9759)*
City of Toledo .... D 419 245-1800
  Toledo *(G-13743)*
Cleveland Elc Illuminating Co .... D 800 589-3101
  Akron *(G-109)*
Consolidated Cooperative .... D 419 947-3055
  Mount Gilead *(G-11459)*
Consumers Energy Company .... E 800 477-5050
  Cincinnati *(G-2499)*
Dayton Power and Light Company ..... C 937 549-2641
  Manchester *(G-10239)*
Dayton Power and Light Company ..... D 937 549-2641
  Manchester *(G-10240)*
Dayton Power and Light Company ..... D 937 642-9100
  Marysville *(G-10482)*
Dayton Power and Light Company ..... E 937 331-3032
  Miamisburg *(G-11047)*
Dayton Power and Light Company ..... C 937 331-3900
  Dayton *(G-7129)*
DPL Inc .... C 937 259-7215
  Dayton *(G-7130)*
Duke Energy Beckjord LLC .... A 513 287-2561
  Cincinnati *(G-2578)*
Duke Energy Ohio Inc .... A 800 544-6900
  Cincinnati *(G-2581)*
Duke Energy Ohio Inc .... A 513 287-1120
  Cincinnati *(G-2582)*
Duke Energy Ohio Inc .... A 513 287-4622
  Monroe *(G-11340)*
Duke Energy Ohio Inc .... A 513 467-5000
  New Richmond *(G-11676)*
▲ Duke Energy Ohio Inc .... D 704 382-3853
  Cincinnati *(G-2583)*
Duke Energy One Inc .... A 980 373-3931
  Cincinnati *(G-2584)*
Dynegy Coml Asset MGT LLC .... C 513 287-5033
  Cincinnati *(G-2590)*
Energy Cooperative Inc .... E 740 348-1206
  Newark *(G-11699)*
Energy Harbor Corp .... E 888 254-6359
  Akron *(G-149)*
Energy Harbor LLC .... A 888 254-6356
  Akron *(G-150)*
Firstenergy Corp .... A 800 736-3402
  Akron *(G-161)*
Frontier Power Company .... E 740 622-6755
  Coshocton *(G-6985)*
Gavin AEP Plant .... E 740 925-3166
  Cheshire *(G-2030)*
Gavin Power LLC .... D 740 925-3140
  Cheshire *(G-2031)*

Guernsy-Muskingum Elc Coop Inc ...... E 740 826-7661
  New Concord *(G-11611)*
Hancock-Wood Electric Coop Inc .... E 419 257-3241
  North Baltimore *(G-11801)*
Hexion Inc .... C 888 443-9466
  Columbus *(G-5989)*
Holmes-Wayne Electric Coop .... E 330 674-1055
  Millersburg *(G-11281)*
Indiana Michigan Power Company ...... D 614 716-1000
  Columbus *(G-6045)*
Jackson & Sons Drilling & Pump .... E 419 756-2758
  Mansfield *(G-10275)*
Jersey Central Pwr & Light Co .... C 740 537-6391
  Stratton *(G-13407)*
▲ Jersey Central Pwr & Light Co .... B 800 736-3402
  Akron *(G-211)*
Licking Rur Elctrification Inc .... D 740 892-2071
  Utica *(G-14328)*
Metropolitan Edison Company .... C 800 736-3402
  Akron *(G-231)*
Mid-Ohio Energy Coop Inc .... E 419 568-5321
  Kenton *(G-9621)*
Moores Electric LLC .... E 614 504-2909
  Columbus *(G-6261)*
National Gas & Oil Corporation .... E 740 344-2102
  Newark *(G-11733)*
North Central Elc Coop Inc .... E 800 426-3072
  Attica *(G-600)*
Ohio Edison Company .... E 740 671-2900
  Shadyside *(G-12970)*
Ohio Edison Company .... E 330 336-9880
  Wadsworth *(G-14445)*
Ohio Edison Company .... C 330 740-7754
  Youngstown *(G-15680)*
Ohio Edison Company .... C 800 736-3402
  Akron *(G-249)*
Ohio Power Company .... C 614 716-1000
  Columbus *(G-6439)*
Ohio Valley Electric Corp .... D 740 289-7200
  Piketon *(G-12425)*
Paulding-Putnam Electric Coop .... E 419 399-5015
  Paulding *(G-12287)*
Pennsylvania Electric Company .... D 800 545-7741
  Akron *(G-263)*
Pennsylvania Power Company .... C 800 720-3600
  Akron *(G-264)*
Pioneer Rural Electric Coop .... E 800 762-0997
  Piqua *(G-12451)*
Public Service Company Okla .... D 888 216-3523
  Canton *(G-1834)*
Reliability First Corporation .... E 216 503-0600
  Cleveland *(G-4821)*
Scana Energy Marketing LLC .... D 803 217-1322
  Dublin *(G-8116)*
South Central Power Company .... D 740 425-4018
  Barnesville *(G-721)*
South Central Power Company .... E 614 837-4351
  Lancaster *(G-9743)*
▲ South Central Power Company ...... C 740 653-4422
  Lancaster *(G-9742)*
Southwestern Electric Power Co .... D 614 716-1000
  Columbus *(G-6699)*
Stg Electric Services LLC .... E 330 650-0513
  Macedonia *(G-10206)*
Toledo Edison Company .... C 800 447-3333
  Akron *(G-335)*
Union Rural Electric Coop Inc .... E 937 642-1826
  Marysville *(G-10515)*
Vectren Energy Dlvry Ohio LLC .... E 937 259-7400
  Fairborn *(G-8383)*
Village of Sycamore .... D 419 927-4262
  Sycamore *(G-13533)*

49 ELECTRIC, GAS AND SANITARY SERVICES

Vistra Corp... C 513 467-5289
  Moscow *(G-11457)*

Vistra Energy Corp................................. C 513 467-4900
  North Bend *(G-11804)*

W T Leones Tri-Area Elc Inc................. E 330 744-0151
  Youngstown *(G-15750)*

Walleye Power LLC............................... D 567 298-7400
  Oregon *(G-12147)*

4922 Natural gas transmission

▲ Duke Energy Ohio Inc....................... D 704 382-3853
  Cincinnati *(G-2583)*

◆ Knight Material Tech LLC.................... D 330 488-1651
  East Canton *(G-8169)*

Ko Transmission Company.................... E 513 287-3553
  Cincinnati *(G-2946)*

National Gas & Oil Corporation.............. E 740 454-7252
  Zanesville *(G-15818)*

National Gas & Oil Corporation.............. E 740 344-2102
  Newark *(G-11733)*

Ohio Gas Company................................ E 419 636-3642
  Bryan *(G-1490)*

4923 Gas transmission and distribution

Aspire Energy of Ohio LLC.................... E 330 682-7726
  Orrville *(G-12156)*

National Gas & Oil Corporation.............. E 740 454-7252
  Zanesville *(G-15818)*

Ngo Development Corporation.............. B 740 622-9560
  Coshocton *(G-6993)*

4924 Natural gas distribution

Bay State Gas Company........................ D 614 460-4292
  Columbus *(G-5423)*

▲ Cinergy Corp.. A 513 421-9500
  Cincinnati *(G-2440)*

City of Lancaster................................... E 740 687-6670
  Lancaster *(G-9701)*

City of Toledo.. D 419 245-1800
  Toledo *(G-13743)*

Columbia Gas of Ohio Inc.................... D 419 562-4003
  Bucyrus *(G-1500)*

Columbia Gas of Ohio Inc.................... D 559 683-1567
  Cambridge *(G-1564)*

Columbia Gas of Ohio Inc.................... C 440 891-2458
  Cleveland *(G-4089)*

Columbia Gas of Ohio Inc.................... D 614 878-6015
  Columbus *(G-5599)*

Columbia Gas of Ohio Inc.................... C 614 481-1000
  Columbus *(G-5600)*

Columbia Gas of Ohio Inc.................... D 614 460-6000
  Columbus *(G-5601)*

Columbia Gas of Ohio Inc.................... D 614 818-2101
  Columbus *(G-5602)*

Columbia Gas of Ohio Inc.................... C 419 435-7725
  Findlay *(G-8523)*

Columbia Gas of Ohio Inc.................... D 419 332-9951
  Fremont *(G-8670)*

Columbia Gas of Ohio Inc.................... D 740 264-5577
  Steubenville *(G-13320)*

Columbia Gas of Ohio Inc.................... D 419 539-6046
  Toledo *(G-13749)*

Columbia Gas of Ohio Inc.................... D 740 450-1215
  Zanesville *(G-15782)*

Columbia Gas of Ohio Inc.................... E 614 460-6000
  Columbus *(G-5598)*

Columbia Gas Transmission LLC......... E 614 460-4704
  Columbus *(G-5603)*

Columbia Gulf Transmission LLC......... D 614 460-6991
  Columbus *(G-5604)*

Columbia Gulf Transmission LLC......... D 740 746-9105
  Sugar Grove *(G-13507)*

Consumers Energy Company................ E 800 477-5050
  Cincinnati *(G-2499)*

▲ Duke Energy Ohio Inc....................... D 704 382-3853
  Cincinnati *(G-2583)*

Dynegy Coml Asset MGT LLC.............. C 513 287-5033
  Cincinnati *(G-2590)*

East Ohio Gas Company....................... D 800 362-7557
  Akron *(G-145)*

East Ohio Gas Company....................... D 216 736-6120
  Ashtabula *(G-534)*

East Ohio Gas Company....................... D 740 439-2721
  Byesville *(G-1534)*

East Ohio Gas Company....................... D 330 266-2161
  Canton *(G-1741)*

East Ohio Gas Company....................... D 330 477-9411
  Canton *(G-1742)*

East Ohio Gas Company....................... D 330 499-2501
  Canton *(G-1743)*

East Ohio Gas Company....................... D 216 736-6959
  Cleveland *(G-4198)*

East Ohio Gas Company....................... D 330 266-2169
  New Franklin *(G-11615)*

East Ohio Gas Company....................... E 216 736-6917
  Wickliffe *(G-15148)*

East Ohio Gas Company....................... D 330 478-3114
  Wooster *(G-15335)*

East Ohio Gas Company....................... A 800 362-7557
  Cleveland *(G-4197)*

Energy Cooperative Inc......................... E 740 348-1206
  Newark *(G-11699)*

National Gas & Oil Corporation.............. E 740 454-7252
  Zanesville *(G-15818)*

National Gas & Oil Corporation.............. E 740 344-2102
  Newark *(G-11733)*

Ohio Gas Company................................ E 419 636-1117
  Bryan *(G-1491)*

Pike Natural Gas Company................... D 937 393-4602
  Hillsboro *(G-9267)*

Scana Energy Marketing LLC............... D 803 217-1322
  Dublin *(G-8116)*

Stand Energy Corporation..................... E 513 621-1113
  Cincinnati *(G-3407)*

Vectren Energy Dlvry Ohio LLC........... E 937 331-3080
  Englewood *(G-8325)*

Volunteer Energy Services Inc.............. E 614 856-3128
  Pickerington *(G-12413)*

4925 Gas production and/or distribution

Heritage Cooperative Inc....................... D 877 240-4393
  Delaware *(G-7804)*

Titan Propane LLC................................ C 419 332-9832
  Fremont *(G-8706)*

4931 Electric and other services combined

Consumers Energy Company................ E 800 477-5050
  Cincinnati *(G-2499)*

Dayton Power and Light Company........ D 937 549-2641
  Manchester *(G-10240)*

Dayton Power and Light Company........ E 937 331-3032
  Miamisburg *(G-11047)*

Dayton Power and Light Company........ C 937 331-3900
  Dayton *(G-7129)*

Duke Energy Kentucky Inc.................... C 704 594-6200
  Cincinnati *(G-2580)*

▲ Duke Energy Ohio Inc....................... D 704 382-3853
  Cincinnati *(G-2583)*

RB Watkins Inc..................................... E 330 688-4061
  Stow *(G-13387)*

4932 Gas and other services combined

Dayton Power and Light Company........ D 937 549-2641
  Manchester *(G-10240)*

Dayton Power and Light Company........ E 937 331-3032
  Miamisburg *(G-11047)*

Duke Energy Kentucky Inc.................... C 704 594-6200
  Cincinnati *(G-2580)*

Duke Energy Ohio Inc........................... A 513 287-4622
  Monroe *(G-11340)*

Heritage Cooperative Inc....................... D 877 240-4393
  Delaware *(G-7804)*

National Gas & Oil Corporation.............. E 740 344-2102
  Newark *(G-11733)*

Tuttle Construction Inc........................... C 419 228-6262
  Lima *(G-9974)*

4939 Combination utilities, nec

City of Lorain... D 440 204-2500
  Lorain *(G-10064)*

Ohio Edison Company........................... E 740 671-2900
  Shadyside *(G-12970)*

4941 Water supply

Aqua Ohio Inc....................................... D 440 255-3984
  Mentor *(G-10912)*

Belmont County of Ohio........................ E 740 695-3144
  Saint Clairsville *(G-12778)*

City of Akron... D 330 678-0077
  Kent *(G-9563)*

City of Avon Lake.................................. E 440 933-6226
  Avon Lake *(G-676)*

City of Cleveland................................... E 216 348-7277
  Newburgh Heights *(G-11757)*

City of Columbus................................... E 614 645-7490
  Columbus *(G-5576)*

City of Cuyahoga Falls.......................... E 330 971-8130
  Cuyahoga Falls *(G-7056)*

City of Dayton....................................... E 937 333-6070
  Dayton *(G-7228)*

City of Dayton....................................... E 937 333-3725
  Dayton *(G-7232)*

City of Lorain... D 440 204-2500
  Lorain *(G-10064)*

City of Middletown................................. D 513 425-7781
  Middletown *(G-11157)*

City of Toledo.. D 419 245-1800
  Toledo *(G-13743)*

Clearwater Services Inc........................ E 330 836-4946
  Akron *(G-106)*

Cleveland Water Department................ E 216 664-3168
  Cleveland *(G-4072)*

County of Guernsey.............................. E 740 439-1269
  Cambridge *(G-1565)*

County of Portage................................. D 330 297-3670
  Ravenna *(G-12624)*

County of Warren.................................. D 513 925-1377
  Lebanon *(G-9762)*

Del-Co Water Company Inc.................. D 740 548-7746
  Delaware *(G-7793)*

Hecla Water Association....................... E 740 533-0526
  Ironton *(G-9507)*

Knox County... D 740 397-7041
  Mount Vernon *(G-11493)*

Mahoning Valley Sanitary Dst............... D 330 799-6315
  Mineral Ridge *(G-11303)*

Northast Ohio Rgonal Sewer Dst.......... C 216 881-6600
  Cleveland *(G-4659)*

Northwestern Water & Sewer Dst......... E 419 354-9090
  Bowling Green *(G-1329)*

Ohio-American Water Co Inc................ E 740 382-3993
  Marion *(G-10449)*

Ross County Water Company Inc......... E 740 774-4117
  Chillicothe *(G-2088)*

Rural Lorain County Water Auth........... D 440 355-5121
  Lagrange *(G-9650)*

49 ELECTRIC, GAS AND SANITARY SERVICES

Scioto County Region Wtr Dst 1............. E 740 259-2301
Lucasville *(G-10180)*

4952 Sewerage systems

Belmont County of Ohio..................... E 740 695-3144
Saint Clairsville *(G-12778)*

City of Akron.. E 330 375-2666
Akron *(G-100)*

City of Alliance................................... E 330 829-2220
Alliance *(G-379)*

City of Avon Lake............................... E 440 933-6226
Avon Lake *(G-676)*

City of Cuyahoga Falls...................... D 330 971-8005
Cuyahoga Falls *(G-7058)*

City of Dayton..................................... D 937 333-1837
Dayton *(G-7229)*

City of Hamilton.................................. E 513 785-7551
Hamilton *(G-9028)*

City of Lorain...................................... D 440 204-2500
Lorain *(G-10064)*

City of Toledo..................................... D 419 245-1800
Toledo *(G-13743)*

City of Toledo..................................... D 419 936-2924
Toledo *(G-13744)*

City of Zanesville............................... E 740 455-0641
Zanesville *(G-15781)*

Clermont Cnty Wtr Rsources Dept.... D 513 732-7970
Batavia *(G-732)*

County of Stark.................................. C 330 451-2303
Canton *(G-1725)*

County of Warren............................... D 513 925-1377
Lebanon *(G-9762)*

Franklin Cnty Bd Commissioners...... C 614 525-3100
Columbus *(G-5885)*

Metropltan Swer Dst Grter Cncn........ A 513 244-1300
Cincinnati *(G-3053)*

North Ohio Regional Sewer............... E 216 299-0312
Cleveland *(G-4649)*

Northast Ohio Rgonal Sewer Dst...... C 216 641-6000
Cleveland *(G-4657)*

Northast Ohio Rgonal Sewer Dst...... C 216 641-3200
Cleveland *(G-4658)*

Northwestern Water & Sewer Dst..... E 419 354-9090
Bowling Green *(G-1329)*

Treatment Technologies LLC............ E 937 802-4883
Clayton *(G-3737)*

4953 Refuse systems

Ace Iron & Metal Company................. E 614 443-5196
Columbus *(G-5305)*

Adams - Brown Counties.................... E 937 544-2650
West Union *(G-14864)*

Adams Brown Cnties Ecnmic Oppr.... E 937 378-3431
Georgetown *(G-8797)*

Agri-Sludge Inc.................................. E 330 567-2500
Shreve *(G-13015)*

American Landfill Inc......................... D 330 866-3265
Waynesburg *(G-14621)*

Avalon Holdings Corporation............ D 330 856-8800
Warren *(G-14501)*

B & B Plastics Recyclers Inc............ C 614 409-2880
Columbus *(G-5411)*

Bluescope Recycling & Mtls LLC...... D 419 747-6522
Mansfield *(G-10247)*

Cecos International Inc..................... E 513 724-6114
Williamsburg *(G-15178)*

Central Ohio Contractors Inc............ D 740 369-7700
Delaware *(G-7784)*

Central Ohio Contractors Inc............ D 614 539-2579
Grove City *(G-8907)*

Chemtron Corporation....................... E 440 937-6348
Avon *(G-644)*

▲ Cirba Solutions Us Inc..................... E 740 653-6290
Lancaster *(G-9700)*

City of Akron.. E 330 375-2650
Akron *(G-101)*

City of Dayton..................................... D 937 333-4860
Dayton *(G-7230)*

City of Lakewood................................ E 216 252-4322
Cleveland *(G-3990)*

City of Perrysburg............................... E 419 872-8020
Perrysburg *(G-12324)*

City of Xenia....................................... E 937 376-7271
Xenia *(G-15501)*

Clean Hrbors Es Indus Svcs Inc....... D 937 425-0512
Dayton *(G-7235)*

Clm Pallet Recycling Inc................... E 614 272-5761
Columbus *(G-5586)*

Cross-Roads Asphalt Recycling Inc...... E 440 236-5066
Columbia Station *(G-5226)*

DMS Recycling LLC............................ E 740 397-0790
Mount Vernon *(G-11484)*

Envirite of Ohio Inc............................ E 330 456-6238
Canton *(G-1747)*

Environmental Enterprises Inc.......... C 513 772-2818
Cincinnati *(G-2627)*

Enviroserve Inc.................................. C 330 361-7764
North Canton *(G-11828)*

▲ Fpt Cleveland LLC........................... C 216 441-3800
Cleveland *(G-4282)*

Fultz & Son Inc................................... E 419 547-9365
Clyde *(G-5201)*

▲ Garden Street Iron & Metal Inc...... E 513 721-4660
Cincinnati *(G-2715)*

Gateway Products Recycling Inc...... E 216 341-8777
Cleveland *(G-4306)*

Global Scrap Management Inc.......... E 513 576-6600
Batavia *(G-741)*

H Hafner & Sons Inc.......................... E 513 321-1895
Cincinnati *(G-2786)*

▼ Hope Timber Pallet Recycl LLC...... E 740 344-1788
Newark *(G-11706)*

Hpj Industries Inc.............................. E 419 278-1000
Bowling Green *(G-1325)*

Industrial Waste Control Inc............. D 330 270-9900
Youngstown *(G-15638)*

▲ Interstate Shredding LLC............... E 330 545-5477
Girard *(G-8817)*

▼ Jasar Recycling Inc........................ D 864 233-5421
East Palestine *(G-8196)*

Kimble Recycl & Disposal Inc........... E 330 963-5493
Twinsburg *(G-14200)*

Kimble Recycl & Disposal Inc........... C 330 343-1226
Dover *(G-7892)*

Liberty Tire Services LLC................. E 330 868-0097
Minerva *(G-11308)*

Mahoning County............................... E 330 793-5514
Youngstown *(G-15656)*

Miles Alloys Inc................................. E 216 295-1000
Cleveland *(G-4581)*

Mondo Polymer Technologies Inc.... E 740 376-9396
Marietta *(G-10391)*

Muskingum Iron & Metal Co.............. E 740 452-9351
Zanesville *(G-15815)*

▲ Novelis Alr Recycling Ohio LLC.... C 740 922-2373
Uhrichsville *(G-14236)*

Novotec Recycling LLC..................... C 614 231-8326
Columbus *(G-6375)*

Plastic Recycling Tech Inc................ E 419 238-9395
Van Wert *(G-14349)*

Plastic Recycling Tech Inc................ E 937 615-9286
Piqua *(G-12456)*

Polychem LLC.................................... D 419 547-1400
Clyde *(G-5207)*

Pratt Paper (oh) LLC......................... E 567 320-3353
Wapakoneta *(G-14490)*

PSC Metals LLC................................. D 330 484-7610
Canton *(G-1833)*

PSC Metals LLC................................. E 614 299-4175
Columbus *(G-6555)*

Rbg Inc... E 513 247-0175
Blue Ash *(G-1233)*

Recycle Waste Services Inc............. D 419 517-1323
Sylvania *(G-13567)*

Republic Services Inc....................... E 330 830-9050
Massillon *(G-10662)*

Republic Services Kentucky LLC..... C 859 824-5466
Williamsburg *(G-15181)*

Republic Services Ohio Hlg LLC...... E 513 771-4200
Cincinnati *(G-3289)*

Ross Consolidated Corp................... D 440 748-5800
Grafton *(G-8841)*

▼ Ross Incineration Services Inc..... C 440 366-2000
Grafton *(G-8842)*

Royal Paper Stock Company Inc...... D 614 851-4714
Columbus *(G-6616)*

RSR Partners LLC.............................. C 440 248-3991
Solon *(G-13140)*

Rumpke Cnsld Companies Inc.......... C 800 828-8171
Cincinnati *(G-3330)*

Rumpke of Ohio Inc........................... C 740 947-7082
Waverly *(G-14618)*

Rumpke Transportation Co LLC....... B 513 242-4600
Cincinnati *(G-3331)*

Rumpke Transportation Co LLC....... B 937 461-0004
Dayton *(G-7597)*

Rumpke Waste Inc............................. C 513 242-4401
Cincinnati *(G-3333)*

Rumpke Waste Inc............................. C 740 474-9790
Circleville *(G-3722)*

Rumpke Waste Inc............................. C 513 851-0122
Columbus *(G-6620)*

Rumpke Waste Inc............................. C 937 378-4126
Georgetown *(G-8801)*

Rumpke Waste Inc............................. C 937 548-1939
Greenville *(G-8883)*

Rumpke Waste Inc............................. C 419 895-0058
Shiloh *(G-13014)*

Rumpke Waste Inc............................. C 740 384-4400
Wellston *(G-14641)*

Rumpke Waste Inc............................. D 513 851-0122
Cincinnati *(G-3332)*

Shredded Bedding Corporation........ D 740 893-3567
Centerburg *(G-1936)*

Shur-Green Farms LLC..................... D 937 547-9633
Ansonia *(G-446)*

Solid Waste Auth Centl Ohio............ C 614 871-5100
Grove City *(G-8956)*

Spring Grove Rsrce Rcovery Inc...... E 513 681-6242
Cincinnati *(G-3398)*

Sustain LLC.. E 888 525-0029
New Waterford *(G-11684)*

Triad Transport Inc............................ E 614 491-9497
Columbus *(G-6788)*

Valicor Environmental Svcs LLC..... D 937 268-6501
Dayton *(G-7698)*

Veolia Es Tchncal Slutions LLC....... E 937 859-6101
Miamisburg *(G-11102)*

Waste Management Michigan Inc.... D 740 787-2327
Glenford *(G-8832)*

Waste Management Ohio Inc............ E 740 787-2327
Glenford *(G-8833)*

Waste Management Ohio Inc............ E 419 221-2029
Lima *(G-9980)*

Waste Management Ohio Inc............ D 740 345-1212
Newark *(G-11752)*

Waste Management Ohio Inc .... E 800 343-6047
  Fairborn *(G-8387)*
Waste-Away Systems LLC .... E 740 349-2783
  Newark *(G-11753)*
Werlor Inc .... E 419 784-4285
  Defiance *(G-7775)*
Wm Ccp Solutions LLC .... D 513 871-9733
  Cincinnati *(G-3676)*

4959 Sanitary services, nec

American Beauty Landscaping .... E 330 788-1501
  Youngstown *(G-15548)*
Bremec Group Inc .... E 440 951-0770
  Chesterland *(G-2032)*
Brunk Excavating Inc .... E 513 360-0308
  Monroe *(G-11335)*
C & K Industrial Services Inc .... D 216 642-0055
  Independence *(G-9414)*
Chemtron Corporation .... E 440 937-6348
  Avon *(G-644)*
City of Lima .... E 419 221-5294
  Lima *(G-9874)*
City of Toledo .... D 419 936-2924
  Toledo *(G-13744)*
Contract Sweepers & Eqp Co .... E 513 577-7900
  West Chester *(G-14675)*
Contract Sweepers & Eqp Co .... E 614 221-7441
  Columbus *(G-5700)*
▲ Cousins Waste Control LLC .... D 419 726-1500
  Toledo *(G-13768)*
Cuyahoga County Sani Engrg Svc .... E 216 443-8211
  Cleveland *(G-4146)*
▼ Diproinduca (usa) Limited LLC .... D 330 722-4442
  Medina *(G-10828)*
Dun Rite Home Improvement Inc .... E 330 650-5322
  Macedonia *(G-10191)*
Environmental Enterprises Inc .... E 513 772-2818
  Cincinnati *(G-2627)*
Green Impressions LLC .... D 440 240-8508
  Sheffield Village *(G-12998)*
Greenscapes Landscape Co Inc .... D 614 837-1869
  Columbus *(G-5955)*
Klamfoth Inc .... E 614 833-5007
  Canal Winchester *(G-1611)*
Mahoning County .... E 330 799-1581
  Youngstown *(G-15655)*
Northast Ohio Rgonal Sewer Dst .... C 216 641-3200
  Cleveland *(G-4658)*
Paramount Lawn Service Inc .... E 513 984-5200
  Loveland *(G-10157)*
Petro Environmental Tech .... E 513 489-6789
  Cincinnati *(G-3202)*
▲ Samsel Rope & Marine Supply Co .... E 216 241-0333
  Cleveland *(G-4875)*
Sand Road Enterprises Inc .... E 419 668-3670
  Norwalk *(G-12026)*
Sca of Ca LLC .... E 216 777-2750
  Seven Hills *(G-12958)*
Sca of Mi LLC .... E 216 777-2750
  Seven Hills *(G-12959)*
Sca of Sc LLC .... E 216 777-2750
  Seven Hills *(G-12960)*
Schill Ldscpg Lawn Care Svcs L .... D 440 327-3030
  North Ridgeville *(G-11936)*
Superior Envmtl Solutions LLC .... E 513 874-8355
  West Chester *(G-14836)*
T O J Inc .... E 440 352-1900
  Mentor *(G-11002)*
TLC Landscaping LLC .... E 440 248-4852
  Cleveland *(G-5021)*
Vns Federal Services LLC .... E 740 443-7005
  Piketon *(G-12431)*

Warstler Bros Landscaping Inc .... E 330 492-9500
  Canton *(G-1883)*
Wells Township .... E 740 598-9602
  Brilliant *(G-1382)*
Yardmaster of Columbus Inc .... E 614 863-4510
  Blacklick *(G-1115)*

4961 Steam and air-conditioning supply

Akron Energy Systems LLC .... E 330 374-0600
  Akron *(G-26)*
Brewer-Garrett Company .... C 440 243-3535
  Middleburg Heights *(G-11113)*
Cleveland Thermal LLC .... E 216 241-3636
  Cleveland *(G-4071)*

4971 Irrigation systems

City of Dayton .... E 937 333-7138
  Dayton *(G-7231)*
Warstler Bros Landscaping Inc .... E 330 492-9500
  Canton *(G-1883)*

50 WHOLESALE TRADE - DURABLE GOODS

5012 Automobiles and other motor vehicles

Aaj Enterprises Inc .... A 614 497-2000
  Obetz *(G-12078)*
Abers Garage Inc .... E 419 281-5500
  Ashland *(G-471)*
Adesa Ohio LLC .... E 330 467-8280
  Northfield *(G-11951)*
▼ Albert Mike Leasing .... C 513 563-1400
  Cincinnati *(G-2158)*
Beechmont Chevrolet Inc .... D 513 624-1100
  Cincinnati *(G-2247)*
Beechmont Motors Inc .... E 513 388-3883
  Cincinnati *(G-2248)*
Beechmont Motors T Inc .... E 513 388-3800
  Cincinnati *(G-2249)*
Bobb Automotive Inc .... E 614 853-3000
  Columbus *(G-5452)*
Broadvue Motors Inc .... E 440 845-6000
  Cleveland *(G-3899)*
Brown Industrial Inc .... E 937 693-3838
  Botkins *(G-1299)*
Bulldawg Holdings LLC .... E 419 423-3131
  Findlay *(G-8519)*
Cerni Leasing LLC .... B 515 967-3300
  Youngstown *(G-15574)*
Cerni Motor Sales Inc .... D 330 652-9917
  Youngstown *(G-15575)*
Cipted Corp .... D 412 829-2120
  Monroe *(G-11336)*
Columbus Truck & Equipmen .... D 614 252-3111
  Columbus *(G-5657)*
Coughlin Chevrolet Inc .... D 740 964-9191
  Pataskala *(G-12271)*
Cronin Auto Inc .... C 419 874-4331
  Perrysburg *(G-12327)*
Dave Knapp Ford Lincoln Inc .... E 937 547-3000
  Greenville *(G-8869)*
Donley Ford-Lincoln Inc .... E 419 281-3673
  Ashland *(G-497)*
Dons Automotive Group Llc .... E 419 337-3010
  Wauseon *(G-14599)*
Doug Bigelow Chevrolet Inc .... D 330 644-7500
  Akron *(G-136)*
Downtown Ford Lincoln Inc .... D 330 456-2781
  Canton *(G-1738)*
Dutro Ford Lincoln-Mercury Inc .... D 740 452-6334
  Zanesville *(G-15786)*

Ed Tomko Chrysler Jeep Ddge In .... E 440 835-5900
  Avon Lake *(G-677)*
Esec Corporation .... E 614 875-3732
  Grove City *(G-8918)*
Fyda Frghtliner Youngstown Inc .... D 330 797-0224
  Youngstown *(G-15615)*
George P Ballas Buick GMC Trck .... E 419 535-1000
  Toledo *(G-13820)*
Girard Equipment Co .... E 330 545-2575
  Girard *(G-8814)*
Graham Chevrolet-Cadillac Co .... C 419 989-4012
  Ontario *(G-12105)*
Haydocy Automotive Inc .... D 614 279-8880
  Columbus *(G-5973)*
Helton Enterprises Inc .... E 419 423-4180
  Findlay *(G-8546)*
Hidy Motors Inc .... D 937 426-9564
  Dayton *(G-7133)*
Interstate Truckway Inc .... D 513 542-5500
  Cincinnati *(G-2883)*
Kenworth of Cincinnati Inc .... E 513 771-5831
  Cincinnati *(G-2937)*
Klaben Lincoln Ford Inc .... D 330 593-6800
  Kent *(G-9585)*
▲ Ktm North America Inc .... D 855 215-6360
  Amherst *(G-430)*
Laria Chevrolet-Buick Inc .... E 330 925-2015
  Rittman *(G-12730)*
Lower Great Lakes Kenworth Inc .... E 419 874-3511
  Perrysburg *(G-12354)*
Mac Manufacturing Inc .... C 330 829-1680
  Salem *(G-12846)*
▲ Mac Manufacturing Inc .... A 330 823-9900
  Alliance *(G-390)*
◆ Mac Trailer Manufacturing Inc .... A 800 795-8454
  Alliance *(G-391)*
Mansfield Truck Sls & Svc Inc .... D 419 522-9811
  Mansfield *(G-10290)*
McCluskey Chevrolet Inc .... C 513 761-1111
  Loveland *(G-10149)*
▼ Midway Inc .... D 419 465-2551
  Monroeville *(G-11357)*
Ohio Truck Sales LLC .... D 419 582-8087
  Sandusky *(G-12923)*
Peterbilt of Cincinnati .... B 513 772-1740
  Cincinnati *(G-3199)*
R & R Inc .... E 330 799-1536
  Youngstown *(G-15705)*
R & R Truck Sales Inc .... E 330 784-5881
  Akron *(G-276)*
Recmv2 Inc .... D 330 367-5461
  Youngstown *(G-15707)*
Rush Truck Leasing Inc .... E 937 264-2365
  Dayton *(G-7599)*
Rush Truck Leasing Inc .... E 419 224-6045
  Lima *(G-9957)*
Rush Truck Leasing Inc .... E 330 798-0600
  Walton Hills *(G-14479)*
Sharpnack Chevrolet Co .... E 800 752-7513
  Vermilion *(G-14408)*
Sims Buick-GMC Truck Inc .... E 330 372-3500
  Warren *(G-14554)*
Slimans Sales & Service Inc .... E 440 988-4484
  Amherst *(G-432)*
Stoops of Lima Inc .... D 419 228-4334
  Lima *(G-9967)*
Stykemain-Buick-Gmc Ltd .... D 419 784-5252
  Defiance *(G-7770)*
◆ Valley Ford Truck Inc .... D 216 524-2400
  Cleveland *(G-5097)*
▲ Venco Venturo Industries LLC .... E 513 772-8448
  Cincinnati *(G-3619)*

50 WHOLESALE TRADE - DURABLE GOODS

Village Motors Inc..................................D 330 674-2055
   Millersburg *(G-11295)*

Voss Auto Network Inc........................E 937 428-2447
   Dayton *(G-7711)*

Voss Chevrolet Inc...............................C 937 428-2500
   Dayton *(G-7713)*

Voss Dodge..E 937 435-7800
   Dayton *(G-7714)*

Wabash National Trlr Ctrs Inc.............D 614 878-6088
   Groveport *(G-9012)*

Warner Buick-Nissan Inc......................E 419 423-7161
   Findlay *(G-8597)*

White Family Companies Inc..............E 937 222-3701
   Dayton *(G-7720)*

Whites Service Center Inc...................E 937 653-5279
   Urbana *(G-14317)*

♦ Wholecycle Inc...................................E 330 929-8123
   Peninsula *(G-12296)*

Worldwide Equipment Inc....................E 614 876-0336
   Columbus *(G-6904)*

5013 Motor vehicle supplies and new parts

♦ Accel Performance Group LLC........C 216 658-6413
   Independence *(G-9394)*

♦ Adelmans Truck Parts Corp.............E 330 456-0206
   Canton *(G-1655)*

▲ Aftermarket Parts Company LLC....D 740 369-1056
   Delaware *(G-7777)*

All Lift Service Company Inc...............E 440 585-1542
   Willoughby *(G-15183)*

ARE Inc..A 330 830-7800
   Massillon *(G-10631)*

Auto Parts Center-Cuyahoga FLS........E 330 928-2149
   Cuyahoga Falls *(G-7045)*

Auto-Wares Inc.....................................D 419 867-1927
   Toledo *(G-13695)*

Autobody Supply Company Inc..........D 614 228-4328
   Columbus *(G-5407)*

Automotive Distributors Co Inc...........E 216 398-2014
   Cleveland *(G-3841)*

Automotive Distributors Co Inc...........D 614 476-1315
   Columbus *(G-5408)*

Autosales Incorporated.......................E 330 630-0888
   Tallmadge *(G-13586)*

♦ Axiom Automotive Tech Inc............A 800 321-8830
   Bedford *(G-954)*

Beechmont Chevrolet Inc....................D 513 624-1100
   Cincinnati *(G-2247)*

Beechmont Ford Inc.............................C 513 752-6611
   Cincinnati *(G-2098)*

Beechmont Motors Inc.........................E 513 388-3883
   Cincinnati *(G-2248)*

Beechmont Motors T Inc......................D 513 388-3800
   Cincinnati *(G-2249)*

♦ Bendix Coml Vhcl Systems LLC.......B 440 329-9000
   Avon *(G-640)*

Bills Battery Company Inc...................E 513 922-0100
   Cincinnati *(G-2262)*

♦ Borgers Ohio Inc................................B 419 663-3700
   Norwalk *(G-12002)*

Bridgeport Auto Parts Inc...................E 740 635-0441
   Bridgeport *(G-1375)*

BTMC Corporation...............................E 614 891-1454
   Thornville *(G-13619)*

▲ Building 8 Inc....................................E 513 771-8000
   Cincinnati *(G-2289)*

Buyers Products Company..................C 440 974-8888
   Mentor *(G-10916)*

♦ Buyers Products Company..............C 440 974-8888
   Mentor *(G-10915)*

♦ Cadna Rubber Company Inc............E 901 566-9090
   Fairlawn *(G-8468)*

Car Parts Warehouse Inc......................E 216 581-4800
   Cleveland *(G-3925)*

Car Parts Warehouse Inc......................E 216 496-6540
   Perry *(G-12304)*

▲ Car Parts Warehouse Inc..................E 216 281-4500
   Brookpark *(G-1429)*

Cedar Elec Holdings Corp....................D 773 804-6288
   West Chester *(G-14662)*

Chagrin Valley Auto Parts Co..............E 216 398-9800
   Cleveland *(G-3960)*

▲ Chemspec Usa Inc.............................D 330 669-8512
   Orrville *(G-12158)*

Columbus City School District............E 614 365-5263
   Columbus *(G-5622)*

Columbus Truck & Equipmen.............D 614 252-3111
   Columbus *(G-5657)*

Cornwell Quality Tools Company........E 330 335-2933
   Wadsworth *(G-14434)*

Crane Carrier Company LLC...............C 918 286-2889
   New Philadelphia *(G-11647)*

Crane Carrier Holdings LLC................C 918 286-2889
   New Philadelphia *(G-11648)*

Cross Truck Equipment Co Inc...........E 330 477-8151
   Canton *(G-1728)*

Ctek Inc..C 330 963-0981
   Twinsburg *(G-14179)*

▲ Dixie Distributing Company.............E 937 322-0033
   Springfield *(G-13247)*

Doran Mfg LLC.....................................D 866 816-7233
   Blue Ash *(G-1163)*

Dp Medina Holdings Inc......................E 216 254-7883
   Medina *(G-10832)*

♦ Dreison International Inc..................C 216 362-0755
   Cleveland *(G-4184)*

▲ Durable Corporation..........................D 800 537-1603
   Norwalk *(G-12008)*

▼ East Manufacturing Corporation......B 330 325-9921
   Randolph *(G-12618)*

▲ Emssons Faurecia Ctrl Systems.......C 812 341-2000
   Toledo *(G-13792)*

Fayette Parts Service Inc.....................E 740 282-4547
   Steubenville *(G-13324)*

Four Wheel Drive Hardware LLC.......C 330 482-4733
   Columbiana *(G-5235)*

Freudenberg-Nok General Partnr......C 419 499-2502
   Milan *(G-11206)*

♦ G-Cor Automotive Corp.....................E 614 443-6735
   Columbus *(G-5907)*

Goodyear Tire & Rubber Company....A 330 796-2121
   Akron *(G-179)*

▲ Grammer Industries LLC..................D 864 284-9616
   Toledo *(G-13823)*

Great Lakes-Ramco Inc.......................E 586 759-5500
   Mentor *(G-10944)*

GTM Service Inc...................................E 440 944-5099
   Wickliffe *(G-15151)*

Hankook Tire America Corp.................E 330 896-6199
   Uniontown *(G-14255)*

Herbert E Orr Company Inc................C 419 399-4866
   Paulding *(G-12284)*

♦ Hy-Tek Material Handling LLC.........D 614 497-2500
   Columbus *(G-6030)*

Ieh Auto Parts LLC...............................E 740 732-2395
   Caldwell *(G-1550)*

Ieh Auto Parts LLC...............................E 740 373-8327
   Marietta *(G-10373)*

Ieh Auto Parts LLC...............................D 740 373-8151
   Marietta *(G-10374)*

Inoac Exterior Systems LLC................C 419 334-8951
   Fremont *(G-8687)*

Inoac Exterior Systems LLC................E 419 334-8951
   Fremont *(G-8688)*

▲ International Brake Inds Inc..............E 419 227-4421
   Lima *(G-9911)*

♦ Interstate Diesel Service Inc.............C 216 881-0015
   Cleveland *(G-4420)*

♦ Interstate-Mcbee LLC........................C 216 881-0015
   Bedford *(G-967)*

Jegs Automotive Inc............................B 614 294-5451
   Columbus *(G-6086)*

♦ Jegs Automotive LLC.........................C 614 294-5050
   Delaware *(G-7808)*

Jobbers Automotive LLC.....................E 216 524-2229
   Eastlake *(G-8203)*

♦ Kaffenbarger Truck Eqp Co..............C 937 845-3804
   New Carlisle *(G-11602)*

Kenworth of Cincinnati Inc..................D 513 771-5831
   Cincinnati *(G-2937)*

Keystone Auto Glass Inc......................D 419 509-0497
   Maumee *(G-10736)*

Knox Auto LLC.....................................E 330 701-5266
   Mount Vernon *(G-11490)*

KOI Enterprises Inc.............................C 513 648-3020
   Cincinnati *(G-2947)*

▲ KOI Enterprises Inc...........................D 513 357-2400
   Cincinnati *(G-2948)*

Kyocera Precision Tools Inc................D 419 738-6652
   Wapakoneta *(G-14486)*

▲ Lake County Parts Warehouse Inc...E 440 259-2991
   Perry *(G-12306)*

♦ Lippert Enterprises Inc......................E 419 281-8084
   Ashland *(G-505)*

Lower Great Lakes Kenworth Inc.......E 419 874-3511
   Perrysburg *(G-12354)*

Lucas Sumitomo Brakes Inc...............E 513 934-0024
   Lebanon *(G-9776)*

♦ Luk-Aftermarket Service Inc............D 330 273-4383
   Valley City *(G-14335)*

♦ Mac Trailer Manufacturing Inc........A 800 795-8454
   Alliance *(G-391)*

♦ Mahle Behr Mt Sterling Inc...............B 740 869-3333
   Mount Sterling *(G-11474)*

▲ Matco Tools Corporation...................B 330 929-4949
   Stow *(G-13382)*

▲ McBee Supply Corporation...............D 216 881-0015
   Bedford *(G-971)*

▼ Midway Inc...D 419 465-2551
   Monroeville *(G-11357)*

Mill Supply Inc......................................E 216 518-5072
   Cleveland *(G-4583)*

▼ Myers Equipment Corporation.........E 330 533-5556
   Canfield *(G-1635)*

Myers Industries Inc...........................E 330 253-5592
   Akron *(G-238)*

N S International Ltd..........................D 248 251-1600
   Dublin *(G-8067)*

National Marketshare Group..............E 513 921-0800
   Cincinnati *(G-3095)*

♦ Nk Parts Industries Inc.....................C 937 498-4651
   Sidney *(G-13041)*

Nu-Di Products Co Inc........................D 216 251-9070
   Cleveland *(G-4672)*

▲ Ohashi Technica USA Inc.................E 740 965-5115
   Sunbury *(G-13523)*

Ohio Auto Kolor Inc............................E 614 272-2255
   Columbus *(G-6393)*

P & M Exhaust Systems Whse Inc....E 513 825-2660
   Cincinnati *(G-3179)*

▲ Pag Mentor A1 Inc............................E 440 951-1040
   Mentor *(G-10982)*

♦ Par International Inc..........................E 614 529-1300
   Obetz *(G-12082)*

▲ Pat Young Service Co Inc................E 216 447-8550
   Cleveland *(G-4729)*

50 WHOLESALE TRADE - DURABLE GOODS

Peterbilt of Cincinnati......................... B 513 772-1740
  Cincinnati *(G-3199)*
◆ Pioneer Automotive Tech Inc............. C 937 746-2293
  Miamisburg *(G-11084)*
◆ Power Train Components Inc............. D 419 636-4430
  Bryan *(G-1493)*
Qualitor Subsidiary H Inc..................... C 419 562-7987
  Bucyrus *(G-1517)*
R & R Inc... E 330 799-1536
  Youngstown *(G-15705)*
▲ R L Morrissey & Assoc Inc................. E 440 498-3730
  Solon *(G-13135)*
▲ Shrader Tire & Oil Inc......................... E 419 472-2128
  Toledo *(G-14012)*
▲ Sims Bros Inc...................................... D 740 387-9041
  Marion *(G-10454)*
Smyth Automotive Inc........................... D 513 528-2800
  Cincinnati *(G-3389)*
▲ Snyders Antique Auto Parts Inc......... E 330 549-5313
  New Springfield *(G-11679)*
◆ Stellar Srkg Acquisition LLC.............. E 330 769-8484
  Seville *(G-12966)*
The E and R Trailer Sales..................... E 419 968-2115
  Middle Point *(G-11111)*
The Glockner Chevrolet Company......... C 740 353-2161
  Portsmouth *(G-12576)*
▲ Thyssenkrupp Bilstein Amer Inc......... C 513 881-7600
  Hamilton *(G-9086)*
Trailines Incorporated........................... E 513 755-7900
  West Chester *(G-14777)*
Transport Services Inc........................... E 440 582-4900
  Cleveland *(G-5032)*
◆ Transtar Industries LLC..................... C 440 232-5100
  Cleveland *(G-5035)*
Truckomat Corporation......................... E 740 467-2818
  Hebron *(G-9155)*
▲ TS Trim Industries Inc........................ B 614 837-4114
  Canal Winchester *(G-1618)*
Turbo Parts LLC................................... D 740 223-1695
  Marion *(G-10457)*
United Wheels Inc.................................. E 937 865-2813
  Miamisburg *(G-11101)*
◆ Valley Ford Truck Inc......................... D 216 524-2400
  Cleveland *(G-5097)*
▲ Ventra Salem LLC............................... A 330 337-8002
  Salem *(G-12856)*
Vgp Holdings LLC.................................. B 513 557-3100
  Cincinnati *(G-3629)*
Wabash National Trlr Ctrs Inc............... D 614 878-6088
  Groveport *(G-9012)*
Whites Service Center Inc...................... E 937 653-5259
  Urbana *(G-14317)*
Worldwide Equipment Inc..................... E 614 876-0336
  Columbus *(G-6904)*
◆ Wz Management Inc........................... E 330 628-4881
  Akron *(G-365)*
Young Truck Sales Inc........................... E 330 477-6271
  Canton *(G-1891)*

5014 Tires and tubes

▲ American Kenda Rbr Indus Ltd........... E 866 536-3287
  Reynoldsburg *(G-12653)*
▲ Best One Tire & Svc Lima Inc............. E 419 229-2380
  Lima *(G-9868)*
Bestdrive LLC....................................... A 614 284-7549
  Urbancrest *(G-14319)*
▲ Capital Tire Inc................................... E 419 241-5111
  Rossford *(G-12765)*
Carrolls LLC... E 330 733-8100
  Akron *(G-81)*
Carrolls LLC... E 513 733-5559
  West Chester *(G-14659)*
Conrads Tire Service Inc....................... E 216 941-3333
  Cleveland *(G-4103)*
▲ Dealer Tire LLC................................... B 216 432-0088
  Cleveland *(G-4155)*
Gateway Tire of Texas Inc..................... E 513 874-2500
  West Chester *(G-14813)*
▲ Grismer Tire Company........................ E 937 643-2526
  Centerville *(G-1945)*
Hankook Tire America Corp.................. E 330 896-6199
  Uniontown *(G-14255)*
▲ Millersburg Tire Service Inc............... E 330 674-1085
  Millersburg *(G-11286)*
Myers Industries Inc.............................. D 330 253-5592
  Akron *(G-238)*
North Gateway Tire Company Inc......... E 330 725-8473
  Medina *(G-10869)*
Reville Tire Co....................................... D 330 468-1900
  Northfield *(G-11965)*
Rush Truck Centers Ohio Inc................ E 513 733-8500
  Cincinnati *(G-3334)*
Rush Truck Leasing Inc........................ E 937 264-2365
  Dayton *(G-7599)*
Rush Truck Leasing Inc........................ E 419 224-6045
  Lima *(G-9957)*
Rush Truck Leasing Inc........................ E 330 798-0600
  Walton Hills *(G-14479)*
Shrader Tire & Oil Inc........................... E 614 445-6601
  Columbus *(G-6675)*
Shrader Tire & Oil Inc........................... E 740 788-8032
  Heath *(G-9139)*
▲ Shrader Tire & Oil Inc........................ E 419 472-2128
  Toledo *(G-14012)*
▲ Stoney Hollow Tire Inc....................... D 740 635-5200
  Martins Ferry *(G-10470)*
◆ Technical Rubber Company Inc.......... C 740 967-9015
  Johnstown *(G-9549)*
◆ The Hercules Tire & Rubber Company.. E 800 677-9535
  Findlay *(G-8592)*
Thyssenkrupp Bilstein Amer Inc............ D 513 881-7600
  Hamilton *(G-9085)*
Treadmaxx Tire Distrs Inc..................... D 404 762-4944
  Wooster *(G-15379)*
▲ W D Tire Warehouse Inc..................... E 614 461-8944
  Columbus *(G-6862)*
Ziegler Tire and Supply Co.................... E 330 834-3332
  Massillon *(G-10676)*

5015 Motor vehicle parts, used

Brims Imports....................................... E 419 675-1099
  Kenton *(G-9611)*
Cedar Elec Holdings Corp..................... D 773 804-6288
  West Chester *(G-14662)*
◆ G-Cor Automotive Corp...................... E 614 443-6735
  Columbus *(G-5907)*
Lkq Tripletttasap Inc............................. C 330 733-6333
  Akron *(G-223)*
Lucas Sumitomo Brakes Inc.................. E 513 934-0024
  Lebanon *(G-9776)*
◆ Mac Trailer Manufacturing Inc........... A 800 795-8454
  Alliance *(G-391)*
Pick Pull Auto Dismantling Inc............. E 614 497-8858
  Columbus *(G-6525)*
Pull-A-Part LLC.................................... E 330 456-8349
  Canton *(G-1835)*
Pull-A-Part LLC.................................... E 330 631-6280
  Cleveland *(G-4798)*
Renascent Salvage Holdings LLC......... E 216 539-1033
  Brecksville *(G-1365)*
▼ Stricker Bros Inc................................. E 513 732-1152
  Batavia *(G-748)*
Zappys Auto Washes.............................. E 844 927-9274
  Mentor *(G-11013)*

5021 Furniture

12985 Snow Holdings Inc...................... E 216 267-5000
  Cleveland *(G-3739)*
◆ American Interiors Inc........................ E 419 535-1808
  Toledo *(G-13683)*
Best Restaurant Equipment & Design.... D 614 488-2378
  Columbus *(G-5433)*
◆ Big Lots Stores LLC........................... A 614 278-6800
  Columbus *(G-5439)*
Business Furniture LLC........................ E 937 293-1010
  Dayton *(G-7207)*
Central Business Equipment Co............ E 513 891-4430
  Cincinnati *(G-2333)*
Collaborative Inc................................... E 419 242-7405
  Toledo *(G-13748)*
Comdoc Inc.. E 513 766-8124
  Blue Ash *(G-1156)*
Commercial Works Inc.......................... D 614 870-2342
  Columbus *(G-5667)*
◆ Cornerstone Brands Inc...................... A 513 603-1000
  West Chester *(G-14676)*
D Yoder Hardwoods LLC...................... D 330 852-8105
  Sugarcreek *(G-13508)*
Dayton Ews Inc...................................... E 937 293-1010
  Moraine *(G-11400)*
Friends Service Co Inc.......................... D 419 427-1704
  Findlay *(G-8534)*
G & P Construction LLC....................... E 855 494-4830
  North Royalton *(G-11941)*
Gasser Chair Co Inc.............................. D 330 742-2234
  Youngstown *(G-15617)*
Jsc Employee Leasing Corp.................. D 330 773-8971
  Akron *(G-212)*
▲ KMC Holdings LLC............................ C 419 238-2442
  Van Wert *(G-14347)*
Loth Inc... E 614 487-4000
  Columbus *(G-6173)*
◆ Mill Distributors Inc........................... D 330 995-9200
  Aurora *(G-618)*
▲ National Electro-Coatings Inc............ D 216 898-0080
  Cleveland *(G-4624)*
Partitions Plus Incorporated.................. E 419 422-2600
  Findlay *(G-8575)*
Retail Service Systems Inc.................... D 614 203-6126
  Dublin *(G-8108)*
◆ Rize Home LLC................................... D 800 333-8333
  Solon *(G-13138)*
S P Richards Company.......................... E 614 497-2270
  Lockbourne *(G-10015)*
◆ Sauder Woodworking Co.................... A 419 446-2711
  Archbold *(G-467)*
Smith & Schaefer Inc............................. E 216 226-6700
  Bethel *(G-1094)*
Space & Asset Management Inc............ E 937 918-1000
  Dayton *(G-7631)*
Springfield Business Eqp Co................. E 937 322-3828
  Springfield *(G-13294)*
The Ohio Desk Company....................... E 216 623-0600
  Cleveland *(G-5005)*
W B Mason Co Inc................................ E 216 267-5000
  North Olmsted *(G-11918)*
◆ Wasserstrom Company........................ B 614 228-6525
  Columbus *(G-6867)*

5023 Homefurnishings

Accent Drapery Co Inc.......................... E 614 488-0741
  Columbus *(G-5300)*
▲ American Frame Corporation.............. D 419 893-5595
  Maumee *(G-10690)*
▼ Americas Floor Source LLC................ D 614 808-3915
  Columbus *(G-5363)*

50 WHOLESALE TRADE - DURABLE GOODS

Artwall LLC .... E 216 476-0635
   Cleveland *(G-3836)*

Black River Group Inc .... E 419 524-4312
   Mansfield *(G-10246)*

▲ Bostwick-Braun Company .... D 419 259-3600
   Toledo *(G-13713)*

Business Furniture LLC .... E 937 293-1010
   Dayton *(G-7207)*

▲ Cdc Distributors Inc .... D 513 771-3100
   Cincinnati *(G-2329)*

Certified Carpet Distrs Inc .... E 216 573-1422
   Cleveland *(G-3957)*

Dayton Ews Inc .... E 937 293-1010
   Moraine *(G-11400)*

▲ Dealers Supply North Inc .... E 614 274-6285
   Lockbourne *(G-10011)*

Decorate With Style Inc .... E 419 621-5577
   Sandusky *(G-12887)*

Famous Distribution Inc .... D 330 762-9621
   Akron *(G-154)*

◆ G & S Metal Products Co Inc .... C 216 441-0700
   Cleveland *(G-4295)*

◆ G G Marck & Associates Inc .... E 419 478-0900
   Toledo *(G-13815)*

◆ Geoglobal Partners LLC .... D 561 598-6000
   Aurora *(G-614)*

Golden Drapery Supply Inc .... E 216 351-3283
   Cleveland *(G-4318)*

Hobby Lobby Stores Inc .... E 330 686-1508
   Stow *(G-13373)*

▲ Inside Outfitters Inc .... E 614 798-3500
   Lewis Center *(G-9824)*

◆ Interdesign Inc .... C 440 248-0178
   Solon *(G-13101)*

JP Flooring Systems Inc .... E 513 346-4300
   West Chester *(G-14715)*

◆ K & K Interiors Inc .... E 419 627-0039
   Sandusky *(G-12907)*

Lumenomics Inc .... E 614 798-3500
   Lewis Center *(G-9827)*

Luminex HM Dcor Frgrnce Hldg C ...... B 513 563-1113
   Blue Ash *(G-1204)*

Messina Floor Covering LLC .... D 216 595-0100
   Cleveland *(G-4557)*

Metro Decor LLC .... C 855 498-5899
   Glenwillow *(G-8834)*

◆ Mill Distributors Inc .... D 330 995-9200
   Aurora *(G-618)*

National Marketshare Group .... E 513 921-0800
   Cincinnati *(G-3095)*

▲ Norwood Hardware and Supply Co .. D 513 733-1175
   Cincinnati *(G-3129)*

Ohio Valley Flooring Inc .... E 216 328-9091
   Cleveland *(G-4691)*

▲ Ohio Valley Flooring Inc .... D 513 271-3434
   Cincinnati *(G-3150)*

Old Time Pottery LLC .... D 513 825-5211
   Cincinnati *(G-3156)*

Old Time Pottery LLC .... D 440 842-1244
   Cleveland *(G-4694)*

Old Time Pottery LLC .... D 614 337-1258
   Columbus *(G-6470)*

Rubbermaid Incorporated .... D 330 733-7771
   Akron *(G-290)*

◆ Standard Textile Co Inc .... B 513 761-9255
   Cincinnati *(G-3409)*

◆ State Crest Carpet & Flooring .... E 440 232-3980
   Bedford *(G-987)*

Style-Line Incorporated .... E 614 291-0600
   Columbus *(G-6725)*

Tri-State Wholesale Build .... E 513 381-1231
   Cincinnati *(G-3505)*

Van Boxel Stor Solutions LLC .... E 440 721-1504
   Chardon *(G-2025)*

Walter F Stephens Jr Inc .... E 937 746-0521
   Franklin *(G-8652)*

Wholesale Decor LLC .... E 330 587-7100
   Hartville *(G-9131)*

◆ Wholesale Decor LLC .... E 877 745-5050
   Seville *(G-12967)*

5031 Lumber, plywood, and millwork

A-E Door Sales and Service Inc .... E 513 742-1984
   Cincinnati *(G-2132)*

Adkins Timber Products Inc .... E 740 984-2768
   Beverly *(G-1099)*

Allegion Access Tech LLC .... E 440 248-2330
   Cleveland *(G-3793)*

Allied Window Inc .... E 513 559-1212
   Cincinnati *(G-2169)*

Alside Inc .... E 330 929-1811
   Cuyahoga Falls *(G-7036)*

American Warming and Vent .... D 419 288-2703
   Bradner *(G-1341)*

Apco Industries Inc .... D 614 224-2345
   Columbus *(G-5371)*

◆ Appalachian Hardwood Lumber Co . E 440 232-6767
   Cleveland *(G-3820)*

Arling Lumber Incorporated .... E 513 451-5700
   Cincinnati *(G-2216)*

▲ Associated Materials LLC .... A 330 929-1811
   Cuyahoga Falls *(G-7041)*

Associated Materials Group Inc .... C 330 929-1811
   Cuyahoga Falls *(G-7043)*

Associated Mtls Holdings LLC .... A 330 929-1811
   Cuyahoga Falls *(G-7044)*

Babin Building Solutions LLC .... E 216 292-2500
   Broadview Heights *(G-1383)*

Baillie Lumber Co LP .... E 419 462-2000
   Galion *(G-8745)*

Boise Cascade Company .... C 740 382-6766
   Marion *(G-10419)*

Buckeye Components LLC .... E 330 482-5163
   Columbiana *(G-5231)*

Carter-Jones Lumber Company .... E 330 784-5441
   Akron *(G-82)*

▲ Carter-Jones Lumber Company ...... C 330 673-6100
   Kent *(G-9561)*

Champion Opco LLC .... E 440 249-6768
   Macedonia *(G-10190)*

Dayton Door Sales Inc .... E 937 253-9181
   Dayton *(G-7280)*

◆ Df Supply Inc .... E 330 650-9226
   Twinsburg *(G-14181)*

◆ Direct Import Home Decor Inc .... E 216 898-9758
   Cleveland *(G-4166)*

Don Walter Kitchen Distrs Inc .... E 330 793-9338
   Youngstown *(G-15600)*

Dortrnic Service-Tallmadge Inc .... E 330 928-2727
   Stow *(G-13364)*

Dortronic Service Inc .... E 216 739-3667
   Cleveland *(G-4180)*

▼ Eagle Hardwoods Inc .... E 330 339-8838
   Newcomerstown *(G-11767)*

Empire Enterprises Inc .... E 330 665-7800
   Akron *(G-147)*

▲ Empire Wholesale Lumber C .... E 330 665-7800
   Akron *(G-148)*

▲ Enclosure Suppliers LLC .... E 513 782-3900
   Cincinnati *(G-2619)*

Enterprise Door & Supply Inc .... E 440 942-3478
   Mentor *(G-10937)*

Famous Distribution Inc .... E 740 282-0951
   Steubenville *(G-13323)*

Famous Enterprises Inc .... E 330 762-9621
   Akron *(G-156)*

Flagship Trading Corporation .... E
   Cleveland *(G-4263)*

Francis-Schulze Co .... E 937 295-3941
   Russia *(G-12770)*

▲ Gilkey Window Company Inc .... D 513 769-4527
   Cincinnati *(G-2732)*

Gorell Enterprises Inc .... B 724 465-1800
   Streetsboro *(G-13414)*

▲ Graves Lumber Co .... C 330 666-1115
   Copley *(G-6958)*

Gunton Corporation .... E 216 831-2420
   Cleveland *(G-4342)*

▲ Hamilton-Parker Company .... D 614 358-7800
   Columbus *(G-5968)*

▼ Hartzell Hardwoods Inc .... D 937 773-7054
   Piqua *(G-12443)*

Holmes Lumber & Bldg Ctr Inc .... E 330 479-8314
   Canton *(G-1775)*

Holmes Lumber & Bldg Ctr Inc .... C 330 674-9060
   Millersburg *(G-11279)*

Installed Building Pdts LLC .... C 614 272-5577
   Columbus *(G-6058)*

Jackpot Pallets LLC .... E 877 770-0005
   Brooklyn Heights *(G-1421)*

Jeld-Wen Inc .... C 513 874-6771
   West Chester *(G-14821)*

Keidel Sup LLC Fka Kdel Sup In .... E 513 351-1600
   Cincinnati *(G-2933)*

Keim Lumber Company .... D 330 893-2251
   Baltic *(G-690)*

▲ Keim Lumber Company .... D 330 893-2251
   Millersburg *(G-11282)*

Khempco Bldg Sup Co Ltd Partnr .... D 740 549-0465
   Delaware *(G-7811)*

Kurtz Bros Inc .... E 216 986-7000
   Independence *(G-9442)*

◆ Litco International Inc .... D 330 539-5433
   Vienna *(G-14421)*

Lowes Home Centers LLC .... C 330 665-9356
   Akron *(G-225)*

Lowes Home Centers LLC .... C 330 829-2700
   Alliance *(G-389)*

Lowes Home Centers LLC .... C 440 998-6555
   Ashtabula *(G-540)*

Lowes Home Centers LLC .... C 740 589-3750
   Athens *(G-582)*

Lowes Home Centers LLC .... C 440 937-3500
   Avon *(G-660)*

Lowes Home Centers LLC .... C 937 427-1110
   Beavercreek *(G-889)*

Lowes Home Centers LLC .... C 216 831-2860
   Bedford *(G-970)*

Lowes Home Centers LLC .... D 937 599-4000
   Bellefontaine *(G-1032)*

Lowes Home Centers LLC .... C 330 497-2720
   Canton *(G-1797)*

Lowes Home Centers LLC .... C 740 773-7777
   Chillicothe *(G-2079)*

Lowes Home Centers LLC .... C 513 598-7050
   Cincinnati *(G-2990)*

Lowes Home Centers LLC .... C 216 351-4723
   Cleveland *(G-4506)*

Lowes Home Centers LLC .... C 614 853-6200
   Columbus *(G-6174)*

Lowes Home Centers LLC .... C 937 235-2920
   Dayton *(G-7460)*

Lowes Home Centers LLC .... C 937 438-4900
   Dayton *(G-7461)*

Lowes Home Centers LLC .... C 937 854-8200
   Dayton *(G-7462)*

50 WHOLESALE TRADE - DURABLE GOODS

Lowes Home Centers LLC............................C..... 419 782-9000
   Defiance *(G-7753)*

Lowes Home Centers LLC............................C..... 614 659-0530
   Dublin *(G-8058)*

Lowes Home Centers LLC............................C..... 440 324-5004
   Elyria *(G-8272)*

Lowes Home Centers LLC............................C..... 419 420-7531
   Findlay *(G-8559)*

Lowes Home Centers LLC............................C..... 419 355-0221
   Fremont *(G-8690)*

Lowes Home Centers LLC............................C..... 937 547-2400
   Greenville *(G-8880)*

Lowes Home Centers LLC............................C..... 513 737-3700
   Hamilton *(G-9061)*

Lowes Home Centers LLC............................C..... 614 529-5900
   Hilliard *(G-9210)*

Lowes Home Centers LLC............................C..... 740 681-3464
   Lancaster *(G-9733)*

Lowes Home Centers LLC............................C..... 419 331-3598
   Lima *(G-9930)*

Lowes Home Centers LLC............................C..... 440 985-5700
   Lorain *(G-10090)*

Lowes Home Centers LLC............................C..... 740 374-2151
   Marietta *(G-10381)*

Lowes Home Centers LLC............................C..... 740 389-9737
   Marion *(G-10433)*

Lowes Home Centers LLC............................C..... 937 578-4440
   Marysville *(G-10492)*

Lowes Home Centers LLC............................C..... 513 336-9741
   Mason *(G-10575)*

Lowes Home Centers LLC............................C..... 330 832-1901
   Massillon *(G-10650)*

Lowes Home Centers LLC............................C..... 440 392-0027
   Mentor *(G-10965)*

Lowes Home Centers LLC............................C..... 513 727-3900
   Middletown *(G-11170)*

Lowes Home Centers LLC............................C..... 513 965-3280
   Milford *(G-11237)*

Lowes Home Centers LLC............................C..... 740 393-5350
   Mount Vernon *(G-11498)*

Lowes Home Centers LLC............................D..... 330 339-1936
   New Philadelphia *(G-11657)*

Lowes Home Centers LLC............................C..... 740 522-0003
   Newark *(G-11723)*

Lowes Home Centers LLC............................D..... 330 908-2750
   Northfield *(G-11960)*

Lowes Home Centers LLC............................C..... 419 747-1920
   Ontario *(G-12113)*

Lowes Home Centers LLC............................C..... 419 874-6758
   Perrysburg *(G-12355)*

Lowes Home Centers LLC............................D..... 614 769-9940
   Reynoldsburg *(G-12668)*

Lowes Home Centers LLC............................C..... 440 331-1027
   Rocky River *(G-12748)*

Lowes Home Centers LLC............................D..... 740 699-3000
   Saint Clairsville *(G-12799)*

Lowes Home Centers LLC............................C..... 419 624-6000
   Sandusky *(G-12912)*

Lowes Home Centers LLC............................C..... 937 498-8400
   Sidney *(G-13039)*

Lowes Home Centers LLC............................C..... 513 445-1000
   South Lebanon *(G-13172)*

Lowes Home Centers LLC............................C..... 740 894-7120
   South Point *(G-13177)*

Lowes Home Centers LLC............................C..... 937 327-6000
   Springfield *(G-13264)*

Lowes Home Centers LLC............................C..... 740 266-3500
   Steubenville *(G-13336)*

Lowes Home Centers LLC............................C..... 330 920-9280
   Stow *(G-13380)*

Lowes Home Centers LLC............................C..... 330 626-2980
   Streetsboro *(G-13420)*

Lowes Home Centers LLC............................C..... 440 239-2630
   Strongsville *(G-13473)*

Lowes Home Centers LLC............................C..... 419 843-9758
   Toledo *(G-13894)*

Lowes Home Centers LLC............................C..... 937 339-2544
   Troy *(G-14145)*

Lowes Home Centers LLC............................C..... 330 335-1900
   Wadsworth *(G-14442)*

Lowes Home Centers LLC............................C..... 419 739-1300
   Wapakoneta *(G-14488)*

Lowes Home Centers LLC............................C..... 330 609-8000
   Warren *(G-14536)*

Lowes Home Centers LLC............................C..... 513 755-4300
   West Chester *(G-14726)*

Lowes Home Centers LLC............................C..... 740 574-6200
   Wheelersburg *(G-15130)*

Lowes Home Centers LLC............................C..... 440 942-2759
   Willoughby *(G-15207)*

Lowes Home Centers LLC............................C..... 937 383-7000
   Wilmington *(G-15260)*

Lowes Home Centers LLC............................C..... 330 287-2261
   Wooster *(G-15352)*

Lowes Home Centers LLC............................C..... 937 347-4000
   Xenia *(G-15524)*

Lowes Home Centers LLC............................C..... 330 965-4500
   Youngstown *(G-15653)*

Lowes Home Centers LLC............................C..... 740 450-5500
   Zanesville *(G-15807)*

Mae Holding Company..................................E..... 513 751-2424
   Cincinnati *(G-3002)*

Mason Structural Steel LLC.........................E..... 440 439-1040
   Walton Hills *(G-14476)*

Mastic Home Exteriors Inc...........................C..... 937 497-7008
   Sidney *(G-13040)*

Mentor Lumber and Supply Co....................C..... 440 255-8814
   Mentor *(G-10970)*

▲ Meyer Decorative Surfaces USA Inc........C..... 800 776-3900
   Hudson *(G-9364)*

Milestone Ventures LLC...............................E..... 317 908-2093
   Newark *(G-11730)*

Modern Builders Supply Inc..........................E..... 513 531-1000
   Cincinnati *(G-3075)*

Mssi Group Inc..D..... 440 439-1040
   Walton Hills *(G-14477)*

▲ Norwood Hardware and Supply Co........D..... 513 733-1175
   Cincinnati *(G-3129)*

OK Interiors Corp..C..... 513 742-3278
   Cincinnati *(G-3153)*

Orrville Trucking & Grading Co....................E..... 330 682-4010
   Orrville *(G-12172)*

Pallet Distributors Inc..................................E..... 888 805-9670
   Lakewood *(G-9681)*

▲ Professional Laminate Mllwk Inc.............E..... 513 891-7858
   Milford *(G-11251)*

Provia Holdings Inc......................................C..... 330 852-4711
   Sugarcreek *(G-13512)*

Provia LLC..E..... 330 852-4711
   Sugarcreek *(G-13513)*

Robert McCabe Company Inc.....................E..... 513 469-2500
   Cincinnati *(G-3314)*

Robertson Plumbing & Heating..................E..... 330 863-0611
   Malvern *(G-10235)*

Rockwood Products Ltd..............................E..... 330 893-2392
   Millersburg *(G-11291)*

Rwlp Corporation..E..... 216 883-2424
   Cleveland *(G-4866)*

S R Door Inc...D..... 740 927-3558
   Hebron *(G-9153)*

Schneider Home Equipment Co..................E..... 513 522-1200
   Cincinnati *(G-3349)*

▲ Sims-Lohman Inc......................................E..... 513 651-3510
   Cincinnati *(G-3379)*

Soft-Lite LLC...C..... 330 528-3400
   Streetsboro *(G-13428)*

SPI LLC...E..... 440 914-1122
   Solon *(G-13148)*

▲ Stephen M Trudick....................................E..... 440 834-1891
   Burton *(G-1533)*

The Cleveland Vicon Co Inc........................E..... 216 341-3300
   Cleveland *(G-4996)*

The F A Requarth Company........................E..... 937 224-1141
   Dayton *(G-7665)*

The Galehouse Companies Inc...................E..... 330 658-2023
   Doylestown *(G-7916)*

Toledo Molding & Die LLC..........................B..... 419 692-6022
   Delphos *(G-7846)*

▲ Tri-State Forest Products Inc..................E..... 937 323-6325
   Springfield *(G-13304)*

Universal Pallets Inc....................................E..... 614 444-1095
   Columbus *(G-6820)*

Universal Windows Direct............................D..... 440 232-9060
   Bedford Heights *(G-1003)*

US Lumber Group LLC................................E..... 330 538-3386
   North Jackson *(G-11879)*

♦ Usavinyl LLC..D..... 614 771-4805
   Groveport *(G-9010)*

Vwc Liquidation Company LLC...................C..... 330 372-6776
   Warren *(G-14573)*

Wappoo Wood Products Inc........................E..... 937 492-1166
   Sidney *(G-13057)*

5032 Brick, stone, and related material

Access Drywall Supply Co Inc.....................E..... 614 890-2111
   Westerville *(G-14955)*

Best Supply Inc..D..... 614 527-7000
   Columbus *(G-5434)*

▲ Clay Burley Products Co..........................E..... 740 452-3633
   Roseville *(G-12763)*

Collinwood Shale Brick Sup Co...................E..... 216 587-2700
   Cleveland *(G-4088)*

Columbus Coal & Lime Co..........................E..... 614 224-9241
   Columbus *(G-5624)*

▲ Direct Import Home Decor Inc.................E..... 216 898-9758
   Cleveland *(G-4166)*

Empire Enterprises Inc.................................E..... 330 665-7800
   Akron *(G-147)*

Encore Precast LLC.....................................E..... 513 726-5678
   Seven Mile *(G-12962)*

▼ Exhibit Concepts Inc.................................D..... 937 890-7000
   Vandalia *(G-14376)*

Grafton Ready Mix Concret Inc...................C..... 440 926-2911
   Grafton *(G-8839)*

▲ Hamilton-Parker Company........................D..... 614 358-7800
   Columbus *(G-5968)*

Haulotte Group Biljax Inc.............................E..... 567 444-4159
   Archbold *(G-460)*

Huron Cement Products Company..............E..... 419 433-4161
   Huron *(G-9390)*

Hwz Distribution Group LLC........................C..... 513 618-0300
   West Chester *(G-14818)*

Hy-Grade Corporation..................................E..... 216 341-7711
   Cleveland *(G-4395)*

▲ Kenmore Construction Co Inc..................C..... 330 762-8936
   Akron *(G-215)*

▲ Kuhlman Corporation.................................E..... 419 897-6000
   Maumee *(G-10737)*

L & W Supply Corporation...........................E..... 513 723-1150
   Cincinnati *(G-2960)*

▲ Lang Stone Company Inc.........................E..... 614 235-4099
   Columbus *(G-6139)*

▲ Maza Inc..D..... 614 760-0003
   Plain City *(G-12486)*

▲ Mees Distributors Inc................................E..... 513 541-2311
   Cincinnati *(G-3035)*

Employee Codes: A=Over 500 employees, B=251-500
C=101-250, D=51-100, E=20-50, F=10-19, G=1-9

50 WHOLESALE TRADE - DURABLE GOODS

Modern Builders Supply Inc.......................... C 419 241-3961
　Toledo (G-13926)
▲ Mont Granite Inc.. E 440 287-0101
　Solon (G-13112)
Most Wrshpful Ereka Grnd Ldge................. E 614 626-4076
　Columbus (G-6263)
Nexgen Enterprises Inc................................. B 513 618-0300
　Cincinnati (G-3112)
◆ Pinney Dock & Transport LLC..................D 440 964-7186
　Ashtabula (G-546)
Quality Block & Supply Inc.......................... E 330 364-4411
　Mount Eaton (G-11458)
R W Sidley Incorporated............................... C 440 298-3232
　Thompson (G-13618)
Robinson Insulation Co Inc.......................... E 937 323-9599
　Springfield (G-13286)
Sewer Rodding Equipment Co..................... C 419 991-2065
　Lima (G-9959)
Smyrna Ready Mix Concrete LLC............... E 937 855-0410
　Germantown (G-8805)
Stoneco Inc... E 419 893-7645
　Maumee (G-10771)
◆ The D S Brown Company............................C 419 257-3561
　North Baltimore (G-11802)
The W L Tucker Supply Company............... E 330 928-2155
　Cuyahoga Falls (G-7107)
Tremco Cpg Inc.. D 216 292-5000
　Beachwood (G-846)
United Building Materials Inc...................... E 937 222-4444
　Dayton (G-7681)
Van Boxel Stor Solutions LLC..................... E 440 721-1504
　Chardon (G-2025)

5033 Roofing, siding, and insulation

Alpine Insulation I LLC............................... D 614 221-3399
　Columbus (G-5339)
Alside Inc... D 419 865-0934
　Maumee (G-10687)
Apco Industries Inc...................................... D 614 224-2345
　Columbus (G-5371)
▲ Associated Materials LLC.......................... A 330 929-1811
　Cuyahoga Falls (G-7041)
Associated Materials Group Inc................... C 330 929-1811
　Cuyahoga Falls (G-7043)
Associated Mtls Holdings LLC.................... A 330 929-1811
　Cuyahoga Falls (G-7044)
Banner Supply Company Inc....................... E 330 782-1171
　Youngstown (G-15555)
Famous Distribution Inc.............................. E 740 282-0951
　Steubenville (G-13323)
Installed Building Pdts Inc........................... C 614 221-3399
　Columbus (G-6057)
Installed Building Pdts LLC........................ C 614 272-5577
　Columbus (G-6058)
Modern Builders Supply Inc........................ E 513 531-1000
　Cincinnati (G-3075)
Modern Builders Supply Inc........................ E 216 273-3605
　Cleveland (G-4593)
Modern Builders Supply Inc........................ E 419 224-4627
　Lima (G-9936)
North Coast Commercial Ro........................ C 330 425-3359
　Twinsburg (G-14208)
Owens Crning Inslting Systm...................... D 419 248-8000
　Toledo (G-13953)
Owens-Corning Fiberglas Corp................... E 419 248-8000
　Toledo (G-13954)
▲ Palmer-Donavin Mfg Co........................... D 800 652-1234
　Urbancrest (G-14322)
Pfb Manufacturing LLC............................... E 513 836-3232
　Lebanon (G-9782)
R E Kramig & Co Inc................................... C 513 761-4010
　Cincinnati (G-3270)

Vinyl Design Corporation........................... E 419 283-4009
　Holland (G-9313)
W Team Company...................................... E 440 942-7939
　Mentor (G-11011)
West Development Group LLC................... D 440 355-4682
　Lagrange (G-9651)

5039 Construction materials, nec

▲ Agratronix LLC... E 330 562-2222
　Streetsboro (G-13409)
American Warming and Vent...................... D 419 288-2703
　Bradner (G-1341)
Apco Industries Inc..................................... D 614 224-2345
　Columbus (G-5371)
Black River Group Inc................................ E 419 524-4312
　Mansfield (G-10246)
Cleveland Glass Block Inc.......................... E 614 252-5888
　Columbus (G-5584)
▼ Cleveland Glass Block Inc........................ E 216 531-6363
　Cleveland (G-4046)
Core & Main Inc... B 419 278-2000
　Deshler (G-7865)
Efficient Services Ohio Inc......................... E 330 627-4440
　Carrollton (G-1907)
Harmon Inc... D 513 645-1550
　West Chester (G-14704)
Harmon Inc... E 513 645-1550
　West Chester (G-14705)
Koebbe Products Inc.................................. D 513 753-4200
　Amelia (G-417)
Marysville Steel Inc.................................... E 937 642-5971
　Marysville (G-10494)
▲ Mills Fence Co LLC................................. E 513 631-0333
　Cincinnati (G-3066)
Modern Builders Supply Inc....................... E 330 376-1031
　Akron (G-236)
Multi Builders Supply Co........................... E 216 831-1121
　Cleveland (G-4609)
Palmer-Donavin Mfg Co............................. E 419 692-5000
　Delphos (G-7843)
▲ Richards Whl Fence Co Inc...................... E 330 773-0423
　Akron (G-282)
Saint-Gobain Glass Corporation................. D 614 777-5867
　Columbus (G-6638)
Schneider Home Equipment Co.................. E 513 522-1200
　Cincinnati (G-3349)
Security Fence Group Inc.......................... E 513 681-3700
　Cincinnati (G-3353)
The Chas E Phipps Company..................... E 216 641-2150
　Cleveland (G-4993)
Trulite GL Alum Solutions LLC................. D 740 929-2443
　Hebron (G-9156)
▲ Will-Burt Company.................................. C 330 682-7015
　Orrville (G-12176)
Williams Scotsman Inc.............................. E 513 874-1280
　Hamilton (G-9092)

5043 Photographic equipment and supplies

Dodd Camera Holdings Inc........................ E 216 361-6811
　Cleveland (G-4173)
▲ KAO Collins Inc...................................... E 513 948-9000
　Cincinnati (G-2929)

5044 Office equipment

12985 Snow Holdings Inc.......................... E 216 267-5000
　Cleveland (G-3739)
American Copy Equipment Inc.................. C 330 722-9555
　Cleveland (G-3801)
Aptos LLC... D 614 840-1400
　Lewis Center (G-9806)
Associated Bank.. E 513 246-2200
　Cincinnati (G-2218)

◆ Big Lots Stores LLC.................................A 614 278-6800
　Columbus (G-5439)
Blue Technologies Inc................................ C 216 271-4800
　Cleveland (G-3877)
Canon Solutions America Inc..................... E 216 446-3830
　Independence (G-9415)
Canon Solutions America Inc..................... E 216 750-2980
　Independence (G-9416)
Canon Solutions America Inc..................... E 513 229-8020
　Mason (G-10525)
Canon Solutions America Inc..................... E 419 897-9244
　Maumee (G-10707)
Canon Solutions America Inc..................... E 937 260-4495
　Miamisburg (G-11031)
Collaborative Inc.. E 419 242-7405
　Toledo (G-13748)
Comdoc Inc.. E 513 766-8124
　Blue Ash (G-1156)
Comdoc Inc.. C 330 896-2346
　North Canton (G-11818)
Diebold Nixdorf Incorporated..................... D 330 899-2510
　North Canton (G-11824)
Dolbey Systems Inc................................... E 440 392-9900
　Concord Township (G-6925)
Donnellon McCarthy Entps Inc.................. E 513 769-7800
　Cincinnati (G-2573)
Donnellon McCarthy Inc............................ E 513 769-7800
　Cincinnati (G-2574)
Electronic Merch Systems LLC.................. C 216 524-0900
　Cleveland (G-4209)
Essendant Co... C 614 876-7774
　Columbus (G-5829)
Essendant Co... C 800 733-4091
　Twinsburg (G-14188)
Friends Service Co Inc............................... D 419 427-1704
　Findlay (G-8534)
▲ Graphic Enterprises Inc........................... D 800 553-6616
　North Canton (G-11835)
Graphic Entps Off Slutions Inc................... C 800 553-6616
　North Canton (G-11836)
Lake Business Products Inc....................... C 440 953-1199
　Highland Heights (G-9168)
Meritech Inc... D 216 459-8333
　Cleveland (G-4556)
Modern Office Methods Inc....................... E 513 791-0909
　Blue Ash (G-1211)
Modern Office Methods Inc....................... D 513 791-0909
　Cincinnati (G-3076)
Mpc Inc... E 440 835-1405
　Cleveland (G-4605)
Mt Business Technologies Inc.................... C 440 933-7682
　Avon Lake (G-681)
Mt Business Technologies Inc.................... C 419 529-6100
　Mansfield (G-10300)
Office World Inc.. E 419 991-4694
　Lima (G-9994)
Ohio Business Machines LLC.................... E 216 485-2000
　Cleveland (G-4683)
Perry Pro Tech Inc..................................... D 419 228-1360
　Lima (G-9948)
Repros Inc... E 330 247-3747
　Akron (G-280)
Springfield Business Eqp Co...................... E 937 322-3828
　Springfield (G-13294)
▲ Tameran Graphic Systems Inc................. E 440 349-7100
　Solon (G-13155)
Visual Edge It Inc......................................A 800 828-4801
　North Canton (G-11870)
Visual Edge Technology Inc....................... C 330 494-9694
　Canton (G-1881)
W B Mason Co Inc..................................... E 216 267-5000
　North Olmsted (G-11918)

50 WHOLESALE TRADE - DURABLE GOODS

5045 Computers, peripherals, and software

Advanced Cmpt Connections LLC......... E 419 668-4080
  Norwalk *(G-11999)*
Advantech Corporation......................... D 513 742-8895
  Blue Ash *(G-1124)*
Aktion Associates Incorporated............ E 419 893-7001
  Maumee *(G-10686)*
Alignement Engine Inc......................... E 330 401-8251
  North Canton *(G-11810)*
Apex Software Technologies Inc........... E 614 932-2167
  Powell *(G-12584)*
Aptos LLC .... D 614 840-1400
  Lewis Center *(G-9806)*
Arctos Mission Solutions LLC.............. E 813 609-5591
  Beavercreek *(G-858)*
Autozone Inc.. E 216 751-0571
  Cleveland *(G-3842)*
Autozone Inc.. E 216 267-6586
  Cleveland *(G-3843)*
Autozone Inc.. E 440 593-6934
  Conneaut *(G-6939)*
Autozone Inc.. E 440 639-2247
  Painesville *(G-12221)*
Autozone Inc.. E 419 872-2813
  Perrysburg *(G-12315)*
Avid Technologies Inc.......................... E 330 487-0770
  Twinsburg *(G-14173)*
Blue Tech Smart Solutions LLC............ E 216 271-4800
  Cleveland *(G-3876)*
Brightedge Technologies Inc................ D 800 578-8023
  Cleveland *(G-3893)*
Bsl - Applied Laser Tech LLC............... E 216 663-8181
  Independence *(G-9413)*
Canon Solutions America Inc............... E 937 260-4495
  Miamisburg *(G-11031)*
Cdw Technologies LLC........................ B 513 677-4100
  Cincinnati *(G-2330)*
Commercial Time Sharing Inc.............. E 330 644-3059
  Akron *(G-115)*
Constructconnect Inc........................... C 800 364-2059
  Cincinnati *(G-2498)*
Cranel Incorporated............................. D 614 431-8000
  Columbus *(G-5255)*
▼ Data Processing Sciences .... D 513 791-7100
  Cincinnati *(G-2539)*
Datavantage Corporation..................... B 440 498-4414
  Cleveland *(G-4150)*
DMC Technology Group Inc................ E 419 535-2900
  Toledo *(G-13782)*
Eci Macola/Max LLC .... C 978 539-6186
  Dublin *(G-8000)*
Envirnmntal Systems RES Inst I........... E 614 933-8698
  Columbus *(G-5820)*
Evanhoe & Associates Inc.................... E 937 235-2995
  Xenia *(G-15505)*
Freedom Usa Inc.................................. E 216 503-6374
  Twinsburg *(G-14192)*
▲ Fscreations Corporation................... D 330 746-3015
  Youngstown *(G-15614)*
Fundriver LLC...................................... E 513 618-8718
  Cincinnati *(G-2712)*
▲ GBS Corp... C 330 494-5330
  North Canton *(G-11833)*
Government Acquisitions Inc............... E 513 721-8700
  Cincinnati *(G-2744)*
Horizon Payroll Services Inc................. B 937 434-8244
  Dayton *(G-7414)*
▲ Interntnal Pdts Srcing Group I........... E 614 850-3000
  Hilliard *(G-9205)*
Legrand North America LLC................ B 937 224-0639
  Dayton *(G-7451)*

Manatron Inc.. E 937 431-4000
  Beavercreek *(G-925)*
Manatron Sabre Systems and Svc......... D 937 431-4000
  Beavercreek *(G-926)*
Mapsys Inc... D 614 255-7258
  Columbus *(G-6193)*
Mediquant LLC.................................... C 440 746-2300
  Independence *(G-9451)*
Micro Center Inc.................................. E 614 850-3000
  Hilliard *(G-9214)*
Micro Center Online Inc....................... D 614 326-8500
  Columbus *(G-6232)*
Micro Electronics Inc............................ C 513 782-8500
  Cincinnati *(G-3057)*
Micro Electronics Inc............................ B 614 334-1430
  Columbus *(G-6233)*
Micro Electronics Inc............................ D 614 850-3410
  Hilliard *(G-9215)*
Microplex Inc....................................... E 330 498-0600
  North Canton *(G-11848)*
Netsmart Technologies Inc................... B 800 434-2642
  Dublin *(G-8074)*
Netwave Corporation........................... E 614 850-6300
  Dublin *(G-8075)*
Office World Inc................................... E 419 991-4694
  Lima *(G-9994)*
PC Connection Inc............................... C 937 382-4800
  Wilmington *(G-15263)*
Pomeroy It Solutions Sls Inc................. E 440 717-1364
  Brecksville *(G-1363)*
Positive Bus Solutions Inc..................... D 513 772-2255
  Cincinnati *(G-3222)*
▼ Provantage LLC................................. D 330 494-3781
  North Canton *(G-11854)*
Radial South LP................................... B 678 584-4047
  Groveport *(G-8997)*
Sadler-Necamp Financial Svcs.............. E 513 489-5477
  Cincinnati *(G-3337)*
▲ Sarcom Inc.. A 614 854-1300
  Lewis Center *(G-9835)*
▲ Startechcom USA LLP....................... B 800 265-1844
  Groveport *(G-9003)*
▲ Systemax Manufacturing Inc............. D 937 368-2300
  Dayton *(G-7658)*
Target Systems Inc.............................. E 440 239-1600
  Cleveland *(G-4977)*
Total Loop Inc..................................... E 888 614-5667
  Uniontown *(G-14268)*
Transoft Inc... D 937 427-6200
  Dayton *(G-7677)*
▲ Vecmar Corporation.......................... E 440 953-1119
  Mentor *(G-11009)*

5046 Commercial equipment, nec

Access Catalog Company LLC............ C 440 572-5377
  Strongsville *(G-13438)*
Acorn Distributors Inc.......................... E 614 294-6444
  Columbus *(G-5307)*
Anchor Hocking Holdings Inc............... E 800 562-7511
  Lancaster *(G-9694)*
AVI Food Systems Inc.......................... E 740 452-9363
  Zanesville *(G-15768)*
◆ Aydelott Equipment Inc.....................E 888 293-3568
  Centerville *(G-1939)*
▲ B-Tek Scales LLC............................. E 330 471-8900
  Canton *(G-1684)*
Bakemark USA LLC............................. D 513 870-0880
  Fairfield *(G-8391)*
Best Restaurant Equipment & Design.... D 614 488-2378
  Columbus *(G-5433)*
Brechbuhler Scales Inc........................ E 330 458-3060
  Canton *(G-1689)*

Buckeye Body and Equipment.............. E 614 299-1136
  Columbus *(G-5472)*
▼ Burkett and Sons Inc......................... E 419 242-7377
  Perrysburg *(G-12321)*
Cmbb LLC.. C 937 652-2151
  Urbana *(G-14304)*
Dtv Inc... E 216 226-5465
  Cleveland *(G-4187)*
◆ Fasteners For Retail Inc.....................B 330 998-7800
  Twinsburg *(G-14191)*
G & P Construction LLC...................... E 855 494-4830
  North Royalton *(G-11941)*
Gen III Inc... D 614 228-5550
  Columbus *(G-5924)*
◆ General Data Company Inc...............B 513 752-7978
  Cincinnati *(G-2105)*
◆ Globe Food Equipment Company......E 937 299-5493
  Moraine *(G-11413)*
▲ Harry C Lobalzo & Sons Inc.............. E 330 666-6758
  Akron *(G-184)*
Hobart International Holdings................ C 937 332-3000
  Troy *(G-14138)*
◆ Hubert Company LLC........................B 513 367-8600
  Harrison *(G-9110)*
ITW Food Equipment Group LLC.......... C 937 393-4271
  Hillsboro *(G-9260)*
◆ ITW Food Equipment Group LLC......A 937 332-2396
  Troy *(G-14141)*
John H Kappus Co................................ E 216 367-6677
  Cleveland *(G-4441)*
◆ N Wasserstrom & Sons Inc................C 614 228-5550
  Columbus *(G-6286)*
Nemco Inc... D 419 542-7751
  Hicksville *(G-9161)*
OK Interiors Corp................................. C 513 742-3278
  Cincinnati *(G-3153)*
Partitions Plus Incorporated.................. E 419 422-2600
  Findlay *(G-8575)*
Quality Supply Co................................ E 937 890-6114
  Cincinnati *(G-3260)*
◆ Russell T Bundy Associates Inc.........D 937 652-2151
  Urbana *(G-14312)*
SS Kemp & Co LLC.............................. D 216 271-7700
  Cleveland *(G-4939)*
▲ Takkt Foodservices LLC.................... C 513 367-8600
  Harrison *(G-9116)*
The Cottingham Paper Co.................... E 614 294-6444
  Columbus *(G-6758)*
The Dean Supply Co............................ E 216 771-3300
  Cleveland *(G-4999)*
Thurman Scale Company..................... C 614 221-9077
  Groveport *(G-9004)*
▲ Trendco Supply Inc........................... E 513 752-1871
  Batavia *(G-750)*
Utility Truck & Equipment Inc............... E 740 474-5151
  Circleville *(G-3728)*
Ventrac.. D 330 682-0159
  Orrville *(G-12174)*
◆ Wasserstrom Company......................B 614 228-6525
  Columbus *(G-6867)*
Wasserstrom Holdings Inc.................... C 614 228-6525
  Columbus *(G-6868)*

5047 Medical and hospital equipment

Advanced Medical Equipment Inc......... E 937 534-1080
  Miamisburg *(G-11020)*
Advantage Appliance Services.............. E 330 498-8101
  Canton *(G-1656)*
Agiliti Inc... D 614 409-2734
  Groveport *(G-8967)*
Alliance Medical Inc............................. E 800 890-3092
  Dublin *(G-7930)*

50 WHOLESALE TRADE - DURABLE GOODS

Alpha Imaging Inc .... D 440 953-3800
   Willoughby *(G-15184)*
Alpha Imaging LLC .... D 440 953-3800
   Willoughby *(G-15185)*
Amerimed LLC .... A 513 942-3670
   West Chester *(G-14650)*
Assuramed Inc .... C 330 963-6998
   Twinsburg *(G-14171)*
Bionix LLC .... D 419 727-8421
   Maumee *(G-10701)*
▲ Bound Tree Medical LLC .... D 614 760-5000
   Dublin *(G-7946)*
◆ Boxout LLC .... C 833 462-7746
   Hudson *(G-9334)*
Braden Med Services Inc .... E 740 732-2356
   Caldwell *(G-1547)*
◆ Capsa Solutions LLC .... C 800 437-6633
   Canal Winchester *(G-1600)*
Cardinal Health Inc .... E 614 497-9552
   Obetz *(G-12079)*
◆ Cardinal Health Inc .... A 614 757-5000
   Dublin *(G-7950)*
Cardinal Health 100 Inc .... B 614 757-5000
   Dublin *(G-7951)*
Cardinal Health 110 Inc .... E 614 717-5000
   Dublin *(G-7952)*
Cardio Partners Inc .... E 614 760-5000
   Dublin *(G-7957)*
Cdc Medical .... E 614 504-5511
   Columbus *(G-5525)*
CHI National Home Care .... D 513 942-3670
   West Chester *(G-14664)*
Clinical Technology Inc .... E 440 526-0160
   Brecksville *(G-1351)*
▲ Coltene/Whaledent Inc .... C 330 916-8800
   Cuyahoga Falls *(G-7063)*
Columbus Prescr Phrms Inc .... E 614 294-1600
   Westerville *(G-14972)*
◆ Compass Health Brands Corp .... C 800 376-7263
   Middleburg Heights *(G-11114)*
Concordnce Hlthcare Sltons LLC .... D 419 447-0222
   Tiffin *(G-13625)*
Cornerstone Med Svcs - Mdwest .... E 330 374-0229
   Akron *(G-123)*
◆ Covetrus North America LLC .... C 614 761-9095
   Dublin *(G-7975)*
Dentronix Inc .... D 330 916-7300
   Cuyahoga Falls *(G-7070)*
▲ Dermamed Coatings Company LLC . E 330 634-9449
   Tallmadge *(G-13591)*
Edwards Health Care Services .... E 330 342-9555
   Hudson *(G-9344)*
Espt Liquidation Inc .... D 330 698-4711
   Apple Creek *(G-450)*
▲ Ethicon Endo-Surgery Inc .... A 513 337-7000
   Blue Ash *(G-1170)*
◆ Ferno-Washington Inc .... C 877 733-0911
   Wilmington *(G-15252)*
Fortec Fibers Inc .... E 800 963-7101
   Hudson *(G-9349)*
Fortec Medical Inc .... E 330 463-1265
   Hudson *(G-9350)*
▲ Fujifilm Hlthcare Amricas Corp .... B 330 425-1313
   Twinsburg *(G-14194)*
▲ Gem Edwards Inc .... D 330 342-8300
   Hudson *(G-9352)*
Genesis Respiratory Svcs Inc .... E 937 393-4423
   Hillsboro *(G-9254)*
Global Medical Products LLC .... E 630 521-9545
   Blue Ash *(G-1179)*
Gulf South Medical Supply Inc .... E 614 501-9080
   Gahanna *(G-8717)*

Haag-Sreit Usa Inc .... C 513 336-7255
   Mason *(G-10558)*
Hardy Diagnostics .... D 937 550-2768
   Springboro *(G-13200)*
▲ Health Care Logistics Inc .... C 740 477-1686
   Circleville *(G-3710)*
Health Care Solutions Inc .... C 304 243-9605
   Barnesville *(G-718)*
Homecare With Heart LLC .... C 330 726-0700
   Youngstown *(G-15632)*
Hursh Drugs Inc .... E 419 524-0521
   Mansfield *(G-10271)*
ICP Inc .... D 419 447-6216
   Tiffin *(G-13628)*
Ineos Hygienics LLC .... E 614 790-5428
   Dublin *(G-8036)*
▲ Innovative Therapies LLC .... D 866 484-6798
   Dublin *(G-8039)*
Integra Lifesciences Corp .... D 513 533-7923
   Cincinnati *(G-2874)*
Interntnal Qlty Halthcare Corp .... E 513 731-3338
   Dayton *(G-7425)*
◆ Invacare Respiratory Corp .... D 440 329-6000
   Elyria *(G-8263)*
JLW - TW Corp .... E 440 937-7775
   Avon *(G-657)*
Jones Metal Products Company .... E 740 545-6341
   West Lafayette *(G-14857)*
▲ Julius Zorn Inc .... D 330 923-4999
   Cuyahoga Falls *(G-7083)*
Lake Erie Med Surgical Sup Inc .... E 734 847-3847
   Holland *(G-9293)*
Lima Medical Supplies Inc .... E 419 226-9581
   Lima *(G-9924)*
Lincare Inc .... E 216 581-9649
   Cleveland *(G-4497)*
Lincotek Medical LLC .... C 435 753-7675
   Vandalia *(G-14382)*
Lion First Responder Ppe Inc .... D 937 898-1949
   Dayton *(G-7456)*
Lion Group Inc .... D 937 898-1949
   Dayton *(G-7457)*
Medpace Inc .... A 513 579-9911
   Cincinnati *(G-3031)*
▲ Mill Rose Laboratories Inc .... E 440 974-6730
   Mentor *(G-10974)*
Modern Medical Inc .... C 800 547-3330
   Westerville *(G-14910)*
Neighborcare Inc .... A 513 719-2600
   Cincinnati *(G-3104)*
Nihon Kohden America Inc .... E 330 935-0184
   Alliance *(G-393)*
Nostress Inc .... E 216 593-0226
   Cleveland *(G-4666)*
▲ O E Meyer Co .... D 419 625-1256
   Sandusky *(G-12921)*
Optum Infusion Svcs 550 LLC .... D 866 442-4679
   Cincinnati *(G-3166)*
Owens & Minor Distribution Inc .... A 614 491-8465
   Groveport *(G-8994)*
Oxymed Inc .... E 513 705-4250
   Middletown *(G-11178)*
Partssource Inc .... C 330 562-9900
   Aurora *(G-620)*
Patterson Dental Supply Inc .... E 440 891-1050
   Middleburg Heights *(G-11120)*
◆ Pdi Communication Systems Inc .... D 937 743-6010
   Springboro *(G-13206)*
Pel LLC .... E 216 267-5775
   Cleveland *(G-4737)*
Pharmed Corporation .... D 440 250-5400
   Westlake *(G-15097)*

◆ Philips Healthcare Cleveland .... E 440 483-3235
   Highland Heights *(G-9169)*
◆ Philips Med Systems Clvland In .... B 440 483-3000
   Cleveland *(G-4746)*
▲ PMI Supply Inc .... D 760 598-1128
   Dublin *(G-8092)*
Precision Products Group Inc .... D 330 698-4711
   Apple Creek *(G-452)*
◆ Prestan Products LLC .... E 440 229-5100
   Solon *(G-13131)*
▲ Progressive Medical Intl Inc .... E 760 957-5500
   Dublin *(G-8098)*
Radebaugh-Fetzer Company .... E 440 878-4700
   Strongsville *(G-13481)*
Radiometer America Inc .... E 440 871-8900
   Westlake *(G-15103)*
RB Sigma LLC .... D 440 290-0577
   Mentor *(G-10988)*
Rehab Medical LLC .... D 513 381-3740
   Cincinnati *(G-3281)*
Reidy Medical Supply Inc .... E 800 398-2723
   Stow *(G-13388)*
Relink Medical LLC .... E 330 954-1199
   Twinsburg *(G-14215)*
▲ Rgh Enterprises LLC .... A 330 963-6996
   Twinsburg *(G-14216)*
Riverain Technologies Inc .... E 937 425-6811
   Miamisburg *(G-11091)*
◆ Roscoe Medical Inc .... E 440 572-1962
   Middleburg Heights *(G-11126)*
▲ Safety Today Inc .... E 614 409-7200
   Grove City *(G-8950)*
Sarnova Inc .... D 614 760-5000
   Dublin *(G-8113)*
Sarnova Holdings Inc .... B 614 760-5000
   Dublin *(G-8114)*
Seeley Medical Oxygen Co .... E 440 255-7163
   Andover *(G-441)*
▲ Seneca Medical LLC .... C 800 447-0225
   Tiffin *(G-13644)*
Siffrin Residential Assn .... C 330 799-8932
   Youngstown *(G-15724)*
Smith & Schaefer Inc .... E 216 226-6700
   Bethel *(G-1094)*
Sourceone Healthcare Tech Inc .... E 440 701-1200
   Mentor *(G-10997)*
Spectrum Surgical Instruments Corp .... C 800 783-9251
   Stow *(G-13390)*
Stable Step LLC .... C 800 491-1571
   Wadsworth *(G-14452)*
Synergy Health North America Inc .... A 813 891-9550
   Mentor *(G-11001)*
▲ Thermedx LLC .... E 440 542-0883
   Solon *(G-13156)*
Thermo Fisher Scientific Inc .... E 800 871-8909
   Oakwood Village *(G-12059)*
◆ Tosoh America Inc .... B 614 539-8622
   Grove City *(G-8959)*
◆ Tri-Anim Health Services Inc .... C 614 760-5000
   Dublin *(G-8143)*
◆ Tri-Tech Medical Inc .... E 800 253-8692
   Avon *(G-666)*
Unfors Raysafe Inc .... E 508 435-5600
   Solon *(G-13157)*
Vega Americas Inc .... A 513 272-0524
   Lebanon *(G-9797)*
▲ Viewray Inc .... D 440 703-3210
   Oakwood Village *(G-12060)*
Viewray Systems Inc .... E 303 339-0500
   Oakwood Village *(G-12061)*
WA Butler Company .... E 614 761-9095
   Dublin *(G-8159)*

SIC SECTION

50 WHOLESALE TRADE - DURABLE GOODS

Ziks Family Pharmacy 100............................ E 937 225-9350
Dayton *(G-7737)*

5048 Ophthalmic goods

Diversified Ophthalmics Inc................... E 803 783-3454
Cincinnati *(G-2570)*

Haag-Sreit Usa Inc.................................... C 513 336-7255
Mason *(G-10558)*

◆ Haag-Streit Usa Inc............................... D 513 398-3937
Mason *(G-10559)*

Walmart Inc... E 740 286-8203
Jackson *(G-9528)*

5049 Professional equipment, nec

Approved Networks LLC.......................... E 216 831-1800
Independence *(G-9406)*

City of Toledo.. D 419 245-3209
Toledo *(G-13742)*

Diebold Nixdorf Incorporated.................. D 330 899-0097
Uniontown *(G-14248)*

▲ Diebold Self Service Systems............. A 330 490-5099
Canton *(G-1736)*

Diversified Ophthalmics Inc.................... E 803 783-3454
Cincinnati *(G-2570)*

Essilor Laboratories Amer Inc................. E 614 274-0840
Columbus *(G-5831)*

◆ Gilson Company Inc............................. E 740 548-7298
Lewis Center *(G-9823)*

▼ ICM Distributing Company Inc............ E 234 212-3030
Twinsburg *(G-14196)*

▲ Key Blue Prints Inc.............................. D 614 228-3285
Columbus *(G-6113)*

▲ Lorenz Corporation.............................. D 937 228-6118
Dayton *(G-7459)*

◆ Mettler-Toledo LLC............................... A 614 438-4511
Columbus *(G-5270)*

▲ Monarch Steel Company Inc................ E 216 587-8000
Cleveland *(G-4598)*

▲ Panini North America Inc..................... E 937 291-2195
Miamisburg *(G-11081)*

Queen City Reprographics........................ C 513 326-2300
Cincinnati *(G-3265)*

Repros Inc.. E 330 247-3747
Akron *(G-280)*

Revvity Health Sciences Inc.................... E 330 825-4525
Akron *(G-281)*

▲ S&V Industries Inc.............................. E 330 666-1986
Medina *(G-10886)*

Shawnee Optical Inc.................................. E 440 997-2020
Ashtabula *(G-549)*

Smith & Schaefer Inc............................... E 216 226-6700
Bethel *(G-1094)*

Teledyne Instruments Inc........................ E 513 229-7000
Mason *(G-10614)*

US Tsubaki Power Transm LLC............... C 419 626-4560
Sandusky *(G-12939)*

▲ Zaner-Bloser Inc.................................. C 614 486-0221
Columbus *(G-6918)*

5051 Metals service centers and offices

Act Acquisition Inc.................................. E 216 292-3800
Cleveland *(G-3765)*

Albco Sales Inc... E 330 424-9446
Lisbon *(G-9996)*

◆ All Foils Inc.. D 440 572-3645
Strongsville *(G-13440)*

Alro Steel Corporation............................. D 513 769-9999
Cincinnati *(G-2172)*

Alro Steel Corporation............................. E 614 878-7271
Columbus *(G-5340)*

Alro Steel Corporation............................. E 330 929-4660
Cuyahoga Falls *(G-7035)*

Alro Steel Corporation............................. E 937 253-6121
Dayton *(G-7167)*

Alro Steel Corporation............................. D 419 720-5300
Toledo *(G-13679)*

Alumalloy Metalcasting Company............. D 440 930-2222
Avon Lake *(G-670)*

◆ Aluminum Line Products Company....... D 440 835-8880
Westlake *(G-15032)*

◆ American Consolidated Inds Inc......... E 216 587-8000
Cleveland *(G-3800)*

American Posts LLC................................ E 419 720-0652
Toledo *(G-13687)*

▲ American Tank & Fabricating Co........ D 216 252-1500
Cleveland *(G-3808)*

▲ Arcelrmttal Tblar Pdts Mrion I............ D 740 382-3979
Marion *(G-10418)*

▲ Atlas Bolt & Screw Company LLC..... C 419 289-6171
Ashland *(G-478)*

▲ Atlas Steel Products Co...................... C 330 425-1600
Twinsburg *(G-14172)*

Aviva Metals Inc....................................... D 440 277-1226
Lorain *(G-10057)*

◆ Beck Aluminum Corporation................ D 440 684-4848
Mayfield Heights *(G-10785)*

◆ Benjamin Steel Company Inc.............. D 937 322-8600
Springfield *(G-13221)*

◆ Bertin Steel Processing Inc................ E 440 943-0094
Wickliffe *(G-15146)*

◆ Bico Akron Inc..................................... D 330 794-1716
Mogadore *(G-11324)*

Blackburns Fabrication Inc..................... E 614 875-0784
Columbus *(G-5444)*

Boston Retail Products Inc..................... E 330 744-8100
Youngstown *(G-15564)*

Byer Steel Inc.. E 513 821-6400
Cincinnati *(G-2295)*

Byer Steel Service Center Inc................. E 513 821-6400
Cincinnati *(G-2296)*

Canfield Metal Coating Corp.................... D 330 702-3876
Canfield *(G-1623)*

Central Steel and Wire Co LLC................ E 513 242-2233
Cincinnati *(G-2338)*

Chillicothe Steel Company....................... E 740 772-2481
Chillicothe *(G-2059)*

Cincinnati Steel Products Co................... E 513 871-4444
Cincinnati *(G-2424)*

Ciralsky & Associates Inc....................... E 419 470-1328
Toledo *(G-13735)*

Clifton Steel Company.............................. E 216 662-6111
Maple Heights *(G-10335)*

◆ Clifton Steel Company......................... C 216 662-6111
Maple Heights *(G-10336)*

Clinton Aluminum Acquisition LLC........... B 330 882-6743
New Franklin *(G-11614)*

Clinton Aluminum Dist Inc....................... E 866 636-7640
Jamestown *(G-9534)*

▲ Clinton Aluminum Dist Inc................. D 330 882-6743
Norton *(G-11992)*

Coilplus Inc.. D 937 778-8884
Piqua *(G-12437)*

Coilplus Inc.. D 614 866-1338
Springfield *(G-13236)*

Coilplus Inc.. E 937 322-4455
Springfield *(G-13237)*

▲ Concast Birmingham LLC.................. D 440 965-4455
Wakeman *(G-14458)*

Conley Group Inc...................................... E 330 372-2030
Warren *(G-14513)*

▲ Contractors Materials Company......... E 513 733-3000
Cincinnati *(G-2502)*

Contractors Steel Company..................... D 330 425-3050
Twinsburg *(G-14178)*

Diamond Metals Dist Inc.......................... E 216 898-7900
Cleveland *(G-4165)*

Earle M Jorgensen Company................... E 513 771-3223
Cincinnati *(G-2597)*

Earle M Jorgensen Company................... D 330 425-1500
Twinsburg *(G-14183)*

Earle M Jorgensen Company................... D 330 425-1500
Twinsburg *(G-14184)*

Fedmet International Corp...................... D 440 248-9500
Solon *(G-13087)*

▲ Ferragon Corporation......................... D 216 671-6161
Cleveland *(G-4249)*

▲ Fisher Cast Steel Products Inc.......... E 614 879-8325
West Jefferson *(G-14851)*

Founders Service & Mfg Inc................... D 330 584-7759
North Benton *(G-11805)*

▲ Fpt Cleveland LLC............................... C 216 441-3800
Cleveland *(G-4282)*

◆ Greer Steel Company........................... C 330 343-8811
Dover *(G-7886)*

▲ H & D Steel Service Inc..................... E 800 666-3390
North Royalton *(G-11942)*

▲ Haverhill Coke Company LLC............. D 740 355-9819
Franklin Furnace *(G-8655)*

Heartland Valley Metals LLC................... D 419 886-0220
Bellville *(G-1050)*

Industrial Pping Spcalists Inc................. D 330 750-2800
Struthers *(G-13500)*

Industrial Tube and Steel Corp................ E 513 777-5512
West Chester *(G-14712)*

▲ Industrial Tube and Steel Corp.......... E 330 474-5530
Kent *(G-9580)*

Infra-Metals Co.. D 740 353-1350
Portsmouth *(G-12556)*

▲ Is Acquisition Inc................................ E 440 287-0150
Streetsboro *(G-13418)*

▲ Jade-Sterling Steel Co Inc................. D 330 425-3141
Bedford *(G-968)*

JSW Steel USA Ohio Inc.......................... B 740 535-8172
Mingo Junction *(G-11314)*

▲ Kenilworth Steel Co............................ E 330 373-1885
Warren *(G-14532)*

◆ Kirtland Capital Partners LP............... E 216 593-0100
Beachwood *(G-806)*

Kloeckner Metals Corporation................. D 513 769-4000
Cincinnati *(G-2943)*

Lapham-Hickey Steel Corp...................... E 614 443-4881
Columbus *(G-6140)*

Lapham-Hickey Steel Corp...................... D 937 236-6940
Dayton *(G-7450)*

◆ Latrobe Spcialty Mtls Dist Inc............ D 330 609-5137
Vienna *(G-14420)*

Liberty Steel Industries Inc.................... C 330 372-6363
Warren *(G-14535)*

◆ Liberty Steel Products Inc.................. E 330 538-2236
North Jackson *(G-11873)*

◆ Loveman Steel Corporation................. D 440 232-6200
Bedford *(G-969)*

◆ Majestic Steel Usa Inc....................... C 440 786-2666
Cleveland *(G-4517)*

Major Metals Company............................. E 419 886-4600
Mansfield *(G-10285)*

Matandy Steel & Metal Pdts LLC........... D 513 844-2277
Hamilton *(G-9063)*

Materion Brush Intl Inc........................... D 216 486-4200
Mayfield Heights *(G-10789)*

Materion Ceramics Inc............................. B 216 486-4200
Mayfield Heights *(G-10790)*

Mazzella Holding Company Inc................ D 513 772-4466
Cleveland *(G-4534)*

McOn Inds Inc... E 937 294-2681
Moraine *(G-11422)*

Employee Codes: A=Over 500 employees, B=251-500
C=101-250, D=51-100, E=20-50, F=10-19, G=1-9

50 WHOLESALE TRADE - DURABLE GOODS

McWane Inc .... B 740 622-6651
  Coshocton (G-6992)
▲ Merit Brass Co .... C 216 261-9800
  Cleveland (G-4554)
▲ Metals USA Crbn Flat Rlled Inc .... D 330 264-8416
  Wooster (G-15355)
▼ Miami Valley Steel Service Inc .... C 937 773-7127
  Piqua (G-12449)
Mid-America Steel Corp .... E 800 282-3466
  Cleveland (G-4575)
Mid-West Materials Inc .... E 440 259-5200
  Perry (G-12309)
Middletown Tube Works Inc .... D 513 727-0080
  Middletown (G-11173)
Mill Steel Co .... E 216 464-4480
  Pepper Pike (G-12301)
▲ Misa Metals Inc .... B 212 660-6000
  West Chester (G-14731)
Modern Welding Co Ohio Inc .... E 740 344-9425
  Newark (G-11731)
▲ Monarch Steel Company Inc .... E 216 587-8000
  Cleveland (G-4598)
▲ National Bronze Mtls Ohio Inc .... E 440 277-1226
  Lorain (G-10094)
▲ New Dimension Metals Corp .... E 937 299-2233
  Moraine (G-11427)
▲ Nimers & Woody II Inc .... C 937 454-0722
  Vandalia (G-14386)
North Jckson Specialty Stl LLC .... E 330 538-9621
  North Jackson (G-11874)
◆ North Star Bluescope Steel LLC .... B 419 822-2200
  Delta (G-7854)
Northwestern Holding LLC .... D 419 726-0850
  Toledo (G-13940)
◆ Nucor Steel Marion Inc .... B 740 383-4011
  Marion (G-10448)
Ohio Steel Sheet and Plate Inc .... E 800 827-2401
  Hubbard (G-9322)
Ohio-Kentucky Steel Corp .... E 937 743-4600
  Franklin (G-8645)
Ohio-Kentucky Steel LLC .... E 937 743-4600
  Franklin (G-8646)
▲ Oliver Steel Plate Co .... D 330 425-7000
  Twinsburg (G-14209)
Olympic Steel Inc .... C 216 292-3800
  Bedford (G-979)
Olympic Steel Inc .... D 330 602-6279
  Dover (G-7898)
Olympic Steel Inc .... D 216 292-3800
  Cleveland (G-4695)
◆ Panacea Products Corporation .... E 614 850-7000
  Columbus (G-6497)
Pennsylvania Steel Company Inc .... E 330 823-7383
  Alliance (G-395)
Pennsylvania Steel Company Inc .... D 440 243-9800
  Cleveland (G-4738)
Phoenix Corporation .... E 513 727-4763
  Middletown (G-11180)
▲ Pipe Products Inc .... C 513 587-7532
  West Chester (G-14742)
Precision Strip Inc .... D 513 423-4166
  Middletown (G-11181)
Precision Strip Inc .... D 419 661-1100
  Perrysburg (G-12364)
▲ Precision Strip Inc .... C 419 628-2343
  Minster (G-11320)
Qualstl Corp .... E 937 294-4133
  Moraine (G-11431)
▲ R L Morrissey & Assoc Inc .... E 440 498-3730
  Solon (G-13135)
Radix Wire Co .... D 216 731-9191
  Solon (G-13136)

▲ Remington Steel Inc .... D 937 322-2414
  Springfield (G-13284)
▲ Riverfront Steel Inc .... D 513 769-9999
  Cincinnati (G-3304)
Rownd Metal Sales Inc .... E
  Alliance (G-400)
▲ Samsel Rope & Marine Supply Co .... E 216 241-0333
  Cleveland (G-4875)
Samuel Son & Co (usa) Inc .... D 740 522-2500
  Heath (G-9138)
Samuel Son & Co (usa) Inc .... D 419 470-7070
  Toledo (G-14004)
Scot Industries Inc .... D 330 262-7585
  Wooster (G-15375)
Scott Steel LLC .... E 937 552-9670
  Piqua (G-12458)
Select Steel Inc .... E 330 652-1756
  Niles (G-11796)
Shaq Inc .... D 770 427-0402
  Beachwood (G-836)
Sheffield Steel Products Company .... E 330 468-0091
  Macedonia (G-10204)
▲ Sims Bros Inc .... D 740 387-9041
  Marion (G-10454)
Singer Steel Company .... E 330 562-7200
  Streetsboro (G-13427)
SL Wellspring LLC .... D 513 948-2339
  Cincinnati (G-3387)
Solman Inc .... E 330 580-5188
  Canton (G-1855)
◆ Special Metals Corporation .... B 216 755-3030
  Warrensville Heights (G-14588)
St Lawrence Holdings LLC .... E 330 562-9000
  Maple Heights (G-10347)
◆ St Lawrence Steel Corporation .... E 330 562-9000
  Maple Heights (G-10348)
Steel Warehouse Cleveland LLC .... E 888 225-3760
  Cleveland (G-4945)
Steel Warehouse Company LLC .... E 216 206-2800
  Cleveland (G-4946)
Steel Warehouse of Ohio LLC .... D 888 225-3760
  Cleveland (G-4947)
Stein Steel Mill Services LLC .... D 440 526-9301
  Warren (G-14557)
Stemcor USA Inc .... E 330 373-1885
  Warren (G-14558)
Stephens Pipe & Steel LLC .... C 740 869-2257
  Mount Sterling (G-11475)
Swagelok Company .... D 440 349-5934
  Solon (G-13154)
Tapco Tube Co Inc .... D 330 576-1750
  Wadsworth (G-14454)
Taylor Steel Inc .... D 330 824-8600
  Warren (G-14563)
▲ Three D Metals Inc .... D 330 220-0451
  Valley City (G-14337)
Thyssenkrupp Materials NA Inc .... C 440 234-7500
  Cleveland (G-5018)
Thyssenkrupp Materials NA Inc .... D 216 883-8100
  Independence (G-9490)
Thyssenkrupp Materials NA Inc .... E 419 662-1845
  Toledo (G-14042)
◆ Timken Corporation .... E 330 471-3378
  North Canton (G-11866)
◆ Titanium Metals Corporation .... E 740 537-5600
  Warrensville Heights (G-14589)
◆ Tricor Industrial Inc .... D 330 264-3299
  Wooster (G-15380)
◆ United Performance Metals LLC .... B 513 860-6500
  Hamilton (G-9090)
United States Steel Corp .... A 440 240-2500
  Lorain (G-10105)

◆ United Steel Service LLC .... C 330 448-4057
  Brookfield (G-1407)
▲ Universal Steel Company .... D 216 883-4972
  Cleveland (G-5069)
◆ Voestlpine Precision Strip LLC .... E 330 220-7800
  Brunswick (G-1472)
◆ Watteredge LLC .... D 440 933-6110
  Avon Lake (G-684)
Westfield Steel Inc .... D 937 322-2414
  Springfield (G-13312)
Wheatland Tube LLC .... C 724 342-6851
  Niles (G-11799)
◆ Wieland Chase LLC .... D 419 485-3193
  Montpelier (G-11387)
▲ Wieland Metal Svcs Foils LLC .... D 330 823-1700
  Alliance (G-405)
Wieland Rolled Pdts N Amer LLC .... B 330 823-1700
  Alliance (G-406)
Worthington Enterprises Inc .... D 513 539-9291
  Monroe (G-11355)
Worthington Industries Inc .... D 216 641-6995
  Cleveland (G-5160)
Worthngton Smuel Coil Proc LLC .... E 330 963-3777
  Twinsburg (G-14231)
Worthngton Stelpac Systems LLC .... C 614 438-3205
  Columbus (G-6908)
Youngstown Pipe & Steel LLC .... E 330 783-2700
  Youngstown (G-15760)

5052 Coal and other minerals and ores

Graphel Corporation .... C 513 779-6166
  West Chester (G-14700)
Marshall County Coal Company .... B 740 338-3100
  Saint Clairsville (G-12801)
Ohio County Coal Company .... D 740 338-3100
  Saint Clairsville (G-12809)
Oxford Mining Company Inc .... C 330 878-5120
  Strasburg (G-13404)
◆ Tosoh America Inc .... B 614 539-8622
  Grove City (G-8959)

5063 Electrical apparatus and equipment

Abb Inc .... E 440 725-2968
  Chardon (G-1993)
ABB Inc .... E 513 860-1749
  West Chester (G-14797)
ABB Inc .... C 614 818-6300
  Westerville (G-14876)
Accurate Mechanical Inc .... D 740 681-1332
  Lancaster (G-9690)
Adalet Enclosure Systems .... E 216 201-2710
  Cleveland (G-3767)
Afc Cable Systems Inc .... E 740 435-3340
  Cambridge (G-1552)
Akron Electric Inc .... E 330 745-8891
  Akron (G-25)
Akron Foundry Co .... C 330 745-3101
  Akron (G-28)
Allen Fields Assoc Inc .... E 513 228-1010
  Lebanon (G-9753)
Allied Power Transmission Co .... E 440 708-1006
  Chagrin Falls (G-1972)
◆ American De Rosa Lamparts LLC .... D
  Cuyahoga Falls (G-7038)
Ametek Tchnical Indus Pdts Inc .... D 330 673-3451
  Kent (G-9559)
Associated Mtls Holdings LLC .... A 330 929-1811
  Cuyahoga Falls (G-7044)
Belting Company of Cincinnati .... D 937 498-2104
  Sidney (G-13021)
Belting Company of Cincinnati .... D 937 498-2104
  Sidney (G-13022)

SIC SECTION

50 WHOLESALE TRADE - DURABLE GOODS

▲ Belting Company of Cincinnati......... C 513 621-9050
  Cincinnati (G-2256)
◆ Best Lighting Products Inc................D 740 964-1198
  Etna (G-8332)
▲ Bostwick-Braun Company................. D 419 259-3600
  Toledo (G-13713)
Brehob Corporation................................. E 513 755-1300
  West Chester (G-14655)
Brohl & Appell Inc................................... E 419 625-6761
  Sandusky (G-12865)
C & E Sales LLC...................................... D 937 434-8830
  Miamisburg (G-11029)
◆ Calvert Wire & Cable Corp...................E 216 433-7600
  Cleveland (G-3919)
Cls Facilities MGT Svcs Inc..................... E 440 602-4600
  Mentor (G-10924)
▲ Connector Manufacturing Co............... C 513 860-4455
  Hamilton (G-9035)
Consolidated Elec Distrs Inc................... E 614 445-8871
  Columbus (G-5682)
Control System Mfg Inc........................... E 330 542-0000
  New Middletown (G-11635)
▲ D & L Lighting Inc............................... D 614 841-1200
  Columbus (G-5256)
Dickman Supply Inc................................ D 937 492-6166
  Sidney (G-13029)
Dkmp Consulting Inc.............................. C 614 733-0979
  Plain City (G-12473)
◆ Dorcy International Inc........................D 614 497-5830
  Columbus (G-5782)
▲ Eaton Aerospace LLC........................... B 216 523-5000
  Cleveland (G-4201)
Eaton Corporation.................................... D 216 265-2799
  Cleveland (G-4203)
Eaton Corporation.................................... D 614 839-4387
  Columbus (G-5802)
Eaton Corporation.................................... E 419 891-7627
  Maumee (G-10719)
Eis Intermediate Holdings LLC............... D 800 228-2790
  Miamisburg (G-11049)
Electric Motor Tech LLC.......................... E 513 821-9999
  Cincinnati (G-2609)
▲ Eye Lighting Intl N Amer Inc............... C 440 350-7000
  Mentor (G-10939)
FDL Automation and Supply Co............. E 937 498-2104
  Sidney (G-13031)
Fenton Bros Electric Co........................... E 330 343-0093
  New Philadelphia (G-11651)
Furbay Electric Supply Co....................... E 330 454-3033
  Canton (G-1758)
GA Business Purchaser LLC................... E 419 255-8400
  Toledo (G-13816)
Gatto Electric Supply Co......................... E 216 641-8400
  Cleveland (G-4307)
Generator One LLC.................................. E 440 942-8449
  Mentor (G-10941)
Graybar Electric Company Inc................ E 216 573-0456
  Cleveland (G-4328)
Graybar Electric Company Inc................ E 419 228-7441
  Lima (G-9893)
Graybar Electric Company Inc................ E 330 526-2800
  North Canton (G-11837)
Graybar Electric Company Inc................ E 419 729-1641
  Toledo (G-13825)
Gross Electric Inc..................................... E 419 537-1818
  Toledo (G-13831)
Handl-It Inc.. E 440 439-9400
  Bedford (G-964)
Hle Company.. C 216 325-0941
  Cleveland (G-4368)
Hubbell Power Systems Inc.................... C 330 335-2361
  Wadsworth (G-14436)

Hughes Corporation................................ E 440 238-2550
  Strongsville (G-13463)
Industrial Power Systems Inc................. B 419 531-3121
  Rossford (G-12767)
Johnson Electric Supply Co.................... E 513 421-3700
  Cincinnati (G-2916)
Ke Gutridge LLC..................................... C 614 885-5200
  Dublin (G-8048)
Kirby Risk Corporation........................... D 419 221-0123
  Lima (G-9915)
▼ Kirk Key Interlock Company LLC........ E 330 833-8223
  North Canton (G-11846)
Laughlin Music & Vending Svc.............. E 740 593-7778
  Athens (G-580)
Legrand North America LLC................. B 937 224-0639
  Dayton (G-7451)
Lighting Services Inc.............................. D 330 405-4879
  Twinsburg (G-14201)
▲ Loeb Electric Company........................ D 800 686-6351
  Columbus (G-6172)
LSI Industries Inc.................................... C 913 281-1100
  Blue Ash (G-1202)
▲ LSI Lightron Inc.................................. A 845 562-5500
  Blue Ash (G-1203)
Machine Drive Company.........................D 513 793-7077
  Cincinnati (G-3000)
Mars Electric Company........................... D 440 946-2250
  Cleveland (G-4529)
▼ Matlock Electric Co Inc....................... E 513 731-9600
  Cincinnati (G-3015)
McNaughton-Mckay Elc Ohio Inc........... E 419 784-0295
  Defiance (G-7756)
McNaughton-Mckay Elc Ohio Inc........... E 419 422-2984
  Findlay (G-8564)
McNaughton-Mckay Elc Ohio Inc........... E 740 929-2727
  Hebron (G-9147)
McNaughton-Mckay Elc Ohio Inc........... E 419 891-0262
  Maumee (G-10747)
▲ McNaughton-Mckay Elc Ohio Inc........ D 614 476-2800
  Columbus (G-6218)
Mjo Industries Inc................................... D 800 590-4055
  Huber Heights (G-9325)
◆ Monarch Electric Service Co................D 216 433-7800
  Cleveland (G-4596)
Motor Systems Incorporated................... E 513 576-1725
  Milford (G-11245)
◆ Multilink Inc..C 440 366-6966
  Elyria (G-8276)
▲ Mwe Investments LLC........................ E 855 944-3571
  Columbus (G-6284)
▲ Myers Controlled Power LLC............. C 330 834-3200
  North Canton (G-11850)
◆ Noco Company.....................................D 216 464-8131
  Solon (G-13119)
◆ Noland Company..................................C 937 396-7980
  Moraine (G-11428)
Optimas Oe Solutions LLC..................... E 440 546-4400
  Solon (G-13122)
Optimas Oe Solutions LLC..................... E 513 881-4600
  West Chester (G-14737)
Powell Electrical Systems Inc................. D 330 966-1750
  North Canton (G-11853)
Powerbilt Mtl Hdlg Sltions LLC.............. D 937 592-5660
  Bellefontaine (G-1036)
Professional Electric Pdts Co................... E 330 896-3790
  Akron (G-272)
Professional Electric Pdts Co................... E 614 563-2504
  Columbus (G-6549)
Professional Electric Pdts Co................... E 800 379-3790
  Elyria (G-8288)
Professional Electric Pdts Co................... E 330 896-3790
  Green (G-8857)

Professional Electric Pdts Co................... E 419 269-3790
  Toledo (G-13967)
Professional Electric Products Co Inc..... D 800 872-7000
  Eastlake (G-8207)
Rexel Usa Inc... E 216 778-6400
  Cleveland (G-4835)
Rexel Usa Inc... E 419 625-6761
  Sandusky (G-12927)
Richard Lawrence Teaberry Inc.............. E
  Youngstown (G-15708)
▲ Richards Electric Sup Co LLC............. E 513 242-8800
  Cincinnati (G-3297)
▼ Riverside Drives Inc............................ E 216 362-1211
  Cleveland (G-4844)
Schneider Electric Usa Inc...................... B 513 523-4171
  Oxford (G-12217)
Schneider Electric Usa Inc...................... D 513 777-4445
  West Chester (G-14761)
Scott Fetzer Company.............................. C 216 267-9000
  Cleveland (G-4885)
▲ Shoemaker Electric Company.............. E 614 294-5626
  Columbus (G-6673)
Signature Control Systems LLC.............. E 614 864-2222
  Columbus (G-6679)
State Alarm Inc.. E 888 726-8111
  Youngstown (G-15730)
Status Solutions LLC............................... E 434 296-1789
  Westerville (G-14938)
Stock Fairfield Corporation..................... C 440 543-6000
  Solon (G-13149)
◆ Technical Consumer Pdts Inc..............B 330 995-6111
  Aurora (G-628)
The F D Lawrence Electric Company..... D 513 542-1100
  Cincinnati (G-3465)
The John A Becker Co.............................. C 937 226-1341
  Dayton (G-7666)
▲ Torq Corporation................................. E 440 232-4100
  Bedford (G-989)
▲ TPC Wire & Cable Corp...................... C 800 211-4520
  Macedonia (G-10208)
◆ Venture Lighting Intl Inc.....................D 800 451-2606
  Solon (G-13159)
Vincent Lighting Systems Co.................. E 216 475-7600
  Solon (G-13161)
Wesco Distribution Inc............................ D 216 741-0441
  Cleveland (G-5131)
Westfield Electric Inc.............................. E 419 862-0078
  Gibsonburg (G-8807)
▲ Winkle Industries Inc.......................... D 330 823-9730
  Alliance (G-407)
Wolff Bros Supply Inc............................. C 330 725-3451
  Medina (G-10904)
Wright State University........................... E 937 775-3333
  Beavercreek (G-916)
Yes Management Inc............................... E 330 747-8593
  Columbiana (G-5242)

5064 Electrical appliances, television and radio

◆ Associated Premium Corporation.......E 513 679-4444
  Cincinnati (G-2219)
C C Mitchell Supply Co Inc..................... E 440 526-2040
  Cleveland (G-3915)
Dayton Appliance Parts LLC.................. E 937 224-0487
  Dayton (G-7270)
Don Walter Kitchen Distrs Inc................ E 330 793-9338
  Youngstown (G-15600)
G D Supply Inc.. E 614 258-1111
  Columbus (G-5904)
◆ GMI Holdings Inc................................B 800 354-3643
  Mount Hope (G-11466)

50 WHOLESALE TRADE - DURABLE GOODS

Great Lakes Telcom Ltd........................ E 330 629-8848
  Youngstown (G-15622)
ITA INC.. E 513 631-7000
  Cincinnati (G-2889)
Lowes Home Centers LLC................... C 330 665-9356
  Akron (G-225)
Lowes Home Centers LLC................... C 330 829-2700
  Alliance (G-389)
Lowes Home Centers LLC................... C 440 998-6555
  Ashtabula (G-540)
Lowes Home Centers LLC................... C 740 589-3750
  Athens (G-582)
Lowes Home Centers LLC................... C 440 937-3500
  Avon (G-660)
Lowes Home Centers LLC................... C 937 427-1110
  Beavercreek (G-889)
Lowes Home Centers LLC................... C 216 831-2860
  Bedford (G-970)
Lowes Home Centers LLC................... D 937 599-4000
  Bellefontaine (G-1032)
Lowes Home Centers LLC................... C 330 497-2720
  Canton (G-1797)
Lowes Home Centers LLC................... C 740 773-7777
  Chillicothe (G-2079)
Lowes Home Centers LLC................... C 513 598-7050
  Cincinnati (G-2990)
Lowes Home Centers LLC................... C 216 351-4723
  Cleveland (G-4506)
Lowes Home Centers LLC................... C 614 853-6200
  Columbus (G-6174)
Lowes Home Centers LLC................... C 937 235-2920
  Dayton (G-7460)
Lowes Home Centers LLC................... C 937 438-4900
  Dayton (G-7461)
Lowes Home Centers LLC................... C 937 854-8200
  Dayton (G-7462)
Lowes Home Centers LLC................... C 419 782-9000
  Defiance (G-7753)
Lowes Home Centers LLC................... C 614 659-0530
  Dublin (G-8058)
Lowes Home Centers LLC................... C 419 420-7531
  Findlay (G-8559)
Lowes Home Centers LLC................... C 419 355-0221
  Fremont (G-8690)
Lowes Home Centers LLC................... C 937 547-2400
  Greenville (G-8880)
Lowes Home Centers LLC................... C 513 737-3700
  Hamilton (G-9061)
Lowes Home Centers LLC................... C 614 529-5900
  Hilliard (G-9210)
Lowes Home Centers LLC................... C 740 681-3464
  Lancaster (G-9733)
Lowes Home Centers LLC................... C 419 331-3598
  Lima (G-9930)
Lowes Home Centers LLC................... C 440 985-5700
  Lorain (G-10090)
Lowes Home Centers LLC................... C 740 374-2151
  Marietta (G-10381)
Lowes Home Centers LLC................... C 740 389-9737
  Marion (G-10433)
Lowes Home Centers LLC................... C 937 578-4440
  Marysville (G-10492)
Lowes Home Centers LLC................... C 513 336-9741
  Mason (G-10575)
Lowes Home Centers LLC................... ..... 330 832-1901
  Massillon (G-10650)
Lowes Home Centers LLC................... C 440 392-0027
  Mentor (G-10965)
Lowes Home Centers LLC................... C 513 727-3900
  Middletown (G-11170)
Lowes Home Centers LLC................... C 513 965-3480
  Milford (G-11237)

Lowes Home Centers LLC................... C 740 393-5350
  Mount Vernon (G-11498)
Lowes Home Centers LLC................... D 330 339-1936
  New Philadelphia (G-11657)
Lowes Home Centers LLC................... C 740 522-0003
  Newark (G-11723)
Lowes Home Centers LLC................... D 330 908-2750
  Northfield (G-11960)
Lowes Home Centers LLC................... C 419 747-1920
  Ontario (G-12113)
Lowes Home Centers LLC................... C 419 874-6758
  Perrysburg (G-12355)
Lowes Home Centers LLC................... D 614 769-9940
  Reynoldsburg (G-12668)
Lowes Home Centers LLC................... C 440 331-1027
  Rocky River (G-12748)
Lowes Home Centers LLC................... D 740 699-3000
  Saint Clairsville (G-12799)
Lowes Home Centers LLC................... C 419 624-6000
  Sandusky (G-12912)
Lowes Home Centers LLC................... C 937 498-8400
  Sidney (G-13039)
Lowes Home Centers LLC................... C 513 445-1000
  South Lebanon (G-13172)
Lowes Home Centers LLC................... C 740 894-7120
  South Point (G-13177)
Lowes Home Centers LLC................... C 937 327-6000
  Springfield (G-13264)
Lowes Home Centers LLC................... C 740 266-3500
  Steubenville (G-13336)
Lowes Home Centers LLC................... C 330 920-9280
  Stow (G-13380)
Lowes Home Centers LLC................... C 330 626-2980
  Streetsboro (G-13420)
Lowes Home Centers LLC................... C 440 239-2630
  Strongsville (G-13473)
Lowes Home Centers LLC................... C 419 843-9758
  Toledo (G-13894)
Lowes Home Centers LLC................... C 937 339-2544
  Troy (G-14145)
Lowes Home Centers LLC................... C 330 335-1900
  Wadsworth (G-14442)
Lowes Home Centers LLC................... C 419 739-1300
  Wapakoneta (G-14488)
Lowes Home Centers LLC................... C 330 609-8000
  Warren (G-14536)
Lowes Home Centers LLC................... C 513 755-4300
  West Chester (G-14726)
Lowes Home Centers LLC................... C 740 574-6200
  Wheelersburg (G-15130)
Lowes Home Centers LLC................... C 440 942-2759
  Willoughby (G-15207)
Lowes Home Centers LLC................... C 937 383-7000
  Wilmington (G-15260)
Lowes Home Centers LLC................... C 330 287-2261
  Wooster (G-15352)
Lowes Home Centers LLC................... C 937 347-4000
  Xenia (G-15524)
Lowes Home Centers LLC................... C 330 965-4500
  Youngstown (G-15653)
Lowes Home Centers LLC................... C 740 450-5500
  Zanesville (G-15807)
▲ Merc Acquisitions Inc......................... C 216 524-4141
  Twinsburg (G-14205)
Mobilcomm Inc..................................... D 513 742-5555
  Cincinnati (G-3072)
Rieman Arszman Cstm Distrs Inc........ E 513 874-5444
  Fairfield (G-8437)
Schaffer Partners Inc........................... D 216 881-3000
  Cleveland (G-4882)
▲ Trumbull Industries Inc....................... D 800 477-1799
  Warren (G-14566)

V and V Appliance Parts Inc................ E 330 743-5144
  Youngstown (G-15745)
VSI Global LLC..................................... E 216 642-8778
  Cleveland (G-5117)
Whirlpool Corporation........................... E 740 383-7122
  Marion (G-10464)

5065 Electronic parts and equipment, nec

Access Catalog Company LLC............ C 440 572-5377
  Strongsville (G-13438)
Acuative Corporation............................ D 440 202-4500
  Strongsville (G-13439)
Arrow Electronics Inc........................... D 440 349-1300
  Solon (G-13068)
Bear Communications Inc.................... D 216 642-1670
  Independence (G-9410)
Cbst Acquisition LLC............................ D 513 361-9600
  Cincinnati (G-2326)
Communications III Inc......................... E 614 901-7720
  Westerville (G-14973)
Comproducts Inc.................................. E 614 276-5552
  Columbus (G-5679)
Convergint Technologies LLC............... C 513 771-1717
  Cincinnati (G-2505)
Cornerstone Controls Inc..................... E 513 489-2500
  Cincinnati (G-2509)
Donnellon Mc Carthy Inc...................... E 937 299-0200
  Moraine (G-11404)
▲ DSI Systems Inc................................. E 614 871-1456
  Grove City (G-8917)
Electra Sound Inc................................. D 216 433-9600
  Avon Lake (G-678)
Enviro It LLC.. E 614 453-0709
  Columbus (G-5821)
FAI Electronics Corp............................. E 937 426-0090
  Dayton (G-7345)
Famous Industries Inc.......................... E 330 535-1811
  Akron (G-157)
▲ Floyd Bell Inc..................................... D 614 294-4000
  Columbus (G-5874)
▼ Fox International Limited Inc.............. C 216 454-1001
  Beachwood (G-793)
◆ Geep USA Inc.....................................E 919 544-1443
  Stow (G-13369)
Graybar Electric Company Inc.............. E 216 573-0456
  Cleveland (G-4328)
Graybar Electric Company Inc.............. E 419 729-1641
  Toledo (G-13825)
Info-Hold Inc... E 513 248-5600
  Cincinnati (G-2870)
▲ Koehlke Components Inc................... D 937 435-5435
  Franklin (G-8643)
Kyocera Precision Tools Inc................. D 419 738-6652
  Wapakoneta (G-14486)
▲ Ladd Distribution LLC........................ D 937 438-2646
  Kettering (G-9630)
Lake Business Products Inc................. C 440 953-1199
  Highland Heights (G-9168)
◆ Mace Personal Def & SEC Inc...........E 440 424-5321
  Cleveland (G-4514)
◆ McM Electronics Inc...........................C 888 235-4692
  Centerville (G-1947)
▲ Meder Electronic Inc.......................... D 508 295-0771
  Fairfield (G-8429)
▲ Midwest Digital Inc............................. D 330 966-4744
  North Canton (G-11849)
Mjo Industries Inc................................. D 800 590-4055
  Huber Heights (G-9325)
Mobilcomm Inc...................................... D 513 742-5555
  Cincinnati (G-3072)
Newark Corporation.............................. B 330 523-4457
  Richfield (G-12704)

50 WHOLESALE TRADE - DURABLE GOODS

P & R Communications Svc Inc............ E 937 512-8100
   Dayton *(G-7543)*
◆ Parts Express International Inc........... D 800 338-0531
   Springboro *(G-13205)*
▲ Pepperl + Fuchs Inc............................. C 330 425-3555
   Twinsburg *(G-14210)*
Pepperl+fuchs Americas Inc................. D 330 425-3555
   Twinsburg *(G-14211)*
Pepperl+fuchs Mfg Inc........................... C 330 425-3555
   Twinsburg *(G-14212)*
Post-Browning Inc.................................. C 513 771-1717
   Cincinnati *(G-3224)*
▲ Pro Oncall Technologies LLC............ E 513 489-7660
   Cincinnati *(G-3234)*
Projects Unlimited Inc............................ C 937 918-2200
   Dayton *(G-7571)*
Quasonix Inc... E 513 942-1287
   West Chester *(G-14751)*
▲ RPC Electronics Inc.......................... E 440 461-4700
   Highland Heights *(G-9170)*
Shawntech Communications Inc........... E 937 898-4900
   Miamisburg *(G-11093)*
Sound Com Corporation......................... D 440 234-2604
   Berea *(G-1081)*
▲ Standex Electronics Inc.................... D 513 871-3777
   Fairfield *(G-8443)*
Tele-Solutions Inc................................... E 330 782-2888
   Youngstown *(G-15733)*
Teletronics Services Inc......................... E 216 778-6500
   Strongsville *(G-13491)*
Visual Edge Technology Inc.................. C 330 494-9694
   Canton *(G-1881)*
▲ Vmetro Inc... D 281 584-0728
   Fairborn *(G-8386)*
Warwick Communications Inc................ E 216 787-0300
   Broadview Heights *(G-1404)*
◆ Wholesale House Inc........................ D 419 542-1315
   Hicksville *(G-9162)*
◆ Winncom Technologies Corp............ C 440 498-9510
   Solon *(G-13165)*
◆ Wurtec Incorporated.........................D 419 726-1066
   Toledo *(G-14110)*
Wurth Electronics Ics Inc....................... E 937 415-7700
   Miamisburg *(G-11104)*

5072 Hardware

◆ A M Leonard Inc...............................D 937 773-2694
   Piqua *(G-12434)*
Ackerman Chacco Company Inc........... E 513 791-4252
   Blue Ash *(G-1121)*
Akron Hardware Consultants Inc........... E 330 644-7167
   Akron *(G-33)*
▲ Atlas Bolt & Screw Company LLC..... C 419 289-6171
   Ashland *(G-478)*
B B I T Inc.. C 419 259-3600
   Toledo *(G-13697)*
Babin Building Solutions LLC................ E 216 292-2500
   Broadview Heights *(G-1383)*
Barnes Group Inc................................... E 419 891-9292
   Maumee *(G-10698)*
▲ Bostwick-Braun Company.................. D 419 259-3600
   Toledo *(G-13713)*
Buckeye Parts Services Inc................... E 614 274-1888
   Columbus *(G-5476)*
Do It Best Corp...................................... B 330 725-3859
   Medina *(G-10831)*
E&H Hardware Group LLC.................... E 330 683-2060
   Orrville *(G-12164)*
Elliott Tool Technologies Ltd.................. D 937 253-6133
   Dayton *(G-7333)*
◆ F & M Mafco Inc...............................C 513 367-2151
   Harrison *(G-9104)*

◆ Facil North America Inc.................... C 330 487-2500
   Twinsburg *(G-14190)*
◆ Fastener Tool & Supply Inc.............. D 440 248-2710
   Solon *(G-13086)*
◆ G & S Metal Products Co Inc............C 216 441-0700
   Cleveland *(G-4295)*
▲ Hardware Suppliers of America Inc.. D 330 644-7167
   Akron *(G-183)*
Hd Supply Facilities Maint Ltd............... D 440 542-9188
   Solon *(G-13094)*
◆ Hillman Companies Inc.....................B 513 851-4900
   Cincinnati *(G-2822)*
◆ Hillman Group Inc............................. E 513 851-4900
   Cincinnati *(G-2823)*
◆ Hillman Solutions Corp..................... E 513 851-4900
   Cincinnati *(G-2824)*
◆ Hodell-Natco Industries Inc..............E 216 447-0165
   Cleveland *(G-4372)*
Khempco Bldg Sup Co Ltd Partnr......... D 740 549-0465
   Delaware *(G-7811)*
◆ L E Smith Company.......................... D 419 636-4555
   Bryan *(G-1486)*
Mae Holding Company........................... E 513 751-2424
   Cincinnati *(G-3002)*
▲ Matco Tools Corporation................... B 330 929-4949
   Stow *(G-13382)*
Mazzella Holding Company Inc............. D 513 772-4466
   Cleveland *(G-4534)*
◆ Mid-State Industrial Pdts Inc............. E 614 253-8631
   Columbus *(G-6240)*
Multi Builders Supply Co........................ E 216 831-1121
   Cleveland *(G-4609)*
◆ Noco Company..................................D 216 464-8131
   Solon *(G-13119)*
◆ Norwood Hardware and Supply Co... D 513 733-1175
   Cincinnati *(G-3129)*
▲ Ohashi Technica USA Inc................. E 740 965-5115
   Sunbury *(G-13523)*
Production Tool Supply Ohio................. D 216 265-0000
   Cleveland *(G-4772)*
Reitter Stucco Inc................................... E 614 291-2212
   Columbus *(G-6575)*
Robert McCabe Company Inc............... E 513 469-2500
   Cincinnati *(G-3314)*
▲ Saw Service and Supply Company... E 216 252-5600
   Cleveland *(G-4880)*
▲ Serv-A-Lite Products Inc................... C 309 762-7741
   Cincinnati *(G-3360)*
State Industrial Products Corp............... D 740 929-6370
   Hebron *(G-9154)*
▲ State Industrial Products Corp.......... B 877 747-6986
   Cleveland *(G-4944)*
The Cleveland Vicon Co Inc.................. E 216 341-3300
   Cleveland *(G-4996)*
The Robert McCabe Company Inc........ D 513 683-2662
   Loveland *(G-10164)*
Waxman Consumer Pdts Group Inc...... E 614 491-0500
   Groveport *(G-9013)*
▲ Waxman Consumer Pdts Group Inc.. D 440 439-1830
   Bedford Heights *(G-1004)*
◆ Waxman Industries Inc......................C 440 439-1830
   Bedford Heights *(G-1005)*
Ziegler Bolt & Parts Co.......................... D 330 478-2542
   Canton *(G-1893)*

5074 Plumbing and hydronic heating supplies

Accurate Mechanical Inc........................ D 740 681-1332
   Lancaster *(G-9690)*
Active Plumbing Supply Co.................... D 440 352-4411
   Painesville *(G-12220)*

Banner Supply Company Inc................. E 330 782-1171
   Youngstown *(G-15555)*
Brohl & Appell Inc.................................. E 419 625-6761
   Sandusky *(G-12865)*
Carter-Jones Lumber Company............. E 440 834-8164
   Middlefield *(G-11139)*
▲ Chandler Systems Incorporated........ D 888 363-9434
   Ashland *(G-491)*
▲ Corrosion Fluid Products Corp.......... E 248 478-0100
   Columbus *(G-5704)*
Eastway Supplies Inc............................. E 614 252-3650
   Columbus *(G-5801)*
◆ Elkay Ohio Plumbing Pdts Co...........B 419 841-1820
   Toledo *(G-13788)*
▲ Enting Water Conditioning Inc.......... E 937 294-5100
   Moraine *(G-11407)*
Famous Distribution Inc......................... E 330 434-5194
   Akron *(G-155)*
Famous Distribution Inc......................... D 330 762-9621
   Akron *(G-154)*
Famous Enterprises Inc......................... E 330 762-9621
   Akron *(G-156)*
Famous Industries Inc........................... E 330 535-1811
   Akron *(G-157)*
Ferguson Enterprises LLC..................... E 513 771-6000
   Cincinnati *(G-2658)*
Ferguson Enterprises LLC..................... E 513 771-6566
   West Chester *(G-14691)*
G D Supply Inc....................................... E 614 258-1111
   Columbus *(G-5904)*
Gordon Brothers Inc............................... E 800 331-7611
   Salem *(G-12842)*
Habegger Corporation............................ D 513 612-4700
   Cincinnati *(G-2787)*
Indelco Custom Products Inc................. E 216 797-7300
   Euclid *(G-8349)*
Keidel Sup LLC Fka Kdel Sup In........... E 513 351-1600
   Cincinnati *(G-2933)*
◆ Kinetico Incorporated........................B 440 564-9111
   Newbury *(G-11761)*
L B Brunk & Sons Inc............................ E 330 332-0359
   Salem *(G-12845)*
Lakeside Supply Co............................... E 216 941-6800
   Cleveland *(G-4478)*
◆ Mansfield Plumbing Pdts LLC........... A 419 938-5211
   Perrysville *(G-12392)*
Mason Structural Steel LLC................... E 440 439-1040
   Walton Hills *(G-14476)*
▲ Merit Brass Co................................... C 216 261-9800
   Cleveland *(G-4554)*
Morrow Control and Supply Inc............. E 330 452-9791
   Canton *(G-1810)*
Mssi Group Inc....................................... D 440 439-1040
   Walton Hills *(G-14477)*
Multi Builders Supply Co........................ E 216 831-1121
   Cleveland *(G-4609)*
◆ Noland Company...............................C 937 396-7980
   Moraine *(G-11428)*
◆ Oatey Supply Chain Svcs Inc............ C 216 267-7100
   Cleveland *(G-4679)*
Palmer-Donavin Mfg Co......................... E 419 692-5000
   Delphos *(G-7843)*
Parker-Hannifin Corporation................... C 614 279-7070
   Columbus *(G-6500)*
Parker-Hannifin Corporation................... D 937 456-5571
   Eaton *(G-8219)*
Pickrel Bros Inc...................................... E 937 461-5960
   Dayton *(G-7552)*
Picoma Industries Inc............................. E 740 432-2146
   Cambridge *(G-1579)*
Rexel Usa Inc... E 419 625-6761
   Sandusky *(G-12927)*

Employee Codes: A=Over 500 employees, B=251-500
C=101-250, D=51-100, E=20-50, F=10-19, G=1-9

50 WHOLESALE TRADE - DURABLE GOODS

Robertson Heating Sup Co Ohio............ C 800 433-9532
  Alliance *(G-397)*
▲ Robertson Htg Sup Aliance Ohio...... D 330 821-9180
  Alliance *(G-398)*
Ssi Fabricated Inc............................. E 513 217-3535
  Middletown *(G-11187)*
The Famous Manufacturing Co............ B 330 762-9621
  Akron *(G-332)*
Trumbull Industries Inc..................... D 330 270-7800
  Youngstown *(G-15737)*
▲ Trumbull Industries Inc.................. D 800 477-1799
  Warren *(G-14566)*
Waxman Consumer Pdts Group Inc...... E 614 491-0500
  Groveport *(G-9013)*
▲ Waxman Consumer Pdts Group Inc... D 440 439-1830
  Bedford Heights *(G-1004)*
◆ Waxman Industries Inc................... C 440 439-1830
  Bedford Heights *(G-1005)*
▲ Wayne/Scott Fetzer Company........... C 800 237-0987
  Harrison *(G-9119)*
Winsupply Inc.................................. D 937 294-5331
  Moraine *(G-11450)*
Wolff Bros Supply Inc........................ C 330 725-3451
  Medina *(G-10904)*
Woodhill Supply Inc........................... E 440 269-1100
  Willoughby *(G-15229)*
Worly Plumbing Supply Inc................. D 614 445-1000
  Columbus *(G-6905)*
Zekelman Industries Inc..................... C 740 432-2146
  Cambridge *(G-1588)*

5075 Warm air heating and air conditioning

2 J Supply Llc................................... E 937 223-0811
  Dayton *(G-7147)*
Airtron Inc....................................... D 614 274-2345
  Columbus *(G-5333)*
Allied Supply Company Inc................. E 937 224-9833
  Dayton *(G-7164)*
Best Aire Compressor Service............. D 419 726-0055
  Millbury *(G-11266)*
Breeze 33 Products LLC..................... D 833 273-3950
  Akron *(G-74)*
▲ Brock Air Products Inc.................... E 937 335-2626
  Troy *(G-14130)*
Buckeye Heating and AC Sup Inc......... E 216 831-0066
  Bedford Heights *(G-996)*
Famous Distribution Inc..................... E 330 434-5194
  Akron *(G-155)*
Famous Distribution Inc..................... E 740 282-0951
  Steubenville *(G-13323)*
Famous Distribution Inc..................... D 330 762-9621
  Akron *(G-154)*
Famous Enterprises Inc..................... E 330 762-9621
  Akron *(G-156)*
G D Supply Inc................................. E 614 258-1111
  Columbus *(G-5904)*
Gardiner Service Company LLC........... C 440 248-3400
  Solon *(G-13091)*
Habegger Corporation....................... D 513 612-4700
  Cincinnati *(G-2787)*
▲ Habegger Corporation..................... E 513 853-6644
  Cincinnati *(G-2788)*
▲ Hamilton-Parker Company............... D 614 358-7800
  Columbus *(G-5968)*
Lakeside Supply Co............................ E 216 941-6800
  Cleveland *(G-4478)*
Luxury Heating Company................... D 440 366-0971
  Sheffield Village *(G-13001)*
◆ Noland Company............................ C 937 396-7980
  Moraine *(G-11428)*
▲ Refrigeration Sales Company LLC..... E 216 525-8200
  Cleveland *(G-4818)*

Resolute Industrial LLC..................... E 513 779-7909
  West Chester *(G-14831)*
Robertson Heating Sup Co Ohio........... C 800 433-9532
  Alliance *(G-397)*
Robertson Htg Sup Clumbus Ohio........ C 330 821-9180
  Alliance *(G-399)*
Style Crest Enterprises Inc................. D 419 355-8586
  Fremont *(G-8705)*
Swift Filters Inc................................ E 440 735-0995
  Oakwood Village *(G-12058)*
The Famous Manufacturing Co............ B 330 762-9621
  Akron *(G-332)*
▼ Verantis Corporation...................... E 440 243-0700
  Middleburg Heights *(G-11133)*
Wadsworth-Slawson Inc..................... E 216 391-7263
  Perrysburg *(G-12385)*
Waibel Energy Systems Inc................. D 937 264-4343
  Vandalia *(G-14403)*
Wolff Bros Supply Inc........................ C 330 725-3451
  Medina *(G-10904)*
Yanfeng US Auto Intr Systems I........... E 419 662-4905
  Northwood *(G-11988)*

5078 Refrigeration equipment and supplies

Allied Supply Company Inc................. E 937 224-9833
  Dayton *(G-7164)*
Buckeye Heating and AC Sup Inc......... E 216 831-0066
  Bedford Heights *(G-996)*
Climate Pros LLC.............................. D 216 881-5200
  Cleveland *(G-4083)*
Climate Pros LLC.............................. D 330 744-2732
  Youngstown *(G-15579)*
Fingles Holdings LLC......................... E 419 468-5321
  Mount Gilead *(G-11460)*
Gordon Brothers Inc.......................... E 800 331-7611
  Salem *(G-12842)*
Gustave A Larson Company................ E 513 681-4089
  Cincinnati *(G-2785)*
◆ Lvd Acquisition LLC....................... D 614 861-1350
  Columbus *(G-6181)*
▲ Refrigeration Sales Company LLC..... E 216 525-8200
  Cleveland *(G-4818)*
The Hattenbach Company................... D 216 881-5200
  Cleveland *(G-5001)*

5082 Construction and mining machinery

Ackerman Chacco Company Inc.......... E 513 791-4252
  Blue Ash *(G-1121)*
Ag-Pro Ohio LLC.............................. E 740 653-6951
  Lancaster *(G-9691)*
Ag-Pro Ohio LLC.............................. E 740 450-7446
  Zanesville *(G-15765)*
All Make Solutions LLC...................... D 800 255-6253
  Middletown *(G-11151)*
American Crane Inc........................... E 614 496-2268
  Reynoldsburg *(G-12651)*
▲ American Producers Sup Co Inc....... D 740 373-5050
  Marietta *(G-10355)*
Bauer Corporation............................. E 800 321-4760
  Wooster *(G-15310)*
▲ Bobcat Enterprises Inc.................... D 513 874-8945
  West Chester *(G-14652)*
Brandsafway Services LLC................. E 614 443-1314
  Columbus *(G-5459)*
Carmichael Equipment Inc.................. E 740 446-2412
  Bidwell *(G-1103)*
▲ Caterpllar Trmble Ctrl Tech LL........ D 937 233-8921
  Dayton *(G-7217)*
CCC Contractors LLC........................ E 937 579-5100
  Lynchburg *(G-10184)*
▼ Columbus Equipment Company........ E 614 437-0352
  Columbus *(G-5633)*

▲ Company Wrench Ltd..................... D 740 654-5304
  Carroll *(G-1900)*
Ebony Construction Co...................... E 419 841-3455
  Sylvania *(G-13542)*
Elder Sales & Service Inc................... E 330 426-2166
  East Palestine *(G-8195)*
Equipment Maintenance Inc............... E 513 353-3518
  Cleves *(G-5188)*
EZ Grout Corporation Inc................... E 740 962-2024
  Malta *(G-10232)*
◆ F & M Mafco Inc............................ C 513 367-2151
  Harrison *(G-9104)*
Gibson 2021 LLC.............................. E 440 439-4000
  Cleveland *(G-4312)*
Global Energy Partners LLC............... E 419 756-8027
  Mansfield *(G-10267)*
▲ Lefeld Implement Inc..................... E 419 678-2375
  Coldwater *(G-5215)*
Leppo Inc.. E 330 633-3999
  Tallmadge *(G-13599)*
Liechty Inc...................................... E 419 298-2302
  Edgerton *(G-8228)*
◆ Mesa Industries Inc....................... E 513 321-2950
  Cincinnati *(G-3048)*
Mountain Supply and Svc LLC............ E 304 547-1119
  Saint Clairsville *(G-12805)*
Murphy Tractor & Eqp Co Inc............. E 316 633-7215
  Rossford *(G-12769)*
◆ Npk Construction Equipment Inc..... D 440 232-7900
  Bedford *(G-976)*
Ohio Machinery Co............................ E 330 874-1003
  Bolivar *(G-1296)*
Ohio Machinery Co............................ D 440 526-0520
  Broadview Heights *(G-1395)*
Ohio Machinery Co............................ D 740 942-4626
  Cadiz *(G-1542)*
Ohio Machinery Co............................ B 614 878-2287
  Columbus *(G-6435)*
Ohio Machinery Co............................ E 614 878-2287
  Columbus *(G-6436)*
Ohio Machinery Co............................ D 419 874-7975
  Perrysburg *(G-12359)*
Ohio Machinery Co............................ D 937 335-7660
  Troy *(G-14149)*
Ohio Machinery Co............................ D 740 453-0563
  Zanesville *(G-15822)*
◆ Ohio Machinery Co........................ C 440 526-6200
  Broadview Heights *(G-1394)*
▲ Reco LLC...................................... E
  Blue Ash *(G-1234)*
◆ Richard Goettle Inc........................ D 513 825-8100
  Cincinnati *(G-3296)*
Seal Aftermarket Products LLC........... E 419 355-1200
  Fremont *(G-8701)*
Shearer Farm Inc.............................. C 330 345-9023
  Wooster *(G-15376)*
Simpson Strong-Tie Company Inc........ C 614 876-8060
  Columbus *(G-6683)*
▲ Southeastern Equipment Co Inc....... E 740 432-6303
  Cambridge *(G-1582)*
The Wagner-Smith Company.............. B 866 338-0398
  Moraine *(G-11444)*
United Rentals North Amer Inc........... E 614 276-5444
  Columbus *(G-6814)*
Vermeer Heartland Inc....................... E 740 335-8571
  Wshngtn Ct Hs *(G-15495)*
Waco Scaffolding & Equipment Inc...... A 216 749-8900
  Cleveland *(G-5119)*
▲ Zink Foodservice Group Inc............. C 800 492-7400
  Columbus *(G-6919)*

5083 Farm and garden machinery

50 WHOLESALE TRADE - DURABLE GOODS

Ag-Pro Ohio LLC .... E 740 389-5458
  Marion *(G-10416)*
Ag-Pro Ohio LLC .... E 937 486-5211
  Wilmington *(G-15238)*
▲ Agrinomix LLC .... D 440 774-2981
  Oberlin *(G-12062)*
Apple Farm Service Inc .... E 937 526-4851
  Covington *(G-7017)*
◆ Arnold Corporation .... C 330 225-2600
  Valley City *(G-14331)*
Bellas Lawn & Landscape LLC .... E 419 536-9003
  Toledo *(G-13703)*
▲ Bostwick-Braun Company .... D 419 259-3600
  Toledo *(G-13713)*
Bryan Equipment Sales Inc .... D 513 248-2000
  Loveland *(G-10129)*
Buckeye Companies .... E 740 452-3641
  Zanesville *(G-15772)*
▼ Buckeye Supply Company .... E 740 452-3641
  Zanesville *(G-15773)*
Century Equipment Inc .... E 419 865-7400
  Toledo *(G-13728)*
◆ Clarke Power Services Inc .... D 513 771-2200
  Cincinnati *(G-2456)*
Coughlin Chevrolet Inc .... E 740 852-1122
  London *(G-10040)*
Deerfield AG Services Inc .... E 330 584-4715
  Massillon *(G-10637)*
Deerfield Farms Service Inc .... D 330 584-4715
  Deerfield *(G-7741)*
Evolution Ag LLC .... E 740 363-1341
  Delaware *(G-7796)*
Franklin Equipment LLC .... E 937 951-3819
  Dayton *(G-7366)*
Franklin Equipment LLC .... D 614 228-2014
  Groveport *(G-8990)*
Gardner-Connell LLC .... E 614 456-4000
  Columbus *(G-5915)*
▲ Hayward Distributing Co .... E 614 272-5953
  Columbus *(G-5974)*
Hull Bros Inc .... E 419 375-2827
  Fort Recovery *(G-8610)*
◆ JD Equipment Inc .... C 614 879-6620
  London *(G-10044)*
◆ Lesco Inc .... C 216 706-9250
  Cleveland *(G-4490)*
Leslie Equipment Co .... E 740 373-5255
  Marietta *(G-10380)*
Liechty Inc .... E 419 592-3075
  Napoleon *(G-11526)*
Liechty Inc .... E 419 445-1565
  Archbold *(G-461)*
Old Meadow Farms Inc .... E 440 632-5590
  Middlefield *(G-11143)*
Rock Pile Inc .... E 440 937-5100
  Avon *(G-664)*
Schmidt Machine Company .... E 419 294-3814
  Upper Sandusky *(G-14292)*
Steinke Tractor Sales Inc .... E 937 456-4271
  Eaton *(G-8224)*
Streacker Tractor Sales Inc .... E 419 422-6973
  Findlay *(G-8589)*
United Rentals North Amer Inc .... E 614 276-5444
  Columbus *(G-6814)*

5084 Industrial machinery and equipment

A & A Safety Inc .... E 513 943-6100
  Amelia *(G-409)*
▲ Absolute Machine Tools Inc .... E 440 960-6911
  Lorain *(G-10052)*
Access Drywall Supply Co Inc .... E 614 890-2111
  Westerville *(G-14955)*
◆ Acd Enterprises Inc .... E 866 252-4395
  Cleveland *(G-3761)*
▲ Adams Elevator Equipment Co .... D 847 581-2900
  Holland *(G-9276)*
▲ Addition Manufacturing Te .... C 513 228-7000
  Lebanon *(G-9752)*
Aerocontrolex Group Inc .... D 216 291-6025
  South Euclid *(G-13170)*
▲ Agrinomix LLC .... D 440 774-2981
  Oberlin *(G-12062)*
▲ Air Technical Industries Inc .... E 440 951-5191
  Mentor *(G-10909)*
Air-Way Manufacturing Company .... C 419 298-2366
  Edgerton *(G-8227)*
Airgas Inc .... D 937 222-8312
  Moraine *(G-11388)*
▲ Airgas Merchant Gases LLC .... E 800 242-0105
  Cleveland *(G-3780)*
Airgas Usa LLC .... B 216 642-6600
  Independence *(G-9399)*
Airtech LLC .... A 614 342-6123
  Columbus *(G-5332)*
Alba Manufacturing Inc .... D 513 874-0551
  Fairfield *(G-8388)*
Albright Welding Supply Co Inc .... E 330 264-2021
  Wooster *(G-15309)*
Aldrich Chemical .... D 937 859-1808
  Miamisburg *(G-11023)*
◆ Alfons Haar Inc .... E 937 560-2031
  Springboro *(G-13192)*
▲ Alkon Corporation .... D 419 355-9111
  Fremont *(G-8665)*
All Lift Service Company Inc .... E 440 585-1542
  Willoughby *(G-15183)*
American Welding & Gas Inc .... C 859 519-8772
  Cincinnati *(G-2188)*
◆ Ampac Packaging LLC .... C 513 671-1777
  Cincinnati *(G-2195)*
Anderson & Vreeland Inc .... D 419 636-5002
  Bryan *(G-1479)*
▲ Argo-Hytos Inc .... A 419 353-6070
  Bowling Green *(G-1303)*
Atlas Machine and Supply Inc .... D 502 584-7262
  Hamilton *(G-9017)*
▲ Ats Systems Oregon Inc .... C 541 738-0932
  Lewis Center *(G-9808)*
▲ Automatic Feed Co .... D 419 592-0050
  Napoleon *(G-11517)*
▲ Automation Tooling Systems .... C 614 781-8063
  Lewis Center *(G-9810)*
Bay Advanced Technologies LLC .... E 510 857-0900
  Cleveland *(G-3856)*
▲ Becker Pumps Corporation .... E 330 928-9966
  Cuyahoga Falls *(G-7049)*
▲ Bettcher Industries Inc .... C 440 965-4422
  Birmingham *(G-1107)*
Bevcorp LLC .... D 440 954-3500
  Eastlake *(G-8200)*
Bionix Safety Technologies Ltd .... E 419 727-0552
  Maumee *(G-10702)*
◆ Blastmaster Holdings Usa LLC .... D 877 725-2781
  Columbus *(G-5445)*
Bohl Crane Inc .... D 419 214-3940
  Toledo *(G-13708)*
◆ Bohl Equipment Company .... D 800 962-4802
  Toledo *(G-13709)*
Bollin & Sons Inc .... E 419 693-6573
  Toledo *(G-13710)*
Bosch Rexroth Corporation .... D 614 527-7400
  Grove City *(G-8898)*
▲ Bostwick-Braun Company .... D 419 259-3600
  Toledo *(G-13713)*

Brennan Equipment Services Co .... E 419 867-6000
  Holland *(G-9282)*
Brown Industrial Inc .... E 937 693-3838
  Botkins *(G-1299)*
▼ Buckeye Supply Company .... E 740 452-3641
  Zanesville *(G-15773)*
C H Bradshaw Co .... E 614 871-2087
  Grove City *(G-8904)*
Cangen Holdings Inc .... B 770 458-4882
  Blue Ash *(G-1140)*
Cascade Corporation .... E 419 425-3675
  Findlay *(G-8521)*
Cbg Biotech Ltd Co .... D 800 941-9484
  Solon *(G-13074)*
◆ Chemineer Inc .... C 937 454-3200
  Dayton *(G-7222)*
▲ Cho Bedford Inc .... E 330 433-2270
  North Canton *(G-11816)*
Cintas Corporation .... D 513 631-5750
  Cincinnati *(G-2443)*
◆ Cintas Corporation .... A 513 459-1200
  Cincinnati *(G-2442)*
Cintas Corporation No 2 .... D 330 966-7800
  Canton *(G-1709)*
Cintas Corporation No 2 .... D 614 878-7313
  Columbus *(G-5572)*
Cintas Corporation No 2 .... A 513 459-1200
  Mason *(G-10534)*
Cintas Corporation No 2 .... C 513 965-0800
  Milford *(G-11223)*
▲ Cintas Corporation No 2 .... A 513 459-1200
  Mason *(G-10535)*
Clarke Fire Prtection Pdts Inc .... E 513 771-2200
  Cincinnati *(G-2455)*
Cleveland Tank & Supply Inc .... E 216 771-8265
  Cleveland *(G-4069)*
▲ Clippard Instrument Lab Inc .... C 513 521-4261
  Cincinnati *(G-2460)*
◆ Cold Jet LLC .... C 513 831-3211
  Loveland *(G-10132)*
Columbus Dnv Inc .... C 614 761-1214
  Dublin *(G-7966)*
Combined Tech Group Inc .... E 937 274-4866
  Dayton *(G-7240)*
Contitech Usa Inc .... D 937 644-8900
  Marysville *(G-10481)*
Contract Sweepers & Eqp Co .... E 513 577-7900
  West Chester *(G-14675)*
Contract Sweepers & Eqp Co .... E 614 221-7441
  Columbus *(G-5700)*
▲ Conveyer & Caster Corp .... E 877 598-8534
  Westlake *(G-15054)*
▲ Corrosion Fluid Products Corp .... E 248 478-0100
  Columbus *(G-5704)*
Cross Truck Equipment Co Inc .... E 330 477-8151
  Canton *(G-1728)*
Ctm Integration Incorporated .... E 330 332-1800
  Salem *(G-12840)*
Cummins Inc .... D 513 563-6670
  West Chester *(G-14681)*
▲ Daihen Inc .... E 937 667-0800
  Tipp City *(G-13656)*
Dearing Compressor and Pu .... E 330 783-2258
  Youngstown *(G-15595)*
▲ Depot Direct Inc .... E 419 661-1233
  Perrysburg *(G-12332)*
Detroit Diesel Corporation .... B 330 430-4300
  Canton *(G-1735)*
Dickman Supply Inc .... D 937 492-6166
  Sidney *(G-13029)*
▲ Double A Trailer Sales Inc .... E 419 692-7626
  Delphos *(G-7840)*

50 WHOLESALE TRADE - DURABLE GOODS

Dreier & Maller Inc .... E 614 575-0065
  Reynoldsburg (G-12661)
Eagle Equipment Corporation .... E 937 746-0510
  Franklin (G-8635)
Ellison Technologies Inc .... E 513 874-2736
  Hamilton (G-9038)
▲ EMI Corp .... D 937 596-5511
  Jackson Center (G-9531)
Equipment Depot Ohio Inc .... E 513 934-2121
  Lebanon (G-9765)
▲ Equipment Mfrs Intl Inc .... E 216 651-6700
  Cleveland (G-4217)
Esec Corporation .... E 614 875-3732
  Grove City (G-8918)
◆ Esko-Graphics Inc .... D 937 454-1721
  Miamisburg (G-11051)
Estabrook Corporation .... E 440 234-8566
  Berea (G-1068)
▲ Eurolink Inc .... E 740 392-1549
  Mount Vernon (G-11486)
Expert Crane Inc .... E 216 451-9900
  Wellington (G-14632)
Fairborn Equipment Co Ohio Inc .... E 614 384-5466
  Worthington (G-15415)
Fairborn Equipment Company Inc ..... E 419 209-0760
  Upper Sandusky (G-14288)
Fairborn Equipment Midwest Inc ...... D 513 492-9422
  Mason (G-10546)
▲ Fallsway Equipment Co Inc .... C 330 633-6000
  Akron (G-152)
Fameccanica North America Inc .... D 513 645-0629
  West Chester (G-14689)
Fastener Industries Inc .... E 440 891-2031
  Berea (G-1069)
▲ Fcx Performance Inc .... E 614 253-1996
  Columbus (G-5853)
◆ Federal Machinery & Eqp Co .... E 800 652-2466
  Cleveland (G-4245)
▲ Feintool Equipment Corporation ...... E 513 791-1118
  Blue Ash (G-1172)
▲ Fischer Pump & Valve Company ..... E 513 583-4800
  Loveland (G-10137)
Fluid Line Products Inc .... C 440 946-9470
  Willoughby (G-15193)
Forney Industries Inc .... D 937 494-6102
  Dayton (G-7362)
Forte Industrial Equipmen .... E 513 398-2800
  Mason (G-10550)
Franklin Equipment LLC .... E 937 951-3819
  Dayton (G-7366)
Freeman Manufacturing & Sup Co ..... E 440 934-1902
  Avon (G-651)
▲ Freeman Schwabe Machinery LLC ... E 513 947-2888
  Batavia (G-740)
▲ Fujitec America Inc .... C 513 755-6100
  Mason (G-10551)
G & P Construction LLC .... E 855 494-4830
  North Royalton (G-11941)
Gateway Products Recycling Inc .... E 216 341-8777
  Cleveland (G-4306)
Gei Wide Format Solutions .... E 330 494-8189
  North Canton (G-11834)
◆ General Data Company Inc .... B 513 752-7978
  Cincinnati (G-2105)
▲ Giant Industries Inc .... E 419 531-4600
  Toledo (G-13821)
Givens Lifting Systems Inc .... E 419 724-9001
  Perrysburg (G-12338)
▲ Global EDM Inc .... D 513 701-0468
  Mason (G-10555)
Gnco Inc .... E 216 706-2349
  Brooklyn Heights (G-1419)

Gold Medal Products Co .... E 614 228-1155
  Columbus (G-5939)
Gorman-Rupp Company .... E 419 886-3001
  Bellville (G-1049)
Gosiger Holdings Inc .... E 734 582-2100
  Solon (G-13093)
Gosiger Holdings Inc .... C 937 228-5174
  Dayton (G-7381)
◆ Gosiger Inc .... B 937 228-5174
  Dayton (G-7382)
Graco Ohio Inc .... E 330 494-1313
  Canton (G-1766)
◆ Great Lakes Power Products Inc ..... D 440 951-5111
  Mentor (G-10943)
◆ Hagglunds Drives Inc .... D 614 527-7400
  Columbus (G-5964)
Hannon Company .... D 330 456-4728
  Canton (G-1770)
Hemly Tool Supply Inc .... E 800 445-1068
  Thompson (G-13617)
Hendrickson International Corp .... D 740 929-5600
  Hebron (G-9143)
◆ Heritage Equipment Company .... E 614 873-3941
  Plain City (G-12480)
▼ Hgr Industrial Surplus Inc .... E 216 486-4567
  Euclid (G-8347)
◆ Hiab USA Inc .... D 419 482-6000
  Perrysburg (G-12343)
Hirsch Holdings Inc .... D 513 733-4111
  Cincinnati (G-2828)
Hy-Tek Material Handling Inc .... E 440 239-9852
  Middleburg Heights (G-11117)
◆ Hy-Tek Material Handling LLC ...... D 614 497-2500
  Columbus (G-6030)
Hydraulic Manifolds USA LLC .... E 973 728-1214
  Stow (G-13376)
Hydraulic Parts Store Inc .... E 330 364-6667
  New Philadelphia (G-11656)
◆ Hydro Systems Company .... E 513 271-8800
  Cincinnati (G-2861)
◆ Hydrotech Inc .... D 888 651-5712
  West Chester (G-14819)
Imco Carbide Tool Inc .... D 419 661-6313
  Perrysburg (G-12346)
◆ Impact Products LLC .... D 419 841-2891
  Toledo (G-13860)
◆ IMS Company .... D 440 543-1615
  Chagrin Falls (G-1980)
Industrial Air Centers Inc .... E 513 770-4161
  Mason (G-10564)
Industrial Air Centers LLC .... D 614 274-9171
  Columbus (G-6050)
Intelligrated Inc .... A 513 874-0788
  West Chester (G-14820)
▲ Intelligrated Systems Inc .... A 866 936-7300
  Mason (G-10565)
Intelligrated Systems LLC .... A 513 701-7300
  Mason (G-10566)
◆ Intelligrated Systems Ohio LLC ..... A 513 701-7300
  Mason (G-10567)
Interstate Lift Trucks Inc .... E 216 328-0970
  Cleveland (G-4421)
◆ Interstate-Mcbee LLC .... C 216 881-0015
  Bedford (G-967)
▲ Interstop Corporation .... E 513 272-1133
  Cincinnati (G-2884)
◆ Jackson International Inc .... E 866 379-2009
  Mineral Ridge (G-11302)
◆ Jergens Inc .... C 216 486-5540
  Cleveland (G-4437)
▲ Joseph Industries Inc .... D 330 528-0091
  Streetsboro (G-13419)

▲ K & M Newspaper Services Inc .... D 845 782-3817
  Elyria (G-8264)
▼ K A Bergquist Inc .... E 419 865-4196
  Toledo (G-13872)
Ka Wanner Inc .... E 740 251-4636
  Marion (G-10432)
◆ Ken Miller Supply Inc .... D 330 264-9146
  Wooster (G-15348)
◆ Kinetics Noise Control Inc .... C 614 889-0480
  Dublin (G-8049)
▲ Kmh Systems Inc .... E 800 962-3178
  Dayton (G-7444)
◆ Kraft Fluid Systems Inc .... E 440 238-5545
  Strongsville (G-13469)
▲ Kyocera SGS Precision Tls Inc ...... E 330 688-6667
  Cuyahoga Falls (G-7086)
◆ Lawrence Industries Inc .... E 216 518-7000
  Cleveland (G-4483)
▲ Lefeld Welding & Stl Sups Inc .... E 419 678-2397
  Coldwater (G-5216)
▲ Leyman Manufacturing Corp .... D 513 891-6210
  Cincinnati (G-2972)
Linde Gas & Equipment Inc .... E 330 376-2242
  Akron (G-222)
Linden-Two Inc .... E 330 928-4064
  Cuyahoga Falls (G-7087)
▲ LNS America Inc .... E 513 528-5674
  Cincinnati (G-2110)
Lorad LLC .... E 800 504-4016
  Westlake (G-15077)
Lord Corporation .... E 440 542-0012
  Solon (G-13107)
M Conley Company .... D 330 456-8243
  Canton (G-1798)
Maag Automatik Inc .... E 330 677-2225
  Kent (G-9586)
Maple Mountain Industries Inc .... E 330 948-2510
  Lodi (G-10020)
McCormick Equipment Co Inc .... E 513 677-8888
  Loveland (G-10150)
Mentor 67 LLC .... D 800 589-5842
  Curtice (G-7031)
Mfh Partners Inc .... B 440 461-4100
  Cleveland (G-4571)
MH Logistics Corp .... D 330 425-2476
  Medina (G-10865)
MH Logistics Corp .... D 513 681-2200
  West Chester (G-14825)
Miami Industrial Trucks Inc .... E 419 424-0042
  Findlay (G-8567)
Miami Industrial Trucks Inc .... E 937 293-4194
  Moraine (G-11425)
▲ Mid-State Sales Inc .... D 614 864-1811
  Columbus (G-6241)
▲ Midwest Industrial Supply Inc .... E 330 456-3121
  Canton (G-1807)
▲ Miller Supply of WvA Inc .... E 330 264-9146
  Wooster (G-15357)
Millwood Inc .... E 513 860-4567
  West Chester (G-14730)
Minerva Welding and Fabg Inc .... E 330 868-7731
  Minerva (G-11310)
Modal Shop Inc .... D 513 351-9919
  Cincinnati (G-3073)
Monode Marking Products Inc .... E 440 975-8802
  Mentor (G-10976)
◆ Multi Products Company .... E 330 674-5981
  Millersburg (G-11287)
National Tool Leasing Inc .... E 866 952-8665
  Eastlake (G-8206)
◆ Nelsen Corporation .... E 330 745-6000
  Norton (G-11996)

SIC SECTION

50 WHOLESALE TRADE - DURABLE GOODS

▲ Newtown Nine Inc.................................. D 440 781-0623
Macedonia *(G-10200)*

Norwalk Custodial Service...................... D 419 668-1517
Norwalk *(G-12018)*

▲ O E Meyer Co... D 419 625-1256
Sandusky *(G-12921)*

O S Walker Company Inc......................... E 614 492-1614
Columbus *(G-6379)*

Oci LLC... D 513 713-3751
Cincinnati *(G-3140)*

Ohio Machinery Co.................................. E 419 423-1447
Findlay *(G-8574)*

◆ Ohio Transmission LLC........................ C 614 342-6247
Columbus *(G-6463)*

Onpoint Group LLC................................. B 567 336-9764
Perrysburg *(G-12361)*

Oracle Elevator Company....................... E 614 781-9731
Columbus *(G-6476)*

Otis Elevator Company........................... C 513 531-7888
Cincinnati *(G-3175)*

Otis Elevator Company........................... E 216 573-2333
Cleveland *(G-4709)*

Otis Elevator Company........................... C 614 777-6500
Columbus *(G-6489)*

Otis Elevator Company........................... E 740 282-1461
Steubenville *(G-13341)*

◆ Park Corporation................................. B 216 267-4870
Medina *(G-10874)*

Parker-Hannifin Corporation.................. D 440 366-5100
Elyria *(G-8285)*

Parker-Hannifin Corporation.................. E 937 644-3915
Marysville *(G-10501)*

Parker-Hannifin Corporation.................. C 330 296-2871
Ravenna *(G-12634)*

Parker-Hannifin Corporation.................. E 610 926-1115
Wickliffe *(G-15159)*

▲ Pennsylvania TI Sls & Svc Inc.............. D 330 758-0845
Youngstown *(G-15692)*

▲ Pines Manufacturing Inc..................... E 440 835-5553
Westlake *(G-15098)*

▲ Power Distributors LLC....................... D 614 876-3533
Columbus *(G-6539)*

Powerbilt Mtl Hdlg Sltions LLC............... D 937 592-5660
Bellefontaine *(G-1036)*

Precision Supply Company Inc............... D 330 225-5530
Brunswick *(G-1468)*

Precision Tools Service Inc.................... D 614 873-8000
Plain City *(G-12490)*

Primetals Technologies USA LLC........... E 419 929-1554
New London *(G-11633)*

▲ Princeton Tool Inc............................... C 440 290-8666
Mentor *(G-10985)*

▲ Pro Quip Inc.. D 330 468-1850
Macedonia *(G-10202)*

Process Pump & Seal Inc........................ E 513 988-7000
Cincinnati *(G-3242)*

Production Tool Supply Ohio.................. E 216 265-0000
Cleveland *(G-4772)*

R A Mueller Inc.. E 513 489-5200
Blue Ash *(G-1228)*

R and J Corporation............................... E 440 871-6009
Westlake *(G-15101)*

◆ R&M Materials Handling Inc............... E 937 328-5100
Springfield *(G-13283)*

R3 Safety LLC.. E 800 421-7081
West Chester *(G-14753)*

Raymond Storage Concepts Inc............. E 614 275-3494
Groveport *(G-8998)*

▲ Raymond Storage Concepts Inc.......... D 513 891-7290
Blue Ash *(G-1232)*

◆ Reduction Engineering Inc.................. E 330 677-2225
Kent *(G-9593)*

Remtec Engineering................................ E 513 860-4299
Mason *(G-10601)*

Ridge Corporation................................... E 740 513-9880
Frazeysburg *(G-8657)*

▲ Robeck Fluid Power Co....................... D 330 562-1140
Aurora *(G-624)*

▲ Rodem Inc... E 513 922-6140
Harrison *(G-9115)*

▲ Rolls-Royce Energy Systems Inc......... A 703 834-1700
Mount Vernon *(G-11506)*

◆ RP Gatta Inc.. D 330 562-2288
Aurora *(G-627)*

▼ RSR Partners LLC................................ D 440 519-1768
Stow *(G-13389)*

▲ Rubber City Machinery Corp............... E 330 434-3500
Akron *(G-288)*

▲ Rumpke/Kenworth Contract................ D 740 774-5111
Chillicothe *(G-2089)*

Safety Solutions Inc................................ E 614 799-9900
Columbus *(G-6634)*

▲ Safety Today Inc.................................. E 614 409-7200
Grove City *(G-8950)*

▲ Salvagnini America Inc....................... E 513 874-8284
Hamilton *(G-9080)*

Samuel Son & Co (usa) Inc..................... D 740 522-2500
Heath *(G-9138)*

Scott Industrial Systems Inc................... D 937 233-8146
Dayton *(G-7612)*

Sentinel Fluid Controls LLC.................... E 419 478-9086
Toledo *(G-14008)*

Shawcor Pipe Protection LLC.................. E 513 683-7800
Loveland *(G-10159)*

South Shore Controls Inc....................... E 440 259-2500
Mentor *(G-10998)*

▲ Sroka Inc... E 440 572-2811
Strongsville *(G-13486)*

Stanwade Metal Products Inc................. E 330 772-2421
Hartford *(G-9123)*

Stolle Machinery Company LLC.............. D 330 493-0444
Canton *(G-1861)*

Stolle Machinery Company LLC.............. D 330 494-6382
North Canton *(G-11863)*

▲ Stuertz Machinery Inc......................... D 330 405-0444
Twinsburg *(G-14221)*

Super Systems Inc.................................. E 513 772-0060
Cincinnati *(G-3428)*

▲ Sylvester Highland Holding Inc........... D 440 473-1640
Cleveland *(G-4971)*

System Seals Inc..................................... E 216 220-1800
Brecksville *(G-1369)*

T J Automation Inc................................. E 419 267-5687
Archbold *(G-468)*

Tech Elevator Inc.................................... D 216 310-3497
Cleveland *(G-4981)*

Tfs Ltd... D 419 868-8853
Perrysburg *(G-12375)*

Tiffin Loader Crane Company................. D 419 448-8156
Tiffin *(G-13646)*

Tk Elevator Corporation.......................... C 440 717-0080
Broadview Heights *(G-1401)*

Tk Elevator Corporation.......................... D 614 895-8930
Westerville *(G-15017)*

Toga-Pak Inc... E 937 294-7311
Dayton *(G-7672)*

▲ Total Fleet Solutions LLC.................... E 419 868-8853
Holland *(G-9309)*

Towlift Inc... E 614 851-1001
Columbus *(G-6774)*

Towlift Inc... E 440 951-9519
Mentor *(G-11004)*

Towlift Inc... E 419 666-1333
Northwood *(G-11985)*

Towlift Inc... E 419 531-6110
Toledo *(G-14072)*

▲ Towlift Inc... C 216 749-6800
Brooklyn Heights *(G-1428)*

Toyota Material Hdlg Ohio Inc................ D 216 328-0970
Cleveland *(G-5027)*

◆ TPC Packaging Solutions Inc.............. D 513 489-8840
Cincinnati *(G-3499)*

Tractor Supply Company......................... E 937 382-2595
Wilmington *(G-15275)*

Transtar Industries Inc........................... D 855 872-6782
Cleveland *(G-5034)*

Trew LLC... E 800 571-8739
Fairfield *(G-8448)*

◆ Trewbric III Inc.................................... E 614 444-2184
Columbus *(G-6785)*

Triad Technologies LLC........................... E 937 832-2861
Vandalia *(G-14395)*

▲ Tripack LLC... E 513 248-1255
Milford *(G-11262)*

▲ Union Process Inc............................... E 330 929-3333
Akron *(G-339)*

▲ United Grinding North Amer Inc......... E 937 859-1975
Miamisburg *(G-11100)*

US Advanced Systems LLC..................... E 330 425-0020
Twinsburg *(G-14226)*

US Safetygear Inc................................... E 330 898-1344
Warren *(G-14570)*

V & P Hydraulic Products LLC................. D 740 203-3600
Delaware *(G-7833)*

▲ Valley Industrial Trucks Inc................. E 330 788-4081
Youngstown *(G-15746)*

Vargo LLC.. E 614 876-1163
Dublin *(G-8147)*

Vargo Solutions Inc................................ D 614 876-1163
Dublin *(G-8148)*

▲ Venco Venturo Industries LLC............. E 513 772-8448
Cincinnati *(G-3619)*

W W Williams Company LLC................... E 330 225-7751
Brunswick *(G-1473)*

W W Williams Midwest Inc..................... E 330 225-7751
Brunswick *(G-1474)*

◆ Wardjet LLC.. D 330 677-9100
Tallmadge *(G-13611)*

Weiler Welding Company Inc.................. D 937 222-8312
Moraine *(G-11448)*

Weld Plus Inc.. E 513 941-4411
Cincinnati *(G-3648)*

Weldco Inc.. E 513 744-9353
Cincinnati *(G-3649)*

Western Branch Diesel LLC.................... E 740 695-6301
Saint Clairsville *(G-12820)*

Williams Super Service Inc..................... E 330 733-7750
East Sparta *(G-8199)*

Winelco Inc... E 513 755-8050
West Chester *(G-14795)*

Wolf Machine Company.......................... E 513 791-5194
Blue Ash *(G-1274)*

▲ Wooster Hydrostatics Inc.................... E 330 263-6555
Wooster *(G-15395)*

◆ Wurtec Incorporated........................... D 419 726-1066
Toledo *(G-14110)*

Yaskawa America Inc............................. E 614 733-3200
Plain City *(G-12498)*

5085 Industrial supplies

3b Holdings Inc....................................... E 800 791-7124
Cleveland *(G-3745)*

Ackerman Chacco Company Inc............. E 513 791-4252
Blue Ash *(G-1121)*

▲ Afc Industries Inc................................ E 513 874-7456
West Chester *(G-14649)*

50 WHOLESALE TRADE - DURABLE GOODS

Albright Welding Supply Co Inc......... E 330 264-2021
  Wooster *(G-15309)*

▲ Alkon Corporation............................. D 419 355-9111
  Fremont *(G-8665)*

▲ All Ohio Threaded Rod Co Inc......... E 216 426-1800
  Cleveland *(G-3791)*

Allen Refractories Company............. C 740 927-8000
  Pataskala *(G-12269)*

Allied Power Transmission Co........... E 440 708-1006
  Chagrin Falls *(G-1972)*

Allied Supply Company Inc................ E 937 224-9833
  Dayton *(G-7164)*

Alro Steel Corporation...................... E 614 878-7271
  Columbus *(G-5340)*

Alro Steel Corporation...................... D 419 720-5300
  Toledo *(G-13679)*

▲ American Producers Sup Co Inc..... D 740 373-5050
  Marietta *(G-10355)*

American Ring..................................... E 414 355-9206
  Solon *(G-13065)*

▲ Anchor Flange Company................. D 513 527-3512
  Cincinnati *(G-2196)*

▲ Applied Indus Tech - CA LLC......... B 216 426-4000
  Cleveland *(G-3825)*

▲ Applied Industrial Tech Inc............ B 216 426-4000
  Cleveland *(G-3827)*

Applied Mint Sups Slutions LLC......... E 216 456-3600
  Strongsville *(G-13443)*

▲ Atlas Bolt & Screw Company LLC... C 419 289-6171
  Ashland *(G-478)*

▲ Atwood Rope Manufacturing Inc.... E 614 920-0534
  Canal Winchester *(G-1598)*

B W Grinding Co.................................. E 419 923-1376
  Lyons *(G-10187)*

▲ Bdi Inc.. C 216 642-9100
  Cleveland *(G-3858)*

Bearing & Drive Systems Inc............ D 440 846-4272
  Strongsville *(G-13445)*

◆ Bearing Distributors Inc................. C 216 642-9100
  Cleveland *(G-3860)*

▲ Bearing Technologies Ltd.............. D 800 597-3486
  Avon Lake *(G-675)*

Belting Company of Cincinnati........... D 937 498-2104
  Sidney *(G-13022)*

▲ Belting Company of Cincinnati...... C 513 621-9050
  Cincinnati *(G-2256)*

Benchmark Industrial Inc.................... D 614 695-6500
  Gahanna *(G-8711)*

Binkelman Corporation....................... E 419 537-9333
  Bowling Green *(G-1308)*

Blackhawk Industrial Dist Inc............. E 918 610-4719
  Brunswick *(G-1451)*

Bonnie Plants LLC.............................. C 937 642-7764
  Marysville *(G-10476)*

Bottle Solutions LLC........................... E 216 889-3330
  Cleveland *(G-3883)*

Brimar Packaging Inc.......................... E 440 934-3080
  Avon *(G-641)*

▲ Buckeye Rubber & Packing Co...... E 216 464-8900
  Beachwood *(G-771)*

▲ C B Mfg & Sls Co Inc...................... D 937 866-5986
  Miamisburg *(G-11030)*

Catensys US Inc.................................. B 330 273-4383
  Strongsville *(G-13447)*

Chandler Products LLC...................... E 216 481-1400
  Brecksville *(G-1347)*

Chardon Tool & Supply Co Inc........... E 440 286-6440
  Chardon *(G-1997)*

Ci Disposition Co................................. D 216 587-5200
  Brooklyn Heights *(G-1414)*

◆ Cincinnati Container Company....... E 513 874-6874
  West Chester *(G-14804)*

◆ Cleveland Supplyone Inc................ E 216 514-7000
  Cleveland *(G-4068)*

Commercial Electric Pdts Corp.......... E 216 241-2886
  Cleveland *(G-4094)*

Continental.. E 937 644-8940
  Marysville *(G-10480)*

Cornerstone Controls Inc................... E 513 489-2500
  Cincinnati *(G-2509)*

Cornwell Quality Tools Company....... D 330 628-2627
  Mogadore *(G-11325)*

Cornwell Quality Tools Company....... E 330 335-2933
  Wadsworth *(G-14434)*

Crane Pumps & Systems Inc............ C 937 773-2442
  Piqua *(G-12440)*

◆ Datwyler Sling Sltions USA Inc..... D 937 387-2800
  Vandalia *(G-14373)*

Dayton Windustrial Co........................ E 937 461-2603
  Dayton *(G-7306)*

Dearing Compressor and Pu.............. E 330 783-2258
  Youngstown *(G-15595)*

Delille Oxygen Company..................... E 614 444-1177
  Columbus *(G-5752)*

Delta Corporate Holdings LLC........... B 216 433-7700
  Cleveland *(G-4161)*

◆ Earnest Machine Products Co....... E 440 895-8400
  Rocky River *(G-12740)*

Evans Adhesive Corporation.............. E 614 451-2665
  Columbus *(G-5833)*

F & M Mafco Inc................................... E 513 367-2151
  Harrison *(G-9105)*

◆ F & M Mafco Inc............................... C 513 367-2151
  Harrison *(G-9104)*

◆ Facil North America Inc.................. C 330 487-2500
  Twinsburg *(G-14190)*

Famous Distribution Inc..................... D 330 762-9621
  Akron *(G-154)*

▲ Fcx Performance Inc...................... E 614 253-1996
  Columbus *(G-5853)*

Ferguson Enterprises LLC................. E 513 771-6000
  Cincinnati *(G-2658)*

Ferry Cap & Set Screw Company...... D 440 783-3126
  Strongsville *(G-13456)*

▲ Ferry Cap & Set Screw Company. C 216 649-7400
  Lakewood *(G-9666)*

Festo Corporation............................... C 513 486-1050
  Mason *(G-10548)*

▲ Fischer Pump & Valve Company... E 513 583-4800
  Loveland *(G-10137)*

▲ Forge Industries Inc....................... A 330 960-2468
  Youngstown *(G-15613)*

Fosbel Wahl Holdings LLC................. D 419 334-2650
  Fremont *(G-8678)*

Fulflo Specialties Company................ E 937 783-2411
  Blanchester *(G-1117)*

▲ G M Industrial LLC......................... C 440 786-1177
  Cleveland *(G-4298)*

General Factory Sups Co Inc............ E 513 681-6300
  Cincinnati *(G-2727)*

◆ Ges Graphite Inc............................. E 216 658-6660
  Parma *(G-12254)*

◆ Gorilla Glue Company LLC............. B 513 271-3300
  Cincinnati *(G-2743)*

Goss Supply Company........................ E 740 454-2571
  Zanesville *(G-15796)*

▲ Great Lakes Fasteners Inc............ D 330 425-4488
  Twinsburg *(G-14195)*

▲ Great Lakes Power Products Inc.. E 440 951-5111
  Mentor *(G-10943)*

▲ H & D Steel Service Inc.................. E 800 666-3390
  North Royalton *(G-11942)*

H3d Tool Corporation.......................... E 740 498-5181
  Newcomerstown *(G-11768)*

▲ Hart Industries Inc.......................... E 513 541-4278
  Middletown *(G-11165)*

Hd Supply Facilities Maint Ltd............ D 440 542-9188
  Solon *(G-13094)*

Hydraulic Manifolds USA LLC............ E 973 728-1214
  Stow *(G-13376)*

Indelco Custom Products Inc............ E 216 797-7300
  Euclid *(G-8349)*

Industrial Cont Svcs - CA LLC............ B 614 864-1900
  Blacklick *(G-1111)*

▼ Japo Inc.. E 614 263-2850
  Columbus *(G-6084)*

Jet Rubber Company.......................... E 330 325-1821
  Rootstown *(G-12760)*

◆ Kaufman Container Company........ C 216 898-2000
  Cleveland *(G-4450)*

Kellermeyer Company......................... D 419 255-3022
  Bowling Green *(G-1326)*

Kirby Risk Corporation....................... D 419 221-0123
  Lima *(G-9915)*

▲ Lake Erie Abrasive & Tool Inc....... E 216 692-2778
  Euclid *(G-8353)*

Lakeside Supply Co............................. E 216 941-6800
  Cleveland *(G-4478)*

◆ Lawrence Industries Inc................. E 216 518-7000
  Cleveland *(G-4483)*

Lincoln Electric Company................... E 216 481-8100
  Euclid *(G-8355)*

◆ Lincoln Electric Intl Holdg Co........ D 216 481-8100
  Euclid *(G-8356)*

▲ Logan Clutch Corporation.............. E 440 808-4258
  Cleveland *(G-4504)*

Mauser Usa LLC.................................. D 740 397-1762
  Mount Vernon *(G-11499)*

Mazzella Holding Company Inc......... D 513 772-4466
  Cleveland *(G-4534)*

McMaster-Carr Supply Company....... A 330 995-5500
  Aurora *(G-617)*

▲ McNeil Industries Inc...................... E 440 951-7756
  Painesville *(G-12236)*

McWane Inc.. B 740 622-6651
  Coshocton *(G-6992)*

▼ Merchandise Inc............................... D 513 353-2200
  Miamitown *(G-11107)*

◆ Mesa Industries Inc......................... E 513 321-2950
  Cincinnati *(G-3048)*

▲ Miba Bearings US LLC.................... B 740 962-4242
  Mcconnelsville *(G-10803)*

◆ Mid-State Industrial Pdts Inc......... E 614 253-8631
  Columbus *(G-6240)*

▲ Mill-Rose Company......................... C 440 255-9171
  Mentor *(G-10975)*

◆ Mirka USA Inc................................... D 330 963-6421
  Twinsburg *(G-14206)*

Motion Industries Inc.......................... E 937 236-7711
  Dayton *(G-7515)*

◆ Noland Company.............................. C 937 396-7980
  Moraine *(G-11428)*

▲ North Coast Bearings LLC............. E 440 930-7600
  Avon *(G-662)*

◆ NSK Industries Inc........................... D 330 923-4112
  Cuyahoga Falls *(G-7091)*

◆ O K I Supply Co................................ C 513 341-4002
  West Chester *(G-14826)*

◆ Ohio Transmission LLC................... C 614 342-6247
  Columbus *(G-6463)*

Optimas Oe Solutions LLC................. E 740 774-4553
  Chillicothe *(G-2081)*

Otp Holding LLC................................... E 614 342-6123
  Columbus *(G-6490)*

Pallet Distributors Inc........................ E 888 805-9670
  Lakewood *(G-9681)*

SIC SECTION

50 WHOLESALE TRADE - DURABLE GOODS

▲ Pennsylvania Tl Sls & Svc Inc............ D 330 758-0845
  Youngstown *(G-15692)*

PHD Manufacturing Inc........................ C 330 482-9256
  Columbiana *(G-5238)*

▲ Pipe Products Inc............................... C 513 587-7532
  West Chester *(G-14742)*

Pipe-Valves Inc..................................... E 614 294-4971
  Columbus *(G-6526)*

Precision Supply Company Inc........... D 330 225-5530
  Brunswick *(G-1468)*

◆ Pressure Connections Corp................ D 614 863-6930
  Columbus *(G-6543)*

Process Pump & Seal Inc.................... E 513 988-7000
  Cincinnati *(G-3242)*

▲ R L Morrissey & Assoc Inc................ E 440 498-3730
  Solon *(G-13135)*

▲ Sabco Industries Inc......................... E 419 531-5347
  Toledo *(G-14002)*

▲ Samsel Rope & Marine Supply Co..... E 216 241-0333
  Cleveland *(G-4875)*

Samuel Son & Co (usa) Inc................. D 740 522-2500
  Heath *(G-9138)*

Scioto LLC.. B 937 644-0888
  Marysville *(G-10507)*

Setech Incorporated............................ C 937 425-9482
  Moraine *(G-11437)*

Shaq Inc.. D 770 427-0402
  Beachwood *(G-836)*

▲ Solution Industries Inc....................... D 440 816-9500
  Strongsville *(G-13485)*

◆ Spencer Products Co.......................... E 330 487-5200
  Twinsburg *(G-14219)*

▲ SSP Fittings Corp............................... D 330 425-4250
  Twinsburg *(G-14220)*

▲ Sst Bearing Corporation.................... D 513 583-5500
  Loveland *(G-10162)*

◆ Stafast Products Inc.......................... E 440 357-5546
  Painesville *(G-12243)*

Steam Trbine Altrntive Rsrces............. E 740 387-5535
  Marion *(G-10455)*

▼ Stud Welding Associates Inc.............. D 440 783-3160
  Strongsville *(G-13490)*

▲ Sunsong North America Inc............... E 919 365-3825
  Moraine *(G-11441)*

Superior Holding LLC........................... E 216 651-9400
  Cleveland *(G-4964)*

Superior Products LLC......................... D 216 651-9400
  Cleveland *(G-4965)*

Supply Technologies LLC..................... D 937 898-5795
  Dayton *(G-7656)*

Supply Technologies LLC..................... D 440 248-8170
  Solon *(G-13151)*

◆ Supply Technologies LLC.................... C 440 947-2100
  Cleveland *(G-4966)*

Swagelok Company.............................. D 440 349-5962
  Solon *(G-13152)*

Swagelok Company.............................. E 440 542-1250
  Solon *(G-13153)*

▲ The Cornwell Quality Tool................... D 330 336-3506
  Wadsworth *(G-14455)*

◆ The Kindt-Collins Company LLC.......... D 216 252-4122
  Cleveland *(G-5003)*

▲ The Voto Manufacturers Sa............... E 740 282-3621
  Steubenville *(G-13345)*

▲ Thermodyn Corporation..................... E 419 841-7782
  Sylvania *(G-13577)*

Timken Company.................................. D 419 563-2200
  Bucyrus *(G-1518)*

Timken Company.................................. E 234 262-3000
  Niles *(G-11797)*

◆ Timken Company................................ A 234 262-3000
  North Canton *(G-11865)*

◆ Timken Corporation........................... E 330 471-3378
  North Canton *(G-11866)*

◆ Tolco Corporation.............................. D 419 241-1113
  Toledo *(G-14048)*

▲ Tricor Industrial Inc........................... D 330 264-3299
  Wooster *(G-15380)*

▲ Trumbull Industries Inc...................... D 800 477-1799
  Warren *(G-14566)*

Vallen Distribution Inc......................... E
  Monroe *(G-11354)*

▲ Victory White Metal Company........... D 216 271-1400
  Cleveland *(G-5104)*

W W Grainger Inc................................. D 330 425-8388
  Macedonia *(G-10209)*

◆ Watteredge LLC................................. D 440 933-6110
  Avon Lake *(G-684)*

▼ Welding Cutting Tls & ACC LLC......... E 216 481-8100
  Cleveland *(G-5128)*

Wesco Distribution Inc........................ D 216 741-0441
  Cleveland *(G-5131)*

Williams Scotsman Inc......................... E 216 399-6285
  Hinckley *(G-9273)*

Winsupply Inc....................................... D 937 294-5331
  Moraine *(G-11450)*

Wulco Inc.. D 513 379-6115
  Hamilton *(G-9093)*

▲ Wulco Inc... D 513 679-2600
  Cincinnati *(G-3682)*

Ziegler Bolt & Parts Co........................ D 330 478-2542
  Canton *(G-1893)*

5087 Service establishment equipment

A-1 Sprinkler Company Inc................. D 937 859-6198
  Miamisburg *(G-11019)*

Acorn Distributors Inc......................... E 614 294-6444
  Columbus *(G-5307)*

▲ Action Coupling & Eqp Inc................. D 330 279-4242
  Holmesville *(G-9316)*

Airgas Usa LLC.................................... B 216 642-6600
  Independence *(G-9399)*

Alco-Chem Inc...................................... E 330 833-8551
  Canton *(G-1658)*

▲ Alco-Chem Inc................................... E 330 253-3535
  Akron *(G-43)*

Baf Holding Company.......................... E 440 287-2200
  Bedford *(G-955)*

▲ Betco Corporation............................. C 419 241-2156
  Bowling Green *(G-1307)*

Brakefire Incorporated........................ E 937 426-9717
  Beavercreek *(G-919)*

Brakefire Incorporated........................ E 330 535-4343
  Akron *(G-73)*

Brakefire Incorporated........................ D 513 733-5655
  Cincinnati *(G-2276)*

Clean Innovations................................ E 614 299-1187
  Columbus *(G-5581)*

Commercial Parts & Ser...................... D 614 221-0057
  Columbus *(G-5666)*

Cooper Enterprises Inc........................ D 419 347-5232
  Shelby *(G-13006)*

▼ Fox International Limited Inc............. C 216 454-1001
  Beachwood *(G-793)*

Friendly Wholesale Co.......................... E 724 224-6580
  Wooster *(G-15338)*

Friends Service Co Inc......................... D 419 427-1704
  Findlay *(G-8534)*

H & H Green LLC.................................. E 419 674-4152
  Kenton *(G-9614)*

Hd Supply Facilities Maint Ltd............. D 440 542-9188
  Solon *(G-13094)*

HP Products Corporation..................... D 513 683-8553
  Cincinnati *(G-2852)*

I Supply Co... C 937 878-5240
  Fairborn *(G-8377)*

◆ Impact Products LLC.......................... D 419 841-2891
  Toledo *(G-13860)*

Imperial Dade Intrmdate Hldngs......... E 800 998-5453
  West Chester *(G-14709)*

J L Wilson Co....................................... E 216 431-4040
  Cleveland *(G-4426)*

Kaleel Bros Inc.................................... D 330 758-0861
  Youngstown *(G-15644)*

Kellermeyer Company.......................... D 419 255-3022
  Bowling Green *(G-1326)*

Laughlin Music & Vending Svc............ E 740 593-7778
  Athens *(G-580)*

M Conley Company............................... D 330 456-8243
  Canton *(G-1798)*

Martin-Brower Company LLC............... C 513 773-2301
  West Chester *(G-14729)*

Mougianis Industries Inc..................... D 740 264-6372
  Steubenville *(G-13340)*

Multi Builders Supply Co...................... E 216 831-1121
  Cleveland *(G-4609)*

National Marketshare Group................ E 513 921-0800
  Cincinnati *(G-3095)*

Nichols Paper & Supply Co.................. D 419 255-3022
  Bowling Green *(G-1328)*

▲ Phillips Supply Company.................... D 513 579-1762
  Cincinnati *(G-3208)*

▲ Pioneer Manufacturing Inc................. D 216 671-5500
  Cleveland *(G-4750)*

Powell Company Inc............................. D 419 228-3552
  Lima *(G-9951)*

Rdp Foodservice Ltd............................ D 614 261-5661
  Hilliard *(G-9228)*

Rhiel Supply Co.................................... E 330 799-7777
  Austintown *(G-636)*

Seaway Sponge & Chamois Co............ E 419 691-4694
  Toledo *(G-14007)*

Solv-All LLC... D 888 765-8255
  Mentor *(G-10996)*

Stewart & Calhoun Fnrl HM Inc........... E 330 535-1543
  Akron *(G-311)*

▼ Sutphen Corporation.......................... C 800 726-7030
  Dublin *(G-8136)*

The Cottingham Paper Co.................... E 614 294-6444
  Columbus *(G-6758)*

The Dean Supply Co............................. E 216 771-3300
  Cleveland *(G-4999)*

▲ Trendco Supply Inc............................. E 513 752-1871
  Batavia *(G-750)*

▲ Vendors Exchange International Inc.. E 216 432-1800
  Cleveland *(G-5098)*

◆ Wasserstrom Company....................... B 614 228-6525
  Columbus *(G-6867)*

5088 Transportation equipment and supplies

▲ Abx Air Inc... B 937 382-5591
  Wilmington *(G-15237)*

▲ Aim Mro LLC...................................... E 513 831-2938
  Camp Dennison *(G-1590)*

▲ Aim Mro Holdings LLC....................... E 513 831-2938
  Miamiville *(G-11108)*

Airborne Maint Engrg Svcs Inc............ C 937 366-2559
  Wilmington *(G-15242)*

Airborne Maint Engrg Svcs Inc............ C 937 382-5591
  Wilmington *(G-15243)*

Amsted Industries Incorporated.......... D 614 836-2323
  Groveport *(G-8969)*

◆ Bendix Coml Vhcl Systems LLC.......... B 440 329-9000
  Avon *(G-640)*

◆ Buck Equipment Inc........................... E 614 539-3039
  Grove City *(G-8901)*

50 WHOLESALE TRADE - DURABLE GOODS

Century Equipment Inc .... E 419 865-7400
   Toledo *(G-13728)*

◆ Djj Holding Corporation .... C 513 419-6200
   Cincinnati *(G-2572)*

▲ Eleet Cryogenics Inc .... E 330 874-4009
   Bolivar *(G-1294)*

▲ GE Engine Services Dist LLC .... C 513 243-2000
   Cincinnati *(G-2720)*

General Electric Company .... A 617 443-3000
   Cincinnati *(G-2725)*

◆ Greenfield Products Inc .... D 937 981-2696
   Greenfield *(G-8865)*

Grimes Aerospace Company .... D 937 484-2001
   Urbana *(G-14308)*

◆ Jilco Industries Inc .... E 330 698-0280
   Kidron *(G-9636)*

◆ Lippert Enterprises Inc .... E 419 281-8084
   Ashland *(G-505)*

Mazzella Holding Company Inc .... D 513 772-4466
   Cleveland *(G-4534)*

Netjets Sales Inc .... C 614 239-5500
   Columbus *(G-6350)*

PCC Airfoils LLC .... B 440 944-1880
   Wickliffe *(G-15160)*

▲ Sportsmans Market Inc .... C 513 735-9100
   Batavia *(G-747)*

Transdigm Group Incorporated .... B 216 706-2960
   Cleveland *(G-5031)*

5091 Sporting and recreation goods

21st Century Health Spa Inc .... E 419 476-5585
   Toledo *(G-13670)*

A K Athletic Equipment Inc .... E 614 920-3069
   Canal Winchester *(G-1597)*

Air Venturi Ltd .... D 216 292-2570
   Solon *(G-13063)*

Artwall LLC .... E 216 476-0635
   Cleveland *(G-3836)*

Aspc Corp .... C 937 593-7010
   Bellefontaine *(G-1019)*

▲ Atwood Rope Manufacturing Inc .... E 614 920-0534
   Canal Winchester *(G-1598)*

Cherry Valley Lodge .... E 740 788-1200
   Newark *(G-11692)*

Competitor Swim Products Inc .... D 800 888-7946
   Columbus *(G-5676)*

◆ Coulter Ventures Llc .... E 614 358-6190
   Columbus *(G-5708)*

Dtv Inc .... E 216 226-5465
   Cleveland *(G-4187)*

Durga Llc .... E 513 771-2080
   Cincinnati *(G-2587)*

▲ Golf Galaxy Golfworks Inc .... C 740 328-4193
   Newark *(G-11702)*

Heritage Pool Supply Group Inc .... D 440 238-2100
   Strongsville *(G-13460)*

Jack Entertainment LLC .... D 313 309-5225
   Cleveland *(G-4430)*

Kames Inc .... E 330 499-4558
   Canton *(G-1789)*

▲ Kohlmyer Sporting Goods Inc .... E 440 277-8296
   Lorain *(G-10079)*

▲ Litehouse Products LLC .... E 440 638-2350
   Strongsville *(G-13471)*

Lmn Development LLC .... C 419 433-7200
   Sandusky *(G-12910)*

Metropolitan Pool Service Co .... E 216 741-9451
   Parma *(G-12257)*

▲ Miami Corporation .... E 800 543-0448
   Cincinnati *(G-3054)*

▲ Micnan Inc .... E 330 920-6200
   Cuyahoga Falls *(G-7088)*

Mke Holdings Inc .... E 440 238-2100
   Strongsville *(G-13476)*

Schaffer Partners Inc .... D 216 881-3000
   Cleveland *(G-4882)*

◆ Schneider Saddlery LLC .... E 440 543-2700
   Chagrin Falls *(G-1989)*

◆ Zebec of North America Inc .... E 513 829-5533
   Fairfield *(G-8455)*

5092 Toys and hobby goods and supplies

Artwall LLC .... E 216 476-0635
   Cleveland *(G-3836)*

▲ AW Faber-Castell Usa Inc .... D 216 643-4660
   Independence *(G-9408)*

Ball Bounce and Sport Inc .... E 614 662-5381
   Columbus *(G-5416)*

◆ Ball Bounce and Sport Inc .... E 419 289-9310
   Ashland *(G-479)*

▲ Bendon Inc .... D 419 207-3600
   Ashland *(G-482)*

◆ Closeout Distribution LLC .... A 614 278-6800
   Westerville *(G-14968)*

▼ Craft Wholesalers Inc .... C 740 964-6210
   Groveport *(G-8980)*

▲ CSC Distribution LLC .... A 614 278-6800
   Columbus *(G-5734)*

▼ ICM Distributing Company Inc .... E 234 212-3030
   Twinsburg *(G-14196)*

◆ K & M International Inc .... D 330 425-2550
   Independence *(G-9439)*

Lancaster Bingo Company LLC .... C 800 866-5001
   Lancaster *(G-9729)*

▲ Miller Fireworks Company Inc .... E 419 865-7329
   Holland *(G-9298)*

Nannicola Wholesale Co .... D 330 799-0888
   Youngstown *(G-15672)*

National Marketshare Group .... E 513 921-0800
   Cincinnati *(G-3095)*

◆ Phantom Fireworks Inc .... B 330 746-1064
   Youngstown *(G-15693)*

Schaffer Partners Inc .... D 216 881-3000
   Cleveland *(G-4882)*

▲ Twin Sisters Productions LLC .... E 330 631-0361
   Stow *(G-13399)*

5093 Scrap and waste materials

◆ Aci Industries Ltd .... E 740 368-4160
   Delaware *(G-7776)*

▲ Agmet LLC .... E 440 439-7400
   Cleveland *(G-3775)*

Bluescope Recycling & Mtls LLC .... C 816 968-3000
   Delta *(G-7849)*

Cohen Brothers Inc .... E 513 422-3696
   Middletown *(G-11158)*

Cohen Electronics Inc .... D 513 425-6911
   Middletown *(G-11159)*

Daniel Cohen Enterprises Inc .... C 513 896-4547
   Oxford *(G-12207)*

David J Joseph Company .... E 513 419-6016
   Cincinnati *(G-2542)*

▼ Diproinduca (usa) Limited LLC .... D 330 722-4442
   Medina *(G-10828)*

◆ Djj Holding Corporation .... C 513 419-6200
   Cincinnati *(G-2572)*

▲ Fpt Cleveland LLC .... C 216 441-3800
   Cleveland *(G-4282)*

◆ Franklin Iron & Metal Corp .... C 937 253-8184
   Dayton *(G-7367)*

◆ G-Cor Automotive Corp .... E 614 443-6735
   Columbus *(G-5907)*

◆ Geep USA Inc .... E 919 544-1443
   Stow *(G-13369)*

◆ Lakeside Scrap Metals Inc .... E 216 458-7150
   Cleveland *(G-4477)*

▲ Legend Smelting and Recycl Inc .... D 740 928-0139
   Hebron *(G-9145)*

Metalx LLC .... D 260 232-3000
   Delta *(G-7852)*

Mw Metals Group LLC .... D 937 222-5992
   Dayton *(G-7522)*

Omnisource LLC .... D 419 537-1631
   Toledo *(G-13950)*

▼ Plezall Wipers Inc .... E 216 535-4300
   Richmond Heights *(G-12721)*

◆ Quantum Metals Inc .... C 513 573-0144
   Lebanon *(G-9784)*

Rm Advisory Group Inc .... E 513 242-2100
   Cincinnati *(G-3309)*

Rnw Holdings Inc .... E 330 792-0600
   Youngstown *(G-15709)*

Shredded Bedding Corporation .... D 740 893-3567
   Centerburg *(G-1936)*

▲ Sims Bros Inc .... D 740 387-9041
   Marion *(G-10454)*

Slesnick Iron & Metal Co .... E 330 453-8475
   Canton *(G-1854)*

◆ The David J Joseph Company .... C 513 419-6200
   Cincinnati *(G-3464)*

◆ Unico Alloys & Metals Inc .... D 614 299-0545
   Columbus *(G-6798)*

◆ United Alloys & Metals Inc .... E 614 299-0545
   Columbus *(G-6803)*

◆ Willoughby Ir & Waste Mtls LLC .... B 440 946-8990
   Willoughby *(G-15227)*

5094 Jewelry and precious stones

▲ Cas-Ker Company Inc .... E 513 674-7700
   Cincinnati *(G-2317)*

Equity Diamond Brokers Inc .... E 513 793-4760
   Montgomery *(G-11367)*

◆ Gottlieb & Sons Inc .... E 216 771-4785
   Beachwood *(G-795)*

Marfo Company .... D 614 276-3352
   Columbus *(G-6197)*

Point Recognition Ltd .... E 330 220-6777
   Brunswick *(G-1467)*

5099 Durable goods, nec

▼ Abco Holdings LLC .... C 216 433-7200
   Cleveland *(G-3757)*

Andrew Distribution Inc .... B 614 824-3123
   Columbus *(G-5369)*

Animal Supply Company LLC .... E 330 642-6037
   Orrville *(G-12155)*

Benchmark Building Supply Inc .... E 513 732-2522
   Batavia *(G-728)*

◆ Dualite Sales & Service Inc .... C 513 724-7100
   Williamsburg *(G-15179)*

◆ Evenflo Company Inc .... E 937 415-3300
   Miamisburg *(G-11053)*

▲ Jatiga Inc .... D 859 817-7100
   Blue Ash *(G-1191)*

Kcc Supply LLC .... E 740 694-6315
   Fredericktown *(G-8661)*

Keidel Sup LLC Fka Kdel Sup In .... E 513 351-1600
   Cincinnati *(G-2933)*

Live Technologies LLC .... D 614 278-7777
   Columbus *(G-6171)*

▼ Merchandise Inc .... D 513 353-2200
   Miamitown *(G-11107)*

Merco Group Inc .... D 937 890-5841
   Dayton *(G-7481)*

PCC Airfoils LLC .... E 216 692-7900
   Cleveland *(G-4732)*

51 WHOLESALE TRADE - NONDURABLE GOODS

Red Bull Media Hse N Amer Inc................. C 614 801-5193
   Grove City *(G-8948)*

▲ Safety Today Inc................................. E 614 409-7200
   Grove City *(G-8950)*

Skeye Wholesale Inc.............................. D 419 720-4440
   Maumee *(G-10766)*

Telarc International Corp....................... E 216 464-2313
   Beachwood *(G-843)*

TS Tech Americas Inc............................ C 740 593-5958
   Athens *(G-595)*

▲ TS Tech Americas Inc........................ B 614 575-4100
   Reynoldsburg *(G-12678)*

▲ Wcm Holdings Inc............................. C 513 705-2100
   Cincinnati *(G-3643)*

▲ West Chester Holdings LLC................ C 513 705-2100
   Cincinnati *(G-3655)*

Windy Hill Ltd Inc................................. D 216 391-4800
   Cleveland *(G-5150)*

51 WHOLESALE TRADE - NONDURABLE GOODS

5111 Printing and writing paper

Catalyst Paper (usa) Inc......................... E 937 528-3800
   Dayton *(G-7216)*

▲ Millcraft Group LLC........................... D 216 441-5500
   Independence *(G-9452)*

Millcraft Paper Company....................... E 614 675-4800
   Columbus *(G-6249)*

▲ Millcraft Paper Company................... D
   Independence *(G-9453)*

▲ Sabin Robbins LLC............................ C 513 874-5270
   West Chester *(G-14760)*

▲ Sterling Paper Co.............................. E 614 443-0303
   Columbus *(G-6718)*

◆ Veritiv Pubg & Print MGT Inc.............. E 614 288-0911
   Stow *(G-13400)*

5112 Stationery and office supplies

12985 Snow Holdings Inc....................... E 216 267-5000
   Cleveland *(G-3739)*

American Business Forms Inc................. E 513 312-2522
   West Chester *(G-14798)*

American Business Forms Inc................. E 614 664-0202
   Westerville *(G-14958)*

▲ AW Faber-Castell Usa Inc.................. D 216 643-4660
   Independence *(G-9408)*

▲ Dexxxon Digital Storage Inc.............. E 740 548-7179
   Lewis Center *(G-9817)*

EMI Enterprises Inc............................... E 419 666-0012
   Northwood *(G-11973)*

Essendant Co....................................... C 614 876-7774
   Columbus *(G-5829)*

Essendant Co....................................... E 330 650-9361
   Hudson *(G-9345)*

Essendant Co....................................... C 800 733-4091
   Twinsburg *(G-14188)*

Essendant Co....................................... E 330 425-7343
   Twinsburg *(G-14189)*

Essendant Co....................................... D 513 942-1354
   West Chester *(G-14810)*

Friends Service Co Inc.......................... D 419 427-1704
   Findlay *(G-8534)*

▲ GBS Corp... C 330 494-5330
   North Canton *(G-11833)*

Highland Computer Forms Inc................ D 937 393-4215
   Hillsboro *(G-9257)*

Indepndence Office Bus Sup Inc............. D 216 398-8880
   Cleveland *(G-4408)*

▲ Jbm Packaging Company................... C 513 933-8333
   Lebanon *(G-9770)*

Lake Business Products Inc.................... C 440 953-1199
   Highland Heights *(G-9168)*

Large & Loving Cards Inc...................... E 440 877-0261
   North Royalton *(G-11943)*

Med-Pass Incorporated......................... E 937 438-8884
   Dayton *(G-7476)*

Optimum System Products Inc............... E 614 885-4464
   Westerville *(G-15009)*

Pac Worldwide Corporation.................... E 800 535-0039
   Monroe *(G-11347)*

Pac Worldwide Holding Company............ E 513 217-3200
   Middletown *(G-11179)*

Pfg Ventures LP................................... D 216 520-8400
   Independence *(G-9466)*

Powell Company Inc............................. D 419 228-3552
   Lima *(G-9951)*

Proforma Inc.. C 800 825-1525
   Independence *(G-9472)*

Queen City Reprographics Inc................ E 513 326-2300
   Cincinnati *(G-3266)*

▼ Quick Tab II Inc................................ D 419 448-6622
   Tiffin *(G-13639)*

Reynolds and Reynolds Holdings............ E 937 485-8125
   Dayton *(G-7590)*

S P Richards Company.......................... E 614 497-2270
   Lockbourne *(G-10015)*

▲ Shamrock Companies Inc.................. D 440 899-9510
   Westlake *(G-15108)*

Staples Contract & Coml LLC................. E 740 845-5600
   London *(G-10051)*

W B Mason Co Inc............................... E 216 267-5000
   North Olmsted *(G-11918)*

◆ Wasserstrom Company....................... B 614 228-6525
   Columbus *(G-6867)*

Western States Envelope Co.................. E 419 666-7480
   Walbridge *(G-14468)*

Westrock Commercial LLC..................... E 419 476-9101
   Toledo *(G-14106)*

Wilmer.. E 419 678-6000
   Coldwater *(G-5221)*

5113 Industrial and personal service paper

Acorn Distributors Inc........................... E 614 294-6444
   Columbus *(G-5307)*

Adapt-A-Pak Inc.................................. E 937 845-0386
   Fairborn *(G-8365)*

Aetna Building Maintenance Inc............. C 937 324-5711
   Springfield *(G-13214)*

Alco-Chem Inc..................................... E 330 833-8551
   Canton *(G-1658)*

Apex Environmental Services L.............. C 513 772-2739
   Cincinnati *(G-2208)*

Avalon Foodservice Inc......................... C 330 854-4551
   Canal Fulton *(G-1592)*

Bath Bdy Wrks Lgstics Svcs LLC............. E 513 435-1643
   Groveport *(G-8974)*

▲ Bath Bdy Wrks Lgstics Svcs LLC......... C 614 415-7500
   Columbus *(G-5421)*

▲ Berk Enterprises Inc......................... D 330 369-1192
   Warren *(G-14506)*

▼ Buckeye Paper Co Inc....................... E 330 477-5925
   Canton *(G-1692)*

◆ Cleveland Supplyone Inc.................... E 216 514-7000
   Cleveland *(G-4068)*

Commerce Paper Company.................... E 419 241-9101
   Toledo *(G-13750)*

▲ Dazpak Flexible Packaging Corp......... C 614 252-2121
   Columbus *(G-5746)*

Espt Liquidation Inc.............................. D 330 698-4711
   Apple Creek *(G-450)*

Friendly Wholesale Co........................... E 724 224-6580
   Wooster *(G-15338)*

Gergelys Mint King Sups Svc In.............. E 440 244-4446
   Lorain *(G-10076)*

Gold Medal Products Co........................ E 614 228-1155
   Columbus *(G-5939)*

I Supply Co.. C 937 878-5240
   Fairborn *(G-8377)*

Kaleel Bros Inc.................................... D 330 758-0861
   Youngstown *(G-15644)*

Kellermeyer Company........................... D 419 255-3022
   Bowling Green *(G-1326)*

M Conley Company............................... D 330 456-8243
   Canton *(G-1798)*

▲ Mailender Inc................................... D 513 942-5453
   West Chester *(G-14728)*

▲ Millcraft Group LLC........................... D 216 441-5500
   Independence *(G-9452)*

Millcraft Paper Company....................... E 614 675-4800
   Columbus *(G-6249)*

▲ Millcraft Paper Company................... D
   Independence *(G-9453)*

Ohio Farmers Wholesale Dealers Inc....... D 216 391-9733
   Cleveland *(G-4688)*

▲ Peck Distributors Inc........................ E 216 587-6814
   Maple Heights *(G-10343)*

◆ Polymer Packaging Inc....................... D 330 832-2000
   North Canton *(G-11852)*

Precision Products Group Inc................. D 330 698-4711
   Apple Creek *(G-452)*

Procter & Gamble Distrg LLC................. B 513 626-2500
   Blue Ash *(G-1224)*

◆ Ranpak Corp..................................... C 440 354-4445
   Concord Township *(G-6934)*

Ricking Holding Co............................... E 513 825-3551
   Cleveland *(G-4839)*

Rvc Inc.. E 330 535-2211
   Akron *(G-291)*

Sofidel America Corp............................ C 740 500-1965
   Circleville *(G-3724)*

Sonoco Products Company.................... D 937 429-0040
   Beavercreek Township *(G-949)*

Sysco Cincinnati LLC............................ B 513 563-6300
   Cincinnati *(G-3430)*

Systems Pack Inc................................. E 330 467-5729
   Macedonia *(G-10207)*

The Cottingham Paper Co...................... E 614 294-6444
   Columbus *(G-6758)*

The Dean Supply Co............................. E 216 771-3300
   Cleveland *(G-4999)*

◆ TPC Packaging Solutions Inc.............. D 513 489-8840
   Cincinnati *(G-3499)*

▲ Trendco Supply Inc........................... E 513 752-1871
   Batavia *(G-750)*

Veritiv Operating Company.................... C 513 285-0999
   Fairfield *(G-8452)*

5122 Drugs, proprietaries, and sundries

Absolute Pharmacy Inc.......................... E 330 498-8200
   Canton *(G-1653)*

American Regent Inc............................ D 614 436-2222
   Hilliard *(G-9178)*

APS Acquisition LLC............................. E 513 719-2600
   Cincinnati *(G-2211)*

Basic Drugs Inc.................................... E 937 898-4010
   Vandalia *(G-14366)*

◆ Beautyavenues LLC........................... C 614 856-6000
   Reynoldsburg *(G-12654)*

Beiersdorf Inc...................................... C 513 682-7300
   West Chester *(G-14800)*

Boehringer Ingelheim Pharma................ C 216 525-0195
   Cleveland *(G-3879)*

◆ Boxout LLC....................................... C 833 462-7746
   Hudson *(G-9334)*

51 WHOLESALE TRADE - NONDURABLE GOODS

Braden Med Services Inc .... E 740 732-2356
 Caldwell *(G-1547)*
◆ Brothers Trading Co Inc .... C 937 746-1010
 Springboro *(G-13194)*
Capital Wholesale Drug Company .... D 614 297-8225
 Columbus *(G-5502)*
Cardinal Health Inc .... D 614 409-6770
 Groveport *(G-8976)*
Cardinal Health Inc .... E 614 497-9552
 Obetz *(G-12079)*
◆ Cardinal Health Inc .... A 614 757-5000
 Dublin *(G-7950)*
Cardinal Health 100 Inc .... B 614 757-5000
 Dublin *(G-7951)*
◆ Cardinal Health 200 LLC .... E 614 757-5000
 Dublin *(G-7953)*
Cardinal Health 201 Inc .... E 614 757-5000
 Dublin *(G-7954)*
▲ Cardinal Health 301 LLC .... A 614 757-5000
 Dublin *(G-7955)*
Cardinal Health Systems Inc .... A 513 874-5940
 West Chester *(G-14802)*
Cencora Inc .... E 610 727-7000
 Columbus *(G-5527)*
◆ Covetrus North America LLC ...... C 614 761-9095
 Dublin *(G-7975)*
▲ Discount Drug Mart Inc .... C 330 725-2340
 Medina *(G-10829)*
Elixir Pharmacy LLC .... C 330 491-4200
 North Canton *(G-11827)*
Evergreen Pharmaceutical LLC ..... B 513 719-2600
 Cincinnati *(G-2641)*
Evergreen Phrm Cal LLC .... E 513 719-2600
 Cincinnati *(G-2642)*
Firelands Tech Ventures LLC .... E 419 616-5115
 Huron *(G-9388)*
▲ Fredrics Corporation .... C 513 874-2226
 West Chester *(G-14695)*
▲ Gem Edwards Inc .... D 330 342-8300
 Hudson *(G-9352)*
Greenfield Hts Oper Group LLC ..... E 312 877-1153
 Lima *(G-9894)*
Heartland Healthcare Svcs LLC .... C 419 535-8435
 Toledo *(G-13842)*
▼ ICM Distributing Company Inc .... E 234 212-3030
 Twinsburg *(G-14196)*
ICP Inc .... D 419 447-6216
 Tiffin *(G-13628)*
Masters Drug Company Inc .... B 800 982-7922
 Lebanon *(G-9777)*
▲ Masters Pharmaceutical LLC ..... C 800 982-7922
 Mason *(G-10579)*
McKesson Corporation .... E 740 636-3500
 Wshngtn Ct Hs *(G-15490)*
McKesson Medical-Surgical Inc .... C 614 539-2600
 Urbancrest *(G-14321)*
Medpace Inc .... A 513 579-9911
 Cincinnati *(G-3031)*
▼ Merchandise Inc .... D 513 353-2200
 Miamitown *(G-11107)*
◆ Mitsubshi Intl Fd Ingrdnts Inc ...... E 614 652-1111
 Dublin *(G-8065)*
Ncs Healthcare LLC .... E 513 719-2600
 Cincinnati *(G-3101)*
Ncs Healthcare Inc .... A 216 514-3350
 Cleveland *(G-4630)*
▲ Nehemiah Manufacturing Co LLC .. D 513 351-5700
 Cincinnati *(G-3103)*
Neighborcare Inc .... A 513 719-2600
 Cincinnati *(G-3104)*
Omnicare LLC .... C 513 719-2600
 Cincinnati *(G-3157)*
Omnicare Distribution Ctr LLC ...... D 419 720-8200
 Cincinnati *(G-3158)*
Omnicare Pharmacies of The GP ... E 513 719-2600
 Cincinnati *(G-3159)*
Omnicare Phrm of Midwest LLC ... D 513 719-2600
 Cincinnati *(G-3160)*
Optum Infusion Svcs 550 LLC ...... D 866 442-4679
 Cincinnati *(G-3166)*
Optumrx Home Delivery Ohio LLC .. D 440 930-5520
 Avon Lake *(G-682)*
Orveon Global US LLC .... B 614 348-4994
 Columbus *(G-6482)*
Pantherx Specialty LLC .... E 855 726-8479
 Canfield *(G-1637)*
Pharmed Corporation .... D 440 250-5400
 Westlake *(G-15097)*
Pharmscript LLC .... D 908 389-1818
 Columbus *(G-6521)*
Prescription Supply Inc .... D 419 661-6600
 Northwood *(G-11982)*
Procter & Gamble Distrg LLC .... B 513 626-2500
 Blue Ash *(G-1224)*
Remedi Seniorcare of Ohio LLC ... E 800 232-4239
 Troy *(G-14155)*
Riser Foods Company .... D 216 292-7000
 Bedford Heights *(G-1001)*
◆ Robert J Matthews Company ..... D 330 834-3000
 Massillon *(G-10664)*
Rxcrossroads 3pl LLC .... C 866 447-9758
 Mason *(G-10604)*
Samuels Products Inc .... E 513 891-4456
 Blue Ash *(G-1239)*
Second Wind Vitamins Inc .... E 330 336-9260
 Wadsworth *(G-14451)*
Specialized Pharmacy Svcs LLC .. E 513 719-2600
 Cincinnati *(G-3396)*
Sysco Guest Supply LLC .... E 614 539-9348
 Urbancrest *(G-14323)*
Teva Womens Health LLC .... C 513 731-9900
 Cincinnati *(G-3460)*
▲ Triplefin LLC .... D 855 877-5346
 Mason *(G-10621)*
WA Butler Company .... E 614 761-9095
 Dublin *(G-8159)*
Walter F Stephens Jr Inc .... E 937 746-0521
 Franklin *(G-8652)*

5131 Piece goods and notions

▲ Checker Notions Company Inc .. C 419 893-3636
 Maumee *(G-10710)*
▲ Custom Products Corporation ... D 440 528-7100
 Solon *(G-13080)*
Everfast Inc .... E 614 789-0900
 Dublin *(G-8008)*
▲ Miami Corporation .... E 800 543-0448
 Cincinnati *(G-3054)*
Style-Line Incorporated .... E 614 291-0600
 Columbus *(G-6725)*
Welspun Usa Inc .... E 614 945-5100
 Grove City *(G-8966)*

5136 Men's and boy's clothing

◆ Abercrombie & Fitch Trading Co .. D 614 283-6500
 New Albany *(G-11551)*
▲ Alsico Usa Inc .... D 330 673-7413
 Kent *(G-9557)*
◆ Barbs Graffiti Inc .... E 216 881-5550
 Cleveland *(G-3849)*
◆ Cintas Corporation No 1 .... A 513 459-1200
 Mason *(G-10533)*
Cintas Sales Corporation .... B 513 459-1200
 Cincinnati *(G-2445)*
◆ For Women Like Me Inc .... E 407 848-7339
 Chagrin Falls *(G-1958)*
Gymnastics World Inc .... E 440 526-2970
 Cleveland *(G-4343)*
▲ J Peterman Company LLC .... E 888 647-2555
 Blue Ash *(G-1189)*
JP Outfitters LLC .... E 513 745-1137
 Blue Ash *(G-1192)*
▲ K Amalia Enterprises Inc .... E 614 733-3800
 Plain City *(G-12483)*
Legend .... D 216 534-1541
 Cleveland *(G-4488)*
▼ Lion-Vallen Ltd Partnership ...... C 937 898-1949
 Dayton *(G-7458)*
◆ MII Brand Import LLC .... C 614 256-7267
 Reynoldsburg *(G-12670)*
▲ Profill Holdings LLC .... A 513 742-4000
 Cincinnati *(G-3247)*
▲ R G Barry Corporation .... A 614 864-6400
 Pickerington *(G-12408)*
Safety Solutions Inc .... D 614 799-9900
 Columbus *(G-6634)*
Walter F Stephens Jr Inc .... E 937 746-0521
 Franklin *(G-8652)*
▲ West Chester Holdings LLC ..... C 513 705-2100
 Cincinnati *(G-3655)*

5137 Women's and children's clothing

1 Natural Way LLC .... E 888 977-2229
 Maumee *(G-10682)*
◆ Abercrombie & Fitch Trading Co .. D 614 283-6500
 New Albany *(G-11551)*
◆ Atrium Buying Corporation .... D 740 966-8200
 Blacklick *(G-1110)*
▲ Barbs Graffiti Inc .... E 216 881-5550
 Cleveland *(G-3849)*
◆ Cintas Corporation No 1 .... A 513 459-1200
 Mason *(G-10533)*
Cintas Corporation No 2 .... D 800 444-2687
 Vandalia *(G-14370)*
Cintas Sales Corporation .... B 513 459-1200
 Cincinnati *(G-2445)*
◆ For Women Like Me Inc .... E 407 848-7339
 Chagrin Falls *(G-1958)*
Gymnastics World Inc .... E 440 526-2970
 Cleveland *(G-4343)*
▲ J Peterman Company LLC .... E 888 647-2555
 Blue Ash *(G-1189)*
▼ Lion-Vallen Ltd Partnership ...... C 937 898-1949
 Dayton *(G-7458)*
Lululemon USA Inc .... E 440 250-0415
 Westlake *(G-15078)*
◆ MII Brand Import LLC .... C 614 256-7267
 Reynoldsburg *(G-12670)*
◆ Philips Med Systems Clvland In .. B 440 483-3000
 Cleveland *(G-4746)*
Procter & Gamble Distrg LLC .... B 513 626-2500
 Blue Ash *(G-1224)*
▲ Profill Holdings LLC .... A 513 742-4000
 Cincinnati *(G-3247)*
▲ R G Barry Corporation .... A 614 864-6400
 Pickerington *(G-12408)*
Sugar & Spice Spa llc .... D 513 319-0112
 Mason *(G-10612)*
▲ TSC Apparel LLC .... D 800 289-5400
 Cincinnati *(G-3534)*
▲ West Chester Holdings LLC ..... C 513 705-2100
 Cincinnati *(G-3655)*

5139 Footwear

▲ Drew Ventures Inc .... E 740 653-4271
 Lancaster *(G-9708)*

SIC SECTION

51 WHOLESALE TRADE - NONDURABLE GOODS

Ebuys Inc .... E 858 831-0839
  Columbus *(G-5803)*
Georgia-Boot Inc .... D 740 753-1951
  Nelsonville *(G-11545)*
◆ Lehigh Outfitters LLC .... C 740 753-1951
  Nelsonville *(G-11549)*
▲ R G Barry Corporation .... A 614 864-6400
  Pickerington *(G-12408)*
Safety Solutions Inc .... D 614 799-9900
  Columbus *(G-6634)*
US Footwear Holdings LLC .... C 740 753-9100
  Nelsonville *(G-11550)*

5141 Groceries, general line

Albert Guarnieri & Co .... D 330 794-9834
  Hudson *(G-9328)*
Anderson and Dubose Inc .... D 440 248-8800
  Warren *(G-14499)*
Artwall LLC .... E 216 476-0635
  Cleveland *(G-3836)*
Atlantic Fish & Distrg Co .... E 330 454-1307
  Canton *(G-1673)*
Brothers Trading Co Inc .... E 937 746-1010
  Springboro *(G-13195)*
◆ Brothers Trading Co Inc .... C 937 746-1010
  Springboro *(G-13194)*
Cantrell Oil Company .... E 937 695-8003
  Winchester *(G-15286)*
Comber Holdings Inc .... E 216 961-8600
  Cleveland *(G-4090)*
Empire Food Brokers Inc .... E 614 889-2322
  Dublin *(G-8003)*
Euclid Fish Company .... D 440 951-6448
  Mentor *(G-10938)*
Food Sample Express LLc .... D 330 225-3550
  Brunswick *(G-1456)*
Foxtail Foods LLC .... A 973 582-4613
  Fairfield *(G-8415)*
Generative Growth II LLC .... B 419 422-8090
  Findlay *(G-8537)*
Giant Eagle Inc .... C 412 968-5300
  Columbus *(G-5933)*
Gummer Wholesale Inc .... D 740 928-0415
  Heath *(G-9133)*
Impact Sales Inc .... D 937 274-1905
  Dayton *(G-7419)*
J M Sealts Company .... E 419 224-8075
  Blue Ash *(G-1188)*
◆ John Zidian Co Inc .... E 330 743-6050
  Youngstown *(G-15642)*
Krlp Inc .... A 513 762-4000
  Cincinnati *(G-2953)*
Larosas Inc .... A 513 347-5660
  Cincinnati *(G-2966)*
Mattingly Foods Inc .... C 740 454-0136
  Zanesville *(G-15811)*
McLane Foodservice Dist Inc .... C 614 771-9660
  Columbus *(G-6217)*
McLane Foodservice Dist Inc .... C 614 662-7700
  Lockbourne *(G-10012)*
Mondelez Global LLC .... E 513 714-0308
  West Chester *(G-14734)*
Mpf Sales and Mktg Group LLC .... C 513 793-6241
  Blue Ash *(G-1213)*
Novelart Manufacturing Company .... D 513 351-7700
  Cincinnati *(G-3132)*
Queensgate Food Group LLC .... D 513 721-5503
  Cincinnati *(G-3269)*
R G Sellers Company .... E 937 299-1545
  Moraine *(G-11432)*
▲ R S Hanline and Co Inc .... C 419 347-8077
  Shelby *(G-13010)*

Ricking Holding Co .... E 513 825-3551
  Cleveland *(G-4839)*
Riser Foods Company .... D 216 292-7000
  Bedford Heights *(G-1001)*
Sommers Market LLC .... D 330 352-7470
  Hartville *(G-9130)*
▲ Sygma Network Inc .... C 614 734-2500
  Dublin *(G-8137)*
Sygma Network Inc .... B 614 771-3801
  Columbus *(G-6740)*
Sysco Central Ohio Inc .... B
  Columbus *(G-6743)*
Sysco Cleveland Inc .... A 216 201-3000
  Cleveland *(G-4973)*
Tasty Pure Food Company .... E 330 434-8141
  Akron *(G-329)*
The Chas G Buchy Packing Company ... E
  Cincinnati *(G-3462)*
The Ellenbee-Leggett Company Inc ..... C 513 874-3200
  Fairfield *(G-8446)*
The H T Hackney Co .... E 614 751-5100
  Gahanna *(G-8733)*
▼ Tusco Grocers Inc .... D 740 922-8721
  Dennison *(G-7859)*
US Foods Inc .... E 330 963-6789
  Twinsburg *(G-14227)*
US Foods Inc .... E 614 539-7993
  West Chester *(G-14843)*
Valley Wholesale Foods Inc .... E 740 354-5216
  Portsmouth *(G-12581)*
Vendors Supply Inc .... E 513 755-2111
  West Chester *(G-14790)*

5142 Packaged frozen goods

A To Z Portion Ctrl Meats Inc .... E 419 358-2926
  Bluffton *(G-1276)*
Anderson and Dubose Inc .... D 440 248-8800
  Warren *(G-14499)*
Avalon Foodservice Inc .... C 330 854-4551
  Canal Fulton *(G-1592)*
Blue Ribbon Meats Inc .... D 216 631-8850
  Cleveland *(G-3875)*
Catanzaro Frank J Sons Dghters .... D 800 827-4020
  Cincinnati *(G-2321)*
Euclid Fish Company .... D 440 951-6448
  Mentor *(G-10938)*
Hillcrest Egg & Cheese Co .... D 216 361-4625
  Cleveland *(G-4363)*
J M Sealts Company .... E 419 224-8075
  Blue Ash *(G-1188)*
Kaleel Bros Inc .... D 330 758-0861
  Youngstown *(G-15644)*
King Kold Inc .... E 937 836-2731
  Englewood *(G-8311)*
Lori Holding Co .... E 740 342-3230
  New Lexington *(G-11628)*
Mattingly Foods Inc .... C 740 454-0136
  Zanesville *(G-15811)*
Northern Frozen Foods Inc .... C 440 439-0600
  Cleveland *(G-4664)*
▲ Peck Distributors Inc .... E 216 587-6814
  Maple Heights *(G-10343)*
Powell Company Inc .... D 419 228-3552
  Lima *(G-9951)*
Produce One Inc .... D 931 253-4749
  Dayton *(G-7569)*
Ritchies Food Distributors Inc .... E 740 443-6303
  Piketon *(G-12429)*
Swd Corporation .... E 419 227-2436
  Lima *(G-9968)*
Sysco Central Ohio Inc .... B
  Columbus *(G-6743)*

Tasty Pure Food Company .... E 330 434-8141
  Akron *(G-329)*
The Ellenbee-Leggett Company Inc ..... C 513 874-3200
  Fairfield *(G-8446)*
US Foods Inc .... E 614 539-7993
  West Chester *(G-14843)*
◆ White Castle System Inc .... B 614 228-5781
  Columbus *(G-6883)*

5143 Dairy products, except dried or canned

Austintown Dairy Inc .... E 330 629-6170
  Youngstown *(G-15553)*
Bfc Inc .... E 330 364-6645
  Dover *(G-7873)*
Borden Dairy Co Cincinnati LLC .... E 513 948-8811
  Cleveland *(G-3881)*
Catanzaro Frank J Sons Dghters .... D 800 827-4020
  Cincinnati *(G-2321)*
Cheese Holdings Inc .... E 330 893-2479
  Millersburg *(G-11275)*
Coblentz Distributing Inc .... C 330 893-3895
  Millersburg *(G-11277)*
Euclid Fish Company .... D 440 951-6448
  Mentor *(G-10938)*
Giant Eagle Inc .... C 412 968-5300
  Columbus *(G-5933)*
◆ Great Lakes Cheese Co Inc .... B 440 834-2500
  Hiram *(G-9274)*
▲ Hans Rothenbuhler & Son Inc .... E 440 632-6000
  Middlefield *(G-11140)*
Hillcrest Egg & Cheese Co .... D 216 361-4625
  Cleveland *(G-4363)*
Instantwhip-Akron Inc .... E 614 488-2536
  Stow *(G-13377)*
Instantwhip-Columbus Inc .... E 614 871-9447
  Grove City *(G-8928)*
Johnsons Real Ice Cream LLC .... C 614 231-0014
  Columbus *(G-6095)*
Lori Holding Co .... E 740 342-3230
  New Lexington *(G-11628)*
S and S Gilardi Inc .... D 740 397-2751
  Mount Vernon *(G-11507)*
Sysco Cincinnati LLC .... B 513 563-6300
  Cincinnati *(G-3430)*
United Dairy Farmers Inc .... C 513 396-8700
  Cincinnati *(G-3553)*
US Foods Inc .... E 614 539-7993
  West Chester *(G-14843)*
Velvet Ice Cream Company .... E 419 562-2009
  Bucyrus *(G-1519)*
▲ Weaver Bros Inc .... D 937 526-3907
  Versailles *(G-14417)*

5144 Poultry and poultry products

▼ Ballas Egg Products Corp .... D 614 453-0386
  Zanesville *(G-15769)*
Bfc Inc .... E 330 364-6645
  Dover *(G-7873)*
Borden Dairy Co Cincinnati LLC .... E 513 948-8811
  Cleveland *(G-3881)*
Catanzaro Frank J Sons Dghters .... D 800 827-4020
  Cincinnati *(G-2321)*
Cooper Hatchery Inc .... E 419 375-5800
  Fort Recovery *(G-8607)*
Euclid Fish Company .... D 440 951-6448
  Mentor *(G-10938)*
Hartford Farms LLC .... A 740 893-7200
  Croton *(G-7030)*
Hillcrest Egg & Cheese Co .... D 216 361-4625
  Cleveland *(G-4363)*
Michaels Finer Meats LLC .... C 614 527-4900
  Columbus *(G-6231)*

Employee Codes: A=Over 500 employees, B=251-500
C=101-250, D=51-100, E=20-50, F=10-19, G=1-9

51 WHOLESALE TRADE - NONDURABLE GOODS

Ohio Farmers Wholesale Dealers Inc......... D 216 391-9733
   Cleveland *(G-4688)*

Ohio Fresh Eggs LLC..................................C 740 499-2352
   La Rue *(G-9648)*

R W Sauder Inc... D 330 359-5440
   Winesburg *(G-15290)*

Sherwood Food Distributors LLC............... D 216 662-8000
   Maple Heights *(G-10346)*

Sysco Cincinnati LLC................................ B 513 563-6300
   Cincinnati *(G-3430)*

5145 Confectionery

Albert Guarnieri & Co................................. D 330 794-9834
   Hudson *(G-9328)*

▲ Bendon Inc... D 419 207-3600
   Ashland *(G-482)*

Bloomer Candy Co....................................C 740 452-7501
   Zanesville *(G-15771)*

Cju Enterprises Inc................................... D 330 493-1800
   Canton *(G-1710)*

Friendly Wholesale Co...............................E 724 224-6580
   Wooster *(G-15338)*

Frito-Lay North America Inc......................E 216 491-4000
   Cleveland *(G-4292)*

Frito-Lay North America Inc......................E 614 508-3004
   Columbus *(G-5899)*

Gold Medal Products Co............................E 614 228-1155
   Columbus *(G-5939)*

◆ Gold Medal Products Co......................... B 513 769-7676
   Cincinnati *(G-2739)*

Gorant Chocolatier LLC............................C 330 726-8821
   Boardman *(G-1288)*

Gummer Wholesale Inc............................. D 740 928-0415
   Heath *(G-9133)*

▲ Hayden Valley Foods Inc....................... D 614 539-7233
   Urbancrest *(G-14320)*

JE Carsten Company................................E 330 794-4440
   Hudson *(G-9359)*

◆ Jml Holdings Inc....................................E 419 866-7500
   Holland *(G-9291)*

Jones Potato Chip Co...............................E 419 529-9424
   Mansfield *(G-10276)*

Lobby Shoppes Inc....................................C 937 324-0002
   Springfield *(G-13263)*

Mike-Sells Potato Chip Co.........................E 937 228-9400
   Dayton *(G-7504)*

Mike-Sells West Virginia Inc...................... D 937 228-9400
   Dayton *(G-7505)*

Multi-Flow Dispensers Ohio Inc................. D 216 641-0200
   Brooklyn Heights *(G-1425)*

Novelart Manufacturing Company............. D 513 351-7700
   Cincinnati *(G-3132)*

Ohio Hckry Hrvest Brnd Pdts In.................E 330 644-6266
   Coventry Township *(G-7014)*

◆ Shearers Foods LLC...............................A 800 428-6843
   Massillon *(G-10669)*

Shearers Foods Phoenix LLC...................E 330 834-4330
   Massillon *(G-10670)*

Tarrier Foods Corp....................................E 614 876-8594
   Columbus *(G-6749)*

5146 Fish and seafoods

101 River Inc...E 440 352-6343
   Grand River *(G-8848)*

Michaels Finer Meats LLC........................C 614 527-4900
   Columbus *(G-6231)*

Ohio Farmers Wholesale Dealers Inc......... D 216 391-9733
   Cleveland *(G-4688)*

Omegasea Ltd Liability Co........................E 440 639-2372
   Painesville *(G-12240)*

Riser Foods Company.............................. D 216 292-7000
   Bedford Heights *(G-1001)*

Ritchies Food Distributors Inc....................E 740 443-6303
   Piketon *(G-12429)*

Sherwood Food Distributors LLC............... D 216 662-8000
   Maple Heights *(G-10346)*

5147 Meats and meat products

Blue Ribbon Meats Inc............................. D 216 631-8850
   Cleveland *(G-3875)*

Carfagnas Incorporated.............................E 614 846-6340
   Columbus *(G-5248)*

Catanzaro Frank J Sons Dghters............... D 800 827-4020
   Cincinnati *(G-2321)*

Cheese Holdings Inc.................................E 330 893-2479
   Millersburg *(G-11275)*

Dutch Creek Foods Inc..............................E 330 852-2631
   Sugarcreek *(G-13509)*

Empire Packing Company LP.................... D 513 942-5400
   West Chester *(G-14809)*

Frank Brunckhorst Co LLC........................C 614 662-5300
   Groveport *(G-8989)*

◆ Fresh Mark Inc....................................... B 330 832-7491
   Massillon *(G-10641)*

Giant Eagle Inc..C 412 968-5300
   Columbus *(G-5933)*

Harvest Sherwood Fd Distrs Inc................ B 216 662-8000
   Maple Heights *(G-10339)*

Hillcrest Egg & Cheese Co........................ D 216 361-4625
   Cleveland *(G-4363)*

Landes Fresh Meats Inc............................E 937 836-3613
   Clayton *(G-3734)*

Lori Holding Co..E 740 342-3230
   New Lexington *(G-11628)*

Michaels Finer Meats LLC........................C 614 527-4900
   Columbus *(G-6231)*

Northern Frozen Foods Inc........................C 440 439-0600
   Cleveland *(G-4664)*

Ohio Farmers Wholesale Dealers Inc......... D 216 391-9733
   Cleveland *(G-4688)*

Produce One Inc....................................... D 931 253-4749
   Dayton *(G-7569)*

Ritchies Food Distributors Inc....................E 740 443-6303
   Piketon *(G-12429)*

S and S Gilardi Inc.................................... D 740 397-2751
   Mount Vernon *(G-11507)*

Sherwood Food Distributors LLC............... D 216 662-8000
   Maple Heights *(G-10346)*

Smithfield Direct LLC................................C 216 267-6196
   Brookpark *(G-1439)*

Smithfield Direct LLC................................ D 419 422-2233
   Findlay *(G-8584)*

Smithfield Direct LLC................................C 614 539-9600
   Grove City *(G-8955)*

Tasty Pure Food Company........................E 330 434-8141
   Akron *(G-329)*

The Ellenbee-Leggett Company Inc...........C 513 874-3200
   Fairfield *(G-8446)*

Weilands Fine Meats Inc...........................E 614 267-9910
   Columbus *(G-6873)*

Winner Corporation...................................E 419 582-4321
   Yorkshire *(G-15538)*

5148 Fresh fruits and vegetables

Al Peake & Sons Inc..................................E 419 243-9284
   Toledo *(G-13677)*

Anselmo Rssis Premier Prod Ltd................E 800 229-5517
   Cleveland *(G-3818)*

Bfc Inc..E 330 364-6645
   Dover *(G-7873)*

Catanzaro Frank J Sons Dghters............... D 800 827-4020
   Cincinnati *(G-2321)*

Cecil T Brinager....................................... D 740 843-5280
   Portland *(G-12542)*

Chefs Garden Inc......................................C 419 433-4947
   Huron *(G-9385)*

Dno Inc... D 614 231-3601
   Columbus *(G-5779)*

Dole Fresh Vegetables Inc........................C 937 525-4300
   Springfield *(G-13248)*

Freshedge LLC.. D 330 298-2222
   Ravenna *(G-12626)*

Freshway Foods Company Inc.................. D 937 498-4664
   Sidney *(G-13034)*

Giant Eagle Inc..C 412 968-5300
   Columbus *(G-5933)*

Hillcrest Egg & Cheese Co........................ D 216 361-4625
   Cleveland *(G-4363)*

Jao Distributors Inc................................... D 513 531-6000
   Cincinnati *(G-2900)*

Kaleel Bros Inc.. D 330 758-0861
   Youngstown *(G-15644)*

Midwest Fresh Foods Inc..........................E 614 469-1492
   Columbus *(G-6243)*

Miles Farmers Market Inc.........................C 440 248-5222
   Solon *(G-13111)*

Powell Company Inc.................................E 419 228-3552
   Lima *(G-9951)*

Produce One Inc....................................... D 931 253-4749
   Dayton *(G-7569)*

Produce Packaging Inc..............................C 216 391-6129
   Willoughby Hills *(G-15234)*

Roth Produce Co......................................E 614 337-2825
   Columbus *(G-6613)*

Sanfillipo Produce Co Inc..........................E 614 237-3300
   Columbus *(G-6642)*

Stv Holdings Inc..C 419 668-4857
   Norwalk *(G-12028)*

The Sanson Company............................... D 216 431-8560
   Cleveland *(G-5006)*

US Foods Inc..E 614 539-7993
   West Chester *(G-14843)*

5149 Groceries and related products, nec

Alfred Nickles Bakery Inc..........................E 216 267-8055
   Cleveland *(G-3786)*

American Bottling Company......................C 614 237-4201
   Columbus *(G-5346)*

▲ Antonio Sofo Son Importing Co..............C 419 476-4211
   Toledo *(G-13690)*

▲ Atlantic Foods Corp............................... D 513 772-3535
   Cincinnati *(G-2227)*

Avalon Foodservice Inc.............................C 330 854-4551
   Canal Fulton *(G-1592)*

Bagel Place Inc...E 419 537-9377
   Toledo *(G-13698)*

Bakemark USA LLC................................. D 513 870-0880
   Fairfield *(G-8391)*

▲ Bendon Inc... D 419 207-3600
   Ashland *(G-482)*

Boston Company Inc.................................A 937 652-0410
   Urbana *(G-14298)*

◆ Brothers Trading Co Inc.........................C 937 746-1010
   Springboro *(G-13194)*

Busken Bakery Inc.................................... D 513 871-2114
   Cincinnati *(G-2294)*

Cassanos Inc..E 937 294-8400
   Dayton *(G-7215)*

Catanzaro Frank J Sons Dghters............... D 800 827-4020
   Cincinnati *(G-2321)*

Central Coca-Cola Btlg Co Inc...................C 419 476-6622
   Toledo *(G-13727)*

Cerelia USA Bakery Inc.............................E 614 471-9994
   Whitehall *(G-15136)*

Cheese Holdings Inc.................................E 330 893-2479
   Millersburg *(G-11275)*

51 WHOLESALE TRADE - NONDURABLE GOODS

Cju Enterprises Inc .... D 330 493-1800
  Canton (G-1710)
Coffee Break Corporation .... E 513 841-1100
  Cincinnati (G-2468)
Dayton Heidelberg Distrg Co .... B 937 220-6450
  Moraine (G-11401)
Distillata Company .... D 216 771-2900
  Cleveland (G-4167)
Ditsch Usa LLC .... E 513 782-8888
  Cincinnati (G-2568)
Dutchman Hospitality Group Inc .... C 614 873-3414
  Plain City (G-12474)
▲ Esber Beverage Company .... E 330 456-4361
  Canton (G-1750)
▲ Euro Usa Inc .... D 216 714-0500
  Cleveland (G-4224)
Flowers Baking Co Ohio LLC .... E 419 661-2586
  Northwood (G-11974)
Frito-Lay North America Inc .... E 216 491-4000
  Cleveland (G-4292)
G & J Pepsi-Cola Bottlers Inc .... E 740 593-3366
  Athens (G-568)
G & J Pepsi-Cola Bottlers Inc .... B 740 354-9191
  Franklin Furnace (G-8654)
G & J Pepsi-Cola Bottlers Inc .... E 740 354-9191
  Zanesville (G-15788)
Griffin Industries LLC .... E 419 257-3560
  North Baltimore (G-11800)
▲ Hayden Valley Foods Inc .... D 614 539-7233
  Urbancrest (G-14320)
Hillcrest Egg & Cheese Co .... D 216 361-4625
  Cleveland (G-4363)
Interbake Foods LLC .... C 614 294-4931
  Columbus (G-6064)
JM Smucker LLC .... D 330 682-3000
  Orrville (G-12169)
Jo-Ann Stores LLC .... E 419 621-8101
  Sandusky (G-12906)
Kaleel Bros Inc .... D 330 758-0861
  Youngstown (G-15644)
Kerry Inc .... E 760 685-2548
  Byesville (G-1535)
Kinetic Nutrition Group LLC .... E 513 279-8966
  Cincinnati (G-2940)
Klosterman Baking Co LLC .... D 513 242-5667
  Cincinnati (G-2944)
▲ Lajd Warehousing & Leasing Inc .... D 330 452-5010
  Canton (G-1793)
Luxfer Magtech Inc .... E 513 772-3066
  Cincinnati (G-2995)
M & M Wine Cellar Inc .... D 330 536-6450
  Lowellville (G-10170)
Made From Scratch Inc .... D 614 873-3444
  Plain City (G-12484)
Magnetic Springs Water Company .... D 614 421-1780
  Columbus (G-6189)
Marzetti Manufacturing Company .... C 856 205-1485
  Westerville (G-14908)
Mattingly Foods Inc .... C 740 454-0136
  Zanesville (G-15811)
Mondelez Global LLC .... E 330 626-6500
  Streetsboro (G-13423)
Mondelez Global LLC .... D 419 691-5200
  Toledo (G-13927)
Mondelez Global LLC .... E 513 714-0308
  West Chester (G-14734)
▲ More Than Gourmet Holdings Inc ...... E 330 762-6652
  Akron (G-237)
Morton Salt Inc .... C 330 925-3015
  Rittman (G-12731)
▲ National Foods Packaging Inc .... E 216 622-2740
  Cleveland (G-4626)

National Marketshare Group .... E 513 921-0800
  Cincinnati (G-3095)
Northern Frozen Foods Inc .... C 440 439-0600
  Cleveland (G-4664)
Ohio Farmers Wholesale Dealers Inc .... D 216 391-9733
  Cleveland (G-4688)
Ohio Hckry Hrvest Brnd Pdts In .... E 330 644-6266
  Coventry Township (G-7014)
Ohio Pizza Products LLC .... D 937 294-6969
  Monroe (G-11346)
Osmans Pies Inc .... E 330 607-9083
  Stow (G-13384)
P & S Bakery Inc .... E 330 707-4141
  Youngstown (G-15687)
▲ Peck Distributors Inc .... E 216 587-6814
  Maple Heights (G-10343)
Pepsi-Cola Metro Btlg Co Inc .... E 937 461-4664
  Dayton (G-7549)
Pepsi-Cola Metro Btlg Co Inc .... C 330 425-8236
  Twinsburg (G-14213)
Powell Company Inc .... D 419 228-3552
  Lima (G-9951)
Procter & Gamble Distrg LLC .... B 513 626-2500
  Blue Ash (G-1224)
Produce One Inc .... D 931 253-4749
  Dayton (G-7569)
▲ R L Lipton Distributing Co .... D 216 475-4150
  Cleveland (G-4805)
Rdp Foodservice Ltd .... D 614 261-5661
  Hilliard (G-9228)
Ritchies Food Distributors Inc .... E 740 443-6303
  Piketon (G-12429)
Servatii Inc .... D 513 271-5040
  Cincinnati (G-3362)
Skallys Old World Bakery Inc .... E 513 931-1411
  Cincinnati (G-3382)
◆ Skidmore Sales & Distrg Co Inc .... E 513 755-4200
  West Chester (G-14766)
▲ Skyline Cem Holdings LLC .... C 513 874-1188
  Fairfield (G-8441)
Superior Beverage Group Ltd .... C 419 529-0702
  Lexington (G-9845)
Sysco Cincinnati LLC .... B 513 563-6300
  Cincinnati (G-3430)
Tarrier Foods Corp .... E 614 876-8594
  Columbus (G-6749)
The Dean Supply Co .... E 216 771-3300
  Cleveland (G-4999)
Tiffin Paper Company .... E 419 447-2121
  Tiffin (G-13647)
Tony Packos Toledo LLC .... E 419 691-6054
  Maumee (G-10775)
US Foods Inc .... C 216 475-7400
  Cleveland (G-5092)
US Foods Inc .... C 513 874-3900
  Fairfield (G-8451)
US Foods Inc .... E 330 963-6789
  Twinsburg (G-14227)
US Foods Inc .... E 614 539-7993
  West Chester (G-14843)
WA Butler Company .... E 614 761-9095
  Dublin (G-8159)
◆ Wine-Art of Ohio Inc .... E 330 678-7733
  Kent (G-9607)

5153 Grain and field beans

Andersons Inc .... C 419 893-5050
  Maumee (G-10692)
◆ Andersons Agriculture Group LP .... E 419 893-5050
  Maumee (G-10694)
Bunge North America East LLC .... A 419 692-6010
  Delphos (G-7837)

Champion Feed and Pet Sup LLC .... E 740 369-3020
  Granville (G-8851)
Consolidated Grain & Barge Co .... E 513 244-7400
  Cincinnati (G-2495)
Cooper Hatchery Inc .... C 419 594-3325
  Oakwood (G-12053)
Deerfield AG Services Inc .... D 330 584-4715
  Massillon (G-10637)
Deerfield Farms Service Inc .... D 330 584-4715
  Deerfield (G-7741)
Fort Recovery Equity Inc .... C 419 942-1148
  Fort Recovery (G-8608)
Fort Recovery Equity Inc .... E 419 375-4119
  Fort Recovery (G-8609)
Hanby Farms Inc .... E 740 763-3554
  Nashport (G-11535)
Heritage Cooperative Inc .... E 330 533-5551
  Canfield (G-1630)
Heritage Cooperative Inc .... E 877 240-4393
  Delaware (G-7804)
Mid-Wood Inc .... E 419 937-2233
  Bascom (G-725)
Milky Acres LLC .... E 419 561-1364
  Sycamore (G-13532)
Minster Farmers Coop Exch .... D 419 628-4705
  Minster (G-11319)
The Andersons Marathon Ethanol LLC .. E 937 316-3700
  Greenville (G-8887)
Trupointe Cooperative Inc .... B 937 575-6780
  Piqua (G-12459)

5154 Livestock

Hord Livestock Company Inc .... E 419 562-0277
  Bucyrus (G-1509)
Mt Hope Auction Inc .... E 330 674-6188
  Mount Hope (G-11467)
United Producers Inc .... D 614 433-2150
  Columbus (G-6813)
Winner Corporation .... E 419 582-4321
  Yorkshire (G-15538)

5162 Plastics materials and basic shapes

Alro Steel Corporation .... E 614 878-7271
  Columbus (G-5340)
Alro Steel Corporation .... D 419 720-5300
  Toledo (G-13679)
▲ American Plastics Inc .... D 330 945-4100
  Akron (G-48)
◆ Avient Corporation .... D 440 930-1000
  Avon Lake (G-672)
▲ Checker Notions Company Inc .... C 419 893-3636
  Maumee (G-10710)
◆ Cleveland Supplyone Inc .... E 216 514-7000
  Cleveland (G-4068)
Curbell Plastics Inc .... E 513 742-9898
  Cincinnati (G-2524)
Epsilyte Holdings LLC .... D 937 778-9500
  Piqua (G-12441)
Hexpol Compounding LLC .... C 440 834-4644
  Burton (G-1528)
HP Manufacturing Company Inc .... D 216 361-6500
  Cleveland (G-4386)
◆ Network Polymers Inc .... E 330 773-2700
  Akron (G-241)
Plastics Family Holdings Inc .... E 330 733-9595
  Stow (G-13385)
Plastics R Unique Inc .... E 330 334-4820
  Wadsworth (G-14448)
◆ Polymer Packaging Inc .... D 330 832-2000
  North Canton (G-11852)
Queen City Polymers Inc .... E 513 779-0990
  West Chester (G-14752)

51 WHOLESALE TRADE - NONDURABLE GOODS

Skybox Packaging LLC................................C 419 525-7209
Mansfield *(G-10317)*

Tahoma Enterprises Inc.............................D 330 745-9016
Barberton *(G-714)*

▼ Tahoma Rubber & Plastics Inc...............D 330 745-9016
Barberton *(G-715)*

United States Plastic Corp.........................D 419 228-2242
Lima *(G-9976)*

5169 Chemicals and allied products, nec

Airgas Inc..D 937 222-8312
Moraine *(G-11388)*

Airgas Usa LLC...B 216 642-6600
Independence *(G-9399)*

◆ Akrochem Corporation...............................D 330 535-2100
Akron *(G-19)*

Anatrace Products LLC..............................E 800 252-1280
Maumee *(G-10691)*

▲ Applied Indus Tech - Dixie Inc..................D 216 426-4546
Cleveland *(G-3826)*

▲ Applied Industrial Tech Inc.......................B 216 426-4000
Cleveland *(G-3827)*

Ashland Chemco Inc...................................D 614 232-8510
Columbus *(G-5393)*

Ashland Chemco Inc...................................C 614 790-3333
Columbus *(G-5394)*

Avalon Foodservice Inc..............................C 330 854-4551
Canal Fulton *(G-1592)*

▲ Bonded Chemicals Inc...............................E 614 777-9240
Columbus *(G-5455)*

Braden Med Services Inc..........................E 740 732-2356
Caldwell *(G-1547)*

▲ Calvary Industries Inc...............................E 513 874-1113
Fairfield *(G-8398)*

Cantrell Oil Company..................................E 937 695-8003
Winchester *(G-15286)*

Cargill Incorporated...................................E 440 716-4664
North Olmsted *(G-11893)*

▼ Ccp Industries Inc......................................B 216 535-4227
Richmond Heights *(G-12716)*

▲ Chemical Associates of Illinois Inc.........E 330 666-7200
Copley *(G-6949)*

Chemical Solvents Inc................................D 216 741-9310
Cleveland *(G-3966)*

▲ Chemical Solvents Inc................................E 216 741-9310
Cleveland *(G-3965)*

▲ Cimcool Industrial Pdts LLC.....................E 513 458-8100
Cincinnati *(G-2389)*

▲ CL Zimmerman Delaware LLC..................E 513 860-9300
West Chester *(G-14667)*

◆ Cleveland FP Inc...D 216 249-4900
Cleveland *(G-4045)*

Consolidated Coatings Corp......................A 216 514-7596
Cleveland *(G-4106)*

Custom Chemical Solutions LLC..............E 800 291-1057
Loveland *(G-10134)*

D W Dickey and Son Inc............................C 330 424-1441
Lisbon *(G-10001)*

Detrex Corporation.....................................E 440 997-6131
Ashtabula *(G-533)*

◆ Dover Chemical Corporation.....................C 330 343-7711
Dover *(G-7880)*

Dubois Chemicals Inc................................E 513 868-9662
Hamilton *(G-9037)*

▼ Dubois Chemicals Inc................................E 800 438-2647
Sharonville *(G-12993)*

▲ Electro Prime Group LLC..........................D 419 476-0100
Toledo *(G-13786)*

▲ Emerald Hilton Davis LLC.........................D 513 841-0057
Cincinnati *(G-2614)*

FBC Chemical Corporation.......................E 330 723-7780
Medina *(G-10833)*

Fisk Kinne Holdings Inc.............................E 937 461-9906
Dayton *(G-7356)*

Flex Technologies Inc................................D 330 897-6311
Baltic *(G-688)*

Formlabs Ohio Inc......................................E 419 837-9783
Millbury *(G-11268)*

◆ Fort Amanda Specialties LLC...................E 419 229-0088
Lima *(G-9890)*

Galaxy Associates Inc...............................C 513 731-6350
Cincinnati *(G-2714)*

Gem City Chemicals Inc............................D 937 224-0711
Dayton *(G-7373)*

Gergelys Mint King Sups Svc In...............E 440 244-4446
Lorain *(G-10076)*

◆ Gorilla Glue Company LLC.......................B 513 271-3300
Cincinnati *(G-2743)*

◆ Harwick Standard Dist Corp.....................D 330 798-9300
Akron *(G-186)*

Hexion Inc..C 888 443-9466
Columbus *(G-5989)*

▲ Imcd Us LLC..E 216 228-8900
Westlake *(G-15069)*

◆ Industrial Chemical Corp..........................E 330 725-0800
Medina *(G-10846)*

Kellermeyer Company................................D 419 255-3022
Bowling Green *(G-1326)*

◆ Knight Material Tech LLC..........................D 330 488-1651
East Canton *(G-8169)*

Kraton Polymers US LLC..........................B 740 423-7571
Belpre *(G-1056)*

Lincare Inc..E 216 581-9649
Cleveland *(G-4497)*

Medi Home Health Agency Inc.................E 740 266-3977
Steubenville *(G-13338)*

◆ Mitsubshi Intl Fd Ingrdnts Inc...................E 614 652-1111
Dublin *(G-8065)*

Morton Salt Inc..C 440 354-9901
Painesville *(G-12237)*

▲ National Biochemicals LLC......................E 330 425-2522
Aurora *(G-619)*

Nouryon Chemicals LLC............................E 419 229-0088
Lima *(G-9943)*

Novagard Solutions Inc.............................C 216 881-8111
Cleveland *(G-4668)*

◆ Palmer Holland Inc.....................................C 440 686-2300
Westlake *(G-15094)*

◆ Phoenix Technologies Intl LLC................E 419 353-7738
Bowling Green *(G-1330)*

◆ Polymer Additives Inc................................D 216 875-7200
Independence *(G-9468)*

Polymer Additives Holdings Inc..............C 216 875-7200
Independence *(G-9469)*

Polymer Solutions Group LLC..................E 229 435-8394
Cleveland *(G-4760)*

Procter & Gamble Distrg LLC...................B 513 626-2500
Blue Ash *(G-1224)*

Procter & Gamble Distrg LLC...................C 513 945-7960
Cincinnati *(G-3243)*

Products Chemical Company LLC..........D 216 281-1155
Cleveland *(G-4773)*

Red Rover LLC..E 330 262-6501
Wooster *(G-15368)*

◆ Rhein Chemie Corporation.......................C 440 279-2367
Chardon *(G-2017)*

Rhiel Supply Co..E 330 799-7777
Austintown *(G-636)*

Santmyer Logistics Inc.............................D 330 262-6501
Wooster *(G-15371)*

◆ Sea-Land Chemical Co..............................E 440 871-7887
Cleveland *(G-4887)*

◆ Shin-Etsu Silicones of America Inc........C 330 630-4600
Akron *(G-299)*

Sigma-Aldrich Corporation.......................D 216 206-5424
Cleveland *(G-4907)*

◆ Skidmore Sales & Distrg Co Inc..............E 513 755-4200
West Chester *(G-14766)*

◆ Spartan Chemical Company Inc..............C 419 897-5551
Maumee *(G-10768)*

▲ Specialty Chemical Sales Inc..................E 216 267-4248
Cleveland *(G-4928)*

◆ Struktol Company America LLC...............E 330 928-5188
Stow *(G-13395)*

◆ Synthomer LLC...D 678 400-6655
Beachwood *(G-842)*

T&L Global Management LLC...................D 614 586-0303
Columbus *(G-6744)*

◆ Tembec Btlsr Inc...E 419 244-5856
Toledo *(G-14037)*

▲ Toagosei America Inc................................D 614 718-3855
West Jefferson *(G-14853)*

◆ Tosoh America Inc.....................................B 614 539-8622
Grove City *(G-8959)*

◆ Tricor Industrial Inc...................................D 330 264-3299
Wooster *(G-15380)*

▲ United McGill Corporation.........................E 614 829-1200
Groveport *(G-9007)*

Veolia Wts Usa Inc.....................................E 330 339-2292
New Philadelphia *(G-11672)*

Wampum Hardware Co..............................E 419 273-2542
Forest *(G-8602)*

▼ Washing Systems LLC..............................C 800 272-1974
Loveland *(G-10166)*

Weiler Welding Company Inc....................D 937 222-8312
Moraine *(G-11448)*

Young Chemical Co LLC...........................E 330 486-4210
Twinsburg *(G-14232)*

5171 Petroleum bulk stations and terminals

Beck Suppliers Inc.....................................E 419 426-3051
Attica *(G-598)*

Cincinnati - Vulcan Company...................D 513 242-5300
Cincinnati *(G-2391)*

Four O Corporation....................................E 513 941-2800
Blue Ash *(G-1176)*

Red Rover LLC..E 330 262-6501
Wooster *(G-15368)*

Santmyer Logistics Inc.............................D 330 262-6501
Wooster *(G-15371)*

Slattery Oil Company Inc..........................E 419 272-3305
Edon *(G-8229)*

Universal Oil Inc...E 216 771-4300
Cleveland *(G-5068)*

5172 Petroleum products, nec

▲ Applied Indus Tech - Dixie Inc..................D 216 426-4546
Cleveland *(G-3826)*

Bazell Oil Co Inc...E 740 385-5420
Logan *(G-10021)*

BP Oil Supply Company.............................E 330 945-4132
Cuyahoga Falls *(G-7051)*

BP Oil Supply Company.............................D 937 434-7008
Dayton *(G-7199)*

Centerra Co-Op..E 419 281-2153
Ashland *(G-490)*

Clay Distributing Co...................................C 419 426-3051
Attica *(G-599)*

D W Dickey and Son Inc............................C 330 424-1441
Lisbon *(G-10001)*

Duncan Oil Co...E 937 426-5945
Dayton *(G-7131)*

Fisk Kinne Holdings Inc.............................E 937 461-9906
Dayton *(G-7356)*

Gfl Environmental Svcs USA Inc..............E 614 441-4001
Columbus *(G-5932)*

SIC SECTION — 51 WHOLESALE TRADE - NONDURABLE GOODS

Glockner Oil Company Inc .... E 740 289-2979
Piketon (G-12420)

Heartland Petroleum LLC .... E 614 441-4001
Columbus (G-5979)

Hightowers Petroleum Company .... E 513 423-4272
Middletown (G-11199)

Holland Oil Company .... D 330 835-1815
Akron (G-194)

◆ Knight Material Tech LLC .... D 330 488-1651
East Canton (G-8169)

Lyden Oil Company .... E 330 792-1100
Youngstown (G-15654)

Lykins Companies Inc .... E 513 831-8820
Milford (G-11238)

Lykins Oil Company .... E 513 831-8820
Milford (G-11239)

▲ Marathon Petroleum Corporation ...... A 419 422-2121
Findlay (G-8561)

Marathon Petroleum Supply LLC .... E 419 422-2121
Findlay (G-8562)

McKinley Air Transport Inc .... E 330 497-6956
Canton (G-1802)

Mighty Mac Investments Inc .... E 937 335-2928
Troy (G-14147)

Minster Farmers Coop Exch .... D 419 628-4705
Minster (G-11319)

Mplx Terminals LLC .... D 330 479-5539
Canton (G-1811)

Nzr Retail of Toledo Inc .... D 419 724-0005
Toledo (G-13943)

Pannu Petroleum Inc .... E 937 599-5454
Bellefontaine (G-1035)

Ports Petroleum Company Inc .... E 330 264-1885
Wooster (G-15367)

Reladyne Florida LLC .... D 904 354-8411
Cincinnati (G-3284)

Reladyne Inc .... C 513 941-2800
Cincinnati (G-3285)

▲ Shrader Tire & Oil Inc .... E 419 472-2128
Toledo (G-14012)

◆ Specialty Lubricants Corp .... E 330 425-2567
Macedonia (G-10205)

Suburban Oil Company .... E 513 459-8100
Mason (G-10611)

Tesoro Refining & Mktg Co LLC .... C 419 421-2159
Findlay (G-8591)

The Glockner Chevrolet Company ..... C 740 353-2161
Portsmouth (G-12576)

Triumph Energy Corporation .... C 513 367-9900
Harrison (G-9118)

True North Energy LLC .... D 330 722-2031
Medina (G-10900)

True North Energy LLC .... E 877 245-9336
Brecksville (G-1370)

Ull Inc .... E 440 543-5195
Chagrin Falls (G-1992)

X F Construction Svcs Inc .... E 614 575-2700
Columbus (G-6911)

5181 Beer and ale

Anheuser-Busch LLC .... E 513 381-3927
Cincinnati (G-2205)

Anheuser-Busch LLC .... E 419 221-2337
Lima (G-9865)

Arrow Wine Stores Inc .... E 937 433-6778
Dayton (G-7180)

▲ Beverage Distributors Inc .... C 216 431-1600
Cleveland (G-3872)

Bonbright Distributors Inc .... E 937 222-1001
Springfield (G-13223)

▲ Bonbright Distributors Inc .... D 937 222-1001
Dayton (G-7196)

▲ Cavalier Distributing Company .... D 513 247-9222
Blue Ash (G-1143)

▲ Central Beverage Group Ltd .... C 614 294-3555
Lewis Center (G-9813)

Columbus Distributing Company .... D 740 726-2211
Waldo (G-14470)

▲ Columbus Distributing Company ..... C 614 846-1000
Columbus (G-5628)

Dayton Heidelberg Distrg Co .... B 513 421-5000
Cincinnati (G-2544)

Dayton Heidelberg Distrg Co .... C 216 520-2626
Cleveland (G-4153)

Dayton Heidelberg Distrg Co .... E 614 308-0400
Columbus (G-5745)

Dayton Heidelberg Distrg Co .... E 937 220-6450
Moraine (G-11401)

Dayton Heidelberg Distrg Co .... C 419 666-9783
Perrysburg (G-12330)

◆ Dayton Heidelberg Distrg LLC .... B 937 222-8692
Moraine (G-11402)

▲ Esber Beverage Company .... E 330 456-4361
Canton (G-1750)

Heidelberg Distributing C .... D 513 771-9370
Cincinnati (G-2816)

House of La Rose Cleveland .... C 440 746-7500
Brecksville (G-1354)

Litter Distributing Co Inc .... D 740 774-2831
Chillicothe (G-2078)

M & A Distributing Co Inc .... E 440 703-4580
Solon (G-13110)

Maple City Ice Company .... E 419 668-2531
Norwalk (G-12016)

▲ Matesich Distributing Co .... D 740 349-8686
Newark (G-11724)

Nwo Beverage Inc .... E 419 725-2162
Northwood (G-11980)

◆ Ohio Valley Wine Company LLC ..... C 513 771-9370
Cincinnati (G-3151)

▲ R L Lipton Distributing Co .... D 216 475-4150
Cleveland (G-4805)

▲ Rhinegeist LLC .... D 513 381-1367
Cincinnati (G-3295)

Southern Glzers Dstrs Ohio LLC .... D 440 542-7000
Solon (G-13147)

▲ Southern Glzers Dstrs Ohio LLC ..... D 614 552-7900
Columbus (G-6696)

The Maple City Ice Company .... E 419 747-4777
Mansfield (G-10319)

Treu House of Munch Inc .... D 419 666-7770
Northwood (G-11986)

▲ Warsteiner Importers Agency .... E 513 942-9872
West Chester (G-14793)

5182 Wine and distilled beverages

Arrow Wine Stores Inc .... E 937 433-6778
Dayton (G-7180)

Dayton Heidelberg Distrg Co .... B 937 220-6450
Moraine (G-11401)

▲ Esber Beverage Company .... E 330 456-4361
Canton (G-1750)

Gervasi Vinyrd Itln Bistro LLC .... D 330 497-1000
Canton (G-1762)

M & A Distributing Co Inc .... E 440 703-4580
Solon (G-13110)

M & M Wine Cellar Inc .... E 330 536-6450
Lowellville (G-10170)

◆ Ohio Valley Wine Company LLC ..... C 513 771-9370
Cincinnati (G-3151)

▲ Paramount Distillers Inc .... B 216 671-6300
Cleveland (G-4718)

▲ Premium Beverage Supply Ltd .... D 614 777-1007
Hilliard (G-9227)

▲ R L Lipton Distributing Co .... D 216 475-4150
Cleveland (G-4805)

Southern Glzers Dstrs Ohio LLC .... D 440 542-7000
Solon (G-13147)

▲ Southern Glzers Dstrs Ohio LLC ..... D 614 552-7900
Columbus (G-6696)

Southern Glzers Wine Sprits TX .... E 513 755-7082
Fairfield (G-8442)

▲ Vanguard Wines LLC .... E 614 291-3493
Columbus (G-6842)

▲ Vintage Wine Distributor Inc .... E 440 248-1750
Solon (G-13162)

Watershed Distillery LLC .... E 614 357-1936
Columbus (G-6869)

Wine Trends .... E 937 222-8692
Moraine (G-11449)

5191 Farm supplies

◆ A M Leonard Inc .... D 937 773-2694
Piqua (G-12434)

Andersons Inc .... C 419 893-5050
Maumee (G-10692)

◆ Bfg Supply Co LLC .... E 800 883-0234
Burton (G-1526)

Cooper Farms Inc .... D 419 375-4116
Fort Recovery (G-8606)

Cover Crop Shop LLC .... D 937 417-3972
Sidney (G-13028)

Custom Agri Systems Inc .... E 419 599-5180
Napoleon (G-11521)

Deerfield AG Services Inc .... E 330 584-4715
Massillon (G-10637)

Deerfield Farms Service Inc .... D 330 584-4715
Deerfield (G-7741)

Edko LLC .... E 614 863-5946
Columbus (G-5808)

Evans Landscaping Inc .... E 513 271-1119
Cincinnati (G-2639)

▲ Express Seed Company .... D 440 774-2259
Oberlin (G-12068)

Family Farm & Home Inc .... E 440 307-1030
Madison (G-10216)

Fort Recovery Equity Inc .... C 419 942-1148
Fort Recovery (G-8608)

Gardenlife Inc .... E 800 241-7333
Chardon (G-1999)

Gardner-Connell LLC .... E 614 456-4000
Columbus (G-5915)

◆ Geoglobal Partners LLC .... D 561 598-6000
Aurora (G-614)

Gerald Grain Center Inc .... E 419 445-2451
Archbold (G-459)

Gerber Feed Service Inc .... E 330 857-4421
Dalton (G-7120)

Green Valley Co-Op Inc .... D 740 374-7741
Marietta (G-10369)

Griffin Industries LLC .... E 419 257-3560
North Baltimore (G-11800)

H Hafner & Sons Inc .... E 513 321-1895
Cincinnati (G-2786)

Hanby Farms Inc .... E 740 763-3554
Nashport (G-11535)

▲ Imcd Us LLC .... E 216 228-8900
Westlake (G-15069)

◆ Jiffy Products America Inc .... D 440 282-2818
Lorain (G-10078)

Keynes Bros Inc .... D 740 385-6824
Logan (G-10030)

◆ Lesco Inc .... C 216 706-9250
Cleveland (G-4490)

Mennel Milling Company .... E 740 385-6824
Logan (G-10034)

51 WHOLESALE TRADE - NONDURABLE GOODS

Minster Farmers Coop Exch................... D 419 628-4705
  Minster *(G-11319)*

Morral Companies LLC............................ E 740 465-3251
  Morral *(G-11454)*

Noxious Vegetation Control Inc............... D 614 486-8994
  Ashville *(G-553)*

▲ Provimi North America Inc..................... B 937 770-2400
  Lewisburg *(G-9842)*

Rj Matthews Company................................ E 330 834-3000
  Massillon *(G-10663)*

Rk Family Inc.. C 740 474-3874
  Circleville *(G-3721)*

Rk Family Inc.. C 419 355-8230
  Fremont *(G-8698)*

Rk Family Inc.. C 513 737-0436
  Hamilton *(G-9079)*

Rk Family Inc.. C 513 934-0015
  Lebanon *(G-9786)*

Rk Family Inc.. C 740 389-2674
  Marion *(G-10452)*

Rk Family Inc.. C 330 308-5075
  New Philadelphia *(G-11665)*

Rk Family Inc.. C 419 660-0363
  Norwalk *(G-12024)*

Rk Family Inc.. B 419 443-1663
  Tiffin *(G-13640)*

Rk Family Inc.. C 330 264-5475
  Wooster *(G-15369)*

Rosens Inc.. D 419 225-7382
  Lima *(G-9956)*

Seed Consultants Inc............................... E 740 333-8644
  Wshngtn Ct Hs *(G-15494)*

Sunrise Cooperative Inc.......................... E 419 683-7340
  Crestline *(G-7026)*

Tractor Supply Company.......................... E 937 320-1855
  Beavercreek Township *(G-951)*

Tractor Supply Company.......................... E 614 878-7170
  Columbus *(G-6779)*

Tractor Supply Company.......................... E 740 288-1079
  Jackson *(G-9526)*

Tractor Supply Company.......................... E 419 673-8900
  Kenton *(G-9623)*

Tractor Supply Company.......................... E 740 456-0000
  Portsmouth *(G-12577)*

Tractor Supply Company.......................... E 937 446-9425
  Sardinia *(G-12941)*

Trupointe Cooperative Inc....................... B 937 575-6780
  Piqua *(G-12459)*

Western Reserve Farm Cooperative Inc .. D 440 632-0271
  Middlefield *(G-11146)*

5192 Books, periodicals, and newspapers

Alliance Medical Inc............................... E 800 890-3092
  Dublin *(G-7930)*

◆ Bookmasters Inc.................................. C 419 281-1802
  Ashland *(G-483)*

◆ Daedalus Books Inc............................. C 800 395-2665
  Hudson *(G-9342)*

Ed Map Inc.. D 740 753-3439
  Nelsonville *(G-11543)*

▲ Findaway World LLC............................ E 440 893-0808
  Solon *(G-13089)*

Hubbard Company................................. E 419 784-4455
  Defiance *(G-7750)*

▲ Kable News Company Inc.................... C 815 734-4151
  West Chester *(G-14716)*

McGraw-Hill Schl Edcatn Hldngs............ A 419 207-7400
  Ashland *(G-507)*

Media Source Inc.................................. D 614 873-7435
  Plain City *(G-12487)*

Murfbooks LLC...................................... E 937 260-3741
  Dayton *(G-7518)*

Windy Hill Ltd Inc................................... D 216 391-4800
  Cleveland *(G-5150)*

▲ Zaner-Bloser Inc................................. C 614 486-0221
  Columbus *(G-6918)*

5193 Flowers and florists supplies

▲ August Corso Sons Inc....................... C 419 626-0765
  Sandusky *(G-12863)*

Autograph Inc.. E 216 881-1911
  Cleveland *(G-3840)*

Claprood Roman J Co............................ E 614 221-5515
  Columbus *(G-5579)*

Cottage Gardens Inc.............................. D 440 259-2900
  Perry *(G-12305)*

Dennis Top Soil & Ldscpg Inc................ E 419 865-5656
  Toledo *(G-13775)*

Dummen USA Inc................................... E 614 850-9551
  Columbus *(G-5790)*

▲ Express Seed Company...................... D 440 774-2259
  Oberlin *(G-12068)*

Flowers Baking Co Ohio LLC................ E 419 661-2586
  Northwood *(G-11974)*

Giant Eagle Inc..................................... D 330 364-5301
  Dover *(G-7885)*

Maria Gardens LLC............................... E 440 238-7637
  Strongsville *(G-13474)*

Millcreek Gardens LLC.......................... E 740 666-7125
  Ostrander *(G-12183)*

North Branch Nursery Inc...................... E 419 287-4679
  Pemberville *(G-12290)*

Pickaway Growers LLC........................... E 614 344-4956
  Orient *(G-12154)*

Rentokil North America Inc................... E 614 837-0099
  Groveport *(G-8999)*

▲ Rwam Bros Inc................................... E 419 826-3671
  Swanton *(G-13528)*

Siebenthaler Company........................... D 937 274-1154
  Beavercreek *(G-905)*

▲ Straders Garden Centers Inc............. C 614 889-1314
  Columbus *(G-6721)*

The Cleveland Plant and F..................... E 216 898-3500
  Cleveland *(G-4995)*

▲ Thorsens Greenhouse LLC.................. E 740 363-5069
  Delaware *(G-7830)*

5194 Tobacco and tobacco products

Albert Guarnieri & Co............................. D 330 794-9834
  Hudson *(G-9328)*

Arrow Wine Stores Inc........................... E 937 433-6778
  Dayton *(G-7180)*

Cju Enterprises Inc................................ D 330 493-1800
  Canton *(G-1710)*

Core-Mark Holding Company Inc............ C 650 589-9445
  Solon *(G-13077)*

Dittman-Adams Company........................ E 513 870-7530
  Harrison *(G-9102)*

Friendly Wholesale Co........................... E 724 224-6580
  Wooster *(G-15338)*

Gummer Wholesale Inc........................... D 740 928-0415
  Heath *(G-9133)*

JE Carsten Company.............................. E 330 794-4440
  Hudson *(G-9359)*

Novelart Manufacturing Company............ D 513 351-7700
  Cincinnati *(G-3132)*

◆ Scandinavian Tob Group Ln Ltd........... C 770 934-4594
  Akron *(G-295)*

Swd Corporation................................... E 419 227-2436
  Lima *(G-9968)*

5198 Paints, varnishes, and supplies

Autobody Supply Company Inc............... D 614 228-4328
  Columbus *(G-5407)*

◆ Comex North America Inc................... D 303 307-2100
  Cleveland *(G-4092)*

Dutch Boy Group................................... E 800 828-5669
  Cleveland *(G-4189)*

▲ Jmac Inc.. E 614 436-2418
  Columbus *(G-6092)*

Matrix Sys Auto Finishes LLC................ B 248 668-8135
  Massillon *(G-10654)*

Miller Bros Wallpaper Company.............. E 513 231-4470
  Cincinnati *(G-3063)*

Nanogate North America LLC................ B 419 747-6639
  Mansfield *(G-10301)*

Ohio Auto Kolor Inc............................... E 614 272-2255
  Columbus *(G-6393)*

◆ Synthomer LLC................................... D 678 400-6655
  Beachwood *(G-842)*

▲ Teknol Inc.. D 937 264-0190
  Dayton *(G-7661)*

◆ The Blonder Company........................ C 216 431-3560
  Cleveland *(G-4992)*

5199 Nondurable goods, nec

▲ A-Roo Company LLC.......................... D 440 238-8850
  Strongsville *(G-13437)*

▲ Acor Orthopaedic LLC....................... E 216 662-4500
  Cleveland *(G-3764)*

▲ Advanced Poly-Packaging Inc............ C 330 785-4000
  Akron *(G-18)*

Aero Industries Inc................................ D 330 626-3246
  Kent *(G-9555)*

Alene Candles LLC................................ C 614 933-4005
  New Albany *(G-11555)*

Amcor Flexibles North Amer Inc............ D 419 334-9465
  Fremont *(G-8666)*

American Business Forms Inc................ E 513 312-2522
  West Chester *(G-14798)*

Ample Industries Inc.............................. C 937 746-9700
  Franklin *(G-8631)*

▼ Armaly LLC.. E 740 852-3621
  London *(G-10037)*

Artwall LLC... E 216 476-0635
  Cleveland *(G-3836)*

◆ Associated Premium Corporation....... E 513 679-4444
  Cincinnati *(G-2219)*

◆ Aurora Wholesalers LLC..................... D 440 248-5200
  Solon *(G-13069)*

◆ B D G Wrap-Tite Inc........................... E 440 349-5400
  Solon *(G-13070)*

▲ Bgr Inc.. D 800 628-9195
  West Chester *(G-14651)*

◆ Boost Engagement LLC...................... E 937 223-2203
  Dayton *(G-7197)*

◆ Bottomline Ink Corporation................ E 419 897-8000
  Perrysburg *(G-12318)*

BP 10 Inc.. E 513 346-3900
  West Chester *(G-14653)*

Bprex Closures LLC............................... D 812 424-2904
  Maumee *(G-10703)*

◆ Buckhorn Inc..................................... E 513 831-4402
  Milford *(G-11219)*

Cambridge Packaging Inc....................... E 740 432-3351
  Cambridge *(G-1560)*

▲ Checker Notions Company Inc........... C 419 893-3636
  Maumee *(G-10710)*

◆ Compass Packaging LLC..................... E 330 274-2001
  Mantua *(G-10329)*

▼ Crown Packaging Corporation............ C 937 294-6580
  Dayton *(G-7263)*

▲ Custom Products Corporation............ D 440 528-7100
  Solon *(G-13080)*

D & D Advertising Entps Inc.................. E 513 921-6827
  Cincinnati *(G-2529)*

52 BUILDING MATERIALS, HARDWARE, GARDEN SUPPLIES & MOBILE HOMES

◆ Dayton Bag & Burlap Co............E 937 258-8000
  Dayton (G-7272)
Dayton Corrugated Packaging Corp....E 937 254-8422
  Dayton (G-7277)
Distribution Data Incorporated............D 216 362-3009
  Brookpark (G-1433)
Dollar Paradise............................E 216 432-0421
  Cleveland (G-4174)
Eastgate Group Ltd........................E 513 228-5522
  Lebanon (G-9764)
Ekco Cleaning Inc.........................C 513 733-8882
  Cincinnati (G-2608)
◆ Flower Factory Inc......................B 330 494-7978
  North Canton (G-11831)
General Commercial Corporation............E 330 938-1000
  Sebring (G-12949)
▲ GK Packaging Inc........................D 614 873-3900
  Plain City (G-12478)
▲ Glow Industries Inc.....................D 419 872-4772
  Perrysburg (G-12339)
Gpax Inc..................................E 614 501-7622
  Reynoldsburg (G-12664)
Graham Packg Plastic Pdts LLC.............E 419 423-3271
  Findlay (G-8539)
Graphic Packaging Intl LLC................D 630 584-2900
  Cincinnati (G-2750)
Greif Inc.................................D 740 549-6000
  Cincinnati (G-2775)
Gummer Wholesale Inc......................D 740 928-0415
  Heath (G-9133)
Halo Branded Solutions Inc................E 855 425-6266
  Cincinnati (G-2793)
Halo Branded Solutions Inc................E 614 434-6275
  Columbus (G-5965)
▲ Hi-Way Distributing Corp Amer..........D 330 645-6633
  Coventry Township (G-7010)
Huhtamaki Inc.............................C 937 987-3078
  New Vienna (G-11680)
▼ ICM Distributing Company Inc...........E 234 212-3030
  Twinsburg (G-14196)
▲ Inno-Pak LLC............................D 740 363-0090
  Delaware (G-7807)
Jlt Packaging Cincinnati Inc..............E 513 933-0250
  Lebanon (G-9771)
Johnson Bros Rubber Co Inc................E 419 752-4814
  Greenwich (G-8892)
◆ Johnson Bros Rubber Co.................D 419 853-4122
  West Salem (G-14863)
Just Candy LLC............................E 201 805-8562
  Fairfield (G-8424)
◆ K & M International Inc................D 330 425-2550
  Independence (G-9439)
▲ Kaeser and Blair Incorporated..........D 513 732-6400
  Batavia (G-742)
Kopco Graphics Inc........................E 513 874-7230
  West Chester (G-14721)
▲ Leader Promotions Inc..................D 614 416-6565
  Columbus (G-6150)
Lineage Logistics LLC.....................E 330 559-4860
  Youngstown (G-15652)
Lori Holding Co...........................E 740 342-3230
  New Lexington (G-11628)
▼ Merchandise Inc........................D 513 353-2200
  Miamitown (G-11107)
Mid-States Packaging Inc..................E 937 843-3243
  Lewistown (G-9843)
▲ Mosser Glass Inc.......................E 740 439-1827
  Cambridge (G-1576)
Nannicola Wholesale Co....................D 330 799-0888
  Youngstown (G-15672)
New Method Packaging LLC..................E 937 324-3838
  Springfield (G-13276)

Next Generation Bag Inc...................E 419 884-1327
  Mansfield (G-10305)
◆ Novelty Advertising Co Inc.............E 740 622-3113
  Coshocton (G-6994)
▲ Nutis Press Inc........................C 614 237-8626
  Columbus (G-6378)
▲ Ohio Packaging.........................D 330 833-2884
  Massillon (G-10660)
Old Forge Services Inc....................E 330 733-5531
  Windham (G-15289)
Pac Worldwide Corporation.................D 800 535-0039
  Monroe (G-11348)
▲ Pacific MGT Holdings LLC...............E 440 324-3339
  Elyria (G-8284)
Packaging & Pads R Us LLC.................E 419 499-2905
  Milan (G-11210)
▲ Papyrus-Recycled Greetings Inc.........D 773 348-6410
  Westlake (G-15095)
▲ Par International Inc..................E 614 529-1300
  Obetz (G-12082)
▲ Pfp Holdings LLC.......................A 419 647-4191
  Spencerville (G-13190)
▲ Pipeline Packaging Corporation.........E 440 349-3200
  Hudson (G-9368)
Plastipak Packaging Inc...................D 937 596-5166
  Jackson Center (G-9532)
Plastipak Packaging Inc...................C 330 725-0205
  Medina (G-10876)
▲ Potter Inc.............................E 419 636-5624
  Bryan (G-1492)
Ppc Flexible Packaging LLC................C 614 876-1204
  Columbus (G-6540)
Pretium Packaging LLC.....................C 419 943-3733
  Leipsic (G-9802)
Primary Packaging Incorporated............D 330 874-3131
  Bolivar (G-1297)
Proampac Holdings Inc.....................D 513 671-1777
  Cincinnati (G-3236)
▲ Profill Holdings LLC...................A 513 742-4000
  Cincinnati (G-3247)
Protective Packg Solutions LLC............E 513 769-5777
  Cincinnati (G-3255)
▼ Questar Solutions LLC..................E 330 966-2070
  North Canton (G-11857)
R D Thompson Paper Pdts Co Inc............E 419 994-3614
  Loudonville (G-10110)
▲ Rdh Ohio LLC...........................E 419 475-8621
  Holland (G-9302)
▲ Regal-Elite Inc........................D 614 873-3800
  Plain City (G-12492)
Riser Foods Company.......................D 216 292-7000
  Bedford Heights (G-1001)
Samuel Son & Co (usa) Inc.................D 740 522-2500
  Heath (G-9138)
Screen Works Inc..........................E 937 264-9111
  Dayton (G-7613)
▲ Shamrock Companies Inc.................D 440 899-9510
  Westlake (G-15108)
▲ Ship-Paq Inc...........................E 513 860-0700
  Fairfield (G-8439)
Skybox Investments Inc....................E 419 525-6013
  Mansfield (G-10316)
Skybox Packaging LLC......................C 419 525-7209
  Mansfield (G-10317)
Star Packaging Inc........................E 614 564-9936
  Columbus (G-6711)
Sterling Paper Co.........................E 614 443-0303
  Columbus (G-6718)
▲ Storopack Inc..........................E 513 874-0314
  West Chester (G-14834)
Sutherland Building Pdts Inc..............D 740 477-2244
  Circleville (G-3725)

Systems Pack Inc..........................E 330 467-5729
  Macedonia (G-10207)
Tahoma Enterprises Inc....................D 330 745-9016
  Barberton (G-714)
▼ Tahoma Rubber & Plastics Inc...........D 330 745-9016
  Barberton (G-715)
▲ Third Dimension Inc....................E 440 466-4040
  Geneva (G-8790)
Toga-Pak Inc..............................E 937 294-7311
  Dayton (G-7672)
▲ Touchstone Mdse Group LLC..............D 513 741-0400
  Mason (G-10617)
▲ Trademark Global LLC...................E 440 960-6200
  Lorain (G-10104)
Versa-Pak Ltd.............................E 419 586-5466
  Celina (G-1931)
Victory Packaging LP......................D 216 898-9130
  Brookpark (G-1442)
▲ Waterbeds n Stuff Inc..................E 614 871-1171
  Grove City (G-8965)
Wayne Signer Enterprises Inc..............E 513 841-1351
  Cincinnati (G-3642)
▲ Weaver Leather LLC.....................D 330 674-7548
  Millersburg (G-11296)
Welch Packaging Group Inc.................C 419 726-3491
  Toledo (G-14100)
Wholesome Pet Co Inc......................D 877 345-7297
  Orrville (G-12175)
Wingate Packaging Inc.....................E 513 745-8600
  Cincinnati (G-3675)
▲ Winston Products LLC...................D 440 945-6912
  Solon (G-13166)

52 BUILDING MATERIALS, HARDWARE, GARDEN SUPPLIES & MOBILE HOMES

5211 Lumber and other building materials

Alpine Insulation I LLC...................D 614 221-3399
  Columbus (G-5339)
Alside Inc................................D 419 865-0934
  Maumee (G-10687)
Apco Industries Inc.......................D 614 224-2345
  Columbus (G-5371)
Babin Building Solutions LLC..............E 216 292-2500
  Broadview Heights (G-1383)
BG Trucking & Cnstr Inc...................E 234 759-3440
  North Lima (G-11884)
Cabinet Restylers Inc.....................D 419 281-8449
  Ashland (G-486)
Carter-Jones Companies Inc................E 330 673-6100
  Kent (G-9560)
Carter-Jones Lumber Company...............E 330 784-5441
  Akron (G-82)
Carter-Jones Lumber Company...............E 440 834-8164
  Middlefield (G-11139)
▲ Carter-Jones Lumber Company............C 330 673-6100
  Kent (G-9561)
Clays Heritage Carpet Inc.................E 330 497-1280
  Canton (G-1711)
Columbus Coal & Lime Co...................E 614 224-9241
  Columbus (G-5624)
Contract Lumber Inc.......................C 740 964-3147
  Pataskala (G-12270)
▲ Contractors Materials Company..........E 513 733-3000
  Cincinnati (G-2502)
◆ Df Supply Inc..........................E 330 650-9226
  Twinsburg (G-14181)
Do It Best Corp...........................B 330 725-3859
  Medina (G-10831)

52 BUILDING MATERIALS, HARDWARE, GARDEN SUPPLIES & MOBILE HOMES — SIC SECTION

Dun Rite Home Improvement Inc............ E 330 650-5322
  Macedonia *(G-10191)*

Encore Precast LLC............................... E 513 726-5678
  Seven Mile *(G-12962)*

Erie Construction Mid-West Inc............... D 937 898-4688
  Dayton *(G-7339)*

Erie Construction Mid-West Inc............... D 419 472-4200
  Toledo *(G-13794)*

Erie Construction Mid-West Inc............... B 419 472-4200
  Toledo *(G-13795)*

▲ Fortune Brands Windows Inc.............. C 614 532-3500
  Columbus *(G-5879)*

Grafton Ready Mix Concret Inc............... C 440 926-2911
  Grafton *(G-8839)*

▲ Graves Lumber Co............................. C 330 666-1115
  Copley *(G-6958)*

▲ Hamilton-Parker Company.................. D 614 358-7800
  Columbus *(G-5968)*

Hercules Led LLC.................................. E 844 437-2533
  Boardman *(G-1289)*

Holmes Lumber & Bldg Ctr Inc............... E 330 479-8314
  Canton *(G-1775)*

Holmes Lumber & Bldg Ctr Inc............... C 330 674-9060
  Millersburg *(G-11279)*

Home Depot USA Inc............................. C 330 245-0280
  Akron *(G-195)*

Home Depot USA Inc............................. C 440 937-2240
  Avon *(G-654)*

Home Depot USA Inc............................. C 330 497-1810
  Canton *(G-1776)*

Home Depot USA Inc............................. C 513 688-1654
  Cincinnati *(G-2835)*

Home Depot USA Inc............................. C 513 661-2413
  Cincinnati *(G-2836)*

Home Depot USA Inc............................. C 513 631-1705
  Cincinnati *(G-2837)*

Home Depot USA Inc............................. C 216 676-9969
  Cleveland *(G-4373)*

Home Depot USA Inc............................. C 216 251-3091
  Cleveland *(G-4374)*

Home Depot USA Inc............................. C 216 297-1303
  Cleveland Heights *(G-5179)*

Home Depot USA Inc............................. B 614 523-0600
  Columbus *(G-5999)*

Home Depot USA Inc............................. C 614 878-9150
  Columbus *(G-6000)*

Home Depot USA Inc............................. C 614 939-5036
  Columbus *(G-6001)*

Home Depot USA Inc............................. C 330 922-3448
  Cuyahoga Falls *(G-7078)*

Home Depot USA Inc............................. C 937 312-9053
  Dayton *(G-7409)*

Home Depot USA Inc............................. D 937 312-9076
  Dayton *(G-7410)*

Home Depot USA Inc............................. C 937 837-1551
  Dayton *(G-7411)*

Home Depot USA Inc............................. C 440 324-7222
  Elyria *(G-8256)*

Home Depot USA Inc............................. C 937 431-7346
  Fairborn *(G-8376)*

Home Depot USA Inc............................. D 513 887-1450
  Hamilton *(G-9053)*

Home Depot USA Inc............................. C 440 684-1343
  Highland Heights *(G-9166)*

Home Depot USA Inc............................. C 419 529-0015
  Mansfield *(G-10269)*

Home Depot USA Inc............................. D 216 581-6611
  Maple Heights *(G-10340)*

Home Depot USA Inc............................. C 440 357-0428
  Mentor *(G-10949)*

Home Depot USA Inc............................. C 614 577-1601
  Reynoldsburg *(G-12666)*

Home Depot USA Inc............................. C 419 626-6493
  Sandusky *(G-12903)*

Home Depot USA Inc............................. D 440 826-9092
  Strongsville *(G-13462)*

Home Depot USA Inc............................. C 419 476-4573
  Toledo *(G-13848)*

Home Depot USA Inc............................. C 419 537-1920
  Toledo *(G-13849)*

Installed Building Pdts Inc...................... C 614 221-3399
  Columbus *(G-6057)*

Installed Building Products LLC.............. C 614 221-3399
  Columbus *(G-6059)*

Keim Lumber Company.......................... D 330 893-2251
  Baltic *(G-690)*

▲ Keim Lumber Company....................... D 330 893-2251
  Millersburg *(G-11282)*

Khempco Bldg Sup Co Ltd Partnr........... D 740 549-0465
  Delaware *(G-7811)*

Kurtz Bros Inc....................................... E 216 986-7000
  Independence *(G-9442)*

L & W Supply Corporation..................... E 513 723-1150
  Cincinnati *(G-2960)*

▲ Lang Stone Company Inc.................... E 614 235-4099
  Columbus *(G-6139)*

Lowes Home Centers LLC..................... C 330 665-9356
  Akron *(G-225)*

Lowes Home Centers LLC..................... C 330 829-2700
  Alliance *(G-389)*

Lowes Home Centers LLC..................... C 440 998-6555
  Ashtabula *(G-540)*

Lowes Home Centers LLC..................... C 740 589-3750
  Athens *(G-582)*

Lowes Home Centers LLC..................... C 440 937-3500
  Avon *(G-660)*

Lowes Home Centers LLC..................... C 937 427-1110
  Beavercreek *(G-889)*

Lowes Home Centers LLC..................... C 216 831-2860
  Bedford *(G-970)*

Lowes Home Centers LLC..................... D 937 599-4000
  Bellefontaine *(G-1032)*

Lowes Home Centers LLC..................... C 330 497-2720
  Canton *(G-1797)*

Lowes Home Centers LLC..................... C 740 773-7777
  Chillicothe *(G-2079)*

Lowes Home Centers LLC..................... C 513 598-7050
  Cincinnati *(G-2990)*

Lowes Home Centers LLC..................... C 216 351-4723
  Cleveland *(G-4506)*

Lowes Home Centers LLC..................... C 614 853-6200
  Columbus *(G-6174)*

Lowes Home Centers LLC..................... C 937 235-2920
  Dayton *(G-7460)*

Lowes Home Centers LLC..................... C 937 438-4900
  Dayton *(G-7461)*

Lowes Home Centers LLC..................... C 937 854-8200
  Dayton *(G-7462)*

Lowes Home Centers LLC..................... C 419 782-9000
  Defiance *(G-7753)*

Lowes Home Centers LLC..................... C 614 659-0530
  Dublin *(G-8058)*

Lowes Home Centers LLC..................... C 440 324-5004
  Elyria *(G-8272)*

Lowes Home Centers LLC..................... C 419 420-7531
  Findlay *(G-8559)*

Lowes Home Centers LLC..................... C 419 355-0221
  Fremont *(G-8690)*

Lowes Home Centers LLC..................... C 937 547-2400
  Greenville *(G-8880)*

Lowes Home Centers LLC..................... C 513 737-3700
  Hamilton *(G-9061)*

Lowes Home Centers LLC..................... C 614 529-5900
  Hilliard *(G-9210)*

Lowes Home Centers LLC..................... C 740 681-3464
  Lancaster *(G-9733)*

Lowes Home Centers LLC..................... C 419 331-3598
  Lima *(G-9930)*

Lowes Home Centers LLC..................... C 440 985-5700
  Lorain *(G-10090)*

Lowes Home Centers LLC..................... C 740 374-2151
  Marietta *(G-10381)*

Lowes Home Centers LLC..................... C 740 389-9737
  Marion *(G-10433)*

Lowes Home Centers LLC..................... C 937 578-4440
  Marysville *(G-10492)*

Lowes Home Centers LLC..................... C 513 336-9741
  Mason *(G-10575)*

Lowes Home Centers LLC..................... C 330 832-1901
  Massillon *(G-10650)*

Lowes Home Centers LLC..................... C 440 392-0027
  Mentor *(G-10965)*

Lowes Home Centers LLC..................... C 513 727-3900
  Middletown *(G-11170)*

Lowes Home Centers LLC..................... C 513 965-3280
  Milford *(G-11237)*

Lowes Home Centers LLC..................... C 740 393-5350
  Mount Vernon *(G-11498)*

Lowes Home Centers LLC..................... D 330 339-1936
  New Philadelphia *(G-11657)*

Lowes Home Centers LLC..................... C 740 522-0003
  Newark *(G-11723)*

Lowes Home Centers LLC..................... D 330 908-2750
  Northfield *(G-11960)*

Lowes Home Centers LLC..................... C 419 747-1920
  Ontario *(G-12113)*

Lowes Home Centers LLC..................... C 419 874-6758
  Perrysburg *(G-12355)*

Lowes Home Centers LLC..................... D 614 769-9940
  Reynoldsburg *(G-12668)*

Lowes Home Centers LLC..................... C 440 331-1027
  Rocky River *(G-12748)*

Lowes Home Centers LLC..................... D 740 699-3000
  Saint Clairsville *(G-12799)*

Lowes Home Centers LLC..................... C 419 624-6000
  Sandusky *(G-12912)*

Lowes Home Centers LLC..................... C 937 498-8400
  Sidney *(G-13039)*

Lowes Home Centers LLC..................... C 513 445-1000
  South Lebanon *(G-13172)*

Lowes Home Centers LLC..................... C 740 894-7120
  South Point *(G-13177)*

Lowes Home Centers LLC..................... C 937 327-6000
  Springfield *(G-13264)*

Lowes Home Centers LLC..................... C 740 266-3500
  Steubenville *(G-13336)*

Lowes Home Centers LLC..................... C 330 920-9280
  Stow *(G-13380)*

Lowes Home Centers LLC..................... C 330 626-2980
  Streetsboro *(G-13420)*

Lowes Home Centers LLC..................... C 440 239-2630
  Strongsville *(G-13473)*

Lowes Home Centers LLC..................... C 419 843-9758
  Toledo *(G-13894)*

Lowes Home Centers LLC..................... C 937 339-2544
  Troy *(G-14145)*

Lowes Home Centers LLC..................... C 330 335-1900
  Wadsworth *(G-14442)*

Lowes Home Centers LLC..................... C 419 739-1300
  Wapakoneta *(G-14488)*

Lowes Home Centers LLC..................... C 330 609-8000
  Warren *(G-14536)*

Lowes Home Centers LLC..................... C 513 755-4300
  West Chester *(G-14726)*

Lowes Home Centers LLC..................... C 740 574-6200
  Wheelersburg *(G-15130)*

54 FOOD STORES

Lowes Home Centers LLC.................C 440 942-2759
   Willoughby *(G-15207)*

Lowes Home Centers LLC.................C 937 383-7000
   Wilmington *(G-15260)*

Lowes Home Centers LLC.................C 330 287-2261
   Wooster *(G-15352)*

Lowes Home Centers LLC.................C 937 347-4000
   Xenia *(G-15524)*

Lowes Home Centers LLC.................C 330 965-4500
   Youngstown *(G-15653)*

Lowes Home Centers LLC.................C 740 450-5500
   Zanesville *(G-15807)*

▲ Maza Inc..D 614 760-0003
   Plain City *(G-12486)*

Menard Inc...D 513 737-2204
   Fairfield Township *(G-8463)*

Menard Inc...D 937 630-3550
   Miamisburg *(G-11072)*

Mentor Lumber and Supply Co...............C 440 255-8814
   Mentor *(G-10970)*

▲ Mills Fence Co LLC.......................E 513 631-0333
   Cincinnati *(G-3066)*

Modern Builders Supply Inc...............E 330 376-1031
   Akron *(G-236)*

Modern Builders Supply Inc...............E 216 273-3605
   Cleveland *(G-4593)*

▼ Nofziger Door Sales Inc..................C 419 337-9900
   Wauseon *(G-14607)*

Overhead Door Co- Cincinnati............C 513 346-4000
   West Chester *(G-14739)*

Overhead Inc.....................................E 419 476-7811
   Toledo *(G-13951)*

Robert McCabe Company Inc..............E 513 469-2500
   Cincinnati *(G-3314)*

Rockwood Products Ltd.....................E 330 893-2392
   Millersburg *(G-11291)*

Schlabach Wood Design Inc...............E 330 897-2600
   Baltic *(G-691)*

Schneider Home Equipment Co..........E 513 522-1200
   Cincinnati *(G-3349)*

Sievers Security Inc...........................E 216 291-2222
   Cleveland *(G-4905)*

Smyrna Ready Mix Concrete LLC........E 937 855-0410
   Germantown *(G-8805)*

The F A Requarth Company................E 937 224-1141
   Dayton *(G-7665)*

The Galehouse Companies Inc............E 330 658-2023
   Doylestown *(G-7916)*

The Robert McCabe Company Inc........D 513 683-2662
   Loveland *(G-10164)*

The W L Tucker Supply Company........E 330 928-2155
   Cuyahoga Falls *(G-7107)*

▲ Thomas Do-It Center Inc.................E 740 446-2002
   Gallipolis *(G-8769)*

United Building Materials Inc............E 937 222-4444
   Dayton *(G-7681)*

Universal Windows Direct Inc............E 614 418-5232
   Columbus *(G-6822)*

◆ Usavinyl LLC..................................D 614 771-4805
   Groveport *(G-9010)*

Western Reserve Farm Cooperative Inc D 440 632-0271
   Middlefield *(G-11146)*

5231 Paint, glass, and wallpaper stores

AWH Holdings Inc..............................D 513 241-2614
   Cincinnati *(G-2230)*

Cleveland Glass Block Inc..................E 614 252-5888
   Columbus *(G-5584)*

▼ Cleveland Glass Block Inc..............E 216 531-6363
   Cleveland *(G-4046)*

◆ Comex North America Inc...............D 303 307-2100
   Cleveland *(G-4092)*

Decorate With Style Inc.....................E 419 621-5577
   Sandusky *(G-12887)*

Miller Bros Wallpaper Company.........E 513 231-4470
   Cincinnati *(G-3063)*

R C Hemm Glass Shops Inc................E 937 773-5591
   Piqua *(G-12457)*

5251 Hardware stores

Bass Family LLC................................C
   Bedford Heights *(G-995)*

Best Aire Compressor Service............D 419 726-0055
   Millbury *(G-11266)*

Carter-Jones Companies Inc..............E 330 673-6100
   Kent *(G-9560)*

Carter-Jones Lumber Company..........E 330 784-5441
   Akron *(G-82)*

▲ Cdc Distributors Inc.......................D 513 771-3100
   Cincinnati *(G-2329)*

▲ De Haven Home and Garden..........E 419 227-7003
   Lima *(G-9883)*

Do It Best Corp.................................B 330 725-3859
   Medina *(G-10831)*

E&H Hardware Group LLC..................C 330 683-2060
   Orrville *(G-12164)*

Lochard Inc.......................................D 937 492-8811
   Sidney *(G-13037)*

▲ Matco Tools Corporation................B 330 929-4949
   Stow *(G-13382)*

National Tool Leasing Inc..................E 866 952-8665
   Eastlake *(G-8206)*

Robert McCabe Company Inc..............E 513 469-2500
   Cincinnati *(G-3314)*

Robertson Plumbing & Heating..........E 330 863-0611
   Malvern *(G-10235)*

The Robert McCabe Company Inc........D 513 683-2662
   Loveland *(G-10164)*

▲ Thomas Do-It Center Inc.................E 740 446-2002
   Gallipolis *(G-8769)*

Tool Testing Lab Inc..........................E 937 898-5696
   Tipp City *(G-13666)*

Tractor Supply Company....................E 937 382-2595
   Wilmington *(G-15275)*

5261 Retail nurseries and garden stores

Ag-Pro Ohio LLC................................E 740 653-6951
   Lancaster *(G-9691)*

Ag-Pro Ohio LLC................................E 937 486-5211
   Wilmington *(G-15238)*

▲ August Corso Sons Inc...................C 419 626-0765
   Sandusky *(G-12863)*

Barnes Nursery Inc............................E 800 421-8722
   Huron *(G-9384)*

◆ Bfg Supply Co LLC.........................E 800 883-0234
   Burton *(G-1526)*

Bonnie Plants LLC.............................C 937 642-7764
   Marysville *(G-10476)*

Carmichael Equipment Inc.................E 740 446-2412
   Bidwell *(G-1103)*

Centerra Co-Op..................................E 419 281-2153
   Ashland *(G-490)*

▲ De Haven Home and Garden..........E 419 227-7003
   Lima *(G-9883)*

Dell Willo Nursery Inc........................E 419 289-0606
   Ashland *(G-496)*

Dennis Top Soil & Ldscpg Inc............E 419 865-5656
   Toledo *(G-13775)*

Equipment Maintenance Inc...............E 513 353-3518
   Cleves *(G-5188)*

Evans Landscaping Inc......................E 513 271-1919
   Cincinnati *(G-2639)*

Fox Services Inc...............................E 513 858-2022
   Fairfield *(G-8414)*

Grandmas Gardens Inc.......................E 937 885-2973
   Waynesville *(G-14623)*

Heil Brothers Incorporated.................E 937 256-3500
   Dayton *(G-7404)*

Heritage Cooperative Inc...................D 877 240-4393
   Delaware *(G-7804)*

HJ Benken Flor & Greenhouses..........E 513 891-1040
   Cincinnati *(G-2830)*

Hull Bros Inc.....................................E 419 375-2827
   Fort Recovery *(G-8610)*

◆ Lesco Inc.......................................C 216 706-9250
   Cleveland *(G-4490)*

Naragon Companies Inc.....................E 330 745-7700
   Norton *(G-11995)*

North Branch Nursery Inc..................E 419 287-4679
   Pemberville *(G-12290)*

▲ Oakland Nursery Inc......................E 614 268-3834
   Columbus *(G-6380)*

Old Meadow Farms Inc......................E 440 632-5590
   Middlefield *(G-11143)*

Rock Pile Inc.....................................E 440 937-5100
   Avon *(G-664)*

Sand Road Enterprises Inc.................E 419 668-3670
   Norwalk *(G-12026)*

Seed Consultants Inc.........................E 740 333-8644
   Wshngtn Ct Hs *(G-15494)*

Siebenthaler Company.......................D 937 274-1154
   Beavercreek *(G-905)*

Steinke Tractor Sales Inc...................E 937 456-4271
   Eaton *(G-8224)*

▲ Straders Garden Centers Inc..........C 614 889-1314
   Columbus *(G-6721)*

Tractor Supply Company....................E 937 382-2595
   Wilmington *(G-15275)*

53 GENERAL MERCHANDISE STORES

5311 Department stores

Centro Properties Group LLC.............E 440 324-6610
   Elyria *(G-8235)*

JC Penney Corporation Inc.................D 419 394-7610
   Saint Marys *(G-12827)*

▲ The Elder-Beerman Stores Corp......A 937 296-2700
   Moraine *(G-11443)*

Walmart Inc......................................E 740 286-8203
   Jackson *(G-9528)*

Walmart Inc......................................C 937 399-0370
   Springfield *(G-13310)*

5331 Variety stores

◆ Big Lots Stores LLC........................A 614 278-6800
   Columbus *(G-5439)*

▲ Discount Drug Mart Inc..................C 330 725-2340
   Medina *(G-10829)*

Dollar Paradise.................................E 216 432-0421
   Cleveland *(G-4174)*

◆ Glow Industries Inc........................D 419 872-4772
   Perrysburg *(G-12339)*

Lululemon USA Inc............................E 440 250-0415
   Westlake *(G-15078)*

Marc Glassman Inc............................C 330 995-9246
   Aurora *(G-616)*

5399 Miscellaneous general merchandise

Goodwill Inds Centl Ohio Inc...............B 614 294-5181
   Columbus *(G-5941)*

54 FOOD STORES

5411 Grocery stores

54 FOOD STORES

Bagel Place Inc.................................... E 419 537-9470
  Toledo *(G-13698)*

Beck Suppliers Inc............................... E 419 426-3051
  Attica *(G-598)*

Buehler Food Markets Inc.................... C 330 364-3079
  Dover *(G-7874)*

Carfagnas Incorporated........................ E 614 846-6340
  Columbus *(G-5248)*

Convenient Food Mart Inc.................... E 800 860-4844
  Mentor *(G-10926)*

▲ Discount Drug Mart Inc.................... C 330 725-2340
  Medina *(G-10829)*

Duncan Oil Co..................................... E 937 426-5945
  Dayton *(G-7131)*

Fisher Foods Marketing Inc.................. C 330 497-3000
  North Canton *(G-11830)*

Fred W Albrecht Grocery Co................ C 330 666-6781
  Akron *(G-169)*

Fred W Albrecht Grocery Co................ C 330 645-6222
  Coventry Township *(G-7008)*

Giant Eagle Inc.................................... C 412 968-5300
  Columbus *(G-5933)*

Giant Eagle Inc.................................... D 330 364-5301
  Dover *(G-7885)*

Holland Oil Company........................... D 330 835-1815
  Akron *(G-194)*

Krlp Inc.. A 513 762-4000
  Cincinnati *(G-2953)*

Lykins Companies Inc.......................... E 513 831-8820
  Milford *(G-11238)*

Mary C Enterprises Inc........................ D 937 253-6169
  Dayton *(G-7467)*

National At/Trckstops Hldngs C........... A 440 808-9100
  Westlake *(G-15081)*

Riser Foods Company.......................... D 216 292-7000
  Bedford Heights *(G-1001)*

Sack n Save Inc................................... E 740 382-2464
  Marion *(G-10453)*

Sommers Market LLC........................... D 330 352-7470
  Hartville *(G-9130)*

Ta Operating LLC................................. B 440 808-9100
  Westlake *(G-15113)*

United Dairy Farmers Inc..................... C 513 396-8700
  Cincinnati *(G-3553)*

Walmart Inc... E 740 286-8203
  Jackson *(G-9528)*

Walmart Inc... C 937 399-0370
  Springfield *(G-13310)*

Weilands Fine Meats Inc...................... E 614 267-9910
  Columbus *(G-6873)*

5421 Meat and fish markets

Euclid Fish Company........................... D 440 951-6448
  Mentor *(G-10938)*

Landes Fresh Meats Inc....................... E 937 836-3613
  Clayton *(G-3734)*

Mary C Enterprises Inc........................ D 937 253-6169
  Dayton *(G-7467)*

S and S Gilardi Inc............................... D 740 397-2751
  Mount Vernon *(G-11507)*

Weilands Fine Meats Inc...................... E 614 267-9910
  Columbus *(G-6873)*

5431 Fruit and vegetable markets

A Brown and Sons Nursery Inc............ D 937 836-5820
  Brookville *(G-1444)*

Euclid Fish Company........................... D 440 951-6448
  Mentor *(G-10938)*

Mapleside Valley LLC........................... D 330 225-5576
  Brunswick *(G-1462)*

Miles Farmers Market Inc.................... C 440 248-5222
  Solon *(G-13111)*

5441 Candy, nut, and confectionery stores

Cleveland Soc For The Blind............... C 216 791-8118
  Cleveland *(G-4067)*

Gorant Chocolatier LLC....................... C 330 726-8821
  Boardman *(G-1288)*

◆ Jml Holdings Inc............................... E 419 866-7500
  Holland *(G-9291)*

5451 Dairy products stores

Austintown Dairy Inc........................... E 330 629-6170
  Youngstown *(G-15553)*

Coblentz Distributing Inc..................... C 330 893-3895
  Millersburg *(G-11277)*

▲ Discount Drug Mart Inc.................... C 330 725-2340
  Medina *(G-10829)*

▲ Hans Rothenbuhler & Son Inc......... E 440 632-6000
  Middlefield *(G-11140)*

S and S Gilardi Inc............................... D 740 397-2751
  Mount Vernon *(G-11507)*

United Dairy Farmers Inc..................... C 513 396-8700
  Cincinnati *(G-3553)*

Youngs Jersey Dairy Inc...................... B 937 325-0629
  Yellow Springs *(G-15537)*

5461 Retail bakeries

Alfred Nickles Bakery Inc..................... E 216 267-8055
  Cleveland *(G-3786)*

Bagel Place Inc.................................... E 419 537-9470
  Toledo *(G-13698)*

Buns of Delaware Inc........................... E 740 363-2867
  Delaware *(G-7781)*

Busken Bakery Inc............................... D 513 871-2114
  Cincinnati *(G-2294)*

▲ Cedar Fair LP................................... A 419 627-2344
  Sandusky *(G-12871)*

Mapleside Valley LLC........................... D 330 225-5576
  Brunswick *(G-1462)*

Mocha House Inc................................. E 330 392-3020
  Warren *(G-14540)*

Osmans Pies Inc.................................. E 330 607-9083
  Stow *(G-13384)*

Servatii Inc.. D 513 271-5040
  Cincinnati *(G-3362)*

5499 Miscellaneous food stores

▲ Antonio Sofo Son Importing Co........ C 419 476-4211
  Toledo *(G-13690)*

Cornucopia Inc.................................... E 216 521-4600
  Lakewood *(G-9662)*

Gold Star Chili Inc............................... E 513 231-4541
  Cincinnati *(G-2740)*

M & M Wine Cellar Inc......................... E 330 536-6450
  Lowellville *(G-10170)*

Magnetic Springs Water Company...... D 614 421-1780
  Columbus *(G-6189)*

Mustard Seed Health Fd Mkt Inc......... E 440 519-3663
  Solon *(G-13115)*

Second Wind Vitamins Inc................... E 330 336-9260
  Wadsworth *(G-14451)*

Superior Beverage Group Ltd............. C 419 529-0702
  Lexington *(G-9845)*

55 AUTOMOTIVE DEALERS AND GASOLINE SERVICE STATIONS

5511 New and used car dealers

Abers Garage Inc................................. E 419 281-5500
  Ashland *(G-471)*

Advantage Ford Lincoln Mercury......... E 419 334-9751
  Fremont *(G-8664)*

Ag-Pro Ohio LLC.................................. E 740 653-6951
  Lancaster *(G-9691)*

Al Spitzer Ford Inc............................... E 330 929-6546
  Cuyahoga Falls *(G-7034)*

▼ Albert Mike Leasing.......................... C 513 563-1400
  Cincinnati *(G-2158)*

Allegiance Administrators LLC............ E 877 895-1414
  Dublin *(G-7929)*

Allstate Trck Sls Estrn Ohio L............. E 330 339-5555
  New Philadelphia *(G-11639)*

Beechmont Chevrolet Inc..................... D 513 624-1100
  Cincinnati *(G-2247)*

Beechmont Ford Inc............................. C 513 752-6611
  Cincinnati *(G-2098)*

Beechmont Motors Inc......................... E 513 388-3883
  Cincinnati *(G-2248)*

Beechmont Motors T Inc...................... D 513 388-3800
  Cincinnati *(G-2249)*

Benedict Enterprises Inc...................... E 513 539-9216
  Monroe *(G-11334)*

Bill Delord Autocenter Inc.................... D 513 932-3000
  Maineville *(G-10225)*

Bob Ford Chapman Inc......................... E 937 642-0015
  Marysville *(G-10475)*

Bob Pulte Chevrolet Inc....................... D 513 932-0303
  Lebanon *(G-9757)*

Bob-Boyd Ford Inc............................... D 614 860-0606
  Lancaster *(G-9697)*

Bobb Automotive Inc............................ E 614 853-3000
  Columbus *(G-5452)*

Bobby Layman Cadillac GMC Inc......... E 740 654-9590
  Carroll *(G-1899)*

Bowling Green Lincoln Inc................... E 419 352-2553
  Bowling Green *(G-1312)*

▲ Brentlinger Enterprises..................... C 614 889-2571
  Dublin *(G-7947)*

Broadvue Motors Inc............................ D 440 845-6000
  Cleveland *(G-3899)*

▼ Brondes Ford.................................... E 419 473-1411
  Toledo *(G-13719)*

Buckeye Ford Inc................................. E 740 852-7842
  London *(G-10038)*

Cain Motors Inc.................................... E 330 494-5588
  Canton *(G-1695)*

▼ Carcorp Inc....................................... C 877 857-2801
  Columbus *(G-5506)*

Central Cadillac Limited....................... D 216 861-5800
  Cleveland *(G-3954)*

Chesrown Oldsmobile GMC Inc........... E 614 846-3040
  Columbus *(G-5554)*

Classic Automotive Group Inc............. E 440 255-5511
  Mentor *(G-10922)*

Classic Bick Oldsmbile Cdliac.............. E 440 639-4500
  Painesville *(G-12222)*

Cole Valley Motor Company Ltd.......... D 330 372-1665
  Warren *(G-14509)*

Columbus SAI Motors LLC................... E 614 851-3273
  Columbus *(G-5653)*

Coughlin Chevrolet Inc........................ E 740 852-1122
  London *(G-10040)*

Coughlin Chevrolet Inc........................ D 740 964-9191
  Pataskala *(G-12271)*

Coughlin Chevrolet Toyota Inc............ D 740 366-1381
  Newark *(G-11696)*

Cronin Auto Inc.................................... C 419 874-4331
  Perrysburg *(G-12327)*

Dave Dennis Inc................................... D 937 429-5566
  Beavercreek Township *(G-935)*

Dave Knapp Ford Lincoln Inc.............. E 937 547-3000
  Greenville *(G-8869)*

Decosky Motor Holdings Inc............... E 740 397-9122
  Mount Vernon *(G-11483)*

55 AUTOMOTIVE DEALERS AND GASOLINE SERVICE STATIONS

Diane Sauer Chevrolet Inc .... E 330 373-1600
   Warren *(G-14518)*

Dick Masheter Ford Inc .... D 614 861-7150
   Columbus *(G-5764)*

Don Wood Inc .... E 740 593-6641
   Athens *(G-566)*

Donley Ford-Lincoln Inc .... E 419 281-3673
   Ashland *(G-497)*

Dons Automotive Group Llc .... E 419 337-3010
   Wauseon *(G-14599)*

Doug Bigelow Chevrolet Inc .... D 330 644-7500
   Akron *(G-136)*

Downtown Ford Lincoln Inc .... D 330 456-2781
   Canton *(G-1738)*

▲ Driverge Vhcl Innovations LLC .... E 330 861-1118
   Akron *(G-141)*

Dunning Motor Sales Inc .... E 740 439-4465
   Cambridge *(G-1568)*

Dutro Ford Lincoln-Mercury Inc .... D 740 452-6334
   Zanesville *(G-15786)*

Ed Mullinax Ford LLC .... C 440 984-2431
   Amherst *(G-427)*

Ed Tomko Chrysler Jeep Ddge In .... E 440 835-5900
   Avon Lake *(G-677)*

Fairborn Buick-GMC Truck Inc .... D 937 878-7371
   Fairborn *(G-8374)*

Falls Motor City Inc .... E 330 929-3066
   Cuyahoga Falls *(G-7074)*

▲ Fallsway Equipment Co Inc .... E 330 633-6000
   Akron *(G-152)*

Fleetpride Inc .... E 740 282-2711
   Steubenville *(G-13326)*

Fred Martin Nissan LLC .... E 330 644-8888
   Akron *(G-168)*

George P Ballas Buick GMC Trck .... E 419 535-1000
   Toledo *(G-13820)*

Germain Ford LLC .... C 614 889-7777
   Columbus *(G-5931)*

Germain of Beavercreek II LLC .... D 937 429-2400
   Beavercreek *(G-880)*

Germain of Sidney III LLC .... E 937 498-4014
   Sidney *(G-13035)*

Graham Chevrolet-Cadillac Co .... C 419 989-4012
   Ontario *(G-12105)*

Greenwood Chevrolet Inc .... C 330 270-1299
   Youngstown *(G-15624)*

▼ Grogans Towne Chrysler Inc .... D 419 476-0761
   Toledo *(G-13830)*

Guess Motors Inc .... E 866 890-0522
   Carrollton *(G-1908)*

Hans Truck and Trlr Repr Inc .... D 216 581-0046
   Cleveland *(G-4349)*

Harry Humphries Auto City Inc .... E 330 343-6681
   Dover *(G-7888)*

Haydocy Automotive Inc .... D 614 279-8880
   Columbus *(G-5973)*

Herrnstein Chrysler Inc .... C 740 773-2203
   Chillicothe *(G-2068)*

Hidy Motors Inc .... D 937 426-9564
   Dayton *(G-7133)*

▼ Hill Intl Trcks NA LLC .... D 330 386-6440
   East Liverpool *(G-8185)*

Honda Dev & Mfg Amer LLC .... C 937 644-0724
   Marysville *(G-10488)*

Hoss II Inc .... E 937 669-4300
   Tipp City *(G-13660)*

Hoss Value Cars & Trucks Inc .... E 937 428-2400
   Dayton *(G-7415)*

I-75 Pierson Automotive Inc .... E 513 424-1881
   Franklin *(G-8642)*

Interstate Ford Inc .... C 937 866-0781
   Miamisburg *(G-11065)*

Jake Sweeney Automotive Inc .... D 513 782-2800
   Cincinnati *(G-2896)*

Jerry Haag Motors Inc .... E 937 402-2090
   Hillsboro *(G-9261)*

Jim Brown Chevrolet Inc .... C 440 255-5511
   Mentor *(G-10955)*

Jim Keim Ford .... D 614 888-3333
   Columbus *(G-6091)*

▲ Jmac Inc .... E 614 436-2418
   Columbus *(G-6092)*

Joyce Buick Inc .... E 419 529-3211
   Ontario *(G-12110)*

Kempthorn Motors Inc .... D 800 451-3877
   Canton *(G-1790)*

Kerry Ford Inc .... E 513 671-6400
   Cincinnati *(G-2939)*

Kings Toyota Inc .... D 513 583-4333
   Cincinnati *(G-2941)*

Klaben Lincoln Ford Inc .... D 330 593-6800
   Kent *(G-9585)*

Knox Auto LLC .... E 330 701-5266
   Mount Vernon *(G-11490)*

▲ Krieger Ford Inc .... C 614 888-3320
   Columbus *(G-6129)*

Lakewood Chrysler-Plymouth .... E 216 521-1000
   Brookpark *(G-1437)*

Laria Chevrolet-Buick Inc .... E 330 925-2015
   Rittman *(G-12730)*

Lariche Chevrolet-Cadillac Inc .... D 419 422-1855
   Findlay *(G-8556)*

Lavery Chevrolet-Buick Inc .... E 330 823-1100
   Alliance *(G-388)*

Lebanon Ford Inc .... D 513 932-1010
   Lebanon *(G-9775)*

Leikin Motor Companies Inc .... D 440 946-6900
   Willoughby *(G-15204)*

Lima Auto Mall Inc .... E 419 993-6000
   Lima *(G-9918)*

Lincoln Mrcury Kings Auto Mall .... E 513 683-3800
   Cincinnati *(G-2979)*

Mansfield Truck Sls & Svc Inc .... D 419 522-9811
   Mansfield *(G-10290)*

Mark Thomas Ford Inc .... E 330 638-1010
   Cortland *(G-6972)*

Mathews Ddge Chrysler Jeep Inc .... E 740 389-2341
   Marion *(G-10443)*

Mathews Ford Sandusky Inc .... E 419 626-4721
   Sandusky *(G-12914)*

Mathews Kennedy Ford L-M Inc .... D 740 387-3673
   Marion *(G-10444)*

Matia Motors Inc .... E 440 365-7311
   Elyria *(G-8273)*

McCluskey Chevrolet Inc .... C 513 761-1111
   Loveland *(G-10149)*

Miami Valley Intl Trcks Inc .... E 937 324-5526
   Springfield *(G-13273)*

Mike Castrucci Ford .... C 513 831-7010
   Milford *(G-11243)*

Mike Ford Bass Inc .... D 440 934-3673
   Sheffield Village *(G-13002)*

Mizar Motors Inc .... D 419 729-2400
   Toledo *(G-13925)*

Montrose Ford Inc .... C 330 666-0711
   Fairlawn *(G-8491)*

Mullinax Ford North Canton Inc .... C 330 238-3206
   Canton *(G-1812)*

Nassief Automotive Inc .... E 440 997-5151
   Austinburg *(G-632)*

Nick Mayer Lincoln-Mercury Inc .... D 877 836-5314
   Westlake *(G-15084)*

Northern Automotive Inc .... E 614 436-2001
   Columbus *(G-6367)*

Northgate Chrysler Ddge Jeep I .... D 513 385-3900
   Cincinnati *(G-3123)*

▲ Pag Mentor A1 Inc .... E 440 951-1040
   Mentor *(G-10982)*

Pallotta Ford Inc .... D 330 345-5051
   Wooster *(G-15365)*

Partners Auto Group Bdford Inc .... D 440 439-2323
   Bedford *(G-980)*

Paul Hrnchar Ford-Mercury Inc .... E 330 533-3673
   Canfield *(G-1638)*

Pete Baur Buick GMC Inc .... E 440 238-5600
   Cleveland *(G-4745)*

R & R Inc .... E 330 799-1536
   Youngstown *(G-15705)*

R & R Truck Sales Inc .... E 330 784-5881
   Akron *(G-276)*

Reineke Ford Inc .... E 888 691-8175
   Fostoria *(G-8622)*

▲ Ricart Ford Inc .... B 614 836-5321
   Groveport *(G-9000)*

Ron Marhofer Auto Family .... E 330 940-4422
   Cuyahoga Falls *(G-7098)*

Ron Marhofer Automall Inc .... C 330 835-6707
   Cuyahoga Falls *(G-7099)*

Ron Marhofer Automall Inc .... E 330 923-5059
   Cuyahoga Falls *(G-7100)*

Rouen Chrysler Plymouth Dodge .... E 419 837-6228
   Woodville *(G-15306)*

Roush Equipment Inc .... C 614 882-1535
   Westerville *(G-15014)*

▲ Rumpke/Kenworth Contract .... D 740 774-5111
   Chillicothe *(G-2089)*

Rush Truck Centers Ohio Inc .... E 513 733-8500
   Cincinnati *(G-3334)*

Schoner Chevrolet Inc .... E 330 877-6731
   Hartville *(G-9129)*

Sharpnack Chevrolet Co .... E 800 752-7513
   Vermilion *(G-14408)*

Sims Buick-GMC Truck Inc .... E 330 372-3500
   Warren *(G-14554)*

Slimans Sales & Service Inc .... E 440 988-4484
   Amherst *(G-432)*

Sonic Automotive .... D 614 870-8200
   Columbus *(G-6692)*

Sorbir Inc .... D 440 449-1000
   Cleveland *(G-4919)*

Spires Motors Inc .... E 614 771-2345
   Hilliard *(G-9233)*

Spitzer Chevrolet Inc .... E 330 467-4141
   Northfield *(G-11966)*

Stoops of Lima Inc .... D 419 228-4334
   Lima *(G-9967)*

Stykemain-Buick-Gmc Ltd .... D 419 784-5252
   Defiance *(G-7770)*

Sunnyside Cars Inc .... E 440 777-9911
   North Olmsted *(G-11917)*

Surfside Motors Inc .... E 419 419-4776
   Galion *(G-8751)*

Tansky Motors Inc .... E 650 322-7069
   Rockbridge *(G-12736)*

Taylor Chevrolet Inc .... E 740 653-2091
   Lancaster *(G-9746)*

The Glockner Chevrolet Company .... C 740 353-2161
   Portsmouth *(G-12576)*

Tim Lally Chevrolet Inc .... D 440 232-2000
   Bedford *(G-988)*

Tom Ahl Chryslr-Plymouth-Dodge .... C 419 227-0202
   Lima *(G-9971)*

Toyota Industries N Amer Inc .... D 937 237-0976
   Dayton *(G-7675)*

◆ Valley Ford Truck Inc .... D 216 524-2400
   Cleveland *(G-5097)*

Employee Codes: A=Over 500 employees, B=251-500
C=101-250, D=51-100, E=20-50, F=10-19, G=1-9

55 AUTOMOTIVE DEALERS AND GASOLINE SERVICE STATIONS

Van Devere Inc .... D 330 253-6137
  Akron *(G-348)*

Village Motors Inc .... D 330 674-2055
  Millersburg *(G-11295)*

Vin Devers Inc .... C 888 847-9535
  Sylvania *(G-13578)*

Volvo BMW Dyton Evans Volkswag .... E 937 890-6200
  Dayton *(G-7710)*

Voss Auto Network Inc .... E 937 428-2447
  Dayton *(G-7711)*

Voss Chevrolet Inc .... C 937 428-2500
  Dayton *(G-7713)*

Voss Dodge .... E 937 435-7800
  Dayton *(G-7714)*

Wabash National Trlr Ctrs Inc .... D 614 878-6088
  Groveport *(G-9012)*

Walker Auto Group Inc .... D 937 433-4950
  Miamisburg *(G-11103)*

Walt Ford Sweeney Inc .... D 513 347-2600
  Cincinnati *(G-3639)*

Warner Buick-Nissan Inc .... E 419 423-7161
  Findlay *(G-8597)*

White Family Companies Inc .... E 937 222-3701
  Dayton *(G-7720)*

Whites Service Center Inc .... E 937 653-5279
  Urbana *(G-14317)*

▲ Wmk LLC .... E 234 312-2000
  Richfield *(G-12714)*

Yark Automotive Group Inc .... B 419 841-7771
  Toledo *(G-14111)*

Young Truck Sales Inc .... E 330 477-6271
  Canton *(G-1891)*

5521 Used car dealers

Aaj Enterprises Inc .... A 614 497-2000
  Obetz *(G-12078)*

Abraham Ford LLC .... E 440 233-7402
  Elyria *(G-8232)*

▼ Albert Mike Leasing .... C 513 563-1400
  Cincinnati *(G-2158)*

Brown Motor Sales Co .... E 419 531-0151
  Toledo *(G-13720)*

Cain Motors Inc .... E 330 494-5588
  Canton *(G-1695)*

▼ Carcorp Inc .... C 877 857-2801
  Columbus *(G-5506)*

Central Cadillac Limited .... D 216 861-5800
  Cleveland *(G-3954)*

Chesrown Oldsmobile GMC Inc .... E 614 846-3040
  Columbus *(G-5554)*

Columbus SAI Motors LLC .... E 614 851-3273
  Columbus *(G-5653)*

Coughlin Chevrolet Inc .... E 740 852-1122
  London *(G-10040)*

Coughlin Chevrolet Toyota Inc .... D 740 366-1381
  Newark *(G-11696)*

Cronin Auto Inc .... C 419 874-4331
  Perrysburg *(G-12327)*

Dons Automotive Group Llc .... E 419 337-3010
  Wauseon *(G-14599)*

Doug Bigelow Chevrolet Inc .... D 330 644-7500
  Akron *(G-136)*

Ed Mullinax Ford LLC .... C 440 984-2431
  Amherst *(G-427)*

George P Ballas Buick GMC Trck .... E 419 535-1000
  Toledo *(G-13820)*

Graham Chevrolet-Cadillac Co .... E 419 989-4012
  Ontario *(G-12105)*

Greenwood Chevrolet Inc .... C 330 270-1299
  Youngstown *(G-15624)*

▼ Grogans Towne Chrysler Inc .... D 419 476-0761
  Toledo *(G-13830)*

Interstate Ford Inc .... C 937 866-0781
  Miamisburg *(G-11065)*

Jake Sweeney Automotive Inc .... D 513 782-2800
  Cincinnati *(G-2896)*

Jim Keim Ford .... D 614 888-3333
  Columbus *(G-6091)*

Kempthorn Motors Inc .... D 800 451-3877
  Canton *(G-1790)*

Laria Chevrolet-Buick Inc .... E 330 925-2015
  Rittman *(G-12730)*

Lariche Chevrolet-Cadillac Inc .... D 419 422-1855
  Findlay *(G-8556)*

Lavery Chevrolet-Buick Inc .... E 330 823-1100
  Alliance *(G-388)*

Lebanon Ford Inc .... D 513 932-1010
  Lebanon *(G-9775)*

Leikin Motor Companies Inc .... D 440 946-6900
  Willoughby *(G-15204)*

Lincoln Mrcury Kings Auto Mall .... E 513 683-3800
  Cincinnati *(G-2979)*

Lkq Triplettasap Inc .... C 330 733-6333
  Akron *(G-223)*

Mark Thomas Ford Inc .... E 330 638-1010
  Cortland *(G-6972)*

McCluskey Chevrolet Inc .... C 513 761-1111
  Loveland *(G-10149)*

Mike Castrucci Ford .... C 513 831-7010
  Milford *(G-11243)*

Modern Finance Company .... E 614 351-7400
  Columbus *(G-6255)*

Montrose Ford Inc .... C 330 666-0711
  Fairlawn *(G-8491)*

Mullinax Ford North Canton Inc .... C 330 238-3206
  Canton *(G-1812)*

Northern Automotive Inc .... E 614 436-2001
  Columbus *(G-6367)*

▼ Premier Truck Sls & Rentl Inc .... E 800 825-1255
  Cleveland *(G-4768)*

Priced Right Cars Inc .... E 614 337-0037
  Columbus *(G-6545)*

Reineke Ford Inc .... E 888 691-8175
  Fostoria *(G-8622)*

Rouen Chrysler Plymouth Dodge .... E 419 837-6228
  Woodville *(G-15306)*

Roush Equipment Inc .... C 614 882-1535
  Westerville *(G-15014)*

Schoner Chevrolet Inc .... E 330 877-6731
  Hartville *(G-9129)*

Sharpnack Chevrolet Co .... E 800 752-7513
  Vermilion *(G-14408)*

Skipco Financial Adjusters Inc .... D 330 854-4800
  Canal Fulton *(G-1594)*

Sonic Automotive .... D 614 870-8200
  Columbus *(G-6692)*

Spitzer Chevrolet Inc .... E 330 467-4141
  Northfield *(G-11966)*

▼ Stricker Bros Inc .... E 513 732-1152
  Batavia *(G-748)*

Sunnyside Cars Inc .... E 440 777-9911
  North Olmsted *(G-11917)*

Surfside Motors Inc .... E 419 419-4776
  Galion *(G-8751)*

Tansky Motors Inc .... E 650 322-7069
  Rockbridge *(G-12736)*

◆ Valley Ford Truck Inc .... D 216 524-2400
  Cleveland *(G-5097)*

Village Motors Inc .... D 330 674-2055
  Millersburg *(G-11295)*

Vin Devers Inc .... C 888 847-9535
  Sylvania *(G-13578)*

Volunteers America Ohio & Ind .... C 614 253-6100
  Columbus *(G-6856)*

Voss Auto Network Inc .... B 937 433-1444
  Dayton *(G-7712)*

Voss Auto Network Inc .... E 937 428-2447
  Dayton *(G-7711)*

Voss Chevrolet Inc .... C 937 428-2500
  Dayton *(G-7713)*

Voss Dodge .... E 937 435-7800
  Dayton *(G-7714)*

Walker Auto Group Inc .... D 937 433-4950
  Miamisburg *(G-11103)*

Warner Buick-Nissan Inc .... E 419 423-7161
  Findlay *(G-8597)*

World Trck Towing Recovery Inc .... E 330 723-1116
  Seville *(G-12968)*

5531 Auto and home supply stores

Abraham Ford LLC .... E 440 233-7402
  Elyria *(G-8232)*

▼ Albert Mike Leasing .... C 513 563-1400
  Cincinnati *(G-2158)*

Allstate Trck Sls Estrn Ohio L .... E 330 339-5555
  New Philadelphia *(G-11639)*

Auto Parts Center-Cuyahoga FLS .... E 330 928-2149
  Cuyahoga Falls *(G-7045)*

Autozone Inc .... E 216 751-0571
  Cleveland *(G-3842)*

Autozone Inc .... E 216 267-6586
  Cleveland *(G-3843)*

Autozone Inc .... E 440 593-6934
  Conneaut *(G-6939)*

Autozone Inc .... E 440 639-2247
  Painesville *(G-12221)*

Autozone Inc .... E 419 872-2813
  Perrysburg *(G-12315)*

Beechmont Ford Inc .... C 513 752-6611
  Cincinnati *(G-2098)*

Belle Tire Distributors Inc .... E 419 535-3033
  Toledo *(G-13704)*

▲ Best One Tire & Svc Lima Inc .... E 419 229-2380
  Lima *(G-9868)*

Bridgeport Auto Parts Inc .... E 740 635-0441
  Bridgeport *(G-1375)*

Brown Motor Sales Co .... E 419 531-0151
  Toledo *(G-13720)*

Bulldawg Holdings LLC .... E 419 423-3131
  Findlay *(G-8519)*

▲ Car Parts Warehouse Inc .... E 216 281-4500
  Brookpark *(G-1429)*

Chagrin Valley Auto Parts Co .... E 216 398-9800
  Cleveland *(G-3960)*

Chesrown Oldsmobile GMC Inc .... E 614 846-3040
  Columbus *(G-5554)*

Cole Valley Motor Company Ltd .... D 330 372-1665
  Warren *(G-14509)*

Conrads Tire Service Inc .... E 216 941-3333
  Cleveland *(G-4103)*

Coughlin Chevrolet Inc .... D 740 964-9191
  Pataskala *(G-12271)*

Coughlin Chevrolet Toyota Inc .... D 740 366-1381
  Newark *(G-11696)*

Cronin Auto Inc .... C 419 874-4331
  Perrysburg *(G-12327)*

Dave Dennis Inc .... D 937 429-5566
  Beavercreek Township *(G-935)*

Dave Knapp Ford Lincoln Inc .... E 937 547-3000
  Greenville *(G-8869)*

▲ Dealer Tire LLC .... B 216 432-0088
  Cleveland *(G-4155)*

▲ Detroit Tire & Auto Supply Inc .... E 937 426-0949
  Xenia *(G-15503)*

Dutro Ford Lincoln-Mercury Inc .... D 740 452-6334
  Zanesville *(G-15786)*

SIC SECTION
56 APPAREL AND ACCESSORY STORES

Esec Corporation............................. E 614 875-3732
  Grove City *(G-8918)*

Fayette Parts Service Inc................. E 724 880-3616
  Wintersville *(G-15294)*

◆ Four Wheel Drive Hardware LLC......... C 330 482-4733
  Columbiana *(G-5235)*

◆ Goodyear Tire & Rubber Company..... A 330 796-2121
  Akron *(G-179)*

▲ Grismer Tire Company..................... E 937 643-2526
  Centerville *(G-1945)*

Haasz Automall LLC........................ E 330 296-2866
  Ravenna *(G-12627)*

Haydocy Automotive Inc................... D 614 279-8880
  Columbus *(G-5973)*

Helton Enterprises Inc..................... E 419 423-4180
  Findlay *(G-8546)*

▼ Hill Intl Trcks NA LLC...................... D 330 386-6440
  East Liverpool *(G-8185)*

◆ Jegs Automotive LLC..................... C 614 294-5050
  Delaware *(G-7808)*

Jerry Haag Motors Inc...................... E 937 402-2090
  Hillsboro *(G-9261)*

Kerry Ford Inc................................ D 513 671-6400
  Cincinnati *(G-2939)*

Keystone Auto Glass Inc.................. D 419 509-0497
  Maumee *(G-10736)*

KOI Enterprises Inc......................... C 513 648-3020
  Cincinnati *(G-2947)*

▲ KOI Enterprises Inc...................... D 513 357-2400
  Cincinnati *(G-2948)*

Leikin Motor Companies Inc.............. D 440 946-6900
  Willoughby *(G-15204)*

Matia Motors Inc............................ E 440 365-7311
  Elyria *(G-8273)*

Miami Valley Intl Trcks Inc................ E 937 324-5526
  Springfield *(G-13273)*

▲ Millersburg Tire Service Inc........... E 330 674-1085
  Millersburg *(G-11286)*

North Gateway Tire Company Inc....... E 330 725-8473
  Medina *(G-10869)*

Orwell Tire Service Inc..................... D 440 437-6515
  Orwell *(G-12179)*

▲ Pat Young Service Co Inc.............. E 216 447-8550
  Cleveland *(G-4729)*

Pep Boys - Mnny Moe Jack Del L........ E 614 864-2092
  Columbus *(G-6515)*

Pete Baur Buick GMC Inc.................. E 440 238-5600
  Cleveland *(G-4745)*

▼ QT Equipment Company................. E 330 724-3055
  Akron *(G-275)*

R & M Leasing Inc............................ C 937 382-6800
  Wilmington *(G-15269)*

Ron Marhofer Auto Family................. E 330 940-4422
  Cuyahoga Falls *(G-7098)*

Rush Truck Centers Ohio Inc............. E 513 733-8500
  Cincinnati *(G-3334)*

Rush Truck Leasing Inc.................... E 937 264-2365
  Dayton *(G-7599)*

Rush Truck Leasing Inc.................... E 419 224-6045
  Lima *(G-9957)*

Rush Truck Leasing Inc.................... E 330 798-0600
  Walton Hills *(G-14479)*

Smyth Automotive Inc...................... D 513 528-2800
  Cincinnati *(G-3389)*

▲ Snyders Antique Auto Parts Inc...... E 330 549-5313
  New Springfield *(G-11679)*

Sonic Automotive............................ D 614 870-8200
  Columbus *(G-6692)*

▼ Stricker Bros Inc.......................... E 513 732-1152
  Batavia *(G-748)*

Sunnyside Cars Inc.......................... E 440 777-9911
  North Olmsted *(G-11917)*

Tansky Motors Inc........................... E 650 322-7069
  Rockbridge *(G-12736)*

Tbc Retail Group Inc........................ E 216 267-8040
  Cleveland *(G-4980)*

Tm Final Ltd.................................. B 419 724-8473
  Toledo *(G-14047)*

Tractor Supply Company................. E 937 382-2595
  Wilmington *(G-15275)*

Treadmaxx Tire Distrs Inc................. D 404 762-4944
  Wooster *(G-15379)*

◆ Valley Ford Truck Inc..................... D 216 524-2400
  Cleveland *(G-5097)*

Wabash National Trlr Ctrs Inc............ D 614 878-6088
  Groveport *(G-9012)*

Walker Auto Group Inc..................... D 937 433-4950
  Miamisburg *(G-11103)*

Weastec Incorporated...................... E 614 734-9645
  Dublin *(G-8161)*

◆ Wz Management Inc....................... E 330 628-4881
  Akron *(G-365)*

Ziebart of Ohio Inc........................... E 440 845-6031
  Cleveland *(G-5175)*

Ziegler Tire and Supply Co............... C 330 343-7739
  Dover *(G-7911)*

Ziegler Tire and Supply Co............... C 330 834-3332
  Massillon *(G-10676)*

5541 Gasoline service stations

1st Stop Inc................................... E 937 695-0318
  Winchester *(G-15283)*

Beck Suppliers Inc.......................... E 419 426-3051
  Attica *(G-598)*

Buehler Food Markets Inc................. C 330 364-3079
  Dover *(G-7874)*

Convenient Food Mart Inc................. E 800 860-4844
  Mentor *(G-10926)*

G J Shue Inc.................................. E 330 722-0082
  Medina *(G-10837)*

Holland Oil Company...................... D 330 835-1815
  Akron *(G-194)*

Irace Inc...................................... E 330 836-7247
  Akron *(G-204)*

Island Service Company................... E 419 285-3695
  Put In Bay *(G-12617)*

Mighty Mac Investments Inc............. E 937 335-2928
  Troy *(G-14147)*

National At/Trckstops Hldngs C......... A 440 808-9100
  Westlake *(G-15081)*

Ports Petroleum Company Inc........... E 330 264-1885
  Wooster *(G-15367)*

Red Rover LLC............................... E 330 262-6501
  Wooster *(G-15368)*

Santmyer Logistics Inc.................... D 330 262-6501
  Wooster *(G-15371)*

Seaway Gas & Petroleum Inc............. E 216 566-9070
  Cleveland *(G-4888)*

Ta Operating LLC............................ B 440 808-9100
  Westlake *(G-15113)*

Travelcenters of America Inc............ A 440 808-9100
  Westlake *(G-15117)*

Trep Ltd....................................... E 419 717-5624
  Napoleon *(G-11533)*

Triumph Energy Corporation............. C 513 367-9900
  Harrison *(G-9118)*

True North Energy LLC.................... D 330 722-2031
  Medina *(G-10900)*

True North Energy LLC.................... E 877 245-9336
  Brecksville *(G-1370)*

United Dairy Farmers Inc.................. C 513 396-8700
  Cincinnati *(G-3553)*

Yorktown Automotive Center Inc....... E 440 885-2803
  Cleveland *(G-5165)*

5551 Boat dealers

Beaver Park Marina Inc.................... E 440 282-6308
  Lorain *(G-10059)*

Bob Pulte Chevrolet Inc................... E 513 932-0303
  Lebanon *(G-9757)*

Lakeside Marine Inc......................... E 419 732-7160
  Port Clinton *(G-12537)*

S B S Transit Inc............................. E 440 288-2222
  Elyria *(G-8292)*

5561 Recreational vehicle dealers

L B Brunk & Sons Inc...................... E 330 332-0359
  Salem *(G-12845)*

Moores Rv Inc................................ E 800 523-1904
  North Ridgeville *(G-11932)*

Sirpilla Recrtl Vhcl Ctr Inc............... E 330 494-2525
  Akron *(G-303)*

Surfside Motors Inc......................... E 419 419-4776
  Galion *(G-8751)*

5571 Motorcycle dealers

AD Farrow LLC............................... E 740 965-9900
  Sunbury *(G-13514)*

▼ Carcorp Inc................................. C 877 857-2801
  Columbus *(G-5506)*

Damarc Inc.................................... E 330 454-6171
  Canton *(G-1731)*

Old Meadow Farms Inc..................... E 440 632-5590
  Middlefield *(G-11143)*

South E Harley Davidson Sls Co......... E 440 439-5300
  Cleveland *(G-4920)*

◆ Wholecycle Inc............................. E 330 929-8123
  Peninsula *(G-12296)*

5599 Automotive dealers, nec

▲ IAC Wauseon LLC......................... E 419 335-1000
  Wauseon *(G-14605)*

◆ Jilco Industries Inc....................... E 330 698-0280
  Kidron *(G-9636)*

Lane Aviation Corporation................ C 614 237-3747
  Columbus *(G-6138)*

McKinley Air Transport Inc............... E 330 497-6956
  Canton *(G-1802)*

Old Meadow Farms Inc..................... E 440 632-5590
  Middlefield *(G-11143)*

Options Flight Support Inc................ A 216 261-3500
  Cleveland *(G-4705)*

▲ Sportsmans Market Inc.................. C 513 735-9100
  Batavia *(G-747)*

Wabash National Trlr Ctrs Inc............ D 614 878-6088
  Groveport *(G-9012)*

56 APPAREL AND ACCESSORY STORES

5611 Men's and boys' clothing stores

◆ Abercrombie & Fitch Trading Co...... D 614 283-6500
  New Albany *(G-11551)*

◆ For Women Like Me Inc.................. E 407 848-7339
  Chagrin Falls *(G-1958)*

▲ J Peterman Company LLC.............. E 888 647-2555
  Blue Ash *(G-1189)*

5621 Women's clothing stores

◆ Abercrombie & Fitch Trading Co...... D 614 283-6500
  New Albany *(G-11551)*

◆ For Women Like Me Inc.................. E 407 848-7339
  Chagrin Falls *(G-1958)*

▲ J Peterman Company LLC.............. E 888 647-2555
  Blue Ash *(G-1189)*

Employee Codes: A=Over 500 employees, B=251-500
C=101-250, D=51-100, E=20-50, F=10-19, G=1-9

56 APPAREL AND ACCESSORY STORES

Jcherie LLC...E 216 453-1051
  Shaker Heights *(G-12979)*

5632 Women's accessory and specialty stores

Lifestages Boutique For Women.............D 937 274-5420
  Englewood *(G-8314)*
◆ Schneider Saddlery LLC.........................E 440 543-2700
  Chagrin Falls *(G-1989)*

5641 Children's and infants' wear stores

◆ Abercrombie & Fitch Trading Co.........D 614 283-6500
  New Albany *(G-11551)*

5661 Shoe stores

Cov-Ro Inc...E 330 856-3176
  Warren *(G-14515)*
◆ Lehigh Outfitters LLC............................C 740 753-1951
  Nelsonville *(G-11549)*
▲ The Elder-Beerman Stores Corp........A 937 296-2700
  Moraine *(G-11443)*

5699 Miscellaneous apparel and accessories

Gymnastics World Inc.................................E 440 526-2970
  Cleveland *(G-4343)*
▲ K Amalia Enterprises Inc......................E 614 733-3800
  Plain City *(G-12483)*
Lifestages Boutique For Women.............D 937 274-5420
  Englewood *(G-8314)*
Lululemon USA Inc.....................................C 614 418-9127
  Columbus *(G-6177)*
◆ Schneider Saddlery LLC.........................E 440 543-2700
  Chagrin Falls *(G-1989)*
Tractor Supply Company...........................E 937 382-2595
  Wilmington *(G-15275)*
▲ TSC Apparel LLC....................................D 800 289-5400
  Cincinnati *(G-3534)*

57 HOME FURNITURE, FURNISHINGS AND EQUIPMENT STORES

5712 Furniture stores

Big Sandy Furniture Inc............................D 740 894-4242
  Chesapeake *(G-2028)*
Big Sandy Furniture Inc............................D 740 775-4244
  Chillicothe *(G-2052)*
Big Sandy Furniture Inc............................D 740 354-3193
  Portsmouth *(G-12546)*
▲ Big Sandy Furniture Inc........................D 740 574-2113
  Franklin Furnace *(G-8653)*
Dtv Inc..E 216 226-5465
  Cleveland *(G-4187)*
Globe Furniture Rentals Inc.....................D 513 771-8287
  Cincinnati *(G-2734)*
Indepndence Office Bus Sup Inc............D 216 398-8880
  Cleveland *(G-4408)*
▲ Litehouse Products LLC.......................E 440 638-2350
  Strongsville *(G-13471)*
Loth Inc..E 614 487-4000
  Columbus *(G-6173)*
Mill Tech LLC...E 614 496-9778
  Canal Winchester *(G-1613)*
▲ Professional Laminate Mllwk Inc........E 513 891-7858
  Milford *(G-11251)*
River City Furniture LLC...........................E 513 612-7303
  West Chester *(G-14756)*
Stationers Inc...E 740 423-1400
  Belpre *(G-1059)*
W Home Collection LLC............................E 440 247-4474
  Chagrin Falls *(G-1971)*

▲ Waterbeds n Stuff Inc..........................E 614 871-1171
  Grove City *(G-8965)*

5713 Floor covering stores

▼ Americas Floor Source LLC................D 614 808-3915
  Columbus *(G-5363)*
Clays Heritage Carpet Inc........................E 330 497-1280
  Canton *(G-1711)*
J L G Co Inc...E 513 248-1755
  Loveland *(G-10144)*
JP Flooring Systems Inc...........................E 513 346-4300
  West Chester *(G-14715)*
Rite Rug Co...E 614 478-3365
  Columbus *(G-6591)*
Schoch Tile & Carpet Inc..........................E 513 922-3466
  Cincinnati *(G-3350)*
▲ Stanley Steemer Intl Inc.......................C 614 764-2007
  Dublin *(G-8124)*

5714 Drapery and upholstery stores

Accent Drapery Co Inc..............................E 614 488-0741
  Columbus *(G-5300)*

5719 Miscellaneous homefurnishings

▲ D & L Lighting Inc.................................D 614 841-1200
  Columbus *(G-5256)*
Gross Electric Inc.......................................E 419 537-1818
  Toledo *(G-13831)*
Mars Electric Company.............................D 440 946-2250
  Cleveland *(G-4529)*
▲ Mosser Glass Inc...................................E 740 439-1827
  Cambridge *(G-1576)*
Nacco Industries Inc..................................E 440 229-5151
  Cleveland *(G-4616)*
Overhead Inc...E 419 476-7811
  Toledo *(G-13951)*
▼ Provantage LLC......................................D 330 494-3781
  North Canton *(G-11854)*
◆ The Blonder Company............................C 216 431-3560
  Cleveland *(G-4992)*
◆ Wasserstrom Company..........................B 614 228-6925
  Columbus *(G-6867)*

5722 Household appliance stores

Big Sandy Furniture Inc............................D 740 775-4244
  Chillicothe *(G-2052)*
Big Sandy Furniture Inc............................D 740 354-3193
  Portsmouth *(G-12546)*
▲ Big Sandy Furniture Inc........................D 740 574-2113
  Franklin Furnace *(G-8653)*
Dayton Appliance Parts LLC.....................E 937 224-0487
  Dayton *(G-7270)*
Hull Bros Inc...E 419 375-2827
  Fort Recovery *(G-8610)*
Kinn Bros Plbg Htg & AC Inc....................E 419 562-1484
  Bucyrus *(G-1511)*
Lowes Home Centers LLC........................C 330 665-9356
  Akron *(G-225)*
Lowes Home Centers LLC........................C 330 829-2700
  Alliance *(G-389)*
Lowes Home Centers LLC........................C 440 998-6555
  Ashtabula *(G-540)*
Lowes Home Centers LLC........................C 740 589-3750
  Athens *(G-582)*
Lowes Home Centers LLC........................C 440 937-3500
  Avon *(G-660)*
Lowes Home Centers LLC........................C 937 427-1110
  Beavercreek *(G-889)*
Lowes Home Centers LLC........................C 216 831-2860
  Bedford *(G-970)*
Lowes Home Centers LLC........................D 937 599-4000
  Bellefontaine *(G-1032)*

Lowes Home Centers LLC........................C 330 497-2720
  Canton *(G-1797)*
Lowes Home Centers LLC........................C 740 773-7777
  Chillicothe *(G-2079)*
Lowes Home Centers LLC........................C 513 598-7050
  Cincinnati *(G-2990)*
Lowes Home Centers LLC........................C 216 351-4723
  Cleveland *(G-4506)*
Lowes Home Centers LLC........................C 614 853-6200
  Columbus *(G-6174)*
Lowes Home Centers LLC........................C 937 235-2920
  Dayton *(G-7460)*
Lowes Home Centers LLC........................C 937 438-4900
  Dayton *(G-7461)*
Lowes Home Centers LLC........................C 937 854-8200
  Dayton *(G-7462)*
Lowes Home Centers LLC........................C 419 782-9000
  Defiance *(G-7753)*
Lowes Home Centers LLC........................C 614 659-0530
  Dublin *(G-8058)*
Lowes Home Centers LLC........................C 440 324-5004
  Elyria *(G-8272)*
Lowes Home Centers LLC........................C 419 420-7531
  Findlay *(G-8559)*
Lowes Home Centers LLC........................C 419 355-0221
  Fremont *(G-8690)*
Lowes Home Centers LLC........................C 937 547-2400
  Greenville *(G-8880)*
Lowes Home Centers LLC........................C 513 737-3700
  Hamilton *(G-9061)*
Lowes Home Centers LLC........................C 614 529-5900
  Hilliard *(G-9210)*
Lowes Home Centers LLC........................C 740 681-3464
  Lancaster *(G-9733)*
Lowes Home Centers LLC........................C 419 331-3598
  Lima *(G-9930)*
Lowes Home Centers LLC........................C 440 985-5700
  Lorain *(G-10090)*
Lowes Home Centers LLC........................C 740 374-2151
  Marietta *(G-10381)*
Lowes Home Centers LLC........................C 740 389-9737
  Marion *(G-10433)*
Lowes Home Centers LLC........................C 937 578-4440
  Marysville *(G-10492)*
Lowes Home Centers LLC........................C 513 336-9741
  Mason *(G-10575)*
Lowes Home Centers LLC........................C 330 832-1901
  Massillon *(G-10650)*
Lowes Home Centers LLC........................C 440 392-0027
  Mentor *(G-10965)*
Lowes Home Centers LLC........................C 513 727-3900
  Middletown *(G-11170)*
Lowes Home Centers LLC........................C 513 965-3280
  Milford *(G-11237)*
Lowes Home Centers LLC........................C 740 393-5350
  Mount Vernon *(G-11498)*
Lowes Home Centers LLC........................D 330 339-1936
  New Philadelphia *(G-11657)*
Lowes Home Centers LLC........................C 740 522-0003
  Newark *(G-11723)*
Lowes Home Centers LLC........................D 330 908-2750
  Northfield *(G-11960)*
Lowes Home Centers LLC........................C 419 747-1920
  Ontario *(G-12113)*
Lowes Home Centers LLC........................C 419 874-6758
  Perrysburg *(G-12355)*
Lowes Home Centers LLC........................D 614 769-9940
  Reynoldsburg *(G-12668)*
Lowes Home Centers LLC........................C 440 331-1027
  Rocky River *(G-12748)*
Lowes Home Centers LLC........................D 740 699-3000
  Saint Clairsville *(G-12799)*

SIC SECTION

58 EATING AND DRINKING PLACES

Lowes Home Centers LLC.................. C 419 624-6000
  Sandusky *(G-12912)*

Lowes Home Centers LLC.................. C 937 498-8400
  Sidney *(G-13039)*

Lowes Home Centers LLC.................. C 513 445-1000
  South Lebanon *(G-13172)*

Lowes Home Centers LLC.................. C 740 894-7120
  South Point *(G-13177)*

Lowes Home Centers LLC.................. C 937 327-6000
  Springfield *(G-13264)*

Lowes Home Centers LLC.................. C 740 266-3500
  Steubenville *(G-13336)*

Lowes Home Centers LLC.................. C 330 920-9280
  Stow *(G-13380)*

Lowes Home Centers LLC.................. C 330 626-2980
  Streetsboro *(G-13420)*

Lowes Home Centers LLC.................. C 440 239-2630
  Strongsville *(G-13473)*

Lowes Home Centers LLC.................. C 419 843-9758
  Toledo *(G-13894)*

Lowes Home Centers LLC.................. C 937 339-2544
  Troy *(G-14145)*

Lowes Home Centers LLC.................. C 330 335-1900
  Wadsworth *(G-14442)*

Lowes Home Centers LLC.................. C 419 739-1300
  Wapakoneta *(G-14488)*

Lowes Home Centers LLC.................. C 330 609-8000
  Warren *(G-14536)*

Lowes Home Centers LLC.................. C 513 755-4300
  West Chester *(G-14726)*

Lowes Home Centers LLC.................. C 740 574-6200
  Wheelersburg *(G-15130)*

Lowes Home Centers LLC.................. C 440 942-2759
  Willoughby *(G-15207)*

Lowes Home Centers LLC.................. C 937 383-7000
  Wilmington *(G-15260)*

Lowes Home Centers LLC.................. C 330 287-2261
  Wooster *(G-15352)*

Lowes Home Centers LLC.................. C 937 347-4000
  Xenia *(G-15524)*

Lowes Home Centers LLC.................. C 330 965-4500
  Youngstown *(G-15653)*

Lowes Home Centers LLC.................. C 740 450-5500
  Zanesville *(G-15807)*

Morrison Inc................................... E 740 373-5869
  Marietta *(G-10392)*

▲ Recker and Boerger Inc................. D 513 942-9663
  West Chester *(G-14830)*

▲ Robertson Htg Sup Aliance Ohio..... D 330 821-9180
  Alliance *(G-398)*

Schmids Service Now Inc................. E 330 499-0157
  Wooster *(G-15374)*

Weaver Appliance Sls & Svc LLC....... C 330 852-4555
  Dover *(G-7910)*

5731 Radio, television, and electronic stores

Cincinnati Bell Wireless Company....... C 513 397-9548
  Cincinnati *(G-2400)*

Dodd Camera Holdings Inc................ E 216 361-6811
  Cleveland *(G-4173)*

Electra Sound Inc............................. D 216 433-9600
  Avon Lake *(G-678)*

▲ Hi-Way Distributing Corp Amer...... D 330 645-6633
  Coventry Township *(G-7010)*

5734 Computer and software stores

Autozone Inc.................................... E 216 751-0571
  Cleveland *(G-3842)*

Autozone Inc.................................... E 216 267-6586
  Cleveland *(G-3843)*

Autozone Inc.................................... E 440 593-6934
  Conneaut *(G-6939)*

Autozone Inc.................................... E 440 639-2247
  Painesville *(G-12221)*

Autozone Inc.................................... E 419 872-2813
  Perrysburg *(G-12315)*

▼ Cbts Technology Solutions LLC...... B 513 841-2287
  Cincinnati *(G-2328)*

Datavantage Corporation.................. B 440 498-4414
  Cleveland *(G-4150)*

Great Lakes Computer Corp.............. D 440 937-1100
  Avon *(G-652)*

Harley-Dvidson Dlr Systems Inc........ D 216 573-1393
  Cleveland *(G-4350)*

Micro Center Inc.............................. E 614 850-3000
  Hilliard *(G-9214)*

Micro Center Online Inc.................... D 614 326-8500
  Columbus *(G-6232)*

Micro Electronics Inc........................ C 513 782-8500
  Cincinnati *(G-3057)*

Micro Electronics Inc........................ B 614 334-1430
  Columbus *(G-6233)*

Micro Electronics Inc........................ D 614 850-3410
  Hilliard *(G-9215)*

Microman Inc.................................. E 614 923-8000
  Dublin *(G-8064)*

Nuonosys Inc.................................. E 888 666-7976
  Independence *(G-9461)*

Office World Inc............................... E 419 991-4694
  Lima *(G-9994)*

Ohio Business Machines LLC........... E 216 485-2000
  Cleveland *(G-4683)*

Personalized Data Corporation.......... E 216 289-2200
  Cleveland *(G-4743)*

▼ Provantage LLC............................ D 330 494-3781
  North Canton *(G-11854)*

RB Sigma LLC................................. D 440 290-0577
  Mentor *(G-10988)*

Resource One Cmpt Systems Inc....... E 614 485-4800
  Worthington *(G-15452)*

Retalix Inc...................................... E 937 384-2277
  Miamisburg *(G-11089)*

▲ Stratacache Inc........................... C 937 224-0485
  Dayton *(G-7646)*

Xtek Partners Inc............................. E 614 973-7400
  Columbus *(G-6913)*

5736 Musical instrument stores

Coyle Music Centers Inc................... E 614 885-6654
  Columbus *(G-5716)*

58 EATING AND DRINKING PLACES

5812 Eating places

101 River Inc................................... E 440 352-6343
  Grand River *(G-8848)*

5901 Pfffer Rd Htels Sites LLC......... E 513 793-4500
  Blue Ash *(G-1120)*

A C Management Inc........................ E 440 461-9200
  Cleveland *(G-3748)*

AK Group Hotels Inc........................ D 937 372-9921
  Xenia *(G-15498)*

Akron Management Corp.................. B 330 644-8441
  Akron *(G-34)*

Amish Door Inc................................ C 330 359-5464
  Wilmot *(G-15281)*

Arbys.. E 740 369-0317
  Sunbury *(G-13517)*

Aurora Hotel Partners LLC............... E 330 562-0767
  Aurora *(G-605)*

Avalon Foodservice Inc.................... C 330 854-4551
  Canal Fulton *(G-1592)*

AVI Food Systems Inc...................... E 740 452-9363
  Zanesville *(G-15768)*

AVI Food Systems Inc...................... B 330 372-6000
  Warren *(G-14505)*

B & I Hotel Management LLC........... C 330 995-0200
  Aurora *(G-607)*

Bagel Place Inc................................ E 419 537-9377
  Toledo *(G-13698)*

Bob-Mor Inc.................................... C 419 485-5555
  Montpelier *(G-11381)*

Broad Street Hotel Assoc LP............. D 614 861-0321
  Columbus *(G-5467)*

Brown Derby Roadhouse................... E 330 528-3227
  Hudson *(G-9335)*

Buehler Food Markets Inc................. C 330 364-3079
  Dover *(G-7874)*

Buns of Delaware Inc....................... E 740 363-2867
  Delaware *(G-7781)*

Buxton Inn Inc................................. E 740 587-0001
  Granville *(G-8849)*

Cameron Mitchell Rest LLC.............. E 614 621-3663
  Columbus *(G-5494)*

Canterbury Golf Club Inc.................. D 216 561-1914
  Cleveland *(G-3923)*

Carpediem Management Company..... E 740 687-1563
  Lancaster *(G-9699)*

Cassanos Inc................................... E 937 294-8400
  Dayton *(G-7215)*

▲ Cedar Fair LP............................... A 419 627-2344
  Sandusky *(G-12871)*

Ch Relty Iv/Clmbus Partners LP........ D 614 885-3334
  Columbus *(G-5550)*

Charter Hotel Group Ltd Partnr........ E 216 772-4538
  Mentor *(G-10920)*

Cherry Jack Ltd Partnership............. C 740 788-1200
  Newark *(G-11691)*

Cherry Valley Lodge......................... E 740 788-1200
  Newark *(G-11692)*

Chgc Inc... E 330 225-6122
  Valley City *(G-14332)*

Chillicothe Bowling Lanes Inc........... E 740 773-3300
  Chillicothe *(G-2055)*

City Life Inc.................................... E 216 523-5899
  Cleveland *(G-3975)*

City of Centerville............................ D 937 438-3585
  Dayton *(G-7227)*

Cleveland Arprt Hspitality LLC.......... D 440 871-6000
  Westlake *(G-15051)*

Cleveland Rest Oper Ltd Partnr........ E 216 328-1121
  Cleveland *(G-4064)*

Columbus Airport Ltd Partnr............ C 614 475-7551
  Columbus *(G-5606)*

▲ Columbus Museum of Art.............. D 614 221-6801
  Columbus *(G-5647)*

Commodore Prry Inns Suites LLC..... E 419 732-2645
  Port Clinton *(G-12520)*

Concord Dayton Hotel II LLC............ E 937 223-1000
  Dayton *(G-7245)*

Connor Concepts Inc........................ E 937 291-1661
  Dayton *(G-7246)*

Country Club of Hudson................... D 330 650-1188
  Hudson *(G-9341)*

Crefiii Wrmaug Sprngfeld Lssee........ E 937 322-3600
  Springfield *(G-13245)*

Dari Pizza Enterprises II Inc............. C 419 534-3000
  Maumee *(G-10717)*

David W Milliken.............................. E 740 998-5023
  Frankfort *(G-8629)*

Davis Construction Management....... E 440 248-7770
  Cleveland *(G-4151)*

Detroit Westfield LLC....................... D 330 666-4131
  Akron *(G-133)*

58 EATING AND DRINKING PLACES

Company	Code	Phone
Dino Persichetti	D	330 821-9600
Alliance *(G-381)*		
Durga Llc	E	513 771-2080
Cincinnati *(G-2587)*		
Dutchman Hospitality Group Inc	C	614 873-3414
Plain City *(G-12474)*		
East of Chicago Pizza Inc	D	419 225-7116
Lima *(G-9885)*		
Emmett Dan House Ltd Partnr	E	740 392-6886
Mount Vernon *(G-11485)*		
Epiqurian Inns	D	614 885-2600
Worthington *(G-15414)*		
Escape Enterprises Inc	D	614 224-0300
Columbus *(G-5828)*		
Fairfield Industries Inc	E	740 409-1539
Carroll *(G-1901)*		
Fairlawn Associates Ltd	C	330 867-5000
Fairlawn *(G-8478)*		
Findlay Country Club	E	419 422-9263
Findlay *(G-8528)*		
Findlay Inn & Conference Ctr	E	419 422-5682
Findlay *(G-8529)*		
First Hotel Associates LP	E	614 228-3800
Columbus *(G-5862)*		
Fred W Albrecht Grocery Co	C	330 645-6222
Coventry Township *(G-7008)*		
Frickers USA LLC	E	937 865-9242
Miamisburg *(G-11056)*		
Fusian Inc	E	937 361-7146
Columbus *(G-5902)*		
Gallipolis Hospitality Inc	C	740 446-0090
Gallipolis *(G-8756)*		
Gioninos Pizzeria Inc	E	330 630-2010
Tallmadge *(G-13592)*		
Glenlaurel Inc	E	740 385-4070
Rockbridge *(G-12735)*		
Gold Star Chili Inc	E	513 231-4541
Cincinnati *(G-2740)*		
Golden Lamb	D	513 932-5065
Lebanon *(G-9767)*		
Gosh Enterprises Inc	E	614 923-4700
Columbus *(G-5943)*		
Granville Hospitality Llc	D	740 587-3333
Granville *(G-8853)*		
Green Township Hospitality LLC	D	513 574-6000
Cincinnati *(G-2774)*		
Greenville Inn Inc	E	937 548-3613
Greenville *(G-8875)*		
Grill Rest At Sheraton Suites	E	614 436-0004
Columbus *(G-5957)*		
Grizzly Golf Center Inc	B	513 398-5200
Mason *(G-10557)*		
Hauck Hospitality LLC	D	513 563-8330
Cincinnati *(G-2805)*		
Henderson Rd Rest Systems Inc	E	614 442-3310
Columbus *(G-5984)*		
Hillbrook Club Inc	E	440 247-4940
Cleveland *(G-4362)*		
Hotel 50 S Front Opco L P	D	614 885-3334
Columbus *(G-6010)*		
◆ Hrm Enterprises Inc	C	330 877-9353
Hartville *(G-9127)*		
Hyatt Corporation	C	216 575-1234
Cleveland *(G-4396)*		
Hyatt Corporation	D	614 463-1234
Columbus *(G-6031)*		
Hyatt Corporation	D	614 228-1234
Columbus *(G-6032)*		
▲ I-X Center Corporation	C	216 265-2675
Cleveland *(G-4398)*		
Island Service Company	E	419 285-3695
Put In Bay *(G-12617)*		
Jackson I-94 Ltd Partnership	D	614 793-2244
Dublin *(G-8042)*		
Johnsons Real Ice Cream LLC	C	614 231-0014
Columbus *(G-6095)*		
Kohler Foods Inc	E	937 291-3600
Dayton *(G-7445)*		
Lancaster Country Club	D	740 654-3535
Lancaster *(G-9730)*		
Larosas Inc	A	513 347-5660
Cincinnati *(G-2966)*		
Lobby Shoppes Inc	C	937 324-0002
Springfield *(G-13263)*		
Lucid Investments Inc	D	216 972-0058
Willoughby *(G-15208)*		
Made From Scratch Inc	E	614 873-3344
Plain City *(G-12484)*		
Mahoning Country Club Inc	E	330 545-2517
Girard *(G-8819)*		
Mapleside Valley LLC	D	330 225-5576
Brunswick *(G-1462)*		
Marcos Inc	D	419 885-4844
Toledo *(G-13910)*		
Marcus Theatres Corporation	D	614 436-9818
Columbus *(G-6196)*		
Marriott Hotel Services Inc	C	216 252-5333
Cleveland *(G-4527)*		
Mason Family Resorts LLC	B	608 237-5871
Mason *(G-10577)*		
Medallion Club	C	614 794-6999
Westerville *(G-14909)*		
Mfbusiness Group	E	216 609-7297
Cleveland *(G-4570)*		
Mocha House Inc	E	330 392-3020
Warren *(G-14540)*		
Mocho Ltd	E	330 832-8807
Massillon *(G-10659)*		
Mohawk Golf Club	E	419 447-5876
Tiffin *(G-13634)*		
Moundbuilders Country Club Co	D	740 344-4500
Newark *(G-11732)*		
Mount Vernon Country Club Co	D	740 392-4216
Mount Vernon *(G-11500)*		
Msr Legacy	D	216 381-0826
Cleveland *(G-4608)*		
Mustard Seed Health Fd Mkt Inc	E	440 519-3663
Solon *(G-13115)*		
N C R Employees Benefit Assn	C	937 299-3571
Dayton *(G-7524)*		
National At/Trckstops Hldngs C	A	440 808-9100
Westlake *(G-15081)*		
Nestle Usa Inc	C	440 349-5757
Solon *(G-13118)*		
OBannon Creek Golf Club	E	513 683-5657
Loveland *(G-10156)*		
Ohio Ski Slopes Inc	D	419 774-9818
Mansfield *(G-10308)*		
Ohio State Parks Inc	D	513 664-3504
College Corner *(G-5222)*		
Pam Johnsonident	E	419 946-4551
Mount Gilead *(G-11464)*		
▲ Paramount Distillers Inc	B	216 671-6300
Cleveland *(G-4718)*		
Parkway Pizza Incorporated	D	937 303-8800
Marysville *(G-10502)*		
Patterson-Erie Corporation	D	440 593-6161
Conneaut *(G-6944)*		
Paul A Ertel	E	216 696-8888
Cleveland *(G-4730)*		
Piqua Country Club Holding Co	E	937 773-7744
Piqua *(G-12452)*		
Playhouse Square Foundation	C	216 615-7500
Cleveland *(G-4758)*		
Plaza Inn Foods Inc	E	937 354-2181
Mount Victory *(G-11512)*		
Premier Broadcasting Co Inc	E	614 866-0700
Reynoldsburg *(G-12672)*		
Quail Hollow Management Inc	C	440 639-4000
Concord Township *(G-6933)*		
▲ R P L Corporation	E	937 335-0021
Troy *(G-14153)*		
Rapps Enterprises Inc	E	330 542-2362
New Middletown *(G-11636)*		
Red Robin Gourmet Burgers Inc	C	330 305-1080
Canton *(G-1841)*		
Refectory Restaurant Inc	E	614 451-9774
Columbus *(G-6570)*		
Ridgehills Hotel Ltd Partnr	D	440 585-0600
Wickliffe *(G-15162)*		
Rivals Sports Grille LLC	E	216 267-0005
Middleburg Heights *(G-11125)*		
Rockwell Springs Trout Club	E	419 684-7971
Clyde *(G-5208)*		
Rocky Fork Hunt and Cntry CLB	D	614 471-7828
Gahanna *(G-8727)*		
Romeos Pizza Franchise LLC	C	234 248-4549
Medina *(G-10885)*		
Roscoe Village Foundation	D	740 622-2222
Coshocton *(G-7000)*		
Roseland Lanes Inc	D	440 439-0097
Bedford *(G-983)*		
S & S Management Inc	D	567 356-4151
Wapakoneta *(G-14491)*		
S & S Realty Ltd	E	419 625-0362
Sandusky *(G-12928)*		
Sabo Inc	E	937 222-7939
Dayton *(G-7603)*		
Sachs Management Corp	D	740 282-0901
Steubenville *(G-13342)*		
Sand Ridge Golf Club	E	440 285-8088
Chardon *(G-2019)*		
Sanese Services Inc	A	614 436-1234
Warren *(G-14550)*		
Savour Hospitality LLC	C	216 308-0018
Cleveland *(G-4879)*		
Saw Mill Creek Ltd	D	419 433-3800
Huron *(G-9392)*		
Sb Hotel LLC	E	614 793-2244
Dublin *(G-8115)*		
SC Resort Ltd	C	419 433-3800
Huron *(G-9393)*		
Schmidt Hsptality Concepts Inc	E	614 878-4527
Columbus *(G-6649)*		
Shady Hollow Cntry CLB Co Inc	D	330 832-1581
Massillon *(G-10668)*		
Shawnee Country Club	D	419 227-7177
Lima *(G-9960)*		
Shelby Golf Course Inc	E	937 492-2883
Sidney *(G-13049)*		
Shoreby Club Inc	D	216 851-2587
Cleveland *(G-4903)*		
Silver Lake Country Club	E	330 688-6066
Silver Lake *(G-13060)*		
Skallys Old World Bakery Inc	E	513 931-1411
Cincinnati *(G-3382)*		
Skylane LLC	E	330 527-9999
Garrettsville *(G-8780)*		
▲ Skyline Cem Holdings LLC	C	513 874-1188
Fairfield *(G-8441)*		
Southwest Sports Center Inc	E	440 234-6448
Berea *(G-1082)*		
Spread Eagle Tavern Inc	C	330 223-1583
Hanoverton *(G-9095)*		
St Johns Villa	C	330 627-4662
Carrollton *(G-1913)*		

59 MISCELLANEOUS RETAIL

Strike Zone Inc .... D 440 235-4420
   Olmsted Twp *(G-12094)*

Sugar Valley Country Club .... E 937 372-4820
   Xenia *(G-15531)*

Swiminc Incorporated .... E 614 885-1619
   Worthington *(G-15460)*

Sycamore Lake Inc .... E 440 729-9775
   Chesterland *(G-2043)*

Ta Operating LLC .... B 440 808-9100
   Westlake *(G-15113)*

Tappan Lake Marina Inc .... E 740 269-2031
   Scio *(G-12943)*

Tartan Fields Golf Club Ltd .... D 614 792-0900
   Dublin *(G-8140)*

The Oaks Lodge .... D 330 769-2601
   Chippewa Lake *(G-2094)*

Tiki Bowling Lanes Inc .... E 740 654-4513
   Lancaster *(G-9747)*

Tippecanoe Country Club Inc .... E 330 758-7518
   Canfield *(G-1644)*

Tony Packos Toledo LLC .... E 419 691-6054
   Maumee *(G-10775)*

Travelcenters of America Inc .... A 440 808-9100
   Westlake *(G-15117)*

Union Club Company .... D 216 621-4230
   Cleveland *(G-5050)*

United Scoto Senior Activities .... E 740 354-6672
   Portsmouth *(G-12579)*

United Skates America Inc .... E 614 431-2751
   Columbus *(G-6815)*

United Skates of America Inc .... E 614 802-2440
   Columbus *(G-6816)*

University of Cincinnati .... D 513 556-6381
   Cincinnati *(G-3590)*

Valley Hospitality Inc .... D 740 374-9660
   Marietta *(G-10409)*

Velvet Ice Cream Company .... D 740 892-3921
   Utica *(G-14330)*

Walden Club .... E 330 995-7162
   Aurora *(G-629)*

◆ Wendys Company .... B 614 764-3100
   Dublin *(G-8163)*

Wendys Restaurants LLC .... E 614 764-3100
   Dublin *(G-8164)*

Western Bowl Inc .... E 513 574-2200
   Cincinnati *(G-3660)*

Westgate Lanes Incorporated .... E 419 229-3845
   Lima *(G-9986)*

Weymouth Valley Inc .... D 440 498-8888
   Solon *(G-13163)*

◆ White Castle System Inc .... B 614 228-5781
   Columbus *(G-6883)*

Whiteys Restaurant Inc .... E 330 659-3600
   Richfield *(G-12713)*

Winking Lizard Inc .... E 330 220-9944
   Brunswick *(G-1476)*

Yankee Lake Inc .... E 330 448-8866
   Brookfield *(G-1408)*

York Temple Country Club .... D 614 885-5459
   Columbus *(G-6916)*

Youngs Jersey Dairy Inc .... B 937 325-0629
   Yellow Springs *(G-15537)*

Youngstown Country Club .... D 330 759-1040
   Youngstown *(G-15757)*

5813 Drinking places

A C Management Inc .... E 440 461-9200
   Cleveland *(G-3748)*

Akron Management Corp .... B 330 644-8441
   Akron *(G-34)*

Avalon Inn Services Inc .... D 330 856-1900
   Warren *(G-14502)*

B & I Hotel Management LLC .... C 330 995-0200
   Aurora *(G-607)*

Big Bang Bar Cleveland LLC .... E 615 264-5650
   Cleveland *(G-3873)*

Brewdog Franchising LLC .... E 614 908-3051
   Canal Winchester *(G-1599)*

Broad Street Hotel Assoc LP .... D 614 861-0321
   Columbus *(G-5467)*

Ch Relty Iv/Clmbus Partners LP .... D 614 885-3334
   Columbus *(G-5550)*

Chillicothe Bowling Lanes Inc .... E 740 773-3300
   Chillicothe *(G-2055)*

City Life Inc .... E 216 523-5899
   Cleveland *(G-3975)*

Cleveland Arprt Hspitality LLC .... D 440 871-6000
   Westlake *(G-15051)*

Columbus Airport Ltd Partnr .... C 614 475-7551
   Columbus *(G-5606)*

Columbus Lintel Inc .... E 614 871-0440
   Grove City *(G-8911)*

Columbus Sq Bowl Palace Inc .... E 614 895-1122
   Columbus *(G-5655)*

Econo Lodge Wooster Inc .... E 330 264-8883
   Wooster *(G-15336)*

Epiqurian Inns .... D 614 885-2600
   Worthington *(G-15414)*

Fairlawn Associates Ltd .... C 330 867-5000
   Fairlawn *(G-8478)*

Findlay Country Club .... E 419 422-9263
   Findlay *(G-8528)*

First Hotel Associates LP .... E 614 228-3800
   Columbus *(G-5862)*

Gallipolis Hospitality Inc .... C 740 446-0090
   Gallipolis *(G-8756)*

Granville Hospitality Llc .... D 740 587-3333
   Granville *(G-8853)*

Hotel 50 S Front Opco L P .... D 614 885-3334
   Columbus *(G-6010)*

Hyatt Corporation .... D 614 463-1234
   Columbus *(G-6031)*

Hyatt Corporation .... D 614 228-1234
   Columbus *(G-6032)*

Island Service Company .... E 419 285-3695
   Put In Bay *(G-12617)*

Marcus Theatres Corporation .... D 614 436-9818
   Columbus *(G-6196)*

Marriott Hotel Services Inc .... C 216 252-5333
   Cleveland *(G-4527)*

Medallion Club .... C 614 794-6999
   Westerville *(G-14909)*

Mohawk Golf Club .... E 419 447-5876
   Tiffin *(G-13634)*

Mount Vernon Country Club Co .... D 740 392-4216
   Mount Vernon *(G-11500)*

Msr Legacy .... D 216 381-0826
   Cleveland *(G-4608)*

OBannon Creek Golf Club .... E 513 683-5657
   Loveland *(G-10156)*

Ohio State Parks Inc .... D 513 664-3504
   College Corner *(G-5222)*

Paul A Ertel .... E 216 696-8888
   Cleveland *(G-4730)*

Quail Hollow Management Inc .... C 440 639-4000
   Concord Township *(G-6933)*

▲ R P L Corporation .... E 937 335-0021
   Troy *(G-14153)*

▲ Rhinegeist LLC .... D 513 381-1367
   Cincinnati *(G-3295)*

Ridgehills Hotel Ltd Partnr .... D 440 585-0600
   Wickliffe *(G-15162)*

Roscoe Village Foundation .... D 740 622-2222
   Coshocton *(G-7000)*

Saw Mill Creek Ltd .... D 419 433-3800
   Huron *(G-9392)*

Sb Hotel LLC .... E 614 793-2244
   Dublin *(G-8115)*

Sps Inc .... E 937 339-7801
   Troy *(G-14160)*

Tartan Fields Golf Club Ltd .... D 614 792-0900
   Dublin *(G-8140)*

Ten Pin Alley .... E 614 876-2475
   Hilliard *(G-9237)*

The Oaks Lodge .... D 330 769-2601
   Chippewa Lake *(G-2094)*

Union Club Company .... D 216 621-4230
   Cleveland *(G-5050)*

Valley Hospitality Inc .... D 740 374-9660
   Marietta *(G-10409)*

Western Bowl Inc .... E 513 574-2200
   Cincinnati *(G-3660)*

Weymouth Valley Inc .... D 440 498-8888
   Solon *(G-13163)*

Whiteys Restaurant Inc .... E 330 659-3600
   Richfield *(G-12713)*

Yankee Lake Inc .... E 330 448-8866
   Brookfield *(G-1408)*

59 MISCELLANEOUS RETAIL

5912 Drug stores and proprietary stores

Buehler Food Markets Inc .... C 330 364-3079
   Dover *(G-7874)*

City of Wooster .... A 330 263-8100
   Wooster *(G-15321)*

Columbus Prescr Phrms Inc .... E 614 294-1600
   Westerville *(G-14972)*

Compass Community Health .... E 740 355-7102
   Portsmouth *(G-12549)*

CVS Revco DS Inc .... D 740 593-8501
   Athens *(G-563)*

CVS Revco DS Inc .... D 440 729-9070
   Chesterland *(G-2034)*

CVS Revco DS Inc .... C 937 393-4218
   Hillsboro *(G-9252)*

CVS Revco DS Inc .... D 330 678-4009
   Kent *(G-9567)*

CVS Revco DS Inc .... E 740 389-1122
   Marion *(G-10424)*

CVS Revco DS Inc .... E 740 383-6244
   Marion *(G-10425)*

CVS Revco DS Inc .... D 513 523-6378
   Oxford *(G-12206)*

Dayton Osteopathic Hospital .... E 937 439-6000
   Dayton *(G-7295)*

Discount Drug Mart Inc .... E 330 343-7700
   Dover *(G-7879)*

▲ Discount Drug Mart Inc .... C 330 725-2340
   Medina *(G-10829)*

Fields Family Enterprises Inc .... E 513 897-1000
   Waynesville *(G-14622)*

Fred W Albrecht Grocery Co .... C 330 666-6781
   Akron *(G-169)*

Fred W Albrecht Grocery Co .... C 330 645-6222
   Coventry Township *(G-7008)*

Giant Eagle Inc .... D 330 364-5301
   Dover *(G-7885)*

Hursh Drugs Inc .... E 419 524-0521
   Mansfield *(G-10271)*

ICP Inc .... E 419 447-6216
   Tiffin *(G-13628)*

Marc Glassman Inc .... C 330 995-9246
   Aurora *(G-616)*

Medical Service Company .... D 440 232-3000
   Bedford *(G-973)*

Employee Codes: A=Over 500 employees, B=251-500
C=101-250, D=51-100, E=20-50, F=10-19, G=1-9

59 MISCELLANEOUS RETAIL

Modern Medical Inc .... C 800 547-3330
  Westerville *(G-14910)*
Ncs Healthcare Inc .... A 216 514-3350
  Cleveland *(G-4630)*
Neighborcare Inc .... A 513 719-2600
  Cincinnati *(G-3104)*
Northast Ohio Nghbrhood Hlth S .... C 216 231-7700
  Cleveland *(G-4653)*
Omnicare Phrm of Midwest LLC .... D 513 719-2600
  Cincinnati *(G-3160)*
Promedica Health System Inc .... A 567 585-9600
  Toledo *(G-13972)*
Rite Aid of Ohio Inc .... E 330 706-1004
  Barberton *(G-705)*
Rite Aid of Ohio Inc .... E 937 833-2174
  Brookville *(G-1448)*
Rite Aid of Ohio Inc .... E 740 942-3101
  Cadiz *(G-1543)*
Rite Aid of Ohio Inc .... E 330 922-4466
  Cuyahoga Falls *(G-7095)*
Rite Aid of Ohio Inc .... E 937 277-1611
  Dayton *(G-7591)*
Rite Aid of Ohio Inc .... E 937 258-8101
  Dayton *(G-7592)*
Rite Aid of Ohio Inc .... E 937 256-3111
  Dayton *(G-7593)*
Rite Aid of Ohio Inc .... E 937 836-5204
  Englewood *(G-8321)*
Rite Aid of Ohio Inc .... E 330 527-2828
  Garrettsville *(G-8779)*
Rite Aid of Ohio Inc .... E 937 687-3456
  New Lebanon *(G-11620)*
St Lukes Hospital .... B 419 893-5911
  Maumee *(G-10769)*
Trumbll-Mahoning Med Group Inc .... E 330 372-8800
  Cortland *(G-6976)*
Walmart Inc .... E 740 286-8203
  Jackson *(G-9528)*
Ziks Family Pharmacy 100 .... E 937 225-9350
  Dayton *(G-7737)*

5921 Liquor stores

Arrow Wine Stores Inc .... E 937 433-6778
  Dayton *(G-7180)*
Dayton Heidelberg Distrg Co .... B 937 220-6450
  Moraine *(G-11401)*
G J Shue Inc .... E 330 722-0082
  Medina *(G-10837)*
Larosas Inc .... A 513 347-5660
  Cincinnati *(G-2966)*
▲ Premium Beverage Supply Ltd .... D 614 777-1007
  Hilliard *(G-9227)*
Yankee Lake Inc .... E 330 448-8866
  Brookfield *(G-1408)*

5932 Used merchandise stores

Goodwill Inds Ashtabula Inc .... D 440 964-3565
  Ashtabula *(G-536)*
Goodwill Inds Centl Ohio Inc .... E 740 439-7000
  Cambridge *(G-1572)*
Goodwill Inds Erie Hron Ottawa .... E 419 625-4744
  Sandusky *(G-12900)*
Goodwill Inds NW Ohio Inc .... D 419 255-0070
  Toledo *(G-13822)*
Goodwill Inds S Centl Ohio .... D 740 702-4000
  Chillicothe *(G-2067)*
Goodwill Inds Wyne Hlmes Cntie .... E 330 264-1300
  Wooster *(G-15341)*
Gw Business Solutions LLC .... C 740 345-9861
  Newark *(G-11703)*
In Youngstown Area Gdwill Inds .... C 330 759-7921
  Youngstown *(G-15637)*

Licking-Knox Goodwill Inds Inc .... D 740 345-9861
  Newark *(G-11721)*
Planet Aid Inc .... E 440 542-1171
  Solon *(G-13127)*
Riverfront Antique Mall Inc .... E 330 339-4448
  New Philadelphia *(G-11663)*
Salvation Army .... E 330 773-3331
  Cleveland *(G-4873)*
Salvation Army .... E 419 447-2252
  Tiffin *(G-13641)*
Student Ln Fnding Rsources LLC .... E 513 763-4300
  Cincinnati *(G-3425)*
Volunteers America Ohio & Ind .... C 614 253-6100
  Columbus *(G-6856)*
Zanesvlle Wlfare Orgnztion Gdw .... E 740 450-6060
  Zanesville *(G-15843)*

5941 Sporting goods and bicycle shops

Akron Management Corp .... B 330 644-8441
  Akron *(G-34)*
Arrowhead Park Golf Club Inc .... E 419 628-2444
  Minster *(G-11315)*
Burnett Pools Inc .... E 330 372-1725
  Cortland *(G-6968)*
Capitol Varsity Sports Inc .... E 513 523-4126
  Oxford *(G-12204)*
Chillicothe Bowling Lanes Inc .... E 740 773-3300
  Chillicothe *(G-2055)*
◆ Coulter Ventures Llc .... E 614 358-6190
  Columbus *(G-5708)*
▲ Golf Galaxy Golfworks Inc .... C 740 328-4193
  Newark *(G-11702)*
Grizzly Golf Center Inc .... B 513 398-5200
  Mason *(G-10557)*
Hof Fitness Center Inc .... D 330 455-0555
  Canton *(G-1773)*
Kames Inc .... E 330 499-4558
  Canton *(G-1789)*
▲ Kohlmyer Sporting Goods Inc .... E 440 277-8296
  Lorain *(G-10079)*
Lakewood Country Club Pro Shop ...... E 440 871-0400
  Cleveland *(G-4480)*
Lancaster Country Club .... D 740 654-3535
  Lancaster *(G-9730)*
Mahoning Country Club Inc .... E 330 545-2517
  Girard *(G-8819)*
Medallion Club .... C 614 794-6999
  Westerville *(G-14909)*
Moundbuilders Country Club Co .... D 740 344-4500
  Newark *(G-11732)*
Mount Vernon Country Club Co .... D 740 392-4216
  Mount Vernon *(G-11500)*
Msr Legacy .... D 216 381-0826
  Cleveland *(G-4608)*
OBannon Creek Golf Club .... E 513 683-5657
  Loveland *(G-10156)*
Ohio Skate Inc .... E 419 476-2808
  Toledo *(G-13948)*
Ohio Ski Slopes Inc .... D 419 774-9818
  Mansfield *(G-10308)*
Quail Hollow Management Inc .... C 440 639-4000
  Concord Township *(G-6933)*
Sand Ridge Golf Club .... E 440 285-8088
  Chardon *(G-2019)*
◆ Schneider Saddlery LLC .... E 440 543-2700
  Chagrin Falls *(G-1989)*
Shady Hollow Cntry CLB Co Inc .... D 330 832-1581
  Massillon *(G-10668)*
Silver Lake Country Club .... E 330 688-6066
  Silver Lake *(G-13060)*
Tartan Fields Golf Club Ltd .... D 614 792-0900
  Dublin *(G-8140)*

Tennis Unlimited Inc .... E 330 928-8763
  Akron *(G-331)*
Tippecanoe Country Club Inc .... E 330 758-7518
  Canfield *(G-1644)*
United Skates America Inc .... E 614 431-2751
  Columbus *(G-6815)*
United Skates of America Inc .... E 614 802-2440
  Columbus *(G-6816)*
Walden Club .... E 330 995-7162
  Aurora *(G-629)*
Youngstown Country Club .... D 330 759-1040
  Youngstown *(G-15757)*

5942 Book stores

◆ Daedalus Books Inc .... C 800 395-2665
  Hudson *(G-9342)*
Emerge Ministries Inc .... E 330 865-8351
  Akron *(G-146)*
Grail .... E 513 683-2340
  Loveland *(G-10139)*
Mile Inc .... D 614 794-2203
  Worthington *(G-15440)*
University of Cincinnati .... C 513 556-4200
  Cincinnati *(G-3582)*

5943 Stationery stores

Comdoc Inc .... D 330 920-3900
  Cuyahoga Falls *(G-7064)*
Hubbard Company .... E 419 784-4455
  Defiance *(G-7750)*
Staples Contract & Coml LLC .... E 740 845-5600
  London *(G-10051)*
Stationers Inc .... E 740 423-1400
  Belpre *(G-1059)*
United Art and Education Inc .... E 800 322-3247
  Dayton *(G-7680)*

5944 Jewelry stores

Equity Diamond Brokers Inc .... E 513 793-4760
  Montgomery *(G-11367)*
◆ Gottlieb & Sons Inc .... E 216 771-4785
  Beachwood *(G-795)*

5945 Hobby, toy, and game shops

Dtv Inc .... E 216 226-5465
  Cleveland *(G-4187)*
Hobby Lobby Stores Inc .... E 419 861-1862
  Holland *(G-9288)*
Hobby Lobby Stores Inc .... E 330 686-1508
  Stow *(G-13373)*

5946 Camera and photographic supply stores

Dodd Camera Holdings Inc .... E 216 361-6811
  Cleveland *(G-4173)*
▲ KAO Collins Inc .... E 513 948-9000
  Cincinnati *(G-2929)*

5947 Gift, novelty, and souvenir shop

AG Interactive Inc .... C 216 889-5000
  Cleveland *(G-3774)*
Amish Door Inc .... C 330 359-5464
  Wilmot *(G-15281)*
Auxiliary St Lukes Hospital .... D 419 893-5911
  Maumee *(G-10697)*
Civic Grdn Ctr Grter Cncinnati .... E 513 221-0981
  Cincinnati *(G-2454)*
Columbus Zoological Park Assn .... C 614 645-3400
  Powell *(G-12589)*
Dutchman Hospitality Group Inc .... C 614 873-3414
  Plain City *(G-12474)*

SIC SECTION
59 MISCELLANEOUS RETAIL

Golden Lamb.. D 513 932-5065
   Lebanon *(G-9767)*
Gorant Chocolatier LLC .... C 330 726-8821
   Boardman *(G-1288)*
◆ Hrm Enterprises Inc .... C 330 877-9353
   Hartville *(G-9127)*
Large & Loving Cards Inc .... E 440 877-0261
   North Royalton *(G-11943)*
Lowes Investments Inc .... E 440 543-5123
   Chagrin Falls *(G-1984)*
Mapleside Valley LLC .... D 330 225-5576
   Brunswick *(G-1462)*
Marriott Hotel Services Inc .... C 216 252-5333
   Cleveland *(G-4527)*
Mohun Health Care Center .... E 614 416-6132
   Columbus *(G-6256)*
S-P Company Inc .... D 330 782-5651
   Columbiana *(G-5240)*
▲ Things Remembered Inc .... A 440 473-2000
   Highland Heights *(G-9172)*
Thirty-One Gifts LLC .... C 614 414-4300
   New Albany *(G-11588)*
Velvet Ice Cream Company .... D 740 892-3921
   Utica *(G-14330)*
▲ Waterbeds n Stuff Inc .... E 614 871-1171
   Grove City *(G-8965)*
Williamsburg of Cincinnati Mgt .... B 513 948-2308
   Cincinnati *(G-3673)*
Youngs Jersey Dairy Inc .... B 937 325-0629
   Yellow Springs *(G-15537)*

5949 Sewing, needlework, and piece goods

▲ Checker Notions Company Inc .... C 419 893-3636
   Maumee *(G-10710)*
Everfast Inc .... E 614 789-0900
   Dublin *(G-8008)*

5961 Catalog and mail-order houses

▲ American Frame Corporation .... D 419 893-5595
   Maumee *(G-10690)*
Amerimark Holdings LLC .... B 440 325-2000
   Cleveland *(G-3809)*
Ampersand Group LLC .... E 330 379-0044
   Akron *(G-49)*
▲ Bendon Inc .... D 419 207-3600
   Ashland *(G-482)*
▼ Cornerstone Brands Group Inc .... A 513 603-1000
   West Chester *(G-14677)*
▲ Cornerstone Consolidated .... A 513 603-1100
   West Chester *(G-14678)*
▼ Craft Wholesalers Inc .... C 740 964-6210
   Groveport *(G-8980)*
E Retailing Associates LLC .... D 614 300-5785
   Columbus *(G-5798)*
Franchise Group Inc .... B 740 363-2222
   Delaware *(G-7799)*
▲ Gem Edwards Inc .... D 330 342-8300
   Hudson *(G-9352)*
◆ Jegs Automotive LLC .... C 614 294-5050
   Delaware *(G-7808)*
Medco Health Solutions Inc .... C 614 822-2000
   Dublin *(G-8061)*
Nextrx LLC .... A 317 532-6000
   Mason *(G-10584)*
Optumrx Home Delivery Ohio LLC .... D 440 930-5520
   Avon Lake *(G-682)*
PC Connection Sales Corp .... D 937 382-4800
   Wilmington *(G-15264)*
Perishable Shipg Solutions LLC .... E 724 944-9024
   Warren *(G-14546)*
▼ Provantage LLC .... D 330 494-3781
   North Canton *(G-11854)*

◆ Schneider Saddlery LLC .... E 440 543-2700
   Chagrin Falls *(G-1989)*
▲ Systemax Manufacturing Inc .... D 937 368-2300
   Dayton *(G-7658)*
▲ Trademark Global LLC .... E 440 960-6200
   Lorain *(G-10104)*
▲ Twin Sisters Productions LLC .... E 330 631-0361
   Stow *(G-13399)*

5962 Merchandising machine operators

AVI Food Systems Inc .... E 740 452-9363
   Zanesville *(G-15768)*
AVI Food Systems Inc .... B 330 372-6000
   Warren *(G-14505)*
Coffee Break Corporation .... E 513 841-1100
   Cincinnati *(G-2468)*
Dtv Inc .... E 216 226-5465
   Cleveland *(G-4187)*
Laughlin Music & Vending Svc .... E 740 593-7778
   Athens *(G-580)*
Sanese Services Inc .... A 614 436-1234
   Warren *(G-14550)*

5963 Direct selling establishments

Mas International Mktg LLC .... D 614 556-7083
   Columbus *(G-6202)*
Universal Marketing Group LLC .... D 419 720-6581
   Toledo *(G-14085)*

5983 Fuel oil dealers

Aim Leasing Company .... D 330 759-0438
   Girard *(G-8809)*
Bazell Oil Co Inc .... E 740 385-5420
   Logan *(G-10021)*
Centerra Co-Op .... E 419 281-2153
   Ashland *(G-490)*
Cincinnati - Vulcan Company .... D 513 242-5300
   Cincinnati *(G-2391)*
Duncan Oil Co .... E 937 426-5945
   Dayton *(G-7131)*
Energy Cooperative Inc .... E 740 348-1206
   Newark *(G-11699)*
Lykins Oil Company .... E 513 831-8820
   Milford *(G-11239)*
Mighty Mac Investments Inc .... E 937 335-2928
   Troy *(G-14147)*
Ports Petroleum Company Inc .... E 330 264-1885
   Wooster *(G-15367)*
Red Rover LLC .... E 330 262-6501
   Wooster *(G-15368)*
Santmyer Logistics Inc .... B 330 262-6501
   Wooster *(G-15371)*
Suburban Oil Company .... E 513 459-8100
   Mason *(G-10611)*
UII Inc .... E 440 543-5195
   Chagrin Falls *(G-1992)*
Western Reserve Farm Cooperative Inc .... D 440 632-0271
   Middlefield *(G-11146)*

5984 Liquefied petroleum gas dealers

Beck Suppliers Inc .... E 419 426-3051
   Attica *(G-598)*
Ngo Development Corporation .... B 740 622-9560
   Coshocton *(G-6993)*
Titan Propane LLC .... C 419 332-9832
   Fremont *(G-8706)*
Welders Supply Inc .... E 216 267-4470
   Brookpark *(G-1443)*

5989 Fuel dealers, nec

▼ Cliffs Logan County Coal LLC .... C 216 694-5700
   Cleveland *(G-4077)*

5992 Florists

Bonnie Plants LLC .... C 937 642-7764
   Marysville *(G-10476)*
Buehler Food Markets Inc .... C 330 364-3079
   Dover *(G-7874)*
Deans Greenhouse Inc .... E 440 871-2050
   Cleveland *(G-4158)*
Fred W Albrecht Grocery Co .... C 330 645-6222
   Coventry Township *(G-7008)*
HJ Benken Flor & Greenhouses .... E 513 891-1040
   Cincinnati *(G-2830)*
Lowes Investments Inc .... E 440 543-5123
   Chagrin Falls *(G-1984)*
Made From Scratch Inc .... E 614 873-3344
   Plain City *(G-12484)*
Maria Gardens LLC .... E 440 238-7637
   Strongsville *(G-13474)*
Pickaway Growers LLC .... E 614 344-4956
   Orient *(G-12154)*
Wilsons Hillview Farm Inc .... E 740 763-2873
   Newark *(G-11755)*

5993 Tobacco stores and stands

Arrow Wine Stores Inc .... E 937 433-6778
   Dayton *(G-7180)*

5994 News dealers and newsstands

Gazette Publishing Company .... D 419 335-2010
   Napoleon *(G-11523)*

5995 Optical goods stores

▲ Big Sandy Furniture Inc .... D 740 574-2113
   Franklin Furnace *(G-8653)*
Cambridge Eye Associates Inc .... C 513 527-9700
   West Chester *(G-14657)*
Shawnee Optical Inc .... E 440 997-2020
   Ashtabula *(G-549)*

5999 Miscellaneous retail stores, nec

Advanced Medical Equipment Inc .... E 937 534-1080
   Miamisburg *(G-11020)*
Ag-Pro Ohio LLC .... E 740 653-6951
   Lancaster *(G-9691)*
Ag-Pro Ohio LLC .... E 740 450-7446
   Zanesville *(G-15765)*
Albright Welding Supply Co Inc .... E 330 264-2021
   Wooster *(G-15309)*
Amerimed LLC .... A 513 942-3670
   West Chester *(G-14650)*
Bath & Body Works LLC .... D 937 439-0350
   Dayton *(G-7186)*
◆ Beautyavenues LLC .... C 614 856-6000
   Reynoldsburg *(G-12654)*
Bell Vault and Monu Works Inc .... E 937 866-2444
   Miamisburg *(G-11025)*
▲ Bendon Inc .... D 419 207-3600
   Ashland *(G-482)*
▲ Big Sandy Furniture Inc .... D 740 574-2113
   Franklin Furnace *(G-8653)*
▲ Boardman Medical Supply Co .... C 330 545-6700
   Girard *(G-8810)*
◆ Boxout LLC .... C 833 462-7746
   Hudson *(G-9334)*
Burnett Pools Inc .... E 330 372-1725
   Cortland *(G-6968)*
Care Medical Inc .... E 513 821-7272
   Cincinnati *(G-2309)*
Carmichael Equipment Inc .... E 740 446-2412
   Bidwell *(G-1103)*
Centerra Co-Op .... E 419 281-2153
   Ashland *(G-490)*

Employee Codes: A=Over 500 employees, B=251-500
C=101-250, D=51-100, E=20-50, F=10-19, G=1-9

59 MISCELLANEOUS RETAIL

▼ Christian Aid Ministries .... E 330 893-2428
  Millersburg (G-11276)
Combined Technologies Inc .... E 513 595-5900
  Cincinnati (G-2478)
Comdoc Inc .... D 330 920-3900
  Cuyahoga Falls (G-7064)
Ctd Investments LLC .... E 614 570-9949
  Columbus (G-5735)
Donnellon Mc Carthy Inc .... E 937 299-0200
  Moraine (G-11404)
Elder Sales & Service Inc .... E 330 426-2166
  East Palestine (G-8195)
▲ Enting Water Conditioning Inc .... E 937 294-5100
  Moraine (G-11407)
Fairfield Medical Center .... A 740 687-8000
  Lancaster (G-9718)
▲ Findaway World LLC .... E 440 893-0808
  Solon (G-13089)
▲ Gem Edwards Inc .... D 330 342-8300
  Hudson (G-9352)
Gordon Brothers Inc .... E 800 331-7611
  Salem (G-12842)
Gross Plumbing Incorporated .... E 440 324-9999
  Elyria (G-8253)
Guardian Protection Svcs Inc .... E 330 797-1570
  Bedford (G-962)
Hanger Prsthtics Orthtics E In .... E 330 633-9807
  Tallmadge (G-13593)
◆ Heading4ward Investment Co .... D 937 293-9994
  Moraine (G-11416)
Health Aid of Ohio Inc .... E 216 252-3900
  Cleveland (G-4353)
Health Services Inc .... E 330 837-7678
  Massillon (G-10644)
Hearinglife Usa Inc .... D 513 759-2999
  West Chester (G-14707)
Hhd Aviation LLC .... D 513 426-8378
  Hamilton (G-9052)
High Line Corporation .... E 330 848-8800
  Akron (G-192)
Hull Bros Inc .... E 419 375-2827
  Fort Recovery (G-8610)
Jani-Source LLC .... E 740 374-6298
  Marietta (G-10376)
◆ JD Equipment Inc .... C 614 879-6620
  London (G-10044)
Jo-Ann Stores LLC .... E 419 621-8101
  Sandusky (G-12906)
Kenneths Hair Slons Day Spas I .... B 614 457-7712
  Columbus (G-6112)
▲ Lefeld Implement Inc .... E 419 678-2375
  Coldwater (G-5215)
Liechty Inc .... E 419 298-2302
  Edgerton (G-8228)
▲ Litehouse Products LLC .... E 440 638-2350
  Strongsville (G-13471)
Lucas Funeral Homes Inc .... E 419 294-1985
  Upper Sandusky (G-14291)
▲ Maza Inc .... D 614 760-0003
  Plain City (G-12486)
McCracken Group Inc .... E 513 697-2000
  Cincinnati (G-3022)
Metropolitan Pool Service Co .... E 216 741-9451
  Parma (G-12257)
▲ Miller Fireworks Company Inc .... E 419 865-7329
  Holland (G-9298)
Millers Rental and Sls Co Inc .... E 330 753-8600
  Akron (G-234)
Mobilcomm Inc .... D 513 742-5555
  Cincinnati (G-3072)
Modern Medical Inc .... C 800 547-3330
  Westerville (G-14910)

Modern Office Methods Inc .... E 937 436-2295
  Dayton (G-7510)
Modern Office Methods Inc .... E 614 891-3693
  Westerville (G-15000)
National Lime and Stone Co .... E 740 387-3485
  Marion (G-10446)
Northwestern Ohio SEC Systems .... E 419 227-1655
  Lima (G-9942)
Old Meadow Farms Inc .... E 440 632-5590
  Middlefield (G-11143)
Old Time Pottery LLC .... D 513 825-5211
  Cincinnati (G-3156)
Old Time Pottery LLC .... D 440 842-1244
  Cleveland (G-4694)
Old Time Pottery LLC .... D 614 337-1258
  Columbus (G-6470)
Our Lady Bellefonte Hosp Inc .... A 606 833-3333
  Cincinnati (G-3176)
◆ Parts Express International Inc .... D 800 338-0531
  Springboro (G-13205)
Paul Peterson Safety Div Inc .... E 614 486-4375
  Columbus (G-6505)
Perry Pro Tech Inc .... D 419 228-1360
  Lima (G-9948)
Petland Inc .... E 740 775-2464
  Chillicothe (G-2082)
Petsmart Inc .... E 513 336-0365
  Mason (G-10591)
Petsmart LLC .... E 614 418-9389
  Columbus (G-6518)
Rentokil North America Inc .... E 440 964-5641
  Ashtabula (G-547)
▲ Rgh Enterprises LLC .... A 330 963-6996
  Twinsburg (G-14216)
▲ Robertson Htg Sup Aliance Ohio .... D 330 821-9180
  Alliance (G-398)
Romitech Inc .... E 937 297-9529
  Franklin (G-8648)
Sarnova Inc .... D 614 760-5000
  Dublin (G-8113)
Sateri Home Inc .... D 330 758-8106
  Youngstown (G-15717)
Seeley Enterprises Company .... E 440 293-6600
  Andover (G-440)
Shawntech Communications Inc .... E 937 898-4900
  Miamisburg (G-11093)
Sievers Security Inc .... E 216 291-2222
  Cleveland (G-4905)
Stable Step LLC .... C 800 491-1571
  Wadsworth (G-14452)
State Alarm Inc .... E 888 726-8111
  Youngstown (G-15730)
Streacker Tractor Sales Inc .... E 419 422-6973
  Findlay (G-8589)
▲ Thomas Do-It Center Inc .... E 740 446-2002
  Gallipolis (G-8769)
Toledo Medical Equipment Co .... E 419 866-7120
  Maumee (G-10774)
Tractor Supply Company .... E 937 382-2595
  Wilmington (G-15275)
United Art and Education Inc .... E 800 322-3247
  Dayton (G-7680)
United Rhbltition Svcs Grter Dy .... D 937 233-1230
  Dayton (G-7683)
Unity Health Network LLC .... E 330 626-0549
  Streetsboro (G-13434)
University Mednet .... B 216 383-0100
  Euclid (G-8363)
University Otlryngologists Inc .... E 614 273-2241
  Columbus (G-6824)
US Safetygear Inc .... E 330 898-1344
  Warren (G-14570)

Vincent Lighting Systems Co .... E 216 475-7600
  Solon (G-13161)
Walter F Stephens Jr Inc .... E 937 746-0521
  Franklin (G-8652)
Welders Supply Inc .... E 216 267-4470
  Brookpark (G-1443)
◆ William R Hague Inc .... D 614 836-2115
  Groveport (G-9014)
Witmers Inc .... E 330 427-2147
  Salem (G-12858)
Wmk LLC .... E 440 951-4335
  Bedford (G-993)
Woodhull LLC .... E 937 294-5311
  Springboro (G-13209)

60 DEPOSITORY INSTITUTIONS

6021 National commercial banks

Banc Amer Prctice Slutions Inc .... D 614 794-8247
  Westerville (G-14878)
Bny Mellon National Assn .... B 216 595-8769
  Beachwood (G-769)
Buckeye State Bancshares Inc .... E 614 796-4747
  Powell (G-12587)
Century National Bank .... E 740 454-2521
  Zanesville (G-15780)
CF Bankshares Inc .... D 614 334-7979
  Worthington (G-15407)
▲ Charter One Bank National .... A 216 277-5326
  Cleveland (G-3963)
▲ Chase Equipment Finance Inc .... C 800 678-2601
  Columbus (G-5252)
Chase Manhattan Mortgage Corp .... A 614 422-6900
  Columbus (G-5553)
Cheviot Financial Corp .... C 513 661-0457
  Cincinnati (G-2353)
Citizens Bank National Assn .... E 419 720-0009
  Toledo (G-13736)
Citizens Nat Bnk of Wdsfeld Th .... E 740 472-1696
  Woodsfield (G-15300)
Citizens Nat Bnk Urbana Ohio .... D 937 653-1200
  Urbana (G-14303)
Citizens State Bnk of Strsburg .... E 330 878-5551
  Strasburg (G-13403)
Colonial Banc Corp .... E 937 456-5544
  Eaton (G-8210)
Consumers National Bank .... E 330 868-7701
  Minerva (G-11305)
Credit First NA .... D 216 362-5000
  Brookpark (G-1432)
Fairfield National Bank .... D 740 653-1422
  Lancaster (G-9719)
Fairfield National Bank .... E 740 653-7242
  Lancaster (G-9720)
Farmers Nat Bnk of Canfield .... E 440 564-1520
  Chesterland (G-2035)
Fcn Bank Corp .... E 513 367-6111
  Harrison (G-9106)
▲ Fifth Third Bank of North .... A 216 274-5533
  Cleveland (G-4250)
First Commonwealth Bank .... C 740 657-7000
  Lewis Center (G-9820)
First Ctzens Nat Bnk of Upper .... E 419 294-2351
  Upper Sandusky (G-14289)
First Nat Bnk of Nelsonville .... E 740 753-1941
  Nelsonville (G-11544)
First National Bank of Pandora .... E 419 384-3221
  Pandora (G-12245)
First National Bank of Waverly .... E 740 947-2136
  Waverly (G-14612)
First National Bnk of Dennison .... E 740 922-2532
  Dennison (G-7855)

First-Knox National Bank .... E 419 289-6137
Ashland *(G-498)*

First-Knox National Bank .... E 740 694-2015
Fredericktown *(G-8659)*

First-Knox National Bank .... C 740 399-5500
Mount Vernon *(G-11488)*

Firstmerit Bank National Association .... A 330 384-7201
Akron *(G-162)*

Firstmerit Corporation .... A 330 996-6300
Akron *(G-163)*

Fnb Inc .... E 740 922-2532
Dennison *(G-7856)*

Greenville National Bank .... E 937 548-1114
Greenville *(G-8877)*

Huntington Bancshares Inc .... A 614 480-2265
Columbus *(G-6016)*

Huntington National Bank .... E 419 281-6020
Ashland *(G-502)*

Huntington National Bank .... E 216 515-0029
Bay Village *(G-760)*

Huntington National Bank .... E 937 848-6861
Bellbrook *(G-1017)*

Huntington National Bank .... E 216 515-0013
Brookpark *(G-1435)*

Huntington National Bank .... E 440 834-4481
Burton *(G-1529)*

Huntington National Bank .... E 614 480-0008
Canal Winchester *(G-1609)*

Huntington National Bank .... E 330 966-5232
Canton *(G-1778)*

Huntington National Bank .... D 513 762-1860
Cincinnati *(G-2857)*

Huntington National Bank .... E 216 515-6401
Cleveland *(G-4392)*

Huntington National Bank .... E 614 480-0005
Columbus *(G-6018)*

Huntington National Bank .... E 614 480-0017
Columbus *(G-6019)*

Huntington National Bank .... D 614 480-0038
Columbus *(G-6020)*

Huntington National Bank .... E 614 480-0004
Columbus *(G-6022)*

Huntington National Bank .... E 614 480-0026
Columbus *(G-6023)*

Huntington National Bank .... E 614 480-0020
Columbus *(G-6024)*

Huntington National Bank .... E 614 480-0060
Columbus *(G-6027)*

Huntington National Bank .... E 937 428-7400
Dayton *(G-7417)*

Huntington National Bank .... E 330 343-6611
Dover *(G-7890)*

Huntington National Bank .... E 937 746-9904
Franklin *(G-8641)*

Huntington National Bank .... E 614 480-4500
Hilliard *(G-9202)*

Huntington National Bank .... E 330 677-8200
Kent *(G-9579)*

Huntington National Bank .... E 419 226-8200
Lima *(G-9908)*

Huntington National Bank .... E 740 852-1234
London *(G-10043)*

Huntington National Bank .... E 330 343-2527
New Philadelphia *(G-11655)*

Huntington National Bank .... E 740 498-8376
Newcomerstown *(G-11769)*

Huntington National Bank .... E 419 747-2265
Ontario *(G-12107)*

Huntington National Bank .... E 419 734-2157
Port Clinton *(G-12534)*

Huntington National Bank .... E 330 296-2214
Ravenna *(G-12629)*

Huntington National Bank .... E 937 390-1779
Springfield *(G-13255)*

Huntington National Bank .... E 330 626-3426
Streetsboro *(G-13416)*

Huntington National Bank .... E 330 334-1591
Wadsworth *(G-14438)*

Huntington National Bank .... E 330 841-0205
Warren *(G-14529)*

Huntington National Bank .... E 614 480-0016
Westerville *(G-14987)*

Huntington National Bank .... E 740 452-8444
Zanesville *(G-15802)*

Huntington National Bank .... E 740 455-7048
Zanesville *(G-15803)*

Icx Corporation .... E 330 656-3611
Cleveland *(G-4400)*

Jpmorgan Chase & Co .... C 614 248-5800
Columbus *(G-5263)*

Jpmorgan Chase Bank Nat Assn .... D 212 270-6000
Columbus *(G-6098)*

Jpmorgan Chase Bank Nat Assn .... E 740 363-8032
Delaware *(G-7810)*

Keybanc Capital Markets Inc .... B 800 553-2240
Cleveland *(G-4458)*

Keybank National Association .... E 330 823-9615
Alliance *(G-385)*

Keybank National Association .... E 800 539-8336
Brooklyn *(G-1410)*

Keybank National Association .... D 330 477-6787
Canton *(G-1791)*

Keybank National Association .... E 440 345-7055
Cleveland *(G-4460)*

Keybank National Association .... E 216 464-4727
Cleveland *(G-4462)*

Keybank National Association .... E 216 382-3000
Cleveland *(G-4463)*

Keybank National Association .... E 216 689-8481
Cleveland *(G-4464)*

Keybank National Association .... E 216 464-6128
Cleveland *(G-4465)*

Keybank National Association .... E 614 460-3415
Columbus *(G-6114)*

Keybank National Association .... E 216 289-7670
Euclid *(G-8352)*

Keybank National Association .... E 216 226-0850
Lakewood *(G-9671)*

Keybank National Association .... E 330 748-8010
Macedonia *(G-10197)*

Keybank National Association .... E 419 893-7696
Maumee *(G-10735)*

Keybank National Association .... E 330 499-2566
North Canton *(G-11845)*

Keybank National Association .... E 440 734-7700
North Olmsted *(G-11908)*

Keybank National Association .... E 216 502-3260
Rocky River *(G-12747)*

Keybank National Association .... E 330 633-5335
Tallmadge *(G-13598)*

Keybank National Association .... E 419 727-6280
Toledo *(G-13876)*

Keybank National Association .... E 419 473-2088
Toledo *(G-13877)*

Keybank National Association .... E 567 455-4022
Toledo *(G-13878)*

Keybank National Association .... E 330 425-4434
Twinsburg *(G-14199)*

Keybank National Association .... B 800 539-2968
Cleveland *(G-4461)*

Lcnb Corp .... E 513 932-1414
Lebanon *(G-9773)*

Lcnb National Bank .... D 513 932-1414
Lebanon *(G-9774)*

Lorain National Bank .... D 440 244-7242
Lorain *(G-10089)*

Lorain National Bank .... C 440 244-6000
Lorain *(G-10088)*

Mahoning Youngstown Community .... E 330 747-7921
Youngstown *(G-15663)*

National Bancshares Corporation .... C 330 682-1010
Orrville *(G-12171)*

NB&t Financial Group Inc .... B 937 382-1441
Wilmington *(G-15261)*

Northwest Bancshares Inc .... C 800 859-1000
Columbus *(G-6371)*

Oreco Inc .... C 724 349-7220
Lewis Center *(G-9833)*

Park National Bank .... C 740 349-8451
Newark *(G-11738)*

Park National Corporation .... C 740 349-8451
Newark *(G-11739)*

Peoples Community Bancorp Inc .... D 513 870-3530
West Chester *(G-14741)*

PNC Banc Corp Ohio .... D 513 981-2420
Liberty Township *(G-9857)*

PNC Banc Corp Ohio .... D 513 651-8738
Cincinnati *(G-3216)*

Second National Bank .... E 937 548-5068
Greenville *(G-8885)*

Second National Bank .... E 937 548-2122
Greenville *(G-8884)*

Security National Bank & Tr Co .... E 937 845-3811
New Carlisle *(G-11605)*

Security National Bank & Tr Co .... E 937 325-0351
Springfield *(G-13290)*

Security National Bank & Tr Co .... C 740 426-6384
Newark *(G-11747)*

Springleaf Fincl Holdings LLC .... B 419 841-0785
Toledo *(G-14021)*

Standing Stone National Bank .... E 740 653-5115
Lancaster *(G-9744)*

Strategic Comp .... D 770 225-3532
Cincinnati *(G-3421)*

United Bank National Assn .... E 419 683-1010
Crestline *(G-7027)*

Unity National Bank .... E 937 773-0752
Piqua *(G-12460)*

◆ **US Bank National Association** .... A 513 632-4234
Cincinnati *(G-3604)*

Wells Fargo Fincl SEC Svcs Inc .... B 513 530-0333
Cincinnati *(G-3651)*

6022 State commercial banks

Andover Bancorp Inc .... E 440 293-7605
Andover *(G-437)*

Buckeye Community Bank .... C 440 233-8800
Elyria *(G-8234)*

Citizens Bank Company .... E 740 984-2381
Beverly *(G-1100)*

Citizens Bank of Ashville Ohio .... E 740 983-2511
Ashville *(G-551)*

Citizens Capital Markets Inc .... E 216 589-0900
Cleveland *(G-3973)*

Civista Bancshares Inc .... E 419 625-4121
Sandusky *(G-12880)*

Civista Bank .... E 419 599-1065
Napoleon *(G-11518)*

Civista Bank .... D 419 625-4121
Sandusky *(G-12881)*

Comenity Capital Bank .... A 614 944-3682
Columbus *(G-5663)*

Commercial Bancshares Inc .... D 419 294-5781
Upper Sandusky *(G-14285)*

Community Bank .... E 740 654-0900
Lancaster *(G-9705)*

60 DEPOSITORY INSTITUTIONS

Community Savings............................. E 740 732-5678
   Caldwell *(G-1548)*

Croghan Colonial Bank....................... E 419 332-7301
   Fremont *(G-8673)*

CSB Bancorp Inc................................... E 330 674-9015
   Millersburg *(G-11278)*

DCB Financial Corp............................... C 740 657-7000
   Lewis Center *(G-9815)*

Exchange Bank Inc.............................. E 419 833-3401
   Luckey *(G-10182)*

Fahey Banking Company...................... E 740 382-8232
   Marion *(G-10426)*

Farmers & Merchants State Bank......... C 419 446-2501
   Archbold *(G-457)*

Farmers Citizens Bank......................... E 419 562-7040
   Bucyrus *(G-1508)*

Farmers Merchants Bancorp Inc.......... D 419 446-2501
   Archbold *(G-458)*

Farmers Nat Bnk of Canfield................ D 330 533-3341
   Canfield *(G-1628)*

Farmers National Banc Corp................ D 330 533-3341
   Canfield *(G-1629)*

Federal Home Ln Bnk Cincinnati.......... C 513 852-5719
   Cincinnati *(G-2655)*

▲ Fifth Third Bancorp........................... A 800 972-3030
   Cincinnati *(G-2662)*

Fifth Third Bank National Assn............ D 513 579-5203
   Cincinnati *(G-2664)*

▲ Fifth Third Bank National Assn......... A 513 579-5203
   Cincinnati *(G-2663)*

Fifth Third Bnk Nrthwstern Ohi............ D 419 259-7820
   Toledo *(G-13805)*

Fifth Third Bnk of Columbus OH.......... A 614 744-7595
   Columbus *(G-5856)*

Fifth Third Bnk of Sthern OH I............. E 937 382-2620
   Wilmington *(G-15253)*

Fifth Third Bnk of Sthern OH I............. E 937 840-5353
   Hillsboro *(G-9253)*

▲ Fifth Third Financial Corp................ B 513 579-5300
   Cincinnati *(G-2666)*

First Financial..................................... E 419 547-7733
   Clyde *(G-5200)*

First Financial Bank............................. A 877 322-9530
   Cincinnati *(G-2671)*

First Financial Bank Nat Assn.............. C 877 322-9530
   Cincinnati *(G-2672)*

First State Bank................................... E 937 695-0331
   Winchester *(G-15287)*

Forcht Bancorp Inc............................... A 513 231-7871
   Cincinnati *(G-2691)*

Forcht Bank National Assn.................. D 513 231-7871
   Cincinnati *(G-2692)*

Genoa Banking Company...................... E 419 855-8381
   Genoa *(G-8794)*

Govplus LLC... E 330 580-1913
   Canton *(G-1765)*

Govplus LLC... E 440 888-0330
   Cleveland *(G-4322)*

Heartland Bank.................................... E 614 337-4600
   Columbus *(G-5978)*

Hicksville Bank Inc............................... E 419 542-7726
   Hicksville *(G-9159)*

Hocking Vly Bnk of Athens Co............. E 740 592-4441
   Athens *(G-572)*

Hometown Bank................................... E 330 673-9827
   Kent *(G-9578)*

Huntington National Bank.................... E 440 992-7342
   Ashtabula *(G-537)*

Huntington National Bank.................... E 937 593-2010
   Bellefontaine *(G-1029)*

Huntington National Bank.................... E 419 636-1164
   Bryan *(G-1485)*

Huntington National Bank.................... E 419 429-4627
   Findlay *(G-8547)*

Huntington National Bank.................... E 330 424-7226
   Lisbon *(G-10003)*

Huntington National Bank.................... E 330 841-0142
   Newton Falls *(G-11776)*

Huntington National Bank.................... E 419 523-6880
   Ottawa *(G-12186)*

Huntington National Bank.................... E 740 695-3323
   Saint Clairsville *(G-12794)*

Huntington National Bank.................... E 419 254-7016
   Toledo *(G-13854)*

Huntington National Bank.................... E 419 254-7052
   Toledo *(G-13855)*

Huntington National Bank.................... E 419 249-3340
   Toledo *(G-13856)*

Huntington National Bank.................... E 330 841-0197
   Warren *(G-14528)*

Huntington National Bank.................... E 330 841-0205
   Warren *(G-14529)*

Independence Bank.............................. E 216 447-1444
   Cleveland *(G-4405)*

JP Morgan Partners LLC..................... E 800 848-9136
   Delaware *(G-7809)*

◆ Jpmorgan Chase Bank Nat Assn...... A 614 436-3055
   Columbus *(G-5264)*

Keybank National Association.............. B 800 539-2968
   Cleveland *(G-4461)*

Killbuck Savings Bank Company.......... E 330 276-4881
   Killbuck *(G-9638)*

Liberty Capital Inc................................ D 937 382-1000
   Wilmington *(G-15258)*

Liberty Savings Bank FSB................... C 937 382-1000
   Wilmington *(G-15259)*

Lnb Bancorp Inc.................................. B 440 244-6000
   Lorain *(G-10083)*

Mechanics Bank.................................. E 419 524-0831
   Mansfield *(G-10291)*

Merchants National Bank..................... E 937 393-1134
   Hillsboro *(G-9263)*

Middlefield Banking Company.............. D 419 634-5015
   Ada *(G-2)*

Minster Bank....................................... E 419 628-2351
   Minster *(G-11318)*

North Side Bank and Trust Co............. D 513 533-8000
   Cincinnati *(G-3120)*

North Side Bank and Trust Co............. D 513 542-7800
   Cincinnati *(G-3119)*

Northwest Ohio Chapter Cfma............. E 419 891-1040
   Maumee *(G-10750)*

Ohio Valley Banc Corp......................... E 740 446-2631
   Gallipolis *(G-8765)*

Ohio Valley Bank Company.................. C 740 446-2631
   Gallipolis *(G-8766)*

Osgood State Bank Inc........................ E 419 582-2681
   Osgood *(G-12181)*

Peoples Bancorp Inc............................. C 740 373-3155
   Marietta *(G-10396)*

Peoples Bank...................................... D 740 354-3177
   Portsmouth *(G-12564)*

Peoples Bank...................................... D 740 373-3155
   Marietta *(G-10397)*

Peoples Nat Bnk of New Lxngton........ E 740 342-5111
   New Lexington *(G-11630)*

Portage Community Bank..................... E 330 296-8090
   Ravenna *(G-12637)*

Premier Bank....................................... E 330 742-0500
   Youngstown *(G-15697)*

Republic Bank & Trust Company.......... E 513 651-3000
   Cincinnati *(G-3288)*

Retirement Corp of America................ D 513 769-4040
   Blue Ash *(G-1237)*

Richland Trust Company...................... C 419 525-8700
   Mansfield *(G-10314)*

Richwood Banking Company................ E 937 390-0470
   Springfield *(G-13285)*

Richwood Banking Company................ E 740 943-2317
   Richwood *(G-12724)*

Rockhold Bank..................................... E 740 634-2331
   Bainbridge *(G-686)*

Savings Bank....................................... E 740 474-3191
   Circleville *(G-3723)*

Sb Financial Group Inc........................ C 419 783-8950
   Defiance *(G-7768)*

Ssb Community Bank........................... E 330 878-5555
   Strasburg *(G-13406)*

◆ State Bank and Trust Company........ E 419 783-8950
   Defiance *(G-7769)*

The Delaware County Bank Inc........... C 740 657-7000
   Lewis Center *(G-9838)*

The Peoples Bank Co Inc.................... E 419 678-2385
   Coldwater *(G-5220)*

Unified Bank....................................... E 740 633-0445
   Martins Ferry *(G-10472)*

Union Savings Bank............................. E 513 247-0300
   Cincinnati *(G-3550)*

Wayne Savings Bancshares Inc........... C 330 264-5767
   Wooster *(G-15383)*

Wayne Savings Community Bank......... D 330 264-5767
   Wooster *(G-15374)*

Westfield Bank Fsb............................. E 800 368-8930
   Westfield Center *(G-15026)*

Wilmington Savings Bank..................... E 937 382-1659
   Wilmington *(G-15280)*

6029 Commercial banks, nec

Farmers Merchants Bancorp Inc.......... D 419 822-9510
   Delta *(G-7850)*

FDS Bank... A 513 573-2265
   Mason *(G-10547)*

First Merchants Bank........................... E 614 486-9000
   Upper Arlington *(G-14278)*

Guardian Savings Bank........................ E 513 842-8900
   Cincinnati *(G-2781)*

Huntington National Bank.................... E 330 786-9950
   Akron *(G-197)*

Huntington National Bank.................... E 330 762-4210
   Akron *(G-198)*

Huntington National Bank.................... E 330 869-5950
   Akron *(G-199)*

Huntington National Bank.................... E 419 281-6020
   Ashland *(G-502)*

Huntington National Bank.................... E 419 281-2541
   Ashland *(G-503)*

Huntington National Bank.................... E 440 992-7342
   Ashtabula *(G-537)*

Huntington National Bank.................... E 440 937-5545
   Avon *(G-655)*

Huntington National Bank.................... E 216 515-0029
   Bay Village *(G-760)*

Huntington National Bank.................... E 937 848-6861
   Bellbrook *(G-1017)*

Huntington National Bank.................... E 937 593-2010
   Bellefontaine *(G-1029)*

Huntington National Bank.................... E 440 202-3050
   Berea *(G-1071)*

Huntington National Bank.................... E 216 515-0013
   Brookpark *(G-1435)*

Huntington National Bank.................... E 330 225-3946
   Brunswick *(G-1457)*

Huntington National Bank.................... E 419 636-1164
   Bryan *(G-1485)*

Huntington National Bank.................... E 440 834-4481
   Burton *(G-1529)*

60 DEPOSITORY INSTITUTIONS

Huntington National Bank .... E 740 439-5533
  Cambridge (G-1574)
Huntington National Bank .... E 614 480-0008
  Canal Winchester (G-1609)
Huntington National Bank .... E 330 966-5232
  Canton (G-1778)
Huntington National Bank .... E 440 285-2111
  Chardon (G-2005)
Huntington National Bank .... D 513 762-1860
  Cincinnati (G-2857)
Huntington National Bank .... E 216 515-0471
  Cleveland (G-4390)
Huntington National Bank .... E 216 290-2445
  Cleveland (G-4391)
Huntington National Bank .... E 216 515-6401
  Cleveland (G-4392)
Huntington National Bank .... E 216 515-0064
  Cleveland (G-4393)
Huntington National Bank .... E 440 236-5011
  Columbia Station (G-5228)
Huntington National Bank .... E 614 480-0005
  Columbus (G-6018)
Huntington National Bank .... E 614 480-0017
  Columbus (G-6019)
Huntington National Bank .... D 614 480-0038
  Columbus (G-6020)
Huntington National Bank .... E 614 480-0004
  Columbus (G-6022)
Huntington National Bank .... E 614 480-0026
  Columbus (G-6023)
Huntington National Bank .... E 614 480-0020
  Columbus (G-6024)
Huntington National Bank .... E 800 480-2265
  Columbus (G-6025)
Huntington National Bank .... D 614 331-9537
  Columbus (G-6026)
Huntington National Bank .... E 330 920-6190
  Cuyahoga Falls (G-7081)
Huntington National Bank .... E 937 428-7400
  Dayton (G-7417)
Huntington National Bank .... E 740 363-9343
  Delaware (G-7805)
Huntington National Bank .... E 330 343-6611
  Dover (G-7890)
Huntington National Bank .... E 440 406-5070
  Elyria (G-8259)
Huntington National Bank .... E 440 365-1890
  Elyria (G-8260)
Huntington National Bank .... E 440 943-3389
  Euclid (G-8348)
Huntington National Bank .... E 330 867-2828
  Fairlawn (G-8484)
Huntington National Bank .... E 419 429-4627
  Findlay (G-8547)
Huntington National Bank .... E 937 746-9904
  Franklin (G-8641)
Huntington National Bank .... E 419 468-6868
  Galion (G-8749)
Huntington National Bank .... E 614 480-4500
  Hilliard (G-9202)
Huntington National Bank .... E 330 653-5161
  Hudson (G-9357)
Huntington National Bank .... E 330 677-8200
  Kent (G-9579)
Huntington National Bank .... E 419 226-8200
  Lima (G-9908)
Huntington National Bank .... E 330 424-7226
  Lisbon (G-10003)
Huntington National Bank .... E 740 852-1234
  London (G-10042)
Huntington National Bank .... E 740 852-1234
  London (G-10043)

Huntington National Bank .... E 440 428-1124
  Madison (G-10217)
Huntington National Bank .... E 419 589-3111
  Mansfield (G-10270)
Huntington National Bank .... E 740 373-2886
  Marietta (G-10371)
Huntington National Bank .... E 330 830-1200
  Massillon (G-10646)
Huntington National Bank .... E 330 721-5555
  Medina (G-10842)
Huntington National Bank .... E 330 723-6666
  Medina (G-10843)
Huntington National Bank .... E 330 722-6762
  Medina (G-10844)
Huntington National Bank .... E 330 725-0593
  Medina (G-10845)
Huntington National Bank .... E 330 343-2527
  New Philadelphia (G-11655)
Huntington National Bank .... E 740 498-8376
  Newcomerstown (G-11769)
Huntington National Bank .... E 330 841-0142
  Newton Falls (G-11776)
Huntington National Bank .... E 330 966-5353
  North Canton (G-11840)
Huntington National Bank .... E 440 327-7054
  North Ridgeville (G-11929)
Huntington National Bank .... E 330 467-7127
  Northfield (G-11957)
Huntington National Bank .... E 419 747-2265
  Ontario (G-12107)
Huntington National Bank .... E 419 523-6880
  Ottawa (G-12186)
Huntington National Bank .... E 440 886-1959
  Parma (G-12255)
Huntington National Bank .... E 330 314-1395
  Poland (G-12504)
Huntington National Bank .... E 419 734-2157
  Port Clinton (G-12534)
Huntington National Bank .... E 419 734-2157
  Port Clinton (G-12535)
Huntington National Bank .... E 330 296-2214
  Ravenna (G-12629)
Huntington National Bank .... E 216 515-0022
  Rocky River (G-12742)
Huntington National Bank .... E 216 515-0022
  Rocky River (G-12743)
Huntington National Bank .... E 740 695-3323
  Saint Clairsville (G-12794)
Huntington National Bank .... E 216 515-0024
  Solon (G-13097)
Huntington National Bank .... E 937 390-1779
  Springfield (G-13255)
Huntington National Bank .... E 330 626-3426
  Streetsboro (G-13416)
Huntington National Bank .... E 330 626-3431
  Streetsboro (G-13417)
Huntington National Bank .... E 330 634-0841
  Tallmadge (G-13595)
Huntington National Bank .... E 419 249-7877
  Toledo (G-13853)
Huntington National Bank .... E 419 254-7016
  Toledo (G-13854)
Huntington National Bank .... E 419 254-7052
  Toledo (G-13855)
Huntington National Bank .... E 419 249-3340
  Toledo (G-13856)
Huntington National Bank .... E 330 334-1091
  Wadsworth (G-14437)
Huntington National Bank .... E 330 334-1591
  Wadsworth (G-14438)
Huntington National Bank .... E 330 609-5029
  Warren (G-14527)

Huntington National Bank .... E 330 841-0197
  Warren (G-14528)
Huntington National Bank .... E 330 841-0205
  Warren (G-14529)
Huntington National Bank .... E 440 647-4533
  Wellington (G-14633)
Huntington National Bank .... E 614 480-0016
  Westerville (G-14987)
Huntington National Bank .... E 330 263-2751
  Wooster (G-15347)
Huntington National Bank .... E 330 314-1410
  Youngstown (G-15635)
Huntington National Bank .... E 330 314-1380
  Youngstown (G-15636)
Huntington National Bank .... E 740 452-8444
  Zanesville (G-15802)
Huntington National Bank .... E 740 455-7048
  Zanesville (G-15803)
▲ Huntington National Bank .... B 614 480-4293
  Columbus (G-6021)
Vinton County National Bank .... E 800 223-4031
  Mc Arthur (G-10799)

6035 Federal savings institutions

Belmont Federal Sav & Ln Assn .... E 740 676-1165
  Bellaire (G-1008)
Centery National Bank .... E 740 454-2521
  Zanesville (G-15779)
Citizens Bank of Delphos .... D 419 692-2010
  Delphos (G-7838)
Fairfield Federal Sav Ln Assn .... E 740 653-3863
  Lancaster (G-9712)
Farmers Merchants Bancorp Inc .... D 419 822-9510
  Delta (G-7850)
Federal Reserve Bank Cleveland .... C 513 721-4787
  Cincinnati (G-2656)
Federal Reserve Bank Cleveland .... A 216 579-2000
  Cleveland (G-4246)
First Fdral Sav Ln Assn Lkwood .... C 216 221-7300
  Lakewood (G-9667)
First Fdral Sav Ln Assn Lorain .... D 440 282-6188
  Lorain (G-10075)
First Fdral Sav Ln Assn Newark .... E 740 345-3494
  Newark (G-11700)
First Federal Bank of Ohio .... E 419 468-1518
  Galion (G-8747)
First Place Bank .... A 330 726-3396
  Warren (G-14519)
Greenville Federal .... E 937 548-4158
  Greenville (G-8874)
Guardian Savings Bank .... E 513 842-8900
  Cincinnati (G-2781)
Guardian Savings Bank .... E 513 528-8787
  Cincinnati (G-2782)
Guardian Savings Bank .... E 513 942-3535
  West Chester (G-14702)
Harrison Building and Ln Assn .... E 513 367-2015
  Harrison (G-9108)
Home Sav & Ln Co Kenton Ohio .... E 419 673-1117
  Kenton (G-9619)
Home Savings Loan Company .... E 304 594-0013
  Youngstown (G-15631)
Park View Federal Savings Bank .... C 440 248-7171
  Solon (G-13124)
Peoples Savings and Loan Co .... E 419 562-6896
  Bucyrus (G-1516)
Premier Financial Corp .... D 419 782-5015
  Defiance (G-7762)
Pvf Capital Corp .... C 440 248-7171
  Solon (G-13133)
Resolute Bank .... E 419 868-1750
  Maumee (G-10761)

60 DEPOSITORY INSTITUTIONS

Tfs Financial Corporation............................. A 216 441-6000
Cleveland *(G-4989)*

Third Fdral Sav Ln Assn Clvlan................. E 440 885-4900
Cleveland *(G-5009)*

Third Fdral Sav Ln Assn Clvlan................. E 216 581-0881
Cleveland *(G-5010)*

Third Fdral Sav Ln Assn Clvlan................. E 440 526-3001
Cleveland *(G-5011)*

Third Fdral Sav Ln Assn Clvlan................. E 440 238-4333
Cleveland *(G-5012)*

Third Fdral Sav Ln Assn Clvlan................. E 440 946-9040
Mentor *(G-11003)*

Third Fdral Sav Ln Assn Clvlan................. E 330 963-3130
Twinsburg *(G-14222)*

Third Fdral Sav Ln Assn Clvlan................. B 800 844-7333
Cleveland *(G-5008)*

Van Wert Federal Sav Bnk Inc.................... E 419 238-9662
Van Wert *(G-14359)*

6036 Savings institutions, except federal

Camco Financial Corporation..................... C 740 435-2020
Cambridge *(G-1562)*

Harrison Building and Ln Assn.................. E 513 367-2015
Harrison *(G-9108)*

Home Sav & Ln Co Kenton Ohio................ E 419 673-1117
Kenton *(G-9619)*

New York Community Bancorp Inc........... C 216 736-3480
Cleveland *(G-4640)*

State Farm General Insur Co..................... D 513 662-7283
Cincinnati *(G-3413)*

The Home Savings and Loan..................... C 330 742-0500
Youngstown *(G-15734)*

United Community Financial Corp........... A 330 742-0500
Youngstown *(G-15742)*

6061 Federal credit unions

Advantage Credit Union Inc..................... E 419 529-5603
Ontario *(G-12098)*

American Chem Soc Fderal Cr Un............ A 614 447-3675
Columbus *(G-5347)*

Aurgroup Financial Cr Un Inc................... E 513 942-4422
Fairfield *(G-8390)*

B F G Federal Credit Union...................... E 330 374-2990
Akron *(G-57)*

Bay Area Credit Union Inc....................... E 419 698-2962
Oregon *(G-12128)*

Bmi Federal Credit Union........................ D 614 707-4000
Dublin *(G-7944)*

Bmi Federal Credit Union........................ E 614 298-8527
Columbus *(G-5451)*

C E S Credit Union Inc............................. E 740 397-1136
Mount Vernon *(G-11478)*

Canton Schl Employees Fdral Cr............. E 330 452-9801
Canton *(G-1705)*

Chaco Credit Union Inc........................... E 513 785-3500
Hamilton *(G-9026)*

Christian Family Credit Union.................. C 513 528-1521
Milford *(G-11222)*

Cinco Credit Union................................. E 513 281-9988
Cincinnati *(G-2437)*

Cinfed Federal Credit Union.................... D 513 333-3800
Cincinnati *(G-2441)*

Columbus Municipal Employees............. E 614 224-8890
Columbus *(G-5646)*

Corporate One Federal Cr Un................. D 614 825-9314
Columbus *(G-5254)*

Credit Union of Ohio Inc........................ E 614 487-6650
Hilliard *(G-9190)*

Day Air Credit Union Inc........................ E 937 643-2160
Dayton *(G-7268)*

Desco Federal Credit Union.................... E 740 354-7791
Portsmouth *(G-12550)*

Directions Credit Union Inc.................... D 419 720-4769
Sylvania *(G-13541)*

Dover Phila Federal Credit Un................ E 330 364-8874
Dover *(G-7884)*

Erie Shores Credit Union Inc.................. E 419 897-8110
Maumee *(G-10723)*

Fairview Hlth Sys Fderal Cr Un............... B 216 476-7000
Cleveland *(G-4237)*

Firelands Federal Credit Union............... E 419 483-4180
Bellevue *(G-1044)*

First Chice Amer Cmnty Fdral C............ E 800 427-4835
Steubenville *(G-13325)*

First Day Fincl Federal Cr Un................. E 937 222-4546
Dayton *(G-7352)*

First Ohio Credit Union.......................... E 419 435-8513
Fostoria *(G-8615)*

General Electric Credit Union................ D 513 243-4328
Cincinnati *(G-2726)*

Greater Cincinnati Credit Un.................. E 513 559-1234
Mason *(G-10556)*

Hancock Federal Credit Union............... E 419 420-0338
Findlay *(G-8542)*

Honda Federal Credit Union.................. E 937 642-6000
Marysville *(G-10489)*

Honda Federal Credit Union.................. E 937 642-6000
Marysville *(G-10490)*

Ih Credit Union Inc............................... E 937 390-1800
Springfield *(G-13256)*

Impact Credit Union Inc........................ E 419 547-7781
Clyde *(G-5203)*

Kemba Credit Union Inc....................... C 513 541-3015
Cincinnati *(G-2934)*

Kemba Credit Union Inc....................... D 513 762-5070
West Chester *(G-14718)*

Lormet Community Federal Cr Un......... E 440 960-6600
Amherst *(G-431)*

Midusa Credit Union............................ E 513 420-8640
Middletown *(G-11175)*

Midwest Cmnty Federal Cr Un............. E 419 599-5522
Napoleon *(G-11529)*

Millstream Area Credit Un Inc.............. E 419 422-5626
Findlay *(G-8570)*

Nationwide Credit Union..................... D 614 249-6226
Columbus *(G-6327)*

Ohio Educational Credit Un Inc............ E 216 621-6296
Seven Hills *(G-12956)*

Pathways Financial Cr Un Inc.............. D 614 416-7588
Columbus *(G-6503)*

Plain Dealer Federal Cr Un Inc............ E 216 999-4270
Cleveland *(G-4754)*

Postal Family Credit Union Inc............ E 513 381-8600
Cincinnati *(G-3225)*

Pse Credit Union Inc.......................... E 330 661-0160
Medina *(G-10880)*

Pse Credit Union Inc.......................... E 440 572-3830
Strongsville *(G-13480)*

School Emplyees Lrain Cnty Cr........... E 440 324-3400
Elyria *(G-8293)*

Seven Seventeen Credit Un Inc........... C 330 372-8100
Warren *(G-14552)*

Sun Federal Credit Union................... E 800 786-0945
Maumee *(G-10772)*

Taleris Credit Union Inc...................... E 216 739-2300
Independence *(G-9489)*

Telhio Credit Union Inc...................... E 614 221-3233
Columbus *(G-6755)*

True Core Federal Credit Union.......... E 740 345-6608
Newark *(G-11751)*

Trupartner Credit Union Inc............... E 513 241-2050
Cincinnati *(G-3532)*

Universal 1 Credit Union Inc.............. D 800 762-9555
Dayton *(G-7687)*

Universal One Inc.............................. D 937 431-3100
Beavercreek *(G-912)*

6062 State credit unions

Buckeye State Credit Union Inc........... E 330 823-7930
Alliance *(G-376)*

Firefighters Cmnty Cr Un Inc.............. E 216 621-4644
Cleveland *(G-4252)*

Homeland Credit Union Inc................ E 740 775-3024
Chillicothe *(G-2069)*

Kemba Financial Credit Un Inc........... D 614 235-2395
Columbus *(G-6110)*

Kemba Financial Credit Union............ E 614 235-2395
Columbus *(G-6111)*

Nationwide Credit Union.................... D 614 249-6226
Columbus *(G-6327)*

Struthers CU A Div Brdge Cr Un......... E 800 434-7300
Columbus *(G-6723)*

Wright-Patt Credit Union Inc............... B 937 912-7000
Beavercreek *(G-917)*

6099 Functions related to depository banking

Allied Cash Advance Cal LLC.............. D 800 528-1974
Cincinnati *(G-2164)*

Allied Cash Advance Ohio LLC........... C 800 528-1974
Cincinnati *(G-2165)*

Allied Cash Holdings LLC................... D
Cincinnati *(G-2166)*

Buckeye Check Cashing Inc................ E 740 851-4073
Chillicothe *(G-2053)*

Buckeye Check Cashing Inc................ E 513 936-9995
Cincinnati *(G-2285)*

Buckeye Check Cashing Inc................ E 513 851-3100
Cincinnati *(G-2286)*

Buckeye Check Cashing Inc................ E 513 931-7300
Cincinnati *(G-2287)*

Buckeye Check Cashing Inc................ E 513 741-3777
Cincinnati *(G-2288)*

Buckeye Check Cashing Inc................ E 740 497-4039
Circleville *(G-3704)*

Buckeye Check Cashing Inc................ E 740 575-4314
Coshocton *(G-6977)*

Buckeye Check Cashing Inc................ E 216 486-3434
Euclid *(G-8338)*

Buckeye Check Cashing Inc................ E 216 289-8462
Euclid *(G-8339)*

Buckeye Check Cashing Inc................ E 937 393-9087
Hillsboro *(G-9250)*

Buckeye Check Cashing Inc................ E 567 371-3497
Lima *(G-9872)*

Buckeye Check Cashing Inc................ E 419 528-1315
Mansfield *(G-10249)*

Buckeye Check Cashing Inc................ E 740 374-6005
Marietta *(G-10358)*

Buckeye Check Cashing Inc................ E 419 382-5385
Toledo *(G-13722)*

Buckeye Check Cashing Inc................ E 614 863-2522
Whitehall *(G-15135)*

Buckeye Check Cashing Inc................ C 614 798-5900
Dublin *(G-7948)*

Check n Go of Florida Inc................... D 513 336-7735
Cincinnati *(G-2349)*

Check n Go of Missouri Inc................. E 513 531-2288
Cincinnati *(G-2350)*

Checksmart Fincl Holdings Corp......... E 614 798-5900
Dublin *(G-7961)*

CNG Financial Corporation................ B 513 336-7735
Cincinnati *(G-2465)*

Community Choice Financial Inc......... C 614 798-5900
Dublin *(G-7968)*

◆ **Jpmorgan Chase Bank Nat Assn**...... A 614 436-3055
Columbus *(G-5264)*

61 NONDEPOSITORY CREDIT INSTITUTIONS

Klarna Inc. .... E 614 615-4705
  Columbus *(G-6118)*

Mary C Enterprises Inc .... D 937 253-6169
  Dayton *(G-7467)*

Nationwide Biweekly ADM Inc .... C 937 376-5800
  Xenia *(G-15529)*

Pls Financial Services Inc .... E 513 421-4200
  Cincinnati *(G-3215)*

Sack n Save Inc .... E 740 382-2464
  Marion *(G-10453)*

61 NONDEPOSITORY CREDIT INSTITUTIONS

6111 Federal and federally sponsored credit

Federal Home Ln Bnk Cincinnati .... C 513 852-7500
  Cincinnati *(G-2654)*

Ferno Group Inc .... C 937 382-1451
  Wilmington *(G-15251)*

National City Credit Corp .... E 216 575-2000
  Cleveland *(G-4621)*

Navient Solutions LLC .... C 513 605-7530
  Mason *(G-10583)*

Student Ln Fnding Rsources LLC ..... E 513 763-4300
  Cincinnati *(G-3425)*

6141 Personal credit institutions

Check N Go of Washington Inc .... E 800 561-2274
  Cincinnati *(G-2351)*

Diebold Global Finance Corp .... D 330 490-6900
  North Canton *(G-11822)*

Equity Resources Inc .... E 614 389-4462
  Dublin *(G-8006)*

Farm Credit Svcs Mid-America .... E 740 335-3306
  Wshngtn Ct Hs *(G-15480)*

First American .... D 330 379-2320
  Akron *(G-159)*

Grange Indemnity Insurance Co .... C 614 445-2900
  Columbus *(G-5946)*

Jpmorgan Chase & Co .... C 614 248-5800
  Columbus *(G-5263)*

Macys Cr & Customer Svcs Inc .... A 513 398-5221
  Mason *(G-10576)*

Modern Finance Company .... E 614 351-7400
  Columbus *(G-6255)*

◆ Mtd Holdings Inc .... B 330 225-2600
  Valley City *(G-14336)*

Ohio Auto Loan Services Inc .... E 614 434-2397
  Columbus *(G-6394)*

Ohio Auto Loan Services Inc .... E 440 716-1710
  North Olmsted *(G-11909)*

Ohio Auto Loan Services Inc .... E 419 982-8013
  Ontario *(G-12118)*

Ohio Auto Loan Services Inc .... E 937 556-4687
  Wilmington *(G-15262)*

Ohio Auto Loan Services Inc .... E 330 272-9488
  Youngstown *(G-15679)*

Ohio Auto Loan Services Inc .... E 740 624-8547
  Zanesville *(G-15821)*

Regional Acceptance Corp .... E 513 398-2106
  Cincinnati *(G-3280)*

Security Nat Auto Accptnce LLC ...... C 513 459-8118
  Mason *(G-10605)*

Splash Financial Inc .... D 216 452-0113
  Cleveland *(G-4935)*

United Consumer Fincl Svcs Co .... C 440 835-3230
  Cleveland *(G-5056)*

6153 Short-term business credit

Lemon Group LLC .... E 614 409-9850
  Obetz *(G-12081)*

Relentless Recovery Inc .... D 216 621-8333
  Cleveland *(G-4820)*

Unifund Ccr LLC .... D 513 489-8877
  Blue Ash *(G-1262)*

Unifund Corporation .... E 513 489-8877
  Blue Ash *(G-1263)*

6159 Miscellaneous business credit

Agri Business Finance Inc .... E 937 663-0186
  Saint Paris *(G-12837)*

BMW Financial Services Na LLC ..... D 614 718-6900
  Dublin *(G-7945)*

BMW Financial Services Na LLC ..... E 614 718-6900
  Hilliard *(G-9184)*

Dana Credit Corporation .... B 419 887-3000
  Maumee *(G-10715)*

Farm Credit Svcs Mid-America .... A 740 373-8211
  Marietta *(G-10367)*

Ford Motor Company .... E 513 573-1101
  Mason *(G-10549)*

Keybank National Association .... B 800 539-2968
  Cleveland *(G-4461)*

Lancaster Pollard Mrtg Co LLC .... D 614 224-8800
  Columbus *(G-6134)*

Momentum Fleet MGT Group Inc ..... D 440 759-2219
  Westlake *(G-15080)*

◆ Ohio Machinery Co .... C 440 526-6200
  Broadview Heights *(G-1394)*

Pfsc Inc .... E 513 221-5080
  Cincinnati *(G-3204)*

Producers Credit Corporation .... C 800 641-7522
  Columbus *(G-6548)*

▲ Reynolds and Reynolds Company .. A 937 485-2000
  Kettering *(G-9632)*

Security Nat Auto Accptnce LLC ...... C 513 459-8118
  Mason *(G-10605)*

Summit Funding Group Inc .... E 513 489-1222
  Mason *(G-10613)*

6162 Mortgage bankers and correspondents

American Midwest Mortgage Corp .... E 440 882-5210
  Cleveland *(G-3804)*

Amerifirst Financial Corp .... D 614 766-5709
  Dublin *(G-7937)*

Amerifirst Financial Corp .... D 216 452-5120
  Lakewood *(G-9657)*

Apex Mortgage Services LLC .... D 614 839-2739
  Columbus *(G-5373)*

C O Howard Hanna Mortgage .... D 412 967-9000
  Cleveland *(G-3917)*

Chase Manhattan Mortgage Corp .... C 614 422-7982
  Columbus *(G-5552)*

Crosscountry Mortgage Inc .... E 440 845-3700
  Cleveland *(G-4139)*

Crosscountry Mortgage LLC .... D 216 314-0107
  Beachwood *(G-785)*

Crosscountry Mortgage LLC .... D 513 373-4240
  Blue Ash *(G-1162)*

Crosscountry Mortgage LLC .... E 419 636-4663
  Bryan *(G-1483)*

Crosscountry Mortgage LLC .... D 440 262-3528
  Cleveland *(G-4140)*

Crosscountry Mortgage LLC .... D 614 779-0316
  Columbus *(G-5731)*

Crosscountry Mortgage LLC .... D 440 413-0867
  Mentor *(G-10928)*

Crosscountry Mortgage LLC .... D 440 354-5206
  Painesville *(G-12225)*

Crosscountry Mortgage LLC .... D 330 655-5626
  Stow *(G-13360)*

Crosscountry Mortgage LLC .... D 330 715-4878
  Stow *(G-13361)*

Crosscountry Mortgage LLC .... B 440 845-3700
  Brecksville *(G-1352)*

Equity Resources Inc .... E 740 363-7300
  Delaware *(G-7795)*

Equity Resources Inc .... E 614 389-4462
  Dublin *(G-8006)*

Fairway Independent Mrtg Corp .... E 614 930-6552
  Columbus *(G-5847)*

Fairway Independent Mrtg Corp .... E 513 833-1973
  Milford *(G-11227)*

Fairway Independent Mrtg Corp .... E 937 304-1443
  Springboro *(G-13198)*

Fairway Independent Mrtg Corp .... E 330 587-9152
  Uniontown *(G-14250)*

Fifth Third Bnk of Sthern OH I .... E 937 840-5353
  Hillsboro *(G-9253)*

First Day Fincl Federal Cr Un .... E 937 222-4546
  Dayton *(G-7352)*

First Ohio Banc & Lending Inc .... D 216 642-8900
  Cleveland *(G-4259)*

Firstmerit Mortgage Corp .... D 330 478-3400
  Canton *(G-1754)*

Guaranteed Rate Inc .... C 513 609-4477
  Cincinnati *(G-2779)*

Guardian Savings Bank .... E 513 842-8900
  Cincinnati *(G-2781)*

Huntington National Bank .... D 513 762-1860
  Cincinnati *(G-2857)*

Huntington National Bank .... E 419 226-8200
  Lima *(G-9908)*

Huntington National Bank .... E 740 852-1234
  London *(G-10043)*

Huntington National Bank .... E 419 734-2157
  Port Clinton *(G-12534)*

Huntington National Bank .... E 419 249-3340
  Toledo *(G-13856)*

Jpmorgan Chase & Co .... C 614 248-5800
  Columbus *(G-5263)*

◆ Jpmorgan Chase Bank Nat Assn .. A 614 436-3055
  Columbus *(G-5264)*

Keller Mortgage LLC .... D 614 310-3100
  Powell *(G-12596)*

Lancaster Pollard Mrtg Co LLC .... D 614 224-8800
  Columbus *(G-6134)*

Liberty Home Mortgage Corp .... C 440 644-0001
  Independence *(G-9443)*

Liberty Mortgage Company Inc .... E 614 224-4000
  Columbus *(G-6157)*

M/I Financial LLC .... D 614 418-8661
  Columbus *(G-6184)*

M/I Homes Inc .... B 614 418-8000
  Columbus *(G-6186)*

Modern Finance Company .... E 614 351-7400
  Columbus *(G-6255)*

Mortgage Now Inc .... E 800 245-1050
  Cleveland *(G-4603)*

National City Mortgage Inc .... A 937 910-1200
  Miamisburg *(G-11075)*

Nations Lending Corporation .... D 877 816-1220
  Independence *(G-9456)*

Nations Lending Corporation .... D 440 785-0963
  Medina *(G-10867)*

Nations Lending Corporation .... D 440 842-4817
  Westlake *(G-15082)*

Nations Lending Corporation .... C 216 363-6901
  Independence *(G-9457)*

Northern Ohio Investment Co .... D 419 885-8300
  Sylvania *(G-13557)*

Old Rpblic Ttle Nthrn Ohio LLC .... C 216 524-5700
  Independence *(G-9464)*

PNC Mortgage Company .... E 412 762-2000
  Miamisburg *(G-11085)*

61 NONDEPOSITORY CREDIT INSTITUTIONS

Priority Mortgage Corp............................. E 614 431-1141
    Worthington *(G-15448)*

Rapid Mortgage Company....................... E 937 748-8888
    Cincinnati *(G-3273)*

Real Estate Mortgage Corp...................... D 440 356-5373
    Chagrin Falls *(G-1964)*

Residential Finance Corp......................... A 614 324-4700
    Columbus *(G-6584)*

River City Mortgage LLC.......................... C 513 631-6400
    Blue Ash *(G-1238)*

Rocket Mortgage LLC............................... E 216 586-8900
    Cleveland *(G-4850)*

Sibcy Cline Inc... C 513 777-8100
    West Chester *(G-14764)*

Sirva Mortgage Inc.................................. D 800 531-3837
    Independence *(G-9483)*

Stockton Mortgage Corporation............... E 513 486-4140
    Mason *(G-10609)*

Union Home Mortgage Corp.................... E 800 767-4684
    Strongsville *(G-13493)*

Van Dyk Mortgage Corporation................ E 419 720-4384
    Toledo *(G-14090)*

Vinton County National Bank.................... E 800 223-4031
    Mc Arthur *(G-10799)*

Western Ohio Mortgage Corp................... E 937 497-9662
    Sidney *(G-13058)*

6163 Loan brokers

Board of Dirs of Wttnberg Clle.................. D 937 327-6310
    Springfield *(G-13222)*

BP Financial Group Inc............................ E 513 851-8525
    Cincinnati *(G-2275)*

Civista Bank... E 419 599-1065
    Napoleon *(G-11518)*

Crosscountry Mortgage LLC.................... B 440 845-3700
    Brecksville *(G-1352)*

Firefighters Cmnty Cr Un Inc.................... E 216 621-4644
    Cleveland *(G-4252)*

Firelands Federal Credit Union................. E 419 483-4180
    Bellevue *(G-1044)*

First Merchants Bank............................... E 614 486-9000
    Upper Arlington *(G-14278)*

Forest City Residential Dev...................... E 216 621-6060
    Cleveland *(G-4275)*

Guardian Savings Bank............................ E 513 842-8900
    Cincinnati *(G-2781)*

Guardian Savings Bank............................ E 513 528-8787
    Cincinnati *(G-2782)*

Guardian Savings Bank............................ E 513 942-3535
    West Chester *(G-14702)*

Impact Credit Union Inc........................... E 419 547-7781
    Clyde *(G-5203)*

Millstream Area Credit Un Inc.................. E 419 422-5626
    Findlay *(G-8570)*

Multi-Fund Inc... E 216 750-2331
    Cleveland *(G-4610)*

Nations Lending Corporation................... C 216 363-6901
    Independence *(G-9457)*

North Coast Capital Funding.................... D 330 923-5333
    Cuyahoga Falls *(G-7090)*

Osgood State Bank Inc............................ E 419 582-2681
    Osgood *(G-12181)*

Premiere Service Mortgage Corp.............. E 513 546-9895
    West Chester *(G-14745)*

Randall Mortgage Services...................... C 614 336-7948
    Dublin *(G-8105)*

Second National Bank.............................. E 937 548-2122
    Greenville *(G-8884)*

◆ State Bank and Trust Company............. E 419 783-4950
    Defiance *(G-7769)*

Struthers CU A Div Brdge Cr Un............... E 800 434-7300
    Columbus *(G-6723)*

Student Ln Fnding Rsources LLC............. E 513 763-4300
    Cincinnati *(G-3425)*

The Home Savings and Loan.................... C 330 742-0500
    Youngstown *(G-15734)*

Total Loan Services LLC.......................... D 937 228-5600
    Oakwood *(G-12052)*

Union Mortgage Services Inc................... E 614 457-4815
    Columbus *(G-6802)*

Welles-Bowen Realty Inc......................... C 419 535-0011
    Toledo *(G-14101)*

62 SECURITY & COMMODITY BROKERS, DEALERS, EXCHANGES & SERVICES

6211 Security brokers and dealers

Capital Securities of America................... E 419 609-9489
    Sandusky *(G-12869)*

Charles Schwab & Co Inc........................ E 330 908-4478
    Richfield *(G-12691)*

Charles Schwab Corporation................... E 800 435-4000
    Beachwood *(G-776)*

Cincinnati Financial Corp......................... A 513 870-2000
    Fairfield *(G-8402)*

Cincinnati Insurance Company................. A 513 870-2000
    Fairfield *(G-8404)*

Corporate Fin Assoc Clmbus Inc............... D 614 457-9219
    Columbus *(G-5703)*

Crosscountry Mortgage LLC.................... B 440 845-3700
    Brecksville *(G-1352)*

Department of Commerce Ohio................ D 614 644-7381
    Columbus *(G-5757)*

Farmers Trust Company........................... E 330 744-4351
    Youngstown *(G-15610)*

Fifth Third Securities Inc.......................... D 513 346-2775
    Cincinnati *(G-2667)*

Fifth Third Securities Inc.......................... D 513 272-7755
    Cincinnati *(G-2668)*

First Source Title Agency Inc................... E 216 986-0970
    North Ridgeville *(G-11927)*

Ifs Financial Services Inc........................ E 513 362-8000
    Westerville *(G-14988)*

◆ Jpmorgan Chase Bank Nat Assn........... A 614 436-3055
    Columbus *(G-5264)*

Key Capital Corporation........................... E 216 828-8154
    Cleveland *(G-4457)*

Keybanc Capital Markets Inc................... B 800 553-2240
    Cleveland *(G-4458)*

Linsalata Cpitl Prtners Fund I................... E 440 684-1400
    Cleveland *(G-4499)*

Marsh Berry & Company LLC.................. E 440 637-8122
    Beachwood *(G-810)*

Merrill Lynch Prce Fnner Smith................ D 440 526-8880
    Broadview Heights *(G-1392)*

Merrill Lynch Prce Fnner Smith................ C 614 225-3000
    Columbus *(G-5269)*

Mm Ascend Life Inv Svcs LLC.................. E 513 333-6030
    Cincinnati *(G-3071)*

Morgan Stnley Smith Barney LLC............. C 216 360-4900
    Cleveland *(G-4600)*

National Associates Inc........................... D 440 333-0222
    Cleveland *(G-4618)*

Nationwide Inv Svcs Corp........................ B 614 249-7111
    Columbus *(G-6333)*

◆ Nationwide Life Insur Co Amer.............. A 800 688-5177
    Columbus *(G-6335)*

Oberlin Investments LLC......................... E 419 636-4001
    Bryan *(G-1489)*

Old Rpblic Ttle Nthrn Ohio LLC................ C 216 524-5700
    Independence *(G-9464)*

R B C Apollo Equity Partners................... E 216 875-2626
    Cleveland *(G-4803)*

Red Capital Markets LLC......................... C 614 857-1400
    Columbus *(G-6566)*

Ross Sinclaire & Assoc LLC.................... E 513 381-3939
    Cincinnati *(G-3320)*

Sirak Financial Services Inc.................... D 330 493-0642
    Canton *(G-1852)*

Skilkengold Development LLC................. E 614 418-3100
    Columbus *(G-6685)*

Stateco Financial Services Inc................. C 614 464-5000
    Columbus *(G-6716)*

Stifel Ind Advisors LLC............................ E 937 293-1220
    Dayton *(G-7643)*

The Cadle Company................................ C 330 872-0918
    Newton Falls *(G-11778)*

The Huntington Investment Co................. C 614 480-3600
    Columbus *(G-6760)*

UBS Financial Services Inc...................... E 513 576-5000
    Cincinnati *(G-3540)*

Valmark Financial Group LLC.................. C 330 576-1234
    Akron *(G-347)*

Van Dyk Mortgage Corporation................ E 419 720-4384
    Toledo *(G-14090)*

Western & Southern Lf Insur Co.............. A 513 629-1800
    Cincinnati *(G-3659)*

Western Southern Mutl Holdg Co............. A 866 832-7719
    Cincinnati *(G-3664)*

Western Sthern Fincl Group Inc............... A 877 367-9734
    Cincinnati *(G-3665)*

Westmnster Fncl Securities Inc................ E 937 898-5010
    Dayton *(G-7719)*

World Group Securities Inc...................... D 513 367-5900
    Harrison *(G-9121)*

6221 Commodity contracts brokers, dealers

Aspen Energy Corporation....................... E 614 884-5300
    Dublin *(G-7941)*

Bakkt Clearing LLC................................. C 614 487-9550
    Columbus *(G-5415)*

Wisewel LLC.. E 440 591-4896
    Cleveland *(G-5153)*

6231 Security and commodity exchanges

Griid Infrastructure Inc............................. E 513 268-6185
    Cincinnati *(G-2778)*

6282 Investment advice

ABN Financial Group............................... E 937 522-0101
    Dayton *(G-7152)*

Allworth Financial LP.............................. E 513 469-7500
    Blue Ash *(G-1128)*

American Financial Network Inc............... E 714 831-4000
    Blacklick *(G-1108)*

Ancora Group LLC.................................. D 216 825-4000
    Cleveland *(G-3815)*

Bartlett & Co LLC.................................... D 513 621-4612
    Cincinnati *(G-2238)*

Beacon Capital Management Inc.............. A 937 203-4025
    Dayton *(G-7188)*

Buckingham & Company.......................... E 937 435-2742
    Dayton *(G-7205)*

C H Dean LLC.. D 937 222-9531
    Beavercreek *(G-867)*

Carnegie Capital Asset MGT LLC.............. E 216 595-1349
    Cleveland *(G-3930)*

Centerfield Insur Fincl Co LLC.................. E 330 501-9719
    Canfield *(G-1625)*

Clearstead Advisors LLC......................... D 216 621-1090
    Cleveland *(G-3999)*

Cleveland Research Company LLC........... E 216 649-7250
    Cleveland *(G-4063)*

SIC SECTION

63 INSURANCE CARRIERS

Cmt II Advisors LLC .... E 937 434-3095
  Centerville *(G-1942)*
Daymark Wealth Partners LLC .... E 513 838-2524
  Montgomery *(G-11366)*
Dbs Financial .... E 440 232-0001
  Bedford *(G-959)*
Diamond Hill Capital MGT Inc .... E 614 255-3333
  Columbus *(G-5761)*
Diamond Hill Funds .... E 614 255-3333
  Columbus *(G-5762)*
Eubel Brady Sttman Asset MGT I .... E 937 291-1223
  Miamisburg *(G-11052)*
Everhart Advisors .... D 614 717-9705
  Dublin *(G-8009)*
Financial Management Group .... D 513 984-6696
  Blue Ash *(G-1173)*
Fort Wash Inv Advisors Inc .... D 513 361-7600
  Cincinnati *(G-2695)*
Foster & Motley Inc .... D 513 561-6640
  Cincinnati *(G-2697)*
Fund Evaluation Group LLC .... E 513 977-4400
  Cincinnati *(G-2711)*
Hamilton Capital MGT Inc .... D 614 273-1000
  Columbus *(G-5967)*
Homeside Financial LLC .... E 614 907-7696
  New Albany *(G-11568)*
Horter Investment MGT LLC .... E 513 984-9933
  Cincinnati *(G-2844)*
Huntington National Bank .... A 614 480-4293
  Columbus *(G-6028)*
Ifs Financial Services Inc .... E 513 362-8000
  Westerville *(G-14988)*
Johnson Investment Counsel Inc .... D 800 541-0170
  Cincinnati *(G-2917)*
Johnson Trust Company .... E 513 598-8859
  Cincinnati *(G-2918)*
Jpmorgan Inv Advisors Inc .... A 614 248-5800
  Columbus *(G-5265)*
Lancaster Pollard Mrtg Co LLC .... D 614 224-8800
  Columbus *(G-6134)*
Lang Financial Group Inc .... E 513 699-2966
  Blue Ash *(G-1199)*
Longbow Research LLC .... D 216 986-0700
  Independence *(G-9448)*
MAI Capital Management LLC .... D 216 920-4800
  Independence *(G-9449)*
Mc Cormack Advisors Intl .... E 216 522-1200
  Cleveland *(G-4535)*
Meeder Asset Management Inc .... D 614 760-2112
  Dublin *(G-8063)*
Merrill Lynch Prce Fnner Smith .... E 614 225-3000
  Columbus *(G-5269)*
Mm Ascend Life Inv Svcs LLC .... E 513 333-6030
  Cincinnati *(G-3071)*
Morgan Stnley Smith Barney LLC .... C 216 344-8700
  Cleveland *(G-4601)*
Mt Washington Care Center Inc .... E 513 231-4561
  Cincinnati *(G-3087)*
National Care Advisors LLC .... E 937 748-9412
  Powell *(G-12601)*
Oak Associates Ltd .... E 330 666-5263
  Akron *(G-245)*
Octavia Wealth Advisors LLC .... E 513 762-7775
  Blue Ash *(G-1216)*
Parkwood LLC .... E 216 875-6500
  Cleveland *(G-4726)*
Parkwood Corporation .... E 216 875-6500
  Cleveland *(G-4727)*
Quickinsured Brokerage .... E 330 722-7070
  Medina *(G-10881)*
Roulston & Company Inc .... E 216 431-3000
  Cleveland *(G-4857)*

Schaeffers Investment Research Inc .... D 513 589-3800
  Blue Ash *(G-1242)*
Sequoia Financial Group LLC .... E 330 375-9480
  Akron *(G-297)*
Sherman Financial Group LLC .... B 513 707-3000
  Cincinnati *(G-3369)*
Stepstone Group Real Estate LP .... E 216 522-0330
  Cleveland *(G-4954)*
Strategic Wealth Partners .... E 216 800-9000
  Independence *(G-9488)*
The Cadle Company .... C 330 872-0918
  Newton Falls *(G-11778)*
Truepoint Wealth Counsel LLC .... E 513 792-6648
  Blue Ash *(G-1259)*
UBS Americas Inc .... D 440 356-5237
  Rocky River *(G-12754)*
Vela Investment Management LLC .... E 614 653-8352
  New Albany *(G-11589)*
Victory Capital Holdings Inc .... E 216 898-2400
  Brooklyn *(G-1412)*
Wealth Bartlett Management .... D 513 345-6217
  Cincinnati *(G-3644)*
Woodsage Corporation .... D 419 866-8000
  Holland *(G-9315)*

63 INSURANCE CARRIERS

6311 Life insurance

21st Century Financial Inc .... D 330 668-9065
  Akron *(G-5)*
Afc Holding Company Inc .... E 513 579-2121
  Cincinnati *(G-2154)*
Allstate Insurance Company .... E 330 650-2917
  Hudson *(G-9330)*
Alpha Investment Partnership .... D 513 621-1826
  Cincinnati *(G-2170)*
American Security Insurance Co .... C 937 327-7700
  Springfield *(G-13216)*
Ameritas Life Insurance Corp .... A 866 696-7478
  Cincinnati *(G-2190)*
Ameritas Life Insurance Corp .... C 513 595-2334
  Cincinnati *(G-2191)*
Andrew Insurance Associates .... D 614 336-8030
  Dublin *(G-7938)*
Buckeye State Mutual Insur Co .... D 937 778-5000
  Piqua *(G-12436)*
Cincinnati Financial Corp .... A 513 870-2000
  Fairfield *(G-8402)*
Cincinnati Insurance Company .... A 513 870-2000
  Fairfield *(G-8404)*
Columbus Life Insurance Co .... C 513 361-6700
  Cincinnati *(G-2477)*
Constellation Insurance Inc .... A 513 794-6100
  Cincinnati *(G-2496)*
Constltion Insur Holdings Inc .... A 513 794-6100
  Cincinnati *(G-2497)*
Crestbrook Insurance Company .... A 614 249-7111
  Columbus *(G-5725)*
Family Heritg Lf Insur Co Amer .... D 440 922-5222
  Broadview Heights *(G-1389)*
Gerber Life Agency LLC .... E 917 765-3572
  Cincinnati *(G-2731)*
Grange Indemnity Insurance Co .... C 614 445-2900
  Columbus *(G-5946)*
◆ Great American Insurance Co .... A 513 369-5000
  Cincinnati *(G-2757)*
Guardian Life Insur Co Amer .... E 513 579-1114
  Cincinnati *(G-2780)*
Hancock Cnty Bd Dvlpmntal Dsbl .... D 419 422-6387
  Findlay *(G-8541)*
Irongate Inc .... D 937 433-3300
  Centerville *(G-1946)*

J P Farley Corporation .... E 440 250-4300
  Westlake *(G-15073)*
Lafayette Life Insurance Co .... C 800 443-8793
  Cincinnati *(G-2963)*
Midland-Guardian Co .... A 513 943-7100
  Amelia *(G-419)*
Modern Finance Company .... E 614 351-7400
  Columbus *(G-6255)*
Nationwide Financial Svcs Inc .... C 614 249-7111
  Columbus *(G-6329)*
Nationwide General Insur Co .... A 614 249-7111
  Columbus *(G-6331)*
Nationwide Insurance .... E 513 341-7221
  Hamilton *(G-9067)*
Nationwide Insurance Co Fla .... A 614 249-7111
  Columbus *(G-6332)*
◆ Nationwide Mutual Insurance Co .... A 614 249-7111
  Columbus *(G-6338)*
Nf Reinsurance Ltd .... C 614 249-7111
  Columbus *(G-6356)*
Ohio Casualty Insurance Co .... A 800 843-6446
  Cincinnati *(G-3143)*
Ohio National Life Asrn Corp .... A 513 794-6100
  Montgomery *(G-11371)*
Pacific Life Insurance Company .... E 513 241-5000
  West Chester *(G-14740)*
Peak Performance Solutions Inc .... E 614 344-4640
  Orient *(G-12153)*
Premier Financial Corp .... D 419 782-5015
  Defiance *(G-7762)*
Standard Insurance Company .... C 513 241-7275
  Cincinnati *(G-3408)*
State Farm General Insur Co .... D 513 662-7283
  Cincinnati *(G-3413)*
Summa Insurance Company Inc .... B 800 996-8411
  Akron *(G-322)*
◆ The Union Central Life In .... A 866 696-7478
  Cincinnati *(G-3472)*
Transamerica Agency Netwrk Inc .... B 614 824-4964
  Columbus *(G-6782)*
Valic Financial Advisor .... E 216 643-6340
  Independence *(G-9495)*
Western & Southern Lf Insur Co .... A 513 629-1800
  Cincinnati *(G-3659)*
Western-Southern Life Asrn Co .... D 513 629-1800
  Cincinnati *(G-3666)*

6321 Accident and health insurance

American Modern Home Svc Co .... E 513 943-7100
  Amelia *(G-412)*
Ameritas Life Insurance Corp .... A 866 696-7478
  Cincinnati *(G-2190)*
Andrew Insurance Associates .... D 614 336-8030
  Dublin *(G-7938)*
Aultcare Insurance Company .... B 330 363-6360
  Canton *(G-1676)*
Caresource .... A 937 224-3300
  Dayton *(G-7211)*
Caresource Management Group Co .... E 614 221-3370
  Hilliard *(G-9188)*
Cincinnati Insurance Company .... A 513 870-2000
  Fairfield *(G-8404)*
◆ Great American Insurance Co .... A 513 369-5000
  Cincinnati *(G-2757)*
J P Farley Corporation .... E 440 250-4300
  Westlake *(G-15073)*
Medical Benefits Mutl Lf Insur .... C 740 522-8425
  Newark *(G-11728)*
Medical Mutual of Ohio .... C 216 292-0400
  Cleveland *(G-4546)*
Nationwide Better Health Inc .... B 614 249-7111
  Columbus *(G-6308)*

63 INSURANCE CARRIERS

◆ Nationwide Corporation.................................E 614 249-7111
  Columbus (G-6326)
◆ Nationwide Mutual Insurance Co..............A 614 249-7111
  Columbus (G-6338)
Oha Holdings Inc..D 614 221-7614
  Columbus (G-6387)
Ohio National Life Asrn Corp.......................A 513 794-6100
  Montgomery (G-11371)
Paramount Care Inc......................................B 419 887-2500
  Maumee (G-10755)
Premier Financial Corp.................................D 419 782-5015
  Defiance (G-7762)
Progressive Casualty Insur Co......................E 440 603-4033
  Cleveland (G-4778)
▼ Progressive Casualty Insur Co..................A 855 347-3939
  Mayfield Village (G-10795)
Sentry Life Insurance Company....................C 513 733-0100
  Cincinnati (G-3359)
State Farm General Insur Co........................D 513 662-7283
  Cincinnati (G-3413)
Summa Insurance Company Inc...................B 800 996-8411
  Akron (G-322)
Superior Dental Care Inc..............................D 937 438-0283
  Dayton (G-7654)
◆ The Union Central Life In..........................A 866 696-7478
  Cincinnati (G-3472)

6324 Hospital and medical service plans

Amerigroup Ohio Inc.....................................C 513 733-2300
  Blue Ash (G-1130)
Anthem Insurance Companies Inc................C 330 492-2151
  Canton (G-1668)
Anthem Insurance Companies Inc................A 614 438-3542
  Columbus (G-5246)
Aultcare Corp..B 330 363-6360
  Canton (G-1674)
Aultcare Holding Company...........................B 330 452-9911
  Canton (G-1675)
Beam Dental Insurance Svcs LLC................C 740 262-1409
  Columbus (G-5427)
Bon Secours Mercy Health Inc.....................E 216 362-2000
  Cleveland (G-3880)
Caresource Management Group Co..............C 216 839-1001
  Cleveland (G-3929)
Centene Corporation.....................................E 513 469-4500
  Columbus (G-5528)
Community Insurance Company...................E 859 282-7888
  Cincinnati (G-2483)
Custom Design Benefits Inc.........................E 513 598-2929
  Cincinnati (G-2527)
Firelands Regional Health Sys.....................E 419 626-7400
  Sandusky (G-12898)
Health Plan of Ohio Inc................................C 330 837-6880
  Massillon (G-10643)
Healthspan Integrated Care.........................A 216 621-5600
  Cincinnati (G-2813)
Humana Health Plan Ohio Inc......................D 513 784-5200
  Cincinnati (G-2856)
Intellihartx LLC..E 419 949-5040
  Findlay (G-8549)
J P Farley Corporation..................................E 440 250-4300
  Westlake (G-15073)
Metrohealth System......................................C 216 778-3867
  Cleveland (G-4567)
Miami Valley Hospitalist Group.....................D 937 208-8394
  Dayton (G-7495)
Molina Healthcare Inc..................................A 800 642-4168
  Columbus (G-6257)
Neo Administration Company......................D 330 864-0690
  Akron (G-240)
Nextrx LLC..A 317 532-6000
  Mason (G-10584)

Ohio Health Choice Inc................................D 800 554-0027
  Akron (G-252)
Promedica Health System Inc......................D 419 355-9209
  Fremont (G-8697)
Promedica Health System Inc......................A 567 585-9600
  Toledo (G-13972)
Qualchoice Health Plan Inc..........................C 440 544-2800
  Euclid (G-8360)
Summa Health System Corp........................E 330 375-4848
  Akron (G-321)
Uc Health Llc..D 513 585-7600
  Cincinnati (G-3541)
United Healthcare Ohio Inc..........................D 513 603-6200
  Cincinnati (G-3554)
United Healthcare Ohio Inc..........................E 216 694-4080
  Cleveland (G-5061)
United Healthcare Ohio Inc..........................B 614 410-7000
  Columbus (G-6806)
Unitedhealthcare Insurance Co....................A 440 282-1357
  Lorain (G-10106)
Vsp Vision Care..D 614 471-1372
  Columbus (G-6861)

6331 Fire, marine, and casualty insurance

Afc Holding Company Inc............................D 513 579-2121
  Cincinnati (G-2154)
American Empire Srpls Lnes Ins..................E 513 369-3000
  Cincinnati (G-2178)
American Financial Corporation...................C 513 579-2121
  Cincinnati (G-2179)
American Money Management Corp............E 513 579-2592
  Cincinnati (G-2183)
American Select Insurance Co.....................D 330 887-0101
  Westfield Center (G-15024)
American Western Home Insur Co...............A 513 943-7100
  Amelia (G-415)
Amtrust North America Inc..........................C 216 328-6100
  Cleveland (G-3813)
Andrew Insurance Associates......................D 614 336-8030
  Dublin (G-7938)
Artisan and Truckers Cslty Co......................D 440 461-5000
  Cleveland (G-3835)
Caret Holdings Inc.......................................A 866 980-9431
  Columbus (G-5510)
Cbiz Inc..A 216 447-9000
  Cleveland (G-3942)
Cbiz Accnting Tax Advsory Wash................E 216 447-9000
  Cleveland (G-3943)
Cbiz Mhm Northern Cal LLC........................E 216 447-9000
  Cleveland (G-3944)
Celina Mutual Insurance Co.........................C 800 552-5181
  Celina (G-1919)
Central Mutual Insurance Co........................B 419 238-1010
  Van Wert (G-14341)
Cincinnati Financial Corp.............................A 513 870-2000
  Fairfield (G-8402)
Cincinnati Insurance Company....................A 513 870-2000
  Fairfield (G-8404)
Compmanagement Inc.................................E 330 782-0363
  Youngstown (G-15586)
Consumers Insurance Usa Inc.....................D 615 896-6133
  Columbus (G-5688)
Crestbrook Insurance Company...................A 614 249-7111
  Columbus (G-5725)
Drive Insurance Company............................D 440 446-5100
  Cleveland (G-4185)
▲ Freedom Specialty Insurance Co.............C 614 249-1545
  Columbus (G-5893)
Globe American Casualty Co.......................C 513 576-3200
  Loveland (G-10138)
Grange Insurance Company........................A 800 422-0550
  Columbus (G-5947)

Great Amercn Aliance Insur Co....................E 513 369-5000
  Cincinnati (G-2754)
Great American Assurance...........................D 513 369-5000
  Cincinnati (G-2755)
Great American Holding Inc.........................D 513 369-3000
  Cincinnati (G-2756)
◆ Great American Insurance Co..................A 513 369-5000
  Cincinnati (G-2757)
Great American SEC Insur Co.....................E 513 369-5000
  Cincinnati (G-2758)
Great Amrcn Fncl Resources Inc.................C 513 333-5300
  Cincinnati (G-2759)
Great Amrcn Plan Admnstrtors I...................E 513 412-2316
  Cincinnati (G-2760)
Great Amrcn Risk Sltons Srpls.....................D 513 369-3000
  Cincinnati (G-2761)
L Calvin Jones & Company..........................E 330 533-1195
  Canfield (G-1634)
Loyal American Life Insur Co.......................C 800 633-6752
  Cincinnati (G-2991)
▲ Massmutual Ascend Lf Insur Co..............E 800 854-3649
  Cincinnati (G-3014)
Matic Insurance Services Inc.......................C 833 382-1304
  Columbus (G-6206)
Midland Company...A 513 947-5503
  Amelia (G-418)
Midland-Guardian Co...................................A 513 943-7100
  Amelia (G-419)
Mitsui Smitomo Mar MGT USA Inc..............D 513 719-8480
  Cincinnati (G-3068)
Motorists Mutual Insurance Co.....................A 614 225-8211
  Columbus (G-6264)
Mountain Laurel Assurance Co.....................B 440 461-5000
  Cleveland (G-4604)
National Continental Insur Co.......................E 631 320-2405
  Cleveland (G-4623)
National Interstate Corp................................B 330 659-8900
  Richfield (G-12701)
National Interstate Insur Co..........................C 330 659-8900
  Richfield (G-12702)
Nationwide General Insur Co.......................A 614 249-7111
  Columbus (G-6331)
Nationwide Insurance...................................E 513 341-7221
  Hamilton (G-9067)
Nationwide Insurance Co Fla........................A 614 249-7111
  Columbus (G-6332)
◆ Nationwide Mutual Insurance Co.............A 614 249-7111
  Columbus (G-6338)
Occupational Health Link.............................E 614 885-0039
  Delaware (G-7820)
Ohic Insurance Company.............................D 614 221-7777
  Columbus (G-6388)
Ohio Bureau Wkrs Compensation................A 800 644-6292
  Columbus (G-6396)
Ohio Casualty Insurance Co.........................A 800 843-6446
  Cincinnati (G-3143)
Ohio Fair Plan Undwrt Assn.........................E 614 839-6446
  Columbus (G-5275)
Ohio Farmers Insurance Company..............A 800 243-0210
  Westfield Center (G-15025)
Ohio Mutual Insurance Company.................C 419 562-3011
  Bucyrus (G-1514)
Pension Associates Inc................................B 614 249-7111
  Columbus (G-6514)
Permanent Gen Asrn Corp Ohio...................E 216 986-3000
  Cleveland (G-4742)
Platinum Rstoration Contrs Inc.....................E 440 327-0699
  Elyria (G-8287)
Premier Financial Corp.................................D 419 782-5015
  Defiance (G-7762)
Progressive Adjusting Co Inc.......................D 440 461-5000
  Cleveland (G-4775)

SIC SECTION

64 INSURANCE AGENTS, BROKERS AND SERVICE

Progressive Bayside Insur Co............... C 440 395-4460
  Cleveland *(G-4777)*

Progressive Casualty Insur Co............... E 440 603-4033
  Cleveland *(G-4778)*

▼ Progressive Casualty Insur Co............... A 855 347-3939
  Mayfield Village *(G-10795)*

Progressive Choice Insur Co............... C 440 461-5000
  Cleveland *(G-4779)*

Progressive Classic Insur Co............... E 440 661-5000
  Cleveland *(G-4780)*

Progressive Coml Cslty Co............... D 440 461-5000
  Cleveland *(G-4781)*

Progressive Freedom Insur Co............... D 440 461-5000
  Cleveland *(G-4783)*

Progressive Paloverde Insur Co............... C 440 461-5000
  Cleveland *(G-4786)*

Progressive Rsc Inc............... D 440 461-5000
  Cleveland *(G-4788)*

Progressive Universal Insur Co............... C 440 461-5000
  Cleveland *(G-4791)*

Rod Lightning Mutual Insur Co............... B 330 262-9060
  Wooster *(G-15370)*

Root Inc............... C 866 980-9431
  Columbus *(G-6610)*

Rtw Inc............... D 952 893-0403
  Columbus *(G-6618)*

Safe Auto Insurance Group Inc............... C 614 231-0200
  Columbus *(G-6627)*

Sequoia Insurance Company............... D 831 655-9612
  Cleveland *(G-4896)*

State Auto Financial Corp............... C 614 464-5000
  Columbus *(G-6713)*

State Automobile Mutl Insur Co............... A 833 724-3577
  Columbus *(G-6714)*

Verti Insurance Company............... D 844 448-3784
  Columbus *(G-6844)*

Western Reserve Group............... B 330 262-9060
  Wooster *(G-15387)*

Westfield Insurance Company............... C 800 243-0210
  Westfield Center *(G-15027)*

Westfield National Insur Co............... D 330 887-0101
  Westfield Center *(G-15028)*

6351 Surety insurance

▼ Progressive Casualty Insur Co............... A 855 347-3939
  Mayfield Village *(G-10795)*

Radian Guaranty Inc............... D 614 847-8300
  Worthington *(G-15450)*

Rockhill Holding Company............... E 816 412-2800
  Columbus *(G-6606)*

State Automobile Mutl Insur Co............... A 833 724-3577
  Columbus *(G-6714)*

6361 Title insurance

Accurate Group Holdings Inc............... D 216 520-1740
  Independence *(G-9395)*

Commonwealth Title Dallas Inc............... A 513 985-0550
  Cincinnati *(G-2481)*

Entitle Direct Group Inc............... E 216 236-7800
  Independence *(G-9430)*

First American Equity Ln Svcs............... C 800 221-8683
  Cleveland *(G-4254)*

Lawyers Title Cincinnati Inc............... D 513 421-1313
  Cincinnati *(G-2967)*

Lawyers Title Insurance Corp............... D 614 221-4523
  Columbus *(G-5266)*

Mercantile Title Agency Inc............... E 614 628-6880
  Columbus *(G-6225)*

Midland Title Security Inc............... D 216 241-6045
  Cleveland *(G-4578)*

Mortgage Information Services............... D 216 514-7480
  Cleveland *(G-4602)*

Ohio Bar Title Insurance Co............... D 614 310-8098
  Columbus *(G-5274)*

Old Republic Nat Title Insur............... E 614 341-1900
  Columbus *(G-6469)*

Omega Title Agency LLC............... D 330 436-0600
  Akron *(G-255)*

Port Lawrence Title and Tr Co............... E 419 244-4605
  Toledo *(G-13965)*

Resource Title Agency Inc............... D 216 520-0050
  Cleveland *(G-4831)*

Resource Title Nat Agcy Inc............... D 216 520-0050
  Independence *(G-9476)*

Signature Closers LLC............... E 614 448-7750
  Columbus *(G-6678)*

Stewart Advnced Land Title Ltd............... E 513 753-2800
  Cincinnati *(G-2113)*

Title First Agency Inc............... E 614 347-8383
  Westerville *(G-14942)*

6371 Pension, health, and welfare funds

City of Cncnnati Emplyees Rtrm............... D 513 591-6000
  Cincinnati *(G-2453)*

County of Gallia............... E 740 446-3222
  Gallipolis *(G-8753)*

Diocese Tledo Prest Retirement............... E 419 244-6711
  Toledo *(G-13781)*

Nationwide Rtrment Sltions Inc............... C 614 854-8300
  Dublin *(G-8072)*

Ohio Pub Emplyees Rtrement Sys............... B 614 228-8471
  Columbus *(G-6440)*

Pharmacy Data Management Inc............... D 330 757-1500
  Youngstown *(G-15694)*

School Emplyees Rtrment Sys OH............... C 614 222-5853
  Columbus *(G-6651)*

Seneca County............... D 419 447-5011
  Tiffin *(G-13642)*

State Tchers Rtrement Sys Ohio............... C 614 227-4090
  Columbus *(G-6715)*

6399 Insurance carriers, nec

Dimension Service Corporation............... C 614 226-7455
  Dublin *(G-7987)*

Hartville Group Inc............... D 330 484-8166
  Akron *(G-185)*

64 INSURANCE AGENTS, BROKERS AND SERVICE

6411 Insurance agents, brokers, and service

▲ 4mybenefits Inc............... E 513 891-6726
  Blue Ash *(G-1119)*

A A Hammersmith Insurance Inc............... E 330 832-7411
  Massillon *(G-10627)*

A J Amer Agency Inc............... E 330 665-9966
  Akron *(G-10)*

A J Amer Agency Inc............... E 330 665-9966
  Akron *(G-9)*

A-1 General Insurance Agency............... D 216 986-3000
  Cleveland *(G-3752)*

Aba Insurance Services Inc............... D 800 274-5222
  Shaker Heights *(G-12972)*

Accurate Group Holdings Inc............... D 216 520-1740
  Independence *(G-9395)*

Acu-Serve Corp............... C 330 923-5258
  Akron *(G-16)*

AFLAC............... E 216 641-8760
  Cleveland *(G-3773)*

Alex N Sill Company LLC............... E 216 524-9999
  Cleveland *(G-3783)*

All America Insurance Company............... B 419 238-1010
  Van Wert *(G-14340)*

Allstate Insurance Company............... E 330 650-2917
  Hudson *(G-9330)*

Alps Services Inc............... E 513 772-4746
  Cincinnati *(G-2171)*

American Family Home Insur Co............... E 513 943-7100
  Amelia *(G-411)*

American Fidelity Assurance Co............... E 800 437-1011
  Columbus *(G-5350)*

American Financial Group Inc............... A 513 579-2121
  Cincinnati *(G-2180)*

American Highways Insur Agcy............... E 330 659-8900
  Richfield *(G-12686)*

American Insurance Strategies............... E 937 221-8896
  Dayton *(G-7171)*

American Modrn Insur Group Inc............... C 800 543-2644
  Amelia *(G-413)*

American Modrn Select Insur Co............... C 513 943-7100
  Amelia *(G-414)*

American Mutl Share Insur Corp............... E 614 764-1900
  Dublin *(G-7936)*

American Risk Services LLC............... E 513 772-3712
  Cincinnati *(G-2187)*

Amtrust North America Inc............... C 216 328-6100
  Cleveland *(G-3813)*

Andrew Insurance Associates............... D 614 336-8030
  Dublin *(G-7938)*

ARC Healthcare LLC............... E 888 552-0677
  Worthington *(G-15405)*

Auto-Owners Life Insurance Co............... E 419 227-1452
  Lima *(G-9866)*

Auto-Owners Life Insurance Co............... E 419 887-1218
  Maumee *(G-10696)*

Bazemore Insurance Group LLC............... E 614 559-8585
  Columbus *(G-5424)*

Beam Technologies Inc............... B 800 648-1179
  Columbus *(G-5428)*

Beecher Carlson Insur Svcs LLC............... D 330 726-8177
  Youngstown *(G-15556)*

Benefit Services Inc............... D 330 666-0337
  Copley *(G-6948)*

Bold Penguin Inc............... D 614 344-1029
  Columbus *(G-5453)*

Brands Insurance Agency Inc............... E 513 777-7775
  West Chester *(G-14654)*

Bridgepoint Risk MGT LLC............... E 419 794-1075
  Maumee *(G-10704)*

Britton-Gallagher & Assoc Inc............... D 216 658-7100
  Cleveland *(G-3897)*

Brooker Insurance Agency Inc............... E 440 238-5454
  Strongsville *(G-13446)*

Brooks & Stafford Co............... E 216 696-3000
  Cleveland *(G-3904)*

Brower Insurance Agency LLC............... C 937 228-4135
  Dayton *(G-7201)*

Brown & Brown of Ohio LLC............... D 513 831-2200
  Terrace Park *(G-13613)*

Brown & Brown of Ohio LLC............... E 419 874-1974
  Perrysburg *(G-12319)*

Brunswick Insurance Agency............... D 330 864-8800
  Cleveland *(G-3907)*

Business Admnstrators Cons Inc............... E 614 863-8780
  Reynoldsburg *(G-12656)*

Businessplans Incorporated............... E 937 865-6501
  Moraine *(G-11393)*

C GI Voluntary............... E 216 401-0081
  Cleveland *(G-3916)*

Cannasure Insurance Svcs LLC............... E 800 420-5757
  Cleveland *(G-3922)*

Careworks of Ohio Inc............... A 614 792-1085
  Dublin *(G-7958)*

Cincinnati Casualty Company............... C 513 870-2000
  Fairfield *(G-8401)*

Employee Codes: A=Over 500 employees, B=251-500
C=101-250, D=51-100, E=20-50, F=10-19, G=1-9

64 INSURANCE AGENTS, BROKERS AND SERVICE

Cincinnati Financial Corp................ A 513 870-2000
　Fairfield *(G-8402)*
Cincinnati Indeminty Co.................. D 513 870-2000
　Fairfield *(G-8403)*
Cincinnati Life Insurance Co............. A 513 870-2000
　Fairfield *(G-8405)*
Clark Theders Insurance Agency......... E 513 779-2800
　West Chester *(G-14669)*
Columbus Life Insurance Co............. C 513 361-6700
　Cincinnati *(G-2477)*
Compmanagement Inc..................... E 614 376-5300
　Dublin *(G-7970)*
Compmed Analysis LLC................... E 330 650-0888
　Hudson *(G-9340)*
Conduent Care Solutions LLC........... E 330 644-0927
　Akron *(G-120)*
Cornerstone Brk Insur Svcs AGC........ E 513 241-7675
　Cincinnati *(G-2508)*
Corporate Plans Inc...................... E 440 542-7800
　Solon *(G-13078)*
CSC Insurance Agency Inc................ C 614 895-2000
　Westerville *(G-14886)*
Dawson Companies....................... D 440 333-9000
　Richfield *(G-12693)*
Donald P Pipino Company Ltd............ D 330 726-8177
　Youngstown *(G-15601)*
Eliza Jennings Inc........................ C 216 226-5000
　Olmsted Twp *(G-12089)*
Erie Indemnity Company.................. C 330 433-6300
　Canton *(G-1748)*
Erie Insur Exch Actvties Assn............ E 330 433-1925
　Canton *(G-1749)*
Erie Insur Exch Actvties Assn............ E 614 430-8530
　Columbus *(G-5826)*
Evarts-Tremaine-Flicker Co............... E 216 621-7183
　Cleveland *(G-4225)*
Explorer Rv Insurance Agcy Inc.......... E 330 659-8900
　Richfield *(G-12697)*
Fairlawn Partners LLC................... E 330 576-1100
　Akron *(G-151)*
Farmers Insurance Columbus Inc........ B 614 799-3200
　Columbus *(G-5851)*
Fedeli Group LLC......................... D 216 328-8080
　Cleveland *(G-4244)*
Firefly Agency LLC....................... E 614 507-7847
　Dublin *(G-8012)*
▲ Forge Industries Inc.................... A 330 960-2468
　Youngstown *(G-15613)*
Galt Enterprises Inc..................... E 216 464-6744
　Moreland Hills *(G-11452)*
Gardiner Allen Drbrts Insur LL........... E 614 221-1500
　Columbus *(G-5913)*
Gates McDonald of Ohio LLC............. E 614 677-3700
　Columbus *(G-5917)*
Geico General Insurance Co............. B 513 794-3426
　Cincinnati *(G-2722)*
Grange Life Insurance Company.......... E 800 445-3030
　Columbus *(G-5948)*
Hagerty Insurance Agency LLC........... D 877 922-9701
　Dublin *(G-8025)*
Hauser Inc................................ D 513 745-9200
　Cincinnati *(G-2806)*
Health Management Solutions............ E 419 536-5690
　Maumee *(G-10730)*
Holtz Agency Ltd......................... E 513 671-7220
　Cincinnati *(G-2832)*
Huntington Insurance Inc................ C 419 720-7900
　Columbus *(G-6017)*
Hylant Administrative Services.......... E 419 255-1020
　Toledo *(G-13857)*
Hylant Group Inc......................... D 419 255-1020
　Toledo *(G-13858)*

Insurance Intermediaries Inc............. A 614 846-1111
　Columbus *(G-6060)*
Insurance Partners Agency LLC.......... E 330 493-3211
　Canton *(G-1781)*
Insurancecom Inc........................ D 440 498-0001
　Solon *(G-13100)*
Insurnce Office Centl Ohio Inc........... E 614 939-5471
　New Albany *(G-11569)*
Insurnce Specialists Group Inc.......... E 440 975-0309
　Chardon *(G-2007)*
Integrity Mutual Insurance Co........... D 920 734-4511
　Columbus *(G-6063)*
International Healthcare Corp........... D 513 731-3338
　Cincinnati *(G-2882)*
Investment Pdts Ffl Inv Svcs............. E 216 529-2700
　Lakewood *(G-9669)*
Kellison & Co............................. E 216 464-5160
　Cleveland *(G-4456)*
Knight Insurance Agency Inc............ E 419 241-5133
　Toledo *(G-13880)*
Lang Financial Group Inc................ E 513 699-2966
　Blue Ash *(G-1199)*
Licking Memorial Hlth Systems........... A 220 564-4000
　Newark *(G-11717)*
Lighthouse Insurance Group LLC........ E 216 503-2439
　Independence *(G-9445)*
LP Insurance Services LLC............... C 877 369-5121
　Solon *(G-13108)*
Marsh & McLennan Agency LLC.......... C 937 228-4135
　Dayton *(G-7466)*
McGohan/Brabender Agency Inc......... E 937 293-1600
　Moraine *(G-11421)*
McGowan & Company Inc................ D 800 545-1538
　Cleveland *(G-4537)*
Medical Mutual of Ohio................... C 216 292-0400
　Cleveland *(G-4546)*
Medical Mutual of Ohio................... C 419 473-7100
　Rossford *(G-12768)*
Medical Mutual of Ohio................... A 216 687-7000
　Cleveland *(G-4545)*
Mennonite Mutual Insurance Co......... D 330 682-2986
　Orrville *(G-12170)*
MetLife Legal Plans Inc.................. D 216 241-0022
　Cleveland *(G-4559)*
Mm Ascend Life Inv Svcs LLC............ E 513 333-6030
　Cincinnati *(G-3071)*
Move Ez Inc.............................. D 844 466-8339
　Columbus *(G-6280)*
Mutual Health Services Company........ B 216 687-7000
　Cleveland *(G-4614)*
National Auto Care Corporation......... E 800 548-1875
　Westerville *(G-14914)*
National Benefit Programs Inc........... E 614 481-9000
　Columbus *(G-6290)*
National General Insurance Co.......... E 212 380-9462
　Cleveland *(G-4627)*
National Interstate Corp................. B 330 659-8900
　Richfield *(G-12701)*
Nationwide................................ E 800 421-3535
　Canton *(G-1818)*
Nationwide Affinity Insur Amer.......... B 614 249-2141
　Columbus *(G-6304)*
Nationwide Bank.......................... C 800 882-2822
　Columbus *(G-6307)*
◆ Nationwide Corporation................. E 614 249-7111
　Columbus *(G-6326)*
Nationwide Financial Svcs Inc........... C 614 249-7111
　Columbus *(G-6329)*
Nationwide Fncl Instn Dstrs AG......... D 614 249-6825
　Columbus *(G-6330)*
Nationwide Insrnce Spnning Ins......... E 408 520-6420
　London *(G-10048)*

Nationwide Lf Annuity Insur Co......... A 614 249-7111
　Columbus *(G-6334)*
◆ Nationwide Life Insur Co Amer......... A 800 688-5177
　Columbus *(G-6335)*
Nationwide Life Insurance Co........... C 877 669-6877
　Columbus *(G-6336)*
Nationwide Mutl Fire Insur Co........... E 614 249-7111
　Columbus *(G-6337)*
Nationwide Mutual Insurance Co........ E 330 489-5000
　Canton *(G-1819)*
Nationwide Mutual Insurance Co........ E 614 249-7654
　Columbus *(G-6339)*
Nationwide Mutual Insurance Co........ E 614 899-6300
　Columbus *(G-6340)*
Nationwide Mutual Insurance Co........ E 614 734-1276
　Dublin *(G-8071)*
Nationwide Mutual Insurance Co........ D 614 430-3047
　Lewis Center *(G-9830)*
Nationwide Prperty Cslty Insur.......... D 614 677-8166
　Columbus *(G-6341)*
Nationwide Rtrment Sltions Inc......... E 614 854-8300
　Dublin *(G-8072)*
Neace Assoc Insur Agcy of Ohio........ E 614 224-0772
　Columbus *(G-6343)*
New York Lf Insur Joe Stich RG......... E 614 793-2121
　Dublin *(G-8076)*
Nirvana Insurance........................ E 330 217-3079
　Columbus *(G-6360)*
NI of Ky Inc.............................. E 614 224-0772
　Columbus *(G-6361)*
Ohic Insurance Company................. D 614 221-7777
　Columbus *(G-6388)*
Ohio Bureau Wkrs Compensation....... E 614 221-4064
　Columbus *(G-6397)*
Ohio Farmers Insurance Company....... A 800 243-0210
　Westfield Center *(G-15025)*
Ohio Mutual Insurance Company......... C 419 562-3011
　Bucyrus *(G-1514)*
Ohio Sers................................. E 614 222-5853
　Columbus *(G-6444)*
Ohio United Agency Inc................. E 419 562-3011
　Bucyrus *(G-1515)*
Old Republic Nat Title Insur............ E 614 341-1900
　Columbus *(G-6469)*
Old Rpblic Ttle Nthrn Ohio LLC......... C 216 524-5700
　Independence *(G-9464)*
One80 Intermediaries Inc................ E 617 330-5700
　Beachwood *(G-823)*
ONeill Insurance Agency Inc............ E 330 334-1561
　Wadsworth *(G-14446)*
Optumrx Inc.............................. A 614 794-3300
　Westerville *(G-14924)*
Order of Untd Coml Trvlers of........... D 614 487-9680
　Columbus *(G-6479)*
Otto Insurance Group LLC............... E 740 278-7888
　Westerville *(G-14927)*
Overmyer Hall Associates................ E 614 453-4400
　Columbus *(G-6494)*
Pasco Inc................................. E 330 650-0613
　Hudson *(G-9367)*
Paul Moss LLC............................ E 216 765-1580
　Solon *(G-13125)*
Progressive Advanced Insur Co......... B 440 461-5000
　Cleveland *(G-4776)*
▼ Progressive Casualty Insur Co......... A 855 347-3939
　Mayfield Village *(G-10795)*
Progressive Express Insur Co........... C 440 461-5000
　Cleveland *(G-4782)*
Progressive Grdn State Insur........... B 440 461-5000
　Cleveland *(G-4784)*
Progressive Hawaii Insur Corp.......... D 440 461-5000
　Cleveland *(G-4785)*

Progressive Medical LLC .... A 614 794-3300
  Westerville *(G-14931)*
Progressive Premier Insur III .... D 440 461-5000
  Cleveland *(G-4787)*
Progressive Select Insur Co .... A 440 461-5000
  Cleveland *(G-4789)*
Progressive Specialty Insur Co .... A 440 461-5000
  Cleveland *(G-4790)*
Progrssive Coml Advntage Agcy .... E 440 461-5000
  Cleveland *(G-4792)*
Progrssive Spclty Insur Agcy I .... C 440 461-5000
  Cleveland *(G-4793)*
R E Whitney Insur Agcy LLC .... D 877 652-7765
  Cincinnati *(G-3271)*
Rod Lightning Mutual Insur Co .... B 330 262-9060
  Wooster *(G-15370)*
S & S Halthcare Strategies Ltd .... C 513 772-8866
  Cincinnati *(G-3335)*
Safe Auto Insurance Company .... B 740 472-1900
  Woodsfield *(G-15302)*
Safe Auto Insurance Company .... B 614 231-0200
  Columbus *(G-6626)*
Safe Auto Insurance Group Inc .... C 614 231-0200
  Columbus *(G-6627)*
◆ Safelite Group Inc .... A 614 210-9000
  Columbus *(G-6632)*
Savage and Associates Inc .... C 419 475-8665
  Maumee *(G-10764)*
Schaeffler Group USA Inc .... A 330 202-6215
  Wooster *(G-15372)*
Schauer Group Incorporated .... E 330 453-7721
  Canton *(G-1849)*
Schiff John J & Thomas R & Co .... E 513 870-2580
  Fairfield *(G-8438)*
Schroeder Associates Inc .... E 419 258-5075
  Antwerp *(G-448)*
Sedgwick CMS Holdings Inc .... B 800 825-6755
  Dublin *(G-8117)*
Sedgwick CMS Holdings Inc .... E 614 658-0900
  Hilliard *(G-9230)*
Seibert-Keck Insurance Agency .... E 330 867-3140
  Fairlawn *(G-8498)*
Self-Funded Plans Inc .... E 216 566-1455
  Seven Hills *(G-12961)*
Selman & Company .... D 440 646-9336
  Cleveland *(G-4893)*
Sentry Life Insurance Company .... C 513 733-0100
  Cincinnati *(G-3359)*
Sirak Financial Services Inc .... D 330 493-0642
  Canton *(G-1852)*
State Automobile Mutl Insur Co .... A 833 724-3577
  Columbus *(G-6714)*
State Farm General Insur Co .... D 513 231-4975
  Cincinnati *(G-3414)*
State Farm General Insur Co .... D 740 364-5000
  Newark *(G-11750)*
State Farm General Insur Co .... D 440 268-0600
  Strongsville *(G-13487)*
State Farm General Insur Co .... D 513 870-0285
  West Chester *(G-14769)*
State Farm Life Insurance Co .... E 937 276-1900
  Dayton *(G-7640)*
Stateside Undwrt Agcy Inc .... E 440 893-9917
  Chagrin Falls *(G-1968)*
Stephens-Matthews Mktg LLC .... E 740 984-8011
  Beverly *(G-1102)*
Stolly Insurance Agency Inc .... E 419 227-2570
  Lima *(G-9966)*
The James B Oswald Company .... D 216 367-8787
  Cleveland *(G-5002)*
The Sheakley Group Inc .... E 513 771-2277
  Cincinnati *(G-3471)*

Travelers Property Cslty Corp .... C 513 639-5300
  Cincinnati *(G-3502)*
United Agencies Inc .... E 216 696-8044
  Cleveland *(G-5052)*
United Financial Casualty Co .... D 440 461-5000
  Cleveland *(G-5060)*
◆ United Trnsp Un Insur Assn .... C 216 228-9400
  Independence *(G-9493)*
USI Insurance Services Nat Inc .... E 513 657-3116
  Cincinnati *(G-3608)*
USI Insurance Services Nat Inc .... E 513 852-6300
  Cincinnati *(G-3609)*
USI Insurance Services Nat Inc .... E 614 228-5565
  Columbus *(G-6839)*
▲ USI Midwest LLC .... C 513 852-6300
  Cincinnati *(G-3610)*
Valmark Financial Group LLC .... C 330 576-1234
  Akron *(G-347)*
Victoria Fire & Casualty Co .... E 513 648-9888
  Cleveland *(G-5103)*
Wabe Maquaw Holdings Inc .... D 419 243-1191
  Toledo *(G-14096)*
Wells Fargo Insurance Ser .... D 614 324-2820
  Columbus *(G-6875)*
Westfield Insurance Company .... C 800 243-0210
  Westfield Center *(G-15027)*
Westfield National Insur Co .... D 330 887-0101
  Westfield Center *(G-15028)*
Whitaker-Myers Insur Agcy Inc .... E 330 345-5000
  Wooster *(G-15388)*
Your Agency Inc .... E 937 550-9596
  Springboro *(G-13211)*

65 REAL ESTATE

6512 Nonresidential building operators

127 PS Fee Owner LLC .... D 216 520-1250
  Cleveland *(G-3738)*
Ad Investments LLC .... E 614 857-2340
  Columbus *(G-5311)*
Airriva LLC .... E 614 345-3996
  Sunbury *(G-13515)*
Anderson Jeffery R RE Inc .... E 513 241-5800
  Cincinnati *(G-2199)*
At Holdings Corporation .... A 216 692-6000
  Cleveland *(G-3837)*
Belvedere Corporation .... B 513 241-3888
  Cincinnati *(G-2257)*
Brookfield Properties LLC .... D 216 621-6060
  Cleveland *(G-3903)*
Brookwood Realty Company .... D 513 530-9555
  Cincinnati *(G-2283)*
Bw Alumni Association .... D 440 826-2104
  Berea *(G-1063)*
Cafaro Company .... C 330 747-2661
  Niles *(G-11783)*
Cafaro Northwest Partnership .... E 419 626-8575
  Sandusky *(G-12867)*
Cararo Co Inc .... E 330 652-6980
  Niles *(G-11784)*
Carnegie Management & Dev Corp .... E 440 892-6800
  Westlake *(G-15046)*
Casto Communities Cnstr Ltd .... B 614 228-5331
  Columbus *(G-5519)*
Cavaliers Holdings LLC .... B 216 420-2000
  Cleveland *(G-3937)*
Central Ohio Associates Ltd .... E 419 342-2045
  Shelby *(G-13005)*
Centro Properties Group LLC .... E 440 324-6610
  Elyria *(G-8235)*
Ch Relty Iv/Clmbus Partners LP .... D 614 885-3334
  Columbus *(G-5550)*

Cincinnati Sports Mall Inc .... C 513 527-4000
  Cincinnati *(G-2423)*
City of Cleveland .... E 216 348-2200
  Cleveland *(G-3984)*
Co Hatch LLC .... D 614 368-1810
  Columbus *(G-5253)*
Coldwell Bnkr Hritg Rltors LLC .... E 937 434-7600
  Dayton *(G-7238)*
Compco Land Company .... D 330 482-0200
  Youngstown *(G-15585)*
Continental Properties .... E 614 221-1800
  Columbus *(G-5694)*
Cornerstone Managed Prpts LLC .... E 440 263-7708
  Westlake *(G-15055)*
Denovo Constructors Inc .... D 419 265-8888
  Findlay *(G-8525)*
Easton Town Center II LLC .... D 614 416-7000
  Columbus *(G-5799)*
Easton Town Center LLC .... C 614 337-2560
  Columbus *(G-5800)*
Emmett Dan House Ltd Partnr .... E 740 392-6886
  Mount Vernon *(G-11485)*
Fairfield Homes Inc .... C 614 873-3533
  Plain City *(G-12477)*
Fairlawn Associates Ltd .... C 330 867-5000
  Fairlawn *(G-8478)*
Findlay Inn & Conference Ctr .... E 419 422-5682
  Findlay *(G-8529)*
First Interstate Prpts Ltd .... E 216 381-2900
  Cleveland *(G-4258)*
Forest City Commercial MGT Inc .... C 216 623-4750
  Cleveland *(G-4270)*
▲ Forest City Enterprises LP .... B 216 621-6060
  Cleveland *(G-4271)*
Forest City Properties LLC .... C 216 621-6060
  Cleveland *(G-4272)*
Garland/Dbs Inc .... C 216 641-7500
  Cleveland *(G-4302)*
Glimcher Realty Trust .... A 614 621-9000
  Columbus *(G-5938)*
Gms Management Co Inc .... E 216 766-6000
  Cleveland *(G-4317)*
Good Inc .... D 740 592-9667
  Athens *(G-569)*
Graham Investment Co .... D 740 382-0902
  Marion *(G-10429)*
Henry H Stmbugh Aditorium Assn ..... E 330 747-5175
  Youngstown *(G-15629)*
Hileman Group .... E 216 926-4365
  Cleveland *(G-4360)*
Hills Property Management Inc .... D 513 984-0300
  Blue Ash *(G-1183)*
Hotel 50 S Front Opco L P .... D 614 885-3334
  Columbus *(G-6010)*
Hoty Enterprises Inc .... E 419 609-7000
  Sandusky *(G-12904)*
Hyatt Corporation .... D 614 228-1234
  Columbus *(G-6032)*
▲ I-X Center Corporation .... C 216 265-2675
  Cleveland *(G-4398)*
Industrial Coml Prpts LLC .... D 440 539-1046
  Solon *(G-13099)*
Infotrust LLC .... D 513 403-2107
  Blue Ash *(G-1184)*
K&D Management LLC .... E 216 624-4686
  Cleveland *(G-4447)*
Kregel Properties LLC .... E 937 885-3250
  Troy *(G-14144)*
▲ L Brands Service Company LLC ...... D 614 415-7000
  Columbus *(G-6130)*
Landmark Properties Group LLC .... E 740 701-7511
  Wellston *(G-14640)*

65 REAL ESTATE

Legacy Properties Inc............................. E 440 349-9000
  Cleveland *(G-4484)*
Manleys Manor Nursing Home Inc........ E 419 424-0402
  Findlay *(G-8560)*
Maple Retail Ltd Partnership.................. D 216 221-6600
  Lakewood *(G-9678)*
Meadowbrook Mall Company................ E 330 747-2661
  Youngstown *(G-15664)*
MEI Hotels Incorporated......................... C 216 589-0441
  Cleveland *(G-4549)*
Meijer Dist DC 804 Corp......................... B 616 791-5821
  Tipp City *(G-13662)*
Miller-Valentine Partners Ltd.................. D 937 293-0900
  Cincinnati *(G-3064)*
Mills Corporation..................................... E 513 671-2882
  Cincinnati *(G-3065)*
▲ Musical Arts Association..................... C 216 231-7300
  Cleveland *(G-4613)*
Nationwide Arena LLC........................... D 614 232-8810
  Columbus *(G-6305)*
Oak Hlth Care Invstors Mssllon.............. E 614 794-8800
  Westerville *(G-14919)*
Ohio Equities LLC.................................. D 614 224-2400
  Columbus *(G-6420)*
Ohio Valley Mall Company..................... E 330 747-2661
  Youngstown *(G-15684)*
◆ Park Corporation................................. B 216 267-4870
  Medina *(G-10874)*
Patterson-Erie Corporation..................... D 440 593-6161
  Conneaut *(G-6944)*
Pfp Columbus LLC................................. E 614 456-0123
  Columbus *(G-5277)*
Phil Giessler.. E 614 888-0307
  Worthington *(G-15446)*
PNC Banc Corp Ohio............................. D 513 651-8738
  Cincinnati *(G-3216)*
Polaris Towne Center LLC..................... E 614 456-0123
  Columbus *(G-5278)*
Premium Outlet Partners LP.................. D 330 562-2000
  Aurora *(G-621)*
Prime Outlets Acquisition LLC............... E 740 948-9090
  Jeffersonville *(G-9542)*
◆ Pubco Corporation.............................. D 216 881-5300
  Cleveland *(G-4797)*
Ricco Enterprises Incorporated............. E 216 883-7775
  Cleveland *(G-4837)*
Riverfront Antique Mall Inc..................... E 330 339-4448
  New Philadelphia *(G-11663)*
Robinson Investments Ltd..................... E 937 593-1849
  Bellefontaine *(G-1037)*
Ron-Joy Nursing Home Inc................... C 330 286-9122
  Youngstown *(G-15712)*
Rvsharecom... E 330 907-9479
  Copley *(G-6962)*
S-P Company Inc................................... D 330 782-5651
  Columbiana *(G-5240)*
Saw Mill Creek Ltd................................. D 419 433-3800
  Huron *(G-9392)*
Simon Property Group........................... E 614 798-3015
  Dublin *(G-8121)*
Smg Holdings LLC................................. E 614 827-2500
  Columbus *(G-6689)*
St Performing Arts LLC......................... E 419 381-8851
  Toledo *(G-14027)*
Threebond International......................... D 513 759-8771
  West Chester *(G-14773)*
Turner Property Svcs Group Inc............ E 937 461-7474
  Dayton *(G-7679)*
U S Development Corp.......................... D 330 673-6900
  Kent *(G-9604)*
Uber Greenlight Hub.............................. E 800 593-7069
  Norwood *(G-12035)*

United Fd Coml Wkrs Un Lcal 88........... E 216 241-5930
  Broadview Heights *(G-1402)*
United Management Inc......................... D 614 228-5331
  Columbus *(G-6807)*
Victoria Theatre Association.................. C 937 461-8190
  Dayton *(G-7706)*
Vora Solution Center LLC..................... A 513 867-7277
  Cincinnati *(G-3634)*
Waldon Management Corp.................... E 330 792-7688
  Youngstown *(G-15751)*
Washington Prime Group Inc................. C 614 621-9000
  Columbus *(G-6866)*
Welded Ring Properties Co.................... E 216 961-3800
  Cleveland *(G-5127)*
Weston Inc... E 440 349-9000
  Cleveland *(G-5143)*
Wsa Studio... E 614 824-1633
  Columbus *(G-6909)*
Z & Sons Limited Partnership................ D 440 249-5164
  Cleveland *(G-5171)*
Zucker Building Company...................... E 216 861-7114
  Cleveland *(G-5176)*
Zvn Properties Inc................................. D 330 854-5890
  Canal Fulton *(G-1596)*

6513 Apartment building operators

A P & P Dev & Cnstr Co......................... E 330 833-8886
  Massillon *(G-10628)*
Abel-Bishop & Clarke Realty Co............ D 614 253-8627
  Columbus *(G-5295)*
Akron Metropolitan Hsing Auth.............. D 330 920-1652
  Stow *(G-13354)*
Alpha PHI Alpha Homes Inc................... E 330 376-2115
  Akron *(G-45)*
Anchor Lodge Ltd Partnership............... D 440 244-2019
  Lorain *(G-10053)*
Andrews Apartments Ltd....................... C 440 946-3600
  Willoughby *(G-15186)*
Aspen Management Usa LLC................ E 419 281-3367
  Ashland *(G-477)*
Aurora Hotel Partners LLC.................... E 330 562-0767
  Aurora *(G-605)*
Brethren Care Inc.................................. C 419 289-0803
  Ashland *(G-484)*
Brewer Holdco Inc................................. B 419 247-2800
  Toledo *(G-13717)*
Brg Realty Group LLC........................... C 513 936-5960
  Cincinnati *(G-2280)*
Brodhead Village Ltd............................. D 614 863-4640
  New Albany *(G-11557)*
Buckeye Cmnty Eighty One LP.............. E 614 942-2020
  Columbus *(G-5473)*
Buckingham Management LLC.............. E 844 361-5559
  Perrysburg *(G-12320)*
C I E Inc... B 419 986-5566
  Burgoon *(G-1523)*
Capital Properties MGT Ltd.................... E 216 991-3057
  Cleveland *(G-3924)*
Cardinal Retirement Village................... E 330 928-7888
  Cuyahoga Falls *(G-7052)*
City of Akron.. E 330 564-4075
  Akron *(G-102)*
Claremont Retirement Village................ D 614 761-2011
  Columbus *(G-5580)*
Community Prpts Ohio MGT Svcs......... D 614 253-0984
  Columbus *(G-5672)*
Copeland Oaks...................................... B 330 938-1050
  Sebring *(G-12946)*
Copeland Oaks...................................... D 330 938-6126
  Sebring *(G-12947)*
Creative Living Inc................................. E 614 421-1131
  Columbus *(G-5721)*

Crestview Manor Nursing Home............. C 740 654-2634
  Lancaster *(G-9706)*
Danbury Woods Ltd............................... E 330 928-6757
  Cuyahoga Falls *(G-7068)*
Eaglewood Care Center........................ C 937 399-7195
  Springfield *(G-13250)*
Ebenezer Road Corporation.................. C 513 941-0099
  Cincinnati *(G-2601)*
Emeritus Corporation............................. D 513 683-9966
  Cincinnati *(G-2615)*
Emeritus Corporation............................. D 419 255-4455
  Toledo *(G-13790)*
Episcopal Retirement Homes Inc........... C 513 871-2090
  Cincinnati *(G-2632)*
Episcopal Retirement Homes Inc........... C 513 561-6363
  Cincinnati *(G-2633)*
Episcpal Rtrment Svcs Affrdbl................ D 513 271-9610
  Cincinnati *(G-2634)*
Evanglcal Rtrment Vllges Inc D............. C 937 837-5581
  Dayton *(G-7340)*
Fairfield Homes Inc................................ E 614 873-3533
  Plain City *(G-12477)*
Fairfield Homes Inc................................ E 740 653-3583
  Lancaster *(G-9713)*
Fath Management Company.................. E 513 662-3724
  Cincinnati *(G-2649)*
Fay Limited Partnership......................... E 513 542-8333
  Cincinnati *(G-2650)*
Fay Limited Partnership......................... E 513 241-1911
  Cincinnati *(G-2651)*
Fieldstone Limited Partnership.............. C 937 293-0900
  Moraine *(G-11410)*
▲ Forest City Enterprises LP................. B 216 621-6060
  Cleveland *(G-4271)*
Forest City Properties LLC.................... C 216 621-6060
  Cleveland *(G-4272)*
Forest City Residential Dev................... E 440 888-8664
  Cleveland *(G-4274)*
Franklin Crossing Oh LP........................ D 216 520-1250
  Kent *(G-9575)*
Garland Group Inc................................. E 614 294-4411
  Columbus *(G-5916)*
Gemini Properties.................................. E 614 764-2800
  Dublin *(G-8020)*
Giffin Management Group Inc................ E 330 758-4695
  Youngstown *(G-15621)*
Glen Wesley Inc..................................... D 614 888-7492
  Columbus *(G-5937)*
Globe Furniture Rentals Inc................... D 513 771-8287
  Cincinnati *(G-2734)*
Gms Management Co Inc...................... E 216 766-6000
  Cleveland *(G-4317)*
Hamlet Village In Chagrin FLS............... E 216 263-6033
  Chagrin Falls *(G-1959)*
Hcf Management Inc............................. D 419 999-2010
  Lima *(G-9896)*
Hills Property Management Inc............. D 513 984-0300
  Blue Ash *(G-1183)*
Interntional Towers I Ohio Ltd............... D 216 520-1250
  Youngstown *(G-15641)*
J Foothills LLC...................................... E 614 445-8461
  Columbus *(G-6077)*
Judson.. D 216 791-2004
  Cleveland *(G-4444)*
K&D Management LLC.......................... E 216 624-4686
  Cleveland *(G-4447)*
K&D Management LLC.......................... B 440 946-3600
  Willoughby *(G-15195)*
Klingbeil Multifamilty Fund IV................ D 415 398-0106
  Columbus *(G-6121)*
Lincoln Pointe....................................... E 614 253-4602
  Columbus *(G-6167)*

SIC SECTION
65 REAL ESTATE

Little Bark View Limited .... E 216 520-1250
  Cleveland *(G-4500)*

Mansfield Memorial Homes .... C 419 774-5100
  Mansfield *(G-10288)*

Massillon Senior Living Ltd .... E 330 833-7229
  Massillon *(G-10653)*

Menorah Pk Ctr For Snior Lving .... A 216 831-6500
  Cleveland *(G-4550)*

Miami Cnty Cmnty Action Cuncil .... E 937 335-7921
  Troy *(G-14146)*

Midtown Investment Co .... D 216 398-7210
  Cleveland *(G-4579)*

Millennia Commercial Group Ltd .... D 216 520-1250
  Cleveland *(G-4584)*

Millennia Housing MGT Ltd .... C 216 520-1250
  Cleveland *(G-4585)*

Mrn Limited Partnership .... E 216 589-5631
  Cleveland *(G-4606)*

Musicians Towers OH Tc LP .... E 216 520-1250
  Cleveland Heights *(G-5182)*

National Church Residences .... C 614 451-2151
  Columbus *(G-6292)*

National Housing Corporation .... E 614 481-8106
  Columbus *(G-6299)*

Neighborhood Properties Inc .... E 419 473-2604
  Toledo *(G-13931)*

Oberer Development Co .... E 937 910-0851
  Miamisburg *(G-11077)*

Ohio Living .... B 330 746-2944
  Youngstown *(G-15682)*

Ohio Living Quaker Heights .... E 937 897-6050
  Waynesville *(G-14626)*

One Lincoln Park .... E 937 298-0594
  Dayton *(G-7538)*

Original Partners Ltd Partnr .... E 513 381-8696
  Cincinnati *(G-3168)*

Otterbein Portage Valley Inc .... C 888 749-4950
  Pemberville *(G-12291)*

Owners Management Company .... D 440 232-6093
  Bedford Heights *(G-1000)*

Owners Management Company .... E 440 439-3800
  Parma *(G-12259)*

Park Lane Manor Akron Inc .... E 330 724-3315
  Akron *(G-261)*

Phoenix Residential Ctrs Inc .... D 440 887-6097
  Cleveland *(G-4747)*

Pickaway Cnty Cmnty Action Org .... E 740 477-1655
  Circleville *(G-3716)*

Plaza Properties Inc .... E 614 237-3726
  Columbus *(G-6532)*

Realmark Property Investors .... E 937 434-7242
  Dayton *(G-7582)*

Royal F & S Holdings LLC .... E 614 402-8422
  Columbus *(G-6615)*

Ryan Senior Care LLC .... D 419 389-0800
  Toledo *(G-14001)*

Sanctary Grnde Snior Lving LLC .... D 330 470-4411
  North Canton *(G-11860)*

Sateri Home Inc .... D 330 758-8106
  Youngstown *(G-15717)*

Shaker House .... D 216 991-6000
  Cleveland *(G-4898)*

Shaker Hts High Schl Crew Prnt .... D 216 991-6138
  Shaker Heights *(G-12984)*

Sherman Thompson Oh Tc LP .... D 216 520-1250
  Ironton *(G-9513)*

Showe Management Corporation .... D 614 492-8111
  Columbus *(G-6674)*

SKW Management LLC .... E 937 382-7938
  Lynchburg *(G-10186)*

Smb Construction Co Inc .... E 419 269-1473
  Toledo *(G-14017)*

South Franklin Circle .... D 440 247-1300
  Chagrin Falls *(G-1991)*

Spectrum Rtrment Cmmnities LLC .... D 440 892-9777
  Westlake *(G-15110)*

Summit Management Services Inc .... E 330 723-0864
  Medina *(G-10895)*

Tgm Associates LP .... E 513 829-8383
  Fairfield *(G-8445)*

The Lochhaven Company .... D 419 227-5450
  Lima *(G-9970)*

Towne Properties Asset MGT .... D 513 381-8696
  Cincinnati *(G-3490)*

Towne Properties Assoc Inc .... E 513 793-6976
  Cincinnati *(G-3491)*

Towne Properties Assoc Inc .... D 513 489-4059
  Cincinnati *(G-3492)*

Towne Properties Assoc Inc .... D 513 874-3737
  Cincinnati *(G-3493)*

Transcon Builders Inc .... E 440 439-3400
  Cleveland *(G-5030)*

Tsmm Management LLC .... E 740 450-1100
  Zanesville *(G-15834)*

Tyrone Townhouses PA Inv LLC .... D 216 520-1250
  Cleveland *(G-5043)*

United Ch Rsdnces Knton Ohio I .... E 740 382-4885
  Kenton *(G-9624)*

Uptown Rental Properties LLC .... E 513 861-9394
  Cincinnati *(G-3599)*

Wallick Construction Co .... D 937 399-7009
  Springfield *(G-13309)*

Wayne Manor II Inc .... E 330 345-2835
  Wooster *(G-15382)*

▲ Welltower Op LLC .... D 419 247-2800
  Toledo *(G-14103)*

Westerville Senior Dev Ltd .... D 614 794-9300
  Westerville *(G-14954)*

Westlake Village Inc .... C 440 892-4200
  Cleveland *(G-5140)*

Whitehurst Company .... E 419 534-6022
  Maumee *(G-10780)*

Worthngton Chrstn Vlg Cngrgate .... E 614 846-6076
  Columbus *(G-6907)*

Zanesville Metro Hsing Auth .... D 740 454-9714
  Zanesville *(G-15841)*

Zepf Housing Corp One Inc .... B 419 531-0019
  Toledo *(G-14120)*

6514 Dwelling operators, except apartments

Birchaven Village .... D 419 424-3000
  Findlay *(G-8512)*

Good Inc .... D 740 592-9667
  Athens *(G-569)*

Homeport Inc .... E 614 221-8889
  Columbus *(G-6003)*

New Life Properties Inc .... D 513 221-3350
  Walnut Hills *(G-14475)*

Norwalk Golf Properties Inc .... E 419 668-8535
  Norwalk *(G-12019)*

Original Partners Ltd Partnr .... E 513 381-8696
  Cincinnati *(G-3168)*

Our House Inc .... E 440 835-2110
  Westlake *(G-15093)*

Towne Properties Assoc Inc .... D 513 874-3737
  Cincinnati *(G-3493)*

6519 Real property lessors, nec

Bessemer and Lake Erie RR Co .... D 440 593-1102
  Conneaut *(G-6940)*

Catawba-Cleveland Dev Corp .... D 419 797-4424
  Port Clinton *(G-12518)*

Cutler Real Estate Inc .... E 614 339-4664
  Dublin *(G-7980)*

Eagle Realty Group LLC .... C 513 361-4000
  Cincinnati *(G-2593)*

Fairlawn Associates Ltd .... C 330 867-5000
  Fairlawn *(G-8478)*

Globe Furniture Rentals Inc .... D 513 771-8287
  Cincinnati *(G-2734)*

J & E LLC .... E 513 241-0429
  Cincinnati *(G-2891)*

Ohio Living .... C 330 638-2420
  Cortland *(G-6974)*

Select Hotels Group LLC .... D 513 754-0003
  Mason *(G-10606)*

6531 Real estate agents and managers

3cre Advisors LLC .... D 513 745-9333
  Cincinnati *(G-2123)*

Ackermann Group .... D 513 480-5204
  Cincinnati *(G-2142)*

Adena Commercial LLC .... E 614 436-9800
  Columbus *(G-5244)*

Al Neyer LLC .... E 513 271-6400
  Cincinnati *(G-2157)*

Alpha PHI Alpha Homes Inc .... E 330 376-9956
  Akron *(G-44)*

American Bulk Commodities Inc .... C 330 758-0841
  Youngstown *(G-15549)*

American Homes 4 Rent .... E 513 429-7174
  Cincinnati *(G-2182)*

Appraisal Research Corporation .... D 419 423-3582
  Findlay *(G-8509)*

Arena Management Holdings LLC .... A 513 421-4111
  Cincinnati *(G-2215)*

Bellwether .... D 949 247-8912
  Cleveland *(G-3862)*

Bellwether Entp RE Capitl LLC .... E 216 820-4500
  Cleveland *(G-3863)*

Big Hill Realty Corp .... E 937 435-1177
  Dayton *(G-7193)*

Bock & Clark Corporation .... E 330 665-4821
  Canton *(G-1688)*

Brunswick Senior Living LLC .... E 330 460-4244
  Brunswick *(G-1452)*

C V Perry & Co .... E 614 221-4131
  Columbus *(G-5490)*

Carleton Realty Inc .... E 740 653-5200
  Lancaster *(G-9698)*

Carleton Realty Inc .... E 614 431-5700
  Westerville *(G-14964)*

Carnegie Companies Inc .... E 440 232-2300
  Solon *(G-13072)*

Cassidy Trley Coml RE Svcs Inc .... D 513 771-2580
  Cincinnati *(G-2319)*

Cassidy Trley Coml RE Svcs Inc .... C 614 241-4700
  Columbus *(G-5518)*

Cavalear Corporation .... E 419 882-7125
  Sylvania *(G-13538)*

Cbre Inc .... E 614 764-4798
  Dublin *(G-7960)*

Century 21 Homestar .... E 440 449-9100
  Cleveland *(G-3956)*

Century 21 Premiere Properties .... E 419 334-2121
  Fremont *(G-8669)*

Choice Properties Real Estate .... D 937 593-7216
  Bellefontaine *(G-1023)*

Coastal Ridge Management LLC .... B 614 339-4608
  Columbus *(G-5588)*

Coldwell Banker First Place RE .... D 330 726-8161
  Poland *(G-12503)*

Coldwell Banker Residential .... E 954 771-2600
  Columbus *(G-5593)*

Coldwell Banker West Shell .... E 513 271-7200
  Cincinnati *(G-2474)*

65 REAL ESTATE

Coldwell Banker West Shell .... E 513 777-7900
West Chester *(G-14672)*

Coldwell Bnkr Hritg Rltors Dyt .... C 937 482-0082
Beavercreek *(G-920)*

Coldwell Bnkr Hritg Rltors LLC .... E 937 426-6060
Beavercreek Township *(G-934)*

Coldwell Bnkr Hritg Rltors LLC .... E 937 435-7759
Springboro *(G-13197)*

Coldwell Bnkr Hritg Rltors LLC .... E 937 434-7600
Dayton *(G-7238)*

Comey & Shepherd LLC .... D 513 489-2100
Cincinnati *(G-2480)*

Community Management Corp .... D 513 761-6339
Cincinnati *(G-2484)*

Connor Group A RE Inv Firm LLC .... B 937 434-3095
Miamisburg *(G-11038)*

Continental Realty Ltd .... E 614 221-6260
Columbus *(G-5697)*

Continental Realty Ltd .... D 614 224-2393
Columbus *(G-5696)*

County of Allen .... E 419 228-6065
Lima *(G-9880)*

Crawford Hoying Ltd .... C 614 335-2020
Dublin *(G-7979)*

Cresco Limited Partnership .... E 216 520-1200
Cleveland *(G-4138)*

Crossroads REO Inc .... E 440 846-0077
Strongsville *(G-13450)*

Cushman Wakefield Holdings Inc .... E 513 241-4880
Cincinnati *(G-2526)*

Cutler Real Estate .... D 330 836-9141
Fairlawn *(G-8472)*

Cutler Real Estate Inc .... E 614 339-4664
Dublin *(G-7980)*

Danberry Co .... E 419 866-8888
Maumee *(G-10716)*

Danbury Wods At Grnfeld Crssin .... D 330 264-0355
Wooster *(G-15333)*

Dari Pizza Enterprises II Inc .... C 419 534-3000
Maumee *(G-10717)*

Dayton Realtors .... E 937 223-0900
Dayton *(G-7301)*

Dehoff Agency Inc .... E 330 499-8153
Canton *(G-1733)*

Design Homes & Development Co .... E 937 438-3667
Dayton *(G-7311)*

Di Salle Real Estate Co .... E 419 255-6909
Toledo *(G-13778)*

E-Merge Real Estate .... D 614 804-5600
Pickerington *(G-12401)*

Eagle Realty Group LLC .... E 513 361-4000
Cincinnati *(G-2593)*

Eagle Realty Group LLC .... C 513 361-7750
Cincinnati *(G-2594)*

Eagle Realty Group LLC .... E 513 361-7700
Cincinnati *(G-2595)*

Ebthcom LLC .... D 513 242-3284
Cincinnati *(G-2602)*

Echoing Hills Village Inc .... C 740 327-2311
Warsaw *(G-14591)*

Essex Healthcare Corporation .... E 614 416-0600
Columbus *(G-5830)*

Exclusive Lifestyles Ohio LLC .... E 740 647-5552
Columbus *(G-5837)*

EZ Sales Teamkeller Willi .... D 216 916-7778
Westlake *(G-15058)*

Fairfield Homes Inc .... C 614 873-3533
Plain City *(G-12477)*

Fairfield Homes Inc .... E 740 653-3583
Lancaster *(G-9714)*

Fay Limited Partnership .... E 513 241-1911
Cincinnati *(G-2651)*

First Realty Property MGT Ltd .... E 440 720-0100
Cleveland *(G-4260)*

Flashhouse Inc .... E 216 600-0504
Beachwood *(G-792)*

Forest City Commercial MGT Inc .... C 216 696-7701
Cleveland *(G-4268)*

Forest City Commercial MGT Inc .... E 216 621-6060
Cleveland *(G-4269)*

Forest Cy Residential MGT Inc .... C 216 621-6060
Cleveland *(G-4276)*

G J Goudreau & Co .... E 216 351-5233
Cleveland *(G-4297)*

Garland Group Inc .... E 614 294-4411
Columbus *(G-5916)*

Geneva Chervenic Realty Inc .... E 330 686-8400
Stow *(G-13370)*

Globe Furniture Rentals Inc .... D 513 771-8287
Cincinnati *(G-2734)*

Hadler Realty Company .... E 614 457-6650
Columbus *(G-5963)*

Hanna Commercial LLC .... D 216 861-7200
Cleveland *(G-4347)*

Haynes Real Estate Inc .... E 419 475-8383
Toledo *(G-13837)*

Her Inc .... E 614 221-7400
Columbus *(G-5985)*

Her Majesty Management Group .... D 614 680-7461
Columbus *(G-5986)*

Hoeting Inc .... E 513 385-5100
Cincinnati *(G-2831)*

Home Experts Realty .... D 937 705-6336
Beavercreek *(G-882)*

Home Experts Realty .... E 937 435-6000
Dayton *(G-7412)*

Homestead America .... B 614 221-5400
Columbus *(G-6005)*

Howard Hanna Real Estate Svcs .... E 440 665-0649
Cleveland *(G-4384)*

Howard Hanna Smythe Cramer .... C 216 447-4477
Cleveland *(G-4385)*

ICP Realty LLC .... E 440 539-1046
Cleveland *(G-4399)*

Ihs Services Inc .... D 419 224-8811
Lima *(G-9909)*

Industrial Coml Prpts LLC .... D 440 539-1046
Solon *(G-13099)*

Integra Cncinnati/Columbus Inc .... E 614 764-8040
Dublin *(G-8040)*

Integra Rlty Rsrces - Cncnnt/D .... C 513 561-2305
Cincinnati *(G-2875)*

Irg Realty Advisors LLC .... E 330 659-4060
Richfield *(G-12699)*

Irongate Inc .... D 937 890-4880
Englewood *(G-8310)*

Irongate Inc .... D 937 432-3432
Dayton *(G-7426)*

Irongate Inc .... D 937 433-3300
Centerville *(G-1946)*

J & W Enterprises Inc .... E 740 774-4500
Chillicothe *(G-2074)*

John Stewart Company .... E 513 703-5412
Cincinnati *(G-2914)*

Johnson Rose LLC .... E 440 785-9892
North Olmsted *(G-11907)*

Keller Williams Bruce .... E 440 888-6800
Middleburg Heights *(G-11118)*

Keller Williams Realty .... E 614 944-5900
Columbus *(G-6109)*

Keller Williams Realty Atlanta .... E 614 406-5461
Hilliard *(G-9208)*

Keller Williams Rlty Suppliers .... E 614 403-2411
Worthington *(G-15425)*

Klingbeil Management Group Co .... E 614 220-8900
Columbus *(G-6120)*

Laclede Development Company .... E 513 702-4391
Wyoming *(G-15496)*

▲ Lenz Inc .... E 937 277-9364
Dayton *(G-7452)*

Link Real Estate Group LLC .... D 614 686-7775
Columbus *(G-6168)*

Luxe Omni Inc .... E 937 929-0511
Oakwood *(G-12050)*

Manatron Sabre Systems and Svc .... D 937 431-4000
Beavercreek *(G-926)*

Manco Real Estate MGT Inc .... E 937 277-9551
Dayton *(G-7465)*

Marcus Mllchap RE Inv Svcs Inc .... E 614 360-9800
Columbus *(G-6195)*

Martin + WD Apprisal Group Ltd .... E 419 241-4998
Toledo *(G-13912)*

Mc Mahon Realestate Co .... E 740 344-2250
Newark *(G-11725)*

McDowell Homes LLC .... E 440 205-2000
Mentor *(G-10967)*

Meadowbrook Mall Company .... E 330 747-2661
Youngstown *(G-15664)*

Millennia Housing MGT Ltd .... C 216 520-1250
Cleveland *(G-4585)*

Miller-Valentine Partners Ltd .... E 513 588-1000
Dayton *(G-7506)*

Miller-Vlentine Operations Inc .... B 513 771-0900
Dayton *(G-7508)*

Miller-Vlentine Operations Inc .... E 937 293-0900
Dayton *(G-7507)*

MJM Management Corporation .... E 330 678-0761
Kent *(G-9588)*

▲ Model Group Inc .... E 513 559-0048
Cincinnati *(G-3074)*

Monarch Inv & MGT Group LLC .... A 216 453-3630
Cleveland *(G-4597)*

Mortgage Information Services .... D 216 514-7480
Cleveland *(G-4602)*

Mri Software LLC .... B 800 321-8770
Solon *(G-13114)*

Murwood Real Estate Group LLC .... E 216 839-5500
Beachwood *(G-820)*

National Church Residences .... C 614 451-2151
Columbus *(G-6292)*

◆ Nationwide Mutual Insurance Co .... A 614 249-7111
Columbus *(G-6338)*

Neighborhood Properties Inc .... E 419 473-2604
Toledo *(G-13931)*

Newmark & Company RE Inc .... E 216 861-3040
Cleveland *(G-4641)*

Neyer Real Estate MGT LLC .... C 513 618-6000
Cincinnati *(G-3116)*

Noneman Real Estate Company .... E 419 531-4020
Toledo *(G-13935)*

North Wood Realty .... D 330 856-3915
Warren *(G-14544)*

Oakwood Management Company .... E 614 866-8702
Reynoldsburg *(G-12671)*

Oberer Residential Cnstr Ltd .... D 937 278-0851
Miamisburg *(G-11078)*

Ohio Equities LLC .... D 614 469-0058
Columbus *(G-6419)*

Ohio Equities LLC .... D 614 224-2400
Columbus *(G-6420)*

Olmsted Residence Corporation .... C 440 235-7100
Olmsted Twp *(G-12093)*

Om Partners LLC .... E 216 861-7200
Cleveland *(G-4696)*

One Lincoln Park .... E 937 298-0594
Dayton *(G-7538)*

SIC SECTION

65 REAL ESTATE

Orum Stair Rsdntl Brkg OH .... E 614 920-8100
   Pickerington *(G-12407)*

Owners Management Company .... E 440 439-3800
   Parma *(G-12259)*

Paran Management Company Ltd .... E 216 921-5663
   Cleveland *(G-4719)*

Phil Giessler .... E 614 888-0307
   Worthington *(G-15446)*

Phillips Edison & Company LLC .... E 513 554-1110
   Cincinnati *(G-3206)*

Pinnacle Realty Management Co .... D 614 430-3678
   Worthington *(G-15447)*

Pizzuti Inc .... E 614 280-4000
   Columbus *(G-6527)*

Pk Management LLC .... C 216 472-1870
   Cleveland *(G-4753)*

Plaza Properties Inc .... E 614 237-3726
   Columbus *(G-6532)*

Plk Communities LLC .... D 513 561-5080
   Cincinnati *(G-3214)*

Port Lawrence Title and Tr Co .... E 419 244-4605
   Toledo *(G-13965)*

Prudential Select Properties .... D 440 255-1111
   Mentor *(G-10986)*

Re/Max .... D 614 694-0255
   Pickerington *(G-12411)*

Re/Max Affiliates Inc .... D 614 891-1661
   Westerville *(G-14932)*

Re/Max Premiere Choice .... E 614 436-0330
   Columbus *(G-6563)*

Real Property Management Inc .... E 614 766-6500
   Dublin *(G-8106)*

Reichle Klein Group Inc .... E 419 861-1100
   Toledo *(G-13986)*

Remax Preferred Associates LLC .... C 419 720-5600
   Toledo *(G-13987)*

Residential HM Assn Marion Inc .... C 740 387-9999
   Marion *(G-10451)*

Residential One Realty Inc .... E 614 436-9830
   Columbus *(G-6585)*

Resource Title Agency Inc .... D 216 520-0050
   Cleveland *(G-4831)*

Resource Title Nat Agcy Inc .... D 216 520-0050
   Independence *(G-9476)*

Reuben Co .... E 419 241-3400
   Toledo *(G-13989)*

Rhm Real Estate Inc .... E 216 360-8333
   Cleveland *(G-4836)*

Rlj Management Co Inc .... C 614 942-2020
   Columbus *(G-6602)*

Robert F Lindsay Co .... D 419 476-6221
   Toledo *(G-13993)*

Roman Catholic Diocese Toledo .... E 419 531-5747
   Toledo *(G-13996)*

Ron Neff Real Estate .... E 740 773-4670
   Chillicothe *(G-2083)*

Rose Community Management LLC ...... C 917 542-3600
   Independence *(G-9479)*

Russell Real Estate Service .... E 440 835-8300
   Cleveland *(G-4863)*

Sawmill Road Management Co LLC ...... E 937 342-9071
   Columbus *(G-6646)*

Saxton Real Estate Co .... E 614 875-2327
   Grove City *(G-8951)*

Schottenstein RE Group LLC .... E 614 418-8900
   Columbus *(G-6653)*

◆ Schroeder Company .... E 419 473-3139
   Perrysburg *(G-12368)*

Sgt Clans Wstlake Holdings LLC .... D 440 653-5146
   Westlake *(G-15107)*

Sharon Gay Phlps - Hward Hnna .... D 216 539-2696
   Cleveland *(G-4900)*

Sibcy Cline Inc .... C 513 793-2121
   Cincinnati *(G-3374)*

Sibcy Cline Inc .... C 513 931-7700
   Cincinnati *(G-3376)*

Sibcy Cline Inc .... C 937 610-3404
   Dayton *(G-7620)*

Sibcy Cline Inc .... D 513 385-3330
   Fairfield *(G-8440)*

Sibcy Cline Inc .... C 513 932-6334
   Lebanon *(G-9787)*

Sibcy Cline Inc .... C 513 793-2700
   Montgomery *(G-11374)*

Sibcy Cline Inc .... C 513 777-8100
   West Chester *(G-14764)*

Sibcy Cline Inc .... C 513 677-1830
   West Chester *(G-14765)*

Sibcy Cline Inc .... D 513 984-4100
   Cincinnati *(G-3375)*

Steve Brown .... E 937 436-2700
   Dayton *(G-7642)*

Stouffer Realty Inc .... E 330 564-0711
   Stow *(G-13392)*

Stouffer Realty Inc .... E 330 835-4900
   Fairlawn *(G-8501)*

Stouffer Realty LLC .... E 440 247-4210
   Chagrin Falls *(G-1969)*

Streamlinemd LLC .... D 330 564-2627
   Cuyahoga Falls *(G-7101)*

Sundance Property MGT LLC .... E 513 489-3363
   Blue Ash *(G-1247)*

T & R Properties .... E 614 923-4000
   Dublin *(G-8138)*

Tiger 2010 LLC .... E 330 236-5100
   North Canton *(G-11864)*

▲ Tipton Group Inc .... E 937 885-6300
   Dayton *(G-7670)*

Towne Properties Assoc Inc .... D 513 874-3737
   Cincinnati *(G-3493)*

Turnserv LLC .... E 216 600-8876
   Akron *(G-338)*

Tyson Group .... E 800 659-1080
   Dublin *(G-8145)*

▲ University Circle Incorporated .... E 216 791-3900
   Cleveland *(G-5071)*

Valucentric LLC .... E 410 912-2085
   Toledo *(G-14089)*

Village Communities LLC .... C 614 540-2400
   Westerville *(G-14951)*

Vinebrook Homes LLC .... B 855 513-5678
   Dayton *(G-7707)*

Vinebrook II LLC .... D 614 783-5573
   Dayton *(G-7708)*

Visconsi Companies Ltd .... E 216 464-5550
   Cleveland *(G-5108)*

Vistula Management Company .... D 419 242-2300
   Toledo *(G-14094)*

Waldon Management Corp .... E 330 792-7688
   Youngstown *(G-15751)*

Wallick Properties Midwest LLC .... A 419 381-7477
   New Albany *(G-11591)*

Welles-Bowen Realty Inc .... C 419 535-0011
   Toledo *(G-14101)*

West Shell Commercial Inc .... D 513 721-4200
   Cincinnati *(G-3657)*

Weston Development Company LLC ..... D 440 914-8427
   Cleveland *(G-5141)*

Whitehurst Company .... E 419 534-6022
   Maumee *(G-10780)*

Wilbur Realty Inc .... D 330 673-5883
   Kent *(G-9606)*

Williamfall Group Inc .... E 419 418-5852
   Toledo *(G-14108)*

Woda Group Inc .... A 614 396-3200
   Columbus *(G-6901)*

Your Home Court Advantage LLC .... E 330 364-6602
   New Philadelphia *(G-11674)*

Zaremba Group LLC .... D 216 221-6600
   Lakewood *(G-9689)*

6541 Title abstract offices

Cleveland Home Title Inc .... E 440 788-7100
   Cleveland *(G-4050)*

Louisvlle Title Agcy For NW OH .... D 419 248-4611
   Toledo *(G-13892)*

Mason Title Agency Ltd .... E 614 446-1151
   Columbus *(G-6203)*

Midland Title Security Inc .... C 513 863-7600
   Hamilton *(G-9065)*

Ohio Real Title Agency LLC .... E 216 373-9900
   Cleveland *(G-4689)*

Revere Title Agency Inc .... E 216 447-4070
   Cleveland *(G-4833)*

Weston Inc .... E 440 349-9000
   Cleveland *(G-5143)*

6552 Subdividers and developers, nec

Bostleman Corp .... E
   Holland *(G-9281)*

C V Perry & Co .... E 614 221-4131
   Columbus *(G-5490)*

Cardida Corporation .... D 740 439-4359
   Kimbolton *(G-9640)*

Carnegie Management & Dev Corp .... E 440 892-6800
   Westlake *(G-15046)*

Carter-Jones Companies Inc .... E 330 673-6100
   Kent *(G-9560)*

Cathedral Holdings Inc .... D 513 271-6400
   Cincinnati *(G-2322)*

Cavalear Corporation .... E 419 882-7125
   Sylvania *(G-13538)*

Columbus Housing Partnr Inc .... D 614 221-8889
   Columbus *(G-5640)*

Coral Company .... E 216 932-8822
   Independence *(G-9425)*

Dehoff Agency Inc .... E 330 499-8153
   Canton *(G-1733)*

Eagle Realty Group LLC .... E 513 361-7700
   Cincinnati *(G-2595)*

Equity Cnstr Solutions LLC .... E 614 802-2900
   Hilliard *(G-9195)*

Equity LLC .... D 614 802-2900
   Hilliard *(G-9196)*

Ford Development Corp .... E 513 207-9118
   Cincinnati *(G-2694)*

▲ Forest City Enterprises LP .... B 216 621-6060
   Cleveland *(G-4271)*

Forest Cy Residential MGT Inc .... C 216 621-6060
   Cleveland *(G-4276)*

George J Igel & Co Inc .... A 614 445-8421
   Columbus *(G-5928)*

Highland Som Development .... E 330 528-3500
   Streetsboro *(G-13415)*

Jack Gray .... D 216 688-0466
   Cincinnati *(G-2892)*

▲ Magnum Management Corporation .... C 419 627-2334
   Sandusky *(G-12913)*

Midwestern Plumbing Svc Inc .... E 513 753-0050
   Cincinnati *(G-3060)*

Miller-Vlentine Operations Inc .... B 513 771-0900
   Dayton *(G-7508)*

Miller-Vlentine Operations Inc .... E 937 293-0900
   Dayton *(G-7507)*

Multicon Builders Inc .... E 614 463-1142
   Columbus *(G-6283)*

Employee Codes: A=Over 500 employees, B=251-500
C=101-250, D=51-100, E=20-50, F=10-19, G=1-9

65 REAL ESTATE

Oberer Development Co................... E 937 910-0851
 Miamisburg (G-11077)
Phillips Edison & Company LLC........... E 513 554-1110
 Cincinnati (G-3206)
Pizzuti Inc................................ E 614 280-4000
 Columbus (G-6527)
Req/Jqh Holdings Inc..................... B 513 891-1066
 Blue Ash (G-1235)
Robert L Stark Enterprises Inc........... E 216 292-0240
 Cleveland (G-4846)
Rockford Homes Inc...................... D 614 785-0015
 Columbus (G-5281)
Seg of Ohio Inc........................... E 614 414-7300
 Columbus (G-6659)
Sunrise Development Co.................. B 216 621-6060
 Cleveland (G-4959)
Sunrise Land Co.......................... E 216 621-6060
 Cleveland (G-4960)
T O J Inc................................. E 440 352-1900
 Mentor (G-11002)
The Daimler Group Inc................... E 614 488-4424
 Columbus (G-6759)
Towne Development Group Ltd........... E 513 381-8696
 Cincinnati (G-3489)
Visconsi Companies Ltd.................. E 216 464-5550
 Cleveland (G-5108)
Vision Development Inc................... E 614 487-1804
 Upper Arlington (G-14283)
Windsor Companies....................... E 740 653-8822
 Lancaster (G-9750)
Zaremba Group LLC....................... D 216 221-6600
 Lakewood (G-9689)

6553 Cemetery subdividers and developers

American Cemetery Services LLP......... D 330 345-8379
 Warren (G-14497)
Archdiocese of Cincinnati................. C 513 489-0300
 Cincinnati (G-2213)
Arlington Memorial Grdns Assn........... E 513 521-7003
 Cincinnati (G-2217)
Catholic Cmtries Assn of The D.......... D 216 641-7575
 Cleveland (G-3936)
City of Cleveland.......................... E 216 348-7210
 Cleveland (G-3979)
Miami Valley Memory Grdns Assn........ E 937 885-7779
 Dayton (G-7497)
Roman Cthlic Docese Youngstown....... E 330 792-4721
 Youngstown (G-15710)
Spring Grove Cmtry & Arboretum........ D 513 681-7526
 Cincinnati (G-3397)

67 HOLDING AND OTHER INVESTMENT OFFICES

6712 Bank holding companies

Greenville National Bancorp.............. E 937 548-1114
 Greenville (G-8876)

6719 Holding companies, nec

◆ 2023 Ventures Inc...................... D
 Archbold (G-454)
Akron Brass Holding Corp................. E 330 264-5678
 Wooster (G-15307)
◆ Ampac Holdings LLC..................... A 513 671-1777
 Cincinnati (G-2194)
Armor Consolidated Inc................... A 513 923-5260
 Mason (G-10520)
AWH Holdings Inc......................... D 513 241-2614
 Cincinnati (G-2230)
Brake Parts Holdings Inc.................. B 216 589-0198
 Cleveland (G-3889)

Cai Holdings LLC........................... D 419 656-3568
 Sandusky (G-12868)
Cauffiel Industries Corp.................... E
 Toledo (G-13725)
CNG Holdings Inc.......................... A 513 336-7735
 Cincinnati (G-2466)
Consoldted Fndries Hldngs Corp......... A 216 772-1041
 Cleveland (G-4105)
Cpp Group Holdings LLC................. E 216 453-4800
 Cleveland (G-4134)
Crane Carrier Holdings LLC.............. C 918 286-2889
 New Philadelphia (G-11648)
Drt Holdings Inc............................ D 937 298-7391
 Dayton (G-7317)
Eci Macola/Max Holding LLC............ E 614 410-2712
 Dublin (G-8001)
Elyria Foundry Holdings LLC............. B 440 322-4657
 Elyria (G-8247)
Entelco Corporation....................... D 419 872-4620
 Maumee (G-10721)
▲ Exochem Corporation................... D 440 277-1246
 Lorain (G-10073)
Fosbel Holding Inc......................... E 216 362-3900
 Cleveland (G-4279)
▼ Hexion Topco LLC...................... D 614 225-4000
 Columbus (G-5990)
Hopkins Acquisition Inc................... A 248 371-1700
 Cleveland (G-4375)
IBP Corporation Holdings Inc............ A 614 692-6360
 Columbus (G-6038)
Lion Group Inc............................. D 937 898-1949
 Dayton (G-7457)
LTV-Trico Inc.............................. B 216 622-5000
 Cleveland (G-4508)
Mbp Holdings Inc.......................... D
 Dayton (G-7471)
Midwest Dairies Inc....................... D 419 678-8059
 Coldwater (G-5219)
Mssl Consolidated Inc..................... B 330 766-5510
 Warren (G-14541)
◆ Nationwide Life Insur Co Amer........ A 800 688-5177
 Columbus (G-6335)
Norse Dairy Systems Inc.................. C 614 294-4931
 Columbus (G-6363)
Parkway Operating Co LLC.............. E 513 530-1600
 Toledo (G-13958)
Qualus Corp................................ D 800 434-0415
 Cincinnati (G-3261)
Sarnova Holdings Inc..................... B 614 760-5000
 Dublin (G-8114)
Scar Holdings LLC......................... E 419 214-0890
 Toledo (G-14006)
Supreme Acquisition Holdg LLC......... D 330 906-2509
 Canton (G-1867)
Vertiv JV Holdings LLC................... A 614 888-0246
 Columbus (G-6846)
Wensminger Holdings Inc................ D 513 563-8822
 Cincinnati (G-3653)

6722 Management investment, open-ended

Keybank Eb Mnged Grnteed Inv C...... C 216 689-3000
 Cleveland (G-4459)
Nationwide Asset MGT LLC.............. C 614 677-7300
 Columbus (G-6306)
Proampac Holdings Inc.................... D 513 671-1777
 Cincinnati (G-3236)
Profunds................................... E 888 776-5717
 Columbus (G-6551)
Strategic Wealth Partners................. E 216 800-9000
 Independence (G-9488)
Touchstone Advisors Inc.................. E 800 638-8194
 Cincinnati (G-3486)

Victory Capital Holdings Inc.............. E 216 898-2400
 Brooklyn (G-1412)

6726 Investment offices, nec

Airborne Acquisition Inc................... E 216 438-6111
 Solon (G-13064)
National Housing Tr Ltd Partnr........... E 614 451-9929
 Columbus (G-6300)
Rockwood Equity Partners LLC.......... E 216 342-1760
 Cleveland (G-4851)
US Capital Inc.............................. E 330 867-4525
 Akron (G-345)
▲ Westlake Dimex LLC................... C 740 374-3100
 Marietta (G-10414)

6732 Trusts: educational, religious, etc.

Altruism Society Inc....................... D 877 283-4001
 Beachwood (G-765)
Cleveland Foundation..................... D 216 861-3810
 Cleveland (G-4044)
Golden Endngs Glden Rtrver RSC....... E 614 486-0773
 Columbus (G-5940)
Mercy Health Foundation................. B 937 523-6670
 Springfield (G-13270)
Miami Vly Cmnty Action Partnr.......... D 937 222-1009
 Dayton (G-7503)
Ncbw Grter Clvland Chpter Wmen...... D 216 232-2992
 Garfield Heights (G-8777)

6733 Trusts, nec

Cleveland Clinic Foundation.............. D 216 444-5000
 Cleveland (G-4030)
Cleveland Clinic Foundation.............. C 216 444-5715
 Cleveland (G-4031)
Colerain Township......................... E 740 633-5778
 Martins Ferry (G-10465)
County of Preble........................... E 937 839-5845
 West Alexandria (G-14643)
Equity Trust Company.................... B 440 323-5491
 Westlake (G-15057)
Huntington Trust Co Nat Assn............ B 614 480-5345
 Columbus (G-6029)
Nestle Usa Inc............................. E 440 349-5757
 Solon (G-13117)
Trust Processing........................... E 513 774-8805
 Cincinnati (G-3533)
Unibilt Inds Hlth & Welfare Tr............ D 937 890-7570
 Vandalia (G-14396)

6794 Patent owners and lessors

Bagel Place Inc............................ E 419 537-9377
 Toledo (G-13698)
Brewdog Franchising LLC................. E 614 908-3051
 Canal Winchester (G-1599)
Cassanos Inc............................... E 937 294-8400
 Dayton (G-7215)
Chemstation International Inc............ E 937 294-8265
 Moraine (G-11397)
Clark Brands LLC.......................... A 330 723-9886
 Medina (G-10821)
Cleveland Rest Oper Ltd Partnr.......... E 216 328-1121
 Cleveland (G-4064)
Convenient Food Mart Inc................ E 800 860-4844
 Mentor (G-10926)
East of Chicago Pizza Inc................. D 419 225-7116
 Lima (G-9885)
Epcon Cmmnties Franchising Inc........ D 614 761-1010
 Dublin (G-8005)
Escape Enterprises Inc.................... D 614 224-0300
 Columbus (G-5828)
Franchise Group Inc....................... B 740 363-2222
 Delaware (G-7799)

SIC SECTION
70 HOTELS, ROOMING HOUSES, CAMPS, AND OTHER LODGING PLACES

Frickers USA LLC .... E 937 865-9242
   Miamisburg *(G-11056)*

Giant Eagle Inc .... C 412 968-5300
   Columbus *(G-5933)*

Gioninos Pizzeria Inc .... E 330 630-2010
   Tallmadge *(G-13592)*

Gold Star Chili Inc .... E 513 231-4541
   Cincinnati *(G-2740)*

Gosh Enterprises Inc .... E 614 923-4700
   Columbus *(G-5943)*

Hobby Lobby Stores Inc .... E 419 861-1862
   Holland *(G-9288)*

Hometeam Inspection Service .... C 513 831-1300
   Milford *(G-11230)*

Larosas Inc .... A 513 347-5660
   Cincinnati *(G-2966)*

Lei Home Enhancements .... C 513 738-4663
   Cincinnati *(G-2970)*

Marcos Inc .... D 419 885-4844
   Toledo *(G-13910)*

Moto Franchise Corporation .... E 937 291-1900
   Dayton *(G-7516)*

Ohio/Oklahoma Hearst TV Inc .... D 513 412-5000
   Cincinnati *(G-3152)*

Parkway Pizza Incorporated .... D 937 303-8800
   Marysville *(G-10502)*

Petland Inc .... E 740 775-2464
   Chillicothe *(G-2082)*

Pfg Ventures LP .... D 216 520-8400
   Independence *(G-9466)*

Premier Broadcasting Co Inc .... E 614 866-0700
   Reynoldsburg *(G-12672)*

Red Robin Gourmet Burgers Inc .... C 330 305-1080
   Canton *(G-1841)*

Red Roof Inns Inc .... A 614 744-2600
   New Albany *(G-11584)*

Romeos Pizza Franchise LLC .... C 234 248-4549
   Medina *(G-10885)*

Sabo Inc .... E 937 222-7939
   Dayton *(G-7603)*

Sakrete Inc .... E 513 242-3644
   Cincinnati *(G-3343)*

▲ Skyline Cem Holdings LLC .... C 513 874-1188
   Fairfield *(G-8441)*

▲ Stanley Steemer Intl Inc .... C 614 764-2007
   Dublin *(G-8124)*

Staymobile Franchising LLC .... D 614 601-3345
   Columbus *(G-6717)*

Ta Operating LLC .... B 440 808-9100
   Westlake *(G-15113)*

▲ The Cornwell Quality Tool .... D 330 336-3506
   Wadsworth *(G-14455)*

Tuffy Associates Corp .... E 419 865-6900
   Toledo *(G-14077)*

Waxxpot Group Franchise LLC .... C 614 622-3018
   Columbus *(G-6871)*

◆ Wendys Company .... B 614 764-3100
   Dublin *(G-8163)*

Wendys Restaurants LLC .... E 614 764-3100
   Dublin *(G-8164)*

6798 Real estate investment trusts

American Cmpus Communities Inc ... E 216 687-5196
   Cleveland *(G-3799)*

Associated Estates Realty Corporation. B 216 261-5000
   Richmond Heights *(G-12715)*

Divine Strings Investment LLC .... D 937 241-0782
   Canton *(G-1737)*

Forest City Realty Trust Inc .... A 216 621-6060
   Cleveland *(G-4273)*

Ohad Investment Group LLC .... E 513 426-5202
   Cincinnati *(G-3141)*

▲ Profill Holdings LLC .... A 513 742-4000
   Cincinnati *(G-3247)*

Site Centers Corp .... C 216 755-5500
   Beachwood *(G-839)*

Washington Prime Acqsition LLC ...... C 614 621-9000
   Columbus *(G-6865)*

Washington Prime Group Inc .... C 614 621-9000
   Columbus *(G-6866)*

Welltower Inc .... D 419 247-2800
   Toledo *(G-14102)*

▲ Welltower Op LLC .... D 419 247-2800
   Toledo *(G-14103)*

6799 Investors, nec

BAIN CAPITAL PRIVATE EQUITY ..... E 614 751-5315
   Columbus *(G-5413)*

Bit Mining Limited .... D 346 204-8537
   Akron *(G-69)*

Camelot Realty Investments .... E 740 357-5291
   Lucasville *(G-10173)*

Capital Investment Group Llc .... E 513 241-5090
   Cincinnati *(G-2306)*

Cke Acquisition Co LLC .... E 614 205-0242
   Columbus *(G-5577)*

Ctd Investments LLC .... E 614 570-9949
   Columbus *(G-5735)*

Dg3 Topco Holdings LLC .... E 216 292-0200
   Cleveland *(G-4163)*

Drive Capital .... E 614 284-9436
   Columbus *(G-5786)*

Elite Investments LLC .... D 419 350-8949
   Maumee *(G-10720)*

Golden Reserve LLC .... E 614 563-2818
   Dublin *(G-8022)*

Greenhuse Sltons Acqsition LLC ...... E 440 236-8332
   Strongsville *(G-13458)*

Horan Capital Advisors LLC .... D 513 745-0707
   Cincinnati *(G-2842)*

Igs Ventures Inc .... C 614 659-5000
   Dublin *(G-8035)*

Imdt Acquisition LLC .... D 937 235-0510
   Dayton *(G-7418)*

◆ Jpmorgan Chase Bank Nat Assn ... A 614 436-3055
   Columbus *(G-5264)*

Kassel Equity Group LLC .... E 614 310-4060
   Dublin *(G-8046)*

Kaulig Capital LLC .... E 330 968-1110
   Hudson *(G-9360)*

◆ Kinetico Incorporated .... B 440 564-9111
   Newbury *(G-11761)*

Klingbeil Capital MGT Ltd .... D 415 398-0106
   Worthington *(G-15427)*

Lazear Capital Partners Ltd .... E 614 221-1616
   Columbus *(G-6148)*

Linsalata Capital Partners Inc .... B 440 684-1400
   Mayfield Heights *(G-10788)*

Lti Inc .... D 614 278-7777
   Columbus *(G-6176)*

Lucid Investments Inc .... D 216 972-0058
   Willoughby *(G-15208)*

Lument Real Estate Capital LLC .... E 614 586-9380
   Columbus *(G-6178)*

McM Capital Partners II LP .... B 216 514-1840
   Beachwood *(G-813)*

National City Capital Corp .... B 216 222-2491
   Cleveland *(G-4619)*

National Financial Svcs LLC .... A 614 841-1790
   Columbus *(G-5271)*

Newmark & Company RE Inc .... E 216 861-3040
   Cleveland *(G-4641)*

Oakdale Estates II Inv LLC .... D 216 520-1850
   West Union *(G-14871)*

Praetorian Holdings Group LLC .... E 440 665-4246
   Cleveland *(G-4764)*

Producers Service LLC .... E 740 454-6253
   Zanesville *(G-15828)*

Rainstar Capital Group .... E 419 801-4113
   Perrysburg *(G-12366)*

Resilience Fund III LP .... E 216 292-0200
   Cleveland *(G-4830)*

Riverside Company .... D 216 344-1040
   Cleveland *(G-4843)*

Riverside Partners LLC .... A 216 344-1040
   Cleveland *(G-4845)*

Shields Capital Corporation .... D 216 767-1340
   Beachwood *(G-837)*

Sotera Health Holdings LLC .... B 440 262-1410
   Broadview Heights *(G-1397)*

Stephens Investments LLC .... E 937 299-4993
   Dayton *(G-7641)*

Stonehenge Capital Company LLC ... E 614 246-2456
   Columbus *(G-6719)*

Stonehenge Fincl Holdings Inc .... E 614 246-2500
   Columbus *(G-6720)*

Styx Acquisition LLC .... A 330 264-9900
   Wooster *(G-15378)*

Ultimus Fund Solutions LLC .... E 513 587-3400
   Cincinnati *(G-3549)*

Verdant Commercial Capital LLC ...... E 513 769-2033
   Blue Ash *(G-1270)*

Weinberg Capital Group Inc .... D 216 503-8307
   Cleveland *(G-5125)*

White Oak Partners Inc .... D 614 855-1155
   Westerville *(G-15021)*

Ws One Investment Usa LLC .... D 855 895-3728
   Aurora *(G-631)*

70 HOTELS, ROOMING HOUSES, CAMPS, AND OTHER LODGING PLACES

7011 Hotels and motels

11689 Sharon West Inc .... E 513 771-2525
   Cincinnati *(G-2118)*

1460 Ninth St Assoc Ltd Partnr .... E 216 241-6600
   Cleveland *(G-3740)*

16644 Snow Rd LLC .... E 216 676-5200
   Beachwood *(G-762)*

1st Stop Inc .... E 937 695-0318
   Winchester *(G-15283)*

5 Star Hotel Management IV LP .... E 614 431-1819
   Columbus *(G-5288)*

506 Phelps Holdings LLC .... E 513 651-1234
   Cincinnati *(G-2124)*

5145 Corporation .... D 330 659-6662
   Richfield *(G-12684)*

5901 Pfffer Rd Htels Sites LLC .... E 513 793-4500
   Blue Ash *(G-1120)*

609 Walnut Hotel LLC .... E 513 578-6600
   Cincinnati *(G-2125)*

6300 Sharonville Assoc LLC .... E 513 489-3636
   Cincinnati *(G-2126)*

631 South Main Street Dev LLC .... D 419 423-0631
   Findlay *(G-8504)*

823 Dayton Hotel Tenant LLC .... E 937 879-2696
   Dayton *(G-7124)*

A & K Ishvar Inc .... D 937 322-0707
   Springfield *(G-13212)*

A C Management Inc .... E 440 461-9200
   Cleveland *(G-3748)*

Aashna Corporation .... E 614 871-0065
   Urbancrest *(G-14318)*

70 HOTELS, ROOMING HOUSES, CAMPS, AND OTHER LODGING PLACES

Aatish Hospitality LLC .... E 937 437-8009
  New Paris *(G-11637)*
AC Hotel Columbus Dublin .... D 614 798-8652
  Dublin *(G-7919)*
AFP 116 Corp .... C 614 536-0500
  Columbus *(G-5328)*
Ahip OH Columbus Entps LLC .... D 614 790-9000
  Dublin *(G-7925)*
AIR Management Group LLC .... E 330 856-1900
  Warren *(G-14495)*
AK Group Hotels Inc .... D 937 372-9921
  Xenia *(G-15498)*
Akron Inn Limited Partnership .... D 330 336-7692
  Wadsworth *(G-14426)*
All Star Mgmt Inc .... E 330 792-9740
  Austintown *(G-635)*
Allen County Property LLC .... E 419 534-4234
  Toledo *(G-13678)*
Alliance Hospitality Inc .... E 614 885-4334
  Columbus *(G-5337)*
Amish Door Inc .... C 330 359-5464
  Wilmot *(G-15281)*
Amlon Ltd .... E 614 431-3670
  Columbus *(G-5366)*
Amoxford Inc .... D 513 523-2722
  Oxford *(G-12200)*
Anishiv Inc .... E 513 932-3034
  Lebanon *(G-9754)*
Ap/Aim Indpndnce Sites Trs LLC .... D 216 986-9900
  Independence *(G-9405)*
Apple Hospitality Five Inc .... E 440 519-9500
  Solon *(G-13066)*
Apple Sven Hospitality MGT Inc .... E 513 248-4663
  Milford *(G-11216)*
Arbys .... E 740 369-0317
  Sunbury *(G-13517)*
Arpita LLC .... E 614 443-6506
  Columbus *(G-5386)*
Arvind Sagar Inc .... D 614 428-8800
  Columbus *(G-5390)*
Ashford Trs Clumbus Easton LLC .... E 614 473-9911
  Columbus *(G-5392)*
At Hospitality LLC .... D 513 527-9962
  Cincinnati *(G-2223)*
Athens OH State 405 LLC .... E 740 593-5600
  Athens *(G-556)*
Aurora Hotel Partners LLC .... E 330 562-0767
  Aurora *(G-605)*
Avalon Inn Services Inc .... D 330 856-1900
  Warren *(G-14502)*
Avalon Resort and Spa LLC .... C 330 856-1900
  Warren *(G-14504)*
Awe Hospitality Group LLC .... E 330 888-8836
  Macedonia *(G-10189)*
B & I Hotel Management LLC .... C 330 995-0200
  Aurora *(G-607)*
Bansi & Pratima Inc .... D 513 735-0453
  Batavia *(G-727)*
Bay Pint Resort Operations LLC .... E 419 798-4434
  Marblehead *(G-10351)*
Beachwood Lodging LLC .... E 216 831-3735
  Beachwood *(G-768)*
Bellefontaine Lodging Inc .... D 937 599-6666
  Bellefontaine *(G-1020)*
Bennett Enterprises Inc .... C 419 893-1004
  Maumee *(G-10699)*
Berlin Grande Hotel Ltd .... E 330 403-3050
  Berlin *(G-1089)*
Best Western Adena Inn .... E 877 722-3422
  Chillicothe *(G-2051)*
Best Western Caldwell Inn Inc .... E 740 732-7599
  Caldwell *(G-1546)*

Best Western Executive Inn .... E 330 794-1050
  Akron *(G-67)*
Best Western Suites .... D 614 870-2378
  Columbus *(G-5435)*
Best Wooster Inc .... E 330 264-7750
  Wooster *(G-15311)*
Bindu Associates LLC Elyria .... E 440 324-0099
  Amherst *(G-424)*
Black Spphire C Clmbus Univ 20 .... D 614 297-9912
  Columbus *(G-5443)*
Blissful Corporation .... D 614 539-3500
  Grove City *(G-8897)*
Blue-Kenwood LLC .... E 513 469-6900
  Blue Ash *(G-1137)*
Bob-Mor Inc .... C 419 485-5555
  Montpelier *(G-11381)*
Boulevard Motel Corp .... C 440 234-3131
  Cleveland *(G-3884)*
Brighton Manor Company .... B 216 241-3123
  Cleveland *(G-3894)*
Broad Street Hotel Assoc LP .... D 614 861-0321
  Columbus *(G-5467)*
Buckeye Hospitality Inc .... E 614 586-1001
  Columbus *(G-5475)*
Buffalo-6305 Eb Associates LLC .... E 614 322-8000
  Columbus *(G-5482)*
Burton Carol Management .... E 216 464-5130
  Cleveland *(G-3912)*
Buxton Inn Inc .... E 740 587-0001
  Granville *(G-8849)*
Ca-Mj Hotel Associates Ltd .... D 330 494-6494
  Canton *(G-1694)*
Cambrdge Prperty Investors Ltd .... E 740 432-7313
  Cambridge *(G-1557)*
Cambria Green Management LLC .... E 330 899-1263
  Uniontown *(G-14244)*
Cambridge Associates Ltd .... E 740 432-7313
  Cambridge *(G-1558)*
Cambridge Surgical Suites LLC .... E 740 421-4455
  Cambridge *(G-1561)*
Cambridge Trs Inc .... E 617 231-3176
  Sharonville *(G-12992)*
Cambridge Trs Inc .... E 617 231-3176
  Westlake *(G-15044)*
Cap City Hotels LLC .... E 614 294-7500
  Columbus *(G-5496)*
Cardida Corporation .... D 740 439-4359
  Kimbolton *(G-9640)*
Carol Ruta .... D 419 663-3501
  Norwalk *(G-12004)*
Castaway Bay Resort .... E 419 627-2500
  Sandusky *(G-12870)*
CD Block K Hotel LLC .... E 440 871-3100
  Westlake *(G-15047)*
Cedar Point Park LLC .... D 419 627-2500
  Sandusky *(G-12875)*
Cedar Point Park LLC .... D 419 627-2106
  Sandusky *(G-12876)*
Cedar Point Park LLC .... E 888 950-5062
  Sandusky *(G-12877)*
Cedar Point Park LLC .... E 419 627-2106
  Sandusky *(G-12878)*
Cedar Point Park LLC .... D 419 626-0830
  Sandusky *(G-12873)*
Central Ohio Gming Vntures LLC .... D 614 308-3333
  Columbus *(G-5538)*
CER Hotels LLC .... E 330 422-1855
  Streetsboro *(G-13411)*
Ch Relty Iv/Clmbus Partners LP .... D 614 885-3334
  Columbus *(G-5550)*
Chandni Inc .... E 419 228-4251
  Lima *(G-9873)*

Charter Hotel Group Ltd Partnr .... E 216 772-4538
  Mentor *(G-10920)*
Cherry Jack Ltd Partnership .... C 740 788-1200
  Newark *(G-11691)*
Cherry Valley Lodge .... E 740 788-1200
  Newark *(G-11692)*
Chester Ave Hotel LLC .... E 216 249-9090
  Cleveland *(G-3967)*
Chillicothe Inn .... E 740 774-2512
  Chillicothe *(G-2056)*
Chillicothe Motel LLC .... D 740 773-3903
  Chillicothe *(G-2058)*
Choice Hotels Intl Inc .... E 330 729-5645
  Berlin *(G-1090)*
Chy Hotel LLC .... E 614 766-7255
  Dublin *(G-7963)*
Cinci Hospitalities Inc .... E 513 398-8075
  Mason *(G-10531)*
Cincinnati Fifth Street Ht LLC .... D 513 579-1234
  Cincinnati *(G-2411)*
Cincinnati Netherland Ht LLC .... B 513 421-9100
  Cincinnati *(G-2417)*
Cincinnatian Hotel .... E 513 381-3000
  Cincinnati *(G-2433)*
Clermont Hills Co LLC .... D 513 752-4400
  Cincinnati *(G-2100)*
Cleveland Arprt Hspitality LLC .... D 440 871-6000
  Westlake *(G-15051)*
Cleveland Bchwood Hsptlity LLC .... D 216 464-5950
  Beachwood *(G-777)*
Cleveland Cbd Hotel LLC .... E 216 377-9000
  Cleveland *(G-4004)*
Cleveland East Hotel LLC .... D 216 378-9191
  Cleveland *(G-4042)*
Cleveland East Htl LLC .... E 513 794-2566
  Cincinnati *(G-2458)*
Cleveland S Hospitality LLC .... D 216 447-1300
  Cleveland *(G-4065)*
Cleveland Westin Downtown .... D 440 730-4338
  Cleveland *(G-4073)*
Clp Gw Sandusky Tenant LP .... B 419 609-6000
  Sandusky *(G-12883)*
Cmp I Blue Ash Owner LLC .... D 513 733-4334
  Blue Ash *(G-1154)*
Cni Thl Ops LLC .... E 937 890-6112
  Dayton *(G-7237)*
Cobb Motel Company LLC .... E 513 336-8871
  Mason *(G-10541)*
Columbia Properties Lima LLC .... C 419 222-0004
  Lima *(G-9875)*
Columbia Sussex Corporation .... E 937 898-4946
  Dayton *(G-7239)*
Columbus Airport Ltd Partnr .... C 614 475-7551
  Columbus *(G-5606)*
Columbus Arprt N Cssady Ht LLC .... D 614 475-7551
  Columbus *(G-5609)*
Columbus Concord Ltd Partnr .... D 614 228-3200
  Columbus *(G-5625)*
Columbus Easton Hotel LLC .... D 614 414-1000
  Columbus *(G-5630)*
Columbus Easton Hotel LLC .... E 614 414-1000
  Columbus *(G-5631)*
Columbus Easton Hotel LLC .... D 614 383-2005
  Columbus *(G-5632)*
Columbus Hilton Downtown .... C 614 384-8600
  Columbus *(G-5636)*
Columbus Hospitality LLC .... E 614 461-2648
  Columbus *(G-5638)*
Columbus Hotel Partnership LLC .... D 614 890-8600
  Columbus *(G-5639)*
Columbus Leasing LLC .... D 614 885-1885
  Columbus *(G-5642)*

70 HOTELS, ROOMING HOUSES, CAMPS, AND OTHER LODGING PLACES

Columbus Lintel Inc.................................E..... 614 871-0440
  Grove City (G-8911)
Columbus OH 0617 LLC.........................E..... 614 855-9766
  Columbus (G-5651)
Columbus Sutheast Ht Group LLC.........E..... 614 491-3800
  Lockbourne (G-10010)
Columbus Worthington Hospitali...........D..... 614 885-3334
  Columbus (G-5659)
Comfort Inn...D..... 740 454-4144
  Zanesville (G-15783)
Commodore Prry Inns Suites LLC..........E..... 419 732-2645
  Port Clinton (G-12520)
Concord Dayton Hotel II LLC................E..... 937 223-1000
  Dayton (G-7245)
Concord Hmltnian Rvrfront Ht L.............E..... 513 896-6200
  Hamilton (G-9034)
Concord Testa Hotel Assoc LLC............D..... 330 252-9228
  Akron (G-119)
Continental RE Companies....................C..... 614 221-1800
  Columbus (G-5695)
Continental/Olentangy Ht LLC...............E..... 614 297-9912
  Columbus (G-5698)
Courtyard By Marriott.............................E..... 937 429-5203
  Beavercreek (G-874)
Courtyard By Marriott.............................E..... 216 765-1900
  Cleveland (G-4132)
Courtyard By Marriott.............................E..... 937 433-3131
  Miamisburg (G-11040)
Courtyard By Marriott.............................E..... 740 344-1800
  Newark (G-11698)
Courtyard By Marriott Rossford..............D..... 419 872-5636
  Rossford (G-12766)
Courtyard By Mrrott Columbus W..........E..... 614 771-8999
  Columbus (G-5712)
Courtyard By Mrrott Dytn-Nvrsi..............E..... 937 220-9060
  Dayton (G-7258)
Courtyard Management Corp.................E..... 216 901-9988
  Cleveland (G-4133)
Courtyard Management Corp.................E..... 614 436-7070
  Columbus (G-5713)
Courtyard Management Corp.................E..... 614 475-8530
  Columbus (G-5714)
Courtyard Management Corp.................E..... 419 866-1001
  Holland (G-9284)
Courtyard Management Corp.................E..... 419 897-2255
  Maumee (G-10713)
CP Dublin LLC.......................................D..... 614 791-1000
  Dublin (G-7976)
CP Mason LLC.......................................D..... 513 459-9800
  Mason (G-10543)
CPX Canton Airport LLC.......................E..... 330 305-0500
  North Canton (G-11819)
Crefiii Wrmaug Sprngfeld Lssee............E..... 937 322-3600
  Springfield (G-13245)
Crossroads Hospitality Co LLC..............E..... 216 241-6600
  Cleveland (G-4141)
Cs Hotels Limited Partnership...............E..... 614 771-8999
  Columbus (G-5733)
Cumberland Gap LLC............................E..... 513 681-9300
  Cincinnati (G-2522)
Das Dutch Village Inn............................E..... 330 482-5050
  Columbiana (G-5234)
Days Inn...D..... 740 695-0100
  Saint Clairsville (G-12789)
Days Inn Htels Athens Clmbus R..........E..... 740 593-6655
  Athens (G-565)
Days Inn Middletown.............................D..... 513 420-9378
  Middletown (G-11194)
Days Inns of America............................E..... 330 345-1500
  Wooster (G-15334)
Dayton Hotels LLC................................E..... 937 965-7500
  Dayton (G-7289)

Dayton V Lw LLC...................................E..... 937 229-9836
  Dayton (G-7303)
Dbp Enterprises LLC.............................D..... 740 513-2399
  Sunbury (G-13519)
Dchm Inc..D..... 330 874-3435
  Bolivar (G-1293)
Detroit Westfield LLC.............................D..... 330 666-4131
  Akron (G-133)
Dev Investments of Ohio Inc.................E..... 740 454-9332
  Zanesville (G-15785)
Dhanlaxmi LLC.......................................D..... 614 871-9617
  Grove City (G-8916)
Dino Persichetti.....................................D..... 330 821-9600
  Alliance (G-381)
Donlen Inc..D..... 216 961-6767
  Cleveland (G-4177)
Doro Inc...E..... 740 695-1994
  Saint Clairsville (G-12790)
Doubletree By Hilton..............................E..... 330 333-8284
  Youngstown (G-15602)
Doubletree Guest Suites Dayton...........E..... 937 436-2400
  Miamisburg (G-11048)
Drury Hotels Company LLC..................E..... 513 771-5601
  Cincinnati (G-2576)
Drury Hotels Company LLC..................E..... 937 454-5200
  Dayton (G-7318)
Drury Hotels Company LLC..................E..... 419 422-9700
  Findlay (G-8526)
Drury Hotels Company LLC..................E..... 513 425-6650
  Franklin (G-8634)
Dublin Hotel Ltd Liability Co..................E..... 513 891-1066
  Dublin (G-7994)
Durga Llc...E..... 513 771-2080
  Cincinnati (G-2587)
Dutchman Hospitality Group Inc...........D..... 330 852-2586
  Sugarcreek (G-13510)
Dutchman Hospitality Group Inc...........D..... 330 893-3636
  Walnut Creek (G-14471)
East End Ro Burton Inc........................E..... 440 942-2742
  Willoughby (G-15190)
Eastlake Lodging LLC..........................A..... 440 953-8000
  Eastlake (G-8202)
Econo Lodge...D..... 216 475-4070
  Cleveland (G-4205)
Econo Lodge...E..... 419 627-8000
  Sandusky (G-12888)
Econo Lodge Wooster Inc....................E..... 330 264-8883
  Wooster (G-15336)
Emmett Dan House Ltd Partnr.............E..... 740 392-6886
  Mount Vernon (G-11485)
Epiqurian Inns......................................D..... 614 885-2600
  Worthington (G-15414)
Equity Lodging LLC.............................E..... 740 435-0427
  Cambridge (G-1570)
F F & W Inc..E..... 419 636-3123
  Bryan (G-1484)
Fairfield Inn Stes Clmbus Arprt............E..... 614 237-2100
  Columbus (G-5844)
Fairfield Inn..E..... 614 267-1111
  Columbus (G-5845)
Fairlawn Associates Ltd.......................C..... 330 867-5000
  Fairlawn (G-8478)
Falcon Plaza LLC................................E..... 419 352-4671
  Bowling Green (G-1319)
Fields Family Enterprises Inc..............E..... 513 897-1000
  Waynesville (G-14622)
Findlay Inn & Conference Ctr..............E..... 419 422-5682
  Findlay (G-8529)
First Group America............................E..... 908 281-4589
  Cincinnati (G-2673)
First Hospitality Company LLC...........D..... 614 864-4555
  Reynoldsburg (G-12663)

First Hotel Associates LP.....................E..... 614 228-3800
  Columbus (G-5862)
First Leveque LLC................................D..... 614 224-9500
  Columbus (G-5863)
First Management Company.................D..... 614 885-9696
  Columbus (G-5864)
First Tdt LLC...D..... 419 244-2444
  Toledo (G-13809)
Frog and Toad Inc................................E..... 419 877-1180
  Whitehouse (G-15142)
Future Lodging Northwood LLC...........E..... 419 666-2600
  Northwood (G-11975)
Gallipolis Hospitality Inc.......................C..... 740 446-0090
  Gallipolis (G-8756)
Ganga Hospitality Ohio LLC................E..... 614 870-3700
  Columbus (G-5909)
Gateway Hotel Ltd...............................E..... 513 772-2837
  Sharonville (G-12994)
Glenlaurel Inc.......................................E..... 740 385-4070
  Rockbridge (G-12735)
Glidden House Associates Ltd............E..... 216 231-8900
  Cleveland (G-4315)
Golden Lamb.......................................D..... 513 932-5065
  Lebanon (G-9767)
Good Venture Enterprises LLC...........E..... 740 282-0901
  Steubenville (G-13327)
Goodnight Inn Inc................................E..... 419 334-9551
  Fremont (G-8682)
Goodnight Inn Inc................................E..... 419 734-2274
  Port Clinton (G-12527)
Grand Heritage Hotel Portland............A..... 440 734-4477
  North Olmsted (G-11903)
Grandview Inn Inc...............................E..... 740 377-4388
  South Point (G-13175)
Granville Hospitality Llc......................D..... 740 587-3333
  Granville (G-8853)
Great Bear Lodge Sandusky LLC......B..... 419 609-6000
  Sandusky (G-12901)
Green Township Hospitality LLC........D..... 513 574-6000
  Cincinnati (G-2774)
Greenville Inn Inc................................E..... 937 548-3613
  Greenville (G-8875)
Grill Rest At Sheraton Suites..............E..... 614 436-0004
  Columbus (G-5957)
Hampton Inn.......................................E..... 513 752-8584
  Cincinnati (G-2106)
Hampton Inn.......................................E..... 937 387-0598
  Dayton (G-7392)
Hampton Inn.......................................E..... 740 282-9800
  Steubenville (G-13329)
Hampton Inn & Suite Inc....................E..... 440 234-0206
  Middleburg Heights (G-11116)
Hampton Inn Columbus East.............D..... 614 864-8383
  Pickerington (G-12402)
Hampton Inn Dry Ridge.....................E..... 859 823-7111
  Cincinnati (G-2797)
Hampton Inn of Huber Heights..........E..... 937 233-4300
  Dayton (G-7393)
Hampton Inn Stow.............................E..... 330 945-4160
  Stow (G-13372)
Hampton Inn Wooster.......................D..... 330 345-4424
  Wooster (G-15342)
Hard Rock Csino Cincinnati LLC......B..... 513 250-3375
  Cincinnati (G-2800)
Hardage Hotels I LLC.......................D..... 614 766-7762
  Dublin (G-8026)
Hariom Associates Medina LLC.....D..... 330 723-4994
  Medina (G-10839)
Hauck Hospitality LLC.....................D..... 513 563-8330
  Cincinnati (G-2805)
Hawkeye Hotels Inc........................E..... 614 782-8292
  Grove City (G-8924)

Employee Codes: A=Over 500 employees, B=251-500
C=101-250, D=51-100, E=20-50, F=10-19, G=1-9

70 HOTELS, ROOMING HOUSES, CAMPS, AND OTHER LODGING PLACES

He Hari Inc .... D 614 436-0700
   Worthington *(G-15419)*

Hilton Garden Inn .... D 614 263-7200
   Columbus *(G-5994)*

Hilton Garden Inn .... E 614 539-8944
   Grove City *(G-8925)*

Hilton Garden Inns MGT LLC .... B 937 247-5850
   Miamisburg *(G-11061)*

Hilton Grdn Inn - Cleveland E .... E 440 646-1777
   Cleveland *(G-4365)*

Hilton Grdn Inn Clumbus Easton ...... E 877 782-9444
   Columbus *(G-5995)*

Hilton Grdn Inn Columbus Arprt .... E 614 231-2869
   Columbus *(G-5996)*

Hilton Polaris .... E 614 885-1600
   Columbus *(G-5261)*

Holiday Inn .... E 440 951-7333
   Mentor *(G-10947)*

Holiday Inn Ex Ht & Suites .... E 330 821-6700
   Alliance *(G-383)*

Holiday Inn Ex Ht Stes Lamalfa .... E 440 357-0384
   Mentor *(G-10948)*

Holiday Inn Express .... E 614 447-1212
   Columbus *(G-5998)*

Holiday Inn Express .... E 937 424-5757
   Dayton *(G-7407)*

Holiday Inn Express .... E 513 860-2900
   Fairfield *(G-8419)*

Holiday Inn Express .... E 740 385-7700
   Logan *(G-10025)*

Hollywood Casino Toledo .... C 419 661-5200
   Toledo *(G-13847)*

Hollywood Gming At Mhning Vly ...... D 330 505-8700
   Youngstown *(G-15630)*

Hopkins Partners .... C 216 267-1500
   Cleveland *(G-4377)*

Horseshoe Cleveland MGT LLC .... D 216 297-4777
   Cleveland *(G-4380)*

Hospitality Inc .... D 419 227-0112
   Lima *(G-9906)*

Host Cincinnati Hotel LLC .... C 513 621-7700
   Cincinnati *(G-2850)*

Hoster Hotels LLC .... E 419 931-8900
   Perrysburg *(G-12345)*

Hotel .... E 614 373-2002
   Columbus *(G-6009)*

Hotel 1100 Carnegie Opco L P .... C 216 658-6400
   Cleveland *(G-4383)*

Hotel 2345 LLC .... E 614 766-7762
   Dublin *(G-8031)*

Hotel 50 S Front Opco L P .... D 614 885-3334
   Columbus *(G-6010)*

Hotel 50 S Front Opco LP .... D 614 228-4600
   Columbus *(G-6011)*

Hotel 75 E State Opco L P .... D 614 365-4500
   Columbus *(G-6012)*

Hotel Dayton Opco L P .... D 937 432-9161
   Miamisburg *(G-11062)*

Hotel Stow LP .... E 330 945-9722
   Stow *(G-13375)*

Hpt Trs Ihg-2 Inc .... E 614 461-4100
   Columbus *(G-6014)*

Hst Lessee Cincinnati LLC .... C 513 852-2702
   Cincinnati *(G-2853)*

Hyatt Corporation .... C 216 575-1234
   Cleveland *(G-4396)*

Hyatt Corporation .... D 614 463-1234
   Columbus *(G-6031)*

Hyatt Corporation .... D 614 228-1234
   Columbus *(G-6032)*

Hyatt Regency Columbus .... B 614 463-1234
   Columbus *(G-6033)*

IA Urban Htels Bchwood Trs LLC .... D 216 765-8066
   Beachwood *(G-801)*

Ihg Management (maryland) LLC ..... C 614 461-4100
   Columbus *(G-6039)*

Impac Hotel Group LLC .... E 440 238-8800
   Strongsville *(G-13465)*

Independent Hotel Partners LLC ...... D 216 524-0700
   Cleveland *(G-4406)*

Indiana Hospitality Group .... D 937 505-1670
   Springfield *(G-13258)*

Indus Airport Hotels I LLC .... D 614 231-2869
   Columbus *(G-6046)*

Indus Airport Hotels II LLC .... D 614 235-0717
   Columbus *(G-6047)*

Indus Hilliard Hotel LLC .... E 614 334-1800
   Hilliard *(G-9204)*

Indus Hotel 77 LLC .... D 614 223-1400
   Columbus *(G-6048)*

Indus Newark Hotel LLC .... E 740 322-6455
   Newark *(G-11709)*

Indus Newark Hotel LLC .... E 740 322-6455
   Columbus *(G-6049)*

Inn At Marietta Ltd .... E 740 373-9600
   Marietta *(G-10375)*

Inn At Olentangy Trail .... E 740 417-9287
   Delaware *(G-7806)*

Inn At Wickliffe LLC .... E 440 585-0600
   Wickliffe *(G-15154)*

Inn Hampton and Suites .... E 614 473-9911
   Columbus *(G-6053)*

Inn Hampton and Suites .... E 440 324-7755
   Elyria *(G-8262)*

Island Hospitality MGT LLC .... E 614 864-8844
   Columbus *(G-6075)*

Ja Htl LLC .... E 330 467-1981
   Macedonia *(G-10194)*

Jack Cleveland Casino LLC .... E 216 297-4777
   Cleveland *(G-4429)*

Jackson I-94 Ltd Partnership .... D 614 793-2244
   Dublin *(G-8042)*

Jag Guru Inc .... D 614 552-2400
   Columbus *(G-6081)*

Jagi Clvland - Indpendence LLC ...... C 216 524-8050
   Cleveland *(G-4431)*

Jagi Springhill LLC .... E 216 264-4190
   Independence *(G-9438)*

Jai Bapa Swami LLC .... E 513 791-2822
   Blue Ash *(G-1190)*

Jai Guru II Inc .... D 614 920-2400
   Columbus *(G-6082)*

Janessa Inc .... D 740 687-4823
   Lancaster *(G-9726)*

Jay Ganesh LLC .... E 740 344-2136
   Newark *(G-11710)*

Kaival Corporation .... E 330 467-1981
   Macedonia *(G-10196)*

Kay Surati .... E 419 727-8725
   Toledo *(G-13875)*

KDM and Associates LLC .... D 614 853-6199
   Columbus *(G-6106)*

Kenyon College .... E 740 427-2202
   Gambier *(G-8774)*

Khodiyar Inc .... E 419 589-2200
   Mansfield *(G-10278)*

Kishan Inc .... D 330 821-5688
   Alliance *(G-386)*

Kmb Management Services Corp .... D 330 263-2660
   Wooster *(G-15349)*

Kribha LLC .... E 740 788-8991
   Newark *(G-11711)*

Krish Hospitality LLC .... D 859 351-1060
   Dayton *(G-7446)*

Lake Erie Hospitality LLC .... D 419 547-6660
   Clyde *(G-5205)*

Lake Hospitality Inc .... E 440 579-0300
   Concord Township *(G-6929)*

Lakeland Motel Inc .... E 419 734-2101
   Port Clinton *(G-12536)*

Lancaster Host LLC .... E 740 654-4445
   Lancaster *(G-9731)*

Lander Hotel Group LLC .... E 330 590-8040
   Medina *(G-10851)*

Landmark Star Properties Inc .... E 937 316-5252
   Greenville *(G-8879)*

Lane Avenue Hotel Holdings LLC .... E 614 486-5433
   Upper Arlington *(G-14279)*

Lawnfield Mentor LLC .... E 440 205-7378
   Mentor *(G-10963)*

Levis Commons Hotel LLC .... D 419 873-3573
   Perrysburg *(G-12353)*

Liberty Ashtabula Holdings .... E 330 872-6000
   Newton Falls *(G-11777)*

Liberty Ctr Lodging Assoc LLC .... E 608 833-4100
   Liberty Township *(G-9854)*

Liberty Hospitality Inc .... E 330 759-3180
   Youngstown *(G-15649)*

Liberty Mahoning LLC .... E 330 549-0070
   North Lima *(G-11891)*

LLC Moon Dye .... E 440 623-9016
   Brecksville *(G-1358)*

Lmn Development LLC .... C 419 433-7200
   Sandusky *(G-12910)*

Lodging Assoc St Clrsville Inc .... E 740 695-5038
   Saint Clairsville *(G-12798)*

Lodging Industry Inc .... E 419 625-7070
   Sandusky *(G-12911)*

Lq Management LLC .... E 513 771-0300
   Cincinnati *(G-2992)*

Lq Management LLC .... E 216 447-1133
   Cleveland *(G-4507)*

Lq Management LLC .... E 419 774-0005
   Mansfield *(G-10283)*

Lytle Park Inn LLC .... E 513 621-4500
   Cincinnati *(G-2997)*

M&C Hotel Interests Inc .... C 937 778-8100
   Piqua *(G-12446)*

Mad River Mountain Resort .... E 937 303-3646
   Zanesfield *(G-15764)*

Main Hospitality Holdings LLC .... E 513 744-9900
   Cincinnati *(G-3004)*

Mansfield Hotel Partnership .... E 419 529-1000
   Mansfield *(G-10287)*

March Investors Ltd .... E 740 373-5353
   Marietta *(G-10382)*

Marcus Hotels Inc .... C 614 228-3800
   Columbus *(G-6194)*

Marion Lodge .... E 740 389-4300
   Marion *(G-10440)*

Marriott .... E 440 243-8785
   Cleveland *(G-4525)*

Marriott .... E 440 234-6688
   Cleveland *(G-4526)*

Marriott Hotel Services Inc .... C 216 252-5333
   Cleveland *(G-4527)*

Marriott International Inc .... E 216 696-9200
   Cleveland *(G-4528)*

Martel Lodging Ltd .... E 740 373-7373
   Marietta *(G-10388)*

Mason Family Resorts LLC .... B 608 237-5871
   Mason *(G-10577)*

Meander Hspitality Group V LLC ..... E 740 948-9305
   Jeffersonville *(G-9540)*

Meander Hsptality Group II LLC ...... E 330 422-0500
   Streetsboro *(G-13422)*

SIC SECTION
70 HOTELS, ROOMING HOUSES, CAMPS, AND OTHER LODGING PLACES

Mentor Hospitality LLC .... E 440 951-7333
 Mentor *(G-10969)*

Mercer Hospitality Inc .... E 937 615-0140
 Piqua *(G-12447)*

Metropolitan Hotel LLC .... D 216 239-1200
 Cleveland *(G-4568)*

Microtel Inn .... D 614 277-0705
 Grove City *(G-8934)*

Middletown Innkeepers Inc .... E 513 942-3440
 Fairfield *(G-8431)*

Mnm Hotels Inc .... D 740 385-1700
 Logan *(G-10035)*

Mohammad Shoaib .... E 513 831-7829
 Milford *(G-11244)*

Moody Nat Cy Dt Clumbus Mt LLC .... E 614 228-3200
 Columbus *(G-6259)*

Motel Investments Marietta Inc .... E 740 374-8190
 Marietta *(G-10393)*

Mrn-Newgar Hotel Ltd .... E 216 443-1000
 Cleveland *(G-4607)*

Mt Vernon Star Properties Inc .... E 740 392-1900
 Mount Vernon *(G-11502)*

N P Motel System Inc .... E 330 492-5030
 Canton *(G-1816)*

N P Motel System Inc .... E 330 339-7731
 New Philadelphia *(G-11660)*

Naffah South LLC .... E 330 420-0111
 Lisbon *(G-10006)*

Natraj Corporation .... E 614 875-7770
 Grove City *(G-8940)*

Neighborhood Hospitality Inc .... E 740 588-9244
 Zanesville *(G-15820)*

Nf II Cleveland Op Co LLC .... E 216 443-9043
 Cleveland *(G-4643)*

Northern Tier Hospitality LLC .... E 570 888-7711
 Westlake *(G-15089)*

Northfield Park Associates LLC .... C 330 908-7625
 Northfield *(G-11961)*

Northland Hotel Inc .... E 614 885-1601
 Columbus *(G-6368)*

Northtowne Square Ltd Partnr .... E 419 691-8911
 Oregon *(G-12137)*

Ntk Hotel Group II LLC .... D 614 559-2000
 Columbus *(G-6376)*

Oakwood Hospitality Corp .... E 440 786-1998
 Bedford *(G-978)*

Oh-16 Clmbus Wrthngton Prprty .... E 614 885-1557
 Columbus *(G-6386)*

Oh-16 Clvland Wstlake Prprty S .... E 440 892-4275
 Westlake *(G-15090)*

Ohio State Parks Inc .... D 513 664-3504
 College Corner *(G-5222)*

Omsagar Hotels Ltd .... D 703 675-7785
 Jeffersonville *(G-9541)*

Optima 777 LLC .... E 216 771-7700
 Cleveland *(G-4704)*

Oxford Hospitality Group Inc .... E 513 524-0114
 Oxford *(G-12214)*

Oxford Motel & LP .... E 513 523-0000
 Oxford *(G-12215)*

Pac Associates Inc .... D 330 869-9000
 Fairlawn *(G-8493)*

Pacific Heritg Inn Polaris LLC .... E 614 880-9080
 Columbus *(G-5276)*

Paradise Hotels LLC .... E 937 836-8339
 Englewood *(G-8317)*

Park & Spruce Acquisitions LLC .... E 614 227-6100
 Columbus *(G-6498)*

Park Hospitality LLC .... E 419 525-6000
 Mansfield *(G-10310)*

Park Hotels & Resorts Inc .... E 513 421-9100
 Cincinnati *(G-3183)*

Park Inn .... D 419 241-3000
 Toledo *(G-13956)*

Parkins Incorporated .... E 614 334-1800
 Hilliard *(G-9226)*

Patel LLC .... E 330 759-3180
 Youngstown *(G-15689)*

Payal Development LLC .... E 937 429-2222
 Beavercreek *(G-892)*

Peacock Hotels LLC .... E 330 725-1395
 Medina *(G-10875)*

Peitro Properties Ltd Partnr .... E 216 328-7777
 Cleveland *(G-4736)*

Penn National Gaming Inc .... E 614 308-3333
 Columbus *(G-6512)*

Penn National Holding Company .... C 419 661-5200
 Toledo *(G-13962)*

PH Fairborn Ht Owner 2800 LLC .... D 937 426-7800
 Beavercreek *(G-894)*

Pikes Inc .... E 440 275-2000
 Austinburg *(G-633)*

Playhouse Square Foundation .... C 216 615-7500
 Cleveland *(G-4758)*

Plaza Inn Foods Inc .... E 937 354-2181
 Mount Victory *(G-11512)*

Polaris Innkeepers LLC .... E 614 568-0770
 Westerville *(G-14928)*

Premier Hotel Group LLC .... D 937 754-9109
 Fairborn *(G-8380)*

Premier Hotels Inc .... E 419 747-2227
 Ontario *(G-12123)*

Primary Dayton Innkeepers LLC .... E 937 938-9550
 Dayton *(G-7565)*

Priya Pvt Ltd .... E 740 389-1998
 Marion *(G-10450)*

Qh Management Company LLC .... E 440 497-1100
 Concord Township *(G-6932)*

Quail Hollow Management Inc .... C 440 639-4000
 Concord Township *(G-6933)*

Quality Inn Toledo Airport .... E 419 867-1144
 Holland *(G-9301)*

Quality Team Management Inc .... E 937 490-2000
 Middletown *(G-11182)*

R & H Service Inc .... E 330 626-2888
 Streetsboro *(G-13425)*

R & K Gorby LLC .... E 419 222-0004
 Lima *(G-9953)*

▲ R P L Corporation .... E 937 335-0021
 Troy *(G-14153)*

Radha Corporation .... D 614 851-5599
 Columbus *(G-6560)*

Rama Inc .... E 614 473-9888
 Columbus *(G-6561)*

Ramada Elyria Rsrvtons Wrld Wl .... E 440 324-5411
 Elyria *(G-8290)*

RB Knoxville LLC .... D 865 523-2300
 Columbus *(G-6562)*

Red Bank Hetzel LP .... E 513 834-9191
 Cincinnati *(G-3276)*

Red Roof Inns Inc .... E 330 644-7748
 Akron *(G-277)*

Red Roof Inns Inc .... E 330 499-1970
 Canton *(G-1842)*

Red Roof Inns Inc .... E 216 447-0030
 Cleveland *(G-4814)*

Red Roof Inns Inc .... E 440 892-7920
 Cleveland *(G-4815)*

Red Roof Inns Inc .... E 440 202-1521
 Cleveland *(G-4816)*

Red Roof Inns Inc .... E 614 267-9941
 Columbus *(G-6567)*

Red Roof Inns Inc .... D 614 224-6539
 Columbus *(G-6568)*

Red Roof Inns Inc .... E 740 288-1200
 Jackson *(G-9524)*

Red Roof Inns Inc .... E 937 866-0705
 Miamisburg *(G-11088)*

Red Roof Inns Inc .... E 330 758-1999
 Poland *(G-12507)*

Red Roof Inns Inc .... E 740 695-4057
 Saint Clairsville *(G-12812)*

Red Roof Inns Inc .... E 419 536-0118
 Toledo *(G-13983)*

Red Roof Inns Inc .... E 440 946-9872
 Willoughby *(G-15220)*

Red Roof Inns Inc .... A 614 744-2600
 New Albany *(G-11584)*

Regal Hospitality LLC .... C 614 436-0004
 Columbus *(G-6572)*

Renaissance Hotel MGT Co LLC .... D 614 882-6800
 Westerville *(G-14934)*

Renaissance Hotel Operating Co .... A 216 696-5600
 Cleveland *(G-4826)*

Renaissance Hotel Operating Co .... B 614 228-5050
 Columbus *(G-6577)*

▲ Renthotel Dayton LLC .... D 937 461-4700
 Dayton *(G-7585)*

Req/Jqh Holdings Inc .... B 513 891-1066
 Blue Ash *(G-1235)*

Residence Inn .... E 614 222-2610
 Columbus *(G-6581)*

Residence Inn By Marriott .... E 513 771-2525
 Cincinnati *(G-3291)*

Residence Inn By Marriott LLC .... E 513 530-5060
 Blue Ash *(G-1236)*

Residence Inn By Marriott LLC .... E 614 222-2610
 Columbus *(G-6582)*

Residence Inn By Marriott LLC .... E 614 885-0799
 Columbus *(G-6583)*

Residence Inn By Marriott LLC .... E 440 392-0800
 Mentor *(G-10992)*

Residence Inn By Marriott LLC .... E 440 638-5856
 Middleburg Heights *(G-11123)*

Residence Inn Toledo Maumee .... E 419 891-2233
 Maumee *(G-10760)*

Rhea Aryan Inc .... C 937 865-0077
 Miamisburg *(G-11090)*

Richfeld Bnquet Cnfrnce Ctr LL .... E 330 659-6151
 Richfield *(G-12708)*

Richfield Inn Inc .... E 248 946-5838
 Maumee *(G-10762)*

Ridgehills Hotel Ltd Partnr .... D 440 585-0600
 Wickliffe *(G-15162)*

Riley Hotel Group LLC .... E 330 590-8040
 Medina *(G-10884)*

Ritz-Carlton Hotel Company LLC .... E 216 623-1300
 Cleveland *(G-4842)*

Riverview Hospitality Corp .... D 330 339-7000
 New Philadelphia *(G-11664)*

Riverview Hotel LLC .... E 614 268-8700
 Columbus *(G-6600)*

Rlj III - Em Clmbus Lessee LLC .... D 614 890-8600
 Columbus *(G-6601)*

Rock Hotel Ltd LLC .... E 216 520-2020
 Cleveland *(G-4848)*

Rockbridge Capital LLC .... D 614 246-2400
 Columbus *(G-6605)*

Rockside Hospitality LLC .... D 216 524-0700
 Independence *(G-9477)*

Roschmans Restaurant ADM .... E 419 225-8300
 Lima *(G-9955)*

Rukh-Jagi Holdings LLC .... D 330 494-2770
 Canton *(G-1848)*

S & S Management Inc .... D 937 235-2000
 Dayton *(G-7601)*

70 HOTELS, ROOMING HOUSES, CAMPS, AND OTHER LODGING PLACES

S & S Management Inc .... D 567 356-4151
 Wapakoneta *(G-14491)*
S & S Management Inc .... D 937 382-5858
 Wilmington *(G-15272)*
S & S Realty Ltd .... E 419 625-0362
 Sandusky *(G-12928)*
S&S Management .... E 937 332-1700
 Troy *(G-14158)*
Sachs Management Corp .... D 740 282-0901
 Steubenville *(G-13342)*
Sage Hospitality Resources LLC .... C 513 771-2080
 Cincinnati *(G-3340)*
Sahaj Hospitality Ltd .... D 740 593-5565
 Athens *(G-588)*
Salt Fork Resort Club Inc .... E 740 498-8116
 Kimbolton *(G-9641)*
Salvation Army .... E 937 461-2769
 Cincinnati *(G-3346)*
Sandy Shores Partners Inc .... D 513 469-6130
 Blue Ash *(G-1240)*
Saw Mill Creek Ltd .... D 419 433-3800
 Huron *(G-9392)*
Sb Hotel LLC .... E 614 793-2244
 Dublin *(G-8115)*
SC Resort Ltd .... C 419 433-3800
 Huron *(G-9393)*
Scioto Lodging Inc .... D 740 851-6140
 Chillicothe *(G-2091)*
Select Hotels Group LLC .... D 513 754-0003
 Mason *(G-10606)*
SGB Management Inc .... E 614 539-1177
 Grove City *(G-8954)*
Shaker House .... D 216 991-6000
 Cleveland *(G-4898)*
Shihasi Starwind Ne Llp .... E 513 683-9700
 Cincinnati *(G-3370)*
Shir-Sath Inc .... D 330 759-9820
 Girard *(G-8825)*
Shree Hospitality Corporation .... E 330 666-9300
 Copley *(G-6963)*
Shree Sava Ltd .... E 440 324-7676
 Elyria *(G-8294)*
Shree Shiv LLC .... E 419 897-5555
 Maumee *(G-10765)*
Shri Guru Inc .... E 614 552-2071
 Columbus *(G-6676)*
Shri Mahalaxmi Inc .... E 614 860-9804
 Pickerington *(G-12412)*
Sidney Host LLC .... E 937 498-8888
 Sidney *(G-13051)*
Sidney Lodges .... E 937 492-3001
 Sidney *(G-13052)*
Six Continents Hotels Inc .... E 216 707-4100
 Cleveland *(G-4911)*
Siya Motel LLC .... E 330 264-6211
 Wooster *(G-15377)*
Sk Hospitality LLC .... C 419 294-3891
 Upper Sandusky *(G-14293)*
Skyline Clvland Rnaissance LLC .... D 216 696-5600
 Cleveland *(G-4913)*
Sns Hospitality LLC .... E 740 522-8499
 Heath *(G-9140)*
Solon Lodging Associates LLC .... C 440 248-9600
 Solon *(G-13144)*
Somnus Corporation .... E 740 695-3961
 Saint Clairsville *(G-12815)*
Sortino Management & Dev Co .... E 419 627-8884
 Sandusky *(G-12933)*
Spread Eagle Tavern Inc .... C 330 223-1583
 Hanoverton *(G-9095)*
Spring Hill Suites .... E 513 381-8300
 Cincinnati *(G-3399)*

Sps Inc .... E 937 339-7801
 Troy *(G-14160)*
Sree SAI Hotels LLC .... E 630 440-0765
 Eastlake *(G-8209)*
Staybridge Suites .... E 330 945-4180
 Stow *(G-13391)*
Strang Corporation .... E 216 961-6767
 Cleveland *(G-4955)*
Strongsvlle Ldging Assoc I Ltd .... D 440 238-8800
 Strongsville *(G-13488)*
Summit Hotel Trs 144 LLC .... E 216 443-9043
 Cleveland *(G-4958)*
Sun Development & Mgt Corp .... C 614 801-9000
 Grove City *(G-8957)*
Sun Lodging LLC .... E 330 670-0888
 Copley *(G-6965)*
Sunrise Hospitality Inc .... E 567 331-8900
 Perrysburg *(G-12372)*
Sunrise Hospitality Inc .... E 567 331-8613
 Perrysburg *(G-12373)*
Sunrise Hospitality Inc .... E 937 492-6010
 Sidney *(G-13056)*
Super 8 .... E 419 529-0444
 Ashland *(G-513)*
Sycamore Lake Inc .... E 440 729-9775
 Chesterland *(G-2043)*
Synergy Hotels LLC .... E 614 492-9000
 Obetz *(G-12084)*
Tharaldson Hospitality MGT .... C 513 947-9402
 Cincinnati *(G-2115)*
TI Resort LLC .... E 216 464-5130
 Cleveland *(G-5019)*
Toledo Inn North LLC .... E 419 476-0170
 Toledo *(G-14059)*
Toledo Inns Inc .... D 440 243-4040
 Cleveland *(G-5023)*
Town Inn Co LLC .... D 614 221-3281
 Columbus *(G-6775)*
Towne Place Suites Worthington .... E 614 885-1557
 Columbus *(G-6776)*
TownePlace Management LLC .... D 419 724-0044
 Oregon *(G-12145)*
TownePlace Suites By Marriott .... E 513 774-0610
 Cincinnati *(G-3496)*
TownePlace Suites By Marriott .... E 419 425-9545
 Findlay *(G-8594)*
TownePlace Suites By Marriott .... E 440 871-3756
 Westlake *(G-15116)*
TownePlace Suites Dayton North .... E 937 898-5700
 Dayton *(G-7674)*
Townplace Suites By Marriott .... E 440 816-9300
 Cleveland *(G-5026)*
Travelodge Zanesville .... E 740 453-0611
 Zanesville *(G-15832)*
Troy Hotel II LLC .... E 937 332-1446
 Troy *(G-14164)*
Troy Motel Assn Inc .... E 614 299-4300
 Columbus *(G-6793)*
Tudor Arms Mstr Subtenant LLC .... D 216 696-6611
 Cleveland *(G-5040)*
Tuttle Inn Developers LLC .... E 614 793-5500
 Dublin *(G-8144)*
Union Centre Hotel LLC .... C 513 874-7335
 West Chester *(G-14786)*
United Hsptality Solutions LLC .... E 800 238-0487
 Buffalo *(G-1521)*
Universal Development MGT Inc .... E 330 759-7017
 Girard *(G-8829)*
Uph Holdings LLC .... D 614 447-9977
 Columbus *(G-6826)*
US Hotel Osp Ventures LLC .... E 740 435-9000
 Cambridge *(G-1586)*

US Hotel Osp Ventures LLC .... D 740 767-2112
 Glouster *(G-8836)*
US Hotel Osp Ventures LLC .... E 440 564-9144
 Newbury *(G-11765)*
US Hotel Osp Ventures LLC .... E 419 836-9009
 Oregon *(G-12146)*
Valam Hospitality Inc .... E 419 232-6040
 Van Wert *(G-14354)*
Valley Hospitality Inc .... D 740 374-9660
 Marietta *(G-10409)*
Valley View Management Co Inc .... E 419 886-4000
 Bellville *(G-1052)*
Value Inn Inc .... E 888 315-2378
 Grove City *(G-8963)*
Velocity A Managed Svcs Co Inc .... D 281 221-4444
 Holland *(G-9312)*
Visicon Inc .... E 937 879-2696
 Fairborn *(G-8385)*
Vjp Hospitality Ltd .... E 614 475-8383
 Columbus *(G-6853)*
W & H Realty Inc .... E 513 891-1066
 Cincinnati *(G-3636)*
Wadsworth Hie Management Inc .... D 330 334-7666
 Wadsworth *(G-14457)*
Welcome Hospitality Corp .... E 937 325-5356
 Springfield *(G-13311)*
West Park Shell .... E 216 252-5086
 Cleveland *(G-5132)*
Westpost Columbus LLC .... E 614 885-1885
 Columbus *(G-6881)*
Widewaters Edr Solon Ht Co LLC .... E 440 542-0400
 Solon *(G-13164)*
Winegrdner Hmmons Ht Group LLC .... C 513 891-1066
 Cincinnati *(G-3674)*
Wingate Inc .... E 216 591-1061
 Cleveland *(G-5151)*
Wingate By Wyndham Dyton Frbor .... E 937 912-9350
 Beavercreek *(G-914)*
Wingate Inn .... E 614 844-5888
 Columbus *(G-5285)*
Wingate Inn .... D 330 422-9900
 Streetsboro *(G-13436)*
Wm Columbus Hotel LLC .... C 614 228-3800
 Columbus *(G-6899)*
Woodson Operations One Ltd .... E 419 420-1776
 Findlay *(G-8598)*
Woodspring Hotels Holdings LLC .... E 614 272-2170
 Columbus *(G-6902)*
Wright Executive Ht Ltd Partnr .... D 937 426-7800
 Beavercreek *(G-915)*
Youngstown Hospitality LLC .... E 330 759-9555
 Youngstown *(G-15758)*
Youngstown Wlcome Hsptlity LLC .... C 330 759-6600
 Girard *(G-8831)*

7021 Rooming and boarding houses

A M Management Inc .... E 937 426-6500
 Beavercreek *(G-855)*
Lodging First LLC .... E 614 792-2770
 Dublin *(G-8056)*

7032 Sporting and recreational camps

Archdiocese of Cincinnati .... E 513 729-1725
 Cincinnati *(G-2212)*
Ashland Training Center .... E 419 281-2767
 Ashland *(G-476)*
Camp Ho Mita Koda Foundation .... E 440 739-4095
 Newbury *(G-11759)*
Camp Patmos Inc .... E 419 746-2214
 Kelleys Island *(G-9552)*
Countryside Yung MNS Chrstn As .... D 513 677-3702
 Maineville *(G-10227)*

SIC SECTION

72 PERSONAL SERVICES

Echoing Hills Village Inc .... D 740 594-3541
   Athens *(G-567)*

Echoing Hills Village Inc .... D 937 854-5151
   Dayton *(G-7326)*

Echoing Hills Village Inc .... D 937 237-7881
   Dayton *(G-7327)*

Echoing Hills Village Inc .... E 440 323-0915
   Elyria *(G-8243)*

Echoing Hills Village Inc .... D 440 989-1400
   Lorain *(G-10071)*

Echoing Hills Village Inc .... E 440 986-3085
   South Amherst *(G-13168)*

Echoing Hills Village Inc .... C 740 327-2311
   Warsaw *(G-14591)*

Family YMCA of LANcstr&fairfld .... D 740 277-7373
   Lancaster *(G-9723)*

Great Mami Vly Yung MNS Chrstn ..... D 513 887-0001
   Hamilton *(G-9046)*

Great Miami Valley YMCA .... D 513 829-3091
   Fairfield *(G-8417)*

Great Miami Valley YMCA .... D 513 892-9622
   Fairfield Township *(G-8461)*

Great Miami Valley YMCA .... D 513 887-0014
   Hamilton *(G-9048)*

Great Miami Valley YMCA .... D 513 868-9622
   Hamilton *(G-9049)*

Joy Outdoor Education Ctr LLC .... E 937 289-2031
   Clarksville *(G-3730)*

Lake Cnty Yung MNS Chrstn Assn .... C 440 352-3303
   Painesville *(G-12231)*

Lake County YMCA .... C 440 428-5125
   Madison *(G-10219)*

Lake County YMCA .... C 440 259-2724
   Perry *(G-12307)*

Lake County YMCA .... C 440 946-1160
   Willoughby *(G-15198)*

Lima Family YMCA .... D 419 223-6055
   Lima *(G-9923)*

Ohio Ffa Camps Inc .... E 330 627-2208
   Carrollton *(G-1911)*

Procamps Inc .... E 513 745-5855
   Blue Ash *(G-1223)*

Rockwell Springs Trout Club .... E 419 684-7971
   Clyde *(G-5208)*

Round Lk Christn Assembly Inc .... E 419 827-2018
   Lakeville *(G-9656)*

Stars Yuth Enrchment Prgram In ...... E 513 978-7735
   Trotwood *(G-14128)*

Sycamore Board of Education .... C 513 489-3937
   Montgomery *(G-11375)*

West Ohio Cnfrnce of Untd Mthd ...... E 614 844-6200
   Worthington *(G-15468)*

Y M C A of Ashland Ohio Inc .... D 419 289-0626
   Ashland *(G-516)*

YMCA .... E 330 823-1930
   Alliance *(G-408)*

Young Mens Christian Assn .... D 330 480-5656
   Youngstown *(G-15754)*

Young MNS Chrstn Assn Cntl STA ... D 330 305-5437
   Canton *(G-1889)*

Young MNS Chrstn Assn Cntl STA ... D 330 498-4082
   Canton *(G-1890)*

Young MNS Chrstn Assn Cntl STA ... D 330 875-1611
   Louisville *(G-10124)*

Young MNS Chrstn Assn Cntl STA ... D 330 830-6275
   Massillon *(G-10675)*

Young MNS Chrstn Assn Grter CL .... E 440 285-7543
   Chardon *(G-2027)*

Young MNS Chrstn Assn Grter CL .... D 216 521-8400
   Lakewood *(G-9688)*

Young MNS Chrstn Assn Grter CN .... D 513 241-9622
   Cincinnati *(G-3694)*

Young MNS Chrstn Assn Grter CN .... C 513 923-4466
   Cincinnati *(G-3695)*

Young MNS Chrstn Assn Grter CN .... C 513 921-0911
   Cincinnati *(G-3696)*

Young MNS Chrstn Assn Grter CN .... A 513 932-1424
   Lebanon *(G-9800)*

Young MNS Chrstn Assn Grter Dy .... C 937 312-1810
   Dayton *(G-7733)*

Young MNS Chrstn Assn Grter Dy .... C 513 932-3756
   Oregonia *(G-12150)*

Young MNS Chrstn Assn Grter NY .... C 740 392-9622
   Mount Vernon *(G-11509)*

Young MNS Chrstn Assn of Akron .... E 330 983-5573
   Akron *(G-372)*

Young MNS Chrstn Assn of Akron .... D 330 376-1335
   Clinton *(G-5197)*

Young MNS Chrstn Assn of Akron .... D 330 923-5223
   Cuyahoga Falls *(G-7119)*

Young MNS Chrstn Assn of Akron .... E 330 467-8366
   Macedonia *(G-10210)*

Young MNS Chrstn Assn of Grter ..... C 419 866-9622
   Maumee *(G-10782)*

Young MNS Chrstn Assn of Grter ..... C 419 691-3523
   Oregon *(G-12148)*

Young MNS Chrstn Assn of Grter ..... D 419 474-3995
   Toledo *(G-14112)*

Young MNS Chrstn Assn of Grter ..... D 419 241-7218
   Toledo *(G-14115)*

Young MNS Chrstn Assn of Grter ..... E 419 729-8135
   Sylvania *(G-13579)*

Young MNS Chrstn Assn of Mt Vr ..... D 740 392-9622
   Mount Vernon *(G-11510)*

Young MNS Chrstn Assn of Van W ... E 419 238-0443
   Van Wert *(G-14362)*

Young Wns Chrstn Assn Clvland ...... E 216 881-6878
   Cleveland *(G-5167)*

Young Wns Chrstn Assn of Cnton .... D 330 453-0789
   Canton *(G-1892)*

Young Womens Christian Assn .... D 614 224-9121
   Columbus *(G-6917)*

YWCA Mahoning Valley .... E 330 746-6361
   Youngstown *(G-15762)*

YWCA of Greater Cincinnati .... D 513 241-7090
   Cincinnati *(G-3697)*

YWCA of Northwest Ohio .... D 419 241-3235
   Toledo *(G-14117)*

7033 Trailer parks and campsites

Big Brthers Big Ssters Cntl OH .... E 614 839-2447
   Columbus *(G-5437)*

Cedar Point Park LLC .... E 419 627-2106
   Sandusky *(G-12878)*

Great Miami Valley YMCA .... D 513 867-0600
   Hamilton *(G-9047)*

Great Parks Forever .... E 513 522-4357
   Cincinnati *(G-2765)*

Muskingum Wtrshed Cnsrvncy Dst ... C 330 343-6780
   Mineral City *(G-11301)*

Muskingum Wtrshed Cnsrvncy Dst ... C 740 685-6013
   Senecaville *(G-12950)*

Muskingum Wtrshed Cnsrvncy Dst ... D 330 343-6647
   New Philadelphia *(G-11659)*

Whiteys Restaurant Inc .... E 330 659-3600
   Richfield *(G-12713)*

7041 Membership-basis organization hotels

Rockwell Springs Trout Club .... E 419 684-7971
   Clyde *(G-5208)*

72 PERSONAL SERVICES

7211 Power laundries, family and commercial

Economy Linen & Towel Service Inc ...... C 937 222-4625
   Dayton *(G-7328)*

Evergreen Cooperative Ldry Inc .... C 216 268-3548
   Cleveland *(G-4227)*

Heights Laundry & Dry Cleaning .... E 216 932-9666
   Cleveland Heights *(G-5178)*

Midwest Laundry Inc .... D 513 563-5560
   Cincinnati *(G-3058)*

Morgan Services Inc .... C 937 223-5241
   Dayton *(G-7514)*

Reino Linen Service Inc .... D 419 637-2151
   Gibsonburg *(G-8806)*

7212 Garment pressing and cleaners' agents

Apc2 Inc .... E 513 231-5540
   Cincinnati *(G-2207)*

C&C Clean Team Enterprises LLC .... C 513 321-5100
   Cincinnati *(G-2299)*

7213 Linen supply

Ameripride Services Inc .... D 859 371-4037
   Cincinnati *(G-2189)*

Barberton Laundry and Clg Inc .... D 330 825-6911
   Barberton *(G-694)*

◆ Cintas Corporation No 1 .... A 513 459-1200
   Mason *(G-10533)*

Cintas Corporation No 2 .... C 513 965-0800
   Milford *(G-11223)*

Cintas Corporation No 2 .... D 800 444-2687
   Vandalia *(G-14370)*

Economy Linen & Towel Service Inc ...... C 937 222-4625
   Dayton *(G-7328)*

◆ G&K Services LLC .... B 513 459-1200
   Mason *(G-10552)*

Kimmel Corporation .... D 419 294-1959
   Upper Sandusky *(G-14290)*

Kramer Enterprises Inc .... D 419 422-7924
   Findlay *(G-8555)*

Midwest Laundry Inc .... D 513 563-5560
   Cincinnati *(G-3058)*

Morgan Services Inc .... C 216 241-3107
   Cleveland *(G-4599)*

Morgan Services Inc .... C 937 223-5241
   Dayton *(G-7514)*

Morgan Services Inc .... D 419 243-2214
   Toledo *(G-13928)*

Nucentury Textile Services LLC .... D 419 241-2267
   Toledo *(G-13942)*

She Is US .... D 863 315-1233
   Cleveland *(G-4901)*

Synergy Health North America Inc .... A 813 891-9550
   Mentor *(G-11001)*

Unifirst Corporation .... E 614 575-9999
   Blacklick *(G-1114)*

Unifirst Corporation .... E 937 746-0531
   Franklin *(G-8651)*

Van Dyne-Crotty Co .... D 440 248-6935
   Solon *(G-13158)*

Vestis Corporation .... C 513 533-1000
   Cincinnati *(G-3625)*

Vestis Corporation .... E 216 341-7400
   Cleveland *(G-5100)*

Vestis Corporation .... E 614 445-8341
   Columbus *(G-6847)*

Vestis Corporation .... E 937 223-6667
   Dayton *(G-7703)*

Vestis Corporation .... E 419 729-5454
   Toledo *(G-14092)*

7215 Coin-operated laundries and cleaning

Fox Cleaners Inc .... E 937 276-4171
   Dayton *(G-7364)*

72 PERSONAL SERVICES

Good Inc... D 740 592-9667
 Athens *(G-569)*

7216 Drycleaning plants, except rugs

A One Fine Dry Cleaners Inc............... E 513 731-7950
 Cincinnati *(G-2130)*
Apc2 Inc... E 513 231-5540
 Cincinnati *(G-2207)*
Dublin Cleaners Inc............................. D 614 764-9934
 Columbus *(G-5788)*
Fox Cleaners Inc................................. E 937 276-4171
 Dayton *(G-7364)*
Good Inc.. D 740 592-9667
 Athens *(G-569)*
Heights Laundry & Dry Cleaning........ E 216 932-9666
 Cleveland Heights *(G-5178)*
Kimmel Corporation............................. D 419 294-1959
 Upper Sandusky *(G-14290)*
Kramer Enterprises Inc........................ D 419 422-7924
 Findlay *(G-8555)*
Midwest Laundry Inc........................... D 513 563-5560
 Cincinnati *(G-3058)*
Miles Cleaning Services Inc................ E 216 626-0040
 Cleveland *(G-4582)*
Prime Valet Cleaners Inc..................... E 513 860-9595
 West Chester *(G-14747)*
Velco Inc.. E 513 772-4226
 Cincinnati *(G-3618)*
Vestis Corporation............................... E 937 223-6667
 Dayton *(G-7703)*
Widmers LLC...................................... C 513 321-5100
 Cincinnati *(G-3670)*
Wilkers Inc... E 513 851-4000
 Cincinnati *(G-3671)*

7217 Carpet and upholstery cleaning

Allen-Keith Construction Co................ D 330 266-2220
 Canton *(G-1659)*
B&L Acquisition Group LLC................ E 216 626-0040
 Bedford Heights *(G-994)*
Best Karpet Klean Ohio LLC.............. E 440 942-2481
 Cleveland *(G-3871)*
C&C Clean Team Enterprises LLC..... C 513 321-5100
 Cincinnati *(G-2299)*
Interfinish LLC..................................... E 216 662-6550
 Cleveland *(G-4418)*
Lazar Brothers Inc............................... E 440 585-9333
 Wickliffe *(G-15156)*
Martin Carpet Cleaning Company....... E 614 443-4655
 Columbus *(G-6199)*
Miles Cleaning Services Inc................ E 216 626-0040
 Cleveland *(G-4582)*
Stanley Steemer Intl Inc....................... E 614 764-2007
 Beavercreek Township *(G-950)*
Stanley Steemer Intl Inc....................... E 513 771-0213
 Cincinnati *(G-3411)*
Stanley Steemer Intl Inc....................... E 614 767-8017
 Cleveland *(G-4942)*
▲ Stanley Steemer Intl Inc................... C 614 764-2007
 Dublin *(G-8124)*
Teasdale Fnton Crpt Clg Rstrtn............ D 513 797-0900
 Cincinnati *(G-3446)*
Velco Inc.. E 513 772-4226
 Cincinnati *(G-3618)*
Widmers LLC...................................... C 513 321-5100
 Cincinnati *(G-3670)*
Wiggins Clg & Crpt Svc Inc................. D 937 279-9080
 Dayton *(G-7722)*

7218 Industrial launderers

Brent Industries Inc............................. E 419 382-8693
 Toledo *(G-13716)*
Cintas Corporation.............................. D 513 631-5750
 Cincinnati *(G-2443)*
◆ Cintas Corporation........................... A 513 459-1200
 Cincinnati *(G-2442)*
Cintas Corporation No 2...................... D 614 878-7313
 Columbus *(G-5572)*
Cintas Corporation No 3...................... E 513 459-1200
 Mason *(G-10536)*
Cintas R US Inc................................... D 513 459-1200
 Cincinnati *(G-2444)*
Cintas Sales Corporation.................... B 513 459-1200
 Cincinnati *(G-2445)*
Cintas-Rus LP..................................... E 513 459-1200
 Mason *(G-10538)*
◆ G&K Services LLC.......................... B 513 459-1200
 Mason *(G-10552)*
Kimmel Corporation............................. D 419 294-1959
 Upper Sandusky *(G-14290)*
Leef Bros Inc....................................... E 952 912-5500
 Mason *(G-10572)*
Midwest Laundry Inc........................... D 513 563-5560
 Cincinnati *(G-3058)*
Morgan Services Inc............................ C 216 241-3107
 Cleveland *(G-4599)*
Morgan Services Inc............................ D 419 243-2214
 Toledo *(G-13928)*
Unifirst Corporation............................. E 614 575-9999
 Blacklick *(G-1114)*
Unifirst Corporation............................. E 937 746-0531
 Franklin *(G-8651)*
Van Dyne-Crotty Co............................ D 740 432-7503
 Cambridge *(G-1587)*
Van Dyne-Crotty Co............................ D 440 248-6935
 Solon *(G-13158)*
Vestis Corporation............................... E 216 341-7400
 Cleveland *(G-5100)*
Vestis Corporation............................... E 614 445-8341
 Columbus *(G-6847)*
Vestis Corporation............................... E 937 223-6667
 Dayton *(G-7703)*
Vestis Corporation............................... C 419 729-5454
 Toledo *(G-14092)*

7219 Laundry and garment services, nec

Central Ohio Medical Textiles............. C 614 453-9274
 Columbus *(G-5540)*
◆ G&K Services LLC.......................... B 513 459-1200
 Mason *(G-10552)*
Hyo Ok Inc... E 614 876-7644
 Hilliard *(G-9203)*

7221 Photographic studios, portrait

Arctos Tech Solutions LLC.................. D 937 426-2808
 Beavercreek *(G-859)*
Fotosav Inc.. E 330 436-6500
 Akron *(G-167)*
Lifetouch Nat Schl Studios Inc............ E 330 497-1291
 Canton *(G-1795)*
Lifetouch Nat Schl Studios Inc............ E 440 234-1337
 Cleveland *(G-4494)*
Lifetouch Nat Schl Studios Inc............ E 423 892-3817
 Ontario *(G-12112)*
Lifetouch Nat Schl Studios Inc............ E 513 772-2110
 West Chester *(G-14723)*
Pam Johnsonident............................... E 419 946-4551
 Mount Gilead *(G-11464)*
Peters Main Street Photography......... E 740 852-2731
 London *(G-10049)*
Rapid Mortgage Company................... E 937 748-8888
 Cincinnati *(G-3273)*
Ripcho Studio Inc................................ E 216 631-0061
 Cleveland *(G-4841)*
Wp7pro Inc.. E 419 483-3364
 Bellevue *(G-1046)*

7231 Beauty shops

845 Yard Street LLC........................... E 614 484-6860
 Columbus *(G-5290)*
AFA Beauty Inc.................................... E 740 331-1655
 Athens *(G-554)*
American Salon Group LLC................ D 330 975-0085
 Medina *(G-10806)*
Bella Capelli Inc.................................. D 440 899-1225
 Westlake *(G-15038)*
Blowout Bar... E 614 732-0965
 Columbus *(G-5448)*
Casals Hair Salon Inc.......................... E 330 533-6766
 Canfield *(G-1624)*
Creative Hair Designs......................... E 419 425-4247
 Findlay *(G-8524)*
Elite Salon Distributors LLC................ E 419 902-0545
 Toledo *(G-13787)*
Face Forward Aesthetics LLC............. E 844 307-5929
 Columbus *(G-5841)*
Frank Santo LLC................................. E 216 831-9374
 Pepper Pike *(G-12299)*
▲ Fredrics Corporation....................... C 513 874-2226
 West Chester *(G-14695)*
Ihs Services Inc................................... D 614 396-9980
 Worthington *(G-15422)*
Jbentley Studio & Spa LLC................. D 614 790-8828
 Powell *(G-12593)*
JC Penney Corporation Inc................. D 419 394-7610
 Saint Marys *(G-12827)*
John Rbrts Hair Studio Spa Inc........... D 216 839-1430
 Mayfield Heights *(G-10787)*
Kenneths Hair Slons Day Spas I......... B 614 457-7712
 Columbus *(G-6112)*
Mato Inc... E 440 729-9008
 Chesterland *(G-2040)*
Mfh Inc... D 937 435-4701
 Dayton *(G-7485)*
Mfh Inc... E 937 435-4701
 Dayton *(G-7484)*
Mitchells Salon & Day Spa.................. C 513 793-0900
 West Chester *(G-14732)*
Mitchells Salon & Day Spa Inc............ D 513 793-0900
 Cincinnati *(G-3067)*
New View Management Group Inc..... D 513 733-4444
 Cincinnati *(G-3110)*
Nurtur Holdings LLC........................... E 614 487-3033
 Loveland *(G-10154)*
Nutur Holdings LLC............................. C 513 576-9333
 Loveland *(G-10155)*
Picasso For Nail LLC.......................... E 440 308-4470
 Solon *(G-13126)*
PS Lifestyle LLC.................................. A 440 600-1595
 Cleveland *(G-4796)*
Pure Concept Salon Inc...................... E 513 770-2120
 Mason *(G-10597)*
Queens Beauty Bar LLC..................... E 216 804-0533
 Cleveland *(G-4802)*
R L O Inc... E 937 620-9998
 Dayton *(G-7577)*
Reve Salon and Spa Inc...................... D 419 885-1140
 Sylvania *(G-13569)*
Salon Lofts.. E 440 356-1062
 Cleveland *(G-4872)*
Sugar & Spice Spa llc......................... D 513 319-0112
 Mason *(G-10612)*
Tanyas Image LLC.............................. E 513 386-9981
 Cincinnati *(G-3443)*
W Nail Bar LLC.................................... E 614 299-9587
 Columbus *(G-6863)*

SIC SECTION

73 BUSINESS SERVICES

Walmart Inc.. C 937 399-0370
   Springfield *(G-13310)*

Waxxpot Group Franchise LLC............ C 614 622-3018
   Columbus *(G-6871)*

7241 Barber shops

Mfh Inc.. E 937 435-4701
   Dayton *(G-7484)*

7261 Funeral service and crematories

Bell Vault and Monu Works Inc............. E 937 866-2444
   Miamisburg *(G-11025)*

Berkowitz Kmin Bkatz Mem Chpel......... E 216 932-7900
   Cleveland Heights *(G-5177)*

E F Boyd & Son Inc................................ E 216 791-0770
   Cleveland *(G-4193)*

Ferfolia Funeral Homes Inc................... E 216 663-4222
   Northfield *(G-11955)*

Keller Ochs Koch Inc............................. E 419 332-8288
   Fremont *(G-8689)*

Lucas Funeral Homes Inc..................... E 419 294-1985
   Upper Sandusky *(G-14291)*

Reed Funeral Home Inc........................ E 330 477-6721
   Canton *(G-1843)*

SCI Shared Resources LLC................. E 614 224-6105
   Columbus *(G-6654)*

SCI Shared Resources LLC................. A 614 875-6333
   Grove City *(G-8952)*

Stewart & Calhoun Fnrl HM Inc............. E 330 535-1543
   Akron *(G-311)*

Sunset Hills Cemetery Corp.................. E 330 494-2051
   Canton *(G-1865)*

Vernon Funeral Homes Inc................... E 937 653-8888
   Urbana *(G-14316)*

7291 Tax return preparation services

Barnes Wendling Cpas Inc.................... E 216 566-9000
   Cleveland *(G-3851)*

Buckingham & Company........................ E 937 435-2742
   Dayton *(G-7205)*

Colonial Banc Corp................................ E 937 456-5544
   Eaton *(G-8210)*

Deloitte & Touche LLP........................... B 513 784-7100
   Cincinnati *(G-2556)*

E T Financial Service Inc....................... E 937 716-1726
   Trotwood *(G-14127)*

Franchise Group Inc.............................. B 740 363-2222
   Delaware *(G-7799)*

Gbq Partners LLC.................................. E 419 885-8338
   Sylvania *(G-13546)*

Gbq Partners LLC.................................. D 614 221-1120
   Columbus *(G-5921)*

H & R Block Estrn Tax Svcs Inc............. E 216 464-7212
   Cleveland *(G-4344)*

Hometown Urgent Care......................... E 937 252-2000
   Wooster *(G-15345)*

Hometown Urgent Care......................... E 330 629-2300
   Youngstown *(G-15633)*

Morgan Tax Service............................... E 614 948-5296
   Columbus *(G-6262)*

Regional Income Tax Agency................ C 800 860-7482
   Brecksville *(G-1364)*

Thornhill Financial Inc........................... E 440 238-0445
   Cleveland *(G-5014)*

7299 Miscellaneous personal services

3sg Plus LLC... E 614 652-0019
   Columbus *(G-5243)*

845 Yard Street LLC.............................. E 614 484-6860
   Columbus *(G-5290)*

Action For Children Inc.......................... E 614 224-0222
   Columbus *(G-5310)*

Akron Metropolitan Hsing Auth.............. D 330 920-1652
   Stow *(G-13354)*

Alpha PHI Alpha Homes Inc.................. E 330 376-2115
   Akron *(G-45)*

APM Management LLC.......................... E 216 468-0050
   Pepper Pike *(G-12297)*

Barberton Laundry and Clg Inc............. D 330 825-6911
   Barberton *(G-694)*

Brown Derby Roadhouse....................... E 330 528-3227
   Hudson *(G-9335)*

Buns of Delaware Inc............................. E 740 363-2867
   Delaware *(G-7781)*

Castaway Bay Resort............................. E 419 627-2500
   Sandusky *(G-12870)*

Cintas Document Management LLC..... E 800 914-1960
   Mason *(G-10537)*

City Life Inc.. E 216 523-5899
   Cleveland *(G-3975)*

City of Centerville.................................. D 937 438-3585
   Dayton *(G-7227)*

Cleveland Metroparks............................ E 216 661-6500
   Cleveland *(G-4057)*

Connor Concepts Inc............................. E 937 291-1661
   Dayton *(G-7246)*

Consumer Cr Cnsling Svc of Mdw......... E 614 552-2222
   Columbus *(G-5687)*

Continntal Mssage Solution Inc............. D 614 224-4534
   Columbus *(G-5699)*

Costume Specialists Inc........................ E 614 464-2115
   Columbus *(G-5706)*

Eagle Industries Ohio Inc...................... E 513 247-2900
   Fairfield *(G-8409)*

Excel Decorators Inc.............................. D 614 522-0056
   Columbus *(G-5835)*

Findlay Inn & Conference Ctr................ E 419 422-5682
   Findlay *(G-8529)*

Formu3 International Inc....................... E 330 668-1461
   Akron *(G-166)*

German Family Society Inc................... E 330 678-8229
   Kent *(G-9576)*

Hkt Teleservices Inc.............................. C 614 652-6300
   Grove City *(G-8926)*

Integrted Wllness Partners LLC............. E 330 762-9102
   Akron *(G-203)*

Irish Envy LLC....................................... E 440 808-8000
   Chagrin Falls *(G-1981)*

Juvly Aesthetic LLC............................... E 800 254-0188
   Columbus *(G-6101)*

Kinetic Renovations LLC....................... E 937 321-1576
   Middletown *(G-11168)*

Kohler Foods Inc.................................... E 937 291-3600
   Dayton *(G-7445)*

Lei Home Enhancements...................... C 513 738-4663
   Cincinnati *(G-2970)*

Life Time Inc.. D 614 428-6000
   Columbus *(G-6159)*

Mason Family Resorts LLC................... B 608 237-5871
   Mason *(G-10577)*

Memorial Hall... D 937 293-2841
   Dayton *(G-7479)*

Michaels Inc... D 440 357-0384
   Mentor *(G-10973)*

Mix Talent LLC....................................... D 614 572-9452
   Lewis Center *(G-9829)*

Mocha House Inc................................... E 330 392-3020
   Warren *(G-14540)*

Mocho Ltd.. E 330 832-8807
   Massillon *(G-10659)*

Mustard Seed Health Fd Mkt Inc........... E 440 519-3663
   Solon *(G-13115)*

Parking Solutions Inc............................. A 614 469-7000
   Columbus *(G-6501)*

R & R Chiropractic................................. E 419 425-2225
   Attica *(G-601)*

Refectory Restaurant Inc....................... E 614 451-9774
   Columbus *(G-6570)*

Research Associates Inc....................... D 440 892-1000
   Cleveland *(G-4828)*

River Financial Inc................................. E 415 878-3375
   Columbus *(G-6593)*

Robert Bettinger Inc.............................. E 419 832-6033
   Grand Rapids *(G-8847)*

Roscoe Village Foundation................... D 740 622-2222
   Coshocton *(G-7000)*

Schmidt Hsptality Concepts Inc............ E 614 878-4527
   Columbus *(G-6649)*

Sugar & Spice Spa llc........................... D 513 319-0112
   Mason *(G-10612)*

Teasdale Fnton Crpt Clg Rstrti.............. D 513 797-0900
   Cincinnati *(G-3446)*

The Oaks Lodge.................................... D 330 769-2601
   Chippewa Lake *(G-2094)*

Valley Hospitality Inc............................. D 740 374-9660
   Marietta *(G-10409)*

Villa Milano Inc...................................... E 614 882-2058
   Columbus *(G-6851)*

Winking Lizard Inc................................. E 330 220-9944
   Brunswick *(G-1476)*

73 BUSINESS SERVICES

7311 Advertising agencies

Advent Media Group LLC..................... E 513 421-2267
   Cincinnati *(G-2152)*

▲ Airmate Co Inc................................... D 419 636-3184
   Bryan *(G-1478)*

BBDO Worldwide Inc............................. E 513 861-3668
   Cincinnati *(G-2241)*

Bbs & Associates Inc............................ E 330 665-5227
   Akron *(G-63)*

Berry Network.. D 513 702-3373
   Dayton *(G-7191)*

Black River Group Inc........................... E 419 524-6699
   Mansfield *(G-10245)*

Brandience LLC..................................... E 513 333-4100
   Cincinnati *(G-2277)*

Brokaw Inc... E 216 241-8003
   Cleveland *(G-3900)*

Charles W Powers & Assoc Inc............. E 513 721-5353
   Cincinnati *(G-2347)*

Clum Media Inc...................................... E 216 239-1525
   Cleveland *(G-4085)*

Comcage LLC.. E 513 549-4003
   Cincinnati *(G-2479)*

Comcast Spotlight LP............................ E 216 575-8016
   Cleveland *(G-4091)*

Cooper-Smith Advertising LLC.............. D 419 470-5900
   Toledo *(G-13761)*

Curiosity LLC... D 513 744-6000
   Cincinnati *(G-2525)*

Deanhouston Creative Group Inc.......... E 513 659-5051
   West Chester *(G-14684)*

Distributor Marketing MGT Inc.............. E 440 236-5534
   Columbia Station *(G-5227)*

Dix & Eaton Incorporated...................... E 216 241-0405
   Cleveland *(G-4168)*

Engauge Holdings LLC......................... D 614 573-1010
   Columbus *(G-5819)*

Epipheo Inc.. E 888 687-7620
   Cincinnati *(G-2631)*

Fahlgren Inc... E 614 383-1500
   Columbus *(G-5843)*

Fruchtman Advertising Inc.................... E 419 539-2770
   Toledo *(G-13814)*

Employee Codes: A=Over 500 employees, B=251-500
C=101-250, D=51-100, E=20-50, F=10-19, G=1-9

73 BUSINESS SERVICES

Gerbig Snell/Weisheimer A .... B 614 848-4848
  Westerville (G-14896)
Guardian Enterprise Group Inc .... E 614 416-6080
  Columbus (G-5959)
Gypc Inc .... C 309 677-0405
  Dayton (G-7390)
Hart Associates Inc .... D 419 893-9600
  Toledo (G-13836)
Hitchcock Fleming & Assoc Inc .... D 330 376-2111
  Akron (G-193)
ICC Lowe Pace LLC .... E 330 823-7223
  Alliance (G-384)
Inquiry Systems Inc .... E 614 464-3800
  Columbus (G-6055)
JWT Action .... E 513 578-6721
  Cincinnati (G-2924)
JWT Action .... D 330 376-6148
  Akron (G-214)
Kreber Graphics Inc .... D 614 529-5701
  Columbus (G-6128)
Lind Outdoor Advertising Co .... E 419 522-2600
  Mansfield (G-10282)
M A M Inc .... E 740 588-9882
  Zanesville (G-15809)
Madison Avenue Mktg Group Inc .... E 419 473-9000
  Toledo (G-13903)
Marcus Thomas Llc .... D 216 292-4700
  Cleveland (G-4524)
▲ Marketing Support Services Inc ...... E 513 752-1200
  Cincinnati (G-3011)
Matrix Media Services Inc .... E 614 228-2200
  Columbus (G-6207)
National Cinemedia LLC .... C 614 297-8933
  Columbus (G-6293)
Nct Retail .... E 937 236-8000
  Dayton (G-7528)
Northlich LLC .... C 513 421-8840
  Cincinnati (G-3126)
Opti LLC .... E 212 651-7317
  Cincinnati (G-3165)
Prodigal Media Company Inc .... E 330 707-2088
  Youngstown (G-15698)
Real Art Design Group Inc .... D 937 223-9955
  Dayton (G-7581)
Rockfish Interactive LLC .... E 513 381-1583
  Cincinnati (G-3315)
Rttw Ltd .... E 614 291-7944
  Columbus (G-6617)
Saatchi & Saatchi X Inc .... E 479 575-0200
  Cincinnati (G-3336)
SBC Advertising Ltd .... C 614 891-7070
  Columbus (G-6648)
Sgk LLC .... C 513 569-9900
  Cincinnati (G-3365)
Skylight Partners Inc .... E 513 381-5555
  Cincinnati (G-3385)
Syneos Health Communications Inc ... D 614 543-6650
  Westerville (G-14939)
The Arras Group Inc .... E 216 621-1601
  Cleveland (G-4991)
Thread Information Design Inc .... E 419 887-6801
  Toledo (G-14041)
◆ Tigerspike Inc .... E 646 330-4636
  Cincinnati (G-3479)
Tri Advertising Inc .... E 614 548-0913
  Westerville (G-14946)
Triad Communications Inc .... D 330 237-3531
  Cuyahoga Falls (G-7111)
Universal Advg Assoc Inc .... E 513 522-5000
  Cincinnati (G-3560)
Whitespace Design Group Inc .... E 330 762-9320
  Akron (G-360)

Wyse Advertising Inc .... E 216 696-2424
  Cleveland (G-5162)
Young & Rubicam LLC .... D 513 345-3400
  Cincinnati (G-3687)
Young & Rubicam LLC .... E 513 419-2300
  Cincinnati (G-3688)

7312 Outdoor advertising services

Kessler Sign Company .... E 740 453-0668
  Zanesville (G-15805)
Lind Outdoor Advertising Co .... E 419 522-2600
  Mansfield (G-10282)
Matrix Media Services Inc .... E 614 228-2200
  Columbus (G-6207)
Orange Barrel Media LLC .... D 614 294-4898
  Columbus (G-6477)

7313 Radio, television, publisher representatives

American City Bus Journals Inc .... B 937 528-4400
  Dayton (G-7170)
Bath & Body Works LLC .... D 937 439-0350
  Dayton (G-7186)
Copley Ohio Newspapers Inc .... C 330 364-5577
  New Philadelphia (G-11643)
Ctv Media Inc .... E 614 848-5800
  Powell (G-12590)
Gazette Publishing Company .... D 419 335-2010
  Napoleon (G-11523)
Madison Avenue Mktg Group Inc .... E 419 473-9000
  Toledo (G-13903)
Manta Media Inc .... E 888 875-5833
  Columbus (G-5268)

7319 Advertising, nec

Atlas Partners LLC .... C 937 439-7970
  Dayton (G-7183)
Berry Network LLC .... C 800 366-1264
  Moraine (G-11391)
Ctv Media Inc .... E 614 848-5800
  Powell (G-12590)
Dismas Distribution Services .... E 614 861-2525
  Columbus (G-5770)
Dispatch Consumer Services .... E 740 548-5555
  Columbus (G-5771)
▲ Downing Displays Inc .... D 513 248-9800
  Milford (G-11225)
Empower Media Partners LLC .... C 513 871-7779
  Cincinnati (G-2618)
Hillman Group Inc .... E 513 874-5905
  West Chester (G-14817)
IMG College LLC .... E 513 556-4532
  Cincinnati (G-2866)
Innomark Communications LLC .... D 513 379-7800
  West Chester (G-14713)
JB Dollar Stretcher .... E 614 436-2800
  Akron (G-209)
News Amer Mktg In-Store Svcs L ...... A 513 333-7373
  Cincinnati (G-3111)
Promotion Exction Partners LLC .... E 513 826-0101
  Cincinnati (G-3253)
Signum LLC .... D 440 248-2233
  Solon (G-13142)
Yp LLC .... C 216 642-4000
  Cleveland (G-5169)

7322 Adjustment and collection services

Apelles LLC .... E 614 899-7322
  Columbus (G-5372)
Associated Credit Service Inc .... E 419 524-6446
  Mansfield (G-10244)

Axcess Rcvery Cr Solutions Inc .... E 513 229-6700
  Cincinnati (G-2232)
C & S Associates Inc .... E 440 461-9661
  Highland Heights (G-9163)
Cbc Companies Inc .... D 614 222-4343
  Columbus (G-5522)
Choice Recovery Inc .... D 614 358-9900
  Columbus (G-5568)
Credit Bur Collectn Svcs Inc .... E 614 223-0688
  Columbus (G-5723)
Credit Bur Collectn Svcs Inc .... E 614 223-0688
  Columbus (G-5724)
Dfs Corporate Services LLC .... E 614 777-7020
  Hilliard (G-9192)
Estate Information Svcs LLC .... D 614 729-1700
  Gahanna (G-8716)
First Federal Credit Control .... E 216 360-2000
  Beachwood (G-791)
General Audit Corporation .... D 419 993-2900
  Lima (G-9891)
General Revenue Corporation .... C 513 469-1472
  Mason (G-10554)
Guardian Water & Power Inc .... E 614 291-3141
  Columbus (G-5960)
Head Mercantile Co Inc .... D 440 847-2700
  Westlake (G-15065)
Hs Financial Group LLC .... E 216 762-1800
  Cleveland (G-4387)
ITM Marketing Inc .... C 740 295-3575
  Coshocton (G-6988)
JP Recovery Services Inc .... C 440 331-2200
  Rocky River (G-12745)
Logan View LLC .... E 937 592-3902
  Bellefontaine (G-1031)
Macys Cr & Customer Svcs Inc .... A 513 398-5221
  Mason (G-10576)
Mammoth Tech Inc .... C 419 782-3709
  Defiance (G-7754)
McCarthy Burgess & Wolff Inc .... C 440 735-5100
  Bedford (G-972)
Media Collections Inc .... D 216 831-5626
  Twinsburg (G-14204)
Millennium Cpitl Recovery Corp .... E 330 805-9063
  Akron (G-233)
National Entp Systems Inc .... C 440 542-1360
  Solon (G-13116)
Ncs Incorporated .... D 440 684-9455
  Cleveland (G-4631)
Oriana House Inc .... C 419 447-1444
  Tiffin (G-13637)
Platinum Recovery LLC .... E 740 373-8811
  Marietta (G-10400)
PRC Medical LLC .... D 330 493-9004
  Cuyahoga Falls (G-7093)
Recovery One LLC .... D 614 336-4207
  Columbus (G-6564)
Reliant Capital Solutions LLC .... C 614 452-6100
  Gahanna (G-8726)
Revenue Assistance Corporation .... C 216 763-2100
  Cleveland (G-4832)
Roddy Group Inc .... E 216 763-0088
  Beachwood (G-831)
Security Check LLC .... C 614 944-5788
  Columbus (G-6658)
Tek-Collect Incorporated .... C 614 299-2766
  Columbus (G-6754)
United Collection Bureau Inc .... C 614 732-5000
  Columbus (G-6804)
United Collection Bureau Inc .... E 419 866-6227
  Maumee (G-10776)
United Collection Bureau Inc .... C 419 866-6227
  Toledo (G-14082)

7323 Credit reporting services

Cbcinnovis International Inc............... E 614 222-4343
  Columbus *(G-5523)*
Fd Holdings LLC................................. B 614 228-5775
  Columbus *(G-5854)*
Innovis Data Solutions Inc.................. E 614 222-4343
  Columbus *(G-6054)*
Kreller Bus Info Group Inc................... E 513 723-8900
  Cincinnati *(G-2951)*
Pasco Inc... E 330 650-0613
  Hudson *(G-9367)*
Safegard Bckgrund Screening LLC...... E 877 700-7345
  Beachwood *(G-834)*

7331 Direct mail advertising services

A W S Inc... B 216 749-0356
  Cleveland *(G-3751)*
A W S Inc... A 440 333-1791
  Rocky River *(G-12738)*
▲ Aero Fulfillment Services Corp......... D 800 225-7145
  Mason *(G-10517)*
American Paper Group Inc.................. B 330 758-4545
  Youngstown *(G-15551)*
Amerimark Holdings LLC..................... B 440 325-2000
  Cleveland *(G-3809)*
Amsive OH LLC.................................. D 937 885-8000
  Miamisburg *(G-11024)*
Angstrom Graphics Inc Midwest.......... C 216 271-5300
  Cleveland *(G-3817)*
Baesman Group Inc............................ D 614 771-2300
  Hilliard *(G-9181)*
Bindery & Spc Pressworks Inc............. D 614 873-4623
  Plain City *(G-12470)*
Clipper Magazine LLC......................... D 513 794-4100
  Blue Ash *(G-1151)*
▲ Consolidated Graphics Group Inc..... C 216 881-9191
  Cleveland *(G-4104)*
Ctrac Inc.. E 440 572-1000
  Cleveland *(G-4144)*
Ddm-Dgtal Imging Data Proc Mli......... D 740 928-1110
  Hebron *(G-9142)*
Deepwood Industries Inc..................... C 440 350-5231
  Mentor *(G-10933)*
Early Express Services Inc.................. E 937 223-5801
  Dayton *(G-7322)*
▲ Fine Line Graphics Corp.................. E 614 486-0276
  Columbus *(G-5857)*
Harte-Hanks Trnsp Svcs..................... D 513 458-7600
  Cincinnati *(G-2803)*
Hkm Drect Mkt Cmmnications Inc........ C 800 860-4456
  Cleveland *(G-4367)*
Mid-West Presort Mailing Services Inc.. C 216 251-2500
  Cleveland *(G-4576)*
Northlich LLC..................................... C 513 421-8840
  Cincinnati *(G-3126)*
▲ Patented Acquisition Corp................ D 937 353-2299
  Miamisburg *(G-11082)*
Promotion Exction Partners LLC........... D 513 826-0101
  Cincinnati *(G-3253)*
Resource Interactive.......................... E 614 621-2888
  Columbus *(G-6586)*
▲ TMR Inc... E 330 220-8564
  Brunswick *(G-1471)*
Traxium LLC...................................... E 330 572-8200
  Stow *(G-13398)*
Valassis Direct Mail Inc....................... D 859 283-2386
  Cincinnati *(G-3612)*
Valassis Direct Mail Inc....................... D 216 573-1400
  Independence *(G-9494)*
Valassis Direct Mail Inc....................... E 614 987-2200
  Worthington *(G-15465)*

Weekleys Mailing Service Inc............... D 440 234-4325
  Berea *(G-1086)*

7334 Photocopying and duplicating services

A-A Blueprint Co Inc........................... E 330 794-8803
  Akron *(G-11)*
ARC Document Solutions Inc............... D 216 281-1234
  Cleveland *(G-3830)*
Comdoc Inc.. D 330 920-3900
  Cuyahoga Falls *(G-7064)*
Ers Digital Inc.................................... D 216 281-1234
  Cleveland *(G-4221)*
▲ Key Blue Prints Inc........................ D 614 228-3285
  Columbus *(G-6113)*
Printers Devil Inc............................... E 330 650-1218
  Hudson *(G-9369)*
Queen City Reprographics.................. C 513 326-2300
  Cincinnati *(G-3265)*
Queen City Reprographics Inc............ E 513 326-2300
  Cincinnati *(G-3266)*
Repros Inc.. E 330 247-3747
  Akron *(G-280)*
▲ TMR Inc... E 330 220-8564
  Brunswick *(G-1471)*

7335 Commercial photography

Aerocon Photogrammetric Svcs.......... E 440 946-6277
  Concord Township *(G-6922)*
AG Interactive Inc.............................. C 216 889-5000
  Cleveland *(G-3774)*
Eclipse 3d/Pi LLC............................... E 614 626-8536
  Columbus *(G-5804)*
Jackson & Sons Drilling & Pump......... E 419 756-2758
  Mansfield *(G-10275)*
Kucera International Inc..................... D 440 975-4230
  Willoughby *(G-15197)*
Marsh Inc.. D 513 421-1234
  Cincinnati *(G-3012)*
Photo-Type Engraving Company.......... E 513 281-0999
  Cincinnati *(G-3209)*
Queen City Reprographics.................. C 513 326-2300
  Cincinnati *(G-3265)*
Rapid Mortgage Company................... E 937 748-8888
  Cincinnati *(G-3273)*
The Photo-Type Engraving Company.... D 513 281-0999
  Cincinnati *(G-3469)*
Tj Metzgers Inc................................. D 419 861-8611
  Toledo *(G-14043)*
Trg Studios Inc.................................. E 216 781-8644
  Brooklyn *(G-1411)*
Wp7pro Inc....................................... E 419 483-3364
  Bellevue *(G-1046)*

7336 Commercial art and graphic design

Adcom Group Inc............................... C 216 574-9100
  Cleveland *(G-3769)*
Bottle Solutions LLC........................... E 216 889-3330
  Cleveland *(G-3883)*
Clarity Retail Services LLC................. D 513 800-9369
  West Chester *(G-14668)*
Concept Imaging Group Inc................ E 888 466-6627
  Miamisburg *(G-11037)*
Container Graphics Corp.................... E 419 531-5133
  Toledo *(G-13760)*
Coyne Graphic Finishing Inc............... E 740 397-6232
  Mount Vernon *(G-11481)*
Dr Alxander C Nnabue Assoc PA......... E 614 499-7687
  Columbus *(G-5785)*
Edward Howard & Co......................... E 216 781-2400
  Cleveland *(G-4207)*
Exhibitpro Inc.................................... E 614 885-9541
  New Albany *(G-11564)*

Fitch Inc... D 614 885-3453
  Columbus *(G-5870)*
▲ General Theming Contrs LLC........... C 614 252-6342
  Columbus *(G-5925)*
Haney Inc... D 513 561-1441
  Cincinnati *(G-2799)*
Hofrichter Brothers Inc...................... E 740 314-5669
  Steubenville *(G-13331)*
Interbrand Hulefeld Inc...................... E 513 421-2210
  Cincinnati *(G-2881)*
Libby Prszyk Kthman Hldngs Inc........ D 513 241-6401
  Cincinnati *(G-2973)*
Marsh Inc... D 513 421-1234
  Cincinnati *(G-3012)*
Mueller Art Cover & Binding Co.......... E 440 238-3303
  Strongsville *(G-13477)*
Nottinghm-Spirk Dsign Assoc In.......... E 216 800-5782
  Cleveland *(G-4667)*
ONeil & Associates Inc....................... C 937 865-0800
  Miamisburg *(G-11079)*
Photo-Type Engraving Company.......... E 513 475-5638
  Cincinnati *(G-3210)*
Real Art Design Group Inc.................. D 937 223-9955
  Dayton *(G-7581)*
Screen Works Inc.............................. E 937 264-9111
  Dayton *(G-7613)*
▲ Shamrock Companies Inc................ D 440 899-9510
  Westlake *(G-15108)*
▲ Suntwist Corp................................ E 800 935-3534
  Maple Heights *(G-10350)*
The Photo-Type Engraving Company.... E 513 281-0999
  Cincinnati *(G-3469)*
▲ Third Dimension Inc....................... E 440 466-4040
  Geneva *(G-8790)*
Univenture Inc................................... D 877 831-9428
  Marysville *(G-10516)*
▲ Univenture Inc............................... E 937 645-4600
  Dublin *(G-8146)*
Whitespace Design Group Inc............ E 330 762-9320
  Akron *(G-360)*
Woodrow Manufacturing Co................ E 937 399-9333
  Springfield *(G-13313)*
Young MNS Chrstn Assn Grter CN...... B 513 791-5000
  Blue Ash *(G-1275)*

7338 Secretarial and court reporting

ABC Scribes Ltd................................. E 937 705-5471
  Centerville *(G-1938)*
Chase Transcriptions Inc.................... E 330 656-3980
  Hudson *(G-9338)*
Edward Allen Company...................... E 216 621-4984
  Cleveland *(G-4206)*
Veritext Holding Company.................. B 216 664-0799
  Cleveland *(G-5099)*

7342 Disinfecting and pest control services

Aabel Exterminating Co...................... E 937 434-4343
  Dayton *(G-7151)*
Apex Pest Control Service Inc............. E 440 461-6530
  Bedford *(G-953)*
Corporate Cleaning Inc...................... E 614 203-6051
  Columbus *(G-5702)*
DCS Sanitation Management Inc......... A 513 891-4980
  Cincinnati *(G-2545)*
Duncan Sales Inc............................... E 614 755-6580
  Columbus *(G-5793)*
Extermital Chemicals Inc.................... E 937 253-6144
  Dayton *(G-7342)*
Greenix Holdings LLC........................ D 614 961-7378
  Hilliard *(G-9197)*
Innovative Cleaning Svcs & Sup.......... D 513 981-1287
  Cincinnati *(G-2872)*

73 BUSINESS SERVICES

◆ J T Eaton & Co Inc .... E 330 425-7801
   Twinsburg *(G-14197)*

Moxie Pest Control LP .... E 513 216-1804
   Fairfield *(G-8433)*

Patton Pest Control Co .... E 440 338-3101
   Novelty *(G-12042)*

Plunketts Pest Control Inc .... D 614 794-8169
   Columbus *(G-6533)*

Rentokil North America Inc .... E 440 964-5641
   Ashtabula *(G-547)*

Scherzinger Corporation .... D 513 531-7848
   Cincinnati *(G-3347)*

▲ Scotts Miracle-Gro Company .... B 937 644-0011
   Marysville *(G-10509)*

7349 Building maintenance services, nec

A B M Inc .... A 419 421-2292
   Findlay *(G-8505)*

AAA Standard Services Inc .... E 419 535-0274
   Toledo *(G-13672)*

ABM Janitorial Services Inc .... D 513 731-1418
   Cincinnati *(G-2135)*

ABM Janitorial Services Inc .... D 216 861-1199
   Cleveland *(G-3759)*

Aetna Building Maintenance Inc .... C 937 324-5711
   Springfield *(G-13214)*

Ajax Commercial Cleaning Inc .... D 330 928-4543
   Cuyahoga Falls *(G-7033)*

Alexis Eppinger .... E 216 509-0475
   Cleveland *(G-3785)*

Allen-Keith Construction Co .... D 330 266-2220
   Canton *(G-1659)*

Alpha & Omega Bldg Svcs Inc .... B 513 429-5082
   Blue Ash *(G-1129)*

Alpha & Omega Bldg Svcs Inc .... E 937 298-2125
   Dayton *(G-7165)*

Apex Environmental Services L .... E 513 772-2739
   Cincinnati *(G-2208)*

Aramark Facility Services LLC .... C 216 687-5000
   Cleveland *(G-3828)*

Ashland Cleaning LLC .... E 419 281-1747
   Ashland *(G-474)*

Atalian US Ohio Valley Inc .... B 614 476-1818
   Columbus *(G-5400)*

▲ Atlantis Security Company .... D 440 717-7050
   Cleveland *(G-3838)*

August Groh & Sons Inc .... E 513 821-0090
   Cincinnati *(G-2229)*

Beneficial Building Svcs Inc .... D 330 848-2556
   Akron *(G-65)*

Blanchard Valley Health System .... A 419 423-4500
   Findlay *(G-8514)*

Blast-All Inc .... E 606 393-5786
   Ironton *(G-9503)*

Blue Chip 2000 Coml Clg Inc .... A 513 561-2999
   Cincinnati *(G-2267)*

Buckeye Commercial Clg Inc .... D 614 866-4700
   Pickerington *(G-12400)*

C & K Industrial Services Inc .... D 216 642-0055
   Independence *(G-9414)*

C & S Cleaning Services Inc .... D 440 349-5907
   Solon *(G-13071)*

C&W Facility Services Inc .... A 614 827-1702
   Columbus *(G-5491)*

Cardinal Group Inc .... C 330 252-1047
   Akron *(G-80)*

▲ Carmens Dist Systems Inc .... E 800 886-8227
   Columbus *(G-5513)*

Caveney Inc .... E 330 497-4600
   North Canton *(G-11815)*

Center Cleaning Services Inc .... D 440 327-5099
   Avon *(G-642)*

Champion Clg Specialists Inc .... E 513 871-2333
   Cincinnati *(G-2344)*

▲ Chemical Solvents Inc .... E 216 741-9310
   Cleveland *(G-3965)*

Circle Building Services Inc .... E 614 228-6090
   Columbus *(G-5574)*

Circle Building Services Inc .... E 614 228-6090
   Columbus *(G-5573)*

Clean All Services Inc .... C 937 498-4146
   Sidney *(G-13023)*

Cleanpro Janitorial Svc LLC .... E 330 592-9860
   Stow *(G-13359)*

CMS Business Services LLC .... D 740 687-0577
   Lancaster *(G-9703)*

Coleman Professional Svcs Inc .... C 330 673-1347
   Kent *(G-9565)*

Corporate Cleaning Inc .... E 614 203-6051
   Columbus *(G-5702)*

County of Cuyahoga .... B 216 443-6954
   Cleveland *(G-4131)*

Csi International Inc .... A 614 781-1571
   Worthington *(G-15411)*

Cummins Facility Services LLC .... B 740 726-9800
   Prospect *(G-12616)*

Custom Cleaning Svcs By Horton .... E 440 774-1222
   Oberlin *(G-12066)*

D&D Foundation LLC .... E 513 291-3191
   Cincinnati *(G-2532)*

DCS Sanitation Management Inc .... A 513 891-4980
   Cincinnati *(G-2545)*

Deaton Enterprises Inc .... C 937 320-6200
   Beavercreek *(G-877)*

Divisions Inc .... C 859 448-9730
   Cincinnati *(G-2571)*

Ecobryt LLC .... E 877 326-2798
   Cincinnati *(G-2605)*

Emcor Facilities Services Inc .... D 888 846-9462
   Cincinnati *(G-2613)*

Environment Ctrl Beachwood Inc .... E 330 405-6201
   Twinsburg *(G-14187)*

Environment Ctrl of Miami Cnty .... D 937 669-9900
   Tipp City *(G-13658)*

Ermc II LP .... D 513 424-8517
   Middletown *(G-11197)*

Executive Management Services .... A 419 529-8800
   Ontario *(G-12104)*

Flawless Janitorial LLC .... E 216 266-1425
   Maple Heights *(G-10338)*

G J Goudreau & Co .... E 216 351-5233
   Cleveland *(G-4297)*

G7 Services Inc .... E 937 256-3473
   Dayton *(G-7372)*

Galaxie Industrial Svcs LLC .... E 330 503-2334
   Youngstown *(G-15616)*

Gca Services Group Inc .... D 800 422-8760
   Cleveland *(G-4308)*

Gergelys Mint King Sups Svc In .... E 440 244-4446
   Lorain *(G-10076)*

Green Clean Ohio LLC .... E 866 853-6337
   Cleveland *(G-4337)*

Green Impressions LLC .... D 440 240-8508
   Sheffield Village *(G-12998)*

Gsf Usa Inc .... C 513 733-1451
   West Chester *(G-14814)*

Hamilton City School District .... E 513 887-5055
   Hamilton *(G-9050)*

Heco Operations Inc .... C 614 888-5700
   Worthington *(G-15420)*

High-TEC Industrial Services .... D 937 667-1772
   Tipp City *(G-13659)*

I E R Inc .... E 440 324-2620
   Elyria *(G-8261)*

Integrity Concepts Llc Inc .... D 614 529-8332
   Columbus *(G-6062)*

J V Janitorial Services Inc .... C 216 749-1150
   Brooklyn Heights *(G-1420)*

Jancoa Janitorial Services Inc .... B 513 351-7200
   Cincinnati *(G-2899)*

Jani-Source LLC .... E 740 374-6298
   Marietta *(G-10376)*

Janitorial Services Inc .... B 216 341-8601
   Cleveland *(G-4433)*

Jantech Building Services Inc .... E 216 661-6102
   Brooklyn Heights *(G-1422)*

Jdd Inc .... D 216 464-8855
   Chagrin Falls *(G-1982)*

Kettering City School District .... E 937 297-1990
   Dayton *(G-7438)*

Kleman Services LLC .... D 419 339-0871
   Lima *(G-9916)*

▲ Leadec Corp .... E 513 731-3590
   Blue Ash *(G-1200)*

Legacy Maintenance Svcs LLC .... E 614 473-8444
   Columbus *(G-6152)*

Lima Sheet Metal Machine & Mfg .... E 419 229-1161
   Lima *(G-9927)*

Logan-Hocking School District .... E 740 385-7844
   Logan *(G-10033)*

Louderback Fmly Invstments Inc .... E 937 845-1762
   New Carlisle *(G-11604)*

M3 Cleaning Services Inc .... C 419 725-2100
   Toledo *(G-13902)*

Maass - Midwest Mfg Inc .... A 419 485-6905
   Pioneer *(G-12433)*

Merry Maids Ltd Partnership .... E 614 430-8441
   Columbus *(G-6227)*

Metropolitan Envmtl Svcs Inc .... D 614 771-1881
   Hilliard *(G-9213)*

Mid-American Clg Contrs Inc .... C 614 291-7170
   Columbus *(G-6235)*

Mid-American Clg Contrs Inc .... C 419 429-6222
   Findlay *(G-8568)*

Mid-American Clg Contrs Inc .... D 419 229-3899
   Lima *(G-9935)*

Miles Cleaning Services Inc .... E 216 626-0040
   Cleveland *(G-4582)*

Montaque Cleaning Services LLC .... E 937 705-0429
   Dayton *(G-7511)*

Mougianis Industries Inc .... D 740 264-6372
   Steubenville *(G-13340)*

▲ MPW Industrial Services Inc .... A 800 827-8790
   Hebron *(G-9149)*

MPW Industrial Svcs Group Inc .... E 740 245-5393
   Bidwell *(G-1105)*

MPW Industrial Svcs Group Inc .... B 740 927-8790
   Hebron *(G-9150)*

Nelbud Services Group Inc .... E 317 202-0360
   Columbus *(G-6344)*

Nicholas D Starr Inc .... C 419 229-3192
   Lima *(G-9940)*

Northpointe Property MGT LLC .... C 614 579-9712
   Columbus *(G-6369)*

Norwalk Custodial Service .... D 419 668-1517
   Norwalk *(G-12018)*

Ohio Custodial Maintenance .... C 614 443-1232
   Columbus *(G-6399)*

Ohio Helping Hands Clg Svc LLC .... E 937 402-0733
   Hillsboro *(G-9264)*

Professional Bldg Maint Inc .... D 440 666-8509
   Warrensville Heights *(G-14586)*

Professional Maint of Columbus .... E 513 579-1762
   Cincinnati *(G-3245)*

Professional Pavement Svcs LLC .... E 740 726-2222
   Delaware *(G-7821)*

73 BUSINESS SERVICES

Professional Restoration Svc............. E 330 825-1803
  Medina *(G-10879)*

Psp Operations Inc.......................... E 614 888-5700
  Worthington *(G-15449)*

Rags Brooms & Mops Inc................. D 440 969-0164
  Jefferson *(G-9539)*

Restoration Resources Inc............... E 330 650-4486
  Hudson *(G-9371)*

Richland Newhope Inds Inc.............. C 419 774-4400
  Mansfield *(G-10313)*

Rwk Services Inc............................ E 440 526-2144
  Cleveland *(G-4865)*

Rwk Services Inc CCI...................... E 216 387-3754
  Independence *(G-9481)*

S-T Acquisition Company LLC.......... E 440 735-1505
  Cleveland *(G-4868)*

Scioto LLC..................................... B 937 644-0888
  Marysville *(G-10507)*

Seaway Sponge & Chamois Co......... E 419 691-4694
  Toledo *(G-14007)*

Service Master Co............................ E 330 864-7300
  Eastlake *(G-8208)*

Solv-All LLC................................... D 888 765-8255
  Mentor *(G-10996)*

Space Management Inc.................... D 937 254-6622
  Moraine *(G-11440)*

Star Inc... C 740 354-1517
  Portsmouth *(G-12575)*

Starlight Enterprises Inc.................. C 330 339-2020
  New Philadelphia *(G-11668)*

Super Shine Inc.............................. E 513 423-8999
  Middletown *(G-11190)*

T & L Enterprises Inc...................... E 440 234-5900
  Berea *(G-1083)*

T&L Global Management LLC............ D 614 586-0303
  Columbus *(G-6744)*

Tdg Facilities LLC........................... C 513 834-6105
  Cincinnati *(G-3445)*

Toledo Building Services Co............. A 419 241-3101
  Toledo *(G-14052)*

Total Maintenance Solution Inc......... E 513 770-0925
  Cincinnati *(G-3484)*

Trg Maintenance LLC....................... A 614 891-4850
  Westerville *(G-14945)*

Trk Investments Montgomery LLC..... E 513 388-0186
  Cincinnati *(G-3529)*

Turn Around Group Inc.................... D 330 372-0064
  Warren *(G-14568)*

Two Men & A Vacuum LLC............... D 614 300-7970
  Columbus *(G-6796)*

United Scoto Senior Activities........... E 740 354-6672
  Portsmouth *(G-12579)*

Universal Services America LP.......... A 937 454-9035
  Vandalia *(G-14398)*

University of Cincinnati.................... D 513 556-6381
  Cincinnati *(G-3590)*

Vadakin Inc.................................... E 740 373-7518
  Marietta *(G-10408)*

Wiggins Clg & Crpt Svc Inc............... D 937 279-9080
  Dayton *(G-7722)*

Wj Service Co Inc............................ E 330 372-5040
  Warren *(G-14576)*

7352 Medical equipment rental

▲ Boardman Medical Supply Co......... C 330 545-6700
  Girard *(G-8810)*

Braden Med Services Inc.................. E 740 732-2356
  Caldwell *(G-1547)*

Care Medical Inc............................. E 513 821-7272
  Cincinnati *(G-2309)*

Cornerstone Med Svcs - Mdwest........ E 330 374-0229
  Akron *(G-123)*

Fairfield Medical Center.................... A 740 687-8000
  Lancaster *(G-9718)*

First Choice Homecare Inc................ E 440 717-1984
  Broadview Heights *(G-1390)*

Health Aid of Ohio Inc...................... E 216 252-3900
  Cleveland *(G-4353)*

Hill-Rom Inc................................... E 513 769-6343
  Cincinnati *(G-2821)*

Integrated Medical Inc..................... E 216 332-1550
  Cleveland *(G-4414)*

Lincare Inc..................................... E 330 928-0884
  Akron *(G-221)*

Lincare Inc..................................... E 304 243-9605
  Barnesville *(G-719)*

Lincare Inc..................................... E 513 272-6050
  Cincinnati *(G-2978)*

Lincare Inc..................................... E 216 581-9649
  Cleveland *(G-4497)*

Lincare Inc..................................... E 419 499-1188
  Milan *(G-11207)*

Lincare Inc..................................... E 937 299-1141
  Moraine *(G-11420)*

Lincare Inc..................................... E 740 349-8236
  Newark *(G-11722)*

Medical Service Company................. D 440 232-3000
  Bedford *(G-973)*

Mercy Hlth - St Rtas Med Ctr L.......... A 419 227-3361
  Lima *(G-9934)*

Millers Rental and Sls Co Inc............ D 330 753-8600
  Akron *(G-234)*

Sateri Home Inc.............................. D 330 758-8106
  Youngstown *(G-15717)*

Seeley Enterprises Company............. E 440 293-6600
  Andover *(G-440)*

Seeley Medical Oxygen Co............... E 440 255-7163
  Andover *(G-441)*

Toledo Medical Equipment Co........... E 419 866-7120
  Maumee *(G-10774)*

7353 Heavy construction equipment rental

All Crane Rental Corp...................... D 614 261-1800
  Columbus *(G-5334)*

All Erection & Crane Rental.............. E 216 524-6550
  Cleveland *(G-3789)*

▼ All Erection & Crane Rental........... C 216 524-6550
  Cleveland *(G-3788)*

American Crane Inc......................... E 614 496-2268
  Reynoldsburg *(G-12651)*

▲ Bobcat Enterprises Inc.................. D 513 874-8945
  West Chester *(G-14652)*

▲ Canton Erectors Inc...................... D 330 453-7363
  Massillon *(G-10634)*

Capital City Group Inc...................... E 614 278-2120
  Columbus *(G-5498)*

▼ Columbus Equipment Company...... E 614 437-0352
  Columbus *(G-5633)*

▲ Eleet Cryogenics Inc..................... E 330 874-4009
  Bolivar *(G-1294)*

◆ F & M Mafco Inc.......................... C 513 367-2151
  Harrison *(G-9104)*

General Crane Rental LLC................ E 330 908-0001
  Macedonia *(G-10192)*

H M Miller Construction Co............... D 330 628-4811
  Mogadore *(G-11327)*

Henry Jergens Contractor Inc........... E 937 233-1830
  Dayton *(G-7405)*

Interstate Lift Trucks Inc.................. E 216 328-0970
  Cleveland *(G-4421)*

Jeffers Crane Service Inc................. E 419 223-9010
  Lima *(G-9912)*

Kelley Steel Erectors Inc.................. D 440 232-1573
  Cleveland *(G-4455)*

▲ Lefeld Welding & Stl Sups Inc......... E 419 678-2397
  Coldwater *(G-5216)*

Leppo Inc....................................... E 330 633-3999
  Tallmadge *(G-13599)*

Messer Construction Co................... C 513 482-7402
  Cincinnati *(G-3051)*

National Tool Leasing Inc.................. E 866 952-8665
  Eastlake *(G-8206)*

◆ Ohio Machinery Co....................... C 440 526-6200
  Broadview Heights *(G-1394)*

Piqua Steel Co................................ D 937 773-3632
  Piqua *(G-12454)*

Pollock Research & Design Inc.......... E 330 332-3300
  Salem *(G-12847)*

RELAM Inc..................................... E 440 232-3354
  Solon *(G-13137)*

Selinsky Force LLC.......................... C 330 477-4527
  Canton *(G-1850)*

Skyworks LLC................................. E 419 662-8630
  Perrysburg *(G-12370)*

Sunbelt Rentals Inc......................... D 614 848-4075
  Columbus *(G-5282)*

Sunbelt Rentals Inc......................... E 614 341-9770
  Columbus *(G-6729)*

The Selinsky Force LLC.................... D 330 477-4527
  Canton *(G-1872)*

The Wagner-Smith Company............ B 866 338-0398
  Moraine *(G-11444)*

Towlift Inc..................................... E 440 951-9519
  Mentor *(G-11004)*

Towlift Inc..................................... E 419 666-1333
  Northwood *(G-11985)*

United Rentals North Amer Inc......... E 614 276-5444
  Columbus *(G-6814)*

United Rentals North Amer Inc......... E 800 877-3687
  Perrysburg *(G-12383)*

7359 Equipment rental and leasing, nec

A & A Safety Inc............................. E 513 943-6100
  Amelia *(G-409)*

Ackerman Chacco Company Inc......... E 513 791-4252
  Blue Ash *(G-1121)*

Ag-Pro Ohio LLC............................. E 740 653-6951
  Lancaster *(G-9691)*

All Erection & Crane Rental.............. E 216 524-6550
  Cleveland *(G-3789)*

▼ All Erection & Crane Rental........... C 216 524-6550
  Cleveland *(G-3788)*

All Lift Service Company Inc............. E 440 585-1542
  Willoughby *(G-15183)*

All Temp Refrigeration Inc................ E 419 692-5016
  Delphos *(G-7836)*

American Roadway Logistics Inc........ E 330 659-2003
  Norton *(G-11989)*

Auto Mall Rental & Leasing LLC........ D 419 874-4331
  Perrysburg *(G-12313)*

Bkg Holdings LLC............................ E 614 252-7455
  Columbus *(G-5442)*

Bnd Rentals Inc.............................. E 937 898-5061
  Vandalia *(G-14367)*

Brandsafway Services LLC............... E 614 443-1314
  Columbus *(G-5459)*

Brennan Equipment Services Co........ E 419 867-6000
  Holland *(G-9282)*

Budget Dumpster LLC...................... E 866 284-6164
  Westlake *(G-15041)*

Celina Enterprises LLC..................... D 419 586-3610
  Celina *(G-1918)*

CFC Investment Company................ E 513 870-2203
  Fairfield *(G-8399)*

Combined Technologies Inc.............. E 513 595-5900
  Cincinnati *(G-2478)*

73 BUSINESS SERVICES

Comdoc Inc .... C 330 896-2346
  North Canton *(G-11818)*
Coyle Music Centers Inc .... E 614 885-6654
  Columbus *(G-5716)*
Cuyahoga Vending Co Inc .... C 440 353-9595
  North Ridgeville *(G-11926)*
◆ De Nora Tech LLC .... D 440 710-5334
  Concord Township *(G-6924)*
Dearing Compressor and Pu .... E 330 783-2258
  Youngstown *(G-15595)*
Diane Sauer Chevrolet Inc .... E 330 373-1600
  Warren *(G-14518)*
Eaton Leasing Corporation .... B 216 382-2292
  Beachwood *(G-788)*
Electronic Merch Systems LLC .... C 216 524-0900
  Cleveland *(G-4209)*
Elliott Tool Technologies Ltd .... D 937 253-6133
  Dayton *(G-7333)*
Enerstar Rentals and Svcs Ltd .... E 570 360-3271
  Bellaire *(G-1011)*
Equipment Depot Ohio Inc .... E 513 934-2121
  Lebanon *(G-9765)*
▲ Fallsway Equipment Co Inc .... C 330 633-6000
  Akron *(G-152)*
▲ Fern Exposition Services LLC .... E 888 621-3376
  Cincinnati *(G-2659)*
▲ Fifth Third Equipment Fin Co .... E 800 972-3030
  Cincinnati *(G-2665)*
Fleming Leasing LLC .... C 703 842-1358
  Girard *(G-8812)*
Flexjet LLC .... C 216 261-3880
  Cleveland *(G-4265)*
Flight Options Inc .... B 216 261-3880
  Richmond Heights *(G-12719)*
Flight Options LLC .... E 216 261-3500
  Cleveland *(G-4266)*
Flight Options Intl Inc .... E 216 261-3500
  Richmond Heights *(G-12720)*
Franklin Equipment LLC .... E 614 389-2161
  Dublin *(G-8015)*
Franklin Equipment LLC .... E 513 893-9105
  West Chester *(G-14694)*
Franklin Equipment LLC .... E 614 948-3409
  Westerville *(G-14980)*
Garda CL Great Lakes Inc .... B 561 939-7000
  Columbus *(G-5911)*
Globe Furniture Rentals Inc .... D 513 771-8287
  Cincinnati *(G-2734)*
Gordon Brothers Inc .... E 800 331-7611
  Salem *(G-12842)*
Great Lakes Crushing Ltd .... D 440 944-5500
  Wickliffe *(G-15150)*
Hogan Truck Leasing Inc .... E 314 802-5995
  Obetz *(G-12080)*
Home Depot USA Inc .... C 330 245-0280
  Akron *(G-195)*
Home Depot USA Inc .... C 440 937-2240
  Avon *(G-654)*
Home Depot USA Inc .... C 330 497-1810
  Canton *(G-1776)*
Home Depot USA Inc .... C 513 688-1654
  Cincinnati *(G-2835)*
Home Depot USA Inc .... C 513 661-2413
  Cincinnati *(G-2836)*
Home Depot USA Inc .... C 513 631-1705
  Cincinnati *(G-2837)*
Home Depot USA Inc .... C 216 676-9969
  Cleveland *(G-4373)*
Home Depot USA Inc .... C 216 251-3091
  Cleveland *(G-4374)*
Home Depot USA Inc .... C 216 297-1303
  Cleveland Heights *(G-5179)*
Home Depot USA Inc .... B 614 523-0600
  Columbus *(G-5999)*
Home Depot USA Inc .... C 614 878-9150
  Columbus *(G-6000)*
Home Depot USA Inc .... C 614 939-5036
  Columbus *(G-6001)*
Home Depot USA Inc .... C 330 922-3448
  Cuyahoga Falls *(G-7078)*
Home Depot USA Inc .... C 937 312-9053
  Dayton *(G-7409)*
Home Depot USA Inc .... D 937 312-9076
  Dayton *(G-7410)*
Home Depot USA Inc .... C 937 837-1551
  Dayton *(G-7411)*
Home Depot USA Inc .... C 440 324-7222
  Elyria *(G-8256)*
Home Depot USA Inc .... C 937 431-7346
  Fairborn *(G-8376)*
Home Depot USA Inc .... D 513 887-1450
  Hamilton *(G-9053)*
Home Depot USA Inc .... C 440 684-1343
  Highland Heights *(G-9166)*
Home Depot USA Inc .... C 419 529-0015
  Mansfield *(G-10269)*
Home Depot USA Inc .... D 216 581-6611
  Maple Heights *(G-10340)*
Home Depot USA Inc .... C 440 357-0428
  Mentor *(G-10949)*
Home Depot USA Inc .... C 614 577-1601
  Reynoldsburg *(G-12666)*
Home Depot USA Inc .... C 419 626-6493
  Sandusky *(G-12903)*
Home Depot USA Inc .... D 440 826-9092
  Strongsville *(G-13462)*
Home Depot USA Inc .... C 419 476-4573
  Toledo *(G-13848)*
Home Depot USA Inc .... C 419 537-1920
  Toledo *(G-13849)*
ITA INC .... E 513 631-7000
  Cincinnati *(G-2889)*
JBK Group Inc .... E 216 901-0000
  Cleveland *(G-4435)*
▲ Kern Inc .... E 614 317-2600
  Grove City *(G-8930)*
▲ Kmh Systems Inc .... E 800 962-3178
  Dayton *(G-7444)*
Lasting Imprsssons Event Pty Rn .... D 614 252-5400
  Columbus *(G-6143)*
Leading Families Home .... E 419 244-2175
  Toledo *(G-13883)*
Live Technologies LLC .... D 614 278-7777
  Columbus *(G-6171)*
Made From Scratch Inc .... E 614 873-3344
  Plain City *(G-12484)*
Maloney & Associates Inc .... E 330 477-7719
  Canton *(G-1799)*
MH Logistics Corp .... D 330 425-2476
  Medina *(G-10865)*
Miami Industrial Trucks Inc .... D 937 293-4194
  Moraine *(G-11425)*
Miller & Co Portable Toil Svcs .... E 330 453-9472
  Canton *(G-1808)*
Mobilcomm Inc .... D 513 742-5555
  Cincinnati *(G-3072)*
Modal Shop Inc .... D 513 351-9919
  Cincinnati *(G-3073)*
Modern Office Methods Inc .... E 513 791-0909
  Blue Ash *(G-1211)*
Modern Office Methods Inc .... D 513 791-0909
  Cincinnati *(G-3076)*
Multi-Flow Dispensers Ohio Inc .... D 216 641-0200
  Brooklyn Heights *(G-1425)*
National Tool Leasing Inc .... E 866 952-8665
  Eastlake *(G-8206)*
Northeast Projections Inc .... E 216 514-5023
  Cleveland *(G-4663)*
Ohio Machinery Co .... D 419 874-7975
  Perrysburg *(G-12359)*
One Sky Flight LLC .... E 877 703-2348
  Cleveland *(G-4698)*
ONeil Tent Co Inc .... E 614 837-6352
  Canal Winchester *(G-1614)*
Paul Peterson Safety Div Inc .... E 614 486-4375
  Columbus *(G-6505)*
Piqua Steel Co .... D 937 773-3632
  Piqua *(G-12454)*
Pncef LLC .... D 513 421-9191
  Cincinnati *(G-3217)*
Prime Time Pty Event Rentl LLC .... E 937 296-9262
  Moraine *(G-11429)*
Priority Equipment Rental Ltd .... E 724 227-3070
  Newark *(G-11743)*
Rentokil North America Inc .... E 513 247-9300
  Cincinnati *(G-3287)*
Resolute Industrial LLC .... E 513 779-7909
  West Chester *(G-14831)*
Robinair Leasing Co LLC .... E 513 530-1600
  Montpelier *(G-11386)*
Rumpke Transportation Co LLC .... B 937 461-0004
  Dayton *(G-7597)*
Rumpke Waste Inc .... C 937 548-1939
  Greenville *(G-8883)*
Smartpay Leasing LLC .... E 800 374-5587
  Cincinnati *(G-3388)*
South I Leasing Co LLC .... E 513 530-1600
  Boardman *(G-1291)*
Sunbelt Rentals Inc .... E 614 341-9770
  Columbus *(G-6729)*
Tempoe LLC .... E 415 390-2620
  Cincinnati *(G-3451)*
▲ Thomas Do-It Center Inc .... E 740 446-2002
  Gallipolis *(G-8769)*
▲ Towlift Inc .... C 216 749-6800
  Brooklyn Heights *(G-1428)*
Two Men & A Vacuum LLC .... D 614 300-7970
  Columbus *(G-6796)*
U Haul Co of Northwestern Ohio .... E 419 478-1101
  Toledo *(G-14078)*
United Rentals North Amer Inc .... E 614 276-5444
  Columbus *(G-6814)*
United Rentals North Amer Inc .... E 800 877-3687
  Perrysburg *(G-12383)*
▲ Valley Industrial Trucks Inc .... E 330 788-4081
  Youngstown *(G-15746)*
Vincent Lighting Systems Co .... E 216 475-7600
  Solon *(G-13161)*
Waco Scaffolding & Equipment Inc ...... A 216 749-8900
  Cleveland *(G-5119)*
Warwick Communications Inc .... E 216 787-0300
  Broadview Heights *(G-1404)*
Williams Scotsman Inc .... D 614 449-8675
  Columbus *(G-6894)*
Wmog Inc .... E 419 334-3801
  Fremont *(G-8709)*

7361 Employment agencies

11th Hour Staffing Inc .... D 937 405-1900
  Tipp City *(G-13650)*
A-1 Hlthcare Stffing Plcements .... C 216 329-3500
  Cleveland *(G-3753)*
Abacus Corporation .... B 614 367-7000
  Reynoldsburg *(G-12649)*
Abilities First Foundation Inc .... D 513 423-9496
  Middletown *(G-11149)*

SIC SECTION
73 BUSINESS SERVICES

Action Management Services............. E 216 642-8777
   Cleveland *(G-3766)*

Ado Professional Solutions Inc........... E 614 681-5050
   Columbus *(G-5314)*

Ado Professional Solutions Inc........... E 216 328-0888
   Independence *(G-9396)*

Advancement LLC............................. C 440 248-8550
   Solon *(G-13062)*

Advantage Resourcing Amer Inc........... E 781 472-8900
   Cincinnati *(G-2149)*

Advantage Rn LLC............................ D 866 301-4045
   West Chester *(G-14647)*

Advantage Tchncal Rsurcing Inc......... B 513 651-1111
   Cincinnati *(G-2150)*

Advantage Technical Svcs Inc............. D 513 852-4891
   Cincinnati *(G-2151)*

Akkodis Inc.................................... C 216 447-1909
   Independence *(G-9400)*

Alexander Mann Solutions Corp........... A 216 336-6756
   Cleveland *(G-3784)*

Alliance Legal Solutions LLC............... D 216 525-0100
   Independence *(G-9401)*

Alliance Solutions Group LLC............. E 216 503-1690
   Independence *(G-9402)*

Alliance Tchncal Solutions LLC............. E 216 548-2290
   Independence *(G-9403)*

Alternate Solutions First LLC............... C 937 298-1111
   Dayton *(G-7169)*

Amotec Inc..................................... E 440 250-4600
   Cleveland *(G-3811)*

Arrc One LLC................................. E 440 754-0855
   Oberlin *(G-12063)*

Beacon Hill Staffing Group LLC........... C 216 447-8900
   Independence *(G-9409)*

Belflex Staffing Network LLC............... C 513 488-8588
   Cincinnati *(G-2255)*

Berkheimer Enterprises LLC............... E 513 884-8702
   Milford *(G-11217)*

Berns Oneill SEC & Safety LLC........... E 330 374-9133
   Akron *(G-66)*

Buckeye Health Staffing LLC............... E 614 706-9437
   Marietta *(G-10359)*

Buckman Enochs Coss & Assoc......... E 614 825-6215
   Columbus *(G-5479)*

Cambridge Home Health Care............. A 330 725-1968
   Medina *(G-10816)*

Cardinalcommerce Corporation............. D 877 352-8444
   Mentor *(G-10918)*

Carestar Inc.................................... C 513 618-8300
   Cincinnati *(G-2313)*

Careworks of Ohio Inc....................... A 614 792-1085
   Dublin *(G-7958)*

Cavalry Staffing LLC......................... E 440 663-9990
   Cleveland *(G-3939)*

CBS Personnel Services LLC............. A 513 651-3600
   Cincinnati *(G-2325)*

Chapter Two Inc.............................. D 513 792-5100
   Blue Ash *(G-1149)*

Childrens Home Care Dayton............. D 937 641-4663
   Dayton *(G-7223)*

Cnsld Humacare- Employee MGT....... E 513 605-3522
   Cincinnati *(G-2467)*

Community Hlth Prfssionals Inc........... E 419 586-6266
   Celina *(G-1921)*

Community Hlth Prfssionals Inc........... C 419 238-9223
   Van Wert *(G-14342)*

Compass Professional Svcs LLC......... D 216 705-2233
   Cleveland *(G-4100)*

Compassnate Hnds Stffing Sltion......... E 216 710-6736
   Highland Heights *(G-9164)*

Comprhnsive Halthcare Svcs Inc......... C 513 245-0100
   Cincinnati *(G-2490)*

Construction Labor Contrs LLC........... C 216 741-3351
   Cleveland *(G-4109)*

Construction Labor Contrs LLC........... C 614 932-9937
   Columbus *(G-5684)*

Construction Labor Contrs LLC........... C 513 539-2904
   Monroe *(G-11337)*

Construction Labor Contrs LLC........... C 330 724-1906
   Uniontown *(G-14246)*

Corecrew LLC................................. E 855 692-6733
   West Chester *(G-14806)*

Creative Fincl Staffing LLC................. E 614 343-7800
   Worthington *(G-15410)*

Daily Services LLC........................... D 614 431-5100
   Columbus *(G-5737)*

Damascus Staffing LLC..................... D 513 954-8941
   Cincinnati *(G-2535)*

Dawson Resources........................... B 614 274-8900
   Columbus *(G-5743)*

Day Star Staffing LLC....................... E 440 481-1060
   North Olmsted *(G-11900)*

Decapua Enterprises Inc.................. E 614 255-1400
   Columbus *(G-5747)*

Dedicated Nursing Assoc Inc............. C 888 465-6929
   Beavercreek *(G-922)*

Dedicated Nursing Assoc Inc............. C 866 450-5550
   Hilliard *(G-9191)*

Dedicated Technologies Inc............... D 614 460-3200
   Columbus *(G-5748)*

Delta Diversified Inc......................... D 440 914-9400
   Solon *(G-13081)*

Dhr International Inc......................... D 513 762-7690
   Cincinnati *(G-2561)*

Diversfied Emplyee Sltions Inc............. E 330 764-4125
   Medina *(G-10830)*

Diversity Search Group LLC............. B 614 352-2988
   Columbus *(G-5775)*

Educare Medical Staffing LLP............. E 216 938-9374
   Woodmere *(G-15298)*

Emerald Resource Group Inc............. E 440 922-9000
   Broadview Heights *(G-1387)*

Endevis LLC................................. E 419 482-4848
   Sylvania *(G-13543)*

Excite It Partners LLC....................... E 216 447-9808
   Cleveland *(G-4230)*

Exodus Integrity Services Inc............. E 440 918-0140
   Willoughby *(G-15192)*

Fast Switch Ltd.............................. B 614 336-1122
   Dublin *(G-8011)*

First Chice Med Stffing Ohio I............. C 419 521-2700
   Mansfield *(G-10264)*

First Chice Med Stffing Ohio I............. B 216 521-2222
   Cleveland *(G-4256)*

First Dvrsity Stffing Group In............. E 937 323-4114
   Springfield *(G-13252)*

Focuscfo LLC................................. C 614 944-5760
   Westerville *(G-14979)*

Foxtrot Aviation Services LLC............. E 330 806-7477
   Canton *(G-1757)*

Gem City Home Care Llc.................. E 937 438-9100
   Dayton *(G-7374)*

Gilman Partners.............................. E 513 272-2400
   Cincinnati *(G-2733)*

Global Exec Slutions Group LLC......... E 330 666-3354
   Akron *(G-178)*

Global Tchnical Recruiters Inc............. D 440 365-1670
   Westlake *(G-15061)*

Gtradvance LLC.............................. C 440 365-1670
   Elyria *(G-8254)*

Gus Perdikakis Associates................. D 513 583-0900
   Cincinnati *(G-2784)*

Healthlinx Inc................................. E 614 542-2228
   Columbus *(G-5976)*

Heitmeyer Group LLC....................... C 614 699-5770
   Westerville *(G-14984)*

Heritage Health Care Services............. C 614 848-6550
   Columbus *(G-5988)*

Home Care Network Inc.................... C 216 378-9011
   Beachwood *(G-800)*

Home Care Network Inc.................... D 800 600-3974
   Dayton *(G-7408)*

Horizon Personnel Resources............. D 440 585-0031
   Wickliffe *(G-15152)*

Hr Services Inc............................... E 419 224-2462
   Lima *(G-9907)*

I-Force LLC................................... C 614 431-5100
   Columbus *(G-6037)*

Independent Personnel Services......... D 216 781-5350
   Cleveland *(G-4407)*

Interex Inc..................................... E 646 905-0091
   Beachwood *(G-803)*

Interim Hlthcare Columbus Inc............. B 330 836-5571
   Fairlawn *(G-8486)*

Interntnal Qlty Halthcare Corp............. E 513 731-3338
   Dayton *(G-7425)*

Its Technologies Inc......................... D 614 901-2265
   Westerville *(G-14990)*

Its Technologies Inc......................... D 419 842-2100
   Holland *(G-9290)*

Jack Black Staffing LLC.................... E 614 629-7614
   Columbus *(G-6079)*

Jarrett Companies Inc....................... E 330 682-0099
   Orrville *(G-12167)*

Job1usa Inc................................... C 419 255-5005
   Toledo *(G-13868)*

Jobsohio....................................... D 614 224-6446
   Columbus *(G-6093)*

Joe Knows Energy LLC.................... E 614 989-2228
   Dublin *(G-8043)*

Judge Group Inc............................. D 614 891-8337
   Westerville *(G-14901)*

Just In Time Staffing Inc.................... C 440 205-2002
   Mentor *(G-10957)*

K&K Technical Group Inc.................. C 513 202-1300
   Cincinnati *(G-2927)*

Kandu Group................................. D 419 425-2638
   Findlay *(G-8553)*

L2 Source LLC............................... E 513 428-4530
   Cincinnati *(G-2961)*

Mancan Inc................................... A 440 884-9675
   Cleveland *(G-4519)*

Mancan Inc................................... A 330 264-5375
   Wooster *(G-15353)*

Medi Home Health Agency Inc............. E 740 266-3977
   Steubenville *(G-13338)*

Medlink of Ohio Inc.......................... B 330 773-9434
   Akron *(G-228)*

Miracle Path Staffing Agcy Inc............. E 234 205-3541
   Fairlawn *(G-8490)*

Murtech Consulting LLC.................... D 216 328-8580
   Cleveland *(G-4611)*

Nesco Inc..................................... A 614 785-9675
   Gahanna *(G-8725)*

Nsc Glbal Mnaged Resources LLC..... E 646 499-9113
   Mason *(G-10585)*

Nurse Staffing Cincinnati LLC............. C 513 984-8414
   Cincinnati *(G-3136)*

Nurses Care Inc.............................. D 513 791-0233
   Milford *(G-11247)*

Nurses Heart Paramedics LLC............. E 614 648-5111
   Columbus *(G-6377)*

Ohio Dept Job & Fmly Svcs................. E 330 484-5402
   Akron *(G-248)*

On Search Partners LLC.................... D 440 318-1006
   Hudson *(G-9365)*

73 BUSINESS SERVICES

Ouicare Rcrtment Stffing Svcs............. E 440 536-4829
  Ashtabula (G-544)
Pathway Inc....................................... E 419 242-7304
  Toledo (G-13961)
Pearl Interactive Network Inc............. B 614 556-4470
  Columbus (G-6507)
Prn Health Services Inc..................... B 513 792-2217
  Cincinnati (G-3232)
Prn Nurse Inc.................................... B 614 864-9292
  Columbus (G-6547)
Professionals Group LLC................... E 330 957-5114
  Akron (G-273)
Prolink Resources LLC...................... D 866 777-3704
  Cincinnati (G-3250)
Promedica Physcn Cntinuum Svcs..... C 419 824-7200
  Sylvania (G-13565)
PSI Associates LLC........................... C 330 425-8474
  Twinsburg (G-14214)
Psychpros Inc................................... E 513 651-9500
  Cincinnati (G-3257)
▲ Quality Associates Inc.................... B 513 242-4477
  West Chester (G-14829)
Randstad Professionals Us LLC......... D 513 791-8600
  Blue Ash (G-1231)
Reserves Network Inc....................... E 440 779-1400
  Cleveland (G-4829)
Residential Care Inc.......................... E 937 299-8090
  Dayton (G-7589)
Rightthing LLC.................................. B 419 420-1830
  Findlay (G-8583)
Ringside Search Partners LLC............ E 614 643-0700
  Columbus (G-6589)
Riverfront Stffing Sltions Inc............... E 330 929-3002
  Cuyahoga Falls (G-7096)
Rumpf Corporation............................ E 419 255-5005
  Toledo (G-13999)
Salo Inc... E 877 759-2106
  Coshocton (G-7002)
SAR Warehouse Staffing LLC............. D 740 963-6235
  Columbus (G-6643)
Search Masters Inc........................... E 216 532-8660
  Independence (G-9482)
Siffrin Residential Assn...................... C 330 799-8932
  Youngstown (G-15724)
Simos Insourcing Solutions LLC......... D 614 470-6088
  Columbus (G-6682)
Staffing Studio LLC............................ E 614 934-1860
  Columbus (G-6708)
Staffmark Group LLC......................... D 513 651-1111
  Cincinnati (G-3404)
◆ Staffmark Investment LLC...............C 513 651-3600
  Cincinnati (G-3405)
Stamper Staffing LLC......................... E 937 938-7010
  Kettering (G-9633)
Surgeforce LLC.................................. A 614 431-4991
  Columbus (G-6736)
Synerfac Inc...................................... E 614 416-6010
  Westerville (G-14940)
Tailored Management Services.......... E 614 859-1500
  Columbus (G-6746)
Temp Tech LLC.................................. D 440 805-6037
  Cleveland (G-4983)
Thinkpath Engineering Svcs LLC........ E 937 291-8374
  Miamisburg (G-11097)
Trades Cnstr Staffing Inc................... C 833 668-0444
  West Chester (G-14776)
Tradesource Inc................................ D 614 824-3883
  Columbus (G-6780)
Tradesource Inc................................ D 216 801-4944
  Parma (G-12266)
Traincroft Inc..................................... E 513 792-0291
  Blue Ash (G-1256)

Triage LLC.. B 513 774-7300
  Loveland (G-10165)
Trustaff Management LLC................. A 513 272-3999
  Blue Ash (G-1260)
Twg Staffing LLC............................... C 877 293-3670
  Cincinnati (G-3538)
Vaco Cincinnati LLC.......................... B 513 239-5674
  Blue Ash (G-1265)
Vaco LLC... D 513 239-5674
  Blue Ash (G-1266)
Vector Technical Inc.......................... C 440 946-8800
  Willoughby (G-15225)
Vocational Guidance Services........... D 614 222-2899
  Columbus (G-6854)
Willcare Inc....................................... C 216 289-5300
  Cleveland (G-5148)
Willory LLC.. E 330 576-5486
  Bath (G-756)
Wtw Delaware Holdings LLC.............. D 216 937-4000
  Cleveland (G-5161)
Xpert Staffing LLC............................. D 330 969-9949
  Akron (G-366)

7363 Help supply services

Acloche LLC...................................... E 888 608-0889
  Columbus (G-5306)
Act I Temporaries Findlay Inc............. E 419 423-0713
  Findlay (G-8506)
Ado Staffing Inc................................ B 330 922-2077
  Cuyahoga Falls (G-7032)
Alliance Solutions Group LLC............ E 216 503-1690
  Independence (G-9402)
Alta It Services LLC........................... C 813 999-3101
  Cincinnati (G-2173)
Alternate Sltons Hlth Ntwrk LL........... D 937 681-9269
  Dayton (G-7168)
Alternate Sltons Hmcare Dyton.......... A 937 298-1111
  Kettering (G-9625)
American Bulk Commodities Inc........ C 330 758-0841
  Youngstown (G-15549)
Amerimed LLC................................... A 513 942-3670
  West Chester (G-14650)
Amotec Inc.. C 440 250-4600
  Cleveland (G-3811)
Arcadia Services Inc......................... E 330 869-9520
  Akron (G-54)
Arcadia Services Inc......................... E 937 912-5800
  Beavercreek (G-857)
Area Temps Inc................................. A 440 842-2100
  Cleveland (G-3833)
Area Temps Inc................................. A 216 227-8200
  Lakewood (G-9658)
Area Temps Inc................................. A 216 518-2000
  Maple Heights (G-10333)
Area Temps Inc................................. A 440 975-4400
  Mentor (G-10913)
Area Temps Inc................................. E 216 781-5350
  Independence (G-9407)
Belcan LLC.. A 513 891-0972
  Blue Ash (G-1132)
Belcan Svcs Group Ltd Partnr............ C 513 891-0972
  Blue Ash (G-1136)
Belflex Staffing Network LLC............. A 513 939-3444
  Fairfield (G-8393)
Belflex Staffing Network LLC............. C 513 488-8588
  Cincinnati (G-2255)
Buckeye Leasing Inc.......................... D 330 758-0841
  Youngstown (G-15567)
Callos Resource LLC......................... E 330 788-3033
  Youngstown (G-15569)
Cavalry Staffing LLC.......................... E 440 663-9990
  Cleveland (G-3939)

CBS Personnel Services LLC............. A 513 651-3600
  Cincinnati (G-2325)
Central Ohio Hospitalists.................. E 614 255-6900
  Columbus (G-5539)
▲ Channel Products Inc..................... D 440 423-0113
  Solon (G-13075)
CHI Health At Home........................... E 513 576-0262
  Milford (G-11221)
Classic Medical Staffing LLC............. D 216 688-0900
  Cleveland (G-3998)
Cohesion Corporation........................ C 813 999-3101
  Cincinnati (G-2469)
Constant Aviation LLC....................... C 800 440-9004
  Cleveland (G-4108)
Corporate Aviation Svcs Inc............... D 740 338-3100
  Saint Clairsville (G-12788)
Creative Fincl Staffing LLC................ E 614 343-7800
  Worthington (G-15410)
Custom Personnel Inc....................... B 330 723-4131
  Medina (G-10826)
Decapua Enterprises Inc................... E 614 255-1400
  Columbus (G-5747)
Dedicated Nursing Assoc Inc............. C 888 465-6929
  Beavercreek (G-922)
Dedicated Nursing Assoc Inc............. C 866 450-5550
  Hilliard (G-9191)
Dedicated Tech Services Inc............. E 614 309-0059
  Dublin (G-7986)
Edge Plastics Inc............................... E 419 522-6696
  Mansfield (G-10260)
Emily Management Inc...................... D 440 354-6713
  Concord Township (G-6926)
Emp Holdings Ltd............................... E 330 493-4443
  Canton (G-1746)
Extras Support Staffing..................... C 740 671-3996
  Bellaire (G-1012)
Falcon Partners LLC.......................... E 216 896-1010
  Cleveland (G-4239)
Flex-Temp Employment Svcs Inc....... C 419 355-9675
  Fremont (G-8677)
Frontline National LLC....................... D 513 528-7823
  Milford (G-11229)
Health Carousel LLC.......................... E 855 665-4544
  Cincinnati (G-2808)
Heiser Staffing Services LLC............. E 614 800-4188
  Columbus (G-5983)
Hogan Truck Leasing Inc................... E 513 454-3500
  Fairfield (G-8418)
Hogan Truck Leasing Inc................... E 937 293-0033
  Moraine (G-11417)
Horizon Personnel Resources........... D 440 585-0031
  Wickliffe (G-15152)
Hr Services Inc.................................. E 419 224-2462
  Lima (G-9907)
▲ Industrial Repair and Mfg............... E 419 822-4232
  Delta (G-7851)
Innovtive Sltons Unlimited LLC.......... C 740 289-3282
  Piketon (G-12423)
Innovtive Sltons Unlimited LLC.......... D 740 289-3282
  Piketon (G-12424)
▲ Integrated Marketing Tech Inc........ D 330 225-3550
  Brunswick (G-1460)
Interim Halthcare Columbus Inc......... B 330 836-5571
  Fairlawn (G-8486)
Interim Hlthcare Cambridge Inc......... E 740 432-2966
  Worthington (G-15423)
Its Technologies Inc.......................... D 419 842-2100
  Holland (G-9290)
Job1usa Inc....................................... C 419 255-5005
  Toledo (G-13868)
Labor Ready Midwest Inc.................. D 419 382-6565
  Toledo (G-13881)

SIC SECTION

73 BUSINESS SERVICES

Locum Medical Group LLC.................. D 216 464-2125
  Independence (G-9447)
Macair Aviation LLC............................ E 937 347-1302
  Xenia (G-15525)
Magnit APC I LLC................................ E 614 252-7300
  Gahanna (G-8721)
Maxim Healthcare Services Inc............. D 330 670-1054
  Akron (G-227)
Maxim Healthcare Services Inc............. D 216 606-3000
  Independence (G-9450)
Med1care Ltd...................................... D 419 866-0555
  Findlay (G-8565)
Medlink of Ohio Inc............................. B 330 773-9434
  Akron (G-228)
Minute Men Inc................................... D 216 426-2225
  Cleveland (G-4589)
Minute Men Select Inc......................... E 216 452-0100
  Cleveland (G-4590)
Netjets Assn Shred Arcft Plots.............. E 614 532-0555
  Columbus (G-6347)
New View Management Group Inc........ D 513 733-4444
  Cincinnati (G-3110)
Nobletek LLC...................................... E 330 287-1500
  Wooster (G-15361)
Nursenow LLC.................................... D 812 868-7732
  Maumee (G-10751)
Ohio Dept Job & Fmly Svcs.................. E 419 334-3891
  Fremont (G-8696)
Paradigm Industrial LLC...................... E 937 224-4415
  Dayton (G-7546)
Physician Staffing Inc.......................... B 440 542-5000
  Cleveland (G-4748)
Planet Healthcare LLC......................... D 888 845-2539
  Westlake (G-15099)
Pontoon Solutions Inc......................... A 855 881-1533
  Maumee (G-10756)
Preferred Temporary Svcs Inc............... E 330 494-5502
  Canton (G-1830)
Prestige Technical Svcs Inc.................. D 513 779-6800
  West Chester (G-14746)
Prn Nurse Inc...................................... B 614 864-9292
  Columbus (G-6547)
Professional Transportation.................. B 419 661-0576
  Walbridge (G-14463)
Prolink Healthcare Staffing................... D 513 489-5300
  Montgomery (G-11373)
Prolink Staffing Services LLC................ A 614 405-9810
  Dublin (G-8099)
Prolink Staffing Services LLC................ D 513 489-5300
  Cincinnati (G-3251)
Promedica Employment Svcs LLC......... A 419 824-7529
  Toledo (G-13968)
Quadax Inc... C 330 759-4600
  Youngstown (G-15702)
Reserves Network Inc......................... E 440 779-1400
  Cleveland (G-4829)
Residential Care Inc............................ B 937 299-8090
  Dayton (G-7589)
Ringside Search Partners LLC............... E 614 643-0700
  Columbus (G-6589)
Rumpf Corporation.............................. E 419 255-5005
  Toledo (G-13999)
Safegard Bckgrund Screening LLC........ E 877 700-7345
  Beachwood (G-834)
Salo Inc.. C 419 419-0038
  Bowling Green (G-1332)
Salo Inc.. E 877 759-2106
  Coshocton (G-7002)
Salo Inc.. C 740 653-5990
  Lancaster (G-9740)
Sequent Inc.. D 614 436-5880
  Westerville (G-14937)

Sfn Group Inc..................................... A 419 727-4104
  Toledo (G-14009)
Spherion of Lima Inc........................... A 567 208-5471
  Findlay (G-8586)
Spherion of Lima Inc........................... E 419 224-8367
  Lima (G-9964)
Staffmark Group LLC........................... D 513 651-1111
  Cincinnati (G-3404)
Stafftech Inc....................................... D 937 228-2667
  Dayton (G-7637)
Super Shine Inc.................................. E 513 423-8999
  Middletown (G-11190)
Supplemental Healthcare..................... E 937 247-0169
  Miamisburg (G-11096)
Technical Aid Corporation.................... E 781 251-8000
  Cincinnati (G-3448)
Transportation Unlimited Inc................ A 216 426-0088
  Cleveland (G-5033)
Tsl Ltd.. A 419 843-3200
  Toledo (G-14075)
Twist Aero Inc..................................... E 937 675-9581
  Jamestown (G-9536)
Universal Express LLC......................... E 404 642-4747
  Dayton (G-7688)
Upshift Work LLC................................ C 513 813-5695
  Cincinnati (G-3598)
Vernovis Ltd....................................... D 513 234-7201
  Mason (G-10623)
Youth Intensive Services Inc................ E 330 318-3436
  Youngstown (G-15761)

7371 Custom computer programming services

121ecommerce LLC............................ E 216 586-6656
  University Heights (G-14274)
1848 Ventures LLC.............................. C 330 887-0187
  Westfield Center (G-15023)
1worldsync Inc................................... D 866 280-4013
  Dayton (G-7146)
2060 Digital LLC................................. E 513 699-5012
  Cincinnati (G-2121)
22nd Century Technologies Inc............. B 866 537-9191
  Beavercreek (G-854)
2immersive4u Corporation................... E 440 570-4055
  North Royalton (G-11937)
3d Systems Inc................................... E 216 229-2040
  Cleveland (G-3746)
Aclara Technologies LLC...................... C 440 528-7200
  Solon (G-13061)
Advanced Prgrm Resources Inc............. E 614 761-9994
  Dublin (G-7920)
Agility Partners LLC............................. D 740 819-2712
  Columbus (G-5330)
Akkodis Inc... C 513 769-9797
  Blue Ash (G-1126)
Aktion Associates Incorporated............. E 419 893-7001
  Maumee (G-10686)
Amcs Group Inc................................... D 419 891-1100
  Toledo (G-13681)
Analex Corporation.............................. E 703 721-6001
  Brook Park (G-1405)
ARC Healthcare LLC............................ E 888 552-0677
  Worthington (G-15405)
Arcos LLC... C 614 396-5500
  Columbus (G-5384)
Assurecare LLC................................... E 513 618-2150
  Cincinnati (G-2220)
Autoway Investors Ltd......................... E 419 841-6691
  Toledo (G-13696)
Avertest LLC....................................... E 330 591-7219
  Medina (G-10812)

▲ B-Tek Scales LLC............................. E 330 471-8900
  Canton (G-1684)
Balaji D Loganathan............................. C 614 918-0411
  Hilliard (G-9182)
Batterii LLC.. E 513 379-3595
  Cincinnati (G-2239)
Belcan Staffing Solution....................... E 513 241-8367
  Cincinnati (G-2254)
▲ Benchmark Digital Partners LLC........ D 513 774-1000
  Mason (G-10523)
Bennett Adelson Prof Svcs LLC............. E 216 369-0140
  Cleveland (G-3870)
Big Red Rooster.................................. E 614 255-0200
  Columbus (G-5440)
▲ Blue Creek Enterprises Inc............... E 937 364-2920
  Lynchburg (G-10183)
Bluespring Software Inc....................... E 513 794-1764
  Blue Ash (G-1138)
Bold Penguin Company LLC................. C 614 344-1029
  Columbus (G-5454)
Briteskies LLC..................................... E 216 369-3600
  Cleveland (G-3895)
Btas Inc.. D 937 431-9431
  Beavercreek (G-866)
Business Equipment Co Inc.................. E 513 948-1500
  Cincinnati (G-2293)
Camgen Ltd.. D 330 204-8636
  Cleveland (G-3920)
Campuseai Inc..................................... C 216 589-9626
  Cleveland (G-3921)
▲ Cdo Technologies Inc...................... D 937 258-0022
  Dayton (G-7128)
Cengage Learning Inc.......................... B 513 229-1000
  Mason (G-10527)
Cerkl Incorporated............................... D 513 813-8425
  Blue Ash (G-1147)
Cerner Corporation.............................. E 740 826-7678
  New Concord (G-11609)
Chesterfield Services Inc...................... E 330 896-9777
  Uniontown (G-14245)
Cimx LLC.. E 513 248-7700
  Cincinnati (G-2390)
▲ Cincom Systems Inc........................ B 513 612-2300
  Cincinnati (G-2438)
Cintech LLC.. E 513 731-6000
  Cincinnati (G-2446)
Click4care Inc..................................... E 614 431-3700
  Powell (G-12588)
Clubessential LLC............................... E 800 448-1475
  Blue Ash (G-1153)
Cochin Technologies LLC..................... E 440 941-4856
  Avon (G-648)
Coleman Professional Svcs Inc.............. C 330 673-1347
  Kent (G-9565)
Command Alkon Incorporated............... E 614 799-0600
  Dublin (G-7967)
Commercial Time Sharing Inc............... E 330 644-3059
  Akron (G-115)
Commsys Inc...................................... E 937 220-4990
  Dayton (G-7241)
Computer Aided Technology LLC.......... D 513 745-2700
  Cincinnati (G-2491)
Constructconnect Inc........................... C 800 364-2059
  Cincinnati (G-2498)
Convention Vstors Bur of Grter.............. E 216 875-6600
  Cleveland (G-4114)
Cott Systems Inc................................. D 614 847-4405
  Columbus (G-5707)
Critical Business Analysis Inc................ E 419 874-0800
  Perrysburg (G-12326)
▲ Crosschx Inc.................................. D 800 501-3161
  Columbus (G-5730)

Employee Codes: A=Over 500 employees, B=251-500
C=101-250, D=51-100, E=20-50, F=10-19, G=1-9

73 BUSINESS SERVICES

Cryptic Vector LLC .... D 513 318-9061
  Liberty Township *(G-9851)*

Csg Cleveland Enterprises Inc .... E 440 918-9341
  Richmond Heights *(G-12717)*

CT Logistics Inc .... C 216 267-1636
  Cleveland *(G-4143)*

Darcie R Clark Lpcc LLC .... E 937 319-4448
  Dayton *(G-7267)*

Dash Technologies Inc .... C 614 593-3274
  Dublin *(G-7981)*

Data Systems Intgrtion Group I .... C 614 344-4600
  Dublin *(G-7982)*

Datavantage Corporation .... B 440 498-4414
  Cleveland *(G-4150)*

Dedicated Tech Services Inc .... E 614 309-0059
  Dublin *(G-7986)*

Deemsys Inc .... D 614 322-9928
  Gahanna *(G-8715)*

Deep Mind Music LLC .... D 440 829-6401
  Lakewood *(G-9664)*

Devcare Solutions Ltd .... E 614 221-2277
  Westerville *(G-14888)*

▲ Dexxxon Digital Storage Inc .... E 740 548-7179
  Lewis Center *(G-9817)*

Dhl Infrmtion Svcs Amricas Inc .... E 614 865-5993
  Westerville *(G-14890)*

Differential Dev Shop LLC .... E 513 205-8930
  Cincinnati *(G-2564)*

Digital Forensics Corp LLC .... E 888 210-1296
  Warrensville Heights *(G-14580)*

Digitek Software Inc .... E 614 764-8875
  Lewis Center *(G-9819)*

Distribution Data Incorporated .... D 216 362-3009
  Brookpark *(G-1433)*

Diversified Systems Inc .... E 614 476-9939
  Westerville *(G-14976)*

Dizer Corp .... C 440 368-0201
  Painesville *(G-12227)*

DMC Technology Group Inc .... E 419 535-2900
  Toledo *(G-13782)*

DOT Net Factory LLC .... D 614 792-0645
  Dublin *(G-7988)*

Dotloop LLC .... E 513 257-0550
  Cincinnati *(G-2575)*

Double A Solutions LLC .... D 256 489-6458
  Toledo *(G-13783)*

Drb Holdings LLC .... B 330 645-3299
  Akron *(G-138)*

Drb Systems LLC .... B 330 645-3299
  Akron *(G-139)*

Drs Signal Technologies Inc .... E 937 429-7470
  Beavercreek *(G-878)*

Drund Ltd .... D 330 402-5944
  Boardman *(G-1287)*

Dynamite Technologies LLC .... E 614 538-0095
  Columbus *(G-5797)*

E2 Infosystems Ltd .... E 833 832-4637
  New Albany *(G-11562)*

Echo 360 Inc .... E 877 324-6360
  Youngstown *(G-15606)*

Eci Macola/Max LLC .... C 978 539-6186
  Dublin *(G-8000)*

Edaptive Computing Inc .... D 937 433-0477
  Dayton *(G-7329)*

Emplifi Inc .... E 614 508-6100
  Columbus *(G-5815)*

Empora Title Inc .... E 937 360-8876
  Columbus *(G-5816)*

Emprise Technologies LLC .... D 419 720-6982
  Toledo *(G-13791)*

Engineering Cons Group Inc .... D 330 869-9949
  Fairlawn *(G-8477)*

◆ Envisionware Inc .... E 678 382-6530
  Columbus *(G-5822)*

Epicor Edi Source Inc .... D 440 519-7800
  Solon *(G-13084)*

Epsilon .... C 513 248-2882
  Milford *(G-11226)*

Evanhoe & Associates Inc .... E 937 235-2995
  Xenia *(G-15505)*

Evolv LLC .... E 440 994-9115
  Hudson *(G-9346)*

Exodus Integrity Services Inc .... E 440 918-0140
  Willoughby *(G-15192)*

Expesite LLC .... E 614 917-1100
  Columbus *(G-5839)*

▲ Fastems LLC .... E 513 779-4614
  West Chester *(G-14690)*

Fenetech LLC .... C 330 995-2830
  Solon *(G-13088)*

First Data Gvrnmnt Solutns Inc .... C 513 489-9599
  Blue Ash *(G-1174)*

First Mobile Trust LLC .... E 855 270-3592
  Miamisburg *(G-11055)*

Flairsoft Ltd .... E 614 888-0700
  Columbus *(G-5872)*

Foresight Corporation .... E 614 791-1600
  Dublin *(G-8013)*

Forge LLC .... E 937 461-6560
  Bellbrook *(G-1016)*

Formfire LLC .... E 866 448-2302
  Cleveland *(G-4277)*

Foundation Software LLC .... B 330 220-8383
  Strongsville *(G-13457)*

Framework Mi Inc .... E 513 444-2165
  Cincinnati *(G-2700)*

Frontier Technology Inc .... E 937 429-3302
  Beavercreek Township *(G-939)*

▲ Fscreations Corporation .... D 330 746-3015
  Youngstown *(G-15614)*

Fund Evaluation Group LLC .... E 513 977-4400
  Cincinnati *(G-2711)*

Fundable LLC .... E 614 364-4523
  Powell *(G-12591)*

Fusian Inc .... E 937 361-7146
  Columbus *(G-5902)*

Fusion Alliance LLC .... C 513 563-8444
  Blue Ash *(G-1177)*

Fusion Alliance LLC .... C 614 852-8000
  Columbus *(G-5259)*

Genomoncology LLC .... E 440 617-6087
  Mentor *(G-10942)*

Geoamps LLC .... E 614 389-4872
  Delaware *(G-7801)*

▼ Gracie Plum Investments Inc .... E 740 355-9029
  Portsmouth *(G-12552)*

Harley-Dvidson Dlr Systems Inc .... D 216 573-1393
  Cleveland *(G-4350)*

Henry Call Inc .... C 216 433-5609
  Cleveland *(G-4358)*

Holo Pundits Inc .... E 614 707-5225
  Dublin *(G-8029)*

Horizon Payroll Services Inc .... B 937 434-8244
  Dayton *(G-7414)*

Humanit Solutions LLC .... D 937 901-7576
  Beavercreek Township *(G-941)*

Icr Inc .... C 513 900-7007
  Mason *(G-10563)*

Ils Technology LLC .... E 800 695-8650
  Cleveland *(G-4404)*

Imflux Inc .... D 513 488-1017
  Cincinnati *(G-2865)*

Infinite Tiers Inc .... B 513 769-1900
  Cincinnati *(G-2869)*

Info-Hold Inc .... E 513 248-5600
  Cincinnati *(G-2870)*

Infovision21 Inc .... E 614 761-8844
  Dublin *(G-8038)*

Insurance Technologies Corp .... E 866 683-6915
  Columbus *(G-6061)*

Intelligrated Inc .... A 513 874-0788
  West Chester *(G-14820)*

▲ Intelligrated Systems Inc .... A 866 936-7300
  Mason *(G-10565)*

Intelligrated Systems LLC .... A 513 701-7300
  Mason *(G-10566)*

International Technegroup Inc .... D 513 576-3900
  Milford *(G-11233)*

Iotco LLC .... E 877 464-6826
  Cincinnati *(G-2887)*

Irth Solutions Inc .... E 614 459-2328
  Columbus *(G-6071)*

Itcube LLC .... E 513 891-7300
  Blue Ash *(G-1186)*

J Becker Solutions Inc .... D 888 421-1155
  Westlake *(G-15072)*

▲ Jenne Inc .... C 440 835-0040
  Avon *(G-656)*

Jifiticom Inc .... C 914 339-5376
  Columbus *(G-6090)*

Jjr Solutions LLC .... E 937 912-0288
  Dayton *(G-7429)*

Jyg Innovations LLC .... D 937 630-3858
  Dayton *(G-7431)*

▲ Keithley Instruments LLC .... C 440 248-0400
  Solon *(G-13103)*

Keyfactor Inc .... C 216 785-2986
  Independence *(G-9440)*

Kk Associates LLC .... E 614 783-7966
  Dublin *(G-8050)*

Knowledge MGT Interactive Inc .... E 614 224-0664
  Columbus *(G-6124)*

Knowledge Support Systems Inc .... E 973 408-9157
  Independence *(G-9441)*

Kognetics LLC .... E 614 591-4416
  Gahanna *(G-8720)*

Krish Services Group Inc .... E 813 784-0039
  Brecksville *(G-1356)*

Lakeland Foundation .... E 440 525-7094
  Willoughby *(G-15202)*

Leidos Inc .... D 937 656-8433
  Beavercreek *(G-886)*

Liberty Comm Sftwr Sltions Inc .... E 614 318-5000
  Columbus *(G-6156)*

Liberty Home Mortgage Corp .... C 440 644-0001
  Independence *(G-9443)*

Lifecycle Solutions Jv LLC .... D 937 938-1321
  Beavercreek *(G-887)*

Lisnr Inc .... E 513 322-8400
  Cincinnati *(G-2981)*

Logic Soft Inc .... D 614 884-5544
  Dublin *(G-8057)*

London Computer Systems Inc .... D 513 583-0840
  Cincinnati *(G-2986)*

Losant Iot Inc .... E 513 381-2947
  Cincinnati *(G-2987)*

Main Sequence Technology Inc .... E 440 946-5214
  Willoughby *(G-15209)*

Main Sequence Technology Inc .... E 440 946-5214
  Mentor On The Lake *(G-11015)*

Manifest Solutions Corp .... D 614 930-2800
  Upper Arlington *(G-14280)*

Mansfeld Ohio Arie No 336 Frtn .... E 419 636-7812
  Bryan *(G-1487)*

Mapsys Inc .... D 614 255-7258
  Columbus *(G-6193)*

73 BUSINESS SERVICES

Marshall Information Svcs LLC............... E 614 430-0355
   Columbus *(G-6198)*

Marxent Labs LLC................................... E 727 851-9522
   Miamisburg *(G-11071)*

▲ Masterbrand Cabinets LLC.................. B 812 482-2527
   Beachwood *(G-812)*

Materials MGT Microsystems.................. D 262 240-9900
   Mentor *(G-10966)*

Mediu Inc... E 614 332-7410
   Delaware *(G-7817)*

Montpelier Exempted Vlg Schl................ E 419 485-3676
   Montpelier *(G-11385)*

Mri Software LLC..................................... B 800 321-8770
   Solon *(G-13114)*

Muc Holdings LLC.................................. E 513 417-8452
   Cincinnati *(G-3088)*

Navistone Inc.. E 844 677-3667
   Cincinnati *(G-3099)*

Netsmart Technologies Inc..................... B 800 434-2642
   Dublin *(G-8074)*

Neumeric Technologies Corp.................. D 614 610-4999
   Lewis Center *(G-9831)*

New Albany Country Club LLC................ C 614 939-8500
   New Albany *(G-11579)*

New Innovations Inc............................... E 330 899-9954
   Uniontown *(G-14260)*

Nextgen Federal Systems LLC................ C 304 413-0208
   Beavercreek Township *(G-944)*

Nuonosys Inc... E 888 666-7976
   Independence *(G-9461)*

Oeconnection LLC................................... D 888 776-5792
   Akron *(G-246)*

Office World Inc...................................... E 419 991-4694
   Lima *(G-9994)*

Onshift Inc... C 216 333-1353
   Cleveland *(G-4700)*

Open Practice Solutions Ltd................... E 234 380-8345
   Hudson *(G-9366)*

Operating Tax Systems LLC.................... A 330 940-3967
   Stow *(G-13383)*

Overdrive Inc.. D 216 573-6886
   Cleveland *(G-4711)*

Pcms Datafit Inc...................................... D 513 587-3100
   Blue Ash *(G-1219)*

Pcms International Inc............................. D 513 587-3100
   Cincinnati *(G-3192)*

Pearl Interactive Network Inc................. B 614 556-4470
   Columbus *(G-6507)*

Pegasus Technical Services Inc.............. D 513 793-0094
   Cincinnati *(G-3194)*

Physna Inc.. D 844 474-9762
   Columbus *(G-6523)*

Playaway Products LLC.......................... D 440 893-0808
   Solon *(G-13128)*

Plumbline Solutions Inc.......................... E 419 581-2963
   Findlay *(G-8577)*

Positive Bus Solutions Inc...................... D 513 772-2255
   Cincinnati *(G-3222)*

Premier Nursing Network LLC................ D 440 563-1586
   Middlefield *(G-11144)*

Projetech Inc... E 513 481-4900
   Cincinnati *(G-3248)*

Pulse Ltd LLC... E 216 570-7732
   Chesterland *(G-2042)*

Q4-2 Inc... E 440 256-3870
   Willoughby *(G-15219)*

Qc Software LLC..................................... E 513 469-1424
   Cincinnati *(G-3259)*

Quality Ip LLC.. D 330 931-4141
   Kent *(G-9592)*

Quick Solutions Inc................................. C 614 825-8000
   Columbus *(G-5280)*

Rainbow Data Systems Inc..................... E 937 431-8000
   Beavercreek *(G-899)*

Ready Set Grow LLC............................... E 513 445-2939
   Cincinnati *(G-3275)*

Reflexis Systems Inc............................... C 614 948-1931
   Westerville *(G-14933)*

Renaissancetech...................................... E 419 569-3999
   Dublin *(G-8107)*

Resource International Inc...................... C 614 823-4949
   Columbus *(G-6587)*

Rhyme Software Corporation.................. D 888 213-3728
   New Albany *(G-11585)*

Rippe & Kingston Systems Inc................ D 513 977-4578
   Cincinnati *(G-3299)*

Robots and Pencils LP............................. C 866 515-9897
   Chagrin Falls *(G-1965)*

Saama Technologies Inc.......................... D 614 652-6100
   Worthington *(G-15454)*

Sacred Hour Inc....................................... D 216 228-9750
   Lakewood *(G-9684)*

Sadler-Necamp Financial Svcs................ E 513 489-5477
   Cincinnati *(G-3337)*

Saec/Kinetic Vision Inc........................... C 513 793-4959
   Cincinnati *(G-3338)*

Sanctuary Software Studio Inc............... E 330 666-9690
   Fairlawn *(G-8496)*

▲ Sarcom Inc... A 614 854-1300
   Lewis Center *(G-9835)*

Sawdey Solution Services Inc................. E 937 490-4060
   Beavercreek *(G-930)*

Scriptdrop Inc.. D 614 641-0648
   Columbus *(G-6656)*

Service Pronet LLC................................. E 614 874-4300
   Columbus *(G-6665)*

Shiftwise... E 513 476-1532
   Columbus *(G-6672)*

Shoptech Industrial Sftwr Corp............... E 513 985-9900
   Cincinnati *(G-3371)*

Siemens Industry Software Inc............... E 513 576-2400
   Milford *(G-11256)*

Siertek Ltd... E 937 623-2466
   Beavercreek Township *(G-948)*

Solutons Thrugh Innvtive Tech............... D 937 320-9994
   Beavercreek *(G-907)*

Spacepointe Inc....................................... E 937 886-7995
   Dayton *(G-7632)*

Starship Technologies Inc...................... C 440 251-7096
   Bowling Green *(G-1333)*

Strategic Data Systems Inc.................... C 513 772-7374
   Cincinnati *(G-3422)*

Sumaria Systems LLC............................. C 937 429-6070
   Beavercreek *(G-909)*

Sumtotal Systems LLC............................ E 352 264-2800
   Columbus *(G-6728)*

Switchbox Inc.. E 614 334-9517
   Columbus *(G-6739)*

Synapse Tech Services Inc..................... E 337 592-3205
   Columbus *(G-6742)*

Systems Evolution Inc............................. E 513 459-1992
   Cincinnati *(G-3431)*

T-Cetra LLC... C 877 956-2359
   Dublin *(G-8139)*

Talis Clinical LLC................................... D 234 284-2399
   Streetsboro *(G-13431)*

Tangram Flex Inc.................................... E 937 985-3199
   Dayton *(G-7659)*

Tata America Intl Corp............................ B 513 677-6500
   Milford *(G-11259)*

Teamdynamix Solutions LLC................... E 877 752-6196
   Columbus *(G-6752)*

Tensure Consulting LLC.......................... D 513 428-4493
   Mason *(G-10615)*

Terillium Inc.. C 513 621-9500
   Cincinnati *(G-3457)*

Tradeglobal LLC...................................... C 866 345-5835
   West Chester *(G-14775)*

Trayak Inc.. E 513 252-8089
   Mason *(G-10618)*

Trz Holdings Inc..................................... E 419 931-0072
   Perrysburg *(G-12381)*

Unicon International Inc......................... D 614 861-7070
   Columbus *(G-6799)*

Vantage Solutions Inc............................ D 330 757-4864
   Poland *(G-12511)*

Vendorinsight... E 800 997-2674
   Blue Ash *(G-1269)*

▼ Ventech Solutions Inc.......................... D 614 757-1167
   Columbus *(G-5284)*

Vertex Computer Systems Inc................ C 513 662-6888
   Cincinnati *(G-3624)*

Virtual Hold Tech Slutions LLC............... E 330 670-2200
   Akron *(G-353)*

Vooks Inc... D 503 694-9217
   Stow *(G-13401)*

Votem Corp... D 216 930-4300
   Cleveland *(G-5116)*

Widepint Intgrted Sltions Corp.............. D 614 410-1587
   Columbus *(G-6890)*

Workstate Consulting LLC...................... E 614 559-3904
   Columbus *(G-6903)*

Wtw Delaware Holdings LLC.................. D 216 937-4000
   Cleveland *(G-5161)*

Xngage LLC... E 440 990-5767
   Middleburg Heights *(G-11136)*

Yardi Systems... E 805 699-2056
   Cleveland *(G-5164)*

Yashco Systems Inc................................ D 614 467-4600
   Hilliard *(G-9247)*

Zaps Technocrats Inc.............................. D 614 664-3199
   Dublin *(G-8167)*

7372 Prepackaged software

Acu-Serve Corp....................................... C 330 923-5258
   Akron *(G-16)*

Advanced Prgrm Resources Inc.............. E 614 761-9994
   Dublin *(G-7920)*

Agile Global Solutions Inc..................... E 916 655-7745
   Independence *(G-9398)*

Avt Technology Solutions LLC............... D 727 539-7429
   Groveport *(G-8973)*

Butler Tech... E 513 867-1028
   Fairfield Township *(G-8458)*

Cbts Technology Solutions LLC.............. B 440 569-2300
   Cleveland *(G-3945)*

Cequence Security Inc........................... C 650 437-6338
   Blue Ash *(G-1146)*

Cerkl Incorporated.................................. D 513 813-8425
   Blue Ash *(G-1147)*

Cerner Corporation................................. D 740 826-7678
   New Concord *(G-11609)*

Check Point Software Tech Inc............... D 440 748-0900
   Cleveland *(G-3964)*

Cimx LLC... E 513 248-7700
   Cincinnati *(G-2390)*

Clinicl Otcms Mngmnt Syst LLC.............. D 330 650-9900
   Broadview Heights *(G-1386)*

Creative Microsystems Inc..................... D 937 836-4499
   Englewood *(G-8304)*

D+h USA Corporation............................. C 513 381-9400
   Cincinnati *(G-2533)*

Dakota Software Corporation.................. D 216 765-7100
   Cleveland *(G-4148)*

Datatrak International Inc....................... E 440 443-0082
   Beachwood *(G-786)*

73 BUSINESS SERVICES

Delphia Consulting LLC .... E 614 421-2000
 Columbus (G-5754)
Delta Media Group Inc .... D 330 493-0350
 North Canton (G-11820)
Drb Holdings LLC .... B 330 645-3299
 Akron (G-138)
Drb Systems LLC .... B 330 645-3299
 Akron (G-139)
Eci Macola/Max LLC .... C 978 539-6186
 Dublin (G-8000)
Edict Systems Inc .... E 937 429-4288
 Beavercreek (G-879)
◆ Esko-Graphics Inc .... D 937 454-1721
 Miamisburg (G-11051)
Facilities Management Ex LLC .... D 614 519-2186
 Columbus (G-5842)
Foundation Software LLC .... B 330 220-8383
 Strongsville (G-13457)
▲ Fscreations Corporation .... D 330 746-3015
 Youngstown (G-15614)
Gaslight Holdings LLC .... E 513 470-3525
 Cincinnati (G-2716)
▼ Gracie Plum Investments Inc .... E 740 355-9029
 Portsmouth (G-12552)
Hyland Software Inc .... A 440 788-5000
 Westlake (G-15068)
Igel Technology America Inc .... E 954 739-9990
 Cincinnati (G-2863)
Mim Software Inc .... C 216 455-0600
 Beachwood (G-817)
Move Ez Inc .... D 844 466-8339
 Columbus (G-6280)
Navistone Inc .... E 844 677-3667
 Cincinnati (G-3099)
Nextmed Systems Inc .... E 216 674-0511
 Cincinnati (G-3113)
Northrop Grmmn Spce & Mssn Sys .... D 937 259-4956
 Dayton (G-7531)
▲ Ohio Cllbrtive Lrng Sltons Inc .... E 216 595-5289
 Strongsville (G-13479)
Onx Acquisition LLC .... B 440 569-2300
 Mayfield Heights (G-10791)
Onx Holdings LLC .... D 866 587-2287
 Cincinnati (G-3164)
Open Text Inc .... E 614 658-3588
 Hilliard (G-9224)
Pamee LLC .... E 216 232-9255
 Rocky River (G-12751)
Parallel Technologies Inc .... D 614 798-9700
 Dublin (G-8087)
Patrick J Burke & Co .... E 513 455-8200
 Cincinnati (G-3189)
Patriot Software LLC .... D 877 968-7147
 Canton (G-1828)
Qc Software LLC .... E 513 469-1424
 Cincinnati (G-3259)
Quest Software Inc .... E 614 336-9223
 Dublin (G-8103)
Rebiz LLC .... E 844 467-3249
 Cleveland (G-4811)
Retalix Inc .... E 937 384-2277
 Miamisburg (G-11089)
Revolution Group Inc .... D 614 212-1111
 Westerville (G-14935)
Rivals Sports Grille LLC .... E 216 267-0005
 Middleburg Heights (G-11125)
Sanctuary Software Studio Inc .... E 330 666-9690
 Fairlawn (G-8496)
▲ Sarcom Inc .... A 614 854-1300
 Lewis Center (G-9835)
SC Strategic Solutions LLC .... C 567 424-6054
 Norwalk (G-12027)

Sigmatek Systems LLC .... D 513 674-0005
 Cincinnati (G-3377)
Snap-On Business Solutions Inc .... B 330 659-1600
 Richfield (G-12710)
Starwin Industries LLC .... E 937 293-8568
 Dayton (G-7639)
Sterling Commerce LLC .... A 614 798-2192
 Dublin (G-8126)
Tata America Intl Corp .... B 513 677-6500
 Milford (G-11259)
To Scale Software LLC .... E 513 253-0053
 Mason (G-10616)
TOA Technologies Inc .... C 216 925-5950
 Beachwood (G-844)
Trimble Trnsp Entp Sltions Inc .... C 216 831-6606
 Mayfield Heights (G-10793)
◆ Turning Technologies LLC .... C 330 746-3015
 Youngstown (G-15740)
Ultraedit Inc .... D 216 464-7465
 Hamilton (G-9088)
Upshift Work LLC .... E 513 813-5695
 Cincinnati (G-3598)
Veeam Software Corporation .... A 614 339-8200
 Columbus (G-5283)
Virtual Hold Tech Slutions LLC .... E 330 670-2200
 Akron (G-353)
Vndly LLC .... E 513 572-2500
 Mason (G-10625)
Zipscene LLC .... D 513 201-5174
 Cincinnati (G-3698)
Zullix LLC .... E 440 536-9300
 Rocky River (G-12758)

7373 Computer integrated systems design

3c Technology Solutions LLC .... E 614 319-4681
 Hilliard (G-9174)
Aclara Technologies LLC .... C 440 528-7200
 Solon (G-13061)
Advanced Prgrm Resources Inc .... E 614 761-9994
 Dublin (G-7920)
Advizex Technologies LLC .... E 513 229-8400
 Blue Ash (G-1125)
Advizex Technologies LLC .... D 614 318-0386
 Columbus (G-5319)
Advizex Technologies LLC .... E 216 901-1818
 Independence (G-9397)
Afidence Inc .... E 513 234-5822
 Mason (G-10518)
Alta It Services LLC .... C 813 999-3101
 Cincinnati (G-2173)
Altamira Technologies Corp .... C 937 490-4804
 Beavercreek (G-856)
▲ Ats Carolina Inc .... C 803 324-9300
 Lewis Center (G-9807)
Baxter Hdell Dnnlly Prston Inc .... C 513 271-1634
 Cincinnati (G-2240)
Belcan Corporation .... E 513 891-0972
 Blue Ash (G-1134)
▲ Blue Creek Enterprises Inc .... E 937 364-2920
 Lynchburg (G-10183)
Bpi Infrmtion Systems Ohio Inc .... E 440 717-4112
 Brecksville (G-1345)
Brandmuscle Inc .... C 216 464-4342
 Cleveland (G-3890)
Caci Mtl Systems Inc .... D 937 429-2771
 Beavercreek (G-868)
Caci Mtl Systems Inc .... D 937 426-3111
 Beavercreek (G-869)
Caci-CMS Info Systems LLC .... C 937 986-3600
 Fairborn (G-8368)
Cameo Solutions Inc .... E 513 645-4220
 West Chester (G-14658)

Career Cnnctons Stffing Svcs I .... E 440 471-8210
 Westlake (G-15045)
Carolinas It LLC .... D 919 856-2300
 Dublin (G-7959)
▲ Cdo Technologies Inc .... D 937 258-0022
 Dayton (G-7128)
◆ Cincinnati Bell Inc .... B 513 397-9900
 Cincinnati (G-2398)
Cincinnati Trning Trml Svcs In .... D 513 563-4474
 Cincinnati (G-2429)
Cohesion Corporation .... C 813 999-3101
 Cincinnati (G-2469)
Commercial Time Sharing Inc .... E 330 644-3059
 Akron (G-115)
Commsys Inc .... E 937 220-4990
 Dayton (G-7241)
Concentrix Cvg Corporation .... A 800 747-0583
 Cincinnati (G-2492)
Contingent Network Services LLC ...... C 513 616-5773
 West Chester (G-14674)
Cott Systems Inc .... D 614 847-4405
 Columbus (G-5707)
Creative Microsystems Inc .... D 937 836-4499
 Englewood (G-8304)
▼ Data Processing Sciences .... D 513 791-7100
 Cincinnati (G-2539)
Dedicated Tech Services Inc .... E 614 309-0059
 Dublin (G-7986)
Deemsys Inc .... D 614 322-9928
 Gahanna (G-8715)
Devcare Solutions Ltd .... E 614 221-2277
 Westerville (G-14888)
Dewesoft LLC .... D 855 339-3669
 Whitehouse (G-15140)
Drb Holdings LLC .... B 330 645-3299
 Akron (G-138)
Drb Systems LLC .... B 330 645-3299
 Akron (G-139)
E-Merging Technologies Group Inc .... D 440 779-5680
 Cleveland (G-4194)
Easy2 Technologies Inc .... E 216 479-0482
 Cleveland (G-4200)
Eosys Group Inc .... E 513 217-7294
 Middletown (G-11163)
Evanhoe & Associates Inc .... E 937 235-2995
 Xenia (G-15505)
Freedom Usa Inc .... E 216 503-6374
 Twinsburg (G-14192)
Humanit Solutions LLC .... D 937 901-7576
 Beavercreek Township (G-941)
ID Networks Inc .... E 440 992-0062
 Ashtabula (G-538)
Jackson Control Co Inc .... E 513 824-9850
 Cincinnati (G-2893)
K&R Network Solutions .... E 858 292-5766
 Dublin (G-8044)
◆ Kc Robotics Inc .... E 513 860-4442
 West Chester (G-14717)
Leidos Inc .... D 937 656-8433
 Beavercreek (G-886)
Logos Communications Systems Inc .. D 440 871-0777
 Westlake (G-15076)
Lucrum Incorporated .... E 513 241-5949
 Cincinnati (G-2993)
Manatron Inc .... E 937 431-4000
 Beavercreek (G-925)
Manifest Solutions Corp .... D 614 930-2800
 Upper Arlington (G-14280)
Mapsys Inc .... D 614 255-7258
 Columbus (G-6193)
Marcus Thomas Llc .... D 216 292-4700
 Cleveland (G-4523)

SIC SECTION
73 BUSINESS SERVICES

Microman Inc .... E 614 923-8000
  Dublin (G-8064)
Mid-America Consulting Group Inc .... D
  Cleveland (G-4574)
Millenium Control Systems LLC .... E 440 510-0050
  Eastlake (G-8205)
Netsmart Technologies Inc .... B 800 434-2642
  Dublin (G-8074)
Northrop Grmman Tchncal Svcs I .... D 937 320-3100
  Beavercreek Township (G-945)
Pantek Incorporated .... E 216 344-1614
  Independence (G-9465)
Pcms Datafit Inc .... D 513 587-3100
  Blue Ash (G-1219)
Pegasus Technical Services Inc .... D 513 793-0094
  Cincinnati (G-3194)
▲ Pinnacle Data Systems Inc .... C 614 748-1150
  Groveport (G-8995)
Pomeroy It Solutions Sls Inc .... E 440 717-1364
  Brecksville (G-1363)
Possible Worldwide LLC .... E 513 381-1380
  Cincinnati (G-3223)
Presidio Infrstrcture Sltons L .... E 614 381-1400
  Dublin (G-8095)
Presidio Infrstrcture Sltons L .... E 419 241-8303
  Toledo (G-13966)
Process Plus Holdings Inc .... D 513 742-7590
  Cincinnati (G-3241)
Rainbow Data Systems Inc .... E 937 431-8000
  Beavercreek (G-899)
▲ Reynolds and Reynolds Company ...... A 937 485-2000
  Kettering (G-9632)
Rockwell Automation Ohio LLC .... D 513 576-6151
  Milford (G-11254)
Rovisys Company .... D 330 562-8600
  Aurora (G-626)
▲ Sarcom Inc .... A 614 854-1300
  Lewis Center (G-9835)
Sentient Studios Ltd .... E 330 204-8636
  Fairlawn (G-8499)
Sgi Matrix LLC .... D 937 438-9033
  Miamisburg (G-11092)
Siertek Ltd .... E 937 623-2466
  Beavercreek Township (G-948)
Sogeti USA LLC .... C 614 847-4477
  Westerville (G-15015)
Sterling Buying Group LLC .... E 513 564-9000
  Cincinnati (G-3416)
Sterling Commerce (america) LLC .... A 614 793-7000
  Dublin (G-8125)
Streamline Technical Svcs LLC .... D 614 441-7448
  Lockbourne (G-10016)
Sumaria Systems LLC .... C 937 429-6070
  Beavercreek (G-909)
▲ Systemax Manufacturing Inc .... D 937 368-2300
  Dayton (G-7658)
Sytronics Inc .... E 937 431-6100
  Beavercreek (G-910)
Talx Corporation .... D 614 527-9404
  Hilliard (G-9235)
Tangram Flex Inc .... E 937 985-3199
  Dayton (G-7659)
Tata America Intl Corp .... B 513 677-6500
  Milford (G-11259)
Teknobility LLC .... E 216 255-9433
  Medina (G-10898)
Thinkpath Engineering Svcs LLC .... E 937 291-8374
  Miamisburg (G-11097)
Twism Enterprises LLC .... E 513 800-1098
  Cincinnati (G-3539)
United Technical Support Svcs .... C 330 562-3330
  Streetsboro (G-13433)

Velocity A Managed Svcs Co Inc .... C 419 868-9983
  Holland (G-9311)
▼ Ventech Solutions Inc .... D 614 757-1167
  Columbus (G-5284)
Vintek Inc .... D 937 382-8986
  Wilmington (G-15277)

7374 Data processing and preparation

1st All File Recovery Usa .... E 800 399-7150
  Cleveland (G-3742)
ACS Computer Services Corp .... D 614 351-8298
  Columbus (G-5309)
ADP Rpo .... E 419 420-1830
  Findlay (G-8507)
▲ Aero Fulfillment Services Corp .... D 800 225-7145
  Mason (G-10517)
Alt Media Studios LLC .... E 440 777-6666
  Novelty (G-12036)
Amsive OH LLC .... D 937 885-8000
  Miamisburg (G-11024)
Bold Penguin Company LLC .... C 614 344-1029
  Columbus (G-5454)
Btas Inc .... D 937 431-9431
  Beavercreek (G-866)
Cash Flow Solutions Inc .... D 513 524-2320
  Oxford (G-12205)
◆ Cincinnati Bell Inc .... B 513 397-9900
  Cincinnati (G-2398)
City of Cleveland .... E 216 664-2430
  Cleveland (G-3985)
Clubessential LLC .... E 800 448-1475
  Blue Ash (G-1153)
Coleman Professional Svcs Inc .... C 330 673-1347
  Kent (G-9565)
Comcage LLC .... E 513 549-4003
  Cincinnati (G-2479)
Concentrix Cvg Corporation .... A 800 747-0583
  Cincinnati (G-2492)
Concentrix Solutions Corp .... E 480 968-2496
  Cincinnati (G-2494)
Continental Broadband PA .... D 877 570-7827
  Columbus (G-5691)
County of Stark .... E 330 451-7232
  Canton (G-1726)
Csi Complete Inc .... E 800 343-0641
  Plain City (G-12472)
Ctrac Inc .... E 440 572-1000
  Cleveland (G-4144)
Datatrak International Inc .... D 440 443-0082
  Beachwood (G-786)
Early Express Services Inc .... E 937 223-5801
  Dayton (G-7322)
▼ Gracie Plum Investments Inc .... E 740 355-9029
  Portsmouth (G-12552)
Great Lakes Publishing Company .... D 216 771-2833
  Cleveland (G-4330)
Hyperquake LLC .... E 513 563-6555
  Cincinnati (G-2862)
Illumination Works LLC .... D 937 938-1321
  Beavercreek (G-884)
Infovision21 Inc .... E 614 761-8844
  Dublin (G-8038)
Integrated Data Services Inc .... E 937 656-5496
  Dayton (G-7422)
▲ Integrated Marketing Tech Inc .... D 330 225-3550
  Brunswick (G-1460)
Interact One Inc .... E 513 469-7042
  Blue Ash (G-1185)
Isaac Instruments LLC .... E 888 658-7520
  Cleveland (G-4424)
ITM Marketing Inc .... C 740 295-3575
  Coshocton (G-6988)

Karcher Group Inc .... E 330 493-6141
  North Canton (G-11843)
Lunar Cow Design Inc .... D 330 836-0911
  Akron (G-226)
Mast Technology Services Inc .... E 614 415-7000
  Columbus (G-6204)
Medical Mutual Services LLC .... C 440 878-4800
  Strongsville (G-13475)
Midland Council Governments .... E 330 264-6047
  Wooster (G-15356)
Mri Software LLC .... B 800 321-8770
  Solon (G-13114)
Northrop Grmmn Spce & Mssn Sys .... D 937 259-4956
  Dayton (G-7531)
Northwest Ohio Computer Assn .... E 419 267-5565
  Archbold (G-464)
Office World Inc .... E 419 991-4694
  Lima (G-9994)
Ohio State University .... D 614 292-3416
  Columbus (G-6457)
Ohio United Agency Inc .... E 419 562-3011
  Bucyrus (G-1515)
Personalized Data Corporation .... E 216 289-2200
  Cleveland (G-4743)
Prisma Integration Corp .... E 330 545-8690
  Girard (G-8823)
Rebiz LLC .... E 844 467-3249
  Cleveland (G-4811)
Relational Solutions Inc .... E 440 899-3296
  North Olmsted (G-11913)
Rurbanc Data Services Inc .... D 419 782-2530
  Defiance (G-7767)
▲ Sarcom Inc .... A 614 854-1300
  Lewis Center (G-9835)
SC Strategic Solutions LLC .... C 567 424-6054
  Norwalk (G-12027)
Sedlak Management Consultants .... E 216 206-4700
  Cleveland (G-4890)
Service Pronet LLC .... E 614 874-4300
  Columbus (G-6665)
Skylight Partners Inc .... E 513 381-5555
  Cincinnati (G-3385)
Southstern Ohio Vlntary Edcatn .... E 740 594-7663
  Athens (G-591)
Spa Performance Inc .... E 216 455-1540
  Cleveland (G-4925)
Speedeon Data LLC .... E 440 264-2100
  Cleveland (G-4932)
Sumaria Systems LLC .... C 937 429-6070
  Beavercreek (G-909)
Thunder Tech Inc .... E 216 391-2255
  Cleveland (G-5017)
Universal Enterprises Inc .... E 419 529-3500
  Ontario (G-12126)
Vndly LLC .... E 513 572-2500
  Mason (G-10625)
Worldpay LLC .... B
  Symmes Twp (G-13583)

7375 Information retrieval services

AGS Custom Graphics Inc .... D 330 963-7770
  Macedonia (G-10188)
Armstrong Utilities Inc .... D 330 723-3536
  Medina (G-10808)
Atlas Partners LLC .... C 937 439-7970
  Dayton (G-7183)
Bluespring Software Inc .... E 513 794-1764
  Blue Ash (G-1138)
Com Net Inc .... D 419 739-3100
  Wapakoneta (G-14481)
Community Isp Inc .... E 419 867-6060
  Toledo (G-13752)

73 BUSINESS SERVICES

End-User Computing Inc .... D 419 292-2200
   Toledo *(G-13793)*

Hkm Drect Mkt Cmmnications Inc .... C 800 860-4456
   Cleveland *(G-4367)*

Innovative Technologies Corp .... D 937 252-2145
   Dayton *(G-7135)*

Lexisnexis Group .... C 937 865-6900
   Miamisburg *(G-11068)*

▲ Lexisnexis Group .... C 937 865-6800
   Miamisburg *(G-11069)*

Medical Mutual Services LLC .... C 440 878-4800
   Strongsville *(G-13475)*

Oclc Inc .... A 614 764-6000
   Dublin *(G-8079)*

Png Telecommunications Inc .... D 513 942-7900
   Cincinnati *(G-3218)*

Relational Solutions Inc .... E 440 899-3296
   North Olmsted *(G-11913)*

Relx Inc .... C 937 865-1012
   Dayton *(G-7141)*

Security Hut Inc .... D 216 226-0461
   Lakewood *(G-9685)*

Simplified Logistics LLC .... E 440 250-8912
   Westlake *(G-15109)*

Title First Agency Inc .... E 614 347-8383
   Westerville *(G-14942)*

TSC Communications Inc .... D 419 739-2200
   Wapakoneta *(G-14492)*

7376 Computer facilities management

ARC Healthcare LLC .... E 888 552-0677
   Worthington *(G-15405)*

Career Cnnctons Stffing Svcs I .... E 440 471-8210
   Westlake *(G-15045)*

City of Cleveland .... E 216 664-2941
   Cleveland *(G-3986)*

Dedicated Tech Services Inc .... E 614 309-0059
   Dublin *(G-7986)*

Evanhoe & Associates Inc .... E 937 235-2995
   Xenia *(G-15505)*

General Electric Company .... C 513 583-3500
   Cincinnati *(G-2724)*

Interactive Payer Network LLC .... E
   Cleveland *(G-4417)*

Jjr Solutions LLC .... E 937 912-0288
   Dayton *(G-7429)*

Jyg Innovations LLC .... D 937 630-3858
   Dayton *(G-7431)*

K&R Network Solutions .... E 858 292-5766
   Dublin *(G-8044)*

Park Place Technologies LLC .... C 877 778-8707
   Cleveland *(G-4724)*

Reliant Technology LLC .... E 404 551-4534
   Cleveland *(G-4822)*

Siertek Ltd .... E 937 623-2466
   Beavercreek Township *(G-948)*

Technical Assurance Inc .... E 440 953-3147
   Willoughby *(G-15222)*

7377 Computer rental and leasing

▼ Data Processing Sciences .... D 513 791-7100
   Cincinnati *(G-2539)*

Pomeroy It Solutions Sls Inc .... E 440 717-1364
   Brecksville *(G-1363)*

Reliant Technology LLC .... E 404 551-4534
   Cleveland *(G-4822)*

Target Systems Inc .... E 440 239-1600
   Cleveland *(G-4977)*

7378 Computer maintenance and repair

Aptos LLC .... D 614 840-1400
   Lewis Center *(G-9806)*

Avnet Integrated Inc .... E 614 851-8700
   Groveport *(G-8972)*

Bpi Infrmtion Systems Ohio Inc .... E 440 717-4112
   Brecksville *(G-1345)*

Bsl - Applied Laser Tech LLC .... E 216 663-8181
   Independence *(G-9413)*

Career Cnnctons Stffing Svcs I .... E 440 471-8210
   Westlake *(G-15045)*

CTS Construction Inc .... D 513 489-8290
   Cincinnati *(G-2521)*

Custom Hdwr Engrg Cnslting LLC .... C 636 305-9669
   Cleveland *(G-4145)*

Datatech Depot (east) Inc .... E 513 860-5651
   West Chester *(G-14682)*

DMC Technology Group Inc .... E 419 535-2900
   Toledo *(G-13782)*

Efix It Solutions LLC .... E 937 476-7533
   Dayton *(G-7330)*

Evanhoe & Associates Inc .... E 937 235-2995
   Xenia *(G-15505)*

Geeks On Call .... D 800 905-4335
   Independence *(G-9433)*

Government Acquisitions Inc .... E 513 721-8700
   Cincinnati *(G-2744)*

Great Lakes Computer Corp .... D 440 937-1100
   Avon *(G-652)*

Mt Business Technologies Inc .... C 419 529-6100
   Mansfield *(G-10300)*

Park Place Technologies LLC .... E 603 617-7123
   Cleveland *(G-4723)*

Park Place Technologies LLC .... B 610 544-0571
   Mayfield Heights *(G-10792)*

Park Place Technologies LLC .... C 877 778-8707
   Cleveland *(G-4724)*

Perry Pro Tech Inc .... D 419 228-1360
   Lima *(G-9948)*

▲ Pinnacle Data Systems Inc .... C 614 748-1150
   Groveport *(G-8995)*

Pomeroy It Solutions Sls Inc .... E 440 717-1364
   Brecksville *(G-1363)*

Positive Bus Solutions Inc .... D 513 772-2255
   Cincinnati *(G-3222)*

Projetech Inc .... E 513 481-4900
   Cincinnati *(G-3248)*

Resource One Cmpt Systems Inc .... E 614 485-4800
   Worthington *(G-15452)*

Sjn Data Center LLC .... E 513 386-7871
   Cincinnati *(G-3381)*

Vertiv Corporation .... C 614 841-6400
   Westerville *(G-14948)*

Vertiv Services Inc .... A 614 841-6400
   Westerville *(G-14950)*

WD Bpi LLC .... E 440 717-4112
   Brecksville *(G-1371)*

Wellington Technologies Inc .... E 440 238-4377
   Westlake *(G-15123)*

Xtek Partners Inc .... E 614 973-7400
   Columbus *(G-6913)*

7379 Computer related services, nec

3sg Corporation .... B 614 761-8394
   Dublin *(G-7918)*

Advanced Prgrm Resources Inc .... E 614 761-9994
   Dublin *(G-7920)*

Affiliated Resource Group Inc .... D 614 889-6555
   Dublin *(G-7922)*

Amazon Data Services Inc .... E 206 617-0149
   Hilliard *(G-9177)*

American Bus Solutions Inc .... D 614 888-2227
   Lewis Center *(G-9804)*

Americas Headquarters .... D 614 339-8200
   Columbus *(G-5245)*

Arcos LLC .... C 614 396-5500
   Columbus *(G-5384)*

Arctos Mission Solutions LLC .... E 813 609-5591
   Beavercreek *(G-858)*

Array Information Tech Inc .... E 937 203-3209
   Beavercreek *(G-860)*

Ascendum Solutions LLC .... E 513 792-5100
   Blue Ash *(G-1131)*

Atos It Solutions and Svcs Inc .... B 513 336-1000
   Mason *(G-10521)*

Blue Chip Consulting Group LLC .... E 216 503-6001
   Seven Hills *(G-12951)*

Cadre Computer Resources Co .... E 513 762-7350
   Cincinnati *(G-2300)*

Calyx LLC .... E 216 916-0639
   Westlake *(G-15043)*

Capgemini America Inc .... B 678 427-6642
   Miamisburg *(G-11032)*

Cardinal Solutions Group Inc .... D 513 984-6700
   Cincinnati *(G-2308)*

Career Cnnctons Stffing Svcs I .... E 440 471-8210
   Westlake *(G-15045)*

Carolinas It LLC .... D 919 856-2300
   Dublin *(G-7959)*

Carpenter & Lee Consulting LLC .... E 614 766-8670
   Delaware *(G-7783)*

Cbiz Technologies LLC .... E 216 447-9000
   Independence *(G-9417)*

Cbts LLC .... E 440 478-8447
   Cincinnati *(G-2327)*

Cbts Technology Solutions LLC .... B 440 569-2300
   Cleveland *(G-3945)*

▼ Cbts Technology Solutions LLC .... B 513 841-2287
   Cincinnati *(G-2328)*

Cgi Technologies Solutions Inc .... C 216 687-1480
   Cleveland *(G-3958)*

Cgi Technologies Solutions Inc .... D 614 880-2200
   Columbus *(G-5251)*

Chapter Two Inc .... D 513 792-5100
   Blue Ash *(G-1149)*

◆ Cincinnati Bell Inc .... B 513 397-9900
   Cincinnati *(G-2398)*

Cincinnati Trning Trml Svcs In .... D 513 563-4474
   Cincinnati *(G-2429)*

Codex Techworks Inc .... E 614 486-9900
   Columbus *(G-5591)*

Comresource Inc .... E 614 221-6348
   Columbus *(G-5680)*

Contingent Network Services LLC .... C 513 616-5773
   West Chester *(G-14674)*

Credence MGT Sltions Ltd Lblty .... C 571 620-7586
   Beavercreek *(G-875)*

Creek Technologies Company .... C 937 272-4581
   Beavercreek *(G-876)*

Data Recovery Services LLC .... D 330 397-0100
   Youngstown *(G-15593)*

Datafield Inc .... C 614 847-9600
   Worthington *(G-15412)*

Datalysys LLC .... E 614 495-0260
   Dublin *(G-7984)*

Dedicated Tech Services Inc .... E 614 309-0059
   Dublin *(G-7986)*

Diversified Systems Inc .... E 614 476-9939
   Westerville *(G-14976)*

DMC Technology Group Inc .... E 419 535-2900
   Toledo *(G-13782)*

▲ E-Mek Technologies LLC .... E 937 424-3166
   Dayton *(G-7320)*

E2b Teknologies Inc .... E 440 352-4700
   Mentor *(G-10934)*

Eight Eleven Group LLC .... C 513 533-7350
   Cincinnati *(G-2607)*

73 BUSINESS SERVICES

Enviro It LLC.................................... E 614 453-0709
   Columbus *(G-5821)*
Epicor Edi Source Inc................... D 440 519-7800
   Solon *(G-13084)*
Erp Analysts Inc............................ B 614 718-9222
   Dublin *(G-8007)*
Evanhoe & Associates Inc............ E 937 235-2995
   Xenia *(G-15505)*
Everest Technologies Inc.............. E 614 436-3120
   Columbus *(G-5834)*
Expedient Tech Solutions LLC....... E 937 535-4300
   Miamisburg *(G-11054)*
Fit Technologies LLC..................... E 216 583-5000
   Cleveland *(G-4261)*
Foxhire LLC................................... E 330 454-3508
   Canton *(G-1756)*
Franklin Cmpt Svcs Group Inc....... E 614 431-3327
   New Albany *(G-11566)*
Freedom Usa Inc........................... E 216 503-6374
   Twinsburg *(G-14192)*
▲ Fscreations Corporation............ D 330 746-3015
   Youngstown *(G-15614)*
G2o LLC... B 614 523-3070
   Dublin *(G-8018)*
Genesis Corp................................. D 330 597-4100
   Akron *(G-175)*
Global Associates Inc................... E 937 312-1204
   Dayton *(G-7376)*
Golden Resources Incorporated... E 513 342-6290
   West Chester *(G-14698)*
GP Strategies Corporation............. E 513 583-8810
   Cincinnati *(G-2745)*
Great Nthrn Cnsulting Svcs Inc...... E 614 890-9999
   Columbus *(G-5951)*
Greentree Group Inc..................... D 937 490-5500
   Dayton *(G-7388)*
Humanit Solutions LLC.................. D 937 901-7576
   Beavercreek Township *(G-941)*
Iler Networking & Cmpt Ltd........... E 440 748-8083
   Sheffield Village *(G-12999)*
Illumination Works LLC................. D 937 938-1321
   Beavercreek *(G-884)*
Indus Valley Consultants Inc......... E 937 660-4748
   Miamisburg *(G-11063)*
Infovision21 Inc............................. E 614 761-8844
   Dublin *(G-8038)*
Innomark Communications LLC.... C 888 466-6627
   Miamisburg *(G-11064)*
Integrated Root Systems LLC........ E 216 282-7470
   Cleveland *(G-4416)*
Interactive Bus Systems Inc.......... D 513 984-2205
   Cincinnati *(G-2879)*
Intralot Inc..................................... E 440 268-2900
   Strongsville *(G-13466)*
Itelligence Outsourcing Inc........... D 513 956-2000
   Cincinnati *(G-2890)*
Ivhr LLC... E 216 445-4315
   Cleveland *(G-4425)*
Jjr Solutions LLC........................... E 937 912-0288
   Dayton *(G-7429)*
Jyg Innovations LLC...................... D 937 630-3858
   Dayton *(G-7431)*
K&R Network Solutions.................. E 858 292-5766
   Dublin *(G-8044)*
Keystone Technology Cons........... E 330 666-6200
   Akron *(G-216)*
Lan Solutions Inc.......................... D 513 469-6500
   Blue Ash *(G-1197)*
Lanco Global Systems Inc............ E 937 660-8090
   Dayton *(G-7449)*
▲ Leadership Circle LLC............... E 801 518-2980
   Whitehouse *(G-15143)*

Leading Edje LLC.......................... E 614 636-3353
   Dublin *(G-8053)*
Leading Edje LLC.......................... E 614 636-3353
   Columbus *(G-5267)*
London Computer Systems Inc.... D 513 583-0840
   Cincinnati *(G-2986)*
Lucrum Incorporated..................... E 513 241-5949
   Cincinnati *(G-2993)*
Main Sail LLC................................ E 216 472-5100
   Chesterland *(G-2039)*
Martin Wilson and Associates...... D 513 772-7284
   Cincinnati *(G-3013)*
Maven LLC..................................... E 614 353-3873
   Columbus *(G-6208)*
Mavennext Inc............................... E 800 850-8708
   Columbus *(G-6209)*
McData Services Corporation........ E 614 272-5529
   Columbus *(G-6214)*
▼ Meyer Hill Lynch Corporation... E 419 897-9797
   Maumee *(G-10748)*
Mt Business Technologies Inc...... C 419 529-6100
   Mansfield *(G-10300)*
Netwave Corporation..................... E 614 850-6300
   Dublin *(G-8075)*
Nextcable Corporation.................. E 330 576-3154
   Akron *(G-242)*
Ntt Data Bus Solutions Inc........... E 513 956-2000
   Cincinnati *(G-3133)*
Olr America Inc............................. E 612 436-4970
   Solon *(G-13120)*
Onx Acquisition LLC...................... B 440 569-2300
   Mayfield Heights *(G-10791)*
Onx Entrprise Solutions US Inc..... C 440 569-2300
   Cleveland *(G-4701)*
Onx Holdings LLC.......................... D 866 587-2287
   Cincinnati *(G-3164)*
Optimum Technology Inc.............. E 614 785-1110
   Powell *(G-12602)*
Park Place Technologies LLC....... C 877 778-8707
   Cleveland *(G-4724)*
Plumbline Consulting LLC............ E 419 581-2973
   Findlay *(G-8576)*
Plus One Communications LLC... B 330 255-4500
   Akron *(G-267)*
Premiere Medical Resources Inc.. E 330 923-5899
   Cuyahoga Falls *(G-7094)*
Pressco Technology Inc................ D 440 715-2559
   Solon *(G-13130)*
Quest Def Systems Slutions Inc... D 513 628-4521
   Blue Ash *(G-1227)*
R Dorsey & Company Inc.............. D 614 486-8900
   Columbus *(G-6558)*
Rainbow Data Systems Inc.......... E 937 431-8000
   Beavercreek *(G-899)*
Resolvit Resources LLC................ E 513 619-5900
   Cincinnati *(G-3292)*
Resource One Solutions LLC........ E 614 485-8500
   Worthington *(G-15453)*
Revel It Inc.................................... D 614 336-1122
   Dublin *(G-8109)*
Revolution Group Inc.................... D 614 212-1111
   Westerville *(G-14935)*
Rippe & Kingston Systems Inc..... D 513 977-4578
   Cincinnati *(G-3299)*
Riverside Computing Inc............... D 937 440-9199
   Dayton *(G-7594)*
Rockwell Automation Ohio LLC.... D 513 576-6151
   Milford *(G-11254)*
Roundtower Technologies LLC..... D 513 247-7900
   Cincinnati *(G-3326)*
▲ Sarcom Inc................................ A 614 854-1300
   Lewis Center *(G-9835)*

Satyam Computer Services Ltd.... C 216 654-1800
   Cleveland *(G-4876)*
Securedata LLC............................ E 323 944-0822
   Mayfield Village *(G-10796)*
Server Suites LLC......................... C 513 831-5528
   Loveland *(G-10158)*
Siertek Ltd.................................... E 937 623-2466
   Beavercreek Township *(G-948)*
Sikich LLP..................................... E 513 482-1127
   Cincinnati *(G-3378)*
Sjn Data Center LLC..................... E 513 386-7871
   Cincinnati *(G-3381)*
Snapblox Hosted Solutions LLC... E 866 524-7707
   Cincinnati *(G-3390)*
Sogeti USA LLC............................. C 513 824-3000
   Blue Ash *(G-1245)*
Sogeti USA LLC............................. D 216 654-2230
   Cleveland *(G-4916)*
Sogeti USA LLC............................. D 937 433-3334
   Dayton *(G-7624)*
Sogeti USA LLC............................. D 937 291-8142
   West Chester *(G-14767)*
Sogeti USA LLC............................. C 614 847-4477
   Westerville *(G-15015)*
Sogeti USA LLC............................. C 937 291-8100
   Miamisburg *(G-11094)*
Speedeon Data LLC...................... E 440 264-2100
   Cleveland *(G-4932)*
Star Seven Six Ltd........................ E 800 669-9623
   Columbus *(G-6712)*
Strategic Systems Inc.................. C 614 717-4774
   Dublin *(G-8132)*
Sudhi Infomatics Inc..................... E 855 200-6650
   Lewis Center *(G-9836)*
Svats Inc....................................... E 614 214-4115
   Lewis Center *(G-9837)*
Synapse Tech Services Inc........... E 337 592-3205
   Columbus *(G-6742)*
Technology Recovery Group Ltd... D 440 250-9970
   Westlake *(G-15114)*
Terillium Inc.................................. C 513 621-9500
   Cincinnati *(G-3457)*
Thunderyard Solutions LLC.......... E 281 222-3644
   Westlake *(G-15115)*
Unicon International Inc............... D 614 861-7070
   Columbus *(G-6799)*
Vana Solutions LLC....................... E 937 242-6399
   Beavercreek *(G-913)*
▼ Ventech Solutions Inc............... D 614 757-1167
   Columbus *(G-5284)*
Vertical Knowledge LLC................ E 216 920-7790
   Chagrin Falls *(G-1970)*
Vigilant LLC.................................. D 513 300-1460
   Liberty Township *(G-9859)*
Vinson Group LLC......................... E 440 283-8832
   Akron *(G-352)*
Vitalyst LLC.................................. C 216 201-9070
   Cleveland *(G-5110)*
Wolters Kluwer Clinical D............. D 330 650-6506
   Hudson *(G-9378)*
Workstate Consulting LLC............ E 614 559-3904
   Columbus *(G-6903)*
World Synergy Enterprises Inc..... E 440 349-4940
   Beachwood *(G-852)*
Zaps Technocrats Inc.................... D 614 664-3199
   Dublin *(G-8167)*
Zin Technologies Inc..................... E 440 625-2200
   Middleburg Heights *(G-11137)*

7381 Detective and armored car services

1st Advnce SEC Invstgtions Inc.... D 937 210-9010
   Dayton *(G-7123)*

Employee Codes: A=Over 500 employees, B=251-500
C=101-250, D=51-100, E=20-50, F=10-19, G=1-9

73 BUSINESS SERVICES

1st Advnce SEC Invstgtions Inc............ E 937 317-4433
  Dayton (G-7145)
1st Choice Security Inc........................ C 513 381-6789
  Cincinnati (G-2120)
Allied Security LLC............................... D 513 771-3776
  Cincinnati (G-2168)
American Svcs & Protection LLC......... D 614 884-0177
  Columbus (G-5362)
▲ Atlantis Security Company................ D 440 717-7050
  Cleveland (G-3838)
Belayusa Corporation........................... E 614 878-8200
  Columbus (G-5431)
City of Cleveland.................................. D 216 664-2625
  Cleveland (G-3987)
Community Crime Patrol....................... E 614 247-1765
  Columbus (G-5669)
Confidential Services Inc...................... E 614 252-4646
  Columbus (G-5681)
Corporate Screening Svcs LLC............. D 440 816-0500
  Cleveland (G-4116)
Danson Inc... C 513 948-0066
  Cincinnati (G-2538)
Darke County Sheriffs Patrol................. E 937 548-3399
  Greenville (G-8868)
Deacon 10 LLC..................................... D 216 731-4000
  Euclid (G-8340)
Dunbar Armored Inc............................. E 330 630-0603
  Akron (G-142)
Dunbar Armored Inc............................. E 513 381-8000
  Cincinnati (G-2585)
Dunbar Armored Inc............................. D 216 642-5700
  Cleveland (G-4188)
Dunbar Armored Inc............................. D 614 475-1969
  Columbus (G-5791)
Dunbar Armored Inc............................. E 614 848-7833
  Columbus (G-5792)
Extract LLC... D 937 732-9495
  Dayton (G-7343)
Falu Corporation................................... E 502 641-8106
  Cincinnati (G-2646)
Garda CL Great Lakes Inc.................... E 614 863-4044
  Columbus (G-5910)
Garda CL Great Lakes Inc.................... B 561 939-7000
  Columbus (G-5911)
Gardaworld Security Corp..................... D 614 963-2098
  Columbus (G-5912)
Genric Inc... B 937 553-9250
  Marysville (G-10486)
Hereford Security Group....................... D 330 644-1371
  Uniontown (G-14257)
Highland SEC Invstigations LLC............ E 614 558-2421
  Columbus (G-5992)
Home State Protective Svcs LLC........... E 513 253-3095
  Cincinnati (G-2839)
Human Resource Profile Inc.................. E 513 388-4300
  Cincinnati (G-2855)
Independent Research Group Inc.......... D 330 273-3380
  Brunswick (G-1459)
Industrial Security Svc Inc..................... E 614 785-7046
  Columbus (G-6051)
Industrial Security Svc Inc..................... D 216 898-9970
  Cleveland (G-4410)
Job1usa Inc.. C 419 255-2005
  Toledo (G-13868)
Kreller Bus Info Group Inc..................... E 513 723-8900
  Cincinnati (G-2951)
McKeen Security Inc............................. D 740 699-1301
  Saint Clairsville (G-12802)
Merchnts SEC Svc Dyton Ohio In.......... E 937 256-9373
  Dayton (G-7480)
Metropolitan Security Svcs Inc.............. C 330 253-6459
  Akron (G-232)
Metropolitan Security Svcs Inc.............. C 216 298-4076
  Cleveland (G-4569)
Midwest Protection Div LLC.................. D 844 844-8200
  Columbus (G-6246)
Moonlight Security Inc.......................... D 937 252-1600
  Dayton (G-7512)
National Alliance SEC Agcy Inc............. E 866 636-3098
  Vandalia (G-14385)
Ohio Support Services Corp.................. E 614 443-0291
  Columbus (G-6460)
Ohio Tctcal Enfrcment Svcs LLC........... D 614 989-9485
  Columbus (G-6462)
Patriot Protection Svcs LLC.................. D 614 379-1333
  Columbus (G-6504)
Patrol Urban Services LLC.................... E 614 620-4672
  Westerville (G-15011)
▲ Professional Security Bur Inc............. D 330 438-6800
  Canton (G-1832)
Rehmann Robson LLC.......................... E 248 952-5000
  Independence (G-9475)
Rmi International Inc............................. E 937 642-5032
  Marysville (G-10504)
Rumpf Corporation................................ E 419 255-5005
  Toledo (G-13999)
Safeguard Properties LLC..................... A 216 739-2900
  Cleveland (G-4869)
Sahara Global Security LLC.................. D 614 448-7940
  Columbus (G-6635)
Sam-Tom Inc.. E 216 426-7752
  Cleveland (G-4874)
Securitas SEC Svcs USA Inc................ E 440 887-6800
  Cleveland (G-4889)
Securitas SEC Svcs USA Inc................ E 614 871-6051
  Grove City (G-8953)
Security Hut Inc.................................... D 216 226-0461
  Lakewood (G-9685)
St Moritz Security Svcs Inc................... D 614 351-8798
  Worthington (G-15459)
St Moritz Security Svcs Inc................... D 330 270-5922
  Youngstown (G-15729)
Sterling Infosystems Inc........................ B 216 685-7600
  Independence (G-9487)
Stifel Ind Advisors LLC.......................... E 740 653-9222
  Lancaster (G-9745)
SW Squared LLC.................................. D 614 300-5304
  Columbus (G-6738)
Tenable Protective Svcs Inc.................. A 216 361-0002
  Cleveland (G-4984)
United Sttes Dept of Hmland SE........... D 937 821-5543
  Dayton (G-7684)
Universal Services America LP............. A 937 454-9035
  Vandalia (G-14398)
US Protection Service LLC................... E 614 794-4950
  Columbus (G-6837)
US Security Associates Inc................... B 937 454-9035
  Cincinnati (G-3607)
US Security Associates Inc................... A 937 454-9035
  Vandalia (G-14400)
Veteran Security Patrol Co.................... C 513 381-4482
  Cincinnati (G-3626)
Veteran Security Patrol Co.................... C 937 222-7333
  Dayton (G-7704)
W William Schmidt & Associates........... C 419 526-4747
  Mansfield (G-10323)
Whitestone Group Inc........................... B 614 501-7007
  Reynoldsburg (G-12682)
Whittguard Security Svcs Inc................ C 440 288-7233
  Avon (G-667)
Willo Security Inc.................................. C 614 481-9456
  Columbus (G-6895)
Willoughby Services Inc........................ D 440 953-9191
  Willoughby (G-15228)

7382 Security systems services

Acree-Daily Corporation........................ E 614 452-7300
  Columbus (G-5308)
ADT LLC.. D 614 793-0861
  Columbus (G-5317)
Bass Family LLC................................... C
  Bedford Heights (G-995)
Bureau Workers Compensation............. D 614 466-5109
  Columbus (G-5484)
Electra Sound Inc................................. C 216 433-1050
  Cleveland (G-4208)
Fe Moran SEC Solutions LLC............... E 217 403-6444
  Uniontown (G-14251)
Fellhauer Mechanical Systems.............. E 419 734-3674
  Port Clinton (G-12525)
Finite State Inc..................................... D 614 639-5107
  Columbus (G-5858)
GA Business Purchaser LLC................. E 419 255-8400
  Toledo (G-13816)
Genric Inc... B 937 553-9250
  Marysville (G-10486)
Gillmore Security Systems Inc............... E 440 232-1000
  Cleveland (G-4313)
Guardian Protection Svcs Inc................ E 330 797-1570
  Bedford (G-962)
Habitec Security Inc............................. D 419 537-6768
  Holland (G-9286)
Integrated Protection Svcs Inc.............. D 513 631-5505
  Cincinnati (G-2876)
▲ Jenne Inc.. C 440 835-0040
  Avon (G-656)
Johnson Cntrls SEC Sltions LLC........... E 330 497-0850
  Canton (G-1786)
Johnson Cntrls SEC Sltions LLC........... E 513 277-4966
  Cincinnati (G-2915)
Johnson Cntrls SEC Sltions LLC........... E 419 243-8400
  Maumee (G-10734)
Koorsen Fire & Security Inc.................. E 513 398-4300
  Blue Ash (G-1196)
Koorsen Fire & Security Inc.................. E 614 878-2228
  Columbus (G-6126)
Koorsen Fire & Security Inc.................. E 419 526-2212
  Mansfield (G-10280)
Macair Aviation LLC.............................. E 937 347-1302
  Xenia (G-15525)
Northwestern Ohio SEC Systems.......... E 419 227-1655
  Lima (G-9942)
Ohio Tctcal Enfrcment Svcs LLC........... D 614 989-9485
  Columbus (G-6462)
Ohio Vly Integration Svcs Inc................ E 937 492-0008
  Sidney (G-13045)
Protegis LLC... E 216 377-3044
  Independence (G-9474)
Safe-N-Sound Security Inc................... D 330 491-1148
  Millersburg (G-11292)
Safeguard Properties LLC..................... A 216 739-2900
  Cleveland (G-4869)
Sahara Global Security LLC.................. D 614 448-7940
  Columbus (G-6635)
Securestate LLC................................... E 216 927-0115
  Novelty (G-12043)
Securitas Technology Corp.................... D 800 548-4478
  Uniontown (G-14264)
Shiver Security Systems LLC................ E 513 719-4000
  Mason (G-10607)
Sievers Security Systems Inc................ E 216 383-1234
  Cleveland (G-4906)
State Alarm Inc..................................... E 888 726-8111
  Youngstown (G-15730)
Tacg LLC.. E 937 203-8201
  Beavercreek (G-931)

SIC SECTION
73 BUSINESS SERVICES

The OGara Group Inc................................... D 513 881-9800
  Cincinnati *(G-3467)*

Turnkey Technology LLC........................... E 513 725-2177
  Cincinnati *(G-3537)*

United Sttes Prtctive Svcs Cor.................. E 216 475-8550
  Independence *(G-9492)*

Vigilant Defense... E 513 309-0672
  Liberty Township *(G-9858)*

Wj Service Co Inc... E 330 372-5040
  Warren *(G-14576)*

Yp LLC.. C 330 896-6000
  Uniontown *(G-14273)*

7384 Photofinish laboratories

Buehler Food Markets Inc.......................... C 330 364-3079
  Dover *(G-7874)*

CVS Revco DS Inc...................................... D 740 593-8501
  Athens *(G-563)*

CVS Revco DS Inc...................................... D 440 729-9070
  Chesterland *(G-2034)*

CVS Revco DS Inc...................................... C 937 393-4218
  Hillsboro *(G-9252)*

CVS Revco DS Inc...................................... D 330 678-4009
  Kent *(G-9567)*

CVS Revco DS Inc...................................... E 740 389-1122
  Marion *(G-10424)*

CVS Revco DS Inc...................................... E 740 383-6244
  Marion *(G-10425)*

CVS Revco DS Inc...................................... D 513 523-6378
  Oxford *(G-12206)*

Discount Drug Mart Inc.............................. E 330 343-7700
  Dover *(G-7879)*

Fred W Albrecht Grocery Co...................... C 330 666-6781
  Akron *(G-169)*

Fred W Albrecht Grocery Co...................... C 330 645-6222
  Coventry Township *(G-7008)*

Marc Glassman Inc..................................... C 330 995-9246
  Aurora *(G-616)*

Marco Photo Service Inc............................ D 419 529-9010
  Ontario *(G-12115)*

Rite Aid of Ohio Inc..................................... E 330 706-1004
  Barberton *(G-705)*

Rite Aid of Ohio Inc..................................... E 937 833-2174
  Brookville *(G-1448)*

Rite Aid of Ohio Inc..................................... E 740 942-3101
  Cadiz *(G-1543)*

Rite Aid of Ohio Inc..................................... E 330 922-4466
  Cuyahoga Falls *(G-7095)*

Rite Aid of Ohio Inc..................................... E 937 277-1611
  Dayton *(G-7591)*

Rite Aid of Ohio Inc..................................... E 937 258-8101
  Dayton *(G-7592)*

Rite Aid of Ohio Inc..................................... E 937 256-3111
  Dayton *(G-7593)*

Rite Aid of Ohio Inc..................................... E 937 836-5204
  Englewood *(G-8321)*

Rite Aid of Ohio Inc..................................... E 330 527-2828
  Garrettsville *(G-8779)*

Rite Aid of Ohio Inc..................................... E 937 687-3456
  New Lebanon *(G-11620)*

7389 Business services, nec

1848 Ventures LLC...................................... C 330 887-0187
  Westfield Center *(G-15023)*

2mc Management LLC............................... E 513 771-1700
  Cincinnati *(G-2122)*

365 Holdings LLC....................................... D 800 403-8182
  Akron *(G-6)*

500 Degrees LLC.. D 786 615-8265
  Columbus *(G-5289)*

A L D Precast Corp..................................... E 614 449-3366
  Columbus *(G-5291)*

A2z Field Services LLC............................... C 614 873-0211
  Plain City *(G-12464)*

ABB Enterprise Software Inc..................... E 440 585-6716
  Painesville *(G-12219)*

▼ Abco Holdings LLC.................................. C 216 433-7200
  Cleveland *(G-3757)*

Ability Works Inc... C 419 626-1048
  Sandusky *(G-12861)*

Abraham Ford LLC..................................... E 440 233-7402
  Elyria *(G-8232)*

▲ Accel Inc.. C 614 656-1100
  New Albany *(G-11552)*

Accucall LLC.. E 440 522-8681
  Elyria *(G-8233)*

Accurate Invntory Clclting Svc.................. B 800 777-9414
  Columbus *(G-5304)*

Acuren Inspection Inc................................ C 513 671-7073
  West Chester *(G-14646)*

ADS Manufacturing Ohio LLC................... D 513 217-4502
  Middletown *(G-11150)*

Advanced Financial Services..................... E 800 320-0000
  Copley *(G-6946)*

Advanced Rhbilitation Tech Ltd................ E 419 636-2684
  Bryan *(G-1477)*

Aerocon Photogrammetric Svcs............... E 440 946-6277
  Concord Township *(G-6922)*

Aghapy Plus Inc.. D 216 820-3996
  Euclid *(G-8336)*

Ai-Media Inc... E 213 337-8552
  Youngstown *(G-15544)*

Ai-Media Technologies LLC....................... E 800 335-0911
  Youngstown *(G-15545)*

Aim Integrated Logistics Inc..................... B 330 759-0438
  Girard *(G-8808)*

Aim Leasing Company............................... E 216 883-6300
  Cleveland *(G-3777)*

▲ Akron-Smmit Cnvntion Vstors Bu......... E 330 374-7560
  Akron *(G-42)*

Aldelano Corporation................................. E 909 861-3970
  Lima *(G-9861)*

Alexis Eppinger... E 216 509-0475
  Cleveland *(G-3785)*

Alexzander Angels LLC.............................. E 678 984-3093
  Cincinnati *(G-2160)*

Allstate Insurance Company..................... E 330 650-2917
  Hudson *(G-9330)*

Alorica Customer Care Inc........................ C 216 525-3311
  Cleveland *(G-3795)*

Alterntive Rsrces Homecare Inc............... D 216 256-3049
  Shaker Heights *(G-12973)*

Ambers Design Studio LLC...................... E 614 221-1837
  Columbus *(G-5344)*

American Crane Inc.................................... E 614 496-2268
  Reynoldsburg *(G-12651)*

Ameridial Inc.. C 330 339-7222
  New Philadelphia *(G-11640)*

Ameridial Inc.. B 234 542-5036
  Canton *(G-1666)*

Aml Rightsource LLC................................. D 216 771-1250
  Cleveland *(G-3810)*

▲ Amos Media Company............................ C 937 638-0967
  Sidney *(G-13018)*

Ampersand Group LLC.............................. E 330 379-0044
  Akron *(G-49)*

Amros Industries Inc.................................. E 216 433-0010
  Cleveland *(G-3812)*

Andydandy Center LLC.............................. E 513 272-6141
  Cincinnati *(G-2203)*

Answernet Inc.. E 978 710-5856
  Akron *(G-51)*

Answernet Inc.. E 877 864-2251
  Akron *(G-52)*

Arrc One LLC... E 440 754-0855
  Oberlin *(G-12063)*

Ashland Aqualon Functiona...................... E 614 790-3333
  Dublin *(G-7940)*

▲ Asm International..................................... D 440 338-5151
  Novelty *(G-12037)*

Atrium Apparel Corporation....................... D 740 966-8200
  Johnstown *(G-9544)*

Balaji D Loganathan................................... C 614 918-0411
  Hilliard *(G-9182)*

Banc One Services Corporation............... A 614 248-5800
  Columbus *(G-5247)*

Barklyn Heights LLC................................... E 216 577-5960
  Cleveland *(G-3850)*

◆ Baumfolder Corporation.......................... E 937 492-1281
  Sidney *(G-13020)*

Bay Mechanical & Elec Corp..................... D 440 282-6816
  Lorain *(G-10058)*

Bbs & Associates Inc................................ E 330 665-5227
  Akron *(G-63)*

Benchmark Craftsman Inc........................ E 866 313-4700
  Seville *(G-12963)*

Benchmark National Corporation............ E 419 843-6691
  Bellevue *(G-1043)*

Benchmark National Corporation............ E 419 424-0900
  Findlay *(G-8511)*

Bermex Inc... B 330 945-7500
  Stow *(G-13355)*

Best Payment Solutions Inc..................... E 630 321-0117
  Symmes Twp *(G-13582)*

Bethesda Foundation Inc.......................... E 513 745-1616
  Montgomery *(G-11361)*

▲ Bgr Inc.. D 800 628-9195
  West Chester *(G-14651)*

Blessing Home Health Care Inc............... E 614 329-2086
  Hilliard *(G-9183)*

Bollin & Sons Inc.. E 419 693-6573
  Toledo *(G-13710)*

◆ Bookmasters Inc....................................... C 419 281-1802
  Ashland *(G-483)*

Boss Display Corporation......................... D 614 443-9495
  Columbus *(G-5456)*

Bpi Acquisition Company LLC................. B 216 589-0198
  Cleveland *(G-3888)*

Brand Protect Plus LLC............................. E 216 539-1880
  Beachwood *(G-770)*

Bread Financial Holdings Inc................... C 614 729-3000
  Columbus *(G-5460)*

Bread Financial Holdings Inc................... D 614 729-5800
  Reynoldsburg *(G-12655)*

Bread Financial Holdings Inc................... E 614 729-5000
  Westerville *(G-14963)*

Bread Financial Holdings Inc................... C 614 729-4000
  Columbus *(G-5461)*

Buckeye Mechanical Contg Inc................ E 740 282-0089
  Toronto *(G-14121)*

Buckeye Pools Inc...................................... E 937 434-7916
  Dayton *(G-7203)*

Burgess & Niple/Heapy LLC..................... D 614 459-2050
  Columbus *(G-5487)*

Burrilla LLC.. E 513 615-9350
  West Chester *(G-14656)*

Byrider Finance Inc.................................... D 513 407-4140
  Cincinnati *(G-2297)*

C M R Inc... E 614 447-7100
  Columbus *(G-5489)*

Cardio Partners Inc.................................... E 614 760-5000
  Dublin *(G-7957)*

Cartruck Packaging Inc............................. E 216 631-7225
  Cleveland *(G-3931)*

Catalyst Recovery La LLC......................... D 513 354-3640
  Cincinnati *(G-2320)*

Employee Codes: A=Over 500 employees, B=251-500
C=101-250, D=51-100, E=20-50, F=10-19, G=1-9

73 BUSINESS SERVICES

Cbiz Inc .... A 216 447-9000
   Cleveland *(G-3942)*

Cbiz Accnting Tax Advsory Wash ..... E 216 447-9000
   Cleveland *(G-3943)*

Cec Combustion Safety LLC .... E 216 749-2992
   Brookpark *(G-1430)*

Ceiba Enterprises Incorporated .... C 614 818-3220
   Westerville *(G-14965)*

Cgh-Global Security LLC .... E 800 376-0655
   Cincinnati *(G-2340)*

Chardon Laboratories Inc .... E 614 860-1000
   Reynoldsburg *(G-12658)*

Chief Delivery LLC .... D 419 277-6190
   Toledo *(G-13732)*

Chute Gerdeman Inc .... D 614 469-1001
   Westerville *(G-14966)*

Cincinnati Financial Corp .... A 513 870-2000
   Fairfield *(G-8402)*

◆ CIP International Inc .... D 513 874-9925
   West Chester *(G-14666)*

Citicorp Credit Services Inc .... B 212 559-1000
   Columbus *(G-5575)*

City of Cleveland .... E 216 664-3922
   Cleveland *(G-3988)*

City of North Olmsted .... E 440 777-0678
   North Olmsted *(G-11895)*

Clarity Retail Services LLC .... D 513 800-9369
   West Chester *(G-14668)*

Clark State Community College .... E 937 328-3841
   Springfield *(G-13235)*

Clearwater Services Inc .... E 330 836-4946
   Akron *(G-106)*

Cleary Company .... E 614 459-4000
   Columbus *(G-5582)*

Cleveland Clinic Foundation .... D 216 444-5000
   Cleveland *(G-4030)*

Clgt Solutions LLC .... E 740 920-4795
   Granville *(G-8852)*

Clovernook Ctr For Blind Vslly .... C 513 522-3860
   Cincinnati *(G-2464)*

▲ CMC Group Inc .... D 419 354-2591
   Bowling Green *(G-1313)*

Collaborative Company .... E 419 242-7405
   Toledo *(G-13748)*

Collections Acquisition Co LLC .... C 614 944-5788
   Columbus *(G-5595)*

Comenity Servicing LLC .... E 614 729-4000
   Columbus *(G-5664)*

Commercial Grounds Care Inc .... E 614 456-3764
   Columbus *(G-5665)*

Commercial Works Inc .... D 614 870-2342
   Columbus *(G-5667)*

Concentrix Cvg Cstmer MGT Intl .... D 513 268-7014
   Cincinnati *(G-2493)*

◆ Continental Office Furn Corp .... C 614 262-5010
   Columbus *(G-5693)*

Continntal Mssage Solution Inc .... D 614 224-4534
   Columbus *(G-5699)*

Contrlled Envmt Crtfction Svcs .... E 513 870-0293
   Columbus *(G-2503)*

Convention Vstors Bur of Grter .... E 216 875-6603
   Cleveland *(G-4115)*

▼ Convergys Cstmer MGT Group Inc .. B 513 723-6104
   Cincinnati *(G-2506)*

▲ Conversion Tech Intl Inc .... E 419 924-5566
   West Unity *(G-14874)*

Corporate Fin Assoc Clmbus Inc ...... D 614 457-9219
   Columbus *(G-5703)*

Corporate Support Inc .... E 419 221-3838
   Lima *(G-9877)*

County Fire Protection LLC .... D 330 633-1014
   Kent *(G-9566)*

Cowans LLC .... D 513 871-1670
   Cincinnati *(G-2513)*

Crain Communications Inc .... E 330 836-9180
   Cuyahoga Falls *(G-7065)*

Crane Consumables Inc .... E 513 539-9980
   Middletown *(G-11160)*

Credit First National Assn .... E 216 362-5300
   Cleveland *(G-4136)*

Crescent Park Corporation .... C 513 759-7000
   West Chester *(G-14679)*

Crimson Design Group LLC .... E 614 444-3743
   Columbus *(G-5729)*

Csa Amrica Tstg Crtfcation LLC .... B 216 524-4990
   Independence *(G-9427)*

Culinary Metz Management LLC .... D 330 684-3368
   Orrville *(G-12159)*

▲ Custom Products Corporation ...... D 440 528-7100
   Solon *(G-13080)*

◆ Custom-Pak Inc .... D 330 725-0800
   Medina *(G-10827)*

Dan & Maria Davis Inc .... E 937 669-2271
   Tipp City *(G-13657)*

Decorate With Style Inc .... E 419 621-5577
   Sandusky *(G-12887)*

Dehart Works LLC .... D 440 600-8003
   Cleveland *(G-4159)*

Delaware North-Sportservice .... E 614 246-3203
   Columbus *(G-5751)*

▲ Depot Direct Inc .... E 419 661-1233
   Perrysburg *(G-12332)*

Design Central Inc .... E 614 890-0202
   Columbus *(G-5758)*

Dfs Corporate Services LLC .... E 614 777-7020
   Hilliard *(G-9192)*

Dfs Corporate Services LLC .... B 614 283-2499
   New Albany *(G-11561)*

Dialamerica Marketing Inc .... B 330 836-5293
   Fairlawn *(G-8475)*

DJ Roofing & Imprvs LLC .... E 419 307-5712
   Fremont *(G-8675)*

Dollries Group LLC .... E 513 834-6105
   North Bend *(G-11803)*

Domino Foods Inc .... C 216 432-3222
   Cleveland *(G-4175)*

◆ Downing Enterprises Inc .... D 330 666-3888
   Copley *(G-6956)*

Dqr 4 Ted .... E 740 264-4323
   Steubenville *(G-13322)*

Dreier & Maller Inc .... E 614 575-0065
   Reynoldsburg *(G-12661)*

Duke Energy Center .... E 513 419-7300
   Cincinnati *(G-2579)*

Dwellworks LLC .... D 216 682-4200
   Cleveland *(G-4190)*

E T Financial Service Inc .... E 937 716-1726
   Trotwood *(G-14127)*

Elevar Design Group Inc .... E 513 721-0600
   Cincinnati *(G-2611)*

Emersion Design LLC .... E 513 841-9100
   Cincinnati *(G-2616)*

Empire One LLC .... E 330 628-9310
   Mogadore *(G-11326)*

Essilor of America Inc .... E 614 492-0888
   Groveport *(G-8986)*

Euclidean Support Services Inc .... E 330 405-8501
   Euclid *(G-8342)*

▼ Exhibit Concepts Inc .... E 937 890-7000
   Vandalia *(G-14376)*

Exhibitpro Inc .... E 614 885-9541
   New Albany *(G-11564)*

Extract LLC .... D 937 732-9495
   Dayton *(G-7343)*

Facts Management Company .... D 440 892-4272
   Westlake *(G-15059)*

Federal Card Services LLC .... E 513 429-4459
   Cincinnati *(G-2653)*

Ferguson Hills Inc .... D 513 539-4497
   Dayton *(G-7351)*

Fiducius .... E 513 645-5400
   Cincinnati *(G-2660)*

Filterfresh Coffee Service Inc .... D 513 681-8911
   West Chester *(G-14811)*

Findaway World LLC .... E 330 794-7758
   Akron *(G-158)*

▲ First Choice Packaging Inc .... C 419 333-4100
   Fremont *(G-8676)*

First Hospital Labs LLC .... C 215 396-5500
   Independence *(G-9432)*

Fis Investor Services LLC .... E 904 438-6000
   Columbus *(G-5866)*

Five Cfc Inc .... E 937 578-3271
   Lewis Center *(G-9821)*

Flamos Enterprises Inc .... E 330 478-0009
   Canton *(G-1755)*

Flawless Janitorial LLC .... E 216 266-1425
   Maple Heights *(G-10338)*

Flexsys Inc .... B 212 605-6000
   Akron *(G-165)*

Flying Pig Logistics Inc .... E 513 300-9331
   West Chester *(G-14692)*

▼ Fox International Limited Inc .... C 216 454-1001
   Beachwood *(G-793)*

Franklin Works Inc .... E 361 215-2300
   Columbus *(G-5890)*

Freudenberg-Nok General Partnr ..... C 419 499-2502
   Milan *(G-11206)*

G and J Automatic Systems Inc .... E 216 741-6070
   Cleveland *(G-4296)*

▼ G Robert Toney & Assoc Inc .... E 216 391-1900
   Cleveland *(G-4299)*

Gabriel Partners LLC .... E 216 771-1250
   Cleveland *(G-4300)*

Garda CL Great Lakes Inc .... B 561 939-7000
   Columbus *(G-5911)*

Gem City Chemicals Inc .... D 937 224-0711
   Dayton *(G-7373)*

Gencraft Designs LLC .... E 330 359-6251
   Navarre *(G-11537)*

▲ General Theming Contrs LLC .... C 614 252-6342
   Columbus *(G-5925)*

Geneva Liberty Steel Ltd .... E 330 740-0103
   Youngstown *(G-15620)*

Genius Solutions Engrg Co .... E 419 794-9914
   Maumee *(G-10727)*

Gerdau McSteel Atmsphere Annli .... E 330 478-0314
   Canton *(G-1761)*

Grand Encore Cincinnati LLC .... E 513 482-7500
   West Chester *(G-14699)*

Grays Trnsp & Logistics LLC .... E 614 656-3460
   Columbus *(G-5949)*

Great Lkes Cmnty Action Partnr ...... E 419 332-8089
   Fremont *(G-8686)*

Greater Clmbus Cnvntion Ctr Fo ...... C 614 827-2500
   Columbus *(G-5953)*

Greater Clmbus Cnvntion Vstors ...... E 614 221-6623
   Columbus *(G-5954)*

Greater Cncnnati Cnvntion Vsto ...... D 513 621-2142
   Cincinnati *(G-2771)*

Greenheart Companies LLC .... E 330 259-3070
   Youngstown *(G-15623)*

Guardian Water & Power Inc .... E 614 291-3141
   Columbus *(G-5960)*

Gws FF&e LLC .... E 513 759-6000
   West Chester *(G-14703)*

73 BUSINESS SERVICES

Hamilton Capital LLC .... D 614 273-1000
  Columbus *(G-5966)*
Hands Enterprises Ltd .... E 419 528-1389
  Ontario *(G-12106)*
Hastings Water Works Inc .... E 440 832-7700
  Brecksville *(G-1353)*
Hd Davis Cpas LLC .... D 330 759-8522
  Youngstown *(G-15626)*
Hdi Landing Gear USA Inc .... C 440 783-5255
  Strongsville *(G-13459)*
High Line Corporation .... E 330 848-8800
  Akron *(G-192)*
Hkt Teleservices Inc .... C 614 652-6300
  Grove City *(G-8926)*
Holloway Ventures LLC .... E 740 641-3592
  Newark *(G-11705)*
Home Inspections .... E 800 241-0133
  Dublin *(G-8030)*
Hometeam Inspection Service .... C 513 831-1300
  Milford *(G-11230)*
◆ Hrm Enterprises Inc .... C 330 877-9353
  Hartville *(G-9127)*
▲ I-X Center Corporation .... C 216 265-2675
  Cleveland *(G-4398)*
Ies Systems Inc .... E 330 533-6683
  Canfield *(G-1632)*
Illuminate USA LLC .... A 614 598-9742
  Pataskala *(G-12275)*
In Terminal Services Corp .... C 216 518-8407
  Maple Heights *(G-10341)*
Incept Corporation .... C 330 649-8000
  Canton *(G-1779)*
▲ Industrial Chemical Corp .... E 330 725-0800
  Medina *(G-10846)*
Industrial Insul Coatings LLC .... E 800 506-1399
  Girard *(G-8816)*
Industrial Power Systems Inc .... B 419 531-3121
  Rossford *(G-12767)*
◆ Ineos ABS (usa) LLC .... C 513 467-2400
  Addyston *(G-4)*
Infocision Management Corp .... C 330 726-0872
  Youngstown *(G-15639)*
Infocision Management Corp .... C 330 544-1400
  Youngstown *(G-15640)*
Infocision Management Corp .... B 330 668-1411
  Akron *(G-201)*
Infotelecom LLC .... B 216 373-4600
  Cleveland *(G-4412)*
Infoverity LLC .... E 614 327-5173
  Dublin *(G-8037)*
Innovairre Communications LLC .... C 330 869-8500
  Fairlawn *(G-8485)*
Inquiry Systems Inc .... E 614 464-3800
  Columbus *(G-6055)*
Interbrand Design Forum LLC .... C 513 421-2210
  Cincinnati *(G-2880)*
Interior Supply Cincinnati LLC .... E 614 424-6611
  Columbus *(G-6066)*
◆ Interscope Manufacturing Inc .... C 513 423-8866
  Middletown *(G-11166)*
Invincible Fire Co Inc .... E 419 647-4615
  Spencerville *(G-13189)*
Iten Defense LLC .... D 440 990-2440
  Ashtabula *(G-539)*
ITM Marketing Inc .... C 740 295-3575
  Coshocton *(G-6988)*
Jackson & Sons Drilling & Pump .... E 419 756-2758
  Mansfield *(G-10275)*
Jcherie LLC .... E 216 453-1051
  Shaker Heights *(G-12979)*
◆ Jck Recycling LLC .... E 419 698-1153
  Fairlawn *(G-8487)*

Jeffers Crane Service Inc .... E 419 223-9010
  Lima *(G-9912)*
◆ Jpmorgan Chase Bank Nat Assn .... A 614 436-3055
  Columbus *(G-5264)*
Juice Technologies Inc .... E 800 518-5576
  Worthington *(G-15424)*
Jumbo Logistics LLC .... E 216 662-5420
  Macedonia *(G-10195)*
▲ Kable News Company Inc .... C 815 734-4151
  West Chester *(G-14716)*
Karlsberger Architecture Inc .... D 614 471-1812
  Columbus *(G-6103)*
Karlsberger Companies .... E 614 461-9500
  Columbus *(G-6104)*
Kaufman Realty & Auctions LLC .... E 330 852-4111
  Sugarcreek *(G-13511)*
Keller Logistics Group Inc .... E 866 276-9486
  Defiance *(G-7751)*
◆ Kent Adhesive Products Co .... D 330 678-1626
  Kent *(G-9583)*
King Tut Logistics LLC .... E 614 538-0509
  Columbus *(G-6117)*
Koinonia Partners Holdings LLC .... E 216 588-8777
  Maple Heights *(G-10342)*
Kucera International Inc .... D 440 975-4230
  Willoughby *(G-15197)*
▲ Kyocera Senco Indus Tls Inc .... D 513 388-2000
  Cincinnati *(G-2958)*
Landor & Fitch LLC .... E 614 843-1766
  Columbus *(G-6136)*
Laserflex Corporation .... D 614 850-9600
  Hilliard *(G-9209)*
Lendly LLC .... E 844 453-6359
  Oakwood *(G-12049)*
Lions Gate SEC Solutions Inc .... E 440 539-8382
  Euclid *(G-8357)*
Logistics Inc .... E 419 478-1514
  Toledo *(G-13891)*
Loth Inc .... D 513 554-4900
  Cincinnati *(G-2989)*
Lowell Mackenzie .... E 614 451-6669
  Sidney *(G-13038)*
M A Folkes Company Inc .... E 513 785-4200
  Hamilton *(G-9062)*
Macys Cr & Customer Svcs Inc .... A 513 398-5221
  Mason *(G-10576)*
Mak Burtnett Inc .... E 440 256-8080
  Willoughby *(G-15210)*
Making Life Easy LLC .... D 513 280-0422
  Cincinnati *(G-3006)*
Manav Enterprises Inc .... E 513 563-4606
  Sharonville *(G-12995)*
Market Day Llc .... B 513 860-1370
  West Chester *(G-14823)*
Marysville Exmpted Vlg Schl Dst .... E 937 645-6733
  Marysville *(G-10495)*
Matic Insurance Services Inc .... C 833 382-1304
  Columbus *(G-6206)*
Mbd Transport LLC .... D 513 449-0777
  Brunswick *(G-1463)*
McConnell Excavating Ltd .... E 440 774-4578
  Oberlin *(G-12072)*
McCracken Group Inc .... E 513 697-2000
  Cincinnati *(G-3022)*
Medigistics Inc .... D 614 430-5700
  Columbus *(G-6221)*
Metropolitan Pool Service Co .... E 216 741-9451
  Parma *(G-12257)*
Metzenbaum Sheltered Inds Inc .... D 440 729-1919
  Chesterland *(G-2041)*
Miami University .... C 513 529-6911
  Oxford *(G-12211)*

Miami University .... D 513 529-1230
  Oxford *(G-12212)*
Michael Schuster Assoc Inc .... E 513 241-5666
  Cincinnati *(G-3056)*
Micro Products Co Inc .... E 440 943-0258
  Willoughby Hills *(G-15233)*
Mid-Ohio Pipeline Services LLC .... E 419 884-3772
  Mansfield *(G-10299)*
Midwest Investors Group Inc .... C 270 887-8888
  Galena *(G-8737)*
Mission Essential Group LLC .... D 614 416-2345
  New Albany *(G-11574)*
Montaque Cleaning Services LLC .... E 937 705-0429
  Dayton *(G-7511)*
Most Wrshpful Ereka Grnd Ldge .... E 614 626-4076
  Columbus *(G-6263)*
MSI Express Inc .... D 740 498-4700
  Newcomerstown *(G-11770)*
Mt Hope Auction Inc .... E 330 674-6188
  Mount Hope *(G-11467)*
Mt Washington Care Center Inc .... E 513 231-4561
  Cincinnati *(G-3087)*
National Bd of Bler Prssure Vs .... D 614 888-8320
  Columbus *(G-6289)*
Nationwide General Insur Co .... A 614 249-7111
  Columbus *(G-6331)*
Ncp Holdings LP .... E 937 228-5600
  Oakwood *(G-12051)*
Neighborcare Inc .... A 513 719-2600
  Cincinnati *(G-3104)*
▲ Nelson Packaging Company Inc .... D 419 229-3471
  Lima *(G-9939)*
Nestle Usa Inc .... C 440 349-5757
  Solon *(G-13118)*
Nexxtshow LLC .... E
  Cincinnati *(G-3114)*
North Bay Construction Inc .... E 440 835-1898
  Westlake *(G-15085)*
Oak Hill Financial Inc .... B 740 286-3283
  Jackson *(G-9523)*
Ohio Fabricators Inc .... D 330 745-4406
  Akron *(G-250)*
Ohio Fundation of Ind Colleges .... E 614 469-1950
  Columbus *(G-6422)*
◆ Ohio Gasket and Shim Co Inc .... D 330 630-0626
  Akron *(G-251)*
Ohio Prsbt Rtrment Svcs Fndtio .... E 614 888-7800
  Westerville *(G-14923)*
Ohio-T-Home Hlth Care Agcy Ltd .... D 614 947-0791
  Columbus *(G-6464)*
Oki Auction LLC .... E 513 679-7910
  Cincinnati *(G-3154)*
Online Liquidation Auction LLC .... E 440 596-8733
  North Royalton *(G-11947)*
Pactiv LLC .... D 614 771-5400
  Columbus *(G-6496)*
Pandora Manufacturing Llc .... D 419 384-3241
  Ottawa *(G-12191)*
▲ Patented Acquisition Corp .... E 937 353-2299
  Miamisburg *(G-11082)*
Payrix Solutions LLC .... E 718 506-9250
  Symmes Township *(G-13580)*
Pedco E & A Services Inc .... D 513 782-4920
  Blue Ash *(G-1220)*
▲ Perfect Cut-Off Inc .... E 440 943-0000
  Wickliffe *(G-15161)*
Persistent Systems Inc .... E 614 763-6500
  Dublin *(G-8090)*
Piada Group LLC .... D 614 397-1339
  Columbus *(G-6524)*
Planet Healthcare LLC .... D 888 845-2539
  Westlake *(G-15099)*

Employee Codes: A=Over 500 employees, B=251-500
C=101-250, D=51-100, E=20-50, F=10-19, G=1-9

2024 Harris Ohio
Services Directory

73 BUSINESS SERVICES

Point Recognition Ltd .... E 330 220-6777
 Brunswick *(G-1467)*
Polaris Automation Inc .... E 614 431-0170
 Columbus *(G-6534)*
Pollock Research & Design Inc .... E 330 332-3300
 Salem *(G-12847)*
Predictive Service LLC .... D 866 772-6770
 Cleveland *(G-4766)*
Premier Hotel Group LLC .... D 937 754-9109
 Fairborn *(G-8380)*
Priority Designs Inc .... D 614 337-9979
 Columbus *(G-6546)*
◆ Pro-Pet LLC .... D 419 394-3374
 Saint Marys *(G-12835)*
Proampac Holdings Inc .... D 513 671-1777
 Cincinnati *(G-3236)*
Process Plus Design Build LLC .... C 513 262-2261
 Cincinnati *(G-3240)*
Producers Credit Corporation .... C 800 641-7522
 Columbus *(G-6548)*
Progressive Quality Care Inc .... E 330 875-7866
 Louisville *(G-10121)*
Progressive Quality Care Inc .... D 216 661-6800
 Parma *(G-12263)*
Promotion Exction Partners LLC .... E 513 826-0101
 Cincinnati *(G-3253)*
Pxp Ohio .... E 614 575-4242
 Reynoldsburg *(G-12673)*
Quadax Inc .... C 330 759-4600
 Youngstown *(G-15702)*
▲ Quality Associates Inc .... B 513 242-4477
 West Chester *(G-14829)*
Quality Control Inspection .... D 440 359-1900
 Cleveland *(G-4799)*
Quality Lines Inc .... C 740 815-1165
 Findlay *(G-8580)*
Queens Beauty Bar LLC .... E 216 804-0533
 Cleveland *(G-4802)*
Quintus Technologies LLC .... E 614 891-2732
 Lewis Center *(G-9834)*
R and J Corporation .... E 440 871-6009
 Westlake *(G-15101)*
R D D Inc .... C 216 781-5858
 Cleveland *(G-4804)*
Rapid Mortgage Company .... E 937 748-8888
 Cincinnati *(G-3273)*
Rdi Corporation .... D 513 524-3320
 Oxford *(G-12216)*
Real Estate Vltion Prtners LLC .... E 281 313-1571
 Toledo *(G-13982)*
Recycling Services Inc .... E 419 381-7762
 Maumee *(G-10758)*
Red Group Limited .... E 440 256-1268
 Mentor *(G-10989)*
Redkey Express LLC .... E 859 393-3221
 Mason *(G-10599)*
Reliance Financial Services NA .... E 419 783-8007
 Defiance *(G-7765)*
Renaissance Hotel Operating Co .... A 216 696-5600
 Cleveland *(G-4826)*
Republic Telcom Worldwide LLC .... E 330 244-8285
 North Canton *(G-11858)*
Republic Telcom Worldwide LLC .... C 330 966-4586
 Canton *(G-1845)*
Resource Interactive .... E 614 621-2888
 Columbus *(G-6586)*
▲ Richardson Printing Corp .... D 800 848-9752
 Marietta *(G-10204)*
Richland Newhope Inds Inc .... C 419 774-4400
 Mansfield *(G-10313)*
Rise Brands .... E 614 754-7522
 Columbus *(G-6590)*

Rite Rug Co .... E 614 478-3365
 Columbus *(G-6591)*
◆ Rittal Corporation .... E 937 399-0500
 Urbana *(G-14310)*
River City Furniture LLC .... E 513 612-7303
 West Chester *(G-14756)*
River Financial Inc .... E 415 878-3375
 Columbus *(G-6593)*
Rustic Pathways LLC .... D 440 497-4166
 Mentor *(G-10994)*
◆ Ryder Last Mile Inc .... D 866 711-3129
 New Albany *(G-11586)*
S&P Data Ohio LLC .... B 216 965-0018
 Cleveland *(G-4867)*
Sacred Hour Inc .... D 216 228-9750
 Lakewood *(G-9684)*
Samuel Joseph Corp .... E 330 983-6557
 Akron *(G-294)*
Sanese Services Inc .... A 614 436-1234
 Warren *(G-14550)*
SAR Warehouse Staffing LLC .... D 740 963-6235
 Columbus *(G-6643)*
Scot Industries Inc .... D 330 262-7585
 Wooster *(G-15375)*
Screen Works Inc .... E 937 264-9111
 Dayton *(G-7613)*
Security Check LLC .... C 614 944-5788
 Columbus *(G-6658)*
Seifert Technologies Inc .... D 330 833-2700
 Massillon *(G-10667)*
Self Mployed .... E 216 408-3280
 Cleveland *(G-4892)*
Sequoia Financial Group LLC .... E 330 375-9480
 Akron *(G-297)*
Service Pronet LLC .... E 614 874-4300
 Columbus *(G-6665)*
Servicelink Field Services LLC .... A 440 424-0058
 Solon *(G-13141)*
▲ Shamrock Companies Inc .... D 440 899-9510
 Westlake *(G-15108)*
Shred-It US JV LLC .... A 937 401-4224
 Dayton *(G-7618)*
Shredded Bedding Corporation .... D 740 893-3567
 Centerburg *(G-1936)*
Siertek Ltd .... E 937 623-2466
 Beavercreek Township *(G-948)*
Signature Closers LLC .... E 614 448-7750
 Columbus *(G-6678)*
Silco Fire Protection Company .... C 330 535-4343
 Akron *(G-301)*
Sirva Relocation LLC .... B 216 606-4000
 Independence *(G-9484)*
Six Sigma Logistics Inc .... E 440 666-6026
 Vermilion *(G-14409)*
Skipco Financial Adjusters Inc .... D 330 854-4800
 Canal Fulton *(G-1594)*
Snapblox Hosted Solutions LLC .... E 866 524-7707
 Cincinnati *(G-3390)*
Soh Trumbul Co Help ME Grow .... E 330 675-6610
 Leavittsburg *(G-9751)*
Solomon Lei & Associates Inc .... E 419 246-6931
 Toledo *(G-14018)*
Sotera Health LLC .... D 440 262-1410
 Broadview Heights *(G-1398)*
Southwood Pallet LLC .... D 330 682-3747
 Orrville *(G-12173)*
▼ Spa LLC .... E 513 733-8800
 Milford *(G-11258)*
Space & Asset Management Inc .... E 937 918-1000
 Dayton *(G-7631)*
Sparkbase Inc .... E 216 867-0877
 Cleveland *(G-4927)*

◆ Specialty Lubricants Corp .... E 330 425-2567
 Macedonia *(G-10205)*
Specialty Pumps Group Inc .... E 216 589-0198
 Cleveland *(G-4930)*
Spend and Send .... E 216 381-5459
 Cleveland *(G-4933)*
Springleaf Fincl Holdings LLC .... B 419 334-9748
 Fremont *(G-8704)*
Springleaf Fincl Holdings LLC .... B 419 841-0785
 Toledo *(G-14021)*
Ssoe Inc .... B 419 255-3830
 Toledo *(G-14023)*
◆ Standard Textile Co Inc .... B 513 761-9255
 Cincinnati *(G-3409)*
Standard Wellness Company LLC .... C 330 931-1037
 Cleveland *(G-4941)*
Startek Inc .... D 419 528-7801
 Ontario *(G-12125)*
Steriltek Inc .... E 615 627-0241
 Concord Township *(G-6935)*
Sterling Buying Group LLC .... E 513 564-9000
 Cincinnati *(G-3416)*
Sterling Infosystems Inc .... B 216 685-7600
 Independence *(G-9487)*
Stifel Ind Advisors LLC .... E 937 312-0111
 Dayton *(G-7644)*
Strive Enterprises Inc .... E 614 593-2840
 Dublin *(G-8133)*
Systems Pack Inc .... E 330 467-5729
 Macedonia *(G-10207)*
T W I International Inc .... C 440 439-1830
 Cleveland *(G-4976)*
T2 Financial LLC .... B 614 697-2021
 Westerville *(G-14941)*
Taylor Steel Inc .... D 330 824-8600
 Warren *(G-14563)*
Tc Architects Inc .... E 330 867-1093
 Akron *(G-330)*
Tebo Financial Services Inc .... E 234 207-2500
 Canton *(G-1869)*
Technical Assurance Inc .... E 440 953-3147
 Willoughby *(G-15222)*
Tekni-Plex Inc .... E 419 491-2399
 Holland *(G-9307)*
Telarc International Corp .... E 216 464-2313
 Beachwood *(G-843)*
Testech Inc .... D 937 435-8584
 Dayton *(G-7663)*
Teva Womens Health LLC .... C 513 731-9900
 Cincinnati *(G-3460)*
▲ The Elder-Beerman Stores Corp .... A 937 296-2700
 Moraine *(G-11443)*
▲ Things Remembered Inc .... A 440 473-2000
 Highland Heights *(G-9172)*
▲ Third Dimension Inc .... E 440 466-4040
 Geneva *(G-8790)*
Thrive Lgbt .... E 440 319-5906
 Cleveland *(G-5016)*
Tipp Machine & Tool Inc .... C 937 890-8428
 Dayton *(G-7669)*
Tm Capture Services LLC .... D 937 728-1781
 Dayton *(G-7671)*
TMC Micrographic Services Inc .... E 614 761-1033
 Columbus *(G-6772)*
Tmt Consolidated Inc .... D 216 781-7016
 Cleveland *(G-5022)*
Total System Services .... E 614 385-9221
 Columbus *(G-6773)*
Tpusa Inc .... D 614 621-5512
 Columbus *(G-6778)*
Traffic Safety Solutions LLC .... E 216 214-3735
 Cuyahoga Falls *(G-7110)*

75 AUTOMOTIVE REPAIR, SERVICES AND PARKING

▼ Tri County Tower LLC .... E 330 538-9874
North Jackson *(G-11878)*

▲ Tripack LLC .... E 513 248-1255
Milford *(G-11262)*

Turocy & Watson LLP .... E 216 696-8730
Cleveland *(G-5042)*

▲ Twin Sisters Productions LLC ..... E 330 631-0361
Stow *(G-13399)*

Uhhs/Csahs - Cuyahoga Inc .... D 440 746-3401
Cleveland *(G-5046)*

▲ Ultra Tech Machinery Inc .... E 330 929-5544
Cuyahoga Falls *(G-7113)*

United Art and Education Inc ...... E 800 322-3247
Dayton *(G-7680)*

▲ Univenture Inc .... D 937 645-4600
Dublin *(G-8146)*

Universal Packg Systems Inc .... C 513 732-2000
Batavia *(G-751)*

Universal Packg Systems Inc .... C 513 735-4777
Batavia *(G-752)*

Universal Packg Systems Inc .... C 513 674-9400
Cincinnati *(G-3563)*

University of Cincinnati .... D 513 556-2389
Cincinnati *(G-3576)*

US Inspection Services Inc .... D 513 671-7073
Cincinnati *(G-3606)*

US Postal Service .... E 614 600-5544
Columbus *(G-6836)*

Valeo North America Inc .... E 248 550-6054
East Liberty *(G-8177)*

◆ Veritiv Pubg & Print MGT Inc ..... E 614 288-0911
Stow *(G-13400)*

Versapay Corporation .... D 216 535-9016
Twinsburg *(G-14229)*

Vigilant Global Trade Svcs LLC .... E 260 417-1825
Shaker Heights *(G-12988)*

Vincent & Vincent .... E 513 617-2089
Cincinnati *(G-3630)*

Vocalink Inc .... B 937 223-1415
Dayton *(G-7709)*

Vocon Design Inc .... E 216 588-0800
Cleveland *(G-5114)*

W Home Collection LLC .... E 440 247-4474
Chagrin Falls *(G-1971)*

Wad Investments Oh Inc .... E 513 891-4477
Cincinnati *(G-3637)*

Weaver Industries Inc .... D 330 379-3606
Akron *(G-355)*

Weaver Industries Inc .... C 330 666-5114
Akron *(G-357)*

Weaver Industries Inc .... E 330 745-2400
Akron *(G-358)*

Weaver Industries Inc .... E 330 379-3660
Tallmadge *(G-13612)*

Weaver Industries Inc .... E 330 379-3660
Akron *(G-356)*

Wegman Construction Company .. E 513 381-1111
Cincinnati *(G-3646)*

Welch Packaging Group Inc .... C 614 870-2000
Columbus *(G-6874)*

Wesbanco Title Agency LLC .... E 866 295-1714
Columbus *(G-6877)*

Western Inventory Service Inc ..... C 419 756-7071
Mansfield *(G-10325)*

▲ White Oak Investments Inc .... D 614 491-1000
Columbus *(G-6885)*

◆ William R Hague Inc .... D 614 836-2115
Groveport *(G-9014)*

Wisewel LLC .... E 440 591-4896
Cleveland *(G-5153)*

Wolseley Industrial Group .... E 513 587-7532
West Chester *(G-14796)*

Wood Investment Property LLC ... E 330 644-5100
Medina *(G-10905)*

Woody Sander Ford Inc .... D 513 541-5586
Cincinnati *(G-3681)*

Worldpay Inc .... A 866 622-2390
Symmes Township *(G-13581)*

Worldpay Holding LLC .... C 513 358-6192
Symmes Twp *(G-13584)*

Worldpay Iso Inc .... C 502 961-5200
Symmes Twp *(G-13585)*

Worthngton Smuel Coil Proc LLC. E 330 963-3777
Twinsburg *(G-14231)*

Xcess Limited .... E 330 347-4901
Wooster *(G-15401)*

75 AUTOMOTIVE REPAIR, SERVICES AND PARKING

7513 Truck rental and leasing, without drivers

Aim Integrated Logistics Inc .... B 330 759-0438
Girard *(G-8808)*

Aim Leasing Company .... D 330 759-0438
Girard *(G-8809)*

▼ Albert Mike Leasing .... C 513 563-1400
Cincinnati *(G-2158)*

Benedict Enterprises Inc .... E 513 539-9216
Monroe *(G-11334)*

Columbus Truck & Equipmen ...... D 614 252-3111
Columbus *(G-5657)*

Diane Sauer Chevrolet Inc .... E 330 373-1600
Warren *(G-14518)*

First Group Investment Partnr ..... D 513 241-2200
Cincinnati *(G-2674)*

Firstgroup Usa Inc .... B 513 241-2200
Cincinnati *(G-2687)*

G J Shue Inc .... E 330 722-0082
Medina *(G-10837)*

Geo Byers Sons Holding Inc .... E 614 239-1084
Columbus *(G-5927)*

Graham Chevrolet-Cadillac Co .... C 419 989-4012
Ontario *(G-12105)*

▼ Grogans Towne Chrysler Inc ..... D 419 476-0761
Toledo *(G-13830)*

Helton Enterprises Inc .... E 419 423-4180
Findlay *(G-8546)*

Hogan Truck Leasing Inc .... E 513 454-3500
Fairfield *(G-8418)*

Hogan Truck Leasing Inc .... E 937 293-0033
Moraine *(G-11417)*

◆ Hy-Tek Material Handling LLC .. D 614 497-2500
Columbus *(G-6030)*

Interstate Truckway Inc .... D 513 542-5500
Cincinnati *(G-2883)*

Kempthorn Motors Inc .... D 800 451-3877
Canton *(G-1790)*

Kenworth of Cincinnati Inc .... D 513 771-5831
Cincinnati *(G-2937)*

Kirk NationaLease Co .... E 937 498-1151
Sidney *(G-13036)*

▲ Krieger Ford Inc .... C 614 888-3320
Columbus *(G-6129)*

McCluskey Chevrolet Inc .... C 513 761-1111
Loveland *(G-10149)*

Miami Valley Intl Trcks Inc .... E 513 733-8500
Cincinnati *(G-3055)*

Miami Valley Intl Trcks Inc .... E 937 324-5526
Springfield *(G-13273)*

Montrose Ford Inc .... C 330 666-0711
Fairlawn *(G-8491)*

◆ Ohio Machinery Co .... C 440 526-6200
Broadview Heights *(G-1394)*

Penske Logistics LLC .... D 216 765-5475
Beachwood *(G-825)*

▼ Premier Truck Sls & Rentl Inc .. E 800 825-1255
Cleveland *(G-4768)*

Reineke Ford Inc .... E 888 691-8175
Fostoria *(G-8622)*

Rouen Chrysler Plymouth Dodge . E 419 837-6228
Woodville *(G-15306)*

Roush Equipment Inc .... C 614 882-1535
Westerville *(G-15014)*

Rush Truck Centers Ohio Inc .... E 513 733-8500
Cincinnati *(G-3334)*

Rush Truck Leasing Inc .... E 937 264-2365
Dayton *(G-7599)*

Rush Truck Leasing Inc .... E 419 224-6045
Lima *(G-9957)*

Rush Truck Leasing Inc .... E 330 798-0600
Walton Hills *(G-14479)*

Schoner Chevrolet Inc .... E 330 877-6731
Hartville *(G-9129)*

Star Leasing Company LLC .... D 614 278-9999
Columbus *(G-6710)*

Triangle Leasing Corp .... E 419 729-3868
Toledo *(G-14074)*

U Haul Co of Northwestern Ohio . E 419 478-1101
Toledo *(G-14078)*

Vin Devers Inc .... C 888 847-9535
Sylvania *(G-13578)*

Voss Auto Network Inc .... E 937 428-2447
Dayton *(G-7711)*

White Family Companies Inc .... E 937 222-3701
Dayton *(G-7720)*

7514 Passenger car rental

Avis Administration .... D 937 898-2581
Vandalia *(G-14364)*

Cartemp USA Inc .... C 440 715-1000
Solon *(G-13073)*

Clerac LLC .... E 440 345-3999
Strongsville *(G-13448)*

Edison Local School District .... E 740 543-4011
Amsterdam *(G-436)*

Enterprise Holdings Inc .... E 513 538-6200
Blue Ash *(G-1169)*

Enterprise Rent-A-Car .... E 419 424-9626
Findlay *(G-8527)*

Falls Motor City Inc .... E 330 929-3066
Cuyahoga Falls *(G-7074)*

Geo Byers Sons Holding Inc .... E 614 239-1084
Columbus *(G-5927)*

George P Ballas Buick GMC Trck . E 419 535-1000
Toledo *(G-13820)*

Leikin Motor Companies Inc .... D 440 946-6900
Willoughby *(G-15204)*

Lincoln Mrcury Kings Auto Mall ... E 513 683-3800
Cincinnati *(G-2979)*

Ohio United Agency Inc .... E 419 562-3011
Bucyrus *(G-1515)*

Rental Concepts Inc .... E 216 525-3870
Hudson *(G-9370)*

Schoner Chevrolet Inc .... E 330 877-6731
Hartville *(G-9129)*

Spirit Rent-A-Car Inc .... A 440 715-1000
Cleveland *(G-4934)*

Taylor Chevrolet Inc .... E 740 653-2091
Lancaster *(G-9746)*

Thrifty LLC .... E 614 237-1500
Columbus *(G-6767)*

7515 Passenger car leasing

75 AUTOMOTIVE REPAIR, SERVICES AND PARKING

▼ Albert Mike Leasing................................ C 513 563-1400
   Cincinnati (G-2158)
Beechmont Ford Inc................................ C 513 752-6611
   Cincinnati (G-2098)
Bob Pulte Chevrolet Inc........................... E 513 932-0303
   Lebanon (G-9757)
Bobb Automotive Inc.............................. E 614 853-3000
   Columbus (G-5452)
Brondes All Makes Auto Leasing............ D 419 887-1511
   Maumee (G-10705)
Brown Motor Sales Co............................ E 419 531-0151
   Toledo (G-13720)
▼ Carcorp Inc... C 877 857-2801
   Columbus (G-5506)
Chesrown Oldsmobile GMC Inc............. E 614 846-3040
   Columbus (G-5554)
Classic Automotive Group Inc................ E 440 255-5511
   Mentor (G-10922)
Classic Bick Oldsmbile Cdliac................ E 440 639-4500
   Painesville (G-12222)
Clerac LLC.. E 440 345-3999
   Strongsville (G-13448)
Columbus SAI Motors LLC..................... E 614 851-3273
   Columbus (G-5653)
Dunning Motor Sales Inc........................ E 740 439-4465
   Cambridge (G-1568)
Ed Tomko Chrysler Jeep Ddge In........... E 440 835-5900
   Avon Lake (G-677)
Enterprise Holdings Inc.......................... E 513 538-6200
   Blue Ash (G-1169)
Graham Chevrolet-Cadillac Co................ C 419 989-4012
   Ontario (G-12105)
▼ Grogans Towne Chrysler Inc................ D 419 476-0761
   Toledo (G-13830)
Hidy Motors Inc...................................... D 937 426-9564
   Dayton (G-7133)
Jake Sweeney Automotive Inc................ D 513 782-2800
   Cincinnati (G-2896)
Jim Brown Chevrolet Inc......................... C 440 255-5511
   Mentor (G-10955)
Kempthorn Motors Inc............................ D 800 451-3877
   Canton (G-1790)
Kerry Ford Inc.. D 513 671-6400
   Cincinnati (G-2939)
Kings Toyota Inc..................................... D 513 583-4333
   Cincinnati (G-2941)
Klaben Lincoln Ford Inc.......................... D 330 593-6800
   Kent (G-9585)
▲ Krieger Ford Inc.................................. C 614 888-3320
   Columbus (G-6129)
Lakewood Chrysler-Plymouth................. E 216 521-1000
   Brookpark (G-1437)
Lariche Chevrolet-Cadillac Inc................ D 419 422-1855
   Findlay (G-8556)
Lavery Chevrolet-Buick Inc.................... E 330 823-1100
   Alliance (G-388)
Lima Auto Mall Inc................................. D 419 993-6000
   Lima (G-9918)
Lincoln Mrcury Kings Auto Mall.............. E 513 683-3800
   Cincinnati (G-2979)
Mathews Ddge Chrysler Jeep Inc............ E 740 389-2341
   Marion (G-10443)
Mathews Kennedy Ford L-M Inc............. D 740 387-3673
   Marion (G-10444)
McCluskey Chevrolet Inc........................ C 513 761-1111
   Loveland (G-10149)
Mike Albert Fleet Solutions..................... C 800 985-3273
   Cincinnati (G-3061)
Montrose Ford Inc.................................. D 330 666-0711
   Fairlawn (G-8491)
Mullinax Ford North Canton Inc.............. C 330 238-3206
   Canton (G-1812)

Nick Mayer Lincoln-Mercury Inc............. D 877 836-5314
   Westlake (G-15084)
Northgate Chrysler Ddge Jeep I.............. D 513 385-3900
   Cincinnati (G-3123)
Partners Auto Group Bdford Inc............. D 440 439-2323
   Bedford (G-980)
Reineke Ford Inc.................................... E 888 691-8175
   Fostoria (G-8622)
Ron Marhofer Automall Inc.................... E 330 923-5059
   Cuyahoga Falls (G-7100)
Rouen Chrysler Plymouth Dodge........... E 419 837-6228
   Woodville (G-15306)
Roush Equipment Inc............................. C 614 882-1535
   Westerville (G-15014)
Schoner Chevrolet Inc............................ E 330 877-6731
   Hartville (G-9129)
Sharpnack Chevrolet Co......................... E 800 752-7513
   Vermilion (G-14408)
Sonic Automotive................................... D 614 870-8200
   Columbus (G-6692)
Sorbir Inc... E 440 449-1000
   Cleveland (G-4919)
Sunnyside Cars Inc................................ E 440 777-9911
   North Olmsted (G-11917)
Swapalease Inc...................................... D 513 381-0100
   Blue Ash (G-1250)
Tansky Motors Inc.................................. E 650 322-7069
   Rockbridge (G-12736)
Tom Ahl Chryslr-Plymouth-Dodge........... C 419 227-0202
   Lima (G-9971)
Van Devere Inc....................................... D 330 253-6137
   Akron (G-348)
Vin Devers Inc.. C 888 847-9535
   Sylvania (G-13578)
Yark Automotive Group Inc.................... B 419 841-7771
   Toledo (G-14111)

7519 Utility trailer rental

A Duie Pyle Inc....................................... D 330 342-7750
   Streetsboro (G-13408)
Benedict Enterprises Inc........................ E 513 539-9216
   Monroe (G-11334)
Brown Gibbons Lang Ltd Ptrship............ E 216 241-2800
   Cleveland (G-3905)
Columbus Truck & Equipmen................. D 614 252-3111
   Columbus (G-5657)
E & J Trailer Sales & Svc Inc.................. E 513 563-2550
   Cincinnati (G-2591)
▲ Eleet Cryogenics Inc.......................... E 330 874-4009
   Bolivar (G-1294)
Transport Services Inc........................... E 440 582-4900
   Cleveland (G-5032)
U Haul Co of Northwestern Ohio............ E 419 478-1101
   Toledo (G-14078)

7521 Automobile parking

ABM Industry Groups LLC..................... E 216 621-6600
   Cleveland (G-3758)
Central Parking System of Ohio............. C 614 224-1320
   Columbus (G-5549)
City of Cincinnati................................... E 513 352-3680
   Cincinnati (G-2451)
City of Springfield.................................. E 937 328-3701
   Springfield (G-13227)
Franklin City Schools............................. E 937 743-8670
   Franklin (G-8637)
Houck Asphalt Maintenance LLC............ E 513 734-4500
   Bethel (G-1092)
Laz Karp Associates LLC....................... D 614 227-0356
   Columbus (G-6147)
Park n Fly Llc... E 404 264-1000
   Cleveland (G-4721)

Park Place Operations Inc..................... E 513 241-0415
   Cincinnati (G-3184)
Park Place Operations Inc..................... E 513 381-2179
   Cincinnati (G-3185)
Park Place Operations Inc..................... E 216 265-0500
   Cleveland (G-4722)
Park Place Operations Inc..................... D 614 224-3827
   Columbus (G-6499)
Park Place Operations Inc..................... E 513 241-0415
   Cincinnati (G-3186)
United Parcel Service Inc...................... E 419 424-9494
   Findlay (G-8595)
USA Parking Systems............................. E 216 621-9255
   Cleveland (G-5093)
Yark Automotive Group Inc.................... B 419 841-7771
   Toledo (G-14111)

7532 Top and body repair and paint shops

Advantage Ford Lincoln Mercury........... E 419 334-9751
   Fremont (G-8664)
Aero Industries Inc................................ D 330 626-3246
   Kent (G-9555)
American Bulk Commodities Inc............ C 330 758-0841
   Youngstown (G-15549)
American Nat Fleet Svc Inc.................... D 216 447-6060
   Cleveland (G-3805)
Auto Body North Inc............................... E 614 436-3700
   Columbus (G-5406)
▼ Brondes Ford..................................... E 419 473-1411
   Toledo (G-13719)
Brown Motor Sales Co........................... E 419 531-0151
   Toledo (G-13720)
Buckeye Collision Service Inc................ E 740 387-5313
   Marion (G-10420)
Chesrown Oldsmobile GMC Inc............. E 614 846-3040
   Columbus (G-5554)
Coughlin Chevrolet Inc.......................... E 740 852-1122
   London (G-10040)
Coughlin Chevrolet Inc.......................... D 740 964-9191
   Pataskala (G-12271)
Coughlin Chevrolet Toyota Inc............... D 740 366-1381
   Newark (G-11696)
Cronin Auto Inc..................................... C 419 874-4331
   Perrysburg (G-12327)
Dave Dennis Inc.................................... D 937 429-5566
   Beavercreek Township (G-935)
Decorative Paint Incorporated............... D 419 485-0632
   Montpelier (G-11384)
Doug Bigelow Chevrolet Inc................... D 330 644-7500
   Akron (G-136)
Downtown Ford Lincoln Inc.................... D 330 456-2781
   Canton (G-1738)
▲ Driverge Vhcl Innovations LLC........... E 330 861-1118
   Akron (G-141)
Dutro Ford Lincoln-Mercury Inc............. D 740 452-6334
   Zanesville (G-15786)
Ed Mullinax Ford LLC............................ C 440 984-2431
   Amherst (G-427)
Excalibur Collision Inc........................... E 440 708-9898
   Chagrin Falls (G-1977)
Fairborn Buick-GMC Truck Inc............... D 937 878-7371
   Fairborn (G-8374)
George P Ballas Buick GMC Trck........... E 419 535-1000
   Toledo (G-13820)
Grandview Fifth Auto Svc Inc................. E 614 488-6106
   Columbus (G-5945)
▼ Grogans Towne Chrysler Inc.............. D 419 476-0761
   Toledo (G-13830)
Haydocy Automotive Inc........................ D 614 279-8880
   Columbus (G-5973)
Highway Auto Center LLC...................... E 440 543-9569
   Chagrin Falls (G-1979)

75 AUTOMOTIVE REPAIR, SERVICES AND PARKING

I-75 Pierson Automotive Inc .... E 513 424-1881
 Franklin *(G-8642)*
Jake Sweeney Automotive Inc .... D 513 782-2800
 Cincinnati *(G-2896)*
Jake Sweeney Body Shop .... D 513 782-1100
 Cincinnati *(G-2897)*
Joyce Buick Inc .... E 419 529-3211
 Ontario *(G-12110)*
Kerry Ford Inc .... D 513 671-6400
 Cincinnati *(G-2939)*
Kumler Collision Inc .... E 740 653-4301
 Lancaster *(G-9728)*
Lavery Chevrolet-Buick Inc .... E 330 823-1100
 Alliance *(G-388)*
Leikin Motor Companies Inc .... D 440 946-6900
 Willoughby *(G-15204)*
Lima Auto Mall Inc .... D 419 993-6000
 Lima *(G-9918)*
Maaco Franchising Inc .... E 937 236-6700
 Dayton *(G-7463)*
Marhofer Development Co LLC .... E 330 686-2262
 Stow *(G-13381)*
Mark Thomas Ford Inc .... E 330 638-1010
 Cortland *(G-6972)*
Mathews Kennedy Ford L-M Inc .... D 740 387-3673
 Marion *(G-10444)*
Matia Motors Inc .... E 440 365-7311
 Elyria *(G-8273)*
Meinkings Service LLC .... E 513 631-5198
 Cincinnati *(G-3037)*
Mike Castrucci Ford .... C 513 831-7010
 Milford *(G-11243)*
Montrose Ford Inc .... C 330 666-0711
 Fairlawn *(G-8491)*
Northgate Chrysler Ddge Jeep l .... D 513 385-3900
 Cincinnati *(G-3123)*
Paul Hrnchar Ford-Mercury Inc .... E 330 533-3673
 Canfield *(G-1638)*
▼ QT Equipment Company .... E 330 724-3055
 Akron *(G-275)*
Roemer Unlimited Inc .... E 216 267-5454
 Cleveland *(G-4852)*
Ron Marhofer Automall Inc .... C 330 835-6707
 Cuyahoga Falls *(G-7099)*
Ron Marhofer Automall Inc .... E 330 923-5059
 Cuyahoga Falls *(G-7100)*
Roush Equipment Inc .... C 614 882-1535
 Westerville *(G-15014)*
S&S / Superior Coach Co Inc .... E 888 324-7895
 Lima *(G-9958)*
Sharpnack Chevrolet Co .... E 800 752-7513
 Vermilion *(G-14408)*
Skinner Diesel Services Inc .... E 614 491-8785
 Columbus *(G-6686)*
Suburban Collision Centers .... E 440 777-1717
 North Olmsted *(G-11916)*
Sunnyside Cars Inc .... E 440 777-9911
 North Olmsted *(G-11917)*
Surfside Motors Inc .... E 419 419-4776
 Galion *(G-8751)*
Tallmadge Collision Center .... E 330 630-2188
 Tallmadge *(G-13608)*
Tansky Motors Inc .... E 650 322-7069
 Rockbridge *(G-12736)*
Tansky Sales Inc .... E 614 793-2080
 Columbus *(G-6748)*
Three C Body Shop Inc .... E 614 885-0900
 Columbus *(G-6766)*
Three C Body Shop Inc .... D 614 274-9700
 Columbus *(G-6765)*
Voss Auto Network Inc .... B 937 433-1444
 Dayton *(G-7712)*

Walker Auto Group Inc .... D 937 433-4950
 Miamisburg *(G-11103)*
Warner Buick-Nissan Inc .... E 419 423-7161
 Findlay *(G-8597)*
Wmk LLC .... E 440 951-4335
 Bedford *(G-993)*
▲ Wmk LLC .... E 234 312-2000
 Richfield *(G-12714)*

7533 Auto exhaust system repair shops

Midas Auto Systems Experts .... A 419 243-7281
 Toledo *(G-13923)*
Tuffy Associates Corp .... E 419 865-6900
 Toledo *(G-14077)*

7534 Tire retreading and repair shops

▲ Best One Tire & Svc Lima Inc .... E 419 229-2380
 Lima *(G-9868)*
Big Oki LLC .... E 513 874-1111
 Fairfield *(G-8394)*
◆ Goodyear Tire & Rubber Company .... A 330 796-2121
 Akron *(G-179)*
▲ Grismer Tire Company .... E 937 643-2526
 Centerville *(G-1945)*
Tbc Retail Group Inc .... E 216 267-8040
 Cleveland *(G-4980)*
Ziegler Tire and Supply Co .... E 330 343-7739
 Dover *(G-7911)*

7536 Automotive glass replacement shops

▲ Advanced Auto Glass Inc .... E 412 373-6675
 Akron *(G-17)*
Belletech Corp .... C 937 599-3774
 Bellefontaine *(G-1021)*
Keystone Auto Glass Inc .... D 419 509-0497
 Maumee *(G-10736)*
Mels Auto Glass Inc .... E 513 563-7771
 Cincinnati *(G-3039)*
Ryans All-Glass Incorporated .... E 513 771-4440
 West Chester *(G-14759)*
Safelite Autoglass Foundation .... C 614 210-9000
 Columbus *(G-6629)*
Safelite Billing Services Corp .... C 614 210-9000
 Columbus *(G-6630)*
Safelite Glass Corp .... E 614 431-4936
 Worthington *(G-15455)*
▲ Safelite Glass Corp .... A 614 210-9000
 Columbus *(G-6631)*
◆ Safelite Group Inc .... E 614 210-9000
 Columbus *(G-6632)*
Wiechart Enterprises Inc .... E 419 227-0027
 Lima *(G-9987)*

7537 Automotive transmission repair shops

Power Acquisition LLC .... D 614 228-5000
 Dublin *(G-8093)*
▲ Tri-W Group Inc .... A 614 228-5000
 Columbus *(G-6786)*
W W Williams Company LLC .... E 330 225-7751
 Brunswick *(G-1473)*
W W Williams Company LLC .... D 614 228-5000
 Dublin *(G-8158)*
W W Williams Midwest Inc .... E 330 225-7751
 Brunswick *(G-1474)*

7538 General automotive repair shops

Abers Garage Inc .... E 419 281-5500
 Ashland *(G-471)*
Abraham Ford LLC .... E 440 233-7402
 Elyria *(G-8232)*
Advantage Ford Lincoln Mercury .... E 419 334-9751
 Fremont *(G-8664)*

Aim Leasing Company .... E 216 883-6300
 Cleveland *(G-3777)*
Aim Leasing Company .... D 330 759-0438
 Girard *(G-8809)*
Al Spitzer Ford Inc .... E 330 929-6546
 Cuyahoga Falls *(G-7034)*
Allstate Trck Sls Estrn Ohio L .... E 330 339-5555
 New Philadelphia *(G-11639)*
American Nat Fleet Svc Inc .... D 216 447-6060
 Cleveland *(G-3805)*
Ashtabula Area City School Dst .... E 440 992-1221
 Ashtabula *(G-517)*
Automotive Rfnish Clor Sltons l .... E 330 461-6067
 Medina *(G-10810)*
Beechmont Ford Inc .... C 513 752-6611
 Cincinnati *(G-2098)*
Belle Tire Distributors Inc .... E 419 535-3033
 Toledo *(G-13704)*
Benedict Enterprises Inc .... E 513 539-9216
 Monroe *(G-11334)*
Bill Delord Autocenter Inc .... D 513 932-3000
 Maineville *(G-10225)*
Bob Ford Chapman Inc .... E 937 642-0015
 Marysville *(G-10475)*
Bob-Boyd Ford Inc .... D 614 860-0606
 Lancaster *(G-9697)*
Bowling Green Lincoln Inc .... E 419 352-2553
 Bowling Green *(G-1312)*
▲ Brentlinger Enterprises .... C 614 889-2571
 Dublin *(G-7947)*
Broadvue Motors Inc .... D 440 845-6000
 Cleveland *(G-3899)*
▼ Brondes Ford .... E 419 473-1411
 Toledo *(G-13719)*
Brown Motor Sales Co .... E 419 531-0151
 Toledo *(G-13720)*
Buckeye Ford Inc .... E 740 852-7842
 London *(G-10038)*
Cain Motors Inc .... E 330 494-5588
 Canton *(G-1695)*
Central Cadillac Limited .... D 216 861-5800
 Cleveland *(G-3954)*
City of Athens .... E 740 592-3343
 Athens *(G-561)*
City of Toledo .... E 419 936-2507
 Toledo *(G-13737)*
Classic Automotive Group Inc .... E 440 255-5511
 Mentor *(G-10922)*
Cole Valley Motor Company Ltd .... D 330 372-1665
 Warren *(G-14509)*
Columbus SAI Motors LLC .... E 614 851-3273
 Columbus *(G-5653)*
Conrads Tire Service Inc .... E 216 941-3333
 Cleveland *(G-4103)*
Coughlin Chevrolet Inc .... D 740 964-9191
 Pataskala *(G-12271)*
Cronin Auto Inc .... C 419 874-4331
 Perrysburg *(G-12327)*
Cronin Automotive Co LLC .... E 513 202-5812
 Harrison *(G-9100)*
D & S Custom Van Inc .... E 440 946-2178
 Mentor *(G-10931)*
D + S Distribution Inc .... D 330 804-5590
 Orrville *(G-12160)*
Dave Dennis Inc .... D 937 429-5566
 Beavercreek Township *(G-935)*
Dcr Systems LLC .... E 440 205-9900
 Mentor *(G-10932)*
Decosky Motor Holdings Inc .... E 740 397-9122
 Mount Vernon *(G-11483)*
Delaware City School District .... D 740 363-5901
 Delaware *(G-7794)*

75 AUTOMOTIVE REPAIR, SERVICES AND PARKING

▲ Detroit Tire & Auto Supply Inc............ E 937 426-0949
  Xenia *(G-15503)*
Dick Masheter Ford Inc........................ D 614 861-7150
  Columbus *(G-5764)*
Don Wood Inc....................................... E 740 593-6641
  Athens *(G-566)*
Doug Bigelow Chevrolet Inc.................. D 330 644-7500
  Akron *(G-136)*
Downtown Ford Lincoln Inc.................. D 330 456-2781
  Canton *(G-1738)*
Dunning Motor Sales Inc...................... E 740 439-4465
  Cambridge *(G-1568)*
Dutro Ford Lincoln-Mercury Inc............ D 740 452-6334
  Zanesville *(G-15786)*
Duvall Automotive LLC.......................... E 513 836-6447
  Blanchester *(G-1116)*
Ed Mullinax Ford LLC............................ C 440 984-2431
  Amherst *(G-427)*
Ed Tomko Chrysler Jeep Ddge In........... E 440 835-5900
  Avon Lake *(G-677)*
Fairborn Buick-GMC Truck Inc.............. D 937 878-7371
  Fairborn *(G-8374)*
FCA US LLC... E 419 727-7285
  Toledo *(G-13804)*
Fleetpride Inc...................................... E 740 282-2711
  Steubenville *(G-13326)*
Fyda Frghtliner Youngstown Inc............ D 330 797-0224
  Youngstown *(G-15615)*
Garner Trucking Inc.............................. E 419 334-4040
  Fremont *(G-8681)*
Germain of Beavercreek II LLC............. D 937 429-2400
  Beavercreek *(G-880)*
Germain of Sidney III LLC..................... E 937 498-4014
  Sidney *(G-13035)*
◆ Goodyear Tire & Rubber Company..... A 330 796-2121
  Akron *(G-179)*
Greenwood Chevrolet Inc..................... C 330 270-1299
  Youngstown *(G-15624)*
▲ Grismer Tire Company........................ E 937 643-2526
  Centerville *(G-1945)*
▼ Grogans Towne Chrysler Inc............... D 419 476-0761
  Toledo *(G-13830)*
Guess Motors Inc................................. E 866 890-0522
  Carrollton *(G-1908)*
Harry Humphries Auto City Inc............. E 330 343-6681
  Dover *(G-7888)*
Hartwig Transit Inc.............................. C 513 563-1765
  Cincinnati *(G-2804)*
Haydocy Automotive Inc...................... D 614 279-8880
  Columbus *(G-5973)*
Highway Auto Center LLC..................... E 440 543-9569
  Chagrin Falls *(G-1979)*
▼ Hill Intl Trcks NA LLC........................... D 330 386-6440
  East Liverpool *(G-8185)*
Hoss Value Cars & Trucks Inc............... E 937 428-2400
  Dayton *(G-7415)*
◆ Hy-Tek Material Handling LLC............ D 614 497-2500
  Columbus *(G-6030)*
I-75 Pierson Automotive Inc................. E 513 424-1881
  Franklin *(G-8642)*
▲ IAC Wauseon LLC............................... E 419 335-1000
  Wauseon *(G-14605)*
Interstate Ford Inc............................... C 937 866-0781
  Miamisburg *(G-11065)*
Irace Inc... E 330 836-7247
  Akron *(G-204)*
Jake Sweeney Automotive Inc............... D 513 782-2800
  Cincinnati *(G-2896)*
Jerry Haag Motors Inc.......................... E 937 402-2090
  Hillsboro *(G-9261)*
Jim Keim Ford...................................... D 614 888-3333
  Columbus *(G-6091)*

Jones Truck & Spring Repr Inc............. D 614 443-4619
  Columbus *(G-6097)*
Kempthorn Motors Inc......................... D 800 451-3877
  Canton *(G-1790)*
Kenworth of Cincinnati Inc................... D 513 771-5831
  Cincinnati *(G-2937)*
Kerry Ford Inc...................................... D 513 671-6400
  Cincinnati *(G-2939)*
Kings Toyota Inc................................... D 513 583-4333
  Cincinnati *(G-2941)*
Kirk NationaLease Co........................... E 937 498-1151
  Sidney *(G-13036)*
Klaben Lincoln Ford Inc....................... D 330 593-6800
  Kent *(G-9585)*
Knox Auto LLC..................................... E 330 701-5266
  Mount Vernon *(G-11490)*
▲ Krieger Ford Inc.................................. C 614 888-3320
  Columbus *(G-6129)*
Lakewood Chrysler-Plymouth............... E 216 521-1000
  Brookpark *(G-1437)*
Lariche Chevrolet-Cadillac Inc.............. D 419 422-1855
  Findlay *(G-8556)*
Lavery Chevrolet-Buick Inc.................. E 330 823-1100
  Alliance *(G-388)*
Lebanon Ford Inc................................. D 513 932-1010
  Lebanon *(G-9775)*
Lima Auto Mall Inc............................... D 419 993-6000
  Lima *(G-9918)*
Lima City School District..................... E 419 996-3400
  Lima *(G-9919)*
Lincoln Mrcury Kings Auto Mall............ E 513 683-3800
  Cincinnati *(G-2979)*
Lower Great Lakes Kenworth Inc.......... E 419 874-3511
  Perrysburg *(G-12354)*
Mansfield Truck Sls & Svc Inc.............. D 419 522-9811
  Mansfield *(G-10290)*
Mark Thomas Ford Inc......................... E 330 638-1010
  Cortland *(G-6972)*
Mathews Ddge Chrysler Jeep Inc......... E 740 389-2341
  Marion *(G-10443)*
Mathews Ford Sandusky Inc................. E 419 626-4721
  Sandusky *(G-12914)*
Mathews Kennedy Ford L-M Inc........... D 740 387-3673
  Marion *(G-10444)*
Matia Motors Inc.................................. E 440 365-7311
  Elyria *(G-8273)*
Meinkings Service LLC........................ E 513 631-5198
  Cincinnati *(G-3037)*
▼ Midway Inc... D 419 465-2551
  Monroeville *(G-11357)*
Mike Castrucci Ford............................. C 513 831-7010
  Milford *(G-11243)*
Mike Ford Bass Inc.............................. D 440 934-3673
  Sheffield Village *(G-13002)*
Mizar Motors Inc.................................. D 419 729-2400
  Toledo *(G-13925)*
Montrose Ford Inc................................ C 330 666-0711
  Fairlawn *(G-8491)*
Moores Rv Inc...................................... E 800 523-1904
  North Ridgeville *(G-11932)*
Nassief Automotive Inc........................ E 440 997-5151
  Austinburg *(G-632)*
National At/Trckstops Hldngs C........... A 440 808-9100
  Westlake *(G-15081)*
National Auto Experts LLC................... C 440 274-5114
  Strongsville *(G-13478)*
Nicholas Auto Elec Rblding LLC........... D 740 373-3861
  Marietta *(G-10395)*
Nick Mayer Lincoln-Mercury Inc........... D 877 836-5314
  Westlake *(G-15084)*
Northern Automotive Inc...................... E 614 436-2001
  Columbus *(G-6367)*

Northgate Chrysler Ddge Jeep I........... D 513 385-3900
  Cincinnati *(G-3123)*
Nvp Warranty....................................... D 888 270-5835
  Independence *(G-9462)*
Ohio Machinery Co............................... E 614 878-2287
  Columbus *(G-6436)*
Ohio Machinery Co............................... E 419 423-1447
  Findlay *(G-8574)*
Orwell Tire Service Inc......................... D 440 437-6515
  Orwell *(G-12179)*
Pallotta Ford Inc.................................. D 330 345-5051
  Wooster *(G-15365)*
Parkman Automotive LLC..................... E 234 223-2806
  Warren *(G-14545)*
Pep Boys - Mnny Moe Jack Del L......... E 614 864-2092
  Columbus *(G-6515)*
Peterbilt of Cincinnati......................... B 513 772-1740
  Cincinnati *(G-3199)*
Power Acquisition LLC......................... D 614 228-5000
  Dublin *(G-8093)*
Priced Right Cars Inc.......................... E 614 337-0037
  Columbus *(G-6545)*
Putnam Cnty Commissioners Off......... E 419 523-6832
  Ottawa *(G-12192)*
R & M Leasing Inc............................... C 937 382-6800
  Wilmington *(G-15269)*
R & R Inc... E 330 799-1536
  Youngstown *(G-15705)*
▲ Ricart Ford Inc................................... B 614 836-5321
  Groveport *(G-9000)*
Ron Marhofer Auto Family.................... E 330 940-4422
  Cuyahoga Falls *(G-7098)*
Ron Marhofer Automall Inc.................. E 330 923-5059
  Cuyahoga Falls *(G-7100)*
Rondy Fleet Services Inc..................... E 330 745-9016
  Barberton *(G-706)*
Roush Equipment Inc........................... C 614 882-1535
  Westerville *(G-15014)*
Rush Truck Centers Ohio Inc................ E 513 733-8500
  Cincinnati *(G-3334)*
Rush Truck Leasing Inc....................... E 937 264-2365
  Dayton *(G-7599)*
Rush Truck Leasing Inc....................... E 419 224-6045
  Lima *(G-9957)*
Rush Truck Leasing Inc....................... E 330 798-0600
  Walton Hills *(G-14479)*
Salem City Schools.............................. E 330 332-2321
  Salem *(G-12851)*
Schoner Chevrolet Inc.......................... E 330 877-6731
  Hartville *(G-9129)*
Seaway Gas & Petroleum Inc................ E 216 566-9070
  Cleveland *(G-4888)*
Sharpnack Chevrolet Co....................... E 800 752-7513
  Vermilion *(G-14408)*
Skinner Diesel Services Inc................. E 614 491-8785
  Columbus *(G-6686)*
Sonic Automotive................................ D 614 870-8200
  Columbus *(G-6692)*
Spires Motors Inc................................ E 614 771-2345
  Hilliard *(G-9233)*
Spitzer Chevrolet Inc........................... E 330 467-4141
  Northfield *(G-11966)*
Sunnyside Cars Inc.............................. E 440 777-9911
  North Olmsted *(G-11917)*
Surfside Motors Inc............................. E 419 419-4776
  Galion *(G-8751)*
Sutphen Towers Inc.............................. D 614 876-1262
  Hilliard *(G-9234)*
T I G Fleet Service Inc......................... E 419 250-6333
  Perrysburg *(G-12374)*
Ta Operating LLC................................. B 440 808-9100
  Westlake *(G-15113)*

75 AUTOMOTIVE REPAIR, SERVICES AND PARKING

Company	Code	Phone
Tansky Motors Inc	E	650 322-7069
Rockbridge (G-12736)		
Taylor Chevrolet Inc	E	740 653-2091
Lancaster (G-9746)		
Tim Lally Chevrolet Inc	D	440 232-2000
Bedford (G-988)		
Tm Final Ltd	B	419 724-8473
Toledo (G-14047)		
Travelcenters of America Inc	A	440 808-9100
Westlake (G-15117)		
▲ Tri-W Group Inc	A	614 228-5000
Columbus (G-6786)		
United Parcel Service Inc	D	419 872-0211
Perrysburg (G-12382)		
◆ Valley Ford Truck Inc	D	216 524-2400
Cleveland (G-5097)		
Vin Devers Inc	C	888 847-9535
Sylvania (G-13578)		
Volvo BMW Dyton Evans Volkswag	E	937 890-6200
Dayton (G-7710)		
Voss Auto Network Inc	E	937 428-2447
Dayton (G-7711)		
W W Williams Company LLC	E	330 225-7751
Brunswick (G-1473)		
W W Williams Company LLC	E	614 527-9400
Hilliard (G-9241)		
W W Williams Company LLC	E	614 228-5000
Dublin (G-8158)		
W W Williams Midwest Inc	E	330 225-7751
Brunswick (G-1474)		
Walker Auto Group Inc	D	937 433-4950
Miamisburg (G-11103)		
Walt Ford Sweeney Inc	D	513 347-2600
Cincinnati (G-3639)		
Warner Buick-Nissan Inc	E	419 423-7161
Findlay (G-8597)		
Yorktown Automotive Center Inc	E	440 885-2803
Cleveland (G-5165)		
Young Truck Sales Inc	E	330 477-6271
Canton (G-1891)		

7539 Automotive repair shops, nec

Company	Code	Phone
Beechmont Chevrolet Inc	D	513 624-1100
Cincinnati (G-2247)		
Beechmont Motors Inc	E	513 388-3883
Cincinnati (G-2248)		
Beechmont Motors T Inc	D	513 388-3800
Cincinnati (G-2249)		
Bobby Layman Cadillac GMC Inc	E	740 654-9590
Carroll (G-1899)		
Coates Car Care Inc	E	330 652-4180
Niles (G-11785)		
▲ Double A Trailer Sales Inc	E	419 692-7626
Delphos (G-7840)		
▼ East Manufacturing Corporation	B	330 325-9921
Randolph (G-12618)		
First Services Inc	A	513 241-2200
Cincinnati (G-2675)		
◆ First Transit Inc	D	513 241-2200
Cincinnati (G-2682)		
Fred Martin Nissan LLC	E	330 644-8888
Akron (G-168)		
Germain Ford LLC	C	614 889-7777
Columbus (G-5931)		
Girard Equipment Co	E	330 545-2575
Girard (G-8814)		
◆ Goodyear Tire & Rubber Company	A	330 796-2121
Akron (G-179)		
Haasz Automall LLC	E	330 296-2866
Ravenna (G-12627)		
Hans Truck and Trlr Repr Inc	D	216 581-0046
Cleveland (G-4349)		
Hoss II Inc	E	937 669-4300
Tipp City (G-13660)		
Irace Inc	E	330 836-7247
Akron (G-204)		
◆ Mac Trailer Manufacturing Inc	A	800 795-8454
Alliance (G-391)		
▲ Miscor Group Ltd	B	330 830-3500
Massillon (G-10658)		
▼ Nelson Manufacturing Company	D	419 523-5321
Ottawa (G-12189)		
Paul Hrnchar Ford-Mercury Inc	E	330 533-3673
Canfield (G-1638)		
◆ RL Best Company	E	330 758-8601
Boardman (G-1290)		
Spitzer Chevrolet Inc	E	330 467-4141
Northfield (G-11966)		
Star Leasing Company LLC	D	614 278-9999
Columbus (G-6710)		
Three C Body Shop Inc	D	614 274-9700
Columbus (G-6765)		
Trailines Incorporated	E	513 755-7900
West Chester (G-14777)		
Transport Services Inc	E	440 582-4900
Cleveland (G-5032)		
Tuffy Associates Corp	E	419 865-6900
Toledo (G-14077)		
Wabash National Trlr Ctrs Inc	D	614 878-6088
Groveport (G-9012)		

7542 Carwashes

Company	Code	Phone
Allied Car Wash Inc	E	513 559-1733
Cincinnati (G-2163)		
Blue Beacon USA LP	D	330 534-4419
Hubbard (G-9319)		
Blue Beacon USA LP II	E	419 643-8146
Beaverdam (G-952)		
Coates Car Care Inc	E	330 652-4180
Niles (G-11785)		
Combined Technologies Inc	E	513 595-5900
Cincinnati (G-2478)		
Expresso Car Wash Systems Inc	E	419 866-7099
Toledo (G-13801)		
Henderson Rd Rest Systems Inc	E	614 442-3310
Columbus (G-5984)		
JKL Development Company	E	937 390-0358
Springfield (G-13261)		
Klean-A-Kar Inc	E	614 221-3145
Columbus (G-6119)		
Matthew T Hovanic Inc	E	330 898-3387
Warren (G-14538)		
Mikes Carwash Inc	E	513 677-4700
Loveland (G-10151)		
Mikescar Wash	E	513 672-6440
Loveland (G-10152)		
Napoleon Wash-N-Fill Inc	C	419 424-1726
Findlay (G-8572)		
Perfect Power Wash	D	330 697-0131
Norton (G-11997)		
Rapps Enterprises Inc	E	330 542-2362
New Middletown (G-11636)		
Roulan Enterprises Inc	E	440 543-2070
Cleveland (G-4856)		
Tri-Valley Equipment Sales Inc	E	740 695-5895
Barnesville (G-723)		
Truckomat Corporation	E	740 467-2818
Hebron (G-9155)		
Waterway Gas & Wash Company	E	330 995-2900
Aurora (G-630)		
Waterway Gas & Wash Company	E	636 537-1111
Hudson (G-9377)		
Zappys Auto Washes	E	844 927-9274
Mentor (G-11013)		

7549 Automotive services, nec

Company	Code	Phone
AAA Ohio Auto Club	D	614 431-7800
Worthington (G-15403)		
Abers Garage Inc	E	419 281-5500
Ashland (G-471)		
▲ Afg Industries Inc	D	614 322-4580
Grove City (G-8893)		
Charlie Towing Service Inc	E	440 234-5300
Berea (G-1064)		
◆ Cintas Corporation No 1	A	513 459-1200
Mason (G-10533)		
City of Athens	E	740 592-3343
Athens (G-561)		
Coates Car Care Inc	E	330 652-4180
Niles (G-11785)		
Dave Marshall Inc	E	937 878-9135
Fairborn (G-8372)		
Dealer Supply and Eqp Ltd	E	419 724-8473
Toledo (G-13772)		
Eitel Towing Service Inc	E	614 877-4139
Orient (G-12151)		
Englewood Truck Inc	E	937 836-5109
Clayton (G-3732)		
Fayette Parts Service Inc	E	724 880-3616
Wintersville (G-15294)		
First Vehicle Services Inc	C	513 241-2200
Cincinnati (G-2683)		
Ground Effects LLC	E	440 565-5925
Westlake (G-15062)		
Herrnstein Chrysler Inc	C	740 773-2203
Chillicothe (G-2068)		
Industrial Sorting Services	E	513 772-6501
West Chester (G-14711)		
Mbd Transport LLC	D	513 449-0777
Brunswick (G-1463)		
Meinkings Service LLC	E	513 631-5198
Cincinnati (G-3037)		
Pete Baur Buick GMC Inc	E	440 238-5600
Cleveland (G-4745)		
Pioneer Quick Lubes Inc	E	419 782-2213
Defiance (G-7761)		
R Robnsons Twing Recovery LLC	E	937 458-3666
Beavercreek (G-897)		
Richs Towing & Service Inc	E	440 234-3435
Middleburg Heights (G-11124)		
Rustys Towing Service Inc	D	614 491-6288
Columbus (G-6622)		
Sandys Auto & Truck Svc Inc	E	937 461-4980
Moraine (G-11436)		
Sandys Towing	E	937 228-6832
Dayton (G-7610)		
SGS North America Inc	E	513 674-7048
Cincinnati (G-3366)		
Southern Express Lubes Inc	E	937 278-5807
Dayton (G-7630)		
Sprandel Enterprises Inc	E	513 777-6622
West Chester (G-14768)		
Star Leasing Company LLC	D	614 278-9999
Columbus (G-6710)		
Team Lubrication Inc	D	614 231-9909
Columbus (G-6751)		
Valvoline Instant Oil Change	C	937 548-0123
Greenville (G-8888)		
Valvoline Instant Oil Chnge Fr	E	330 453-4549
Canton (G-1879)		
Valvoline Instant Oil Chnge Fr	E	419 589-5396
Mansfield (G-10321)		
Valvoline Instant Oil Chnge Fr	E	513 422-4980
Middletown (G-11191)		
Valvoline Instant Oil Chnge Fr	E	937 773-0112
Piqua (G-12461)		

75 AUTOMOTIVE REPAIR, SERVICES AND PARKING

Valvoline Instant Oil Chnge Fr............. D 614 452-4682
  Reynoldsburg (G-12679)
Valvoline Instant Oil Chnge Fr............. E 330 372-4416
  Warren (G-14571)
Valvoline Instant Oil Chnge Fr............. E 330 726-5676
  Youngstown (G-15747)
Valvoline LLC.. C 513 557-3100
  Cincinnati (G-3614)
Westfall Towing LLC............................ E 740 371-5185
  Marietta (G-10413)
World Trck Towing Recovery Inc......... E 330 723-1116
  Seville (G-12968)
Ziebart of Ohio Inc............................... E 440 845-6031
  Cleveland (G-5175)

76 MISCELLANEOUS REPAIR SERVICES

7622 Radio and television repair

Cbst Acquisition LLC........................... D 513 361-9600
  Cincinnati (G-2326)
Combined Technologies Inc................. E 513 595-5900
  Cincinnati (G-2478)
Comproducts Inc.................................. E 614 276-5552
  Columbus (G-5679)
Electra Sound Inc................................. C 216 433-1050
  Cleveland (G-4208)
Electra Sound Inc................................. D 216 433-9600
  Avon Lake (G-678)
Mobilcomm Inc..................................... D 513 742-5555
  Cincinnati (G-3072)
Office World Inc................................... E 419 991-4694
  Lima (G-9994)
P & R Communications Svc Inc........... E 937 512-8100
  Dayton (G-7543)

7623 Refrigeration service and repair

Cac Group LLC.................................... E 740 369-4328
  Delaware (G-7782)
Columbus/Worthington Htg AC Inc...... E 614 771-5381
  Columbus (G-5605)
Cov-Ro Inc... E 330 856-3176
  Warren (G-14515)
Electrical Appl Repr Svc Inc................. E 216 459-8700
  Brooklyn Heights (G-1417)
Gardiner Service Company LLC........... C 440 248-3400
  Solon (G-13091)
McPhillips Plbg Htg & AC Co................ E 216 481-1400
  Cleveland (G-4542)
Refrigeration Systems Company........... D 614 263-0913
  Columbus (G-6571)
Smith & Oby Service Co....................... E 440 735-5322
  Bedford (G-985)
The Geiler Company............................ E 513 574-1200
  Cincinnati (G-3466)

7629 Electrical repair shops

Alco-Chem Inc...................................... E 330 833-8551
  Canton (G-1658)
▲ Amko Service Company.................... E 330 364-8857
  Midvale (G-11203)
Appliance Warehouse Amer Inc........... D 614 623-3131
  Columbus (G-5375)
▲ Automation & Control Tech Ltd......... E 419 661-6400
  Perrysburg (G-12314)
Brehob Corporation.............................. E 513 755-1300
  West Chester (G-14655)
Cbst Acquisition LLC........................... D 513 361-9600
  Cincinnati (G-2326)
◆ Ceramic Holdings Inc....................... C 216 362-3900
  Brookpark (G-1431)

City of Wadsworth................................ E 330 334-1581
  Wadsworth (G-14430)
Cornerstone Wauseon Inc.................... C 419 337-0940
  Wauseon (G-14598)
CP Redi LLC.. C 866 682-7462
  Columbus (G-5717)
DTE Inc.. E 419 522-3428
  Mansfield (G-10259)
Electric Motor Tech LLC...................... E 513 821-9999
  Cincinnati (G-2609)
Electric Service Co Inc......................... E 513 271-6387
  Cincinnati (G-2610)
Electrical Appl Repr Svc Inc................. E 216 459-8700
  Brooklyn Heights (G-1417)
Fak Group Inc...................................... E 440 498-8465
  Solon (G-13085)
General Electric Company.................... E 513 977-1500
  Cincinnati (G-2723)
General Electric Company.................... E 216 883-1000
  Cleveland (G-4310)
Generator One LLC............................. E 440 942-8449
  Mentor (G-10941)
High Line Corporation.......................... E 330 848-8800
  Akron (G-192)
▲ Instrmntation Ctrl Systems Inc......... E 513 662-2600
  Cincinnati (G-2873)
Kiemle-Hankins Company.................... E 419 661-2430
  Perrysburg (G-12349)
Leppo Inc... E 330 633-3999
  Tallmadge (G-13599)
▲ Miscor Group Ltd.............................. B 330 830-3500
  Massillon (G-10658)
Mmi-Cpr LLC.. E 216 674-0645
  Independence (G-9454)
Modern Office Methods Inc.................. E 513 791-0909
  Blue Ash (G-1211)
Modern Office Methods Inc.................. E 614 891-3693
  Westerville (G-15000)
Modern Office Methods Inc.................. D 513 791-0909
  Cincinnati (G-3076)
Narrow Way Custom Tech Inc............. E 937 743-1611
  Carlisle (G-1898)
Ohio Business Machines LLC............. E 216 485-2000
  Cleveland (G-4683)
Ohio Machinery Co.............................. D 740 453-0563
  Zanesville (G-15822)
Qualus Corp... D 800 434-0415
  Cincinnati (G-3261)
▲ Rubber City Machinery Corp............ E 330 434-3500
  Akron (G-288)
S D Myers Inc...................................... C 330 630-7000
  Tallmadge (G-13602)
▲ Steel Eqp Specialists Inc.................. D 330 823-8260
  Alliance (G-401)
Tegam Inc.. E 440 466-6100
  Geneva (G-8789)
◆ Vertiv Corporation............................ A 614 888-0246
  Westerville (G-14949)
◆ Vertiv Energy Systems Inc............... A 440 288-1122
  Lorain (G-10107)
VSI Global LLC.................................... E 216 642-8778
  Cleveland (G-5117)
Weaver Appliance Sls & Svc LLC........ D 330 852-4555
  Dover (G-7910)
Winner Aviation Corporation................. C 330 856-5000
  Vienna (G-14424)

7631 Watch, clock, and jewelry repair

Family Liquidation Company Inc.......... D 937 780-3075
  Wshngtn Ct Hs (G-15479)
R S Stoll and Company........................ E 937 434-7800
  Dayton (G-7578)

SIC SECTION

Sunrise Senior Living MGT Inc............. C 614 235-3900
  Columbus (G-6731)

7641 Reupholstery and furniture repair

Business Furniture LLC....................... E 937 293-1010
  Dayton (G-7207)
▲ Casco Mfg Solutions Inc.................. D 513 681-0003
  Cincinnati (G-2318)
Dayton Ews Inc.................................... E 937 293-1010
  Moraine (G-11400)
Integrated Whse Solutions Inc............. E 614 899-5080
  Westerville (G-14900)
▲ National Electro-Coatings Inc........... D 216 898-0080
  Cleveland (G-4624)
Soft Touch Wood LLC......................... E 330 545-4204
  Girard (G-8826)

7692 Welding repair

▲ A & G Manufacturing Co Inc............. E 419 468-7433
  Galion (G-8740)
Abbott Tool Inc..................................... E 419 476-6742
  Toledo (G-13673)
All-Type Welding & Fabrication............ E 440 439-3990
  Cleveland (G-3792)
Allied Fabricating & Wldg Co................ E 614 751-6664
  Columbus (G-5338)
Arctech Fabricating Inc........................ E 937 525-9353
  Springfield (G-13219)
Athens Mold and Machine Inc............. D 740 593-6613
  Athens (G-559)
Bayloff Stmped Pdts Knsman Inc......... D 330 876-4511
  Kinsman (G-9644)
Breitinger Company.............................. C 419 526-4255
  Mansfield (G-10248)
Brown Industrial Inc............................. E 937 693-3838
  Botkins (G-1299)
▲ Byron Products Inc........................... D 513 870-9111
  Fairfield (G-8397)
C & R Inc... E 614 497-1130
  Groveport (G-8975)
C-N-D Industries Inc............................ E 330 478-8811
  Massillon (G-10633)
◆ Ceramic Holdings Inc....................... C 216 362-3900
  Brookpark (G-1431)
▲ Combs Manufacturing Inc................. D 330 784-3151
  Akron (G-114)
Crest Bending Inc................................ E 419 492-2108
  New Washington (G-11682)
Dynamic Weld Corporation................... E 419 582-2900
  Osgood (G-12180)
▲ East End Welding LLC..................... C 330 677-6000
  Kent (G-9573)
Falls Stamping & Welding Co............... C 330 928-1191
  Cuyahoga Falls (G-7075)
Fleetpride Inc....................................... E 740 282-2711
  Steubenville (G-13326)
Gaspar Inc... D 330 477-2222
  Canton (G-1759)
▲ General Tool Company..................... C 513 733-5500
  Cincinnati (G-2728)
George Steel Fabricating Inc............... E 513 932-2887
  Lebanon (G-9766)
▲ Glenridge Machine Co...................... E 440 975-1055
  Solon (G-13092)
▲ Hi-Tek Manufacturing Inc.................. C 513 459-1094
  Mason (G-10562)
▲ Industry Products Co........................ B 937 778-0585
  Piqua (G-12445)
J & S Industrial Mch Pdts Inc............... D 419 691-1380
  Toledo (G-13865)
Jerl Machine Inc.................................. D 419 873-0270
  Perrysburg (G-12348)

76 MISCELLANEOUS REPAIR SERVICES

JMw Welding and Mfg Inc............................ E 330 484-2428
　Canton (G-1785)
Kinninger Prod Wldg Co Inc........................ D 419 629-3491
　New Bremen (G-11598)
Laserflex Corporation................................... D 614 850-9600
　Hilliard (G-9209)
Lima Sheet Metal Machine & Mfg................ E 419 229-1161
　Lima (G-9927)
Lincoln Electric Automtn Inc....................... B 937 295-2120
　Fort Loramie (G-8605)
▲ Long-Stanton Mfg Company..................... E 513 874-8020
　West Chester (G-14725)
Lunar Tool & Mold Inc................................. E 440 237-2141
　North Royalton (G-11944)
▲ McGregor Mtal Leffel Works LLC............. D 937 325-5561
　Springfield (G-13265)
Meta Manufacturing Corporation................ E 513 793-6382
　Blue Ash (G-1210)
Paulo Products Company............................ E 440 942-0153
　Willoughby (G-15218)
◆ Pentaflex Inc... C 937 325-5551
　Springfield (G-13281)
Phillips Mfg and Tower Co........................... D 419 347-1720
　Shelby (G-13008)
Precision Mtal Fabrication Inc..................... D 937 235-9261
　Dayton (G-7559)
Precision Welding Corporation................... E 216 524-6110
　Cleveland (G-4765)
Prout Boiler Htg & Wldg Inc........................ E 330 744-0293
　Youngstown (G-15699)
▲ R K Industries Inc...................................... D 419 523-5001
　Ottawa (G-12195)
Schmidt Machine Company........................ E 419 294-3814
　Upper Sandusky (G-14292)
Stan-Kell LLC... E 440 998-1116
　Ashtabula (G-550)
Triangle Precision Industries...................... D 937 299-6776
　Dayton (G-7678)
Turn-Key Industrial Svcs LLC..................... D 614 274-1128
　Grove City (G-8960)
Valley Machine Tool Inc.............................. E 513 899-2737
　Morrow (G-11456)
Welders Supply Inc..................................... E 216 267-4470
　Brookpark (G-1443)
Worthington Industries Inc......................... E 614 438-3028
　Columbus (G-6906)

7694 Armature rewinding shops

▲ 3-D Service Ltd... C 330 830-3500
　Massillon (G-10626)
E-Z Electric Motor Svc Corp....................... E 216 581-8820
　Cleveland (G-4195)
Fenton Bros Electric Co.............................. E 330 343-0093
　New Philadelphia (G-11651)
Integrated Power Services LLC.................. D 216 433-7808
　Cleveland (G-4415)
Integrated Power Services LLC.................. E 513 863-8816
　Hamilton (G-9055)
Kiemle-Hankins Company........................... E 419 661-2430
　Perrysburg (G-12349)
▲ Magnetech Industrial Svcs Inc................. D 330 830-3500
　Massillon (G-10651)
▼ Matlock Electric Co Inc............................ E 513 731-9600
　Cincinnati (G-3015)
◆ National Electric Coil Inc.......................... B 614 488-1151
　Columbus (G-6296)
▲ Shoemaker Electric Company.................. E 614 294-5626
　Columbus (G-6673)
Whelco Industrial Ltd.................................. D 419 385-4627
　Perrysburg (G-12387)
Yaskawa America Inc.................................. C 937 847-6200
　Miamisburg (G-11105)

7699 Repair services, nec

21st Century Solutions Ltd......................... E 877 439-5377
　Miamisburg (G-11017)
▲ 3-D Service Ltd... C 330 830-3500
　Massillon (G-10626)
AAA Pipe Cleaning Corporation.................. C 216 341-2900
　Cleveland (G-3756)
AD Farrow LLC.. E 740 965-9900
　Sunbury (G-13514)
Advanced Rhbilitation Tech Ltd................. E 419 636-2684
　Bryan (G-1477)
Ag-Pro Ohio LLC.. E 937 486-5211
　Wilmington (G-15238)
Aim Integrated Logistics Inc...................... B 330 759-0438
　Girard (G-8808)
Aim Leasing Company................................ E 330 759-0438
　Girard (G-8809)
Aimhi Inc... E 614 939-0112
　New Albany (G-11554)
Airborne Maint Engrg Svcs Inc................... C 937 366-2559
　Wilmington (G-15242)
Airborne Maint Engrg Svcs Inc................... C 937 382-5591
　Wilmington (G-15243)
◆ Ajax Tocco Magnethermic Corp................ C 800 547-1527
　Warren (G-14496)
AKD Cleaning Service of Texas.................. D 937 521-3900
　Springfield (G-13215)
▲ All American Sports Corp......................... E 440 366-8225
　North Ridgeville (G-11921)
All Lift Service Company Inc...................... E 440 585-1542
　Willoughby (G-15183)
Alpha Imaging LLC...................................... E 440 953-3800
　Willoughby (G-15185)
Altaquip LLC.. E 513 674-6464
　Harrison (G-9097)
▲ American Frame Corporation.................... D 419 893-5595
　Maumee (G-10690)
▲ American Hydraulic Svcs Inc................... E 606 739-8680
　Ironton (G-9502)
American Suncraft Co Inc........................... E 937 849-9475
　Medway (G-10907)
▲ Amko Service Company............................ E 330 364-8857
　Midvale (G-11203)
▲ Apph Wichita Inc....................................... E 316 943-5752
　Strongsville (G-13442)
Apple Farm Service Inc.............................. E 937 526-4851
　Covington (G-7017)
▲ Applied Industrial Tech Inc...................... B 216 426-4000
　Cleveland (G-3827)
Aptos LLC.. D 614 840-1400
　Lewis Center (G-9806)
Atm Solutions Inc.. D 513 742-4900
　Cincinnati (G-2228)
B M Machine... E 419 595-2898
　New Riegel (G-11677)
◆ Babcock & Wilcox Company...................... A 330 753-4511
　Akron (G-59)
Best Aire Compressor Service.................... D 419 726-0055
　Millbury (G-11266)
Brakefire Incorporated................................ D 513 733-5655
　Cincinnati (G-2276)
Brechbuhler Scales Inc............................... E 330 458-3060
　Canton (G-1689)
C H Bradshaw Co.. E 614 871-2087
　Grove City (G-8904)
Canton-Stark Cnty Swer Clg Inc................. C 330 456-7890
　North Canton (G-11814)
Capitol Varsity Sports Inc........................... E 513 523-4126
　Oxford (G-12204)
Chemed Corporation................................... C 513 762-6690
　Cincinnati (G-2352)

Clean Team Inc.. E 419 537-8770
　Toledo (G-13746)
Cleveland Electric Labs Co......................... E 800 447-2207
　Twinsburg (G-14177)
Cmbb LLC.. C 937 652-2151
　Urbana (G-14304)
Columbs/Worthington Htg AC Inc.............. E 614 771-5381
　Columbus (G-5605)
Comdoc Inc.. C 330 896-2346
　North Canton (G-11818)
Commercial Electric Pdts Corp................... E 216 241-2886
　Cleveland (G-4094)
Component Repair Technologies Inc.......... B 440 255-1793
　Mentor (G-10925)
Convergint Technologies LLC..................... E 513 771-1717
　Cincinnati (G-2505)
Corporate Cleaning Inc............................... E 614 203-6051
　Columbus (G-5702)
Corrotec Inc... E 937 325-3585
　Springfield (G-13242)
Cov-Ro Inc... E 330 856-3176
　Warren (G-14515)
Coyle Music Centers Inc............................. E 614 885-6654
　Columbus (G-5716)
Crane America Services Inc....................... B 937 293-6526
　Miamisburg (G-11041)
Damarc Inc... E 330 454-6171
　Canton (G-1731)
Dayton Door Sales Inc................................ E 937 253-9181
　Dayton (G-7280)
Dearing Compressor and Pu....................... E 330 783-2258
　Youngstown (G-15595)
Diebold Nixdorf Incorporated..................... D 330 899-1300
　North Canton (G-11823)
Donnellon McCarthy Entps Inc................... E 513 769-7800
　Cincinnati (G-2573)
Dortrnic Service-Tallmadge Inc.................. E 330 928-2727
　Stow (G-13364)
Dortronic Service Inc.................................. E 216 739-3667
　Cleveland (G-4180)
▲ Dover Hydraulics Inc................................. D 330 364-1617
　Dover (G-7882)
Dp Medina Holdings Inc.............................. E 216 254-7883
　Medina (G-10832)
Dreier & Maller Inc...................................... E 614 575-0065
　Reynoldsburg (G-12661)
Dtv Inc... E 216 226-5465
　Cleveland (G-4187)
▲ Eagleburgmann Ke Inc.............................. E 859 746-0091
　Cincinnati (G-2596)
Eaton Industrial Corporation...................... C 216 692-5456
　Cleveland (G-4204)
▲ Emsco Inc... E 330 830-7125
　Massillon (G-10638)
Equipment Maintenance Inc....................... E 513 353-3518
　Cleves (G-5188)
▲ Equipment MGT Svc & Repr Inc............... E 937 383-1052
　Wilmington (G-15250)
Estabrook Corporation................................ E 440 234-8566
　Berea (G-1068)
Expert Crane Inc... E 216 451-9900
　Wellington (G-14632)
▲ Fallsway Equipment Co Inc...................... C 330 633-6000
　Akron (G-152)
Famous Enterprises Inc.............................. E 330 762-9621
　Akron (G-156)
Fire Foe Corp.. E 330 759-9834
　Girard (G-8811)
Fleet Team.. E 614 699-2500
　Brooklyn Heights (G-1418)
▲ Forge Industries Inc.................................. A 330 960-2468
　Youngstown (G-15613)

76 MISCELLANEOUS REPAIR SERVICES

Fortuna Construction Co Inc .... E 440 892-3834
  Cleveland (G-4278)
French Company LLC .... D 330 963-4344
  Twinsburg (G-14193)
◆ GE Engine Services LLC .... C 513 243-2000
  Cincinnati (G-2721)
Graphic Systems Services Inc .... E 937 746-0708
  Springboro (G-13199)
Great Lakes-Ramco Inc .... E 586 759-5500
  Mentor (G-10944)
Grimes Aerospace Company .... D 937 484-2001
  Urbana (G-14308)
◆ Grob Systems Inc .... A 419 358-9015
  Bluffton (G-1281)
Hans Truck and Trlr Repr Inc .... D 216 581-0046
  Cleveland (G-4349)
▲ Harry C Lobalzo & Sons Inc .... E 330 666-6758
  Akron (G-184)
Heil Brothers Incorporated .... E 937 256-3500
  Dayton (G-7404)
◆ Hillman Companies Inc .... B 513 851-4900
  Cincinnati (G-2822)
▲ Industrial Repair and Mfg .... E 419 822-4232
  Delta (G-7851)
Inertial Airline Services Inc .... E 440 995-6555
  Cleveland (G-4411)
Integrity Processing LLC .... E 330 285-6937
  Barberton (G-699)
Interstate Lift Trucks Inc .... E 216 328-0970
  Cleveland (G-4421)
JJ&pl Services-Consulting LLC .... E 330 923-5783
  Cuyahoga Falls (G-7082)
Kelco Enterprises Inc .... E 440 926-4357
  Grafton (G-8840)
Kone Inc .... E 330 762-8886
  Cleveland (G-4470)
Kone Inc .... E 513 755-6195
  West Chester (G-14720)
Lance A1 Cleaning Services LLC .... D 614 370-0550
  Columbus (G-6135)
Laserflex Corporation .... D 614 850-9600
  Hilliard (G-9209)
◆ Lawrence Industries Inc .... E 216 518-7000
  Cleveland (G-4483)
Liechty Inc .... E 419 298-2302
  Edgerton (G-8228)
Lw Equipment LLC .... E 614 475-7376
  Columbus (G-6182)
Lyco Corporation .... E 412 973-9176
  Lowellville (G-10169)
Mannys Cleaning Co .... E 614 596-1919
  Dublin (G-8060)
McJ Holdings Inc .... C 937 592-5025
  Columbus (G-6216)
McNational Inc .... D 740 377-4391
  South Point (G-13179)
Metro Design Inc .... E 440 458-4200
  Elyria (G-8274)
◆ Mettler-Toledo LLC .... A 614 438-4511
  Columbus (G-5270)
Miami Industrial Trucks Inc .... D 937 293-4194
  Moraine (G-11425)
Modern Office Methods Inc .... E 937 436-2295
  Dayton (G-7510)
◆ Monarch Electric Service Co .... D 216 433-7800
  Cleveland (G-4596)
▲ Moyno Inc .... C 937 327-3111
  Springfield (G-13275)
National Heat Exch Clg Corp .... E 330 482-0893
  Youngstown (G-15673)
Nbw Inc .... E 216 377-1700
  Cleveland (G-4629)

Norris Brothers Co Inc .... C 216 771-2233
  Cleveland (G-4647)
Nurotoco Massachusetts Inc .... E 513 762-6690
  Cincinnati (G-3135)
Obr Cooling Towers Inc .... E 419 243-3443
  Northwood (G-11981)
▼ Ohio Broach & Machine Company .... E 440 946-1040
  Willoughby (G-15214)
Ohio Machinery Co .... E 330 874-1003
  Bolivar (G-1296)
◆ Ohio Machinery Co .... C 440 526-6200
  Broadview Heights (G-1394)
Ohio State Taxidermy Supply .... E 330 674-8600
  Killbuck (G-9639)
◆ OKL Can Line Inc .... E
  Cincinnati (G-3155)
Omni Cart Services Inc .... E 440 205-8363
  Mentor (G-10981)
Otis Elevator Company .... C 513 531-7888
  Cincinnati (G-3175)
Otis Elevator Company .... C 614 777-6500
  Columbus (G-6489)
Paradigm Industrial LLC .... E 937 224-4415
  Dayton (G-7546)
Pas Technologies Inc .... D 937 840-1053
  Hillsboro (G-9266)
▲ Pennsylvania TI Sls & Svc Inc .... D 330 758-0845
  Youngstown (G-15692)
Petro-Com Corp .... E 440 327-6900
  North Ridgeville (G-11933)
Post-Browning Inc .... C 513 771-1717
  Cincinnati (G-3224)
Precision Endoscopy Amer Inc .... E 410 527-9598
  Stow (G-13386)
Primetals Technologies USA LLC .... E 419 929-1554
  New London (G-11633)
Quality Assured Cleaning Inc .... E 614 798-1505
  Columbus (G-6556)
Quintus Technologies LLC .... E 614 891-2732
  Lewis Center (G-9834)
Raymond Storage Concepts Inc .... E 614 275-3494
  Groveport (G-8998)
▲ Raymond Storage Concepts Inc .... D 513 891-7290
  Blue Ash (G-1232)
Red Carpet Janitorial Service .... B 513 242-7575
  Cincinnati (G-3277)
Rmf Nooter LLC .... D 419 727-1970
  Toledo (G-13992)
Roto Rt Inc .... E 513 762-6690
  Cincinnati (G-3321)
Roto-Rooter Development Co .... D 513 762-6690
  Cincinnati (G-3322)
Roto-Rooter Group Inc .... C 513 762-6690
  Cincinnati (G-3323)
Roto-Rooter Services Company .... D 513 762-6690
  Cincinnati (G-3324)
Rudd Equipment Company Inc .... D 513 321-7833
  Cincinnati (G-3329)
◆ Russell T Bundy Associates Inc .... D 937 652-2151
  Urbana (G-14312)
Rwlp Company .... E 216 883-2424
  Cleveland (G-4866)
▲ Sabco Industries Inc .... E 419 531-5347
  Toledo (G-14002)
▲ Saw Service and Supply Company .... E 216 252-5600
  Cleveland (G-4880)
Schaefer Group Inc .... E 513 489-2420
  Blue Ash (G-1241)
Schindler Elevator Corporation .... C 419 867-5100
  Holland (G-9303)
◆ Scott Fetzer Company .... E 440 892-3000
  Westlake (G-15105)

Seilkop Industries Inc .... E 513 761-1035
  Cincinnati (G-3356)
Serex Corporation .... E 330 726-6062
  Youngstown (G-15721)
Service Experts LLC .... E 614 334-3192
  Columbus (G-6664)
Siemens Industry Inc .... E 800 879-8079
  Lebanon (G-9788)
Siemens Med Solutions USA Inc .... B 937 859-5413
  Dayton (G-7621)
Sievers Security Inc .... E 216 291-2222
  Cleveland (G-4905)
Sirpilla Recrtl Vhcl Ctr Inc .... C 330 494-2525
  Akron (G-303)
Smith & Oby Service Co .... E 440 735-5322
  Bedford (G-985)
Spartan Supply Co .... E 513 932-6954
  Lebanon (G-9790)
Spectrum Surgical Instruments Corp .... C 800 783-9251
  Stow (G-13390)
Ssi Fabricated Inc .... E 513 217-3535
  Middletown (G-11187)
Standrdaero Component Svcs Inc .... D 513 618-9588
  Cincinnati (G-3410)
▲ Steel Eqp Specialists Inc .... D 330 823-8260
  Alliance (G-401)
Steinke Tractor Sales Inc .... E 937 456-4271
  Eaton (G-7807)
Superior Marine Ways Inc .... C 740 894-6224
  Proctorville (G-12613)
Tk Elevator Corporation .... C 440 717-0080
  Broadview Heights (G-1401)
Tk Elevator Corporation .... C 513 241-6000
  Cincinnati (G-3481)
Tk Elevator Corporation .... D 614 895-8930
  Westerville (G-15017)
Towlift Inc .... E 614 851-1001
  Columbus (G-6774)
Towlift Inc .... E 440 951-9519
  Mentor (G-11004)
Towlift Inc .... E 419 666-1333
  Northwood (G-11985)
▲ Towlift Inc .... C 216 749-6800
  Brooklyn Heights (G-1428)
Toyota Industries N Amer Inc .... D 937 237-0976
  Dayton (G-7675)
U S Molding Machinery Co Inc .... E 440 918-1701
  Willoughby (G-15224)
▲ Vendors Exchange International Inc .... D 216 432-1800
  Cleveland (G-5098)
Vertneys LLC .... E 937 272-0585
  Dayton (G-7702)
◆ Walker National Inc .... E 614 492-1614
  Columbus (G-6864)
Walts Cleaning Contrs Inc .... E 330 899-0040
  Akron (G-354)
Waterworks LLC .... C 614 253-7246
  Columbus (G-6870)
Williams Super Service Inc .... E 330 733-7750
  East Sparta (G-8199)
Winelco Inc .... E 513 755-8050
  West Chester (G-14795)
▲ Winkle Industries Inc .... D 330 823-9730
  Alliance (G-407)
Witmers Inc .... E 330 427-2147
  Salem (G-12858)
Wm Plotz Machine and Forge Co .... E 216 861-0441
  Cleveland (G-5156)
◆ Wood Graphics Inc .... E 513 771-6300
  Cincinnati (G-3680)
Wood Investment Property LLC .... E 330 644-5100
  Medina (G-10905)

79 AMUSEMENT AND RECREATION SERVICES

Woodhull LLC .... E 937 294-5311
  Springboro *(G-13209)*
▲ Wooster Hydrostatics Inc .... E 330 263-6555
  Wooster *(G-15395)*
Worthington Analytical Svcs .... D 614 599-5254
  Lucas *(G-10172)*

78 MOTION PICTURES

7812 Motion picture and video production

Arctos Tech Solutions LLC .... D 937 426-2808
  Beavercreek *(G-859)*
Bkg Holdings LLC .... E 614 252-7455
  Columbus *(G-5442)*
Boxcast Inc .... E 888 392-2278
  Cleveland *(G-3885)*
For Women Like Me Inc .... E 407 848-7339
  Cleveland *(G-4267)*
◆ For Women Like Me Inc .... E 407 848-7339
  Chagrin Falls *(G-1958)*
Greater Cncnnati TV Edctl Fndt ...... D 513 381-4033
  Cincinnati *(G-2773)*
Icon World Entertainment LLC .... D 330 615-7008
  Barberton *(G-698)*
Live Media Group Holdings LLC ..... D 614 297-0001
  Columbus *(G-6170)*
Madison Avenue Mktg Group Inc .... E 419 473-9000
  Toledo *(G-13903)*
Mills/James Inc .... E 614 777-9933
  Hilliard *(G-9217)*
P Dakota Inc .... B 833 325-6827
  Northfield *(G-11963)*
Strategy Group For Media Inc .... E 740 201-5500
  Delaware *(G-7829)*
▲ Video Duplication Services Inc ...... E 614 871-3827
  Columbus *(G-6850)*
World Harvest Church Inc .... C 614 837-1990
  Canal Winchester *(G-1620)*

7819 Services allied to motion pictures

Ai-Media Technologies LLC .... E 800 335-0911
  Youngstown *(G-15545)*
Live Technologies LLC .... D 614 278-7777
  Columbus *(G-6171)*
Mills/James Inc .... E 614 777-9933
  Hilliard *(G-9217)*
P Dakota Inc .... B 833 325-6827
  Northfield *(G-11963)*

7822 Motion picture and tape distribution

Arconic Wheel Wheel Forge .... E 479 750-6359
  Cleveland *(G-3832)*
Billie Lawless .... E 714 851-6372
  Cleveland *(G-3874)*
Enterprise Pdts Partners LP .... D 513 423-2122
  Middletown *(G-11162)*
Spray Products Corporation .... D 610 277-1010
  Medina *(G-10892)*
Vooks Inc .... D 503 694-9217
  Stow *(G-13401)*

7832 Motion picture theaters, except drive-in

American Multi-Cinema Inc .... E 614 889-0580
  Dublin *(G-7935)*
American Multi-Cinema Inc .... E 614 801-9130
  Grove City *(G-8896)*
American Multi-Cinema Inc .... E 440 331-2826
  Rocky River *(G-12739)*
Beachwood Cinema LLC .... E 954 840-8150
  Beachwood *(G-767)*
Carmike Cinemas LLC .... E 419 423-7414
  Findlay *(G-8520)*

Carmike Cinemas LLC .... D 740 695-3919
  Saint Clairsville *(G-12783)*
▲ Cedar Fair Southwest Inc .... E 419 626-0830
  Sandusky *(G-12872)*
Cincinnati Museum Center .... B 513 287-7000
  Cincinnati *(G-2416)*
City Base Cincinnati LLC .... E 210 907-7197
  Cincinnati *(G-2449)*
Cleveland Cinemas MGT Co Ltd ...... E 440 528-0355
  Cleveland *(G-4007)*
Gateway Film Foundation .... E 614 247-4968
  Columbus *(G-5918)*
Great Eastern Theatre Company ..... E 419 691-9668
  Oregon *(G-12134)*
Marcus Theatres Corporation .... D 614 436-9818
  Columbus *(G-6196)*
Northgate Ops LLC .... D 812 945-4006
  Cincinnati *(G-3124)*
Profit Track Ltd .... E 330 848-2730
  Barberton *(G-704)*

7841 Video tape rental

Emerge Ministries Inc .... E 330 865-8351
  Akron *(G-146)*
Mile Inc .... C 614 252-6724
  Columbus *(G-6247)*
Mile Inc .... D 614 794-2203
  Worthington *(G-15440)*

79 AMUSEMENT AND RECREATION SERVICES

7911 Dance studios, schools, and halls

Ballet Metropolitan Inc .... C 614 229-4860
  Columbus *(G-5417)*
Cincinnati Ballet Company Inc .... E 513 621-5219
  Cincinnati *(G-2397)*
Piqua Country Club Holding Co ...... E 937 773-7744
  Piqua *(G-12452)*
The Fine Arts Association .... E 440 951-7500
  Willoughby *(G-15223)*
University of Cincinnati .... D 513 556-2700
  Cincinnati *(G-3577)*
Yankee Lake Inc .... E 330 448-8866
  Brookfield *(G-1408)*

7922 Theatrical producers and services

Ballet Metropolitan Inc .... C 614 229-4860
  Columbus *(G-5417)*
Beck Center For Arts .... C 216 521-2540
  Lakewood *(G-9659)*
Cincinnati Lndmark Productions ..... E 513 241-6550
  Cincinnati *(G-2414)*
Cincinnati Opera Association .... E 513 768-5500
  Cincinnati *(G-2418)*
Cleveland Ballet .... E 216 320-9000
  Bedford Heights *(G-997)*
Columbus Assn For Prfrmg Arts ..... E 614 469-1045
  Columbus *(G-5612)*
Columbus Assn For The Prfrmg A ... B 614 469-0939
  Columbus *(G-5614)*
▲ Columbus Assn For The Prfrmg A ... A 614 469-1045
  Columbus *(G-5613)*
Dayton Performing Arts Aliance ...... E 937 224-3521
  Dayton *(G-7297)*
Ensemble Theatre Cincinnati .... E 513 421-3555
  Cincinnati *(G-2625)*
Hanson Productions Inc .... E 419 327-6100
  Toledo *(G-13833)*
Hob Entertainment LLC .... D 216 523-2583
  Cleveland *(G-4370)*

◆ Interntnal MGT Group Ovrseas L ... B 216 522-1200
  Cleveland *(G-4419)*
Jeanne B McCoy Cmnty Ctr For A ... E 614 469-0939
  Columbus *(G-6085)*
Playhouse Square Foundation .... C 216 771-4444
  Cleveland *(G-4757)*
Playhouse Square Holdg Co LLC .... C 216 771-4444
  Cleveland *(G-4759)*
Rock Roll Hall of Fame Mseum I ..... D 216 781-7625
  Cleveland *(G-4849)*
Shadoart Productions Inc .... E 614 416-7625
  Columbus *(G-6668)*
The Cincinnati Playhouse .... E 513 345-2242
  Cincinnati *(G-3463)*

7929 Entertainers and entertainment groups

Big Bang Bar Cleveland LLC .... E 615 264-5650
  Cleveland *(G-3873)*
Blue Wtr Chamber Orchestra Inc .... E 440 781-6215
  Cleveland *(G-3878)*
Cincinnati Circus Company LLC ..... E 513 921-5454
  Cincinnati *(G-2403)*
Cincinnati Symphony Orchestra ...... D 513 381-3300
  Cincinnati *(G-2426)*
Cincinnati Symphony Orchestra ...... E 513 621-1919
  Cincinnati *(G-2425)*
Cleveland Jazz Orchestra .... E 419 908-8858
  Medina *(G-10823)*
Columbus Assn For The Prfrmg A ... B 614 469-0939
  Columbus *(G-5614)*
Columbus Symphony Orchstra Inc ... D 614 228-9600
  Columbus *(G-5656)*
Fountain Square MGT Group LLC ... E 513 621-4400
  Cincinnati *(G-2698)*
Four Entertainment Group .... E 513 721-0083
  Cincinnati *(G-2699)*
Henrys King Touring Company .... E 330 628-1886
  Mogadore *(G-11328)*
Ingram Entertainment Holdings ...... C 419 662-3132
  Perrysburg *(G-12347)*
Jack Entertainment LLC .... D 313 309-5225
  Cleveland *(G-4430)*
▲ Musical Arts Association .... C 216 231-7300
  Cleveland *(G-4613)*
Musical Upcming Stars In Clssi .... E 216 702-7047
  Chagrin Falls *(G-1963)*
NBD International Inc .... E 330 296-0221
  Ravenna *(G-12633)*
Otherworld Inc .... E 614 868-3631
  Columbus *(G-6488)*
Philo Band Boosters .... E 740 221-3023
  Zanesville *(G-15827)*
Pro Audio Video Inc .... D 330 494-2100
  Canton *(G-1831)*
▲ Rock House Entrmt Group Inc ...... C 440 232-7625
  Oakwood Village *(G-12057)*
Rollhouse Entertainment S .... D 440 248-4080
  Solon *(G-13139)*
Sliddy Ent LLC .... E 419 376-1797
  Toledo *(G-14016)*
Sugar & Spice Spa llc .... D 513 319-0112
  Mason *(G-10612)*
Wqkt 1045 FM .... B 330 264-5122
  Wooster *(G-15399)*
Y & E Entertainment Group LLC ..... E 440 385-5500
  Parma *(G-12268)*

7933 Bowling centers

AMF Bowling Centers Inc .... E 614 889-0880
  Columbus *(G-5365)*
AMF Bowling Centers Inc .... E 330 725-4548
  Medina *(G-10807)*

Employee Codes: A=Over 500 employees, B=251-500
C=101-250, D=51-100, E=20-50, F=10-19, G=1-9

2024 Harris Ohio
Services Directory

79 AMUSEMENT AND RECREATION SERVICES

Chillicothe Bowling Lanes Inc .... E 740 773-3300
  Chillicothe *(G-2055)*
Columbus Sq Bowl Palace Inc .... E 614 895-1122
  Columbus *(G-5655)*
Roseland Lanes Inc .... D 440 439-0097
  Bedford *(G-983)*
Sequoia Pro Bowl Inc .... E 614 885-7043
  Columbus *(G-6662)*
Skylane LLC .... E 330 527-9999
  Garrettsville *(G-8780)*
Ten Pin Alley .... E 614 876-2475
  Hilliard *(G-9237)*
Tiki Bowling Lanes Inc .... E 740 654-4513
  Lancaster *(G-9747)*
Western Bowl Inc .... E 513 574-2200
  Cincinnati *(G-3660)*
Westgate Lanes Incorporated .... E 419 229-3845
  Lima *(G-9986)*

7941 Sports clubs, managers, and promoters

Akron Rubberducks .... D 330 253-5151
  Akron *(G-37)*
Arena Horse Shows Ocala LLC .... D 239 275-2314
  Wilmington *(G-15246)*
Arena Management Holdings LLC .... A 513 421-4111
  Cincinnati *(G-2215)*
Brimstone & Fire LLC .... E 937 776-5182
  Wilmington *(G-15247)*
Cavaliers Holdings LLC .... B 216 420-2000
  Cleveland *(G-3937)*
Cavaliers Operating Co LLC .... A 216 420-2000
  Cleveland *(G-3938)*
Cincinnati Bengals Inc .... A 513 621-3550
  Cincinnati *(G-2401)*
Cincinnati Cyclones LLC .... E 513 421-7825
  Cincinnati *(G-2407)*
Cincinnati Reds LLC .... C 513 765-7923
  Cincinnati *(G-2421)*
◆ Cincinnati Reds LLC .... C 513 765-7000
  Cincinnati *(G-2420)*
Cleveland Browns .... D 216 261-3401
  Cleveland *(G-4003)*
Cleveland Browns Football LLC .... C 440 891-5000
  Berea *(G-1065)*
Cleveland Guardians Basbal LLC .... D 216 420-4487
  Cleveland *(G-4048)*
Cleveland Indians Inc .... B 216 420-4487
  Cleveland *(G-4052)*
Crew SC Team Company LLC .... D 614 447-2739
  Columbus *(G-5727)*
Crew Soccer Stadium LLC .... D 614 447-2739
  Columbus *(G-5728)*
Dayton Prof Basbal CLB LLC .... E 937 228-2287
  Dayton *(G-7300)*
Fc Cincinnati Ltd .... C 513 977-5425
  Cincinnati *(G-2652)*
◆ Interntnal MGT Group Ovrseas L .... B 216 522-1200
  Cleveland *(G-4419)*
Milestone Football League LLC .... D 513 479-7602
  Cincinnati *(G-3062)*
National Football Museum Inc .... E 330 456-8207
  Canton *(G-1817)*
Pffa Acquisition LLC .... D 859 835-6088
  Cincinnati *(G-3203)*
Pro Football Fcs .... E 513 381-3404
  Cincinnati *(G-3233)*
Towne Properties Assoc Inc .... D 513 489-9700
  Cincinnati *(G-3494)*
Towne Properties Associates Inc .... D 513 381-8696
  Cincinnati *(G-3495)*

7948 Racing, including track operation

Eldora Speedway Inc .... E 317 299-6066
  New Weston *(G-11685)*
Kaulig Racing Inc .... D 815 382-8007
  Hudson *(G-9361)*
Park Northfield Associates LLC .... C 330 467-4101
  Northfield *(G-11964)*
Pnk (ohio) LLC .... A 513 232-8000
  Cincinnati *(G-3219)*
Scioto Downs Inc .... A 614 295-4700
  Columbus *(G-6655)*
◆ Team Rahal Inc .... D 614 529-7000
  Hilliard *(G-9236)*
Thorsport Inc .... E 419 621-8800
  Sandusky *(G-12936)*

7991 Physical fitness facilities

Amboy Rifle Club .... D 440 228-9366
  Conneaut *(G-6937)*
Avalon Holdings Corporation .... D 330 856-8800
  Warren *(G-14501)*
B & I Hotel Management LLC .... C 330 995-0200
  Aurora *(G-607)*
Beechmont Racquet Club Inc .... E 513 528-5700
  Cincinnati *(G-2250)*
Body Alive Corporate LLC .... D 513 834-8043
  Cincinnati *(G-2269)*
Broad Street Hotel Assoc LP .... D 614 861-0321
  Columbus *(G-5467)*
Centerville Fitness Inc .... E 937 291-7990
  Centerville *(G-1940)*
Chillicothe Motel LLC .... D 740 773-3903
  Chillicothe *(G-2058)*
Cincinnati Sports Mall Inc .... C 513 527-4000
  Cincinnati *(G-2423)*
City of Brecksville .... E 440 526-4109
  Brecksville *(G-1349)*
City of Westlake .... D 440 808-5700
  Westlake *(G-15050)*
Compel Fitness LLC .... D 216 965-5694
  Westlake *(G-15052)*
Corazon Country Club LLC .... E 614 504-5250
  Dublin *(G-7973)*
◆ Coulter Ventures Llc .... E 614 358-6190
  Columbus *(G-5708)*
Countryside Yung MNS Chrstn As .... D 513 677-3702
  Maineville *(G-10227)*
Cycle-Logik LLC .... D 937 381-7055
  Dayton *(G-7266)*
Emh Regional Medical Center .... D 440 988-6800
  Avon *(G-650)*
Family YMCA Lncster Frfeld CNT .... E 740 654-0616
  Lancaster *(G-9722)*
Family YMCA of LANcstr&fairfld .... D 740 277-7373
  Lancaster *(G-9723)*
Findlay Country Club .... E 419 422-9263
  Findlay *(G-8528)*
Fitworks Holding LLC .... E 513 923-9931
  Cincinnati *(G-2688)*
Fitworks Holding LLC .... E 513 531-1500
  Cincinnati *(G-2689)*
Fitworks Holding LLC .... E 440 842-1499
  Cleveland *(G-4262)*
Fitworks Holding LLC .... E 440 333-4141
  Rocky River *(G-12741)*
Fitworks Holding LLC .... E 330 688-2329
  Stow *(G-13368)*
Great Mami Vly Yung MNS Chrstn .... D 513 887-0001
  Hamilton *(G-9046)*
Great Miami Valley YMCA .... D 513 829-3091
  Fairfield *(G-8417)*
Great Miami Valley YMCA .... D 513 892-9622
  Fairfield Township *(G-8461)*

Great Miami Valley YMCA .... D 513 887-0014
  Hamilton *(G-9048)*
Great Miami Valley YMCA .... D 513 868-9622
  Hamilton *(G-9049)*
Holzer Clinic LLC .... E 740 446-5412
  Gallipolis *(G-8757)*
Island Hospitality MGT LLC .... E 614 864-8844
  Columbus *(G-6075)*
Jbentley Studio & Spa LLC .... D 614 790-8828
  Powell *(G-12593)*
Jto Club Corp .... E 440 352-1900
  Mentor *(G-10956)*
Kinsale Golf & Fitnes CLB LLC .... C 740 881-6500
  Powell *(G-12597)*
Lake Cnty Yung MNS Chrstn Assn .... C 440 352-3303
  Painesville *(G-12231)*
Lake County YMCA .... C 440 428-5125
  Madison *(G-10219)*
Lake County YMCA .... C 440 259-2724
  Perry *(G-12307)*
Lake County YMCA .... C 440 946-1160
  Willoughby *(G-15198)*
Life Time Inc .... D 614 428-6000
  Columbus *(G-6159)*
Life Time Inc .... D 614 789-7824
  Dublin *(G-8054)*
Life Time Inc .... C 513 234-0660
  Mason *(G-10574)*
Life Time Fitness Inc .... D 614 326-1500
  Columbus *(G-6160)*
Lifecenter Plus Inc .... E 330 342-9021
  Hudson *(G-9363)*
Lima Family YMCA .... D 419 223-6055
  Lima *(G-9923)*
Lima Family YMCA .... D 419 223-6045
  Lima *(G-9922)*
Lululemon USA Inc .... C 614 418-9127
  Columbus *(G-6177)*
Mansfield Hotel Partnership .... E 419 529-1000
  Mansfield *(G-10287)*
Medallion Club .... C 614 794-6999
  Westerville *(G-14909)*
Mercy Healthplex Anderson LLC .... E 513 624-1871
  Cincinnati *(G-3043)*
Metro Fitness Hilliard .... D 614 850-0070
  Hilliard *(G-9211)*
Mitchells Salon & Day Spa Inc .... D 513 793-0900
  Cincinnati *(G-3067)*
Moores Fitness World Inc .... C 513 424-0000
  Middletown *(G-11176)*
Mount Vernon Country Club Co .... D 740 392-4216
  Mount Vernon *(G-11500)*
Movement Fitness LLC .... E 419 410-5733
  Marietta *(G-10394)*
N C R Employees Benefit Assn .... C 937 299-3571
  Dayton *(G-7524)*
Paragon Salons Inc .... E 513 574-7610
  Cincinnati *(G-3182)*
Perry Fitness Center .... E 440 259-9499
  Perry *(G-12311)*
Prescribe Fit Inc .... E 614 598-8788
  Columbus *(G-6542)*
Progrssive Fghting Systems LLC .... E 216 520-0271
  Independence *(G-9473)*
Queen City Racquet Club LLC .... D 513 771-2835
  Cincinnati *(G-3264)*
Racquet Club Columbus Ltd .... E 614 457-5671
  Columbus *(G-6559)*
Redefine Enterprises LLC .... E 330 952-2024
  Medina *(G-10883)*
Sacred Hour Inc .... D 216 228-9750
  Lakewood *(G-9684)*

79 AMUSEMENT AND RECREATION SERVICES

Scioto Reserve Inc .... D 740 881-9082
   Powell *(G-12604)*

Shady Hollow Cntry CLB Co Inc .... D 330 832-1581
   Massillon *(G-10668)*

Southern Ohio Medical Center .... D 740 356-6160
   Portsmouth *(G-12574)*

Spa Fitness Centers Inc .... E 419 476-6018
   Toledo *(G-14019)*

Sps Inc .... E 937 339-7801
   Troy *(G-14160)*

Swiminc Incorporated .... E 614 885-1619
   Worthington *(G-15460)*

Sycamore Board of Education .... C 513 489-3937
   Montgomery *(G-11375)*

Synergy Hotels LLC .... E 614 492-9000
   Obetz *(G-12084)*

T O J Inc .... E 440 352-1900
   Mentor *(G-11002)*

Tippecanoe Country Club Inc .... E 330 758-7518
   Canfield *(G-1644)*

Troy Hotel II LLC .... E 937 332-1446
   Troy *(G-14164)*

Vermilion Family YMCA .... E 440 967-4208
   Vermilion *(G-14410)*

Vio Med Spa Strongsville LLC .... E 440 268-6100
   Strongsville *(G-13495)*

Washington Twnship Mntgmery CN .... E 937 433-0130
   Dayton *(G-7715)*

Western Rsrve Racquet CLB Corp .... E 330 653-3103
   Streetsboro *(G-13435)*

Woodson Operations One Ltd .... E 419 420-1776
   Findlay *(G-8598)*

Y M C A of Ashland Ohio Inc .... D 419 289-0626
   Ashland *(G-516)*

YMCA .... E 330 823-1930
   Alliance *(G-408)*

Young Mens Christian Assn .... D 330 480-5656
   Youngstown *(G-15754)*

Young MNS Christn Assn Findlay .... D 419 422-4424
   Findlay *(G-8599)*

Young MNS Chrstn Assn Cntl STA .... D 330 305-5437
   Canton *(G-1889)*

Young MNS Chrstn Assn Cntl STA .... D 330 498-4082
   Canton *(G-1890)*

Young MNS Chrstn Assn Cntl STA .... D 330 875-1611
   Louisville *(G-10124)*

Young MNS Chrstn Assn Cntl STA .... C 330 830-6275
   Massillon *(G-10675)*

Young MNS Chrstn Assn Grter CL .... E 440 285-7543
   Chardon *(G-2027)*

Young MNS Chrstn Assn Grter CL .... D 216 521-8400
   Lakewood *(G-9688)*

Young MNS Chrstn Assn Grter CL .... E 440 808-8150
   Westlake *(G-15126)*

Young MNS Chrstn Assn Grter CN .... D 513 961-3510
   Cincinnati *(G-3691)*

Young MNS Chrstn Assn Grter CN .... C 513 731-0115
   Cincinnati *(G-3692)*

Young MNS Chrstn Assn Grter CN .... B 513 474-1400
   Cincinnati *(G-3693)*

Young MNS Chrstn Assn Grter CN .... D 513 241-9622
   Cincinnati *(G-3694)*

Young MNS Chrstn Assn Grter CN .... C 513 923-4466
   Cincinnati *(G-3695)*

Young MNS Chrstn Assn Grter CN .... C 513 921-0911
   Cincinnati *(G-3696)*

Young MNS Chrstn Assn Grter CN .... A 513 932-1424
   Lebanon *(G-9800)*

Young MNS Chrstn Assn Grter Dy .... E 937 228-9622
   Dayton *(G-7732)*

Young MNS Chrstn Assn Grter Dy .... C 937 312-1810
   Dayton *(G-7733)*

Young MNS Chrstn Assn Grter Dy .... C 937 223-5201
   Springboro *(G-13210)*

Young MNS Chrstn Assn Grter NY .... C 740 392-9622
   Mount Vernon *(G-11509)*

Young MNS Chrstn Assn Mtro Los .... D 740 286-7008
   Jackson *(G-9530)*

Young MNS Chrstn Assn of Akron .... E 330 983-5573
   Akron *(G-372)*

Young MNS Chrstn Assn of Akron .... D 330 923-5223
   Cuyahoga Falls *(G-7119)*

Young MNS Chrstn Assn of Akron .... E 330 467-8366
   Macedonia *(G-10210)*

Young MNS Chrstn Assn of Grter .... C 419 866-9622
   Maumee *(G-10782)*

Young MNS Chrstn Assn of Grter .... C 419 691-3523
   Oregon *(G-12148)*

Young MNS Chrstn Assn of Grter .... D 419 474-3995
   Toledo *(G-14112)*

Young MNS Chrstn Assn of Grter .... D 419 241-7218
   Toledo *(G-14115)*

Young MNS Chrstn Assn of Grter .... E 419 729-8135
   Sylvania *(G-13579)*

Young MNS Chrstn Assn of Mt Vr .... D 740 392-9622
   Mount Vernon *(G-11510)*

Young MNS Chrstn Assn of Van W .... E 419 238-0443
   Van Wert *(G-14362)*

Young MNS Chrstn Assn Wster OH ...... E 330 264-3131
   Wooster *(G-15402)*

Young Wns Chrstn Assn Clvland .... E 216 881-6878
   Cleveland *(G-5167)*

Young Wns Chrstn Assn of Cnton .... D 330 453-0789
   Canton *(G-1892)*

Young Womens Christian Assn .... D 614 224-9121
   Columbus *(G-6917)*

Youngstown Area Jwish Fdration .... C 330 746-3251
   Youngstown *(G-15756)*

YWCA Mahoning Valley .... E 330 746-6361
   Youngstown *(G-15762)*

YWCA of Greater Cincinnati .... D 513 241-7090
   Cincinnati *(G-3697)*

7992 Public golf courses

▲ Aboutgolf Limited .... E 419 482-9095
   Maumee *(G-10683)*

American Golf Corporation .... E 419 726-9353
   Toledo *(G-13682)*

Arrowhead Park Golf Club Inc .... E 419 628-2444
   Minster *(G-11315)*

Avalon Lakes Golf Inc .... E 330 856-8898
   Warren *(G-14503)*

Boulder Creek Golf Club .... E 330 626-2828
   Streetsboro *(G-13410)*

Bowling Green Country Club Inc .... E 419 352-5546
   Bowling Green *(G-1311)*

Brassboys Enterprises Inc .... E 740 545-7796
   West Lafayette *(G-14855)*

Brookwood Management Co LLC .... E 330 499-7721
   Canton *(G-1690)*

Championship Management Co Inc .... E 740 524-4653
   Sunbury *(G-13518)*

Chardon Lakes Golf Course Inc .... E 440 285-4653
   Chardon *(G-1996)*

Chgc Inc .... E 330 225-6122
   Valley City *(G-14332)*

Chippewa Golf Corp .... E 330 658-2566
   Doylestown *(G-7913)*

City of Cuyahoga Falls .... E 330 971-8416
   Cuyahoga Falls *(G-7061)*

City of Springfield .... E 937 324-7725
   Springfield *(G-13228)*

City of Westlake .... E 440 835-6442
   Westlake *(G-15049)*

Columbus Zoological Park Assn .... C 614 645-3400
   Powell *(G-12589)*

Creekside Golf Ltd .... E 513 785-2999
   Fairfield Township *(G-8459)*

Creekside Ltd LLC .... D 513 583-4977
   Loveland *(G-10133)*

Diamondback Golf LLC .... D 614 410-1313
   Sunbury *(G-13520)*

Edgewater Golf Inc .... E 330 862-2630
   Minerva *(G-11306)*

Ganzfair Investment Inc .... E 614 792-6630
   Delaware *(G-7800)*

Grizzly Golf Center Inc .... B 513 398-5200
   Mason *(G-10557)*

Hawthorne Hills Cntry CLB Inc .... E 419 221-1891
   Lima *(G-9895)*

Heather Downs Cntry CLB Assoc .... E 419 385-0248
   Toledo *(G-13844)*

Hickory Woods Golf Course Inc .... E 513 575-3900
   Loveland *(G-10142)*

Kinsale Golf & Fitnes CLB LLC .... C 740 881-6500
   Powell *(G-12597)*

Mahoning Country Club Inc .... E 330 545-2517
   Girard *(G-8819)*

Mayfair Country Club Inc .... D 330 699-2209
   Uniontown *(G-14258)*

Miami Valley Golf Club .... D 937 278-7381
   Dayton *(G-7487)*

Mill Creek Golf Course Corp .... E 740 666-7711
   Ostrander *(G-12182)*

Mill Creek Metropolitan Park .... E 330 740-7112
   Youngstown *(G-15667)*

Moss Creek Golf Course .... E 937 837-4653
   Clayton *(G-3735)*

Moundbuilders Country Club Co .... D 740 344-4500
   Newark *(G-11732)*

Mount Vernon Country Club Co .... D 740 392-4216
   Mount Vernon *(G-11500)*

New Albany Links Dev Co Ltd .... E 614 939-5914
   New Albany *(G-11580)*

Norwalk Golf Properties Inc .... E 419 668-8535
   Norwalk *(G-12019)*

Ohio State Parks Inc .... D 513 664-3504
   College Corner *(G-5222)*

Pine Hills Golf Club Inc .... E 330 225-4477
   Hinckley *(G-9271)*

Quail Hollow Management Inc .... C 440 639-4000
   Concord Township *(G-6933)*

Reserve Run Golf Club LLC .... D 330 758-1017
   Poland *(G-12508)*

Scioto Reserve Inc .... E 740 881-6500
   Powell *(G-12605)*

Scioto Reserve Inc .... D 740 881-9082
   Powell *(G-12604)*

Shady Hollow Cntry CLB Co Inc .... D 330 832-1581
   Massillon *(G-10668)*

Silver Lake Country Club .... E 330 688-6066
   Silver Lake *(G-13060)*

Sugar Valley Country Club .... E 937 372-4820
   Xenia *(G-15531)*

Table Rock Golf Club Inc .... E 740 625-6859
   Centerburg *(G-1937)*

Valleywood Golf Club Inc .... E 419 826-3991
   Swanton *(G-13531)*

Wryneck Development LLC .... E 419 354-2535
   Bowling Green *(G-1339)*

7993 Coin-operated amusement devices

Edwards Realty & Inv Corp .... C 330 253-9171
   Copley *(G-6957)*

Good Inc .... D 740 592-9667
   Athens *(G-569)*

79 AMUSEMENT AND RECREATION SERVICES

Pnk (ohio) LLC .... A 513 232-8000
  Cincinnati *(G-3219)*
Strike Zone Inc .... D 440 235-4420
  Olmsted Twp *(G-12094)*

7996 Amusement parks

▲ Beach At Mason Ltd Partnership .... E 513 398-7946
  Lebanon *(G-9756)*
▲ Cedar Fair LP .... A 419 627-2344
  Sandusky *(G-12871)*
Cedar Point Park LLC .... E 419 627-2350
  Sandusky *(G-12874)*
Cedar Point Park LLC .... D 419 627-2500
  Sandusky *(G-12875)*
Cedar Point Park LLC .... D 419 626-0830
  Sandusky *(G-12873)*
▲ Kings Dominion LLC .... E 419 626-0830
  Sandusky *(G-12908)*
◆ Kings Island Company .... C 513 754-5700
  Kings Mills *(G-9642)*
Kings Island Park LLC .... C 513 754-5901
  Kings Mills *(G-9643)*
Kings Island Park LLC .... E 419 626-0830
  Sandusky *(G-12909)*
Lmn Development LLC .... C 419 433-7200
  Sandusky *(G-12910)*
▲ Magnum Management Corporation ... C 419 627-2334
  Sandusky *(G-12913)*
Millennium Operations LLC .... E 419 626-0830
  Sandusky *(G-12915)*
Muskingum Wtrshed Cnsrvncy Dst .... C 330 343-6780
  Mineral City *(G-11301)*
Paramounts Kings Island .... C 513 754-5700
  Mason *(G-10590)*
Strongville Recreation Complex .... C 440 580-3230
  Strongsville *(G-13489)*
Sugar & Spice Spa llc .... D 513 319-0112
  Mason *(G-10612)*
Willo Putt-Putt Course Inc .... E 440 951-7888
  Willoughby *(G-15226)*

7997 Membership sports and recreation clubs

Akron Management Corp .... B 330 644-8441
  Akron *(G-34)*
Athens Golf & Country Club .... E 740 592-1655
  Athens *(G-558)*
Avalon Golf and Cntry CLB Inc .... C 330 856-8898
  Warren *(G-14500)*
Avon-Oaks Country Club .... D 440 892-0660
  Avon *(G-639)*
B-W Baseball .... E 440 826-2182
  Berea *(G-1062)*
Barrington Golf Club Inc .... D 330 995-0821
  Aurora *(G-609)*
Barrington Golf Club Inc .... D 330 995-0600
  Aurora *(G-608)*
Beechmont Racquet Club Inc .... E 513 528-5700
  Cincinnati *(G-2250)*
Belmont Country Club .... D 419 666-1472
  Perrysburg *(G-12316)*
Belmont Hills Country Club .... D 740 695-2181
  Saint Clairsville *(G-12779)*
Bowling Green Country Club Inc .... E 419 352-5546
  Bowling Green *(G-1311)*
Boys and Girls CLB Wooster Inc .... D 330 988-1616
  Wooster *(G-15314)*
Brook Plum Country Club .... D 419 625-5394
  Sandusky *(G-12866)*
Brookside Golf & Cntry CLB Co .... C 614 889-2581
  Columbus *(G-5469)*

Browns Run Country Club .... E 513 423-6291
  Middletown *(G-11154)*
Camargo Club .... C 513 561-9292
  Cincinnati *(G-2302)*
Canterbury Golf Club Inc .... D 216 561-1914
  Cleveland *(G-3923)*
Catawba-Cleveland Dev Corp .... D 419 797-4424
  Port Clinton *(G-12518)*
Chagrin Valley Athc CLB Inc .... D 440 543-5141
  Chagrin Falls *(G-1974)*
Chagrin Valley Country Club Co .... D 440 248-4310
  Chagrin Falls *(G-1955)*
Chagrin Valley Hunt Club .... E 440 423-4414
  Gates Mills *(G-8782)*
Chiller LLC .... E 614 246-3380
  Columbus *(G-5566)*
Cincinnati Country Club .... C 513 533-5200
  Cincinnati *(G-2405)*
Cincinnati Sports Mall Inc .... C 513 527-4000
  Cincinnati *(G-2423)*
City of Sylvania .... E 419 885-1167
  Sylvania *(G-13539)*
City of Tallmadge .... E 330 634-2349
  Tallmadge *(G-13588)*
Cleveland Skating Club .... D 216 791-2800
  Cleveland *(G-4066)*
Cleveland Yachting Club Inc .... D 440 333-1155
  Cleveland *(G-4074)*
Clovernook Country Club .... D 513 521-0333
  Cincinnati *(G-2463)*
Coldstream Country Club .... D 513 231-3900
  Cincinnati *(G-2473)*
Columbia Hills Country CLB Inc .... D 440 236-5051
  Columbia Station *(G-5225)*
Congress Lake Club Company .... E 330 877-9318
  Hartville *(G-9124)*
Country Club Inc .... C 216 831-9200
  Cleveland *(G-4121)*
Country Club At Muirfield Vlg .... E 614 764-1714
  Dublin *(G-7974)*
Country Club of Hudson .... D 330 650-1188
  Hudson *(G-9341)*
County of Perry .... E 740 342-0416
  New Lexington *(G-11624)*
Dayton Classics Basbal CLB Inc .... E 937 974-6722
  West Carrollton *(G-14645)*
Dayton Country Club Company .... D 937 294-3352
  Dayton *(G-7278)*
Dry Run Limited Partnership .... E 513 561-9119
  Cincinnati *(G-2577)*
East Liverpool Country Club .... E 330 385-7197
  East Liverpool *(G-8181)*
Eastern Ohio Conservation Club .... D 330 799-7393
  Salem *(G-12841)*
Elyria Country Club Company .... D 440 322-6391
  Elyria *(G-8245)*
Escalante - Cntry CLB of N LLC .... E 937 374-5000
  Xenia *(G-15504)*
Family YMCA Lncster Frfeld CNT .... E 740 654-0616
  Lancaster *(G-9722)*
Findlay Country Club .... E 419 422-9263
  Findlay *(G-8528)*
Fitworks Holding LLC .... E 440 333-4141
  Rocky River *(G-12741)*
Four Bridges Country Club Ltd .... D 513 759-4620
  Liberty Township *(G-9852)*
Futbol Club Cincinnati LLC .... C 513 977-5425
  Cincinnati *(G-2713)*
Game Haus LLC .... E 513 490-1799
  Franklin *(G-8638)*
Ganzfair Investment Inc .... E 614 792-6632
  Delaware *(G-7800)*

Geneva Area Rcrtl Edctl Athc T .... E 440 466-1002
  Geneva *(G-8785)*
German Family Society Inc .... E 330 678-8229
  Kent *(G-9576)*
Golf Club Co .... D 614 855-7326
  New Albany *(G-11567)*
Heil and Hornik LLC .... E 614 873-8749
  Plain City *(G-12479)*
Heritage Club .... D 513 459-7711
  Mason *(G-10560)*
Highland Meadows Golf Club .... E 419 882-7153
  Sylvania *(G-13550)*
Hillbrook Club Inc .... D 440 247-4940
  Cleveland *(G-4362)*
Hof Fitness Center Inc .... D 330 455-0555
  Canton *(G-1773)*
Hyde Park Golf & Country Club .... D 513 871-3111
  Cincinnati *(G-2858)*
Inverness Club .... D 419 578-9000
  Toledo *(G-13864)*
Island Service Company .... E 419 285-3695
  Put In Bay *(G-12617)*
Jefferson Golf & Country Club .... D 614 759-7500
  Blacklick *(G-1112)*
Kirtland Country Club Company .... D 440 942-4400
  Willoughby *(G-15196)*
Lake Club .... C 330 549-3996
  Poland *(G-12505)*
Lake Erie Monsters .... E 216 420-0000
  Cleveland *(G-4475)*
Lake Township Trustees .... E 419 836-1143
  Millbury *(G-11270)*
Lakes Golf & Country Club Inc .... E 614 882-2582
  Westerville *(G-14904)*
Lakewood Country Club Company .... D 440 871-0400
  Cleveland *(G-4479)*
Lancaster Country Club .... D 740 654-3535
  Lancaster *(G-9730)*
Lenau Park .... E 440 235-2646
  Olmsted Twp *(G-12091)*
Little Leag Bsbal Englwood Inc .... E 937 545-2670
  Englewood *(G-8315)*
Losantiville Country Club .... D 513 631-4133
  Cincinnati *(G-2988)*
M&C Hotel Interests Inc .... C 440 543-1331
  Chagrin Falls *(G-1985)*
Macair Aviation LLC .... E 937 347-1302
  Xenia *(G-15525)*
Maketewah Country Club Company ..... D 513 242-9333
  Cincinnati *(G-3005)*
Mayfield Cntry CLB Schlrship F .... E 216 381-0826
  Cleveland *(G-4532)*
Medallion Club .... C 614 794-6999
  Westerville *(G-14909)*
Medina Country Club LLC .... D 330 725-6621
  Medina *(G-10855)*
Meyers Lake Sportsmans CLB Inc .... D 330 456-1025
  Canton *(G-1805)*
Mill Creek Golf Course Corp .... E 740 666-7711
  Ostrander *(G-12182)*
Mohawk Golf Club .... E 419 447-5876
  Tiffin *(G-13634)*
Moraine Country Club .... E 937 294-6200
  Dayton *(G-7513)*
Moundbuilders Country Club Co .... D 740 344-4500
  Newark *(G-11732)*
Mount Vernon Country Club Co .... D 740 392-4216
  Mount Vernon *(G-11500)*
Msr Legacy .... D 216 381-0826
  Cleveland *(G-4608)*
Muirfield Village Golf Club .... E 614 889-6700
  Dublin *(G-8066)*

2024 Harris Ohio Services Directory

79 AMUSEMENT AND RECREATION SERVICES

N C R Employees Benefit Assn............. C 937 299-3571
  Dayton *(G-7524)*

New Albany Cntry CLB Cmnty Ass........ C 614 939-8500
  New Albany *(G-11578)*

New Albany Country Club LLC.............. C 614 939-8500
  New Albany *(G-11579)*

New London Hills Club Inc.................... E 513 868-9026
  Hamilton *(G-9068)*

Normandy Swim & Tennis Club............. E 513 683-0232
  Loveland *(G-10153)*

Oakland Pk Cnservation CLB Inc........... D 614 989-8739
  Dublin *(G-8078)*

OBannon Creek Golf Club..................... E 513 683-5657
  Loveland *(G-10156)*

Palisdes Bsbal A Cal Ltd Prtnr............... E 330 505-0000
  Niles *(G-11795)*

Pepper Pike Club Company Inc............. D 216 831-9400
  Cleveland *(G-4739)*

Piqua Country Club Holding Co............ E 937 773-7744
  Piqua *(G-12452)*

Portage Country Club Company............ D 330 836-8565
  Akron *(G-268)*

Quail Hollow Management Inc.............. C 440 639-4000
  Concord Township *(G-6933)*

Racquet Club Columbus Ltd................. E 614 457-5671
  Columbus *(G-6559)*

Raintree Country Club Inc.................... E 330 699-3232
  Uniontown *(G-14262)*

Rawiga Country Club Inc...................... E 330 336-2220
  Seville *(G-12964)*

River Oaks Rcquet CLB Assoc In.......... E 440 331-4980
  Rocky River *(G-12752)*

Rocky Fork Hunt and Cntry CLB............ D 614 471-7828
  Gahanna *(G-8727)*

Salt Fork Resort Club Inc..................... E 740 498-8116
  Kimbolton *(G-9641)*

Sand Ridge Golf Club........................... E 440 285-8088
  Chardon *(G-2019)*

Sandusky Yacht Club Inc...................... E 419 625-6567
  Sandusky *(G-12930)*

Scioto Reserve Inc.............................. D 740 881-3903
  Powell *(G-12606)*

Scioto Reserve Inc.............................. D 740 881-9082
  Powell *(G-12604)*

Shady Hollow Cntry CLB Co Inc............ D 330 832-1581
  Massillon *(G-10668)*

Shaker Heights Country Club Co........... C 216 991-3660
  Shaker Heights *(G-12983)*

Shawnee Country Club......................... D 419 227-7177
  Lima *(G-9960)*

Shelby Golf Course Inc........................ E 937 492-2883
  Sidney *(G-13049)*

Sightless Children Club Inc................... E 937 671-9162
  Franklin *(G-8649)*

Silver Lake Country Club...................... E 330 688-6066
  Silver Lake *(G-13060)*

Steubenville Country Club Inc............... E 740 264-0521
  Steubenville *(G-13343)*

Stone Oak Country Club....................... D 419 867-0969
  Holland *(G-9306)*

Sugar Valley Country Club.................... E 937 372-4820
  Xenia *(G-15531)*

Swiminc Incorporated........................... E 614 885-1619
  Worthington *(G-15460)*

Sycamore Creek Country Club.............. C 937 748-0791
  Springboro *(G-13208)*

Sylvania Country Club.......................... D 419 392-0530
  Sylvania *(G-13575)*

Tartan Fields Golf Club Ltd.................. D 614 792-0900
  Dublin *(G-8140)*

Tennis Unlimited Inc............................. E 330 928-8763
  Akron *(G-331)*

Terrace Park Country Club Inc.............. D 513 965-4061
  Milford *(G-11260)*

Tiffin Cmnty YMCA Rcration Ctr........... D 419 447-8711
  Tiffin *(G-13645)*

Tippecanoe Country Club Inc............... E 330 758-7518
  Canfield *(G-1644)*

Toledo Club.. D 419 243-2200
  Toledo *(G-14058)*

Toledo Mud Hens Basbal CLB Inc......... D 419 725-4367
  Toledo *(G-14062)*

Toledo Walleye Prof Hockey CLB.......... D 419 725-4350
  Toledo *(G-14067)*

Troy Country Club................................ E 937 335-5691
  Troy *(G-14163)*

Turtle Golf Management Ltd................ D 614 882-5920
  Westerville *(G-15019)*

Union Country Club............................... E 330 343-5544
  Dover *(G-7905)*

Urbana Country Club............................ E 937 653-1690
  Urbana *(G-14314)*

Vermilion Family YMCA......................... E 440 967-4208
  Vermilion *(G-14410)*

Vertical Adventures Inc....................... D 614 888-8393
  Columbus *(G-6845)*

Walden Club... E 330 995-7162
  Aurora *(G-629)*

Wedgewood Golf & Country Club......... C 614 793-9600
  Powell *(G-12609)*

Western Hills Country Club.................. D 513 922-0011
  Cincinnati *(G-3662)*

Western Hills Sportsplex Inc................ D 513 451-4900
  Cincinnati *(G-3663)*

Westwood Country Club Company........ D 440 331-3016
  Rocky River *(G-12756)*

Wetherngton Golf Cntry CLB Inc.......... E 513 755-2582
  West Chester *(G-14794)*

Weymouth Valley Inc............................ D 440 498-8888
  Solon *(G-13163)*

William Henry Harrison Jr Hs................ E 513 367-4831
  Harrison *(G-9120)*

York Temple Country Club.................... D 614 885-5459
  Columbus *(G-6916)*

Young MNS Christn Assn Findlay......... D 419 422-4424
  Findlay *(G-8599)*

Young MNS Chrstn Assn Grter CN....... B 513 791-5000
  Blue Ash *(G-1275)*

Young MNS Chrstn Assn Grter CN....... B 513 521-7112
  Cincinnati *(G-3690)*

Young MNS Chrstn Assn Grter CN....... D 513 961-3510
  Cincinnati *(G-3691)*

Young MNS Chrstn Assn Grter CN....... D 513 731-0115
  Cincinnati *(G-3692)*

Young MNS Chrstn Assn Grter CN....... B 513 474-1400
  Cincinnati *(G-3693)*

Young MNS Chrstn Assn Grter Dy........ C 937 228-9622
  Dayton *(G-7732)*

Young MNS Chrstn Assn Grter Dy........ D 937 426-9622
  Dayton *(G-7734)*

Young MNS Chrstn Assn Grter Dy........ D 937 836-9622
  Englewood *(G-8327)*

Young MNS Chrstn Assn Grter Dy........ C 937 223-5201
  Springboro *(G-13210)*

Young MNS Chrstn Assn Mtro Los........ D 740 286-7008
  Jackson *(G-9530)*

Young MNS Chrstn Assn Wster OH...... E 330 264-3131
  Wooster *(G-15402)*

Young MNS Chrstn Assn Yngstown..... D 330 744-8411
  Youngstown *(G-15755)*

Youngstown Country Club..................... D 330 759-1040
  Youngstown *(G-15757)*

Zanesville Country Club........................ D 740 452-2726
  Zanesville *(G-15840)*

7999 Amusement and recreation, nec

A Grade Ahead Inc............................... D 614 389-3830
  Powell *(G-12582)*

Aimhi Inc... E 614 939-0112
  New Albany *(G-11554)*

Allwell Behavioral Health Svcs.............. E 740 432-7155
  Cambridge *(G-1553)*

Amusements of America Inc................. C 614 297-8863
  Columbus *(G-5367)*

Anderson Township Park Dst................ D 513 474-0003
  Cincinnati *(G-2201)*

Arena Horse Shows LLC....................... E 937 382-0985
  Wilmington *(G-15245)*

▲ Asm International.............................. D 440 338-5151
  Novelty *(G-12037)*

Avalon Holdings Corporation................. D 330 856-8800
  Warren *(G-14501)*

Bates Bros Amusement Co................... E 740 266-2950
  Wintersville *(G-15292)*

Cedar Point Park LLC........................... E 419 627-2350
  Sandusky *(G-12874)*

Chiller LLC.. E 614 475-7575
  Columbus *(G-5567)*

Chiller LLC.. E 740 549-0009
  Lewis Center *(G-9814)*

Chiller LLC.. E 614 433-9600
  Worthington *(G-15408)*

Chiller LLC.. D 614 764-1000
  Dublin *(G-7962)*

City of Moraine..................................... E 937 535-1100
  Dayton *(G-7234)*

City of North Olmsted........................... D 440 734-8200
  North Olmsted *(G-11896)*

City of Seven Hills................................ D 216 524-6262
  Seven Hills *(G-12952)*

City of South Euclid.............................. E 216 381-7674
  Cleveland *(G-3993)*

City of Sylvania.................................... E 419 885-1167
  Sylvania *(G-13539)*

City of Westlake................................... D 440 808-5700
  Westlake *(G-15050)*

City of Willowick................................... E 440 516-3011
  Willowick *(G-15235)*

Cleveland Destination........................... E 216 875-6652
  Cleveland *(G-4041)*

Cleveland Metroparks........................... B 216 635-3200
  Cleveland *(G-4056)*

Columbus Frkln Cnty Pk....................... E 614 891-0700
  Westerville *(G-14970)*

Columbus Frnklin Cnty Mtro Pk............ E 614 891-0700
  Reynoldsburg *(G-12659)*

Columbus Frnklin Cnty Mtro Pk............ E 614 895-6219
  Westerville *(G-14971)*

▲ Coney Island Inc............................... E 513 232-8230
  Milford *(G-11224)*

Cuyahoga County AG Soc..................... E 440 243-0090
  Berea *(G-1067)*

Dayton History..................................... C 937 293-2841
  Dayton *(G-7287)*

Erie Metroparks General Info................ E 419 621-4220
  Huron *(G-9387)*

Five Rivers Metroparks......................... E 937 278-2601
  Dayton *(G-7357)*

Five Rivers Metroparks......................... E 937 228-2088
  Dayton *(G-7358)*

Friends Five Rivers Metroparks............ C 937 275-7275
  Dayton *(G-7369)*

Goodrich Gnnett Nghborhood Ctr......... E 216 432-1717
  Cleveland *(G-4320)*

Goofy Golf II Inc................................... E 419 732-6671
  Port Clinton *(G-12528)*

79 AMUSEMENT AND RECREATION SERVICES

Great Parks Hamilton County............... C 513 521-7275
  Cincinnati (G-2766)
Gymnastics World Inc...................... E 440 526-2970
  Cleveland (G-4343)
Hard Knocks................................ E 614 407-1444
  Columbus (G-5971)
Hickory Hill Lakes Inc.................... E 937 295-3000
  Fort Loramie (G-8604)
Hof Village Newco LLC.................... C 330 458-9176
  Canton (G-1774)
◆ Interntnal MGT Group Ovrseas L.......B 216 522-1200
  Cleveland (G-4419)
Jack Entertainment LLC................... D 313 309-5225
  Cleveland (G-4430)
Jewish Cmnty Ctr of Grter Clmb.......... C 614 231-2731
  Columbus (G-6088)
▲ Jmac Inc................................. E 614 436-2418
  Columbus (G-6092)
Kissel Entertainment LLC................. E 513 266-4505
  Okeana (G-12086)
Lake Metroparks........................... E 440 256-2122
  Kirtland (G-9645)
Lake Metroparks........................... C 440 639-7275
  Painesville (G-12233)
Lakewood Country Club Pro Shop....... E 440 871-0400
  Cleveland (G-4480)
Metropolitan Pool Service Co............. E 216 741-9451
  Parma (G-12257)
Miami Valley Gaming & Racg LLC...... C 513 934-7070
  Lebanon (G-9778)
Mill Creek Metropolitan Park............. E 330 740-7116
  Youngstown (G-15668)
Moss Creek Golf Course.................. E 937 837-4653
  Clayton (G-3735)
National Concession Company............ E 216 881-9911
  Cleveland (G-4622)
Nexxtshow LLC............................. E
  Cincinnati (G-3114)
Ohio Caverns Inc.......................... E 937 465-4017
  West Liberty (G-14861)
Ohio Skate Inc............................. E 419 476-2808
  Toledo (G-13948)
Ohio Ski Slopes Inc....................... D 419 774-9818
  Mansfield (G-10308)
◆ Park Corporation......................... B 216 267-4870
  Medina (G-10874)
Paul A Ertel................................ E 216 696-8888
  Cleveland (G-4730)
Progrssive Fghting Systems LLC........ E 216 520-0271
  Independence (G-9473)
Quest Gymnstics Extreme Spt CT....... E 937 426-3547
  Beavercreek (G-896)
Rec Center.................................. E 330 721-6900
  Medina (G-10882)
Rockin Jump Holdings LLC.............. B 513 373-4260
  Cincinnati (G-3316)
Roto Group LLC........................... D 614 760-8690
  Dublin (G-8110)
S & S Management Inc.................... D 567 356-4151
  Wapakoneta (G-14491)
Skateworld Inc............................. E 937 890-6550
  Vandalia (G-14392)
Society of The Transfiguration.......... D 513 771-7462
  Cincinnati (G-3391)
South E Harley Davidson Sls Co......... E 440 439-5300
  Cleveland (G-4920)
Southwest Sports Center Inc............. E 440 234-6448
  Berea (G-1082)
Stark County Park District............... C 330 477-3552
  Canton (G-1860)
Strike Zone Inc............................. D 440 235-4420
  Olmsted Twp (G-12094)

Strongville Recreation Complex......... E 440 878-6000
  Cleveland (G-4957)
Troy City School District................. E 937 339-0457
  Troy (G-14162)
United Skates America Inc............... E 614 431-2751
  Columbus (G-6815)
United Skates of America Inc............ E 614 802-2440
  Columbus (G-6816)
Vertical Adventures Inc................... D 614 888-8393
  Columbus (G-6845)
Village of Sycamore....................... D 419 927-2357
  Sycamore (G-13534)
Washington Twnship Mntgmery CN..... E 937 433-0130
  Dayton (G-7715)
Western Hills Sportsplex Inc............. D 513 451-4900
  Cincinnati (G-3663)
Willo Putt-Putt Course Inc................ E 440 951-7888
  Willoughby (G-15226)
Wonderworker Inc.......................... D 234 249-3030
  Hudson (G-9379)
Young MNS Chrstn Assn Grter Dy...... C 937 228-9622
  Dayton (G-7732)
Young MNS Chrstn Assn Wster OH..... E 330 264-3131
  Wooster (G-15402)
Youngs Jersey Dairy Inc.................. B 937 325-0629
  Yellow Springs (G-15537)

80 HEALTH SERVICES

8011 Offices and clinics of medical doctors

3rd Street Community Clinic............. D 419 522-6191
  Ontario (G-12095)
88th Mdss/Sgsm Mm-Ht1135............ A 937 257-8935
  Wright Patterson Afb (G-15473)
A-1 Hlthcare Stffing Plcements.......... C 216 329-3500
  Cleveland (G-3753)
Access Urgent Medical Care Pic........ E 614 306-0116
  Pickerington (G-12396)
Adel Youssef MD........................... E 330 399-7215
  Warren (G-14494)
Adena Health System...................... E 740 779-4300
  Chillicothe (G-2045)
Advanced Csmtc Srgery Lser Ctr....... E 513 351-3223
  Cincinnati (G-2148)
Advanced Drmtlogy Skin Cncer C...... E 330 965-8760
  Youngstown (G-15541)
Advanced Eye Care Center Inc.......... E 419 521-3937
  Ontario (G-12097)
Advanced Neurologic Assoc Inc........ E 419 483-2403
  Bellevue (G-1040)
Advanced Surgical Associates........... E 937 578-2650
  Marysville (G-10473)
Advanced Urology Inc..................... E 330 758-9787
  Youngstown (G-15542)
Akron General Health System........... A 330 344-3030
  Hudson (G-9327)
Albert T Domingo Ms MD Inc........... E 330 452-9460
  Canton (G-1657)
Allergy & Asthma Inc..................... E 740 654-8623
  Lancaster (G-9693)
Alta Partners LLC......................... E 440 808-3654
  Westlake (G-15031)
Ambulatory Medical Care Inc........... E 513 831-8555
  Cincinnati (G-2175)
American Health Network Inc........... E 614 794-4500
  Dublin (G-7933)
American Hlth Netwrk Ohio LLC........ E 740 344-5437
  Newark (G-11686)
American Hlth Netwrk Ohio LLC........ D 614 794-4500
  Dublin (G-7934)
Americas Urgent Care..................... C 614 929-2721
  Upper Arlington (G-14275)

Ameriwound................................. D 216 273-9800
  Mayfield Heights (G-10784)
Anders Dermatology Inc.................. E 419 473-3257
  Toledo (G-13688)
Anderson Hills Pediatrics Inc............ D 513 232-8100
  Cincinnati (G-2198)
Anesthesia Associates PLL.............. C 440 350-0832
  Cleveland (G-3816)
Anesthesiology Assoc of Akron......... E 330 344-6401
  Akron (G-50)
Anesthesiology Svcs Netwrk Ltd....... E 937 208-6173
  Dayton (G-7175)
Anesthsia Assoc Cincinnati Inc......... A 513 585-0577
  Cincinnati (G-2204)
AP Cchmc................................... D 513 636-4200
  Cincinnati (G-2206)
Ashland Hospital Corporation........... D 740 894-2080
  South Point (G-13173)
Ashtabula Clinic Inc....................... D 440 997-6980
  Ashtabula (G-518)
Ashtabula County Medical Ctr.......... B 440 997-6960
  Ashtabula (G-523)
Associates In Dermatology Inc.......... E 440 249-0274
  Westlake (G-15035)
Associates In Nephrology Ltd........... E 330 729-1355
  Youngstown (G-15552)
Assocted Spclsts of Intrnal MD......... E 937 208-7272
  Dayton (G-7182)
Athens Surgery Center Ltd............... E 740 566-4504
  Athens (G-560)
Atrium Medical Center..................... E 513 424-2111
  Dayton (G-7184)
Aultman North Canton Med Group...... E 330 363-6333
  Canton (G-1682)
Aultman North Inc......................... D 330 305-6999
  Canton (G-1683)
Avita Health System....................... E 419 468-7059
  Galion (G-8742)
Avita Health System....................... D 419 468-4841
  Galion (G-8743)
Beacon Orthpaedcs & Sprts Med....... B 513 354-3700
  Cincinnati (G-2243)
Beacon Orthpdics Spt Mdcine Lt....... A 513 985-2252
  Cincinnati (G-2244)
Beacon Orthpdics Spt Mdcine Lt....... D 513 354-3700
  Cincinnati (G-2245)
Bel-Park Anesthesia....................... E 330 480-3658
  Youngstown (G-15557)
Belmont Bhc Pines Hospital Inc......... D 330 759-2700
  Youngstown (G-15558)
Bethesda Hospital Inc..................... D 513 563-1505
  Cincinnati (G-2259)
Bethesda Hospital Inc..................... D 513 248-8800
  Milford (G-11218)
Blanchard Valley Med Assoc Inc....... D 419 424-0380
  Findlay (G-8515)
Blanchard Valley Wns Care LLC....... E 419 420-0904
  Perrysburg (G-12317)
Blood & Cancer Center Inc............... E 330 533-3040
  Canfield (G-1621)
Bon Secours Mercy Health Inc.......... C 330 729-1420
  Youngstown (G-15563)
Brigids Path Inc............................ E 937 350-1785
  Moraine (G-11392)
Bucyrus Community Physicians......... C 419 492-2200
  New Washington (G-11681)
Butler Cnty Cmnty Hlth Cnsrtiu......... C 513 454-1468
  Hamilton (G-9023)
Canal Physician Group.................... E 330 344-4000
  Akron (G-79)
Canton Ophthalmology Assoc Inc...... E 330 456-0047
  Canton (G-1703)

80 HEALTH SERVICES

Canyon Medical Center Inc .... E 614 864-6010
Columbus (G-5495)

Capitol City Cardiology Inc .... E 614 464-0884
Columbus (G-5503)

Cardiac Vsclar Thrcic Surgeons .... D 513 421-3494
Cincinnati (G-2307)

Cardilgist of Clark Chmpign CN .... C 937 653-8897
Urbana (G-14299)

Cardinal Orthopaedic Group Inc .... E 614 759-1186
Columbus (G-5508)

Cardinal Orthopedic Institute .... E 614 488-1816
Hilliard (G-9187)

Cardiology Ctr of Cincinnati .... E 513 745-9800
Montgomery (G-11364)

Cardiovascular Associates Inc .... E 330 747-6446
Youngstown (G-15571)

Cardiovascular Clinic Inc .... E 440 882-0075
Cleveland (G-3926)

Care Alliance .... E 216 781-6228
Cleveland (G-3927)

Carefirst Urgent Care LLC .... D 513 868-2345
Cincinnati (G-2311)

Carp Cosmetic Surgery Ctr Inc .... E 216 416-1221
Beachwood (G-773)

Cei Physicians PSC LLC .... C 513 984-5133
Blue Ash (G-1144)

Cei Vision Partners LLC .... D 513 569-3114
Blue Ash (G-1145)

Center For Dialysis Care .... E 440 286-4103
Chardon (G-1995)

Center For Srgcal Drmtlogy Inc .... E 614 847-4100
Westerville (G-14879)

Center For Urologic Health LLC .... E 330 375-0924
Akron (G-85)

Central Ohio Geriatrics LLC .... E 614 530-4077
Granville (G-8850)

Central Ohio Primary Care .... E 614 834-8042
Canal Winchester (G-1601)

Central Ohio Primary Care .... E 614 268-8164
Columbus (G-5541)

Central Ohio Primary Care .... C 614 552-2300
Reynoldsburg (G-12657)

Central Ohio Prmry Care Physca .... D 614 442-7550
Columbus (G-5542)

Central Ohio Prmry Care Physca .... C 614 451-9229
Columbus (G-5543)

Central Ohio Prmry Care Physca .... C 614 473-1300
Columbus (G-5544)

Central Ohio Prmry Care Physca .... D 614 882-0708
Westerville (G-14880)

Central Ohio Prmry Care Physca .... E 614 891-9505
Westerville (G-14881)

Central Ohio Prmry Care Physca .... E 614 326-2672
Westerville (G-14882)

Central Ohio Surgical Assoc .... E 614 222-8000
Grove City (G-8908)

Chagrin Surgery Center LLC .... E 216 839-1800
Beachwood (G-775)

Child Adlscent Spclty Care Dyt .... E 937 667-7711
Tipp City (G-13655)

Childrens Anesthesia Assoc Inc .... E 614 722-4200
Columbus (G-5561)

Childrens Hosp Med Ctr Akron .... D 330 253-4931
Akron (G-89)

Childrens Hosp Med Ctr Akron .... D 330 543-8004
Akron (G-90)

Childrens Hosp Med Ctr Akron .... D 330 543-8639
Akron (G-91)

Childrens Hosp Med Ctr Akron .... D 330 543-8503
Akron (G-92)

Childrens Hosp Med Ctr Akron .... D 330 746-8040
Boardman (G-1286)

Childrens Hosp Med Ctr Akron .... D 330 342-5437
Hudson (G-9339)

Childrens Hosp Med Ctr Akron .... D 419 529-6285
Ontario (G-12102)

Childrens Hosp Med Ctr Akron .... D 330 345-1100
Wooster (G-15319)

Childrens Hospital .... C 513 636-9900
Cincinnati (G-2358)

Childrens Hospital Medical Ctr .... A 513 803-9600
Liberty Township (G-9848)

Childrens Hospital Medical Ctr .... B 513 636-6800
Mason (G-10529)

Childrens Rdiological Inst Inc .... A 614 722-2363
Columbus (G-5565)

Christ Hospital .... D 513 561-7809
Cincinnati (G-2384)

▲ Christian Community Hlth Svcs .... E 513 381-2247
Cincinnati (G-2386)

Christian Hlthcare Mnstries In .... E 330 848-1511
Barberton (G-696)

Cincinnati Aesthetics LLC .... E 513 204-3490
Mason (G-10532)

Cincinnati Ctr For Psychthrapy .... E 513 961-8484
Cincinnati (G-2406)

Cincinnati Dermatology Ctr LLC .... E 513 984-4800
Cincinnati (G-2409)

Cincinnati Hand Surgery Cons .... E 513 961-4263
Montgomery (G-11365)

Cleveland Clinic .... A 440 366-9444
Elyria (G-8236)

Cleveland Clinic Foundation .... E 216 442-3412
Cleveland (G-4024)

Cleveland Clinic Foundation .... E 216 444-5540
Cleveland (G-4025)

Cleveland Clinic Foundation .... E 216 444-6618
Cleveland (G-4026)

Cleveland Clinic Foundation .... E 216 444-2273
Cleveland (G-4027)

Cleveland Clinic Foundation .... E 614 358-4223
Columbus (G-5583)

Cleveland Clinic Foundation .... D 216 986-4312
Independence (G-9421)

Cleveland Clinic Foundation .... D 419 609-2812
Sandusky (G-12882)

Cleveland Clinic Foundation .... D 330 287-4930
Wooster (G-15323)

Cleveland Clinic Mercy Hosp .... B 330 627-7641
Carrollton (G-1904)

Cleveland Clnic Chgrin FLS FML .... B 440 893-9393
Chagrin Falls (G-1956)

Cleveland Clnic Hlth Systm-Wst .... C 216 476-7606
Cleveland (G-4038)

Cleveland Ear Nose Throat Ctr .... E 330 723-6673
Medina (G-10822)

Cleveland Eye Lser Srgery Ctr .... E 440 777-8400
Cleveland (G-4043)

Clevland Clinic Foundation .... A 216 445-5121
Cleveland (G-4076)

Clyo Internal Medicine Inc .... E 937 435-5857
Centerville (G-1941)

Coleman Professional Svcs Inc .... C 330 673-1347
Kent (G-9565)

Columbus Arthritis Center Inc .... E 614 486-5200
Columbus (G-5610)

Columbus Cancer Clinic Inc .... E 614 263-5006
Columbus (G-5616)

Columbus Dermatologists-Grtr .... E 614 268-2748
Columbus (G-5627)

Columbus Neighborhood Health C .... E 614 445-0685
Columbus (G-5648)

Columbus Nghbrhood Hlth Ctr In .... E 614 859-1947
Columbus (G-5649)

Community and Rural Hlth Svcs .... D 419 334-8943
Fremont (G-8671)

Community Hlh Ctr of Gtr Daton .... E 937 461-4336
Dayton (G-7242)

Community Hlth Ctrs Grter Dyto .... E 937 558-0180
Dayton (G-7243)

Community Mental Health Svc .... D 740 695-9344
Saint Clairsville (G-12787)

Compass Community Health .... E 740 355-7102
Portsmouth (G-12549)

Comprhnsve Eycare Cntl Ohio I .... E 614 890-5692
Westerville (G-14883)

Copcp .... E 614 865-6570
Westerville (G-14884)

County of Delaware .... D 740 203-2040
Delaware (G-7789)

County of Lucas .... C 419 248-3585
Toledo (G-13765)

County of Lucas .... B 419 213-4018
Toledo (G-13766)

County of Lucas .... C 419 213-3903
Toledo (G-13767)

County of Montgomery .... E 937 225-4156
Dayton (G-7256)

County of Wayne .... E 330 345-5891
Wooster (G-15331)

Covenant Care Ohio Inc .... A 937 526-5570
Versailles (G-14415)

Cranley Surgical Associates .... E 513 961-4335
Cincinnati (G-2515)

Crossroads Health .... D 440 255-1700
Mentor (G-10929)

Crystal Clinic Inc .... E 330 644-7436
Akron (G-126)

Crystal Clinic Inc .... E 330 929-9136
Cuyahoga Falls (G-7066)

Crystal Clinic Surgery Ctr LLC .... E 330 668-4040
Akron (G-127)

Crystal Clnic Orthpdic Ctr LLC .... D 330 535-3396
Akron (G-128)

Davis Eye Center Inc .... D 330 923-5676
Cuyahoga Falls (G-7069)

Dayton Childrens Hospital .... D 513 424-2850
Middletown (G-11195)

Dayton Childrens Hospital .... D 937 398-5464
Springfield (G-13246)

Dayton Eye Surgery Center .... E 937 431-9531
Dayton (G-7281)

Dayton Fmly Practice Assoc Inc .... E 937 254-5661
Dayton (G-7282)

Dayton Gastroenterology LLC .... D 937 320-5050
Dayton (G-7285)

Dayton Heart Center Inc .... E 937 277-4274
Dayton (G-7286)

Dayton Medical Imaging .... E 937 439-0390
Dayton (G-7290)

Dayton Ob Gyn .... E 937 439-7550
Centerville (G-1943)

Dayton Orthpdic Srgery Spt Mdc .... E 937 436-5763
Dayton (G-7291)

Dayton Physicians LLC .... E 937 208-2636
Dayton (G-7299)

Dayton Physicians LLC .... D 937 547-0563
Greenville (G-8870)

Dayton Physicians LLC .... D 937 440-4210
Troy (G-14133)

Dayton Physicians LLC .... E 937 280-8400
Dayton (G-7298)

Dayton Surgeons Inc .... D 937 228-4126
Englewood (G-8305)

Dayton Vtreo-Retinal Assoc Inc .... E 937 228-5015
Dayton (G-7304)

80 HEALTH SERVICES

Defiance Family Physicians Ltd............ E 419 785-3281
   Defiance *(G-7744)*

Dermatlgists of Southwest Ohio............ E 937 435-2094
   Dayton *(G-7310)*

Dermatlogists Centl States LLC............ A 888 414-3627
   Cincinnati *(G-2558)*

Dickman Kettler & Bruner Ltd............... E 419 678-3016
   Coldwater *(G-5212)*

Digest Health Center Ltd...................... E 330 869-0178
   Akron *(G-134)*

Digestive Care Inc................................ D 937 320-5050
   Dayton *(G-7313)*

Digestive Disease Consultants............. E 330 225-6468
   Brunswick *(G-1455)*

Digestive Hlth Cre Cnsltnts of............... E 419 843-7996
   Toledo *(G-13779)*

▲ Digestive Specialists Inc.................. E 937 534-7330
   Dayton *(G-7314)*

Doctors Office...................................... E 740 622-3016
   Coshocton *(G-6983)*

Doctors Ohiohealth Corporation............ A 614 544-5424
   Columbus *(G-5781)*

Drs Weinberger and Visy LLC.............. E 216 765-1180
   Cleveland *(G-4186)*

Dublin Family Care Inc........................ E 614 761-2244
   Dublin *(G-7992)*

Dublin Internal Medicine Inc................. E 614 764-1777
   Dublin *(G-7995)*

Dublin Surgery Center LLC.................. E 614 932-9548
   Dublin *(G-7998)*

Dunlap Fmly Physcans Inc Prof............ E 330 684-2015
   Orrville *(G-12163)*

Eastern Ohio Plmonary Cons Inc.......... E 330 726-3357
   Youngstown *(G-15604)*

Elizabeth Place Holdings LLC.............. E 323 300-3700
   Dayton *(G-7331)*

Emerald Pediatrics............................... E 614 932-5050
   Dublin *(G-8002)*

Emergency Medicine Specialists.......... D 937 438-8910
   Miamisburg *(G-11050)*

Emergency Physicians of Northw......... C 419 291-4101
   Toledo *(G-13789)*

Emergency Services Inc....................... D 614 224-6420
   Columbus *(G-5814)*

Endoscopy Ctr of W Cntl Ohio L........... E 419 879-3636
   Lima *(G-9990)*

Ent Realty Corp.................................... C 888 881-4368
   Van Wert *(G-14343)*

Equitas Health Inc............................... D 614 299-2437
   Columbus *(G-5825)*

Evokes LLC... E 513 947-8433
   Mason *(G-10545)*

Eye Care Associates Inc...................... D 330 746-7691
   Youngstown *(G-15608)*

Eye Laser & Surgery Center................ E 937 427-7800
   Dayton *(G-7344)*

Fairfield Internal Medicine.................... E 740 681-9447
   Lancaster *(G-9716)*

Fairview Eye Center Inc...................... D 440 333-3060
   Cleveland *(G-4236)*

Fairview Hospital................................. A 216 476-7000
   Cleveland *(G-4238)*

Fairway Family Physicians Inc............. E 614 861-7051
   Columbus *(G-5846)*

Family Hlth Care NW Ohio Inc.............. E 419 238-6747
   Van Wert *(G-14344)*

Family Hlth Svcs Drke Cnty Inc............ C 937 548-3806
   Greenville *(G-8873)*

Family Medical Care Inc....................... E 330 633-3883
   Hudson *(G-9347)*

Family Medical Ctr of Aliance............... E 330 823-3856
   Alliance *(G-382)*

Family Medicine Stark County.............. E 330 499-5600
   Canton *(G-1751)*

Family Physicians Inc.......................... E 330 494-7099
   Canton *(G-1752)*

Family Physicians Associates.............. E 440 449-1014
   Cleveland *(G-4240)*

Family Physicians of Gahanna............. E 614 471-9654
   Columbus *(G-5849)*

Family Practice Associates.................. E 513 424-7291
   Franklin *(G-8636)*

Family Practice Associates.................. E 330 832-3188
   Massillon *(G-10639)*

Family Prctice Assoc Sprngfeld............ E 937 399-6650
   Springfield *(G-13251)*

Far Hills Open Mri Inc.......................... D 937 435-6674
   Dayton *(G-7346)*

Far Hills Surgical Center LLC.............. E 937 208-8000
   Dayton *(G-7347)*

Far Oaks Orthopedists Inc................... E 937 433-5309
   Dayton *(G-7349)*

Far Oaks Orthopedists Inc................... E 937 298-0452
   Vandalia *(G-14377)*

Fauster-Cameron Inc........................... B 419 784-1414
   Defiance *(G-7746)*

Fayette Medical Center........................ E 740 335-1210
   Wshngtn Ct Hs *(G-15484)*

Fersenius Medical Center.................... C 330 746-2860
   Youngstown *(G-15611)*

First Priority Urgent Care LLC.............. E 937 723-7230
   Dayton *(G-7353)*

First Settlement Orthopaedics.............. E 740 373-8756
   Marietta *(G-10368)*

Fisher-Titus Medical Center................. D 440 839-2226
   Wakeman *(G-14459)*

Forum Health....................................... A 330 841-9011
   Warren *(G-14521)*

Fresenius Vascular Care Inc................ E 513 351-2494
   Norwood *(G-12033)*

Gastrnterology Specialists Inc.............. E 330 455-5011
   Canton *(G-1760)*

Gastrntrlogy Assoc Clvland Inc............ E 216 593-7700
   Bay Village *(G-759)*

Gastro-Intestinal Assoc Inc.................. E 419 227-8209
   Lima *(G-9991)*

Geisinger Health Plan.......................... E 570 271-6211
   Cleveland *(G-4309)*

Gem City Surgical Associates.............. E 254 400-1783
   Englewood *(G-8307)*

Gem City Urologist Inc......................... E 937 832-8400
   Englewood *(G-8308)*

Getinge Usa Inc................................... D 440 449-1540
   Cleveland *(G-4311)*

Gloria Gadmack Do.............................. E 216 363-2353
   Cleveland *(G-4316)*

Good Samaritan Hosp Cincinnati.......... E 513 569-6251
   Cincinnati *(G-2742)*

Grandview Family Practice Inc............. E 740 258-9267
   Columbus *(G-5944)*

Grandvlle Pike Fmly Physicians........... E 740 687-0793
   Lancaster *(G-9724)*

Greater Cin Cardi Consults In.............. E 513 751-4222
   Cincinnati *(G-2767)*

Greater Cincinnati Gastro Assc............ D 513 336-8636
   Cincinnati *(G-2768)*

Greater Cincinnati Ob/Gyn Inc.............. D 513 245-3103
   Cincinnati *(G-2769)*

Greater Dayton Surgery Ctr LLC.......... E 937 535-2200
   Dayton *(G-7385)*

H B Magruder Memorial Hosp.............. C 419 734-3131
   Oak Harbor *(G-12045)*

H B Magruder Memorial Hosp.............. C 419 732-6520
   Port Clinton *(G-12532)*

Hand & Reconstructive Surgeons......... E 937 298-2262
   Dayton *(G-7394)*

Hand Amblatory Surgery Ctr LLC......... E 513 961-4263
   Cincinnati *(G-2798)*

Hand Rcnstructive Surgeons Inc........... E 937 435-4263
   Dayton *(G-7395)*

Health Collaborative............................. D 513 618-3600
   Cincinnati *(G-2809)*

Healthcare 2000 Cmnty Clnic In........... E 330 262-2500
   Wooster *(G-15343)*

Healthsource of Ohio Inc...................... E 513 753-2820
   Cincinnati *(G-2812)*

Healthsource of Ohio Inc...................... E 513 575-1444
   Loveland *(G-10140)*

Healthsource of Ohio Inc...................... E 937 386-0049
   Seaman *(G-12944)*

Hearinglife Usa Inc.............................. D 513 759-2999
   West Chester *(G-14707)*

Heart Center of N Eastrn Ohio.............. E 330 758-7703
   Youngstown *(G-15628)*

Hematogy Oncology Toledo Clinc......... E 419 794-7720
   Maumee *(G-10732)*

Hematology Oncology Center............... E 440 324-0401
   Elyria *(G-8255)*

Heritage Family Medical Inc................. E 513 867-9000
   Hamilton *(G-9051)*

Heritage Valley Health Sys Inc............. D 724 773-8209
   East Liverpool *(G-8183)*

Highland Health Providers Corp........... D 937 981-1121
   Greenfield *(G-8866)*

Highland Health Providers Corp........... D 937 393-4899
   Hillsboro *(G-9258)*

Highland Health Providers Corp........... D 937 364-2346
   Lynchburg *(G-10185)*

Hilliard Family Medicine Inc................. E 614 876-8989
   Hilliard *(G-9199)*

Holzer Clinic LLC................................. E 740 446-5412
   Gallipolis *(G-8757)*

Holzer Clinic LLC................................. E 740 886-9403
   Proctorville *(G-12612)*

Holzer Clinic LLC................................. A 740 446-5411
   Gallipolis *(G-8759)*

Home Health Connection Inc................ E 614 839-4545
   Lancaster *(G-9725)*

Hometown Urgent Care......................... E 513 831-5900
   Milford *(G-11231)*

Hometown Urgent Care......................... D 937 342-9520
   Springfield *(G-13254)*

Hometown Urgent Care......................... E 937 252-2000
   Wooster *(G-15345)*

Hometown Urgent Care......................... D 937 372-6012
   Xenia *(G-15521)*

Hometown Urgent Care......................... E 330 629-2300
   Youngstown *(G-15633)*

Hometown Urgent Care of K................. E 614 505-7601
   Columbus *(G-6006)*

Hopewell Health Centers Inc................ E 740 342-4192
   New Lexington *(G-11626)*

Hopewell Health Centers Inc................ E 740 773-1006
   Chillicothe *(G-2070)*

Hudson L Surgcenter L C.................... E 330 655-5460
   Akron *(G-196)*

Immediate Health Associates............... E 614 794-0481
   Westerville *(G-14989)*

Internal Mdcine Cons of Clmbus........... D 614 878-6413
   Columbus *(G-6067)*

Internal Medical Physicians.................. D 330 868-3711
   Minerva *(G-11307)*

Internal Revenue Service..................... D 937 643-1494
   Dayton *(G-7424)*

Ironton Lwrnce Cnty Area Cmnty.......... B 740 532-3534
   Ironton *(G-9508)*

SIC SECTION
80 HEALTH SERVICES

James Center .... C 614 410-5615
  Columbus *(G-6083)*
Jewish Hospital .... E 513 569-2434
  Cincinnati *(G-2907)*
John E Brunner MD .... E 419 537-5111
  Toledo *(G-13869)*
Joint Implant Surgeons Inc .... E 614 221-6331
  New Albany *(G-11570)*
Joint Implant Surgeons Inc A .... E 740 566-4640
  Athens *(G-578)*
Jyg Innovations LLC .... D 937 630-3858
  Dayton *(G-7431)*
Kaiser Foundation Hospitals .... E 216 524-7377
  Avon *(G-658)*
Kaiser Foundation Hospitals .... E 216 524-7377
  Brooklyn Heights *(G-1423)*
Kaiser Foundation Hospitals .... E 800 524-7377
  Brooklyn Heights *(G-1424)*
Kaiser Foundation Hospitals .... E 800 524-7377
  Fairlawn *(G-8488)*
Kaiser Foundation Hospitals .... E 800 524-7377
  Kent *(G-9582)*
Kaiser Foundation Hospitals .... E 800 524-7377
  Medina *(G-10850)*
Kaiser Foundation Hospitals .... E 800 524-7377
  Mentor *(G-10958)*
Kaiser Foundation Hospitals .... E 800 524-7377
  North Canton *(G-11842)*
Kaiser Foundation Hospitals .... E 216 524-7377
  Strongsville *(G-13467)*
Kaiser Foundation Hospitals .... E 330 486-2800
  Twinsburg *(G-14198)*
Kentucky Heart Institute Inc .... C 740 353-8100
  Portsmouth *(G-12560)*
Kettering Anesthesia Assoc .... E 937 225-3429
  Dayton *(G-7436)*
Kidney Care Specialists LLC .... E 937 643-0015
  Dayton *(G-7441)*
Kidney Group Inc .... E 330 746-1488
  Youngstown *(G-15646)*
Kindred Healthcare LLC .... E 937 222-5963
  Dayton *(G-7443)*
Kolczun Klczun Orthpd Assoc In .... A 440 985-3113
  Lorain *(G-10080)*
Kunesh Eye Center Inc .... E 937 298-1703
  Oakwood *(G-12048)*
Lake Health .... E 440 816-2225
  Cleveland *(G-4476)*
Lake Hospital System Inc .... C 440 352-0646
  Concord Township *(G-6928)*
Lakewood Hospital Association .... C 216 228-5437
  Cleveland *(G-4481)*
Lancaster Radiation Oncology .... E 740 687-8554
  Lancaster *(G-9732)*
Lca-Vision Inc .... E 513 792-9292
  Cincinnati *(G-2968)*
Libbey Inc .... C 419 671-6000
  Toledo *(G-13887)*
Licking Memorial Hospital .... B 740 348-1750
  Newark *(G-11718)*
Lifecare Fmly Hlth Dntl Ctr In .... E 330 454-2000
  Canton *(G-1794)*
Lifestages Boutique For Women .... D 937 274-5420
  Englewood *(G-8314)*
Lifestges Smrtan Ctrs For Wmen .... E 937 277-8988
  Dayton *(G-7454)*
Lu-Jean Feng Clinic LLC .... E 216 831-7007
  Cleveland *(G-4509)*
Lutheran Medical Center Inc .... C 216 696-4300
  Cleveland *(G-4511)*
Lutheran Medical Center Inc .... B 440 519-6800
  Solon *(G-13109)*

Mahoning Vly Hmtlogy Onclogy A ...... E 330 318-1100
  Youngstown *(G-15659)*
Manheim Auctions Inc .... D 216 539-1701
  Cleveland *(G-4520)*
Marietta Hlth Care Physicians .... E 740 376-5044
  Marietta *(G-10383)*
Marietta Occptnal Hlth Prtners .... D 740 374-9954
  Marietta *(G-10385)*
Marietta Surgery Center .... E 740 373-7207
  Marietta *(G-10387)*
Marion Ancillary Services LLC .... E 740 383-7983
  Marion *(G-10435)*
Marysvlle Ohio Srgical Ctr LLC .... C 937 578-4200
  Marysville *(G-10496)*
Maternohio Clinical Assoicates .... E 614 457-7660
  Columbus *(G-6205)*
Maumee Eye Clinic Inc .... E 419 893-4883
  Maumee *(G-10746)*
Maxim Healthcare Services Inc .... C 614 880-1210
  Columbus *(G-6210)*
Mayfield Clinic Inc .... D 513 221-1100
  Cincinnati *(G-3020)*
Medcentral Health System .... B 419 526-8900
  Ontario *(G-12117)*
Medical and Surgical Assoc .... E 740 522-7600
  Newark *(G-11727)*
Medical Assessments LLC .... E 216 397-0917
  Cleveland *(G-4544)*
Medical Assoc Cambridge Inc .... D 740 439-3515
  Cambridge *(G-1575)*
Medical Cllege Ohio Physcans L .... D 419 383-7100
  Toledo *(G-13913)*
Medical Diagnostic Lab Inc .... E 440 333-1375
  Avon *(G-661)*
Medical Group Associates Inc .... E 740 283-4773
  Steubenville *(G-13339)*
Medical Mutual of Ohio .... E 614 621-4585
  Dublin *(G-8062)*
Medin-Smmit Ambltory Srgery CT ..... E 330 952-0014
  Medina *(G-10854)*
Medplus Inc .... B 513 229-5500
  Mason *(G-10581)*
Mentor Surgery Center Ltd .... E 440 205-5725
  Mentor *(G-10972)*
Mercer Cnty Jint Twnship Cmnty .... D 419 586-1611
  Celina *(G-1926)*
Mercy Hlth - Clermont Hosp LLC .... A 513 732-8200
  Batavia *(G-743)*
Mercy Hlth - Rgnal Med Ctr LLC .... A 440 960-4000
  Lorain *(G-10092)*
Mercy Hlth - St Vncent Med Ctr .... A 419 475-5433
  Toledo *(G-13920)*
Metrohealth System .... C 216 957-9000
  Brecksville *(G-1359)*
Metrohealth System .... C 216 598-9908
  Cleveland *(G-4565)*
Metrohealth System .... E 216 778-8446
  Cleveland *(G-4566)*
Metrohealth System .... E 216 524-7377
  Parma *(G-12256)*
Metropolitian Family Care Inc .... E 614 237-1067
  Reynoldsburg *(G-12669)*
Miami Valley Hospital .... B 937 208-7396
  Dayton *(G-7488)*
Mid-Ohio Onclgy/Hematology Inc ...... E 614 383-6000
  Columbus *(G-6237)*
Mid-Ohio Oncology/Hematology Inc .. E 614 383-6000
  Columbus *(G-6238)*
Midwest Physcans Ansthsia Svcs ...... D 614 884-0641
  Columbus *(G-6245)*
Milltown Family Physicians .... E 330 345-8060
  Wooster *(G-15358)*

Montgomery Family Medicine .... E 513 891-2211
  Cincinnati *(G-3078)*
Mount Carmel Health .... C 614 234-4060
  Westerville *(G-14912)*
Mount Carmel Health System .... B 614 866-3703
  Columbus *(G-6277)*
Mount Carmel Health System .... B 614 445-6215
  Columbus *(G-6278)*
Mount Carmel Health System .... C 614 876-1260
  Hilliard *(G-9219)*
Mount Crmel Cntl Ohio Nrlgcal .... E 614 268-9561
  Westerville *(G-15003)*
Mount Notre Dame Health Center ...... E 513 821-7448
  Cincinnati *(G-3082)*
Mrp Inc .... E 513 965-9700
  Milford *(G-11246)*
Mvhe Inc .... C 937 208-7575
  Dayton *(G-7521)*
Mvhe Inc .... E 937 499-8211
  Dayton *(G-7520)*
My Community Health Center .... E 330 363-6242
  Canton *(G-1814)*
Nadine El Asmar MD - Uh Clvlan .... E 216 844-3400
  Cleveland *(G-4617)*
National Hospice Cooperative .... E 937 256-9507
  Dayton *(G-7527)*
National Rgstry of Emrgncy Med .... E 614 888-4484
  Columbus *(G-6301)*
Nationwide Childrens Hospital .... C 614 355-7000
  Dublin *(G-8070)*
Nationwide Childrens Hospital .... C 740 522-3221
  Newark *(G-11734)*
Neighborhood Health Care Inc .... E 216 281-8945
  Cleveland *(G-4633)*
Neurological Associates Inc .... D 614 544-4455
  Columbus *(G-6351)*
New Horizons Surgery Ctr LLC .... E 740 375-5854
  Marion *(G-10447)*
Niagara Health Corporation .... A 614 855-4878
  New Albany *(G-11582)*
Noms Internal Medicine .... D 419 626-6891
  Sandusky *(G-12919)*
North Coast Prof Co LLC .... E 419 557-5541
  Sandusky *(G-12920)*
North Ohio Heart Center Inc .... E 440 204-4000
  Elyria *(G-8281)*
North Shore Gastroenterology .... E 216 663-7064
  Westlake *(G-15087)*
North Shore Gstrenterology Inc .... E 440 808-1212
  Westlake *(G-15088)*
Northeast Ohio Nephrology Assoc ..... E 330 252-0600
  Akron *(G-244)*
Northast Ohio Nghbrhood Hlth S .... E 216 851-2600
  Cleveland *(G-4654)*
Northast Ohio Nghbrhood Hlth S .... E 216 851-1500
  Cleveland *(G-4656)*
Northast Ohio Nghbrhood Hlth S .... C 216 231-7700
  Cleveland *(G-4653)*
Northast Srgcal Wound Care Inc .... E 216 643-2780
  Independence *(G-9460)*
Northeast Obgyn .... E 614 875-4191
  Grove City *(G-8942)*
Northwest Eye Surgeons Inc .... E 614 451-7550
  Columbus *(G-6372)*
Northwest Obsttrics Gynclogy A .... E 614 777-4801
  Hilliard *(G-9221)*
Northwest Ohio Cardiology Cons .... D 419 842-3000
  Toledo *(G-13938)*
Northwest Ohio Gstrntrlgsts As .... E 419 471-1350
  Toledo *(G-13939)*
Northwest Ohio Orthpdics Spt M .... C 419 427-1984
  Findlay *(G-8573)*

80 HEALTH SERVICES

Norwood Endoscopy Center............... E 513 731-5600
Cincinnati *(G-3128)*

Novus Clinic... D 330 630-9699
Tallmadge *(G-13601)*

Nuerological & Sleep Disorders........... E 513 721-7533
Cincinnati *(G-3134)*

Ob-Gyn Specialists Lima Inc............... E 419 227-0610
Lima *(G-9944)*

▲ **Obstetric Anesthesia Assoc Inc**........ C 513 862-1400
Cincinnati *(G-3139)*

Occupational Health Services............... E 937 492-7296
Sidney *(G-13042)*

Occupational Services........................... E 419 891-8003
Maumee *(G-10752)*

Occuptnal Mdcine Assoc Wyne CN..... D 330 263-7270
Wooster *(G-15362)*

Offor Health Inc..................................... D 877 789-8583
Columbus *(G-6385)*

Ohio Allergy Associates Inc................ E 937 435-8999
Centerville *(G-1948)*

Ohio Chest Physicians Ltd................... E 216 267-5139
Cleveland *(G-4684)*

Ohio Eye Alliance Inc............................ E 330 823-1680
Alliance *(G-394)*

Ohio Eye Associates Inc....................... D 800 423-0694
Mansfield *(G-10307)*

Ohio Eye Care Consultants LLC........... E 330 722-8300
Medina *(G-10871)*

Ohio Gstroenterology Group Inc......... E 614 754-5500
Columbus *(G-6423)*

Ohio Gstroenterology Group Inc......... E 614 754-5500
Dublin *(G-8080)*

Ohio Gstroenterology Group Inc......... E 614 754-5500
Columbus *(G-6424)*

Ohio Head & Neck Surgeons Inc........ E 330 492-2844
Canton *(G-1822)*

Ohio Health Center Inc......................... E 614 252-3636
Columbus *(G-6425)*

Ohio Health Group LLC......................... E 614 566-0010
Columbus *(G-6426)*

Ohio Heart Group Inc........................... E 740 348-0012
Newark *(G-11737)*

Ohio Heart Health Center Inc............. C 513 792-7800
Montgomery *(G-11370)*

Ohio Heart Health Center Inc............. E 513 351-9900
Cincinnati *(G-3146)*

Ohio Hills Health Services................... D 740 425-5165
Barnesville *(G-720)*

Ohio Minority Medical........................... E 513 400-5011
East Liverpool *(G-8189)*

Ohio Orthpd Surgery Inst LLC............. E 614 827-8777
Columbus *(G-6438)*

Ohio Pediatrics Inc............................... E 937 299-2743
Dayton *(G-7534)*

Ohio Reproductive Medicine................ E 614 451-2280
Columbus *(G-6441)*

Ohio State Univ Physicians Inc........... E 614 947-3700
Columbus *(G-6449)*

Ohio State Univ Wexner Med Ctr........ C 614 293-6255
Columbus *(G-6450)*

Ohio State Univ Wexner Med Ctr........ C 614 293-7521
Columbus *(G-6452)*

Ohio State University............................ C 614 257-3000
Columbus *(G-6453)*

Ohio State University............................ D 614 293-3860
Columbus *(G-6456)*

Ohio Surgery Center Ltd...................... D 614 451-0500
Columbus *(G-6461)*

Ohio Vly Ambltory Srgery Ctr L.......... E 740 423-4684
Belpre *(G-1058)*

Olympic Urogynecology LLC................ E 330 953-3414
Fairlawn *(G-8492)*

Omni Medical Center............................ E 330 492-5565
Canton *(G-1825)*

Oncolgy/Hmatology Care Inc PSC...... D 513 751-2145
Cincinnati *(G-3163)*

Ophthlmic Srgons Cons Ohio Inc........ E 614 221-7464
Columbus *(G-6473)*

Optivue Inc.. E 419 891-1391
Oregon *(G-12138)*

Oregon Clinic Inc.................................. D 419 691-8132
Oregon *(G-12140)*

Orthoneuro... E 614 890-6555
Westerville *(G-15010)*

Orthopaedic & Trauma Surgeons Inc... D 614 827-8700
Upper Arlington *(G-14281)*

Orthopaedic Associates Inc................ E 440 892-1440
Westlake *(G-15092)*

Orthopaedic Institute Ohio Inc............ D 419 222-6622
Lima *(G-9945)*

Orthopaedic Surgery Cente.................. E 330 758-1065
Youngstown *(G-15686)*

Orthpdic Assoc Zanesville Inc............ D 740 454-3273
Zanesville *(G-15823)*

Orthpdic Spine Ctr At Plris L.............. E 937 707-4662
Grove City *(G-8943)*

Orthopedic Assoc SW Ohio Inc........... E 937 415-9100
Centerville *(G-1949)*

Orthopedic Associates......................... D 800 824-9861
Liberty Township *(G-9856)*

Orthopedic Associates Dayton............ E 937 280-4988
Dayton *(G-7541)*

Orthopedic Cons Cincinnati.................. E 513 753-7488
Cincinnati *(G-3170)*

Orthopedic Cons Cincinnati.................. E 513 232-6677
Cincinnati *(G-3171)*

Orthopedic Cons Cincinnati.................. E 513 245-2500
Cincinnati *(G-3172)*

Orthopedic Cons Cincinnati.................. E 513 347-9999
Cincinnati *(G-3173)*

Orthopedic Cons Cincinnati.................. E 937 393-6169
Hillsboro *(G-9265)*

▲ **Orthopedic Cons Cincinnati**.............. E 513 733-8894
West Chester *(G-14738)*

Orthopedic One Inc.............................. D 614 827-8700
Columbus *(G-6480)*

Orthopedic One Inc.............................. E 614 570-4419
Dublin *(G-8083)*

Orthopedic One Inc.............................. E 614 488-1816
Hilliard *(G-9225)*

Orthopedic One Inc.............................. E 614 839-2300
Westerville *(G-14925)*

Orthopedic One Inc.............................. E 614 545-7900
Columbus *(G-6481)*

Orthorpdics Mltspcialty Netwrk.......... E 330 493-1630
Canton *(G-1826)*

Osu Internal Medicine LLC................... D 614 688-6400
Columbus *(G-6484)*

OSu Spt Mdcine Physcians Inc............ E 614 293-3600
Columbus *(G-6486)*

Osu Surgery LLC.................................. C 614 261-1141
Columbus *(G-6487)*

Our Lady Bellefonte Hosp Inc.............. A 606 833-3333
Cincinnati *(G-3176)*

P C Vpa.. E 614 840-1688
Columbus *(G-6495)*

Pain Care Specialists LLC..................... E 614 865-2120
Dublin *(G-8086)*

Pain Evlation MGT Ctr Ohio Inc........... E 937 439-4949
Dayton *(G-7545)*

Pain Management Group LLC............... E 419 462-4547
Galion *(G-8750)*

Pain Spcialists Cincinnati LLC............. E 513 922-2204
Cincinnati *(G-3181)*

Pajka Eye Center Inc........................... E 419 228-7432
Lima *(G-9946)*

Paragon Obstetrics & Gyne Asso....... D 330 665-8270
Akron *(G-260)*

Parkway Surgery Center Inc................ D
Toledo *(G-13959)*

Passport Health LLC............................. C 614 453-3920
Dublin *(G-8088)*

Patricia A Dickerson MD....................... E 937 436-1117
Dayton *(G-7547)*

Pediatric Adlscent Mdicine Inc............ E 614 326-1600
Columbus *(G-6509)*

Pediatric Assoc Youngstown............... E 330 965-7454
Youngstown *(G-15691)*

Pediatric Associates Inc...................... E 614 501-7337
Columbus *(G-6510)*

Pediatric Ophthlmlogy Assoc In.......... D 614 224-6222
Columbus *(G-6511)*

Pediatric Services Inc.......................... E 440 845-1500
Cleveland *(G-4735)*

Peri Natal Partners LLC........................ D 937 208-6970
Dayton *(G-7550)*

Perry County Fmly Practice Inc........... D 740 342-3435
New Lexington *(G-11631)*

Physicans Srgons For Women Inc....... E 937 323-7340
Springfield *(G-13282)*

Physicians Care of Marietta................ D 740 373-2519
Marietta *(G-10398)*

Piqua Family Practice........................... E 937 773-6314
Dayton *(G-7554)*

Plastic Srgery Inst Dayton Inc............ E 937 886-2980
Dayton *(G-7556)*

Polaris Pkwy Intrnal Mdcine Pd.......... E 614 865-4800
Westerville *(G-14929)*

Portsmouth Hospital Corp.................... A 740 991-4000
Portsmouth *(G-12565)*

Premier Integrated Med Assoc............ D 937 291-6813
Dayton *(G-7561)*

Premier Sports Medicine...................... E 937 312-1661
Centerville *(G-1950)*

Preterm Foundation.............................. E 216 991-4577
Cleveland *(G-4770)*

Primary Care Ntwrk Prmier Hlth......... E 937 424-9800
Dayton *(G-7562)*

Primary Care Ntwrk Prmier Hlth......... E 937 836-5170
Englewood *(G-8319)*

Primary Care Ntwrk Prmier Hlth......... E 937 743-5965
Franklin *(G-8647)*

Primary Care Ntwrk Prmier Hlth......... E 513 988-6369
Trenton *(G-14124)*

Primary Care Ntwrk Prmier Hlth......... E 937 278-5854
Vandalia *(G-14387)*

Primary Care Nursing Services............ E 614 764-0960
Dublin *(G-8096)*

Primary Cr Ntwrk Prmr Hlth Prt......... E 937 208-7000
Beavercreek *(G-895)*

Primary Cr Ntwrk Prmr Hlth Prt......... E 937 208-9090
Dayton *(G-7564)*

Primary Cr Ntwrk Prmr Hlth Prt......... E 513 492-5940
Mason *(G-10595)*

Primary Cr Ntwrk Prmr Hlth Prt......... E 513 420-5233
Middletown *(G-11201)*

Primary Cr Ntwrk Prmr Hlth Prt......... E 937 890-6644
Vandalia *(G-14388)*

Primary Cr Ntwrk Prmr Hlth Prt......... E 937 226-7085
Dayton *(G-7563)*

Primed Kettering Pediatrics................. E 937 433-7991
Dayton *(G-7566)*

Primed Physicians................................. D 937 237-4945
Dayton *(G-7567)*

Primed Physicians................................. E 937 298-8058
Dayton *(G-7568)*

80 HEALTH SERVICES

Professional Radiology Inc .... E 513 872-4500
  Blue Ash *(G-1225)*
Professionals For Womens Hlth .... E 614 268-8800
  Columbus *(G-6550)*
Professnl Psychiatric Svcs LLC .... E 513 229-7585
  Mason *(G-10596)*
Promedica Health System Inc .... B 419 534-6600
  Toledo *(G-13971)*
Promedica Toledo Hospital .... A 419 291-4000
  Toledo *(G-13976)*
Proscan Imaging LLC .... D 513 281-3400
  Cincinnati *(G-3254)*
Psycare Inc .... E 330 856-6663
  Warren *(G-14549)*
Pulmonary Critical Care and SL .... E 513 893-5864
  Hamilton *(G-9076)*
Pulmonary Crtcal Care Cons Inc .... E 937 461-5815
  Dayton *(G-7573)*
Pulmonary Rehabilitation .... E 330 758-7575
  Youngstown *(G-15701)*
Queen City Physicians .... A 513 872-2061
  Cincinnati *(G-3263)*
Quick Med Urgent Care LLC .... C 234 320-7770
  Salem *(G-12850)*
Radiology Associates Athens .... E 740 593-5551
  Athens *(G-586)*
Radiology Physicians Inc .... E 614 717-9840
  Delaware *(G-7822)*
Rakesh Ranjan MD & Assoc Inc .... D 440 324-4555
  Elyria *(G-8289)*
Regency Park Surgery Ctr LLC .... E 419 882-0003
  Toledo *(G-13984)*
Reid Physician Associates Inc .... B 937 456-4400
  Eaton *(G-8222)*
Retina Associate of Cleveland .... E 216 831-5700
  Beachwood *(G-830)*
Reynolds Road Surgical Ctr LLC .... E 419 578-7500
  Toledo *(G-13990)*
▲ Rgh Enterprises LLC .... A 330 963-6996
  Twinsburg *(G-14216)*
Richmond Medical Center .... B 440 585-6500
  Richmond Heights *(G-12722)*
Riverhills Healthcare Inc .... E 513 241-2370
  Cincinnati *(G-3306)*
Riverside Nephrology Assoc Inc .... E 614 538-2250
  Columbus *(G-6596)*
Riverside Pulmonary Assoc Inc .... E 614 267-8585
  Columbus *(G-6597)*
Riverside Rdlgy Intrvntnal Ass .... E 614 340-7747
  Columbus *(G-6598)*
Riverside Surgical Associates .... E 614 261-1900
  Columbus *(G-6599)*
Riverview Health Institute .... D 937 222-5390
  Dayton *(G-7595)*
Robert Wiley MD Inc .... E 216 621-3211
  Cleveland *(G-4847)*
Robinson Health System Inc .... A 330 562-3169
  Aurora *(G-625)*
Robinson Health System Inc .... A 330 626-3455
  Streetsboro *(G-13426)*
Robinson Health System Inc .... A 330 297-0811
  Ravenna *(G-12643)*
Roholt Vision Institute Inc .... E 330 702-8755
  Canfield *(G-1639)*
Roosevelt Surgical Associates .... E 513 424-0941
  Middletown *(G-11185)*
Russell Weisman Jr MD .... E 216 844-3127
  Cleveland *(G-4864)*
Salem Community Hospital .... E 330 482-2265
  Columbiana *(G-5241)*
Sandusky Orthopedic Surgeons .... E 419 625-4900
  Sandusky *(G-12929)*

Saras Garden .... D 419 335-7272
  Wauseon *(G-14608)*
Schoenbrunn Healthcare .... A 330 339-3595
  New Philadelphia *(G-11666)*
Scottcare Crdvscular Solutions .... E 216 362-0550
  Cleveland *(G-4886)*
Seven Hill Anesthesia LLC .... E 513 865-5204
  Cincinnati *(G-3363)*
Shawneespring Hlth Cre Cntr Rl .... D 513 943-4000
  Loveland *(G-10160)*
Shriners International Hdqtr .... D 800 875-8580
  Cincinnati *(G-3373)*
Signature Dermatology LLC .... E 614 777-1200
  Hilliard *(G-9231)*
Skgai Holdings Inc .... D 330 493-1480
  Canton *(G-1853)*
Sleepmed Incorporated .... E 440 716-8139
  North Olmsted *(G-11915)*
South Dayton Family Physicians .... E 937 208-7400
  Dayton *(G-7627)*
South Dyton Acute Care Cons In .... C 937 433-8990
  Dayton *(G-7628)*
South Dyton Urlgcal Asscations .... E 937 294-1489
  Dayton *(G-7629)*
Southast Cmnty Mental Hlth Ctr .... C 614 225-0980
  Columbus *(G-6694)*
Southern Ohio Medical Center .... D 740 947-7662
  Waverly *(G-14619)*
Southstern Ohio Physicians Inc .... E 740 432-5685
  Cambridge *(G-1583)*
Southwest Anesthesia Svcs Inc .... E 419 897-8370
  Maumee *(G-10767)*
Southwest Fmly Physicians Inc .... E 440 816-2750
  Cleveland *(G-4922)*
Southwest Ohio Ambltory Srgery .... E 513 425-0930
  Middletown *(G-11186)*
Southwest Urology LLC .... E 440 845-0900
  Cleveland *(G-4924)*
Spectrum Eye Care Inc .... E 419 423-8665
  Findlay *(G-8585)*
Spectrum Orthpedics Inc Canton .... D 330 455-5367
  North Canton *(G-11862)*
Springdale Family Medicine PC .... E 513 771-7213
  Cincinnati *(G-3400)*
Springfeld Ctr For Fmly Mdcine .... E 937 399-7777
  Springfield *(G-13292)*
Stahl Vision Laser Surgery Ctr .... E 937 643-2020
  Dayton *(G-7638)*
Stark County Neurologists Inc .... E 330 494-2097
  Canton *(G-1859)*
Summit Ophthalmology Inc .... D 330 899-9641
  Uniontown *(G-14266)*
Surgery Center Canfield LLC .... E 330 449-0030
  Canfield *(G-1642)*
Surgery Ctr An Ohio Ltd Partnr .... C 440 826-3240
  Cleveland *(G-4968)*
Surgery Ctr At Southwoods LLC .... C 330 729-8000
  Youngstown *(G-15732)*
Surgical Assoc Springfield Inc .... E 937 521-1111
  Springfield *(G-13297)*
Surgical Partners Inc .... E 419 841-6600
  Toledo *(G-14030)*
Swrh Physicians Inc .... D 330 923-5899
  Stow *(G-13397)*
System Optics Csmt Srgcal Arts .... E 330 630-9699
  Tallmadge *(G-13607)*
Taylor Stn Surgical Ctr Ltd .... D 614 751-4466
  Columbus *(G-6750)*
Theken Spine LLC .... C 330 733-7600
  Akron *(G-333)*
Three Gables Surgery Ctr LLC .... C 740 886-9911
  Proctorville *(G-12615)*

Toledo Cardiology Cons Inc .... E 419 251-6183
  Toledo *(G-14053)*
Toledo Clinic Inc .... D 419 841-1600
  Toledo *(G-14055)*
Toledo Clinic Inc .... D 419 330-5288
  Wauseon *(G-14609)*
▲ Toledo Clinic Inc .... B 419 473-3561
  Toledo *(G-14054)*
Township of Colerain .... D 513 741-7551
  Cincinnati *(G-3497)*
Tri County Family Physicians .... E 614 837-6363
  Canal Winchester *(G-1617)*
Tri County Mental Health Svcs .... D 740 592-3091
  Athens *(G-593)*
Tri State Urlogic Svcs PSC Inc .... D 513 841-7400
  Cincinnati *(G-3503)*
Tri State Urologic Svcs PSC .... C 513 681-2700
  Cincinnati *(G-3504)*
Trihealth Inc .... C 513 891-1627
  Blue Ash *(G-1257)*
Trihealth Inc .... B 513 481-9700
  Cincinnati *(G-3506)*
Trihealth Inc .... C 513 931-2400
  Cincinnati *(G-3507)*
Trihealth Inc .... C 513 389-1400
  Cincinnati *(G-3508)*
Trihealth Inc .... E 513 853-4900
  Cincinnati *(G-3515)*
Trihealth Inc .... C 513 867-0015
  Fairfield Township *(G-8466)*
Trihealth Inc .... C 513 874-3990
  Hamilton *(G-9087)*
Trihealth Inc .... C 513 282-7300
  Lebanon *(G-9794)*
Trihealth Inc .... A 513 985-0900
  Montgomery *(G-11378)*
Trihealth G LLC .... C 513 862-1888
  Cincinnati *(G-3521)*
Trihealth G LLC .... E 513 922-1200
  Cincinnati *(G-3522)*
Trihealth G LLC .... E 513 792-4700
  Cincinnati *(G-3523)*
Trihealth G LLC .... E 513 398-3445
  Mason *(G-10619)*
Trihealth G LLC .... D 513 732-0700
  Cincinnati *(G-3520)*
Trihealth Oncology Inst LLC .... D 513 451-4033
  Cincinnati *(G-3524)*
Trihealth Os LLC .... E 513 985-3700
  Cincinnati *(G-3525)*
Trinity Health System .... B 740 283-7000
  Steubenville *(G-13346)*
Trinity Hospital Twin City .... B 740 922-2800
  Dennison *(G-7858)*
Trumbll-Mahoning Med Group Inc .... E 330 372-8800
  Cortland *(G-6976)*
Uc Health Llc .... D 513 475-7880
  Cincinnati *(G-3542)*
Uc Health Llc .... D 513 271-5111
  Cincinnati *(G-3543)*
Uc Health Llc .... D 513 648-9077
  Cincinnati *(G-3544)*
Uc Health Llc .... D 513 584-6999
  Mason *(G-10622)*
Uc Health Llc .... D 513 475-8050
  Milford *(G-11264)*
Uc Health Llc .... D 513 475-7777
  West Chester *(G-14781)*
Uc Health Llc .... A 513 585-6000
  Cincinnati *(G-3546)*
Uc Health Partners LLC .... E 513 475-8524
  Cincinnati *(G-3547)*

Employee Codes: A=Over 500 employees, B=251-500
C=101-250, D=51-100, E=20-50, F=10-19, G=1-9

80 HEALTH SERVICES

Uhmg Department of Urologist.............. E 216 844-3009
   Cleveland *(G-5047)*

Union County Physician Corp............... C 800 686-4677
   Marysville *(G-10514)*

Union Hospital Association..................... A 330 343-3311
   Dover *(G-7907)*

Unity Health Network LLC................... E 330 678-7782
   Kent *(G-9605)*

Unity Health Network LLC................... E 330 626-0549
   Streetsboro *(G-13434)*

Univ Dermatology................................... E 513 475-7630
   Cincinnati *(G-3559)*

University Cncnnati Physcans I.............. E 513 475-8521
   Cincinnati *(G-3565)*

University Ear Nose Throat Spc............. C 513 475-8403
   Cincinnati *(G-3566)*

University Family Physicians.................. E 513 929-0104
   Cincinnati *(G-3568)*

University Family Physicians.................. E 513 475-7505
   Cincinnati *(G-3569)*

University GYN&ob Cnsltnts Inc............ E 614 293-8697
   Columbus *(G-6823)*

University Hsptals Clvland Med.............. A 216 378-6240
   Beachwood *(G-849)*

University Hsptals Clvland Med.............. A 216 342-5556
   Beachwood *(G-850)*

University Hsptals Clvland Med.............. A 440 499-5900
   Broadview Heights *(G-1403)*

University Hsptals Clvland Med.............. A 440 205-5755
   Mentor *(G-11007)*

University Mednet.................................... C 440 285-9079
   Bedford *(G-992)*

University Mednet.................................... C 440 255-0800
   Mentor *(G-11008)*

University Neurology Inc........................ E 513 475-8730
   Cincinnati *(G-3571)*

University of Cincinnati........................... E 513 558-4194
   Cincinnati *(G-3572)*

University of Cincinnati........................... B 513 558-1200
   Cincinnati *(G-3573)*

University of Cincinnati........................... D 513 584-0618
   Cincinnati *(G-3574)*

University of Cincinnati........................... C 513 475-8771
   Cincinnati *(G-3575)*

University of Cincinnati Phys.................. C 513 475-7934
   Cincinnati *(G-3595)*

University of Cincinnati Phys.................. D 513 475-8000
   West Chester *(G-14788)*

University of Toledo................................ E 419 383-5322
   Toledo *(G-14087)*

University Ophthlmlogy Assoc I............ E 216 382-8022
   Cleveland *(G-5084)*

University Otlryngologists Inc............... E 614 273-2241
   Columbus *(G-6824)*

University Prmry Care Prctices............... E 440 808-1283
   Westlake *(G-15122)*

University Radiology Assoc.................... D 513 475-8760
   Cincinnati *(G-3596)*

University Suburban Health Ctr............. E 216 382-8920
   Cleveland *(G-5087)*

Universty of Cincinnti Medcl C.............. A 513 475-8000
   Cincinnati *(G-3597)*

Upper Valley Medical Center.................. B 937 440-7107
   Dayton *(G-7694)*

Upper Valley Medical Center.................. A 937 440-4000
   Troy *(G-14166)*

Uppervalley Professional Corp............... E 937 440-4000
   Troy *(G-14168)*

UPS Family Health Center North........... D 330 364-8038
   Dover *(G-7908)*

Urgent Care Specialists LLC.................... D 614 472-2880
   Columbus *(G-6831)*

Urgent Care Specialists LLC.................... D 614 272-1100
   Columbus *(G-6832)*

Urgent Care Specialists LLC.................... D 614 263-4400
   Columbus *(G-6833)*

Urgent Care Specialists LLC.................... D 614 505-7601
   Columbus *(G-6834)*

Urgent Care Specialists LLC.................... D 937 236-8630
   Dayton *(G-7696)*

Urgent Care Specialists LLC.................... D 614 835-0400
   Groveport *(G-9009)*

Urgent Care Specialists LLC.................... D 937 322-6222
   Springfield *(G-13308)*

Urgent Care Specialists LLC.................... D 330 505-9400
   Warren *(G-14569)*

Urology Center LLC................................ E 513 841-7500
   Cincinnati *(G-3601)*

Urology Group Inc.................................. E 513 662-0222
   Cincinnati *(G-3602)*

US Acute Care Solutions LLC................. C 800 828-0898
   Canton *(G-1876)*

US Healthcare System............................. D 513 585-1821
   Cincinnati *(G-3605)*

US Teleradiology LLC............................. E 678 904-2599
   Hudson *(G-9376)*

Usacs Management Group Ltd.............. D 330 493-4443
   Canton *(G-1877)*

Usacs Medical Group Ltd...................... D 330 493-4443
   Canton *(G-1878)*

Van Wert Family Physicians LLC............ E 419 238-6251
   Van Wert *(G-14358)*

Vein Clinics of America Inc.................... E 630 725-2700
   Cincinnati *(G-3617)*

Veterans Health Administration............. A 740 773-1141
   Chillicothe *(G-2093)*

Veterans Health Administration............. A 513 861-3100
   Cincinnati *(G-3627)*

Veterans Health Administration............. A 216 791-3800
   Cleveland *(G-5101)*

Veterans Health Administration............. D 614 257-5200
   Columbus *(G-6848)*

Veterans Health Administration............. C 614 257-5524
   Columbus *(G-6849)*

Veterans Health Administration............. A 937 268-6511
   Dayton *(G-7705)*

Vision Associates Inc............................. E 419 578-7598
   Toledo *(G-14093)*

▲ Volk Optical Inc.................................... D 440 942-6161
   Mentor *(G-11010)*

Waterville Fmly Physicians Inc............... E 419 878-2026
   Waterville *(G-14596)*

Wellcare Physicians Group LLC............. E 419 891-8541
   Maumee *(G-10779)*

Wellnow Urgent Care PC........................ D 937 236-8630
   Dayton *(G-7716)*

West Central Ohio Group Ltd................ D 419 224-7586
   Lima *(G-9981)*

West Chster Dntstry Dr Jffrey................. E 330 753-7734
   Akron *(G-359)*

West Cntl Ohio Srgery Endscopy........... E 419 226-8700
   Lima *(G-9982)*

West Market St Fmly Physicians............. E 419 229-4747
   Lima *(G-9983)*

West Side Pediatrics Inc......................... E 513 922-8200
   Cincinnati *(G-3658)*

Westerville Family Physicians................ E 614 899-2700
   Westerville *(G-14952)*

Westerville Internal Medicine................. E 614 891-8080
   Westerville *(G-14953)*

White Fnce Surgical Suites LLC.............. E 614 289-6282
   New Albany *(G-11592)*

Whole Health Management Inc............. E 216 921-8601
   Cleveland *(G-5146)*

Wlkop LLC... C 440 892-2100
   Westlake *(G-15125)*

Womens Care Inc.................................... E 419 756-6000
   Mansfield *(G-10326)*

Wood Health Company LLC.................. D 419 353-7069
   Bowling Green *(G-1337)*

Wooster Ambltory Srgery Ctr LL........... E 330 804-2000
   Wooster *(G-15389)*

Wooster Cmnty Hosp Blmngton ME..... D 330 263-8100
   Wooster *(G-15392)*

Wooster Community Hosp Aux Inc....... D 330 263-8389
   Wooster *(G-15393)*

Wooster Ent Associates Inc................... E 330 264-9699
   Wooster *(G-15394)*

Wooster Ophthalmologists Inc.............. E 330 345-7800
   Wooster *(G-15397)*

Wooster Orthpdics Sprtsmdcine............ E 330 804-9712
   Wooster *(G-15398)*

Wpafb Medical Center............................ E 937 522-2778
   Wright Patterson Afb *(G-15475)*

Wright State Physcans Drmtlogy........... D 937 401-1100
   Dayton *(G-7727)*

Wright State Physicians Inc.................. C 937 208-3999
   Dayton *(G-7728)*

Wright State University........................... D 937 208-2177
   Dayton *(G-7729)*

Yeater Alene K MD................................. E 740 348-4694
   Newark *(G-11756)*

Yellow Springs Primary Care.................. E 937 767-1088
   Yellow Springs *(G-15536)*

Youngstown Orthopedic Assoc Ltd....... E 330 726-1466
   Canfield *(G-1646)*

Zanesville Surgery Center LLC............... E 740 453-5713
   Zanesville *(G-15842)*

8021 Offices and clinics of dentists

Advance Implant Dentistry Inc.............. D 513 271-0821
   Cincinnati *(G-2146)*

▲ Ashtabula Dental Assoc Inc............... E 440 992-3146
   Ashtabula *(G-525)*

Blue Tooth Dental................................... D 937 432-6677
   Dayton *(G-7195)*

Buckeye Oral & Maxillofacial.................. E 740 392-2000
   Mount Vernon *(G-11477)*

Cabi C Aydin DDS Inc............................. E 330 562-1644
   Aurora *(G-610)*

Childrens Dntl Spclsts Lk Cnty.............. E 440 266-1740
   Mentor *(G-10921)*

Cincinnati Dental Services..................... D 513 721-8888
   Cincinnati *(G-2408)*

Cleveland Dental Institute LLC.............. E 216 727-0234
   Cleveland *(G-4040)*

Concorde Therapy Group Inc................ C 330 493-4210
   Canton *(G-1721)*

Courtney W Fleming DDS L.................. E 614 263-4040
   Columbus *(G-5711)*

David Harnett DDS Inc........................... E 330 638-3065
   Cortland *(G-6971)*

Dean A Carmichael.................................. E 216 524-8481
   Cleveland *(G-4156)*

Dental Assoc Newton FLS Inc................ E 330 872-5737
   Newton Falls *(G-11774)*

Dental Center Northwest Ohio............... E 419 241-6215
   Toledo *(G-13776)*

Dental Group At North Hamilton........... D 614 351-0555
   Columbus *(G-5755)*

Dental Health Assoc............................... E 419 882-4510
   Sylvania *(G-13540)*

▲ Dental Health Services........................ E 330 864-9090
   Fairlawn *(G-8474)*

Dental Support Specialties LLC.............. E 330 639-1333
   Canton *(G-1734)*

SIC SECTION 80 HEALTH SERVICES

Dentalcare Partners Inc............................... A 216 584-1000
  Independence *(G-9428)*
Dentalone Partners Inc............................... C 440 934-0147
  Avon *(G-649)*
Dentalone Partners Inc............................... C 614 356-7245
  Columbus *(G-5257)*
Dentalone Partners Inc............................... C 844 214-4179
  Stow *(G-13363)*
Dentalone Partners Inc............................... C 440 238-1591
  Strongsville *(G-13452)*
Dentalone Partners Inc............................... C 419 534-3005
  Toledo *(G-13777)*
Dr Gerald F Johnson DDS Inc................... D 513 683-8333
  Loveland *(G-10136)*
Empire Dental Arts LLC................................ E 216 410-1331
  Mentor *(G-10936)*
Equitas Health Inc.. D 614 299-2437
  Columbus *(G-5825)*
Eric W Warnock.. E 419 228-2233
  Lima *(G-9887)*
Family Dental Team Inc................................ E 330 733-7911
  Akron *(G-153)*
Frankel Dental.. E 419 474-9611
  Toledo *(G-13812)*
Gordon W Womack DDS............................. E 937 426-2653
  Beavercreek *(G-881)*
Grove City Ctr For Dentistry........................ E 614 875-3141
  Grove City *(G-8922)*
Hani Ashqar DDS & Partners LLC.............. E 203 560-3131
  Euclid *(G-8344)*
Healthsource of Ohio Inc............................. E 937 386-0049
  Seaman *(G-12944)*
Henry J Fioritto DDS Inc.............................. E 440 951-5511
  Mentor *(G-10946)*
Institute of Jaw Fcial Srgery....................... D 330 493-1605
  Canton *(G-1780)*
J Clarke Sanders DDS Inc........................... E 614 864-3196
  Pickerington *(G-12404)*
John A Hudec DDS Inc................................ D 216 398-8900
  Cleveland *(G-4439)*
Joshua M Halderman DDS LLC.................. E 614 309-1474
  Galloway *(G-8772)*
Lake Hospital System Inc............................. C 440 255-8133
  Mentor *(G-10961)*
Lakireddy Dental LLC.................................. D 330 439-0355
  Macedonia *(G-10198)*
Langstonmc Kenna Lesia........................... E 937 393-1472
  Hillsboro *(G-9262)*
Lawrence M Shell DDS............................... E 614 235-3444
  Columbus *(G-6146)*
Merkley Professionals Inc........................... E 419 447-9541
  Tiffin *(G-13633)*
Merrill Swanson DDS LLC........................... E 419 884-3411
  Mansfield *(G-10296)*
Metro Health Dental Associates................. C 216 778-4982
  Cleveland *(G-4560)*
Metrohealth System.................................... A 216 957-1500
  Cleveland *(G-4562)*
Monarch Dental Corp.................................. E 440 324-2310
  Elyria *(G-8275)*
Monarch Dental Corp.................................. E 440 282-6677
  Lorain *(G-10093)*
Monarch Dental Corp.................................. E 937 684-4845
  Miamisburg *(G-11073)*
Monarch Dental Corp.................................. E 937 778-0150
  Piqua *(G-12450)*
Morris Kent Orthodontics Inc..................... E 513 226-0459
  Montgomery *(G-11369)*
North American Dental MGT LLC............... A 330 721-0606
  Medina *(G-10868)*
North American Dental MGT LLC............... A 740 498-5155
  Newcomerstown *(G-11773)*

Ollom Dental Group LLC............................. C 614 392-8090
  Westerville *(G-15008)*
Oral & Facial Surgery Assoc....................... E 513 791-0550
  Montgomery *(G-11372)*
Oral Fcial Srgons Ohio Rchard.................. E 614 764-9455
  Dublin *(G-8082)*
Orthodontic Associates LLC....................... E 419 229-8771
  Celina *(G-1929)*
Periodontal Associates Inc......................... E 440 461-3400
  Cleveland *(G-4740)*
Rahn Dental Group Inc............................... E 937 435-0324
  Dayton *(G-7579)*
Rankin Wiesenburger and Otto................... D 419 539-2160
  Toledo *(G-13981)*
Raymond A Greiner DDS Inc...................... E 440 951-6688
  Mentor *(G-10987)*
Raymond H Vecchio.................................... E 440 365-9580
  Elyria *(G-8291)*
Rinaldi Orthodontics Inc............................. E 513 831-6160
  Milford *(G-11253)*
Robert E Davis DDS Ms Inc........................ E 614 878-7887
  Columbus *(G-6603)*
Rogers Family Dentistry Inc....................... D 513 231-1012
  Cincinnati *(G-3317)*
Rummell Dvid G Schmcher Mike R............ E 614 451-1110
  Columbus *(G-6619)*
Ryan G Harris DMD..................................... E 937 426-5411
  Beavercreek *(G-903)*
Smiley Samuel E DDS PC........................... E 614 889-0726
  Dublin *(G-8122)*
Stow Dental Group Inc................................ E 330 688-6456
  Stow *(G-13393)*
Strauss Gerald DDS Inc.............................. E 937 642-8500
  Marysville *(G-10512)*
Streem-Rsnick Ttelman Young PC............. E 440 461-8200
  Cleveland *(G-4956)*
Testerman Dental.. E 513 932-4806
  Lebanon *(G-9793)*
Trio Orthodontics... E 614 889-7613
  Plain City *(G-12496)*
Tuscarwas Oral Mxllfcial Srger................... E 330 364-8665
  New Philadelphia *(G-11670)*
West Chster Dntstry Dr Jffrey..................... E 330 753-7734
  Akron *(G-359)*
William J Hagerty DDS Inc.......................... E 937 434-3987
  Dayton *(G-7723)*

8031 Offices and clinics of osteopathic physicians

Adena Health System.................................. E 740 779-7201
  Chillicothe *(G-2046)*
Childrens Hosp Med Ctr Akron.................. D 330 253-4931
  Akron *(G-89)*
Childrens Hosp Med Ctr Akron.................. D 330 543-8639
  Akron *(G-91)*
Childrens Hosp Med Ctr Akron.................. D 330 746-8040
  Boardman *(G-1286)*
Christ Hospital... D 513 561-7809
  Cincinnati *(G-2384)*
Cleveland Clinic Foundation....................... E 614 358-4223
  Columbus *(G-5583)*
Cleveland Clinic Foundation....................... E 419 660-6946
  Norwalk *(G-12006)*
Davis Eye Center Inc.................................. D 330 923-5676
  Cuyahoga Falls *(G-7069)*
Dayton Childrens Hospital.......................... D 513 424-2850
  Middletown *(G-11195)*
Dayton Fmly Practice Assoc Inc................ E 937 254-5661
  Dayton *(G-7282)*
Doctors Pain Center LLC........................... D 330 629-2888
  Youngstown *(G-15599)*

Grandview Family Practice Inc................... E 740 258-9267
  Columbus *(G-5944)*
Healthsource of Ohio Inc............................ E 937 386-0049
  Seaman *(G-12944)*
Heritage Valley Health Sys Inc.................... D 724 773-8209
  East Liverpool *(G-8183)*
Hometown Urgent Care............................... D 937 372-6012
  Xenia *(G-15521)*
Internal Mdcine Cons of Clmbus................ D 614 878-6413
  Columbus *(G-6067)*
Lake Hospital System Inc........................... C 440 352-0646
  Concord Township *(G-6928)*
Medical Assessments LLC.......................... E 216 397-0917
  Cleveland *(G-4544)*
Ohio Heart Group Inc.................................. E 740 348-0012
  Newark *(G-11737)*
Robinson Health System Inc...................... A 330 562-3169
  Aurora *(G-625)*
Southern Ohio Medical Center................... D 740 947-7662
  Waverly *(G-14619)*
Sports Medicine Grant Inc......................... E 614 461-8174
  Columbus *(G-6705)*

8041 Offices and clinics of chiropractors

◆ Boxout LLC.. C 833 462-7746
  Hudson *(G-9334)*
Healthquest Fields Ertel Inc....................... D 513 774-9800
  Cincinnati *(G-2811)*
Healthsource Chiropractic Inc................... E 440 934-5858
  Avon *(G-653)*
Lbi Starbucks DC 3...................................... D 614 415-6363
  Columbus *(G-6149)*
Medquest Health Center Inc...................... E 740 417-4567
  Delaware *(G-7818)*
Miami Valley Hospital.................................. B 937 208-7450
  Dayton *(G-7489)*
R & R Chiropractic....................................... E 419 425-2225
  Attica *(G-601)*

8042 Offices and clinics of optometrists

Cambridge Eye Associates Inc.................. C 513 527-9700
  West Chester *(G-14657)*
Cleveland Clinic Foundation...................... D 216 636-7400
  Independence *(G-9420)*
Dickman Kettler & Bruner Ltd.................... E 419 678-3016
  Coldwater *(G-5212)*
Eyemed Vision.. D 330 995-0597
  Aurora *(G-612)*
Optivue Inc... E 419 891-1391
  Oregon *(G-12138)*
Ottivue.. D 419 693-4444
  Oregon *(G-12141)*
Shawnee Optical Inc................................... D 440 997-2020
  Ashtabula *(G-549)*
Student Vol Opt Serv To Humnty............... D 614 292-9086
  Columbus *(G-6724)*
Thomas Ritter Od Inc.................................. E 513 984-0202
  Blue Ash *(G-1254)*
Toledo Society For The Blind..................... E 419 720-3937
  Toledo *(G-14066)*

8043 Offices and clinics of podiatrists

Medicine Midwest LLC................................ E 937 435-8786
  Dayton *(G-7477)*
Toledo Clinic Inc.. D 419 381-9977
  Toledo *(G-14056)*
Unity Health Network LLC.......................... E 330 626-0549
  Streetsboro *(G-13434)*

8049 Offices of health practitioner

Aaris Therapy Group Inc............................. E 330 505-1606
  Niles *(G-11780)*

80 HEALTH SERVICES

Abilities First Foundation Inc................ D 513 423-9496
  Middletown *(G-11149)*
Accelerated Health Systems LLC........ E 614 334-5135
  Hilliard *(G-9175)*
Akron General Health System................ A 330 665-8200
  Akron *(G-30)*
Appleseed Cmnty Mntal Hlth Ctr............ D 419 281-3716
  Ashland *(G-472)*
Barrie G Glvin Otr/L Assoc Ltd............... E 216 514-1600
  Cleveland *(G-3852)*
Bittersweet Inc.. D 419 999-9174
  Lima *(G-9869)*
◆ Boxout LLC.. C 833 462-7746
  Hudson *(G-9334)*
Carington Health Systems..................... B 513 961-8881
  Cincinnati *(G-2315)*
Center For Cgntive Bhvral Thra............. E 614 459-4490
  Columbus *(G-5529)*
Center For Fmly Safety Healing............. E 614 722-5985
  Columbus *(G-5532)*
Central Ohio Prmry Care Physca........... D 614 442-7550
  Columbus *(G-5542)*
Christ Hospital... D 513 688-1111
  Cincinnati *(G-2379)*
Cleveland Clinic Foundation.................. E 419 660-6946
  Norwalk *(G-12006)*
Concorde Therapy Group Inc................ C 330 493-4210
  Canton *(G-1721)*
Correctnal Hlth Care Group Inc............. E 330 454-6766
  Canton *(G-1722)*
County of Cuyahoga................................ C 216 698-6526
  Cleveland *(G-4127)*
County of Hamilton.................................. E 513 946-8757
  Blue Ash *(G-1161)*
County of Wayne..................................... E 330 345-5891
  Wooster *(G-15331)*
Dietary Solutions Inc............................... D 614 985-6567
  Lewis Center *(G-9818)*
Encompass Care Inc.............................. C 419 999-2030
  Lima *(G-9886)*
Equitas Health Inc................................... D 614 299-2437
  Columbus *(G-5825)*
First Settlement Orthopaedics................ E 740 373-8756
  Marietta *(G-10368)*
Fulton County Health Center.................. D 419 335-1919
  Wauseon *(G-14600)*
Gemcare Wellness Inc............................ D 800 294-9176
  Hudson *(G-9353)*
Health Services Inc................................. E 330 837-7678
  Massillon *(G-10644)*
Healthquest Fields Ertel Inc................... D 513 774-9800
  Cincinnati *(G-2811)*
Hearinglife Usa Inc.................................. D 513 759-2999
  West Chester *(G-14707)*
Herman Bair Enterprise........................... E 330 262-4449
  Wooster *(G-15344)*
Hilty Memorial Home Inc........................ E 419 384-3218
  Pandora *(G-12246)*
Holzer Clinic LLC.................................... E 740 886-9403
  Proctorville *(G-12612)*
Homecare With Heart LLC..................... C 330 726-0700
  Youngstown *(G-15632)*
Hometown Urgent Care........................... E 513 831-5900
  Milford *(G-11231)*
Hometown Urgent Care........................... D 937 342-9520
  Springfield *(G-13254)*
Hometown Urgent Care........................... E 937 252-2000
  Wooster *(G-15345)*
Hometown Urgent Care........................... E 330 629-2300
  Youngstown *(G-15633)*
Jewish Home Cincinnati Inc................... B 513 754-3100
  Mason *(G-10569)*

Kettering Adventist Healthcare............... D 937 506-3112
  Tipp City *(G-13661)*
Knapp Ctr For Chldhood Dev LLC........ E 330 629-2955
  Youngstown *(G-15647)*
Maryhaven Inc... E 614 626-2432
  Columbus *(G-6201)*
Maxim Healthcare Services Inc............. C 740 772-4100
  Columbus *(G-6211)*
Medcentral Health System..................... B 419 683-1040
  Crestline *(G-7025)*
Medcentral Health System..................... C 419 342-5015
  Shelby *(G-13007)*
Medlink of Ohio Inc................................. B 216 751-5900
  Cleveland *(G-4547)*
Midwest Rehab Inc.................................. D 419 692-3405
  Ada *(G-3)*
Milan Skilled Nursing LLC...................... D 216 727-3996
  Milan *(G-11208)*
Mount Carmel Health.............................. C 614 234-4060
  Westerville *(G-14912)*
Nationwide Childrens Hospital............... C 614 355-7000
  Dublin *(G-8070)*
Ncs Healthcare Inc.................................. A 216 514-3350
  Cleveland *(G-4630)*
Newcomerstown Progress Corp............ C 740 498-5165
  Newcomerstown *(G-11772)*
Nova Care.. E 614 864-1089
  Columbus *(G-6273)*
Occupational Health Services................ E 937 492-7296
  Sidney *(G-13042)*
Ohio Living... C 614 228-8888
  Columbus *(G-6431)*
Ohio State University.............................. C 614 257-3000
  Columbus *(G-6453)*
Ohio-T-Home Hlth Care Agcy Ltd......... D 614 947-0791
  Columbus *(G-6464)*
Oxford Physcl Thrapy Rhblttion.............. E 513 549-1927
  Maineville *(G-10229)*
Oxford Physcl Thrapy Rhblttion.............. E 513 229-7560
  Mason *(G-10587)*
Oxford Physical Therapy Inc.................. E 513 745-9877
  Blue Ash *(G-1218)*
Oxford Physical Therapy Inc.................. E 513 469-1444
  Cincinnati *(G-3178)*
Oxford Physical Therapy Inc.................. E 513 229-7560
  Mason *(G-10588)*
Pastoral Cnsling Svc Smmit CNT.......... C 330 996-4600
  Akron *(G-262)*
Prohealth Partners Inc............................ D 419 491-7150
  Perrysburg *(G-12365)*
PSI Associates LLC................................ C 330 425-8474
  Twinsburg *(G-14214)*
Rehab Center.. C 330 297-2770
  Ravenna *(G-12641)*
Robinson Health System Inc.................. A 330 297-8844
  Ravenna *(G-12642)*
Salo Inc.. C 513 984-1110
  Cincinnati *(G-3345)*
Samaritan Regional Health Sys............. D 419 281-1330
  Ashland *(G-511)*
St Lukes Hospital.................................... A 419 441-1002
  Waterville *(G-14595)*
Steward Trumbull Mem Hosp Inc.......... A 330 841-9011
  Warren *(G-14561)*
Temenos... D 513 791-7022
  Blue Ash *(G-1252)*
Tky Associates LLC................................ E 419 535-7777
  Toledo *(G-14045)*
Toledo Clinic Inc..................................... D 419 479-5960
  Toledo *(G-14057)*
Trihealth Inc... C 513 751-5900
  Cincinnati *(G-3516)*

Trihealth G LLC....................................... E 513 922-1200
  Cincinnati *(G-3522)*
United Rhblttion Svcs Grter Dy.............. D 937 233-1230
  Dayton *(G-7683)*
Willcare Inc.. C 216 289-5300
  Cleveland *(G-5148)*
Wings of Change Therapy Inc............... E 330 715-6046
  Cuyahoga Falls *(G-7117)*
Wooster Cmnty Hosp Blmngton ME...... D 330 263-8100
  Wooster *(G-15392)*

8051 Skilled nursing care facilities

204 W Main Street Oper Co LLC........... E 419 929-1563
  New London *(G-11632)*
Addison Leasing Co LLC....................... E 513 530-1600
  Masury *(G-10677)*
Ahf Ohio Inc... D 937 256-4663
  Dayton *(G-7160)*
Ahf Ohio Inc... D 614 760-8870
  Dublin *(G-7923)*
Ahf Ohio Inc... D 740 532-6188
  Ironton *(G-9501)*
Ahf Ohio Inc... D 330 725-4123
  Medina *(G-10805)*
Ahf/Central States Inc............................ C 724 941-7150
  Dublin *(G-7924)*
Alexson Services Inc.............................. D 513 874-0423
  Fairfield *(G-8389)*
Algart Health Care Inc............................ D 216 631-1550
  Cleveland *(G-3787)*
Altenheim Foundation Inc....................... E 440 238-3361
  Strongsville *(G-13441)*
Altercare Inc.. E 330 929-4231
  Cuyahoga Falls *(G-7037)*
Altercare Inc.. E 330 335-2555
  Wadsworth *(G-14427)*
Altercare Inc.. E 440 327-5285
  North Ridgeville *(G-11922)*
Altercare Lsvlle Ctr For Rhblt................. E 330 875-4224
  Louisville *(G-10112)*
Altercare Nobles Pond Inc..................... E 330 834-4800
  Canton *(G-1663)*
Altercare of Bucyrus Inc......................... E 419 562-7644
  Bucyrus *(G-1495)*
Altercare of Mntor Ctr For Rhb.............. E 440 953-4421
  Mentor *(G-10910)*
Altercare of Ohio Inc............................... D 330 767-3458
  Navarre *(G-11536)*
American Eagle Hlth Care Svcs............ D 440 428-5103
  Madison *(G-10211)*
American Nursing Care Inc.................... B 513 731-4600
  Cincinnati *(G-2184)*
American Nursing Care Inc.................... C 513 245-1500
  Cincinnati *(G-2185)*
American Nursing Care Inc.................... B 937 438-3844
  Dayton *(G-7172)*
American Nursing Care Inc.................... B 614 847-0555
  Zanesville *(G-15767)*
American Nursing Care Inc.................... C 513 576-0262
  Loveland *(G-10126)*
American Retirement Corp..................... C 216 291-6140
  Cleveland *(G-3807)*
Amherst Manor Inc................................. B 440 988-4415
  Amherst *(G-422)*
Anchor Lodge Nursing Home Inc........... E 440 244-2019
  Lorain *(G-10054)*
Anderson Healthcare Ltd....................... E 513 474-6200
  Cincinnati *(G-2197)*
Andover Vlg Rtrement Cmnty Ltd......... D 440 293-5416
  Andover *(G-438)*
Anna Maria of Aurora Inc....................... D 330 562-3120
  Aurora *(G-604)*

SIC SECTION   80 HEALTH SERVICES

Anna Maria of Aurora Inc .... C 330 562-6171
　Aurora *(G-603)*

Apostolic Christian Home Inc .... D 330 927-1010
　Rittman *(G-12729)*

April Enterprises Inc .... C 937 293-7703
　Moraine *(G-11389)*

Arbors East LLC .... E 614 575-9003
　Columbus *(G-5377)*

Arbors West LLC .... E 614 879-7661
　West Jefferson *(G-14848)*

Aristocrat W Nursing Hm Corp .... C 216 252-7730
　Cleveland *(G-3834)*

Arlington Care Ctr .... B 740 344-0303
　Newark *(G-11688)*

Arlington Crt Nrsing HM Svc In .... D 614 545-5502
　Upper Arlington *(G-14276)*

Ashley Enterprises LLC .... D 330 726-5790
　Boardman *(G-1284)*

Assisted Living Concepts LLC .... E 419 334-6962
　Fremont *(G-8667)*

Assumption Village .... C 330 549-2434
　North Lima *(G-11882)*

Astoria Healthcare Group LLC .... D 937 855-2363
　Germantown *(G-8803)*

Astoria Place Columbus LLC .... D 614 228-5900
　Columbus *(G-5398)*

Astoria Place of Clyde LLC .... D 419 547-9595
　Clyde *(G-5198)*

Astoria Snf Inc .... E 330 455-5500
　Canton *(G-1671)*

Atrium Centers Inc .... E 614 416-0600
　Columbus *(G-5404)*

Atrium Living Centers of .... E 614 416-2662
　Columbus *(G-5405)*

Aurora Manor Ltd Partnership .... B 330 562-5000
　Aurora *(G-606)*

Autumn Aegis Inc .... B 440 282-6768
　Lorain *(G-10056)*

Autumn Court Operating Co LLC .... D 419 523-4370
　Ottawa *(G-12185)*

Autumn Hills Care Center Inc .... D 330 652-2053
　Niles *(G-11781)*

Aventura At Oakwood Vlg LLC .... C 937 390-9000
　Springfield *(G-13220)*

Avenue At Medina .... E 330 721-7001
　Medina *(G-10811)*

Balanced Care Corporation .... E 330 908-1166
　Northfield *(G-11952)*

Bath Manor Limited Partnership .... B 330 836-1006
　Akron *(G-62)*

Beaver Dam Health Care Center .... D 330 762-6486
　Akron *(G-64)*

Beaver Dam Health Care Center .... E 440 247-4200
　Chagrin Falls *(G-1953)*

Beaver Dam Health Care Center .... E 614 861-6666
　Columbus *(G-5429)*

Beaver Dam Health Care Center .... E 419 227-2154
　Lima *(G-9867)*

Beaver Dam Health Care Center .... E 330 335-1558
　Wadsworth *(G-14429)*

Beechwood Home .... E 513 321-9294
　Cincinnati *(G-2251)*

Beechwood Terrace Care Ctr Inc .... E 513 578-6200
　Cincinnati *(G-2252)*

Beeghly Nursing LLC .... D 330 884-2300
　Boardman *(G-1285)*

Bellevue Healthcare Group LLC .... E 419 483-6225
　Bellevue *(G-1041)*

Belmont County Home .... D 740 695-4925
　Saint Clairsville *(G-12775)*

Belmore Leasing Co LLC .... E 216 268-3600
　Cleveland *(G-3864)*

Bentley Leasing Co LLC .... A 330 337-9503
　Salem *(G-12839)*

Best Care Nrsing Rhblttion Ctr .... A 740 574-2558
　Wheelersburg *(G-15127)*

Bethany Nursing Home Inc .... E 330 492-7171
　Canton *(G-1686)*

Birchaven Village .... D 419 424-3000
　Findlay *(G-8512)*

Blossom Hills Nursing Home .... E 440 635-5567
　Huntsburg *(G-9381)*

Blue Ash Healthcare Group Inc .... E 513 793-3362
　Cincinnati *(G-2266)*

Blue Creek Healthcare LLC .... D 419 877-5338
　Whitehouse *(G-15139)*

Bluesky Healthcare Inc .... E 440 989-5200
　Lorain *(G-10061)*

Brecksville Leasing Co LLC .... E 330 659-6166
　Richfield *(G-12689)*

Brentwood Life Care Company .... C 330 468-2273
　Northfield *(G-11953)*

Brethren Care Inc .... E 419 289-0803
　Ashland *(G-484)*

Brethren Care Village LLC .... D 419 289-1585
　Ashland *(G-485)*

Brewster Parke Inc .... D 330 767-4179
　Brewster *(G-1373)*

Briar Hl Hlth Care Rsdence Inc .... D 440 632-5241
　Middlefield *(G-11138)*

Briarfield Manor LLC .... C 330 270-3468
　Youngstown *(G-15565)*

Briarwood Inc .... D 330 688-1828
　Stow *(G-13356)*

Broadview Nursing Home Inc .... D 216 661-5084
　Parma *(G-12250)*

Brook Willow Chrstn Cmmunities .... C 614 885-3300
　Columbus *(G-5468)*

Brookdale Lving Cmmunities Inc .... B 330 666-4545
　Akron *(G-76)*

Brookview Healthcare Ctr .... D 419 784-1014
　Defiance *(G-7742)*

Brookville Enterprises Inc .... C 937 833-2133
　Brookville *(G-1445)*

Brookwood Realty Company .... D 513 530-9555
　Cincinnati *(G-2283)*

Bryant Health Center Inc .... D 740 532-6188
　Ironton *(G-9504)*

Buckeye Frest Rsmount Pavilion .... C 740 354-4505
　Portsmouth *(G-12547)*

Burlington House Inc .... E 513 851-7888
　Cincinnati *(G-2292)*

Butler County of Ohio .... D 513 887-3728
　Hamilton *(G-9020)*

C Micah Rand Inc .... E 513 605-2000
　Cincinnati *(G-2298)*

Canterbury Vlla Oprations Corp .... E 330 821-4000
　Alliance *(G-377)*

Canton Asssted Lving Rhblttion .... E 330 492-7131
　Canton *(G-1697)*

Canton Christian Home Inc .... D 330 456-0004
　Canton *(G-1698)*

Capital Health Services Inc .... E 937 277-0505
　Miamisburg *(G-11033)*

Caprice Health Care Inc .... E 330 965-9200
　North Lima *(G-11885)*

Care One LLC .... E 937 236-6707
　Dayton *(G-7210)*

Carefor Place Nursing Home Inc .... E 513 481-2201
　Cincinnati *(G-2312)*

Careserve .... C 740 454-4000
　Zanesville *(G-15776)*

Caring Place Healthcare Group .... D 513 771-1779
　Cincinnati *(G-2314)*

Carington Health Systems .... A 513 732-6500
　Batavia *(G-730)*

Carington Health Systems .... B 513 961-8881
　Cincinnati *(G-2315)*

Carington Health Systems .... B 937 743-2754
　Franklin *(G-8632)*

Carington Health Systems .... E 513 682-2700
　Hamilton *(G-9025)*

Caritas Inc .... E 419 332-2589
　Fremont *(G-8668)*

Carlton Manor Nursing and .... C 740 335-7143
　Wshngtn Ct Hs *(G-15477)*

Carriage Inn Bowerston Inc .... E 740 269-8001
　Bowerston *(G-1301)*

Carriage Inn of Cadiz Inc .... D 740 942-8084
　Cadiz *(G-1538)*

Carriage Inn of Steubenville .... C 740 264-7161
　Steubenville *(G-13318)*

Carriage Inn of Trotwood Inc .... E 937 277-0505
　Miamisburg *(G-11034)*

Carriage Inn Rtrment Cmnty of .... D 937 278-0404
　Dayton *(G-7213)*

Carriage Inn Trotwood Inc .... E 937 854-1180
　Dayton *(G-7214)*

Cch Healthcare Oh LLC .... E 513 932-1121
　Lebanon *(G-9758)*

Cedar Hill Opco LLC .... D 740 454-6823
　Zanesville *(G-15777)*

Cedar Medical Group .... E 513 729-2300
　Cincinnati *(G-2331)*

Center Ridge Nursing Home Inc .... C 440 808-5500
　North Ridgeville *(G-11924)*

Centerburg Pnte Hlthcare Group .... C 740 625-5401
　Centerburg *(G-1932)*

Centerburg Two LLC .... D 740 625-5774
　Centerburg *(G-1933)*

CHI Living Communities .... C 419 627-2273
　Sandusky *(G-12879)*

Chillicothe Long-Term Care Inc .... C 740 773-6161
　Chillicothe *(G-2057)*

Chillicothe Long-Term Care Inc .... D 740 773-6470
　Cincinnati *(G-2372)*

CHS Norwood Inc .... E 513 242-1360
　Cincinnati *(G-2387)*

Chs-Norwood Inc .... C 513 351-7007
　Cincinnati *(G-2388)*

Church of God Retirement Cmnty .... E 513 422-5600
　Middletown *(G-11156)*

City View Nursing & Rehab LLC .... C 216 361-1414
　Cleveland *(G-3995)*

Clifton Care Center Inc .... E 513 530-1600
　Cincinnati *(G-2459)*

Clovernook Inc .... D 513 605-4000
　Cincinnati *(G-2462)*

Clovernook Inc .... E 513 605-4000
　Cincinnati *(G-2461)*

CMS & Co Management Svcs Inc .... D 440 989-5200
　Lorain *(G-10067)*

Coal Grove Long Term Care Inc .... E 740 532-0449
　Ironton *(G-9506)*

Colon Leasing Co LLC .... E 513 530-1600
　Tallmadge *(G-13589)*

Colonial Mnor Hlth Care Ctr In .... E 419 994-4191
　Loudonville *(G-10108)*

Columbus Alzheimers Care Ctr .... D 614 459-7050
　Columbus *(G-5607)*

Columbus Clny For Eldrly Care .... C 614 891-5055
　Westerville *(G-14969)*

Communi Care Inc .... E 419 382-2200
　Toledo *(G-13751)*

Communicare Health Svcs Inc .... D 440 234-0454
　Berea *(G-1066)*

Employee Codes: A=Over 500 employees, B=251-500
C=101-250, D=51-100, E=20-50, F=10-19, G=1-9

2024 Harris Ohio
Services Directory

80 HEALTH SERVICES

Communicare Health Svcs Inc .... E 330 454-6508
  Canton *(G-1719)*
Communicare Health Svcs Inc .... C 614 443-7210
  Columbus *(G-5668)*
Communicare Health Svcs Inc .... C 330 659-6166
  Richfield *(G-12692)*
Community Hlth Prfssionals Inc .... E 419 634-7443
  Ada *(G-1)*
Community Sklled Hlth Care CNT .... C 330 373-1160
  Warren *(G-14512)*
Concord Care Center of Toledo .... D 419 385-6616
  Toledo *(G-13757)*
Concord Care Ctr Cortland Inc .... E 330 637-7906
  Cortland *(G-6969)*
Concord Health Care Inc .... E 419 626-5373
  Sandusky *(G-12885)*
Concord Health Care Inc .... E 330 759-2357
  Youngstown *(G-15588)*
Concordia of Ohio .... E 330 664-1000
  Copley *(G-6952)*
Congregate Living of America .... D 937 393-6700
  Hillsboro *(G-9251)*
Congregate Living of America .... D 513 899-2801
  Morrow *(G-11455)*
Consulate Healthcare Inc .... E 419 865-1248
  Maumee *(G-10711)*
Consulate Management Co LLC .... C 419 886-3922
  Bellville *(G-1047)*
Consulate Management Co LLC .... B 440 237-7966
  Cleveland *(G-4110)*
Consulate Management Co LLC .... C 419 683-3255
  Crestline *(G-7020)*
Consulate Management Co LLC .... B 740 259-2351
  Lucasville *(G-10174)*
Consulate Management Co LLC .... B 330 837-1001
  Massillon *(G-10636)*
Consulate Management Co LLC .... C 419 867-7926
  Maumee *(G-10712)*
Contining Hlthcare Sltions Inc .... B 440 466-1181
  Geneva *(G-8784)*
Copley Health Center Inc .... C 330 666-0980
  Copley *(G-6953)*
Cortland Healthcare Group Inc .... C 330 638-4015
  Cortland *(G-6970)*
Cottingham Rtirement Cmnty Inc .... D 513 563-3600
  Cincinnati *(G-2511)*
Country CLB Retirement Ctr LLC .... D 440 992-0022
  Ashtabula *(G-530)*
Country CLB Retirement Ctr LLC .... D 740 671-9330
  Bellaire *(G-1010)*
Country Club Center Homes Inc .... D 330 343-6351
  Dover *(G-7876)*
Country Club Center II Ltd .... C 740 397-2350
  Mount Vernon *(G-11479)*
Country Court .... B 740 397-4125
  Mount Vernon *(G-11480)*
County of Allen .... E 419 221-1103
  Lima *(G-9881)*
County of Erie .... E 419 627-8733
  Huron *(G-9386)*
County of Logan .... C 937 592-2901
  Bellefontaine *(G-1027)*
County of Monroe .... D 740 472-0144
  Woodsfield *(G-15301)*
County of Montgomery .... C 937 264-0460
  Dayton *(G-7257)*
County of Ottawa .... C 567 262-3600
  Oak Harbor *(G-12044)*
County of Perry .... E 740 342-0416
  New Lexington *(G-11624)*
County of Shelby .... D 937 492-6900
  Sidney *(G-13027)*

County of Wood .... D 419 353-8411
  Bowling Green *(G-1314)*
Covenant Care Ohio Inc .... D 937 878-7046
  Fairborn *(G-8370)*
Covenant Care Ohio Inc .... D 937 378-0188
  Georgetown *(G-8800)*
Covenant Care Ohio Inc .... D 419 898-5506
  Port Clinton *(G-12521)*
Covenant Care Ohio Inc .... D 937 399-5551
  Springfield *(G-13244)*
Covenant Care Ohio Inc .... B 419 531-4201
  Toledo *(G-13769)*
Covenant Care Ohio Inc .... A 937 526-5570
  Versailles *(G-14415)*
Crandall Medical Center .... E 330 938-6126
  Sebring *(G-12948)*
Creative Foundations Inc .... D 614 832-2121
  Delaware *(G-7791)*
Cred-Kap Inc .... D 330 755-1466
  Struthers *(G-13499)*
Crestline Nursing Center LLC .... E 419 683-3255
  Crestline *(G-7021)*
Crestmont Nursing Home N Corp .... C 216 228-9550
  Lakewood *(G-9663)*
Crestview Manor Nursing Home .... C 740 654-2634
  Lancaster *(G-9706)*
Cridersville Health Care Ctr .... D 419 645-4468
  Cridersville *(G-7028)*
Crotinger Nursing Home Inc .... E 937 968-5284
  Union City *(G-14239)*
Crystal Care Centers Inc .... D 419 747-2666
  Mansfield *(G-10256)*
Csji-Tiffin Inc .... D 419 447-2723
  Tiffin *(G-13626)*
Cw Opco LLC .... E 440 428-5103
  Madison *(G-10214)*
D James Incorporated .... C 513 574-4550
  Cincinnati *(G-2530)*
Daniel Drake Ctr For PST-Cute .... A 513 418-2500
  Cincinnati *(G-2536)*
Danridge Nursing Home Inc .... E 330 746-5157
  Youngstown *(G-15592)*
Dayspring Health Care Center .... E 937 864-5800
  Fairborn *(G-8373)*
Deaconess Long Term Care of MI .... A 513 487-3600
  Cincinnati *(G-2551)*
Dearth Management Company .... D 419 253-0144
  Marengo *(G-10352)*
Dearth Management Company .... D 330 339-3595
  New Philadelphia *(G-11649)*
Debmar Inc .... D 419 728-7010
  Bowling Green *(G-1317)*
Dedicated Nursing Assoc Inc .... C 888 465-6929
  Beavercreek *(G-922)*
Dedicated Nursing Assoc Inc .... C 866 450-5550
  Hilliard *(G-9191)*
Diversicare St Theresa LLC .... D 513 271-7010
  Cincinnati *(G-2569)*
DMD Management Inc .... C 216 371-3600
  Cleveland *(G-4172)*
DMD Management Inc .... C 330 405-6040
  Twinsburg *(G-14182)*
Doctors Hospital Cleveland Inc .... C 740 753-7300
  Nelsonville *(G-11542)*
Dover Nursing Center Llc .... D 330 364-4436
  Dover *(G-7883)*
Dublin Geriatric Care Co LP .... E 614 761-1188
  Dublin *(G-7993)*
Eagle Creek Hlthcare Group Inc .... B 937 544-5531
  West Union *(G-14869)*
Eagle Pointe Skilled Rehab LLC .... E 440 437-7171
  Orwell *(G-12178)*

Eaglewood Care Center .... C 937 399-7195
  Springfield *(G-13250)*
East Water Leasing Co LLC .... E 419 278-6921
  Deshler *(G-7866)*
Eastgate Health Care Center .... D 513 752-3710
  Cincinnati *(G-2103)*
Eaton Grdns Rhbltion Hlth Car .... D 937 456-5537
  Eaton *(G-8213)*
Ebenezer Road Corporation .... C 513 941-0099
  Cincinnati *(G-2601)*
Echoing Hills Village Inc .... D 937 854-5151
  Dayton *(G-7326)*
Echoing Hills Village Inc .... C 440 989-1400
  Lorain *(G-10071)*
Echoing Hills Village Inc .... C 740 327-2311
  Warsaw *(G-14591)*
Edgewood Manor of Lucasville .... E 740 259-5536
  Lucasville *(G-10176)*
Edgewood Manor Westerville LLC .... E 614 882-4055
  Westerville *(G-14977)*
Edgewood Mnor Lucasville I LLC .... D 740 259-5536
  Lucasville *(G-10177)*
Edgewood Mnor Rhbltion Hlthca .... D 732 730-7360
  Port Clinton *(G-12524)*
Eliza Jnnngs Snior Care Netwrk .... C 216 226-5000
  Olmsted Twp *(G-12090)*
Elms Retirement Village Inc .... B 440 647-2414
  Wellington *(G-14631)*
Elmwood Centers Inc .... D 419 332-3378
  Green Springs *(G-8858)*
Embassy Healthcare Inc .... E 513 868-6500
  Fairfield *(G-8411)*
Embassy Healthcare MGT Inc .... E 216 378-2050
  Beachwood *(G-789)*
Embassy Winchester LLC .... D 614 834-2273
  Canal Winchester *(G-1605)*
Emeritus Corporation .... C 330 477-5727
  Canton *(G-1745)*
Emeritus Corporation .... C 440 201-9200
  Cleveland *(G-4211)*
Emeritus Corporation .... C 614 836-5990
  Groveport *(G-8985)*
Emeritus Corporation .... D 330 342-0934
  Stow *(G-13365)*
Emeritus Corporation .... C 440 269-8600
  Willoughby *(G-15191)*
Emery Leasing Co LLC .... B 216 475-8880
  Cleveland *(G-4212)*
Esop Realty Inc .... C 216 361-0718
  Cleveland *(G-4223)*
Euclid Health Care Inc .... C 513 561-6400
  Cincinnati *(G-2638)*
Evanglcal Lthran Good Smrtan S .... C 419 365-5115
  Arlington *(G-469)*
Fairchild MD Leasing Co LLC .... C 330 678-4912
  Kent *(G-9574)*
Fairfeld Grdns Rhbltion Care .... E 740 536-7381
  Thornville *(G-13620)*
Fairhope Hspice Plltive Care I .... D 740 654-7077
  Lancaster *(G-9721)*
Fairlawn Opco LLC .... D 502 429-8062
  Fairlawn *(G-8479)*
Fairmount Nursing Home Inc .... D 440 338-8220
  Newbury *(G-11760)*
Falling Leasing Co LLC .... E 440 238-1100
  Strongsville *(G-13455)*
Falls Vlg Retirement Cmnty Ltd .... D 330 945-9797
  Cuyahoga Falls *(G-7076)*
Fhs Carington Inc .... E 440 964-8446
  Ashtabula *(G-535)*
First Community Village .... B 614 324-4455
  Columbus *(G-5861)*

80 HEALTH SERVICES

Fisher - Titus Health .... A 419 668-8101
  Norwalk (G-12010)
Five Star Senior Living Inc .... E 614 451-6793
  Columbus (G-5871)
Flower Hospital .... B 419 824-1000
  Sylvania (G-13545)
Fountains At Canterbury .... E 405 751-3600
  Toledo (G-13810)
Four Seasons Washington LLC .. D 740 895-6101
  Wshngtn Ct Hs (G-15486)
Franciscan Care Ctr Sylvania ..... A 419 882-2087
  Toledo (G-13811)
Franciscan Sisters of Chicago ..... B 440 843-7800
  Cleveland (G-4283)
Friends Health Care Assn .... C 937 767-7363
  Yellow Springs (G-15535)
Friendship Vlg of Clumbus Ohio .. D 614 890-8287
  Columbus (G-5897)
Friendship Vlg of Clumbus Ohio .. C 614 890-8282
  Columbus (G-5898)
Friendship Vlg of Dublin Ohio ..... C 614 764-1600
  Dublin (G-8016)
Front Leasing Co LLC .... E 440 243-4000
  Berea (G-1070)
Fulton County Health Center ...... C 419 335-2017
  Wauseon (G-14601)
Gables At Green Pastures .... E 937 642-3893
  Marysville (G-10485)
Gables Care Center Inc .... E 740 937-2900
  Hopedale (G-9318)
Garden Manor Extended Care Cen .. C 513 420-5972
  Middletown (G-11164)
Gardens Wapakoneta Oper Co LLC .. E 419 738-0725
  Wapakoneta (G-14484)
Gateway Health Care Center ..... D 216 486-4949
  Cleveland (G-4305)
Gaymont Leasing LLC .... E 419 668-8258
  Norwalk (G-12014)
Generation Health Corp .... E 614 337-1066
  Columbus (G-5926)
Genertion Hlth Rhblttion Ctr L ..... D 740 348-1300
  Newark (G-11701)
Genesis Healthcare .... A 937 875-4604
  Troy (G-14136)
Genesis Healthcare LLC .... B 419 666-0935
  Perrysburg (G-12336)
GFS Leasing Inc .... D 330 877-2666
  Hartville (G-9126)
GFS Leasing Inc .... D 330 296-6415
  Kent (G-9577)
Gillette Nursing Home Inc .... D 330 372-1960
  Warren (G-14524)
Glen Wesley Inc .... D 614 888-7492
  Columbus (G-5937)
Glendora Health Care Center ..... E 330 264-0912
  Wooster (G-15340)
Glenward Inc .... E 513 863-3100
  Fairfield Township (G-8460)
Golden Years Nursing Home Inc .. C 513 893-0471
  Hamilton (G-9045)
Good Samaritan Health Group Inc .. C
  Cleveland (G-4319)
Good Shepherd Home .... C 419 937-1801
  Fostoria (G-8618)
Good Shepherd Home For Aged . C 614 228-5200
  Ashland (G-499)
Good Shepherd Village LLC .... E 937 322-1911
  Springfield (G-13253)
Governors Village LLC .... D 440 449-8788
  Cleveland (G-4321)
Grace Brethren Village .... E 937 836-4011
  Englewood (G-8309)

Graceworks Lutheran Services ... A 937 433-2140
  Dayton (G-7383)
Greenbrier Senior Living Cmnty .. D 440 888-0400
  Cleveland (G-4338)
Greenbrier Senior Living Cmnty .. C 440 888-5900
  Cleveland (G-4339)
Greens of Lyndhurst The Inc ...... E 440 460-1000
  Cleveland (G-4340)
Guardian Hlthcare HM Off I LLC . B 330 549-0898
  North Lima (G-11888)
H & G Nursery Home Inc .... E 513 734-7401
  Bethel (G-1091)
H & G Nursing Homes Inc .... D 937 544-2205
  West Union (G-14870)
Hackensack Meridian Health Inc . D 513 792-9697
  Cincinnati (G-2791)
Hanover House Inc .... E 330 837-1741
  Massillon (G-10642)
Harbor Operator LLC .... E 330 399-8997
  Warren (G-14525)
Harborside Clveland Ltd Partnr ... C 440 871-5900
  Westlake (G-15063)
Harborside Clveland Ltd Partnr ... D 440 871-5900
  Westlake (G-15064)
Harborside Dayton Ltd Partnr ..... A 937 224-0793
  Dayton (G-7396)
Harborside Dayton Ltd Partnr ..... A 937 687-1311
  New Lebanon (G-11619)
Harborside Healthcare LLC .... C 937 436-6155
  Dayton (G-7397)
Harborside Healthcare LLC .... C 419 825-1111
  Swanton (G-13526)
Harborside Healthcare LLC .... E 937 335-7161
  Troy (G-14137)
Harborside Pointe Place LLC ..... C 419 727-7870
  Toledo (G-13835)
Harborside Sylvania LLC .... D 419 882-1875
  Sylvania (G-13548)
Hcf Management Inc .... E 419 435-8112
  Fostoria (G-8619)
Hcf Management Inc .... D 419 999-2055
  Lima (G-9897)
Hcf Management Inc .... E 740 289-2394
  Piketon (G-12422)
Hcf Management Inc .... D 419 999-2010
  Lima (G-9896)
Hcf of Bowl Green Care Ctr Inc .. C 419 352-7558
  Bowling Green (G-1321)
Hcf of Bowling Green Inc .... C 419 352-4694
  Bowling Green (G-1322)
Hcf of Briarwood Inc .... C 419 678-2311
  Coldwater (G-5213)
Hcf of Celina Inc .... B 419 999-2010
  Lima (G-9898)
Hcf of Celina Inc .... D 419 586-6645
  Celina (G-1925)
Hcf of Court House Inc .... C 740 335-9290
  Wshngtn Ct Hs (G-15487)
Hcf of Crestview Inc .... E 937 426-5033
  Beavercreek (G-924)
Hcf of Findlay Inc .... D 419 999-2010
  Findlay (G-8545)
Hcf of Lima Inc .... D 419 999-2010
  Lima (G-9899)
Hcf of Lima Inc .... E 419 227-2611
  Lima (G-9900)
Hcf of Perrysburg Inc .... D 419 874-0306
  Perrysburg (G-12340)
Hcf of Piqua Inc .... C 937 773-0040
  Piqua (G-12444)
Hcf of Roselawn Inc .... C 419 647-4115
  Spencerville (G-13188)

Hcf of Shawnee Inc .... E 419 999-2055
  Lima (G-9901)
Hcf of Van Wert Inc .... C 419 999-2010
  Van Wert (G-14346)
Hcf of Wapakoneta Inc .... E 419 738-3711
  Wapakoneta (G-14485)
Hcr Manorcare Inc .... E 419 252-5500
  Toledo (G-13838)
Hcr Manorcare Med Svcs Fla LLC .. C 419 252-5500
  Toledo (G-13839)
Health Care Opportunities Inc .... E 513 932-0300
  Lebanon (G-9768)
Health Care Rtrement Corp Amer .. D 937 644-8836
  Marysville (G-10487)
Health Care Rtrement Corp Amer .. C 419 252-5500
  Toledo (G-13840)
Healthcare Walton Group LLC ... D 440 439-4433
  Cleveland (G-4355)
Heartland Miamisburg Oh LLC ... E 937 866-8885
  Miamisburg (G-11060)
Heartland Perrysburg Oh LLC ... E 419 874-3578
  Perrysburg (G-12341)
Heartland Vlg Wstrvlle OH RC L . A 614 895-1038
  Westerville (G-14983)
Heath Nursing Care Center .... D 740 522-1171
  Newark (G-11704)
Heather Knoll Rtrement Vlg Inc . D 330 688-8600
  Tallmadge (G-13594)
Heatherdowns Operating Co LLC .. D 419 382-5050
  Toledo (G-13845)
Heatherhill Care Communities ... E 440 285-4040
  Chardon (G-2004)
Hempstead Manor .... E 740 354-8150
  Portsmouth (G-12553)
Hennis Nursing Home .... C 330 364-8849
  Dover (G-7889)
Heritage Corner Nursing HM LLC .. E 419 728-7010
  Bowling Green (G-1324)
Hickory Creek Hlthcare Fndtion . E 419 542-7795
  Hicksville (G-9158)
Highbanks Care Center LLC ...... E 614 888-2021
  Columbus (G-5991)
Hill Side Plaza .... D 216 486-6300
  Cleveland (G-4361)
Hillandale Health Care Inc .... E 513 777-1400
  West Chester (G-14708)
Hilliard Hlth Rhbilitation Inc .... D 614 777-6001
  Hilliard (G-9200)
Hillspring Health Care Center .... D 937 748-1100
  Springboro (G-13201)
Hilty Memorial Home Inc .... E 419 384-3218
  Pandora (G-12246)
Holzer Senior Care Center .... E 740 446-5001
  Bidwell (G-1104)
Home At Hearthstone .... E 513 521-2700
  Cincinnati (G-2833)
Home Echo Club Inc .... D 614 864-1718
  Pickerington (G-12403)
Home The Friends Inc .... D 513 897-6050
  Waynesville (G-14624)
Homefront Nursing LLC .... E 513 404-1189
  Cincinnati (G-2840)
Homestead I Hlthcare Group LLC .. C 440 226-8869
  Painesville (G-12229)
Homestead II Hlthcare Group LL .. D 440 352-0788
  Painesville (G-12230)
Hooberry & Associates Inc .... E 330 872-1991
  Newton Falls (G-11775)
Horizon Health Management LLC .. E 513 793-5220
  Cincinnati (G-2843)
Hospice Cincinnati Inc .... D 513 891-7700
  Cincinnati (G-2848)

80 HEALTH SERVICES

Hospice North Central Ohio Inc............. E 419 281-7107
  Ashland *(G-501)*
Hospice of Genesis Health................. E 740 454-5381
  Zanesville *(G-15801)*
Hosser Assisted Living..................... E 740 286-8785
  Jackson *(G-9521)*
Humility House................................. D 330 505-0144
  Youngstown *(G-15634)*
Huron Health Care Center Inc............. E 419 433-4990
  Huron *(G-9391)*
Hyde Park Health Center..................... E 513 272-0600
  Cincinnati *(G-2859)*
I Vrable Inc.................................... C 614 545-5500
  Columbus *(G-6036)*
Independence Care Community........... E 419 435-8505
  Fostoria *(G-8620)*
Indian Hlls Hlthcare Group Inc............ A 216 486-8880
  Euclid *(G-8350)*
Indian Lk Healthcare Group LLC.......... C 937 843-4929
  Lakeview *(G-9655)*
Inner City Nursing Home Inc............... C 216 795-1363
  Cleveland *(G-4413)*
Isabelle Ridgway Care Ctr Inc............. D 614 252-4931
  Columbus *(G-6074)*
Jackson Cnty Hlth Fclities Inc............. D 740 384-0722
  Wellston *(G-14639)*
Jennings Eliza Home Inc.................... C 216 226-0282
  Cleveland *(G-4436)*
Jewish Fdrtion Grter Dyton Inc............ D 937 837-2651
  Dayton *(G-7428)*
Jewish Home Cincinnati Inc............... B 513 754-3100
  Mason *(G-10569)*
Jma Healthcare LLC........................... E 440 439-7976
  Cleveland *(G-4438)*
Jo-Lin Health Center Inc.................... E 740 532-0860
  Ironton *(G-9510)*
Joint Township Dst Mem Hosp............ B 419 394-3335
  Saint Marys *(G-12829)*
Judson Care Center Inc..................... A 513 662-5880
  Cincinnati *(G-2922)*
Jwj Investments Inc.......................... C 419 643-3161
  Delphos *(G-7841)*
Karl Hc LLC...................................... B 614 846-5420
  Columbus *(G-6102)*
Karrington Operating Co Inc............... B 614 875-0514
  Grove City *(G-8929)*
Kendal At Oberlin.............................. C 440 775-0094
  Oberlin *(G-12071)*
Kenton Nrsing Rhblttion Ctr LL............ E 419 674-4197
  Kenton *(G-9620)*
Kenwood Ter Hlth Care Ctr Inc............ C 513 793-2255
  Cincinnati *(G-2936)*
Kimes Convalescent Center Ltd........... D 740 593-3391
  Athens *(G-579)*
Kindred Healthcare LLC..................... E 937 222-5963
  Dayton *(G-7443)*
Kindred Nursing Centers E LLC........... D 614 837-9666
  Canal Winchester *(G-1610)*
Kindred Nursing Centers E LLC........... C 740 772-5900
  Chillicothe *(G-2077)*
Kindred Nursing Centers E LLC........... E 614 276-8222
  Columbus *(G-6116)*
Kindred Nursing Centers E LLC........... D 314 631-3000
  Pickerington *(G-12405)*
Kingston Healthcare Company............ E 419 289-3859
  Ashland *(G-504)*
Kingston Healthcare Company............ E 440 967-1800
  Vermilion *(G-14407)*
Kingston of Miamisburg LLC............... D 937 866-9089
  Miamisburg *(G-11067)*
Kingston Rsdnce Perrysburg LLC........ C 419 872-6200
  Perrysburg *(G-12350)*

Kinston Care Center Sylvani............... E 419 517-8200
  Sylvania *(G-13555)*
Lakewood Health Care Center............ D 216 226-3103
  Lakewood *(G-9673)*
Lakewood Senior Campus LLC........... E 216 228-7650
  Lakewood *(G-9677)*
Lancia Nursing Homes Inc................. C 740 264-7101
  Steubenville *(G-13334)*
Laurel Health Care Company.............. D 740 264-5042
  Steubenville *(G-13335)*
Laurel Health Care Company.............. D 614 794-8800
  Westerville *(G-14905)*
Laurel Healthcare............................. D 419 782-7879
  Defiance *(G-7752)*
Laurel Hlth Care Battle Creek............. E 614 794-8800
  Westerville *(G-14906)*
Laurel Hlth Care of Mt Plasant............ D 614 794-8800
  Westerville *(G-14907)*
Laurels of Athens............................. E 740 592-1000
  Athens *(G-581)*
Laurels of Worthington...................... D 614 885-0408
  Worthington *(G-15430)*
Lexington Court Care Center.............. E 419 884-2000
  Mansfield *(G-10281)*
Liberty Nrsing Ctr of Jmestown........... E 937 675-3311
  Jamestown *(G-9535)*
Liberty Nrsing Ctr Rvrside LLC........... E 513 557-3621
  Cincinnati *(G-2974)*
Liberty Nursing Center....................... E 937 836-5143
  Englewood *(G-8313)*
Liberty Nursing Home Inc................... E 937 376-2121
  Xenia *(G-15523)*
Liberty Nursing of Willard................... D 419 935-0148
  Willard *(G-15170)*
Liberty Retirement Cmnty Lima........... E 419 331-2273
  Lima *(G-9917)*
Life Care Centers America Inc............ D 614 889-6320
  Columbus *(G-6158)*
Life Care Centers America Inc............ D 440 365-5200
  Elyria *(G-8268)*
Life Care Centers America Inc............ D 330 483-3131
  Valley City *(G-14334)*
Life Care Centers America Inc............ C 440 871-3030
  Westlake *(G-15075)*
Lima Cnvlscent HM Fndation Inc......... D 419 227-5450
  Lima *(G-9920)*
Lincoln Park Associates II LP.............. D 937 297-4300
  Dayton *(G-7455)*
Little Ssters of Poor Bltmore............... D 419 698-4331
  Oregon *(G-12135)*
Little Ssters of Poor Bltmore............... D 216 464-1221
  Warrensville Heights *(G-14584)*
Locust Ridge Nursing Home Inc.......... C 937 444-2920
  Williamsburg *(G-15180)*
Lodge Care Center Inc....................... E 513 683-9966
  Loveland *(G-10147)*
Logan Elm Health Care Center........... B 740 474-3121
  Circleville *(G-3712)*
Logan Healthcare Leasing LLC........... D 216 367-1214
  Logan *(G-10032)*
London Health & Rehab Ctr LLC......... C 740 852-3100
  London *(G-10045)*
Longmeadow Care Center Inc............ E 330 297-5781
  Ravenna *(G-12632)*
Lorain Manor Inc.............................. D 440 277-8173
  Lorain *(G-10087)*
Lorantffy Care Center Inc................... D 330 666-2631
  Copley *(G-6960)*
Lost Creek Hlth Care Rhblttion............ C 419 225-9040
  Lima *(G-9929)*
Loveland Health Care Center.............. C 513 605-6000
  Loveland *(G-10148)*

LP Coshocton LLC............................ E 470 622-1220
  Coshocton *(G-6991)*
LP Opco LLC.................................... D 440 593-6266
  Conneaut *(G-6943)*
Lutheran Home................................. B 440 871-0090
  Cleveland *(G-4510)*
Lutheran Homes Society Inc............... C 419 861-2233
  Holland *(G-9295)*
Lutheran Scial Svcs Centl Ohio.......... E 419 289-3523
  Ashland *(G-506)*
Lutheran Senior City Inc.................... B 614 228-5200
  Columbus *(G-6180)*
Lutheran Village At Wolf Creek............ E 419 861-2233
  Holland *(G-9296)*
Madison Care Inc............................. B 440 428-1492
  Madison *(G-10220)*
Main Street Terrace Care Ctr.............. D 740 653-8767
  Lancaster *(G-9734)*
Mallard Cove Senior Dev LLC............. C 513 772-6655
  Cincinnati *(G-3007)*
Manleys Manor Nursing Home Inc...... E 419 424-0402
  Findlay *(G-8560)*
Manor Care Inc................................. D 419 252-5500
  Toledo *(G-13905)*
Manor Care Barberton Oh LLC........... E 330 753-5005
  Barberton *(G-701)*
Manor Care Wilmington De LLC......... A 567 585-9600
  Toledo *(G-13906)*
Manor Cr-Pike Creek Wlmngton D...... C 567 585-9600
  Toledo *(G-13907)*
Manorcare Health Services LLC.......... E 419 252-5500
  Toledo *(G-13908)*
Manorcare Health Svcs VA Inc............ D 419 252-5500
  Toledo *(G-13909)*
Mansfield Memorial Homes LLC......... C 419 774-5100
  Mansfield *(G-10289)*
Maple Knoll Communities Inc............ C 513 524-7990
  Oxford *(G-12209)*
Maple Knoll Communities Inc............ B 513 782-2400
  Cincinnati *(G-3008)*
Mapleview Country Villa..................... D 440 286-8176
  Chardon *(G-2011)*
Marion Care Leasing LLC.................. D 740 387-7537
  Marion *(G-10436)*
Marion Manor................................... E 740 387-9545
  Marion *(G-10441)*
Mary Scott Nursing Home Inc............. D 937 278-0761
  Dayton *(G-7468)*
▲ Marymount Hospital Inc................. B 216 581-0500
  Cleveland *(G-4531)*
Mason Health Care Center................. E 513 398-2881
  Mason *(G-10578)*
Mayfair Nursing Care Centers............. D 614 889-6320
  Columbus *(G-6212)*
Mayflower Nursing Home Inc............. E 330 492-7131
  Canton *(G-1801)*
McClellan Management Inc............... E 419 855-7755
  Genoa *(G-8795)*
McGregor Foundation........................ B 216 851-8200
  Cleveland *(G-4538)*
McKinley Hall Inc............................. E 937 328-5300
  Springfield *(G-13266)*
McV Health Care Facilities Inc............ E 513 398-1486
  Mason *(G-10580)*
MD Omg Emp LLC........................... D 513 489-7100
  Blue Ash *(G-1207)*
Meadow Wind Hlth Care Ctr Inc.......... D 330 833-2026
  Massillon *(G-10656)*
Meadowbrook Manor of Hartford........ E 330 772-5253
  Fowler *(G-8628)*
Medina Meadows.............................. E 330 725-1550
  Medina *(G-10862)*

80 HEALTH SERVICES

Medina Medical Investors Ltd.................. D 330 483-3131
   Medina *(G-10863)*

Megco Management Inc.......................... C 330 874-9999
   Bolivar *(G-1295)*

Meigs County Care Center LLC.............. C 740 992-6472
   Middleport *(G-11148)*

Mennonite Memorial Home...................... D 419 358-7654
   Bluffton *(G-1282)*

Mennonite Memorial Home...................... C 419 358-1015
   Bluffton *(G-1283)*

Menorah Pk Ctr For Snior Lving................ A 216 831-6500
   Cleveland *(G-4550)*

Mercy St Theresa Center Inc.................... E 513 271-7010
   Cincinnati *(G-3047)*

Merit House LLC.. C 419 478-5131
   Toledo *(G-13921)*

Merit Leasing Co LLC............................... D 216 261-9592
   Cleveland *(G-4555)*

Mff Somerset LLC.................................... E 216 752-5600
   Shaker Heights *(G-12982)*

Milcrest Healthcare Inc............................. D 937 642-0218
   Marysville *(G-10499)*

Mill Run Care Center LLC........................ E 614 527-3000
   Hilliard *(G-9216)*

Minerva Elder Care Inc............................. E 330 868-4147
   Minerva *(G-11309)*

Mkjb Inc.. D 513 851-8400
   West Chester *(G-14733)*

Mon Health Care Inc................................ E 304 285-2700
   Westerville *(G-14911)*

Montefiore Home....................................... B 216 360-9080
   Beachwood *(G-819)*

Mount Vernon Elderly Svcs LLC............. D 740 397-2350
   Mount Vernon *(G-11501)*

Mountain Crest OH Opco LLC................ D 419 882-1875
   Sylvania *(G-13556)*

Mt Airy Grdns Rhblttion Care.................. E 513 591-0400
   Cincinnati *(G-3085)*

Mt Washington Care Center Inc............. E 513 231-4561
   Cincinnati *(G-3087)*

Multi-Care Inc... C 440 352-0788
   Painesville *(G-12238)*

Multi-Care Inc... D 440 357-6181
   Painesville *(G-12239)*

Multicare Management Group Inc........... D 513 868-6500
   Fairfield *(G-8434)*

National Ch Rsdnces Pmbroke GA........ D 614 451-2151
   Columbus *(G-6291)*

National Church Residences.................. C 614 451-2151
   Columbus *(G-6292)*

Nentwick Convalescent Home................ E 330 385-5001
   East Liverpool *(G-8187)*

New Albany Care Center LLC................ E 614 855-8866
   Columbus *(G-6352)*

New Dawn Health Care Inc.................... C 330 343-5521
   Dover *(G-7895)*

New Life Hospice Inc............................... C 440 934-1458
   Lorain *(G-10095)*

New Scotland Health Care LLC............. E 513 861-2044
   Cincinnati *(G-3109)*

Newark Leasing LLC................................ C 740 344-0357
   Newark *(G-11736)*

Newcomerstown Development Inc......... E 740 498-5165
   Newcomerstown *(G-11771)*

Newcomerstown Progress Corp............. C 740 498-5165
   Newcomerstown *(G-11772)*

Nightingale Holdings LLC....................... B 330 645-0200
   Akron *(G-243)*

Nightingale Holdings LLC....................... A 513 489-7100
   Blue Ash *(G-1215)*

Normandy II Ltd Partnership.................. C 440 333-5401
   Rocky River *(G-12750)*

North Park Retirement Cmnty................ E 216 267-0555
   Cleveland *(G-4650)*

Northcrest Nursing & Rehab.................. E 419 599-4070
   Napoleon *(G-11531)*

Northwesterly Ltd.................................... E 216 228-2266
   Cleveland *(G-4665)*

Norwood Health Care Center LLC......... D 513 351-0153
   Cincinnati *(G-3130)*

Norwood Hghlnds Healthcare LLC........ D 513 351-0153
   Cincinnati *(G-3131)*

Norwood Towers Healthcare LLC......... D 513 631-6800
   Norwood *(G-12034)*

Nova Passport Home Care Llc.............. E 419 531-9060
   Toledo *(G-13941)*

Oak Creek Terrace Inc............................ C 937 439-1454
   Dayton *(G-7533)*

Oak Grove Manor Inc............................... E 419 589-6222
   Mansfield *(G-10306)*

Oak Hlth Care Invstors Dfnce I............... E 614 794-8800
   Westerville *(G-14918)*

Oak Hlth Care Invstors of Mt V.............. D 740 397-3200
   Mount Vernon *(G-11503)*

Oakhill Manor Care Center..................... E 330 875-5060
   Louisville *(G-10118)*

Oaktree LLC... D 513 598-8000
   Cincinnati *(G-3138)*

Oakwood Health Care Svcs Inc.............. C 440 439-7976
   Cleveland *(G-4677)*

October Enterprises Inc.......................... D 937 456-9535
   Eaton *(G-8218)*

Ohio Living.. B 330 867-2150
   Akron *(G-253)*

Ohio Living.. B 513 681-4230
   Cincinnati *(G-3147)*

Ohio Living.. B 513 539-7391
   Monroe *(G-11345)*

Ohio Living.. B 937 498-2391
   Sidney *(G-13043)*

Ohio Living.. B 330 746-2944
   Youngstown *(G-15682)*

Ohio Living Communities........................ D 614 888-7800
   Columbus *(G-6432)*

Ohio Living Holdings................................ E 330 533-4350
   Canfield *(G-1636)*

Ohio Living Holdings................................ D 614 433-0031
   Columbus *(G-6433)*

Ohio Living Holdings................................ D 937 415-5666
   Sidney *(G-13044)*

Ohio Living Holdings................................ D 419 865-1499
   Toledo *(G-13947)*

Ohio Valley Manor Inc............................. C 937 392-4318
   Ripley *(G-12727)*

Ohioguidestone... B 440 234-2006
   Berea *(G-1078)*

Ohioguidestone... E 440 234-2006
   Berea *(G-1079)*

Ohiohealth Corporation........................... A 614 788-8860
   Columbus *(G-6465)*

Olmsted Manor Ltd................................. D 440 777-8444
   North Olmsted *(G-11910)*

Omni Manor Inc.. A 330 793-5648
   Youngstown *(G-15685)*

Omni Manor Inc.. C 330 545-1550
   Girard *(G-8821)*

Optum Infusion Svcs 550 LLC............... D 866 442-4679
   Cincinnati *(G-3166)*

Orchard Villa Inc...................................... D 419 697-4100
   Oregon *(G-12139)*

Orion Care Services LLC........................ E 216 752-3600
   Cleveland *(G-4707)*

Otterbein Homes...................................... D 419 645-5114
   Cridersville *(G-7029)*

Otterbein Homes...................................... E 513 696-8565
   Lebanon *(G-9780)*

Otterbein Homes...................................... E 419 943-4376
   Leipsic *(G-9801)*

Otterbein Homes...................................... E 513 260-7690
   Middletown *(G-11200)*

Otterbein Homes...................................... E 419 394-1622
   Saint Marys *(G-12833)*

Otterbein Homes...................................... E 419 394-2366
   Saint Marys *(G-12834)*

Otterbein Homes...................................... B 513 933-5400
   Lebanon *(G-9781)*

Otterbein Portage Valley Inc.................. C 888 749-4950
   Pemberville *(G-12291)*

Otterbein Snior Lfstyle Chices................ E 937 885-5426
   Dayton *(G-7542)*

Ovm Investment Group LLC.................. C 937 392-0145
   Ripley *(G-12728)*

Park View Manor Inc............................... D 937 296-1550
   Englewood *(G-8318)*

Park Vlg Assisted Living LLC................ E 330 364-4436
   Dover *(G-7899)*

Parkview Manor Inc.................................. C 419 243-5191
   Toledo *(G-13957)*

Parma Care Center Inc.......................... C 216 661-6800
   Cleveland *(G-4728)*

Patrician Inc... C 440 237-3104
   Brunswick *(G-1466)*

Pearl Leasing Co LLC............................. E 513 530-1600
   Parma *(G-12261)*

Peregrine Health Services Inc................ D 330 823-9005
   Alliance *(G-396)*

Personacare of Ohio Inc.......................... C 440 357-1311
   Painesville *(G-12241)*

Pgn Op Summit LLC............................... E 614 252-4987
   Columbus *(G-6519)*

Pickaway Manor Inc................................. C 740 474-5400
   Circleville *(G-3717)*

Piketon Nursing Center Inc.................... A 740 289-4074
   Piketon *(G-12427)*

Pleasant Hill Leasing LLC...................... C 740 289-2394
   Piketon *(G-12428)*

Pleasant Ridge Care Center Inc............. C 513 631-1310
   Cincinnati *(G-3213)*

Pleasant View Nursing Home Inc........... D 330 745-6028
   Barberton *(G-703)*

Pomeroy Opco LLC................................. D 740 992-6606
   Pomeroy *(G-12515)*

Preble Cnty Bd Dvlpmntal Dsblt............ E 937 456-5891
   Eaton *(G-8220)*

Progressive Aurora LLC......................... E 330 995-0094
   Aurora *(G-622)*

Progressive Green Meadows LLC......... D 330 875-1456
   Louisville *(G-10120)*

Progressive Macedonia LLC.................. E 330 748-8800
   Macedonia *(G-10203)*

Provide-A-Care Inc.................................. C 330 828-2278
   Dalton *(G-7121)*

Quality Care Nursing Svc Inc................. C 740 377-9095
   South Point *(G-13182)*

R & J Investment Co Inc......................... C 440 934-5204
   Avon *(G-663)*

Rae-Ann Center Inc................................ E 440 466-5733
   Geneva *(G-8788)*

Rapids Nursing Homes Inc..................... E 216 292-5706
   Grand Rapids *(G-8846)*

Red Carpet Health Care Center............. D 740 439-4401
   Cambridge *(G-1580)*

Regency Leasing Co LLC....................... B 614 542-3100
   Columbus *(G-6574)*

Reichart Leasing Co LLC....................... E 513 530-1600
   Wintersville *(G-15296)*

80 HEALTH SERVICES

Residence At Kensington Place............ C 513 863-4218
  Hamilton *(G-9078)*
Rest Haven Nursing Home Inc............ D 937 548-1138
  Greenville *(G-8882)*
Ridge-Pleasant Valley Inc.................... C 440 845-0200
  Cleveland *(G-4840)*
Ridgecrest Healthcare Group In............ E 216 292-5706
  Bedford *(G-982)*
River Vista Hlth Wellness LLC................ D 614 643-5454
  Columbus *(G-6594)*
Rivers Bend Health Care LLC................ D 740 894-3476
  South Point *(G-13183)*
Rocky River Leasing Co LLC................ E 440 243-5688
  Berea *(G-1080)*
Rolling Hlls Rhab Wellness Ctr.............. E 330 225-9121
  Brunswick *(G-1469)*
Roman Cthlic Docese Youngstown........ C 330 875-5562
  Louisville *(G-10122)*
Rose Ln Hlth Rhabilitation Inc................ C 330 833-3174
  Massillon *(G-10665)*
Rossford Grtric Care Ltd Prtnr................ E 614 459-0445
  Columbus *(G-6612)*
Royal Manor Health Care Inc................ E 216 752-3600
  Cleveland *(G-4859)*
Royal Oak Nrsing Rhblttion Ctr.............. E 440 884-9191
  Cleveland *(G-4860)*
S Meridian Leasing Co LLC.................. E 513 530-1600
  Youngstown *(G-15715)*
Saber Healthcare Group LLC................ E 216 464-4300
  Beachwood *(G-832)*
Saber Healthcare Group LLC................ D 740 852-3100
  London *(G-10050)*
Saber Healthcare Group LLC................ E 216 292-5706
  Beachwood *(G-833)*
Saber Healthcare Holdings LLC............ E 216 292-5706
  Bedford Heights *(G-1002)*
Salem Community Hospital.................... A 330 332-1551
  Salem *(G-12854)*
Salem Healthcare MGT LLC.................. E 330 332-1588
  Salem *(G-12855)*
Salutary Providers Inc............................ C 440 964-8446
  Ashtabula *(G-548)*
Samaritan Care Center Inc.................... D 330 725-4123
  Medina *(G-10887)*
Sanctuary At Tuttle Crossing.................. D 614 408-0182
  Dublin *(G-8112)*
Sanctuary Medina LLC.......................... E 330 725-3393
  Medina *(G-10888)*
Sateri Home Inc...................................... D 330 758-8106
  Youngstown *(G-15717)*
Schoenbrunn Healthcare........................ A 330 339-3595
  New Philadelphia *(G-11666)*
Select Spclty Hosp - Yngstown.............. C 330 480-3488
  Youngstown *(G-15720)*
Select Spclty Hsptal-Akron LLC.............. D 330 761-7500
  Akron *(G-296)*
Senior Lifestyle Evergreen Ltd................ E 513 948-2308
  Cincinnati *(G-3357)*
Serenity Center Inc................................ E 614 891-1111
  Columbus *(G-6663)*
Shelby County Mem Hosp Assn............ E 937 492-9591
  Sidney *(G-13047)*
Shepherd of Vly Lthran Rtrment............ E 330 726-9061
  Youngstown *(G-15723)*
Shg Whitehall Holdings LLC.................. E 614 501-8271
  Columbus *(G-6671)*
Siffrin Residential Assn.......................... C 330 799-8932
  Youngstown *(G-15724)*
Singleton Health Care Ctr Inc................ D 216 231-0076
  Cleveland *(G-4909)*
Sisters of Chrity Cncnnati Ohi................ C 513 347-5200
  Cincinnati *(G-3380)*

Sisters of St Jseph St Mark PR.............. B 216 531-7426
  Euclid *(G-8362)*
Skilled In Management Co LLC............ D 513 489-7100
  Blue Ash *(G-1244)*
Slovene Home For The Aged................ C 216 486-0268
  Cleveland *(G-4915)*
Snf Wadsworth LLC................................ E 330 336-3472
  Solon *(G-13143)*
Solon Pnte At Emrald Ridge LLC.......... E 440 498-3000
  Solon *(G-13145)*
South Brdway Hlthcare Group In............ B 330 339-2151
  New Philadelphia *(G-11667)*
Southeastern Health Care Ctr................ D 740 425-3648
  Barnesville *(G-722)*
Southern Hlls Hlth Rhblttion C................ D 614 545-5502
  Columbus *(G-6697)*
Spring Hills Health Care LLC................ D 937 274-1400
  Dayton *(G-7634)*
Spring Hills Health Care LLC................ D 513 424-9999
  Middletown *(G-11202)*
Spring Mdow Extnded Care Ctr F.......... D 419 866-6124
  Holland *(G-9305)*
Springfeld Halthcare Group Inc.............. C 937 399-8311
  Springfield *(G-13293)*
Springview Manor Nursing Home.......... E 419 227-3661
  Lima *(G-9965)*
St Catherines Care Ctr Findlay.............. E 419 422-3978
  Findlay *(G-8587)*
St Clare Commons................................ E 419 931-0050
  Perrysburg *(G-12371)*
St Cthrnes Care Ctrs Fstria I.................. E 419 435-8112
  Fostoria *(G-8626)*
St Edward Home.................................... C 330 668-2828
  Fairlawn *(G-8500)*
Steubnvlle Cntry CLB Manor Inc............ E 740 266-6118
  Steubenville *(G-13344)*
Stone Crssing Asssted Lving LL............ C 330 492-7131
  Canton *(G-1862)*
Stow Opco LLC...................................... D 502 429-8062
  Stow *(G-13394)*
Streetsboro Opco LLC.......................... E 502 429-8062
  Streetsboro *(G-13430)*
Summerville Senior Living Inc................ E 440 354-5499
  Mentor *(G-11000)*
Summit Facility Operations LLC............ A 330 633-0555
  Tallmadge *(G-13606)*
Summitt Ohio Leasing Co LLC.............. D 937 436-2273
  Dayton *(G-7651)*
Sumner Home For The Aged Inc.......... C 330 666-2952
  Copley *(G-6964)*
Sunbridge Marion Hlth Care LLC.......... D 740 389-6306
  Marion *(G-10456)*
Sunrise Connecticut Ave Assn.............. A 614 451-6766
  Columbus *(G-6730)*
Sunrise Healthcare Group LLC............ C 216 662-3343
  Maple Heights *(G-10349)*
Sunrise Senior Living LLC.................... E 216 447-8909
  Cleveland *(G-4961)*
Sunrise Senior Living LLC.................... E 216 751-0930
  Cleveland *(G-4962)*
Sunrise Senior Living LLC.................... E 330 929-8500
  Cuyahoga Falls *(G-7104)*
Sunrise Senior Living LLC.................... E 937 438-0054
  Dayton *(G-7653)*
Sunrise Senior Living LLC.................... E 614 718-2062
  Dublin *(G-8135)*
Sunrise Senior Living LLC.................... E 937 836-9617
  Englewood *(G-8323)*
Sunrise Senior Living LLC.................... E 419 425-3440
  Findlay *(G-8590)*
Sunrise Senior Living LLC.................... E 614 418-9775
  Gahanna *(G-8731)*

Sunrise Senior Living LLC.................... E 513 893-9000
  Hamilton *(G-9084)*
Sunrise Senior Living LLC.................... E 330 707-1313
  Poland *(G-12510)*
Sunrise Senior Living LLC.................... E 440 895-2383
  Rocky River *(G-12753)*
Sunrise Senior Living LLC.................... E 614 457-3500
  Upper Arlington *(G-14282)*
Sunrise Senior Living LLC.................... E 440 808-0074
  Westlake *(G-15112)*
Sunrise Senior Living MGT Inc.............. C 614 235-3900
  Columbus *(G-6731)*
Sunset Mnor Hlthcare Group Inc............ E 216 795-5710
  Cleveland *(G-4963)*
Swa Inc.. E 440 243-7888
  Cleveland *(G-4970)*
Swanton Hlth Care Rtrment Ctr.............. D 419 825-1145
  Swanton *(G-13529)*
Talbert House.. D 513 629-2303
  Cincinnati *(G-3440)*
The Community Hospital of.................... A 937 325-0531
  Springfield *(G-13300)*
The Maria-Joseph Center...................... B 937 278-2692
  Dayton *(G-7667)*
Tlevay Inc.. C 419 385-3958
  Toledo *(G-14046)*
Traditions At Bath Rd Inc...................... D 330 929-6272
  Cuyahoga Falls *(G-7109)*
Traditions At Stygler Road.................... E 614 475-8778
  Columbus *(G-6781)*
Tri County Extended Care Ctr.............. C 513 829-3555
  Fairfield *(G-8449)*
Trilogy Health Services LLC................ D 419 935-6511
  Willard *(G-15174)*
Trilogy Healthcare Putnam LLC............ A 419 532-2961
  Kalida *(G-9551)*
Trilogy Rehab Services LLC................ C 740 452-3000
  Zanesville *(G-15833)*
Troy Rhblttion Hlthcare Ctr LL.............. D 937 335-7161
  Troy *(G-14165)*
Twilight Grdns Hlthcare Group.............. E 419 668-2086
  Norwalk *(G-12029)*
Uhrichsville Hlth Care Ctr Inc................ E 740 922-2208
  Uhrichsville *(G-14237)*
United Church Homes Inc.................... C 937 426-8481
  Dayton *(G-7682)*
United Church Homes Inc.................... D 937 878-0262
  Fairborn *(G-8382)*
United Church Homes Inc.................... E 740 286-7551
  Jackson *(G-9527)*
United Church Homes Inc.................... E 740 376-5600
  Marietta *(G-10406)*
University Hsptals Hlth Systm-.............. B 440 285-4040
  Chardon *(G-2024)*
University Manor Hlth Care Ctr............ E 216 721-1400
  Cleveland *(G-5082)*
University Mnor Hlthcare Group............ C 216 721-1400
  Cleveland *(G-5083)*
Urbana Healthcare Group LLC............ C 937 652-1381
  Urbana *(G-14315)*
Uvmc Management Corporation............ C 937 440-4000
  Troy *(G-14169)*
Uvmc Nursing Care Inc........................ C 937 473-2075
  Covington *(G-7019)*
Uvmc Nursing Care Inc........................ C 937 667-7500
  Tipp City *(G-13668)*
Uvmc Nursing Care Inc........................ C 937 440-7663
  Troy *(G-14170)*
Valley View Mnor Nrsing HM Inc.......... E 740 998-2948
  Frankfort *(G-8630)*
Van Rue Incorporated............................ D 419 238-0715
  Van Wert *(G-14355)*

Vancare Inc .... D ..... 937 898-4202 Vandalia *(G-14401)*	Windsor Medical Center Inc .... D ..... 330 499-8300 Canton *(G-1886)*	Bittersweet Inc .... D ..... 419 875-6986 Whitehouse *(G-15138)*
Vancrest Ltd .... E ..... 419 695-2871 Delphos *(G-7847)*	Wlkop LLC .... C ..... 440 892-2100 Westlake *(G-15125)*	Blossom Hill Inc .... E ..... 440 652-6749 North Royalton *(G-11938)*
Vancrest Ltd .... E ..... 937 456-3010 Eaton *(G-8225)*	Womens Welsh Clubs of America .... D ..... 440 331-0420 Rocky River *(G-12757)*	Blossom Hills Nursing Home .... E ..... 440 635-5567 Huntsburg *(G-9381)*
Vancrest Management Corp .... D ..... 419 238-0715 Van Wert *(G-14361)*	Woodland Country Manor Inc .... D ..... 513 523-4449 Somerville *(G-13167)*	Brethren Care Inc .... C ..... 419 289-0803 Ashland *(G-484)*
Village Green Healthcare Ctr .... E ..... 937 548-1993 Greenville *(G-8889)*	Woodlands Healthcare Group LLC .... E ..... 330 297-4564 Ravenna *(G-12646)*	Brewster Parke Inc .... D ..... 330 767-4179 Brewster *(G-1373)*
Vista Centre .... E ..... 330 424-5852 Lisbon *(G-10007)*	Woodsfield Opco LLC .... D ..... 740 472-1678 Woodsfield *(G-15304)*	Brook Willow Chrstn Cmmunities .... C ..... 614 885-3300 Columbus *(G-5468)*
Voa Rehabilitation Centers Inc .... E ..... 419 447-7151 Tiffin *(G-13648)*	Woodside Properties I Ltd .... E ..... 419 396-7287 Carey *(G-1897)*	Brookville Enterprises Inc .... C ..... 937 833-2133 Brookville *(G-1445)*
Voluntors Amer Care Facilities .... C ..... 419 225-9040 Lima *(G-9978)*	Woodside Village Care Center .... D ..... 419 947-2015 Mount Gilead *(G-11465)*	Brookwood Realty Company .... D ..... 513 530-9555 Cincinnati *(G-2283)*
Voluntors Amer Care Facilities .... C ..... 419 447-7151 Tiffin *(G-13649)*	Woodstock Healthcare Group Inc .... E ..... 937 826-3351 Woodstock *(G-15305)*	Brown Memorial Home Inc .... D ..... 740 474-6238 Circleville *(G-3703)*
Vrable Healthcare Inc .... E ..... 614 889-8585 Dublin *(G-8157)*	Wyant Leasing Co LLC .... E ..... 330 836-7953 Akron *(G-364)*	Butler County of Ohio .... D ..... 513 887-3728 Hamilton *(G-9020)*
Vrable Healthcare Inc .... E ..... 614 545-5500 Columbus *(G-6859)*	Zandex Health Care Corporation .... C ..... 740 454-1400 New Concord *(G-11613)*	Butler Cnty Bd Dvlpmntal Dsblt .... D ..... 513 867-5913 Fairfield *(G-8396)*
Vrable IV Inc .... D ..... 614 545-5502 Columbus *(G-6860)*	Zandex Health Care Corporation .... C ..... 740 695-7233 Saint Clairsville *(G-12823)*	Canton Asssted Lving Rhbltton .... E ..... 330 492-7131 Canton *(G-1697)*
Walnut Creek Snior Lving Cmpus .... E ..... 937 293-7703 Moraine *(G-11447)*	Zandex Health Care Corporation .... C ..... 740 454-9747 Zanesville *(G-15837)*	Caprice Health Care Inc .... E ..... 330 965-9200 North Lima *(G-11885)*
Walnut Hills Inc .... E ..... 330 852-2457 Walnut Creek *(G-14472)*	Zandex Health Care Corporation .... C ..... 740 452-4636 Zanesville *(G-15838)*	▲ Cardinal Health 414 LLC .... C ..... 614 757-5000 Dublin *(G-7956)*
Washington MD Leasing Co LLC .... E ..... 513 489-7100 Blue Ash *(G-1273)*	Zandex Health Care Corporation .... C ..... 740 454-9769 Zanesville *(G-15839)*	Cardinal Retirement Village .... E ..... 330 928-7888 Cuyahoga Falls *(G-7052)*
Water Leasing Co LLC .... C ..... 440 285-9400 Chardon *(G-2026)*	**8052 Intermediate care facilities**	Carington Health Systems .... B ..... 937 743-2754 Franklin *(G-8632)*
Watermark Rtrment Cmmnties Inc .... D ..... 405 751-3600 Toledo *(G-14098)*	599 W Main Corporation .... E ..... 440 466-1079 Geneva *(G-8783)*	Carlton Manor Nursing and .... C ..... 740 335-7143 Wshngtn Ct Hs *(G-15477)*
Wayside Farm Inc .... D ..... 330 666-7716 Peninsula *(G-12295)*	Alexson Services Inc .... D ..... 513 874-0423 Fairfield *(G-8389)*	Carriage Crt-Mrysvlle Ltd Prtn .... E ..... 937 642-2202 Marysville *(G-10478)*
Wellington Place LLC .... D ..... 440 734-9933 North Olmsted *(G-11920)*	Altercare Inc .... E ..... 330 335-2555 Wadsworth *(G-14427)*	Center For Eating Disorders .... E ..... 614 896-8222 Columbus *(G-5531)*
Wessell Generations Inc .... D ..... 440 775-1491 Oberlin *(G-12077)*	Altercare Nobles Pond Inc .... E ..... 330 834-4800 Canton *(G-1663)*	Center For Rhbltton At Hmpton .... E ..... 330 792-7681 Poland *(G-12502)*
West Park Care Center LLC .... B ..... 614 274-4222 Columbus *(G-6880)*	Alternative Residences Two Inc .... C ..... 740 526-0514 Saint Clairsville *(G-12773)*	Center Ridge Nursing Home Inc .... C ..... 440 808-5500 North Ridgeville *(G-11924)*
West Park Retirement Community .... E ..... 513 451-8900 Cincinnati *(G-3656)*	American Retirement Corp .... C ..... 216 291-6140 Cleveland *(G-3807)*	Choices In Community Living .... C ..... 937 898-3655 Dayton *(G-7225)*
West Side Dtscher Fruen Verein .... B ..... 440 238-3361 Berea *(G-1087)*	Anchor Lodge Nursing Home Inc .... E ..... 440 244-2019 Lorain *(G-10054)*	Church of God Retirement Cmnty .... E ..... 513 422-5600 Middletown *(G-11156)*
West View Manor Inc .... C ..... 330 264-8640 Wooster *(G-15386)*	Anne Grady Corporation .... C ..... 419 380-8985 Holland *(G-9278)*	Clovernook Inc .... D ..... 513 605-4000 Cincinnati *(G-2462)*
Western Hills Care Center .... D ..... 513 941-0099 Cincinnati *(G-3661)*	Apostolic Christian Home Inc .... D ..... 330 927-1010 Rittman *(G-12729)*	Columbus Center For Human Svcs .... C ..... 614 278-9362 Columbus *(G-5617)*
Western Rsrve Msonic Cmnty Inc .... C ..... 330 721-3000 Medina *(G-10903)*	ARA-Bexley LLC .... E ..... 614 253-3300 Columbus *(G-5376)*	Compassus .... D ..... 440 249-6036 Seven Hills *(G-12953)*
Wexner Heritage Village .... B ..... 614 231-4900 Columbus *(G-6882)*	Arbors East LLC .... E ..... 614 575-9003 Columbus *(G-5377)*	Concord Health Care Inc .... E ..... 330 759-2357 Youngstown *(G-15588)*
Whitehouse Operator LLC .... D ..... 419 877-5338 Whitehouse *(G-15144)*	Arlington Care Ctr .... B ..... 740 344-0303 Newark *(G-11688)*	Congregate Living of America .... D ..... 937 393-6700 Hillsboro *(G-9251)*
Wickliffe Country Place Ltd .... C ..... 440 944-9400 Wickliffe *(G-15165)*	Arlington Crt Nrsing HM Svc In .... D ..... 614 545-5502 Upper Arlington *(G-14276)*	Congregate Living of America .... D ..... 513 899-2801 Morrow *(G-11455)*
Widows Home of Dayton Ohio .... D ..... 937 252-1661 Dayton *(G-7721)*	Asana Hospice Cleveland LLC .... E ..... 419 903-0300 Berea *(G-1061)*	Connecting Dots Cnncting To SL .... E ..... 216 356-2362 Cleveland *(G-4101)*
Willow Brook Christian Svcs .... E ..... 740 201-5640 Delaware *(G-7834)*	Assisted Living Concepts LLC .... E ..... 419 334-6962 Fremont *(G-8667)*	Consulate Healthcare Inc .... E ..... 419 865-1248 Maumee *(G-10711)*
Willow Brook Chrstn Cmmunities .... D ..... 740 369-0048 Delaware *(G-7835)*	Atrium Living Centers of .... E ..... 614 416-2662 Columbus *(G-5405)*	Consulate Management Co LLC .... B ..... 440 237-7966 Cleveland *(G-4110)*
Willowood Care Center .... C ..... 330 225-3156 Brunswick *(G-1475)*	Aws .... E ..... 513 648-9360 Cincinnati *(G-2231)*	Continuum Care Home Health LLC .... E ..... 216 898-8399 Parma *(G-12252)*
Wilmington Hathcare Group Inc .... E ..... 937 382-1621 Wilmington *(G-15278)*	Beaver Dam Health Care Center .... E ..... 614 861-6666 Columbus *(G-5429)*	Country CLB Retirement Ctr LLC .... D ..... 740 671-9330 Bellaire *(G-1010)*
Winchester Place Leasing LLC .... D ..... 614 834-2273 Canal Winchester *(G-1619)*	Beaver Dam Health Care Center .... E ..... 419 227-2154 Lima *(G-9867)*	Country Club Center Homes Inc .... D ..... 330 343-6351 Dover *(G-7876)*
Windsong Healthcare Group LLC .... D ..... 216 292-5706 Akron *(G-362)*	Beaver Dam Health Care Center .... E ..... 330 335-1558 Wadsworth *(G-14429)*	Country Club Center II Ltd .... C ..... 740 397-2350 Mount Vernon *(G-11479)*

80 HEALTH SERVICES

County of Montgomery.................................... C 937 264-0460
   Dayton *(G-7257)*

County of Shelby.. D 937 492-6900
   Sidney *(G-13027)*

Covenant Care Ohio Inc................................... D 937 878-7046
   Fairborn *(G-8370)*

Cridersville Health Care Ctr............................. D 419 645-4468
   Cridersville *(G-7028)*

Crossrads Sleep Dsrders Ctr LL...................... E 330 965-0220
   Youngstown *(G-15590)*

Crystalwood Inc... E 513 605-1000
   Cincinnati *(G-2519)*

Dayspring Health Care Center....................... E 937 864-5800
   Fairborn *(G-8373)*

Dayton Hospice Incorporated........................ C 513 422-0300
   Franklin *(G-8633)*

Dayton Hospice Incorporated........................ B 937 256-4490
   Dayton *(G-7288)*

Deaconess Long Term Care of MI................. A 513 487-3600
   Cincinnati *(G-2551)*

Dearth Management Company..................... D 419 253-0144
   Marengo *(G-10352)*

Dearth Management Company..................... D 330 339-3595
   New Philadelphia *(G-11649)*

Debmar Inc.. D 419 728-7010
   Bowling Green *(G-1317)*

Dover Nursing Center Llc............................... D 330 364-4436
   Dover *(G-7883)*

Eagle Creek Hlthcare Group Inc..................... B 937 544-5531
   West Union *(G-14869)*

Earley & Ross Ltd... D 740 634-3301
   Sabina *(G-12771)*

East Lverpool Convalescent Ctr.................... D 330 382-0101
   East Liverpool *(G-8182)*

Ebenezer Road Corporation.......................... C 513 941-0099
   Cincinnati *(G-2601)*

Echoing Hills Village Inc................................. D 440 989-1400
   Lorain *(G-10071)*

Edgewood Manor of Wellston........................ D 740 384-5611
   Wellston *(G-14637)*

Elms Retirement Village Inc........................... B 440 647-2414
   Wellington *(G-14631)*

Emeritus Corporation....................................... D 513 683-9966
   Cincinnati *(G-2615)*

Fairmount Nursing Home Inc......................... D 440 338-8220
   Newbury *(G-11760)*

Falls Vlg Retirement Cmnty Ltd...................... D 330 945-9797
   Cuyahoga Falls *(G-7076)*

Fayette Hospice County Inc........................... E 740 335-0149
   Wshngtn Ct Hs *(G-15483)*

Fc Compassus LLC.. E 380 207-1526
   West Jefferson *(G-14850)*

Filling Memorial Home of Mercy.................... B 419 592-6451
   Napoleon *(G-11522)*

Fisher-Titus Medical Center........................... D 419 668-4228
   Norwalk *(G-12012)*

▲ Fisher-Titus Medical Center....................... A 419 668-8101
   Norwalk *(G-12013)*

Flower Hospital... B 419 824-1000
   Sylvania *(G-13545)*

Fountains At Canterbury................................ E 405 751-3600
   Toledo *(G-13810)*

Franciscan At St Leonard................................ D 937 433-0480
   Dayton *(G-7365)*

Friends of Good Shepherd Manor................ E 740 289-2861
   Lucasville *(G-10178)*

Gateway Health Care Center......................... D 216 486-4949
   Cleveland *(G-4305)*

Genertion Hlth Rhbittion Ctr L....................... D 740 348-1300
   Newark *(G-11701)*

Genesis Healthcare LLC................................... B 419 666-0935
   Perrysburg *(G-12336)*

Gentry Health Services Inc............................ D 330 721-1077
   Avon Lake *(G-679)*

Gillette Nursing Home Inc............................. D 330 372-1960
   Warren *(G-14524)*

Good Shepherd Home.................................... C 419 937-1801
   Fostoria *(G-8618)*

Grace Hospice LLC... C 513 458-5545
   Cincinnati *(G-2746)*

Grace Hospice LLC... D 216 288-7413
   Cleveland *(G-4323)*

Grace Hospice LLC... C 440 826-0350
   Cleveland *(G-4324)*

Grace Hospice LLC... C 937 293-1381
   Moraine *(G-11414)*

Greens of Lyndhurst The Inc......................... E 440 460-1000
   Cleveland *(G-4340)*

Guernsey Health Systems............................... A 740 439-3561
   Cambridge *(G-1573)*

H & G Nursery Home Inc................................ E 513 734-7401
   Bethel *(G-1091)*

H & G Nursing Homes Inc.............................. D 937 544-2205
   West Union *(G-14870)*

Harborside Sylvania LLC................................. D 419 882-1875
   Sylvania *(G-13548)*

Hattie Lrlham Ctr For Chldren....................... C 330 274-2272
   Mantua *(G-10331)*

Hcrmc-Promedica LLC...................................... A 419 540-6000
   Sylvania *(G-13549)*

Heinzerling Foundation................................... C 614 272-8888
   Columbus *(G-5981)*

Hempstead Manor.. E 740 354-8150
   Portsmouth *(G-12553)*

Hennis Nursing Home..................................... C 330 364-8849
   Dover *(G-7889)*

Heritage Professional Services....................... E 740 456-8245
   New Boston *(G-11594)*

Hill Side Plaza.. D 216 486-6300
   Cleveland *(G-4361)*

Holzer Clinic LLC... E 740 446-5074
   Gallipolis *(G-8758)*

Home Echo Club Inc.. D 614 864-1718
   Pickerington *(G-12403)*

Hospice Cincinnati Inc..................................... D 513 389-5528
   Cincinnati *(G-2845)*

Hospice Cincinnati Inc..................................... D 513 598-5093
   Cincinnati *(G-2846)*

Hospice Cincinnati Inc..................................... D 513 386-6000
   Cincinnati *(G-2847)*

Hospice of Central Ohio................................. D 740 344-0311
   Newark *(G-11707)*

Hospice of Darke County Inc........................ E 937 548-2999
   Greenville *(G-8878)*

Hospice of Hope Inc.. D 937 444-4900
   Mount Orab *(G-11471)*

Hospice of Miami County Inc........................ E 937 335-5191
   Troy *(G-14139)*

Hospice of Miami Valley LLC.......................... E 937 458-6028
   Beavercreek *(G-883)*

Hospice of Northwest Ohio........................... D 419 661-4001
   Toledo *(G-13851)*

Hospice of Northwest Ohio........................... B 419 661-4001
   Perrysburg *(G-12344)*

Hospice of The Western Reserve.................. C 216 227-9048
   Cleveland *(G-4381)*

Hospice of The Western Reserve.................. E 440 414-7349
   Westlake *(G-15066)*

Hospice of Western Reserve Inc................... C 216 383-2222
   Cleveland *(G-4382)*

Hospice Tuscarawas County Inc................... E 330 627-4796
   Carrollton *(G-1909)*

Hospice Tuscarawas County Inc................... D 330 343-7605
   New Philadelphia *(G-11654)*

Humility House.. D 330 505-0144
   Youngstown *(G-15634)*

Indian Hlls Hlthcare Group Inc...................... A 216 486-8880
   Euclid *(G-8350)*

Inn At Marietta Ltd... E 740 373-9600
   Marietta *(G-10375)*

Isabelle Ridgway Care Ctr Inc........................ D 614 252-4931
   Columbus *(G-6074)*

Jennings Eliza Home Inc................................ C 216 226-0282
   Cleveland *(G-4436)*

Judson... D 216 791-2004
   Cleveland *(G-4444)*

Judson Care Center Inc................................... A 513 662-5880
   Cincinnati *(G-2922)*

Kendal At Oberlin.. C 440 775-0094
   Oberlin *(G-12071)*

Lakeside Manor Inc.. E 330 549-2545
   North Lima *(G-11890)*

Leeda Services Inc.. E 330 392-6006
   Warren *(G-14534)*

Lexington Court Care Center......................... E 419 884-2000
   Mansfield *(G-10281)*

Liberty Nursing Center.................................... E 937 836-5143
   Englewood *(G-8313)*

Liberty Nursing of Willard.............................. D 419 935-0148
   Willard *(G-15170)*

Life Care Centers America Inc....................... D 330 483-3131
   Valley City *(G-14334)*

Lifecare Hospice... E 330 674-8448
   Millersburg *(G-11283)*

Lifecare Hospice... E 330 264-4899
   Wooster *(G-15351)*

Lifeservices Management Corp..................... D 440 257-3866
   Mentor *(G-10964)*

Light of Hearts Villa Inc.................................. D 440 232-1991
   Cleveland *(G-4495)*

Lincoln Park Associates II LP......................... D 937 297-4300
   Dayton *(G-7455)*

Little Ssters of Poor Bltmore.......................... D 513 281-8001
   Cincinnati *(G-2982)*

Little Ssters of Poor Bltmore.......................... D 216 464-1222
   Warrensville Heights *(G-14584)*

Living Care Altrntves of Utica....................... E 740 892-3414
   Utica *(G-14329)*

Lorain Manor Inc.. D 440 277-8173
   Lorain *(G-10087)*

Lutheran Home.. B 440 871-0090
   Cleveland *(G-4510)*

Lutheran Memorial Home Inc........................ D 419 502-5700
   Toledo *(G-13900)*

Lutheran Village At Wolf Creek..................... E 419 861-2233
   Holland *(G-9296)*

Madison Village Manor Inc............................ D 440 428-1519
   Madison *(G-10222)*

Main Street Terrace Care Ctr......................... D 740 653-8767
   Lancaster *(G-9734)*

Mansfield Memorial Homes LLC.................... C 419 774-5100
   Mansfield *(G-10289)*

Maple Knoll Communities Inc....................... B 513 782-2400
   Cincinnati *(G-3008)*

McClellan Management Inc........................... E 419 855-7755
   Genoa *(G-8795)*

McKinley Health Care Ctr LLC........................ D 330 456-1014
   Canton *(G-1803)*

McV Health Care Facilities Inc....................... E 513 398-1486
   Mason *(G-10580)*

Meigs County Care Center LLC..................... C 740 992-6472
   Middleport *(G-11148)*

Mennonite Memorial Home.......................... C 419 358-1015
   Bluffton *(G-1283)*

Miami Valley Hsing Assn I Inc....................... E 937 263-4449
   Dayton *(G-7496)*

80 HEALTH SERVICES

Mill Run Care Center LLC .... E 614 527-3000
   Hilliard *(G-9216)*

Mount Aloysius Corp .... D 740 342-3343
   New Lexington *(G-11629)*

Mount Carmel Health System .... B 614 636-6290
   Columbus *(G-6276)*

New Dawn Health Care Inc .... C 330 343-5521
   Dover *(G-7895)*

Northcrest Nursing & Rehab .... E 419 599-4070
   Napoleon *(G-11531)*

Northeast Care Center Inc .... D 440 234-9407
   Berea *(G-1075)*

Northeast Care Center Inc .... D 440 888-9320
   North Royalton *(G-11946)*

Norwood Health Care Center LLC .... D 513 351-0153
   Cincinnati *(G-3130)*

Oak Hlth Care Invstors of Mt V .... D 740 397-3200
   Mount Vernon *(G-11503)*

October Enterprises Inc .... D 937 456-9535
   Eaton *(G-8218)*

Ohio Department of Mental Health .... A 614 466-2337
   Columbus *(G-6401)*

Ohio Dept Dvlpmntal Dsbilities .... C 614 272-0509
   Columbus *(G-6405)*

Ohio Dept Dvlpmntal Dsbilities .... C 740 446-1642
   Gallipolis *(G-8764)*

Ohio Living .... B 513 681-4230
   Cincinnati *(G-3147)*

Ohio Living .... B 513 539-7391
   Monroe *(G-11345)*

Ohio Living .... B 937 498-2391
   Sidney *(G-13043)*

Ohio Living .... B 330 746-2944
   Youngstown *(G-15682)*

Ohio Living Holdings .... D 614 433-0031
   Columbus *(G-6434)*

Ohio Valley Manor Inc .... C 937 392-4318
   Ripley *(G-12727)*

Ohios Hospice Inc .... D 937 256-4490
   Dayton *(G-7535)*

Ohios Hospice Foundation 0 .... E 937 256-4490
   Dayton *(G-7536)*

Orchard Villa Inc .... D 419 697-4100
   Oregon *(G-12139)*

Orion Care Services LLC .... E 216 752-3600
   Cleveland *(G-4707)*

Otterbein Homes .... B 513 933-5400
   Lebanon *(G-9781)*

Otterbein Portage Valley Inc .... C 888 749-4950
   Pemberville *(G-12291)*

Park Creek Rtirement Cmnty Inc .... E 440 842-5100
   Cleveland *(G-4720)*

Park View Manor Inc .... D 937 296-1550
   Englewood *(G-8318)*

Parma Care Center Inc .... C 216 661-6800
   Cleveland *(G-4728)*

Pickaway Manor Inc .... E 740 474-5400
   Circleville *(G-3717)*

Pleasant View Nursing Home Inc .... D 330 848-5028
   Barberton *(G-702)*

Promedica Health System Inc .... B 513 831-5800
   Cincinnati *(G-3252)*

Provide-A-Care Inc .... C 330 828-2278
   Dalton *(G-7121)*

R & G Nursing Care Inc .... C 330 562-3120
   Aurora *(G-623)*

Rae-Ann Center Inc .... E 440 466-5733
   Geneva *(G-8788)*

Renaissance House Inc .... E 419 626-1110
   Sandusky *(G-12926)*

RES-Care Inc .... D 330 627-7552
   Carrollton *(G-1912)*

RES-Care Inc .... D 513 271-0708
   Cincinnati *(G-3290)*

RES-Care Inc .... D 419 435-6620
   Fostoria *(G-8623)*

RES-Care Inc .... D 937 298-6276
   Moraine *(G-11433)*

RES-Care Inc .... D 740 941-1178
   Waverly *(G-14617)*

Rescare Ohio Inc .... E 513 724-1177
   Mount Orab *(G-11473)*

Residence of Chardon .... E 440 286-2277
   Chardon *(G-2016)*

Rest Haven Nursing Home Inc .... D 937 548-1138
   Greenville *(G-8882)*

Ridge-Pleasant Valley Inc .... C 440 845-0200
   Cleveland *(G-4840)*

Rivers Bend Health Care LLC .... D 740 894-3476
   South Point *(G-13183)*

Roman Cthlic Docese Youngstown ..... C 330 875-5562
   Louisville *(G-10122)*

Rose Mary Johanna Grassell .... D 216 481-4823
   Cleveland *(G-4854)*

Royal Manor Health Care Inc .... E 216 752-3600
   Cleveland *(G-4859)*

Salutary Providers Inc .... C 440 964-8446
   Ashtabula *(G-548)*

Samaritan Care Center Inc .... D 330 725-4123
   Medina *(G-10887)*

Sarah Moore Hlth Care Ctr Inc .... D 740 362-9641
   Delaware *(G-7824)*

Sateri Home Inc .... D 330 758-8106
   Youngstown *(G-15717)*

Singleton Health Care Ctr Inc .... D 216 231-0076
   Cleveland *(G-4909)*

Society For Hndcpped Ctzens of .... E 330 722-1900
   Seville *(G-12965)*

Southeastern Health Care Ctr .... D 740 425-3648
   Barnesville *(G-722)*

Southern Care Inc .... D 419 774-0555
   Ontario *(G-12124)*

Spring Mdow Extnded Care Ctr F .... D 419 866-6124
   Holland *(G-9305)*

Spring Meadow Extended Care Ce ..... E 419 866-6124
   Mansfield *(G-10318)*

St Johns Villa .... C 330 627-4662
   Carrollton *(G-1913)*

St Joseph Infant Maternity HM .... C 513 563-2520
   Cincinnati *(G-3403)*

St Luke Lutheran Community .... E 330 644-3914
   New Franklin *(G-11616)*

▲ Stein Hospice Service Inc .... E 800 625-5269
   Sandusky *(G-12934)*

Stratford Commons Inc .... D 440 914-0900
   Solon *(G-13150)*

Summit Acres Inc .... C 740 732-2364
   Caldwell *(G-1551)*

Summit Facility Operations LLC .... A 330 633-0555
   Tallmadge *(G-13606)*

Sunset House Inc .... D 419 536-4645
   Toledo *(G-14029)*

Sunshine Communities .... B 419 865-0251
   Maumee *(G-10773)*

Swanton Hlth Care Rtrment Ctr .... D 419 825-1145
   Swanton *(G-13529)*

The Maria-Joseph Center .... B 937 278-2692
   Dayton *(G-7667)*

Tridia Hospice Care Inc .... D 614 915-8882
   Westerville *(G-14947)*

Twilight Grdns Hlthcare Group .... E 419 668-2086
   Norwalk *(G-12029)*

United Church Homes Inc .... C 937 426-8481
   Dayton *(G-7682)*

United Church Homes Inc .... D 937 878-0262
   Fairborn *(G-8382)*

United Church Homes Inc .... E 740 286-7551
   Jackson *(G-9527)*

United Church Homes Inc .... E 419 294-4973
   Upper Sandusky *(G-14294)*

United Crbral Plsy Assn Grter .... E 216 381-9993
   Cleveland *(G-5058)*

University Hsptals Hlth Systm- .... B 440 285-4040
   Chardon *(G-2024)*

University Manor Hlth Care Ctr .... E 216 721-1400
   Cleveland *(G-5082)*

Valley Hospice Inc .... E 740 859-5041
   Rayland *(G-12648)*

Vancare Inc .... D 937 898-4202
   Vandalia *(G-14401)*

Villa Vista Royale LLC .... E 740 264-7301
   Steubenville *(G-13350)*

Vista Centre .... E 330 424-5852
   Lisbon *(G-10007)*

Vitas Healthcare Corp Midwest .... C 614 822-2700
   Dublin *(G-8156)*

Vitas Healthcare Corporation .... C 513 742-6310
   Cincinnati *(G-3632)*

Vitas Healthcare Corporation .... D 937 299-5379
   Moraine *(G-11446)*

Voiers Enterprises Inc .... E 740 259-2838
   Mc Dermott *(G-10800)*

Volunters Amer Care Facilities .... C 419 225-9040
   Lima *(G-9978)*

Walnut Hills Inc .... E 330 852-2457
   Walnut Creek *(G-14472)*

Warren Cnty Bd Dvlpmntal Dsblt .... C 513 925-1813
   Lebanon *(G-9798)*

Wedgewood Estates .... E 419 756-7400
   Mansfield *(G-10324)*

Wesley Ridge Inc .... D 614 759-0023
   Reynoldsburg *(G-12681)*

West Park Retirement Community .... E 513 451-8900
   Cincinnati *(G-3656)*

Western Rsrve Msonic Cmnty Inc .... C 330 721-3000
   Medina *(G-10903)*

Wexner Heritage Village .... B 614 231-4900
   Columbus *(G-6882)*

Willow Brook Chrstn Cmmunities .... D 740 369-0048
   Delaware *(G-7835)*

Windsor Medical Center Inc .... D 330 499-8300
   Canton *(G-1886)*

Wood Lane Residential Svcs Inc .... D 419 353-9577
   Bowling Green *(G-1338)*

Woodside Village Care Center .... D 419 947-2015
   Mount Gilead *(G-11465)*

Zandex Health Care Corporation .... C 740 454-1400
   Johnstown *(G-9550)*

Zandex Health Care Corporation .... D 740 392-1099
   Mount Vernon *(G-11511)*

Zandex Health Care Corporation .... C 740 454-1400
   New Concord *(G-11613)*

Zandex Health Care Corporation .... C 740 695-7233
   Saint Clairsville *(G-12823)*

Zandex Health Care Corporation .... C 740 454-9747
   Zanesville *(G-15837)*

Zandex Health Care Corporation .... C 740 452-4636
   Zanesville *(G-15838)*

Zandex Health Care Corporation .... C 740 454-9769
   Zanesville *(G-15839)*

8059 Nursing and personal care, nec

8001 Red Buckeye Landlord LLC .... D 937 506-4733
   North Canton *(G-11806)*

Altercare Inc .... E 330 929-4231
   Cuyahoga Falls *(G-7037)*

80 HEALTH SERVICES

Amara Homecare Bedford Tel No............ D 440 353-0600
  North Ridgeville *(G-11923)*
Antioch Cnnction Canton MI LLC............ E 614 531-9285
  Pickerington *(G-12398)*
Antioch Salem Fields Frederick............. E 614 531-9285
  Pickerington *(G-12399)*
Apostolic Christian Home Inc................ D 330 927-1010
  Rittman *(G-12729)*
Arbors West LLC....................................... E 614 879-7661
  West Jefferson *(G-14848)*
Astoria Place Silverton LLC.................... D 513 793-2090
  Cincinnati *(G-2222)*
Beaver Dam Health Care Center............ E 330 762-6486
  Akron *(G-64)*
Beaver Dam Health Care Center............ E 614 861-6666
  Columbus *(G-5429)*
Beaver Dam Health Care Center............ E 419 227-2154
  Lima *(G-9867)*
Beaver Dam Health Care Center............ E 330 335-1558
  Wadsworth *(G-14429)*
Beaver Dam Health Care Center............ E 440 256-8100
  Willoughby *(G-15187)*
Birchaven Village....................................... C 419 424-3000
  Findlay *(G-8513)*
Blue Ash Healthcare Group Inc.............. E 513 793-3362
  Cincinnati *(G-2266)*
Boy-Ko Management Inc......................... E 513 677-4900
  Loveland *(G-10128)*
Brewster Parke Inc.................................. D 330 767-4179
  Brewster *(G-1373)*
Briarwood Inc... D 330 688-1828
  Stow *(G-13356)*
Broken Arrow Inc..................................... E 419 562-3480
  Bucyrus *(G-1496)*
Brookside Extended Care Center.......... E 513 398-1020
  Mason *(G-10524)*
Brookview Healthcare Ctr....................... D 419 784-1014
  Defiance *(G-7742)*
Bryant Health Center Inc........................ D 740 532-6188
  Ironton *(G-9504)*
Buckeye Community Services Inc......... C 740 941-1639
  Waverly *(G-14611)*
Capital Health Services Inc.................... E 937 277-0505
  Miamisburg *(G-11033)*
Careworks of Ohio Inc............................. A 614 792-1085
  Dublin *(G-7958)*
Carriage Court Company Inc.................. C 614 871-8000
  Grove City *(G-8905)*
Center Ridge Nursing Home Inc............ C 440 808-5500
  North Ridgeville *(G-11924)*
Center Street Cmnty Clinic Inc.............. E 740 751-6380
  Marion *(G-10421)*
Columbana Cnty For Dvlpmntal D.......... C 330 424-0404
  Lisbon *(G-9998)*
Columbus Alzheimers Care Ctr.............. D 614 459-7050
  Columbus *(G-5607)*
Columbus Alzheimers Oper LLC............ D 614 459-7050
  Columbus *(G-5608)*
Columbus Ctr For Humn Svcs Inc......... D 614 245-8180
  New Albany *(G-11559)*
Columbus Ctr For Humn Svcs Inc......... C 614 641-2904
  Columbus *(G-5626)*
Community Concepts Inc........................ D 513 398-8181
  Mason *(G-10542)*
Connecting Dots Cnncting To SL.......... E 216 356-2362
  Cleveland *(G-4101)*
Consulate Management Co LLC............. B 740 259-2351
  Lucasville *(G-10174)*
Consumer Support Services Inc............ D 330 764-4785
  Medina *(G-10825)*
Cotter House Worthington LLC............. D 614 540-2414
  Westerville *(G-14885)*

Country CLB Retirement Ctr LLC.......... D 740 671-9330
  Bellaire *(G-1010)*
Country Club Center Homes Inc............ D 330 343-6351
  Dover *(G-7876)*
Country Meadow Care Center LLC........ E 419 886-3922
  Bellville *(G-1048)*
County of Auglaize................................... D 419 738-3816
  Wapakoneta *(G-14482)*
County of Richland.................................. B 419 774-4200
  Mansfield *(G-10255)*
County of Shelby..................................... D 937 492-6900
  Sidney *(G-13027)*
County of Wayne..................................... D 330 262-1786
  Wooster *(G-15328)*
County of Wyandot.................................. D 419 294-1714
  Upper Sandusky *(G-14286)*
Crystal Care Centers Inc....................... D 419 747-2666
  Mansfield *(G-10256)*
Crystalwood Inc....................................... E 513 605-1000
  Cincinnati *(G-2519)*
Deaconess Associations Inc.................. B 513 559-2100
  Cincinnati *(G-2548)*
Deaconess Long Term Care Inc............ D 513 861-0400
  Cincinnati *(G-2550)*
Deaconess Long Term Care of MI........ A 513 487-3600
  Cincinnati *(G-2551)*
Debmar Inc... D 419 728-7010
  Bowling Green *(G-1317)*
Dhl Home Care LLC................................. E 614 987-5813
  Columbus *(G-5760)*
Dublin Cnvlarium Operating LLC........... D 614 761-1188
  Dublin *(G-7991)*
Dublin Geriatric Care Co LP.................. E 614 761-1188
  Dublin *(G-7993)*
East Glbrith Hlth Care Ctr Inc............... B 513 984-5220
  Cincinnati *(G-2598)*
Echoing Hills Village Inc........................ D 937 237-7881
  Dayton *(G-7327)*
Echoing Hills Village Inc........................ E 440 323-0915
  Elyria *(G-8243)*
Echoing Hills Village Inc........................ E 440 986-3085
  South Amherst *(G-13168)*
Edgewood Manor Lucasville LLC.......... D 740 259-5536
  Lucasville *(G-10175)*
Elixir Vi LLC... C 419 884-9808
  Mansfield *(G-10262)*
Elms Retirement Village Inc.................. B 440 647-2414
  Wellington *(G-14631)*
Evanglcal Lthran Good Smrtan S........ C 419 365-5115
  Arlington *(G-469)*
First Choice Medical Staffing................ D 216 521-2222
  Cleveland *(G-4257)*
First Community Village......................... B 614 324-4455
  Columbus *(G-5861)*
Franciscan At St Leonard...................... D 937 433-0480
  Dayton *(G-7365)*
Friendship Vlg of Dublin Ohio................ C 614 764-1600
  Dublin *(G-8016)*
Gardens At Celina Oper Co LLC........... E 419 584-0100
  Celina *(G-1924)*
Gardens At Paulding Oper LLC............. D 419 399-4940
  Paulding *(G-12283)*
Gardens At St Henry Oper LLC............ D 419 678-9800
  Saint Henry *(G-12825)*
Gardens Western Reserve Inc.............. E 330 342-9100
  Streetsboro *(G-13412)*
Gillette Associates LP............................ E 330 372-1960
  Warren *(G-14523)*
Graceworks Enhanced Living................ D 513 825-3333
  Cincinnati *(G-2748)*
Guardian Elder Care Columbus.............. D 614 868-9306
  Columbus *(G-5958)*

Guiding Fndtons Spport Svcs LL......... D 440 485-3772
  Bedford *(G-963)*
H C F Inc.. E 740 289-2528
  Piketon *(G-12421)*
Hamlet Village In Chagrin FLS............... C 440 247-4200
  Chagrin Falls *(G-1960)*
Hardin County Home................................ D 419 673-0961
  Kenton *(G-9616)*
Harrison Pavilion..................................... E 513 662-5800
  Cincinnati *(G-2802)*
Hcf of Washington Inc........................... E 419 999-2010
  Wshngtn Ct Hs *(G-15488)*
Health Care Solutions Inc...................... C 330 729-9491
  Youngstown *(G-15627)*
Heath Nursing Care Center.................... D 740 522-1171
  Newark *(G-11704)*
Heinzerling Foundation........................... B 614 272-2000
  Columbus *(G-5982)*
Heinzerling Foundation........................... C 614 272-8888
  Columbus *(G-5981)*
Home At Hearthstone............................. E 513 521-2700
  Cincinnati *(G-2833)*
Home Health Connection Inc................ E 614 839-4545
  Lancaster *(G-9725)*
Hospice North Central Ohio Inc............. E 419 281-7107
  Ashland *(G-501)*
Hudson Elms Opco LLC........................... E 330 650-0436
  Hudson *(G-9355)*
Judson... D 216 791-2004
  Cleveland *(G-4444)*
Jwj Investments Inc.............................. C 419 643-3161
  Delphos *(G-7841)*
Karrington Operating Co Inc.................. B 614 875-0514
  Grove City *(G-8929)*
Karrington Operating Co Inc.................. D 614 324-5951
  Columbus *(G-6105)*
Kingston Healthcare Company............... E 440 967-1800
  Vermilion *(G-14407)*
Kingston Healthcare Company............... E 419 247-2880
  Toledo *(G-13879)*
Lcd Agency Services LLC....................... E 513 497-0441
  Hamilton *(G-9059)*
Lima Cnvlscent HM Fndation Inc.......... D 419 227-5450
  Lima *(G-9920)*
Lincoln Park Associates II LP................ D 937 297-4300
  Dayton *(G-7455)*
Lutheran Memorial Home Inc.................. D 419 502-5700
  Toledo *(G-13900)*
Lutheran Village At Wolf Creek............. E 419 861-2233
  Holland *(G-9296)*
Mahoning County..................................... E 330 797-2925
  Youngstown *(G-15657)*
Mahoning Vly Infusioncare Inc.............. C 330 759-9487
  Youngstown *(G-15660)*
Marion Manor... E 740 387-9545
  Marion *(G-10441)*
Marymount Health Care Systems.......... A 216 332-1100
  Cleveland *(G-4530)*
Mayflower Nursing Home Inc.................. E 330 492-7131
  Canton *(G-1801)*
McCrea Operating Company LLC......... D 330 823-9055
  Alliance *(G-392)*
McV Health Care Facilities Inc.............. E 513 398-1486
  Mason *(G-10580)*
Medina Medical Investors Ltd................ D 330 483-3131
  Medina *(G-10863)*
Mennonite Memorial Home..................... C 419 358-1015
  Bluffton *(G-1283)*
Mikouis Enterprise Inc........................... D 330 424-1418
  Lisbon *(G-10005)*
Mill Run Care Center LLC....................... E 614 527-3000
  Hilliard *(G-9216)*

Minamyer Rsdntial Care Svcs In............ E 614 802-0190
  Columbus (G-6251)
Mkjb Inc... D 513 851-8400
  West Chester (G-14733)
Mohun Health Care Center.................. E 614 416-6132
  Columbus (G-6256)
Morning View Delaware Inc................ C 740 965-3984
  Sunbury (G-13522)
Multi-Care Inc.................................... D 440 357-6181
  Painesville (G-12239)
National Church Residences................ C 614 451-2151
  Columbus (G-6292)
Nentwick Convalescent Home............. E 330 385-5001
  East Liverpool (G-8187)
Niles Residential Care LLC................. D 216 727-3996
  Niles (G-11794)
Northcrest Nursing & Rehab................ E 419 599-4070
  Napoleon (G-11531)
Northeast Care Center Inc................... D 440 234-9407
  Berea (G-1075)
Norwood Health Care Center LLC......... D 513 351-0153
  Cincinnati (G-3130)
Ohio Living.. B 937 498-2391
  Sidney (G-13043)
Ohio Mentor Inc.................................. C 216 525-1885
  Independence (G-9463)
Ohio Valley Manor Inc........................ C 937 392-4318
  Ripley (G-12727)
Orchard Villa Inc................................ D 419 697-4100
  Oregon (G-12139)
Otterbein Homes................................. E 513 260-7690
  Middletown (G-11200)
Otterbein Snior Lfstyle Chices.............. E 937 885-5426
  Dayton (G-7542)
Ouicare Rcrtment Stffing Svcs............. E 440 536-4829
  Ashtabula (G-544)
Phillips Hthcare LLC DBA Cring........... E 330 531-6110
  Warren (G-14547)
Pristine Senior Living of...................... E 419 935-0148
  Willard (G-15173)
Provider Services Inc.......................... E 614 888-2021
  Columbus (G-6553)
Pure Health Care Llc........................... E 937 668-7873
  Centerville (G-1951)
Rae-Ann Enterprises Inc...................... D 440 249-5092
  Cleveland (G-4807)
Red Carpet Health Care Center............. E 740 439-4401
  Cambridge (G-1580)
RES-Care Inc...................................... D 419 523-4981
  Moraine (G-11434)
Rest Haven Nursing Home Inc.............. C 937 548-1138
  Greenville (G-8882)
Rittenhouse.. E 513 423-2322
  Middletown (G-11183)
Salutary Providers Inc........................ C 440 964-8446
  Ashtabula (G-548)
Samaritan Care Center Inc................... D 330 725-4123
  Medina (G-10887)
Sarah Moore Hlth Care Ctr Inc.............. D 740 362-9641
  Delaware (G-7824)
Schoenbrunn Healthcare...................... A 330 339-3595
  New Philadelphia (G-11666)
Society of The Transfiguration............. D 513 771-7462
  Cincinnati (G-3391)
Springhills LLC.................................. E 937 705-5002
  Dayton (G-7636)
Stratford Commons Inc........................ D 440 914-0900
  Solon (G-13150)
Sunrise Senior Living LLC................... E 614 457-3500
  Upper Arlington (G-14282)
Team Health Holdings Inc.................... E 937 252-2000
  Dayton (G-7660)

United Church Homes Inc.................... E 419 294-4973
  Upper Sandusky (G-14294)
United Crbral Plsy Assn Grter............... E 216 381-9993
  Cleveland (G-5058)
University Hsptals Hlth Systm-............. B 440 285-4040
  Chardon (G-2024)
Uvmc Nursing Care Inc........................ C 937 473-2075
  Covington (G-7019)
Valley View Mnor Nrsing HM Inc........... E 740 998-2948
  Frankfort (G-8630)
Wedgewood Estates............................ E 419 756-7400
  Mansfield (G-10324)
Wesley Ridge Inc................................ E 614 759-0023
  Reynoldsburg (G-12681)
Western Rsrve Msonic Cmnty Inc.......... C 330 721-3000
  Medina (G-10903)
Wickshire Deer Park Opco LLC............. E 513 745-7600
  Cincinnati (G-3669)
Williamsburg of Cincinnati Mgt............. B 513 948-2308
  Cincinnati (G-3673)
Windsor Medical Center Inc................. D 330 499-8300
  Canton (G-1886)
Wings of Love Services LLC................. E 937 789-8192
  Dayton (G-7144)
Youngstown Area Jwish Fdration.......... C 330 746-3251
  Youngstown (G-15756)
Zandex Health Care Corporation............ C 740 454-1400
  Johnstown (G-9550)
Zandex Health Care Corporation............ C 740 695-7233
  Saint Clairsville (G-12823)
Zandex Health Care Corporation............ C 740 454-9747
  Zanesville (G-15837)

8062 General medical and surgical hospitals

Acute Care Specialty Hospital............... E 330 363-4860
  Canton (G-1654)
Adams County Regional Med Ctr........... C 937 900-2316
  West Union (G-14865)
Adena Health System.......................... E 740 779-8700
  Chillicothe (G-2044)
Adena Health System.......................... E 740 779-4300
  Chillicothe (G-2045)
Adena Health System.......................... E 740 779-7201
  Chillicothe (G-2046)
Adena Health System.......................... E 740 779-4801
  Chillicothe (G-2048)
Adena Health System.......................... E 740 420-3000
  Circleville (G-3702)
Adena Health System.......................... E 937 981-9444
  Greenfield (G-8863)
Adena Health System.......................... E 937 383-1040
  Hillsboro (G-9248)
Adena Health System.......................... E 740 947-2186
  Waverly (G-14610)
Adena Health System.......................... E 740 779-7500
  Wshngtn Ct Hs (G-15476)
Adena Health System.......................... A 740 779-7500
  Chillicothe (G-2047)
Adena Regional Medical Center............. E 740 779-4050
  Chillicothe (G-2049)
After Hours Family Care Inc................. E 937 667-2614
  Tipp City (G-13651)
Akron Children S Hospital.................... D 330 310-0157
  Doylestown (G-7912)
Akron City Hospital Inc........................ A 330 253-5046
  Akron (G-23)
Akron General Health System............... A 330 896-5070
  Uniontown (G-14240)
Akron General Medical Center.............. A 330 344-6000
  Akron (G-32)
Akron Radiology Inc............................ E 330 375-3043
  Akron (G-35)

Alliance Citizens Health Assn............... D 330 596-6000
  Alliance (G-374)
Alliance Community Hospital............... D 330 596-6000
  Alliance (G-375)
Ambulatory Care Pharmacy.................. D 419 251-2545
  Toledo (G-13680)
Amherst Hospital Association............... C 440 988-6000
  Amherst (G-421)
Appalchian Cmnty Vsting Nrse A.......... E 740 594-8226
  Athens (G-555)
Arthur G Jmes Cncer Hosp RES I........... E 614 293-3300
  Columbus (G-5389)
Ashland Hospital Corporation............... D 740 894-2080
  South Point (G-13173)
Ashtabula County Medical Ctr.............. B 440 997-6960
  Ashtabula (G-523)
Ashtabula County Medical Ctr.............. B 440 997-6680
  Ashtabula (G-524)
Ashtabula County Medical Ctr.............. A 440 997-2262
  Ashtabula (G-522)
Atrium Medical Center......................... A 513 424-2111
  Middletown (G-11153)
Aultman Health Foundation.................. B 330 305-6999
  Canton (G-1677)
Aultman Health Foundation.................. C 330 875-6050
  Louisville (G-10113)
Aultman Health Foundation.................. A 330 682-3010
  Orrville (G-12157)
Aultman Health Foundation.................. E 330 452-9911
  Canton (G-1678)
Aultman Hospital................................ A 330 452-9911
  Canton (G-1679)
Aultman Mso Inc................................. E 330 479-8705
  Canton (G-1680)
Aultman North Canton Med Group......... C 330 433-1200
  Canton (G-1681)
Aultman North Inc............................... D 330 305-6999
  Canton (G-1683)
Auxiliary Bd Fairview Gen Hosp............ A 216 476-7000
  Cleveland (G-3844)
Baptist Health Hardin.......................... C 419 673-0761
  Kenton (G-9609)
Barnesville Hospital Assn Inc............... B 740 425-3941
  Barnesville (G-717)
Bay Park Community Hospital.............. E 419 690-7900
  Oregon (G-12129)
Bay Park Community Hospital.............. E 419 690-8725
  Toledo (G-13700)
Bay Park Community Hospital.............. B 567 585-9600
  Toledo (G-13701)
Beavercreek Medical Center................. C 937 702-4000
  Beavercreek (G-863)
Bellevue Hospital................................ B 419 483-4040
  Bellevue (G-1042)
Belmont Bhc Pines Hospital Inc............ D 330 759-2700
  Youngstown (G-15558)
Belmont Community Hospital............... B 740 671-1200
  Bellaire (G-1007)
Bethesda Inc....................................... D 513 563-1505
  Cincinnati (G-2259)
Bethesda Hospital Inc.......................... C 513 894-8888
  Fairfield Township (G-8456)
Bethesda Hospital Inc.......................... B 513 745-1111
  Montgomery (G-11363)
Bethesda Hospital Inc.......................... A 513 569-6100
  Cincinnati (G-2258)
Bethesda Hospital Association............. B 740 454-4000
  Zanesville (G-15770)
Blanchard Vly Rgional Hlth Ctr............. C 419 358-9010
  Bluffton (G-1277)
▲ Blanchard Vly Rgional Hlth Ctr......... A 419 423-4500
  Findlay (G-8516)

80 HEALTH SERVICES

Bluffton Community Hospital..................C 419 358-9010
  Bluffton *(G-1278)*
Bon Scurs Mrcy Hlth Foundation..........D 513 952-4019
  Cincinnati *(G-2270)*
Bon Secours Mercy Health Inc..............A 440 233-1000
  Amherst *(G-425)*
Bon Secours Mercy Health Inc..............E 513 639-2800
  Cincinnati *(G-2271)*
Bon Secours Mercy Health Inc..............E 513 624-1950
  Cincinnati *(G-2272)*
Bon Secours Mercy Health Inc..............A 513 639-2800
  Cincinnati *(G-2273)*
Bon Secours Mercy Health Inc..............E 419 991-7805
  Lima *(G-9870)*
Bon Secours Mercy Health Inc..............D 440 774-6800
  Oberlin *(G-12064)*
Bon Secours Mercy Health Inc..............E 419 251-2659
  Toledo *(G-13712)*
Bon Secours Mercy Health Inc..............E 330 746-7211
  Youngstown *(G-15562)*
Bon Secours Mercy Health Inc..............D 513 956-3729
  Cincinnati *(G-2274)*
Bowling Green Clinic Inc.......................E 419 352-1121
  Bowling Green *(G-1310)*
Bridgeshome Health Care Inc................B 330 764-1000
  Medina *(G-10815)*
Bucyrus Community Hospital Inc.........C 419 562-4677
  Bucyrus *(G-1497)*
Bucyrus Community Hospital LLC........D 419 562-4677
  Bucyrus *(G-1498)*
C C F Vsclar Srgery At Mrymunt............C 216 475-1551
  Cleveland *(G-3914)*
Canton Altman Emrgncy Physcans.......E 330 456-2695
  Canton *(G-1696)*
Catholic Hlthcare Prtners Fndt...............D 513 639-2800
  Cincinnati *(G-2324)*
Cha - Community Health Affairs.............D 800 362-2628
  Cleveland *(G-3959)*
Chester West Medical Center................A 513 298-3000
  West Chester *(G-14663)*
Childrens H Cincinnati............................C 513 803-2707
  Cincinnati *(G-2356)*
Childrens Hosp Med Ctr Akron..............D 330 543-8521
  Akron *(G-93)*
Childrens Hosp Med Ctr Akron..............D 330 375-3528
  Akron *(G-94)*
Childrens Hosp Med Ctr Akron..............D 330 865-1252
  Akron *(G-95)*
Childrens Hosp Med Ctr Akron..............D 330 543-1000
  Akron *(G-96)*
Childrens Hosp Med Ctr Akron..............D 330 543-8260
  Akron *(G-97)*
Childrens Hosp Med Ctr Akron..............D 330 543-8530
  Akron *(G-99)*
Childrens Hosp Med Ctr Akron..............D 330 823-7311
  Alliance *(G-378)*
Childrens Hosp Med Ctr Akron..............D 419 281-3077
  Ashland *(G-493)*
Childrens Hosp Med Ctr Akron..............D 330 746-8040
  Boardman *(G-1286)*
Childrens Hosp Med Ctr Akron..............D 440 526-4543
  Brecksville *(G-1348)*
Childrens Hosp Med Ctr Akron..............D 330 676-1020
  Kent *(G-9562)*
Childrens Hosp Med Ctr Akron..............D 419 521-2900
  Mansfield *(G-10253)*
Childrens Hosp Med Ctr Akron..............D 330 308-5432
  New Philadelphia *(G-11642)*
Childrens Hosp Med Ctr Akron..............D 419 529-6285
  Ontario *(G-12102)*
Childrens Hosp Med Ctr Akron..............D 330 425-3344
  Twinsburg *(G-14176)*
Childrens Hosp Med Ctr Akron..............A 330 543-1000
  Akron *(G-98)*
Childrens Hospital..................................C 513 636-9900
  Cincinnati *(G-2358)*
Childrens Hospital..................................D 513 636-4051
  Cincinnati *(G-2359)*
Childrens Hospital Medical Ctr..............B 513 636-6036
  Cincinnati *(G-2099)*
Childrens Hospital Medical Ctr..............A 513 541-4500
  Cincinnati *(G-2360)*
Childrens Hospital Medical Ctr..............A 513 636-4200
  Cincinnati *(G-2361)*
Childrens Hospital Medical Ctr..............A 513 803-1751
  Cincinnati *(G-2362)*
Childrens Hospital Medical Ctr..............A 513 636-4200
  Cincinnati *(G-2363)*
Childrens Hospital Medical Ctr..............A 513 636-4366
  Cincinnati *(G-2364)*
Childrens Hospital Medical Ctr..............A 513 636-4288
  Cincinnati *(G-2365)*
Childrens Hospital Medical Ctr..............B 513 636-8778
  Cincinnati *(G-2366)*
Childrens Hospital Medical Ctr..............A 513 803-9600
  Liberty Township *(G-9848)*
Chirst Hospital Surgery Center..............E 513 272-3448
  Cincinnati *(G-2374)*
Chmc Cmnty Hlth Svcs Netwrk..............A 513 636-8778
  Cincinnati *(G-2375)*
Christ Hospital.......................................D 513 631-3300
  Cincinnati *(G-2376)*
Christ Hospital.......................................D 513 351-0800
  Cincinnati *(G-2377)*
Christ Hospital.......................................E 513 585-2000
  Cincinnati *(G-2378)*
Christ Hospital.......................................D 513 688-1111
  Cincinnati *(G-2379)*
Christ Hospital.......................................D 513 651-0094
  Cincinnati *(G-2381)*
Christ Hospital.......................................D 513 272-3448
  Cincinnati *(G-2382)*
Christ Hospital.......................................D 513 347-2300
  Cincinnati *(G-2383)*
Christ Hospital.......................................D 513 561-7809
  Cincinnati *(G-2384)*
Christ Hospital.......................................D 513 648-7950
  Liberty Township *(G-9849)*
Christ Hospital.......................................D 513 648-7800
  Liberty Township *(G-9850)*
Christ Hospital.......................................D 513 648-7900
  Mason *(G-10530)*
Christ Hospital.......................................D 513 755-4700
  West Chester *(G-14665)*
Christ Hospital.......................................A 513 585-2000
  Cincinnati *(G-2380)*
Christus Hlth Southeast Texas.............C 330 726-0771
  Youngstown *(G-15577)*
City Hospital Association.......................A 330 385-7200
  East Liverpool *(G-8179)*
City of Wooster......................................A 330 263-8100
  Wooster *(G-15321)*
Cleveland Anesthesia Group.................E 216 901-5706
  Independence *(G-9419)*
Cleveland Clinic Avon Hospital..............D 440 695-5000
  Avon *(G-645)*
Cleveland Clinic Cole Eye Inst...............E 216 444-4508
  Cleveland *(G-4009)*
Cleveland Clinic Foundation..................E 330 864-8060
  Akron *(G-107)*
Cleveland Clinic Foundation..................E 440 937-9099
  Avon *(G-647)*
Cleveland Clinic Foundation..................D 216 831-0120
  Beachwood *(G-780)*
Cleveland Clinic Foundation..................E 216 448-0116
  Beachwood *(G-781)*
Cleveland Clinic Foundation..................D 800 223-2273
  Beachwood *(G-782)*
Cleveland Clinic Foundation..................E 216 455-6400
  Beachwood *(G-783)*
Cleveland Clinic Foundation..................E 440 986-4000
  Broadview Heights *(G-1384)*
Cleveland Clinic Foundation..................E 440 717-1370
  Broadview Heights *(G-1385)*
Cleveland Clinic Foundation..................E 330 533-8350
  Canfield *(G-1626)*
Cleveland Clinic Foundation..................E 440 729-9000
  Chesterland *(G-2033)*
Cleveland Clinic Foundation..................B 800 223-2273
  Cleveland *(G-4010)*
Cleveland Clinic Foundation..................D 800 223-2273
  Cleveland *(G-4011)*
Cleveland Clinic Foundation..................D 216 444-5755
  Cleveland *(G-4012)*
Cleveland Clinic Foundation..................B 216 444-5715
  Cleveland *(G-4013)*
Cleveland Clinic Foundation..................B 216 448-4325
  Cleveland *(G-4014)*
Cleveland Clinic Foundation..................E 866 223-8100
  Cleveland *(G-4015)*
Cleveland Clinic Foundation..................D 216 444-1764
  Cleveland *(G-4016)*
Cleveland Clinic Foundation..................D 216 442-6700
  Cleveland *(G-4017)*
Cleveland Clinic Foundation..................E 216 444-5600
  Cleveland *(G-4018)*
Cleveland Clinic Foundation..................E 216 445-4500
  Cleveland *(G-4019)*
Cleveland Clinic Foundation..................E 216 445-6888
  Cleveland *(G-4021)*
Cleveland Clinic Foundation..................D 216 986-4000
  Cleveland *(G-4022)*
Cleveland Clinic Foundation..................B 216 444-2200
  Cleveland *(G-4023)*
Cleveland Clinic Foundation..................E 216 444-6618
  Cleveland *(G-4026)*
Cleveland Clinic Foundation..................E 234 815-5100
  Copley *(G-6950)*
Cleveland Clinic Foundation..................E 330 923-9585
  Cuyahoga Falls *(G-7062)*
Cleveland Clinic Foundation..................E 833 427-5634
  Fairlawn *(G-8471)*
Cleveland Clinic Foundation..................E 330 948-5523
  Lodi *(G-10018)*
Cleveland Clinic Foundation..................E 440 988-5651
  Lorain *(G-10065)*
Cleveland Clinic Foundation..................E 440 282-7420
  Lorain *(G-10066)*
Cleveland Clinic Foundation..................E 440 428-1111
  Madison *(G-10212)*
Cleveland Clinic Foundation..................D 440 250-5737
  North Olmsted *(G-11897)*
Cleveland Clinic Foundation..................E 440 327-1050
  North Ridgeville *(G-11925)*
Cleveland Clinic Foundation..................E 419 660-6946
  Norwalk *(G-12006)*
Cleveland Clinic Foundation..................D 419 609-2812
  Sandusky *(G-12882)*
Cleveland Clinic Foundation..................D 216 444-2200
  Solon *(G-13076)*
Cleveland Clinic Foundation..................A 440 878-2500
  Strongsville *(G-13449)*
Cleveland Clinic Foundation..................E 330 334-4620
  Wadsworth *(G-14432)*
Cleveland Clinic Foundation..................E 440 647-0004
  Wellington *(G-14629)*

80 HEALTH SERVICES

Cleveland Clinic Foundation................ E 440 516-8896
  Willoughby Hills *(G-15231)*
Cleveland Clinic Foundation................ B 330 287-4500
  Wooster *(G-15322)*
Cleveland Clinic Foundation................ E 330 287-4930
  Wooster *(G-15323)*
▲ Cleveland Clinic Foundation................ A 216 636-8335
  Cleveland *(G-4020)*
Cleveland Clinic Mercy Hosp................ B 330 823-3856
  Alliance *(G-380)*
Cleveland Clinic Mercy Hosp................ B 330 966-8884
  Canton *(G-1712)*
Cleveland Clinic Mercy Hosp................ B 330 588-4892
  Canton *(G-1713)*
Cleveland Clinic Mercy Hosp................ B 330 649-4380
  Canton *(G-1714)*
Cleveland Clinic Mercy Hosp................ B 330 489-1329
  Canton *(G-1715)*
Cleveland Clinic Mercy Hosp................ B 330 492-8803
  Canton *(G-1716)*
Cleveland Clinic Mercy Hosp................ E 330 489-1000
  Canton *(G-1717)*
Cleveland Clnic Chld Hosp For................ C 216 721-5400
  Cleveland *(G-4033)*
Cleveland Clnic Hlth Systm-AST................ E 440 449-4500
  Cleveland *(G-4035)*
Cleveland Clnic Hlth Systm-AST................ D 216 692-7555
  Cleveland *(G-4036)*
Cleveland Clnic Hlth Systm-AST................ E 330 468-0190
  Northfield *(G-11954)*
Cleveland Clnic Hlth Systm-AST................ D 330 287-4830
  Wooster *(G-15324)*
Cleveland Clnic Hlth Systm-Wst................ D 216 518-3444
  Cleveland *(G-4037)*
Cleveland Clnic Hlth Systm-Wst................ C 216 491-6000
  Warrensville Heights *(G-14579)*
Cleveland Clnic Lrner Cllege M................ C 216 445-3853
  Cleveland *(G-4039)*
Clinton Memorial Hospital................ B 937 382-6611
  Wilmington *(G-15249)*
Columbus Cardiology Cons Inc................ C 614 224-2281
  Grove City *(G-8910)*
Community Health Systems Inc................ D 330 841-9011
  Warren *(G-14511)*
Community Hlth Prtners Rgnal F................ A 440 960-4000
  Lorain *(G-10068)*
Community Hospitals................ B 419 636-1131
  Bryan *(G-1480)*
Community Hospitals Wellness................ D 419 636-1131
  Bryan *(G-1481)*
Community Hsptals Wllness Ctrs................ E 419 445-2015
  Archbold *(G-456)*
Community Hsptals Wllness Ctrs................ E 419 485-3154
  Montpelier *(G-11383)*
Community Hsptals Wllness Ctrs................ C 419 636-1131
  Bryan *(G-1482)*
Community Mercy Health System................ D 937 523-5500
  Springfield *(G-13238)*
Community Mercy Hlth Partners................ E 937 523-6670
  Springfield *(G-13239)*
Convalescent Hospital For Chil................ E 513 636-4415
  Cincinnati *(G-2504)*
Copc Hospitals................ C 614 268-8164
  Columbus *(G-5701)*
Cuyahoga Falls General Hospital................ A 330 971-7000
  Cuyahoga Falls *(G-7067)*
Dayton Childrens Cardiology................ E 937 641-3418
  Dayton *(G-7273)*
Dayton Childrens Hospital................ D 937 641-5760
  Dayton *(G-7274)*
Dayton Childrens Hospital................ D 937 641-3500
  Dayton *(G-7275)*

Dayton Childrens Hospital................ D 513 424-2850
  Middletown *(G-11195)*
Dayton Osteopathic Hospital................ E 937 401-6400
  Centerville *(G-1944)*
Dayton Osteopathic Hospital................ E 937 558-0200
  Dayton *(G-7292)*
Dayton Osteopathic Hospital................ E 937 558-3800
  Dayton *(G-7294)*
Dayton Osteopathic Hospital................ E 937 439-6000
  Dayton *(G-7295)*
Dayton Osteopathic Hospital................ E 937 401-6503
  Dayton *(G-7296)*
Dayton Osteopathic Hospital................ E 937 456-8300
  Eaton *(G-8212)*
Dayton Osteopathic Hospital................ E 513 696-1200
  Lebanon *(G-9763)*
Dayton Osteopathic Hospital................ E 937 898-9729
  Vandalia *(G-14374)*
Dayton Osteopathic Hospital................ A 937 762-1629
  Dayton *(G-7293)*
Deaconess Hospital of Cincinna................ C 513 559-2100
  Cincinnati *(G-2549)*
Defiance Hospital Inc................ B 419 783-6955
  Toledo *(G-13774)*
Doctors Hospital Cleveland Inc................ C 740 753-7300
  Nelsonville *(G-11542)*
Doctors Ohiohealth Corporation................ A 614 297-4000
  Columbus *(G-5780)*
Doctors Ohiohealth Corporation................ A 614 544-5424
  Columbus *(G-5781)*
East Ohio Hospital LLC................ C 740 633-1100
  Martins Ferry *(G-10467)*
East Ohio Hospital LLC................ C 740 695-5955
  Saint Clairsville *(G-12791)*
East Ohio Hospital LLC................ E 740 633-1100
  Martins Ferry *(G-10468)*
Emh Regional Medical Center................ D 440 988-6800
  Avon *(G-650)*
Emh Regional Medical Center................ A 440 329-7500
  Elyria *(G-8249)*
Equitas Health Inc................ E 937 424-1440
  Dayton *(G-7338)*
Euclid Hospital................ B 216 531-9000
  Euclid *(G-8341)*
Fairfield Diagnstc Imaging LLC................ E 740 654-6312
  Lancaster *(G-9711)*
Fairfield Medical Associates................ E 740 687-8377
  Lancaster *(G-9717)*
Fairfield Medical Center................ A 740 687-8000
  Lancaster *(G-9718)*
Fairview Hospital................ A 216 476-7000
  Cleveland *(G-4238)*
Falls Family Practice Inc................ E 330 923-9585
  Cuyahoga Falls *(G-7072)*
Family Birth Center Lima Mem................ E 419 998-4570
  Lima *(G-9888)*
Family Physicians of Coshocton................ D 740 622-0332
  Coshocton *(G-6984)*
Far Oaks Orthopedists Inc................ E 937 433-5309
  Dayton *(G-7348)*
Fayette County Memorial Hosp................ C 740 335-1210
  Wshngtn Ct Hs *(G-15482)*
Findlay Surgery Center Ltd................ E 419 421-1845
  Findlay *(G-8530)*
Firelands Regional Health Sys................ E 419 557-6161
  Sandusky *(G-12894)*
Firelands Regional Health Sys................ E 419 557-7455
  Sandusky *(G-12895)*
Firelands Regional Health Sys................ A 419 557-7485
  Sandusky *(G-12896)*
Fisher - Titus Health................ A 419 668-8101
  Norwalk *(G-12010)*

Fisher-Titus Medical Center................ D 419 663-6464
  Norwalk *(G-12011)*
▲ Fisher-Titus Medical Center................ A 419 668-8101
  Norwalk *(G-12013)*
Flower Hospital................ A 419 824-1444
  Sylvania *(G-13544)*
Fort Hamilton Hospital................ C 513 867-2382
  Hamilton *(G-9042)*
Fort Hamilton Hospital................ B 513 867-2280
  Hamilton *(G-9043)*
Fort Hamilton Hospital................ D 513 867-2000
  Hamilton *(G-9041)*
Fostoria Hospital Association................ B 419 435-7734
  Fostoria *(G-8616)*
Foundtion Srgery Afflate Mddlb................ E 440 743-8400
  Middleburg Heights *(G-11115)*
Frederick C Smith Clinic Inc................ B 740 383-7000
  Marion *(G-10427)*
Fulton County Health Center................ C 419 335-2017
  Wauseon *(G-14601)*
Fulton County Health Center................ B 419 335-2015
  Wauseon *(G-14602)*
Garden II Leasing Co LLC................ D 419 381-0037
  Toledo *(G-13817)*
Geauga Regional Hosp HM Care................ E 440 285-6834
  Chardon *(G-2002)*
Genesis Healthcare System................ D 740 454-5922
  Zanesville *(G-15790)*
Genesis Healthcare System................ D 740 454-5913
  Zanesville *(G-15792)*
Genesis Healthcare System................ D 740 454-4585
  Zanesville *(G-15793)*
Genesis Healthcare System................ E 740 586-6732
  Zanesville *(G-15794)*
Genesis Healthcare System................ E 740 454-4566
  Zanesville *(G-15795)*
Genesis Healthcare System................ A 740 454-5000
  Zanesville *(G-15791)*
Gerlach John J Ctr For Snior H................ E 614 566-5858
  Columbus *(G-5930)*
Good Samaritan Hosp Cincinnati................ E 513 569-6251
  Cincinnati *(G-2742)*
Good Samaritan Hospital................ A 937 278-2612
  Dayton *(G-7378)*
Grace Hospital................ D 216 687-4013
  Amherst *(G-429)*
Grace Hospital................ D 216 687-1500
  Bedford *(G-961)*
Grace Hospital................ D 216 476-2704
  Cleveland *(G-4325)*
Grace Hospital................ E 216 687-1500
  Warrensville Heights *(G-14581)*
Grady Memorial Hospital................ B 740 615-1000
  Delaware *(G-7802)*
Greene Memorial Hospital Inc................ A 937 352-2000
  Xenia *(G-15517)*
Greene Oaks................ D 937 352-2800
  Xenia *(G-15518)*
Greenfield Area Medical Ctr................ B 937 981-9400
  Greenfield *(G-8864)*
Guernsey Health Systems................ A 740 439-3561
  Cambridge *(G-1573)*
H B Magruder Memorial Hosp................ C 419 734-3131
  Oak Harbor *(G-12045)*
H B Magruder Memorial Hosp................ C 419 732-6520
  Port Clinton *(G-12532)*
H B Magruder Memorial Hosp................ C 419 734-4539
  Port Clinton *(G-12533)*
Harrison Community Hospital Inc................ C 740 942-4631
  Cadiz *(G-1539)*
Hcl of Dayton Inc................ C 937 384-8300
  Miamisburg *(G-11059)*

80 HEALTH SERVICES

Health Care Specialists............................ E 740 454-4530
  Zanesville *(G-15799)*
Heart Care.. E..... 614 533-5000
  Gahanna *(G-8718)*
Henry County Hospital Inc .... B 419 592-4015
  Napoleon *(G-11525)*
Highland Cnty Jnt Twnship Dst............. B 937 393-6100
  Hillsboro *(G-9256)*
Hillcrest Hospital Auxiliary...................... D 440 449-4500
  Cleveland *(G-4364)*
Hocking Vly Cmnty Hosp Mem Fun........ B 740 380-8389
  Logan *(G-10023)*
Holzer Clinic LLC..................................... E 740 589-3100
  Athens *(G-574)*
Holzer Clinic LLC..................................... E 304 746-3701
  Gallipolis *(G-8760)*
Holzer Health System............................. A 740 446-5000
  Gallipolis *(G-8761)*
Holzer Hospital Foundation................... A 740 446-5000
  Gallipolis *(G-8762)*
Holzer Medical Ctr - Jackson .... D 740 288-4625
  Jackson *(G-9520)*
Hometown Urgent Care .... D 937 342-9520
  Springfield *(G-13254)*
Hospice of Genesis Health..................... E 740 454-5381
  Zanesville *(G-15801)*
Internists of Fairfield Inc .... E 513 896-9595
  Fairfield *(G-8420)*
Jewish Hospital .... E 513 569-2434
  Cincinnati *(G-2907)*
Jewish Hospital LLC................................ B 513 686-5970
  Cincinnati *(G-2908)*
Jewish Hospital LLC................................ B 513 585-2668
  Cincinnati *(G-2909)*
Jewish Hospital LLC................................ E 513 988-6067
  Trenton *(G-14123)*
▲ Jewish Hospital LLC............................ A 513 686-3000
  Cincinnati *(G-2910)*
▲ Jewish Hospital Cincinnati Inc........... A 513 686-3303
  Cincinnati *(G-2911)*
Joint Township Dst Mem Hosp............... E 419 394-3335
  Saint Marys *(G-12828)*
Joint Township Dst Mem Hosp............... E 419 394-9959
  Saint Marys *(G-12830)*
Joint Township Dst Mem Hosp............... B 419 394-3335
  Saint Marys *(G-12829)*
Joint Township Home Health................ D 419 394-3335
  Saint Marys *(G-12831)*
Jtd Health Systems Inc .... D 419 394-3335
  Saint Marys *(G-12832)*
Junior Coop Soc Chldren S Hosp........... E 513 636-4310
  Cincinnati *(G-2923)*
Kettering Adventist Healthcare.............. A 937 298-4331
  Dayton *(G-7435)*
Kettering Health Hamilton...................... A 513 867-2000
  Hamilton *(G-9056)*
Kettering Medical Center........................ E 937 384-8750
  Dayton *(G-7439)*
Kettering Medical Center........................ B 937 866-0551
  Miamisburg *(G-11066)*
Kettering Medical Center........................ A 937 298-4331
  Kettering *(G-9629)*
Kettering Pathology Assoc Inc............... D 937 298-4331
  Dayton *(G-7440)*
Khn Pharmacy Huber............................. C 937 558-3333
  Huber Heights *(G-9324)*
Kindred Healthcare LLC......................... E 937 222-5963
  Dayton *(G-7442)*
Kindred Healthcare LLC......................... E 937 222-5963
  Dayton *(G-7443)*
Kindred Healthcare LLC......................... E 419 224-1888
  Lima *(G-9914)*

Knox Cardiology Associates................... E 740 397-0108
  Mount Vernon *(G-11491)*
Knox Community Hospital...................... A 740 393-9000
  Mount Vernon *(G-11492)*
Lake Health Inc....................................... D 440 279-1500
  Chardon *(G-2009)*
Lake Hospital System Inc...................... C 216 545-4800
  Beachwood *(G-807)*
Lake Hospital System Inc...................... C 440 205-8818
  Mentor *(G-10962)*
Lake Hospital System Inc...................... C 440 953-9600
  Willoughby *(G-15199)*
Lake Hospital System Inc...................... C 440 975-0027
  Willoughby *(G-15200)*
Lake Hospital System Inc...................... C 440 942-4226
  Willoughby *(G-15201)*
Lake Hospital System Inc...................... C 440 833-2095
  Willowick *(G-15236)*
Lake Hospital System Inc...................... A 440 375-8100
  Concord Township *(G-6927)*
Lakewood Hospital Association.............. C 216 228-5437
  Cleveland *(G-4481)*
Lakewood Hospital Association.............. A 216 529-7201
  Lakewood *(G-9674)*
Licking Memorial Hospital...................... B 740 348-7915
  Heath *(G-9135)*
Licking Memorial Hospital...................... B 740 348-1750
  Newark *(G-11718)*
Licking Memorial Hospital...................... B 740 348-4870
  Newark *(G-11719)*
Licking Memorial Hospital...................... E 740 348-4137
  Newark *(G-11720)*
Lima Memorial Hospital.......................... A 419 228-3335
  Lima *(G-9925)*
Lima Memorial Hospital La..................... B 419 738-5151
  Wapakoneta *(G-14487)*
Lima Memorial Joint Oper Co................ A 419 228-5165
  Lima *(G-9926)*
Lodi Community Hospital....................... D 330 948-1222
  Lodi *(G-10019)*
Ltac Investors LLC.................................. C 740 346-2600
  Steubenville *(G-13337)*
Lutheran Medical Center Inc.................. C 216 696-4300
  Cleveland *(G-4511)*
Lutheran Medical Center Inc.................. B 440 519-6800
  Solon *(G-13109)*
Macdonald Hospital Resear................... E 216 844-3888
  Cleveland *(G-4513)*
Madison County Community Hospital... B 740 845-7000
  London *(G-10046)*
Madison Family Health Corp.................. E 740 845-7000
  London *(G-10047)*
Madison Medical Campus...................... D 440 428-6800
  Madison *(G-10221)*
Manor Care Inc....................................... D 419 252-5500
  Toledo *(G-13905)*
Marietta Memorial Hospital.................... D 740 401-0362
  Belpre *(G-1057)*
Marietta Memorial Hospital.................... A 740 374-1400
  Marietta *(G-10384)*
Marion General Hospital Inc.................. A 740 383-8400
  Marion *(G-10439)*
Mark Mlford Hcksvlle Jint Twn............... C 419 542-6692
  Hicksville *(G-9160)*
Mary Rutan Hospital............................... E 937 599-1411
  West Liberty *(G-14860)*
Mary Rutan Hospital............................... A 937 592-4015
  Bellefontaine *(G-1034)*
▲ Marymount Hospital Inc..................... B 216 581-0500
  Cleveland *(G-4531)*
Mayfield Spine Surgery Ctr LLC............ D 513 619-4535
  Cincinnati *(G-3021)*

McCullough-Hyde Mem Hosp Inc........... E 513 863-2215
  Hamilton *(G-9064)*
McCullough-Hyde Mem Hosp Inc........... B 513 523-2111
  Oxford *(G-12210)*
MCN Health LLC..................................... C 740 788-6000
  Newark *(G-11726)*
Med America Hlth Systems Corp.......... A 937 223-6192
  Dayton *(G-7475)*
Medcentral Health System.................... B 419 683-1040
  Crestline *(G-7025)*
Medcentral Health System.................... C 419 526-8442
  Mansfield *(G-10292)*
Medcentral Health System.................... E 419 526-8970
  Mansfield *(G-10294)*
Medcentral Health System.................... B 419 526-8900
  Ontario *(G-12117)*
Medcentral Health System.................... C 419 342-5015
  Shelby *(G-13007)*
Medcentral Health System.................... A 419 526-8000
  Mansfield *(G-10293)*
Medical Assoc of Zanesville................... D 740 454-8551
  Zanesville *(G-15812)*
Medina Hospital...................................... E 330 723-3117
  Medina *(G-10861)*
Medina Hospital...................................... A 330 725-1000
  Medina *(G-10860)*
Medone Hospital Physicians.................. C 314 255-6900
  Columbus *(G-6223)*
Memorial Hosp Aux Un Cnty Ohio........ A 937 644-6115
  Marysville *(G-10497)*
Memorial Hospital................................... C 419 547-6419
  Clyde *(G-5206)*
Memorial Hospital................................... B 419 334-6657
  Fremont *(G-8693)*
Memorial Hospital Union County........... C 937 644-1001
  Marysville *(G-10498)*
Mep Health LLC...................................... E 330 492-4559
  Canton *(G-1804)*
Mercer Cnty Jint Twnship Cmnty.......... D 419 586-1611
  Celina *(G-1926)*
Mercer Cnty Joint Townshp Hosp.......... C 419 678-2341
  Coldwater *(G-5217)*
Mercer Health... D 419 678-4300
  Coldwater *(G-5218)*
Mercy Franciscan Hosp Mt Airy............. A 513 853-5101
  Cincinnati *(G-3040)*
Mercy Hamilton Hospital........................ E 513 603-8600
  Fairfield *(G-8430)*
Mercy Health - Tiffin Hosp LLC............. B 419 455-7000
  Tiffin *(G-13632)*
Mercy Health.. B 513 639-2800
  Perrysburg *(G-12356)*
Mercy Health Anderson Hospital........... A 513 624-4500
  Cincinnati *(G-3041)*
Mercy Health Cincinnati LLC................. D 513 952-5000
  Cincinnati *(G-3042)*
Mercy Health Dermatology.................... E 567 225-3407
  Toledo *(G-13915)*
Mercy Health North LLC........................ A 419 251-1359
  Toledo *(G-13916)*
Mercy Health Youngstown LLC.............. D 440 960-4389
  Springfield *(G-13271)*
Mercy Health Youngstown LLC.............. D 330 841-4000
  Warren *(G-14539)*
Mercy Health Youngstown LLC.............. A 330 746-7211
  Youngstown *(G-15665)*
Mercy Hlth - Clermont Hosp LLC........... A 513 732-8200
  Batavia *(G-743)*
Mercy Hlth - Defiance Hosp LLC........... C 419 782-8444
  Defiance *(G-7757)*
Mercy Hlth - Sprngfeld Cncer C........... A 937 323-5001
  Springfield *(G-13272)*

SIC SECTION
80 HEALTH SERVICES

Mercy Hlth - St Anne Hosp LLC.............. D 419 407-2663
  Toledo *(G-13917)*
Mercy Hlth - St Chrles Hosp LL................ A 419 696-7200
  Oregon *(G-12136)*
Mercy Hlth - St Rtas Med Ctr L................. A 419 227-3361
  Lima *(G-9934)*
Mercy Hlth - St Vncent Med Ctr................ A 419 251-0580
  Toledo *(G-13918)*
Mercy Hlth - St Vncent Med Ctr................ A 419 251-3232
  Toledo *(G-13919)*
Mercy Hlth - Willard Hosp LLC.................. C 419 964-5000
  Willard *(G-15171)*
Mercy Hospital.. C 513 870-7767
  Cincinnati *(G-3044)*
Mercy Hospital.. D 513 624-4590
  Cincinnati *(G-3045)*
Metrohealth System.................................... B 216 765-0733
  Beachwood *(G-815)*
Metrohealth System.................................... C 216 591-0523
  Beachwood *(G-816)*
Metrohealth System.................................... B 216 957-4000
  Cleveland *(G-4561)*
Metrohealth System.................................... A 216 957-1500
  Cleveland *(G-4562)*
Metrohealth System.................................... C 216 696-3876
  Cleveland Heights *(G-5181)*
Miami Valley Hospital................................ B 937 208-7396
  Dayton *(G-7488)*
Miami Valley Hospital................................ B 937 208-4076
  Dayton *(G-7490)*
Miami Valley Hospital................................ A 937 438-2400
  Dayton *(G-7491)*
Miami Valley Hospital................................ B 937 208-4673
  Dayton *(G-7493)*
Miami Valley Hospital................................ B 937 208-7065
  Vandalia *(G-14384)*
Miami Valley Hospital................................ A 937 208-8000
  Dayton *(G-7492)*
Mid-Ohio Heart Clinic Inc......................... E 419 524-8151
  Mansfield *(G-10297)*
Midohio Crdiolgy Vascular Cons............... E 740 420-8174
  Circleville *(G-3713)*
Midohio Crdiolgy Vascular Cons............... D 614 262-6772
  Columbus *(G-6242)*
Midwest Cmnty Hlth Assoc Inc................. C 419 633-4034
  Bryan *(G-1488)*
Mill Pond Family Physicians..................... E 330 928-3111
  Cuyahoga Falls *(G-7089)*
Morrow County Hospital........................... B 419 949-3085
  Mount Gilead *(G-11463)*
Mount Carmel East Hospital..................... A 614 234-6000
  Columbus *(G-6265)*
Mount Carmel Health................................ C 614 308-1803
  Columbus *(G-6266)*
Mount Carmel Health................................ D 614 986-7752
  Columbus *(G-6267)*
Mount Carmel Health................................ C 614 234-0034
  Groveport *(G-8993)*
Mount Carmel Health................................ C 614 527-8674
  Hilliard *(G-9218)*
Mount Carmel Health................................ C 614 855-4878
  New Albany *(G-11575)*
Mount Carmel Health................................ C 614 234-0100
  Westerville *(G-15002)*
Mount Carmel Health................................ C 614 234-9889
  Worthington *(G-15441)*
Mount Carmel Health................................ A 614 234-5000
  Grove City *(G-8936)*
Mount Carmel Health Plan Inc................. D 614 546-4300
  Columbus *(G-6268)*
Mount Carmel Health System................... A 614 856-0700
  Columbus *(G-6269)*

Mount Carmel Health System................... E 734 343-4551
  Columbus *(G-6270)*
Mount Carmel Health System................... B 614 860-0659
  Columbus *(G-6271)*
Mount Carmel Health System................... A 614 234-3355
  Columbus *(G-6272)*
Mount Carmel Health System................... A 614 679-2184
  Columbus *(G-6273)*
Mount Carmel Health System................... A 614 221-1009
  Columbus *(G-6275)*
Mount Carmel Health System................... E 614 663-5300
  Grove City *(G-8937)*
Mount Carmel Health System................... A 614 775-6600
  New Albany *(G-11576)*
Mount Carmel Health System................... A 614 234-9889
  Worthington *(G-15442)*
Mount Carmel Health System................... A 614 234-6000
  Columbus *(G-6274)*
Mt Carmel East Urgent Care.................... D 614 355-8150
  Columbus *(G-6281)*
Nationwide Childrens.............................. E 407 782-0053
  Columbus *(G-6309)*
Nationwide Childrens Hospital................. C 513 636-6000
  Cincinnati *(G-2111)*
Nationwide Childrens Hospital................. B 614 722-5750
  Columbus *(G-6310)*
Nationwide Childrens Hospital................. B 614 355-1100
  Columbus *(G-6311)*
Nationwide Childrens Hospital................. C 614 355-9300
  Columbus *(G-6312)*
Nationwide Childrens Hospital................. C 614 355-9900
  Columbus *(G-6314)*
Nationwide Childrens Hospital................. C 614 722-5175
  Columbus *(G-6315)*
Nationwide Childrens Hospital................. C 614 355-8100
  Columbus *(G-6316)*
Nationwide Childrens Hospital................. C 614 355-9200
  Columbus *(G-6317)*
Nationwide Childrens Hospital................. C 614 355-9400
  Columbus *(G-6318)*
Nationwide Childrens Hospital................. C 614 355-6850
  Columbus *(G-6319)*
Nationwide Childrens Hospital................. C 614 355-8737
  Dublin *(G-8069)*
Nationwide Childrens Hospital................. D 419 221-3177
  Lima *(G-9938)*
Nationwide Childrens Hospital................. D 419 528-3140
  Mansfield *(G-10303)*
Nationwide Childrens Hospital................. C 614 355-6100
  Westerville *(G-14916)*
Nationwide Childrens Hospital................. B 614 866-3473
  Westerville *(G-15005)*
Nationwide Childrens Hospital................. D 614 355-8315
  Westerville *(G-15006)*
Nationwide Childrens Hospital................. C 740 588-0237
  Zanesville *(G-15819)*
◆ Nationwide Childrens Hospital............. A 614 722-2000
  Columbus *(G-6313)*
Nationwide Chld Hosp Fundation............ E 614 355-5400
  Columbus *(G-6324)*
New Albany Surgery Center LLC............. C 614 775-1616
  New Albany *(G-11581)*
Newark Family Physicians Inc................. E 740 348-1788
  Newark *(G-11735)*
Niagara Health Corporation...................... C 614 898-4000
  Columbus *(G-6357)*
Northeast Ohio Heart Assoc LLC............. D 440 352-9554
  Concord Township *(G-6930)*
Northwest Ohio Srgcal Spcalist................ E 419 998-8207
  Lima *(G-9941)*
Oak Tree Physicians Inc........................... E 440 816-8000
  Cleveland *(G-4676)*

Ohio Dept Mntal Hlth Addction................. C 614 752-0333
  Columbus *(G-6409)*
Ohio Heart and Vascular........................... E 513 206-1800
  Cincinnati *(G-3145)*
Ohio Hlth Physcn Group Hritg C.............. E 740 594-8819
  Athens *(G-584)*
Ohio Medical Group................................... E 440 414-9400
  Westlake *(G-15091)*
Ohio State Univ Wexner Med Ctr............ A 614 293-8000
  Columbus *(G-6451)*
Ohio State University................................ C 614 257-3000
  Columbus *(G-6453)*
Ohio Valley Medical Center LLC.............. D 937 521-3900
  Springfield *(G-13279)*
Ohiohealth Corporation............................. D 614 566-5977
  Columbus *(G-6466)*
Ohiohealth Corporation............................. B 614 544-8000
  Dublin *(G-8081)*
Ohiohealth Corporation............................. A 614 788-8860
  Columbus *(G-6465)*
Ohiohealth Group Ltd.............................. E 614 566-0056
  Columbus *(G-6467)*
Ohiohealth Physician Group Inc.............. E 567 241-7000
  Mansfield *(G-10309)*
Ohiohlth Rverside Methdst Hosp............. A 614 566-5000
  Columbus *(G-6468)*
Osu Nephrology Medical Ctr.................... A 614 293-8300
  Columbus *(G-6485)*
Our Lady Bellefonte Hosp Inc.................. A 606 833-3333
  Cincinnati *(G-3176)*
Pam Specialty Hosp Dayton LLC............. B 937 384-8300
  Miamisburg *(G-11080)*
Parma Community General Hosp............. A 440 743-3000
  Parma *(G-12260)*
Patientpoint LLC...................................... D 513 936-6800
  Cincinnati *(G-3188)*
Paulding County Hospital......................... C 419 399-4080
  Paulding *(G-12285)*
Poison Information Center....................... E 513 636-5111
  Cincinnati *(G-3220)*
Pomerene Hospital.................................... B 330 674-1015
  Millersburg *(G-11289)*
Primary Care Ntwrk Prmier Hlth.............. D 937 237-9575
  Huber Heights *(G-9326)*
Prime Healthcare Foundation................... B 740 623-4178
  Coshocton *(G-6997)*
Prime Hlthcare Fndtn-Cshcton L............. C 740 623-4013
  Coshocton *(G-6998)*
Promedica Cntning Care Svcs Co............ A 419 885-1715
  Sylvania *(G-13561)*
Promedica Gnt-Urinary Surgeons............. E 419 531-8558
  Toledo *(G-13969)*
Promedica Health System Inc................. C 419 783-6802
  Defiance *(G-7763)*
Promedica Health System Inc................. C 419 891-6201
  Maumee *(G-10757)*
Promedica Health System Inc................. B 419 291-6720
  Sylvania *(G-13562)*
Promedica Health System Inc................. C 419 291-2121
  Toledo *(G-13970)*
Promedica Health Systems Inc............... D 419 690-7700
  Oregon *(G-12142)*
Promedica Health Systems Inc............... A 419 824-1444
  Sylvania *(G-13563)*
Promedica Health Systems Inc............... B 419 578-7036
  Toledo *(G-13973)*
Promedica Health Systems Inc............... A 419 291-4000
  Toledo *(G-13974)*
Promedica of Sylvania Oh LLC................ A 844 247-5337
  Sylvania *(G-13564)*
Promedica Toledo Hospital....................... D 419 291-2051
  Toledo *(G-13977)*

Employee Codes: A=Over 500 employees, B=251-500
C=101-250, D=51-100, E=20-50, F=10-19, G=1-9

80 HEALTH SERVICES

Promedica Toledo Hospital............................ E 419 291-8701
  Toledo *(G-13978)*
Promedica Toledo Hospital............................ A 419 291-4000
  Toledo *(G-13976)*
Promedica Wldwood Orthpdic SPI......... C 419 578-7107
  Toledo *(G-13979)*
Providence Care Center................................. C 419 627-2273
  Sandusky *(G-12924)*
Regency Hospital Company LLC............... C 614 456-0300
  Columbus *(G-6573)*
Regency Hospital Company LLC............... D 440 202-4200
  Middleburg Heights *(G-11122)*
Regency Hospital Company LLC............... C 216 910-3800
  Warrensville Heights *(G-14587)*
Regency Hospital Toledo LLC..................... E 419 318-5700
  Sylvania *(G-13568)*
Research Inst At Ntnwide Chld..................... C 614 722-2700
  Columbus *(G-6580)*
Richmond Medical Center............................ B 440 585-6500
  Richmond Heights *(G-12722)*
Riverside Hospital... E 614 566-5000
  Columbus *(G-6595)*
Riverview Surgery Center............................. E 740 681-2700
  Lancaster *(G-9739)*
Robinson Health System Inc....................... A 330 562-3169
  Aurora *(G-625)*
Robinson Health System Inc....................... A 330 677-3434
  Kent *(G-9594)*
Robinson Health System Inc....................... A 330 678-0900
  Kent *(G-9595)*
Robinson Health System Inc....................... A 330 297-0811
  Kent *(G-9596)*
Robinson Health System Inc....................... A 330 678-4100
  Kent *(G-9597)*
Robinson Health System Inc....................... A 330 297-8844
  Ravenna *(G-12642)*
Robinson Health System Inc....................... A 330 626-3455
  Streetsboro *(G-13426)*
Robinson Health System Inc....................... A 330 297-0811
  Ravenna *(G-12643)*
Salem Community Hospital......................... E 330 337-9922
  Salem *(G-12853)*
Salem Community Hospital......................... A 330 332-1551
  Salem *(G-12854)*
Samaritan Health Partners........................... A 937 208-8400
  Dayton *(G-7608)*
Samaritan N Surgery Ctr Ltd....................... E 937 567-6100
  Englewood *(G-8322)*
Samaritan Professional Corp...................... E 419 289-0491
  Ashland *(G-509)*
Samaritan Regional Health Sys................. D 419 281-1330
  Ashland *(G-511)*
Samaritan Regional Health Sys................. D 419 289-0491
  Ashland *(G-512)*
Samaritan Regional Health Sys................. B 419 289-0491
  Ashland *(G-510)*
Selby General Hospital.................................. C 740 568-2000
  Marietta *(G-10405)*
Select Medical Corporation........................ E 216 983-8030
  Cleveland *(G-4891)*
Select Spcalty Hosp - Boardman............. E 330 729-1750
  Youngstown *(G-15719)*
Select Spclty Hosp - Clmbs/AST............. B 614 293-6931
  Columbus *(G-6660)*
Select Spclty Hosp - Clmbus In................ A 614 291-8467
  Columbus *(G-6661)*
Shelby County Mem Hosp Assn.............. E 937 492-9591
  Sidney *(G-13047)*
Shelby County Mem Hosp Assn.............. A 937 498-2311
  Sidney *(G-13048)*
Sheltring Arms Hosp Fndtion In................ B 740 592-9300
  Athens *(G-589)*

Shriners Hspitals For Children..................... B 513 872-6000
  Cincinnati *(G-3372)*
Southast Ohio Srgcal Sites LLC................. E 740 856-9044
  Athens *(G-590)*
Southern Ohio Medical Center................... D 740 259-5699
  Lucasville *(G-10181)*
Southern Ohio Medical Center................... D 740 820-2141
  Minford *(G-11312)*
Southern Ohio Medical Center................... A 740 354-5000
  Portsmouth *(G-12569)*
Southern Ohio Medical Center................... D 740 356-8171
  Portsmouth *(G-12570)*
Southern Ohio Medical Center................... D 740 356-5600
  Portsmouth *(G-12572)*
Southern Ohio Medical Center................... E 740 356-5000
  Portsmouth *(G-12573)*
Southern Ohio Medical Center................... C 937 544-8989
  West Union *(G-14873)*
Southern Ohio Medical Center................... C 740 574-9090
  Wheelersburg *(G-15132)*
Southern Ohio Medical Center................... C 740 574-4022
  Wheelersburg *(G-15133)*
▲ Southern Ohio Medical Center............... C 740 354-5000
  Portsmouth *(G-12571)*
Southstern Ohio Rgonal Med Ctr............. E 740 439-3561
  Cambridge *(G-1584)*
Southwest Community Health Sys........... A 440 816-8000
  Middleburg Heights *(G-11128)*
Southwest General Health Ctr................... A 440 816-8000
  Cleveland *(G-4923)*
Southwest General Med Group................. A 440 816-8000
  Middleburg Heights *(G-11129)*
Southwest Hlthcare Brown Cnty................ C 937 378-7800
  Georgetown *(G-8802)*
Specialty Hosp Cleveland LLC................... E 216 592-2830
  Cleveland *(G-4929)*
Specialty Hospital of Lorain........................ E 440 988-6088
  Amherst *(G-433)*
Springboro Family Health Care.................. E 937 748-4211
  Springboro *(G-13207)*
St Anne Mercy Hospital................................ C 419 407-2663
  Toledo *(G-14025)*
St Elzabeth Boardman Hlth Ctr................. E 330 729-4580
  Boardman *(G-1292)*
St Johns West Shore Hosp Phrm.............. E 440 835-8000
  Westlake *(G-15111)*
St Joseph Riverside Hospital...................... A 330 841-4000
  Warren *(G-14555)*
St Lukes Hospital... B 419 893-5911
  Maumee *(G-10769)*
St Vincent Charity Med Ctr......................... D 216 861-6200
  Cleveland *(G-4940)*
Steward Hllside Rhblttion Hosp.................. D 330 841-3700
  Warren *(G-14559)*
Steward Northside Med Ctr Inc.................. C 330 884-1000
  Warren *(G-14560)*
Steward Trumbull Mem Hosp Inc............. A 330 841-9011
  Warren *(G-14561)*
Stlukes Medical Imagery.............................. E 419 893-4856
  Maumee *(G-10770)*
Stress Care/Bridges...................................... D 937 723-3200
  Dayton *(G-7647)*
Summa Akron Cy St Thmas Hsptal......... A 330 375-3159
  Akron *(G-313)*
Summa Barberton Citizens Hospital........ A 330 615-3000
  Barberton *(G-710)*
Summa Health... C 330 375-3315
  Akron *(G-314)*
Summa Health... D 330 864-8060
  Akron *(G-315)*
Summa Health... A 330 615-5200
  Barberton *(G-711)*

Summa Health... D 330 753-3649
  Barberton *(G-712)*
Summa Health... D 330 926-0384
  Cuyahoga Falls *(G-7102)*
Summa Health... D 330 836-9023
  Fairlawn *(G-8502)*
Summa Health... D 330 688-4531
  Stow *(G-13396)*
Summa Health... D 330 899-5599
  Uniontown *(G-14265)*
Summa Health Center Lk Medina............. D 330 952-0014
  Medina *(G-10894)*
Summa Health System.................................. C 330 375-3000
  Akron *(G-317)*
Summa Health System.................................. B 330 535-7319
  Akron *(G-318)*
Summa Health System.................................. C 330 798-5026
  Akron *(G-319)*
Summa Health System.................................. D 330 928-8700
  Akron *(G-320)*
Summa Health System.................................. A 330 615-3000
  Barberton *(G-713)*
Summa Health System.................................. A 330 334-1504
  Wadsworth *(G-14453)*
Summa Health System.................................. D 330 375-3000
  Akron *(G-316)*
Summa Western Reserve Hosp LLC...... E 330 926-0384
  Cuyahoga Falls *(G-7103)*
Summa Western Reserve Hosp LLC...... E 330 650-5110
  Hudson *(G-9374)*
Summa Western Reserve Hosp LLC...... E 330 926-3337
  Kent *(G-9600)*
Summa Western Reserve Hosp LLC...... E 330 633-7782
  Tallmadge *(G-13605)*
Superior Med LLC.. E 740 439-8839
  Cambridge *(G-1585)*
Surgery Alliance Ltd..................................... E 330 821-7997
  Alliance *(G-403)*
Surgical Associates Inc............................... D 740 453-0661
  Zanesville *(G-15831)*
Teater Orthopedic Surgeons...................... E 330 343-3335
  Dover *(G-7903)*
The Berger Hospital....................................... A 740 474-2126
  Circleville *(G-3727)*
The Community Hospital of......................... A 937 325-0531
  Springfield *(G-13300)*
The Medical Center At Eli........................... C 937 223-6237
  Dayton *(G-7668)*
The Metrohealth System.............................. A 216 778-7800
  Cleveland *(G-5004)*
The Wadsworth-Rittman Are....................... A 330 334-1504
  Wadsworth *(G-14456)*
Thornville Family Med Ctr Inc.................... E 740 246-6361
  Thornville *(G-13623)*
Trihealth Inc... B 513 624-5558
  Cincinnati *(G-3514)*
Trihealth Inc... B 513 794-5600
  Montgomery *(G-11376)*
Trihealth Inc... E 513 569-5400
  Cincinnati *(G-3517)*
Trihealth Evendale Hospital........................ C 513 454-2222
  Cincinnati *(G-3519)*
Trinity Health System.................................... B 740 283-7000
  Steubenville *(G-13346)*
Trinity Hospital Holding Co......................... A 740 264-8000
  Steubenville *(G-13347)*
Trinity Hospital Twin City............................. B 740 922-2800
  Dennison *(G-7858)*
Trinity School of Nursing............................. E 740 283-7525
  Steubenville *(G-13348)*
Trinity West.. A 740 264-8000
  Steubenville *(G-13349)*

SIC SECTION   80 HEALTH SERVICES

Tripoint Medical Center............................ A 440 375-8100
  Concord Township *(G-6936)*
Trumbull Mem Hosp Foundation............... D 330 841-9376
  Warren *(G-14567)*
Twin City Hospital....................................... E 740 922-6675
  Dennison *(G-7860)*
U Hcmc.. D 216 721-3405
  Cleveland *(G-5044)*
Uc Health Llc... C 513 584-8600
  Cincinnati *(G-3545)*
Uc Health Llc... D 513 475-8300
  West Chester *(G-14782)*
Uc Health Llc... C 513 475-7458
  West Chester *(G-14783)*
Uh Regional Hospitals................................. D 440 735-3900
  Bedford *(G-991)*
Uh Regional Hospitals................................. A 440 285-6000
  Chardon *(G-2022)*
Uh Regional Hospitals................................. D 440 585-6439
  Richmond Heights *(G-12723)*
Uhhs Westlake Medical Center.................. E 440 250-2070
  Westlake *(G-15118)*
Uhhs-Memorial Hosp of Geneva................ B 440 466-1141
  Geneva *(G-8791)*
Union Hospital Association......................... E 330 602-0719
  Dover *(G-7906)*
Union Hospital Association......................... A 330 343-3311
  Dover *(G-7907)*
University Cncnnati Med Ctr LL................. A 513 475-8300
  West Chester *(G-14787)*
▲ University Cncnnati Med Ctr LL............. B 513 584-1000
  Cincinnati *(G-3564)*
University Hosp Geneva Med Ctr............... D 440 415-0159
  Geneva *(G-8792)*
University Hospital..................................... D 513 584-1000
  Cincinnati *(G-3570)*
University Hospital..................................... D 330 486-9610
  Twinsburg *(G-14225)*
University Hospital..................................... D 440 835-8922
  Westlake *(G-15120)*
University Hospitals.................................... D 216 536-3020
  Cleveland *(G-5072)*
University Hospitals Cleveland................... D 440 646-2626
  Beachwood *(G-848)*
University Hospitals Cleveland................... A 216 844-1000
  Cleveland *(G-5073)*
University Hsptals Clvland Med.................. A 216 378-6240
  Beachwood *(G-849)*
University Hsptals Clvland Med.................. A 216 342-5556
  Beachwood *(G-850)*
University Hsptals Clvland Med.................. A 216 844-1369
  Cleveland *(G-5075)*
University Hsptals Clvland Med.................. A 216 358-2346
  Cleveland *(G-5076)*
University Hsptals Clvland Med.................. A 216 675-6640
  Cleveland *(G-5077)*
University Hsptals Clvland Med.................. A 216 844-4663
  Cleveland *(G-5079)*
University Hsptals Clvland Med.................. A 216 844-1767
  Cleveland *(G-5080)*
University Hsptals Clvland Med.................. A 216 844-3528
  Cleveland *(G-5081)*
University Hsptals Clvland Med.................. A 440 205-5755
  Mentor *(G-11007)*
University Hsptals Clvland Med.................. A 216 844-3323
  Shaker Heights *(G-12986)*
▲ University Hsptals Clvland Med............. A 216 844-1000
  Cleveland *(G-5078)*
University Hsptals Cnnaut Med.................. D 440 593-1131
  Conneaut *(G-6945)*
▲ University Hsptals Hlth Sys In............... A 216 767-8900
  Shaker Heights *(G-12987)*

University Hsptals St John Med.................. A 440 835-8000
  Westlake *(G-15121)*
University Medical Assoc Inc...................... D 740 593-0753
  Athens *(G-597)*
University of Cincinnati............................... B 513 584-1000
  Cincinnati *(G-3578)*
University of Cincinnati............................... A 513 584-7522
  Cincinnati *(G-3579)*
University of Cincinnati............................... C 513 584-1000
  Cincinnati *(G-3580)*
University of Cincinnati............................... B 513 584-4396
  Cincinnati *(G-3581)*
University of Toledo.................................... A 419 383-4000
  Toledo *(G-14086)*
University Primary Care Prac..................... D 216 844-1000
  Cleveland *(G-5085)*
Upper Valley Medical Center...................... A 937 440-4000
  Troy *(G-14166)*
Uvmc Management Corporation................. C 937 440-4000
  Troy *(G-14169)*
Van Wert County Hospital Assn................. B 419 238-2390
  Van Wert *(G-14357)*
Van Wert Medical Services Ltd.................. C 419 238-7727
  Van Wert *(G-14360)*
Vibra Hosp Mahoning Vly LLC................... D 330 726-5000
  Youngstown *(G-15748)*
Wayne Health Corporation......................... A 919 736-1110
  Greenville *(G-8890)*
Wayne Healthcare....................................... B 937 548-1141
  Greenville *(G-8891)*
Western Reserve Hospital LLC.................. A 330 971-7000
  Cuyahoga Falls *(G-7115)*
Western Rsrve Hosp Prtners LLC.............. C 330 971-7000
  Cuyahoga Falls *(G-7116)*
Wheeling Hospital Inc................................. C 740 942-4631
  Cadiz *(G-1544)*
Whetstone Medical Clinic Inc..................... E 740 467-2787
  Millersport *(G-11300)*
Wilmington Medical Associates.................. D 937 382-1616
  Wilmington *(G-15279)*
Wood County Hospital................................ A 419 354-8900
  Bowling Green *(G-1336)*

8063 Psychiatric hospitals

Adriel School Inc.. D 937 465-0010
  West Liberty *(G-14859)*
Arrowhead Behavioral Hlth LLC................. C 419 891-9333
  Maumee *(G-10695)*
Belmont Bhc Pines Hospital Inc................. D 330 759-2700
  Youngstown *(G-15558)*
Bethesda Hospital Association.................. B 740 454-4000
  Zanesville *(G-15770)*
Bhc Fox Run Hospital Inc.......................... E 740 695-2131
  Saint Clairsville *(G-12781)*
Bon Secours Mercy Health Inc.................. A 440 233-1000
  Amherst *(G-425)*
Cambridge Behavioral Hospital.................. C 740 432-4906
  Cambridge *(G-1559)*
Center For Addiction Treatment................. D 513 381-6672
  Cincinnati *(G-2332)*
Central Cmnty Hlth Bd Hmlton C............... D 513 559-2000
  Cincinnati *(G-2335)*
Community Health Alliance........................ E 513 896-3458
  Fairfield *(G-8406)*
Eastway Corporation.................................. C 937 496-2000
  Dayton *(G-7324)*
Focus Healthcare of Ohio LLC................... E 419 891-9333
  Maumee *(G-10725)*
Genertons Bhvral Hlth - Yngsto................. E 234 855-0523
  Youngstown *(G-15619)*
Heartland Bhavioral Healthcare................. D 330 833-3135
  Massillon *(G-10645)*

Laurelwood Hospital................................... C 440 953-3000
  Willoughby *(G-15203)*
Magnolia Clubhouse Inc............................ E 216 721-3030
  Cleveland *(G-4515)*
▲ Marymount Hospital Inc........................ B 216 581-0500
  Cleveland *(G-4531)*
Mental Hlth Svcs For Clark CNT................ C 937 399-9500
  Springfield *(G-13269)*
Mt Airy Development LLC......................... E 855 537-2301
  Cincinnati *(G-3084)*
Oglethorpe Middlepoint LLC...................... E 419 968-2950
  Middle Point *(G-11110)*
Ohio Dept Dvlpmntal Dsbilities................... C 614 272-0509
  Columbus *(G-6405)*
Ohio Dept Dvlpmntal Dsbilities................... C 740 446-1642
  Gallipolis *(G-8764)*
Ohio Dept Mntal Hlth Addction.................... C 513 948-3600
  Cincinnati *(G-3144)*
Ohio Dept Mntal Hlth Addction.................... C 614 752-0333
  Columbus *(G-6408)*
Ohio Dept Mntal Hlth Addction.................... D 614 752-0333
  Columbus *(G-6410)*
Ohio Dept Mntal Hlth Addction.................... C 330 467-7131
  Northfield *(G-11962)*
Ohio Dept Mntal Hlth Addction.................... C 419 381-1881
  Toledo *(G-13945)*
Osu Harding Hospital.................................. A 614 293-9600
  Columbus *(G-6483)*
Rescue Incorporated.................................. C 419 255-9585
  Toledo *(G-13988)*

8069 Specialty hospitals, except psychiatric

Abraxas Cornell Group LLC....................... C 419 747-3322
  Shelby *(G-13004)*
Akron-Rban Mnrity Alchlism DRG.............. E 330 379-3467
  Akron *(G-41)*
Alcohol DRG Addction Mntal Svc............... E 937 443-0416
  Dayton *(G-7161)*
Anderson Healthcare Ltd........................... E 513 474-6200
  Cincinnati *(G-2197)*
Arthur G Jmes Cncer Hosp Rchar.............. B 614 293-4878
  Columbus *(G-5388)*
Aultman Hospital.. A 330 452-9911
  Canton *(G-1679)*
Behavral Cnnctions WD Cnty Inc............... E 419 352-5561
  Bowling Green *(G-1305)*
Behavral Cnnctions WD Cnty Inc............... E 419 352-5387
  Bowling Green *(G-1306)*
Cambridge Behavioral Hospital.................. C 740 432-4906
  Cambridge *(G-1559)*
Center For Addiction Treatment................. D 513 381-6672
  Cincinnati *(G-2332)*
Childrens Hosp Med Ctr Akron.................. D 330 253-4931
  Akron *(G-89)*
Childrens Hosp Med Ctr Akron.................. D 330 543-8004
  Akron *(G-90)*
Childrens Hosp Med Ctr Akron.................. D 330 746-8040
  Boardman *(G-1286)*
Childrens Hosp Med Ctr Akron.................. D 330 308-5432
  New Philadelphia *(G-11642)*
Childrens Hosp Med Ctr Akron.................. D 330 345-1100
  Wooster *(G-15319)*
Childrens Hosp Med Ctr Akron.................. D 330 629-6085
  Youngstown *(G-15576)*
Childrens Hospital Inc................................ D 614 355-0616
  Columbus *(G-5563)*
Childrens Hospital Medical Ctr................... A 513 636-4200
  Cincinnati *(G-2369)*
Childrens Hospital Medical Ctr................... B 513 636-6800
  Mason *(G-10529)*
Childrens Hospital Medical Ctr................... A 513 636-4200
  Cincinnati *(G-2368)*

Employee Codes: A=Over 500 employees, B=251-500
C=101-250, D=51-100, E=20-50, F=10-19, G=1-9

80 HEALTH SERVICES

Cleveland Clinic Foundation .... E 216 444-5437
   Cleveland *(G-4028)*
Community Counseling Svcs Inc .... E 419 562-2000
   Bucyrus *(G-1501)*
Community Health Alliance .... E 513 896-3458
   Fairfield *(G-8406)*
Compass Corp For Recovery Svcs .... D 419 241-8827
   Toledo *(G-13753)*
County of Clermont .... D 513 732-5400
   Batavia *(G-737)*
County of Stark .... C 330 455-6644
   Canton *(G-1727)*
Covenant Care Ohio Inc .... D 937 878-7046
   Fairborn *(G-8370)*
Crossroads Center .... C 513 475-5300
   Cincinnati *(G-2517)*
▲ Dayton Childrens Hospital .... A 937 641-3000
   Dayton *(G-7276)*
Dublin Springs LLC .... C 614 717-1800
   Dublin *(G-7997)*
Edwin Shaw Rehab LLC .... D 330 436-0910
   Cuyahoga Falls *(G-7071)*
Glenbeigh Health Sources Inc .... C 440 951-7000
   Rock Creek *(G-12734)*
Greenbrier Senior Living Cmnty .... D 440 888-5900
   Cleveland *(G-4339)*
Health Recovery Services Inc .... C 740 592-6720
   Athens *(G-571)*
Hospice of Medina County .... D 330 725-1900
   Medina *(G-10840)*
Hospice of The Western Reserve .... E 330 800-2240
   Medina *(G-10841)*
Hospice of Valley Inc .... D 330 788-1992
   Girard *(G-8815)*
Laurelwood Hospital .... C 440 953-3000
   Willoughby *(G-15203)*
Liberty Nrsing Ctr Rvrside LLC .... E 513 557-3621
   Cincinnati *(G-2974)*
Lutheran Medical Center Inc .... C 216 696-4300
   Cleveland *(G-4511)*
Lutheran Medical Center Inc .... B 440 519-6800
   Solon *(G-13109)*
Marietta Memorial Hospital .... A 740 374-1400
   Marietta *(G-10384)*
Maryhaven Inc .... E 419 562-1740
   Bucyrus *(G-1512)*
Maryhaven Inc .... E 740 375-5550
   Marion *(G-10442)*
Maryhaven Inc .... E 937 644-9192
   Marysville *(G-10493)*
McKinley Hall Inc .... E 937 328-5300
   Springfield *(G-13266)*
Metrohealth System .... B 216 957-2100
   Cleveland *(G-4563)*
Metrohealth System .... C 216 778-3867
   Cleveland *(G-4567)*
Muskingum Cnty DRG Alchol Sbst .... E 740 454-1266
   Zanesville *(G-15813)*
Nationwide Childrens Hospital .... C 330 253-5200
   Akron *(G-239)*
Nationwide Childrens Hospital .... C 614 722-2000
   Columbus *(G-6320)*
Nationwide Childrens Hospital .... B 614 722-8200
   Columbus *(G-6321)*
Nationwide Childrens Hospital .... C 614 355-0802
   Columbus *(G-6322)*
Nationwide Childrens Hospital .... C 614 355-8000
   Columbus *(G-6323)*
Nationwide Childrens Hospital .... C 614 355-8200
   Hilliard *(G-9220)*
Nationwide Childrens Hospital .... C 614 864-9216
   Pickerington *(G-12406)*

Nationwide Childrens Hospital .... C 614 355-8300
   Westerville *(G-14915)*
Ohio Department Youth Services .... C 614 466-4314
   Columbus *(G-6403)*
Oriana House Inc .... D 330 996-7730
   Akron *(G-258)*
Pickaway Area Rcovery Svcs Inc .... E 740 477-1745
   Circleville *(G-3715)*
Pike County Recovery Council .... D 740 835-8437
   Waverly *(G-14616)*
Salvation Army .... E 330 773-3331
   Cleveland *(G-4873)*
Scioto Pnt Vly Mental Hlth Ctr .... C 740 335-6935
   Wshngtn Ct Hs *(G-15493)*
Select Spclty Hosp - Yngstown .... C 330 480-3488
   Youngstown *(G-15720)*
Select Spclty Hsptal-Akron LLC .... D 330 761-7500
   Akron *(G-296)*
Sleepmed Incorporated .... E 440 716-8139
   North Olmsted *(G-11915)*
Southeast Inc .... B 614 225-0990
   Columbus *(G-6695)*
Stein Hospice Services Inc .... C 419 502-0019
   Sandusky *(G-12935)*
Stella Maris Inc .... D 216 781-0550
   Cleveland *(G-4948)*
Summit County .... E 330 762-3500
   Akron *(G-324)*
Talbert House .... D 513 751-7747
   Cincinnati *(G-3436)*
Talbert House .... D 513 684-7968
   Cincinnati *(G-3441)*
Transitional Living LLC .... D 513 863-6383
   Fairfield Township *(G-8465)*
Trihealth Os LLC .... A 513 791-6611
   Montgomery *(G-11379)*
University Ear Nose Throat Spc .... E 513 558-4158
   Cincinnati *(G-3567)*
▲ University Hsptals Clvland Med .... A 216 844-1000
   Cleveland *(G-5078)*
University Hsptals Hlth Systm .... B 440 285-4040
   Chardon *(G-2024)*
University Mednet .... B 216 383-0100
   Euclid *(G-8363)*
Uvmc Nursing Care Inc .... C 937 473-2075
   Covington *(G-7019)*
Zepf Center .... D 419 841-7701
   Toledo *(G-14119)*

8071 Medical laboratories

Alliance Imaging Inc .... D 330 493-5100
   Canton *(G-1660)*
Amerathon LLC .... E 419 230-9108
   Euclid *(G-8337)*
Amerathon LLC .... E 216 409-7201
   Uniontown *(G-14241)*
Amerathon LLC .... B 513 752-7300
   Cincinnati *(G-2096)*
American Health Imaging S LLC .... A 513 752-7300
   Cincinnati *(G-2097)*
Arbor View Family Medicine Inc .... E 740 687-3386
   Lancaster *(G-9695)*
Avertest LLC .... E 330 591-7219
   Medina *(G-10812)*
Belmont Manor Inc .... E 740 695-4404
   Saint Clairsville *(G-12780)*
Berkebile Russell & Associates .... E 440 989-9480
   Lorain *(G-10060)*
Bon Secours Mercy Health Inc .... C 330 729-1420
   Youngstown *(G-15563)*
Cadx Systems Inc .... D 937 431-1464
   Beavercreek *(G-870)*

Cavalier Mobile X-Ray Co .... E 330 726-0202
   Youngstown *(G-15573)*
Cellular Technology Limited .... E 216 791-5084
   Shaker Heights *(G-12975)*
Center For Dialysis Care .... E 440 286-4103
   Chardon *(G-1995)*
Childrens Hosp Reference Lab .... E 614 722-5477
   Columbus *(G-5562)*
Childrens Hospital Medical Ctr .... B 513 636-6400
   Fairfield *(G-8400)*
Cleveland Clinic Foundation .... E 216 445-6636
   Cleveland *(G-4029)*
Cleveland Clnic Hlth Systm-Wst .... D 440 716-9810
   North Olmsted *(G-11898)*
▼ Cleveland Heartlab Inc .... D 866 358-9828
   Cleveland *(G-4049)*
Community Blood Center .... D 800 684-7783
   Kettering *(G-9627)*
Compunet Clinical Labs LLC .... E 937 912-9017
   Beavercreek *(G-873)*
Compunet Clinical Labs LLC .... E 937 427-2655
   Beavercreek *(G-921)*
Compunet Clinical Labs LLC .... E 937 208-3555
   Dayton *(G-7244)*
Compunet Clinical Labs LLC .... E 937 342-0015
   Springfield *(G-13240)*
Compunet Clinical Labs LLC .... E 937 372-9681
   Xenia *(G-15502)*
Compunet Clinical Labs LLC .... C 937 296-0844
   Moraine *(G-11399)*
Connie Parks .... E 330 759-8334
   Hubbard *(G-9320)*
Consultants Laboratory Medici .... E 419 535-9629
   Toledo *(G-13759)*
County of Lake .... E 440 350-2793
   Painesville *(G-12224)*
Dayton Medical Imaging .... E 937 439-0390
   Dayton *(G-7290)*
Drew Medical Inc .... E 407 363-6700
   Hudson *(G-9343)*
FMI Medical Systems Inc .... E 440 600-5952
   Solon *(G-13090)*
Kettering Pathology Assoc Inc .... D 937 298-4331
   Dayton *(G-7440)*
Kilbourne Medical Laboratories Inc ...... C 513 385-5457
   Cincinnati *(G-2109)*
Laboratory of Dermatopathology .... E 937 434-2351
   Dayton *(G-7448)*
Medical Diagnostic Lab Inc .... E 440 333-1375
   Avon *(G-661)*
Medpace Bioanalytical Labs LLC .... E 513 366-3260
   Cincinnati *(G-3032)*
Mercy Health Youngstown LLC .... D 440 960-4389
   Springfield *(G-13271)*
Mercy Health Youngstown LLC .... A 330 746-7211
   Youngstown *(G-15665)*
Mp Biomedicals LLC .... C 440 337-1200
   Solon *(G-13113)*
Nationwide Childrens Hospital .... C 614 355-8200
   Hilliard *(G-9220)*
Nationwide Childrens Hospital .... D 419 528-3140
   Mansfield *(G-10303)*
Northast Ohio Nghbrhood Hlth S .... C 216 231-7700
   Cleveland *(G-4653)*
Oncodiagnostic Laboratory Inc .... E
   Cleveland *(G-4697)*
P C Vpa .... E 614 840-1688
   Columbus *(G-6495)*
Pathology Laboratories Inc .... C 419 255-4600
   Toledo *(G-13960)*
Perry County Fmly Practice Inc .... D 740 342-3435
   New Lexington *(G-11631)*

Precision Diagnostic Imaging............... D 216 360-8300
  Beachwood *(G-826)*
	Advance Home Care LLC................... D 937 723-6335
	  Dayton *(G-7157)*
		Beyond Homecare LLC..................... E 937 704-4002
		  Urbana *(G-14297)*

Q Medical LLC....................................... B 440 903-1827
  Pepper Pike *(G-12302)*
	Advance Home Care LLC................... D 614 436-3611
	  Columbus *(G-5318)*
		Black Stone Cincinnati LLC............... D 513 924-1370
		  Cincinnati *(G-2264)*

Senior Touch Solution......................... E 216 862-4841
  Cleveland *(G-4895)*
	Advantage Home Health Svcs Inc........ E 330 491-8161
	  North Canton *(G-11807)*
		Blessing Home Health Care Inc.......... E 614 329-2086
		  Hilliard *(G-9183)*

Smithers Group Inc............................... D 330 833-8548
  Massillon *(G-10671)*
	Advantage Skilled Care LLC............... E 740 353-9200
	  Portsmouth *(G-12543)*
		Blu Diamond Home Care LLC............. D 937 723-7836
		  Kettering *(G-9626)*

Sotera Health Topco Parent LP........... A 440 262-1410
  Broadview Heights *(G-1400)*
	Aide For You LLC................................. E 419 214-0111
	  Toledo *(G-13676)*
		Braden Med Services Inc..................... E 740 732-2356
		  Caldwell *(G-1547)*

Southwest Urology LLC....................... E 440 845-0900
  Cleveland *(G-4924)*
	Aims Supported Living LLC................. E 614 805-1507
	  Westerville *(G-14957)*
		Bradley Bay Assisted Living................ E 440 871-4509
		  Bay Village *(G-758)*

St Lukes Hospital................................. A 419 441-1002
  Waterville *(G-14595)*
	Alexson Services Inc............................. D 614 889-5837
	  Dublin *(G-7928)*
		Briarfield of Boardman LLC................. E 330 259-9393
		  Youngstown *(G-15566)*

Summa Health.. D 330 753-3649
  Barberton *(G-712)*
	Alexzander Angels LLC......................... E 678 984-3093
	  Cincinnati *(G-2160)*
		Bridgeshome Health Care Inc............. B 330 764-1000
		  Medina *(G-10815)*

Summa Health.. D 330 688-4531
  Stow *(G-13396)*
	All About Home Care Svcs LLC............ E 937 222-2980
	  Dayton *(G-7162)*
		Buckeye Home Health Care................ C 513 791-6446
		  Blue Ash *(G-1139)*

Summit County...................................... D 330 643-2101
  Akron *(G-325)*
	All Gods Graces Inc............................. D 419 222-8109
	  Lima *(G-9862)*
		Buckeye Homecare Services Inc......... D 216 321-9300
		  Cleveland *(G-3908)*

Symphony Dagnstc Svcs No 1 LLC........ A 614 888-2226
  Columbus *(G-6741)*
	All Heart Home Care LLC.................... E 419 298-0034
	  Wauseon *(G-14597)*
		Buckeye Rsdntial Solutions LLC......... D 330 235-9183
		  Ravenna *(G-12620)*

University Hsptals Clvland Med........... A 216 844-1369
  Cleveland *(G-5075)*
	All Hearts Home Health Care............... E 440 342-2026
	  Cleveland *(G-3790)*
		C K Franchising Inc............................. D 937 264-1933
		  Dayton *(G-7209)*

University of Cincinnati......................... C 513 558-4444
  Cincinnati *(G-3587)*
	Alliance HM Hlth Care Svcs LLC.......... D 614 928-3053
	  Columbus *(G-5336)*
		Cambridge Home Health Care............ A 419 775-1253
		  Mansfield *(G-10250)*

University of Cincinnati......................... C 513 584-5331
  Cincinnati *(G-3588)*
	Alpine Nursing Care Inc...................... D 216 662-7096
	  Cleveland *(G-3796)*
		Cambridge Home Health Care............ A 330 725-1968
		  Medina *(G-10816)*

Vet Path Services Inc........................... E 513 469-0777
  Mason *(G-10624)*
	Alternate Solutions First LLC............... C 937 298-1111
	  Dayton *(G-7169)*
		Capital City Hospice............................ E 614 441-9300
		  Columbus *(G-5499)*

X-Ray Industries Inc............................ D 216 642-0100
  Cleveland *(G-5163)*
	Amara Homecare Bedford Tel No......... D 440 353-0600
	  North Ridgeville *(G-11923)*
		Caprice Health Care Inc...................... E 330 965-9200
		  North Lima *(G-11885)*

8072 Dental laboratories	Amazing Grace HM Hlth Care LLC....... D 937 825-4862
	  Huber Heights *(G-9323)*
		Carestar Inc... C 513 618-8300
		  Cincinnati *(G-2313)*

Dental Ceramics Inc............................ E 330 523-5240
  Richfield *(G-12694)*
	Amber Home Care LLC........................ E 614 523-0668
	  Columbus *(G-5343)*
		Caring Hearts HM Hlth Care Inc.......... C 513 339-1237
		  Mason *(G-10526)*

Greater Cncnnati Dntl Labs Inc............ E 513 385-4222
  Cincinnati *(G-2772)*
	American Cmpassionate Care LLC...... E 513 443-8156
	  Cincinnati *(G-2177)*
		Centerwell Health Services Inc........... D 419 482-6519
		  Maumee *(G-10709)*

Lantz Dental Prosthetics Inc................ E 419 866-1515
  Maumee *(G-10738)*
	American Nursing Care Inc.................. B 513 731-4600
	  Cincinnati *(G-2184)*
		Central Star... B 419 756-9449
		  Ontario *(G-12100)*

National Dentex LLC............................ D 216 671-0577
  Brunswick *(G-1464)*
	American Nursing Care Inc.................. B 937 438-3844
	  Dayton *(G-7172)*
		Chemed Corporation........................... C 513 762-6690
		  Cincinnati *(G-2352)*

Roe Dental Laboratory Inc.................. D 216 663-2233
  Independence *(G-9478)*
	Amorso At HM Snior Dsblity Car......... E 513 761-6500
	  Cincinnati *(G-2193)*
		Cherished Companions Home Care..... D 440 273-7230
		  Chagrin Falls *(G-1975)*

United Dental Laboratories.................. E 330 253-1810
  Tallmadge *(G-13609)*
	Angels In Waiting Home Care.............. E 440 946-0349
	  Mentor *(G-10911)*
		Chesterfield Services Inc.................... E 330 896-9777
		  Uniontown *(G-14245)*

8082 Home health care services	Answercare LLC................................... D 855 213-1511
	  Canton *(G-1667)*
		CHI National Home Care..................... D 513 576-0262
		  Loveland *(G-10131)*

1-888-Ohiocomp Inc............................. D 888 644-6266
  Mansfield *(G-10241)*
	Arcadia Services Inc............................ E 330 869-9520
	  Akron *(G-54)*
		Childrens Home Care Dayton............... D 937 641-4663
		  Dayton *(G-7223)*

17322 Euclid Avenue Co LLC................ E 216 486-2280
  Cleveland *(G-3741)*
	Arcadia Services Inc............................ E 937 912-5800
	  Beavercreek *(G-857)*
		Childrens Home Care Group............... B 330 543-5000
		  Akron *(G-88)*

A Loving Hart HM Hlth Care LLC......... C 937 549-4484
  Manchester *(G-10238)*
	Area Agcy On Aging Plg Svc Are........ C 800 258-7277
	  Dayton *(G-7179)*
		Choice Healthcare Limited.................. E 937 254-6220
		  Beavercreek *(G-871)*

A Touch of Grace Inc.......................... E 567 560-2350
  Mansfield *(G-10242)*
	Area Office On Aging Nrthwster........... D 419 382-0624
	  Toledo *(G-13693)*
		Christian Home Care LLC................... E 419 254-2840
		  Toledo *(G-13734)*

Abcap Foundation................................ E 937 378-6041
  Georgetown *(G-8796)*
	Ash Brothers Home Health Care........... E 614 882-3600
	  Westerville *(G-14960)*
		Cincinnati Aml Refl Emer C LLC......... E 937 610-0414
		  Dayton *(G-7226)*

Academic Bhvral Lrng Enrchment....... E 513 544-4991
  Columbus *(G-5298)*
	Ashtabula Rgional Hm Hlth Svcs......... E 440 992-4663
	  Ashtabula *(G-526)*
		Cincinnati Home Care Inc................... D 513 771-2760
		  Cincinnati *(G-2412)*

Adams Hlping Hands HM Care LLC..... E 419 298-0034
  Edgerton *(G-8226)*
	Associated Home Health Inc................ E 740 264-6311
	  Steubenville *(G-13316)*
		Circle J Home Health Care Inc........... D 330 482-0877
		  Salineville *(G-12859)*

Addus Healthcare Inc........................... D 614 407-0677
  Columbus *(G-5312)*
	Assurecare LLC.................................... E 513 618-2150
	  Cincinnati *(G-2220)*
		Clearpath HM Hlth Hospice LLC.......... E 330 784-2162
		  Akron *(G-105)*

Addus Healthcare Inc........................... D 630 296-3400
  Steubenville *(G-13315)*
	Avita Home Health and Hospice........... E 419 468-7985
	  Galion *(G-8744)*
		Cleveland Clnic Akron Gen Vsti........... D 330 677-4666
		  Kent *(G-9564)*

Addus Homecare Corporation.............. C 440 219-0245
  Perry *(G-12303)*
	Bayada Home Health Care Inc............. D 330 929-5512
	  Cuyahoga Falls *(G-7048)*
		Cleveland Clnic Akron Gen Vsti........... B 330 745-1601
		  Akron *(G-108)*

Addus Homecare Corporation.............. C 866 684-0385
  Wintersville *(G-15291)*
	Benjamin Rose Institute....................... D 216 791-8000
	  Cleveland *(G-3867)*
		Columbus Home Health Svcs LLC....... E 614 985-1464
		  Columbus *(G-5637)*

Adult Comfort Care Inc....................... E 440 320-3335
  Vermilion *(G-14404)*
	Bethesda Hospital Association............. B 740 454-4000
	  Zanesville *(G-15770)*
		Comfort Keepers.................................. E 419 229-1031
		  Lima *(G-9876)*

80 HEALTH SERVICES

Company	Location	Code	Phone
Community Caregivers	Wadsworth (G-14433)	D	330 725-9800
Community Concepts Inc	Mason (G-10542)	C	513 398-8181
Community Hlth Prfssionals Inc	Ada (G-1)	E	419 634-7443
Community Hlth Prfssionals Inc	Archbold (G-455)	E	419 445-5128
Community Hlth Prfssionals Inc	Celina (G-1920)	E	419 586-1999
Community Hlth Prfssionals Inc	Celina (G-1921)	E	419 586-6266
Community Hlth Prfssionals Inc	Delphos (G-7839)	E	419 695-8101
Community Hlth Prfssionals Inc	Lima (G-9989)	E	419 991-1822
Community Hlth Prfssionals Inc	Paulding (G-12281)	E	419 399-4708
Community Hlth Prfssionals Inc	Van Wert (G-14342)	C	419 238-9223
Companion Care Services Inc	Mentor On The Lake (G-11014)	E	440 257-0075
Companions of Ashland LLC	Ashland (G-494)	E	419 281-2273
Comprhnsive Healthcare Svcs Inc	Cincinnati (G-2490)	C	513 245-0100
Connections In Ohio Inc	Cleveland (G-4102)	D	216 228-9760
Consumer Support Services Inc	Niles (G-11786)	D	330 652-8800
Continental Home Health Care	Mansfield (G-10254)	E	419 521-2470
Continental Home Health Care	Springfield (G-13241)	E	937 323-4499
Counting Blessings HM Care LLC	Ashtabula (G-529)	E	440 850-1050
Crawford Cnty Shared Hlth Svcs	Galion (G-8746)	E	419 468-7985
D&J Quality Care Entps Inc	Strongsville (G-13451)	D	440 638-7001
Daynas Homecare LLC	Maple Heights (G-10337)	E	216 323-0323
Ddc Group Inc	Dayton (G-7307)	C	937 619-3111
Decahealth Inc	Toledo (G-13773)	D	866 908-3514
Detox Health Care Corp Ohio	Cincinnati (G-2560)	D	513 742-6310
Diamonds Pearls Hlth Svcs LLC	Beachwood (G-787)	D	216 752-8500
Dillon Holdings LLC	West Chester (G-14685)	C	513 942-5600
▲ Discount Drug Mart Inc	Medina (G-10829)	C	330 725-2340
Diversified Health MGT Inc	Columbus (G-5774)	D	614 338-8888
Ecumencal Shlter Ntwrk Lk Cnty	Painesville (G-12228)	E	440 354-6417
Ember Complete Care	Uhrichsville (G-14233)	D	740 922-6968
Ember Complete Care Inc	Uhrichsville (G-14234)	E	740 922-6888
Every Child Succeeds Inc	Cincinnati (G-2643)	E	513 636-2830
Everyday Homecare LLC	Mount Orab (G-11470)	E	937 444-1672
Excellence Home Healthcare LLC	Columbus (G-5836)	E	614 755-6502
Fairfield Community Health Ctr	Lancaster (G-9710)	E	740 277-6043
Fairhope Hspice Plltive Care I	Lancaster (G-9721)	D	740 654-7077
Family Service of NW Ohio	Toledo (G-13803)	D	419 321-6455
Fidelity Health Care	Moraine (G-11409)	A	937 208-6400
First Assist Health Care LLC	Cleveland (G-4255)	E	440 421-9256
First Choice Medical Staffing	Toledo (G-13807)	D	419 861-2722
First Community Village	Columbus (G-5861)	B	614 324-4455
Firsticare Inc	Columbus (G-5865)	E	614 721-2273
Fns Inc	Chillicothe (G-2065)	E	740 775-5463
Freedom Caregivers	Mansfield (G-10265)	E	567 560-8277
Friends In Deed Inc	Wooster (G-15339)	E	330 345-9222
Gaash Home Health Care LLC	Mansfield (G-10266)	D	419 775-4823
Good Samaritan Hosp Cincinnati	Cincinnati (G-2742)	E	513 569-6251
Goods Hands Supported Living	Chillicothe (G-2066)	E	740 773-4170
Graves Care Services LLC	Westerville (G-14982)	E	614 392-2820
Great Home Healthcare LLC	Columbus (G-5950)	E	614 475-4026
Greater Clvland HM Hlth Care I	Beachwood (G-796)	D	440 232-4995
Greenville Nursing Services	Xenia (G-15519)	E	937 736-2272
Guardian Angels HM Hlth Care I	Sylvania (G-13547)	D	419 517-7797
Hanson Services Inc	Lakewood (G-9668)	C	216 226-5425
Healing Touch Agency LLC	Dayton (G-7400)	E	937 813-8333
Health Care Plus	Marietta (G-10370)	C	740 373-9446
Health Care Rtrment Corp Amer	Toledo (G-13841)	C	304 925-4771
Health Partners Western Ohio	Lima (G-9902)	E	419 221-3072
Health With Hart Snior Svcs LL	West Chester (G-14706)	E	513 229-8888
Hearty Hearts Home Health LLC	Cleveland (G-4356)	E	216 898-5533
Heavenly Home Health LLC	Rayland (G-12647)	E	740 859-4735
Helping Hands Healthcare Inc	West Chester (G-14816)	C	513 755-4181
Helping U Home Health Care LLC	Beachwood (G-798)	E	440 724-3754
Heritage Health Care Services	Columbus (G-5988)	C	614 848-6550
Heritage Health Care Services	Lima (G-9905)	C	419 867-2002
HH Franchising Systems Inc	Blue Ash (G-1181)	D	513 563-8339
Holistic Hlpers HM Hlth Care L	Shaker Heights (G-12978)	D	216 331-5014
Holzer Home Care Services	Jackson (G-9519)	D	740 288-4287
Home Care Network Inc	Beachwood (G-800)	C	216 378-9011
Home Care Network Inc	Dayton (G-7134)	C	937 258-1111
Home Care Network Inc	Portsmouth (G-12555)	C	740 353-2329
Home Care Network Inc	Dayton (G-7408)	D	800 600-3974
Home Instead Senior Care	Bedford (G-965)	E	440 914-1400
Home Instead Senior Care	Canal Winchester (G-1608)	E	614 432-8524
Home Instead Senior Care	Wadsworth (G-14435)	E	330 334-4664
Home Is Where Hart Is HM Care	Wintersville (G-15295)	E	740 457-5240
Homecare With Heart LLC	Youngstown (G-15632)	C	330 726-0700
Hometown Care LLC	Cuyahoga Falls (G-7079)	E	330 926-1118
Honorworth Homecare LLC	Cincinnati (G-2841)	E	513 557-0093
Hope Homes Inc	Stow (G-13374)	E	330 688-4935
Horizon HM Hlth Care Agcy LLC	Columbus (G-6008)	E	614 279-2933
Horizon Home Health Care LLC	Vandalia (G-14381)	C	937 410-3838
Hospice Care Ohio	Fairlawn (G-8483)	D	330 665-1455
Hospice Cincinnati Inc	Cincinnati (G-2848)	D	513 891-7700
Hospice North Central Ohio Inc	Ashland (G-501)	E	419 281-7107
Hospice of Genesis Health	Zanesville (G-15801)	E	740 454-5381
Hospice of Knox County	Mount Vernon (G-11489)	E	740 397-5188
Hospice of Medina County	Medina (G-10840)	D	330 725-1900
Hospice of Memorial Hospita L	Clyde (G-5202)	E	419 334-6626
Hospice of The Western Reserve	Medina (G-10841)	E	330 800-2240
Hospice Southwest Ohio Inc	Cincinnati (G-2849)	D	513 770-0820
Hospital HM Hlth Svcs Hghland	Hillsboro (G-9259)	E	937 393-6371
In Home Health Inc	Toledo (G-13862)	C	419 252-5500
Infinity Health Services Inc	Westlake (G-15070)	D	440 614-0145
Infusion Partners Inc	Sylvania (G-13551)	E	419 843-2100
▲ Infusion Partners Inc	Cincinnati (G-2871)	E	513 396-6060
Interim Halthcare Columbus Inc	Heath (G-9134)	B	740 349-8700
Interim Halthcare Columbus Inc	Marion (G-10431)	C	740 387-0301
Interim Halthcare Columbus Inc	Gahanna (G-8719)	E	614 888-3130
Interim Healthcare	Portsmouth (G-12557)	D	740 354-5550
Interim Healthcare Inc	Columbus (G-6065)	D	614 552-3400
Interim Healthcare Inc	Kent (G-9581)	D	330 677-8010
Interim Healthcare of Dayton	Dayton (G-7423)	A	937 291-5330
Interim Hlth Care of Nrthwster	Findlay (G-8550)	D	419 422-5328
Interim Hlth Care of Nrthwster	Lima (G-9993)	D	419 228-9345
Interim Hlth Care of Nrthwster	New Lexington (G-11627)	D	740 343-4112
Interim Hlth Care of Nrthwster	Zanesville (G-15804)	D	740 453-5130
Interim Hlthcare Cambridge Inc	Coshocton (G-6987)	D	740 623-2949

80 HEALTH SERVICES

Interim Hlthcare Cambridge Inc............ E 740 432-2966
   Worthington *(G-15423)*

International Healthcare Corp.................. D 513 731-3338
   Cincinnati *(G-2882)*

Interntnal Qlty Halthcare Corp................. E 513 731-3338
   Dayton *(G-7425)*

Intervention For Peace Inc..................... E 330 725-1298
   Medina *(G-10848)*

Jag Healthcare Inc................................... A 440 385-4370
   Rocky River *(G-12744)*

Jmo & Dsl Llc... E 216 785-9375
   Lakewood *(G-9670)*

Joint Township Dst Mem Hosp................ E 419 394-3335
   Saint Marys *(G-12828)*

Kentix Developmental Hlth Inc................ E 330 949-0131
   Cuyahoga Falls *(G-7084)*

Khc Inc.. D 740 775-5463
   Chillicothe *(G-2076)*

Knox County.. E 740 392-2200
   Mount Vernon *(G-11494)*

L JC Home Care LLC.............................. D 614 495-0276
   Worthington *(G-15429)*

Labelle Hmhealth Care Svcs LLC........... D 740 392-1405
   Mount Vernon *(G-11497)*

Ladneir Healthcare Service LLC............. E 216 744-7296
   South Euclid *(G-13171)*

Lake Hospital Sys HM Hlth Svcs............. E 440 639-0900
   Painesville *(G-12232)*

Lbs International Inc............................... E 614 866-3688
   Reynoldsburg *(G-12667)*

Liberty Provider LLC............................... D 419 517-7000
   Toledo *(G-13888)*

Lifecare Alliance..................................... C 614 278-3130
   Columbus *(G-6161)*

Lincare Inc.. E 513 705-4250
   Middletown *(G-11169)*

Living Assistance Services Inc................ E 330 733-1532
   Tallmadge *(G-13600)*

Lizzies Hse Senior HM Care LLC........... E 216 816-4188
   Cleveland *(G-4501)*

Lorain County Senior Care Inc............... E 440 353-3080
   North Ridgeville *(G-11931)*

Loving Family Home Care Inc................ D 888 469-2178
   Toledo *(G-13893)*

Mahoning Vly Infusioncare Inc................ C 330 759-9487
   Youngstown *(G-15660)*

Manor Care Inc....................................... D 419 252-5500
   Toledo *(G-13905)*

Maple Grove Enterprises Inc.................. D 440 286-1342
   Chardon *(G-2010)*

Maple Knoll Communities Inc................. B 513 782-2400
   Cincinnati *(G-3008)*

▲ Marymount Hospital Inc...................... B 216 581-0500
   Cleveland *(G-4531)*

Maxim Healthcare Services Inc.............. C 513 793-6444
   Cincinnati *(G-3018)*

Maxim Healthcare Services Inc.............. C 614 986-3001
   Gahanna *(G-8723)*

Maxim Healthcare Services Inc.............. C 740 526-2222
   Hebron *(G-9146)*

Maxim Healthcare Services Inc.............. C 419 747-8040
   Ontario *(G-12116)*

McGregor Pace.. E 216 361-0917
   Cleveland *(G-4539)*

McGregor Pace.. E 216 791-3580
   Cleveland *(G-4540)*

Mch Services Inc.................................... C 260 432-9699
   Dayton *(G-7473)*

Med America Hlth Systems Corp............ A 937 223-6192
   Dayton *(G-7475)*

Medcentral Health System...................... C 419 526-8442
   Mansfield *(G-10292)*

Medcorp Inc.. C 419 425-9700
   Findlay *(G-8566)*

Medi Home Health Agency Inc............... E 740 441-1779
   Gallipolis *(G-8763)*

Medi Home Health Agency Inc............... E 740 266-3977
   Steubenville *(G-13338)*

Medical Housecalls LLC......................... E 513 699-9090
   Cincinnati *(G-3027)*

Medlink of Ohio Inc................................ B 216 751-5900
   Cleveland *(G-4547)*

Memorial Hospital................................... C 419 547-6419
   Clyde *(G-5206)*

Mercer Cnty Joint Townshp Hosp........... D 419 584-0143
   Celina *(G-1927)*

Mobile Hyperbaric Centers LLC............. E 216 443-0430
   Cleveland *(G-4591)*

Multicare Hlth Eductl Svcs Inc................ E 216 731-8900
   Euclid *(G-8358)*

National Mentor Holdings Inc................. B 419 443-0867
   Fostoria *(G-8621)*

National Mentor Holdings Inc................. B 234 806-5361
   Warren *(G-14542)*

Nationwide Childrens Hospital................ C 740 522-3221
   Newark *(G-11734)*

Nationwide Childrens Hospital................ C 614 355-8300
   Westerville *(G-14915)*

Nationwide Chld Hosp Homecare............ A 614 355-1100
   Columbus *(G-6325)*

Nationwide Health MGT LLC................... C 440 888-8888
   Parma *(G-12258)*

NC Hha Inc... C 216 593-7750
   Elyria *(G-8279)*

Ncs Healthcare Inc................................. A 216 514-3350
   Cleveland *(G-4630)*

New Life Hospice Inc.............................. C 440 934-1458
   Lorain *(G-10095)*

Northcoast Health Care Group................ E 330 856-2656
   Beachwood *(G-822)*

Northeast Professional Hm Care............. D 330 966-2311
   Canton *(G-1821)*

Nurses Care Inc...................................... D 513 424-1141
   Miamisburg *(G-11076)*

Ohio North E Hlth Systems Inc............... E 330 747-9551
   Youngstown *(G-15683)*

Ohio Valley Home Health Inc.................. E 740 249-4219
   Athens *(G-585)*

Ohio Valley Home Health Inc.................. E 740 441-1393
   Gallipolis *(G-8767)*

Ohio-T-Home Hlth Care Agcy Ltd........... D 614 947-0791
   Columbus *(G-6464)*

Ohioans Home Healthcare Inc............... D 419 843-4422
   Perrysburg *(G-12360)*

Ohiohealth Corporation........................... A 614 788-8860
   Columbus *(G-6465)*

Open Arms Health Systems Llc.............. D 614 385-8354
   Columbus *(G-6472)*

Option Care Brecksville O....................... E 440 627-2031
   Brecksville *(G-1361)*

Options Home Services LLC.................. E 614 203-6340
   Columbus *(G-6475)*

Our Lady Bellefonte Hosp Inc................. A 606 833-3333
   Cincinnati *(G-3176)*

P C Vpa... D 513 841-0777
   Cincinnati *(G-3180)*

Pace Plus Corp....................................... D 419 754-1897
   Toledo *(G-13955)*

Paramount Spport Svc of St Clrs............ E 740 526-0540
   Saint Clairsville *(G-12811)*

Paris Home Health Care LLC................. E 888 416-9889
   Warrensville Heights *(G-14585)*

Parkside Care Corporation...................... D 440 286-2273
   Chardon *(G-2014)*

Patriot Homecare Inc.............................. C 330 306-9651
   Girard *(G-8822)*

Peoplfrst Hmcare Hspice Ohio L............ E 937 433-2400
   Dayton *(G-7548)*

Personal Touch HM Care IPA Inc........... C 513 984-9600
   Cincinnati *(G-3198)*

Personal Touch HM Care IPA Inc........... C 614 227-6952
   Columbus *(G-6517)*

Personal Touch HM Care IPA Inc........... C 513 868-2272
   Hamilton *(G-9072)*

Personal Touch HM Care IPA Inc........... C 330 263-1112
   Wooster *(G-15366)*

Phillips Hthcare LLC DBA Cring............. E 330 531-6110
   Warren *(G-14547)*

Preferred Medical Group Inc.................. C 404 403-8310
   Beachwood *(G-827)*

Premier Health Partners......................... A 937 499-9596
   Dayton *(G-7560)*

Primary Care Nursing Services............... E 614 764-0960
   Dublin *(G-8096)*

Prime Home Care LLC........................... E 513 340-4183
   Maineville *(G-10230)*

Private Duty Services Inc....................... C 419 238-3714
   Van Wert *(G-14350)*

Pro Health Care Services Ltd................. C 614 856-9111
   Groveport *(G-8996)*

Promedica Toledo Hospital..................... D 419 291-2273
   Sylvania *(G-13566)*

Prompt Prvate Nursing Care Inc............. D 614 834-1105
   Canal Winchester *(G-1615)*

Pulmonary Solutions Inc........................ E 937 393-0991
   Blue Ash *(G-1226)*

Pure Health Care Llc.............................. E 937 668-7873
   Centerville *(G-1951)*

Pure Healthcare...................................... E 937 668-7873
   Dayton *(G-7574)*

Putnam Cnty Homecare & Hospice........ D 419 523-4449
   Ottawa *(G-12193)*

Quality Care Nursing Svc Inc................. C 740 377-9095
   South Point *(G-13182)*

Quality Cmfort Living Svcs LLC.............. D 330 280-7659
   Canton *(G-1836)*

Quantum Health Inc............................... A 800 257-2038
   Dublin *(G-8102)*

Queen City Hospice LLC........................ A 513 510-4406
   Mason *(G-10598)*

Queen City Skilled Care LLC................. D 513 802-5010
   Cincinnati *(G-3267)*

Reliable Home Healthcare LLC.............. E 937 274-2900
   Dayton *(G-7584)*

REM Corp... C 740 828-2601
   Frazeysburg *(G-8656)*

Res Care Home Care.............................. D 937 436-3966
   Dayton *(G-7586)*

RES-Care Inc.. D 740 782-1476
   Bethesda *(G-1097)*

RES-Care Inc.. D 330 452-2913
   Canton *(G-1846)*

RES-Care Inc.. D 740 446-7549
   Gallipolis *(G-8768)*

RES-Care Inc.. D 740 526-0285
   Saint Clairsville *(G-12813)*

RES-Care Inc.. C 740 695-4931
   Saint Clairsville *(G-12814)*

RES-Care Inc.. D 513 858-4550
   West Chester *(G-14755)*

Rescue91 Healthcare Svcs LLC............. E 937 500-5371
   Dayton *(G-7587)*

Resource Alliance Homecare LLC.......... D 216 465-9977
   Cleveland Heights *(G-5184)*

Richard Health Systems LLC................. C 419 534-2371
   Toledo *(G-13991)*

Employee Codes: A=Over 500 employees, B=251-500
C=101-250, D=51-100, E=20-50, F=10-19, G=1-9

80 HEALTH SERVICES

Rose Health Care Services Ltd.............. E 937 277-7518
   Dayton (G-7596)
Rosmansearch Inc.............................. E 216 256-9020
   Cleveland (G-4855)
Ross County Health District.................. E 740 775-1114
   Chillicothe (G-2086)
Ross County Home Health LLC............ D 740 775-1114
   Chillicothe (G-2087)
Royalty Care Nursing LLC..................... D 216 386-8762
   Cleveland (G-4861)
Safe and Secure Homecare Corp........... D 614 808-0164
   Columbus (G-6625)
Salo Inc... C 419 419-0038
   Bowling Green (G-1332)
Salo Inc... B 740 432-2966
   Cambridge (G-1581)
Salo Inc... C 513 984-1110
   Cincinnati (G-3345)
Salo Inc... C 740 623-2331
   Coshocton (G-7001)
Salo Inc... C 330 836-5571
   Fairlawn (G-8495)
Salo Inc... C 740 653-5990
   Lancaster (G-9740)
Salo Inc... C 740 651-5209
   Mcconnelsville (G-10804)
Salo Inc... C 740 964-2904
   Pataskala (G-12276)
Salo Inc... D 614 436-9404
   Columbus (G-6639)
Sar Enterprises LLC............................ E 419 472-8181
   Toledo (G-14005)
Schroer Properties Navarre Inc............. D 330 498-8200
   North Canton (G-11861)
Scriptdrop Inc..................................... D 614 641-0648
   Columbus (G-6656)
Sdx Home Care Operations LLC........... D 937 322-6288
   Springfield (G-13289)
Senior Touch Solution.......................... E 216 862-4841
   Cleveland (G-4895)
Source Diagnostics LLC....................... E 440 542-9481
   Solon (G-13146)
Southern Care Inc................................ D 330 797-8940
   Youngstown (G-15727)
Specilzed HM Care Prviders LLC........... E 330 758-8740
   Youngstown (G-15728)
St Augustine Manor.............................. C 440 888-7722
   Parma (G-12265)
Summit Acres Inc................................. C 740 732-2364
   Caldwell (G-1551)
Summit Ortho Home Care..................... D 513 898-3375
   Blue Ash (G-1246)
Sunrise Nursing Healthcare LLC............ D 513 797-5144
   Amelia (G-420)
Supreme Touch Home Health Svcs........ E 614 783-1115
   Columbus (G-6732)
Synergy Homecare................................ D 937 610-0555
   Dayton (G-7657)
Tender Hrts At HM Snior Care I............. D 513 234-0805
   Cincinnati (G-3453)
The Berger Hospital.............................. A 740 474-2126
   Circleville (G-3727)
Tk Homecare Llc................................... C 419 517-7000
   Toledo (G-14044)
Tky Associates LLC............................. E 419 535-7777
   Toledo (G-14045)
Toledo Society For The Blind................. E 419 720-3937
   Toledo (G-14066)
Total Homecare Solutions LLC.............. E 513 277-0915
   Cincinnati (G-3483)
Trucare Provider Services LLC............. C 513 201-5611
   Cincinnati (G-3531)

Tsk Assisted Living Svcs Inc.................. D 330 297-2000
   Ravenna (G-12645)
Turning Point Residential Inc................. E 330 788-0669
   Youngstown (G-15738)
Ultimate Home Services LLC.................. E 614 888-8698
   Worthington (G-15464)
Union Healthcare Services Inc............... E 614 686-2322
   Columbus (G-6801)
Unity I Home Healthcare LLC................. E 740 351-0500
   Portsmouth (G-12580)
Universal Nursing Services.................... E 330 434-7318
   Akron (G-343)
University Hsptals Clvland Med.............. A 216 844-4663
   Cleveland (G-5079)
University Mednet................................. B 216 383-0100
   Euclid (G-8363)
Vandalia Butler Emrgncy Fd Ctr............ D 937 898-4202
   Vandalia (G-14402)
Viaquest Behavioral Health LLC............. E 614 339-0868
   Dublin (G-8153)
Viaquest Residential Svcs LLC............... C 216 446-2650
   Independence (G-9496)
Viaquest Residential Svcs LLC............... E 614 889-5837
   Dublin (G-8154)
Vision Home Health Care LLC................ E 614 338-8100
   Pataskala (G-12279)
Visiting Nrse Assn Hlthcare PR.............. C 216 931-1300
   Independence (G-9497)
Visiting Nrse Assn Hspice Nrth.............. D 330 841-5440
   Warren (G-14572)
Visiting Nrse Assn of Clveland............... C 419 281-2480
   Ashland (G-515)
Visiting Nrse Assn of Clveland............... E 419 522-4969
   Mansfield (G-10322)
Visiting Nrse Assn of Grter CN.............. E 513 345-8000
   Cincinnati (G-3631)
Visiting Nrse Assn of Mid-Ohio.............. E 216 931-1300
   Cleveland (G-5109)
Vna Comprehensive Services Inc........... D 419 695-8101
   Delphos (G-7848)
Walton Home Health Care LLC.............. E 513 270-0555
   Cincinnati (G-3640)
West Branch Nursing Home Ltd............ D 330 537-4621
   Salem (G-12857)
Western Rsrve Area Agcy On Agi........... C 216 621-0303
   Cleveland (G-5138)
Whitney Home Care LLC....................... E 440 647-2200
   Wellington (G-14635)
Willcare Inc... C 216 289-5300
   Cleveland (G-5148)
Willglo Services Inc.............................. E 614 443-3020
   Columbus (G-6893)
Ziks Family Pharmacy 100..................... E 937 225-9350
   Dayton (G-7737)
Ziks Home Healthcare LLC.................... D 937 225-9350
   Dayton (G-7738)
Zimohana LLC..................................... D 330 922-4721
   Medina (G-10906)

8092 Kidney dialysis centers

022808 Kenwood LLC............................ E 513 745-0800
   Cincinnati (G-2117)
Bio-Mdcal Applcations Ohio Inc............. E 330 376-4905
   Akron (G-68)
Borrego Dialysis LLC............................ E 513 737-0158
   Hamilton (G-9018)
Columbus-Rna-Davita LLC.................... E 614 501-7224
   Columbus (G-5660)
Columbus-Rna-Davita LLC.................... E 614 228-1773
   Columbus (G-5661)
Columbus-Rna-Davita LLC.................... E 614 985-1732
   Columbus (G-5662)

Community Dialysis Center.................... C 216 295-7000
   Cleveland (G-4098)
Community Dialysis Center.................... C 216 229-6170
   Cleveland (G-4099)
Community Dialysis Center.................... C 330 609-0370
   Warren (G-14510)
Court Dialysis LLC............................... E 740 773-3733
   Chillicothe (G-2063)
Desoto Dialysis LLC............................. E 419 691-1514
   Oregon (G-12132)
Dialysis Centers Dayton LLC................. D 937 208-7900
   Dayton (G-7312)
Dialysis Centers Dayton LLC................. D 937 548-7019
   Greenville (G-8871)
Dialysis Clinic Inc................................ D 513 281-0091
   Cincinnati (G-2562)
Dialysis Clinic Inc................................ E 740 351-0596
   Portsmouth (G-12551)
Dva Hlthcare - Sthwest Ohio LL............. E 513 733-8215
   Blue Ash (G-1165)
Dva Hlthcare - Sthwest Ohio LL............. E 513 347-0444
   Cincinnati (G-2588)
Dva Hlthcare - Sthwest Ohio LL............. E 513 591-2900
   Cincinnati (G-2589)
Dva Hlthcare - Sthwest Ohio LL............. E 513 939-1110
   Fairfield (G-8408)
Dva Hlthcare - Sthwest Ohio LL............. E 513 422-1467
   Middletown (G-11196)
Fields Dialysis LLC.............................. E 513 531-2111
   Cincinnati (G-2661)
Fresenius Med Care Butler Cty.............. E 513 737-1415
   Hamilton (G-9044)
Fresenius Med Care Milford LLC............ E 513 248-1690
   Milford (G-11228)
Fresenius Med Care S Grove Cy............ E 614 801-2505
   Grove City (G-8920)
Fresenius Med Care Wlmngton HM........ E 937 382-3379
   Wilmington (G-15254)
Garrett Dialysis LLC............................. D 216 398-6029
   Cleveland (G-4303)
Greenfield Health Systems Corp............ E 419 389-9681
   Toledo (G-13829)
Kidney Center of Bexley LLC................. D 614 231-2200
   Columbus (G-6115)
Kidney Group Inc................................. E 330 746-1488
   Youngstown (G-15646)
Kidney Services W Centl Ohio............... E 419 227-0918
   Lima (G-9913)
Nxstage Cincinnati LLC......................... E 513 712-1300
   Cincinnati (G-3137)
Ohio Renal Care Supply Co LLC............ E 216 739-0500
   Cleveland (G-4690)
Ohio River Dialysis LLC........................ E 513 385-3580
   Cincinnati (G-3148)
River Valley Dialysis LLC...................... E 513 922-5900
   Cincinnati (G-3301)
River Valley Dialysis LLC...................... E 513 793-0555
   Cincinnati (G-3302)
River Valley Dialysis LLC...................... E 513 741-1062
   Cincinnati (G-3303)
River Valley Dialysis LLC...................... E 513 934-0272
   Lebanon (G-9785)
Storrie Dialysis LLC............................. E 937 390-3125
   Springfield (G-13296)
Tenack Dialysis LLC............................. E 513 810-4369
   Cincinnati (G-3452)
Warren Dialysis Center LLC.................. E 330 609-5502
   Warren (G-14575)

8093 Specialty outpatient clinics, nec

A W S Inc.. A 216 941-8800
   Cleveland (G-3750)

SIC SECTION   80 HEALTH SERVICES

Access Counseling Services LLC .... C 513 649-8008
  Middletown *(G-11193)*
Access Hospital Dayton LLC .... D 937 228-0579
  Dayton *(G-7153)*
Adamhscc Board .... E 216 241-3400
  Cleveland *(G-3768)*
Alcohol DRG Addction Mntal Svc .... E 937 443-0416
  Dayton *(G-7161)*
Allwell Behavioral Health Svcs .... E 740 432-7155
  Cambridge *(G-1553)*
Alta Care Group Inc .... E 330 793-2487
  Youngstown *(G-15547)*
American Kidney Stone MGT Ltd .... E 800 637-5188
  Columbus *(G-5352)*
Appleseed Cmnty Mntal Hlth Ctr .... D 419 281-3716
  Ashland *(G-472)*
Applewood Centers Inc .... D 440 324-1300
  Lorain *(G-10055)*
Aultman North Canton Med Group .... E 330 363-6333
  Canton *(G-1682)*
Aurora Manor Ltd Partnership .... B 330 562-5000
  Aurora *(G-606)*
Baymark Health Services La Inc .... C 440 328-4213
  Amherst *(G-423)*
Baymark Health Services La Inc .... C 937 203-2017
  Dayton *(G-7187)*
Bayshore Counseling Svcs Inc .... E 419 626-9156
  Sandusky *(G-12864)*
Beacon Health .... C 440 354-9924
  Mentor *(G-10914)*
Behavral Cnnctions WD Cnty Inc .... E 419 352-5387
  Bowling Green *(G-1304)*
Behavral Cnnctions WD Cnty Inc .... E 419 352-5561
  Bowling Green *(G-1305)*
Behavral Cnnctions WD Cnty Inc .... E 419 352-5387
  Bowling Green *(G-1306)*
Behavral Hlthcare Prtners Cntl .... C 740 522-8477
  Newark *(G-11690)*
Behavrial Hlthcare Prtners CNT .... E 740 397-0442
  Mount Vernon *(G-11476)*
Belmont Bhc Pines Hospital Inc .... D 330 759-2700
  Youngstown *(G-15558)*
Best Care Nrsing Rhblttion Ctr .... A 740 574-2558
  Wheelersburg *(G-15127)*
Bhc Fox Run Hospital Inc .... E 740 695-2131
  Saint Clairsville *(G-12781)*
Blick Clinic Inc .... C 330 762-5425
  Akron *(G-71)*
Blick Clinic Inc .... D 330 762-5425
  Akron *(G-70)*
Brecksvlle Hlthcare Group Inc .... E 440 546-0643
  Brecksville *(G-1346)*
Bridge .... E 513 244-3985
  Cincinnati *(G-2281)*
Bridgeway Inc .... C 216 688-4114
  Cleveland *(G-3892)*
Bryans Treatment Center .... E 216 208-0634
  Toledo *(G-13721)*
Buckeye Ranch Foundation Inc .... E 614 875-2371
  Grove City *(G-8903)*
Butler Bhavioral Hlth Svcs Inc .... E 513 896-7887
  Hamilton *(G-9021)*
Caprice Health Care Inc .... E 330 965-9200
  North Lima *(G-11885)*
Cedar Ridge Behavioral He .... E 740 801-0655
  Zanesville *(G-15778)*
Center For Addiction Treatment .... D 513 381-6672
  Cincinnati *(G-2332)*
Center For Families & Children .... E 216 252-5800
  Cleveland *(G-3950)*
Center For Indvdual Fmly Svcs .... C 419 522-4357
  Mansfield *(G-10251)*

Central Cmnty Hlth Bd Hmlton C .... D 513 559-2000
  Cincinnati *(G-2335)*
Central Ohio Mental Health Ctr .... D 740 368-7837
  Delaware *(G-7785)*
Century Health Inc .... D 419 425-5050
  Findlay *(G-8522)*
CHI Health At Home .... E 513 576-0262
  Milford *(G-11221)*
Child Adlscent Behavioral Hlth .... E 330 454-7917
  Cantor. *(G-1708)*
Child Focus Inc .... D 513 752-1555
  Cincinnati *(G-2355)*
Childrens Advantage .... E 330 296-5552
  Ravenna *(G-12621)*
Childrens Hospital Medical Ctr .... B 513 636-6100
  Cincinnati *(G-2367)*
Childrens Hospital Medical Ctr .... B 513 636-6800
  Mason *(G-10529)*
Choices Behavioral Health Care .... E 419 960-4009
  Port Clinton *(G-12519)*
Christian Chld HM Ohio Inc .... D 330 345-7949
  Wooster *(G-15320)*
Cincinnati Speech Hearing Ctr .... E 513 221-0527
  Cincinnati *(G-2422)*
Clermont Recovery Center Inc .... E 513 735-8100
  Batavia *(G-734)*
Cleveland Clinic Foundation .... E 440 988-5651
  Lorain *(G-10065)*
Cleveland Clinic Mercy Hosp .... B 330 627-7641
  Carrollton *(G-1904)*
Cleveland Clnc Bchwd Fmly Ctr .... A 216 839-3100
  Cleveland *(G-4032)*
Cleveland Clinic Hlth Systm-AST .... E 330 468-0190
  Northfield *(G-11954)*
Cleveland Clinic Hlth Systm-AST .... D 330 287-4830
  Wooster *(G-15324)*
Cleveland Clnic Rhbltion Physc .... C 440 516-5400
  Willoughby Hills *(G-15232)*
Coleman Professional Services .... E 330 394-8831
  Akron *(G-112)*
Coleman Professional Svcs Inc .... D 330 744-2991
  Akron *(G-113)*
Coleman Professional Svcs Inc .... C 330 673-1347
  Kent *(G-9565)*
Community Action Agnst Addctio .... E 216 881-0765
  Cleveland *(G-4096)*
Community Asssment Trtmnt Svc .... E 216 441-0200
  Cleveland *(G-4097)*
Community Behavioral Hlth Inc .... C 513 887-8500
  Hamilton *(G-9033)*
Community Cnsling Ctr Ashtbula .... E 440 998-4210
  Ashtabula *(G-528)*
Community Cnsling Wllness Ctrs .... E 740 387-5210
  Marion *(G-10422)*
Community Counseling Svcs Inc .... E 419 562-2000
  Bucyrus *(G-1501)*
Community Drug Board Inc .... D 330 996-5114
  Akron *(G-117)*
Community Drug Board Inc .... D 330 315-5590
  Akron *(G-116)*
Community Mental Health Svc .... E 740 633-2161
  Martins Ferry *(G-10466)*
Community Mental Health Svc .... D 740 695-9344
  Saint Clairsville *(G-12787)*
Community Support Services Inc .... C 330 253-9388
  Akron *(G-118)*
Compass Community Health .... E 740 355-7102
  Portsmouth *(G-12549)*
Compass Family and Cmnty Svcs .... E 330 782-5664
  Youngstown *(G-15584)*
Comprehensive Behavioral Hlth .... C 330 385-8800
  East Liverpool *(G-8180)*

Comprhnsive Addction Svc Syste .... D 419 241-8827
  Toledo *(G-13755)*
Concept Rehab Inc .... D 419 843-6002
  Toledo *(G-13756)*
Cornerstone Support Services .... D 330 339-7850
  New Philadelphia *(G-11644)*
Counseling Source Inc .... E 513 984-9838
  Blue Ash *(G-1160)*
Country Meadow Care Center LLC .... E 419 886-3922
  Bellville *(G-1048)*
County of Carroll .... D 330 627-7651
  Carrollton *(G-1906)*
Crossroads Center .... C 513 475-5300
  Cincinnati *(G-2517)*
Crossroads Health .... D 440 255-1700
  Mentor *(G-10929)*
De Coach Team LLC .... D 513 942-4673
  Cincinnati *(G-2546)*
E Home Behavioral LLC .... E 513 530-1600
  Springfield *(G-13249)*
East Way Behavioral Hlth Care .... D 937 222-4900
  Dayton *(G-7323)*
Easter Seal Society of .... D 330 743-1168
  Youngstown *(G-15603)*
Education Alternatives .... D 216 332-9360
  Brookpark *(G-1434)*
Encore Rehabilitation Services .... E 614 459-6901
  Dublin *(G-8004)*
Equitas Health Inc .... D 614 299-2437
  Columbus *(G-5825)*
Family Rsource Ctr NW Ohio Inc .... E 419 222-1168
  Lima *(G-9889)*
Firelands Regional Health Sys .... E 419 557-5177
  Sandusky *(G-12897)*
First Alnce Hlathcare Ohio Inc .... D 216 417-8813
  Cleveland *(G-4253)*
First Step Recovery LLC .... E 330 369-8022
  Warren *(G-14520)*
Formu3 International Inc .... E 330 668-1461
  Akron *(G-166)*
Fort Hamilton Hospital .... B 513 867-2280
  Hamilton *(G-9043)*
Foundtons Bhvral Hlth Svcs Inc .... D 419 584-1000
  Celina *(G-1923)*
Franklin Cnty Bd Commissioners .... D 614 261-3196
  Columbus *(G-5881)*
Fulton County Health Dept .... E 419 337-0915
  Wauseon *(G-14603)*
Giving Tree Inc .... E 419 734-2942
  Port Clinton *(G-12526)*
Glenbeigh .... E 440 563-3400
  Rock Creek *(G-12733)*
Greater Cncnnati Bhvral Hlth S .... C 513 354-7000
  Walnut Hills *(G-14474)*
Harbor .... D 419 479-3233
  Toledo *(G-13834)*
Hcf of Roselawn Inc .... C 419 647-4115
  Spencerville *(G-13188)*
Healthsource of Ohio Inc .... E 513 753-2820
  Cincinnati *(G-2812)*
Healthsource of Ohio Inc .... E 513 575-1444
  Loveland *(G-10140)*
Healthsource of Ohio Inc .... E 937 386-0049
  Seaman *(G-12944)*
▲ Healthsource of Ohio Inc .... E 513 576-7700
  Loveland *(G-10141)*
Heartland Rhblitation Svcs Inc .... D 419 537-0764
  Toledo *(G-13843)*
Highland Springs LLC .... D 216 591-9433
  Beachwood *(G-799)*
Hitchcock Center For Women Inc .... E 216 421-0662
  Cleveland *(G-4366)*

Employee Codes: A=Over 500 employees, B=251-500
C=101-250, D=51-100, E=20-50, F=10-19, G=1-9

80 HEALTH SERVICES

Hopebridge LLC .... E 513 831-2578
   Milford *(G-11232)*

Hopebridge LLC .... E 855 324-0885
   Westerville *(G-14986)*

Hopewell Health Centers Inc .... D 740 594-5045
   Athens *(G-575)*

Hopewell Health Centers Inc .... E 740 592-3504
   Athens *(G-576)*

Hopewell Health Centers Inc .... E 740 757-2352
   Athens *(G-577)*

Hopewell Health Centers Inc .... E 740 385-8468
   Logan *(G-10026)*

Hopewell Health Centers Inc .... D 740 385-6594
   Logan *(G-10027)*

Hopewell Health Centers Inc .... E 740 385-2555
   Logan *(G-10028)*

Hopewell Health Centers Inc .... E 740 596-4809
   Mc Arthur *(G-10798)*

Ironton Lwrnce Cnty Area Cmnty .... B 740 532-3534
   Ironton *(G-9508)*

Lake-Geauga Recovery Ctrs Inc .... E 440 354-2848
   Painesville *(G-12234)*

Landmark Recovery Ohio LLC .... B 855 950-5035
   Euclid *(G-8354)*

Lorain Cnty Alchol DRG Abuse S .... D 440 323-6122
   Lorain *(G-10084)*

Lorain Cnty Bd Dvlpmntal Dsblt .... E 440 329-3734
   Elyria *(G-8271)*

Lorain County Alcohol and Drug .... D 440 246-0109
   Lorain *(G-10086)*

Lumiere Detox Center .... E 513 644-2275
   West Chester *(G-14727)*

Mahoning Vly Hmtlogy Onclogy A ..... E 330 318-1100
   Youngstown *(G-15659)*

Maryhaven Inc .... E 614 626-2432
   Columbus *(G-6201)*

Maryhaven Inc .... E 740 203-3800
   Delaware *(G-7816)*

Maryhaven Inc .... E 419 946-6734
   Mount Gilead *(G-11462)*

Maryhaven Inc .... D 614 449-1530
   Columbus *(G-6200)*

Maumee Valley Guidance Ctr Inc .... E 419 782-8856
   Defiance *(G-7755)*

Mayfield Spine Surgery Ctr LLC .... D 513 619-5899
   Cincinnati *(G-3021)*

McKinley Hall Inc .... E 937 328-5300
   Springfield *(G-13266)*

Medcentral Health System .... B 419 683-1040
   Crestline *(G-7025)*

Medcentral Health System .... C 419 526-8442
   Mansfield *(G-10292)*

Meigs County Care Center LLC .... C 740 992-6472
   Middleport *(G-11148)*

Mental Health Service .... E 937 399-9500
   Springfield *(G-13268)*

Mental Hlth Svcs For Hmless PR .... C 216 623-6555
   Cleveland *(G-4551)*

Meridian Healthcare .... D 330 797-0070
   Youngstown *(G-15666)*

Metrohealth System .... C 216 957-5000
   Cleveland *(G-4564)*

Metrohealth System .... C 216 778-8446
   Cleveland *(G-4566)*

Mid-Ohio Psychlogical Svcs Inc .... E 740 687-0042
   Lancaster *(G-9735)*

Muskingum Cnty DRG Alchol Sbst ...... E 740 454-1266
   Zanesville *(G-15813)*

N Market Behavioral Hosp LLC .... E 513 530-1600
   Canton *(G-1815)*

National Mentor Holdings Inc .... B 330 491-4331
   Youngstown *(G-15675)*

Nationwide Childrens Hospital .... C 614 355-8000
   Columbus *(G-6323)*

Nationwide Childrens Hospital .... C 614 355-7000
   Dublin *(G-8070)*

Ncs Healthcare Inc .... A 216 514-3350
   Cleveland *(G-4630)*

Neighbrhood Hlth Assn Tledo In .... E 419 720-7883
   Toledo *(G-13932)*

Netcare Corporation .... D 614 274-9500
   Columbus *(G-6346)*

Norcare Enterprises Inc .... C 440 233-7232
   Lorain *(G-10096)*

Nord Center .... E 440 233-7232
   Lorain *(G-10097)*

▲ Nord Center Associates Inc .... C 440 233-7232
   Lorain *(G-10098)*

North Cntl Mntal Hlth Svcs Inc .... D 614 227-6865
   Columbus *(G-6366)*

North East Ohio Health Svcs .... D 216 831-6466
   Beachwood *(G-821)*

Oak Clinic .... E 330 896-9625
   Uniontown *(G-14261)*

Ohio Dept Mntal Hlth Addction .... C 740 594-5000
   Athens *(G-583)*

Ohio Dept Mntal Hlth Addction .... C 614 752-0333
   Columbus *(G-6409)*

Ohio Dept Mntal Hlth Addction .... C 740 947-7581
   Waverly *(G-14614)*

Ohio Heart Institute Inc .... E 330 747-6446
   Youngstown *(G-15681)*

Ohio Hosp For Psychiatry LLC .... E 614 449-9664
   Columbus *(G-6429)*

Ohio State University .... C 614 257-3000
   Columbus *(G-6453)*

Osu Harding Hospital .... A 614 293-9600
   Columbus *(G-6483)*

P T Svcs Rehabilitation Inc .... B 419 455-8600
   Tiffin *(G-13638)*

Pain Management Associates Inc .... B 937 252-2000
   Dayton *(G-7138)*

Peregrine Health Services Inc .... D 330 823-9005
   Alliance *(G-396)*

Philio Inc .... E 419 531-5544
   Toledo *(G-13963)*

Pickaway Area Rcovery Svcs Inc .... E 740 477-1745
   Circleville *(G-3715)*

Pinnacle Trtmnt Ctrs Oh-I LLC .... E 330 577-5881
   Ravenna *(G-12635)*

Planned Parenthood Association .... E 937 226-0780
   Dayton *(G-7555)*

Planned Prenthood Greater Ohio .... E 614 224-2235
   Columbus *(G-6529)*

Planned Prnthood Sthwest Ohio .... E 513 721-7635
   Cincinnati *(G-3212)*

Pomegranate Development Ltd .... E 614 223-1650
   Columbus *(G-6535)*

Portage Path Behavioral Health .... D 330 253-3100
   Akron *(G-269)*

Portage Path Behavorial Health .... E 330 762-6110
   Akron *(G-270)*

Portage Path Behavorial Health .... E 330 928-2324
   Cuyahoga Falls *(G-7092)*

Positive Education Program .... E 440 471-8200
   Cleveland *(G-4763)*

Preserve Operating Co LLC .... E 513 471-8667
   Cincinnati *(G-3229)*

Preterm Foundation .... E 216 991-4577
   Cleveland *(G-4770)*

Project CURE Inc .... E 937 262-3500
   Dayton *(G-7570)*

Providers For Healthy Living .... D 614 664-3595
   Columbus *(G-6554)*

Psycare Inc .... E 330 856-6663
   Warren *(G-14549)*

Psycare Inc .... D 330 318-3078
   Struthers *(G-13502)*

Psycare Inc .... D 330 759-2310
   Youngstown *(G-15700)*

Pulmonary Solutions Inc .... E 937 393-0991
   Blue Ash *(G-1226)*

Quadco Rehabilitation Center .... E 419 782-0389
   Defiance *(G-7764)*

Ravenwood Mental Hlth Ctr Inc .... D 440 632-5355
   Middlefield *(G-11145)*

Ravenwood Mental Hlth Ctr Inc .... E 440 285-3568
   Chardon *(G-2015)*

Recovery Center .... E 740 687-4500
   Lancaster *(G-9738)*

Recovery Prevention Resources .... E 740 369-6811
   Delaware *(G-7823)*

Recovery Resources .... D 216 431-4131
   Cleveland *(G-4812)*

Recovery Resources .... E 216 431-4131
   Cleveland *(G-4813)*

Regard Recovery Florida LLC .... D 330 866-0900
   Sherrodsville *(G-13012)*

Rehab Center .... C 330 297-2770
   Ravenna *(G-12641)*

Rehabcare Group East Inc .... C 330 220-8950
   Cleveland *(G-4819)*

Rehabilitation Support Svcs .... E 330 252-9012
   Akron *(G-278)*

Rehabltion Ctr At Mrietta Mem .... E 740 374-1407
   Marietta *(G-10403)*

Rescue Incorporated .... C 419 255-9585
   Toledo *(G-13988)*

Ridge Ohio .... E 513 804-2204
   Milford *(G-11252)*

River Centre Clinic .... E 419 885-8800
   Sylvania *(G-13570)*

Robinson Health System Inc .... A 330 678-4100
   Kent *(G-9597)*

Samaritan Behavioral Hlth Inc .... C 937 456-1915
   Eaton *(G-8223)*

Samaritan Behavioral Hlth Inc .... E 937 734-8333
   Dayton *(G-7607)*

Sciot-Pint Vly Mental Hlth Ctr .... C 740 775-1260
   Chillicothe *(G-2090)*

Scioto Pnt Vly Mental Hlth Ctr .... C 740 335-6935
   Wshngtn Ct Hs *(G-15493)*

Select Spclty Hosp - Yngstown .... C 330 480-3488
   Youngstown *(G-15720)*

Shawnee Mental Health Ctr Inc .... E 740 533-6280
   Coal Grove *(G-5211)*

Shawnee Mental Health Ctr Inc .... E 937 544-5581
   West Union *(G-14872)*

Signature Health Inc .... A 440 953-9999
   Willoughby *(G-15221)*

Sleep Care Inc .... E 614 901-8989
   Columbus *(G-6688)*

Sojourner Recovery Svcs LLC .... E 513 868-7654
   Hamilton *(G-9082)*

South Community Inc .... E 937 252-0100
   Dayton *(G-7625)*

South Community Inc .... E 937 293-1115
   Dayton *(G-7626)*

South Community Inc .... C 937 293-8300
   Moraine *(G-11439)*

Southast Cmnty Mental Hlth Ctr .... C 614 225-0980
   Columbus *(G-6694)*

Southern Ohio Bhvoral Hlth LLC .... E 740 533-0055
   Ironton *(G-9514)*

Springvale Health Centers Inc .... E 330 343-6631
   Dover *(G-7902)*

SIC SECTION
80 HEALTH SERVICES

St Vincent Family Services............. C 614 252-0731
  Columbus *(G-6707)*

Stark County Board of Developm.......... A 330 477-5200
  Canton *(G-1858)*

Summa Rehab Hospital LLC................ D 330 572-7300
  Akron *(G-323)*

Summit Acres Inc........................ C 740 732-2364
  Caldwell *(G-1551)*

Sunbridge Marion Hlth Care LLC.......... D 740 389-6306
  Marion *(G-10456)*

Sunrise Treatment Center LLC............ E 513 595-5340
  Cincinnati *(G-3427)*

Sunrise Treatment Center LLC............ E 513 217-4676
  Middletown *(G-11189)*

Sunrise Treatment Center LLC............ E 513 941-4999
  Cincinnati *(G-3426)*

Taylor Murtis Human Svcs Sys............ E 216 283-4400
  Cleveland *(G-4979)*

Taylor Murtis Human Svcs Sys............ D 216 283-4400
  Cleveland *(G-4978)*

Tcn Behavioral Health Svcs Inc.......... C 937 376-8700
  Xenia *(G-15532)*

Therapy Advantage Group LLC............. D 614 784-0400
  Worthington *(G-15461)*

Thompkins Child Adlescent Svcs.......... D 740 622-4470
  Coshocton *(G-7003)*

Tri County Mental Health Svcs........... C 740 594-5045
  Athens *(G-594)*

Tri County Mental Health Svcs........... D 740 592-3091
  Athens *(G-593)*

Trihealth Inc........................... A 513 569-6777
  Cincinnati *(G-3512)*

Trinity Rhabilitation Svcs LLC.......... D 740 695-0069
  Saint Clairsville *(G-12817)*

Tuscarwas Ambltory Srgery Ctr........... D 330 365-2101
  Dover *(G-7904)*

Ultimate Rehab Ltd...................... D 513 563-8777
  Blue Ash *(G-1261)*

Unison Bhvioral Hlth Group Inc.......... D 419 214-4673
  Toledo *(G-14081)*

United Disability Services Inc.......... D 330 379-3337
  Akron *(G-340)*

United Disability Services Inc.......... D 330 374-1169
  Akron *(G-341)*

United Rhblttion Svcs Grter Dy.......... D 937 233-1230
  Dayton *(G-7683)*

Univ Dermatology........................ E 513 475-7630
  Cincinnati *(G-3559)*

University Hospitals Cleveland.......... A 216 983-3066
  Cleveland *(G-5074)*

University Mednet....................... C 440 255-0800
  Mentor *(G-11008)*

University of Cincinnati................ E 513 584-3200
  Cincinnati *(G-3594)*

University Radiology Assoc.............. D 513 475-8760
  Cincinnati *(G-3596)*

Upper Valley Medical Center............. C 937 440-4820
  Troy *(G-14167)*

Urbana Healthcare Group LLC............. D 937 652-1381
  Urbana *(G-14315)*

Wendt-Bristol Health Services........... C 614 403-9966
  Columbus *(G-6876)*

Wood County Chld Svcs Assn.............. E 419 352-7588
  Bowling Green *(G-1335)*

Woodland Centers Inc.................... D 740 446-5500
  Gallipolis *(G-8770)*

Wsb Rehabilitation Svcs Inc............. A 330 847-7819
  Warren *(G-14577)*

Wsb Rehabilitation Svcs Inc............. D 330 533-1338
  Canfield *(G-1645)*

Zepf Center............................. D 419 841-7701
  Toledo *(G-14119)*

8099 Health and allied services, nec

Akron General Health System............. A 330 344-3030
  Hudson *(G-9327)*

Akron General Health System............. A 330 945-9300
  Stow *(G-13353)*

Alta Behavioral Healthcare.............. D 330 793-2487
  Youngstown *(G-15546)*

Baptist Health.......................... D 502 253-4700
  Westlake *(G-15036)*

Behavior Key Services LLC............... D 937 952-6379
  Dayton *(G-7189)*

Bio-Blood Components Inc................ C 614 294-3183
  Columbus *(G-5441)*

BioLife Plasma Services LP.............. E 419 313-3406
  Toledo *(G-13705)*

Biotest Pharmaceuticals Corp............ E 419 819-3068
  Bowling Green *(G-1309)*

Blood Services Centl Ohio Reg........... C 614 253-7981
  Columbus *(G-5447)*

Bon Secours Mercy Health Inc............ D 513 956-3729
  Cincinnati *(G-2274)*

Brecksvlle Hlthcare Group Inc........... E 440 546-0643
  Brecksville *(G-1346)*

Bucyrus Community Physicians............ D 419 563-9801
  Bucyrus *(G-1499)*

Butler County of Ohio................... E 513 757-4683
  Oxford *(G-12202)*

Canfield Leasing Co LLC................. D 513 530-1600
  Youngstown *(G-15570)*

Carespring Health Care MGT LLC.......... E 513 943-4000
  Loveland *(G-10130)*

Catholic Health Initiatives............. A 614 871-3047
  Grove City *(G-8906)*

Centauri Health Solutions............... D 216 431-5200
  Cleveland *(G-3947)*

Center Al Health........................ E 216 831-8118
  Beachwood *(G-774)*

Central Clinic Outpatient Svcs.......... D 513 558-9005
  Cincinnati *(G-2334)*

Christmas Home Health LLC............... E 440 708-6442
  Ravenna *(G-12622)*

CHS Therapy Rehab Holdings LLC.......... E 888 995-1305
  Brunswick *(G-1453)*

Cincinnati Speech Hearing Ctr........... E 513 221-0527
  Cincinnati *(G-2422)*

Cleveland Clinic........................ D 216 374-0239
  Lakewood *(G-9661)*

Cleveland Clinic Fndtn-Cardio........... E 440 695-4000
  Avon *(G-646)*

Cleveland Clinic Foundation............. D 216 839-3000
  Beachwood *(G-778)*

Cleveland Clinic Foundation............. D 216 448-0770
  Beachwood *(G-779)*

Cleveland Clinic Foundation............. E 614 358-4223
  Columbus *(G-5583)*

Cleveland Clnic Edctl Fndtion........... E 216 444-1157
  Cleveland *(G-4034)*

Clinix Healthcare LLC................... E 614 792-5422
  Dublin *(G-7965)*

Cloudbreak Health LLC................... D 614 468-6110
  Columbus *(G-5587)*

Columbus Womens Wellness................ E 614 532-8370
  Gahanna *(G-8713)*

Compassion Health Toledo................ E 419 537-9185
  Toledo *(G-13754)*

▼ Contining Hlthcare Sltions Inc........ D 419 529-7272
  Brunswick *(G-1454)*

Cornerstone Hlthcare Sltons LL.......... D 937 985-4011
  Lebanon *(G-9761)*

County of Clark......................... E 937 390-5600
  Springfield *(G-13243)*

County of Cuyahoga...................... E 216 941-8800
  Cleveland *(G-4128)*

Crn Healthcare Inc...................... D 937 250-1412
  Dayton *(G-7261)*

Cuyahoga County of Board Hlth........... C 216 201-2000
  Parma *(G-12253)*

Dayton Childrens Hospital............... D 937 641-3000
  Miamisburg *(G-11046)*

District Board Health Mahoning.......... E 330 270-2855
  Youngstown *(G-15598)*

Donor Care Center Inc................... E 330 497-4888
  North Canton *(G-11826)*

Engage Healthcare Svcs Corp............. E 614 457-8180
  Columbus *(G-5818)*

Everside Health LLC..................... E 216 672-0211
  Beachwood *(G-790)*

Excelas LLC............................. E 440 442-7310
  Cleveland *(G-4229)*

First Chice Med Stffing Ohio I.......... D 330 867-1409
  Fairlawn *(G-8480)*

Foundtion For Cmnty Blood Cntr.......... C 937 461-3450
  Dayton *(G-7363)*

Franklin County Adamh Board............. E 614 224-1057
  Columbus *(G-5887)*

Franklin County Public Health........... C 614 525-3160
  Columbus *(G-5889)*

Health At Home LLC...................... E 937 436-7717
  Dayton *(G-7401)*

Health Crousel Trvl Netwrk LLC.......... E 513 665-4544
  Cincinnati *(G-2810)*

Health Data MGT Solutions Inc........... D 216 595-1232
  Beachwood *(G-797)*

Health Partners Western Ohio............ E 419 679-5994
  Kenton *(G-9617)*

Health Partners Western Ohio............ E 937 667-1122
  New Carlisle *(G-11601)*

Heartspring Home Hlth Care LLC.......... E 937 531-6920
  Dayton *(G-7403)*

Heritage Corner Health Care CA.......... E 419 353-3759
  Bowling Green *(G-1323)*

Heritage Valley Health Sys Inc.......... E 724 773-1995
  East Liverpool *(G-8184)*

High Point Home Health Ltd.............. E 419 674-4090
  Kenton *(G-9618)*

Hospitlist Svcs Med Group of M.......... A 937 644-6115
  Marysville *(G-10491)*

Insight Cunseling Wellness LLC.......... E 330 635-0638
  Mentor *(G-10951)*

Integrated Health Services Inc.......... E 440 856-5475
  Warrensville Heights *(G-14582)*

Ironton Lwrnce Cnty Area Cmnty.......... B 740 532-3534
  Ironton *(G-9508)*

Itx Healthcare LLC...................... E 844 489-2273
  Findlay *(G-8551)*

Jennings Assisted Living................ E 216 581-2900
  Garfield Heights *(G-8775)*

Kettering Health Network................ E 513 585-6000
  Hamilton *(G-9057)*

Larlham Care Hattie Group............... D 330 274-2272
  Mantua *(G-10332)*

Life Connection of Ohio................. D 419 893-4891
  Maumee *(G-10740)*

Life Line Screening Amer Ltd............ C 216 581-6556
  Independence *(G-9444)*

Lifebanc................................ D 216 752-5433
  Cleveland *(G-4492)*

Lifecenter Organ Donor Network.......... E 513 558-5555
  Cincinnati *(G-2976)*

Lifeshare Cmnty Blood Svcs Inc.......... E 440 322-5700
  Elyria *(G-8270)*

Lifestges Smrtan Ctrs For Wmen.......... E 937 277-8988
  Dayton *(G-7454)*

80 HEALTH SERVICES

Loving Care Home Hlth Agcy LLC........... D 216 322-9316
  Garfield Heights *(G-8776)*
Maxim Healthcare Services Inc................ C 740 772-4100
  Columbus *(G-6211)*
Medical Urgency Prep Svcs Inc................ E 937 374-2420
  Xenia *(G-15526)*
Medone Health LLC................................. E 614 255-6900
  Columbus *(G-6222)*
Metrohealth System.................................. C 216 957-5000
  Cleveland *(G-4564)*
Mindfully LLC... D 513 939-0300
  Fairfield *(G-8432)*
Mobile Hyperbaric Centers LLC............... E 216 443-0430
  Cleveland *(G-4592)*
Molina Healthcare Inc.............................. E 216 606-1400
  Independence *(G-9455)*
Mount Carmel Health................................ D 614 776-5164
  Westerville *(G-15001)*
Mount Carmel Health System.................. C 614 235-4039
  Columbus *(G-6279)*
Mvhe Inc... E 937 499-8211
  Dayton *(G-7520)*
Northast Ohio Nghbrhood Hlth S.............. E 216 851-2600
  Cleveland *(G-4654)*
Northast Ohio Nghbrhood Hlth S.............. E 216 541-5600
  Cleveland *(G-4655)*
Northast Ohio Nghbrhood Hlth S.............. E 216 851-1500
  Cleveland *(G-4656)*
Northast Ohio Nghbrhood Hlth S.............. C 216 231-7700
  Cleveland *(G-4653)*
Ohio Living Holdings................................. D 440 953-1256
  Willoughby *(G-15216)*
Ohio North E Hlth Systems Inc................. E 330 747-9551
  Youngstown *(G-15683)*
Omni Wellness Group LLC....................... E 937 540-9920
  Troy *(G-14150)*
P C Vpa.. E 440 826-0500
  Cleveland *(G-4714)*
P N P Inc.. D 330 386-1231
  East Liverpool *(G-8190)*
Paladina Health LLC................................ E 440 368-0900
  Mentor *(G-10983)*
Paladina Health LLC................................ E 440 368-0930
  Seven Hills *(G-12957)*
Palestine Chld Relief Fund....................... D 330 678-2645
  Kent *(G-9590)*
Paramont Care of Michigan...................... D 419 887-2728
  Maumee *(G-10754)*
Plasmacare Inc.. D 614 231-5322
  Columbus *(G-6531)*
Premier Home Health LLC....................... E 740 403-6806
  Newark *(G-11742)*
Premier Nursing Network LLC................. D 440 563-1586
  Middlefield *(G-11144)*
Primary Cr Ntwrk Prmr Hlth Prt................ E 513 204-5785
  Mason *(G-10594)*
Providence Healthcare MGT Inc.............. B 216 200-5917
  Cleveland *(G-4794)*
Providence Medical Group LLC.............. E 513 897-0085
  Waynesville *(G-14627)*
Putnam County Public Hlth Dept............. E 419 523-5608
  Ottawa *(G-12194)*
Rehab Medical LLC................................. D 513 381-3740
  Cincinnati *(G-3281)*
Renaissance Home Health Care............. E 216 662-8702
  Bedford *(G-981)*
Right Drction Bhvral Hlth Svcs................ E 216 260-9022
  Cleveland Heights *(G-5185)*
River Valley Physicians LLC................... D 330 386-3610
  East Liverpool *(G-8192)*
Riverhills Healthcare Inc.......................... E 513 624-6031
  Cincinnati *(G-3305)*

Rock Medical Orthopedics Inc................. D 216 496-3168
  Hudson *(G-9372)*
Shelby Health & Wellness Ctr.................. E 419 525-6795
  Shelby *(G-13011)*
Signature Health Inc................................ C 440 578-8200
  Mentor *(G-10995)*
Southwest Lithotripsy............................... D 614 447-0281
  Columbus *(G-6698)*
St Elzabeth Boardman Hlth Ctr................ E 330 729-4580
  Boardman *(G-1292)*
Sterling Medical Associates..................... D 513 984-1800
  Cincinnati *(G-3417)*
Toledo Clinic Inc...................................... D 419 865-3111
  Holland *(G-9308)*
Toledo Clinic Cancer Centers.................. D 419 691-4235
  Oregon *(G-12143)*
Trihealth Inc... C 513 734-9050
  Bethel *(G-1095)*
Trihealth Inc... C 513 221-4848
  Cincinnati *(G-3518)*
Trihealth Hf LLC...................................... E 513 398-3445
  Mason *(G-10620)*
Trihealth Os LLC..................................... E 513 985-3700
  Cincinnati *(G-3525)*
Trinity Health... E 614 227-0197
  Columbus *(G-6790)*
Uc Health Llc... D 513 475-8050
  Milford *(G-11264)*
Uc Health Llc... D 513 475-8282
  West Chester *(G-14780)*
Union Healthcare Services Inc................ E 614 686-2322
  Columbus *(G-6801)*
Unity Health Network LLC....................... E 330 655-3820
  Hudson *(G-9375)*
Unity Health Network LLC....................... E 330 633-7782
  Tallmadge *(G-13610)*
University of Cincinnati............................ C 513 558-1243
  Cincinnati *(G-3589)*
University Tledo Physcians LLC.............. E 419 931-0030
  Toledo *(G-14088)*
Vincent & Vincent.................................... E 513 617-2089
  Cincinnati *(G-3630)*
Vitalant.. E 440 322-8720
  Elyria *(G-8299)*
Webmd Health Corp................................ E 419 324-8000
  Toledo *(G-14099)*
Wellness Iq Inc.. E 216 264-2727
  Independence *(G-9499)*
Wellness Residential Svc LLC................. E 513 969-4160
  Cincinnati *(G-3650)*
Western Reserve Health Sys LLC........... E 330 923-8660
  Cuyahoga Falls *(G-7114)*

81 LEGAL SERVICES

8111 Legal services

Advoctes For Bsic Lgal Eqlity.................. E 419 255-0814
  Toledo *(G-13675)*
Amin Turocy & Watson LLP.................... E 216 696-8730
  Beachwood *(G-766)*
▲ Anspach Meeks Ellenberger LLP....... E 419 447-6181
  Toledo *(G-13689)*
Arthur Mddlton Cpitl Hldngs In................ D 330 966-9000
  North Canton *(G-11812)*
Bailey Cavalieri LLC................................ D 614 221-3258
  Columbus *(G-5412)*
Baker & Hostetler LLP............................. D 513 929-3400
  Cincinnati *(G-2236)*
Baker & Hostetler LLP............................. E 216 430-2960
  Cleveland *(G-3848)*
Baker & Hostetler LLP............................. D 614 228-1541
  Columbus *(G-5414)*

Baker & Hostetler LLP............................. B 216 621-0200
  Cleveland *(G-3847)*
Barkan & Neff Co Lpa.............................. E 614 221-4221
  Columbus *(G-5418)*
Barkan Mzlish Drose Wntz McNrv........... E 614 221-4221
  Columbus *(G-5419)*
Benesch Frdlnder Cplan Arnoff................ E 216 363-4686
  Cleveland *(G-3865)*
Benesch Frdlnder Cplan Arnoff................ E 614 223-9300
  Columbus *(G-5432)*
Benesch Friedlander Copla...................... C 216 363-4500
  Cleveland *(G-3866)*
Bieser Greer & Landis LLP...................... D 937 223-3277
  Dayton *(G-7192)*
Bordas & Bordas Pllc.............................. D 740 695-8141
  Saint Clairsville *(G-12782)*
Brennan Manna & Diamond LLC............. E 330 253-5060
  Akron *(G-75)*
Bricker & Eckler LLP............................... B 614 227-2300
  Columbus *(G-5465)*
Buckingham Dlttle Brroughs LLC............. E 330 492-8717
  Canton *(G-1693)*
Buckingham Dlttle Brroughs LLC............. E 216 621-5300
  Cleveland *(G-3909)*
Buckingham Dlttle Brroughs LLC............. C 330 376-5300
  Akron *(G-77)*
Burke Manley Lpa................................... E 513 721-5525
  Cincinnati *(G-2291)*
Calfee Halter & Griswold LLP.................. E 513 693-4880
  Cincinnati *(G-2301)*
Calfee Halter & Griswold LLP.................. E 614 621-1500
  Columbus *(G-5493)*
Calfee Halter & Griswold LLP.................. B 216 622-8200
  Cleveland *(G-3918)*
Carlile Patchen & Murphy LLP................ D 614 228-6135
  Columbus *(G-5512)*
Carlisle McNllie Rini Krmer Ul................. E 216 360-7200
  Beachwood *(G-772)*
Carpenter Lipps LLP............................... D 614 365-4100
  Columbus *(G-5514)*
Cavitch Familo & Durkin Co Lpa.............. E 216 621-7860
  Cleveland *(G-3941)*
Chambrlain Hrdlcka White Wllam............ D 216 589-9280
  Avon *(G-643)*
City of Lakewood..................................... E 216 529-6170
  Cleveland *(G-3991)*
City of Pepper Pike.................................. E 216 831-9604
  Pepper Pike *(G-12298)*
Cleveland Metro Bar Assn....................... E 216 696-3525
  Cleveland *(G-4055)*
Cleveland Teachers Union Inc................. E 216 861-7676
  Cleveland *(G-4070)*
Climaco Wlcox Peca Grofoli Lpa............. D 216 621-8484
  Cleveland *(G-4082)*
Clunk Hoose Co Lpa............................... E 330 922-5492
  Akron *(G-110)*
Coolidge Wall Co LPA............................. D 937 223-8177
  Dayton *(G-7247)*
▲ Cors & Bassett LLC........................... D 513 852-8200
  Cincinnati *(G-2510)*
County of Lucas...................................... D 419 213-4700
  Toledo *(G-13764)*
County of Ottawa.................................... C 567 262-3600
  Oak Harbor *(G-12044)*
County of Portage................................... E 330 297-3850
  Ravenna *(G-12625)*
Crabbe Brown & James LLP.................. E 614 229-4509
  Columbus *(G-5718)*
Criminal Jstice Crdnting Cncil.................. E 567 200-6850
  Toledo *(G-13770)*
Critchfeld Crtchfeld Jhnston L.................. E 330 264-4444
  Wooster *(G-15332)*

SIC SECTION

81 LEGAL SERVICES

Dagger Jhnston Mller Oglvie HM............ E 740 653-6464
   Lancaster *(G-9707)*

David L Barth Lwyr.................................. D 513 852-8228
   Cincinnati *(G-2543)*

Davis Young A Legal Prof Assn............... E 216 348-1700
   Cleveland *(G-4152)*

Day Ketterer Ltd...................................... D 330 455-0173
   Canton *(G-1732)*

Deedscom Inc... E 330 606-0119
   Fairlawn *(G-8473)*

Dickie McCamey & Chilcote PC............... B 412 281-7272
   Columbus *(G-5765)*

Dinsmore & Shohl LLP............................. D 614 628-6880
   Columbus *(G-5766)*

Dinsmore & Shohl LLP............................. E 937 449-6400
   Dayton *(G-7315)*

Dinsmore & Shohl LLP............................. B 513 977-8200
   Cincinnati *(G-2565)*

Dungan & Lefevre Co LPA....................... E 937 339-0511
   Troy *(G-14134)*

Dworken & Bernstein Co Lpa................... E 216 230-5170
   Cleveland *(G-4191)*

Dyer Grfalo Mann Schltz A Lga............... D 937 223-8888
   Dayton *(G-7319)*

Eastman & Smith Ltd................................ C 419 241-6000
   Toledo *(G-13785)*

Elk & Elk Co Lpa....................................... E 800 355-6446
   Mayfield Heights *(G-10786)*

Ernest V Thomas Jr.................................. E 513 961-5311
   Cincinnati *(G-2635)*

Fairfield Federal Sav Ln Assn.................. E 740 653-3863
   Lancaster *(G-9712)*

Faust Hrrlson Flker McCrthy SC............. E 937 335-8324
   Troy *(G-14135)*

Fay Sharpe LLP.. E 216 363-9000
   Cleveland *(G-4243)*

Finney Law Firm LLC............................... E 513 943-6650
   Cincinnati *(G-2104)*

Flanagan Lberman Hoffman Swaim........ E 937 223-5200
   Dayton *(G-7359)*

Flannery Georgalis LLC........................... E 216 367-2095
   Cleveland *(G-4264)*

Frantz Ward LLP....................................... E 216 515-1660
   Cleveland *(G-4286)*

Freking Myers & Reul LLC....................... E 513 721-1975
   Cincinnati *(G-2707)*

Freund Freze Arnold A Lgal Pro............... D 937 222-2424
   Dayton *(G-7368)*

Friedman Domiano Smith Co Lpa............ E 216 621-0070
   Cleveland *(G-4289)*

Frost Brown Todd LLC............................. B 513 651-6800
   Cincinnati *(G-2709)*

Gallagher Gams Pryor Tllan Ltt............... D 614 228-5151
   Columbus *(G-5908)*

Gallagher Sharp.. C 216 241-5310
   Cleveland *(G-4301)*

Gallon Tkacs Bssnult Schffer L............... D 419 843-2001
   Maumee *(G-10726)*

Garden City Group LLC........................... C 631 470-5000
   Dublin *(G-8019)*

Gbd Legacy LLC....................................... E 330 441-0785
   Akron *(G-172)*

General Audit Corporation....................... D 419 993-2900
   Lima *(G-9891)*

Gottlieb Jhnson Beam Dal Pnte............... E 740 452-7555
   Zanesville *(G-15797)*

Graydon Head & Ritchey LLP.................. C 513 621-6464
   Cincinnati *(G-2753)*

Hahn Loeser & Parks LLP........................ C 216 621-0150
   Cleveland *(G-4346)*

Hammond Neal Moore Llc....................... D 513 381-2011
   Cincinnati *(G-2796)*

Hanna Cambell & Powell.......................... E 330 670-7300
   Akron *(G-182)*

Hoover Kacyon LLC.................................. E 330 922-4491
   Cuyahoga Falls *(G-7080)*

Horenstein Nchlson Blmnthal A............... E 937 224-7200
   Dayton *(G-7413)*

Ibold & OBrien Inc.................................... E 440 279-0688
   Chardon *(G-2006)*

Isaac Brant Ledman Teetor LLP............... E 614 221-2121
   Columbus *(G-6072)*

Isaac Wiles & Burkholder LLC................. D 614 221-2121
   Columbus *(G-6073)*

Janik LLP... E 440 838-7600
   Cleveland *(G-4432)*

Javitch Block LLC..................................... D 513 381-3051
   Cincinnati *(G-2901)*

Javitch Block LLC..................................... C 216 623-0000
   Cleveland *(G-4434)*

Jones Day Limited Partnership................ D 614 469-3939
   Columbus *(G-6096)*

Jones Day Limited Partnership................ A 216 586-3939
   Cleveland *(G-4442)*

Kademenos Wisehart Hines..................... E 419 524-6011
   Mansfield *(G-10277)*

Kademnos Wshart Hnes Dlyk Zher........ E 440 967-6136
   Vermilion *(G-14406)*

Katz Teller Brant Hild Co Lpa................... D 513 721-4532
   Cincinnati *(G-2931)*

Keating Muething & Klekamp Pll.............. B 513 579-6400
   Cincinnati *(G-2932)*

Kegler Brown Hl Ritter Co Lpa.................. C 614 462-5400
   Columbus *(G-6107)*

▲ Keis George LLP................................... E 216 241-4100
   Cleveland *(G-4452)*

Kelley Ferraro LLC.................................... E 216 575-0777
   Cleveland *(G-4454)*

Kohrman Jackson & Krantz LLP............... D 216 696-8700
   Cleveland *(G-4468)*

Krugliak Wlkins Grffths Dghrty................. D 330 497-0700
   Canton *(G-1792)*

Lane Alton & Horst LLC........................... E 614 228-6885
   Columbus *(G-6137)*

Larrimer & Larrimer LLC.......................... E 614 221-7548
   Columbus *(G-6142)*

Law Offces of John D Clunk A L.............. D 330 436-0300
   Akron *(G-219)*

Law Offces Rbert A Schrger Lpa............ E 614 824-5731
   Wilmington *(G-15256)*

Legal Aid Society Cincinnati.................... D 513 241-9400
   Cincinnati *(G-2969)*

Legal Aid Society of Cleveland................ E 440 324-1121
   Elyria *(G-8267)*

Legal Aid Society of Cleveland................ D 216 861-5500
   Cleveland *(G-4486)*

Legal Aid Society of Columbus............... E 614 737-0139
   Columbus *(G-6153)*

Legal Aid Southeast Centl Ohio.............. D 740 354-7563
   Portsmouth *(G-12561)*

Legal Aid Western Ohio Inc..................... E 419 724-0030
   Toledo *(G-13884)*

Legal Dfnders Off Smmit Cnty O............ D 330 434-3461
   Akron *(G-220)*

Legal Support Simplified LLC.................. E 440 546-3368
   Cleveland *(G-4487)*

Levy & Associates LLC........................... E 614 898-5200
   Columbus *(G-6155)*

Lewis Brsbois Bsgard Smith LLP........... E 859 663-9830
   Cincinnati *(G-2971)*

Lindhorst & Dreidame Co Lpa................. E 513 421-6630
   Cincinnati *(G-2980)*

Linebrger Gggan Blair Smpson L.......... E 614 210-8100
   Dublin *(G-8055)*

Litigation Management Inc....................... C 440 484-2000
   Chesterland *(G-2038)*

LLP Gallagher Sharp................................ E 216 241-5310
   Cleveland *(G-4502)*

LLP Ziegler Metzger.................................. E 216 781-5470
   Cleveland *(G-4503)*

Luper Neidental & Logan A Leg.............. E 614 221-7663
   Columbus *(G-6179)*

Lupo & Koczkur PC.................................. E 419 897-7931
   Maumee *(G-10743)*

Maguire & Schneider LLP........................ E 614 224-1222
   Columbus *(G-6190)*

Manley Deas & Kochalski LLC................. C 614 220-5611
   Columbus *(G-6192)*

Mansour Gavin Lpa.................................. D 216 523-1501
   Cleveland *(G-4521)*

Marshall & Melhorn LLC.......................... D 419 249-7100
   Toledo *(G-13911)*

Mazanec Raskin & Ryder Co Lpa............ D 440 248-7906
   Cleveland *(G-4533)*

MCDONALD HOPKINS LLC..................... C 216 348-5400
   Cleveland *(G-4536)*

McGlinchey Stafford Pllc......................... E 216 378-9905
   Shaker Heights *(G-12981)*

Millikin and Fitton Law Firm..................... E 513 863-6700
   Hamilton *(G-9066)*

Murray & Murray Co LPA......................... E 419 624-3000
   Sandusky *(G-12916)*

Musillo Unkenholt LLC............................. E 513 744-4080
   Cincinnati *(G-3091)*

Nicholas E Davis....................................... E 937 228-2838
   Dayton *(G-7530)*

Nicola Gudbranson & Cooper LLC.......... E 216 621-7227
   Cleveland *(G-4644)*

Northern Kentucky.................................... D 513 563-7555
   Cincinnati *(G-3122)*

Nurenberg Prls Hller McCrthy L.............. D 440 423-0750
   Cleveland *(G-4674)*

OGara Group Inc....................................... A 513 275-8456
   West Chester *(G-14736)*

Ohio Dsblity Rghts Law Plicy C............... E 614 466-7264
   Columbus *(G-6414)*

OToole McLghlin Dley Pcora LP............. E 440 930-4001
   Sheffield Village *(G-13003)*

Pickrel Schaeffer Ebeling Lpa.................. D 937 223-1130
   Dayton *(G-7553)*

Porter Wrght Morris Arthur LLP............... E 513 381-4700
   Cincinnati *(G-3221)*

Porter Wrght Morris Arthur LLP............... E 216 443-2506
   Cleveland *(G-4761)*

Porter Wrght Morris Arthur LLP............... E 937 449-6810
   Dayton *(G-7558)*

Porter Wright Morris & Arthur LLP........... B 614 227-2000
   Columbus *(G-6537)*

Rathbone Group LLC............................... E 800 870-5521
   Cleveland *(G-4809)*

Recovery One LLC................................... D 614 336-4207
   Columbus *(G-6564)*

Reese Pyle Drake & Meyer...................... E 740 345-3431
   Newark *(G-11745)*

Reisenfeld & Assoc Lpa LLC................... C 513 322-7000
   Cincinnati *(G-3283)*

Reminger Co LPA..................................... C 216 687-1311
   Cleveland *(G-4825)*

Rendigs Fry Kiely & Dennis LLP.............. E 513 381-9200
   Cincinnati *(G-3286)*

Renner Knner Greve Bbak Tylor............. E 330 376-1242
   Akron *(G-279)*

Renner Otto Boiselle & Sklar.................... E 216 621-1113
   Cleveland *(G-4827)*

Robbins Kelly Patterson Tucker............... E 513 721-3330
   Cincinnati *(G-3312)*

Employee Codes: A=Over 500 employees, B=251-500
C=101-250, D=51-100, E=20-50, F=10-19, G=1-9

81 LEGAL SERVICES

Robert Kelly & Bucio LLP .... E 937 332-9300
  Troy (G-14156)
Roderick Linton Belfance LLP............. E 330 434-3000
  Akron (G-285)
Roetzel Andress A Lgal Prof As............ E 216 623-0150
  Cleveland (G-4853)
Roetzel Andress A Lgal Prof As............ C 330 376-2700
  Akron (G-286)
Rohrbchers Light Crone Trimble........... E 419 471-1160
  Toledo (G-13994)
Rolfes Henry Co LPA........................ E 513 579-0080
  Cincinnati (G-3318)
Rose & Dobyns An Ohio Partnr............. E 740 335-4700
  Wshngtn Ct Hs (G-15492)
Rose & Dobyns An Ohio Partnr............. E 937 382-2838
  Wilmington (G-15271)
Ross Brittain Schonberg Lpa............... E 216 447-1551
  Independence (G-9480)
Schneder Smltz Spieth Bell LLP............ E 216 535-1001
  Cleveland (G-4883)
Scott S Duko Attorney At Law.............. E 800 593-6676
  Fairlawn (G-8497)
Sebaly Shllito Dyer A Lgal Pro............. D 937 222-2500
  Dayton (G-7614)
Seeley Svdge Ebert Gourash Lpa........... E 216 566-8200
  Westlake (G-15106)
Shumaker Loop & Kendrick LLP.......... D 614 463-9441
  Columbus (G-6677)
Shumaker Loop & Kendrick LLP.......... E 419 241-9000
  Toledo (G-14013)
Sierra Lobo Inc.................................. E 301 345-1386
  Milan (G-11212)
Singerman Mlls Dsberg Kntz Lpa.......... D 216 292-5807
  Cleveland (G-4908)
Sonkin & Koberna Co Lpa................... E 216 514-8300
  Cleveland (G-4918)
Sottile & Barile LLC........................... E 513 345-0592
  Loveland (G-10161)
Spangenberg Shibley Liber LLP........... E 216 215-7445
  Cleveland (G-4926)
Spengler Nathanson PLL.................... E 419 241-2201
  Toledo (G-14020)
Spitz Law Firm LLC.......................... D 216 291-4744
  Beachwood (G-840)
Squire Patton Boggs (us) LLP.............. E 513 361-1200
  Cincinnati (G-3402)
Squire Patton Boggs (us) LLP.............. B 216 479-8500
  Cleveland (G-4938)
Stagnaro Saba Patterson Co Lpa.......... E 513 533-2700
  Cincinnati (G-3406)
Sutter OConnell Co............................ E 216 928-4504
  Cleveland (G-4969)
Taft Stettinius Hollister LLP................ B 513 381-2838
  Cincinnati (G-3433)
Teating Mueting & Klekamp Pll............ E 513 579-6462
  Cincinnati (G-3447)
The Garretson Firm Resolu.................. C 513 794-0400
  Loveland (G-10163)
Thompson Dunlap Heydinger Ltd......... E 937 593-6065
  Bellefontaine (G-1039)
Thompson Hine LLP.......................... D 614 469-3200
  Columbus (G-6763)
Thompson Hine LLP.......................... D 614 469-3200
  Columbus (G-6764)
Thompson Hine LLP.......................... D 937 443-6859
  Miamisburg (G-11098)
Thompson Hine LLP.......................... B 216 566-5500
  Cleveland (G-5013)
Toledo Bar Association Inc................. E 419 242-7363
  Toledo (G-14051)
Troy Strauss Co Lpa.......................... C 513 621-2120
  Cincinnati (G-3530)

Tucker Ellis LLP............................... C 216 592-5000
  Cleveland (G-5039)
Turocy & Watson LLP........................ E 216 696-8730
  Cleveland (G-5042)
Tzangas Plakas Mannos Recupero........ E 330 453-5466
  Canton (G-1874)
Ulmer & Berne LLP........................... E 513 698-5000
  Cincinnati (G-3548)
Ulmer & Berne LLP........................... D 614 229-0000
  Columbus (G-6797)
Ulmer & Berne LLP........................... B 216 583-7000
  Cleveland (G-5049)
United Scoto Senior Activities.............. E 740 354-6672
  Portsmouth (G-12579)
Volpini Law LLC.............................. E 216 956-4133
  Strongsville (G-13496)
Vorys Sater Seymour and Pease LLP.... B 614 464-6400
  Columbus (G-6858)
Vorys Sater Seymour Pease LLP.......... E 513 723-4000
  Cincinnati (G-3635)
Vorys Sater Seymour Pease LLP.......... D 216 479-6100
  Cleveland (G-5115)
Waite Schnder Byless Chsley LP.......... D 513 621-0267
  Cincinnati (G-3638)
Walter Haverfield LLP........................ D 216 781-1212
  Cleveland (G-5121)
Wegman Hessler Vanderburg............... D 216 642-3342
  Cleveland (G-5124)
Weiner Keith D Co L P A Inc............... E 216 771-6500
  Cleveland (G-5126)
Weltman Weinberg & Reis Co Lpa....... C 513 723-2200
  Cincinnati (G-3652)
Weltman Weinberg & Reis Co Lpa....... B 216 459-8633
  Cleveland (G-5129)
Weltman Weinberg & Reis Co Lpa....... B 614 801-2600
  Dublin (G-8162)
Weltman Weinberg & Reis Co Lpa....... C 216 685-1000
  Independence (G-9500)
Weston Hurd LLP.............................. D 216 241-6602
  Cleveland (G-5142)
Wickens Herzer Panza Co................... D 440 695-8000
  Avon (G-668)
Wiles Boyle Burkholder &.................. D 614 221-5216
  Columbus (G-6892)
Willis Spangler Starling..................... D 614 586-7900
  Hilliard (G-9243)
Wong Margaret W Assoc Co Lpa.......... E 313 527-9989
  Cleveland (G-5158)
Wood Herron & Evans LLP................. D 513 241-2324
  Cincinnati (G-3678)
Wood & Lamping LLP....................... D 513 852-6000
  Cincinnati (G-3679)
Young & Alexander Co LPA............... E 513 326-5555
  Cincinnati (G-3686)
Zaremba Group LLC.......................... D 216 221-6600
  Lakewood (G-9689)
Zashin & Rich Co LPA...................... E 216 696-4441
  Cleveland (G-5172)

82 EDUCATIONAL SERVICES

8211 Elementary and secondary schools

Abilities First Foundation Inc.............. D 513 423-9496
  Middletown (G-11149)
Adriel School Inc.............................. D 937 465-0010
  West Liberty (G-14859)
Akron Metropolitan Hsing Auth............ D 330 920-1652
  Stow (G-13354)
Ashland City School District............... D 419 289-7967
  Ashland (G-473)
Ashtabula Area City School Dst........... E 440 992-1221
  Ashtabula (G-517)

Ashtabula Cnty Eductl Svc Ctr............. E 440 576-4085
  Ashtabula (G-520)
Bay Village City School Dst................ D 440 617-7330
  Cleveland (G-3857)
Boardman Local Schools..................... D 330 726-3409
  Youngstown (G-15560)
Brown Co Ed Service Center............... E 937 378-6118
  Georgetown (G-8799)
Butler Tech..................................... E 513 867-1028
  Fairfield Township (G-8458)
Canton Country Day School................ E 330 453-8279
  Canton (G-1700)
Catholic Charities Corporation............ D 419 289-7456
  Ashland (G-487)
Catholic Chrties Sthstern Ohio............. D 740 432-6751
  Cambridge (G-1563)
Catholic Chrties Sthstern Ohio............. C 740 695-3189
  Saint Clairsville (G-12784)
Catholic Chrties Sthstern Ohio............. B 740 676-4932
  Steubenville (G-13319)
Childrens Lab Schools Inc.................. E 937 274-7195
  Dayton (G-7224)
Christian Schools Inc........................ D 330 857-7311
  Kidron (G-9635)
Church On North Coast...................... E 440 960-1100
  Lorain (G-10063)
Cleveland Municipal School Dst.......... D 216 459-4200
  Cleveland (G-4059)
Cleveland Municipal School Dst.......... E 216 838-8700
  Cleveland (G-4061)
Colonial Senior Services Inc.............. D 513 856-8600
  Hamilton (G-9030)
Colonial Senior Services Inc.............. E 513 867-4006
  Hamilton (G-9031)
Columbus City School District............ D 614 365-5456
  Columbus (G-5621)
County of Lucas.............................. C 419 248-3585
  Toledo (G-13765)
D-R Training Center & Workshop......... D 419 289-0470
  Ashland (G-495)
David Evangelical Lutheran Ch........... E 614 920-3517
  Canal Winchester (G-1603)
Delaware City School District............. D 740 363-5901
  Delaware (G-7794)
Discovery School.............................. E 419 756-8880
  Mansfield (G-10258)
Dover City Schools........................... E 330 343-8880
  Dover (G-7881)
East Dayton Christian School............. E 937 252-5400
  Dayton (G-7132)
Edison Local School District.............. E 740 543-4011
  Amsterdam (G-436)
Education Alternatives....................... D 216 332-9360
  Brookpark (G-1434)
Educatonal Svc Ctr Lorain Cnty........... C 440 244-1659
  Elyria (G-8244)
Fairmount Montessori Assn................ D 216 321-7571
  Cleveland (G-4235)
First Assembly of God....................... E 330 836-1436
  Akron (G-160)
Forest Park Christian School.............. E 614 888-5282
  Columbus (G-5878)
Franklin City Schools........................ E 937 743-8670
  Franklin (G-8637)
Great Oaks Inst Tech Creer Dev.......... E 513 771-8840
  Cincinnati (G-2763)
Great Oaks Inst Tech Creer Dev.......... D 513 613-3657
  Cincinnati (G-2764)
Hamilton City School District............. E 513 887-5055
  Hamilton (G-9050)
Hanna Perkins School....................... C 216 991-4472
  Cleveland (G-4348)

Harrison Avenue Assembly God............ E 513 367-6109
   Harrison *(G-9107)*

Heartland Christian School Inc............ C 330 482-2331
   Columbiana *(G-5236)*

Hudson Montessori Association............ E 330 650-0424
   Hudson *(G-9356)*

Interval Brotherhood Homes Inc............ D 330 644-4095
   Coventry Township *(G-7011)*

Jewish Day Schl Assn Grter Clv............ D 216 763-1400
   Pepper Pike *(G-12300)*

Kelna Inc.. E 330 729-0167
   Youngstown *(G-15645)*

Kettering City School District................ E 937 499-1770
   Dayton *(G-7437)*

Kettering City School District................ E 937 297-1990
   Dayton *(G-7438)*

Laurel School.. C 216 464-1441
   Shaker Heights *(G-12980)*

Leo Yssnoff Jwish Cmnty Ctr Gr............ C 614 775-0312
   New Albany *(G-11572)*

Lillian and Betty Ratner Schl.................. E 216 464-0033
   Cleveland *(G-4496)*

Lima City School District....................... E 419 996-3400
   Lima *(G-9919)*

Lincolnview Local Schools.................... C 419 968-2226
   Van Wert *(G-14348)*

Logan-Hocking School District.............. E 740 385-7844
   Logan *(G-10033)*

Madison Local School District............... E 419 589-7851
   Mansfield *(G-10284)*

Miami Valley School.............................. D 937 434-4444
   Dayton *(G-7499)*

Midland Council Governments............... E 330 264-6047
   Wooster *(G-15356)*

Montpelier Exempted Vlg Schl............... E 419 485-3676
   Montpelier *(G-11385)*

Muskingum Starlight Industries............. D 740 453-4622
   Zanesville *(G-15817)*

New Hope Christian Academy................ E 740 477-6427
   Circleville *(G-3714)*

Nightingale Montessori Inc.................... E 937 324-0336
   Springfield *(G-13277)*

Northwest Local School Dst................... E 513 923-1000
   Cincinnati *(G-3127)*

Northwest Ohio Computer Assn............. E 419 267-5565
   Archbold *(G-464)*

Oesterlen - Svcs For Youth Inc............... D 937 399-6101
   Springfield *(G-13278)*

Ohio Arson School Inc........................... E 740 881-4467
   Galena *(G-8738)*

Old Trail School.................................... D 330 666-1118
   Bath *(G-754)*

Open Door Christn Schools Inc.............. E 440 322-6386
   Elyria *(G-8283)*

Our Lady Bethlehem Schools Inc........... E 614 459-8285
   Columbus *(G-6491)*

Paulding Exempted Vlg Schl Dst............ E 419 594-3309
   Paulding *(G-12286)*

Positive Education Program................... E 216 227-2730
   Cleveland *(G-4762)*

Positive Education Program................... E 440 471-8200
   Cleveland *(G-4763)*

Preble Cnty Bd Dvlpmntal Dsblt............. E 937 456-5891
   Eaton *(G-8220)*

Royal Rdmer Lthran Ch N Rylton........... E 440 237-7958
   North Royalton *(G-11949)*

Royalmont Academy.............................. E 513 754-0555
   Mason *(G-10602)*

Saint Cecilia Church.............................. E 614 878-5353
   Columbus *(G-6637)*

Seton Catholic School Hudson............... D 330 342-4200
   Hudson *(G-9373)*

Small World Childrens Center................ E 513 867-9963
   Hamilton *(G-9081)*

Society of The Transfiguration............... D 513 771-7462
   Cincinnati *(G-3391)*

St Francis De Sales Church................... D 740 345-9874
   Newark *(G-11749)*

St Jhns Evang Lthran Ch Mrysv............. E 937 644-5540
   Marysville *(G-10510)*

St Marys City Board Education.............. C 419 394-2616
   Saint Marys *(G-12836)*

St Pauls Catholic Church....................... E 330 724-1263
   Akron *(G-308)*

Sycamore Board of Education............... C 513 489-3937
   Montgomery *(G-11375)*

Talawanda City School District.............. D 513 273-3200
   Oxford *(G-12218)*

Thomas Edson Erly Chldhood Ctr.......... D 419 238-1514
   Van Wert *(G-14352)*

Troy Christian Schools Inc..................... E 937 339-5692
   Troy *(G-14161)*

Upper Arlington City Schl Dst................ E 614 487-5133
   Columbus *(G-6827)*

West Side Montessori............................ D 419 866-1931
   Toledo *(G-14104)*

Whitehall City Schools.......................... E 614 417-5680
   Columbus *(G-6887)*

Wooster Christian School Inc................ E 330 345-6436
   Wooster *(G-15390)*

8221 Colleges and universities

Antioch University................................ C 937 769-1366
   Yellow Springs *(G-15534)*

Aultman Hospital.................................. A 330 452-9911
   Canton *(G-1679)*

Board of Dirs of Wttnberg Clle............... D 937 327-6310
   Springfield *(G-13222)*

Cleveland Clnic Lrner Cllege M.............. C 216 445-3853
   Cleveland *(G-4039)*

Cleveland Municipal School Dst............. D 216 459-4200
   Cleveland *(G-4059)*

Devry University Inc............................. D 614 251-6969
   Columbus *(G-5759)*

Hebrew Un Cllg-Jwish Inst Rlgi.............. E 513 221-1875
   Cincinnati *(G-2815)*

Kenyon College..................................... E 740 427-2202
   Gambier *(G-8774)*

Miami University................................... B 513 727-3200
   Middletown *(G-11172)*

Miami University................................... C 513 529-6911
   Oxford *(G-12211)*

Miami University................................... D 513 529-1230
   Oxford *(G-12212)*

Oberlin College..................................... E 440 775-8665
   Oberlin *(G-12074)*

Ohio State Univ Wexner Med Ctr........... C 614 293-6255
   Columbus *(G-6450)*

Ohio State Univ Wexner Med Ctr........... C 614 293-7521
   Columbus *(G-6452)*

Ohio State University............................ E 614 292-6661
   Columbus *(G-6455)*

Ohio State University............................ D 614 293-3860
   Columbus *(G-6456)*

Ohio State University............................ D 614 292-3416
   Columbus *(G-6457)*

Ohio State University............................ E 614 292-1284
   Columbus *(G-6458)*

Ohio State University............................ C 614 688-0857
   Columbus *(G-6459)*

Ohio State University............................ D 330 263-3700
   Wooster *(G-15363)*

University Ear Nose Throat Spc............. C 513 475-8403
   Cincinnati *(G-3566)*

University Hospital................................ D 330 486-9610
   Twinsburg *(G-14225)*

University Hospital................................ D 440 835-8922
   Westlake *(G-15120)*

University of Cincinnati......................... E 513 556-6932
   Blue Ash *(G-1264)*

University of Cincinnati......................... E 513 558-4194
   Cincinnati *(G-3572)*

University of Cincinnati......................... B 513 558-1200
   Cincinnati *(G-3573)*

University of Cincinnati......................... C 513 475-8771
   Cincinnati *(G-3575)*

University of Cincinnati......................... D 513 556-2389
   Cincinnati *(G-3576)*

University of Cincinnati......................... D 513 556-2700
   Cincinnati *(G-3577)*

University of Cincinnati......................... B 513 584-1000
   Cincinnati *(G-3578)*

University of Cincinnati......................... A 513 584-7522
   Cincinnati *(G-3579)*

University of Cincinnati......................... C 513 584-1000
   Cincinnati *(G-3580)*

University of Cincinnati......................... B 513 584-4396
   Cincinnati *(G-3581)*

University of Cincinnati......................... C 513 558-4231
   Cincinnati *(G-3583)*

University of Cincinnati......................... E 513 556-2263
   Cincinnati *(G-3584)*

University of Cincinnati......................... E 513 558-4110
   Cincinnati *(G-3585)*

University of Cincinnati......................... C 513 556-4603
   Cincinnati *(G-3586)*

University of Cincinnati......................... C 513 558-4444
   Cincinnati *(G-3587)*

University of Cincinnati......................... C 513 584-5331
   Cincinnati *(G-3588)*

University of Cincinnati......................... D 513 556-6381
   Cincinnati *(G-3590)*

University of Cincinnati......................... D 513 556-4054
   Cincinnati *(G-3591)*

University of Cincinnati......................... D 513 556-3732
   Cincinnati *(G-3592)*

University of Cincinnati......................... E 513 556-3803
   Cincinnati *(G-3593)*

University of Cincinnati......................... E 513 584-3200
   Cincinnati *(G-3594)*

University of Dayton.............................. C 937 229-2113
   Dayton *(G-7690)*

University of Dayton.............................. B 937 229-3822
   Dayton *(G-7691)*

University of Dayton.............................. D 937 255-3141
   Dayton *(G-7692)*

University of Dayton.............................. B 937 229-3913
   Dayton *(G-7693)*

▲ University of Dayton.......................... A 937 229-1000
   Dayton *(G-7689)*

University of Toledo.............................. A 419 383-4000
   Toledo *(G-14086)*

University of Toledo.............................. E 419 383-5322
   Toledo *(G-14087)*

Wright State University......................... E 937 775-3333
   Beavercreek *(G-916)*

Wright State University......................... D 937 208-2177
   Dayton *(G-7729)*

Wright State University......................... D 937 298-4331
   Kettering *(G-9634)*

Xavier University................................... E 513 745-3335
   Cincinnati *(G-3683)*

8222 Junior colleges

Cleveland Municipal School Dst............. D 216 459-4200
   Cleveland *(G-4059)*

82 EDUCATIONAL SERVICES

8231 Libraries

Cincinnati Museum Center............................ B 513 287-7000
  Cincinnati *(G-2416)*
Rthrford B Hayes Prsdntial Ctr.................... E 419 332-2081
  Fremont *(G-8699)*
Western Reserve Historical Soc.................. D 216 721-5722
  Cleveland *(G-5136)*
Worthington Public Library........................... C 614 807-2626
  Worthington *(G-15472)*

8243 Data processing schools

Critical Business Analysis Inc...................... E 419 874-0800
  Perrysburg *(G-12326)*
Pomeroy It Solutions Sls Inc....................... E 440 717-1364
  Brecksville *(G-1363)*

8249 Vocational schools, nec

East Way Behavioral Hlth Care................... D 937 222-4900
  Dayton *(G-7323)*
Great Oaks Inst Tech Creer Dev................. E 513 771-8840
  Cincinnati *(G-2763)*
Great Oaks Inst Tech Creer Dev................. D 513 613-3657
  Cincinnati *(G-2764)*
Griffings Flying Service Inc.......................... E 419 734-5400
  Port Clinton *(G-12530)*
Lcd Agency Services LLC........................... E 513 497-0441
  Hamilton *(G-9059)*
New View Management Group Inc............. D 513 733-4444
  Cincinnati *(G-3110)*
▲ Zaner-Bloser Inc..................................... C 614 486-0221
  Columbus *(G-6918)*

8299 Schools and educational services

▲ Abx Air Inc... B 937 382-5591
  Wilmington *(G-15237)*
Allen County Eductl Svc Ctr........................ E 419 222-1836
  Lima *(G-9863)*
▲ Cincinnati Museum Association.............. E 513 721-5204
  Cincinnati *(G-2415)*
Columbus Literacy Council......................... E 614 282-7661
  Columbus *(G-5643)*
Columbus Mntessori Educatn Ctr............... E 614 231-3790
  Columbus *(G-5645)*
County of Lorain... D 440 324-5777
  Elyria *(G-8239)*
Coyle Music Centers Inc............................. E 614 885-6654
  Columbus *(G-5716)*
Deemsys Inc.. D 614 322-9928
  Gahanna *(G-8715)*
Grail.. E 513 683-2340
  Loveland *(G-10139)*
Great Oaks Inst Tech Creer Dev................. E 513 771-8840
  Cincinnati *(G-2763)*
Great Oaks Inst Tech Creer Dev................. D 513 613-3657
  Cincinnati *(G-2764)*
Jo-Ann Stores LLC..................................... E 419 621-8101
  Sandusky *(G-12906)*
Knowledgeworks Foundation...................... E 513 929-4777
  Cincinnati *(G-2945)*
Lakeland Foundation................................... E 440 525-7094
  Willoughby *(G-15202)*
Macair Aviation LLC................................... E 937 347-1302
  Xenia *(G-15525)*
Osu Nephrology Medical Ctr....................... A 614 293-8300
  Columbus *(G-6485)*
Roundtable Learning LLC........................... E 440 220-5252
  Chagrin Falls *(G-1988)*
South Central Ohio Eductl Ctr.................... D 740 456-0517
  New Boston *(G-11595)*
Temenos... D 513 791-7022
  Blue Ash *(G-1252)*

Upper Valley Medical Center...................... C 937 440-4820
  Troy *(G-14167)*

83 SOCIAL SERVICES

8322 Individual and family services

A W S Inc... E 216 486-0600
  Euclid *(G-8335)*
Abilities Connection................................... E 937 525-7400
  Springfield *(G-13213)*
Ability Works Inc.. C 419 626-1048
  Sandusky *(G-12861)*
Abuse Refuge Inc....................................... D 614 686-2121
  Lewis Center *(G-9803)*
Access Inc.. E 330 535-2999
  Akron *(G-13)*
Achievement Ctrs For Children................... D 440 250-2520
  Westlake *(G-15029)*
Achievement Ctrs For Children................... D 216 292-9700
  Cleveland *(G-3763)*
Action For Children Inc............................... E 614 224-0222
  Columbus *(G-5310)*
Active Day Inc.. E 513 984-8000
  Cincinnati *(G-2143)*
Addiction Services Council......................... E 513 281-7880
  Cincinnati *(G-2144)*
ADS Alliance Data Systems Inc................. D 513 707-6800
  Columbus *(G-5316)*
Agape For Youth Inc.................................. E 937 439-4406
  Dayton *(G-7159)*
Aids Tskfrce Grter Clvland Inc................... E 216 357-3131
  Cleveland *(G-3776)*
Akron Cmnty Svc Ctr Urban Leag............. E 234 542-4141
  Akron *(G-24)*
Akron Family Institute Inc.......................... E 330 644-3469
  Akron *(G-27)*
Akron General Foundation......................... C 330 344-6888
  Akron *(G-29)*
Akron-Canton Regional Foodbank............. E 330 535-6900
  Akron *(G-40)*
Akron-Rban Mnrity Alchlism DRG............. D 330 379-3467
  Akron *(G-41)*
Als Assction Nthrn Ohio Chpter................ E 216 592-2572
  Independence *(G-9404)*
Altercare Inc... E 330 929-4231
  Cuyahoga Falls *(G-7037)*
Altercare Inc... E 330 677-4550
  Kent *(G-9558)*
Altercare of Ohio Inc.................................. E 330 498-8110
  Canton *(G-1664)*
Alterntive Rsrces Homecare Inc................ D 216 256-3049
  Shaker Heights *(G-12973)*
Altruism Society Inc................................... D 877 283-4001
  Beachwood *(G-765)*
Always With US Chrties Awu CHR............ E 800 675-4710
  Columbus *(G-5341)*
Amazing Grace HM Hlth Care LLC........... D 937 825-4862
  Huber Heights *(G-9323)*
American National Red Cross................... D 330 535-6131
  Akron *(G-46)*
American National Red Cross................... E 330 535-6131
  Akron *(G-47)*
American National Red Cross................... E 330 452-1111
  Canton *(G-1665)*
American National Red Cross................... E 614 253-2740
  Columbus *(G-5355)*
American National Red Cross................... E 614 326-2337
  Columbus *(G-5356)*
American National Red Cross................... E 800 448-3543
  Columbus *(G-5357)*
American National Red Cross................... E 614 334-0425
  Columbus *(G-5358)*

American National Red Cross................... E 614 473-3783
  Gahanna *(G-8710)*
American National Red Cross................... E 614 436-3862
  Lewis Center *(G-9805)*
American National Red Cross................... E 740 344-2510
  Newark *(G-11687)*
American National Red Cross................... E 216 303-5476
  Parma *(G-12249)*
American National Red Cross................... C 419 382-2707
  Toledo *(G-13684)*
American National Red Cross................... E 800 733-2767
  Toledo *(G-13685)*
American National Red Cross................... D 419 329-2900
  Toledo *(G-13686)*
American National Red Cross................... E 330 469-6403
  Warren *(G-14498)*
American National Red Cross................... E 330 726-6063
  Youngstown *(G-15550)*
American Red Cross.................................. A 513 579-3000
  Cincinnati *(G-2186)*
American Red Cross of Grtr Col................ E 614 253-7981
  Columbus *(G-5360)*
Antonine Ssters Adult Day Care................ C 330 538-9822
  North Jackson *(G-11871)*
Applewood Centers Inc............................. E 216 696-5800
  Cleveland *(G-3822)*
Applewood Centers Inc............................. E 216 521-6511
  Cleveland *(G-3823)*
Applewood Centers Inc............................. D 216 741-2241
  Cleveland *(G-3824)*
Applewood Centers Inc............................. D 216 696-6815
  Cleveland *(G-3821)*
Arbor Rehabilitation & Healtcr................... B 440 423-0206
  Gates Mills *(G-8781)*
ARC Indstries Inc Frnklin Cnty.................. C 614 836-0700
  Groveport *(G-8971)*
Archdiocese of Cincinnati.......................... E 937 325-8715
  Springfield *(G-13218)*
Area Agcy On Aging Plg Svc Are.............. C 800 258-7277
  Dayton *(G-7179)*
Area Agency On Aging Dst 7 Inc.............. D 740 446-7000
  Gallipolis *(G-8752)*
Area Agency On Aging Dst 7 Inc.............. D 740 245-5306
  West Union *(G-14866)*
Area Agency On Aging Dst 7 Inc.............. E 800 582-7277
  Rio Grande *(G-12726)*
Area Agency On Aging Reg 9 Inc.............. D 740 439-4478
  Cambridge *(G-1554)*
Area Office On Aging Nrthwster................ D 419 382-0624
  Toledo *(G-13693)*
Artemis Ctr For Altrntves To D................... E 937 461-5091
  Dayton *(G-7181)*
Ashtabula Cnty Cmnty Action AG.............. E 440 997-1721
  Ashtabula *(G-519)*
Assoction For Dvlpmntlly Dsble................. E 614 486-4361
  Westerville *(G-14961)*
Athens County Board of Dev..................... E 740 594-3539
  Athens *(G-557)*
Avalon Foodservice Inc............................. C 330 854-4551
  Canal Fulton *(G-1592)*
Battered Womens Shelter......................... E 330 723-3900
  Medina *(G-10814)*
Battle Bullying Hotline Inc......................... D 216 731-1976
  Cleveland *(G-3855)*
Beech Acres Parenting Center.................. D 513 231-6630
  Cincinnati *(G-2246)*
Bellefaire Jewish Chld Bur......................... B 216 932-2800
  Shaker Heights *(G-12974)*
Benjamin Rose Institute............................. C 216 791-3580
  Cleveland *(G-3868)*
Benjamin Rose Institute............................. D 216 791-8000
  Cleveland *(G-3867)*

83 SOCIAL SERVICES

Big Brthers Big Ssters Cntl OH............. E 614 839-2447
  Columbus *(G-5437)*

Blanchard Vly Rsdntial Svcs In............ D 419 422-6503
  Findlay *(G-8517)*

Blick Clinic Inc................................... D 330 762-5425
  Akron *(G-70)*

Blossom Hill Inc................................. E 440 250-9182
  Westlake *(G-15039)*

Bluestone Counseling LLC.................. E 614 406-0299
  Columbus *(G-5450)*

Bobby Tripodi Foundation Inc............. E 216 524-3787
  Independence *(G-9412)*

Bridges To Independence Inc............. C 740 362-1996
  Delaware *(G-7780)*

Bridgeway Inc..................................... C 216 688-4114
  Cleveland *(G-3892)*

Broken Arrow Inc................................ E 419 562-3480
  Bucyrus *(G-1496)*

Brook Beech.. C 216 391-4069
  Cleveland *(G-3901)*

Brook Beech.. C 216 831-2255
  Cleveland *(G-3902)*

Brookwood Management Company...... E 330 497-8718
  Canton *(G-1691)*

Butler County of Ohio......................... D 513 887-3728
  Hamilton *(G-9020)*

Cadence Care Network...................... E 330 544-8005
  Niles *(G-11782)*

Cambridge Counseling Center............ C 740 450-7790
  Zanesville *(G-15775)*

Camelot Community Care Inc............ C 513 961-5900
  Cincinnati *(G-2303)*

Cancer Family Care Inc..................... E 513 731-3346
  Cincinnati *(G-2305)*

Caring For Kids Inc............................ D 330 928-0044
  Cuyahoga Falls *(G-7053)*

Carriage Inn of Cadiz Inc................... D 740 942-8084
  Cadiz *(G-1538)*

Casleo Corporation............................. C 614 252-6508
  Columbus *(G-5515)*

Catalyst Counseling LLC................... E 937 219-7770
  Middletown *(G-11155)*

Catholic Charities Corporation............ D 419 289-1903
  Ashland *(G-488)*

Catholic Charities Corporation............ D 216 939-3713
  Cleveland *(G-3933)*

Catholic Charities Corporation............ D 216 268-4006
  Cleveland *(G-3934)*

Catholic Charities Corporation............ D 330 723-9615
  Medina *(G-10817)*

Catholic Charities Corporation............ D 330 262-7836
  Wooster *(G-15317)*

Catholic Charities Corporation............ E 216 334-2900
  Cleveland *(G-3935)*

Catholic Charities of Southwst............ D 937 325-8715
  Springfield *(G-13224)*

Catholic Chrties of Sthwstern............. D 513 241-7745
  Cincinnati *(G-2323)*

Catholic Chrties Regional Agcy.......... E 330 744-3320
  Youngstown *(G-15572)*

Catholic Chrties Sthstern Ohio........... D 740 432-6751
  Cambridge *(G-1563)*

Catholic Chrties Sthstern Ohio........... C 740 695-3189
  Saint Clairsville *(G-12784)*

Catholic Chrties Sthstern Ohio........... B 740 676-4932
  Steubenville *(G-13319)*

Catholic Scial Svcs of Mami Vl........... E 937 223-7217
  Dayton *(G-7218)*

Catholic Social Services Inc............... E 614 221-5891
  Columbus *(G-5520)*

Center For Cognitv Behav Psych........ E 614 459-4490
  Columbus *(G-5530)*

Center For Families & Children........... E 216 252-5800
  Cleveland *(G-3950)*

Center For Families & Children........... E 216 671-1919
  Cleveland *(G-3951)*

Center For Indvdual Fmly Svcs.......... C 419 522-4357
  Mansfield *(G-10251)*

Centers For Families Children............ D 216 432-7200
  Cleveland *(G-3953)*

Central Community Hse Columbus..... E 614 252-3157
  Columbus *(G-5534)*

Central Ohio Area Agcy On Agin........ C 614 645-7250
  Columbus *(G-5535)*

Champaign Cnty Board of Dd............. B 937 653-5217
  Urbana *(G-14300)*

Child Focus Inc................................... E 513 732-8800
  Batavia *(G-731)*

Child Focus Inc................................... E 937 444-1613
  Mount Orab *(G-11469)*

Child Focus Inc................................... D 513 752-1555
  Cincinnati *(G-2355)*

Childrens Cmprhensive Svcs Inc........ D 419 589-5511
  Mansfield *(G-10252)*

Childrens HM of Cncinnati Ohio......... C 513 272-2800
  Cincinnati *(G-2357)*

Childrens Hosp Med Ctr Akron.......... D 330 633-2055
  Tallmadge *(G-13587)*

Childrens Hunger Alliance.................. E 614 341-7700
  Columbus *(G-5564)*

Choices In Community Living............. D 937 325-0344
  Springfield *(G-13226)*

▼ Christian Aid Ministries.................. E 330 893-2428
  Millersburg *(G-11276)*

Christian Chld HM Ohio Inc................ D 330 345-7949
  Wooster *(G-15320)*

Cincinnati Area Snior Svcs Inc........... D 513 721-4330
  Cincinnati *(G-2394)*

▲ Cincinnati Assn For The Blind....... C 513 221-8558
  Cincinnati *(G-2395)*

Cincinnati Youth Collaborative............ E 513 475-4165
  Cincinnati *(G-2432)*

Cincinnt-Hmlton Cnty Cmnty Act........ E 513 354-3900
  Cincinnati *(G-2435)*

Cincinnt-Hmlton Cnty Cmnty Act........ C 513 569-1840
  Cincinnati *(G-2434)*

Cincysmiles Foundation Inc............... E 513 621-0248
  Cincinnati *(G-2439)*

Circle Health Services........................ E 216 721-4010
  Cleveland *(G-3972)*

City Mission.. E 216 431-3510
  Cleveland *(G-3976)*

City of Brecksville.............................. E 440 526-4109
  Brecksville *(G-1349)*

City of Brooklyn.................................. D 216 635-4222
  Cleveland *(G-3977)*

City of Canal Winchester.................... D 614 837-8276
  Canal Winchester *(G-1602)*

City of Cincinnati................................ E 513 471-9844
  Cincinnati *(G-2452)*

City of Cuyahoga Falls....................... D 330 971-8425
  Cuyahoga Falls *(G-7057)*

City of Lakewood............................... E 216 521-1515
  Lakewood *(G-9660)*

City of Lyndhurst................................ E 440 449-5011
  Cleveland *(G-3992)*

City of Maple Heights......................... E 216 587-5451
  Maple Heights *(G-10334)*

City of Westlake................................. D 440 808-5700
  Westlake *(G-15050)*

Clark Cnty Bd Dvlpmntal Dsblti........... D 937 328-5240
  Springfield *(G-13231)*

Clark County Board of Developm....... E 937 328-2675
  Springfield *(G-13232)*

Clermont Cnty Bd Dvlpmntal DSB...... E 513 732-7015
  Owensville *(G-12199)*

Clermont Counseling Center.............. D 513 345-8555
  Cincinnati *(G-2457)*

Clermont Counseling Center.............. E 513 947-7000
  Amelia *(G-416)*

Clermont County Cmnty Svcs Inc...... E 513 732-2277
  Batavia *(G-733)*

Clermont Senior Services Inc............. D 513 724-1255
  Batavia *(G-735)*

Cleveland Christian Home Inc............ E 216 671-0977
  Cleveland *(G-4006)*

Cleveland Municipal School Dst......... E 216 521-6511
  Cleveland *(G-4060)*

Cleveland Soc For The Blind............. C 216 791-8118
  Cleveland *(G-4067)*

Clintnvlle Bchwold Cmnty Rsrce......... E 614 268-3539
  Columbus *(G-5585)*

Clossman Catering Incorporated......... E 513 942-7744
  Hamilton *(G-9029)*

Clovernook Ctr For Blind Vslly........... D 513 522-3860
  Cincinnati *(G-2464)*

College Now Grter Clveland Inc......... E 216 241-5587
  Cleveland *(G-4087)*

Columbus Literacy Council................. E 614 282-7661
  Columbus *(G-5643)*

Columbus Speech & Hearing Ctr....... D 614 263-5151
  Columbus *(G-5654)*

Columbus Urban League.................... E 614 257-6300
  Columbus *(G-5658)*

Commquest Services Inc................... C 330 455-0374
  Canton *(G-1718)*

Community Action - Wyne/Medina...... D 330 264-8677
  Wooster *(G-15325)*

Community Action Cmmttee Pike....... C 740 289-2371
  Piketon *(G-12416)*

Community Action Comm Blmont C... D 740 676-0800
  Bellaire *(G-1009)*

Community Action Comm Blmont C... E 740 695-0293
  Saint Clairsville *(G-12786)*

Community Action Comm Erie Hro..... E 419 935-6481
  Willard *(G-15166)*

Community Action Comm Fytte CN.... D 740 335-7282
  Wshngtn Ct Hs *(G-15478)*

Community Action Orgnztion Sco....... C 740 354-7541
  Portsmouth *(G-12548)*

Community Action Prgram Comm O... D 740 345-8750
  Newark *(G-11693)*

Community Action Prgram Comm O... D 740 653-1711
  Lancaster *(G-9704)*

Community Action Prgram Corp O..... C 740 373-6016
  Marietta *(G-10363)*

Community Cnsling Wllness Ctrs........ E 740 387-5210
  Marion *(G-10422)*

Community Counseling Svcs Inc........ E 419 562-2000
  Bucyrus *(G-1501)*

Community Drug Board Inc................ D 330 315-5590
  Akron *(G-116)*

Community For New Drction Incr........ E 614 272-1464
  Columbus *(G-5670)*

Community Rfgee Immgrtion Svcs..... D 614 235-5747
  Columbus *(G-5673)*

Compass Family and Cmnty Svcs...... D 330 743-9275
  Youngstown *(G-15583)*

Compass Family and Cmnty Svcs...... E 330 782-5664
  Youngstown *(G-15584)*

Compdrug... D 614 224-4506
  Columbus *(G-5675)*

Comprhnsive Cmnty Child Care O..... E 513 221-0033
  Cincinnati *(G-2489)*

Concerned Ctzens Agnst Vlnce A..... E 740 382-8988
  Marion *(G-10423)*

83 SOCIAL SERVICES

Concord Counseling Services .... E 614 882-9338
  Westerville *(G-14974)*
Connecting Kids To Meals Inc .... D 419 720-1106
  Toledo *(G-13758)*
Consumer Support Services Inc .... D 216 447-1521
  Independence *(G-9423)*
Consumer Support Services Inc .... D 330 764-4785
  Medina *(G-10825)*
Consumer Support Services Inc .... D 740 522-5464
  Newark *(G-11694)*
Consumer Support Services Inc .... D 740 344-3600
  Newark *(G-11695)*
Consumer Support Services Inc .... D 440 354-7082
  Painesville *(G-12223)*
Corportion For Ohio Applchian .... E 740 594-8499
  Athens *(G-562)*
Council On Aging Sthwstern Ohi .... C 513 721-1025
  Blue Ash *(G-1159)*
Council On Rur Svc Prgrams Inc .... D 937 773-0773
  Piqua *(G-12439)*
Counsling Ctr of Wyne Hlmes CN .... D 330 264-9029
  Wooster *(G-15327)*
Country Neighbor Program Inc .... E 440 437-6311
  Orwell *(G-12177)*
Countryside Yung MNS Chrstn As .... D 513 677-3702
  Maineville *(G-10227)*
County of Adams .... E 937 544-5067
  West Union *(G-14868)*
County of Allen .... E 419 227-8590
  Lima *(G-9878)*
County of Allen .... E 419 228-2120
  Lima *(G-9879)*
County of Ashtabula .... C 440 998-1811
  Ashtabula *(G-531)*
County of Clermont .... E 513 732-7265
  Batavia *(G-736)*
County of Coshocton .... E 740 622-1020
  Coshocton *(G-6982)*
County of Crawford .... E 419 562-3050
  Bucyrus *(G-1503)*
County of Cuyahoga .... E 216 420-6750
  Cleveland *(G-4122)*
County of Cuyahoga .... E 216 443-5100
  Cleveland *(G-4123)*
County of Cuyahoga .... E 216 681-4433
  Cleveland *(G-4124)*
County of Cuyahoga .... E 216 941-8800
  Cleveland *(G-4128)*
County of Cuyahoga .... D 216 431-4500
  Cleveland *(G-4129)*
County of Cuyahoga .... E 216 432-2621
  Cleveland *(G-4130)*
County of Cuyahoga .... E 419 399-8260
  Paulding *(G-12282)*
County of Geauga .... D 440 285-9141
  Chardon *(G-1998)*
County of Guernsey .... E 740 439-6681
  Cambridge *(G-1566)*
County of Hamilton .... E 513 946-1800
  Cincinnati *(G-2512)*
County of Logan .... E 937 599-7290
  Bellefontaine *(G-1028)*
County of Lorain .... D 440 329-3734
  Elyria *(G-8238)*
County of Lorain .... D 440 329-5340
  Elyria *(G-8240)*
County of Lorain .... E 440 326-4700
  Elyria *(G-8241)*
County of Lorain .... E 440 233-2020
  Lorain *(G-10069)*
County of Lucas .... D 419 213-3000
  Toledo *(G-13763)*

County of Meigs .... E 740 992-2117
  Middleport *(G-11147)*
County of Perry .... E 740 342-1213
  New Lexington *(G-11621)*
County of Perry .... E 740 342-4264
  New Lexington *(G-11622)*
County of Pickaway .... E 740 474-7588
  Ashville *(G-552)*
County of Preble .... E 937 456-2085
  Eaton *(G-8211)*
County of Summit .... A 330 634-8000
  Tallmadge *(G-13590)*
County of Tuscarawas .... D 330 339-7791
  New Philadelphia *(G-11646)*
Crawford County Children Svcs .... E 419 562-1200
  Bucyrus *(G-1506)*
Creative Foundations Inc .... E 877 345-6733
  Delaware *(G-7790)*
Creative Options LLC .... E 614 868-1231
  Columbus *(G-5722)*
Crossroads Health .... D 440 255-1700
  Mentor *(G-10929)*
Custom Clg Svcs Disaster LLC .... E 440 774-1222
  Oberlin *(G-12067)*
Cyo & Community Services Inc .... E 330 762-2961
  Akron *(G-130)*
Dan Sechkar Sech Kar C .... E 740 753-9955
  Nelsonville *(G-11541)*
Darcie R Clark Lpcc LLC .... E 937 319-4448
  Dayton *(G-7267)*
Dave Thmas Fndtion For Adption .... E 614 764-8454
  Dublin *(G-7985)*
Daybreak Inc .... E 937 395-4600
  Dayton *(G-7269)*
Deepwood Industries Inc .... C 440 350-5231
  Mentor *(G-10933)*
Defiance Cnty Bd Commissioners .... E 419 782-3233
  Defiance *(G-7743)*
Delaware Cnty Bd Dvlpmntal DSB .... C 740 201-3600
  Lewis Center *(G-9816)*
Delhi Township .... D 513 922-0060
  Cincinnati *(G-2555)*
Direction HM Akron Cnton Area .... C 330 896-9172
  Uniontown *(G-14249)*
Direction Home Eastrn Ohio Inc .... C 330 505-2355
  Youngstown *(G-15597)*
Directions For Youth Families .... E 614 258-8043
  Columbus *(G-5767)*
Directions For Youth Families .... E 614 694-0203
  Columbus *(G-5768)*
Directions For Youth Families .... E 614 294-2661
  Columbus *(G-5769)*
DMD Management Inc .... C 216 371-3600
  Cleveland *(G-4172)*
East Community Learning Center .... D 330 814-7412
  Akron *(G-144)*
Easter Seal Society of .... D 330 743-1168
  Youngstown *(G-15603)*
Easter Seals Tristate LLC .... D 513 281-2316
  Cincinnati *(G-2600)*
Easter Seals Tristate .... C 513 985-0515
  Cincinnati *(G-2599)*
Eastern Ohio Correction Center .... E 740 765-4324
  Wintersville *(G-15293)*
Eastersals Cntl Southeast Ohio .... C 614 228-5523
  Hilliard *(G-9193)*
Eastway Corporation .... C 937 496-2000
  Dayton *(G-7324)*
Echoing Hills Village Inc .... C 740 327-2311
  Warsaw *(G-14591)*
Elizabeths New Life Center Inc .... D 937 226-7414
  Dayton *(G-7332)*

Emerge Ministries Inc .... E 330 865-8351
  Akron *(G-146)*
Employee Services LLC .... D 585 593-9870
  Cleveland *(G-4213)*
Epilepsy Ctr of Nrthwstern Ohi .... E 419 867-5950
  Maumee *(G-10722)*
Equitas Health Inc .... D 614 299-2437
  Columbus *(G-5825)*
Faith Mission Inc .... D 614 224-6617
  Columbus *(G-5848)*
Family Child Abuse Prvntion CT .... E 419 244-3053
  Toledo *(G-13802)*
Family Service .... E 513 381-6300
  Cincinnati *(G-2648)*
Family Service Association .... E 937 222-9481
  Moraine *(G-11408)*
Family Service of NW Ohio .... D 419 321-6455
  Toledo *(G-13803)*
Family Vlnce Prvntion Ctr Gren .... E 937 372-4552
  Xenia *(G-15506)*
Family YMCA of LANcstr&fairfld .... D 740 277-7373
  Lancaster *(G-9723)*
Far West Center .... E 440 835-6212
  Westlake *(G-15060)*
Fayette Progressive Inds Inc .... E 740 335-7453
  Wshngtn Ct Hs *(G-15485)*
Feli .... E 216 421-6262
  Cleveland *(G-4247)*
First Community Village .... B 614 324-4455
  Columbus *(G-5861)*
Focus On Youth Inc .... E 513 644-1030
  West Chester *(G-14693)*
Foodbank Inc .... E 937 461-0265
  Dayton *(G-7360)*
Franklin Cnty Bd Commissioners .... E 614 462-3275
  Columbus *(G-5882)*
Franklin Cnty Bd Commissioners .... B 614 229-7100
  Columbus *(G-5883)*
Franklin Cnty Bd Commissioners .... C 614 275-2571
  Columbus *(G-5884)*
Free Store/Food Bank Inc .... E 513 241-1064
  Cincinnati *(G-2705)*
Free Store/Food Bank Inc .... E 513 482-4526
  Cincinnati *(G-2704)*
Freedom Recovery LLC .... E 614 754-8051
  Columbus *(G-5892)*
Freestore Foodbank Inc .... E 513 482-4500
  Cincinnati *(G-2706)*
Friendly Inn Settlement Inc .... E 216 431-7656
  Cleveland *(G-4290)*
Friends For Lf Rhbltition Svcs .... E 440 558-2859
  Cleveland *(G-4291)*
Friends of Casa Frnklin Cnty O .... E 614 525-7450
  Columbus *(G-5896)*
Front Steps Housing & Svcs Inc .... E 216 781-2250
  Cleveland *(G-4293)*
G M N Tri Cnty Cmnty Action CM .... E 740 732-2388
  Caldwell *(G-1549)*
Galli-Migs Cmnty Action Agcy I .... E 740 367-7341
  Cheshire *(G-2029)*
Ganzhorn Suites Inc .... D 614 356-9810
  Powell *(G-12592)*
Gardens Western Reserve Inc .... E 330 342-9100
  Streetsboro *(G-13412)*
Golden Age Senior Citizens .... E 937 376-4353
  Xenia *(G-15509)*
Goodrich Gnnett Nghborhood Ctr .... E 216 432-1717
  Cleveland *(G-4320)*
Goods Hands Supported Living .... E 740 474-2646
  Circleville *(G-3709)*
Goodwill Ester Seals Miami Vly .... C 937 461-4800
  Dayton *(G-7379)*

83 SOCIAL SERVICES

Goodwill Inds Erie Hron Ottawa............. D 419 334-7566
   Fremont *(G-8683)*

Goodwill Inds Erie Hron Ottawa............. E 419 625-4744
   Sandusky *(G-12900)*

Goodwill Inds Rhbilitation Ctr................. C 330 454-9461
   Canton *(G-1764)*

Great Lkes Cmnty Action Partnr.............. E 419 729-8035
   Toledo *(G-13828)*

Great Lkes Cmnty Action Partnr.............. D 419 333-6068
   Fremont *(G-8684)*

Great Mami Vly Yung MNS Chrstn........... D 513 887-0001
   Hamilton *(G-9046)*

Great Miami Valley YMCA...................... D 513 829-3091
   Fairfield *(G-8417)*

Great Miami Valley YMCA...................... D 513 892-9622
   Fairfield Township *(G-8461)*

Great Miami Valley YMCA...................... D 513 887-0014
   Hamilton *(G-9048)*

Great Miami Valley YMCA...................... D 513 868-9622
   Hamilton *(G-9049)*

Greater Cleveland Food Bnk Inc............. C 216 738-2265
   Cleveland *(G-4331)*

Greene County.. E 937 562-5266
   Xenia *(G-15511)*

Greene County.. E 937 562-6000
   Xenia *(G-15512)*

Greene County Board of Dd.................... E 937 562-6500
   Xenia *(G-15515)*

Greene County Council On Aging............ E 937 374-5600
   Xenia *(G-15516)*

Greenleaf Family Center......................... E 330 376-9494
   Akron *(G-181)*

Grow Well Cleveland Corp...................... E 216 282-3838
   Cleveland *(G-4341)*

Handson Central Ohio Inc...................... E 614 221-2255
   Columbus *(G-5969)*

Harcatus Tr-Cnty Cmnty Action............... E 740 922-3600
   Dennison *(G-7857)*

Harcatus Tr-Cnty Cmnty Action............... E 740 922-0933
   Dover *(G-7887)*

Hardin Cnty Cncil On Aging Inc.............. E 419 673-1102
   Kenton *(G-9615)*

Harrison Pavilion.................................... E 513 662-5800
   Cincinnati *(G-2802)*

Harrison Township.................................. E 740 942-2171
   Cadiz *(G-1540)*

Hattie Larlham Community Svcs............. E 330 274-2272
   Mantua *(G-10330)*

Hattie Lrlham Ctr For Chldren................. C 330 274-2272
   Mantua *(G-10331)*

Havar Inc.. D 740 594-3533
   Athens *(G-570)*

Haven Bhavioral Healthcare Inc.............. C 937 234-0100
   Dayton *(G-7399)*

Haven Rest Ministries Inc....................... D 330 535-1563
   Akron *(G-190)*

Hcf Management Inc.............................. E 740 289-2394
   Piketon *(G-12422)*

Hcf of Roselawn Inc............................... C 419 647-4115
   Spencerville *(G-13188)*

Healing Hrts Cunseling Ctr Inc................ E 419 528-5993
   Mansfield *(G-10268)*

Health Services (adamhs) Brd O............. E 216 241-3400
   Cleveland *(G-4354)*

Hearing Spech Deaf Ctr Grter C............. E 513 221-0527
   Cincinnati *(G-2814)*

Heartbeat International Inc..................... E 614 885-7577
   Columbus *(G-5977)*

Heinzerling Community........................... A 614 272-8888
   Columbus *(G-5980)*

Help Foundation Inc............................... E 216 432-4810
   Northfield *(G-11956)*

Helpline Del Mrrow Cunties Inc............... E 740 369-3316
   Delaware *(G-7803)*

Heritage Day Health Centers.................. D 614 451-2151
   Columbus *(G-5987)*

Highland Cnty Cmnty Action Org............ E 937 393-3060
   Hillsboro *(G-9255)*

Highlands Community Lrng Ctr................ E 614 210-0830
   Columbus *(G-5993)*

Hilty Memorial Home Inc........................ E 419 384-3218
   Pandora *(G-12246)*

Hockingthensperry Cmnty Action........... E 740 385-6813
   Logan *(G-10024)*

Hockingthensperry Cmnty Action........... E 740 767-4500
   Glouster *(G-8835)*

Hockins Athens Prry Cmnty Acti.............. C 740 753-3062
   Nelsonville *(G-11547)*

Hockins Athens Prry Cmnty Acti.............. E 740 385-3644
   Athens *(G-573)*

Home Instead Senior Care...................... E 330 334-4664
   Wadsworth *(G-14435)*

Homefull... D 937 293-1945
   Moraine *(G-11418)*

Homeless Families Foundation............... D 614 461-9247
   Columbus *(G-6002)*

Homelife Residential Svcs Inc................. E 440 964-2419
   Geneva *(G-8786)*

Hopewell Health Centers Inc.................. E 740 596-4809
   Mc Arthur *(G-10798)*

Horizon Education Centers..................... E 440 277-5437
   Lorain *(G-10077)*

Horizon Education Centers..................... E 440 779-6536
   North Olmsted *(G-11906)*

Hospice of Knox County......................... E 740 397-5188
   Mount Vernon *(G-11489)*

Hospice of Valley Inc............................. D 330 788-1992
   Girard *(G-8815)*

House of New Hope................................ E 740 345-5437
   Saint Louisville *(G-12826)*

Huckleberry House Inc........................... D 614 294-5553
   Columbus *(G-6015)*

Impact Community Action....................... D 614 252-2799
   Columbus *(G-6042)*

Inside Out... E 937 525-7880
   Springfield *(G-13259)*

Integrted Svcs For Bhvral Hlth................ D 740 216-4093
   Logan *(G-10029)*

Integrted Svcs For Bhvral Hlth................ E 740 300-0225
   Nelsonville *(G-11548)*

Jackson County Bd On Aging Inc........... E 740 286-2909
   Jackson *(G-9522)*

Jay Hash LLC.. D 740 353-4673
   Portsmouth *(G-12559)*

Jewish Cmnty Ctr of Cincinnati............... D 513 761-7500
   Cincinnati *(G-2905)*

Jewish Cmnty Ctr of Toledo.................... E 419 885-4485
   Sylvania *(G-13554)*

Jewish Family Service............................ C 614 231-1890
   Columbus *(G-6089)*

Jewish Fdrtion Grter Dyton Inc............... D 937 830-7904
   Dayton *(G-7427)*

Jewish Fdrtion Grter Dyton Inc............... E 937 837-2651
   Dayton *(G-7428)*

Jewish Fmly Svc Assn Clvland O............ B 216 292-3999
   Beachwood *(G-805)*

Jewish Fmly Svc Assn Clvland O............ E 216 292-3999
   Beachwood *(G-804)*

Jewish Fmly Svc of Cncnnati AR............. E 513 469-1188
   Cincinnati *(G-2906)*

Kinnect.. E 216 692-1161
   Cleveland *(G-4467)*

Lake Cnty Yung MNS Chrstn Assn.......... C 440 352-3303
   Painesville *(G-12231)*

Lake County Council On Aging............... E 440 205-8111
   Mentor *(G-10959)*

Lake County YMCA................................ C 440 428-5125
   Madison *(G-10219)*

Lake County YMCA................................ C 440 259-2724
   Perry *(G-12307)*

Lake County YMCA................................ C 440 946-1160
   Willoughby *(G-15198)*

Lake Hospital System Inc...................... C 440 375-8590
   Perry *(G-12308)*

Lakewood Recreation Department.......... E 216 529-4081
   Lakewood *(G-9675)*

Landmark Recovery Ohio LLC................ B 855 950-5035
   Willard *(G-15169)*

Lark Residential Support Inc.................. E 614 582-9721
   Columbus *(G-6141)*

Lawrence Cnty Bd Dev Dsblities............. E 740 377-2356
   South Point *(G-13176)*

Leeda Services Inc................................ C 330 325-1560
   Rootstown *(G-12761)*

Licking County Adult Crt Svcs................ E 740 670-5734
   Newark *(G-11714)*

Licking County Aging Program............... D 740 345-0821
   Newark *(G-11715)*

Licking County Board of Mrdd................ C 740 349-6588
   Newark *(G-11716)*

Lifecare Hospice.................................... D 330 336-6595
   Wadsworth *(G-14440)*

Lifeline Partners Inc.............................. E 330 501-6316
   Girard *(G-8818)*

Lifespan Incorporated............................ D 513 868-3210
   Hamilton *(G-9060)*

Lifeway For Youth.................................. E 937 845-3625
   New Carlisle *(G-11603)*

Light of Hearts Villa Inc........................ D 440 232-1991
   Cleveland *(G-4495)*

Lighthouse Youth Services Inc............... E 740 634-3094
   Bainbridge *(G-685)*

Lighthouse Youth Services Inc............... E 513 221-3350
   Cincinnati *(G-2977)*

Lighthuse Bhvral Hlth Sltons L.............. D 614 334-6903
   Columbus *(G-6163)*

Lima Family YMCA................................. D 419 223-6055
   Lima *(G-9923)*

Lima Family YMCA................................. D 419 223-6045
   Lima *(G-9922)*

Long Term Care Ombudsman................. E 216 696-2719
   Cleveland *(G-4505)*

Lucas Cnty Bd Dvlpmntal Dsblti............. C 419 380-4000
   Toledo *(G-13895)*

Lucas County Children Services............. B 419 213-3247
   Toledo *(G-13897)*

Lutheran Scial Svcs Centl Ohio.............. E 419 289-3523
   Worthington *(G-15434)*

Lyman W Lggins Urban Affirs CT........... E 419 385-2532
   Toledo *(G-13901)*

Mahoning County Childrens Svcs........... E 330 941-8888
   Youngstown *(G-15658)*

Mahoning Yngstown Cmnty Action.......... D 330 747-7921
   Youngstown *(G-15661)*

Mandel Jcc.. E 781 934-5774
   Beachwood *(G-808)*

Mandel Jwish Cmnty Ctr of Clvl............. C 216 831-0700
   Beachwood *(G-809)*

Marion Cnty Bd Dev Dsabilities.............. D 740 387-1035
   Marion *(G-10437)*

Marion Family YMCA.............................. D 740 725-9622
   Marion *(G-10438)*

Maryhaven Inc....................................... E 614 626-2432
   Columbus *(G-6201)*

Maxim Healthcare Services Inc.............. C 614 880-1210
   Columbus *(G-6210)*

83 SOCIAL SERVICES

Medassist Incorporated............................ C 614 367-9416
  Gahanna (G-8724)
Mended Reeds Services Inc..................... C 740 532-6220
  Ironton (G-9511)
Menorah Pk Ctr For Snior Lving................. A 216 831-6500
  Cleveland (G-4550)
Mentor REM... A 216 642-5339
  Cleveland (G-4552)
Miami Vly Cmnty Action Partnr.................. D 937 222-1009
  Dayton (G-7503)
Miami Vly Jvnile Rhblttion Ctr.................... E 937 562-4000
  Xenia (G-15527)
Mid-Ohio Foodbank................................. C 614 277-3663
  Grove City (G-8935)
Mid-Ohio Psychlogical Svcs Inc................. E 740 687-0042
  Lancaster (G-9735)
Middltown Area Snior Ctzens In................. E 513 423-1734
  Middletown (G-11174)
Mobile Meals... D 330 376-7717
  Akron (G-235)
Mount Carmel Health.............................. C 614 234-4060
  Westerville (G-14912)
Mt Washington Care Center Inc................. E 513 231-4561
  Cincinnati (G-3087)
Multi-Cnty Jvnile Attntion Sys.................... D 330 339-7775
  New Philadelphia (G-11658)
Multi-Cnty Jvnile Attntion Sys.................... D 330 484-6471
  Canton (G-1813)
Murray Ridge Prod Ctr Inc........................ C 440 329-3734
  Elyria (G-8277)
Muskingum Cnty DRG Alchol Sbst............. E 740 454-1266
  Zanesville (G-15813)
Nami of Preble County Ohio..................... E 937 456-4947
  Eaton (G-8216)
National Exch CLB Fndtion For.................. E 419 535-3232
  Toledo (G-13930)
National Youth Advcate Prgram I................ E 614 487-8758
  Columbus (G-6303)
Nationwide Childrens Hospital................... C 614 355-7000
  Dublin (G-8070)
Nationwide Chld Hosp Homecare............... A 614 355-1100
  Columbus (G-6325)
Ncc Harvest Inc..................................... D 440 582-3300
  North Royalton (G-11945)
Near W Side Multi-Service Corp................ D 216 631-5800
  Cleveland (G-4632)
New Hrzons Mntal Hlth Svcs Inc................ D 740 901-3150
  Lancaster (G-9736)
Nick Amster Inc..................................... D 330 264-9667
  Wooster (G-15360)
North East Ohio Health Svcs.................... D 216 831-6466
  Beachwood (G-821)
Northwestern Ohio Cmnty Action................ C 419 784-2150
  Defiance (G-7758)
Nueva Luz Urban Resource Ctr................. E 216 651-8236
  Cleveland (G-4673)
Ocali.. E 614 410-0321
  Columbus (G-6382)
Ohio Addiction Recovery Center................. E 800 481-8457
  Columbus (G-6389)
Ohio Assn Cnty Brds Srving Ppl................. E 614 431-0616
  Worthington (G-15443)
Ohio Association of Foodbanks.................. D 614 221-4336
  Columbus (G-6392)
Ohio Department Rehabilitat..................... E 614 877-4516
  Orient (G-12152)
Ohio Department Youth Services................ C 419 245-3040
  Cleveland (G-4686)
Ohio Department Youth Services................ C 419 875-6965
  Liberty Center (G-9846)
Ohio Dept Dvlpmntal Dsbilities................... C 513 732-9200
  Batavia (G-744)

Ohio Dept Job & Fmly Svcs...................... E 614 466-1213
  Columbus (G-6407)
Ohio Dept Job & Fmly Svcs...................... E 740 295-7516
  Coshocton (G-6995)
Ohio Dept Job & Fmly Svcs...................... E 419 626-6781
  Sandusky (G-12922)
Ohio Dept Mntal Hlth Addction.................. D 740 773-2283
  Chillicothe (G-2080)
Ohio Dept Rhbilitation Corectn.................. D 614 274-9000
  Columbus (G-6411)
Ohio Dept Rhbilitation Corectn.................. D 614 752-0800
  Columbus (G-6412)
Ohio Dept Rhbilitation Corectn.................. E 419 782-3385
  Defiance (G-7759)
Ohio Dept Rhbilitation Corectn.................. D 419 448-0004
  Tiffin (G-13636)
Ohio Domestic Violence Network............... E 614 406-7274
  Columbus (G-6413)
Ohio Dst 5 Area Agcy On Aging................. C 419 522-5612
  Ontario (G-12119)
Ohio Mentor Inc..................................... C 216 525-1885
  Independence (G-9463)
Ohio Prsbt Rtrment Svcs Dev Co................ E 614 888-7800
  Westerville (G-14922)
Ohioguidestone...................................... C 440 234-2006
  Canton (G-1824)
Ohioguidestone...................................... B 440 260-8900
  Cleveland (G-4693)
Ohioguidestone...................................... C 440 234-2006
  Berea (G-1079)
Olmsted Residence Corporation................ C 440 235-7100
  Olmsted Twp (G-12093)
Oneeighty Inc.. D 330 263-6021
  Wooster (G-15364)
Opportunities For Ohioans....................... E 614 438-1200
  Columbus (G-6474)
Oriana House Inc................................... B 330 374-9610
  Akron (G-256)
Oriana House Inc................................... D 330 996-7730
  Akron (G-258)
Oriana House Inc................................... D 330 535-8116
  Akron (G-257)
Oriana House Inc................................... E 216 881-7882
  Burton (G-1532)
Otterbein Homes.................................... E 419 394-2366
  Saint Marys (G-12834)
Our Town Studios Inc............................. E 614 832-2121
  Columbus (G-6492)
Over Rainbow Adult Daycare.................... E 330 638-9599
  Cortland (G-6975)
Partners In Prime................................... E 513 867-1998
  Hamilton (G-9071)
Pastoral Cnsling Svc Smmit CNT............... C 330 996-4600
  Akron (G-262)
Pathway Inc.. E 419 242-7304
  Toledo (G-13961)
Pathways of Central Ohio........................ E 740 345-6166
  Newark (G-11740)
Person Centered Services Inc................... E 419 874-4900
  Perrysburg (G-12363)
Personal Fmly Cnsling Svcs of.................. E 330 343-8171
  New Philadelphia (G-11661)
Phillips Hthcare LLC DBA Cring................. E 330 531-6110
  Warren (G-14547)
Pickaway Cnty Cmnty Action Org.............. E 740 477-1655
  Circleville (G-3716)
Planned Parenthood Association............... E 937 226-0780
  Dayton (G-7555)
Portage Cnty Bd Dvlpmntal Dsbl................ C 330 678-2400
  Ravenna (G-12636)
Positive Education Program..................... E 216 227-2730
  Cleveland (G-4762)

Pregnancy Decision Health Ctr................. E 614 888-8774
  Columbus (G-6541)
Pressley Ridge Foundation...................... C 513 752-4548
  Cincinnati (G-2112)
Pressley Ridge Foundation...................... C 216 763-0800
  Cleveland (G-4769)
Pressley Ridge Foundation...................... C 513 737-0400
  Hamilton (G-9073)
Prevention Action Alliance....................... D 614 540-9985
  Columbus (G-6544)
Private Duty Services Inc........................ C 419 238-3714
  Van Wert (G-14350)
Pro Seniors Inc..................................... E 513 345-4160
  Cincinnati (G-3235)
Prokids.. E 513 281-2000
  Cincinnati (G-3249)
Providence House Inc............................ E 216 651-5982
  Cleveland (G-4795)
Providers For Healthy Living.................... D 614 664-3595
  Columbus (G-6554)
Quest Recovery Prevention Svcs............... C 330 453-8252
  Canton (G-1837)
Rainbow Rascals Lrng Ctr Inc.................. D 513 769-7529
  Blue Ash (G-1230)
Rehab Resources Inc............................. E 513 474-4123
  Cincinnati (G-3282)
Ronald McDonald Hse Chrties CNT............ E 614 227-3700
  Columbus (G-6609)
Ronald McDonald Hse Chrties Grt............. E 513 636-7642
  Cincinnati (G-3319)
Ronald McDonald Hse Chrties NW............. E 419 471-4663
  Toledo (G-13998)
Ross County Children Svcs Ctr................. E 740 773-2651
  Chillicothe (G-2085)
Royal Rdmer Lthran Ch N Rylton............... E 440 237-7958
  North Royalton (G-11949)
Salem Community Center Inc................... D 330 332-5885
  Salem (G-12852)
Salvation Army...................................... E 614 252-7171
  Columbus (G-6640)
Salvation Army...................................... E 800 728-7825
  Columbus (G-6641)
Salvation Army...................................... E 937 528-5100
  Dayton (G-7606)
Sateri Home Inc.................................... D 330 758-8106
  Youngstown (G-15717)
Sciot-Pint Vly Mental Hlth Ctr................... C 740 775-1260
  Chillicothe (G-2090)
Scioto Cnty Counseling Ctr Inc................. C 740 354-6685
  Portsmouth (G-12567)
Scioto Pnt Vly Mental Hlth Ctr.................. C 740 335-6935
  Wshngtn Ct Hs (G-15493)
Second Hrvest Fdbank of Mhning.............. E 330 792-5522
  Youngstown (G-15718)
Self Reliance Inc................................... E 937 525-0809
  Springfield (G-13291)
Seneca County Board Mr/Dd -.................. E 419 447-7521
  Tiffin (G-13643)
Senior Citizens Resources Inc.................. E 216 459-2870
  Cleveland (G-4894)
Senior Resource Connection.................... C 937 223-8246
  Dayton (G-7615)
Senior Star Management Company............ D 513 271-1747
  Cincinnati (G-3358)
Senior Touch Solution............................ E 216 862-4841
  Cleveland (G-4895)
Seven Hlls Neighborhood Houses.............. E 513 407-5362
  Cincinnati (G-3364)
Shaw Jewish Community Center............... D 330 867-7850
  Akron (G-298)
Sheconna L Daniels................................ D 216 370-0256
  Euclid (G-8361)

83 SOCIAL SERVICES

Shelterhouse Vlntr Group Inc............... E 513 721-0643
 Cincinnati *(G-3368)*
Sidney-Shelby County YMCA................ E 937 492-9134
 Sidney *(G-13053)*
Siffrin Residential Assn........................ C 330 799-8932
 Youngstown *(G-15724)*
Simply EZ HM Dlvred Mals Nrtha........... D 330 633-7490
 Akron *(G-302)*
Sourcepoint... D 740 363-6677
 Delaware *(G-7827)*
Southstern Ohio Cnsling Ctr LL............. E 740 260-9440
 Old Washington *(G-12087)*
Specialized Alternatives For F................ C 513 771-7239
 Cincinnati *(G-3395)*
Specialized Alternatives For F................ C 419 222-1527
 Lima *(G-9963)*
Specialized Alternatives For F................ C 216 295-7239
 Shaker Heights *(G-12985)*
Specilzed Altrntves For Fmlies............... D 419 695-8010
 Delphos *(G-7844)*
Specilzed Altrntves For Fmlies............... E 419 695-8010
 Delphos *(G-7845)*
Spectrum Supportive Services.............. E 216 875-0460
 Cleveland *(G-4931)*
St Joseph Infant Maternity HM.............. C 513 563-2520
 Cincinnati *(G-3403)*
St Pauls Community Center................. E 419 255-5520
 Toledo *(G-14026)*
St Stphens Cmnty Hmes Ltd Prt............ D 614 294-6347
 Columbus *(G-6706)*
St Vincent Family Services................... C 614 252-0731
 Columbus *(G-6707)*
Steady Care Behavioral LLC................. E 330 956-1190
 Akron *(G-310)*
Step Forward..................................... D 216 696-9077
 Cleveland *(G-4949)*
Sunshine Communities........................ B 419 865-0251
 Maumee *(G-10773)*
Sycamore Board of Education............... C 513 489-3937
 Montgomery *(G-11375)*
Sycamore Senior Center...................... D 513 984-1234
 Blue Ash *(G-1251)*
Sylvania Cmnty Svcs Ctr Inc................. E 419 885-2451
 Sylvania *(G-13574)*
Talbert House..................................... D 513 872-8870
 Cincinnati *(G-3434)*
Talbert House..................................... E 513 541-1184
 Cincinnati *(G-3435)*
Talbert House..................................... E 513 541-0127
 Cincinnati *(G-3437)*
Talbert House..................................... E 513 221-2398
 Cincinnati *(G-3438)*
Talbert House..................................... D 513 933-9304
 Lebanon *(G-9792)*
Talbert House..................................... D 513 872-5863
 Cincinnati *(G-3439)*
Talbert House Health........................... E 513 541-7577
 Cincinnati *(G-3442)*
Taylor Murtis Human Svcs Sys............. D 216 283-4400
 Cleveland *(G-4978)*
Tcn Behavioral Health Svcs Inc............. C 937 376-8700
 Xenia *(G-15532)*
Tender Mercies Inc............................. D 513 721-8666
 Cincinnati *(G-3454)*
Tender Mercies Inc............................. E 513 721-8666
 Cincinnati *(G-3455)*
Tennessee Centerstone Inc.................. E 740 779-4888
 Chillicothe *(G-2092)*
The East Toledo Family Ctr Inc.............. D 419 691-1429
 Toledo *(G-14040)*
Tom Paige Catering Company.............. E 216 431-4236
 Cleveland *(G-5024)*

Towards Employment Inc...................... E 216 696-5750
 Cleveland *(G-5025)*
Townhall 2... E 330 678-3006
 Kent *(G-9603)*
Tri-County Help Center Inc................... E 740 695-5441
 Saint Clairsville *(G-12816)*
Trihealth Rehabilitation Hosp................ C 513 601-0600
 Cincinnati *(G-3526)*
Trillium Family Solutions Inc................. E 330 454-7066
 Cuyahoga Falls *(G-7112)*
Turning Pt Counseling Svcs Inc............. D 330 744-2991
 Youngstown *(G-15739)*
United Crbral Plsy Assn Grter............... E 216 351-4888
 Cleveland *(G-5059)*
United Disability Services Inc................ D 330 379-3337
 Akron *(G-340)*
United Disability Services Inc................ D 330 374-1169
 Akron *(G-341)*
United Mthdst Chld HM W Ohio C.......... D 614 885-5020
 Columbus *(G-6808)*
United Rhbltton Svcs Grter Dy.............. D 937 233-1230
 Dayton *(G-7683)*
United Scoto Senior Activities............... E 740 354-6672
 Portsmouth *(G-12579)*
United Way Central Ohio Inc................ D 614 227-2700
 Columbus *(G-6819)*
United Way Greater Cincinnati.............. D 513 762-7100
 Cincinnati *(G-3558)*
United Way Grter Stark Cnty In............. E 330 491-0445
 Canton *(G-1875)*
United Way of Greater Toledo............... E 419 254-4742
 Toledo *(G-14084)*
United Way of Lake County Inc............. E 440 639-4420
 Mentor *(G-11006)*
United Way of The Grter Dyton............. E 937 225-3060
 Dayton *(G-7686)*
United Way of Yngstown The Mhn......... E 330 746-8494
 Youngstown *(G-15744)*
United Way Summit and Medina........... D 330 762-7601
 Akron *(G-342)*
University of Cincinnati........................ E 513 556-3803
 Cincinnati *(G-3593)*
University Settlement Inc..................... E 216 641-8948
 Cleveland *(G-5086)*
Untd Elderly Clark C Sprngfld............... D 937 323-4948
 Springfield *(G-13307)*
Upreach LLC...................................... E 614 442-7702
 Columbus *(G-6828)*
Urban Leag Grter Sthwstern Ohi........... D 513 281-9955
 Cincinnati *(G-3600)*
US Together Inc.................................. C 614 437-9941
 Columbus *(G-6838)*
Vantage Aging.................................... B 330 785-9770
 Akron *(G-350)*
Vantage Aging.................................... B 513 924-9100
 Cincinnati *(G-3615)*
Vantage Aging.................................... B 440 324-3588
 Elyria *(G-8298)*
Vantage Aging.................................... D 330 253-4597
 Akron *(G-349)*
Vermilion Family YMCA....................... E 440 967-4208
 Vermilion *(G-14410)*
Victim Assistance Program Inc.............. E 330 376-7022
 Akron *(G-351)*
Volunteers America Ohio & Ind............. C 614 253-6100
 Columbus *(G-6856)*
Volunteers of America Inc.................... D 513 381-1954
 Cincinnati *(G-3633)*
Volunteers of America Inc.................... C 513 420-1887
 Middletown *(G-11192)*
Volunteers of America NW Ohio............ E 419 248-3733
 Columbus *(G-6857)*

Volunters Amer Care Facilities.............. C 419 334-9521
 Fremont *(G-8707)*
Wellness Grove LLC........................... E 330 244-1566
 Canton *(G-1885)*
Wesley Community Services LLC.......... C 513 661-2777
 Cincinnati *(G-3654)*
West Ohio Cmnty Action Partnr............. E 419 227-2586
 Lima *(G-9985)*
West Ohio Cmnty Action Partnr............. C 419 227-2586
 Lima *(G-9984)*
West Side Community House................ E 216 771-7297
 Cleveland *(G-5133)*
West Side Ecumenical Ministry............. C 216 325-9369
 Cleveland *(G-5134)*
Westcare Ohio Inc.............................. E 937 259-1898
 Dayton *(G-7718)*
Western Rsrve Area Agcy On Agi.......... E 216 621-0303
 Cleveland *(G-5139)*
Western Rsrve Area Agcy On Agi.......... C 216 621-0303
 Cleveland *(G-5138)*
Wings of Love Services LLC................. E 937 789-8192
 Dayton *(G-7144)*
Wood Cnty Cmmttee On Aging Inc......... E 419 353-5661
 Bowling Green *(G-1334)*
Wood County Chld Svcs Assn............... E 419 352-7588
 Bowling Green *(G-1335)*
Wyandot Cnty Cncil On Aging In........... E 419 294-5733
 Upper Sandusky *(G-14295)*
Y M C A of Ashland Ohio Inc................ D 419 289-0626
 Ashland *(G-516)*
YMCA.. E 330 823-1930
 Alliance *(G-408)*
Young Mens Christian Assn.................. D 330 480-5656
 Youngstown *(G-15754)*
Young MNS Chrstn Assn Cntl STA........ D 330 305-5437
 Canton *(G-1889)*
Young MNS Chrstn Assn Cntl STA........ D 330 498-4082
 Canton *(G-1890)*
Young MNS Chrstn Assn Cntl STA........ D 330 875-1611
 Louisville *(G-10124)*
Young MNS Chrstn Assn Cntl STA........ C 330 830-6275
 Massillon *(G-10675)*
Young MNS Chrstn Assn Grter CL......... E 440 285-7543
 Chardon *(G-2027)*
Young MNS Chrstn Assn Grter CL......... D 216 521-8400
 Lakewood *(G-9688)*
Young MNS Chrstn Assn Grter CL......... E 440 808-8150
 Westlake *(G-15126)*
Young MNS Chrstn Assn Grter CN......... D 513 241-9622
 Cincinnati *(G-3694)*
Young MNS Chrstn Assn Grter CN......... C 513 923-4466
 Cincinnati *(G-3695)*
Young MNS Chrstn Assn Grter CN......... C 513 921-0911
 Cincinnati *(G-3696)*
Young MNS Chrstn Assn Grter CN......... A 513 932-1424
 Lebanon *(G-9800)*
Young MNS Chrstn Assn Grter Dy.......... C 937 312-1810
 Dayton *(G-7733)*
Young MNS Chrstn Assn Grter Dy.......... C 937 223-5201
 Springboro *(G-13210)*
Young MNS Chrstn Assn Grter NY......... C 740 392-9622
 Mount Vernon *(G-11509)*
Young MNS Chrstn Assn of Akron......... E 330 983-5573
 Akron *(G-372)*
Young MNS Chrstn Assn of Akron......... D 330 923-5223
 Cuyahoga Falls *(G-7119)*
Young MNS Chrstn Assn of Akron......... E 330 467-8366
 Macedonia *(G-10210)*
Young MNS Chrstn Assn of Grter........... C 419 866-9622
 Maumee *(G-10782)*
Young MNS Chrstn Assn of Grter........... C 419 691-3523
 Oregon *(G-12148)*

83 SOCIAL SERVICES

Young MNS Chrstn Assn of Grter........... D 419 474-3995
   Toledo *(G-14112)*

Young MNS Chrstn Assn of Grter........... D 419 241-7218
   Toledo *(G-14115)*

Young MNS Chrstn Assn of Grter........... E 419 729-8135
   Sylvania *(G-13579)*

Young MNS Chrstn Assn of Mt Vr........... D 740 392-9622
   Mount Vernon *(G-11510)*

Young MNS Chrstn Assn of Van W........... E 419 238-0443
   Van Wert *(G-14362)*

Young MNS Chrstn Assn Yngstown........... D 330 744-8411
   Youngstown *(G-15755)*

Young Wns Chrstn Assn Clvland........... E 216 881-6878
   Cleveland *(G-5167)*

Young Wns Chrstn Assn of Cnton........... D 330 453-0789
   Canton *(G-1892)*

Young Womens Christian Assn........... D 614 224-9121
   Columbus *(G-6917)*

Youngstown Area Jwish Fdration........... C 330 746-3251
   Youngstown *(G-15756)*

Youngstown Nghborhood Dev Corp........... E 330 480-0423
   Youngstown *(G-15759)*

YWCA Mahoning Valley........... E 330 746-6361
   Youngstown *(G-15762)*

YWCA of Greater Cincinnati........... D 513 241-7090
   Cincinnati *(G-3697)*

YWCA of Northwest Ohio........... D 419 241-3235
   Toledo *(G-14117)*

8331 Job training and related services

A W S Inc........... A 216 941-8800
   Cleveland *(G-3750)*

A W S Inc........... B 216 749-0356
   Cleveland *(G-3751)*

A W S Inc........... E 216 486-0600
   Euclid *(G-8335)*

A W S Inc........... A 440 333-1791
   Rocky River *(G-12738)*

Abilities First Foundation Inc........... D 513 423-9496
   Middletown *(G-11149)*

Ability Works Inc........... C 419 626-1048
   Sandusky *(G-12861)*

Akron Blind Center & Workshop........... E 330 253-2555
   Akron *(G-21)*

Alpha Group of Delaware Inc........... D 740 368-5820
   Delaware *(G-7778)*

Alpha Group of Delaware Inc........... D 740 368-5810
   Delaware *(G-7779)*

Angeline Industries Inc........... E 419 294-4488
   Upper Sandusky *(G-14284)*

Anne Grady Corporation........... C 419 867-7501
   Holland *(G-9279)*

ARC Indstries Inc Frnklin Cnty........... C 614 436-4800
   Columbus *(G-5379)*

ARC Indstries Inc Frnklin Cnty........... C 614 864-2406
   Columbus *(G-5380)*

ARC Indstries Inc Frnklin Cnty........... C 614 267-1207
   Columbus *(G-5381)*

ARC Indstries Inc Frnklin Cnty........... C 614 836-0700
   Groveport *(G-8971)*

ARC Indstries Inc Frnklin Cnty........... C 614 479-2500
   Columbus *(G-5378)*

Belco Works Inc........... D 740 695-0500
   Saint Clairsville *(G-12774)*

Boundless Cmnty Pathways Inc........... A 937 461-0034
   West Carrollton *(G-14644)*

Brown Cnty Bd Mntal Rtardation........... E 937 378-4891
   Georgetown *(G-8798)*

Butler Cnty Bd Dvlpmntal Dsblt........... D 513 785-2870
   Fairfield Township *(G-8457)*

Careerbuilder LLC........... E 513 297-3707
   Cincinnati *(G-2310)*

Center of Voctnl Altrntvs Mntl........... D 614 294-7117
   Columbus *(G-5533)*

▲ Cincinnati Assn For The Blind........... C 513 221-8558
   Cincinnati *(G-2395)*

Cincinnati Works Corp........... C 513 744-9675
   Cincinnati *(G-2431)*

Cleveland Christian Home Inc........... E 216 671-0977
   Cleveland *(G-4006)*

Cleveland Job Corps Center........... C 216 541-2500
   Cleveland *(G-4053)*

CLI Incorporated........... E 419 668-8840
   Norwalk *(G-12007)*

Columbus Literacy Council........... E 614 282-7661
   Columbus *(G-5643)*

Community Action Orgnztion Sco........... C 740 354-7541
   Portsmouth *(G-12548)*

Community Support Services Inc........... C 330 253-9388
   Akron *(G-118)*

Cornucopia Inc........... E 216 521-4600
   Lakewood *(G-9662)*

County of Crawford........... E 419 562-0015
   Bucyrus *(G-1502)*

County of Hardin........... E 419 674-4158
   Kenton *(G-9613)*

County of Lake........... D 440 350-5100
   Mentor *(G-10927)*

County of Sandusky........... D 419 637-2243
   Fremont *(G-8672)*

Creative Learning Workshop LLC........... E 330 393-5929
   Warren *(G-14516)*

D-R Training Center & Workshop........... D 419 289-0470
   Ashland *(G-495)*

Deepwood Industries Inc........... C 440 350-5231
   Mentor *(G-10933)*

Dynamic Eductl Systems Inc........... E 602 995-0116
   Columbus *(G-5796)*

Easter Seals Tristate........... C 513 985-0515
   Cincinnati *(G-2599)*

Employment Development Inc........... E 330 424-7711
   Lisbon *(G-10002)*

Esc of Cuyahoga County........... E 216 524-3000
   Independence *(G-9431)*

Fairhaven Industries Inc........... C 330 505-3644
   Niles *(G-11790)*

Fairhaven Sheltered Workshop........... C 330 652-1116
   Niles *(G-11791)*

▲ Findaway World LLC........... E 440 893-0808
   Solon *(G-13089)*

First Capital Enterprises Inc........... D 740 773-2166
   Chillicothe *(G-2064)*

Goodwill Inds Ashtabula Inc........... D 440 964-3565
   Ashtabula *(G-536)*

Goodwill Inds Centl Ohio Inc........... E 740 439-7000
   Cambridge *(G-1572)*

Goodwill Inds Centl Ohio Inc........... D 614 274-5296
   Columbus *(G-5942)*

Goodwill Inds Centl Ohio Inc........... B 614 294-5181
   Columbus *(G-5941)*

Goodwill Inds NW Ohio Inc........... D 419 255-0070
   Toledo *(G-13822)*

Goodwill Inds Rhbilitation Ctr........... C 330 454-9461
   Canton *(G-1764)*

Goodwill Inds S Centl Ohio........... D 740 702-4000
   Chillicothe *(G-2067)*

Goodwill Inds Wyne Hlmes Cntie........... E 330 264-1300
   Wooster *(G-15341)*

GP Strategies Corporation........... E 513 583-8810
   Cincinnati *(G-2745)*

Great Lkes Cmnty Action Partnr........... E 419 334-8511
   Fremont *(G-8685)*

Great Lkes Cmnty Action Partnr........... E 419 332-8089
   Fremont *(G-8686)*

Great Lkes Cmnty Action Partnr........... E 419 732-7007
   Port Clinton *(G-12529)*

Great Lkes Cmnty Action Partnr........... D 419 333-6068
   Fremont *(G-8684)*

Great Oaks Inst Tech Creer Dev........... E 513 771-8840
   Cincinnati *(G-2763)*

Great Oaks Inst Tech Creer Dev........... D 513 613-3657
   Cincinnati *(G-2764)*

Greene Inc........... D 937 562-4200
   Xenia *(G-15510)*

Gw Business Solutions LLC........... C 740 345-9861
   Newark *(G-11703)*

Handson Central Ohio Inc........... E 614 221-2255
   Columbus *(G-5969)*

Hocking Valley Industries Inc........... E 740 385-2118
   Logan *(G-10022)*

Hockingthensperry Cmnty Action........... E 740 767-4500
   Glouster *(G-8835)*

Hockins Athens Prry Cmnty Acti........... E 740 385-3644
   Athens *(G-573)*

▼ Hunter Defense Tech Inc........... E 216 438-6111
   Solon *(G-13096)*

In Youngstown Area Gdwill Inds........... C 330 759-7921
   Youngstown *(G-15637)*

Integrted Svcs For Bhvral Hlth........... D 740 216-4093
   Logan *(G-10029)*

Integrted Svcs For Bhvral Hlth........... E 740 300-0225
   Nelsonville *(G-11548)*

Ironton Lwrnce Cnty Area Cmnty........... B 740 532-3534
   Ironton *(G-9508)*

Jewish Family Service........... C 614 231-1890
   Columbus *(G-6089)*

Knox New Hope Industries Inc........... C 740 397-4601
   Mount Vernon *(G-11496)*

L & M Products Inc........... E 937 456-7141
   Eaton *(G-8214)*

Licking-Knox Goodwill Inds Inc........... D 740 345-9861
   Newark *(G-11721)*

Linking Emplyment Ablties Ptnt........... E 216 696-2716
   Cleveland *(G-4498)*

Lorain Cnty Bd Dvlpmntal Dsblt........... E 440 329-3734
   Elyria *(G-8271)*

Lott Industries Incorporated........... B 419 891-5215
   Maumee *(G-10741)*

Mahoning Clmbana Training Assn........... E 330 420-9675
   Lisbon *(G-10004)*

Marca Industries Inc........... D 740 387-1035
   Marion *(G-10434)*

Marimor Industries Inc........... D 419 221-1226
   Lima *(G-9933)*

Medina Cnty Sheltered Inds Inc........... E 330 334-4491
   Wadsworth *(G-14443)*

Metzenbaum Sheltered Inds Inc........... D 440 729-1919
   Chesterland *(G-2041)*

Miami University........... B 513 727-3200
   Middletown *(G-11172)*

Midwest Investors Group Inc........... C 270 887-8888
   Galena *(G-8737)*

Moresteamcom LLC........... E 614 602-8190
   Powell *(G-12600)*

Murray Ridge Prod Ctr Inc........... C 440 329-3734
   Elyria *(G-8277)*

Muskingum Starlight Industries........... D 740 453-4622
   Zanesville *(G-15816)*

Nick Amster Inc........... E 330 264-9667
   Wooster *(G-15359)*

Ohio Arson School Inc........... E 740 881-4467
   Galena *(G-8738)*

Ohio Dept Job & Fmly Svcs........... E 614 752-9494
   Columbus *(G-6406)*

Opportnties For Indvdual Chnge........... E 937 323-6461
   Springfield *(G-13280)*

SIC SECTION
83 SOCIAL SERVICES

Portage Prvate Indust Cncil In................ D 330 297-7795
   Ravenna *(G-12639)*

Production Svcs Unlimited Inc................ E 513 695-1658
   Lebanon *(G-9783)*

Quadco Rehabilitation Ctr Inc................ E 419 445-1950
   Archbold *(G-466)*

Quadco Rehabilitation Ctr Inc................ B 419 682-1011
   Stryker *(G-13505)*

Richland Newhope Inds Inc................... E 419 774-4200
   Mansfield *(G-10311)*

Richland Newhope Inds Inc................... E 419 774-4496
   Mansfield *(G-10312)*

Richland Newhope Inds Inc................... E 419 774-4400
   Mansfield *(G-10313)*

Riverview Industries Inc........................ D 419 898-5250
   Oak Harbor *(G-12047)*

RT Industries Inc................................... C 937 339-8313
   Troy *(G-14157)*

Sandco Industries.................................. E 419 547-3273
   Clyde *(G-5209)*

Seneca County....................................... E 419 435-0729
   Fostoria *(G-8625)*

Software Craftsmanship Guild................ E 330 888-8519
   Akron *(G-307)*

Spectrum Supportive Services................ E 216 875-0460
   Cleveland *(G-4931)*

Star Inc.. C 740 354-1517
   Portsmouth *(G-12575)*

Stark County Board of Developm............ A 330 477-5200
   Canton *(G-1858)*

Starlight Enterprises Inc......................... C 330 339-2020
   New Philadelphia *(G-11668)*

TAC Industries Inc.................................. D 937 328-5200
   Springfield *(G-13298)*

TAC Industries Inc.................................. B 937 328-5200
   Springfield *(G-13299)*

U-Co Industries Inc................................ E 937 644-3021
   Marysville *(G-10513)*

United Crbral Plsy Assn Grter................ D 216 791-8363
   Cleveland *(G-5057)*

United Disability Services Inc................ E 330 374-1169
   Akron *(G-341)*

Vgs Inc... C 216 431-7800
   Cleveland *(G-5102)*

Vocational Guidance Services................ B 440 322-1123
   Elyria *(G-8300)*

Vocational Guidance Services................ A 216 431-7800
   Cleveland *(G-5112)*

Vocational Services Inc.......................... E 216 431-8085
   Cleveland *(G-5113)*

Wasco Inc... D 740 373-3418
   Marietta *(G-10411)*

Waycraft Inc... C 419 563-0550
   Bucyrus *(G-1520)*

Weaver Industries Inc............................ C 330 666-5114
   Akron *(G-357)*

Weaver Industries Inc............................ E 330 379-3660
   Akron *(G-356)*

Workshops Inc....................................... D 330 479-3958
   Canton *(G-1887)*

Zanesvlle Wlfare Orgnztion Gdw............ E 740 450-6060
   Zanesville *(G-15843)*

8351 Child day care services

A Childs Hope Intl Inc............................ E 513 771-2244
   Cincinnati *(G-2129)*

Abilities First Foundation Inc................. D 513 423-9496
   Middletown *(G-11149)*

▲ Academy Kids Learning Ctr Inc......... E 614 258-5437
   Columbus *(G-5299)*

Accs Day Care Centers Inc................... E 513 841-2227
   Cincinnati *(G-2139)*

Action For Children Inc......................... E 614 224-0222
   Columbus *(G-5310)*

Advanced Solutions For Educatn........... E 224 518-3111
   Mentor *(G-10908)*

Akron Summit Cmnty Action Agcy......... B 330 376-7730
   Akron *(G-38)*

All About Children Inc........................... C 330 339-9519
   New Philadelphia *(G-11638)*

Allen County Eductl Svc Ctr................... E 419 222-1836
   Lima *(G-9863)*

Anderson Little...................................... E 513 474-7800
   Cincinnati *(G-2200)*

Ashland City School District.................. D 419 289-7967
   Ashland *(G-473)*

Ashland Training Center........................ E 419 281-2767
   Ashland *(G-476)*

Assoction For Dvlpmntlly Dsble............. C 614 447-0606
   Columbus *(G-5397)*

Baco LLC... E 740 454-4840
   South Zanesville *(G-13186)*

Barrington School.................................. E 614 336-3000
   Dublin *(G-7942)*

Bay Village City School Dst................... D 440 617-7330
   Cleveland *(G-3857)*

Brecksvll-Brdview Hts Cy Schl............... E 419 885-8103
   Sylvania *(G-13536)*

Butler Cnty Bd Dvlpmntal Dsblt.............. D 513 785-2815
   Hamilton *(G-9022)*

Canton Country Day School.................... E 330 453-8279
   Canton *(G-1700)*

Canton Montessori Association.............. E 330 452-0148
   Canton *(G-1702)*

Catholic Scial Svcs of Mami Vl.............. E 937 223-7217
   Dayton *(G-7218)*

Child Care Resource Center................... E 216 575-0061
   Cleveland *(G-3969)*

Child Dev Cncil Frnklin Cnty I............... D 614 221-1694
   Columbus *(G-5555)*

Child Dev Cncil Frnklin Cnty I............... E 614 262-8190
   Columbus *(G-5556)*

Child Dev Cncil Frnklin Cnty I............... D 614 416-5178
   Columbus *(G-5558)*

Child Dev Cncil Frnklin Cnty I............... E 614 457-2811
   Columbus *(G-5559)*

Child Dev Cncil Frnklin Cnty I............... E 614 221-1709
   Columbus *(G-5557)*

Child Dev Ctr Jackson Cnty................... E 740 286-3995
   Jackson *(G-9517)*

Child Focus Inc..................................... E 937 444-1613
   Mount Orab *(G-11469)*

Child Focus Inc..................................... D 513 752-1555
   Cincinnati *(G-2355)*

Childrens Hosp Med Ctr Akron.............. D 330 543-8503
   Akron *(G-92)*

Childrens House LLC............................ E 513 451-4551
   Cincinnati *(G-2371)*

Childrens Lab Schools Inc..................... E 937 274-7195
   Dayton *(G-7224)*

Childvine Inc... E 937 748-1260
   Springboro *(G-13196)*

Chillcth-Ross Child Care Ctr I................ E 740 775-7772
   Chillicothe *(G-2054)*

Chippewa School District...................... E 330 658-4868
   Doylestown *(G-7914)*

Christ King Catholic Church.................. E 614 236-8838
   Columbus *(G-5569)*

Christian Missionary Alliance................ E 614 457-4085
   Columbus *(G-5570)*

Christian Rivertree School.................... D 330 494-1860
   Massillon *(G-10635)*

Christian Schools Inc........................... D 330 857-7311
   Kidron *(G-9635)*

Church On North Coast.......................... E 440 960-1100
   Lorain *(G-10063)*

Cincinnati Early Learning Ctr................ D 513 367-2129
   Harrison *(G-9099)*

Cincinnati Early Learning Ctr................ E 513 961-2690
   Cincinnati *(G-2410)*

City of Lakewood.................................. E 216 226-0080
   Cleveland *(G-3989)*

Cleveland Child Care Inc...................... E 216 631-3211
   Cleveland *(G-4005)*

Colerain Dry Rdge Chldcare Ltd............ E 513 923-4300
   Cincinnati *(G-2476)*

Colonial Senior Services Inc................. D 513 856-8600
   Hamilton *(G-9030)*

Colonial Senior Services Inc................. E 513 867-4006
   Hamilton *(G-9031)*

Columbus Christian Center Inc.............. E 614 416-9673
   Columbus *(G-5619)*

Columbus City School District............... E 614 421-2305
   Columbus *(G-5620)*

Columbus City School District............... D 614 365-5456
   Columbus *(G-5621)*

Columbus Early Learning Ctrs............... E 614 253-5525
   Columbus *(G-5629)*

Columbus Mntessori Educatn Ctr.......... E 614 231-3790
   Columbus *(G-5645)*

Community Action Agcy Clmbana.......... D 330 424-7221
   Lisbon *(G-9999)*

Community Action Comm Blmont C...... E 740 695-0293
   Saint Clairsville *(G-12786)*

Community Action Comm Erie Hro........ E 419 935-6481
   Willard *(G-15166)*

Community Action Prgram Corp O........ C 740 962-3792
   Malta *(G-10231)*

Compass School Waterstone LLC......... E 513 683-8833
   Cincinnati *(G-2486)*

Consolidated Learning Ctrs Inc............. E 614 791-0050
   Dublin *(G-7972)*

Corporation For OH Appalachian........... E 330 364-8882
   New Philadelphia *(G-11645)*

Coshocton Cnty Head Start Inc.............. E 740 622-3667
   Coshocton *(G-6981)*

Council On Rur Svc Prgrams Inc........... D 937 452-1090
   Camden *(G-1589)*

Council On Rur Svc Prgrams Inc........... D 937 773-0773
   Piqua *(G-12439)*

Council On Rur Svc Prgrams Inc........... D 937 492-8787
   Sidney *(G-13025)*

Countryside Yung MNS Chrstn As........ D 513 677-3702
   Maineville *(G-10227)*

County of Guernsey............................... E 740 439-5555
   Cambridge *(G-1567)*

Creative Child Care Inc......................... E 614 863-3500
   Columbus *(G-5720)*

Creative Connections LLC.................... D 513 389-0213
   Cincinnati *(G-2516)*

Creative Playroom................................. E 440 248-3100
   Solon *(G-13079)*

Creative Playroom................................. D 216 475-6464
   Cleveland *(G-4135)*

Crossroad Health................................... C 440 358-7370
   Painesville *(G-12226)*

Cwcc Inc.. D 937 236-6116
   Dayton *(G-7265)*

CWff Child Development Ctr.................. E 513 569-5660
   Cincinnati *(G-2528)*

David Evangelical Lutheran Ch.............. E 614 920-3517
   Canal Winchester *(G-1603)*

Discovery School................................... E 419 756-8880
   Mansfield *(G-10258)*

Dover City Schools................................ E 330 343-8880
   Dover *(G-7881)*

Employee Codes: A=Over 500 employees, B=251-500
C=101-250, D=51-100, E=20-50, F=10-19, G=1-9

83 SOCIAL SERVICES

Company	Phone
Dublin Latchkey — Dublin (G-7996)	E 614 793-0871
Early Chldhood Enrchment Ctr I — Cleveland (G-4196)	E 216 991-9761
East Dayton Christian School — Dayton (G-7132)	E 937 252-5400
Empower Learn Create Inc — Cincinnati (G-2617)	E 513 961-2825
Fairmount Montessori Assn — Cleveland (G-4235)	D 216 321-7571
Family YMCA of LANcstr&fairfld — Lancaster (G-9723)	D 740 277-7373
First Assembly Child Care — Mansfield (G-10263)	E 419 529-6501
First Assembly of God — Akron (G-160)	E 330 836-1436
First Christian Church — Canton (G-1753)	E 330 445-2700
First Community Church — Columbus (G-5860)	E 614 488-0681
Forest Park Christian School — Columbus (G-5878)	E 614 888-5282
G M N Tri Cnty Cmnty Action CM — Cambridge (G-1571)	E 740 732-2388
Gateway To Grace Fundation Inc — Fairfield (G-8416)	E 513 869-4645
Geary Fmly Yung MNS Chrstn Ass — Fostoria (G-8617)	E 419 435-6608
Goddard School — Cincinnati (G-2735)	E 513 271-6311
Goddard School — Westerville (G-14981)	E 614 865-2100
Grace Brthren Ch Columbus Ohio — Westerville (G-14897)	E 614 888-7733
Great Lkes Cmnty Action Partnr — Fremont (G-8685)	E 419 334-8511
Great Lkes Cmnty Action Partnr — Port Clinton (G-12529)	E 419 732-7007
Great Lkes Cmnty Action Partnr — Fremont (G-8684)	D 419 333-6068
Great Mami Vly Yung MNS Chrstn — Hamilton (G-9046)	D 513 887-0001
Great Miami Valley YMCA — Fairfield (G-8417)	D 513 829-3091
Great Miami Valley YMCA — Fairfield Township (G-8461)	D 513 892-9622
Great Miami Valley YMCA — Hamilton (G-9048)	D 513 887-0014
Great Miami Valley YMCA — Hamilton (G-9049)	D 513 868-9622
Hamilton County Eductl Svc Ctr — Cincinnati (G-2795)	B 513 674-4200
Hanna Perkins School — Cleveland (G-4348)	C 216 991-4472
Harcatus Tr-Cnty Cmnty Action — New Philadelphia (G-11652)	D 330 602-5442
Harrison Avenue Assembly God — Harrison (G-9107)	E 513 367-6109
Heartland Christian School Inc — Columbiana (G-5236)	C 330 482-2331
Heathers Day Care LLC — Defiance (G-7748)	E 419 784-9600
Hershey Montessori School Inc — Huntsburg (G-9382)	D 440 357-0918
Hewlettco Inc — Strongsville (G-13461)	E 440 238-4600
Hockingthensperry Cmnty Action — Nelsonville (G-11546)	D 740 753-9404
Hockingthensperry Cmnty Action — New Lexington (G-11625)	D 740 342-1333
Horizon Education Centers — Elyria (G-8257)	E 440 322-0288
Horizon Education Centers — Elyria (G-8258)	E 440 458-5115
Horizon Education Centers — Lorain (G-10077)	E 440 277-5437
Hudson Montessori Association — Hudson (G-9356)	E 330 650-0424
Hugs Hearts Early Lrng Ctr Inc — Columbus (G-5262)	E 614 848-6777
Hunt Tiffani — Cleveland (G-4389)	E 216 258-1923
Intergncy Emplyees Child Care — Chillicothe (G-2073)	E 740 772-7086
Ironton Lwrnce Cnty Area Cmnty — Ironton (G-9508)	B 740 532-3534
J-Nan Enterprises Llc — Hudson (G-9358)	E 330 653-3766
Jewish Cmnty Ctr of Grter Clmb — Columbus (G-6088)	C 614 231-2731
Jewish Day Schl Assn Grter Clv — Pepper Pike (G-12300)	D 216 763-1400
Karing 4 Kids Learning Center — Cincinnati (G-2930)	E 513 931-5273
Kelna Inc — Youngstown (G-15645)	E 330 729-0167
Kennedy Heights Montessori Ctr — Cincinnati (G-2935)	E 513 631-8135
Kiddie Day Care of Champion — Warren (G-14533)	E 330 847-9393
Kids First Academy LLC — Cincinnati (G-2108)	E 513 752-2811
Kids World Daycare — Wheelersburg (G-15129)	E 740 776-4548
Kids-Play Inc — Mogadore (G-11329)	E 330 896-2400
Kids-Play Inc — Stow (G-13379)	E 330 678-5554
Kinder Garden School — Blue Ash (G-1195)	E 513 791-4300
Kindercare Learning Ctrs LLC — Cleveland (G-4466)	E 440 442-8067
Kindercare Learning Ctrs LLC — Westerville (G-14991)	E 614 901-4000
Kleptz Early Learning Center — Englewood (G-8312)	D 937 832-6750
Knox County Head Start Inc — Mount Vernon (G-11495)	E 740 397-1344
Ladan Learning Center LLC — Columbus (G-6133)	E 614 426-4306
Lake Cnty Yung MNS Chrstn Assn — Painesville (G-12231)	C 440 352-3303
Lake County YMCA — Madison (G-10219)	C 440 428-5125
Lake County YMCA — Perry (G-12307)	C 440 259-2724
Lake County YMCA — Willoughby (G-15198)	C 440 946-1160
Lakewood Catholic Academy — Lakewood (G-9672)	E 216 521-4352
Laurel School — Shaker Heights (G-12980)	C 216 464-1441
Lawrence Cnty Bd Dev Dsblities — South Point (G-13176)	E 740 377-2356
Learning Spectrum Ltd — Lewis Center (G-9825)	E 614 316-1160
Learning Spectrum Ltd — Columbus (G-6151)	E 614 844-5433
Liberty Community Center — Delaware (G-7814)	E 740 369-3876
Lillian and Betty Ratner Schl — Cleveland (G-4496)	E 216 464-0033
Lima Family YMCA — Lima (G-9923)	D 419 223-6055
Lima Family YMCA — Lima (G-9922)	D 419 223-6045
Little Drmers Big Blievers LLC — Columbus (G-6169)	E 614 824-4666
Little Scholars Inc — Willoughby (G-15206)	E 440 951-3596
Lorain Cnty Cmnty Action Agcy — Lorain (G-10085)	C 440 246-0480
Loving Care Day Care Ottawa LL — Ottawa (G-12188)	E 419 523-3133
Madison Local School District — Mansfield (G-10284)	E 419 589-7851
Mahoning Youngstown Community — Youngstown (G-15662)	E 330 747-0236
Mangos Place — Powell (G-12598)	D 614 499-1611
Mercy Montessori Center — Cincinnati (G-3046)	E 513 475-6700
Miami Valley Hospital — Dayton (G-7494)	B 937 224-3916
Miami Valley School — Dayton (G-7499)	D 937 434-4444
Miami Vly Child Dev Ctrs Inc — Brookville (G-1446)	E 937 833-6600
Miami Vly Child Dev Ctrs Inc — Dayton (G-7501)	E 937 228-1644
Miami Vly Child Dev Ctrs Inc — Dayton (G-7502)	E 937 258-2470
Miami Vly Child Dev Ctrs Inc — Springfield (G-13274)	E 937 325-2559
Miami Vly Child Dev Ctrs Inc — Dayton (G-7500)	D 937 226-5664
Mini University Inc — Oxford (G-12213)	D 513 275-5184
Mini University Inc — Dayton (G-7509)	D 937 426-1414
Ministerial Day Care Assn — Cleveland (G-4587)	E 216 881-6924
Ministerial Day Care-Headstart — Cleveland (G-4588)	C 216 707-0344
Mk Childcare Warsaw Ave LLC — Cincinnati (G-3069)	E 513 922-6279
Mlm Childcare LLC — Cincinnati (G-3070)	E 513 623-8243
Montessori School Bowl Green — Bowling Green (G-1327)	E 419 352-4203
Mount Washington Baptist Ch — Cincinnati (G-3083)	E 513 231-4334
N & E Learning LLC — Grove City (G-8939)	E 614 270-1559
Nbdc II LLC — Cincinnati (G-3100)	E 513 681-5439
New Dawn Health Care Inc — Dover (G-7895)	C 330 343-5521
New Hope Christian Academy — Circleville (G-3714)	E 740 477-6427
Nichalex Inc — Youngstown (G-15676)	E 330 726-1422
Nicoles Child Care Center — Cleveland (G-4645)	E 216 991-2416
Nightingale Montessori Inc — Springfield (G-13277)	E 937 324-0336
North Broadway Childrens Ctr — Columbus (G-6365)	E 614 262-6222
Northwest Child Development An — Dayton (G-7532)	E 937 559-9565
Northwest Local School Dst — Cincinnati (G-3127)	E 513 923-1000
Nurtury — Medina (G-10870)	E 330 723-1800
Ohio Dept Job & Fmly Svcs — Columbus (G-6407)	E 614 466-1213

SIC SECTION — 83 SOCIAL SERVICES

Ohioguidestone .... C 216 433-4136
  Cleveland (G-4692)
Ohioguidestone .... E 440 234-2006
  Berea (G-1079)
Old Trail School .... D 330 666-1118
  Bath (G-754)
Open Door Christn Schools Inc .... D 440 322-6386
  Elyria (G-8283)
Orange Early Childhood Center .... E 216 831-4909
  Cleveland (G-4706)
Our Lady Bethlehem Schools Inc .... E 614 459-8285
  Columbus (G-6491)
Overfeld Erly Chldhood Program .... E 937 339-5111
  Troy (G-14151)
P J & R J Connection Inc .... E 513 398-2777
  Mason (G-10589)
Paulding Exempted Vlg Schl Dst .... E 419 594-3309
  Paulding (G-12286)
Playland Day Care Ltd .... E 419 625-8200
  Castalia (G-1915)
Portage Prvate Indust Cncil In .... D 330 297-7795
  Ravenna (G-12639)
Potential Development Program .... C 330 746-7641
  Youngstown (G-15696)
Powell Enterprises Inc .... E 614 882-0111
  Westerville (G-14930)
Preble County Head Start .... C 937 456-2800
  Eaton (G-8221)
Primrose School Lewis Cente .... E 740 548-5808
  Powell (G-12603)
Professional Maint of Columbus .... E 513 579-1762
  Cincinnati (G-3245)
Promedica Health System Inc .... A 567 585-9600
  Toledo (G-13972)
R & J Investment Co Inc .... C 440 934-5204
  Avon (G-663)
Rainbow Rascals Lrng Ctr Inc .... D 513 769-7529
  Blue Ash (G-1230)
Rainbow Station Day Care Inc .... E 614 759-8667
  Pickerington (G-12409)
Rainbow Station Day Care Inc .... E 614 575-5040
  Reynoldsburg (G-12674)
Rainbow Station Day Care Inc .... E 614 759-8667
  Pickerington (G-12410)
Roman Catholic Diocese Toledo .... D 419 243-7255
  Toledo (G-13995)
Royal Rdmer Lthran Ch N Rylton .... E 440 237-7958
  North Royalton (G-11949)
Royalmont Academy .... E 513 754-0555
  Mason (G-10602)
Saint Cecilia Church .... E 614 878-5353
  Columbus (G-6637)
Seton Catholic School Hudson .... D 330 342-4200
  Hudson (G-9373)
Share and Kare Inc .... D 330 493-6600
  Canton (G-1851)
Sisters of Ntre Dame of Chrdon .... E 440 279-0575
  Chardon (G-2020)
Small Hnds Big Drams Lrng Ctrs .... E 440 708-0559
  Chagrin Falls (G-1990)
Small World Childrens Center .... E 513 867-9963
  Hamilton (G-9081)
Something Special Lrng Ctr Inc .... E 419 878-4190
  Waterville (G-14594)
South Side Learning & Dev Ctr .... D 614 212-4696
  Columbus (G-6693)
South Suburban Montessori Assn .... E 440 526-1966
  Brecksville (G-1367)
Southwest Lcking Kndrgrten Ctr .... E 740 927-1130
  Pataskala (G-12277)
St Francis De Sales Church .... D 740 345-9874
  Newark (G-11749)

St Jhns Evang Lthran Ch Mrysv .... E 937 644-5540
  Marysville (G-10510)
St Johns Villa .... C 330 627-4662
  Carrollton (G-1913)
St Marys City Board Education .... C 419 394-2616
  Saint Marys (G-12836)
St Pauls Catholic Church .... E 330 724-1263
  Akron (G-308)
St Stphens Cmnty Hmes Ltd Prt .... D 614 294-6347
  Columbus (G-6706)
St Thomas Episcopal Church .... E 513 831-6908
  Terrace Park (G-13614)
Step Forward .... D 216 696-9077
  Cleveland (G-4949)
Stepforward .... D 216 736-2934
  Cleveland (G-4953)
Sycamore Board of Education .... C 513 489-3937
  Montgomery (G-11375)
Sylvania Cmnty Svcs Ctr Inc .... E 419 885-2451
  Sylvania (G-13574)
Texas Migrant Council Inc .... E 937 846-0699
  New Carlisle (G-11608)
Thrive Ministries Inc .... E 419 873-0870
  Perrysburg (G-12376)
Trinity United Methodist Ch .... E 614 488-3659
  Columbus (G-6792)
Troy Christian Schools Inc .... E 937 339-5692
  Troy (G-14161)
Tutor Time Learning Ctrs LLC .... C 513 755-6690
  West Chester (G-14779)
United Rhblttion Svcs Grter Dy .... D 937 233-1230
  Dayton (G-7683)
Upper Arlington City Schl Dst .... E 614 487-5133
  Columbus (G-6827)
Upper Arlington Lutheran Ch .... E 614 451-3736
  Hilliard (G-9238)
Van Wert Cnty Day Care Ctr Inc .... E 419 238-9918
  Van Wert (G-14356)
Vermilion Family YMCA .... E 440 967-4208
  Vermilion (G-14410)
Wenzler Day Learning Ctr Inc .... E 937 435-8200
  Dayton (G-7717)
West After School Center .... E 740 653-5678
  Lancaster (G-9749)
West Branch Local School Dst .... E 330 938-1122
  Alliance (G-404)
West Ohio Cmnty Action Partnr .... C 419 227-2586
  Lima (G-9984)
West Side Montessori .... D 419 866-1931
  Toledo (G-14104)
Whitehall City Schools .... E 614 417-5680
  Columbus (G-6887)
Whitehead Falana .... E 513 742-1766
  Cincinnati (G-3668)
Wishing Well Acquisition Ltd .... E 440 237-5000
  Cleveland (G-5154)
Wooster Christian School Inc .... E 330 345-6436
  Wooster (G-15390)
Y M C A Hilltop Educare Inc .... E 614 752-8877
  Columbus (G-6915)
Y M C A of Ashland Ohio Inc .... E 419 289-0626
  Ashland (G-516)
YMCA .... E 330 823-1930
  Alliance (G-408)
Young Mens Christian Assn .... D 740 373-2250
  Marietta (G-10415)
Young Mens Christian Assn .... D 330 480-5656
  Youngstown (G-15754)
Young MNS Chrstn Assn Cntl STA .... D 330 305-5437
  Canton (G-1889)
Young MNS Chrstn Assn Cntl STA .... D 330 498-4082
  Canton (G-1890)

Young MNS Chrstn Assn Cntl STA .... D 330 875-1611
  Louisville (G-10124)
Young MNS Chrstn Assn Cntl STA .... C 330 830-6275
  Massillon (G-10675)
Young MNS Chrstn Assn Grter CL .... E 440 285-7543
  Chardon (G-2027)
Young MNS Chrstn Assn Grter CL .... D 216 521-8400
  Lakewood (G-9688)
Young MNS Chrstn Assn Grter CN .... B 513 791-5000
  Blue Ash (G-1275)
Young MNS Chrstn Assn Grter CN .... C 513 731-0115
  Cincinnati (G-3692)
Young MNS Chrstn Assn Grter CN .... B 513 474-1400
  Cincinnati (G-3693)
Young MNS Chrstn Assn Grter CN .... C 513 241-9622
  Cincinnati (G-3694)
Young MNS Chrstn Assn Grter CN .... C 513 923-4466
  Cincinnati (G-3695)
Young MNS Chrstn Assn Grter CN .... C 513 921-0911
  Cincinnati (G-3696)
Young MNS Chrstn Assn Grter CN .... A 513 932-1424
  Lebanon (G-9800)
Young MNS Chrstn Assn Grter Dy .... C 937 228-9622
  Dayton (G-7732)
Young MNS Chrstn Assn Grter Dy .... C 937 312-1810
  Dayton (G-7733)
Young MNS Chrstn Assn Grter Dy .... C 937 223-5201
  Springboro (G-13210)
Young MNS Chrstn Assn Grter NY .... C 740 392-9622
  Mount Vernon (G-11509)
Young MNS Chrstn Assn of Akron .... D 330 376-1335
  Akron (G-368)
Young MNS Chrstn Assn of Akron .... E 330 724-1255
  Akron (G-371)
Young MNS Chrstn Assn of Akron .... E 330 983-5573
  Akron (G-372)
Young MNS Chrstn Assn of Akron .... D 330 923-5223
  Cuyahoga Falls (G-7119)
Young MNS Chrstn Assn of Akron .... E 330 467-8366
  Macedonia (G-10210)
Young MNS Chrstn Assn of Akron .... D 419 523-5233
  Ottawa (G-12196)
Young MNS Chrstn Assn of Akron .... E 330 899-9622
  Uniontown (G-14272)
Young MNS Chrstn Assn of Grter .... C 419 866-9622
  Maumee (G-10782)
Young MNS Chrstn Assn of Grter .... C 419 691-3523
  Oregon (G-12148)
Young MNS Chrstn Assn of Grter .... D 419 474-3995
  Toledo (G-14112)
Young MNS Chrstn Assn of Grter .... D 419 241-7218
  Toledo (G-14115)
Young MNS Chrstn Assn of Grter .... E 419 729-8135
  Sylvania (G-13579)
Young MNS Chrstn Assn of Mt Vr .... D 740 392-9622
  Mount Vernon (G-11510)
Young MNS Chrstn Assn of Van W .... E 419 238-0443
  Van Wert (G-14362)
Young Wns Chrstn Assn Clvland .... E 216 881-6878
  Cleveland (G-5167)
Young Wns Chrstn Assn of Cnton .... D 330 453-0789
  Canton (G-1892)
Young Womens Christian Assn .... D 614 224-9121
  Columbus (G-6917)
Younglearnersworld .... E 937 426-5437
  Beavercreek (G-918)
YWCA Mahoning Valley .... E 330 746-6361
  Youngstown (G-15762)
YWCA of Greater Cincinnati .... D 513 241-7090
  Cincinnati (G-3697)
YWCA of Northwest Ohio .... D 419 241-3235
  Toledo (G-14117)

Employee Codes: A=Over 500 employees, B=251-500
C=101-250, D=51-100, E=20-50, F=10-19, G=1-9

83 SOCIAL SERVICES

8361 Residential care

Abbewood Limited Partnership............ E 440 366-8980
   Elyria *(G-8231)*
Abilities First Foundation Inc................ D 513 423-9496
   Middletown *(G-11149)*
Ability Ctr of Greater Toledo................. E 419 517-7123
   Sylvania *(G-13535)*
Abraxas Cornell Group LLC................. C 419 747-3322
   Shelby *(G-13004)*
Adriel School Inc.................................. D 937 465-0010
   West Liberty *(G-14859)*
Ahf Ohio Inc... D 937 256-4663
   Dayton *(G-7160)*
Ahf Ohio Inc... D 614 760-8870
   Dublin *(G-7923)*
Ahf Ohio Inc... D 330 725-4123
   Medina *(G-10805)*
Alexson Services Inc............................ D 513 874-0423
   Fairfield *(G-8389)*
Altercare Inc.. E 330 929-4231
   Cuyahoga Falls *(G-7037)*
Alternative Residences Two Inc............ D 740 425-1565
   Barnesville *(G-716)*
Alternative Residences Two Inc............ D 330 627-7552
   Carrollton *(G-1902)*
Alternative Residences Two Inc............ D 330 833-5564
   Massillon *(G-10630)*
Alternative Residences Two Inc............ C 740 526-0514
   Saint Clairsville *(G-12773)*
American Health Foundation Inc........... A 614 798-5110
   Chillicothe *(G-2050)*
American Nursing Care Inc................... B 614 847-0555
   Zanesville *(G-15767)*
Anne Grady Corporation....................... C 419 380-8985
   Holland *(G-9278)*
Antwerp Mnor Asssted Lving LLC......... E 419 258-1500
   Antwerp *(G-447)*
Ardmore Inc... D 330 535-2601
   Akron *(G-55)*
Ashtabula Cnty Rsdntial Svcs C............ E 440 593-6404
   Conneaut *(G-6938)*
Assoction For Dvlpmntlly Dsble............. C 614 447-0606
   Columbus *(G-5397)*
Assoction For Dvlpmntlly Dsble............. E 614 486-4361
   Westerville *(G-14961)*
Atrium Living Centers of .... E 614 416-2662
   Columbus *(G-5405)*
Basinger Lfe Enhncmnt Sprt Svc.......... D 614 557-5461
   Marysville *(G-10474)*
Bellefaire Jewish Chld Bur.................... B 216 932-2800
   Shaker Heights *(G-12974)*
Benjamin Rose Institute....................... C 216 791-3580
   Cleveland *(G-3868)*
Bittersweet Inc..................................... D 419 875-6986
   Whitehouse *(G-15138)*
Blue Stream LLC.................................. D 330 659-6166
   Richfield *(G-12688)*
Bradley Bay Assisted Living.................. E 440 871-4509
   Bay Village *(G-758)*
Brittany Residential Inc........................ E 216 692-3212
   Cleveland *(G-3896)*
Browning Mesonic Community.............. E 419 878-4055
   Waterville *(G-14593)*
Buckeye Community Services Inc......... E 740 797-4166
   The Plains *(G-13615)*
Buckeye Ranch Inc............................... D 614 543-1380
   Columbus *(G-5478)*
Buckeye Ranch Inc............................... C 614 875-2371
   Grove City *(G-8902)*
Butler Cnty Bd Dvlpmntal Dsblt............. D 513 867-5913
   Fairfield *(G-8396)*

Butler Cnty Bd Dvlpmntal Dsblt............. D 513 785-2870
   Fairfield Township *(G-8457)*
Butler Cnty Bd Dvlpmntal Dsblt............. D 513 785-2815
   Hamilton *(G-9022)*
Butterfield Recovery Group LLC........... E 513 932-4673
   Oregonia *(G-12149)*
C I E Inc... B 419 986-5566
   Burgoon *(G-1523)*
Cardinal Retirement Village.................. E 330 928-7888
   Cuyahoga Falls *(G-7052)*
Caritas Inc.. E 419 332-2589
   Fremont *(G-8668)*
Carlton Manor Nursing and.................. C 740 335-7143
   Wshngtn Ct Hs *(G-15477)*
Carriage Court Company Inc................ C 614 871-8000
   Grove City *(G-8905)*
Carriage Crt-Mrysvlle Ltd Prtn.............. E 937 642-2202
   Marysville *(G-10478)*
Catholic Charities Corporation............. D 216 432-0680
   Cleveland *(G-3932)*
Champaign Residential Svcs Inc........... A 740 852-3850
   London *(G-10039)*
Champaign Residential Svcs Inc........... D 937 653-1320
   Urbana *(G-14301)*
Cherry St Mission Ministries................. E 419 242-5141
   Toledo *(G-13731)*
Childrens Cmprhensive Svcs Inc........... D 419 589-5511
   Mansfield *(G-10252)*
Choices In Community Living............... D 937 325-0344
   Springfield *(G-13226)*
Choices In Community Living............... C 937 898-3655
   Dayton *(G-7225)*
Christian Chld HM Ohio Inc.................. D 330 345-7949
   Wooster *(G-15320)*
Christian Worthington Vlg Inc.............. D 614 846-6076
   Columbus *(G-5571)*
Church of God Retirement Cmnty......... E 513 422-5600
   Middletown *(G-11156)*
Cincinntis Optmum Rsdntial Env.......... C 513 771-2673
   Cincinnati *(G-2436)*
City Mission... E 216 431-3510
   Cleveland *(G-3976)*
Clark Cnty Bd Dvlpmntal Dsblti............. E 937 328-5200
   Springfield *(G-13230)*
Clark Memorial Home Assn.................. E 937 399-4262
   Springfield *(G-13234)*
Cleveland Christian Home Inc.............. E 216 671-0977
   Cleveland *(G-4006)*
College Park Inc................................... C 740 623-4607
   Coshocton *(G-6978)*
Columbus Nghbrhood Hlth Ctr In.......... D 614 645-2300
   Columbus *(G-5650)*
Community Living Experiences............ E 614 588-0320
   Columbus *(G-5671)*
Community Rstrtion Ctrs Inc St............ D 330 456-3565
   Canton *(G-1720)*
Community Support Services Inc......... C 330 253-9388
   Akron *(G-118)*
Compass Family and Cmnty Svcs......... E 330 782-5664
   Youngstown *(G-15582)*
Compass Family and Cmnty Svcs......... E 330 782-5664
   Youngstown *(G-15584)*
Compdrug.. D 614 224-4506
   Columbus *(G-5675)*
Comprhnsive Addction Svc Syste........ D 419 241-8827
   Toledo *(G-13755)*
Concord Reserve.................................. E 440 871-0090
   Westlake *(G-15053)*
County of Allen..................................... E 419 221-1103
   Lima *(G-9881)*
County of Auglaize............................... D 419 629-2419
   New Bremen *(G-11596)*

County of Cuyahoga............................. A 216 241-8230
   Cleveland *(G-4126)*
County of Logan................................... C 937 592-2901
   Bellefontaine *(G-1027)*
County of Lorain.................................. D 440 329-3734
   Elyria *(G-8238)*
County of Lorain.................................. D 440 329-5340
   Elyria *(G-8240)*
County of Ross.................................... E 740 773-4169
   Chillicothe *(G-2062)*
County of Wayne.................................. D 330 345-5340
   Wooster *(G-15329)*
Crossroads Center............................... C 513 475-5300
   Cincinnati *(G-2517)*
Crystalwood Inc................................... E 513 605-1000
   Cincinnati *(G-2519)*
D-R Training Center & Workshop......... D 419 289-0470
   Ashland *(G-495)*
Dag-Dell Inc... E 740 754-2600
   Dresden *(G-7917)*
Deaconess Long Term Care of MI......... A 513 487-3600
   Cincinnati *(G-2551)*
Department of Health Ohio................... E 419 447-1450
   Tiffin *(G-13627)*
Dtac of Ohio LLC................................. E 614 443-5454
   Columbus *(G-5787)*
Early Childhood Resource Ctr............... D 330 491-3272
   Canton *(G-1740)*
Eastwood Residential Svcs Inc............. E 440 428-8169
   Madison *(G-10215)*
Echoing Hills Village Inc....................... D 740 594-3541
   Athens *(G-567)*
Echoing Hills Village Inc....................... C 740 327-2311
   Warsaw *(G-14591)*
Echos Haven LLC................................. E 513 715-1189
   Harrison *(G-9103)*
Embracing Autism Inc........................... E 614 559-0077
   Columbus *(G-5812)*
Evant... E 330 920-1517
   Stow *(G-13367)*
Fairhaven Industries............................. E 330 652-6168
   Niles *(G-11789)*
Feridean Commons LLC........................ E 614 898-7488
   Westerville *(G-14895)*
First Community Village........................ B 614 324-4455
   Columbus *(G-5861)*
Flat Rock Care Center.......................... D 419 483-7330
   Flat Rock *(G-8600)*
Fountains At Canterbury...................... E 405 751-3600
   Toledo *(G-13810)*
Friends of Good Shepherd Manor......... E 740 289-2861
   Lucasville *(G-10178)*
Friendship Vlg of Clumbus Ohio............ C 614 890-8282
   Columbus *(G-5898)*
Garden Manor Extended Care Cen....... C 513 420-5972
   Middletown *(G-11164)*
Gardens Western Reserve Inc.............. E 330 928-4500
   Cuyahoga Falls *(G-7077)*
Gateways To Better Living Inc.............. E 330 792-2854
   Youngstown *(G-15618)*
Gentlebrook Inc.................................... D 330 877-3694
   Hartville *(G-9125)*
Glen Wesley Inc................................... D 614 888-7492
   Columbus *(G-5937)*
Greenbrier Senior Living Cmnty............ D 440 888-0400
   Cleveland *(G-4338)*
Harbor Retirement Assoc LLC.............. D 216 925-4898
   Shaker Heights *(G-12977)*
Hattie Lrlham Ctr For Chldren.............. E 330 274-2272
   Akron *(G-189)*
Hattie Lrlham Ctr For Chldren.............. E 440 232-9320
   Bedford Heights *(G-998)*

SIC SECTION
83 SOCIAL SERVICES

Hattie Lrlham Ctr For Chldren............ E 330 274-2272
  Uniontown *(G-14256)*

Hattie Lrlham Ctr For Chldren............ C 330 274-2272
  Mantua *(G-10331)*

Havar Inc.. D 740 594-3533
  Athens *(G-570)*

Hcf Management Inc........................... D 419 999-2055
  Lima *(G-9897)*

Health Recovery Services Inc............ C 740 592-6720
  Athens *(G-571)*

Heinzerling Foundation......................... B 614 272-2000
  Columbus *(G-5982)*

Helen Purcell Home............................. E 740 453-1745
  Zanesville *(G-15800)*

Help Foundation Inc............................ E 216 486-5258
  Cleveland *(G-4357)*

Heritage Crossing................................. E 330 510-3110
  Akron *(G-191)*

Heritage Legacy Hlth Svcs LLC......... E 740 456-8245
  New Boston *(G-11593)*

Hill View Retirement Center................. C 740 354-3135
  Portsmouth *(G-12554)*

Hilliard Operator LLC.......................... A 614 503-4414
  Hilliard *(G-9201)*

Hitchcock Center For Women Inc....... E 216 421-0662
  Cleveland *(G-4366)*

Hopewell.. E 440 426-2000
  Middlefield *(G-11141)*

Horizons Tuscarawas/Carroll.............. C 330 262-4183
  Wooster *(G-15346)*

I AM Boundless Inc.............................. B 614 844-3800
  Worthington *(G-15421)*

Interval Brotherhood Homes Inc......... C 330 644-4095
  Coventry Township *(G-7011)*

Jefferson Rehab & Wellness LLC....... C 440 576-0043
  Andover *(G-439)*

Jo-Lin Health Center Inc..................... E 740 532-0860
  Ironton *(G-9510)*

Josina Lott Foundation........................ E 419 866-9013
  Toledo *(G-13871)*

Judson.. B 216 791-2555
  Cleveland *(G-4445)*

Judson Services Inc............................ E 216 791-2004
  Chagrin Falls *(G-1983)*

Kemper Hse Hghland Hts Oper LL..... D 440 461-0600
  Highland Heights *(G-9167)*

Kentridge At Golden Pond Ltd............ E 330 677-4040
  Kent *(G-9584)*

Kingston Rsdnce Perrysburg LLC...... C 419 872-6200
  Perrysburg *(G-12350)*

Koinonia Homes Inc............................ B 216 588-8777
  Cleveland *(G-4469)*

Ladd Inc.. E 513 861-4089
  Cincinnati *(G-2962)*

Lakeside Manor Inc.............................. E 330 549-2545
  North Lima *(G-11890)*

Lantern of Chagrin Valley.................... E 440 996-5084
  Chagrin Falls *(G-1962)*

Lighthouse Youth Services Inc........... E 740 634-3094
  Bainbridge *(G-685)*

Little Ssters of Poor Bltmore................ D 513 281-8001
  Cincinnati *(G-2982)*

Living Arrngmnts For Dvlpmntll........... C 513 861-5233
  Cincinnati *(G-2983)*

Lutheran Home..................................... D 419 724-1414
  Toledo *(G-13898)*

Lutheran Homes Society Inc.............. C 419 334-5500
  Fremont *(G-8691)*

Lutheran Homes Society Inc.............. C 419 724-1525
  Holland *(G-9294)*

Lutheran Homes Society Inc.............. C 419 591-4060
  Napoleon *(G-11527)*

Lutheran Homes Society Inc.............. E 419 861-4990
  Toledo *(G-13899)*

Lutheran Village At Wolf Creek........... E 419 861-2233
  Holland *(G-9296)*

Maple Knoll Communities Inc............ C 513 524-7990
  Oxford *(G-12209)*

Mason Health Care Center................. E 513 398-2881
  Mason *(G-10578)*

Medina County..................................... E 330 723-9553
  Medina *(G-10856)*

Mentor Senior Living LLC................... D 440 701-4560
  Mentor *(G-10971)*

Methodist Rtrment Ctr of Cntl.............. C 614 888-7492
  Columbus *(G-6229)*

Mid-Western Childrens Home.............. E 513 877-2141
  Pleasant Plain *(G-12499)*

Midwest Health Services Inc............... C 330 828-0779
  Massillon *(G-10657)*

Mount Aloysius Corp............................ D 740 342-3343
  New Lexington *(G-11629)*

Mt Healthy Christian Home Inc........... D 513 931-5000
  Cincinnati *(G-3086)*

National Ch Rsdnces Pmbroke GA..... D 614 451-2151
  Columbus *(G-6291)*

National Mentor Holdings Inc.............. B 440 657-5658
  Elyria *(G-8278)*

National Mentor Holdings Inc.............. B 419 443-0867
  Fostoria *(G-8621)*

New Avnues To Independence Inc..... D 440 259-4300
  Perry *(G-12310)*

New Avnues To Independence Inc..... D 216 481-1907
  Cleveland *(G-4637)*

New Dawn Health Care Inc................ C 330 343-5521
  Dover *(G-7895)*

New Directions Inc............................... D 216 591-0324
  Cleveland *(G-4638)*

New Mercy Outreach Inc..................... E 567 560-9021
  Mansfield *(G-10304)*

New Nghbors Rsdential Svcs Inc....... E 937 717-5731
  Saint Paris *(G-12838)*

North Cntl Mntal Hlth Svcs Inc............ D 614 227-6865
  Columbus *(G-6366)*

Northeast Care Center Inc.................. D 440 234-9407
  Berea *(G-1075)*

Northeast Care Center Inc.................. D 440 888-9320
  North Royalton *(G-11946)*

Northgate Pk Retirement Cmnty......... E 513 923-3711
  Cincinnati *(G-3125)*

Oak Hills Manor LLC........................... E 330 875-5060
  Louisville *(G-10117)*

Oesterlen - Svcs For Youth Inc........... D 937 399-6101
  Springfield *(G-13278)*

Ohio Dept Dvlpmntal Dsbilities............ C 330 544-2231
  Columbus *(G-6404)*

Ohio Dept Dvlpmntal Dsbilities............ C 419 385-0231
  Toledo *(G-13944)*

Ohio Living.. B 513 681-4230
  Cincinnati *(G-3147)*

Ohio Living.. B 513 539-7391
  Monroe *(G-11345)*

Ohio Living.. B 419 865-4445
  Toledo *(G-13946)*

Ohio Living.. A 440 942-4342
  Willoughby *(G-15215)*

Ohio Living.. E 614 888-7800
  Westerville *(G-14921)*

Ohioguidestone.................................... D 440 235-0918
  Olmsted Falls *(G-12088)*

Ohioguidestone.................................... E 440 234-2006
  Berea *(G-1079)*

Osu Harding Hospital.......................... A 614 293-9600
  Columbus *(G-6483)*

Otterbein Homes................................... D 419 645-5114
  Cridersville *(G-7029)*

Otterbein Homes................................... E 513 260-7690
  Middletown *(G-11200)*

Otterbein Homes................................... E 419 394-2366
  Saint Marys *(G-12834)*

Otterbein Homes................................... B 513 933-5400
  Lebanon *(G-9781)*

Otterbein Snior Lfstyle Chices............ E 419 833-7000
  Pemberville *(G-12292)*

Pathway Caring For Children............... D 330 493-0083
  Canton *(G-1827)*

Phillips Hthcare LLC DBA Cring.......... E 330 531-6110
  Warren *(G-14547)*

Pines Alf Inc... E 330 856-4232
  Hiram *(G-9275)*

Portage County Board.......................... E 330 297-6209
  Ravenna *(G-12638)*

Premier Estates 525 LLC.................... D 513 631-6800
  Cincinnati *(G-3227)*

Premier Estates 526 LLC.................... D 513 922-1440
  Cincinnati *(G-3228)*

Primrose Rtrment Cmmnities LLC...... D 419 422-6200
  Findlay *(G-8578)*

Primrose Rtrment Cmmnities LLC...... D 740 653-3900
  Lancaster *(G-9737)*

Primrose Rtrment Cmmnities LLC...... D 419 224-1200
  Lima *(G-9952)*

Primrose Senior Holdings LLC........... D 605 226-3300
  Findlay *(G-8579)*

Pristine Senior Living........................... D 513 471-8667
  Cincinnati *(G-3231)*

Pristine Snior Lving Englewood.......... C 937 836-5143
  Englewood *(G-8320)*

Promedica Toledo Hospital.................. D 419 291-2273
  Sylvania *(G-13566)*

Providence House Inc......................... E 216 651-5982
  Cleveland *(G-4795)*

Provision Living LLC........................... D 513 970-9201
  Batavia *(G-746)*

Provision Living LLC........................... D 513 847-9050
  West Chester *(G-14749)*

Regard Recovery Florida LLC............ D 330 866-0900
  Sherrodsville *(G-13012)*

Rehablttion Ctr At Mrietta Mem.......... E 740 374-1407
  Marietta *(G-10403)*

REM-Ohio Inc....................................... E 937 335-8267
  Troy *(G-14154)*

REM-Ohio Inc....................................... E 330 644-9730
  Coventry Township *(G-7015)*

REM-Ohio Inc....................................... E 614 367-1370
  Reynoldsburg *(G-12675)*

Renaissance House Inc...................... D 419 425-0633
  Findlay *(G-8581)*

Renaissance House Inc...................... E 419 663-1316
  Norwalk *(G-12023)*

RES-Care Inc....................................... E 740 968-0181
  Flushing *(G-8601)*

Rescare Ohio Inc................................. E 513 724-1177
  Mount Orab *(G-11473)*

Rescue Incorporated........................... C 419 255-9585
  Toledo *(G-13988)*

Resident HM Assn Grter Dyton I........ D 937 278-0791
  Dayton *(G-7588)*

Residential HM Assn Marion Inc........ C 740 387-9999
  Marion *(G-10451)*

Residential MGT Systems Inc............ E 614 880-6009
  Worthington *(G-15451)*

Residntial HM For Dvlpmntlly D.......... E 740 677-0500
  The Plains *(G-13616)*

Residntial HM For Dvlpmntlly D.......... C 740 622-9778
  Coshocton *(G-6999)*

83 SOCIAL SERVICES

Rhc Inc .... D 513 389-7501
   Cincinnati *(G-3294)*

RMS of Ohio Inc .... C 513 841-0990
   Cincinnati *(G-3310)*

Roman Cthlic Docese Youngstown .... C 330 875-5562
   Louisville *(G-10122)*

Rose Mary Johanna Grassell .... D 216 481-4823
   Cleveland *(G-4854)*

Saint Joseph Orphanage .... D 513 231-5010
   Cincinnati *(G-3342)*

Saint Joseph Orphanage .... D 937 643-0398
   Dayton *(G-7605)*

Saint Joseph Orphanage .... D 513 741-3100
   Cincinnati *(G-3341)*

Scioto Residential Services .... E 740 353-0288
   Portsmouth *(G-12568)*

Select Spclty Hsptal-Akron LLC .... D 330 761-7500
   Akron *(G-296)*

Shalom House Inc .... E 614 239-1999
   Columbus *(G-6669)*

Shepherd of Vly Lthran Rtrment .... E 330 544-0771
   Girard *(G-8824)*

Shepherd of Vly Lthran Rtrment .... E 330 726-7110
   Poland *(G-12509)*

Shepherd of Vly Lthran Rtrment .... E 330 856-9232
   Warren *(G-14553)*

Shepherd of Vly Lthran Rtrment .... E 330 530-4038
   Youngstown *(G-15722)*

Shining Star Rsdntial Svcs LLC .... D 419 318-0932
   Toledo *(G-14010)*

Shurmer Place At Altenheim .... D 440 238-9001
   Strongsville *(G-13484)*

Simple Journey Inc .... D 513 360-2678
   Monroe *(G-11351)*

Sisters of Mrcy of The Amrcas .... D 419 332-8208
   Fremont *(G-8703)*

SL Seasons LLC .... D 513 984-9400
   Cincinnati *(G-3386)*

Society For Hndcpped Ctzens of .... E 330 722-1900
   Seville *(G-12965)*

Southast Cmnty Mental Hlth Ctr .... C 614 225-0980
   Columbus *(G-6694)*

Spencer Half-Way House Inc .... E 740 345-5074
   Newark *(G-11748)*

St Edward Home .... C 330 668-2828
   Fairlawn *(G-8500)*

St Johns Villa .... C 330 627-4662
   Carrollton *(G-1913)*

St Vincent Family Services .... C 614 252-0731
   Columbus *(G-6707)*

Stone Creek Alliance Inc .... C 330 856-4232
   Alliance *(G-402)*

Sunrise Senior Living LLC .... E 216 447-8909
   Cleveland *(G-4961)*

Sunrise Senior Living LLC .... E 419 425-3440
   Findlay *(G-8590)*

Sunrise Senior Living LLC .... E 614 418-9775
   Gahanna *(G-8731)*

Sunrise Senior Living LLC .... E 440 895-2383
   Rocky River *(G-12753)*

Sunset House Inc .... D 419 536-4645
   Toledo *(G-14029)*

Sunshine Communities .... B 419 865-0251
   Maumee *(G-10773)*

Sylvania Franciscan Health .... B 419 824-3674
   Toledo *(G-14031)*

Talbert House .... D 513 872-8870
   Cincinnati *(G-3434)*

Tender Hrts At HM Snior Care I .... D 513 234-0805
   Cincinnati *(G-3453)*

The Lochhaven Company .... D 419 227-5450
   Lima *(G-9970)*

Thomas Edson Erly Chldhood Ctr .... D 419 238-1514
   Van Wert *(G-14352)*

Toward Independence Inc .... C 513 531-0804
   Cincinnati *(G-3487)*

Traditions At Bath Rd Inc .... D 330 929-6272
   Cuyahoga Falls *(G-7109)*

Tri County Mental Health Svcs .... D 740 592-3091
   Athens *(G-593)*

Trilogy Health Services LLC .... D 419 935-6511
   Willard *(G-15174)*

Twin Lakes Senior Living Cmnty .... D 360 933-0741
   Montgomery *(G-11380)*

Ucc Ix DBA Barrington Square .... D 740 382-4885
   Marion *(G-10458)*

United Ch Residences Goshen .... D 740 382-4885
   Marion *(G-10459)*

United Ch Rsdnces Immklee Cypr .... D 740 382-4885
   Marion *(G-10460)*

United Ch Rsdnces Immklee Fla .... D 740 382-4885
   Marion *(G-10461)*

United Church Homes Inc .... C 937 426-8481
   Dayton *(G-7682)*

United Church Homes Inc .... D 419 621-1900
   Sandusky *(G-12938)*

United Church Homes Inc .... D 800 837-2211
   Marion *(G-10462)*

United Church Homes Inc .... E 740 376-5600
   Marietta *(G-10406)*

United Crbral Plsy Assn Grter .... E 216 381-9993
   Cleveland *(G-5058)*

United Crbral Plsy Assn Grter .... E 440 835-5511
   Westlake *(G-15119)*

United Crbral Plsy Assn Grter .... D 216 791-8363
   Cleveland *(G-5057)*

United Mthdst Chld HM W Ohio C .... D 614 885-5020
   Columbus *(G-6808)*

Uvmc Nursing Care Inc .... C 937 667-7500
   Tipp City *(G-13668)*

Village Network .... C 330 264-3232
   Wooster *(G-15381)*

Volunteers America Ohio & Ind .... C 614 253-6100
   Columbus *(G-6856)*

Volunteers of America Inc .... D 513 381-1954
   Cincinnati *(G-3633)*

Wallick Construction Co .... D 937 399-7009
   Springfield *(G-13309)*

Walnut Hlls Rtrment Cmmnties I .... C 330 893-3200
   Walnut Creek *(G-14473)*

Walton Retirement Home .... E 740 425-2344
   Barnesville *(G-724)*

Watermark Rtrment Cmmnties Inc .... D 405 751-3600
   Toledo *(G-14098)*

Welcome House Inc .... D 440 471-7601
   North Olmsted *(G-11919)*

Wesley Glen Rtrement Cmnty LLC .... E 614 888-7492
   Columbus *(G-6878)*

West View Manor Inc .... C 330 264-8640
   Wooster *(G-15386)*

White Lght Bhvral Hlth Clmbus .... D 614 350-4010
   Columbus *(G-6884)*

Widows Home of Dayton Ohio .... D 937 252-1661
   Dayton *(G-7721)*

Womens Welsh Clubs of America .... D 440 331-0420
   Rocky River *(G-12757)*

Wood County Chld Svcs Assn .... E 419 352-7588
   Bowling Green *(G-1335)*

Wynn-Reeth Inc .... E 419 639-2094
   Green Springs *(G-8862)*

Zandex Health Care Corporation .... C 740 454-1400
   New Concord *(G-11613)*

8399 Social services, nec

Adams & Brown Counties Economi .... E 937 695-0316
   Winchester *(G-15284)*

Adams Brown Cnties Ecnmic Oppr .... D 937 695-0316
   Winchester *(G-15285)*

ARC Indstries Inc Frnklin Cnty .... C 614 836-6050
   Groveport *(G-8970)*

Ashtabula County Commnty Actn .... C 440 997-1721
   Ashtabula *(G-521)*

Catholic Charities Corporation .... D 419 289-7456
   Ashland *(G-487)*

Catholic Charities Corporation .... D 419 289-1903
   Ashland *(G-488)*

Catholic Charities Corporation .... D 216 432-0680
   Cleveland *(G-3932)*

Catholic Charities Corporation .... D 216 939-3713
   Cleveland *(G-3933)*

Catholic Charities Corporation .... D 216 268-4006
   Cleveland *(G-3934)*

Catholic Charities Corporation .... D 330 262-7836
   Wooster *(G-15317)*

Center For Community Solutions .... E 216 781-2944
   Cleveland *(G-3949)*

Childrens Hunger Alliance .... E 614 341-7700
   Columbus *(G-5564)*

Cleveland Municipal School Dst .... E 216 838-8700
   Cleveland *(G-4061)*

Clinton Cnty Cmnty Action Prgr .... D 937 382-8365
   Wilmington *(G-15248)*

Colonial Senior Services Inc .... E 513 856-8600
   Hamilton *(G-9030)*

Columbus Jewish Federation .... E 614 237-7686
   Columbus *(G-5641)*

Community Action Comm Erie Hro .... E 419 626-6540
   Sandusky *(G-12884)*

Community Action Prgram Corp O .... C 740 962-3792
   Malta *(G-10231)*

Community Action Prgram Corp O .... E 740 373-6016
   Marietta *(G-10363)*

Community Action Prgram Corp O .... D 740 373-3745
   Marietta *(G-10362)*

Concord Counseling Services .... E 614 882-9338
   Westerville *(G-14974)*

Council On Aging Sthwstern Ohi .... C 513 721-1025
   Blue Ash *(G-1159)*

Council On Rur Svc Prgrams Inc .... D 937 773-0773
   Piqua *(G-12439)*

Council On Rur Svc Prgrams Inc .... D 937 492-8787
   Sidney *(G-13025)*

Council On Rur Svc Prgrams Inc .... E 937 778-5220
   Piqua *(G-12438)*

County of Lucas .... C 419 248-3585
   Toledo *(G-13765)*

County of Montgomery .... D 937 225-4192
   Dayton *(G-7255)*

County of Tuscarawas .... D 330 343-5555
   Dover *(G-7877)*

County of Wood .... D 419 352-8402
   Bowling Green *(G-1315)*

Eastgate Rgnal Cncil Gvrnments .... E 330 779-3800
   Youngstown *(G-15605)*

Economic & Cmnty Dev Inst Inc .... E 614 559-0104
   Columbus *(G-5806)*

Fairfax Renaissance Dev Corp .... E 216 361-8400
   Cleveland *(G-4234)*

Fairfield Cnty Job & Fmly Svcs .... E 800 450-8845
   Lancaster *(G-9709)*

Far West Center .... E 440 835-6212
   Westlake *(G-15060)*

Fugees Family Inc .... E 678 358-0547
   Columbus *(G-5901)*

Great Lkes Cmnty Action Partnr .... E 419 639-2802
   Green Springs *(G-8859)*

SIC SECTION   86 MEMBERSHIP ORGANIZATIONS

Greater Cleveland Food Bnk Inc............ C 216 738-2265
   Cleveland *(G-4331)*
Habitat For Hmnity E Cntl Ohio............... E 330 915-5888
   Canton *(G-1767)*
Habitat For Hmnity Grter Cncnn............. C 513 389-1792
   Cincinnati *(G-2789)*
Habitat For Hmnity Grter Cncnn............. E 513 721-4483
   Cincinnati *(G-2790)*
Hancock-Hrdn-Wyndt-ptnam Cmnty...... C 419 423-3755
   Findlay *(G-8543)*
Health Partners Western Ohio................ E 419 221-3072
   Lima *(G-9903)*
Hockingthensperry Cmnty Action........... E 740 767-4500
   Glouster *(G-8835)*
Integrted Svcs For Bhvral Hlth................ D 740 216-4093
   Logan *(G-10029)*
Integrted Svcs For Bhvral Hlth................ E 740 300-0225
   Nelsonville *(G-11548)*
Interact For Health................................... E 513 458-6600
   Cincinnati *(G-2878)*
Jacksn-Vinton Cmnty Action Inc............ E 740 384-3722
   Wellston *(G-14638)*
Jefferson Cnty Cmnty Action CN............ C 740 282-0971
   Steubenville *(G-13332)*
Jewish Edcatn Ctr of Cleveland.............. D 216 371-0446
   Cleveland Heights *(G-5180)*
Licking County Aging Program................ D 740 345-0821
   Newark *(G-11715)*
Lifeservices Management Corp.............. E 440 257-3866
   Mentor *(G-10964)*
Mahoning Yngstown Cmnty Action......... D 330 747-7921
   Youngstown *(G-15661)*
Medina County.. C 330 722-9511
   Medina *(G-10857)*
Miami Cnty Cmnty Action Cuncil............ E 937 335-7921
   Troy *(G-14146)*
Miami Vly Cmnty Action Partnr............... D 937 222-1009
   Dayton *(G-7503)*
National Affrdbl Hsing Tr Inc................... E 614 451-9929
   Columbus *(G-6288)*
National Yuth Advcate Prgram I.............. E 614 487-8758
   Columbus *(G-6303)*
Nationwide Childrens Hospital................ B 614 722-8200
   Columbus *(G-6321)*
Nextchapter... E 888 861-7122
   Columbus *(G-6355)*
Northwestern Ohio Cmnty Action........... C 419 784-2150
   Defiance *(G-7758)*
Occupational Health Link........................ E 614 885-0039
   Delaware *(G-7820)*
Ohio Citizen Action.................................. E 216 861-5200
   Cleveland *(G-4685)*
Ohio Community Dev Fin Fund............... E 614 221-1114
   Columbus *(G-6398)*
Pavilion At Pkton For Nrsing R................ D 740 289-2394
   Piketon *(G-12426)*
Planet Aid Inc... E 440 542-1171
   Solon *(G-13127)*
Playhouse Square Holdg Co LLC........... C 216 771-4444
   Cleveland *(G-4759)*
Potential Development Program............. C 330 746-7641
   Youngstown *(G-15696)*
Provider Services Inc.............................. E 614 888-2021
   Columbus *(G-6553)*
Randall R Leab....................................... E 330 689-6263
   Ashland *(G-508)*
Ross Cnty Cmnty Action Comm In......... D 740 702-7222
   Chillicothe *(G-2084)*
Salvation Army.. E 614 252-7171
   Columbus *(G-6640)*
Salvation Army.. E 800 728-7825
   Columbus *(G-6641)*

Shawnee Mental Health Ctr Inc.............. E 937 544-5581
   West Union *(G-14872)*
Solidarity Health Network Inc................. E 216 831-1220
   Cleveland *(G-4917)*
Springfield Masonic Community............. E 937 325-1531
   Springfield *(G-13295)*
Step Forward... D 216 692-4010
   Cleveland *(G-4950)*
Step Forward... D 216 696-9077
   Cleveland *(G-4949)*
Stepforward... D 216 541-7878
   Cleveland *(G-4951)*
Transportation Resources Inc................. D 614 253-7948
   Columbus *(G-6784)*
Trumbull Cmnty Action Program............ D 330 393-2507
   Warren *(G-14564)*
Union First Care Inc............................... E 614 396-6192
   Columbus *(G-6800)*
United Labor Agency Inc........................ C 216 664-3446
   Cleveland *(G-5062)*
United Rhblttion Svcs Grter Dy............... E 937 233-1230
   Dayton *(G-7683)*
United Way Greater Cleveland............... C 216 436-2100
   Cleveland *(G-5067)*
United Way of The Grter Dyton.............. E 937 225-3060
   Dayton *(G-7686)*
Warren County Cmnty Svcs Inc............. C 513 695-2100
   Lebanon *(G-9799)*
Waymaker Medstaff LLC....................... E 330 526-8594
   Canton *(G-1884)*
West Ohio Cmnty Action Partnr............. C 419 227-2586
   Lima *(G-9984)*
Westcare Ohio Inc.................................. E 937 259-1898
   Dayton *(G-7718)*

84 MUSEUMS, ART GALLERIES AND BOTANICAL AND ZOOLOGICAL GARDENS

8412 Museums and art galleries

Air Frce Museum Foundation Inc........... E 937 258-1218
   Dayton *(G-7126)*
Akron Art Museum................................... D 330 376-9185
   Akron *(G-20)*
Anderson Twnship Hstrcal Soc I............ E 513 231-2114
   Cincinnati *(G-2202)*
Butler Institute American Art.................. E 330 743-1711
   Youngstown *(G-15568)*
Childrens Museum of Cleveland............ E 216 791-7114
   Cleveland *(G-3970)*
▲ Cincinnati Museum Association........ C 513 721-5204
   Cincinnati *(G-2415)*
Cincinnati Museum Center..................... B 513 287-7000
   Cincinnati *(G-2416)*
▲ Cleveland Mseum of Ntral Hstor....... D 216 231-4600
   Cleveland *(G-4058)*
▲ Columbus Museum of Art.................. D 614 221-6801
   Columbus *(G-5647)*
Contemporary Arts Center..................... E 513 721-0390
   Cincinnati *(G-2501)*
Dayton History.. C 937 293-2841
   Dayton *(G-7287)*
Entertrainment Inc.................................. E 513 898-8000
   West Chester *(G-14687)*
Fairfield Industries Inc............................ E 740 409-1539
   Carroll *(G-1901)*
◆ Franklin County Historical Soc.......... C 614 228-2674
   Columbus *(G-5888)*
Hall of Fame Village................................ E 714 337-0333
   Canton *(G-1768)*

Holden Arboretum................................... D 440 946-4400
   Willoughby *(G-15194)*
▲ Museum Cntmprary Art Cleveland... E 216 421-8671
   Cleveland *(G-4612)*
National Undgrd RR Frdom Ctr I............ E 513 333-7500
   Cincinnati *(G-3098)*
National Vtrans Mem Mseum Oper........ E 614 362-2800
   Columbus *(G-6302)*
Oberlin College....................................... E 440 775-8665
   Oberlin *(G-12074)*
Ohio Historic Preservation Off................ E 614 298-2000
   Columbus *(G-6427)*
Ohio Historical Society........................... C 614 297-2300
   Columbus *(G-6428)*
Rock Roll Hall of Fame Mseum I........... E 216 781-7625
   Cleveland *(G-4849)*
Rthrford B Hayes Prsdntial Ctr............... E 419 332-2081
   Fremont *(G-8699)*
Stan Hywet Hall and Grdns Inc.............. D 330 836-5533
   Akron *(G-309)*
Taft Museum of Art................................. E 513 241-0343
   Cincinnati *(G-3432)*
▲ The Cleveland Museum of Art........... B 216 421-7340
   Cleveland *(G-4994)*
The United States Dept A Force............. B 937 255-3286
   Dayton *(G-7142)*
▲ Toledo Museum of Art....................... C 419 255-8000
   Toledo *(G-14063)*
Toledo Science Center........................... E 419 244-2674
   Toledo *(G-14065)*
Velvet Ice Cream Company................... D 740 892-3921
   Utica *(G-14330)*
Western Reserve Historical Soc............. E 330 666-3711
   Bath *(G-755)*
Western Reserve Historical Soc............. D 216 721-5722
   Cleveland *(G-5136)*

8422 Botanical and zoological gardens

Akron Zoological Park............................. E 330 375-2550
   Akron *(G-39)*
Animal Mgt Svcs Ohio Inc...................... E 248 398-6533
   Port Clinton *(G-12517)*
Cleveland Metroparks............................. E 216 661-6500
   Cleveland *(G-4057)*
Columbus Zoological Park Assn............. C 614 645-3400
   Powell *(G-12589)*
Cox Arboretum....................................... C 937 434-9005
   Dayton *(G-7259)*
Stan Hywet Hall and Grdns Inc.............. D 330 836-5533
   Akron *(G-309)*
Toledo Zoo.. E 419 385-5721
   Toledo *(G-14068)*
Toledo Zoological Society...................... B 419 385-4040
   Toledo *(G-14070)*
Toledo Zoological Society...................... C 419 385-4040
   Toledo *(G-14069)*
Zoo Cincinnati... E 513 961-0041
   Cincinnati *(G-3699)*
▲ Zoological Society Cincinnati............. B 513 281-4700
   Cincinnati *(G-3700)*

86 MEMBERSHIP ORGANIZATIONS

8611 Business associations

Allied Construction Industries................. D 513 221-8020
   Cincinnati *(G-2167)*
Altruism Society Inc................................ D 877 283-4001
   Beachwood *(G-765)*
American Jersey Cattle Assn................. E 614 861-3636
   Reynoldsburg *(G-12652)*
Archdiocese of Cincinnati...................... E 513 779-6585
   Middletown *(G-11152)*

Employee Codes: A=Over 500 employees, B=251-500
C=101-250, D=51-100, E=20-50, F=10-19, G=1-9

86 MEMBERSHIP ORGANIZATIONS

Better Bus Bur Centl Ohio Inc .... E 614 486-6336
  Columbus *(G-5436)*
Better Bus Bur Srving Cnton RE .... E 330 454-9401
  Canton *(G-1687)*
Blue Chip Pavement Maintenance Inc .... D 513 321-9595
  Cincinnati *(G-2268)*
Buckeye Power Inc .... E 614 781-0573
  Columbus *(G-5477)*
Builders Exchange Inc .... E 216 393-6300
  Cleveland *(G-3910)*
Certified Angus Beef LLC .... D 330 345-2333
  Wooster *(G-15318)*
Cincinnati USA Rgional Chamber .... D 513 579-3100
  Cincinnati *(G-2430)*
City of Kenton .... E 419 674-4850
  Kenton *(G-9612)*
City of Louisville .... E 330 875-3321
  Louisville *(G-10114)*
City of Oberlin .... E 440 775-1531
  Oberlin *(G-12065)*
City of Toledo .... E 419 245-1400
  Toledo *(G-13739)*
City of Toledo .... E 419 245-1001
  Toledo *(G-13741)*
Columbus Chamber of Commerce .... E 614 225-6943
  Columbus *(G-5618)*
Consolidated Cooperative .... D 419 947-3055
  Mount Gilead *(G-11459)*
Council Dev Fin Agencies .... E 614 705-1300
  Columbus *(G-5709)*
County Commissioners Assn Ohio .... E 614 220-0636
  Columbus *(G-5710)*
County of Logan .... E 937 292-3031
  Bellefontaine *(G-1025)*
County of Montgomery .... C 937 225-4010
  Dayton *(G-7254)*
Dayton Area Chamber Commerce .... E 937 226-1444
  Dayton *(G-7271)*
Dayton Realtors .... E 937 223-0900
  Dayton *(G-7301)*
Department of Commerce Ohio .... D 614 728-8400
  Columbus *(G-5756)*
Energy Cooperative Inc .... E 740 348-1206
  Newark *(G-11699)*
Greater Cleveland Partnership .... D 216 621-3300
  Cleveland *(G-4332)*
Greater Clmbus Chmber Commerce ...... E 614 221-1321
  Columbus *(G-5952)*
Gs1 Us Inc .... C 609 620-0200
  Dayton *(G-7389)*
Home Bldrs Assn Grter Cncnnati .... D 513 851-6300
  Cincinnati *(G-2834)*
Hospital Council of NW Ohio .... E 419 842-0800
  Toledo *(G-13852)*
Interstate Contractors LLC .... E 513 372-5393
  Mason *(G-10568)*
Lucas County Ohio .... D 419 213-4808
  Toledo *(G-13896)*
Mid-Ohio Regional Plg Comm .... D 614 228-2663
  Columbus *(G-6239)*
National Assn Cllege Stres Inc .... D 440 775-7777
  Oberlin *(G-12073)*
National Federation Ind Bus .... D 614 221-4107
  Columbus *(G-6297)*
National Ground Water Assn Inc .... E 614 898-7791
  Westerville *(G-15004)*
Oak Harbor Lions Club Inc .... E 419 898-3828
  Oak Harbor *(G-12046)*
Ohio Civl Svc Employees Assn AF .... D 614 865-4700
  Westerville *(G-14920)*
Ohio Hospital Association .... D 614 221-7614
  Columbus *(G-6430)*

Ohio Restaurant Association .... E 614 442-3535
  Columbus *(G-6442)*
Ohio Utilities Protection Svc .... D 800 311-3692
  North Jackson *(G-11875)*
▲ Precision Metalforming Assn .... E 216 901-8800
  Independence *(G-9471)*
Prime Outlets Acquisition LLC .... E 740 948-9090
  Jeffersonville *(G-9542)*
Redi Cincinnati LLC .... E 513 562-8474
  Cincinnati *(G-3278)*
Toledo Rgonal Chamber Commerce ...... D 419 243-8191
  Toledo *(G-14064)*
Union Rural Electric Coop Inc .... E 937 642-1826
  Marysville *(G-10515)*
United States Trotting Assn .... D 614 224-2291
  Westerville *(G-15020)*
Universal Advg Assoc Inc .... E 513 522-5000
  Cincinnati *(G-3560)*
Vigilant Global Trade Svcs LLC .... E 260 417-1825
  Shaker Heights *(G-12988)*

8621 Professional organizations

Action Bar LLC .... E 419 250-1938
  Bowling Green *(G-1302)*
Almo Distributing PA Inc .... A 267 350-2726
  Groveport *(G-8968)*
American Ceramic Society .... E 614 890-4700
  Westerville *(G-14877)*
American Cllege Crdlgy Fndtion .... E 614 442-5950
  Dublin *(G-7932)*
American Heart Association Inc .... E 614 848-6676
  Columbus *(G-5351)*
Balanced Care Corporation .... E 330 908-1166
  Northfield *(G-11952)*
Breathing Association .... E 614 457-4570
  Columbus *(G-5462)*
Caresource Ohio Inc .... C 937 224-3300
  Dayton *(G-7212)*
CCI Engineering .... E 614 485-0670
  Columbus *(G-5524)*
Center For Health Affairs .... D 216 696-6900
  Cleveland *(G-3952)*
Central Ohio Diabetes Assn .... E 614 884-4400
  Columbus *(G-5537)*
Clark County Combined Hlth Dst .... D 937 390-5600
  Springfield *(G-13233)*
Columbus Bar Association .... E 614 221-4112
  Columbus *(G-5615)*
Columbus Medical Association .... D 614 240-7410
  Columbus *(G-5644)*
Community Tissue Services .... E 937 222-0228
  Kettering *(G-9628)*
County of Crawford .... E 419 562-5871
  Bucyrus *(G-1504)*
Dnv Healthcare USA Inc .... E 281 396-1610
  Cincinnati *(G-2102)*
Egp 2022 Vehicle Inc .... E 866 538-1909
  Cincinnati *(G-2606)*
Health Collaborative .... D 513 618-3600
  Cincinnati *(G-2809)*
Healthspot Inc .... D 614 361-1193
  Dublin *(G-8028)*
Jefferson Behavioral Hlth Sys .... D 740 535-1314
  Mingo Junction *(G-11313)*
Lake County General Health Dst .... D 440 350-2543
  Mentor *(G-10960)*
Lakeside Association .... E 419 798-4461
  Lakeside *(G-9654)*
Music Teachers Nat Assn Inc .... E 513 421-1420
  Cincinnati *(G-3090)*
Ohio Assn Cmnty Hlth Ctrs Inc .... E 614 884-3101
  Columbus *(G-6390)*

Ohio Domestic Violence Network .... E 614 406-7274
  Columbus *(G-6413)*
Ohio Education Association .... D 614 228-4526
  Columbus *(G-6416)*
Ohio Soc of Crtif Pub Accntnts .... D 614 764-2727
  Columbus *(G-6445)*
Ohio State Bar Association .... D 614 487-2050
  Columbus *(G-6446)*
Ohio State Medical Association .... D 614 527-6762
  Columbus *(G-6447)*
Toledo Bar Association Inc .... E 419 242-9363
  Toledo *(G-14051)*
Wingspan Care Group .... E 216 932-2800
  Highland Heights *(G-9173)*

8631 Labor organizations

Civil Service Personnel Assn .... E 330 434-2772
  Akron *(G-104)*
Cleveland Teachers Union Inc .... E 216 861-7676
  Cleveland *(G-4070)*
Esi Employee Assistance Group .... C 800 535-4841
  Cleveland *(G-4222)*
Laborers Intl Un N Amer Lcal 3 .... D 216 881-5901
  Cleveland *(G-4472)*
Laborers Local Union No 860 .... E 216 432-1022
  Cleveland *(G-4473)*
National Pstal Mail Hndlers Un .... D 513 625-7192
  Cincinnati *(G-3096)*
Ohio Assn Pub Schl Employees .... E 614 890-4770
  Columbus *(G-6391)*
Ohio Cvil Svc Emplyees Assn AF .... D 614 865-4700
  Westerville *(G-14920)*
Plumbers Lcal 55 Federal Cr Un .... E 216 459-0099
  Independence *(G-9467)*
United Fd Coml Wkrs Un Lcal 10 .... E 614 235-3635
  Columbus *(G-6805)*
United Fd Coml Wkrs Un Lcal 88 .... E 216 241-5930
  Broadview Heights *(G-1402)*
◆ United Trnsp Un Insur Assn .... C 216 228-9400
  Independence *(G-9493)*

8641 Civic and social associations

Aladdin Temple .... E 614 475-2609
  Grove City *(G-8894)*
American Heritage Girls Inc .... D 513 771-2025
  Cincinnati *(G-2181)*
Avon Heritage Boosters .... E 440 934-5111
  Avon *(G-638)*
Beta Theta Pi Fraternity .... E 513 523-7591
  Oxford *(G-12201)*
Boys & Girls Club of Toledo .... E 419 241-4258
  Toledo *(G-13715)*
Boys Girls Clubs Columbus Inc .... E 614 221-8830
  Columbus *(G-5458)*
Buckeye Trls Girl Scout Cncil .... E 937 275-7601
  Dayton *(G-7204)*
Cincinnati Assn For The Prfrmg .... D 513 744-3344
  Cincinnati *(G-2396)*
Civic Grdn Ctr Grter Cncinnati .... E 513 221-0981
  Cincinnati *(G-2454)*
Cleveland Municipal School Dst .... D 216 459-4200
  Cleveland *(G-4059)*
Communties In Schols Cntl Ohio .... E 614 268-2472
  Columbus *(G-5674)*
Countryside Yung MNS Chrstn As .... D 513 677-3702
  Maineville *(G-10227)*
Cuyahoga County AG Soc .... E 440 243-0090
  Berea *(G-1067)*
Delta Gamma Fraternity .... E 614 481-8169
  Upper Arlington *(G-14277)*
Disabled American Veterans .... D 937 644-1907
  Marysville *(G-10483)*

86 MEMBERSHIP ORGANIZATIONS

Eagles CLB At Qail Hllow Cndo............. E 419 734-1000
  Port Clinton (G-12523)
Emerald Transformer Ppm LLC............. B 330 425-3825
  Twinsburg (G-14186)
Envirocore Inc.................................... E 614 263-6554
  Plain City (G-12476)
Erie Shres Cncil Inc Boy Scuts.............. A 419 241-7293
  Toledo (G-13797)
Family Motor Coach Assn Inc............... E 513 474-3622
  Cincinnati (G-2647)
Family YMCA of LANcstr&fairfld........... D 740 277-7373
  Lancaster (G-9723)
Fayette Cnty Fmly Yung MNS CHR....... D 740 335-0477
  Wshngtn Ct Hs (G-15481)
Fraternal Order of Plice of OH.............. E 614 224-5700
  Columbus (G-5891)
Fred Crdnal Athc Schlrship Fun............. E 812 801-7641
  Barberton (G-697)
Geary Fmly Yung MNS Chrstn Ass........ E 419 435-6608
  Fostoria (G-8617)
Geauga Park District............................. D 440 415-5661
  Chardon (G-2001)
Girl Scouts North East Ohio.................. D 330 864-9933
  Macedonia (G-10193)
Girl Scouts of Western Ohio.................. E 567 225-3557
  Maumee (G-10729)
Girl Scouts of Western Ohio.................. E 513 489-1025
  Blue Ash (G-1178)
Girl Scuts Ohios Hrtland Cncil............... D 614 340-8829
  Columbus (G-5935)
Grand Aerie of The Fraternal................. E 419 227-1566
  Lima (G-9892)
Grand Arie of The Frtnrl Order............... E 614 883-2200
  Grove City (G-8921)
Great Mami Vly Yung MNS Chrstn........ D 513 217-5501
  Middletown (G-11198)
Great Mami Vly Yung MNS Chrstn........ D 513 887-0001
  Hamilton (G-9046)
Great Miami Valley YMCA..................... D 513 829-3091
  Fairfield (G-8417)
Great Miami Valley YMCA..................... D 513 892-9622
  Fairfield Township (G-8461)
Great Miami Valley YMCA..................... D 513 867-0600
  Hamilton (G-9047)
Great Miami Valley YMCA..................... D 513 887-0014
  Hamilton (G-9048)
Great Miami Valley YMCA..................... D 513 868-9622
  Hamilton (G-9049)
Guiding Fndtons Spport Svcs LL........... D 440 485-3772
  Bedford (G-963)
Help Foundation Inc............................. E 216 289-7710
  Euclid (G-8345)
Independence Foundation Inc.............. C 330 296-2851
  Ravenna (G-12630)
International Dev Assn Africa................ E 314 629-2431
  Columbus (G-6068)
Jack Jseph Mrton Mndel Fndtio............ E 216 875-6511
  Cleveland (G-4428)
Jewish Cmnty Ctr of Grter Clmb............ C 614 231-2731
  Columbus (G-6088)
Jobsohio.. D 614 224-6446
  Columbus (G-6093)
Kappa Kappa Gamma Foundation........ E 614 228-6515
  Dublin (G-8045)
Kensington Intrmdiate Schl Pta............. E 440 356-6770
  Rocky River (G-12746)
Lady Warriors Summer Softball............. C 614 668-6329
  Etna (G-8333)
Lake Cnty Yung MNS Chrstn Assn........ C 440 352-3303
  Painesville (G-12231)
Lake County YMCA............................... C 440 428-5125
  Madison (G-10219)

Lake County YMCA............................... C 440 259-2724
  Perry (G-12307)
Lake County YMCA............................... C 440 946-1160
  Willoughby (G-15198)
Lake Erie Cncil Boy Scuts Amer............ E 216 861-6060
  Cleveland (G-4474)
Lake Wynoka Prprty Owners Assn........ E 937 446-3774
  Lake Waynoka (G-9653)
Lenau Park... E 440 235-2646
  Olmsted Twp (G-12091)
Leo Yssnoff Jwish Cmnty Ctr Gr........... C 614 775-0312
  New Albany (G-11572)
Liberty Twnship Powell Y M C A........... D 740 938-2007
  Lewis Center (G-9826)
Licking Area Computer Assn................ D 740 345-3400
  Newark (G-11713)
Lima Family YMCA............................... D 419 223-6055
  Lima (G-9923)
Lima Family YMCA............................... D 419 223-6045
  Lima (G-9922)
Lorain Cnty Bys Girls CLB Inc.............. E 330 773-3375
  Akron (G-224)
Lutz Pto.. E 419 332-0091
  Fremont (G-8692)
Mansfield Ohio Arie No 336 Frtn........... E 419 636-7812
  Bryan (G-1487)
Marion Family YMCA............................ D 740 725-9622
  Marion (G-10438)
Meridian Condominiums Inc................. E 216 228-4211
  Lakewood (G-9679)
Miami Co YMCA Child Care.................. E 937 778-5241
  Piqua (G-12448)
Ohio Environmental Council................. E 614 487-7506
  Columbus (G-6417)
Ohio State Univ Alumni Assn................ D 614 292-2200
  Columbus (G-6448)
Parallax Advanced RES Corp............... E 937 775-2620
  Dayton (G-7139)
Ptao Sffeld Elem Ohio Congress........... E 330 628-3430
  Mogadore (G-11331)
Riverfront YMCA Schl Age - Ech........... E 330 733-2551
  Cuyahoga Falls (G-7097)
Salvation Army..................................... E 419 447-2252
  Tiffin (G-13641)
Say Yes Clvland Schlarship Inc............ D 216 273-6350
  Cleveland (G-4881)
Shriners International.......................... C 855 206-2096
  Dayton (G-7619)
Sidney-Shelby County YMCA............... E 937 492-9134
  Sidney (G-13053)
Simon Knton Cncil Byscuts Amer......... D 614 436-7200
  Columbus (G-6681)
Star House... E 614 826-5868
  Columbus (G-6709)
Sycamore Board of Education.............. C 513 489-3937
  Montgomery (G-11375)
The Community Mercy Foundation....... A 937 328-7000
  Springfield (G-13301)
The Young Mens Christian................... A 614 389-4409
  Columbus (G-6762)
Three Village Condominium.................. E 440 461-1483
  Cleveland (G-5015)
Tiffin Cmnty YMCA Rcration Ctr........... D 419 447-8711
  Tiffin (G-13645)
Toledo Club.. D 419 243-2200
  Toledo (G-14058)
Trilegiant Corporation........................... B 614 823-5215
  Westerville (G-15018)
Union Club Company........................... D 216 621-4230
  Cleveland (G-5050)
United Sttes Sprtsmens Alnce F........... E 614 888-4868
  Columbus (G-6818)

University of Cincinnati......................... E 513 556-2263
  Cincinnati (G-3584)
Urban Leag Grter Cleveland Inc........... E 216 622-0999
  Cleveland (G-5089)
Vermilion Family YMCA........................ E 440 967-4208
  Vermilion (G-14410)
Veterans of Foreign Wars of US............ D 740 698-8841
  Albany (G-373)
Veterans of Foreign Wars of US............ D 513 563-6830
  Cincinnati (G-3628)
Veterans of Foreign Wars of US............ D 937 864-2361
  Fairborn (G-8384)
Veterans of Foreign Wars of US............ D 740 653-1516
  Lancaster (G-9748)
Veterans of Foreign Wars of US............ D 937 773-9122
  Piqua (G-12462)
Veterans of Foreign Wars of US............ D 419 899-2775
  Sherwood (G-13013)
Veterans of Foreign Wars of US............ D 440 349-1863
  Solon (G-13160)
Veterans of Foreign Wars of US............ D 330 532-1423
  Wellsville (G-14642)
Veterans of Foreign Wars of US............ D 740 472-1199
  Woodsfield (G-15303)
Village of Cuyahoga Heights................. D 216 641-7020
  Cleveland (G-5105)
Wapakneta Fmly Yung MNS Chrstn...... D 419 739-9622
  Wapakoneta (G-14493)
Y M C A of Ashland Ohio Inc................ D 419 289-0626
  Ashland (G-516)
YMCA.. E 330 823-1930
  Alliance (G-408)
YMCA of Massillon............................... D 330 837-5116
  Massillon (G-10674)
Young Mens Christian Assn................. D 740 373-2250
  Marietta (G-10415)
Young Mens Christian Assn................. D 330 480-5656
  Youngstown (G-15754)
Young Mens Christian Asso................. E 513 651-2100
  Cincinnati (G-3689)
Young MNS Chrstn Assn Findlay......... D 419 422-4424
  Findlay (G-8599)
Young MNS Chrstn Assn Cntl STA....... D 330 305-5437
  Canton (G-1889)
Young MNS Chrstn Assn Cntl STA....... D 330 498-4082
  Canton (G-1890)
Young MNS Chrstn Assn Cntl STA....... D 330 875-1611
  Louisville (G-10124)
Young MNS Chrstn Assn Cntl STA....... C 330 830-6275
  Massillon (G-10675)
Young MNS Chrstn Assn Cntl STA....... D 330 868-5988
  Minerva (G-11311)
Young MNS Chrstn Assn Grter CL....... D 440 285-7543
  Chardon (G-2027)
Young MNS Chrstn Assn Grter CL....... E 216 344-7700
  Cleveland (G-5166)
Young MNS Chrstn Assn Grter CL....... D 216 521-8400
  Lakewood (G-9688)
Young MNS Chrstn Assn Grter CL....... E 440 808-8150
  Westlake (G-15126)
Young MNS Chrstn Assn Grter CN....... B 513 791-5000
  Blue Ash (G-1275)
Young MNS Chrstn Assn Grter CN....... B 513 521-7112
  Cincinnati (G-3690)
Young MNS Chrstn Assn Grter CN....... D 513 961-3510
  Cincinnati (G-3691)
Young MNS Chrstn Assn Grter CN....... E 513 731-0115
  Cincinnati (G-3692)
Young MNS Chrstn Assn Grter CN....... B 513 474-1400
  Cincinnati (G-3693)
Young MNS Chrstn Assn Grter CN....... D 513 241-9622
  Cincinnati (G-3694)

86 MEMBERSHIP ORGANIZATIONS

Young MNS Chrstn Assn Grter CN......... C 513 923-4466
  Cincinnati *(G-3695)*
Young MNS Chrstn Assn Grter CN......... C 513 921-0911
  Cincinnati *(G-3696)*
Young MNS Chrstn Assn Grter CN......... A 513 932-1424
  Lebanon *(G-9800)*
Young MNS Chrstn Assn Grter Dy........... C 937 228-9622
  Dayton *(G-7732)*
Young MNS Chrstn Assn Grter Dy........... C 937 312-1810
  Dayton *(G-7733)*
Young MNS Chrstn Assn Grter Dy........... D 937 426-9622
  Dayton *(G-7734)*
Young MNS Chrstn Assn Grter Dy........... C 937 836-9622
  Englewood *(G-8327)*
Young MNS Chrstn Assn Grter Dy........... C 513 932-3756
  Oregonia *(G-12150)*
Young MNS Chrstn Assn Grter Dy........... C 937 223-5201
  Springboro *(G-13210)*
Young MNS Chrstn Assn Grter NY........... C 740 392-9622
  Mount Vernon *(G-11509)*
Young MNS Chrstn Assn of Akron........... E 330 376-1335
  Akron *(G-368)*
Young MNS Chrstn Assn of Akron........... E 330 434-5900
  Akron *(G-369)*
Young MNS Chrstn Assn of Akron........... E 330 376-1335
  Akron *(G-370)*
Young MNS Chrstn Assn of Akron........... E 330 724-1255
  Akron *(G-371)*
Young MNS Chrstn Assn of Akron........... E 330 983-5573
  Akron *(G-372)*
Young MNS Chrstn Assn of Akron........... D 330 376-1335
  Clinton *(G-5197)*
Young MNS Chrstn Assn of Akron........... D 330 923-5223
  Cuyahoga Falls *(G-7119)*
Young MNS Chrstn Assn of Akron........... E 330 467-8366
  Macedonia *(G-10210)*
Young MNS Chrstn Assn of Akron........... D 419 523-5233
  Ottawa *(G-12196)*
Young MNS Chrstn Assn of Akron........... E 330 899-9622
  Uniontown *(G-14272)*
Young MNS Chrstn Assn of E Lvr............ D 330 385-0663
  East Liverpool *(G-8194)*
Young MNS Chrstn Assn of Grter........... C 419 866-9622
  Maumee *(G-10782)*
Young MNS Chrstn Assn of Grter........... D 419 794-7304
  Maumee *(G-10783)*
Young MNS Chrstn Assn of Grter........... C 419 691-3523
  Oregon *(G-12148)*
Young MNS Chrstn Assn of Grter........... D 419 251-9622
  Perrysburg *(G-12390)*
Young MNS Chrstn Assn of Grter........... D 419 474-3995
  Toledo *(G-14112)*
Young MNS Chrstn Assn of Grter........... D 419 475-3496
  Toledo *(G-14113)*
Young MNS Chrstn Assn of Grter........... D 419 381-7980
  Toledo *(G-14114)*
Young MNS Chrstn Assn of Grter........... D 419 241-7218
  Toledo *(G-14115)*
Young MNS Chrstn Assn of Grter........... E 419 729-8135
  Sylvania *(G-13579)*
Young MNS Chrstn Assn of Mnsfe.......... E 419 522-3511
  Mansfield *(G-10327)*
Young MNS Chrstn Assn of Mt Vr........... D 740 392-9622
  Mount Vernon *(G-11510)*
Young MNS Chrstn Assn of Van W......... E 419 238-0443
  Van Wert *(G-14362)*
Young MNS Chrstn Assn Wster OH........ E 330 264-3131
  Wooster *(G-15402)*
Young MNS Chrstn Assn Yngstown........ D 330 744-8411
  Youngstown *(G-15755)*
Young Wns Chrstn Assn Clvland............ E 216 881-6878
  Cleveland *(G-5167)*

Young Wns Chrstn Assn of Cnton.......... D 330 453-0789
  Canton *(G-1892)*
Young Wns Chrstn Assn of Lima........... E 419 241-3230
  Toledo *(G-14116)*
Young Womens Christian Assn.............. D 614 224-9121
  Columbus *(G-6917)*
Youth For Christ/Usa Inc......................... E 216 252-9883
  Cleveland *(G-5168)*
YWCA Mahoning Valley......................... E 330 746-6361
  Youngstown *(G-15762)*
YWCA of Greater Cincinnati................... D 513 241-7090
  Cincinnati *(G-3697)*

8651 Political organizations

America Votes... E 614 236-3410
  Columbus *(G-5345)*
City of Westlake..................................... E 440 871-3300
  Cleveland *(G-3994)*
Ohio Democratic Party........................... D 614 221-6563
  Columbus *(G-6400)*
Republican State Cntl Exec Cmmt........ E 614 228-2481
  Columbus *(G-6579)*
Strategy Network LLC........................... E 614 595-0688
  Columbus *(G-6722)*

8661 Religious organizations

Catholic Charities Corporation............... D 419 289-7456
  Ashland *(G-487)*
Catholic Charities Corporation............... D 216 432-0680
  Cleveland *(G-3932)*
Christ King Catholic Church................... E 614 236-8838
  Columbus *(G-5569)*
Church On North Coast.......................... E 440 960-1100
  Lorain *(G-10063)*
Columbus Christian Center Inc.............. E 614 416-9673
  Columbus *(G-5619)*
Comfort Inn... D 740 454-4144
  Zanesville *(G-15783)*
Community Ambulance Service............. C 740 454-6800
  Zanesville *(G-15784)*
Cyo & Community Services Inc............. E 330 762-2961
  Akron *(G-130)*
First Assembly Child Care...................... E 419 529-6501
  Mansfield *(G-10263)*
First Christian Church............................. E 330 445-2700
  Canton *(G-1753)*
First Community Church......................... E 614 488-0681
  Columbus *(G-5860)*
Grace Brthren Ch Columbus Ohio......... E 614 888-7733
  Westerville *(G-14897)*
Harrison Avenue Assembly God............ E 513 367-6109
  Harrison *(G-9107)*
Haven Rest Ministries Inc....................... D 330 535-1563
  Akron *(G-190)*
Heartbeat International Inc..................... E 614 885-7577
  Columbus *(G-5977)*
Oesterlen - Svcs For Youth Inc.............. D 937 399-6101
  Springfield *(G-13278)*
Ohio State Univ Alumni Assn................. D 614 292-2200
  Columbus *(G-6448)*
Our Lady Bethlehem Schools Inc.......... E 614 459-8285
  Columbus *(G-6491)*
Pillar of Fire.. E 513 542-1212
  Cincinnati *(G-3211)*
Royal Rdmer Lthran Ch N Rylton.......... E 440 237-7958
  North Royalton *(G-11949)*
Saint Cecilia Church............................... E 614 878-5353
  Columbus *(G-6637)*
Salvation Army....................................... E 937 461-2769
  Cincinnati *(G-3346)*
Salvation Army....................................... E 937 528-5100
  Dayton *(G-7606)*

Sidney-Shelby County YMCA................ E 937 492-9134
  Sidney *(G-13053)*
Sisters of Chrity Cncnnati Ohi................ C 513 347-5200
  Cincinnati *(G-3380)*
Society of The Transfiguration............... D 513 771-7462
  Cincinnati *(G-3391)*
St Francis De Sales Church................... D 740 345-9874
  Newark *(G-11749)*
St Jhns Evang Lthran Ch Mrysv............ E 937 644-5540
  Marysville *(G-10510)*
St Pauls Catholic Church....................... E 330 724-1263
  Akron *(G-308)*
St Thomas Episcopal Church................. E 513 831-6908
  Terrace Park *(G-13614)*
The Sisters of Charity of......................... E 216 696-5560
  Cleveland *(G-5007)*
Trinity United Methodist Ch.................... E 614 488-3659
  Columbus *(G-6792)*
United Church Homes Inc...................... E 419 294-4973
  Upper Sandusky *(G-14294)*
Upper Arlington Lutheran Ch................. E 614 451-3736
  Hilliard *(G-9238)*
Wapakneta Fmly Yung MNS Chrstn...... D 419 739-9622
  Wapakoneta *(G-14493)*
West Ohio Cnfrnce of Untd Mthd.......... E 614 844-6200
  Worthington *(G-15468)*
West Side Ecumenical Ministry.............. C 216 325-9369
  Cleveland *(G-5134)*
Windsor Medical Center Inc................... D 330 499-8300
  Canton *(G-1886)*
Young MNS Chrstn Assn Grter CL........ E 440 808-8150
  Westlake *(G-15126)*
Young MNS Chrstn Assn Grter Dy......... C 937 836-9622
  Englewood *(G-8327)*
Youth For Christ/Usa Inc......................... E 216 252-9883
  Cleveland *(G-5168)*

8699 Membership organizations, nec

A Blessed Path Inc................................ D 330 244-0657
  Canton *(G-1651)*
AAA Club Alliance Inc............................ E 513 984-3553
  Cincinnati *(G-2133)*
AAA Club Alliance Inc............................ A 513 762-3301
  Cincinnati *(G-2134)*
AAA Club Alliance Inc............................ D 419 843-1200
  Toledo *(G-13671)*
AAA East Central................................... E 330 652-6466
  Niles *(G-11779)*
AAA Miami Valley................................... D 937 224-2896
  Dayton *(G-7150)*
Affinion Group LLC................................. A 614 895-1803
  Westerville *(G-14956)*
Als Assction Nthrn Ohio Chpter............. E 216 592-2572
  Independence *(G-9404)*
Alternacare... B 740 454-4248
  Zanesville *(G-15766)*
▲ American Motorcycle Assn................ D 614 856-1900
  Pickerington *(G-12397)*
Applewood Centers Inc.......................... D 216 696-6815
  Cleveland *(G-3821)*
Ardmore Inc... D 330 535-2601
  Akron *(G-55)*
Aspca... E 646 596-0321
  Columbus *(G-5396)*
Athletes In Action Spt Cmplex................ D 937 352-1000
  Xenia *(G-15499)*
Athletic Trining Solutions LLC................ E 513 295-1756
  Cincinnati *(G-2225)*
Auxiliary St Lukes Hospital..................... D 419 893-5911
  Maumee *(G-10697)*
Belmont County of Ohio......................... E 740 695-4708
  Saint Clairsville *(G-12776)*

87 ENGINEERING, ACCOUNTING, RESEARCH, AND MANAGEMENT SERVICES

Broken Arrow Inc............................... E 419 562-3480
  Bucyrus *(G-1496)*

Cha - Community Health Affairs......... D 800 362-2628
  Cleveland *(G-3959)*

Childhood League Cent....................... E 614 253-6933
  Columbus *(G-5560)*

Chiquita Brnds Intl Foundation............ D 980 636-5000
  Cincinnati *(G-2373)*

Cincinnati Institute Fine Arts................ E 513 871-2787
  Cincinnati *(G-2413)*

Clark State Community College........... E 937 328-3841
  Springfield *(G-13235)*

Cleveland America Scores................... E 216 881-7988
  Cleveland *(G-4002)*

Columbus Humane................................ C 614 777-7387
  Hilliard *(G-9189)*

Conservncy For Cyhoga Vly Nat............ D 330 657-2909
  Peninsula *(G-12293)*

Damascus Cthlic Mission Campus......... E 740 480-1288
  Centerburg *(G-1935)*

Downtown Akron Partnership Inc.......... E 330 374-7676
  Akron *(G-137)*

Echoing Hills Village Inc....................... E 800 419-6513
  Dayton *(G-7325)*

Envision.. E 513 389-7500
  Cincinnati *(G-2629)*

Equality Ohio Education Fund............... E 614 224-0400
  Columbus *(G-5824)*

Evanston Blldogs Yuth Ftball A............. E 513 254-9500
  Cincinnati *(G-2640)*

Fairfield Industries Inc......................... E 740 409-1539
  Carroll *(G-1901)*

First Capital Enterprises Inc.................. D 740 773-2166
  Chillicothe *(G-2064)*

Fitton Ctr For Creative Arts.................. E 513 863-8873
  Hamilton *(G-9039)*

Geauga County Humane Soc Inc........... E 440 338-4819
  Novelty *(G-12038)*

Goodwill Inds Centl Ohio Inc................ E 740 439-7000
  Cambridge *(G-1572)*

Grail... E 513 683-2340
  Loveland *(G-10139)*

H N S Sports Group Ltd....................... E 614 764-4653
  Dublin *(G-8024)*

Hamilton Cnty Soc For The Prvn............ E 513 541-6100
  Cincinnati *(G-2794)*

Hearing Spech Deaf Ctr Grter C............ E 513 221-0527
  Cincinnati *(G-2814)*

Humane Society Greater Dayton........... E 937 268-7387
  Dayton *(G-7416)*

Irish Youth Sports Inc.......................... E 859 257-7910
  Bellaire *(G-1013)*

Jewish Cmnty Ctr of Grter Clmb............ C 614 231-2731
  Columbus *(G-6088)*

Mid-Ohio Foodbank............................. C 614 277-3663
  Grove City *(G-8935)*

Nami of Preble County Ohio................. E 937 456-4947
  Eaton *(G-8216)*

Nwoca West... E 419 267-2544
  Archbold *(G-465)*

Ohio Automobile Club.......................... D 330 762-0631
  Akron *(G-247)*

Ohio Automobile Club.......................... C 614 431-7901
  Worthington *(G-15444)*

Ohio Farm Bur Federation Inc.............. D 614 249-2400
  Columbus *(G-6421)*

▲ Ohio School Boards Association...... E 614 540-4000
  Columbus *(G-6443)*

Ohio Vly Athc Conference Inc............... E 740 671-3269
  Bellaire *(G-1014)*

People Developed Systems Inc............ D 330 479-7823
  Canton *(G-1829)*

Pepper Pike Club Company Inc............ D 216 831-9400
  Cleveland *(G-4739)*

Professnl Glfers Assn of Amer.............. E 419 882-3197
  Sylvania *(G-13560)*

Recovery Center................................... E 740 687-4500
  Lancaster *(G-9738)*

Rotary International Inc....................... E 740 385-8575
  Logan *(G-10036)*

Shoreby Club Inc................................. D 216 851-2587
  Cleveland *(G-4903)*

Sisters of Charity................................. E 216 696-5560
  Cleveland *(G-4910)*

Stepforward... E 216 476-3201
  Cleveland *(G-4952)*

Strivetogether Inc................................ E 513 929-1150
  Cincinnati *(G-3424)*

University of Cincinnati........................ C 513 556-4603
  Cincinnati *(G-3586)*

Volunteers of America NW Ohio............ E 419 248-3733
  Columbus *(G-6857)*

Wapakneta Fmly Yung MNS Chrstn...... D 419 739-9622
  Wapakoneta *(G-14493)*

White Gorilla Corporation..................... E 202 384-6486
  Hilliard *(G-9242)*

Youngstown Area Jwish Fdration.......... C 330 746-3251
  Youngstown *(G-15756)*

Youngstown Nghborhood Dev Corp...... E 330 480-0423
  Youngstown *(G-15759)*

87 ENGINEERING, ACCOUNTING, RESEARCH, AND MANAGEMENT SERVICES

8711 Engineering services

7nt Enterprises LLC............................. E 614 961-2026
  Miamisburg *(G-11018)*

Accelerant Technologies LLC................ D 419 236-8768
  Maumee *(G-10684)*

Acpi Systems Inc................................. E 513 738-3840
  Hamilton *(G-9016)*

Actalent Services LLC......................... C 614 328-4900
  New Albany *(G-11553)*

▲ Advanced Design Industries Inc....... E 440 277-4141
  Sheffield Village *(G-12997)*

▲ Advanced Engrg Solutions Inc......... D 937 743-6900
  Springboro *(G-13191)*

Advancement LLC................................ C 440 248-8550
  Solon *(G-13062)*

Aerospace Corporation......................... E 937 657-9634
  Dayton *(G-7125)*

▲ Alexander & Associates Co.............. C 513 731-7800
  Cincinnati *(G-2159)*

♦ Alfons Haar Inc................................ E 937 560-2031
  Springboro *(G-13192)*

▲ American Electric Pwr Svc Corp....... B 614 716-1000
  Columbus *(G-5348)*

American Structurepoint Inc................. E 614 901-2235
  Columbus *(G-5361)*

Amg Inc.. E 937 274-0736
  Dayton *(G-7173)*

Apec Engineering Inc........................... E 440 708-2303
  Chagrin Falls *(G-1973)*

Applied Technology Integration............ E 419 537-9052
  Toledo *(G-13691)*

Arcadis A California Partnr.................... E 614 818-4900
  Columbus *(G-5382)*

Arcadis Engrg Svcs USA Inc................ D 614 818-4900
  Columbus *(G-5383)*

Arctos Tech Solutions LLC.................... D 937 426-2808
  Beavercreek *(G-859)*

Ardent Technologies Inc....................... D 937 312-1345
  Dayton *(G-7178)*

Associated Prof Engrg Cons LLC........... E 937 746-4600
  Springboro *(G-13193)*

Atmos360 Inc....................................... E 513 772-4777
  West Chester *(G-14799)*

Austin Building and Design Inc............. C 440 544-2600
  Cleveland *(G-3839)*

Automation Zone Inc............................ E 419 684-8050
  Castalia *(G-1914)*

Avid Technologies Inc.......................... E 330 487-0770
  Twinsburg *(G-14173)*

Awp Inc.. A 330 677-7401
  North Canton *(G-11813)*

Azimuth Corporation............................ C 937 256-8571
  Beavercreek *(G-861)*

B&N Coal Inc.. E 740 783-3575
  Dexter City *(G-7867)*

Babcock & Wilcox Holdings Inc............. A 704 625-4900
  Akron *(G-60)*

Bae Systems Science & Tec.................. A
  Beavercreek *(G-862)*

Bair Goodie and Assoc Inc................... E 330 343-3499
  New Philadelphia *(G-11641)*

Barr Engineering Incorporated.............. E 614 714-0299
  Columbus *(G-5420)*

Basic Systems Inc................................ D 740 432-3001
  Cambridge *(G-1555)*

Bayer & Becker Inc.............................. E 513 492-7401
  Mason *(G-10522)*

BBC&m Engineering Inc....................... D 614 793-2226
  Dublin *(G-7943)*

Bbs Professional Corporation................ D 614 888-8616
  Columbus *(G-5426)*

Belcan LLC... E 513 985-7777
  Blue Ash *(G-1133)*

Belcan LLC... C 513 277-3100
  Cincinnati *(G-2253)*

Belcan LLC... A 513 891-0972
  Blue Ash *(G-1132)*

Belcan Engineering Group LLC............ A 513 891-0972
  Blue Ash *(G-1135)*

Bi-Con Engineering LLC...................... E 740 685-9217
  Derwent *(G-7863)*

Bowen Engineering Corporation........... D 614 536-0273
  Columbus *(G-5457)*

Bowser-Morner Inc............................... C 937 236-8805
  Dayton *(G-7198)*

Brewer-Garrett Company...................... C 440 243-3535
  Middleburg Heights *(G-11113)*

Brilligent Solutions LLC........................ E 937 879-4148
  Fairborn *(G-8367)*

Brown and Caldwell.............................. E 614 410-6144
  Columbus *(G-5470)*

BSI Engineering LLC............................ C 513 201-3100
  Cincinnati *(G-2284)*

Buehrer Group Arch & Engrg................ E 419 893-9021
  Maumee *(G-10706)*

Burgess & Niple Inc............................. D 703 631-6041
  Columbus *(G-5486)*

Burgess & Niple Inc............................. B 614 459-2050
  Columbus *(G-5485)*

Burgess & Niple/Heapy LLC................. D 614 459-2050
  Columbus *(G-5487)*

Capablity Anlis Msrment Orgnzt........... E 937 260-9373
  Beavercreek Township *(G-933)*

▲ Cbn Westside Technologies Inc........ B 513 772-7000
  West Chester *(G-14660)*

Cec Combustion Safety LLC.................. E 216 749-2992
  Brookpark *(G-1430)*

Ceso Inc... E 937 435-8584
  Miamisburg *(G-11035)*

87 ENGINEERING, ACCOUNTING, RESEARCH, AND MANAGEMENT SERVICES

Ch2m Hill Inc .... D 513 243-5070
  Cincinnati *(G-2342)*
Ch2m Hill Engineers Inc .... C 513 530-5520
  Blue Ash *(G-1148)*
Ch2m Hill Engineers Inc .... D 720 286-2000
  Cincinnati *(G-2343)*
Chagrin Valley Engineering Ltd .... E 440 439-1999
  Cleveland *(G-3961)*
Chemstress Consultant Company .... C 330 535-5591
  Akron *(G-87)*
Circle Prime Manufacturing .... E 330 923-0019
  Cuyahoga Falls *(G-7054)*
City of Akron .... C 330 375-2355
  Akron *(G-103)*
City of Cuyahoga Falls .... E 330 971-8230
  Cuyahoga Falls *(G-7059)*
City of Toledo .... D 419 936-2275
  Toledo *(G-13740)*
Civil & Environmental Cons Inc .... E 513 985-0226
  Blue Ash *(G-1150)*
Civil & Environmental Cons Inc .... D 614 540-6633
  Worthington *(G-15409)*
Clarkdietrich Engrg Svcs LLC .... A 513 870-1100
  West Chester *(G-14670)*
▼ Clarkwstern Dtrich Bldg System .... C 513 870-1100
  West Chester *(G-14671)*
Clear Creek Applied Tech .... E 937 912-5438
  Beavercreek *(G-872)*
Coal Services Inc .... B 740 795-5220
  Powhatan Point *(G-12610)*
Colas Construction USA Inc .... C 513 272-5648
  Cincinnati *(G-2471)*
Columbus Dnv Inc .... C 614 761-1214
  Dublin *(G-7966)*
County of Champaign .... D 937 653-4848
  Urbana *(G-14305)*
County of Crawford .... D 419 562-7731
  Bucyrus *(G-1505)*
County of Cuyahoga .... B 216 348-3800
  Cleveland *(G-4125)*
County of Delaware .... C 740 833-2400
  Delaware *(G-7788)*
County of Erie .... E 419 627-7710
  Sandusky *(G-12886)*
County of Gallia .... E 740 446-4009
  Gallipolis *(G-8754)*
County of Logan .... E 937 592-2791
  Bellefontaine *(G-1024)*
County of Lucas .... C 419 213-2892
  Holland *(G-9283)*
County of Montgomery .... D 937 854-4576
  Dayton *(G-7253)*
County of Perry .... E 740 342-2191
  New Lexington *(G-11623)*
County of Stark .... C 330 477-6781
  Canton *(G-1724)*
County of Washington .... E 740 376-7430
  Marietta *(G-10364)*
County of Wayne .... D 330 287-5500
  Wooster *(G-15330)*
Crown Solutions Co LLC .... C 937 890-4075
  Vandalia *(G-14272)*
CT Consultants Inc .... C 440 951-9000
  Mentor *(G-10930)*
CTI Engineers Inc .... D 330 294-5996
  Akron *(G-129)*
Ctl Engineering Inc .... C 614 276-8123
  Columbus *(G-5736)*
Curtiss-Wright Controls .... E 937 252-5001
  Fairborn *(G-8371)*
▲ Custom Materials Inc .... D 440 543-8284
  Chagrin Falls *(G-1976)*

DCS Corporation .... D 937 306-7180
  Beavercreek Township *(G-937)*
DCS Corporation .... C 781 419-6370
  Beavercreek Township *(G-938)*
Dctech Ltd .... E 330 687-3977
  Twinsburg *(G-14180)*
Design Engners Cnsulting Assoc .... E 419 891-0022
  Maumee *(G-10718)*
Design Homes & Development Co .... E 937 438-3667
  Dayton *(G-7311)*
Deskey Associates Inc .... D 513 721-6800
  Cincinnati *(G-2559)*
Dillin Engineered Systems Corp .... E 419 666-6789
  Perrysburg *(G-12333)*
Dizer Corp .... C 440 368-0201
  Painesville *(G-12227)*
Dlr Group Inc .... D 216 522-1350
  Cleveland *(G-4169)*
Dlz Construction Services Inc .... E 614 888-0040
  Columbus *(G-5777)*
Dlz Ohio Inc .... E 330 923-0401
  Akron *(G-135)*
Dlz Ohio Inc .... C 614 888-0040
  Columbus *(G-5778)*
◆ Dms Inc .... C 440 951-9838
  Willoughby *(G-15189)*
E-Technologies Group LLC .... D 513 771-7271
  West Chester *(G-14686)*
E-Volve Systems LLC .... E 765 543-8123
  Blue Ash *(G-1166)*
Eco Engineering Inc .... D 513 985-8300
  Cincinnati *(G-2604)*
▲ Edison Welding Institute Inc .... C 614 688-5000
  Columbus *(G-5807)*
Elevar Design Group Inc .... E 513 721-0600
  Cincinnati *(G-2611)*
Emersion Design LLC .... E 513 841-9100
  Cincinnati *(G-2616)*
Engineering Associates Inc .... D 330 345-6556
  Wooster *(G-15337)*
EP Ferris & Associates Inc .... E 614 299-2999
  Columbus *(G-5823)*
Equity Engineering Group Inc .... D 216 283-9519
  Shaker Heights *(G-12976)*
Euthenics Inc .... E 440 260-1555
  Strongsville *(G-13454)*
Evans McHwart Hmblton Tlton In .... B 614 775-4500
  New Albany *(G-11563)*
Feller Finch & Associates Inc .... E 419 893-3680
  Maumee *(G-10724)*
Fishbeck Thmpson Carr Hber Inc .... C 513 469-2370
  Blue Ash *(G-1175)*
Fishel Company .... C 614 850-4400
  Columbus *(G-5867)*
Fishel Company .... D 614 274-8100
  Columbus *(G-5869)*
Floyd Browne International Ltd .... D 740 363-6792
  Columbus *(G-5875)*
Forte Industrial Equipmen .... E 513 398-2800
  Mason *(G-10550)*
Fosdick & Hilmer Inc .... D 513 241-5640
  Cincinnati *(G-2696)*
Fredrick Frdrick Hller Engners .... E 440 546-9696
  Cleveland *(G-4287)*
Frontier Technology Inc .... E 937 429-3302
  Beavercreek Township *(G-939)*
Frost Engineering Inc .... E 513 541-6330
  Cincinnati *(G-2710)*
Fulton & Assoc Balance Co LLC .... E 440 943-9450
  Mentor *(G-10940)*
Garmann/Miller & Assoc Inc .... E 419 628-4240
  Minster *(G-11316)*

Gbc Design Inc .... E 330 836-0228
  Akron *(G-171)*
Geiger Brothers Inc .... B 740 286-0800
  Jackson *(G-9518)*
Genius Solutions Engrg Co .... E 419 794-9914
  Maumee *(G-10727)*
Genpact LLC .... E 513 763-7660
  Cincinnati *(G-2729)*
Glaus Pyle Schmer Brns Dhven I .... E 216 518-5544
  Cleveland *(G-4314)*
Glaus Pyle Schmer Brns Dhven I .... D 614 210-0751
  Columbus *(G-5936)*
Glaus Pyle Schmer Brns Dhven I .... E 330 645-2131
  Coventry Township *(G-7009)*
Glaus Pyle Schmer Brns Dhven I .... E 740 382-6840
  Marion *(G-10428)*
Glaus Pyle Schmer Brns Dhven I .... B 330 572-2100
  Akron *(G-176)*
Gohypersonic Incorporated .... E 937 331-9460
  Dayton *(G-7377)*
Greene County .... D 937 562-7500
  Xenia *(G-15514)*
Gus Perdikakis Associates .... D 513 583-0900
  Cincinnati *(G-2784)*
Hahn Automation Group Us Inc .... D 937 886-3232
  Miamisburg *(G-11058)*
Haley & Aldrich Inc .... D 216 739-0555
  Independence *(G-9435)*
▲ Hamilton Manufacturing Corp .... E 419 867-4858
  Holland *(G-9287)*
Hammontree & Associates Ltd .... E 330 499-8817
  Canton *(G-1769)*
Hawa Incorporated .... E 614 451-1711
  Westerville *(G-14898)*
Hdr Inc .... E 614 839-5770
  Columbus *(G-5260)*
Hdt Global Inc .... A 216 438-6111
  Solon *(G-13095)*
Heapy Engineering Inc .... C 937 224-0861
  Dayton *(G-7402)*
Hexion Inc .... C 888 443-9466
  Columbus *(G-5989)*
High Voltage Maintenance Corp .... E 937 278-0811
  Dayton *(G-7406)*
Hill Technical Services Inc .... E 330 494-3656
  Canton *(G-1771)*
Hntb Corporation .... E 216 522-1140
  Cleveland *(G-4369)*
Hokuto USA Inc .... E 614 782-6200
  Grove City *(G-8927)*
Houston Interests LLC .... A 614 890-3456
  Columbus *(G-6013)*
▼ Hunter Defense Tech Inc .... E 216 438-6111
  Solon *(G-13096)*
HWH Archtcts-Ngnrs-Plnners Inc .... D 216 875-4000
  Cleveland *(G-4394)*
▲ Hydro-Dyne Inc .... E 330 832-5076
  Massillon *(G-10647)*
Icr Inc .... C 513 900-7007
  Mason *(G-10563)*
Iet Inc .... E 419 385-1233
  Toledo *(G-13859)*
Ijus LLC .... D 614 470-9882
  Columbus *(G-6040)*
Illumination Works LLC .... D 937 938-1321
  Beavercreek *(G-884)*
Imeg Consultants Corp .... E 614 443-1178
  Columbus *(G-6041)*
Industrial Origami Inc .... E 440 260-0000
  Cleveland *(G-4409)*
Innovative Controls Corp .... E 419 691-6684
  Toledo *(G-13863)*

87 ENGINEERING, ACCOUNTING, RESEARCH, AND MANAGEMENT SERVICES

Innovtive Sltons Unlimited LLC............ C 740 289-3282
  Piketon *(G-12423)*

Innovtive Sltons Unlimited LLC............ D 740 289-3282
  Piketon *(G-12424)*

Integris Composites Inc......................... D 740 928-0326
  Hebron *(G-9144)*

Interbrand Design Forum LLC................ C 513 421-2210
  Cincinnati *(G-2880)*

Intren Inc... E 815 482-0651
  Cincinnati *(G-2885)*

Jacobs Engineering Group Inc............... E 513 595-7500
  Cincinnati *(G-2894)*

Jdi Group Inc.. D 419 725-7161
  Maumee *(G-10733)*

Jdrm Engineering Inc............................ E 419 824-2400
  Sylvania *(G-13553)*

Jedson Engineering Inc......................... D 513 965-5999
  Cincinnati *(G-2902)*

Jetson Engineering................................ E 513 965-5999
  Cincinnati *(G-2904)*

Jjr Solutions LLC................................... E 937 912-0288
  Dayton *(G-7429)*

Jones & Henry Engineers Ltd................ E 419 473-9611
  Toledo *(G-13870)*

Juice Technologies Inc.......................... E 800 518-5576
  Worthington *(G-15424)*

Jumporg LLC... E 216 250-4678
  Cleveland *(G-4446)*

Karpinski Engineering Inc..................... E 216 391-3700
  Cleveland *(G-4449)*

Kemron Environmental Svcs Inc............ E 740 373-4071
  Marietta *(G-10378)*

◆ Keuchel & Associates Inc.................. E 330 945-9455
  Cuyahoga Falls *(G-7085)*

Kleingers Group Inc.............................. D 614 882-4311
  Westerville *(G-14903)*

Kleingers Group Inc.............................. D 513 779-7851
  West Chester *(G-14719)*

▲ Koehlke Components Inc................... D 937 435-5435
  Franklin *(G-8643)*

Kokosing Construction Co Inc............... D 440 322-2685
  Elyria *(G-8265)*

KS Associates Inc.................................. D 440 365-4730
  Elyria *(G-8266)*

Kucera International Inc........................ D 440 975-4230
  Willoughby *(G-15197)*

Kudu Dynamics LLC............................. D 973 209-0305
  Worthington *(G-15428)*

KZF Design Inc..................................... D 513 621-6211
  Cincinnati *(G-2959)*

L-3 Cmmncations Nova Engrg Inc......... C 877 282-1168
  Mason *(G-10571)*

L&T Technology Services Ltd............... B 732 688-4402
  Dublin *(G-8052)*

Leantrak Inc.. E 419 482-0797
  Maumee *(G-10739)*

Linquest Corporation............................. D 937 306-6040
  Beavercreek *(G-888)*

Ljb Incorporated.................................... E 440 683-4504
  Independence *(G-9446)*

Louis Perry & Associates Inc................. C 330 334-1585
  Wadsworth *(G-14441)*

LSI Adl Technology LLC........................ E 614 345-9040
  Columbus *(G-6175)*

M Retail Engineering Inc....................... E 614 818-2323
  Westerville *(G-14997)*

Macaulay-Brown Inc.............................. A 937 426-3421
  Beavercreek Township *(G-943)*

Mahoning County.................................. E 330 799-1581
  Youngstown *(G-15655)*

Majidzadeh Enterprises Inc................... E 614 823-4949
  Columbus *(G-6191)*

Mannik & Smith Group Inc.................... C 419 891-2222
  Maumee *(G-10744)*

Martin Control Systems Inc................... E 614 761-5600
  Plain City *(G-12485)*

Matrix Research Inc.............................. D 937 427-8433
  Beavercreek *(G-927)*

Matrix Technologies Inc........................ D 419 897-7200
  Maumee *(G-10745)*

Matthews International Corp.................. E 513 679-7400
  Cincinnati *(G-3017)*

◆ Maval Industries LLC........................ C 330 405-1600
  Twinsburg *(G-14203)*

McGill Smith Punshon Inc..................... E 513 759-0004
  Cincinnati *(G-3023)*

Melink Corporation................................ D 513 685-0958
  Milford *(G-11242)*

Michael Baker Intl Inc............................ E 330 453-3110
  Canton *(G-1806)*

Michael Baker Intl Inc............................ E 412 269-6300
  Cleveland *(G-4573)*

Micro Industries Corporation................. D 740 548-7878
  Westerville *(G-14999)*

Middough Inc.. B 216 367-6000
  Cleveland *(G-4577)*

Mkc Associates Inc............................... E 740 657-3202
  Powell *(G-12599)*

Modal Shop Inc..................................... D 513 351-9919
  Cincinnati *(G-3073)*

Mole Constructors Inc........................... A 440 248-0616
  Beachwood *(G-818)*

Moody-Nolan Inc.................................. C 614 461-4664
  Columbus *(G-6260)*

Morris Technologies Inc........................ E 513 733-1611
  Cincinnati *(G-3080)*

Mote and Associates Inc....................... E 937 548-7511
  Greenville *(G-8881)*

Mrl Materials Resources LLC................. E 937 531-6657
  Xenia *(G-15528)*

Ms Consultants Inc............................... C 330 744-5321
  Youngstown *(G-15669)*

Muskingum County Ohio....................... E 740 453-0381
  Zanesville *(G-15814)*

Neesai Cad Designs LLC....................... E 614 822-7701
  New Albany *(G-11577)*

Neundorfer Inc...................................... E 440 942-8990
  Willoughby *(G-15213)*

Nexus Engineering Group Inc............... D 216 404-7867
  Cleveland *(G-4642)*

Northast Ohio Rgonal Sewer Dst........... C 216 961-2187
  Cleveland *(G-4660)*

Northrop Grmman Tchncal Svcs I......... D 937 320-3100
  Beavercreek Township *(G-945)*

Nottinghm-Spirk Dsign Assoc In........... E 216 800-5782
  Cleveland *(G-4667)*

Nova Engineering & Envmtl LLC........... D 614 325-8092
  Columbus *(G-6374)*

Nu Waves Ltd....................................... E 513 360-0800
  Middletown *(G-11177)*

Ohio Blow Pipe Company..................... E 216 681-7379
  Cleveland *(G-4682)*

Onpower Inc.. E 513 228-2100
  Lebanon *(G-9779)*

Onyx Creative Inc................................. D 216 223-3200
  Cleveland *(G-4702)*

Osborn Engineering Company............... D 216 861-2020
  Cleveland *(G-4708)*

P E Systems Inc.................................... C 937 258-0141
  Dayton *(G-7137)*

Panelmatic Inc....................................... E 330 782-8007
  Youngstown *(G-15688)*

Pedco E & A Services Inc..................... D 513 782-4920
  Blue Ash *(G-1220)*

Pegasus Technical Services Inc............ D 513 793-0094
  Cincinnati *(G-3194)*

Phantom Technical Services Inc........... E 614 868-9920
  Columbus *(G-6520)*

Phoenix Group Holding Co.................... C 937 704-9850
  Dayton *(G-7551)*

Pike County.. E 740 947-9339
  Waverly *(G-14615)*

▼ Plastic Safety Systems Inc................ E 216 231-8590
  Cleveland *(G-4755)*

PMC Systems Limited........................... E 330 538-2268
  North Jackson *(G-11876)*

Poggemeyer Design Group Inc.............. C 419 244-8074
  Bowling Green *(G-1331)*

Polaris Automation Inc.......................... E 614 431-0170
  Columbus *(G-6534)*

Pollock Research & Design Inc............. E 330 332-3300
  Salem *(G-12847)*

Power Engineers Incorporated.............. E 234 678-9875
  Akron *(G-271)*

Power Engineers Incorporated.............. E 513 326-1500
  Cincinnati *(G-3226)*

Power System Engineering Inc............. E 740 568-9220
  Marietta *(G-10401)*

Prater Engineering Assoc Inc................ D 614 766-4896
  Dublin *(G-8094)*

Precision Engrg & Contg Inc................. D 440 349-1204
  Solon *(G-13129)*

Prime Ae Group Inc.............................. E 614 839-0250
  Columbus *(G-5279)*

Process Plus LLC.................................. D 513 742-7590
  Cincinnati *(G-3239)*

Professional Service Inds Inc................ E 216 447-1335
  Cleveland *(G-4774)*

Pta Engineering Inc.............................. E 330 666-3702
  Akron *(G-274)*

Quality Control Services LLC................ E 216 862-9264
  Cleveland *(G-4800)*

Qualus Corp.. D 800 434-0415
  Cincinnati *(G-3261)*

R E Warner & Associates Inc................ D 440 835-9400
  Westlake *(G-15102)*

Ra Consultants LLC.............................. E 513 469-6600
  Blue Ash *(G-1229)*

RCT Engineering Inc............................. E 561 684-7534
  Beachwood *(G-829)*

Red Barn Group Inc.............................. E 419 625-7838
  Sandusky *(G-12925)*

Reed Westlake Leskosky Ltd................. C 216 522-0449
  Cleveland *(G-4817)*

Resonant Sciences LLC........................ E 937 431-8180
  Beavercreek *(G-929)*

Resource International Inc.................... C 614 823-4949
  Columbus *(G-6587)*

Richard L Bowen & Assoc Inc............... D 216 491-9300
  Cleveland *(G-4838)*

Ridge & Associates Inc......................... E 419 423-3641
  Findlay *(G-8582)*

River Consulting LLC............................ D 614 797-2480
  Columbus *(G-6592)*

Roger D Fields Associates Inc.............. E 614 451-2248
  Columbus *(G-6608)*

◆ Rolls-Royce Energy Systems Inc...... A 703 834-1700
  Mount Vernon *(G-11506)*

Saec/Kinetic Vision Inc......................... C 513 793-4959
  Cincinnati *(G-3338)*

Safran Humn Rsrces Support Inc.......... D 513 552-3230
  Cincinnati *(G-3339)*

Safran Power Usa LLC.......................... D 330 487-2000
  Twinsburg *(G-14218)*

Sawdey Solution Services Inc............... E 937 490-4060
  Beavercreek *(G-930)*

Employee Codes: A=Over 500 employees, B=251-500
C=101-250, D=51-100, E=20-50, F=10-19, G=1-9

87 ENGINEERING, ACCOUNTING, RESEARCH, AND MANAGEMENT SERVICES

Scheeser Buckley Mayfield LLC............ E 330 896-4664
   Uniontown *(G-14263)*

Schooley Caldwell Assoc Inc................ D 614 628-0300
   Columbus *(G-6652)*

Sea Ltd... D 614 888-4160
   Columbus *(G-6657)*

SEI Engineers Inc................................ E 740 657-1860
   Powell *(G-12607)*

Sgi Matrix LLC.................................... D 937 438-9033
   Miamisburg *(G-11092)*

Shirk Odnvan Cnslting Engneers.......... E 614 436-6465
   Worthington *(G-15456)*

Shive-Hattery Inc................................. E 216 532-7143
   Cleveland *(G-4902)*

Shively Brothers Inc............................ E 419 626-5091
   Sandusky *(G-12931)*

▲ Si Liquidating Inc............................ E 513 388-2076
   Milford *(G-11255)*

Sierra Lobo Inc................................... C 419 621-3367
   Cleveland *(G-4904)*

Sierra Lobo Inc................................... E 419 332-7101
   Fremont *(G-8702)*

Siertek Ltd.. E 937 623-2466
   Beavercreek Township *(G-948)*

Sigma Technologies Ltd...................... E 419 874-9262
   Perrysburg *(G-12369)*

Solutons Thrugh Innvtive Tech............ D 937 320-9994
   Beavercreek *(G-907)*

Sponseller Group Inc.......................... E 419 861-3000
   Holland *(G-9304)*

Ssoe Inc.. B 419 255-3830
   Toledo *(G-14023)*

Stantec Consulting Svcs Inc................ E 216 621-2407
   Cleveland *(G-4943)*

Star Distribution and Mfg LLC.............. E 513 860-3573
   West Chester *(G-14833)*

Steven Schaefer Associates Inc.......... D 513 542-3300
   Cincinnati *(G-3420)*

Stock Fairfield Corporation.................. C 440 543-6000
   Solon *(G-13149)*

Straight 72 Inc.................................... D 740 943-5730
   Marysville *(G-10511)*

Stress Engineering Svcs Inc................ D 513 336-6701
   Mason *(G-10610)*

Sumaria Systems LLC........................ C 937 429-6070
   Beavercreek *(G-909)*

Summit County.................................... C 330 643-2850
   Akron *(G-326)*

Sunpower Inc...................................... D 740 594-2221
   Athens *(G-592)*

Sutton & Associates Inc...................... E 614 487-9096
   Columbus *(G-6737)*

T J Neff Holdings Inc........................... E 440 884-3100
   Cleveland *(G-4975)*

Technical Assurance Inc..................... E 440 953-3147
   Willoughby *(G-15222)*

Techsolve Inc...................................... D 513 948-2000
   Cincinnati *(G-3449)*

Tecoglas Inc....................................... D 419 537-9750
   Toledo *(G-14034)*

Terracon Consultants Inc.................... C 513 321-5816
   Cincinnati *(G-3458)*

Terracon Consultants Inc.................... D 614 863-3113
   Gahanna *(G-8732)*

Terracon Consultants Inc.................... B 513 321-5816
   Cincinnati *(G-3459)*

Testech Inc... D 937 435-8584
   Dayton *(G-7663)*

Thermal Treatment Center Inc............. E 216 881-8100
   Wickliffe *(G-15164)*

Thermaltech Engineering Inc............... D 513 561-2471
   Cincinnati *(G-3473)*

Thinkpath Engineering Svcs LLC......... E 937 291-8374
   Miamisburg *(G-11097)*

Thorson Baker & Assoc Inc................. E 513 579-8200
   Cincinnati *(G-3476)*

Thorson Baker & Assoc Inc................. E 614 389-3144
   Dublin *(G-8141)*

Thorson Baker & Associates Inc.......... D 330 659-6688
   Richfield *(G-12712)*

Thp Limited Inc................................... D 513 241-3222
   Cincinnati *(G-3477)*

Thrasher Group Inc............................. D 330 620-4790
   Canton *(G-1873)*

TL Industries Inc................................. C 419 666-8144
   Perrysburg *(G-12377)*

Toogann Technologies LLC................. D 614 973-9266
   Dublin *(G-8142)*

Triad Engineering & Contg Co............. E 440 786-1000
   Cleveland *(G-5037)*

Trumbull County Engineering.............. D 330 675-2640
   Warren *(G-14565)*

Ttl Associates Inc................................ D 419 241-4556
   Toledo *(G-14076)*

Twism Enterprises LLC....................... E 513 800-1098
   Cincinnati *(G-3539)*

Underground Services Inc................... E 330 323-0166
   Uniontown *(G-14269)*

University of Cincinnati........................ D 513 556-3732
   Cincinnati *(G-3592)*

URS Group Inc.................................... B 330 836-9111
   Akron *(G-344)*

URS Group Inc.................................... B 513 651-3440
   Cincinnati *(G-3603)*

URS Group Inc.................................... B 216 622-2300
   Cleveland *(G-5090)*

URS Group Inc.................................... B 614 464-4500
   Columbus *(G-6835)*

◆ Uti Corp..D 614 879-7316
   West Jefferson *(G-14854)*

Utility Technologies Intl Corp............... E 614 879-7624
   Groveport *(G-9011)*

Vanner Inc... D 614 771-2718
   Hilliard *(G-9239)*

Varo Engineers Inc.............................. E 740 587-2228
   Granville *(G-8856)*

Varo Engineers Inc.............................. E 513 729-9313
   West Chester *(G-14789)*

Varo Engineers Inc.............................. D 614 459-0424
   Dublin *(G-8149)*

Verdantas LLC.................................... C 614 793-8777
   Dublin *(G-8151)*

Vns Federal Services LLC................... E 740 443-7005
   Piketon *(G-12431)*

Wade Trim... E 216 363-0300
   Cleveland *(G-5120)*

Weastec Incorporated......................... E 614 734-9645
   Dublin *(G-8161)*

Wellert Corporation............................. E 330 239-2699
   Medina *(G-10901)*

Werks Kraft Engineering LLC............... E 330 721-7374
   Medina *(G-10902)*

Whs Engineering Inc........................... E 216 227-8505
   Cleveland *(G-5147)*

◆ Winncom Technologies Corp...........C 440 498-9510
   Solon *(G-13165)*

Woolpert Inc.. C 937 461-5660
   Dayton *(G-7725)*

◆ Xaloy LLC.......................................C 330 726-4000
   Austintown *(G-637)*

Zin Technologies Inc........................... E 440 625-2200
   Middleburg Heights *(G-11137)*

8712 Architectural services

A D A Architects Inc............................ E 216 521-5134
   Cleveland *(G-3749)*

Abbot Stdios Archtcts + Plnner............ E 614 461-0101
   Columbus *(G-5293)*

Andrews Architects Inc....................... E 614 766-1117
   Worthington *(G-15404)*

Arcadis A California Partnr.................. E 614 818-4900
   Columbus *(G-5382)*

ASC Group Inc.................................... E 614 268-2514
   Columbus *(G-5391)*

Austin Building and Design Inc............ C 440 544-2600
   Cleveland *(G-3839)*

Baxter Hdell Dnnlly Prston Inc............. C 513 271-1634
   Cincinnati *(G-2240)*

Big Red Rooster.................................. E 614 255-0200
   Columbus *(G-5440)*

Bostwick Design Partnr Inc................. E 216 621-7900
   Cleveland *(G-3882)*

Buehrer Group Arch & Engrg............... E 419 893-9021
   Maumee *(G-10706)*

Burgess & Niple Inc............................. D 703 631-6041
   Columbus *(G-5486)*

Burgess & Niple Inc............................. B 614 459-2050
   Columbus *(G-5485)*

Burgess & Niple/Heapy LLC................ D 614 459-2050
   Columbus *(G-5487)*

Ceso Inc.. E 937 435-8584
   Miamisburg *(G-11035)*

Champlin Haupt Architects Inc............ E 513 241-4474
   Cincinnati *(G-2346)*

Chemstress Consultant Company........ C 330 535-5591
   Akron *(G-87)*

Chute Gerdeman Inc........................... D 614 469-1001
   Westerville *(G-14966)*

City Architecture Inc............................ E 216 881-2444
   Cleveland *(G-3974)*

Collaborative Inc................................. E 419 242-7405
   Toledo *(G-13748)*

◆ Continental Office Furn Corp...........C 614 262-5010
   Columbus *(G-5693)*

Cornelia C Hodgson - Architec............ E 216 593-0057
   Beachwood *(G-784)*

Csa America Inc.................................. D 513 791-6918
   Cincinnati *(G-2520)*

CT Consultants Inc............................. C 440 951-9000
   Mentor *(G-10930)*

David A Levy Inc.................................. E 330 352-1289
   Akron *(G-132)*

Davis-Mcmackin Inc............................ E 614 824-1587
   Columbus *(G-5742)*

Dei Incorporated................................. D 513 825-5800
   Cincinnati *(G-2554)*

Dlr Group Inc....................................... D 216 522-1350
   Cleveland *(G-4169)*

Dlz Ohio Inc.. C 614 888-0040
   Columbus *(G-5778)*

Dorsky Hodgson + Partners Inc........... D 216 464-8600
   Cleveland *(G-4179)*

Elevar Design Group Inc..................... E 513 721-0600
   Cincinnati *(G-2611)*

Emersion Design LLC......................... E 513 841-9100
   Cincinnati *(G-2616)*

Fanning/Howey Associates Inc............ D 614 764-4661
   Dublin *(G-8010)*

Fanning/Howey Associates Inc............ E 419 586-2292
   Celina *(G-1922)*

Frch Design Worldwide - Cincin........... B 513 241-3000
   Cincinnati *(G-2701)*

Garland/Dbs Inc.................................. C 216 641-7500
   Cleveland *(G-4302)*

Garmann/Miller & Assoc Inc................ E 419 628-4240
   Minster *(G-11316)*

SIC SECTION 87 ENGINEERING, ACCOUNTING, RESEARCH, AND MANAGEMENT SERVICES

Gbc Design Inc.. E 330 836-0228
   Akron *(G-171)*

Glaus Pyle Schmer Brns Dhven I.............. E 216 518-5544
   Cleveland *(G-4314)*

Glaus Pyle Schmer Brns Dhven I.............. D 614 210-0751
   Columbus *(G-5936)*

Glaus Pyle Schmer Brns Dhven I.............. B 330 572-2100
   Akron *(G-176)*

Gpd Services Company Inc......................... C 330 572-2100
   Akron *(G-180)*

Harris Day Architects Inc........................... E 330 493-3722
   North Canton *(G-11838)*

Hasenstab Architects Inc........................... E 330 434-4464
   Akron *(G-187)*

Hixson Incorporated................................... C 513 241-1230
   Cincinnati *(G-2829)*

HWH Archtcts-Ngnrs-Plnners Inc.............. D 216 875-4000
   Cleveland *(G-4394)*

Jdi Group Inc.. D 419 725-7161
   Maumee *(G-10733)*

K4 Architecture LLC................................... D 513 455-5005
   Cincinnati *(G-2928)*

Karlsberger Architecture Inc..................... D 614 471-1812
   Columbus *(G-6103)*

Karlsberger Companies.............................. C 614 461-9500
   Columbus *(G-6104)*

KZF Design Inc... D 513 621-6211
   Cincinnati *(G-2959)*

Ljb Inc... C 937 259-5000
   Miamisburg *(G-11070)*

Ljb Incorporated... E 440 683-4504
   Independence *(G-9446)*

Loth Inc... D 513 554-4900
   Cincinnati *(G-2989)*

Louis Perry & Associates Inc.................... C 330 334-1585
   Wadsworth *(G-14441)*

Luminaut Inc... E 513 984-1070
   Cincinnati *(G-2994)*

Makovich Pusti Architects Inc................... E 440 891-8910
   Berea *(G-1073)*

McGill Smith Punshon Inc.......................... E 513 759-0004
   Cincinnati *(G-3023)*

Meacham & Apel Architects Inc................ D 614 764-0407
   Columbus *(G-6220)*

Meyers + Associates Arch LLC................. E 614 221-9433
   Columbus *(G-6230)*

Michael Schuster Assoc Inc...................... E 513 241-5666
   Cincinnati *(G-3056)*

Middough Inc.. B 216 367-6000
   Cleveland *(G-4577)*

Mkc Associates Inc.................................... E 740 657-3202
   Powell *(G-12599)*

Moody-Nolan Inc.. C 614 461-4664
   Columbus *(G-6260)*

Ms Consultants Inc.................................... C 330 744-5321
   Youngstown *(G-15669)*

NBBJ LLC... C 206 223-5026
   Columbus *(G-6342)*

Nelson... C 216 781-9144
   Seven Hills *(G-12955)*

New Republic Architecture....................... E 513 800-8075
   Cincinnati *(G-3108)*

Neyer Architects Engineers Inc................ E 513 271-6400
   Cincinnati *(G-3115)*

Onyx Creative Inc...................................... D 216 223-3200
   Cleveland *(G-4702)*

Orchard Hiltz & McCliment Inc.................. E 614 418-0600
   Columbus *(G-6478)*

Osborn Engineering Company................... D 216 861-2020
   Cleveland *(G-4708)*

Pedco E & A Services Inc......................... D 513 782-4920
   Blue Ash *(G-1220)*

Perspectus Architecture LLC.................... E 216 752-1800
   Cleveland *(G-4744)*

Poggemeyer Design Group Inc.................. C 419 244-8074
   Bowling Green *(G-1331)*

Prime Ae Group Inc.................................... D 614 839-0250
   Columbus *(G-5279)*

R E Warner & Associates Inc.................... D 440 835-9400
   Westlake *(G-15102)*

Red Architecture LLC................................ D 614 487-8770
   Columbus *(G-6565)*

Reed Westlake Leskosky Ltd..................... C 216 522-0449
   Cleveland *(G-4817)*

Richard L Bowen & Assoc Inc................... E 216 491-9300
   Cleveland *(G-4838)*

Rvc Architects Inc..................................... E 740 592-5615
   Athens *(G-587)*

Schooley Caldwell Assoc Inc.................... D 614 628-0300
   Columbus *(G-6652)*

Shremshock Architects Inc....................... D 614 545-4550
   New Albany *(G-11587)*

Ssoe Inc... B 419 255-3830
   Toledo *(G-14023)*

Steed Hammond Paul Inc.......................... D 513 381-2112
   Cincinnati *(G-3415)*

Strollo Architects Inc................................ E 330 743-1177
   Youngstown *(G-15731)*

Sullivan Bruck Architects Inc................... D 614 464-9800
   Columbus *(G-6726)*

Tc Architects Inc....................................... E 330 867-1093
   Akron *(G-330)*

Technical Assurance Inc........................... E 440 953-3147
   Willoughby *(G-15222)*

Triad Architects Ltd................................... E 614 942-1050
   Columbus *(G-6787)*

Trinity Health Group Ltd........................... E 614 899-4830
   Columbus *(G-6791)*

Twism Enterprises LLC............................. E 513 800-1098
   Cincinnati *(G-3539)*

United Architectural Mtls Inc.................... E 330 433-9220
   North Canton *(G-11868)*

URS Group Inc... B 330 836-9111
   Akron *(G-344)*

URS Group Inc... B 614 464-4500
   Columbus *(G-6835)*

WD Partners Inc... B 614 634-7000
   Dublin *(G-8160)*

8713 Surveying services

7nt Enterprises LLC................................... E 614 961-2026
   Miamisburg *(G-11018)*

▲ American Electric Pwr Svc Corp........... B 614 716-1000
   Columbus *(G-5348)*

ASC Group Inc.. E 614 268-2514
   Columbus *(G-5391)*

Bair Goodie and Assoc Inc....................... E 330 343-3499
   New Philadelphia *(G-11641)*

Barr Engineering Incorporated................. E 614 714-0299
   Columbus *(G-5420)*

Bayer & Becker Inc................................... E 513 492-7401
   Mason *(G-10522)*

Burgess & Niple Inc................................... D 703 631-6041
   Columbus *(G-5486)*

CT Consultants Inc.................................... C 440 951-9000
   Mentor *(G-10930)*

Ctl Engineering Inc.................................... C 614 276-8123
   Columbus *(G-5736)*

Division of Geological Survey................... E 614 265-6576
   Columbus *(G-5776)*

Dlz Ohio Inc.. C 614 888-0040
   Columbus *(G-5778)*

Evans McHwart Hmblton Tlton In............. B 614 775-4500
   New Albany *(G-11563)*

Feller Finch & Associates Inc................... E 419 893-3680
   Maumee *(G-10724)*

Gbc Design Inc... E 330 836-0228
   Akron *(G-171)*

Hammontree & Associates Ltd.................. E 330 499-8817
   Canton *(G-1769)*

Kleingers Group Inc................................... D 513 779-7851
   West Chester *(G-14719)*

KS Associates Inc...................................... D 440 365-4730
   Elyria *(G-8266)*

Kucera International Inc........................... D 440 975-4230
   Willoughby *(G-15197)*

Ljb Incorporated... E 440 683-4504
   Independence *(G-9446)*

McGill Smith Punshon Inc.......................... E 513 759-0004
   Cincinnati *(G-3023)*

McSteen & Associates Inc........................ D 440 585-9800
   Wickliffe *(G-15157)*

Millman Surveying Inc............................... E 330 342-0723
   Uniontown *(G-14259)*

Millman Surveying Inc............................... E 330 296-9017
   Cleveland *(G-4586)*

Mote and Associates Inc........................... E 937 548-7511
   Greenville *(G-8881)*

Poggemeyer Design Group Inc.................. C 419 244-8074
   Bowling Green *(G-1331)*

Pve Sheffler LLC.. D 330 332-5200
   Salem *(G-12848)*

R E Warner & Associates Inc.................... D 440 835-9400
   Westlake *(G-15102)*

Resource International Inc....................... C 614 823-4949
   Columbus *(G-6587)*

Surveying and Mapping LLC..................... D 512 447-0575
   Westerville *(G-15016)*

T J Neff Holdings Inc................................. E 440 884-3100
   Cleveland *(G-4975)*

Testech Inc... D 937 435-8584
   Dayton *(G-7663)*

Usic Locating Services LLC...................... D 330 733-9393
   Akron *(G-346)*

Wade Trim... E 216 363-0300
   Cleveland *(G-5120)*

Wellert Corporation................................... E 330 239-2699
   Medina *(G-10901)*

8721 Accounting, auditing, and bookkeeping

415 Group Inc... E 330 492-0094
   Canton *(G-1648)*

Advocate Rcm LLC.................................... D 614 210-1885
   Dublin *(G-7921)*

Ahola Corporation...................................... D 440 717-7620
   Brecksville *(G-1342)*

Akron-Canton Regional Airport................ E 330 499-4059
   North Canton *(G-11809)*

▲ American Electric Pwr Svc Corp........... B 614 716-1000
   Columbus *(G-5348)*

▲ Apple Growth Partners Inc................... D 330 867-7350
   Akron *(G-53)*

APS Medical Billing.................................... D 419 866-1804
   Toledo *(G-13692)*

ARC Healthcare LLC.................................. E 888 552-0677
   Worthington *(G-15405)*

Arthur Mddlton Cpitl Hldngs In................. D 330 966-9000
   North Canton *(G-11812)*

AT&T Teleholdings Inc............................... C 330 385-9967
   East Liverpool *(G-8178)*

Barnes Dennig & Co Ltd............................ E 513 241-8313
   Cincinnati *(G-2237)*

Barnes Wendling Cpas Inc........................ E 216 566-9000
   Cleveland *(G-3851)*

Battelle Rippe Kingston LLP...................... C 937 853-1470
   Moraine *(G-11390)*

Employee Codes: A=Over 500 employees, B=251-500
C=101-250, D=51-100, E=20-50, F=10-19, G=1-9

87 ENGINEERING, ACCOUNTING, RESEARCH, AND MANAGEMENT SERVICES

BCI Mississippi Broadband LLC .... E 419 724-7295
  Toledo *(G-13702)*
Blue & Co LLC .... D 513 241-4507
  Cincinnati *(G-2265)*
Bober Markey Fedorovich & Co .... D 330 762-9785
  Fairlawn *(G-8467)*
Bodine Perry LLC .... E 330 702-8100
  Canfield *(G-1622)*
Brady Ware & Schoenfeld Inc .... D 937 223-5247
  Miamisburg *(G-11026)*
Breen Winkel & Co .... E 614 261-1494
  Columbus *(G-5463)*
Brixey and Meyer Inc .... E 937 291-4110
  Miamisburg *(G-11027)*
C H Dean LLC .... D 937 222-9531
  Beavercreek *(G-867)*
Cassady Schiller & Assoc Inc .... C 513 483-6699
  Blue Ash *(G-1142)*
Cavcapital Ltd .... E 216 831-8900
  Cleveland *(G-3940)*
Cbiz Accnting Tax Advsory Ohio .... C 330 668-6500
  Akron *(G-84)*
Chard Snyder & Associates LLC .... C 513 459-9997
  Mason *(G-10528)*
Chicago Mso Inc .... E 513 624-8300
  Cincinnati *(G-2354)*
City of Cleveland .... E 216 664-2640
  Cleveland *(G-3978)*
City of Wellston .... D 740 384-2428
  Wellston *(G-14636)*
Ciulla Smith & Dale LLP .... E 440 439-4700
  Bedford *(G-956)*
Ciulla Smith & Dale LLP .... E 440 884-2036
  Cleveland *(G-3996)*
Ciuni & Panichi Inc .... D 216 831-7171
  Cleveland *(G-3997)*
Clark Schaefer Hackett & Co .... E 937 399-2000
  Springfield *(G-13229)*
Clark Schaefer Hackett & Co .... E 937 226-0070
  Miamisburg *(G-11036)*
Cohen & Company Ltd .... C 330 374-1040
  Akron *(G-111)*
Cohen & Company Ltd .... C 330 743-1040
  Youngstown *(G-15581)*
County of Champaign .... E 937 653-2711
  Urbana *(G-14306)*
County of Lucas .... D 419 213-4500
  Toledo *(G-13762)*
Defense Fin & Accounting Svc .... A 614 693-6700
  Columbus *(G-5750)*
Deloitte & Touche LLP .... B 513 784-7100
  Cincinnati *(G-2556)*
Deloitte & Touche LLP .... A 216 589-1300
  Cleveland *(G-4160)*
Deloitte & Touche LLP .... A 614 221-1000
  Columbus *(G-5753)*
Deloitte & Touche LLP .... E 937 223-8821
  Dayton *(G-7308)*
Doyle Hcm Inc .... E 614 322-9310
  Columbus *(G-5784)*
E T Financial Service Inc .... E 937 716-1726
  Trotwood *(G-14127)*
Ernst & Young LLP .... E 513 612-1594
  Cincinnati *(G-2636)*
Ernst & Young LLP .... E 513 612-1400
  Cincinnati *(G-2637)*
Ernst & Young LLP .... D 216 861-5000
  Cleveland *(G-4218)*
Ernst & Young LLP .... E 216 583-1823
  Cleveland *(G-4219)*
Ernst & Young LLP .... C 614 224-5678
  Columbus *(G-5827)*

Ernst & Young LLP .... E 419 244-8000
  Toledo *(G-13798)*
Ernst & Young US LLP .... D 216 583-1893
  Cleveland *(G-4220)*
First-Knox National Bank .... C 740 399-5500
  Mount Vernon *(G-11488)*
Flagel Huber Flagel & Co .... E 937 299-3400
  Moraine *(G-11411)*
Flynn Crtif Pub Accntnts PSC I .... E 513 530-9200
  Cincinnati *(G-2690)*
Forvis LLP .... E 330 650-1752
  Hudson *(G-9351)*
Fully Accountable LLC .... E 330 940-1440
  Fairlawn *(G-8482)*
Gbq Holdings LLC .... E 614 221-1120
  Columbus *(G-5920)*
Gbq Partners LLC .... C 513 871-3033
  Cincinnati *(G-2719)*
Gbq Partners LLC .... E 419 885-8338
  Sylvania *(G-13546)*
Gbq Partners LLC .... D 614 221-1120
  Columbus *(G-5921)*
Gilmore Jasion Mahler Ltd .... E 419 423-4481
  Findlay *(G-8538)*
Gilmore Jasion Mahler Ltd .... E 419 794-2000
  Maumee *(G-10728)*
Grant Thornton LLP .... E 513 762-5000
  Cincinnati *(G-2749)*
Hammerman Graf Hughes & Co Inc .... E 937 320-1262
  Dayton *(G-7391)*
Healthpro Medical Billing Inc .... D 419 223-2717
  Lima *(G-9904)*
Hill Barth & King LLC .... E 330 758-8613
  Canfield *(G-1631)*
Hobe Lcas Crtif Pub Accntnts I .... E 216 524-7167
  Cleveland *(G-4371)*
Holbrook & Manter .... E 740 387-8620
  Marion *(G-10430)*
Howard Wershbale & Co .... E 614 794-8710
  Westerville *(G-14899)*
Howard Wershbale & Co .... D 216 831-1200
  Woodmere *(G-15299)*
Hr Butler LLC .... E 614 923-2900
  Dublin *(G-8032)*
Jones Cochenour & Co Inc .... E 740 653-9581
  Lancaster *(G-9727)*
Julian & Grube Inc .... E 614 846-1899
  Westerville *(G-14902)*
Kaiser Consulting LLC .... D 614 378-5361
  Powell *(G-12594)*
Kaiser Technology LLC .... D 614 300-1088
  Powell *(G-12595)*
Klingbeil Management Group Co .... E 614 220-8900
  Columbus *(G-6120)*
Kpmg LLP .... D 614 249-2300
  Columbus *(G-6127)*
Lbk Health Care Inc .... E 937 296-1550
  Bellbrook *(G-1018)*
Lipari Foods Operating Co LLC .... E 330 893-2479
  Millersburg *(G-11284)*
Maloney + Novotny LLC .... D 216 363-0100
  Cleveland *(G-4518)*
Marcum LLP .... E 440 459-5700
  Mayfield Village *(G-10794)*
Martin Wilson and Associates .... D 513 772-7284
  Cincinnati *(G-3013)*
MBI Solutions Inc .... A 937 619-4000
  Dayton *(G-7470)*
Meaden & Moore LLP .... D 216 241-3272
  Cleveland *(G-4543)*
Medic Management Group LLC .... D 330 670-5316
  Beachwood *(G-814)*

Medicount Management Inc .... E 513 612-3144
  Cincinnati *(G-3029)*
Medigistics Inc .... D 614 430-5700
  Columbus *(G-6221)*
Mellott & Mellott Pll .... E 513 241-2940
  Cincinnati *(G-3038)*
Nationwide Childrens Hospital .... C 330 253-5200
  Akron *(G-239)*
Novogradac & Company LLP .... E 415 356-8000
  Dover *(G-7897)*
Ohio Bell Telephone Company .... A 216 822-9700
  Brecksville *(G-1360)*
Patrick J Burke & Co .... E 513 455-8200
  Cincinnati *(G-3189)*
Paychex Inc .... D 800 939-2462
  Lima *(G-9947)*
Paychex Advance LLC .... D 216 831-8900
  Cleveland *(G-4731)*
Paycom Software Inc .... C 888 678-0796
  Cincinnati *(G-3190)*
Paycor Inc .... C 513 381-0505
  Cincinnati *(G-3191)*
Pease Bell Cpas LLC .... E 216 348-9600
  Cleveland *(G-4734)*
Physicians Professional Mgt .... E 207 782-7494
  Dublin *(G-8091)*
Plante & Moran Pllc .... A 614 849-3000
  Columbus *(G-6530)*
Premiere Medical Resources Inc .... E 330 923-5899
  Cuyahoga Falls *(G-7094)*
Promedica Health Systems Inc .... B 800 477-4035
  Toledo *(G-13975)*
Promedica Physcn Cntinuum Svcs ..... C 419 824-7200
  Sylvania *(G-13565)*
Quadax Inc .... C 216 765-1144
  Beachwood *(G-828)*
Quadax Inc .... C 330 759-4600
  Youngstown *(G-15702)*
Quadax Inc .... E 440 777-6300
  Middleburg Heights *(G-11121)*
Radiology Assoc Canton Inc .... E 330 363-2842
  Canton *(G-1840)*
REA & Associates Inc .... D 330 339-6651
  New Philadelphia *(G-11662)*
Real Property Management Inc .... E 614 766-6500
  Dublin *(G-8106)*
Rehmann Robson LLC .... E 248 952-5000
  Independence *(G-9475)*
REM-Ohio Inc .... E 330 644-9730
  Coventry Township *(G-7015)*
Reynolds & Co Inc .... E 740 353-1040
  Portsmouth *(G-12566)*
Richland Trust Company .... C 419 525-8700
  Mansfield *(G-10314)*
Rlj Management Co Inc .... C 614 942-2020
  Columbus *(G-6602)*
RSM US LLP .... E 216 523-1900
  Cleveland *(G-4862)*
Schneider Downs & Co Inc .... E 614 621-4060
  Columbus *(G-6650)*
Schroedel Scullin & Bestic LLC .... E 330 533-1131
  Canfield *(G-1640)*
Sheakley-Uniservice Inc .... E 513 771-2277
  Cincinnati *(G-3367)*
Specilzed Med Blling Rvnue Rcv .... E 614 461-8154
  Worthington *(G-15458)*
Specilzed Med Blling Rvnue Rcv .... E 614 461-8154
  Worthington *(G-15457)*
THE COMMERCIAL TRAFFIC CO .... C 216 267-2000
  Cleveland *(G-4998)*
The Peoples Bank Co Inc .... E 419 678-2385
  Coldwater *(G-5220)*

87 ENGINEERING, ACCOUNTING, RESEARCH, AND MANAGEMENT SERVICES

The Sheakley Group Inc .... E 513 771-2277
   Cincinnati *(G-3471)*

Thomas Packer & Co .... E 330 533-9777
   Canfield *(G-1643)*

Thornhill Financial Inc .... E 440 238-0445
   Cleveland *(G-5014)*

Vonlehman & Company Inc .... E 513 891-5911
   Blue Ash *(G-1271)*

Walthall LLP .... E 216 573-2330
   Cleveland *(G-5122)*

Warren Bros & Sons Inc .... E 740 373-1430
   Marietta *(G-10410)*

Whalen and Company Cpas Inc .... D 614 396-4200
   Worthington *(G-15469)*

William Vaughan Company .... D 419 891-1040
   Maumee *(G-10781)*

Wilson Shannon & Snow Inc .... E 740 345-6611
   Newark *(G-11754)*

Zinner & Co .... E 216 831-0733
   Beachwood *(G-853)*

8731 Commercial physical research

Acrt Inc .... E 800 622-2562
   Stow *(G-13352)*

Aerospace Corporation .... E 937 657-9634
   Dayton *(G-7125)*

Alliance Imaging Inc .... D 330 493-5100
   Canton *(G-1660)*

American Showa Inc .... E 740 965-4040
   Sunbury *(G-13516)*

Amplifybio LLC .... D 833 641-2006
   West Jefferson *(G-14847)*

Antioch University .... C 937 769-1366
   Yellow Springs *(G-15534)*

Apex Software Technologies Inc .... E 614 932-2167
   Powell *(G-12584)*

Applied Medical Technology Inc .... E 440 717-4000
   Brecksville *(G-1343)*

Arthur G Jmes Cncer Hosp Rchar .... B 614 293-4878
   Columbus *(G-5388)*

ASC Group Inc .... E 614 268-2514
   Columbus *(G-5391)*

Azimuth Corporation .... C 937 256-8571
   Beavercreek *(G-861)*

Bae Systems Iap Research LLC .... E 937 296-1806
   Dayton *(G-7185)*

BASF Catalysts LLC .... C 216 360-5005
   Cleveland *(G-3853)*

▲ Battelle Memorial Institute .... A 614 424-6424
   Columbus *(G-5422)*

Berriehill Research Corp .... E 937 435-1016
   Dayton *(G-7190)*

◆ Borchers Americas Inc .... D 440 899-2950
   Westlake *(G-15040)*

Brilligent Solutions LLC .... E 937 879-4148
   Fairborn *(G-8367)*

▲ Caterpllar Trmble Ctrl Tech LL .... D 937 233-8921
   Dayton *(G-7217)*

Center For Eating Disorders .... E 614 896-8222
   Columbus *(G-5531)*

Charles River Laboratories Inc .... E 419 647-4196
   Spencerville *(G-13187)*

Charles River Labs Ashland LLC .... A 419 282-8700
   Ashland *(G-492)*

Charles Rver Labs Clveland Inc .... D 216 332-1665
   Cleveland *(G-3962)*

Chemimage Filter Tech LLC .... E 330 686-2726
   Stow *(G-13358)*

Childrens Hosp Reference Lab .... E 614 722-5477
   Columbus *(G-5562)*

Childrens Hospital Medical Ctr .... A 513 636-4200
   Cincinnati *(G-2369)*

Childrens Hospital Medical Ctr .... A 513 636-4200
   Cincinnati *(G-2368)*

Circle Prime Manufacturing .... E 330 923-0019
   Cuyahoga Falls *(G-7054)*

Columbus Dnv Inc .... C 614 761-1214
   Dublin *(G-7966)*

Concord Biosciences LLC .... D 440 357-3200
   Concord Township *(G-6923)*

Conwed Plas Acquisition V LLC .... D 877 542-7699
   Dover *(G-7875)*

Ctl Engineering Inc .... E 614 276-8123
   Columbus *(G-5736)*

Curtiss-Wright Controls .... E 937 252-5601
   Fairborn *(G-8371)*

▲ Edison Welding Institute Inc .... C 614 688-5000
   Columbus *(G-5807)*

EMD Millipore Corporation .... C 513 631-0445
   Norwood *(G-12032)*

Energy Harbor Nuclear Corp .... D 440 604-9836
   Cleveland *(G-4214)*

◆ Flexsys America LP .... D 330 666-4111
   Akron *(G-164)*

▲ Guild Associates Inc .... D 614 798-8215
   Dublin *(G-8023)*

▲ Heraeus Epurio LLC .... E 937 264-1000
   Vandalia *(G-14380)*

Hii Mission Technologies Corp .... C 937 426-3421
   Beavercreek Township *(G-940)*

Icon Government .... B 330 278-2343
   Hinckley *(G-9270)*

Imarc Research Inc .... D 440 801-1540
   Strongsville *(G-13464)*

Infinity Labs LLC .... E 937 317-0030
   Xenia *(G-15522)*

Innovest Global Inc .... D 216 815-1122
   Chesterland *(G-2036)*

Kbr Wyle Services LLC .... C 937 320-2713
   Dayton *(G-7433)*

Kemron Environmental Svcs Inc .... E 740 373-4071
   Marietta *(G-10378)*

Kenmore Research Company .... D 330 297-1407
   Ravenna *(G-12631)*

Lazurite Inc .... E 216 334-3127
   Warrensville Heights *(G-14583)*

Leidos Inc .... D 937 656-8433
   Beavercreek *(G-886)*

Leidos Inc .... E 614 575-4900
   Columbus *(G-6154)*

Lyondell Chemical Company .... C 513 530-4000
   Cincinnati *(G-2996)*

Medpace Inc .... A 513 579-9911
   Cincinnati *(G-3031)*

Medpace Holdings Inc .... C 513 579-9911
   Cincinnati *(G-3033)*

Morris Technologies Inc .... E 513 733-1611
   Cincinnati *(G-3080)*

Mp Biomedicals LLC .... C 440 337-1200
   Solon *(G-13113)*

Muskingum Starlight Industries .... D 740 453-4622
   Zanesville *(G-15817)*

Nokia of America Corporation .... D 614 860-2000
   Dublin *(G-8077)*

North Amercn Science Assoc LLC .... C 419 666-9455
   Northwood *(G-11979)*

Ohio State University .... D 330 263-3700
   Wooster *(G-15363)*

Oleco Inc .... E 937 223-3000
   Dayton *(G-7537)*

Olon USA LLC .... D 440 357-3300
   Concord Township *(G-6931)*

Peak Nanosystems LLC .... D 216 264-4818
   Cleveland *(G-4733)*

Peerless Technologies Corp .... D 937 490-5000
   Beavercreek Township *(G-946)*

Phoenix Technology Services .... E 740 325-1138
   Bellaire *(G-1015)*

▲ Plastic Technologies Inc .... D 419 867-5400
   Holland *(G-9300)*

Q Labs LLC .... C 513 471-1300
   Cincinnati *(G-3258)*

Quality Construction MGT Inc .... D 513 779-8425
   West Chester *(G-14750)*

R & D Nestle Center Inc .... D 440 264-2200
   Solon *(G-13134)*

▲ R & D Nestle Center Inc .... D 937 642-7015
   Marysville *(G-10503)*

Radiance Technologies Inc .... C 937 425-0747
   Beavercreek *(G-898)*

RGBSI Aerospace & Defense LLC .... D 248 761-0412
   Beavercreek *(G-900)*

Sierra Nevada Corporation .... C 937 431-2800
   Beavercreek *(G-906)*

Smithers MSE Inc .... D 330 762-7441
   Akron *(G-305)*

Solutons Through Innvtive Tech .... D 937 320-9994
   Beavercreek *(G-907)*

Spr Therapeutics Inc .... E 216 378-2658
   Cleveland *(G-4936)*

Steiner Eoptics Inc .... E 937 264-2341
   Miamisburg *(G-11095)*

Sunpower Inc .... D 740 594-2221
   Athens *(G-592)*

Synthomer Inc .... D 330 794-6300
   Akron *(G-328)*

Sytronics Inc .... C 937 431-6100
   Beavercreek *(G-910)*

Taitech Inc .... E 937 255-4141
   Fairborn *(G-8381)*

Terracon Consultants Inc .... D 614 863-3113
   Gahanna *(G-8732)*

Terracon Consultants Inc .... B 513 321-5816
   Cincinnati *(G-3459)*

◆ Trico Products Corporation .... C 248 371-1700
   Cleveland *(G-5038)*

Trucent Renewable Chem LLC .... D 877 280-7212
   Van Wert *(G-14353)*

Velocys Inc .... D 614 733-3300
   Plain City *(G-12497)*

▲ Wiley Companies .... C 740 622-0755
   Coshocton *(G-7005)*

Zin Technologies Inc .... E 440 625-2200
   Middleburg Heights *(G-11137)*

8732 Commercial nonphysical research

8451 LLC .... D 513 632-1020
   Cincinnati *(G-2127)*

Alphamicron Incorporated .... E 330 676-0648
   Kent *(G-9556)*

Alta360 Research Inc .... E 419 535-5757
   Maumee *(G-10688)*

Big Village Insights Inc .... D 513 772-7580
   Cincinnati *(G-2261)*

Big Village Insights Inc .... D 419 893-0029
   Maumee *(G-10700)*

Burke Inc .... D 513 576-5700
   Milford *(G-11220)*

Burke Inc .... C 513 241-5663
   Cincinnati *(G-2290)*

Cbg Biotech Ltd Co .... D 800 941-9484
   Solon *(G-13074)*

Circana Inc .... C 513 651-0500
   Cincinnati *(G-2448)*

▼ Convergys Cstmer MGT Group Inc ...... B 513 723-6104
   Cincinnati *(G-2506)*

Employee Codes: A=Over 500 employees, B=251-500
C=101-250, D=51-100, E=20-50, F=10-19, G=1-9

87 ENGINEERING, ACCOUNTING, RESEARCH, AND MANAGEMENT SERVICES

Cushman Wakefield Holdings Inc............ E 513 241-4880
   Cincinnati *(G-2526)*
Data Recognition Corporation................ E 513 588-7260
   Cincinnati *(G-2540)*
Deskey Associates Inc............................ D 513 721-6800
   Cincinnati *(G-2559)*
Directions Research Inc........................... D 513 651-2990
   Cincinnati *(G-2567)*
EMC Research Incorporated................... E 614 268-1660
   Columbus *(G-5813)*
Freedonia Publishing LLC........................ C 440 684-9600
   Cleveland *(G-4288)*
Great Lakes Mktg Assoc Inc.................... E 419 534-4700
   Toledo *(G-13827)*
Icon Government..................................... B 330 278-2343
   Hinckley *(G-9270)*
Impact Sales Solutions Inc...................... E 419 466-0131
   Toledo *(G-13861)*
Independent Research Group Inc............ D 330 273-3380
   Brunswick *(G-1459)*
Infocision Management Corp................... C 330 544-1400
   Youngstown *(G-15640)*
Ipsos-Asi LLC.. C 513 872-4300
   Cincinnati *(G-2888)*
Kantar Media Research Inc..................... D 419 666-8800
   Northwood *(G-11976)*
Lerner RES Inst Clvland Clinic.................. D 216 444-3900
   Cleveland *(G-4489)*
Lightspeed LLC.. D 419 666-8800
   Northwood *(G-11977)*
Mahoning Yngstown Cmnty Action.......... D 330 747-7921
   Youngstown *(G-15661)*
Mahoning Youngstown Community.......... E 330 747-0236
   Youngstown *(G-15662)*
Marketing Research Services................... D 513 579-1555
   Cincinnati *(G-3009)*
Marketing Research Svcs Inc................... C 513 772-7580
   Cincinnati *(G-3010)*
Marketvision Research Inc...................... D 513 791-3100
   Blue Ash *(G-1206)*
National Rgstry of Emrgncy Med.............. D 614 888-4484
   Columbus *(G-6301)*
Procter Gamble US Bus Svcs Co.............. C 513 983-7777
   Cincinnati *(G-3244)*
Quality Solutions Inc................................ E 440 933-9946
   Cleveland *(G-4801)*
Sytronics Inc.. E 937 431-6100
   Beavercreek *(G-910)*
The Rdi Corporation................................ A 513 984-5927
   Cincinnati *(G-3470)*
University of Cincinnati............................ D 513 556-4054
   Cincinnati *(G-3591)*
Various Views Research Inc.................... D 513 489-9000
   Blue Ash *(G-1268)*
Vogt Santer Insights Ltd.......................... E 614 224-4300
   Columbus *(G-6855)*

8733 Noncommercial research organizations

Aerospace Corporation............................ E 937 657-9634
   Dayton *(G-7125)*
Air Force Research Laboratory................ D 937 255-9209
   Wright Patterson Afb *(G-15474)*
Applied Research Solutions Inc............... D 937 912-6100
   Dayton *(G-7177)*
Aramark... D 614 921-7495
   Hilliard *(G-9179)*
Arthur G Jmes Cncer Hosp Rchar............ B 614 293-4878
   Columbus *(G-5388)*
ASC Group Inc... E 614 268-2514
   Columbus *(G-5391)*
Aventiv Research Inc.............................. E 614 495-8970
   Columbus *(G-5410)*

Benjamin Rose Institute........................... E 216 791-8000
   Cleveland *(G-3869)*
Childrens Hosp Med Ctr Akron................ D 330 633-2055
   Tallmadge *(G-13587)*
Childrens Hospital Medical Ctr................. B 513 636-6100
   Cincinnati *(G-2367)*
Childrens Hospital Medical Ctr................. A 513 636-4200
   Cincinnati *(G-2369)*
Childrens Hospital Medical Ctr................. B 513 636-6400
   Fairfield *(G-8400)*
Childrens Hospital Medical Ctr................. B 513 636-6800
   Mason *(G-10529)*
Childrens Hospital Medical Ctr................. A 513 636-4200
   Cincinnati *(G-2368)*
Cornerstone Research Group Inc............ C 937 320-1877
   Miamisburg *(G-11039)*
Hebrew Un Cllg-Jwish Inst Rlgi................ E 513 221-1875
   Cincinnati *(G-2815)*
Help Foundation Inc................................ E 216 432-4810
   Northfield *(G-11956)*
Jjr Solutions LLC.................................... E 937 912-0288
   Dayton *(G-7429)*
Kumho Tire Co Inc.................................. E 330 666-4030
   Fairlawn *(G-8489)*
Lazurite Inc... E 216 334-3127
   Warrensville Heights *(G-14583)*
Lerner RES Inst Clvland Clinic.................. D 216 444-3900
   Cleveland *(G-4489)*
Macaulay-Brown Inc................................ A 937 426-3421
   Beavercreek Township *(G-943)*
Mp Biomedicals LLC................................ C 440 337-1200
   Solon *(G-13113)*
NASA/Glenn Research Center................. A 419 625-1123
   Sandusky *(G-12918)*
Nationwide Childrens Hospital................. C 614 722-2000
   Columbus *(G-6320)*
Ohio Aerospace Institute.......................... E 440 962-3000
   Cleveland *(G-4681)*
Ohio State University............................... C 614 688-0857
   Columbus *(G-6459)*
Phillips Edison Institutional...................... E 513 554-1110
   Cincinnati *(G-3207)*
Prologue Research Intl Inc....................... C 614 324-1500
   Columbus *(G-6552)*
Quasonix Inc.. E 513 942-1287
   West Chester *(G-14751)*
Research Inst At Ntnwide Chld................ C 614 722-2700
   Columbus *(G-6580)*
Riverside Research Institute.................... C 937 431-3810
   Beavercreek *(G-901)*
Src Inc... E 937 431-0717
   Beavercreek *(G-908)*
Sunpower Inc... D 740 594-2221
   Athens *(G-592)*
The Sisters of Charity of.......................... E 216 696-5560
   Cleveland *(G-5007)*
Trihealth Inc.. C 513 985-3700
   Cincinnati *(G-3509)*
Trihealth Inc.. C 513 246-7000
   Cincinnati *(G-3510)*
Trihealth Inc.. C 513 860-6820
   West Chester *(G-14778)*
Uc Health Llc.. A 513 585-6000
   Cincinnati *(G-3546)*
Universities Space Res Assn.................... E 216 368-0750
   Cleveland *(G-5070)*
University of Dayton................................ C 937 229-2113
   Dayton *(G-7690)*
University of Dayton................................ B 937 229-3822
   Dayton *(G-7691)*
▲ University of Dayton............................ A 937 229-1000
   Dayton *(G-7689)*

Within3 Inc.. B 855 948-4463
   Lakewood *(G-9687)*
Wright State University............................ D 937 298-4331
   Kettering *(G-9634)*

8734 Testing laboratories

Advanced Testing Lab Inc........................ C 513 489-8447
   Blue Ash *(G-1122)*
Advanced Testing MGT Group Inc........... D 513 489-8447
   Blue Ash *(G-1123)*
Agrana Fruit Us Inc................................. C 937 693-3821
   Anna *(G-442)*
Akron Rubber Dev Lab Inc....................... E 330 794-6600
   Barberton *(G-692)*
Akron Rubber Dev Lab Inc....................... D 330 794-6600
   Akron *(G-36)*
Als Group Usa Corp................................ D 281 530-5656
   Cleveland *(G-3797)*
Analytical Pace Services LLC................... D 937 832-8242
   Englewood *(G-8303)*
Andritz Inc... C 937 390-3400
   Springfield *(G-13217)*
Aqua Tech Envmtl Labs Inc..................... E 740 389-5991
   Marion *(G-10417)*
Asnt Certification Svcs LLC..................... D 614 274-6003
   Columbus *(G-5395)*
Balancing Company Inc........................... E 937 898-9111
   Vandalia *(G-14365)*
Barr Engineering Incorporated................ E 614 714-0299
   Columbus *(G-5420)*
Bowser-Morner Inc.................................. E 419 691-4800
   Toledo *(G-13714)*
Bowser-Morner Inc.................................. C 937 236-8805
   Dayton *(G-7198)*
Bwi Chassis Dynamics NA Inc.................. E 937 455-5230
   Moraine *(G-11394)*
Bwi North America Inc............................. E 937 212-2892
   Moraine *(G-11395)*
Cincinnati Prcision Instrs Inc................... E 513 874-2122
   West Chester *(G-14805)*
Cincinnati Testing Laboratories Inc......... E 513 851-3313
   Cincinnati *(G-2427)*
Cincinnati Testing Labs Inc...................... E 513 851-3313
   Cincinnati *(G-2428)*
Columbus Dnv Inc.................................... C 614 761-1214
   Dublin *(G-7966)*
County of Lake.. E 440 350-2793
   Painesville *(G-12224)*
Csa America Standards Inc..................... C 216 524-4990
   Cleveland *(G-4142)*
Ctl Engineering Inc.................................. C 614 276-8123
   Columbus *(G-5736)*
Curtiss-Wright Flow Ctrl Corp.................. D 513 528-7900
   Cincinnati *(G-2101)*
Dna Diagnostics Center Inc..................... D 513 881-7800
   Fairfield *(G-8407)*
Electro-Analytical Inc.............................. E 440 951-3514
   Mentor *(G-10935)*
Element Materials Technol....................... E 216 524-1450
   Cleveland *(G-4210)*
Element Mtls Tech Cncnnati Inc.............. E 513 984-4112
   Fairfield *(G-8410)*
Energy Harbor Nuclear Corp.................... D 440 604-9836
   Cleveland *(G-4214)*
Envirite of Ohio Inc.................................. E 330 456-6238
   Canton *(G-1747)*
Environmental Enterprises Inc................. C 513 772-2818
   Cincinnati *(G-2627)*
Enviroscience Inc.................................... D 330 688-0111
   Stow *(G-13366)*
Eurofins Testoil Inc.................................. D 216 251-2510
   Strongsville *(G-13453)*

SIC SECTION
87 ENGINEERING, ACCOUNTING, RESEARCH, AND MANAGEMENT SERVICES

Food Safety Net Services Ltd................ E 614 274-2070
Columbus (G-5876)
General Electric Company.................... C 937 587-2631
Peebles (G-12288)
Gentherm Medical LLC....................... D 513 326-5252
Cincinnati (G-2730)
▲ Godfrey & Wing Inc............................ E 330 562-1440
Aurora (G-615)
Headwinds LP..................................... E 724 209-5543
Steubenville (G-13330)
High Voltage Maintenance Corp........... E 937 278-0811
Dayton (G-7406)
Ics Laboratories Inc............................. E 330 220-0515
Brunswick (G-1458)
Intertek Testing Svcs NA Inc................ E 614 279-8090
Columbus (G-6070)
Isomedix Operations Inc...................... D 614 836-5757
Groveport (G-8992)
Isomedix Operations Inc...................... E 877 783-7497
Mentor (G-10953)
Juice Technologies Inc........................ E 800 518-5576
Worthington (G-15424)
◆ Kaplan Industries Inc.......................... D 856 779-8181
Harrison (G-9111)
Kbr Wyle Services LLC........................ E 937 912-3470
Beavercreek (G-885)
Kemron Environmental Svcs Inc........... E 740 373-4071
Marietta (G-10378)
Kenmore Research Company............... D 330 297-1407
Ravenna (G-12631)
Lexamed Ltd.. E 419 693-5307
Toledo (G-13886)
Lmsi LLC... E 800 838-0602
Toledo (G-13890)
McCloy Engineering LLC..................... E 513 984-4112
Fairfield (G-8428)
Merieux Nutrisciences Corp................. D 614 486-0150
Columbus (G-6226)
Metcut Research Associates Inc.......... D 513 271-5100
Cincinnati (G-3052)
Microbac Laboratories Inc................... E 740 373-4071
Marietta (G-10389)
◆ Microtek Laboratories Inc................... E 937 236-2213
Moraine (G-11426)
Mistras Group Inc................................ C 740 788-9188
Heath (G-9136)
Mrl Materials Resources LLC............... E 937 531-6657
Xenia (G-15528)
National Testing Laboratories............... E 440 449-2525
Cleveland (G-4628)
Nelson Labs Fairfield Inc..................... E 973 227-6882
Broadview Heights (G-1393)
Nestle Usa Inc..................................... B 614 526-5300
Dublin (G-8073)
North Amercn Science Assoc LLC....... C 419 666-9455
Northwood (G-11979)
Northast Ohio Rgonal Sewer Dst......... E 216 641-6000
Cleveland (G-4657)
Nsl Analytical Services Inc................... D 216 438-5200
Cleveland (G-4671)
Ohio Department Transportation.......... E 614 275-1300
Columbus (G-6402)
Omega Laboratories Inc...................... D 330 628-5748
Mogadore (G-11330)
▲ Plastic Technologies Inc..................... D 419 867-5400
Holland (G-9300)
Prime NDT Services Inc...................... D 330 878-4202
Strasburg (G-13405)
Q Labs LLC... C 513 471-1300
Cincinnati (G-3258)
Resource International Inc................... C 614 823-4949
Columbus (G-6587)

S D Myers Inc..................................... C 330 630-7000
Tallmadge (G-13602)
Sample Machining Inc......................... E 937 258-3338
Dayton (G-7609)
SD Myers LLC..................................... C 330 630-7000
Tallmadge (G-13603)
Silliker Laboratories Ohio Inc............... E 614 486-0150
Columbus (G-6680)
Smithers Group Inc............................. D 330 833-8548
Massillon (G-10671)
Smithers MSE Inc................................ E 330 297-1495
Ravenna (G-12644)
Smithers MSE Inc................................ D 330 762-7441
Akron (G-305)
Smithers Tire Auto Tstg of Txa............ C 330 762-7441
Akron (G-306)
Sotera Health Company....................... E 440 262-1410
Broadview Heights (G-1396)
Sotera Health Holdings LLC................ B 440 262-1410
Broadview Heights (G-1397)
Sotera Health Services LLC................. D 440 262-1410
Broadview Heights (G-1399)
◆ Steris Isomedix Services Inc............... B 440 354-2600
Mentor (G-10999)
Technology Recovery Group Ltd.......... D 440 250-9970
Westlake (G-15114)
Teledyne Brown Engineering Inc.......... D 419 470-3000
Toledo (G-14036)
Tensile Tstg A Div J T Adams I............ E 216 641-3290
Cleveland (G-4985)
Terracon Consultants Inc..................... B 513 321-5816
Cincinnati (G-3459)
Tool Testing Lab Inc............................ E 937 898-5696
Tipp City (G-13666)
Transportation Research Center Inc..... A 937 666-2011
East Liberty (G-8176)
◆ Trico Products Corporation................. C 248 371-1700
Cleveland (G-5038)
University of Cincinnati......................... E 513 558-4110
Cincinnati (G-3585)
▲ US Inspection Services Inc................. E 937 660-9879
Dayton (G-7697)
US Tubular Products Inc..................... D 330 832-1734
North Lawrence (G-11880)
Wallover Enterprises Inc...................... E 440 238-9250
Strongsville (G-13497)
X-Ray Industries Inc............................ D 216 642-0100
Cleveland (G-5163)
Yoder Industries Inc............................. C 937 278-5769
Dayton (G-7731)

8741 Management services

Acme Dynamite.................................... E 313 867-5309
Toledo (G-13674)
Act For Health Inc................................ B 740 443-5000
Piketon (G-12414)
Adaptive Development Corp................. E 937 890-3388
Dayton (G-7156)
Agile Pursuits Inc................................ D 513 945-9908
Cincinnati (G-2156)
Aim Integrated Logistics Inc................ B 330 759-0438
Girard (G-8808)
Akron General Health System.............. B 330 344-6000
Akron (G-31)
Amend Consulting LLC....................... D 513 399-6300
Cincinnati (G-2176)
American Hospitality Group Inc............ B 330 336-6684
Wadsworth (G-14428)
Arthur Mddlton Cpitl Hldngs In............ D 330 966-9000
North Canton (G-11812)
Ashland Home Towne Phrm Inc........... E 419 281-4040
Ashland (G-475)

Atrium Living Centers of...................... E 614 416-2662
Columbus (G-5405)
◆ Babcock & Wilcox Company............... A 330 753-4511
Akron (G-59)
Balanced Care Corporation.................. E 330 908-1166
Northfield (G-11952)
Balanced Care Corporation.................. D 330 296-4545
Ravenna (G-12619)
Baxter Hdell Dnnlly Prston Inc............. C 513 271-1634
Cincinnati (G-2240)
Benjamin Rose Institute....................... C 216 791-3580
Cleveland (G-3868)
Bethesda Hospital Inc......................... E 513 247-0224
Montgomery (G-11362)
Bionix Development Corporation.......... E 800 551-7096
Toledo (G-13706)
Blanchard Valley Health System.......... A 419 423-4500
Findlay (G-8514)
Bon Appetit Management Co............... C 614 823-1880
Westerville (G-14962)
Bostleman Corp................................... E
Holland (G-9281)
Bravo Wellness LLC............................ E 216 658-9500
Cleveland (G-3891)
Bridgepoint Risk MGT LLC.................. E 419 794-1075
Maumee (G-10704)
Brown Co Ed Service Center............... E 937 378-6118
Georgetown (G-8799)
C M M Inc... E 216 789-7480
Hudson (G-9336)
Cameron Mitchell Rest LLC................. D 724 824-7558
Dublin (G-7949)
Cameron Mitchell Rest LLC................. E 614 621-3663
Columbus (G-5494)
Canton Rhbltition Nrsing Ctr LL........... E 330 456-2842
Canton (G-1704)
Cardinal Health Inc.............................. E 614 497-9552
Obetz (G-12079)
◆ Cardinal Health Inc............................. A 614 757-5000
Dublin (G-7950)
Carespring Health Care MGT LLC....... E 513 943-4000
Loveland (G-10130)
Careworks of Ohio Inc......................... A 614 792-1085
Dublin (G-7958)
Cargotec Services USA Inc................. E 419 482-6000
Perrysburg (G-12322)
Carington Health Systems................... E 513 682-2700
Hamilton (G-9025)
Carpediem Management Company...... E 740 687-1563
Lancaster (G-9699)
Catastrophe MGT Solutions Inc........... D 800 959-2630
Hudson (G-9337)
Ccf Health Care Ventures Inc.............. B 216 295-1959
Cleveland (G-3946)
Central Coca-Cola Btlg Co Inc............. E 330 875-1487
Akron (G-86)
Central Coca-Cola Btlg Co Inc............. E 740 474-2180
Circleville (G-3705)
CFC Mansfield LLC............................. E 216 328-1121
Ontario (G-12101)
CFM Religion Pubg Group LLC........... D 513 931-4050
Cincinnati (G-2339)
Chemstress Consultant Company........ C 330 535-5591
Akron (G-87)
Christian Benevolent Assn................... C 513 931-5000
Cincinnati (G-2385)
Chronic Care Management Inc............. C 440 248-6500
Independence (G-9418)
Chu Management Co Inc..................... E 330 725-4571
Medina (G-10820)
City of Youngstown.............................. B 330 742-8700
Youngstown (G-15578)

87 ENGINEERING, ACCOUNTING, RESEARCH, AND MANAGEMENT SERVICES

▲ CK Construction Group Inc............... B 614 901-8844
  Westerville (G-14967)
Cks & Associates MGT LLC................ E 614 621-9710
  Columbus (G-5578)
Clevelan Clinic Hlth Sys W Reg............ A 216 476-7000
  Cleveland (G-4001)
Cleveland Clinic Foundation................ D 419 609-2812
  Sandusky (G-12882)
Cleveland Clnic Hlth Systm-Wst............ C 216 476-7606
  Cleveland (G-4038)
Cleveland Clnic Hlth Systm-Wst............ D 440 716-9810
  North Olmsted (G-11898)
Cleveland Clnic Hlth Systm-Wst............ C 216 491-6000
  Warrensville Heights (G-14579)
Clinical Management Cons Inc.............. D 440 638-5000
  Cleveland (G-4084)
Coal Services Inc................................ B 740 795-5220
  Powhatan Point (G-12610)
Collins Assoc Tchncal Svcs Inc............. C 740 574-2320
  Wheelersburg (G-15128)
Colonial Senior Services Inc................ D 513 856-8600
  Hamilton (G-9030)
Colonial Senior Services Inc................ E 513 867-4006
  Hamilton (G-9031)
Colonial Senior Services Inc................ D 513 844-8004
  Hamilton (G-9032)
Communicare Health Svcs Inc.............. E 513 530-1654
  Blue Ash (G-1157)
Communications Buying Group............ D 216 377-3000
  Cleveland (G-4095)
Complete General Cnstr Co................. D 614 258-9515
  Columbus (G-5678)
Comprhnsive Hlth Care Ohio Inc........... A 440 329-7500
  Elyria (G-8237)
Connecting Dots Cnncting To SL.......... E 216 356-2362
  Cleveland (G-4101)
Consoldted Fndries Hldngs Corp.......... A 216 772-1041
  Cleveland (G-4105)
Cook Paving and Cnstr Co................... E 216 267-7705
  Independence (G-9424)
Core Resources Inc........................... D 513 731-1771
  Cincinnati (G-2507)
Corvel Corporation............................. E 800 275-6463
  Cleveland (G-4119)
County of Lucas................................. C 419 248-3585
  Toledo (G-13765)
Cpca Manufacturing LLC..................... D 937 723-9031
  Dayton (G-7260)
CPS Medmanagement LLC.................. D 901 748-0470
  Dublin (G-7977)
CPS Solutions LLC............................. C 901 748-0470
  Dublin (G-7978)
Crane Group Co................................. E 614 754-3000
  Columbus (G-5719)
Crescent Park Corporation................... C 513 759-7000
  West Chester (G-14679)
Critical Business Analysis Inc.............. E 419 874-0800
  Perrysburg (G-12326)
Crown Group Incorporated.................. E 586 558-5311
  Lima (G-9882)
Danis Building Construction Co............ E 513 984-9696
  Cincinnati (G-2537)
Danis Building Construction Co............ C 614 761-8385
  Columbus (G-5739)
◆ Dco LLC...E 419 931-9086
  Perrysburg (G-12331)
DE Foxx & Associates Inc................... B 513 621-5522
  Cincinnati (G-2547)
Distribution Data Incorporated.............. D 216 362-3009
  Brookpark (G-1433)
DMD Management Inc......................... C 216 749-4010
  Cleveland (G-4170)

DMD Management Inc......................... C 440 944-9400
  Wickliffe (G-15147)
DMD Management Inc......................... E 216 898-8399
  Cleveland (G-4171)
EDM Management Inc......................... E 330 726-5790
  Youngstown (G-15607)
Educatonal Svc Ctr Lorain Cnty............ C 440 244-1659
  Elyria (G-8244)
▲ Eleet Cryogenics Inc....................... E 330 874-4009
  Bolivar (G-1294)
Elford Inc.. C 614 488-4000
  Columbus (G-5811)
Ensemble Health Partners Inc.............. A 704 765-3715
  Cincinnati (G-2623)
Ensemble RCM LLC............................ A 704 765-3715
  Cincinnati (G-2624)
Erie Indemnity Company..................... C 330 433-6300
  Canton (G-1748)
Excellence In Motivation Inc................ C 763 445-3000
  Dayton (G-7341)
Executive Jet Management Inc............. B 513 979-6600
  Cincinnati (G-2644)
▲ Fedex Supplychain Systems Inc........ A
  Hudson (G-9348)
First Hospital Labs LLC....................... C 215 396-5500
  Independence (G-9432)
First Services Inc...............................A 513 241-2200
  Cincinnati (G-2675)
◆ First Transit Inc..............................D 513 241-2200
  Cincinnati (G-2682)
Fisher Foods Marketing Inc.................. C 330 497-3000
  North Canton (G-11830)
Flat Rock Care Center......................... D 419 483-7330
  Flat Rock (G-8600)
Forum Health..................................... A 330 841-9011
  Warren (G-14521)
French Company LLC.......................... D 330 963-4344
  Twinsburg (G-14193)
G Stephens Inc.................................. D 614 227-0304
  Columbus (G-5906)
Genesis.. E 740 453-3122
  Zanesville (G-15789)
Gentlebrook Inc.................................. D 330 877-3694
  Hartville (G-9125)
Gilbane Building Company................... E 614 948-4000
  Columbus (G-5934)
Grace Management Inc....................... B 763 971-9271
  Cincinnati (G-2747)
Hammond Construction Inc.................. D 330 455-7039
  Uniontown (G-14254)
Hanger Prsthtics Orthtics E In.............. E 330 633-9807
  Tallmadge (G-13593)
Hat White Management LLC................ C 800 525-7967
  Akron (G-188)
Help Foundation Inc........................... E 216 432-4810
  Euclid (G-8346)
Hill Barth & King LLC......................... E 330 758-8613
  Canfield (G-1631)
Hills Developers Inc........................... C 513 984-0300
  Blue Ash (G-1182)
Holzer Clinic LLC............................... A 740 446-5411
  Gallipolis (G-8759)
Holzer Senior Care Center................... E 740 446-5001
  Bidwell (G-1104)
Imflux Inc.. D 513 488-1017
  Cincinnati (G-2865)
Ingle-Barr Inc.................................... D 740 702-6117
  Chillicothe (G-2072)
Instantwhip-Columbus Inc.................... E 614 871-9447
  Grove City (G-8928)
Integrated Resources Inc..................... E 419 885-7122
  Sylvania (G-13552)

Interservice Corporation...................... C 216 272-3519
  Novelty (G-12039)
Ironwood Development Corp................. C 440 895-1200
  Cleveland (G-4422)
Island Service Company...................... E 419 285-3695
  Put In Bay (G-12617)
ITW Air Management.......................... E 513 891-7474
  Blue Ash (G-1187)
J & P Asset Management Inc............... D 216 408-7693
  Akron (G-205)
Jack Gibson Construction Co................ D 330 394-5280
  Warren (G-14530)
Jake Sweeney Automotive Inc.............. D 513 782-2800
  Cincinnati (G-2896)
Jance & Company Incorporated............ E 440 255-5800
  Mentor (G-10954)
▲ Jmac Inc.. E 614 436-2418
  Columbus (G-6092)
Jordan Hospitality Group LLC............... E 614 406-5139
  New Albany (G-11571)
JP Compass Cnsulting Cnstr Inc........... E 440 635-0500
  Chesterland (G-2037)
Juice Technologies Inc........................ E 800 518-5576
  Worthington (G-15424)
Kaiser Logistics LLC........................... D 937 534-0213
  Monroe (G-11342)
Kaleidoscope Innovation...................... C 513 791-3009
  Blue Ash (G-1193)
KHD Company LLC............................. E 614 935-9939
  Worthington (G-15426)
Kingston Healthcare Company.............. E 419 247-2880
  Toledo (G-13879)
Klingbeil Capital MGT Ltd.................... D 415 398-0106
  Worthington (G-15427)
Knowlton Development Corp................ E 614 656-1130
  Johnstown (G-9547)
Lathrop Company Inc.......................... E 419 893-7000
  Toledo (G-13882)
▲ Leadec Corp................................... E 513 731-3590
  Blue Ash (G-1200)
Leatherman Nursing Ctrs Corp.............. B 330 336-6684
  Wadsworth (G-14439)
Legacy Village Management LLC.......... D 216 382-3871
  Cleveland (G-4485)
Lendkey Technologies Inc.................... C 646 626-7396
  Blue Ash (G-1201)
Liberty Technology Company LLC......... E 740 363-1941
  Delaware (G-7815)
Licking Memorial Hlth Systems............. A 220 564-4000
  Newark (G-11717)
Licking-Knox Goodwill Inds Inc............. D 740 345-9861
  Newark (G-11721)
Lincolnview Local Schools................... C 419 968-2226
  Van Wert (G-14348)
Locus Management LLC...................... D 888 510-0004
  Solon (G-13106)
M A Folkes Company Inc..................... E 513 785-4200
  Hamilton (G-9062)
M&C Hotel Interests Inc...................... C 440 543-1331
  Chagrin Falls (G-1985)
Majidzadeh Enterprises Inc.................. E 614 823-4949
  Columbus (G-6191)
Management and Netwrk Svcs LLC........ D 800 949-2159
  Dublin (G-8059)
Marsh Berry & Company LLC............... E 440 637-8122
  Beachwood (G-810)
Mary Rtan Hlth Assn Logan Cnty.......... E 937 592-4015
  Bellefontaine (G-1033)
Marymount Health Care Systems.......... A 216 332-1100
  Cleveland (G-4530)
McDaniels Cnstr Corp Inc..................... D 614 252-5852
  Columbus (G-6213)

87 ENGINEERING, ACCOUNTING, RESEARCH, AND MANAGEMENT SERVICES

McR LLC .... E 937 879-5055
  Beavercreek *(G-891)*

Med America Hlth Systems Corp .... A 937 223-6192
  Dayton *(G-7475)*

MEI Hotels Incorporated .... C 216 589-0441
  Cleveland *(G-4549)*

Mercy Franciscan Hosp Mt Airy .... A 513 853-5101
  Cincinnati *(G-3040)*

Mfbusiness Group .... E 216 609-7297
  Cleveland *(G-4570)*

Michael Baker Intl Inc .... E 330 453-3110
  Canton *(G-1806)*

Michael Baker Intl Inc .... E 412 269-6300
  Cleveland *(G-4573)*

Ministerial Day Care Assn .... E 216 881-6924
  Cleveland *(G-4587)*

Momentum Fleet MGT Group Inc .... D 440 759-2219
  Westlake *(G-15080)*

Munich RE America Services .... E 609 480-6596
  Cincinnati *(G-3089)*

Mvah Management LLC .... E 513 964-1140
  West Chester *(G-14735)*

National Dcp LLC .... D 216 410-3215
  Twinsburg *(G-14207)*

National Heritg Academies Inc .... E 937 223-2889
  Dayton *(G-7525)*

National Heritg Academies Inc .... E 937 278-6671
  Dayton *(G-7526)*

National Heritg Academies Inc .... E 330 792-4806
  Youngstown *(G-15674)*

Nationwide General Insur Co .... A 614 249-7111
  Columbus *(G-6331)*

Niagara Health Corporation .... A 614 855-4878
  New Albany *(G-11582)*

Niagara Health Corporation .... C 614 898-4000
  Columbus *(G-6357)*

Niederst Management Ltd .... C 440 331-8800
  Rocky River *(G-12749)*

Niederst Management Ltd .... C 440 331-8800
  Cleveland *(G-4646)*

Nms Wealth Management LLC .... E 440 286-5222
  Chardon *(G-2013)*

North Randall Village .... E 216 663-1112
  Cleveland *(G-4651)*

Novotec Recycling LLC .... C 614 231-8326
  Columbus *(G-6375)*

Nrp Management LLC .... E 216 475-8900
  Cleveland *(G-4670)*

Ohc Ohio Co-Manager LLC .... E 513 751-2273
  Cincinnati *(G-3142)*

▲ Ohio Cllbrtive Lrng Sltons Inc .... E 216 595-5289
  Strongsville *(G-13479)*

Ohio Shared Info Svcs Inc .... C 513 677-5600
  Cincinnati *(G-3149)*

◆ Oki Bering Management Co .... D 513 341-4002
  West Chester *(G-14827)*

Omnicare Purch Ltd Partner Inc .... A 800 990-6664
  Cincinnati *(G-3161)*

Osu Internal Medicine LLC .... D 614 293-0080
  Dublin *(G-8084)*

Outreach Professional Svcs Inc .... D 216 472-4094
  Cleveland *(G-4710)*

P I & I Motor Express Inc .... C 330 448-4035
  Masury *(G-10679)*

Parker-Hannifin Intl Corp .... B 216 896-3000
  Cleveland *(G-4725)*

Perduco Group Inc .... E 937 401-0268
  Beavercreek *(G-893)*

Permedion Inc .... C 614 895-9900
  Dublin *(G-8089)*

Pharmacy Data Management .... D 330 757-0724
  Poland *(G-12506)*

Phoenix Administrators LLC .... E 440 628-4235
  Avon Lake *(G-683)*

Piada Group LLC .... D 614 397-1339
  Columbus *(G-6524)*

Plus Management Services Inc .... E 419 331-2273
  Lima *(G-9949)*

Plus Management Services Inc .... C 419 225-9018
  Lima *(G-9950)*

Pro-Model & Talent Mgmt Inc .... E 330 665-0723
  Fairlawn *(G-8494)*

Promedica Health System Inc .... A 567 585-9600
  Toledo *(G-13972)*

Promedica Physcn Cntinuum Svcs .... C 419 824-7200
  Sylvania *(G-13565)*

Providence Medical Group Inc .... E 937 297-8999
  Moraine *(G-11430)*

Purple Land Management LLC .... D 740 238-4259
  North Canton *(G-11856)*

Quality Construction MGT Inc .... D 513 779-8425
  West Chester *(G-14750)*

Quality Control Inspection .... D 440 359-1900
  Cleveland *(G-4799)*

Quality Supply Chain Co-Op Inc .... E 614 764-3124
  Dublin *(G-8101)*

RB Sigma LLC .... D 440 290-0577
  Mentor *(G-10988)*

Renaissance House Inc .... E 419 626-1110
  Sandusky *(G-12926)*

Renier Construction Corp .... E 614 866-4580
  Columbus *(G-6578)*

Resource International Inc .... C 614 823-4949
  Columbus *(G-6587)*

Revolution Group Inc .... D 614 212-1111
  Westerville *(G-14935)*

RGT Management Inc .... E 513 715-4640
  Harrison *(G-9114)*

Ricco Enterprises Incorporated .... E 216 883-7775
  Cleveland *(G-4837)*

Richard L Bowen & Assoc Inc .... D 216 491-9300
  Cleveland *(G-4838)*

Richter & Associates Inc .... D 216 593-7140
  Twinsburg *(G-14217)*

Ridgewood Government Svcs LLC .... E 740 294-7261
  West Lafayette *(G-14858)*

RJ Runge Company Inc .... E 419 740-5781
  Port Clinton *(G-12539)*

RMS of Ohio Inc .... C 440 617-6605
  Westlake *(G-15104)*

Ross Consolidated Corp .... D 440 748-5800
  Grafton *(G-8841)*

Roth Roofing Products LLC .... D 800 872-7684
  Youngstown *(G-15714)*

Roundstone Management Ltd .... C 440 617-0333
  Lakewood *(G-9683)*

Ruscilli Construction Co Inc .... D 614 876-9484
  Dublin *(G-8111)*

Saber Healthcare Group LLC .... E 216 292-5706
  Beachwood *(G-833)*

Safeguard Properties LLC .... A 216 739-2900
  Cleveland *(G-4869)*

Safran Power Usa LLC .... D 330 487-2000
  Twinsburg *(G-14218)*

Salvation Army .... E 330 773-3331
  Cleveland *(G-4873)*

Salvation Army .... E 419 447-2252
  Tiffin *(G-13641)*

Savour Hospitality LLC .... C 216 308-0018
  Cleveland *(G-4879)*

SEI Engineers Inc .... E 740 657-1860
  Powell *(G-12607)*

Select Hotels Group LLC .... D 513 754-0003
  Mason *(G-10606)*

Serco Services Inc .... C 937 369-4066
  Dayton *(G-7616)*

Shook Construction Co .... D 937 276-6666
  Moraine *(G-11438)*

Shook National Corporation .... C 937 276-6666
  Dayton *(G-7617)*

Signature Inc .... E 614 766-5101
  Dublin *(G-8119)*

Skanska USA Building Inc .... D 513 421-0082
  Cincinnati *(G-3383)*

Sleep Network Inc .... E 419 535-9282
  Toledo *(G-14015)*

Smg Holdings LLC .... E 614 827-2500
  Columbus *(G-6689)*

Sprenger Enterprises Inc .... D 630 529-0700
  Lorain *(G-10102)*

Stat Integrated Tech Inc .... E 440 286-7663
  Chardon *(G-2021)*

Sterling Medical Corporation .... C 513 984-1800
  Cincinnati *(G-3419)*

Sterling Medical Corporation .... C 513 984-1800
  Cincinnati *(G-3418)*

Stonespring Trnstnal Care Ctr .... E 937 415-8000
  Dayton *(G-7645)*

Summa Health System Corp .... E 330 375-4848
  Akron *(G-321)*

Surge Management LLC .... E 614 431-5100
  Columbus *(G-6735)*

TAC Industries Inc .... B 937 328-5200
  Springfield *(G-13299)*

Talawanda City School District .... D 513 273-3200
  Oxford *(G-12218)*

The Sheakley Group Inc .... E 513 771-2277
  Cincinnati *(G-3471)*

Tjm Clmbus LLC Tjm Clumbus LLC .... D 614 885-1885
  Columbus *(G-6771)*

Tm Capture Services LLC .... D 937 728-1781
  Dayton *(G-7671)*

Toledo Innvtion Ctr Lndlord LL .... C 419 585-3684
  Toledo *(G-14060)*

Transinternational System Inc .... E 614 891-4942
  Worthington *(G-15463)*

Tri-C Construction Company Inc .... E 330 836-2722
  Akron *(G-337)*

Trihealth Inc .... C 513 891-1627
  Blue Ash *(G-1257)*

Trihealth Inc .... D 513 241-4135
  Cincinnati *(G-3511)*

Trihealth Inc .... A 513 569-6777
  Cincinnati *(G-3512)*

Trihealth Inc .... D 513 871-2340
  Cincinnati *(G-3513)*

Trihealth Inc .... B 513 865-1111
  Montgomery *(G-11377)*

Trihealth Inc .... A 513 985-0900
  Montgomery *(G-11378)*

Trihealth Inc .... E 513 569-5400
  Cincinnati *(G-3517)*

Trinity Hospital Holding Co .... A 740 264-8000
  Steubenville *(G-13347)*

Triversity Construction Co LLC .... D 513 733-0046
  Cincinnati *(G-3528)*

Ttl Associates Inc .... D 419 241-4556
  Toledo *(G-14076)*

Turnbull-Wahlert Construction Inc .... D 513 731-7300
  Cincinnati *(G-3535)*

Turnserv LLC .... E 216 600-8876
  Akron *(G-338)*

Uc Health Llc .... C 513 584-8600
  Cincinnati *(G-3545)*

Uc Health Llc .... E 513 298-3000
  West Chester *(G-14785)*

Employee Codes: A=Over 500 employees, B=251-500
C=101-250, D=51-100, E=20-50, F=10-19, G=1-9

87 ENGINEERING, ACCOUNTING, RESEARCH, AND MANAGEMENT SERVICES

Uc Health Llc .... A 513 585-6000
Cincinnati *(G-3546)*

United Telemanagement Corp .... E 937 454-1888
Dayton *(G-7685)*

University Hsptals Clvland Med .... A 216 844-3528
Cleveland *(G-5081)*

University of Cincinnati .... E 513 556-6932
Blue Ash *(G-1264)*

University of Cincinnati .... C 513 556-4200
Cincinnati *(G-3582)*

University of Cincinnati .... C 513 558-4231
Cincinnati *(G-3583)*

Urban Retail Properties LLC .... E 937 433-0957
Dayton *(G-7695)*

Usacs Management Group Ltd .... D 330 493-4443
Canton *(G-1877)*

Value Add Management LLC .... E 614 291-2600
Columbus *(G-6841)*

Vanguard Property Management .... E 216 521-8222
Lakewood *(G-9686)*

Vein Clinics of America Inc .... E 630 725-2700
Cincinnati *(G-3617)*

Verst Group Logistics Inc .... E 513 772-2494
Cincinnati *(G-3621)*

Verst Group Logistics Inc .... D 859 379-1230
West Chester *(G-14844)*

Viaquest LLC .... E 614 889-5837
Dublin *(G-8152)*

Village of Valley View .... E 216 524-6511
Cleveland *(G-5106)*

Vora Ventures LLC .... B 513 792-5100
Blue Ash *(G-1272)*

Vrc Companies LLC .... D 614 299-2122
Grove City *(G-8964)*

Vrc Companies LLC .... E 419 381-7762
Maumee *(G-10778)*

Walnut Ridge Strgc MGT Co LLC ..... D 234 678-3900
Beachwood *(G-851)*

Wayne Street Development LLC .... E 740 373-5455
Marietta *(G-10412)*

Welty Building Company Ltd .... E 330 867-2400
Fairlawn *(G-8503)*

Western Management Inc .... E 216 941-3333
Cleveland *(G-5135)*

Westlake Ten Inc .... E 440 250-9804
Westlake *(G-15124)*

Weston and Associates LLC .... C 330 791-7118
Massillon *(G-10672)*

Wolf Creek Federal Svcs Inc .... A 216 433-5609
Cleveland *(G-5157)*

8742 Management consulting services

1st Advnce SEC Invstgtions Inc .... E 937 317-4433
Dayton *(G-7145)*

30 Lines .... D 614 859-5030
Columbus *(G-5286)*

3sg Plus LLC .... E 614 652-0019
Columbus *(G-5243)*

▲ 4mybenefits Inc .... E 513 891-6726
Blue Ash *(G-1119)*

5me LLC .... E 513 719-1600
Cincinnati *(G-2095)*

A-1 Hlthcare Stffing Plcements .... C 216 329-3500
Cleveland *(G-3753)*

Accelerant Technologies LLC .... D 419 236-8768
Maumee *(G-10684)*

Accenture LLP .... C 513 455-1000
Cincinnati *(G-2137)*

Accenture LLP .... E 513 651-2444
Cincinnati *(G-2138)*

Accenture LLP .... C 216 685-1435
Cleveland *(G-3760)*

Accenture LLP .... C 614 629-2000
Columbus *(G-5301)*

Accurate Invntory Clclting Svc .... B 800 777-9414
Columbus *(G-5304)*

Acloche LLC .... E 888 608-0889
Columbus *(G-5306)*

Adept Marketing Outsourced LLC ..... E 614 360-3132
Columbus *(G-5313)*

Adroit Assoc Cnslting Svcs LLC .... D 614 966-6925
Columbus *(G-5315)*

Advanced Prgrm Resources Inc .... E 614 761-9994
Dublin *(G-7920)*

Advocate Solutions LLC .... E 614 444-5144
Columbus *(G-5320)*

Agar LLC .... E 513 549-4576
Cincinnati *(G-2155)*

Agri Business Finance Inc .... E 937 663-0186
Saint Paris *(G-12837)*

Aileron .... E 937 669-6500
Tipp City *(G-13652)*

Aldelano Corporation .... E 909 861-3970
Lima *(G-9861)*

All In Staffing .... E 330 315-1530
Parma *(G-12248)*

Allstar Financial Group Inc .... D 866 484-2583
Copley *(G-6947)*

Allworth Financial LP .... E 513 469-7500
Blue Ash *(G-1128)*

Alt Media Studios LLC .... E 440 777-6666
Novelty *(G-12036)*

Alta It Services LLC .... C 813 999-3101
Cincinnati *(G-2173)*

AMG Consultants Inc .... E 917 600-3773
Cincinnati *(G-2192)*

◆ Applied Specialties Inc .... E 440 933-9442
Avon Lake *(G-671)*

ARC Healthcare LLC .... E 888 552-0677
Worthington *(G-15405)*

Archway Marketing Services Inc .... D 440 572-0725
Strongsville *(G-13444)*

Ardmore Power Logistics LLC .... E 216 502-0640
Westlake *(G-15034)*

Armada Ltd .... D 614 505-7256
Powell *(G-12585)*

Astoria Place Cincinnati LLC .... C 513 961-8881
Cincinnati *(G-2221)*

Austin Building and Design Inc .... C 440 544-2600
Cleveland *(G-3839)*

Avaap USA LLC .... E 732 710-3425
Columbus *(G-5409)*

AVI Food Systems Inc .... B 330 372-6000
Warren *(G-14505)*

Azimuth Corporation .... C 937 256-8571
Beavercreek *(G-861)*

Barium Holdings Company Inc .... E 740 282-9776
Steubenville *(G-13317)*

Barrett & Associates Inc .... E 330 928-2323
Cuyahoga Falls *(G-7047)*

Baxter Hdell Dnnlly Prston Inc .... C 513 271-1634
Cincinnati *(G-2240)*

Belcap Inc .... E 330 456-0031
Canton *(G-1685)*

Benchmark National Corporation .... E 419 843-6691
Bellevue *(G-1043)*

Bodine Perry LLC .... E 330 702-8100
Canfield *(G-1622)*

Booz Allen Hamilton Inc .... E 937 912-6400
Beavercreek *(G-864)*

Booz Allen Hamilton Inc .... D 937 429-5580
Beavercreek *(G-865)*

Brandmuscle Inc .... C 216 464-4342
Cleveland *(G-3890)*

Btas Inc .... D 937 431-9431
Beavercreek *(G-866)*

Buckeye Elm Contracting LLC .... E 888 315-8663
Gahanna *(G-8712)*

Buckingham & Company .... E 937 435-2742
Dayton *(G-7205)*

Budros Ruhlin & Roe Inc .... D 614 481-6900
Columbus *(G-5481)*

Burke LLC .... C 513 241-5663
Cincinnati *(G-2290)*

Burrilla LLC .... E 513 615-9350
West Chester *(G-14656)*

C H Dean LLC .... D 937 222-9531
Beavercreek *(G-867)*

Caff LLC .... E 440 918-4570
Westlake *(G-15042)*

Calyx LLC .... E 216 916-0639
Westlake *(G-15043)*

Career Partners Intl LLC .... E 919 401-4260
Columbus *(G-5509)*

Careercurve LLC .... D 800 314-8230
Cleveland *(G-3928)*

Cass Information Systems Inc .... D 614 839-4500
Columbus *(G-5516)*

Cbiz Inc .... A 216 447-9000
Cleveland *(G-3942)*

Cbiz Accnting Tax Advsory Wash ..... E 216 447-9000
Cleveland *(G-3943)*

Cbiz Mhm Northern Cal LLC .... E 216 447-9000
Cleveland *(G-3944)*

Cha - Community Health Affairs .... D 800 362-2628
Cleveland *(G-3959)*

Choicelocal LLC .... D 855 867-5622
Westlake *(G-15048)*

Cincinnati Cnslting Consortium .... E 513 233-0011
Cincinnati *(G-2404)*

Clarity Retail Services LLC .... D 513 800-9369
West Chester *(G-14668)*

Clearstead Advisors LLC .... D 216 621-1090
Cleveland *(G-3999)*

Clearsulting LLC .... D 440 488-4274
Cleveland *(G-4000)*

Clgt Solutions LLC .... E 740 920-4795
Granville *(G-8852)*

Clinlogix LLC .... E 215 855-9054
Northwood *(G-11972)*

Cohesion Corporation .... C 813 999-3101
Cincinnati *(G-2469)*

Coho Creative LLC .... E 513 751-7500
Cincinnati *(G-2470)*

Colliers International .... E 614 436-9800
Columbus *(G-5597)*

Comcage LLC .... E 513 549-4003
Cincinnati *(G-2479)*

◆ Comex North America Inc .... D 303 307-2100
Cleveland *(G-4092)*

Commquest Services Inc .... C 330 455-0374
Canton *(G-1718)*

Comprehensive Hr Solutions LLC ..... C 513 771-2277
Cincinnati *(G-2488)*

Concept Services Limited .... D 330 336-2571
Copley *(G-6951)*

Consoliplex Holding LLC .... E 216 202-3499
Cleveland *(G-4107)*

Consumer Credit Counseling Ser ...... E 800 254-4100
Cleveland *(G-4111)*

Cooper Adel Vu & Assoc Lpa .... D 740 625-4220
Centerburg *(G-1934)*

Corbus LLC .... A 937 226-7724
Dayton *(G-7248)*

▼ Cornerstone Brands Group Inc ...... A 513 603-1000
West Chester *(G-14677)*

87 ENGINEERING, ACCOUNTING, RESEARCH, AND MANAGEMENT SERVICES

Corporate Fin Assoc Clmbus Inc............... D 614 457-9219
  Columbus *(G-5703)*
Corporate Plans Inc................................. E 440 542-7800
  Solon *(G-13078)*
Cosmic Concepts Ltd............................... D 614 228-1104
  Columbus *(G-5705)*
Cost Sharing Solutions LLC..................... E 330 915-6800
  Canton *(G-1723)*
CPS Solutions LLC.................................. C 901 748-0470
  Dublin *(G-7978)*
Critical Business Analysis Inc................... E 419 874-0800
  Perrysburg *(G-12326)*
Crown Associates LLC............................ D 419 629-2220
  New Bremen *(G-11597)*
Cushman Wakefield Holdings Inc............. E 513 241-4880
  Cincinnati *(G-2526)*
D L Ryan Companies LLC....................... D 614 436-6558
  Westerville *(G-14887)*
Dari Pizza Enterprises II Inc..................... C 419 534-3000
  Maumee *(G-10717)*
▲ Darko Inc... E 330 425-9805
  Bedford *(G-958)*
Dataeconomy Inc..................................... E 614 356-8153
  Dublin *(G-7983)*
Dayton Aerospace Inc.............................. E 937 426-4300
  Beavercreek Township *(G-936)*
Dayton Dev Coalition Inc.......................... E 937 222-4422
  Dayton *(G-7279)*
DE Foxx & Associates Inc....................... B 513 621-5522
  Cincinnati *(G-2547)*
Debtnext Solutions LLC........................... D 330 665-0400
  Copley *(G-6954)*
Dedicated Tech Services Inc.................... E 614 309-0059
  Dublin *(G-7986)*
Dedicated Technologies Inc..................... E 614 460-3200
  Columbus *(G-5748)*
Deloitte & Touche LLP............................. B 513 784-7100
  Cincinnati *(G-2556)*
Deloitte & Touche LLP............................. A 216 589-1300
  Cleveland *(G-4160)*
Deloitte & Touche LLP............................. E 937 223-8821
  Dayton *(G-7308)*
Deloitte Consulting LLP........................... E 937 223-8821
  Dayton *(G-7309)*
Delphia Consulting LLC........................... E 614 421-2000
  Columbus *(G-5754)*
Devry University Inc................................. D 614 251-6969
  Columbus *(G-5759)*
Direct Options Inc.................................... E 513 779-4416
  Cincinnati *(G-2566)*
Distribution Data Incorporated................. D 216 362-3009
  Brookpark *(G-1433)*
Diversified Systems Inc............................ E 614 476-9939
  Westerville *(G-14976)*
Djd Express Inc....................................... D 740 676-7464
  Shadyside *(G-12969)*
◆ Dms Inc.. C 440 951-9838
  Willoughby *(G-15189)*
Dunnhumby Inc.. C 513 579-3400
  Cincinnati *(G-2586)*
E-Volve Systems LLC............................. E 765 543-8123
  Blue Ash *(G-1166)*
East Way Behavioral Hlth Care................ D 937 222-4900
  Dayton *(G-7323)*
Eaton Corp... C 216 523-5000
  Cleveland *(G-4202)*
Efficient Collaborative Retail.................... D 440 498-0500
  Solon *(G-13082)*
Elixir Rx Options LLC.............................. D 330 405-8080
  Twinsburg *(G-14185)*
Emerald Health Network Inc.................... E 216 479-2030
  Fairlawn *(G-8476)*

Emprise Technologies LLC...................... E 419 720-6982
  Toledo *(G-13791)*
Engage Healthcare Svcs Corp................. E 614 457-8180
  Columbus *(G-5818)*
Engauge Holdings LLC............................ D 614 573-1010
  Columbus *(G-5819)*
EP Ferris & Associates Inc...................... E 614 299-2999
  Columbus *(G-5823)*
Epipheo Inc.. .... 888 687-7620
  Cincinnati *(G-2631)*
Ernst & Young LLP.................................. C 513 612-1400
  Cincinnati *(G-2637)*
Ernst & Young LLP.................................. C 614 224-5678
  Columbus *(G-5827)*
Everstream Holding Company LLC.......... C 216 923-2260
  Cleveland *(G-4228)*
Extreme Mktg & Promotions Inc.............. D 440 237-8400
  Broadview Heights *(G-1388)*
▲ Fedex Supplychain Systems Inc.......... A
  Hudson *(G-9348)*
Financial Management Group................. D 513 984-6696
  Blue Ash *(G-1173)*
Findley Inc.. D 419 255-1360
  Toledo *(G-13806)*
Finit Group LLC....................................... D 513 793-4648
  Cincinnati *(G-2669)*
First Chice Med Stffing Ohio I.................. E 419 626-9740
  Sandusky *(G-12899)*
◆ First Transit Inc................................... D 513 241-2200
  Cincinnati *(G-2682)*
Fortune Brnds Wtr Innvtons LLC.............. D 440 962-2782
  North Olmsted *(G-11902)*
Frank Gates Service Company................ B 614 793-8000
  Dublin *(G-8014)*
Full Spectrum Marketing LLC................... E 330 541-9456
  Akron *(G-170)*
Gardner Insurance Partners LLC............. E 614 221-1500
  Columbus *(G-5914)*
Gbq Consulting LLC................................ E 614 221-1120
  Columbus *(G-5919)*
Goering Ctr For Fmly/Prvate Bu............... D 513 556-7185
  Cincinnati *(G-2736)*
Goken America LLC................................ D 614 495-8104
  Dublin *(G-8021)*
GP Strategies Corporation....................... E 513 583-8810
  Cincinnati *(G-2745)*
Grants Plus LLC...................................... E 216 916-7376
  Cleveland *(G-4326)*
Greentree Group Inc................................ D 937 490-5500
  Dayton *(G-7388)*
H T V Industries Inc................................. D 216 514-0060
  Cleveland *(G-4345)*
H7 Network.. E 513 526-5139
  Franklin *(G-8639)*
Hayneedle Inc.. B 402 715-3000
  Monroe *(G-11341)*
Health and Safety Sciences LLC.............. E 513 488-1952
  Fairfield Township *(G-8462)*
Healthlinx Inc... E 614 542-2228
  Columbus *(G-5976)*
Henry Call Inc.. C 216 433-5609
  Cleveland *(G-4358)*
Hmt Associates Inc................................. E 216 369-0109
  Broadview Heights *(G-1391)*
Honda Dev & Mfg Amer LLC................... C 937 644-0724
  Marysville *(G-10488)*
Hr Butler LLC.. E 614 923-2900
  Dublin *(G-8032)*
Human ARC Corporation........................ B 216 431-5200
  Cleveland *(G-4388)*
Humanit Solutions LLC........................... D 937 901-7576
  Beavercreek Township *(G-941)*

Hyperion Companies Inc.......................... B 949 309-2409
  Columbus *(G-6034)*
I and T Holdings Inv Group Inc................ E 269 207-7773
  Holland *(G-9289)*
Ignite Philanthropy................................... E 513 381-1848
  Cincinnati *(G-2864)*
Imarc Research Inc................................. D 440 801-1540
  Strongsville *(G-13464)*
Innovative Technologies Corp.................. D 937 252-2145
  Dayton *(G-7135)*
Inquiry Systems Inc................................. E 614 464-3800
  Columbus *(G-6055)*
Integrated Prj Resources LLC................. E 330 272-0998
  Salem *(G-12844)*
Intellihartx LLC.. E 419 949-5040
  Findlay *(G-8549)*
Interbrand Design Forum LLC................. C 513 421-2210
  Cincinnati *(G-2880)*
Interchez Lgistics Systems Inc................ E 330 923-5080
  Stow *(G-13378)*
Iotco LLC... E 877 464-6826
  Cincinnati *(G-2887)*
Isaac Fair Consulting Inc......................... E 216 643-6790
  Cleveland *(G-4423)*
Island Hospitality MGT LLC..................... E 614 864-8844
  Columbus *(G-6075)*
ITM Marketing Inc.................................... C 740 295-3575
  Coshocton *(G-6988)*
Jarrett Logistics Systems Inc................... C 330 682-0099
  Orrville *(G-12168)*
Jjr Solutions LLC..................................... E 937 912-0288
  Dayton *(G-7429)*
Jyg Innovations LLC................................ D 937 630-3858
  Dayton *(G-7431)*
Kaiser Consulting LLC............................. D 614 378-5361
  Powell *(G-12594)*
Kaleidoscope Project Inc.......................... D 330 702-1822
  Canfield *(G-1633)*
Kaleidoscope Prototyping LLC................. E 513 206-9137
  Blue Ash *(G-1194)*
Karlsberger Architecture Inc.................... D 614 471-1812
  Columbus *(G-6103)*
Karlsberger Companies........................... C 614 461-9500
  Columbus *(G-6104)*
Keene Inc... D 440 605-1020
  Cleveland *(G-4451)*
Kings Medical Company.......................... C 330 653-3968
  Richfield *(G-12700)*
Klingbeil Management Group Co............. E 614 220-8900
  Columbus *(G-6120)*
Km2 Solutions LLC.................................. B 610 213-1408
  Columbus *(G-6122)*
Knowledgeworks Foundation................... E 513 929-4777
  Cincinnati *(G-2945)*
Kreller Consulting Group Inc.................... E 513 723-8900
  Cincinnati *(G-2952)*
Kuno Creative Group Inc.......................... E 440 261-5002
  Lorain *(G-10081)*
Landrum & Brown Incorporated............... E 513 530-5333
  Blue Ash *(G-1198)*
Lang Financial Group Inc......................... E 513 699-2966
  Blue Ash *(G-1199)*
Leidos Inc.. D 937 656-8433
  Beavercreek *(G-886)*
Level Seven... D 216 524-9055
  Brecksville *(G-1357)*
Levitan Enterprise LLC............................ D 628 208-7016
  Toledo *(G-13885)*
LLC A Haystack Mssion Essntial............. D 614 750-1908
  New Albany *(G-11573)*
Logistical Resource Group Inc................. D 330 283-3733
  Macedonia *(G-10199)*

87 ENGINEERING, ACCOUNTING, RESEARCH, AND MANAGEMENT SERVICES

Madison Avenue Mktg Group Inc............ E 419 473-9000
   Toledo *(G-13903)*

◆ Malco Products Inc.............................. C 330 753-0361
   Barberton *(G-700)*

Managed Care Advisory Group.............. E 800 355-0466
   Toledo *(G-13904)*

Mancan Inc... A 440 884-9675
   Cleveland *(G-4519)*

Manufacturing Advocacy & .... E 216 391-7002
   Cleveland *(G-4522)*

Marcus Thomas Llc............................... D 216 292-4700
   Cleveland *(G-4523)*

Maritain Health..................................... D 440 249-5750
   Westlake *(G-15079)*

Marsh Berry & Company LLC................ E 440 637-8122
   Beachwood *(G-810)*

Mas International Mktg LLC.................. D 614 556-7083
   Columbus *(G-6202)*

Matrix Claims Management LLC............ D 513 351-1222
   Cincinnati *(G-3016)*

Med-Pass Incorporated......................... E 937 438-8884
   Dayton *(G-7476)*

Medco Health Solutions Inc.................. C 614 822-2000
   Dublin *(G-8061)*

Medcor Safety LLC............................... E 740 876-4003
   Wheelersburg *(G-15131)*

Medical Recovery Systems Inc.............. E 513 872-7000
   Cincinnati *(G-3028)*

Medisync Midwest Ltd Lblty Co............. D 513 533-1199
   Dayton *(G-7478)*

Medpace... D 513 254-1232
   Cincinnati *(G-3030)*

Menard Inc... D 937 318-2831
   Fairborn *(G-8379)*

Merchandising Services Co.................. D 866 479-8246
   Blue Ash *(G-1209)*

Merrill Lynch Prce Fnner Smith............. C 614 225-3000
   Columbus *(G-5269)*

Miami University................................... B 513 727-3200
   Middletown *(G-11172)*

Mid-America Consulting Group Inc........ D
   Cleveland *(G-4574)*

Midwest Investors Group Inc................. C 270 887-8888
   Galena *(G-8737)*

Midwest Mfg Solutions LLC................... E 513 381-7200
   Cincinnati *(G-3059)*

▲ Midwest Motor Supply Co.................. C 800 233-1294
   Columbus *(G-6244)*

Miracle Path Staffing Agcy Inc............... E 234 205-3541
   Fairlawn *(G-8490)*

Modern Business Associates Inc........... D 727 563-1500
   Cleveland *(G-4594)*

Motion Controls Robotics Inc................ D 419 334-5886
   Fremont *(G-8695)*

Muransky Companies LLC.................... E 330 729-7400
   Youngstown *(G-15670)*

Murtech Consulting LLC....................... D 216 328-8580
   Cleveland *(G-4611)*

Naked Lime.. E 855 653-5463
   Beavercreek *(G-928)*

National City Cmnty Dev Corp.............. C 216 575-2000
   Cleveland *(G-4620)*

Nationwide Financial Svcs Inc............... C 614 249-7111
   Columbus *(G-6329)*

Nationwide Rtrment Sltions Inc............. C 614 854-8300
   Dublin *(G-8072)*

NBD International Inc............................ E 330 296-0221
   Ravenna *(G-12633)*

Ncs Healthcare Inc................................ A 216 514-3450
   Cleveland *(G-4630)*

Nesco Inc... C 513 772-5870
   Cincinnati *(G-3106)*

Nesco Inc... C 419 794-7452
   Toledo *(G-13933)*

Netsmart Technologies Inc.................... B 800 434-2642
   Dublin *(G-8074)*

Northwest Country Place Inc................. C 440 488-2700
   Mentor *(G-10980)*

Nova Passport Home Care Llc.............. E 419 531-9060
   Toledo *(G-13941)*

Ohic Insurance Company..................... D 614 221-7777
   Columbus *(G-6388)*

Ohio Custodial Maintenance................. C 614 443-1232
   Columbus *(G-6399)*

Ohio Diversified Services Inc................. E 440 356-7000
   Cleveland *(G-4687)*

Ohio Equities LLC................................ D 614 207-1805
   Columbus *(G-6418)*

Ohio Health Info Partnr Inc.................... E 614 664-2600
   Hilliard *(G-9222)*

Ologie Inc.. D 614 221-1107
   Columbus *(G-6471)*

Omni Property Companies LLC............. E 216 514-1950
   Solon *(G-13121)*

Oncall LLC... D 513 381-4320
   Cincinnati *(G-3162)*

Onefifteen Recovery............................. E 937 223-5609
   Dayton *(G-7539)*

Opti LLC... E 212 651-7317
   Cincinnati *(G-3165)*

Optiem LLC.. E 216 574-9100
   Cleveland *(G-4703)*

Paragon Consulting Inc......................... E 440 684-3101
   Cleveland *(G-4716)*

Paragon Tec Inc................................... E 216 361-5555
   Cleveland *(G-4717)*

Parman Group Inc................................ E 513 673-0077
   Columbus *(G-6502)*

Patientpint Hosp Solutions LLC............. C 513 936-6800
   Cincinnati *(G-3187)*

Pension Corporation America............... D 513 281-3366
   Cincinnati *(G-3195)*

Perduco Group Inc............................... E 937 401-0268
   Beavercreek *(G-893)*

Pharmacy Consultants LLC................... E 864 578-8788
   Cincinnati *(G-3205)*

Piada Group LLC................................. D 614 397-1339
   Columbus *(G-6524)*

Plante & Moran Pllc.............................. A 614 849-3000
   Columbus *(G-6530)*

Platinumtele Solutions LLC................... E 216 609-5804
   Cleveland *(G-4756)*

Plus Management Services Inc............. E 419 331-2273
   Lima *(G-9949)*

Plus Management Services Inc............. C 419 225-9018
   Lima *(G-9950)*

Pope & Associates Inc......................... E 513 671-1277
   West Chester *(G-14744)*

Premiere Medical Resources Inc........... E 330 923-5899
   Cuyahoga Falls *(G-7094)*

Prime Hlthcare Fndton- E Lvrpo............ D 330 385-7200
   East Liverpool *(G-8191)*

Print Management Partners Inc............. E 513 942-9202
   West Chester *(G-14748)*

Professional Review Netwrk Inc............. E 614 791-2700
   Dublin *(G-8097)*

Promedica Health System Inc............... B 419 534-6600
   Toledo *(G-13971)*

PSI Supply Chain Solutions LLC........... B 614 389-4717
   Dublin *(G-8100)*

Quality Solutions Inc............................. E 440 933-9946
   Cleveland *(G-4801)*

Quality Too Good Mktg Group LL.......... D 877 202-6245
   Columbus *(G-6557)*

R D D Inc.. C 216 781-5858
   Cleveland *(G-4804)*

Redwood Living Inc.............................. C 216 360-9441
   Maumee *(G-10759)*

Remesh Inc.. D 561 809-9885
   Cleveland *(G-4824)*

Remtec Automation LLC...................... E 877 759-8151
   Mason *(G-10600)*

Residential HM Assn Marion Inc............ C 740 387-9999
   Marion *(G-10451)*

Revlocal... D 800 456-7470
   Granville *(G-8854)*

Ride Share Information......................... E 513 621-6300
   Cincinnati *(G-3298)*

Ringside Search Partners LLC.............. E 614 643-0700
   Columbus *(G-6589)*

Risque Soles LLC................................. E 216 965-5261
   Akron *(G-283)*

Rls & Associates Inc............................. E 937 299-5007
   Moraine *(G-11435)*

RMS of Ohio Inc................................... C 440 617-6605
   Westlake *(G-15104)*

Robex LLC... E 419 270-0770
   Maumee *(G-10763)*

Root LLC.. D 419 874-0077
   Sylvania *(G-13571)*

Rttw Ltd... E 614 291-7944
   Columbus *(G-6617)*

Sacs Cnslting Training Ctr Inc............... E 330 255-1101
   Akron *(G-293)*

Safegard Bckgrund Screening LLC....... E 877 700-7345
   Beachwood *(G-834)*

Safelite Solutions LLC.......................... A 614 210-9000
   Columbus *(G-6633)*

Salesfuel Inc... D 614 794-0500
   Westerville *(G-14936)*

Sb Capital Acquisitions LLC.................. A 614 443-4080
   Columbus *(G-6647)*

SBC Advertising Ltd............................. C 614 891-7070
   Columbus *(G-6648)*

Scrogginsgrear Inc............................... C 513 672-4281
   Cincinnati *(G-3352)*

Sedlak Management Consultants.......... E 216 206-4700
   Cleveland *(G-4890)*

SEI - Cincinnati LLC............................. D 513 459-1992
   Cincinnati *(G-3354)*

Senior Touch Solution........................... E 216 862-4841
   Cleveland *(G-4895)*

Sequoia Financial Group LLC............... E 330 375-9480
   Akron *(G-297)*

Setech Incorporated............................. C 937 425-9482
   Moraine *(G-11437)*

Sheakley-Uniservice Inc....................... E 513 771-2277
   Cincinnati *(G-3367)*

Signature Inc.. D 614 766-5101
   Dublin *(G-8120)*

Signature Closers LLC......................... E 614 448-7750
   Columbus *(G-6678)*

Signet Management Co Ltd.................. C 330 762-9102
   Akron *(G-300)*

Silver Spruce Holding LLC................... E 937 259-1200
   Dayton *(G-7622)*

Skylight Financial Group LLC............... D 513 579-8555
   Cincinnati *(G-3384)*

Skylight Financial Group LLC............... D 419 885-0011
   Toledo *(G-14014)*

Smithers Group Inc............................... D 330 762-7441
   Akron *(G-304)*

Smithers MSE Inc................................. D 330 762-7441
   Akron *(G-305)*

Socius1 LLC... D 614 280-9880
   Dublin *(G-8123)*

SIC SECTION
87 ENGINEERING, ACCOUNTING, RESEARCH, AND MANAGEMENT SERVICES

Ssoe Inc.. B 419 255-3830
  Toledo *(G-14023)*

Star Distribution and Mfg LLC................ E 513 860-3573
  West Chester *(G-14833)*

Startupscom LLC.................................... D 800 799-6998
  Delaware *(G-7828)*

Stepstone Group Real Estate LP............. E 216 522-0330
  Cleveland *(G-4954)*

◆ Steris Isomedix Services Inc................. B 440 354-2600
  Mentor *(G-10999)*

Sterling Check Corp................................ D 212 736-5100
  Independence *(G-9485)*

Sterling Infosystems Inc......................... B 212 736-5100
  Independence *(G-9486)*

Stratos Wealth Partners......................... E 330 666-8131
  Akron *(G-312)*

Stratos Wealth Partners Ltd................... C 440 519-2500
  Beachwood *(G-841)*

Sugar & Spice Spa llc............................. D 513 319-0112
  Mason *(G-10612)*

Summit Fincl Strategies Inc.................... E 614 885-1115
  Columbus *(G-6727)*

Supernova Lgstic Solutions LLC............. E 937 369-8618
  Dayton *(G-7655)*

Sureshot Communications LLC.............. D 216 496-6100
  Cleveland *(G-4967)*

Surgere LLC.. D 330 966-3746
  Uniontown *(G-14267)*

Tabco Consulting Services LLC.............. E 740 217-0010
  Columbus *(G-6745)*

Tacg LLC... E 937 203-8201
  Beavercreek *(G-931)*

Techsolve Inc.. D 513 948-2000
  Cincinnati *(G-3449)*

Teradata International Inc...................... C 866 548-8348
  Dayton *(G-7662)*

The Arras Group Inc............................... E 216 621-1601
  Cleveland *(G-4991)*

The Sheakley Group Inc......................... E 513 771-2277
  Cincinnati *(G-3471)*

Tiaa-Cref Indvdual Instnl Svcs................ E 614 659-1000
  Cincinnati *(G-3478)*

Tm Capture Services LLC....................... D 937 728-1781
  Dayton *(G-7671)*

Toledo Rgonal Chamber Commerce...... D 419 243-8191
  Toledo *(G-14064)*

Topre America Corporation.................... C 256 339-8407
  Springfield *(G-13302)*

Tower Real Estate Group LLC................ A 216 520-1250
  Beachwood *(G-845)*

TPC and Thomas LLC............................. D 614 354-0717
  Westerville *(G-14943)*

Tradeone Marketing Inc......................... D 512 343-2002
  Cleveland *(G-5028)*

Transtech Consulting Inc........................ C 614 751-0575
  Westerville *(G-14944)*

Trilogy Fulfillment LLC............................ D 614 491-0553
  Groveport *(G-9005)*

Truepoint Inc.. E 513 792-6648
  Blue Ash *(G-1258)*

Turtle Golf Management Ltd................. D 614 882-5920
  Westerville *(G-15019)*

TV Minority Company Inc....................... E 937 832-9350
  Englewood *(G-8324)*

TVC Group LLC....................................... E 919 241-7830
  Grove City *(G-8961)*

Tyto Government Solutions Inc.............. E 937 306-3030
  Beavercreek *(G-911)*

Uhc United Heating & Coolg LLC........... D 866 931-0118
  Northfield *(G-11967)*

United Audit Systems Inc....................... C 513 723-1122
  Cincinnati *(G-3552)*

Universal Marketing Group LLC............. D 419 720-6581
  Toledo *(G-14085)*

Universal Transportation Syste.............. C 513 829-1287
  Fairfield *(G-8450)*

University of Dayton............................... D 937 255-3141
  Dayton *(G-7692)*

University of Dayton............................... B 937 229-3913
  Dayton *(G-7693)*

Untapped Potentials LLC........................ E 888 811-1469
  Columbus *(G-6825)*

Vartek Services Inc................................ E 937 438-3550
  Donnelsville *(G-7870)*

Versatex LLC.. E 513 639-3119
  Cincinnati *(G-3620)*

Vintek Inc... D 937 382-8986
  Wilmington *(G-15277)*

Visteon Corporation................................ E 419 627-3600
  Sandusky *(G-12940)*

Ward Financial Group Inc....................... E 513 791-0303
  Cincinnati *(G-3641)*

Whiteboard Marketing............................ E 614 562-1912
  Dublin *(G-8165)*

William O Cleverley & Assoc.................. E 614 543-7777
  Worthington *(G-15470)*

William Thomas Group Inc.................... D 800 582-3107
  Cincinnati *(G-3672)*

Willowood Care Center.......................... C 330 225-3156
  Brunswick *(G-1475)*

Worthington Public Library..................... C 614 807-2626
  Worthington *(G-15472)*

Wpmi Inc.. E 440 392-2171
  Mentor *(G-11012)*

Wtw Delaware Holdings LLC................. D 216 937-4000
  Cleveland *(G-5161)*

Xlc Srvces Cincinnati Ohio Inc................ E 513 621-3912
  Cincinnati *(G-3684)*

Young and Associates Inc...................... E 330 678-0524
  Kent *(G-9608)*

8743 Public relations services

Campbell Sales Company....................... B 513 697-2900
  Cincinnati *(G-2304)*

City of Kettering..................................... E 937 296-2486
  Dayton *(G-7233)*

Consolidus LLC...................................... E 330 319-7200
  Akron *(G-121)*

Cosmic Concepts Ltd............................. D 216 696-4230
  Cleveland *(G-4120)*

County of Logan..................................... E 937 599-7252
  Bellefontaine *(G-1026)*

County of Montgomery........................... C 937 225-4990
  Dayton *(G-7252)*

D L Ryan Companies LLC....................... D 614 436-6558
  Westerville *(G-14887)*

Distributor Marketing MGT Inc............... E 440 236-5534
  Columbia Station *(G-5227)*

Dix & Eaton Incorporated....................... E 216 241-0405
  Cleveland *(G-4168)*

Domestic Relations................................ E 937 225-4063
  Dayton *(G-7316)*

Edward Howard & Co............................. E 216 781-2400
  Cleveland *(G-4207)*

▲ L Brands Service Company LLC........ D 614 415-7000
  Columbus *(G-6130)*

Marketing Essentials LLC....................... E 419 629-0080
  New Bremen *(G-11599)*

Marsh Inc... D 513 421-1234
  Cincinnati *(G-3012)*

Northlich LLC... E 513 421-8840
  Cincinnati *(G-3126)*

▲ RA Staff Company............................. E 440 891-9900
  Cleveland *(G-4806)*

SBC Advertising Ltd............................... C 614 891-7070
  Columbus *(G-6648)*

United States Trotting Assn................... D 614 224-2291
  Columbus *(G-6817)*

Ver-A-Fast Corp...................................... E 440 331-0250
  Rocky River *(G-12755)*

Whitespace Design Group Inc................ E 330 762-9320
  Akron *(G-360)*

8744 Facilities support services

Aetna Building Maintenance Inc............ C 937 324-5711
  Springfield *(G-13214)*

Alcyon Tchncal Svcs Ats JV LLC............ B 216 433-2488
  Cleveland *(G-3782)*

Aramark Facility Services LLC............... C 216 687-5000
  Cleveland *(G-3828)*

Aztec Services Group Inc...................... E 513 541-2002
  Cincinnati *(G-2233)*

City of Xenia.. E 937 376-7260
  Xenia *(G-15500)*

Community Education Ctrs Inc.............. E 330 424-4065
  Lisbon *(G-10000)*

Corecivic Inc.. D 330 746-3777
  Youngstown *(G-15589)*

Correction Commission NW Ohio.......... C 419 428-3800
  Stryker *(G-13504)*

County of Miami.................................... E 937 335-1314
  Troy *(G-14132)*

Disinfection MGT Tech LLC.................... E 440 212-1061
  Copley *(G-6955)*

Enviroserve Inc...................................... C 330 361-7764
  North Canton *(G-11828)*

Firstgroup America Inc.......................... C 513 241-2200
  Cincinnati *(G-2684)*

Franklin Cnty Bd Commissioners........... C 614 462-3800
  Columbus *(G-5880)*

Green Clean Ohio LLC............................ E 866 853-6337
  Cleveland *(G-4337)*

Greene County....................................... E 937 562-7800
  Xenia *(G-15513)*

Henry Call Inc... C 216 433-5609
  Cleveland *(G-4358)*

Katmai Government Services LLC.......... B 740 314-5432
  Steubenville *(G-13333)*

L B & B Associates Inc........................... E 216 451-2672
  Cleveland *(G-4471)*

◆ Ltccorp Government Services-Oh Inc... B 419 794-3500
  Maumee *(G-10742)*

Midwest Environmental Inc.................... E 419 382-9200
  Perrysburg *(G-12357)*

MPW Industrial Svcs Group Inc............. B 740 927-8790
  Hebron *(G-9150)*

Neocap/Cbcf... E 330 675-2669
  Warren *(G-14543)*

Serco Inc.. D 502 364-8157
  Beavercreek *(G-904)*

Servus LLC... A 844 737-8871
  Beachwood *(G-835)*

Sunohio Inc.. D 330 477-6769
  Canton *(G-1864)*

Technical Assurance Inc......................... E 440 953-3147
  Willoughby *(G-15222)*

Uscg Station Cleveland Harbor.............. E 216 937-0141
  Cleveland *(G-5094)*

Vns Federal Services LLC...................... E 740 443-7005
  Piketon *(G-12431)*

Wastren - Enrgx Mssion Spport............. C 740 897-3724
  Piketon *(G-12432)*

8748 Business consulting, nec

3e Company Environmental Ecolo......... C 330 451-4900
  Canton *(G-1647)*

87 ENGINEERING, ACCOUNTING, RESEARCH, AND MANAGEMENT SERVICES

Abdouni Enterprises LLC................................ E 419 345-6713
  Ottawa Hills *(G-12197)*
ABS Transitions LLC...................................... E 513 832-2884
  Cincinnati *(G-2136)*
Accenture LLP.. C 216 685-1435
  Cleveland *(G-3760)*
Accenture LLP.. C 614 629-2000
  Columbus *(G-5301)*
Acrt Inc... E 800 622-2562
  Stow *(G-13352)*
Actionlink LLC.. A 888 737-8757
  Akron *(G-15)*
Advanced Solutions For Educatn.................. E 224 518-3111
  Mentor *(G-10908)*
Aecom... D 513 651-3440
  Cincinnati *(G-2153)*
Aeroseal LLC.. E 937 428-9300
  Dayton *(G-7158)*
▲ Aeroseal LLC... E 937 428-9300
  Miamisburg *(G-11021)*
Akkodis Inc... C 614 781-6070
  Dublin *(G-7927)*
Allegiance Administrators LLC...................... E 877 895-1414
  Dublin *(G-7929)*
Allendevaux & Company LLC........................ E 937 657-1270
  Englewood *(G-8302)*
Allied Environmental Svcs Inc....................... E 419 227-4004
  Lima *(G-9864)*
♦ Alpha Technologies Svcs LLC................... D 330 745-1641
  Hudson *(G-9331)*
Altix Corporation.. E 513 216-8386
  Mason *(G-10519)*
American Broadband Telecom Co................. E 419 824-5800
  Maumee *(G-10689)*
▲ American Envmtl Group Ltd..................... B 330 659-5930
  Richfield *(G-12685)*
Apex Control Systems Inc............................. D 330 938-2588
  Sebring *(G-12945)*
▲ Apple Growth Partners Inc...................... D 330 867-7350
  Akron *(G-53)*
Aptim Corp... B 419 423-3526
  Findlay *(G-8510)*
Ardent Technologies Inc............................... D 937 312-1345
  Dayton *(G-7178)*
Ashtabula Cnty Eductl Svc Ctr...................... E 440 576-4085
  Ashtabula *(G-520)*
August Mack Environmental Inc................... C 740 548-1500
  Lewis Center *(G-9809)*
Avantia Inc... E 216 901-9366
  Cleveland *(G-3845)*
Bbs & Associates Inc.................................... E 330 665-5227
  Akron *(G-63)*
Bechtold Enterprises Inc............................... E 440 791-7177
  Grafton *(G-8838)*
Benchmark National Corporation.................. E 419 843-6691
  Bellevue *(G-1043)*
Bhe Environmental Inc.................................. C
  Cincinnati *(G-2260)*
BHP Energy LLC.. B 866 720-2700
  Walbridge *(G-14460)*
Big Red Rooster.. E 614 255-0200
  Columbus *(G-5440)*
Bjaam Environmental Inc.............................. E 330 854-5300
  Canal Fulton *(G-1593)*
Blue Chip Consulting Group......................... E 216 503-6000
  Independence *(G-9411)*
Boundless Strgc Resources Inc................... E 614 844-3800
  Worthington *(G-15406)*
Bowser-Morner Inc.. C 937 236-8805
  Dayton *(G-7198)*
Bravo Wellness LLC..................................... E 216 658-9500
  Cleveland *(G-3891)*

Brownflynn Ltd... E 216 303-6000
  Cleveland *(G-3906)*
Buckeye Hills-Hck Vly Reg Dev..................... E 740 373-0087
  Marietta *(G-10360)*
Bureau Veritas North Amer Inc..................... E 330 252-5100
  Akron *(G-78)*
Business Volunteers Unlimited.................... E 216 736-7711
  Cleveland *(G-3913)*
C & W Tank Cleaning Company..................... D 419 691-1995
  Oregon *(G-12131)*
Cardiosolution LLC....................................... E 513 618-2394
  Blue Ash *(G-1141)*
Cash Flow Solutions Inc............................... D 513 524-2320
  Oxford *(G-12205)*
Cavu Group.. E 937 429-2114
  Moraine *(G-11396)*
Centric Consulting LLC................................ D 888 781-7567
  Dayton *(G-7220)*
Cgh-Global Technologies LLC...................... E 800 376-0655
  Cincinnati *(G-2341)*
Cleveland Clnic Hlth Systm-Wst................... D 440 716-9810
  North Olmsted *(G-11898)*
Clgt Solutions LLC.. E 740 920-4795
  Granville *(G-8852)*
Cmbf Products Inc.. C 330 725-4941
  Medina *(G-10824)*
Coact Associates Ltd.................................... E 866 646-4400
  Toledo *(G-13747)*
Cohesion Consulting LLC............................. D 513 587-7700
  Blue Ash *(G-1155)*
Colia Group LLC.. E 614 270-4545
  Columbus *(G-5594)*
Commcapp America Inc................................ E 678 780-0937
  Cleveland *(G-4093)*
Communications III Inc................................. E 614 901-7720
  Westerville *(G-14973)*
Compass Clinical Consulting Co................... E 513 241-0142
  Cincinnati *(G-2485)*
Compmanagement Inc.................................. E 440 546-7100
  Seven Hills *(G-12954)*
Controlsoft Inc... E 440 443-3900
  Cleveland *(G-4113)*
Corbus LLC.. A 937 226-7724
  Dayton *(G-7248)*
CTS Construction Inc................................... D 513 489-8290
  Cincinnati *(G-2521)*
Cwm Envronmental Cleveland LLC............... E 216 663-0808
  Cleveland *(G-4147)*
Dancor Inc... E 614 340-2155
  Columbus *(G-5738)*
Datavantage Corporation.............................. B 440 498-4414
  Cleveland *(G-4150)*
Db Consulting Group Inc.............................. D 216 433-5132
  Cleveland *(G-4154)*
Dedicated Technologies Inc......................... D 614 460-3200
  Columbus *(G-5748)*
Deemsys Inc... D 614 322-9928
  Gahanna *(G-8715)*
Deloitte & Touche LLP................................... B 513 784-7100
  Cincinnati *(G-2556)*
Deloitte Consulting LLP................................ E 937 223-8821
  Dayton *(G-7309)*
Devcare Solutions Ltd.................................. E 614 221-2277
  Westerville *(G-14888)*
E Retailing Associates LLC........................... D 614 300-5785
  Columbus *(G-5798)*
Eagle Certification Group............................. D 937 293-2000
  Dayton *(G-7321)*
Eastwood Local Schools............................... E 419 833-1196
  Bowling Green *(G-1318)*
Eco Engineering Inc..................................... D 513 985-8300
  Cincinnati *(G-2604)*

Ellipse Solutions LLC.................................... E 937 312-1547
  Dayton *(G-7334)*
Emergncy Rspnse Trning Sltons.................. E 440 349-2700
  Solon *(G-13083)*
Emersion Design LLC................................... E 513 841-9100
  Cincinnati *(G-2616)*
Emprise Technologies LLC........................... E 419 720-6982
  Toledo *(G-13791)*
Envirnmntal Sltons Innvtons In.................... E 513 451-1777
  Cincinnati *(G-2626)*
Environmental Quality MGT.......................... D 513 825-7500
  Cincinnati *(G-2628)*
Enviroscience Inc.. D 330 688-0111
  Stow *(G-13366)*
Envision Corporation.................................... D 513 772-5437
  Cincinnati *(G-2630)*
Evergreen Cooperative Corp......................... B 216 268-5399
  Cleveland *(G-4226)*
Excellence In Motivation Inc........................ C 763 445-3000
  Dayton *(G-7341)*
Fanning/Howey Associates Inc.................... E 419 586-2292
  Celina *(G-1922)*
Fass Management & Consulting L................ E 330 405-0545
  Cleveland *(G-4242)*
First Choice Sourcing Solution.................... E 419 359-4002
  Findlay *(G-8532)*
▲ First Communications LLC....................... D 330 835-2323
  Fairlawn *(G-8481)*
First Hospital Labs LLC................................ C 215 396-5500
  Independence *(G-9432)*
Flexential Corp.. E 513 645-2900
  Hamilton *(G-9040)*
For Impact Suddes Gro................................. E 614 352-2505
  Columbus *(G-5877)*
Geo Global Partners LLC.............................. E 561 598-6000
  Aurora *(G-613)*
Go Sustainable Energy LLC.......................... E 614 268-4263
  Worthington *(G-15417)*
Gray & Pape Inc... E 513 287-7700
  Cincinnati *(G-2751)*
Guardian Environmental Inc........................ E 304 224-2011
  North Olmsted *(G-11904)*
Haley & Aldrich Inc....................................... D 216 739-0555
  Independence *(G-9435)*
Hercules Led LLC.. E 844 437-2533
  Boardman *(G-1289)*
Hhd Aviation LLC... D 513 426-8378
  Hamilton *(G-9052)*
High Score Mentor LLC................................. E 513 485-2848
  Cincinnati *(G-2820)*
Hinge Consulting LLC................................... E 513 404-1547
  Cincinnati *(G-2827)*
HPM America LLC.. D 419 946-0222
  Mount Gilead *(G-11461)*
Humanit Solutions LLC................................. D 937 901-7576
  Beavercreek Township *(G-941)*
Humantics Innvtive Sltions Inc.................... C 567 265-5200
  Huron *(G-9389)*
Hzw Environmental Cons LLC...................... E 800 804-8484
  Mentor *(G-10950)*
Idillnire Cnslting Sltions LLC....................... D 305 413-8522
  Cleveland *(G-4402)*
Illumination Works LLC................................ D 937 938-1321
  Beavercreek *(G-884)*
Impact Sales Solutions Inc.......................... E 419 466-0131
  Toledo *(G-13861)*
Informtion Applied Lrng Evltio..................... C 214 329-9100
  Rootstown *(G-12759)*
Infoverity LLC.. E 614 327-5173
  Dublin *(G-8037)*
Insight2profit LLC... E 440 646-9490
  Beachwood *(G-802)*

89 SERVICES, NOT ELSEWHERE CLASSIFIED

Interex Inc .... E 646 905-0091
  Beachwood *(G-803)*
▲ Its Traffic Systems Inc .... D 440 892-4500
  Westlake *(G-15071)*
J V Enviroserve Limited Partnership ...... E 216 642-1311
  Cleveland *(G-4427)*
Jubilee Limited Partnership .... A 614 221-9200
  Columbus *(G-6099)*
Juice Technologies Inc .... E 800 518-5576
  Worthington *(G-15424)*
Jyg Innovations LLC .... D 937 630-3858
  Dayton *(G-7431)*
Kalogerou Enterprises Inc .... D 330 544-9696
  Niles *(G-11792)*
Kemper Company .... D 440 846-1100
  Strongsville *(G-13468)*
Kemron Environmental Svcs Inc .... E 740 373-4071
  Marietta *(G-10378)*
Landrum & Brown Incorporated .... E 513 530-5333
  Blue Ash *(G-1198)*
Lawhon and Associates Inc .... E 614 481-8600
  Columbus *(G-6145)*
Leadfirstai LLC .... E 419 424-6647
  Findlay *(G-8557)*
Learning Spectrum Ltd .... E 614 844-5433
  Columbus *(G-6151)*
Life Safety Enterprises Inc .... E 440 918-1641
  Willoughby *(G-15205)*
Lifetime Value LLC .... E 216 544-3215
  Cleveland *(G-4493)*
Logtec Inc .... E 937 878-8450
  Fairborn *(G-8378)*
Long Business Systems Inc .... E 440 846-8500
  Strongsville *(G-13472)*
Mannik & Smith Group Inc .... C 419 891-2222
  Maumee *(G-10744)*
Massillon Cable TV Inc .... D 330 833-4134
  Massillon *(G-10652)*
Melink Corporation .... D 513 685-0958
  Milford *(G-11242)*
Metropltan Edctl Tchnical Assn .... C 740 389-4798
  Marion *(G-10445)*
▲ Miami Valley Regional Plg Comm .... E 937 223-6323
  Dayton *(G-7498)*
Mission Essential Group LLC .... D 614 416-2345
  New Albany *(G-11574)*
Modern Hire Inc .... E 216 292-0202
  Cleveland *(G-4595)*
Municipal Building Inspection .... C 440 399-0850
  Bedford Heights *(G-999)*
National Associates Inc .... D 440 333-0222
  Cleveland *(G-4618)*
National Premier Protective .... D 216 731-4000
  Euclid *(G-8359)*
Nationwide Energy Partners LLC .... E 614 918-2031
  Columbus *(G-6328)*
Nationwide Rtrment Sltions Inc .... C 614 854-8300
  Dublin *(G-8072)*
Navigate360 LLC .... C 330 661-0106
  Richfield *(G-12703)*
Nor-Com LLC .... E 859 689-7451
  Cincinnati *(G-3118)*
Northast Ohio Arwide Crdnting .... D 216 621-3055
  Cleveland *(G-4652)*
Northcoast Consult LLC .... E 440 291-8987
  Ashtabula *(G-543)*
Occupational Health Services .... E 937 492-7296
  Sidney *(G-13042)*
Ohio State University .... E 614 292-1284
  Columbus *(G-6458)*
Ohio Utilities Protection Svc .... D 800 311-3692
  North Jackson *(G-11875)*

Opocus .... C 800 724-8802
  Worthington *(G-15445)*
Optum Infusion Svcs 550 LLC .... D 866 442-4679
  Cincinnati *(G-3166)*
▼ Orton Edward Jr Crmic Fndation .... E 614 895-2663
  Westerville *(G-14926)*
Oxford Harriman & Co AM LLC .... E 216 755-7150
  Beachwood *(G-824)*
P C Guru Inc .... E 216 292-4878
  Cleveland *(G-4713)*
Pdmi .... D 330 757-0724
  Youngstown *(G-15690)*
Peq Services + Solutions Inc .... D 937 610-4800
  Miamisburg *(G-11083)*
Pg .... D 513 698-6901
  Mason *(G-10592)*
Poggemeyer Design Group Inc .... C 419 244-8074
  Bowling Green *(G-1331)*
Premise Solutions LLC .... E 440 703-8200
  Walton Hills *(G-14478)*
Price For Profit LLC .... D 440 646-9490
  Cleveland *(G-4771)*
Profit Track Ltd .... E 330 848-2730
  Barberton *(G-704)*
Q4-2 Inc .... E 440 256-3870
  Willoughby *(G-15219)*
Qwaide Enterprises LLC .... E 614 209-0551
  New Albany *(G-11583)*
Rainbow Station Day Care Inc .... E 614 759-8667
  Pickerington *(G-12409)*
Rainbow Station Day Care Inc .... E 614 575-5040
  Reynoldsburg *(G-12674)*
RJ Runge Company Inc .... E 419 740-5781
  Port Clinton *(G-12539)*
Romitech Inc .... E 937 297-9529
  Franklin *(G-8648)*
Rosewind Limited Partnership .... C 614 421-6000
  Columbus *(G-6611)*
Rsw/Us GP .... E 513 898-0940
  Cincinnati *(G-3328)*
Sadler-Necamp Financial Svcs .... E 513 489-5477
  Cincinnati *(G-3337)*
Sawdey Solution Services Inc .... E 937 490-4060
  Beavercreek *(G-930)*
Schooley Caldwell Assoc Inc .... D 614 628-0300
  Columbus *(G-6652)*
Sequent Inc .... D 614 436-5880
  Westerville *(G-14937)*
Setech Incorporated .... C 937 425-9482
  Moraine *(G-11437)*
Sjn Data Center LLC .... E 513 386-7871
  Cincinnati *(G-3381)*
Sk Food Group Inc .... B 614 409-0666
  Groveport *(G-9001)*
Solar Testing Laboratories Inc .... D 216 741-7007
  Brooklyn Heights *(G-1427)*
Solutons Thrugh Innvtive Tech .... E 937 320-9994
  Beavercreek *(G-907)*
South Central Ohio Eductl Ctr .... D 740 456-0517
  New Boston *(G-11595)*
Staffworks Group 2 Inc .... E 419 515-0655
  Toledo *(G-14028)*
Stores Consulting Group LLC .... E 717 309-5302
  Wilmington *(G-15274)*
Strategy Network LLC .... E 614 595-0688
  Columbus *(G-6722)*
Summit Solutions Inc .... E 937 291-4333
  Dayton *(G-7650)*
Superior Envmtl Solutions LLC .... D 937 593-0425
  Bellefontaine *(G-1038)*
Tangoe Us Inc .... C 614 842-9998
  Columbus *(G-6747)*

Tata Consultancy Services Ltd .... D 515 553-8300
  Cincinnati *(G-2114)*
Techsolve Inc .... D 513 948-2000
  Cincinnati *(G-3449)*
Telco Pros Inc .... E 877 244-0182
  Cleveland *(G-4982)*
The Payne Firm Inc .... E 513 489-2255
  Blue Ash *(G-1253)*
Toledo Mtro Area Cncil Gvrnmnt .... E 419 241-9155
  Toledo *(G-14061)*
Ttl Associates Inc .... D 419 241-4556
  Toledo *(G-14076)*
Twism Enterprises LLC .... E 513 800-1098
  Cincinnati *(G-3539)*
Uc Health Llc .... E 513 475-7630
  West Chester *(G-14784)*
▲ Valicor Environmental Svcs LLC .... E 513 733-4666
  Monroe *(G-11353)*
Velosio LLC .... E 614 280-9880
  Dublin *(G-8150)*
Verdantas LLC .... C 614 793-8777
  Dublin *(G-8151)*
Warstler Bros Landscaping Inc .... E 330 492-9500
  Canton *(G-1883)*
Wellert Corporation .... E 330 239-2699
  Medina *(G-10901)*
Westlake Ten Inc .... E 440 250-9804
  Westlake *(G-15124)*
Wideopenwest Networks LLC .... D 614 948-4600
  Columbus *(G-6889)*
Wolcott Systems Group LLC .... C 330 666-5900
  Akron *(G-363)*
Workstate Consulting LLC .... E 614 559-3904
  Columbus *(G-6903)*
Yashco Systems Inc .... D 614 467-4600
  Hilliard *(G-9247)*
Zappia Enterprises LLC .... E 937 277-3010
  Dayton *(G-7735)*
Zone Safety LLC .... D 440 752-9545
  Columbia Station *(G-5230)*

89 SERVICES, NOT ELSEWHERE CLASSIFIED

8999 Services, nec

Accelerant Technologies LLC .... D 419 236-8768
  Maumee *(G-10684)*
ASC Group Inc .... E 614 268-2514
  Columbus *(G-5391)*
Center For Arts-Inspired Lrng .... E 216 561-5005
  Cleveland *(G-3948)*
Central Ohio Prmry Care Physca .... E 614 882-0708
  Westerville *(G-14880)*
City of Toledo .... D 419 936-2875
  Toledo *(G-13738)*
Cleveland Clinic Childrens .... A 440 826-0102
  Cleveland *(G-4008)*
Clinical Management Cons Inc .... D 440 638-5000
  Cleveland *(G-4084)*
Coleman Professional Svcs Inc .... C 330 673-1347
  Kent *(G-9565)*
County of Clermont .... E 513 732-7661
  Batavia *(G-739)*
County of Gallia .... E 740 446-6902
  Gallipolis *(G-8755)*
Daily Services LLC .... C 740 326-6130
  Mount Vernon *(G-11482)*
▼ Diproinduca (usa) Limited LLC .... D 330 722-4442
  Medina *(G-10828)*
Dispatch Productions Inc .... C 614 460-3700
  Columbus *(G-5772)*

89 SERVICES, NOT ELSEWHERE CLASSIFIED

Drips Holdings LLC............................... D 512 643-7477
   Akron *(G-140)*

Madison Avenue Mktg Group Inc............ E 419 473-9000
   Toledo *(G-13903)*

Marsden Holding LLC........................... E 440 973-7774
   Middleburg Heights *(G-11119)*

Medina County Park District................... E 330 722-9364
   Medina *(G-10858)*

Mid Ohio Emergency Svcs LLC.............. E 614 566-5070
   Columbus *(G-6234)*

Mrl Materials Resources LLC................. E 937 531-6657
   Xenia *(G-15528)*

Nobleinvestments LLC........................... E 216 856-6555
   Bedford *(G-974)*

ONeil & Associates Inc........................... C 937 865-0800
   Miamisburg *(G-11079)*

Person Centered Services Inc................ E 419 782-7274
   Defiance *(G-7760)*

Quantech Services Inc........................... C 937 490-8461
   Beavercreek Township *(G-947)*

Siemens Government Tech Inc............... D 513 492-7759
   Mason *(G-10608)*

Solutons Thrugh Innvtive Tech................ D 937 320-9994
   Beavercreek *(G-907)*

Superior Envmtl Sltons SES Inc.............. C 513 874-6910
   West Chester *(G-14835)*

Thinkpath Engineering Svcs LLC............ E 937 291-8374
   Miamisburg *(G-11097)*

Wtw Delaware Holdings LLC................. D 216 937-4000
   Cleveland *(G-5161)*

91 EXECUTIVE, LEGISLATIVE & GENERAL GOVERNMENT, EXCEPT FINANCE

9111 Executive offices

Alpha Group of Delaware Inc................. D 740 368-5820
   Delaware *(G-7778)*

Alpha Group of Delaware Inc................. D 740 368-5810
   Delaware *(G-7779)*

Butler County of Ohio............................. D 513 887-3728
   Hamilton *(G-9020)*

Butler Cnty Bd Dvlpmntal Dsblt.............. D 513 867-5913
   Fairfield *(G-8396)*

Butler Cnty Bd Dvlpmntal Dsblt.............. D 513 785-2870
   Fairfield Township *(G-8457)*

City of Akron... C 330 375-2355
   Akron *(G-103)*

City of Aurora... E 330 562-8662
   Aurora *(G-611)*

City of Canal Winchester....................... D 614 837-8276
   Canal Winchester *(G-1602)*

City of Cuyahoga Falls........................... E 330 971-8425
   Cuyahoga Falls *(G-7057)*

City of Cuyahoga Falls........................... E 330 971-8416
   Cuyahoga Falls *(G-7061)*

City of Kenton.. E 419 674-4850
   Kenton *(G-9612)*

City of Lebanon..................................... E 513 228-3200
   Lebanon *(G-9759)*

City of Louisville.................................... E 330 875-3321
   Louisville *(G-10114)*

City of Oberlin.. E 440 775-1531
   Oberlin *(G-12065)*

City of Perrysburg................................. E 419 872-8020
   Perrysburg *(G-12324)*

City of Toledo... E 419 245-1001
   Toledo *(G-13741)*

City of Toledo... D 419 245-1800
   Toledo *(G-13743)*

City of Toledo... D 419 936-2924
   Toledo *(G-13744)*

City of Wadsworth.................................. E 330 334-1581
   Wadsworth *(G-14430)*

City of Wellston..................................... D 740 384-2428
   Wellston *(G-14636)*

Clermont County Cmnty Svcs Inc.......... E 513 732-2277
   Batavia *(G-733)*

County of Auglaize................................. D 419 629-2419
   New Bremen *(G-11596)*

County of Clermont................................ E 513 732-7265
   Batavia *(G-736)*

County of Coshocton............................. E 740 622-1020
   Coshocton *(G-6982)*

County of Cuyahoga............................... C 216 698-6526
   Cleveland *(G-4127)*

County of Erie....................................... E 419 627-8933
   Huron *(G-9386)*

County of Erie....................................... E 419 627-7710
   Sandusky *(G-12886)*

County of Gallia..................................... E 740 446-3222
   Gallipolis *(G-8753)*

County of Guernsey............................... E 740 439-1269
   Cambridge *(G-1565)*

County of Guernsey............................... E 740 439-5555
   Cambridge *(G-1567)*

County of Lucas.................................... D 419 213-3000
   Toledo *(G-13763)*

County of Lucas.................................... D 419 213-4700
   Toledo *(G-13764)*

County of Lucas.................................... C 419 248-3585
   Toledo *(G-13765)*

County of Lucas.................................... C 419 213-3903
   Toledo *(G-13767)*

County of Meigs.................................... E 740 992-2117
   Middleport *(G-11147)*

County of Montgomery........................... C 937 225-4010
   Dayton *(G-7254)*

County of Ottawa................................... C 567 262-3600
   Oak Harbor *(G-12044)*

County of Pickaway............................... E 740 474-7588
   Ashville *(G-552)*

County of Richland................................ B 419 774-4200
   Mansfield *(G-10255)*

County of Stark..................................... E 330 451-7232
   Canton *(G-1726)*

County of Trumbull................................ E 330 675-2640
   Warren *(G-14514)*

County of Tuscarawas........................... D 330 343-5555
   Dover *(G-7877)*

County of Wayne................................... D 330 262-1786
   Wooster *(G-15328)*

County of Wayne................................... D 330 345-5340
   Wooster *(G-15329)*

County of Wood..................................... D 419 353-8411
   Bowling Green *(G-1314)*

Delhi Township...................................... D 513 922-0060
   Cincinnati *(G-2555)*

Harrison Township................................. E 740 942-2171
   Cadiz *(G-1540)*

Jacksn-Vinton Cmnty Action Inc............ E 740 384-3722
   Wellston *(G-14638)*

Jefferson Cnty Cmnty Action CN........... C 740 282-0971
   Steubenville *(G-13332)*

Knox County.. D 740 397-7041
   Mount Vernon *(G-11493)*

Lake Township Trustees........................ E 419 836-1143
   Millbury *(G-11270)*

Medina County...................................... E 330 723-9553
   Medina *(G-10856)*

Medina County...................................... C 330 722-9511
   Medina *(G-10857)*

Oriana House Inc................................... D 330 535-8116
   Akron *(G-257)*

Pike County... E 740 947-9339
   Waverly *(G-14615)*

RT Industries Inc................................... C 937 339-8313
   Troy *(G-14157)*

Summit County...................................... E 330 762-3500
   Akron *(G-324)*

Summit County...................................... C 330 643-2850
   Akron *(G-326)*

Township of Copley............................... E 330 666-1853
   Copley *(G-6967)*

Village of Cuyahoga Heights................. D 216 641-7020
   Cleveland *(G-5105)*

9121 Legislative bodies

County of Auglaize................................. D 419 738-3816
   Wapakoneta *(G-14482)*

County of Clermont................................ E 513 732-7661
   Batavia *(G-739)*

County of Lucas.................................... D 419 213-4500
   Toledo *(G-13762)*

9199 General government, nec

City of Cleveland................................... E 216 664-2430
   Cleveland *(G-3985)*

City of Springfield.................................. E 937 328-3701
   Springfield *(G-13227)*

County of Lorain.................................... E 440 233-2020
   Lorain *(G-10069)*

County of Perry..................................... E 740 342-0416
   New Lexington *(G-11624)*

County of Tuscarawas........................... D 330 339-7791
   New Philadelphia *(G-11646)*

County of Wayne................................... E 330 345-5891
   Wooster *(G-15331)*

Ohio Bureau Wkrs Compensation.......... A 800 644-6292
   Columbus *(G-6396)*

Ohio Department Transportation............ E 614 275-1300
   Columbus *(G-6402)*

92 JUSTICE, PUBLIC ORDER AND SAFETY

9211 Courts

County of Logan.................................... E 937 599-7252
   Bellefontaine *(G-1026)*

9221 Police protection

City of Lakewood................................... E 216 529-6170
   Cleveland *(G-3991)*

City of Toledo... D 419 936-2875
   Toledo *(G-13738)*

County of Montgomery........................... D 937 225-4192
   Dayton *(G-7255)*

Greene County...................................... D 937 562-7500
   Xenia *(G-15514)*

Metrohealth System............................... C 216 957-5000
   Cleveland *(G-4564)*

Wells Township..................................... E 740 598-9602
   Brilliant *(G-1382)*

9222 Legal counsel and prosecution

County of Portage.................................. E 330 297-3850
   Ravenna *(G-12625)*

9223 Correctional institutions

County of Ross...................................... E 740 773-4169
   Chillicothe *(G-2062)*

Greene County...................................... E 937 562-5266
   Xenia *(G-15511)*

Ohio Department Youth Services............ C 419 245-3040
Cleveland *(G-4686)*

Ohio Department Youth Services............ C 419 875-6965
Liberty Center *(G-9846)*

Ohio Dept Rhbilitation Corectn................ D 614 274-9000
Columbus *(G-6411)*

Ohio Dept Rhbilitation Corectn................ D 614 752-0800
Columbus *(G-6412)*

Ohio Dept Rhbilitation Corectn................ E 419 782-3385
Defiance *(G-7759)*

Ohio Dept Rhbilitation Corectn................ D 419 448-0004
Tiffin *(G-13636)*

9224 Fire protection

Butler County of Ohio.............................. E 513 757-4683
Oxford *(G-12202)*

Township of Colerain................................ D 513 741-7551
Cincinnati *(G-3497)*

9229 Public order and safety, nec

City of Cleveland..................................... E 216 664-2555
Cleveland *(G-3981)*

93 PUBLIC FINANCE, TAXATION AND MONETARY POLICY

9311 Finance, taxation, and monetary policy

City of Cleveland..................................... E 216 664-2640
Cleveland *(G-3978)*

Department of Commerce Ohio............... D 614 644-7381
Columbus *(G-5757)*

94 ADMINISTRATION OF HUMAN RESOURCE PROGRAMS

9431 Administration of public health programs

Champaign Cnty Board of Dd.................. B 937 653-5217
Urbana *(G-14300)*

City of Akron.. E 330 564-4075
Akron *(G-102)*

County of Carroll...................................... D 330 627-7651
Carrollton *(G-1906)*

County of Cuyahoga................................. A 216 241-8230
Cleveland *(G-4126)*

County of Cuyahoga................................. C 216 698-6526
Cleveland *(G-4127)*

County of Cuyahoga................................. E 216 432-2621
Cleveland *(G-4130)*

County of Cuyahoga................................. B 216 443-6954
Cleveland *(G-4131)*

County of Summit..................................... A 330 634-8000
Tallmadge *(G-13590)*

County of Wood.. D 419 352-8402
Bowling Green *(G-1315)*

Department of Health Ohio...................... E 419 447-1450
Tiffin *(G-13627)*

Franklin Cnty Bd Commissioners............ D 614 261-3196
Columbus *(G-5881)*

Knox County... E 740 392-2200
Mount Vernon *(G-11494)*

Ohio Department Youth Services............ C 614 466-4314
Columbus *(G-6403)*

Ohio Dept Dvlpmntal Dsbilities................ C 513 732-9200
Batavia *(G-744)*

Ohio Dept Dvlpmntal Dsbilities................ C 330 544-2231
Columbus *(G-6404)*

Ohio Dept Dvlpmntal Dsbilities................ C 614 272-0509
Columbus *(G-6405)*

Ohio Dept Dvlpmntal Dsbilities................ C 740 446-1642
Gallipolis *(G-8764)*

Ohio Dept Dvlpmntal Dsbilities................ C 419 385-0231
Toledo *(G-13944)*

Ohio Dept Mntal Hlth Addction................ C 740 594-5000
Athens *(G-583)*

Ohio Dept Mntal Hlth Addction................ C 513 948-3600
Cincinnati *(G-3144)*

Ohio Dept Mntal Hlth Addction................ C 614 752-0333
Columbus *(G-6408)*

Ohio Dept Mntal Hlth Addction................ C 614 752-0333
Columbus *(G-6409)*

Ohio Dept Mntal Hlth Addction................ D 614 752-0333
Columbus *(G-6410)*

Ohio Dept Mntal Hlth Addction................ C 330 467-7131
Northfield *(G-11962)*

Ohio Dept Mntal Hlth Addction................ C 419 381-1881
Toledo *(G-13945)*

Ohio Dept Mntal Hlth Addction................ C 740 947-7581
Waverly *(G-14614)*

9441 Administration of social and manpower programs

County of Cuyahoga................................. E 216 420-6750
Cleveland *(G-4122)*

County of Cuyahoga................................. E 216 443-5100
Cleveland *(G-4123)*

County of Cuyahoga................................. E 216 681-4433
Cleveland *(G-4124)*

County of Cuyahoga................................. D 216 431-4500
Cleveland *(G-4129)*

County of Hamilton................................... E 513 946-1800
Cincinnati *(G-2512)*

Ohio Dept Job & Fmly Svcs..................... E 330 484-5402
Akron *(G-248)*

Ohio Dept Job & Fmly Svcs..................... E 614 752-9494
Columbus *(G-6406)*

Ohio Dept Job & Fmly Svcs..................... E 614 466-1213
Columbus *(G-6407)*

Ohio Dept Job & Fmly Svcs..................... E 419 334-3891
Fremont *(G-8696)*

Ohio Pub Employees Rtrement Sys........ B 614 228-8471
Columbus *(G-6440)*

School Emplyees Rtrment Sys OH......... C 614 222-5853
Columbus *(G-6651)*

9451 Administration of veterans' affairs

Veterans Health Administration............... A 740 773-1141
Chillicothe *(G-2093)*

Veterans Health Administration............... A 513 861-3100
Cincinnati *(G-3627)*

Veterans Health Administration............... A 216 791-3800
Cleveland *(G-5101)*

Veterans Health Administration............... D 614 257-5200
Columbus *(G-6848)*

Veterans Health Administration............... C 614 257-5524
Columbus *(G-6849)*

Veterans Health Administration............... A 937 268-6511
Dayton *(G-7705)*

95 ADMINISTRATION OF ENVIRONMENTAL QUALITY AND HOUSING PROGRAMS

9511 Air, water, and solid waste management

City of Lakewood..................................... E 216 252-4322
Cleveland *(G-3990)*

Mahoning County...................................... E 330 793-5514
Youngstown *(G-15656)*

Village of Sycamore................................. D 419 927-2357
Sycamore *(G-13534)*

9512 Land, mineral, and wildlife conservation

City of Cleveland..................................... E 216 348-7210
Cleveland *(G-3979)*

City of Cleveland..................................... E 216 348-2200
Cleveland *(G-3984)*

9531 Housing programs

Akron Metropolitan Hsing Auth................ D 330 920-1652
Stow *(G-13354)*

City of Toledo... E 419 245-1400
Toledo *(G-13739)*

9532 Urban and community development

County of Cuyahoga................................. B 216 348-3800
Cleveland *(G-4125)*

96 ADMINISTRATION OF ECONOMIC PROGRAMS

9611 Administration of general economic programs

Department of Commerce Ohio............... D 614 728-8400
Columbus *(G-5756)*

9621 Regulation, administration of transportation

City of Cleveland..................................... A 216 265-6000
Cleveland *(G-3980)*

City of Hamilton....................................... E 513 785-7551
Hamilton *(G-9028)*

Ohio Tpk & Infrastructure Comm............ D 440 234-2081
Berea *(G-1077)*

Ohio Tpk & Infrastructure Comm............ E 440 234-2081
Richfield *(G-12705)*

Ohio Tpk & Infrastructure Comm............ D 330 527-2169
Windham *(G-15288)*

Putnam Cnty Commissioners Off............ E 419 523-6832
Ottawa *(G-12192)*

97 NATIONAL SECURITY AND INTERNATIONAL AFFAIRS

9711 National security

Defense Fin & Accounting Svc................ A 614 693-6700
Columbus *(G-5750)*

The United States Dept A Force.............. B 937 255-3286
Dayton *(G-7142)*

ALPHABETIC SECTION

R & R Sealants (HQ)..999 999-9999
  651 Tally Blvd, Yourtown (99999) *(G-458)*
Ready Box Co..999 999-9999
  704 Lawrence Rd, Anytown (99999) *(G-1723)*
Rendall Mfg Inc, Anytown Also Called RMI *(G-1730)*

- Address, city & ZIP
- Designates this location as a headquarters
- Business phone
- Geographic Section entry number where full company information appears

See footnotes for symbols and codes identification.
- Companies listed alphabetically.
- Complete physical or mailing address.

(Board Of Governors Of The Federal Reserve System, The, Washington, DC), Cleveland
Also Called: Federal Reserve Bank Cleveland (G-4246)

022808 Kenwood LLC... 513 745-0800
  8251 Pine Rd Ste 110 Cincinnati (45236) *(G-2117)*

1 866 Plumber, Milford Also Called: 1 Tom Plumber LLC *(G-11214)*

1 Cochran Buick GMC, Youngstown Also Called: Recmv2 Inc *(G-15707)*

1 Edi Source, Solon Also Called: Epicor Edi Source Inc *(G-13084)*

1 Natural Way LLC... 888 977-2229
  4064 Technology Dr Ste B Maumee (43537) *(G-10682)*

1 Tom Plumber LLC... 866 758-6237
  24 Whitney Dr Ste A Milford (45150) *(G-11214)*

1-888-Ohiocomp Inc.. 888 644-6266
  1495 W Longview Ave Mansfield (44906) *(G-10241)*

101 River Inc... 440 352-6343
  101 River St Grand River (44045) *(G-8848)*

11689 Sharon West Inc... 513 771-2525
  11689 Chester Rd Cincinnati (45246) *(G-2118)*

11th Hour Staffing Inc.. 937 405-1900
  5108 Summerset Dr Tipp City (45371) *(G-13650)*

121ecommerce LLC... 216 586-6656
  2447 Bromley Rd University Heights (44118) *(G-14274)*

127 PS Fee Owner LLC.. 216 520-1250
  1300 Key Tower 127 Public Square Cleveland (44114) *(G-3738)*

12985 Snow Holdings Inc... 216 267-5000
  12985 Snow Rd Cleveland (44130) *(G-3739)*

1460 Ninth St Assoc Ltd Partnr.. 216 241-6600
  1460 E 9th St Cleveland (44114) *(G-3740)*

151 W 4th Cincinnati LLC.. 312 283-3683
  151 W 4th St Cincinnati (45202) *(G-2119)*

16644 Snow Rd LLC... 216 676-5200
  26949 Chagrin Blvd Beachwood (44122) *(G-762)*

17322 Euclid Avenue Co LLC... 216 486-2280
  17322 Euclid Ave Cleveland (44112) *(G-3741)*

1848 Ventures LLC.. 330 887-0187
  1 Park Cir Westfield Center (44251) *(G-15023)*

1hvac, Troy Also Called: Brock Air Products Inc *(G-14130)*

1st Advnce SEC Invstgtions Inc.. 937 210-9010
  1675 Woodman Dr Dayton (45432) *(G-7123)*

1st Advnce SEC Invstgtions Inc.. 937 317-4433
  111 W 1st St Ste 101 Dayton (45402) *(G-7145)*

1st All File Recovery Usa.. 800 399-7150
  4400 Renaissance Pkwy # 1 Cleveland (44128) *(G-3742)*

1st Carrier Corp... 740 477-2587
  177 Neville St Circleville (43113) *(G-3701)*

1st Choice Roofing Company... 216 227-7755
  10311 Berea Rd Cleveland (44102) *(G-3743)*

1st Choice Security Inc... 513 381-6789
  2245 Gilbert Ave Ste 400 Cincinnati (45206) *(G-2120)*

1st Stop Inc (PA)... 937 695-0318
  18856 State Route 136 Winchester (45697) *(G-15283)*

1worldsync Inc.. 866 280-4013
  7777 Washington Village Dr Ste 360 Dayton (45459) *(G-7146)*

2 J Supply Llc (PA)... 937 223-0811
  1456 N Keowee St Dayton (45404) *(G-7147)*

2023 Ventures Inc
  595 E Lugbill Rd Archbold (43502) *(G-454)*

204 W Main Street Oper Co LLC.................................... 419 929-1563
  204 W Main St New London (44851) *(G-11632)*

2060 Digital LLC.. 513 699-5012
  4800 Kennedy Ave Cincinnati (45209) *(G-2121)*

21c Museum Hotel Cincinnati, Cincinnati Also Called: 609 Walnut Hotel LLC *(G-2125)*

21st Century Con Cnstr Inc.. 216 362-0900
  2344 Canal Rd Cleveland (44113) *(G-3744)*

21st Century Financial Inc... 330 668-9065
  130 Springside Dr Ste 100 Akron (44333) *(G-5)*

21st Century Health Spa Inc (PA).................................. 419 476-5585
  343 New Towne Square Dr Toledo (43612) *(G-13670)*

21st Century Solutions Ltd (PA).................................... 877 439-5377
  955 Mound Rd Miamisburg (45342) *(G-11017)*

22nd Century Technologies Inc..................................... 866 537-9191
  2601 Commons Blvd Ste 130 Beavercreek (45431) *(G-854)*

2immersive4u Corporation.. 440 570-4055
  3661 Wallings Rd North Royalton (44133) *(G-11937)*

2mc Management LLC... 513 771-1700
  7660 School Rd Cincinnati (45249) *(G-2122)*

3 D Disaster Kleenup Columbus, Columbus Also Called: 3d Building Systems LLC *(G-5287)*

3-D Service Ltd (PA).. 330 830-3500
  800 Nave Rd Se Massillon (44646) *(G-10626)*

30 Lines.. 614 859-5030
  52 E Lynn St Ste 400 Columbus (43215) *(G-5286)*

365 Holdings LLC.. 800 403-8182
  115 W Bartges St Akron (44311) *(G-6)*

3b Holdings Inc (PA).. 800 791-7124
  11470 Euclid Ave Ste 407 Cleveland (44106) *(G-3745)*

3b Supply, Cleveland Also Called: 3b Holdings Inc *(G-3745)*

3c Technology Solutions LLC....................................... 614 319-4681
  2786 Walcutt Rd Hilliard (43026) *(G-9174)*

3cre Advisors LLC... 513 745-9333
  7815 Cooper Rd Ste C Cincinnati (45242) *(G-2123)*

3d Building Systems LLC.. 614 351-9695
  4110 Perimeter Dr Columbus (43228) *(G-5287)*

3d Systems Inc.. 216 229-2040
  7100 Euclid Ave Cleveland (44103) *(G-3746)*

3dvision Technologies, Cincinnati Also Called: Computer Aided Technology LLC *(G-2491)*

3e Company Environmental Ecolo................................ 330 451-4900
  4450 Belden Village St Nw Ste 407 Canton (44718) *(G-1647)*

3E COMPANY ENVIRONMENTAL, ECOLOGICAL AND ENGINEERING, Canton Also Called: 3e Company Environmental Ecolo *(G-1647)*

3rd Street Community Clinic... 419 522-6191
  1404 Park Ave W Ontario (44906) *(G-12095)*

3RD STREET FAMILY HEALTH SERVI, Ontario Also Called: 3rd Street Community Clinic *(G-12095)*

3sg Corporation... 614 761-8394
  344 Cramer Creek Ct Dublin (43017) *(G-7918)*

ALPHABETIC SECTION

3sg Plus, Columbus *Also Called: 3sg Plus LLC (G-5243)*

3sg Plus LLC..614 652-0019
8415 Pulsar Pl Ste 100 Columbus (43240) *(G-5243)*

4 Paws For Ability Inc..............................937 374-0385
207 Dayton Ave Xenia (45385) *(G-15497)*

4 PAWS FOR ABILITY INC, Xenia *Also Called: 4 Paws For Ability Inc (G-15497)*

415 Group Inc (PA)...................................330 492-0094
4300 Munson St Nw Ste 100 Canton (44718) *(G-1648)*

4859 Hills & Dales Inc.............................330 479-9175
4150 Belden Village St Nw Ste 108 Canton (44718) *(G-1649)*

4C FOR CHILDREN, Cincinnati *Also Called: Comprhnsive Cmnty Child Care O (G-2489)*

4mybenefits Inc..513 891-6726
4665 Cornell Rd Ste 331 Blue Ash (45241) *(G-1119)*

4wd, Columbiana *Also Called: Four Wheel Drive Hardware LLC (G-5235)*

5 Rivers Park, Dayton *Also Called: Cox Arboretum (G-7259)*

5 Star Hotel Management IV LP...........614 431-1819
6191 Quarter Horse Dr Columbus (43229) *(G-5288)*

50 X 20 Holding Company Inc.............330 865-4663
779 White Pond Dr Akron (44320) *(G-7)*

50 X 20 Holding Company Inc.............740 238-4262
41201 Bond Dr Belmont (43718) *(G-1053)*

50 X 20 Holding Company Inc (PA)....330 478-4500
2715 Wise Ave Nw Canton (44708) *(G-1650)*

500 Degrees LLC.....................................786 615-8265
4030 Easton Sta Columbus (43219) *(G-5289)*

506 Phelps Holdings LLC......................513 651-1234
506 E 4th St Cincinnati (45202) *(G-2124)*

5145 Corporation.....................................330 659-6662
4860 Brecksville Rd Richfield (44286) *(G-12684)*

5901 Pfffer Rd Htels Sites LLC............513 793-4500
5901 Pfeiffer Rd Blue Ash (45242) *(G-1120)*

599 W Main Corporation........................440 466-1079
599 W Main St Geneva (44041) *(G-8783)*

5me LLC...513 719-1600
4270 Ivy Pointe Blvd Ste 100 Cincinnati (45245) *(G-2095)*

609 Walnut Hotel LLC.............................513 578-6600
609 Walnut St Ste 2 Cincinnati (45202) *(G-2125)*

6300 Sharonville Assoc LLC.................513 489-3636
6300 E Kemper Rd Cincinnati (45241) *(G-2126)*

631 South Main Street Dev LLC...........419 423-0631
631 S Main St Findlay (45840) *(G-8504)*

7 Up / R C/Canada Dry Btlg Co, Columbus *Also Called: American Bottling Company (G-5346)*

76 Auto, Westlake *Also Called: National At/Trckstops Hldngs C (G-15081)*

7nt, Miamisburg *Also Called: 7nt Enterprises LLC (G-11018)*

7nt Enterprises LLC (PA)......................614 961-2026
3090 S Tech Blvd Miamisburg (45342) *(G-11018)*

80 Acres Urban Agriculture Inc...........888 547-1569
7415 Hamilton Enterprise Park Dr, Hamilton (45011) *(G-9015)*

8001 Red Buckeye Landlord LLC........937 506-4733
8230 Pittsburg Ave Nw North Canton (44720) *(G-11806)*

823 Dayton Hotel Tenant LLC..............937 879-2696
10823 Chidlaw Rd Dayton (45433) *(G-7124)*

845 Yard Street LLC...............................614 484-6860
775 Yard St Columbus (43212) *(G-5290)*

8451 LLC (HQ)...513 632-1020
100 W 5th St Cincinnati (45202) *(G-2127)*

88th Mdss/Sgsm Mm-Ht1135...............937 257-8935
4881 Sugar Maple Dr Wright Patterson Afb (45433) *(G-15473)*

8motel, Canton *Also Called: N P Motel System Inc (G-1816)*

937 Delivers Cooperative.....................937 802-0709
840 Germantown St Dayton (45402) *(G-7148)*

A & A Safety Inc (PA)............................513 943-6100
1126 Ferris Rd Amelia (45102) *(G-409)*

A & A Wall Systems Inc........................513 489-0086
11589 Deerfield Rd Cincinnati (45242) *(G-2128)*

A & G Manufacturing Co Inc (PA)........419 468-7433
280 Gelsanliter Rd Galion (44833) *(G-8740)*

A & K Ishvar Inc......................................937 322-0707
121 Raydo Cir Springfield (45506) *(G-13212)*

A A Hammersmith Insurance Inc (PA)...330 832-7411
210 Erie St N Massillon (44646) *(G-10627)*

A B M Inc..419 421-2292
119 E Sandusky St Findlay (45840) *(G-8505)*

A Bee C Service Inc (PA)......................440 735-1505
7589 First Pl Ste 1 Cleveland (44146) *(G-3747)*

A Blessed Path Inc................................330 244-0657
2380 Nimishillen Church Rd Ne Canton (44721) *(G-1651)*

A Brown and Sons Nursery Inc...........937 836-5826
11506 Dayton Greenville Pike Brookville (45309) *(G-1444)*

A C Management Inc.............................440 461-9200
780 Beta Dr Cleveland (44143) *(G-3748)*

A Childs Hope Intl Inc...........................513 771-2244
2430 E Kemper Rd Unit A Cincinnati (45241) *(G-2129)*

A Crano Excavating Inc........................330 630-1061
1505 Industrial Pkwy Akron (44310) *(G-8)*

A D A Architects Inc..............................216 521-5134
17710 Detroit Ave Cleveland (44107) *(G-3749)*

A D D, Westerville *Also Called: Assoction For Dvlpmntlly Dsble (G-14961)*

A D M Crisis Center, Akron *Also Called: Oriana House Inc (G-258)*

A Duie Pyle Inc.......................................330 342-7750
10225 Philipp Pkwy Streetsboro (44241) *(G-13408)*

A E D Inc..419 661-9999
2845 Crane Way Northwood (43619) *(G-11968)*

A E I, Centerville *Also Called: Aydelott Equipment Inc (G-1939)*

A G Mercury, Galion *Also Called: A & G Manufacturing Co Inc (G-8740)*

A G S Ohio, Macedonia *Also Called: AGS Custom Graphics Inc (G-10188)*

A Grade Ahead Inc................................614 389-3830
10202 Sawmill Pkwy Powell (43065) *(G-12582)*

A H G, Wadsworth *Also Called: American Hospitality Group Inc (G-14428)*

A J Amer Agency Inc (HQ)....................330 665-9966
3737 Embassy Pkwy Ste 260 Akron (44333) *(G-9)*

A J Amer Agency Inc.............................330 665-9966
231 Springside Dr Ste 205 Akron (44333) *(G-10)*

A J Goulder Electric Co.........................440 942-4026
4307 Hamann Pkwy Willoughby (44094) *(G-15182)*

A J Stockmeister Inc (PA)....................740 286-2106
702 E Main St Jackson (45640) *(G-9515)*

A K Athletic Equipment Inc..................614 920-3069
8015 Howe Industrial Pkwy Canal Winchester (43110) *(G-1597)*

A L D Precast Corp................................614 449-3366
1600 Haul Rd Columbus (43207) *(G-5291)*

A L Smith Trucking Inc.........................937 526-3651
8984 Murphy Rd Versailles (45380) *(G-14412)*

A Loving Hart HM Hlth Care LLC.........937 549-4484
255 Cabin Creek Rd Manchester (45144) *(G-10238)*

A M & O Towing Inc...............................330 385-0639
11341 State Route 170 Negley (44441) *(G-11540)*

A M Communications Ltd (PA)............419 528-3051
5707 State Route 309 Galion (44833) *(G-8741)*

A M Leonard Inc.....................................937 773-2694
241 Fox Dr Piqua (45356) *(G-12434)*

A M Management Inc.............................937 426-6500
2000 Zink Rd Beavercreek (45324) *(G-855)*

A One Fine Dry Cleaners Inc...............513 731-7950
6211 Montgomery Rd Cincinnati (45213) *(G-2130)*

A P & P Dev & Cnstr Co (PA)...............330 833-8886
2851 Lincoln Way E Massillon (44646) *(G-10628)*

A P OHoro Company.............................330 759-9317
3130 Belmont Ave Youngstown (44505) *(G-15539)*

A P S Medical Billing, Toledo *Also Called: APS Medical Billing (G-13692)*

A P T, Worthington *Also Called: Datafield Inc (G-15412)*

A Plus Expediting & Logistics.............937 424-0220
2947 Boulder Ave Dayton (45414) *(G-7149)*

A R C, Cleveland *Also Called: ARC Document Solutions Inc (G-3830)*

A S I, Plain City *Also Called: Asi Commercial Roofg Maint Inc (G-12468)*

A T & F Co, Cleveland *Also Called: American Tank & Fabricating Co (G-3808)*

A T Emmett LLC......................................419 734-2520
2028 E State Rd Port Clinton (43452) *(G-12516)*

A T V Inc...614 252-5060
2047 Leonard Ave Columbus (43219) *(G-5292)*

A Techniplas Company, Mansfield *Also Called: Nanogate North America LLC (G-10302)*

ALPHABETIC SECTION

A To Z Portion Ctrl Meats Inc 419 358-2926
201 N Main St Bluffton (45817) *(G-1276)*

A Touch of Grace Inc 567 560-2350
787 Lexington Ave Ste 303 Mansfield (44907) *(G-10242)*

A W Farrell & Son Inc 513 334-0715
745 Us Route 50 Milford (45150) *(G-11215)*

A W S Inc 216 941-8800
10991 Memphis Ave Cleveland (44144) *(G-3750)*

A W S Inc 216 749-0356
4720 Hinckley Industrial Pkwy Cleveland (44109) *(G-3751)*

A W S Inc 216 486-0600
1490 E 191st St Euclid (44117) *(G-8335)*

A W S Inc 440 333-1791
20120 Detroit Rd Rocky River (44116) *(G-12738)*

A-1 Advanced Plumbing Inc 614 873-0548
8299 Memorial Dr Plain City (43064) *(G-12363)*

A-1 Best Locksmith, Cincinnati Also Called: Serv-A-Lite Products Inc *(G-3360)*

A-1 General Insurance Agency (DH) 216 986-3000
9700 Rockside Rd Ste 250 Cleveland (44125) *(G-3752)*

A-1 Hlthcare Stffing Plcements (PA) 216 329-3500
11811 Shaker Blvd Ste 330 Cleveland (44120) *(G-3753)*

A-1 Qlity Lgstcal Slutions LLC (PA) 513 353-0173
3055 Blue Rock Rd Cincinnati (45239) *(G-2131)*

A-1 Sprinkler Company Inc 937 859-6198
2383 Northpointe Dr Miamisburg (45342) *(G-11019)*

A-A Blueprint Co Inc 330 794-8803
2757 Gilchrist Rd Akron (44305) *(G-11)*

A-Advnced Mvg Stor Systms-Self, Akron Also Called: Cotter Moving & Storage Co *(G-125)*

A-E Door and Window Sales, Cincinnati Also Called: A-E Door Sales and Service Inc *(G-2132)*

A-E Door Sales and Service Inc (PA) 513 742-1984
1260 W Sharon Rd Cincinnati (45240) *(G-2132)*

A-Roo Company LLC (HQ) 440 238-8850
22360 Royalton Rd Strongsville (44149) *(G-13437)*

A1 Complete Inc 216 691-0363
1383 Sheffield Rd Cleveland (44121) *(G-3754)*

A1 Industrial Painting Inc 330 750-9441
894 Coitsville Hubbard Rd Youngstown (44505) *(G-15540)*

A2z Field Services LLC 614 873-0211
7450 Industrial Pkwy Ste 105 Plain City (43064) *(G-12464)*

AAA, Niles Also Called: AAA East Central *(G-11779)*

AAA, Worthington Also Called: Ohio Automobile Club *(G-15444)*

AAA Advanced Plbg & Drain Clg, Cleveland Also Called: AAA Pipe Cleaning Corporation *(G-3756)*

AAA Auto Wash, Cincinnati Also Called: Allied Car Wash Inc *(G-2163)*

AAA Club Alliance Inc 513 984-3553
8176 Montgomery Rd Cincinnati (45236) *(G-2133)*

AAA Club Alliance Inc 513 762-3301
15 W Central Pkwy Cincinnati (45202) *(G-2134)*

AAA Club Alliance Inc (PA) 419 843-1200
3201 Meijer Dr Toledo (43617) *(G-13671)*

AAA East Central 330 652-6466
937 Youngstown Warren Rd Niles (44446) *(G-11779)*

AAA Emergency Service 513 554-6473
1279 Lebnon Loveland (45140) *(G-10125)*

AAA Flexible Pipe Clg Corp 216 341-2900
7277 Bessemer Ave Cleveland (44127) *(G-3755)*

AAA Miami Valley (PA) 937 224-2896
825 S Ludlow St Dayton (45402) *(G-7150)*

AAA Mid-Atlantic, Toledo Also Called: AAA Club Alliance Inc *(G-13671)*

AAA Ohio Auto Club 614 431-7800
90 E Wilson Bridge Rd Worthington (43085) *(G-15403)*

AAA Pipe Cleaning Corporation (PA) 216 341-2900
7277 Bessemer Ave Cleveland (44127) *(G-3756)*

AAA Standard Services Inc 419 535-0274
4117 South Ave Toledo (43615) *(G-13672)*

AAA Travel Agency, Dayton Also Called: AAA Miami Valley *(G-7150)*

AAA Worldwide Travel Service, Cincinnati Also Called: AAA Club Alliance Inc *(G-2133)*

Aabel Exterminating Co 937 434-4343
440 Congress Park Dr Dayton (45459) *(G-7151)*

Aacs Consulting, Columbus Also Called: Adroit Assoc Cnslting Svcs LLC *(G-5315)*

Aaj Enterprises Inc 614 497-2000
4700 Groveport Rd Obetz (43207) *(G-12078)*

Aaris Therapy Group Inc 330 505-1606
950 Youngstown Warren Rd Niles (44446) *(G-11780)*

Aashna Corporation 614 871-0065
3131 Broadway Urbancrest (43123) *(G-14318)*

Aatish Hospitality LLC 937 437-8009
9797 Us Route 40 W New Paris (45347) *(G-11637)*

Aatsi, Fort Loramie Also Called: Aviation Auto Trnsp Spclsts In *(G-8603)*

AB Tube Company, Twinsburg Also Called: Atlas Steel Products Co *(G-14172)*

Aba Insurance Services Inc 800 274-5222
3401 Tuttle Rd Ste 300 Shaker Heights (44122) *(G-12972)*

Abacus Corporation 614 367-7000
1676 Brice Rd Reynoldsburg (43068) *(G-12649)*

Abb Inc 440 725-2968
9145 Cambridge Rd Chardon (44024) *(G-1993)*

ABB Enterprise Software Inc 440 585-6716
29801 Eucland Ave Painesville (44077) *(G-12219)*

ABB ENTERPRISE SOFTWARE INC., Painesville Also Called: ABB Enterprise Software Inc *(G-12219)*

ABB Inc 513 860-1749
4828 Business Center Way West Chester (45246) *(G-14797)*

ABB Inc 614 818-6300
579 Executive Campus Dr Frnt Westerville (43082) *(G-14876)*

ABB Industrial Systems, Westerville Also Called: ABB Inc *(G-14876)*

ABB, INC., Chardon Also Called: Abb Inc *(G-1993)*

Abbewood Limited Partnership 440 366-8980
1210 Abbe Rd S Ofc Elyria (44035) *(G-8231)*

Abbot Stdios Archtcts + Plnner 614 461-0101
471 E Broad St Fl 17 Columbus (43215) *(G-5293)*

Abbott Electric Inc (PA) 330 452-6601
1935 Allen Ave Se Canton (44707) *(G-1652)*

Abbott Electric Inc 330 343-8941
610 S Tuscarawas Ave Rear Dover (44622) *(G-7871)*

Abbott Laboratories 847 937-6100
2900 Easton Square Pl Columbus (43219) *(G-5294)*

Abbott Tool Inc 419 476-6742
405 Dura Ave Toledo (43612) *(G-13673)*

Abbruzzese Brothers Inc (PA) 614 873-1550
7775 Smith Calhoun Rd Plain City (43064) *(G-12465)*

ABC, Grafton Also Called: Bechtold Enterprises Inc *(G-8838)*

ABC Early Childhood Lrng Ctr, Cincinnati Also Called: Colerain Dry Rdge Chldcare Ltd *(G-2476)*

ABC Scribes Ltd 937 705-5471
6784 Loop Rd Ste 210 Centerville (45459) *(G-1938)*

Abcap Foundation 937 378-6041
406 W Plum St Georgetown (45121) *(G-8796)*

Abco Fire Protection, Cleveland Also Called: Abco Holdings LLC *(G-3757)*

Abco Holdings LLC 216 433-7200
4545 W 160th St Cleveland (44135) *(G-3757)*

Abdouni Enterprises LLC 419 345-6773
3945 Hillandale Rd Apt W Ottawa Hills (43606) *(G-12197)*

Abel-Bishop & Clarke Realty Co 614 253-8627
1035 Atcheson St Ofc Columbus (43203) *(G-5295)*

Aber's Truck Center, Ashland Also Called: Abers Garage Inc *(G-471)*

Abercrombie & Fitch, New Albany Also Called: Abercrombie & Fitch Trading Co *(G-11551)*

Abercrombie & Fitch Trading Co (DH) 614 283-6500
6301 Fitch Path New Albany (43054) *(G-11551)*

Abers Garage Inc (PA) 419 281-5500
1729 Claremont Ave Ashland (44805) *(G-471)*

ABG Advisors, Cincinnati Also Called: Pension Corporation America *(G-3195)*

Abilities Connection 937 525-7400
2160 Old Selma Rd Springfield (45505) *(G-13213)*

Abilities First Foundation Inc (PA) 513 423-9496
4710 Timber Trail Dr Middletown (45044) *(G-11149)*

Ability Ctr of Greater Toledo (PA) 419 517-7123
5605 Monroe St Sylvania (43560) *(G-13535)*

Ability Works Inc 419 626-1048
3920 Columbus Ave Sandusky (44870) *(G-12861)*

Able, Toledo Also Called: Advoctes For Bsic Lgal Eqlity *(G-13675)*

Able Roofing LLC (PA) 614 444-2253
4777 Westerville Rd Columbus (43231) *(G-5296)*

ABM Industry Groups LLC 216 621-6600
1459 Hamilton Ave Cleveland (44114) *(G-3758)*

ABM Janitorial Services Inc 513 731-1418
354 Gest St Cincinnati (45203) *(G-2135)*

ABM Janitorial Services Inc 216 861-1199
1501 Euclid Ave Ste 320 Cleveland (44115) *(G-3759)*

ABN Financial Group 937 522-0101
8911 Shadycreek Dr Dayton (45458) *(G-7152)*

Aboutgolf Limited (PA) 419 482-9095
352 Tomahawk Dr Maumee (43537) *(G-10683)*

Abraham Ford LLC 440 233-7402
1115 E Broad St Elyria (44035) *(G-8232)*

Abraxas Cornell Group LLC 419 747-3322
2775 State Route 39 Shelby (44875) *(G-13004)*

Abraxas Foundation of Ohio, Shelby *Also Called: Abraxas Cornell Group LLC (G-13004)*

ABS Business Products, Cincinnati *Also Called: Donnellon McCarthy Entps Inc (G-2573)*

ABS Coastal Insulating LLC 843 360-1045
495 S High St Ste 50 Columbus (43215) *(G-5297)*

ABS Communication LLC 419 293-5026
51 E Main St Ste B Norwalk (44857) *(G-11998)*

ABS Transitions LLC 513 832-2884
4861 Duck Creek Rd Cincinnati (45227) *(G-2136)*

Absolute Health Services, Canton *Also Called: Advantage Appliance Services (G-1656)*

Absolute Machine Tools Inc (PA) 440 960-6911
7420 Industrial Parkway Dr Lorain (44053) *(G-10052)*

Absolute Pharmacy Inc 330 498-8200
7167 Keck Park Cir Nw Canton (44720) *(G-1653)*

Absolute Prfmce For Abslute VI, Lorain *Also Called: Absolute Machine Tools Inc (G-10052)*

Abuse Refuge Inc 614 686-2121
928 Polaris Grand Dr Apt G Lewis Center (43035) *(G-9803)*

Abuse Refuge Org, Lewis Center *Also Called: Abuse Refuge Inc (G-9803)*

Abx Air Inc (HQ) 937 382-5591
145 Hunter Dr Wilmington (45177) *(G-15237)*

AC Banks, Cincinnati *Also Called: Main Hospitality Holdings LLC (G-3004)*

AC Hotel Columbus Dublin 614 798-8652
6540 Riverside Dr Dublin (43017) *(G-7919)*

AC Hotels, Dublin *Also Called: AC Hotel Columbus Dublin (G-7919)*

Academic Bhvral Lrng Enrchment 513 544-4991
20 S 3rd St Ste 210 Columbus (43215) *(G-5298)*

Academy Kids Learning Ctr Inc 614 258-5437
289 Woodland Ave Columbus (43203) *(G-5299)*

ACCAA, Ashtabula *Also Called: Ashtabula County Commnty Actn (G-521)*

Accel Inc 614 656-1100
9000 Smiths Mill Rd New Albany (43054) *(G-11552)*

Accel Performance Group LLC (DH) 216 658-6413
6100 Oak Tree Blvd Ste 200 Independence (44131) *(G-9394)*

Accel Schools Ohio LLC 330 535-7728
107 S Arlington St Akron (44306) *(G-12)*

Accelerant Solutions, Maumee *Also Called: Accelerant Technologies LLC (G-10684)*

Accelerant Technologies LLC 419 236-8768
1715 Indian Wood Cir Ste 200 Maumee (43537) *(G-10684)*

Accelerated Health Systems LLC 614 334-5135
3780 Ridge Mill Dr Hilliard (43026) *(G-9175)*

Accent Drapery Co Inc 614 488-0741
1180 Goodale Blvd Columbus (43212) *(G-5300)*

Accent Drapery Supply Co, Columbus *Also Called: Accent Drapery Co Inc (G-5300)*

Accenture, Columbus *Also Called: Accenture LLP (G-5301)*

Accenture LLP 513 455-1000
201 E 4th St Ste 1600 Cincinnati (45202) *(G-2137)*

Accenture LLP 513 651-2444
425 Walnut St Ste 1200 Cincinnati (45202) *(G-2138)*

Accenture LLP 216 685-1435
1400 W 10th St Ste 401 Cleveland (44113) *(G-3760)*

Accenture LLP 614 629-2000
400 W Nationwide Blvd Ste 100 Columbus (43215) *(G-5301)*

Access, Columbus *Also Called: Access Information MGT Corp (G-5303)*

Access Inc 330 535-2999
230 W Market St Akron (44303) *(G-13)*

Access Catalog Company LLC 440 572-5377
21848 Commerce Pkwy Ste 100 Strongsville (44149) *(G-13438)*

Access Counseling Services LLC 513 649-8008
4464 S Dixie Hwy Middletown (45005) *(G-11193)*

Access Drywall Supply Co Inc 614 890-2111
297 Old County Line Rd Westerville (43081) *(G-14955)*

Access Hospital Dayton LLC 937 228-0579
2611 Wayne Ave Bldg 61 Dayton (45420) *(G-7153)*

ACCESS HOSPITAL FOR PSYCHIATRY DAYTON, Dayton *Also Called: Access Hospital Dayton LLC (G-7153)*

Access Info Holdings LLC 614 777-1701
2500 Charter St Columbus (43228) *(G-5302)*

Access Information MGT Corp 614 777-1701
2500 Charter St Ste B Columbus (43228) *(G-5303)*

Access Urgent Medical Care Plc 614 306-0116
1797 Hill Rd N Pickerington (43147) *(G-12396)*

Accessibility, Ashland *Also Called: Randall R Leab (G-508)*

Accessmd Ancillary Services, Columbus *Also Called: Urgent Care Specialists LLC (G-6834)*

Accf Accreditation, Dublin *Also Called: American Cllege Crdlgy Fndtion (G-7932)*

Acclaim Hspice Plltive Care Dy, Dayton *Also Called: Peoplfrst Hmcare Hspice Ohio L (G-7548)*

Accounts Pyble Sso Mrcy AP Shr, Cincinnati *Also Called: Bon Secours Mercy Health Inc (G-2271)*

Accs Day Care Centers Inc 513 841-2227
1705 Section Rd Cincinnati (45237) *(G-2139)*

Accu Grind, Kent *Also Called: Reduction Engineering Inc (G-9593)*

Accucall LLC 440 522-8681
144 Keep Ct Elyria (44035) *(G-8233)*

Acculube, Dayton *Also Called: Fisk Kinne Holdings Inc (G-7356)*

Accurate Electric Cnstr Inc 614 863-1844
6901 Americana Pkwy Reynoldsburg (43068) *(G-12650)*

Accurate Group Holdings Inc (PA) 216 520-1740
6000 Freedom Square Dr Ste 300 Independence (44131) *(G-9395)*

Accurate Invntory Clclting Svc 800 777-9414
4284 N High St Columbus (43214) *(G-5304)*

Accurate It Services, Columbus *Also Called: Enviro It LLC (G-5821)*

Accurate Mechanical Inc 740 681-1332
566 Mill Park Dr Lancaster (43130) *(G-9690)*

Accutek Testing Laboratory, Fairfield *Also Called: McCloy Engineering LLC (G-8428)*

Acd Enterprises Inc 866 252-4395
9601 Granger Rd Cleveland (44125) *(G-3761)*

Ace Disposal, Dover *Also Called: Kimble Recycl & Disposal Inc (G-7892)*

Ace Doran Hauling & Rigging Co 513 681-7900
10765 Medallion Dr Cincinnati (45241) *(G-2140)*

Ace Hardware, Orrville *Also Called: E&H Hardware Group LLC (G-12164)*

Ace Iron & Metal Company (PA) 614 443-5196
2515 Groveport Rd Columbus (43207) *(G-5305)*

Ace Mitchell Bowlers Mart, Cuyahoga Falls *Also Called: Micnan Inc (G-7088)*

Ace Taxi Service Inc 216 361-4700
1798 E 55th St Cleveland (44103) *(G-3762)*

Achievement Ctrs For Children (PA) 216 292-9700
4255 Northfield Rd Cleveland (44128) *(G-3763)*

Achievement Ctrs For Children 440 250-2520
24211 Center Ridge Rd Westlake (44145) *(G-15029)*

Aci Industries Ltd (PA) 740 368-4160
970 Pittsburgh Dr Frnt Delaware (43015) *(G-7776)*

Ackerman Chacco Company Inc 513 791-4252
10770 Kenwood Rd Blue Ash (45242) *(G-1121)*

Ackermann Enterprises Inc 513 842-3100
5801 Madison Rd Cincinnati (45227) *(G-2141)*

Ackermann Group 513 480-5204
5801 Madison Rd Cincinnati (45227) *(G-2142)*

Aclara Technologies LLC 440 528-7200
30400 Solon Rd Solon (44139) *(G-13061)*

Acloche LLC (PA) 888 608-0889
1800 Watermark Dr Ste 430 Columbus (43215) *(G-5306)*

Acloche Medical Staffing Svc, Columbus *Also Called: Acloche LLC (G-5306)*

Acme, Akron *Also Called: Fred W Albrecht Grocery Co (G-169)*

Acme, Coventry Township *Also Called: Fred W Albrecht Grocery Co (G-7008)*

Acme Dynamite 313 867-5309
3816 Hoiles Ave Toledo (43612) *(G-13674)*

ALPHABETIC SECTION — Adena Health System

Acnr River Towing Inc.. 740 338-3100
   46226 National Rd Saint Clairsville (43950) *(G-12772)*
Acor Orthopaedic LLC (PA).. 216 662-4500
   18530 S Miles Rd Cleveland (44128) *(G-3764)*
Acorn Distributors Inc... 614 294-6444
   5310 Crosswind Dr Columbus (43228) *(G-5307)*
Acpi Systems Inc... 513 738-3840
   3445 Hamilton New London Rd Hamilton (45013) *(G-9016)*
Acree-Daily Corporation... 614 452-7300
   771 Dearborn Park Ln Ste N Columbus (43085) *(G-5308)*
Acro Tool & Die Company... 330 773-5173
   325 Morgan Ave Akron (44311) *(G-14)*
Acrt Inc (PA).. 800 622-2562
   4500 Courthouse Blvd Ste 150 Stow (44224) *(G-13352)*
ACS Computer Services Corp.. 614 351-8298
   4238 Westview Center Plz Columbus (43228) *(G-5309)*
Act Acquisition Inc (HQ)... 216 292-3800
   22901 Millcreek Blvd Ste 650 Cleveland (44122) *(G-3765)*
Act For Health Inc.. 740 443-5000
   1862 Shyville Rd Piketon (45661) *(G-12414)*
Act I Temporaries Findlay Inc....................................... 419 423-0713
   2017 Tiffin Ave Findlay (45840) *(G-8506)*
Actalent Services LLC... 614 328-4900
   8100 Walton Pkwy New Albany (43054) *(G-11553)*
Action Bar LLC... 419 250-1938
   238 N Main St Bowling Green (43402) *(G-1302)*
Action Coupling & Eqp Inc... 330 279-4242
   8248 County Road 245 Holmesville (44633) *(G-9316)*
Action Door, Cleveland *Also Called: Dortronic Service Inc (G-4180)*
Action Door of Stow, Stow *Also Called: Dortrnic Service-Tallmadge Inc (G-13364)*
Action For Children Inc (PA).. 614 224-0222
   78 Jefferson Ave Columbus (43215) *(G-5310)*
Action Management Services....................................... 216 642-8777
   6055 Rockside Woods Blvd N Ste 160 Cleveland (44131) *(G-3766)*
Action Stainless, Cleveland *Also Called: Act Acquisition Inc (G-3765)*
Actionlink LLC.. 888 737-8757
   286 N Cleveland Massillon Rd # 200 Akron (44333) *(G-15)*
Active Day Inc... 513 984-8000
   2600 Civic Center Dr Cincinnati (45231) *(G-2143)*
Active Electric Incorporated.. 937 299-1885
   1885 Southtown Blvd Dayton (45439) *(G-7154)*
Active Plumbing Supply Co (PA)................................... 440 352-4411
   216 Richmond St Painesville (44077) *(G-12220)*
Activity Training, Cleveland *Also Called: County of Cuyahoga (G-4124)*
Acu-Serve Corp (PA).. 330 923-5258
   121 S Main St Ste 102 Akron (44308) *(G-16)*
Acuative Corporation.. 440 202-4500
   8237 Dow Cir Strongsville (44136) *(G-13439)*
Acuren Inspection, Dayton *Also Called: US Inspection Services Inc (G-7697)*
Acuren Inspection Inc... 513 671-7073
   4692 Brate Dr # 200 West Chester (45011) *(G-14646)*
Acute Care Consultants, Dayton *Also Called: South Dyton Acute Care Cons In (G-7628)*
Acute Care Specialty Hospital....................................... 330 363-4860
   2600 6th St Sw Canton (44710) *(G-1654)*
AD Farrow LLC... 740 965-9900
   7754 E State Route 37 Sunbury (43074) *(G-13514)*
Ad Investments LLC... 614 857-2340
   375 N Front St Ste 200 Columbus (43215) *(G-5311)*
Ada Visiting Nurses, Ada *Also Called: Community Hlth Prfssionals Inc (G-1)*
Adalet Enclosure Systems... 216 201-2710
   4801 W 150th St Cleveland (44135) *(G-3767)*
Adamhs Bd For Montgomery Cnty, Dayton *Also Called: Alcohol DRG Addction Mntal Svc (G-7161)*
Adamhscc Board... 216 241-3400
   2012 W 25th St Fl 6 Cleveland (44113) *(G-3768)*
Adams - Brown Counties... 937 544-2650
   95 Trefz Rd West Union (45693) *(G-14864)*
Adams - Brown Counties Economic Opportunities, Inc, West Union *Also Called: Adams - Brown Counties (G-14864)*
Adams & Brown Counties Economi................................ 937 695-0316
   19221 State Route 136 Winchester (45697) *(G-15284)*
Adams Brown Cnties Ecnmic Oppr................................ 937 378-3431
   9262 Mount Orab Pike Georgetown (45121) *(G-8797)*
Adams Brown Cnties Ecnmic Oppr................................ 937 695-0316
   19211 Main St Winchester (45697) *(G-15285)*
Adams Brown Wthrzation Program, Winchester *Also Called: Adams Brown Cnties Ecnmic Oppr (G-15285)*
Adams County Manor, West Union *Also Called: H & G Nursing Homes Inc (G-14870)*
Adams County Regional Med Ctr................................... 937 900-2316
   11110 State Rte 41 West Union (45693) *(G-14865)*
Adams Elevator Equipment Co (DH)............................... 847 581-2900
   1530 Timber Wolf Dr Holland (43528) *(G-9276)*
Adams Hlping Hands HM Care LLC................................ 419 298-0034
   143 N Michigan Ave Edgerton (43517) *(G-8226)*
Adams Lane Care Center, Zanesville *Also Called: Zandex Health Care Corporation (G-15839)*
Adams Robinson Construction, Dayton *Also Called: Adams-Robinson Enterprises Inc (G-7155)*
Adams Signs, Massillon *Also Called: Identitek Systems Inc (G-10648)*
Adams-Robinson Enterprises Inc (PA)........................... 937 274-5318
   2735 Needmore Rd Dayton (45414) *(G-7155)*
Adapt-A-Pak Inc.. 937 845-0386
   678 Yellow Springs Fairfield Rd Ste 100 Fairborn (45324) *(G-8365)*
Adaptive Development Corp... 937 890-3388
   6060 Milo Rd Dayton (45414) *(G-7156)*
Adcom Group Inc.. 216 574-9100
   1468 W 9th St Ste 600 Cleveland (44113) *(G-3769)*
Addiction Services Council... 513 281-7880
   2828 Vernon Pl Cincinnati (45219) *(G-2144)*
Addison Healthcare Center, Masury *Also Called: Addison Leasing Co LLC (G-10677)*
Addison Leasing Co LLC.. 513 530-1600
   8055 Addison Rd Masury (44438) *(G-10677)*
Addisonmckee, Lebanon *Also Called: Addition Manufacturing Technologies LLC (G-9752)*
Addition Manufacturing Technologies LLC..................... 513 228-7000
   1637 Kingsview Dr Lebanon (45036) *(G-9752)*
ADDUS, Mason *Also Called: Queen City Hospice LLC (G-10598)*
Addus Healthcare, Columbus *Also Called: Addus Healthcare Inc (G-5312)*
Addus Healthcare Inc.. 614 407-0677
   1395 E Dublin Granville Rd Columbus (43229) *(G-5312)*
Addus Healthcare Inc.. 630 296-3400
   1406 Cadiz Rd Steubenville (43953) *(G-13315)*
Addus Home Care, Wintersville *Also Called: Addus Homecare Corporation (G-15291)*
Addus Homecare Corporation....................................... 440 219-0245
   3721 N Ridge Rd Perry (44081) *(G-12303)*
Addus Homecare Corporation....................................... 866 684-0385
   1406 Cadiz Rd Wintersville (43953) *(G-15291)*
Adel Youssef MD.. 330 399-7215
   1622 E Market St Warren (44483) *(G-14494)*
Adelman's Truck Sales, Canton *Also Called: Adelmans Truck Parts Corp (G-1655)*
Adelmans Truck Parts Corp (PA)................................... 330 456-0206
   2000 Waynesburg Dr Se Canton (44707) *(G-1655)*
Adelphia, Cleveland *Also Called: Comcast Spotlight LP (G-4091)*
Adena Commercial LLC... 614 436-9800
   8800 Lyra Dr Ste 650 Columbus (43240) *(G-5244)*
Adena Corp Mansfield Ohio, Ontario *Also Called: Adena Corporation (G-12096)*
Adena Corporation... 419 529-4456
   1310 W 4th St Ontario (44906) *(G-12096)*
Adena Fmly Medicine-Greenfield, Greenfield *Also Called: Adena Health System (G-8863)*
Adena Health System... 740 779-8700
   4437 State Route 159 Ste 240 Chillicothe (45601) *(G-2044)*
Adena Health System... 740 779-4300
   4439 State Route 159 Ste 204 Chillicothe (45601) *(G-2045)*
Adena Health System... 740 779-7201
   4439 State Route 159 Ste 120 Chillicothe (45601) *(G-2046)*
Adena Health System (PA).. 740 779-7500
   272 Hospital Rd Chillicothe (45601) *(G-2047)*
Adena Health System... 740 779-4801
   445 Shawnee Ln Chillicothe (45601) *(G-2048)*
Adena Health System... 740 420-3000
   798 N Court St Circleville (43113) *(G-3702)*
Adena Health System... 937 981-9444
   1075 N Washington St Greenfield (45123) *(G-8863)*

Adena Health System — ALPHABETIC SECTION

Adena Health System 937 383-1040
  160 Roberts Ln Ste A Hillsboro (45133) *(G-9248)*
Adena Health System 740 947-2186
  100 Dawn Ln Waverly (45690) *(G-14610)*
Adena Health System 740 779-7500
  308 Highland Ave Unit C Wshngtn Ct Hs (43160) *(G-15476)*
Adena Pike Medical Center, Waverly Also Called: Adena Health System *(G-14610)*
Adena Plmnlogy Crtcal Care Sle, Chillicothe Also Called: Adena Health System *(G-2044)*
Adena Regional Medical Center 740 779-4050
  Western Ave. Chillicothe (45601) *(G-2049)*
ADENA REGIONAL MEDICAL CENTER, Chillicothe Also Called: Adena Health System *(G-2047)*
ADENA REGIONAL MEDICAL CENTER, Greenfield Also Called: Greenfield Area Medical Ctr *(G-8864)*
Adena Rhblitation Wellness Ctr, Chillicothe Also Called: Adena Health System *(G-2048)*
Adept, Columbus Also Called: Adept Marketing Outsourced LLC *(G-5313)*
Adept Marketing Outsourced LLC 614 360-3132
  855 Grandview Ave Ste 140 Columbus (43215) *(G-5313)*
Adesa Cleveland, Northfield Also Called: Adesa Ohio LLC *(G-11951)*
Adesa Ohio LLC 330 467-8280
  210 E Twinsburg Rd Northfield (44067) *(G-11951)*
ADI, Sheffield Village Also Called: Advanced Design Industries Inc *(G-12997)*
Adkins Timber Products Inc 740 984-2768
  22180 State Rte 60 Beverly (45715) *(G-1099)*
Adleta Construction, Cincinnati Also Called: Adleta Inc *(G-2145)*
Adleta Inc 513 554-1469
  389 S Wayne Ave Cincinnati (45215) *(G-2145)*
ADM Facilities, Lancaster Also Called: Singleton Construction LLC *(G-9741)*
Administration Services Dept, Cincinnati Also Called: University of Cincinnati *(G-3590)*
Admirals Pnte Nrsing Rhblttion, Huron Also Called: Huron Health Care Center Inc *(G-9391)*
Ado Professional Solutions Inc 614 681-5050
  445 Hutchinson Ave Ste 330 Columbus (43235) *(G-5314)*
Ado Professional Solutions Inc 216 328-0888
  6150 Oak Tree Blvd Ste 490 Independence (44131) *(G-9396)*
Ado Staffing Inc 330 922-2077
  3773 State Rd Cuyahoga Falls (44223) *(G-7032)*
ADP, Findlay Also Called: ADP Rpo *(G-8507)*
ADP Rpo 419 420-1830
  3401 Technology Dr Findlay (45840) *(G-8507)*
ADRIEL, West Liberty Also Called: Adriel School Inc *(G-14859)*
Adriel School Inc (PA) 937 465-0010
  414 N Detroit St West Liberty (43357) *(G-14859)*
Adroit Assoc Cnslting Svcs LLC 614 966-6925
  4809 Moreland Dr W Columbus (43220) *(G-5315)*
ADS, Columbus Also Called: Pomeroy It Solutions Sls Inc *(G-6536)*
ADS Alliance Data Systems Inc 513 707-6800
  3095 Loyalty Cir Columbus (43219) *(G-5316)*
ADS ALLIANCE DATA SYSTEMS, INC., Columbus Also Called: ADS Alliance Data Systems Inc *(G-5316)*
ADS Manufacturing Ohio LLC 513 217-4502
  1701 Reinartz Blvd Middletown (45042) *(G-11150)*
ADT LLC 614 793-0861
  4245 Diplomacy Dr Columbus (43228) *(G-5317)*
Adult Comfort Care Inc 440 320-3335
  5710 Lake St Vermilion (44089) *(G-14404)*
Adult Parole Authority, Tiffin Also Called: Ohio Dept Rhbilitation Corectn *(G-13636)*
Adult Probation, Xenia Also Called: Greene County *(G-15511)*
Adult Probation Department, Elyria Also Called: County of Lorain *(G-8241)*
Advance Home Care LLC (PA) 614 436-3611
  1191 S James Rd Columbus (43227) *(G-5318)*
Advance Home Care LLC 937 723-6335
  1250 W Dorothy Ln Dayton (45409) *(G-7157)*
Advance Implant Dentistry Inc 513 271-0821
  5823 Wooster Pike Cincinnati (45227) *(G-2146)*
Advance Ohio Media LLC 216 999-3900
  4800 Tiedeman Rd Cleveland (44144) *(G-3770)*
Advance Partners, Cleveland Also Called: Paychex Advance LLC *(G-4731)*
Advance Payroll Funding Ltd., Cleveland Also Called: Cavcapital Ltd *(G-3940)*
Advance Trnsp Systems Inc 513 818-4311
  2 Crowne Point Ct Ste 300 Cincinnati (45241) *(G-2147)*

Advanced Auto Glass Inc (PA) 412 373-6675
  44 N Union St Akron (44304) *(G-17)*
Advanced Bar Technology, Canton Also Called: Gerdau McSteel Atmsphere Annli *(G-1761)*
Advanced Cmpt Connections LLC 419 668-4080
  166 Milan Ave Norwalk (44857) *(G-11999)*
Advanced Cnstr Group Inc 419 891-1505
  205 W Sophia St Maumee (43537) *(G-10685)*
Advanced Csmtc Srgery Lser Ctr 513 351-3223
  3805 Edwards Rd Ste 100 Cincinnati (45209) *(G-2148)*
Advanced Design Industries Inc 440 277-4141
  4686 French Creek Rd Sheffield Village (44054) *(G-12997)*
Advanced Drmtlogy Skin Cncer C 330 965-8760
  987 Boardman Canfield Rd Youngstown (44512) *(G-15541)*
Advanced Elec Specialists Inc 330 237-9930
  1258 Industrial Pkwy N # 2 Brunswick (44212) *(G-1449)*
Advanced Engrg Solutions Inc 937 743-6900
  250 Advanced Dr Springboro (45066) *(G-13191)*
Advanced Eye Care Center Inc 419 521-3937
  1991 Park Ave W Ontario (44906) *(G-12097)*
Advanced Eye Care Csmtc Lser C, Ontario Also Called: Advanced Eye Care Center Inc *(G-12097)*
Advanced Fastener, West Chester Also Called: Afc Industries Inc *(G-14649)*
Advanced Financial Services 800 320-0000
  1234 S Cleveland Massillon Rd Copley (44321) *(G-6946)*
Advanced Health Care Center, Toledo Also Called: Communi Care Inc *(G-13751)*
Advanced Healthcare, Toledo Also Called: Parkway Operating Co LLC *(G-13958)*
Advanced Industrial Products, Columbus Also Called: Otp Holding LLC *(G-6490)*
Advanced Industrial Roofg Inc 330 837-1999
  1330 Erie St S Massillon (44646) *(G-10629)*
Advanced Mechanical Svcs Inc 937 879-7426
  575 Sports St Fairborn (45324) *(G-8366)*
Advanced Medical Equipment Inc (PA) 937 534-1080
  426 Alexandersville Rd Miamisburg (45342) *(G-11020)*
Advanced Neurologic Assoc Inc 419 483-2403
  5433 State Route 113 Bellevue (44811) *(G-1040)*
Advanced Plumbing, Plain City Also Called: A-1 Advanced Plumbing Inc *(G-12463)*
Advanced Poly-Packaging Inc (PA) 330 785-4000
  1331 Emmitt Rd Akron (44306) *(G-18)*
Advanced Prgrm Resources Inc (PA) 614 761-9994
  2715 Tuller Pkwy Dublin (43017) *(G-7920)*
Advanced Rhbilitation Tech Ltd 419 636-2684
  525 Winzeler Dr # 1 Bryan (43506) *(G-1477)*
Advanced Roofing Services, Maumee Also Called: Advanced Cnstr Group Inc *(G-10685)*
Advanced Solutions For Educatn 224 518-3111
  8303 Tyler Blvd Mentor (44060) *(G-10908)*
Advanced Surgical Associates 937 578-2650
  388 Damascus Rd Marysville (43040) *(G-10473)*
Advanced Testing Lab Inc 513 489-8447
  6954 Cornell Rd Ste 200 Blue Ash (45242) *(G-1122)*
Advanced Testing Laboratories, Blue Ash Also Called: Advanced Testing Lab Inc *(G-1122)*
Advanced Testing MGT Group Inc 513 489-8447
  6954 Cornell Rd Ste 200 Blue Ash (45242) *(G-1123)*
Advanced Urology Inc (PA) 330 758-9787
  904 Sahara Trl Ste 1 Youngstown (44514) *(G-15542)*
Advanced Welding Division, Tipp City Also Called: Daihen Inc *(G-13656)*
Advancement LLC 440 248-8550
  32200 Solon Rd Solon (44139) *(G-13062)*
Advantage Appliance Services 330 498-8101
  7235 Whipple Ave Nw Canton (44720) *(G-1656)*
Advantage Credit Union Inc (PA) 419 529-5603
  700 Stumbo Rd Ontario (44906) *(G-12098)*
Advantage Ford Lincoln Mercury 419 334-9751
  885 Hagerty Dr Fremont (43420) *(G-8664)*
Advantage Home Health Svcs Inc 330 491-8161
  7951 Pittsburg Ave Nw North Canton (44720) *(G-11807)*
Advantage Local, West Chester Also Called: Advantage Rn LLC *(G-14647)*
Advantage Resourcing Amer Inc (HQ) 781 472-8900
  201 E 4th St Ste 800 Cincinnati (45202) *(G-2149)*
Advantage Rn LLC (PA) 866 301-4045
  9021 Meridian Way West Chester (45069) *(G-14647)*

Advantage Skilled Care LLC..740 353-9200
1656 Coles Blvd Portsmouth (45662) *(G-12543)*

Advantage Staffing, Cincinnati Also Called: Advantage Resourcing Amer Inc *(G-2149)*

Advantage Tank Lines Inc (HQ)..330 491-0474
4366 Mount Pleasant St Nw North Canton (44720) *(G-11808)*

Advantage Tchncal Rsurcing Inc.......................................513 651-1111
201 E 4th St Ste 800 Cincinnati (45202) *(G-2150)*

Advantage Technical Svcs Inc...513 852-4891
191 Rosa Parks St Cincinnati (45202) *(G-2151)*

Advantech Corporation..513 742-8895
4445 Lake Forest Dr Ste 200 Blue Ash (45242) *(G-1124)*

Advantech Indus Automtn Group, Blue Ash Also Called: Advantech Corporation *(G-1124)*

Advent Media Group LLC..513 421-2267
537 E Pete Rose Way Cincinnati (45202) *(G-2152)*

Advizex Technologies, Independence Also Called: Advizex Technologies LLC *(G-9397)*

Advizex Technologies LLC..513 229-8400
10260 Alliance Rd Ste 205 Blue Ash (45242) *(G-1125)*

Advizex Technologies LLC..614 318-0386
1103 Schrock Rd Ste 100 Columbus (43229) *(G-5319)*

Advizex Technologies LLC (PA).......................................216 901-1818
6480 Rockside Woods Blvd S Ste 190 Independence (44131) *(G-9397)*

Advocate Rcm LLC..614 210-1885
5475 Rings Rd Ste 300 Dublin (43017) *(G-7921)*

Advocate Solutions LLC...614 444-5144
762 S Pearl St Columbus (43206) *(G-5320)*

Advoctes For Bsic Lgal Eqlity (PA)..................................419 255-0814
525 Jefferson Ave Toledo (43604) *(G-13675)*

Aecom..513 651-3440
525 Vine St Ste 1800 Cincinnati (45202) *(G-2153)*

Aecom Energy & Cnstr Inc..216 622-2300
1300 E 9th St Ste 500 Cleveland (44114) *(G-3771)*

Aegco, Columbus Also Called: AEP Generating Company *(G-5322)*

Aegis Protective Services, Cincinnati Also Called: Danson Inc *(G-2538)*

AEP, Columbus Also Called: Ohio Power Company *(G-6439)*

AEP Energy Partners Inc...614 716-1000
1 Riverside Plz Fl 1 Columbus (43215) *(G-5321)*

AEP Generating Company (HQ).......................................614 223-1000
1 Riverside Plz Ste 1600 Columbus (43215) *(G-5322)*

AEP Investments Holding Co Inc.....................................614 583-2900
155 W Nationwide Blvd Columbus (43215) *(G-5323)*

AEP Power Marketing Inc (HQ)..614 716-1000
1 Riverside Plz Fl 1 Columbus (43215) *(G-5324)*

AEP Service, Columbus Also Called: American Electric Pwr Svc Corp *(G-5349)*

AEP Texas, Columbus Also Called: AEP Texas Inc *(G-5326)*

AEP Texas Central Company..614 716-1000
1 Riverside Plz Columbus (43215) *(G-5325)*

AEP Texas Inc (HQ)...614 716-1000
1 Riverside Plz Columbus (43215) *(G-5326)*

AEP Texas North Company...614 716-1000
1 Riverside Plz Columbus (43215) *(G-5327)*

Aerco Sandblasting Company..419 224-2464
429 N Jackson St Lima (45801) *(G-9860)*

Aero Communications Inc..734 467-8121
25101 Chagrin Blvd # 350 Beachwood (44122) *(G-763)*

Aero Fulfillment, West Chester Also Called: Aero Fulfillment Services Corp *(G-14648)*

Aero Fulfillment Services Corp (PA)...............................800 225-7145
3900 Aero Dr Mason (45040) *(G-10517)*

Aero Fulfillment Services Corp..513 874-4112
6023 Union Centre Blvd Steb West Chester (45069) *(G-14648)*

Aero Industries Inc..330 626-3246
4240 Sunnybrook Rd Kent (44240) *(G-9555)*

Aero Propulsion Support Inc..513 367-9452
108 May Dr Ste A Harrison (45030) *(G-9096)*

Aero Propulsion Support Group, Harrison Also Called: Aero Propulsion Support Inc *(G-9096)*

Aerobarrier, Dayton Also Called: Aeroseal LLC *(G-7158)*

Aerocon Photogrammetric Svcs (PA).............................440 946-6277
7294 Hunting Lake Dr Concord Township (44077) *(G-6922)*

Aerocontrolex, South Euclid Also Called: Aerocontrolex Group Inc *(G-13170)*

Aerocontrolex Group Inc..216 291-6025
4223 Monticello Blvd South Euclid (44121) *(G-13170)*

Aerodynmics Inc Ardynamics Inc....................................404 596-8751
25700 Science Park Dr Ste 210 Beachwood (44122) *(G-764)*

Aeroseal LLC...937 428-9300
1851 S Metro Pkwy Dayton (45459) *(G-7158)*

Aeroseal LLC (PA)...937 428-9300
225 Byers Rd # 1 Miamisburg (45342) *(G-11021)*

Aerospace Corporation..937 657-9634
4180 Watson Way Dayton (45433) *(G-7125)*

AES, Brunswick Also Called: Advanced Elec Specialists Inc *(G-1449)*

AES, Dayton Also Called: DPL Inc *(G-7130)*

AES Ohio, Dayton Also Called: Dayton Power and Light Company *(G-7129)*

Aesi, Springboro Also Called: Advanced Engrg Solutions Inc *(G-13191)*

Aetna Building Maintenance Inc......................................937 324-5711
525 N Yellow Springs St Springfield (45504) *(G-13214)*

Aetna Integrated Services, Columbus Also Called: Atalian US Ohio Valley Inc *(G-5400)*

Aetna Integrated Services, Springfield Also Called: Aetna Building Maintenance Inc *(G-13214)*

Aey Electric Inc..330 792-5745
801 N Meridian Rd Youngstown (44509) *(G-15543)*

AFA Beauty Inc...740 331-1655
385 Richland Ave Athens (45701) *(G-554)*

Afc Cable Systems Inc..740 435-3340
829 Georgetown Rd Cambridge (43725) *(G-1552)*

Afc Holding Company Inc (HQ)..513 579-2121
1 E 4th St Cincinnati (45202) *(G-2154)*

Afc Industries Inc (HQ)...513 874-7456
9030 Port Union Rialto Rd West Chester (45069) *(G-14649)*

Affilate Ntons Roof LLC Lthia, Springboro Also Called: Nations Roof of Ohio LLC *(G-13204)*

Affiliated Resource Group Inc..614 889-6555
5700 Perimeter Dr Ste H Dublin (43017) *(G-7922)*

Affinion Group LLC..614 895-1803
300 W Schrock Rd Westerville (43081) *(G-14956)*

Affordable Dem & Hlg Inc...216 429-1874
4980 Mead Ave Cleveland (44127) *(G-3772)*

Afg Industries Inc..614 322-4580
4000 Gantz Rd Ste A Grove City (43123) *(G-8893)*

Afidence Inc..513 234-5822
5412 Courseview Dr Ste 122 Mason (45040) *(G-10518)*

AFLAC..216 641-8760
4712 E 90th St Cleveland (44125) *(G-3773)*

AFP 116 Corp..614 536-0500
2886 Airport Dr Columbus (43219) *(G-5328)*

African Safari Wildlife Park, Port Clinton Also Called: Animal Mgt Svcs Ohio Inc *(G-12517)*

Afrl/Rx, Wright Patterson Afb Also Called: Air Force Research Laboratory *(G-15474)*

After Hours Family Care Inc...937 667-2614
450 N Hyatt St Ste 204 Tipp City (45371) *(G-13651)*

After Market Products, Avon Also Called: North Coast Bearings LLC *(G-662)*

Aftermarket Parts Company LLC (HQ)............................740 369-1056
3229 Sawmill Pkwy Delaware (43015) *(G-7777)*

AFTERSCHOOL PROGRAMS OF LANCAS, Lancaster Also Called: West After School Center *(G-9749)*

AG Container Transport LLC...740 862-8866
433 London Groveport Rd Lockbourne (43137) *(G-10009)*

AG Interactive Inc (DH)...216 889-5000
1 American Rd Cleveland (44144) *(G-3774)*

AG Trucking Inc...937 497-7770
798 S Vandemark Rd Sidney (45365) *(G-13017)*

Ag-Pro Ohio LLC..740 653-6951
1200 Delmont Rd Sw Lancaster (43130) *(G-9691)*

Ag-Pro Ohio LLC..740 389-5458
219 Columbus Sandusky Rd N Marion (43302) *(G-10416)*

Ag-Pro Ohio LLC..937 486-5211
7550 N Us Highway 68 Wilmington (45177) *(G-15238)*

Ag-Pro Ohio LLC..740 450-7446
4394 Northpointe Dr Zanesville (43701) *(G-15765)*

Agape For Youth Inc..937 439-4406
2300 S Edwin C Moses Blvd Ste 140 Dayton (45417) *(G-7159)*

Agar LLC...513 549-4576
1205 Walnut St Cincinnati (45202) *(G-2155)*

AGC Automotive Americas, Grove City Also Called: Afg Industries Inc *(G-8893)*

Aggressive Mechanical Inc...614 443-3280
638 Greenlawn Ave Columbus (43223) *(G-5329)*

ALPHABETIC SECTION

Aghapy Plus Inc..216 820-3996
    25451 Euclid Ave Euclid (44117) *(G-8336)*
Agile Global Solutions Inc..................................916 655-7745
    5755 Granger Rd Ste 610 Independence (44131) *(G-9398)*
Agile Pursuits Inc...513 945-9908
    One Procter & Gamble Plaza Cincinnati (45202) *(G-2156)*
Agilit, Dayton *Also Called: Riverside Computing Inc (G-7594)*
Agiliti Inc...614 409-2734
    4391 Professional Pkwy Groveport (43125) *(G-8967)*
Agility Partners LLC...740 819-2712
    175 S 3rd St Ste 360 Columbus (43215) *(G-5330)*
Agmet LLC (PA)..440 439-7400
    7800 Medusa Rd Cleveland (44146) *(G-3775)*
Agrana Fruit Us Inc..937 693-3821
    16197 County Road 25a Anna (45302) *(G-442)*
Agratronix LLC..330 562-2222
    1790 Miller Pkwy Streetsboro (44241) *(G-13409)*
Agri Business Finance Inc..................................937 663-0186
    11921 Wick Ct Saint Paris (43072) *(G-12837)*
Agri-Sludge Inc..330 567-2500
    8047 State Route 754 Shreve (44676) *(G-13015)*
Agrinomix LLC...440 774-2981
    300 Creekside Dr Oberlin (44074) *(G-12062)*
AGS Custom Graphics Inc..................................330 963-7770
    8107 Bavaria Dr E Macedonia (44056) *(G-10188)*
Ahf Ohio Inc...937 256-4663
    264 Wilmington Ave Dayton (45420) *(G-7160)*
Ahf Ohio Inc...614 760-8870
    4880 Tuttle Rd Dublin (43017) *(G-7923)*
Ahf Ohio Inc...740 532-6188
    2932 S 5th St Ironton (45638) *(G-9501)*
Ahf Ohio Inc...330 725-4123
    806 E Washington St Medina (44256) *(G-10805)*
Ahf/Central States Inc......................................724 941-7150
    5920 Venture Dr Ste 100 Dublin (43017) *(G-7924)*
AHG, Cincinnati *Also Called: American Heritage Girls Inc (G-2181)*
Ahip OH Columbus Entps LLC..............................614 790-9000
    5100 Upper Metro Pl Dublin (43017) *(G-7925)*
Ahola Corporation...440 717-7620
    6820 W Snowville Rd Brecksville (44141) *(G-1342)*
Ahsland Cleaning, Ashland *Also Called: Ashland Cleaning LLC (G-474)*
Ai-Media Inc..213 337-8552
    241 W Federal St Youngstown (44503) *(G-15544)*
Ai-Media Technologies LLC.................................800 335-0911
    241 W Federal St Ste 201-B Youngstown (44503) *(G-15545)*
Aide For You LLC...419 214-0111
    3131 Executive Pkwy Ste 220 Toledo (43606) *(G-13676)*
Aids Tskfrce Grter Clvland Inc...............................216 357-3131
    2829 Euclid Ave Cleveland (44115) *(G-3776)*
Aileron..937 669-6500
    8860 Wildcat Rd Tipp City (45371) *(G-13652)*
Aim Integrated Logistics Inc................................330 759-0438
    1500 Trumbull Ave Girard (44420) *(G-8808)*
Aim Leasing Company.......................................216 883-6200
    8150 Old Granger Rd Cleveland (44125) *(G-3777)*
Aim Leasing Company (PA).................................330 759-0438
    1500 Trumbull Ave Girard (44420) *(G-8809)*
Aim Mro LLC..513 831-2938
    8500 Glendale Milford Rd Camp Dennison (45111) *(G-1590)*
Aim Mro Holdings LLC (PA)................................513 831-2938
    375 Center St 175 Miamiville (45147) *(G-11108)*
Aimhi Inc..614 939-0112
    10299 Johnstown Rd New Albany (43054) *(G-11554)*
Aims Supported Living LLC..................................614 805-1507
    948 Cross Country Dr W Westerville (43081) *(G-14957)*
Air Cargo Department, Grove City *Also Called: Nippon Express USA Inc (G-8941)*
Air Evac Ems Inc..417 274-6754
    2929 Lancaster Thornville Rd Ne Lancaster (43130) *(G-9692)*
Air Evac Lifeteam, Lancaster *Also Called: Air Evac Ems Inc (G-9692)*
Air Force One Inc (PA)......................................614 889-0121
    5810 Shier Rings Rd Ste B Dublin (43016) *(G-7926)*

Air Force Research Laboratory..............................937 255-9209
    2977 Hobson Way Bldg 653 Wright Patterson Afb (45433) *(G-15474)*
Air Frce Museum Foundation Inc...........................937 258-1218
    1100 Spaatz St Bldg 489 Dayton (45433) *(G-7126)*
Air General Inc..216 501-5643
    6090 Cargo Rd Cleveland (44135) *(G-3778)*
AIR Management Group LLC...............................330 856-1900
    1 American Way Ne # 20 Warren (44484) *(G-14495)*
Air Tahoma Inc (PA)..614 774-0728
    2615 Carriage Rd Powell (43065) *(G-12583)*
Air Technical Industries Inc................................440 951-5191
    7501 Clover Ave Mentor (44060) *(G-10909)*
Air Transport Intl Inc..937 382-5591
    145 Hunter Dr Ste 2 Wilmington (45177) *(G-15239)*
Air Transport Intl Ltd Lblty.................................501 615-3500
    1750 Eber Rd Ste A Holland (43528) *(G-9277)*
Air Transport Svcs Group Inc (PA)..........................937 382-5591
    145 Hunter Dr Ste 2 Wilmington (45177) *(G-15240)*
Air Venturi, Solon *Also Called: Air Venturi Ltd (G-13063)*
Air Venturi Ltd...216 292-2570
    5135 Naiman Pkwy Solon (44139) *(G-13063)*
Air-Temp Climate Control Inc..............................216 579-1552
    3013 Payne Ave Cleveland (44114) *(G-3779)*
Air-Temp Mechanical, Cleveland *Also Called: Air-Temp Climate Control Inc (G-3779)*
Air-Way Manufacturing Company...........................419 298-2366
    303 W River St Edgerton (43517) *(G-8227)*
Airborne, Wilmington *Also Called: Airborne Maint Engrg Svcs Inc (G-15242)*
Airborne Acquisition Inc (HQ)..............................216 438-6111
    30500 Aurora Rd Ste 100 Solon (44139) *(G-13064)*
Airborne Global Solutions Inc...............................937 382-5591
    145 Hunter Dr Wilmington (45177) *(G-15241)*
Airborne Maint Engrg Svcs Inc..............................937 366-2559
    1111 Airport Rd Wilmington (45177) *(G-15242)*
Airborne Maint Engrg Svcs Inc (HQ)........................937 382-5591
    145 Hunter Dr Wilmington (45177) *(G-15243)*
Airgas, Moraine *Also Called: Airgas Inc (G-11388)*
Airgas Inc..937 222-8312
    2400 Sandridge Dr Moraine (45439) *(G-11388)*
Airgas Merchant Gases LLC (DH)..........................800 242-0105
    6055 Rockside Woods Blvd N Ste 500 Cleveland (44131) *(G-3780)*
Airgas Usa LLC..216 642-6600
    6055 Rockside Woods Blvd N Ste 500 Independence (44131) *(G-9399)*
Airmate Co Inc..419 636-3184
    16280 County Road D Bryan (43506) *(G-1478)*
Airnet, Columbus *Also Called: Airnet Systems Inc (G-5331)*
Airnet Systems Inc (DH)....................................614 409-4900
    7250 Star Check Dr Columbus (43217) *(G-5331)*
Airplaco Equipment Company, Cincinnati *Also Called: Mesa Industries Inc (G-3048)*
Airport Fast Park, Cincinnati *Also Called: Park Place Operations Inc (G-3186)*
Airport Pass Park, Cleveland *Also Called: Park Place Operations Inc (G-4722)*
Airriva LLC..614 345-3996
    970 Joe Walker Rd Sunbury (43074) *(G-13515)*
Airtech LLC..614 342-6123
    1900 Jetway Blvd Columbus (43219) *(G-5332)*
Airtron Inc...614 274-2345
    3021 International St Columbus (43228) *(G-5333)*
Airtron Inc...859 371-7780
    2485 Belvo Rd Miamisburg (45342) *(G-11022)*
Ajax Commercial Cleaning Inc..............................330 928-4543
    3566 State Rd 5 Cuyahoga Falls (44223) *(G-7033)*
Ajax Tocco Magnethermic Corp (HQ)......................800 547-1527
    1745 Overland Ave Ne Warren (44483) *(G-14496)*
AK Group Hotels Inc..937 372-9921
    300 Xenia Towne Sq Xenia (45385) *(G-15498)*
Aka Team Inc..216 751-2000
    1306 E 55th St Cleveland (44103) *(G-3781)*
AKD Cleaning Service of Texas.............................937 521-3900
    100 W Main St Springfield (45502) *(G-13215)*
Akkodis Inc..513 769-9797
    4665 Cornell Rd Ste 155 Blue Ash (45241) *(G-1126)*
Akkodis Inc..614 781-6070
    495 Metro Pl S Ste 200 Dublin (43017) *(G-7927)*

Akkodis Inc 216 447-1909
6150 Oak Tree Blvd Ste 490 Independence (44131) *(G-9400)*

Akro-Plastics, Kent *Also Called: U S Development Corp (G-9604)*

Akrochem Corporation (PA) 330 535-2100
3770 Embassy Pkwy Akron (44333) *(G-19)*

Akron Art Museum 330 376-9185
1 S High St Akron (44308) *(G-20)*

Akron Automobile Club, Akron *Also Called: Ohio Automobile Club (G-247)*

Akron Blind Center & Workshop (PA) 330 253-2555
325 E Market St Akron (44304) *(G-21)*

Akron Board of Education 330 761-1660
10 N Main St Akron (44308) *(G-22)*

Akron Brass Holding Corp (HQ) 330 264-5678
343 Venture Blvd Wooster (44691) *(G-15307)*

Akron Canton Airport, North Canton *Also Called: Akron-Canton Regional Airport (G-11809)*

Akron Children S Hospital 330 310-0157
105 Franklin Dr Doylestown (44230) *(G-7912)*

AKRON CHILDREN'S HOSPITAL, Akron *Also Called: Childrens Hosp Med Ctr Akron (G-98)*

Akron Childrens Hospital, Akron *Also Called: Childrens Hosp Med Ctr Akron (G-92)*

AKRON CITIZEN'S COALITION FOR, Akron *Also Called: Access Inc (G-13)*

Akron City Hospital, Akron *Also Called: Summa Health (G-314)*

Akron City Hospital Inc 330 253-5046
525 E Market St Akron (44304) *(G-23)*

Akron Cmnty Svc Ctr Urban Leag 234 542-4141
440 Vernon Odom Blvd Akron (44307) *(G-24)*

AKRON COMMUNITY SERV CENTER, Akron *Also Called: Akron Cmnty Svc Ctr Urban Leag (G-24)*

Akron Electric Inc 330 745-8891
1025 Eaton Ave Akron (44303) *(G-25)*

Akron Energy Systems LLC 330 374-0600
222 Opportunity Pkwy Akron (44307) *(G-26)*

Akron Family Institute Inc 330 644-3469
3469 Fortuna Dr Akron (44312) *(G-27)*

Akron First Academy Preschool, Akron *Also Called: First Assembly of God (G-160)*

Akron Foundry Co (PA) 330 745-3101
2728 Wingate Ave Akron (44314) *(G-28)*

Akron Gen Spt & Physcl Therapy, Akron *Also Called: Akron General Health System (G-30)*

Akron General Foundation 330 344-6888
400 Wabash Ave Akron (44307) *(G-29)*

Akron General Health System 330 665-8200
4125 Medina Rd Ofc Akron (44333) *(G-30)*

Akron General Health System (HQ) 330 344-6000
1 Akron General Ave Akron (44307) *(G-31)*

Akron General Health System 330 344-3030
1310 Corporate Dr Hudson (44236) *(G-9327)*

Akron General Health System 330 945-9300
4300 Allen Rd Stow (44224) *(G-13353)*

Akron General Health System 330 896-5070
1940 Town Park Blvd Uniontown (44685) *(G-14240)*

Akron General Lodi Hospital, Lodi *Also Called: Cleveland Clinic Foundation (G-10018)*

Akron General Medical Center (DH) 330 344-6000
1 Akron General Ave Akron (44307) *(G-32)*

Akron Hardware Consultants Inc (PA) 330 644-7167
1100 Killian Rd Akron (44312) *(G-33)*

Akron Homecare Adult, Akron *Also Called: Maxim Healthcare Services Inc (G-227)*

Akron Inn Limited Partnership 330 336-7692
5 Park Centre Dr Wadsworth (44281) *(G-14426)*

Akron Management Corp 330 644-8441
452 E Warner Rd Akron (44319) *(G-34)*

Akron Metropolitan Hsing Auth 330 920-1652
500 Hardman Dr Stow (44224) *(G-13354)*

Akron Radiology Inc 330 375-3043
525 E Market St Akron (44304) *(G-35)*

Akron Rubber Dev Lab Inc (PA) 330 794-6600
2887 Gilchrist Rd Akron (44305) *(G-36)*

Akron Rubber Dev Lab Inc 330 794-6600
75 Robinson Ave Barberton (44203) *(G-692)*

Akron Rubberducks 330 253-5151
300 S Main St Akron (44308) *(G-37)*

Akron Summit Cmnty Action Agcy (PA) 330 376-7730
55 E Mill St Akron (44308) *(G-38)*

Akron Welding & Spring Co, Akron *Also Called: Brakefire Incorporated (G-73)*

AKRON ZOO, Akron *Also Called: Akron Zoological Park (G-39)*

Akron Zoological Park 330 375-2550
500 Edgewood Ave Akron (44307) *(G-39)*

Akron-Canton Regional Airport 330 499-4059
5400 Lauby Rd Ste 9 North Canton (44720) *(G-11809)*

Akron-Canton Regional Foodbank (PA) 330 535-6900
350 Opportunity Pkwy Akron (44307) *(G-40)*

Akron-Rban Mnrity Alchlism DRG 330 379-3467
665 W Market St Ste 2d Akron (44303) *(G-41)*

Akron-Smmit Cnvntion Vstors Bu 330 374-7560
77 E Mill St Akron (44308) *(G-42)*

Aksm, Columbus *Also Called: American Kidney Stone MGT Ltd (G-5352)*

Aksm/Southwest Lithotripsy, Columbus *Also Called: Southwest Lithotripsy (G-6698)*

Aktion Associates Incorporated (PA) 419 893-7001
1687 Woodlands Dr Maumee (43537) *(G-10686)*

Al Neyer LLC (PA) 513 271-6400
302 W 3rd St Cincinnati (45202) *(G-2157)*

Al Peake & Sons Inc 419 243-9284
4949 Stickney Ave Toledo (43612) *(G-13677)*

Al Spitzer Ford Inc 330 929-6546
3737 State Rd Cuyahoga Falls (44223) *(G-7034)*

ALADDIN SHRINE TEMPLE, Grove City *Also Called: Aladdin Temple (G-8894)*

Aladdin Temple 614 475-2609
1801 Gateway Cir Grove City (43123) *(G-8894)*

Alamo Local Market, Cleveland *Also Called: Spirit Rent-A-Car Inc (G-4934)*

Alan Manufacturing Inc 330 262-1555
3927 E Lincoln Way Wooster (44691) *(G-15308)*

Alba Manufacturing Inc 513 874-0551
8950 Seward Rd Fairfield (45011) *(G-8388)*

Albco Sales Inc (PA) 330 424-9446
230 Maple St Lisbon (44432) *(G-9996)*

Albert Guarnieri & Co 330 794-9834
7481 Herrick Park Dr Hudson (44236) *(G-9328)*

Albert Mike Leasing (PA) 513 563-1400
10340 Evendale Dr Cincinnati (45241) *(G-2158)*

Albert T Domingo Ms MD Inc 330 452-9460
3120 Parkway St Nw Ste A Canton (44708) *(G-1657)*

Albright Welding Supply Co Inc (PA) 330 264-2021
3132 E Lincoln Way Wooster (44691) *(G-15309)*

Alco, Akron *Also Called: Alco-Chem Inc (G-43)*

Alco-Chem Inc (PA) 330 253-3535
45 N Summit St Akron (44308) *(G-43)*

Alco-Chem Inc 330 833-8551
1303 Park Ave Sw Canton (44706) *(G-1658)*

Alcohol DRG Addction Mntal Svc 937 443-0416
409 E Monument Ave Ste 102 Dayton (45402) *(G-7161)*

Alcohol, Drug Addiction, Akron *Also Called: City of Akron (G-102)*

ALCOHOLIC DROP-IN CENTER, Cincinnati *Also Called: Shelterhouse Vlntr Group Inc (G-3368)*

Alcyon Tchncal Svcs Ats JV LLC 216 433-2488
21000 Brookpark Rd Cleveland (44135) *(G-3782)*

Aldelano Corporation (PA) 909 861-3970
2050 Spencerville Rd Lima (45805) *(G-9861)*

Aldrich Chemical 937 859-1808
3858 Benner Rd Miamisburg (45342) *(G-11023)*

Alec, Rootstown *Also Called: Informtion Applied Lrng Evltio (G-12759)*

Alego Health, Westlake *Also Called: Caff LLC (G-15042)*

Alene Candles LLC 614 933-4005
8860 Smiths Mill Rd Ste 100 New Albany (43054) *(G-11555)*

Alex N Sill Company LLC (HQ) 216 524-9999
6000 Lombardo Ctr Ste 600 Cleveland (44131) *(G-3783)*

Alexander & Associates Co (PA) 513 731-7800
4625 Este Ave Cincinnati (45232) *(G-2159)*

Alexander and Bebout Inc 419 238-9567
10098 Lincoln Hwy Van Wert (45891) *(G-14339)*

Alexander Great Distributing, Steubenville *Also Called: Mougianis Industries Inc (G-13340)*

Alexander Mann Solutions Corp 216 336-6756
1300 E 9th St Ste 400 Cleveland (44114) *(G-3784)*

Alexis Eppinger 216 509-0475
3878 E 177th St Cleveland (44128) *(G-3785)*

Alexson Services Inc — 525 Metro Pl N Ste 300 Dublin (43017) *(G-7928)* — 614 889-5837

Alexson Services Inc — 350 Kolb Dr Fairfield (45014) *(G-8389)* — 513 874-0423

Alexzander Angels LLC — 478 Maple Circle Dr Cincinnati (45246) *(G-2160)* — 678 984-3093

Alfons Haar Inc — 150 Advanced Dr Springboro (45066) *(G-13192)* — 937 560-2031

Alfred Nickles Bakery Inc — 13500 Snow Rd Cleveland (44142) *(G-3786)* — 216 267-8055

Algart Health Care Inc — 8902 Detroit Ave Cleveland (44102) *(G-3787)* — 216 631-1550

Alignement Engine Inc — 8050 Freedom Ave Nw North Canton (44720) *(G-11810)* — 330 401-8251

Alkon Corporation (PA) — 728 Graham Dr Fremont (43420) *(G-8665)* — 419 355-9111

All About Children Inc — 217 Commercial Ave Se New Philadelphia (44663) *(G-11638)* — 330 339-9519

All About Home Care Svcs LLC — 70 Birch Aly Ste 240 Dayton (45440) *(G-7162)* — 937 222-2980

All America Insurance Company (HQ) — 800 S Washington St Van Wert (45891) *(G-14340)* — 419 238-1010

All American Sports Corp (HQ) — 7501 Performance Ln North Ridgeville (44039) *(G-11921)* — 440 366-8225

All American Trnsp Svcs LLC — 575 Beer Rd Ontario (44906) *(G-12099)* — 419 589-7433

All Amrcan Gtter Protection LL — 800 N Main St North Canton (44720) *(G-11811)* — 330 470-4100

All Construction Services Inc — 945 Industrial Pkwy N Brunswick (44212) *(G-1450)* — 330 225-1653

All Construction/Mooney Moses, Brunswick Also Called: All Construction Services Inc *(G-1450)*

All Crane Rental Corp (PA) — 683 Oakland Park Ave Columbus (43224) *(G-5334)* — 614 261-1800

All Erection & Crane Rental (PA) — 4700 Acorn Dr Ste 100 Cleveland (44131) *(G-3788)* — 216 524-6550

All Erection & Crane Rental — 7809 Old Rockside Rd Cleveland (44131) *(G-3789)* — 216 524-6550

All Foils Inc — 16100 Imperial Pkwy Strongsville (44149) *(G-13440)* — 440 572-3645

All Gods Graces Inc (PA) — 1142 W North St Lima (45805) *(G-9862)* — 419 222-8109

All Heart Home Care LLC — 132 S Fulton St Wauseon (43567) *(G-14597)* — 419 298-0034

All Hearts Home Health Care — 6009 Landerhaven Dr Ste D Cleveland (44124) *(G-3790)* — 440 342-2026

All In Staffing — 5561 Ridge Rd Parma (44129) *(G-12248)* — 330 315-1530

All Industrial Engine Service, Willoughby Also Called: All Lift Service Company Inc *(G-15183)*

All Lift Service Company Inc — 4607 Hamann Pkwy Willoughby (44094) *(G-15183)* — 440 585-1542

All Make Solutions LLC — 2710 S Main St Middletown (45044) *(G-11151)* — 800 255-6253

All My Sons Moving & Storage, Cincinnati Also Called: All My Sons Mvg Stor Cncnnati *(G-2161)*

All My Sons Mvg Stor Cncnnati — 3010 Harris Ave Cincinnati (45212) *(G-2161)* — 513 440-5924

All Ohio Landscaping Inc — 5649 Akron Cleveland Rd Hudson (44236) *(G-9329)* — 330 650-2226

All Ohio Threaded Rod Co Inc — 5349 Saint Clair Ave Cleveland (44103) *(G-3791)* — 216 426-1800

All Phase Power and Ltg Inc — 3501 Cleveland Rd Sandusky (44870) *(G-12862)* — 419 624-9640

All Pro Freight Systems Inc (PA) — 1006 Crocker Rd Westlake (44145) *(G-15030)* — 440 934-2222

All Saints Academy Pre School, Columbus Also Called: Christ King Catholic Church *(G-5569)*

All Service Glass, Lima Also Called: Wiechart Enterprises Inc *(G-9987)*

All Star Mgmt Inc — 5425 Clarkins Dr Austintown (44515) *(G-635)* — 330 792-9740

All Temp Refrigeration Inc — 18996 State Route 66 Delphos (45833) *(G-7836)* — 419 692-5016

All Trucks Inc — 5185 Tarlton Blvd Hilliard (43026) *(G-9176)* — 614 800-4595

All-Type Welding & Fabrication — 7690 Bond St Cleveland (44139) *(G-3792)* — 440 439-3990

Allan Miller Do, Toledo Also Called: Surgical Partners Inc *(G-14030)*

Allard Excavation LLC — 8336 Bennett School House Rd South Webster (45682) *(G-13185)* — 740 778-2242

Allegiance Administrators LLC — 5500 Frantz Rd Ste 100 Dublin (43017) *(G-7929)* — 877 895-1414

Allegiance Select, Dublin Also Called: Allegiance Administrators LLC *(G-7929)*

Allegiant Plumbing LLC — 2162 Mckinley Ave Columbus (43204) *(G-5335)* — 614 824-5002

Allegion Access Tech LLC — 14574 Neo Pkwy Cleveland (44128) *(G-3793)* — 440 248-2330

Allegion S&S Holding Co Inc — 9017 Blue Ash Rd Blue Ash (45242) *(G-1127)* — 513 766-4300

Allen County Childrens Svcs Bd, Lima Also Called: County of Allen *(G-9878)*

Allen County Eductl Svc Ctr — 1920 Slabtown Rd Lima (45801) *(G-9863)* — 419 222-1836

Allen County Health Care Ctr, Lima Also Called: County of Allen *(G-9881)*

Allen County Property LLC — 457 S Reynolds Rd Toledo (43615) *(G-13678)* — 419 534-4234

Allen Fields Assoc Inc — 3525 Grant Ave Ste D Lebanon (45036) *(G-9753)* — 513 228-1010

Allen Horizon Center, Elyria Also Called: Horizon Education Centers *(G-8258)*

Allen Memorial Art Museum, Oberlin Also Called: Oberlin College *(G-12074)*

Allen Metro Housinig Auth, Lima Also Called: County of Allen *(G-9880)*

Allen Refractories Company — 131 Shackelford Rd Pataskala (43062) *(G-12269)* — 740 927-8000

Allen-Keith Construction Co (PA) — 2735 Greensburg Rd Canton (44720) *(G-1659)* — 330 266-2220

Allendevaux & Company LLC — 35 Rockridge Rd Englewood (45322) *(G-8302)* — 937 657-1270

Allens Ronnell Trnsp LLC — 1611 E 79th St Apt 1511 Cleveland (44103) *(G-3794)* — 440 453-2273

Allergy & Asthma Inc — 2405 N Columbus St Ste 270 Lancaster (43130) *(G-9693)* — 740 654-8623

Allergy & Asthma Centre Dayton, Centerville Also Called: Ohio Allergy Associates Inc *(G-1948)*

Allgood Home Improvements, Fairfield Also Called: Eagle Industries Ohio Inc *(G-8409)*

Alliance Citizens Health Assn — 200 E State St Alliance (44601) *(G-374)* — 330 596-6000

Alliance Community Hospital (PA) — 200 E State St Alliance (44601) *(G-375)* — 330 596-6000

Alliance Crane & Rigging Inc — 2321 Energy Dr Louisville (44641) *(G-10111)* — 330 823-8823

Alliance Customs Clearance — 4010 Executive Park Dr Ste 300 Cincinnati (45241) *(G-2162)* — 513 794-9400

Alliance Health, Cincinnati Also Called: Uc Health Llc *(G-3545)*

Alliance HM Hlth Care Svcs LLC — 611 E Weber Rd Ste 200 Columbus (43211) *(G-5336)* — 614 928-3053

Alliance Hospitality Inc — 1221 E Dublin Granville Rd Columbus (43229) *(G-5337)* — 614 885-4334

Alliance Imaging Inc — 4825 Higbee Ave Nw Ste 201 Canton (44718) *(G-1660)* — 330 493-5100

Alliance Legal Solutions LLC — 6161 Oak Tree Blvd Ste 300 Independence (44131) *(G-9401)* — 216 525-0100

Alliance Medical Inc — 5000 Tuttle Crossing Blvd Dublin (43016) *(G-7930)* — 800 890-3092

Alliance Solutions Group LLC (PA) — 6161 Oak Tree Blvd Ste 130 Independence (44131) *(G-9402)* — 216 503-1690

Alliance Super 8, Alliance Also Called: Kishan Inc *(G-386)*

Alliance Tchncal Solutions LLC — 6161 Oak Tree Blvd Ste 300 Independence (44131) *(G-9403)* — 216 548-2290

Allied Builders Inc (PA) — 1644 Kuntz Rd Dayton (45404) *(G-7163)* — 937 226-0311

Allied Car Wash Inc — 3330 Central Pkwy Cincinnati (45225) *(G-2163)* — 513 559-1733

Allied Cash Advance, Cincinnati Also Called: Allied Cash Advance Ohio LLC *(G-2165)*

Allied Cash Advance, Cincinnati Also Called: Allied Cash Holdings LLC *(G-2166)*

Allied Cash Advance Cal LLC.. 800 528-1974
   7755 Montgomery Rd Ste 400 Cincinnati (45236) *(G-2164)*
Allied Cash Advance Ohio LLC.. 800 528-1974
   7755 Montgomery Rd Ste 400 Cincinnati (45236) *(G-2165)*
Allied Cash Holdings LLC (HQ) 7755 Montgomery Rd Ste 400 Cincinnati (45236) *(G-2166)*
Allied Communications Corp... 614 588-3370
   4300 Tuller Rd Dublin (43017) *(G-7931)*
Allied Construction Industries.. 513 221-8020
   3 Kovach Dr Cincinnati (45215) *(G-2167)*
Allied Environmental Svcs Inc.. 419 227-4004
   585 Liberty Commons Pkwy Lima (45804) *(G-9864)*
Allied Fabricating & Wldg Co... 614 751-6664
   5699 Chantry Dr Columbus (43232) *(G-5338)*
Allied Fence Builders, Dayton Also Called: Allied Builders Inc *(G-7163)*
Allied Power Transmission Co.. 440 708-1006
   10160 Queens Way Unit 3 Chagrin Falls (44023) *(G-1972)*
Allied Security LLC.. 513 771-3776
   110 Boggs Ln Ste 140 Cincinnati (45246) *(G-2168)*
Allied Supply Company Inc (PA)... 937 224-9833
   1100 E Monument Ave Dayton (45402) *(G-7164)*
Allied Universal, Vandalia Also Called: Universal Services America LP *(G-14398)*
Allied Window Inc.. 513 559-1212
   11111 Canal Rd Cincinnati (45241) *(G-2169)*
Allmed, Dublin Also Called: Alliance Medical Inc *(G-7930)*
Allshred Services, Maumee Also Called: Recycling Services Inc *(G-10758)*
Allstar Financial Group Inc... 866 484-2583
   202 Montrose West Ave Ste 200 Copley (44321) *(G-6947)*
Allstars Travel Group Inc.. 614 901-4100
   7775 Walton Pkwy Ste 100 New Albany (43054) *(G-11556)*
Allstate, Cleveland Also Called: Evarts-Tremaine-Flicker Co *(G-4225)*
Allstate, Hudson Also Called: Allstate Insurance Company *(G-9330)*
Allstate, Springboro Also Called: Your Agency Inc *(G-13211)*
Allstate Insurance Company... 330 650-2917
   75 Milford Dr Ste 222 Hudson (44236) *(G-9330)*
Allstate Trck Sls Estrn Ohio L.. 330 339-5555
   327 Stonecreek Rd Nw New Philadelphia (44663) *(G-11639)*
Allure Scents LLC... 330 312-2019
   1405 22nd St Ne Canton (44714) *(G-1661)*
Allwell Behavioral Health Svcs.. 740 432-7155
   917 Batte Ave Cambridge (43725) *(G-1553)*
Allworth Financial LP... 513 469-7500
   9987 Carver Rd Blue Ash (45242) *(G-1128)*
Almo Distributing PA Inc.. 267 350-2726
   6500 Port Rd Groveport (43125) *(G-8968)*
Almost Family, Cincinnati Also Called: Active Day Inc *(G-2143)*
Almost Family, Medina Also Called: Cambridge Home Health Care *(G-10816)*
Aloft Columbus University Area, Columbus Also Called: Cap City Hotels LLC *(G-5496)*
Alois Alzheimer Center, The, Cincinnati Also Called: Crystalwood Inc *(G-2519)*
Alorica Customer Care Inc.. 216 525-3311
   9525 Sweet Valley Dr Cleveland (44125) *(G-3795)*
Alpco, Westlake Also Called: Aluminum Line Products Company *(G-15032)*
Alpha & Omega Bldg Svcs Inc... 513 429-5082
   11319 Grooms Rd Blue Ash (45242) *(G-1129)*
Alpha & Omega Bldg Svcs Inc (PA)... 937 298-2125
   2843 Culver Ave Ste A Dayton (45429) *(G-7165)*
Alpha Group of Delaware Inc.. 740 368-5820
   1000 Alpha Dr Delaware (43015) *(G-7778)*
Alpha Group of Delaware Inc (PA)... 740 368-5810
   1000 Alpha Dr Delaware (43015) *(G-7779)*
Alpha Imaging Inc.. 440 953-3800
   4455 Glenbrook Rd Willoughby (44094) *(G-15184)*
Alpha Imaging LLC (PA)... 440 953-3800
   4455 Glenbrook Rd Willoughby (44094) *(G-15185)*
Alpha Investment Partnership (PA).. 513 621-1826
   525 Vine St Ste 1925 Cincinnati (45202) *(G-2170)*
Alpha Media LLC... 330 456-7166
   550 Market Ave S Canton (44702) *(G-1662)*
Alpha Media LLC... 937 294-5858
   717 E David Rd Dayton (45429) *(G-7166)*
Alpha PHI Alpha Homes Inc... 330 376-9956
   695 Dunbar Dr Akron (44311) *(G-44)*
Alpha PHI Alpha Homes Inc... 330 376-2115
   730 Callis Dr Akron (44311) *(G-45)*
Alpha Technologies Svcs LLC (DH)... 330 745-1641
   6279 Hudson Crossing Pkwy Ste 200 Hudson (44236) *(G-9331)*
Alphamicron Incorporated... 330 676-0648
   1950 State Route 59 Ste 100 Kent (44240) *(G-9556)*
Alphera Financial Services, Hilliard Also Called: BMW Financial Services Na LLC *(G-9184)*
Alpine Homehealth Care, Cleveland Also Called: Alpine Nursing Care Inc *(G-3796)*
Alpine Insulation I LLC... 614 221-3399
   495 S High St Ste 50 Columbus (43215) *(G-5339)*
Alpine Nursing Care Inc.. 216 662-7096
   4753 Northfield Rd Ste 5 Cleveland (44128) *(G-3796)*
Alpine Valley Ski Area, Chesterland Also Called: Sycamore Lake Inc *(G-2043)*
Alps Services Inc.. 513 772-4746
   12073 Sheraton Ln Cincinnati (45246) *(G-2171)*
Alro Steel, Cuyahoga Falls Also Called: Alro Steel Corporation *(G-7035)*
Alro Steel Corporation.. 513 769-9999
   10310 S Medallion Dr Cincinnati (45241) *(G-2172)*
Alro Steel Corporation.. 614 878-7271
   555 Hilliard Rome Rd Columbus (43228) *(G-5340)*
Alro Steel Corporation.. 330 929-4660
   4787 State Rd Cuyahoga Falls (44223) *(G-7035)*
Alro Steel Corporation.. 937 253-6121
   821 Springfield St Dayton (45403) *(G-7167)*
Alro Steel Corporation.. 419 720-5300
   3003 Airport Hwy Toledo (43609) *(G-13679)*
Als Assction Nthrn Ohio Chpter... 216 592-2572
   6155 Rockside Rd Ste 403 Independence (44131) *(G-9404)*
Als Group Usa Corp... 281 530-5656
   6180 Halle Dr Ste D Cleveland (44125) *(G-3797)*
Alsico Usa Inc (PA).. 330 673-7413
   333 Martinel Dr Kent (44240) *(G-9557)*
Alside Inc (HQ).. 330 929-1811
   3773 State Rd Cuyahoga Falls (44223) *(G-7036)*
Alside Inc.. 419 865-0934
   3510 Briarfield Blvd Maumee (43537) *(G-10687)*
Alside Supply Center, Cuyahoga Falls Also Called: Associated Materials LLC *(G-7041)*
Alside Window Company, Cuyahoga Falls Also Called: Alside Inc *(G-7036)*
Alstate-Peterbilt-Trucks, New Philadelphia Also Called: Allstate Trck Sls Estrn Ohio L *(G-11639)*
Alt, Independence Also Called: Bsl - Applied Laser Tech LLC *(G-9413)*
Alt Media Studios LLC... 440 777-6666
   13572 Chillicothe Rd Novelty (44072) *(G-12036)*
Alta, Canton Also Called: Bock & Clark Corporation *(G-1688)*
Alta Behavioral Healthcare.. 330 793-2487
   711 Belmont Ave Youngstown (44502) *(G-15546)*
Alta Care Group Inc.. 330 793-2487
   711 Belmont Ave Youngstown (44502) *(G-15547)*
Alta It Services LLC.. 813 999-3101
   511 W Bay St Ste 480 Cincinnati (45242) *(G-2173)*
Alta Partners LLC.. 440 808-3654
   902 Westpoint Pkwy Ste 320 Westlake (44145) *(G-15031)*
Alta360 Research Inc.. 419 535-5757
   1690 Woodlands Dr Ste 103 Maumee (43537) *(G-10688)*
Altafiber, Cincinnati Also Called: Cincinnati Bell Inc *(G-2398)*
Altamira Technologies Corp... 937 490-4804
   2850 Presidential Dr Ste 200 Beavercreek (45324) *(G-856)*
Altaquip LLC (HQ).. 513 674-6464
   100 Production Dr Harrison (45030) *(G-9097)*
ALTENHEIM, Berea Also Called: West Side Dtscher Fruen Verein *(G-1087)*
Altenheim Foundation, Strongsville Also Called: Altenheim Foundation Inc *(G-13441)*
Altenheim Foundation Inc.. 440 238-3361
   18627 Shurmer Rd Strongsville (44136) *(G-13441)*
Altercare Inc.. 330 929-4231
   2728 Bailey Rd Cuyahoga Falls (44221) *(G-7037)*
Altercare Inc.. 330 677-4550
   1463 Tallmadge Rd Kent (44240) *(G-9558)*
Altercare Inc (PA)... 440 327-5285
   35990 Westminister Ave North Ridgeville (44039) *(G-11922)*
Altercare Inc.. 330 335-2555
   147 Garfield St Wadsworth (44281) *(G-14427)*

Altercare Hartville, Hartville Also Called: GFS Leasing Inc (G-9126)

Altercare Lsvlle Ctr For Rhblt... 330 875-4224
7187 Saint Francis St Louisville (44641) (G-10112)

Altercare Nobles Pond Inc.. 330 834-4800
7006 Fulton Dr Nw Canton (44718) (G-1663)

Altercare of Bucyrus Inc.. 419 562-7644
1929 Whetstone St Bucyrus (44820) (G-1495)

Altercare of Mntor Ctr For Rhb... 440 953-4421
9901 Johnnycake Ridge Rd Mentor (44060) (G-10910)

Altercare of Navarre, North Canton Also Called: Schroer Properties Navarre Inc (G-11861)

Altercare of Ohio, Canton Also Called: Altercare Nobles Pond Inc (G-1663)

Altercare of Ohio Inc... 330 498-8110
7235 Whipple Ave Nw Canton (44720) (G-1664)

Altercare of Ohio Inc... 330 767-3458
7222 Day Ave Sw Navarre (44662) (G-11536)

Altercare of Ravenna, Kent Also Called: GFS Leasing Inc (G-9577)

Altercare of Wadsworth, Wadsworth Also Called: Altercare Inc (G-14427)

Alternacare.. 740 454-4248
2951 Maple Ave Zanesville (43701) (G-15766)

Alternate Sltons Hlth Ntwrk LL (PA)..................................937 681-9269
1050 Forrer Blvd Dayton (45420) (G-7168)

Alternate Sltons Hmcare Dyton... 937 298-1111
1050 Forrer Blvd Kettering (45420) (G-9625)

Alternate Solutions First LLC.. 937 298-1111
1251 E Dorothy Ln Dayton (45419) (G-7169)

Alternative Residences Two Inc.. 740 425-1565
320 E Main St Barnesville (43713) (G-716)

Alternative Residences Two Inc.. 330 627-7552
520 S Lisbon St Carrollton (44615) (G-1902)

Alternative Residences Two Inc.. 330 833-5564
1865 Tremont Ave Se Massillon (44646) (G-10630)

Alternative Residences Two Inc (PA)................................ 740 526-0514
100 W Main St Lowr Saint Clairsville (43950) (G-12773)

Alterntive Rsrces Homecare Inc.. 216 256-3049
3445 Menlo Rd Shaker Heights (44120) (G-12973)

Altivity Packaging, Cincinnati Also Called: Graphic Packaging Intl LLC (G-2750)

Altix Corporation.. 513 216-8386
6402 Thornberry Ct Mason (45040) (G-10519)

Altoria Solutions LLC.. 513 612-2007
600 Vine St Ste 1904 Cincinnati (45202) (G-2174)

Altruism Society Inc.. 877 283-4001
3695 Green Rd Unit 22896 Beachwood (44122) (G-765)

Alumalloy Metalcasting Company..................................... 440 930-2222
33665 Walker Rd Avon Lake (44012) (G-670)

Aluminum Line Products Company (PA)...........................440 835-8880
24460 Sperry Cir Westlake (44145) (G-15032)

ALUMNI ASSOCIATION, THE, Columbus Also Called: Ohio State Univ Alumni Assn (G-6448)

Alvada Const Inc.. 419 595-4224
1700 Fostoria Ave Ste 800 Findlay (45840) (G-8508)

Alvada Construction, Findlay Also Called: Alvada Const Inc (G-8508)

Always With US Chrties Awu CHR.................................... 800 675-4710
4449 Easton Way Ste 200 Columbus (43219) (G-5341)

Alzheimer Center, Beachwood Also Called: University Hsptals Clvland Med (G-850)

AM Industrial Group LLC... 216 267-6783
4680 Grayton Rd Cleveland (44135) (G-3798)

Amara Homecare Bedford Tel No..................................... 440 353-0600
35136 Center Ridge Rd North Ridgeville (44039) (G-11923)

Amark Logistics Inc.. 440 892-4500
28915 Clemens Rd Westlake (44145) (G-15033)

Amazing Grace HM Hlth Care LLC.................................... 937 825-4862
7039 Taylorsville Rd Huber Heights (45424) (G-9323)

Amazon... 951 733-5325
6366 Downwing Ln Columbus (43230) (G-5342)

Amazon Data Services Inc... 206 617-0149
5101 Hayden Run Rd Hilliard (43026) (G-9177)

Amber Home Care LLC... 614 523-0668
150 E Campus View Blvd Ste 160 Columbus (43235) (G-5343)

Ambers Design Studio LLC.. 614 221-5711
175 S 3rd St Ste 1090 Columbus (43215) (G-5344)

Amberwood Manor, New Philadelphia Also Called: South Brdway Hlthcare Group In (G-11667)

Ambius, Cincinnati Also Called: Rentokil North America Inc (G-3287)

Amboy Rifle Club.. 440 228-9366
100 Hawthorne Dr Conneaut (44030) (G-6937)

Ambrose Asphalt Inc... 419 774-1780
2251 Marion Avenue Rd Mansfield (44903) (G-10243)

Ambulatory Care Pharmacy... 419 251-2545
2213 Cherry St Toledo (43608) (G-13680)

Ambulatory Medical Care Inc (PA)................................... 513 831-8555
7312 Beechmont Ave Cincinnati (45230) (G-2175)

AMC, Dublin Also Called: American Multi-Cinema Inc (G-7935)

AMC, Grove City Also Called: American Multi-Cinema Inc (G-8896)

AMC, Rocky River Also Called: American Multi-Cinema Inc (G-12739)

Amcor Flexibles North Amer Inc....................................... 419 334-9465
730 Industrial Dr Fremont (43420) (G-8666)

Amcs Group Inc... 419 891-1100
2942 Centennial Rd Toledo (43617) (G-13681)

AMEDISYS, Dayton Also Called: Gem City Home Care Llc (G-7374)

Amend Consulting LLC.. 513 399-6300
538 Reading Rd Ste 300 Cincinnati (45202) (G-2176)

Amer Insurance, Akron Also Called: A J Amer Agency Inc (G-9)

Amerathon LLC (HQ).. 513 752-7300
671 Ohio Pike Ste K Cincinnati (45245) (G-2096)

Amerathon LLC.. 419 230-9108
26300 Euclid Ave Ste 810 Euclid (44132) (G-8337)

Amerathon LLC.. 216 409-7201
3575 Forest Lake Dr Ste 500 Uniontown (44685) (G-14241)

Ameri-Line Inc.. 440 316-4500
27060 Royalton Rd Columbia Station (44028) (G-5223)

America Electric Power Texas, Columbus Also Called: AEP Power Marketing Inc (G-5324)

America Votes.. 614 236-3410
5 E Long St Fl 8 Columbus (43215) (G-5345)

America's Best Medical, Akron Also Called: Lincare Inc (G-221)

AMERICA'S URGENT CARE, Upper Arlington Also Called: Americas Urgent Care (G-14275)

American Air Comfort Tech, Grove City Also Called: American Air Furnace Company (G-8895)

American Air Furnace Company....................................... 614 876-1702
3945 Brookham Dr Grove City (43123) (G-8895)

American Airlines Inc.. 937 890-6668
3600 Terminal Rd Vandalia (45377) (G-14363)

American Airlines/Eagle, North Canton Also Called: Piedmont Airlines Inc (G-11851)

American Ambulette & Ambulance Service Inc................... 937 237-1105
729 6th St Portsmouth (45662) (G-12544)

American Beauty Landscaping... 330 788-1501
5415 South Ave Youngstown (44512) (G-15548)

American Bottling Company.. 614 237-4201
950 Stelzer Rd Columbus (43219) (G-5346)

American Broadband Telecom Co.................................... 419 824-5800
1480 Ford St Maumee (43537) (G-10689)

American Brzing Div Paulo Pdts, Willoughby Also Called: Paulo Products Company (G-15218)

American Bulk Commodities Inc (PA)............................... 330 758-0841
8063 Southern Blvd Youngstown (44512) (G-15549)

American Bus Solutions Inc... 614 888-2227
8850 Whitney Dr Lewis Center (43035) (G-9804)

American Business Forms Inc.. 513 312-2522
10000 International Blvd West Chester (45246) (G-14798)

American Business Forms Inc.. 614 664-0202
178 Granby Pl W Westerville (43081) (G-14958)

AMERICAN CAMPUS COMMUNITIES, INC., Cleveland Also Called: American Cmpus Communities Inc (G-3799)

American Cemetery Services LLP..................................... 330 345-8379
4049 Youngstown Rd Se Warren (44484) (G-14497)

American Ceramic Society (PA)....................................... 614 890-4700
550 Polaris Pkwy Ste 510 Westerville (43082) (G-14877)

American Chem Soc Fderal Cr Un.................................... 614 447-3675
2540 Olentangy River Rd Columbus (43202) (G-5347)

American City Bus Journals Inc.. 937 528-4400
40 N Main St Ste 810 Dayton (45423) (G-7170)

American Cllege Crdlgy Fndtion....................................... 614 442-5950
5600 Blazer Pkwy Ste 220 # 320 Dublin (43017) (G-7932)

American Cmpassionate Care LLC.................................... 513 443-8156
5960 Glenway Ave Cincinnati (45238) (G-2177)

ALPHABETIC SECTION — American Nat Red Cross - Blood

American Cmpus Communities Inc.. 216 687-5196
1983 E 24th St Cleveland (44115) *(G-3799)*

American Coatings Corporation... 614 335-1000
7510 Montgomery Rd Plain City (43064) *(G-12466)*

American Consolidated Inds Inc (PA)... 216 587-8000
4650 Johnston Pkwy Cleveland (44128) *(G-3800)*

American Copy Equipment Inc... 330 722-9555
6599 Granger Rd Cleveland (44131) *(G-3801)*

American Court & DRG Tstg Svcs, Medina *Also Called: Avertest LLC* *(G-10812)*

American Crane Inc.. 614 496-2268
7791 Taylor Rd Sw Ste A Reynoldsburg (43068) *(G-12651)*

American Crane & Lift Trck Svc, Reynoldsburg *Also Called: American Crane Inc* *(G-12651)*

American De Rosa Lamparts LLC (HQ) 370 Falls Commerce Pkwy Cuyahoga Falls (44224) *(G-7038)*

American Diesel, Cleveland *Also Called: Interstate Diesel Service Inc* *(G-4420)*

American Dream Solar & Win Inc.. 513 543-5645
4007 Bach Buxton Rd Amelia (45102) *(G-410)*

American Eagle Hlth Care Svcs... 440 428-5103
6831 Chapel Rd Madison (44057) *(G-10211)*

American Eagle Mortgage, Cleveland *Also Called: Crosscountry Mortgage LLC* *(G-4140)*

American Electric Power, Columbus *Also Called: American Electric Pwr Svc Corp* *(G-5348)*

American Electric Pwr Svc Corp (HQ).. 614 716-1000
1 Riverside Plz Columbus (43215) *(G-5348)*

American Electric Pwr Svc Corp... 614 582-1742
825 Tech Center Dr Columbus (43230) *(G-5349)*

American Empire Insurance, Cincinnati *Also Called: American Empire Srpls Lnes Ins* *(G-2178)*

American Empire Srpls Lnes Ins... 513 369-3000
515 Main St Cincinnati (45202) *(G-2178)*

American Empire Srpls Lnes Ins, Cincinnati *Also Called: Great Amrcn Risk Sltons Srpls* *(G-2761)*

American Envmtl Group Ltd... 330 659-5930
3600 Brecksville Rd Ste 100 Richfield (44286) *(G-12685)*

American Ex Trvl Rlted Svcs In.. 330 922-5700
911 Graham Rd Ste 24 Cuyahoga Falls (44221) *(G-7039)*

American Excelsior Company... 419 663-3241
180 Cleveland Rd Norwalk (44857) *(G-12000)*

American Express, Cuyahoga Falls *Also Called: American Ex Trvl Rlted Svcs In* *(G-7039)*

American Family Home Insur Co.. 513 943-7100
7000 Midland Blvd Amelia (45102) *(G-411)*

American Fidelity Assurance Co... 800 437-1011
90 Northwoods Blvd Ste B Columbus (43235) *(G-5350)*

American Financial Corporation.. 513 579-2121
580 Walnut St Fl 9 Cincinnati (45202) *(G-2179)*

American Financial Group Inc (PA).. 513 579-2121
301 E 4th St Cincinnati (45202) *(G-2180)*

American Financial Network Inc... 714 831-4000
6833 Clark State Rd Blacklick (43004) *(G-1108)*

American Fleet Services, Cleveland *Also Called: American Nat Fleet Svc Inc* *(G-3805)*

American Frame Corporation (PA).. 419 893-5595
400 Tomahawk Dr Maumee (43537) *(G-10690)*

American Golf Corporation... 419 726-9353
4001 N Summit St Toledo (43611) *(G-13682)*

American Greetings, Cleveland *Also Called: AG Interactive Inc* *(G-3774)*

American Health Associates, Cincinnati *Also Called: American Health Imaging S LLC* *(G-2097)*

American Health Foundation Inc.. 614 798-5110
1839 Western Ave Chillicothe (45601) *(G-2050)*

American Health Imaging S LLC... 513 752-7300
665 Ohio Pike Cincinnati (45245) *(G-2097)*

American Health Network, Newark *Also Called: Newark Family Physicians Inc* *(G-11735)*

American Health Network Inc... 614 794-4500
5900 Parkwood Pl Dublin (43016) *(G-7933)*

American Health Packaging, Columbus *Also Called: Amerisource Health Svcs LLC* *(G-5364)*

American Heart Association Inc... 614 848-6676
118 Graceland Blvd Columbus (43214) *(G-5351)*

American Heritage Girls Inc.. 513 771-2025
35 Tri County Pkwy Cincinnati (45246) *(G-2181)*

American Highways Insur Agcy.. 330 659-8900
3250 Interstate Dr Richfield (44286) *(G-12686)*

American Hlth Netwrk Ohio LLC (DH).. 614 794-4500
5900 Parkwood Pl Dublin (43016) *(G-7934)*

American Hlth Netwrk Ohio LLC... 740 344-5437
1920 Tamarack Rd Newark (43055) *(G-11686)*

American Home Health Services,, Westlake *Also Called: Infinity Health Services Inc* *(G-15070)*

American Homes 4 Rent.. 513 429-7174
11802 Conrey Rd Ste 100 Cincinnati (45249) *(G-2182)*

American Hospitality Group Inc (HQ).. 330 336-6684
200 Smokerise Dr Wadsworth (44281) *(G-14428)*

American Hydraulic Svcs Inc.. 606 739-8680
1912 S 1st St Ironton (45638) *(G-9502)*

American Insurance Strategies.. 937 221-8896
78 Marco Ln Dayton (45458) *(G-7171)*

American Interiors Inc (PA)... 419 535-1808
302 S Byrne Rd Bldg 100 Toledo (43615) *(G-13683)*

American Jersey Cattle Assn (PA).. 614 861-3636
6486 E Main St Reynoldsburg (43068) *(G-12652)*

American Kenda Rbr Indus Ltd (HQ).. 866 536-3287
7095 Americana Pkwy Reynoldsburg (43068) *(G-12653)*

American Kidney Stone MGT Ltd (PA)... 800 637-5188
100 W 3rd Ave Ste 350 Columbus (43201) *(G-5352)*

American Landfill Inc... 330 866-3265
7916 Chapel St Se Waynesburg (44688) *(G-14621)*

American Limousine Service, Cleveland *Also Called: American Livery Service Inc* *(G-3802)*

American Livery Service Inc.. 216 221-9330
11723 Detroit Ave Cleveland (44107) *(G-3802)*

American Marine Express Inc... 216 268-3005
765 E 140th St Ste A Cleveland (44110) *(G-3803)*

American Mechanical Group Inc... 614 575-3720
5729 Westbourne Ave Columbus (43213) *(G-5353)*

American Midwest Mortgage Corp (PA)....................................... 440 882-5210
6363 York Rd Ste 300 Cleveland (44130) *(G-3804)*

American Modern Home Insur Co, Amelia *Also Called: American Modrn Insur Group Inc* *(G-413)*

American Modern Home Svc Co.. 513 943-7100
7000 Midland Blvd Amelia (45102) *(G-412)*

American Modrn Insur Group Inc (DH).. 800 543-2644
7000 Midland Blvd Amelia (45102) *(G-413)*

American Modrn Select Insur Co... 513 943-7100
7000 Midland Blvd Amelia (45102) *(G-414)*

American Money Management Corp... 513 579-2592
301 E 4th St 27th Fl Cincinnati (45202) *(G-2183)*

American Motorcycle Assn (PA)... 614 856-1900
13515 Yarmouth Dr Pickerington (43147) *(G-12397)*

American Motorcyclist Assn, Pickerington *Also Called: American Motorcycle Assn* *(G-12397)*

American Multi-Cinema Inc... 614 889-0580
6700 Village Pkwy Dublin (43017) *(G-7935)*

American Multi-Cinema Inc... 614 801-9130
4218 Buckeye Pkwy Grove City (43123) *(G-8896)*

American Multi-Cinema Inc... 440 331-2826
21653 Center Ridge Rd Rocky River (44116) *(G-12739)*

American Municipal Power Inc (PA)... 614 540-1111
1111 Schrock Rd Ste 100 Columbus (43229) *(G-5354)*

American Mutl Share Insur Corp (PA).. 614 764-1900
5656 Frantz Rd Dublin (43017) *(G-7936)*

American Nat Fleet Svc Inc... 216 447-6060
7714 Commerce Park Oval Cleveland (44131) *(G-3805)*

American Nat Red Cross - Blood, Akron *Also Called: American National Red Cross* *(G-46)*

American Nat Red Cross - Blood, Columbus *Also Called: American National Red Cross* *(G-5355)*

American Nat Red Cross - Blood, Columbus *Also Called: American National Red Cross* *(G-5356)*

American Nat Red Cross - Blood, Columbus *Also Called: American National Red Cross* *(G-5358)*

American Nat Red Cross - Blood, Parma *Also Called: American National Red Cross* *(G-12249)*

American Nat Red Cross - Blood, Toledo *Also Called: American National Red Cross* *(G-13684)*

American Nat Red Cross - Blood, Toledo *Also Called: American National Red Cross* *(G-13685)*

American National Red Cross — ALPHABETIC SECTION

American National Red Cross.. 330 535-6131
501 W Market St Akron (44303) *(G-46)*

American National Red Cross.. 330 535-6131
501 W Market St Akron (44303) *(G-47)*

American National Red Cross.. 330 452-1111
408 9th St Sw Canton (44707) *(G-1665)*

American National Red Cross.. 614 253-2740
995 E Broad St Columbus (43205) *(G-5355)*

American National Red Cross.. 614 326-2337
4820 Sawmill Rd Columbus (43235) *(G-5356)*

American National Red Cross.. 800 448-3543
1 W Nationwide Blvd Columbus (43215) *(G-5357)*

American National Red Cross.. 614 334-0425
4327 Equity Dr Columbus (43228) *(G-5358)*

American National Red Cross.. 614 473-3783
337 Stoneridge Ln Gahanna (43230) *(G-8710)*

American National Red Cross.. 614 436-3862
1327 Cameron Ave Lewis Center (43035) *(G-9805)*

American National Red Cross.. 740 344-2510
1272 W Main St Ste 505 Newark (43055) *(G-11687)*

American National Red Cross.. 216 303-5476
5585 Pearl Rd Parma (44129) *(G-12249)*

American National Red Cross.. 419 382-2707
1111 Research Dr Toledo (43614) *(G-13684)*

American National Red Cross.. 800 733-2767
3510 Executive Pkwy Toledo (43606) *(G-13685)*

American National Red Cross.. 419 329-2900
3100 W Central Ave Ste 200 Toledo (43606) *(G-13686)*

American National Red Cross.. 330 469-6403
126 Valley Cir Ne Warren (44484) *(G-14498)*

American National Red Cross.. 330 726-6063
8392 Tod Ave Youngstown (44512) *(G-15550)*

American Nursing Care, Zanesville *Also Called: American Nursing Care Inc (G-15767)*

American Nursing Care Inc.. 513 731-4600
4750 Wesley Ave Ste Q Cincinnati (45212) *(G-2184)*

American Nursing Care Inc.. 513 245-1500
4460 Red Bank Rd Ste 100 Cincinnati (45227) *(G-2185)*

American Nursing Care Inc.. 937 438-3844
6450 Poe Ave Ste 118 Dayton (45414) *(G-7172)*

American Nursing Care Inc (DH).. 513 576-0262
6281 Tri Ridge Blvd Ste 300 Loveland (45140) *(G-10126)*

American Nursing Care Inc.. 614 847-0555
1206 Brandywine Blvd Ste A Zanesville (43701) *(G-15767)*

American Paper Group Inc.. 330 758-4545
8401 Southern Blvd Youngstown (44512) *(G-15551)*

American Paper Products Co Div, Youngstown *Also Called: American Paper Group Inc (G-15551)*

American Pavements Inc.. 614 873-2191
7475 Montgomery Rd Plain City (43064) *(G-12467)*

American Plastics Inc.. 330 945-4100
1914 Akron Peninsula Rd Akron (44313) *(G-48)*

American Plumbing.. 440 871-8293
31400 Fairwin Dr Bay Village (44140) *(G-757)*

American Posts LLC (PA).. 419 720-0652
810 Chicago St Toledo (43611) *(G-13687)*

American Power Tower LLC.. 440 261-2245
538 Goodale Rd Jefferson (44047) *(G-9537)*

American Precast Refractories.. 614 876-8416
2700 Scioto Pkwy Columbus (43221) *(G-5359)*

American Procomm, Marietta *Also Called: Davis Pickering & Company Inc (G-10365)*

American Producers Sup Co Inc (PA).. 740 373-5050
119 2nd St Marietta (45750) *(G-10355)*

American Prservation Bldrs LLC.. 216 236-2007
127 Public Sq Ste 1300 Cleveland (44114) *(G-3806)*

American Red Cross.. 513 579-3000
2111 Dana Ave Cincinnati (45207) *(G-2186)*

American Red Cross, Akron *Also Called: American National Red Cross (G-47)*

American Red Cross, Columbus *Also Called: American National Red Cross (G-5357)*

American Red Cross, Columbus *Also Called: American Red Cross of Grtr Col (G-5360)*

American Red Cross, Gahanna *Also Called: American National Red Cross (G-8710)*

American Red Cross, Lewis Center *Also Called: American National Red Cross (G-9805)*

American Red Cross, Newark *Also Called: American National Red Cross (G-11687)*

American Red Cross Med Educa, Warren *Also Called: American National Red Cross (G-14498)*

American Red Cross of Grtr Col (PA).. 614 253-7981
995 E Broad St Columbus (43205) *(G-5360)*

American Regent Inc.. 614 436-2222
4150 Lyman Dr Hilliard (43026) *(G-9178)*

AMERICAN RENAL, Columbus *Also Called: Kidney Center of Bexley LLC (G-6115)*

AMERICAN RENAL, Warren *Also Called: Warren Dialysis Center LLC (G-14575)*

American Retirement Corp.. 216 291-6140
3 Homewood Way Cleveland (44143) *(G-3807)*

American Ring.. 414 355-9206
30450 Bruce Industrial Pkwy Solon (44139) *(G-13065)*

American Ring & Tool Co, Solon *Also Called: R L Morrissey & Assoc Inc (G-13135)*

American Risk Services LLC.. 513 772-3712
1130 Congress Ave Ste A Cincinnati (45246) *(G-2187)*

American Roadway Logistics Inc.. 330 659-2003
2661 Barber Rd Norton (44203) *(G-11989)*

American Salon Group LLC.. 330 975-0085
4081 N Jefferson St Medina (44256) *(G-10806)*

American Sand & Gravel Div, Massillon *Also Called: Kenmore Construction Co Inc (G-10649)*

American Seaway, Bedford Heights *Also Called: Riser Foods Company (G-1001)*

American Security Insurance Co.. 937 327-7700
1 Assurant Way Springfield (45505) *(G-13216)*

American Select Insurance Co.. 330 887-0101
1 Park Cir Westfield Center (44251) *(G-15024)*

American Services, Columbus *Also Called: American Svcs & Protection LLC (G-5362)*

AMERICAN SHARE INSURANCE, Dublin *Also Called: American Mutl Share Insur Corp (G-7936)*

American Showa Inc.. 740 965-4040
677 W Cherry St Sunbury (43074) *(G-13516)*

American Solutions For Bus, West Chester *Also Called: American Business Forms Inc (G-14798)*

American Solutions For Bus, Westerville *Also Called: American Business Forms Inc (G-14958)*

American Structurepoint Inc.. 614 901-2235
2550 Corporate Exchange Dr Ste 300 Columbus (43231) *(G-5361)*

American Suncraft Cnstr Co, Medway *Also Called: American Suncraft Co Inc (G-10907)*

American Suncraft Co Inc.. 937 849-9475
10836 Schiller Rd Medway (45341) *(G-10907)*

American Svcs & Protection LLC.. 614 884-0177
2572 Oakstone Dr Ste 1 Columbus (43231) *(G-5362)*

American Tank & Fabricating Co (PA).. 216 252-1500
12314 Elmwood Ave Cleveland (44111) *(G-3808)*

American Warming and Vent.. 419 288-2703
120 Plin St Bradner (43406) *(G-1341)*

American Welding & Gas Inc.. 859 519-8772
1210 Glendale Milford Rd Cincinnati (45215) *(G-2188)*

American Western Home Insur, Amelia *Also Called: Midland Company (G-418)*

American Western Home Insur Co.. 513 943-7100
7000 Midland Blvd Amelia (45102) *(G-415)*

Americas Best Value Inn, Saint Clairsville *Also Called: Lodging Assoc St Clrsville Inc (G-12798)*

Americas Best Value Inn, Streetsboro *Also Called: R & H Service Inc (G-13425)*

Americas Floor Source LLC (PA).. 614 808-3915
3442 Millenium Ct Columbus (43219) *(G-5363)*

Americas Headquarters.. 614 339-8200
8800 Lyra Dr Ste 350 Columbus (43240) *(G-5245)*

Americas Urgent Care.. 614 929-2721
4661 Sawmill Rd Ste 101 Upper Arlington (43220) *(G-14275)*

Americoat, Plain City *Also Called: American Coatings Corporation (G-12466)*

Americold Logistics LLC.. 419 599-5015
1175 Independence Dr Napoleon (43545) *(G-11515)*

Americold Logistics LLC.. 419 599-5015
1800 Industrial Dr Napoleon (43545) *(G-11516)*

Ameridial Inc (HQ).. 234 542-5036
4877 Higbee Ave Nw Fl 2 Canton (44718) *(G-1666)*

Ameridial Inc.. 330 339-7222
521 W High Ave New Philadelphia (44663) *(G-11640)*

Amerifirst Financial Corp.. 614 766-5709
5930 Venture Dr Dublin (43017) *(G-7937)*

ALPHABETIC SECTION — Anderson Healthcare Ltd

Amerifirst Financial Corp 216 452-5120
  14701 Detroit Avenue Ste 750 Lakewood (44107) *(G-9657)*
Amerigroup Ohio Inc 513 733-2300
  10123 Alliance Rd Ste 140 Blue Ash (45242) *(G-1130)*
Amerihost Inn, Zanesville *Also Called: Dev Investments of Ohio Inc (G-15785)*
Amerihost Inn Suites, Concord Township *Also Called: Lake Hospitality Inc (G-6929)*
Amerihost Mt. Vernon, Mount Vernon *Also Called: Emmett Dan House Ltd Partnr (G-11485)*
Amerimark Direct, Cleveland *Also Called: Amerimark Holdings LLC (G-3809)*
Amerimark Holdings LLC (HQ) 440 325-2000
  6864 Engle Rd Cleveland (44130) *(G-3809)*
Amerimed LLC 513 942-3670
  9961 Cincinnati Dayton Rd West Chester (45069) *(G-14650)*
Amerimed, Inc., West Chester *Also Called: Amerimed LLC (G-14650)*
Ameripride Services Inc 859 371-4037
  4936 Montgomery Rd Cincinnati (45212) *(G-2189)*
AMERIPRIDE SERVICES, INC., Cincinnati *Also Called: Ameripride Services Inc (G-2189)*
Ameriprise Financial Services, Dublin *Also Called: Amerifirst Financial Corp (G-7937)*
Ameriscape Inc 614 863-5400
  6751 Taylor Rd Unit D1 Blacklick (43004) *(G-1109)*
Amerisource Health Svcs LLC 614 492-8177
  2550 John Glenn Ave Ste A Columbus (43217) *(G-5364)*
Ameritas Life Insurance Corp 866 696-7478
  1876 Waycross Rd Cincinnati (45240) *(G-2190)*
Ameritas Life Insurance Corp 513 595-2334
  1876 Waycross Rd Cincinnati (45240) *(G-2191)*
Ameritech Ohio, Columbus *Also Called: Ohio Bell Telephone Company (G-6395)*
Ameriwound 216 273-9800
  5800 Landerbrook Dr Ste 100 Mayfield Heights (44124) *(G-10784)*
Ames Material Services Inc 937 382-5591
  145 Hunter Dr Wilmington (45177) *(G-15244)*
Ametek Electromechanical Group, Kent *Also Called: Ametek Tchnical Indus Pdts Inc (G-9559)*
Ametek Tchnical Indus Pdts Inc (HQ) 330 673-3451
  100 E Erie St Ste 130 Kent (44240) *(G-9559)*
AMF, Columbus *Also Called: AMF Bowling Centers Inc (G-5365)*
AMF, Medina *Also Called: AMF Bowling Centers Inc (G-10807)*
AMF Bowling Centers Inc 614 889-0880
  4825 Sawmill Rd Columbus (43235) *(G-5365)*
AMF Bowling Centers Inc 330 725-4548
  201 Harding St Medina (44256) *(G-10807)*
Amg Inc (PA) 937 274-0736
  1497 Shoup Mill Rd Dayton (45414) *(G-7173)*
AMG Consultants Inc 917 600-3773
  700 W Pete Rose Way Cincinnati (45203) *(G-2192)*
AMG-Eng, Dayton *Also Called: Amg Inc (G-7173)*
Amherst Hospital Association 440 988-6000
  254 Cleveland Ave Amherst (44001) *(G-421)*
Amherst Maintenance Bldg, Berea *Also Called: Ohio Tpk & Infrastructure Comm (G-1077)*
Amherst Manor Inc 440 988-4415
  175 N Lake St Amherst (44001) *(G-422)*
Amherst Manor Nursing Home, Amherst *Also Called: Amherst Manor Inc (G-422)*
AMI, Mayfield Heights *Also Called: Park Place Technologies LLC (G-10792)*
Amin Turocy & Watson LLP (PA) 216 696-8730
  200 Park Ave Ste 300 Beachwood (44122) *(G-766)*
Amish Door Inc (PA) 330 359-5464
  1210 Winesburg St Wilmot (44689) *(G-15281)*
Amish Door Restaurant, Wilmot *Also Called: Amish Door Inc (G-15281)*
Amko Service Company (DH) 330 364-8857
  3211 Brightwood Rd Midvale (44653) *(G-11203)*
Aml Rightsource LLC (PA) 216 771-1250
  1300 E 9th St Fl 2 Cleveland (44114) *(G-3810)*
Amlon Ltd 614 431-3670
  4875 Sinclair Rd Columbus (43229) *(G-5366)*
Amorso At HM Snior Dsblity Car 513 761-6500
  1821 Summit Rd Ste 113 Cincinnati (45237) *(G-2193)*
Amos Media Company (PA) 937 638-0967
  1660 Campbell Rd Ste A Sidney (45365) *(G-13018)*
Amotec Inc (PA) 440 250-4600
  3133 Chester Ave Cleveland (44114) *(G-3811)*
Amoxford Inc 513 523-2722
  5190 College Corner Pike Oxford (45056) *(G-12200)*

AMP, Columbus *Also Called: American Municipal Power Inc (G-5354)*
Ampac, Cincinnati *Also Called: Ampac Packaging LLC (G-2195)*
Ampac Holdings LLC (HQ) 513 671-1777
  12025 Tricon Rd Cincinnati (45246) *(G-2194)*
Ampac Packaging LLC (HQ) 513 671-1777
  12025 Tricon Rd Cincinnati (45246) *(G-2195)*
Ampco System Parking, Cleveland *Also Called: ABM Industry Groups LLC (G-3758)*
Ampersand Group LLC 330 379-0044
  1946 S Arlington St Akron (44306) *(G-49)*
Ample Industries Inc 937 746-9700
  4000 Commerce Center Dr Franklin (45005) *(G-8631)*
Amplifybio LLC (PA) 833 641-2006
  1425 Plain-City Georgesville Rd West Jefferson (43162) *(G-14847)*
Amros Industries Inc 216 433-0010
  14701 Industrial Pkwy Cleveland (44135) *(G-3812)*
AMS, Dayton *Also Called: Applied Mechanical Systems Inc (G-7176)*
AMS Construction Inc (PA) 513 794-0410
  10670 Loveland Madeira Rd Loveland (45140) *(G-10127)*
AMS Construction Inc 513 398-6689
  7431 Windsor Park Dr Maineville (45039) *(G-10224)*
AMS Construction Parts, Middletown *Also Called: All Make Solutions LLC (G-11151)*
Amsc, Cleveland *Also Called: Northast Ohio Rgonal Sewer Dst (G-4657)*
Amsive OH LLC 937 885-8000
  3303 W Tech Blvd Miamisburg (45342) *(G-11024)*
Amstan Logistics, Liberty Township *Also Called: As Logistics Inc (G-9847)*
Amsted Industries Incorporated 614 836-2323
  3900 Bixby Rd Groveport (43125) *(G-8969)*
Amsurg, Akron *Also Called: Digest Health Center Ltd (G-134)*
Amt, Brecksville *Also Called: Applied Medical Technology Inc (G-1343)*
Amtrac Railroad Contrs Ohio, Orrville *Also Called: Gg Ohio Inc (G-12165)*
Amtrust Financial Services, Cleveland *Also Called: Amtrust North America Inc (G-3813)*
Amtrust North America Inc (DH) 216 328-6100
  59 Maiden Ln Flr 43 Cleveland (44114) *(G-3813)*
Amusements of America Inc 614 297-8863
  717 E 17th Ave Columbus (43211) *(G-5367)*
Amx, Cleveland *Also Called: American Marine Express Inc (G-3803)*
Analex Corporation 703 721-6001
  1000 Apollo Dr Brook Park (44142) *(G-1405)*
Analytical Pace Services LLC 937 832-8242
  25 Holiday Dr Englewood (45322) *(G-8303)*
Anatrace Products LLC (HQ) 800 252-1280
  434 W Dussel Dr Maumee (43537) *(G-10691)*
Anchor Flange Company (PA) 513 527-3512
  5553 Murray Ave Cincinnati (45227) *(G-2196)*
Anchor Fluid Power, Cincinnati *Also Called: Anchor Flange Company (G-2196)*
Anchor Hocking Holdings Inc 800 562-7511
  519 N Pierce Ave Lancaster (43130) *(G-9694)*
Anchor Lodge Ltd Partnership 440 244-2019
  3756 W Erie Ave Lorain (44053) *(G-10053)*
Anchor Lodge Nursing Home Inc 440 244-2019
  3756 W Erie Ave Ofc Lorain (44053) *(G-10054)*
Anchor Metal Processing Inc (PA) 216 362-1850
  11830 Brookpark Rd Cleveland (44130) *(G-3814)*
Anchor Security and Logistics, Columbus *Also Called: SW Squared LLC (G-6738)*
ANCHOR TRADER, Upper Arlington *Also Called: Delta Gamma Fraternity (G-14277)*
Ancora Group LLC 216 825-4000
  6060 Parkland Blvd Ste 200 Cleveland (44124) *(G-3815)*
Anders Dermatology Inc 419 473-3257
  4126 N Holland Sylvania Rd Ste 200 Toledo (43623) *(G-13688)*
Anders Medical, Toledo *Also Called: Anders Dermatology Inc (G-13688)*
Anderson & Vreeland Inc 419 636-5002
  15348 Us Highway 127 Ew Bryan (43506) *(G-1479)*
Anderson Aluminum Corporation 614 476-4877
  2816 Morse Rd Columbus (43231) *(G-5368)*
Anderson and Dubose Inc 440 248-8800
  5300 Tod Ave Sw Warren (44481) *(G-14499)*
Anderson Autmtc Htg & AC Inc 512 574-0005
  6085 Hamilton Cleves Rd Cleves (45002) *(G-5186)*
Anderson Healthcare Ltd 513 474-6200
  8139 Beechmont Ave Cincinnati (45255) *(G-2197)*

(PA)=Parent Co (HQ)=Headquarters (DH)=Div Headquarters

Anderson Hills Pediatrics Inc 513 232-8100
  7400 Jager Ct Cincinnati (45230) *(G-2198)*

Anderson Jeffery R RE Inc 513 241-5800
  3805 Edwards Rd Ste 700 Cincinnati (45209) *(G-2199)*

Anderson Little 513 474-7800
  8516 Beechmont Ave Cincinnati (45255) *(G-2200)*

Anderson Nrsing Rhbltation Ctr, Cincinnati Also Called: Anderson Healthcare Ltd *(G-2197)*

Anderson Properties, Columbus Also Called: Anderson Aluminum Corporation *(G-5368)*

Anderson Township Park Dst 513 474-0003
  6910 Salem Rd Cincinnati (45230) *(G-2201)*

Anderson Twnship Hstrcal Soc I 513 231-2114
  6550 Clough Pike Cincinnati (45244) *(G-2202)*

Anderson Vreeland Midwest, Bryan Also Called: Anderson & Vreeland Inc *(G-1479)*

Anderson-Dubose Co, The, Warren Also Called: Anderson and Dubose Inc *(G-14499)*

Anderson's Farm, Maumee Also Called: Andersons Agriculture Group LP *(G-10694)*

Andersons Inc (PA) 419 893-5050
  1947 Briarfield Blvd Maumee (43537) *(G-10692)*

Andersons Inc 419 891-6479
  1380 Ford St Maumee (43537) *(G-10693)*

Andersons Agriculture Group LP (HQ) 419 893-5050
  1947 Briarfield Blvd Maumee (43537) *(G-10694)*

Andersons Tireman Auto Centers, Toledo Also Called: Belle Tire Distributors Inc *(G-13704)*

Andersons, The, Maumee Also Called: Andersons Inc *(G-10692)*

Anderzack-Pitzen Cnstr Inc 419 644-2111
  424 E Main St Metamora (43540) *(G-11016)*

Andover Bancorp Inc (PA) 440 293-7605
  19 Public Sq Andover (44003) *(G-437)*

Andover Vlg Rtrement Cmnty Ltd 440 293-5416
  486 S Main St Andover (44003) *(G-438)*

Andrew Casey Electric LLC 937 765-4210
  4008 N Dixie Dr Dayton (45414) *(G-7174)*

Andrew Distribution Inc 614 824-3123
  509 Industry Dr Columbus (43204) *(G-5369)*

Andrew Insurance Associates 614 336-8030
  545 Metro Pl S Ste 150 Dublin (43017) *(G-7938)*

Andrews Apartments Ltd 440 946-3600
  4420 Sherwin Rd Willoughby (44094) *(G-15186)*

Andrews Architects Inc 614 766-1117
  130 E Wilson Bridge Rd Ste 50 Worthington (43085) *(G-15404)*

Andrews William Architct/ Bldg, Worthington Also Called: Andrews Architects Inc *(G-15404)*

Andritz Inc 937 390-3400
  3200 Upper Valley Pike Springfield (45504) *(G-13217)*

Andritz Sprout Bauer, Springfield Also Called: Andritz Inc *(G-13217)*

Andy Russo Jr Inc 440 585-1456
  29200 Anderson Rd Wickliffe (44092) *(G-15145)*

Andy's Mirror and Glass, Cincinnati Also Called: Diers2018co Inc *(G-2563)*

Andydandy Center LLC 513 272-6141
  3804 Church St Cincinnati (45244) *(G-2203)*

Anesthesia Associates PLL 440 350-0832
  835 Ford Rd Cleveland (44143) *(G-3816)*

Anesthesiology Assoc of Akron 330 344-6401
  1 Akron General Ave Akron (44307) *(G-50)*

Anesthesiology Svcs Netwrk Ltd 937 208-6173
  1 Wyoming St Dayton (45409) *(G-7175)*

Anesthsia Assoc Cincinnati Inc 513 585-0577
  2139 Auburn Ave Cincinnati (45219) *(G-2204)*

Angeline Industries Inc 419 294-4488
  210 N Sandusky Ave Upper Sandusky (43351) *(G-14284)*

Angels In Waiting Home Care 440 946-0349
  8336 Tyler Blvd Mentor (44060) *(G-10911)*

Angstrom Graphics Inc Midwest (HQ) 216 271-5300
  4437 E 49th St Cleveland (44125) *(G-3817)*

Anheuser-Busch, Cincinnati Also Called: Anheuser-Busch LLC *(G-2205)*

Anheuser-Busch, Lima Also Called: Anheuser-Busch LLC *(G-9865)*

Anheuser-Busch LLC 513 381-3927
  600 Vine St Ste 1002 Cincinnati (45202) *(G-2205)*

Anheuser-Busch LLC 419 221-2337
  3535 Saint Johns Rd Lima (45804) *(G-9865)*

Animal Care Unlimited Inc 614 766-2317
  2665 Billingsley Rd Columbus (43235) *(G-5370)*

Animal Hospital Inc 440 946-2800
  2735 Som Center Rd Willoughby Hills (44094) *(G-15230)*

Animal Mgt Svcs Ohio Inc 248 398-6533
  267 S Lightner Rd Port Clinton (43452) *(G-12517)*

Animal Shelter Blemont CN, Saint Clairsville Also Called: Belmont County of Ohio *(G-12776)*

Animal Supply Company LLC 330 642-6037
  1630 Commerce Dr Orrville (44667) *(G-12155)*

Anishiv Inc 513 932-3034
  725 E Main St Lebanon (45036) *(G-9754)*

Anna Maria of Aurora (PA) 330 562-6171
  889 N Aurora Rd Aurora (44202) *(G-603)*

Anna Maria of Aurora Inc 330 562-3120
  849 Rural Rd Aurora (44202) *(G-604)*

Anne Camm, Psy.d., Company, Middletown Also Called: Primary Cr Ntwrk Prmr Hlth Prt *(G-11201)*

Anne Grady Corporation (PA) 419 380-8985
  1525 Eber Rd Holland (43528) *(G-9278)*

Anne Grady Corporation 419 867-7501
  1645 Trade Rd Holland (43528) *(G-9279)*

Annehurst Veterinary Hospital 614 818-4221
  25 Collegeview Rd Westerville (43081) *(G-14959)*

ANR Electric LLC 330 644-4454
  3783 State Rd Coventry Township (44203) *(G-7006)*

Anselmo Rssis Premier Prod Ltd 800 229-5517
  4500 Willow Pkwy Cleveland (44125) *(G-3818)*

Anspach Meeks Ellenberger LLP (PA) 419 447-6181
  25 S Huron St Toledo (43604) *(G-13689)*

Answercare LLC 855 213-1511
  4150 Belden Village St Nw Ste 307 Canton (44718) *(G-1667)*

Answernet Inc 978 710-5856
  411 Wolf Ledges Pkwy Ste 201 Akron (44311) *(G-51)*

Answernet Inc 877 864-2251
  120 E Mill St Akron (44308) *(G-52)*

Antares Management Solutions, Cleveland Also Called: Medical Mutual of Ohio *(G-4546)*

Antares Management Solutions, Strongsville Also Called: Medical Mutual Services LLC *(G-13475)*

Antero Resources Corporation 303 357-7310
  44510 Marietta Rd Caldwell (43724) *(G-1545)*

Antero Resources Corporation 740 760-1000
  27841 State Route 7 Marietta (45750) *(G-10356)*

Anthem, Cincinnati Also Called: Community Insurance Company *(G-2483)*

Anthem Insurance Companies Inc 330 492-2151
  4150 Belden Village St Nw Ste 506 Canton (44718) *(G-1668)*

Anthem Insurance Companies Inc 614 438-3542
  8940 Lyra Dr Columbus (43240) *(G-5246)*

Anthony Allega Cem Contr Inc 216 447-0814
  5146 Allega Way Richfield (44286) *(G-12687)*

Anthony Wayne Local Schools 419 877-0451
  6320 Industrial Pkwy Whitehouse (43571) *(G-15137)*

Anthony Wayne Trnsp Dept, Whitehouse Also Called: Anthony Wayne Local Schools *(G-15137)*

Antioch Cnnction Canton MI LLC 614 531-9285
  799 Windmiller Dr Pickerington (43147) *(G-12398)*

Antioch Salem Fields Frederick 614 531-9285
  799 Windmiller Dr Pickerington (43147) *(G-12399)*

Antioch University 937 769-1366
  1 Morgan Pl Yellow Springs (45387) *(G-15534)*

Antonine Ssters Adult Day Care 330 538-9822
  2675 N Lipkey Rd North Jackson (44451) *(G-11871)*

Antonio Sofo Son Importing Co (PA) 419 476-4211
  253 Waggoner Blvd Toledo (43612) *(G-13690)*

Antwerp Mnor Asssted Lving LLC 419 258-1500
  204 Archer Dr Antwerp (45813) *(G-447)*

Anytime Collect, Mentor Also Called: E2b Teknologies Inc *(G-10934)*

AP Cchmc 513 636-4200
  3333 Burnet Ave Cincinnati (45229) *(G-2206)*

Ap-Alternatives, Ridgeville Corners Also Called: APA Solar LLC *(G-12725)*

Ap/Aim Indpndnce Sites Trs LLC 216 986-9900
  5800 Rockside Woods Blvd N Independence (44131) *(G-9405)*

APA Solar LLC 419 267-5280
  20 345 County Road X Ridgeville Corners (43555) *(G-12725)*

ALPHABETIC SECTION — Arbors At Stow

Apbn Inc.. 724 964-8252
   670 Robinson Rd Campbell (44405) *(G-1591)*

Apc2 Inc (PA).. 513 231-5540
   6812 Clough Pike Cincinnati (45244) *(G-2207)*

Apco Industries Inc... 614 224-2345
   2030 Dividend Dr Columbus (43228) *(G-5371)*

Apco Window & Door Company, Columbus *Also Called: Apco Industries Inc (G-5371)*
Apec, Springboro *Also Called: Associated Prof Engrg Cons LLC (G-13193)*

Apec Engineering Inc.. 440 708-2303
   7416 Pettibone Rd Chagrin Falls (44023) *(G-1973)*

Apelles LLC.. 614 899-7322
   3700 Corporate Dr Ste 240 Columbus (43231) *(G-5372)*

Apex Control Systems Inc.. 330 938-2588
   751 N Johnson Rd Sebring (44672) *(G-12945)*

Apex Environmental LLC (PA)... 740 543-4389
   11 County Road 78 Amsterdam (43903) *(G-435)*

Apex Environmental Services L.. 513 772-2739
   19 E 72nd St Cincinnati (45216) *(G-2208)*

Apex Mortgage Services LLC.. 614 839-2739
   2550 Corporate Exchange Dr Ste 102 Columbus (43231) *(G-5373)*

Apex Payroll, Powell *Also Called: Apex Software Technologies Inc (G-12584)*

Apex Pest Control Service Inc... 440 461-6530
   26118 Broadway Ave Ste E Bedford (44146) *(G-953)*

Apex Restoration Contrs Ltd (PA)..................................... 513 489-1795
   6315 Warrick St Cincinnati (45227) *(G-2209)*

Apex Software Technologies Inc...................................... 614 932-2167
   445 Village Park Dr Powell (43065) *(G-12584)*

Apex Transit Solutions LLC... 216 938-5606
   805 E 70th St Cleveland (44103) *(G-3819)*

APM Management LLC.. 216 468-0050
   30195 Chagrin Blvd Ste 320n Pepper Pike (44124) *(G-12297)*

Apollo Heating & AC Inc... 513 271-3600
   4538 Camberwell Rd Cincinnati (45209) *(G-2210)*

Apostolic Christian Home Inc... 330 927-1010
   10680 Steiner Rd Rittman (44270) *(G-12729)*

Appalachian Fuels LLC (PA)... 606 928-0460
   6375 Riverside Dr Ste 200 Dublin (43017) *(G-7939)*

Appalachian Hardwood Lumber Co................................. 440 232-6767
   5433 Perkins Rd Cleveland (44146) *(G-3820)*

Appalachian Inc... 937 444-3043
   2280 Hales Way Williamsburg (45176) *(G-15176)*

Appalachian Power Company... 330 438-7102
   301 Cleveland Ave Sw Canton (44702) *(G-1669)*

Appalachian Power Company (HQ)................................... 614 716-1000
   1 Riverside Plz Columbus (43215) *(G-5374)*

Appalchian Bhvioral Healthcare, Athens *Also Called: Ohio Dept Mntal Hlth Addction (G-583)*

Appalchian Cmnty Vsting Nrse A...................................... 740 594-8226
   444 W Union St Ste C Athens (45701) *(G-555)*

Appearance Plus, Cincinnati *Also Called: Apc2 Inc (G-2207)*

Appelgren Ltd.. 330 945-6402
   3772 Wyoga Lake Rd Cuyahoga Falls (44224) *(G-7040)*

Apph, Strongsville *Also Called: Apph Wichita Inc (G-13442)*

Apph Wichita Inc... 316 943-5752
   15900 Foltz Pkwy Strongsville (44149) *(G-13442)*

Apple Farm Service Inc (PA)... 937 526-4851
   10120 W Versailles Rd Covington (45318) *(G-7017)*

Apple Farm Service Infc, Covington *Also Called: Apple Farm Service Inc (G-7017)*

Apple Growth Partners Inc (PA)....................................... 330 867-7350
   1540 W Market St Akron (44313) *(G-53)*

Apple Hospitality Five Inc.. 440 519-9500
   6085 Enterprise Pkwy Solon (44139) *(G-13066)*

Apple Sven Hospitality MGT Inc.. 513 248-4663
   600 Chamber Dr Milford (45150) *(G-11216)*

Apple Tree Homes, Mount Vernon *Also Called: Zandex Health Care Corporation (G-11511)*

Appleseed Cmnty Mntal Hlth Ctr....................................... 419 281-3716
   2233 Rocky Ln Ashland (44805) *(G-472)*

APPLESEED COUNSELING, Ashland *Also Called: Appleseed Cmnty Mntal Hlth Ctr (G-472)*

Applewood Centers Inc (PA).. 216 696-6815
   10427 Detroit Ave Cleveland (44102) *(G-3821)*

Applewood Centers Inc.. 216 696-5800
   2525 E 22nd St Cleveland (44115) *(G-3822)*

Applewood Centers Inc.. 216 521-6511
   10427 Detroit Ave Cleveland (44102) *(G-3823)*

Applewood Centers Inc.. 216 741-2241
   3518 W 25th St Cleveland (44109) *(G-3824)*

Applewood Centers Inc.. 440 324-1300
   1865 N Ridge Rd E Ste A Lorain (44055) *(G-10055)*

Appliance Warehouse Amer Inc.. 614 623-3131
   536 E Starr Ave Columbus (43201) *(G-5375)*

Applied Indus Tech - CA LLC (HQ)..................................... 216 426-4000
   1 Applied Plz Cleveland (44115) *(G-3825)*

Applied Indus Tech - Dixie Inc (HQ)................................. 216 426-4546
   1 Applied Plz Cleveland (44115) *(G-3826)*

Applied Industrial Tech, Cleveland *Also Called: Applied Indus Tech - CA LLC (G-3825)*
Applied Industrial Tech, Cleveland *Also Called: Applied Indus Tech - Dixie Inc (G-3826)*

Applied Industrial Tech Inc (PA)....................................... 216 426-4000
   1 Applied Plz Cleveland (44115) *(G-3827)*

Applied Mechanical Systems Inc (PA).............................. 937 854-3073
   5598 Wolf Creek Pike Dayton (45426) *(G-7176)*

Applied Medical Technology Inc.. 440 717-4000
   8006 Katherine Blvd Brecksville (44141) *(G-1343)*

Applied Mint Sups Slutions LLC (HQ)............................... 216 456-3600
   14790 Foltz Pkwy Strongsville (44149) *(G-13443)*

Applied Research Solutions Inc.. 937 912-6100
   51 Plum St Ste 240 Dayton (45440) *(G-7177)*

Applied Specialties Inc.. 440 933-9442
   33555 Pin Oak Pkwy Avon Lake (44012) *(G-671)*

Applied Technology Integration.. 419 537-9052
   3130 Executive Pkwy Fl 5 Toledo (43606) *(G-13691)*

Appraisal Research Corporation (PA).............................. 419 423-3582
   101 E Sandusky St Ste 408 Findlay (45840) *(G-8509)*

APPRISEN, Columbus *Also Called: Consumer Cr Cnsling Svc of Mdw (G-5687)*

Approved Networks LLC... 216 831-1800
   7575 E Pleasant Valley Rd Independence (44131) *(G-9406)*

April Enterprises Inc.. 937 293-7703
   5070 Lamme Rd Moraine (45439) *(G-11389)*

APS Acquisition LLC (DH)... 513 719-2600
   201 E 4th St Ste 900 Cincinnati (45202) *(G-2211)*

APS Medical Billing... 419 866-1804
   5620 Southwyck Blvd Toledo (43614) *(G-13692)*

Aptim Corp.. 419 423-3526
   16406 E Us Route 224 Findlay (45840) *(G-8510)*

Aptos LLC.. 614 840-1400
   400 Venture Dr Lewis Center (43035) *(G-9806)*

Aqua Doc Lake & Pond MGT, Chardon *Also Called: Stat Integrated Tech Inc (G-2021)*

Aqua Ohio Inc.. 440 255-3984
   8644 Station St Mentor (44060) *(G-10912)*

Aqua Tech Envmtl Labs Inc (PA).. 740 389-5991
   1776 Marion Waldo Rd Marion (43302) *(G-10417)*

ARA-Bexley LLC.. 614 253-3300
   1805 E Main St Columbus (43205) *(G-5376)*

Aramark... 614 921-7495
   2800 Walker Rd Hilliard (43026) *(G-9179)*

Aramark, Cincinnati *Also Called: Vestis Corporation (G-3625)*
Aramark, Cleveland *Also Called: Aramark Facility Services LLC (G-3828)*
Aramark, Cleveland *Also Called: Vestis Corporation (G-5100)*
Aramark, Columbus *Also Called: Vestis Corporation (G-6847)*
Aramark, Dayton *Also Called: Vestis Corporation (G-7703)*
Aramark, Hilliard *Also Called: Aramark (G-9179)*
Aramark, Toledo *Also Called: Vestis Corporation (G-14092)*

Aramark Facility Services LLC.. 216 687-5000
   2121 Euclid Ave Cleveland (44115) *(G-3828)*

Arbor Construction Co Inc... 216 360-8989
   1350 W 3rd St Cleveland (44113) *(G-3829)*

Arbor Rehabilitation & Healtcr.. 440 423-0206
   45125 Fairmount Blvd Gates Mills (44040) *(G-8781)*

Arbor View Family Medicine Inc....................................... 740 687-3386
   1941 W Fair Ave Lancaster (43130) *(G-9695)*

Arbors At Fairlawn, Fairlawn *Also Called: Fairlawn Opco LLC (G-8479)*
Arbors At London, London *Also Called: Saber Healthcare Group LLC (G-10050)*
Arbors At Stow, Stow *Also Called: Stow Opco LLC (G-13394)*

Arbors At Streetsboro, Streetsboro *Also Called: Streetsboro Opco LLC* **(G-13430)**

Arbors At Woodsfield, Woodsfield *Also Called: Woodsfield Opco LLC* **(G-15304)**

Arbors East LLC... 614 575-9003
5500 E Broad St Columbus (43213) **(G-5377)**

Arbors West LLC... 614 879-7661
375 W Main St West Jefferson (43162) **(G-14848)**

ARBORS WEST SUBACUTE & REHABIL, West Jefferson *Also Called: Arbors West LLC* **(G-14848)**

Arbys... 740 369-0317
7259 E State Route 37 Sunbury (43074) **(G-13517)**

ARC Document Solutions Inc... 216 281-1234
3666 Carnegie Ave Cleveland (44115) **(G-3830)**

ARC Healthcare LLC... 888 552-0677
6877 N High St Ste 100 Worthington (43085) **(G-15405)**

ARC Indstries Inc Frnklin Cnty (PA).................................... 614 479-2500
2780 Airport Dr Columbus (43219) **(G-5378)**

ARC Indstries Inc Frnklin Cnty... 614 436-4800
6633 Doubletree Ave Columbus (43229) **(G-5379)**

ARC Indstries Inc Frnklin Cnty... 614 864-2406
909 Taylor Station Rd Columbus (43230) **(G-5380)**

ARC Indstries Inc Frnklin Cnty... 614 267-1207
250 W Dodridge St Columbus (43202) **(G-5381)**

ARC Indstries Inc Frnklin Cnty... 614 836-6050
4200 Bixby Rd Groveport (43125) **(G-8970)**

ARC Indstries Inc Frnklin Cnty... 614 836-0700
4395 Marketing Pl Groveport (43125) **(G-8971)**

ARC Industreis East, Columbus *Also Called: ARC Indstries Inc Frnklin Cnty* **(G-5380)**

ARC Industries North, Columbus *Also Called: ARC Indstries Inc Frnklin Cnty* **(G-5379)**

ARC Industries South, Groveport *Also Called: ARC Indstries Inc Frnklin Cnty* **(G-8971)**

ARC Industries West, Columbus *Also Called: ARC Indstries Inc Frnklin Cnty* **(G-5381)**

Arcadia Health Care, Akron *Also Called: Arcadia Services Inc* **(G-54)**

Arcadia Services Inc... 330 869-9520
1650 W Market St Ste 27 Akron (44313) **(G-54)**

Arcadia Services Inc... 937 912-5800
2440 Dayton Xenia Rd Ste C Beavercreek (45434) **(G-857)**

Arcadis A California Partnr... 614 818-4900
8101 N High St Ste 100 Columbus (43235) **(G-5382)**

Arcadis Engrg Svcs USA Inc (DH)...................................... 614 818-4900
8101 N High St Ste 100 Columbus (43235) **(G-5383)**

Arcelormittal Tubular Pdts USA, Marion *Also Called: Arcelrmttal Tblar Pdts Mrion I* **(G-10418)**

Arcelrmttal Tblar Pdts Mrion I... 740 382-3979
686 W Fairground St Marion (43302) **(G-10418)**

Arcfield, Brook Park *Also Called: Analex Corporation* **(G-1405)**

Archbishop Leibold Home, Cincinnati *Also Called: Little Ssters of Poor Bltmore* **(G-2982)**

Archbold Hospital, Archbold *Also Called: Community Hsptals Wllness Ctrs* **(G-456)**

Archdiocese of Cincinnati.. 513 729-1725
9375 Winton Rd Cincinnati (45231) **(G-2212)**

Archdiocese of Cincinnati.. 513 489-0300
11000 Montgomery Rd Cincinnati (45249) **(G-2213)**

Archdiocese of Cincinnati.. 513 779-6585
6085 Jackie Dr Middletown (45044) **(G-11152)**

Archdiocese of Cincinnati.. 937 325-8715
701 E Columbia St Springfield (45503) **(G-13218)**

Archer Corporation.. 330 455-9955
1917 Henry Ave Sw Canton (44706) **(G-1670)**

Archer Sign, Canton *Also Called: Archer Corporation* **(G-1670)**

Archiable Electric Company.. 513 621-1707
3803 Ford Cir Cincinnati (45227) **(G-2214)**

Architctral Intr Rstrtions Inc... 216 241-2455
2401 Train Ave Ste 100 Cleveland (44113) **(G-3831)**

Archway Marketing Services Inc....................................... 440 572-0725
20770 Westwood Dr Strongsville (44149) **(G-13444)**

Arco Heating & AC Co (PA).. 216 663-3211
5325 Naiman Pkwy Ste J Solon (44139) **(G-13067)**

Arconic Wheel Wheel Forge... 479 750-6359
5801 Postal Rd Cleveland (44181) **(G-3832)**

Arcos LLC (PA)... 614 396-5500
445 Hutchinson Ave Ste 600 Columbus (43235) **(G-5384)**

Arctech Fabricating Inc (PA).. 937 525-9363
1317 Lagonda Ave Springfield (45503) **(G-13219)**

Arctic Express Inc... 614 876-4008
4277 Lyman Dr Hilliard (43026) **(G-9180)**

Arctos Mission Solutions LLC... 813 609-5591
2601 Mission Point Blvd Beavercreek (45431) **(G-858)**

Arctos Tech Solutions LLC (DH)....................................... 937 426-2808
2601 Mission Point Blvd Ste 300 Beavercreek (45431) **(G-859)**

Ardent Technologies Inc.. 937 312-1345
6234 Far Hills Ave Dayton (45459) **(G-7178)**

Ardmore Inc... 330 535-2601
981 E Market St Akron (44305) **(G-55)**

Ardmore Logistics, Westlake *Also Called: Ardmore Power Logistics LLC* **(G-15034)**

Ardmore Power Logistics LLC... 216 502-0640
24610 Detroit Rd Ste 1200 Westlake (44145) **(G-15034)**

ARE Inc... 330 830-7800
400 Nave Rd Sw Massillon (44646) **(G-10631)**

Area Agcy On Aging Plg Svc Are....................................... 800 258-7277
40 W 2nd St Ste 400 Dayton (45402) **(G-7179)**

Area Agency On Aging, Cambridge *Also Called: Area Agency On Aging Reg 9 Inc* **(G-1554)**

Area Agency On Aging, Marietta *Also Called: Buckeye Hills-Hck Vly Reg Dev* **(G-10360)**

Area Agency On Aging Dst 7 Inc.. 740 446-7000
1167 State Route 160 Gallipolis (45631) **(G-8752)**

Area Agency On Aging Dst 7 Inc (PA)................................ 800 582-7277
160 Dorsey Dr Rio Grande (45674) **(G-12726)**

Area Agency On Aging Dst 7 Inc.. 740 245-5306
123 W Main St West Union (45693) **(G-14866)**

AREA AGENCY ON AGING P S A 2, Dayton *Also Called: Area Agcy On Aging Plg Svc Are* **(G-7179)**

Area Agency On Aging Reg 9 Inc....................................... 740 439-4478
710 Wheeling Ave Cambridge (43725) **(G-1554)**

Area Energy & Electric Inc (PA)... 937 498-4784
2001 Commerce Dr Sidney (45365) **(G-13019)**

Area Office On Aging Nrthwster.. 419 382-0624
2155 Arlington Ave Toledo (43609) **(G-13693)**

Area Temps, Independence *Also Called: Area Temps Inc* **(G-9407)**

Area Temps Inc.. 440 842-2100
5805 Pearl Rd Cleveland (44130) **(G-3833)**

Area Temps Inc (PA).. 216 781-5350
4511 Rockside Rd Ste 190 Independence (44131) **(G-9407)**

Area Temps Inc.. 216 227-8200
14801 Detroit Ave Lakewood (44107) **(G-9658)**

Area Temps Inc.. 216 518-2000
15689 Broadway Ave Maple Heights (44137) **(G-10333)**

Area Temps Inc.. 440 975-4400
7288 Mentor Ave Mentor (44060) **(G-10913)**

Area Wide Protective, North Canton *Also Called: Awp Inc* **(G-11813)**

Arena Horse Shows LLC (PA).. 937 382-0985
4095 State Route 730 Wilmington (45177) **(G-15245)**

Arena Horse Shows Ocala LLC... 239 275-2314
600 Gilliam Rd Wilmington (45177) **(G-15246)**

Arena Management Holdings LLC.................................... 513 421-4111
100 Broadway St Ste 300 Cincinnati (45202) **(G-2215)**

Arett Sales Corp.. 937 552-2005
1261 Brukner Dr Troy (45373) **(G-14129)**

ARETT SALES CORP, Troy *Also Called: Arett Sales Corp* **(G-14129)**

Argo Tech Fluid Elec Dist Div, Cleveland *Also Called: Eaton Industrial Corporation* **(G-4204)**

Argo-Hytos Inc... 419 353-6070
1835 N Research Dr Bowling Green (43402) **(G-1303)**

Aris Horticulture Inc (PA)... 330 745-2143
115 3rd St Se Barberton (44203) **(G-693)**

Arise Incorporated.. 440 746-8860
7000 S Edgerton Rd Ste 100 Brecksville (44141) **(G-1344)**

Arista Home Care Solutions, Toledo *Also Called: Pace Plus Corp* **(G-13955)**

Aristcrat Brea Sklled Nrsing R, Berea *Also Called: Front Leasing Co LLC* **(G-1070)**

Aristocrat W Nursing Hm Corp.. 216 252-7730
4401 W 150th St Cleveland (44135) **(G-3834)**

Ark of Medina County, The, Seville *Also Called: Society For Hndcpped Ctzens of* **(G-12965)**

Arledge Construction Inc... 614 732-4258
2460 Performance Way Columbus (43207) **(G-5385)**

Arlette Child Family Rese, Cincinnati *Also Called: University of Cincinnati* **(G-3593)**

Arling Lumber Incorporated... 513 451-5700
771 Neeb Rd Cincinnati (45233) **(G-2216)**

ALPHABETIC SECTION

Ashtabula County Medical Ctr

Arlington Care Ctr.. 740 344-0303
98 S 30th St Newark (43055) *(G-11688)*

Arlington Commercial Supply, Toledo *Also Called: Wichman Co (G-14107)*

Arlington Crt Nrsing HM Svc In (PA)...................... 614 545-5502
1605 Nw Professional Plz Upper Arlington (43220) *(G-14276)*

Arlington Crt Sklled Nrsing Rh, Upper Arlington *Also Called: Arlington Crt Nrsing HM Svc In (G-14276)*

ARLINGTON MEMORIAL GARDENS, TH, Cincinnati *Also Called: Arlington Memorial Grdns Assn (G-2217)*

Arlington Memorial Grdns Assn................................ 513 521-7003
2145 Compton Rd Cincinnati (45231) *(G-2217)*

Arlington Nursing Home, Newark *Also Called: Arlington Care Ctr (G-11688)*

Arlington-Blaine Lumber Co, Delaware *Also Called: Khempco Bldg Sup Co Ltd Partnr (G-7811)*

Armada Ltd.. 614 505-7256
23 Clairedan Dr Powell (43065) *(G-12585)*

Armaly Brands, London *Also Called: Armaly LLC (G-10037)*

Armaly LLC... 740 852-3621
110 W 1st St London (43140) *(G-10037)*

Armcorp Construction Inc....................................... 419 778-7024
8511 State Route 703 Celina (45822) *(G-1916)*

Armeton US Co... 419 660-9296
205 Republic St Norwalk (44857) *(G-12001)*

Armor Consolidated Inc (PA)................................. 513 923-5260
4600 N Mason Montgomery Rd Mason (45040) *(G-10520)*

Armour, Brookpark *Also Called: Smithfield Direct LLC (G-1439)*

Arms Trucking Co Inc (PA).................................... 800 362-1343
14818 Mayfield Rd Huntsburg (44046) *(G-9380)*

Armstrong Cable Service, Medina *Also Called: Armstrong Utilities Inc (G-10808)*

Armstrong Cable Services, North Lima *Also Called: Armstrong Utilities Inc (G-11881)*

Armstrong Steel Erectors Inc................................. 740 345-4503
50 S 4th St Newark (43055) *(G-11689)*

Armstrong Utilities Inc... 330 723-3536
1141 Lafayette Rd Medina (44256) *(G-10808)*

Armstrong Utilities Inc... 330 758-6411
9328 Woodworth Rd North Lima (44452) *(G-11881)*

Arnold Company, Valley City *Also Called: Arnold Corporation (G-14331)*

Arnold Corporation.. 330 225-2600
5965 Grafton Rd Valley City (44280) *(G-14331)*

Arnold's Landscaping, Ontario *Also Called: Dta Inc (G-12103)*

Arpita LLC.. 614 443-6506
920 S High St Columbus (43206) *(G-5386)*

Array Information Tech Inc..................................... 937 203-3209
2689 Commons Blvd Ste 105 Beavercreek (45431) *(G-860)*

Arrc One LLC... 440 754-0855
55 S Main St Pmb 107 Oberlin (44074) *(G-12063)*

Arrow Electronics Inc.. 440 349-1300
5440 Naiman Pkwy Solon (44139) *(G-13068)*

Arrow Wine & Spirits, Dayton *Also Called: Arrow Wine Stores Inc (G-7180)*

Arrow Wine Stores Inc... 937 433-6778
615 Lyons Rd Dayton (45459) *(G-7180)*

Arrowhead Behavioral Hlth LLC............................ 419 891-9333
1725 Timber Line Rd Maumee (43537) *(G-10695)*

Arrowhead Park Golf Club Inc.............................. 419 628-2444
2211 Dirksen Rd Minster (45865) *(G-11315)*

ARS, Cincinnati *Also Called: American Risk Services LLC (G-2187)*

ARS Aleut Construction LLC................................. 225 381-2991
1071 Fishinger Rd Ste 102& Columbus (43221) *(G-5387)*

Art, Bryan *Also Called: Advanced Rhbilitation Tech Ltd (G-1477)*

Artemis Ctr For Altrntves To D (PA)..................... 937 461-5091
310 W Monument Ave Dayton (45402) *(G-7181)*

Artemis Fine Art Services, Akron *Also Called: Artemis Fine Arts Inc (G-56)*

Artemis Fine Arts Inc... 214 357-2577
320 Ely Rd Akron (44313) *(G-56)*

Arthur G Jmes Cncer Hosp Rchar........................ 614 293-4878
460 W 10th Ave Columbus (43210) *(G-5388)*

Arthur G Jmes Cncer Hosp RES I........................ 614 293-3300
300 W 10th Ave Columbus (43210) *(G-5389)*

Arthur Mddlton Cpitl Hldngs In (PA)..................... 330 966-9000
8000 Freedom Ave Nw North Canton (44720) *(G-11812)*

Artisan and Truckers Cslty Co............................... 440 461-5000
6300 Wilson Mills Rd Cleveland (44143) *(G-3835)*

ARTSWAVE, Cincinnati *Also Called: Cincinnati Institute Fine Arts (G-2413)*

Artwall LLC.. 216 476-0635
4700 Lakeside Ave E Fl 3 Cleveland (44114) *(G-3836)*

Arvind Sagar Inc.. 614 428-8800
2880 Airport Dr Columbus (43219) *(G-5390)*

As Automotive Systems, Valley City *Also Called: Luk-Aftermarket Service Inc (G-14335)*

As Logistics Inc (DH)... 513 863-4627
7570 Bales St Ste 310 Liberty Township (45069) *(G-9847)*

Asana Hospice Cleveland LLC............................... 419 903-0300
885 W Bagley Rd Berea (44017) *(G-1061)*

Asana Hospice Palliative Care, Berea *Also Called: Asana Hospice Cleveland LLC (G-1061)*

ASC Group Inc (PA)... 614 268-2514
800 Freeway Dr N Ste 101 Columbus (43229) *(G-5391)*

ASC of Cincinnati Inc... 513 886-7100
4028 Binion Way Lebanon (45036) *(G-9755)*

ASC- Orrville, Orrville *Also Called: Animal Supply Company LLC (G-12155)*

ASC/Auxano, Columbus *Also Called: ASC Group Inc (G-5391)*

Ascendum Solutions, Blue Ash *Also Called: Ascendum Solutions LLC (G-1131)*

Ascendum Solutions LLC (HQ)............................ 513 792-5100
10290 Alliance Rd Blue Ash (45242) *(G-1131)*

Ascent Global Logistics LLC................................. 330 342-8700
5876 Darrow Rd Hudson (44236) *(G-9332)*

Ascent Globl Lgstics Hldngs In (PA).................... 603 881-3350
5876 Darrow Rd Hudson (44236) *(G-9333)*

Ash Brothers Home Health Care........................... 614 882-3600
635 Park Meadow Rd Ste 115 Westerville (43081) *(G-14960)*

Ashford Trs Clumbus Easton LLC........................ 614 473-9911
4150 Stelzer Rd Columbus (43230) *(G-5392)*

Ashland Aqualon Functional Ingredients............. 614 790-3333
5200 Blazer Pkwy Dublin (43017) *(G-7940)*

Ashland Chemco Inc... 614 232-8510
802 Harmon Ave Columbus (43223) *(G-5393)*

Ashland Chemco Inc... 614 790-3333
1979 Atlas St Columbus (43228) *(G-5394)*

Ashland City School District................................. 419 289-7967
850 Jackson Dr Ashland (44805) *(G-473)*

Ashland Cleaning LLC.. 419 281-1747
1965 S Baney Rd Ashland (44805) *(G-474)*

Ashland Distribution, Columbus *Also Called: Ashland Chemco Inc (G-5394)*

Ashland Home Towne Phrm Inc............................ 419 281-4040
849 Smith Rd Ashland (44805) *(G-475)*

Ashland Hospital Corporation................................ 740 894-2080
384 County Road 120 S South Point (45680) *(G-13173)*

Ashland Performance Materials, Columbus *Also Called: Ashland Chemco Inc (G-5393)*

Ashland Training Center.. 419 281-2767
228 Maple St Ashland (44805) *(G-476)*

Ashley Enterprises LLC (PA)................................. 330 726-5790
1419 Boardman Canfield Rd Ste 500 Boardman (44512) *(G-1284)*

Ashtabula Area City School Dst............................ 440 992-1221
5921 Gerald Rd Ashtabula (44004) *(G-517)*

Ashtabula Clinic Inc (PA)...................................... 440 997-6980
2422 Lake Ave Ashtabula (44004) *(G-518)*

Ashtabula Cnty Chldren Svcs Bd, Ashtabula *Also Called: County of Ashtabula (G-531)*

Ashtabula Cnty Cmnty Action AG......................... 440 997-1721
6920 Austinburg Rd Ashtabula (44004) *(G-519)*

Ashtabula Cnty Eductl Svc Ctr............................. 440 576-4085
2630 W 13th St Ste A Ashtabula (44004) *(G-520)*

Ashtabula Cnty Rsdntial Svcs C (PA)................... 440 593-6404
29 Parrish Rd Conneaut (44030) *(G-6938)*

Ashtabula County Commnty Actn (PA)................ 440 997-1721
6920 Austinburg Rd Ashtabula (44004) *(G-521)*

Ashtabula County Highway Dept, Jefferson *Also Called: County of Ashtabula (G-9538)*

Ashtabula County Medical Ctr (PA)...................... 440 997-2262
2420 Lake Ave Ashtabula (44004) *(G-522)*

Ashtabula County Medical Ctr.............................. 440 997-6960
2422 Lake Ave Ashtabula (44004) *(G-523)*

Ashtabula County Medical Ctr.............................. 440 997-6680
2515 Lake Ave Ashtabula (44004) *(G-524)*

Ashtabula Dental Assoc Inc 440 992-3146
5005 State Rd Ashtabula (44004) *(G-525)*

Ashtabula Rgional Hm Hlth Svcs 440 992-4663
2131 Lake Ave Ste 2 Ashtabula (44004) *(G-526)*

Asi Chemical Company, Avon Lake *Also Called: Applied Specialties Inc (G-671)*

Asi Commercial Roofg Maint Inc 614 873-2057
8633 Memorial Dr Plain City (43064) *(G-12468)*

Asi Technical Services, Cincinnati *Also Called: Atm Solutions Inc (G-2228)*

Ask Childrens, Akron *Also Called: Childrens Hosp Med Ctr Akron (G-90)*

Asm International 440 338-5151
9639 Kinsman Rd Novelty (44073) *(G-12037)*

Asnt Certification Svcs LLC 614 274-6003
1711 Arlingate Ln Columbus (43228) *(G-5395)*

Aspc Corp 937 593-7010
1 Hunter Pl Bellefontaine (43311) *(G-1019)*

Aspca 646 596-0321
782 Wager St Columbus (43206) *(G-5396)*

Aspen Dental, Macedonia *Also Called: Lakireddy Dental LLC (G-10198)*

Aspen Energy Corporation 614 884-5300
4789 Rings Rd Ste 100 Dublin (43017) *(G-7941)*

Aspen Management Usa LLC (PA) 419 281-3367
1566 County Road 1095 Ashland (44805) *(G-477)*

Aspen Village Apartments, Cincinnati *Also Called: Fath Management Company (G-2649)*

Aspire Energy of Ohio LLC (HQ) 330 682-7726
300 Tracy Bridge Rd Orrville (44667) *(G-12156)*

Asplundh, Millersport *Also Called: Asplundh Tree Expert LLC (G-11297)*

Asplundh Tree Expert LLC 740 467-1028
12488 Lancaster St Bldg 94 Millersport (43046) *(G-11297)*

Assembly Child Care, Mansfield *Also Called: First Assembly Child Care (G-10263)*

Asset Solutions, Cincinnati *Also Called: Loth Inc (G-2989)*

Assisted Care By Black Stone, Cincinnati *Also Called: Black Stone Cincinnati LLC (G-2264)*

Assisted Living Apartments, Lorain *Also Called: Autumn Aegis Inc (G-10056)*

Assisted Living Concepts LLC 419 334-6962
805 S Buchanan St Ofc Fremont (43420) *(G-8667)*

Associated Bank 513 246-2200
312 Walnut St Ste 3450 Cincinnati (45202) *(G-2218)*

Associated Credit Service Inc 419 524-6446
6 Plymouth St Mansfield (44904) *(G-10244)*

Associated Estates Realty Corporation 216 261-5000
1 Integrity Pkwy Richmond Heights (44143) *(G-12715)*

Associated Home Health Inc 740 264-6311
2199 Ste B Steubenville (43952) *(G-13316)*

Associated Materials LLC (PA) 330 929-1811
3773 State Rd Cuyahoga Falls (44223) *(G-7041)*

Associated Materials Fin Inc 330 922-7624
3773 State Rd Cuyahoga Falls (44223) *(G-7042)*

Associated Materials Group Inc (PA) 330 929-1811
3773 State Rd Cuyahoga Falls (44223) *(G-7043)*

Associated Mtls Holdings LLC 330 929-1811
3773 State Rd Cuyahoga Falls (44223) *(G-7044)*

Associated Premium Corporation 513 679-4444
1870 Summit Rd Cincinnati (45237) *(G-2219)*

Associated Prof Engrg Cons LLC 937 746-4600
204 Hiawatha Trl Springboro (45066) *(G-13193)*

Associates In Dermatology Inc (PA) 440 249-0274
2205 Crocker Rd Westlake (44145) *(G-15035)*

Associates In Nephrology Ltd 330 729-1355
7153 Tiffany Blvd Youngstown (44514) *(G-15552)*

Assocted Spclsts of Intrnal MD 937 208-7272
7707 Paragon Rd Ste 101 Dayton (45459) *(G-7182)*

Assoction For Dvlpmntlly Dsble 614 447-0606
1915 E Cooke Rd Columbus (43224) *(G-5397)*

Assoction For Dvlpmntlly Dsble (PA) 614 486-4361
769 Brooksedge Blvd Westerville (43081) *(G-14961)*

Assumption Village 330 549-2434
9800 Market St North Lima (44452) *(G-11882)*

Assuramed, Twinsburg *Also Called: Assuramed Inc (G-14171)*

Assuramed Inc (HQ) 330 963-6998
1810 Summit Commerce Park Twinsburg (44087) *(G-14171)*

Assurecare LLC 513 618-2150
250 W Court St Ste 450e Cincinnati (45202) *(G-2220)*

Assured Performance Coop, Akron *Also Called: Oeconnection LLC (G-246)*

Astoria Health & Rehab Center, Germantown *Also Called: Astoria Healthcare Group LLC (G-8803)*

Astoria Healthcare Group LLC 937 855-2363
300 Astoria Rd Germantown (45327) *(G-8803)*

Astoria Place Cincinnati LLC 513 961-8881
3627 Harvey Ave Cincinnati (45229) *(G-2221)*

Astoria Place Columbus LLC 614 228-5900
44 S Souder Ave Columbus (43222) *(G-5398)*

Astoria Place of Clyde LLC 419 547-9595
700 Helen St Clyde (43410) *(G-5198)*

Astoria Place Silverton LLC 513 793-2090
6922 Ohio Ave Cincinnati (45236) *(G-2222)*

Astoria Snf Inc 330 455-5500
3537 12th St Nw Canton (44708) *(G-1671)*

Asw Akron Logistic, Canton *Also Called: Asw Global LLC (G-1672)*

Asw Global LLC 330 899-1003
2150 International Pkwy Canton (44720) *(G-1672)*

Asw Global LLC (PA) 330 733-6291
3375 Gilchrist Rd Mogadore (44260) *(G-11322)*

Asw Global LLC 330 798-5184
3325 Gilchrist Rd Mogadore (44260) *(G-11323)*

Asw Supply Chain Service, Mogadore *Also Called: Asw Global LLC (G-11323)*

At Holdings Corporation 216 692-6000
23555 Euclid Ave Cleveland (44117) *(G-3837)*

At Hospitality LLC 513 527-9962
5375 Medpace Way Cincinnati (45227) *(G-2223)*

At Systems, Columbus *Also Called: Garda CL Great Lakes Inc (G-5910)*

AT&T, Beavercreek *Also Called: Tyto Government Solutions Inc (G-911)*

AT&T, Columbus *Also Called: AT&T Corp (G-5399)*

AT&T, Elyria *Also Called: New Cingular Wireless Svcs Inc (G-8280)*

AT&T, Independence *Also Called: New Cingular Wireless Svcs Inc (G-9458)*

AT&T, Mentor *Also Called: New Cingular Wireless Svcs Inc (G-10979)*

AT&T, Toledo *Also Called: New Cingular Wireless Svcs Inc (G-13934)*

AT&T, Uniontown *Also Called: Yp LLC (G-14273)*

AT&T, Vickery *Also Called: AT&T Corp (G-14418)*

AT&T Corp 513 407-4446
11711 Princeton Pike Cincinnati (45246) *(G-2224)*

AT&T Corp 614 223-8236
150 E Gay St Ste 4a Columbus (43215) *(G-5399)*

AT&T Corp 419 547-0578
1591 County Road 260 Vickery (43464) *(G-14418)*

AT&T Corp., Cincinnati *Also Called: AT&T Corp (G-2224)*

AT&T Ohio, Brecksville *Also Called: Ohio Bell Telephone Company (G-1360)*

AT&T Teleholdings Inc 330 385-9967
214 W 5th St East Liverpool (43920) *(G-8178)*

AT&T Wireless, Columbus *Also Called: New Cingular Wireless Svcs Inc (G-5272)*

Atalian US Ohio Valley Inc (DH) 614 476-1818
646 Parsons Ave Columbus (43206) *(G-5400)*

Atech Motorsports, Tallmadge *Also Called: Autosales Incorporated (G-13586)*

Atel, Marion *Also Called: Aqua Tech Envmtl Labs Inc (G-10417)*

Aten & Mennetti Insurance Agcy, Wooster *Also Called: Whitaker-Myers Insur Agcy Inc (G-15388)*

Athens OH State 405 LLC 740 593-5600
986 E State St Athens (45701) *(G-556)*

ATHENS COUNTRY CLUB, Athens *Also Called: Athens Golf & Country Club (G-558)*

Athens County Board of Dev (PA) 740 594-3539
801 W Union St Athens (45701) *(G-557)*

Athens Golf & Country Club (PA) 740 592-1655
7606 Country Club Rd Athens (45701) *(G-558)*

Athens Mold and Machine Inc 740 593-6613
180 Mill St Athens (45701) *(G-559)*

Athens Surgery Center Ltd 740 566-4504
75 Hospital Dr Ste 100 Athens (45701) *(G-560)*

Athletes In Action, Xenia *Also Called: Athletes In Action Spt Cmplex (G-15499)*

Athletes In Action Spt Cmplex (HQ) 937 352-1000
651 Taylor Dr Xenia (45385) *(G-15499)*

Athletic Trining Solutions LLC 513 295-1756
7430 Bridge Point Pass Cincinnati (45248) *(G-2225)*

ALPHABETIC SECTION   Automated Control & Power

Athletics Dept, Cincinnati *Also Called: University of Cincinnati (G-3586)*

ATI, Toledo *Also Called: Abbott Tool Inc (G-13673)*

ATI, Toledo *Also Called: Applied Technology Integration (G-13691)*

Atkins & Stang Inc 513 242-8300
1031 Meta Dr Cincinnati (45237) *(G-2226)*

Atlantic Fish & Distrg Co 330 454-1307
430 6th St Se Canton (44702) *(G-1673)*

Atlantic Food Distributors, Canton *Also Called: Atlantic Fish & Distrg Co (G-1673)*

Atlantic Foods Corp 513 772-3535
1999 Section Rd Cincinnati (45237) *(G-2227)*

Atlantis Company, The, Cleveland *Also Called: Atlantis Security Company (G-3838)*

Atlantis Security Company (PA) 440 717-7050
105 Ken Mar Industrial Pkwy Cleveland (44147) *(G-3838)*

Atlas Bolt & Screw Company LLC (DH) 419 289-6171
1628 Troy Rd Ashland (44805) *(G-478)*

Atlas Butler Heating & Cooling, Columbus *Also Called: Atlas Capital Services Inc (G-5401)*

Atlas Capital Services Inc (PA) 614 294-7373
4849 Evanswood Dr Columbus (43229) *(G-5401)*

Atlas Construction Company 614 475-2282
4672 Friendship Dr Columbus (43230) *(G-5402)*

Atlas Fasteners For Cnstr, Ashland *Also Called: Atlas Bolt & Screw Company LLC (G-478)*

Atlas Industrial Contractors, Columbus *Also Called: Atlas Industrial Contrs LLC (G-5403)*

Atlas Industrial Contrs LLC (HQ) 614 841-4500
5275 Sinclair Rd Columbus (43229) *(G-5403)*

Atlas Machine and Supply Inc 502 584-7262
8556 Trade Center Dr # 250 Hamilton (45011) *(G-9017)*

Atlas Partners LLC 937 439-7970
7750 Paragon Rd Dayton (45459) *(G-7183)*

Atlas Steel Products Co (PA) 330 425-1600
7990 Bavaria Rd Twinsburg (44087) *(G-14172)*

Atlas Transportation LLC 202 963-4241
799 N Court St Ste 16 Medina (44256) *(G-10809)*

Atm Solutions Inc (PA) 513 742-4900
551 Northland Blvd Cincinnati (45240) *(G-2228)*

Atmos 360 A Systems Solutions, West Chester *Also Called: Atmos360 Inc (G-14799)*

Atmos360 Inc 513 772-4777
4690 Interstate Dr Ste A West Chester (45246) *(G-14799)*

Atos It Solutions and Svcs Inc 513 336-1000
4705 Duke Dr Mason (45040) *(G-10521)*

Atrium Apparel Corporation 740 966-8200
188 Commerce Blvd Johnstown (43031) *(G-9544)*

Atrium Buying Corporation 740 966-8200
1010 Jackson Hole Dr Ste 100 Blacklick (43004) *(G-1110)*

Atrium Centers Inc (PA) 614 416-0600
2550 Corporate Exchange Dr Ste 200 Columbus (43231) *(G-5404)*

Atrium Living Centers of Eastern Indiana Inc (HQ) ... 614 416-2662
2780 Airport Dr Columbus (43219) *(G-5405)*

Atrium Living Ctrs Eastrn In, Columbus *Also Called: Atrium Living Centers of Eastern Indiana Inc (G-5405)*

Atrium Medical Center 513 424-2111
40 W 4th St Ste 525 Dayton (45402) *(G-7184)*

Atrium Medical Center (DH) 513 424-2111
1 Medical Center Dr Middletown (45044) *(G-11153)*

Ats Carolina Inc 803 324-9300
425 Enterprise Dr Lewis Center (43035) *(G-9807)*

Ats Ohio, Lewis Center *Also Called: Automation Tooling Systems (G-9810)*

Ats Systems Oregon Inc 541 738-0932
425 Enterprise Dr Lewis Center (43035) *(G-9808)*

Ats Transportation Services, Cincinnati *Also Called: Advance Trnsp Systems Inc (G-2147)*

ATSG, Wilmington *Also Called: Air Transport Svcs Group Inc (G-15240)*

Attari Delivery LLC 443 251-8172
5533 Southwyck Blvd Ste 101 Toledo (43614) *(G-13694)*

Attorneys-At-Law, Dayton *Also Called: Porter Wrght Morris Arthur LLP (G-7558)*

Atwood Lake Park, Mineral City *Also Called: Muskingum Wtrshed Cnsrvncy Dst (G-11301)*

Atwood Rope Manufacturing Inc 614 920-0534
121 N Trine St Canal Winchester (43110) *(G-1598)*

Audi Willoughby, Mentor *Also Called: Pag Mentor A1 Inc (G-10982)*

Auglaize County Board of Mr/Dd, New Bremen *Also Called: County of Auglaize (G-11596)*

August Corso Sons Inc 419 626-0765
3404 Milan Rd Sandusky (44870) *(G-12863)*

August Groh & Sons Inc 513 821-0090
8832 Reading Rd Cincinnati (45215) *(G-2229)*

August Mack Environmental Inc 740 548-1500
7830 N Central Dr Ste B Lewis Center (43035) *(G-9809)*

Aultcare, Canton *Also Called: Aultcare Insurance Company (G-1676)*

Aultcare Corp 330 363-6360
2600 6th St Sw Canton (44710) *(G-1674)*

Aultcare Holding Company 330 452-9911
2600 6th St Sw Canton (44710) *(G-1675)*

Aultcare Insurance Company 330 363-6360
2600 6th St Sw Canton (44710) *(G-1676)*

Aultman Health Foundation 330 305-6999
6100 Whipple Ave Nw Canton (44720) *(G-1677)*

Aultman Health Foundation (PA) 330 452-9911
2600 6th St Sw Canton (44710) *(G-1678)*

Aultman Health Foundation 330 875-6050
1925 Williamsburg Way Ne Louisville (44641) *(G-10113)*

Aultman Health Foundation 330 682-3010
832 S Main St Orrville (44667) *(G-12157)*

Aultman Hospital (HQ) 330 452-9911
2600 6th St Sw Canton (44710) *(G-1679)*

Aultman Mso, Canton *Also Called: Aultman Mso Inc (G-1680)*

Aultman Mso Inc 330 479-8705
4455 Dressler Rd Nw Ste 201 Canton (44718) *(G-1680)*

Aultman North Canton Med Group (PA) 330 433-1200
6046 Whipple Ave Nw Canton (44720) *(G-1681)*

Aultman North Canton Med Group 330 363-6333
2600 6th St Sw Canton (44710) *(G-1682)*

Aultman North Inc 330 305-6999
6100 Whipple Ave Nw Canton (44720) *(G-1683)*

AUNTIE ANNE'S, Sandusky *Also Called: Cedar Fair LP (G-12871)*

Aurgroup Financial Cr Un Inc (PA) 513 942-4422
8811 Holden Blvd Fairfield (45014) *(G-8390)*

Aurgroup Financial Credit Un, Fairfield *Also Called: Aurgroup Financial Cr Un Inc (G-8390)*

Aurora Hotel Partners LLC 330 562-0767
30 Shawnee Trl Aurora (44202) *(G-605)*

Aurora Inn Hotel & Event Ctr, Aurora *Also Called: Aurora Hotel Partners LLC (G-605)*

Aurora Manor Ltd Partnership 330 562-5000
101 S Bissell Rd Aurora (44202) *(G-606)*

Aurora Mnor Spcial Care Centre, Aurora *Also Called: Aurora Manor Ltd Partnership (G-606)*

Aurora Wholesalers LLC (PA) 440 248-5200
31000 Aurora Rd Solon (44139) *(G-13069)*

Austin Building and Design Inc (DH) 440 544-2600
6095 Parkland Blvd Ste 100 Cleveland (44124) *(G-3839)*

Austin Company, The, Cleveland *Also Called: Austin Building and Design Inc (G-3839)*

Austintown Dairy Inc 330 629-6170
780 Bev Rd Youngstown (44512) *(G-15553)*

Austintown Healthcare Center, Youngstown *Also Called: S Meridian Leasing Co LLC (G-15715)*

Auto Body Mill Run, Columbus *Also Called: Auto Body North Inc (G-5406)*

Auto Body North Inc (PA) 614 436-3700
8675 N High St Columbus (43235) *(G-5406)*

Auto Crushers, Canton *Also Called: Slesnick Iron & Metal Co (G-1854)*

Auto Mall Rental & Leasing LLC 419 874-4331
26875 Dixie Hwy Perrysburg (43551) *(G-12313)*

Auto Parts Center-Cuyahoga FLS 330 928-2149
2990 Oakwood Dr Cuyahoga Falls (44221) *(G-7045)*

Auto Plus, Marietta *Also Called: Ieh Auto Parts LLC (G-10373)*

Auto-Owners Life Insurance Co 419 227-1452
2325 N Cole St Lima (45801) *(G-9866)*

Auto-Owners Life Insurance Co 419 887-1218
1645 Indian Wood Cir Ste 202 Maumee (43537) *(G-10696)*

Auto-Wares Inc 419 867-1927
3404 N Holland Sylvania Rd Toledo (43615) *(G-13695)*

Autobody Supply Company Inc 614 228-4328
212 N Grant Ave Columbus (43215) *(G-5407)*

Autograph Inc 216 881-1911
4419 Perkins Ave Cleveland (44103) *(G-3840)*

Autograph Foliages, Cleveland *Also Called: Autograph Inc (G-3840)*

Automated Control & Power, Hamilton *Also Called: Acpi Systems Inc (G-9016)*

(PA)=Parent Co (HQ)=Headquarters (DH)=Div Headquarters

Automatic Feed Co (HQ).. 419 592-0050
   476 E Riverview Ave Napoleon (43545) *(G-11517)*
Automatic Feed Company, Napoleon Also Called: Automatic Feed Co *(G-11517)*
Automation & Control Tech Ltd....................................... 419 661-6400
   28210 Cedar Park Blvd Perrysburg (43551) *(G-12314)*
Automation Tooling Systems (HQ)................................... 614 781-8063
   425 Enterprise Dr Lewis Center (43035) *(G-9810)*
Automation Tooling Systems, Lewis Center Also Called: Ats Carolina Inc *(G-9807)*
Automation Zone Inc.. 419 684-8050
   508 Lucas St E Castalia (44824) *(G-1914)*
Automotive Distributors Co Inc....................................... 216 398-2014
   990 Valley Belt Rd Cleveland (44109) *(G-3841)*
Automotive Distributors Co Inc (PA)............................... 614 476-1315
   2981 Morse Rd Columbus (43231) *(G-5408)*
Automotive Distributors Whse, Columbus Also Called: Automotive Distributors Co Inc *(G-5408)*
Automotive Div Of,, Cincinnati Also Called: SGS North America Inc *(G-3366)*
Automotive Part Supplier, Fremont Also Called: Inoac Exterior Systems LLC *(G-8687)*
Automtive Rfnish Clor Sltons I... 330 461-6067
   2771 Sunburst Dr Medina (44256) *(G-10810)*
Autonation Ford Amherst, Amherst Also Called: Ed Mullinax Ford LLC *(G-427)*
Autonation Ford North Canton, Canton Also Called: Mullinax Ford North Canton Inc *(G-1812)*
Autosales Incorporated.. 330 630-0888
   1234 Southeast Ave Tallmadge (44278) *(G-13586)*
Autoway Investors Ltd... 419 841-6691
   6800 W Central Ave Toledo (43617) *(G-13696)*
Autozone, Cleveland Also Called: Autozone Inc *(G-3842)*
Autozone, Cleveland Also Called: Autozone Inc *(G-3843)*
Autozone, Conneaut Also Called: Autozone Inc *(G-6939)*
Autozone, Painesville Also Called: Autozone Inc *(G-12221)*
Autozone, Perrysburg Also Called: Autozone Inc *(G-12315)*
Autozone Inc.. 216 751-0571
   11414 Kinsman Rd Cleveland (44104) *(G-3842)*
Autozone Inc.. 216 267-6586
   15427 Snow Rd Cleveland (44142) *(G-3843)*
Autozone Inc.. 440 593-6934
   199 Gateway Ave Ste D Conneaut (44030) *(G-6939)*
Autozone Inc.. 440 639-2247
   1487 Mentor Ave Painesville (44077) *(G-12221)*
Autozone Inc.. 419 872-2813
   650 E South Boundary St Perrysburg (43551) *(G-12315)*
Autumn Aegis Inc... 440 282-6768
   1130 Tower Blvd Ste A Lorain (44052) *(G-10056)*
AUTUMN COURT, Ottawa Also Called: Autumn Court Operating Co LLC *(G-12185)*
Autumn Court Operating Co LLC.................................... 419 523-4370
   1925 E 4th St Ottawa (45875) *(G-12185)*
Autumn Hills Care Center Inc.. 330 652-2053
   2565 Niles Vienna Rd Niles (44446) *(G-11781)*
Autumn Years Nursing Center, Sabina Also Called: Earley & Ross Ltd *(G-12771)*
Auxiliary Bd Fairview Gen Hosp..................................... 216 476-7000
   18101 Lorain Ave Cleveland (44111) *(G-3844)*
Auxiliary St Lukes Hospital.. 419 893-5911
   5901 Monclova Rd Maumee (43537) *(G-10697)*
Avaap USA LLC (PA)... 732 710-3425
   1400 Goodale Blvd Ste 100 Columbus (43212) *(G-5409)*
Avadirect.com, Twinsburg Also Called: Freedom Usa Inc *(G-14192)*
Avalon, Warren Also Called: Avalon Holdings Corporation *(G-14501)*
Avalon Foodservice Inc.. 330 854-4551
   1 Avalon Dr Canal Fulton (44614) *(G-1592)*
Avalon Golf and Cntry CLB Inc....................................... 330 856-8898
   1 American Way Ne Warren (44484) *(G-14500)*
Avalon Holdings Corporation (PA)................................ 330 856-8800
   1 American Way Ne Warren (44484) *(G-14501)*
Avalon Inn, Warren Also Called: Avalon Inn Services Inc *(G-14502)*
Avalon Inn and Resort, Warren Also Called: AIR Management Group LLC *(G-14495)*
Avalon Inn Services Inc.. 330 856-1900
   9519 E Market St Warren (44484) *(G-14502)*
Avalon Lakes Golf Inc (HQ).. 330 856-8898
   1 American Way Ne Warren (44484) *(G-14503)*
Avalon Lakes Pro Shop, Warren Also Called: Avalon Lakes Golf Inc *(G-14503)*
Avalon Resort and Spa LLC... 330 856-1900
   9519 E Market St Warren (44484) *(G-14504)*
Avanti Salon, Chesterland Also Called: Mato Inc *(G-2040)*
Avantia Inc... 216 901-9366
   9655 Sweet Valley Dr Ste 1 Cleveland (44125) *(G-3845)*
Aventiv Research Inc.. 614 495-8970
   3600 Olentangy River Rd Ste A Columbus (43214) *(G-5410)*
Aventivs Womens Health RES, Columbus Also Called: Aventiv Research Inc *(G-5410)*
Aventura At Oakwood Vlg LLC...................................... 937 390-9000
   1500 Villa Rd Springfield (45503) *(G-13220)*
Avenue At Aurora, Aurora Also Called: Progressive Aurora LLC *(G-622)*
Avenue At Macedonia, The, Macedonia Also Called: Progressive Macedonia LLC *(G-10203)*
Avenue At Medina... 330 721-7001
   699 E Smith Rd Medina (44256) *(G-10811)*
Avertest LLC... 330 591-7219
   124 N Court St Medina (44256) *(G-10812)*
AVI Food Systems Inc (PA).. 330 372-6000
   2590 Elm Rd Ne Warren (44483) *(G-14505)*
AVI Food Systems Inc.. 740 452-9363
   333 Richards Rd Zanesville (43701) *(G-15768)*
Aviation Auto Trnsp Spclsts In...................................... 502 785-4657
   1100 Tower Dr Fort Loramie (45845) *(G-8603)*
Aviation, Department of, Vandalia Also Called: City of Dayton *(G-14371)*
Avid Technologies Inc.. 330 487-0770
   2112 Case Pkwy Ste 1 Twinsburg (44087) *(G-14173)*
Avient, Avon Lake Also Called: Avient Corporation *(G-672)*
Avient Corporation (PA).. 440 930-1000
   33587 Walker Rd Avon Lake (44012) *(G-672)*
Avis Administration.. 937 898-2581
   3300 Valet Dr Vandalia (45377) *(G-14364)*
Avita Health System... 419 468-7059
   955 Hosford Rd Galion (44833) *(G-8742)*
Avita Health System (PA)... 419 468-4841
   269 Portland Way S Galion (44833) *(G-8743)*
Avita Health System, Galion Also Called: Avita Health System *(G-8743)*
Avita Home Health and Hospice.................................... 419 468-7985
   1220 N Market St Galion (44833) *(G-8744)*
Aviva Metals, Lorain Also Called: National Bronze Mtls Ohio Inc *(G-10094)*
Aviva Metals Inc... 440 277-1226
   5311 W River Rd Lorain (44055) *(G-10057)*
Avizent, Dublin Also Called: Frank Gates Service Company *(G-8014)*
Avnet, Groveport Also Called: Avnet Integrated Inc *(G-8972)*
Avnet Integrated Inc... 614 851-8700
   5300 Centerpoint Pkwy Groveport (43125) *(G-8972)*
Avon Branch, Avon Also Called: Huntington National Bank *(G-655)*
Avon Heritage Boosters.. 440 934-5111
   37545 Detroit Rd Avon (44011) *(G-638)*
Avon Lake Animal Care Center, Avon Lake Also Called: Avon Lake Vet Holdings Inc *(G-674)*
Avon Lake Sheet Metal Co... 440 933-3505
   33574 Pin Oak Pkwy Avon Lake (44012) *(G-673)*
Avon Lake Vet Holdings Inc... 440 933-5297
   124 Miller Rd Avon Lake (44012) *(G-674)*
Avon Medical Offices, Avon Also Called: Kaiser Foundation Hospitals *(G-658)*
Avon Oaks Nursing Home, Avon Also Called: R & J Investment Co Inc *(G-663)*
Avon-Oaks Country Club... 440 892-0660
   32300 Detroit Rd Avon (44011) *(G-639)*
Avt Technology Solutions LLC...................................... 727 539-7429
   5350 Centerpoint Pkwy Groveport (43125) *(G-8973)*
AW Faber-Castell Usa Inc.. 216 643-4660
   9000 Rio Nero Dr Independence (44131) *(G-9408)*
Awe Hospitality Group LLC... 330 888-8836
   9652 N Bedford Rd Macedonia (44056) *(G-10189)*
AWH Holdings Inc.. 513 241-2614
   125 E 9th St Cincinnati (45202) *(G-2230)*
Awl Transport Inc... 330 899-3444
   4626 State Route 82 Mantua (44255) *(G-10328)*
Awp Inc (PA)... 330 677-7401
   4244 Mount Pleasant St Nw Ste 100 North Canton (44720) *(G-11813)*
Aws.. 513 648-9360
   2718 E Camp Rd Cincinnati (45241) *(G-2231)*

ALPHABETIC SECTION — Band, The

Awu Charities, Columbus Also Called: Always With US Chrties Awu CHR *(G-5341)*

Axcess Rcvery Cr Solutions Inc..513 229-6700
4540 Cooper Rd Ste 305 Cincinnati (45242) *(G-2232)*

Axiom Automotive Tech Inc..800 321-8830
7350 Young Dr Bedford (44146) *(G-954)*

Axiom Wireless Llc..330 863-4410
3323 Magnolia Rd Nw Magnolia (44643) *(G-10223)*

Aydelott Equipment Inc..888 293-3568
119 Compark Rd Centerville (45459) *(G-1939)*

Ayrshire Inc (PA)..440 286-9507
191 5th Ave Chardon (44024) *(G-1994)*

Azimuth Corporation..937 256-8571
2970 Presidential Dr Ste 200 Beavercreek (45324) *(G-861)*

Aztec Demolition & Envmtl Co, Cincinnati Also Called: Aztec Services Group Inc *(G-2233)*

Aztec Services Group Inc..513 541-2002
3814 William P Dooley Byp Cincinnati (45223) *(G-2233)*

B & A, Cuyahoga Falls Also Called: Barrett & Associates Inc *(G-7047)*

B & B Contrs & Developers Inc..330 270-5020
4531 Belmont Ave Ste A Youngstown (44505) *(G-15554)*

B & B Plastics Recyclers Inc..614 409-2880
3300 Lockbourne Rd Columbus (43207) *(G-5411)*

B & B Wrecking & Excvtg Inc...216 429-1700
4510 E 71st St Ste 6 Cleveland (44105) *(G-3846)*

B & C Communications, Columbus Also Called: Comproducts Inc *(G-5679)*

B & I Hotel Management LLC...330 995-0200
600 N Aurora Rd Aurora (44202) *(G-607)*

B & J Electrical Company Inc...513 351-7100
6265 Wiehe Rd Cincinnati (45237) *(G-2234)*

B & L Transport Inc (PA)...866 848-2888
3149 State Route 39 Millersburg (44654) *(G-11272)*

B & T Express Inc (PA)...330 549-0000
400 Miley Rd North Lima (44452) *(G-11883)*

B B & E Inc..740 354-5469
1630 Kendall Ave Portsmouth (45662) *(G-12545)*

B B I T Inc..419 259-3600
1946 N 13th St Ste 101 Toledo (43604) *(G-13697)*

B C E, Derwent Also Called: Bi-Con Engineering LLC *(G-7863)*

B C M, Cleveland Also Called: Burton Carol Management *(G-3912)*

B D G Wrap-Tite Inc (PA)..440 349-5400
6200 Cochran Rd Solon (44139) *(G-13070)*

B D S Inc (PA)...513 921-8441
3500 Southside Ave Cincinnati (45204) *(G-2235)*

B D Transportation Inc..937 773-9280
9590 Looney Rd Piqua (45356) *(G-12435)*

B Dry System Inc..513 724-3444
3481 Concord Hennings Mill Rd Williamsburg (45176) *(G-15177)*

B F G Federal Credit Union (PA)..330 374-2990
445 S Main St Ste B Akron (44311) *(G-57)*

B M Machine..419 595-2898
27 S Perry St New Riegel (44853) *(G-11677)*

B P Products North America, Cuyahoga Falls Also Called: BP Oil Supply Company *(G-7051)*

B W Grinding Co..419 923-1376
15048 County Rd 10-3 Lyons (43533) *(G-10187)*

B-Dry System, Williamsburg Also Called: B Dry System Inc *(G-15177)*

B-Tek Scales LLC..330 471-8900
1510 Metric Ave Sw Canton (44706) *(G-1684)*

B-W Baseball...440 826-2182
275 Eastland Rd Berea (44017) *(G-1062)*

B&L Acquisition Group LLC..216 626-0040
23580 Miles Rd Bedford Heights (44128) *(G-994)*

B&N Coal Inc...740 783-3575
38455 Marietta Rt Dexter City (45727) *(G-7867)*

Babcock & Wilcox Cnstr Co LLC (HQ)...................................330 753-9750
1200 E Market St Ste 651 Akron (44305) *(G-58)*

Babcock & Wilcox Company (HQ)..330 753-4511
1200 E Market St Ste 650 Akron (44305) *(G-59)*

Babcock & Wilcox Holdings Inc..704 625-4900
1200 E Market St Ste 650 Akron (44305) *(G-60)*

Babin Building Solutions LLC...216 292-2500
4101 E Royalton Rd Broadview Heights (44147) *(G-1383)*

Bachmans Inc..513 943-5300
4058 Clough Woods Dr Batavia (45103) *(G-726)*

Backbone Power Systems, Cleves Also Called: North Amrcn Utlity Sltions LLC *(G-5191)*

Backyard Storage Solutions LLC..330 723-4412
2648 Medina Rd Unit 13 Medina (44256) *(G-10813)*

Baco LLC..740 454-4840
3921 Northpointe Dr South Zanesville (43701) *(G-13186)*

Badilad LLC..330 805-3173
1015 Howe Ave Apt 11 Cuyahoga Falls (44221) *(G-7046)*

Badl Logistics, Columbus Also Called: Geist Logistics LLC *(G-5923)*

Bae Systems Iap Research LLC..937 296-1806
2763 Culver Ave Dayton (45429) *(G-7185)*

Bae Systems Science & Technology Inc
3725 Pentagon Blvd Ste 110 Beavercreek (45431) *(G-862)*

Baesman Group Inc (PA)..614 771-2300
4477 Reynolds Dr Hilliard (43026) *(G-9181)*

Baf Holding Company...440 287-2200
26050 Richmond Rd Bedford (44146) *(G-955)*

Bagel Place Inc (PA)...419 537-9377
3444 Secor Rd Toledo (43606) *(G-13698)*

Bagpack, West Chester Also Called: BP 10 Inc *(G-14653)*

Bailey Cavalieri LLC (PA)...614 221-3258
10 West Broad St Ste 2100 Columbus (43215) *(G-5412)*

Baillie Lumber Co LP..419 462-2000
3953 County Road 51 Galion (44833) *(G-8745)*

BAIN CAPITAL PRIVATE EQUITY..614 751-5315
6055 E Main St Columbus (43213) *(G-5413)*

Bair Goodie and Assoc Inc..330 343-3499
153 N Broadway St Ste 5 New Philadelphia (44663) *(G-11641)*

Bakemark USA LLC...513 870-0880
9250 Seward Rd # D Fairfield (45014) *(G-8391)*

Baker & Hostetler LLP..513 929-3400
312 Walnut St Ste 3200 Cincinnati (45202) *(G-2236)*

Baker & Hostetler LLP (PA)..216 621-0200
127 Public Sq Ste 2000 Cleveland (44114) *(G-3847)*

Baker & Hostetler LLP..216 430-2960
1375 E 9th St Ste 2100 Cleveland (44114) *(G-3848)*

Baker & Hostetler LLP..614 228-1541
200 Civic Center Dr Ste 12 Columbus (43215) *(G-5414)*

Baker & Taylor Publisher Svcs, Ashland Also Called: Bookmasters Inc *(G-483)*

Baker Equipment and Mtls Ltd..513 422-6697
990 N Garver Rd Monroe (45050) *(G-11333)*

Bakkt Clearing LLC..614 487-9550
1500 Lake Shore Dr Ste 450 Columbus (43204) *(G-5415)*

Balaji D Loganathan...614 918-0411
6352 Pinefield Dr Hilliard (43026) *(G-9182)*

Balanced Care Corporation...330 908-1166
997 W Aurora Rd Northfield (44067) *(G-11952)*

Balanced Care Corporation...330 296-4545
141 Chestnut Hill Dr Apt 213 Ravenna (44266) *(G-12619)*

Balanced Logistics Brkg LLC..216 296-4817
3601 Shady Timber Dr Twinsburg (44087) *(G-14174)*

Balancing Company Inc (PA)...937 898-9111
898 Center Dr Vandalia (45377) *(G-14365)*

Baldwin International, Solon Also Called: Fedmet International Corp *(G-13087)*

Ball Bounce and Sport Inc (PA)..419 289-9310
1 Hedstrom Dr Ashland (44805) *(G-479)*

Ball Bounce and Sport Inc..614 662-5381
3275 Alum Creek Dr Columbus (43207) *(G-5416)*

Ballas Egg Products Corp...614 453-0386
40 N 2nd St Zanesville (43701) *(G-15769)*

Ballet Metropolitan Inc...614 229-4860
322 Mount Vernon Ave Columbus (43215) *(G-5417)*

BALLETMET COLUMBUS, Columbus Also Called: Ballet Metropolitan Inc *(G-5417)*

Ballreich Bros Inc...419 447-1814
186 Ohio Ave Tiffin (44883) *(G-13624)*

Ballreichs Potato Chips Snacks, Tiffin Also Called: Ballreich Bros Inc *(G-13624)*

Banc Amer Prctice Slutions Inc...614 794-8247
600 N Cleveland Ave Ste 300 Westerville (43082) *(G-14878)*

Banc One, Columbus Also Called: Banc One Services Corporation *(G-5247)*

Banc One Services Corporation (HQ)....................................614 248-5800
1111 Polaris Pkwy Ste B3 Columbus (43240) *(G-5247)*

Band, The, Cincinnati Also Called: University of Cincinnati *(G-3584)*

Baney Rd Medical Office Bldg, Ashland *Also Called: Samaritan Regional Health Sys* *(G-512)*
Banfield Pet Hospital 1299, Vandalia *Also Called: Medical Management Intl Inc* *(G-14383)*
Banner Supply Company Inc (PA) 330 782-1171
   103 E Indianola Ave Youngstown (44507) *(G-15555)*
Bansal Construction Inc 513 874-5410
   3263 Homeward Way Ste A Fairfield (45014) *(G-8392)*
Bansi & Pratima Inc 513 735-0453
   1839 Clough Pike Batavia (45103) *(G-727)*
Banta Electrical Contrs Inc (PA) 513 353-4446
   5701 Hamilton Cleves Rd Cleves (45002) *(G-5187)*
Baptist Health 502 253-4700
   Westlake (44145) *(G-15036)*
Baptist Health Hardin (HQ) 419 673-0761
   921 E Franklin St Kenton (43326) *(G-9609)*
Barberton Laundry and Clg Inc 330 825-6911
   1050 Northview Ave Barberton (44203) *(G-694)*
Barberton Tree, Norton *Also Called: Barberton Tree Service Inc* *(G-11990)*
Barberton Tree Service Inc 330 848-2344
   3307 Clark Mill Rd Norton (44203) *(G-11990)*
Barbicas Construction Co 330 733-9101
   124 Darrow Rd Ste 1 Akron (44305) *(G-61)*
Barbs Graffiti Inc (PA) 216 881-5550
   3111 Carnegie Ave Cleveland (44115) *(G-3849)*
Bareminerals, Columbus *Also Called: Orveon Global US LLC* *(G-6482)*
Barium Holdings Company Inc 740 282-9776
   515 Kingsdale Rd Steubenville (43952) *(G-13317)*
Barkan & Neff Co Lpa (PA) 614 221-4221
   4200 Regent St Ste 210 Columbus (43219) *(G-5418)*
Barkan Mzlish Drose Wntz McNrv 614 221-4221
   4200 Regent St Ste 210 Columbus (43219) *(G-5419)*
Barklyn Heights LLC 216 577-5960
   247 Old Brookpark Rd Cleveland (44109) *(G-3850)*
Barnes Dennig & Co Ltd (PA) 513 241-8313
   150 E 4th St Ste 300 Cincinnati (45202) *(G-2237)*
Barnes Group Inc 419 891-9292
   370 W Dussel Dr Ste A Maumee (43537) *(G-10698)*
Barnes Nursery Inc (PA) 800 421-8722
   3511 Cleveland Rd W Huron (44839) *(G-9384)*
Barnes Wendling Cpas Inc (PA) 216 566-9000
   1350 Euclid Ave Ste 1400 Cleveland (44115) *(G-3851)*
Barnesville Health Care Center, Barnesville *Also Called: Southeastern Health Care Ctr* *(G-722)*
Barnesville Hospital Assn Inc (PA) 740 425-3941
   639 W Main St Barnesville (43713) *(G-717)*
Barr Engineering Incorporated (PA) 614 714-0299
   2800 Corporate Exchange Dr Ste 240 Columbus (43231) *(G-5420)*
Barrett & Associates Inc (PA) 330 928-2323
   1060 Graham Rd Ste C Cuyahoga Falls (44224) *(G-7047)*
Barrie G Glvin Otr/L Assoc Ltd 216 514-1600
   25221 Miles Rd Unit F Cleveland (44128) *(G-3852)*
Barrington Golf Club Inc (PA) 330 995-0600
   350 N Aurora Rd Aurora (44202) *(G-608)*
Barrington Golf Club Inc 330 995-0821
   680 N Aurora Rd Aurora (44202) *(G-609)*
Barrington School 614 336-3000
   6046 Tara Hill Dr Dublin (43017) *(G-7942)*
Barrington Toledo LLC 419 535-0024
   300 S Byrne Rd Toledo (43615) *(G-13699)*
Barry Bagels, Toledo *Also Called: Bagel Place Inc* *(G-13698)*
Bartha Audio Visual, Columbus *Also Called: Bkg Holdings LLC* *(G-5442)*
Bartlett & Co LLC 513 621-4612
   600 Vine St Ste 2100 Cincinnati (45202) *(G-2238)*
Basement Dctor HM Imprv Ctr CP 800 880-8324
   13659 National Rd Sw Etna (43068) *(G-8328)*
BASF, Cleveland *Also Called: BASF Catalysts LLC* *(G-3853)*
BASF Catalysts LLC 216 360-5005
   23800 Mercantile Rd Cleveland (44122) *(G-3853)*
Basic Drugs Inc 937 898-4010
   300 Corporate Center Dr Vandalia (45377) *(G-14366)*
Basic Systems Inc 740 432-3001
   9255 Cadiz Rd Cambridge (43725) *(G-1555)*

Basic Vitamins, Vandalia *Also Called: Basic Drugs Inc* *(G-14366)*
Basinger Lfe Enhncmnt Sprt Svc (PA) 614 557-5461
   941 E 5th St Marysville (43040) *(G-10474)*
Basista Furniture Inc 216 398-5900
   5340 Brookpark Rd Cleveland (44134) *(G-3854)*
Bass Family LLC
   26701 Richmond Rd Bedford Heights (44146) *(G-995)*
Bass Truck Center, Sheffield Village *Also Called: Mike Ford Bass Inc* *(G-13002)*
Bassett Nut Company, Holland *Also Called: Jml Holdings Inc* *(G-9291)*
Batavia Nrsing Cnvalescent Inn, Batavia *Also Called: Carington Health Systems* *(G-730)*
Bates Bros Amusement Co 740 266-2950
   1506 Fernwood Rd Wintersville (43953) *(G-15292)*
Bates Metal Products Inc 740 498-8371
   403 E Mn St Port Washington (43837) *(G-12541)*
Bath & Body Works, Dayton *Also Called: Bath & Body Works LLC* *(G-7186)*
Bath & Body Works LLC 937 439-0350
   2700 Miamisburg Centerville Rd Unit 1 Dayton (45459) *(G-7186)*
Bath and Body Works, Reynoldsburg *Also Called: Beautyavenues LLC* *(G-12654)*
Bath Bdy Wrks Lgstics Svcs LLC (HQ) 614 415-7500
   2 Limited Pkwy Columbus (43230) *(G-5421)*
Bath Bdy Wrks Lgstics Svcs LLC 513 435-1643
   4400 S Hamilton Rd Groveport (43125) *(G-8974)*
Bath Manor Limited Partnership 330 836-1006
   2330 Smith Rd Akron (44333) *(G-62)*
Bath Manor Special Care Centre, Akron *Also Called: Bath Manor Limited Partnership* *(G-62)*
Battelle, Columbus *Also Called: Battelle Memorial Institute* *(G-5422)*
Battelle Memorial Institute (PA) 614 424-6424
   505 King Ave Columbus (43201) *(G-5422)*
Battelle Rippe Kingston LLP 937 853-1470
   2000 W Dorothy Ln Moraine (45439) *(G-11390)*
Battered Womens Shelter 330 723-3900
   696 E Washington St Ste 1a Medina (44256) *(G-10814)*
Batterii LLC 513 379-3595
   1008 Race St Ste 4 Cincinnati (45202) *(G-2239)*
Battle Bullying Hotline Inc 216 731-1976
   3185 Warren Rd Cleveland (44111) *(G-3855)*
Bauer Corporation (PA) 800 321-4760
   2540 Progress Dr Wooster (44691) *(G-15310)*
Bauer Ladder, Wooster *Also Called: Bauer Corporation* *(G-15310)*
Baumfolder Corporation (DH) 937 492-1281
   1660 Campbell Rd Sidney (45365) *(G-13020)*
Baxter Hdell Dnnlly Prston Inc (PA) 513 271-1634
   302 W 3rd St Ste 500 Cincinnati (45202) *(G-2240)*
Bay Advanced Technologies LLC 510 857-0900
   1 Applied Plz Cleveland (44115) *(G-3856)*
Bay Area Credit Union Inc 419 698-2962
   4202 Navarre Ave Oregon (43616) *(G-12128)*
Bay Furnace Sheet Metal Co 440 871-3777
   24530 Sperry Dr Westlake (44145) *(G-15037)*
Bay Heating & Air Conditioning, Westlake *Also Called: Bay Furnace Sheet Metal Co* *(G-15037)*
Bay Mechanical & Elec Corp 440 282-6816
   2221 W Park Dr Lorain (44053) *(G-10058)*
Bay Park Community Hospital 419 690-7900
   2801 Bay Park Dr Oregon (43616) *(G-12129)*
Bay Park Community Hospital 419 690-8725
   2142 N Cove Blvd Toledo (43606) *(G-13700)*
Bay Park Community Hospital (HQ) 567 585-9600
   100 Madison Ave Toledo (43604) *(G-13701)*
Bay Pint Resort Operations LLC 419 798-4434
   10948 E Bayshore Rd Marblehead (43440) *(G-10351)*
Bay Point Yacht Club, Marblehead *Also Called: Bay Pint Resort Operations LLC* *(G-10351)*
Bay State Gas Company 614 460-4292
   200 Civic Center Dr Columbus (43215) *(G-5423)*
Bay Village City School Dst 440 617-7330
   28727 Wolf Rd Cleveland (44140) *(G-3857)*
Bayada Home Health Care Inc 330 929-5512
   2251 Front St Ste 202 Cuyahoga Falls (44221) *(G-7048)*
Bayer & Becker Inc (PA) 513 492-7401
   6900 Tylersville Rd Ste A Mason (45040) *(G-10522)*

Bayer Becker, Mason Also Called: Bayer & Becker Inc (G-10522)

Bayloff Stmped Pdts Knsman Inc.. 330 876-4511
  8091 State Route 5 Kinsman (44428) (G-9644)

Baymark Health Services La Inc.. 440 328-4213
  530 N Leavitt Rd Amherst (44001) (G-423)

Baymark Health Services La Inc.. 937 203-2017
  4201 N Main St Dayton (45405) (G-7187)

Baymont Inn & Suites, Fairborn Also Called: Premier Hotel Group LLC (G-8380)

Baymont Inn & Suites, Logan Also Called: Mnm Hotels Inc (G-10035)

Baymont Inn & Suites, Oxford Also Called: Amoxford Inc (G-12200)

Bayshore Counseling Svcs Inc (PA).. 419 626-9156
  1634 Sycamore Line Sandusky (44870) (G-12864)

Bazell Oil Co Inc.. 740 385-5420
  14371 State Route 328 Logan (43138) (G-10021)

Bazemore Insurance Group LLC.. 614 559-8585
  800 Cross Pointe Rd Ste F Columbus (43230) (G-5424)

BBC&m Engineering Inc (PA).. 614 793-2226
  6190 Enterprise Ct Dublin (43016) (G-7943)

BBDO, Cincinnati Also Called: BBDO Worldwide Inc (G-2241)

BBDO Worldwide Inc.. 513 861-3668
  700 W Pete Rose Way Cincinnati (45203) (G-2241)

Bbi Logistics LLC.. 800 809-2172
  80 E Rich St Ste 200 Columbus (43215) (G-5425)

Bbs & Associates Inc.. 330 665-5227
  130 Springside Dr Ste 200 Akron (44333) (G-63)

Bbs Professional Corporation.. 614 888-8616
  1103 Schrock Rd Ste 400 Columbus (43229) (G-5426)

Bcbd, West Chester Also Called: Cameo Solutions Inc (G-14658)

BCI Mississippi Broadband LLC.. 419 724-7295
  5552 Southwyck Blvd Toledo (43614) (G-13702)

Bcrta, Hamilton Also Called: Butler Cnty Rgional Trnst Auth (G-9024)

BCU Electric Inc.. 419 281-8944
  1019 Us Highway 250 N Ashland (44805) (G-480)

BD Oil Gathering Corp.. 740 374-9355
  649 Mitchells Ln Marietta (45750) (G-10357)

Bdi Inc (HQ).. 216 642-9100
  8000 Hub Pkwy Cleveland (44125) (G-3858)

Bdi-USA, Cleveland Also Called: Bearing Distributors Inc (G-3860)

Beach At Mason Ltd Partnership.. 513 398-7946
  3000 Henkle Dr Lebanon (45036) (G-9756)

Beach Waterpark, Lebanon Also Called: Beach At Mason Ltd Partnership (G-9756)

Beachwood Cinema LLC.. 954 840-8150
  10 Park Ave Ste 218 Beachwood (44122) (G-767)

Beachwood City Schools.. 216 464-6609
  23757 Commerce Park Cleveland (44122) (G-3859)

Beachwood Family Health Center, Beachwood Also Called: Cleveland Clinic Foundation (G-778)

Beachwood Lodging LLC.. 216 831-3735
  3840 Orange Pl Beachwood (44122) (G-768)

Beachwood Medical Center, Beachwood Also Called: Lake Hospital System Inc (G-807)

Beacon Capital Management Inc.. 937 203-4025
  7777 Washington Village Dr Ste 280 Dayton (45459) (G-7188)

Beacon Electric Company.. 513 851-0711
  7815 Redsky Dr Cincinnati (45249) (G-2242)

Beacon Electrical Contractors, Cincinnati Also Called: Beacon Electric Company (G-2242)

Beacon Health.. 440 354-9924
  9220 Mentor Ave Mentor (44060) (G-10914)

Beacon Hill Staffing Group LLC.. 216 447-8900
  6155 Rockside Rd Ste 305 Independence (44131) (G-9409)

Beacon Hill Technologies, Independence Also Called: Beacon Hill Staffing Group LLC (G-9409)

Beacon of Light Health Agency, Toledo Also Called: Nova Passport Home Care Llc (G-13941)

Beacon Orthopedics, Cincinnati Also Called: Beacon Orthpdics Spt Mdcine Lt (G-2245)

Beacon Orthpaedcs & Sprts Med.. 513 354-3700
  6480 Harrison Ave Ste 100 Cincinnati (45247) (G-2243)

Beacon Orthpdics Spt Mdcine Lt.. 513 985-2252
  8099 Cornell Rd Cincinnati (45249) (G-2244)

Beacon Orthpdics Spt Mdcine Lt (PA).. 513 354-3700
  500 E Business Way Cincinnati (45241) (G-2245)

Beacon Point Rehab, Uhrichsville Also Called: Uhrichsville Hlth Care Ctr Inc (G-14237)

Beam Dental Insurance Svcs LLC.. 740 262-1409
  226 N 5th St Ste 300 Columbus (43215) (G-5427)

Beam Technologies Inc.. 800 648-1179
  80 E Rich St Ste 400 Columbus (43215) (G-5428)

Bear Communications Inc.. 216 642-1670
  900 Resource Dr Ste 8 Independence (44131) (G-9410)

Bearing & Drive Systems Inc.. 440 846-4272
  15157 Foltz Pkwy Strongsville (44149) (G-13445)

Bearing Distributors, Cleveland Also Called: Bdi Inc (G-3858)

Bearing Distributors Inc (HQ).. 216 642-9100
  8000 Hub Pkwy Cleveland (44125) (G-3860)

Bearing Technologies Ltd (PA).. 800 597-3486
  33554 Pin Oak Pkwy Avon Lake (44012) (G-675)

Beary Land, Piqua Also Called: Council On Rur Svc Prgrams Inc (G-12439)

Beautyavenues LLC (HQ).. 614 856-6000
  7 Limited Pkwy E Reynoldsburg (43068) (G-12654)

Beaver Dam Health Care Center.. 330 762-6486
  721 Hickory St Akron (44303) (G-64)

Beaver Dam Health Care Center.. 440 247-4200
  150 Cleveland St Chagrin Falls (44022) (G-1953)

Beaver Dam Health Care Center.. 614 861-6666
  1425 Yorkland Rd Columbus (43232) (G-5429)

Beaver Dam Health Care Center.. 419 227-2154
  599 S Shawnee St Lima (45804) (G-9867)

Beaver Dam Health Care Center.. 330 335-1558
  365 Johnson Rd Wadsworth (44281) (G-14429)

Beaver Dam Health Care Center.. 440 256-8100
  9679 Chillicothe Rd Willoughby (44094) (G-15187)

Beaver Park Marina Inc.. 440 282-6308
  6101 W Erie Ave Lorain (44053) (G-10059)

Beavercreek Fmly Mdcine Obsttr, Dayton Also Called: Mvhe Inc (G-7521)

Beavercreek Medical Center.. 937 702-4000
  3535 Pentagon Blvd Beavercreek (45431) (G-863)

Beavercreek YMCA Sch's Out I, Dayton Also Called: Young MNS Chrstn Assn Grter Dy (G-7734)

Beazer East Inc.. 937 364-2311
  4281 Roush Rd Hillsboro (45133) (G-9249)

Bechtel Jacobs Company LLC.. 740 897-2700
  3930 Us Highway 23 Anx Piketon (45661) (G-12415)

Bechtold Enterprises Inc.. 440 791-7177
  951 Main St Grafton (44044) (G-8838)

Beck Aluminum Corporation.. 440 684-4848
  6150 Parkland Blvd Ste 260 Mayfield Heights (44124) (G-10785)

Beck Center For Arts.. 216 521-2540
  17801 Detroit Ave Lakewood (44107) (G-9659)

Beck Company.. 216 883-0909
  10701 Broadway Ave Cleveland (44125) (G-3861)

Beck Suppliers Inc.. 419 426-3051
  15025 E. Us 224 Attica (44807) (G-598)

Becker Electric Supply, Dayton Also Called: The John A Becker Co (G-7666)

Becker Pumps Corporation.. 330 928-9966
  100 E Ascot Ln Cuyahoga Falls (44223) (G-7049)

Beckett House At New Concord, New Concord Also Called: Zandex Health Care Corporation (G-11613)

Beckjord Power Station, New Richmond Also Called: Duke Energy Ohio Inc (G-11676)

Beco Legal Systems, Cincinnati Also Called: Business Equipment Co Inc (G-2293)

Bedford Medical Offices, Brooklyn Heights Also Called: Kaiser Foundation Hospitals (G-1423)

Beds N Stuff, Grove City Also Called: Waterbeds n Stuff Inc (G-8965)

Beech Acres Parenting Center (PA).. 513 231-6630
  615 Elsinore Pl Cincinnati (45202) (G-2246)

Beech Acres Park, Cincinnati Also Called: Anderson Township Park Dst (G-2201)

BEECH ACRES THERAPUTIC FOSTER, Cincinnati Also Called: Beech Acres Parenting Center (G-2246)

Beecher Carlson Insur Svcs LLC.. 330 726-8177
  7600 Market St Youngstown (44512) (G-15556)

Beechmont Chevrolet, Cincinnati Also Called: Beechmont Chevrolet Inc (G-2247)

Beechmont Chevrolet Inc.. 513 624-1100
  7600 Beechmont Ave Cincinnati (45255) (G-2247)

Beechmont Ford Inc (PA).. 513 752-6611
600 Ohio Pike Cincinnati (45245) *(G-2098)*

Beechmont Motors Inc (PA).. 513 388-3883
8639 Beechmont Ave Cincinnati (45255) *(G-2248)*

Beechmont Motors T Inc.. 513 388-3800
8667 Beechmont Ave Cincinnati (45255) *(G-2249)*

Beechmont Porsche, Cincinnati *Also Called: Beechmont Motors Inc (G-2248)*

Beechmont Racquet and Fitness, Cincinnati *Also Called: Beechmont Racquet Club Inc (G-2250)*

Beechmont Racquet Club Inc.. 513 528-5700
435 Ohio Pike Cincinnati (45255) *(G-2250)*

Beechmont Urgent Care, Cincinnati *Also Called: Carefirst Urgent Care LLC (G-2311)*

Beechwold Veterinary Hospital (PA).. 614 268-8666
4590 Indianola Ave Columbus (43214) *(G-5430)*

Beechwood Home.. 513 321-9294
2140 Pogue Ave Cincinnati (45208) *(G-2251)*

Beechwood Terrace Care Ctr Inc.. 513 578-6200
8700 Moran Rd Cincinnati (45244) *(G-2252)*

Beeghly Nursing LLC.. 330 884-2300
6505 Market St Bldg D Boardman (44512) *(G-1285)*

Beeghly Oaks Ctr For Rhbltiton, Boardman *Also Called: Beeghly Nursing LLC (G-1285)*

Beem Construction Inc.. 937 693-3176
225 S Mill St Botkins (45306) *(G-1298)*

Behavior Key Services LLC.. 937 952-6379
5963a Kentshire Dr Dayton (45440) *(G-7189)*

BEHAVORIAL HEALTHCARE PARTNERS OF CENTRAL OHIO, INC., Mount Vernon *Also Called: Behavrial Hlthcare Prtners CNT (G-11476)*

Behavral Cnnctions WD Cnty Inc.. 419 352-5387
1010 N Prospect St Bowling Green (43402) *(G-1304)*

Behavral Cnnctions WD Cnty Inc.. 419 352-5561
1033 Devlac Grv Bowling Green (43402) *(G-1305)*

Behavral Cnnctions WD Cnty Inc.. 419 352-5387
320 W Gypsy Lane Rd Ste A Bowling Green (43402) *(G-1306)*

Behavral Hlthcare Prtners Cntl (PA).. 740 522-8477
65 Messimer Dr Unit 2 Newark (43055) *(G-11690)*

Behavrial Hlthcare Prtners CNT.. 740 397-0442
8402 Blackjack Road Ext Mount Vernon (43050) *(G-11476)*

Beidt Health, Cleveland *Also Called: A-1 Hlthcare Stffing Plcements (G-3753)*

Beiersdorf Inc.. 513 682-7300
5232 E Provident Dr West Chester (45246) *(G-14800)*

Bel-Park Anesthesia.. 330 480-3658
1044 Belmont Ave Youngstown (44504) *(G-15557)*

Belayusa Corporation.. 614 878-8200
5197 Trabue Rd Columbus (43228) *(G-5431)*

Belcan, Blue Ash *Also Called: Belcan LLC (G-1132)*

Belcan LLC (PA).. 513 891-0972
10151 Carver Rd Ste 105 Blue Ash (45242) *(G-1132)*

Belcan LLC.. 513 985-7777
10151 Carver Rd Ste 105 Blue Ash (45242) *(G-1133)*

Belcan LLC.. 513 277-3100
7785 E Kemper Rd Cincinnati (45249) *(G-2253)*

Belcan Corporation.. 513 891-0972
10151 Carver Rd Ste 105 Blue Ash (45242) *(G-1134)*

Belcan Engineering Group LLC (HQ).. 513 891-0972
10151 Carver Rd Blue Ash (45242) *(G-1135)*

Belcan Engineering Services, Cincinnati *Also Called: Belcan LLC (G-2253)*

Belcan Staffing Solution.. 513 241-8367
127 W 4th St Cincinnati (45202) *(G-2254)*

Belcan Svcs Group Ltd Partnr (HQ).. 513 891-0972
10151 Carver Rd Blue Ash (45242) *(G-1136)*

Belcap Inc.. 330 456-0031
700 Tuscarawas St W Canton (44702) *(G-1685)*

BELCO WORKS, Saint Clairsville *Also Called: Belco Works Inc (G-12774)*

Belco Works Inc.. 740 695-0500
68425 Hammond Rd Saint Clairsville (43950) *(G-12774)*

Belcourt Terracenursing Home, Dublin *Also Called: Ahf/Central States Inc (G-7924)*

Belflex Staffing Network, Blue Ash *Also Called: Belcan Svcs Group Ltd Partnr (G-1136)*

Belflex Staffing Network LLC (HQ).. 513 488-8758
11591 Goldcoast Dr Cincinnati (45249) *(G-2255)*

Belflex Staffing Network LLC.. 513 939-3444
4757 Dixie Hwy Fairfield (45014) *(G-8393)*

Bell & Blaire LLC.. 330 794-5647
103 S Main St Munroe Falls (44262) *(G-11513)*

Bell Vault and Monu Works Inc.. 937 866-2444
1019 S Main St Miamisburg (45342) *(G-11025)*

Bella Capelli Inc.. 440 899-1225
24350 Center Ridge Rd Westlake (44145) *(G-15038)*

Bella Capelli Salon, Westlake *Also Called: Bella Capelli Inc (G-15038)*

Bellaire Harbor Service LLC.. 740 676-4305
4102 Jefferson St Bellaire (43906) *(G-1006)*

Bellas Lawn & Landscape LLC.. 419 536-9003
3017 Hill Ave Ste A Toledo (43607) *(G-13703)*

Belle Tire Distributors Inc.. 419 535-3033
750 S Reynolds Rd Toledo (43615) *(G-13704)*

Bellefaire Jewish Chld Bur (PA).. 216 932-2800
22001 Fairmount Blvd Shaker Heights (44118) *(G-12974)*

Bellefaire Jewish Chld Bur, Shaker Heights *Also Called: Bellefaire Jewish Chld Bur (G-12974)*

Bellefontaine Lodging Inc.. 937 599-6666
260 Northview Dr Bellefontaine (43311) *(G-1020)*

Belletech Corp.. 937 599-3774
20 Hunter Pl Bellefontaine (43311) *(G-1021)*

Bellevue Care Center, Bellevue *Also Called: Bellevue Healthcare Group LLC (G-1041)*

Bellevue Healthcare Group LLC.. 419 483-6225
1 Audrich Sq Bellevue (44811) *(G-1041)*

Bellevue Hospital (PA).. 419 483-4040
1400 W Main St Frnt Bellevue (44811) *(G-1042)*

Bellwether.. 949 247-8912
1375 E 9th St Ste 2440 Cleveland (44114) *(G-3862)*

Bellwether Entp RE Capitl LLC (PA).. 216 820-4500
1360 E 9th St Ste 300 Cleveland (44114) *(G-3863)*

Belmont Bhc Pines Hospital Inc.. 330 759-2700
615 Churchill Hubbard Rd Youngstown (44505) *(G-15558)*

Belmont Community Hospital (DH).. 740 671-1200
4697 Harrison St Bellaire (43906) *(G-1007)*

Belmont Country Club.. 419 666-1472
29601 Bates Rd Perrysburg (43551) *(G-12316)*

Belmont County Engineering, Saint Clairsville *Also Called: Belmont County of Ohio (G-12777)*

Belmont County Home.. 740 695-4925
100 Pine Ave Saint Clairsville (43950) *(G-12775)*

Belmont County of Ohio.. 740 695-4708
45244 National Rd Saint Clairsville (43950) *(G-12776)*

Belmont County of Ohio.. 740 695-1580
101 W Main St Saint Clairsville (43950) *(G-12777)*

Belmont County of Ohio.. 740 695-3144
67711 Oak View Rd Saint Clairsville (43950) *(G-12778)*

Belmont County Sani Sewer Dst, Saint Clairsville *Also Called: Belmont County of Ohio (G-12778)*

Belmont Division, Barnesville *Also Called: South Central Power Company (G-721)*

Belmont Federal Sav & Ln Assn (PA).. 740 676-1165
3301 Guernsey St Bellaire (43906) *(G-1008)*

Belmont Hills Country Club.. 740 695-2181
47080 National Rd Saint Clairsville (43950) *(G-12779)*

Belmont Manor Inc.. 740 695-4404
51999 Guirino Dr Saint Clairsville (43950) *(G-12780)*

Belmont Physicians, Dayton *Also Called: Miami Valley Hospital (G-7488)*

Belmore Leasing Co LLC.. 216 268-3600
1835 Belmore Rd Cleveland (44112) *(G-3864)*

Belting Company of Cincinnati (PA).. 513 621-9050
5500 Ridge Ave Cincinnati (45213) *(G-2256)*

Belting Company of Cincinnati.. 937 498-2104
301 Stolle Ave Sidney (45365) *(G-13021)*

Belting Company of Cincinnati.. 937 498-2104
2450 Ross St Sidney (45365) *(G-13022)*

Belvedere Corporation.. 513 241-3888
35 W 5th St Cincinnati (45202) *(G-2257)*

Benchmark Building Supply Inc.. 513 732-2522
4701 State Route 276 Batavia (45103) *(G-728)*

Benchmark Craftsman Inc.. 866 313-4700
4700 Greenwich Rd Seville (44273) *(G-12963)*

Benchmark Craftsmen, Seville *Also Called: Benchmark Craftsman Inc (G-12963)*

Benchmark Digital Partners LLC (PA).. 513 774-1000
5181 Natorp Blvd Ste 610 Mason (45040) *(G-10523)*

Benchmark Industrial Inc (PA) 614 695-6500
950 Claycraft Rd Gahanna (43230) *(G-8711)*

Benchmark Landscape Cnstr Inc 614 873-8080
9600 Industrial Pkwy Plain City (43064) *(G-12469)*

Benchmark National Corporation 419 843-6691
400 N Buckeye St Bellevue (44811) *(G-1043)*

Benchmark National Corporation 419 424-0900
1800 Industrial Dr Findlay (45840) *(G-8511)*

Bendix, Avon *Also Called: Bendix Coml Vhcl Systems LLC (G-640)*

Bendix Coml Vhcl Systems LLC (DH) 440 329-9000
35500 Chester Rd Avon (44011) *(G-640)*

Bendon Inc 419 903-0403
1191 Commerce Pkwy Ashland (44805) *(G-481)*

Bendon Inc (PA) 419 207-3600
1840 S Baney Rd Ashland (44805) *(G-482)*

Bendon Publishing Intl, Ashland *Also Called: Bendon Inc (G-482)*

Benedict Enterprises Inc (PA) 513 539-9216
750 Lakeview Rd Monroe (45050) *(G-11334)*

Beneficial Building Svcs Inc (PA) 330 848-2556
1830 13th St Sw Akron (44314) *(G-65)*

Beneficial Talent Source, Milford *Also Called: Berkheimer Enterprises LLC (G-11217)*

Benefit Services Inc (PA) 330 666-0337
3636 Copley Rd Ste 201 Copley (44321) *(G-6948)*

Benesch FrdInder Cplan Arnoff 216 363-4686
127 Public Sq Cleveland (44114) *(G-3865)*

Benesch FrdInder Cplan Arnoff 614 223-9300
41 S High St Ste 2600 Columbus (43215) *(G-5432)*

Benesch Friedlander Coplan & Aronoff LLP (PA) 216 363-4500
200 Public Sq Ste 2300 Cleveland (44114) *(G-3866)*

Benjamin Rose Institute (PA) 216 791-8000
11890 Fairhill Rd Cleveland (44120) *(G-3867)*

Benjamin Rose Institute 216 791-3580
2373 Euclid Heights Blvd 2nd Fl Cleveland (44106) *(G-3868)*

Benjamin Rose Institute 216 791-8000
850 Euclid Ave Ste 1100 Cleveland (44114) *(G-3869)*

Benjamin Steel, Springfield *Also Called: Benjamin Steel Company Inc (G-13221)*

Benjamin Steel Company Inc (PA) 937 322-8600
777 Benjamin Dr Springfield (45502) *(G-13221)*

Benmit Division, North Lawrence *Also Called: US Tubular Products Inc (G-11880)*

Bennett Adelson Prof Svcs LLC 216 369-0140
6050 Oak Tree Blvd Ste 150 Cleveland (44131) *(G-3870)*

Bennett Enterprises Inc 419 893-1004
1409 Reynolds Rd Maumee (43537) *(G-10699)*

Bennington Glen Nursing Home, Marengo *Also Called: Dearth Management Company (G-10352)*

Benny's Pizza, Marysville *Also Called: Parkway Pizza Incorporated (G-10502)*

Bentley Leasing Co LLC 330 337-9503
2511 Bentley Dr Salem (44460) *(G-12839)*

Berea Alzheimer's Care Center, Berea *Also Called: Communicare Health Svcs Inc (G-1066)*

Berger Health System, Circleville *Also Called: The Berger Hospital (G-3727)*

Bergholz 7, Bergholz *Also Called: Rosebud Mining Company (G-1088)*

Bergquist, Toledo *Also Called: K A Bergquist Inc (G-13872)*

Berk Enterprises Inc (PA) 330 369-1192
1554 Thomas Rd Se Warren (44484) *(G-14506)*

Berk Paper & Supply, Warren *Also Called: Berk Enterprises Inc (G-14506)*

Berkebile Russell & Associates 440 989-4480
1720 Cooper Foster Park Rd W Ste B Lorain (44053) *(G-10060)*

Berkeley Square Retirement Ctr, Hamilton *Also Called: Colonial Senior Services Inc (G-9030)*

Berkheimer Enterprises LLC 513 884-8702
2 Crestview Dr Milford (45150) *(G-11217)*

Berkowitz Kmin Bkatz Mem Chpel 216 932-7900
1985 S Taylor Rd Cleveland Heights (44118) *(G-5177)*

Berkshire Local School Dst 440 834-4123
14259 Claridon Troy Rd Burton (44021) *(G-1525)*

Berkshire Realty Group, Cincinnati *Also Called: Brg Realty Group LLC (G-2280)*

Berlin Grande Hotel Ltd 330 403-3050
4787 Township Rd 366 Berlin (44610) *(G-1089)*

Berlin Transportation LLC 330 674-3395
7576 State Rte 241 Millersburg (44654) *(G-11273)*

Bermex Inc 330 945-7500
4500 Courthouse Blvd Ste 150 Stow (44224) *(G-13355)*

Bermis, Fremont *Also Called: Amcor Flexibles North Amer Inc (G-8666)*

Berner Trucking Inc 330 343-5812
5885 Crown Rd Nw Dover (44622) *(G-7872)*

Berns Oneill SEC & Safety LLC 330 374-9133
1000 N Main St Akron (44310) *(G-66)*

Berriehill Research Corp 937 435-1016
7735 Paragon Rd Dayton (45459) *(G-7190)*

Berry Insurance Group, Terrace Park *Also Called: Brown & Brown of Ohio LLC (G-13613)*

Berry Network 513 702-3373
6 N Main St Ste 610 Dayton (45402) *(G-7191)*

Berry Network LLC (DH) 800 366-1264
3100 Kettering Blvd Moraine (45439) *(G-11391)*

Bertin Steel Processing Inc 440 943-0094
1271 E 289th St Ste 1 Wickliffe (44092) *(G-15146)*

Bertram Inn, Aurora *Also Called: B & I Hotel Management LLC (G-607)*

Bessemer and Lake Erie RR Co 440 593-1102
950 Ford Ave Conneaut (44030) *(G-6940)*

Best Aire, Millbury *Also Called: Best Aire Compressor Service (G-11266)*

Best Aire Compressor Service (DH) 419 726-0055
3648 Rockland Cir Millbury (43447) *(G-11266)*

Best Care Nrsing Rhblttion Ctr 740 574-2558
2159 Dogwood Ridge Rd Wheelersburg (45694) *(G-15127)*

Best Communications Inc 440 758-5854
213 S Ridge Rd W Conneaut (44030) *(G-6941)*

Best Controls Company, Ashland *Also Called: Chandler Systems Incorporated (G-491)*

Best Frnds Veterinary Hosp Inc 614 889-7387
275 W Olentangy St Powell (43065) *(G-12586)*

Best Karpet Klean Ohio LLC 440 942-2481
5525 Canal Rd Unit A Cleveland (44125) *(G-3871)*

Best Lighting Products, Etna *Also Called: Best Lighting Products Inc (G-8332)*

Best Lighting Products Inc (HQ) 740 964-1198
1213 Etna Pkwy Etna (43062) *(G-8332)*

Best One Tire & Svc Lima Inc (PA) 419 229-2380
701 E Hanthorn Rd Lima (45804) *(G-9868)*

Best Payment Solutions Inc (HQ) 630 321-0117
8500 Governors Hill Dr Symmes Twp (45249) *(G-13582)*

Best Restaurant Equipment & Design 614 488-2378
4020 Business Park Dr Columbus (43204) *(G-5433)*

Best Supply Inc 614 527-7000
1885 Obrien Rd Columbus (43228) *(G-5434)*

Best Value Inn, Columbus *Also Called: Amlon Ltd (G-5366)*

Best Western, Akron *Also Called: Best Western Executive Inn (G-67)*

Best Western, Caldwell *Also Called: Best Western Caldwell Inn Inc (G-1546)*

Best Western, Chillicothe *Also Called: Best Western Adena Inn (G-2051)*

Best Western, Columbus *Also Called: Best Western Suites (G-5435)*

Best Western, Copley *Also Called: Sun Lodging LLC (G-6965)*

Best Western, Grove City *Also Called: Natraj Corporation (G-8940)*

Best Western, Norwalk *Also Called: Carol Ruta (G-12004)*

Best Western, Port Clinton *Also Called: Goodnight Inn Inc (G-12527)*

Best Western Adena Inn 877 722-3422
1250 N Bridge St Chillicothe (45601) *(G-2051)*

Best Western Caldwell Inn Inc 740 732-7599
44128 Fairground Rd Caldwell (43724) *(G-1546)*

Best Western Executive Inn 330 794-1050
2677 Gilchrist Rd Unit 1 Akron (44305) *(G-67)*

Best Western Falcon Plaza Mtl, Bowling Green *Also Called: Falcon Plaza LLC (G-1319)*

Best Western Grnd Victoria Inn, Westlake *Also Called: Northern Tier Hospitality LLC (G-15089)*

Best Western Suites 614 870-2378
1133 Evans Way Ct Columbus (43228) *(G-5435)*

Best Western Sycamore Inn, Oxford *Also Called: Oxford Motel & LP (G-12215)*

Best Western Wooster Plaza, Wooster *Also Called: Best Wooster Inc (G-15311)*

Best Wooster Inc 330 264-7750
243 E Liberty St Ste 11 Wooster (44691) *(G-15311)*

Bestdrive, Urbancrest *Also Called: Bestdrive LLC (G-14319)*

Bestdrive LLC 614 284-7549
3315 Urbancrest Industrial Dr Urbancrest (43123) *(G-14319)*

Bestrateusa, Brecksville *Also Called: Crosscountry Mortgage LLC (G-1352)*

Bestway Transport Co (PA) 419 687-2000
2040 Sandusky St Rt 61n Plymouth (44865) *(G-12501)*

Beta Lab & Technical Svcs — ALPHABETIC SECTION

Beta Lab & Technical Svcs, Cleveland *Also Called: Energy Harbor Nuclear Corp* **(G-4214)**
Beta Theta PI Fraternity (PA) 513 523-7591
  5134 Bonham Rd Oxford (45056) **(G-12201)**
Betco Corporation (PA) 419 241-2156
  400 Van Camp Rd Bowling Green (43402) **(G-1307)**
Bethany Nursing Home Inc 330 492-7171
  626 34th St Nw Canton (44709) **(G-1686)**
Bethel Rgional Fmly Healthcare, Bethel *Also Called: Trihealth Inc* **(G-1095)**
Bethesda Butler Hospital, Fairfield Township *Also Called: Bethesda Hospital Inc* **(G-8456)**
BETHESDA CARE, Zanesville *Also Called: Community Ambulance Service* **(G-15784)**
BETHESDA CARE, Zanesville *Also Called: Genesis Healthcare System* **(G-15791)**
Bethesda Care Butler County, Hamilton *Also Called: Trihealth Inc* **(G-9087)**
Bethesda Care Center, Fremont *Also Called: Volunters Amer Care Facilities* **(G-8707)**
Bethesda Corp Communications, Montgomery *Also Called: Bethesda Hospital Inc* **(G-11362)**
Bethesda Foundation Inc 513 745-1616
  10500 Montgomery Rd Montgomery (45242) **(G-11361)**
Bethesda Group Practice, Milford *Also Called: Bethesda Hospital Inc* **(G-11218)**
Bethesda Hospital Inc (DH) 513 569-6100
  4750 Wesley Ave Cincinnati (45212) **(G-2258)**
Bethesda Hospital Inc 513 563-1505
  3801 Hauck Rd Frnt Cincinnati (45241) **(G-2259)**
Bethesda Hospital Inc 513 894-8888
  3125 Hamilton Mason Rd Fairfield Township (45011) **(G-8456)**
Bethesda Hospital Inc 513 248-8800
  5861 Cinema Dr Milford (45150) **(G-11218)**
Bethesda Hospital Inc 513 247-0224
  10700 Montgomery Rd Ste 315 Montgomery (45242) **(G-11362)**
Bethesda Hospital Inc 513 745-1111
  10500 Montgomery Rd Montgomery (45242) **(G-11363)**
Bethesda Hospital Association 740 454-4000
  2951 Maple Ave Zanesville (43701) **(G-15770)**
Bethesda North Hospital, Cincinnati *Also Called: Bethesda Hospital Inc* **(G-2258)**
Bethesda North Hospital, Montgomery *Also Called: Bethesda Hospital Inc* **(G-11363)**
Bethesda North Hospital, Montgomery *Also Called: Trihealth Inc* **(G-11377)**
Bettcher Industries, Birmingham *Also Called: Bettcher Industries Inc* **(G-1107)**
Bettcher Industries Inc (PA) 440 965-4422
  6801 State Rte 60 Birmingham (44816) **(G-1107)**
Better Bus Bur Centl Ohio I, Columbus *Also Called: Better Bus Bur Centl Ohio Inc* **(G-5436)**
Better Bus Bur Centl Ohio Inc 614 486-6336
  1169 Dublin Rd Columbus (43215) **(G-5436)**
Better Bus Bur Srving Cnton RE 330 454-9401
  1434 Cleveland Ave Nw Canton (44703) **(G-1687)**
BETTER BUSINESS BUREAU, Canton *Also Called: Better Bus Bur Srving Cnton RE* **(G-1687)**
Bevcorp LLC (HQ) 440 954-3500
  37200 Research Dr Eastlake (44095) **(G-8200)**
Beverage Distributors Inc 216 431-1600
  3800 King Ave Cleveland (44114) **(G-3872)**
Beverly, Akron *Also Called: Beaver Dam Health Care Center* **(G-64)**
Beverly, Columbus *Also Called: Beaver Dam Health Care Center* **(G-5429)**
Beverly, Lima *Also Called: Beaver Dam Health Care Center* **(G-9867)**
Beverly, Wadsworth *Also Called: Beaver Dam Health Care Center* **(G-14429)**
Beverly, Willoughby *Also Called: Beaver Dam Health Care Center* **(G-15187)**
Bexley Plaza Apartments, Columbus *Also Called: Plaza Properties Inc* **(G-6532)**
Beyond Homecare LLC 937 704-4002
  31 1/2 Monument Sq Urbana (43078) **(G-14297)**
Bfc Inc (PA) 330 364-6645
  1213 E 3rd St Dover (44622) **(G-7873)**
Bfg Supply Co LLC (PA) 800 883-0234
  14500 Kinsman Rd Burton (44021) **(G-1526)**
Bfg Supply Co., Burton *Also Called: Bfg Supply Co LLC* **(G-1526)**
Bfs Supply, Cincinnati *Also Called: Frederick Steel Company LLC* **(G-2703)**
BG Trucking & Cnstr Inc 234 759-3440
  11330 Market St North Lima (44452) **(G-11884)**
Bgr Inc (PA) 800 628-9195
  6392 Gano Rd West Chester (45069) **(G-14651)**
Bhc Fox Run Hospital Inc 740 695-2131
  67670 Traco Dr Saint Clairsville (43950) **(G-12781)**
Bhdp Architecture, Cincinnati *Also Called: Baxter Hdell Dnnlly Prston Inc* **(G-2240)**

Bhe Environmental Inc
  11733 Chesterdale Rd Cincinnati (45246) **(G-2260)**
BHP Energy LLC 866 720-2700
  6842 Commodore Dr Walbridge (43465) **(G-14460)**
Bi-Con Engineering LLC 740 685-9217
  10901 Clay Pike Rd Derwent (43733) **(G-7863)**
Bi-Con Services Inc 740 685-2542
  10901 Clay Pike Rd Derwent (43733) **(G-7864)**
Bico Akron Inc 330 794-1716
  3100 Gilchrist Rd Mogadore (44260) **(G-11324)**
Bico Steel Service Centers, Mogadore *Also Called: Bico Akron Inc* **(G-11324)**
Bieser Greer & Landis LLP 937 223-3277
  6 N Main St Ste 400 Dayton (45402) **(G-7192)**
Big Bang Bar Cleveland LLC 615 264-5650
  1163 Front Ave Cleveland (44113) **(G-3873)**
Big Bang, The, Cleveland *Also Called: Big Bang Bar Cleveland LLC* **(G-3873)**
Big Blue Trucking Inc 330 372-1421
  518 Perkins Jones Rd Ne Warren (44483) **(G-14507)**
Big Brthers Big Ssters Cntl OH (PA) 614 839-2447
  1855 E Dublin Granville Rd Fl 1 Columbus (43229) **(G-5437)**
Big Creek Surgery Center, Middleburg Heights *Also Called: Foundtion Srgery Afflate Mddlb* **(G-11115)**
Big Grens Lawn Svc Snow Plwing 937 539-8163
  914 Township Road 219 W Bellefontaine (43311) **(G-1022)**
Big Hill Realty Corp (PA) 937 435-1177
  5580 Far Hills Ave Dayton (45429) **(G-7193)**
Big Lots, Columbus *Also Called: Big Lots Stores Inc* **(G-5438)**
Big Lots, Columbus *Also Called: Big Lots Stores LLC* **(G-5439)**
Big Lots, Westerville *Also Called: Closeout Distribution LLC* **(G-14968)**
Big Lots Stores Inc 614 278-6800
  300 Phillipi Rd Bldg 500 Columbus (43228) **(G-5438)**
Big Lots Stores LLC (HQ) 614 278-6800
  4900 E Dublin Granville Rd Columbus (43081) **(G-5439)**
Big Oki LLC 513 874-1111
  6500 Dixie Hwy # 4 Fairfield (45014) **(G-8394)**
Big Red Rooster (HQ) 614 255-0200
  121 Thurman Ave Columbus (43206) **(G-5440)**
Big Sandy Furniture Inc 740 894-4242
  45 County Rd 407 Chesapeake (45619) **(G-2028)**
Big Sandy Furniture Inc 740 775-4244
  1404 N Bridge St Chillicothe (45601) **(G-2052)**
Big Sandy Furniture Inc (HQ) 740 574-2113
  8375 Gallia Pike Franklin Furnace (45629) **(G-8653)**
Big Sandy Furniture Inc 740 354-3193
  730 10th St Portsmouth (45662) **(G-12546)**
Big Sandy Furniture Store 5, Portsmouth *Also Called: Big Sandy Furniture Inc* **(G-12546)**
Big Sandy Service Company, Franklin Furnace *Also Called: Big Sandy Furniture Inc* **(G-8653)**
Big Sandy Superstore, Chesapeake *Also Called: Big Sandy Furniture Inc* **(G-2028)**
Big Village Insights Inc 513 772-7580
  110 Boggs Ln Ste 380 Cincinnati (45246) **(G-2261)**
Big Village Insights Inc 419 893-0029
  1900 Indian Wood Cir Ste 200 Maumee (43537) **(G-10700)**
Bigger Road Veterinary Clinic (PA) 937 435-3262
  5655 Bigger Rd Dayton (45440) **(G-7194)**
Bijoe Development Inc 330 674-5981
  7188 State Rte 62 & 39 Millersburg (44654) **(G-11274)**
Bill Delord Autocenter Inc 513 932-3000
  5455 Grandin Pass Ct Maineville (45039) **(G-10225)**
Bill Hawk Inc 330 833-5558
  2200 Venture Cir Se Massillon (44646) **(G-10632)**
Billie Lawless 714 851-6372
  4533 Payne Ave Cleveland (44103) **(G-3874)**
Billing Department, Toledo *Also Called: Promedica Health Systems Inc* **(G-13975)**
Bills Battery Company Inc 513 922-0100
  5221 Crookshank Rd Cincinnati (45238) **(G-2262)**
Billy Royal, Chagrin Falls *Also Called: Schneider Saddlery LLC* **(G-1989)**
Bindery & Spc Pressworks Inc 614 873-4623
  351 W Bigelow Ave Plain City (43064) **(G-12470)**
Bindley Western Drug, Dublin *Also Called: Cardinal Health 100 Inc* **(G-7951)**

ALPHABETIC SECTION

Bindu Associates LLC Elyria.. 440 324-0099
  99 Cortland Cir Amherst (44001) *(G-424)*

Bingo Division, Youngstown *Also Called: Nannicola Wholesale Co* *(G-15672)*

Binkelman Corporation (PA)... 419 537-9333
  828 Van Camp Rd Bowling Green (43402) *(G-1308)*

Bio-Blood Components Inc.. 614 294-3183
  1393 N High St Columbus (43201) *(G-5441)*

Bio-Mdcal Applcations Ohio Inc.. 330 376-4905
  345 Bishop St Akron (44307) *(G-68)*

BioLife Plasma Services LP.. 419 313-3406
  4711 Talmadge Rd Toledo (43623) *(G-13705)*

Biomedical Laboratory, Hubbard *Also Called: Connie Parks* *(G-9320)*

Bionix LLC.. 419 727-8421
  1670 Indian Wood Cir Maumee (43537) *(G-10701)*

Bionix Development Corporation.. 800 551-7096
  5154 Enterprise Blvd Toledo (43612) *(G-13706)*

Bionix Safety Technologies Ltd (HQ)..................................... 419 727-0552
  1670 Indian Wood Cir Maumee (43537) *(G-10702)*

Biotest Pharmaceuticals Corp... 419 819-3068
  1616 E Wooster St Unit 39 Bowling Green (43402) *(G-1309)*

Biotest Plasma Center, Bowling Green *Also Called: Biotest Pharmaceuticals Corp* *(G-1309)*

Birchaven Village (PA).. 419 424-3000
  15100 Birchaven Ln Ofc C Findlay (45840) *(G-8512)*

Birchaven Village.. 419 424-3000
  415 College St Findlay (45840) *(G-8513)*

Bit Mining Limited.. 346 204-8537
  428 Seiberling St Akron (44306) *(G-69)*

Bitec, Dayton *Also Called: Sample Machining Inc* *(G-7609)*

BITTERSWEET FARMS, Whitehouse *Also Called: Bittersweet Inc* *(G-15138)*

Bittersweet Inc.. 419 999-9174
  4640 Fort Amanda Rd Lima (45805) *(G-9869)*

Bittersweet Inc (PA).. 419 875-6986
  12660 Archbold Whitehouse Rd Whitehouse (43571) *(G-15138)*

Bixby Living Skills Center, Groveport *Also Called: ARC Indstries Inc Frnklin Cnty* *(G-8970)*

Biz Com Electric LLC.. 513 961-7200
  682 Tuxedo Pl Cincinnati (45206) *(G-2263)*

Bjaam Environmental, Canal Fulton *Also Called: Bjaam Environmental Inc* *(G-1593)*

Bjaam Environmental Inc... 330 854-5300
  472 Elm Ridge Ave Canal Fulton (44614) *(G-1593)*

Bkg Holdings LLC.. 614 252-7455
  600 N Cassady Ave Ofc Columbus (43219) *(G-5442)*

Bkp Ambulance District... 419 674-4574
  439 S Main St Kenton (43326) *(G-9610)*

Black Horse Brothers Inc.. 267 265-0013
  141 Broad Blvd Ste 108 Cuyahoga Falls (44221) *(G-7050)*

Black River Display, Mansfield *Also Called: Black River Group Inc* *(G-10246)*

Black River Display Group, Mansfield *Also Called: Black River Group Inc* *(G-10245)*

Black River Group Inc (PA).. 419 524-6699
  195 E 4th St Mansfield (44902) *(G-10245)*

Black River Group Inc... 419 524-4312
  195 E 4th St Mansfield (44902) *(G-10246)*

Black Spphire C Clmbus Univ 20.. 614 297-9912
  1421 Olentangy River Rd Columbus (43212) *(G-5443)*

Black Stone Cincinnati LLC (DH).. 513 924-1370
  4700 E Galbraith Rd Fl 3 Cincinnati (45236) *(G-2264)*

Black Swamp Steel Inc... 419 867-8050
  1761 Commerce Rd Holland (43528) *(G-9280)*

Blackburns Fabrication Inc.. 614 875-0784
  2467 Jackson Pike Columbus (43223) *(G-5444)*

Blackhawk Industrial Dist Inc... 918 610-4719
  2845 Interstate Pkwy Brunswick (44212) *(G-1451)*

Blacklick Woods Metro Park, Reynoldsburg *Also Called: Columbus Frnklin Cnty Mtro Pk* *(G-12659)*

Blanchard Valley Center, Findlay *Also Called: Hancock Cnty Bd Dvlpmntal Dsbl* *(G-8541)*

Blanchard Valley Health System (PA).................................... 419 423-4500
  1900 S Main St Findlay (45840) *(G-8514)*

Blanchard Valley Hospital, Findlay *Also Called: Blanchard Vly Rgional Hlth Ctr* *(G-8516)*

Blanchard Valley Med Assoc Inc.. 419 424-0380
  200 W Pearl St Findlay (45840) *(G-8515)*

Blanchard Valley Wns Care LLC.. 419 420-0904
  1103 Village Square Dr Perrysburg (43551) *(G-12317)*

Blanchard Vly Rgional Hlth Ctr... 419 358-9010
  139 Garau St Bluffton (45817) *(G-1277)*

Blanchard Vly Rgional Hlth Ctr (HQ)..................................... 419 423-4500
  1900 S Main St Findlay (45840) *(G-8516)*

Blanchard Vly Rsdntial Svcs In.. 419 422-6503
  1701 E Main Cross St Findlay (45840) *(G-8517)*

Blast-All Inc.. 606 393-5786
  541 Private Road 908 Ironton (45638) *(G-9503)*

Blastmaster Holdings Usa LLC (PA)...................................... 877 725-2781
  4510 Bridgeway Ave Columbus (43219) *(G-5445)*

Blastone International, Columbus *Also Called: Blastmaster Holdings Usa LLC* *(G-5445)*

Bleckmann Logistics, Columbus *Also Called: Bleckmann USA LLC* *(G-5446)*

Bleckmann USA LLC... 740 809-2645
  10 W Broad St Ste 2100 Columbus (43215) *(G-5446)*

Blendon Gardens, Lewis Center *Also Called: Blendon Gardens Inc* *(G-9811)*

Blendon Gardens Inc... 614 840-0500
  9590 S Old State Rd Lewis Center (43035) *(G-9811)*

Blendonwoods Metro Park, Westerville *Also Called: Columbus Frnklin Cnty Mtro Pk* *(G-14971)*

Bless, Marysville *Also Called: Basinger Lfe Enhncmnt Sprt Svc* *(G-10474)*

Blessing Home Health Care Inc... 614 329-2086
  5214 Tarlmeadows Ln Hilliard (43026) *(G-9183)*

Blick Clinic Inc (PA)... 330 762-5425
  640 W Market St Akron (44303) *(G-70)*

Blick Clinic Inc... 330 762-5425
  682 W Market St Akron (44303) *(G-71)*

Blind & Son LLC.. 330 753-7711
  344 4th St Nw Barberton (44203) *(G-695)*

Blink Marketing Logistics, Perrysburg *Also Called: Bottomline Ink Corporation* *(G-12318)*

Blissful Corporation... 614 539-3500
  4197 Marlane Dr Grove City (43123) *(G-8897)*

Block Communications Inc.. 419 724-2539
  2700 Oregon Rd Northwood (43619) *(G-11969)*

Blonder Home Accents, Cleveland *Also Called: The Blonder Company* *(G-4992)*

Blood & Cancer Center Inc... 330 533-3040
  3695 Boardman Canfield Rd Canfield (44406) *(G-1621)*

Blood Center, Cincinnati *Also Called: University of Cincinnati* *(G-3573)*

Blood Services Centl Ohio Reg (PA)...................................... 614 253-7981
  995 E Broad St Columbus (43205) *(G-5447)*

Bloomer Candy Co... 740 452-7501
  3610 National Rd Zanesville (43701) *(G-15771)*

BLOOMFIELD COTTAGES, Ashland *Also Called: Brethren Care Inc* *(G-484)*

Blossom Hill Inc (PA)... 440 652-6749
  10983 Abbey Rd North Royalton (44133) *(G-11938)*

Blossom Hill Inc... 440 250-9182
  28700 Center Ridge Rd Westlake (44145) *(G-15039)*

Blossom Hill Care Center, Huntsburg *Also Called: Blossom Hills Nursing Home* *(G-9381)*

Blossom Hills Nursing Home.. 440 635-5567
  12496 Princeton Rd Huntsburg (44046) *(G-9381)*

Blowout Bar... 614 732-0965
  1378 Grandview Ave Columbus (43212) *(G-5448)*

Bls Trucking Inc... 937 224-0494
  1730 Dalton Dr New Carlisle (45344) *(G-11600)*

Blu Diamond Home Care LLC... 937 723-7836
  3481 Office Park Dr Ste 120 Kettering (45439) *(G-9626)*

Blue & Co LLC... 513 241-4507
  720 E Pete Rose Way Ste 100 Cincinnati (45202) *(G-2265)*

BLUE ASH CARE CENTER, Cincinnati *Also Called: Blue Ash Healthcare Group Inc* *(G-2266)*

Blue Ash Dialysis, Blue Ash *Also Called: Dva Hlthcare - Sthwest Ohio LL* *(G-1165)*

Blue Ash Healthcare Group Inc... 513 793-3362
  4900 Cooper Rd Cincinnati (45242) *(G-2266)*

Blue Ash Roofing Co, Blue Ash *Also Called: Molloy Roofing Company* *(G-1212)*

Blue Ash YMCA, Blue Ash *Also Called: Young MNS Chrstn Assn Grter CN* *(G-1275)*

Blue Beacon of Beaverdam, Beaverdam *Also Called: Blue Beacon USA LP II* *(G-952)*

Blue Beacon Truck Wash, Hubbard *Also Called: Blue Beacon USA LP* *(G-9319)*

Blue Beacon USA LP.. 330 534-4419
  7044 Truck World Blvd Hubbard (44425) *(G-9319)*

Blue Beacon USA LP II.. 419 643-8146
  413 E Main St Beaverdam (45808) *(G-952)*

Blue Chip 2000 Coml Clg Inc... 513 561-2999
  7250 Edington Dr Cincinnati (45249) *(G-2267)*

Blue Chip Consulting Group | ALPHABETIC SECTION

Blue Chip Consulting Group 216 503-6000
   6050 Oak Tree Blvd Ste 290 Independence (44131) *(G-9411)*
Blue Chip Consulting Group LLC 216 503-6001
   6000 Lombardo Ctr Ste 650 Seven Hills (44131) *(G-12951)*
Blue Chip Pavement Maintenance Inc 513 321-9595
   4320 Mount Carmel Rd Cincinnati (45244) *(G-2268)*
Blue Chip Pros, Cincinnati *Also Called: Blue Chip 2000 Coml Clg Inc (G-2267)*
Blue Creek Enterprises Inc (PA) 937 364-2920
   316 N Main St Lynchburg (45142) *(G-10183)*
Blue Creek Healthcare LLC 419 877-5338
   11239 Waterville St Whitehouse (43571) *(G-15139)*
Blue Cross, Canton *Also Called: Anthem Insurance Companies Inc (G-1668)*
Blue Cross, Columbus *Also Called: Anthem Insurance Companies Inc (G-5246)*
Blue Flag Logistics LLC 502 975-8473
   5365 Valley Ln E Columbus (43231) *(G-5449)*
Blue Racer Midstream LLC 740 630-7556
   11388 E Pike Rd Unit B Cambridge (43725) *(G-1556)*
Blue Ribbon Meats Inc (PA) 216 631-8850
   3316 W 67th Pl Cleveland (44102) *(G-3875)*
Blue Sky Therapy, Canfield *Also Called: Wsb Rehabilitation Svcs Inc (G-1645)*
Blue Stream LLC (PA) 330 659-6166
   4360 Brecksville Rd Richfield (44286) *(G-12688)*
Blue Tech Smart Solutions LLC 216 271-4800
   5885 Grant Ave Cleveland (44105) *(G-3876)*
Blue Technologies Inc (PA) 216 271-4800
   5885 Grant Ave Cleveland (44105) *(G-3877)*
Blue Tooth Dental 937 432-6677
   2198 Hewitt Ave Dayton (45440) *(G-7195)*
Blue Wtr Chamber Orchestra Inc 440 781-6215
   3631 Perkins Ave Ste 4c Cleveland (44114) *(G-3878)*
Blue-Kenwood LLC 513 469-6900
   5300 Cornell Rd Blue Ash (45242) *(G-1137)*
Bluescope Recycling & Mtls LLC 816 968-3000
   7300 State Route 109 Delta (43515) *(G-7849)*
Bluescope Recycling & Mtls LLC 419 747-6522
   2384 Springmill Rd Mansfield (44903) *(G-10247)*
Bluesky Healthcare Inc (PA) 440 989-5200
   3885 Oberlin Ave Lorain (44053) *(G-10061)*
Bluespring Software Inc (HQ) 513 794-1764
   10290 Alliance Rd Blue Ash (45242) *(G-1138)*
Bluestone Counseling LLC 614 406-0299
   3748 Kilmuir Dr Columbus (43221) *(G-5450)*
Bluestreak Consulting, Cleveland *Also Called: Onyx Creative Inc (G-4702)*
Bluffton Campus, Bluffton *Also Called: Blanchard Vly Rgional Hlth Ctr (G-1277)*
Bluffton Community Hospital 419 358-9010
   139 Garau St Bluffton (45817) *(G-1278)*
Bluffton Stone Co 419 358-6941
   310 Quarry Dr Bluffton (45817) *(G-1279)*
Bmf, Fairlawn *Also Called: Bober Markey Fedorovich & Co (G-8467)*
Bmi Federal Credit Union (PA) 614 298-8527
   760 Kinnear Rd Frnt Columbus (43212) *(G-5451)*
Bmi Federal Credit Union 614 707-4000
   6165 Emerald Pkwy Dublin (43016) *(G-7944)*
Bmu77 LLC 740 652-1679
   10 Whiley Rd Lancaster (43130) *(G-9696)*
BMW Financial Services Na LLC 614 718-6900
   5515 Parkcenter Cir Dublin (43017) *(G-7945)*
BMW Financial Services Na LLC (DH) 614 718-6900
   5550 Britton Pkwy Hilliard (43026) *(G-9184)*
Bmwc Constructors Inc 419 490-2000
   913 Madison Ave Toledo (43604) *(G-13707)*
Bnd Rentals Inc 937 898-5061
   950 Engle Rd Vandalia (45377) *(G-14367)*
Bnsf Logistics LLC 937 526-3141
   611 Marker Rd Versailles (45380) *(G-14413)*
Bny Mellon National Assn 216 595-8769
   3333 Richmond Rd Ste 110 Beachwood (44122) *(G-769)*
Boak & Sons Inc 330 793-5646
   75 Victoria Rd Youngstown (44515) *(G-15559)*
Board Lucas Cnty Commissioners, Toledo *Also Called: County of Lucas (G-13762)*
Board of Dirs of Wttnberg Clle 937 327-6310
   225 N Fountain Ave Springfield (45504) *(G-13222)*
Board of Mental Health, Lorain *Also Called: County of Lorain (G-10069)*
Board of Mental Retardation, Carrollton *Also Called: County of Carroll (G-1906)*
Boardman Local Schools 330 726-3409
   7777 Glenwood Ave Youngstown (44512) *(G-15560)*
Boardman Medical Supply Co (HQ) 330 545-6700
   300 N State St Girard (44420) *(G-8810)*
Boardman School Bus Garage, Youngstown *Also Called: Boardman Local Schools (G-15560)*
Bob Chapman Ford, Marysville *Also Called: Bob Ford Chapman Inc (G-10475)*
Bob Ford Chapman Inc 937 642-0015
   1255 Columbus Ave Marysville (43040) *(G-10475)*
Bob Miller Rigging Inc 419 422-7477
   11758 Township Road 100 Findlay (45840) *(G-8518)*
Bob Pulte Chevrolet Inc 513 932-0303
   909 Columbus Ave Lebanon (45036) *(G-9757)*
Bob-Boyd Ford Inc (PA) 614 860-0606
   2840 N Columbus St Lancaster (43130) *(G-9697)*
Bob-Mor Inc 419 485-5555
   13508 State Route 15 Montpelier (43543) *(G-11381)*
Bobb Automotive Inc 614 853-3000
   4639 W Broad St Columbus (43228) *(G-5452)*
Bobb Suzuki, Columbus *Also Called: Bobb Automotive Inc (G-5452)*
Bobboyd Auto Family, Lancaster *Also Called: Bob-Boyd Ford Inc (G-9697)*
Bobby Layman Cadillac, Carroll *Also Called: Bobby Layman Cadillac GMC Inc (G-1899)*
Bobby Layman Cadillac GMC Inc 740 654-9590
   3733 Claypool Dr Carroll (43112) *(G-1899)*
Bobby Tripodi Foundation Inc (PA) 216 524-3787
   5905 Brecksville Rd Independence (44131) *(G-9412)*
Bobcat Enterprises, West Chester *Also Called: Bobcat Enterprises Inc (G-14652)*
Bobcat Enterprises Inc (PA) 513 874-8945
   9605 Princeton Glendale Rd West Chester (45011) *(G-14652)*
Bober Markey Fedorovich & Co (PA) 330 762-9785
   3421 Ridgewood Rd Ste 300 Fairlawn (44333) *(G-8467)*
Bock & Clark Corporation (HQ) 330 665-4821
   4580 Stephens Cir Nw Ste 300 Canton (44718) *(G-1688)*
Bodie Electric Inc 419 435-3672
   1109 N Main St Fostoria (44830) *(G-8613)*
Bodine Perry LLC (PA) 330 702-8100
   3711 Starrs Centre Dr Ste 2 Canfield (44406) *(G-1622)*
Body Alive Corporate LLC 513 834-8043
   8110 Montgomery Rd Ste 3 Cincinnati (45236) *(G-2269)*
Body Alive Fitness, Cincinnati *Also Called: Body Alive Corporate LLC (G-2269)*
Boehringer Ingelheim Pharma 216 525-0195
   5005 Rockside Rd Cleveland (44131) *(G-3879)*
Bogie Industries Inc Ltd 330 745-3105
   1100 Home Ave Akron (44310) *(G-72)*
Bogner Construction Company 330 262-6730
   305 Mulberry St Wooster (44691) *(G-15312)*
Bogner Corporation 330 262-6393
   427 S Grant St Wooster (44691) *(G-15313)*
Bohl Crane Inc 419 214-3940
   1104 Custer Dr Toledo (43612) *(G-13708)*
Bohl Equipment Company (PA) 800 962-4802
   534 W Laskey Rd Toledo (43612) *(G-13709)*
Boise Cascade, Marion *Also Called: Boise Cascade Company (G-10419)*
Boise Cascade Company 740 382-6766
   3007 Harding Hwy E Bldg 203b Marion (43302) *(G-10419)*
Bold Penguin, Columbus *Also Called: Bold Penguin Company LLC (G-5454)*
Bold Penguin Inc (HQ) 614 344-1029
   100 E Broad St Fl 15 Columbus (43215) *(G-5453)*
Bold Penguin Company LLC 614 344-1029
   100 E Broad St Fl 15 Columbus (43215) *(G-5454)*
Bollin & Sons Inc 419 693-6573
   6001 Brent Dr Toledo (43611) *(G-13710)*
Bollin Label Systems, Toledo *Also Called: Bollin & Sons Inc (G-13710)*
Bolt Construction Inc 330 549-0349
   10422 South Ave Youngstown (44514) *(G-15561)*
Bolt Construction Co, Youngstown *Also Called: Bolt Construction Inc (G-15561)*
Bolt Express LLC (PA) 419 729-6698
   7255 Crossleigh Ct Ste 108 Toledo (43617) *(G-13711)*
Bon Appetit Management Co 614 823-1880
   100 W Home St Westerville (43081) *(G-14962)*

ALPHABETIC SECTION

Bon Scurs Mrcy Hlth Foundation...............513 952-4019
1701 Mercy Health Pl Cincinnati (45237) *(G-2270)*

Bon Secours Mercy Health Inc...............440 233-1000
360 Cleveland Ave Amherst (44001) *(G-425)*

Bon Secours Mercy Health Inc...............513 639-2800
1701 Mercy Health Pl Cincinnati (45237) *(G-2271)*

Bon Secours Mercy Health Inc...............513 624-1950
7520 State Rd Cincinnati (45255) *(G-2272)*

Bon Secours Mercy Health Inc...............513 639-2800
1701 Mercy Health Pl Cincinnati (45237) *(G-2273)*

Bon Secours Mercy Health Inc (PA)...............513 956-3729
1701 Mercy Health Pl Cincinnati (45237) *(G-2274)*

Bon Secours Mercy Health Inc...............216 362-2000
12301 Snow Rd Cleveland (44130) *(G-3880)*

Bon Secours Mercy Health Inc...............419 991-7805
2875 W Elm St Lima (45805) *(G-9870)*

Bon Secours Mercy Health Inc...............440 774-6800
200 W Lorain St Oberlin (44074) *(G-12064)*

Bon Secours Mercy Health Inc...............419 251-2659
2213 Cherry St Toledo (43608) *(G-13712)*

Bon Secours Mercy Health Inc...............330 746-7211
1044 Belmont Ave Youngstown (44504) *(G-15562)*

Bon Secours Mercy Health Inc...............330 729-1420
8401 Market St Youngstown (44512) *(G-15563)*

BON SECURE MERCY HEALTH, Maumee Also Called: *St Lukes Hospital (G-10769)*

Bon Secure Mercy Health, Perrysburg Also Called: *Mercy Health (G-12356)*

Bonbright, Dayton Also Called: *Bonbright Distributors Inc (G-7196)*

Bonbright Distributors Inc (PA)...............937 222-1001
1 Arena Park Dr Dayton (45417) *(G-7196)*

Bonbright Distributors Inc...............937 222-1001
2024 Selma Rd Springfield (45505) *(G-13223)*

Bonded Chemicals Inc (HQ)...............614 777-9240
2645 Charter St Columbus (43228) *(G-5455)*

Bonnie Plants LLC...............937 642-7764
21109 Cotton Slash Rd Marysville (43040) *(G-10476)*

Bontrager Excavating Co Inc...............330 499-8775
11087 Cleveland Ave Nw Uniontown (44685) *(G-14242)*

Bookmasters Inc (HQ)...............419 281-1802
30 Amberwood Pkwy Ashland (44805) *(G-483)*

Boonshoft Ctr For Jwish Clture, Dayton Also Called: *Jewish Fdrtion Grter Dyton Inc (G-7427)*

Boost Engagement LLC...............937 223-2203
811 E 4th St Dayton (45402) *(G-7197)*

Booz Allen Hamilton Inc...............937 912-6400
3800 Pentagon Blvd Ste 110 Beavercreek (45431) *(G-864)*

Booz Allen Hamilton Inc...............937 429-5580
3800 Pentagon Blvd Ste 110 Beavercreek (45431) *(G-865)*

Borchers Americas Inc (HQ)...............440 899-2950
811 Sharon Dr Westlake (44145) *(G-15040)*

Bordas & Bordas Pllc...............740 695-8141
106 E Main St Saint Clairsville (43950) *(G-12782)*

Borden Dairy Co Cincinnati LLC (DH)...............513 948-8811
3068 W 106th St Cleveland (44111) *(G-3881)*

Borderless Logistics, Hooven Also Called: *Gozal Incorporated (G-9317)*

Borgers Ohio Inc...............419 663-3700
400 Industrial Pkwy Norwalk (44857) *(G-12002)*

Borrego Dialysis LLC...............513 737-0158
1532 Main St Hamilton (45013) *(G-9018)*

Bosch Rexroth Corporation...............614 527-7400
3940 Gantz Rd Ste F Grove City (43123) *(G-8898)*

Boss Display Corporation...............614 443-9495
1975 Galaxie St Columbus (43207) *(G-5456)*

Boss Investigations, Akron Also Called: *Berns Oneill SEC & Safety LLC (G-66)*

Bostleman Corp
7142 Nightingale Dr Ste 1 Holland (43528) *(G-9281)*

Boston Company Inc...............937 652-0410
121 N Main St Urbana (43078) *(G-14298)*

Boston Maintenance Bldg, Richfield Also Called: *Ohio Tpk & Infrastructure Comm (G-12705)*

Boston Retail Products Inc...............330 744-8100
225 Hubbard Rd Youngstown (44505) *(G-15564)*

Bostwick Design Partnr Inc (PA)...............216 621-7900
2729 Prospect Ave E Cleveland (44115) *(G-3882)*

Bostwick-Braun Company (PA)...............419 259-3600
7349 Crossleigh Ct Toledo (43617) *(G-13713)*

Botha Trucking LLC...............330 695-2296
5421 County Road 229 Fredericksburg (44627) *(G-8658)*

Bottle Solutions LLC...............216 889-3330
12201 Elmwood Ave Cleveland (44111) *(G-3883)*

Bottomline Ink Corporation...............419 897-8000
7829 Ponderosa Rd Perrysburg (43551) *(G-12318)*

Boulder Creek Golf Club...............330 626-2828
9700 Page Rd Streetsboro (44241) *(G-13410)*

Boulevard Motel Corp...............440 234-3131
17550 Rosbough Blvd Cleveland (44130) *(G-3884)*

Bound Tree Medical LLC (DH)...............614 760-5000
5000 Tuttle Crossing Blvd Dublin (43016) *(G-7946)*

Boundless Cmnty Pathways Inc (PA)...............937 461-0034
700 Liberty Ln West Carrollton (45449) *(G-14644)*

Boundless Strgc Resources Inc...............614 844-3800
445 E Dublin Granville Rd Ste H Worthington (43085) *(G-15406)*

Bowen Engineering Corporation...............614 536-0273
355 E Campus View Blvd Ste 110 Columbus (43235) *(G-5457)*

Bowling Green Clinic Inc...............419 352-1121
1039 Haskins Rd Unit A Bowling Green (43402) *(G-1310)*

Bowling Green Country Club Inc...............419 352-5546
923 Fairview Ave Bowling Green (43402) *(G-1311)*

Bowling Green Lincoln Inc...............419 352-2553
1079 N Main St Bowling Green (43402) *(G-1312)*

Bowling Green Lincoln Auto SL, Bowling Green Also Called: *Bowling Green Lincoln Inc (G-1312)*

Bowling Transportation Inc (PA)...............419 436-9590
1827 Sandusky St Fostoria (44830) *(G-8614)*

Bowser Morner and Associates, Toledo Also Called: *Bowser-Morner Inc (G-13714)*

Bowser-Morner Inc...............419 691-4800
1419 Miami St Toledo (43605) *(G-13714)*

Bowser-Morner Inc (PA)...............937 236-8805
4518 Taylorsville Rd Dayton (45424) *(G-7198)*

Bowstring Advisors, Cleveland Also Called: *Citizens Capital Markets Inc (G-3973)*

Boxcast Inc...............888 392-2278
2401 Superior Via Ste 5 Cleveland (44113) *(G-3885)*

Boxout LLC (PA)...............833 462-7746
6333 Hudson Crossing Pkwy Hudson (44236) *(G-9334)*

Boy Scouts of America, Cleveland Also Called: *Lake Erie Cncil Boy Scuts Amer (G-4474)*

BOY SCOUTS OF AMERICA, Columbus Also Called: *Simon Knton Cncil Byscuts Amer (G-6681)*

Boy Scouts Of America, Toledo Also Called: *Erie Shres Cncil Inc Boy Scuts (G-13797)*

Boy-Ko Management Inc...............513 677-4900
9370 Union Cemetery Rd Loveland (45140) *(G-10128)*

Boyas Enterprises I Inc...............216 524-3620
11311 Rockside Rd Cleveland (44125) *(G-3886)*

Boyas Excavating, Inc., Cleveland Also Called: *Boyas Enterprises I Inc (G-3886)*

Boyd Funeral Home, Cleveland Also Called: *E F Boyd & Son Inc (G-4193)*

Boys & Girls Club of Columbus, Columbus Also Called: *Boys Girls Clubs Columbus Inc (G-5458)*

Boys & Girls Club of Toledo (PA)...............419 241-4258
2250 N Detroit Ave Toledo (43606) *(G-13715)*

Boys and Girls CLB Wooster Inc...............330 988-1616
124 N Walnut St Wooster (44691) *(G-15314)*

BOYS CLUB CAMP ASSOCIATION, Toledo Also Called: *Boys & Girls Club of Toledo (G-13715)*

Boys Girls Clubs Columbus Inc...............614 221-8830
1108 City Park Ave Ste 301 Columbus (43206) *(G-5458)*

BP, Aurora Also Called: *Waterway Gas & Wash Company (G-630)*

BP 10 Inc...............513 346-3900
9486 Sutton Pl West Chester (45011) *(G-14653)*

BP Financial Group Inc...............513 851-8525
415 Glensprings Dr Ste 201 Cincinnati (45246) *(G-2275)*

BP Oil Pipeline Company...............216 398-8685
4421 Bradley Rd Cleveland (44109) *(G-3887)*

BP Oil Supply Company...............330 945-4132
1205 Main St Cuyahoga Falls (44221) *(G-7051)*

BP Oil Supply Company...............937 434-7008
1580 Miamisburg Centerville Rd Dayton (45459) *(G-7199)*

Bpi Acquisition Company LLC (DH)...............216 589-0198
127 Public Sq Ste 5110 Cleveland (44114) *(G-3888)*

Bpi Information Systems — ALPHABETIC SECTION

Bpi Information Systems, Brecksville Also Called: WD Bpi LLC (G-1371)
Bpi Infrmtion Systems Ohio Inc 440 717-4112
6055 W Snowville Rd Brecksville (44141) (G-1345)

Bprex Closures LLC 812 424-2904
1695 Indian Circle Ste 116 Maumee (43537) (G-10703)

Brackett Builders Inc (PA) 937 339-7505
418 E 1st St Dayton (45402) (G-7200)

Braden Med Services Inc 740 732-2356
44519 Marietta Rd Caldwell (43724) (G-1547)

Bradford Fire Rescue Svcs Inc 937 448-2686
200 S Miami Ave Bradford (45308) (G-1340)

Bradley Bay Assisted Living 440 871-4509
605 Bradley Rd Bay Village (44140) (G-758)

Brady Ware & Schoenfeld Inc (DH) 937 223-5247
3601 Rigby Rd Ste 400 Miamisburg (45342) (G-11026)

Brady Ware & Company, Miamisburg Also Called: Brady Ware & Schoenfeld Inc (G-11026)
Brake Parts Holdings Inc (DH) 216 589-0198
127 Public Sq Ste 5110 Cleveland (44114) (G-3889)

Brakefire Incorporated 937 426-9717
4099 Industrial Ln Beavercreek (45430) (G-919)

Brakefire Incorporated 330 535-4343
451 Kennedy Rd Akron (44305) (G-73)

Brakefire Incorporated (PA) 513 733-5655
10200 Reading Rd Cincinnati (45241) (G-2276)

Brampton Inn, Cleveland Also Called: 1460 Ninth St Assoc Ltd Partnr (G-3740)
Brand Protect Plus LLC 216 539-1880
23945 Mercantile Rd Beachwood (44122) (G-770)

Brandience LLC 513 333-4100
3251 Riverside Dr Cincinnati (45226) (G-2277)

Brandmuscle, Cleveland Also Called: Tradeone Marketing Inc (G-5028)
Brandmuscle Inc (HQ) 216 464-4342
1100 Superior Ave E Ste 500 Cleveland (44114) (G-3890)

Brands Insurance Agency Inc 513 777-7775
6449 Allen Rd Ste 1 West Chester (45069) (G-14654)

Brandsafway Services LLC 614 443-1314
1250 Emig Rd Columbus (43223) (G-5459)

Brassboys Enterprises Inc 740 545-7796
54188 Township Road 155 West Lafayette (43845) (G-14855)

Brasspack Packing Supply, Mansfield Also Called: Skybox Investments Inc (G-10316)
Bravo Wellness LLC (HQ) 216 658-9500
20445 Emerald Pkwy Ste 400 Cleveland (44135) (G-3891)

BRC Rail Car Company, Columbus Also Called: Cathcart Repair Facilities LLC (G-5250)
Brcom Inc (DH) 513 397-9900
201 E 4th St Cincinnati (45202) (G-2278)

Bread Financial Holdings Inc 614 729-3000
4590 E Broad St Columbus (43213) (G-5460)

Bread Financial Holdings Inc (PA) 614 729-4000
3095 Loyalty Cir Columbus (43219) (G-5461)

Bread Financial Holdings Inc 614 729-5800
6939 Americana Pkwy Reynoldsburg (43068) (G-12655)

Bread Financial Holdings Inc 614 729-5000
220 W Schrock Rd Westerville (43081) (G-14963)

Breakers Express Hotel, Sandusky Also Called: Cedar Point Park LLC (G-12877)
Breakthrough Media Ministries, Canal Winchester Also Called: World Harvest Church Inc (G-1620)
Breast Consultation Center, Cincinnati Also Called: University of Cincinnati (G-3588)
Breast Health Center, Coshocton Also Called: Prime Healthcare Foundation (G-6997)
Breathing Association 614 457-4570
788 Mount Vernon Ave Columbus (43203) (G-5462)

Brechbuhler Scales Inc (PA) 330 458-3060
1424 Scales St Sw Canton (44706) (G-1689)

Breckenridge Village, Willoughby Also Called: Ohio Living (G-15215)
Brecksville City Service Dept, Brecksville Also Called: City of Brecksville (G-1350)
Brecksville Community Center, Brecksville Also Called: City of Brecksville (G-1349)
Brecksville Leasing Co LLC 330 659-6766
4360 Brecksville Rd Richfield (44286) (G-12689)

Brecksvll-Brdview Hts Cy Schl 419 885-8103
7240 Erie St Sylvania (43560) (G-13536)

Brecksvlle Halthcare Group Inc 440 546-0643
8757 Brecksville Rd Brecksville (44141) (G-1346)

Brecon Distribution Center, Cincinnati Also Called: Duke Energy Ohio Inc (G-2582)
Breen Winkel & Co 614 261-1494
3752 N High St Columbus (43214) (G-5463)

Breeze 33 Products LLC 833 273-3950
2620 Ridgewood Rd Akron (44313) (G-74)

Breeze33, Akron Also Called: Breeze 33 Products LLC (G-74)
Brehob Corporation 513 755-1300
9790 Windisch Rd West Chester (45069) (G-14655)

Brehob Crane and Hoist Div, West Chester Also Called: Brehob Corporation (G-14655)
Breitinger Company 419 526-4255
595 Oakenwaldt St Mansfield (44905) (G-10248)

Bremec Group, Chesterland Also Called: Bremec Group Inc (G-2032)
Bremec Group Inc 440 951-0770
12265 Chillicothe Rd Chesterland (44026) (G-2032)

Brendamour Moving & Stor Inc 800 354-9715
2630 Glendale Milford Rd Ste D Cincinnati (45241) (G-2279)

Brenmar Construction Inc 740 286-2151
900 Morton St Jackson (45640) (G-9516)

Brennan Manna & Diamond LLC (PA) 330 253-5060
75 E Market St Akron (44308) (G-75)

Brennan Equipment Services, Holland Also Called: Brennan Equipment Services Co (G-9282)
Brennan Equipment Services Co 419 867-6000
6940 Hall St Holland (43528) (G-9282)

Brent Industries Inc 419 382-8693
2922 South Ave Toledo (43609) (G-13716)

Brentlinger Enterprises 614 889-2571
6335 Perimeter Loop Rd Dublin (43017) (G-7947)

Brentwood Health Care Center, Northfield Also Called: Brentwood Life Care Company (G-11953)
Brentwood Life Care Company 330 468-2273
907 W Aurora Rd Northfield (44067) (G-11953)

Brethren Care Inc 419 289-0803
2140 Center St Ofc Ashland (44805) (G-484)

Brethren Care Village LLC 419 289-1585
2140 Center St Ashland (44805) (G-485)

Brewdog, Canal Winchester Also Called: Brewdog Franchising LLC (G-1599)
Brewdog Franchising LLC 614 908-3051
96 Gender Rd Canal Winchester (43110) (G-1599)

Brewer Holdco Inc 419 247-2800
4500 Dorr St Toledo (43615) (G-13717)

Brewer-Garrett Company (PA) 440 243-3535
6800 Eastland Rd Middleburg Heights (44130) (G-11113)

Brewster Convalescent Center, Brewster Also Called: Brewster Parke Inc (G-1373)
Brewster Parke Inc 330 767-4179
264 Mohican St Ne Brewster (44613) (G-1373)

Brexton Construction LLC 614 441-4110
1123 Goodale Blvd Ste 500 Columbus (43212) (G-5464)

Brg Realty Group LLC (PA) 513 936-5960
7265 Kenwood Rd Ste 111 Cincinnati (45236) (G-2280)

Briar Hl Hlth Care Rsdence Inc 440 632-5241
15950 Pierce St Middlefield (44062) (G-11138)

Briar-Gate Realty Inc (PA) 614 299-2121
3827 Brookham Dr Grove City (43123) (G-8899)

Briarfield At Ashley Circle, Boardman Also Called: Ashley Enterprises LLC (G-1284)
Briarfield At Glanzman Road, Toledo Also Called: Concord Care Center of Toledo (G-13757)
Briarfield Manor LLC 330 270-3468
461 S Canfield Niles Rd Youngstown (44515) (G-15565)

Briarfield of Boardman LLC 330 259-9393
830 Boardman Canfield Rd Youngstown (44512) (G-15566)

Briarfield of Sandusky, Sandusky Also Called: Concord Health Care Inc (G-12885)
Briarwood Inc 330 688-1828
3700 Englewood Dr Stow (44224) (G-13356)

BRIARWOOD HEALTHCARE CENTER, T, Stow Also Called: Briarwood Inc (G-13356)
Briarwood Mano, Coldwater Also Called: Hcf of Briarwood Inc (G-5213)
Brick Loft At Historic W Tech, Cleveland Also Called: Monarch Inv & MGT Group LLC (G-4597)
Bricker & Eckler LLP (PA) 614 227-2300
100 S 3rd St Ste B Columbus (43215) (G-5465)

Bridge 513 244-3985
1515 Carll St Cincinnati (45225) (G-2281)

ALPHABETIC SECTION — Brown & Brown of Ohio LLC

Bridge Logistics Inc.. 513 874-7444
5 Circle Freeway Dr West Chester (45246) *(G-14801)*

Bridge The, Youngstown *Also Called: Siffrin Residential Assn (G-15724)*

Bridgepoint Risk MGT LLC.. 419 794-1075
1440 Arrowhead Dr Maumee (43537) *(G-10704)*

Bridgeport Auto Parts Inc (PA).................................. 740 635-0441
56104 National Rd Ste 110 Bridgeport (43912) *(G-1375)*

Bridges To Independence Inc (PA)............................ 740 362-1996
106 Stover Dr Delaware (43015) *(G-7780)*

Bridgeshome Health Care, Medina *Also Called: Bridgeshome Health Care Inc (G-10815)*

Bridgeshome Health Care Inc.................................... 330 764-1000
5075 Windfall Rd Medina (44256) *(G-10815)*

Bridgeway Inc (PA).. 216 688-4114
2202 Prame Ave Cleveland (44109) *(G-3892)*

Bright Bginnings Childcare Ctr, South Zanesville *Also Called: Baco LLC (G-13186)*

Bright Now Dental, Lorain *Also Called: Monarch Dental Corp (G-10093)*

Brightedge, Cleveland *Also Called: Brightedge Technologies Inc (G-3893)*

Brightedge Technologies Inc..................................... 800 578-8023
1500 W 3rd St Ste 405 Cleveland (44113) *(G-3893)*

Brighton Gardens of Westlake, Westlake *Also Called: Sunrise Senior Living LLC (G-15112)*

Brighton Gardens Wash Township, Dayton *Also Called: Sunrise Senior Living LLC (G-7653)*

Brighton Manor Company... 216 241-3123
1625 E 31st St Cleveland (44114) *(G-3894)*

Brightstar Care, Dayton *Also Called: Ddc Group Inc (G-7307)*

Brightview Landscape Svcs Inc.................................. 614 478-2085
3001 Innis Rd Columbus (43224) *(G-5466)*

Brigids Path Inc.. 937 350-1785
3601 S Dixie Dr Moraine (45439) *(G-11392)*

Brilliant Electric Sign Co Ltd..................................... 216 741-3800
4811 Van Epps Rd Brooklyn Heights (44131) *(G-1413)*

Brilligent Solutions LLC (PA)..................................... 937 879-4148
1130 Channingway Dr Fairborn (45324) *(G-8367)*

Brimar Packaging Inc... 440 934-3080
37520 Colorado Ave Avon (44011) *(G-641)*

Brims Imports.. 419 675-1099
County 140 E Kenton (43326) *(G-9611)*

Brims Imports Auto Salvage, Kenton *Also Called: Brims Imports (G-9611)*

Brimstone & Fire LLC.. 937 776-5182
317 Brimstone Rd Wilmington (45177) *(G-15247)*

Brinager, Tye & Sons Produce, Portland *Also Called: Cecil T Brinager (G-12542)*

Brint Electric Inc... 419 841-3326
7825 W Central Ave Sylvania (43560) *(G-13537)*

Briskey Concrete Inc... 517 403-9869
100 B's And K Rd Galena (43021) *(G-8735)*

Briteskies LLC.. 216 369-3600
2658 Scranton Rd Ste 3 Cleveland (44113) *(G-3895)*

Brittany Residential Inc... 216 692-3212
427 Richmond Rd Cleveland (44143) *(G-3896)*

Britton-Gallagher & Assoc Inc................................... 216 658-7100
1375 E 9th St Cleveland (44114) *(G-3897)*

Brixey & Meyer, Miamisburg *Also Called: Brixey and Meyer Inc (G-11027)*

Brixey and Meyer Inc (PA)... 937 291-4110
2991 Newmark Dr Miamisburg (45342) *(G-11027)*

Broad Street Hotel Assoc LP..................................... 614 861-0321
4801 E Broad St Columbus (43213) *(G-5467)*

Broadband Express LLC.. 513 834-8085
11359 Mosteller Rd Cincinnati (45241) *(G-2282)*

Broadband Express LLC.. 216 712-7505
14200 Broadway Ave Cleveland (44125) *(G-3898)*

Broadband Express LLC.. 419 536-9127
1915 Nebraska Ave Toledo (43607) *(G-13718)*

BROADBAND HOSPITALITY, Youngstown *Also Called: Great Lakes Telcom Ltd (G-15622)*

Broadview Health Center, Columbus *Also Called: Generation Health Corp (G-5926)*

BROADVIEW MULTI-CARE CENTER, Parma *Also Called: Broadview Nursing Home Inc (G-12250)*

Broadview Nursing Home Inc..................................... 216 661-5084
5520 Broadview Rd Parma (44134) *(G-12250)*

Broadvue Motors Inc.. 440 845-6000
6930 Pearl Rd Cleveland (44130) *(G-3899)*

Brock & Sons Inc.. 513 874-4555
8731 N Gilmore Rd Fairfield (45014) *(G-8395)*

Brock Air Products Inc (PA)...................................... 937 335-2626
2331 W State Route 55 Troy (45373) *(G-14130)*

Brocon Construction Inc.. 614 871-7300
2120 Hardy Parkway St Grove City (43123) *(G-8900)*

Brodhead Village Ltd (PA)... 614 863-4640
160 W Main St New Albany (43054) *(G-11557)*

Brohl & Appell, Sandusky *Also Called: Rexel Usa Inc (G-12927)*

Brohl & Appell Inc... 419 625-6761
140 Lane St Sandusky (44870) *(G-12865)*

Brokaw Inc.. 216 241-8003
1213 W 6th St Cleveland (44113) *(G-3900)*

Broken Arrow Inc.. 419 562-3480
1649 Marion Rd Bucyrus (44820) *(G-1496)*

Brondes All Makes Auto Leasing............................... 419 887-1511
1511 Reynolds Rd Maumee (43537) *(G-10705)*

BRONDES ALL MAKES AUTO LEASING INC, Maumee *Also Called: Brondes All Makes Auto Leasing (G-10705)*

Brondes Ford (PA)... 419 473-1411
5545 Secor Rd Toledo (43623) *(G-13719)*

Brondes Ford Toledo, Toledo *Also Called: Brondes Ford (G-13719)*

Brook Beech.. 216 391-4069
6001 Woodland Ave Ste 2260 Cleveland (44104) *(G-3901)*

Brook Beech (PA).. 216 831-2255
13201 Granger Rd Cleveland (44125) *(G-3902)*

Brook Plum Country Club.. 419 625-5394
3712 Galloway Rd Sandusky (44870) *(G-12866)*

Brook Willow Chrstn Cmmunities.............................. 614 885-3300
55 Lazelle Rd Columbus (43235) *(G-5468)*

Brookdale Lving Cmmunities Inc............................... 330 666-4545
100 Brookmont Rd Ofc Akron (44333) *(G-76)*

Brooker Insurance Agency Inc................................... 440 238-5454
10749 Pearl Rd Ste 1a Strongsville (44136) *(G-13446)*

Brookfield Properties LLC... 216 621-6060
127 Public Sq Ste 3200 Cleveland (44114) *(G-3903)*

BROOKHAVEN NURSING & CARE CENT, Brookville *Also Called: Brookville Enterprises Inc (G-1445)*

Brookledge Golf Club, Cuyahoga Falls *Also Called: City of Cuyahoga Falls (G-7061)*

Brooklyn Adult Activity Center, Cleveland *Also Called: A W S Inc (G-3750)*

Brooks & Stafford Co... 216 696-3000
55 Public Sq Ste 1650 Cleveland (44113) *(G-3904)*

Brookside Extended Care Center............................... 513 398-1020
780 Snider Rd Mason (45040) *(G-10524)*

Brookside Golf & Cntry CLB Co................................. 614 889-2581
2770 W Dublin Granville Rd Columbus (43235) *(G-5469)*

Brookside Healthcare Center, Cincinnati *Also Called: Preserve Operating Co LLC (G-3229)*

Brookside Holdings LLC (PA).................................... 419 925-4457
8022 State Route 119 Maria Stein (45860) *(G-10353)*

Brookside Trucking, Maria Stein *Also Called: Brookside Holdings LLC (G-10353)*

Brookview Healthcare Center, Defiance *Also Called: Brookview Healthcare Ctr (G-7742)*

Brookview Healthcare Ctr.. 419 784-1014
214 Harding St Defiance (43512) *(G-7742)*

Brookville Enterprises Inc.. 937 833-2133
1 Country Ln Brookville (45309) *(G-1445)*

Brookwood Management Co LLC............................... 330 499-7721
2017 Applegrove St Nw Canton (44720) *(G-1690)*

Brookwood Management Company............................ 330 497-8718
181 Applegrove St Ne Canton (44720) *(G-1691)*

Brookwood Realty Company...................................... 513 530-9555
12100 Reed Hartman Hwy Apt 118 Cincinnati (45241) *(G-2283)*

Brookwood Retirement Community, Cincinnati *Also Called: Brookwood Realty Company (G-2283)*

Brookwood Retirement Community, Cincinnati *Also Called: C Micah Rand Inc (G-2298)*

Brothers Auto Transport LLC..................................... 330 824-0082
2188 Lyntz Townline Rd Sw Warren (44481) *(G-14508)*

Brothers Trading Co Inc (PA).................................... 937 746-1010
400 Victory Ln Springboro (45066) *(G-13194)*

Brothers Trading Co Inc.. 937 746-1010
425 Victory Ln Springboro (45066) *(G-13195)*

Brower Insurance Agency LLC................................... 937 228-4135
409 E Monument Ave Ste 400 Dayton (45402) *(G-7201)*

Brown & Brown of Ohio LLC (HQ)............................. 419 874-1974
360 3 Meadows Dr Perrysburg (43551) *(G-12319)*

Brown & Brown of Ohio LLC — ALPHABETIC SECTION

Brown & Brown of Ohio LLC 513 831-2200
706 Indian Hill Rd Terrace Park (45174) *(G-13613)*

Brown and Caldwell 614 410-6144
445 Hutchinson Ave Ste 540 Columbus (43235) *(G-5470)*

Brown Cnty Bd Mntal Rtardation 937 378-4891
325 W State St Bldg A Georgetown (45121) *(G-8798)*

Brown Co Ed Service Center 937 378-6118
9231b Hamer Rd Georgetown (45121) *(G-8799)*

Brown Derby Roadhouse 330 528-3227
72 N Main St Ste 208 Hudson (44236) *(G-9335)*

Brown Gibbons Lang Ltd Ptrship 216 241-2800
1111 Superior Ave E # 900 Cleveland (44114) *(G-3905)*

Brown Industrial Inc 937 693-3838
311 W South St Botkins (45306) *(G-1299)*

Brown Logistics Solutions Inc (PA) 614 866-9111
2100 Cloverleaf St E Columbus (43232) *(G-5471)*

Brown Memorial Home Inc 740 474-6238
158 E Mound St Circleville (43113) *(G-3703)*

Brown Motor Sales Co (PA) 419 531-0151
5625 W Central Ave Toledo (43615) *(G-13720)*

Brown Motors, Toledo *Also Called: Brown Motor Sales Co (G-13720)*

Brownflynn Ltd (DH) 216 303-6000
50 Public Sq Fl 36 Cleveland (44113) *(G-3906)*

Browning Mesonic Community (PA) 419 878-4055
8883 Browning Dr Waterville (43566) *(G-14593)*

Browns Run Country Club 513 423-6291
6855 Sloebig Rd Middletown (45042) *(G-11154)*

Brumbaugh Construction Inc 937 692-5107
3520 State Route 49 Arcanum (45304) *(G-453)*

Bruner Corporation (PA) 614 334-9000
3637 Lacon Rd Hilliard (43026) *(G-9185)*

Brunk Excavating, Monroe *Also Called: Brunk Excavating Inc (G-11335)*

Brunk Excavating Inc 513 360-0308
301 Breaden Dr Monroe (45050) *(G-11335)*

Brunk's Stoves, Salem *Also Called: L B Brunk & Sons Inc (G-12845)*

Bruns Building & Dev Corp Inc 419 925-4095
1429 Cranberry Rd Saint Henry (45883) *(G-12824)*

Bruns Construction Enterprises Inc 937 339-2300
3050 S Tipp Cowlesville Rd Tipp City (45371) *(G-13653)*

Bruns Construction Entps LLC 419 586-9367
6781 Hellwarth Rd Celina (45822) *(G-1917)*

Brunswick Insurance Agency 330 864-8800
5309 Transportation Blvd Cleveland (44125) *(G-3907)*

Brunswick Senior Living LLC 330 460-4244
3430 Brunswick Lake Pkwy Brunswick (44212) *(G-1452)*

Bruss, Mark R MD, Waterville *Also Called: Waterville Fmly Physicians Inc (G-14596)*

Bryan Equipment Sales Inc 513 248-2000
6300 Smith Rd Loveland (45140) *(G-10129)*

Bryan Systems, Montpelier *Also Called: Bryan Truck Line Inc (G-11382)*

Bryan Truck Line Inc 419 485-8373
14020 Us Hwy 20 Ste A Montpelier (43543) *(G-11382)*

Bryans Treatment Center 216 208-0634
1701 W Sylvania Ave Toledo (43613) *(G-13721)*

Bryant Health Center Inc 740 532-6188
2932 S 5th St Ironton (45638) *(G-9504)*

BSI Engineering LLC (PA) 513 201-3100
300 E Business Way Ste 300 Cincinnati (45241) *(G-2284)*

BSI Group, The, Derwent *Also Called: Bi-Con Services Inc (G-7864)*

BsI - Applied Laser Tech LLC (PA) 216 663-8181
1100 Resource Dr Independence (44131) *(G-9413)*

Btas Inc (PA) 937 431-9431
4391 Dayton Xenia Rd Beavercreek (45432) *(G-866)*

BTMC Corporation 614 891-1454
15056 Harbor Point Dr W Thornville (43076) *(G-13619)*

Buchy Food Service, Cincinnati *Also Called: The Chas G Buchy Packing Company (G-3462)*

Buck and Sons Ldscp Svc Inc 614 876-5359
7147 Hayden Run Rd Hilliard (43026) *(G-9186)*

Buck Equipment Inc 614 539-3039
1720 Feddern Ave Grove City (43123) *(G-8901)*

Buckeye Ambulance, Dayton *Also Called: Ems Team LLC (G-7335)*

Buckeye Body and Equipment 614 299-1136
939 E Starr Ave Columbus (43201) *(G-5472)*

Buckeye Broadband, Northwood *Also Called: Block Communications Inc (G-11969)*

Buckeye Charter Service Inc 937 879-3000
8240 Expansion Way Dayton (45424) *(G-7202)*

Buckeye Charter Service Inc (PA) 419 222-2455
1235 E Hanthorn Rd Lima (45804) *(G-9871)*

Buckeye Charters, Dayton *Also Called: Buckeye Charter Service Inc (G-7202)*

Buckeye Check Cashing Inc 740 851-4073
860 N Bridge St Chillicothe (45601) *(G-2053)*

Buckeye Check Cashing Inc 513 936-9995
7680 Montgomery Rd Cincinnati (45236) *(G-2285)*

Buckeye Check Cashing Inc 513 851-3100
10990 Hamilton Ave Cincinnati (45231) *(G-2286)*

Buckeye Check Cashing Inc 513 931-7300
2003 W Galbraith Rd Cincinnati (45239) *(G-2287)*

Buckeye Check Cashing Inc 513 741-3777
9385 Colerain Ave Cincinnati (45251) *(G-2288)*

Buckeye Check Cashing Inc 740 497-4039
513 E Main St Circleville (43113) *(G-3704)*

Buckeye Check Cashing Inc 740 575-4314
105 S 2nd Street Coshocton (43812) *(G-6977)*

Buckeye Check Cashing Inc (HQ) 614 798-5900
5165 Emerald Pkwy Ste 100 Dublin (43017) *(G-7948)*

Buckeye Check Cashing Inc 216 486-3434
22641 Euclid Ave # 5 Euclid (44117) *(G-8338)*

Buckeye Check Cashing Inc 216 289-8462
22318a Lake Shore Blvd Euclid (44123) *(G-8339)*

Buckeye Check Cashing Inc 937 393-9087
583 Harry Sauner Rd Hillsboro (45133) *(G-9250)*

Buckeye Check Cashing Inc 567 371-3497
1980 Elida Rd Lima (45805) *(G-9872)*

Buckeye Check Cashing Inc 419 528-1315
801 N Lexington Springmill Rd Mansfield (44906) *(G-10249)*

Buckeye Check Cashing Inc 740 374-6005
234 Pike St Marietta (45750) *(G-10358)*

Buckeye Check Cashing Inc 419 382-5385
1221 S Reynolds Rd Toledo (43615) *(G-13722)*

Buckeye Check Cashing Inc 614 863-2522
4100 E Broad St Whitehall (43213) *(G-15135)*

Buckeye Cmnty Eighty One LP 614 942-2020
3021 E Dublin Granville Rd Columbus (43231) *(G-5473)*

Buckeye Cmnty Hope Foundation (PA) 614 942-2014
3021 E Dublin Granville Rd Ste 200 Columbus (43231) *(G-5474)*

Buckeye Collision Service Inc 740 387-5313
1770 Harding Hwy E Marion (43302) *(G-10420)*

Buckeye Collision Towing, Marion *Also Called: Buckeye Collision Service Inc (G-10420)*

Buckeye Commercial Clg Inc 614 866-4700
12936 Stonecreek Dr Ste F Pickerington (43147) *(G-12400)*

Buckeye Community Bank 440 233-8800
42935 N Ridge Rd Elyria (44035) *(G-8234)*

Buckeye Community Services Inc 740 797-4166
33 Hartman Rd The Plains (45780) *(G-13615)*

Buckeye Community Services Inc 740 941-1639
207 Remy Ct Waverly (45690) *(G-14611)*

Buckeye Companies (PA) 740 452-3641
999 Zane St Zanesville (43701) *(G-15772)*

Buckeye Components LLC 330 482-5163
1340 State Route 14 Columbiana (44408) *(G-5231)*

Buckeye Ecocare 937 435-4727
2550 Belvo Rd Miamisburg (45342) *(G-11028)*

Buckeye Egg Farm Lp-Main Off, Croton *Also Called: Hartford Farms LLC (G-7030)*

Buckeye Elm Contracting LLC 888 315-8663
1333 Research Rd Gahanna (43230) *(G-8712)*

Buckeye Excavating & Cnstr Inc 419 663-3113
191 State Route 61 Norwalk (44857) *(G-12003)*

BUCKEYE FASTENERS COMPANY, Streetsboro *Also Called: Joseph Industries Inc (G-13419)*

Buckeye Ford Inc 740 852-7842
110 Us Highway 42 Se London (43140) *(G-10038)*

Buckeye Frest Rsmount Pavilion 740 354-4505
20 Easter Dr Portsmouth (45662) *(G-12547)*

Buckeye Health Staffing LLC 614 706-9337
125 Putnam St Ste 110 Marietta (45750) *(G-10359)*

ALPHABETIC SECTION — Burd Brothers Inc

Buckeye Heating and AC Sup Inc (PA) 216 831-0066
5075 Richmond Rd Bedford Heights (44146) *(G-996)*

Buckeye Hills-Hck Vly Reg Dev (HQ) 740 373-0087
1400 Pike St Marietta (45750) *(G-10360)*

Buckeye Hlth Stffng/Bckeye Src, Marietta *Also Called: Buckeye Health Staffing LLC* *(G-10359)*

Buckeye Home Health Care 513 791-6446
10921 Reed Hartman Hwy Ste 310 Blue Ash (45242) *(G-1139)*

Buckeye Homecare Services Inc 216 321-9300
14077 Cedar Rd Ste 103 Cleveland (44118) *(G-3908)*

Buckeye Honda, Hilliard *Also Called: Spires Motors Inc (G-9233)*

Buckeye Hospitality Inc 614 586-1001
1690 Clara St Columbus (43211) *(G-5475)*

Buckeye Insurance Group, Piqua *Also Called: Buckeye State Mutual Insur Co (G-12436)*

Buckeye Leasing Inc 330 758-0841
8063 Southern Blvd Youngstown (44512) *(G-15567)*

Buckeye Mechanical Contg Inc 740 282-0089
2325 Township Rd 370 Toronto (43964) *(G-14121)*

Buckeye Oral & Maxillofacial 740 392-2000
1650 Coshocton Ave Ste D Mount Vernon (43050) *(G-11477)*

Buckeye Paper Co Inc 330 477-5925
5233 Southway St Sw Ste 523 Canton (44706) *(G-1692)*

Buckeye Parts Services Inc 614 274-1888
4221 Westward Ave Columbus (43228) *(G-5476)*

Buckeye Pipe Line Services Co 419 698-8770
3321 York St Oregon (43616) *(G-12130)*

Buckeye Pipeline Cnstr Inc 330 804-0101
7835 Millersburg Rd Wooster (44691) *(G-15315)*

Buckeye Pools Inc 937 434-7916
671 Miamisburg Centerville Rd Dayton (45459) *(G-7203)*

Buckeye Power Inc 740 598-6534
306 County Road 7e Brilliant (43913) *(G-1378)*

Buckeye Power Inc (PA) 614 781-0573
6677 Busch Blvd Columbus (43229) *(G-5477)*

Buckeye Ranch Inc 614 543-1380
2865 W Broad St Columbus (43204) *(G-5478)*

Buckeye Ranch Inc (PA) 614 875-2371
5665 Hoover Rd Grove City (43123) *(G-8902)*

Buckeye Ranch Foundation Inc 614 875-2371
5665 Hoover Rd Grove City (43123) *(G-8903)*

Buckeye Real Estate, Columbus *Also Called: Garland Group Inc (G-5916)*

Buckeye Rsdntial Solutions LLC 330 235-9183
320 E Main St Ste 301 Ravenna (44266) *(G-12620)*

Buckeye Rubber & Packing Co 216 464-8900
23940 Mercantile Rd Beachwood (44122) *(G-771)*

Buckeye Rural Elc Coop Inc 740 379-2025
4848 State Route 325 Patriot (45658) *(G-12280)*

Buckeye Sales, Columbus *Also Called: Jegs Automotive Inc (G-6086)*

Buckeye State Bancshares Inc 614 796-4747
9494 Wedgewood Blvd Powell (43065) *(G-12587)*

Buckeye State Credit Union Inc 330 823-7930
1010 W State St Alliance (44601) *(G-376)*

Buckeye State Mutual Insur Co (PA) 937 778-5000
1 Heritage Pl Piqua (45356) *(G-12436)*

Buckeye Supply Company (HQ) 740 452-3641
999 Zane St Ste A Zanesville (43701) *(G-15773)*

Buckeye Telesystem Inc (HQ) 419 724-9898
2700 Oregon Rd Northwood (43619) *(G-11970)*

BUCKEYE TERRACE REHABILITATION, Westerville *Also Called: Edgewood Manor Westerville LLC (G-14977)*

Buckeye Transfer LLC 330 719-0375
44626 State Rte 154 Lisbon (44432) *(G-9997)*

Buckeye Trls Girl Scout Cncil (PA) 937 275-7601
450 Shoup Mill Rd Dayton (45415) *(G-7204)*

Buckeye Truck Equipment, Columbus *Also Called: Buckeye Body and Equipment (G-5472)*

Buckhorn, Milford *Also Called: Buckhorn Inc (G-11219)*

Buckhorn Inc (HQ) 513 831-4402
400 Techne Center Dr Ste 215 Milford (45150) *(G-11219)*

Buckingham & Company 937 435-2742
6856 Loop Rd Dayton (45459) *(G-7205)*

Buckingham Coal Company LLC
11 N 4th St Zanesville (43701) *(G-15774)*

Buckingham Dlttle Brroughs LLC (PA) 330 376-5300
3800 Embassy Pkwy Ste 300 Akron (44333) *(G-77)*

Buckingham Dlttle Brroughs LLC 330 492-8717
4277 Munson St Nw Canton (44718) *(G-1693)*

Buckingham Dlttle Brroughs LLC 216 621-5300
1375 E 9th St Ste 1700 Cleveland (44114) *(G-3909)*

Buckingham Doolittle Burroughs, Cleveland *Also Called: Buckingham Dlttle Brroughs LLC (G-3909)*

Buckingham Financial Group, Dayton *Also Called: Buckingham & Company (G-7205)*

Buckingham Management LLC 844 361-5559
1000 Hollister Ln Perrysburg (43551) *(G-12320)*

Buckman Enochs Coss & Assoc 614 825-6215
4449 Easton Way Ste 130 Columbus (43219) *(G-5479)*

Bucyrus Community Hospital Inc 419 562-4677
629 N Sandusky Ave Bucyrus (44820) *(G-1497)*

Bucyrus Community Hospital LLC 419 562-4677
629 N Sandusky Ave Bucyrus (44820) *(G-1498)*

Bucyrus Community Physicians 419 563-9801
140 Hill St Ste A Bucyrus (44820) *(G-1499)*

Bucyrus Community Physicians 419 492-2200
120 W Main St New Washington (44854) *(G-11681)*

Bucyrus Ice Company, Bucyrus *Also Called: Velvet Ice Cream Company (G-1519)*

Bucyrus Radio Group 614 451-2191
4401 Carriage Hill Ln Columbus (43220) *(G-5480)*

Budget Dumpster LLC (PA) 866 284-6164
830 Canterbury Rd Westlake (44145) *(G-15041)*

Budget Dumpster Rental, Westlake *Also Called: Budget Dumpster LLC (G-15041)*

Budget Rent-A-Car, Toledo *Also Called: George P Ballas Buick GMC Trck (G-13820)*

Budros Ruhlin & Roe Inc 614 481-6900
1801 Watermark Dr Ste 300 Columbus (43215) *(G-5481)*

Buehler 10, Dover *Also Called: Buehler Food Markets Inc (G-7874)*

Buehler Food Markets Inc 330 364-3079
3000 N Wooster Ave Dover (44622) *(G-7874)*

Buehrer Group Arch & Engrg 419 893-9021
314 Conant St Maumee (43537) *(G-10706)*

Buffalo Mfg Works BMW, Columbus *Also Called: Edison Welding Institute Inc (G-5807)*

Buffalo-6305 Eb Associates LLC 614 322-8000
6305 E Broad St Columbus (43213) *(G-5482)*

Builder Services Group Inc 614 263-9378
2365 Scioto Harper Dr Columbus (43204) *(G-5483)*

Builder Services Group Inc 513 942-2204
28 Kiesland Ct Hamilton (45015) *(G-9019)*

Builders Exchange Inc (PA) 216 393-6300
9555 Rockside Rd Ste 300 Cleveland (44125) *(G-3910)*

Builders Installed Products, Columbus *Also Called: Installed Building Products LLC (G-6059)*

Building & Grounds Maintenance, Dayton *Also Called: Mad River Local School Dst (G-7464)*

Building 8 Inc 513 771-8000
10995 Canal Rd Cincinnati (45241) *(G-2289)*

Building Integrated Svcs LLC 330 733-9191
7777 First Pl Oakwood Village (44146) *(G-12055)*

BUILDING LABORERS LOCAL 310, Cleveland *Also Called: Laborers Intl Un N Amer Lcal 3 (G-4472)*

Building Management Services, East Liberty *Also Called: Reliant Mechanical Inc (G-8175)*

Building/Engineering Dept, Cuyahoga Falls *Also Called: City of Cuyahoga Falls (G-7059)*

Buildinglogix, Vandalia *Also Called: Waibel Energy Systems Inc (G-14403)*

Bulk Transit Corporation (PA) 614 873-4632
7177 Indl Pkwy Plain City (43064) *(G-12471)*

Bulldawg Holdings LLC (PA) 419 423-3131
151 Stanford Pkwy Findlay (45840) *(G-8519)*

Bundy Baking Solutions, Urbana *Also Called: Cmbb LLC (G-14304)*

Bundy Baking Solutions, Urbana *Also Called: Russell T Bundy Associates Inc (G-14312)*

Bunge North America East LLC 419 692-6010
234 S Jefferson St Delphos (45833) *(G-7837)*

Buns of Delaware Inc 740 363-2867
14 W Winter St Delaware (43015) *(G-7781)*

Buns Restaurant & Bakery, Delaware *Also Called: Buns of Delaware Inc (G-7781)*

Burbank Inc 419 698-3434
623 Burbank Dr Toledo (43607) *(G-13723)*

Burd Brothers Inc (PA) 800 538-2873
4294 Armstrong Blvd Batavia (45103) *(G-729)*

(PA)=Parent Co (HQ)=Headquarters (DH)=Div Headquarters

Burd Brothers Inc 513 708-7787
1789 Stanley Ave Dayton (45404) *(G-7206)*

Bureau Labor Market Info, Columbus *Also Called: Ohio Dept Job & Fmly Svcs (G-6406)*

Bureau of Sanitation, Perrysburg *Also Called: City of Perrysburg (G-12324)*

Bureau Veritas North Amer Inc 330 252-5100
520 S Main St Ste 2444 Akron (44311) *(G-78)*

Bureau Workers Compensation 614 466-5109
30 W Spring St Fl 25 Columbus (43215) *(G-5484)*

Burge Service, Columbus *Also Called: Willglo Services Inc (G-6893)*

Burge, Ron, Burbank *Also Called: Ron Burge Trucking Inc (G-1522)*

Burger King, Conneaut *Also Called: Patterson-Erie Corporation (G-6944)*

Burger Plant, Shadyside *Also Called: Ohio Edison Company (G-12970)*

Burgess & Niple Inc (PA) 614 459-2050
330 Rush Aly Ste 700 Columbus (43215) *(G-5485)*

Burgess & Niple Inc (HQ) 703 631-6041
330 Rush Aly Ste 700 Columbus (43215) *(G-5486)*

Burgess & Niple/Heapy LLC 614 459-2050
330 Rush Aly Ste 700 Columbus (43215) *(G-5487)*

Burke Inc (PA) 513 241-5663
500 W 7th St Cincinnati (45203) *(G-2290)*

Burke Inc 513 576-5700
25 Whitney Dr Ste 110 Milford (45150) *(G-11220)*

Burke & Company, Cincinnati *Also Called: Patrick J Burke & Co (G-3189)*

Burke Institute, Cincinnati *Also Called: Burke Inc (G-2290)*

Burke Manley Lpa 513 721-5525
225 W Court St Cincinnati (45202) *(G-2291)*

Burke Milford, Milford *Also Called: Burke Inc (G-11220)*

Burkett and Sons Inc 419 242-7377
28740 Glenwood Rd Perrysburg (43551) *(G-12321)*

Burkett Restaurant Equipment, Perrysburg *Also Called: Burkett and Sons Inc (G-12321)*

Burkshire Construction Company 440 885-9700
6033 State Rd Cleveland (44134) *(G-3911)*

Burlington Coat Factory, Columbus *Also Called: BAIN CAPITAL PRIVATE EQUITY (G-5413)*

Burlington House Inc 513 851-7888
2222 Springdale Rd Cincinnati (45231) *(G-2292)*

Burnett Pools Inc (PA) 330 372-1725
2498 State Route 5 Cortland (44410) *(G-6968)*

Burnett Pools and Spas, Cortland *Also Called: Burnett Pools Inc (G-6968)*

BURNS INTERNATIONAL STAFFING, Mansfield *Also Called: Lexington Court Care Center (G-10281)*

Burr Oak State Park Lodge, Glouster *Also Called: US Hotel Osp Ventures LLC (G-8836)*

Burrilla LLC 513 615-9350
7969 Cincinnati Dayton Rd Ste F West Chester (45069) *(G-14656)*

Burton Carol Management (PA) 216 464-5130
4832 Richmond Rd Ste 200 Cleveland (44128) *(G-3912)*

Burton Rubber Processing, Burton *Also Called: Hexpol Compounding LLC (G-1528)*

Bus Garage, Franklin *Also Called: Franklin City Schools (G-8637)*

Bus Garage, Girard *Also Called: Girard City School District (G-8813)*

Bus Garage, Liberty Township *Also Called: Lakota Local School District (G-9853)*

Bus Garage & Maintenance Dept, Toledo *Also Called: Washington Local Schools (G-14097)*

Bushra Transportation LLC 614 745-1584
4200 Westview Center Plz # 101 Columbus (43228) *(G-5488)*

Business Admnstrators Cons Inc (PA) 614 863-8780
6331 E Livingston Ave Reynoldsburg (43068) *(G-12656)*

Business Community Section, Cincinnati *Also Called: Universal Advg Assoc Inc (G-3560)*

Business Equipment Co, Springfield *Also Called: Springfield Business Eqp Co (G-13294)*

Business Equipment Co Inc 513 948-1500
11590 Century Blvd Cincinnati (45246) *(G-2293)*

Business Furniture LLC 937 293-1010
607 E 3rd St Ste 200 Dayton (45402) *(G-7207)*

Business Tech & Solutions, Beavercreek *Also Called: Btas Inc (G-866)*

Business Volunteers Unlimited 216 736-7711
1300 E 9th St Ste 1220 Cleveland (44114) *(G-3913)*

Businessplans Incorporated 937 865-6501
1 Tyler Way Moraine (45439) *(G-11393)*

Busken Bakery Inc (PA) 513 871-2114
2675 Madison Rd Cincinnati (45208) *(G-2294)*

Butler County of Ohio 513 887-3728
315 High St Hamilton (45011) *(G-9020)*

Butler County of Ohio 513 757-4683
6093 Reily Millville Rd Oxford (45056) *(G-12202)*

Butler Bhavioral Hlth Svcs Inc (PA) 513 896-7887
1502 University Blvd Hamilton (45011) *(G-9021)*

Butler Cnty Bd Dvlpmntal Dsblt 513 867-5913
441 Patterson Blvd Fairfield (45014) *(G-8396)*

Butler Cnty Bd Dvlpmntal Dsblt 513 785-2870
5645 Liberty Fairfield Rd Fairfield Township (45011) *(G-8457)*

Butler Cnty Bd Dvlpmntal Dsblt 513 785-2815
282 N Fair Ave Hamilton (45011) *(G-9022)*

Butler Cnty Cmnty Hlth Cnsrtiu 513 454-1468
300 High St Fl 4 Hamilton (45011) *(G-9023)*

Butler Cnty Rgional Trnst Auth 513 785-5237
3045 Moser Ct Hamilton (45011) *(G-9024)*

Butler County Care Facility, Hamilton *Also Called: Butler County of Ohio (G-9020)*

Butler County Dialysis, Middletown *Also Called: Dva Hlthcare - Sthwest Ohio LL (G-11196)*

Butler Heating & AC, Dayton *Also Called: Butler Heating Company (G-7208)*

Butler Heating Company 937 253-8871
120 Springfield St Dayton (45403) *(G-7208)*

Butler Institute American Art (PA) 330 743-1711
524 Wick Ave Youngstown (44502) *(G-15568)*

Butler Rural Electric Coop 513 867-4400
3888 Stillwell Beckett Rd Oxford (45056) *(G-12203)*

Butler Tech 513 867-1028
3611 Hamilton Middletown Rd Fairfield Township (45011) *(G-8458)*

Butt Construction Company Inc 937 426-1313
3858 Germany Ln Dayton (45431) *(G-7127)*

Butterfield Recovery Group LLC 513 932-4673
5778 State Route 350 Oregonia (45054) *(G-12149)*

Buxton Inn, Granville *Also Called: Buxton Inn Inc (G-8849)*

Buxton Inn Inc 740 587-0001
313 Broadway E Granville (43023) *(G-8849)*

Buyers Products Company (PA) 440 974-8888
9049 Tyler Blvd Mentor (44060) *(G-10915)*

Buyers Products Company 440 974-8888
8200 Tyler Blvd Mentor (44060) *(G-10916)*

BVRSI, Findlay *Also Called: Blanchard Vly Rsdntial Svcs In (G-8517)*

Bw Alumni Association 440 826-2104
279 Front St Berea (44017) *(G-1063)*

Bw Supply Co., Lyons *Also Called: B W Grinding Co (G-10187)*

BWC Trucking Company Inc 740 532-5188
164 State Route 650 Ironton (45638) *(G-9505)*

Bwi Chassis Dynamics NA Inc 937 455-5230
2582 E River Rd Moraine (45439) *(G-11394)*

Bwi Group NA, Moraine *Also Called: Bwi North America Inc (G-11395)*

Bwi North America Inc 937 212-2892
2582 E River Rd Moraine (45439) *(G-11395)*

BX OHIO, Cleveland *Also Called: Builders Exchange Inc (G-3910)*

By Design, Sandusky *Also Called: Decorate With Style Inc (G-12887)*

By-Line Transit Inc 937 642-2500
16505 Springdale Rd Marysville (43040) *(G-10477)*

Byer Steel, Cincinnati *Also Called: Byer Steel Service Center Inc (G-2296)*

Byer Steel Inc 513 821-6400
200 W North Bend Rd Cincinnati (45216) *(G-2295)*

Byer Steel Service Center Inc 513 821-6400
200 Wn Bend Rd Cincinnati (45216) *(G-2296)*

Byrider Finance Inc 513 407-4140
8581 Beechmont Ave Cincinnati (45255) *(G-2297)*

Byron Products Inc 513 870-9111
3781 Port Union Rd Fairfield (45014) *(G-8397)*

C & E Advanced Technologies, Miamisburg *Also Called: C & E Sales LLC (G-11029)*

C & E Sales LLC 937 434-8830
2400 Technical Dr Miamisburg (45342) *(G-11029)*

C & G Transportation Inc 419 288-2653
11100 Wayne Rd Wayne (43466) *(G-14620)*

C & K Industrial Services Inc (PA) 216 642-0055
5617 E Schaaf Rd Independence (44131) *(G-9414)*

C & L Supply, Logan *Also Called: Kilbarger Construction Inc (G-10031)*

C & R Inc (PA) 614 497-1130
5600 Clyde Moore Dr Groveport (43125) *(G-8975)*

ALPHABETIC SECTION — Camargo Club

C & S Associates Inc 440 461-9661
729 Miner Rd Highland Heights (44143) *(G-9163)*

C & S Cleaning Services Inc 440 349-5907
31200 Solon Rd Ste 10 Solon (44139) *(G-13071)*

C & W Tank Cleaning Company 419 691-1995
50 N Lallendorf Rd Oregon (43616) *(G-12131)*

C A C Distributing, Cincinnati *Also Called: Habegger Corporation (G-2787)*

C A S, Napoleon *Also Called: Custom Agri Systems Inc (G-11521)*

C B Mfg & Sls Co Inc (PA) 937 866-5986
4455 Infirmary Rd Miamisburg (45342) *(G-11030)*

C C, Mentor *Also Called: Cardinalcommerce Corporation (G-10918)*

C C F Vsclar Srgery At Mrymunt 216 475-1551
99 Northline Cir Ste 201 Cleveland (44119) *(G-3914)*

C C H, Canton *Also Called: Canton Christian Home Inc (G-1698)*

C C I, Broadview Heights *Also Called: Warwick Communications Inc (G-1404)*

C C Mitchell Supply Co Inc 440 526-2040
3001 E Royalton Rd Cleveland (44147) *(G-3915)*

C D O, Dayton *Also Called: Cdo Technologies Inc (G-7128)*

C E I, Massillon *Also Called: Canton Erectors Inc (G-10634)*

C E S Credit Union Inc (PA) 740 397-1136
1215 Yauger Rd Mount Vernon (43050) *(G-11478)*

C GI Voluntary 216 401-0081
3500 Woodridge Rd Cleveland (44121) *(G-3916)*

C H Bradshaw Co 614 871-2087
2004 Hendrix Dr Grove City (43123) *(G-8904)*

C H Dean LLC (PA) 937 222-9531
3500 Pentagon Blvd Ste 200 Beavercreek (45431) *(G-867)*

C I E Inc 419 986-5566
2704 County Road 13 Burgoon (43407) *(G-1523)*

C K Franchising Inc 937 264-1933
111 W 1st St Ste 910 Dayton (45402) *(G-7209)*

C M C, Hamilton *Also Called: Connector Manufacturing Co (G-9035)*

C M I Group, Chagrin Falls *Also Called: Custom Materials Inc (G-1976)*

C M M Inc 216 789-7480
546 Meadowridge Way Hudson (44236) *(G-9336)*

C M R Inc 614 447-7100
4449 Easton Way Ste 200 Columbus (43219) *(G-5489)*

C Micah Rand Inc 513 605-2000
12100 Reed Hartman Hwy Cincinnati (45241) *(G-2298)*

C O Howard Hanna Mortgage 412 967-9000
6000 Parkland Blvd Ste 200 Cleveland (44124) *(G-3917)*

C P W, Brookpark *Also Called: Car Parts Warehouse Inc (G-1429)*

C R G, Miamisburg *Also Called: Cornerstone Research Group Inc (G-11039)*

C R M, Clyde *Also Called: Chaney Roofing Maintenance Inc (G-5199)*

C R T, Mentor *Also Called: Component Repair Technologies Inc (G-10925)*

C Ray Wllams Erly Chldhood Ctr, Columbus *Also Called: Whitehall City Schools (G-6887)*

C Rst Specialized Trnsp, Cincinnati *Also Called: CRST International Inc (G-2518)*

C T I, Akron *Also Called: Commercial Time Sharing Inc (G-115)*

C V Perry & Co (PA) 614 221-4131
370 S 5th St Columbus (43215) *(G-5490)*

C-N-D Industries Inc 330 478-8811
359 State Ave Nw Massillon (44647) *(G-10633)*

C. P. I., West Chester *Also Called: Cincinnati Prcision Instrs Inc (G-14805)*

C.H.P., Columbus *Also Called: Columbus Housing Partnr Inc (G-5640)*

C.J. Mahan Construction Co, Grove City *Also Called: CJ Mahan Construction Co LLC (G-8909)*

C&C Clean Team Enterprises LLC 513 321-5100
2016 Madison Rd Cincinnati (45208) *(G-2299)*

C&E Advanced Technologies, Miamisburg *Also Called: Eis Intermediate Holdings LLC (G-11049)*

C&W Facility Services Inc 614 827-1702
325 John H Mcconnell Blvd Columbus (43215) *(G-5491)*

C2g, Dayton *Also Called: Legrand North America LLC (G-7451)*

CA Bulding - Tussig Cancer Ctr, Cleveland *Also Called: Cleveland Clinic Foundation (G-4024)*

Ca-Mj Hotel Associates Ltd 330 494-6494
4375 Metro Cir Nw Canton (44720) *(G-1694)*

Cabi C Aydin DDS, Aurora *Also Called: Cabi C Aydin DDS Inc (G-610)*

Cabi C Aydin DDS Inc 330 562-1644
485 N Aurora Rd Aurora (44202) *(G-610)*

Cabinet and Granite Direct, Cleveland *Also Called: Direct Import Home Decor Inc (G-4166)*

Cabinet Restylers, Ashland *Also Called: Cabinet Restylers Inc (G-486)*

Cabinet Restylers Inc 419 281-8449
419 E 8th St Ashland (44805) *(G-486)*

Cable System, The, Sandusky *Also Called: Erie County Cablevision Inc (G-12891)*

Cac Group LLC 740 369-4328
2097 London Rd Delaware (43015) *(G-7782)*

Caci Mtl Systems Inc 937 429-2771
2685 Hibiscus Way Ste 200 Beavercreek (45431) *(G-868)*

Caci Mtl Systems Inc 937 426-3111
3481 Dayton Xenia Rd Ste A Beavercreek (45432) *(G-869)*

Caci-CMS Info Systems LLC 937 986-3600
2600 Paramount Pl Ste 300 Fairborn (45324) *(G-8368)*

Cadence Care Network 330 544-8005
165 E Park Ave Niles (44446) *(G-11782)*

Cadle Company, The, Newton Falls *Also Called: The Cadle Company (G-11778)*

Cadna Automotive, Fairlawn *Also Called: Cadna Rubber Company Inc (G-8468)*

Cadna Rubber Company Inc 901 566-9090
703 S Cleveland Massillon Rd Fairlawn (44333) *(G-8468)*

Cadre Computer Resources Co (PA) 513 762-7350
625 Eden Park Dr Cincinnati (45202) *(G-2300)*

Cadre Information Security, Cincinnati *Also Called: Cadre Computer Resources Co (G-2300)*

Cadx Systems Inc 937 431-1464
2689 Commons Blvd Ste 100 Beavercreek (45431) *(G-870)*

Caesar Creek Flea Market, Dayton *Also Called: Ferguson Hills Inc (G-7351)*

Cafaro, Niles *Also Called: Cafaro Company (G-11783)*

Cafaro Company (PA) 330 747-2661
5577 Youngstown Warren Rd Niles (44446) *(G-11783)*

Cafaro Northwest Partnership 419 626-8575
4314 Milan Rd Sandusky (44870) *(G-12867)*

Caff LLC 440 918-4570
24651 Center Ridge Rd Ste 400 Westlake (44145) *(G-15042)*

Cahill Cnstr Inc Cahill Cnstr 614 442-8570
6331 Fiesta Dr Columbus (43235) *(G-5492)*

Cahill Corporation 330 724-1224
3951 Creek Wood Ln Uniontown (44685) *(G-14243)*

Cai Holdings LLC 419 656-3568
1707 George St Sandusky (44870) *(G-12868)*

Cain B M W, Canton *Also Called: Cain Motors Inc (G-1695)*

Cain Motors Inc 330 494-5588
6527 Whipple Ave Nw Canton (44720) *(G-1695)*

Cal-Maine Foods Inc 937 337-9576
3078 Washington Rd Rossburg (45362) *(G-12764)*

Calcutta Health Care Center, East Liverpool *Also Called: P N P Inc (G-8190)*

Calfee, Cleveland *Also Called: Calfee Halter & Griswold LLP (G-3918)*

Calfee Halter & Griswold LLP 513 693-4880
255 E 5th St Cincinnati (45202) *(G-2301)*

Calfee Halter & Griswold LLP (PA) 216 622-8200
The Calfee Building 1405 E Sixth St Cleveland (44114) *(G-3918)*

Calfee Halter & Griswold LLP 614 621-1500
41 S High St Ste 1200 Columbus (43215) *(G-5493)*

Calibre Scientific, Maumee *Also Called: Anatrace Products LLC (G-10691)*

Call Management Resources, Columbus *Also Called: C M R Inc (G-5489)*

Call Traditions, Cleveland *Also Called: Aristocrat W Nursing Hm Corp (G-3834)*

Callos Prof Employment II, Youngstown *Also Called: Callos Resource LLC (G-15569)*

Callos Resource LLC (PA) 330 788-3033
755 Boardman Canfield Rd Ste N2-Up Youngstown (44512) *(G-15569)*

Calvary Cemetery, Youngstown *Also Called: Roman Cthlic Docese Youngstown (G-15710)*

Calvary Contracting Inc 937 754-0300
4125 Gibson Dr Tipp City (45371) *(G-13654)*

Calvary Industries Inc (PA) 513 874-1113
9233 Seward Rd Fairfield (45014) *(G-8398)*

Calvert Wire & Cable Corp (DH) 216 433-7600
17909 Cleveland Pkwy Dr Ste 180 Cleveland (44142) *(G-3919)*

Calvin Electric LLC 937 670-2558
7272 Pleasant Plain Rd Clayton (45315) *(G-3731)*

Calyx LLC 216 916-0639
909 Canterbury Rd Ste O Westlake (44145) *(G-15043)*

Camargo Club 513 561-9292
8605 Shawnee Run Rd Cincinnati (45243) *(G-2302)*

Cambrdge Prperty Investors Ltd 740 432-7313
  2248 Southgate Pkwy Cambridge (43725) *(G-1557)*
Cambria Green Management LLC 330 899-1263
  1787 Thorn Dr Uniontown (44685) *(G-14244)*
Cambria Stes Akrn-Canton Arprt, Uniontown Also Called: Cambria Green Management LLC *(G-14244)*
Cambridge Associates Ltd 740 432-7313
  2248 Southgate Pkwy Cambridge (43725) *(G-1558)*
Cambridge Behavioral Hospital 740 432-4906
  66755 State St Cambridge (43725) *(G-1559)*
Cambridge Box & Gift Shop, Cambridge Also Called: Cambridge Packaging Inc *(G-1560)*
Cambridge Counseling Center 740 450-7790
  326 Main St Zanesville (43701) *(G-15775)*
Cambridge Eye Associates Inc 513 527-9700
  8100 Beckett Center Dr West Chester (45069) *(G-14657)*
Cambridge Eye Doctors, West Chester Also Called: Cambridge Eye Associates Inc *(G-14657)*
Cambridge Home Health Care 419 775-1253
  780 Park Ave W Unit B Mansfield (44906) *(G-10250)*
Cambridge Home Health Care 330 725-1968
  750 E Washington St Ste B1 Medina (44256) *(G-10816)*
Cambridge Packaging Inc 740 432-3351
  60794 Southgate Rd Cambridge (43725) *(G-1560)*
Cambridge Savings Bank, Cambridge Also Called: Huntington National Bank *(G-1574)*
Cambridge Surgical Suites LLC 740 421-4455
  61605 Southgate Rd Cambridge (43725) *(G-1561)*
Cambridge Trs Inc 617 231-3176
  2670 E Kemper Rd Sharonville (45241) *(G-12992)*
Cambridge Trs Inc 617 231-3176
  30100 Clemens Rd Westlake (44145) *(G-15044)*
Camco Financial Corporation 740 435-2020
  814 Wheeling Ave Cambridge (43725) *(G-1562)*
Camden Health Center, Cincinnati Also Called: Deaconess Long Term Care of MI *(G-2551)*
Camelot Community Care Inc 513 961-5900
  7162 Reading Rd Ste 300 Cincinnati (45237) *(G-2303)*
Camelot East Apartments, Fairfield Also Called: Tgm Associates LP *(G-8445)*
Camelot Realty Investments 740 357-5291
  10689 Us-23 Lucasville (45648) *(G-10173)*
Cameo Solutions Inc 513 645-4220
  9078 Union Centre Blvd Ste 200 West Chester (45069) *(G-14658)*
Cameron Mitchell Rest LLC (PA) 614 621-3663
  390 W Nationwide Blvd Ste 300 # 3 Columbus (43215) *(G-5494)*
Cameron Mitchell Rest LLC 724 824-7558
  6644 Riverside Dr Dublin (43017) *(G-7949)*
Camgen Ltd 330 204-8636
  1621 Euclid Ave Ste 220-314 Cleveland (44115) *(G-3920)*
Camo, Beavercreek Township Also Called: Capablity Anlis Msrment Orgnzt *(G-933)*
Camp Bow Wow, Hilliard Also Called: Wolf and Woof LLC *(G-9246)*
Camp Ho Mita Koda Foundation 440 739-4095
  14040 Auburn Rd Newbury (44065) *(G-11759)*
CAMP JOY, Clarksville Also Called: Joy Outdoor Education Ctr LLC *(G-3730)*
Camp Patmos Inc 419 746-2214
  920 Monaghan Rd Kelleys Island (43438) *(G-9552)*
Camp Y-Noah, Clinton Also Called: Young MNS Chrstn Assn of Akron *(G-5197)*
Campbell Inc (PA) 419 476-4444
  2875 Crane Way Northwood (43619) *(G-11971)*
Campbell Construction Inc (PA) 330 262-5186
  1159 Blachleyville Rd Wooster (44691) *(G-15316)*
Campbell Sales Company 513 697-2900
  8805 Governors Hill Dr Ste 300 Cincinnati (45249) *(G-2304)*
Campus Life, Cleveland Also Called: Youth For Christ/Usa Inc *(G-5168)*
Campuseai Inc 216 589-9626
  1111 Superior Ave E Ste 310 Cleveland (44114) *(G-3921)*
Camtaylor Co Realtors, Worthington Also Called: Phil Giessler *(G-15446)*
Canaan Companies Inc 419 842-8373
  328 21st St Toledo (43604) *(G-13724)*
Canal Physician Group 330 344-4000
  1 Akron General Ave Akron (44307) *(G-79)*
Canal Square Branch, Akron Also Called: Young MNS Chrstn Assn of Akron *(G-368)*
Cancer Care Center, Youngstown Also Called: Mahoning Vly Hmtlogy Onclogy A *(G-15659)*
Cancer Center, Canton Also Called: Aultman North Canton Med Group *(G-1682)*

Cancer Center, Cincinnati Also Called: University of Cincinnati *(G-3594)*
Cancer Centre, Cleveland Also Called: Cleveland Clinic Foundation *(G-4021)*
Cancer Family Care Inc 513 731-3346
  4790 Red Bank Rd Ste 128 Cincinnati (45227) *(G-2305)*
Candlewood Park Healthcare Ctr, Cleveland Also Called: Belmore Leasing Co LLC *(G-3864)*
Canfield Healthcare Center, Youngstown Also Called: Canfield Leasing Co LLC *(G-15570)*
Canfield Leasing Co LLC 513 530-1600
  2958 Canfield Rd Youngstown (44511) *(G-15570)*
Canfield Metal Coating Corp 330 702-3876
  460 W Main St Canfield (44406) *(G-1623)*
Cangen Holdings Inc 770 458-4882
  10200 Alliance Rd Ste 200 Blue Ash (45242) *(G-1140)*
Caniano Bsner Pdiatrics Clinic, Columbus Also Called: Nationwide Childrens Hospital *(G-6310)*
Cannasure Insurance Svcs LLC 800 420-5757
  1468 W 9th St Ste 805 Cleveland (44113) *(G-3922)*
Canon Solutions America Inc 216 446-3830
  6000 Freedom Square Dr Ste 240 Independence (44131) *(G-9415)*
Canon Solutions America Inc 216 750-2980
  6161 Oak Tree Blvd Ste 301 Independence (44131) *(G-9416)*
Canon Solutions America Inc 513 229-8020
  4900 Parkway Dr Ste 170 Mason (45040) *(G-10525)*
Canon Solutions America Inc 419 897-9244
  1724 Indian Wood Cir Ste F Maumee (43537) *(G-10707)*
Canon Solutions America Inc 937 260-4495
  1 Prestige Pl Miamisburg (45342) *(G-11031)*
Canterbury Enterprises, Canton Also Called: 4859 Hills & Dales Inc *(G-1649)*
Canterbury Golf Club Inc 216 561-1914
  22000 S Woodland Rd Cleveland (44122) *(G-3923)*
Canterbury Retirement Cmnty, Toledo Also Called: Fountains At Canterbury *(G-13810)*
Canterbury Villa of Alliance Center, Alliance Also Called: Canterbury Vlla Oprations Corp *(G-377)*
Canterbury Vlla Oprations Corp 330 821-4000
  1785 N Freshley Ave Alliance (44601) *(G-377)*
Canton Allergy Lab, Canton Also Called: Ohio Head & Neck Surgeons Inc *(G-1822)*
Canton Altman Emrgncy Physcans 330 456-2695
  2600 6th St Sw Canton (44710) *(G-1696)*
Canton Asssted Lving Rhblttion 330 492-7131
  836 34th St Nw Canton (44709) *(G-1697)*
Canton Chair Rental, Canton Also Called: Maloney & Associates Inc *(G-1799)*
Canton Christian Home Inc 330 456-0004
  2550 Cleveland Ave Nw Canton (44709) *(G-1698)*
Canton City School District 330 456-6710
  2030 Cleveland Ave Sw Canton (44707) *(G-1699)*
Canton Country Day School 330 453-8279
  3000 Demington Ave Nw Canton (44718) *(G-1700)*
Canton Erectors Inc 330 453-7363
  1369 Sanders Ave Sw Massillon (44647) *(G-10634)*
Canton Floors Inc 330 492-1121
  3944 Fulton Dr Nw Canton (44718) *(G-1701)*
Canton Montessori Association 330 452-0148
  125 15th St Nw Canton (44703) *(G-1702)*
Canton Montessori School, Canton Also Called: Canton Montessori Association *(G-1702)*
Canton Ophthalmology Assoc Inc 330 456-0047
  2600 Tuscarawas St W Ste 200 Canton (44708) *(G-1703)*
Canton Rhblttion Nrsing Ctr LL 330 456-2842
  2714 13th St Nw Canton (44708) *(G-1704)*
Canton Schl Emplyees Fdral Cr (PA) 330 452-9801
  1380 Market Ave N Canton (44714) *(G-1705)*
Canton School Trnsp Dept, Canton Also Called: Canton City School District *(G-1699)*
Canton-Stark Cnty Swer Clg Inc 330 456-7890
  7300 Freedom Ave Nw North Canton (44720) *(G-11814)*
Cantrell Oil Company 937 695-8003
  18856 State Route 136 Winchester (45697) *(G-15286)*
Cantrell's Motel, Winchester Also Called: 1st Stop Inc *(G-15283)*
Canyon Medical Center Inc 614 864-6010
  5969 E Broad St Ste 200 Columbus (43213) *(G-5495)*
Cap City Hotels LLC 614 294-7500
  1295 Olentangy River Rd Columbus (43212) *(G-5496)*
Capa, Columbus Also Called: Columbus Assn For The Prfrmg A *(G-5613)*

ALPHABETIC SECTION — Careerbuilder LLC

Capablity Anlis Msrment Orgnzt.. 937 260-9373
4027 Colonel Glenn Hwy Ste 100 Beavercreek Township (45431) *(G-933)*

Capgemini America Inc.. 678 427-6642
10100 Innovation Dr Ste 200 Miamisburg (45342) *(G-11032)*

Capital City Aviation Inc.. 614 459-2541
2160 West Case Rd Unit 15 Columbus (43235) *(G-5497)*

Capital City Crane Rental, Columbus Also Called: Capital City Group Inc *(G-5498)*

Capital City Electric Inc.. 614 933-8700
9798 Karmar Ct Ste B New Albany (43054) *(G-11558)*

Capital City Group Inc (HQ).. 614 278-2120
2299 Performance Way Columbus (43207) *(G-5498)*

Capital City Hospice.. 614 441-9300
2800 Corporate Exchange Dr Ste 170 Columbus (43231) *(G-5499)*

Capital City Medical Assoc, Columbus Also Called: Central Ohio Prmry Care Physca *(G-5544)*

Capital Drug, Columbus Also Called: Capital Wholesale Drug Company *(G-5502)*

Capital Fire Protection Co (PA).. 614 279-9448
3360 Valleyview Dr Columbus (43204) *(G-5500)*

Capital Health Services, Miamisburg Also Called: Capital Health Services Inc *(G-11033)*

Capital Health Services Inc (PA).. 937 277-0505
3015 Newmark Dr Miamisburg (45342) *(G-11033)*

Capital Investment Group Llc.. 513 241-5090
525 Vine St Ste 1605 Cincinnati (45202) *(G-2306)*

Capital Land Services Inc.. 330 338-4709
3665 Brookside Dr Norton (44203) *(G-11991)*

Capital Lighting, Columbus Also Called: D & L Lighting Inc *(G-5256)*

Capital Properties MGT Ltd.. 216 991-3057
12929 Shaker Blvd Cleveland (44120) *(G-3924)*

Capital Securities of America.. 419 609-9489
233 E Water St Sandusky (44870) *(G-12869)*

Capital Tire Inc (PA).. 419 241-5111
7001 Integrity Dr Rossford (43460) *(G-12765)*

Capital Transportation Inc.. 614 258-0400
1170 N Cassady Ave Columbus (43219) *(G-5501)*

Capital Wholesale Drug Company.. 614 297-8225
873 Williams Ave Columbus (43212) *(G-5502)*

Capitol City Cardiology Inc (PA).. 614 464-0884
5825 Westbourne Ave Columbus (43213) *(G-5503)*

Capitol Express Entps Inc (PA).. 614 279-2819
3815 Twin Creeks Dr Columbus (43204) *(G-5504)*

Capitol Tunneling Inc.. 614 444-0255
2216 Refugee Rd Columbus (43207) *(G-5505)*

Capitol Varsity Sports Inc.. 513 523-4126
6723 Ringwood Rd Oxford (45056) *(G-12204)*

Capo Preble County, Eaton Also Called: Preble County Head Start *(G-8221)*

CAPRICE HEALTH CARE CENTER, North Lima Also Called: Caprice Health Care Inc *(G-11885)*

Caprice Health Care Inc.. 330 965-9200
9184 Market St North Lima (44452) *(G-11885)*

Capsa Healthcare, Canal Winchester Also Called: Capsa Solutions LLC *(G-1600)*

Capsa Solutions LLC (PA).. 800 437-6633
8170 Dove Pkwy Canal Winchester (43110) *(G-1600)*

Car Parts Warehouse Inc (PA).. 216 281-4500
5200 W 130th St Brookpark (44142) *(G-1429)*

Car Parts Warehouse Inc.. 216 581-4800
18525 Miles Rd Cleveland (44128) *(G-3925)*

Car Parts Warehouse Inc.. 216 496-6540
3382 N Ridge Rd Perry (44081) *(G-12304)*

Car-X Muffler & Brake, Cincinnati Also Called: P & M Exhaust Systems Whse Inc *(G-3179)*

Cararo Co Inc.. 330 652-6980
492 Wood Ave Niles (44446) *(G-11784)*

Carbon Products, West Chester Also Called: Graphel Corporation *(G-14700)*

Carcorp Inc.. 877 857-2801
2900 Morse Rd Columbus (43231) *(G-5506)*

Cardiac Vsclar Thrcic Surgeons.. 513 421-3494
4030 Smith Rd Ste 300 Cincinnati (45209) *(G-2307)*

Cardida Corporation.. 740 439-4359
74978 Broadhead Rd Kimbolton (43749) *(G-9640)*

Cardilgist of Clark Chmpign CN.. 937 653-8897
900 E Court St Urbana (43078) *(G-14299)*

Cardinal Builders Inc.. 614 237-1000
4409 E Main St Columbus (43213) *(G-5507)*

Cardinal Commercecom Inc.. 440 352-8444
6119 Heisley Rd Mentor (44060) *(G-10917)*

Cardinal Group Inc.. 330 252-1047
180 E Miller Ave Akron (44301) *(G-80)*

Cardinal Health, Dublin Also Called: Cardinal Health 110 Inc *(G-7952)*

Cardinal Health, West Chester Also Called: Cardinal Health Systems Inc *(G-14802)*

Cardinal Health Inc (PA).. 614 757-5000
7000 Cardinal Pl Dublin (43017) *(G-7950)*

Cardinal Health Inc.. 614 409-6770
5995 Commerce Center Dr Groveport (43125) *(G-8976)*

Cardinal Health Inc.. 614 497-9552
2320 Mcgaw Rd Obetz (43207) *(G-12079)*

Cardinal Health 100 Inc (HQ).. 614 757-5000
7000 Cardinal Pl Dublin (43017) *(G-7951)*

Cardinal Health 110 Inc.. 614 717-5000
7000 Cardinal Pl Dublin (43017) *(G-7952)*

Cardinal Health 200 LLC (HQ).. 614 757-5000
7000 Cardinal Pl Dublin (43017) *(G-7953)*

Cardinal Health 201 Inc (HQ).. 614 757-5000
7000 Cardinal Pl Dublin (43017) *(G-7954)*

Cardinal Health 301 LLC (HQ).. 614 757-5000
7000 Cardinal Pl Dublin (43017) *(G-7955)*

Cardinal Health 414 LLC (HQ).. 614 757-5000
7000 Cardinal Pl Dublin (43017) *(G-7956)*

Cardinal Health At Home, Twinsburg Also Called: Rgh Enterprises LLC *(G-14216)*

Cardinal Health Systems Inc.. 513 874-5940
5532 Spellmire Dr West Chester (45246) *(G-14802)*

Cardinal Operating Company.. 740 598-4164
306 County Road 7e Brilliant (43913) *(G-1379)*

Cardinal Orthopaedic Group Inc.. 614 759-1186
170 Taylor Station Rd Columbus (43213) *(G-5508)*

Cardinal Orthopaedic Institute, Columbus Also Called: Orthopedic One Inc *(G-6481)*

Cardinal Orthopedic Institute.. 614 488-1816
3777 Trueman Ct Hilliard (43026) *(G-9187)*

Cardinal Plant, Brilliant Also Called: Buckeye Power Inc *(G-1378)*

Cardinal Retirement Village.. 330 928-7888
171 Graham Rd Cuyahoga Falls (44223) *(G-7052)*

Cardinal Solutions Group Inc (HQ).. 513 984-6700
7755 Montgomery Rd Ste 510 Cincinnati (45236) *(G-2308)*

Cardinal Wds Skilled Nursing, Madison Also Called: American Eagle Hlth Care Svcs *(G-10211)*

Cardinal Wods Sklled Nrsing Rh, Madison Also Called: Cw Opco LLC *(G-10214)*

Cardinalcommerce Corporation.. 877 352-8444
8100 Tyler Blvd Ste 100 Mentor (44060) *(G-10918)*

Cardinalhealth, Dublin Also Called: Cardinal Health Inc *(G-7950)*

Cardio Partners Inc (DH).. 614 760-5000
5000 Tuttle Crossing Blvd Dublin (43016) *(G-7957)*

Cardiology Center Cincinnati, Montgomery Also Called: Cardiology Ctr of Cincinnati *(G-11364)*

Cardiology Ctr of Cincinnati (PA).. 513 745-9800
10525 Montgomery Rd # A Montgomery (45242) *(G-11364)*

Cardiosolution LLC.. 513 618-2394
4675 Cornell Rd Ste 100 Blue Ash (45241) *(G-1141)*

Cardiovascular Associates Inc.. 330 747-6446
1001 Belmont Ave Youngstown (44504) *(G-15571)*

Cardiovascular Clinic Inc.. 440 882-0075
6525 Powers Blvd Rm 301 Cleveland (44129) *(G-3926)*

Care Alliance.. 216 781-6228
2163 Payne Ave Cleveland (44114) *(G-3927)*

Care Center, Cincinnati Also Called: Cincinnati Anmal Rfrral Emrgnc *(G-2393)*

Care Heating and Cooling Inc.. 614 841-1555
397 Venture Dr Ste B Lewis Center (43035) *(G-9812)*

Care Medical Inc.. 513 821-7272
8340 Reading Rd Cincinnati (45237) *(G-2309)*

Care One LLC.. 937 236-6707
5440 Charlesgate Rd Dayton (45424) *(G-7210)*

Career Cnnctons Stffing Svcs I.. 440 471-8210
26260 Center Ridge Rd Westlake (44145) *(G-15045)*

Career Partners Intl LLC (PA).. 919 401-4260
20 S 3rd St Ste 210 Columbus (43215) *(G-5509)*

Careerbuilder LLC.. 513 297-3707
8044 Montgomery Rd Ste 505 Cincinnati (45236) *(G-2310)*

Careercurve LLC — ALPHABETIC SECTION

Careercurve LLC (HQ) 800 314-8230
5005 Rockside Rd Ste 600 Cleveland (44131) *(G-3928)*

Carefirst Urgent Care LLC 513 868-2345
7300 Beechmont Ave Cincinnati (45230) *(G-2311)*

Carefor Place Nursing Home Inc 513 481-2201
3904 N Bend Rd Cincinnati (45211) *(G-2312)*

Careserve (HQ) 740 454-4000
2991 Maple Ave Zanesville (43701) *(G-15776)*

Caresource (PA) 937 224-3300
230 N Main St Dayton (45402) *(G-7211)*

Caresource Management Group Co 216 839-1001
5900 Landerbrook Dr Ste 300 Cleveland (44124) *(G-3929)*

Caresource Management Group Co 614 221-3370
3455 Mill Run Dr Hilliard (43026) *(G-9188)*

CARESOURCE MANAGEMENT GROUP CO., Cleveland Also Called: Caresource Management Group Co *(G-3929)*

Caresource Ohio Inc (HQ) 937 224-3300
230 N Main St Dayton (45402) *(G-7212)*

CareSource USA Holding, Dayton Also Called: Caresource Ohio Inc *(G-7212)*

CARESPRING, Cincinnati Also Called: Eastgate Health Care Center *(G-2103)*

Carespring, Loveland Also Called: Carespring Health Care MGT LLC *(G-10130)*

CARESPRING, Springboro Also Called: Hillspring Health Care Center *(G-13201)*

Carespring Health Care MGT LLC (PA) 513 943-4000
390 Wards Corner Rd Loveland (45140) *(G-10130)*

Carestar, Cincinnati Also Called: Carestar Inc *(G-2313)*

Carestar Inc (PA) 513 618-8300
5566 Cheviot Rd Cincinnati (45247) *(G-2313)*

Caret Holdings Inc 866 980-9431
80 E Rich St Ste 500 Columbus (43215) *(G-5510)*

Careworks of Ohio Inc 614 792-1085
5555 Glendon Ct Ste 300 Dublin (43016) *(G-7958)*

Carey Electric Co 937 669-3399
3925 Vanco Ln Vandalia (45377) *(G-14368)*

Carfagna's Cleve Meats, Columbus Also Called: Carfagnas Incorporated *(G-5248)*

Carfagnas Incorporated 614 846-6340
1440 Gemini Pl Columbus (43240) *(G-5248)*

Cargill, North Olmsted Also Called: Cargill Incorporated *(G-11893)*

Cargill Incorporated 440 716-4664
24950 Country Club Blvd Ste 450 North Olmsted (44070) *(G-11893)*

Cargill Premix and Nutrition, Lewisburg Also Called: Provimi North America Inc *(G-9842)*

Cargo Solution Express Inc 614 980-0351
4540 Fisher Rd Columbus (43228) *(G-5511)*

Cargotec Services USA Inc 419 482-6000
12233 Williams Rd Perrysburg (43551) *(G-12322)*

CARILLON HISTORICAL PARK, Dayton Also Called: Dayton History *(G-7287)*

Caring For Kids Inc 330 928-0044
650 Graham Rd Ste 101 Cuyahoga Falls (44221) *(G-7053)*

Caring Hearts HM Hlth Care Inc (PA) 513 339-1237
6677 Summer Field Dr Mason (45040) *(G-10526)*

Caring Place Healthcare Group 513 771-1779
779 Glendale Milford Rd Cincinnati (45215) *(G-2314)*

Carington Health Systems 513 732-6500
4000 Golden Age Dr Batavia (45103) *(G-730)*

Carington Health Systems 513 961-8881
3627 Harvey Ave Cincinnati (45229) *(G-2315)*

Carington Health Systems 937 743-2754
421 Mission Ln Franklin (45005) *(G-8632)*

Carington Health Systems (PA) 513 682-2700
8200 Beckett Park Dr Hamilton (45011) *(G-9025)*

Carington Park, Ashtabula Also Called: Fhs Carington Inc *(G-535)*

Carington Park, Ashtabula Also Called: Salutary Providers Inc *(G-548)*

Caritas Inc 419 332-2589
1406 Oak Harbor Rd Fremont (43420) *(G-8668)*

Carl B Stokes Head Start Ctr, Cleveland Also Called: Step Forward *(G-4950)*

Carleton Realty Inc 740 653-5200
826 N Memorial Dr Lancaster (43130) *(G-9698)*

Carleton Realty Inc (PA) 614 431-5700
580 W Schrock Rd Westerville (43081) *(G-14964)*

Carlile Patchen & Murphy LLP (PA) 614 228-6135
950 Goodale Blvd Ste 200 Columbus (43212) *(G-5512)*

Carlisle McNllie Rini Krmer Ul 216 360-7200
24755 Chagrin Blvd Beachwood (44122) *(G-772)*

Carlisle Msnry/Cnstruction Inc 740 966-5045
6300 Van Fossen Rd Johnstown (43031) *(G-9545)*

Carlson Quality Brake, Lima Also Called: International Brake Inds Inc *(G-9911)*

Carlson, L D Company, Kent Also Called: Wine-Art of Ohio Inc *(G-9607)*

Carlton Manor, Wshngtn Ct Hs Also Called: Carlton Manor Nursing and Rehabilitation Center Inc *(G-15477)*

Carlton Manor Nursing and Rehabilitation Center Inc 740 335-7143
726 Rawlings St Wshngtn Ct Hs (43160) *(G-15477)*

Carmens Dist Systems Inc 800 886-8227
4585 Poth Rd Columbus (43213) *(G-5513)*

Carmeuse Lime Inc 419 986-5200
1967 W County Rd 42 Bettsville (44815) *(G-1098)*

Carmeuse Natural Chemicals, Bettsville Also Called: Carmeuse Lime Inc *(G-1098)*

Carmichael Equipment Inc (PA) 740 446-2412
668 Pinecrest Dr Bidwell (45614) *(G-1103)*

Carmike Cinemas, Findlay Also Called: Carmike Cinemas LLC *(G-8520)*

Carmike Cinemas, Saint Clairsville Also Called: Carmike Cinemas LLC *(G-12783)*

Carmike Cinemas LLC 419 423-7414
906 Interstate Dr Findlay (45840) *(G-8520)*

Carmike Cinemas LLC 740 695-3919
700 Banfield Rd Saint Clairsville (43950) *(G-12783)*

Carnegie Capital Asset MGT LLC 216 595-1349
30300 Chagrin Blvd Cleveland (44124) *(G-3930)*

Carnegie Companies Inc 440 232-2300
6190 Cochran Rd Ste A Solon (44139) *(G-13072)*

Carnegie Investment Counsel, Cleveland Also Called: Carnegie Capital Asset MGT LLC *(G-3930)*

Carnegie Management & Dev Corp 440 892-6800
27500 Detroit Rd Ste 300 Westlake (44145) *(G-15046)*

Carney McNicholas, Youngstown Also Called: Nicholas Carney-Mc Inc *(G-15677)*

Carol Ruta 419 663-3501
351 Milan Ave Norwalk (44857) *(G-12004)*

Carolinas It LLC 919 856-2300
5747 Perimeter Dr Dublin (43017) *(G-7959)*

Carp Cosmetic Surgery Ctr Inc 216 416-1221
24300 Chagrin Blvd Beachwood (44122) *(G-773)*

Carpe Diem Industries LLC 419 358-0129
505 E Jefferson St Bluffton (45817) *(G-1280)*

Carpe Diem Industries LLC (PA) 419 659-5639
4599 Campbell Rd Columbus Grove (45830) *(G-6921)*

Carpediem Management Company 740 687-1563
800 E Main St Lancaster (43130) *(G-9699)*

Carpenter & Lee Consulting LLC 614 766-8670
2237 Hyatts Rd Delaware (43015) *(G-7783)*

Carpenter Lipps LLP (PA) 614 365-4100
280 N High St Ste 1300 Columbus (43215) *(G-5514)*

Carrara Companies Inc (PA) 330 659-2800
2406 Farmstead Rd Richfield (44286) *(G-12690)*

Carriage Court Company Inc 614 871-8000
2320 Sonora Dr Grove City (43123) *(G-8905)*

Carriage Court of Kenwood, Cincinnati Also Called: Hackensack Meridian Health Inc *(G-2791)*

Carriage Crt Snior Communities, Grove City Also Called: Carriage Court Company Inc *(G-8905)*

Carriage Crt-Mrysvlle Ltd Prtn 937 642-2202
717 S Walnut St Marysville (43040) *(G-10478)*

Carriage House, Norwalk Also Called: Fisher-Titus Medical Center *(G-12012)*

Carriage Inn Bowerston Inc 740 269-8001
102 Boyce Dr Bowerston (44695) *(G-1301)*

Carriage Inn of Cadiz Inc 740 942-8084
308 W Warren St Cadiz (43907) *(G-1538)*

Carriage Inn of Dayton, Dayton Also Called: Carriage Inn Rtrment Cmnty of *(G-7213)*

Carriage Inn of Steubenville 740 264-7161
3102 Saint Charles Dr Steubenville (43952) *(G-13318)*

Carriage Inn of Trotwood Inc 937 277-0505
3015 Newmark Dr Miamisburg (45342) *(G-11034)*

Carriage Inn Rtrment Cmnty of 937 278-0404
5040 Philadelphia Dr Dayton (45415) *(G-7213)*

Carriage Inn Trotwood Inc 937 854-1180
5020 Philadelphia Dr Dayton (45415) *(G-7214)*

ALPHABETIC SECTION

Catholic Chrties Sthstern Ohio

Carroll Electric Coop Inc.. 330 627-2116
 250 Canton Rd Nw Carrollton (44615) *(G-1903)*

Carrolls LLC.. 330 733-8100
 2880 Gilchrist Rd Akron (44305) *(G-81)*

Carrolls LLC.. 513 733-5559
 2939 Crescentville Rd West Chester (45069) *(G-14659)*

Carrollton Habilitation Center, Carrollton *Also Called: Alternative Residences Two Inc* *(G-1902)*

Cartcom Inc... 740 644-0912
 200 Arrowhead Blvd Hebron (43025) *(G-9141)*

Cartemp USA Inc (PA)... 440 715-1000
 29100 Aurora Rd Solon (44139) *(G-13073)*

Carter Heath Care, Steubenville *Also Called: Associated Home Health Inc (G-13316)*

Carter Lumber, Akron *Also Called: Carter-Jones Lumber Company (G-82)*

Carter Lumber, Kent *Also Called: Carter-Jones Companies Inc (G-9560)*

Carter Lumber, Kent *Also Called: Carter-Jones Lumber Company (G-9561)*

Carter Lumber, Middlefield *Also Called: Carter-Jones Lumber Company (G-11139)*

Carter Site Development LLC... 513 831-8843
 106 Glendale Milford Rd Miamiville (45147) *(G-11109)*

Carter-Jones Companies Inc (PA).................................. 330 673-6100
 601 Tallmadge Rd Kent (44240) *(G-9560)*

Carter-Jones Lumber Company...................................... 330 784-5441
 172 N Case Ave Akron (44305) *(G-82)*

Carter-Jones Lumber Company (HQ).............................. 330 673-6100
 601 Tallmadge Rd Kent (44240) *(G-9561)*

Carter-Jones Lumber Company...................................... 440 834-8164
 14601 Kinsman Rd Middlefield (44062) *(G-11139)*

Cartruck Packaging Inc... 216 631-7225
 7315 Associate Ave Cleveland (44144) *(G-3931)*

Caruso Inc (PA)... 513 860-9200
 3465 Hauck Rd Cincinnati (45241) *(G-2316)*

Carwas, The, Cleveland *Also Called: Roulan Enterprises Inc (G-4856)*

Cas-Ker Company Inc... 513 674-7700
 2550 Civic Center Dr Cincinnati (45231) *(G-2317)*

CASA, Cincinnati *Also Called: Addiction Services Council (G-2144)*

CASA OF FRANKLIN COUNTY, Columbus *Also Called: Friends of Casa Frnklin Cnty O (G-5896)*

Casal Day Spa and Salon, Canfield *Also Called: Casals Hair Salon Inc (G-1624)*

Casals Hair Salon Inc (PA).. 330 533-6766
 4030 Boardman Canfield Rd Canfield (44406) *(G-1624)*

Cascade Corporation... 419 425-3675
 2000 Production Dr Findlay (45840) *(G-8521)*

Casco Mfg Solutions Inc.. 513 681-0003
 3107 Spring Grove Ave Cincinnati (45225) *(G-2318)*

Cash Flow Solutions Inc.. 513 524-2320
 5166 College Corner Pike Oxford (45056) *(G-12205)*

Casleo Corporation.. 614 252-6508
 2741 E 4th Ave Columbus (43219) *(G-5515)*

Casnet, Akron *Also Called: High Line Corporation (G-192)*

Casod Industrial Properties, Marion *Also Called: Graham Investment Co (G-10429)*

Cass Information Systems Inc.. 614 839-4500
 2675 Corporate Exchange Dr Columbus (43231) *(G-5516)*

Cass Information Systems Inc.. 614 839-4503
 2644 Kirkwood Hyw Newark Columbus (43218) *(G-5517)*

Cass Logistics, Columbus *Also Called: Cass Information Systems Inc (G-5516)*

Cassady Altrntive Elmntary Sch, Columbus *Also Called: Columbus City School District (G-5621)*

Cassady Schiller & Assoc Inc.. 513 483-6699
 4555 Lake Forest Dr Ste 400 Blue Ash (45242) *(G-1142)*

Cassano's Pizza & Subs, Dayton *Also Called: Cassanos Inc (G-7215)*

Cassanos Inc (PA)... 937 294-8400
 1700 E Stroop Rd Dayton (45429) *(G-7215)*

Cassidy Trley Coml RE Svcs Inc..................................... 513 771-2580
 300 E Business Way Ste 190 Cincinnati (45241) *(G-2319)*

Cassidy Trley Coml RE Svcs Inc..................................... 614 241-4700
 325 John H Mcconnell Blvd Ste 250 Columbus (43215) *(G-5518)*

Castaway Bay, Sandusky *Also Called: Cedar Point Park LLC (G-12875)*

Castaway Bay Resort.. 419 627-2500
 2001 Cleveland Rd Sandusky (44870) *(G-12870)*

Castaways On The River, The, Wilmington *Also Called: RLR Investments LLC (G-15270)*

Casto, Columbus *Also Called: United Management Inc (G-6807)*

Casto Communities Cnstr Ltd (PA)................................. 614 228-5331
 191 W Nationwide Blvd Ste 200 Columbus (43215) *(G-5519)*

Casto Health Care, Mansfield *Also Called: Wedgewood Estates (G-10324)*

Catalyst Counseling LLC... 937 219-7770
 5104 Sandhurst Ct Middletown (45044) *(G-11155)*

Catalyst Life Services, Mansfield *Also Called: Center For Indvdual Fmly Svcs (G-10251)*

Catalyst Paper (usa) Inc... 937 528-3800
 7777 Washington Village Dr Ste 210 Dayton (45459) *(G-7216)*

Catalyst Recovery La LLC (PA)...................................... 513 354-3640
 1 Landy Ln Cincinnati (45215) *(G-2320)*

Catanzaro Frank J Sons Dghters.................................... 800 827-4020
 535 Shepherd Ave Cincinnati (45215) *(G-2321)*

Catastrophe MGT Solutions Inc...................................... 800 959-2630
 280 Executive Pkwy W Hudson (44236) *(G-9337)*

Catawba Island Marina, Port Clinton *Also Called: Catawba-Cleveland Dev Corp (G-12518)*

Catawba-Cleveland Dev Corp (PA)................................. 419 797-4424
 4235 E Beachclub Rd Port Clinton (43452) *(G-12518)*

Catensys US Inc.. 330 273-4383
 21487 Royalton Rd Strongsville (44149) *(G-13447)*

Caterpillar, Broadview Heights *Also Called: Ohio Machinery Co (G-1395)*

Caterpillar, Columbus *Also Called: Ohio Machinery Co (G-6436)*

Caterpillar Authorized Dealer, Bolivar *Also Called: Ohio Machinery Co (G-1296)*

Caterpillar Authorized Dealer, Broadview Heights *Also Called: Ohio Machinery Co (G-1394)*

Caterpillar Authorized Dealer, Dayton *Also Called: Caterpllar Trmble Ctrl Tech LL (G-7217)*

Caterpillar Authorized Dealer, Perrysburg *Also Called: Ohio Machinery Co (G-12359)*

Caterpillar Authorized Dealer, Zanesville *Also Called: Ohio Machinery Co (G-15822)*

Caterpllar Trmble Ctrl Tech LL.. 937 233-8921
 5475 Kellenburger Rd Dayton (45424) *(G-7217)*

Cathcart Rail LLC (PA)... 380 390-2058
 8940 Lyra Dr Ste 200 Columbus (43240) *(G-5249)*

Cathcart Repair Facilities LLC (DH) 8940 Lyra Dr Ste 200 Columbus (43240) *(G-5250)*

Cathedral Holdings Inc.. 513 271-6400
 302 W 3rd St Ste 800 Cincinnati (45202) *(G-2322)*

CATHOLIC CHARITIES, Cincinnati *Also Called: Catholic Chrties of Sthwstern (G-2323)*

Catholic Charities, Medina *Also Called: Catholic Charities Corporation (G-10817)*

Catholic Charities, Springfield *Also Called: Catholic Charities of Southwst (G-13224)*

Catholic Charities, Wooster *Also Called: Catholic Charities Corporation (G-15317)*

Catholic Charities, Youngstown *Also Called: Catholic Chrties Regional Agcy (G-15572)*

Catholic Charities Corporation... 419 289-7456
 433 Cottage St Ashland (44805) *(G-487)*

Catholic Charities Corporation... 419 289-1903
 34 W 2nd St Ste 18 Ashland (44805) *(G-488)*

Catholic Charities Corporation... 216 432-0680
 3135 Euclid Ave Ste 202 Cleveland (44115) *(G-3932)*

Catholic Charities Corporation... 216 939-3713
 7800 Detroit Ave Cleveland (44102) *(G-3933)*

Catholic Charities Corporation... 216 268-4006
 1264 E 123rd St Cleveland (44108) *(G-3934)*

Catholic Charities Corporation (PA)................................ 216 334-2900
 7911 Detroit Ave Cleveland (44102) *(G-3935)*

Catholic Charities Corporation... 330 723-9615
 4210 N Jefferson St Medina (44256) *(G-10817)*

Catholic Charities Corporation... 330 262-7836
 521 Beall Ave Wooster (44691) *(G-15317)*

CATHOLIC CHARITIES DIOCESE OF, Cleveland *Also Called: Catholic Charities Corporation (G-3935)*

Catholic Charities of Southwst.. 937 325-8715
 701 E Columbia St Springfield (45503) *(G-13224)*

Catholic Chrties of Sthwstern (PA).................................. 513 241-7745
 7162 Reading Rd Ste 604 Cincinnati (45237) *(G-2323)*

Catholic Chrties Regional Agcy....................................... 330 744-3320
 319 W Rayen Ave Youngstown (44502) *(G-15572)*

Catholic Chrties Sthstern Ohio.. 740 432-6751
 220 N 7th St Cambridge (43725) *(G-1563)*

Catholic Chrties Sthstern Ohio.. 740 695-3189
 226 W Main St Saint Clairsville (43950) *(G-12784)*

Catholic Chrties Sthstern Ohio.. 740 676-4932
 422 Washington St # 1 Steubenville (43952) *(G-13319)*

(PA)=Parent Co (HQ)=Headquarters (DH)=Div Headquarters

Catholic Chrties Svcs Ashland — ALPHABETIC SECTION

Catholic Chrties Svcs Ashland, Ashland *Also Called: Catholic Charities Corporation* *(G-488)*

Catholic Chrties Svcs Cyhoga C, Cleveland *Also Called: Catholic Charities Corporation* *(G-3933)*

Catholic Club, Toledo *Also Called: Roman Catholic Diocese Toledo* *(G-13995)*

Catholic Cmtries Assn of The D (PA) 216 641-7575
10000 Miles Ave Cleveland (44105) *(G-3936)*

Catholic Health Initiatives 614 871-3047
2160 Southwest Blvd Grove City (43123) *(G-8906)*

Catholic Hlthcare Prtners Fndt 513 639-2800
1701 Mercy Health Pl Cincinnati (45237) *(G-2324)*

Catholic Scial Svcs of Mami VI (PA) 937 223-7217
922 W Riverview Ave Dayton (45402) *(G-7218)*

Catholic Scial Svcs Sprngfield, Springfield *Also Called: Archdiocese of Cincinnati* *(G-13218)*

Catholic Social Services Inc 614 221-5891
197 E Gay St Columbus (43215) *(G-5520)*

Cattrell Companies Inc 740 537-2481
906 Franklin St Toronto (43964) *(G-14122)*

Cauffiel Industries Corp
3171 N Republic Blvd Ste 102 Toledo (43615) *(G-13725)*

Cauffiel Technologies Corporation 419 843-7262
3171 N Republic Blvd Ste 207 Toledo (43615) *(G-13726)*

Caufiel Technology, Toledo *Also Called: Cauffiel Industries Corp* *(G-13725)*

Cavalear Corporation 419 882-7125
6444 Monroe St Sylvania (43560) *(G-13538)*

Cavalier Distributing Company (PA) 513 247-9222
4650 Lake Forest Dr Ste 580 Blue Ash (45242) *(G-1143)*

Cavalier Mobile X-Ray Co 330 726-0202
590 E Western Reserve Rd Bldg 10d Youngstown (44514) *(G-15573)*

Cavalier Tele Mid-Atlantic LLC 614 884-0000
180 E Broad St Fl 9 Columbus (43215) *(G-5521)*

Cavaliers Holdings LLC (PA) 216 420-2000
1 Center Ct Cleveland (44115) *(G-3937)*

Cavaliers Operating Co LLC 216 420-2000
1 Center Ct Cleveland (44115) *(G-3938)*

Cavalry Staffing LLC 440 663-9990
5400 Transportation Blvd Ste 12b Cleveland (44125) *(G-3939)*

Cavanaugh Building Corporation 330 753-6658
1744 Collier Rd Akron (44320) *(G-83)*

Cavcapital Ltd 216 831-8900
23000 Millcreek Blvd Cleveland (44122) *(G-3940)*

Caveney Inc 330 497-4600
7801 Cleveland Ave Nw North Canton (44720) *(G-11815)*

Cavins Trucking & Garage LLC (PA) 419 661-9947
100 J St # C Perrysburg (43551) *(G-12323)*

Cavitch Familo & Durkin Co Lpa 216 621-7860
1300 E 9th St Cleveland (44114) *(G-3941)*

Cavu Group 937 429-2114
2400 E River Rd Moraine (45439) *(G-11396)*

CB Richard Ellis, Toledo *Also Called: Reichle Klein Group Inc* *(G-13986)*

CBA, Perrysburg *Also Called: Critical Business Analysis Inc* *(G-12326)*

Cbc Companies Inc (PA) 614 222-4343
250 E Broad St Fl 21 Columbus (43215) *(G-5522)*

Cbc Global 330 482-3373
200 W Railroad St Columbiana (44408) *(G-5232)*

Cbcinnovis, Columbus *Also Called: Cbcinnovis International Inc* *(G-5523)*

Cbcinnovis International Inc (HQ) 614 222-4343
250 E Broad St Fl 21 Columbus (43215) *(G-5523)*

Cbcs, Columbus *Also Called: Credit Bur Collectn Svcs Inc* *(G-5723)*

Cbcs, Columbus *Also Called: Credit Bur Collectn Svcs Inc* *(G-5724)*

Cbg Biotech Ltd Co 800 941-9484
30175 Solon Industrial Pkwy Solon (44139) *(G-13074)*

Cbiz Inc (PA) 216 447-9000
5959 Rockside Woods Blvd N Ste 600 Cleveland (44131) *(G-3942)*

Cbiz Accnting Tax Advsory Ohio 330 668-6500
4040 Embassy Pkwy Ste 100 Akron (44333) *(G-84)*

Cbiz Accnting Tax Advsory Wash 216 447-9000
6050 Oak Tree Blvd Ste 500 Cleveland (44131) *(G-3943)*

Cbiz Mhm Northern Cal LLC 216 447-9000
6050 Oak Tree Blvd Ste 500 Cleveland (44131) *(G-3944)*

Cbiz Technologies LLC 216 447-9000
6050 Oak Tree Blvd Ste 500 Independence (44131) *(G-9417)*

Cbkb Inc 440 946-6019
8669 Twinbrook Rd Mentor (44060) *(G-10919)*

Cbn Westside Technologies Inc 513 772-7000
8800 Global Way West Chester (45069) *(G-14660)*

Cbre Inc 614 764-4798
5175 Emerald Pkwy Dublin (43017) *(G-7960)*

CBS Personnel Services LLC 513 651-3600
201 E 4th St Cincinnati (45202) *(G-2325)*

Cbst Acquisition LLC 513 361-9600
6900 Steger Dr Cincinnati (45237) *(G-2326)*

Cbt Company, Cincinnati *Also Called: Belting Company of Cincinnati* *(G-2256)*

Cbt Company, Sidney *Also Called: Belting Company of Cincinnati* *(G-13021)*

Cbt Company, Sidney *Also Called: Belting Company of Cincinnati* *(G-13022)*

Cbtk Group Inc 330 359-9111
17201 Dover Rd Dundee (44624) *(G-8168)*

Cbts, Cincinnati *Also Called: Cbts Technology Solutions LLC* *(G-2328)*

Cbts LLC 440 478-8447
25 Merchant St Cincinnati (45246) *(G-2327)*

Cbts Technology Solutions, Cincinnati *Also Called: Cintech LLC* *(G-2446)*

Cbts Technology Solutions LLC (DH) 513 841-2287
25 Merchant St Cincinnati (45246) *(G-2328)*

Cbts Technology Solutions LLC 440 569-2300
5910 Landerbrook Dr Ste 250 Cleveland (44124) *(G-3945)*

CCAO, Columbus *Also Called: County Commissioners Assn Ohio* *(G-5710)*

CCC Contractors LLC 937 579-5100
6951 State Route 134 Lynchburg (45142) *(G-10184)*

Ccems, Coshocton *Also Called: Coshocton Cnty Emrgncy Med Svc* *(G-6980)*

Ccf Health Care Ventures Inc 216 295-1959
9775 Rockside Rd Ste 200 Cleveland (44125) *(G-3946)*

Cch Healthcare Oh LLC 513 932-1121
115 Oregonia Rd Lebanon (45036) *(G-9758)*

CCHS JOHNSTOWN HOME, Columbus *Also Called: Columbus Ctr For Humn Svcs Inc* *(G-5626)*

CCI, Mentor *Also Called: Cleveland Construction Inc* *(G-10923)*

CCI Engineering 614 485-0670
2323 W 5th Ave Ste 220 Columbus (43204) *(G-5524)*

Ccj, Wooster *Also Called: Critchfeld Crtchfeld Jhnston L* *(G-15332)*

Ccp Industries, Richmond Heights *Also Called: Ccp Industries Inc* *(G-12716)*

Ccp Industries Inc 216 535-4227
26301 Curtiss Wright Pkwy Ste 200 Richmond Heights (44143) *(G-12716)*

CD Block K Hotel LLC 440 871-3100
2020 Crocker Rd Westlake (44145) *(G-15047)*

Cd102.5, Columbus *Also Called: Wwcd Ltd* *(G-6910)*

Cdc Capital Park Head St Ctr, Columbus *Also Called: Child Dev Cncil Frnklin Cnty I* *(G-5558)*

Cdc Distributors Inc (PA) 513 771-3100
10511 Medallion Dr Cincinnati (45241) *(G-2329)*

Cdc Marburn Head Start Ctr, Columbus *Also Called: Child Dev Cncil Frnklin Cnty I* *(G-5559)*

Cdc Medical 614 504-5511
1300 Dublin Rd Columbus (43215) *(G-5525)*

Cdc of Warren, Warren *Also Called: Community Dialysis Center* *(G-14510)*

Cdcscn Linden, Columbus *Also Called: Child Dev Cncil Frnklin Cnty I* *(G-5556)*

CDK Perforating LLC 817 862-9834
2167 State Route 821 Marietta (45750) *(G-10361)*

Cdo Technologies Inc (PA) 937 258-0022
5200 Springfield St Ste 320 Dayton (45431) *(G-7128)*

Cdw Technologies LLC 513 677-4100
9349 Waterstone Blvd Ste 150 Cincinnati (45249) *(G-2330)*

Cec Combustion Safety LLC (DH) 216 749-2992
2100 Apollo Dr Brookpark (44142) *(G-1430)*

Cecil T Bringer (PA) 740 843-5280
53640 Portland Rd Portland (45770) *(G-12542)*

Ceco Concrete Construction, West Chester *Also Called: Ceco Concrete Construction LLC* *(G-14661)*

Ceco Concrete Construction LLC 513 874-6953
4535 Port Union Rd West Chester (45011) *(G-14661)*

Cecos International Inc 513 724-6114
5092 Aber Rd Williamsburg (45176) *(G-15178)*

Cedar Elec Holdings Corp 773 804-6288
5440 W Chester Rd West Chester (45069) *(G-14662)*

Cedar Fair LP (PA) 419 627-2344
1 Cedar Point Dr Sandusky (44870) *(G-12871)*

ALPHABETIC SECTION — Centers For Families Children

Cedar Fair Southwest Inc (HQ) 419 626-0830
1 Cedar Point Dr Sandusky (44870) *(G-12872)*

Cedar Hill Opco LLC 740 454-6823
1136 Adair Ave Zanesville (43701) *(G-15777)*

Cedar Hlls Hlthcare Rhblttion, Zanesville *Also Called: Cedar Hill Opco LLC (G-15777)*

CEDAR HOUSE, Cleveland *Also Called: Rose Mary Johanna Grassell (G-4854)*

Cedar Medical Group 513 729-2300
7220 Pippin Rd Cincinnati (45239) *(G-2331)*

Cedar Oaks Wellness Center, Oregonia *Also Called: Butterfield Recovery Group LLC (G-12149)*

Cedar Point Park LLC (HQ) 419 626-0830
1 Cedar Point Dr Sandusky (44870) *(G-12873)*

Cedar Point Park LLC 419 627-2350
1 Cedar Point Dr Sandusky (44870) *(G-12874)*

Cedar Point Park LLC 419 627-2500
2001 Cleveland Rd Sandusky (44870) *(G-12875)*

Cedar Point Park LLC 419 627-2106
1 Cedar Point Dr Sandusky (44870) *(G-12876)*

Cedar Point Park LLC 888 950-5062
1201 Cedar Point Dr Sandusky (44870) *(G-12877)*

Cedar Point Park LLC 419 627-2106
1201 Cedar Point Dr Sandusky (44870) *(G-12878)*

Cedar Ridge Behavioral He 740 801-0655
56 N 5th St Zanesville (43701) *(G-15778)*

Cedar Village, Mason *Also Called: Jewish Home Cincinnati Inc (G-10569)*

Cedars of Lebanon Nursing Home, Lebanon *Also Called: Health Care Opportunities Inc (G-9768)*

Cedarview Rhblttion Nrsing Car, Lebanon *Also Called: Cch Healthcare Oh LLC (G-9758)*

Ceder Hill, Zanesville *Also Called: Zandex Health Care Corporation (G-15838)*

Cei Physicians PSC LLC (PA) 513 984-5133
1945 Cei Dr Blue Ash (45242) *(G-1144)*

Cei Vision Partners LLC 513 569-3114
1945 Cei Dr Blue Ash (45242) *(G-1145)*

Ceiba Enterprises Incorporated 614 818-3220
159 Baranof W Westerville (43081) *(G-14965)*

Celebrate Vitamins, Wadsworth *Also Called: Second Wind Vitamins Inc (G-14451)*

Celebrations, Plain City *Also Called: Made From Scratch Inc (G-12484)*

Celina Area Vsting Nurses Assn, Van Wert *Also Called: Community Hlth Prfssionals Inc (G-14342)*

Celina Enterprises LLC (PA) 419 586-3610
5481 State Route 29 Celina (45822) *(G-1918)*

Celina Insurance Group, Celina *Also Called: Celina Mutual Insurance Co (G-1919)*

Celina Mutual Insurance Co (PA) 800 552-5181
1 Insurance Sq Celina (45822) *(G-1919)*

Celina Visting Nurses, Celina *Also Called: Community Hlth Prfssionals Inc (G-1920)*

Cellco Partnership 419 281-1714
1441 Claremont Ave Ashland (44805) *(G-489)*

Cellco Partnership 440 893-6100
16 S Main St Chagrin Falls (44022) *(G-1954)*

Cellco Partnership 330 697-2211
3750 W Market St Unit A Fairlawn (44333) *(G-8469)*

Cellco Partnership 330 764-7380
1231 N Court St Medina (44256) *(G-10818)*

Cellco Partnership 440 886-5461
7779 Day Dr Parma (44129) *(G-12251)*

Cellular Technology Limited 216 791-5084
20521 Chagrin Blvd Ste 200 Shaker Heights (44122) *(G-12975)*

Cem-Base Inc 330 405-4105
8530 N Boyle Pkwy Twinsburg (44087) *(G-14175)*

Cems of Ohio Inc 614 751-6651
2827 W Dublin Granville Rd Columbus (43235) *(G-5526)*

Cencora Inc 610 727-7000
1200 E 5th Ave Columbus (43219) *(G-5527)*

Cengage Learning Inc 513 229-1000
5191 Natorp Blvd Lowr Mason (45040) *(G-10527)*

Centaur Associates, Maumee *Also Called: Centaur Mail Inc (G-10708)*

Centaur Mail Inc 419 887-5857
4064 Technology Dr Ste A Maumee (43537) *(G-10708)*

Centauri Health Solutions 216 431-5200
1457 E 40th St Cleveland (44103) *(G-3947)*

Centene Corporation 513 469-4500
4349 Easton Way Ste 300 Columbus (43219) *(G-5528)*

Center AI Health 216 831-8118
3690 Orange Pl Ste 320 Beachwood (44122) *(G-774)*

Center Cleaning Services Inc 440 327-5099
34100 Mills Rd Avon (44011) *(G-642)*

Center For Addiction Treatment 513 381-6672
830 Ezzard Charles Dr Cincinnati (45214) *(G-2332)*

Center For Arts-Inspired Lrng 216 561-5005
10917 Magnolia Dr Cleveland (44106) *(G-3948)*

CENTER FOR BALANCED LIVING, TH, Columbus *Also Called: Center For Eating Disorders (G-5531)*

Center For Cgntive Bhvral Thra (HQ) 614 459-4490
4624 Sawmill Rd Columbus (43220) *(G-5529)*

Center For Cognitv Behav Psych 614 459-4490
4624 Sawmill Rd Columbus (43220) *(G-5530)*

Center For Community Solutions 216 781-2944
1300 E 9th St Ste 1703 Cleveland (44114) *(G-3949)*

Center For Dialysis Care 440 286-4103
12340 Bass Lake Rd Chardon (44024) *(G-1995)*

Center For Dialysis Care, Cleveland *Also Called: Community Dialysis Center (G-4098)*

Center For Dialysis Care, Cleveland *Also Called: Community Dialysis Center (G-4099)*

Center For Eating Disorders 614 896-8222
8001 Ravines Edge Ct Ste 201 Columbus (43235) *(G-5531)*

Center For Employment Resource, Cincinnati *Also Called: Great Oaks Inst Tech Creer Dev (G-2763)*

Center For Executive Education, Blue Ash *Also Called: University of Cincinnati (G-1264)*

Center For Families & Children 216 252-5800
3929 Rocky River Dr Cleveland (44111) *(G-3950)*

Center For Families & Children 216 671-1919
4400 Euclid Ave Cleveland (44103) *(G-3951)*

CENTER FOR FAMILIES AND CHILDREN, Cleveland *Also Called: Center For Families & Children (G-3950)*

Center For Fmly Safety Healing 614 722-5985
655 E Livingston Ave Columbus (43205) *(G-5532)*

Center For Health Affairs 216 696-6900
1226 Huron Rd E Ste 2 Cleveland (44115) *(G-3952)*

Center For Indvdual Fmly Svcs (PA) 419 522-4357
741 Scholl Rd Mansfield (44907) *(G-10251)*

Center For Occptional Medicine, Wooster *Also Called: Occuptnal Mdcine Assoc Wyne CN (G-15362)*

Center For Rhblttion At Hmpton 330 792-7681
1517 E Western Reserve Rd Poland (44514) *(G-12502)*

Center For Srgcal Drmtlogy Drm, Westerville *Also Called: Center For Srgcal Drmtlogy Inc (G-14879)*

Center For Srgcal Drmtlogy Inc 614 847-4100
428 County Line Rd W Westerville (43082) *(G-14879)*

Center For Urologic Health LLC (PA) 330 375-0924
95 Arch St Ste 165 Akron (44304) *(G-85)*

Center of Hope, Union City *Also Called: Crotinger Nursing Home Inc (G-14239)*

Center of Voctnl Altrntvs Mntl (PA) 614 294-7117
3770 N High St Columbus (43214) *(G-5533)*

Center Ridge House, Westlake *Also Called: Blossom Hill Inc (G-15039)*

Center Ridge Nursing Home Inc 440 808-5500
38600 Center Ridge Rd North Ridgeville (44039) *(G-11924)*

Center Seeds, Sidney *Also Called: Cover Crop Shop LLC (G-13028)*

Center Street Cmnty Clinic Inc 740 751-6380
136 W Center St Marion (43302) *(G-10421)*

Centerburg Pnte Hlthcare Group 740 625-5401
4531 Columbus Rd Centerburg (43011) *(G-1932)*

Centerburg Pointe, Centerburg *Also Called: Centerburg Pnte Hlthcare Group (G-1932)*

Centerburg Respiratory and Specialty Rehab Center, Centerburg *Also Called: Centerburg Two LLC (G-1933)*

Centerburg Two LLC 740 625-5774
212 Fairview St Centerburg (43011) *(G-1933)*

Centerfield Insur Fincl Co LLC (PA) 330 501-9719
900 Blueberry Hill Dr Canfield (44406) *(G-1625)*

Centerra Co-Op (PA) 419 281-2153
813 Clark Ave Ashland (44805) *(G-490)*

Centers For Families Children (PA) 216 432-7200
4500 Euclid Ave Cleveland (44103) *(G-3953)*

CENTERS, THE — ALPHABETIC SECTION

CENTERS, THE, Cleveland Also Called: *Centers For Families Children* **(G-3953)**
CENTERS, THE, Cleveland Also Called: *Circle Health Services* **(G-3972)**

Centerville Fitness Inc... 937 291-7990
51 E Spring Valley Pike Centerville (45458) **(G-1940)**

Centerville Landscaping Inc.. 937 433-5395
1082 W Spring Valley Pike Dayton (45458) **(G-7219)**

Centerwell Health Services Inc.. 419 482-6519
1900 Indian Wood Cir Ste 100 Maumee (43537) **(G-10709)**

Centery National Bank.. 740 454-2521
14 S 5th St Zanesville (43701) **(G-15779)**

Centimark Corporation... 330 920-3560
700 Alpha Pkwy Stow (44224) **(G-13357)**

Central Allied Enterprises Inc (PA)...................................... 330 477-6751
1243 Raff Rd Sw Canton (44710) **(G-1706)**

Central Beverage Group Ltd.. 614 294-3555
8133 Highfield Dr Lewis Center (43035) **(G-9813)**

Central Billing Office, Akron Also Called: *Nationwide Childrens Hospital* **(G-239)**

Central Business Equipment Co.. 513 891-4430
10321 S Medallion Dr Cincinnati (45241) **(G-2333)**

Central Cadillac Limited... 216 861-5800
2801 Carnegie Ave Cleveland (44115) **(G-3954)**

Central Cadillac-Hummer, Cleveland Also Called: *Central Cadillac Limited* **(G-3954)**

Central Christian School, Kidron Also Called: *Christian Schools Inc* **(G-9635)**

Central Clinic Outpatient Svcs... 513 558-9005
311 Albert Sabin Way Cincinnati (45229) **(G-2334)**

Central Cmnty Hlth Bd Hmlton C (PA).................................. 513 559-2000
532 Maxwell Ave Cincinnati (45219) **(G-2335)**

Central Coca-Cola Btlg Co Inc... 330 875-1487
1560 Triplett Blvd Akron (44306) **(G-86)**

Central Coca-Cola Btlg Co Inc... 740 474-2180
387 Walnut St Circleville (43113) **(G-3705)**

Central Coca-Cola Btlg Co Inc... 419 476-6722
3970 Catawba St Toledo (43612) **(G-13727)**

Central Community Hse Columbus (PA)............................. 614 252-3157
1150 E Main St Columbus (43205) **(G-5534)**

Central Environmental Systems, Cincinnati Also Called: *Central Insulation Systems Inc* **(G-2336)**

Central Fire Protection Co Inc... 937 322-0713
583 Selma Rd Springfield (45505) **(G-13225)**

Central Hamilton YMCA, Hamilton Also Called: *Great Miami Valley YMCA* **(G-9048)**

Central Insulation Systems Inc.. 513 242-0600
300 Murray Rd Cincinnati (45217) **(G-2336)**

Central Insurance Companies, Van Wert Also Called: *Central Mutual Insurance Co* **(G-14341)**

Central Mutual Insurance Co (PA).. 419 238-1010
800 S Washington St Van Wert (45891) **(G-14341)**

Central Ohio Area Agcy On Agin.. 614 645-7250
3776 S High St Columbus (43207) **(G-5535)**

Central Ohio Associates Ltd.. 419 342-2045
18 Allison Dr Shelby (44875) **(G-13005)**

Central Ohio Building Co Inc... 614 475-6392
3756 Agler Rd Columbus (43219) **(G-5536)**

Central Ohio Contractors Inc... 740 369-7700
888 Us Highway 42 N Delaware (43015) **(G-7784)**

Central Ohio Contractors Inc (PA).. 614 539-2579
2879 Jackson Pike Grove City (43123) **(G-8907)**

Central Ohio Diabetes Assn... 614 884-4400
1699 W Mound St Columbus (43223) **(G-5537)**

Central Ohio Geriatrics LLC... 614 530-4077
590 Newark Granville Rd Granville (43023) **(G-8850)**

Central Ohio Gming Vntures LLC.. 614 308-3333
200 Georgesville Rd Columbus (43228) **(G-5538)**

Central Ohio Hospitalists... 614 255-6900
3525 Olentangy River Rd Ste 4330 Columbus (43214) **(G-5539)**

Central Ohio Medical Textiles.. 614 453-9274
575 Harmon Ave Columbus (43223) **(G-5540)**

Central Ohio Mental Health Ctr (PA).................................... 740 368-7837
250 S Henry St Delaware (43015) **(G-7785)**

Central Ohio Primary Care... 614 834-8042
6201 Gender Rd Canal Winchester (43110) **(G-1601)**

Central Ohio Primary Care... 614 268-8164
3535 Olentangy River Rd Columbus (43214) **(G-5541)**

Central Ohio Primary Care... 614 552-2300
6488 E Main St Ste C Reynoldsburg (43068) **(G-12657)**

Central Ohio Primary Care, Westerville Also Called: *Central Ohio Prmry Care Physca* **(G-14882)**

Central Ohio Prmry Care Physca... 614 442-7550
4030 Henderson Rd Columbus (43220) **(G-5542)**

Central Ohio Prmry Care Physca... 614 451-9229
4885 Olentangy River Rd Columbus (43214) **(G-5543)**

Central Ohio Prmry Care Physca... 614 473-1300
2489 Stelzer Rd # 101 Columbus (43219) **(G-5544)**

Central Ohio Prmry Care Physca... 614 882-0708
400 Altair Pkwy Westerville (43082) **(G-14880)**

Central Ohio Prmry Care Physca... 614 891-9505
507 Executive Campus Dr Ste 160 Westerville (43082) **(G-14881)**

Central Ohio Prmry Care Physca (PA).................................. 614 326-2672
655 Africa Rd Westerville (43082) **(G-14882)**

Central Ohio Surgical Assoc (PA).. 614 222-8000
5500 N Meadows Dr Ste 210 Grove City (43123) **(G-8908)**

Central Ohio Transit Authority... 614 275-5800
1333 Fields Ave Columbus (43201) **(G-5545)**

Central Ohio Transit Authority (PA)...................................... 614 275-5800
33 N High St Columbus (43215) **(G-5546)**

Central Ohio Transit Authority... 614 228-1776
1600 Mckinley Ave Columbus (43222) **(G-5547)**

Central Ohio Transit Authority... 614 275-5800
33 N High St Ste 749 Columbus (43215) **(G-5548)**

Central Parking System, Columbus Also Called: *Central Parking System of Ohio* **(G-5549)**

Central Parking System of Ohio.. 614 224-1320
107 S High St Ste 400 Columbus (43215) **(G-5549)**

Central Power Systems, Columbus Also Called: *Power Distributors LLC* **(G-6539)**

Central Railroad of Indiana, Cincinnati Also Called: *Indiana & Ohio Rail Corp* **(G-2867)**

Central Ready Mix LLC (PA).. 513 402-5001
6310 E Kemper Rd Ste 125 Cincinnati (45241) **(G-2337)**

Central Services Department, Cleveland Also Called: *County of Cuyahoga* **(G-4131)**

Central Star.. 419 756-9449
2003 W 4th St Ste 116 Ontario (44906) **(G-12100)**

Central Star Home Health Svcs, Ontario Also Called: *Central Star* **(G-12100)**

Central Steel and Wire Co LLC.. 513 242-2233
525 Township Ave Cincinnati (45216) **(G-2338)**

Central Whse Operations Inc... 330 453-3709
2207 Kimball Rd Se Canton (44707) **(G-1707)**

Centran Logistics Inc.. 216 271-7100
6707 Bessemer Ave Cleveland (44127) **(G-3955)**

Centric Consulting LLC (PA).. 888 781-7567
1215 Lyons Rd # F Dayton (45458) **(G-7220)**

Centro Properties Group LLC.. 440 324-6610
3343 Midway Mall Elyria (44035) **(G-8235)**

Centruy Securities Associates, Dayton Also Called: *Stifel Ind Advisors LLC* **(G-7643)**

Centura X-Ray, Cleveland Also Called: *Nostress Inc* **(G-4666)**

Century 21, Cleveland Also Called: *Century 21 Homestar* **(G-3956)**

Century 21, Fremont Also Called: *Century 21 Premiere Properties* **(G-8669)**

Century 21, Kent Also Called: *Wilbur Realty Inc* **(G-9606)**

Century 21, Mentor Also Called: *Prudential Select Properties* **(G-10986)**

Century 21, Warren Also Called: *North Wood Realty* **(G-14544)**

Century 21 Homestar... 440 449-9100
6151 Wilson Mills Rd Ste 110 Cleveland (44143) **(G-3956)**

Century 21 Premiere Properties.. 419 334-2121
308 E State St Fremont (43420) **(G-8669)**

Century Equipment Inc (PA)... 419 865-7400
5959 Angola Rd Toledo (43615) **(G-13728)**

Century Health Inc (PA).. 419 425-5050
1918 N Main St Findlay (45840) **(G-8522)**

Century National Bank (HQ).. 740 454-2521
14 S 5th St Zanesville (43701) **(G-15780)**

Century Oak Care Center, Cleveland Also Called: *Swa Inc* **(G-4970)**

Century Tel of Odon Inc (HQ).. 440 244-8544
203 W 9th St Lorain (44052) **(G-10062)**

Centurylink, Lorain Also Called: *Century Tel of Odon Inc* **(G-10062)**

Cequence Security Inc... 650 437-6338
10805 Indeco Dr Ste B Blue Ash (45241) **(G-1146)**

CER Hotels LLC 330 422-1855
795 Mondial Pkwy Streetsboro (44241) *(G-13411)*

Ceramic Holdings Inc (DH) 216 362-3900
20600 Sheldon Rd Brookpark (44142) *(G-1431)*

Cerelia USA Bakery Inc 614 471-9994
430 N Yearling Rd Whitehall (43213) *(G-15136)*

Cerkl, Blue Ash *Also Called: Cerkl Incorporated (G-1147)*

Cerkl Incorporated 513 813-8425
11126 Kenwood Rd Blue Ash (45242) *(G-1147)*

Cerner Corporation 740 826-7678
140 S Friendship Dr New Concord (43762) *(G-11609)*

Cerni Leasing LLC 515 967-3300
5751 Cerni Pl Youngstown (44515) *(G-15574)*

Cerni Motor Sales Inc (HQ) 330 652-9917
5751 Cerni Pl Youngstown (44515) *(G-15575)*

Certified Angus Beef LLC (HQ) 330 345-2333
206 Riffel Rd Wooster (44691) *(G-15318)*

Certified Carpet Distrs Inc 216 573-1422
9090 Bank St Cleveland (44125) *(G-3957)*

Ceso, Miamisburg *Also Called: Ceso Inc (G-11035)*

Ceso Inc (PA) 937 435-8584
3601 Rigby Rd Ste 300 Miamisburg (45342) *(G-11035)*

Cetek, Brookpark *Also Called: Ceramic Holdings Inc (G-1431)*

Ceva Logistics, Groveport *Also Called: Ceva Logistics LLC (G-8977)*

Ceva Logistics LLC 614 482-5000
2727 London Groveport Rd Groveport (43125) *(G-8977)*

CF Bankshares Inc (PA) 614 334-7979
7000 N High St Worthington (43085) *(G-15407)*

CFC Investment Company 513 870-2203
6200 S Gilmore Rd Fairfield (45014) *(G-8399)*

CFC Mansfield LLC 216 328-1121
900 N Lexington Springmill Rd Ontario (44906) *(G-12101)*

CFI Interiors, Canton *Also Called: Canton Floors Inc (G-1701)*

CFM Religion Pubg Group LLC (PA) 513 931-4050
8805 Governors Hill Dr Ste 400 Cincinnati (45249) *(G-2339)*

CFS Family Holdings Inc 740 492-0595
500 Enterprise Dr Newcomerstown (43832) *(G-11766)*

CFS Services, Worthington *Also Called: Creative Fincl Staffing LLC (G-15410)*

Cgh-Global Security LLC 800 376-0655
4957 Cinnamon Cir Cincinnati (45244) *(G-2340)*

Cgh-Global Technologies LLC 800 376-0655
4957 Cinnamon Cir Cincinnati (45244) *(G-2341)*

Cgi, Cleveland *Also Called: Cgi Technologies Solutions Inc (G-3958)*

Cgi Technologies Solutions Inc 216 687-1480
1001 Lakeside Ave E Ste 800 Cleveland (44114) *(G-3958)*

Cgi Technologies Solutions Inc 614 880-2200
2000 Polaris Pkwy Ste 110 Columbus (43240) *(G-5251)*

Ch Relty Iv/Clmbus Partners LP 614 885-3334
175 Hutchinson Ave Columbus (43235) *(G-5550)*

Ch2m Hill Inc 513 243-5070
1880 Waycross Rd Cincinnati (45240) *(G-2342)*

Ch2m Hill Engineers Inc 513 530-5520
10123 Alliance Rd Ste 300 Blue Ash (45242) *(G-1148)*

Ch2m Hill Engineers Inc 720 286-2000
1880 Waycross Rd Cincinnati (45240) *(G-2343)*

Cha - Community Health Affairs 800 362-2628
1226 Huron Rd E Cleveland (44115) *(G-3959)*

Chaco Credit Union Inc (PA) 513 785-3500
601 Park Ave Hamilton (45013) *(G-9026)*

Chagrin Surgery Center LLC 216 839-1800
3755 Orange Pl Ste 102 Beachwood (44122) *(G-775)*

Chagrin Valley Athc CLB Inc 440 543-5141
17260 Snyder Rd Chagrin Falls (44023) *(G-1974)*

Chagrin Valley Auto Parts Co 216 398-9800
8550 Brookpark Rd Cleveland (44129) *(G-3960)*

Chagrin Valley Country Club Co 440 248-4310
4700 Som Center Rd Chagrin Falls (44022) *(G-1955)*

Chagrin Valley Engineering Ltd 440 439-1999
22999 Forbes Rd Ste B Cleveland (44146) *(G-3961)*

Chagrin Valley Hunt Club 440 423-4414
7620 Old Mill Rd Gates Mills (44040) *(G-8782)*

Chalmers P Wylie VA Ambltory C, Columbus *Also Called: Veterans Health Administration (G-6848)*

Chalmers P Wylie VA Otptent Cl, Columbus *Also Called: Veterans Health Administration (G-6849)*

Chamberlin Healthcare Center, Cincinnati *Also Called: East Glbrith Hlth Care Ctr Inc (G-2598)*

Chambers Leasing Systems Corp 937 547-9777
5187 Childrens Home Bradford Rd Greenville (45331) *(G-8867)*

Chambers Leasing Systems Corp 937 642-4260
23198 Northwest Pkwy Marysville (43040) *(G-10479)*

Chambers Leasing Systems Corp (PA) 419 726-9747
3100 N Summit St Toledo (43611) *(G-13729)*

Chambrlain Hrdlcka White Wllam 216 589-9280
36368 Detroit Rd Ste A Avon (44011) *(G-643)*

Champaign Cnty Board of Dd 937 653-5217
1250 E Us Highway 36 Urbana (43078) *(G-14300)*

Champaign County Auditor, Urbana *Also Called: County of Champaign (G-14306)*

Champaign County Board of Mrdd, Urbana *Also Called: Champaign Cnty Board of Dd (G-14300)*

Champaign County Engineer, Urbana *Also Called: County of Champaign (G-14305)*

Champaign Residential, London *Also Called: Champaign Residential Svcs Inc (G-10039)*

Champaign Residential Svcs Inc 740 852-3850
117 W High St Ste 104 London (43140) *(G-10039)*

Champaign Residential Svcs Inc (PA) 937 653-1320
1150 Scioto St Ste 201 Urbana (43078) *(G-14301)*

Champaign Transit System 937 653-8777
1512 S Us Highway 68 Ste K100 Urbana (43078) *(G-14302)*

Champion, Cincinnati *Also Called: Enclosure Suppliers LLC (G-2619)*

Champion Clg Specialists Inc 513 871-2333
8391 Blue Ash Rd Cincinnati (45236) *(G-2344)*

Champion Feed and Pet Sup LLC 740 369-3020
400 S Main St Granville (43023) *(G-8851)*

Champion One, Independence *Also Called: Approved Networks LLC (G-9406)*

Champion Opco LLC (DH) 513 327-7338
12121 Champion Way Cincinnati (45241) *(G-2345)*

Champion Opco LLC 440 249-6768
9011 Freeway Dr Macedonia (44056) *(G-10190)*

Champion Windows, Cincinnati *Also Called: Champion Opco LLC (G-2345)*

Championship Management Co Inc 740 524-4653
1150 Wilson Rd Sunbury (43074) *(G-13518)*

Champlin Architecture, Cincinnati *Also Called: Champlin Haupt Architects Inc (G-2346)*

Champlin Haupt Architects Inc (PA) 513 241-4474
720 E Pete Rose Way Ste 140 Cincinnati (45202) *(G-2346)*

Chandler Products LLC 216 481-4400
10147 Brecksville Rd Brecksville (44141) *(G-1347)*

Chandler Systems Incorporated 888 363-9434
710 Orange St Ashland (44805) *(G-491)*

Chandni Inc 419 228-4251
1210 Neubrecht Rd Ste 106206 Lima (45801) *(G-9873)*

Chaney Roofing Maintenance Inc 419 639-2761
7040 State Route 101 N Clyde (43410) *(G-5199)*

Change 4 Growth, Westerville *Also Called: TPC and Thomas LLC (G-14943)*

CHANNEL 48, Cincinnati *Also Called: Greater Cncnnati TV Edctl Fndt (G-2773)*

Channel Products Inc (PA) 440 423-0113
30700 Solon Industrial Pkwy Solon (44139) *(G-13075)*

Chapel Electric Co LLC 937 222-2290
1985 Founders Dr Dayton (45420) *(G-7221)*

Chapel Electric Co., Dayton *Also Called: Quebe Holdings Inc (G-7575)*

CHAPEL HILL COMMUNITY, Kenton *Also Called: United Ch Rsdnces Knton Ohio I (G-9624)*

CHAPEL HILL COMMUNITY, Marion *Also Called: Ucc Ix DBA Barrington Square (G-10458)*

CHAPEL HILL COMMUNITY, Marion *Also Called: United Ch Residences Goshen (G-10459)*

CHAPEL HILL COMMUNITY, Marion *Also Called: United Ch Rsdnces Immklee Cypr (G-10460)*

Chapel Hill Community, Marion *Also Called: United Church Homes Inc (G-10462)*

Chapter 55, Marysville *Also Called: Disabled American Veterans (G-10483)*

Chapter Two Inc (PA) 513 792-5100
4555 Lake Forest Dr Ste 220 Blue Ash (45242) *(G-1149)*

Charak Ctr For Hlth & Wellness, Elyria *Also Called: Rakesh Ranjan MD & Assoc Inc (G-8289)*

Chard Snyder & Associates LLC 513 459-9997
6867 Cintas Blvd Mason (45040) *(G-10528)*

Chard Snyder, Mason *Also Called: Chard Snyder & Associates LLC (G-10528)*

CHARDON HEALTHCARE CENTER — ALPHABETIC SECTION

CHARDON HEALTHCARE CENTER, Chardon *Also Called: Water Leasing Co LLC (G-2026)*

Chardon Laboratories Inc 614 860-1000
7300 Tussing Rd Reynoldsburg (43068) *(G-12658)*

Chardon Lakes Golf Course Inc (PA) 440 285-4653
470 South St Chardon (44024) *(G-1996)*

Chardon Tool & Supply Co Inc 440 286-6440
115 Parker Ct Chardon (44024) *(G-1997)*

Charles Drew Health Center, Dayton *Also Called: Community Hlh Ctr of Gtr Daton (G-7242)*

CHARLES F KETTERING MEMORIAL H, Hamilton *Also Called: Fort Hamilton Hospital (G-9041)*

Charles H Hamilton Co 513 683-2442
5875 S State Route 48 Maineville (45039) *(G-10226)*

Charles Rewinding Div, Canton *Also Called: Hannon Company (G-1770)*

Charles River Laboratories Inc 419 647-4196
640 N Elizabeth St Spencerville (45887) *(G-13187)*

Charles River Labs Ashland LLC 419 282-8700
1407 George Rd Ashland (44805) *(G-492)*

Charles Rver Labs Clveland Inc 216 332-1665
14656 Neo Pkwy Cleveland (44128) *(G-3962)*

Charles Schwab, Beachwood *Also Called: Charles Schwab Corporation (G-776)*
Charles Schwab, Richfield *Also Called: Charles Schwab & Co Inc (G-12691)*

Charles Schwab & Co Inc 330 908-4478
4150 Kinross Lakes Pkwy Richfield (44286) *(G-12691)*

Charles Schwab Corporation 800 435-4000
511 Park Ave Ste 145 Beachwood (44122) *(G-776)*

Charles W Powers & Assoc Inc 513 721-5353
151 W 4th St Unit 36 Cincinnati (45202) *(G-2347)*

Charleston Ordnance Center, Medina *Also Called: Park Corporation (G-10874)*
Charley's Steakery, Columbus *Also Called: Gosh Enterprises Inc (G-5943)*

Charlie Towing Service Inc 440 234-5300
55 Lou Groza Blvd Berea (44017) *(G-1064)*

Charlie's Towing Svc, Berea *Also Called: Charlie Towing Service Inc (G-1064)*
Charnan Div, Ontario *Also Called: Lake Erie Electric Inc (G-12111)*
Charter Bus Service, Cincinnati *Also Called: Queen City Transportation LLC (G-3268)*

Charter Communications 614 588-5036
1600 Dublin Rd Ste 800 Columbus (43215) *(G-5551)*

Charter Hotel Group Ltd Partnr (PA) 216 772-4538
5966 Heisley Rd Mentor (44060) *(G-10920)*

Charter One, Cleveland *Also Called: Charter One Bank National Association (G-3963)*

Charter One Bank National Association 216 277-5326
1215 Superior Ave E Ste 245 Cleveland (44114) *(G-3963)*

Chas F Mann Painting Co 419 385-7151
3638 Marine Rd Toledo (43609) *(G-13730)*

Chase, Columbus *Also Called: Jpmorgan Chase Bank Nat Assn (G-5264)*
Chase, Delaware *Also Called: JP Morgan Partners LLC (G-7809)*
Chase Doors, West Chester *Also Called: Chase Industries Inc (G-14803)*

Chase Equipment Finance Inc (HQ) 800 678-2601
1111 Polaris Pkwy Ste A3 Columbus (43240) *(G-5252)*

Chase HM Mrtgages Florence Off, Columbus *Also Called: Jpmorgan Chase Bank Nat Assn (G-6098)*

Chase Industries Inc (DH) 513 860-5565
10021 Commerce Park Dr West Chester (45246) *(G-14803)*

Chase Manhattan, Columbus *Also Called: Chase Manhattan Mortgage Corp (G-5552)*
Chase Manhattan, Columbus *Also Called: Chase Manhattan Mortgage Corp (G-5553)*

Chase Manhattan Mortgage Corp 614 422-7982
200 E Campus View Blvd 3rd Fl Columbus (43235) *(G-5552)*

Chase Manhattan Mortgage Corp 614 422-6900
3415 Vision Dr Columbus (43219) *(G-5553)*

Chase Suite Hotel, Dublin *Also Called: Hardage Hotels I LLC (G-8026)*

Chase Transcriptions Inc (PA) 330 656-3980
1737 Georgetown Rd Ste G Hudson (44236) *(G-9338)*

Chavez Properties, Cincinnati *Also Called: J & E LLC (G-2891)*

Chc Fabricating Corp (PA) 513 821-7757
10270 Wayne Ave Cincinnati (45215) *(G-2348)*

Che Consulting, Cleveland *Also Called: Custom Hdwr Engrg Cnslting LLC (G-4145)*
Check N Go, Cincinnati *Also Called: Check n Go of Missouri Inc (G-2350)*
Check N Go, Cincinnati *Also Called: Check N Go of Washington Inc (G-2351)*
Check N Go, Cincinnati *Also Called: CNG Financial Corporation (G-2465)*

Check n Go of Florida Inc 513 336-7735
7755 Montgomery Rd Ste 400 Cincinnati (45236) *(G-2349)*

Check n Go of Missouri Inc 513 531-2288
7755 Montgomery Rd Ste 400 Cincinnati (45236) *(G-2350)*

Check N Go of Washington Inc 800 561-2274
7755 Montgomery Rd Ste 400 Cincinnati (45236) *(G-2351)*

Check Point Software Tech Inc 440 748-0900
6100 Oak Tree Blvd Ste 200 Cleveland (44131) *(G-3964)*

Checker Distributors, Maumee *Also Called: Checker Notions Company Inc (G-10710)*

Checker Notions Company Inc (PA) 419 893-3636
400 W Dussel Dr Ste B Maumee (43537) *(G-10710)*

Checksmart, Coshocton *Also Called: Buckeye Check Cashing Inc (G-6977)*
Checksmart, Mansfield *Also Called: Buckeye Check Cashing Inc (G-10249)*
Checksmart, Whitehall *Also Called: Buckeye Check Cashing Inc (G-15135)*

Checksmart Fincl Holdings Corp (HQ) 614 798-5900
6785 Bobcat Way Ste 200 Dublin (43016) *(G-7961)*

Cheese Holdings Inc 330 893-2479
6597 County Road 625 Millersburg (44654) *(G-11275)*

Cheeseman, Fort Recovery *Also Called: Zumstein Inc (G-8612)*

Chefs Garden Inc 419 433-4947
9009 Huron Avery Rd Huron (44839) *(G-9385)*

Chelsea Court Apartments, Youngstown *Also Called: Giffin Management Group Inc (G-15621)*
Chelsea House Fabrics, Columbus *Also Called: Style-Line Incorporated (G-6725)*
Chemed, Cincinnati *Also Called: Chemed Corporation (G-2352)*

Chemed Corporation (PA) 513 762-6690
255 E 5th St Ste 2600 Cincinnati (45202) *(G-2352)*

Chemgroup, Columbus *Also Called: Bonded Chemicals Inc (G-5455)*
Chemical Associates, Copley *Also Called: Chemical Associates of Illinois Inc (G-6949)*

Chemical Associates of Illinois Inc 330 666-7200
1270 S Cleveland Massillon Rd Copley (44321) *(G-6949)*

Chemical Solvents Inc (PA) 216 741-9310
3751 Jennings Rd Cleveland (44109) *(G-3965)*

Chemical Solvents Inc 216 741-9310
1010 Denison Ave Cleveland (44109) *(G-3966)*

Chemimage Filter Tech LLC 330 686-2726
1100 Campus Dr Ste 500 Stow (44224) *(G-13358)*

Chemineer Inc 937 454-3200
5870 Poe Ave Dayton (45414) *(G-7222)*

Chempower Sheetmetal, Canton *Also Called: Global Insulation Inc (G-1763)*
Chemsafe International, Cleveland *Also Called: G M Industrial LLC (G-4298)*

Chemspec Usa Inc 330 669-8512
9287 Smucker Rd Orrville (44667) *(G-12158)*

Chemstation, Moraine *Also Called: Chemstation International Inc (G-11397)*

Chemstation International Inc (PA) 937 294-8265
3400 Encrete Ln Moraine (45439) *(G-11397)*

Chemstress Consultant Company (PA) 330 535-5591
39 S Main St Ste 315 Akron (44308) *(G-87)*

Chemtron, Avon *Also Called: Chemtron Corporation (G-644)*

Chemtron Corporation (PA) 440 937-6348
35850 Schneider Ct Avon (44011) *(G-644)*

Cherished Companions Home Care 440 273-7230
7181 Chagrin Rd Ste 200 Chagrin Falls (44023) *(G-1975)*

Cherokee Hills Golf Club, Valley City *Also Called: Chgc Inc (G-14332)*

Cherry Jack Ltd Partnership 740 788-1200
2299 Cherry Valley Rd Se Newark (43055) *(G-11691)*

Cherry St Mission Ministries (PA) 419 242-5141
1501 Monroe St Toledo (43604) *(G-13731)*

Cherry Valley Lodge 740 788-1200
2299 Cherry Valley Rd Se Newark (43055) *(G-11692)*

Cherry Valley Lodge, Newark *Also Called: Cherry Jack Ltd Partnership (G-11691)*
Cherry Valley Lodge and Coco, Newark *Also Called: Cherry Valley Lodge (G-11692)*

Chesrown Oldsmobile GMC Inc 614 846-3040
4675 Karl Rd Columbus (43229) *(G-5554)*

Chessrown Kia Town, Columbus *Also Called: Chesrown Oldsmobile GMC Inc (G-5554)*

Chester Ave Hotel LLC 216 249-9090
1914 E 101st St Cleveland (44106) *(G-3967)*

Chester West Medical Center 513 298-3000
7700 University Dr West Chester (45069) *(G-14663)*

Chesterfield Claims Services, Uniontown *Also Called: Chesterfield Services Inc (G-14245)*

Chesterfield Services Inc 330 896-9777
3520 Forest Lake Dr Uniontown (44685) *(G-14245)*

ALPHABETIC SECTION

Chesterwood Village, West Chester Also Called: Hillandale Health Care Inc *(G-14708)*

Cheviot Financial Corp.. 513 661-0457
3723 Glenmore Ave Cincinnati (45211) *(G-2353)*

Chevrolet Buick GMC Mt Vernon, Mount Vernon Also Called: Knox Auto LLC *(G-11490)*

Chewy Inc.. 937 669-4839
3280 Lightner Rd Vandalia (45377) *(G-14369)*

Chgc Inc.. 330 225-6122
5740 Center Rd Valley City (44280) *(G-14332)*

CHI Health At Home (DH).. 513 576-0262
1700 Edison Dr Ste 300 Milford (45150) *(G-11221)*

CHI Living Communities.. 419 627-2273
2025 Hayes Ave Sandusky (44870) *(G-12879)*

CHI National Home Care (DH)... 513 576-0262
6281 Tri Ridge Blvd Ste 300 Loveland (45140) *(G-10131)*

CHI National Home Care.. 513 942-3670
9031 Meridian Way West Chester (45069) *(G-14664)*

Chicago Mso Inc (PA)... 513 624-8300
6136 Campus Ln Cincinnati (45230) *(G-2354)*

Chick Master Incubator Company (PA)......................... 330 722-5591
1093 Medina Rd Medina (44256) *(G-10819)*

Chief Delivery LLC.. 419 277-6190
7620 W Bancroft St Toledo (43617) *(G-13732)*

Chieftain Trucking & Excav Inc.. 216 485-8034
3926 Valley Rd Ste 300 Cleveland (44109) *(G-3968)*

Child Adlscent Behavioral Hlth (PA)............................... 330 454-7917
919 2nd St Ne Canton (44704) *(G-1708)*

Child Adlscent Spclty Care Dyt....................................... 937 667-7711
1483 W Main St Tipp City (45371) *(G-13655)*

Child Care Center, Dayton Also Called: Miami Valley Hospital *(G-7494)*

Child Care Resource Center (PA)................................... 216 575-0061
6001 Euclid Ave Cleveland (44103) *(G-3969)*

Child Dev Cncil Frnklin Cnty I.. 614 221-1694
398 S Grant Ave Columbus (43215) *(G-5555)*

Child Dev Cncil Frnklin Cnty I.. 614 262-8190
1718 E Cooke Rd Columbus (43224) *(G-5556)*

Child Dev Cncil Frnklin Cnty I (PA)................................. 614 221-1709
999 Crupper Ave Columbus (43229) *(G-5557)*

Child Dev Cncil Frnklin Cnty I.. 614 416-5178
2150 Agler Rd Columbus (43224) *(G-5558)*

Child Dev Cncil Frnklin Cnty I.. 614 457-2811
4141 Rudy Rd Columbus (43214) *(G-5559)*

Child Dev Ctr Jackson Cnty.. 740 286-3995
692 Pattonsville Rd Jackson (45640) *(G-9517)*

Child Development, Port Clinton Also Called: Great Lkes Cmnty Action Partnr *(G-12529)*

Child Focus Inc.. 513 732-8800
2337 Clermont Center Dr Batavia (45103) *(G-731)*

Child Focus Inc (PA)... 513 752-1555
4629 Aicholtz Rd Cincinnati (45244) *(G-2355)*

Child Focus Inc.. 937 444-1613
710 N High St Mount Orab (45154) *(G-11469)*

Child Support Agency, Coshocton Also Called: County of Coshocton *(G-6982)*

Child Support Enforcement Agcy, Cleveland Also Called: County of Cuyahoga *(G-4123)*

Child Support Enforcement Agcy, Columbus Also Called: Franklin Cnty Bd Commissioners *(G-5882)*

Child Support Enforcement Agcy, Toledo Also Called: County of Lucas *(G-13763)*

Childern's Hospital Gift Shop, Cincinnati Also Called: Junior Coop Soc Chldren S Hosp *(G-2923)*

Childhood League Cent.. 614 253-6933
674 Cleveland Ave Columbus (43215) *(G-5560)*

Children and Family Services, Cleveland Also Called: County of Cuyahoga *(G-4129)*

Children Services, West Union Also Called: County of Adams *(G-14868)*

Children's Aid Society, Cleveland Also Called: Cleveland Municipal School Dst *(G-4060)*

Children's Aide Society Campus, Cleveland Also Called: Applewood Centers Inc *(G-3823)*

CHILDREN'S HOME CARE, Dayton Also Called: Childrens Home Care Dayton *(G-7223)*

Children's Home Healthcare, Cincinnati Also Called: Childrens Hospital Medical Ctr *(G-2368)*

CHILDREN'S HOME HEALTHCARE, Cincinnati Also Called: Chmc Cmnty Hlth Svcs Netwrk *(G-2375)*

CHILDREN'S HOME SCHOOL, Cincinnati Also Called: Childrens HM of Cncinnati Ohio *(G-2357)*

Children's Homecare Services, Columbus Also Called: Nationwide Chld Hosp Homecare *(G-6325)*

Children's Hospital Outpatient, Hilliard Also Called: Nationwide Childrens Hospital *(G-9220)*

Children's Medical Center, Dayton Also Called: Dayton Childrens Hospital *(G-7276)*

Children's Outpatient North, Mason Also Called: Childrens Hospital Medical Ctr *(G-10529)*

CHILDREN'S RESOURCE CENTER, Bowling Green Also Called: Wood County Chld Svcs Assn *(G-1335)*

Children's Service Board, Bucyrus Also Called: Crawford County Children Svcs *(G-1506)*

Childrens Advantage... 330 296-5552
771 N Freedom St Ravenna (44266) *(G-12621)*

Childrens Anesthesia Assoc Inc..................................... 614 722-4200
700 Childrens Dr Columbus (43205) *(G-5561)*

Childrens Cmprhensive Svcs Inc.................................... 419 589-5511
1451 Lucas Rd Mansfield (44903) *(G-10252)*

Childrens Dntl Spclsts Lk Cnty....................................... 440 266-1740
8484 Market St Mentor (44060) *(G-10921)*

Childrens H Cincinnati.. 513 803-2707
3244 Burnet Ave Cincinnati (45229) *(G-2356)*

Childrens HM of Cncinnati Ohio..................................... 513 272-2800
5050 Madison Rd Cincinnati (45227) *(G-2357)*

Childrens Home Care Dayton.. 937 641-4663
18 Childrens Plz Dayton (45404) *(G-7223)*

Childrens Home Care Group... 330 543-5000
185 W Cedar St Ste 203 Akron (44307) *(G-88)*

Childrens Hosp Guidance Ctrs, Columbus Also Called: Nationwide Childrens Hospital *(G-6323)*

Childrens Hosp Med Ctr Akron....................................... 330 253-4931
1463 Canton Rd # A Akron (44312) *(G-89)*

Childrens Hosp Med Ctr Akron....................................... 330 543-8004
1 Perkins Sq Akron (44308) *(G-90)*

Childrens Hosp Med Ctr Akron....................................... 330 543-8639
1 Perkins Sq Akron (44308) *(G-91)*

Childrens Hosp Med Ctr Akron....................................... 330 543-8503
214 W Bowery St Akron (44308) *(G-92)*

Childrens Hosp Med Ctr Akron....................................... 330 543-8521
6100 Whipple Ave. Nw Ste 5200 Akron (44308) *(G-93)*

Childrens Hosp Med Ctr Akron....................................... 330 375-3528
525 E Market St Akron (44304) *(G-94)*

Childrens Hosp Med Ctr Akron....................................... 330 865-1252
701 White Pond Dr Ste 100 Akron (44320) *(G-95)*

Childrens Hosp Med Ctr Akron....................................... 330 543-1000
1 Perkins Sq Ste 214 Akron (44308) *(G-96)*

Childrens Hosp Med Ctr Akron....................................... 330 543-8260
215 W Bowery St Ste 2200 Akron (44308) *(G-97)*

Childrens Hosp Med Ctr Akron (PA).............................. 330 543-1000
1 Perkins Sq Akron (44308) *(G-98)*

Childrens Hosp Med Ctr Akron....................................... 330 543-8530
300 Locust St Akron (44302) *(G-99)*

Childrens Hosp Med Ctr Akron....................................... 330 823-7311
1826 S Arch Ave Alliance (44601) *(G-378)*

Childrens Hosp Med Ctr Akron....................................... 419 281-3077
2212 Mifflin Ave Ashland (44805) *(G-493)*

Childrens Hosp Med Ctr Akron....................................... 330 746-8040
6505 Market St Ste 2100 Boardman (44512) *(G-1286)*

Childrens Hosp Med Ctr Akron....................................... 440 526-4543
7001 S Edgerton Rd Ste 1 Brecksville (44141) *(G-1348)*

Childrens Hosp Med Ctr Akron....................................... 330 342-5437
5655 Hudson Dr Hudson (44236) *(G-9339)*

Childrens Hosp Med Ctr Akron....................................... 330 676-1020
1951 State Route 59 Ste A Kent (44240) *(G-9562)*

Childrens Hosp Med Ctr Akron....................................... 419 521-2900
371 Cline Ave Mansfield (44907) *(G-10253)*

Childrens Hosp Med Ctr Akron....................................... 330 308-5432
1045 W High Ave New Philadelphia (44663) *(G-11642)*

Childrens Hosp Med Ctr Akron....................................... 419 529-6285
2003 W 4th St Ontario (44906) *(G-12102)*

Childrens Hosp Med Ctr Akron....................................... 330 633-2055
143 Northwest Ave Bldg A Tallmadge (44278) *(G-13587)*

Childrens Hosp Med Ctr Akron....................................... 330 425-3344
8054 Darrow Rd Twinsburg (44087) *(G-14176)*

Childrens Hosp Med Ctr Akron....................................... 330 345-1100
128 E Milltown Rd Wooster (44691) *(G-15319)*

Childrens Hosp Med Ctr Akron....................................... 330 629-6085
8423 Market St Ste 300 Youngstown (44512) *(G-15576)*

Childrens Hosp Reference Lab 614 722-5477
525 Kennedy Dr Columbus (43215) *(G-5562)*

Childrens Hospital 513 636-9900
5642 Hamilton Ave 1flr Cincinnati (45224) *(G-2358)*

Childrens Hospital 513 636-4051
3373 Burnet Ave Cincinnati (45229) *(G-2359)*

Childrens Hospital Inc 614 355-0616
154 W 12th Ave Columbus (43210) *(G-5563)*

Childrens Hospital Medical Ctr 513 636-6036
796 Cincinnati Batavia Pike Cincinnati (45245) *(G-2099)*

Childrens Hospital Medical Ctr 513 541-4500
2750 Beekman St Cincinnati (45225) *(G-2360)*

Childrens Hospital Medical Ctr 513 636-4200
6941 Moorfield Dr Cincinnati (45230) *(G-2361)*

Childrens Hospital Medical Ctr 513 803-1751
240 Albert Sabin Way Rm S4.381 Cincinnati (45229) *(G-2362)*

Childrens Hospital Medical Ctr 513 636-4200
2900 Vernon Pl Cincinnati (45219) *(G-2363)*

Childrens Hospital Medical Ctr 513 636-4366
2800 Winslow Ave Fl 3 Cincinnati (45206) *(G-2364)*

Childrens Hospital Medical Ctr 513 636-4288
3333 Burnet Ave Fl 6 Cincinnati (45229) *(G-2365)*

Childrens Hospital Medical Ctr 513 636-8778
3333 Burnet Ave Cincinnati (45229) *(G-2366)*

Childrens Hospital Medical Ctr 513 636-6100
7495 State Rd Ste 355 Cincinnati (45255) *(G-2367)*

Childrens Hospital Medical Ctr (PA) 513 636-4200
3333 Burnet Ave Cincinnati (45229) *(G-2368)*

Childrens Hospital Medical Ctr 513 636-4200
3401 Burnet Ave Cincinnati (45229) *(G-2369)*

Childrens Hospital Medical Ctr 513 636-4200
3350 Elland Ave Cincinnati (45229) *(G-2370)*

Childrens Hospital Medical Ctr 513 636-6400
3050 Mack Rd Ste 105 Fairfield (45014) *(G-8400)*

Childrens Hospital Medical Ctr 513 803-9600
7777 Yankee Rd Liberty Township (45044) *(G-9848)*

Childrens Hospital Medical Ctr 513 636-6800
9560 Children Dr Mason (45040) *(G-10529)*

Childrens House LLC 513 451-4551
11161 Montgomery Rd Cincinnati (45249) *(G-2371)*

Childrens Hunger Alliance (PA) 614 341-7700
1105 Schrock Rd Ste 505 Columbus (43229) *(G-5564)*

Childrens Lab Schools Inc 937 274-7195
615 Shiloh Dr Dayton (45415) *(G-7224)*

Childrens Museum of Cleveland 216 791-7114
3813 Euclid Ave Cleveland (44115) *(G-3970)*

Childrens Rdiological Inst Inc 614 722-2363
700 Childrens Dr Columbus (43205) *(G-5565)*

Childvine Inc 937 748-1260
790 N Main St Springboro (45066) *(G-13196)*

Chillcth-Ross Child Care Ctr I 740 775-7772
369 N High St Chillicothe (45601) *(G-2054)*

Chiller, Dublin *Also Called: Chiller LLC (G-7962)*

Chiller LLC 614 246-3380
200 W Nationwide Blvd Columbus (43215) *(G-5566)*

Chiller LLC 614 475-7575
3600 Chiller Ln Columbus (43219) *(G-5567)*

Chiller LLC (PA) 614 764-1000
7001 Dublin Park Dr Dublin (43016) *(G-7962)*

Chiller LLC 740 549-0009
8144 Highfield Dr Lewis Center (43035) *(G-9814)*

Chiller LLC 614 433-9600
401 E Wilson Bridge Rd Worthington (43085) *(G-15408)*

Chillicothe Bowling Lanes Inc 740 773-3300
1680 N Bridge St Chillicothe (45601) *(G-2055)*

Chillicothe Inn 740 774-2512
24 N Bridge St Chillicothe (45601) *(G-2056)*

Chillicothe Long-Term Care Inc 740 773-6161
230 Cherry St Chillicothe (45601) *(G-2057)*

Chillicothe Long-Term Care Inc (PA) 740 773-6470
7265 Kenwood Rd Ste 300 Cincinnati (45236) *(G-2372)*

Chillicothe Motel LLC 740 773-3903
20 N Plaza Blvd Chillicothe (45601) *(G-2058)*

Chillicothe Steel Company 740 772-2481
1393 Industrial Dr Chillicothe (45601) *(G-2059)*

Chillicothe Telephone Company (HQ) 740 772-8200
68 E Main St Chillicothe (45601) *(G-2060)*

Chillicothe VA Medical Center, Chillicothe *Also Called: Veterans Health Administration (G-2093)*

Chima Travel Bureau Inc (PA) 330 867-4770
55 Merz Blvd Unit B Fairlawn (44333) *(G-8470)*

Chippewa Golf Club, Doylestown *Also Called: Chippewa Golf Corp (G-7913)*

Chippewa Golf Corp 330 658-2566
12147 Shank Rd Doylestown (44230) *(G-7913)*

Chippewa School District 330 658-4868
165 Brooklyn Ave Doylestown (44230) *(G-7914)*

Chiquita Brnds Intl Foundation 980 636-5000
250 E 5th St Cincinnati (45202) *(G-2373)*

Chirst Hospital Surgery Center 513 272-3448
4850 Red Bank Rd Fl 1 Cincinnati (45227) *(G-2374)*

Chmc Cmnty Hlth Svcs Netwrk 513 636-8778
3333 Burnet Ave Cincinnati (45229) *(G-2375)*

Cho Bedford Inc 330 433-2270
320 Witwer St Ne North Canton (44720) *(G-11816)*

Choice Healthcare Limited 937 254-6220
1257 N Fairfield Rd Beavercreek (45432) *(G-871)*

Choice Hotels Intl Inc 330 729-5645
4810 Tr 366 N St Berlin (44610) *(G-1090)*

Choice Properties Real Estate 937 593-7216
245 S Main St Bellefontaine (43311) *(G-1023)*

Choice Recovery Inc 614 358-9900
1105 Schrock Rd Ste 700 Columbus (43229) *(G-5568)*

Choicelocal LLC 855 867-5622
24960 Center Ridge Rd Westlake (44145) *(G-15048)*

Choices Behavioral Health Care 419 960-4009
201 Madison St Port Clinton (43452) *(G-12519)*

Choices In Community Living (PA) 937 898-3655
1651 Needmore Rd Ste B Dayton (45414) *(G-7225)*

Choices In Community Living 937 325-0344
2100 E High St Ste 113 Springfield (45505) *(G-13226)*

Cholesterol Center, The, Cincinnati *Also Called: Jewish Hospital (G-2907)*

Chop House Restaurant, Dayton *Also Called: Connor Concepts Inc (G-7246)*

Chores Unlimited Inc 440 439-5455
4889 Neo Pkwy Cleveland (44128) *(G-3971)*

Christ Hosp Physcans - Obsttri, Liberty Township *Also Called: Christ Hospital (G-9849)*

Christ Hosp Spcial Chmstry Lab, Mason *Also Called: Christ Hospital (G-10530)*

Christ Hospital 513 631-3300
4803 Montgomery Rd Ste 114 Cincinnati (45212) *(G-2376)*

Christ Hospital 513 351-0800
2355 Norwood Ave Ste 1 Cincinnati (45212) *(G-2377)*

Christ Hospital 513 585-2000
2139 Auburn Ave Cincinnati (45219) *(G-2378)*

Christ Hospital 513 688-1111
7545 Beechmont Ave Ste E Cincinnati (45255) *(G-2379)*

Christ Hospital (PA) 513 585-2000
2139 Auburn Ave Cincinnati (45219) *(G-2380)*

Christ Hospital 513 651-0094
2123 Auburn Ave Ste 722 Cincinnati (45219) *(G-2381)*

Christ Hospital 513 272-3448
4850 Red Bank Rd Fl 1 Cincinnati (45227) *(G-2382)*

Christ Hospital 513 347-2300
5649 Harrison Rd Ste C Cincinnati (45248) *(G-2383)*

Christ Hospital 513 561-7809
11140 Montgomery Rd Cincinnati (45249) *(G-2384)*

Christ Hospital 513 648-7950
7335 Yankee Rd Ste 202 Liberty Township (45044) *(G-9849)*

Christ Hospital 513 648-7800
6939 Cox Rd Liberty Township (45069) *(G-9850)*

Christ Hospital 513 648-7900
7450 S Mason Montgomery Rd Mason (45040) *(G-10530)*

Christ Hospital 513 755-4700
7589 Tylers Place Blvd West Chester (45069) *(G-14665)*

ALPHABETIC SECTION

Christ Hospital Health Network, Cincinnati *Also Called: Christ Hospital* *(G-2380)*
Christ Hospital, The, Cincinnati *Also Called: Christ Hospital* *(G-2377)*
Christ King Catholic Church..614 236-8838
  2855 E Livingston Ave Columbus (43209) *(G-5569)*
Christen & Sons Company (PA)...419 243-4161
  714 George St Toledo (43608) *(G-13733)*
Christen Detroit, Toledo *Also Called: Christen & Sons Company (G-13733)*
Christian Aid Ministries (PA)...330 893-2428
  4464 State Route 39 Millersburg (44654) *(G-11276)*
Christian Benevolent Assn (PA)..513 931-5000
  8097 Hamilton Ave Cincinnati (45231) *(G-2385)*
CHRISTIAN BENEVOLENT ASSOCIATION OF GREATER CINCINNATI, THE, Cincinnati *Also Called: Mt Healthy Christian Home Inc (G-3086)*
Christian Chld HM Ohio Inc...330 345-7949
  2685 Armstrong Rd Wooster (44691) *(G-15320)*
Christian Community Hlth Svcs..513 381-2247
  5 E Liberty St Ste 4 Cincinnati (45202) *(G-2386)*
Christian Family Credit Union..513 528-1521
  410 Chamber Dr Milford (45150) *(G-11222)*
Christian Hlthcare Mnstries In..330 848-1511
  127 Hazelwood Ave Barberton (44203) *(G-696)*
Christian Home Care LLC..419 254-2840
  5555 Airport Hwy Ste 200 Toledo (43615) *(G-13734)*
Christian Missionary Alliance...614 457-4085
  3750 Henderson Rd Columbus (43220) *(G-5570)*
Christian Rivertree School..330 494-1860
  7373 Portage St Nw Massillon (44646) *(G-10635)*
Christian Schools Inc...330 857-7311
  3970 Kidron Rd Kidron (44636) *(G-9635)*
Christian Worthington Vlg Inc..614 846-6076
  165 Highbluffs Blvd Columbus (43235) *(G-5571)*
Christmas Home Health LLC..440 708-6442
  4300 Lynn Rd Ste 203b Ravenna (44266) *(G-12622)*
Christndtroit Div of Fred Chrs, Toledo *Also Called: Fred Christen & Sons Company (G-13813)*
Christopher Burkey...330 770-9607
  1185 W Pine Lake Rd North Lima (44452) *(G-11886)*
Christopher Burkey Plumbing, North Lima *Also Called: Christopher Burkey (G-11886)*
Christus Hlth Southeast Texas...330 726-0771
  7000 South Ave Ste 4 Youngstown (44512) *(G-15577)*
Chronic Care Management Inc..440 248-6500
  6505 Rockside Rd Ste 200 Independence (44131) *(G-9418)*
CHS, Sylvania *Also Called: Infusion Partners Inc (G-13551)*
CHS Norwood Inc..513 242-1360
  1171 Towne St Cincinnati (45216) *(G-2387)*
CHS Therapy Rehab Holdings LLC...................................888 995-1305
  2875 Center Rd Brunswick (44212) *(G-1453)*
Chs-Norwood Inc..513 351-7007
  6969 Glenmeadow Ln Cincinnati (45237) *(G-2388)*
Chu Management Co Inc (PA)..330 725-4571
  2875 Medina Rd Medina (44256) *(G-10820)*
Chugach, Cleveland *Also Called: Wolf Creek Federal Svcs Inc (G-5157)*
Church of God Retirement Cmnty....................................513 422-5600
  4400 Vannest Ave Middletown (45042) *(G-11156)*
Church On North Coast (PA)...440 960-1100
  4125 Leavitt Rd Lorain (44053) *(G-10063)*
Chute Gerdeman Inc...614 469-1001
  501 W Schrock Rd Ste 201 Westerville (43081) *(G-14966)*
Chwc, Bryan *Also Called: Community Hsptals Wllness Ctrs (G-1482)*
Chy Hotel LLC..614 766-7255
  4475 Bridge Park Ave Dublin (43017) *(G-7963)*
Ci Disposition Co..216 587-5200
  1000 Valley Belt Rd Brooklyn Heights (44131) *(G-1414)*
Cima, Hamilton *Also Called: Wulco Inc (G-9093)*
Cimarron Express Inc...419 855-7713
  21611 State Route 51 W Genoa (43430) *(G-8793)*
Cimcool, Cincinnati *Also Called: Cimcool Industrial Pdts LLC (G-2389)*
Cimcool Industrial Pdts LLC (DH).....................................513 458-8100
  3000 Disney St Cincinnati (45209) *(G-2389)*
Cimx LLC...513 248-7700
  2368 Victory Pkwy Ste 120 Cincinnati (45206) *(G-2390)*

Cimx Software, Cincinnati *Also Called: Cimx LLC (G-2390)*
Cinc Transit Whs 1103, Fairfield *Also Called: US Foods Inc (G-8451)*
Cinci Hospitalities Inc..513 398-8075
  5589 State Route 741 Mason (45040) *(G-10531)*
Cincinatti Chld Hosp Med Ctr, Fairfield *Also Called: Childrens Hospital Medical Ctr (G-8400)*
Cincinnati - Vulcan Company...513 242-5300
  5353 Spring Grove Ave Cincinnati (45217) *(G-2391)*
Cincinnati & Ohio Rlwy Svc LLC.......................................513 371-3277
  561 Main St Hamilton (45013) *(G-9027)*
Cincinnati 007, Cincinnati *Also Called: Stanley Steemer Intl Inc (G-3411)*
Cincinnati Aesthetics LLC...513 204-3490
  8381 Oakdale Ct Mason (45040) *(G-10532)*
Cincinnati Air Conditioning Co...513 721-5622
  2080 Northwest Dr Cincinnati (45231) *(G-2392)*
Cincinnati Aml Refl Emer C LLC......................................937 610-0414
  6405 Clyo Rd Dayton (45459) *(G-7226)*
Cincinnati Anmal Rfrral Emrgnc......................................513 530-0911
  6995 East Kimper Rd Cincinnati (45249) *(G-2393)*
Cincinnati Area Chapter, Cincinnati *Also Called: American Red Cross (G-2186)*
Cincinnati Area Snior Svcs Inc (PA).................................513 721-4330
  644 Linn St Ste 304 Cincinnati (45203) *(G-2394)*
CINCINNATI ART MUSEUM, Cincinnati *Also Called: Cincinnati Museum Association (G-2415)*
Cincinnati Asphalt Corporation..513 367-0250
  6000 Madden Way Harrison (45030) *(G-9098)*
Cincinnati Assn For The Blind...513 221-8558
  2045 Gilbert Ave Cincinnati (45202) *(G-2395)*
Cincinnati Assn For The Prfrmg (PA)..............................513 744-3344
  650 Walnut St Cincinnati (45202) *(G-2396)*
Cincinnati Ballet, Cincinnati *Also Called: Cincinnati Ballet Company Inc (G-2397)*
Cincinnati Ballet Company Inc..513 621-5219
  1801 Gilbert Ave Cincinnati (45202) *(G-2397)*
Cincinnati Bell Inc (DH)..513 397-9900
  221 E 4th St Cincinnati (45202) *(G-2398)*
Cincinnati Bell Tele Co LLC (DH)....................................513 397-9900
  221 E 4th St 103-710 Cincinnati (45202) *(G-2399)*
Cincinnati Bell Telephone Co, Cincinnati *Also Called: Cincinnati Bell Tele Co LLC (G-2399)*
Cincinnati Bell Wireless Company..................................513 397-9548
  221 E 4th St Ste 113 Cincinnati (45202) *(G-2400)*
Cincinnati Bengals Inc (PA)..513 621-3550
  1 Paycor Stadium Cincinnati (45202) *(G-2401)*
Cincinnati Bulk Terminals, Cincinnati *Also Called: Cincinnati Bulk Terminals LLC (G-2402)*
Cincinnati Bulk Terminals LLC..513 621-4800
  895 Mehring Way Cincinnati (45203) *(G-2402)*
Cincinnati Casualty Company...513 870-2000
  6200 S Gilmore Rd Fairfield (45014) *(G-8401)*
Cincinnati Children's Hospital, Cincinnati *Also Called: Childrens Hospital Medical Ctr (G-2370)*
Cincinnati Childrens Hospital, Cincinnati *Also Called: Childrens Hospital Medical Ctr (G-2369)*
Cincinnati Chld Hosp Med Ctr, Cincinnati *Also Called: Childrens Hospital Medical Ctr (G-2361)*
Cincinnati Circus Company LLC....................................513 921-5454
  6433 Wiehe Rd Cincinnati (45237) *(G-2403)*
Cincinnati Cnslting Consortium......................................513 233-0011
  220 Wyoming Ave Cincinnati (45215) *(G-2404)*
Cincinnati Container Company (PA)..............................513 874-6874
  5060 Duff Dr West Chester (45246) *(G-14804)*
Cincinnati Country Club...513 533-5200
  2348 Grandin Rd Cincinnati (45208) *(G-2405)*
Cincinnati Ctr For Psychthrapy.......................................513 961-8484
  3001 Highland Ave Cincinnati (45219) *(G-2406)*
Cincinnati Cyclones LLC..513 421-7825
  100 Broadway St Fl 3 Cincinnati (45202) *(G-2407)*
Cincinnati Dental Services (PA)......................................513 721-8888
  121 E Mcmillan St Cincinnati (45219) *(G-2408)*
Cincinnati Dermatology Ctr LLC.....................................513 984-4800
  7730 Montgomery Rd Ste 200 Cincinnati (45236) *(G-2409)*
Cincinnati Early Learning Ctr (PA)..................................513 961-2690
  1301 E Mcmillan St Cincinnati (45206) *(G-2410)*
Cincinnati Early Learning Ctr....513 367-2129
  498 S State St Harrison (45030) *(G-9099)*

Cincinnati Equitable Insurance — ALPHABETIC SECTION

Cincinnati Equitable Insurance, Cincinnati *Also Called: Alpha Investment Partnership* *(G-2170)*

Cincinnati Eye Institute, Blue Ash *Also Called: Cei Physicians PSC LLC* *(G-1144)*

Cincinnati Fifth Street Ht LLC.. 513 579-1234
151 W 5th St Cincinnati (45202) *(G-2411)*

Cincinnati Financial Corp (PA).. 513 870-2000
6200 S Gilmore Rd Fairfield (45014) *(G-8402)*

CINCINNATI HABITAT FOR HUMANIT, Cincinnati *Also Called: Habitat For Hmnity Grter Cncnn* *(G-2790)*

Cincinnati Hand Surgery Cons (PA).. 513 961-4263
10700 Montgomery Rd Ste 150 Montgomery (45242) *(G-11365)*

Cincinnati Home Care Inc.. 513 771-2760
742 Waycross Rd Cincinnati (45240) *(G-2412)*

Cincinnati Home Healthcare, Cincinnati *Also Called: Maxim Healthcare Services Inc* *(G-3018)*

Cincinnati Hyatt Regency, Cincinnati *Also Called: Cincinnati Fifth Street Ht LLC* *(G-2411)*

Cincinnati Indeminty Co.. 513 870-2000
6200 S Gilmore Rd Fairfield (45014) *(G-8403)*

Cincinnati Institute Fine Arts (PA).. 513 871-2787
20 East Central Pkwy Ste 2 Cincinnati (45202) *(G-2413)*

Cincinnati Insurance, Fairfield *Also Called: Cincinnati Insurance Company* *(G-8404)*

Cincinnati Insurance Company (HQ).. 513 870-2000
6200 S Gilmore Rd Fairfield (45014) *(G-8404)*

Cincinnati Life Insurance Co.. 513 870-2000
6200 S Gilmore Rd Fairfield (45014) *(G-8405)*

Cincinnati Lndmark Productions (PA).. 513 241-6550
4990 Glenway Ave Cincinnati (45238) *(G-2414)*

Cincinnati Marriott Northeast, Mason *Also Called: CP Mason LLC* *(G-10543)*

Cincinnati Mechanical Svcs LLC, Blue Ash *Also Called: Complete Mechanical Svcs LLC* *(G-1158)*

Cincinnati Municipal Garage, Cincinnati *Also Called: City of Cincinnati* *(G-2451)*

Cincinnati Museum Association (PA).. 513 721-5204
953 Eden Park Dr Cincinnati (45202) *(G-2415)*

Cincinnati Museum Center (PA).. 513 287-7000
1301 Western Ave Ste 2253 Cincinnati (45203) *(G-2416)*

Cincinnati Netherland Ht LLC.. 513 421-9100
35 W 5th St Cincinnati (45202) *(G-2417)*

Cincinnati Opera Association.. 513 768-5500
1243 Elm St Cincinnati (45202) *(G-2418)*

CINCINNATI PLAYHOUSE, Cincinnati *Also Called: The Cincinnati Playhouse In The Park Inc* *(G-3463)*

Cincinnati Port Union Facility, West Chester *Also Called: Dawson Logistics LLC* *(G-14683)*

Cincinnati Prcision Instrs Inc.. 513 874-2122
253 Circle Freeway Dr West Chester (45246) *(G-14805)*

Cincinnati Public Radio Inc.. 513 352-9185
1223 Central Pkwy Cincinnati (45214) *(G-2419)*

Cincinnati Reds LLC (PA).. 513 765-7000
100 Joe Nuxhall Way Cincinnati (45202) *(G-2420)*

Cincinnati Reds LLC.. 513 765-7923
100 Main Street Cincinnati (45202) *(G-2421)*

Cincinnati Speech Hearing Ctr (PA).. 513 221-0527
2825 Burnet Ave Ste 401 Cincinnati (45219) *(G-2422)*

Cincinnati Sports Club, Cincinnati *Also Called: Cincinnati Sports Mall Inc* *(G-2423)*

Cincinnati Sports Mall Inc.. 513 527-4000
3950 Red Bank Rd Ste A Cincinnati (45227) *(G-2423)*

Cincinnati Steel Products Co.. 513 871-4444
4540 Steel Pl Cincinnati (45209) *(G-2424)*

Cincinnati Sub-Zero Products, Cincinnati *Also Called: Gentherm Medical LLC* *(G-2730)*

Cincinnati Symphony Orchestra (PA).. 513 621-1919
1241 Elm St Cincinnati (45202) *(G-2425)*

Cincinnati Symphony Orchestra.. 513 381-3300
1229 Elm St Cincinnati (45202) *(G-2426)*

Cincinnati Testing Laboratories Inc (HQ).. 513 851-3313
1775 Carillion Blvd Cincinnati (45240) *(G-2427)*

Cincinnati Testing Labs, Cincinnati *Also Called: Cincinnati Testing Laboratories Inc* *(G-2427)*

Cincinnati Testing Labs Inc.. 513 851-3313
417 Northland Blvd Cincinnati (45240) *(G-2428)*

Cincinnati Trning Trml Svcs In (PA).. 513 563-4474
4000 Executive Park Dr Ste 402 Cincinnati (45241) *(G-2429)*

Cincinnati USA Rgional Chamber.. 513 579-3100
3 E 4th St Ste 200 Cincinnati (45202) *(G-2430)*

Cincinnati V A Medical Center, Cincinnati *Also Called: Veterans Health Administration* *(G-3627)*

Cincinnati Works Corp.. 513 744-9675
708 Walnut St Ste 200 Cincinnati (45202) *(G-2431)*

CINCINNATI YOUNG PEOPLE'S THEA, Cincinnati *Also Called: Cincinnati Lndmark Productions* *(G-2414)*

Cincinnati Youth Collaborative.. 513 475-4165
301 Oak St Cincinnati (45219) *(G-2432)*

CINCINNATI ZOO & BOTANICAL GAR, Cincinnati *Also Called: Zoological Society Cincinnati* *(G-3700)*

Cincinnatian Hotel.. 513 381-3000
601 Vine St Cincinnati (45202) *(G-2433)*

Cincinnatian Hotel, The, Cincinnati *Also Called: Cincinnatian Hotel* *(G-2433)*

Cincinnatti Processing, West Chester *Also Called: Empire Packing Company LP* *(G-14809)*

Cincinnt-Hmlton Cnty Cmnty Act (PA).. 513 569-1840
1740 Langdon Farm Rd Ste 300 Cincinnati (45237) *(G-2434)*

Cincinnt-Hmlton Cnty Cmnty Act.. 513 354-3900
880 W Court St Cincinnati (45203) *(G-2435)*

Cincinntis Optmum Rsdntial Env.. 513 771-2673
75 Tri County Pkwy Cincinnati (45246) *(G-2436)*

Cinco Credit Union (PA).. 513 281-9988
49 William Howard Taft Rd Cincinnati (45219) *(G-2437)*

CINCO FAMILY FINANCIAL CENTER, Cincinnati *Also Called: Cinco Credit Union* *(G-2437)*

Cincom, Cincinnati *Also Called: Cincom Systems Inc* *(G-2438)*

Cincom Systems Inc (PA).. 513 612-2300
55 Merchant St Cincinnati (45246) *(G-2438)*

Cincysavers, Cincinnati *Also Called: Hubbard Radio Cincinnati LLC* *(G-2854)*

Cincysmiles Foundation Inc.. 513 621-0248
5310 Rapid Run Rd Ste 101 Cincinnati (45238) *(G-2439)*

Cinergy Corp (DH).. 513 421-9500
139 E 4th St Cincinnati (45202) *(G-2440)*

CINergy-Ulh&p, Cincinnati *Also Called: Duke Energy Kentucky Inc* *(G-2580)*

CINFED CREDIT UNION, Cincinnati *Also Called: Cinfed Federal Credit Union* *(G-2441)*

Cinfed Federal Credit Union (PA).. 513 333-3800
4801 Kennedy Ave Cincinnati (45209) *(G-2441)*

Cintas, Canton *Also Called: Cintas Corporation No 2* *(G-1709)*

Cintas, Cincinnati *Also Called: Cintas Corporation* *(G-2442)*

Cintas, Cincinnati *Also Called: Cintas Sales Corporation* *(G-2445)*

Cintas, Columbus *Also Called: Cintas Corporation No 2* *(G-5572)*

Cintas, Mason *Also Called: Cintas Corporation No 2* *(G-10534)*

Cintas, Milford *Also Called: Cintas Corporation No 2* *(G-11223)*

Cintas, Vandalia *Also Called: Cintas Corporation No 2* *(G-14370)*

Cintas Corporation (PA).. 513 459-1200
6800 Cintas Blvd Cincinnati (45262) *(G-2442)*

Cintas Corporation.. 513 631-5750
5570 Ridge Ave Cincinnati (45213) *(G-2443)*

Cintas Corporation No 1 (HQ).. 513 459-1200
6800 Cintas Blvd Mason (45040) *(G-10533)*

Cintas Corporation No 2.. 330 966-7800
3865 Highland Park Nw Canton (44720) *(G-1709)*

Cintas Corporation No 2.. 614 878-7313
1300 Boltonfield St Columbus (43228) *(G-5572)*

Cintas Corporation No 2.. 513 459-1200
5800 Cintas Blvd Mason (45040) *(G-10534)*

Cintas Corporation No 2 (HQ).. 513 459-1200
6800 Cintas Blvd Mason (45040) *(G-10535)*

Cintas Corporation No 2.. 513 965-0800
27 Whitney Dr Milford (45150) *(G-11223)*

Cintas Corporation No 2.. 800 444-2687
850 Center Dr Vandalia (45377) *(G-14370)*

Cintas Corporation No 3 (HQ).. 513 459-1200
6800 Cintas Blvd Mason (45040) *(G-10536)*

Cintas Document Management LLC (HQ).. 800 914-1960
6800 Cintas Blvd Mason (45040) *(G-10537)*

Cintas Fire Protection, Mason *Also Called: Cintas Corporation No 2* *(G-10535)*

Cintas R US Inc.. 513 459-1200
6800 Cintas Blvd Cincinnati (45262) *(G-2444)*

Cintas Sales Corporation (HQ).. 513 459-1200
6800 Cintas Blvd Cincinnati (45262) *(G-2445)*

Cintas Uniforms AP Fcilty Svcs, Cincinnati *Also Called: Cintas Corporation* *(G-2443)*

ALPHABETIC SECTION — City of Cuyahoga Falls

Cintas-Rus LP (HQ) 513 459-1200
  6800 Cintas Blvd Mason (45040) *(G-10538)*
Cintech LLC 513 731-6000
  3280 Hageman Ave Cincinnati (45241) *(G-2446)*
Cintech Construction Inc 513 563-1991
  4865 Duck Creek Rd Cincinnati (45227) *(G-2447)*
CIP International Inc 513 874-9925
  9575 Le Saint Dr West Chester (45014) *(G-14666)*
Cipted Corp 412 829-2120
  301 Lawton Ave Monroe (45050) *(G-11336)*
Ciralsky & Associates Inc 419 470-1328
  1604 Prosperity Rd Toledo (43612) *(G-13735)*
Ciralsky Steel, Toledo Also Called: Ciralsky & Associates Inc *(G-13735)*
Cirba Solutions Us Inc (PA) 740 653-6290
  265 Quarry Rd Se Lancaster (43130) *(G-9700)*
Circana Inc 513 651-0500
  250 E 5th St Ste 700 Cincinnati (45202) *(G-2448)*
CIRCANA, INC., Cincinnati Also Called: Circana Inc *(G-2448)*
Circle Building Services Inc (PA) 614 228-6090
  742 Harmon Ave Columbus (43223) *(G-5573)*
Circle Building Services Inc 614 228-6090
  793 Harmon Ave Columbus (43223) *(G-5574)*
Circle Health Services 216 721-4010
  12201 Euclid Ave Cleveland (44106) *(G-3972)*
Circle J Home Health Care Inc (PA) 330 482-0877
  412 State Route 164 Salineville (43945) *(G-12859)*
Circle Prime Manufacturing 330 923-0019
  2114 Front St Cuyahoga Falls (44221) *(G-7054)*
Cisco Capitol Express, Columbus Also Called: Capitol Express Entps Inc *(G-5504)*
Citgo, Medina Also Called: G J Shue Inc *(G-10837)*
Citicorp, Columbus Also Called: Citicorp Credit Services Inc *(G-5575)*
Citicorp Credit Services Inc 212 559-1000
  1500 Boltonfield St Columbus (43228) *(G-5575)*
Citizens Bank, Ashville Also Called: Citizens Bank of Ashville Ohio *(G-551)*
CITIZENS BANK, Beverly Also Called: Citizens Bank Company *(G-1100)*
Citizens Bank, Delphos Also Called: Citizens Bank of Delphos *(G-7838)*
CITIZENS BANK, Martins Ferry Also Called: Unified Bank *(G-10472)*
Citizens Bank, Strasburg Also Called: Citizens State Bnk of Strsburg *(G-13403)*
Citizens Bank Company (HQ) 740 984-2381
  501 5th St Beverly (45715) *(G-1100)*
Citizens Bank National Assn 419 720-0009
  3410 Secor Rd Ste 510 Toledo (43606) *(G-13736)*
Citizens Bank of Ashville Ohio 740 983-2511
  26 Main St E Ashville (43103) *(G-551)*
Citizens Bank of Delphos 419 692-2010
  114 E 3rd St Delphos (45833) *(G-7838)*
Citizens Capital Markets Inc 216 589-0900
  200 Public Sq Ste 3750 Cleveland (44114) *(G-3973)*
Citizens Nat Bnk of Wdsfeld Th (HQ) 740 472-1696
  143 S Main St Woodsfield (43793) *(G-15300)*
Citizens Nat Bnk Urbana Ohio 937 653-1200
  1 Monument Sq Urbana (43078) *(G-14303)*
Citizens State Bnk of Strsburg 330 878-5551
  202 N Wooster Ave Strasburg (44680) *(G-13403)*
City Architecture Inc 216 881-2444
  12205 Larchmere Blvd Cleveland (44120) *(G-3974)*
City Base Cincinnati LLC 210 907-7197
  5901 E Galbraith Rd Ste 200 Cincinnati (45236) *(G-2449)*
City Dash, Cincinnati Also Called: City Dash LLC *(G-2450)*
City Dash LLC 513 562-2000
  949 Laidlaw Ave Cincinnati (45237) *(G-2450)*
City Dayton Waste Collection, Dayton Also Called: City of Dayton *(G-7230)*
City Dayton Water Distribution, Dayton Also Called: City of Dayton *(G-7231)*
City Dept Streets and Sewers, Hamilton Also Called: City of Hamilton *(G-9028)*
City Garage, Athens Also Called: City of Athens *(G-561)*
City Hospital Association 330 385-7200
  425 W 5th St East Liverpool (43920) *(G-8179)*
City Laundry & Dry Cleaning Co, Findlay Also Called: Kramer Enterprises Inc *(G-8555)*
City Life Inc (PA) 216 523-5899
  1382 W 9th St Ste 310 Cleveland (44113) *(G-3975)*

City Mission (PA) 216 431-3510
  5310 Carnegie Ave Cleveland (44103) *(G-3976)*
City of Akron 330 375-2666
  2460 Akron Peninsula Rd Akron (44313) *(G-100)*
City of Akron 330 375-2650
  1180 S Main St Ste 110 Akron (44301) *(G-101)*
City of Akron 330 564-4075
  100 W Cedar St Ste 300 Akron (44307) *(G-102)*
City of Akron 330 375-2355
  166 S High St Rm 701 Akron (44308) *(G-103)*
City of Akron 330 678-0077
  1570 Ravenna Rd Kent (44240) *(G-9563)*
City of Alliance 330 829-2220
  12251 Rockhill Ave Ne Alliance (44601) *(G-379)*
City of Athens 740 592-3343
  387 W State St Athens (45701) *(G-561)*
City of Aurora 330 562-8662
  158 W Pioneer Trl Aurora (44202) *(G-611)*
City of Avon Lake 440 933-6226
  201 Miller Rd Avon Lake (44012) *(G-676)*
City of Brecksville 440 526-4109
  1 Community Dr Brecksville (44141) *(G-1349)*
City of Brecksville 440 526-1384
  9069 Brecksville Rd Brecksville (44141) *(G-1350)*
City of Brooklyn 216 635-4222
  7727 Memphis Ave Cleveland (44144) *(G-3977)*
City of Canal Winchester 614 837-8276
  22 S Trine St Canal Winchester (43110) *(G-1602)*
City of Centerville 937 438-3585
  10000 Yankee St Dayton (45458) *(G-7227)*
City of Cincinnati 513 352-3680
  1106 Bates Ave Cincinnati (45225) *(G-2451)*
City of Cincinnati 513 471-9844
  4356 Dunham Ln Cincinnati (45238) *(G-2452)*
City of Cincinnati, Cincinnati Also Called: City of Cincinnati *(G-2452)*
City of Cleveland 216 664-2640
  601 Lakeside Ave E Rm 19 Cleveland (44114) *(G-3978)*
City of Cleveland 216 348-7210
  21400 Chagrin Blvd Cleveland (44122) *(G-3979)*
City of Cleveland 216 265-6000
  5300 Riverside Dr Ste 15 Cleveland (44135) *(G-3980)*
City of Cleveland 216 664-2555
  1708 Southpoint Cleveland (44109) *(G-3981)*
City of Cleveland 216 664-2555
  2001 Payne Ave Cleveland (44114) *(G-3982)*
City of Cleveland 216 664-4277
  1300 Lakeside Ave E Cleveland (44114) *(G-3983)*
City of Cleveland 216 348-2200
  500 Lakeside Ave E Cleveland (44114) *(G-3984)*
City of Cleveland 216 664-2430
  205 W Saint Clair Ave 4th Fl Cleveland (44113) *(G-3985)*
City of Cleveland 216 664-2941
  205 W Saint Clair Ave Fl 4 Cleveland (44113) *(G-3986)*
City of Cleveland 216 664-2625
  205 W Saint Clair Ave Fl 5 Cleveland (44113) *(G-3987)*
City of Cleveland 216 664-3922
  1300 Lakeside Ave E Cleveland (44114) *(G-3988)*
City of Cleveland 216 348-7277
  4600 Harvard Ave Newburgh Heights (44105) *(G-11757)*
City of Cncnnati Emplyees Rtrm 513 591-6000
  801 Plum St Cincinnati (45202) *(G-2453)*
City of Columbus 614 645-7490
  910 Dublin Rd Ste 4050 Columbus (43215) *(G-5576)*
City of Cuyahoga Falls 330 971-8000
  2550 Bailey Rd Cuyahoga Falls (44221) *(G-7055)*
City of Cuyahoga Falls 330 971-8130
  2310 2nd St Cuyahoga Falls (44221) *(G-7056)*
City of Cuyahoga Falls 330 971-8425
  1201 Grant Ave Cuyahoga Falls (44223) *(G-7057)*
City of Cuyahoga Falls 330 971-8005
  2560 Bailey Rd Cuyahoga Falls (44221) *(G-7058)*

City of Cuyahoga Falls — ALPHABETIC SECTION

City of Cuyahoga Falls 330 971-8230
2310 2nd St Cuyahoga Falls (44221) *(G-7059)*

City of Cuyahoga Falls 330 971-8030
2560 Bailey Rd Cuyahoga Falls (44221) *(G-7060)*

City of Cuyahoga Falls 330 971-8416
1621 Bailey Rd Cuyahoga Falls (44221) *(G-7061)*

City of Dayton 937 333-6070
3210 Chuck Wagner Ln Dayton (45414) *(G-7228)*

City of Dayton 937 333-1837
2800 Guthrie Rd Ste A Dayton (45417) *(G-7229)*

City of Dayton 937 333-4860
1010 Ottawa St Bldg 7 Dayton (45402) *(G-7230)*

City of Dayton 937 333-7138
945 Ottawa St Dayton (45402) *(G-7231)*

City of Dayton 937 333-3725
320 W Monument Ave Dayton (45402) *(G-7232)*

City of Dayton 937 454-8200
3600 Terminal Rd Ste 300 Vandalia (45377) *(G-14371)*

City of Dublin 614 410-4750
6555 Shier Rings Rd Dublin (43016) *(G-7964)*

City of Hamilton 513 785-7551
2210 S Erie Hwy Hamilton (45011) *(G-9028)*

City of Kenton (PA) 419 674-4850
111 W Franklin St Kenton (43326) *(G-9612)*

City of Kettering 937 296-2486
3170 Valleywood Dr Dayton (45429) *(G-7233)*

City of Lakewood 216 226-0080
2019 Woodward Ave Cleveland (44107) *(G-3989)*

City of Lakewood 216 252-4322
12920 Berea Rd Cleveland (44111) *(G-3990)*

City of Lakewood 216 529-6170
12650 Detroit Ave Cleveland (44107) *(G-3991)*

City of Lakewood 216 521-1515
16024 Madison Ave Lakewood (44107) *(G-9660)*

City of Lancaster 740 687-6670
1424 Campground Rd Lancaster (43130) *(G-9701)*

City of Lebanon 513 228-3200
125 S Sycamore St Lebanon (45036) *(G-9759)*

City of Lima 419 221-5294
50 Town Sq 3rd Fl Lima (45801) *(G-9874)*

City of Lorain 440 204-2500
1106 W 1st St Lorain (44052) *(G-10064)*

City of Louisville (PA) 330 875-3321
215 S Mill St Louisville (44641) *(G-10114)*

City of Lyndhurst 440 449-5011
1341 Parkview Dr Ste 1 Cleveland (44124) *(G-3992)*

City of Maple Heights 216 587-5451
15901 Libby Rd Maple Heights (44137) *(G-10334)*

City of Middletown 513 425-7781
805 Columbia Ave Middletown (45042) *(G-11157)*

City of Moraine 937 535-1100
3800 Main St Dayton (45439) *(G-7234)*

City of North Olmsted 440 777-8000
5200 Dover Center Rd North Olmsted (44070) *(G-11894)*

City of North Olmsted 440 777-0678
5873 Canterbury Rd North Olmsted (44070) *(G-11895)*

City of North Olmsted 440 734-8200
26000 Lorain Rd North Olmsted (44070) *(G-11896)*

City of Oberlin (PA) 440 775-1531
85 S Main St Oberlin (44074) *(G-12065)*

City of Pepper Pike (PA) 216 831-9804
28000 Shaker Blvd Pepper Pike (44124) *(G-12298)*

City of Perrysburg 419 872-8020
11980 Route Roached Rd Perrysburg (43551) *(G-12324)*

City of Seven Hills 216 524-6262
7777 Summitview Dr Seven Hills (44131) *(G-12952)*

City of South Euclid 216 381-7674
711 S Belvoir Blvd Cleveland (44121) *(G-3993)*

City of Springfield 937 328-3701
50 E Columbia St Springfield (45502) *(G-13227)*

City of Springfield 937 324-7725
1325 S Bird Rd Springfield (45505) *(G-13228)*

City of Sylvania 419 885-1167
7060 Sylvania Ave Sylvania (43560) *(G-13539)*

City of Tallmadge 330 634-2349
46 N Munroe Rd Tallmadge (44278) *(G-13588)*

City of Toledo 419 936-2507
555 N Expressway Dr Toledo (43608) *(G-13737)*

City of Toledo 419 936-2875
2201 Ottawa Dr Toledo (43606) *(G-13738)*

City of Toledo 419 245-1400
1 Government Ctr Ste 1800 Toledo (43604) *(G-13739)*

City of Toledo 419 936-2275
600 Jefferson Ave Ste 300 Toledo (43604) *(G-13740)*

City of Toledo 419 245-1001
1 Government Ctr Ste 2200 Toledo (43604) *(G-13741)*

City of Toledo 419 245-3209
525 N Erie St Ste 2 Toledo (43604) *(G-13742)*

City of Toledo 419 245-1800
420 Madison Ave Ste 100 Toledo (43604) *(G-13743)*

City of Toledo 419 936-2924
4032 Creekside Ave Toledo (43612) *(G-13744)*

City of Wadsworth 330 334-1581
365 College St Wadsworth (44281) *(G-14430)*

City of Wadsworth 330 334-1581
311 Broad St Wadsworth (44281) *(G-14431)*

City of Wellston 740 384-2428
203 E Broadway St Wellston (45692) *(G-14636)*

City of Westlake 440 871-3300
27216 Hilliard Blvd Cleveland (44145) *(G-3994)*

City of Westlake 440 835-6442
29800 Center Ridge Rd Westlake (44145) *(G-15049)*

City of Westlake 440 808-5700
28955 Hilliard Blvd Westlake (44145) *(G-15050)*

City of Willowick 440 516-3011
30100 Arnold Rd Willowick (44095) *(G-15235)*

City of Wooster 330 263-8100
1761 Beall Ave Wooster (44691) *(G-15321)*

City of Xenia 937 376-7260
966 Towler Rd Xenia (45385) *(G-15500)*

City of Xenia 937 376-7271
779 Ford Rd Xenia (45385) *(G-15501)*

City of Youngstown (PA) 330 742-8700
26 S Phelps St Bsmt Youngstown (44503) *(G-15578)*

City of Zanesville 740 455-0641
401 Market St Rm 1 Zanesville (43701) *(G-15781)*

City Service, Loveland *Also Called: Dill-Elam Inc (G-10135)*

City View Nursing & Rehab LLC 216 361-1414
6606 Carnegie Ave Cleveland (44103) *(G-3995)*

City Wide Fclty Sltons - Clmbu, Columbus *Also Called: Duncan Sales Inc (G-5793)*

Cityview Nrsing Rhbltation Ctr, Cleveland *Also Called: City View Nursing & Rehab LLC (G-3995)*

Ciulla Smith & Dale, Cleveland *Also Called: Ciulla Smith & Dale LLP (G-3996)*

Ciulla Smith & Dale LLP 440 439-4700
25 Tarbell Ave Bedford (44146) *(G-956)*

Ciulla Smith & Dale LLP (PA) 440 884-2036
6364 Pearl Rd Ste 4 Cleveland (44130) *(G-3996)*

Ciuni & Panichi Inc 216 831-7171
25201 Chagrin Blvd Ste 200 Cleveland (44122) *(G-3997)*

Civic Grdn Ctr Grter Cncinnati 513 221-0981
2715 Reading Rd Cincinnati (45206) *(G-2454)*

Civica CMI, Englewood *Also Called: Creative Microsystems Inc (G-8304)*

Civil & Environmental Cons Inc 513 985-0220
10300 Alliance Rd Blue Ash (45242) *(G-1150)*

Civil & Environmental Cons Inc 614 540-6633
250 W Old Wilson Bridge Rd Ste 260 Worthington (43085) *(G-15409)*

Civil Service Personnel Assn 330 434-2772
720 Wolf Ledges Pkwy Ste 203 Akron (44311) *(G-104)*

Civista Bancshares Inc (PA) 419 625-4121
100 E Water St Sandusky (44870) *(G-12880)*

Civista Bank 419 599-1065
122 E Washington St Napoleon (43545) *(G-11518)*

Civista Bank (HQ) 419 625-4121
100 E Water St Sandusky (44870) *(G-12881)*

ALPHABETIC SECTION

CJ Logistics America LLC.. 847 390-6800
   1260 W Laskey Rd Toledo (43612) *(G-13745)*

CJ LOGISTICS HOLDINGS AMERICA CORPORATION, West Jefferson *Also Called: CJ Logstics Holdings Amer Corp (G-14849)*

CJ Logstics Holdings Amer Corp.. 614 879-9659
   125 Enterprise Pkwy West Jefferson (43162) *(G-14849)*

CJ Mahan Construction Co LLC (PA).. 614 277-4545
   3458 Lewis Centre Way Grove City (43123) *(G-8909)*

Cjm Technologies, Dublin *Also Called: WD Partners Inc (G-8160)*

Cju Enterprises Inc.. 330 493-1800
   2830 Cleveland Ave Nw Canton (44709) *(G-1710)*

CK Construction Group Inc.. 614 901-8844
   6245 Westerville Rd Westerville (43081) *(G-14967)*

Cke Acquisition Co LLC.. 614 205-0242
   10 W Broad St Ste 2100 Columbus (43215) *(G-5577)*

Ckp Heating and Cooling LLC.. 330 791-3029
   555 N Main St Ste 5 North Canton (44720) *(G-11817)*

Cks & Associates MGT LLC.. 614 621-9710
   399 S Grant Ave Columbus (43215) *(G-5578)*

CL Zimmerman Delaware LLC.. 513 860-9300
   5115 Excello Ct West Chester (45069) *(G-14667)*

Claprood Roman J Co.. 614 221-5515
   242 N Grant Ave Columbus (43215) *(G-5579)*

Claremont Retirement Village.. 614 761-2011
   7041 Bent Tree Blvd Columbus (43235) *(G-5580)*

Clarion Hotel Suites, Blue Ash *Also Called: 5901 Pfffer Rd Htels Sites LLC (G-1120)*

Clarity Retail Services LLC.. 513 800-9369
   5115 Excello Ct West Chester (45069) *(G-14668)*

Clark Schaefer Hackett & Co (PA).. 937 226-0070
   10100 Innovation Dr Ste 400 Miamisburg (45342) *(G-11036)*

Clark Schaefer Hackett & Co.. 937 399-2000
   14 E Main St Ste 500 Springfield (45502) *(G-13229)*

Clark Brands LLC.. 330 723-9886
   427 N Court St Medina (44256) *(G-10821)*

Clark Cnty Bd Dvlpmntal Dsblti.. 937 328-5200
   110 W Leffel Ln Springfield (45506) *(G-13230)*

Clark Cnty Bd Dvlpmntal Dsblti.. 937 328-5240
   50 W Leffel Ln Springfield (45506) *(G-13231)*

Clark County Board of Developm (PA).. 937 328-2675
   2527 Kenton St Springfield (45505) *(G-13232)*

Clark County Combined Hlth Dst (PA).. 937 390-5600
   529 E Home Rd Springfield (45503) *(G-13233)*

Clark County Mrdd Trnsp, Springfield *Also Called: Clark Cnty Bd Dvlpmntal Dsblti (G-13231)*

Clark County Office, Springfield *Also Called: Miami Vly Child Dev Ctrs Inc (G-13274)*

Clark Memorial Home Assn.. 937 399-4262
   106 Kewbury Rd Springfield (45504) *(G-13234)*

Clark State Community College.. 937 328-3841
   300 S Fountain Ave Springfield (45506) *(G-13235)*

CLARK STATE COMMUNITY COLLEGE, Springfield *Also Called: Clark State Community College (G-13235)*

Clark Theders Insurance Agency.. 513 779-2800
   9938 Crescent Park Dr West Chester (45069) *(G-14669)*

Clark Trucking Inc.. 937 642-0335
   11590 Township Road 157 East Liberty (43319) *(G-8171)*

Clarkdietrich, West Chester *Also Called: Clarkwstern Dtrich Bldg System (G-14671)*

Clarkdietrich Engrg Svcs LLC.. 513 870-1100
   9050 Centre Pointe Dr Ste 400 West Chester (45069) *(G-14670)*

Clarke Detroit Diesel-Allison, Cincinnati *Also Called: Clarke Power Services Inc (G-2456)*

Clarke Fire Prtection Pdts Inc.. 513 771-2200
   11407 Rockfield Ct Cincinnati (45241) *(G-2455)*

Clarke Power Services Inc (PA).. 513 771-2200
   3133 E Kemper Rd Cincinnati (45241) *(G-2456)*

Clarkwstern Dtrich Bldg System (HQ).. 513 870-1100
   9050 Centre Pointe Dr Ste 400 West Chester (45069) *(G-14671)*

Clarkwstern Dtrich Bldg System, West Chester *Also Called: Clarkdietrich Engrg Svcs LLC (G-14670)*

Classic Accident Repair Center, Mentor *Also Called: Dcr Systems LLC (G-10932)*

Classic Automotive Group Inc.. 440 255-5511
   6877 Center St Mentor (44060) *(G-10922)*

Classic Bick Oldsmbile Cdliac.. 440 639-4500
   1700 Mentor Ave Painesville (44077) *(G-12222)*

Classic Brands, Chillicothe *Also Called: Litter Distributing Co Inc (G-2078)*

Classic Carriers, Versailles *Also Called: Classic Carriers Inc (G-14414)*

Classic Carriers Inc (PA).. 937 604-8118
   151 Industrial Pkwy Versailles (45380) *(G-14414)*

Classic Chevrolet, Mentor *Also Called: Classic Automotive Group Inc (G-10922)*

Classic Growers Co, Perry *Also Called: Cottage Gardens Inc (G-12305)*

Classic Medical Staffing LLC.. 216 688-0900
   15703 Lorain Ave Cleveland (44111) *(G-3998)*

Classic Oldsmobile, Painesville *Also Called: Classic Bick Oldsmbile Cdliac (G-12222)*

Classical Glass & Mirror, Mansfield *Also Called: J & B Acoustical Inc (G-10273)*

Claust LLC.. 440 783-2847
   27457 Royalton Rd Columbia Station (44028) *(G-5224)*

Clay Burley Products Co (PA).. 740 452-3633
   455 Gordon St Roseville (43777) *(G-12763)*

Clay Distributing Co.. 419 426-3051
   15025 E Us 224 Attica (44807) *(G-599)*

Claypool Electric Inc.. 740 653-5683
   1275 Lancaster Kirkersville Rd Nw Lancaster (43130) *(G-9702)*

Claypool Electrical Contg, Lancaster *Also Called: Claypool Electric Inc (G-9702)*

Clays Heritage Carpet Inc (PA).. 330 497-1280
   1440 N Main St Canton (44720) *(G-1711)*

Clayton Railroad Cnstr LLC.. 937 549-2952
   500 Lane Rd West Union (45693) *(G-14867)*

CLC, Columbus *Also Called: Construction Labor Contrs LLC (G-5684)*

Cle Transportation Company.. 567 805-4008
   203 Republic St Norwalk (44857) *(G-12005)*

Clean All Services, Sidney *Also Called: Clean All Services Inc (G-13023)*

Clean All Services Inc.. 937 498-4146
   324 Adams St Bldg 1 Sidney (45365) *(G-13023)*

Clean Hrbors Es Indus Svcs Inc.. 937 425-0512
   6151 Executive Blvd Dayton (45424) *(G-7235)*

Clean Innovations (PA).. 614 299-1187
   575 E 11th Ave Columbus (43211) *(G-5581)*

Clean Team Inc.. 419 537-8770
   419 N Westwood Ave Toledo (43607) *(G-13746)*

Cleanpro Janitorial Svc LLC.. 330 592-9860
   5026 Hudson Dr Stow (44224) *(G-13359)*

Clear Creek Applied Tech (PA).. 937 912-5438
   3855 Colonel Glenn Hwy Ste 100 Beavercreek (45324) *(G-872)*

Clearpath HM Hlth Hospice LLC.. 330 784-2162
   577 Grant St Ste C Akron (44311) *(G-105)*

Clearpath Home Health, Akron *Also Called: Clearpath HM Hlth Hospice LLC (G-105)*

Clearstead Advisors LLC.. 216 621-1090
   1100 Superior Ave E Ste 700 Cleveland (44114) *(G-3999)*

Clearsulting LLC (PA).. 440 488-4274
   1621 Euclid Ave Ste 2150 Cleveland (44115) *(G-4000)*

Clearwater Services Inc (PA).. 330 836-4946
   1411 Vernon Odom Blvd Akron (44320) *(G-106)*

Clearwater Systems, Akron *Also Called: Clearwater Services Inc (G-106)*

Cleary Company.. 614 459-4000
   989a Old Henderson Rd Columbus (43220) *(G-5582)*

Cleopatra Trucking, Columbus *Also Called: King Tut Logistics LLC (G-6117)*

Clerac LLC (DH).. 440 345-3999
   8249 Mohawk Dr Strongsville (44136) *(G-13448)*

Clermont Cnty Bd Dvlpmntal DSB.. 513 732-7015
   204 State Rte Hwy 50 Benton Rd Owensville (45160) *(G-12199)*

Clermont Cnty Cmmon Pleas Crt, Batavia *Also Called: County of Clermont (G-736)*

Clermont Cnty Hlth Recovery Bd, Batavia *Also Called: County of Clermont (G-737)*

Clermont Cnty Wtr Rsources Dept.. 513 732-7970
   4400 Haskell Ln Batavia (45103) *(G-732)*

Clermont Counseling Center (PA).. 513 947-7000
   43 E Main St Amelia (45102) *(G-416)*

Clermont Counseling Center.. 513 345-8555
   3730 Glenway Ave Cincinnati (45205) *(G-2457)*

Clermont County Cmnty Svcs Inc (PA).. 513 732-2277
   3003 Hospital Dr Batavia (45103) *(G-733)*

Clermont Hills Co LLC.. 513 752-4400
   4501 Eastgate Blvd Cincinnati (45245) *(G-2100)*

Clermont Recovery Center Inc.. 513 735-8100
   1088 Wasserman Way Ste C Batavia (45103) *(G-734)*

CLERMONT SENIOR SERVICES, Batavia *Also Called: Clermont Senior Services Inc (G-735)*
Clermont Senior Services Inc (PA)..513 724-1255
2085 James E Sauls Sr Dr Batavia (45103) *(G-735)*
Clevelan Clinic Hlth Sys W Reg (HQ)..................................216 476-7000
18101 Lorain Ave Cleveland (44111) *(G-4001)*
Cleveland 094, Cleveland *Also Called: Stanley Steemer Intl Inc (G-4942)*
Cleveland America Scores..216 881-7988
3631 Perkins Ave Ste 2ce Cleveland (44114) *(G-4002)*
Cleveland Anesthesia Group..216 901-5706
6161 Oak Tree Blvd Independence (44131) *(G-9419)*
Cleveland Arprt Hspitality LLC..440 871-6000
1100 Crocker Rd Westlake (44145) *(G-15051)*
Cleveland Ballet..216 320-9000
23020 Miles Rd Bedford Heights (44128) *(G-997)*
Cleveland Bchwood Hsptlity LLC..216 464-5950
3663 Park East Dr Beachwood (44122) *(G-777)*
Cleveland Browns..216 261-3401
26500 Curtiss Wright Pkwy Cleveland (44143) *(G-4003)*
Cleveland Browns, Berea *Also Called: Cleveland Browns Football LLC (G-1065)*
Cleveland Browns Football LLC..440 891-5000
76 Lou Groza Blvd Berea (44017) *(G-1065)*
Cleveland Cbd Hotel LLC..216 377-9000
651 Huron Rd E Cleveland (44115) *(G-4004)*
Cleveland Cement Contractors, Brooklyn Heights *Also Called: Cleveland Concrete Cnstr Inc (G-1415)*
Cleveland Child Care Inc..216 631-3211
3274 W 58th St Fl 1 Cleveland (44102) *(G-4005)*
CLEVELAND CHILDREN'S MUSEUM, Cleveland *Also Called: Childrens Museum of Cleveland (G-3970)*
Cleveland Christian Home Inc..216 671-0977
4500 Euclid Ave Cleveland (44103) *(G-4006)*
Cleveland Cinemas MGT Co Ltd..440 528-0355
13116 Shaker Sq Cleveland (44120) *(G-4007)*
Cleveland Clini, Cleveland *Also Called: Cleveland Clinic Foundation (G-4027)*
Cleveland Clinic..440 366-9444
303 Chestnut Commons Dr Elyria (44035) *(G-8236)*
Cleveland Clinic..216 374-0239
1508 Lauderdale Ave Lakewood (44107) *(G-9661)*
Cleveland Clinic, Beachwood *Also Called: Cleveland Clinic Foundation (G-781)*
Cleveland Clinic, Beachwood *Also Called: Cleveland Clinic Foundation (G-783)*
Cleveland Clinic, Cleveland *Also Called: C C F Vsclar Srgery At Mrymunt (G-3914)*
Cleveland Clinic, Cleveland *Also Called: Cleveland Clinic Cole Eye Inst (G-4009)*
Cleveland Clinic, Cleveland *Also Called: Cleveland Clinic Foundation (G-4010)*
Cleveland Clinic, Cleveland *Also Called: Cleveland Clinic Foundation (G-4013)*
Cleveland Clinic, Cleveland *Also Called: Cleveland Clinic Foundation (G-4018)*
Cleveland Clinic, Cleveland *Also Called: Cleveland Clinic Foundation (G-4019)*
Cleveland Clinic, Cleveland *Also Called: Cleveland Clinic Foundation (G-4023)*
Cleveland Clinic, Cleveland *Also Called: Lutheran Medical Center Inc (G-4511)*
Cleveland Clinic, Lorain *Also Called: Kolczun Klczun Orthpd Assoc In (G-10080)*
Cleveland Clinic, Norwalk *Also Called: Cleveland Clinic Foundation (G-12006)*
Cleveland Clinic, Strongsville *Also Called: Cleveland Clinic Foundation (G-13449)*
Cleveland Clinic ADM Campus, Beachwood *Also Called: Cleveland Clinic Foundation (G-782)*
Cleveland Clinic Avon Hospital..440 695-5000
33300 Cleveland Clinic Blvd Avon (44011) *(G-645)*
Cleveland Clinic Breast Center, Cleveland *Also Called: Cleveland Clinic Foundation (G-4026)*
Cleveland Clinic Childrens..440 826-0102
17800 Jefferson Park Rd Ste 101 Cleveland (44130) *(G-4008)*
Cleveland Clinic Cole Eye Inst..216 444-4508
9500 Euclid Ave Cleveland (44195) *(G-4009)*
Cleveland Clinic Fndtn-Cardio..440 695-4000
33100 Cleveland Clinic Blvd Avon (44011) *(G-646)*
Cleveland Clinic Foundation..330 864-8060
1 Park West Blvd Ste 150 Akron (44320) *(G-107)*
Cleveland Clinic Foundation..440 937-9099
33355 Health Campus Blvd Avon (44011) *(G-647)*
Cleveland Clinic Foundation..216 839-3000
26900 Cedar Rd Beachwood (44122) *(G-778)*
Cleveland Clinic Foundation..216 448-0770
3050 Science Park Dr Bldg 3 Beachwood (44122) *(G-779)*
Cleveland Clinic Foundation..216 831-0120
2000 Auburn Dr Ste 300 Beachwood (44122) *(G-780)*
Cleveland Clinic Foundation..216 448-0116
3025 Science Park Dr Beachwood (44122) *(G-781)*
Cleveland Clinic Foundation..800 223-2273
25900 Science Park Dr Bldg 2 Beachwood (44122) *(G-782)*
Cleveland Clinic Foundation..216 455-6400
3025 Science Park Dr Beachwood (44122) *(G-783)*
Cleveland Clinic Foundation..440 986-4000
2001 E Royalton Rd Broadview Heights (44147) *(G-1384)*
Cleveland Clinic Foundation..440 717-1370
2525 E Royalton Rd Ste 1 Broadview Heights (44147) *(G-1385)*
Cleveland Clinic Foundation..330 533-8350
3736 Boardman Canfield Rd Ste 1 Canfield (44406) *(G-1626)*
Cleveland Clinic Foundation..440 729-9000
8254 Mayfield Rd Ste 4 Chesterland (44026) *(G-2033)*
Cleveland Clinic Foundation..800 223-2273
2049 E 100th St Cleveland (44106) *(G-4010)*
Cleveland Clinic Foundation..800 223-2273
2111 E 96th St Cleveland (44106) *(G-4011)*
Cleveland Clinic Foundation..216 444-5755
10300 Carnegie Ave Bldg LI Cleveland (44106) *(G-4012)*
Cleveland Clinic Foundation..216 444-5715
2035 E 86th St Cleveland (44106) *(G-4013)*
Cleveland Clinic Foundation..216 448-4325
1950 Richmond Rd Cleveland (44124) *(G-4014)*
Cleveland Clinic Foundation..866 223-8100
10201 Carnegie Ave Ca Bldg Cleveland (44106) *(G-4015)*
Cleveland Clinic Foundation..216 444-1764
9500 Euclid Ave Cleveland (44195) *(G-4016)*
Cleveland Clinic Foundation..216 442-6700
315 Euclid Ave Cleveland (44114) *(G-4017)*
Cleveland Clinic Foundation..216 444-5600
2050 E 96th St Cleveland (44106) *(G-4018)*
Cleveland Clinic Foundation..216 445-4500
9105 Cedar Ave Cleveland (44106) *(G-4019)*
Cleveland Clinic Foundation (PA)..216 636-8335
9500 Euclid Ave Cleveland (44195) *(G-4020)*
Cleveland Clinic Foundation..216 445-6888
9500 Euclid Ave Fl 3r35 Cleveland (44195) *(G-4021)*
Cleveland Clinic Foundation..216 986-4000
5001 Rockside Rd Fl 1 Cleveland (44131) *(G-4022)*
Cleveland Clinic Foundation..216 444-2200
9500 Euclid Ave Cleveland (44195) *(G-4023)*
Cleveland Clinic Foundation..216 442-3412
10201 Carnegie Ave Cleveland (44106) *(G-4024)*
Cleveland Clinic Foundation..216 444-5540
9500 Euclid Ave Ste S51 Cleveland (44195) *(G-4025)*
Cleveland Clinic Foundation..216 444-6618
9500 Euclid Ave Aq2 Cleveland (44195) *(G-4026)*
Cleveland Clinic Foundation..216 444-2273
9500 Euclid Ave Cleveland (44195) *(G-4027)*
Cleveland Clinic Foundation..216 444-5437
9500 Euclid Ave Cleveland (44195) *(G-4028)*
Cleveland Clinic Foundation..216 445-6636
13333 Gerald Dr Ste Nb5 Cleveland (44130) *(G-4029)*
Cleveland Clinic Foundation..216 444-5000
9500 Euclid Ave Cleveland (44195) *(G-4030)*
Cleveland Clinic Foundation..216 444-5715
2045 E 89th St Cleveland (44106) *(G-4031)*
Cleveland Clinic Foundation..614 358-4223
425 Beecher Rd Ste B Columbus (43230) *(G-5583)*
Cleveland Clinic Foundation..234 815-5100
4389 Medina Rd Copley (44321) *(G-6950)*
Cleveland Clinic Foundation..330 923-9585
857 Graham Rd Cuyahoga Falls (44221) *(G-7062)*
Cleveland Clinic Foundation..833 427-5634
3600 W Market St Ste 200 Fairlawn (44333) *(G-8471)*
Cleveland Clinic Foundation..216 636-7400
6801 Brecksville Rd Ste 10 Independence (44131) *(G-9420)*
Cleveland Clinic Foundation..216 986-4312
5001 Rockside Rd Ste 700 Independence (44131) *(G-9421)*

ALPHABETIC SECTION — Cleveland Glass Block Inc

Cleveland Clinic Foundation 330 948-5523
225 Elyria St Lodi (44254) *(G-10018)*

Cleveland Clinic Foundation 440 988-5651
5700 Cooper Foster Park Rd W Ste A Lorain (44053) *(G-10065)*

Cleveland Clinic Foundation 440 282-7420
5172 Leavitt Rd Ste B Lorain (44053) *(G-10066)*

Cleveland Clinic Foundation 440 428-1111
2999 Mcmackin Rd Ste Ec1 Madison (44057) *(G-10212)*

Cleveland Clinic Foundation 440 250-5737
24700 Lorain Rd Ste 207 North Olmsted (44070) *(G-11897)*

Cleveland Clinic Foundation 440 327-1050
35105 Center Ridge North Ridgeville (44039) *(G-11925)*

Cleveland Clinic Foundation 419 660-6946
272 Benedict Ave Norwalk (44857) *(G-12006)*

Cleveland Clinic Foundation 419 609-2812
417 Quarry Lakes Dr Sandusky (44870) *(G-12882)*

Cleveland Clinic Foundation 216 444-2200
33001 Solon Rd Ste 112 Solon (44139) *(G-13076)*

Cleveland Clinic Foundation 440 878-2500
16761 Southpark Ctr Strongsville (44136) *(G-13449)*

Cleveland Clinic Foundation 330 334-4620
1 Park Centre Dr Wadsworth (44281) *(G-14432)*

Cleveland Clinic Foundation 440 647-0004
805 Patriot Dr Ste E Wellington (44090) *(G-14629)*

Cleveland Clinic Foundation 440 516-8896
2570 Som Center Rd Willoughby Hills (44094) *(G-15231)*

Cleveland Clinic Foundation 330 287-4500
1740 Cleveland Rd Wooster (44691) *(G-15322)*

Cleveland Clinic Foundation 330 287-4930
1739 Cleveland Rd Wooster (44691) *(G-15323)*

Cleveland Clinic Foundation, Cleveland *Also Called: Cleveland Clinic Foundation (G-4016)*

Cleveland Clinic Foundation, North Olmsted *Also Called: Cleveland Clinic Foundation (G-11897)*

CLEVELAND CLINIC HEALTH SYSTEM, Cleveland *Also Called: Cleveland Clinic Foundation (G-4020)*

CLEVELAND CLINIC HEALTH SYSTEM, Cleveland *Also Called: Marymount Health Care Systems (G-4530)*

CLEVELAND CLINIC HEALTH SYSTEM, Euclid *Also Called: Euclid Hospital (G-8341)*

Cleveland Clinic Health System, Independence *Also Called: Cleveland Clinic Foundation (G-9420)*

Cleveland Clinic Health System, North Ridgeville *Also Called: Cleveland Clinic Foundation (G-11925)*

Cleveland Clinic HM Care Svcs, Cleveland *Also Called: Ccf Health Care Ventures Inc (G-3946)*

Cleveland Clinic Mercy Hosp 330 823-3856
149 E Simpson St Alliance (44601) *(G-380)*

Cleveland Clinic Mercy Hosp 330 966-8884
6200 Whipple Ave Nw Canton (44720) *(G-1712)*

Cleveland Clinic Mercy Hosp 330 588-4892
1459 Superior Ave Ne Canton (44705) *(G-1713)*

Cleveland Clinic Mercy Hosp 330 649-4380
4369 Whipple Ave Nw Canton (44718) *(G-1714)*

Cleveland Clinic Mercy Hosp 330 489-1329
1320 Mercy Dr Nw Canton (44708) *(G-1715)*

Cleveland Clinic Mercy Hosp 330 492-8803
1320 Mercy Dr Nw Canton (44708) *(G-1716)*

Cleveland Clinic Mercy Hosp (HQ) 330 489-1000
1320 Mercy Dr Nw Canton (44708) *(G-1717)*

Cleveland Clinic Mercy Hosp 330 627-7641
125 Canton Rd Nw Carrollton (44615) *(G-1904)*

Cleveland Clinic Pain MGT Dept, Solon *Also Called: Cleveland Clinic Foundation (G-13076)*

Cleveland Clinic Star Imaging, Columbus *Also Called: Cleveland Clinic Foundation (G-5583)*

Cleveland Clinic Wooster, Wooster *Also Called: Cleveland Clinic Foundation (G-15322)*

Cleveland Clinic Wooster, Wooster *Also Called: Cleveland Clnic Hlth Systm-AST (G-15324)*

Cleveland Clinic, The, Chesterland *Also Called: Cleveland Clinic Foundation (G-2033)*

Cleveland Clnc Bchwd Fmly Ctr 216 839-3100
26900 Cedar Rd Lbby Cleveland (44122) *(G-4032)*

Cleveland Clnic Akron Gen Smmi, Fairlawn *Also Called: Cleveland Clinic Foundation (G-8471)*

Cleveland Clnic Akron Gen Vsti (PA) 330 745-1601
1 Home Care Pl Akron (44320) *(G-108)*

Cleveland Clnic Akron Gen Vsti 330 677-4666
4080 Brimfield Plz Kent (44240) *(G-9564)*

Cleveland Clnic Chgrin FLS FML 440 893-9393
551 Washington St Chagrin Falls (44022) *(G-1956)*

Cleveland Clnic Chld Hosp For (HQ) 216 721-5400
2801 Martin Luther King Jr Dr Cleveland (44104) *(G-4033)*

Cleveland Clnic Chld Inptent H, Cleveland *Also Called: Cleveland Clinic Foundation (G-4028)*

Cleveland Clnic Ctr For Cntnue, Beachwood *Also Called: Cleveland Clinic Foundation (G-779)*

Cleveland Clnic Edctl Fndtion 216 444-1157
9500 Euclid Ave Cleveland (44195) *(G-4034)*

Cleveland Clnic Hlth Systm-AST 440 449-4500
6780 Mayfield Rd Cleveland (44124) *(G-4035)*

Cleveland Clnic Hlth Systm-AST 216 692-7555
18901 Lake Shore Blvd Cleveland (44119) *(G-4036)*

Cleveland Clnic Hlth Systm-AST 330 468-0190
863 W Aurora Rd Northfield (44067) *(G-11954)*

Cleveland Clnic Hlth Systm-AST 330 287-4830
721 E Milltown Rd Wooster (44691) *(G-15324)*

Cleveland Clnic Hlth Systm-Wst 216 518-3444
5555 Transportation Blvd Cleveland (44125) *(G-4037)*

Cleveland Clnic Hlth Systm-Wst 216 476-7606
18200 Lorain Ave Cleveland (44111) *(G-4038)*

Cleveland Clnic Hlth Systm-Wst 440 716-9810
24700 Lorain Rd Ste 100 North Olmsted (44070) *(G-11898)*

Cleveland Clnic Hlth Systm-Wst 216 491-6000
20000 Harvard Ave Warrensville Heights (44122) *(G-14579)*

Cleveland Clnic HSP Fincl Dept, Cleveland *Also Called: Cleveland Clinic Foundation (G-4030)*

Cleveland Clnic Jurnl Medicine, Cleveland *Also Called: Cleveland Clnic Edctl Fndtion (G-4034)*

Cleveland Clnic Lrner Cllege M 216 445-3853
9500 Euclid Ave Cleveland (44195) *(G-4039)*

Cleveland Clnic Lyndhrst Cmpus, Cleveland *Also Called: Cleveland Clinic Foundation (G-4014)*

Cleveland Clnic Rhbltion Physc 440 516-5400
29017 Chardon Rd Willoughby Hills (44092) *(G-15232)*

Cleveland Clnic Tssig Cncer Ct, Cleveland *Also Called: Cleveland Clinic Foundation (G-4015)*

Cleveland Concrete Cnstr Inc (PA) 216 741-3954
4823 Van Epps Rd Brooklyn Heights (44131) *(G-1415)*

Cleveland Construction Inc 440 255-8000
5390 Courseview Dr Ste 200 Mason (45040) *(G-10539)*

Cleveland Construction Inc (PA) 440 255-8000
8620 Tyler Blvd Mentor (44060) *(G-10923)*

Cleveland Dental Institute LLC 216 727-0234
4071 Lee Rd Ste 260 Cleveland (44128) *(G-4040)*

Cleveland Destination 216 875-6652
334 Euclid Ave Cleveland (44114) *(G-4041)*

CLEVELAND DEVELOPMENT FOUNDATI, Cleveland *Also Called: Greater Cleveland Partnership (G-4332)*

Cleveland Ear Nose Throat Ctr 330 723-6673
970 E Washington St Ste 6a Medina (44256) *(G-10822)*

Cleveland East Hotel LLC 216 378-9191
26300 Harvard Rd Cleveland (44122) *(G-4042)*

Cleveland East Htl LLC 513 794-2566
8044 Montgomery Rd Ste 385 Cincinnati (45236) *(G-2458)*

Cleveland Elc Illuminating Co (HQ) 800 589-3101
76 S Main St Akron (44308) *(G-109)*

Cleveland Electric Labs, Twinsburg *Also Called: Cleveland Electric Labs Co (G-14177)*

Cleveland Electric Labs Co (PA) 800 447-2207
1776 Enterprise Pkwy Twinsburg (44087) *(G-14177)*

Cleveland Emergency Med Svc, Cleveland *Also Called: City of Cleveland (G-3982)*

Cleveland Eye Clinic, Cleveland *Also Called: Robert Wiley MD Inc (G-4847)*

Cleveland Eye Lser Srgery Ctr 440 777-8400
22715 Fairview Center Dr Cleveland (44126) *(G-4043)*

Cleveland Foundation 216 861-3810
6601 Euclid Ave Cleveland (44103) *(G-4044)*

Cleveland FP Inc (PA) 216 249-4900
12819 Coit Rd Cleveland (44108) *(G-4045)*

Cleveland Glass Block Inc (PA) 216 531-6363
4566 E 71st St Cleveland (44105) *(G-4046)*

Cleveland Glass Block Inc 614 252-5888
3091 E 14th Ave Columbus (43219) *(G-5584)*

Cleveland Granite & Marble LLC 216 291-7637
   4121 Carnegie Ave Cleveland (44103) *(G-4047)*

Cleveland Guardians Basbal LLC (PA) 216 420-4487
   2401 Ontario St Cleveland (44115) *(G-4048)*

Cleveland Heartlab Inc 866 358-9828
   6701 Carnegie Ave Ste 500 Cleveland (44103) *(G-4049)*

Cleveland Heights Medical Ctr, Cleveland Heights *Also Called: Metrohealth System* *(G-5181)*

Cleveland Home Title Inc 440 788-7100
   2035 Crocker Rd Ste 201 Cleveland (44145) *(G-4050)*

Cleveland Hopkins Intl Arprt 216 265-6000
   5300 Riverside Dr Cleveland (44135) *(G-4051)*

Cleveland Idealease East, Walton Hills *Also Called: Rush Truck Leasing Inc* *(G-14479)*

Cleveland Indians Inc 216 420-4487
   2401 Ontario St Cleveland (44115) *(G-4052)*

Cleveland Jazz Orchestra 419 908-8858
   6027 Triple Crown Dr Medina (44256) *(G-10823)*

Cleveland Job Corps Center 216 541-2500
   13421 Coit Rd Cleveland (44110) *(G-4053)*

Cleveland Magazine, Cleveland *Also Called: Great Lakes Publishing Company* *(G-4330)*

Cleveland Marble Mosaic Co (PA) 216 749-2840
   4595 Hinckley Industrial Pkwy Cleveland (44109) *(G-4054)*

Cleveland Metro Bar Assn 216 696-3525
   1375 E 9th St Fl 2 Cleveland (44114) *(G-4055)*

Cleveland Metroparks (PA) 216 635-3200
   4101 Fulton Pkwy Cleveland (44144) *(G-4056)*

Cleveland Metroparks 216 661-6500
   3900 Wildlife Way Cleveland (44109) *(G-4057)*

Cleveland Metroparks Zoo, Cleveland *Also Called: Cleveland Metroparks* *(G-4057)*

Cleveland Motor Carrier Inc 440 901-9192
   204 Parkway Blvd Madison (44057) *(G-10213)*

Cleveland Mseum of Ntral Hstor 216 231-4600
   1 Wade Oval Dr Cleveland (44106) *(G-4058)*

Cleveland Municipal School Dst 216 459-4200
   5100 Biddulph Ave Cleveland (44144) *(G-4059)*

Cleveland Municipal School Dst 216 521-6511
   10427 Detroit Ave Cleveland (44102) *(G-4060)*

Cleveland Municipal School Dst 216 838-8700
   11801 Worthington Ave Cleveland (44111) *(G-4061)*

Cleveland Municipal School Dst 216 634-7005
   3832 Ridge Rd Cleveland (44144) *(G-4062)*

Cleveland Orchestra, The, Cleveland *Also Called: Musical Arts Association* *(G-4613)*

Cleveland Plant & Flower Co, Cleveland *Also Called: The Cleveland Plant and Flower Company* *(G-4995)*

Cleveland Quarries, Vermilion *Also Called: Irg Operating LLC* *(G-14405)*

Cleveland Research Company LLC 216 649-7250
   1375 E 9th St Ste 2700 Cleveland (44114) *(G-4063)*

Cleveland Rest Oper Ltd Partnr 216 328-1121
   9700 Rockside Rd Ste 150 Cleveland (44125) *(G-4064)*

Cleveland S Hospitality LLC 216 447-1300
   6200 Quarry Ln Cleveland (44131) *(G-4065)*

CLEVELAND SIGHT CENTER, Cleveland *Also Called: Cleveland Soc For The Blind* *(G-4067)*

Cleveland Skating Club 216 791-2800
   2500 Kemper Rd Cleveland (44120) *(G-4066)*

Cleveland Soc For The Blind 216 791-8118
   1909 E 101st St Cleveland (44106) *(G-4067)*

Cleveland Supplyone Inc (DH) 216 514-7000
   26801b Fargo Ave Cleveland (44146) *(G-4068)*

Cleveland Tank & Supply Inc 216 771-8265
   6560 Juniata Ave Cleveland (44103) *(G-4069)*

Cleveland Teachers Union Inc 216 861-7676
   1228 Euclid Ave Ste 300 Cleveland (44115) *(G-4070)*

Cleveland Thermal LLC 216 241-3636
   1921 Hamilton Ave Cleveland (44114) *(G-4071)*

Cleveland Unlimited Inc
   7165 E Pleasant Valley Rd Independence (44131) *(G-9422)*

Cleveland Water Department 216 664-3168
   5953 Deering Ave Cleveland (44130) *(G-4072)*

Cleveland Westin Downtown 440 730-4338
   777 Saint Clair Ave Ne Cleveland (44114) *(G-4073)*

Cleveland Yachting Club Inc 440 333-1155
   200 Yacht Club Dr Cleveland (44116) *(G-4074)*

Cleveland-Cliffs Intl Holdg Co 216 694-5700
   1100 Superior Ave E Fl 18 Cleveland (44114) *(G-4075)*

Clevland Business Consultants, Cleveland *Also Called: Independent Personnel Services* *(G-4407)*

Clevland Clinic Foundation 216 445-5121
   9500 Uclid Ave Desk 100 Cleveland (44195) *(G-4076)*

Clgt Solutions LLC 740 920-4795
   1670 Columbus Rd Ste C Granville (43023) *(G-8852)*

CLI Incorporated 419 668-8840
   306 S Norwalk Rd W Norwalk (44857) *(G-12007)*

Click4care Inc 614 431-3700
   50 S Liberty St Ste 200 Powell (43065) *(G-12588)*

Cliff Viessman Inc 937 454-6490
   5560 Brentlinger Dr Dayton (45414) *(G-7236)*

Cliffs Logan County Coal LLC 216 694-5700
   200 Public Sq Ste 3300 Cleveland (44114) *(G-4077)*

Cliffs Mining Services Company 218 262-5913
   1100 Superior Ave E Ste 1500 Cleveland (44114) *(G-4078)*

Cliffs Natural Resources Explo 216 694-5700
   200 Public Sq Ste 3300 Cleveland (44114) *(G-4079)*

Cliffs Resources Inc (HQ) 216 694-5700
   200 Public Sq Ste 200 Cleveland (44114) *(G-4080)*

Cliffs UTAC Holding LLC 216 694-5700
   200 Public Sq Ste 3300 Cleveland (44114) *(G-4081)*

Clifton Care Center Inc 513 530-1600
   625 Probasco St Cincinnati (45220) *(G-2459)*

Clifton Heat Treating, Maple Heights *Also Called: Clifton Steel Company* *(G-10335)*

Clifton Steel Company 216 662-6111
   16500 Rockside Rd Maple Heights (44137) *(G-10335)*

Clifton Steel Company (HQ) 216 662-6111
   16500 Rockside Rd Maple Heights (44137) *(G-10336)*

Climaco Wlcox Peca Grofoli Lpa (PA) 216 621-8484
   1001 Lakeside Ave E Cleveland (44114) *(G-4082)*

Climate Pros LLC 216 881-5200
   5309 Hamilton Ave Cleveland (44114) *(G-4083)*

Climate Pros LLC 330 744-2732
   52 E Myrtle Ave Youngstown (44507) *(G-15579)*

Clinical Management Cons Inc 440 638-5000
   1400 W 10th St Ste 301 Cleveland (44113) *(G-4084)*

Clinical Technology Inc 440 526-0160
   7005 S Edgerton Rd Brecksville (44141) *(G-1351)*

Clinicl Otcms Mngmnt Syst LLC 330 650-9900
   9200 S Hills Blvd Ste 200 Broadview Heights (44147) *(G-1386)*

Clinix Healthcare LLC 614 792-5422
   5080 Tuttle Crossing Blvd Ste 300 Dublin (43016) *(G-7965)*

Clinlogix LLC (HQ) 215 855-9054
   6750 Wales Rd Northwood (43619) *(G-11972)*

Clintnvlle Bchwold Cmnty Rsrce 614 268-3539
   3222 N High St Columbus (43202) *(G-5585)*

Clinton Alum & Stainless Stl, New Franklin *Also Called: Clinton Aluminum Acquisition LLC* *(G-11614)*

Clinton Aluminum, Norton *Also Called: Clinton Aluminum Dist Inc* *(G-11992)*

Clinton Aluminum Acquisition LLC 330 882-6743
   6270 Van Buren Rd New Franklin (44216) *(G-11614)*

Clinton Aluminum Dist Inc 866 636-7640
   5120 Waynesville Jamestown Rd Jamestown (45335) *(G-9534)*

Clinton Aluminum Dist Inc (PA) 330 882-6743
   2811 Eastern Rd Norton (44203) *(G-11992)*

Clinton Cnty Cmnty Action Prgr (PA) 937 382-8365
   789 N Nelson Ave Wilmington (45177) *(G-15248)*

Clinton Memorial Hospital (PA) 937 382-6611
   610 W Main St Wilmington (45177) *(G-15249)*

Clippard Instrument Lab Inc (PA) 513 521-4261
   7390 Colerain Ave Cincinnati (45239) *(G-2460)*

CLIPPARD MINIMATIC, Cincinnati *Also Called: Clippard Instrument Lab Inc* *(G-2460)*

Clipper Magazine LLC 513 794-4100
   4601 Malsbary Rd # 1 Blue Ash (45242) *(G-1151)*

Clm Pallet Recycling Inc 614 272-5761
   4311 Janitrol Rd Ste 150 Columbus (43228) *(G-5586)*

Clopay Corporation (HQ) 800 282-2260
   8585 Duke Blvd Mason (45040) *(G-10540)*

ALPHABETIC SECTION

Clopay Transportation Company.. 937 440-6790
   1400 W Market St Troy (45373) *(G-14131)*

Close To Home Health Care Ctr, Columbus *Also Called: Nationwide Childrens Hospital (G-6316)*

Close To Home Health Care Ctr, Westerville *Also Called: Nationwide Childrens Hospital (G-14915)*

Closeout Distribution LLC (HQ).. 614 278-6800
   4900 E Dublin Granville Rd Westerville (43081) *(G-14968)*

Closets By Design.. 513 469-6130
   11275 Deerfield Rd Blue Ash (45242) *(G-1152)*

Clossman Catering Incorporated... 513 942-7744
   3725 Symmes Rd Hamilton (45015) *(G-9029)*

Cloudbreak Health LLC.. 614 468-6110
   6400 Huntley Rd Columbus (43229) *(G-5587)*

Clouse Construction Corp (PA)... 419 448-1365
   4382 Township Road 90 New Riegel (44853) *(G-11678)*

Clovehitch, Granville *Also Called: Clgt Solutions LLC (G-8852)*

Cloverleaf Suites, Dublin *Also Called: Hotel 2345 LLC (G-8031)*

Cloverleaf Transport Co.. 419 599-5015
   1165 Independence Dr Napoleon (43545) *(G-11519)*

Clovernook Inc (PA).. 513 605-4000
   7025 Clovernook Ave Cincinnati (45231) *(G-2461)*

Clovernook Inc.. 513 605-4000
   7025 Clovernook Ave Cincinnati (45231) *(G-2462)*

Clovernook Country Club.. 513 521-0333
   2035 W Galbraith Rd Cincinnati (45239) *(G-2463)*

Clovernook Ctr For Blind Vslly (PA).. 513 522-3860
   7000 Hamilton Ave Cincinnati (45231) *(G-2464)*

Clovernook Hlth Care Pavilion, Cincinnati *Also Called: Clovernook Inc (G-2461)*

Clovernook Nursing Center, Cincinnati *Also Called: Clovernook Inc (G-2462)*

Clovervale Farms LLC (DH).. 440 960-0146
   8133 Cooper Foster Park Rd Amherst (44001) *(G-426)*

Clovervale Foods, Amherst *Also Called: Clovervale Farms LLC (G-426)*

Clp Gw Sandusky Tenant LP... 419 609-6000
   4600 Milan Rd Sandusky (44870) *(G-12883)*

Cls Facilities Management Svcs, Mentor *Also Called: Cls Facilities MGT Svcs Inc (G-10924)*

Cls Facilities MGT Svcs Inc... 440 602-4600
   8061 Tyler Blvd Mentor (44060) *(G-10924)*

Cls Group, Norton *Also Called: Capital Land Services Inc (G-11991)*

Club 51 Fitness, Centerville *Also Called: Centerville Fitness Inc (G-1940)*

Clubessential LLC (PA).. 800 448-1475
   9987 Carver Rd Blue Ash (45242) *(G-1153)*

Clubessential Holdings, Blue Ash *Also Called: Clubessential LLC (G-1153)*

Clum Creative, Cleveland *Also Called: Clum Media Inc (G-4085)*

Clum Media Inc... 216 239-1525
   1419 E 40th St Cleveland (44103) *(G-4085)*

Clunk Hoose Co Lpa... 330 922-5492
   495 Wolf Ledges Pkwy Ste 1 Akron (44311) *(G-110)*

Clutch Interactive, Dublin *Also Called: G2o LLC (G-8018)*

Clyo Internal Medicine Inc... 937 435-5857
   7073 Clyo Rd Centerville (45459) *(G-1941)*

Cmbb LLC.. 937 652-2151
   417 E Water St Urbana (43078) *(G-14304)*

Cmbf Products Inc... 330 725-4941
   111 S Elmwood Ave Medina (44256) *(G-10824)*

CMC Group Inc (PA)... 419 354-2591
   12836 S Dixie Hwy Bowling Green (43402) *(G-1313)*

Cmdm, Dublin *Also Called: Advocate Rcm LLC (G-7921)*

Cmp I Blue Ash Owner LLC.. 513 733-4334
   4625 Lake Forest Dr Blue Ash (45242) *(G-1154)*

CMS, Stow *Also Called: Custom Movers Services Inc (G-13462)*

CMS & Co Management Svcs Inc.. 440 989-5200
   3905 Oberlin Ave Lorain (44053) *(G-10067)*

CMS Business Services LLC... 740 687-0577
   416 N Mount Pleasant Ave Lancaster (43130) *(G-9703)*

CMS Customer Solutions, Columbus *Also Called: Continntal Mssage Solution Inc (G-5699)*

CMS Mortgage Services, Independence *Also Called: Sirva Mortgage Inc (G-9483)*

Cmso, Cincinnati *Also Called: Chicago Mso Inc (G-2354)*

Cmt II Advisors LLC.. 937 434-3095
   6485 Centerville Business Pkwy Centerville (45459) *(G-1942)*

Cnd Machine, Massillon *Also Called: C-N-D Industries Inc (G-10633)*

CNG Financial Corporation (PA)... 513 336-7735
   7755 Montgomery Rd Ste 400 Cincinnati (45236) *(G-2465)*

CNG Holdings Inc.. 513 336-7735
   7755 Montgomery Rd Ste 400 Cincinnati (45236) *(G-2466)*

Cni Thl Ops LLC.. 937 890-6112
   7087 Miller Ln Dayton (45414) *(G-7237)*

Cnsld Humacare- Employee MGT (PA)... 513 605-3522
   9435 Waterstone Blvd Ste 250 Cincinnati (45249) *(G-2467)*

Co Hatch LLC.. 614 368-1810
   1554 Polaris Pkwy Columbus (43240) *(G-5253)*

Coact Associates Ltd... 866 646-4400
   2748 Centennial Rd Toledo (43617) *(G-13747)*

COAD, Athens *Also Called: Corportion For Ohio Applchian (G-562)*

Coal Grove Long Term Care Inc... 740 532-0449
   813 1/2 Marion Pike Ironton (45638) *(G-9506)*

Coal Resources Inc (PA)... 216 765-1240
   46226 National Rd Saint Clairsville (43950) *(G-12785)*

Coal Services Inc.. 740 795-5220
   155 Highway 7 S Powhatan Point (43942) *(G-12610)*

Coal Services Group, Powhatan Point *Also Called: Coal Services Inc (G-12610)*

Coalition For Enrgy Ecnmic Rvt, Columbus *Also Called: Appalachian Power Company (G-5374)*

Coast To Coast, Avon Lake *Also Called: Bearing Technologies Ltd (G-675)*

Coastal Ridge Management LLC.. 614 339-4608
   80 E Rich St Ste 220 Columbus (43215) *(G-5588)*

Coastal Ridge Real Estate, Columbus *Also Called: Coastal Ridge Management LLC (G-5588)*

Coates Car Care Inc... 330 652-4180
   59 Youngstown Warren Rd Niles (44446) *(G-11785)*

Coaxial Cmmnctons of Sthern OH (PA).. 513 797-4400
   700 Ackerman Rd Ste 280 Columbus (43202) *(G-5589)*

Coba/Select Sires Inc (PA)... 614 878-5333
   1224 Alton Darby Creek Rd Columbus (43228) *(G-5590)*

Cobb Motel Company LLC... 513 336-8871
   9665 S Mason Montgomery Rd Mason (45040) *(G-10541)*

Coblentz Distributing Inc (PA)... 330 893-3895
   3850 State Route 39 Millersburg (44654) *(G-11277)*

Coca-Cola, Akron *Also Called: Central Coca-Cola Btlg Co Inc (G-86)*

Coca-Cola, Circleville *Also Called: Central Coca-Cola Btlg Co Inc (G-3705)*

Coca-Cola, Toledo *Also Called: Central Coca-Cola Btlg Co Inc (G-13727)*

Cocca Development Ltd.. 330 729-1010
   100 Debartolo Pl Ste 400 Youngstown (44512) *(G-15580)*

Cochin Technologies LLC... 440 941-4856
   37854 Briar Lakes Dr Avon (44011) *(G-648)*

Coda, Columbus *Also Called: Central Ohio Diabetes Assn (G-5537)*

Codex Techworks Inc... 614 486-9900
   1500 W 3rd Ave Columbus (43212) *(G-5591)*

Coffee Break Corporation.. 513 841-1100
   1940 Losantiville Ave Cincinnati (45237) *(G-2468)*

Coffman Branch, Springboro *Also Called: Young MNS Chrstn Assn Grter Dy (G-13210)*

Cogun Inc... 330 549-5321
   11369 Market St North Lima (44452) *(G-11887)*

Cohen & Company Ltd.. 330 374-1040
   3500 Embassy Pkwy Ste 100 Akron (44333) *(G-111)*

Cohen & Company Ltd.. 330 743-1040
   201 E Commerce St Ste 400 Youngstown (44503) *(G-15581)*

Cohen Brothers Inc (PA)... 513 422-3696
   1520 14th Ave Middletown (45044) *(G-11158)*

Cohen Electronics Inc... 513 425-6911
   3120 S Verity Pkwy Middletown (45044) *(G-11159)*

Cohen Middletown, Middletown *Also Called: Cohen Electronics Inc (G-11159)*

Cohesion, Cincinnati *Also Called: Cohesion Corporation (G-2469)*

Cohesion Consulting LLC.. 513 587-7700
   5151 Pfeiffer Rd Ste 105 Blue Ash (45242) *(G-1155)*

Cohesion Corporation... 813 999-3101
   511 W Bay St Ste 480 Cincinnati (45242) *(G-2469)*

Coho Creative LLC.. 513 751-7500
   2331 Victory Pkwy Cincinnati (45206) *(G-2470)*

Coilplus Inc.. 937 778-8884
   100 Steelway Dr Piqua (45356) *(G-12437)*

Coilplus Inc 614 866-1338
  4801 Gateway Blvd Springfield (45502) *(G-13236)*

Coilplus Inc 937 322-4455
  4801 Gateway Blvd Springfield (45502) *(G-13237)*

Coilplus Berwick, Piqua *Also Called: Coilplus Inc (G-12437)*

Coin World, Sidney *Also Called: Amos Media Company (G-13018)*

Coit, Cincinnati *Also Called: Velco Inc (G-3618)*

Coit, Cleveland *Also Called: Miles Cleaning Services Inc (G-4582)*

Coit Clg & Restoration Svcs, Bedford Heights *Also Called: B&L Acquisition Group LLC (G-994)*

Colaianni Construction Inc 740 769-2362
  2141 State Route 150 Dillonvale (43917) *(G-7869)*

Colas Construction USA Inc 513 272-5648
  7374 Main St Cincinnati (45244) *(G-2471)*

Colas Solutions LLC 513 272-5648
  7374 Main St Cincinnati (45244) *(G-2472)*

Cold Jet, Loveland *Also Called: Cold Jet LLC (G-10132)*

Cold Jet LLC (PA) 513 831-3211
  6283 Tri Ridge Blvd Pmb 100 Loveland (45140) *(G-10132)*

Coldliner Express, Columbus *Also Called: Coldliner Express Inc (G-5592)*

Coldliner Express Inc 614 570-0836
  4921 Vulcan Ave Columbus (43228) *(G-5592)*

Coldstream Country Club 513 231-3900
  400 Asbury Rd Cincinnati (45255) *(G-2473)*

Coldwell Banker, Beavercreek Township *Also Called: Coldwell Bnkr Hrtg Rltors LLC (G-934)*

Coldwell Banker, Columbus *Also Called: Coldwell Banker Residential (G-5593)*

Coldwell Banker, Dayton *Also Called: Coldwell Bnkr Hrtg Rltors LLC (G-7238)*

Coldwell Banker, Newark *Also Called: Mc Mahon Realestate Co (G-11725)*

Coldwell Banker, Poland *Also Called: Coldwell Banker First Place RE (G-12503)*

Coldwell Banker, Springboro *Also Called: Coldwell Bnkr Hrtg Rltors LLC (G-13197)*

Coldwell Banker, Toledo *Also Called: Haynes Real Estate Inc (G-13837)*

Coldwell Banker, West Chester *Also Called: Coldwell Banker West Shell (G-14672)*

Coldwell Banker First Place RE 330 726-8161
  1275 Boardman Poland Rd Ste 1 Poland (44514) *(G-12503)*

Coldwell Banker Residential 954 771-2600
  5975 Cleveland Ave Columbus (43231) *(G-5593)*

Coldwell Banker West Shell 513 271-7200
  7203 Wooster Pike Cincinnati (45227) *(G-2474)*

Coldwell Banker West Shell 513 777-7900
  7311 Tylers Corner Dr West Chester (45069) *(G-14672)*

Coldwell Bnkr Hrtg Rltors Dyt 937 482-0082
  4060 Executive Dr Beavercreek (45430) *(G-920)*

Coldwell Bnkr Hrtg Rltors LLC 937 426-6060
  4139 Colonel Glenn Hwy Beavercreek Township (44431) *(G-934)*

Coldwell Bnkr Hrtg Rltors LLC (PA) 937 434-7600
  4486 Indian Ripple Rd Dayton (45440) *(G-7238)*

Coldwell Bnkr Hrtg Rltors LLC 937 435-7759
  20 S Main St Springboro (45066) *(G-13197)*

Cole Eye Institute, Beachwood *Also Called: Cleveland Clinic Foundation (G-780)*

Cole Valley Motor Company Ltd 330 372-1665
  4111 Elm Rd Ne Warren (44483) *(G-14509)*

Cole, Benton DDS, Cleveland *Also Called: Periodontal Associates Inc (G-4740)*

Coleman Data Solutions, Kent *Also Called: Coleman Professional Svcs Inc (G-9565)*

Coleman Professional Services 330 394-8831
  3043 Sanitarium Rd Ste 2 Akron (44312) *(G-112)*

Coleman Professional Svcs Inc 330 744-2991
  3043 Sanitarium Rd Ste 2 Akron (44312) *(G-113)*

Coleman Professional Svcs Inc (PA) 330 673-1347
  5982 Rhodes Rd Kent (44240) *(G-9565)*

Coleman Spohn Corporation (PA) 216 431-8070
  1775 E 45th St Cleveland (44103) *(G-4086)*

Colerain Animal Clinic Inc (PA) 513 923-4400
  6340 Colerain Ave Cincinnati (45239) *(G-2475)*

Colerain Dry Rdge Chldcare Ltd 513 923-4300
  3998 Dry Ridge Rd Cincinnati (45252) *(G-2476)*

Colerain Township 740 633-5778
  53979 Colerain Pike Martins Ferry (43935) *(G-10465)*

Colia Group LLC 614 270-4545
  3271 Kady Ln Columbus (43232) *(G-5594)*

Collaborative Inc 419 242-7405
  1 Seagate Ste 118 Toledo (43604) *(G-13748)*

Collections Acquisition Co LLC 614 944-5788
  2 Easton Oval Ste 210 Columbus (43219) *(G-5595)*

Collector Wells Intl Inc 614 888-6263
  6360 Huntley Rd Columbus (43229) *(G-5596)*

College Conservatory of Music, Cincinnati *Also Called: University of Cincinnati (G-3577)*

College Now Grter Clveland Inc (PA) 216 241-5587
  1500 W 3rd St Ste 125 Cleveland (44113) *(G-4087)*

College of Optometry, Columbus *Also Called: Student Vol Opt Serv To Humnty (G-6724)*

College Park HM Hlth Care Plus, Coshocton *Also Called: College Park Inc (G-6978)*

College Park Inc 740 623-4607
  380 Browns Ln Ste 7 Coshocton (43812) *(G-6978)*

Colliers International 614 436-9800
  2 Miranova Pl Ste 900 Columbus (43215) *(G-5597)*

Colliers International, Cincinnati *Also Called: West Shell Commercial Inc (G-3657)*

Colliers International, Columbus *Also Called: Adena Commercial LLC (G-5244)*

Colliers Turley Martin Tucker, Cincinnati *Also Called: Cassidy Trley Coml RE Svcs Inc (G-2319)*

Collins Assoc Tchncal Svcs Inc 740 574-2320
  7991 Ohio River Rd Wheelersburg (45694) *(G-15128)*

Collinwood Shale Brick Sup Co (PA) 216 587-2700
  16219 Saranac Rd Cleveland (44110) *(G-4088)*

Colloquy, Milford *Also Called: Epsilon (G-11226)*

Coloma Emergency Ambulance Inc (PA) 269 343-2224
  3771 Township Road 221 Huntsville (43324) *(G-9383)*

Colon Leasing Co LLC 513 530-1600
  563 Colony Park Dr Tallmadge (44278) *(G-13589)*

Colonial Banc Corp (PA) 937 456-5544
  110 W Main St Eaton (45320) *(G-8210)*

Colonial Manor Motel, Bryan *Also Called: F F & W Inc (G-1484)*

Colonial Mnor Hlth Care Ctr In 419 994-4191
  747 S Mount Vernon Ave Loudonville (44842) *(G-10108)*

Colonial Senior Services Inc 513 856-8600
  100 Berkley Dr Hamilton (45013) *(G-9030)*

Colonial Senior Services Inc 513 867-4006
  855 Stahlheber Rd Hamilton (45013) *(G-9031)*

Colonial Senior Services Inc 513 844-8004
  855 Stahlheber Rd Hamilton (45013) *(G-9032)*

Colonial Surface Solutions, Columbus Grove *Also Called: Carpe Diem Industries LLC (G-6921)*

Colony Healthcare Center, The, Tallmadge *Also Called: Colon Leasing Co LLC (G-13589)*

Coltene/Whaledent Inc (HQ) 330 916-8800
  235 Ascot Pkwy Cuyahoga Falls (44223) *(G-7063)*

Columbana Cnty For Dvlpmntal D 330 424-0404
  35947 State Route 172 Lisbon (44432) *(G-9998)*

Columbia, Bucyrus *Also Called: Columbia Gas of Ohio Inc (G-1500)*

Columbia, Cambridge *Also Called: Columbia Gas of Ohio Inc (G-1564)*

Columbia, Cleveland *Also Called: Columbia Gas of Ohio Inc (G-4089)*

Columbia, Columbus *Also Called: Columbia Gas of Ohio Inc (G-5598)*

Columbia, Columbus *Also Called: Columbia Gas of Ohio Inc (G-5599)*

Columbia, Columbus *Also Called: Columbia Gas of Ohio Inc (G-5600)*

Columbia, Columbus *Also Called: Columbia Gas of Ohio Inc (G-5601)*

Columbia, Columbus *Also Called: Columbia Gas of Ohio Inc (G-5602)*

Columbia, Findlay *Also Called: Columbia Gas of Ohio Inc (G-8523)*

Columbia, Fremont *Also Called: Columbia Gas of Ohio Inc (G-8670)*

Columbia, Steubenville *Also Called: Columbia Gas of Ohio Inc (G-13320)*

Columbia, Toledo *Also Called: Columbia Gas of Ohio Inc (G-13749)*

Columbia, Vandalia *Also Called: Datwyler Sling Sltions USA Inc (G-14373)*

Columbia Energy, Columbus *Also Called: Columbia Gas Transmission LLC (G-5603)*

Columbia Energy, Sugar Grove *Also Called: Columbia Gulf Transmission LLC (G-13507)*

Columbia Gas of Ohio Inc 419 562-4003
  231 S Poplar St Bucyrus (44820) *(G-1500)*

Columbia Gas of Ohio Inc 559 683-1567
  98 Steubenville Ave Cambridge (43725) *(G-1564)*

Columbia Gas of Ohio Inc 440 891-2458
  7080 Fry Rd Cleveland (44130) *(G-4089)*

Columbia Gas of Ohio Inc (HQ) 614 460-6000
  290 W Nationwide Blvd Unit 114 Columbus (43215) *(G-5598)*

ALPHABETIC SECTION

Columbia Gas of Ohio Inc 614 878-6015
  601 Manor Park Dr Columbus (43228) *(G-5599)*
Columbia Gas of Ohio Inc 614 481-1000
  290 W Nationwide Blvd Columbus (43215) *(G-5600)*
Columbia Gas of Ohio Inc 614 460-6000
  200 Civic Center Dr Ste 110 Columbus (43215) *(G-5601)*
Columbia Gas of Ohio Inc 614 818-2101
  3550 Johnny Appleseed Ct Columbus (43231) *(G-5602)*
Columbia Gas of Ohio Inc 419 435-7725
  1800 Broad Ave Findlay (45840) *(G-8523)*
Columbia Gas of Ohio Inc 419 332-9951
  1208 Dickinson St Fremont (43420) *(G-8670)*
Columbia Gas of Ohio Inc 740 264-5577
  300 Luray Dr Steubenville (43953) *(G-13320)*
Columbia Gas of Ohio Inc 419 539-6046
  2901 E Manhattan Blvd Toledo (43611) *(G-13749)*
Columbia Gas of Ohio Inc 740 450-1215
  2429 Linden Ave Zanesville (43701) *(G-15782)*
Columbia Gas Transmission LLC 614 460-4704
  290 W Nationwide Blvd Unit 114 Columbus (43215) *(G-5603)*
Columbia Gulf Transmission LLC 614 460-6991
  200 Civic Center Dr Columbus (43215) *(G-5604)*
Columbia Gulf Transmission LLC 740 746-9105
  6175 Old Logan Rd Sugar Grove (43155) *(G-13507)*
Columbia Hills Country CLB Inc 440 236-5051
  16200 East River Rd Columbia Station (44028) *(G-5225)*
Columbia Properties Lima LLC 419 222-0004
  1920 Roschman Ave Lima (45804) *(G-9875)*
Columbia Sussex Corporation 937 898-4946
  7470 Miller Ln Dayton (45414) *(G-7239)*
Columbiana Boiler Company, LLC, Columbiana *Also Called: Cbc Global (G-5232)*
Columbs/Worthington Htg AC Inc 614 771-5381
  6363 Fiesta Dr Columbus (43235) *(G-5605)*
Columbus & Ohio River RR Co 740 622-8092
  47849 Papermill Rd Coshocton (43812) *(G-6979)*
Columbus Air Center, Columbus *Also Called: Industrial Air Centers LLC (G-6050)*
Columbus Airport Ltd Partnr 614 475-7551
  1375 N Cassady Ave Columbus (43219) *(G-5606)*
Columbus Airport Marriott, Columbus *Also Called: Columbus Airport Ltd Partnr (G-5606)*
Columbus Airport Marriott, Columbus *Also Called: Columbus Arprt N Cssady Ht LLC (G-5609)*
Columbus Alzheimers, Columbus *Also Called: Columbus Alzheimers Oper LLC (G-5608)*
Columbus Alzheimers Care Ctr 614 459-7050
  700 Jasonway Ave Columbus (43214) *(G-5607)*
Columbus Alzheimers Oper LLC 614 459-7050
  700 Jasonway Ave Columbus (43214) *(G-5608)*
Columbus Arprt N Cssady Ht LLC 614 475-7551
  1375 N Cassady Ave Columbus (43219) *(G-5609)*
Columbus Arthritis Center, Columbus *Also Called: Columbus Arthritis Center Inc (G-5610)*
Columbus Arthritis Center Inc 614 486-5200
  1211 Dublin Rd Columbus (43215) *(G-5610)*
Columbus Asphalt Paving Inc 614 759-9800
  5715 Westbourne Ave Columbus (43213) *(G-5611)*
Columbus Assn For Prfrmg Arts (PA) 614 469-1045
  21 E Main St Columbus (43215) *(G-5612)*
Columbus Assn For The Prfrmg A (PA) 614 469-1045
  55 E State St Columbus (43215) *(G-5613)*
Columbus Assn For The Prfrmg A 614 469-0939
  39 E State St Columbus (43215) *(G-5614)*
Columbus Bar Association 614 221-4112
  175 S 3rd St Ste 1100 Columbus (43215) *(G-5615)*
Columbus Cancer Clinic Inc 614 263-5006
  1699 W Mound St Columbus (43223) *(G-5616)*
Columbus Cardiology Cons Inc 614 224-2281
  5350 N Meadows Dr Grove City (43123) *(G-8910)*
Columbus Center For Human Serv, Columbus *Also Called: Columbus Center For Human Svcs (G-5617)*
Columbus Center For Human Svcs 614 278-9362
  540 Industrial Mile Rd Columbus (43228) *(G-5617)*
Columbus Chamber of Commerce 614 225-6943
  150 S Front St Ste 220 Columbus (43215) *(G-5618)*

Columbus Childrens Hospital, Columbus *Also Called: Nationwide Childrens Hospital (G-6321)*
Columbus Christian Center Inc (PA) 614 416-9673
  2300 N Cassady Ave Columbus (43219) *(G-5619)*
Columbus City School District 614 421-2305
  1077 Lexington Ave Columbus (43201) *(G-5620)*
Columbus City School District 614 365-5456
  2500 N Cassady Ave Columbus (43219) *(G-5621)*
Columbus City School District 614 365-5263
  889 E 17th Ave Columbus (43211) *(G-5622)*
Columbus City School District 614 365-6542
  4001 Appian Way Columbus (43230) *(G-5623)*
Columbus Clny For Eldrly Care 614 891-5055
  1150 Colony Dr Westerville (43081) *(G-14969)*
Columbus Coach Supreme Limosne, Columbus *Also Called: Supreme Ventures LLC (G-6733)*
Columbus Coal & Lime Co (PA) 614 224-9241
  1150 Sullivant Ave Columbus (43223) *(G-5624)*
COLUMBUS COLONY ELDERLY CARE, Westerville *Also Called: Columbus Clny For Eldrly Care (G-14969)*
Columbus Concord Ltd Partnr 614 228-3200
  35 W Spring St Columbus (43215) *(G-5625)*
Columbus Crew SC, Columbus *Also Called: Crew SC Team Company LLC (G-5727)*
Columbus Ctr For Humn Svcs Inc (PA) 614 641-2904
  540 Industrial Mile Rd Columbus (43228) *(G-5626)*
Columbus Ctr For Humn Svcs Inc 614 245-8180
  6227 Harlem Rd New Albany (43054) *(G-11559)*
Columbus Dermatologists-Grtr 614 268-2748
  3555 Olentangy River Rd Ste 4000 Columbus (43214) *(G-5627)*
Columbus Developmental Center, Columbus *Also Called: Ohio Dept Dvlpmntal Dsbilities (G-6405)*
Columbus Dialysis, Columbus *Also Called: Columbus-Rna-Davita LLC (G-5662)*
Columbus Distributing Company (PA) 614 846-1000
  4949 Freeway Dr E Columbus (43229) *(G-5628)*
Columbus Distributing Company 740 726-2211
  6829 Waldo Delaware Rd Waldo (43356) *(G-14470)*
Columbus Division, Columbus *Also Called: Millcraft Paper Company (G-6249)*
Columbus Dnv Inc 614 761-1214
  5777 Frantz Rd Dublin (43017) *(G-7966)*
Columbus Downtown Dialysis, Columbus *Also Called: Columbus-Rna-Davita LLC (G-5661)*
Columbus Early Learning Ctrs 614 253-5525
  162 N Ohio Ave Columbus (43203) *(G-5629)*
Columbus East Dialysis, Columbus *Also Called: Columbus-Rna-Davita LLC (G-5660)*
Columbus Easton Hotel LLC 614 414-1000
  3999 Easton Loop W Columbus (43219) *(G-5630)*
Columbus Easton Hotel LLC 614 414-1000
  3999 Easton Loop W Columbus (43219) *(G-5631)*
Columbus Easton Hotel LLC 614 383-2005
  3900 Morse Xing Columbus (43219) *(G-5632)*
Columbus Equipment Company (PA) 614 437-0352
  2323 Performance Way Columbus (43207) *(G-5633)*
Columbus Foam Products, Westerville *Also Called: Integrated Whse Solutions Inc (G-14900)*
Columbus Frkln Cnty Pk (PA) 614 891-0700
  1069 W Main St Unit B Westerville (43081) *(G-14970)*
Columbus Frnklin Cnty Mtro Pk 614 891-0700
  6975 E Livingston Ave Reynoldsburg (43068) *(G-12659)*
Columbus Frnklin Cnty Mtro Pk 614 895-6219
  4265 E Dublin Granville Rd Westerville (43081) *(G-14971)*
Columbus Glass Block, Columbus *Also Called: Cleveland Glass Block Inc (G-5584)*
Columbus Green Cabs Inc (PA) 614 783-3663
  1989 Camaro Ave Columbus (43207) *(G-5634)*
Columbus Heating & Vent Co 614 274-1177
  182 N Yale Ave Columbus (43222) *(G-5635)*
Columbus Hilton Downtown 614 384-8600
  401 N High St Columbus (43215) *(G-5636)*
Columbus Home Health Svcs LLC 614 985-1464
  1150 Morse Rd Ste 101 Columbus (43229) *(G-5637)*
Columbus Homecare Adult Svcs, Columbus *Also Called: Maxim Healthcare Services Inc (G-6210)*
Columbus Hospitality LLC 614 461-2648
  775 Yard St Ste 180 Columbus (43212) *(G-5638)*

Columbus Hotel Partnership LLC.................................. 614 890-8600
  2700 Corporate Exchange Dr Columbus (43231) *(G-5639)*
Columbus Housing Partnr Inc.. 614 221-8889
  3443 Agler Rd Ste 200 Columbus (43219) *(G-5640)*
Columbus Humane.. 614 777-7387
  3015 Scioto Darby Executive Ct Hilliard (43026) *(G-9189)*
Columbus Jan Healthnet Svcs, Columbus *Also Called: Clean Innovations (G-5581)*
Columbus Jewish Federation.. 614 237-7686
  1175 College Ave Columbus (43209) *(G-5641)*
Columbus Leasing LLC... 614 885-1885
  6500 Doubletree Ave Columbus (43229) *(G-5642)*
Columbus Life Insurance Co... 513 361-6700
  400 Broadway St Cincinnati (45202) *(G-2477)*
Columbus Lintel Inc.. 614 871-0440
  1849 Stringtown Rd Grove City (43123) *(G-8911)*
Columbus Literacy Council.. 614 282-7661
  5825 Chantry Dr Columbus (43232) *(G-5643)*
Columbus Marriott Northwest, Dublin *Also Called: CP Dublin LLC (G-7976)*
Columbus Medical Association................................... 614 240-7410
  1390 Dublin Rd Columbus (43215) *(G-5644)*
Columbus Mntessori Educatn Ctr................................ 614 231-3790
  979 S James Rd Columbus (43227) *(G-5645)*
Columbus Municipal Employees (PA)........................ 614 224-8890
  365 S 4th St Columbus (43215) *(G-5646)*
Columbus Museum of Art... 614 221-6801
  480 E Broad St Columbus (43215) *(G-5647)*
Columbus Neighborhood Health, Columbus *Also Called: Columbus Neighborhood Health C (G-5648)*
Columbus Neighborhood Health C............................. 614 445-0685
  1905 Parsons Ave Columbus (43207) *(G-5648)*
Columbus Nghbrhood Hlth Ctr In................................ 614 859-1947
  3433 Agler Rd Ste 2800 Columbus (43219) *(G-5649)*
Columbus Nghbrhood Hlth Ctr In................................ 614 645-2300
  2300 W Broad St Columbus (43204) *(G-5650)*
Columbus OH 0617 LLC.. 614 855-9766
  4976 E Dublin Granville Rd Columbus (43081) *(G-5651)*
Columbus Peterbilt, Grove City *Also Called: Esec Corporation (G-8918)*
Columbus Prescr Phrms Inc.. 614 294-1600
  975 Eastwind Dr Ste 155 Westerville (43081) *(G-14972)*
Columbus Pub Schl Vhcl Maint, Columbus *Also Called: Columbus City School District (G-5622)*
Columbus Regional Airport Auth (PA)........................ 614 239-4000
  4600 International Gtwy Ste 25 Columbus (43219) *(G-5652)*
Columbus Regional Office, Columbus *Also Called: Ohio Dept Rhbilitation Corectn (G-6412)*
Columbus Rhbilitation Subacute, Columbus *Also Called: Astoria Place Columbus LLC (G-5398)*
Columbus SAI Motors LLC... 614 851-3273
  1400 Auto Mall Dr Columbus (43228) *(G-5653)*
Columbus Schl Dst Bus Compound, Columbus *Also Called: Columbus City School District (G-5623)*
Columbus Speech & Hearing Ctr................................. 614 263-5151
  510 E North Broadway St Columbus (43214) *(G-5654)*
Columbus Sq Bowl Palace Inc..................................... 614 895-1122
  5707 Forest Hills Blvd Columbus (43231) *(G-5655)*
Columbus Sutheast Ht Group LLC............................... 614 491-3800
  5950 S High St Lockbourne (43137) *(G-10010)*
Columbus Symphony Orchstra Inc.............................. 614 228-9600
  55 E State St Fl 5 Columbus (43215) *(G-5656)*
Columbus Truck & Equipment Center LLC (PA)....... 614 252-3111
  1688 E 5th Ave Columbus (43219) *(G-5657)*
Columbus Urban League.. 614 257-6300
  788 Mount Vernon Ave Columbus (43203) *(G-5658)*
Columbus Womens Wellness...................................... 614 532-8370
  4625 Morse Rd Ste 200 Gahanna (43230) *(G-8713)*
Columbus Worthington Hospitali.................................. 614 885-3334
  175 Hutchinson Ave Columbus (43235) *(G-5659)*
Columbus Zoo and Aquarium, Powell *Also Called: Columbus Zoological Park Assn (G-12589)*
Columbus Zoological Park Assn (PA).......................... 614 645-3400
  4850 Powell Rd Powell (43065) *(G-12589)*
Columbus-Gatehouse Inn, Columbus *Also Called: Island Hospitality MGT LLC (G-6075)*
Columbus-Marriott NW, Dublin *Also Called: Dublin Hotel Ltd Liability Co (G-7994)*
Columbus-Rna-Davita LLC.. 614 501-7224
  299 Outerbelt St Columbus (43213) *(G-5660)*
Columbus-Rna-Davita LLC.. 614 228-1773
  415 E Mound St Columbus (43215) *(G-5661)*
Columbus-Rna-Davita LLC.. 614 985-1732
  226 Graceland Blvd Ste 3-09a Columbus (43214) *(G-5662)*
Columbus/Worthington Htg & AC, Columbus *Also Called: Columbs/Worthington Htg AC Inc (G-5605)*
Com Doc, Blue Ash *Also Called: Comdoc Inc (G-1156)*
Com Net Inc... 419 739-3100
  1720 Willipie St Wapakoneta (45895) *(G-14481)*
Comber Holdings Inc... 216 961-8600
  3304 W 67th Pl Cleveland (44102) *(G-4090)*
Combined Tech Group Inc.. 937 274-4866
  6061 Milo Rd Dayton (45414) *(G-7240)*
Combined Technologies Inc (PA)................................ 513 595-5900
  1211 W Sharon Rd Cincinnati (45240) *(G-2478)*
Combs Interior Specialties Inc.................................... 937 879-2047
  475 W Funderburg Rd Fairborn (45324) *(G-8369)*
Combs Manufacturing Inc.. 330 784-3151
  380 Kennedy Rd Akron (44305) *(G-114)*
Comcage LLC.. 513 549-4003
  2345 Ashland Ave Cincinnati (45206) *(G-2479)*
Comcast Spotlight LP.. 216 575-8016
  3300 Lakeside Ave E Cleveland (44114) *(G-4091)*
Comdoc, North Canton *Also Called: Comdoc Inc (G-11818)*
Comdoc Inc.. 513 766-8124
  9999 Carver Rd Ste 100 Blue Ash (45242) *(G-1156)*
Comdoc Inc.. 330 920-3900
  220 Ascot Pkwy Cuyahoga Falls (44223) *(G-7064)*
Comdoc Inc (DH)... 330 896-2346
  8247 Pittsburg Ave Nw North Canton (44720) *(G-11818)*
Comenity Capital Bank... 614 944-3682
  3100 Easton Square Pl Columbus (43219) *(G-5663)*
Comenity Servicing LLC.. 614 729-4000
  3095 Loyalty Cir Columbus (43219) *(G-5664)*
Comex Group, Cleveland *Also Called: Comex North America Inc (G-4092)*
Comex North America Inc (HQ).................................... 303 307-2100
  101 W Prospect Ave Ste 1020 Cleveland (44115) *(G-4092)*
Comey & Shepherd LLC.. 513 489-2100
  7870 E Kemper Rd Ste 100 Cincinnati (45249) *(G-2480)*
Comforcare Home Care, Strongsville *Also Called: D&J Quality Care Entps Inc (G-13451)*
Comfort Express Inc.. 740 389-4400
  3527 State Route 37 W Delaware (43015) *(G-7786)*
Comfort In Northeast, Cincinnati *Also Called: Shihasi Starwind Ne Llp (G-3370)*
Comfort Inn... 740 454-4144
  500 Monroe St Zanesville (43701) *(G-15783)*
Comfort Inn, Austintown *Also Called: All Star Mgmt Inc (G-635)*
Comfort Inn, Bellefontaine *Also Called: Bellefontaine Lodging Inc (G-1020)*
Comfort Inn, Bellville *Also Called: Valley View Management Co Inc (G-1052)*
Comfort Inn, Cambridge *Also Called: Equity Lodging LLC (G-1570)*
Comfort Inn, Chillicothe *Also Called: Chillicothe Motel LLC (G-2058)*
Comfort Inn, Cleveland *Also Called: Boulevard Motel Corp (G-3884)*
Comfort Inn, Cleveland *Also Called: Peitro Properties Ltd Partnr (G-4736)*
Comfort Inn, Grove City *Also Called: Blissful Corporation (G-8897)*
Comfort Inn, Lima *Also Called: Chandni Inc (G-9873)*
Comfort Inn, Maumee *Also Called: Shree Shiv LLC (G-10765)*
Comfort Inn, Northwood *Also Called: Future Lodging Northwood LLC (G-11975)*
Comfort Inn, Oregon *Also Called: Northtowne Square Ltd Partnr (G-12137)*
Comfort Inn, Oxford *Also Called: Oxford Hospitality Group Inc (G-12214)*
Comfort Inn, Sidney *Also Called: Sidney Lodges (G-13052)*
Comfort Inn, Toledo *Also Called: Toledo Inn North LLC (G-14059)*
Comfort Inn, Youngstown *Also Called: Liberty Hospitality Inc (G-15649)*
Comfort Inn, Zanesville *Also Called: Comfort Inn (G-15783)*
Comfort Inn Greenville, Greenville *Also Called: Landmark Star Properties Inc (G-8879)*
Comfort Keepers.. 419 229-1031
  1726 Allentown Rd Lima (45805) *(G-9876)*
Comfort Keepers, Springfield *Also Called: Sdx Home Care Operations LLC (G-13289)*

ALPHABETIC SECTION

Comfort Keepers, Toledo Also Called: Tky Associates LLC *(G-14045)*
Comfort Suites, Springfield Also Called: A & K Ishvar Inc *(G-13212)*
Comfort Suites Berlin, Berlin Also Called: Choice Hotels Intl Inc *(G-1090)*
Comfort Systems USA, Bedford Also Called: Comfort Systems USA Ohio Inc *(G-957)*
Comfort Systems USA Ohio Inc (HQ).................................... 440 703-1600
  7401 First Pl Ste A Bedford (44146) *(G-957)*
Command Alkon Incorporated... 614 799-0600
  6750 Crosby Ct Dublin (43016) *(G-7967)*
Command Roofing Co.. 937 298-1155
  2485 Arbor Blvd Moraine (45439) *(G-11398)*
Commcapp America Inc... 678 780-0937
  1300 E 9th St Fl 22 Cleveland (44114) *(G-4093)*
Commerce Paper, Toledo Also Called: Commerce Paper Company *(G-13750)*
Commerce Paper Company.. 419 241-9101
  302 S Byrne Rd Bldg 200 Toledo (43615) *(G-13750)*
Commercial Bancshares Inc... 419 294-5781
  118 S Sandusky Ave Upper Sandusky (43351) *(G-14285)*
Commercial Comfort Systems Inc.................................... 419 481-4444
  26610 Eckel Rd Ste 3a Perrysburg (43551) *(G-12325)*
Commercial Electric Pdts Corp (PA)................................. 216 241-2886
  1821 E 40th St Cleveland (44103) *(G-4094)*
Commercial Fluid Power, North Canton Also Called: Cho Bedford Inc *(G-11816)*
Commercial Grounds Care Inc... 614 456-3764
  1901 Dividend Dr Columbus (43228) *(G-5665)*
Commercial Installers, Cincinnati Also Called: Valley Interior Systems Inc *(G-3613)*
Commercial Interior Products, West Chester Also Called: CIP International Inc *(G-14666)*
Commercial Maintenance & Repr, Akron Also Called: Ohio Maint & Renovation Inc *(G-254)*
Commercial Parts & Ser.. 614 221-0057
  5033 Transamerica Dr Columbus (43228) *(G-5666)*
Commercial Radiator, Columbus Also Called: Skinner Diesel Services Inc *(G-6686)*
Commercial Time Sharing Inc.. 330 644-3059
  2740 Cory Ave Akron (44314) *(G-115)*
Commercial Warehouse & Cartage.................................. 614 409-3901
  6295 Commerce Center Dr Groveport (43125) *(G-8978)*
Commercial Works Inc (PA)... 614 870-2342
  1299 Boltonfield St Columbus (43228) *(G-5667)*
Commission On Partransit, North Olmsted Also Called: City of North Olmsted *(G-11894)*
Commodore Prry Inns Suites LLC.................................... 419 732-2645
  255 W Lakeshore Dr Port Clinton (43452) *(G-12520)*
Commonwealth Container, Dayton Also Called: Dayton Corrugated Packaging Corp *(G-7277)*
Commonwealth Land Title, Cincinnati Also Called: Commonwealth Title Dallas Inc *(G-2481)*
Commonwealth Title Dallas Inc....................................... 513 985-0550
  30 Garfield Pl Ste 720 Cincinnati (45202) *(G-2481)*
Commonwealth Warehouse Inc (PA)................................ 513 791-1966
  400 Murray Rd Cincinnati (45217) *(G-2482)*
Commquest Services Inc... 330 455-0374
  625 Cleveland Ave Nw Canton (44702) *(G-1718)*
Commsys Inc... 937 220-4990
  7887 Washington Village Dr Ste 220 Dayton (45459) *(G-7241)*
Communcare Clfton Pstcute Rhbl, Cincinnati Also Called: Clifton Care Center Inc *(G-2459)*
Communi Care Inc.. 419 382-2200
  955 Garden Lake Pkwy Toledo (43614) *(G-13751)*
Communicare, Blue Ash Also Called: Skilled In Management Co LLC *(G-1244)*
Communicare Family of Company, Blue Ash Also Called: MD Omg Emp LLC *(G-1207)*
Communicare Health Services, Blue Ash Also Called: Communicare Health Svcs Inc *(G-1157)*
COMMUNICARE HEALTH SERVICES, Dayton Also Called: Summitt Ohio Leasing Co LLC *(G-7651)*
Communicare Health Services, Deshler Also Called: East Water Leasing Co LLC *(G-7866)*
COMMUNICARE HEALTH SERVICES, Toledo Also Called: Garden II Leasing Co LLC *(G-13817)*
Communicare Health Svcs Inc... 440 234-0454
  49 Sheldon Rd Berea (44017) *(G-1066)*
Communicare Health Svcs Inc (PA)................................. 513 530-1654
  10123 Alliance Rd Blue Ash (45242) *(G-1157)*
Communicare Health Svcs Inc... 330 454-6508
  3015 17th St Nw Canton (44708) *(G-1719)*
Communicare Health Svcs Inc... 614 443-7210
  2000 Regency Manor Cir Columbus (43207) *(G-5668)*
Communicare Health Svcs Inc... 330 659-6166
  4360 Brecksville Rd Richfield (44286) *(G-12692)*

Communication Options Inc.. 614 901-7095
  4689 Reynoldsburg New Albany Rd New Albany (43054) *(G-11560)*
Communications Buying Group....................................... 216 377-3000
  6060 Rockside Woods Blvd Cleveland (44131) *(G-4095)*
Communications III Inc (PA)... 614 901-7720
  921 Eastwind Dr Ste 104 Westerville (43081) *(G-14973)*
Community Action - Wyne/Medina (PA)........................... 330 264-8677
  905 Pittsburgh Ave Wooster (44691) *(G-15325)*
Community Action Agcy Clmbana (PA)............................ 330 424-7221
  7880 Lincole Pl Lisbon (44432) *(G-9999)*
Community Action Agnst Addctio................................... 216 881-0765
  5209 Euclid Ave Cleveland (44103) *(G-4096)*
COMMUNITY ACTION AKRON SUMMIT, Akron Also Called: Akron Summit Cmnty Action Agcy *(G-38)*
Community Action Cmmttee Pike (PA)............................. 740 289-2371
  941 Market St Piketon (45661) *(G-12416)*
Community Action Comm Blmont C................................. 740 676-0800
  4129 Noble St Bellaire (43906) *(G-1009)*
Community Action Comm Blmont C (PA)......................... 740 695-0293
  153 1/2 W Main St Saint Clairsville (43950) *(G-12786)*
Community Action Comm Erie Hro (PA).......................... 419 626-6540
  908 Seavers Way Sandusky (44870) *(G-12884)*
Community Action Comm Erie Hro................................. 419 935-6481
  1530 S Conwell Ave Willard (44890) *(G-15166)*
Community Action Comm Fytte CN (PA)......................... 740 335-7282
  1400 Us Highway 22 Nw Wshngtn Ct Hs (43160) *(G-15478)*
COMMUNITY ACTION COMMISSION OF, Saint Clairsville Also Called: Community Action Comm Blmont C *(G-12786)*
Community Action Orgnztion Sco (PA)........................... 740 354-7541
  433 3rd St Portsmouth (45662) *(G-12548)*
Community Action Prgram Comm O (PA)....................... 740 653-1711
  1743 E Main St Lancaster (43130) *(G-9704)*
Community Action Prgram Comm O.............................. 740 345-8750
  986 E Main St Newark (43055) *(G-11693)*
Community Action Prgram Corp O................................. 740 962-3792
  320 S Main St Malta (43758) *(G-10231)*
Community Action Prgram Corp O (PA)......................... 740 373-3745
  218 Putnam St Marietta (45750) *(G-10362)*
Community Action Prgram Corp O................................. 740 373-6016
  205 Phillips St Marietta (45750) *(G-10363)*
Community Ambulance Service...................................... 740 454-6800
  952 Linden Ave Zanesville (43701) *(G-15784)*
Community and Rural Hlth Svcs (PA).............................. 419 334-8943
  2221 Hayes Ave Fremont (43420) *(G-8671)*
Community Assssment Trtmnt Svc (PA).......................... 216 441-0200
  8411 Broadway Ave Cleveland (44105) *(G-4097)*
Community Bank... 740 654-0900
  201 N Columbus St Lancaster (43130) *(G-9705)*
Community Behavioral Hlth Inc...................................... 513 887-8500
  824 S Martin Luther King Jr Blvd Hamilton (45011) *(G-9033)*
Community Blood Center... 800 684-7783
  2900 College Dr Kettering (45420) *(G-9627)*
Community Care Amblance Netwrk (PA)......................... 440 992-1401
  115 E 24th St Ashtabula (44004) *(G-527)*
Community Care Center, Alliance Also Called: Alliance Community Hospital *(G-375)*
Community Care Rehabilitation, Marion Also Called: Marion Care Leasing LLC *(G-10436)*
Community Caregivers... 330 725-9800
  230 Quadral Dr Ste D Wadsworth (44281) *(G-14433)*
Community Choice Financial Inc (PA)............................. 614 798-5900
  6785 Bobcat Way Ste 200 Dublin (43016) *(G-7968)*
Community Christian School, Hamilton Also Called: Small World Childrens Center *(G-9081)*
Community Cnsling Ctr Ashtbula (PA)............................. 440 998-4210
  2801 C Ct Unit 2 Ashtabula (44004) *(G-528)*
Community Cnsling Wllness Ctrs (PA)............................. 740 387-5210
  320 Executive Dr Marion (43302) *(G-10422)*
Community Concepts Inc (PA).. 513 398-8181
  6699 Tri Way Dr Mason (45040) *(G-10542)*
Community Concepts & Options, Mason Also Called: Community Concepts Inc *(G-10542)*
Community Correctional Center, Lebanon Also Called: Talbert House *(G-9792)*
Community Counseling Svcs Inc.................................... 419 562-2000
  2458 Stetzer Rd Bucyrus (44820) *(G-1501)*

Community Crime Patrol — ALPHABETIC SECTION

Community Crime Patrol 614 247-1765
  248 E 11th Ave Columbus (43201) *(G-5669)*
Community Dialysis Center 216 295-7000
  11717 Euclid Ave Cleveland (44106) *(G-4098)*
Community Dialysis Center 216 229-6170
  11717 Euclid Ave Cleveland (44106) *(G-4099)*
Community Dialysis Center 330 609-0370
  1950 Niles Cortland Rd Ne Ste 12 Warren (44484) *(G-14510)*
Community Drug Board Inc (PA) 330 315-5590
  725 E Market St Akron (44305) *(G-116)*
Community Drug Board Inc 330 996-5114
  380 S Portage Path Akron (44320) *(G-117)*
Community Education Ctrs Inc 330 424-4065
  8473 County Home Rd Lisbon (44432) *(G-10000)*
Community Employment Services, Newark Also Called: Licking County Board of Mrdd *(G-11716)*
  Community For New Drction Incr 614 272-1464
    993 E Main St Columbus (43205) *(G-5670)*
  Community Health Alliance (PA) 513 896-3458
    1020 Symmes Rd Fairfield (45014) *(G-8406)*
Community Health Professionals, Archbold Also Called: Community Hlth Prfssionals Inc *(G-455)*
COMMUNITY HEALTH SERVICES, Fremont Also Called: Community and Rural Hlth Svcs *(G-8671)*
  Community Health Systems Inc 330 841-9011
    1350 E Market St Warren (44483) *(G-14511)*
  Community Hlh Ctr of Gtr Daton 937 461-4336
    1323 W 3rd St Dayton (45402) *(G-7242)*
  Community Hlth Ctrs Grter Dyto 937 558-0180
    165 S Edwin C Moses Blvd Dayton (45402) *(G-7243)*
  Community Hlth Prfssionals Inc 419 634-7443
    1200 S Main St Ada (45810) *(G-1)*
  Community Hlth Prfssionals Inc 419 445-5128
    230 Westfield Dr Archbold (43502) *(G-455)*
  Community Hlth Prfssionals Inc 419 586-1999
    816 Pro Dr Celina (45822) *(G-1920)*
  Community Hlth Prfssionals Inc 419 586-6266
    816 Pro Dr Celina (45822) *(G-1921)*
  Community Hlth Prfssionals Inc 419 695-8101
    1500 E 5th St Delphos (45833) *(G-7839)*
  Community Hlth Prfssionals Inc 419 991-1822
    3739 Shawnee Rd # A Lima (45806) *(G-9989)*
  Community Hlth Prfssionals Inc 419 399-4708
    250 Dooley Dr Ste A Paulding (45879) *(G-12281)*
  Community Hlth Prfssionals Inc (PA) 419 238-9223
    1159 Westwood Dr Van Wert (45891) *(G-14342)*
  Community Hlth Prtners Rgnal F (HQ) 440 960-4000
    3700 Kolbe Rd Lorain (44053) *(G-10068)*
Community Hosp Schl Nursing, Springfield Also Called: The Community Hospital of Springfield and Clark County *(G-13300)*
COMMUNITY HOSPICE, New Philadelphia Also Called: Hospice Tuscarawas County Inc *(G-11654)*
Community Hospice Carroll Cnty, Carrollton Also Called: Hospice Tuscarawas County Inc *(G-1909)*
  Community Hospitals 419 636-1131
    433 W High St Bryan (43506) *(G-1480)*
  Community Hospitals Wellness 419 636-1131
    442 W High St Bryan (43506) *(G-1481)*
  Community Hsptals Wllness Ctrs 419 445-2015
    121 Westfield Dr Ste 1 Archbold (43502) *(G-456)*
  Community Hsptals Wllness Ctrs (PA) 419 636-1131
    433 W High St Bryan (43506) *(G-1482)*
  Community Hsptals Wllness Ctrs 419 485-3154
    909 E Snyder Ave Montpelier (43543) *(G-11383)*
  Community Insurance Company 859 282-7888
    1351 William Howard Taft Rd Cincinnati (45206) *(G-2483)*
  Community Isp Inc 419 867-6060
    3035 Moffat Rd Toledo (43615) *(G-13752)*
  Community Living Experiences 614 588-0350
    2939 Donnylane Blvd Columbus (43235) *(G-5671)*
  Community Management Corp 513 761-6339
    375 W Galbraith Rd Cincinnati (45215) *(G-2484)*

Community Medical Center, Celina Also Called: Mercer Cnty Jint Twnship Cmnty *(G-1926)*
COMMUNITY MEMORIAL HOSPITAL, Hicksville Also Called: Mark Mlford Hcksvlle Jint Twn *(G-9160)*
  Community Mental Health Svc 740 633-2161
    301 Walnut St Martins Ferry (43935) *(G-10466)*
  Community Mental Health Svc (PA) 740 695-9344
    68353 Bannock Rd Saint Clairsville (43950) *(G-12787)*
Community Mental Health Svcs, Saint Clairsville Also Called: Community Mental Health Svc *(G-12787)*
  Community Mercy Health System (HQ) 937 523-5500
    100 Medical Center Dr Springfield (45504) *(G-13238)*
  Community Mercy Hlth Partners (DH) 937 523-6670
    100 Medical Center Dr Springfield (45504) *(G-13239)*
Community Mobile Health, Grove City Also Called: Superior Ar-Grund Amblnce Svc *(G-8958)*
COMMUNITY NETWORK THE, Xenia Also Called: Tcn Behavioral Health Svcs Inc *(G-15532)*
  Community Prpts Ohio MGT Svcs 614 253-0984
    910 E Broad St Columbus (43205) *(G-5672)*
  Community Rfgee Immgrtion Svcs 614 235-5747
    4645 Executive Dr Columbus (43220) *(G-5673)*
  Community Rstrtion Ctrs Inc St 330 456-3565
    1432 Tuscarawas St E Canton (44707) *(G-1720)*
  Community Savings 740 732-5678
    425 Main St Caldwell (43724) *(G-1548)*
COMMUNITY SERVICES OF STARK CO, Canton Also Called: Commquest Services Inc *(G-1718)*
  Community Sklled Hlth Care CNT 330 373-1160
    1320 Mahoning Ave Nw Warren (44483) *(G-14512)*
  Community Support Services Inc (PA) 330 253-9388
    47 N Arlington St Akron (44305) *(G-118)*
Community Supports Services, Fairfield Also Called: Butler Cnty Bd Dvlpmntal Dsblt *(G-8396)*
  Community Tissue Services 937 222-0228
    2900 College Dr Kettering (45420) *(G-9628)*
Community Tissue Services, Dayton Also Called: Foundtion For Cmnty Blood Cntr *(G-7363)*
  Communties In Schols Cntl Ohio 614 268-2472
    6500 Busch Blvd Ste 105 Columbus (43229) *(G-5674)*
Commutair, North Olmsted Also Called: Commuteair LLC *(G-11899)*
  Commuteair LLC (PA) 440 779-4588
    24950 Country Club Blvd Ste 200 North Olmsted (44070) *(G-11899)*
  Compak Inc 330 345-5666
    1130 Riffel Rd Wooster (44691) *(G-15326)*
  Companion Care Services Inc (PA) 440 257-0075
    7618 Miami Rd Mentor On The Lake (44060) *(G-11014)*
  Companions of Ashland LLC (PA) 419 281-2273
    1241 E Main St Ashland (44805) *(G-494)*
  Company Wrench Ltd (PA) 740 654-5304
    4805 Scooby Ln Carroll (43112) *(G-1900)*
Comparisonmarket Insur Agcy, Solon Also Called: Insurancecom Inc *(G-13100)*
Compass, Toledo Also Called: Comprhnsive Addction Svc Syste *(G-13755)*
  Compass Clinical Consulting Co 513 241-0142
    2181 Victory Pkwy Ste 200 Cincinnati (45206) *(G-2485)*
  Compass Community Health 740 355-7102
    1634 11th St Portsmouth (45662) *(G-12549)*
  Compass Construction Inc 614 761-7800
    7670 Fishel Dr S Dublin (43016) *(G-7969)*
  Compass Corp For Recovery Svcs 419 241-8827
    2005 Ashland Ave Toledo (43620) *(G-13753)*
  Compass Family and Cmnty Svcs 330 782-5664
    246 Broadway Ave Youngstown (44504) *(G-15582)*
  Compass Family and Cmnty Svcs 330 743-9275
    284 Broadway Ave Youngstown (44504) *(G-15583)*
  Compass Family and Cmnty Svcs (PA) 330 782-5664
    535 Marmion Ave Youngstown (44502) *(G-15584)*
Compass Health, Middleburg Heights Also Called: Compass Health Brands Corp *(G-11114)*
  Compass Health Brands Corp (PA) 800 376-7263
    6753 Engle Rd Ste A Middleburg Heights (44130) *(G-11114)*
  Compass Packaging LLC 330 274-2001
    10585 Main St Mantua (44255) *(G-10329)*
  Compass Professional Svcs LLC 216 705-2233
    1536 Saint Clair Ave Ne # 58 Cleveland (44114) *(G-4100)*
Compass S&S, Norton Also Called: Compass Systems & Sales LLC *(G-11993)*

ALPHABETIC SECTION — Coney Island Inc

Compass School Waterstone LLC 513 683-8833
   9370 Waterstone Blvd Cincinnati (45249) *(G-2486)*

Compass Systems & Sales LLC 330 733-2111
   5185 New Haven Cir Norton (44203) *(G-11993)*

Compassion Health Toledo 419 537-9185
   1638n Broadway St Toledo (43609) *(G-13754)*

Compassnate Hnds Stffing Slton 216 710-6736
   675 Alpha Dr Ste E Highland Heights (44143) *(G-9164)*

Compassus 440 249-6036
   6000 Lombardo Ctr Ste 140 Seven Hills (44131) *(G-12953)*

Compassus- W Jefferson Hospice, West Jefferson Also Called: Fc Compassus LLC *(G-14850)*

Compco Land Company (PA) 330 482-0200
   85 E Hylda Ave Youngstown (44507) *(G-15585)*

Compdrug (PA) 614 224-4506
   547 E 11th Ave Columbus (43211) *(G-5675)*

Compel Fitness LLC 216 965-5694
   25935 Detroit Rd Westlake (44145) *(G-15052)*

Competitive Interiors Inc 330 297-1281
   625 Enterprise Pkwy Ravenna (44266) *(G-12623)*

Competitor Swim Products Inc 800 888-7946
   5310 Career Ct Columbus (43213) *(G-5676)*

Complete Care Providers Inc 937 825-4698
   9888 Reading Rd Cincinnati (45241) *(G-2487)*

Complete Dntl Care Nwcmerstown, Newcomerstown Also Called: North American Dental MGT LLC *(G-11773)*

Complete General Cnstr Co (PA) 614 258-9515
   1221 E 5th Ave Columbus (43219) *(G-5677)*

Complete General Cnstr Co 614 258-9515
   1275 E 5th Ave Columbus (43219) *(G-5678)*

Complete Home Care, Massillon Also Called: Health Services Inc *(G-10644)*

Complete Mechanical Svcs LLC 513 489-3080
   11399 Grooms Rd Blue Ash (45242) *(G-1158)*

Compmanagement Inc (HQ) 614 376-5300
   6377 Emerald Pkwy Dublin (43016) *(G-7970)*

Compmanagement Inc 440 546-7100
   5700 Lombardo Ctr Ste 150 Seven Hills (44131) *(G-12954)*

Compmanagement Inc 330 782-0363
   4706 Brookwood Rd Youngstown (44512) *(G-15586)*

Compmed Analysis LLC (PA) 330 650-0888
   1742 Georgetown Rd Ste G Hudson (44236) *(G-9340)*

Component Repair Technologies Inc 440 255-1793
   8507 Tyler Blvd Mentor (44060) *(G-10925)*

Composite Advantage, Dayton Also Called: Cpca Manufacturing LLC *(G-7260)*

Compounded Eps, Piqua Also Called: Epsilyte Holdings LLC *(G-12441)*

COMPREHENSIVE BEHAVIORAL HEALTH, East Liverpool Also Called: Comprehensive Behavioral Hlth *(G-8180)*

Comprehensive Behavioral Hlth 330 385-8800
   321 W 5th St East Liverpool (43920) *(G-8180)*

Comprehensive Health Care Svcs, Cincinnati Also Called: Comprhnsive Halthcare Svcs Inc *(G-2490)*

Comprehensive Hr Solutions LLC 513 771-2277
   1 Sheakley Way Cincinnati (45246) *(G-2488)*

Comprehensive Logistics Co Inc 563 445-6001
   4944 Belmont Ave Ste 201 Youngstown (44505) *(G-15587)*

Comprhnsive Addction Svc Syste 419 241-8827
   2005 Ashland Ave Toledo (43620) *(G-13755)*

Comprhnsive Cmnty Child Care O (PA) 513 221-0033
   2100 Sherman Ave Ste 300 Cincinnati (45212) *(G-2489)*

Comprhnsive Eyecare Cntl Ohio I 614 890-5692
   450 Alkyre Run Ste 100 Westerville (43082) *(G-14883)*

Comprhnsive Halthcare Svcs Inc 513 245-0100
   18 E 4th St Ste 100 Cincinnati (45202) *(G-2490)*

Comprhnsive Hlth Care Ohio Inc (HQ) 440 329-7500
   630 E River St Elyria (44035) *(G-8237)*

Comproducts Inc (PA) 614 276-5552
   1740 Harmon Ave Ste F Columbus (43223) *(G-5679)*

Compunet Clinical Labs, Moraine Also Called: Compunet Clinical Labs LLC *(G-11399)*

Compunet Clinical Labs LLC 937 912-9017
   3535 Pentagon Blvd Beavercreek (45431) *(G-873)*

Compunet Clinical Labs LLC 937 427-2655
   75 Sylvania Dr Beavercreek (45440) *(G-921)*

Compunet Clinical Labs LLC 937 208-3555
   2508 Sandridge Dr Dayton (45439) *(G-7244)*

Compunet Clinical Labs LLC (HQ) 937 296-0844
   2308 Sandridge Dr Moraine (45439) *(G-11399)*

Compunet Clinical Labs LLC 937 342-0015
   2100 Emmanuel Way Springfield (45502) *(G-13240)*

Compunet Clinical Labs LLC 937 372-9681
   1214 N Monroe Dr Xenia (45385) *(G-15502)*

Computer Aided Technology LLC 513 745-2700
   11500 Northlake Dr Ste 122 Cincinnati (45249) *(G-2491)*

Comresource Inc 614 221-6348
   1159 Dublin Rd Ste 200 Columbus (43215) *(G-5680)*

Coms Interactive, Broadview Heights Also Called: Clinicl Otcms Mngmnt Syst LLC *(G-1386)*

Comtex, Columbus Also Called: Central Ohio Medical Textiles *(G-5540)*

Comwavz, Findlay Also Called: Midwest Communications LLC *(G-8569)*

Con-Way Multimodal Inc (DH) 614 923-1400
   5165 Emerald Pkwy Dublin (43017) *(G-7971)*

Concast Birmingham LLC 440 965-4455
   14315 State Route 113 Wakeman (44889) *(G-14458)*

Concast Birmingham, Inc., Wakeman Also Called: Concast Birmingham LLC *(G-14458)*

Concentrix, Cincinnati Also Called: Concentrix Cvg Corporation *(G-2492)*

Concentrix Cvg Corporation (HQ) 800 747-0583
   201 E 4th St Cincinnati (45202) *(G-2492)*

Concentrix Cvg Cstmer MGT Intl (DH) 513 268-7014
   201 E 4th St Bsmt Cincinnati (45202) *(G-2493)*

Concentrix Solutions Corp 480 968-2496
   201 E 4th St Cincinnati (45202) *(G-2494)*

Concept Imaging Group Inc 888 466-6627
   3233 S Tech Blvd Miamisburg (45342) *(G-11037)*

Concept Rehab Inc (PA) 419 843-6002
   6591 W Central Ave Toledo (43617) *(G-13756)*

Concept Services Limited 330 336-2571
   202 Montrose West Ave Ste 100 Copley (44321) *(G-6951)*

Concerned Ctzens Agnst VInce A 740 382-8988
   330 Barks Rd W Marion (43302) *(G-10423)*

Concord Biosciences LLC 440 357-3200
   10845 Wellness Way Concord Township (44077) *(G-6923)*

Concord Care Center of Toledo 419 385-6616
   3121 Glanzman Rd Toledo (43614) *(G-13757)*

Concord Care Ctr Cortland Inc 330 637-7906
   4250 Sodom Hutchings Rd Cortland (44410) *(G-6969)*

Concord Counseling Services 614 882-9338
   700 Brooksedge Blvd Westerville (43081) *(G-14974)*

Concord Dayton Hotel II LLC 937 223-1000
   1414 S Patterson Blvd Dayton (45409) *(G-7245)*

Concord Express Inc (HQ) 718 656-7821
   5905 Green Pointe Dr S Ste D Groveport (43125) *(G-8979)*

Concord Health Care Inc 419 626-5373
   620 W Strub Rd Sandusky (44870) *(G-12885)*

Concord Health Care Inc (PA) 330 759-2357
   202 Churchill Hubbard Rd Youngstown (44505) *(G-15588)*

Concord Health Center Hartford, Fowler Also Called: Meadowbrook Manor of Hartford *(G-8628)*

Concord Hmltnian Rvrfront Ht L 513 896-6200
   1 Riverfront Plz Hamilton (45011) *(G-9034)*

Concord Reserve 440 871-0090
   2116 Dover Center Rd Westlake (44145) *(G-15053)*

Concord Steel of Ohio, Warren Also Called: Conley Group Inc *(G-14513)*

Concord Testa Hotel Assoc LLC 330 252-9228
   41 Furnace St Akron (44308) *(G-119)*

Concorde Therapy Group Inc (PA) 330 493-4210
   4645 Belpar St Nw Canton (44718) *(G-1721)*

CONCORDIA AT SUMNER, Copley Also Called: Concordia of Ohio *(G-6952)*

Concordia of Ohio 330 664-1000
   970 Sumner Pkwy Copley (44321) *(G-6952)*

Concordnce Hlthcare Sltons LLC (PA) 419 447-0222
   85 Shaffer Park Dr Tiffin (44883) *(G-13625)*

Concrete Protector The, Lima Also Called: Incredible Products LLC *(G-9910)*

Conduent Care Solutions LLC 330 644-0927
   2717 S Arlington Rd Ste B Akron (44312) *(G-120)*

Coney Island Inc 513 232-8230
   502 Techne Center Dr Milford (45150) *(G-11224)*

Confidential Services Inc 614 252-4646
1156 Alum Creek Dr Columbus (43209) *(G-5681)*

Conger Construction Group Inc 513 932-1206
2020 Mckinley Blvd Lebanon (45036) *(G-9760)*

Congregate Living of America 937 393-6700
141 Willetsville Pike Hillsboro (45133) *(G-9251)*

Congregate Living of America (PA) 513 899-2801
463 E Pike St Morrow (45152) *(G-11455)*

CONGRESS LAKE CLUB, Hartville Also Called: Congress Lake Club Company *(G-9124)*

Congress Lake Club Company 330 877-9318
1 East Dr Ne Hartville (44632) *(G-9124)*

Conie Construction Company, Columbus Also Called: Jack Conie & Sons Corp *(G-6080)*

Conley Group Inc 330 372-2030
197 W Market St Ste 202 Warren (44481) *(G-14513)*

Conneaut Telephone Company 440 593-7140
224 State St Conneaut (44030) *(G-6942)*

Connect Trnsp Svcs LLC 740 656-5042
1338 Delano Rd Chillicothe (45601) *(G-2061)*

Connecting Dots Cnncting To SL 216 356-2362
3030 Euclid Ave Cleveland (44115) *(G-4101)*

Connecting Kids To Meals Inc 419 720-1106
1501 Monroe St Toledo (43604) *(G-13758)*

Connection, Wilmington Also Called: PC Connection Inc *(G-15263)*

Connections In Ohio Inc 216 228-9760
8001 Sweet Valley Dr Ste 4 Cleveland (44125) *(G-4102)*

Connectons Hlth Wllness Advcac, Beachwood Also Called: North East Ohio Health Svcs *(G-821)*

Connector Manufacturing Co (DH) 513 860-4455
3501 Symmes Rd Hamilton (45015) *(G-9035)*

Connie Parks (PA) 330 759-8334
4504 Logan Way Ste B Hubbard (44425) *(G-9320)*

Connor Concepts Inc 937 291-1661
7727 Washington Village Dr Dayton (45459) *(G-7246)*

Connor Group A RE Inv Firm LLC 937 434-3095
10510 Springboro Pike Miamisburg (45342) *(G-11038)*

Conrad's Total Car Care, Cleveland Also Called: Conrads Tire Service Inc *(G-4103)*

Conrads Tire Service Inc (PA) 216 941-3333
14577 Lorain Ave Cleveland (44111) *(G-4103)*

Conservncy For Cyhoga Vly Nat 330 657-2909
1403 W Hines Hill Rd Peninsula (44264) *(G-12293)*

Consoldated Graphics Group Inc 216 881-9191
1614 E 40th St Cleveland (44103) *(G-4104)*

Consoldted Fndries Hldngs Corp 216 772-1041
1621 Euclid Ave Ste 1850 Cleveland (44115) *(G-4105)*

Consolidated Coatings Corp 216 514-7596
3735 Green Rd Cleveland (44122) *(G-4106)*

Consolidated Cooperative 419 947-3055
5255 State Route 95 Mount Gilead (43338) *(G-11459)*

CONSOLIDATED COOPERATIVE, Mount Gilead Also Called: Consolidated Cooperative *(G-11459)*

Consolidated Elec Distrs Inc 614 445-8871
265 N Hamilton Rd Columbus (43213) *(G-5682)*

Consolidated Grain & Barge Co 513 244-7400
3164 Southside Ave Cincinnati (45204) *(G-2495)*

Consolidated Learning Ctrs Inc 614 791-0050
7100 Muirfield Dr Ste 200 Dublin (43017) *(G-7972)*

Consolidated Management, Cleveland Also Called: TI Resort LLC *(G-5019)*

Consolidated Solutions, Cleveland Also Called: Consoldated Graphics Group Inc *(G-4104)*

Consolidus LLC 330 319-7200
526 S Main St Ste 804 Akron (44311) *(G-121)*

Consoliplex Holding LLC (PA) 216 202-3499
9555 Rockside Rd Ste 300c Cleveland (44125) *(G-4107)*

Constant Aviation LLC (DH) 800 440-9004
18601 Cleveland Pkwy Dr Ste 1b Cleveland (44135) *(G-4108)*

Constellation Insurance Inc (HQ) 513 794-6100
1 Financial Way Ste 100 Cincinnati (45242) *(G-2496)*

Constlltion Insur Holdings Inc (PA) 513 794-6100
1 Financial Way Ste 100 Cincinnati (45242) *(G-2497)*

Constrction Wste Hlg Prtners L 614 683-0001
1575 Harmon Ave Columbus (43223) *(G-5683)*

Constructconnect, Cincinnati Also Called: Constructconnect Inc *(G-2498)*

Constructconnect Inc (HQ) 800 364-2059
3825 Edwards Rd Ste 800 Cincinnati (45209) *(G-2498)*

Construction, Niles Also Called: Danessa Construction Llc *(G-11787)*

Construction First, Columbus Also Called: Construction One Inc *(G-5685)*

Construction Labor Contrs LLC 216 741-3351
981 Keynote Cir Ste 25 Cleveland (44131) *(G-4109)*

Construction Labor Contrs LLC 614 932-9937
6155 Huntley Rd Ste G Columbus (43229) *(G-5684)*

Construction Labor Contrs LLC 513 539-2904
60 American Way Ste B Monroe (45050) *(G-11337)*

Construction Labor Contrs LLC 330 724-1906
3755 Boettler Oaks Dr Ste F Uniontown (44685) *(G-14246)*

Construction Mechanics Inc 330 630-9239
1025 S Broadway St Akron (44311) *(G-122)*

Construction One Inc 614 235-0057
101 E Town St Ste 401 Columbus (43215) *(G-5685)*

Construction Systems Inc (PA) 614 252-0708
2865 E 14th Ave Columbus (43219) *(G-5686)*

CONSULATE HEALTHCARE, Wellston Also Called: Edgewood Manor of Wellston *(G-14637)*

Consulate Healthcare Inc (PA) 419 865-1248
3231 Manley Rd Maumee (43537) *(G-10711)*

Consulate Management Co LLC 419 886-3922
4910 Algire Rd Bellville (44813) *(G-1047)*

Consulate Management Co LLC 440 237-7966
13900 Bennett Rd Cleveland (44133) *(G-4110)*

Consulate Management Co LLC 419 683-3255
327 W Main St Crestline (44827) *(G-7020)*

Consulate Management Co LLC 740 259-2351
10098 Big Bear Creek Rd Lucasville (45648) *(G-10174)*

Consulate Management Co LLC 330 837-1001
2311 Nave Rd Sw Massillon (44646) *(G-10636)*

Consulate Management Co LLC 419 867-7926
3600 Butz Rd Maumee (43537) *(G-10712)*

Consultants In Lab Medicine, Toledo Also Called: Promedica Health System Inc *(G-13971)*

Consultants Laboratory Medici 419 535-9629
2130 W Central Ave Ste 300 Toledo (43606) *(G-13759)*

Consumer Cr Cnsling Svc of Mdw (PA) 614 552-2222
700 Taylor Rd Ste 190 Columbus (43230) *(G-5687)*

Consumer Credit Counseling Ser (PA) 800 254-4100
1228 Euclid Ave Ste 390 Cleveland (44115) *(G-4111)*

Consumer Support Services Inc 216 447-1521
6505 Rockside Rd Ste 400 Independence (44131) *(G-9423)*

Consumer Support Services Inc 330 764-4785
2575 Medina Rd Ste A Medina (44256) *(G-10825)*

Consumer Support Services Inc 740 522-5464
640 Industrial Pkwy Newark (43056) *(G-11694)*

Consumer Support Services Inc 740 344-3600
100 James St Newark (43055) *(G-11695)*

Consumer Support Services Inc 330 652-8800
1254 Youngstown Warren Rd Ste B Niles (44446) *(G-11786)*

Consumer Support Services Inc 440 354-7082
368 Blackbrook Rd Ste 100 Painesville (44077) *(G-12223)*

Consumers Energy Company 800 477-5050
Cincinnati (45274) *(G-2499)*

Consumers Insurance Usa Inc 615 896-6133
471 E Broad St Fl 12 Columbus (43215) *(G-5688)*

Consumers National Bank (HQ) 330 868-7701
614 E Lincolnway Minerva (44657) *(G-11305)*

Container Graphics Corp 419 531-5133
305 Ryder Rd Toledo (43607) *(G-13760)*

Containerport Group Inc (HQ) 440 333-1330
1340 Depot St Fl 2 Cleveland (44116) *(G-4112)*

Containerport Group Inc 440 333-1330
2400 Creekway Dr Columbus (43207) *(G-5689)*

Contanda Terminals LLC 513 921-8441
3500 Southside Ave Cincinnati (45204) *(G-2500)*

Contech Trckg & Logistics LLC 513 645-7000
9025 Centre Pointe Dr Ste 400 West Chester (45069) *(G-14673)*

Contemporary Arts Center 513 721-0390
44 E 6th St Cincinnati (45202) *(G-2501)*

Contemporary Electric Inc 440 975-9965
38150 Strumbly Pl Willoughby (44094) *(G-15188)*

Continental 937 644-8940
  13601 Industrial Pkwy Marysville (43040) *(G-10480)*
Continental Airlines, Cleveland *Also Called: United Airlines Inc (G-5053)*
Continental Airlines, Cleveland *Also Called: United Airlines Inc (G-5054)*
Continental Airlines, Vandalia *Also Called: United Airlines Inc (G-14397)*
Continental Bldg Systems LLC 614 221-1818
  150 E Broad St Columbus (43215) *(G-5690)*
Continental Broadband PA 877 570-7827
  5000 Arlington Centre Blvd Columbus (43220) *(G-5691)*
Continental Building Company 614 221-1800
  150 E Broad St Columbus (43215) *(G-5692)*
Continental Building Company, Columbus *Also Called: Continental RE Companies (G-5695)*
Continental Contitech, Marysville *Also Called: Contitech Usa Inc (G-10481)*
Continental Express, Cleveland *Also Called: United Airlines Inc (G-5055)*
Continental Express Inc 937 497-2100
  10450 State Route 47 W Sidney (45365) *(G-13024)*
Continental Home Health Care 419 521-2470
  1495 W Longview Ave Ste 103 Mansfield (44906) *(G-10254)*
Continental Home Health Care 937 323-4499
  2100 E High St Ste 112 Springfield (45505) *(G-13241)*
Continental Office Furn Corp (PA) 614 262-5010
  5061 Freeway Dr E Columbus (43229) *(G-5693)*
Continental Properties 614 221-1800
  150 E Broad St Ste 700 Columbus (43215) *(G-5694)*
Continental RE Companies (PA) 614 221-1800
  150 E Broad St Ste 200 Columbus (43215) *(G-5695)*
Continental Realty Ltd (HQ) 614 224-2393
  150 E Gay St Columbus (43215) *(G-5696)*
Continental Realty Ltd 614 221-6260
  180 E Broad St Ste 1708 Columbus (43215) *(G-5697)*
Continental/Olentangy Ht LLC 614 297-9912
  1421 Olentangy River Rd Columbus (43212) *(G-5698)*
Contingent Network Services LLC 513 616-5773
  4400 Port Union Rd West Chester (45011) *(G-14674)*
Contining Hlthcare Sltions Inc 419 529-7272
  2875 Center Rd Ste 6 Brunswick (44212) *(G-1454)*
Contining Hlthcare Sltions Inc 440 466-1181
  60 West St Geneva (44041) *(G-8784)*
Continntal Mssage Solution Inc 614 224-4534
  41 S Grant Ave Fl 2 Columbus (43215) *(G-5699)*
Continntal Office Environments, Columbus *Also Called: Continental Office Furn Corp (G-5693)*
Continuing Healthcare of Milan, Milan *Also Called: Milan Skilled Nursing LLC (G-11208)*
Continuum Care Home Health LLC 216 898-8399
  12380 Plaza Dr Ste 103 Parma (44130) *(G-12252)*
Contitech Usa Inc 937 644-8900
  13601 Industrial Pkwy Marysville (43040) *(G-10481)*
Contract Lumber Inc (PA) 740 964-3147
  3245 Hazelton Etna Rd Sw Pataskala (43062) *(G-12270)*
Contract Sweepers & Eqp Co (PA) 614 221-7441
  2137 Parkwood Ave Columbus (43219) *(G-5700)*
Contract Sweepers & Eqp Co 513 577-7900
  10136 Mosteller Ln West Chester (45069) *(G-14675)*
Contractors Materials Company 513 733-3000
  10320 S Medallion Dr Cincinnati (45241) *(G-2502)*
Contractors Steel Company 330 425-3050
  8383 Boyle Pkwy Twinsburg (44087) *(G-14178)*
Contrlled Chaos Enrgy Svcs LLC 740 257-0724
  43510 National Rd Belmont (43718) *(G-1054)*
Contrlled Envmt Crtfction Svcs 513 870-0293
  171 Container Pl Cincinnati (45246) *(G-2503)*
Control System Mfg Inc 330 542-0000
  10725 Struthers Rd New Middletown (44442) *(G-11635)*
Controlsoft Inc 440 443-3900
  5387 Avion Park Dr Cleveland (44143) *(G-4113)*
Convalarium At Indian Run, Dublin *Also Called: Dublin Geriatric Care Co LP (G-7993)*
Convalescent Center Lucasville, Lucasville *Also Called: Edgewood Manor of Lucasville (G-10176)*
Convalescent Hospital For Chil 513 636-4415
  3333 Burnet Ave Cincinnati (45229) *(G-2504)*
Convenient Food Mart, Mentor *Also Called: Convenient Food Mart Inc (G-10926)*

Convenient Food Mart Inc (HQ) 800 860-4844
  6078 Pinecone Dr Mentor (44060) *(G-10926)*
Convenient Tire Service, Columbus *Also Called: W D Tire Warehouse Inc (G-6862)*
CONVENTION & VISITORS BUREAU, Cleveland *Also Called: Convention Vstors Bur of Grter (G-4115)*
Convention Vstors Bur of Grter 216 875-6600
  334 Euclid Ave Cleveland (44114) *(G-4114)*
Convention Vstors Bur of Grter (PA) 216 875-6603
  50 Public Sq Ste 3100 Cleveland (44113) *(G-4115)*
Convergint Technologies LLC 513 771-1717
  7812 Redsky Dr Cincinnati (45249) *(G-2505)*
Convergys Cstmer MGT Group Inc (DH) 513 723-6104
  201 E 4th St Bsmt Cincinnati (45202) *(G-2506)*
Convergys Cstomer MGT Intl Inc, Cincinnati *Also Called: Concentrix Cvg Cstmer MGT Intl (G-2493)*
Converse Electric Inc 614 808-4377
  3783 Gantz Rd Grove City (43123) *(G-8912)*
Conversion Tech Intl Inc 419 924-5566
  700 Oak St West Unity (43570) *(G-14874)*
Conveyer & Caster Corp (PA) 877 598-8534
  29570 Clemens Rd Westlake (44145) *(G-15054)*
Conveyer Cstr-Qpment For Indus, Westlake *Also Called: Conveyer & Caster Corp (G-15054)*
Conwed Plas Acquisition V LLC 877 542-7699
  2243 State Route 516 Nw Dover (44622) *(G-7875)*
Cook Paving and Cnstr Co 216 267-7705
  4545 Spring Rd Independence (44131) *(G-9424)*
Coolidge Wall Co LPA (PA) 937 223-8177
  33 W 1st St Ste 600 Dayton (45402) *(G-7247)*
Coon Caulking & Restoration, Louisville *Also Called: Coon Caulking & Sealants Inc (G-10115)*
Coon Caulking & Sealants Inc 330 875-2100
  7349 Ravenna Ave Louisville (44641) *(G-10115)*
Cooper Adel Vu & Assoc Lpa 740 625-4220
  36 W Main St Centerburg (43011) *(G-1934)*
Cooper Enterprises Inc 419 347-5232
  89 Curtis Dr Shelby (44875) *(G-13006)*
Cooper Farms, Oakwood *Also Called: Cooper Hatchery Inc (G-12053)*
Cooper Farms Inc (PA) 419 375-4116
  2321 State Route 49 Fort Recovery (45846) *(G-8606)*
Cooper Farms Liquid Egg Pdts, Fort Recovery *Also Called: Cooper Hatchery Inc (G-8607)*
Cooper Foods, Fort Recovery *Also Called: V H Cooper & Co Inc (G-8611)*
Cooper Hatchery Inc 419 375-5800
  2360 Wabash Rd Fort Recovery (45846) *(G-8607)*
Cooper Hatchery Inc (PA) 419 594-3325
  22348 Rd 140 Oakwood (45873) *(G-12053)*
Cooper-Smith Advertising LLC 419 470-5900
  3500 Granite Cir Toledo (43617) *(G-13761)*
Copac, Monroe *Also Called: Pac Worldwide Corporation (G-11348)*
Copc Hospitals 614 268-8164
  3555 Olentangy River Rd Columbus (43214) *(G-5701)*
Copc-Radiology, Columbus *Also Called: Central Ohio Prmry Care Physca (G-5543)*
Copcp 614 865-6570
  570 Polaris Pkwy Ste 200 Westerville (43082) *(G-14884)*
Copeland Oaks 330 938-1050
  715 S Johnson Rd Sebring (44672) *(G-12946)*
Copeland Oaks (PA) 330 938-6126
  800 S 15th St Sebring (44672) *(G-12947)*
Copley Health Center Inc 330 666-0980
  155 Heritage Woods Dr Copley (44321) *(G-6953)*
Copley Ohio Newspapers Inc 330 364-5577
  629 Wabash Ave Nw New Philadelphia (44663) *(G-11643)*
Copper and Brass Sales Div, Northwood *Also Called: Thyssenkrupp Logistics Inc (G-11984)*
Coral Company (PA) 216 932-8822
  4401 Rockside Rd Ste 390 Independence (44131) *(G-9425)*
Corazon Country Club LLC 614 504-5250
  7155 Corazon Dr Dublin (43016) *(G-7973)*
Corbus LLC (HQ) 937 226-7724
  9059 Springboro Pike Ste B Dayton (45449) *(G-7248)*
Corcoran Global Living, Columbus *Also Called: Exclusive Lifestyles Ohio LLC (G-5837)*
Cordelia Mrtin Hlth Ctr At Lbb, Toledo *Also Called: Libbey Inc (G-13887)*

Cordell Transportation Co LLC 937 277-7271
2942 Boulder Ave Dayton (45414) *(G-7249)*

Cordell Transportation Co., Dayton *Also Called: Cordell Transportation Co LLC (G-7249)*

Core, Cincinnati *Also Called: Cincinntis Optmum Rsdntial Env (G-2436)*

Core & Main Inc 419 278-2000
300 S Chestnut St Ste C Deshler (43516) *(G-7865)*

Core Resources Inc 513 731-1771
7795 5 Mile Rd Cincinnati (45230) *(G-2507)*

Core-Mark Holding Company Inc 650 589-9445
30300 Emerald Valley Pkwy Solon (44139) *(G-13077)*

Corecivic Inc 330 746-3777
2240 Hubbard Rd Youngstown (44505) *(G-15589)*

Corecrew LLC 855 692-6733
4670 Dues Dr West Chester (45246) *(G-14806)*

Corna Kokosing, Westerville *Also Called: CK Construction Group Inc (G-14967)*

Cornelia C Hodgson - Architec (PA) 216 593-0057
23240 Chagrin Blvd Ste 350 Beachwood (44122) *(G-784)*

Cornerstone, West Chester *Also Called: Cornerstone Brands Inc (G-14676)*

Cornerstone Brands Inc (DH) 513 603-1000
5568 W Chester Rd West Chester (45069) *(G-14676)*

Cornerstone Brands Group Inc 513 603-1000
5568 W Chester Rd West Chester (45069) *(G-14677)*

Cornerstone Brk Insur Svcs AGC (PA) 513 241-7675
2101 Florence Ave Cincinnati (45206) *(G-2508)*

Cornerstone Brkg Insur Svc Agc, Cincinnati *Also Called: Cornerstone Brk Insur Svcs AGC (G-2508)*

Cornerstone Brnds Group, West Chester *Also Called: Cornerstone Consolidated Services Group Inc (G-14678)*

Cornerstone Consolidated Services Group Inc 513 603-1000
5568 W Chester Rd West Chester (45069) *(G-14678)*

Cornerstone Controls Inc (PA) 513 489-2500
7131 E Kemper Rd Cincinnati (45249) *(G-2509)*

Cornerstone Hlthcare Sltons LL 937 985-4011
301 S Mechanic St Lebanon (45036) *(G-9761)*

Cornerstone Hope Bravement Ctr, Independence *Also Called: Bobby Tripodi Foundation Inc (G-9412)*

Cornerstone Managed Prprts LLC 440 263-7708
25255 Center Ridge Rd Westlake (44145) *(G-15055)*

Cornerstone Med Svcs - Mdwest 330 374-0229
453 S High St Ste 201 Akron (44311) *(G-123)*

Cornerstone Research Group Inc 937 320-1877
510 Earl Blvd Miamisburg (45342) *(G-11039)*

Cornerstone Support Services (PA) 330 339-7850
344 W High Ave New Philadelphia (44663) *(G-11644)*

Cornerstone Wauseon Inc 419 337-0940
995 Enterprise Ave Wauseon (43567) *(G-14598)*

Cornucopia Inc 216 521-4600
18120 Sloane Ave Lakewood (44107) *(G-9662)*

Cornwell Quality Tools, Mogador *Also Called: Cornwell Quality Tools Company (G-11325)*

Cornwell Quality Tools, Wadsworth *Also Called: The Cornwell Quality Tools Company (G-14455)*

Cornwell Quality Tools Company 330 628-2627
200 N Cleveland Ave Mogadore (44260) *(G-11325)*

Cornwell Quality Tools Company 330 335-2933
635 Seville Rd Wadsworth (44281) *(G-14434)*

Coroner, Dayton *Also Called: County of Montgomery (G-7256)*

Coroner's Office, Akron *Also Called: Summit County (G-325)*

Coroner's Office, Cleveland *Also Called: County of Cuyahoga (G-4127)*

Corporate Aviation Svcs Inc 740 338-3100
46226 National Rd Saint Clairsville (43950) *(G-12788)*

Corporate Cleaning Inc 614 203-6051
1720 Zollinger Rd Ste 99 Columbus (43221) *(G-5702)*

Corporate Fin Assoc Clmbus Inc 614 457-9219
671 Camden Yard Ct Columbus (43235) *(G-5703)*

Corporate One, Columbus *Also Called: Corporate One Federal Cr Un (G-5254)*

Corporate One Federal Cr Un (PA) 614 825-9314
8700 Orion Pl Columbus (43240) *(G-5254)*

Corporate Plans Inc 440 542-7800
6830 Cochran Rd Solon (44139) *(G-13078)*

Corporate Screening, Cleveland *Also Called: Corporate Screening Svcs LLC (G-4116)*

Corporate Screening Svcs LLC (HQ) 440 816-0500
16530 Commerce Ct Ste 3 Cleveland (44130) *(G-4116)*

Corporate Support Inc (PA) 419 221-3838
2262 Baton Rouge Lima (45805) *(G-9877)*

Corporate Wngs - Cleveland LLC 216 261-9000
355 Richmond Rd Ste A Cleveland (44143) *(G-4117)*

Corporation For OH Appalachian 330 364-8882
1260 Monroe St Nw Ste 39s New Philadelphia (44663) *(G-11645)*

Corportion For Ohio Applchian (PA) 740 594-8499
1 Pinchot Pl Athens (45701) *(G-562)*

Correction Commission NW Ohio 419 428-3800
3151 County Road 2425 Stryker (43557) *(G-13504)*

Correctnal Hlth Care Group Inc 330 454-6766
4500 Atlantic Blvd Ne Canton (44705) *(G-1722)*

Corrigan Moving Systems 440 243-5860
13900 Keystone Pkwy Cleveland (44135) *(G-4118)*

Corrosion Fluid Products Corp (DH) 248 478-0100
3000 E 14th Ave Columbus (43219) *(G-5704)*

Corrotec Inc 937 325-3585
1125 W North St Springfield (45504) *(G-13242)*

Cors & Bassett LLC (PA) 513 852-8200
537 E Pete Rose Way Ste 400 Cincinnati (45202) *(G-2510)*

Corso's Flower & Garden Center, Sandusky *Also Called: August Corso Sons Inc (G-12863)*

Cortland Dental Technology Ctr, Cortland *Also Called: David Harnett DDS Inc (G-6971)*

Cortland Healthcare Center, Cortland *Also Called: Cortland Healthcare Group Inc (G-6970)*

Cortland Healthcare Group Inc 330 638-4015
369 N High St Cortland (44410) *(G-6970)*

Corvel, Cleveland *Also Called: Corvel Corporation (G-4119)*

Corvel Corporation 800 275-6463
7530 Lucerne Dr Ste 400 Cleveland (44130) *(G-4119)*

Corwin M. Nixon Health Center, Lebanon *Also Called: Dayton Osteopathic Hospital (G-9763)*

Cosan Group, Independence *Also Called: Chronic Care Management Inc (G-9418)*

Coshocton Cnty Emrgncy Med Svc 740 622-4294
513 Chestnut St Coshocton (43812) *(G-6980)*

Coshocton Cnty Head Start Inc 740 622-3667
3201 County Road 16 Coshocton (43812) *(G-6981)*

Cosi, Columbus *Also Called: Franklin County Historical Soc (G-5888)*

Cosmic Concepts, Columbus *Also Called: Cosmic Concepts Ltd (G-5705)*

Cosmic Concepts Ltd 216 696-4230
5000 Euclid Ave Cleveland (44103) *(G-4120)*

Cosmic Concepts Ltd 614 228-1104
399 E Main St Ste 140 Columbus (43215) *(G-5705)*

Cost Sharing Solutions LLC 330 915-6800
2824 Woodlawn Ave Nw Canton (44708) *(G-1723)*

Costume Specialists Inc 614 464-2115
1801 Lone Eagle St Columbus (43228) *(G-5706)*

Cota, Columbus *Also Called: Central Ohio Transit Authority (G-5546)*

Cota, Columbus *Also Called: Central Ohio Transit Authority (G-5547)*

Cott Systems Inc 614 847-4405
2800 Corporate Exchange Dr Ste 300 Columbus (43231) *(G-5707)*

Cottage Gardens Inc 440 259-2900
4992 Middle Ridge Rd Perry (44081) *(G-12305)*

Cotter House Worthington LLC 614 540-2414
470 Olde Worthington Rd Ste 100 Westerville (43082) *(G-14885)*

Cotter Mdse Stor of Ohio 330 773-9177
1564 Firestone Pkwy Akron (44301) *(G-124)*

Cotter Moving & Storage Co 330 535-5115
265 W Bowery St Akron (44308) *(G-125)*

Cottingham Party Savers, Columbus *Also Called: The Cottingham Paper Co (G-6758)*

Cottingham Rtirement Cmnty Inc 513 563-3600
3995 Cottingham Dr Cincinnati (45241) *(G-2511)*

Coughlin Automotive, Newark *Also Called: Coughlin Chevrolet Toyota Inc (G-11696)*

Coughlin Automotive Group, Pataskala *Also Called: Coughlin Chevrolet Inc (G-12271)*

Coughlin Chevrolet Inc 740 852-1122
255 Lafayette St London (43140) *(G-10040)*

Coughlin Chevrolet Inc (PA) 740 964-9191
9000 Broad St Sw Pataskala (43062) *(G-12271)*

Coughlin Chevrolet Toyota Inc 740 366-1381
1850 N 21st St Newark (43055) *(G-11696)*

Coulter Ventures Llc (PA) 614 358-6190
545 E 5th Ave Columbus (43201) *(G-5708)*

ALPHABETIC SECTION

Council Dev Fin Agencies.. 614 705-1300
100 E Broad St Ste 1200 Columbus (43215) *(G-5709)*

Council On Aging Sthwstern Ohi.................................. 513 721-1025
4601 Malsbary Rd Blue Ash (45242) *(G-1159)*

Council On Rur Svc Prgrams Inc................................... 937 452-1090
8263 Us Route 127 Camden (45311) *(G-1589)*

Council On Rur Svc Prgrams Inc (PA).......................... 937 778-5220
201 Robert M Davis Pkwy Ste B Piqua (45356) *(G-12438)*

Council On Rur Svc Prgrams Inc................................... 937 773-0773
285 Robert M Davis Pkwy Piqua (45356) *(G-12439)*

Council On Rur Svc Prgrams Inc................................... 937 492-8787
1502 N Main Ave Sidney (45365) *(G-13025)*

Counsel, North Canton Also Called: Visual Edge It Inc *(G-11870)*

COUNSELING CENTER, THE, Portsmouth Also Called: Scioto Cnty Counseling Ctr Inc *(G-12567)*

Counseling Source Inc... 513 984-9838
10921 Reed Hartman Hwy Ste 133 Blue Ash (45242) *(G-1160)*

Counsling Ctr of Wyne Hlmes CN (PA)....................... 330 264-9029
2285 Benden Dr Wooster (44691) *(G-15327)*

Counting Blessings HM Care LLC................................ 440 850-1050
4310 Main Ave Ashtabula (44004) *(G-529)*

Country Butcher, The, Coldwater Also Called: I-O Properties LLC *(G-5214)*

Country CLB Retirement Ctr LLC................................. 440 992-0022
925 E 26th St Ashtabula (44004) *(G-530)*

Country CLB Retirement Ctr LLC (PA)........................ 740 671-9330
55801 Conno Mara Dr Bellaire (43906) *(G-1010)*

Country Club Inc... 216 831-9200
2825 Lander Rd Cleveland (44124) *(G-4121)*

Country Club At Muirfield Vlg..................................... 614 764-1714
8715 Muirfield Dr Dublin (43017) *(G-7974)*

Country Club Center Homes Inc.................................. 330 343-6351
860 E Iron Ave Dover (44622) *(G-7876)*

Country Club Center II Ltd.. 740 397-2350
1350 Yauger Rd Mount Vernon (43050) *(G-11479)*

Country Club Center III, Ashtabula Also Called: Country CLB Retirement Ctr LLC *(G-530)*

Country Club of Hudson... 330 650-1188
2155 Middleton Rd Hudson (44236) *(G-9341)*

Country Club of The North, Xenia Also Called: Escalante - Cntry CLB of N LLC *(G-15504)*

COUNTRY CLUB RETIREMENT CAMPUS, Mount Vernon Also Called: Country Club Center II Ltd *(G-11479)*

Country Club Retirement Ctr IV, Dover Also Called: Country Club Center Homes Inc *(G-7876)*

COUNTRY CLUB, THE, Dublin Also Called: Country Club At Muirfield Vlg *(G-7974)*

Country Concert, Fort Loramie Also Called: Hickory Hill Lakes Inc *(G-8604)*

Country Court.. 740 397-4125
1076 Coshocton Ave Mount Vernon (43050) *(G-11480)*

Country Ln Grdns Rhbltion Nrs, Thornville Also Called: Fairfeld Grdns Rhbltion Care *(G-13620)*

Country Mdow Rhbltion Nrsing, Bellville Also Called: Country Meadow Care Center LLC *(G-1048)*

Country Meadow Care Center, Bellville Also Called: Consulate Management Co LLC *(G-1047)*

Country Meadow Care Center LLC............................. 419 886-3922
4910 Algire Rd Bellville (44813) *(G-1048)*

Country Neighbor Program Inc (PA)........................... 440 437-6311
39 S Maple St Orwell (44076) *(G-12177)*

Country Suites By Carlson, Amherst Also Called: Bindu Associates LLC Elyria *(G-424)*

Country Suites By Carlson, Beavercreek Also Called: Payal Development LLC *(G-892)*

Country Suites By Carlson, Ontario Also Called: Premier Hotels Inc *(G-12123)*

Country View of Sunbury, Sunbury Also Called: Morning View Delaware Inc *(G-13522)*

Countryside Yung MNS Chrstn As............................... 513 677-3702
6246 Turning Leaf Way Maineville (45039) *(G-10227)*

County Commissioners Assn Ohio.............................. 614 220-0636
209 E State St Columbus (43215) *(G-5710)*

County Fire Protection LLC.. 330 633-1014
4620 Crystal Pkwy Kent (44240) *(G-9566)*

County Garage, Ottawa Also Called: Putnam Cnty Commissioners Off *(G-12192)*

County of Adams.. 937 544-5067
300 N Wilson Dr West Union (45693) *(G-14868)*

County of Allen... 419 227-8590
123 W Spring St Lima (45801) *(G-9878)*

County of Allen... 419 228-2120
951 Commerce Pkwy Ste 100 Lima (45804) *(G-9879)*

County of Allen... 419 228-6065
600 S Main St Lima (45804) *(G-9880)*

County of Allen... 419 221-1103
3125 Ada Rd Lima (45801) *(G-9881)*

County of Ashtabula... 440 998-1811
3914 C Ct Ashtabula (44004) *(G-531)*

County of Ashtabula... 440 576-2816
186 E Satin St Jefferson (44047) *(G-9538)*

County of Auglaize... 419 629-2419
20 E 1st St New Bremen (45869) *(G-11596)*

County of Auglaize... 419 738-3816
13093 Infirmary Rd Wapakoneta (45895) *(G-14482)*

County of Carroll.. 330 627-1900
2205 Commerce Dr Carrollton (44615) *(G-1905)*

County of Carroll.. 330 627-7651
2167 Kensington Rd Ne Carrollton (44615) *(G-1906)*

County of Champaign... 937 653-4848
428 Beech St Urbana (43078) *(G-14305)*

County of Champaign... 937 653-2711
1512 S Us Highway 68 Ste B300 Urbana (43078) *(G-14306)*

County of Clark... 937 390-5600
529 E Home Rd Springfield (45503) *(G-13243)*

County of Clermont.. 513 732-7265
270 E Main St Ste 8 Batavia (45103) *(G-736)*

County of Clermont.. 513 732-5400
2337 Clermont Center Dr Batavia (45103) *(G-737)*

County of Clermont.. 513 732-7970
4400 Haskell Ln Batavia (45103) *(G-738)*

County of Clermont.. 513 732-7661
2279 Clermont Center Dr Batavia (45103) *(G-739)*

County of Coshocton.. 740 622-1020
725 Pine St Coshocton (43812) *(G-6982)*

County of Crawford.. 419 562-0015
224 Norton Way Bucyrus (44820) *(G-1502)*

County of Crawford.. 419 562-3050
200 S Spring St Bucyrus (44820) *(G-1503)*

County of Crawford.. 419 562-5871
1520 Isaac Beal Rd Bucyrus (44820) *(G-1504)*

County of Crawford.. 419 562-7731
815 Whetstone St Bucyrus (44820) *(G-1505)*

County of Cuyahoga... 216 420-6750
1701 E 12th St Ste 11 Cleveland (44114) *(G-4122)*

County of Cuyahoga... 216 443-5100
1640 Superior Ave E Cleveland (44114) *(G-4123)*

County of Cuyahoga... 216 681-4433
13231 Euclid Ave Cleveland (44112) *(G-4124)*

County of Cuyahoga... 216 348-3800
2100 Superior Via Cleveland (44113) *(G-4125)*

County of Cuyahoga... 216 241-8230
1275 Lakeside Ave E Cleveland (44114) *(G-4126)*

County of Cuyahoga... 216 698-6526
11001 Cedar Ave Ste 400 Cleveland (44106) *(G-4127)*

County of Cuyahoga... 216 941-8800
5202 Memphis Ave Cleveland (44144) *(G-4128)*

County of Cuyahoga... 216 431-4500
3955 Euclid Ave Cleveland (44115) *(G-4129)*

County of Cuyahoga... 216 432-2621
3955 Euclid Ave Rm 344 Cleveland (44115) *(G-4130)*

County of Cuyahoga... 216 443-6954
2079 E 9th St Cleveland (44115) *(G-4131)*

County of Cuyahoga... 419 399-8260
112 N Williams St Paulding (45879) *(G-12282)*

County of Delaware.. 740 833-2240
50 Channing St Delaware (43015) *(G-7787)*

County of Delaware.. 740 833-2400
50 Channing St Delaware (43015) *(G-7788)*

County of Delaware.. 740 203-2040
1 W Winter St 2nd Fl Delaware (43015) *(G-7789)*

County of Erie... 419 627-8733
3916 Perkins Ave Huron (44839) *(G-9386)*

County of Erie... 419 627-7710
2700 Columbus Ave Sandusky (44870) *(G-12886)*

County of Gallia — 848 3rd Ave Gallipolis (45631) *(G-8753)*	740 446-3222
County of Gallia — 1167 State Route 160 Gallipolis (45631) *(G-8754)*	740 446-4009
County of Gallia — 77 Mill Creek Rd Gallipolis (45631) *(G-8755)*	740 446-6902
County of Geauga — 12611 Ravenwood Dr Ste 150 Chardon (44024) *(G-1998)*	440 285-9141
County of Guernsey — 11272 E Pike Rd Cambridge (43725) *(G-1565)*	740 439-1269
County of Guernsey — 1022 Carlisle Ave Cambridge (43725) *(G-1566)*	740 439-6681
County of Guernsey — 274 Highland Ave Cambridge (43725) *(G-1567)*	740 439-5555
County of Hamilton — 4477 Carver Woods Dr Blue Ash (45242) *(G-1161)*	513 946-8757
County of Hamilton — 222 East Central Pkwy Cincinnati (45202) *(G-2512)*	513 946-1800
County of Hardin — 705 N Ida St Kenton (43326) *(G-9613)*	419 674-4158
County of Lake — 8121 Deepwood Blvd Mentor (44060) *(G-10927)*	440 350-5100
County of Lake — 235 Fairgrounds Rd Painesville (44077) *(G-12224)*	440 350-2793
County of Logan — 1991 County Road 13 Bellefontaine (43311) *(G-1024)*	937 592-2791
County of Logan — 1851 State Route 47 W Bellefontaine (43311) *(G-1025)*	937 292-3031
County of Logan — 101 S Main St Rm 1 Bellefontaine (43311) *(G-1026)*	937 599-7252
County of Logan — 2739 County Road 91 Bellefontaine (43311) *(G-1027)*	937 592-2901
County of Logan — 1100 S Detroit St Bellefontaine (43311) *(G-1028)*	937 599-7290
County of Lorain — 1091 Infirmary Rd Elyria (44035) *(G-8238)*	440 329-3734
County of Lorain — 1885 Lake Ave Elyria (44035) *(G-8239)*	440 324-5777
County of Lorain — 226 Middle Ave 4th Fl Elyria (44035) *(G-8240)*	440 329-5340
County of Lorain — 308 2nd St Elyria (44035) *(G-8241)*	440 326-4700
County of Lorain — 1173 N Ridge Rd E Ste 101 Lorain (44055) *(G-10069)*	440 233-2020
County of Lorain — 179 E Herrick Ave Wellington (44090) *(G-14630)*	440 647-5803
County of Lucas — 1049 S Mccord Rd Bldg A Holland (43528) *(G-9283)*	419 213-2892
County of Lucas — 1 Government Ctr Ste 800 Toledo (43604) *(G-13762)*	419 213-4500
County of Lucas — 701 Adams St Toledo (43604) *(G-13763)*	419 213-3000
County of Lucas — 700 Adams St Ste 250 Toledo (43604) *(G-13764)*	419 213-4700
County of Lucas — 2001 Collingwood Blvd Toledo (43620) *(G-13765)*	419 248-3585
County of Lucas — 635 N Erie St Toledo (43604) *(G-13766)*	419 213-4018
County of Lucas — 2595 Arlington Ave Toledo (43614) *(G-13767)*	419 213-3903
County of Meigs — 175 Race St Middleport (45760) *(G-11147)*	740 992-2117
County of Meigs — Mulburry Heights Stn 11 Pomeroy (45769) *(G-12513)*	740 992-6617
County of Miami — 2100 N County Road 25a Troy (45373) *(G-14132)*	937 335-1314
County of Monroe — 47045 Moore Ridge Rd Woodsfield (43793) *(G-15301)*	740 472-0144
County of Montgomery — 451 W 3rd St Dayton (45422) *(G-7250)*	937 225-6140
County of Montgomery — 451 W 3rd St Dayton (45422) *(G-7251)*	937 225-6294
County of Montgomery — 361 W 3rd St Dayton (45402) *(G-7252)*	937 225-4990
County of Montgomery — 5625 Little Richmond Rd Dayton (45426) *(G-7253)*	937 854-4576
County of Montgomery — 451 W 3rd St Fl 2 Dayton (45422) *(G-7254)*	937 225-4010
County of Montgomery — 345 W 2nd St Dayton (45422) *(G-7255)*	937 225-4192
County of Montgomery — 361 W 3rd St Dayton (45402) *(G-7256)*	937 225-4156
County of Montgomery — 8100 N Main St Dayton (45415) *(G-7257)*	937 264-0460
County of Ottawa — 8180 W State Route 163 Oak Harbor (43449) *(G-12044)*	567 262-3600
County of Perry — 5550 State Route 37 E New Lexington (43764) *(G-11621)*	740 342-1213
County of Perry — 520 1st St New Lexington (43764) *(G-11622)*	740 342-4264
County of Perry — 2645 Old Somerset Rd New Lexington (43764) *(G-11623)*	740 342-2191
County of Perry — 601 Senior Dr New Lexington (43764) *(G-11624)*	740 342-0416
County of Pickaway — 16405 Us Highway 23 Ashville (43103) *(G-552)*	740 474-7588
County of Portage — 8116 Infirmary Rd Ravenna (44266) *(G-12624)*	330 297-3670
County of Portage — 466 S Chestnut St Ravenna (44266) *(G-12625)*	330 297-3850
County of Preble — 116 E Main St Ste B Eaton (45320) *(G-8211)*	937 456-2085
County of Preble — 1251 State Route 503 N West Alexandria (45381) *(G-14643)*	937 839-5845
County of Richland — 314 Cleveland Ave Mansfield (44902) *(G-10255)*	419 774-4200
County of Ross — 184 Cattail Rd Chillicothe (45601) *(G-2062)*	740 773-4169
County of Sandusky — 1001 Castalia St Fremont (43420) *(G-8672)*	419 637-2243
County of Shelby — 500 Gearhart Rd Sidney (45365) *(G-13026)*	937 498-7244
County of Shelby — 2901 Fair Rd Sidney (45365) *(G-13027)*	937 492-6900
County of Stark — 5165 Southway St Sw Canton (44706) *(G-1724)*	330 477-6781
County of Stark — 1701 Mahoning Rd Ne Canton (44705) *(G-1725)*	330 451-2303
County of Stark — 225 4th St Ne Canton (44702) *(G-1726)*	330 451-7232
County of Stark — 121 Cleveland Ave Sw Canton (44702) *(G-1727)*	330 455-6644
County of Summit — 89 E Howe Rd Tallmadge (44278) *(G-13590)*	330 634-8000
County of Trumbull — 650 N River Rd Nw Warren (44483) *(G-14514)*	330 675-2640
County of Tuscarawas — 897 E Iron Ave Dover (44622) *(G-7877)*	330 343-5555
County of Tuscarawas — 389 16th St Sw New Philadelphia (44663) *(G-11646)*	330 339-7791
County of Warren — 903 N Broadway St Lebanon (45036) *(G-9762)*	513 925-1377
County of Washington — 103 Westview Ave Marietta (45750) *(G-10364)*	740 376-7430
County of Wayne — 876 S Geyers Chapel Rd Wooster (44691) *(G-15328)*	330 262-1786
County of Wayne — 2534 Burbank Rd Wooster (44691) *(G-15329)*	330 345-5340
County of Wayne — 3151 W Old Lincoln Way Wooster (44691) *(G-15330)*	330 287-5500
County of Wayne — 128 E Milltown Rd Ste 105 Wooster (44691) *(G-15331)*	330 345-5891
County of Wood — 1965 E Gypsy Lane Rd Bowling Green (43402) *(G-1314)*	419 353-8411

ALPHABETIC SECTION — Crane America Services Inc

County of Wood 419 352-8402
　1840 E Gypsy Lane Rd Bowling Green (43402) *(G-1315)*

County of Wyandot 419 294-1714
　7830 State Highway 199 Upper Sandusky (43351) *(G-14286)*

Court Dialysis LLC 740 773-3733
　1180 N Bridge St Chillicothe (45601) *(G-2063)*

Courtesy Ambulance Inc 740 522-8588
　1890 W Main St Newark (43055) *(G-11697)*

Courtney W Fleming DDS L 614 263-4040
　3701 N High St Columbus (43214) *(G-5711)*

Courtyard By Marriott 937 429-5203
　2777 Fairfield Commons Blvd Beavercreek (45431) *(G-874)*

Courtyard By Marriott 216 765-1900
　3695 Orange Pl Cleveland (44122) *(G-4132)*

Courtyard By Marriott 937 433-3131
　100 Prestige Pl Miamisburg (45342) *(G-11040)*

Courtyard By Marriott 740 344-1800
　500 Highland Blvd Newark (43055) *(G-11698)*

Courtyard By Marriott, Akron *Also Called: Concord Testa Hotel Assoc LLC (G-119)*

Courtyard By Marriott, Beavercreek *Also Called: Courtyard By Marriott (G-874)*

Courtyard By Marriott, Cleveland *Also Called: Courtyard Management Corp (G-4133)*

Courtyard By Marriott, Columbus *Also Called: Columbus Concord Ltd Partnr (G-5625)*

Courtyard By Marriott, Columbus *Also Called: Courtyard By Mrrott Columbus W (G-5712)*

Courtyard By Marriott, Columbus *Also Called: Courtyard Management Corp (G-5714)*

Courtyard By Marriott, Dayton *Also Called: Courtyard By Mrrott Dytn-Nvrsi (G-7258)*

Courtyard By Marriott, Hamilton *Also Called: Concord Hmltnian Rvrfront Ht L (G-9034)*

Courtyard By Marriott, Holland *Also Called: Courtyard Management Corp (G-9284)*

Courtyard By Marriott, Maumee *Also Called: Courtyard Management Corp (G-10713)*

Courtyard By Marriott, Mentor *Also Called: Charter Hotel Group Ltd Partnr (G-10920)*

Courtyard By Marriott, Miamisburg *Also Called: Courtyard By Marriott (G-11040)*

Courtyard By Marriott, Newark *Also Called: Courtyard By Marriott (G-11698)*

Courtyard By Marriott, Rossford *Also Called: Courtyard By Marriott Rossford (G-12766)*

Courtyard By Marriott, Stow *Also Called: Hotel Stow LP (G-13375)*

Courtyard By Marriott Canton, Canton *Also Called: Ca-Mj Hotel Associates Ltd (G-1694)*

Courtyard By Marriott Rossford 419 872-5636
　9789 Clark Dr Rossford (43460) *(G-12766)*

Courtyard By Mrrott Clmbus Dwn, Columbus *Also Called: Moody Nat Cy Dt Clumbus Mt LLC (G-6259)*

Courtyard By Mrrott Columbus W 614 771-8999
　2350 Westbelt Dr Columbus (43228) *(G-5712)*

Courtyard By Mrrott Dytn-Nvrsi 937 220-9060
　2006 S Edwin C Moses Blvd Dayton (45417) *(G-7258)*

Courtyard Cincinnati Blue Ash, Blue Ash *Also Called: Cmp I Blue Ash Owner LLC (G-1154)*

Courtyard Cleveland Beach, Cleveland *Also Called: Courtyard By Marriott (G-4132)*

Courtyard Columbus West, Columbus *Also Called: Cs Hotels Limited Partnership (G-5733)*

Courtyard Dayton, Dayton *Also Called: Cni Thl Ops LLC (G-7237)*

Courtyard Management Corp 216 901-9988
　5051 W Creek Rd Cleveland (44131) *(G-4133)*

Courtyard Management Corp 614 436-7070
　7411 Vantage Dr Columbus (43235) *(G-5713)*

Courtyard Management Corp 614 475-8530
　2901 Airport Dr Columbus (43219) *(G-5714)*

Courtyard Management Corp 419 866-1001
　1435 E Mall Dr Holland (43528) *(G-9284)*

Courtyard Management Corp 419 897-2255
　415 W Dussel Dr Maumee (43537) *(G-10713)*

Courtyard Springfield Downtown, Springfield *Also Called: Crefiii Wrmaug Sprngfeld Lssee (G-13245)*

Courtyard Toledo Maumee, Maumee *Also Called: Richfield Inn Inc (G-10762)*

Cousins Waste Control LLC (HQ) 419 726-1500
　1701 E Matzinger Rd Toledo (43612) *(G-13768)*

Cov-Ro Inc 330 856-3176
　3900 E Market St Ste 1 Warren (44484) *(G-14515)*

Cova, Columbus *Also Called: Center of Voctnl Altrntvs Mntl (G-5533)*

Covenant Care Ohio Inc 937 878-7046
　829 Yellow Springs Fairborn Rd Fairborn (45324) *(G-8370)*

Covenant Care Ohio Inc 937 378-0188
　8065 Doctor Faul Rd Georgetown (45121) *(G-8800)*

Covenant Care Ohio Inc 419 898-5506
　1330 Fulton St Port Clinton (43452) *(G-12521)*

Covenant Care Ohio Inc 937 399-5551
　701 Villa Rd Springfield (45503) *(G-13244)*

Covenant Care Ohio Inc 419 531-4201
　4420 South Ave Toledo (43615) *(G-13769)*

Covenant Care Ohio Inc 937 526-5570
　200 Marker Rd Versailles (45380) *(G-14415)*

Covenant House, Dayton *Also Called: Jewish Fdrtion Grter Dyton Inc (G-7428)*

Covenant Transport Inc 423 821-1212
　3825 Aries Brook Dr Columbus (43207) *(G-5715)*

Cover Crop Shop LLC 937 417-3972
　739 S Vandemark Rd Sidney (45365) *(G-13028)*

Covetrus North America, Dublin *Also Called: Covetrus North America LLC (G-7975)*

Covetrus North America, Dublin *Also Called: WA Butler Company (G-8159)*

Covetrus North America LLC (HQ) 614 761-9095
　400 Metro Pl N Ste 100 Dublin (43017) *(G-7975)*

Covia Holdings LLC (PA) 800 255-7263
　3 Summit Park Dr Ste 700 Independence (44131) *(G-9426)*

Covington Care Center, Covington *Also Called: Uvmc Nursing Care Inc (G-7019)*

Cowan's Auctions, Cincinnati *Also Called: Cowans LLC (G-2513)*

Cowans LLC 513 871-1670
　5030 Oaklawn Dr Ste 1 Cincinnati (45227) *(G-2513)*

Cowen Truck Line Inc 419 938-3401
　2697 State Rte 39 Perrysville (44864) *(G-12391)*

Cox Arboretum 937 434-9005
　6733 Springboro Pike Dayton (45449) *(G-7259)*

Cox Institute, Kettering *Also Called: Wright State University (G-9634)*

Coy Bros Inc 330 533-6864
　433 Fairground Blvd Canfield (44406) *(G-1627)*

Coyle Music, Columbus *Also Called: Coyle Music Centers Inc (G-5716)*

Coyle Music Centers Inc 614 885-6654
　137 Graceland Blvd Columbus (43214) *(G-5716)*

Coyne Finishing, Mount Vernon *Also Called: Coyne Graphic Finishing Inc (G-11481)*

Coyne Graphic Finishing Inc 740 397-6232
　1301 Newark Rd Mount Vernon (43050) *(G-11481)*

CP Dublin LLC 614 791-1000
　5605 Blazer Pkwy Dublin (43017) *(G-7976)*

CP Mason LLC 513 459-9800
　9664 S Mason Montgomery Rd Mason (45040) *(G-10543)*

CP Redi LLC 866 682-7462
　1030 Freeway Dr N Bldg 6 Columbus (43229) *(G-5717)*

Cpca Manufacturing LLC 937 723-9031
　750 Rosedale Dr Dayton (45402) *(G-7260)*

Cpg, Columbus *Also Called: Containerport Group Inc (G-5689)*

CPI-Hr, Solon *Also Called: Corporate Plans Inc (G-13078)*

Cpo Managment Services, Columbus *Also Called: Community Prpts Ohio MGT Svcs (G-5672)*

Cpp Group Holdings LLC (PA) 216 453-4800
　1621 Euclid Ave Ste 1850 Cleveland (44115) *(G-4134)*

Cpr, Independence *Also Called: Mmi-Cpr LLC (G-9454)*

CPS Medmanagement LLC 901 748-0470
　655 Metro Pl S Ste 450 Dublin (43017) *(G-7977)*

CPS Solutions LLC (HQ) 901 748-0470
　655 Metro Pl S Ste 450 Dublin (43017) *(G-7978)*

CPW-32, Perry *Also Called: Car Parts Warehouse Inc (G-12304)*

CPX Canton Airport LLC 330 305-0500
　7883 Freedom Ave Nw North Canton (44720) *(G-11819)*

Crabbe Brown & James LLP (PA) 614 229-4509
　500 S Front St Ste 1200 Columbus (43215) *(G-5718)*

Crabbe, Brown & James, Columbus *Also Called: Crabbe Brown & James LLP (G-5718)*

Craft Wholesalers Inc 740 964-6210
　4600 S Hamilton Rd Groveport (43125) *(G-8980)*

Craftsman Electric Inc 513 891-4426
　3855 Alta Ave Ste 1 Cincinnati (45236) *(G-2514)*

Craig Smith Auto Group, Galion *Also Called: Surfside Motors Inc (G-8751)*

Craig Transportation Co 419 874-7981
　819 Kingsbury St Ste 102 Maumee (43537) *(G-10714)*

Crain Communications Inc 330 836-9180
　2291 Riverfront Pkwy Ste 1000 Cuyahoga Falls (44221) *(G-7065)*

Crandall Medical Center 330 938-6126
　800 S 15th St Ste A Sebring (44672) *(G-12948)*

Crane America Services Inc 937 293-6526
　1027 Byers Rd Miamisburg (45342) *(G-11041)*

Crane Carrier Company LLC — ALPHABETIC SECTION

Crane Carrier Company LLC (HQ) 918 286-2889
  1951 Reiser Ave Se New Philadelphia (44663) *(G-11647)*
Crane Carrier Holdings LLC 918 286-2889
  1951 Reiser Ave Se New Philadelphia (44663) *(G-11648)*
Crane Consumables Inc 513 539-9980
  155 Wright Dr Middletown (45044) *(G-11160)*
Crane Group Co (PA) 614 754-3000
  330 W Spring St Ste 200 Columbus (43215) *(G-5719)*
Crane Pumps & Systems Inc 937 773-2442
  420 3rd St Piqua (45356) *(G-12440)*
Crane Renovation Group, Columbus *Also Called: Able Roofing LLC (G-5296)*
Crane Service Div, Lima *Also Called: Jeffers Crane Service Inc (G-9912)*
Cranel Imaging, Columbus *Also Called: Cranel Incorporated (G-5255)*
Cranel Incorporated (PA) 614 431-8000
  8999 Gemini Pkwy Ste A Columbus (43240) *(G-5255)*
Cranley Surgical Associates 513 961-4335
  3747 W Fork Rd Cincinnati (45247) *(G-2515)*
Crawford Cnty Council On Aging, Bucyrus *Also Called: County of Crawford (G-1503)*
Crawford Cnty Job & Fmly Svcs, Bucyrus *Also Called: County of Crawford (G-1502)*
Crawford Cnty Shared Hlth Svcs 419 468-7985
  1220 N Market St Galion (44833) *(G-8746)*
Crawford County Children Svcs (PA) 419 562-1200
  224 Norton Way Bucyrus (44820) *(G-1506)*
Crawford Hoying Ltd (PA) 614 335-2020
  6640 Riverside Dr Ste 500 Dublin (43017) *(G-7979)*
Crawford Manor Healthcare Ctr, Cleveland *Also Called: Sunset Mnor Hlthcare Group Inc (G-4963)*
Crawford Mechanical Svcs Inc 614 478-9424
  9464 Jersey Mill Rd Nw Pataskala (43062) *(G-12272)*
CRC, Columbus *Also Called: Clintnvlle Bchwold Cmnty Rsrce (G-5585)*
Creative Child Care, Columbus *Also Called: Creative Child Care Inc (G-5720)*
Creative Child Care Inc 614 863-3500
  1601 Shanley Dr Columbus (43224) *(G-5720)*
Creative Connections LLC 513 389-0213
  5558 Cheviot Rd Cincinnati (45247) *(G-2516)*
Creative Fincl Staffing LLC 614 343-7800
  150 E Wilson Bridge Rd Ste 340 Worthington (43085) *(G-15410)*
Creative Foundations Inc (PA) 877 345-6733
  20 Troy Rd Delaware (43015) *(G-7790)*
Creative Foundations Inc 614 832-2121
  20 Troy Rd Delaware (43015) *(G-7791)*
Creative Hair Designs 419 425-4247
  212 E Sandusky St Findlay (45840) *(G-8524)*
Creative Learning Workshop LLC (PA) 330 393-5929
  1268 N River Rd Ne Ste 1 Warren (44483) *(G-14516)*
Creative Living Inc 614 421-1131
  150 W 10th Ave Columbus (43201) *(G-5721)*
Creative Microsystems Inc 937 836-4499
  52 Hillside Ct Englewood (45322) *(G-8304)*
Creative Options LLC 614 868-1231
  605 Claycraft Rd Columbus (43230) *(G-5722)*
Creative Playroom (PA) 216 475-6464
  16574 Broadway Ave Cleveland (44137) *(G-4135)*
Creative Playroom 440 248-3100
  32750 Solon Rd Ste 3 Solon (44139) *(G-13079)*
Creativity For Kids, Independence *Also Called: AW Faber-Castell Usa Inc (G-9408)*
Cred-Kap Inc 330 755-1466
  400 Sexton St Struthers (44471) *(G-13499)*
Credence MGT Sltions Ltd Lblty 571 620-7586
  2940 Presidential Dr Ste 230 Beavercreek (45324) *(G-875)*
Credit Adjustments, Defiance *Also Called: Mammoth Tech Inc (G-7754)*
Credit Bur Collectn Svcs Inc 614 223-0688
  250 E Broad St Ste 1250 Columbus (43215) *(G-5723)*
Credit Bur Collectn Svcs Inc (HQ) 614 223-0688
  236 E Town St Columbus (43215) *(G-5724)*
Credit Care, Bellefontaine *Also Called: Logan View LLC (G-1031)*
Credit First NA 216 362-5000
  6275 Eastland Rd Brookpark (44142) *(G-1432)*
Credit First National Assn (DH) 216 362-5300
  6275 Eastland Rd Cleveland (44142) *(G-4136)*

Credit Union of Ohio Inc (PA) 614 487-6650
  5500 Britton Pkwy Hilliard (43026) *(G-9190)*
Creek At Hicksburg, Hicksville *Also Called: Hickory Creek Hlthcare Fndtion (G-9158)*
Creek Tech, Beavercreek *Also Called: Creek Technologies Company (G-876)*
Creek Technologies Company 937 272-4581
  2372 Lakeview Dr Ste H Beavercreek (45431) *(G-876)*
Creekside Cargo Inc 216 688-1770
  15416 Industrial Pkwy Cleveland (44135) *(G-4137)*
CREEKSIDE CONDOMINIUMS, Holland *Also Called: Lutheran Village At Wolf Creek (G-9296)*
Creekside Golf Ltd 513 785-2999
  6090 Golf Club Ln Fairfield Township (45011) *(G-8459)*
Creekside Ltd LLC 513 583-4977
  902 Loveland Miamiville Rd Loveland (45140) *(G-10133)*
Crefiii Wrmaug Sprngfeld Lssee 937 322-3600
  100 S Fountain Ave Springfield (45502) *(G-13245)*
Crescent Park Corporation (PA) 513 759-7000
  9817 Crescent Park Dr West Chester (45069) *(G-14679)*
Cresco Limited Partnership 216 520-1200
  3 Summit Park Dr Cleveland (44131) *(G-4138)*
Crest Bending Inc 419 492-2108
  108 John St New Washington (44854) *(G-11682)*
Crestbrook Insurance Company 614 249-7111
  1 W Nationwide Blvd Columbus (43215) *(G-5725)*
Crestline Agronomy, Crestline *Also Called: Sunrise Cooperative Inc (G-7026)*
Crestline Hospital, Crestline *Also Called: Medcentral Health System (G-7025)*
Crestline Nursing Center, Crestline *Also Called: Consulate Management Co LLC (G-7020)*
Crestline Nursing Center LLC 419 683-3255
  327 W Main St Crestline (44827) *(G-7021)*
Crestmont North, Lakewood *Also Called: Crestmont Nursing Home N Corp (G-9663)*
Crestmont Nursing Home N Corp 216 228-9550
  13330 Detroit Ave Lakewood (44107) *(G-9663)*
Crestview Manor II, Lancaster *Also Called: Crestview Manor Nursing Home (G-9706)*
Crestview Manor Nursing Home (PA) 740 654-2634
  957 Becks Knob Rd Lancaster (43130) *(G-9706)*
Crestwood Rdge Sklled Nrsing R, Hillsboro *Also Called: Congregate Living of America (G-9251)*
Crete Carrier, Columbus *Also Called: Crete Carrier Corporation (G-5726)*
Crete Carrier Corporation 614 853-4500
  5400 Crosswind Dr Columbus (43228) *(G-5726)*
Crew SC Team Company LLC 614 447-2739
  1 Black And Gold Blvd Columbus (43211) *(G-5727)*
Crew Soccer Stadium LLC 614 447-2739
  1 Black And Gold Blvd Columbus (43211) *(G-5728)*
Cricket Construction Ltd 330 536-8773
  400 E Water St Lowellville (44436) *(G-10167)*
Cridersville Health Care Ctr 419 645-4468
  603 E Main St Frnt Cridersville (45806) *(G-7028)*
CRIDERSVILLE NURSING HOME, Cridersville *Also Called: Cridersville Health Care Ctr (G-7028)*
Criminal Jstice Crdnting Cncil 567 200-6850
  1 Government Ctr Ste 1720 Toledo (43604) *(G-13770)*
Crimson Design Group LLC 614 444-3743
  825 Grandview Ave Columbus (43215) *(G-5729)*
Crisis Nursery, Cleveland *Also Called: Providence House Inc (G-4795)*
Cristo Homes 513 755-0570
  7594 Tylers Place Blvd Ste A West Chester (45069) *(G-14680)*
Critchfeld Crtchfeld Jhnston L (PA) 330 264-4444
  225 N Market St Wooster (44691) *(G-15332)*
Critical Business Analysis Inc 419 874-0800
  133 W 2nd St Ste 1 Perrysburg (43551) *(G-12326)*
Critical Care, Akron *Also Called: Childrens Hosp Med Ctr Akron (G-91)*
Crn Healthcare Inc 937 250-1412
  519 Xenia Ave Dayton (45410) *(G-7261)*
Croghan Colonial Bank (HQ) 419 332-7301
  323 Croghan St Fremont (43420) *(G-8673)*
Cronin Auto Inc 419 874-4331
  26875 Dixie Hwy Perrysburg (43551) *(G-12327)*
Cronin Automotive Co LLC 513 202-5812
  10700 New Haven Rd Harrison (45030) *(G-9100)*
Cross Creek Day Treatment, Columbus *Also Called: Buckeye Ranch Inc (G-5478)*

ALPHABETIC SECTION

Cross Roads Head Start, Painesville Also Called: Crossroad Health (G-12226)
Cross Truck Equipment Co Inc 330 477-8151
  1801 Perry Dr Sw Canton (44706) (G-1728)
Cross-Roads Asphalt Recycling Inc 440 236-5066
  13421 Hawke Rd Columbia Station (44028) (G-5226)
Crosschx Inc 800 501-3161
  99 E Main St Columbus (43215) (G-5730)
Crosscountry Mortgage Inc 440 845-3700
  12000 Snow Rd Ste 9 Cleveland (44130) (G-4139)
Crosscountry Mortgage LLC 216 314-0107
  29225 Chagrin Blvd Ste 350 Beachwood (44122) (G-785)
Crosscountry Mortgage LLC 513 373-4240
  4700 Ashwood Dr Blue Ash (45241) (G-1162)
Crosscountry Mortgage LLC (PA) 440 845-3700
  6850 Miller Rd Brecksville (44141) (G-1352)
Crosscountry Mortgage LLC 419 636-4663
  1607 W High St Bryan (43506) (G-1483)
Crosscountry Mortgage LLC 440 262-3528
  2160 Superior Ave E Cleveland (44114) (G-4140)
Crosscountry Mortgage LLC 614 779-0316
  2 Miranova Pl Ste 320 Columbus (43215) (G-5731)
Crosscountry Mortgage LLC 440 413-0867
  9179 Mentor Ave Ste H Mentor (44060) (G-10928)
Crosscountry Mortgage LLC 440 354-5206
  2709 N Ridge Rd Painesville (44077) (G-12225)
Crosscountry Mortgage LLC 330 655-5626
  4704 Darrow Rd Ste 1 Stow (44224) (G-13360)
Crosscountry Mortgage LLC 330 715-4878
  3226 Kent Rd Ste 105 Stow (44224) (G-13361)
Crossrads Sleep Dsrders Ctr LL 330 965-0220
  721 Boardman Poland Rd Ste 204 Youngstown (44512) (G-15590)
Crossroad Health 440 358-7370
  1083 Mentor Ave Painesville (44077) (G-12226)
CROSSROAD HEALTH CENTER, Cincinnati Also Called: Christian Community Hlth Svcs (G-2386)
Crossroads Center 513 475-5300
  311 Martin Luther King Dr E Cincinnati (45219) (G-2517)
Crossroads Health (PA) 440 255-1700
  8445 Munson Rd Mentor (44060) (G-10929)
Crossroads Hospitality Co LLC 216 241-6600
  1460 E 9th St Cleveland (44114) (G-4141)
Crossroads REO Inc 440 846-0077
  17075 Pearl Rd Ste 1 Strongsville (44136) (G-13450)
Crosswoods Ultrascreen Cinema, Columbus Also Called: Marcus Theatres Corporation (G-6196)
Croswell of Williamsburg LLC 800 782-8747
  4828 Wolf Creek Pike Dayton (45417) (G-7262)
Crotinger Nursing Home Inc 937 968-5284
  907 E Central St Union City (45390) (G-14239)
CROWN, Dayton Also Called: Crown Packaging Corporation (G-7263)
Crown Associates LLC 419 629-2220
  40 S Washington St New Bremen (45869) (G-11597)
Crown Associates of Ohio, New Bremen Also Called: Crown Associates LLC (G-11597)
Crown Group Incorporated 586 558-5311
  1340 Neubrecht Rd Lima (45801) (G-9882)
Crown Packaging Corporation (PA) 937 294-6580
  1885 Woodman Center Dr Dayton (45420) (G-7263)
Crown Solutions, Vandalia Also Called: Crown Solutions Co LLC (G-14372)
Crown Solutions Co LLC 937 890-4075
  913 Industrial Park Dr Vandalia (45377) (G-14372)
Crowne Plaza Cleveland, Cleveland Also Called: Playhouse Square Foundation (G-4758)
Crowne Plaza Cleveland Airport, Cleveland Also Called: Toledo Inns Inc (G-5023)
Crowne Plaza Columbus Downtown, Columbus Also Called: Ihg Management (maryland) LLC (G-6039)
Crowne Plaza Columbus North, Columbus Also Called: Columbus Leasing LLC (G-5642)
Crowne Plz Clvland Sth/Ndpndnc, Independence Also Called: Rockside Hospitality LLC (G-9477)
Crowne Plz Cnncnnati Nrth-Coco, Cincinnati Also Called: Sage Hospitality Resources LLC (G-3340)
Crp Contracting 614 338-8501
  4477 E 5th Ave Columbus (43219) (G-5732)

CRST International Inc 513 552-1935
  11677 Chesterdale Rd Cincinnati (45246) (G-2518)
Crw Inc 330 264-3785
  3716 S Elyria Rd Shreve (44676) (G-13016)
Cryptic Vector LLC 513 318-9061
  7570 Bales St Ste 400 Liberty Township (45069) (G-9851)
Crystal Care Centers Inc (PA) 419 747-2666
  1159 Wyandotte Ave Mansfield (44906) (G-10256)
Crystal Care of Mansfield, Mansfield Also Called: Crystal Care Centers Inc (G-10256)
Crystal Clinic Inc 330 644-7436
  1622 E Turkeyfoot Lake Rd Ste 200 Akron (44312) (G-126)
Crystal Clinic Inc 330 929-9136
  437 Portage Trl Cuyahoga Falls (44221) (G-7066)
Crystal Clinic Surgery Ctr LLC 330 668-4040
  3975 Embassy Pkwy Ste 202 Akron (44333) (G-127)
Crystal Clnic Orthpdic Ctr - F, Cuyahoga Falls Also Called: Crystal Clinic Inc (G-7066)
Crystal Clnic Orthpdic Ctr LLC 330 535-3396
  20 Olive St Ste 200 Akron (44310) (G-128)
Crystalwood Inc 513 605-1000
  70 Damon Rd Cincinnati (45218) (G-2519)
Cs Hotels Limited Partnership 614 771-8999
  2350 Westbelt Dr Columbus (43228) (G-5733)
Cs Trucking LLC 330 878-1990
  6531 Mckracken Dr Nw Dover (44622) (G-7878)
Csa America Inc 513 791-6918
  635 W 7th St Ste 406 Cincinnati (45203) (G-2520)
Csa America Standards Inc 216 524-4990
  8501 E Pleasant Valley Rd Cleveland (44131) (G-4142)
Csa Amrica Tstg Crtfcation LLC 216 524-4990
  8501 E Pleasant Valley Rd Independence (44131) (G-9427)
Csa Animal Nutrition, Dayton Also Called: Csa Animal Nutrition LLC (G-7264)
Csa Animal Nutrition LLC 866 615-8084
  6640 Poe Ave Ste 225 Dayton (45414) (G-7264)
Csa Group, Cincinnati Also Called: Csa America Inc (G-2520)
Csa Group, Independence Also Called: Csa Amrica Tstg Crtfcation LLC (G-9427)
Csa International Services, Cleveland Also Called: Csa America Standards Inc (G-4142)
CSB, Millersburg Also Called: CSB Bancorp Inc (G-11278)
CSB Bancorp Inc (PA) 330 674-9015
  91 N Clay St Millersburg (44654) (G-11278)
CSC Distribution LLC 614 278-6800
  4900 E Dublin Granville Rd Columbus (43081) (G-5734)
CSC Insurance Agency Inc 614 895-2000
  550 Polaris Pkwy Ste 300 Westerville (43082) (G-14886)
Csg Cleveland Enterprises Inc (PA) 440 918-9341
  26301 Curtiss Wright Pkwy Ste 115 Richmond Heights (44143) (G-12717)
Csi Complete Inc 800 343-0641
  8080 Corporate Blvd Plain City (43064) (G-12472)
Csi International Inc 614 781-1571
  690 Lakeview Plaza Blvd Ste C Worthington (43085) (G-15411)
Csji-Tiffin Inc 419 447-2723
  182 Saint Francis Ave Tiffin (44883) (G-13626)
Cspa, Akron Also Called: Civil Service Personnel Assn (G-104)
CST Utilities L L C 614 801-9600
  2136 Hardy Parkway St Grove City (43123) (G-8913)
CSX, Delaware Also Called: CSX Transportation Inc (G-7792)
CSX, Lorain Also Called: CSX Transportation Inc (G-10070)
CSX Transportation Inc 740 362-7924
  770 Hills Miller Rd Delaware (43015) (G-7792)
CSX Transportation Inc 440 245-3930
  311 Broadway Rear Lorain (44052) (G-10070)
CT Consultants Inc (PA) 440 951-9000
  8150 Sterling Ct Mentor (44060) (G-10930)
CT Logistics, Cleveland Also Called: THE COMMERCIAL TRAFFIC COMPANY (G-4998)
CT Logistics Inc 216 267-1636
  12487 Plaza Dr Cleveland (44130) (G-4143)
Ctd, Columbus Also Called: Ctd Investments LLC (G-5735)
Ctd Investments LLC (PA) 614 570-9949
  630 E Broad St Columbus (43215) (G-5735)
Ctek Inc 330 963-0981
  9347 Ravenna Rd Ste B Twinsburg (44087) (G-14179)

CTI Engineers Inc 330 294-5996
17 S Main St Akron (44308) *(G-129)*

Ctl Analyzers, Shaker Heights *Also Called: Cellular Technology Limited (G-12975)*

Ctl Engineering Inc (PA) 614 276-8123
2860 Fisher Rd Columbus (43204) *(G-5736)*

Ctm Integration Incorporated 330 332-1800
1318 Quaker Cir Salem (44460) *(G-12840)*

Ctrac Inc 440 572-1000
2222 W 110th St Cleveland (44102) *(G-4144)*

CTS Construction Inc 513 489-8290
7275 Edington Dr Cincinnati (45249) *(G-2521)*

CTS Telecommunications, Cincinnati *Also Called: CTS Construction Inc (G-2521)*

Ctts, Cincinnati *Also Called: Cincinnati Trning Trml Svcs In (G-2429)*

Ctv Media Inc (PA) 614 848-5800
1490 Manning Pkwy Powell (43065) *(G-12590)*

Cui, Cleveland *Also Called: Chores Unlimited Inc (G-3971)*

Culinary Metz Management LLC 330 684-3368
1 Strawberry Ln Orrville (44667) *(G-12159)*

Cumberland Gap LLC 513 681-9300
2285 Banning Rd Cincinnati (45239) *(G-2522)*

Cummins Facility Services LLC 740 726-9800
5202 Marion Waldo Rd Prospect (43342) *(G-12616)*

Cummins Inc 513 563-6670
5400 Rialto Rd West Chester (45069) *(G-14681)*

Cumulus Media Inc 513 241-9898
4805 Montgomery Rd Ste 300 Cincinnati (45212) *(G-2523)*

Cumulus Media Inc 419 725-5700
3225 Arlington Ave Toledo (43614) *(G-13771)*

Curbell Plastics, Cincinnati *Also Called: Curbell Plastics Inc (G-2524)*

Curbell Plastics Inc 513 742-9898
11145 Ashburn Rd Cincinnati (45240) *(G-2524)*

Curiosity LLC 513 744-6000
1140 Main St Cincinnati (45202) *(G-2525)*

Curiosity Advertising, Cincinnati *Also Called: Curiosity LLC (G-2525)*

Curtiss-Wright Controls 937 252-5601
2600 Paramount Pl Ste 200 Fairborn (45324) *(G-8371)*

Curtiss-Wright Controls, Fairborn *Also Called: Curtiss-Wright Controls (G-8371)*

Curtiss-Wright Flow Ctrl Corp 513 528-7900
4600 E Tech Dr Cincinnati (45245) *(G-2101)*

Cushman Wakefield Holdings Inc 513 241-4880
221 E 4th St Fl 26 Cincinnati (45202) *(G-2526)*

Custar Stone Co 419 669-4327
9072 County Road 424 Napoleon (43545) *(G-11520)*

Custom AC & Htg Co 614 552-4822
935 Claycraft Rd Gahanna (43230) *(G-8714)*

Custom Agri Systems Inc 419 209-0940
1289 N Warpole St Upper Sandusky (43351) *(G-14287)*

Custom Agri Systems Inc (PA) 419 599-5180
255 County Road R Napoleon (43545) *(G-11521)*

Custom Cable Construction Inc 330 351-1207
3670 Progress St Ne Canton (44705) *(G-1729)*

Custom Chemical Solutions LLC 800 291-1057
167 Commerce Dr Loveland (45140) *(G-10134)*

Custom Cleaning Svcs By Horton 440 774-1222
305 Artino St Unit A Oberlin (44074) *(G-12066)*

Custom Clg Svcs Disaster LLC 440 774-1222
305 Artino St Unit A Oberlin (44074) *(G-12067)*

Custom Design Benefits Inc 513 598-2929
5589 Cheviot Rd Cincinnati (45247) *(G-2527)*

Custom Distributors, Fairfield *Also Called: Rieman Arszman Cstm Distrs Inc (G-8437)*

Custom Glass & Doors, Columbus *Also Called: Wilson Insulation Company LLC (G-6897)*

Custom Hdwr Engrg Cnslting LLC 636 305-9669
5910 Landerbrook Dr Ste 300 Cleveland (44124) *(G-4145)*

Custom Materials Inc 440 543-8284
16865 Park Circle Dr Chagrin Falls (44023) *(G-1976)*

Custom Movers Services Inc 330 564-0507
3290 Kent Rd Stow (44224) *(G-13362)*

Custom Pak, Medina *Also Called: Industrial Chemical Corp (G-10846)*

Custom Personnel Inc 330 723-4131
190 Highland Dr Medina (44256) *(G-10826)*

Custom Products Corporation (PA) 440 528-7100
7100 Cochran Rd Solon (44139) *(G-13080)*

Custom Utilicom, Canton *Also Called: Custom Cable Construction Inc (G-1729)*

Custom-Pak Inc 330 725-0800
885 W Smith Rd Medina (44256) *(G-10827)*

Customer Service, Columbus *Also Called: Central Ohio Transit Authority (G-5548)*

Customized Girl, Columbus *Also Called: E Retailing Associates LLC (G-5798)*

Custompak, Medina *Also Called: Custom-Pak Inc (G-10827)*

Cuthbert Greenhouse Inc (PA) 614 836-3866
4900 Hendron Rd Groveport (43125) *(G-8981)*

Cutler Real Estate (PA) 330 836-9141
2800 W Market St Fairlawn (44333) *(G-8472)*

Cutler Real Estate Inc 614 339-4664
6375 Riverside Dr Ste 210 Dublin (43017) *(G-7980)*

Cutting Edge Countertops Inc 419 873-9500
1300 Flagship Dr Perrysburg (43551) *(G-12328)*

Cuyahoga Cnty Bd Dvlpmntal Dsb, Cleveland *Also Called: County of Cuyahoga (G-4126)*

Cuyahoga County AG Soc 440 243-0090
164 Eastland Rd Berea (44017) *(G-1067)*

Cuyahoga County Dept Pub Works, Cleveland *Also Called: County of Cuyahoga (G-4125)*

Cuyahoga County Fair, Berea *Also Called: Cuyahoga County AG Soc (G-1067)*

Cuyahoga County of Board Hlth 216 201-2000
5550 Venture Dr Parma (44130) *(G-12253)*

Cuyahoga County Sani Engrg Svc 216 443-8211
6100 W Canal Rd Cleveland (44125) *(G-4146)*

Cuyahoga Falls General Hospital 330 971-7000
1900 23rd St Cuyahoga Falls (44223) *(G-7067)*

Cuyahoga Group, The, North Ridgeville *Also Called: Cuyahoga Vending Co Inc (G-11926)*

Cuyahoga Vending Co Inc 440 353-9595
39405 Taylor Pkwy North Ridgeville (44035) *(G-11926)*

CVNPA, Peninsula *Also Called: Conservncy For Cyhoga Vly Nat (G-12293)*

Cvp Health, Blue Ash *Also Called: Cei Vision Partners LLC (G-1145)*

CVS, Athens *Also Called: CVS Revco DS Inc (G-563)*

CVS, Chesterland *Also Called: CVS Revco DS Inc (G-2034)*

CVS, Hillsboro *Also Called: CVS Revco DS Inc (G-9252)*

CVS, Kent *Also Called: CVS Revco DS Inc (G-9567)*

CVS, Marion *Also Called: CVS Revco DS Inc (G-10424)*

CVS, Marion *Also Called: CVS Revco DS Inc (G-10425)*

CVS, Oxford *Also Called: CVS Revco DS Inc (G-12206)*

CVS Revco DS Inc 740 593-8501
555 E State St Athens (45701) *(G-563)*

CVS Revco DS Inc 440 729-9070
8519 Mayfield Rd Chesterland (44026) *(G-2034)*

CVS Revco DS Inc 937 393-4218
1400 N High St Hillsboro (45133) *(G-9252)*

CVS Revco DS Inc 330 678-4009
500 S Water St Kent (44240) *(G-9567)*

CVS Revco DS Inc 740 389-1122
137 Mcmahan Blvd Marion (43302) *(G-10424)*

CVS Revco DS Inc 740 383-6244
535 Delaware Ave Marion (43302) *(G-10425)*

CVS Revco DS Inc 513 523-6378
123 W Spring St Oxford (45056) *(G-12206)*

Cw Opco LLC 440 428-5103
6831 Chapel Rd Madison (44057) *(G-10214)*

Cwcc Inc 937 236-6116
5030 Nebraska Ave Dayton (45424) *(G-7265)*

CWff Child Development Ctr 513 569-5660
434 Forest Ave Cincinnati (45229) *(G-2528)*

Cwi, Columbus *Also Called: Commercial Works Inc (G-5667)*

Cwm Envronmental Cleveland LLC 216 663-0808
4450 Johnston Pkwy Ste B Cleveland (44128) *(G-4147)*

Cwv Family Housing, Akron *Also Called: Alpha PHI Alpha Homes Inc (G-44)*

Cycle-Logik LLC 937 381-7055
4242 Clyo Rd Dayton (45440) *(G-7266)*

Cynergies Solutions Group, Richmond Heights *Also Called: Csg Cleveland Enterprises Inc (G-12717)*

Cyo, Akron *Also Called: Cyo & Community Services Inc (G-130)*

Cyo & Community Services Inc (PA) 330 762-2961
795 Russell Ave Akron (44307) *(G-130)*

ALPHABETIC SECTION

Cypress Run, Marion *Also Called: United Ch Rsdnces Immklee Fla* **(G-10461)**

D & A Plumbing & Heating Inc 330 499-8733
 11197 Cleveland Ave Nw Uniontown (44685) **(G-14247)**

D & D Advertising Entps Inc 513 921-6827
 801 Evans St Ste 203 Cincinnati (45204) **(G-2529)**

D & G Focht Construction Co 419 732-2412
 2040 E State Rd Port Clinton (43452) **(G-12522)**

D & L Energy Inc 330 270-1201
 3930 Fulton Dr Nw Ste 200 Canton (44718) **(G-1730)**

D & L Lighting Inc 614 841-1200
 901 Polaris Pkwy Columbus (43240) **(G-5256)**

D & S Auto Collision Restyling, Mentor *Also Called: D & S Custom Van Inc* **(G-10931)**

D & S Custom Van Inc 440 946-2178
 7588 Tyler Blvd Mentor (44060) **(G-10931)**

D & V Trucking Inc 330 482-9440
 12803 Columbiana Canfield Rd Columbiana (44408) **(G-5233)**

D + S Distribution Inc 330 804-5590
 425 Collins Blvd Orrville (44667) **(G-12160)**

D + S Distribution Inc 800 752-5993
 175 Allen Ave Orrville (44667) **(G-12161)**

D E Williams Electric Inc 440 543-1222
 168 Solon Rd Ste B Chagrin Falls (44022) **(G-1957)**

D J J, Cincinnati *Also Called: The David J Joseph Company* **(G-3464)**

D James Incorporated 513 574-4550
 4320 Bridgetown Rd Cincinnati (45211) **(G-2530)**

D L Ryan Companies LLC 614 436-6558
 440 Polaris Pkwy Ste 350 Westerville (43082) **(G-14887)**

D M I, Reynoldsburg *Also Called: Dimensional Metals Inc* **(G-12660)**

D R S, Youngstown *Also Called: Data Recovery Services LLC* **(G-15593)**

D S C, Dublin *Also Called: Dimension Service Corporation* **(G-7987)**

D S Dstrbution Inc Smith Foods, Orrville *Also Called: D + S Distribution Inc* **(G-12161)**

D W Dickey, Lisbon *Also Called: D W Dickey and Son Inc* **(G-10001)**

D W Dickey and Son Inc (PA) 330 424-1441
 7896 Dickey Dr Lisbon (44432) **(G-10001)**

D Yoder Hardwoods LLC 330 852-8105
 2131 County Road 70 Sugarcreek (44681) **(G-13508)**

D-R Training Center & Workshop 419 289-0470
 1256 Center St Ashland (44805) **(G-495)**

D&A Transport LLC 513 570-7153
 1410 Springfield Pike Apt 33 Cincinnati (45215) **(G-2531)**

D&D Foundation LLC 513 291-3191
 412 Dayton St Cincinnati (45214) **(G-2532)**

D&J Quality Care Entps Inc 440 638-7001
 13315 Prospect Rd Strongsville (44149) **(G-13451)**

D+h USA Corporation 513 381-9400
 312 Plum St Ste 500 Cincinnati (45202) **(G-2533)**

Daedalus Books Inc 800 395-2665
 5581 Hudson Industrial Pkwy Hudson (44236) **(G-9342)**

Daedalus Books Warehouse Outl, Hudson *Also Called: Daedalus Books Inc* **(G-9342)**

DAG Construction Co Inc 513 542-8597
 447 Ivy Trails Dr Cincinnati (45244) **(G-2534)**

Dag-Dell Inc 740 754-2600
 507 Main St Dresden (43821) **(G-7917)**

Dagger Jhnston Mller Oglvie HM (PA) 740 653-6464
 144 E Main St Lancaster (43130) **(G-9707)**

Dahlberg Learning Center, Columbus *Also Called: Assoction For Dvlpmntlly Dsble* **(G-5397)**

Daihen Inc (HQ) 937 667-0800
 1400 Blauser Dr Tipp City (45371) **(G-13656)**

Daily Services LLC (PA) 614 431-5100
 4 Easton Oval Columbus (43219) **(G-5737)**

Daily Services LLC 740 326-6130
 12 E Gambier St Mount Vernon (43050) **(G-11482)**

DAILY SERVICES LLC, Mount Vernon *Also Called: Daily Services LLC* **(G-11482)**

Dairy Farm, Polk *Also Called: Falling Star Farm Ltd* **(G-12512)**

Dairy Queen, Berea *Also Called: Southwest Sports Center Inc* **(G-1082)**

Dairy Queen, New Middletown *Also Called: Rapps Enterprises Inc* **(G-11636)**

Dak P Kids, Northfield *Also Called: P Dakota Inc* **(G-11963)**

Dakota Software Corporation (PA) 216 765-7100
 1375 Euclid Ave Ste 500 Cleveland (44115) **(G-4148)**

DALE-ROY SCHOOL & TRAINING CEN, Ashland *Also Called: D-R Training Center & Workshop* **(G-495)**

Damarc Inc 330 454-6171
 4330 Kirby Ave Ne Canton (44705) **(G-1731)**

Damascus Cthlic Mission Campus 740 480-1288
 3 Township Road 200 Centerburg (43011) **(G-1935)**

Damascus Staffing LLC 513 954-8941
 1832 Freeman Ave Cincinnati (45214) **(G-2535)**

Damschroder Roofing Inc 419 332-5000
 2625 E State St Fremont (43420) **(G-8674)**

Dan & Maria Davis Inc 937 669-2271
 135 S Garber Dr Tipp City (45371) **(G-13657)**

Dan Marchetta Cnstr Co Inc 330 668-4800
 525 N Cleveland Massillon Rd Ste 109 Akron (44333) **(G-131)**

Dan Sechkar Sech Kar C 740 753-9955
 4831 2nd St Nelsonville (45764) **(G-11541)**

Dana Credit Corporation 419 887-3000
 3939 Technology Dr Maumee (43537) **(G-10715)**

Danberry Co 419 866-8888
 3555 Briarfield Blvd Maumee (43537) **(G-10716)**

Danbury Brunswick, Brunswick *Also Called: Brunswick Senior Living LLC* **(G-1452)**

Danbury Huber Heights, North Canton *Also Called: 8001 Red Buckeye Landlord LLC* **(G-11806)**

Danbury Massillon, Massillon *Also Called: Massillon Senior Living Ltd* **(G-10653)**

Danbury Mentor, Mentor *Also Called: Mentor Senior Living LLC* **(G-10971)**

Danbury Sanctuary Grande, North Canton *Also Called: Sanctary Grnde Snior Lving LLC* **(G-11860)**

Danbury Senior Living, Canton *Also Called: Brookwood Management Company* **(G-1691)**

Danbury Wods At Grnfeld Crssin 330 264-0355
 939 Portage Rd Wooster (44691) **(G-15333)**

Danbury Woods Ltd 330 928-6757
 1691 Queens Gate Cir Cuyahoga Falls (44221) **(G-7068)**

Danbury Woods Cuyahoga Falls, Cuyahoga Falls *Also Called: Danbury Woods Ltd* **(G-7068)**

Danbury Wooster, Wooster *Also Called: Danbury Wods At Grnfeld Crssin* **(G-15333)**

Dancor Inc 614 340-2155
 2155 Dublin Rd Columbus (43228) **(G-5738)**

Danessa Construction Llc 330 219-1212
 620 Sophia Ct Niles (44446) **(G-11787)**

Daniel A Terreri & Sons Inc 330 538-2950
 1091 N Meridian Rd Youngstown (44509) **(G-15591)**

Daniel Cohen Enterprises Inc 513 896-4547
 152 Stone Creek Dr Oxford (45056) **(G-12207)**

Daniel Drake Ctr For PST-Cute 513 418-2500
 151 W Galbraith Rd Cincinnati (45216) **(G-2536)**

Daniel N Rizek 614 895-0006
 93 E Broadway Ave Westerville (43081) **(G-14975)**

Danis, Miamisburg *Also Called: Danis Building Construction Co* **(G-11042)**

Danis Building Construction Co 513 984-9696
 50 E-Business Way Cincinnati (45241) **(G-2537)**

Danis Building Construction Co 614 761-8385
 777 Goodale Blvd Ste 100 Columbus (43212) **(G-5739)**

Danis Building Construction Co (PA) 937 228-1225
 3233 Newmark Dr Miamisburg (45342) **(G-11042)**

Danis Companies 937 228-1225
 3233 Newmark Dr Miamisburg (45342) **(G-11043)**

Danis Industrial Cnstr Co 937 228-1225
 3233 Newmark Dr Miamisburg (45342) **(G-11044)**

Danite Holdings Ltd 614 444-3333
 1640 Harmon Ave Columbus (43223) **(G-5740)**

Danite Sign Co, Columbus *Also Called: Danite Holdings Ltd* **(G-5740)**

Danny Veghs Home Entertainment, Cleveland *Also Called: Dtv Inc* **(G-4187)**

Danridge Nursing Home Inc 330 746-5157
 31 Maranatha Ct Youngstown (44505) **(G-15592)**

Danson Inc 513 948-0066
 3033 Robertson Ave Cincinnati (45209) **(G-2538)**

Darana Hybrid Inc (PA) 513 860-4490
 903 Belle Ave Hamilton (45015) **(G-9036)**

Darby Creek Excavating Inc 740 477-8600
 19524 London Rd Circleville (43113) **(G-3706)**

Darby Creek Nursery, Plain City *Also Called: R & S Halley and Company Inc* **(G-12491)**

DARBY GLENN NURSING AND REHABI, Hilliard *Also Called: Hilliard Hlth Rhbilitation Inc* **(G-9200)**

Darcie R Clark Lpcc LLC.. 937 319-4448
 11 W Monument Ave Ste 100 Dayton (45402) (G-7267)
Dari Pizza Enterprises II Inc.. 419 534-3000
 1683 Woodlands Dr Ste A Maumee (43537) (G-10717)
Darke County Sheriffs Patrol.. 937 548-3399
 5185 County Home Rd Greenville (45331) (G-8868)
Darko Inc.. 330 425-9805
 26401 Richmond Rd Bedford (44146) (G-958)
Darling International, North Baltimore Also Called: Griffin Industries LLC (G-11800)
Das Aviation, Solon Also Called: Jet East Inc (G-13102)
Das Dutch Village Inn... 330 482-5050
 150 E State Route 14 Columbiana (44408) (G-5234)
Dash Technologies Inc... 614 593-3274
 565 Metro Pl S Ste 400 Dublin (43017) (G-7981)
DAT, Akron Also Called: Downtown Akron Partnership Inc (G-137)
DATA Den Inc... 216 622-0900
 1901 Train Ave Cleveland (44113) (G-4149)
Data Processing, Canton Also Called: County of Stark (G-1726)
Data Processing Sciences Corporation........................... 513 791-7100
 2 Camargo Cyn Cincinnati (45243) (G-2539)
Data Recognition Corporation... 513 588-7260
 3645 Park 42 Dr Cincinnati (45241) (G-2540)
Data Recovery, Cleveland Also Called: 1st All File Recovery Usa (G-3742)
Data Recovery Services LLC... 330 397-0100
 1343 Belmont Ave Youngstown (44504) (G-15593)
Data Systems Intgrtion Group I.. 614 344-4600
 485 Metro Pl S Ste 101 Dublin (43017) (G-7982)
Dataeconomy Inc.. 614 356-8153
 565 Metro Pl S Dublin (43017) (G-7983)
Datafield Inc... 614 847-9600
 25 W New England Ave Worthington (43085) (G-15412)
Datalysys LLC.. 614 495-0260
 5200 Upper Metro Pl Ste 120 # 125 Dublin (43017) (G-7984)
Datatech Depot (east) Inc... 513 860-5651
 4750 Ashley Dr West Chester (45011) (G-14682)
Datatrak International Inc.. 440 443-0082
 3690 Orange Pl Ste 375 Beachwood (44122) (G-786)
Datavantage Corporation (DH).. 440 498-4414
 30500 Bruce Industrial Pkwy Ste A Cleveland (44139) (G-4150)
Datwyler Sling Sltions USA Inc.. 937 387-2800
 875 Center Dr Vandalia (45377) (G-14373)
Dave Dennis Inc... 937 429-5566
 4232 Colonel Glenn Hwy Beavercreek Township (45431) (G-935)
Dave Dennis Auto Group, Beavercreek Township Also Called: Dave Dennis Inc (G-935)
Dave Knapp Ford Lincoln Inc (PA)................................. 937 547-3000
 500 Wagner Ave Greenville (45331) (G-8869)
Dave Marshall Inc (PA)... 937 878-9135
 1448 Kauffman Ave Fairborn (45324) (G-8372)
Dave Sugar Excavating LLC... 330 542-1100
 11640 S State Line Rd Petersburg (44454) (G-12394)
Dave Thmas Fndtion For Adption................................... 614 764-8454
 4900 Tuttle Crossing Blvd Dublin (43016) (G-7985)
Davey Resource Group Inc.. 859 630-9879
 1230 W 8th St Cincinnati (45203) (G-2541)
Davey Resource Group Inc (HQ)................................... 330 673-5685
 295 S Water St Ste 300 Kent (44240) (G-9568)
Davey Tree Expert Company.. 330 673-9511
 3567 Westerville Rd Columbus (43224) (G-5741)
Davey Tree Expert Company.. 330 678-5818
 1550 Franklin Ave Kent (44240) (G-9569)
Davey Tree Expert Company (PA).................................. 330 673-9511
 1500 N Mantua St Kent (44240) (G-9570)
David A Levy Inc.. 330 352-1289
 345 Springside Dr Akron (44333) (G-132)
David Evangelical Lutheran Ch....................................... 614 920-3517
 300 Groveport Pike Canal Winchester (43110) (G-1603)
David Harnett DDS Inc... 330 638-3065
 500 Wakefield Dr Ste 4 Cortland (44410) (G-6971)
David J Joseph Company.. 513 419-6016
 300 Pike St Cincinnati (45202) (G-2542)
David J Joseph Company, The, Cincinnati Also Called: Djj Holding Corporation (G-2572)

David J. Joseph Co-Metals, The, Cincinnati Also Called: David J Joseph Company (G-2542)
David L Barth Lwyr... 513 852-8228
 537 E Pete Rose Way Cincinnati (45202) (G-2543)
David Lutheran Chrn Pre-School, Canal Winchester Also Called: David Evangelical Lutheran Ch (G-1603)
David R White Services Inc (PA)................................... 740 594-8381
 5315 Hebbardsville Rd Athens (45701) (G-564)
David W Milliken (PA).. 740 998-5023
 2 S Main St Frankfort (45628) (G-8629)
Davis Construction Co, Cleveland Also Called: Davis Construction Management (G-4151)
Davis Construction Management..................................... 440 248-7770
 32000 Solon Rd Cleveland (44139) (G-4151)
Davis Eye Center Inc... 330 923-5676
 789 Graham Rd Cuyahoga Falls (44221) (G-7069)
Davis H Elliot Cnstr Co Inc.. 937 847-8025
 1 S Gebhart Church Rd Miamisburg (45342) (G-11045)
Davis Pickering & Company Inc...................................... 740 373-5896
 165 Enterprise Dr Marietta (45750) (G-10365)
Davis Young A Legal Prof Assn (PA)............................. 216 348-1700
 600 Superior Ave E Ste 1200 Cleveland (44114) (G-4152)
Davis-Mcmackin Inc... 614 824-1587
 1880 Mackenzie Dr Ste 101 Columbus (43220) (G-5742)
DAVITA, Chillicothe Also Called: Court Dialysis LLC (G-2063)
Dawson Companies.. 440 333-9000
 3900 Kinross Lakes Pkwy Richfield (44286) (G-12693)
Dawson Logistics LLC... 217 689-2610
 4350 Port Union Rd Ste B West Chester (45011) (G-14683)
Dawson Personnel, Columbus Also Called: Dawson Resources (G-5743)
Dawson Personnel Systems, Columbus Also Called: Decapua Enterprises Inc (G-5747)
Dawson Resources.. 614 274-8900
 4184 W Broad St Columbus (43228) (G-5743)
Day Air Credit Union Inc (PA).. 937 643-2160
 3501 Wilmington Pike Dayton (45429) (G-7268)
Day Care Center, Columbus Also Called: Y M C A Hilltop Educare Inc (G-6915)
Day Ketterer Ltd (PA)... 330 455-0173
 200 Market Ave N Ste 300 Canton (44702) (G-1732)
Day Star Staffing LLC... 440 481-1060
 26697 Brookpark Road Ext North Olmsted (44070) (G-11900)
Daybreak Inc (PA)... 937 395-4600
 605 S Patterson Blvd Dayton (45402) (G-7269)
Daylay Egg Farm Inc... 937 355-6531
 11177 Township Road 133 West Mansfield (43358) (G-14862)
Daymark Safety Systems.. 419 353-2458
 12830 S Dixie Hwy Bowling Green (43402) (G-1316)
Daymark Wealth Partners LLC....................................... 513 838-2524
 9675 Montgomery Rd Montgomery (45242) (G-11366)
Daynas Homecare LLC... 216 323-0323
 14616 Tabor Ave Maple Heights (44137) (G-10337)
Days Inn... 740 695-0100
 52601 Holiday Dr Saint Clairsville (43950) (G-12789)
Days Inn, Athens Also Called: Days Inn Htels Athens Clmbus R (G-565)
Days Inn, Columbus Also Called: First Management Company (G-5864)
Days Inn, Fremont Also Called: Goodnight Inn Inc (G-8682)
Days Inn, Girard Also Called: Shir-Sath Inc (G-8825)
Days Inn, Grove City Also Called: Columbus Lintel Inc (G-8911)
Days Inn, Lisbon Also Called: Naffah South LLC (G-10006)
Days Inn, Sandusky Also Called: Sortino Management & Dev Co (G-12933)
Days Inn Htels Athens Clmbus R..................................... 740 593-6655
 330 Columbus Rd Athens (45701) (G-565)
Days Inn Middletown.. 513 420-9378
 3458 Commerce Dr Middletown (45005) (G-11194)
Days Inn Saint Clairsville, Saint Clairsville Also Called; Days Inn (G-12789)
Days Inn-Dayton North, Dayton Also Called: Columbia Sussex Corporation (G-7239)
Days Inns of America.. 330 345-1500
 789 E Milltown Rd Wooster (44691) (G-15334)
Dayspring Health Care Center.. 937 864-5800
 8001 Dayton Springfield Rd Fairborn (45324) (G-8373)
Daystar Transportation LLC.. 740 852-9202
 271 W High St London (43140) (G-10041)
Dayton 009, Beavercreek Township Also Called: Stanley Steemer Intl Inc (G-950)

ALPHABETIC SECTION — Dayton Surgeons Inc

Dayton Aerospace Inc 937 426-4300
4141 Colonel Glenn Hwy Ste 252 Beavercreek Township (45431) *(G-936)*

Dayton Appliance Parts LLC (DH) 937 224-0487
122 Sears St Dayton (45402) *(G-7270)*

Dayton Area Chamber Commerce 937 226-1444
8 N Main St # 100 Dayton (45402) *(G-7271)*

Dayton Bag & Burlap, Dayton Also Called: Dayton Bag & Burlap Co *(G-7272)*

Dayton Bag & Burlap Co (PA) 937 258-8000
322 Davis Ave Dayton (45403) *(G-7272)*

Dayton Business Journal, Dayton Also Called: American City Bus Journals Inc *(G-7170)*

Dayton Care Center, Dayton Also Called: Cincinnati Aml Refl Emer C LLC *(G-7226)*

Dayton Childrens - S Campus, Miamisburg Also Called: Dayton Childrens Hospital *(G-11046)*

Dayton Childrens Cardiology 937 641-3418
1 Childrens Plz Dayton (45404) *(G-7273)*

Dayton Childrens Hospital 937 641-5760
4475 Far Hills Ave Dayton (45429) *(G-7274)*

Dayton Childrens Hospital 937 641-3500
730 Valley St Ste C Dayton (45404) *(G-7275)*

Dayton Childrens Hospital (PA) 937 641-3000
1 Childrens Plz Dayton (45404) *(G-7276)*

Dayton Childrens Hospital 937 641-3000
3333 W Tech Blvd Miamisburg (45342) *(G-11046)*

Dayton Childrens Hospital 513 424-2850
100 Campus Loop Rd Middletown (45005) *(G-11195)*

Dayton Childrens Hospital 937 398-5464
1644 N Limestone St Springfield (45503) *(G-13246)*

Dayton City Water Department, Dayton Also Called: City of Dayton *(G-7228)*

Dayton Classics Basbal CLB Inc 937 974-6722
165 S Alex Rd West Carrollton (45449) *(G-14645)*

Dayton Corrugated Packaging Corp (PA) 937 254-8422
1300 Wayne Ave Dayton (45410) *(G-7277)*

Dayton Country Club Company 937 294-3352
555 Kramer Rd Dayton (45419) *(G-7278)*

Dayton Dev Coalition Inc 937 222-4422
900 Kettering Tower Dayton (45402) *(G-7279)*

Dayton Door Sales Inc (PA) 937 253-9181
1112 Springfield St Dayton (45403) *(G-7280)*

Dayton Dragons Baseball, Dayton Also Called: Dayton Prof Basbal CLB LLC *(G-7300)*

Dayton Ews Inc 937 293-1010
3050 Springboro Pike Moraine (45439) *(G-11400)*

Dayton Eye Surgery Center 937 431-9531
81 Sylvania Dr Dayton (45440) *(G-7281)*

Dayton Fmly Practice Assoc Inc 937 254-5661
3328 S Smithville Rd Dayton (45420) *(G-7282)*

Dayton Freight, Dayton Also Called: Dayton Freight Lines Inc *(G-7284)*

Dayton Freight Lines Inc 614 860-1080
1406 Blatt Blvd Columbus (43230) *(G-5744)*

Dayton Freight Lines Inc 937 236-4880
6265 Executive Blvd Ste A Dayton (45424) *(G-7283)*

Dayton Freight Lines Inc 330 346-0750
280 Progress Blvd Kent (44240) *(G-9571)*

Dayton Freight Lines Inc 419 589-0350
103 Cairns Rd Mansfield (44903) *(G-10257)*

Dayton Freight Lines Inc 419 661-8600
28240 Oregon Rd Perrysburg (43551) *(G-12329)*

Dayton Freight Lines Inc (PA) 937 264-4060
6450 Poe Ave Ste 311 Dayton (45414) *(G-7284)*

Dayton Gastroenterology LLC 937 320-5050
75 Sylvania Dr Dayton (45440) *(G-7285)*

Dayton Heart Center Inc (PA) 937 277-4274
1530 Needmore Rd Ste 300 Dayton (45414) *(G-7286)*

Dayton Heidelberg Distrg Co 513 421-5000
1518 Dalton Ave Cincinnati (45214) *(G-2544)*

Dayton Heidelberg Distrg Co, Dayton 216 520-2626
9101 E Pleasant Valley Rd Cleveland (44131) *(G-4153)*

Dayton Heidelberg Distrg Co 614 308-0400
3801 Parkwest Dr Columbus (43228) *(G-5745)*

Dayton Heidelberg Distrg Co 937 220-6450
3601 Dryden Rd Moraine (45439) *(G-11401)*

Dayton Heidelberg Distrg Co 419 666-9783
912 3rd St Perrysburg (43551) *(G-12330)*

Dayton Heidelberg Distrg LLC (HQ) 937 222-8692
3601 Dryden Rd Moraine (45439) *(G-11402)*

Dayton Heidelberg Distributing Co., Columbus Also Called: Dayton Heidelberg Distrg Co *(G-5745)*

Dayton History 937 293-2841
1000 Carillon Blvd Dayton (45409) *(G-7287)*

Dayton Hospice Incorporated (PA) 937 256-4490
324 Wilmington Ave Dayton (45420) *(G-7288)*

Dayton Hospice Incorporated 513 422-0300
5940 Long Meadow Dr Franklin (45005) *(G-8633)*

Dayton Hotels LLC 937 965-7500
124 Madison St Dayton (45402) *(G-7289)*

Dayton Live, Dayton Also Called: Victoria Theatre Association *(G-7706)*

Dayton Loudspeaker Co., Springboro Also Called: Parts Express International Inc *(G-13205)*

Dayton Marriott, Dayton Also Called: Concord Dayton Hotel II LLC *(G-7245)*

Dayton Medical Imaging 937 439-0390
7901 Schatz Pointe Dr Dayton (45459) *(G-7290)*

Dayton Medical Imaging, Vandalia Also Called: Dayton Osteopathic Hospital *(G-14374)*

Dayton Ob Gyn 937 439-7550
330 N Main St Ste 200 Centerville (45459) *(G-1943)*

Dayton Orthpdic Srgery Spt Mdc 937 436-5763
5491 Far Hills Ave Dayton (45429) *(G-7291)*

Dayton Osteopathic Hospital 937 401-6400
7677 Yankee St Ste 110 Centerville (45459) *(G-1944)*

Dayton Osteopathic Hospital 937 558-0200
165 S Edwin C Moses Blvd Dayton (45402) *(G-7292)*

Dayton Osteopathic Hospital (HQ) 937 762-1629
405 W Grand Ave Dayton (45405) *(G-7293)*

Dayton Osteopathic Hospital 937 558-3800
6438 Wilmington Pike Dayton (45459) *(G-7294)*

Dayton Osteopathic Hospital 937 439-6000
1997 Miamisburg Centerville Rd Dayton (45459) *(G-7295)*

Dayton Osteopathic Hospital 937 401-6503
7677 Yankee St Dayton (45459) *(G-7296)*

Dayton Osteopathic Hospital 937 456-8300
450b Washington Jackson Rd Eaton (45320) *(G-8212)*

Dayton Osteopathic Hospital 513 696-1200
1470 N Broadway St Lebanon (45036) *(G-9763)*

Dayton Osteopathic Hospital 937 898-9729
113 W National Rd Vandalia (45377) *(G-14374)*

Dayton Outpatien Practice, Dayton Also Called: Pain Management Associates Inc *(G-7138)*

Dayton Performing Arts Aliance 937 224-3521
126 N Main St Ste 210 Dayton (45402) *(G-7297)*

Dayton Pharmacy, Dayton Also Called: Equitas Health Inc *(G-7338)*

Dayton Physicians LLC (PA) 937 280-8400
6680 Poe Ave Ste 200 Dayton (45414) *(G-7298)*

Dayton Physicians LLC 937 208-2636
8881 N Main St Dayton (45415) *(G-7299)*

Dayton Physicians LLC 937 547-0563
1111 Sweitzer St Ste C Greenville (45331) *(G-8870)*

Dayton Physicians LLC 937 440-4210
3130 N County Road 25a Troy (45373) *(G-14133)*

Dayton Power and Light Company (DH) 937 331-3900
1065 Woodman Dr Dayton (45432) *(G-7129)*

Dayton Power and Light Company 937 549-2641
745 Us Highway 52 Unit 1 Manchester (45144) *(G-10239)*

Dayton Power and Light Company 937 549-2641
14869 Us Highway 52 Manchester (45144) *(G-10240)*

Dayton Power and Light Company 937 642-9100
1201 W 5th St Marysville (43040) *(G-10482)*

Dayton Power and Light Company 937 331-3032
1 S Gebhart Church Rd Miamisburg (45342) *(G-11047)*

Dayton Prof Basbal CLB LLC 937 228-2287
220 N Patterson Blvd 1st Fl Dayton (45402) *(G-7300)*

Dayton Realtors 937 223-0900
1515 S Main St Dayton (45409) *(G-7301)*

Dayton Sports Medicine Preble, Eaton Also Called: Dayton Osteopathic Hospital *(G-8212)*

Dayton Spt Mdicine Centerville, Centerville Also Called: Dayton Osteopathic Hospital *(G-1944)*

Dayton Surgeons Inc 937 228-4126
9000 N Main St Ste 233 Englewood (45415) *(G-8305)*

(PA)=Parent Co (HQ)=Headquarters (DH)=Div Headquarters

Dayton Synchrnous Spport Ctr I 937 226-1559
  1700 E Monument Ave Dayton (45402) (G-7302)
Dayton V A Medical Center, Dayton Also Called: Veterans Health Administration (G-7705)
Dayton V Lw LLC 937 229-9836
  33 E 5th St Dayton (45402) (G-7303)
Dayton Vtreo-Retinal Assoc Inc 937 228-5015
  301 W 1st St Ste 300 Dayton (45402) (G-7304)
Dayton Walls & Ceilings Inc 937 277-0531
  4328 Webster St Dayton (45414) (G-7305)
Dayton Wastewater Trtmnt Plant, Dayton Also Called: City of Dayton (G-7229)
Dayton Windustrial Co 937 461-2603
  137 E Helena St Dayton (45404) (G-7306)
Dayton YMCA Camp Kern, Oregonia Also Called: Young MNS Chrstn Assn Grter Dy (G-12750)
Daytonidealease, Dayton Also Called: Rush Truck Leasing Inc (G-7599)
Dazpak Flexible Packaging Corp (PA) 614 252-2121
  2901 E 4th Ave Columbus (43219) (G-5746)
Db Consulting Group Inc 216 433-5132
  21000 Brookpark Rd Ms142-1 Cleveland (44135) (G-4154)
Dbi Services LLC 410 590-4181
  2393 County Road 1 South Point (45680) (G-13174)
Dbp Enterprises LLC 740 513-2399
  7301 E State Route 37 Sunbury (43074) (G-13519)
Dbs Financial 440 232-0001
  424 Broadway Ave Bedford (44146) (G-959)
DCB Financial Corp 740 657-7000
  110 Riverbend Ave Lewis Center (43035) (G-9815)
Dchm Inc 330 874-3435
  11155 State Route 212 Ne Bolivar (44612) (G-1293)
Dco LLC (DH) 419 931-9086
  900 E Boundary St Ste 8a Perrysburg (43551) (G-12331)
Dcr Systems LLC (PA) 440 205-9900
  8697 Tyler Blvd Mentor (44060) (G-10932)
DCS Corporation 937 306-7180
  4027 Colonel Glenn Hwy Ste 210 Beavercreek Township (45431) (G-937)
DCS Corporation 781 419-6370
  4027 Colonel Glenn Hwy Ste 210 Beavercreek Township (45431) (G-938)
DCS Sanitation Management Inc 513 891-4980
  7864 Camargo Rd Cincinnati (45243) (G-2545)
Dct Telecom Group LLC 440 892-0300
  27877 Clemens Rd Westlake (44145) (G-15056)
Dctech Ltd 330 687-3977
  2241 Pinnacle Pkwy Twinsburg (44087) (G-14180)
Ddc, Fairfield Also Called: Dna Diagnostics Center Inc (G-8407)
Ddc Group Inc 937 619-3111
  10536 Success Ln Dayton (45458) (G-7307)
Ddi, Brookpark Also Called: Distribution Data Incorporated (G-1433)
Ddm Direct of Ohio, Hebron Also Called: Ddm-Dgtal Imging Data Proc Mli (G-9142)
Ddm-Dgtal Imging Data Proc Mli 740 928-1110
  190 Milliken Dr Hebron (43025) (G-9142)
Ddw Consulting Inc (PA) 937 299-9920
  3176 Kettering Blvd Moraine (45439) (G-11403)
De Bra - Kuempel, Cincinnati Also Called: Debra-Kuempel Inc (G-2552)
De Coach Team LLC 513 942-4673
  100 Crowne Point Pl Cincinnati (45241) (G-2546)
DE Foxx & Associates Inc (PA) 513 621-5522
  324 W 9th St Fl 5 Cincinnati (45202) (G-2547)
De Haven Home and Garden Centers Inc 419 227-7003
  775 Shawnee Rd Lima (45805) (G-9883)
De Nora Tech LLC (DH) 440 710-5334
  7590 Discovery Ln Concord Township (44077) (G-6924)
De-Cal Inc 330 272-0021
  8392 Tod Ave Ste 1 Youngstown (44512) (G-15594)
Deacon 10 LLC 216 731-4000
  1353 E 260th St Ste 110 Euclid (44132) (G-8340)
Deaconess Associations Inc (PA) 513 559-2100
  615 Elsinore Pl Ste 900 Cincinnati (45202) (G-2548)
DEACONESS HOSPITAL, Cincinnati Also Called: Deaconess Hospital of Cincinna (G-2549)
Deaconess Hospital of Cincinna (PA) 513 559-2100
  615 Elsinore Pl Ste 900 Cincinnati (45202) (G-2549)
Deaconess Long Term Care Inc (HQ) 513 861-0400
  330 Straight St Ste 310 Cincinnati (45219) (G-2550)

Deaconess Long Term Care of MI (PA) 513 487-3600
  330 Straight St Ste 310 Cincinnati (45219) (G-2551)
DEACONESS-KRAFFT CENTER, Cleveland Also Called: Senior Citizens Resources Inc (G-4894)
Dealer Supply and Eqp Ltd 419 724-8473
  1549 Campbell St Toledo (43607) (G-13772)
Dealer Tire LLC (PA) 216 432-0088
  7012 Euclid Ave Cleveland (44103) (G-4155)
Dealers Supply North Inc (HQ) 614 274-6285
  2315 Creekside Pkwy Ste 500 Lockbourne (43137) (G-10011)
Dean A Carmichael 216 524-8481
  6132 W Creek Rd Cleveland (44131) (G-4156)
Dean Contracting Inc 440 260-7590
  19100 Holland Rd Cleveland (44142) (G-4157)
Dean Financial Management, Beavercreek Also Called: C H Dean LLC (G-867)
Dean Houston, West Chester Also Called: Deanhouston Inc (G-14807)
Dean Supply Company, Cleveland Also Called: The Dean Supply Co (G-4999)
Deanhouston Inc 740 646-2914
  4612 Interstate Dr West Chester (45246) (G-14807)
Deanhouston Creative Group Inc 513 659-5051
  9393 Princeton Glendale Rd West Chester (45011) (G-14684)
Deans Greenhouse Inc 440 871-2050
  3984 Porter Rd Cleveland (44145) (G-4158)
Dearing Compressor and Pump Company (PA) 330 783-2258
  3974 Simon Rd Youngstown (44512) (G-15595)
Dearman Moving and Storage, Mansfield Also Called: J-Trac Inc (G-10274)
Dearth Management Company 419 253-0144
  825 State Route 61 Marengo (43334) (G-10352)
Dearth Management Company 330 339-3595
  2594 E High Ave New Philadelphia (44663) (G-11649)
Deaton Enterprises Inc 937 320-6200
  1619 Mardon Dr Beavercreek (45432) (G-877)
Debmar Inc 419 728-7010
  1069 Klotz Rd Bowling Green (43402) (G-1317)
Debra Kuempel, Cincinnati Also Called: Kuempel Service Inc (G-2956)
Debra-Kuempel Inc (HQ) 513 271-6500
  3976 Southern Ave Cincinnati (45227) (G-2552)
Debtnext Solutions LLC 330 665-0400
  175 Montrose West Ave Ste 170 Copley (44321) (G-6954)
Decahealth Inc 866 908-3514
  5151 Monroe St Ste 104 Toledo (43623) (G-13773)
Decapua Enterprises Inc (PA) 614 255-1400
  1114 Dublin Rd Columbus (43215) (G-5747)
Decker Forklifts, Cleveland Also Called: Acd Enterprises Inc (G-3761)
Deckers Nursery Inc 614 836-2130
  6239 Rager Rd Groveport (43125) (G-8982)
Deco-Crete Supply Inc 330 682-5678
  133 N Kohler Rd Orrville (44667) (G-12162)
Decoach Rehabilitation Centre, Cincinnati Also Called: De Coach Team LLC (G-2546)
Decora, Beachwood Also Called: Masterbrand Cabinets LLC (G-812)
Decorate With Style Inc 419 621-5577
  2419 E Perkins Ave Ste E Sandusky (44870) (G-12887)
Decorative Paint Incorporated 419 485-0632
  700 Randolph St Montpelier (43543) (G-11384)
Decosky GM Center, Mount Vernon Also Called: Decosky Motor Holdings Inc (G-11483)
Decosky Motor Holdings Inc 740 397-9122
  510 Harcourt Rd # 550 Mount Vernon (43050) (G-11483)
Dedicated Nursing Assoc Inc 888 465-6929
  70 Birch Aly Ste 240 Beavercreek (45440) (G-922)
Dedicated Nursing Assoc Inc 866 450-5550
  3535 Fishinger Blvd Ste 140 Hilliard (43026) (G-9191)
Dedicated Tech Services Inc 614 309-0059
  545 Metro Pl S Ste 100 Dublin (43017) (G-7986)
Dedicated Technologies Inc 614 460-3200
  175 S 3rd St Ste 200 Columbus (43215) (G-5748)
Dedicated Transport LLC (HQ) 216 641-2500
  700 W Resource Dr Brooklyn Heights (44131) (G-1416)
Deedscom Inc 330 606-0119
  3094 W Market St Ste 242 Fairlawn (44333) (G-8473)
Deemsys Inc (PA) 614 322-9928
  800 Cross Pointe Rd Ste A Gahanna (43230) (G-8715)

ALPHABETIC SECTION — Department Job and Family Svcs

Deep Mind Music LLC 440 829-6401
11850 Edgewater Dr Apt 904 Lakewood (44107) *(G-9664)*

Deepwood Center, Mentor *Also Called: County of Lake (G-10927)*

Deepwood Industries Inc 440 350-5231
8121 Deepwood Blvd Mentor (44060) *(G-10933)*

Deer Park Roofing Inc (PA) 513 891-9151
7201 Blue Ash Rd Cincinnati (45236) *(G-2553)*

Deerfield AG Services Inc 330 584-4715
411 Oberlin Ave Sw Massillon (44647) *(G-10637)*

Deerfield AG Services, Inc., Massillon *Also Called: Deerfield AG Services Inc (G-10637)*

Deerfield Family Practice, Lebanon *Also Called: Trihealth Inc (G-9794)*

Deerfield Farms 330 584-4715
9041 State Route 224 Deerfield (44411) *(G-7740)*

Deerfield Farms Service Inc 330 584-4715
9041 State Route 224 Deerfield (44411) *(G-7741)*

Defabco Inc 614 231-2700
3765 E Livingston Ave Columbus (43227) *(G-5749)*

Defense Fin & Accounting Svc 614 693-6700
3990 E Broad St Columbus (43213) *(G-5750)*

Defiance Clinic, Defiance *Also Called: Fauster-Cameron Inc (G-7746)*

Defiance Cnty Bd Commissioners 419 782-3233
140 E Broadway St Defiance (43512) *(G-7743)*

Defiance County Senior Center, Defiance *Also Called: Defiance Cnty Bd Commissioners (G-7743)*

Defiance Family Physicians Ltd 419 785-3281
1250 Ralston Ave Ste 104 Defiance (43512) *(G-7744)*

Defiance Hospital Inc 419 783-6955
300 N Summit St Toledo (43604) *(G-13774)*

Defiance Regional Medical Ctr, Toledo *Also Called: Defiance Hospital Inc (G-13774)*

Definity Partners, Cincinnati *Also Called: Midwest Mfg Solutions LLC (G-3059)*

Degen Excavating Inc 419 225-6871
1920 Bible Rd Lima (45801) *(G-9884)*

Degussa Construction, Beachwood *Also Called: Master Builders LLC (G-811)*

Dehart Works LLC 440 600-8003
15210 Industrial Pkwy Cleveland (44135) *(G-4159)*

Dehoff Agency Inc 330 499-8153
821 S Main St Canton (44720) *(G-1733)*

Dei Incorporated 513 825-5800
1550 Kemper Meadow Dr Cincinnati (45240) *(G-2554)*

Del-Co Water Company Inc (PA) 740 548-7746
6658 Olentangy River Rd Delaware (43015) *(G-7793)*

Delaware City School District 740 363-5901
2462 Liberty Rd Delaware (43015) *(G-7794)*

Delaware City School Garage, Delaware *Also Called: Delaware City School District (G-7794)*

Delaware Cnty Bd Dvlpmntal DSB 740 201-3600
7991 Columbus Pike Lewis Center (43035) *(G-9816)*

Delaware County Bank & Tr Co, Lewis Center *Also Called: The Delaware County Bank Inc (G-9838)*

Delaware County Engineers, Delaware *Also Called: County of Delaware (G-7788)*

DELAWARE COURT, Mount Vernon *Also Called: Country Court (G-11480)*

Delaware General Health Dst, Delaware *Also Called: County of Delaware (G-7789)*

Delaware North-Sportservice 614 246-3203
200 W Nationwide Blvd Columbus (43215) *(G-5751)*

Delhi Dialysis, Cincinnati *Also Called: River Valley Dialysis LLC (G-3301)*

Delhi Township (PA) 513 922-0060
934 Neeb Rd Cincinnati (45233) *(G-2555)*

Delight Connection, Avon *Also Called: Cochin Technologies LLC (G-648)*

Delille Oxygen Company (PA) 614 444-1177
772 Marion Rd Columbus (43207) *(G-5752)*

Dell Willo Nursery Inc (PA) 419 289-0606
1398 Us Highway 42 Ashland (44805) *(G-496)*

Delmar Distributing, Columbus *Also Called: Columbus Distributing Company (G-5628)*

Deloitte & Touche LLP 513 784-7100
250 E 5th St Fl 1600 Cincinnati (45202) *(G-2556)*

Deloitte & Touche LLP 216 589-1300
127 Public Sq Ste 3300 Cleveland (44114) *(G-4160)*

Deloitte & Touche LLP 614 221-1000
180 E Broad St Ste 1400 Columbus (43215) *(G-5753)*

Deloitte & Touche LLP 937 223-8821
220 E Monument Ave Ste 500 Dayton (45402) *(G-7308)*

Deloitte Consulting, Cincinnati *Also Called: Deloitte & Touche LLP (G-2556)*

Deloitte Consulting LLP 937 223-8821
711 E Monument Ave Ste 201 Dayton (45402) *(G-7309)*

Delphia Consulting LLC 614 421-2000
250 E Broad St Ste 1150 Columbus (43215) *(G-5754)*

Delphos Plant 2, Delphos *Also Called: Toledo Molding & Die LLC (G-7846)*

Delta Corporate Holdings LLC 216 433-7700
12420 Plaza Dr Cleveland (44130) *(G-4161)*

Delta Diversified Inc 440 914-9400
30625 Solon Rd Ste F Solon (44139) *(G-13081)*

Delta Electrical Contrs Ltd 513 421-7744
4890 Gray Rd Cincinnati (45232) *(G-2557)*

Delta Gamma Fraternity (PA) 614 481-8169
3250 Riverside Dr Upper Arlington (43221) *(G-14277)*

Delta Media Group Inc 330 493-0350
7015 Sunset Strip Ave Nw North Canton (44720) *(G-11820)*

Delta Railroad Cnstr Inc (DH) 440 992-2997
2648 W Prospect Rd Frnt Ashtabula (44004) *(G-532)*

Delta Shipping Inc 619 261-7456
3971 Hoover Rd Ste 254 Grove City (43123) *(G-8914)*

Deltacraft, Independence *Also Called: Millcraft Group LLC (G-9452)*

Delventhal Company 419 244-5570
3796 Rockland Cir Millbury (43447) *(G-11267)*

Denier, Grove City *Also Called: Denier Electric Co Inc (G-8915)*

Denier Electric Co Inc 614 338-4664
4000 Gantz Rd Ste C Grove City (43123) *(G-8915)*

Denier Electric Co Inc (PA) 513 738-2641
7266 New Haven Rd Harrison (45030) *(G-9101)*

Denier Technologies Div, Harrison *Also Called: Denier Electric Co Inc (G-9101)*

Dennis Mitsubishi, Columbus *Also Called: Carcorp Inc (G-5506)*

Dennis Top Soil & Ldscpg Inc 419 865-5656
6340 Dorr St Toledo (43615) *(G-13775)*

Denovo Constructors Inc 419 265-8888
853 Tarra Oaks Dr Findlay (45840) *(G-8525)*

Dental Assoc Newton FLS Inc 330 872-5737
2000 Milton Blvd Newton Falls (44444) *(G-11774)*

Dental Associates, Columbus *Also Called: Lawrence M Shell DDS (G-6146)*

Dental Care One, Piqua *Also Called: Monarch Dental Corp (G-12450)*

Dental Center Northwest Ohio 419 241-6215
2138 Madison Ave Toledo (43604) *(G-13776)*

Dental Ceramics Inc 330 523-5240
3404 Brecksville Rd Richfield (44286) *(G-12694)*

Dental Group At North Hamilton 614 351-0555
1531 W Broad St Columbus (43222) *(G-5755)*

Dental Group West, Toledo *Also Called: Rankin Wiesenburger and Otto (G-13981)*

Dental Health Assoc 419 882-4510
3924 Sylvan Lakes Blvd Sylvania (43560) *(G-13540)*

Dental Health Services 330 864-9090
110 N Miller Rd Ste 200 Fairlawn (44333) *(G-8474)*

Dental Support Specialties LLC 330 639-1333
4774 Munson St Nw Canton (44718) *(G-1734)*

Dentalcare Partners Inc 216 584-1000
6200 Oak Tree Blvd Ste 200 Independence (44131) *(G-9428)*

Dentalone Partners Inc 440 934-0147
36050 Detroit Rd Avon (44011) *(G-649)*

Dentalone Partners Inc 614 356-7245
1099 Polaris Pkwy Columbus (43240) *(G-5257)*

Dentalone Partners Inc 844 214-4179
4176 Kent Rd Stow (44224) *(G-13363)*

Dentalone Partners Inc 440 238-1591
13339 Pearl Rd Strongsville (44136) *(G-13452)*

Dentalone Partners Inc 419 534-3005
3504 Secor Rd Ste 330 Toledo (43606) *(G-13777)*

Dentalworks, Avon *Also Called: Dentalone Partners Inc (G-649)*

Dentalworks, Columbus *Also Called: Dentalone Partners Inc (G-5257)*

Dentronix Inc 330 916-7300
235 Ascot Pkwy Cuyahoga Falls (44223) *(G-7070)*

Department Children Services, Cleveland *Also Called: County of Cuyahoga (G-4130)*

Department Dvelopment-Research, Columbus *Also Called: Ohio State University (G-6459)*

Department Job and Family Svcs, Cadiz *Also Called: Harrison Township (G-1540)*

Department of Anesthetia — ALPHABETIC SECTION

Department of Anesthetia, Cincinnati *Also Called: University of Cincinnati (G-3572)*

Department of Commerce Ohio 614 728-8400
77 S High St Fl 21 Columbus (43215) *(G-5756)*

Department of Commerce Ohio 614 644-7381
77 S High St Fl 22 Columbus (43215) *(G-5757)*

Department of Health Ohio 419 447-1450
600 N River Rd Tiffin (44883) *(G-13627)*

Department of Ob/Gyn, Cleveland *Also Called: Metrohealth System (G-4566)*

Department of Public Utilities, Cleveland *Also Called: City of Cleveland (G-3988)*

Department of Surgery, Dayton *Also Called: Wright State University (G-7729)*

Department Senior Adult S, Cleveland *Also Called: County of Cuyahoga (G-4122)*

Dependable Painting Co (PA) 216 431-4470
4403 Superior Ave Cleveland (44103) *(G-4162)*

Deporres Mrtin Emrgncy Assstnc, Cleveland *Also Called: Catholic Charities Corporation (G-3934)*

Depot Direct Inc 419 661-1233
487 J St Perrysburg (43551) *(G-12332)*

Dept of Human Service, Ashville *Also Called: County of Pickaway (G-552)*

Dept of Laboratory Medicine, Columbus *Also Called: Nationwide Childrens Hospital (G-6313)*

DEPT OF LABORATORY MEDICINE, Columbus *Also Called: Research Inst At Ntnwide Chld (G-6580)*

Dept of Neighborhoods, Toledo *Also Called: City of Toledo (G-13739)*

Dept of Public Utilities, Columbus *Also Called: City of Columbus (G-5576)*

Der Dutchman's Restaurant, Plain City *Also Called: Dutchman Hospitality Group Inc (G-12474)*

Dermamed Coatings Company LLC 330 634-9449
381 Geneva Ave Tallmadge (44278) *(G-13591)*

Dermatlgists of Southwest Ohio (PA) 937 435-2094
5300 Far Hills Ave Ste 100 Dayton (45429) *(G-7310)*

Dermatlogists Centl States LLC 888 414-3627
9349 Waterstone Blvd Fl 3 Cincinnati (45249) *(G-2558)*

Desalvo Construction Company 330 759-8145
1491 W Liberty St Hubbard (44425) *(G-9321)*

Desco Federal Credit Union (PA) 740 354-7791
401 Chillicothe St Portsmouth (45662) *(G-12550)*

Design Build Plus, Cincinnati *Also Called: Process Plus Design Build LLC (G-3240)*

Design Built Construction Inc 419 563-0185
825 E Mansfield St Bucyrus (44820) *(G-1507)*

Design Central Inc 614 890-0202
6464 Presidential Gtwy Columbus (43231) *(G-5758)*

Design Concrete Surfaces, Kent *Also Called: Don Wartko Construction Co (G-9572)*

Design Engners Cnsulting Assoc 419 891-0022
415 Conant St Maumee (43537) *(G-10718)*

Design Homes & Development Co 937 438-3667
8534 Yankee St Ste A Dayton (45458) *(G-7311)*

Design Rstrtion Rcnstrction In 330 563-0010
4305 Mount Pleasant St Nw Ste 103 North Canton (44720) *(G-11821)*

Deskey Associates Inc 513 721-6800
120 E 8th St Cincinnati (45202) *(G-2559)*

Desoto Dialysis LLC 419 691-1514
2702 Navarre Ave Ste 203 Oregon (43616) *(G-12132)*

Detox Health Care Corp Ohio 513 742-6310
11500 Northlake Dr Ste 400 Cincinnati (45249) *(G-2560)*

Detrex Corporation 440 997-6131
1100 State Rd Ashtabula (44004) *(G-533)*

Detroit Diesel Corporation 330 430-4300
515 11th St Se Canton (44707) *(G-1735)*

Detroit Tire, Xenia *Also Called: Detroit Tire & Auto Supply Inc (G-15503)*

Detroit Tire & Auto Supply Inc 937 426-0949
968 W 2nd St Xenia (45385) *(G-15503)*

Detroit Westfield LLC 330 666-4131
4073 Medina Rd Akron (44333) *(G-133)*

Detwiler Park Golf Course, Toledo *Also Called: American Golf Corporation (G-13682)*

Dev Investments of Ohio Inc 740 454-9332
320 Scenic Crest Dr Zanesville (43701) *(G-15785)*

Devcare Solutions Ltd 614 221-2277
579 Executive Campus Dr Ste 370 Westerville (43082) *(G-14888)*

Devry University, Columbus *Also Called: Devry University Inc (G-5759)*

Devry University Inc 614 251-6969
2 Easton Oval Ste 310 # 210 Columbus (43219) *(G-5759)*

Devs United, Cleveland *Also Called: Marcus Thomas Llc (G-4523)*

Dewesoft, Whitehouse *Also Called: Dewesoft LLC (G-15140)*

Dewesoft LLC 855 339-3669
10730 Logan St Whitehouse (43571) *(G-15140)*

Dexxxon Digital Storage Inc 740 548-7179
7611 Green Meadows Dr Lewis Center (43035) *(G-9817)*

Df Supply, Twinsburg *Also Called: Df Supply Inc (G-14181)*

Df Supply Inc 330 650-9226
8500 Hadden Rd Twinsburg (44087) *(G-14181)*

Dfs Corporate Services LLC 614 777-7020
3311 Mill Meadow Dr Hilliard (43026) *(G-9192)*

Dfs Corporate Services LLC 614 283-2499
6500 New Albany Rd E New Albany (43054) *(G-11561)*

Dg3 Topco Holdings LLC 216 292-0200
25101 Chagrin Blvd Ste 350 Cleveland (44122) *(G-4163)*

Dgperry, Pllc, Canfield *Also Called: Bodine Perry LLC (G-1622)*

DH, Cincinnati *Also Called: D+h USA Corporation (G-2533)*

Dhanlaxmi LLC 614 871-9617
4055 Jackpot Rd Grove City (43123) *(G-8916)*

Dhdc, Dayton *Also Called: Design Homes & Development Co (G-7311)*

Dhl Ecommerce, Stow *Also Called: Global Mail Inc (G-13371)*

Dhl Express (usa) Inc 614 865-8325
570 Polaris Pkwy Ste 110 Westerville (43082) *(G-14889)*

Dhl Home Care LLC 614 987-5813
2580 Oakstone Dr Ste A Columbus (43231) *(G-5760)*

Dhl Infrmtion Svcs Amricas Inc (HQ) 614 865-5993
550 Polaris Pkwy Westerville (43082) *(G-14890)*

Dhl Supply Chain USA, Westerville *Also Called: Exel Inc (G-14893)*

Dhr International Inc 513 762-7690
312 Walnut St Ste 1600 Cincinnati (45202) *(G-2561)*

Di Salle Real Estate Co 419 255-6909
405 Madison Ave Toledo (43604) *(G-13778)*

Di Santo Companies Inc 216 292-7772
25111 Emery Rd Cleveland (44128) *(G-4164)*

Dialamerica Marketing Inc 330 836-5293
3090 W Market St Ste 210 Fairlawn (44333) *(G-8475)*

Dialysis Center Dayton- North, Dayton *Also Called: Dialysis Centers Dayton LLC (G-7312)*

Dialysis Centers Dayton LLC 937 208-7900
455 Turner Rd Dayton (45415) *(G-7312)*

Dialysis Centers Dayton LLC 937 548-7019
1111 Sweitzer St Ste B Greenville (45331) *(G-8871)*

Dialysis Clinic Inc 513 281-0091
499 E Mcmillan St Cincinnati (45206) *(G-2562)*

Dialysis Clinic Inc 740 351-0596
1207 17th St Portsmouth (45662) *(G-12551)*

Dialysis Ctr Dyton- Darke Cnty, Greenville *Also Called: Dialysis Centers Dayton LLC (G-8871)*

Dialysis Partners of NW Ohio, Toledo *Also Called: Greenfield Health Systems Corp (G-13829)*

Diamond Hill Capital MGT Inc 614 255-3333
325 John H Mcconnell Blvd Ste 200 Columbus (43215) *(G-5761)*

Diamond Hill Funds 614 255-3333
325 John H Mcconnell Blvd Ste 200 Columbus (43215) *(G-5762)*

Diamond Logistics Inc 614 274-9750
745 N Wilson Rd Columbus (43204) *(G-5763)*

Diamond Machine and Mfg, Bluffton *Also Called: Carpe Diem Industries LLC (G-1280)*

Diamond Metals Dist Inc 216 898-7900
4635 W 160th St Cleveland (44135) *(G-4165)*

Diamond Roofing Systems, Warren *Also Called: Diamond Roofing Systems LLP (G-14517)*

Diamond Roofing Systems LLP 330 856-2500
8600 E Market St Ste 4 Warren (44484) *(G-14517)*

Diamond Steel Construction 330 549-5500
8270 Raupp Ave Youngstown (44512) *(G-15596)*

Diamond W LLC 970 434-9435
50817 State Route 556 Clarington (43915) *(G-3729)*

Diamondback Golf LLC 614 410-1313
1 Rattlesnake Dr Sunbury (43074) *(G-13520)*

DIAMONDS & PEARLS RCH, Beachwood *Also Called: Diamonds Pearls Hlth Svcs LLC (G-787)*

Diamonds Pearls Hlth Svcs LLC 216 752-8500
23611 Chagrin Blvd Ste 226 Beachwood (44122) *(G-787)*

Diane Sauer Chevrolet Inc 330 373-1600
700 Niles Rd Se Warren (44483) *(G-14518)*

ALPHABETIC SECTION — Dittman-Adams Company

Diaz Construction Inc 740 289-4898
  535 Seif Rd Piketon (45661) *(G-12417)*

Dick Masheter Ford Inc 614 861-7150
  1100 S Hamilton Rd Columbus (43227) *(G-5764)*

Dickie McCamey & Chilcote PC (PA) 412 281-7272
  10 W Broad St Ste 1950 Columbus (43215) *(G-5765)*

Dickman Kettler & Bruner Ltd 419 678-3016
  201 S 2nd St Coldwater (45828) *(G-5212)*

Dickman Supply Inc (PA) 937 492-6166
  1991 St Marys Ave Sidney (45365) *(G-13029)*

Diebold Direct, North Canton *Also Called: Diebold Nixdorf Incorporated (G-11824)*

Diebold Global Finance Corp 330 490-6900
  350 Orchard Ave Ne North Canton (44720) *(G-11822)*

Diebold Nixdorf Incorporated 330 899-1300
  5995 Mayfair Rd North Canton (44720) *(G-11823)*

Diebold Nixdorf Incorporated 330 899-2510
  5995 Mayfair Rd North Canton (44720) *(G-11824)*

Diebold Nixdorf Incorporated 330 899-0097
  3800 Tabs Dr Uniontown (44685) *(G-14248)*

Diebold Self Service Systems (PA) 330 490-5099
  5995 Mayfair Rd Canton (44720) *(G-1736)*

Diers2018co Inc 513 242-9250
  5618 Center Hill Ave Cincinnati (45216) *(G-2563)*

Dietary Solutions Inc 614 985-6567
  171 Green Meadows Dr S Lewis Center (43035) *(G-9818)*

Differential Dev Shop LLC 513 205-8930
  815 Main St Cincinnati (45202) *(G-2564)*

Digest Health Center Ltd 330 869-0178
  570 White Pond Dr Ste 150 Akron (44320) *(G-134)*

Digestive Care Inc 937 320-5050
  75 Sylvania Dr Dayton (45440) *(G-7313)*

Digestive Disease Consultants 330 225-6468
  1299 Industrial Pkwy N Ste 110 Brunswick (44212) *(G-1455)*

Digestive Endoscopy Center, Dayton *Also Called: Digestive Specialists Inc (G-7314)*

Digestive Hlth Cre Cnsltnts of 419 843-7996
  3439 Granite Cir Toledo (43617) *(G-13779)*

Digestive Specialists Inc 937 534-7330
  999 Brubaker Dr Ste 1 Dayton (45429) *(G-7314)*

Digi Satellite, Dayton *Also Called: Sun Yer Bunz LLC (G-7652)*

Digioia-Suburban Excvtg LLC 440 237-1978
  11293 Royalton Rd North Royalton (44133) *(G-11939)*

Digital Forensics Corp LLC 888 210-1296
  4400 Renaissance Pkwy Warrensville Heights (44128) *(G-14580)*

Digitek Software Inc 614 764-8875
  650 Radio Dr Lewis Center (43035) *(G-9819)*

Dill-Elam Inc 513 575-0017
  1461 State Route 28 Loveland (45140) *(G-10135)*

Dillin Engineered Systems Corp 419 666-6789
  8030 Broadstone Rd Perrysburg (43551) *(G-12333)*

Dillon Group Homes, Fostoria *Also Called: RES-Care Inc (G-8623)*

Dillon Holdings LLC 513 942-5600
  8050 Beckett Center Dr Ste 103 West Chester (45069) *(G-14685)*

Dimech Services Inc 419 727-0111
  5505 Enterprise Blvd Toledo (43612) *(G-13780)*

Dimension Service Corporation 614 226-7455
  5500 Frantz Rd Ste 100 Dublin (43017) *(G-7987)*

Dimensional Metals Inc (PA) 740 927-3633
  58 Klema Dr N Reynoldsburg (43068) *(G-12660)*

Dimex LLC, Marietta *Also Called: Westlake Dimex LLC (G-10414)*

Dino Persichetti 330 821-9600
  20040 Harrisburg Westville Rd Alliance (44601) *(G-381)*

Dinsmore & Shohl LLP (PA) 513 977-8200
  255 E 5th St Ste 1900 Cincinnati (45202) *(G-2565)*

Dinsmore & Shohl LLP 614 628-6880
  191 W Nationwide Blvd Ste 300 Columbus (43215) *(G-5766)*

Dinsmore & Shohl LLP 937 449-6400
  1 S Main St Ste 1300 Dayton (45402) *(G-7315)*

Diocese Tld/Catholic Cmtry Off, Toledo *Also Called: Roman Catholic Diocese Toledo (G-13996)*

Diocese Tledo Prest Retirement 419 244-6711
  1933 Spielbusch Ave Toledo (43604) *(G-13781)*

Diplomat Spclty Infusion Group, Cincinnati *Also Called: Optum Infusion Svcs 550 LLC (G-3166)*

Diproinduca (usa) Limited LLC 330 722-4442
  2528 Medina Rd Medina (44256) *(G-10828)*

Diproinduca USA, Medina *Also Called: Diproinduca (usa) Limited LLC (G-10828)*

Direct Air, Columbus *Also Called: Airtech LLC (G-5332)*

Direct Expediting Llc 877 880-3400
  5311 Bentley Oak Dr Mason (45040) *(G-10544)*

Direct Health Care Supply, Hudson *Also Called: Edwards Health Care Services (G-9344)*

Direct Import Home Decor Inc (PA) 216 898-9758
  4979 W 130th St Cleveland (44135) *(G-4166)*

Direct Options, Cincinnati *Also Called: Direct Options Inc (G-2566)*

Direct Options Inc 513 779-4416
  1325 Glendale Milford Rd Cincinnati (45215) *(G-2566)*

Direction HM Akron Cnton Area (PA) 330 896-9172
  1550 Corporate Woods Pkwy Uniontown (44685) *(G-14249)*

Direction Home Eastrn Ohio Inc 330 505-2355
  1030 N Meridian Rd Youngstown (44509) *(G-15597)*

Directions Credit Union Inc (PA) 419 720-4769
  5121 Whiteford Rd Sylvania (43560) *(G-13541)*

Directions For Youth Families 614 258-8043
  657 S Ohio Ave Columbus (43205) *(G-5767)*

Directions For Youth Families 614 694-0203
  3860 Kimberly Pkwy N Columbus (43232) *(G-5768)*

Directions For Youth Families (PA) 614 294-2661
  1515 Indianola Ave Columbus (43201) *(G-5769)*

Directions Research Inc (PA) 513 651-2990
  401 E Court St Ste 200 Cincinnati (45202) *(G-2567)*

Dirtworks Drainage, Louisville *Also Called: Alliance Crane & Rigging Inc (G-10111)*

DISABILLITY RIGHTS OHIO, Columbus *Also Called: Ohio Dsblity Rghts Law Plicy C (G-6414)*

Disabled American Veterans 937 644-1907
  209 Prairie Dr Marysville (43040) *(G-10483)*

Discount Drug Mart Inc 330 343-7700
  3015 N Wooster Ave Dover (44622) *(G-7879)*

Discount Drug Mart Inc (HQ) 330 725-2340
  211 Commerce Dr Medina (44256) *(G-10829)*

Discover Card Services, Hilliard *Also Called: Dfs Corporate Services LLC (G-9192)*

Discover Financial Services, New Albany *Also Called: Dfs Corporate Services LLC (G-11561)*

Discovery School 419 756-8880
  855 Millsboro Rd Mansfield (44903) *(G-10258)*

Disinfection MGT Tech LLC 440 212-1061
  1245 S Cleveland Massillon Rd Ste 1 Copley (44321) *(G-6955)*

Dismas Distribution Services 614 861-2525
  450 Mccormick Blvd Columbus (43213) *(G-5770)*

Dispatch Color Press, Columbus *Also Called: Dispatch Consumer Services (G-5771)*

Dispatch Consumer Services (HQ) 740 548-5555
  5300 Crosswind Dr Columbus (43228) *(G-5771)*

Dispatch Productions Inc 614 460-3700
  770 Twin Rivers Dr Columbus (43215) *(G-5772)*

Dist-Trans Inc 614 497-1660
  1580 Williams Rd Columbus (43207) *(G-5773)*

Distillata Company (PA) 216 771-2900
  1608 E 24th St Cleveland (44114) *(G-4167)*

Distribution Center, West Chester *Also Called: Martin-Brower Company LLC (G-14729)*

Distribution Data Incorporated (PA) 216 362-3009
  16101 Snow Rd Ste 200 Brookpark (44142) *(G-1433)*

Distribution Service Company, Wadsworth *Also Called: Cornwell Quality Tools Company (G-14434)*

Distributor Marketing MGT Inc 440 236-5534
  14147 Station Rd Columbia Station (44028) *(G-5227)*

District Board Health Mahoning 330 270-2855
  50 Westchester Dr Youngstown (44515) *(G-15598)*

Distrubution Center, Columbus *Also Called: Ohiohealth Corporation (G-6466)*

Disttech, North Canton *Also Called: Disttech Inc (G-11825)*

Disttech Inc 800 969-5419
  4366 Mount Pleasant St Nw North Canton (44720) *(G-11825)*

Ditsch Usa LLC 513 782-8888
  311 Northland Blvd Cincinnati (45246) *(G-2568)*

Dittman-Adams Company 513 870-7530
  10080 Crosby Rd Harrison (45030) *(G-9102)*

Div of Refuse and Recycling — ALPHABETIC SECTION

Div of Refuse and Recycling, Cleveland *Also Called: City of Lakewood* **(G-3990)**

Diversfied Emplyee Sltions Inc 330 764-4125
  3745 Medina Rd Medina (44256) **(G-10830)**

DIVERSICARE, Cincinnati *Also Called: Diversicare St Theresa LLC* **(G-2569)**

Diversicare St Theresa LLC 513 271-7010
  7010 Rowan Hill Dr Cincinnati (45227) **(G-2569)**

Diversified Fall Protection, Westlake *Also Called: Lorad LLC* **(G-15077)**

Diversified Health MGT Inc 614 338-8888
  3569 Refugee Rd Ste C Columbus (43232) **(G-5774)**

Diversified Ophthalmics Inc 803 783-3454
  250 Mccullough St Cincinnati (45226) **(G-2570)**

Diversified Production LLC 740 373-8771
  111 Industry Rd Unit 206 Marietta (45750) **(G-10366)**

Diversified SE Division, Cincinnati *Also Called: Diversified Ophthalmics Inc* **(G-2570)**

Diversified Systems Inc 614 476-9939
  100 Dorchester Sq N Ste 103 Westerville (43081) **(G-14976)**

Diversity Search Group LLC 614 352-2988
  2550 Corporate Exchange Dr Ste 15 Columbus (43231) **(G-5775)**

Divine Rhblttion Nrsing At Syl, Sylvania *Also Called: Mountain Crest OH Opco LLC* **(G-13556)**

Divine Strings Investment LLC 937 241-0782
  6545 Market Ave N Ste 100 Canton (44721) **(G-1737)**

Division Gorman-Rupp Company, Bellville *Also Called: Gorman-Rupp Company* **(G-1049)**

Division Gstrntrlogy Hptlogy N, Columbus *Also Called: Ohio State Univ Wexner Med Ctr* **(G-6450)**

Division of Geological Survey 614 265-6576
  2045 Morse Rd Bldg C Columbus (43229) **(G-5776)**

Division of Selling Materials, Dover *Also Called: Smith Concrete Co* **(G-7901)**

Division of Water Resources, Batavia *Also Called: County of Clermont* **(G-738)**

Division Streets & Utilities, Dublin *Also Called: City of Dublin* **(G-7964)**

Divisions Inc (PA) 859 448-9730
  50 W 5th St Cincinnati (45202) **(G-2571)**

Divisions Maintenance Group, Cincinnati *Also Called: Divisions Inc* **(G-2571)**

Dix & Eaton Incorporated 216 241-0405
  200 Public Sq Ste 3900 Cleveland (44114) **(G-4168)**

Dixie Distributing Company 937 322-0033
  200 W High St Springfield (45506) **(G-13247)**

Dixon Healthcare Center, Wintersville *Also Called: Reichart Leasing Co LLC* **(G-15296)**

Dizer Corp 440 368-0201
  1912 Mentor Ave Painesville (44077) **(G-12227)**

DJ Roofing & Imprvs LLC 419 307-5712
  1043 County Road 99 Fremont (43420) **(G-8675)**

Djd Express Inc 740 676-7464
  56461 Ferry Landing Rd Shadyside (43947) **(G-12969)**

Djj Holding Corporation (HQ) 513 419-6200
  300 Pike St Cincinnati (45202) **(G-2572)**

DKM Construction Inc 740 289-3006
  W Perimeter Rd Piketon (45661) **(G-12418)**

Dkmp Consulting Inc 614 733-0979
  8000 Corporate Blvd Plain City (43064) **(G-12473)**

DLC Transport Inc 740 282-1763
  320 N 5th St Steubenville (43952) **(G-13321)**

Dlr Group Inc 216 522-1350
  1422 Euclid Ave Ste 300 Cleveland (44115) **(G-4169)**

Dlz, Akron *Also Called: Dlz Ohio Inc* **(G-135)**

Dlz Construction Services Inc 614 888-0040
  6121 Huntley Rd Columbus (43229) **(G-5777)**

Dlz Ohio Inc 330 923-0401
  1 Canal Square Plz Ste 1300 Akron (44308) **(G-135)**

Dlz Ohio Inc (HQ) 614 888-0040
  6121 Huntley Rd Columbus (43229) **(G-5778)**

DMC Consulting, Toledo *Also Called: DMC Technology Group Inc* **(G-13782)**

DMC Technology Group Inc 419 535-2900
  7657 Kings Pointe Rd Toledo (43617) **(G-13782)**

DMD Management Inc 216 749-4010
  5520 Broadview Rd Cleveland (44134) **(G-4170)**

DMD Management Inc (PA) 216 898-8399
  12380 Plaza Dr Cleveland (44130) **(G-4171)**

DMD Management Inc 216 371-3600
  12504 Cedar Rd Cleveland (44106) **(G-4172)**

DMD Management Inc 330 405-6040
  2463 Sussex Blvd Twinsburg (44087) **(G-14182)**

DMD Management Inc 440 944-9400
  1919 Bishop Rd Wickliffe (44092) **(G-15147)**

Dms Inc 440 951-9838
  37121 Euclid Ave Ste 1 Willoughby (44094) **(G-15189)**

DMS Recycling LLC 740 397-0790
  350 Pittsburgh Ave Mount Vernon (43050) **(G-11484)**

Dmt Certified, Copley *Also Called: Disinfection MGT Tech LLC* **(G-6955)**

Dna Diagnostics Center Inc (DH) 513 881-7800
  1 Ddc Way Fairfield (45014) **(G-8407)**

Dno Inc 614 231-3601
  3650 E 5th Ave Columbus (43219) **(G-5779)**

Dnv Healthcare USA Inc 281 396-1610
  4435 Aicholtz Rd Ste 900 Cincinnati (45245) **(G-2102)**

Do It Best, Medina *Also Called: Do It Best Corp* **(G-10831)**

Do It Best, Middlefield *Also Called: Western Reserve Farm Cooperative Inc* **(G-11146)**

Do It Best, Sidney *Also Called: Lochard Inc* **(G-13037)**

Do It Best Corp 330 725-3859
  444 Independence Dr Medina (44256) **(G-10831)**

Doan Pyramid Electric, Cleveland *Also Called: Northeast Ohio Electric LLC* **(G-4662)**

Doan, Randall, New Philadelphia *Also Called: Tuscarwas Oral Mxllfcial Srger* **(G-11670)**

Docs, Cincinnati *Also Called: Dermatlogists Centl States LLC* **(G-2558)**

Doctor's Pain Clinic, Youngstown *Also Called: Doctors Pain Center LLC* **(G-15599)**

Doctor's Urgent Care Offices, Cincinnati *Also Called: Ambulatory Medical Care Inc* **(G-2175)**

Doctors Hospital Cleveland Inc 740 753-7300
  11 John Lloyd Evans Memorial Dr Nelsonville (45764) **(G-11542)**

Doctors Hospital North, Columbus *Also Called: Doctors Ohiohealth Corporation* **(G-5781)**

Doctors Office 740 622-3016
  1460 Orange St Coshocton (43812) **(G-6983)**

Doctors Ohiohealth Corporation 614 297-4000
  5100 W Broad St Columbus (43228) **(G-5780)**

Doctors Ohiohealth Corporation (HQ) 614 544-5424
  5100 W Broad St Columbus (43228) **(G-5781)**

Doctors Pain Center LLC 330 629-2888
  1011 Boardman Canfield Rd Youngstown (44512) **(G-15599)**

DOCUMENT SOLUTIONS, Xenia *Also Called: Greene Inc* **(G-15510)**

Dodd Camera, Cleveland *Also Called: Dodd Camera Holdings Inc* **(G-4173)**

Dodd Camera Holdings Inc (PA) 216 361-6811
  2077 E 30th St Cleveland (44115) **(G-4173)**

Dog Warden, Wadsworth *Also Called: City of Wadsworth* **(G-14431)**

DOGGY DAY CARE, Mantua *Also Called: Hattie Larlham Community Svcs* **(G-10330)**

Dolbey Systems Inc (PA) 440 392-9900
  7280 Auburn Rd Concord Township (44077) **(G-6925)**

Dold Homes Inc (PA) 419 874-2535
  26610 Eckel Rd Perrysburg (43551) **(G-12334)**

Dole, Springfield *Also Called: Dole Fresh Vegetables Inc* **(G-13248)**

Dole Fresh Vegetables Inc 937 525-4300
  600 Benjamin Dr Springfield (45502) **(G-13248)**

Dollar Paradise (PA) 216 432-0421
  1240 E 55th St Cleveland (44103) **(G-4174)**

Dollar Thrifty, Columbus *Also Called: Thrifty LLC* **(G-6767)**

Dollries Group LLC 513 834-6105
  3284 Cherryridge Dr North Bend (45052) **(G-11803)**

Domestic Relations 937 225-4063
  301 W 3rd St Ste 500 Dayton (45402) **(G-7316)**

Dominion Energy Ohio, Akron *Also Called: East Ohio Gas Company* **(G-145)**

Dominion Energy Ohio, Ashtabula *Also Called: East Ohio Gas Company* **(G-534)**

Dominion Energy Ohio, Byesville *Also Called: East Ohio Gas Company* **(G-1534)**

Dominion Energy Ohio, Canton *Also Called: East Ohio Gas Company* **(G-1741)**

Dominion Energy Ohio, Cleveland *Also Called: East Ohio Gas Company* **(G-4197)**

Dominion Energy Ohio, Cleveland *Also Called: East Ohio Gas Company* **(G-4198)**

Dominion Energy Ohio, New Franklin *Also Called: East Ohio Gas Company* **(G-11615)**

Dominion Energy Ohio, Wickliffe *Also Called: East Ohio Gas Company* **(G-15148)**

Dominion Energy Ohio, Wooster *Also Called: East Ohio Gas Company* **(G-15335)**

Domino Foods Inc 216 432-3222
  2075 E 65th St Cleveland (44103) **(G-4175)**

Domino Sugar, Cleveland *Also Called: Domino Foods Inc* **(G-4175)**

Don Walter Kitchen Distrs Inc (PA) 330 793-9338
  260 Victoria Rd Youngstown (44515) **(G-15600)**

ALPHABETIC SECTION — Drew Medical Inc

Don Wartko Construction Co 330 673-5252
975 Tallmadge Rd Kent (44240) *(G-9572)*

Don Wood Inc 740 593-6641
900 E State St Athens (45701) *(G-566)*

Don Wood Bick Oldsmbile Pntiac, Athens *Also Called: Don Wood Inc (G-566)*

Don's Lighthouse Inn, Cleveland *Also Called: Strang Corporation (G-4955)*

Donald Mrtens Sons Ambince Svc (PA) 216 265-4211
10830 Brookpark Rd Cleveland (44130) *(G-4176)*

Donald P Pipino Company Ltd 330 726-8177
7600 Market St Youngstown (44512) *(G-15601)*

Donald R Kenney & Co Rlty LLC (PA) 614 540-2404
470 Olde Worthington Rd Ste 101 Westerville (43082) *(G-14891)*

DONAUSCHWABEN'S GERMANAMERICAN, Olmsted Twp *Also Called: Lenau Park (G-12091)*

Donlen Inc 216 961-6767
8905 Lake Ave Cleveland (44102) *(G-4177)*

Donley Ford-Lincoln Inc (PA) 419 281-3673
1641 Claremont Ave Ashland (44805) *(G-497)*

Donleys Inc (PA) 216 524-6800
5430 Warner Rd Cleveland (44125) *(G-4178)*

Donnellon Mc Carthy Inc 937 299-0200
2580 Lance Dr Moraine (45409) *(G-11404)*

DONNELLON MC CARTHY, INC., Moraine *Also Called: Donnellon Mc Carthy Inc (G-11404)*

Donnellon McCarthy Entps Inc (PA) 513 769-7800
10855 Medallion Dr Cincinnati (45241) *(G-2573)*

Donnellon McCarthy Inc (PA) 513 769-7800
10855 Medallion Dr Cincinnati (45241) *(G-2574)*

Donor Care Center Inc 330 497-4888
4535 Strausser St Nw North Canton (44720) *(G-11826)*

Dons Automotive Group Llc 419 337-3010
720 N Shoop Ave Wauseon (43567) *(G-14599)*

Doran Mfg LLC 866 816-7233
4362 Glendale Milford Rd Blue Ash (45242) *(G-1163)*

Dorcy International Inc (PA) 614 497-5830
2700 Port Rd Columbus (43217) *(G-5782)*

Doro Inc 740 695-1994
68400 Matthews Dr Saint Clairsville (43950) *(G-12790)*

Dorsky Hodgson + Partners Inc (PA) 216 464-8600
23240 Chagrin Blvd Ste 300 Cleveland (44122) *(G-4179)*

Dorsky Hodgson Parrish Yue, Cleveland *Also Called: Dorsky Hodgson + Partners Inc (G-4179)*

Dortrnic Service-Tallmadge Inc 330 928-2727
3878 Hudson Dr Stow (44224) *(G-13364)*

Dortronic Service Inc (PA) 216 739-3667
201 E Granger Rd Cleveland (44131) *(G-4180)*

DOT Diamond Core Drilling Inc (PA) 440 322-6466
780 Sugar Ln Elyria (44035) *(G-8242)*

DOT Net Factory LLC 614 792-0645
4393 Tuller Rd Ste A Dublin (43017) *(G-7988)*

Dotloop LLC 513 257-0550
700 W Pete Rose Way Ste 436 Cincinnati (45203) *(G-2575)*

Dots Market, Dayton *Also Called: Mary C Enterprises Inc (G-7467)*

Double A Solutions LLC 256 489-6458
3139 N Republic Blvd Toledo (43615) *(G-13783)*

Double A Trailer Sales Inc (PA) 419 692-7626
1750 E 5th St Delphos (45833) *(G-7840)*

Double Tree, Columbus *Also Called: Columbus Worthington Hospitali (G-5659)*

Double Z Construction Company 614 274-9334
2550 Harrison Rd Columbus (43204) *(G-5783)*

Doubletree, Fairlawn *Also Called: Pac Associates Inc (G-8493)*

Doubletree By Hilton 330 333-8284
44 E Federal St Youngstown (44503) *(G-15602)*

Doubletree By Hilton, Cleveland *Also Called: Tudor Arms Mstr Subtenant LLC (G-5040)*

Doubletree By Hilton Newark, Columbus *Also Called: Indus Newark Hotel LLC (G-6049)*

Doubletree Columbus, Columbus *Also Called: Hotel 50 S Front Opco L P (G-6010)*

Doubletree Columbus Hotel, Columbus *Also Called: Ch Relty Iv/Clmbus Partners LP (G-5550)*

Doubletree Guest Suites Dayton 937 436-2400
300 Prestige Pl Miamisburg (45342) *(G-11048)*

Doubletree Hotel, Cincinnati *Also Called: 6300 Sharonville Assoc LLC (G-2126)*

Doubletree Hotel, Cleveland *Also Called: Cleveland S Hospitality LLC (G-4065)*

Doubletree Hotel, Dayton *Also Called: Renthotel Dayton LLC (G-7585)*

Doug Bigelow Chevrolet Inc 330 644-7500
894 Robinwood Hills Dr Akron (44333) *(G-136)*

Doug Chevrolet, Akron *Also Called: Doug Bigelow Chevrolet Inc (G-136)*

Dover Chemical Corporation (HQ) 330 343-7711
3676 Davis Rd Nw Dover (44622) *(G-7880)*

Dover City Schools 330 343-8880
865 1/2 E Iron Ave Dover (44622) *(G-7881)*

Dover Cryogenics, Midvale *Also Called: Amko Service Company (G-11203)*

Dover Hydraulics Inc (PA) 330 364-1617
2996 Progress St Dover (44622) *(G-7882)*

Dover Hydraulics South, Dover *Also Called: Dover Hydraulics Inc (G-7882)*

Dover Nursing Center Llc 330 364-4436
1525 N Crater Ave Dover (44622) *(G-7883)*

Dover Phila Federal Credit Un (PA) 330 364-8874
119 Fillmore Ave Dover (44622) *(G-7884)*

Dovetail Construction Co Inc (PA) 740 592-1800
26055 Emery Rd Cleveland (44128) *(G-4181)*

Dovetail Solar and Wind, Cleveland *Also Called: Dovetail Construction Co Inc (G-4181)*

Downing Displays Inc (PA) 513 248-9800
550 Techne Center Dr Milford (45150) *(G-11225)*

Downing Enterprises Inc 330 666-3888
1287 Centerview Cir Copley (44321) *(G-6956)*

Downing Exhibits, Copley *Also Called: Downing Enterprises Inc (G-6956)*

Downtown Akron Partnership Inc 330 374-7676
103 S High St Fl 4 Akron (44308) *(G-137)*

Downtown Fast Park, Cincinnati *Also Called: Park Place Operations Inc (G-3185)*

Downtown Ford Lincoln Inc 330 456-2781
1423 Tuscarawas St W Canton (44702) *(G-1738)*

Doyle Hcm Inc 614 322-9310
735 Taylor Rd Ste 100 Columbus (43230) *(G-5784)*

Doyle Ja Corporation 419 705-1091
10075 Waterville St Whitehouse (43571) *(G-15141)*

Doylestown Communications, Doylestown *Also Called: Doylestown Telephone Company (G-7915)*

Doylestown Telephone Company (PA) 330 658-2121
81 N Portage St Doylestown (44230) *(G-7915)*

Dp Medina Holdings Inc 216 254-7883
1291 Medina Rd Medina (44256) *(G-10832)*

DPL, Manchester *Also Called: Dayton Power and Light Company (G-10239)*

DPL Inc (HQ) 937 259-7215
1065 Woodman Dr Dayton (45432) *(G-7130)*

Dps, Independence *Also Called: Canon Solutions America Inc (G-9416)*

Dpsciences, Cincinnati *Also Called: Data Processing Sciences Corporation (G-2539)*

Dqr 4 Ted 740 264-4323
108 S Hollywood Blvd Steubenville (43952) *(G-13322)*

DQR 4 TED, Steubenville *Also Called: Dqr 4 Ted (G-13322)*

Dr Alxander C Nnabue Assoc PA 614 499-7687
825 Dennison Ave Columbus (43215) *(G-5785)*

Dr Gerald F Johnson DDS Inc 513 683-8333
11050 S Lebanon Rd Loveland (45140) *(G-10136)*

Dr Heuker, Cincinnati *Also Called: Trihealth Inc (G-3508)*

Dr Transportation Inc 216 588-6110
3184 E 79th St Cleveland (44104) *(G-4182)*

Drake Center, LLC, Cincinnati *Also Called: Daniel Drake Ctr For PST-Cute (G-2536)*

Drake Construction Company (PA) 216 664-6500
1545 E 18th St Cleveland (44114) *(G-4183)*

Drb Holdings LLC 330 645-3299
3245 Pickle Rd Akron (44312) *(G-138)*

Drb Systems LLC (HQ) 330 645-3299
3245 Pickle Rd Akron (44312) *(G-139)*

Drb Tunnel Solutions, Akron *Also Called: Drb Systems LLC (G-139)*

Dreier & Maller Inc (PA) 614 575-0065
6508 Taylor Rd Sw Reynoldsburg (43068) *(G-12661)*

Dreison International Inc (PA) 216 362-0755
4540 W 160th St Cleveland (44135) *(G-4184)*

Drew Ag-Transport Inc 937 548-3200
5450 Sebring Warner Rd Greenville (45331) *(G-8872)*

Drew Medical Inc (PA) 407 363-6700
75 Milford Dr Ste 201 Hudson (44236) *(G-9343)*

Drew Shoe, Lancaster *Also Called: Drew Ventures Inc (G-9708)*
Drew Ventures Inc (PA).. 740 653-4271
  252 Quarry Rd Se Lancaster (43130) *(G-9708)*
Drips Holdings LLC... 512 643-7477
  1700 W Market St Ste 173 Akron (44313) *(G-140)*
Drive Capital.. 614 284-9436
  629 N High St Columbus (43215) *(G-5786)*
Drive Insurance Company... 440 446-5100
  6300 Wilson Mills Rd Cleveland (44143) *(G-4185)*
Driverge Vhcl Innovations LLC (HQ)... 330 861-1118
  2000 Brittain Rd Ste 200 Akron (44310) *(G-141)*
Drivers On Call LLC... 330 867-5193
  1263 Norton Ave Norton (44203) *(G-11994)*
Drs Signal Technologies Inc... 937 429-7470
  4393 Dayton Xenia Rd Beavercreek (45432) *(G-878)*
Drs Weinberger and Visy LLC.. 216 765-1180
  3690 Orange Pl Ste 230 Cleveland (44122) *(G-4186)*
Drt Holdings Inc (PA)...937 298-7391
  618 Greenmount Blvd Dayton (45419) *(G-7317)*
Drug & Poison Information Ctr, Cincinnati *Also Called: Poison Information Center (G-3220)*
DRUG FREE ACTION ALLIANCE, Columbus *Also Called: Prevention Action Alliance (G-6544)*
Drug Mart, Medina *Also Called: Discount Drug Mart Inc (G-10829)*
Drund Ltd... 330 402-5944
  945 Boardman Canfield Rd Ste 8 Boardman (44512) *(G-1287)*
Drury Hotels Company LLC.. 513 771-5601
  2265 E Sharon Rd Cincinnati (45241) *(G-2576)*
Drury Hotels Company LLC.. 937 454-5200
  6616 Miller Ln Dayton (45414) *(G-7318)*
Drury Hotels Company LLC.. 419 422-9700
  820 Trenton Ave Findlay (45840) *(G-8526)*
Drury Hotels Company LLC.. 513 425-6650
  3320 Village Dr Franklin (45005) *(G-8634)*
Drury Inn & Suites Dayton N, Dayton *Also Called: Drury Hotels Company LLC (G-7318)*
Drury Inn & Suites Findlay, Findlay *Also Called: Drury Hotels Company LLC (G-8526)*
Drury Inn & Suites Middletown, Franklin *Also Called: Drury Hotels Company LLC (G-8634)*
Drury Inn Suites Cincinnati N, Cincinnati *Also Called: Drury Hotels Company LLC (G-2576)*
Dry Run Limited Partnership.. 513 561-9119
  7711 Ivy Hills Dr Cincinnati (45244) *(G-2577)*
Dsg Canusa, Loveland *Also Called: Shawcor Pipe Protection LLC (G-10159)*
DSI Systems Inc... 614 871-1456
  3650 Brookham Dr Ste K Grove City (43123) *(G-8917)*
Dsn, Lockbourne *Also Called: Dealers Supply North Inc (G-10011)*
Dss, Canton *Also Called: Dental Support Specialties LLC (G-1734)*
Dssc, Dayton *Also Called: Dayton Synchrnous Spport Ctr I (G-7302)*
DSV Builders Inc.. 330 652-3784
  1544 N Main St Niles (44446) *(G-11788)*
DSV Solutions LLC.. 740 989-1200
  251 Arrowhead Rd Little Hocking (45742) *(G-10008)*
Dta Inc... 419 529-2920
  3180 Park Ave W Ontario (44906) *(G-12103)*
Dtac of Ohio LLC.. 614 443-5454
  774 Internet Dr Columbus (43207) *(G-5787)*
DTE Inc.. 419 522-3428
  110 Baird Pkwy Mansfield (44903) *(G-10259)*
Dtv Inc... 216 226-5465
  4070 Mayfield Rd Cleveland (44121) *(G-4187)*
Dtz, Columbus *Also Called: C&W Facility Services Inc (G-5491)*
Dualite, Williamsburg *Also Called: Dualite Sales & Service Inc (G-15179)*
Dualite Sales & Service Inc (PA)..513 724-7100
  1 Dualite Ln Williamsburg (45176) *(G-15179)*
Dublin, Dublin *Also Called: Integra Cncinnati/Columbus Inc (G-8040)*
Dublin Building Systems Co.. 614 760-5831
  6233 Avery Rd Dublin (43016) *(G-7989)*
Dublin City Schools... 614 764-5926
  6371 Shier Rings Rd Dublin (43016) *(G-7990)*
Dublin Cleaners Inc (PA).. 614 764-9934
  6845 Caine Rd Columbus (43235) *(G-5788)*
Dublin Cnvlarium Operating LLC... 614 761-1188
  6430 Post Rd Dublin (43016) *(G-7991)*
Dublin Family Care Inc.. 614 761-2244
  250 W Bridge St Dublin (43017) *(G-7992)*
Dublin Geriatric Care Co LP... 614 761-1188
  6430 Post Rd Dublin (43016) *(G-7993)*
Dublin Hotel Ltd Liability Co.. 513 891-1066
  5605 Paul G Blazer Memorial Pkwy Dublin (43017) *(G-7994)*
Dublin Internal Medicine Inc.. 614 764-1777
  5070 Bradenton Ave Dublin (43017) *(G-7995)*
Dublin Latchkey... 614 793-0871
  5970 Venture Dr Ste A Dublin (43017) *(G-7996)*
Dublin Methodist Hospital, Dublin *Also Called: Ohiohealth Corporation (G-8081)*
DUBLIN SPRINGS, Dublin *Also Called: Dublin Springs LLC (G-7997)*
Dublin Springs LLC.. 614 717-1800
  7625 Hospital Dr Dublin (43016) *(G-7997)*
Dublin Sprnghill Stes By Mrrot, Dublin *Also Called: Chy Hotel LLC (G-7963)*
Dublin Surgery Center LLC.. 614 932-9548
  5005 Parkcenter Ave Dublin (43017) *(G-7998)*
Dubois Chemicals Inc... 513 868-9662
  2550 Bobmeyer Rd Hamilton (45015) *(G-9037)*
Dubois Chemicals Inc (HQ)..800 438-2647
  3630 E Kemper Rd Sharonville (45241) *(G-12993)*
Ductbreeze, Cleveland *Also Called: Rwk Services Inc (G-4865)*
Dugan & Meyers Cnstr Svcs Ltd.. 614 257-7430
  8740 Orion Pl Ste 220 Columbus (43240) *(G-5258)*
Dugan & Meyers Industrial LLC... 513 539-4000
  900 N Garver Rd Monroe (45050) *(G-11338)*
Dugan & Meyers LLC (PA).. 513 891-4300
  11110 Kenwood Rd Blue Ash (45242) *(G-1164)*
Dugan & Meyers LLC... 513 891-4300
  900 N Garver Rd Monroe (45050) *(G-11339)*
DUKE ENERGY, Cincinnati *Also Called: Duke Energy Ohio Inc (G-2583)*
Duke Energy Beckjord LLC.. 513 287-2561
  139 E 4th St Cincinnati (45202) *(G-2578)*
Duke Energy Center.. 513 419-7300
  525 Elm St Cincinnati (45202) *(G-2579)*
Duke Energy Kentucky Inc... 704 594-6200
  139 E 4th St Cincinnati (45202) *(G-2580)*
Duke Energy Ohio Inc... 800 544-6900
  5445 Audro Dr Cincinnati (45247) *(G-2581)*
Duke Energy Ohio Inc... 513 287-1120
  7600 E Kemper Rd Cincinnati (45249) *(G-2582)*
Duke Energy Ohio Inc (HQ)..704 382-3853
  139 E 4th St Cincinnati (45202) *(G-2583)*
Duke Energy Ohio Inc... 513 287-4622
  593 Todhunter Rd Monroe (45050) *(G-11340)*
Duke Energy Ohio Inc... 513 467-5000
  757 Us Highway 52 New Richmond (45157) *(G-11676)*
Duke Energy One Inc.. 980 373-3931
  139 E 4th St Cincinnati (45202) *(G-2584)*
Dummen Na Inc (PA)... 614 850-9551
  250 S High St Ste 650 Columbus (43215) *(G-5789)*
Dummen USA Inc (PA)..614 850-9551
  250 S High St Ste 650 Columbus (43215) *(G-5790)*
Dun Rite Home Improvement Inc.. 330 650-5322
  8601 Freeway Dr Macedonia (44056) *(G-10191)*
Dunbar Armored Inc... 330 630-0603
  830 Moe Dr Ste C Akron (44310) *(G-142)*
Dunbar Armored Inc... 513 381-8000
  1257 W 7th St Cincinnati (45203) *(G-2585)*
Dunbar Armored Inc... 216 642-5700
  5505 Cloverleaf Pkwy Cleveland (44125) *(G-4188)*
Dunbar Armored Inc... 614 475-1969
  2300 Citygate Dr Unit B Columbus (43219) *(G-5791)*
Dunbar Armored Inc... 614 848-7833
  1421 Alpine Dr Columbus (43229) *(G-5792)*
Dunbar Mechanical Inc.. 440 220-2000
  1884 E 337th St Eastlake (44095) *(G-8201)*
Dunbar Mechanical Inc (PA).. 419 537-1900
  2806 N Reynolds Rd Toledo (43615) *(G-13784)*
Duncan Oil Co (PA)..937 426-5945
  849 Factory Rd Dayton (45434) *(G-7131)*
Duncan Oil Co., Dayton *Also Called: Duncan Oil Co (G-7131)*
Duncan Sales Inc.. 614 755-6580
  350 Mccormick Blvd Ste E Columbus (43213) *(G-5793)*

Dungan & Lefevre Co LPA (PA) 937 339-0511
210 W Main St Troy (45373) *(G-14134)*

Dunlap & Kyle, West Chester *Also Called: Gateway Tire of Texas Inc (G-14813)*

Dunlap Fmly Physcans Inc Prof (PA) 330 684-2015
830 S Main St Ste Rear Orrville (44667) *(G-12163)*

Dunlop and Johnston Inc 330 220-2700
5498 Innovation Dr Valley City (44280) *(G-14333)*

Dunnhumby Inc 513 579-3400
3825 Edwards Rd Ste 600 Cincinnati (45209) *(G-2586)*

Dunning Motor Sales Inc 740 439-4465
9108 Southgate Rd Cambridge (43725) *(G-1568)*

Dupree House, Cincinnati *Also Called: Episcopal Retirement Homes Inc (G-2633)*

Durable Corporation 800 537-1603
75 N Pleasant St Norwalk (44857) *(G-12008)*

Durable Materials Company, The, Columbus *Also Called: Durable Slate Co (G-5794)*

Durable Slate Co (PA) 614 299-5522
3933 Groves Rd Columbus (43232) *(G-5794)*

Durango Boot, Nelsonville *Also Called: Georgia-Boot Inc (G-11545)*

Durant Dc LLC 614 278-6800
4900 E Dublin Granville Rd Columbus (43081) *(G-5795)*

Durga Llc 513 771-2080
11320 Chester Rd Cincinnati (45246) *(G-2587)*

Dutch Boy Group 800 828-5669
101 W Prospect Ave Ste 1020 Cleveland (44115) *(G-4189)*

Dutch Creek Foods Inc 330 852-2631
1411 Old Route 39 Ne Sugarcreek (44681) *(G-13509)*

Dutch Maid Logistics Inc 419 935-0136
3377 State Rte 224 E Willard (44890) *(G-15167)*

Dutch Valley Home Inc 330 273-8322
222 Concord Ln Hinckley (44233) *(G-9269)*

Dutchman Hospitality Group Inc 614 873-3414
445 S Jefferson Ave Plain City (43064) *(G-12474)*

Dutchman Hospitality Group Inc 330 852-2586
1357 Old Route 39 Ne Sugarcreek (44681) *(G-13510)*

Dutchman Hospitality Group Inc 330 893-3636
4949 State Rte 515 Walnut Creek (44687) *(G-14471)*

Dutro Ford Lincoln-Mercury Inc (PA) 740 452-6334
132 S 5th St Zanesville (43701) *(G-15786)*

Dutro Lincoln Mercury, Zanesville *Also Called: Dutro Ford Lincoln-Mercury Inc (G-15786)*

Dutro, John A MD, Englewood *Also Called: Gem City Surgical Associates (G-8307)*

Duvall Automotive LLC 513 836-6447
805 E Center St Blanchester (45107) *(G-1116)*

Dva Hlthcare - Sthwest Ohio LL 513 733-8215
10600 Mckinley Rd Blue Ash (45242) *(G-1165)*

Dva Hlthcare - Sthwest Ohio LL 513 347-0444
3267 Westbourne Dr Cincinnati (45248) *(G-2588)*

Dva Hlthcare - Sthwest Ohio LL 513 591-2900
6550 Winton Rd Cincinnati (45224) *(G-2589)*

Dva Hlthcare - Sthwest Ohio LL 513 939-1110
1210 Hicks Blvd Fairfield (45014) *(G-8408)*

Dva Hlthcare - Sthwest Ohio LL 513 422-1467
3497 S Dixie Hwy Middletown (45005) *(G-11196)*

Dwellworks LLC (PA) 216 682-4200
1317 Euclid Ave Cleveland (44115) *(G-4190)*

Dworken & Bernstein Co Lpa 216 230-5170
1468 W 9th St Ste 135 Cleveland (44113) *(G-4191)*

Dworkin Inc (PA) 216 271-5318
5400 Harvard Ave Cleveland (44105) *(G-4192)*

Dworkin Trucking, Cleveland *Also Called: Dworkin Inc (G-4192)*

Dyer Grfalo Mann Schltz A Lga (PA) 937 223-8888
131 N Ludlow St Ste 1400 Dayton (45402) *(G-7319)*

Dynamerican, Medina *Also Called: Wood Investment Property LLC (G-10905)*

Dynamex, Columbus *Also Called: Tforce Logistics East LLC (G-6757)*

Dynamic Construction, Pataskala *Also Called: Dynamic Construction Inc (G-12273)*

Dynamic Construction Inc 740 927-8898
172 Coors Blvd Pataskala (43062) *(G-12273)*

Dynamic Eductl Systems Inc 602 995-0116
329 S Front St Columbus (43215) *(G-5796)*

Dynamic Weld, Osgood *Also Called: Dynamic Weld Corporation (G-12180)*

Dynamic Weld Corporation 419 582-2900
242 N St Osgood (45351) *(G-12180)*

Dynamite Technologies LLC (PA) 614 538-0095
274 Marconi Blvd Ste 300 Columbus (43215) *(G-5797)*

Dynegy Coml Asset MGT LLC 513 287-5033
139 E 4th St Cincinnati (45202) *(G-2590)*

Dyno Nobel Transportation 740 439-5050
850 Woodlawn Ave Cambridge (43725) *(G-1569)*

Dyno Transportation, Cambridge *Also Called: Dyno Nobel Transportation (G-1569)*

Dynus Technologies, Cincinnati *Also Called: Cbst Acquisition LLC (G-2326)*

Dysart Corporation 614 837-1201
48 Elm St Canal Winchester (43110) *(G-1604)*

E & C Div, Cleveland *Also Called: Greater Clvland Rgnal Trnst Au (G-4336)*

E & J Trailer Sales & Svc Inc 513 563-2550
610 Wayne Park Dr Ste 5 Cincinnati (45215) *(G-2591)*

E & V Ventures Inc (PA) 330 794-6683
1511 E Market St Akron (44305) *(G-143)*

E A Group, Mentor *Also Called: Electro-Analytical Inc (G-10935)*

E B Miller Contracting Inc 513 531-7030
1701 Mills Ave Cincinnati (45212) *(G-2592)*

E E I, Cincinnati *Also Called: Environmental Enterprises Inc (G-2627)*

E E M C O, Cleveland *Also Called: Eaton Aerospace LLC (G-4201)*

E F Boyd & Son Inc (PA) 216 791-0770
2165 E 89th St Cleveland (44106) *(G-4193)*

E Home Behavioral LLC 513 530-1600
2317 E Home Rd Springfield (45503) *(G-13249)*

E M H & T, New Albany *Also Called: Evans McHwart Hmblton Tlton In (G-11563)*

E M H Regional Medical Center, Amherst *Also Called: Amherst Hospital Association (G-421)*

E M I, Cleveland *Also Called: Equipment Mfrs Intl Inc (G-4217)*

E M I Plastic Equipment, Jackson Center *Also Called: EMI Corp (G-9531)*

E N T, Columbus *Also Called: University Otlryngologists Inc (G-6824)*

E Q M, Cincinnati *Also Called: Environmental Quality MGT (G-2628)*

E Retailing Associates LLC 614 300-5785
2282 Westbrooke Dr Columbus (43228) *(G-5798)*

E S I Inc 937 298-7481
3178 Encrete Ln Moraine (45439) *(G-11405)*

E S I Inc (DH) 513 454-3741
4696 Devitt Dr West Chester (45246) *(G-14808)*

E T Financial Service Inc 937 716-1726
4550 Salem Ave Trotwood (45416) *(G-14127)*

E Technologies Group, West Chester *Also Called: E-Technologies Group LLC (G-14686)*

E-Mek Technologies, Dayton *Also Called: E-Mek Technologies LLC (G-7320)*

E-Mek Technologies LLC (PA) 937 424-3166
7410 Webster St Dayton (45414) *(G-7320)*

E-Merge Real Estate 614 804-5600
12910 Stonecreek Dr Pickerington (43147) *(G-12401)*

E-Merging Technologies Group Inc 440 779-5680
22021 Brookpark Rd Ste 130 Cleveland (44126) *(G-4194)*

E-Pallet, Lakewood *Also Called: Pallet Distributors Inc (G-9681)*

E-Technologies Group LLC (HQ) 513 771-7271
8614 Jacquemin Dr West Chester (45069) *(G-14686)*

E-Volve Systems LLC (DH) 765 543-8123
4600 Mcauley Pl Ste 120 Blue Ash (45242) *(G-1166)*

E-Volve Systems An E Tech Grou, Blue Ash *Also Called: E-Volve Systems LLC (G-1166)*

E-Z Electric Motor Svc Corp 216 581-8820
8510 Bessemer Ave Cleveland (44127) *(G-4195)*

E-Z Pack, Cincinnati *Also Called: Wayne Signer Enterprises Inc (G-3642)*

E&H Hardware Group LLC 330 683-2060
1400 W High St Orrville (44667) *(G-12164)*

E2 Infosystems Ltd 833 832-4637
7775 Walton Pkwy New Albany (43054) *(G-11562)*

E2b Teknologies Inc (PA) 440 352-4700
9325 Progress Pkwy # A Mentor (44060) *(G-10934)*

Eagle Bridge Co 937 492-5654
800 S Vandemark Rd Sidney (45365) *(G-13030)*

Eagle Burgmann EXT Joint Sol, Cincinnati *Also Called: Eagleburgmann Ke Inc (G-2596)*

Eagle Certification Group 937 293-2000
40 N Main St Dayton (45423) *(G-7321)*

Eagle Chemicals, Hamilton *Also Called: Dubois Chemicals Inc (G-9037)*

Eagle Creek Golf Club, Norwalk *Also Called: Norwalk Golf Properties Inc (G-12019)*

Eagle Creek Hlthcare Group Inc 937 544-5531
141 Spruce Ln West Union (45693) *(G-14869)*

Eagle Creek Nursing Center — ALPHABETIC SECTION

Eagle Creek Nursing Center, West Union Also Called: Eagle Creek Hlthcare Group Inc *(G-14869)*

- **Eagle Equipment Corporation**..937 746-0510
  245 Industrial Dr Franklin (45005) *(G-8635)*
- **Eagle Hardwoods Inc**..330 339-8838
  6138 Stonecreek Rd Newcomerstown (43832) *(G-11767)*
- **Eagle Industrial Painting LLC**...330 866-5965
  1311 Chantilly Cir Ne Canton (44721) *(G-1739)*
- **Eagle Industries Ohio Inc**..513 247-2900
  275 Commercial Dr Fairfield (45014) *(G-8409)*
- **Eagle Pointe Skilled Rehab LLC**.....................................440 437-7171
  87 Staley Rd Orwell (44076) *(G-12178)*
- **Eagle Realty Group LLC**..513 361-4000
  301 E 4th St Cincinnati (45202) *(G-2593)*
- **Eagle Realty Group LLC**..513 361-7750
  2501 Erie Ave Cincinnati (45208) *(G-2594)*
- **Eagle Realty Group LLC (DH)**...513 361-7700
  421 E 4th St Cincinnati (45202) *(G-2595)*
- **Eagleburgmann Ke Inc**..859 746-0091
  3478 Hauck Rd Cincinnati (45241) *(G-2596)*
- **Eagles CLB At Qail Hllow Cndo**......................................419 734-1000
  219 Madison St Port Clinton (43452) *(G-12523)*
- **Eaglewood Care Center**...937 399-7195
  2000 Villa Rd Springfield (45503) *(G-13250)*

Eaglewood Care Center, Carey Also Called: Woodside Properties I Ltd *(G-1897)*

Eaglewood Villa, Springfield Also Called: Wallick Construction Co *(G-13309)*

- **Earle M Jorgensen Company**...513 771-3223
  601 Redna Ter Cincinnati (45215) *(G-2597)*
- **Earle M Jorgensen Company**...330 425-1500
  2060 Enterprise Pkwy Twinsburg (44087) *(G-14183)*
- **Earle M Jorgensen Company**...330 425-1500
  2060 Enterprise Pkwy Twinsburg (44087) *(G-14184)*
- **Earley & Ross Ltd**..740 634-3301
  580 E Washington St Sabina (45169) *(G-12771)*

EARLY CHILDHOOD EDUCATION, Akron Also Called: Shaw Jewish Community Center *(G-298)*

- **Early Childhood Resource Ctr**..330 491-3272
  1718 Cleveland Ave Nw Canton (44703) *(G-1740)*
- **Early Chldhood Enrchment Ctr I**.....................................216 991-9761
  19824 Sussex Rd Rm 178 Cleveland (44122) *(G-4196)*

Early Express Mail Services, Dayton Also Called: Early Express Services Inc *(G-7322)*

- **Early Express Services Inc**..937 223-5801
  1333 E 2nd St Dayton (45403) *(G-7322)*

Early Learning Center, Columbus Also Called: Hugs Hearts Early Lrng Ctr Inc *(G-5262)*

Earnest Machine, Rocky River Also Called: Earnest Machine Products Co *(G-12740)*

- **Earnest Machine Products Co (PA)**................................440 895-8400
  1250 Linda St Ste 301 Rocky River (44116) *(G-12740)*

Ease Logistics, Dublin Also Called: Ease Logistics Services LLC *(G-7999)*

- **Ease Logistics Services LLC**..614 553-7007
  5725 Avery Rd Dublin (43016) *(G-7999)*

East Butler County YMCA, Fairfield Township Also Called: Great Miami Valley YMCA *(G-8461)*

East Central Region, Grove City Also Called: Securitas SEC Svcs USA Inc *(G-8953)*

East Coast Region, Cleveland Also Called: Securitas SEC Svcs USA Inc *(G-4889)*

- **East Community Learning Center**...................................330 814-7412
  80 Brittain Rd Akron (44305) *(G-144)*
- **East Dayton Christian School**..937 252-5400
  999 Spinning Rd Dayton (45431) *(G-7132)*

East Elementary School, Saint Marys Also Called: St Marys City Board Education *(G-12836)*

East End Community Services, Dayton Also Called: Westcare Ohio Inc *(G-7718)*

- **East End Ro Burton Inc**..440 942-2742
  792 Mentor Ave Willoughby (44094) *(G-15190)*
- **East End Welding LLC**..330 677-6000
  357 Tallmadge Rd Kent (44240) *(G-9573)*

East End YMCA Pre School, Madison Also Called: Lake County YMCA *(G-10219)*

East Gate Pediatric Center, Cincinnati Also Called: Healthsource of Ohio Inc *(G-2812)*

- **East Glbrith Hlth Care Ctr Inc (PA)**..................................513 984-5220
  3889 E Galbraith Rd Cincinnati (45236) *(G-2598)*
- **East Inc**...330 609-1339
  3976 King Graves Rd Vienna (44473) *(G-14419)*

EAST LIVERPOOL CITY HOSPITAL, East Liverpool Also Called: City Hospital Association *(G-8179)*

- **East Liverpool Country Club**...330 385-7197
  2485 Park Way East Liverpool (43920) *(G-8181)*
- **East Lverpool Convalescent Ctr (PA)**.............................330 382-0101
  709 Armstrong Ln East Liverpool (43920) *(G-8182)*
- **East Manufacturing Corporation (PA)**............................330 325-9921
  1871 State Rte 44 Randolph (44265) *(G-12618)*

East Mental Health, Cleveland Also Called: Center For Families & Children *(G-3951)*

- **East of Chicago Pizza Inc (PA)**.......................................419 225-7116
  121 W High St Fl 12 Lima (45801) *(G-9885)*
- **East Ohio Gas Company**..800 362-7557
  2100 Eastwood Ave Akron (44305) *(G-145)*
- **East Ohio Gas Company**..216 736-6120
  7001 Center Rd Ashtabula (44004) *(G-534)*
- **East Ohio Gas Company**..740 439-2721
  60755 Country Club Rd Byesville (43723) *(G-1534)*
- **East Ohio Gas Company**..330 266-2161
  5433 West Blvd Nw Canton (44718) *(G-1741)*
- **East Ohio Gas Company**..330 477-9411
  4725 Southway St Sw Canton (44706) *(G-1742)*
- **East Ohio Gas Company**..330 499-2501
  7015 Freedom Ave Nw Canton (44720) *(G-1743)*
- **East Ohio Gas Company (DH)**...800 362-7557
  1201 E 55th St Cleveland (44103) *(G-4197)*
- **East Ohio Gas Company**..216 736-6959
  21200 Miles Rd Cleveland (44128) *(G-4198)*
- **East Ohio Gas Company**..330 266-2169
  6500 Hampsher Rd New Franklin (44216) *(G-11615)*
- **East Ohio Gas Company**..216 736-6917
  29555 Clayton Ave Wickliffe (44092) *(G-15148)*
- **East Ohio Gas Company**..330 478-3114
  1049 Heyl Rd Wooster (44691) *(G-15335)*
- **East Ohio Hospital LLC**...740 633-1100
  90 N 4th St Martins Ferry (43935) *(G-10467)*
- **East Ohio Hospital LLC (PA)**...740 633-1100
  90 N 4th St Martins Ferry (43935) *(G-10468)*
- **East Ohio Hospital LLC**...740 695-5955
  106 Plaza Dr Saint Clairsville (43950) *(G-12791)*

East Side Branch, Marion Also Called: Fahey Banking Company *(G-10426)*

- **East Water Leasing Co LLC**..419 278-6921
  620 E Water St Deshler (43516) *(G-7866)*
- **East Way Behavioral Hlth Care**.......................................937 222-4900
  600 Wayne Ave Dayton (45410) *(G-7323)*

EASTBROOK HEALTHCARE CENTER, Cleveland Also Called: 17322 Euclid Avenue Co LLC *(G-3741)*

Easter Sals Cntl Sthast Ohio I, Hilliard Also Called: Eastersals Cntl Southeast Ohio *(G-9193)*

- **Easter Seal Society of (PA)**...330 743-1168
  299 Edwards St Youngstown (44502) *(G-15603)*

Easter Seals, Cincinnati Also Called: Easter Seals Tristate *(G-2599)*

EASTER SEALS, Youngstown Also Called: Easter Seal Society of *(G-15603)*

- **Easter Seals Tristate (HQ)**..513 985-0515
  8740 Montgomery Rd Cincinnati (45236) *(G-2599)*
- **Easter Seals Tristate LLC (PA)**.......................................513 281-2316
  2901 Gilbert Ave Cincinnati (45206) *(G-2600)*

Eastern Community YMCA, Oregon Also Called: Young MNS Chrstn Assn of Grter *(G-12148)*

- **Eastern Express Inc**..513 267-1212
  30 Enterprise Dr Middletown (45044) *(G-11161)*

EASTERN EXPRESS INC, Middletown Also Called: Eastern Express Inc *(G-11161)*

- **Eastern Express Logistics Inc (PA)**...............................800 348-6514
  8777 Rockside Rd Cleveland (44125) *(G-4199)*
- **Eastern Ohio Conservation Club**....................................330 799-7393
  10366 W Calla Rd Salem (44460) *(G-12841)*
- **Eastern Ohio Correction Center**.....................................740 765-4324
  470 State Rte 43 Wintersville (43953) *(G-15293)*
- **Eastern Ohio Plmonary Cons Inc**....................................330 726-3357
  960 Windham Ct Ste 1 Youngstown (44512) *(G-15604)*
- **Eastersals Cntl Southeast Ohio**......................................614 228-5523
  3830 Trueman Ct Hilliard (43026) *(G-9193)*

Eastgate Graphics, Lebanon Also Called: Eastgate Group Ltd *(G-9764)*

- **Eastgate Group Ltd**...513 228-5522
  611 Norgal Dr Lebanon (45036) *(G-9764)*

ALPHABETIC SECTION — Eddie Bauer LLC

Eastgate Health Care Center.. 513 752-3710
   4400 Glen Este Withamsville Rd Cincinnati (45245) *(G-2103)*

Eastgate Rgnal Cncil Gvrnments.. 330 779-3800
   100 E Federal St Ste 1000 Youngstown (44503) *(G-15605)*

Eastgate Sod, Maineville *Also Called: Mike Ward Landscaping LLC (G-10228)*

Eastlake Lodging LLC.. 440 953-8000
   35000 Curtis Blvd Eastlake (44095) *(G-8202)*

Eastman & Smith Ltd... 419 241-6000
   1 Seagate Ste 2400 Toledo (43604) *(G-13785)*

Easton Town Center Guest Svcs, Columbus *Also Called: Easton Town Center LLC (G-5800)*

Easton Town Center II LLC... 614 416-7000
   160 Easton Town Ctr Columbus (43219) *(G-5799)*

Easton Town Center LLC... 614 337-2560
   4016 Townsfair Way Ste 201 Columbus (43219) *(G-5800)*

EASTWAY BEHAVORIAL HEALTHCARE, Dayton *Also Called: Eastway Corporation (G-7324)*

Eastway Corporation (PA).. 937 496-2000
   600 Wayne Ave Dayton (45410) *(G-7324)*

Eastway Supplies Inc.. 614 252-3650
   1561 Alum Creek Dr Columbus (43209) *(G-5801)*

Eastwood Local Schools.. 419 833-1196
   10142 Dowling Rd Bowling Green (43402) *(G-1318)*

Eastwood Mall, Niles *Also Called: Cararo Co Inc (G-11784)*

Eastwood Residential Svcs Inc (PA)... 440 428-8169
   6455 N Ridge Rd # 1 Madison (44057) *(G-10215)*

Easy 2 Technologies, Cleveland *Also Called: Easy2 Technologies Inc (G-4200)*

Easy Money, Dublin *Also Called: Community Choice Financial Inc (G-7968)*

Easy2 Technologies Inc.. 216 479-0482
   1111 Chester Ave Cleveland (44114) *(G-4200)*

Eaton Aerospace LLC (HQ)... 216 523-5000
   1000 Eaton Blvd Cleveland (44122) *(G-4201)*

Eaton Construction Co Inc... 740 474-3414
   653 Island Rd Circleville (43113) *(G-3707)*

Eaton Corp.. 216 523-5000
   1111 Superior Ave E Cleveland (44114) *(G-4202)*

Eaton Corporation.. 216 265-2799
   6055 Rockside Woods Blvd N Cleveland (44131) *(G-4203)*

Eaton Corporation.. 614 839-4387
   Columbus (43218) *(G-5802)*

Eaton Corporation.. 419 891-7627
   1660 Indian Wood Cir Maumee (43537) *(G-10719)*

Eaton Grdns Rhblttion Hlth Car.. 937 456-5537
   515 S Maple St Eaton (45320) *(G-8213)*

Eaton Industrial Corporation.. 216 692-5456
   1000 Eaton Blvd Cleveland (44122) *(G-4204)*

Eaton Leasing Corporation.. 216 382-2292
   1000 Eaton Blvd Beachwood (44122) *(G-788)*

Ebenezer Road Corporation... 513 941-0099
   6210 Cleves Warsaw Pike Cincinnati (45233) *(G-2601)*

Eblueprints, Cleveland *Also Called: Ers Digital Inc (G-4221)*

Ebony Construction Co... 419 841-3455
   3510 Centennial Rd Sylvania (43560) *(G-13542)*

Ebs Asset Management, Miamisburg *Also Called: Eubel Brady Sttman Asset MGT I (G-11052)*

Ebthcom LLC.. 513 242-3284
   697 Wilmer Ave Cincinnati (45226) *(G-2602)*

Ebuys Inc... 858 831-0839
   810 Dsw Dr Columbus (43219) *(G-5803)*

ECDI, Columbus *Also Called: Economic & Cmnty Dev Inst Inc (G-5806)*

Echo 24 Inc (PA).. 740 964-7081
   167 Cypress St Sw Ste A Reynoldsburg (43068) *(G-12662)*

Echo 360 Inc (PA).. 877 324-6360
   6000 Mahoning Ave Youngstown (44515) *(G-15606)*

Echo Mnor Nrsing Rhblttion Ctr, Pickerington *Also Called: Home Echo Club Inc (G-12403)*

Echoing Hills Village Inc... 740 594-3541
   507 Richland Ave Athens (45701) *(G-567)*

Echoing Hills Village Inc... 800 419-6513
   3400 Stop 8 Rd Dayton (45414) *(G-7325)*

Echoing Hills Village Inc... 937 854-5151
   5455 Salem Bend Dr Dayton (45426) *(G-7326)*

Echoing Hills Village Inc... 937 237-7881
   7040 Union Schoolhouse Rd Dayton (45424) *(G-7327)*

Echoing Hills Village Inc... 440 323-0915
   175 Chadwick Ct Elyria (44035) *(G-8243)*

Echoing Hills Village Inc... 440 989-1400
   3295 Leavitt Rd Lorain (44053) *(G-10071)*

Echoing Hills Village Inc... 440 986-3085
   235 W Main St South Amherst (44001) *(G-13168)*

Echoing Hills Village Inc (PA)... 740 327-2311
   36272 County Road 79 Warsaw (43844) *(G-14591)*

Echoing Lake Residential Home, Lorain *Also Called: Echoing Hills Village Inc (G-10071)*

Echoing Lake/Renouard Home, South Amherst *Also Called: Echoing Hills Village Inc (G-13168)*

Echoing Meadows, Athens *Also Called: Echoing Hills Village Inc (G-567)*

Echoing Ridge Residential Ctr, Warsaw *Also Called: Echoing Hills Village Inc (G-14591)*

Echoing Valley, Dayton *Also Called: Echoing Hills Village Inc (G-7327)*

Echoing Wood Residential Cntr, Dayton *Also Called: Echoing Hills Village Inc (G-7326)*

Echols Heating and AC Inc.. 330 773-3500
   85 Hanna Pkwy Coventry Township (44319) *(G-7007)*

Echos Haven LLC.. 513 715-1189
   114 Broadway St Harrison (45030) *(G-9103)*

Eci Macola/Max LLC (DH).. 978 539-6186
   5455 Rings Rd Ste 100 Dublin (43017) *(G-8000)*

Eci Macola/Max Holding LLC... 614 410-2712
   5455 Rings Rd Ste 400 Dublin (43017) *(G-8001)*

Ecke Ranch, Columbus *Also Called: Dummen Na Inc (G-5789)*

Eckinger Construction Company.. 330 453-2566
   2340 Shepler Church Ave Sw Canton (44706) *(G-1744)*

Eckstein Roofing Company.. 513 941-1511
   264 Stille Dr Cincinnati (45233) *(G-2603)*

Eclipse 3d/Pi LLC... 614 626-8536
   825 Taylor Rd Columbus (43230) *(G-5804)*

Eclipse Midco, Dublin *Also Called: Eci Macola/Max Holding LLC (G-8001)*

Eclipse Resources - Ohio LLC.. 740 452-4503
   4900 Boggs Rd Zanesville (43701) *(G-15787)*

Eco Engineering Inc... 513 985-8300
   11815 Highway Dr Ste 600 Cincinnati (45241) *(G-2604)*

Ecobryt LLC.. 877 326-2798
   7747 Reinhold Dr Cincinnati (45237) *(G-2605)*

Ecohouse LLC... 614 456-7641
   4350 Equity Dr Columbus (43228) *(G-5805)*

Ecohouse Solar, Columbus *Also Called: Ecohouse LLC (G-5805)*

Ecomed Medical Linen Service, Dayton *Also Called: Economy Linen & Towel Service Inc (G-7328)*

Econic, A Duke Energy Company, Cincinnati *Also Called: Duke Energy One Inc (G-2584)*

Econo Lodge.. 216 475-4070
   4353 Northfield Rd Cleveland (44128) *(G-4205)*

Econo Lodge.. 419 627-8000
   1904 Cleveland Rd Sandusky (44870) *(G-12888)*

Econo Lodge, Wooster *Also Called: Econo Lodge Wooster Inc (G-15336)*

Econo Lodge Wooster Inc.. 330 264-8883
   2137 E Lincoln Way Wooster (44691) *(G-15336)*

Economic & Cmnty Dev Inst Inc... 614 559-0104
   1655 Old Leonard Ave Columbus (43219) *(G-5806)*

Economy Linen & Towel Service Inc (PA)................................ 937 222-4625
   80 Mead St Dayton (45402) *(G-7328)*

Ecoplumbers LLC... 614 299-9903
   4691 Northwest Pkwy Hilliard (43026) *(G-9194)*

Ecrm, Solon *Also Called: Efficient Collaborative Retail (G-13082)*

Ecumencal Shlter Ntwrk Lk Cnty... 440 354-6417
   25 Freedom Rd Painesville (44077) *(G-12228)*

Ed Map Inc... 740 753-3439
   296 S Harper St Ste 1 Nelsonville (45764) *(G-11543)*

Ed Mullinax Ford LLC.. 440 984-2431
   8000 Leavitt Rd Amherst (44001) *(G-427)*

Ed Tomko, Avon Lake *Also Called: Ed Tomko Chrysler Jeep Ddge In (G-677)*

Ed Tomko Chrysler Jeep Ddge In.. 440 835-5900
   33725 Walker Rd Avon Lake (44012) *(G-677)*

Edaptive Computing Inc.. 937 433-0477
   1245 Lyons Rd Ste G Dayton (45458) *(G-7329)*

Eddie Bauer, Groveport *Also Called: Eddie Bauer LLC (G-8983)*

Eddie Bauer LLC.. 614 497-8200
   6600 Alum Creek Dr Groveport (43125) *(G-8983)*

Eddie Buer Flfillment Svcs Inc 614 497-8200
  6600 Alum Creek Dr Groveport (43125) *(G-8984)*

Eddie Lane's Diamond Showroom, Montgomery *Also Called: Equity Diamond Brokers Inc (G-11367)*

Eden Vista of Willoughby, Willoughby *Also Called: Emeritus Corporation (G-15191)*

Edendale House, Cleveland *Also Called: United Crbral Plsy Assn Grter (G-5058)*

Edgar Trent Cnstr Co LLC 419 683-4939
  1301 Freese Works Pl Crestline (44827) *(G-7022)*

Edgar Trent Construction Co, Crestline *Also Called: Edgar Trent Cnstr Co LLC (G-7022)*

Edge Plastics Inc 419 522-6696
  449 Newman St Mansfield (44902) *(G-10260)*

Edgewater Golf Club, Minerva *Also Called: Edgewater Golf Inc (G-11306)*

Edgewater Golf Inc 330 862-2630
  2401 Fox Ave Se Minerva (44657) *(G-11306)*

Edgewood Manor Lucasville II, Lucasville *Also Called: Edgewood Manor Lucasville LLC (G-10175)*

Edgewood Manor Lucasville LLC 740 259-5536
  10098a Big Bear Creek Rd Lucasville (45648) *(G-10175)*

Edgewood Manor Nursing Center, Port Clinton *Also Called: Covenant Care Ohio Inc (G-12521)*

Edgewood Manor of Lucasville 740 259-5536
  10098 Big Bear Creek Rd Lucasville (45648) *(G-10176)*

Edgewood Manor of Lucasville, Lucasville *Also Called: Consulate Management Co LLC (G-10174)*

Edgewood Manor of Wellston 740 384-5611
  405 N Park Ave Wellston (45692) *(G-14637)*

EDGEWOOD MANOR OF WESTERVILLE, Piketon *Also Called: Piketon Nursing Center Inc (G-12427)*

EDGEWOOD MANOR OF WESTERVILLE, Tallmadge *Also Called: Summit Facility Operations LLC (G-13606)*

Edgewood Manor Westerville LLC 614 882-4055
  140 N State St Westerville (43081) *(G-14977)*

Edgewood Mnor Lucasville I LLC 740 259-5536
  10098 Big Bear Creek Rd Lucasville (45648) *(G-10177)*

Edgewood Mnor Rhblttion Hlthca 732 730-7360
  1330 Fulton St Port Clinton (43452) *(G-12524)*

Edict Systems Inc 937 429-4288
  2434 Esquire Dr Beavercreek (45431) *(G-879)*

Edison Bus Garage, Amsterdam *Also Called: Edison Local School District (G-436)*

Edison Local School District 740 543-4011
  8235 Amsterdam Rd Se Amsterdam (43903) *(G-436)*

Edison Welding Institute Inc (PA) 614 688-5000
  1250 Arthur E Adams Dr Columbus (43221) *(G-5807)*

Edko LLC 614 863-5946
  5743 Westbourne Ave Columbus (43213) *(G-5808)*

EDM Management Inc 330 726-5790
  1419 Boardman Canfield Rd Ste 500 Youngstown (44512) *(G-15607)*

Edora Logistics Inc 937 573-9090
  212 W National Rd Vandalia (45377) *(G-14375)*

Educaption, Youngstown *Also Called: Ai-Media Technologies LLC (G-15545)*

Educare Medical Staffing LLP 216 938-9374
  27600 Chagrin Blvd Ste 240 Woodmere (44122) *(G-15298)*

Education Alternatives (PA) 216 332-9360
  5445 Smith Rd Brookpark (44142) *(G-1434)*

Educatonal Svc Ctr Lorain Cnty (PA) 440 244-1659
  1885 Lake Ave Elyria (44035) *(G-8244)*

Edward Allen Company 216 621-4984
  1100 Superior Ave E Ste 1820 Cleveland (44114) *(G-4206)*

Edward Howard & Co (PA) 216 781-2400
  1100 Superior Ave E Ste 1600 Cleveland (44114) *(G-4207)*

Edwards Mooney & Moses 614 351-1439
  1320 Mckinley Ave Ste B Columbus (43222) *(G-5809)*

Edwards Health Care Services (PA) 330 342-9555
  5640 Hudson Industrial Pkwy Hudson (44236) *(G-9344)*

Edwards Land Clearing Inc 440 988-4477
  49090 Cooper Foster Park Rd Amherst (44001) *(G-428)*

Edwards Mooney & Moses of Ohio, Columbus *Also Called: Edwards Mooney & Moses (G-5809)*

Edwards Realty & Inv Corp 330 253-9171
  1314 Centerview Cir Copley (44321) *(G-6957)*

Edwards Tree Service, Amherst *Also Called: Edwards Land Clearing Inc (G-428)*

Edwin Shaw Rehab LLC 330 436-0910
  405 Tallmadge Rd Ste 1 Cuyahoga Falls (44221) *(G-7071)*

Edwin Shaw Rehabilitation Hosp, Akron *Also Called: Akron General Medical Center (G-32)*

Eech Brook Family Drop-In Ctr, Cleveland *Also Called: Brook Beech (G-3901)*

Efficient Collaborative Retail (PA) 440 498-0500
  27070 Miles Rd Ste A Solon (44139) *(G-13082)*

Efficient Services Ohio Inc 330 627-4440
  277 Steubenville Rd Se Carrollton (44615) *(G-1907)*

Efix It Solutions LLC 937 476-7533
  3920 Kittyhawk Dr Dayton (45403) *(G-7330)*

Ego of Indiana, Akron *Also Called: American Plastics Inc (G-48)*

Egp 2022 Vehicle Inc (PA) 866 538-1909
  3874 Paxton Ave Unit 9299 Cincinnati (45209) *(G-2606)*

Eight Eleven Group LLC 513 533-7300
  455 Delta Ave Fl 4 Cincinnati (45226) *(G-2607)*

Eighth Day Sound Systems Inc 440 995-2647
  5450 Avion Park Dr Highland Heights (44143) *(G-9165)*

Einheit Electric Co 216 661-6000
  240 Tuxedo Ave Independence (44131) *(G-9429)*

Einstruction Corporation, Youngstown *Also Called: Fscreations Corporation (G-15614)*

Eis, Gahanna *Also Called: Estate Information Svcs LLC (G-8716)*

Eis, Willoughby *Also Called: Exodus Integrity Services Inc (G-15192)*

Eis Intermediate Holdings LLC 800 228-2790
  2400 Technical Dr Miamisburg (45342) *(G-11049)*

Eitel Towing Service Inc 614 877-4139
  7111 Stahl Rd Orient (43146) *(G-12151)*

Eitels Amrcas Towing Trnsp Svc, Orient *Also Called: Eitel Towing Service Inc (G-12151)*

Ej Therapy, Wooster *Also Called: Herman Bair Enterprise (G-15344)*

Ekco Cleaning Inc 513 733-8882
  4055 Executive Park Dr Ste 240 Cincinnati (45241) *(G-2608)*

El-Bee, Moraine *Also Called: The Elder-Beerman Stores Corp (G-11443)*

Elastizell Systems Inc 937 298-1313
  2475 Arbor Blvd Moraine (45439) *(G-11406)*

Elder Sales & Service Inc 330 426-2166
  49290 State Route 14 East Palestine (44413) *(G-8195)*

Eldora Speedway Inc 317 299-6066
  13929 State Route 118 New Weston (45348) *(G-11685)*

Eldorado Stone LLC 330 698-3931
  167 Maple St Apple Creek (44606) *(G-449)*

Elect General Contractors Inc 740 420-3437
  27634 Jackson Rd Circleville (43113) *(G-3708)*

Electra Sound Inc (PA) 216 433-9600
  32483 English Turn Avon Lake (44012) *(G-678)*

Electra Sound Inc 216 433-1050
  10779 Brookpark Rd Ste A Cleveland (44130) *(G-4208)*

Electrasound TV & Appl Svc, Avon Lake *Also Called: Electra Sound Inc (G-678)*

Electric Connection Inc 614 436-1121
  6510 Huntley Rd Columbus (43229) *(G-5810)*

Electric Department, Lebanon *Also Called: City of Lebanon (G-9759)*

Electric Melting Services Co, Massillon *Also Called: Emsco Inc (G-10638)*

Electric Motor Tech LLC (PA) 513 821-9999
  5217 Beech St Cincinnati (45217) *(G-2609)*

Electric Service Co Inc 513 271-6387
  5331 Hetzcell St Cincinnati (45227) *(G-2610)*

Electric Services, Cuyahoga Falls *Also Called: City of Cuyahoga Falls (G-7055)*

Electric Sweeper Service Co, Twinsburg *Also Called: Merc Acquisitions Inc (G-14205)*

Electrical Accents LLC 440 988-2852
  104 N Lake St Ste C South Amherst (44001) *(G-13169)*

Electrical Appl Repr Svc Inc 216 459-8700
  5805 Valley Belt Rd Brooklyn Heights (44131) *(G-1417)*

Electrical Contractor, Warren *Also Called: Main Lite Electric Co Inc (G-14537)*

Electrical Corp America Inc 440 245-3007
  3807 W Erie Ave Lorain (44053) *(G-10072)*

Electrical Design & Engrg Svcs, Columbus *Also Called: Polaris Automation Inc (G-6534)*

Electrical Service Dept, Wadsworth *Also Called: City of Wadsworth (G-14430)*

Electro Prime, Toledo *Also Called: Electro Prime Group LLC (G-13786)*

Electro Prime Group LLC (PA) 419 476-0100
  4510 Lint Ave Ste B Toledo (43612) *(G-13786)*

Electro-Analytical Inc 440 951-3514
  7118 Industrial Park Blvd Mentor (44060) *(G-10935)*

ALPHABETIC SECTION — Emeritus Corporation

Electronic Merch Systems LLC (PA) 216 524-0900
250 W Huron Rd Ste 300 Cleveland (44113) *(G-4209)*

Electronic Merchant Systems, Cleveland Also Called: Electronic Merch Systems LLC *(G-4209)*

Eleet Cryogenics Inc (PA) 330 874-4009
11132 Industrial Pkwy Nw Bolivar (44612) *(G-1294)*

Element, Fairfield Also Called: Element Mtls Tech Cncnnati Inc *(G-8410)*

Element Materials Technology Cleveland Inc (DH) 216 524-1450
5405 E Schaaf Rd Cleveland (44131) *(G-4210)*

Element Mtls Tech Cncnnati Inc (DH) 513 984-4112
3701 Port Union Rd Fairfield (45014) *(G-8410)*

Elements IV Interiors, Dayton Also Called: Space & Asset Management Inc *(G-7631)*

Elevar Design Group Inc 513 721-0600
555 Carr St Cincinnati (45203) *(G-2611)*

Elford Inc 614 488-4000
1220 Dublin Rd Columbus (43215) *(G-5811)*

Elford Construction Services, Columbus Also Called: Elford Inc *(G-5811)*

Elite Excavating Company Inc 419 683-4200
4500 Snodgrass Rd Mansfield (44903) *(G-10261)*

Elite Excavating Ohio Company, Mansfield Also Called: Elite Excavating Company Inc *(G-10261)*

Elite Expediting Corp (PA) 614 279-1181
450 W Wilson Bridge Rd Ste 345 Worthington (43085) *(G-15413)*

Elite Investments LLC 419 350-8949
644 Dussel Dr Maumee (43537) *(G-10720)*

Elite Salon Distributors LLC 419 902-0545
1038 N Holland Sylvania Rd Toledo (43615) *(G-13787)*

Elite Southern Cnstr LLC 614 441-1285
480 Emmaus Rd Marysville (43040) *(G-10484)*

Elixir Pharmacy LLC 330 491-4200
7835 Freedom Ave Nw North Canton (44720) *(G-11827)*

Elixir Rx Options LLC (DH) 330 405-8080
2181 E Aurora Rd Ste 101 Twinsburg (44087) *(G-14185)*

Elixir Vi LLC 419 884-9808
3117 Kings Corners Rd W Mansfield (44904) *(G-10262)*

Eliza Jennings Inc 216 226-5000
26376 John Rd Ofc Olmsted Twp (44138) *(G-12089)*

Eliza Jnnngs Snior Care Netwrk (PA) 216 226-5000
26376 John Rd Ofc C Olmsted Twp (44138) *(G-12090)*

Elizabeth Place Holdings LLC 323 300-3700
1 Elizabeth Pl Dayton (45417) *(G-7331)*

ELIZABETH'S NEW LIFE WOMEN'S C, Dayton Also Called: Elizabeths New Life Center Inc *(G-7332)*

Elizabeths New Life Center Inc 937 226-7414
2201 N Main St Dayton (45405) *(G-7332)*

Elk & Elk Co Lpa (PA) 800 355-6446
6105 Parkland Blvd Ste 200 Mayfield Heights (44124) *(G-10786)*

Elkay Ohio Plumbing Pdts Co (DH) 419 841-1820
7634 New West Rd Toledo (43617) *(G-13788)*

Elliott, Dayton Also Called: Elliott Tool Technologies Ltd *(G-7333)*

Elliott Tool Technologies Ltd (PA) 937 253-6133
1760 Tuttle Ave Dayton (45403) *(G-7333)*

Ellipse Solutions LLC 937 312-1547
7917 Washington Woods Dr Dayton (45459) *(G-7334)*

Ellison Technologies Inc 513 874-2736
5333 Mulhauser Rd Hamilton (45011) *(G-9038)*

Elm Road Rhbltton Svcs A Svc, Warren Also Called: Steward Hllside Rhbltton Hosp *(G-14559)*

Elm Springs, Green Springs Also Called: Elmwood Centers Inc *(G-8858)*

Elms Retirement Village Inc 440 647-2414
136 S Main St Rear Wellington (44090) *(G-14631)*

Elmwood Centers Inc (PA) 419 332-3378
441 N Broadway St Green Springs (44836) *(G-8858)*

Elts Broadcasting, Elyria Also Called: Elyria-Lorain Broadcasting Co *(G-8248)*

Elyria Country Club Company 440 322-6391
41625 Oberlin Elyria Rd Elyria (44035) *(G-8245)*

Elyria Fmly Hlth & Surgery Ctr, Elyria Also Called: Cleveland Clinic *(G-8236)*

Elyria Ford, Elyria Also Called: Abraham Ford LLC *(G-8232)*

Elyria Foundry Company LLC 440 322-4657
745 Leo Bullocks Pkwy Elyria (44035) *(G-8246)*

Elyria Foundry Holdings LLC 440 322-4657
120 Filbert St Elyria (44035) *(G-8247)*

Elyria-Lorain Broadcasting Co (HQ) 440 322-3761
538 Broad St Ste 400 Elyria (44035) *(G-8248)*

Elysium Tennis, Plain City Also Called: Heil and Hornik LLC *(G-12479)*

Embassy Healthcare, Beachwood Also Called: Embassy Healthcare MGT Inc *(G-789)*

Embassy Healthcare Inc 513 868-6500
908 Symmes Rd Fairfield (45014) *(G-8411)*

Embassy Healthcare MGT Inc (PA) 216 378-2050
25201 Chagrin Blvd Ste 190 Beachwood (44122) *(G-789)*

Embassy Stes Akrn-Canton Arprt, North Canton Also Called: CPX Canton Airport LLC *(G-11819)*

Embassy Stes By Hlton Clmbus A, Columbus Also Called: AFP 116 Corp *(G-5328)*

Embassy Suites, Beachwood Also Called: IA Urban Htels Bchwood Trs LLC *(G-801)*

Embassy Suites, Independence Also Called: Ap/Aim Indpndnce Sites Trs LLC *(G-9405)*

Embassy Suites Columbus, Columbus Also Called: Columbus Hotel Partnership LLC *(G-5639)*

Embassy Suites Columbus, Columbus Also Called: Rlj III - Em Clmbus Lessee LLC *(G-6601)*

Embassy Suites Columbus Dublin, Dublin Also Called: Ahip OH Columbus Entps LLC *(G-7925)*

Embassy Winchester LLC 614 834-2273
36 Lehman Dr Canal Winchester (43110) *(G-1605)*

Ember Complete Care 740 922-6968
730 N Water St Uhrichsville (44683) *(G-14233)*

EMBER COMPLETE CARE, Uhrichsville Also Called: Ember Complete Care *(G-14233)*

Ember Complete Care Inc (PA) 740 922-6888
1800 N Water Street Ext Uhrichsville (44683) *(G-14234)*

Embracing Autism Inc 614 559-0077
2491 W Dublin Granville Rd Columbus (43235) *(G-5812)*

EMC Research Incorporated 614 268-1660
3857 N High St Columbus (43214) *(G-5813)*

Emcor Facilities Services Inc 513 948-8469
15 W Voorhees St Cincinnati (45215) *(G-2612)*

Emcor Facilities Services Inc (HQ) 888 846-9462
9655 Reading Rd Cincinnati (45215) *(G-2613)*

EMD Millipore Corporation 513 631-0445
2909 Highland Ave Norwood (45212) *(G-12032)*

Emerald Health Network Inc (HQ) 216 479-2030
3320 W Market St # 100 Fairlawn (44333) *(G-8476)*

Emerald Hilton Davis LLC 513 841-0057
2235 Langdon Farm Rd Cincinnati (45237) *(G-2614)*

Emerald Pediatrics 614 932-5050
5695 Innovation Dr Dublin (43016) *(G-8002)*

Emerald Resource Group Inc 440 922-9000
1 Eagle Valley Ct Broadview Heights (44147) *(G-1387)*

Emerald Specialties Group, Cincinnati Also Called: Emerald Hilton Davis LLC *(G-2614)*

Emerald Transformer Ppm LLC 330 425-3825
1672 Highland Rd Twinsburg (44087) *(G-14186)*

Emerge Ministries Inc 330 865-8351
900 Mull Ave Akron (44313) *(G-146)*

Emergency Medicine Physicians, Canton Also Called: Usacs Management Group Ltd *(G-1877)*

Emergency Medicine Specialists 937 438-8910
3131 Newmark Dr Ste 210 Miamisburg (45342) *(G-11050)*

Emergency Physicians of Northw 419 291-4101
2142 N Cove Blvd Toledo (43606) *(G-13789)*

Emergency Psychiatric Svc, Akron Also Called: Portage Path Behavorial Health *(G-270)*

Emergency Services Inc 614 224-6420
2323 W 5th Ave Ste 220 Columbus (43204) *(G-5814)*

Emergncy Rspnse Trning Sltons 440 349-2700
6001 Cochran Rd Ste 300 Solon (44139) *(G-13083)*

Emeritus Assisted Living, Canton Also Called: Emeritus Corporation *(G-1745)*

Emeritus At Brookside Estates, Cleveland Also Called: Emeritus Corporation *(G-4211)*

Emeritus At Lakeview, Groveport Also Called: Emeritus Corporation *(G-8985)*

Emeritus At Stow, Stow Also Called: Emeritus Corporation *(G-13365)*

Emeritus Corporation 330 477-5727
4507 22nd St Nw Apt 33 Canton (44708) *(G-1745)*

Emeritus Corporation 513 683-9966
12050 Montgomery Rd Ofc Cincinnati (45249) *(G-2615)*

Emeritus Corporation 440 201-9200
15435 Bagley Rd Ste 1 Cleveland (44130) *(G-4211)*

Emeritus Corporation 614 836-5990
4000 Lakeview Xing Groveport (43125) *(G-8985)*

Emeritus Corporation   **ALPHABETIC SECTION**

Emeritus Corporation..330 342-0934
   5511 Fishcreek Rd Stow (44224) *(G-13365)*

Emeritus Corporation..419 255-4455
   142 23rd St Ofc Toledo (43604) *(G-13790)*

Emeritus Corporation..440 269-8600
   35300 Kaiser Ct Willoughby (44094) *(G-15191)*

Emeritus Parklane, Toledo *Also Called: Emeritus Corporation (G-13790)*

Emersion Design, Cincinnati *Also Called: Emersion Design LLC (G-2616)*

Emersion Design LLC..513 841-9100
   310 Culvert St Ste 100 Cincinnati (45202) *(G-2616)*

Emerson Academy, Dayton *Also Called: National Heritg Academies Inc (G-7525)*

Emery Leasing Co LLC..216 475-8880
   20265 Emery Rd Cleveland (44128) *(G-4212)*

Emh Regional Healthcare System, Elyria *Also Called: Comprhnsive Hlth Care Ohio Inc (G-8237)*

Emh Regional Medical Center..440 988-6800
   1997 Healthway Dr Avon (44011) *(G-650)*

Emh Regional Medical Center (DH).....................................440 329-7500
   630 E River St Elyria (44035) *(G-8249)*

EMI Corp (PA)...937 596-5511
   801 W Pike St Jackson Center (45334) *(G-9531)*

EMI Enterprises Inc..419 666-0012
   2639 Tracy Rd Northwood (43619) *(G-11973)*

Emil Pawuk & Associates, Richfield *Also Called: Empaco Equipment Corporation (G-12695)*

Emily Management Inc..440 354-6713
   10280 Pinecrest Rd Concord Township (44077) *(G-6926)*

EMJ Cincinnati, Cincinnati *Also Called: Earle M Jorgensen Company (G-2597)*

EMJ Cleveland, Twinsburg *Also Called: Earle M Jorgensen Company (G-14184)*

EMJ Cleveland Plate, Twinsburg *Also Called: Earle M Jorgensen Company (G-14183)*

Emmett Dan House Ltd Partnr...740 392-6886
   150 Howard St Mount Vernon (43050) *(G-11485)*

Emp Holdings Ltd...330 493-4443
   4535 Dressler Rd Nw Canton (44718) *(G-1746)*

Empaco Equipment Corporation (PA)..................................330 659-9393
   2958 Brecksville Rd Richfield (44286) *(G-12695)*

Empire Dental Arts LLC (PA)...216 410-1331
   9140 Lake Shore Blvd Mentor (44060) *(G-10936)*

Empire Enterprises Inc..330 665-7800
   3677 Embassy Pkwy Akron (44333) *(G-147)*

Empire Food Brokers Inc...614 889-2322
   6131 Avery Rd Dublin (43016) *(G-8003)*

Empire One LLC..330 628-9310
   1532 State Route 43 Mogadore (44260) *(G-11326)*

Empire Packing Company LP..513 942-5400
   113 Circle Freeway Dr West Chester (45246) *(G-14809)*

Empire Transportation, Fairfield *Also Called: Eric Boeppler Fmly Ltd Partnr (G-8412)*

Empire Wholesale Lumber Co, Akron *Also Called: Empire Enterprises Inc (G-147)*

Empire Wholesale Lumber Company...................................330 665-7800
   3677 Embassy Pkwy Akron (44333) *(G-148)*

Emplifi, Columbus *Also Called: Emplifi Inc (G-5815)*

Emplifi Inc (PA)..614 508-6100
   4400 Easton Cmns Columbus (43219) *(G-5815)*

Employee Benefits Sls Svc Off, Cincinnati *Also Called: Standard Insurance Company (G-3408)*

Employee Services LLC..585 593-9870
   100 American Rd Cleveland (44144) *(G-4213)*

Employment Development Inc...330 424-7711
   8330 County Home Rd Lisbon (44432) *(G-10002)*

Empora Title Inc..937 360-8876
   1362 Cole St Columbus (43205) *(G-5816)*

Empower Learn Create Inc...513 961-2825
   3310 Ruther Ave Cincinnati (45220) *(G-2617)*

Empower Media Partners LLC (PA)....................................513 871-7779
   15 E 14th St Cincinnati (45202) *(G-2618)*

Emprise Technologies LLC..419 720-6982
   5693 Swan Creek Dr Toledo (43614) *(G-13791)*

Ems, Cleveland *Also Called: Energy MGT Specialists Inc (G-4215)*

Ems Team LLC..800 735-8190
   1371 W Rahn Rd Dayton (45459) *(G-7335)*

Emsar, Wilmington *Also Called: Equipment MGT Svc & Repr Inc (G-15250)*

Emsco Inc (HQ)..330 830-7125
   1000 Nave Rd Se Massillon (44646) *(G-10638)*

Emsco Distributors, Strongsville *Also Called: Heritage Pool Supply Group Inc (G-13460)*

Emsi Inc (PA)...614 876-9988
   8220 Industrial Pkwy Plain City (43064) *(G-12475)*

Emssons Faurecia Ctrl Systems (DH).................................812 341-2000
   543 Matzinger Rd Toledo (43612) *(G-13792)*

Emt, Cincinnati *Also Called: Electric Motor Tech LLC (G-2609)*

Enclosure Suppliers LLC..513 782-3900
   12119 Champion Way Cincinnati (45241) *(G-2619)*

Encompass Care Inc...419 999-2030
   1100 Shawnee Rd Lima (45805) *(G-9886)*

Encore Label & Packaging, West Chester *Also Called: Grand Encore Cincinnati LLC (G-14699)*

Encore Precast LLC...513 726-5678
   416 W Ritter Seven Mile (45062) *(G-12962)*

Encore Rehabilitation Services...614 459-6901
   6479 Reflections Dr Ste 230 Dublin (43017) *(G-8004)*

Encore Technologies, Cincinnati *Also Called: Sjn Data Center LLC (G-3381)*

End-User Computing Inc..419 292-2200
   4841 Monroe St Ste 307 Toledo (43623) *(G-13793)*

Endevis LLC..419 482-4848
   9313 Bowman Farms Ln Sylvania (43560) *(G-13543)*

Endocrine & Diabetes Care Ctr, Toledo *Also Called: John E Brunner MD (G-13869)*

Endocrine Lab, Cincinnati *Also Called: University of Cincinnati (G-3587)*

Endoscopy Center W Centl Ohio, Lima *Also Called: Gastro-Intestinal Assoc Inc (G-9991)*

Endoscopy Ctr of W Cntl Ohio L..419 879-3636
   2793 Shawnee Rd Lima (45806) *(G-9990)*

Enerfab LLC (PA)...513 641-0500
   4430 Chickering Ave Cincinnati (45232) *(G-2620)*

Enerfab Power & Industrial Inc...513 470-5526
   4955 Spring Grove Ave Cincinnati (45232) *(G-2621)*

Enerfab Process Solutions LLC...513 641-0500
   4430 Chickering Ave Cincinnati (45232) *(G-2622)*

Energy Cooperative Inc (HQ)..740 348-1206
   1500 Granville Rd Newark (43055) *(G-11699)*

Energy Corportive, Coshocton *Also Called: Ngo Development Corporation (G-6993)*

Energy Harbor Corp (HQ)..888 254-6359
   168 E Market St Akron (44308) *(G-149)*

Energy Harbor LLC..888 254-6356
   168 E Market St Akron (44308) *(G-150)*

Energy Harbor Nuclear Corp...440 604-9836
   6670 Beta Dr Cleveland (44143) *(G-4214)*

Energy MGT Specialists Inc..216 676-9045
   15800 Industrial Pkwy Cleveland (44135) *(G-4215)*

Energy Power Services Inc..330 343-2312
   3251 Brightwood Rd Se New Philadelphia (44663) *(G-11650)*

Energy Trucking, Pataskala *Also Called: Energy Trucking LLC (G-12274)*

Energy Trucking LLC (PA)..740 240-2204
   24 Front St Ste 210 Pataskala (43062) *(G-12274)*

Enerstar Rentals and Svcs Ltd..570 360-3271
   55643 High Ridge Rd Bellaire (43906) *(G-1011)*

Enertech Electrical Inc..330 536-2131
   101 Youngstown Lowellville Rd Lowellville (44436) *(G-10168)*

Enervise LLC...614 885-9800
   6663 Huntley Rd Ste K Columbus (43229) *(G-5817)*

Enervise Incorporated (PA)...513 761-6000
   10226 Alliance Rd Blue Ash (45242) *(G-1167)*

Engage Healthcare Svcs Corp..614 457-8180
   4619 Kenny Rd Ste 100 Columbus (43220) *(G-5818)*

Engauge Holdings LLC..614 573-1010
   375 N Front St Ste 400 Columbus (43215) *(G-5819)*

Engineered Con Structures Corp
   14510 Broadway Ave Cleveland (44125) *(G-4216)*

Engineering Associates Inc...330 345-6556
   1935 Eagle Pass Wooster (44691) *(G-15337)*

Engineering Chain Div, Sandusky *Also Called: US Tsubaki Power Transm LLC (G-12939)*

Engineering Cons Group Inc..330 869-9949
   3394 W Market St Fairlawn (44333) *(G-8477)*

Engineering Department, Dayton *Also Called: County of Montgomery (G-7253)*

Engineering Office, Waverly *Also Called: Pike County (G-14615)*
Enginring Exclince Nat Accnts... 844 969-3923
  4360 Glendale Milford Rd Blue Ash (45242) *(G-1168)*
Englewood Manor, Englewood *Also Called: Liberty Nursing Center (G-8313)*
Englewood Trck Towing Recovery, Clayton *Also Called: Englewood Truck Inc (G-3732)*
Englewood Truck Inc... 937 836-5109
  7510 Jacks Ln Clayton (45315) *(G-3732)*
Engram Home, Elyria *Also Called: Echoing Hills Village Inc (G-8243)*
ENNIS COURT, Lakewood *Also Called: Lakewood Health Care Center (G-9673)*
Enpro, West Chester *Also Called: Hydrotech Inc (G-14819)*
Enrichment Center, Grove City *Also Called: Karrington Operating Co Inc (G-8929)*
Ensemble Health Partners, Cincinnati *Also Called: Ensemble RCM LLC (G-2624)*
Ensemble Health Partners Inc... 704 765-3715
  11511 Reed Hartman Hwy Cincinnati (45241) *(G-2623)*
Ensemble RCM LLC.. 704 765-3715
  11511 Reed Hartman Hwy Cincinnati (45241) *(G-2624)*
Ensemble Theatre Cincinnati... 513 421-3555
  1127 Vine St Cincinnati (45202) *(G-2625)*
Ent Realty Corp... 888 881-4368
  140 Fox Rd Van Wert (45891) *(G-14343)*
Entelco Corporation.. 419 872-4620
  6528 Weatherfield Ct Maumee (43537) *(G-10721)*
Enterprise Door & Supply Co., Mentor *Also Called: Enterprise Door & Supply Inc (G-10937)*
Enterprise Door & Supply Inc... 440 942-3478
  7673 Saint Clair Ave Mentor (44060) *(G-10937)*
Enterprise Hill Farm Inc... 419 668-0242
  5264 Huber Rd Norwalk (44857) *(G-12009)*
Enterprise Holdings Inc... 513 538-6200
  4600 Mcauley Pl Ste 150 Blue Ash (45242) *(G-1169)*
Enterprise Pdts Partners LP... 513 423-2122
  3590 Yankee Rd Middletown (45044) *(G-11162)*
Enterprise Rent-A-Car... 419 424-9626
  2028 Tiffin Ave Findlay (45840) *(G-8527)*
Enterprise Rent-A-Car, Blue Ash *Also Called: Enterprise Holdings Inc (G-1169)*
Enterprise Rent-A-Car, Findlay *Also Called: Enterprise Rent-A-Car (G-8527)*
Entertrainment Inc... 513 898-8000
  7379 Squire Ct West Chester (45069) *(G-14687)*
Entertrainment Junction, West Chester *Also Called: Entertrainment Inc (G-14687)*
Enting Water Conditioning Inc (PA)... 937 294-5100
  3211 Dryden Rd Frnt Moraine (45439) *(G-11407)*
Entitle Direct Group Inc... 216 236-7800
  6100 Oak Tree Blvd Ste 200 Independence (44131) *(G-9430)*
Envelope Mart, Northwood *Also Called: EMI Enterprises Inc (G-11973)*
Envirite of Ohio Inc... 330 456-6238
  2050 Central Ave Se Canton (44707) *(G-1747)*
Envirnmental Engrg Systems Inc.. 937 228-6492
  17 Creston Ave Dayton (45404) *(G-7336)*
Envirnmntal Sltons Innvtons In (PA).. 513 451-1777
  4525 Este Ave Cincinnati (45232) *(G-2626)*
Envirnmntal Systems RES Inst I.. 614 933-8698
  1085 Beecher Xing N Ste A Columbus (43230) *(G-5820)*
Enviro It LLC... 614 453-0709
  3854 Fisher Rd Columbus (43228) *(G-5821)*
Envirocare Lawn & Ldscp LLC.. 419 874-6779
  24112 Lime City Rd Perrysburg (43551) *(G-12335)*
Envirocontrol Systems Inc.. 937 275-4718
  165 E Helena St Dayton (45404) *(G-7337)*
Envirocore, Plain City *Also Called: Envirocore Inc (G-12476)*
Envirocore Inc.. 614 263-6554
  8250 Estates Pkwy Plain City (43064) *(G-12476)*
Environment Control, Tipp City *Also Called: Environment Ctrl of Miami Cnty (G-13658)*
Environment Control, Twinsburg *Also Called: Environment Ctrl Beachwood Inc (G-14187)*
Environment Ctrl Beachwood Inc.. 330 405-6201
  1897 E Aurora Rd Twinsburg (44087) *(G-14187)*
Environment Ctrl of Miami Cnty... 937 669-9900
  7939 S County Road 25a Ste A Tipp City (45371) *(G-13658)*
Environmental Conditioning Sys, Mentor *Also Called: Hank Bloom Services Inc (G-10945)*
Environmental Division, Cincinnati *Also Called: Power Engineers Incorporated (G-3226)*
Environmental Enterprises Inc (PA)... 513 772-2818
  10163 Cincinnati Dayton Rd Cincinnati (45241) *(G-2627)*

Environmental Health & Safety, Columbus *Also Called: Ohio State University (G-6458)*
Environmental Health Dept, Springfield *Also Called: County of Clark (G-13243)*
Environmental Quality MGT (DH)... 513 825-7500
  1800 Carillion Blvd Cincinnati (45240) *(G-2628)*
Enviroscience Inc (PA)... 330 688-0111
  5070 Stow Rd Stow (44224) *(G-13366)*
Enviroserve, Cleveland *Also Called: Savage Companies (G-4877)*
Enviroserve, North Canton *Also Called: Enviroserve Inc (G-11828)*
Enviroserve Inc (HQ).. 330 361-7764
  7640 Whipple Ave Nw North Canton (44720) *(G-11828)*
Envision.. 513 389-7500
  3030 W Fork Rd Cincinnati (45211) *(G-2629)*
Envision Children, Cincinnati *Also Called: Envision Corporation (G-2630)*
Envision Corporation.. 513 772-5437
  8 Enfield St Cincinnati (45218) *(G-2630)*
Envision Pharmaceutical Svcs, Twinsburg *Also Called: Elixir Rx Options LLC (G-14185)*
Envision Rx Options, North Canton *Also Called: Elixir Pharmacy LLC (G-11827)*
Envisionware Inc (PA).. 678 382-6530
  861 Taylor Rd Unit H Columbus (43230) *(G-5822)*
Eosys Group Inc.. 513 217-7294
  2660 Towne Blvd Middletown (45044) *(G-11163)*
EP Ferris & Associates Inc... 614 299-2999
  2130 Quarry Trails Dr # 2 Columbus (43228) *(G-5823)*
Epcon Cmmnties Franchising Inc.. 614 761-1010
  500 Stonehenge Pkwy Dublin (43017) *(G-8005)*
Epcor Foundries, Cincinnati *Also Called: Seilkop Industries Inc (G-3356)*
Epicor Edi Source Inc.. 440 519-7800
  31875 Solon Rd Solon (44139) *(G-13084)*
Epilepsy Ctr of Nrthwstern Ohi... 419 867-5950
  1701 Holland Rd Maumee (43537) *(G-10722)*
Epipheo, Cincinnati *Also Called: Epipheo Inc (G-2631)*
Epipheo Inc.. 888 687-7620
  2681 Cyclorama Dr Cincinnati (45211) *(G-2631)*
Epiqurian Inns... 614 885-2600
  649 High St Worthington (43085) *(G-15414)*
Episcopal Retirement Homes Inc.. 513 871-2090
  3550 Shaw Ave Ofc Cincinnati (45208) *(G-2632)*
Episcopal Retirement Homes Inc.. 513 561-6363
  3939 Erie Ave Cincinnati (45208) *(G-2633)*
Episcpal Rtrment Svcs Affrdbl.. 513 271-9610
  3870 Virginia Ave Cincinnati (45227) *(G-2634)*
Epsilon... 513 248-2882
  1000 Summit Dr Unit 200 Milford (45150) *(G-11226)*
Epsilyte Holdings LLC... 937 778-9500
  555 E Statler Rd Piqua (45356) *(G-12441)*
Eq Ohio, Canton *Also Called: Envirite of Ohio Inc (G-1747)*
Equality Ohio Education Fund.. 614 224-0400
  370 S 5th St Ste G3 Columbus (43215) *(G-5824)*
Equipment Depot Ohio Inc... 513 934-2121
  1000 Kingsview Dr Lebanon (45036) *(G-9765)*
Equipment Maintenance Inc... 513 353-3518
  5885 Hamilton Cleves Rd Cleves (45002) *(G-5188)*
Equipment Maintenance & Repair, Cleves *Also Called: Equipment Maintenance Inc (G-5188)*
Equipment Mfrs Intl Inc... 216 651-6700
  16151 Puritas Ave Cleveland (44135) *(G-4217)*
Equipment MGT Svc & Repr Inc... 937 383-1052
  270 Davids Dr Wilmington (45177) *(G-15250)*
Equitas Health Inc (PA).. 614 299-2437
  1105 Schrock Rd Ste 400 Columbus (43229) *(G-5825)*
Equitas Health Inc.. 937 424-1440
  1222 S Patterson Blvd Ste 110 Dayton (45402) *(G-7338)*
Equity Cnstr Solutions LLC (PA).. 614 802-2900
  4653 Trueman Blvd Ste 100 Hilliard (43026) *(G-9195)*
Equity Diamond Brokers Inc (PA).. 513 793-4760
  9563 Montgomery Rd Bsmt Montgomery (45242) *(G-11367)*
Equity Engineering Group Inc (PA)... 216 283-9519
  20600 Chagrin Blvd Ste 1200 Shaker Heights (44122) *(G-12976)*
Equity LLC... 614 802-2900
  4653 Trueman Blvd Ste 100 Hilliard (43026) *(G-9196)*
Equity Lodging LLC.. 740 435-0427
  2327 Southgate Pkwy Cambridge (43725) *(G-1570)*

Equity Real Estate — ALPHABETIC SECTION

Equity Real Estate, Hilliard Also Called: Equity Cnstr Solutions LLC (G-9195)

Equity Resources Inc.. 740 363-7300
15 W Central Ave Ste 103 Delaware (43015) (G-7795)

Equity Resources Inc.. 614 389-4462
7251 Sawmill Rd Ste 100 Dublin (43016) (G-8006)

Equity Trust Company.. 440 323-5491
1 Equity Way Westlake (44145) (G-15057)

ERA, Chillicothe Also Called: J & W Enterprises Inc (G-2074)

Erb Electric Co.. 740 633-5055
500 Hall St Ste 1 Bridgeport (43912) (G-1376)

Ergon, Delaware Also Called: Alpha Group of Delaware Inc (G-7778)

Eric Boeppler Fmly Ltd Partnr..................................... 513 860-3324
9331 Seward Rd Ste A Fairfield (45014) (G-8412)

Eric W Warnock.. 419 228-2233
230 N Eastown Rd Lima (45807) (G-9887)

Erie Blacktop, Sandusky Also Called: Erie Trucking Inc (G-12892)

Erie Blacktop Inc... 419 625-7374
4507 Tiffin Ave Sandusky (44870) (G-12889)

Erie Construction, Toledo Also Called: Erie Construction Mid-West Inc (G-13795)

Erie Construction Co, Dayton Also Called: Erie Construction Mid-West Inc (G-7339)

Erie Construction Group Inc....................................... 419 625-7374
4507 Tiffin Ave Sandusky (44870) (G-12890)

Erie Construction Mid-West Inc.................................. 937 898-4688
3520 Sudachi Dr Dayton (45414) (G-7339)

Erie Construction Mid-West Inc.................................. 419 472-4200
4271 Monroe St Toledo (43606) (G-13794)

Erie Construction Mid-West Inc.................................. 419 472-4200
3516 Granite Cir Toledo (43617) (G-13795)

Erie Construction Mid-West LLC (PA)........................ 567 408-2145
3516 Granite Cir Toledo (43617) (G-13796)

Erie Construction Mid-west, Inc., Toledo Also Called: Erie Construction Mid-West Inc (G-13794)

Erie County Cablevision Inc....................................... 419 627-0800
409 E Market St Sandusky (44870) (G-12891)

Erie County Care Facility, Huron Also Called: County of Erie (G-9386)

Erie County Hwy Dept, Sandusky Also Called: County of Erie (G-12886)

Erie Indemnity Company.. 330 433-6300
4690 Munson St Nw Canton (44718) (G-1748)

Erie Insur Exch Actvties Assn..................................... 330 433-1925
4690 Munson St Nw Ste A Canton (44718) (G-1749)

Erie Insur Exch Actvties Assn..................................... 614 430-8530
445 Hutchinson Ave Columbus (43235) (G-5826)

Erie Metroparks General Info..................................... 419 621-4220
3109 Hull Rd Huron (44839) (G-9387)

Erie Shores Credit Union Inc (PA).............................. 419 897-8110
1688 Woodlands Dr Maumee (43537) (G-10723)

Erie Shres Cncil Inc Boy Scuts................................... 419 241-7293
5600 W Sylvania Ave Toledo (43623) (G-13797)

Erie Trucking Inc.. 419 625-7374
4507 Tiffin Ave Sandusky (44870) (G-12892)

Ermc II LP... 513 424-8517
3461 Towne Blvd Unit 250 Middletown (45005) (G-11197)

Ernest V Thomas Jr (PA)... 513 961-5311
2323 Park Ave Cincinnati (45206) (G-2635)

Ernst & Young, Cleveland Also Called: Ernst & Young US LLP (G-4220)

Ernst & Young LLP... 513 612-1594
1900 Scripps Ctr Cincinnati (45202) (G-2636)

Ernst & Young LLP... 513 612-1400
221 E 4th St Ste 2900 Cincinnati (45202) (G-2637)

Ernst & Young LLP... 216 861-5000
950 Main Ave Ste 1800 Cleveland (44113) (G-4218)

Ernst & Young LLP... 216 583-1823
1660 W 2nd St Ste 200 Cleveland (44113) (G-4219)

Ernst & Young LLP... 614 224-5678
800 Yard St Ste 200 Columbus (43212) (G-5827)

Ernst & Young LLP... 419 244-8000
1 Seagate Ste 2510 Toledo (43604) (G-13798)

Ernst & Young US LLP... 216 583-1893
950 Main Ave Ste 1800 Cleveland (44113) (G-4220)

Erp Analysts Inc... 614 718-9222
425 Metro Pl N Ste 510 Dublin (43017) (G-8007)

Erp Suites, Loveland Also Called: Server Suites Llc (G-10158)

Ers Digital Inc... 216 281-1234
3666 Carnegie Ave Cleveland (44115) (G-4221)

Esber Beverage Company.. 330 456-4361
2217 Bolivar Rd Sw Canton (44706) (G-1750)

Esc of Cuyahoga County... 216 524-3000
6393 Oak Tree Blvd Ste 300 Independence (44131) (G-9431)

Escalante - Cntry CLB of N LLC................................. 937 374-5000
1 Club North Dr Xenia (45385) (G-15504)

Escape Enterprises Inc.. 614 224-0300
222 Neilston St Columbus (43215) (G-5828)

Esec Corporation... 614 875-3732
6240 Enterprise Pkwy Grove City (43123) (G-8918)

Esi Electrical Contractors, Moraine Also Called: E S I Inc (G-11405)

Esi Employee Assistance Group................................ 800 535-4841
100 American Rd Cleveland (44144) (G-4222)

Esj Carrier Corporation... 513 728-7388
3240 Production Dr Fairfield (45014) (G-8413)

Esko-Graphics Inc (HQ)... 937 454-1721
8535 Gander Creek Dr Miamisburg (45342) (G-11051)

Eskoartwork, Miamisburg Also Called: Esko-Graphics Inc (G-11051)

Eslich Wrecking Company... 330 488-8300
3525 Broadway Ave Louisville (44641) (G-10116)

Eso, Carrollton Also Called: Efficient Services Ohio Inc (G-1907)

ESOP, Cleveland Also Called: Esop Realty Inc (G-4223)

Esop Realty Inc.. 216 361-0718
11890 Fairhill Rd Cleveland (44120) (G-4223)

Espt Liquidation Inc... 330 698-4711
339 Mill St Apple Creek (44606) (G-450)

Esri, Columbus Also Called: Envirnmntal Systems RES Inst I (G-5820)

Essendant Co.. 614 876-7774
1634 Westbelt Dr Columbus (43228) (G-5829)

Essendant Co.. 330 650-9361
100 E Highland Rd Hudson (44236) (G-9345)

Essendant Co.. 800 733-4091
2100 Highland Rd Twinsburg (44087) (G-14188)

Essendant Co.. 330 425-7343
2477 Edison Blvd Twinsburg (44087) (G-14189)

Essendant Co.. 513 942-1354
9775 International Blvd West Chester (45246) (G-14810)

Essex Healthcare Corporation (PA)........................... 614 416-0600
2780 Airport Dr Ste 400 Columbus (43219) (G-5830)

Essilor Laboratories Amer Inc................................... 614 274-0840
3671 Interchange Rd Columbus (43204) (G-5831)

Essilor of America Inc... 614 492-0888
2400 Spiegel Dr Ste A Groveport (43125) (G-8986)

Estabrook Corporation (PA)....................................... 440 234-8566
700 W Bagley Rd Berea (44017) (G-1068)

Estate Information Svcs LLC.................................... 614 729-1700
670 Morrison Rd Ste 300 Gahanna (43230) (G-8716)

Estephenson Brenda & John, Maineville Also Called: AMS Construction Inc (G-10224)

Estes, Columbus Also Called: Estes Express Lines (G-5832)

Estes Express Lines.. 614 275-6000
1009 Frank Rd Columbus (43223) (G-5832)

Estes Express Lines.. 330 659-9750
2755 Brecksville Rd Richfield (44286) (G-12696)

Estes Express Lines.. 419 531-1500
5330 Angola Rd Ste B Toledo (43615) (G-13799)

Estes Express Lines.. 513 779-9581
6459 Allen Rd West Chester (45069) (G-14688)

Estes Express Lines 92, Toledo Also Called: Estes Express Lines (G-13799)

Esther Marie Nursing Home, Geneva Also Called: Contining Hlthcare Sltions Inc (G-8784)

Esw, Oregon Also Called: ESwagner Company Inc (G-12133)

ESwagner Company Inc.. 419 691-8651
840 Patchen Rd Oregon (43616) (G-12133)

ETC, Cincinnati Also Called: Ensemble Theatre Cincinnati (G-2625)

Etchen Co, The, Holland Also Called: Rdh Ohio LLC (G-9302)

Ethan Crossing Recovery Center, Springfield Also Called: E Home Behavioral LLC (G-13249)

Ethicon Endo-Surgery Inc (HQ)................................. 513 337-7000
4545 Creek Rd Blue Ash (45242) (G-1170)

ALPHABETIC SECTION — Expert Crane

Etl, Columbus *Also Called: Intertek Testing Svcs NA Inc* **(G-6070)**
Eubel Brady Sttman Asset MGT I 937 291-1223
  10100 Innovation Dr Ste 410 Miamisburg (45342) **(G-11052)**
Euclid Adult Training Center, Euclid *Also Called: A W S Inc* **(G-8335)**
Euclid Fish Company 440 951-6448
  7839 Enterprise Dr Mentor (44060) **(G-10938)**
Euclid Health Care Inc (PA) 513 561-6400
  7885 Camargo Rd Cincinnati (45243) **(G-2638)**
Euclid Hospital (HQ) 216 531-9000
  18901 Lake Shore Blvd Euclid (44119) **(G-8341)**
Euclid Hospital, Cleveland *Also Called: Cleveland Clnic Hlth Systm-AST* **(G-4036)**
Euclid Medical Products, Apple Creek *Also Called: Precision Products Group Inc* **(G-452)**
Euclid Vidaro Mfg. Co., Kent *Also Called: Alsico Usa Inc* **(G-9557)**
Euclidean Support Services Inc 330 405-8501
  26250 Euclid Ave Euclid (44132) **(G-8342)**
Euro Usa Inc (PA) 216 714-0500
  4481 Johnston Pkwy Cleveland (44128) **(G-4224)**
Eurofins Testoil Inc 216 251-2510
  20338 Progress Dr Strongsville (44149) **(G-13453)**
Eurolink Inc 740 392-1549
  106 W Ohio Ave Mount Vernon (43050) **(G-11486)**
Euthenics Inc (PA) 440 260-1555
  8235 Mohawk Dr Strongsville (44136) **(G-13454)**
Evanglcal Lthran Good Smrtan S 419 365-5115
  100 Powell Dr Arlington (45814) **(G-469)**
Evanglcal Rtrment Vllges Inc D 937 837-5581
  5790 Denlinger Rd Dayton (45426) **(G-7340)**
Evanhoe & Associates Inc 937 235-2995
  492 W 2nd St Ste 208 Xenia (45385) **(G-15505)**
Evans Adhesive Corporation (HQ) 614 451-2665
  925 Old Henderson Rd Columbus (43220) **(G-5833)**
Evans Construction 330 305-9355
  4585 Aultman Ave Nw North Canton (44720) **(G-11829)**
Evans Landscaping Inc 513 271-1119
  3700 Round Bottom Rd Cincinnati (45244) **(G-2639)**
Evans McHwart Hmblton Tlton In (PA) 614 775-4500
  5500 New Albany Rd Ste 100 New Albany (43054) **(G-11563)**
Evans Motor Works, Dayton *Also Called: Volvo BMW Dyton Evans Volkswag* **(G-7710)**
Evans, Jonathon P, Chardon *Also Called: Ibold & OBrien Inc* **(G-2006)**
Evanston Blldogs Yuth Ftball A 513 254-9500
  3060 Durrell Ave Cincinnati (45207) **(G-2640)**
Evant (PA) 330 920-1517
  1221 Commerce Dr Stow (44224) **(G-13367)**
Evarts-Tremaine-Flicker Co 216 621-7183
  1111 Superior Ave E Ste 420 Cleveland (44114) **(G-4225)**
Evenflo, Miamisburg *Also Called: Evenflo Company Inc* **(G-11053)**
Evenflo Company Inc (DH) 937 415-3300
  3131 Newmark Dr Ste 300 Miamisburg (45342) **(G-11053)**
Event Source, Cleveland *Also Called: JBK Group Inc* **(G-4435)**
Ever Dry of Cincinnati, West Chester *Also Called: Riverfront Diversified Inc* **(G-14757)**
Everdry Waterproofing, Mansfield *Also Called: Salvanalle Inc* **(G-10315)**
Everdry Waterproofing Toledo, Toledo *Also Called: Rusk Industries Inc* **(G-14000)**
Everest Technologies Inc 614 436-3120
  1105 Schrock Rd Ste 500 Columbus (43229) **(G-5834)**
Everfast Inc 614 789-0900
  6315 Sawmill Rd Dublin (43017) **(G-8008)**
Evergreen Cooperative Corp (PA) 216 268-5399
  4205 Saint Clair Ave Cleveland (44103) **(G-4226)**
Evergreen Cooperative Ldry Inc 216 268-3548
  540 E 105th St Cleveland (44108) **(G-4227)**
Evergreen Healthcare Center, Montpelier *Also Called: Robinair Leasing Co LLC* **(G-11386)**
Evergreen Kindervelt Gift Shop, Cincinnati *Also Called: Williamsburg of Cincinnati Mgt* **(G-3673)**
Evergreen Pharmaceutical LLC (DH) 513 719-2600
  201 E 4th St Ste 900 Cincinnati (45202) **(G-2641)**
Evergreen Phrm Cal LLC (DH) 513 719-2600
  201 E 4th St Ste 900 Cincinnati (45202) **(G-2642)**
Evergreen Plastics, Clyde *Also Called: Polychem LLC* **(G-5207)**
Everhart Advisors 614 717-9705
  535 Metro Pl S Dublin (43017) **(G-8009)**

Everside Health LLC 216 672-0211
  25700 Science Park Dr Ste 120 Beachwood (44122) **(G-790)**
Everstream Holding Company LLC 216 923-2260
  1228 Euclid Ave Ste 250 Cleveland (44115) **(G-4228)**
Every Child Succeeds Inc 513 636-2830
  3333 Burnet Ave Cincinnati (45229) **(G-2643)**
Everybodys Workplace Solutions, Moraine *Also Called: Dayton Ews Inc* **(G-11400)**
Everyday Homecare LLC 937 444-1672
  711 S High St Mount Orab (45154) **(G-11470)**
Evokes LLC 513 947-8433
  8118 Corporate Way Ste 212 Mason (45040) **(G-10545)**
Evolution Ag LLC 740 363-1341
  5565 State Route 37 E Delaware (43015) **(G-7796)**
Evolv LLC 440 994-9115
  5171 Hudson Dr Hudson (44236) **(G-9346)**
Ewers Utility Service LLC 740 326-4451
  301 Columbus Rd Mount Vernon (43050) **(G-11487)**
Excalibur Collision Inc 440 708-9898
  9935 Washington St Chagrin Falls (44023) **(G-1977)**
Excel Decorators Inc 614 522-0056
  3910 Groves Rd Ste A Columbus (43232) **(G-5835)**
Excelas LLC 440 442-7310
  387 Golfview Ln Ste 200 Cleveland (44143) **(G-4229)**
Excellence Home Healthcare LLC 614 755-6502
  2238 S Hamilton Rd Ste 102 Columbus (43232) **(G-5836)**
Excellence In Motivation Inc 763 445-3000
  6 N Main St Ste 370 Dayton (45402) **(G-7341)**
Exchange Bank Inc (HQ) 419 833-3401
  235 Main St Luckey (43443) **(G-10182)**
Excite Health Partners, Cleveland *Also Called: Excite It Partners LLC* **(G-4230)**
Excite It Partners LLC 216 447-9808
  6133 Rockside Rd Ste 307 Cleveland (44131) **(G-4230)**
Exclusive Lifestyles Ohio LLC 740 647-5552
  4449 Easton Way Columbus (43219) **(G-5837)**
Executive Jet Management Inc (DH) 513 979-6600
  4556 Airport Rd Cincinnati (45226) **(G-2644)**
Executive Management Services 419 529-8800
  1225 Home Rd N Ontario (44906) **(G-12104)**
EXECUTIVE OFFICE, Berea *Also Called: Ohio Tpk & Infrastructure Comm* **(G-1076)**
EXECUTIVE OFFICE, Columbus *Also Called: Ohio Pub Emplyees Rtrement Sys* **(G-6440)**
Exel Global Logistics Inc 440 243-5900
  21500 Aerospace Pkwy Cleveland (44142) **(G-4231)**
Exel Global Logistics Inc 614 409-4500
  2144a John Glenn Ave Columbus (43217) **(G-5838)**
Exel Holdings (usa) Inc (DH) 614 865-8500
  570 Polaris Pkwy Ste 110 Westerville (43082) **(G-14892)**
Exel Inc 614 836-1265
  6390 Commerce Ct Groveport (43125) **(G-8987)**
Exel Inc (DH) 614 865-5819
  360 Westar Blvd 4th Fl Westerville (43082) **(G-14893)**
Exel Inc 614 865-8294
  570 Polaris Pkwy Ste 110 Westerville (43082) **(G-14894)**
Exel N Amercn Logistics Inc (DH) 800 272-1052
  570 Players Pkwy Westerville (43081) **(G-14978)**
Exhibit Concepts Inc (PA) 937 890-7000
  700 Crossroads Ct Vandalia (45377) **(G-14376)**
Exhibitpro Inc 614 885-9541
  8900 Smiths Mill Rd New Albany (43054) **(G-11564)**
Exochem Corporation 440 277-1246
  2421 E 28th St Lorain (44055) **(G-10073)**
Exodus Integrity Services Inc 440 918-0140
  37111 Euclid Ave Ste F Willoughby (44094) **(G-15192)**
Expedient, Columbus *Also Called: Continental Broadband PA* **(G-5691)**
Expedient Tech Solutions LLC 937 535-4300
  8561 Gander Creek Dr Miamisburg (45342) **(G-11054)**
Expeditors Intl Wash Inc 440 243-9900
  18029 Cleveland Pkwy Dr Cleveland (44135) **(G-4232)**
Expeditus, Toledo *Also Called: Expeditus Transport LLC* **(G-13800)**
Expeditus Transport LLC 419 464-9450
  7644 Kings Pointe Rd Toledo (43617) **(G-13800)**
Expert Crane, Wellington *Also Called: Expert Crane Inc* **(G-14632)**

ALPHABETIC SECTION

Expert Crane Inc..216 451-9900
720 Shiloh Ave Wellington (44090) *(G-14632)*

Expesite LLC (DH)..614 917-1100
278 N 5th St Columbus (43215) *(G-5839)*

Explorer Rv Insurance Agcy Inc......................330 659-8900
3250 Interstate Dr Richfield (44286) *(G-12697)*

Express Script, Dublin *Also Called: Medco Health Solutions Inc (G-8061)*

Express Seed, Oberlin *Also Called: Express Seed Company (G-12068)*

Express Seed Company......................................440 774-2259
51051 Us Highway 20 Oberlin (44074) *(G-12068)*

Expresso Car Wash 5, Toledo *Also Called: Expresso Car Wash Systems Inc (G-13801)*

Expresso Car Wash Systems Inc......................419 866-7099
1750 S Reynolds Rd Toledo (43614) *(G-13801)*

Extermital Chemicals Inc..................................937 253-6144
1026 Wayne Ave Dayton (45410) *(G-7342)*

Extermital Pest Control, Dayton *Also Called: Extermital Chemicals Inc (G-7342)*

Extract LLC..937 732-9495
425 N Findlay St Ste 218 Dayton (45404) *(G-7343)*

Extras Support Staffing....................................740 671-3996
3494 Noble St Bellaire (43906) *(G-1012)*

Extreme Mktg & Promotions Inc......................440 237-8400
9403 Scottsdale Dr Broadview Heights (44147) *(G-1388)*

Exxcel, Columbus *Also Called: Exxcel Project Management LLC (G-5840)*

Exxcel Project Management LLC......................614 621-4500
328 Civic Center Dr Columbus (43215) *(G-5840)*

Ey, Cincinnati *Also Called: Ernst & Young LLP (G-2637)*

Ey, Cleveland *Also Called: Ernst & Young LLP (G-4218)*

Ey, Cleveland *Also Called: Ernst & Young LLP (G-4219)*

Ey, Columbus *Also Called: Ernst & Young LLP (G-5827)*

Ey, Toledo *Also Called: Ernst & Young LLP (G-13798)*

Eye Care Associates Inc (PA)............................330 746-7691
10 Dutton Dr Youngstown (44502) *(G-15608)*

Eye Laser & Surgery Center..............................937 427-7800
4235 Indian Ripple Rd Dayton (45440) *(G-7344)*

Eye Lighting Intl N Amer Inc.............................440 350-7000
9150 Hendricks Rd Mentor (44060) *(G-10939)*

Eye Surgery Center of Wooster, Wooster *Also Called: Wooster Ophthalmologists Inc (G-15397)*

Eyemed Vision..330 995-0597
295 Westview Dr Aurora (44202) *(G-612)*

EZ Dumper, Cleveland *Also Called: Olympic Steel Inc (G-4695)*

EZ Grout Corporation Inc..................................740 962-2024
1833 N Riverview Rd Malta (43758) *(G-10232)*

EZ Sales Teamkeller Willi..................................216 916-7778
2001 Crocker Rd Westlake (44145) *(G-15058)*

Ezg Manufacturing, Malta *Also Called: EZ Grout Corporation Inc (G-10232)*

F & M Contractors, Clayton *Also Called: Ideal Company Inc (G-3733)*

F & M Mafco Inc (HQ).......................................513 367-2151
9149 Dry Fork Rd Harrison (45030) *(G-9104)*

F & M Mafco Inc..513 367-2151
651 Enterprise Dr Harrison (45030) *(G-9105)*

F C Franchising Systems Inc............................513 563-8339
10700 Montgomery Rd Ste 300 Montgomery (45242) *(G-11368)*

F C Skinner Painting Service, Piqua *Also Called: Francis C Skinner Painting Svc (G-12442)*

F E E, Canal Winchester *Also Called: Feecorp Corporation (G-1606)*

F F & W Inc..419 636-3123
924 E High St Bryan (43506) *(G-1484)*

F F A CAMP MUSKINGUM, Carrollton *Also Called: Ohio Ffa Camps Inc (G-1911)*

F F and H, Cleveland *Also Called: Fredrick Frdrick Hller Engners (G-4287)*

F L Emmert Company..513 721-5808
2007 Dunlap St Cincinnati (45214) *(G-2645)*

F S, Batavia *Also Called: Freeman Schwabe Machinery LLC (G-740)*

F&M Bank, Archbold *Also Called: Farmers & Merchants State Bank (G-457)*

F+w Media Inc..513 531-2690
9912 Carver Rd Ste 100 Blue Ash (45242) *(G-1171)*

Fab3 Group, The, Akron *Also Called: Ohio Fabricators Inc (G-250)*

Fabrizi Trucking & Pav Co Inc..........................440 234-1284
6751 Eastland Rd Cleveland (44128) *(G-4233)*

Fabrizi Trucking & Pav Co Inc..........................440 277-0127
2140 E 28th St Lorain (44055) *(G-10074)*

Fabrizi Trucking & Paving Co, Lorain *Also Called: Fabrizi Trucking & Pav Co Inc (G-10074)*

Face Forward Aesthetics LLC............................844 307-5929
1335 Dublin Rd Ste 110f Columbus (43215) *(G-5841)*

Facil North America Inc (HQ)............................330 487-2500
2242 Pinnacle Pkwy Ste 100 Twinsburg (44087) *(G-14190)*

Facilities Management Ex LLC..........................614 519-2186
800 Yard St Ste 115 Columbus (43212) *(G-5842)*

Facility 1, Toledo *Also Called: Midwest Trmnals Tledo Intl Inc (G-13924)*

Facility Connect, Twinsburg *Also Called: French Company LLC (G-14193)*

Facts Management Company............................440 892-4272
28446 W Preston Pl Westlake (44145) *(G-15059)*

Fahey Banking Company....................................740 382-8232
949 E Center St Marion (43302) *(G-10426)*

Fahlgren Inc (PA)..614 383-1500
4030 Easton Sta Ste 300 Columbus (43219) *(G-5843)*

Fahlgren Mortine, Columbus *Also Called: Fahlgren Inc (G-5843)*

FAI Electronics Corp..937 426-0090
4407 Walnut St Ste 250 Dayton (45440) *(G-7345)*

Fair Haven Shelby County Home, Sidney *Also Called: County of Shelby (G-13027)*

Fairborn Buick-GMC Truck Inc..........................937 878-7371
1105 N Central Ave Fairborn (45324) *(G-8374)*

Fairborn City School District............................937 878-1772
200 N Wright Ave Fairborn (45324) *(G-8375)*

Fairborn Equipment Co Ohio Inc......................614 384-5466
670 Lakeview Plaza Blvd Worthington (43085) *(G-15415)*

Fairborn Equipment Company Inc (PA)............419 209-0760
225 Tarhe Trl Upper Sandusky (43351) *(G-14288)*

Fairborn Equipment Midwest Inc......................513 492-9422
5155 Financial Way Mason (45040) *(G-10546)*

Fairborn Pontiac, Fairborn *Also Called: Fairborn Buick-GMC Truck Inc (G-8374)*

Fairchild MD Leasing Co LLC............................330 678-4912
1290 Fairchild Ave Kent (44240) *(G-9574)*

Fairfax Health Care Center, Cleveland *Also Called: Inner City Nursing Home Inc (G-4413)*

Fairfax Renaissance Dev Corp..........................216 361-8400
8111 Quincy Ave Ste 100 Cleveland (44104) *(G-4234)*

Fairfeld Grdns Rhblttion Care..........................740 536-7381
7820 Pleasantville Rd Ne Thornville (43076) *(G-13620)*

Fairfield Inn Stes Clmbs/New Al, Columbus *Also Called: Columbus OH 0617 LLC (G-5651)*

Fairfield Inn Stes Clmbus Arprt........................614 237-2100
4300 International Gtwy Columbus (43219) *(G-5844)*

Fairfield Center, Fairfield *Also Called: Alexson Services Inc (G-8389)*

Fairfield Cnty Job & Fmly Svcs........................800 450-8845
239 W Main St Lancaster (43130) *(G-9709)*

Fairfield Community Health Ctr........................740 277-6043
220 E Walnut St Lancaster (43130) *(G-9710)*

Fairfield Diagnstc Imaging LLC........................740 654-6312
1241 River Valley Blvd Lancaster (43130) *(G-9711)*

Fairfield Dialysis, Fairfield *Also Called: Dva Hlthcare - Sthwest Ohio LL (G-8408)*

Fairfield Federal Sav Ln Assn (PA)..................740 653-3863
111 E Main St Lancaster (43130) *(G-9712)*

Fairfield Homes Inc (PA)..................................740 653-3583
603 W Wheeling St Lancaster (43130) *(G-9713)*

Fairfield Homes Inc (PA)..................................740 653-3583
603 W Wheeling St Lancaster (43130) *(G-9714)*

Fairfield Homes Inc..614 873-3533
445 Fairfield Dr Ofc Plain City (43064) *(G-12477)*

Fairfield Industries Inc....................................740 409-1539
4465 Coonpath Rd Carroll (43112) *(G-1901)*

Fairfield Inn..614 267-1111
3031 Olentangy River Rd Columbus (43202) *(G-5845)*

Fairfield Inn, Cincinnati *Also Called: Tharaldson Hospitality MGT (G-2115)*

Fairfield Inn, Columbus *Also Called: Fairfield Inn Stes Clmbus Arprt (G-5844)*

Fairfield Inn, Jeffersonville *Also Called: Meander Hspitality Group V LLC (G-9540)*

Fairfield Inn, New Paris *Also Called: Aatish Hospitality LLC (G-11637)*

Fairfield Inn, Reynoldsburg *Also Called: First Hospitality Company LLC (G-12663)*

Fairfield Inn, Westerville *Also Called: Polaris Innkeepers LLC (G-14928)*

Fairfield Inn & Suites Columbu, Columbus *Also Called: Fairfield Inn (G-5845)*

Fairfield Inn & Suites Troy, Troy *Also Called: Troy Hotel II LLC (G-14164)*

Fairfield Insul & Drywall LLC............................740 654-8811
1655 Election House Rd Nw Lancaster (43130) *(G-9715)*

ALPHABETIC SECTION

Fairfield Internal Medicine..740 681-9447
  135 N Ewing St Ste 305 Lancaster (43130) *(G-9716)*

Fairfield Medical Associates..740 687-8377
  1781 Countryside Dr Lancaster (43130) *(G-9717)*

Fairfield Medical Center (PA)...740 687-8000
  401 N Ewing St Lancaster (43130) *(G-9718)*

Fairfield Medical Center, Lancaster Also Called: Fairfield Diagnstc Imaging LLC *(G-9711)*

Fairfield National Bank..740 653-1422
  1280 N Memorial Dr Lancaster (43130) *(G-9719)*

Fairfield National Bank (HQ)..740 653-7242
  143 W Main St Lancaster (43130) *(G-9720)*

Fairfield YMCA, Hamilton Also Called: Great Mami Vly Yung MNS Chrstn *(G-9046)*

Fairfield YMCA Pre-School, Fairfield Also Called: Great Miami Valley YMCA *(G-8417)*

Fairhaven Community, Upper Sandusky Also Called: United Church Homes Inc *(G-14294)*

Fairhaven Industries...330 652-6168
  45 North Rd Niles (44446) *(G-11789)*

Fairhaven Industries Inc (PA)..330 505-3644
  45 North Rd Niles (44446) *(G-11790)*

Fairhaven Sheltered Workshop..330 652-1116
  6000 Youngstown Warren Rd Niles (44446) *(G-11791)*

FAIRHAVEN SHELTERED WORKSHOP INC, Niles Also Called: Fairhaven Sheltered Workshop *(G-11791)*

Fairhope Hspice Plltive Care I...740 654-7077
  282 Sells Rd Lancaster (43130) *(G-9721)*

Fairlawn Associates Ltd...330 867-5000
  3180 W Market St Fairlawn (44333) *(G-8478)*

Fairlawn Medical Offices, Fairlawn Also Called: Kaiser Foundation Hospitals *(G-8488)*

Fairlawn Obgyn Assocs, Akron Also Called: Paragon Obstetrics & Gyne Asso *(G-260)*

Fairlawn Opco LLC...502 429-8062
  575 S Cleveland Massillon Rd Fairlawn (44333) *(G-8479)*

Fairlawn Partners LLC..330 576-1100
  3600 Embassy Pkwy Ste 100 Akron (44333) *(G-151)*

Fairmount Montessori Assn..216 321-7571
  3380 Fairmount Blvd Cleveland (44118) *(G-4235)*

Fairmount Nursing Home Inc..440 338-8220
  10190 Fairmount Rd Newbury (44065) *(G-11760)*

Fairport Asset Management, Cleveland Also Called: Roulston & Company Inc *(G-4857)*

Fairview Eye Center Inc..440 333-3060
  21375 Lorain Rd Cleveland (44126) *(G-4236)*

Fairview Hlth Sys Fderal Cr Un...216 476-7000
  18101 Lorain Ave Cleveland (44111) *(G-4237)*

Fairview Hospital (HQ)..216 476-7000
  18101 Lorain Ave Cleveland (44111) *(G-4238)*

Fairview Sklled Nrsing Rhbltti, Toledo Also Called: Covenant Care Ohio Inc *(G-13769)*

FAIRVIEW WEST PHYSICIAN CENTER, Cleveland Also Called: Auxiliary Bd Fairview Gen Hosp *(G-3844)*

Fairview West Physician Center, Cleveland Also Called: Fairview Hospital *(G-4238)*

Fairway Family Physicians Inc..614 861-7051
  1171 Fairway Blvd Columbus (43213) *(G-5846)*

Fairway Independent Mortgage, Columbus Also Called: Fairway Independent Mrtg Corp *(G-5847)*

Fairway Independent Mrtg Corp..614 930-6552
  4215 Worth Ave Ste 220 Columbus (43219) *(G-5847)*

Fairway Independent Mrtg Corp..513 833-1973
  5989 Meijer Dr Ste 1 Milford (45150) *(G-11227)*

Fairway Independent Mrtg Corp..937 304-1443
  40 Remick Blvd Springboro (45066) *(G-13198)*

Fairway Independent Mrtg Corp..330 587-9152
  1840 Town Park Blvd Ste D Uniontown (44685) *(G-14250)*

Faith Christian Accademy, Columbus Also Called: Columbus Christian Center Inc *(G-5619)*

Faith Mission Inc...614 224-6617
  245 N Grant Ave Columbus (43215) *(G-5848)*

Fak Group Inc...440 498-8465
  6750 Arnold Miller Pkwy Solon (44139) *(G-13085)*

Falcon Partners LLC..216 896-1010
  737 Bolivar Rd Ste 4000 Cleveland (44115) *(G-4239)*

Falcon Plaza LLC..419 352-4671
  1450 E Wooster St Ste 401 Bowling Green (43402) *(G-1319)*

Falcon Transport Co..330 793-1345
  4944 Belmont Ave Youngstown (44505) *(G-15609)*

Falling Leasing Co LLC..440 238-1100
  18840 Falling Water Rd Strongsville (44136) *(G-13455)*

Falling Star Farm Ltd...419 945-2651
  626 State Route 89 Polk (44866) *(G-12512)*

FALLING WATER HEALTHCARE CENTE, Strongsville Also Called: Falling Leasing Co LLC *(G-13455)*

Falls Chrysler Jeep Dodge, Cuyahoga Falls Also Called: Falls Motor City Inc *(G-7074)*

Falls Dermatology, Cuyahoga Falls Also Called: Falls Family Practice Inc *(G-7072)*

Falls Family Practice Inc (PA)..330 923-9585
  857 Graham Rd Cuyahoga Falls (44221) *(G-7072)*

Falls Heating & Cooling Inc...330 929-8777
  461 Munroe Falls Ave Cuyahoga Falls (44221) *(G-7073)*

Falls Motor City Inc...330 929-3066
  4100 State Rd Cuyahoga Falls (44223) *(G-7074)*

Falls Stamping & Welding Co (PA).....................................330 928-1191
  2900 Vincent St Cuyahoga Falls (44221) *(G-7075)*

Falls Vlg Retirement Cmnty Ltd...330 945-9797
  330 Broadway St E Cuyahoga Falls (44221) *(G-7076)*

Fallsway Equipment Co Inc (PA).......................................330 633-6000
  1277 Devalera St Akron (44310) *(G-152)*

Fallsway Equipment Company, Akron Also Called: Fallsway Equipment Co Inc *(G-152)*

Falu Corporation...502 641-8106
  9435 Waterstone Blvd Ste 140 Cincinnati (45249) *(G-2646)*

Falu Security, Cincinnati Also Called: Falu Corporation *(G-2646)*

Fameccanica North America, West Chester Also Called: Fameccanica North America Inc *(G-14689)*

Fameccanica North America Inc..513 645-0629
  8511 Trade Center Dr Bldg 4 West Chester (45011) *(G-14689)*

Family & Children First, Cincinnati Also Called: County of Hamilton *(G-2512)*

Family Birth Center Lima Mem..419 998-4570
  1001 Bellefontaine Ave Lima (45804) *(G-9888)*

Family Child Abuse Prvntion CT (PA).................................419 244-3053
  2460 Cherry St Toledo (43608) *(G-13802)*

Family Child Learning Center, Tallmadge Also Called: Childrens Hosp Med Ctr Akron *(G-13587)*

Family Cnsling Svcs Cntl Stark, Cuyahoga Falls Also Called: Trillium Family Solutions Inc *(G-7112)*

Family Dental Team Inc (PA)..330 733-7911
  620 Ridgewood Xing Ste K Akron (44333) *(G-153)*

Family Farm & Home Inc...419 783-1702
  1500 N Clinton St Defiance (43512) *(G-7745)*

Family Farm & Home Inc...440 307-1030
  6600 N Ridge Rd Madison (44057) *(G-10216)*

FAMILY HEALTH, Greenville Also Called: Family Hlth Svcs Drke Cnty Inc *(G-8873)*

Family Heritg Lf Insur Co Amer (HQ)..................................440 922-5222
  6001 E Royalton Rd Ste 200 Broadview Heights (44147) *(G-1389)*

Family Hlth Care NW Ohio Inc..419 238-6747
  1191 Westwood Dr Van Wert (45891) *(G-14344)*

Family Hlth Svcs Drke Cnty Inc (PA).................................937 548-3806
  5735 Meeker Rd Greenville (45331) *(G-8873)*

FAMILY HOME HEALTH PLUS, Gallipolis Also Called: Ohio Valley Home Health Inc *(G-8767)*

Family Life Center Brook Park, Cleveland Also Called: Ohioguidestone *(G-4692)*

Family Liquidation Company Inc..937 780-3075
  2754 Us Highway 22 Nw Wshngtn Ct Hs (43160) *(G-15479)*

Family Medical Care Inc..330 633-3883
  1320 Corporate Dr Ste 200 Hudson (44236) *(G-9347)*

Family Medical Ctr of Aliance...330 823-3856
  149 E Simpson St Alliance (44601) *(G-382)*

Family Medicine Residency, Toledo Also Called: Promedica Toledo Hospital *(G-13977)*

Family Medicine Stark County..330 499-5600
  6512 Whipple Ave Nw Canton (44720) *(G-1751)*

Family Motor Coach Assn Inc (PA)...................................513 474-3622
  8291 Clough Pike Cincinnati (45244) *(G-2647)*

Family Nursing Services, Chillicothe Also Called: Fns Inc *(G-2065)*

Family Physicians Inc...330 494-7099
  4860 Frank Ave Nw Canton (44720) *(G-1752)*

Family Physicians Associates (PA)..................................440 449-1014
  5187 Mayfield Rd Ste 102 Cleveland (44124) *(G-4240)*

Family Physicians of Coshocton......................................740 622-0332
  440 Browns Ln Coshocton (43812) *(G-6984)*

Family Physicians of Gahanna   **ALPHABETIC SECTION**

Family Physicians of Gahanna..614 471-9654
725 Buckles Ct N Columbus (43230) *(G-5849)*

Family Practice Associates...513 424-7291
5275 State Route 122 # 100 Franklin (45005) *(G-8636)*

Family Practice Associates...330 832-3188
2300 Wales Ave Nw Ste 100 Massillon (44646) *(G-10639)*

Family Prctice Assoc Sprngfield..937 399-6650
2701 Moorefield Rd Springfield (45502) *(G-13251)*

Family Rsource Ctr NW Ohio Inc (PA)..419 222-1168
530 S Main St Lima (45804) *(G-9889)*

Family Service (PA)...513 381-6300
3730 Glenway Ave Cincinnati (45205) *(G-2648)*

Family Service Agency, Youngstown *Also Called: Compass Family and Cmnty Svcs (G-15584)*

Family Service Association...937 222-9481
2211 Arbor Blvd Moraine (45439) *(G-11408)*

Family Service of NW Ohio (PA)...419 321-6455
701 Jefferson Ave Ste 301 Toledo (43604) *(G-13803)*

FAMILY SERVICES AND COMMUNITY, Moraine *Also Called: Family Service Association (G-11408)*

FAMILY VIOLENCE PREVENTION CEN, Xenia *Also Called: Family Vlnce Prvntion Ctr Gren (G-15506)*

Family Vlnce Prvntion Ctr Gren..937 372-4552
380 Bellbrook Ave Xenia (45385) *(G-15506)*

Family YMCA Lncster Frfeld CNT (PA)......................................740 654-0616
465 W 6th Ave Lancaster (43130) *(G-9722)*

Family YMCA of LANcstr&fairfld...740 277-7373
1180 E Locust St Lancaster (43130) *(G-9723)*

Famous Distribution Inc (HQ)..330 762-9621
2620 Ridgewood Rd Akron (44313) *(G-154)*

Famous Distribution Inc..330 434-5194
166 N Union St Akron (44304) *(G-155)*

Famous Distribution Inc..740 282-0951
934 Adams St Steubenville (43952) *(G-13323)*

Famous Enterprises Inc (PA)..330 762-9621
2620 Ridgewood Rd Ste 200 Akron (44313) *(G-156)*

Famous Industries Inc (DH)..330 535-1811
2620 Ridgewood Rd Ste 200 Akron (44313) *(G-157)*

Famous Supply, Akron *Also Called: Famous Enterprises Inc (G-156)*

Famous Supply Companies, Akron *Also Called: Famous Distribution Inc (G-154)*

Fanning Howey, Celina *Also Called: Fanning/Howey Associates Inc (G-1922)*

Fanning/Howey Associates Inc..614 764-4661
4930 Bradenton Ave Ste 200 Dublin (43017) *(G-8010)*

Fanning/Howey Associates Inc (PA)..419 586-2292
1200 Irmscher Blvd Celina (45822) *(G-1922)*

FANTON Logistics Inc (PA)..216 341-2400
10801 Broadway Ave Cleveland (44125) *(G-4241)*

Far Hills Open Mri Inc...937 435-6674
5529 Far Hills Ave Dayton (45429) *(G-7346)*

Far Hills Surgical Center LLC (PA)...937 208-8000
2400 Miami Valley Dr # 2000 Dayton (45459) *(G-7347)*

Far Oaks Orthopedists Inc (PA)...937 433-5309
6438 Wilmington Pike Ste 220 Dayton (45459) *(G-7348)*

Far Oaks Orthopedists Inc...937 433-5309
3737 Southern Blvd Ste 2100 Dayton (45429) *(G-7349)*

Far Oaks Orthopedists Inc...937 298-0452
55 Elva Ct Ste 100 Vandalia (45377) *(G-14377)*

Far West Center (PA)...440 835-6212
29133 Health Campus Dr Westlake (44145) *(G-15060)*

Farber Corporation...614 294-1626
800 E 12th Ave Columbus (43211) *(G-5850)*

Farm Credit Svcs Mid-America..740 373-8211
470 Pike St Marietta (45750) *(G-10367)*

Farm Credit Svcs Mid-America (PA)..740 335-3306
1540 Us Highway 62 Sw Wshngtn Ct Hs (43160) *(G-15480)*

Farmer Smiths Market, Dover *Also Called: Bfc Inc (G-7873)*

Farmer's and Savings Bank, Ashland *Also Called: First-Knox National Bank (G-498)*

Farmers & Merchants State Bank (HQ)......................................419 446-2501
307-11 N Defiance St Archbold (43502) *(G-457)*

Farmers & Merchants State Bank, Delta *Also Called: Farmers Merchants Bancorp Inc (G-7850)*

Farmers Citizens Bank (DH)...419 562-7040
105 Washington Sq Bucyrus (44820) *(G-1508)*

Farmers Insurance, Columbus *Also Called: Farmers Insurance Columbus Inc (G-5851)*

Farmers Insurance Columbus Inc (DH)......................................614 799-3200
7400 Skyline Dr E Columbus (43235) *(G-5851)*

Farmers Merchants Bancorp Inc (PA).......................................419 446-2501
307 N Defiance St Archbold (43502) *(G-458)*

Farmers Merchants Bancorp Inc..419 822-9510
101 Main St Delta (43515) *(G-7850)*

Farmers Nat Bnk of Canfield (HQ)..330 533-3341
20 S Broad St Canfield (44406) *(G-1628)*

Farmers Nat Bnk of Canfield..440 564-1520
8389 Mayfield Rd Ste B-1 Chesterland (44026) *(G-2035)*

Farmers National Banc Corp (PA)..330 533-3341
20 S Broad St Canfield (44406) *(G-1629)*

Farmers National Bank, Canfield *Also Called: Farmers Nat Bnk of Canfield (G-1628)*

Farmers National Bank, Chesterland *Also Called: Farmers Nat Bnk of Canfield (G-2035)*

Farmers Produce Auction, Mount Hope *Also Called: Mt Hope Auction Inc (G-11467)*

Farmers Trust Company...330 744-4351
City Ctr One Bldg Ste 700 Youngstown (44501) *(G-15610)*

Faro Services Inc (PA)..614 497-1700
7070 Pontius Rd Groveport (43125) *(G-8988)*

Farris Enterprises Inc (PA)...614 367-9611
7465 Worthington Galena Rd Ste A Worthington (43085) *(G-15416)*

Fass Management & Consulting L...330 405-0545
3705 Lee Rd Ste 1 Cleveland (44120) *(G-4242)*

Fast Switch Ltd..614 336-1122
4900 Blazer Pkwy Dublin (43017) *(G-8011)*

Fast Track It, Cincinnati *Also Called: 2mc Management LLC (G-2122)*

Fastems LLC..513 779-4614
9850 Windisch Rd West Chester (45069) *(G-14690)*

Fastenal, Chillicothe *Also Called: Optimas Oe Solutions LLC (G-2081)*

Fastener Industries Inc..440 891-2031
33 Lou Groza Blvd Berea (44017) *(G-1069)*

Fastener Tool & Supply Inc (PA)..440 248-2710
42500 Victory Pkwy Solon (44139) *(G-13086)*

Fasteners For Retail Inc (PA)...330 998-7800
8181 Darrow Rd Twinsburg (44087) *(G-14191)*

Fath Management Company..513 662-3724
2703 Erlene Dr Ofc Cincinnati (45238) *(G-2649)*

Faust Hrrlson Flker McCrthy SC..937 335-8324
12 S Cherry St Troy (45373) *(G-14135)*

Fauster-Cameron Inc (PA)...419 784-1414
1400 E 2nd St Defiance (43512) *(G-7746)*

Favret Company...614 488-5211
1296 Dublin Rd Columbus (43215) *(G-5852)*

Favret Heating & Cooling, Columbus *Also Called: Favret Company (G-5852)*

Fay Apartments, Cincinnati *Also Called: Fay Limited Partnership (G-2650)*

Fay Limited Partnership...513 542-8333
3710 President Dr Cincinnati (45225) *(G-2650)*

Fay Limited Partnership...513 241-1911
36 E 4th St # 1320 Cincinnati (45202) *(G-2651)*

Fay Sharpe LLP...216 363-9000
1228 Euclid Ave Ste 500 Cleveland (44115) *(G-4243)*

Fayette Cnty Fmly Yung MNS CHR...740 335-0477
100 Civic Dr Wshngtn Ct Hs (43160) *(G-15481)*

FAYETTE COUNTY FAMILY YMCA, Wshngtn Ct Hs *Also Called: Fayette Cnty Fmly Yung MNS CHR (G-15481)*

Fayette County Memorial Hosp (PA)..740 335-1210
1430 Columbus Ave Wshngtn Ct Hs (43160) *(G-15482)*

FAYETTE COUNTY MRDD, Wshngtn Ct Hs *Also Called: Fayette Progressive Inds Inc (G-15485)*

Fayette Hospice County Inc...740 335-0149
222 N Oakland Ave Wshngtn Ct Hs (43160) *(G-15483)*

Fayette Medical Center..740 335-1210
1430 Columbus Ave Wshngtn Ct Hs (43160) *(G-15484)*

Fayette Parts Service Inc..740 282-4547
1512 Sunset Blvd Steubenville (43952) *(G-13324)*

Fayette Parts Service Inc..724 880-3616
618 Canton Rd Wintersville (43953) *(G-15294)*

Fayette Progressive Inds Inc...740 335-7453
1330 Robinson Rd Se Wshngtn Ct Hs (43160) *(G-15485)*

ALPHABETIC SECTION — Fields Dialysis LLC

FAYETTE RECOVERY CENTER, Circleville Also Called: Pickaway Area Rcovery Svcs Inc *(G-3715)*

FBC Chemical Corporation 330 723-7780
900 W Smith Rd Medina (44256) *(G-10833)*

Fc Cincinnati Ltd 513 977-5425
14 E 4th St 3rd Fl Cincinnati (45202) *(G-2652)*

Fc Compassus LLC 380 207-1526
487 W Main St Ste B West Jefferson (43162) *(G-14850)*

FCA US LLC 419 727-7285
4400 Chrysler Dr Toledo (43608) *(G-13804)*

Fchc, Lancaster Also Called: Fairfield Community Health Ctr *(G-9710)*

Fcn Bank Corp 513 367-6111
590 Ring Rd Harrison (45030) *(G-9106)*

Fcx Performance Inc (HQ) 614 253-1996
3000 E 14th Ave Columbus (43219) *(G-5853)*

Fd Holdings LLC 614 228-5775
250 E Broad St Fl O Columbus (43215) *(G-5854)*

FDL Automation and Supply Co 937 498-2104
301 Stolle Ave Sidney (45365) *(G-13031)*

FDS Bank 513 573-2265
9111 Duke Blvd Ste 100 Mason (45040) *(G-10547)*

Fe Moran SEC Solutions LLC (DH) 217 403-6444
3800 Tabs Dr Uniontown (44685) *(G-14251)*

Feazel Roofing LLC 614 898-7663
7895 Walton Pkwy New Albany (43054) *(G-11565)*

Fechko Excavating Inc 330 722-2890
865 W Liberty St Ste 120 Medina (44256) *(G-10834)*

Fechko Excavating LLC 330 722-2890
865 W Liberty St Ste 120 Medina (44256) *(G-10835)*

Fedeli Group LLC (PA) 216 328-8080
5005 Rockside Rd Ste 500 Cleveland (44131) *(G-4244)*

Federal Card Services LLC 513 429-4459
263 Stille Dr Cincinnati (45233) *(G-2653)*

Federal Equipment Company, Cleveland Also Called: Federal Machinery & Eqp Co *(G-4245)*

Federal Express Corporation 800 463-3339
3605 Concorde Dr Vandalia (45377) *(G-14378)*

Federal Home Ln Bnk Cincinnati (PA) 513 852-7500
221 E 4th St Cincinnati (45201) *(G-2654)*

Federal Home Ln Bnk Cincinnati 513 852-5719
1000 Atrium 2 Cincinnati (45202) *(G-2655)*

Federal Machinery & Eqp Co (PA) 800 652-2466
8200 Bessemer Ave Cleveland (44127) *(G-4245)*

Federal Reserve Bank Cleveland 513 721-4787
150 E 4th St Fl 1 Cincinnati (45202) *(G-2656)*

Federal Reserve Bank Cleveland (HQ) 216 579-2000
1455 E 6th St Cleveland (44114) *(G-4246)*

FEDERAL SAVINGS BANK, West Chester Also Called: Guardian Savings Bank *(G-14702)*

Federated Auto Parts, Cuyahoga Falls Also Called: Auto Parts Center-Cuyahoga FLS *(G-7045)*

Federer Homes and Gardens RE, Dayton Also Called: Big Hill Realty Corp *(G-7193)*

Fedex, Grove City Also Called: Fedex Ground Package Sys Inc *(G-8919)*

Fedex, Hudson Also Called: Fedex Supplychain Systems Inc *(G-9348)*

Fedex, Richfield Also Called: Fedex Custom Critical Inc *(G-12698)*

Fedex, Vandalia Also Called: Federal Express Corporation *(G-14378)*

Fedex Custom Critical Inc (HQ) 234 310-4090
4205 Highlander Pkwy Richfield (44286) *(G-12698)*

Fedex Ground Package Sys Inc 800 463-3339
6120 S Meadows Dr Grove City (43123) *(G-8919)*

Fedex Supplychain Systems Inc
5455 Darrow Rd Hudson (44236) *(G-9348)*

Fedex Truckload Brokerage Inc 800 463-3339
1475 Boettler Rd Uniontown (44685) *(G-14252)*

Fedmet International Corp 440 248-9500
30403 Bruce Industrial Pkwy Solon (44139) *(G-13087)*

Feecorp Corporation (PA) 614 837-3010
7995 Allen Rd Nw Canal Winchester (43110) *(G-1606)*

Feick Contractors Inc 419 625-3241
224 E Water St Sandusky (44870) *(G-12893)*

Feintool Equipment Corporation 513 791-1118
6833 Creek Rd Blue Ash (45242) *(G-1172)*

Feli 216 421-6262
15105 Saint Clair Ave Cleveland (44110) *(G-4247)*

Feller Finch & Associates Inc (PA) 419 893-3680
1683 Woodlands Dr Ste A Maumee (43537) *(G-10724)*

Fellhauer In-Focus, Port Clinton Also Called: Fellhauer Mechanical Systems *(G-12525)*

Fellhauer Mechanical Systems 419 734-3674
2435 E Gill Rd Port Clinton (43452) *(G-12525)*

Fellows Riverside Gardens, Youngstown Also Called: Mill Creek Metropolitan Park *(G-15668)*

Fender Construction, Dayton Also Called: R L Fender Construction Co *(G-7576)*

Fenetech LLC 330 995-2830
32125 Solon Rd Ste 100 Solon (44139) *(G-13088)*

Fenton, Cincinnati Also Called: Fenton Rigging & Contg Inc *(G-2657)*

Fenton Bros Electric Co 330 343-0093
235 Ray Ave Ne New Philadelphia (44663) *(G-11651)*

Fenton Rigging & Contg Inc 513 631-5500
2150 Langdon Farm Rd Cincinnati (45237) *(G-2657)*

Fenton's Festival of Lights, New Philadelphia Also Called: Fenton Bros Electric Co *(G-11651)*

Ferenc/Lakeside Electric Inc 216 426-1880
1192 E 40th St Ste 303/305 Cleveland (44114) *(G-4248)*

Ferfolia Funeral Homes Inc 216 663-4222
356 W Aurora Rd Northfield (44067) *(G-11955)*

Ferguson Construction Company 614 876-8496
3595 Johnny Appleseed Ct Columbus (43231) *(G-5855)*

Ferguson Construction Company 937 274-1173
825 S Ludlow St Dayton (45402) *(G-7350)*

Ferguson Construction Company (PA) 937 498-2381
400 Canal St Sidney (45365) *(G-13032)*

Ferguson Enterprises LLC 513 771-6000
11860 Mosteller Rd Ste B Cincinnati (45241) *(G-2658)*

Ferguson Enterprises LLC 513 771-6566
2945 Crescentville Rd West Chester (45069) *(G-14691)*

Ferguson Hills Inc (PA) 513 539-4497
7812 Mcewen Rd Ste 200 Dayton (45459) *(G-7351)*

Ferguson Integrated Services, West Chester Also Called: Ferguson Enterprises LLC *(G-14691)*

Ferguson Supply, Cincinnati Also Called: Ferguson Enterprises LLC *(G-2658)*

Feridean Commons LLC 614 898-7488
6885 Freeman Rd Westerville (43082) *(G-14895)*

Fern Exposition Services LLC (HQ) 888 621-3376
645 Linn St Cincinnati (45203) *(G-2659)*

Ferno, Wilmington Also Called: Ferno-Washington Inc *(G-15252)*

Ferno Group Inc (PA) 937 382-1451
Weil Way 70 Wilmington (45177) *(G-15251)*

Ferno Washington, Wilmington Also Called: Ferno Group Inc *(G-15251)*

Ferno-Washington Inc (PA) 877 733-0911
70 Weil Way Wilmington (45177) *(G-15252)*

Ferragon Corporation (PA) 216 671-6161
11103 Memphis Ave Cleveland (44144) *(G-4249)*

Ferrous Metal Processing Co., Cleveland Also Called: Ferragon Corporation *(G-4249)*

Ferrous Metal Transfer Co 216 671-8500
11103 Memphis Ave Brooklyn (44144) *(G-1409)*

Ferrous Processing and Trading, Cleveland Also Called: Fpt Cleveland LLC *(G-4282)*

Ferry Cap & Set Screw Company 440 315-9291
2180 Halstead Ave Lakewood (44107) *(G-9665)*

Ferry Cap & Set Screw Company (HQ) 216 649-7400
13300 Bramley Ave Lakewood (44107) *(G-9666)*

Ferry Cap & Set Screw Company 440 783-3126
12200 Alameda Dr Strongsville (44149) *(G-13456)*

Fersenius Medical Center 330 746-2860
1340 Belmont Ave Youngstown (44504) *(G-15611)*

Festo Corporation 513 486-1050
7777 Columbia Rd Mason (45039) *(G-10548)*

Fetter Son Farms Ltd Lblty Co 740 465-2961
2421 Morral Kirkpatrick Rd W Morral (43337) *(G-11453)*

Fhs Carington Inc 440 964-8446
2217 West Ave Ashtabula (44004) *(G-535)*

Fiber Systems, Dayton Also Called: Industrial Fiberglass Spc Inc *(G-7421)*

Fidelity Health Care 937 208-6400
3170 Kettering Blvd Moraine (45439) *(G-11409)*

Fiducius 513 645-5400
151 W 4th St Ste 300 Cincinnati (45202) *(G-2660)*

Fields Dialysis LLC 513 531-2111
2300 Wall St Ste 0 Cincinnati (45212) *(G-2661)*

Fields Excavating Inc 740 532-1780
  177 Township Road 191 Kitts Hill (45645) *(G-9647)*
Fields Family Enterprises Inc 513 897-1000
  415 S Main St Waynesville (45068) *(G-14622)*
Fieldstone Limited Partnership (PA) 937 293-0900
  4000 Miller Valentine Ct Moraine (45439) *(G-11410)*
Fifth Third Bancorp (PA) 800 972-3030
  38 Fountain Square Plz Cincinnati (45263) *(G-2662)*
Fifth Third Bank, Cincinnati *Also Called: Fifth Third Bank National Assn (G-2663)*
Fifth Third Bank, Cleveland *Also Called: Fifth Third Bank of Northeastern Ohio (G-4250)*
Fifth Third Bank, Columbus *Also Called: Fifth Third Bnk of Columbus OH (G-5856)*
Fifth Third Bank, Hillsboro *Also Called: Fifth Third Bnk of Sthern OH I (G-9253)*
Fifth Third Bank, Toledo *Also Called: Fifth Third Bnk Nrthwstern Ohi (G-13805)*
Fifth Third Bank, Wilmington *Also Called: Fifth Third Bnk of Sthern OH I (G-15253)*
Fifth Third Bank National Assn (DH) 513 579-5203
  38 Fountain Square Plz Cincinnati (45202) *(G-2663)*
Fifth Third Bank National Assn 513 579-5203
  38 Fountain Square Plz Cincinnati (45263) *(G-2664)*
Fifth Third Bank of Northeastern Ohio 216 274-5533
  600 Superior Ave E Fl 5 Cleveland (44114) *(G-4250)*
Fifth Third Bnk Nrthwstern Ohi 419 259-7820
  1 Seagate Ste 2200 Toledo (43604) *(G-13805)*
Fifth Third Bnk of Columbus OH 614 744-7595
  21 E State St Columbus (43215) *(G-5856)*
Fifth Third Bnk of Sthern OH I (HQ) 937 840-5353
  511 N High St Hillsboro (45133) *(G-9253)*
Fifth Third Bnk of Sthern OH I 937 382-2620
  995 Rombach Ave Frnt Frnt Wilmington (45177) *(G-15253)*
Fifth Third Business Capital, Cincinnati *Also Called: Fifth Third Bank National Assn (G-2664)*
Fifth Third Equipment Fin Co (DH) 800 972-3030
  38 Fountain Square Plz Ste 1090a4 Cincinnati (45202) *(G-2665)*
Fifth Third Financial Corp (HQ) 513 579-5300
  38 Fountain Square Plz Cincinnati (45202) *(G-2666)*
Fifth Third Securities Inc 513 346-2775
  2998 Cunningham Rd Cincinnati (45241) *(G-2667)*
Fifth Third Securities Inc 513 272-7755
  7101 Miami Ave Cincinnati (45243) *(G-2668)*
Filling Memorial Home of Mercy (PA) 419 592-6451
  N160 State Route 108 Napoleon (43545) *(G-11522)*
Filterfresh, West Chester *Also Called: Filterfresh Coffee Service Inc (G-14811)*
Filterfresh Coffee Service Inc 513 681-8911
  4890 Duff Dr Ste D West Chester (45246) *(G-14811)*
Filtrexx International, Dover *Also Called: Conwed Plas Acquisition V LLC (G-7875)*
Final Assembly and Whse Fcilty, Edgerton *Also Called: Air-Way Manufacturing Company (G-8227)*
Finance Dept, Cleveland *Also Called: City of Cleveland (G-3978)*
Finance Dept, Cleveland *Also Called: City of Cleveland (G-3985)*
FINANCE FUND, Columbus *Also Called: Ohio Community Dev Fin Fund (G-6398)*
Financial Management Group 513 984-6696
  4665 Cornell Rd Ste 160 Blue Ash (45241) *(G-1173)*
Find Your Ohio, Columbus *Also Called: Jobsohio (G-6093)*
Findaway World LLC 330 794-7758
  354 Ely Rd Akron (44313) *(G-158)*
Findaway World LLC (PA) 440 893-0808
  31999 Aurora Rd Solon (44139) *(G-13089)*
Findlay Country Club 419 422-9263
  1500 Country Club Dr Findlay (45840) *(G-8528)*
Findlay Distribution Center, Findlay *Also Called: Kohls Department Stores Inc (G-8554)*
Findlay Inn & Conference Ctr 419 422-5682
  200 E Main Cross St Findlay (45840) *(G-8529)*
Findlay Retirement Community, Findlay *Also Called: Primrose Rtrment Cmmnities LLC (G-8578)*
FINDLAY STREET NEIGHBORHOOD, Cincinnati *Also Called: Seven Hlls Neighborhood Houses (G-3364)*
Findlay Surgery Center Ltd 419 421-4845
  1709 Medical Blvd Findlay (45840) *(G-8530)*
Findlay Truck Line Inc 419 422-1945
  106 W Front St Findlay (45840) *(G-8531)*
Findley Inc (PA) 419 255-1360
  200 N Saint Clair St Toledo (43604) *(G-13806)*

Fine Line Graphics, Columbus *Also Called: Fine Line Graphics Corp (G-5857)*
Fine Line Graphics Corp 614 486-0276
  2364 Featherwood Dr Columbus (43228) *(G-5857)*
Finelli Architectural Iron Co, Cleveland *Also Called: Finelli Ornamental Iron Co (G-4251)*
Finelli Ornamental Iron Co 440 248-0050
  30815 Solon Rd Cleveland (44139) *(G-4251)*
Finer Services, Beavercreek *Also Called: Deaton Enterprises Inc (G-877)*
Fingles Holdings LLC 419 468-5321
  5707 State Route 61 Mount Gilead (43338) *(G-11460)*
Finit Group LLC 513 793-4648
  8050 Hosbrook Rd Ste 326 Cincinnati (45236) *(G-2669)*
Finit Solutions, Cincinnati *Also Called: Finit Group LLC (G-2669)*
Finite State Inc 614 639-5107
  800 N High St Columbus (43215) *(G-5858)*
Finley's Facilities Services, Mount Gilead *Also Called: Fingles Holdings LLC (G-11460)*
Finney Law Firm LLC 513 943-6650
  4270 Ivy Pointe Blvd Ste 225 Cincinnati (45245) *(G-2104)*
Fiorilli Construction, Medina *Also Called: Fiorilli Construction Co Inc (G-10836)*
Fiorilli Construction Co Inc 216 696-5845
  1247 Medina Rd Medina (44256) *(G-10836)*
Fire Dept, Cincinnati *Also Called: Township of Colerain (G-3497)*
Fire Foe Corp 330 759-9834
  999 Trumbull Ave Girard (44420) *(G-8811)*
Fire Guard LLC 740 625-5181
  35 E Granville St Sunbury (43074) *(G-13521)*
Fire Place For Embers Only, Athens *Also Called: David R White Services Inc (G-564)*
Fire-Seal LLC 614 454-4440
  850 Science Blvd Columbus (43230) *(G-5859)*
Firefighters Cmnty Cr Un Inc 216 621-4644
  2300 Saint Clair Ave Ne Cleveland (44114) *(G-4252)*
Firefly Agency LLC 614 507-7847
  655 Metro Pl S Ste 330 Dublin (43017) *(G-8012)*
Firelands Federal Credit Union (PA) 419 483-4180
  300 North St Bellevue (44811) *(G-1044)*
Firelands Physicians Group, Sandusky *Also Called: North Coast Prof Co LLC (G-12920)*
Firelands Regional Health Sys 419 557-6161
  703 Tyler St Ste 352 Sandusky (44870) *(G-12894)*
Firelands Regional Health Sys 419 557-7455
  1912 Hayes Ave Sandusky (44870) *(G-12895)*
Firelands Regional Health Sys (PA) 419 557-7485
  1111 Hayes Ave Sandusky (44870) *(G-12896)*
Firelands Regional Health Sys 419 557-5177
  1925 Hayes Ave Sandusky (44870) *(G-12897)*
Firelands Regional Health Sys 419 626-7400
  1101 Decatur St Sandusky (44870) *(G-12898)*
Firelands Regional Medical Ctr, Sandusky *Also Called: Firelands Regional Health Sys (G-12896)*
Firelands Scientific, Huron *Also Called: Firelands Tech Ventures LLC (G-9388)*
Firelands Tech Ventures LLC 419 616-5115
  2300 University Dr E Huron (44839) *(G-9388)*
Firelnds Cnsling Recovery Svcs, Sandusky *Also Called: Firelands Regional Health Sys (G-12897)*
Firelnds Rgnal Med Ctr S Cmpus, Sandusky *Also Called: Firelands Regional Health Sys (G-12895)*
Fireproof Record Center, Grove City *Also Called: Briar-Gate Realty Inc (G-8899)*
Firestone Country Club, Akron *Also Called: Akron Management Corp (G-34)*
First Alnce Halthcare Ohio Inc 216 417-8813
  11201 Shaker Blvd Ste 308 Cleveland (44104) *(G-4253)*
First American 330 379-2320
  50 S Main St Ste 1210 Akron (44308) *(G-159)*
First American Equity Ln Svcs (DH) 800 221-8683
  1100 Superior Ave E Lbby 3 Cleveland (44114) *(G-4254)*
First Amrcn Ttle Midland Title, Cleveland *Also Called: Midland Title Security Inc (G-4578)*
First Assembly Child Care 419 529-6501
  1000 Mcpherson St Mansfield (44903) *(G-10263)*
First Assembly of God 330 836-1436
  1175 W Market St Akron (44313) *(G-160)*
First Assist Health Care LLC 440 421-9256
  5432 Mayfield Rd Ste 205 Cleveland (44124) *(G-4255)*
First Capital Enterprises Inc 740 773-2166
  505 E 7th St Chillicothe (45601) *(G-2064)*

ALPHABETIC SECTION

First Care Ohio LLC.. 513 563-8811
  955 Redna Ter Ste 1 Cincinnati (45215) *(G-2670)*

First Chice Amer Cmnty Fdral C.. 800 427-4835
  762 Canton Rd Ste 3 Steubenville (43953) *(G-13325)*

First Chice Med Stffing Ohio I (PA).. 216 521-2222
  1457 W 117th St Cleveland (44107) *(G-4256)*

First Chice Med Stffing Ohio I.. 330 867-1409
  3200 W Market St Ste 1 Fairlawn (44333) *(G-8480)*

First Chice Med Stffing Ohio I.. 419 521-2700
  90 W 2nd St Mansfield (44902) *(G-10264)*

First Chice Med Stffing Ohio I.. 419 626-9740
  1164 Cleveland Rd Sandusky (44870) *(G-12899)*

First Choice Communications... 330 439-5440
  648 Marshall St Youngstown (44502) *(G-15612)*

First Choice Homecare Inc.. 440 717-1984
  601 Towpath Trl Ste C Broadview Heights (44147) *(G-1390)*

First Choice Medical Staffing... 216 521-2222
  1457 W 117th St Cleveland (44107) *(G-4257)*

First Choice Medical Staffing... 419 861-2722
  5445 Southwyck Blvd Ste 208 Toledo (43614) *(G-13807)*

First Choice Medical Staffing, Mansfield Also Called: First Chice Med Stffing Ohio I *(G-10264)*

First Choice Packaging Inc (PA).. 419 333-4100
  1501 W State St Fremont (43420) *(G-8676)*

First Choice Packg Solutions, Fremont Also Called: First Choice Packaging Inc *(G-8676)*

First Choice Sourcing Solution.. 419 359-4002
  15757 Forest Ln Findlay (45840) *(G-8532)*

First Christian Church.. 330 445-2700
  6900 Market Ave N Canton (44721) *(G-1753)*

First Commonwealth Bank... 740 657-7000
  110 Riverbend Ave Lewis Center (43035) *(G-9820)*

First Communications, Fairlawn Also Called: First Communications LLC *(G-8481)*

First Communications LLC (PA).. 330 835-2323
  3340 W Mkt St Fairlawn (44333) *(G-8481)*

First Community Church (PA).. 614 488-0681
  1320 Cambridge Blvd Columbus (43212) *(G-5860)*

First Community Mortgage Svcs, Columbus Also Called: Union Mortgage Services Inc *(G-6802)*

First Community Village... 614 324-4455
  1800 Riverside Dr Ofc Columbus (43212) *(G-5861)*

First Ctzens Nat Bnk of Upper (PA)... 419 294-2351
  100 N Sandusky Ave Upper Sandusky (43351) *(G-14289)*

First Data Gvrnmnt Solutns Inc (DH)... 513 489-9599
  11311 Cornell Park Dr Ste 300 Blue Ash (45242) *(G-1174)*

First Day Fincl Federal Cr Un (PA).. 937 222-4546
  1030 N Main St Dayton (45405) *(G-7352)*

First Dvrsity Stffing Group In... 937 323-4114
  560 E High St Springfield (45505) *(G-13252)*

First Fdral Sav Ln Assn Lkwood (PA).. 216 221-7300
  14806 Detroit Ave Lakewood (44107) *(G-9667)*

First Fdral Sav Ln Assn Lorain (PA).. 440 282-6188
  3721 Oberlin Ave Lorain (44053) *(G-10075)*

First Fdral Sav Ln Assn Newark (PA).. 740 345-3494
  2 N 2nd St Newark (43055) *(G-11700)*

First Federal Bank of Ohio (PA).. 419 468-1518
  140 N Columbus St Galion (44833) *(G-8747)*

First Federal Credit Control... 216 360-2000
  25700 Science Park Dr Beachwood (44122) *(G-791)*

FIRST FEDERAL SAVINGS, Newark Also Called: First Fdral Sav Ln Assn Newark *(G-11700)*

First Financial.. 419 547-7733
  137 W Buckeye St Ste B Clyde (43410) *(G-5200)*

First Financial Bank... 877 322-9530
  255 E 5th St Ste 1100 Cincinnati (45202) *(G-2671)*

First Financial Bank Nat Assn (HQ)... 877 322-9530
  255 E 5th St Ste 700 Cincinnati (45202) *(G-2672)*

First Group America.. 908 281-4589
  4105 Hoffman Ave Cincinnati (45236) *(G-2673)*

First Group America, Cincinnati Also Called: First Student Inc *(G-2680)*

First Group Investment Partnr (DH).. 513 241-2200
  600 Vine St Ste 1200 Cincinnati (45202) *(G-2674)*

First Group of America, Cincinnati Also Called: Firstgroup America Inc *(G-2684)*

First Hospital Labs LLC... 215 396-5500
  6150 Oak Tree Blvd Independence (44131) *(G-9432)*

First Hospitality Company LLC.. 614 864-4555
  2826 Taylor Road Ext Reynoldsburg (43068) *(G-12663)*

First Hotel Associates LP.. 614 228-3800
  310 S High St Columbus (43215) *(G-5862)*

First Interstate Prpts Ltd.. 216 381-2900
  25333 Cedar Rd Ste 300 Cleveland (44124) *(G-4258)*

First Leveque LLC... 614 224-9500
  50 W Broad St Columbus (43215) *(G-5863)*

First Light Home Care, Chardon Also Called: Maple Grove Enterprises Inc *(G-2010)*

First Management Company... 614 885-9696
  1212 E Dublin Granville Rd Columbus (43229) *(G-5864)*

First Merchants Bank.. 614 486-9000
  2130 Tremont Ctr Upper Arlington (43221) *(G-14278)*

First Mobile Trust LLC... 855 270-3592
  2835 Miami Village Dr Ste 203 Miamisburg (45342) *(G-11055)*

First Nat Bnk of Nelsonville (PA)... 740 753-1941
  11 Public Sq Nelsonville (45764) *(G-11544)*

First National Bank, Dennison Also Called: First National Bnk of Dennison *(G-7855)*

First National Bank, Nelsonville Also Called: First Nat Bnk of Nelsonville *(G-11544)*

First National Bank, Pandora Also Called: First National Bank of Pandora *(G-12245)*

First National Bank, Waverly Also Called: First National Bank of Waverly *(G-14612)*

First National Bank of Pandora (DH)... 419 384-3221
  102 E Main St Pandora (45877) *(G-12245)*

First National Bank of Waverly (PA).. 740 947-2136
  107 N Market St Waverly (45690) *(G-14612)*

First National Bnk of Dennison (HQ)... 740 922-2532
  105 Grant St Dennison (44621) *(G-7855)*

First Ohio Banc & Lending Inc.. 216 642-8900
  6100 Rockside Woods Blvd N Cleveland (44131) *(G-4259)*

First Ohio Credit Union (PA)... 419 435-8513
  1650 N Countyline St Fostoria (44830) *(G-8615)*

First Page, Dayton Also Called: P & R Communications Svc Inc *(G-7543)*

First Place Bank.. 330 726-3396
  185 E Market St Warren (44481) *(G-14519)*

First Priority Urgent Care LLC... 937 723-7230
  1 Elizabeth Pl Ste 100 Dayton (45417) *(G-7353)*

First Realty Property MGT Ltd.. 440 720-0100
  5001 Mayfield Rd Cleveland (44124) *(G-4260)*

First Services Inc.. 513 241-2200
  600 Vine St Ste 1200 Cincinnati (45202) *(G-2675)*

First Settlement Orthopaedics (PA).. 740 373-8756
  611 2nd St Ste A Marietta (45750) *(G-10368)*

First Source Title Agency Inc.. 216 986-0970
  7717 Victory Ln Ste B North Ridgeville (44039) *(G-11927)*

First Star Logistics LLC (PA).. 812 637-3251
  11461 Northlake Dr Cincinnati (45249) *(G-2676)*

First State Bank (PA).. 937 695-0331
  19230 State Route 136 Winchester (45697) *(G-15287)*

FIRST STATE BANK, Winchester Also Called: First State Bank *(G-15287)*

First Step Recovery LLC... 330 369-8022
  2737 Youngstown Rd Se Warren (44484) *(G-14520)*

First Student, Elyria Also Called: S B S Transit Inc *(G-8292)*

First Student Inc.. 513 531-6888
  1801 Transpark Dr Cincinnati (45229) *(G-2677)*

First Student Inc.. 513 761-6100
  100 Hamilton Blvd Cincinnati (45215) *(G-2678)*

First Student Inc.. 513 554-0105
  11786 Highway Dr Cincinnati (45241) *(G-2679)*

First Student Inc.. 513 761-5136
  100 Hamilton Blvd Cincinnati (45215) *(G-2680)*

First Student Inc (PA).. 513 241-2200
  191 Rosa Parks St Ste 800 Cincinnati (45202) *(G-2681)*

First Student Inc.. 937 645-0201
  301 Gaddis Blvd Dayton (45403) *(G-7354)*

First Student Inc.. 440 284-8030
  42242 Albrecht Rd Elyria (44035) *(G-8250)*

First Student Inc.. 216 767-7600
  393 Babbitt Rd Euclid (44123) *(G-8343)*

First Student Inc.. 419 382-9915
  419 N Westwood Toledo (43607) *(G-13808)*

First Tdt LLC... 419 244-2444
  444 N Summit St Toledo (43604) *(G-13809)*

First Transit

First Transit, Cincinnati *Also Called: Firstgroup Usa Inc (G-2687)*
First Transit Inc..440 834-1020
  13571 W Spring St Burton (44021) *(G-1527)*
First Transit Inc (DH)..513 241-2200
  600 Vine St Ste 1400 Cincinnati (45202) *(G-2682)*
First Transit Inc..440 365-0224
  530 Abbe Rd S Elyria (44035) *(G-8251)*
First Transit Inc..513 524-2877
  203 S Locust St Oxford (45056) *(G-12208)*
First Transit Inc..937 652-4175
  2200 S Us Highway 68 Urbana (43078) *(G-14307)*
First Transit Inc..937 374-6402
  1180 S Patton St Xenia (45385) *(G-15507)*
First Vehicle Services Inc (DH)...........................513 241-2200
  600 Vine St Ste 1400 Cincinnati (45202) *(G-2683)*
First Virginia, Dublin *Also Called: Buckeye Check Cashing Inc (G-7948)*
First Wellington Bank Branch, Wellington *Also Called: Huntington National Bank (G-14633)*
First-Knox National Bank....................................419 289-6137
  1000 Sugarbush Dr Ashland (44805) *(G-498)*
First-Knox National Bank....................................740 694-2015
  137 N Main St Fredericktown (43019) *(G-8659)*
First-Knox National Bank (HQ)............................740 399-5500
  1 S Main St Mount Vernon (43050) *(G-11488)*
First-Knox National Division, Mount Vernon *Also Called: First-Knox National Bank (G-11488)*
Firstenergy, Akron *Also Called: Firstenergy Corp (G-161)*
FIRSTENERGY, Akron *Also Called: Jersey Central Pwr & Light Co (G-211)*
FIRSTENERGY, Akron *Also Called: Toledo Edison Company (G-335)*
Firstenergy, Stratton *Also Called: Jersey Central Pwr & Light Co (G-13407)*
Firstenergy Corp (PA)...800 736-3402
  76 S Main St Akron (44308) *(G-161)*
Firstenterprises Inc...740 369-5100
  2000 Nutter Farms Ln Delaware (43015) *(G-7797)*
Firstgroup America Inc (DH)................................513 241-2200
  191 Rosa Parks St Cincinnati (45202) *(G-2684)*
Firstgroup America Inc.......................................513 419-8611
  191 Rosa Parks St Cincinnati (45202) *(G-2685)*
Firstgroup America Inc.......................................513 241-2200
  705 Central Ave Cincinnati (45202) *(G-2686)*
Firstgroup America Inc.......................................937 372-3876
  921 Yellowstone Rd Xenia (45385) *(G-15508)*
Firstgroup Usa Inc (HQ)......................................513 241-2200
  191 Rosa Parks St Cincinnati (45202) *(G-2687)*
Firsticare Inc..614 721-2273
  3280 Morse Rd Ste 213 Columbus (43231) *(G-5865)*
FIRSTICARE INC, Columbus *Also Called: Firsticare Inc (G-5865)*
Firstlght HM Care Dblin Hliard, Worthington *Also Called: L JC Home Care LLC (G-15429)*
Firstmerit, Mansfield *Also Called: Huntington National Bank (G-10270)*
Firstmerit Bank, Akron *Also Called: Firstmerit Bank National Association (G-162)*
Firstmerit Bank, Akron *Also Called: Huntington National Bank (G-198)*
Firstmerit Bank, Chardon *Also Called: Huntington National Bank (G-2005)*
Firstmerit Bank, Galion *Also Called: Huntington National Bank (G-8749)*
Firstmerit Bank, Medina *Also Called: Huntington National Bank (G-10842)*
Firstmerit Bank National Association..................330 384-7201
  106 S Main St Fl 5 Akron (44308) *(G-162)*
Firstmerit Corporation..330 996-6300
  Iii Cascade Plz Fl 7 Akron (44308) *(G-163)*
Firstmerit Mortgage Corp...................................330 478-3400
  4455 Hills And Dales Rd Nw Canton (44708) *(G-1754)*
Fis Investor Services LLC (HQ)............................904 438-6000
  4249 Easton Way Ste 400 Columbus (43219) *(G-5866)*
Fischer Process Industries, Loveland *Also Called: Fischer Pump & Valve Company (G-10137)*
Fischer Pump & Valve Company (PA)..................513 583-4800
  155 Commerce Dr Loveland (45140) *(G-10137)*
Fishbeck Thmpson Carr Hber Inc.........................513 469-2370
  11353 Reed Hartman Hwy Ste 500 Blue Ash (45241) *(G-1175)*
Fishel Company...614 850-4400
  1600 Walcutt Rd Columbus (43228) *(G-5867)*
Fishel Company...614 921-8504
  1600 Walcutt Rd Columbus (43228) *(G-5868)*

Fishel Company (PA)..614 274-8100
  1366 Dublin Rd Columbus (43215) *(G-5869)*
Fishel Company...937 233-2268
  7651 Center Point 70 Blvd Dayton (45424) *(G-7355)*
Fishel Company...513 956-5210
  4740 Interstate Dr Ste R West Chester (45246) *(G-14812)*
Fishel Technologies, Columbus *Also Called: Fishel Company (G-5869)*
Fisher - Titus Affiliated Svcs................................419 663-1367
  12513 Us Highway 250 N Milan (44846) *(G-11205)*
Fisher - Titus Health (PA)....................................419 668-8101
  272 Benedict Ave Norwalk (44857) *(G-12010)*
Fisher Cast Steel Products Inc (PA)......................614 879-8325
  6 W Town St West Jefferson (43162) *(G-14851)*
Fisher Foods Marketing Inc (PA).........................330 497-3000
  4855 Frank Ave Nw North Canton (44720) *(G-11830)*
Fisher-Titus Medical Center.................................419 663-6464
  368 Milan Ave Ste D Norwalk (44857) *(G-12011)*
Fisher-Titus Medical Center.................................419 668-4228
  175 Shady Lane Dr Ofc Norwalk (44857) *(G-12012)*
Fisher-Titus Medical Center (PA)..........................419 668-8101
  272 Benedict Ave Norwalk (44857) *(G-12013)*
Fisher-Titus Medical Center.................................440 839-2226
  24 Hyde St Wakeman (44889) *(G-14459)*
Fisk Kinne Holdings Inc......................................937 461-9906
  403 Homestead Ave Dayton (45417) *(G-7356)*
Fit Technologies LLC..216 583-5000
  1375 Euclid Ave Cleveland (44115) *(G-4261)*
Fitch Inc (DH)..614 885-3453
  585 S Front St Ste 300 Columbus (43215) *(G-5870)*
Fitness Center, Avon *Also Called: Emh Regional Medical Center (G-650)*
Fitton Ctr For Creative Arts.................................513 863-8873
  101 S Monument Ave Hamilton (45011) *(G-9039)*
Fitton Family YMCA, Hamilton *Also Called: Great Miami Valley YMCA (G-9049)*
Fitworks Fitness & Spt Therapy, Cincinnati *Also Called: Fitworks Holding LLC (G-2689)*
Fitworks Holding LLC...513 923-9931
  5840 Cheviot Rd Cincinnati (45247) *(G-2688)*
Fitworks Holding LLC...513 531-1500
  4600 Smith Rd Ste G Cincinnati (45212) *(G-2689)*
Fitworks Holding LLC...440 842-1499
  8555 Day Dr Cleveland (44129) *(G-4262)*
Fitworks Holding LLC...440 333-4141
  20001 Center Ridge Rd Rocky River (44116) *(G-12741)*
Fitworks Holding LLC...330 688-2329
  4301 Kent Rd Ste 26 Stow (44224) *(G-13368)*
Fitzenrider Inc..419 784-0828
  827 Perry St Defiance (43512) *(G-7747)*
Five Cfc Inc...937 578-3271
  6416 Pullman Dr Lewis Center (43035) *(G-9821)*
Five Rivers Metroparks......................................937 278-2601
  2222 N James H Mcgee Blvd Dayton (45417) *(G-7357)*
Five Rivers Metroparks......................................937 228-2088
  600 E 2nd St Dayton (45402) *(G-7358)*
Five Seasons Landscape MGT Inc.......................740 964-2915
  9886 Mink St Sw Rear Etna (43068) *(G-8329)*
Five Star Senior Living Inc..................................614 451-6793
  4590 Knightsbridge Blvd Columbus (43214) *(G-5871)*
Flag City Exterior Wash, Findlay *Also Called: Napoleon Wash-N-Fill Inc (G-8572)*
Flag City Mack, Findlay *Also Called: Bulldawg Holdings LLC (G-8519)*
Flagel Huber Flagel & Co (PA)............................937 299-3400
  3400 S Dixie Dr Moraine (45439) *(G-11411)*
Flagship Trading Corporation
  734 Alpha Dr Ste J Cleveland (44143) *(G-4263)*
Flairsoft Ltd (PA)...614 888-0700
  7720 Rivers Edge Dr Ste 200 Columbus (43235) *(G-5872)*
Flamos Enterprises Inc......................................330 478-0009
  1501 Raff Rd Sw Ste 1 Canton (44710) *(G-1755)*
Flanagan Lberman Hoffman Swaim....................937 223-5200
  10 N Ludlow St Ste 200 Dayton (45402) *(G-7359)*
Flannery Georgalis LLC......................................216 367-2095
  1301 E 9th St Ste 3500 Cleveland (44114) *(G-4264)*
Flashhouse Inc..216 600-0504
  29225 Chagrin Blvd Ste 300 Beachwood (44122) *(G-792)*

ALPHABETIC SECTION — Forest City Properties LLC

Flat Rock Care Center.. 419 483-7330
7353 County Rd 29 Flat Rock (44828) *(G-8600)*

Flawless Janitorial LLC... 216 266-1425
5165 Joseph St Maple Heights (44137) *(G-10338)*

Fleet Management Institute, Cincinnati Also Called: Nuerological & Sleep Disorders *(G-3134)*

Fleet Operations, Toledo Also Called: City of Toledo *(G-13737)*

Fleet Response, Hudson Also Called: Rental Concepts Inc *(G-9370)*

Fleet Team... 614 699-2500
1425 Valley Belt Rd Brooklyn Heights (44131) *(G-1418)*

Fleetmaster Express Inc.. 419 420-1835
1531 Harvard Ave Findlay (45840) *(G-8533)*

Fleetpride Inc.. 740 282-2711
620 South St Steubenville (43952) *(G-13326)*

Fleming Heating S/M & Roofing, Zanesville Also Called: Hartley Company *(G-15798)*

Fleming Leasing LLC... 703 842-1358
1500 Trumbull Ave Girard (44420) *(G-8812)*

Flex Technologies Inc.. 330 897-6311
3430 State Route 93 Baltic (43804) *(G-688)*

Flex-N-Gate, Sandusky Also Called: Visteon Corporation *(G-12940)*

Flex-Temp Employment Svcs Inc............................. 419 355-9675
524 W State St Fremont (43420) *(G-8677)*

Flexential Corp.. 513 645-2900
5307 Mulhauser Rd Hamilton (45011) *(G-9040)*

Flexjet, Cleveland Also Called: Flexjet LLC *(G-4265)*

Flexjet Inc... 866 309-2214
355 Richmond Rd Richmond Heights (44143) *(G-12718)*

Flexjet LLC (HQ).. 216 261-3880
26180 Curtiss Wright Pkwy Cleveland (44143) *(G-4265)*

Flexsys America, Akron Also Called: Flexsys America LP *(G-164)*

Flexsys America LP (HQ)... 330 666-4111
260 Springside Dr Akron (44333) *(G-164)*

Flexsys Inc (PA)... 212 605-6000
260 Springside Dr Akron (44333) *(G-165)*

Flick Lumber Co Inc... 419 468-6278
340 S Columbus St Galion (44833) *(G-8748)*

Flick Packaging, Galion Also Called: Flick Lumber Co Inc *(G-8748)*

Flight Express Inc (HQ)... 305 379-8686
7250 Star Check Dr Columbus (43217) *(G-5873)*

Flight Options Inc (PA).. 216 261-3880
26180 Curtiss Wright Pkwy Richmond Heights (44143) *(G-12719)*

Flight Options LLC (HQ).. 216 261-3500
26180 Curtiss Wright Pkwy Cleveland (44143) *(G-4266)*

Flight Options Intl Inc (HQ)....................................... 216 261-3500
355 Richmond Rd Richmond Heights (44143) *(G-12720)*

Flint Ridge Nursing & Rehab, Newark Also Called: Genertion Hlth Rhblttion Ctr L *(G-11701)*

Flooring Specialties Div, Cleveland Also Called: Frank Novak & Sons Inc *(G-4285)*

Flow Control Technology, Cincinnati Also Called: Interstop Corporation *(G-2884)*

Flower Factory Inc... 330 494-7978
5655 Whipple Ave Nw North Canton (44720) *(G-11831)*

Flower Factory Super Store, North Canton Also Called: Flower Factory Inc *(G-11831)*

Flower Hospital (HQ)... 419 824-1444
5200 Harroun Rd Sylvania (43560) *(G-13544)*

Flower Hospital.. 419 824-1000
5100 Harroun Rd Sylvania (43560) *(G-13545)*

Flowers Baking Co Ohio LLC................................... 419 661-2586
8071 Wales Rd Northwood (43619) *(G-11974)*

Floyd Bell Inc (PA).. 614 294-4000
720 Dearborn Park Ln Columbus (43085) *(G-5874)*

Floyd Browne Group, Columbus Also Called: Floyd Browne International Ltd *(G-5875)*

Floyd Browne International Ltd............................... 740 363-6792
7965 N High St Ste 340 Columbus (43235) *(G-5875)*

Fluid Line Products Inc.. 440 946-9470
38273 Western Pkwy Willoughby (44094) *(G-15193)*

Fluid Power Components, Franklin Also Called: Eagle Equipment Corporation *(G-8635)*

Fluor-Bwxt Portsmouth LLC..................................... 866 706-6992
3930 Us Highway 23 Anx Piketon (45661) *(G-12419)*

Flush Payment, Symmes Township Also Called: Payrix Solutions LLC *(G-13580)*

Flux Staffing, Cuyahoga Falls Also Called: Ado Staffing Inc *(G-7032)*

Flying Pig Logistics Inc... 513 300-9331
9047 Sutton Pl West Chester (45011) *(G-14692)*

Flynn Crtif Pub Accntnts PSC I................................. 513 530-9200
7800 E Kemper Rd Ste 150 Cincinnati (45249) *(G-2690)*

FM 91 Point 5, Bainbridge Also Called: Wkhr Radio Inc *(G-687)*

FMI Medical Systems Inc.. 440 600-5952
29001 Solon Rd Unit A Solon (44139) *(G-13090)*

Fms Construction Company..................................... 330 225-9320
13821 Progress Pkwy North Royalton (44133) *(G-11940)*

Fnb Inc (PA)... 740 922-2532
105 Grant St Dennison (44621) *(G-7856)*

Fns Inc... 740 775-5463
24 Star Dr Chillicothe (45601) *(G-2065)*

Foam Pac Materials Company, West Chester Also Called: Storopack Inc *(G-14834)*

Foam Seal, Cleveland Also Called: Novagard Solutions Inc *(G-4668)*

Focus Healthcare of Ohio LLC................................. 419 891-9333
1725 Timber Line Rd Maumee (43537) *(G-10725)*

Focus On Youth Inc... 513 644-1030
8904 Brookside Ave West Chester (45069) *(G-14693)*

Focuscfo LLC... 614 944-5760
575 Charring Cross Dr Ste 102 Westerville (43081) *(G-14979)*

Foe 2233, Bryan Also Called: Mansfield Ohio Arie No 336 Frtn *(G-1487)*

Foe 370, Lima Also Called: Grand Aerie of The Fraternal *(G-9892)*

Foill Inc.. 740 947-1117
201 E North St Waverly (45690) *(G-14613)*

Fojournerf Title Agency, Cincinnati Also Called: Reisenfeld & Assoc Lpa LLC *(G-3283)*

Fontaine Bleu', Cleveland Also Called: Mfbusiness Group *(G-4570)*

Food Safety Net Services Ltd.................................. 614 274-2070
4130 Fisher Rd Columbus (43228) *(G-5876)*

Food Sample Express LLc....................................... 330 225-3550
2945 Carquest Dr Brunswick (44212) *(G-1456)*

Foodbank Inc... 937 461-0265
56 Armor Pl Dayton (45417) *(G-7360)*

Foodliner Inc.. 937 898-0075
5560 Brentlinger Dr Dayton (45414) *(G-7361)*

Foor Concrete Co Inc (PA).. 740 513-4346
5361 State Route 37 E Delaware (43015) *(G-7798)*

For Hire Carrier, Cincinnati Also Called: Hc Transport Inc *(G-2807)*

For Impact Suddes Gro... 614 352-2505
1500 Lake Shore Dr Columbus (43204) *(G-5877)*

For Women Like Me Inc (PA).................................... 407 848-7339
46 Shopping Plz Ste 155 Chagrin Falls (44022) *(G-1958)*

For Women Like Me Inc.. 407 848-7339
8800 Woodland Ave Cleveland (44104) *(G-4267)*

Forcht Bancorp Inc... 513 231-7871
2110 Beechmont Ave Cincinnati (45230) *(G-2691)*

Forcht Bank, Cincinnati Also Called: Forcht Bank National Assn *(G-2692)*

Forcht Bank National Assn...................................... 513 231-7871
3549 Columbia Pkwy Cincinnati (45226) *(G-2692)*

Ford, Dover Also Called: Harry Humphries Auto City Inc *(G-7888)*

Ford, Mason Also Called: Ford Motor Company *(G-10549)*

Ford, Ontario Also Called: Graham Chevrolet-Cadillac Co *(G-12105)*

Ford Development Corp (PA)................................... 513 772-1521
11148 Woodward Ln Cincinnati (45241) *(G-2693)*

Ford Development Corp... 513 207-9118
11260 Chester Rd Ste 100 Cincinnati (45246) *(G-2694)*

Ford Development Real Estate, Cincinnati Also Called: Ford Development Corp *(G-2694)*

Ford Motor Company.. 513 573-1101
4680 Parkway Dr Ste 420 Mason (45040) *(G-10549)*

Ford Rental System, Fostoria Also Called: Reineke Ford Inc *(G-8622)*

Foresight Corporation.. 614 791-1600
655 Metro Pl S Ste 900 Dublin (43017) *(G-8013)*

Forest City Commercial MGT Inc............................ 216 696-7701
1228 Euclid Ave Ste 151 Cleveland (44115) *(G-4268)*

Forest City Commercial MGT Inc (DH)................... 216 621-6060
50 Public Sq Apt 1410 Cleveland (44113) *(G-4269)*

Forest City Commercial MGT Inc............................ 216 623-4750
230 W Huron Rd Ofc Ofc Cleveland (44113) *(G-4270)*

Forest City Enterprises LP (HQ)............................. 216 621-6060
127 Public Sq Ste 3200 Cleveland (44114) *(G-4271)*

Forest City Properties LLC (DH)............................ 216 621-6060
127 Public Sq Ste 3100 Cleveland (44114) *(G-4272)*

Forest City Realty Trust Inc 216 621-6060
127 Public Sq Ste 3100 Cleveland (44114) *(G-4273)*

Forest City Residential Dev 440 888-8664
9233 Independence Blvd Apt 114 Cleveland (44130) *(G-4274)*

Forest City Residential Dev (DH) 216 621-6060
1170 Terminal Tower 50 Public Square Cleveland (44113) *(G-4275)*

Forest Cy Residential MGT Inc (DH) 216 621-6060
50 Public Sq Ste 1200 Cleveland (44113) *(G-4276)*

Forest Fair Mall, Cincinnati *Also Called: Mills Corporation (G-3065)*

Forest Hill Retirement Cmnty, Saint Clairsville *Also Called: Zandex Health Care Corporation (G-12823)*

Forest Hills Care Center, Cincinnati *Also Called: Beechwood Terrace Care Ctr Inc (G-2252)*

FOREST HILLS CENTER, Columbus *Also Called: Serenity Center Inc (G-6663)*

Forest Park Christian School 614 888-5282
5600 Karl Rd Columbus (43229) *(G-5878)*

Forest View Care Rhbltttion Ctr, Dayton *Also Called: Harborside Dayton Ltd Partnr (G-7396)*

Forevergreen Lawn Care 440 327-8987
38601 Sugar Ridge Rd North Ridgeville (44039) *(G-11928)*

Forevergreen Lawn Care Inc 440 376-7515
1313 Taylor St Elyria (44035) *(G-8252)*

Forge LLC 937 461-6560
15 N Main St Bellbrook (45305) *(G-1016)*

Forge Industries Inc (PA) 330 960-2468
4450 Market St Youngstown (44512) *(G-15613)*

Forklift of Toledo, Toledo *Also Called: Towlift Inc (G-14072)*

Formation V Consulting, Beachwood *Also Called: World Synergy Enterprises Inc (G-852)*

Formfire, Cleveland *Also Called: Formfire LLC (G-4277)*

Formfire LLC 866 448-2302
1100 Superior Ave E Ste 1650 Cleveland (44114) *(G-4277)*

Formlabs Ohio Inc 419 837-9783
27800 Lemoyne Rd Ste J Millbury (43447) *(G-11268)*

Formu3 International Inc (PA) 330 668-1461
395 Springside Dr Akron (44333) *(G-166)*

Forney Industries Inc 937 494-6102
3435 Stop 8 Rd Dayton (45414) *(G-7362)*

Forrest Trucking Company 614 879-8642
540 Taylor Blair Rd West Jefferson (43162) *(G-14852)*

Fort Amanda Specialties LLC 419 229-0088
1747 Fort Amanda Rd Lima (45804) *(G-9890)*

Fort Hamilton Hospital (DH) 513 867-2000
630 Eaton Ave Hamilton (45013) *(G-9041)*

Fort Hamilton Hospital 513 867-2382
630 Eaton Ave Hamilton (45013) *(G-9042)*

Fort Hamilton Hospital 513 867-2280
630 Eaton Ave Hamilton (45013) *(G-9043)*

Fort Recovery Equity Inc 419 942-1148
5458 State Route 49 Fort Recovery (45846) *(G-8608)*

Fort Recovery Equity Inc (PA) 419 375-4119
2351 Wabash Rd Fort Recovery (45846) *(G-8609)*

Fort Wash Inv Advisors Inc (DH) 513 361-7600
303 Broadway St Ste 1100 Cincinnati (45202) *(G-2695)*

Forte Industrial Equipment Systems Inc 513 398-2800
6037 Commerce Ct Mason (45040) *(G-10550)*

Forte Industries, Mason *Also Called: Forte Industrial Equipment Systems Inc (G-10550)*

Fortec Fibers Inc 800 963-7101
6245 Hudson Crossing Pkwy Hudson (44236) *(G-9349)*

Fortec Medical Inc (PA) 330 463-1265
6245 Hudson Crossing Pkwy Hudson (44236) *(G-9350)*

Fortis Energy Services Inc 248 283-7100
66999 Executive Dr Saint Clairsville (43950) *(G-12792)*

Fortney & Weygandt, North Olmsted *Also Called: R L Fortney Management Inc (G-11912)*

Fortney & Weygandt Inc 440 716-4000
31269 Bradley Rd North Olmsted (44070) *(G-11901)*

Fortuna Construction Co Inc 440 892-3834
3133 Waterfall Way Cleveland (44145) *(G-4278)*

Fortune Brands Windows Inc (DH) 614 532-3500
3948 Townsfair Way Ste 200 Columbus (43219) *(G-5879)*

Fortune Brnds Wtr Innvtons LLC 440 962-2782
25300 Al Moen Dr North Olmsted (44070) *(G-11902)*

Forum At Knightsbridge, Columbus *Also Called: Five Star Senior Living Inc (G-5871)*

Forum At Knightsbridge, Columbus *Also Called: Sunrise Connecticut Ave Assn (G-6730)*

Forum Health 330 841-9011
1350 E Market St 302 Warren (44483) *(G-14521)*

Forum Health At Home-Hospice, Warren *Also Called: Visiting Nrse Assn Hspice Nrth (G-14572)*

Forum Manufacturing Inc 937 349-8685
77 Brown St Milford Center (43045) *(G-11265)*

Forvis LLP 330 650-1752
102 1st St Ste 201 Hudson (44236) *(G-9351)*

Fosbel Holding Inc (HQ) 216 362-3900
20600 Sheldon Rd Cleveland (44142) *(G-4279)*

Fosbel Wahl Holdings LLC 419 334-2650
767 S State Route 19 Fremont (43420) *(G-8678)*

Fosdick & Hilmer Inc 513 241-5640
525 Vine St Ste 1100 Cincinnati (45202) *(G-2696)*

Foster & Motley Inc 513 561-6640
7755 Montgomery Rd Ste 100 Cincinnati (45236) *(G-2697)*

Fostoria Hospital Association 419 435-7734
501 Van Buren St Fostoria (44830) *(G-8616)*

Foti Contracting LLC 330 656-3454
1164 Lloyd Rd Wickliffe (44092) *(G-15149)*

Fotosav Inc 330 436-6500
1479 Exeter Rd Akron (44306) *(G-167)*

Foundation Pk Alzheimers Care, Toledo *Also Called: Tlevay Inc (G-14046)*

Foundation Software LLC (PA) 330 220-8383
17999 Foltz Pkwy Strongsville (44149) *(G-13457)*

Foundation Steel, Swanton *Also Called: Foundation Steel LLC (G-13525)*

Foundation Steel LLC 419 402-4241
12525 Airport Hwy Swanton (43558) *(G-13525)*

Founders Service & Mfg Inc 330 584-7759
10535 12th St North Benton (44449) *(G-11805)*

Foundtion For Cmnty Blood Cntr (PA) 937 461-3450
349 S Main St Dayton (45402) *(G-7363)*

Foundtion Srgery Afflate Mddlb 440 743-8400
15345 Bagley Rd Middleburg Heights (44130) *(G-11115)*

Foundtons Bhvral Hlth Svcs Inc 419 584-1000
4761 State Route 29 Celina (45822) *(G-1923)*

Fountain Square MGT Group LLC 513 621-4400
1203 Walnut St 4th Fl Cincinnati (45202) *(G-2698)*

Fountains At Canterbury 405 751-3600
4500 Dorr St Toledo (43615) *(G-13810)*

Fountains At Canterbury, Toledo *Also Called: Watermark Rtrment Cmmnties Inc (G-14098)*

Four Bridges Country Club Ltd 513 759-4620
8300 Four Bridges Dr Liberty Township (45044) *(G-9852)*

Four Entertainment Group 513 721-0083
1502 Vine St Cincinnati (45202) *(G-2699)*

Four O Corporation (DH) 513 941-2800
9395 Kenwood Rd Blue Ash (45242) *(G-1176)*

Four Pnts By Shrton Clmbus Ohi, Columbus *Also Called: Vjp Hospitality Ltd (G-6853)*

Four Seasons Washington LLC 740 895-6101
201 Courthouse Pkwy Wshngtn Ct Hs (43160) *(G-15486)*

Four Wheel Drive Hardware LLC 330 482-4733
44488 State Route 14 Columbiana (44408) *(G-5235)*

Four Winds Nursing Facility, Jackson *Also Called: United Church Homes Inc (G-9527)*

Fowler Company, The, Oakwood Village *Also Called: Rgt Services LLC (G-12056)*

Fowler Electric Co 440 735-2385
26185 Broadway Ave Bedford (44146) *(G-960)*

Fowler, Gary J DDS Ms, Celina *Also Called: Orthodontic Associates LLC (G-1929)*

Fox 419 352-1673
1010 N Main St Bowling Green (43402) *(G-1320)*

Fox 8, Cleveland *Also Called: Fox Television Stations Inc (G-4281)*

Fox Cleaners Inc (PA) 937 276-4171
4333 N Main St Dayton (45405) *(G-7364)*

Fox Enterprise Services, North Canton *Also Called: Rock Homes Inc (G-11859)*

Fox Hunt Apts, Dayton *Also Called: Realmark Property Investors (G-7582)*

Fox International Limited Inc 216 454-1001
23645 Mercantile Rd Ste B Beachwood (44122) *(G-793)*

Fox Run Apartments, Moraine *Also Called: Fieldstone Limited Partnership (G-11410)*

Fox Run Ctr For Chldren Adlscn, Saint Clairsville *Also Called: Bhc Fox Run Hospital Inc (G-12781)*

ALPHABETIC SECTION — Freedom Rv

Fox Run Manor, Findlay Also Called: Hcf of Findlay Inc *(G-8545)*
Fox Services Inc 513 858-2022
4660 Industry Dr Fairfield (45014) *(G-8414)*
Fox Sports Net Ohio LLC 216 415-3300
200 Public Sq Ste 2510 Cleveland (44114) *(G-4280)*
Fox Television Stations Inc 216 431-8888
5800 S Marginal Rd Cleveland (44103) *(G-4281)*
Foxhire LLC 330 454-3508
4883 Dressler Rd Nw Ste 103 Canton (44718) *(G-1756)*
Foxtail Foods LLC 973 582-4613
6880 Fairfield Business Ctr Fairfield (45014) *(G-8415)*
Foxtrot Aviation Services LLC 330 806-7477
5440 Fulton Dr Nw Ste 201 Canton (44718) *(G-1757)*
Fpt Cleveland LLC (DH) 216 441-3800
8550 Aetna Rd Cleveland (44105) *(G-4282)*
Fraley & Schilling Inc 740 598-4118
708 Dandy Ln Brilliant (43913) *(G-1380)*
Frameco, Cleveland Also Called: Metal Framing Enterprises LLC *(G-4558)*
Framework Mi Inc 513 444-2165
9435 Waterstone Blvd Ste 140 Cincinnati (45249) *(G-2700)*
Franchise Group Inc (HQ) 740 363-2222
109 Innovation Ct Ste J Delaware (43015) *(G-7799)*
Francis C Skinner Painting Svc 937 773-3858
4633 W State Route 36 Piqua (45356) *(G-12442)*
Francis-Schulze Co 937 295-3941
3880 Rangeline Rd Russia (45363) *(G-12770)*
Franciscan At St Leonard 937 433-0480
8100 Clyo Rd Dayton (45458) *(G-7365)*
Franciscan Care Ctr Sylvania 419 882-2087
4111 N Holland Sylvania Rd Toledo (43623) *(G-13811)*
Franciscan Sisters of Chicago 440 843-7800
6765 State Rd Cleveland (44134) *(G-4283)*
Franck and Fric Incorporated 216 524-4451
7919 Old Rockside Rd Cleveland (44131) *(G-4284)*
Frank Brunckhorst Co LLC 614 662-5300
2225 Spiegel Dr Groveport (43125) *(G-8989)*
Frank Gates Service Company (DH) 614 793-8000
5000 Bradenton Ave Ste 100 Dublin (43017) *(G-8014)*
Frank Messer & Sons Cnstr Co, Cincinnati Also Called: Messer Construction Co *(G-3050)*
Frank Novak & Sons Inc 216 475-2495
23940 Miles Rd Cleveland (44128) *(G-4285)*
Frank Santo LLC 216 831-9374
31100 Pinetree Rd Ste 100 Pepper Pike (44124) *(G-12299)*
Frankel Dental 419 474-9611
5012 Talmadge Rd Ste 100 Toledo (43623) *(G-13812)*
Franklin City Schools 937 743-8670
136 E 6th St Franklin (45005) *(G-8637)*
Franklin Cmpt Svcs Group Inc 614 431-3327
6650 Walnut St New Albany (43054) *(G-11566)*
Franklin Cnty Bd Commissioners 614 462-3800
373 S High St Fl 2 Columbus (43215) *(G-5880)*
Franklin Cnty Bd Commissioners 614 261-3196
1855 E Dublin Granville Rd Ste 204 Columbus (43229) *(G-5881)*
Franklin Cnty Bd Commissioners 614 462-3275
80 E Fulton St Columbus (43215) *(G-5882)*
Franklin Cnty Bd Commissioners 614 229-7100
4071 E Main St Columbus (43213) *(G-5883)*
Franklin Cnty Bd Commissioners 614 275-2571
855 W Mound St Columbus (43223) *(G-5884)*
Franklin Cnty Bd Commissioners 614 525-3100
280 E Broad St Rm 201 Columbus (43215) *(G-5885)*
Franklin Communications Inc 614 459-9769
4401 Carriage Hill Ln Columbus (43220) *(G-5886)*
Franklin County Adamh Board 614 224-1057
447 E Broad St Columbus (43215) *(G-5887)*
Franklin County Childrens Svcs, Columbus Also Called: Franklin Cnty Bd Commissioners *(G-5883)*
Franklin County Coal Company 740 338-3100
46226 National Rd Saint Clairsville (43950) *(G-12793)*
Franklin County Historical Soc 614 228-2674
333 W Broad St Columbus (43215) *(G-5888)*

Franklin County Public Health 614 525-3160
280 E Broad St Rm 200 Columbus (43215) *(G-5889)*
Franklin County Sani Engg Dept, Columbus Also Called: Franklin Cnty Bd Commissioners *(G-5885)*
Franklin Crossing Oh LP 216 520-1250
1214 Anita Dr Kent (44240) *(G-9575)*
Franklin Equipment, Dayton Also Called: Franklin Equipment LLC *(G-7366)*
Franklin Equipment LLC 937 951-3819
1500 Kuntz Rd Dayton (45404) *(G-7366)*
Franklin Equipment LLC 614 389-2161
7570 Fishel Dr S Dublin (43016) *(G-8015)*
Franklin Equipment LLC (HQ) 614 228-2014
4141 Hamilton Square Blvd Groveport (43125) *(G-8990)*
Franklin Equipment LLC 513 893-9105
4764 Ashley Dr West Chester (45011) *(G-14694)*
Franklin Equipment LLC 614 948-3409
5755 Westerville Rd Westerville (43081) *(G-14980)*
Franklin Iron & Metal Corp 937 253-8184
1939 E 1st St Dayton (45403) *(G-7367)*
Franklin Park Pediatrics, Toledo Also Called: Mercy Hlth - St Vncent Med Ctr *(G-13920)*
Franklin Ridge Care Facility, Franklin Also Called: Carington Health Systems *(G-8632)*
Franklin Ridge Care Facility, Hamilton Also Called: Carington Health Systems *(G-9025)*
FRANKLIN RIDGE CARE FACILITY, Madison Also Called: Madison Care Inc *(G-10220)*
Franklin Works Inc 361 215-2300
1563 Westbelt Dr Columbus (43228) *(G-5890)*
Franklinton Dental Group, Columbus Also Called: Dental Group At North Hamilton *(G-5755)*
Frantz Ward LLP 216 515-1660
200 Public Sq Ste 3020 Cleveland (44114) *(G-4286)*
Fraternal Insurance, Columbus Also Called: Order of Untd Coml Trvlers of *(G-6479)*
Fraternal Order of Plice of OH (PA) 614 224-5700
222 E Town St Fl 1e Columbus (43215) *(G-5891)*
Frch Design Worldwide - Cincin 513 241-3000
311 Elm St Ste 600 Cincinnati (45202) *(G-2701)*
Fred A Nemann Co 513 467-9400
6480 Bender Rd Cincinnati (45233) *(G-2702)*
Fred Christen & Sons Company (PA) 419 243-4161
714 George St Toledo (43608) *(G-13813)*
Fred Crdnal Athc Schlrship Fun 812 801-7641
39 20th St Sw Barberton (44203) *(G-697)*
Fred Martin Nissan LLC 330 644-8888
3388 S Arlington Rd Akron (44312) *(G-168)*
Fred Olivieri Construction Co (PA) 330 494-1007
6315 Promway Ave Nw North Canton (44720) *(G-11832)*
Fred Olivieri Construction Co, North Canton Also Called: Fred Olivieri Construction Co *(G-11832)*
Fred W Albrecht Grocery Co 330 666-6781
3979 Medina Rd Akron (44333) *(G-169)*
Fred W Albrecht Grocery Co 330 645-6222
3235 Manchester Rd Unit A Coventry Township (44319) *(G-7008)*
Frederick C Smith Clinic Inc (HQ) 740 383-7000
1040 Delaware Ave Marion (43302) *(G-10427)*
Frederick Steel Company LLC 513 821-6400
630 Glendale Milford Rd Cincinnati (45215) *(G-2703)*
Fredrick Frdrick Hller Engners 440 546-9696
672 E Royalton Rd Cleveland (44147) *(G-4287)*
Fredrics Corporation (PA) 513 874-2226
7664 Voice Of America Centre Dr West Chester (45069) *(G-14695)*
Free Store/Food Bank Inc (PA) 513 482-4526
3401 Rosenthal Way Cincinnati (45204) *(G-2704)*
Free Store/Food Bank Inc 513 241-1064
3401 Rosenthal Way Cincinnati (45204) *(G-2705)*
Freedom Caregivers 567 560-8277
1069 Lexington Ave # B Mansfield (44907) *(G-10265)*
FREEDOM CENTER, Cincinnati Also Called: National Undgrd RR Frdom Ctr I *(G-3098)*
Freedom Center, Columbus Also Called: Ohio Department Youth Services *(G-6403)*
Freedom Construction Entps Inc 740 255-5818
60500 Patch Rd New Concord (43762) *(G-11610)*
Freedom Recovery LLC 614 754-8051
4998 W Broad St Ste 104 Columbus (43228) *(G-5892)*
Freedom Rv, Akron Also Called: Sirpilla Recrtl Vhcl Ctr Inc *(G-303)*

Freedom Specialty Insurance Co (DH) 614 249-1545
  1 W Nationwide Blvd Columbus (43215) *(G-5893)*
Freedom Usa Inc 216 503-6374
  2045 Midway Dr Twinsburg (44087) *(G-14192)*
Freedonia Publishing LLC 440 684-9600
  767 Beta Dr Cleveland (44143) *(G-4288)*
Freeland Contracting Co 614 443-2718
  2100 Integrity Dr S Columbus (43209) *(G-5894)*
Freeman Manufacturing & Sup Co (PA) 440 934-1902
  1101 Moore Rd Avon (44011) *(G-651)*
Freeman Schwabe Machinery LLC 513 947-2888
  4064 Clough Woods Dr Batavia (45103) *(G-740)*
Freestore Foodbank Inc 513 482-4500
  3401 Rosenthal Way Cincinnati (45204) *(G-2706)*
Freking Myers & Reul LLC 513 721-1975
  600 Vine St Ste 900 Cincinnati (45202) *(G-2707)*
Fremont City Schools 419 332-6454
  1100 North St Fremont (43420) *(G-8679)*
Fremont City Schools, Fremont *Also Called: Fremont City Schools (G-8679)*
Fremont Logistics LLC 419 333-0669
  1301 Heinz Rd Fremont (43420) *(G-8680)*
Fremont Plant Operations, Fremont *Also Called: Goodwill Inds Erie Hron Ottawa (G-8683)*
Fremont TMC Head Start, Fremont *Also Called: Great Lkes Cmnty Action Partnr (G-8685)*
French Company LLC 330 963-4344
  8289 Darrow Rd Twinsburg (44087) *(G-14193)*
Frenchies of Ig LLC 513 445-2841
  8730 Cincinnati Dayton Rd Apt 1001 West Chester (45069) *(G-14696)*
Fresenius Kdney Care S Grove C, Grove City *Also Called: Fresenius Med Care S Grove Cy (G-8920)*
Fresenius Kdney Care W Hmilton, Hamilton *Also Called: Fresenius Med Care Butler Cty (G-9044)*
Fresenius Kdney Care Wlmngton, Wilmington *Also Called: Fresenius Med Care Wlmngton HM (G-15254)*
FRESENIUS KIDNEY CARE MILFORD, Milford *Also Called: Fresenius Med Care Milford LLC (G-11228)*
Fresenius Med Care Butler Cty 513 737-1415
  890 Nw Washington Blvd Hamilton (45013) *(G-9044)*
Fresenius Med Care Milford LLC 513 248-1690
  5890 Meadow Creek Dr Milford (45150) *(G-11228)*
Fresenius Med Care S Grove Cy 614 801-2505
  5775 N Meadows Dr Ste B Grove City (43123) *(G-8920)*
Fresenius Med Care Wlmngton HM 937 382-3379
  164 Holiday Dr Wilmington (45177) *(G-15254)*
Fresenius Vascular Care Inc 513 351-2494
  4600 Smith Rd Norwood (45212) *(G-12033)*
Fresh and Limited, Sidney *Also Called: Freshway Foods Company Inc (G-13034)*
Fresh Coat Painters, Montgomery *Also Called: F C Franchising Systems Inc (G-11368)*
Fresh Mark Inc 330 833-9870
  950 Cloverleaf St Se Massillon (44646) *(G-10640)*
Fresh Mark Inc (PA) 330 832-7491
  1888 Southway St Sw Massillon (44646) *(G-10641)*
Fresh Transportation Co Ltd 937 492-9876
  2695 Hidden Ridge Dr Sidney (45365) *(G-13033)*
Freshealth LLC 614 231-3601
  3650 E 5th Ave Columbus (43219) *(G-5895)*
Freshedge LLC 330 298-2222
  7176 State Route 88 Ravenna (44266) *(G-12626)*
Freshway Foods Company Inc (DH) 937 498-4664
  601 Stolle Ave Sidney (45365) *(G-13034)*
Freudenberg-Nok General Partnr 419 499-2502
  11617 State Route 13 Milan (44846) *(G-11206)*
Freund Freze Arnold A Lgal Pro (PA) 937 222-2424
  10 N Ludlow St Dayton (45402) *(G-7368)*
Freund, Freeze & Arnold, Dayton *Also Called: Freund Freze Arnold A Lgal Pro (G-7368)*
Frey Electric Inc 513 385-0700
  5700 Cheviot Rd Ste A Cincinnati (45247) *(G-2708)*
Fricker's Restaurant, Miamisburg *Also Called: Frickers USA LLC (G-11056)*
Frickers USA LLC (PA) 937 865-9242
  228 Byers Rd Ste 100 Miamisburg (45342) *(G-11056)*
Friedman Domiano Smith Co Lpa 216 621-0070
  55 Public Sq Ste 1055 Cleveland (44113) *(G-4289)*

Friendly Care Agency, Reynoldsburg *Also Called: Lbs International Inc (G-12667)*
Friendly Inn Settlement Inc 216 431-7656
  2386 Unwin Rd Cleveland (44104) *(G-4290)*
Friendly Wholesale Co 724 224-6580
  655 Cushman St Wooster (44691) *(G-15338)*
FRIENDS BOARDING HOME, Waynesville *Also Called: Home The Friends Inc (G-14624)*
Friends Business Source, Findlay *Also Called: Friends Service Co Inc (G-8534)*
FRIENDS CARE CENTER, Yellow Springs *Also Called: Friends Health Care Assn (G-15535)*
Friends Five Rivers Metroparks (PA) 937 275-7275
  1375 E Siebenthaler Ave Dayton (45414) *(G-7369)*
Friends For Lf Rhbltition Svcs 440 558-2859
  6444 Pearl Rd Cleveland (44130) *(G-4291)*
Friends Health Care Assn (PA) 937 767-7363
  150 E Herman St Yellow Springs (45387) *(G-15535)*
Friends In Deed Inc 330 345-9222
  365 Riffel Rd Ste E Wooster (44691) *(G-15339)*
Friends of Casa Frnklin Cnty O 614 525-7450
  373 S High St Fl 15 Columbus (43215) *(G-5896)*
Friends of Good Shepherd Manor 740 289-2861
  374 Good Manor Rd Lucasville (45648) *(G-10178)*
Friends Service Co Inc (PA) 419 427-1704
  2300 Bright Rd Findlay (45840) *(G-8534)*
Friendship Village of Dayton, Dayton *Also Called: Evanglcal Rtrment Vllges Inc D (G-7340)*
Friendship Village of Dublin, Dublin *Also Called: Friendship Vlg of Dublin Ohio (G-8016)*
Friendship Vlg of Clumbus Ohio 614 890-8287
  5757 Ponderosa Dr Columbus (43231) *(G-5897)*
Friendship Vlg of Clumbus Ohio (PA) 614 890-8282
  5800 Forest Hills Blvd Ofc Columbus (43231) *(G-5898)*
Friendship Vlg of Dublin Ohio 614 764-1600
  6000 Riverside Dr Ofc Dublin (43017) *(G-8016)*
Frito-Lay, Cleveland *Also Called: Frito-Lay North America Inc (G-4292)*
Frito-Lay, Columbus *Also Called: Frito-Lay North America Inc (G-5899)*
Frito-Lay North America Inc 216 491-4000
  4580 Hinckley Industrial Pkwy Cleveland (44109) *(G-4292)*
Frito-Lay North America Inc 614 508-3004
  6611 Broughton Ave Columbus (43213) *(G-5899)*
Fritz-Rumer-Cooke Co Inc (PA) 614 444-8844
  1879 Federal Pkwy Fl 2 Columbus (43207) *(G-5900)*
Frog and Toad Inc 419 877-1180
  10835 Waterville St Whitehouse (43571) *(G-15142)*
Front Leasing Co LLC 440 243-4000
  255 Front St Berea (44017) *(G-1070)*
Front Steps Housing & Svcs Inc 216 781-2250
  1545 W 25th St Cleveland (44113) *(G-4293)*
Frontier Power Company 740 622-6755
  770 S 2nd St Coshocton (43812) *(G-6985)*
Frontier Technology Inc (PA) 937 429-3302
  4141 Colonel Glenn Hwy Ste 140 Beavercreek Township (45431) *(G-939)*
Frontline National LLC 513 528-7823
  502 Techne Center Dr Ste G Milford (45150) *(G-11229)*
FRONTLINE SERVICE, Cleveland *Also Called: Mental Hlth Svcs For Hmless PR (G-4551)*
Frost Brown Todd LLC (PA) 513 651-6800
  3300 Great American Tower 301 E 4th St Cincinnati (45202) *(G-2709)*
Frost Engineering Inc 513 541-6330
  3408 Beekman St Cincinnati (45223) *(G-2710)*
Frost Roofing Inc 419 739-2701
  2 Broadway St Wapakoneta (45895) *(G-14483)*
Fruchtman Advertising Inc 419 539-2770
  6800 W Central Ave Ste F3 Toledo (43617) *(G-13814)*
Fruchtman Marketing, Toledo *Also Called: Fruchtman Advertising Inc (G-13814)*
Frye Mechanical Inc 937 222-8750
  1500 Humphrey Ave Dayton (45410) *(G-7370)*
Fryman-Kuck General Contrs Inc 937 274-2892
  5150 Webster St Dayton (45414) *(G-7371)*
Fscreations Corporation (HQ) 330 746-3015
  255 W Federal St Youngstown (44503) *(G-15614)*
FSI Disposal, Clyde *Also Called: Fultz & Son Inc (G-5201)*
Fsmg, Cincinnati *Also Called: Fountain Square MGT Group LLC (G-2698)*
Fssolutions, Independence *Also Called: First Hospital Labs LLC (G-9432)*
Fst Brokerage Services Inc (HQ) 614 529-7900
  5025 Bradenton Ave Ste B Dublin (43017) *(G-8017)*

ALPHABETIC SECTION
Gallia County Human Services

Fti, Beavercreek Township *Also Called: Frontier Technology Inc* **(G-939)**
Fuel Mart, Wooster *Also Called: Ports Petroleum Company Inc* **(G-15367)**
Fugees Family Inc... 678 358-0547
   1933 E Dublin Granville Rd Ste 117 Columbus (43229) **(G-5901)**
Fujifilm Hlthcare Amricas Corp (DH).. 330 425-1313
   1959 Summit Commerce Park Twinsburg (44087) **(G-14194)**
Fujitec, Mason *Also Called: Fujitec America Inc* **(G-10551)**
Fujitec America Inc (HQ)... 513 755-6100
   7258 Innovation Way Mason (45040) **(G-10551)**
Fulflo Specialties Company.. 937 783-2411
   459 E Fancy St Blanchester (45107) **(G-1117)**
Full Spectrum Marketing LLC... 330 541-9456
   50 S Main St Akron (44308) **(G-170)**
Fully Accountable LLC... 330 940-1440
   2725 Abington Rd Ste 100 Fairlawn (44333) **(G-8482)**
Fulton & Assoc Balance Co LLC... 440 943-9450
   9045 Osborne Dr Mentor (44060) **(G-10940)**
Fulton County Expositor, Napoleon *Also Called: Gazette Publishing Company* **(G-11523)**
Fulton County Health Center.. 419 335-1919
   138 E Elm St Wauseon (43567) **(G-14600)**
Fulton County Health Center.. 419 335-2017
   725 S Shoop Ave Wauseon (43567) **(G-14601)**
Fulton County Health Center (PA).. 419 335-2015
   725 S Shoop Ave Wauseon (43567) **(G-14602)**
Fulton County Health Dept... 419 337-0915
   606 S Shoop Ave Wauseon (43567) **(G-14603)**
Fulton Manor Nursing Home, Wauseon *Also Called: Fulton County Health Center* **(G-14601)**
Fultz & Son Inc.. 419 547-9365
   100 S Main St Clyde (43410) **(G-5201)**
Fund Evaluation Group LLC (PA).. 513 977-4400
   201 E 5th St Ste 1600 Cincinnati (45202) **(G-2711)**
Fundable LLC.. 614 364-4523
   1322 Manning Pkwy Unit A Powell (43065) **(G-12591)**
Fundriver LLC.. 513 618-8718
   1114 Belvedere St Cincinnati (45202) **(G-2712)**
Furbay Electric Supply Co (PA).. 330 454-3033
   208 Schroyer Ave Sw Canton (44702) **(G-1758)**
Fusian Inc (PA).. 937 361-7146
   1391 W 5th Ave Columbus (43212) **(G-5902)**
Fusion Alliance LLC... 513 563-8444
   4555 Lake Forest Dr Ste 325 Blue Ash (45242) **(G-1177)**
Fusion Alliance LLC... 614 852-8000
   8940 Lyra Dr # 220 Columbus (43240) **(G-5259)**
Futbol Club Cincinnati LLC.. 513 977-5425
   14 E 4th St Fl 3 Cincinnati (45202) **(G-2713)**
Future Active Industrial Elec, Dayton *Also Called: FAI Electronics Corp* **(G-7345)**
Future Lodging Northwood LLC... 419 666-2600
   2426 Oregon Rd Northwood (43619) **(G-11975)**
Fuyao Glass America Inc... 937 951-9263
   800 Fuyao Ave Moraine (45439) **(G-11412)**
Fwlm, Chagrin Falls *Also Called: For Women Like Me Inc* **(G-1958)**
Fyda Frghtliner Youngstown Inc... 330 797-0224
   5260 76 Dr Youngstown (44515) **(G-15615)**
Fyda Truck & Equipment, Youngstown *Also Called: Fyda Frghtliner Youngstown Inc* **(G-15615)**
G & G Concrete Cnstr LLC.. 614 475-4151
   2849 Switzer Ave Columbus (43219) **(G-5903)**
G & J Packaging, Cleveland *Also Called: G and J Automatic Systems Inc* **(G-4296)**
G & J Pepsi-Cola Bottlers Inc.. 740 593-3366
   2001 E State St Athens (45701) **(G-568)**
G & J Pepsi-Cola Bottlers Inc.. 740 354-9191
   4587 Gallia Pike Franklin Furnace (45629) **(G-8654)**
G & J Pepsi-Cola Bottlers Inc.. 740 354-9191
   336 N Sixth St Zanesville (43701) **(G-15788)**
G & P Construction LLC... 855 494-4830
   10139 Royalton Rd Ste D North Royalton (44133) **(G-11941)**
G & S Metal Products Co Inc... 216 831-2388
   26840 Fargo Ave Cleveland (44146) **(G-4294)**
G & S Metal Products Co Inc (PA)... 216 441-0700
   3330 E 79th St Cleveland (44127) **(G-4295)**
G and J Automatic Systems Inc... 216 741-6070
   14701 Industrial Pkwy Cleveland (44135) **(G-4296)**

G D Supply Inc (PA).. 614 258-1111
   700 Parkwood Ave Columbus (43219) **(G-5904)**
G E S, Parma *Also Called: Ges Graphite Inc* **(G-12254)**
G G Marck & Associates Inc (PA).. 419 478-0900
   300 Phillips Ave Toledo (43612) **(G-13815)**
G H A T Inc.. 330 392-8838
   219 N River Rd Nw Warren (44483) **(G-14522)**
G J Goudreau & Co (PA)... 216 351-5233
   9701 Brookpark Rd Ste 200 Cleveland (44129) **(G-4297)**
G J Shue Inc.. 330 722-0082
   2855 Medina Rd Medina (44256) **(G-10837)**
G M A C Insurance Center, Hudson *Also Called: Pasco Inc* **(G-9367)**
G M Industrial LLC... 440 786-1177
   1 Zenex Cir Cleveland (44146) **(G-4298)**
G M N, Cambridge *Also Called: G M N Tri Cnty Cmnty Action CM* **(G-1571)**
G M N Tri Cnty Cmnty Action CM (PA)................................... 740 732-2388
   615 North St Caldwell (43724) **(G-1549)**
G M N Tri Cnty Cmnty Action CM.. 740 732-2388
   60901 Beech Grove Ln Cambridge (43725) **(G-1571)**
G M Z, West Chester *Also Called: CL Zimmerman Delaware LLC* **(G-14667)**
G Mechanical Inc.. 614 844-6750
   6635 Singletree Dr Columbus (43229) **(G-5905)**
G P M C, Dublin *Also Called: Gemini Properties* **(G-8020)**
G R C, Mason *Also Called: General Revenue Corporation* **(G-10554)**
G Robert Toney & Assoc Inc (PA).. 216 391-1900
   5401 N Marginal Rd Cleveland (44114) **(G-4299)**
G S M, Batavia *Also Called: Global Scrap Management Inc* **(G-741)**
G S S, Springboro *Also Called: Graphic Systems Services Inc* **(G-13199)**
G Stephens Inc... 614 227-0304
   1175 Dublin Rd Ste 2 Columbus (43215) **(G-5906)**
G W S, West Chester *Also Called: Global Workplace Solutions LLC* **(G-14697)**
G-Cor, Columbus *Also Called: G-Cor Automotive Corp* **(G-5907)**
G-Cor Automotive Corp (PA)... 614 443-6735
   2100 Refugee Rd Columbus (43207) **(G-5907)**
G.L.R., Inc. Alabama Division, Dayton *Also Called: L R G Inc* **(G-7447)**
G&K Services LLC (HQ).. 513 459-1200
   6800 Cintas Blvd Mason (45040) **(G-10552)**
G2o LLC... 614 523-3070
   5455 Rings Rd Ste 500 Dublin (43017) **(G-8018)**
G7 Services Inc... 937 256-3473
   1524 E 2nd St Dayton (45403) **(G-7372)**
GA Business Purchaser LLC... 419 255-8400
   3222 W Central Ave Toledo (43606) **(G-13816)**
Gaash Home Health Care LLC... 419 775-4823
   911 S Main St Mansfield (44907) **(G-10266)**
Gables At Green Pastures... 937 642-3893
   390 Gables Dr Marysville (43040) **(G-10485)**
Gables Care Center Inc.. 740 937-2900
   351 Lahm Dr Hopedale (43976) **(G-9318)**
Gabriel Partners LLC... 216 771-1250
   1300 E 9th St Fl 2 Cleveland (44114) **(G-4300)**
Gade Nursing Home 2, Greenville *Also Called: Village Green Healthcare Ctr* **(G-8889)**
Galaxie Industrial Svcs LLC.. 330 503-2334
   837 E Western Reserve Rd Youngstown (44514) **(G-15616)**
Galaxy Associates Inc... 513 731-6350
   3630 E Kemper Rd Cincinnati (45241) **(G-2714)**
Gale Insulation, Columbus *Also Called: Builder Services Group Inc* **(G-5483)**
Gale Insulation, Hamilton *Also Called: Builder Services Group Inc* **(G-9019)**
Galehouse Lumber, Doylestown *Also Called: The Galehouse Companies Inc* **(G-7916)**
Galia County Council On Aging, Gallipolis *Also Called: Area Agency On Aging Dst 7 Inc* **(G-8752)**
Gallagher Gams Pryor Tllan Ltt.. 614 228-5151
   471 E Broad St Fl 19 Columbus (43215) **(G-5908)**
Gallagher Sharp... 216 241-5310
   1215 Superior Ave E Fl 7 Cleveland (44114) **(G-4301)**
Galli-Migs Cmnty Action Agcy I (PA)...................................... 740 367-7341
   8317 State Route 7 N Cheshire (45620) **(G-2029)**
Gallia County Engineer, Gallipolis *Also Called: County of Gallia* **(G-8754)**
Gallia County Human Services, Gallipolis *Also Called: County of Gallia* **(G-8753)**

Gallipolis Developmental Ctr, Gallipolis Also Called: Ohio Dept Dvlpmntal Dsbilities *(G-8764)*

Gallipolis Hospitality Inc.. 740 446-0090
577 State Route 7 N Gallipolis (45631) *(G-8756)*

Gallon Tkacs Bssnult Schffer L (PA)..............................419 843-2001
1450 Arrowhead Dr Maumee (43537) *(G-10726)*

Galt, Moreland Hills Also Called: Galt Enterprises Inc *(G-11452)*

Galt Enterprises Inc.. 216 464-6744
34555 Chagrin Blvd Ste 100 Moreland Hills (44022) *(G-11452)*

Galvin Edcatn Rsrce Ctr For Fm, Cleveland Also Called: Barrie G Glvin Ctr/L Assoc Ltd *(G-3852)*

Game Haus LLC.. 513 490-1799
3455 Renaissance Blvd Franklin (45005) *(G-8638)*

Ganga Hospitality Ohio LLC... 614 870-3700
4530 W Broad St Columbus (43228) *(G-5909)*

Ganley Lincoln Middleburg Hts, Cleveland Also Called: Broadvue Motors Inc *(G-3899)*

Ganzfair Investment Inc... 614 792-6630
231 Clubhouse Dr Delaware (43015) *(G-7800)*

Ganzhorn Suites Inc.. 614 356-9810
1322 Manning Pkwy Unit B Powell (43065) *(G-12592)*

Garber Connect, Englewood Also Called: Garber Electrical Contrs Inc *(G-8306)*

Garber Electrical Contrs Inc... 937 771-5202
100 Rockridge Rd Englewood (45322) *(G-8306)*

Garda CL Great Lakes Inc... 614 863-4044
201 Schofield Dr Columbus (43213) *(G-5910)*

Garda CL Great Lakes Inc (HQ)..................................... 561 939-7000
201 Schofield Dr Columbus (43213) *(G-5911)*

Gardaworld Security Corp... 614 963-2098
300 Marconi Blvd Ste 310 Columbus (43215) *(G-5912)*

GARDAWORLD SECURITY CORPORATION, Columbus Also Called: Gardaworld Security Corp *(G-5912)*

Garden City Group LLC (DH).. 631 470-5000
5151 Blazer Pkwy Ste A Dublin (43017) *(G-8019)*

Garden II Leasing Co LLC.. 419 381-0037
1015 Garden Lake Pkwy Toledo (43614) *(G-13817)*

Garden Manor Extended Care Cen................................. 513 420-5972
6898 Hamilton Middletown Rd Middletown (45044) *(G-11164)*

Garden Street Iron & Metal Inc (PA)............................... 513 721-4660
2885 Spring Grove Ave Cincinnati (45225) *(G-2715)*

Gardeners Edge, Piqua Also Called: A M Leonard Inc *(G-12434)*

Gardenland, Toledo Also Called: Dennis Top Soil & Ldscpg Inc *(G-13775)*

Gardenlife Inc... 800 241-7333
10010 Mitchells Mill Rd Chardon (44024) *(G-1999)*

GARDENS AT CELINA, Celina Also Called: Gardens At Celina Oper Co LLC *(G-1924)*

Gardens At Celina Oper Co LLC..................................... 419 584-0100
1301 Myers Rd Celina (45822) *(G-1924)*

Gardens At Paulding Oper LLC...................................... 419 399-4940
199 Road 103 Paulding (45879) *(G-12283)*

Gardens At St Henry Oper LLC...................................... 419 678-9800
522 Western Ave Saint Henry (45883) *(G-12825)*

GARDENS AT ST. HENRY, THE, Saint Henry Also Called: Gardens At St Henry Oper LLC *(G-12825)*

Gardens At Wapskoneta, The, Wapakoneta Also Called: Gardens Wapakoneta Oper Co LLC *(G-14484)*

Gardens Wapakoneta Oper Co LLC................................ 419 738-0725
505 Walnut St Wapakoneta (45895) *(G-14484)*

Gardens Western Reserve Inc....................................... 330 928-4500
45 Chart Rd Cuyahoga Falls (44223) *(G-7077)*

Gardens Western Reserve Inc (PA)................................ 330 342-9100
9975 Greentree Pkwy Streetsboro (44241) *(G-13412)*

Gardiner, Solon Also Called: Gardiner Service Company LLC *(G-13091)*

Gardiner Allen Drbrts Insur LL....................................... 614 221-1500
325 John H Mcconnell Blvd Ste 415 Columbus (43215) *(G-5913)*

Gardiner Service Company LLC (PA)............................. 440 248-3400
31200 Bainbridge Rd Ste 1 Solon (44139) *(G-13091)*

Gardiner Service Company LLC..................................... 330 896-9358
1530 Corporate Woods Pkwy Ste 200 Uniontown (44685) *(G-14253)*

Gardner, Toledo Also Called: Gardner Cement Contractors *(G-13818)*

Gardner Cement Contractors... 419 389-0768
821 Warehouse Rd Toledo (43615) *(G-13818)*

Gardner Insurance Partners LLC................................... 614 221-1500
777 Goodale Blvd Ste 200 Columbus (43212) *(G-5914)*

Gardner-Connell LLC... 614 456-4000
3641 Interchange Rd Columbus (43204) *(G-5915)*

Gareat Sports Complex, Geneva Also Called: Geneva Area Rcrtl Edctl Athc T *(G-8785)*

Garland Group Inc... 614 294-4411
48 E 15th Ave Frnt Columbus (43201) *(G-5916)*

Garland/Dbs Inc... 216 641-7500
3800 E 91st St Cleveland (44105) *(G-4302)*

Garmann Miller Architects, Minster Also Called: Garmann/Miller & Assoc Inc *(G-11316)*

Garmann/Miller & Assoc Inc (PA)..................................419 628-4240
38 S Lincoln Dr Minster (45865) *(G-11316)*

Garner Transportation Group, Findlay Also Called: Garner Trucking Inc *(G-8536)*

Garner Trnsp Group Inc... 419 422-5742
9231 County Rd 313 Findlay (45840) *(G-8535)*

Garner Trucking Inc (PA)... 419 422-5742
9291 County Road 313 Findlay (45839) *(G-8536)*

Garner Trucking Inc... 419 334-4040
2673 E State St Fremont (43420) *(G-8681)*

Garretson Resolution Group, Loveland Also Called: The Garretson Firm Resolution Group Inc *(G-10163)*

Garrett Dialysis LLC... 216 398-6029
4805 Pearl Rd Cleveland (44109) *(G-4303)*

Garrison Brewer, Belpre Also Called: Stationers Inc *(G-1059)*

Gasgas North America, Amherst Also Called: Ktm North America Inc *(G-430)*

Gaslight, Cincinnati Also Called: Gaslight Holdings LLC *(G-2716)*

Gaslight Holdings LLC... 513 470-3525
5910 Hamilton Ave Cincinnati (45224) *(G-2716)*

Gaspar, Canton Also Called: Gaspar Inc *(G-1759)*

Gaspar Inc... 330 477-2222
1545 Whipple Ave Sw Canton (44710) *(G-1759)*

Gasser Chair Co Inc... 330 742-2234
2547 Logan Ave Youngstown (44505) *(G-15617)*

Gastoenterology Clinic, Warren Also Called: Adel Youssef MD *(G-14494)*

Gastrnterology Specialists Inc...................................... 330 455-5011
2726 Fulton Dr Nw Canton (44718) *(G-1760)*

Gastrntrlogy Assoc Clvland Inc (PA)............................. 216 593-7700
428 Bassett Rd Bay Village (44140) *(G-759)*

Gastro-Intestinal Assoc Inc... 419 227-8209
2793 Shawnee Rd Lima (45806) *(G-9991)*

Gates McDonald of Ohio LLC... 614 677-3700
215 N Front St Columbus (43215) *(G-5917)*

Gatesair Inc (HQ).. 513 459-3400
5300 Kings Island Dr Ste 101 Mason (45040) *(G-10553)*

Gateway Con Forming Svcs Inc..................................... 513 353-2000
5938 Hamilton-Cleves Rd Miamitown (45041) *(G-11106)*

Gateway Distribution, Cincinnati Also Called: Gateway Distribution LLC *(G-2717)*

Gateway Distribution LLC.. 888 806-8206
11755 Lebanon Rd Cincinnati (45241) *(G-2717)*

Gateway Electric LLC... 216 518-5500
4450 Johnston Pkwy Ste A Cleveland (44128) *(G-4304)*

GATEWAY FILM CENTER, Columbus Also Called: Gateway Film Foundation *(G-5918)*

Gateway Film Foundation.. 614 247-4968
1550 N High St Columbus (43201) *(G-5918)*

Gateway Freight Forwarding Inc................................... 513 248-1514
11755 Lebanon Rd Cincinnati (45241) *(G-2718)*

Gateway Health Care Center... 216 486-4949
3 Gateway Cleveland (44119) *(G-4305)*

Gateway Hotel Ltd.. 513 772-2837
11149 Dowlin Dr Sharonville (45241) *(G-12994)*

Gateway Products Recycling Inc (PA)........................... 216 341-8777
4223 E 49th St Cleveland (44125) *(G-4306)*

Gateway Recycling, Cleveland Also Called: Gateway Products Recycling Inc *(G-4306)*

Gateway Tire of Texas Inc... 513 874-2500
4 W Crescentville Rd West Chester (45246) *(G-14813)*

Gateway To Grace Fundation Inc.................................. 513 869-4645
1260 Hicks Blvd Fairfield (45014) *(G-8416)*

Gateways To Better Living Inc (PA)...............................330 792-2854
6000 Mahoning Ave Ste 234 Youngstown (44515) *(G-15618)*

Gatto Electric Supply Co.. 216 641-8400
4501 Willow Pkwy Cleveland (44125) *(G-4307)*

Gavin AEP Plant... 740 925-3166
7397 State Route 7 N Cheshire (45620) *(G-2030)*

ALPHABETIC SECTION

General Temperature Ctrl Inc

Gavin Generating Station, Cheshire *Also Called: Gavin Power LLC (G-2031)*
Gavin Power LLC.. 740 925-3140
  7397 State Route 7 N Cheshire (45620) *(G-2031)*
Gaymont Care & Rehabilitation, Norwalk *Also Called: Gaymont Leasing LLC (G-12014)*
Gaymont Leasing LLC.. 419 668-8258
  66 Norwood Ave Norwalk (44857) *(G-12014)*
Gayston Corporation... 937 743-6050
  721 Richard St Miamisburg (45342) *(G-11057)*
Gazette Publishing Company... 419 335-2010
  595 E Riverview Ave Napoleon (43545) *(G-11523)*
Gbc Design Inc... 330 836-0228
  565 White Pond Dr Akron (44320) *(G-171)*
Gbd Legacy LLC... 330 441-0785
  1050 Ghent Rd Akron (44333) *(G-172)*
Gbq Consulting LLC... 614 221-1120
  230 West St Ste 700 Columbus (43215) *(G-5919)*
Gbq Holdings LLC (PA).. 614 221-1120
  230 West St Ste 700 Columbus (43215) *(G-5920)*
Gbq Partners LLC... 513 871-3033
  5086 Wooster Rd Cincinnati (45226) *(G-2719)*
Gbq Partners LLC (PA)... 614 221-1120
  230 West St Ste 700 Columbus (43215) *(G-5921)*
Gbq Partners LLC... 419 885-8338
  5580 Monroe St Ste 210 Sylvania (43560) *(G-13546)*
GBS Corp (PA)... 330 494-5330
  7233 Freedom Ave Nw North Canton (44720) *(G-11833)*
GBS Filing Solutions, North Canton *Also Called: GBS Corp (G-11833)*
Gca Services Group Inc (HQ).. 800 422-8760
  1350 Euclid Ave Ste 1500 Cleveland (44115) *(G-4308)*
GCCVB, Columbus *Also Called: Greater Clmbus Cnvntion Vstors (G-5954)*
Gcg Loudoun Co, Dublin *Also Called: Garden City Group LLC (G-8019)*
GCI Construction LLC (HQ)... 216 831-6100
  25101 Chagrin Blvd Beachwood (44122) *(G-794)*
GCR TIRES & SERVICE, Cleveland *Also Called: Credit First National Assn (G-4136)*
Gcrta, Cleveland *Also Called: Rapid Transit Line (G-4808)*
GE, Cincinnati *Also Called: GE Engine Services LLC (G-2721)*
GE, Cincinnati *Also Called: General Electric Company (G-2723)*
GE, Cincinnati *Also Called: General Electric Company (G-2724)*
GE, Cleveland *Also Called: General Electric Company (G-4310)*
GE, Peebles *Also Called: General Electric Company (G-12288)*
GE Engine Services Dist LLC (DH).. 513 243-2000
  1 Neumann Way Cincinnati (45215) *(G-2720)*
GE Engine Services LLC (HQ)... 513 243-2000
  1 Neumann Way Cincinnati (45215) *(G-2721)*
GE Water & Process Tech, New Philadelphia *Also Called: Veolia Wts Usa Inc (G-11672)*
Geary Fmly Yung MNS Chrstn Ass.. 419 435-6608
  154 W Center St Fostoria (44830) *(G-8617)*
Geauga County Humane Soc Inc... 440 338-4819
  15463 Chillicothe Rd Novelty (44072) *(G-12038)*
Geauga County Jobs & Fmly Svcs, Chardon *Also Called: County of Geauga (G-1998)*
Geauga Mechanical Company.. 440 285-2000
  12585 Chardon Windsor Rd Chardon (44024) *(G-2000)*
Geauga Park District.. 440 415-5661
  9160 Robinson Rd Chardon (44024) *(G-2001)*
Geauga Regional Hosp HM Care... 440 285-6834
  13207 Ravenna Rd Chardon (44024) *(G-2002)*
Geben Communications LLC... 614 327-2102
  143 E Main St Apt B Columbus (43215) *(G-5922)*
Gecu, Cincinnati *Also Called: General Electric Credit Union (G-2726)*
Geeks On Call.. 800 905-4335
  7100 E Pleasant Valley Rd Ste 300 Independence (44131) *(G-9433)*
Geep, Stow *Also Called: Geep USA Inc (G-13369)*
Geep USA Inc... 919 544-1443
  4550 Darrow Rd Stow (44224) *(G-13369)*
Gei Wide Format Solutions.. 330 494-8189
  3874 Highland Park Nw North Canton (44720) *(G-11834)*
Geico, Cincinnati *Also Called: Geico General Insurance Co (G-2722)*
Geico General Insurance Co.. 513 794-3426
  8044 Montgomery Rd Cincinnati (45236) *(G-2722)*

Geiger Brothers, Jackson *Also Called: Geiger Brothers Inc (G-9518)*
Geiger Brothers Inc.. 740 286-0800
  317 Ralph St Jackson (45640) *(G-9518)*
Geis Companies LLC... 330 528-3500
  10020 Aurora Hudson Rd Streetsboro (44241) *(G-13413)*
GEIS COMPANY, Streetsboro *Also Called: Highland Som Development (G-13415)*
Geisinger Health Plan... 570 271-6211
  10121 Broadway Ave Cleveland (44125) *(G-4309)*
Geist, Westerville *Also Called: Vertiv Corporation (G-14949)*
Geist Logistics LLC.. 954 463-6910
  3030 Old Horn Lake Rd Columbus (43215) *(G-5923)*
Gem City Chemicals Inc.. 937 224-0711
  1287 Air City Ave Dayton (45404) *(G-7373)*
Gem City Home Care Llc (HQ).. 937 438-9100
  8534 Yankee St Ste 2a Dayton (45458) *(G-7374)*
Gem City Surgical Associates.. 254 400-1783
  9000 N Main St Ste 233 Englewood (45415) *(G-8307)*
Gem City Urologist Inc (PA)... 937 832-8400
  9000 N Main St Ste 333 Englewood (45415) *(G-8308)*
Gem Edwards Inc... 330 342-8300
  5640 Hudson Industrial Pkwy Hudson (44236) *(G-9352)*
Gem Electric... 440 286-6200
  12577 Gar Hwy Chardon (44024) *(G-2003)*
GEM ENERGY, Walbridge *Also Called: BHP Energy LLC (G-14460)*
Gem Industrial Inc (HQ)... 419 666-6554
  6842 Commodore Dr Walbridge (43465) *(G-14461)*
Gemcare Wellness Inc... 800 294-9176
  5640 Hudson Industrial Pkwy Hudson (44236) *(G-9353)*
Gemco Medical, Hudson *Also Called: Gem Edwards Inc (G-9352)*
Gemini Properties... 614 764-2800
  6470 Post Rd Ofc Dublin (43016) *(G-8020)*
Gemini Solar LLC... 833 339-2097
  4433 Professional Pkwy Groveport (43125) *(G-8991)*
Gen III Inc... 614 228-5550
  2300 Lockbourne Rd Columbus (43207) *(G-5924)*
Genacross Lthran Svcs - Wolf C, Holland *Also Called: Lutheran Homes Society Inc (G-9295)*
Genacross Lthran Svcs Bthany P, Fremont *Also Called: Lutheran Homes Society Inc (G-8691)*
Genacross Lutheran Services, Toledo *Also Called: Lutheran Homes Society Inc (G-13899)*
Gencraft Designs LLC... 330 359-6251
  7412 Massillon Rd Sw Navarre (44662) *(G-11537)*
Gene's Refrigeration, Medina *Also Called: Genes Rfrgn Htg & AC Inc (G-10838)*
General Audit Corporation.. 419 993-2900
  2348 Baton Rouge Ste A Lima (45805) *(G-9891)*
General Clinical Research Ctr, Cleveland *Also Called: University Hsptals Clvland Med (G-5075)*
General Commercial Corporation (PA)................................... 330 938-1000
  110 S 15th St Sebring (44672) *(G-12949)*
General Crane Rental LLC... 330 908-0001
  9680 Freeway Dr Macedonia (44056) *(G-10192)*
General Data Company Inc (PA).. 513 752-7978
  4354 Ferguson Dr Cincinnati (45245) *(G-2105)*
General Electric, Cincinnati *Also Called: General Electric Company (G-2725)*
General Electric Company... 513 977-1500
  201 W Crescentville Rd Cincinnati (45246) *(G-2723)*
General Electric Company... 513 583-3500
  8700 Governors Hill Dr Cincinnati (45249) *(G-2724)*
General Electric Company (PA).. 617 443-3000
  1 Aviation Way Cincinnati (45215) *(G-2725)*
General Electric Company... 216 883-1000
  4477 E 49th St Cleveland (44125) *(G-4310)*
General Electric Company... 937 587-2631
  1200 Jaybird Rd Peebles (45660) *(G-12288)*
General Electric Credit Union (PA).. 513 243-4328
  10485 Reading Rd Cincinnati (45241) *(G-2726)*
General Factory Sups Co Inc... 513 681-6300
  4811 Winton Rd Cincinnati (45232) *(G-2727)*
General Revenue Corporation.. 513 469-1472
  4660 Duke Dr Ste 200 Mason (45040) *(G-10554)*
General Temperature Ctrl Inc... 614 837-3888
  970 W Walnut St Canal Winchester (43110) *(G-1607)*

General Theming Contrs LLC ... 614 252-6342
3750 Courtright Ct Columbus (43227) *(G-5925)*

General Tool Company (PA) ... 513 733-5500
101 Landy Ln Cincinnati (45215) *(G-2728)*

General Transport & Cons Inc ... 330 645-6055
1100 Jenkins Blvd Akron (44306) *(G-173)*

General Transport Incorporated ... 330 786-3400
1100 Jenkins Blvd Akron (44306) *(G-174)*

Generation Health Corp ... 614 337-1066
5151 N Hamilton Rd Columbus (43230) *(G-5926)*

Generative Growth II LLC (PA) ... 419 422-8090
317 W Main Cross St Findlay (45840) *(G-8537)*

Generator One LLC ... 440 942-8449
7487 Tyler Blvd Mentor (44060) *(G-10941)*

Genertion Hlth Rhbltion Ctr L ... 740 348-1300
1450 W Main St Newark (43055) *(G-11701)*

Genertons Bhvral Hlth - Yngsto ... 234 855-0523
196 Colonial Dr Youngstown (44505) *(G-15619)*

Genes Rfrgn Htg & AC Inc ... 330 723-4104
6222 Norwalk Rd Medina (44256) *(G-10838)*

Genesis ... 740 453-3122
3287 Maple Ave Zanesville (43701) *(G-15789)*

Genesis, Zanesville Also Called: Genesis (G-15789)

Genesis 10, Akron Also Called: Genesis Corp (G-175)

Genesis Corp ... 330 597-4100
1 Cascade Plz Ste 1230 Akron (44308) *(G-175)*

Genesis Healthcare ... 937 875-4604
2 Crescent Dr Troy (45373) *(G-14136)*

Genesis Healthcare LLC ... 419 666-0935
28546 Starbright Blvd Perrysburg (43551) *(G-12336)*

Genesis Healthcare System ... 740 454-5922
800 Forest Ave Zanesville (43701) *(G-15790)*

Genesis Healthcare System (PA) ... 740 454-5000
2951 Maple Ave Zanesville (43701) *(G-15791)*

Genesis Healthcare System ... 740 454-5913
2529 Maple Ave Zanesville (43701) *(G-15792)*

Genesis Healthcare System ... 740 454-4585
2800 Maple Ave Zanesville (43701) *(G-15793)*

Genesis Healthcare System ... 740 586-6732
2800 Maple Ave Ste A Zanesville (43701) *(G-15794)*

Genesis Healthcare System ... 740 454-4566
2951 Maple Ave Zanesville (43701) *(G-15795)*

Genesis Hospital, New Lexington Also Called: Perry County Fmly Practice Inc (G-11631)

Genesis Hspces Pallitaive Care, Zanesville Also Called: Hospice of Genesis Health (G-15801)

Genesis Logistics, Westerville Also Called: Exel Inc (G-14894)

Genesis Police Department, Zanesville Also Called: Genesis Healthcare System (G-15790)

Genesis Respiratory Svcs Inc ... 937 393-4423
109 W Main St Hillsboro (45133) *(G-9254)*

Geneva Area Rcrtl Edctl Athc T ... 440 466-1002
1822 S Broadway Geneva (44041) *(G-8785)*

Geneva Chervenic Realty Inc ... 330 686-8400
3589 Darrow Rd Stow (44224) *(G-13370)*

Geneva Liberty Steel Ltd (PA) ... 330 740-0103
947 Martin Luther King Jr Blvd Youngstown (44502) *(G-15620)*

Genie Company, The, Baltic Also Called: GMI Holdings Inc (G-689)

Genie Company, The, Mount Hope Also Called: GMI Holdings Inc (G-11466)

Genius Solutions Engrg Co (HQ) ... 419 794-9914
6421 Monclova Rd Maumee (43537) *(G-10727)*

Genmak Geneva Liberty, Youngstown Also Called: Geneva Liberty Steel Ltd (G-15620)

Genoa Bank, Genoa Also Called: Genoa Banking Company (G-8794)

Genoa Banking Company (HQ) ... 419 855-8381
801 Main St Genoa (43430) *(G-8794)*

Genoa Care Center, Genoa Also Called: McClellan Management Inc (G-8795)

Genomoncology LLC ... 440 617-6087
4790 Farley Dr Mentor (44060) *(G-10942)*

Genox Transportation Inc ... 419 837-2023
25750 Oregon Rd Perrysburg (43551) *(G-12337)*

Genpact LLC ... 513 763-7660
100 Tri County Pkwy Ste 200 Cincinnati (45246) *(G-2729)*

Genric Inc ... 937 553-9250
883 London Ave Ste A Marysville (43040) *(G-10486)*

Gentherm Medical LLC ... 513 326-5252
12011 Mosteller Rd Cincinnati (45241) *(G-2730)*

Gentile Bros, Cincinnati Also Called: Jao Distributors Inc (G-2900)

Gentlebrook Inc (PA) ... 330 877-3694
880 Sunnyside St Sw Hartville (44632) *(G-9125)*

Gentlebrook Inc ... 740 545-7487
21990 Orchard St West Lafayette (43845) *(G-14856)*

Gentry Health Services Inc (PA) ... 330 721-1077
33381 Walker Rd Ste A Avon Lake (44012) *(G-679)*

Geo Byers Sons Holding Inc ... 614 239-1084
4185 E 5th Ave Columbus (43219) *(G-5927)*

Geo Global Partners LLC ... 561 598-6000
125 Lena Dr Aurora (44202) *(G-613)*

Geo Gradel Co ... 419 691-7123
3135 Front St Toledo (43605) *(G-13819)*

Geoamps LLC ... 614 389-4872
1707 Hyatts Rd Delaware (43015) *(G-7801)*

Geoglobal Partners LLC ... 561 598-6000
125 Lena Dr Aurora (44202) *(G-614)*

Geological Department, Cincinnati Also Called: University of Cincinnati (G-3592)

Geopfert Company, The, Akron Also Called: J W Geopfert Co Inc (G-208)

George Fern Company, Cincinnati Also Called: Fern Exposition Services LLC (G-2659)

George J Igel & Co Inc ... 614 445-8421
2040 Alum Creek Dr Columbus (43207) *(G-5928)*

George P Ballas Buick GMC Trck (PA) ... 419 535-1000
5715 W Central Ave Toledo (43615) *(G-13820)*

George Steel Fabricating Inc ... 513 932-2887
1207 Us Route 42 S Lebanon (45036) *(G-9766)*

Georgia-Boot Inc ... 740 753-1951
39 E Canal St Nelsonville (45764) *(G-11545)*

Geotex Construction Svcs Inc ... 614 444-5690
1025 Stimmel Rd Columbus (43223) *(G-5929)*

Gerald Grain Center Inc ... 419 445-2451
3265 County Road 24 Archbold (43502) *(G-459)*

Gerber Feed Service Inc ... 330 857-4421
3094 Moser Rd Dalton (44618) *(G-7120)*

Gerber Life Agency LLC ... 917 765-3572
400 Broadway St Cincinnati (45202) *(G-2731)*

Gerbig Snell/Weisheimer Advertising LLC ... 614 848-4848
500 Olde Worthington Rd Westerville (43082) *(G-14896)*

Gerdau McSteel Atmsphere Annli ... 330 478-0314
1501 Raff Rd Sw Canton (44710) *(G-1761)*

Gergelys Mint King Sups Svc In ... 440 244-4446
947 Broadway Ste 201 Lorain (44052) *(G-10076)*

GERIATRICS CENTER OF MANSFIELD, Mansfield Also Called: Mansfield Memorial Homes LLC (G-10289)

Gerken Materials Inc (PA) ... 419 533-2421
9072 County Road 424 Napoleon (43545) *(G-11524)*

Gerlach John J Ctr For Snior H ... 614 566-5858
180 E Broad St Fl 34 Columbus (43215) *(G-5930)*

Germain Ford LLC ... 614 889-7777
7250 Sawmill Rd Columbus (43235) *(G-5931)*

Germain Ford of Sidney, Sidney Also Called: Germain of Sidney III LLC (G-13035)

Germain Honda of Beavercreek, Beavercreek Also Called: Germain of Beavercreek II LLC (G-880)

Germain of Beavercreek II LLC ... 937 429-2400
2300 Heller Dr Beavercreek (45434) *(G-880)*

Germain of Sidney III LLC ... 937 498-4014
2343 Michigan St Sidney (45365) *(G-13035)*

German American Family Society, Kent Also Called: German Family Society Inc (G-9576)

German Family Society Inc ... 330 678-8229
3871 Ranfield Rd Kent (44240) *(G-9576)*

Germann Bros LLC ... 614 905-7314
774 Peachblow Rd Lewis Center (43035) *(G-9822)*

Gervasi Vineyard, Canton Also Called: Gervasi Vinyrd Itln Bistro LLC (G-1762)

Gervasi Vinyrd Itln Bistro LLC ... 330 497-1000
1700 55th St Ne Canton (44721) *(G-1762)*

Ges Graphite Inc (PA) ... 216 658-6660
12300 Snow Rd Parma (44130) *(G-12254)*

Getgo Transportation Co LLC ... 419 666-6850
28500 Lemoyne Rd Millbury (43447) *(G-11269)*

ALPHABETIC SECTION — Global Medical Products LLC

Getinge Usa Inc 440 449-1540
   6559 Wilson Mills Rd Ste 106 Cleveland (44143) *(G-4311)*

Gexpro, Cleveland *Also Called: Rexel Usa Inc (G-4835)*

Gfl Environmental Svcs USA Inc 614 441-4001
   4001 E 5th Ave Columbus (43219) *(G-5932)*

GFS Leasing Inc 330 877-2666
   1420 Smith Kramer St Ne Hartville (44632) *(G-9126)*

GFS Leasing Inc (PA) 330 296-6415
   1463 Tallmadge Rd Kent (44240) *(G-9577)*

Gfwd Supply, Cincinnati *Also Called: General Factory Sups Co Inc (G-2727)*

Gg Ohio Inc 330 683-7206
   11842 Lincoln Way E Orrville (44667) *(G-12165)*

Ghi, Dayton *Also Called: Gohypersonic Incorporated (G-7377)*

Giambrone Masonry Inc
   10000 Aurora Hudson Rd Hudson (44236) *(G-9354)*

Giant Eagle, Columbus *Also Called: Giant Eagle Inc (G-5933)*

Giant Eagle, Dover *Also Called: Giant Eagle Inc (G-7885)*

Giant Eagle Inc 412 968-5300
   6660 Broughton Ave Columbus (43213) *(G-5933)*

Giant Eagle Inc 330 364-5301
   515 Union Ave Ste 243 Dover (44622) *(G-7885)*

Giant Industries Inc 419 531-4600
   900 N Westwood Ave Toledo (43607) *(G-13821)*

Gibson 2021 LLC 440 439-4000
   181 Oak Leaf Oval Cleveland (44146) *(G-4312)*

Giffin Management Group Inc 330 758-4695
   6300 South Ave Apt 1200 Youngstown (44512) *(G-15621)*

Gilbane Building Company 614 948-4000
   145 E Rich St Fl 4 Columbus (43215) *(G-5934)*

Gilkey Window Company Inc (PA) 513 769-4527
   3625 Hauck Rd Cincinnati (45241) *(G-2732)*

Gill Podiatry Supply Co, Strongsville *Also Called: Radebaugh-Fetzer Company (G-13481)*

Gillespie Drug, Caldwell *Also Called: Braden Med Services Inc (G-1547)*

Gillette Associates LP 330 372-1960
   3310 Elm Rd Ne Warren (44483) *(G-14523)*

Gillette Nursing Home Inc 330 372-1960
   3310 Elm Rd Ne Warren (44483) *(G-14524)*

Gillmore Security Systems Inc 440 232-1000
   26165 Broadway Ave Cleveland (44146) *(G-4313)*

Gillson Solutions Inc 937 751-0119
   3100 Research Blvd Ste 260 Dayton (45420) *(G-7375)*

Gilman Partners 513 272-2400
   3960 Red Bank Rd Ste 200 Cincinnati (45227) *(G-2733)*

Gilmore Jasion Mahler Ltd 419 423-4481
   551 Lake Cascade Pkwy Findlay (45840) *(G-8538)*

Gilmore Jasion Mahler Ltd (PA) 419 794-2000
   1715 Indian Wood Cir Ste 100 Maumee (43537) *(G-10728)*

Gilson Company Inc (PA) 740 548-7298
   7975 N Central Dr Lewis Center (43035) *(G-9823)*

Gioninos Pizzeria Inc 330 630-2010
   676 Eastwood Ave Tallmadge (44278) *(G-13592)*

Girard City School District 330 545-6407
   130 W Broadway Ave Girard (44420) *(G-8813)*

Girard Equipment Co 330 545-2575
   1745 N State St Girard (44420) *(G-8814)*

Girl Scouts, Columbus *Also Called: Girl Scuts Ohios Hrtland Cncil (G-5935)*

Girl Scouts North East Ohio (PA) 330 864-9933
   1 Girl Scout Way Macedonia (44056) *(G-10193)*

Girl Scouts of Western Ohio (PA) 513 489-1025
   4930 Cornell Rd Blue Ash (45242) *(G-1178)*

Girl Scouts of Western Ohio 567 225-3557
   460 W Dussel Dr # A Maumee (43537) *(G-10729)*

Girl Scuts Ohios Hrtland Cncil 614 340-8829
   1700 Watermark Dr Columbus (43215) *(G-5935)*

Girl Scuts Wstn Ohio Tledo Div, Maumee *Also Called: Girl Scouts of Western Ohio (G-10729)*

Givens Lifting Systems Inc 419 724-9001
   26437 Southpoint Rd Perrysburg (43551) *(G-12338)*

Giving Tre, The, Port Clinton *Also Called: Giving Tree Inc (G-12526)*

Giving Tree Inc 419 734-2942
   335 Buckeye Blvd Port Clinton (43452) *(G-12526)*

GK Packaging Inc (PA) 614 873-3900
   7680 Commerce Pl Plain City (43064) *(G-12478)*

Glaus Pyle Schmer Brns Dhven I (PA) 330 572-2100
   520 S Main St Ste 2531 Akron (44311) *(G-176)*

Glaus Pyle Schmer Brns Dhven I 216 518-5544
   5595 Transportation Blvd Cleveland (44125) *(G-4314)*

Glaus Pyle Schmer Brns Dhven I 614 210-0751
   1801 Watermark Dr Ste 210 Columbus (43215) *(G-5936)*

Glaus Pyle Schmer Brns Dhven I 330 645-2131
   470 Portage Lakes Dr Ste 212 Coventry Township (44319) *(G-7009)*

Glaus Pyle Schmer Brns Dhven I 740 382-6840
   286 Summit St Marion (43302) *(G-10428)*

Glazer's of Ohio, Columbus *Also Called: Southern Glzers Dstrs Ohio LLC (G-6696)*

Gleason Construction Co Inc 419 865-7480
   540 S Centennial Rd Holland (43528) *(G-9285)*

GLEN MEADOWS, Fairfield Township *Also Called: Glenward Inc (G-8460)*

Glen Wesley Inc 614 888-7492
   5155 N High St Columbus (43214) *(G-5937)*

Glenbeigh (PA) 440 563-3400
   2863 State Route 45 N Rock Creek (44084) *(G-12733)*

Glenbeigh Health Sources Inc (PA) 440 951-7000
   2863 State Route 45 N Rock Creek (44084) *(G-12734)*

Glencare Center, Cincinnati *Also Called: Carington Health Systems (G-2315)*

Glencoe Restoration Group LLC 330 752-1244
   513 James Ave Akron (44312) *(G-177)*

Glendale Assisted Living, The, Toledo *Also Called: Ryan Senior Care LLC (G-14001)*

Glendora Health Care Center 330 264-0912
   1552 N Honeytown Rd Wooster (44691) *(G-15340)*

Glenellen, North Lima *Also Called: Lakeside Manor Inc (G-11890)*

Glenlaurel Inc 740 385-4070
   14940 Mount Olive Rd Rockbridge (43149) *(G-12735)*

Glenlurel-A Scottish Cntry Inn, Rockbridge *Also Called: Glenlaurel Inc (G-12735)*

Glenridge Machine Co 440 975-1055
   37435 Fawn Path Dr Solon (44139) *(G-13092)*

Glenview Ctr For Child Care Lr, Cleveland *Also Called: Bay Village City School Dst (G-3857)*

Glenward Inc 513 863-3100
   3472 Hamilton Mason Rd Fairfield Township (45011) *(G-8460)*

Glenway Family Medicine, Cincinnati *Also Called: Christ Hospital (G-2383)*

Glenwood Assisted Living, Canton *Also Called: Stone Crssing Asssted Lving LL (G-1862)*

Glenwood Behavioral Hlth Hosp, Cincinnati *Also Called: Mt Airy Development LLC (G-3084)*

GLENWOOD GARDENS, Cincinnati *Also Called: Great Parks Hamilton County (G-2766)*

Glic Electrical, Toledo *Also Called: Great Lakes Indus Contg Ltd (G-13826)*

Glickfield, W Scott MD, Trenton *Also Called: Primary Care Ntwrk Prmier Hlth (G-14124)*

Glidden House Associates Ltd 216 231-8900
   1901 Ford Dr Cleveland (44106) *(G-4315)*

Glidden House Inn, Cleveland *Also Called: Glidden House Associates Ltd (G-4315)*

Glimcher, Columbus *Also Called: Washington Prime Group Inc (G-6866)*

Glimcher Realty Trust 614 621-9000
   180 E Broad St Columbus (43215) *(G-5938)*

Glimscher Retail Properties, Dayton *Also Called: Urban Retail Properties LLC (G-7695)*

Glm Transport Inc (PA) 419 363-2041
   1300 Production Dr Van Wert (45891) *(G-14345)*

Global Associates Inc 937 312-1204
   7106 Corporate Way Dayton (45459) *(G-7376)*

Global E.D.M. Supplies, Inc, Mason *Also Called: Global EDM Inc (G-10555)*

Global EDM Inc 513 701-0468
   7697 Innovation Way Mason (45040) *(G-10555)*

Global Energy Partners LLC 419 756-8027
   3401 State Route 13 Mansfield (44904) *(G-10267)*

Global Exec Slutions Group LLC 330 666-3354
   3505 Embassy Pkwy Ste 200 Akron (44333) *(G-178)*

Global Ground, Cleveland *Also Called: Servisair LLC (G-4897)*

Global Insulation Inc (PA) 330 479-3100
   4450 Belden Village St Nw Ste 406 Canton (44718) *(G-1763)*

Global Mail Inc 330 849-3248
   542 Seasons Rd Stow (44224) *(G-13371)*

Global Meals, Columbus *Also Called: Casleo Corporation (G-5515)*

Global Medical Products LLC 630 521-9545
   11253 Williamson Rd Blue Ash (45241) *(G-1179)*

Global Scrap Management Inc.. 513 576-6600
 4340 Batavia Rd Batavia (45103) *(G-741)*

Global Tchnical Recruiters Inc.. 440 365-1670
 27887 Clemens Rd Ste 1 Westlake (44145) *(G-15061)*

Global Technology Center, Holland *Also Called: Tekni-Plex Inc (G-9307)*

Global Workplace Solutions LLC (PA).. 513 759-6000
 9823 Cincinnati Dayton Rd West Chester (45069) *(G-14697)*

Globe American Casualty Co... 513 576-3200
 6281 Tri Ridge Blvd Unit 1 Loveland (45140) *(G-10138)*

Globe Food Equipment Company... 937 299-5493
 2153 Dryden Rd Moraine (45439) *(G-11413)*

Globe Furniture Rentals Inc (PA).. 513 771-8287
 11745 Commons Dr Cincinnati (45246) *(G-2734)*

Glockner Chvrlet Oldsmbile Cdl, Portsmouth *Also Called: The Glockner Chevrolet Company (G-12576)*

Glockner Oil Company Inc.. 740 289-2979
 4407 Us Highway 23 Piketon (45661) *(G-12420)*

GLORIA DEI MONTESSORI SCHOOL, Dayton *Also Called: Childrens Lab Schools Inc (G-7224)*

Gloria Gadmack Do.. 216 363-2353
 17800 Shaker Blvd Cleveland (44120) *(G-4316)*

Glow Industries Inc.. 419 872-4772
 12962 Eckel Junction Rd Perrysburg (43551) *(G-12339)*

Glt Products, Solon *Also Called: SPI LLC (G-13148)*

GM Mechanical Inc (PA).. 937 473-3006
 4263 N State Route 48 Covington (45318) *(G-7018)*

GMAC Insurance, Richfield *Also Called: Explorer Rv Insurance Agcy Inc (G-12697)*

GMI Holdings Inc... 330 897-4424
 606 N Ray St Baltic (43804) *(G-689)*

GMI Holdings Inc (DH)... 800 354-3643
 1 Door Dr Mount Hope (44660) *(G-11466)*

Gms Management Co Inc (PA)... 216 766-6000
 4645 Richmond Rd Ste 101 Cleveland (44128) *(G-4317)*

Gms Realty, Cleveland *Also Called: Gms Management Co Inc (G-4317)*

GNB Banking Centers, Greenville *Also Called: Greenville National Bank (G-8877)*

Gnco Inc (PA)... 216 706-2349
 1395 Valley Belt Rd Brooklyn Heights (44131) *(G-1419)*

Gng Music Instruction, New Albany *Also Called: Qwaide Enterprises LLC (G-11583)*

Go Reliant LLC, Cleveland *Also Called: Reliant Technology LLC (G-4822)*

Go Sustainable Energy LLC.. 614 268-4263
 5701 N High St Ste 112 Worthington (43085) *(G-15417)*

Go2it Group, Westlake *Also Called: Career Cnnctons Stffing Svcs I (G-15045)*

Goddard School... 513 271-6311
 4430 Red Bank Rd Cincinnati (45227) *(G-2735)*

Goddard School... 614 865-2100
 1260 County Line Rd Westerville (43081) *(G-14981)*

Goddard School, Strongsville *Also Called: Hewlettco Inc (G-13461)*

Goddard School, The, Mason *Also Called: P J & R J Connection Inc (G-10589)*

Goddard School, The, Westerville *Also Called: Powell Enterprises Inc (G-14930)*

Goddard School, The, Westerville *Also Called: Goddard School (G-14981)*

Goddard Schools, Hudson *Also Called: J-Nan Enterprises Llc (G-9358)*

Godfrey & Wing Inc (PA).. 330 562-1440
 220 Campus Dr Aurora (44202) *(G-615)*

Goering Ctr For Fmly/Prvate Bu... 513 556-7185
 225 Calhoun St Ste 360 Cincinnati (45219) *(G-2736)*

Goettle Co.. 513 825-8100
 12071 Hamilton Ave Cincinnati (45231) *(G-2737)*

Goettle Construction, Cincinnati *Also Called: Goettle Holding Company Inc (G-2738)*

Goettle Holding Company Inc (PA).. 513 825-8100
 12071 Hamilton Ave Cincinnati (45231) *(G-2738)*

Gofs, Mansfield *Also Called: Global Energy Partners LLC (G-10267)*

Gohypersonic Incorporated.. 937 331-9460
 848 E Monument Ave Dayton (45402) *(G-7377)*

Goken America, Dublin *Also Called: Goken America LLC (G-8021)*

Goken America LLC... 614 495-8104
 5100 Parkcenter Ave Ste 100 Dublin (43017) *(G-8021)*

Gokeyless, Miamisburg *Also Called: 21st Century Solutions Ltd (G-11017)*

Gold Key Homes, Miamisburg *Also Called: Oberer Residential Cnstr Ltd (G-11078)*

Gold Medal Products Co (PA)... 513 769-7676
 10700 Medallion Dr Cincinnati (45241) *(G-2739)*

Gold Medal Products Co.. 614 228-1155
 787 Harrison Dr Columbus (43204) *(G-5939)*

Gold Medal-Carolina, Cincinnati *Also Called: Gold Medal Products Co (G-2739)*

Gold Star Chili, Cincinnati *Also Called: Gold Star Chili Inc (G-2740)*

Gold Star Chili Inc (PA).. 513 231-4541
 650 Lunken Park Dr Cincinnati (45226) *(G-2740)*

Golden Age Senior Citizens... 937 376-4353
 338 S Progress Dr Xenia (45385) *(G-15509)*

Golden Drapery Supply Inc... 216 351-3283
 2500 Brookpark Rd Unit 3 Cleveland (44134) *(G-4318)*

Golden Endngs Glden Rtrver RSC... 614 486-0773
 1043 Elmwood Ave Columbus (43212) *(G-5940)*

Golden Hawk Inc... 419 683-3304
 4594 Lincoln Hwy 30 Crestline (44827) *(G-7023)*

Golden Hawk Transportation Co (PA)... 419 683-3304
 4594 Lincoln Hwy Crestline (44827) *(G-7024)*

Golden Jersey Inn, Yellow Springs *Also Called: Youngs Jersey Dairy Inc (G-15537)*

Golden Lamb... 513 932-5065
 27 S Broadway St Lebanon (45036) *(G-9767)*

Golden Lamb Rest Ht & Gift Sp, Lebanon *Also Called: Golden Lamb (G-9767)*

Golden Leaf, Solon *Also Called: Snf Wadsworth LLC (G-13143)*

Golden Reserve LLC.. 614 563-2818
 270 Bradenton Ave Dublin (43017) *(G-8022)*

Golden Resources Incorporated.. 513 342-6290
 7681 Tylers Place Blvd West Chester (45069) *(G-14698)*

Golden Technology, West Chester *Also Called: Golden Resources Incorporated (G-14698)*

Golden Window Fashions, Cleveland *Also Called: Golden Drapery Supply Inc (G-4318)*

Golden Years Health Care, Hamilton *Also Called: Golden Years Nursing Home Inc (G-9045)*

Golden Years Nursing Home Inc... 513 893-0471
 2436 Old Oxford Rd Hamilton (45013) *(G-9045)*

Goldway Trans, Cincinnati *Also Called: Goldway Trans LLC (G-2741)*

Goldway Trans LLC.. 330 828-0008
 11811 Enterprise Dr Cincinnati (45241) *(G-2741)*

Golf Center At Kings Island, Mason *Also Called: Grizzly Golf Center Inc (G-10557)*

Golf Club Co.. 614 855-7326
 4522 Kitzmiller Rd New Albany (43054) *(G-11567)*

Golf Course At Yankee Trace, Dayton *Also Called: City of Centerville (G-7227)*

Golf Course Branch, Clayton *Also Called: Moss Creek Golf Course (G-3735)*

Golf Galaxy Golfworks Inc.. 740 328-4193
 4820 Jacksontown Rd Newark (43056) *(G-11702)*

Golfworks, The, Newark *Also Called: Golf Galaxy Golfworks Inc (G-11702)*

Gonda Lawn Care LLC.. 330 701-7232
 7822 2nd St Masury (44438) *(G-10678)*

Good Inc.. 740 592-9667
 21 W State St Athens (45701) *(G-569)*

Good Cleaners Laundry, Athens *Also Called: Good Inc (G-569)*

Good Life, Cincinnati *Also Called: Making Life Easy LLC (G-3006)*

Good Samaritan Health Group Inc
 4110 Rocky River Dr Cleveland (44135) *(G-4319)*

Good Samaritan Hosp Cincinnati (HQ).. 513 569-6251
 375 Dixmyth Ave Cincinnati (45220) *(G-2742)*

Good Samaritan Hospital.. 937 278-2612
 2222 Philadelphia Dr Dayton (45406) *(G-7378)*

Good Samaritan Hospital, Cincinnati *Also Called: Obstetric Anesthesia Assoc Inc (G-3139)*

Good Samaritan Soc - Arlington, Arlington *Also Called: Evanglcal Lthran Good Smrtan S (G-469)*

GOOD SAMARITAN, THE, Millersburg *Also Called: Christian Aid Ministries (G-11276)*

Good Shepard Village, Springfield *Also Called: Good Shepherd Village LLC (G-13253)*

Good Shepard, The, Ashland *Also Called: Lutheran Scial Svcs Centl Ohio (G-506)*

Good Shepherd Home.. 419 937-1801
 725 Columbus Ave Fostoria (44830) *(G-8618)*

Good Shepherd Home For Aged.. 614 228-5200
 622 Center St Ashland (44805) *(G-499)*

GOOD SHEPHERD MANOR, Lucasville *Also Called: Friends of Good Shepherd Manor (G-10178)*

Good Shepherd Village LLC... 937 322-1911
 422 N Burnett Rd Springfield (45503) *(G-13253)*

Good Venture Enterprises LLC... 740 282-0901
 1235 University Blvd Steubenville (43952) *(G-13327)*

Goodnight Inn Inc.. 419 334-9551
3701 N State Route 53 Fremont (43420) *(G-8682)*

Goodnight Inn Inc.. 419 734-2274
1734 E Perry St Port Clinton (43452) *(G-12527)*

Goodrich Gannett Headstart, Cleveland *Also Called: Goodrich Gnnett Nghborhood Ctr (G-4320)*

Goodrich Gnnett Nghborhood Ctr......................... 216 432-1717
1801 E 9th St Ste 920 Cleveland (44114) *(G-4320)*

Goods Hands Supported Living............................. 740 773-4170
263 Delano Ave Chillicothe (45601) *(G-2066)*

Goods Hands Supported Living............................. 740 474-2646
2489 N Court St Circleville (43113) *(G-3709)*

GOODS HANDS SUPPORTED LIVING, Chillicothe *Also Called: Goods Hands Supported Living (G-2066)*

GOODS HANDS SUPPORTED LIVING, Circleville *Also Called: Goods Hands Supported Living (G-3709)*

Goodwill Columbus, Columbus *Also Called: Goodwill Inds Centl Ohio Inc (G-5941)*

Goodwill Ester Seals Miami Vly (PA).................... 937 461-4800
660 S Main St Dayton (45402) *(G-7379)*

Goodwill Ester Seals Miami Vly............................ 937 461-4800
660 S Main St Dayton (45402) *(G-7380)*

Goodwill Inds Ashtabula Inc (PA)......................... 440 964-3565
621 Goodwill Dr Ashtabula (44004) *(G-536)*

Goodwill Inds Centl Ohio Inc................................. 740 439-7000
1712 Southgate Pkwy Cambridge (43725) *(G-1572)*

Goodwill Inds Centl Ohio Inc (PA)........................ 614 294-5181
605 S Front St Columbus (43215) *(G-5941)*

Goodwill Inds Centl Ohio Inc................................. 614 274-5296
890 N Hague Ave Columbus (43204) *(G-5942)*

Goodwill Inds Erie Hron Ottawa............................ 419 334-7566
1597 Pontiac Ave Fremont (43420) *(G-8683)*

Goodwill Inds Erie Hron Ottawa (PA)................... 419 625-4744
419 W Market St Sandusky (44870) *(G-12900)*

Goodwill Inds NW Ohio Inc (PA)........................... 419 255-0070
1120 Madison Ave Toledo (43604) *(G-13822)*

Goodwill Inds Rhbilitation Ctr (PA)....................... 330 454-9461
408 9th St Sw Canton (44707) *(G-1764)*

Goodwill Inds S Centl Ohio (PA)........................... 740 702-4000
1285 Industrial Dr Chillicothe (45601) *(G-2067)*

Goodwill Inds Wyne Hlmes Cntie (PA)................. 330 264-1300
1034 Nold Ave Wooster (44691) *(G-15341)*

Goodwill Industries, Cambridge *Also Called: Goodwill Inds Centl Ohio Inc (G-1572)*

Goodwill Industries, Chillicothe *Also Called: Goodwill Inds S Centl Ohio (G-2067)*

GOODWILL INDUSTRIES OF ERIE, H, Sandusky *Also Called: Goodwill Inds Erie Hron Ottawa (G-12900)*

Goodwill Industry, Ashtabula *Also Called: Goodwill Inds Ashtabula Inc (G-536)*

GOODWILL RETAIL STORE, Zanesville *Also Called: Zanesvlle Wlfare Orgnztion Gdw (G-15843)*

Goodyear, Akron *Also Called: Goodyear Tire & Rubber Company (G-179)*

Goodyear Tire & Rubber Company (PA)................ 330 796-2121
200 E Innovation Way Akron (44316) *(G-179)*

Goofy Golf II Inc.. 419 732-6671
1530 S Danbury North Rd Port Clinton (43452) *(G-12528)*

Gorant Chocolatier LLC (PA).................................. 330 726-8821
8301 Market St Boardman (44512) *(G-1288)*

Gorant's Yum Yum Tree, Boardman *Also Called: Gorant Chocolatier LLC (G-1288)*

Gordon Bros Water, Salem *Also Called: Gordon Brothers Inc (G-12842)*

Gordon Brothers Inc (PA)...................................... 800 331-7611
776 N Ellsworth Ave Salem (44460) *(G-12842)*

Gordon W Womack DDS.. 937 426-2653
3300 Kemp Rd Beavercreek (45431) *(G-881)*

Gorell Enterprises Inc (DH).................................. 724 465-1800
10250 Philipp Pkwy Streetsboro (44241) *(G-13414)*

Gorell Windows & Doors, Streetsboro *Also Called: Gorell Enterprises Inc (G-13414)*

Gorilla Glue Company LLC (PA)............................ 513 271-3300
2101 E Kemper Rd Cincinnati (45241) *(G-2743)*

Gorman-Rupp Company.. 419 886-3001
180 Hines Ave Bellville (44813) *(G-1049)*

Gorsuch Management, Lancaster *Also Called: Fairfield Homes Inc (G-9713)*

Gorsuch Management, Lancaster *Also Called: Fairfield Homes Inc (G-9714)*

Gosh Enterprises Inc (PA)..................................... 614 923-4700
5000 Arlington Centre Blvd Columbus (43220) *(G-5943)*

Goshen Family Practice, Loveland *Also Called: Healthsource of Ohio Inc (G-10140)*

Gosiger, Dayton *Also Called: Gosiger Holdings Inc (G-7381)*

Gosiger Holdings Inc (PA)..................................... 937 228-5174
108 Mcdonough St Dayton (45402) *(G-7381)*

Gosiger Holdings Inc... 734 582-2100
30600 Solon Industrial Pkwy Solon (44139) *(G-13093)*

Gosiger Inc... 937 228-5174
108 Mcdonough St Dayton (45402) *(G-7382)*

Gosiger Machine Tools, Solon *Also Called: Gosiger Holdings Inc (G-13093)*

Goss Supply Company (PA)................................... 740 454-2571
620 Marietta St Zanesville (43701) *(G-15796)*

Gottlieb & Sons Inc (PA)....................................... 216 771-4785
25201 Chagrin Blvd Beachwood (44122) *(G-795)*

Gottlieb Jhnson Beam Dal Pnte............................ 740 452-7555
320 Main St Zanesville (43701) *(G-15797)*

Goudreau Management, Cleveland *Also Called: G J Goudreau & Co (G-4297)*

Govana Hospital, Newark *Also Called: Yeater Alene K MD (G-11756)*

Government Acquisitions Inc................................ 513 721-8700
2060 Reading Rd Fl 4 Cincinnati (45202) *(G-2744)*

Government Payment Solutions, Symmes Twp *Also Called: Worldpay Iso Inc (G-13585)*

Governor's Village Assisted LI, Cleveland *Also Called: Governors Village LLC (G-4321)*

Governors Village LLC... 440 449-8788
280 N Commons Blvd Apt 101 Cleveland (44143) *(G-4321)*

Govplus LLC.. 330 580-1913
400 Tuscarawas St W Ste 1 Canton (44702) *(G-1765)*

Govplus LLC.. 440 888-0330
5907 Ridge Rd Cleveland (44129) *(G-4322)*

GOVPLUS LLC, Canton *Also Called: Govplus LLC (G-1765)*

GOVPLUS LLC, Cleveland *Also Called: Govplus LLC (G-4322)*

Gozal Incorporated.. 833 603-0303
4450 Monroe Ave Hooven (45033) *(G-9317)*

GP Strategies Corporation.................................... 513 583-8810
3794 E Galbraith Rd Cincinnati (45236) *(G-2745)*

GPA, Cincinnati *Also Called: Gus Perdikakis Associates (G-2784)*

Gpax Inc.. 614 501-7622
555 Lancaster Ave Reynoldsburg (43068) *(G-12664)*

Gpd Associates, Akron *Also Called: Gpd Services Company Inc (G-180)*

Gpd Group, Akron *Also Called: Glaus Pyle Schmer Brns Dhven I (G-176)*

Gpd Group, Cleveland *Also Called: Glaus Pyle Schmer Brns Dhven I (G-4314)*

Gpd Group, Columbus *Also Called: Glaus Pyle Schmer Brns Dhven I (G-5936)*

Gpd Group, Coventry Township *Also Called: Glaus Pyle Schmer Brns Dhven I (G-7009)*

Gpd Group, Marion *Also Called: Glaus Pyle Schmer Brns Dhven I (G-10428)*

Gpd Services Company Inc (PA)........................... 330 572-2100
520 S Main St Ste 2531 Akron (44311) *(G-180)*

Grabill Plumbing & Heating.................................. 330 756-2075
10235 Manchester Ave Sw Beach City (44608) *(G-761)*

Grace Brethren Village.. 937 836-4011
1010 Taywood Rd Ofc Englewood (45322) *(G-8309)*

Grace Brthren Ch Columbus Ohio (PA)................ 614 888-7733
8724 Olde Worthington Rd Westerville (43082) *(G-14897)*

Grace Hospice LLC.. 513 458-5545
4850 Smith Rd Ste 100 Cincinnati (45212) *(G-2746)*

Grace Hospice LLC.. 216 288-7413
16600 W Sprague Rd Cleveland (44130) *(G-4323)*

Grace Hospice LLC.. 440 826-0350
16600 W Sprague Rd Ste 35 Cleveland (44130) *(G-4324)*

Grace Hospice LLC.. 937 293-1381
3033 Kettering Blvd Ste 210 Moraine (45439) *(G-11414)*

Grace Hospice of Middleburg, Cleveland *Also Called: Grace Hospice LLC (G-4324)*

Grace Hospital... 216 687-4013
254 Cleveland Ave Amherst (44001) *(G-429)*

Grace Hospital... 216 687-1500
44 Blaine Ave Bedford (44146) *(G-961)*

Grace Hospital... 216 476-2704
18101 Lorain Ave Cleveland (44111) *(G-4325)*

Grace Hospital... 216 687-1500
20000 Harvard Ave Warrensville Heights (44122) *(G-14581)*

Grace Management Inc 763 971-9271
9191 Round Top Rd Cincinnati (45251) *(G-2747)*

Grace Polaris Church, Westerville *Also Called: Grace Brthren Ch Columbus Ohio (G-14897)*

Graceworks Enhanced Living 513 825-3333
11430 Hamilton Ave Cincinnati (45231) *(G-2748)*

Graceworks Lutheran Services (PA) 937 433-2140
6430 Inner Mission Way Dayton (45459) *(G-7383)*

Gracie Plum Investments, Portsmouth *Also Called: Gracie Plum Investments Inc (G-12552)*

Gracie Plum Investments Inc 740 355-9029
609 2nd St Unit 2 Portsmouth (45662) *(G-12552)*

Graco Ohio Inc 330 494-1313
8400 Port Jackson Ave Nw Canton (44720) *(G-1766)*

Gracor Language Services, Westerville *Also Called: Ceiba Enterprises Incorporated (G-14965)*

Grady Memorial Hospital (PA) 740 615-1000
561 W Central Ave Delaware (43015) *(G-7802)*

Grae-Con Construction Inc (PA) 740 282-6830
880 Kingsdale Rd Steubenville (43952) *(G-13328)*

Grae-Con Contructions, Steubenville *Also Called: Grae-Con Construction Inc (G-13328)*

Graffiti Co, Cleveland *Also Called: Barbs Graffiti Inc (G-3849)*

Graftech Holdings Inc 216 676-2000
6100 Oak Tree Blvd Ste 300 Independence (44131) *(G-9434)*

Grafton Ready Mix Concret Inc 440 926-2911
1155 Elm St Grafton (44044) *(G-8839)*

Graham Chevrolet-Cadillac Co 419 989-4012
1515 W 4th St Ontario (44906) *(G-12105)*

Graham Investment Co (PA) 740 382-0902
3007 Harding Hwy Bldg 203 Marion (43302) *(G-10429)*

Graham Packg Plastic Pdts LLC (DH) 419 423-3271
170 Stanford Pkwy Findlay (45840) *(G-8539)*

Grail 513 683-2340
931 Obannonville Rd Loveland (45140) *(G-10139)*

GRAILVILLE, Loveland *Also Called: Grail (G-10139)*

Grainger 165, Macedonia *Also Called: W W Grainger Inc (G-10209)*

Grammer Industries LLC (DH) 864 284-9616
1429 Coining Dr Toledo (43612) *(G-13823)*

Grand Aerie of The Fraternal 419 227-1566
800 W Robb Ave Lima (45801) *(G-9892)*

Grand Arie of The Frtnrl Order (PA) 614 883-2200
1623 Gateway Cir Grove City (43123) *(G-8921)*

Grand Encore Cincinnati LLC 513 482-7500
9230 Port Union Rialto Rd West Chester (45069) *(G-14699)*

Grand Heritage Hotel Portland 440 734-4477
25105 Country Club Blvd North Olmsted (44070) *(G-11903)*

Grand Lake Health System, Saint Marys *Also Called: Joint Township Dst Mem Hosp (G-12828)*

GRAND LAKE HEALTH SYSTEM, Saint Marys *Also Called: Joint Township Dst Mem Hosp (G-12829)*

Grand Lake Primary Care, Saint Marys *Also Called: Joint Township Dst Mem Hosp (G-12830)*

Grand Rapids Care Center, Grand Rapids *Also Called: Rapids Nursing Homes Inc (G-8846)*

Grand River Health & Rehab Ctr, Painesville *Also Called: Homestead I Hlthcare Group LLC (G-12229)*

Grand River Seafood Supply, Grand River *Also Called: 101 River Inc (G-8848)*

Grand, The, Dublin *Also Called: Vrable Healthcare Inc (G-8157)*

Grande Oaks & Grande Pavillion, Cleveland *Also Called: Oakwood Health Care Svcs Inc (G-4677)*

Grande Pointe Healthcare Cmnty, Cleveland *Also Called: Merit Leasing Co LLC (G-4555)*

Grandmas Gardens Inc 937 885-2973
8107 State Route 48 Waynesville (45068) *(G-14623)*

Grandview Avenue Home, Waverly *Also Called: Buckeye Community Services Inc (G-14611)*

Grandview Family Practice Inc 740 258-9267
1550 W 5th Ave Lowr Columbus (43212) *(G-5944)*

Grandview Fifth Auto Svc Inc 614 488-6106
2300 Cardigan Ave Columbus (43215) *(G-5945)*

GRANDVIEW HOSPITAL, Dayton *Also Called: Stress Care/Bridges (G-7647)*

Grandview Hospital & Med Ctr, Dayton *Also Called: Dayton Osteopathic Hospital (G-7293)*

GRANDVIEW HOSPITAL & MEDICAL C, Beavercreek *Also Called: Beavercreek Medical Center (G-863)*

Grandview Inn, South Point *Also Called: Grandview Inn Inc (G-13175)*

Grandview Inn Inc 740 377-4388
154 County Road 450 South Point (45680) *(G-13175)*

Grandvlle Pike Fmly Physicians 740 687-0793
1800 Granville Pike Lancaster (43130) *(G-9724)*

Grange Indemnity Insurance Co 614 445-2900
671 S High St Columbus (43206) *(G-5946)*

Grange Insurance Companies, Columbus *Also Called: Grange Insurance Company (G-5947)*

Grange Insurance Company (PA) 800 422-0550
671 S High St Columbus (43206) *(G-5947)*

Grange Life Insurance Company 800 445-3030
671 S High St Columbus (43206) *(G-5948)*

Grange Mutual Casualty Company, Columbus *Also Called: Grange Indemnity Insurance Co (G-5946)*

Grant Thornton LLP 513 762-5000
4000 Smith Rd Ste 500 Cincinnati (45209) *(G-2749)*

Grants Plus LLC 216 916-7376
1422 Euclid Ave Ste 970 Cleveland (44115) *(G-4326)*

Granville Builders Supply, Columbus *Also Called: Columbus Coal & Lime Co (G-5624)*

Granville Hospitality Llc 740 587-3333
314 Broadway E Granville (43023) *(G-8853)*

Graphel Corporation 513 779-6166
6115 Centre Park Dr West Chester (45069) *(G-14700)*

Graphic Communications, Stow *Also Called: Veritiv Pubg & Print MGT Inc (G-13400)*

Graphic Enterprises, North Canton *Also Called: Graphic Entps Off Slutions Inc (G-11836)*

Graphic Enterprises Inc 800 553-6616
3874 Highland Park Nw North Canton (44720) *(G-11835)*

Graphic Entps Off Slutions Inc 800 553-6616
3874 Highland Park Nw North Canton (44720) *(G-11836)*

Graphic Packaging Intl LLC 630 584-2900
4500 Beech St Cincinnati (45212) *(G-2750)*

Graphic Systems Services Inc 937 746-0708
400 S Pioneer Blvd Springboro (45066) *(G-13199)*

Grasscor Lawn & Landscapes, Blue Ash *Also Called: Schill Ldscpg Lawn Care Svcs L (G-1243)*

Graves Care Services LLC 614 392-2820
100 Dorchester Sq N Ste 101 Westerville (43081) *(G-14982)*

Graves Lumber Co 330 666-1115
1315 S Cleveland Massillon Rd Copley (44321) *(G-6958)*

Gray & Pape Inc (PA) 513 287-7700
1318 Main St Fl 1 Cincinnati (45202) *(G-2751)*

Gray Media Group Inc 513 421-1919
635 W 7th St Ste 200 Cincinnati (45203) *(G-2752)*

Gray Media Group Inc 216 367-7300
1717 E 12th St Cleveland (44114) *(G-4327)*

Gray Media Group Inc 419 534-3886
4247 Dorr St Toledo (43607) *(G-13824)*

Graybar Electric Company Inc 216 573-0456
6161 Halle Dr Cleveland (44125) *(G-4328)*

Graybar Electric Company Inc 419 228-7441
990 W Grand Ave Lima (45801) *(G-9893)*

Graybar Electric Company Inc 330 526-2800
3805 Highland Park Nw North Canton (44720) *(G-11837)*

Graybar Electric Company Inc 419 729-1641
1333 E Manhattan Blvd Toledo (43608) *(G-13825)*

Graybill Gallery Kitchens Bath, Beach City *Also Called: Grabill Plumbing & Heating (G-761)*

Graydon Head & Ritchey LLP (PA) 513 621-6464
312 Walnut St Ste 1800 Cincinnati (45202) *(G-2753)*

Grays Trnsp & Logistics LLC 614 656-3460
470 W Broad St Unit 1074 Columbus (43215) *(G-5949)*

Gre Insurance Group, Loveland *Also Called: Globe American Casualty Co (G-10138)*

Great Amercn Aliance Insur Co (DH) 513 369-5000
301 E 4th St Fl 24 Cincinnati (45202) *(G-2754)*

Great American, Cincinnati *Also Called: Great American Insurance Co (G-2757)*

Great American, Cincinnati *Also Called: Great Amrcn Fncl Resources Inc (G-2759)*

Great American, Cincinnati *Also Called: Massmutual Ascend Lf Insur Co (G-3014)*

Great American Advisors, Cincinnati *Also Called: Mm Ascend Life Inv Svcs LLC (G-3071)*

Great American Assurance 513 369-5000
301 E 4th St Fl 8 Cincinnati (45202) *(G-2755)*

Great American Holding Inc (HQ) 513 369-3000
301 E 4th St Cincinnati (45202) *(G-2756)*

Great American Insurance Co (HQ) 513 369-5000
301 E 4th St Cincinnati (45202) *(G-2757)*

ALPHABETIC SECTION

Great American SEC Insur Co (DH).. 513 369-5000
    580 Walnut St Ste S900 Cincinnati (45202) *(G-2758)*
Great American Woodies, Columbus *Also Called: Competitor Swim Products Inc (G-5676)*
Great Amrcn Fncl Resources Inc (HQ).. 513 333-5300
    250 E 5th St Ste 1000 Cincinnati (45202) *(G-2759)*
Great Amrcn Plan Admnstrtors I.. 513 412-2316
    525 Vine St Fl 7 Cincinnati (45202) *(G-2760)*
Great Amrcn Risk Sltons Srpls (DH).. 513 369-3000
    580 Walnut St Cincinnati (45202) *(G-2761)*
Great Bear Lodge Sandusky LLC.. 419 609-6000
    4600 Milan Rd Sandusky (44870) *(G-12901)*
Great Clips, Dayton *Also Called: R L O Inc (G-7577)*
Great Eastern Theatre Company... 419 691-9668
    4500 Navarre Ave Oregon (43616) *(G-12134)*
Great Home Healthcare LLC... 614 475-4026
    2999 E Dublin Granville Rd Ste 215 Columbus (43231) *(G-5950)*
Great Lakes Cheese Co Inc (PA)... 440 834-2500
    17825 Great Lakes Pkwy Hiram (44234) *(G-9274)*
Great Lakes Companies Inc... 513 554-0720
    925 Laidlaw Ave Cincinnati (45237) *(G-2762)*
Great Lakes Computer Corp... 440 937-1100
    33675 Lear Industrial Pkwy Avon (44011) *(G-652)*
Great Lakes Crushing Ltd.. 440 944-5500
    30831 Euclid Ave Wickliffe (44092) *(G-15150)*
Great Lakes Fasteners Inc (PA)... 330 425-4488
    2204 E Enterprise Pkwy Twinsburg (44087) *(G-14195)*
Great Lakes Fasteners & Sup Co, Twinsburg *Also Called: Great Lakes Fasteners Inc (G-14195)*
Great Lakes Group... 216 621-4854
    4500 Division Ave Cleveland (44102) *(G-4329)*
Great Lakes Indus Contg Ltd... 419 945-4542
    3060 South Ave Toledo (43609) *(G-13826)*
Great Lakes Marketing, Toledo *Also Called: Great Lakes Mktg Assoc Inc (G-13827)*
Great Lakes Mktg Assoc Inc... 419 534-4700
    3361 Executive Pkwy Ste 201 Toledo (43606) *(G-13827)*
Great Lakes Packers Inc (PA)... 419 483-2956
    400 Great Lakes Pkwy Bellevue (44811) *(G-1045)*
Great Lakes Power Products Inc (PA).. 440 951-5111
    7455 Tyler Blvd Mentor (44060) *(G-10943)*
Great Lakes Publishing Company (PA).. 216 771-2833
    1422 Euclid Ave Ste 730 Cleveland (44115) *(G-4330)*
Great Lakes Record Center, Mentor *Also Called: Moving Solutions Inc (G-10977)*
Great Lakes Shipyard, Cleveland *Also Called: The Great Lakes Towing Company (G-5000)*
Great Lakes Telcom Ltd (PA)... 330 629-8848
    590 E Western Reserve Rd Bldg 9c Youngstown (44514) *(G-15622)*
Great Lakes Towing, Cleveland *Also Called: Great Lakes Group (G-4329)*
Great Lakes Western Star, Toledo *Also Called: Mizar Motors Inc (G-13925)*
Great Lakes-Ramco Inc.. 586 759-5500
    7455 Tyler Blvd Mentor (44060) *(G-10944)*
Great Lkes Cmnty Action Partnr (PA)... 419 333-6068
    127 S Front St Fremont (43420) *(G-8684)*
Great Lkes Cmnty Action Partnr.. 419 334-8511
    765 S Buchanan St Fremont (43420) *(G-8685)*
Great Lkes Cmnty Action Partnr.. 419 332-8089
    1071 N 5th St Fremont (43420) *(G-8686)*
Great Lkes Cmnty Action Partnr.. 419 639-2802
    1518 E County Road 113 Green Springs (44836) *(G-8859)*
Great Lkes Cmnty Action Partnr.. 419 732-7007
    1854 E Perry St Ste 500 Port Clinton (43452) *(G-12529)*
Great Lkes Cmnty Action Partnr.. 419 729-8035
    1500 N Superior St Ste 303 Toledo (43604) *(G-13828)*
Great Mami Vly Yung MNS Chrstn (PA)... 513 887-0001
    105 N 2nd St Hamilton (45011) *(G-9046)*
Great Mami Vly Yung MNS Chrstn... 513 217-5501
    5750 Innovation Dr Middletown (45005) *(G-11198)*
Great Miami Valley YMCA... 513 829-3091
    5220 Bibury Rd Fairfield (45014) *(G-8417)*
Great Miami Valley YMCA... 513 892-9622
    6645 Morris Rd Fairfield Township (45011) *(G-8461)*
Great Miami Valley YMCA... 513 867-0600
    4803 Augspurger Rd Hamilton (45011) *(G-9047)*

Great Miami Valley YMCA... 513 887-0014
    105 N 2nd St Hamilton (45011) *(G-9048)*
Great Miami Valley YMCA... 513 868-9622
    1307 Nw Washington Blvd Hamilton (45013) *(G-9049)*
Great Nthrn Cnsulting Svcs Inc (PA).. 614 890-9999
    200 E Campus View Blvd Ste 200 Columbus (43235) *(G-5951)*
Great Oaks Inst Tech Creer Dev... 513 771-8840
    3254 E Kemper Rd Cincinnati (45241) *(G-2763)*
Great Oaks Inst Tech Creer Dev (PA)... 513 613-3657
    110 Great Oaks Dr Cincinnati (45241) *(G-2764)*
Great Parks Forever.. 513 522-4357
    10245 Winton Rd Cincinnati (45231) *(G-2765)*
Great Parks Hamilton County... 513 521-7275
    377 Sheffield Rd Cincinnati (45240) *(G-2766)*
Great Wolf Lodge, Mason *Also Called: Mason Family Resorts LLC (G-10577)*
Great Wolf Lodge, Sandusky *Also Called: Clp Gw Sandusky Tenant LP (G-12883)*
Great Wolf Lodge, Sandusky *Also Called: Great Bear Lodge Sandusky LLC (G-12901)*
Greater Akron Dialysis Center, Akron *Also Called: Bio-Mdcal Applcations Ohio Inc (G-68)*
Greater Cin Cardi Consults In.. 513 751-4222
    2123 Auburn Ave Cincinnati (45219) *(G-2767)*
Greater Cincinnati Credit Un.. 513 559-1234
    7948 S Mason Montgomery Rd Mason (45040) *(G-10556)*
GREATER CINCINNATI CREDIT UNION, Mason *Also Called: Greater Cincinnati Credit Un (G-10556)*
Greater Cincinnati Gastro Assc (PA).. 513 336-8636
    2925 Vernon Pl Ste 100 Cincinnati (45219) *(G-2768)*
Greater Cincinnati Ob/Gyn Inc (PA)... 513 245-3103
    2830 Victory Pkwy Ste 140 Cincinnati (45206) *(G-2769)*
Greater Cincinnati Water Works.. 513 591-7700
    4747 Spring Grove Ave Cincinnati (45232) *(G-2770)*
Greater Cleveland Food Bnk Inc.. 216 738-2265
    13815 Coit Rd Cleveland (44110) *(G-4331)*
Greater Cleveland Hosp Assn, Cleveland *Also Called: Cha - Community Health Affairs (G-3959)*
Greater Cleveland Partnership (PA)... 216 621-3300
    1240 Huron Rd E Ste 300 Cleveland (44115) *(G-4332)*
Greater Cleveland Regional... 216 575-3932
    1240 W 6th St Cleveland (44113) *(G-4333)*
Greater Cleveland Regional Transit Authority (PA)............................ 216 566-5100
    1240 W 6th St Cleveland (44113) *(G-4334)*
Greater Clmbus Chmber Commerce.. 614 221-1321
    150 S Front St Ste 220 Columbus (43215) *(G-5952)*
Greater Clmbus Cnvntion Ctr Fo... 614 827-2500
    400 N High St Fl 4 Columbus (43215) *(G-5953)*
Greater Clmbus Cnvntion Vstors (PA).. 614 221-6623
    277 W Nationwide Blvd Ste 125 Columbus (43215) *(G-5954)*
Greater Clmbus Convention Ctr, Columbus *Also Called: Smg Holdings LLC (G-6689)*
Greater Clvland HM Hlth Care I.. 440 232-4995
    23811 Chagrin Blvd Ste 280 Beachwood (44122) *(G-796)*
Greater Clvland Rgnal Trnst Au... 216 781-1110
    4601 Euclid Ave Cleveland (44103) *(G-4335)*
Greater Clvland Rgnal Trnst Au... 216 566-5107
    1240 W 6th St 6th Fl Cleveland (44113) *(G-4336)*
Greater Cncnnati Bhvral Hlth S (PA).. 513 354-7000
    1501 Madison Rd Fl 2 Walnut Hills (45206) *(G-14474)*
Greater Cncnnati Cnvntion Vsto... 513 621-2142
    525 Vine St Ste 1200 Cincinnati (45202) *(G-2771)*
Greater Cncnnati Dntl Labs Inc... 513 385-4222
    3719 Struble Rd Cincinnati (45251) *(G-2772)*
Greater Cncnnati Oral Hlth Cnc, Cincinnati *Also Called: Cincysmiles Foundation Inc (G-2439)*
Greater Cncnnati TV Edctl Fndt... 513 381-4033
    1223 Central Pkwy Cincinnati (45214) *(G-2773)*
Greater Cnti Crdovascular Cons, Cincinnati *Also Called: Greater Cin Cardi Consults In (G-2767)*
Greater Dayton Cnstr Ltd.. 937 426-3577
    4197 Research Blvd Beavercreek (45430) *(G-923)*
Greater Dayton Public TV Inc... 937 220-1600
    110 S Jefferson St Dayton (45402) *(G-7384)*
Greater Dayton Surgery Ctr LLC.. 937 535-2200
    1625 Delco Park Dr Dayton (45420) *(G-7385)*
Greater Dyton Rgnal Trnst Auth (PA)... 937 425-8310
    4 S Main St Ste C Dayton (45402) *(G-7386)*

ALPHABETIC SECTION

Greater Dyton Rgnal Trnst Auth... 937 425-8400
600 Campus 600 Longworth St Dayton (45401) *(G-7387)*

Greater Ohio Orthpd Surgeons, Hilliard *Also Called: Cardinal Orthopedic Institute (G-9187)*

Green Again Turf Inc.. 937 203-0693
109 Helke Rd Vandalia (45377) *(G-14379)*

Green Circle Growers Inc (PA)..440 775-1411
51051 Us Highway 20 Oberlin (44074) *(G-12069)*

Green Circle Growers Inc... 440 775-1411
15650 State Route 511 Oberlin (44074) *(G-12070)*

Green Clean Janitorial, Cleveland *Also Called: Green Clean Ohio LLC (G-4337)*

Green Clean Ohio LLC... 866 853-6337
2580 E 93rd St Cleveland (44104) *(G-4337)*

Green County Engineer, Xenia *Also Called: Greene County (G-15514)*

Green Impressions LLC... 440 240-8508
842 Abbe Rd Sheffield Village (44054) *(G-12998)*

Green King Company Inc.. 614 861-4132
9562 Taylor Rd Sw Reynoldsburg (43068) *(G-12665)*

Green Lawn Specialists, Lewis Center *Also Called: Germann Bros LLC (G-9822)*

Green Legacy, Orient *Also Called: Pickaway Growers LLC (G-12154)*

Green Lines Transportation Inc (PA).....................................330 863-2111
7089 Alliance Rd Nw Malvern (44644) *(G-10233)*

Green Madows Hlth Wellness Ctr, Louisville *Also Called: Progressive Green Meadows LLC (G-10120)*

Green Township Hospitality LLC (PA)................................... 513 574-6000
5505 Rybolt Rd Cincinnati (45248) *(G-2774)*

Green Valley Co-Op Inc... 740 374-7741
219 3rd St Marietta (45750) *(G-10369)*

Greenbriar Boardman, Boardman *Also Called: South I Leasing Co LLC (G-1291)*

Greenbriar Nursing Center, The, Eaton *Also Called: October Enterprises Inc (G-8218)*

Greenbriar Retirement Center, Cleveland *Also Called: Greenbrier Senior Living Cmnty (G-4339)*

Greenbrier Healthcare Center, Parma *Also Called: Pearl Leasing Co LLC (G-12261)*

Greenbrier Retirement Cmnty, Cleveland *Also Called: Greenbrier Senior Living Cmnty (G-4338)*

Greenbrier Senior Living Cmnty... 440 888-0400
6457 Pearl Rd Cleveland (44130) *(G-4338)*

Greenbrier Senior Living Cmnty... 440 888-5900
6455 Pearl Rd Cleveland (44130) *(G-4339)*

Greene Inc.. 937 562-4200
121 Fairground Rd Xenia (45385) *(G-15510)*

Greene County... 937 562-5266
45 N Detroit St Rm 7 Xenia (45385) *(G-15511)*

Greene County... 937 562-6000
541 Ledbetter Rd Xenia (45385) *(G-15512)*

Greene County... 937 562-7800
641 Dayton Xenia Rd Xenia (45385) *(G-15513)*

Greene County... 937 562-7500
615 Dayton Xenia Rd Xenia (45385) *(G-15514)*

Greene County Board of Dd.. 937 562-6500
245 N Valley Rd Xenia (45385) *(G-15515)*

Greene County Council On Aging... 937 374-5600
360 Wilson Dr Xenia (45385) *(G-15516)*

GREENE COUNTY PUBLIC HEALTH, Xenia *Also Called: Greene County Council On Aging (G-15516)*

Greene County Services, Xenia *Also Called: Greene County (G-15513)*

Greene Memorial Hospital Inc (DH)..937 352-2000
1141 N Monroe Dr Xenia (45385) *(G-15517)*

Greene Oaks.. 937 352-2800
164 Office Park Dr Xenia (45385) *(G-15518)*

Greene Oaks Health Center, Xenia *Also Called: Greene Oaks (G-15518)*

Greenfield Area Medical Ctr... 937 981-9400
550 Mirabeau St Greenfield (45123) *(G-8864)*

Greenfield Health Systems Corp (PA)...................................419 389-9681
3401 Glendale Ave Ste 110 Toledo (43614) *(G-13829)*

Greenfield Hts Oper Group LLC.. 312 877-1153
1318 Chestnut St Lima (45804) *(G-9894)*

Greenfield Products Inc.. 937 981-2696
1230 N Washington St Greenfield (45123) *(G-8865)*

Greenheart Companies LLC... 330 259-3070
6001 Southern Blvd Ste 105 Youngstown (44512) *(G-15623)*

Greenhuse Sltons Acqsition LLC.. 440 236-8332
14800 Foltz Pkwy Strongsville (44149) *(G-13458)*

Greenix Holdings LLC... 614 961-7378
4635 Oracle Ln Hilliard (43026) *(G-9197)*

Greenleaf Family Center (PA)... 330 376-9494
580 Grant St Akron (44311) *(G-181)*

Greens of Lyndhurst The Inc... 440 460-1000
1555 Brainard Rd Apt 305 Cleveland (44124) *(G-4340)*

Greenscapes Landscape Co Inc... 614 837-1869
4220 Winchester Pike Columbus (43232) *(G-5955)*

Greenscpes Ldscp Archtcts Cntr, Columbus *Also Called: Greenscapes Landscape Co Inc (G-5955)*

Greentree Group Inc (PA)..937 490-5500
1360 Technology Ct Ste 100 Dayton (45430) *(G-7388)*

Greenville Federal... 937 548-4158
690 Wagner Ave Greenville (45331) *(G-8874)*

Greenville Inn Inc.. 937 548-3613
851 Martin St Unit 1 Greenville (45331) *(G-8875)*

Greenville National Bancorp (PA).. 937 548-1114
446 S Broadway St Greenville (45331) *(G-8876)*

Greenville National Bank (HQ).. 937 548-1114
446 S Broadway St Greenville (45331) *(G-8877)*

Greenville Nursing Services... 937 736-2272
1142 N Monroe Dr Xenia (45385) *(G-15519)*

Greenwood Chevrolet Inc... 330 270-1299
4695 Mahoning Ave Youngstown (44515) *(G-15624)*

Greenwood Motor Lines Inc (HQ)...800 543-5589
600 Gilliam Rd Wilmington (45177) *(G-15255)*

Greer Steel Company.. 330 343-8811
1 Boat St Dover (44622) *(G-7886)*

Greif Inc... 740 549-6000
5500 Wooster Pike Cincinnati (45226) *(G-2775)*

Greiner Dental & Associates, Mentor *Also Called: Raymond A Greiner DDS Inc (G-10987)*

Grey Matter, Cincinnati *Also Called: Ready Set Grow LLC (G-3275)*

Greyhound Lines Inc... 513 721-4450
600 Vine St Ste 1400 Cincinnati (45202) *(G-2776)*

Greyhound Lines Inc... 513 421-7442
1005 Gilbert Ave Cincinnati (45202) *(G-2777)*

Greyhound Lines Inc... 614 221-0577
111 E Town St Columbus (43215) *(G-5956)*

Grgstormpro, Akron *Also Called: Glencoe Restoration Group LLC (G-177)*

Grieser Logistics LLC... 419 445-9256
19230 County Road F Wauseon (43567) *(G-14604)*

Griffin Industries LLC... 419 257-3560
12850 Quarry Rd North Baltimore (45872) *(G-11800)*

Griffing's Airport, Port Clinton *Also Called: Griffings Flying Service Inc (G-12530)*

Griffings Flying Service Inc.. 419 734-5400
3255 E State Rd Port Clinton (43452) *(G-12530)*

Griid Infrastructure Inc... 513 268-6185
2577 Duck Creek Rd Cincinnati (45212) *(G-2778)*

Grill Rest At Sheraton Suites... 614 436-0004
201 Hutchinson Ave Columbus (43235) *(G-5957)*

Grimes Aerospace Company.. 937 484-2001
550 State Route 55 Urbana (43078) *(G-14308)*

Grimes Seeds, Chardon *Also Called: Gardenlife Inc (G-1999)*

Grismer Tire Company (PA)..937 643-2526
1099 S Main St Centerville (45458) *(G-1945)*

Grizzly Golf Center Inc... 513 398-5200
6042 Fairway Dr Mason (45040) *(G-10557)*

Grob Systems Inc... 419 358-9015
1070 Navajo Dr Bluffton (45817) *(G-1281)*

Grocery Outlet Supermarket, Hartville *Also Called: Sommers Market LLC (G-9130)*

Grogans Towne Chrysler Inc (PA)...419 476-0761
6100 Telegraph Rd Toledo (43612) *(G-13830)*

Gross Electric Inc (PA)..419 537-1818
2807 N Reynolds Rd Toledo (43615) *(G-13831)*

Gross Plumbing Incorporated.. 440 324-9999
6843 Lake Ave Elyria (44035) *(G-8253)*

Gross Residential, Cleveland *Also Called: I & M J Gross Company (G-4397)*

Gross Supply, Elyria *Also Called: Gross Plumbing Incorporated (G-8253)*

Ground Effects LLC.. 440 565-5925
31000 Viking Pkwy Westlake (44145) *(G-15062)*

ALPHABETIC SECTION

Ground Rund Grill Bar Prrysbur, Perrysburg *Also Called: Sunrise Hospitality Inc (G-12373)*
Ground Tech Inc.. 330 270-0700
 240 Sinter Ct Youngstown (44510) *(G-15625)*
Groundspro LLC... 513 242-1700
 9405 Sutton Pl West Chester (45011) *(G-14701)*
Groundsystems Inc.. 937 903-5325
 2929 Northlawn Ave Moraine (45439) *(G-11415)*
Groundsystems LLC (PA)... 800 570-0213
 11315 Williamson Rd Blue Ash (45241) *(G-1180)*
GROUNDSYSTEMS, INC., Moraine *Also Called: Groundsystems Inc (G-11415)*
Group Health Associates, Cincinnati *Also Called: Trihealth Inc (G-3514)*
Group Health Associates, Cincinnati *Also Called: Trihealth G LLC (G-3520)*
Group Health Associates, Cincinnati *Also Called: Trihealth G LLC (G-3522)*
Grove City Ctr For Dentistry... 614 875-3141
 4104 Broadway Grove City (43123) *(G-8922)*
Grow Well Cleveland Corp... 216 282-3838
 3000 Bridge Ave Ste 4 Cleveland (44113) *(G-4341)*
Growthplay, Dayton *Also Called: Silver Spruce Holding LLC (G-7622)*
Gs Engineering, Maumee *Also Called: Genius Solutions Engrg Co (G-10727)*
Gs1 Us Inc... 609 620-0200
 7887 Washington Village Dr Ste 300 Dayton (45459) *(G-7389)*
Gsf Usa Inc.. 513 733-1451
 9850 Princeton Glendale Rd Ste B West Chester (45246) *(G-14814)*
Gsw Worldwide, Westerville *Also Called: Gerbig Snell/Weisheimer Advertising LLC (G-14896)*
GTC Artist With Machines, Columbus *Also Called: General Theming Contrs LLC (G-5925)*
GTM Service Inc (PA).. 440 944-5099
 1366 Rockefeller Rd Wickliffe (44092) *(G-15151)*
Gtradvance LLC.. 440 365-1670
 366 Chestnut Commons Dr Elyria (44035) *(G-8254)*
GTS, Hudson *Also Called: Ascent Globl Lgstics Hldngs In (G-9333)*
Guaranteed Rate Inc.. 513 609-4477
 2654 Madison Rd Cincinnati (45208) *(G-2779)*
Guardian Alarm, Toledo *Also Called: GA Business Purchaser LLC (G-13816)*
Guardian Angels HM Hlth Care I... 419 517-7797
 8553 Sylvania Metamora Rd Sylvania (43560) *(G-13547)*
Guardian Angels Senior HM Svc, Sylvania *Also Called: Guardian Angels HM Hlth Care I (G-13547)*
Guardian Elder Care Columbus... 614 868-9306
 2425 Kimberly Pkwy E Columbus (43232) *(G-5958)*
Guardian Enterprise Group Inc.. 614 416-6080
 3948 Townsfair Way Ste 220 Columbus (43219) *(G-5959)*
Guardian Environmental Inc... 304 224-2011
 29510 Lorain Rd North Olmsted (44070) *(G-11904)*
Guardian Hlthcare HM Off I LLC... 330 549-0898
 9625 Market St North Lima (44452) *(G-11888)*
Guardian Home Technology, Bedford *Also Called: Guardian Protection Svcs Inc (G-962)*
Guardian Life Insur Co Amer.. 513 579-1114
 419 Plum St Cincinnati (45202) *(G-2780)*
Guardian Protection Svcs Inc... 330 797-1570
 7710 First Pl Ste H Bedford (44146) *(G-962)*
Guardian Savings Bank.. 513 842-8900
 11333 Princeton Pike Cincinnati (45246) *(G-2781)*
Guardian Savings Bank.. 513 528-8787
 560 Ohio Pike Cincinnati (45255) *(G-2782)*
Guardian Savings Bank (PA)... 513 942-3535
 6100 W Chester Rd West Chester (45069) *(G-14702)*
Guardian Water & Power Inc (PA)... 614 291-3141
 1650 Watermark Dr Ste 170 Columbus (43215) *(G-5960)*
Gudenkauf LLC (HQ).. 614 488-1776
 2679 Mckinley Ave Columbus (43204) *(G-5961)*
Guenther Mechanical Inc.. 419 289-6900
 1248 Middle Rowsburg Rd Ashland (44805) *(G-500)*
Guerbet, Cincinnati *Also Called: Liebel-Flarsheim Company LLC (G-2975)*
Guernsey Cnty Children Svcs Bd, Cambridge *Also Called: County of Guernsey (G-1567)*
Guernsey Cnty Wtr & Sewer Dept, Cambridge *Also Called: County of Guernsey (G-1565)*
Guernsey County Senior Center, Cambridge *Also Called: County of Guernsey (G-1566)*
Guernsey Health Systems (HQ)... 740 439-3561
 1341 Clark St Cambridge (43725) *(G-1573)*
GUERNSEY-MUSKINGUM ELECTRIC CO, New Concord *Also Called: Guernsy-Muskingum Elc Coop Inc (G-11611)*

Guernsy-Muskingum Elc Coop Inc (PA).. 740 826-7661
 17 S Liberty St New Concord (43762) *(G-11611)*
Guess Motors Inc (PA).. 866 890-0522
 457 Steubenville Rd Se Carrollton (44615) *(G-1908)*
Guest Supply Services, Urbancrest *Also Called: Sysco Guest Supply LLC (G-14323)*
Guiding Fndtons Spport Svcs LL... 440 485-3772
 466 Northfield Rd Ste 100 Bedford (44146) *(G-963)*
Guild Associates Inc (PA)... 614 798-8215
 5750 Shier Rings Rd Dublin (43016) *(G-8023)*
Gulf South Medical Supply Inc... 614 501-9080
 915 Taylor Rd Unit A Gahanna (43230) *(G-8717)*
Gummer Wholesale Inc (PA).. 740 928-0415
 1945 James Pkwy Heath (43056) *(G-9133)*
Gundlach Sheet Metal Works Inc.. 419 734-7351
 2439 E Gill Rd Port Clinton (43452) *(G-12531)*
Gundlach Sheet Metal Works Inc (PA)... 419 626-4525
 910 Columbus Ave Sandusky (44870) *(G-12902)*
Gunton Corporation (PA).. 216 831-2420
 26150 Richmond Rd Cleveland (44146) *(G-4342)*
Gus Holthaus Signs Inc... 513 861-0060
 817 Ridgeway Ave Cincinnati (45229) *(G-2783)*
Gus Perdikakis Associates... 513 583-0900
 9155 Governors Way Unit A Cincinnati (45249) *(G-2784)*
Gusco Energy, Sylvania *Also Called: Brint Electric Inc (G-13537)*
Gustave A Larson Company... 513 681-4089
 1201 Harrison Ave Cincinnati (45214) *(G-2785)*
Gutknecht Construction, Columbus *Also Called: Gutknecht Construction Company (G-5962)*
Gutknecht Construction Company... 614 532-5410
 2280 Citygate Dr Columbus (43219) *(G-5962)*
Guyler Automotive, Franklin *Also Called: I-75 Pierson Automotive Inc (G-8642)*
Gw Business Solutions LLC... 740 345-9861
 65 S 5th St Newark (43055) *(G-11703)*
Gws FF&e LLC... 513 759-6000
 9823 Cincinnati Dayton Rd West Chester (45069) *(G-14703)*
Gxo Logistics Supply Chain Inc... 614 305-1705
 3650 Brooklyn Dr Ste B2 Grove City (43123) *(G-8923)*
Gymnastics Center, Canton *Also Called: Young MNS Chrstn Assn Cntl STA (G-1890)*
Gymnastics World Inc... 440 526-2970
 6630 Harris Rd Cleveland (44147) *(G-4343)*
Gypc Inc... 309 677-0405
 475 Stonehaven Rd Dayton (45429) *(G-7390)*
H & C Building Supplies, Huron *Also Called: Huron Cement Products Company (G-9390)*
H & D Steel Service Inc.. 800 666-3390
 9960 York Alpha Dr North Royalton (44133) *(G-11942)*
H & D Steel Service Center, North Royalton *Also Called: H & D Steel Service Inc (G-11942)*
H & G Nursery Home Inc.. 513 734-7401
 322 S Charity St Bethel (45106) *(G-1091)*
H & G Nursing Homes Inc... 937 544-2205
 10856 State Route 41 West Union (45693) *(G-14870)*
H & H Custom Homes LLC... 419 994-4070
 16573 State Route 3 Loudonville (44842) *(G-10109)*
H & H Green LLC... 419 674-4152
 13670 Us Highway 68 Kenton (43326) *(G-9614)*
H & R Block, Cleveland *Also Called: H & R Block Estrn Tax Svcs Inc (G-4344)*
H & R Block Estrn Tax Svcs Inc.. 216 464-7212
 23811 Chagrin Blvd Ste 340 Cleveland (44122) *(G-4344)*
H A Dorsten Inc.. 419 628-2327
 146 N Main St Minster (45865) *(G-11317)*
H B Magruder Memorial Hosp... 419 734-3131
 11697 W State Route 163 Oak Harbor (43449) *(G-12045)*
H B Magruder Memorial Hosp... 419 732-6520
 621 Fulton St Port Clinton (43452) *(G-12532)*
H B Magruder Memorial Hosp... 419 734-4539
 611 Fulton St Port Clinton (43452) *(G-12533)*
H C F Inc... 740 289-2528
 7143 Us Rte 23 Piketon (45661) *(G-12421)*
H F A, Akron *Also Called: Hitchcock Fleming & Assoc Inc (G-193)*
H G C, Cincinnati *Also Called: Hgc Construction Co (G-2818)*
H G R, Euclid *Also Called: Hgr Industrial Surplus Inc (G-8347)*
H Hafner & Sons Inc.. 513 321-1895
 5445 Wooster Pike Cincinnati (45226) *(G-2786)*

H K M | ALPHABETIC SECTION

H K M, Cleveland *Also Called: Hkm Drect Mkt Cmmnications Inc (G-4367)*
H M Miller Construction Co..330 628-4811
   1225 Waterloo Rd Mogadore (44260) *(G-11327)*
H N S Sports Group Ltd..614 764-4653
   6085 Memorial Dr Dublin (43017) *(G-8024)*
H P H Plumbing, Toledo *Also Called: Hanks Plumbing & Heating Co (G-13832)*
H T V Industries Inc...216 514-0060
   30100 Chagrin Blvd Ste 210 Cleveland (44124) *(G-4345)*
H. Meyer Dairy, Cleveland *Also Called: Borden Dairy Co Cincinnati LLC (G-3881)*
H3d Tool Corporation..740 498-5181
   295 Enterprise Dr Newcomerstown (43832) *(G-11768)*
H7 Network..513 526-5139
   610 Harpwood Dr Franklin (45005) *(G-8639)*
Haag-Sreit Usa Inc...513 336-7255
   3535 Kings Mills Rd Mason (45040) *(G-10558)*
Haag-Streit Usa Inc (DH)..513 398-3937
   3535 Kings Mills Rd Mason (45040) *(G-10559)*
Haas Doors, Wauseon *Also Called: Nofziger Door Sales Inc (G-14607)*
Haasz Automall, Ravenna *Also Called: Haasz Automall LLC (G-12627)*
Haasz Automall LLC (PA)..330 296-2866
   4886 State Route 59 Ravenna (44266) *(G-12627)*
Habegger Corporation..513 612-4700
   11413 Enterprise Park Dr Cincinnati (45241) *(G-2787)*
Habegger Corporation (PA)......................................513 853-6644
   4995 Winton Rd Cincinnati (45232) *(G-2788)*
Habitat For Hmnity E Cntl Ohio................................330 915-5888
   1400 Raff Rd Sw Canton (44710) *(G-1767)*
Habitat For Hmnity Grter Cncnn...............................513 389-1792
   3970 N Bend Rd Cincinnati (45211) *(G-2789)*
Habitat For Hmnity Grter Cncnn (PA)......................513 721-4483
   4910 Para Dr Cincinnati (45237) *(G-2790)*
Habitec, Holland *Also Called: Habitec Security Inc (G-9286)*
Habitec Security Inc (PA)..419 537-6768
   1545 Timber Wolf Dr Holland (43528) *(G-9286)*
Hackensack Meridian Health Inc..............................513 792-9697
   4650 E Galbraith Rd Cincinnati (45236) *(G-2791)*
Hadler Company, Columbus *Also Called: Hadler Realty Company (G-5963)*
Hadler Realty Company..614 457-6650
   2000 Henderson Rd Ste 500 Columbus (43220) *(G-5963)*
Hagerty Insurance Agency LLC................................877 922-9701
   555 Metro Pl N Dublin (43017) *(G-8025)*
Haggerty Logistics Inc...734 713-9800
   95 W Crescentville Rd Cincinnati (45246) *(G-2792)*
Hagglunds Drives Inc..614 527-7400
   2275 International St Columbus (43228) *(G-5964)*
Hague Quality Water Intl, Groveport *Also Called: William R Hague Inc (G-9014)*
Hahn Automation Group Us Inc................................937 886-3232
   10909 Industry Ln Miamisburg (45342) *(G-11058)*
Hahn Loeser, Cleveland *Also Called: Hahn Loeser & Parks LLP (G-4346)*
Hahn Loeser & Parks LLP (PA)................................216 621-0150
   200 Public Sq Ste 2800 Cleveland (44114) *(G-4346)*
Hale Farm & Village, Bath *Also Called: Western Reserve Historical Soc (G-755)*
Haley & Aldrich Inc..216 739-0555
   6500 Rockside Rd Ste 200 Independence (44131) *(G-9435)*
Hall Fame Rhblttion Nrsing Ctr, Canton *Also Called: Canton Rhblttion Nrsing Ctr LL (G-1704)*
Hall of Fame Fitness Center, Canton *Also Called: Hof Fitness Center Inc (G-1773)*
Hall of Fame Village...714 337-0333
   2626 Fulton Dr Nw Canton (44718) *(G-1768)*
Halo Branded Solutions Inc......................................855 425-6266
   7800 E Kemper Rd Ste 100 Cincinnati (45249) *(G-2793)*
Halo Branded Solutions Inc......................................614 434-6275
   2550 Corporate Exchange Dr Ste 203 Columbus (43231) *(G-5965)*
Hamilton Capital LLC..614 273-1000
   5025 Arlington Centre Blvd Ste 300 Columbus (43220) *(G-5966)*
Hamilton Capital MGT Inc..614 273-1000
   5025 Arlington Centre Blvd Ste 300 Columbus (43220) *(G-5967)*
Hamilton City School District...................................513 887-5055
   1315 Chestnut St Hamilton (45011) *(G-9050)*
Hamilton Cnty Soc For The Prvn..............................513 541-6100
   11900 Conrey Rd Cincinnati (45249) *(G-2794)*

HAMILTON COUNSELING CENTER T/S, Hamilton *Also Called: Butler Bhavioral Hlth Svcs Inc (G-9021)*
Hamilton County Coroner, Blue Ash *Also Called: County of Hamilton (G-1161)*
Hamilton County Eductl Svc Ctr...............................513 674-4200
   924 Waycross Rd Cincinnati (45240) *(G-2795)*
Hamilton Creek Apartments, Columbus *Also Called: Showe Management Corporation (G-6674)*
Hamilton Manufacturing Corp..................................419 867-4858
   1026 Hamilton Dr Holland (43528) *(G-9287)*
Hamilton-Parker Company (PA)...............................614 358-7800
   1865 Leonard Ave Columbus (43219) *(G-5968)*
Hamlet Manor, Chagrin Falls *Also Called: Beaver Dam Health Care Center (G-1953)*
Hamlet Nursing Home, Chagrin Falls *Also Called: Hamlet Village In Chagrin FLS (G-1960)*
Hamlet Village In Chagrin FLS (PA).........................216 263-6033
   200 Hamlet Hills Dr Ofc Chagrin Falls (44022) *(G-1959)*
Hamlet Village In Chagrin FLS.................................440 247-4200
   150 Cleveland St Chagrin Falls (44022) *(G-1960)*
Hammerman Graf Hughes & Co Inc..........................937 320-1262
   4486 Indian Ripple Rd Dayton (45440) *(G-7391)*
Hammond Construction Inc.....................................330 455-7039
   1550 Corporate Woods Pkwy Uniontown (44685) *(G-14254)*
Hammond Kinetics, Dublin *Also Called: Kinetics Noise Control Inc (G-8049)*
Hammond Neal Moore Llc.......................................513 381-2011
   441 Vine St Ste 3200 Cincinnati (45202) *(G-2796)*
Hammontree & Associates Ltd (PA).........................330 499-8817
   5233 Stoneham Rd Canton (44720) *(G-1769)*
Hampton By Hilton, Cincinnati *Also Called: Hampton Inn Dry Ridge (G-2797)*
Hampton By Hilton, Stow *Also Called: Hampton Inn Stow (G-13372)*
Hampton Inn..513 752-8584
   858 Eastgate North Dr Cincinnati (45245) *(G-2106)*
Hampton Inn..937 387-0598
   7043 Miller Ln Dayton (45414) *(G-7392)*
Hampton Inn..740 282-9800
   820 University Blvd Steubenville (43952) *(G-13329)*
Hampton Inn, Athens *Also Called: Athens OH State 405 LLC (G-556)*
Hampton Inn, Austinburg *Also Called: Pikes Inc (G-633)*
Hampton Inn, Cleveland *Also Called: Rock Hotel Ltd LLC (G-4848)*
Hampton Inn, Columbus *Also Called: Indus Airport Hotels II LLC (G-6047)*
Hampton Inn, Columbus *Also Called: Inn Hampton and Suites (G-6053)*
Hampton Inn, Columbus *Also Called: Jag Guru Inc (G-6081)*
Hampton Inn, Columbus *Also Called: Ntk Hotel Group II LLC (G-6376)*
Hampton Inn, Columbus *Also Called: Riverview Hotel LLC (G-6600)*
Hampton Inn, Dayton *Also Called: Hampton Inn of Huber Heights (G-7393)*
Hampton Inn, Grove City *Also Called: SGB Management Inc (G-8954)*
Hampton Inn, Hilliard *Also Called: Parkins Incorporated (G-9226)*
Hampton Inn, Lima *Also Called: Roschmans Restaurant ADM (G-9955)*
Hampton Inn, Marietta *Also Called: March Investors Ltd (G-10382)*
Hampton Inn, Maumee *Also Called: Bennett Enterprises Inc (G-10699)*
Hampton Inn, Middleburg Heights *Also Called: Hampton Inn & Suite Inc (G-11116)*
Hampton Inn, New Philadelphia *Also Called: Riverview Hospitality Corp (G-11664)*
Hampton Inn, Pickerington *Also Called: Hampton Inn Columbus East (G-12402)*
Hampton Inn, Richfield *Also Called: 5145 Corporation (G-12684)*
Hampton Inn, Saint Clairsville *Also Called: Somnus Corporation (G-12815)*
Hampton Inn, Sidney *Also Called: Sidney Host LLC (G-13051)*
Hampton Inn, Streetsboro *Also Called: Meander Hsptality Group II LLC (G-13422)*
Hampton Inn, Toledo *Also Called: Kay Surati (G-13875)*
Hampton Inn, Troy *Also Called: Sps Inc (G-14160)*
Hampton Inn, Wooster *Also Called: Hampton Inn Wooster (G-15342)*
Hampton Inn, Youngstown *Also Called: Youngstown Hospitality LLC (G-15758)*
Hampton Inn & Suite Inc..440 234-0206
   7074 Engle Rd Middleburg Heights (44130) *(G-11116)*
Hampton Inn & Suites Beachwood, Beachwood *Also Called: Beachwood Lodging LLC (G-768)*
Hampton Inn Cleveland, Cleveland *Also Called: Crossroads Hospitality Co LLC (G-4141)*
Hampton Inn Cleveland, North Olmsted *Also Called: Grand Heritage Hotel Portland (G-11903)*
Hampton Inn Cncinnati Blue Ash, Blue Ash *Also Called: Jai Bapa Swami LLC (G-1190)*
Hampton Inn Cncnnati Nrthwst/F, Fairfield *Also Called: Middletown Innkeepers Inc (G-8431)*

ALPHABETIC SECTION   Hardware Suppliers of America Inc

Hampton Inn Columbus East.. 614 864-8383
   1890 Winderly Ln Pickerington (43147) *(G-12402)*

Hampton Inn Dry Ridge.. 859 823-7111
   310 Culvert St Ste 500 Cincinnati (45202) *(G-2797)*

Hampton Inn of Huber Heights... 937 233-4300
   5588 Merily Way Dayton (45424) *(G-7393)*

Hampton Inn Stes Clmbs-Ston Ar, Columbus *Also Called: Ashford Trs Clumbus Easton LLC*
(G-5392)

Hampton Inn Stes Clmbus Hllard, Hilliard *Also Called: Indus Hilliard Hotel LLC (G-9204)*

Hampton Inn Stow... 330 945-4160
   4331 Lakepointe Corporate Dr Stow (44224) *(G-13372)*

Hampton Inn West, Columbus *Also Called: Radha Corporation (G-6560)*

Hampton Inn Wooster... 330 345-4424
   4253 Burbank Rd Wooster (44691) *(G-15342)*

Hampton Inn-Newark/Heath, Newark *Also Called: Kribha LLC (G-11711)*

Hanby Farms Inc.. 740 763-3554
   10790 Newark Rd Nashport (43830) *(G-11535)*

Hanco Ambulance Inc.. 419 423-2912
   417 6th St Findlay (45840) *(G-8540)*

Hancock Cnty Bd Dvlpmntal Dsbl... 419 422-6387
   1700 E Sandusky St Findlay (45840) *(G-8541)*

Hancock Federal Credit Union.. 419 420-0338
   1701 E Melrose Ave Findlay (45840) *(G-8542)*

Hancock Hotel, Findlay *Also Called: 631 South Main Street Dev LLC (G-8504)*

Hancock-Hrdn-Wyndt-ptnam Cmnty (PA).............................. 419 423-3755
   1637 Tiffin Ave Findlay (45840) *(G-8543)*

Hancock-Wood Electric Coop Inc (PA)................................. 419 257-3241
   1399 Business Park Dr S North Baltimore (45872) *(G-11801)*

Hand & Reconstructive Surgeons.. 937 298-2262
   2400 Miami Valley Dr Dayton (45459) *(G-7394)*

Hand Amblatory Surgery Ctr LLC.. 513 961-4263
   2800 Winslow Ave # 201 Cincinnati (45206) *(G-2798)*

Hand Rcnstructive Surgeons Inc.. 937 435-4263
   2400 Miami Valley Dr Dayton (45459) *(G-7395)*

Hand Surgery Center, Cincinnati *Also Called: Hand Amblatory Surgery Ctr LLC (G-2798)*

Handl-It Inc... 440 439-9400
   7120 Krick Rd Ste 1a Bedford (44146) *(G-964)*

Hands Enterprises Ltd... 419 528-1389
   575 Urwin Pkwy Ontario (44906) *(G-12106)*

Handson Central Ohio Inc... 614 221-2255
   1105 Schrock Rd Ste 107 Columbus (43229) *(G-5969)*

Haney Inc.. 513 561-1441
   5657 Wooster Pike Cincinnati (45227) *(G-2799)*

Haney PRC, Cincinnati *Also Called: Haney Inc (G-2799)*

Hanger Prsthtics Orthtics E In (HQ)................................... 330 633-9807
   33 North Ave Ste 101 Tallmadge (44278) *(G-13593)*

Hani Ashqar DDS & Partners LLC....................................... 203 560-3131
   19551 Euclid Ave Euclid (44117) *(G-8344)*

Hank Bloom Services Inc... 440 946-7823
   7567 Tyler Blvd Mentor (44060) *(G-10945)*

Hankook Tire Akron Office, Uniontown *Also Called: Hankook Tire America Corp (G-14255)*

Hankook Tire America Corp... 330 896-6199
   3535 Forest Lake Dr Uniontown (44685) *(G-14255)*

Hanks Plumbing & Heating Co.. 419 843-2222
   2000 The Blfs Toledo (43615) *(G-13832)*

Hanlin-Rainaldi Construction... 614 436-4204
   1060 Kingsmill Pkwy Columbus (43229) *(G-5970)*

Hanline Fresh, Shelby *Also Called: R S Hanline and Co Inc (G-13010)*

Hanna Cambell & Powell.. 330 670-7300
   3737 Embassy Pkwy Ste 100 Akron (44333) *(G-182)*

Hanna Commercial LLC.. 216 861-7200
   1350 Euclid Ave Ste 700 Cleveland (44115) *(G-4347)*

Hanna Commercial Real Estate, Cleveland *Also Called: Hanna Commercial LLC (G-4347)*

Hanna Perkin Center, Cleveland *Also Called: Hanna Perkins School (G-4348)*

Hanna Perkins School... 216 991-4472
   19910 Malvern Rd Cleveland (44122) *(G-4348)*

Hannah Farm LLC.. 419 295-3929
   8240 S Township Road 171 Bloomville (44818) *(G-1118)*

Hannon Company (PA).. 330 456-4728
   1605 Waynesburg Dr Se Canton (44707) *(G-1770)*

Hanover House Inc.. 330 837-1741
   435 Avis Ave Nw Massillon (44646) *(G-10642)*

Hans Rothenbuhler & Son Inc.. 440 632-6000
   15815 Nauvoo Rd Middlefield (44062) *(G-11140)*

Hans Truck and Trlr Repr Inc... 216 581-0046
   14520 Broadway Ave Cleveland (44125) *(G-4349)*

Hans' Freightliner Cleveland, Cleveland *Also Called: Hans Truck and Trlr Repr Inc (G-4349)*

Hansen Adkins Auto Trnspt Inc... 562 430-4100
   200 W Crescentville Rd West Chester (45246) *(G-14815)*

Hanser Music Group, Blue Ash *Also Called: Jatiga Inc (G-1191)*

Hanson McClain Advisors, Blue Ash *Also Called: Allworth Financial LP (G-1128)*

Hanson Productions Inc... 419 327-6100
   200 N Saint Clair St Ste 100 Toledo (43604) *(G-13833)*

Hanson Services Inc (PA).. 216 226-5425
   17017 Madison Ave Lakewood (44107) *(G-9668)*

Happy Day School, Ravenna *Also Called: Portage Cnty Bd Dvlpmntal Dsbl (G-12636)*

Harbor (PA)... 419 479-3233
   3909 Woodley Rd Toledo (43606) *(G-13834)*

Harbor Operator LLC.. 330 399-8997
   202 Washington St Nw Warren (44483) *(G-14525)*

Harbor Retirement Assoc LLC... 216 925-4898
   17000 Van Aken Blvd Shaker Heights (44120) *(G-12977)*

Harbor Services, Bellaire *Also Called: Bellaire Harbor Service LLC (G-1006)*

Harborchase of Shaker Heights, Shaker Heights *Also Called: Harbor Retirement Assoc LLC (G-12977)*

Harborside Clveland Ltd Partnr... 440 871-5900
   27601 Westchester Pkwy Westlake (44145) *(G-15063)*

Harborside Clveland Ltd Partnr... 440 871-5900
   27601 Westchester Pkwy Westlake (44145) *(G-15064)*

Harborside Dayton Ltd Partnr.. 937 224-0793
   323 Forest Ave Dayton (45405) *(G-7396)*

Harborside Dayton Ltd Partnr.. 937 687-1311
   101 Mills Pl New Lebanon (45345) *(G-11619)*

Harborside Healthcare LLC.. 937 436-6155
   3797 Summit Glen Dr Frnt Dayton (45449) *(G-7397)*

Harborside Healthcare LLC.. 419 825-1111
   401 W Airport Hwy Swanton (43558) *(G-13526)*

Harborside Healthcare LLC.. 937 335-7161
   512 Crescent Dr Troy (45373) *(G-14137)*

Harborside Pointe Place LLC... 419 727-7870
   6101 N Summit St Toledo (43611) *(G-13835)*

Harborside Sylvania LLC.. 419 882-1875
   5757 Whiteford Rd Sylvania (43560) *(G-13548)*

Harcatus Tr-Cnty Cmnty Action... 740 922-3600
   108 N 2nd St Dennison (44621) *(G-7857)*

Harcatus Tr-Cnty Cmnty Action (PA).................................. 740 922-0933
   821 Anola St Dover (44622) *(G-7887)*

Harcatus Tr-Cnty Cmnty Action... 330 602-5442
   504 Bowers Ave Nw New Philadelphia (44663) *(G-11652)*

Harcatus Tr-Cnty Cmnty Action, Dover *Also Called: Harcatus Tr-Cnty Cmnty Action (G-7887)*

Hard Knocks.. 614 407-1444
   100 Dillmont Dr Columbus (43235) *(G-5971)*

Hard Rock Csino Cincinnati LLC... 513 250-3375
   1000 Broadway St Cincinnati (45202) *(G-2800)*

Hardage Hotels I LLC.. 614 766-7762
   4130 Tuller Rd Dublin (43017) *(G-8026)*

Hardin Cnty Cncil On Aging Inc... 419 673-1102
   100 Memorial Dr Kenton (43326) *(G-9615)*

Hardin Cnty Dept Mntal Rtrdtio, Kenton *Also Called: County of Hardin (G-9613)*

Hardin County Home.. 419 673-0961
   1211 W Lima St Kenton (43326) *(G-9616)*

HARDIN HILLS HEALTH CENTER, Kenton *Also Called: Hardin County Home (G-9616)*

Hardin Memorial Hospital, Kenton *Also Called: Baptist Health Hardin (G-9609)*

Hardin Street Marine LLC... 419 672-6500
   200 E Hardin St Findlay (45840) *(G-8544)*

Harding Hospital, Columbus *Also Called: Osu Harding Hospital (G-6483)*

Harding Park Cycle, Canton *Also Called: Damarc Inc (G-1731)*

Hardware Now, Cincinnati *Also Called: Hillman Group Inc (G-2823)*

Hardware Suppliers of America Inc.................................... 330 644-7167
   1100 Killian Rd Akron (44312) *(G-183)*

Hardwood Lumber Co, Burton Also Called: Stephen M Trudick *(G-1533)*

Hardy Diagnostics.. 937 550-2768
429 S Pioneer Blvd Springboro (45066) *(G-13200)*

Hariom Associates Medina LLC... 330 723-4994
2850 Medina Rd Medina (44256) *(G-10839)*

Harley-Dvidson Dlr Systems Inc... 216 573-1393
8555 Sweet Valley Dr Ste Q Cleveland (44125) *(G-4350)*

Harmer Place, Marietta Also Called: United Church Homes Inc *(G-10406)*

Harmon Inc... 513 645-1550
4290 Port Union Rd West Chester (45011) *(G-14704)*

Harmon Inc... 513 645-1550
9111 Meridian Way West Chester (45069) *(G-14705)*

Harmon Road Group Home, The Plains Also Called: Buckeye Community Services Inc *(G-13615)*

Harmony Court, Cincinnati Also Called: Chs-Norwood Inc *(G-2388)*

Harold J Becker Company Inc... 614 279-1414
3946 Indian Ripple Rd Dayton (45440) *(G-7398)*

Harold K Phllips Rstration Inc.. 614 443-5699
972 Harmon Ave Columbus (43223) *(G-5972)*

Harrington Electric Company.. 216 361-5101
3800 Perkins Ave Cleveland (44114) *(G-4351)*

Harris & Heavener Excvtg Inc.. 740 927-1423
149 Humphries Dr Etna (43068) *(G-8330)*

Harris Day Architects Inc.. 330 493-3722
6677 Frank Ave Nw North Canton (44720) *(G-11838)*

Harris Distributing Co... 513 541-4222
4261 Crawford Ave Cincinnati (45223) *(G-2801)*

Harrison Avenue Assembly God.. 513 367-6109
949 Harrison Ave Harrison (45030) *(G-9107)*

Harrison Building and Ln Assn (PA)...................................... 513 367-2015
10490 New Haven Rd Harrison (45030) *(G-9108)*

Harrison Community Hospital, Cadiz Also Called: Wheeling Hospital Inc *(G-1544)*

Harrison Community Hospital Inc.. 740 942-4631
951 E Market St Cadiz (43907) *(G-1539)*

Harrison Hub, Scio Also Called: M3 Midstream LLC *(G-12942)*

Harrison Pavilion... 513 662-5800
2171 Harrison Ave Cincinnati (45211) *(G-2802)*

Harrison Township... 740 942-2171
520 N Main St Cadiz (43907) *(G-1540)*

Harry C Lobalzo & Sons Inc.. 330 666-6758
61 N Cleveland Massillon Rd Unit A Akron (44333) *(G-184)*

Harry Humphries Auto City Inc.. 330 343-6681
311 Commercial Pkwy Dover (44622) *(G-7888)*

Hart, Toledo Also Called: Hart Associates Inc *(G-13836)*

Hart Associates Inc.. 419 893-9600
811 Madison Ave Toledo (43604) *(G-13836)*

Hart Industrial Products Div, Middletown Also Called: Hart Industries Inc *(G-11165)*

Hart Industries Inc (PA)... 513 541-4278
931 Jeanette St Middletown (45042) *(G-11165)*

Harte-Hanks Trnsp Svcs.. 513 458-7600
2950 Robinson Ave Cincinnati (45209) *(G-2803)*

Hartford Farms LLC... 740 893-7200
11212 Croton Rd Croton (43013) *(G-7030)*

Hartland Advsors Llc-Cancelled, Cleveland Also Called: Clearstead Advisors LLC *(G-3999)*

Hartley Company.. 740 439-6668
1950 East Pike Zanesville (43701) *(G-15798)*

Hartsfield Atlanta Intl Arprt, Cincinnati Also Called: Park Place Operations Inc *(G-3184)*

Hartville Group Inc (PA).. 330 484-8166
1210 Massillon Rd Akron (44306) *(G-185)*

Hartwig Transit Inc... 513 563-1765
11971 Reading Rd Cincinnati (45241) *(G-2804)*

Hartzell Hardwoods Inc (PA)... 937 773-7054
1025 S Roosevelt Ave Piqua (45356) *(G-12443)*

Harvest Sherwood Fd Distrs Inc... 216 662-8000
16625 Granite Rd Maple Heights (44137) *(G-10339)*

Harwick Standard Dist Corp (PA).. 330 798-9300
60 S Seiberling St Akron (44305) *(G-186)*

Hasenstab Architects Inc.. 330 434-4464
190 N Union St Ste 400 Akron (44304) *(G-187)*

Haslett Heating & Cooling Inc.. 614 299-2133
7686 Fishel Dr N # A Dublin (43016) *(G-8027)*

Hasselkus Farms Inc... 419 862-3735
2673 Hessville Rd Elmore (43416) *(G-8230)*

Hassler Medical Center, Cleveland Also Called: Cleveland Clnic Hlth Systm-Wst *(G-4038)*

Hastings Water Works Inc... 440 832-7700
10331 Brecksville Rd Brecksville (44141) *(G-1353)*

Hat White Management LLC... 800 525-7967
121 S Main St Ste 500 Akron (44308) *(G-188)*

Hatifield Hyundai, Columbus Also Called: Columbus SAI Motors LLC *(G-5653)*

Hattenbach, Cleveland Also Called: The Hattenbach Company *(G-5001)*

Hattie Larlham Community Svcs.. 330 274-2272
9772 Diagonal Rd Mantua (44255) *(G-10330)*

Hattie Lrlham Ctr For Chldren.. 330 274-2272
540 S Main St Ste 412 Akron (44311) *(G-189)*

Hattie Lrlham Ctr For Chldren.. 440 232-9320
26901 Cannon Rd Bedford Heights (44146) *(G-998)*

Hattie Lrlham Ctr For Chldren (PA)....................................... 330 274-2272
9772 Diagonal Rd Mantua (44255) *(G-10331)*

Hattie Lrlham Ctr For Chldren.. 330 274-2272
1402 Boettler Rd, Ste B Uniontown (44685) *(G-14256)*

HATTIE'S PRE-SCHOOL, Mantua Also Called: Hattie Lrlham Ctr For Chldren *(G-10331)*

Hatzel and Buehler Inc.. 216 777-6000
1200 Resource Dr Ste 10 Cleveland (44131) *(G-4352)*

Hauck Hospitality LLC.. 513 563-8330
3855 Hauck Rd Cincinnati (45241) *(G-2805)*

Haulotte Group Biljax Inc.. 567 444-4159
125 Taylor Pkwy Archbold (43502) *(G-460)*

Hauser Inc.. 513 745-9200
8260 Northcreek Dr Ste 200 Cincinnati (45236) *(G-2806)*

Hauser Group, The, Cincinnati Also Called: Hauser Inc *(G-2806)*

Havar Inc (PA).. 740 594-3533
396 Richland Ave Athens (45701) *(G-570)*

Haven Behavioral Hosp Dayton, Dayton Also Called: Haven Bhaviroal Healthcare Inc *(G-7399)*

Haven Bhaviroal Healthcare Inc... 937 234-0100
1 Elizabeth Pl Ste A Dayton (45417) *(G-7399)*

HAVEN HILL HOME, North Royalton Also Called: Blossom Hill Inc *(G-11938)*

Haven Rest Ministries Inc (PA)... 330 535-1563
175 E Market St Akron (44308) *(G-190)*

Haverhill Coke Company LLC.. 740 355-9819
2446 Gallia Pike Franklin Furnace (45629) *(G-8655)*

Hawa Incorporated (PA).. 614 451-1711
570 Polaris Pkwy Westerville (43082) *(G-14898)*

Hawkeye Hotels Inc.. 614 782-8292
1668 Buckeye Pl Grove City (43123) *(G-8924)*

Hawkins, Terrence Do, Maumee Also Called: Maumee Eye Clinic Inc *(G-10746)*

Hawthorne Hills Cntry CLB Inc... 419 221-1891
1000 Fetter Rd Lima (45801) *(G-9895)*

Hayden Valley Foods Inc (PA).. 614 539-7233
3150 Urbancrest Industrial Dr Urbancrest (43123) *(G-14320)*

Haydocy Automotive Inc.. 614 279-8880
3865 W Broad St Columbus (43228) *(G-5973)*

Haydocy Automotors, Columbus Also Called: Haydocy Automotive Inc *(G-5973)*

Haymaker Tree & Lawn Inc.. 330 499-5037
6854 Wales Ave Nw North Canton (44720) *(G-11839)*

Haymaker Tree and Lawn, North Canton Also Called: Haymaker Tree & Lawn Inc *(G-11839)*

Hayneedle Inc.. 402 715-3000
1003 Logistics Way Monroe (45044) *(G-11341)*

Haynes Manufacturing Company, Westlake Also Called: R and J Corporation *(G-15101)*

Haynes Real Estate Inc... 419 475-8383
4349 Talmadge Rd Ste 4 Toledo (43623) *(G-13837)*

Hayward Distributing Co (PA).. 614 272-5953
4061 Perimeter Dr Columbus (43228) *(G-5974)*

Hazama Ando Corporation... 614 985-4906
500 W Wilson Bridge Rd Ste 130 Worthington (43085) *(G-15418)*

Hbk, Canfield Also Called: Hill Barth & King LLC *(G-1631)*

Hc Solutions Management, Toledo Also Called: Acme Dynamite *(G-13674)*

Hc Transport Inc.. 513 574-1800
6045 Bridgetown Rd Cincinnati (45248) *(G-2807)*

HCCAO, Hillsboro Also Called: Highland Cnty Cmnty Action Org *(G-9255)*

Hcf Management, Fostoria Also Called: Hcf Management Inc *(G-8619)*

ALPHABETIC SECTION

Hcf Management Inc...419 435-8112
25 Christopher Dr Fostoria (44830) *(G-8619)*

Hcf Management Inc (PA)..419 999-2010
1100 Shawnee Rd Lima (45805) *(G-9896)*

Hcf Management Inc...419 999-2055
2535 Fort Amanda Rd Lima (45804) *(G-9897)*

Hcf Management Inc...740 289-2394
7143 Us Highway 23 Piketon (45661) *(G-12422)*

Hcf of Bowl Green Care Ctr Inc................................419 352-7558
850 W Poe Rd Bowling Green (43402) *(G-1321)*

Hcf of Bowling Green Inc..419 352-4694
1021 W Poe Rd Bowling Green (43402) *(G-1322)*

Hcf of Briarwood Inc...419 678-2311
100 Don Desch Dr Coldwater (45828) *(G-5213)*

Hcf of Celina Inc (HQ)...419 586-6645
1001 Myers Rd Celina (45822) *(G-1925)*

Hcf of Celina Inc...419 999-2010
1100 Shawnee Rd Lima (45805) *(G-9898)*

Hcf of Court House Inc...740 335-9290
555 N Glenn Ave Wshngtn Ct Hs (43160) *(G-15487)*

Hcf of Crestview Inc..937 426-5033
4381 Tonawanda Trl Beavercreek (45430) *(G-924)*

Hcf of Findlay Inc..419 999-2010
11745 Township Road 145 Findlay (45840) *(G-8545)*

Hcf of Lima Inc...419 999-2010
1100 Shawnee Rd Lima (45805) *(G-9899)*

Hcf of Lima Inc (PA)..419 227-2611
750 Brower Rd Lima (45801) *(G-9900)*

Hcf of Perrysburg Inc..419 874-0306
250 Manor Dr Perrysburg (43551) *(G-12340)*

Hcf of Piqua Inc..937 773-0040
1840 W High St Piqua (45356) *(G-12444)*

Hcf of Roselawn Inc..419 647-4115
420 E 4th St Spencerville (45887) *(G-13188)*

Hcf of Shawnee Inc..419 999-2055
2535 Fort Amanda Rd Lima (45804) *(G-9901)*

Hcf of Van Wert Inc..419 999-2010
160 Fox Rd Van Wert (45891) *(G-14346)*

Hcf of Wapakoneta Inc...419 738-3711
1010 Lincoln Hwy Wapakoneta (45895) *(G-14485)*

Hcf of Washington Inc...419 999-2010
555 N Glenn Ave Wshngtn Ct Hs (43160) *(G-15488)*

Hcfw, Cleveland *Also Called: Hitchcock Center For Women Inc (G-4366)*

Hcl of Dayton Inc..937 384-8300
4000 Miamisburg Centerville Rd Ste 410 Miamisburg (45342) *(G-11059)*

Hcr Manorcare Inc (HQ)...419 252-5500
333 N Summit Toledo (43604) *(G-13838)*

Hcr Manorcare Med Svcs Fla LLC (PA)....................419 252-5500
333 N Summit St Ste 100 Toledo (43604) *(G-13839)*

Hcrmc-Promedica LLC..419 540-6000
5360 Harroun Rd Sylvania (43560) *(G-13549)*

Hd Davis Cpas LLC..330 759-8522
4308 Belmont Ave Ste 1 Youngstown (44505) *(G-15626)*

Hd Supply Facilities Maint Ltd..................................440 542-9188
30311 Emerald Valley Pkwy Solon (44139) *(G-13094)*

Hdi Landing Gear USA Inc.......................................440 783-5255
15900 Foltz Pkwy Strongsville (44149) *(G-13459)*

HDR, Columbus *Also Called: Hdr Inc (G-5260)*

Hdr Inc..614 839-5770
8890 Lyra Dr Ste 100 Columbus (43240) *(G-5260)*

Hdt Global, Solon *Also Called: Hunter Defense Tech Inc (G-13096)*

Hdt Global Inc..216 438-6111
30500 Aurora Rd Ste 100 Solon (44139) *(G-13095)*

He Hari Inc..614 436-0700
7007 N High St Worthington (43085) *(G-15419)*

Head Inc...614 338-8501
4477 E 5th Ave Columbus (43219) *(G-5975)*

Head Alabama, Columbus *Also Called: Head Inc (G-5975)*

Head Mercantile Co Inc..440 847-2700
29065 Clemens Rd Ste 200 Westlake (44145) *(G-15065)*

Head Start, Lima *Also Called: West Ohio Cmnty Action Partnr (G-9984)*

Head Start Program, Youngstown *Also Called: Mahoning Youngstown Community (G-15662)*

Heading4ward Investment Co (PA)..........................937 293-9994
2425 W Dorothy Ln Moraine (45439) *(G-11416)*

Heads Start Program, Columbus *Also Called: Columbus City School District (G-5620)*

Headstart, Nelsonville *Also Called: Hockingthensperry Cmnty Action (G-11546)*

Headwinds LP...724 209-5543
1294 Bantam Ridge Rd Steubenville (43953) *(G-13330)*

Healing Hrts Cunseling Ctr Inc..................................419 528-5993
680 Park Ave W Ste 204 Mansfield (44906) *(G-10268)*

Healing Touch Agency LLC.......................................937 813-8333
201 Riverside Dr Ste 1d Dayton (45405) *(G-7400)*

Health Aid of Ohio Inc (PA)......................................216 252-3900
5230 Hauserman Rd Ste B Cleveland (44130) *(G-4353)*

Health Alliance Jewish Hosp, Cincinnati *Also Called: Jewish Hospital LLC (G-2908)*

Health and Safety Sciences LLC..............................513 488-1952
3189 Princeton Rd Fairfield Township (45011) *(G-8462)*

Health At Home LLC...937 436-7717
6445 Far Hills Ave Dayton (45459) *(G-7401)*

Health Care, Mansfield *Also Called: Gaash Home Health Care LLC (G-10266)*

HEALTH CARE FACILITIES, Bowling Green *Also Called: Hcf of Bowl Green Care Ctr Inc (G-1321)*

HEALTH CARE FACILITIES, Celina *Also Called: Hcf of Celina Inc (G-1925)*

Health Care Facilities, Lima *Also Called: Hcf Management Inc (G-9896)*

HEALTH CARE FACILITIES, Piqua *Also Called: Hcf of Piqua Inc (G-12444)*

HEALTH CARE FACILITIES, Van Wert *Also Called: Hcf of Van Wert Inc (G-14346)*

HEALTH CARE FACILITIES, Wshngtn Ct Hs *Also Called: Hcf of Court House Inc (G-15487)*

Health Care Logistics Inc..800 848-1633
6106 Bausch Rd Galloway (43119) *(G-8771)*

Health Care Logistics Inc (PA)..................................740 477-1686
450 Town St Circleville (43113) *(G-3710)*

Health Care Opportunities Inc (PA)..........................513 932-0300
102 E Silver St Lebanon (45036) *(G-9768)*

Health Care Personnel, Columbus *Also Called: Pm Nurse Inc (G-6547)*

Health Care Plus..740 373-9446
125 Putnam St Ste 300 Marietta (45750) *(G-10370)*

Health Care Rtrement Corp Amer............................937 644-8836
755 S Plum St Marysville (43040) *(G-10487)*

Health Care Rtrement Corp Amer (DH)...................419 252-5500
333 N Summit St Ste 103 Toledo (43604) *(G-13840)*

Health Care Rtrment Corp Amer..............................304 925-4771
333 N Summit St Toledo (43604) *(G-13841)*

Health Care Solutions, Barnesville *Also Called: Lincare Inc (G-719)*

Health Care Solutions Inc...304 243-9605
114 Mill St Barnesville (43713) *(G-718)*

Health Care Solutions Inc...330 729-9491
6961 Southern Blvd Ste B Youngstown (44512) *(G-15627)*

HEALTH CARE SOLUTIONS, INC, Barnesville *Also Called: Health Care Solutions Inc (G-718)*

HEALTH CARE SOLUTIONS, INC, Youngstown *Also Called: Health Care Solutions Inc (G-15627)*

Health Care Specialists..740 454-4530
945 Bethesda Dr Ste 300 Zanesville (43701) *(G-15799)*

Health Carousel LLC (PA).......................................855 665-4544
4000 Smith Rd Ste 410 Cincinnati (45209) *(G-2808)*

Health Collaborative...513 618-3600
615 Elsinore Pl Cincinnati (45202) *(G-2809)*

Health Crousel Trvl Netwrk LLC...............................513 665-4544
3805 Edwards Rd Ste 700 Cincinnati (45209) *(G-2810)*

Health Data MGT Solutions Inc................................216 595-1232
3201 Enterprise Pkwy Beachwood (44122) *(G-797)*

Health Department, Bucyrus *Also Called: County of Crawford (G-1504)*

Health Dept, Dover *Also Called: County of Tuscarawas (G-7877)*

Health First Physicians - Masn, Mason *Also Called: Trihealth G LLC (G-10619)*

Health Fndtion of Grter Cncnna, Cincinnati *Also Called: Interact For Health (G-2878)*

Health Management Solutions.................................419 536-5690
1901 Indian Wood Cir Maumee (43537) *(G-10730)*

Health Mart, Portsmouth *Also Called: Compass Community Health (G-12549)*

Health Orders, Cleveland *Also Called: Cleveland Clinic Foundation (G-4025)*

Health Partners Western Ohio..................................419 679-5994
111 W Espy St Kenton (43326) *(G-9617)*

Health Partners Western Ohio 419 221-3072
  329 Nw St 2nd Fl Lima (45801) *(G-9902)*
Health Partners Western Ohio (PA) 419 221-3072
  329 N West St Lima (45801) *(G-9903)*
Health Partners Western Ohio 937 667-1122
  106 N Main St New Carlisle (45344) *(G-11601)*
Health Plan of Ohio Inc 330 837-6880
  100 Lillian Gish Blvd Sw Ste 301 Massillon (44647) *(G-10643)*
Health Recovery Services Inc (PA) 740 592-6720
  224 Columbus Rd Ste 102 Athens (45701) *(G-571)*
Health Science Campus, Toledo *Also Called: University of Toledo (G-14087)*
Health Services (adamhs) Brd O 216 241-3400
  2012 W 25th St Ste 600 Cleveland (44113) *(G-4354)*
Health Services Inc 330 837-7678
  2520 Wales Ave Nw Ste 120 Massillon (44646) *(G-10644)*
Health With Hart Snior Svcs LL 513 229-8888
  7368 Kingsgate Way Unit A West Chester (45069) *(G-14706)*
Healthcare 2000 Cmnty Clnic In 330 262-2500
  1874 Cleveland Rd Wooster (44691) *(G-15343)*
Healthcare Walton Group LLC 440 439-4433
  19859 Alexander Rd Cleveland (44146) *(G-4355)*
Healthlinx Inc 614 542-2228
  1391 W 5th Ave Ste 138 Columbus (43212) *(G-5976)*
Healthpro Medical Billing Inc 419 223-2717
  4132 Elida Rd Lima (45807) *(G-9904)*
Healthquest, Cincinnati *Also Called: Healthquest Fields Ertel Inc (G-2811)*
Healthquest Fields Ertel Inc 513 774-9800
  8390 E Kemper Rd Ste 310 Cincinnati (45249) *(G-2811)*
Healthsource Chiropractic Inc 440 934-5858
  36901 American Way Ste 7 Avon (44011) *(G-653)*
Healthsource of Delaware, Delaware *Also Called: Medquest Health Center Inc (G-7818)*
Healthsource of Ohio Inc 513 753-2820
  559 Old State Route 74 Cincinnati (45244) *(G-2812)*
Healthsource of Ohio Inc 513 575-1444
  1507 State Route 28 Loveland (45140) *(G-10140)*
Healthsource of Ohio Inc 937 386-0049
  218 Stern Rd Seaman (45679) *(G-12944)*
Healthsource of Ohio Inc (PA) 513 576-7700
  424 Wards Corner Rd Ste 200 Loveland (45140) *(G-10141)*
Healthspan, Cincinnati *Also Called: Healthspan Integrated Care (G-2813)*
Healthspan Integrated Care 216 621-5600
  1701 Mercy Health Pl Cincinnati (45237) *(G-2813)*
Healthspot Inc 614 361-1193
  545 Metro Pl S Ste 430 Dublin (43017) *(G-8028)*
Heapy Engineering Inc (PA) 937 224-0861
  1400 W Dorothy Ln Dayton (45409) *(G-7402)*
Hearing Spech Deaf Ctr Grter C 513 221-0527
  2825 Burnet Ave Ste 330 Cincinnati (45219) *(G-2814)*
Hearinglife Usa Inc 513 759-2999
  7735 Tylers Place Blvd West Chester (45069) *(G-14707)*
Heart Care 614 533-5000
  765 N Hamilton Rd Ste 120 Gahanna (43230) *(G-8718)*
Heart Center Northeastern Ohio, Youngstown *Also Called: Heart Center of N Eastrn Ohio (G-15628)*
Heart Center of N Eastrn Ohio (PA) 330 758-7703
  250 Debartolo Pl Ste 2750 Youngstown (44512) *(G-15628)*
Heartbeat International Inc 614 885-7577
  5000 Arlington Centre Blvd Ste 2241 Columbus (43220) *(G-5977)*
Heartland Bank (HQ) 614 337-4600
  430 N Hamilton Rd Columbus (43213) *(G-5978)*
Heartland Bhavioral Healthcare 330 833-3135
  3000 Erie St S Massillon (44646) *(G-10645)*
Heartland Christian School Inc 330 482-2331
  28 Pittsburgh St Columbiana (44408) *(G-5236)*
Heartland Employment Svcs LLC, Toledo *Also Called: Promedica Employment Svcs LLC (G-13968)*
Heartland Healthcare Svcs LLC (PA) 419 535-8435
  4755 South Ave Toledo (43615) *(G-13842)*
Heartland HM Hlth Care Hospice, Fremont *Also Called: Promedica Health System Inc (G-8697)*
Heartland Hospice Services, Cincinnati *Also Called: Promedica Health System Inc (G-3252)*

Heartland Miamisburg Oh LLC 937 866-8885
  450 Oak Ridge Blvd Miamisburg (45342) *(G-11060)*
Heartland of Charleston 4109, Toledo *Also Called: Health Care Rtrment Corp Amer (G-13841)*
Heartland of Marysville, Marysville *Also Called: Health Care Rtrment Corp Amer (G-10487)*
Heartland Perrysburg Oh LLC 419 874-3578
  10540 Fremont Pike Perrysburg (43551) *(G-12341)*
Heartland Petroleum, Columbus *Also Called: Gfl Environmental Svcs USA Inc (G-5932)*
Heartland Petroleum LLC 614 441-4001
  4001 E 5th Ave Columbus (43219) *(G-5979)*
Heartland Rhblitation Svcs Inc (DH) 419 537-0764
  3425 Executive Pkwy Ste 128 Toledo (43606) *(G-13843)*
Heartland Valley Metals LLC 419 886-0220
  500 Main St Bellville (44813) *(G-1050)*
Heartland Vlg Wstrvlle OH RC L 614 895-1038
  1060 Eastwind Dr Westerville (43081) *(G-14983)*
Heartspring Home Hlth Care LLC 937 531-6920
  1251 E Dorothy Ln Dayton (45419) *(G-7403)*
Hearty Hearts Home Health LLC 216 898-5533
  4161 Ridge Rd Cleveland (44144) *(G-4356)*
Heat and Frost Insulators Jatc, Toledo *Also Called: Toledo Area Insulator Wkrs Jac (G-14049)*
Heatermeals, Cincinnati *Also Called: Luxfer Magtech Inc (G-2995)*
Heath Nursing Care Center 740 522-1171
  717 S 30th St Newark (43056) *(G-11704)*
Heather Downs Cntry CLB Assoc 419 385-0248
  3910 Heatherdowns Blvd Toledo (43614) *(G-13844)*
Heather Hl Rehabilitation Hosp, Chardon *Also Called: University Hsptals Hlth Systm- (G-2024)*
HEATHER KNOLL NURSING CENTER, Tallmadge *Also Called: Heather Knoll Rtrement Vlg Inc (G-13594)*
Heather Knoll Rtrement Vlg Inc 330 688-8600
  1134 North Ave Tallmadge (44278) *(G-13594)*
Heatherdowns Nursing Center, Columbus *Also Called: Rossford Grtric Care Ltd Prtnr (G-6612)*
Heatherdowns Operating Co LLC 419 382-5050
  2401 Cass Rd Toledo (43614) *(G-13845)*
Heathergreene Nursing Homes, Xenia *Also Called: Liberty Nursing Home Inc (G-15523)*
Heatherhill Care Communities 440 285-4040
  12340 Bass Lake Rd Chardon (44024) *(G-2004)*
Heathers Day Care LLC 419 784-9600
  121 Hopkins St Defiance (43512) *(G-7748)*
Heathrdwns Rhblttion Rsdntial, Toledo *Also Called: Heatherdowns Operating Co LLC (G-13845)*
Heavenly Home Health LLC 740 859-4735
  1800 Old State Route 7 Rayland (43943) *(G-12647)*
Hebrew Un Cllg-Jwish Inst Rlgi 513 221-1875
  3101 Clifton Ave Cincinnati (45220) *(G-2815)*
Hecla Water Association (PA) 740 533-0526
  3190 State Route 141 Ironton (45638) *(G-9507)*
Heco Operations Inc 614 888-5700
  7440 Pingue Dr Worthington (43085) *(G-15420)*
Hedstrom Entertainment, Ashland *Also Called: Ball Bounce and Sport Inc (G-479)*
Heidelberg Distributing C 513 771-9370
  10975 Medallion Dr Cincinnati (45241) *(G-2816)*
Heidelberg Distributing Co, Cincinnati *Also Called: Dayton Heidelberg Distrg Co (G-2544)*
Heights Laundry & Dry Cleaning (PA) 216 932-9666
  1863 Coventry Rd Cleveland Heights (44118) *(G-5178)*
Heil and Hornik LLC 614 873-8749
  7637c Commerce Pl Plain City (43064) *(G-12479)*
Heil Brothers Incorporated 937 256-3500
  2218 Wilmington Pike Dayton (45420) *(G-7404)*
Heil Brothers Lawn & Grdn Eqp, Dayton *Also Called: Heil Brothers Incorporated (G-7404)*
Heimerl Farms Ltd 740 967-0063
  3891 Mink St Johnstown (43031) *(G-9546)*
HEINZERLING 1605, Columbus *Also Called: Heinzerling Community (G-5980)*
Heinzerling Community 614 272-8888
  1800 Heinzerling Dr Columbus (43223) *(G-5980)*
Heinzerling Developmental Ctr, Columbus *Also Called: Heinzerling Foundation (G-5982)*
Heinzerling Foundation (PA) 614 272-8888
  1800 Heinzerling Dr Columbus (43223) *(G-5981)*
Heinzerling Foundation 614 272-2000
  1755 Heinzerling Dr Columbus (43223) *(G-5982)*

Heinzerling Mem Foundation, Columbus Also Called: Heinzerling Foundation *(G-5981)*
Heiser Staffing Services LLC.. 614 800-4188
  330 W Spring St Ste 205 Columbus (43215) *(G-5983)*
Heitmeyer Group LLC... 614 699-5770
  501 W Schrock Rd Ste 410 Westerville (43081) *(G-14984)*
Helen Purcell Home.. 740 453-1745
  1854 Norwood Blvd Zanesville (43701) *(G-15800)*
Helios, Westerville Also Called: Progressive Medical LLC *(G-14931)*
Helm and Associates Inc.. 419 893-1480
  501 W Sophia St Unit 8 Maumee (43537) *(G-10731)*
Help Foundation Inc.. 216 486-5258
  17702 Nottingham Rd Cleveland (44119) *(G-4357)*
Help Foundation Inc.. 216 289-7710
  27348 Oak Ct Euclid (44132) *(G-8345)*
Help Foundation Inc (PA)... 216 432-4810
  26900 Euclid Ave Euclid (44132) *(G-8346)*
Help Foundation Inc.. 216 432-4810
  10333 Northfield Rd Ste 20b Northfield (44067) *(G-11956)*
Helping Hands, Lima Also Called: Community Hlth Prfssionals Inc *(G-9989)*
Helping Hands Healthcare Inc... 513 755-4181
  9692 Cincinnati Columbus Rd West Chester (45241) *(G-14816)*
Helping U Home Health Care LLC... 440 724-3754
  23533 Mercantile Rd Ste 106 Beachwood (44122) *(G-798)*
Helpline, Delaware Also Called: Helpline Del Mrrow Cunties Inc *(G-7803)*
Helpline Del Mrrow Cunties Inc.. 740 369-3316
  11 N Franklin St Delaware (43015) *(G-7803)*
Helton Enterprises Inc (PA).. 419 423-4180
  151 Stanford Pkwy Findlay (45840) *(G-8546)*
Hematogy Oncology Toledo Clinc....................................... 419 794-7720
  5805 Monclova Rd Maumee (43537) *(G-10732)*
Hematology Oncology Center... 440 324-0401
  41201 Schadden Rd Ste 2 Elyria (44035) *(G-8255)*
Hemlock Landscapes Inc.. 440 247-3631
  7209 Chagrin Rd Ste A Chagrin Falls (44023) *(G-1978)*
Hemly Tool Supply Inc... 800 445-1068
  16600 Thompson Rd Thompson (44086) *(G-13617)*
Hemm Glass, Piqua Also Called: R C Hemm Glass Shops Inc *(G-12457)*
Hempstead Manor.. 740 354-8150
  727 8th St Portsmouth (45662) *(G-12553)*
Henderson Rd Rest Systems Inc (PA)................................ 614 442-3310
  1615 Old Henderson Rd Columbus (43220) *(G-5984)*
Henderson Roofing & Cnstr Inc... 330 323-1500
  8045 Dawnwood Ave Ne Middlebranch (44652) *(G-11112)*
Henderson Turf Farm Inc.. 937 748-1559
  2969 Beal Rd Franklin (45005) *(G-8640)*
Hendrickson Auxiliary Axles, Hebron Also Called: Hendrickson International Corp *(G-9143)*
Hendrickson International Corp... 740 929-5600
  277 N High St Hebron (43025) *(G-9143)*
Hennis Care Center of Bolivar, Bolivar Also Called: Megco Management Inc *(G-1295)*
Hennis Care Centre At Dover, Dover Also Called: Hennis Nursing Home *(G-7889)*
Hennis Nursing Home.. 330 364-8849
  1720 N Cross St Dover (44622) *(G-7889)*
Henry Call Inc.. 216 433-5609
  308 Pines St Ste 100 Cleveland (44135) *(G-4358)*
Henry County Hospital Inc.. 419 592-4015
  1600 E Riverview Ave Frnt Napoleon (43545) *(G-11525)*
Henry Gurtzweiler Inc.. 419 729-3955
  921 Galena St Toledo (43611) *(G-13846)*
Henry H Stmbugh Aditorium Assn...................................... 330 747-5175
  1000 5th Ave Frnt Youngstown (44504) *(G-15629)*
Henry J Fioritto DDS Inc... 440 951-5511
  6303 Center St Mentor (44060) *(G-10946)*
Henry Jergens Contractor Inc.. 937 233-1830
  1280 Brandt Pike Dayton (45404) *(G-7405)*
Henrys King Touring Company.. 330 628-1886
  1369 Burbridge Dr Mogadore (44260) *(G-11328)*
Hensley Industries, Cincinnati Also Called: Hensley Industries Inc *(G-2817)*
Hensley Industries Inc (PA).. 513 769-6666
  2150 Langdon Farm Rd Cincinnati (45237) *(G-2817)*
Her Inc (PA)... 614 221-7400
  4261 Morse Rd Columbus (43230) *(G-5985)*

Her Majesty Management Group... 614 680-7461
  3737 Easton Market Ste 1339 Columbus (43219) *(G-5986)*
Heraeus Epurio LLC... 937 264-1000
  970 Industrial Park Dr Vandalia (45377) *(G-14380)*
Heraeus Prcous Mtls N Amer Dyc, Vandalia Also Called: Heraeus Epurio LLC *(G-14380)*
Herb Thyme Farms Inc... 866 386-0854
  8600 S Wilkinson Way Ste G Perrysburg (43551) *(G-12342)*
Herbert E Orr Company Inc.. 419 399-4866
  335 W Wall St Paulding (45879) *(G-12284)*
Herbst Electric LLC.. 216 621-5890
  5171 Grant Ave Cleveland (44125) *(G-4359)*
Herbst Electric Company, Cleveland Also Called: Herbst Electric LLC *(G-4359)*
Hercules Led LLC... 844 437-2533
  5411 Market St Boardman (44512) *(G-1289)*
Hereford Group, Uniontown Also Called: Hereford Security Group *(G-14257)*
Hereford Security Group... 330 644-1371
  3280 Parfoure Blvd Uniontown (44685) *(G-14257)*
Heritage Bank Center, Cincinnati Also Called: Arena Management Holdings LLC *(G-2215)*
Heritage Butlr Fmly Physicians, Fairfield Township Also Called: Trihealth Inc *(G-8466)*
Heritage Carpet & HM Dctg Ctrs, Canton Also Called: Clays Heritage Carpet Inc *(G-1711)*
Heritage Club.. 513 459-7711
  6690 Heritage Club Dr Mason (45040) *(G-10560)*
Heritage Cooperative, Delaware Also Called: Heritage Cooperative Inc *(G-7804)*
Heritage Cooperative Inc... 330 533-5551
  364 Lisbon St Canfield (44406) *(G-1630)*
Heritage Cooperative Inc (PA).. 877 240-4393
  59 Greif Pkwy Ste 200 Delaware (43015) *(G-7804)*
Heritage Corner Health Care CA... 419 353-3759
  1069 Klotz Rd Bowling Green (43402) *(G-1323)*
Heritage Corner Nursing HM LLC....................................... 419 728-7010
  1069 Klotz Rd Ste B Bowling Green (43402) *(G-1324)*
Heritage Crossing... 330 510-3110
  251 N Cleveland Massillon Rd Akron (44333) *(G-191)*
Heritage Day Health Centers (HQ)..................................... 614 451-2151
  2335 N Bank Dr Columbus (43220) *(G-5987)*
Heritage Equipment Company.. 614 873-3941
  9000 Heritage Dr Plain City (43064) *(G-12480)*
Heritage Family Medical Inc.. 513 867-9000
  435 Park Ave Hamilton (45013) *(G-9051)*
Heritage Health Care Services... 614 848-6550
  1625 Bethel Rd Ste 102 Columbus (43220) *(G-5988)*
Heritage Health Care Services (PA).................................. 419 867-2002
  1100 Shawnee Rd Lima (45805) *(G-9905)*
HERITAGE HOUSE NURSING HOME, Columbus Also Called: Wexner Heritage Village *(G-6882)*
Heritage Legacy Hlth Svcs LLC... 740 456-8245
  3304 Rhodes Ave New Boston (45662) *(G-11593)*
Heritage Mnor Jwish HM For Age, Youngstown Also Called: Youngstown Area Jwish Fdration *(G-15756)*
Heritage Mnor Sklled Nrsing Rh, Columbus Also Called: I Vrable Inc *(G-6036)*
Heritage Pinte Assisted Living, New Boston Also Called: Heritage Legacy Hlth Svcs LLC *(G-11593)*
Heritage Pool Supply Group Inc... 440 238-2100
  22350 Royalton Rd Strongsville (44149) *(G-13460)*
Heritage Professional Services... 740 456-8245
  3304 Rhodes Ave New Boston (45662) *(G-11594)*
Heritage Square New Boston, New Boston Also Called: Heritage Professional Services *(G-11594)*
Heritage Valley Health Sys Inc.. 724 773-8209
  48462 Bell School Rd Ste C East Liverpool (43920) *(G-8183)*
Heritage Valley Health Sys Inc.. 724 773-1995
  16280 Dresden Ave East Liverpool (43920) *(G-8184)*
Heritage Village of Clyde, Clyde Also Called: Astoria Place of Clyde LLC *(G-5198)*
HERITAGE, THE, Findlay Also Called: Manleys Manor Nursing Home Inc *(G-8560)*
Herman Bair Enterprise.. 330 262-4449
  2714 Akron Rd Wooster (44691) *(G-15344)*
Herratige Inn, Bowling Green Also Called: Debmar Inc *(G-1317)*
Herrnstein Auto Group, Chillicothe Also Called: Herrnstein Chrysler Inc *(G-2068)*
Herrnstein Chrysler Inc.. 740 773-2203
  133 Marietta Rd Chillicothe (45601) *(G-2068)*

Hershey Montessori School Inc 440 357-0918
11530 Madison Rd Huntsburg (44046) *(G-9382)*

Hertz, Columbus *Also Called: Geo Byers Sons Holding Inc (G-5927)*

Hertzfeld Poultry Farms Inc 419 832-2070
15799 Milton Rd Grand Rapids (43522) *(G-8845)*

Hewlettco Inc 440 238-4600
13590 Falling Water Rd Strongsville (44136) *(G-13461)*

Hexion, Columbus *Also Called: Hexion Inc (G-5989)*

Hexion Inc (PA) 888 443-9466
180 E Broad St Columbus (43215) *(G-5989)*

Hexion Topco LLC (PA) 614 225-4000
180 E Broad St Columbus (43215) *(G-5990)*

Hexpol Compounding LLC 440 834-4644
14330 Kinsman Rd Burton (44021) *(G-1528)*

Hgc Construction Co (PA) 513 861-8866
2814 Stanton Ave Cincinnati (45206) *(G-2818)*

Hgr Industrial Surplus Inc (PA) 216 486-4567
20001 Euclid Ave Euclid (44117) *(G-8347)*

HH Franchising Systems Inc 513 563-8339
10101 Alliance Rd Ste 300 Blue Ash (45242) *(G-1181)*

HH STAMBAUGH, Youngstown *Also Called: Henry H Stmbugh Aditorium Assn (G-15629)*

Hhd Aviation LLC 513 426-8378
2820 Bobmeyer Rd Hngr C7-210 Hamilton (45015) *(G-9052)*

HHWPCAC, Findlay *Also Called: Hancock-Hrdn-Wyndt-ptnam Cmnty (G-8543)*

Hi-Five Development Svcs Inc 513 336-9280
202 W Main St Ste C Mason (45040) *(G-10561)*

Hi-Tek Manufacturing Inc 513 459-1094
6050 Hi Tek Ct Mason (45040) *(G-10562)*

Hi-Way Distributing Corp Amer 330 645-6633
3716 E State St Coventry Township (44203) *(G-7010)*

Hi-Way Paving Inc 614 876-1700
4343 Weaver Ct N Hilliard (43026) *(G-9198)*

Hiab USA Inc (HQ) 419 482-6000
12233 Williams Rd Perrysburg (43551) *(G-12343)*

Hickey Metal Fabrication, Salem *Also Called: Hickey Metal Fabrication Roofg (G-12843)*

Hickey Metal Fabrication Roofg 330 337-9329
873 Georgetown Rd Salem (44460) *(G-12843)*

Hickory Creek Hlthcare Fndtion 419 542-7795
401 Fountain St Hicksville (43526) *(G-9158)*

Hickory Flat Golf Course, West Lafayette *Also Called: Brassboys Enterprises Inc (G-14855)*

Hickory Harvest Foods, Coventry Township *Also Called: Ohio Hckry Hrvest Brnd Pdts In (G-7014)*

Hickory Hill Lakes Inc 937 295-3000
7103 State Route 66 Fort Loramie (45845) *(G-8604)*

Hickory Rver Smkehouse Tipp Cy, Tipp City *Also Called: Dan & Maria Davis Inc (G-13657)*

Hickory Woods Golf Course Inc 513 575-3900
1240 Hickory Woods Dr Loveland (45140) *(G-10142)*

Hicks Industrial Roofing, New Philadelphia *Also Called: Hicks Roofing Inc (G-11653)*

Hicks Roofing Inc 330 364-7737
2162 Pleasant Valley Rd Ne New Philadelphia (44663) *(G-11653)*

Hicksville Bank Inc (HQ) 419 542-7726
144 E High St Hicksville (43526) *(G-9159)*

Hicon Inc 513 242-3612
93 Caldwell Dr # A Cincinnati (45216) *(G-2819)*

Hidy Honda, Dayton *Also Called: Hidy Motors Inc (G-7133)*

Hidy Motors Inc (PA) 937 426-9564
2300 Heller Drive Beaver Creek Dayton (45434) *(G-7133)*

High Banks Care Centre, Columbus *Also Called: Provider Services Inc (G-6553)*

High Definition Tooling, Newcomerstown *Also Called: H3d Tool Corporation (G-11768)*

High Line Corporation 330 848-8800
2420 Wedgewood Dr Ste 20 Akron (44312) *(G-192)*

High Point Home Health Ltd 419 674-4090
118 S Main St Kenton (43326) *(G-9618)*

High Score Mentor LLC 513 485-2848
1172 W Galbraith Rd Ste 211 Cincinnati (45231) *(G-2820)*

High Voltage Maintenance Corp (DH) 937 278-0811
5100 Energy Dr Dayton (45414) *(G-7406)*

High-TEC Industrial Services 937 667-1772
15 Industry Park Ct Tipp City (45371) *(G-13659)*

High-Tech Pools Inc 440 979-5070
31330 Industrial Pkwy North Olmsted (44070) *(G-11905)*

HIGHBANKS CARE CENTER, Columbus *Also Called: Highbanks Care Center LLC (G-5991)*

Highbanks Care Center LLC 614 888-2021
111 Lazelle Rd Columbus (43235) *(G-5991)*

Highland Cnty Cmnty Action Org (PA) 937 393-3060
1487 N High St Ste 500 Hillsboro (45133) *(G-9255)*

Highland Cnty Jint Twnship Dst 937 393-6100
1275 N High St Hillsboro (45133) *(G-9256)*

Highland Computer Forms Inc (PA) 937 393-4215
1025 W Main St Hillsboro (45133) *(G-9257)*

Highland District Hospital, Hillsboro *Also Called: Highland Cnty Jint Twnship Dst (G-9256)*

Highland Health Providers Corp 937 981-1121
1092 Jefferson St Greenfield (45123) *(G-8866)*

Highland Health Providers Corp 937 393-4899
1402 N High St Hillsboro (45133) *(G-9258)*

Highland Health Providers Corp 937 364-2346
8900 State Route 134 Lynchburg (45142) *(G-10185)*

Highland House, Cleveland *Also Called: Brittany Residential Inc (G-3896)*

Highland Meadows Golf Club (PA) 419 882-7153
7455 Erie St Sylvania (43560) *(G-13550)*

Highland SEC Invstigations LLC 614 558-2421
4197 Shoppers Ln Columbus (43228) *(G-5992)*

Highland Som Development (PA) 330 528-3500
10020 Aurora Hudson Rd Streetsboro (44241) *(G-13415)*

Highland Springs LLC 216 591-9433
4199 Millpond Dr Beachwood (44122) *(G-799)*

Highlands Community Lrng Ctr 614 210-0830
5120 Godown Rd Columbus (43220) *(G-5993)*

Highlands Post Acute, Cincinnati *Also Called: Norwood Hghlnds Healthcare LLC (G-3131)*

Hightowers Petroleum Company 513 423-4272
3577 Commerce Dr Middletown (45005) *(G-11199)*

Hightowers Petroleum Company, Middletown *Also Called: Hightowers Petroleum Company (G-11199)*

Highway Auto Body, Chagrin Falls *Also Called: Highway Auto Center LLC (G-1979)*

Highway Auto Center LLC 440 543-9569
8410 Washington St Chagrin Falls (44023) *(G-1979)*

Hii Mission Technologies Corp 937 426-3421
2310 National Rd Beavercreek Township (45324) *(G-940)*

Hileman Group 216 926-4365
1100 W 9th St Cleveland (44113) *(G-4360)*

Hill Barth & King LLC (PA) 330 758-8613
6603 Summit Dr Canfield (44406) *(G-1631)*

Hill & Associates, Canton *Also Called: Hill Technical Services Inc (G-1771)*

Hill Intl Trcks NA LLC (PA) 330 386-6440
47866 Y & O Rd East Liverpool (43920) *(G-8185)*

Hill Rom, Cincinnati *Also Called: Hill-Rom Inc (G-2821)*

Hill Side Plaza 216 486-6300
18220 Euclid Ave Cleveland (44112) *(G-4361)*

Hill Technical Services Inc 330 494-3656
4791 Munson St Nw Canton (44718) *(G-1771)*

Hill View Retirement Center 740 354-3135
1610 28th St Portsmouth (45662) *(G-12554)*

Hill-Rom Inc 513 769-6343
3478 Hauck Rd Cincinnati (45241) *(G-2821)*

Hillandale Health Care Inc 513 777-1400
8073 Tylersville Rd Ofc West Chester (45069) *(G-14708)*

Hillbrook Club Inc 440 247-4940
17200 S Woodland Rd Cleveland (44120) *(G-4362)*

Hillcrest Egg & Cheese Co (PA) 216 361-4625
2735 E 40th St Cleveland (44115) *(G-4363)*

Hillcrest Foodservice, Cleveland *Also Called: Hillcrest Egg & Cheese Co (G-4363)*

Hillcrest Hospital, Cleveland *Also Called: Cleveland Clnic Hlth Systm-AST (G-4035)*

Hillcrest Hospital Auxiliary 440 449-4500
6780 Mayfield Rd Cleveland (44124) *(G-4364)*

Hillebrand Nrsing Rhblttion Ct, Cincinnati *Also Called: D James Incorporated (G-2530)*

Hilliard Asssted Lving Mmory C, Hilliard *Also Called: Hilliard Operator LLC (G-9201)*

Hilliard Family Dentistry, Hilliard *Also Called: Hilliard Family Medicine Inc (G-9199)*

Hilliard Family Medicine Inc 614 876-8989
3958 Leap Rd Ste 101 Hilliard (43026) *(G-9199)*

Hilliard Hlth Rhbilitation Inc 614 777-6001
4787 Tremont Club Dr Hilliard (43026) *(G-9200)*

ALPHABETIC SECTION

Hilliard Operator LLC..614 503-4414
4303 Trueman Blvd Hilliard (43026) *(G-9201)*

Hillman, Cincinnati *Also Called: Hillman Companies Inc (G-2822)*

Hillman Companies Inc (DH).......................................513 851-4900
10590 Hamilton Ave Cincinnati (45231) *(G-2822)*

Hillman Group (DH)..513 851-4900
1280 Kemper Meadow Dr Cincinnati (45240) *(G-2823)*

Hillman Group Inc..513 874-5905
9950 Princeton Glendale Rd West Chester (45246) *(G-14817)*

Hillman Solutions Corp (PA)......................................513 851-4900
10590 Hamilton Ave Cincinnati (45231) *(G-2824)*

Hills Developers Inc..513 984-0300
4901 Hunt Rd Ste 300 Blue Ash (45242) *(G-1182)*

Hills Property Management Inc (PA).........................513 984-0300
4901 Hunt Rd Ste 300 Blue Ash (45242) *(G-1183)*

Hills Real Estate Group, Blue Ash *Also Called: Hills Property Management Inc (G-1183)*

Hillsboro Transportation Co......................................513 772-9223
2889 E Crescentville Rd Cincinnati (45246) *(G-2825)*

Hillside Acres Nursing Home, Willard *Also Called: Liberty Nursing of Willard (G-15170)*

Hillside Plaza, Cleveland *Also Called: Hill Side Plaza (G-4361)*

Hillspring Health Care Center...................................937 748-1100
325 E Central Ave Springboro (45066) *(G-13201)*

Hilltop Basic Resources Inc......................................513 621-1500
511 W Water St Cincinnati (45202) *(G-2826)*

Hilltop Concrete, Cincinnati *Also Called: Hilltop Basic Resources Inc (G-2826)*

Hilltop Health Center, Columbus *Also Called: Columbus Nghbrhood Hlth Ctr In (G-5650)*

Hilltop Nursery School, Harrison *Also Called: Harrison Avenue Assembly God (G-9107)*

Hilltrux Tank Lines Inc..330 538-3700
200 Rosemont Rd North Jackson (44451) *(G-11872)*

Hilscher-Clarke, Canton *Also Called: Hilscher-Clarke Electric Co (G-1772)*

Hilscher-Clarke Electric Co (PA)...............................330 452-9806
519 4th St Nw Canton (44703) *(G-1772)*

Hilscher-Clarke Electric Co......................................740 622-5557
572 S 3rd St Coshocton (43812) *(G-6986)*

Hilton, Blue Ash *Also Called: Blue-Kenwood LLC (G-1137)*

Hilton, Cincinnati *Also Called: Cincinnati Netherland Ht LLC (G-2417)*

Hilton, Cleveland *Also Called: Hotel 1100 Carnegie Opco L P (G-4383)*

Hilton, Columbus *Also Called: Hilton Polaris (G-5261)*

Hilton, Columbus *Also Called: Hilton Garden Inn (G-5994)*

Hilton, Grove City *Also Called: Hilton Garden Inn (G-8925)*

Hilton, Miamisburg *Also Called: Hilton Garden Inns MGT LLC (G-11061)*

Hilton, Sharonville *Also Called: Gateway Hotel Ltd (G-12994)*

Hilton Akron Fairlawn, Fairlawn *Also Called: Fairlawn Associates Ltd (G-8478)*

Hilton Cleveland/Beachwood, Beachwood *Also Called: Cleveland Bchwood Hsptlity LLC (G-777)*

Hilton Cncnnati Netherland Plz, Cincinnati *Also Called: Park Hotels & Resorts Inc (G-3183)*

Hilton Garden Inn...614 263-7200
3232 Olentangy River Rd Columbus (43202) *(G-5994)*

Hilton Garden Inn...614 539-8944
3928 Jackpot Rd Grove City (43123) *(G-8925)*

Hilton Garden Inn Perrysburg, Perrysburg *Also Called: Levis Commons Hotel LLC (G-12353)*

Hilton Garden Inns, Cleveland *Also Called: Hilton Grdn Inn - Cleveland E (G-4365)*

Hilton Garden Inns, Columbus *Also Called: Hilton Grdn Inn Columbus Arprt (G-5996)*

Hilton Garden Inns MGT LLC......................................937 247-5850
12000 Innovation Dr Miamisburg (45342) *(G-11061)*

Hilton Grdn Inn - Cleveland E....................................440 646-1777
700 Beta Dr Cleveland (44143) *(G-4365)*

Hilton Grdn Inn Clumbus Easton...............................877 782-9444
3600 Morse Rd Ste A Columbus (43219) *(G-5995)*

Hilton Grdn Inn Columbus Arprt................................614 231-2869
4265 Sawyer Rd Columbus (43219) *(G-5996)*

Hilton Grdn Inn Columbus Arprt, Columbus *Also Called: Indus Airport Hotels I LLC (G-6046)*

Hilton Knoxville, Columbus *Also Called: RB Knoxville LLC (G-6562)*

Hilton Polaris..614 885-1600
8700 Lyra Dr Columbus (43240) *(G-5261)*

Hilty Memorial Home Inc...419 384-3218
304 Hilty Dr Pandora (45877) *(G-12246)*

Hinge Consulting LLC..513 404-1547
310 Culvert St Ste 301 Cincinnati (45202) *(G-2827)*

Hinson Roofing & Shtmtl Inc.....................................513 367-4477
6191 Kilby Rd Harrison (45030) *(G-9109)*

Hiram Maintenance Bldg, Windham *Also Called: Ohio Tpk & Infrastructure Comm (G-15288)*

Hirsch Division, Chagrin Falls *Also Called: Lake Horry Electric (G-1961)*

Hirsch Holdings Inc...513 733-4111
4 Kovach Dr Ste 470a Cincinnati (45215) *(G-2828)*

Hirzel Transfer Co..419 287-3288
115 Columbus St Pemberville (43450) *(G-12289)*

Hitchcock Center For Women Inc..............................216 421-0662
1227 Ansel Rd Cleveland (44108) *(G-4366)*

Hitchcock Fleming & Assoc Inc.................................330 376-2111
388 S Main St Ste 350 Akron (44311) *(G-193)*

Hittle House, Columbus *Also Called: Dtac of Ohio LLC (G-5787)*

Hiwthi Home Care LLC, Wintersville *Also Called: Home Is Where Hart Is HM Care (G-15295)*

Hixson Archtcts/Ngnrs/Nteriors, Cincinnati *Also Called: Hixson Incorporated (G-2829)*

Hixson Incorporated..513 241-1230
659 Van Meter St Ste 300 Cincinnati (45202) *(G-2829)*

Hiyes Logistics...614 558-0198
8400 Industrial Pkwy Ste C Plain City (43064) *(G-12481)*

HJ Benken Flor & Greenhouses.................................513 891-1040
6000 Plainfield Rd Cincinnati (45213) *(G-2830)*

Hj Services, Cincinnati *Also Called: Advanced Csmtc Srgery Lser Ctr (G-2148)*

Hkm Drect Mkt Cmmnications Inc (PA)......................800 860-4456
5501 Cass Ave Cleveland (44102) *(G-4367)*

Hkt Teleservices, Grove City *Also Called: Hkt Teleservices Inc (G-8926)*

Hkt Teleservices Inc (PA)..614 652-6300
3400 Southpark Pl Ste F Grove City (43123) *(G-8926)*

Hle Company...216 325-0941
4700 Spring Rd Cleveland (44131) *(G-4368)*

Hmhp Sleep Lab, Youngstown *Also Called: Christus Hlth Southeast Texas (G-15577)*

Hmt Associates Inc..216 369-0109
335 Treeworth Blvd Broadview Heights (44147) *(G-1391)*

Hntb Corporation..216 522-1140
1100 Superior Ave E Ste 1701 Cleveland (44114) *(G-4369)*

Hob Entertainment LLC..216 523-2583
308 Euclid Ave Cleveland (44114) *(G-4370)*

Hobart, Hillsboro *Also Called: ITW Food Equipment Group LLC (G-9260)*

Hobart, Troy *Also Called: ITW Food Equipment Group LLC (G-14141)*

Hobart International Holdings...................................937 332-3000
701 S Ridge Ave Troy (45373) *(G-14138)*

Hobart Sales & Service, Akron *Also Called: Harry C Lobalzo & Sons Inc (G-184)*

Hobby Lobby, Stow *Also Called: Hobby Lobby Stores Inc (G-13373)*

Hobby Lobby Stores Inc...419 861-1862
6645 Airport Hwy Holland (43528) *(G-9288)*

Hobby Lobby Stores Inc...330 686-1508
4332 Kent Rd Ste 3 Stow (44224) *(G-13373)*

Hobe Lcas Crtif Pub Accntnts I..................................216 524-7167
4807 Rockside Rd Ste 510 Cleveland (44131) *(G-4371)*

Hocking Valley Community Hosp, Logan *Also Called: Hocking Vly Cmnty Hosp Mem Fun (G-10023)*

Hocking Valley Industries Inc...................................740 385-2118
1369 E Front St Logan (43138) *(G-10022)*

Hocking Vly Bnk of Athens Co (HQ)..........................740 592-4441
7 W Stimson Ave Athens (45701) *(G-572)*

Hocking Vly Cmnty Hosp Mem Fun (PA)...................740 380-8389
601 State Route 664 N Logan (43138) *(G-10023)*

Hockingthensperry Cmnty Action (PA).....................740 767-4500
3 Cardaras Dr Glouster (45732) *(G-8835)*

Hockingthensperry Cmnty Action.............................740 385-6813
1005 C I C Dr Logan (43138) *(G-10024)*

Hockingthensperry Cmnty Action.............................740 753-9404
40 Saint Charles St Nelsonville (45764) *(G-11546)*

Hockingthensperry Cmnty Action.............................740 342-1333
228 W Jefferson St New Lexington (43764) *(G-11625)*

Hockins Athens Prry Cmnty Acti (PA).......................740 385-3644
11100 State Route 550 Athens (45701) *(G-573)*

Hockins Athens Prry Cmnty Acti...............................740 753-3062
50 Saint Charles St Nelsonville (45764) *(G-11547)*

Hodell-Natco Industries Inc (PA)..............................216 447-0165
7825 Hub Pkwy Cleveland (44125) *(G-4372)*

Hodges Trucking Company LLC

Hodges Trucking Company LLC.. 405 947-7764
  5368 Biery St Sw Navarre (44662) *(G-11538)*
Hoeting Inc.. 513 385-5100
  7601 Cheviot Rd Cincinnati (45247) *(G-2831)*
Hoeting Realtors, Cincinnati *Also Called: Hoeting Inc (G-2831)*
Hof Fitness Center Inc... 330 455-0555
  2700 Roberts Ave Nw Canton (44709) *(G-1773)*
Hof Village Newco LLC... 330 458-9176
  2014 Champions Gateway Canton (44708) *(G-1774)*
Hof Vllage Cnstlltion Ctr For, Canton *Also Called: Hof Village Newco LLC (G-1774)*
Hoffman Products, Macedonia *Also Called: TPC Wire & Cable Corp (G-10208)*
Hoffman, Debbie, Toledo *Also Called: West Toledo Animal Hosp Ltd (G-14105)*
Hofrichter Brothers Inc.. 740 314-5669
  680 Lovers Ln Steubenville (43953) *(G-13331)*
Hogan Services Inc... 614 491-8402
  1500 Obetz Rd Columbus (43207) *(G-5997)*
Hogan Truck Leasing Inc... 513 454-3500
  2001 Ddc Way Fairfield (45014) *(G-8418)*
Hogan Truck Leasing Inc... 937 293-0033
  1860 Cardington Rd Moraine (45409) *(G-11417)*
Hogan Truck Leasing Inc... 314 802-5995
  2499 Mcgaw Rd Obetz (43207) *(G-12080)*
Hoge Brush, New Knoxville *Also Called: Hoge Lumber Company (G-11617)*
Hoge Lumber Company (PA)... 419 753-2263
  701 S Main St State New Knoxville (45871) *(G-11617)*
Hokuto USA Inc... 614 782-6200
  2200 Southwest Blvd Ste K Grove City (43123) *(G-8927)*
Holbrook & Manter (PA).. 740 387-8620
  181 E Center St Marion (43302) *(G-10430)*
Holdco LLC.. 614 255-7285
  4151 Executive Pkwy Ste 150 Westerville (43081) *(G-14985)*
Holden Arboretum.. 440 946-4400
  9500 Sperry Rd Willoughby (44094) *(G-15194)*
Holiday Inn.. 440 951-7333
  7701 Reynolds Rd Mentor (44060) *(G-10947)*
Holiday Inn, Akron *Also Called: Detroit Westfield LLC (G-133)*
Holiday Inn, Alliance *Also Called: Holiday Inn Ex Ht & Suites (G-383)*
Holiday Inn, Beavercreek *Also Called: PH Fairborn Ht Owner 2800 LLC (G-894)*
Holiday Inn, Bedford *Also Called: Oakwood Hospitality Corp (G-978)*
Holiday Inn, Cambridge *Also Called: Cambrdge Prperty Investors Ltd (G-1557)*
Holiday Inn, Cambridge *Also Called: Cambridge Associates Ltd (G-1558)*
Holiday Inn, Chillicothe *Also Called: Scioto Lodging Inc (G-2091)*
Holiday Inn, Cincinnati *Also Called: Clermont Hills Co LLC (G-2100)*
Holiday Inn, Cincinnati *Also Called: Green Township Hospitality LLC (G-2774)*
Holiday Inn, Cincinnati *Also Called: Hauck Hospitality LLC (G-2805)*
Holiday Inn, Cincinnati *Also Called: Red Bank Hetzel LP (G-3276)*
Holiday Inn, Cincinnati *Also Called: W & H Realty Inc (G-3636)*
Holiday Inn, Cleveland *Also Called: A C Management Inc (G-3748)*
Holiday Inn, Cleveland *Also Called: Brighton Manor Company (G-3894)*
Holiday Inn, Cleveland *Also Called: Jagi Clvland - Indpendence LLC (G-4431)*
Holiday Inn, Cleveland *Also Called: Mrn-Newgar Hotel Ltd (G-4607)*
Holiday Inn, Columbus *Also Called: Ganga Hospitality Ohio LLC (G-5909)*
Holiday Inn, Columbus *Also Called: Holiday Inn Express (G-5998)*
Holiday Inn, Columbus *Also Called: Jai Guru II Inc (G-6082)*
Holiday Inn, Columbus *Also Called: Town Inn Co LLC (G-6775)*
Holiday Inn, Dayton *Also Called: Holiday Inn Express (G-7407)*
Holiday Inn, Dayton *Also Called: S & S Management Inc (G-7601)*
Holiday Inn, Dublin *Also Called: Tuttle Inn Developers LLC (G-8144)*
Holiday Inn, Fairfield *Also Called: Holiday Inn Express (G-8419)*
Holiday Inn, Findlay *Also Called: Woodson Operations One Ltd (G-8598)*
Holiday Inn, Gallipolis *Also Called: Gallipolis Hospitality Inc (G-8756)*
Holiday Inn, Grove City *Also Called: Sun Development & Mgt Corp (G-8957)*
Holiday Inn, Heath *Also Called: Sns Hospitality LLC (G-9140)*
Holiday Inn, Lima *Also Called: Columbia Properties Lima LLC (G-9875)*
Holiday Inn, Logan *Also Called: Holiday Inn Express (G-10025)*
Holiday Inn, Mansfield *Also Called: Park Hospitality LLC (G-10310)*
Holiday Inn, Marietta *Also Called: Valley Hospitality Inc (G-10409)*
Holiday Inn, Marion *Also Called: Marion Lodge (G-10440)*
Holiday Inn, Medina *Also Called: Hariom Associates Medina LLC (G-10839)*
Holiday Inn, Mentor *Also Called: Holiday Inn Ex Ht Stes Lamalfa (G-10948)*
Holiday Inn, New Philadelphia *Also Called: N P Motel System Inc (G-11660)*
Holiday Inn, Newton Falls *Also Called: Liberty Ashtabula Holdings (G-11777)*
Holiday Inn, North Lima *Also Called: Liberty Mahoning LLC (G-11891)*
Holiday Inn, Obetz *Also Called: Synergy Hotels LLC (G-12084)*
Holiday Inn, Steubenville *Also Called: Good Venture Enterprises LLC (G-13327)*
Holiday Inn, Steubenville *Also Called: Sachs Management Corp (G-13342)*
Holiday Inn, Strongsville *Also Called: Strongsvlle Ldging Assoc I Ltd (G-13488)*
Holiday Inn, Sunbury *Also Called: Dbp Enterprises LLC (G-13519)*
Holiday Inn, Troy *Also Called: S&S Management (G-14158)*
Holiday Inn, Van Wert *Also Called: Valam Hospitality Inc (G-14354)*
Holiday Inn, Wadsworth *Also Called: Wadsworth Hie Management Inc (G-14457)*
Holiday Inn, Wapakoneta *Also Called: S & S Management Inc (G-14491)*
Holiday Inn, Wickliffe *Also Called: Ridgehills Hotel Ltd Partnr (G-15162)*
Holiday Inn, Wilmington *Also Called: S & S Management Inc (G-15272)*
Holiday Inn, Worthington *Also Called: He Hari Inc (G-15419)*
Holiday Inn Canton, Canton *Also Called: Rukh-Jagi Holdings LLC (G-1848)*
Holiday Inn Clvland Nrthst-Mnt, Mentor *Also Called: Mentor Hospitality LLC (G-10969)*
Holiday Inn Ex Ht & Suites.. 330 821-6700
  2341 W State St Alliance (44601) *(G-383)*
Holiday Inn Ex Ht & Suites, Lancaster *Also Called: Lancaster Host LLC (G-9731)*
Holiday Inn Ex Ht Stes Lamalfa... 440 357-0384
  5785 Heisley Rd Mentor (44060) *(G-10948)*
Holiday Inn Ex Stes Clmbus Arp, Columbus *Also Called: Buffalo-6305 Eb Associates LLC (G-5482)*
Holiday Inn Ex Stes Sprngfeld, Springfield *Also Called: Indiana Hospitality Group (G-13258)*
Holiday Inn Express.. 614 447-1212
  3045 Olentangy River Rd Columbus (43202) *(G-5998)*
Holiday Inn Express.. 937 424-5757
  5655 Wilmington Pike Dayton (45459) *(G-7407)*
Holiday Inn Express.. 513 860-2900
  6755 Fairfield Business Ctr Fairfield (45014) *(G-8419)*
Holiday Inn Express.. 740 385-7700
  12916 Grey St Logan (43138) *(G-10025)*
Holiday Inn Express & Suites, Sidney *Also Called: Sunrise Hospitality Inc (G-13056)*
Holiday Inn Express Mt. Vernon, Mount Vernon *Also Called: Mt Vernon Star Properties Inc (G-11502)*
Holiday Inn Slect Strongsville, Strongsville *Also Called: Impac Hotel Group LLC (G-13465)*
Holiday Inn Stes Tledo Sthwst-, Perrysburg *Also Called: Sunrise Hospitality Inc (G-12372)*
Holistic Hlpers HM Hlth Care L... 216 331-5014
  3570 Warrensville Center Rd Ste 210 Shaker Heights (44122) *(G-12978)*
Holland Oil Company (PA).. 330 835-1815
  1485 Marion Ave Akron (44313) *(G-194)*
Holloway Ventures LLC... 740 641-3592
  76 Fairfield Dr Newark (43055) *(G-11705)*
Holly Hill Nursing Home, Newbury *Also Called: Fairmount Nursing Home Inc (G-11760)*
Hollywood Casino, Columbus *Also Called: Penn National Gaming Inc (G-6512)*
Hollywood Casino Columbus, Columbus *Also Called: Central Ohio Gming Vntures LLC (G-5538)*
Hollywood Casino Toledo... 419 661-5200
  1968 Miami St Toledo (43605) *(G-13847)*
Hollywood Gming At Mhning Vly... 330 505-8700
  655 N Canfield Niles Rd Youngstown (44515) *(G-15630)*
Holmes Lumber & Bldg Ctr Inc.. 330 479-8314
  1532 Perry Dr Sw Canton (44710) *(G-1775)*
Holmes Lumber & Bldg Ctr Inc (PA)... 330 674-9060
  6139 S R 39 Millersburg (44654) *(G-11279)*
Holmes Lumber & Supply, Millersburg *Also Called: Holmes Lumber & Bldg Ctr Inc (G-11279)*
Holmes Siding Contractors Ltd (PA)... 330 674-3382
  6767 County Road 624 Millersburg (44654) *(G-11280)*
Holmes-Wayne Electric Coop (PA)... 330 674-1055
  6060 State Route 83 Millersburg (44654) *(G-11281)*
Holo Pundits Inc.. 614 707-5225
  425 Metro Pl N Ste 440 Dublin (43017) *(G-8029)*
Holthaus Lackner Signs, Cincinnati *Also Called: Gus Holthaus Signs Inc (G-2783)*
Holthouse Farms of Ohio Inc (PA)... 419 935-0151
  4373 State Route 103 S Willard (44890) *(G-15168)*

ALPHABETIC SECTION

Holtz Agency Ltd... 513 671-7220
  4015 Executive Park Dr Ste 400 Cincinnati (45241) *(G-2832)*
Holy Family, Lakewood *Also Called: Lakewood Catholic Academy (G-9672)*
Holy Family Home and Hospice, Parma *Also Called: St Augustine Manor (G-12265)*
Holzer, Gallipolis *Also Called: Holzer Health System (G-8761)*
Holzer Clinic Lawrence County, Proctorville *Also Called: Holzer Clinic LLC (G-12612)*
Holzer Clinic LLC.. 740 589-3100
  2131 E State St Athens (45701) *(G-574)*
Holzer Clinic LLC.. 740 446-5412
  90 Jackson Pike Gallipolis (45631) *(G-8757)*
Holzer Clinic LLC.. 740 446-5074
  1086 Jackson Pike Gallipolis (45631) *(G-8758)*
Holzer Clinic LLC (HQ).. 740 446-5411
  90 Jackson Pike Gallipolis (45631) *(G-8759)*
Holzer Clinic LLC.. 304 746-3701
  100 Jackson Pike Gallipolis (45631) *(G-8760)*
Holzer Clinic LLC.. 740 886-9403
  98 State St Proctorville (45669) *(G-12612)*
HOLZER CONSOLIDATED HEALTH SYS, Gallipolis *Also Called: Holzer Clinic LLC (G-8759)*
Holzer Health System (PA).................................... 740 446-5000
  100 Jackson Pike Gallipolis (45631) *(G-8761)*
Holzer Home Care Services................................... 740 288-4287
  100 Jackson Hill Rd Jackson (45640) *(G-9519)*
Holzer Hospital, Gallipolis *Also Called: Holzer Clinic LLC (G-8757)*
Holzer Hospital Foundation (HQ)........................... 740 446-5000
  100 Jackson Pike Gallipolis (45631) *(G-8762)*
Holzer Medical Center, Gallipolis *Also Called: Holzer Hospital Foundation (G-8762)*
Holzer Medical Ctr - Jackson................................. 740 288-4625
  500 Burlington Rd Jackson (45640) *(G-9520)*
Holzer Senior Care Center..................................... 740 446-5001
  380 Colonial Dr Bidwell (45614) *(G-1104)*
Homac Auto & Van Wash, Warren *Also Called: Matthew T Hovanic Inc (G-14538)*
Home At Hearthstone.. 513 521-2700
  8028 Hamilton Ave Cincinnati (45231) *(G-2833)*
Home Bldrs Assn Grter Cncnnati............................ 513 851-6300
  11260 Chester Rd Ste 800 Cincinnati (45246) *(G-2834)*
Home Care Network Inc.. 216 378-9011
  3601 Green Rd Ste 202 Beachwood (44122) *(G-800)*
Home Care Network Inc.. 937 258-1111
  4130 Linden Ave Ste 350 Dayton (45432) *(G-7134)*
Home Care Network Inc (PA)................................. 800 600-3974
  1191 Lyons Rd Dayton (45458) *(G-7408)*
Home Care Network Inc.. 740 353-2329
  1716 11th St Portsmouth (45662) *(G-12555)*
Home Depot USA Inc.. 330 245-0280
  2811 S Arlington Rd Akron (44312) *(G-195)*
Home Depot USA Inc.. 440 937-2240
  35930 Detroit Rd Avon (44011) *(G-654)*
Home Depot USA Inc.. 330 497-1810
  4873 Portage St Nw Canton (44720) *(G-1776)*
Home Depot USA Inc.. 513 688-1654
  520 Ohio Pike Cincinnati (45255) *(G-2835)*
Home Depot USA Inc.. 513 661-2413
  6300 Glenway Ave Cincinnati (45211) *(G-2836)*
Home Depot USA Inc.. 513 631-1705
  3400 Highland Ave Cincinnati (45213) *(G-2837)*
Home Depot USA Inc.. 216 676-9969
  10800 Brookpark Rd Cleveland (44130) *(G-4373)*
Home Depot USA Inc.. 216 251-3091
  11901 Berea Rd Cleveland (44111) *(G-4374)*
Home Depot USA Inc.. 216 297-1303
  3460 Mayfield Rd Cleveland Heights (44118) *(G-5179)*
Home Depot USA Inc.. 614 523-0600
  6333 Cleveland Ave Columbus (43231) *(G-5999)*
Home Depot USA Inc.. 614 878-9150
  100 S Grener Ave Columbus (43228) *(G-6000)*
Home Depot USA Inc.. 614 939-5036
  5200 N Hamilton Rd Columbus (43230) *(G-6001)*
Home Depot USA Inc.. 330 922-3440
  325 Howe Ave Cuyahoga Falls (44221) *(G-7078)*
Home Depot USA Inc.. 937 312-9053
  345 Springboro Pike Dayton (45449) *(G-7409)*
Home Depot USA Inc.. 937 312-9076
  5860 Wilmington Pike Dayton (45459) *(G-7410)*
Home Depot USA Inc.. 937 837-1551
  5200 Salem Ave Unit A Dayton (45426) *(G-7411)*
Home Depot USA Inc.. 440 324-7222
  150 Market Dr Elyria (44036) *(G-8256)*
Home Depot USA Inc.. 937 431-7346
  3775 Presidential Dr Fairborn (45324) *(G-8376)*
Home Depot USA Inc.. 513 887-1450
  6562 Winford Ave Hamilton (45011) *(G-9053)*
Home Depot USA Inc.. 440 684-1343
  6199 Wilson Mills Rd Highland Heights (44143) *(G-9166)*
Home Depot USA Inc.. 419 529-0015
  2000 August Dr Mansfield (44906) *(G-10269)*
Home Depot USA Inc.. 216 581-6611
  21000 Libby Rd Maple Heights (44137) *(G-10340)*
Home Depot USA Inc.. 440 357-0428
  9615 Diamond Centre Dr Mentor (44060) *(G-10949)*
Home Depot USA Inc.. 614 577-1601
  2480 Brice Rd Reynoldsburg (43068) *(G-12666)*
Home Depot USA Inc.. 419 626-6493
  715 Crossings Rd Sandusky (44870) *(G-12903)*
Home Depot USA Inc.. 440 826-9092
  8199 Pearl Rd Strongsville (44136) *(G-13462)*
Home Depot USA Inc.. 419 476-4573
  1035 W Alexis Rd Toledo (43612) *(G-13848)*
Home Depot USA Inc.. 419 537-1920
  3200 Secor Rd Toledo (43606) *(G-13849)*
Home Depot USA Inc.. 419 299-2000
  1989 Allen Township 142 Van Buren (45889) *(G-14338)*
Home Depot, The, Akron *Also Called: Home Depot USA Inc (G-195)*
Home Depot, The, Avon *Also Called: Home Depot USA Inc (G-654)*
Home Depot, The, Canton *Also Called: Home Depot USA Inc (G-1776)*
Home Depot, The, Cincinnati *Also Called: Home Depot USA Inc (G-2835)*
Home Depot, The, Cincinnati *Also Called: Home Depot USA Inc (G-2836)*
Home Depot, The, Cincinnati *Also Called: Home Depot USA Inc (G-2837)*
Home Depot, The, Cleveland *Also Called: Home Depot USA Inc (G-4373)*
Home Depot, The, Cleveland *Also Called: Home Depot USA Inc (G-4374)*
Home Depot, The, Cleveland Heights *Also Called: Home Depot USA Inc (G-5179)*
Home Depot, The, Columbus *Also Called: Home Depot USA Inc (G-5999)*
Home Depot, The, Columbus *Also Called: Home Depot USA Inc (G-6000)*
Home Depot, The, Columbus *Also Called: Home Depot USA Inc (G-6001)*
Home Depot, The, Cuyahoga Falls *Also Called: Home Depot USA Inc (G-7078)*
Home Depot, The, Dayton *Also Called: Home Depot USA Inc (G-7409)*
Home Depot, The, Dayton *Also Called: Home Depot USA Inc (G-7410)*
Home Depot, The, Dayton *Also Called: Home Depot USA Inc (G-7411)*
Home Depot, The, Elyria *Also Called: Home Depot USA Inc (G-8256)*
Home Depot, The, Fairborn *Also Called: Home Depot USA Inc (G-8376)*
Home Depot, The, Hamilton *Also Called: Home Depot USA Inc (G-9053)*
Home Depot, The, Highland Heights *Also Called: Home Depot USA Inc (G-9166)*
Home Depot, The, Mansfield *Also Called: Home Depot USA Inc (G-10269)*
Home Depot, The, Maple Heights *Also Called: Home Depot USA Inc (G-10340)*
Home Depot, The, Mentor *Also Called: Home Depot USA Inc (G-10949)*
Home Depot, The, Reynoldsburg *Also Called: Home Depot USA Inc (G-12666)*
Home Depot, The, Sandusky *Also Called: Home Depot USA Inc (G-12903)*
Home Depot, The, Strongsville *Also Called: Home Depot USA Inc (G-13462)*
Home Depot, The, Toledo *Also Called: Home Depot USA Inc (G-13848)*
Home Depot, The, Toledo *Also Called: Home Depot USA Inc (G-13849)*
Home Depot, The, Van Buren *Also Called: Home Depot USA Inc (G-14338)*
Home Echo Club Inc... 614 864-1718
  10270 Blacklick Eastern Rd Pickerington (43147) *(G-12403)*
Home Experts Realty.. 937 705-6336
  4230 Dayton Xenia Rd Beavercreek (45432) *(G-882)*
Home Experts Realty.. 937 435-6000
  93 W Franklin St Ste 106 Dayton (45459) *(G-7412)*
Home Green Home Inc.. 513 900-1702
  1435 Vine St Cincinnati (45202) *(G-2838)*
Home Health Connection Inc................................. 614 839-4545
  3062 Columbus Lancaster Rd Nw Lancaster (43130) *(G-9725)*

Home Health Plus — ALPHABETIC SECTION

Home Health Plus, Toledo *Also Called: In Home Health Inc (G-13862)*

Home Helpers Home Care, Blue Ash *Also Called: HH Franchising Systems Inc (G-1181)*

Home Inspections 800 241-0133
715 Shawan Falls Dr Unit 1954 Dublin (43017) *(G-8030)*

Home Instead Senior Care 440 914-1400
7650 First Pl Ste H Bedford (44146) *(G-965)*

Home Instead Senior Care 614 432-8524
9263 Lithopolis Rd Nw Canal Winchester (43110) *(G-1608)*

Home Instead Senior Care 330 334-4664
1 Park Centre Dr Ste 15 Wadsworth (44281) *(G-14435)*

Home Instead Senior Care, Lima *Also Called: All Gods Graces Inc (G-9862)*

Home Instead Senior Care, North Ridgeville *Also Called: Lorain County Senior Care Inc (G-11931)*

Home Instead Senior Care, Toledo *Also Called: Sar Enterprises LLC (G-14005)*

Home Is Where Hart Is HM Care 740 457-5240
105 N Avalon Dr Wintersville (43953) *(G-15295)*

Home Mortgage, Findlay *Also Called: Huntington National Bank (G-8547)*

Home Mortgage, Lima *Also Called: Huntington National Bank (G-9908)*

Home Mortgage, London *Also Called: Huntington National Bank (G-10043)*

Home Mortgage, North Canton *Also Called: Huntington National Bank (G-11840)*

Home Mortgage, Port Clinton *Also Called: Huntington National Bank (G-12534)*

Home Mortgage, Toledo *Also Called: Huntington National Bank (G-13856)*

Home Run Inc (PA) 800 543-9198
1299 Lavelle Dr Xenia (45385) *(G-15520)*

Home Sav & Ln Co Kenton Ohio 419 673-1117
116 E Franklin St Kenton (43326) *(G-9619)*

Home Savings & Loan, Kenton *Also Called: Home Sav & Ln Co Kenton Ohio (G-9619)*

Home Savings Loan Company 304 594-0013
275 W Federal St Youngstown (44503) *(G-15631)*

Home State Protective Svcs LLC 513 253-3095
250 E 5th St 15th Fl Cincinnati (45202) *(G-2839)*

Home The Friends Inc 513 897-6050
514 High St Waynesville (45068) *(G-14624)*

Home2 Suites, The, Perrysburg *Also Called: Hoster Hotels LLC (G-12345)*

Homecare, Cleveland *Also Called: Senior Touch Solution (G-4895)*

Homecare With Heart LLC 330 726-0700
821 Kentwood Dr Ste B Youngstown (44512) *(G-15632)*

Homefront Nursing LLC 513 404-1189
149 Northland Blvd Cincinnati (45246) *(G-2840)*

Homefull 937 293-1945
2621 Dryden Rd # 302 Moraine (45439) *(G-11418)*

Homeland Credit Union Inc (PA) 740 775-3024
310 Caldwell St Chillicothe (45601) *(G-2069)*

Homeless Families Foundation 614 461-9247
33 N Grubb St Columbus (43215) *(G-6002)*

Homelife Residential Svcs Inc 440 964-2419
4933 N Myers Rd Geneva (44041) *(G-8786)*

Homeport Inc 614 221-8889
3443 Agler Rd Ste 200 Columbus (43219) *(G-6003)*

Homes America Inc 614 848-8551
83 E Stanton Ave Columbus (43214) *(G-6004)*

Homes By Josh Doyle, Whitehouse *Also Called: Doyle Ja Corporation (G-15141)*

Homeside Financial LLC 614 907-7696
7775 Walton Pkwy Ste 400 New Albany (43054) *(G-11568)*

Homestead, Geneva *Also Called: 599 W Main Corporation (G-8783)*

Homestead 1, Painesville *Also Called: Multi-Care Inc (G-12239)*

Homestead America 614 221-5400
369 E Livingston Ave Columbus (43215) *(G-6005)*

Homestead Finishing, Sugarcreek *Also Called: D Yoder Hardwoods LLC (G-13508)*

Homestead I Hlthcare Group LLC 440 226-8869
1515 Brookstone Blvd Painesville (44077) *(G-12229)*

Homestead II, Painesville *Also Called: Homestead II Hlthcare Group LL (G-12230)*

Homestead II, Painesville *Also Called: Multi-Care Inc (G-12238)*

Homestead II Hlthcare Group LL 440 352-0788
60 Wood St Painesville (44077) *(G-12230)*

Hometeam Inspection Service 513 831-1300
575 Chamber Dr Milford (45150) *(G-11230)*

Hometeam Properties, Columbus *Also Called: Value Add Management LLC (G-6841)*

Hometown Bank (PA) 330 673-9827
142 N Water St Kent (44240) *(G-9578)*

Hometown Care LLC 330 926-1118
2040 Front St Cuyahoga Falls (44221) *(G-7079)*

Hometown Urgent Care 513 831-5900
1068 State Route 28 Ste C Milford (45150) *(G-11231)*

Hometown Urgent Care 937 342-9520
1200 Vester Ave Springfield (45503) *(G-13254)*

Hometown Urgent Care 937 252-2000
4164 Burbank Rd Wooster (44691) *(G-15345)*

Hometown Urgent Care 937 372-6012
101 S Orange St Xenia (45385) *(G-15521)*

Hometown Urgent Care 330 629-2300
1305 Boardman Poland Rd Youngstown (44514) *(G-15633)*

HOMETOWN URGENT CARE, Milford *Also Called: Hometown Urgent Care (G-11231)*

HOMETOWN URGENT CARE, Springfield *Also Called: Hometown Urgent Care (G-13254)*

HOMETOWN URGENT CARE, Wooster *Also Called: Hometown Urgent Care (G-15345)*

HOMETOWN URGENT CARE, Xenia *Also Called: Hometown Urgent Care (G-15521)*

HOMETOWN URGENT CARE, Youngstown *Also Called: Hometown Urgent Care (G-15633)*

Hometown Urgent Care of Kentucky PSC 614 505-7601
1105 Schrock Rd Columbus (43229) *(G-6006)*

Homewood Builders, Columbus *Also Called: Homewood Corporation (G-6007)*

Homewood Corporation (PA) 614 898-7200
2700 E Dublin Granville Rd Ste 300a Columbus (43231) *(G-6007)*

HOMEWOOD RESIDENCE, Cleveland *Also Called: Westlake Village Inc (G-5140)*

Homewood Rsdnce At Rchmond Hts, Cleveland *Also Called: American Retirement Corp (G-3807)*

Homewood Suites, Beavercreek *Also Called: Wright Executive Ht Ltd Partnr (G-915)*

Homewood Suites, Columbus *Also Called: Arvind Sagar Inc (G-5390)*

Homewood Suites, Solon *Also Called: Apple Hospitality Five Inc (G-13066)*

Homewood Suites Hotel Dayton S, Miamisburg *Also Called: Hotel Dayton Opco L P (G-11062)*

Homewood Suties - Milford, Milford *Also Called: Apple Sven Hospitality MGT Inc (G-11216)*

Honda Dev & Mfg Amer LLC 937 644-0724
19900 State Route 739 Marysville (43040) *(G-10488)*

Honda Federal Credit Union 937 642-6000
24000 Honda Pkwy Marysville (43040) *(G-10489)*

Honda Federal Credit Union 937 642-6000
17655 Echo Dr Marysville (43040) *(G-10490)*

Honda Logistics North Amer Inc (DH) 937 642-0335
11590 Township Road 298 East Liberty (43319) *(G-8172)*

Honda Support Office, Marysville *Also Called: Honda Dev & Mfg Amer LLC (G-10488)*

Honeywell, Urbana *Also Called: Grimes Aerospace Company (G-14308)*

Honeywell Authorized Dealer, Anna *Also Called: Wells Brothers Inc (G-445)*

Honeywell Authorized Dealer, Batavia *Also Called: Bachmans Inc (G-726)*

Honeywell Authorized Dealer, Bedford *Also Called: Smylie One Heating & Cooling (G-986)*

Honeywell Authorized Dealer, Canton *Also Called: Miracle Plumbing & Heating Co (G-1809)*

Honeywell Authorized Dealer, Cincinnati *Also Called: Cincinnati Air Conditioning Co (G-2392)*

Honeywell Authorized Dealer, Cincinnati *Also Called: Mechancal/Industrial Contg Inc (G-3025)*

Honeywell Authorized Dealer, Cincinnati *Also Called: Perfection Group Inc (G-3196)*

Honeywell Authorized Dealer, Cincinnati *Also Called: TP Mechanical Contractors LLC (G-3498)*

Honeywell Authorized Dealer, Cleveland *Also Called: Gillmore Security Systems Inc (G-4313)*

Honeywell Authorized Dealer, Cleveland *Also Called: McPhillips Plbg Htg & AC Co (G-4542)*

Honeywell Authorized Dealer, Columbus *Also Called: American Mechanical Group Inc (G-5353)*

Honeywell Authorized Dealer, Columbus *Also Called: Farber Corporation (G-5850)*

Honeywell Authorized Dealer, Coventry Township *Also Called: K Company Incorporated (G-7012)*

Honeywell Authorized Dealer, Cuyahoga Falls *Also Called: Falls Heating & Cooling Inc (G-7073)*

Honeywell Authorized Dealer, Dayton *Also Called: Envirnmental Engrg Systems Inc (G-7336)*

Honeywell Authorized Dealer, Defiance *Also Called: Fitzenrider Inc (G-7747)*

Honeywell Authorized Dealer, Delaware *Also Called: Comfort Express Inc (G-7786)*

Honeywell Authorized Dealer, Dublin *Also Called: Air Force One Inc (G-7926)*

Honeywell Authorized Dealer, Dublin *Also Called: Haslett Heating & Cooling Inc (G-8027)*

Honeywell Authorized Dealer, Fairborn *Also Called: Advanced Mechanical Svcs Inc (G-8366)*

Honeywell Authorized Dealer, Gahanna *Also Called: Custom AC & Htg Co (G-8714)*

Honeywell Authorized Dealer, Hilliard *Also Called: Bruner Corporation (G-9185)*

ALPHABETIC SECTION

Honeywell Authorized Dealer, Marietta *Also Called: Morrison Inc* **(G-10392)**

Honeywell Authorized Dealer, North Canton *Also Called: Ckp Heating and Cooling LLC* **(G-11817)**

Honeywell Authorized Dealer, Sandusky *Also Called: Gundlach Sheet Metal Works Inc* **(G-12902)**

Honeywell Authorized Dealer, Sidney *Also Called: Area Energy & Electric Inc* **(G-13019)**

Honeywell Authorized Dealer, Toledo *Also Called: Noron Inc* **(G-13936)**

Honeywell Authorized Dealer, Uniontown *Also Called: Fe Moran SEC Solutions LLC* **(G-14251)**

Honeywell Authorized Dealer, Worthington *Also Called: Wentz Hc Holdings Inc* **(G-15467)**

Honeywell Intelligrated, Mason *Also Called: Intelligrated Systems Inc* **(G-10565)**

Honorworth Homecare, Cincinnati *Also Called: Honorworth Homecare LLC* **(G-2841)**

Honorworth Homecare LLC 513 557-0093
4101 Spring Grove Ave Cincinnati (45223) **(G-2841)**

Hooberry & Associates Inc 330 872-1991
2200 Milton Blvd Newton Falls (44444) **(G-11775)**

Hoover & Wells Inc 419 691-9220
2011 Seaman St Toledo (43605) **(G-13850)**

Hoover Kacyon LLC 330 922-4491
527 Portage Trl Cuyahoga Falls (44221) **(G-7080)**

Hope Acadamies, Akron *Also Called: Accel Schools Ohio LLC* **(G-12)**

Hope Early Care & Educatn Ctr, Akron *Also Called: Young MNS Chrstn Assn of Akron* **(G-369)**

Hope Hling Srvvor Resource Ctr, Medina *Also Called: Battered Womens Shelter* **(G-10814)**

Hope Homes Inc 330 688-4935
2044 Bryn Mawr Dr Stow (44224) **(G-13374)**

Hope Hotel & Conference Center, Dayton *Also Called: 823 Dayton Hotel Tenant LLC* **(G-7124)**

Hope Hotel & Conference Center, Fairborn *Also Called: Visicon Inc* **(G-8385)**

Hope Timber, Newark *Also Called: Hope Timber Pallet Recycl LLC* **(G-11706)**

Hope Timber Pallet Recycl LLC 740 344-1788
141 Union St Newark (43055) **(G-11706)**

Hopebridge LLC 513 831-2578
1001 Ford Cir Ste A Milford (45150) **(G-11232)**

Hopebridge LLC 855 324-0885
773 Brooksedge Blvd Westerville (43081) **(G-14986)**

Hopebridge Autism Therapy Ctr, Milford *Also Called: Hopebridge LLC* **(G-11232)**

Hopesource, Portsmouth *Also Called: Jay Hash LLC* **(G-12559)**

Hopewell (PA) 440 426-2000
9637 State Route 534 Middlefield (44062) **(G-11141)**

Hopewell Day Treatment Center, Cleveland *Also Called: Positive Education Program* **(G-4762)**

Hopewell Health Centers, Athens *Also Called: Hopewell Health Centers Inc* **(G-575)**

Hopewell Health Centers, Athens *Also Called: Hopewell Health Centers Inc* **(G-576)**

Hopewell Health Centers, Logan *Also Called: Hopewell Health Centers Inc* **(G-10026)**

Hopewell Health Centers Inc 740 594-5045
90 Hospital Dr Athens (45701) **(G-575)**

Hopewell Health Centers Inc 740 592-3504
25 Hocking St Athens (45701) **(G-576)**

Hopewell Health Centers Inc 740 757-2352
315 W Union St Athens (45701) **(G-577)**

Hopewell Health Centers Inc (PA) 740 773-1006
1049 Western Ave Chillicothe (45601) **(G-2070)**

Hopewell Health Centers Inc 740 385-8468
460 E 2nd St Logan (43138) **(G-10026)**

Hopewell Health Centers Inc 740 385-6594
541 State Route 664 N Ste C Logan (43138) **(G-10027)**

Hopewell Health Centers Inc 740 385-2555
1383 W Turner St Logan (43138) **(G-10028)**

Hopewell Health Centers Inc 740 596-4809
313 1/2 W Main St Mc Arthur (45651) **(G-10798)**

Hopewell Health Centers Inc 740 342-4192
2541 Panther Dr Ne New Lexington (43764) **(G-11626)**

HOPEWELL THERAPEUTIC FARM, Middlefield *Also Called: Hopewell* **(G-11141)**

Hopkins Acquisition Inc 248 371-1700
127 Public Sq Ste 5300 Cleveland (44114) **(G-4375)**

Hopkins Airport Limousine Svc (PA) 216 267-8810
13315 Brookpark Rd Cleveland (44142) **(G-4376)**

Hopkins Partners 216 267-1500
5300 Riverside Dr Ste 30 Cleveland (44135) **(G-4377)**

Hopkins Transportation Svcs, Cleveland *Also Called: Hopkins Airport Limousine Svc* **(G-4376)**

Hoppes Construction LLC 580 310-0090
4036 Coral Rd Nw Malvern (44644) **(G-10234)**

Horan Capital Advisors LLC 513 745-0707
4990 E Galbraith Rd Cincinnati (45236) **(G-2842)**

Hord Livestock Company Inc 419 562-0277
887 State Route 98 Bucyrus (44820) **(G-1509)**

Horenstein Nchlson Blmnthal A 937 224-7200
124 E 3rd St Fl 5 Dayton (45402) **(G-7413)**

Horizon Activities Center, Lorain *Also Called: Horizon Education Centers* **(G-10077)**

Horizon Education Centers 440 322-0288
233 Bond St Elyria (44035) **(G-8257)**

Horizon Education Centers 440 458-5115
10347 Dewhurst Rd Elyria (44035) **(G-8258)**

Horizon Education Centers 440 277-5437
4911 Grove Ave Lorain (44055) **(G-10077)**

Horizon Education Centers 440 779-6536
4001 David Dr North Olmsted (44070) **(G-11906)**

Horizon Education Centers, Elyria *Also Called: Horizon Education Centers* **(G-8257)**

Horizon Freight System Inc (PA) 216 341-7410
8777 Rockside Rd Cleveland (44125) **(G-4378)**

Horizon Health Management LLC 513 793-5220
3889 E Galbraith Rd Cincinnati (45236) **(G-2843)**

Horizon HM Hlth Care Agcy LLC 614 279-2933
3079 W Broad St Ste 6 Columbus (43204) **(G-6008)**

Horizon Home Health Care LLC 937 410-3838
410 Corporate Center Dr Vandalia (45377) **(G-14381)**

Horizon Mid Atlantic Inc 800 480-6829
8777 Rockside Rd Cleveland (44125) **(G-4379)**

Horizon Payroll Services Inc 937 434-8244
2700 Miamisburg Centerville Rd Ste 580 Dayton (45459) **(G-7414)**

Horizon Pcs Inc (HQ) 740 772-8200
68 E Main St Chillicothe (45601) **(G-2071)**

Horizon Personnel Resources (PA) 440 585-0031
1516 Lincoln Rd Wickliffe (44092) **(G-15152)**

HORIZONS OF TUSCARAWAS/CARROLL, Wooster *Also Called: Horizons Tuscarawas/Carroll* **(G-15346)**

Horizons Tuscarawas/Carroll 330 262-4183
527 N Market St Wooster (44691) **(G-15346)**

Horseshoe Cleveland MGT LLC 216 297-4777
100 Public Sq Ste 100 Cleveland (44113) **(G-4380)**

Horter Investment MGT LLC 513 984-9933
11726 7 Gables Rd Cincinnati (45249) **(G-2844)**

Hospice Care of Bethesda, Zanesville *Also Called: Genesis Healthcare System* **(G-15795)**

Hospice Care Ohio 330 665-1455
3358 Ridgewood Rd Fairlawn (44333) **(G-8483)**

Hospice Cincinnati Inc 513 389-5528
5343 Hamilton Ave Apt 402 Cincinnati (45224) **(G-2845)**

Hospice Cincinnati Inc 513 598-5093
5343 Hamilton Ave Cincinnati (45224) **(G-2846)**

Hospice Cincinnati Inc 513 386-6000
7691 5 Mile Rd Ste 100 Cincinnati (45230) **(G-2847)**

Hospice Cincinnati Inc (DH) 513 891-7700
4360 Cooper Rd Ste 200 Cincinnati (45242) **(G-2848)**

Hospice North Central Ohio Inc (PA) 419 281-7107
1021 Dauch Dr Ashland (44805) **(G-501)**

HOSPICE OF BUTLER AND WARREN C, Dayton *Also Called: Dayton Hospice Incorporated* **(G-7288)**

Hospice of Care, Chardon *Also Called: Parkside Care Corporation* **(G-2014)**

Hospice of Central Ohio (PA) 740 344-0311
2269 Cherry Valley Rd Se Newark (43055) **(G-11707)**

Hospice of Darke County Inc (PA) 937 548-2999
1350 N Broadway St Greenville (45331) **(G-8878)**

Hospice of Genesis Health 740 454-5381
713 Forest Ave Zanesville (43701) **(G-15801)**

Hospice of Hope Inc 937 444-4900
215 Hughes Blvd Mount Orab (45154) **(G-11471)**

Hospice of Knox County 740 397-5188
17700 Coshocton Rd Mount Vernon (43050) **(G-11489)**

Hospice of Medina County (HQ) 330 725-1900
5075 Windfall Rd Medina (44256) **(G-10840)**

Hospice of Memorial Hospita L 419 334-6626
430 S Main St Clyde (43410) **(G-5202)**

Hospice of Miami County Inc.. 937 335-5191
  3230 N County Road 25a Troy (45373) *(G-14139)*
Hospice of Miami Valley LLC.. 937 458-6028
  2601 Mission Point Blvd Ste 300 Beavercreek (45431) *(G-883)*
Hospice of Northwest Ohio (PA)... 419 661-4001
  30000 E River Rd Perrysburg (43551) *(G-12344)*
Hospice of Northwest Ohio... 419 661-4001
  800 S Detroit Ave Toledo (43609) *(G-13851)*
Hospice of The Western Reserve... 216 227-9048
  22730 Fairview Center Dr Ste 100 Cleveland (44126) *(G-4381)*
Hospice of The Western Reserve... 330 800-2240
  5075 Windfall Rd Medina (44256) *(G-10841)*
Hospice of The Western Reserve... 440 414-7349
  30080 Hospice Way Westlake (44145) *(G-15066)*
HOSPICE OF THE WESTERN RESERVE, INC, Cleveland Also Called: Hospice of The Western Reserve *(G-4381)*
HOSPICE OF THE WESTERN RESERVE, INC, Medina Also Called: Hospice of The Western Reserve *(G-10841)*
HOSPICE OF THE WESTERN RESERVE, INC, Westlake Also Called: Hospice of The Western Reserve *(G-15066)*
Hospice of Valley Inc (PA)... 330 788-1992
  979 Tibbetts Wick Rd Ste A Girard (44420) *(G-8815)*
Hospice of Western Reserve Inc (PA).. 216 383-2222
  17876 Saint Clair Ave Cleveland (44110) *(G-4382)*
Hospice Southwest Ohio Inc... 513 770-0820
  7625 Camargo Rd Cincinnati (45243) *(G-2849)*
Hospice Tuscarawas County Inc... 330 627-4796
  789 N Lisbon St Carrollton (44615) *(G-1909)*
Hospice Tuscarawas County Inc (PA).. 330 343-7605
  716 Commercial Ave Sw New Philadelphia (44663) *(G-11654)*
Hospice Visiting Nurse Service, Fairlawn Also Called: Hospice Care Ohio *(G-8483)*
Hospital Council of NW Ohio... 419 842-0800
  3231 Central Park W Ste 200 Toledo (43617) *(G-13852)*
Hospital HM Hlth Svcs Hghland.. 937 393-6371
  1275 N High St Hillsboro (45133) *(G-9259)*
Hospitality Inc... 419 227-0112
  1250 Neubrecht Rd Lima (45801) *(G-9906)*
Hospitlist Svcs Med Group of M.. 937 644-6115
  500 London Ave Marysville (43040) *(G-10491)*
Hospitlst Srvcs Med Grp Mrysvl, Marysville Also Called: Hospitlist Svcs Med Group of M *(G-10491)*
Hoss, Dayton Also Called: Voss Auto Network Inc *(G-7711)*
Hoss II Inc... 937 669-4300
  155 S Garber Dr Tipp City (45371) *(G-13660)*
Hoss Value Cars & Trucks Inc (PA).. 937 428-2400
  766 Miamisburg Centerville Rd Dayton (45459) *(G-7415)*
Hosser Assisted Living.. 740 286-8785
  101 Markham Dr Jackson (45640) *(G-9521)*
Host Cincinnati Hotel LLC... 513 621-7700
  21 E 5th St Ste A Cincinnati (45202) *(G-2850)*
Hoster Hotels LLC.. 419 931-8900
  5995 Levis Commons Blvd Perrysburg (43551) *(G-12345)*
Hostetler Trucking Inc.. 614 873-8885
  6495 Converse Huff Rd Plain City (43064) *(G-12482)*
Hotel... 614 373-2002
  337 S Ogden Ave Columbus (43204) *(G-6009)*
Hotel 1100 Carnegie Opco L P... 216 658-6400
  1100 Carnegie Ave Cleveland (44115) *(G-4383)*
Hotel 2345 LLC... 614 766-7762
  4130 Tuller Rd Dublin (43017) *(G-8031)*
Hotel 50 S Front Opco L P.. 614 885-3334
  50 S Front St Columbus (43215) *(G-6010)*
Hotel 50 S Front Opco LP... 614 228-4600
  50 S Front St Columbus (43215) *(G-6011)*
Hotel 75 E State Opco L P.. 614 365-4500
  75 E State St Columbus (43215) *(G-6012)*
Hotel Breakers, Sandusky Also Called: Cedar Point Park LLC *(G-12876)*
Hotel Dayton Opco L P.. 937 432-9161
  3100 Contemporary Ln Miamisburg (45342) *(G-11062)*
Hotel Leveque, Columbus Also Called: First Leveque LLC *(G-5863)*
Hotel Stow LP... 330 945-9722
  4047 Bridgewater Pkwy Stow (44224) *(G-13375)*

Hoty Enterprises Inc (PA)... 419 609-7000
  5003 Milan Rd Sandusky (44870) *(G-12904)*
Houck Asphalt Maintenance LLC.. 513 734-4500
  2656 State Route 222 Bethel (45106) *(G-1092)*
House of La Rose, Brecksville Also Called: House of La Rose Cleveland *(G-1354)*
House of La Rose Cleveland.. 440 746-7500
  6745 Southpointe Pkwy Brecksville (44141) *(G-1354)*
House of New Hope.. 740 345-5437
  8135 Mount Vernon Rd Saint Louisville (43071) *(G-12826)*
House of Plastics, Cleveland Also Called: HP Manufacturing Company Inc *(G-4386)*
Houston Dick Plbg & Htg Inc.. 740 763-3961
  724 Montgomery Rd Ne Newark (43055) *(G-11708)*
Houston Interests LLC.. 614 890-3456
  445 Hutchinson Ave Ste 740 Columbus (43235) *(G-6013)*
Houston Plumbing & Heating, Newark Also Called: Houston Dick Plbg & Htg Inc *(G-11708)*
Howard Wershbale & Co... 614 794-8710
  460 Polaris Pkwy # 310 Westerville (43082) *(G-14899)*
Howard Wershbale & Co (PA).. 216 831-1200
  28601 Chagrin Blvd Ste 210 Woodmere (44122) *(G-15299)*
Howard Hanna Real Estate, Cleveland Also Called: Howard Hanna Real Estate Svcs *(G-4384)*
Howard Hanna Real Estate, Cleveland Also Called: Sharon Gay Phlps - Hward Hnna *(G-4900)*
Howard Hanna Real Estate Svcs... 440 665-0649
  14284 W Sprague Rd Cleveland (44130) *(G-4384)*
Howard Hanna Smythe Cramer (HQ)... 216 447-4477
  6000 Parkland Blvd Cleveland (44124) *(G-4385)*
Howard Johnson, Beachwood Also Called: 16644 Snow Rd LLC *(G-762)*
Howard Johnson, Girard Also Called: Universal Development MGT Inc *(G-8829)*
Howard Johnson Lima, Lima Also Called: R & K Gorby LLC *(G-9953)*
Howard Painting Inc... 419 782-7786
  1740 Spruce St Defiance (43512) *(G-7749)*
Howland Crners Twne Cntry Vtrn... 330 856-1862
  8000 E Market St Warren (44484) *(G-14526)*
Howland Logistics LLC... 513 469-5263
  930 Tennessee Ave Cincinnati (45229) *(G-2851)*
Hoxworth Blood Center, Cincinnati Also Called: University of Cincinnati *(G-3589)*
HP Manufacturing Company Inc (PA)... 216 361-6500
  3705 Carnegie Ave Cleveland (44115) *(G-4386)*
HP Products Corporation.. 513 683-8553
  7135 E Kemper Rd Cincinnati (45249) *(G-2852)*
Hpj Industries Inc (PA)... 419 278-1000
  118 N Main St Bowling Green (43402) *(G-1325)*
HPM America LLC.. 419 946-0222
  820 W Marion Rd Mount Gilead (43338) *(G-11461)*
Hpt Trs Ihg-2 Inc... 614 461-4100
  33 E Nationwide Blvd Columbus (43215) *(G-6014)*
Hr Butler LLC.. 614 923-2900
  63 Corbins Mill Dr Ste A Dublin (43017) *(G-8032)*
Hr Profile, Cincinnati Also Called: Human Resource Profile Inc *(G-2855)*
Hr Services Inc... 419 224-2462
  675 W Market St Ste 200 Lima (45801) *(G-9907)*
Hrm Enterprises Inc (PA).. 330 877-9353
  1015 Edison St Nw Ste 3 Hartville (44632) *(G-9127)*
Hrm Leasing, Findlay Also Called: Bob Miller Rigging Inc *(G-8518)*
Hrnchar's Fairway Ford, Canfield Also Called: Paul Hrnchar Ford-Mercury Inc *(G-1638)*
Hs Financial Group LLC (PA)... 216 762-1800
  18013 Cleveland Pkwy Dr Ste 170 Cleveland (44135) *(G-4387)*
Hs Services, Westlake Also Called: Imcd Us LLC *(G-15069)*
Hsi, Akron Also Called: Hardware Suppliers of America Inc *(G-183)*
Hsps Special Operations, Cincinnati Also Called: Home State Protective Svcs LLC *(G-2839)*
Hst Lessee Cincinnati LLC.. 513 852-2702
  21 E 5th St Cincinnati (45202) *(G-2853)*
Hubbard Company.. 419 784-4455
  612 Clinton St Defiance (43512) *(G-7750)*
Hubbard Radio Cincinnati LLC... 513 699-5100
  4800 Kennedy Ave Cincinnati (45209) *(G-2854)*
Hubbell Power Systems Inc... 330 335-2361
  8711 Wadsworth Rd Wadsworth (44281) *(G-14436)*
Hubert, Harrison Also Called: Hubert Company LLC *(G-9110)*
Hubert Company LLC (DH).. 513 367-8600
  9555 Dry Fork Rd Harrison (45030) *(G-9110)*

ALPHABETIC SECTION — Huntington National Bank

Huckleberry House Inc 614 294-5553
1421 Hamlet St Columbus (43201) *(G-6015)*

Hudson Elms Nrsing HM Asssted, Hudson *Also Called: Hudson Elms Opco LLC (G-9355)*

Hudson Elms Opco LLC 330 650-0436
563 W Streetsboro St Hudson (44236) *(G-9355)*

Hudson L Surgcenter L C 330 655-5460
2215 E Waterloo Rd Ste 313 Akron (44312) *(G-196)*

Hudson Montessori Association 330 650-0424
7545 Darrow Rd Hudson (44236) *(G-9356)*

Hudson Montessori School, Hudson *Also Called: Hudson Montessori Association (G-9356)*

Hudson Specialty Center, Hudson *Also Called: Summa Western Reserve Hosp LLC (G-9374)*

Hueston Woods Lodge,, College Corner *Also Called: Ohio State Parks Inc (G-5222)*

Hughes Corporation (PA) 440 238-2550
16900 Foltz Pkwy Strongsville (44149) *(G-13463)*

Hughes Kitchens and Bath LLC 330 455-5269
1258 Cleveland Ave Nw Canton (44703) *(G-1777)*

Hughes-Peters, Huber Heights *Also Called: Mjo Industries Inc (G-9325)*

Hugs Hearts Early Lrng Ctr Inc 614 848-6777
8989 Antares Ave Columbus (43240) *(G-5262)*

Huhtamaki Inc 937 987-3078
5566 New Vienna Rd New Vienna (45159) *(G-11680)*

Huhtamaki Plastics, New Vienna *Also Called: Huhtamaki Inc (G-11680)*

Hull Bros Inc 419 375-2827
520 E Boundary St Fort Recovery (45846) *(G-8610)*

Human ARC, Cleveland *Also Called: Human ARC Corporation (G-4388)*

Human ARC Corporation (HQ) 216 431-5200
1457 E 40th St Cleveland (44103) *(G-4388)*

Human Resource Profile Inc 513 388-4300
8506 Beechmont Ave Cincinnati (45255) *(G-2855)*

Human Services, Xenia *Also Called: Greene County (G-15512)*

Humana, Cincinnati *Also Called: Humana Health Plan Ohio Inc (G-2856)*

Humana Health Plan Ohio Inc 513 784-5200
111 Merchant St Cincinnati (45246) *(G-2856)*

Humane Society Greater Dayton 937 268-7387
1661 Nicholas Rd Dayton (45417) *(G-7416)*

HUMANE SOCIETY SHELTER GEAUGA, Novelty *Also Called: Geauga County Humane Soc Inc (G-12038)*

Humanetics, Huron *Also Called: Humantics Innvtive Sltions Inc (G-9389)*

Humanit Solutions LLC 937 901-7576
4058 Colonel Glenn Hwy Beavercreek Township (45431) *(G-941)*

Humantics Innvtive Sltions Inc 567 265-5200
900 Denton Dr Huron (44839) *(G-9389)*

Hume Supply Inc 419 991-5751
2685 Summer Rambo Ct Lima (45806) *(G-9992)*

Humility House 330 505-0144
755 Ohltown Rd Youngstown (44515) *(G-15634)*

Humility House Assisted Living, Youngstown *Also Called: Humility House (G-15634)*

Hummel Construction Company 330 274-8584
127 E Main St Ravenna (44266) *(G-12628)*

Hunt Tiffani 216 258-1923
17324 Wayne Dr Cleveland (44128) *(G-4389)*

Hunt Real Estate Capital, Columbus *Also Called: Lument Real Estate Capital LLC (G-6178)*

Hunter Defense Tech Inc (PA) 216 438-6111
30500 Aurora Rd Ste 100 Solon (44139) *(G-13096)*

Huntington, Columbus *Also Called: Huntington Bancshares Inc (G-6016)*

Huntington, Columbus *Also Called: Huntington National Bank (G-6020)*

Huntington, Westerville *Also Called: Huntington National Bank (G-14987)*

Huntington, Zanesville *Also Called: Huntington National Bank (G-15803)*

Huntington Bancshares Inc (PA) 614 480-2265
41 S High St Columbus (43287) *(G-6016)*

Huntington Insurance Inc (DH) 419 720-7900
37 W Broad St Ste 1100 Columbus (43215) *(G-6017)*

Huntington National Bank 330 786-9950
1411 S Arlington St Akron (44306) *(G-197)*

Huntington National Bank 330 762-4210
855 W Market St Akron (44303) *(G-198)*

Huntington National Bank 330 869-5950
1525 S Hawkins Ave Akron (44320) *(G-199)*

Huntington National Bank 419 281-6020
308 Eastern Ave Ashland (44805) *(G-502)*

Huntington National Bank 419 281-2541
132 W Main St Ashland (44805) *(G-503)*

Huntington National Bank 440 992-7342
4366 Main Ave Ashtabula (44004) *(G-537)*

Huntington National Bank 440 937-5545
2085 Center Rd Avon (44011) *(G-655)*

Huntington National Bank 216 515-0029
355 Dover Center Rd Bay Village (44140) *(G-760)*

Huntington National Bank 937 848-6861
2010 S Lakeman Dr Bellbrook (45305) *(G-1017)*

Huntington National Bank 937 593-2010
201 E Columbus Ave Bellefontaine (43311) *(G-1029)*

Huntington National Bank 440 202-3050
31 E Bridge St Ste 203 Berea (44017) *(G-1071)*

Huntington National Bank 216 515-0013
5881 Smith Rd Brookpark (44142) *(G-1435)*

Huntington National Bank 330 225-3946
1344 Pearl Rd Brunswick (44212) *(G-1457)*

Huntington National Bank 419 636-1164
310 S Main St Bryan (43506) *(G-1485)*

Huntington National Bank 440 834-4481
14522 Main St Burton (44021) *(G-1529)*

Huntington National Bank 740 439-5533
175 N 11th St Cambridge (43725) *(G-1574)*

Huntington National Bank 614 480-0008
37 S High St Canal Winchester (43110) *(G-1609)*

Huntington National Bank 330 966-5232
3315 Cleveland Ave Nw Canton (44709) *(G-1778)*

Huntington National Bank 440 285-2111
376 Center St Chardon (44024) *(G-2005)*

Huntington National Bank 513 762-1860
525 Vine St Cincinnati (45202) *(G-2857)*

Huntington National Bank 216 515-0471
200 Public Sq Ste 600 Cleveland (44114) *(G-4390)*

Huntington National Bank 216 290-2445
10001 Chester Ave Ste A Cleveland (44106) *(G-4391)*

Huntington National Bank 216 515-6401
917 Euclid Ave 925 Cleveland (44115) *(G-4392)*

Huntington National Bank 216 515-0064
4260 Ridge Rd Cleveland (44144) *(G-4393)*

Huntington National Bank 440 236-5011
26570 Royalton Rd Columbia Station (44028) *(G-5228)*

Huntington National Bank 614 480-0005
3424 Cleveland Ave Columbus (43224) *(G-6018)*

Huntington National Bank 614 480-0017
4661 Reed Rd Columbus (43220) *(G-6019)*

Huntington National Bank 614 480-0038
3464 S High St Columbus (43207) *(G-6020)*

Huntington National Bank (HQ) 614 480-4293
41 S High St Columbus (43215) *(G-6021)*

Huntington National Bank 614 480-0004
1531 W Lane Ave Columbus (43221) *(G-6022)*

Huntington National Bank 614 480-0026
1928 N High St Columbus (43201) *(G-6023)*

Huntington National Bank 614 480-0020
1555 W 5th Ave Columbus (43212) *(G-6024)*

Huntington National Bank 800 480-2265
4780 W Broad St Columbus (43228) *(G-6025)*

Huntington National Bank 614 331-9537
5155 N High St Columbus (43214) *(G-6026)*

Huntington National Bank 614 480-0060
7840 Olentangy River Rd Columbus (43235) *(G-6027)*

Huntington National Bank 614 480-4293
17 S High St Fl 1 Columbus (43215) *(G-6028)*

Huntington National Bank 330 920-6190
2305 2nd St Cuyahoga Falls (44221) *(G-7081)*

Huntington National Bank 937 428-7400
500 Miamisburg Centerville Rd Dayton (45459) *(G-7417)*

Huntington National Bank 740 363-9343
95 E William St Delaware (43015) *(G-7805)*

Huntington National Bank 330 343-6611
232 W 3rd St Ste 207 Dover (44622) *(G-7890)*

(PA)=Parent Co (HQ)=Headquarters (DH)=Div Headquarters

Huntington National Bank — ALPHABETIC SECTION

Huntington National Bank.. 440 406-5070
111 Antioch Dr Elyria (44035) *(G-8259)*

Huntington National Bank.. 440 365-1890
248 Abbe Rd N Elyria (44035) *(G-8260)*

Huntington National Bank.. 440 943-3389
1545 E 260th St Euclid (44132) *(G-8348)*

Huntington National Bank.. 330 867-2828
2700 W Market St Fairlawn (44333) *(G-8484)*

Huntington National Bank.. 419 429-4627
236 S Main St Findlay (45840) *(G-8547)*

Huntington National Bank.. 937 746-9904
340 S Main St Franklin (45005) *(G-8641)*

Huntington National Bank.. 419 468-6868
260 Portland Way N Galion (44833) *(G-8749)*

Huntington National Bank.. 614 480-4500
1880 Hilliard Rome Rd Hilliard (43026) *(G-9202)*

Huntington National Bank.. 330 653-5161
116 W Streetsboro St Ste 1 Hudson (44236) *(G-9357)*

Huntington National Bank.. 330 677-8200
1729 E Main St Kent (44240) *(G-9579)*

Huntington National Bank.. 419 226-8200
631 W Market St Lima (45801) *(G-9908)*

Huntington National Bank.. 330 424-7226
24 N Park Ave Lisbon (44432) *(G-10003)*

Huntington National Bank.. 740 852-1234
2 E High St London (43140) *(G-10042)*

Huntington National Bank.. 740 852-1234
61 S Main St London (43140) *(G-10043)*

Huntington National Bank.. 440 428-1124
6565 N Ridge Rd Madison (44057) *(G-10217)*

Huntington National Bank.. 419 589-3111
1277 Ashland Rd Mansfield (44905) *(G-10270)*

Huntington National Bank.. 740 373-2886
226 3rd St Marietta (45750) *(G-10371)*

Huntington National Bank.. 330 830-1200
5338 Wales Ave Nw Massillon (44646) *(G-10646)*

Huntington National Bank.. 330 721-5555
39 Public Sq Ste 100 Medina (44256) *(G-10842)*

Huntington National Bank.. 330 723-6666
3460 Medina Rd Medina (44256) *(G-10843)*

Huntington National Bank.. 330 722-6762
125 W Washington St Medina (44256) *(G-10844)*

Huntington National Bank.. 330 725-0593
975 N Court St Medina (44256) *(G-10845)*

Huntington National Bank.. 330 343-2527
205 N Broadway St New Philadelphia (44663) *(G-11655)*

Huntington National Bank.. 740 498-8376
100 W Main St Newcomerstown (43832) *(G-11769)*

Huntington National Bank.. 330 841-0142
215 E Broad St Newton Falls (44444) *(G-11776)*

Huntington National Bank.. 330 966-5353
4879 Portage St Nw North Canton (44720) *(G-11840)*

Huntington National Bank.. 440 327-7054
35621 Center Ridge Rd North Ridgeville (44039) *(G-11929)*

Huntington National Bank.. 330 467-7127
8300 Golden Link Blvd Northfield (44067) *(G-11957)*

Huntington National Bank.. 419 747-2265
2313 Village Park Ct Ontario (44906) *(G-12107)*

Huntington National Bank.. 419 523-6880
332 E Main St Ottawa (45875) *(G-12186)*

Huntington National Bank.. 440 886-1959
6690 Ridge Rd Parma (44129) *(G-12255)*

Huntington National Bank.. 330 314-1395
2 S Main St Poland (44514) *(G-12504)*

Huntington National Bank.. 419 734-2157
120 Madison St Port Clinton (43452) *(G-12534)*

Huntington National Bank.. 419 734-2157
123 Monroe St Port Clinton (43452) *(G-12535)*

Huntington National Bank.. 330 296-2214
230 Cedar Ave Ravenna (44266) *(G-12629)*

Huntington National Bank.. 216 515-0022
19975 Center Ridge Rd Rocky River (44116) *(G-12742)*

Huntington National Bank.. 216 515-0022
19880 Detroit Rd Rocky River (44116) *(G-12743)*

Huntington National Bank.. 740 695-3323
154 W Main St Saint Clairsville (43950) *(G-12794)*

Huntington National Bank.. 216 515-0024
33175 Aurora Rd Solon (44139) *(G-13097)*

Huntington National Bank.. 937 390-1779
5 W North St Springfield (45504) *(G-13255)*

Huntington National Bank.. 330 626-3426
9240 Market Square Dr Streetsboro (44241) *(G-13416)*

Huntington National Bank.. 330 626-3431
9717 State Route 14 Streetsboro (44241) *(G-13417)*

Huntington National Bank.. 330 634-0841
27 Northwest Ave Tallmadge (44278) *(G-13595)*

Huntington National Bank.. 419 249-7877
800 Madison Ave Toledo (43604) *(G-13853)*

Huntington National Bank.. 419 254-7016
4773 Glendale Ave Toledo (43614) *(G-13854)*

Huntington National Bank.. 419 254-7052
4105 Talmadge Rd Toledo (43623) *(G-13855)*

Huntington National Bank.. 419 249-3340
519 Madison Ave Toledo (43604) *(G-13856)*

Huntington National Bank.. 330 334-1091
1081 Williams Reserve Blvd Wadsworth (44281) *(G-14437)*

Huntington National Bank.. 330 334-1591
129 High St Wadsworth (44281) *(G-14438)*

Huntington National Bank.. 330 609-5029
8202 E Market St Warren (44484) *(G-14527)*

Huntington National Bank.. 330 841-0197
525 Niles Cortland Rd Warren (44484) *(G-14528)*

Huntington National Bank.. 330 841-0205
108 Main Ave Sw Lbby Warren (44481) *(G-14529)*

Huntington National Bank.. 440 647-4533
817 N Main St Wellington (44090) *(G-14633)*

Huntington National Bank.. 614 480-0016
630 S State St Westerville (43081) *(G-14987)*

Huntington National Bank.. 330 263-2751
135 E Liberty St Wooster (44691) *(G-15347)*

Huntington National Bank.. 330 314-1410
4682 Belmont Ave Youngstown (44505) *(G-15635)*

Huntington National Bank.. 330 314-1380
3939 Market St Youngstown (44512) *(G-15636)*

Huntington National Bank.. 740 452-8444
428 Main St Zanesville (43701) *(G-15802)*

Huntington National Bank.. 740 455-7048
2801 Maple Ave Zanesville (43701) *(G-15803)*

Huntington National Bank, Cleveland *Also Called: Huntington National Bank (G-4391)*

Huntington Trust Co Nat Assn.. 614 480-5345
41 S High St Columbus (43215) *(G-6029)*

Huntley Trucking Co... 740 385-7615
23525 Pumpkin Ridge Rd New Plymouth (45654) *(G-11675)*

Huron Cement Products Company (PA)................................ 419 433-4161
617 Main St Huron (44839) *(G-9390)*

Huron Health Care Center Inc... 419 433-4990
1920 Cleveland Rd W Huron (44839) *(G-9391)*

Hursh Drug, Mansfield *Also Called: Hursh Drugs Inc (G-10271)*

Hursh Drugs Inc... 419 524-0521
90 N Diamond St Mansfield (44902) *(G-10271)*

Hurst Construction Inc... 440 234-5656
26185 Center Ridge Rd Westlake (44145) *(G-15067)*

Husky Energy, Dublin *Also Called: Husky Marketing and Supply Co (G-8033)*

Husky Marketing and Supply Co.. 614 210-2300
5550 Blazer Pkwy Ste 200 Dublin (43017) *(G-8033)*

Hvac, Mentor *Also Called: Cbkb Inc (G-10919)*

Hvac Mech Cntrcto Plbg Ppfttin, Cincinnati *Also Called: Jfdb Ltd (G-2912)*

HWH Archtcts-Ngnrs-Plnners Inc... 216 875-4000
600 Superior Ave E Ste 1100 Cleveland (44114) *(G-4394)*

Hwz Distribution Group LLC... 513 618-0300
40 W Crescentville Rd West Chester (45246) *(G-14818)*

Hy-Grade Corporation (PA).. 216 341-7711
3993 E 93rd St Cleveland (44105) *(G-4395)*

ALPHABETIC SECTION

Hy-Tek Material Handling Inc 440 239-9852
  7550 Lucerne Dr Ste 204 Middleburg Heights (44130) *(G-11117)*
Hy-Tek Material Handling LLC (HQ) 614 497-2500
  2222 Rickenbacker Pkwy W Columbus (43217) *(G-6030)*
HY-TEK MATERIAL HANDLING, INC., Middleburg Heights *Also Called: Hy-Tek Material Handling Inc (G-11117)*
Hyatt Corporation 216 575-1234
  420 Superior Ave E Cleveland (44114) *(G-4396)*
Hyatt Corporation 614 463-1234
  350 N High St Columbus (43215) *(G-6031)*
Hyatt Corporation 614 228-1234
  75 E State St Columbus (43215) *(G-6032)*
Hyatt Hotel, Cleveland *Also Called: Hyatt Corporation (G-4396)*
Hyatt Hotel, Columbus *Also Called: Hyatt Corporation (G-6031)*
Hyatt Hotel, Columbus *Also Called: Hyatt Corporation (G-6032)*
Hyatt Hotel, Columbus *Also Called: Hyatt Regency Columbus (G-6033)*
Hyatt Legal Plans, Inc., Cleveland *Also Called: MetLife Legal Plans Inc (G-4559)*
Hyatt Pl Cincinnati-Northeast, Mason *Also Called: Select Hotels Group LLC (G-10606)*
Hyatt Place, Westlake *Also Called: CD Block K Hotel LLC (G-15047)*
Hyatt Regency Columbus 614 463-1234
  350 N High St Columbus (43215) *(G-6033)*
Hyde Park Golf & Country Club 513 871-3111
  3740 Erie Ave Cincinnati (45208) *(G-2858)*
Hyde Park Grille, Columbus *Also Called: Henderson Rd Rest Systems Inc (G-5984)*
Hyde Park Health Center 513 272-0600
  3763 Hopper Hill Rd Cincinnati (45255) *(G-2859)*
Hyde Park Landscaping, Cincinnati *Also Called: Hyde Park Ldscp & Tree Svc Inc (G-2860)*
Hyde Park Ldscp & Tree Svc Inc 513 731-1334
  5055 Wooster Rd Cincinnati (45226) *(G-2860)*
Hydraulic Manifolds USA LLC 973 728-1214
  4540 Boyce Pkwy Stow (44224) *(G-13376)*
Hydraulic Parts Store Inc 330 364-6667
  145 1st Dr Ne New Philadelphia (44663) *(G-11656)*
Hydraulic Pump Pwr Systems Div, Marysville *Also Called: Parker-Hannifin Corporation (G-10501)*
Hydro Systems Company (DH) 513 271-8800
  3798 Round Bottom Rd Cincinnati (45244) *(G-2861)*
Hydro-Dyne Inc 330 832-5076
  225 Wetmore Ave Se Massillon (44646) *(G-10647)*
Hydrotech Inc (PA) 888 651-5712
  10052 Commerce Park Dr West Chester (45246) *(G-14819)*
Hyland Software Inc (HQ) 440 788-5000
  28105 Clemens Rd Westlake (44145) *(G-15068)*
Hylant Administrative Services (PA) 419 255-1020
  811 Madison Ave Fl 11 Toledo (43604) *(G-13857)*
Hylant Group Inc (PA) 419 255-1020
  811 Madison Ave Toledo (43604) *(G-13858)*
Hyo Ok Inc 614 876-7644
  4315 Cosgray Rd Hilliard (43026) *(G-9203)*
Hyperion Companies Inc 949 309-2409
  5300 Crosswind Dr Columbus (43228) *(G-6034)*
Hyperlogistics Group Inc (PA) 614 497-0800
  9301 Intermodal Ct N Columbus (43217) *(G-6035)*
Hyperquake LLC 513 563-6555
  310 Culvert St, Ste-401 Cincinnati (45202) *(G-2862)*
Hyway Trucking Company 419 423-7145
  10060 W Us Route 224 Findlay (45840) *(G-8548)*
Hzw Environmental Cons LLC (PA) 800 804-8484
  6105 Heisley Rd Mentor (44060) *(G-10950)*
I & M J Gross Company (PA) 440 237-1681
  14300 Ridge Rd Ste 100 Cleveland (44133) *(G-4397)*
I AM Boundless Inc 614 844-3800
  445 E Dublin Granville Rd Ste G Worthington (43085) *(G-15421)*
I and T Holdings Inv Group Inc 269 207-7773
  7050 Spring Meadows Dr W Ste A Holland (43528) *(G-9289)*
I C S, Cincinnati *Also Called: Industrial Comm & Sound Inc (G-2868)*
I E R Inc 440 324-2620
  6856 Lake Ave Elyria (44035) *(G-8261)*
I L S, Cleveland *Also Called: Supply Technologies LLC (G-4966)*
I L S, Solon *Also Called: Supply Technologies LLC (G-13151)*
I P S, Cincinnati *Also Called: Integrated Protection Svcs Inc (G-2876)*
I P S, Rossford *Also Called: Industrial Power Systems Inc (G-12767)*
I Supply Co 937 878-5240
  1255 Spangler Rd Fairborn (45324) *(G-8377)*
I Vrable Inc 614 545-5500
  3248 Henderson Rd Columbus (43220) *(G-6036)*
I-75 Pierson Automotive Inc 513 424-1881
  5001 Sebald Dr Franklin (45005) *(G-8642)*
I-Force LLC 614 431-5100
  4 Easton Oval Columbus (43219) *(G-6037)*
I-O Properties LLC 419 852-7836
  4260 Burrville Rd Coldwater (45828) *(G-5214)*
I-X Center Corporation 216 265-2675
  6200 Riverside Dr Cleveland (44135) *(G-4398)*
IA Urban Htels Bchwood Trs LLC 216 765-8066
  3775 Park East Dr Beachwood (44122) *(G-801)*
IAC Wauseon LLC 419 335-1000
  555 W Linfoot St Wauseon (43567) *(G-14605)*
IBH, Coventry Township *Also Called: Interval Brotherhood Homes Inc (G-7011)*
Ibi, Chillicothe *Also Called: Ingle-Barr Inc (G-2072)*
Ibi Group Engrg Svcs USA Inc, Columbus *Also Called: Arcadis Engrg Svcs USA Inc (G-5383)*
Ibold & OBrien Inc 440 279-0688
  401 South St Ste 1a Chardon (44024) *(G-2006)*
IBP, Columbus *Also Called: Installed Building Pdts Inc (G-6057)*
IBP Corporation Holdings Inc 614 692-6360
  495 S High St Ste 50 Columbus (43215) *(G-6038)*
Ic Holding Company 440 746-9200
  10060 Brecksville Rd Brecksville (44141) *(G-1355)*
Ic Roofing, Mason *Also Called: Interstate Contractors LLC (G-10568)*
ICC Lowe Pace LLC 330 823-7223
  1641 S Arch Ave Alliance (44601) *(G-384)*
Icg Netcom, Cleveland *Also Called: Communications Buying Group (G-4095)*
ICM Distributing Company Inc 234 212-3030
  1755 Enterprise Pkwy Ste 200 Twinsburg (44087) *(G-14196)*
Icon Government (HQ) 330 278-2343
  1265 Ridge Rd Ste A Hinckley (44233) *(G-9270)*
Icon World Entertainment LLC 330 615-7008
  467 W Paige Ave Ste A Barberton (44203) *(G-698)*
ICP Inc (PA) 419 447-6216
  1815 W County Road 54 Tiffin (44883) *(G-13628)*
ICP Realty LLC 440 539-1046
  4780 Hinckley Industrial Pkwy Ste 100 Cleveland (44109) *(G-4399)*
Icr Inc 513 900-7007
  4770 Duke Dr Ste 300 Mason (45040) *(G-10563)*
Icr Engineering, Mason *Also Called: Icr Inc (G-10563)*
Ics Electrical Services, Cincinnati *Also Called: Instrmntation Ctrl Systems Inc (G-2873)*
Ics Laboratories Inc 330 220-0515
  1072 Industrial Pkwy N Brunswick (44212) *(G-1458)*
Icx Corporation (DH) 330 656-3611
  2 Summit Park Dr Ste 105 Cleveland (44131) *(G-4400)*
ID Networks Inc 440 992-0062
  7720 Jefferson Rd Ashtabula (44004) *(G-538)*
Iddings Trucking Inc 740 568-1780
  741 Blue Knob Rd Marietta (45750) *(G-10372)*
Ideal Company Inc (PA) 937 836-8683
  8313 Kimmel Rd Clayton (45315) *(G-3733)*
Idealease Miami Valley Intl, Cincinnati *Also Called: Miami Valley Intl Trcks Inc (G-3055)*
Ideastream (PA) 216 916-6100
  1375 Euclid Ave Cleveland (44115) *(G-4401)*
Identitek Systems Inc 330 832-9844
  1100 Industrial Ave Sw Massillon (44647) *(G-10648)*
Idillnire Cnslting Sltions LLC 305 413-8522
  1300 E 9th St Ste 800 Cleveland (44114) *(G-4402)*
IDM Computer Solutions, Hamilton *Also Called: Ultraedit Inc (G-9088)*
Ieh Auto Parts LLC 740 732-2395
  218 West St Caldwell (43724) *(G-1550)*
Ieh Auto Parts LLC 216 351-2560
  4565 Hinckley Industrial Pkwy Cleveland (44109) *(G-4403)*
Ieh Auto Parts LLC 740 373-8327
  123 Tennis Center Dr Marietta (45750) *(G-10373)*

Ieh Auto Parts LLC 740 373-8151
   121 Tennis Center Dr Marietta (45750) *(G-10374)*

Ies Systems Inc 330 533-6683
   464 Lisbon St Canfield (44406) *(G-1632)*

Iet Inc 419 385-1233
   3539 Glendale Ave Ste C Toledo (43614) *(G-13859)*

Iforce, Columbus *Also Called: I-Force LLC (G-6037)*

Ifs Financial Services Inc (DH) 513 362-8000
   370 S Cleveland Ave Westerville (43081) *(G-14988)*

Igel Technology America LLC 954 739-9990
   2106 Florence Ave Cincinnati (45206) *(G-2863)*

Ignite Philanthropy 513 381-1848
   308 E 8th St Fl 6 Cincinnati (45202) *(G-2864)*

Igs Solar LLC 844 447-7652
   6100 Emerald Pkwy Dublin (43016) *(G-8034)*

Igs Ventures Inc 614 659-5000
   6100 Emerald Pkwy Dublin (43016) *(G-8035)*

Ih Credit Union Inc (PA) 937 390-1800
   5000 Urbana Rd Springfield (45502) *(G-13256)*

Ihg Management (maryland) LLC 614 461-4100
   33 E Nationwide Blvd Columbus (43215) *(G-6039)*

IHS Enterprise LLC (PA) 216 588-9078
   5755 Granger Rd Ste 905 Independence (44131) *(G-9436)*

Ihs Services Inc 419 224-8811
   3225 W Elm St Ste D Lima (45805) *(G-9909)*

Ihs Services Inc 614 396-9980
   667 Lakeview Plaza Blvd Ste D Worthington (43085) *(G-15422)*

Ijus LLC (PA) 614 470-9882
   781 Science Blvd # 200 Columbus (43230) *(G-6040)*

Ikps, Fredericktown *Also Called: Integrity Kksing Ppline Svcs L (G-8660)*

Iler Networking & Cmpt Ltd 440 748-8083
   5061 N Abbe Rd Ste 3 Sheffield Village (44035) *(G-12999)*

Illuminate USA LLC 614 598-9742
   3600 Etna Pkwy Pataskala (43062) *(G-12275)*

Illumination Works LLC 937 938-1321
   2689 Commons Blvd Ste 120 Beavercreek (45431) *(G-884)*

Ils Technology LLC 800 695-8650
   6065 Parkland Blvd Cleveland (44124) *(G-4404)*

Ilt Toyota-Lift, Cleveland *Also Called: Interstate Lift Trucks Inc (G-4421)*

IMAGINATION STATION, Toledo *Also Called: Toledo Science Center (G-14065)*

Imagine Networks LLC 937 552-2340
   1100 Wayne St Troy (45373) *(G-14140)*

Imarc Research Inc 440 801-1540
   22560 Lunn Rd Strongsville (44149) *(G-13464)*

Imcd Us LLC 216 228-8900
   1779 Marvo Dr Akron (44306) *(G-200)*

Imcd Us LLC (HQ) 216 228-8900
   2 Equity Way Ste 210 Westlake (44145) *(G-15069)*

Imco Carbide Tool Inc 419 661-6313
   28170 Cedar Park Blvd Perrysburg (43551) *(G-12346)*

Imco Recycling, Uhrichsville *Also Called: Novelis Alr Recycling Ohio LLC (G-14236)*

Imdt Acquisition LLC 937 235-0510
   4490 Brandt Pike Dayton (45424) *(G-7418)*

Imeg Consultants Corp 614 443-1178
   855 Grandview Ave Ste 300 Columbus (43215) *(G-6041)*

Imflux Inc 513 488-1017
   1 Procter And Gamble Plz Cincinnati (45202) *(G-2865)*

IMG College LLC 513 556-4532
   2751 O Varsity Way Ste 870 Cincinnati (45221) *(G-2866)*

IMG Sports, Cincinnati *Also Called: IMG College LLC (G-2866)*

Imhoff Construction, Orrville *Also Called: Imhoff Construction Svcs Inc (G-12166)*

Imhoff Construction Svcs Inc 330 683-4498
   315 E Market St Orrville (44667) *(G-12166)*

Immaculate Landscapers LLC 440 724-1024
   1221 E 305th St Wickliffe (44092) *(G-15153)*

Immediate Health Associates 614 794-0481
   575 Copeland Mill Rd Ste 1d Westerville (43081) *(G-14989)*

Impac Hotel Group LLC 440 238-8800
   15471 Royalton Rd Strongsville (44136) *(G-13465)*

Impact Community Action 614 252-2799
   711 Southwood Ave Columbus (43207) *(G-6042)*

Impact Credit Union Inc (PA) 419 547-7781
   1455 W Mcpherson Hwy Clyde (43410) *(G-5203)*

Impact Fulfillment Svcs LLC 614 262-8911
   2035 Innis Rd Columbus (43224) *(G-6043)*

Impact Products LLC (HQ) 419 841-2891
   2840 Centennial Rd Toledo (43617) *(G-13860)*

Impact Sales Inc 937 274-1905
   2501 Neff Rd Dayton (45414) *(G-7419)*

Impact Sales Solutions Inc 419 466-0131
   5241 Southwyck Blvd Ste 104 Toledo (43614) *(G-13861)*

Imperial Dade Intrmdate Hldngs 800 998-5453
   9500 Glades Dr West Chester (45011) *(G-14709)*

Imperial Express Inc 937 399-9400
   202 N Limestone St Ste 300 Springfield (45503) *(G-13257)*

Imperial Heating and Coolg Inc (PA) 440 498-1788
   30685 Solon Industrial Pkwy Ste A Solon (44139) *(G-13098)*

Improveit HM Rmdlg An Ohio Enr, Columbus *Also Called: Improveit Home Remodeling Inc (G-6044)*

Improveit HM Rmdlg An Ohio Enr, West Chester *Also Called: Improveit Home Remodeling Inc (G-14710)*

Improveit Hme Rmdlng OH Enrgy, Dayton *Also Called: Improveit Home Remodeling Inc (G-7420)*

Improveit Home Remodeling Inc (PA) 614 297-5121
   4580 Bridgeway Ave Ste B Columbus (43219) *(G-6044)*

Improveit Home Remodeling Inc 937 204-1551
   7200 Poe Ave Ste 102 Dayton (45414) *(G-7420)*

Improveit Home Remodeling Inc 937 514-7546
   8930 Global Way West Chester (45069) *(G-14710)*

Impullitti Landscaping LLC 440 834-1866
   14659 Ravenna Rd Burton (44021) *(G-1530)*

IMS Company 440 543-1615
   10373 Stafford Rd Chagrin Falls (44023) *(G-1980)*

IMT, Brunswick *Also Called: Integrated Marketing Tech Inc (G-1460)*

In Home Health Inc (PA) 419 252-5500
   333 N Summit St Toledo (43604) *(G-13862)*

In Place, The, Cambridge *Also Called: Allwell Behavioral Health Svcs (G-1553)*

In Terminal Services Corp 216 518-8407
   5300 Greenhurst Ext Maple Heights (44137) *(G-10341)*

In Youngstown Area Gdwill Inds (PA) 330 759-7921
   2747 Belmont Ave Youngstown (44505) *(G-15637)*

Inc, Stearns-Stafford, Strongsville *Also Called: Bearing & Drive Systems Inc (G-13445)*

Incept Corporation 330 649-8000
   4150 Belden Village St Nw Ste 205 Canton (44718) *(G-1779)*

Incredible Products LLC 567 297-3700
   1221 Stewart Rd Lima (45801) *(G-9910)*

Indelco Custom Products Inc 216 797-7300
   25861 Tungsten Rd Euclid (44132) *(G-8349)*

Independence Bank 216 447-1444
   4401 Rockside Rd Cleveland (44131) *(G-4405)*

Independence Business Supply, Cleveland *Also Called: Indepndence Office Bus Sup Inc (G-4408)*

Independence Care Community 419 435-8505
   1000 Independence Ave Fostoria (44830) *(G-8620)*

Independence Excavating, Independence *Also Called: Independence Excavating Inc (G-9437)*

Independence Excavating Inc (PA) 216 524-1700
   5720 E Schaaf Rd Independence (44131) *(G-9437)*

Independence Foundation Inc 330 296-2851
   575 E Lake St Ravenna (44266) *(G-12630)*

Independence House, Fostoria *Also Called: Independence Care Community (G-8620)*

Independence Place, Cleveland *Also Called: Forest City Residential Dev (G-4274)*

Independent Hotel Partners LLC 216 524-0700
   5300 Rockside Rd Cleveland (44131) *(G-4406)*

Independent Personnel Services 216 781-5350
   1148 Euclid Ave Ste 405 Cleveland (44115) *(G-4407)*

Independent Research Group Inc 330 273-3380
   1575 Pearl Rd Brunswick (44212) *(G-1459)*

Indepndence Office Bus Sup Inc 216 398-8880
   4550 Hinckley Industrial Pkwy Cleveland (44109) *(G-4408)*

Indepndnce Fmly Hlth RES Cntre, Cleveland *Also Called: Cleveland Clinic Foundation (G-4022)*

ALPHABETIC SECTION — Innomark Communications

Indian Creek Apartments, Cincinnati Also Called: Towne Properties Assoc Inc **(G-3491)**
Indian Hlls Hlthcare Group Inc..216 486-8880
  1500 E 191st St Euclid (44117) **(G-8350)**
Indian Lake Rehabilitation Center, Lakeview Also Called: Indian Lk Healthcare Group LLC **(G-9655)**
Indian Learning Head Start, Bellaire Also Called: Community Action Comm Blmont C **(G-1009)**
Indian Lk Healthcare Group LLC..937 843-4929
  14442 Us Highway 33 Lakeview (43331) **(G-9655)**
Indiana & Ohio Rail Corp (DH)..513 860-1000
  2856 Cypress Way Cincinnati (45212) **(G-2867)**
Indiana Hospitality Group...937 505-1670
  204 Raydo Cir Springfield (45506) **(G-13258)**
Indiana Michigan Power Company (HQ).....................................614 716-1000
  1 Riverside Plz Columbus (43215) **(G-6045)**
Indus Airport Hotels I LLC..614 231-2869
  4265 Sawyer Rd Columbus (43219) **(G-6046)**
Indus Airport Hotels II LLC...614 235-0717
  4280 International Gtwy Columbus (43219) **(G-6047)**
Indus Hilliard Hotel LLC..614 334-1800
  3950 Lyman Dr Hilliard (43026) **(G-9204)**
Indus Hotel 77 LLC..614 223-1400
  77 E Nationwide Blvd Columbus (43215) **(G-6048)**
Indus Newark Hotel LLC (PA)..740 322-6455
  4265 Sawyer Rd Columbus (43219) **(G-6049)**
Indus Newark Hotel LLC..740 322-6455
  50 N 2nd St Newark (43055) **(G-11709)**
Indus Valley Consultants Inc (PA)..937 660-4748
  9049 Springboro Pike Miamisburg (45342) **(G-11063)**
Industrial Air Centers Inc..513 770-4161
  6428 Castle Dr Mason (45040) **(G-10564)**
INDUSTRIAL AIR CENTERS INC., Mason Also Called: Industrial Air Centers Inc **(G-10564)**
Industrial Air Centers Inc..614 274-9171
  2824 Fisher Rd Columbus (43204) **(G-6050)**
Industrial Chemical Corp (PA)...330 725-0800
  885 W Smith Rd Medina (44256) **(G-10846)**
Industrial Coml Prpts LLC..440 539-1046
  6675 Parkland Blvd Ste 100 Solon (44139) **(G-13099)**
Industrial Comm & Sound Inc...614 276-8123
  2105 Schappelle Ln Cincinnati (45240) **(G-2868)**
Industrial Cont Svcs - CA LLC...614 864-1900
  1385 Blatt Blvd Blacklick (43004) **(G-1111)**
Industrial Fiberglass Spc Inc...937 222-9000
  351 Deeds Ave Dayton (45404) **(G-7421)**
Industrial First Inc (PA)..216 991-8605
  25840 Miles Rd Ste 2 Bedford (44146) **(G-966)**
Industrial Insul Coatings LLC..800 506-1399
  142 E 2nd St Girard (44420) **(G-8816)**
Industrial Millwright Svcs LLC...419 523-9147
  1024 Heritage Trl Ottawa (45875) **(G-12187)**
Industrial Origami Inc..440 260-0000
  6755 Engle Rd Ste A Cleveland (44130) **(G-4409)**
Industrial Power Systems Inc..419 531-3121
  146 Dixie Hwy Rossford (43460) **(G-12767)**
Industrial Pping Spcalists Inc..330 750-2800
  100 S Bridge St Ste 3 Struthers (44471) **(G-13500)**
Industrial Repair and Mfg (PA)...419 822-4232
  1140 E Main St Delta (43515) **(G-7851)**
Industrial Security Svc Inc (HQ)...216 898-9970
  4525 W 160th St Cleveland (44135) **(G-4410)**
Industrial Security Svc Inc..614 785-7046
  2021 E Dublin Granville Rd Ste 130 Columbus (43229) **(G-6051)**
Industrial Sorting Services..513 772-6501
  9220 Glades Dr West Chester (45011) **(G-14711)**
Industrial Tube and Steel Corp (PA)...330 474-5530
  4658 Crystal Pkwy Kent (44240) **(G-9580)**
Industrial Tube and Steel Corp..513 777-5512
  9206 Port Union Rialto Rd West Chester (45069) **(G-14712)**
Industrial Waste Control Inc...330 270-9900
  240 Sinter Ct Youngstown (44510) **(G-15638)**
Industry Products Co (PA)...937 778-0585
  500 W Statler Rd Piqua (45356) **(G-12445)**

Ineos, Addyston Also Called: Ineos ABS (usa) LLC **(G-4)**
Ineos ABS (usa) LLC..513 467-2400
  356 Three Rivers Pkwy Addyston (45001) **(G-4)**
Ineos Hygienics LLC..614 790-5428
  5220 Blazer Pkwy Dublin (43017) **(G-8036)**
Inertial Aerospace Services, Cleveland Also Called: Inertial Airline Services Inc **(G-4411)**
Inertial Airline Services Inc..440 995-6555
  375 Alpha Park Cleveland (44143) **(G-4411)**
Infinite Tiers Inc..513 769-1900
  4055 Executive Park Dr Ste 140 Cincinnati (45241) **(G-2869)**
Infinity Health Services Inc (PA)...440 614-0145
  975 Crocker Rd # A Westlake (44145) **(G-15070)**
Infinity Labs LLC..937 317-0030
  171 E Krepps Rd Xenia (45385) **(G-15522)**
Info-Hold Inc..513 248-5600
  4120 Airport Rd Cincinnati (45226) **(G-2870)**
Infocision, Akron Also Called: Infocision Management Corp **(G-201)**
Infocision Management Corp (PA)...330 668-1411
  325 Springside Dr Akron (44333) **(G-201)**
Infocision Management Corp..330 726-0872
  6951 Southern Blvd Ste E Youngstown (44512) **(G-15639)**
Infocision Management Corp..330 544-1400
  5740 Patriot Blvd Youngstown (44515) **(G-15640)**
Information & Referral Center, Lima Also Called: County of Allen **(G-9879)**
Information Systems Dept, Batavia Also Called: County of Clermont **(G-739)**
Informtion Applied Lrng Evltio..214 329-9100
  4332 Tallmadge Rd Rootstown (44272) **(G-12759)**
Infotelecom LLC..216 373-4600
  75 Erieview Plz Fl 4 Cleveland (44114) **(G-4412)**
Infotrust LLC..513 403-2107
  4340 Glendale Milford Rd Ste 200 Blue Ash (45242) **(G-1184)**
Infoverity LLC (PA)..614 327-5173
  5131 Post Rd Ste 220 Dublin (43017) **(G-8037)**
Infovision21 Inc...614 761-8844
  6077 Frantz Rd Ste 105 Dublin (43017) **(G-8038)**
Infra-Metals Co..740 353-1350
  1 Sturgill Way Portsmouth (45662) **(G-12556)**
Infusion Partners Inc (HQ)..513 396-6060
  4623 Wesley Ave Ste H Cincinnati (45212) **(G-2871)**
Infusion Partners Inc..419 843-2100
  3315 Centennial Rd Ste Aa Sylvania (43560) **(G-13551)**
Ingersoll-Rand, Bryan Also Called: Trane Technologies Company LLC **(G-1494)**
Ingle-Barr Inc (PA)..740 702-6117
  20 Plyleys Ln Chillicothe (45601) **(G-2072)**
Ingle-Barr Inc..614 421-0201
  1444 Goodale Blvd Columbus (43212) **(G-6052)**
Ingram Entertainment, Perrysburg Also Called: Ingram Entertainment Holdings **(G-12347)**
Ingram Entertainment Holdings..419 662-3132
  668 1st St Perrysburg (43551) **(G-12347)**
Initial Tropical Plant Svcs, Groveport Also Called: Rentokil North America Inc **(G-8999)**
Injection Molders Supply, Chagrin Falls Also Called: IMS Company **(G-1980)**
Inloes Heating and Cooling, Hamilton Also Called: Inloes Mechanical Inc **(G-9054)**
Inloes Mechanical Inc..513 896-9499
  157 N B St Hamilton (45013) **(G-9054)**
Inmotion Promotion, Columbus Also Called: Brown Logistics Solutions Inc **(G-5471)**
Inn At Marietta Ltd..740 373-9600
  150 Browns Rd Ofc Marietta (45750) **(G-10375)**
Inn At Olentangy Trail..740 417-9287
  36 Corduroy Rd Delaware (43015) **(G-7806)**
Inn At Wickliffe LLC..440 585-0600
  28600 Ridgehills Dr Wickliffe (44092) **(G-15154)**
Inn Hampton and Suites..614 473-9911
  4100 Regent St Ste G Columbus (43219) **(G-6053)**
Inn Hampton and Suites..440 324-7755
  1795 Lorain Blvd Elyria (44035) **(G-8262)**
Inner City Nursing Home Inc...216 795-1363
  9014 Cedar Ave Cleveland (44106) **(G-4413)**
Inno-Pak LLC (PA)...740 363-0090
  100 Founders Ct Delaware (43015) **(G-7807)**
Innomark Communications, Miamisburg Also Called: Concept Imaging Group Inc **(G-11037)**

Innomark Communications LLC 888 466-6627
  3005 W Tech Blvd Miamisburg (45342) *(G-11064)*
Innomark Communications LLC 513 379-7800
  8531 Trade Ctr Dr West Chester (45011) *(G-14713)*
Innovairre Communications LLC 330 869-8500
  3200 W Market St Ste 302 Fairlawn (44333) *(G-8485)*
Innovative Cleaning Svcs & Sup 513 981-1287
  4903 Vine St Ste 2 Cincinnati (45217) *(G-2872)*
Innovative Concept, Girard *Also Called: Boardman Medical Supply Co (G-8810)*
Innovative Controls Corp 419 691-6684
  1354 E Bdwy St Toledo (43605) *(G-13863)*
Innovative Joint Utility Svcs, Columbus *Also Called: Ijus LLC (G-6040)*
Innovative Labor Clg Svcs Sup, Cincinnati *Also Called: Innovative Cleaning Svcs & Sup (G-2872)*
Innovative Logistics Svcs Inc 330 468-6422
  201 E Twinsburg Rd Northfield (44067) *(G-11958)*
Innovative Technologies Corp (PA) 937 252-2145
  1020 Woodman Dr Ste 100 Dayton (45432) *(G-7135)*
Innovative Therapies LLC 866 484-6798
  7000 Cardinal Pl Dublin (43017) *(G-8039)*
Innovest Global Inc (PA) 216 815-1122
  8834 Mayfield Rd Ste A Chesterland (44026) *(G-2036)*
Innovis, Columbus *Also Called: Innovis Data Solutions Inc (G-6054)*
Innovis Data Solutions Inc 614 222-4343
  250 E Broad St Columbus (43215) *(G-6054)*
Innovtive Sltons Unlimited LLC 740 289-3282
  7040 Us 23 Piketon (45661) *(G-12423)*
Innovtive Sltons Unlimited LLC (PA) 740 289-3282
  1862 Shyville Rd Piketon (45661) *(G-12424)*
Inoac Exterior Systems LLC 419 334-8951
  1410 Motor Ave Fremont (43420) *(G-8687)*
Inoac Exterior Systems LLC (DH) 419 334-8951
  1410 Motor Ave Fremont (43420) *(G-8688)*
Inquiry Systems Inc 614 464-3800
  1195 Goodale Blvd Columbus (43212) *(G-6055)*
Inside Out (PA) 937 525-7880
  501 S Wittenberg Ave Springfield (45506) *(G-13259)*
INSIDE OUT CHILD CARE, Springfield *Also Called: Inside Out (G-13259)*
Inside Outfitters, Lewis Center *Also Called: Lumenomics Inc (G-9827)*
Inside Outfitters Inc 614 798-3500
  8333 Green Meadows Dr N Ste B Lewis Center (43035) *(G-9824)*
Insight Cunseling Wellness LLC 330 635-0638
  8031 Middlesex Rd Mentor (44060) *(G-10951)*
Insight Technical Services, Sandusky *Also Called: All Phase Power and Ltg Inc (G-12862)*
Insight2profit, Beachwood *Also Called: Insight2profit LLC (G-802)*
Insight2profit LLC (PA) 440 646-9490
  3333 Richmond Rd Ste 200 Beachwood (44122) *(G-802)*
Installed Building Pdts II LLC (HQ) 626 812-6070
  495 S High St Ste 50 Columbus (43215) *(G-6056)*
Installed Building Pdts Inc (PA) 614 221-3399
  495 S High St Ste 50 Columbus (43215) *(G-6057)*
Installed Building Pdts LLC 330 798-9640
  2783 Gilchrist Rd Unit B Akron (44305) *(G-202)*
Installed Building Pdts LLC 614 272-5577
  2660 Fisher Rd Ste A Columbus (43204) *(G-6058)*
Installed Building Pdts LLC 419 884-0676
  303 E Main St Mansfield (44904) *(G-10272)*
Installed Building Products LLC (HQ) 614 221-3399
  495 S High St Ste 150 Columbus (43215) *(G-6059)*
Instantwhip, Stow *Also Called: Instantwhip-Akron Inc (G-13377)*
Instantwhip-Akron Inc 614 488-2536
  4870 Hudson Dr Stow (44224) *(G-13377)*
Instantwhip-Columbus Inc (HQ) 614 871-9447
  3855 Marlane Dr Grove City (43123) *(G-8928)*
Institute For Orthpdic Surgery, Lima *Also Called: West Central Ohio Group Ltd (G-9981)*
Institute of Jaw Fcial Srgery 330 493-1605
  4181 Holiday St Nw Canton (44718) *(G-1780)*
Institutional Care Pharmacy, Tiffin *Also Called: ICP Inc (G-13628)*
Instrmntation Ctrl Systems Inc 513 662-2600
  11355 Sebring Dr Cincinnati (45240) *(G-2873)*

Insulation Northwest, Columbus *Also Called: Installed Building Pdts II LLC (G-6056)*
Insurance Intermediaries Inc 614 846-1111
  280 N High St Ste 300 Columbus (43215) *(G-6060)*
Insurance Partners Agency LLC 330 493-3211
  4700 Dressler Rd Nw Canton (44718) *(G-1781)*
Insurance Technologies Corp 866 683-6915
  580 N 4th St Ste 500 Columbus (43215) *(G-6061)*
Insurancecom Inc (PA) 440 498-0001
  30775 Bainbridge Rd Ste 210 Solon (44139) *(G-13100)*
Insurnce Office Centl Ohio Inc 614 939-5471
  165 W Main St New Albany (43054) *(G-11569)*
Insurnce Specialists Group Inc 440 975-0309
  373 Center St Ste A Chardon (44024) *(G-2007)*
Integra Cncinnati/Columbus Inc 614 764-8040
  6241 Riverside Dr Dublin (43017) *(G-8040)*
Integra Lifesciences, Cincinnati *Also Called: Integra Lifesciences Corp (G-2874)*
Integra Lifesciences Corp 513 533-7923
  4900 Charlemar Dr Bldg A Cincinnati (45227) *(G-2874)*
Integra Rlty Rsrces - Cncnnt/D 513 561-2305
  8241 Cornell Rd Ste 210 Cincinnati (45249) *(G-2875)*
Integra Svcs Intermediate LLC 317 409-2130
  9045 Osborne Dr Mentor (44060) *(G-10952)*
Integrated Data Services Inc 937 656-5496
  111 Harries St Apt 202 Dayton (45402) *(G-7422)*
Integrated Health Services Inc 440 856-5475
  19201 Cranwood Pkwy Warrensville Heights (44128) *(G-14582)*
Integrated Marketing Tech Inc 330 225-3550
  2945 Carquest Dr Brunswick (44212) *(G-1460)*
Integrated Medical Inc 216 332-1550
  15627 Neo Pkwy Cleveland (44128) *(G-4414)*
Integrated Power Services LLC 216 433-7808
  5325 W 130th St Cleveland (44130) *(G-4415)*
Integrated Power Services LLC 513 863-8816
  2175a Schlichter Dr Hamilton (45015) *(G-9055)*
Integrated Prj Resources LLC 330 272-0998
  542 E State St Salem (44460) *(G-12844)*
Integrated Protection Svcs Inc (PA) 513 631-5505
  5303 Lester Rd Cincinnati (45213) *(G-2876)*
Integrated Resources Inc 419 885-7122
  7901 Sylvania Ave Sylvania (43560) *(G-13552)*
Integrated Root Systems LLC 216 282-7470
  8400 Sweet Valley Dr Ste 401 Cleveland (44125) *(G-4416)*
Integrated Whse Solutions Inc 614 899-5080
  700 Northfield Rd Westerville (43082) *(G-14900)*
Integres Fast Forward Shipping, Medina *Also Called: Integres Global Logistics Inc (G-10847)*
Integres Global Logistics Inc (DH) 866 347-2101
  84 Medina Rd Medina (44256) *(G-10847)*
Integris Composites Inc 740 928-0326
  1051 O Neill Dr Hebron (43025) *(G-9144)*
Integrity, Columbus *Also Called: Integrity Mutual Insurance Co (G-6063)*
Integrity Concepts Llc Inc 614 529-8332
  3500 Millikin Ct Ste A Columbus (43228) *(G-6062)*
Integrity Ex Logistics LLC (DH) 888 374-5138
  4420 Cooper Rd Ste 400 Cincinnati (45242) *(G-2877)*
Integrity Kksing Ppline Svcs L 740 694-6315
  17531 Waterford Rd Fredericktown (43019) *(G-8660)*
Integrity Mutual Insurance Co (PA) 920 734-4511
  671 S High St Columbus (43206) *(G-6063)*
Integrity Pipeline Services LLC 419 886-9907
  500 S Mn St Bellville (44813) *(G-1051)*
Integrity Processing LLC (PA) 330 285-6937
  1055 Wooster Rd N Barberton (44203) *(G-699)*
Integrity Stainless, Streetsboro *Also Called: Is Acquisition Inc (G-13418)*
Integrted Svcs For Bhvral Hlth 740 216-4093
  33 W 2nd St Logan (43138) *(G-10029)*
Integrted Svcs For Bhvral Hlth (PA) 740 300-0225
  1950 Mount Saint Marys Dr Nelsonville (45764) *(G-11548)*
Integrted Wllness Partners LLC 330 762-9102
  19 N High St Akron (44308) *(G-203)*
Intelligrated Inc 513 874-0788
  10045 International Blvd West Chester (45246) *(G-14820)*

ALPHABETIC SECTION — Interstate Truckway Inc

Intelligrated Systems Inc (HQ) 866 936-7300
7901 Innovation Way Mason (45040) *(G-10565)*

Intelligrated Systems LLC 513 701-7300
7901 Innovation Way Mason (45040) *(G-10566)*

Intelligrated Systems Ohio LLC (DH) 513 701-7300
7901 Innovation Way Mason (45040) *(G-10567)*

Intellihartx LLC (PA) 419 949-5040
129 E Crawford St Findlay (45840) *(G-8549)*

Intellinet Corporation (PA) 216 289-4100
150 Center St Chardon (44024) *(G-2008)*

Intellitarget Marketing Svcs, Coshocton *Also Called: ITM Marketing Inc (G-6988)*

Interact For Health 513 458-6600
8230 Montgomery Rd Ste 300 Cincinnati (45236) *(G-2878)*

Interact One Inc 513 469-7042
4665 Cornell Rd Ste 255 Blue Ash (45241) *(G-1185)*

Interactive Bus Systems Inc 513 984-2205
130 Tri County Pkwy Ste 208 Cincinnati (45246) *(G-2879)*

Interactive Payer Network LLC
5910 Landerbrook Dr Ste 110 Cleveland (44124) *(G-4417)*

Interbake Foods LLC 614 294-4931
1700 E 17th Ave Columbus (43219) *(G-6064)*

Interbrand Design Forum LLC 513 421-2210
700 W Pete Rose Way Ste 460 Cincinnati (45203) *(G-2880)*

Interbrand Hulefeld Inc 513 421-2210
700 W Pete Rose Way Ste 460 Cincinnati (45203) *(G-2881)*

Interchez Lgistics Systems Inc 330 923-5080
600 Alpha Pkwy Stow (44224) *(G-13378)*

Intercity Line, Cleveland *Also Called: DATA Den Inc (G-4149)*

Intercontinental, Cleveland *Also Called: Six Continents Hotels Inc (G-4911)*

Interdesign Inc (PA) 440 248-0178
30725 Solon Industrial Pkwy Solon (44139) *(G-13101)*

Interex Inc 646 905-0091
3700 Park East Dr Ste 250 Beachwood (44122) *(G-803)*

Interfinish LLC 216 662-6550
9500 Midwest Ave Cleveland (44125) *(G-4418)*

Intergncy Emplyees Child Care 740 772-7086
17273 State Route 104 Chillicothe (45601) *(G-2073)*

Interim Hlthcare Columbus Inc 330 836-5571
3040 W Market St Ste 1 Fairlawn (44333) *(G-8486)*

Interim Hlthcare Columbus Inc (HQ) 614 888-3130
784 Morrison Rd Gahanna (43230) *(G-8719)*

Interim Hlthcare Columbus Inc 740 349-8700
675 Hopewell Dr Heath (43056) *(G-9134)*

Interim Hlthcare Columbus Inc 740 387-0301
298 E Center St Ste D Marion (43302) *(G-10431)*

Interim Healthcare (PA) 740 354-5550
4130 Gallia St Portsmouth (45662) *(G-12557)*

Interim Healthcare, Bowling Green *Also Called: Salo Inc (G-1332)*

Interim Healthcare, Fairlawn *Also Called: Salo Inc (G-8495)*

Interim Healthcare, Zanesville *Also Called: Interim Hlth Care of Nrthwster (G-15804)*

Interim Healthcare Inc 614 552-3400
784 Morrison Rd Columbus (43230) *(G-6065)*

Interim Healthcare Inc 330 677-8010
184 Currie Hall Pkwy Ste 1 Kent (44240) *(G-9581)*

Interim Healthcare of Dayton 937 291-5330
30 W Rahn Rd Ste 2 Dayton (45429) *(G-7423)*

Interim Hlth Care of Nrthwster 419 422-5328
2129 Stephen Avnue Ste 3 Findlay (45840) *(G-8550)*

Interim Hlth Care of Nrthwster 419 228-9345
3745 Shawnee Rd Ste 108 Lima (45806) *(G-9993)*

Interim Hlth Care of Nrthwster 740 343-4112
445 W Broadway St New Lexington (43764) *(G-11627)*

Interim Hlth Care of Nrthwster 740 453-5130
2809 Bell St Ste D Zanesville (43701) *(G-15804)*

Interim Hlthcare Cambridge Inc 740 623-2949
232 Chestnut St Coshocton (43812) *(G-6987)*

Interim Hlthcare Cambridge Inc (PA) 740 432-2966
300 W Wilson Bridge Rd Ste 250 Worthington (43085) *(G-15423)*

Interim Services, Cambridge *Also Called: Salo Inc (G-1581)*

Interim Services, Cincinnati *Also Called: Salo Inc (G-3345)*

Interim Services, Columbus *Also Called: Salo Inc (G-6639)*

Interim Services, Coshocton *Also Called: Salo Inc (G-7002)*

Interim Services, Dayton *Also Called: Interim Healthcare of Dayton (G-7423)*

Interim Services, Fairlawn *Also Called: Interim Halthcare Columbus Inc (G-8486)*

Interim Services, Findlay *Also Called: Interim Hlth Care of Nrthwster (G-8550)*

INTERIM SERVICES, Gahanna *Also Called: Interim Halthcare Columbus Inc (G-8719)*

Interim Services, Heath *Also Called: Interim Halthcare Columbus Inc (G-9134)*

Interim Services, Kent *Also Called: Interim Healthcare Inc (G-9581)*

Interim Services, Lancaster *Also Called: Salo Inc (G-9740)*

Interim Services, Lima *Also Called: Interim Hlth Care of Nrthwster (G-9993)*

Interim Services, Worthington *Also Called: Interim Hlthcare Cambridge (G-15423)*

Interior Supply Cincinnati LLC 614 424-6611
481 E 11th Ave Columbus (43211) *(G-6066)*

Internal Mdcine Cons of Clmbus 614 878-6413
104 N Murray Hill Rd Columbus (43228) *(G-6067)*

Internal Medical Physicians 330 868-3711
1168 Alliance Rd Nw Minerva (44657) *(G-11307)*

Internal Revenue Service 937 643-1494
3100 Big Hill Rd Dayton (45419) *(G-7424)*

International Brake Inds Inc (DH) 419 227-4421
1840 Mccullough St Lima (45801) *(G-9911)*

International Dev Assn Africa 314 629-2431
341 S 3rd St Ste 100 Columbus (43215) *(G-6068)*

International Exposition Ctr, Cleveland *Also Called: I-X Center Corporation (G-4398)*

International Fuel Systems, Findlay *Also Called: Ohio Machinery Co (G-8574)*

International Healthcare Corp 513 731-3338
2837 Burnet Ave Cincinnati (45219) *(G-2882)*

INTERNATIONAL HEALTHCARE CORPORATION, Cincinnati *Also Called: International Healthcare Corp (G-2882)*

International Masonry Inc 614 469-8338
135 Spruce St Columbus (43215) *(G-6069)*

International Merchants, Blue Ash *Also Called: Req/Jqh Holdings Inc (G-1235)*

International Paper, Fairfield *Also Called: Veritiv Operating Company (G-8452)*

International Qulty Healthcare, Dayton *Also Called: Interntnal Qlty Healthcare Corp (G-7425)*

International Technegroup Inc (HQ) 513 576-3900
5303 Dupont Cir Milford (45150) *(G-11233)*

International Truck & Eng Corp 937 390-4045
6125 Urbana Rd Springfield (45502) *(G-13260)*

Internists of Fairfield Inc 513 896-9595
5150 Sandy Ln Fairfield (45014) *(G-8420)*

Interntional Towers I Ohio Ltd 216 520-1250
25 Market St Youngstown (44503) *(G-15641)*

Interntnal Excess Prgram Mnger, Beachwood *Also Called: One80 Intermediaries Inc (G-823)*

Interntnal MGT Group Ovrseas L (DH) 216 522-1200
1360 E 9th St Ste 100 Cleveland (44114) *(G-4419)*

Interntnal Pckg Pallets Crates, Sidney *Also Called: Wappoo Wood Products Inc (G-13057)*

Interntnal Pdts Srcing Group I (HQ) 614 850-3000
4119 Leap Rd Hilliard (43026) *(G-9205)*

Interntnal Qlty Hlthcare Corp (PA) 513 731-3338
6927 N Main St Ste 101 Dayton (45415) *(G-7425)*

Interntnal Spcial Adit Systems, Beachwood *Also Called: First Federal Credit Control (G-791)*

Interscope Manufacturing Inc 513 423-8866
2901 Carmody Blvd Middletown (45042) *(G-11166)*

Interservice Corporation 216 272-3519
7301 Wharton Rd Novelty (44072) *(G-12039)*

Interstate Coml GL & Door, Northwood *Also Called: A E D Inc (G-11968)*

Interstate Contractors LLC 513 372-5393
762 Reading Rd # G Mason (45040) *(G-10568)*

Interstate Diesel Service Inc (PA) 216 881-0015
5300 Lakeside Ave E Cleveland (44114) *(G-4420)*

Interstate Ford Inc 937 866-0781
125 Alexandersville Rd Miamisburg (45342) *(G-11065)*

Interstate Gas Supply, Dublin *Also Called: Interstate Gas Supply LLC (G-8041)*

Interstate Gas Supply LLC (PA) 877 995-4447
6100 Emerald Pkwy Dublin (43016) *(G-8041)*

Interstate Lift Trucks Inc 216 328-0970
5667 E Schaaf Rd Cleveland (44131) *(G-4421)*

Interstate Shredding LLC 330 545-5477
27 Furnace Ln Girard (44420) *(G-8817)*

Interstate Truckway Inc (PA) 513 542-5500
1755 Dreman Ave Cincinnati (45223) *(G-2883)*

Interstate-Mcbee, Bedford *Also Called: McBee Supply Corporation (G-971)*

Interstate-Mcbee LLC (PA).. 216 881-0015
7440 Oak Leaf Rd Bedford (44146) *(G-967)*

Interstop Corporation... 513 272-1133
3956 Virginia Ave Cincinnati (45227) *(G-2884)*

Intertek Testing Svcs NA Inc.. 614 279-8090
1717 Arlingate Ln Columbus (43228) *(G-6070)*

Interval Brotherhood Homes Inc.. 330 644-4095
3445 S Main St Coventry Township (44319) *(G-7011)*

Intervention For Peace Inc... 330 725-1298
689 W Liberty St Ste 7 Medina (44256) *(G-10848)*

Intralot Inc.. 440 268-2900
13500 Darice Pkwy Ste C Strongsville (44149) *(G-13466)*

Intren Inc.. 815 482-0651
1267 Tennessee Ave Cincinnati (45229) *(G-2885)*

INTREPID USA HEALTHCARE SERVIC, Elyria *Also Called: NC Hha Inc (G-8279)*

Intrust It, Blue Ash *Also Called: Lan Solutions Inc (G-1197)*

Invacare, Elyria *Also Called: Invacare Respiratory Corp (G-8263)*

Invacare Respiratory Corp... 440 329-6000
899 Cleveland St Elyria (44035) *(G-8263)*

Inventory Controlled Mdsg, Twinsburg *Also Called: ICM Distributing Company Inc (G-14196)*

Inverness Club... 419 578-9000
4601 Dorr St Toledo (43615) *(G-13864)*

Investment Pdts Ffl Inv Svcs... 216 529-2700
14806 Detroit Ave Lakewood (44107) *(G-9669)*

Invincible Fire Co Inc... 419 647-4615
204 S Canal St Spencerville (45887) *(G-13189)*

Invision Technologies Dist, Cincinnati *Also Called: Eco Engineering Inc (G-2604)*

Ion Media Stations Inc... 561 659-4122
312 Walnut St Ste 2800 Cincinnati (45202) *(G-2886)*

Iotco LLC.. 877 464-6826
250 E 5th St Ste 1500 Cincinnati (45202) *(G-2887)*

Iowa 80 Group, Hebron *Also Called: Truckomat Corporation (G-9155)*

Ipn, Interpaynet, Cleveland *Also Called: Interactive Payer Network LLC (G-4417)*

Ips, Avon Lake *Also Called: Optumrx Home Delivery Ohio LLC (G-682)*

Ipsg / Micro Center, Hilliard *Also Called: Interntnal Pdts Srcing Group I (G-9205)*

Ipsos Understanding Unlimited, Cincinnati *Also Called: Ipsos-Asi LLC (G-2888)*

Ipsos-Asi LLC (DH).. 513 872-4300
3505 Columbia Pkwy Ste 300 Cincinnati (45226) *(G-2888)*

Irace Inc.. 330 836-7247
2265 W Market St Akron (44313) *(G-204)*

Irace Automotive, Akron *Also Called: Irace Inc (G-204)*

Irg Operating LLC.. 440 963-4008
850 W River Rd Vermilion (44089) *(G-14405)*

Irg Realty Advisors LLC (PA)... 330 659-4060
4020 Kinross Lakes Pkwy Ste 200 Richfield (44286) *(G-12699)*

Irish Envy LLC... 440 808-8000
48 Windward Way Chagrin Falls (44023) *(G-1981)*

Irish Youth Sports Inc... 859 257-7910
5120 Guernsey St Bellaire (43906) *(G-1013)*

Iron Gate Realtors, Englewood *Also Called: Irongate Inc (G-8310)*

Irongate Inc.. 937 890-4880
16 W Wenger Rd Ste E Englewood (45322) *(G-8310)*

Irongate Inc (PA).. 937 433-3300
122 N Main St Centerville (45459) *(G-1946)*

Irongate Inc.. 937 432-3432
1353 Lyons Rd Dayton (45458) *(G-7426)*

Irongate Realtors, Centerville *Also Called: Irongate Inc (G-1946)*

Ironrock Capital Incorporated.. 330 484-4887
1201 Millerton St Se Canton (44707) *(G-1782)*

Irons Fruit Farm... 513 932-2853
1640 Stubbs Mill Rd Lebanon (45036) *(G-9769)*

Ironsite Inc... 740 965-4616
72 Holmes St Galena (43021) *(G-8736)*

Ironton Lwrnce Cnty Area Cmnty (PA).................................. 740 532-3534
305 N 5th St Ironton (45638) *(G-9508)*

Ironwood Development Corp... 440 895-1200
20595 Lorain Rd Ste 300 Cleveland (44126) *(G-4422)*

Irth Solutions Inc (PA)... 614 459-2328
5009 Horizons Dr Ste 100 Columbus (43220) *(G-6071)*

Is Acquisition Inc (HQ)... 440 287-0150
3000 Crane Centre Dr Streetsboro (44241) *(G-13418)*

Isaac Brant Ledman Teetor LLP... 614 221-2121
2 Miranova Pl Ste 700 Columbus (43215) *(G-6072)*

Isaac Fair Consulting Inc... 216 643-6790
6100 Oak Tree Blvd Cleveland (44131) *(G-4423)*

Isaac Foster Mack Co (PA).. 419 625-5500
314 W Market St Sandusky (44870) *(G-12905)*

Isaac Instruments LLC.. 888 658-7520
3121 Bridge Ave Cleveland (44113) *(G-4424)*

Isaac Wiles & Burkholder LLC... 614 221-2121
2 Miranova Pl Ste 700 Columbus (43215) *(G-6073)*

Isaac Wiles Burkholder & Teeto, Columbus *Also Called: Isaac Wiles & Burkholder LLC (G-6073)*

Isabelle Ridgway Care Ctr Inc... 614 252-4931
1520 Hawthorne Ave Columbus (43203) *(G-6074)*

ISI Systems Inc (PA).. 740 942-0050
43029 Industrial Park Rd Cadiz (43907) *(G-1541)*

Island Hospitality MGT LLC.. 614 864-8844
2084 S Hamilton Rd Columbus (43232) *(G-6075)*

Island Service Company.. 419 285-3695
341 Bayview Ave Put In Bay (43456) *(G-12617)*

Isomedix Operations Inc.. 614 836-5757
4405 Marketing Pl Groveport (43125) *(G-8992)*

Isomedix Operations Inc (DH)... 877 783-7497
5960 Heisley Rd Mentor (44060) *(G-10953)*

It Services, Dayton *Also Called: Efix It Solutions LLC (G-7330)*

Ita Audio Visual Solutions, Cincinnati *Also Called: ITA INC (G-2889)*

ITA INC (PA)... 513 631-7000
2162 Dana Ave Cincinnati (45207) *(G-2889)*

Itc, Dayton *Also Called: Innovative Technologies Corp (G-7135)*

Itcube LLC.. 513 891-7300
10999 Reed Hartman Hwy Ste 237 Blue Ash (45242) *(G-1186)*

Itelligence Outsourcing Inc (DH)... 513 956-2000
10856 Reed Hartman Hwy Cincinnati (45242) *(G-2890)*

Iten Defense LLC... 440 990-2440
3500 N Ridge Rd W Ashtabula (44004) *(G-539)*

ITM Marketing Inc.. 740 295-3575
331 Main St Coshocton (43812) *(G-6988)*

Its Technologies Inc (PA).. 419 842-2100
7060 Spring Meadows Dr W Ste D Holland (43528) *(G-9290)*

Its Technologies Inc.. 614 901-2265
4111 Executive Pkwy Ste 201 Westerville (43081) *(G-14990)*

Its Traffic Systems Inc.. 440 892-4500
28915 Clemens Rd Ste 200 Westlake (44145) *(G-15071)*

ITW Air Management... 513 891-7474
10125 Carver Rd Blue Ash (45242) *(G-1187)*

ITW Food Equipment Group LLC.. 937 393-4271
1495 N High St Hillsboro (45133) *(G-9260)*

ITW Food Equipment Group LLC (HQ)................................. 937 332-2396
701 S Ridge Ave Troy (45374) *(G-14141)*

Itx Healthcare LLC... 844 489-2273
129 E Crawford St Ste 360 Findlay (45840) *(G-8551)*

Ivhr Inc., Cleveland *Also Called: Ivhr LLC (G-4425)*

Ivhr LLC.. 216 445-4315
10000 Cedar Ave Ste 2136 Cleveland (44106) *(G-4425)*

Ivy Hills Country Club, Cincinnati *Also Called: Dry Run Limited Partnership (G-2577)*

Ivy League Academy, Mentor *Also Called: Advanced Solutions For Educatn (G-10908)*

J & B Acoustical Inc.. 419 884-1155
2750 Lexington Ave Mansfield (44904) *(G-10273)*

J & D Home Improvement Inc (PA)...................................... 800 288-0831
4400 Easton Cmns Columbus (43219) *(G-6076)*

J & E LLC.. 513 241-0429
250 W Court St Ste 200e Cincinnati (45202) *(G-2891)*

J & F Construction, Bucyrus *Also Called: J & F Construction and Dev Inc (G-1510)*

J & F Construction and Dev Inc.. 419 562-6662
2141 State Route 19 Bucyrus (44820) *(G-1510)*

J & H Erectors, Portsmouth *Also Called: J&H Rnfrcing Strl Erectors Inc (G-12558)*

J & J General Maintenance Inc... 740 533-9729
2430 S 3rd St Ironton (45638) *(G-9509)*

J & J Schlaegel Inc.. 937 652-2045
1250 E Us Highway 36 Urbana (43078) *(G-14309)*

ALPHABETIC SECTION

Jagi Clvland - Indpendence LLC

J & N, Cincinnati *Also Called: Building 8 Inc (G-2289)*

J & P Asset Management Inc 216 408-7693
   4737 Arbour Green Dr Akron (44333) *(G-205)*

J & R Door LLC 740 623-2782
   46700 County Road 405 Coshocton (43812) *(G-6989)*

J & S Industrial Mch Pdts Inc 419 691-1380
   123 Oakdale Ave Toledo (43605) *(G-13865)*

J & W Enterprises Inc (PA) 740 774-4500
   159 E Main St Chillicothe (45601) *(G-2074)*

J B & Company Incorporated 419 447-1716
   1480 S County Road 594 Tiffin (44883) *(G-13629)*

J B Express Inc 740 702-9830
   27311 Old Route 35 Chillicothe (45601) *(G-2075)*

J B Hunt Transport Inc 419 547-2777
   600 N Woodland Ave Clyde (43410) *(G-5204)*

J Becker Solutions Inc 888 421-1155
   1762 Mendelsohn Dr Westlake (44145) *(G-15072)*

J C Buckles Transfer Co, Cincinnati *Also Called: Verst Group Logistics Inc (G-3622)*

J Clarke Sanders DDS Inc 614 864-3196
   11295 Stonecreek Dr Ste C Pickerington (43147) *(G-12404)*

J D Williamson Cnstr Co Inc 330 633-1258
   441 Geneva Ave Tallmadge (44278) *(G-13596)*

J Daniel & Company Inc 513 575-3100
   1975 Phoenix Drive Loveland (45140) *(G-10143)*

J F Painting Co, Columbus *Also Called: Johnson & Fischer Incorporated (G-6094)*

J Foothills LLC 614 445-8461
   4300 E 5th Ave Columbus (43219) *(G-6077)*

J I T, Lebanon *Also Called: Jlt Packaging Cincinnati Inc (G-9771)*

J Kuhn Enterprises Inc 614 481-8838
   2200 Mckinley Ave Columbus (43204) *(G-6078)*

J L G Co Inc 513 248-1755
   419 Wards Corner Rd Loveland (45140) *(G-10144)*

J L Wilson Co 216 431-4040
   3800 Lakeside Ave E Ste 100 Cleveland (44114) *(G-4426)*

J M Sealts Company 419 224-8075
   4755 Lake Forest Dr Ste 100 Blue Ash (45242) *(G-1188)*

J P Farley Corporation (PA) 440 250-4300
   29055 Clemens Rd Westlake (44145) *(G-15073)*

J P Jenks Inc 440 428-4500
   4493 S Madison Rd Madison (44057) *(G-10218)*

J P Transportation Co Inc 513 424-6978
   2518 Oxford State Rd Middletown (45044) *(G-11167)*

J Peterman Company LLC 888 647-2555
   5345 Creek Rd Blue Ash (45242) *(G-1189)*

J R Metals, West Chester *Also Called: Misa Metals Inc (G-14731)*

J Rayl Transport Inc (PA) 330 784-1134
   1016 Triplett Blvd # 1 Akron (44306) *(G-206)*

J T Eaton & Co Inc 330 425-7801
   1393 Highland Rd Twinsburg (44087) *(G-14197)*

J V Enviroserve Limited Partnership 216 642-1311
   4600 Brookpark Rd Cleveland (44134) *(G-4427)*

J V Janitorial Services Inc 216 749-1150
   1000 Resource Dr Brooklyn Heights (44131) *(G-1420)*

J W Didado Electric Inc 330 374-0070
   1033 Kelly Ave Akron (44306) *(G-207)*

J W Geopfert Co Inc 330 762-2293
   1024 Home Ave Akron (44310) *(G-208)*

J-Mak Industries, Columbus *Also Called: Panacea Products Corporation (G-6497)*

J-Nan Enterprises Llc 330 653-3766
   5601 Darrow Rd Hudson (44236) *(G-9358)*

J-Trac Inc 419 524-3456
   961 N Main St Mansfield (44903) *(G-10274)*

J. Peterman, Blue Ash *Also Called: J Peterman Company LLC (G-1189)*

J.M.D. Architectural Products, Hilliard *Also Called: JMd Architectural Pdts Inc (G-9206)*

J.W. Didado Electric, Akron *Also Called: JW Didado Electric LLC (G-213)*

J&B Steel Contractors, West Chester *Also Called: J&B Steel Erectors Inc (G-14714)*

J&B Steel Erectors Inc 513 874-1722
   9430 Sutton Pl West Chester (45011) *(G-14714)*

J&H Rnfrcing Strl Erectors Inc 740 355-0141
   55 River Ave Portsmouth (45662) *(G-12558)*

Ja Htl LLC 330 467-1981
   240 Highland Rd E Macedonia (44056) *(G-10194)*

Jack Jseph Mrton Mndel Fndtio 216 875-6511
   1000 Lakeside Ave E Cleveland (44114) *(G-4428)*

Jack Black Staffing LLC 614 629-7614
   985 Linwood Ave Columbus (43206) *(G-6079)*

Jack Cleveland Casino LLC 216 297-4777
   100 Public Sq Cleveland (44113) *(G-4429)*

Jack Conie & Sons Corp 614 291-5931
   1340 Windsor Ave Columbus (43211) *(G-6080)*

Jack Cooper Transport Co Inc 440 949-2044
   5211 Oster Rd Sheffield Village (44054) *(G-13000)*

Jack Cooper Transport Company, Inc., Sheffield Village *Also Called: Jack Cooper Transport Co Inc (G-13000)*

Jack Entertainment, Cleveland *Also Called: Horseshoe Cleveland MGT LLC (G-4380)*

Jack Entertainment LLC (PA) 313 309-5225
   100 Public Sq Fl 3 Cleveland (44113) *(G-4430)*

Jack Gibson Construction Co 330 394-5280
   2460 Parkman Rd Nw Warren (44485) *(G-14530)*

Jack Gray 216 688-0466
   8044 Montgomery Rd Cincinnati (45236) *(G-2892)*

Jack Matia Honda, Elyria *Also Called: Matia Motors Inc (G-8273)*

Jack, The, Cincinnati *Also Called: Jack Gray (G-2892)*

Jackpot Pallets LLC 877 770-0005
   4770 Van Epps Rd Ste 107 Brooklyn Heights (44131) *(G-1421)*

Jackpot Pallets Wholesale, Brooklyn Heights *Also Called: Jackpot Pallets LLC (G-1421)*

Jacksn-Vinton Cmnty Action Inc (PA) 740 384-3722
   118 S New York Ave Wellston (45692) *(G-14638)*

Jackson & Sons Drilling & Pump 419 756-2758
   3401 State Route 13 Mansfield (44904) *(G-10275)*

Jackson Area YMCA, Jackson *Also Called: Young MNS Chrstn Assn Mtro Los (G-9530)*

Jackson Bluford and Son Inc (PA) 513 831-6231
   910 Us Route 50 Milford (45150) *(G-11234)*

Jackson Cnty Hlth Fclities Inc 740 384-0722
   142 Jenkins Memorial Rd Wellston (45692) *(G-14639)*

Jackson Comfort Htg Coolg Sys, Northfield *Also Called: Jackson Comfort Systems Inc (G-11959)*

Jackson Comfort Systems Inc 330 468-3111
   499 E Twinsburg Rd Northfield (44067) *(G-11959)*

Jackson Community YMCA, Massillon *Also Called: Young MNS Chrstn Assn Cntl STA (G-10675)*

Jackson Control Co Inc 513 824-9850
   2710 E Kemper Rd Cincinnati (45241) *(G-2893)*

Jackson Corporation 419 525-0170
   4135 Park Ave W Ontario (44903) *(G-12108)*

Jackson County Bd On Aging Inc (PA) 740 286-2909
   25 E Mound St Jackson (45640) *(G-9522)*

JACKSON COUNTY SENIOR CITIZENS, Jackson *Also Called: Jackson County Bd On Aging Inc (G-9522)*

Jackson Hewitt Tax Service, Trotwood *Also Called: E T Financial Service Inc (G-14127)*

Jackson I-94 Ltd Partnership 614 793-2244
   6059 Frantz Rd Ste 205 Dublin (43017) *(G-8042)*

Jackson International Inc 866 379-2009
   3714 Union St Mineral Ridge (44440) *(G-11302)*

JACKSON VINTON COMMUNITY ACTIO, Wellston *Also Called: Jacksn-Vinton Cmnty Action Inc (G-14638)*

Jaco Waterproofing LLC 513 738-0084
   4350 Wade Mill Rd Fairfield (45014) *(G-8421)*

Jacobs, Cincinnati *Also Called: Jacobs Mechanical Co (G-2895)*

Jacobs Engineering Group Inc 513 595-7500
   2 Crowne Point Ct Ste 100 Cincinnati (45241) *(G-2894)*

Jacobs Mechanical Co 513 681-6800
   4500 W Mitchell Ave Cincinnati (45232) *(G-2895)*

Jade-Sterling Steel Co Inc (PA) 330 425-3141
   26400 Richmond Rd Bedford (44146) *(G-968)*

Jag Guru Inc 614 552-2400
   2093 S Hamilton Rd Columbus (43232) *(G-6081)*

Jag Healthcare Inc 440 385-4370
   220 Buckingham Rd Rocky River (44116) *(G-12744)*

Jagi Clvland - Indpendence LLC 216 524-8050
   6001 Rockside Rd Cleveland (44131) *(G-4431)*

Jagi Springhill LLC 216 264-4190
  6060 Rockside Pl Independence (44131) *(G-9438)*

Jaguar Volvo, Canton Also Called: *Kempthorn Motors Inc (G-1790)*

Jai Bapa Swami LLC 513 791-2822
  4761 Creek Rd Blue Ash (45242) *(G-1190)*

Jai Guru II Inc 614 920-2400
  3045 Olentangy River Rd Columbus (43202) *(G-6082)*

Jake Sweeney Automotive Inc 513 782-2800
  33 W Kemper Rd Cincinnati (45246) *(G-2896)*

Jake Sweeney Body Shop 513 782-1100
  169 Northland Blvd Ste 1 Cincinnati (45246) *(G-2897)*

Jake Sweeney Chevrolet Imports, Cincinnati Also Called: *Jake Sweeney Body Shop (G-2897)*

James Bower Home, Cincinnati Also Called: *Toward Independence Inc (G-3487)*

James Center 614 410-5615
  2050 Kenny Rd Columbus (43221) *(G-6083)*

James Dickman & Jillyn Bruner, Coldwater Also Called: *Dickman Kettler & Bruner Ltd (G-5212)*

James Hunt Construction Co Inc 513 721-0559
  1865 Summit Rd Cincinnati (45237) *(G-2898)*

James Mc Lean MD, Port Clinton Also Called: *H B Magruder Memorial Hosp (G-12532)*

Jamesway Chick Mstr Incubator, Medina Also Called: *Chick Master Incubator Company (G-10819)*

Jamison Cnstr Solutions Inc 513 377-0705
  96 Arndt Ct Fairfield (45014) *(G-8422)*

Janat Clemmons Center, Hamilton Also Called: *Butler Cnty Bd Dvlpmntal Dsblt (G-9022)*

Jance & Company Incorporated 440 255-5800
  8666 Tyler Blvd Mentor (44060) *(G-10954)*

Jancoa Janitorial Services Inc 513 351-7200
  525 Vine St Ste 1600 Cincinnati (45202) *(G-2899)*

Janessa Inc 740 687-4823
  1327 River Valley Blvd Lancaster (43130) *(G-9726)*

Jani-Source Inc 740 374-6298
  478 Bramblewood Heights Rd Marietta (45750) *(G-10376)*

Janik LLP (PA) 440 838-7600
  9200 S Hills Blvd Ste 300 Cleveland (44147) *(G-4432)*

Janitorial Manager, Toledo Also Called: *Double A Solutions LLC (G-13783)*

Janitorial Services Inc 216 341-8601
  4830 E 49th St Cleveland (44125) *(G-4433)*

Janotta & Herner, Monroeville Also Called: *Jhi Group Inc (G-11356)*

Janson Industries 330 455-7029
  1200 Garfield Ave Sw Canton (44706) *(G-1783)*

Jantech Building Services Inc 216 661-6102
  4963 Schaaf Ln Brooklyn Heights (44131) *(G-1422)*

Jao Distributors Inc 513 531-6000
  10310 Julian Dr Cincinnati (45215) *(G-2900)*

Japo Inc 614 263-2850
  3902 Indianola Ave Columbus (43214) *(G-6084)*

Jaro Transportation Svcs Inc (PA) 330 393-5659
  975 Post Rd Nw Warren (44483) *(G-14531)*

Jarrett Companies Inc 330 682-0099
  1781 N Main St Orrville (44667) *(G-12167)*

Jarrett Logistics Systems Inc 330 682-0099
  1347 N Main St Orrville (44667) *(G-12168)*

Jarrett Warehousing, Orrville Also Called: *Jarrett Companies Inc (G-12167)*

Jasar Recycling Inc 864 233-5421
  183 Edgeworth Ave East Palestine (44413) *(G-8196)*

Jatiga Inc (PA) 859 817-7100
  9933 Alliance Rd Ste 1 Blue Ash (45242) *(G-1191)*

Javitch Block LLC 513 381-3051
  700 Walnut St Ste 300 Cincinnati (45202) *(G-2901)*

Javitch Block LLC (PA) 216 623-0000
  1100 Superior Ave E Cleveland (44114) *(G-4434)*

Jaxon, Mineral Ridge Also Called: *Jackson International Inc (G-11302)*

Jay Ganesh LLC 740 344-2136
  1219 W Church St Newark (43055) *(G-11710)*

Jay Hash LLC 740 353-4673
  800 Gallia St Ste 600 Portsmouth (45662) *(G-12559)*

Jay-Mac, Canton Also Called: *Young Truck Sales Inc (G-1891)*

JB Dollar Stretcher 614 436-2800
  1653 Merriman Rd Ste 203 Akron (44313) *(G-209)*

JB Roofing A Tecta Amer Co LLC 419 447-1716
  1480 S County Road 594 Tiffin (44883) *(G-13630)*

Jbentley Studio & Spa LLC 614 790-8828
  8882 Moreland St Powell (43065) *(G-12593)*

JBK Group Inc (PA) 216 901-0000
  6001 Towpath Dr Cleveland (44125) *(G-4435)*

Jbm Packaging, Lebanon Also Called: *Jbm Packaging Company (G-9770)*

Jbm Packaging Company 513 933-8333
  2850 Henkle Dr Lebanon (45036) *(G-9770)*

JC Penney, Columbus Also Called: *Penney Opco LLC (G-6513)*

JC Penney, Saint Marys Also Called: *JC Penney Corporation Inc (G-12827)*

JC Penney Corporation Inc 419 394-7610
  1170 Indiana Ave Saint Marys (45885) *(G-12827)*

Jc's 5 Star Outlet, Columbus Also Called: *Sb Capital Acquisitions LLC (G-6647)*

JCC, Sylvania Also Called: *Jewish Cmnty Ctr of Toledo (G-13554)*

Jcherie LLC 216 453-1051
  3645 Norwood Rd Shaker Heights (44122) *(G-12979)*

Jck Recycling LLC 419 698-1153
  3090 W Market St Fairlawn (44333) *(G-8487)*

JD Equipment Inc 614 879-6620
  1660 Us Highway 42 Ne London (43140) *(G-10044)*

JD Music Tile Co 740 420-9611
  105 E Ohio St Circleville (43113) *(G-3711)*

Jdd Inc (PA) 216 464-8855
  17800 Chillicothe Rd Ste 250a Chagrin Falls (44023) *(G-1982)*

Jdi Group Inc 419 725-7161
  360 W Dussel Dr Maumee (43537) *(G-10733)*

Jdrm Engineering Inc 419 824-2400
  5604 Main St Ste 200 Sylvania (43560) *(G-13553)*

JE Carsten Company (PA) 330 794-4440
  7481 Herrick Park Dr Hudson (44236) *(G-9359)*

Jeanne B McCoy Cmnty Ctr For A 614 469-0939
  39 E State St Columbus (43215) *(G-6085)*

Jeannie Hughes, Westerville Also Called: *Westerville Family Physicians (G-14952)*

Jedson Engineering Inc (PA) 513 965-5999
  705 Central Ave Cincinnati (45202) *(G-2902)*

Jeffers Crane Service Inc 419 223-9010
  1119 S Metcalf St Lima (45804) *(G-9912)*

Jefferson Behavioral Hlth Sys 740 535-1314
  220 Murdock St Mingo Junction (43938) *(G-11313)*

Jefferson Cnty Cmnty Action CN (PA) 740 282-0971
  114 N 4th St Steubenville (43952) *(G-13332)*

Jefferson Golf & Country Club 614 759-7500
  7271 Jefferson Meadows Dr Blacklick (43004) *(G-1112)*

Jefferson Rehab & Wellness LLC 440 576-0043
  6752 Twitchell Rd Andover (44003) *(G-439)*

Jeg's High-Performance Center, Delaware Also Called: *Jegs Automotive LLC (G-7808)*

Jegs Automotive Inc 614 294-5451
  752 Bonham Ave Columbus (43211) *(G-6086)*

Jegs Automotive LLC (HQ) 614 294-5050
  101 Jegs Pl Delaware (43015) *(G-7808)*

Jeld-Wen Inc 513 874-6771
  400 Circle Freeway Dr West Chester (45246) *(G-14821)*

Jelly Bean Junction Lrng Ctr, Dublin Also Called: *Consolidated Learning Ctrs Inc (G-7972)*

JENKINS MEMORIAL HEALTH FACILI, Wellston Also Called: *Jackson Cnty Hlth Fclities Inc (G-14639)*

Jenne, Avon Also Called: *Jenne Inc (G-656)*

Jenne Inc 440 835-0040
  33665 Chester Rd Avon (44011) *(G-656)*

Jennings Eliza Home Inc (HQ) 216 226-0282
  10603 Detroit Ave Cleveland (44102) *(G-4436)*

Jennings Assisted Living 216 581-2900
  10204 Granger Rd Garfield Heights (44125) *(G-8775)*

Jennings Heating & Cooling, Akron Also Called: *Jennings Heating Company Inc (G-210)*

Jennings Heating Company Inc 330 784-1286
  2279 Romig Rd Akron (44320) *(G-210)*

Jennite Co 419 531-1791
  4694 W Bancroft St Toledo (43615) *(G-13866)*

Jergens Inc (PA) 216 486-5540
  15700 S Waterloo Rd Cleveland (44110) *(G-4437)*

ALPHABETIC SECTION — John Deere Authorized Dealer

Jerl Machine Inc 419 873-0270
   11140 Avenue Rd Perrysburg (43551) *(G-12348)*

Jerry Haag Motors Inc 937 402-2090
   1475 N High St Hillsboro (45133) *(G-9261)*

Jersey Central Pwr & Light Co (HQ) 800 736-3402
   76 S Main St Akron (44308) *(G-211)*

Jersey Central Pwr & Light Co 740 537-6391
   29503 State Route 7 Stratton (43961) *(G-13407)*

Jess Hauer Masonry Inc 513 521-2178
   2400 W Kemper Rd Cincinnati (45231) *(G-2903)*

Jess Howard Electric Company 614 864-2167
   6630 Taylor Rd Blacklick (43004) *(G-1113)*

Jet East Inc 215 937-9020
   32405 Aurora Rd Solon (44139) *(G-13102)*

Jet Machine & Manufacturing, Cincinnati *Also Called: Wulco Inc (G-3682)*

Jet Rubber Company 330 325-1821
   4457 Tallmadge Rd Rootstown (44272) *(G-12760)*

Jetselect LLC 954 648-0998
   4130 E 5th Ave Columbus (43219) *(G-6087)*

Jetson Engineering 513 965-5999
   705 Central Ave Cincinnati (45202) *(G-2904)*

Jewish Cmnty Ctr of Cincinnati 513 761-7500
   8485 Ridge Rd Cincinnati (45236) *(G-2905)*

Jewish Cmnty Ctr of Grter Clmb (PA) 614 231-2731
   1125 College Ave Columbus (43209) *(G-6088)*

Jewish Cmnty Ctr of Toledo 419 885-4485
   6465 Sylvania Ave Sylvania (43560) *(G-13554)*

JEWISH COMMUNITY CARE AT HOME, Beachwood *Also Called: Jewish Fmly Svc Assn Clvland O (G-804)*

Jewish Day Schl Assn Grter Clv (PA) 216 763-1400
   27601 Fairmount Blvd Pepper Pike (44124) *(G-12300)*

Jewish Edcatn Ctr of Cleveland 216 371-0446
   2030 S Taylor Rd Cleveland Heights (44118) *(G-5180)*

Jewish Family Service 614 231-1890
   1070 College Ave Ste A Columbus (43209) *(G-6089)*

Jewish Fdrtion Grter Dyton Inc 937 830-7904
   525 Versailles Dr Dayton (45459) *(G-7427)*

Jewish Fdrtion Grter Dyton Inc 937 837-2651
   4911 Covenant House Dr Dayton (45426) *(G-7428)*

Jewish Fmly Svc Assn Clvland O (PA) 216 292-3999
   29125 Chagrin Blvd Beachwood (44122) *(G-804)*

Jewish Fmly Svc Assn Clvland O 216 292-3999
   29125 Chagrin Blvd Beachwood (44122) *(G-805)*

Jewish Fmly Svc of Cncnnati AR 513 469-1188
   8487 Ridge Rd Cincinnati (45236) *(G-2906)*

Jewish Home Cincinnati Inc 513 754-3100
   5467 Cedar Village Dr Mason (45040) *(G-10569)*

Jewish Hospital 513 569-2434
   3200 Burnet Ave Fl 5 Cincinnati (45229) *(G-2907)*

Jewish Hospital LLC 513 686-5970
   4777 E Galbraith Rd Cincinnati (45236) *(G-2908)*

Jewish Hospital LLC 513 585-2668
   5310 Rapid Run Rd Cincinnati (45238) *(G-2909)*

Jewish Hospital LLC (PA) 513 686-3000
   4777 E Galbraith Rd Cincinnati (45236) *(G-2910)*

Jewish Hospital LLC 513 988-6067
   841 W State St Trenton (45067) *(G-14123)*

Jewish Hospital Cincinnati Inc 513 686-3303
   4777 E Galbraith Rd Cincinnati (45236) *(G-2911)*

Jfdb Ltd 513 870-0601
   10036 Springfield Pike Cincinnati (45215) *(G-2912)*

Jh Instruments, Columbus *Also Called: Fcx Performance Inc (G-5853)*

Jhi Group Inc (PA) 419 465-4611
   309 Monroe St Monroeville (44847) *(G-11356)*

Jiffy Lube, Columbus *Also Called: Team Lubrication Inc (G-6751)*

Jiffy Products America Inc 440 282-2818
   5401 Baumhart Rd Ste B Lorain (44053) *(G-10078)*

Jifiticom Inc (PA) 914 339-5376
   1985 Henderson Rd Pmb 63255 Columbus (43220) *(G-6090)*

Jilco Industries Inc (PA) 330 698-0280
   11234 Hackett Rd Kidron (44636) *(G-9636)*

Jim Brown Chevrolet Inc (PA) 440 255-5511
   6877 Center St Mentor (44060) *(G-10955)*

Jim Keim Ford 614 888-3333
   5575 Keim Cir Columbus (43228) *(G-6091)*

Jims Electric Inc 440 327-8800
   39221 Center Ridge Rd North Ridgeville (44039) *(G-11930)*

Jlt Packaging Cincinnati Inc (PA) 513 933-0250
   1550 Kingsview Dr Lebanon (45036) *(G-9771)*

JJ&pl Services-Consulting LLC 330 923-5783
   1474 Main St Cuyahoga Falls (44221) *(G-7082)*

JJO Construction Inc 216 347-7802
   30047 Regent Rd Wickliffe (44092) *(G-15155)*

Jjr Solutions, Dayton *Also Called: Jjr Solutions LLC (G-7429)*

Jjr Solutions LLC 937 912-0288
   607 E 3rd St Ste 400 Dayton (45402) *(G-7429)*

Jk Services 419 843-2608
   7868 W Central Ave Toledo (43617) *(G-13867)*

Jk-Co LLC 419 422-5240
   16960 E State Route 12 Findlay (45840) *(G-8552)*

JKL Development Company (PA) 937 390-0358
   2101 E Home Rd Springfield (45503) *(G-13261)*

Jkrg Construction Services, West Chester *Also Called: Clarity Retail Services LLC (G-14668)*

JLJI Enterprises Inc 216 481-2175
   21711 Tungsten Rd Euclid (44117) *(G-8351)*

JLW - TW Corp 440 937-7775
   35350 Chester Rd Avon (44011) *(G-657)*

JM Smucker LLC (HQ) 330 682-3000
   1 Strawberry Ln Orrville (44667) *(G-12169)*

Jma Healthcare LLC 440 439-7976
   24579 Broadway Ave Cleveland (44146) *(G-4438)*

Jmac Inc (PA) 614 436-2418
   200 W Nationwide Blvd Unit 1 Columbus (43215) *(G-6092)*

JMd Architectural Pdts Inc 614 527-0306
   2240 Venus Dr Hilliard (43026) *(G-9206)*

Jml Holdings Inc 419 866-7500
   6210 Merger Dr Holland (43528) *(G-9291)*

Jmo & Dsl Llc 216 785-9375
   13702 Detroit Ave Lakewood (44107) *(G-9670)*

JMS Express Inc 855 267-4242
   5055 Duff Dr # 2 West Chester (45246) *(G-14822)*

Jmt Cartage Inc 330 478-2430
   1712 N Park Ave Nw Canton (44708) *(G-1784)*

JMw Welding and Mfg Inc 330 484-2428
   512 45th St Sw Canton (44706) *(G-1785)*

Jo-Ann Stores LLC 419 621-8101
   756 Crossings Rd Sandusky (44870) *(G-12906)*

Jo-Lin Health Center Inc 740 532-0860
   1050 Clinton St Ironton (45638) *(G-9510)*

Joann Stores, Sandusky *Also Called: Jo-Ann Stores LLC (G-12906)*

Job Service of Ohio, Akron *Also Called: Ohio Dept Job & Fmly Svcs (G-248)*

Job1usa, Toledo *Also Called: Rumpf Corporation (G-13999)*

Job1usa Inc (HQ) 419 255-5005
   701 Jefferson Ave Ste 202 Toledo (43604) *(G-13868)*

Jobbers Automotive LLC 216 524-2229
   34600 Lakeland Blvd Eastlake (44095) *(G-8203)*

Jobs On Site, Mansfield *Also Called: Edge Plastics Inc (G-10260)*

Jobsohio 614 224-6446
   41 S High St Ste 1500 Columbus (43215) *(G-6093)*

Joe Dickey Electric Inc 330 549-3976
   180 W South Range Rd North Lima (44452) *(G-11889)*

Joe Knows Energy LLC 614 989-2228
   5880 Venture Dr Ste D Dublin (43017) *(G-8043)*

Joe's Landscaping, Beavercreek Township *Also Called: Joes Ldscpg Beavercreek Inc (G-942)*

Joes Ldscpg Beavercreek Inc 937 427-1133
   2500 National Rd Beavercreek Township (45324) *(G-942)*

John A Hudec DDS Inc 216 398-8900
   3329 Broadview Rd Cleveland (44109) *(G-4439)*

John Deere Authorized Dealer, Coldwater *Also Called: Lefeld Implement Inc (G-5215)*

John Deere Authorized Dealer, East Palestine *Also Called: Elder Sales & Service Inc (G-8195)*

John Deere Authorized Dealer   **ALPHABETIC SECTION**

John Deere Authorized Dealer, Edgerton *Also Called: Liechty Inc* *(G-8228)*
John Deere Authorized Dealer, Lancaster *Also Called: Ag-Pro Ohio LLC* *(G-9691)*
John Deere Authorized Dealer, London *Also Called: JD Equipment Inc* *(G-10044)*
John Deere Authorized Dealer, Marietta *Also Called: Leslie Equipment Co* *(G-10380)*
John Deere Authorized Dealer, Mentor *Also Called: Great Lakes Power Products Inc* *(G-10943)*
John Deere Authorized Dealer, Saint Clairsville *Also Called: Western Branch Diesel LLC* *(G-12820)*
John Deere Authorized Dealer, Wilmington *Also Called: Ag-Pro Ohio LLC* *(G-15238)*
John Deere Authorized Dealer, Wooster *Also Called: Shearer Farm Inc* *(G-15376)*
John Deere Authorized Dealer, Zanesville *Also Called: Ag-Pro Ohio LLC* *(G-15765)*
John E Brunner MD 419 537-5111
   3140 W Central Ave Toledo (43606) *(G-13869)*
John Eramo & Sons Inc 614 777-0020
   3670 Lacon Rd Hilliard (43026) *(G-9207)*
John F Gallagher Plumbing Co 440 946-4256
   36360 Lakeland Blvd Eastlake (44095) *(G-8204)*
John Frankel DDS, Toledo *Also Called: Frankel Dental* *(G-13812)*
John G Johnson Construction Co 216 938-5050
   1284 Riverbed St Cleveland (44113) *(G-4440)*
John H Kappus Co (PA) 216 367-6677
   4755 W 150th St Cleveland (44135) *(G-4441)*
John Hudec DDS & Associates, Cleveland *Also Called: John A Hudec DDS Inc* *(G-4439)*
John R Jurgensen Co (PA) 513 771-0820
   11641 Mosteller Rd Cincinnati (45241) *(G-2913)*
John Rbrts Hair Studio Spa Inc (PA) 216 839-1430
   6727 Eastgate Dr Mayfield Heights (44124) *(G-10787)*
JOHN S KNIGHT CENTER, Akron *Also Called: Akron-Smmit Cnvntion Vstors Bu* *(G-42)*
John Stewart Company 513 703-5412
   6819 Montgomery Rd Cincinnati (45236) *(G-2914)*
John Zidian Co Inc (HQ) 330 743-6050
   574 Mcclurg Rd Youngstown (44512) *(G-15642)*
Johnny Appleseed Brdcstg Co 419 529-5900
   2900 Park Ave W Ontario (44906) *(G-12109)*
Johnson & Fischer Incorporated 614 276-8868
   5303 Trabue Rd Columbus (43228) *(G-6094)*
Johnson Bros Greenwich, Greenwich *Also Called: Johnson Bros Rubber Co Inc* *(G-8892)*
Johnson Bros Rubber Co (PA) 419 853-4122
   42 W Buckeye St West Salem (44287) *(G-14863)*
Johnson Bros Rubber Co Inc 419 752-4814
   41 Center St Greenwich (44837) *(G-8892)*
Johnson Cntrls SEC Sltions LLC 330 497-0850
   5590 Lauby Rd Ste 6 Canton (44720) *(G-1786)*
Johnson Cntrls SEC Sltions LLC 513 277-4966
   4750 Wesley Ave Ste Q Cincinnati (45212) *(G-2915)*
Johnson Cntrls SEC Sltions LLC 419 243-8400
   1722 Indian Wood Cir Ste F Maumee (43537) *(G-10734)*
Johnson Contrls Authorized Dlr, Akron *Also Called: Famous Distribution Inc* *(G-155)*
Johnson Contrls Authorized Dlr, Akron *Also Called: Famous Industries Inc* *(G-157)*
Johnson Contrls Authorized Dlr, Canton *Also Called: Morrow Control and Supply Inc* *(G-1810)*
Johnson Contrls Authorized Dlr, Cincinnati *Also Called: Habegger Corporation* *(G-2788)*
Johnson Contrls Authorized Dlr, Dayton *Also Called: Allied Supply Company Inc* *(G-7164)*
Johnson Contrls Authorized Dlr, Northwood *Also Called: Yanfeng US Auto Intr Systems I* *(G-11988)*
Johnson Contrls Authorized Dlr, Steubenville *Also Called: Famous Distribution Inc* *(G-13323)*
Johnson Electric Supply Co (PA) 513 421-3700
   1841 Riverside Dr Cincinnati (45202) *(G-2916)*
Johnson Institutional MGT, Cincinnati *Also Called: Johnson Trust Company* *(G-2918)*
Johnson Investment Counsel Inc (PA) 800 541-0170
   3777 W Fork Rd Cincinnati (45247) *(G-2917)*
Johnson Restoration LLC 937 907-5056
   9411 Oak Brook Dr Dayton (45458) *(G-7430)*
Johnson Rose LLC 440 785-9892
   27997 Terrace Dr North Olmsted (44070) *(G-11907)*
Johnson Trust Company 513 598-8859
   3777 W Fork Rd Fl 2 Cincinnati (45247) *(G-2918)*
Johnsons Real Ice Cream LLC 614 231-0014
   2728 E Main St Columbus (43209) *(G-6095)*

Johnstone Supply, Columbus *Also Called: G D Supply Inc* *(G-5904)*
Joint Development & Hsing Corp 513 381-8696
   1055 Saint Paul Pl Cincinnati (45202) *(G-2919)*
Joint Implant Surgeons, Martins Ferry *Also Called: East Ohio Hospital LLC* *(G-10467)*
Joint Implant Surgeons Inc 614 221-6331
   7727 Smiths Mill Rd 200 New Albany (43054) *(G-11570)*
Joint Implant Surgeons Inc A 740 566-4640
   20 University Estates Blvd Unit 100 Athens (45701) *(G-578)*
Joint Township Dst Mem Hosp 419 394-3335
   200 Saint Clair Ave Saint Marys (45885) *(G-12828)*
Joint Township Dst Mem Hosp (PA) 419 394-3335
   200 Saint Clair Ave Saint Marys (45885) *(G-12829)*
Joint Township Dst Mem Hosp 419 394-9959
   1140 S Knoxville Ave # A Saint Marys (45885) *(G-12830)*
Joint Township Home Health 419 394-3335
   1122 E Spring St Saint Marys (45885) *(G-12831)*
Jones & Henry Engineers Ltd (PA) 419 473-9611
   3103 Executive Pkwy Ste 300 Toledo (43606) *(G-13870)*
Jones Cochenour & Co Inc (PA) 740 653-9581
   125 W Mulberry St Lancaster (43130) *(G-9727)*
Jones Day, Cleveland *Also Called: Jones Day Limited Partnership* *(G-4442)*
Jones Day Limited Partnership (PA) 216 586-3939
   901 Lakeside Ave E Cleveland (44114) *(G-4442)*
Jones Day Limited Partnership 614 469-3939
   325 John H Mcconnell Blvd Ste 600 Columbus (43215) *(G-6096)*
Jones Metal Products Company 740 545-6341
   305 N Center St West Lafayette (43845) *(G-14857)*
Jones Potato Chip Co (PA) 419 529-9424
   823 Bowman St Mansfield (44903) *(G-10276)*
Jones Truck & Spring Repr Inc 614 443-4619
   350 Frank Rd Columbus (43207) *(G-6097)*
Jonle Co Inc 513 662-2282
   4117 Bridgetown Rd Cincinnati (45211) *(G-2920)*
Jonle Heating & Cooling, Cincinnati *Also Called: Jonle Co Inc* *(G-2920)*
Jordan Hospitality Group LLC 614 406-5139
   6891 Jersey Dr New Albany (43054) *(G-11571)*
Joseph Industries Inc 330 528-0091
   10039 Aurora Hudson Rd Streetsboro (44241) *(G-13419)*
Joseph, Mann & Creed, Twinsburg *Also Called: Media Collections Inc* *(G-14204)*
Joshua M Halderman DDS LLC 614 309-1474
   1101 Norton Rd Galloway (43119) *(G-8772)*
Joshua Tree Care Center, North Olmsted *Also Called: Olmsted Manor Ltd* *(G-11910)*
Josina Lott Foundation 419 866-9013
   120 S Holland Sylvania Rd Toledo (43615) *(G-13871)*
JOSINA LOTT RESIDENTIAL HOME, Toledo *Also Called: Josina Lott Foundation* *(G-13871)*
Jostin, Cincinnati *Also Called: Jostin Construction Inc* *(G-2921)*
Jostin Construction Inc 513 559-9390
   2335 Florence Ave Cincinnati (45206) *(G-2921)*
Joy Outdoor Education Ctr LLC 937 289-2031
   10117 Old 3 C Clarksville (45113) *(G-3730)*
Joyce Buick Inc 419 529-3211
   1400 Park Ave W Ontario (44906) *(G-12110)*
Joyce Buick GMC of Mansfield, Ontario *Also Called: Joyce Buick Inc* *(G-12110)*
JP Compass, Chesterland *Also Called: JP Compass Cnsulting Cnstr Inc* *(G-2037)*
JP Compass Cnsulting Cnstr Inc 440 635-0500
   7948 Mayfield Rd Chesterland (44026) *(G-2037)*
JP Flooring Systems Inc 513 346-4300
   9097 Union Centre Blvd West Chester (45069) *(G-14715)*
JP Morgan Partners LLC 800 848-9136
   61 N Sandusky St Delaware (43015) *(G-7809)*
JP Outfitters LLC 513 745-1137
   5345 Creek Rd Blue Ash (45242) *(G-1192)*
JP Recovery Services Inc 440 331-2200
   20220 Center Ridge Rd Ste 200 Rocky River (44116) *(G-12745)*
Jpmorgan Chase & Co 614 248-5800
   1000 Polaris Pkwy Columbus (43240) *(G-5263)*
Jpmorgan Chase Bank Nat Assn (HQ) 614 436-3055
   1111 Polaris Pkwy Columbus (43240) *(G-5264)*
Jpmorgan Chase Bank Nat Assn 212 270-6000
   3415 Vision Dr Columbus (43219) *(G-6098)*

ALPHABETIC SECTION — Kaiser Foundation Hospitals

Jpmorgan Chase Bank Nat Assn.. 740 363-8032
  61 N Sandusky St Delaware (43015) *(G-7810)*

Jpmorgan Inv Advisors Inc (HQ).. 614 248-5800
  1111 Polaris Pkwy Columbus (43240) *(G-5265)*

JS Bova Excavating LLC... 234 254-4040
  235 State St Struthers (44471) *(G-13501)*

JS Paris Excavating Inc.. 330 538-9876
  185 Industrial Rd Youngstown (44509) *(G-15643)*

Jsc Employee Leasing Corp (PA).. 330 773-8971
  1560 Firestone Pkwy Akron (44301) *(G-212)*

JSW Steel USA Ohio Inc.. 740 535-8172
  1500 Commercial St Mingo Junction (43938) *(G-11314)*

Jsw USA, Mingo Junction *Also Called: JSW Steel USA Ohio Inc (G-11314)*

Jtc Contracting Inc.. 216 635-0745
  7635 Hub Pkwy Ste C Cleveland (44125) *(G-4443)*

Jtc Office Services, Cleveland *Also Called: Jtc Contracting Inc (G-4443)*

Jtd Health Systems Inc.. 419 394-3335
  200 Saint Clair Ave Saint Marys (45885) *(G-12832)*

Jtf Construction Inc.. 513 860-9835
  4235 Mulhauser Rd Fairfield (45014) *(G-8423)*

Jto Club Corp... 440 352-1900
  6011 Heisley Rd Mentor (44060) *(G-10956)*

Jubilee Limited Partnership... 614 221-9200
  4300 E 5th Ave Columbus (43219) *(G-6099)*

Judge Group Inc... 614 891-8337
  440 Polaris Pkwy Ste 290 Westerville (43082) *(G-14901)*

Judson (PA).. 216 791-2004
  2181 Ambleside Dr Apt 411 Cleveland (44106) *(G-4444)*

Judson.. 216 791-2555
  1890 E 107th St Cleveland (44106) *(G-4445)*

Judson Care Center Inc... 513 662-5880
  2386 Kemper Ln Cincinnati (45206) *(G-2922)*

Judson Manor, Cleveland *Also Called: Judson (G-4445)*

Judson Services Inc.. 216 791-2004
  16600 Warren Ct Chagrin Falls (44023) *(G-1983)*

JUDSON UNIVERSITY CIRCLE, Cleveland *Also Called: Judson (G-4444)*

Juice Technologies Inc... 800 518-5576
  640 Lakeview Plaza Blvd Ste J Worthington (43085) *(G-15424)*

Julian & Grube Inc.. 614 846-1899
  333 County Line Rd W Ste A Westerville (43082) *(G-14902)*

Julian Speer Co.. 614 261-6331
  5255 Sinclair Rd Columbus (43229) *(G-6100)*

Julius Zorn Inc.. 330 923-4999
  3690 Zorn Dr Cuyahoga Falls (44223) *(G-7083)*

Jumbo Logistics LLC... 216 662-5420
  1229 Deepwood Dr Macedonia (44056) *(G-10195)*

Jumporg LLC.. 216 250-4678
  12709 Watterson Ave Cleveland (44105) *(G-4446)*

Junction Tavern Inc.. 330 477-4694
  2925 Westdale Rd Nw Canton (44708) *(G-1787)*

Junior Coop Soc Chldren S Hosp... 513 636-4310
  3333 Burnet Ave Cincinnati (45229) *(G-2923)*

Just Candy LLC... 201 805-8562
  6820 Fairfield Business Ctr Dr Fairfield (45014) *(G-8424)*

Just Cheking Cash, Fairfield *Also Called: Southern Glzers Wine Sprits TX (G-8442)*

Just In Time Staffing Inc... 440 205-2002
  8130 Tyler Blvd Mentor (44060) *(G-10957)*

Justin Center, North Olmsted *Also Called: Cleveland Clnic Hlth Systm-Wst (G-11898)*

Justin Doyle Homes... 513 623-1418
  5378a Cox Smith Rd Mason (45040) *(G-10570)*

Juvly Aesthetic LLC.. 800 254-0188
  40 W Gay St Columbus (43215) *(G-6101)*

Juzo USA, Cuyahoga Falls *Also Called: Julius Zorn Inc (G-7083)*

JW Didado Electric LLC... 330 374-0070
  1033 Kelly Ave Akron (44306) *(G-213)*

Jwj Investments Inc... 419 643-3161
  800 Ambrose Dr Delphos (45833) *(G-7841)*

JWT Action (DH).. 330 376-6148
  388 S Main St Ste 410 Akron (44311) *(G-214)*

JWT Action... 513 578-6721
  35 E 7th St Ste 620 Cincinnati (45202) *(G-2924)*

JWT Action, Akron *Also Called: JWT Action (G-214)*

Jyg Innovations LLC... 937 630-3858
  6450 Poe Ave Ste 103 Dayton (45414) *(G-7431)*

K & K Interiors Inc (PA).. 419 627-0039
  2230 Superior St Sandusky (44870) *(G-12907)*

K & M Construction Company.. 330 723-3681
  230 E Smith Rd Medina (44256) *(G-10849)*

K & M International Inc (PA).. 330 425-2550
  7711 E Pleasant Valley Rd Independence (44131) *(G-9439)*

K & M Newspaper Services Inc.. 845 782-3817
  827 Walnut St Elyria (44035) *(G-8264)*

K A Bergquist Inc (PA).. 419 865-4196
  1100 King Rd Toledo (43617) *(G-13872)*

K A P C O, Kent *Also Called: Kent Adhesive Products Co (G-9583)*

K Amalia Enterprises Inc... 614 733-3800
  8025 Corporate Blvd Plain City (43064) *(G-12483)*

K C P, Beachwood *Also Called: Kirtland Capital Partners LP (G-806)*

K Company Incorporated... 330 773-5125
  2234 S Arlington Rd Coventry Township (44319) *(G-7012)*

K F T Inc.. 513 241-5910
  726 Mehring Way Cincinnati (45203) *(G-2925)*

K Hovnanian Summit Homes LLC (HQ)..................................... 330 454-4048
  2000 10th St Ne Canton (44705) *(G-1788)*

K Kern Painting LLC... 419 966-0812
  211 N Reynolds Rd Ste A Toledo (43615) *(G-13873)*

K O I, Cincinnati *Also Called: KOI Enterprises Inc (G-2948)*

K R Drenth Trucking Inc... 708 983-6340
  119 E Court St Cincinnati (45202) *(G-2926)*

K-Limited Carrier Ltd (HQ)... 419 269-0002
  131 Matzinger Rd Toledo (43612) *(G-13874)*

K&D Management LLC... 216 624-4686
  1701 E 12th St Ste 35 Cleveland (44114) *(G-4447)*

K&D Management LLC (PA)... 440 946-3600
  4420 Sherwin Rd Ste 1 Willoughby (44094) *(G-15195)*

K&K Painting Company, Inc., Youngstown *Also Called: North Star Painting Co Inc (G-15678)*

K&K Technical Group Inc.. 513 202-1300
  3554 Blue Rock Rd Cincinnati (45239) *(G-2927)*

K&R Network Solutions.. 858 292-5766
  5747 Perimeter Dr Dublin (43017) *(G-8044)*

K4 Architecture LLC... 513 455-5005
  555 Gest St Cincinnati (45203) *(G-2928)*

Ka Architecture, Seven Hills *Also Called: Nelson (G-12955)*

Ka Wanner Inc... 740 251-4636
  370 W Fairground St Marion (43302) *(G-10432)*

Kable News Company Inc (HQ).. 815 734-4151
  4275 Thunderbird Ln West Chester (45014) *(G-14716)*

Kademenos Wisehart Hines (PA).. 419 524-6011
  6 W 3rd St Ste 200 Mansfield (44902) *(G-10277)*

Kademnos Wshart Hnes Dlyk Zher... 440 967-6136
  1513 State Rd Vermilion (44089) *(G-14406)*

Kaeser and Blair Incorporated (PA)... 513 732-6400
  4236 Grissom Dr Batavia (45103) *(G-742)*

Kaffenbarger Truck Eqp Co (PA)... 937 845-3804
  10100 Ballentine Pike New Carlisle (45344) *(G-11602)*

Kag Specialty Products Group LLC (HQ).................................... 330 409-1124
  4366 Mount Pleasant St Nw North Canton (44720) *(G-11841)*

Kaiser Consulting LLC.. 614 378-5361
  818 Riverbend Ave Powell (43065) *(G-12594)*

Kaiser Foundation Health Plan, Cleveland *Also Called: Bon Secours Mercy Health Inc (G-3880)*

Kaiser Foundation Hospitals... 216 524-7377
  36711 American Way Avon (44011) *(G-658)*

Kaiser Foundation Hospitals... 216 524-7377
  5400 Lancaster Dr Brooklyn Heights (44131) *(G-1423)*

Kaiser Foundation Hospitals... 800 524-7377
  5400 Lancaster Dr Brooklyn Heights (44131) *(G-1424)*

Kaiser Foundation Hospitals... 800 524-7377
  4055 Embassy Pkwy Ste 110 Fairlawn (44333) *(G-8488)*

Kaiser Foundation Hospitals... 800 524-7377
  2500 State Route 59 Kent (44240) *(G-9582)*

Kaiser Foundation Hospitals... 800 524-7377
  3443 Medina Rd Medina (44256) *(G-10850)*

Kaiser Foundation Hospitals 800 524-7377
  7695 Mentor Ave Mentor (44060) *(G-10958)*
Kaiser Foundation Hospitals 800 524-7377
  4914 Portage St Nw North Canton (44720) *(G-11842)*
Kaiser Foundation Hospitals 216 524-7377
  17406 Royalton Rd Strongsville (44136) *(G-13467)*
Kaiser Foundation Hospitals 330 486-2800
  8920 Canyon Falls Blvd Twinsburg (44087) *(G-14198)*
Kaiser Logistics LLC 937 534-0213
  201 Lawton Ave Monroe (45050) *(G-11342)*
Kaiser Technology LLC 614 300-1088
  34 Grace Dr Powell (43065) *(G-12595)*
Kaival Corporation 330 467-1981
  240 Highland Rd E Macedonia (44056) *(G-10196)*
Kaiyuh Services LLC 907 569-9599
  4123 Arcadia Blvd Dayton (45420) *(G-7432)*
Kalahari Resort, Sandusky *Also Called: Lmn Development LLC (G-12910)*
Kaleel Bros Inc 330 758-0861
  761 Bev Rd Youngstown (44512) *(G-15644)*
Kaleel Brothers, Youngstown *Also Called: Kaleel Bros Inc (G-15644)*
Kaleidoscope Innovation 513 791-3009
  4362 Creek Rd Blue Ash (45241) *(G-1193)*
Kaleidoscope Project Inc 330 702-1822
  6610 Pheasant Run Dr Canfield (44406) *(G-1633)*
Kaleidoscope Prototyping LLC 513 206-9737
  4362 Creek Rd Blue Ash (45241) *(G-1194)*
Kalibrate Technologies, Independence *Also Called: Knowledge Support Systems Inc (G-9441)*
Kalogerou Enterprises Inc 330 544-9696
  430 Youngstown Warren Rd Niles (44446) *(G-11792)*
Kame's Sports Center, Canton *Also Called: Kames Inc (G-1789)*
Kames Inc 330 499-4558
  8516 Cleveland Ave Nw Canton (44720) *(G-1789)*
Kandel Cold Storage Inc 330 798-4111
  365 Munroe Falls Rd Tallmadge (44278) *(G-13597)*
Kandu Group 419 425-2638
  318 W Main Cross St Findlay (45840) *(G-8553)*
Kantar Media Research Inc 419 666-8800
  2700 Oregon Rd Northwood (43619) *(G-11976)*
KAO Collins Inc (HQ) 513 948-9000
  1201 Edison Dr Cincinnati (45216) *(G-2929)*
Kaplan Industries Inc 856 779-8181
  6255 Kilby Rd Harrison (45030) *(G-9111)*
Kaplan Trucking Company (PA) 216 341-3722
  8777 Rockside Rd Cleveland (44125) *(G-4448)*
Kapp Construction, Springfield *Also Called: Kapp Construction Inc (G-13262)*
Kapp Construction Inc 937 324-0134
  329 Mount Vernon Ave Springfield (45503) *(G-13262)*
Kappa Kappa Gamma Foundation (PA) 614 228-6515
  6640 Riverside Dr Ste 200 Dublin (43017) *(G-8045)*
KAPPA KAPPA GAMMA FRATERNITY, Dublin *Also Called: Kappa Kappa Gamma Foundation (G-8045)*
Kappus Company, Cleveland *Also Called: John H Kappus Co (G-4441)*
Karcher Group Inc 330 493-6141
  5590 Lauby Rd Ste 8 North Canton (44720) *(G-11843)*
Karing 4 Kids Learning Center 513 931-5273
  9495 Coogan Dr Cincinnati (45231) *(G-2930)*
Karl Hc LLC 614 846-5420
  5700 Karl Rd Columbus (43229) *(G-6102)*
Karlsberger & Associates, Columbus *Also Called: Karlsberger Architecture Inc (G-6103)*
Karlsberger Architecture Inc (HQ) 614 471-1812
  99 E Main St Columbus (43215) *(G-6103)*
Karlsberger Companies (PA) 614 461-9500
  99 E Main St Columbus (43215) *(G-6104)*
Karpinski Engineering Inc (PA) 216 391-3700
  3135 Euclid Ave Ste 200 Cleveland (44115) *(G-4449)*
Karrington, Columbus *Also Called: Karrington Operating Co Inc (G-6105)*
Karrington Operating Co Inc (DH) 614 324-5951
  919 Old Henderson Rd Columbus (43220) *(G-6105)*
Karrington Operating Co Inc 614 875-0514
  4200 Kelnor Dr Grove City (43123) *(G-8929)*
Kassel Equity Group LLC (PA) 614 310-4060
  7686 Fishel Dr N Ste B Dublin (43016) *(G-8046)*

Kastle Electric Company 937 254-2681
  4501 Kettering Blvd Moraine (45439) *(G-11419)*
Kathman Electric Co Inc 513 353-3365
  8969 Harrison Pike Cleves (45002) *(G-5189)*
Katmai Government Services LLC 740 314-5432
  100 Welday Ave Ste D Steubenville (43953) *(G-13333)*
Katz Teller, Cincinnati *Also Called: Katz Teller Brant Hild Co Lpa (G-2931)*
Katz Teller Brant Hild Co Lpa 513 721-4532
  255 E 5th St Fl 24 Cincinnati (45202) *(G-2931)*
Kauffman Tire Co, Orwell *Also Called: Orwell Tire Service Inc (G-12179)*
Kaufman Container Company (PA) 216 898-2000
  1000 Keystone Pkwy Ste 100 Cleveland (44135) *(G-4450)*
Kaufman Realty & Auctions LLC 330 852-4111
  1047 W Main St Sugarcreek (44681) *(G-13511)*
Kaulig Capital LLC 330 968-1110
  1521 Georgetown Rd Ste 101 Hudson (44236) *(G-9360)*
Kaulig Racing Inc (PA) 815 382-8007
  1521 Georgetown Rd Hudson (44236) *(G-9361)*
Kay Surati 419 727-8725
  5865 Hagman Rd Toledo (43612) *(G-13875)*
Kbec Fort Hamilton Hospital, Hamilton *Also Called: Fort Hamilton Hospital (G-9042)*
Kbr Wyle Services LLC 937 912-3470
  2601 Mission Point Blvd Ste 300 Beavercreek (45431) *(G-885)*
Kbr Wyle Services LLC 937 320-2713
  2700 Indian Ripple Rd Dayton (45440) *(G-7433)*
Kc Robotics Inc 513 860-4442
  9000 Le Saint Dr West Chester (45014) *(G-14717)*
Kcc Supply LLC (DH) 740 694-6315
  700 Salem Ave Ext Fredericktown (43019) *(G-8661)*
Kda Lighting Services, Twinsburg *Also Called: Lighting Services Inc (G-14201)*
KDM and Associates LLC 614 853-6199
  5505 Keim Cir Columbus (43228) *(G-6106)*
Ke Gutridge LLC 614 299-2133
  7686 Fishel Dr N Apt A Dublin (43016) *(G-8047)*
Ke Gutridge LLC 614 885-5200
  7686 Fishel Dr N # B Dublin (43016) *(G-8048)*
Keating Muething & Klekamp Pll (PA) 513 579-6400
  1 E 4th St Ste 1400 Cincinnati (45202) *(G-2932)*
Keene Inc 440 605-1020
  2926 Chester Ave Cleveland (44114) *(G-4451)*
Keene Family Holdings Corp, Cleveland *Also Called: Keene Inc (G-4451)*
Kegler Brown Hl Ritter Co Lpa (PA) 614 462-5400
  65 E State St Ste 1800 Columbus (43215) *(G-6107)*
Keidel, Cincinnati *Also Called: Keidel Sup LLC Fka Kdel Sup In (G-2933)*
Keidel Sup LLC Fka Kdel Sup In (HQ) 513 351-1600
  1150 Tennessee Ave Cincinnati (45229) *(G-2933)*
Keim Lumber Company 330 893-2251
  State Rte 557 Baltic (43804) *(G-690)*
Keim Lumber Company 330 893-2251
  4465 State Route 557 Millersburg (44654) *(G-11282)*
Keim, Jim Ford Sales, Columbus *Also Called: Jim Keim Ford (G-6091)*
Keis George LLP (PA) 216 241-4100
  55 Public Sq Ste 1900 Cleveland (44113) *(G-4452)*
Keith D Weiner & Assoc Lpa, Cleveland *Also Called: Weiner Keith D Co L P A Inc (G-5126)*
Keith E Huston DVM Llc 440 461-2226
  6529 Wilson Mills Rd Cleveland (44143) *(G-4453)*
Keithley Instruments LLC (DH) 440 248-0400
  28775 Aurora Rd Solon (44139) *(G-13103)*
Kelchner Inc 330 476-9737
  47443 National Rd Saint Clairsville (43950) *(G-12795)*
Kelchner Inc (DH) 937 704-9890
  50 Advanced Dr Springboro (45066) *(G-13202)*
Kelco Enterprises Inc 440 926-4357
  36300 Grafton Eastern Rd Grafton (44044) *(G-8840)*
Keller Farms Landscape & Nurs, Columbus *Also Called: Keller Group Limited (G-6108)*
Keller Group Limited 614 866-9551
  3909 Groves Rd Columbus (43232) *(G-6108)*
Keller Logistics Group Inc (PA) 866 276-9486
  24862 Elliott Rd Ste 101 Defiance (43512) *(G-7751)*
Keller Marketing, Sebring *Also Called: General Commercial Corporation (G-12949)*

ALPHABETIC SECTION — Kettering Health Hamilton

Keller Mortgage LLC 614 310-3100
9482 Wedgewood Blvd Ste 200 Powell (43065) *(G-12596)*

Keller Ochs Koch Inc 419 332-8288
416 S Arch St Fremont (43420) *(G-8689)*

Keller Williams Bruce 440 888-6800
7087 Pearl Rd D Middleburg Heights (44130) *(G-11118)*

Keller Williams Realtors, Beachwood *Also Called: Murwood Real Estate Group LLC* *(G-820)*

Keller Williams Realtors, Columbus *Also Called: Keller Williams Realty* *(G-6109)*

Keller Williams Realtors, Hilliard *Also Called: Keller Williams Realty Atlanta* *(G-9208)*

Keller Williams Realty 614 944-5900
1 Easton Oval Ste 100 Columbus (43219) *(G-6109)*

Keller Williams Realty Atlanta 614 406-5461
3535 Fishinger Blvd Ste 100 Hilliard (43026) *(G-9208)*

Keller Williams Rlty Suppliers 614 403-2411
100 E Wilson Bridge Rd Ste 100 Worthington (43085) *(G-15425)*

Kellermeyer Company 419 255-3022
475 W Woodland Cir Bowling Green (43402) *(G-1326)*

Kelley Brothers Roofing Inc 513 829-7717
4905 Factory Dr Fairfield (45014) *(G-8425)*

Kelley Ferraro LLC 216 575-0777
950 Main Ave Ste 1300 Cleveland (44113) *(G-4454)*

Kelley Steel Erectors Inc (PA) 440 232-1573
7220 Division St Cleveland (44146) *(G-4455)*

Kellison & Co (PA) 216 464-5160
4925 Galaxy Pkwy Ste U Cleveland (44128) *(G-4456)*

Kellstone, Kelleys Island *Also Called: Kellstone Inc* *(G-9553)*

Kellstone Inc 419 746-2396
Lake Shore Drive Kelleys Island (43438) *(G-9553)*

Kelly Paving Inc 740 373-6495
20220 State Rte 7 Marietta (45750) *(G-10377)*

Kelna Inc 330 729-0167
8388 Tod Ave Youngstown (44512) *(G-15645)*

Kemba Credit Union Inc 513 541-3015
6230 Hamilton Ave Cincinnati (45224) *(G-2934)*

Kemba Credit Union Inc (PA) 513 762-5070
5600 Chappell Crossing Blvd West Chester (45069) *(G-14718)*

Kemba Financial Credit Un Inc 614 235-2395
4311 N High St Columbus (43214) *(G-6110)*

Kemba Financial Credit Union 614 235-2395
4220 E Broad St Columbus (43213) *(G-6111)*

Kemper Company 440 846-1100
10890 Prospect Rd Strongsville (44149) *(G-13468)*

Kemper House of Strongsville, Strongsville *Also Called: Kemper Company* *(G-13468)*

Kemper Hse Hghland Hts Oper LL 440 461-0600
407 Golfview Ln Highland Heights (44143) *(G-9167)*

Kempthorn Motors Inc (PA) 800 451-3877
1449 Cleveland Ave Nw Canton (44703) *(G-1790)*

Kemron Environmental Svcs Inc 740 373-4071
2343 State Route 821 Marietta (45750) *(G-10378)*

Ken Miller Supply Inc 330 264-9146
1537 Blachleyville Rd Wooster (44691) *(G-15348)*

Ken Neyer Plumbing Inc 513 353-3311
4895 Hamilton Cleves Rd Cleves (45002) *(G-5190)*

Ken-Mac Metals, Cleveland *Also Called: Thyssenkrupp Materials NA Inc* *(G-5018)*

Kenakore Solutions, Perrysburg *Also Called: Depot Direct Inc* *(G-12332)*

Kenakore Solutions, Perrysburg *Also Called: TRT Management Corporation* *(G-12380)*

Kenamerican Resources Inc 740 338-3100
46226 National Rd Saint Clairsville (43950) *(G-12796)*

Kenan Advantage Group Inc (PA) 800 969-5419
4366 Mount Pleasant St Nw North Canton (44720) *(G-11844)*

Kenda USA, Reynoldsburg *Also Called: American Kenda Rbr Indus Ltd* *(G-12653)*

Kendal At Oberlin 440 775-0094
600 Kendal Dr Oberlin (44074) *(G-12071)*

Kendal Home Care, Chillicothe *Also Called: Khc Inc* *(G-2076)*

Kenics, Dayton *Also Called: Chemineer Inc* *(G-7222)*

Kenilworth Steel Co 330 373-1885
8700 E Market St Ste 11 Warren (44484) *(G-14532)*

Kenmore Construction Co Inc (PA) 330 762-8936
700 Home Ave Akron (44310) *(G-215)*

Kenmore Construction Co Inc 330 832-8888
9500 Forty Corners Rd Nw Massillon (44647) *(G-10649)*

Kenmore Research Company 330 297-1407
935 N Freedom St Ravenna (44266) *(G-12631)*

Kennedy Heights Montessori Ctr 513 631-8135
6620 Montgomery Rd Cincinnati (45213) *(G-2935)*

Kennedy Manufacturing, Van Wert *Also Called: KMC Holdings LLC* *(G-14347)*

Kenneth G Myers Cnstr Co Inc 419 639-2051
201 Smith St Green Springs (44836) *(G-8860)*

Kenneth's Design Group, Columbus *Also Called: Kenneths Hair Slons Day Spas I* *(G-6112)*

Kenneths Hair Slons Day Spas I (PA) 614 457-7712
5151 Reed Rd Ste 250b Columbus (43220) *(G-6112)*

Kensington At Anna Maria, Aurora *Also Called: R & G Nursing Care Inc* *(G-623)*

Kensington Care Center, Aurora *Also Called: Anna Maria of Aurora Inc* *(G-603)*

Kensington Intrmdiate Schl Pta 440 356-6770
20140 Lake Rd Rocky River (44116) *(G-12746)*

Kensington Plant, Kensington *Also Called: M3 Midstream LLC* *(G-9554)*

Kent Adhesive Products Co 330 678-1626
1000 Cherry St Kent (44240) *(G-9583)*

KENT HEALTHCARE CENTER, Kent *Also Called: Fairchild MD Leasing Co LLC* *(G-9574)*

Kent Mammography Center, Kent *Also Called: Robinson Health System Inc* *(G-9595)*

Kent Medical Offices, Kent *Also Called: Kaiser Foundation Hospitals* *(G-9582)*

Kentix Developmental Hlth Inc 330 949-0131
3439 Atterbury St Cuyahoga Falls (44221) *(G-7084)*

Kenton Community Health Center, Kenton *Also Called: Health Partners Western Ohio* *(G-9617)*

Kenton Nrsing Rhblttion Ctr LL 419 674-4197
117 Jacob Parrot Rd Kenton (43326) *(G-9620)*

Kentridge At Golden Pond Ltd 330 677-4040
5241 Sunnybrook Rd Kent (44240) *(G-9584)*

Kentucky Heart Institute Inc 740 353-8100
2001 Scioto Trl Ste 200 Portsmouth (45662) *(G-12560)*

Kenwood Office, Cincinnati *Also Called: Sibcy Cline Inc* *(G-3374)*

Kenwood Ter Hlth Care Ctr Inc 513 793-2255
7450 Keller Rd Cincinnati (45243) *(G-2936)*

Kenwood Terrace Care Center, Cincinnati *Also Called: Kenwood Ter Hlth Care Ctr Inc* *(G-2936)*

Kenworth of Cincinnati Inc 513 771-5831
65 Partnership Way Cincinnati (45241) *(G-2937)*

Kenworth Truck Co, Chillicothe *Also Called: Rumpke/Kenworth Contract* *(G-2089)*

Kenyon Co, Coshocton *Also Called: Novelty Advertising Co Inc* *(G-6994)*

Kenyon College 740 427-2202
100 W Wegan St Gambier (43022) *(G-8774)*

Kenyon Inn, Gambier *Also Called: Kenyon College* *(G-8774)*

Kerkan, Cincinnati *Also Called: Kerkan Roofing Inc* *(G-2938)*

Kerkan Roofing Inc 513 821-0556
721 W Wyoming Ave Cincinnati (45215) *(G-2938)*

Kern Inc (HQ) 614 317-2600
3940 Gantz Rd Ste A Grove City (43123) *(G-8930)*

Keroam Transportation Inc (PA) 937 274-7033
4518 Webster St Dayton (45414) *(G-7434)*

Kerry Ford Inc (PA) 513 671-6400
155 W Kemper Rd Cincinnati (45246) *(G-2939)*

Kerry Inc 760 685-2548
100 Hope Ave Byesville (43723) *(G-1535)*

Kerry Ingredients, Byesville *Also Called: Kerry Inc* *(G-1535)*

Kerry Mitsubishi, Cincinnati *Also Called: Kerry Ford Inc* *(G-2939)*

Kessler Outdoor Advertising, Zanesville *Also Called: Kessler Sign Company* *(G-15805)*

Kessler Sign Company (PA) 740 453-0668
2669 National Rd Zanesville (43701) *(G-15805)*

Kettering Adventist Healthcare (PA) 937 298-4331
3535 Southern Blvd Dayton (45429) *(G-7435)*

Kettering Adventist Healthcare 937 506-3112
70 Weller Dr Tipp City (45371) *(G-13661)*

Kettering Anesthesia Assoc 937 225-3429
3533 Southern Blvd Ste 3400 Dayton (45429) *(G-7436)*

Kettering City School District 937 499-1770
2640 Wilmington Pike Dayton (45419) *(G-7437)*

Kettering City School District 937 297-1990
2636 Wilmington Pike Dayton (45419) *(G-7438)*

Kettering Health Hamilton (HQ) 513 867-2000
630 Eaton Ave Hamilton (45013) *(G-9056)*

Kettering Health Network

ALPHABETIC SECTION

Kettering Health Network... 513 585-6000
  630 Eaton Ave Hamilton (45013) *(G-9057)*
Kettering Health Network, Dayton *Also Called: Kettering Adventist Healthcare (G-7435)*
Kettering Health Network, Dayton *Also Called: Kettering Medical Center (G-7439)*
KETTERING HEALTH NETWORK, Kettering *Also Called: Kettering Medical Center (G-9629)*
Kettering Health Network, Tipp City *Also Called: Kettering Adventist Healthcare (G-13661)*
Kettering Medical Center... 937 384-8750
  1251 E Dorothy Ln Dayton (45419) *(G-7439)*
Kettering Medical Center (HQ)...937 298-4331
  3535 Southern Blvd Kettering (45429) *(G-9629)*
Kettering Medical Center... 937 866-0551
  4000 Miamisburg Centerville Rd Miamisburg (45342) *(G-11066)*
Kettering Pathology Assoc Inc... 937 298-4331
  3535 Southern Blvd Dayton (45429) *(G-7440)*
Kettering School Maintainence, Dayton *Also Called: Kettering City School District (G-7438)*
Keuchel & Associates Inc... 330 945-9455
  175 Muffin Ln Cuyahoga Falls (44223) *(G-7085)*
Kevin D Arnold, Columbus *Also Called: Center For Cgntive Bhvral Thra (G-5529)*
Key, Cleveland *Also Called: Keybank National Association (G-4464)*
Key Bank, Toledo *Also Called: Keybank National Association (G-13878)*
Key Blue Prints Inc (PA)..614 228-3285
  195 E Livingston Ave Columbus (43215) *(G-6113)*
Key Capital Corporation... 216 828-8154
  127 Public Sq Ste 5600 Cleveland (44114) *(G-4457)*
Key Color, Columbus *Also Called: Key Blue Prints Inc (G-6113)*
Keybanc Capital Markets Inc (HQ)... 800 553-2240
  127 Public Sq Cleveland (44114) *(G-4458)*
Keybank, Brooklyn *Also Called: Keybank National Association (G-1410)*
Keybank, Canton *Also Called: Keybank National Association (G-1791)*
Keybank, Cleveland *Also Called: Keybank National Association (G-4461)*
Keybank, North Canton *Also Called: Keybank National Association (G-11845)*
Keybank Eb Mnged Grnteed Inv C.. 216 689-3000
  127 Public Sq Cleveland (44114) *(G-4459)*
Keybank National Association... 330 823-9615
  960 W State St Ste 210 Alliance (44601) *(G-385)*
Keybank National Association... 800 539-8336
  4900 Tiedeman Rd Brooklyn (44144) *(G-1410)*
Keybank National Association... 330 477-6787
  4428 Tuscarawas St W Canton (44708) *(G-1791)*
Keybank National Association... 440 345-7055
  6912 Pearl Rd Cleveland (44130) *(G-4460)*
Keybank National Association (HQ).. 800 539-2968
  127 Public Sq Ste 5600 Cleveland (44114) *(G-4461)*
Keybank National Association... 216 464-4727
  24600 Chagrin Blvd Cleveland (44122) *(G-4462)*
Keybank National Association... 216 382-3000
  4461 Mayfield Rd Cleveland (44121) *(G-4463)*
Keybank National Association... 216 689-8481
  100 Public Sq Ste 600 Cleveland (44113) *(G-4464)*
Keybank National Association... 216 464-6128
  30200 Chagrin Blvd Cleveland (44124) *(G-4465)*
Keybank National Association... 614 460-3415
  88 E Broad St Columbus (43215) *(G-6114)*
Keybank National Association... 216 289-7670
  22481 Lake Shore Blvd Euclid (44123) *(G-8352)*
Keybank National Association... 216 226-0850
  1435 Warren Rd Lakewood (44107) *(G-9671)*
Keybank National Association... 330 748-8010
  640 E Aurora Rd Ste A Macedonia (44056) *(G-10197)*
Keybank National Association... 419 893-7696
  409 Conant St Maumee (43537) *(G-10735)*
Keybank National Association... 330 499-2566
  932 N Main St North Canton (44720) *(G-11845)*
Keybank National Association... 440 734-7700
  26380 Brookpark Road North Olmsted (44070) *(G-11908)*
Keybank National Association... 216 502-3260
  19234 Detroit Rd Rocky River (44116) *(G-12747)*
Keybank National Association... 330 633-5735
  76 Tallmadge Cir Tallmadge (44278) *(G-13598)*
Keybank National Association... 419 727-6280
  5037 Suder Ave Toledo (43611) *(G-13876)*

Keybank National Association... 419 473-2088
  4106 Talmadge Rd Toledo (43623) *(G-13877)*
Keybank National Association... 567 455-4022
  7350 W Central Ave Toledo (43617) *(G-13878)*
Keybank National Association... 330 425-4434
  2566 E Aurora Rd Twinsburg (44087) *(G-14199)*
Keybridge Medical Revenue MGT, Lima *Also Called: General Audit Corporation (G-9891)*
Keyfactor Inc (PA)...216 785-2986
  6150 Oak Tree Blvd Ste 200 Independence (44131) *(G-9440)*
Keynes Bros Inc... 740 385-6824
  1 W Front St Logan (43138) *(G-10030)*
Keystone Auto Glass Inc.. 419 509-0497
  2255 Linden Ct Maumee (43537) *(G-10736)*
Keystone Business Solutions, Akron *Also Called: Keystone Technology Cons (G-216)*
Keystone Technology Cons... 330 666-6200
  787 Wye Rd Akron (44333) *(G-216)*
Kgbo Holdings Inc (PA)..513 831-2600
  4289 Ivy Pointe Blvd Cincinnati (45245) *(G-2107)*
Khc Inc... 740 775-5463
  24 Star Dr Chillicothe (45601) *(G-2076)*
KHD Company LLC.. 614 935-9939
  5878 N High St Fl 2 Worthington (43085) *(G-15426)*
Khempco Bldg Sup Co Ltd Partnr (PA).................................... 740 549-0465
  130 Johnson Dr Delaware (43015) *(G-7811)*
Khm Consulting Inc... 330 460-5635
  50 Pearl Rd Ste 300 Brunswick (44212) *(G-1461)*
Khm Travel Group, Brunswick *Also Called: Khm Consulting Inc (G-1461)*
Khn Pharmacy Huber.. 937 558-3333
  8701 Troy Pike Ste 4 Huber Heights (45424) *(G-9324)*
Khodiyar Inc... 419 589-2200
  880 Laver Rd Mansfield (44905) *(G-10278)*
Khol Family YMCA, Akron *Also Called: Young MNS Chrstn Assn of Akron (G-370)*
Kiddie Day Care of Champion... 330 847-9393
  5033 Mahoning Ave Nw Warren (44483) *(G-14533)*
Kidney Care Specialists LLC.. 937 643-0015
  1362 E Stroop Rd Dayton (45429) *(G-7441)*
Kidney Center of Bexley LLC... 614 231-2200
  1151 College Ave Columbus (43209) *(G-6115)*
Kidney Group Inc.. 330 746-1488
  1340 Belmont Ave Ste 2300 Youngstown (44504) *(G-15646)*
Kidney Services W Centl Ohio.. 419 227-0918
  750 W High St Ste 100 Lima (45801) *(G-9913)*
Kidron Electric Inc.. 330 857-2871
  5358 Kidron Rd Kidron (44636) *(G-9637)*
Kidron Electric & Mech Contrs, Kidron *Also Called: Kidron Electric Inc (G-9637)*
Kids 'r' Kids 3 OH, Springboro *Also Called: Childvine Inc (G-13196)*
Kids First Academy LLC.. 513 752-2811
  756 Ohio Pike Cincinnati (45245) *(G-2108)*
Kids Play Green, Mogadore *Also Called: Kids-Play Inc (G-11329)*
Kids World Daycare... 740 776-4548
  191 Hansgen Morgan Rd Wheelersburg (45694) *(G-15129)*
Kids-Play Inc.. 330 896-2400
  2096 Creeks Crossing Trl Mogadore (44260) *(G-11329)*
Kids-Play Inc.. 330 678-5554
  4530 Kent Rd Stow (44224) *(G-13379)*
Kiemle-Hankins, Perrysburg *Also Called: Kiemle-Hankins Company (G-12349)*
Kiemle-Hankins Company (PA)... 419 661-2430
  94 H St Perrysburg (43551) *(G-12349)*
Kilbarger Construction Inc... 740 385-6019
  450 Gallagher Ave Logan (43138) *(G-10031)*
Kilbourne Medical Laboratories Inc... 513 385-5457
  665 Ohio Pike Cincinnati (45245) *(G-2109)*
Kilbourne Medical Labs, Cincinnati *Also Called: Kilbourne Medical Laboratories Inc (G-2109)*
Killbuck Savings Bank Company (HQ)..................................... 330 276-4881
  165 N Main St Killbuck (44637) *(G-9638)*
Kimball Midwest, Columbus *Also Called: Midwest Motor Supply Co (G-6244)*
Kimble Clay & Limestone, Dover *Also Called: Kimble Company (G-7891)*
Kimble Company (PA)... 330 343-1226
  3596 State Route 39 Nw Dover (44622) *(G-7891)*
Kimble Recycl & Disposal Inc (PA).. 330 343-1226
  3596 State Route 39 Nw Dover (44622) *(G-7892)*

ALPHABETIC SECTION

Kimble Recycl & Disposal Inc.. 330 963-5493
  8500 Chamberlin Rd Twinsburg (44087) *(G-14200)*

Kimes Convalescent Center Ltd... 740 593-3391
  75 Kimes Ln Athens (45701) *(G-579)*

Kimmel Corporation (PA)... 419 294-1959
  225 N Sandusky Ave Upper Sandusky (43351) *(G-14290)*

Kin Care, Lima Also Called: Comfort Keepers *(G-9876)*

Kinder Garden School.. 513 791-4300
  10969 Reed Hartman Hwy Blue Ash (45242) *(G-1195)*

Kindercare, Westerville Also Called: Kindercare Learning Ctrs LLC *(G-14991)*

Kindercare Child Care Network, Cleveland Also Called: Kindercare Learning Ctrs LLC *(G-4466)*

Kindercare Learning Ctrs LLC.. 440 442-8067
  5684 Mayfield Rd Cleveland (44124) *(G-4466)*

Kindercare Learning Ctrs LLC.. 614 901-4000
  1255 County Line Rd Westerville (43081) *(G-14991)*

Kindred Healthcare LLC... 937 222-5963
  601 S Edwin C Moses Blvd Dayton (45417) *(G-7442)*

Kindred Healthcare LLC... 937 222-5963
  707 S Edwin C Moses Blvd Dayton (45417) *(G-7443)*

Kindred Healthcare LLC... 419 224-1888
  730 W Market St Lima (45801) *(G-9914)*

Kindred Hosp - Clveland - Gtwy, Cleveland Also Called: Specialty Hosp Cleveland LLC *(G-4929)*

Kindred Hospital, Dayton Also Called: Kindred Healthcare LLC *(G-7443)*

Kindred Hospital Lima, Lima Also Called: Kindred Healthcare LLC *(G-9914)*

Kindred Hospital-Dayton, Dayton Also Called: Kindred Healthcare LLC *(G-7442)*

Kindred Nursing Centers E LLC.. 614 837-9666
  36 Lehman Dr Canal Winchester (43110) *(G-1610)*

Kindred Nursing Centers E LLC.. 740 772-5900
  60 Marietta Rd Chillicothe (45601) *(G-2077)*

Kindred Nursing Centers E LLC.. 614 276-8222
  2770 Clime Rd Columbus (43223) *(G-6116)*

Kindred Nursing Centers E LLC.. 314 631-3000
  1300 Hill Rd N Pickerington (43147) *(G-12405)*

Kindred Trnstnal Care Rhblttio, Painesville Also Called: Personacare of Ohio Inc *(G-12241)*

Kindred Trnstnal Care Rhbltton, Chillicothe Also Called: Kindred Nursing Centers E LLC *(G-2077)*

Kindred Trnstnal Care Rhbltton, Columbus Also Called: Kindred Nursing Centers E LLC *(G-6116)*

Kindred Trnstnal Care Rhbltton, Pickerington Also Called: Kindred Nursing Centers E LLC *(G-12405)*

Kinetic Nutrition Group LLC.. 513 279-8966
  10270 Spartan Dr Ste S Cincinnati (45215) *(G-2940)*

Kinetic Renovations Inc... 937 321-1576
  616 Moore St Middletown (45044) *(G-11168)*

Kinetic Vision, Cincinnati Also Called: Saec/Kinetic Vision Inc *(G-3338)*

Kinetico Incorporated (HQ)... 440 564-9111
  10845 Kinsman Rd Newbury (44065) *(G-11761)*

Kinetics Noise Control Inc (PA)... 614 889-0480
  6300 Irelan Pl Dublin (43016) *(G-8049)*

King Daughters Family Care Ctr, South Point Also Called: Ashland Hospital Corporation *(G-13173)*

King Kold Inc.. 937 836-2731
  331 N Main St Englewood (45322) *(G-8311)*

King Saver, Marion Also Called: Sack n Save Inc *(G-10453)*

King Tut Logistics LLC... 614 538-0509
  3600 Enterprise Ave Columbus (43228) *(G-6117)*

KING'S DAUGHTERS' MEDICAL CENT, Portsmouth Also Called: Portsmouth Hospital Corp *(G-12565)*

King's Electric Services, Lebanon Also Called: Kween Industries Inc *(G-9772)*

Kings Dominion LLC (HQ)... 419 626-0830
  1 Cedar Point Dr Sandusky (44870) *(G-12908)*

Kings Island, Kings Mills Also Called: Kings Island Park LLC *(G-9643)*

Kings Island Company.. 513 754-5700
  6300 Kings Island Dr Kings Mills (45034) *(G-9642)*

Kings Island Park LLC.. 513 754-5901
  6300 Kings Island Dr Kings Mills (45034) *(G-9643)*

Kings Island Park LLC (HQ)... 419 626-0830
  1 Cedar Point Dr Sandusky (44870) *(G-12909)*

Kings Medical Company.. 330 653-3968
  4125 Highlander Pkwy Ste 150 Richfield (44286) *(G-12700)*

Kings Toyota Inc... 513 583-4333
  4700 Fields Ertel Rd Cincinnati (45249) *(G-2941)*

Kings Toyota Scion, Cincinnati Also Called: Kings Toyota Inc *(G-2941)*

Kings Veterinary Hospital.. 513 697-0400
  3335 W State Route 22 3 Loveland (45140) *(G-10145)*

Kingston Healthcare Company... 419 289-3859
  20 Amberwood Pkwy Ashland (44805) *(G-504)*

Kingston Healthcare Company (PA).. 419 247-2880
  1 Seagate Ste 1960 Toledo (43604) *(G-13879)*

Kingston Healthcare Company... 440 967-1800
  4210 Telegraph Ln Vermilion (44089) *(G-14407)*

Kingston of Ashland, Ashland Also Called: Kingston Healthcare Company *(G-504)*

Kingston of Miamisburg LLC... 937 866-9089
  1120 Dunaway St Miamisburg (45342) *(G-11067)*

Kingston of Vermilion, Vermilion Also Called: Kingston Healthcare Company *(G-14407)*

Kingston Residence, Toledo Also Called: Kingston Healthcare Company *(G-13879)*

Kingston Rsdnce Perrysburg LLC... 419 872-6200
  333 E Boundary St Perrysburg (43551) *(G-12350)*

Kingsway Farm & Storage Inc... 330 877-6241
  1555 Andrews St Ne Hartville (44632) *(G-9128)*

Kinn Bros Plbg Htg & AC Inc.. 419 562-1484
  527 Whetstone St Bucyrus (44820) *(G-1511)*

Kinnect.. 216 692-1161
  1427 E 36th St Ste 4203f Cleveland (44114) *(G-4467)*

Kinninger Prod Wldg Co Inc... 419 629-3491
  710 Kuenzel Dr New Bremen (45869) *(G-11598)*

Kinsale Golf & Fitnes CLB LLC... 740 881-6500
  3737 Village Club Dr Powell (43065) *(G-12597)*

Kinston Care Center Sylvani.. 419 517-8200
  4121 King Rd Sylvania (43560) *(G-13555)*

Kirby Risk Corporation.. 419 221-0123
  1249 Stewart Rd Lima (45801) *(G-9915)*

Kirby Vacuum Cleaner, Westlake Also Called: Scott Fetzer Company *(G-15105)*

Kirila Contractors Inc... 330 448-4055
  505 Bedford Rd Se Brookfield (44403) *(G-1406)*

Kirk & Blum Manufacturing Co (DH).. 513 458-2600
  4625 Red Bank Rd Ste 200 Cincinnati (45227) *(G-2942)*

Kirk Key Interlock Company LLC.. 330 833-8223
  9048 Meridian Cir Nw North Canton (44720) *(G-11846)*

Kirk NationaLease Co (PA).. 937 498-1151
  3885 Michigan St Sidney (45365) *(G-13036)*

Kirk Williams Company Inc.. 614 875-9023
  2734 Home Rd Grove City (43123) *(G-8931)*

Kirk Williams Piping & Plbg Co... 614 875-9023
  2734 Home Rd Grove City (43123) *(G-8932)*

Kirtland Capital Partners LP (PA)... 216 593-0100
  3201 Enterprise Pkwy Ste 200 Beachwood (44122) *(G-806)*

Kirtland Country Club Company... 440 942-4400
  39438 Kirtland Rd Willoughby (44094) *(G-15196)*

Kishan Inc.. 330 821-5688
  2330 W State St Alliance (44601) *(G-386)*

Kissel Entertainment LLC... 513 266-4505
  3748 State Line Rd Okeana (45053) *(G-12086)*

Kissel Rides & Shows, Okeana Also Called: Kissel Entertainment LLC *(G-12086)*

Kk Associates, Dublin Also Called: Kk Associates LLC *(G-8050)*

Kk Associates LLC (PA)... 614 783-7966
  555 Metro Pl N Ste 100 Dublin (43017) *(G-8050)*

Klaben Auto Group, Kent Also Called: Klaben Lincoln Ford Inc *(G-9585)*

Klaben Lincoln Ford Inc (PA)... 330 593-6800
  1080 W Main St Kent (44240) *(G-9585)*

Klamfoth Inc... 614 833-5007
  6630 Hill Rd Canal Winchester (43110) *(G-1611)*

Klarna Inc.. 614 615-4705
  629 N High St Fl 300 Columbus (43215) *(G-6118)*

Klean-A-Kar Inc (PA).. 614 221-3145
  3383 S High St Columbus (43207) *(G-6119)*

Kleingers Group, West Chester Also Called: Kleingers Group Inc *(G-14719)*

Kleingers Group Inc (PA)... 513 779-7851
  6219 Centre Park Dr West Chester (45069) *(G-14719)*

Kleingers Group Inc..614 882-4311
350 Worthington Rd Westerville (43082) *(G-14903)*

Kleman Services LLC..419 339-0871
2150 Baty Rd Lima (45807) *(G-9916)*

Kleptz Early Learning Center...937 832-6750
1100 W National Rd Englewood (45315) *(G-8312)*

Klingbeil Capital MGT Ltd (PA)..415 398-0106
500 W Wilson Bridge Rd Ste 145 Worthington (43085) *(G-15427)*

Klingbeil Management Group Co (PA).................................614 220-8900
21 W Broad St Fl 10 Columbus (43215) *(G-6120)*

Klingbeil Multifamilty Fund IV..415 398-0106
21 W Broad St Fl 11 Columbus (43215) *(G-6121)*

Klingshirn & Sons Trucking..937 338-5000
14884 St Rt 118 S Burkettsville (45310) *(G-1524)*

Klingshirn, Tom & Sons Trckng, Burkettsville Also Called: Klingshirn & Sons Trucking *(G-1524)*

Kloeckner Metals Corporation..513 769-4000
11501 Reading Rd Cincinnati (45241) *(G-2943)*

Klosterman Baking Co LLC..513 242-5667
1000 E Ross Ave Cincinnati (45217) *(G-2944)*

Klumm Bros..419 829-3166
9241 W Bancroft St Holland (43528) *(G-9292)*

Klx Energy Services LLC..740 922-1155
3571 Brighwood Rd Midvale (44653) *(G-11204)*

Km2 Solutions LLC..610 213-1408
2400 Corporate Exchange Dr Ste 120 Columbus (43231) *(G-6122)*

Kmb Management Services Corp..330 263-2660
801 E Wayne Ave Wooster (44691) *(G-15349)*

KMC Holdings LLC...419 238-2442
1260 Industrial Dr Van Wert (45891) *(G-14347)*

Kmh Systems Inc (PA)..800 962-3178
6900 Poe Ave Dayton (45414) *(G-7444)*

Kmk, Cincinnati Also Called: Keating Muething & Klekamp Pll *(G-2932)*

KMu Trucking & Excvtg LLC...440 934-1008
4436 Center Rd Avon (44011) *(G-659)*

Knapke Cabinets Inc..937 335-8383
2 E Main St Troy (45373) *(G-14142)*

Knapp Ctr For Chldhood Dev LLC..330 629-2955
1051 Tiffany S Youngstown (44514) *(G-15647)*

Knapp Veterinary Hospital Inc..614 267-3124
596 Oakland Park Ave Columbus (43214) *(G-6123)*

Knight Insurance Agency Inc..419 241-5133
22 N Erie St Toledo (43604) *(G-13880)*

Knight Material Tech LLC (PA)...330 488-1651
5385 Orchardview Dr Se East Canton (44730) *(G-8169)*

Knights Inn, Columbus Also Called: Shri Guru Inc *(G-6676)*

Knights Inn, Lancaster Also Called: Janessa Inc *(G-9726)*

Knights Inn, Lebanon Also Called: Anishiv Inc *(G-9754)*

Knights Inn, Macedonia Also Called: Kaival Corporation *(G-10196)*

Knights Inn, Urbancrest Also Called: Aashna Corporation *(G-14318)*

Knoch Corporation..330 244-1440
30505 Bainbridge Rd Solon (44139) *(G-13104)*

Knose Concrete Constructn Inc..513 738-8200
4926 Cincinnati Brookville Rd Hamilton (45013) *(G-9058)*

Knowledge MGT Interactive Inc..614 224-0664
330 W Spring St Ste 320 Columbus (43215) *(G-6124)*

Knowledge Support Systems Inc (PA)..................................973 408-9157
6133 Rockside Rd Ste 302 Independence (44131) *(G-9441)*

Knowledgeworks Foundation (PA).......................................513 929-4777
312 Plum St Ste 950 Cincinnati (45202) *(G-2945)*

Knowlton Development Corp..614 656-1130
8825 Smiths Mill Rd Johnstown (43031) *(G-9547)*

Knox Auto LLC..330 701-5266
510 Harcourt Rd Mount Vernon (43050) *(G-11490)*

Knox Cardiology Associates..740 397-0108
7 Woodlake Trl Ste A Mount Vernon (43050) *(G-11491)*

Knox Cnty Dept Wtr Waste Waste, Mount Vernon Also Called: Knox County *(G-11493)*

Knox Community Hospital (PA)...740 393-9000
1330 Coshocton Ave Mount Vernon (43050) *(G-11492)*

Knox County..740 397-7041
17602 Coshocton Rd Mount Vernon (43050) *(G-11493)*

Knox County..740 392-2200
11660 Upper Gilchrist Rd Mount Vernon (43050) *(G-11494)*

Knox County Head Start Inc (PA)...740 397-1344
11700 Upper Gilchrist Rd Ste B Mount Vernon (43050) *(G-11495)*

Knox County Health Department, Mount Vernon Also Called: Knox County *(G-11494)*

Knox New Hope Industries Inc..740 397-4601
1375 Newark Rd Mount Vernon (43050) *(G-11496)*

Ko Transmission Company (DH)..513 287-3553
139 E 4th St Rm 405-A Cincinnati (45202) *(G-2946)*

Koebbe Products Inc (PA)..513 753-4200
1132 Ferris Rd Amelia (45102) *(G-417)*

Koehlke Components Inc...937 435-5435
1201 Commerce Center Dr Franklin (45005) *(G-8643)*

Koester Pavilion Nursing Home, Troy Also Called: Uvmc Nursing Care Inc *(G-14170)*

Kognetics LLC..614 591-4416
147 N High St Gahanna (43230) *(G-8720)*

Kohler Catering, Dayton Also Called: Kohler Foods Inc *(G-7445)*

Kohler Foods Inc (PA)..937 291-3600
4572 Presidential Way Dayton (45429) *(G-7445)*

Kohlmyer Sporting Goods Inc..440 277-8296
5000 Grove Ave Lorain (44055) *(G-10079)*

Kohlmyer Sports, Lorain Also Called: Kohlmyer Sporting Goods Inc *(G-10079)*

Kohls Department Stores Inc..419 421-5301
7855 County Road 140 Findlay (45840) *(G-8554)*

Kohrman Jackson & Krantz LLP..216 696-8700
1375 E 9th St Fl 29 Cleveland (44114) *(G-4468)*

KOI Enterprises Inc..513 648-3020
11849 Kemper Springs Dr Ste 1 Cincinnati (45240) *(G-2947)*

KOI Enterprises Inc (HQ)...513 357-2400
2701 Spring Grove Ave Cincinnati (45225) *(G-2948)*

Koinonia Homes Inc...216 588-8777
6161 Oak Tree Blvd Ste 400 Cleveland (44131) *(G-4469)*

Koinonia Partners Holdings LLC..216 588-8777
5041 Lee Rd Maple Heights (44137) *(G-10342)*

Kokosing Inc (PA)..614 212-5700
6235 Westerville Rd Ste 200 Westerville (43081) *(G-14992)*

Kokosing Construction Inc..330 263-4168
1516 Timken Rd Wooster (44691) *(G-15350)*

Kokosing Construction Co Inc..440 322-2685
1539 Lowell St Elyria (44035) *(G-8265)*

Kokosing Construction Co Inc..740 694-6315
17531 Waterford Rd Fredericktown (43019) *(G-8662)*

Kokosing Construction Co Inc..419 524-5656
606 N Main St Mansfield (44902) *(G-10279)*

Kokosing Construction Co Inc (HQ).....................................614 228-1029
6235 Westerville Rd Westerville (43081) *(G-14993)*

Kokosing Construction Co Inc..614 228-1029
6235 Westerville Rd Westerville (43081) *(G-14994)*

Kokosing Industrial Inc (HQ)..614 212-5700
6235 Westerville Rd Westerville (43081) *(G-14995)*

Kokosing Mosser Joint Venture..740 848-4955
6235 Westerville Rd Westerville (43081) *(G-14996)*

Kokosing Solar, Westerville Also Called: Kokosing Industrial Inc *(G-14995)*

Kolczun Klczun Orthpd Assoc In..440 985-3113
5800 Cooper Foster Park Rd W Lorain (44053) *(G-10080)*

Komyo America Co Inc..937 339-0157
151 Commerce Center Blvd Troy (45373) *(G-14143)*

Kone Inc...330 762-8886
6670 W Snowville Rd Ste 7 Cleveland (44141) *(G-4470)*

Kone Inc...513 755-6195
6323 Centre Park Dr West Chester (45069) *(G-14720)*

Konkus Marble & Granite, Columbus Also Called: Konkus Marble & Granite Inc *(G-6125)*

Konkus Marble & Granite Inc...614 876-4000
3737 Zane Trace Dr Columbus (43228) *(G-6125)*

Koorsen Fire & Security, Columbus Also Called: Koorsen Fire & Security Inc *(G-6126)*

Koorsen Fire & Security Inc...513 398-4300
10608 Millington Ct Blue Ash (45242) *(G-1196)*

Koorsen Fire & Security Inc...614 878-2228
727 Manor Park Dr Columbus (43228) *(G-6126)*

Koorsen Fire & Security Inc...419 526-2212
100 Swarn Pkwy Mansfield (44903) *(G-10280)*

ALPHABETIC SECTION — L P K

Kopco Graphics Inc (PA) 513 874-7230
9750 Crescent Prk Dr West Chester (45069) *(G-14721)*

Kopf Construction Corporation (PA) 440 933-6908
420 Avon Belden Rd Ste A Avon Lake (44012) *(G-680)*

Koroseal Interior Products LLC 855 753-5474
700 Bf Goodrich Rd Marietta (45750) *(G-10379)*

Kozmos Grille, Massillon *Also Called: Mocho Ltd (G-10659)*

Kp Creek Gifts, Groveport *Also Called: Craft Wholesalers Inc (G-8980)*

Kpa, Dayton *Also Called: Kettering Pathology Assoc Inc (G-7440)*

Kpmg LLP 614 249-2300
191 W Nationwide Blvd Ste 500 Columbus (43215) *(G-6127)*

Kraft Electrical & Telecom Svs, Cincinnati *Also Called: Kraft Electrical Contg Inc (G-2949)*

Kraft Electrical Contg Inc (PA) 513 467-0500
5710 Hillside Ave Cincinnati (45233) *(G-2949)*

Kraft Fluid Systems Inc 440 238-5545
14300 Foltz Pkwy Strongsville (44149) *(G-13469)*

Kraft Foods, Toledo *Also Called: Mondelez Global LLC (G-13927)*

Kraftmaid Trucking Inc (PA) 440 632-2531
16052 Industrial Pkwy Middlefield (44062) *(G-11142)*

Kramer & Feldman Inc 513 821-7444
7636 Production Dr Cincinnati (45237) *(G-2950)*

Kramer Enterprises Inc (PA) 419 422-7924
1800 Westfield Dr Findlay (45840) *(G-8555)*

Kraton Polymers, Belpre *Also Called: Kraton Polymers US LLC (G-1056)*

Kraton Polymers US LLC 740 423-7571
2419 State Route 618 Belpre (45714) *(G-1056)*

Krazy Glue, West Jefferson *Also Called: Toagosei America Inc (G-14853)*

Kreber Graphics Inc (PA) 614 529-5701
2580 Westbelt Dr Columbus (43228) *(G-6128)*

Kregel Properties LLC 937 885-3250
66 Industry Ct Troy (45373) *(G-14144)*

Kreller Bus Info Group Inc (PA) 513 723-8900
817 Main St Ste 300 Cincinnati (45202) *(G-2951)*

Kreller Consulting Group Inc 513 723-8900
817 Main St Ste 700 Cincinnati (45202) *(G-2952)*

Kreller Group, Cincinnati *Also Called: Kreller Bus Info Group Inc (G-2951)*

Kreller Group, Cincinnati *Also Called: Kreller Consulting Group Inc (G-2952)*

Kribha LLC 740 788-8991
1008 Hebron Rd Newark (43056) *(G-11711)*

Krieger Ford Inc (PA) 614 888-3320
1800 Morse Rd Columbus (43229) *(G-6129)*

Krish Hospitality LLC 859 351-1060
3661 Maxton Rd Dayton (45414) *(G-7446)*

Krish Services Group Inc 813 784-0039
10091 Brecksville Rd Brecksville (44141) *(G-1356)*

Krlp Inc 513 762-4000
1014 Vine St Cincinnati (45202) *(G-2953)*

Kroger, Delaware *Also Called: Kroger Company (G-7813)*

Kroger Co 859 630-6959
2000 Nutter Farms Ln Delaware (43015) *(G-7812)*

Kroger Co 859 630-6959
401 Milford Pkwy Milford (45150) *(G-11235)*

Kroger Company 740 657-2124
2000 Nutter Farms Ln Delaware (43015) *(G-7813)*

Kroger Dedicated Logistics Co (HQ) 309 691-9670
1014 Vine St Ste 1000 Cincinnati (45202) *(G-2954)*

Kroger Seasonal - Spa DC, Milford *Also Called: Kroger Co (G-11235)*

Kronis Coatings, Mansfield *Also Called: Nanogate North America LLC (G-10301)*

Krugliak Wlkins Grffths Dghrty (PA) 330 497-0700
4775 Munson St Nw Canton (44718) *(G-1792)*

Krumroy-Cozad Cnstr Corp 330 376-4136
376 W Exchange St Akron (44302) *(G-217)*

Krush Technology, Kettering *Also Called: Oovoo LLC (G-9631)*

KS Associates Inc 440 365-4730
260 Burns Rd Ste 100 Elyria (44035) *(G-8266)*

KS Energy Services LLC 513 271-0276
4320 Mount Carmel Rd Cincinnati (45244) *(G-2955)*

Ktm North America Inc (PA) 855 215-6360
1119 Milan Ave Amherst (44001) *(G-430)*

Kubota Authorized Dealer, Columbus *Also Called: Columbus Equipment Company (G-5633)*

Kubota Authorized Dealer, Delaware *Also Called: Evolution Ag LLC (G-7796)*

Kubota Authorized Dealer, Findlay *Also Called: Streacker Tractor Sales Inc (G-8589)*

Kubota Authorized Dealer, Fort Recovery *Also Called: Hull Bros Inc (G-8610)*

Kucera International Inc (PA) 440 975-4230
38133 Western Pkwy Willoughby (44094) *(G-15197)*

Kucera South, Willoughby *Also Called: Kucera International Inc (G-15197)*

Kudu Dynamics LLC 973 209-0305
500 W Wilson Bridge Rd Ste 316 Worthington (43085) *(G-15428)*

Kuehne + Nagel Inc 440 243-6070
1 Berea Cmns Ste 3 Berea (44017) *(G-1072)*

Kuempel Service Inc 513 271-6500
3976 Southern Ave Cincinnati (45227) *(G-2956)*

Kuhlman Construction Products, Maumee *Also Called: Kuhlman Corporation (G-10737)*

Kuhlman Corporation (PA) 419 897-6000
1845 Indian Wood Cir Maumee (43537) *(G-10737)*

Kuhnle Bros Trucking, Newbury *Also Called: Kuhnle Brothers Inc (G-11762)*

Kuhnle Brothers Inc 440 564-7168
14905 Cross Creek Pkwy Newbury (44065) *(G-11762)*

Kumho Tire Co Inc 330 666-4030
711 Kumho Dr Fairlawn (44333) *(G-8489)*

Kumler Automotive, Lancaster *Also Called: Kumler Collision Inc (G-9728)*

Kumler Collision Inc 740 653-4301
2313 E Main St Lancaster (43130) *(G-9728)*

Kunesh Eye Center Inc 937 298-1703
2601 Far Hills Ave Ste 2 Oakwood (45419) *(G-12048)*

Kuno Creative, Lorain *Also Called: Kuno Creative Group Inc (G-10081)*

Kuno Creative Group Inc 440 261-5002
3248 W Erie Ave Lorain (44053) *(G-10081)*

Kuntzman Trucking Inc (PA) 330 821-9160
13515 Oyster Rd Alliance (44601) *(G-387)*

Kurtz Bros Central Ohio LLC 614 873-2000
6279 Houchard Rd Dublin (43016) *(G-8051)*

Kurtz Bros Inc (PA) 216 986-7000
6415 Granger Rd Independence (44131) *(G-9442)*

Kw International Inc 513 942-8999
500 W Kemper Rd Cincinnati (45246) *(G-2957)*

Kween Industries Inc 513 932-2293
2964 S Us Route 42 Lebanon (45036) *(G-9772)*

Kyocera Precision Tools, Cuyahoga Falls *Also Called: Kyocera SGS Precision Tls Inc (G-7086)*

Kyocera Precision Tools Inc 419 738-6652
321 Commerce Rd Wapakoneta (45895) *(G-14486)*

Kyocera Senco Indus Tls Inc (HQ) 513 388-2000
8450 Broadwell Rd Cincinnati (45244) *(G-2958)*

Kyocera SGS Precision Tls Inc (PA) 330 688-6667
150 Marc Dr Cuyahoga Falls (44223) *(G-7086)*

KZF Design Inc 513 621-6211
700 Broadway St Cincinnati (45202) *(G-2959)*

L & H Wholesale & Supply, Sheffield Village *Also Called: Luxury Heating Company (G-13001)*

L & M Products Inc 937 456-7141
1308 N Maple St Eaton (45320) *(G-8214)*

L & W Supply Corporation 513 723-1150
3274 Spring Grove Ave Cincinnati (45225) *(G-2960)*

L A D D, Cincinnati *Also Called: Living Arrngmnts For Dvlpmntll (G-2983)*

L B & B Associates Inc 216 451-2672
555 E 88th St Cleveland (44108) *(G-4471)*

L B Brunk & Sons Inc 330 332-0359
10460 Salem Warren Rd Salem (44460) *(G-12845)*

L Brands, Reynoldsburg *Also Called: MII Brand Import LLC (G-12670)*

L Brands Service Company LLC (HQ) 614 415-7000
3 Limited Pkwy Columbus (43230) *(G-6130)*

L Brands Store Dsign Cnstr Inc 614 415-7000
3 Ltd Pkwy Columbus (43230) *(G-6131)*

L Calvin Jones & Company 330 533-1195
3744 Starrs Centre Dr Canfield (44406) *(G-1634)*

L E Smith Company (PA) 419 636-4555
1030 E Wilson St Bryan (43506) *(G-1486)*

L JC Home Care LLC 614 495-0276
130 E Wilson Bridge Rd Ste 300 Worthington (43085) *(G-15429)*

L P K, Cincinnati *Also Called: Libby Prszyk Kthman Hldngs Inc (G-2973)*

L R G Inc... 937 890-0510
   3795 Wyse Rd Dayton (45414) *(G-7447)*
L S R, Hebron *Also Called: Legend Smelting and Recycl Inc (G-9145)*
L V I, Dayton *Also Called: Lion-Vallen Ltd Partnership (G-7458)*
L V Trckng, Columbus *Also Called: L V Trucking Inc (G-6132)*
L V Trucking Inc.. 614 275-4994
   2440 Harrison Rd Columbus (43204) *(G-6132)*
L-3 Cmmncations Nova Engrg Inc... 877 282-1168
   4393 Digital Way Mason (45040) *(G-10571)*
L'U Vabella, Lowellville *Also Called: M & M Wine Cellar Inc (G-10170)*
L&T Technology Services Ltd... 732 688-4402
   5550 Blazer Pkwy Ste 125 Dublin (43017) *(G-8052)*
L2 Source, Cincinnati *Also Called: L2 Source LLC (G-2961)*
L2 Source LLC... 513 428-4530
   4620 Wesley Ave Ste 200 Cincinnati (45212) *(G-2961)*
La Quinta Inn, Cincinnati *Also Called: Lq Management LLC (G-2992)*
La Quinta Inn, Cleveland *Also Called: Lq Management LLC (G-4507)*
La Quinta Inn, Mansfield *Also Called: Lq Management LLC (G-10283)*
La Quinta Inn, Piqua *Also Called: Mercer Hospitality Inc (G-12447)*
Lab Care, Barberton *Also Called: Summa Health (G-712)*
Lab Care, Stow *Also Called: Summa Health (G-13396)*
Labelle Hmhealth Care Svcs LLC.. 740 392-1405
   314 S Main St Ste B Mount Vernon (43050) *(G-11497)*
Labor Ready, Toledo *Also Called: Labor Ready Midwest Inc (G-13881)*
Labor Ready Midwest Inc.. 419 382-6565
   3606 W Sylvania Ave Ste 8 Toledo (43623) *(G-13881)*
Laboratory of Dermatopathology.. 937 434-2351
   7835 Paragon Rd Dayton (45459) *(G-7448)*
Laboratory Services, Kent *Also Called: Summa Western Reserve Hosp LLC (G-9600)*
Laborers Intl Un N Amer Lcal 3... 216 881-5901
   3250 Euclid Ave Ste 100 Cleveland (44115) *(G-4472)*
Laborers Local Union No 860... 216 432-1022
   3334 Prospect Ave E Cleveland (44115) *(G-4473)*
Lacca, Lima *Also Called: West Ohio Cmnty Action Partnr (G-9985)*
Laclede Development Company... 513 702-4391
   220 Elm Ave Wyoming (45215) *(G-15496)*
Ladan Learning Center LLC... 614 426-4306
   6028 Cleveland Ave Columbus (43231) *(G-6133)*
Ladd Inc.. 513 861-4089
   3603 Victory Pkwy Cincinnati (45229) *(G-2962)*
Ladd Distribution LLC (DH).. 937 438-2646
   4849 Hempstead Station Dr Kettering (45429) *(G-9630)*
Ladneir Healthcare Service LLC... 216 744-7296
   4225 Mayfield Rd Ste 201 South Euclid (44121) *(G-13171)*
Lads N' Lasses, Youngstown *Also Called: Kelna Inc (G-15645)*
Lady Warriors Summer Softball... 614 668-6329
   8868 Watkins Rd Sw Etna (43062) *(G-8333)*
Lafayette Life Insurance Co (DH)... 800 443-8793
   400 Broadway St Cincinnati (45202) *(G-2963)*
Laidlaw Education Services, Cincinnati *Also Called: First Student Inc (G-2678)*
Laidlaw Transit Services Inc (DH).. 513 241-2200
   600 Vine St Ste 1400 Cincinnati (45202) *(G-2964)*
Laidlaw Transportation, Cincinnati *Also Called: Firstgroup America Inc (G-2685)*
Lajd Warehousing & Leasing Inc.. 330 452-5010
   935 Mckinley Ave Nw Canton (44703) *(G-1793)*
Lake Business Products Inc (PA)... 440 953-1199
   653 Miner Rd Highland Heights (44143) *(G-9168)*
Lake Club.. 330 549-3996
   1140 Paulin Rd Poland (44514) *(G-12505)*
Lake Cnty Yung MNS Chrstn Assn (PA).. 440 352-3303
   933 Mentor Ave Fl 2 Painesville (44077) *(G-12231)*
Lake County Council On Aging (PA).. 440 205-8111
   8520 East Ave Mentor (44060) *(G-10959)*
Lake County Crime Laboratory, Painesville *Also Called: County of Lake (G-12224)*
Lake County General Health Dst.. 440 350-2543
   5966 Heisley Rd Mentor (44060) *(G-10960)*
Lake County Parts Warehouse Inc... 440 259-2991
   3382 N Ridge Rd Perry (44081) *(G-12306)*
Lake County YMCA... 440 428-5125
   730 N Lake St Madison (44057) *(G-10219)*

Lake County YMCA... 440 259-2724
   4540 River Rd Perry (44081) *(G-12307)*
Lake County YMCA... 440 946-1160
   37100 Euclid Ave Willoughby (44094) *(G-15198)*
Lake Erie Abrasive & Tool Inc.. 216 692-2778
   24811 Rockwell Dr Euclid (44117) *(G-8353)*
Lake Erie Cncil Boy Scuts Amer... 216 861-6060
   2241 Woodland Ave Cleveland (44115) *(G-4474)*
Lake Erie Construction Co.. 419 668-3302
   25 S Norwalk Rd E Norwalk (44857) *(G-12015)*
Lake Erie Eductl Cmpt Assn, Elyria *Also Called: County of Lorain (G-8239)*
Lake Erie Electric Inc... 330 724-1241
   1888 Brown St Akron (44301) *(G-218)*
Lake Erie Electric Inc... 937 743-1220
   360 Industrial Dr Franklin (45005) *(G-8644)*
Lake Erie Electric Inc... 419 529-4611
   539 Home Rd N Ontario (44906) *(G-12111)*
LAKE ERIE ELECTRIC INC (PA).. 440 835-5565
   25730 1st St Westlake (44145) *(G-15074)*
Lake Erie Hospitality LLC... 419 547-6660
   1363 W Mcpherson Hwy Clyde (43410) *(G-5205)*
Lake Erie Med Surgical Sup Inc... 734 847-3847
   6920 Hall St Holland (43528) *(G-9293)*
Lake Erie Monsters... 216 420-0000
   1 Center Ice Cleveland (44115) *(G-4475)*
Lake Farm Park, Kirtland *Also Called: Lake Metroparks (G-9645)*
Lake Health... 440 816-2225
   7215 Old Oak Blvd Ste A421 Cleveland (44130) *(G-4476)*
Lake Health, Concord Township *Also Called: Tripoint Medical Center (G-6936)*
Lake Health Inc... 440 279-1500
   510 5th Ave Ste C130 Chardon (44024) *(G-2009)*
Lake Horry Electric (PA)... 440 808-8791
   255 Bramley Ct Chagrin Falls (44022) *(G-1961)*
Lake Hospital Sys HM Hlth Svcs.. 440 639-0900
   9485 Painesville (44077) *(G-12232)*
Lake Hospital System Inc.. 216 545-4800
   25501 Chagrin Blvd Beachwood (44122) *(G-807)*
Lake Hospital System Inc (HQ).. 440 375-8100
   7590 Auburn Rd Concord Township (44077) *(G-6927)*
Lake Hospital System Inc.. 440 352-0646
   7580 Auburn Rd Ste 314 Concord Township (44077) *(G-6928)*
Lake Hospital System Inc.. 440 255-8133
   9485 Mentor Ave Mentor (44060) *(G-10961)*
Lake Hospital System Inc.. 440 205-8818
   8316 Yellowbrick Rd Mentor (44060) *(G-10962)*
Lake Hospital System Inc.. 440 375-8590
   2 Success Blvd Perry (44081) *(G-12308)*
Lake Hospital System Inc.. 440 953-9600
   36000 Euclid Ave Willoughby (44094) *(G-15199)*
Lake Hospital System Inc.. 440 975-0027
   34881 Euclid Ave Willoughby (44094) *(G-15200)*
Lake Hospital System Inc.. 440 942-4226
   36060 Euclid Ave Ste 202 Willoughby (44094) *(G-15201)*
Lake Hospital System Inc.. 440 833-2095
   29804 Lake Shore Blvd Willowick (44095) *(G-15236)*
Lake Hospital Systems, Madison *Also Called: Madison Medical Campus (G-10221)*
Lake Hospitality Inc.. 440 579-0300
   7581 Auburn Rd Concord Township (44077) *(G-6929)*
Lake Metroparks... 440 256-2122
   8800 Euclid Chardon Rd Kirtland (44094) *(G-9645)*
Lake Metroparks (PA)... 440 639-7275
   11211 Spear Rd Painesville (44077) *(G-12233)*
Lake Park At Flower Hospital, Sylvania *Also Called: Flower Hospital (G-13545)*
Lake Pnte Rhbltion Nrsing Ctr, Conneaut *Also Called: LP Opco LLC (G-6943)*
Lake Rdge Vlla Hlth Care Rehab, Cincinnati *Also Called: Cedar Medical Group (G-2331)*
Lake Township Trustees... 419 836-1143
   3800 Ayers Rd Millbury (43447) *(G-11270)*
Lake Univ Ireland Cancer Ctr, Mentor *Also Called: University Hsptals Clvland Med (G-11007)*
Lake Wynoka Prprty Owners Assn... 937 446-3774
   1 Waynoka Dr Lake Waynoka (45171) *(G-9653)*
Lake-Geauga Recovery Ctrs Inc.. 440 354-2848
   796 Oak St Painesville (44077) *(G-12234)*

ALPHABETIC SECTION — Larlham Care Hattie Group

Lake-West Hospital, Willoughby *Also Called: Lake Hospital System Inc (G-15199)*
Lakefront Lines Inc (DH).. 216 267-8810
  13315 Brookpark Rd Brookpark (44142) *(G-1436)*
Lakeland Foundation.. 440 525-7094
  7700 Clocktower Dr C2089 Willoughby (44094) *(G-15202)*
Lakeland Glass Co (PA).. 440 277-4527
  4994 Grove Ave Lorain (44055) *(G-10082)*
Lakeland Motel Inc... 419 734-2101
  121 E Perry St Port Clinton (43452) *(G-12536)*
Lakeland Motel & Charter Svc, Port Clinton *Also Called: Lakeland Motel Inc (G-12536)*
Lakes Golf & Country Club Inc.. 614 882-2582
  6740 Worthington Rd Westerville (43082) *(G-14904)*
Lakeside Association... 419 798-4461
  236 Walnut Ave Lakeside (43440) *(G-9654)*
Lakeside Interior Contractors Inc..................................... 419 867-1300
  26970 Eckel Rd Perrysburg (43551) *(G-12351)*
Lakeside Manor Inc... 330 549-2545
  9661 Market St North Lima (44452) *(G-11890)*
Lakeside Marine Boat Sales, Port Clinton *Also Called: Lakeside Marine Inc (G-12537)*
Lakeside Marine Inc (PA).. 419 732-7160
  650 Se Catawba Rd Port Clinton (43452) *(G-12537)*
Lakeside Scrap Metals Inc.. 216 458-7150
  15000 Miles Ave Cleveland (44128) *(G-4477)*
Lakeside Supply Co... 216 941-6800
  3000 W 117th St Cleveland (44111) *(G-4478)*
Laketran... 440 350-1000
  555 Lakeshore Blvd Painesville (44077) *(G-12235)*
Lakewood Animal Hospital, Lakewood *Also Called: Robert C Barney Dvm Inc (G-9682)*
Lakewood Catholic Academy.. 216 521-4352
  14808 Lake Ave Lakewood (44107) *(G-9672)*
Lakewood Chrysler-Plymouth.. 216 521-1000
  13001 Brookpark Rd Brookpark (44142) *(G-1437)*
Lakewood Community Care Center, Cleveland *Also Called: City of Lakewood (G-3989)*
Lakewood Country Club Company.................................... 440 871-0400
  2613 Bradley Rd Cleveland (44145) *(G-4479)*
Lakewood Country Club Pro Shop.................................... 440 871-0400
  2613 Bradley Rd Cleveland (44145) *(G-4480)*
Lakewood Greenhouse Inc... 419 691-3541
  29800 Sussex Rd Perrysburg (43551) *(G-12352)*
Lakewood Health Care Center.. 216 226-3103
  13315 Detroit Ave Lakewood (44107) *(G-9673)*
Lakewood Hospital Association.. 216 228-5437
  1450 Belle Ave Cleveland (44107) *(G-4481)*
Lakewood Hospital Association (HQ)............................... 216 529-7201
  14519 Detroit Ave Lakewood (44107) *(G-9674)*
Lakewood Police Dept, Cleveland *Also Called: City of Lakewood (G-3991)*
Lakewood Recreation Department................................... 216 529-4081
  13701 Lake Ave Lakewood (44107) *(G-9675)*
Lakewood Rngers Edcatn Fndtion.................................... 216 521-2100
  14100 Franklin Blvd Lakewood (44107) *(G-9676)*
Lakewood Senior Campus LLC.. 216 228-7650
  13900 Detroit Ave Lakewood (44107) *(G-9677)*
Lakewood Y, Lakewood *Also Called: Young MNS Chrstn Assn Grter CL (G-9688)*
Lakireddy Dental LLC.. 330 439-0355
  545 E Aurora Rd Macedonia (44056) *(G-10198)*
Lakota Local School District... 513 777-2150
  6947 Yankee Rd Liberty Township (45044) *(G-9853)*
Lalac One LLC... 216 432-4422
  18451 Euclid Ave Cleveland (44112) *(G-4482)*
Lamalfa Party Center, Mentor *Also Called: Michaels Inc (G-10973)*
Lan Solutions Inc... 513 469-6500
  9850 Redhill Dr Blue Ash (45242) *(G-1197)*
Lancaster Bingo Company LLC.. 800 866-5001
  200 Quarry Rd Se Lancaster (43130) *(G-9729)*
Lancaster Country Club... 740 654-3535
  3100 Country Club Rd Sw Lancaster (43130) *(G-9730)*
Lancaster Host LLC... 740 654-4445
  1861 Riverway Dr Lancaster (43130) *(G-9731)*
Lancaster Municipal Gas, Lancaster *Also Called: City of Lancaster (G-9701)*
Lancaster Pollard Mrtg Co LLC (DH)................................ 614 224-8800
  10 W Broad St Ste 800 Columbus (43215) *(G-6134)*

Lancaster Radiation Oncology.. 740 687-8554
  401 N Ewing St Lancaster (43130) *(G-9732)*
Lancaster Transportation, Cincinnati *Also Called: Mv Transportation Inc (G-3094)*
LANCASTER-FAIRFIELD COMMUNITY, Lancaster *Also Called: Community Action Prgram Comm O (G-9704)*
Lance A1 Cleaning Services LLC...................................... 614 370-0550
  342 Hanton Way Columbus (43213) *(G-6135)*
Lance Global Logistics LLC... 440 522-3822
  3825 E Lake Rd Sheffield Lake (44054) *(G-12996)*
Lancia Nursing Homes Inc.. 740 264-7101
  1852 Sinclair Ave Steubenville (43953) *(G-13334)*
Lancia Villa Royal, Steubenville *Also Called: Lancia Nursing Homes Inc (G-13334)*
Lanco Global Systems Inc... 937 660-8090
  1430c Yankee Park Pl Dayton (45458) *(G-7449)*
Land Management Group, Kent *Also Called: Davey Resource Group Inc (G-9568)*
Lander Hotel Group LLC... 330 590-8040
  387 Medina Rd Ste 600 Medina (44256) *(G-10851)*
Landes Fresh Meats Inc.. 937 836-3613
  9476 Haber Rd Clayton (45315) *(G-3734)*
Landis, Gregory C Od, Westerville *Also Called: Comprhnsive Eycare Cntl Ohio I (G-14883)*
Landmark Properties Group LLC...................................... 740 701-7511
  23 S Ohio Ave Wellston (45692) *(G-14640)*
Landmark Recovery Ohio LLC.. 855 950-5035
  19350 Euclid Ave Euclid (44117) *(G-8354)*
Landmark Recovery Ohio LLC.. 855 950-5035
  725 Wessor Ave Willard (44890) *(G-15169)*
Landmark Star Properties Inc... 937 316-5252
  1190 E Russ Rd Greenville (45331) *(G-8879)*
Landor & Fitch LLC.. 614 843-1766
  191 W Nationwide Blvd Ste 175 Columbus (43215) *(G-6136)*
Landrum & Brown Incorporated (PA)................................ 513 530-5333
  4445 Lake Forest Dr Ste 700 Blue Ash (45242) *(G-1198)*
Landstar Global Logistics Inc.. 740 575-4700
  1247 E Main St Coshocton (43812) *(G-6990)*
Lane Alton & Horst LLC... 614 228-6885
  2 Miranova Pl Ste 220 Columbus (43215) *(G-6137)*
Lane Avenue Hotel Holdings LLC..................................... 614 486-5433
  1640 W Lane Ave Upper Arlington (43221) *(G-14279)*
Lane Aviation, Columbus *Also Called: Lane Aviation Corporation (G-6138)*
Lane Aviation Corporation... 614 237-3747
  4389 International Gtwy Ste 228 Columbus (43219) *(G-6138)*
Lang Financial Group Inc.. 513 699-2966
  4225 Malsbary Rd Ste 100 Blue Ash (45242) *(G-1199)*
Lang Masonry Contractors Inc.. 740 749-3512
  405 Watertown Rd Waterford (45786) *(G-14592)*
Lang Stone Company Inc (PA).. 614 235-4099
  4099 E 5th Ave Columbus (43219) *(G-6139)*
Langdon Inc.. 513 733-5955
  9865 Wayne Ave Cincinnati (45215) *(G-2965)*
Langston Family Dental Clinic, Hillsboro *Also Called: Langstonmc Kenna Lesia (G-9262)*
Langstonmc Kenna Lesia.. 937 393-1472
  321 Chillicothe Ave Hillsboro (45133) *(G-9262)*
Lannings Foods, Mount Vernon *Also Called: S and S Gilardi Inc (G-11507)*
Lantern of Chagrin Valley... 440 996-5084
  5277 Chillicothe Rd Chagrin Falls (44022) *(G-1962)*
Lantz Dental Prosthetics Inc... 419 866-1515
  6490 Wheatstone Ct Maumee (43537) *(G-10738)*
Lapham-Hickey Steel Corp.. 614 443-4881
  753 Marion Rd Columbus (43207) *(G-6140)*
Lapham-Hickey Steel Corp.. 937 236-6940
  3911 Dayton Park Dr Dayton (45414) *(G-7450)*
Large & Loving Cards Inc.. 440 877-0261
  13676 York Rd # 1 North Royalton (44133) *(G-11943)*
Laria Chevrolet-Buick Inc.. 330 925-2015
  112 E Ohio Ave Rittman (44270) *(G-12730)*
Lariche Chevrolet-Cadillac, Findlay *Also Called: Lariche Chevrolet-Cadillac Inc (G-8556)*
Lariche Chevrolet-Cadillac Inc.. 419 422-1855
  215 E Main Cross St Findlay (45840) *(G-8556)*
Lark Residential Support Inc... 614 582-9721
  5026 Sinclair Rd Columbus (43229) *(G-6141)*
Larlham Care Hattie Group.. 330 274-2272
  9772 Diagonal Rd Mantua (44255) *(G-10332)*

(PA)=Parent Co (HQ)=Headquarters (DH)=Div Headquarters

Larosas Inc   ALPHABETIC SECTION

Larosas Inc (PA).. 513 347-5660
   2334 Boudinot Ave Cincinnati (45238) *(G-2966)*

Larrimer & Larrimer LLC (PA)........................ 614 221-7548
   165 N High St Fl 3 Columbus (43215) *(G-6142)*

Larry Lang Excavating Inc................................. 740 984-4750
   19371 State Route 60 Beverly (45715) *(G-1101)*

Laserflex, Hilliard *Also Called: Laserflex Corporation (G-9209)*

Laserflex Corporation (HQ).............................. 614 850-9600
   3649 Parkway Ln Hilliard (43026) *(G-9209)*

Lasikplus, Cincinnati *Also Called: Lca-Vision Inc (G-2968)*

Lasting Imprssions Event Rentl, Columbus *Also Called: Lasting Imprssons Event Pty Rn (G-6143)*

Lasting Imprssons Event Pty Rn...................... 614 252-5400
   5080 Sinclair Rd Ste 200 Columbus (43229) *(G-6143)*

Latent Heat Solution, Moraine *Also Called: Cavu Group (G-11396)*

Lathrop Company Inc (DH)............................... 419 893-7000
   28 N Saint Clair St Toledo (43604) *(G-13882)*

Latorre Concrete Cnstr Inc................................ 614 257-1401
   850 N Cassady Ave Columbus (43219) *(G-6144)*

Latrobe Spcialty Mtls Dist Inc (HQ)................. 330 609-5137
   1551 Vienna Pkwy Vienna (44473) *(G-14420)*

Laughlin Music & Vending Svc (PA)............... 740 593-7778
   148 W Union St Athens (45701) *(G-580)*

Laughlin Music and Vending Svc, Athens *Also Called: Laughlin Music & Vending Svc (G-580)*

Laukhuf, Gary DDS, Ashtabula *Also Called: Ashtabula Dental Assoc Inc (G-525)*

Laurel Health Care Company............................ 740 264-5042
   500 Stanton Blvd Steubenville (43952) *(G-13335)*

Laurel Health Care Company (HQ).................. 614 794-8800
   8181 Worthington Rd Uppr Westerville (43082) *(G-14905)*

Laurel Healthcare... 419 782-7879
   1701 Jefferson Ave Defiance (43512) *(G-7752)*

Laurel Hlth Care Battle Creek (HQ)................. 614 794-8800
   8181 Worthington Rd Westerville (43082) *(G-14906)*

Laurel Hlth Care of Mt Plasant (HQ)............... 614 794-8800
   8181 Worthington Rd Lowr 2 Westerville (43082) *(G-14907)*

Laurel School (PA)... 216 464-1441
   1 Lyman Cir Shaker Heights (44120) *(G-12980)*

Laurels of Athens... 740 592-1000
   70 Columbus Circle Athens (45701) *(G-581)*

Laurels of Bedford, The, Westerville *Also Called: Laurel Hlth Care Battle Creek (G-14906)*

Laurels of Defiance, The, Westerville *Also Called: Oak Hlth Care Invstors Dfnce I (G-14918)*

Laurels of Mt Pleasant, Westerville *Also Called: Laurel Hlth Care of Mt Plasant (G-14907)*

Laurels of Mt Vernon, Mount Vernon *Also Called: Oak Hlth Care Invstors of Mt V (G-11503)*

Laurels of Steubenville, The, Steubenville *Also Called: Laurel Health Care Company (G-13335)*

Laurels of Worthington...................................... 614 885-0408
   1030 High St Worthington (43085) *(G-15430)*

Laurelwood Ctr For Bhvral Hlth, Willoughby *Also Called: Laurelwood Hospital (G-15203)*

Laurelwood Hospital (PA)................................. 440 953-3000
   35900 Euclid Ave Willoughby (44094) *(G-15203)*

Laurelwood, The, Dayton *Also Called: Harborside Healthcare LLC (G-7397)*

Laurie Ann Nursing Home, Newton Falls *Also Called: Hooberry & Associates Inc (G-11775)*

LAURRELS OF DEFIANCE, Defiance *Also Called: Laurel Healthcare (G-7752)*

Lavery Buick, Alliance *Also Called: Lavery Chevrolet-Buick Inc (G-388)*

Lavery Chevrolet-Buick Inc (PA)...................... 330 823-1100
   1096 W State St Alliance (44601) *(G-388)*

Law Offces of John D Clunk A L...................... 330 436-0300
   495 Wolf Ledges Pkwy Ste 1 Akron (44311) *(G-219)*

Law Offces Rbert A Schrger Lpa..................... 614 824-5731
   1113 Airport Rd Wilmington (45177) *(G-15256)*

Lawhon and Associates Inc (PA)..................... 614 481-8600
   1441 King Ave Columbus (43212) *(G-6145)*

Lawnfield Inn and Suites, Mentor *Also Called: Lawnfield Mentor LLC (G-10963)*

Lawnfield Mentor LLC....................................... 440 205-7378
   8434 Mentor Ave Mentor (44060) *(G-10963)*

Lawo, Toledo *Also Called: Legal Aid Western Ohio Inc (G-13884)*

Lawrence Cnty Bd Dev Dsblities...................... 740 377-2356
   1749 County Road 1 South Point (45680) *(G-13176)*

Lawrence Cnty Erly Chldhood Ct, South Point *Also Called: Lawrence Cnty Bd Dev Dsblities (G-13176)*

Lawrence Industries Inc (PA)........................... 216 518-7000
   4500 Lee Rd Ste 120 Cleveland (44128) *(G-4483)*

Lawrence M Shell DDS...................................... 614 235-3444
   2862 E Main St Ste A Columbus (43209) *(G-6146)*

Lawyers Title Cincinnati Inc (HQ).................... 513 421-1313
   3500 Red Bank Rd Cincinnati (45227) *(G-2967)*

Lawyers Title Insurance Corp........................... 614 221-4523
   8425 Pulsar Pl Ste 310 Columbus (43240) *(G-5266)*

Layton Inc (PA)... 740 349-7101
   169 Dayton Rd Ne Newark (43055) *(G-11712)*

Laz Karp Associates LLC.................................. 614 227-0356
   245 Marconi Blvd Columbus (43215) *(G-6147)*

Lazar Brothers Inc... 440 585-9333
   30030 Lakeland Blvd Wickliffe (44092) *(G-15156)*

Lazear Capital Partners Ltd (PA)..................... 614 221-1616
   401 N Front St Ste 250 Columbus (43215) *(G-6148)*

Lazurite Inc.. 216 334-3127
   4760 Richmond Rd Ste 400 Warrensville Heights (44128) *(G-14583)*

Lbi Starbucks DC 3.. 614 415-6363
   3 Limited Pkwy Columbus (43230) *(G-6149)*

Lbk Health Care Inc (PA).................................. 937 296-1550
   4336 W Franklin St Ste A Bellbrook (45305) *(G-1018)*

Lbs, Strongsville *Also Called: Long Business Systems Inc (G-13472)*

Lbs International Inc... 614 866-3688
   6501 E Livingston Ave Ste 4 Reynoldsburg (43068) *(G-12667)*

Lc, Cleveland *Also Called: Logan Clutch Corporation (G-4504)*

Lca-Vision Inc (HQ)... 513 792-9292
   7840 Montgomery Rd Cincinnati (45236) *(G-2968)*

Lcada, Lorain *Also Called: Lorain Cnty Alchol DRG Abuse S (G-10084)*

Lccaa-Hopkins Locke-Head Start, Lorain *Also Called: Lorain Cnty Cmnty Action Agcy (G-10085)*

Lcd Agency Services LLC................................. 513 497-0441
   6 S 2nd St Ste 409 Hamilton (45011) *(G-9059)*

Lcd Nrse Aide Acdemy HM Hlth A, Hamilton *Also Called: Lcd Agency Services LLC (G-9059)*

Lcnb Corp (PA)... 513 932-1414
   2 N Broadway St Lebanon (45036) *(G-9773)*

Lcnb National Bank (HQ).................................. 513 932-1414
   2 N Broadway St Lowr Lebanon (45036) *(G-9774)*

Lcs, Cincinnati *Also Called: London Computer Systems Inc (G-2986)*

Leadec Corp (DH).. 513 731-3590
   9395 Kenwood Rd Ste 200 Blue Ash (45242) *(G-1200)*

Leadec Services, Blue Ash *Also Called: Leadec Corp (G-1200)*

Leader Drug Store, Huber Heights *Also Called: Khn Pharmacy Huber (G-9324)*

Leader Promotions Inc (PA)............................. 614 416-6565
   790 E Johnstown Rd Columbus (43230) *(G-6150)*

Leaderpromos.com, Columbus *Also Called: Leader Promotions Inc (G-6150)*

Leaders Moving & Storage Co, Worthington *Also Called: Leaders Moving Company (G-15431)*

Leaders Moving Company................................ 614 785-9595
   7455 Alta View Blvd Worthington (43085) *(G-15431)*

Leadership Circle LLC....................................... 801 518-2980
   10918 Springbrook Ct Whitehouse (43571) *(G-15143)*

Leadfirstai LLC (PA).. 419 424-6647
   1219 W Main Cross St Ste 205 Findlay (45840) *(G-8557)*

Leading Edje LLC (PA)...................................... 614 636-3353
   1491 Polaris Pkwy Ste 191 Columbus (43240) *(G-5267)*

Leading Edje LLC.. 614 636-3353
   5555 Perimeter Dr Ste 101 Dublin (43017) *(G-8053)*

Leading Families Home.................................... 419 244-2175
   2283 Ashland Ave Toledo (43620) *(G-13883)*

Leads Eastland Center, Newark *Also Called: Community Action Prgram Comm O (G-11693)*

Leaf Home LLC (PA)... 800 290-6106
   1595 Georgetown Rd Hudson (44236) *(G-9362)*

Leantrak Inc... 419 482-0797
   1645 Indian Wood Cir Ste 101 Maumee (43537) *(G-10739)*

Leap, Cleveland *Also Called: Linking Emplyment Ablties Ptnt (G-4498)*

Learning Spectrum Ltd (PA)............................. 614 844-5433
   6660 Doubletree Ave Ste 1 Columbus (43229) *(G-6151)*

Learning Spectrum Ltd..................................... 614 316-1160
   2630 Aikin Cir N Lewis Center (43035) *(G-9825)*

ALPHABETIC SECTION

Leatherman Nursing Ctrs Corp (PA)... 330 336-6684
  200 Smokerise Dr Ste 300 Wadsworth (44281) *(G-14439)*
Lebanon Dialysis Center, Lebanon *Also Called: River Valley Dialysis LLC (G-9785)*
Lebanon Ford, Lebanon *Also Called: Lebanon Ford Inc (G-9775)*
Lebanon Ford Inc... 513 932-1010
  770 Columbus Ave Lebanon (45036) *(G-9775)*
Lectroetch Company, The, Mentor *Also Called: Monode Marking Products Inc (G-10976)*
Lederer Term 1104, Cleveland *Also Called: US Foods Inc (G-5092)*
Ledger 6031, Columbus *Also Called: Eaton Corporation (G-5802)*
Lee House, Maple Heights *Also Called: Koinonia Partners Holdings LLC (G-10342)*
Leeda Services Inc.. 330 325-1560
  4123 Tallmadge Rd Rootstown (44272) *(G-12761)*
Leeda Services Inc (PA).. 330 392-6006
  1441 Parkman Rd Nw Warren (44485) *(G-14534)*
Leef Bros Inc.. 952 912-5500
  6800 Cintas Blvd Mason (45040) *(G-10572)*
Leef Services, Mason *Also Called: Leef Bros Inc (G-10572)*
Lefeld Implement Inc... 419 678-2375
  5228 State Route 118 Coldwater (45828) *(G-5215)*
Lefeld Supplies Rental, Coldwater *Also Called: Lefeld Welding & Stl Sups Inc (G-5216)*
Lefeld Welding & Stl Sups Inc (PA)... 419 678-2397
  600 N 2nd St Coldwater (45828) *(G-5216)*
Leff Electric, Cleveland *Also Called: Hle Company (G-4368)*
Lefke Tree Experts LLC.. 513 325-1783
  10900 Loveland Madeira Rd Loveland (45140) *(G-10146)*
Legacy Commercial Roofing, Coventry Township *Also Called: Legacy Roofing Services LLC (G-7013)*
Legacy Health Services, Cleveland *Also Called: DMD Management Inc (G-4170)*
Legacy Health Services, Cleveland *Also Called: DMD Management Inc (G-4171)*
Legacy Health Services, Wickliffe *Also Called: DMD Management Inc (G-15147)*
LEGACY HEALTH SERVICES, Wickliffe *Also Called: Wickliffe Country Place Ltd (G-15165)*
Legacy Maintenance Svcs LLC.. 614 473-8444
  2475 Scioto Harper Dr Columbus (43204) *(G-6152)*
Legacy Marble and Granite, Findlay *Also Called: Legacy Ntral Stone Srfaces LLC (G-8558)*
Legacy Ntral Stone Srfaces LLC.. 419 420-7440
  235 Stanford Pkwy Findlay (45840) *(G-8558)*
Legacy Place, Twinsburg *Also Called: DMD Management Inc (G-14182)*
Legacy Properties Inc (HQ)... 440 349-9000
  29300 Aurora Rd Cleveland (44139) *(G-4484)*
Legacy Roofing Services LLC... 330 645-6000
  800 Killian Rd Coventry Township (44319) *(G-7013)*
Legacy Village Management LLC... 216 382-3871
  25333 Cedar Rd Ste 303 Cleveland (44124) *(G-4485)*
Legal Aid Society Cincinnati (PA).. 513 241-9400
  215 E 9th St Ste 200 Cincinnati (45202) *(G-2969)*
Legal Aid Society of Cleveland (PA).. 216 861-5500
  1223 W 6th St Fl 4 Cleveland (44113) *(G-4486)*
Legal Aid Society of Cleveland.. 440 324-1121
  1530 W River Rd N Elyria (44035) *(G-8267)*
Legal Aid Society of Columbus (PA).. 614 737-0139
  1108 City Park Ave Ste 100 Columbus (43206) *(G-6153)*
LEGAL AID SOCIETY OF GREATER C, Cincinnati *Also Called: Legal Aid Society Cincinnati (G-2969)*
Legal Aid Southeast Centl Ohio... 740 354-7563
  800 Gallia St Ste 700 Portsmouth (45662) *(G-12561)*
Legal Aid Western Ohio Inc... 419 724-0030
  525 Jefferson Ave # 400 Toledo (43604) *(G-13884)*
Legal Dfnders Off Smmit Cnty O.. 330 434-3461
  1 Cascade Plz 1940 Akron (44308) *(G-220)*
Legal Support Simplified LLC.. 440 546-3368
  7703 Treelawn Dr Cleveland (44141) *(G-4487)*
Legend.. 216 534-1541
  3111 Carnegie Ave Cleveland (44115) *(G-4488)*
Legend Smelting and Recycl Inc (HQ)....................................... 740 928-0139
  717 O Neill Dr Hebron (43025) *(G-9145)*
Legends Care Center, Massillon *Also Called: Consulate Management Co LLC (G-10636)*
Legrand North America LLC... 937 224-0639
  6500 Poe Ave Dayton (45414) *(G-7451)*
Lehigh Outfitters LLC (HQ).. 740 753-1951
  39 E Canal St Nelsonville (45764) *(G-11549)*

Lei Cbus LLC... 614 302-8830
  7492 Sancus Blvd Worthington (43085) *(G-15432)*
Lei Home Enhancements.. 513 738-4663
  11880 Kemper Springs Dr Cincinnati (45240) *(G-2970)*
Leidos Inc.. 937 656-8433
  3745 Pentagon Blvd Beavercreek (45431) *(G-886)*
Leidos Inc.. 614 575-4900
  77 Outerbelt St Columbus (43213) *(G-6154)*
Leikin Motor Companies Inc.. 440 946-6900
  38750 Mentor Ave Willoughby (44094) *(G-15204)*
Lemon Group LLC... 614 409-9850
  2195 Broehm Rd Obetz (43207) *(G-12081)*
Lenau Park.. 440 235-2646
  7370 Columbia Rd Olmsted Twp (44138) *(G-12091)*
Lencyk Masonry Co Inc... 330 729-9780
  7671 South Ave Youngstown (44512) *(G-15648)*
Lendkey Technologies Inc... 646 626-7396
  9999 Carver Rd Ste 400 Blue Ash (45242) *(G-1201)*
Lendly LLC.. 844 453-6359
  105 Sugar Camp Cir Oakwood (45409) *(G-12049)*
Lenz Inc... 937 277-9364
  3301 Klepinger Rd Dayton (45406) *(G-7452)*
Lenz Company, Dayton *Also Called: Lenz Inc (G-7452)*
Leo Yssnoff Jwish Cmnty Ctr Gr.. 614 775-0312
  150 E Dublin Granville Rd New Albany (43054) *(G-11572)*
Lepi Enterprises Inc.. 740 453-2980
  630 Gw Morse St Zanesville (43701) *(G-15806)*
Leppo Inc (PA).. 330 633-3999
  176 West Ave Tallmadge (44278) *(G-13599)*
Leppo Rents, Tallmadge *Also Called: Leppo Inc (G-13599)*
Lerner RES Inst Clvland Clinic.. 216 444-3900
  9500 Euclid Ave Cleveland (44195) *(G-4489)*
Lesaint Logistics Inc... 513 874-3900
  4487 Le Saint Ct West Chester (45014) *(G-14722)*
Lesaint Logistics Trnsp Inc... 513 942-3056
  200 Northpointe Dr Fairfield (45014) *(G-8426)*
Lesco Inc (HQ).. 216 706-9250
  1385 E 36th St Cleveland (44114) *(G-4490)*
Leslie Equipment Co... 740 373-5255
  105 Tennis Center Dr Marietta (45750) *(G-10380)*
Level Seven... 216 524-9055
  8803 Brecksville Rd Unit 7 Brecksville (44141) *(G-1357)*
Level Up Custom Cnstr Inc... 888 505-9676
  1588 E 40th St Ste C Cleveland (44103) *(G-4491)*
Levis Commons Hotel LLC... 419 873-3573
  6165 Levis Commons Blvd Perrysburg (43551) *(G-12353)*
Levitan Enterprise LLC... 628 208-7016
  6020 W Bancroft St Unit 350061 Toledo (43635) *(G-13885)*
Levy & Associates, Akron *Also Called: David A Levy Inc (G-132)*
Levy & Associates, Columbus *Also Called: Levy & Associates LLC (G-6155)*
Levy & Associates LLC... 614 898-5200
  4645 Executive Dr Columbus (43220) *(G-6155)*
Lewis & Michael Inc (PA).. 937 252-6683
  3920 Image Dr Dayton (45414) *(G-7453)*
Lewis Brsbois Bsgard Smith LLP.. 859 663-9830
  250 E 5th St Ste 2000 Cincinnati (45202) *(G-2971)*
Lewis Landscaping & Nurs Inc.. 330 666-2655
  3606 Minor Rd Copley (44321) *(G-6959)*
Lexamed Ltd.. 419 693-5307
  705 Front St Toledo (43605) *(G-13886)*
Lexington Court Care Center.. 419 884-2000
  250 Delaware Ave Mansfield (44904) *(G-10281)*
Lexisnexis Group... 937 865-6900
  4700 Lyons Rd Miamisburg (45342) *(G-11068)*
Lexisnexis Group (DH).. 937 865-6800
  9443 Springboro Pike Miamisburg (45342) *(G-11069)*
Lexisnexis Group, Miamisburg *Also Called: Lexisnexis Group (G-11069)*
Leyman Liftgates, Cincinnati *Also Called: Leyman Manufacturing Corp (G-2972)*
Leyman Manufacturing Corp... 513 891-6210
  10335 Wayne Ave Cincinnati (45215) *(G-2972)*
Lgstx Services Inc (HQ)... 866 931-2337
  145 Hunter Dr Wilmington (45177) *(G-15257)*

Lh Trucking Inc.. 513 398-1682
  6589 Bunker Oak Trl Mason (45040) *(G-10573)*

Libbey Inc.. 419 671-6000
  1250 Western Ave Toledo (43609) *(G-13887)*

Libby Prszyk Kthman Hldngs Inc... 513 241-6401
  19 Garfield Pl Cincinnati (45202) *(G-2973)*

Liberty Ashtabula Holdings.. 330 872-6000
  4185 State Route 5 Newton Falls (44444) *(G-11777)*

Liberty Capital Inc (PA)... 937 382-1000
  3435 Airborne Rd Ste B Wilmington (45177) *(G-15258)*

Liberty Center AC By Marriott, Liberty Township *Also Called: Liberty Ctr Lodging Assoc LLC (G-9854)*

Liberty Comm Sftwr Sltions Inc.. 614 318-5000
  1050 Kingsmill Pkwy Columbus (43229) *(G-6156)*

Liberty Community Center... 740 369-3876
  207 London Rd Delaware (43015) *(G-7814)*

LIBERTY COMMUNITY CHILDRENS CE, Delaware *Also Called: Liberty Community Center (G-7814)*

Liberty Ctr Lodging Assoc LLC.. 608 833-4100
  7505 Gibson St Liberty Township (45069) *(G-9854)*

Liberty Dialysis - Kenwood, Cincinnati *Also Called: 022808 Kenwood LLC (G-2117)*

Liberty Home Mortgage Corp.. 440 644-0001
  6225 Oak Tree Blvd Independence (44131) *(G-9443)*

Liberty Hospitality Inc.. 330 759-3180
  4055 Belmont Ave Youngstown (44505) *(G-15649)*

Liberty Insulation Co Inc... 513 621-0108
  5782 Deerfield Rd Milford (45150) *(G-11236)*

Liberty Mahoning LLC... 330 549-0070
  10111 Market St North Lima (44452) *(G-11891)*

Liberty Maintenance Inc.. 330 755-7711
  777 N Meridian Rd Youngstown (44509) *(G-15650)*

Liberty Mortgage Company Inc... 614 224-4000
  473 E Rich St Columbus (43215) *(G-6157)*

Liberty Mutual, Cincinnati *Also Called: Ohio Casualty Insurance Co (G-3143)*

Liberty Nrsing Ctr of Jmestown.. 937 675-3311
  4960 Old Us Route 35 E Jamestown (45335) *(G-9535)*

Liberty Nrsing Ctr Rvrside LLC.. 513 557-3621
  315 Lilienthal St Cincinnati (45204) *(G-2974)*

Liberty Nursing Center... 937 836-5143
  425 Lauricella Ct Englewood (45322) *(G-8313)*

Liberty Nursing Home Inc.. 937 376-2121
  126 Wilson Dr Xenia (45385) *(G-15523)*

Liberty Nursing of Willard... 419 935-0148
  370 E Howard St Willard (44890) *(G-15170)*

Liberty Provider LLC... 419 517-7000
  7110 W Central Ave Ste A Toledo (43617) *(G-13888)*

Liberty Retirement Cmnty Lima... 419 331-2273
  2440 Baton Rouge Lima (45805) *(G-9917)*

Liberty Savings Bank FSB (HQ).. 937 382-1000
  2251 Rombach Ave Wilmington (45177) *(G-15259)*

Liberty Steel Industries Inc (PA).. 330 372-6363
  2207 Larchmont Ave Ne Warren (44483) *(G-14535)*

Liberty Steel Products Inc (PA)... 330 538-2236
  11650 Mahoning Ave North Jackson (44451) *(G-11873)*

Liberty Technology Company LLC.. 740 363-1941
  620 Liberty Rd Delaware (43015) *(G-7815)*

Liberty Tire Services LLC.. 330 868-0097
  14864 Lincoln St Se Minerva (44657) *(G-11308)*

Liberty Township, Liberty Township *Also Called: Four Bridges Country Club Ltd (G-9852)*

Liberty Twnship Powell Y M C A.. 740 938-2007
  814 Shanahan Rd Ste 100 Lewis Center (43035) *(G-9826)*

Liberty Village Senior Cmnty, Chillicothe *Also Called: American Health Foundation Inc (G-2050)*

Liberty West Nursing Center, Toledo *Also Called: Parkview Manor Inc (G-13957)*

Liberty-Sps JV Ltd Partnership... 330 755-7711
  777 N Meridian Rd Youngstown (44509) *(G-15651)*

Licking Area Computer Assn.. 740 345-3400
  150 S Quentin Rd 3rd Fl Newark (43055) *(G-11713)*

Licking County Adult Crt Svcs... 740 670-5734
  1 Courthouse Sq Newark (43055) *(G-11714)*

Licking County Aging Program... 740 345-0821
  1058 E Main St Newark (43055) *(G-11715)*

Licking County Board of Mrdd... 740 349-6588
  116 N 22nd St Newark (43055) *(G-11716)*

Licking Mem Fmly Prctice Heath, Heath *Also Called: Licking Memorial Hospital (G-9135)*

Licking Memorial Health Systems, Newark *Also Called: Licking Memorial Hospital (G-11720)*

Licking Memorial Hlth Systems (PA).. 220 564-4000
  1320 W Main St Newark (43055) *(G-11717)*

Licking Memorial Hospital.. 740 348-7915
  687 Hopewell Dr Ste 2 Heath (43056) *(G-9135)*

Licking Memorial Hospital.. 740 348-1750
  1320 W Main St Newark (43055) *(G-11718)*

Licking Memorial Hospital.. 740 348-4870
  200 Messimer Dr Newark (43055) *(G-11719)*

Licking Memorial Hospital (HQ).. 740 348-4137
  1320 W Main St Newark (43055) *(G-11720)*

Licking Rur Elctrification Inc (PA)... 740 892-2071
  11339 Mount Vernon Rd Utica (43080) *(G-14328)*

Licking-Knox Goodwill Inds Inc (PA).. 740 345-9861
  65 S 5th St Newark (43055) *(G-11721)*

Liebel-Flarsheim Company LLC... 513 761-2700
  2111 E Galbraith Rd Cincinnati (45237) *(G-2975)*

Liechty Inc (DH)... 419 445-1565
  1701 S Defiance St Archbold (43502) *(G-461)*

Liechty Inc... 419 298-2302
  2773 Us Highway 6 Edgerton (43517) *(G-8228)*

Liechty Inc... 419 592-3075
  20 Interstate Dr Napoleon (43545) *(G-11526)*

Life Ambulance Service Inc... 740 354-6169
  729 6th St Portsmouth (45662) *(G-12562)*

Life Brand, Willard *Also Called: Holthouse Farms of Ohio Inc (G-15168)*

Life Care Center of Cleveland, Westlake *Also Called: Life Care Centers America Inc (G-15075)*

Life Care Center of Medina, Medina *Also Called: Medina Medical Investors Ltd (G-10863)*

Life Care Centers America Inc... 614 889-6320
  3000 Bethel Rd Columbus (43220) *(G-6158)*

Life Care Centers America Inc... 440 365-5200
  1212 Abbe Rd S Elyria (44035) *(G-8268)*

Life Care Centers America Inc... 330 483-3131
  2400 Columbia Rd Valley City (44280) *(G-14334)*

Life Care Centers America Inc... 440 871-3030
  26520 Center Ridge Rd Westlake (44145) *(G-15075)*

Life Care Centers of Medina, Valley City *Also Called: Life Care Centers America Inc (G-14334)*

Life Connection of Ohio (PA).. 419 893-4891
  3661 Briarfield Blvd Ste 105 Maumee (43537) *(G-10740)*

Life Line Screening Amer Ltd.. 216 581-6556
  6150 Oak Tree Blvd Ste 200 Independence (44131) *(G-9444)*

Life Safety Enterprises Inc.. 440 918-1641
  4699 Hamann Pkwy Willoughby (44094) *(G-15205)*

Life Skills Center, Akron *Also Called: Hat White Management LLC (G-188)*

Life Time Inc... 614 428-6000
  3900 Easton Sta Columbus (43219) *(G-6159)*

Life Time Inc... 614 789-7824
  3825 Hard Rd Dublin (43016) *(G-8054)*

Life Time Inc... 513 234-0660
  8310 Wilkens Blvd Mason (45040) *(G-10574)*

Life Time Fitness Inc... 614 326-1500
  1860 Henderson Rd Columbus (43220) *(G-6160)*

Lifebanc... 216 752-5433
  4775 Richmond Rd Cleveland (44128) *(G-4492)*

Lifecare Alliance... 614 278-3130
  1699 W Mound St Columbus (43223) *(G-6161)*

Lifecare Ambulance Inc.. 440 323-2527
  598 Cleveland St Elyria (44035) *(G-8269)*

Lifecare Family Health, Canton *Also Called: Lifecare Fmly Hlth Dntl Ctr In (G-1794)*

Lifecare Fmly Hlth Dntl Ctr In... 330 454-2000
  2725 Lincoln St E Canton (44707) *(G-1794)*

Lifecare Hospice.. 330 674-8448
  1263 Glen Dr Ste B Millersburg (44654) *(G-11283)*

Lifecare Hospice.. 330 336-6595
  102 Main St Wadsworth (44281) *(G-14440)*

Lifecare Hospice (PA)... 330 264-4899
  1900 Akron Rd Wooster (44691) *(G-15351)*

ALPHABETIC SECTION

Lifecare Pallivative Medicine, Wadsworth *Also Called: Lifecare Hospice (G-14440)*
LIFECARE PALLIVATIVE MEDICINE, Wooster *Also Called: Lifecare Hospice (G-15351)*
Lifecenter Organ Donor Network (PA)..513 558-5555
   615 Elsinore Pl Ste 400 Cincinnati (45202) *(G-2976)*
Lifecenter Plus Inc...330 342-9021
   5133 Darrow Rd Hudson (44236) *(G-9363)*
Lifecycle Solutions Jv LLC..937 938-1321
   2689 Commons Blvd Ste 120 Beavercreek (45431) *(G-887)*
Lifefleet LLC..330 549-9716
   11000 Market St Ste 4 North Lima (44452) *(G-11892)*
Lifegear, Columbus *Also Called: Dorcy International Inc (G-5782)*
Lifeline Hospital, Steubenville *Also Called: Ltac Investors LLC (G-13337)*
Lifeline Partners Inc..330 501-6316
   1825 Tibbetts Wick Rd Girard (44420) *(G-8818)*
Lifepoint Solutions, Amelia *Also Called: Clermont Counseling Center (G-416)*
Lifeservices Management Corp..440 257-3866
   7685 Lake Shore Blvd Mentor (44060) *(G-10964)*
Lifeshare Cmnty Blood Svcs Inc (PA)...440 322-5700
   105 Cleveland St Elyria (44035) *(G-8270)*
LIFESPAN, Hamilton *Also Called: Lifespan Incorporated (G-9060)*
Lifespan Incorporated (PA)...513 868-3210
   1900 Fairgrove Ave Hamilton (45011) *(G-9060)*
Lifestages Boutique For Women...937 274-5420
   9000 N Main St Ste 232 Englewood (45415) *(G-8314)*
Lifestar Ambulance Inc...419 245-6210
   2200 Jefferson Ave Fl 5 Toledo (43604) *(G-13889)*
Lifestges Smrtan Ctrs For Wmen..937 277-8988
   2200 Philadelphia Dr # 101 Dayton (45406) *(G-7454)*
Lifestgs-Smrtan Ctrs For Women, Dayton *Also Called: Lifestges Smrtan Ctrs For Wmen (G-7454)*
Lifestyle Communities Ltd (PA)..614 918-2000
   230 West St Ste 200 Columbus (43215) *(G-6162)*
Lifetime, Mason *Also Called: Life Time Inc (G-10574)*
Lifetime Fitness, Columbus *Also Called: Life Time Inc (G-6159)*
Lifetime Fitness, Columbus *Also Called: Life Time Fitness Inc (G-6160)*
Lifetime Value LLC...216 544-3215
   486 Richmond Rd Cleveland (44143) *(G-4493)*
Lifetouch, Canton *Also Called: Lifetouch Nat Schl Studios Inc (G-1795)*
Lifetouch, Cleveland *Also Called: Lifetouch Nat Schl Studios Inc (G-4494)*
Lifetouch, Ontario *Also Called: Lifetouch Nat Schl Studios Inc (G-12112)*
Lifetouch, West Chester *Also Called: Lifetouch Nat Schl Studios Inc (G-14723)*
Lifetouch Nat Schl Studios Inc...330 497-1291
   1300 S Main St Ste 300 Canton (44720) *(G-1795)*
Lifetouch Nat Schl Studios Inc...440 234-1337
   18683 Sheldon Rd Cleveland (44130) *(G-4494)*
Lifetouch Nat Schl Studios Inc...423 892-3817
   2291 W 4th St Ontario (44906) *(G-12112)*
Lifetouch Nat Schl Studios Inc...513 772-2110
   9782 Windisch Rd West Chester (45069) *(G-14723)*
Lifeway For Youth (PA)...937 845-3625
   127 Quick Rd New Carlisle (45344) *(G-11603)*
Lig Solutions, Independence *Also Called: Lighthouse Insurance Group LLC (G-9445)*
Light of Hearts Villa Inc..440 232-1991
   283 Union St Ofc Cleveland (44146) *(G-4495)*
Light Speed Lgistics Ltd Lblty..330 412-0567
   2516 3rd St Ne Canton (44704) *(G-1796)*
Lighthouse Insurance Group LLC (HQ)..216 503-2439
   6100 Rockside Woods Blvd N Ste 300 Independence (44131) *(G-9445)*
Lighthouse Lab Services, Toledo *Also Called: Lmsi LLC (G-13890)*
Lighthouse Point, Sandusky *Also Called: Cedar Point Park LLC (G-12878)*
LIGHTHOUSE YOUTH SERVICES, Cincinnati *Also Called: Lighthouse Youth Services Inc (G-2977)*
   Lighthouse Youth Services Inc...740 634-3094
      1071 Tong Hollow Rd Bainbridge (45612) *(G-685)*
   Lighthouse Youth Services Inc (PA)...513 221-3350
      401 E Mcmillan St Cincinnati (45206) *(G-2977)*
Lighthuse Bhvral Hlth Sltons L...614 334-6903
   4000 E Main St Columbus (43213) *(G-6163)*
Lighting Services Inc...330 405-4879
   9001 Dutton Dr Twinsburg (44087) *(G-14201)*

Lightspeed LLC...419 666-8800
   2700 Oregon Rd Northwood (43619) *(G-11977)*
Lillian and Betty Ratner Schl..216 464-0033
   27575 Shaker Blvd Cleveland (44124) *(G-4496)*
Lima Auto Mall Inc..419 993-6000
   2200 N Cable Rd Lima (45807) *(G-9918)*
Lima Cdllac Pntiac Olds Nissan, Lima *Also Called: Lima Auto Mall Inc (G-9918)*
Lima City School Central Svcs, Lima *Also Called: Lima City School District (G-9919)*
Lima City School District..419 996-3400
   600 E Wayne St Lima (45801) *(G-9919)*
Lima Cnvlscent HM Fndation Inc (PA)..419 227-5450
   1650 Allentown Rd Lima (45805) *(G-9920)*
Lima Communications Corp..419 228-8835
   1424 Rice Ave Lima (45805) *(G-9921)*
LIMA COMMUNITY HEALTH CENTER, Lima *Also Called: Health Partners Western Ohio (G-9903)*
LIMA CONVALESCENT HOME, Lima *Also Called: Lima Cnvlscent HM Fndation Inc (G-9920)*
Lima Family YMCA (PA)..419 223-6045
   345 S Elizabeth St Lima (45801) *(G-9922)*
Lima Family YMCA..419 223-6055
   136 S West St Lima (45801) *(G-9923)*
Lima Manor, Lima *Also Called: Hcf of Lima Inc (G-9899)*
LIMA MANOR, Lima *Also Called: Hcf of Lima Inc (G-9900)*
Lima Medical Supplies Inc...419 226-9581
   770 W North St Lima (45801) *(G-9924)*
Lima Memorial Health System, Lima *Also Called: Lima Memorial Hospital (G-9925)*
Lima Memorial Hospital (HQ)..419 228-3335
   1001 Bellefontaine Ave Lima (45804) *(G-9925)*
Lima Memorial Hospital La...419 738-5151
   1251 Lincoln Hwy Wapakoneta (45895) *(G-14487)*
Lima Memorial Joint Oper Co (PA)...419 228-5165
   1001 Bellefontaine Ave Lima (45804) *(G-9926)*
Lima Sheet Metal, Lima *Also Called: Lima Sheet Metal Machine & Mfg (G-9927)*
Lima Sheet Metal Machine & Mfg...419 229-1161
   1001 Bowman Rd Lima (45804) *(G-9927)*
Limaidealease, Lima *Also Called: Rush Truck Leasing Inc (G-9957)*
Limbach Company LLC..614 299-2175
   851 Williams Ave Columbus (43212) *(G-6164)*
Limbach Company LLC..614 299-2175
   822 Cleveland Ave Columbus (43201) *(G-6165)*
Lincare Inc..330 928-0884
   1566 Akron Peninsula Rd Ste 2 Akron (44313) *(G-221)*
Lincare Inc..304 243-9605
   114 Mill St Barnesville (43713) *(G-719)*
Lincare Inc..513 272-6050
   10720 Makro Dr Ste A Cincinnati (45241) *(G-2978)*
Lincare Inc..216 581-9649
   9545 Midwest Ave Ste F Cleveland (44125) *(G-4497)*
Lincare Inc..513 705-4250
   4765 Emerald Way Middletown (45044) *(G-11169)*
Lincare Inc..419 499-1188
   11001 Us Highway 250 N Ste E15 Milan (44846) *(G-11207)*
Lincare Inc..937 299-1141
   1948 W Dorothy Ln Moraine (45439) *(G-11420)*
Lincare Inc..740 349-8236
   1961 Tamarack Rd Newark (43055) *(G-11722)*
Lincoln Construction Inc..614 457-6015
   4790 Shuster Rd Columbus (43214) *(G-6166)*
LINCOLN CRAWFORD CARE CENTER, Cincinnati *Also Called: New Scotland Health Care LLC (G-3109)*
Lincoln Electric Automtn Inc (HQ)..937 295-2120
   407 S Main St Fort Loramie (45845) *(G-8605)*
Lincoln Electric Company..216 481-8100
   26250 Bluestone Blvd Euclid (44132) *(G-8355)*
Lincoln Electric Intl Holdg Co (HQ)...216 481-8100
   22801 Saint Clair Ave Euclid (44117) *(G-8356)*
Lincoln Memorial Behavioral, Newark *Also Called: Licking Memorial Hospital (G-11719)*
Lincoln Moving & Storage Co...216 741-5500
   20036 Progress Dr Strongsville (44149) *(G-13470)*
Lincoln Mrcury Kings Auto Mall (PA)..513 683-3800
   9600 Kings Auto Mall Rd Cincinnati (45249) *(G-2979)*

Lincoln Park Associates II LP 937 297-4300
   694 Isaac Prugh Way Dayton (45429) *(G-7455)*
Lincoln Park Manor, Dayton *Also Called: Lincoln Park Associates II LP (G-7455)*
Lincoln Pointe 614 253-4602
   40 Hutchinson Ave Columbus (43235) *(G-6167)*
Lincolnview Local Schools (PA) 419 968-2226
   15945 Middle Point Rd Van Wert (45891) *(G-14348)*
Lincotek Medical LLC 435 753-7675
   811 Northwoods Blvd Vandalia (45377) *(G-14382)*
Lind Media Company, Mansfield *Also Called: Lind Outdoor Advertising Co (G-10282)*
Lind Outdoor Advertising Co 419 522-2600
   409 N Main St 411 Mansfield (44902) *(G-10282)*
Linde Gas & Equipment Inc 330 376-2242
   1760 E Market St Akron (44305) *(G-222)*
Linden-Two Inc 330 928-4064
   137 Ascot Pkwy Cuyahoga Falls (44223) *(G-7087)*
Lindhorst & Dreidame, Cincinnati *Also Called: Lindhorst & Dreidame Co Lpa (G-2980)*
Lindhorst & Dreidame Co Lpa 513 421-6630
   312 Walnut St Ste 3100 Cincinnati (45202) *(G-2980)*
Lineage Logistics LLC 330 559-4860
   1130 Performance Pl Youngstown (44502) *(G-15652)*
Linebrger Gggan Blair Smpson L 614 210-8100
   5080 Tuttle Crossing Blvd Ste 340 Dublin (43016) *(G-8055)*
Liniform Service, Barberton *Also Called: Barberton Laundry and Clg Inc (G-694)*
Link Construction Group Inc 937 292-7774
   895 County Road 32 N Bellefontaine (43311) *(G-1030)*
Link Real Estate Group LLC 614 686-7775
   2500 Farmers Dr Ste 250 Columbus (43235) *(G-6168)*
Linking Emplyment Ablties Ptnt (PA) 216 696-2716
   2545 Lorain Ave Cleveland (44113) *(G-4498)*
Linquest Corporation 937 306-6040
   2647 Commons Blvd Beavercreek (45431) *(G-888)*
Linsalata Capital Partners Inc 440 684-1400
   5900 Landerbrook Dr Ste 280 Mayfield Heights (44124) *(G-10788)*
Linsalata Cpitl Prtners Fund I 440 684-1400
   5900 Landerbrook Dr Ste 280 Cleveland (44124) *(G-4499)*
Lion First Responder Ppe Inc 937 898-1949
   7200 Poe Ave Ste 400 Dayton (45414) *(G-7456)*
Lion Group Inc (HQ) 937 898-1949
   7200 Poe Ave Ste 400 Dayton (45414) *(G-7457)*
Lion-Vallen Ltd Partnership (DH) 937 898-1949
   7200 Poe Ave Ste 400 Dayton (45414) *(G-7458)*
Lion's Den, Worthington *Also Called: Mile Inc (G-15440)*
Lion's Gate Trning SEC Sltions, Euclid *Also Called: Lions Gate SEC Solutions Inc (G-8357)*
Lions Den, Columbus *Also Called: Mile Inc (G-6247)*
Lions Gate SEC Solutions Inc 440 539-8382
   2073 E 221st St Euclid (44117) *(G-8357)*
Lipari Foods Operating Co LLC 330 893-2479
   6597 County Road 625 Millersburg (44654) *(G-11284)*
Lippert Enterprises Inc (PA) 419 281-8084
   1327 Faultless Dr Ashland (44805) *(G-505)*
Lippincott Plmbng-Hting AC Inc 419 222-0856
   872 Saint Johns Ave Lima (45804) *(G-9928)*
Lisnr, Cincinnati *Also Called: Lisnr Inc (G-2981)*
Lisnr Inc (PA) 513 322-8400
   1203 Main St 2nd Fl Cincinnati (45202) *(G-2981)*
Litco International Inc (PA) 330 539-5433
   1 Litco Dr Vienna (44473) *(G-14421)*
Litehouse Pools & Spas, Strongsville *Also Called: Litehouse Products LLC (G-13471)*
Litehouse Products LLC (PA) 440 638-2350
   10883 Pearl Rd Ste 301 Strongsville (44136) *(G-13471)*
Lithchem, Lancaster *Also Called: Cirba Solutions Us Inc (G-9700)*
Lithko, West Chester *Also Called: Lithko Contracting LLC (G-14724)*
Lithko Contracting LLC (PA) 513 564-2000
   2958 Crescentville Rd West Chester (45069) *(G-14724)*
Lithko Restoration Tech LLC (PA) 513 863-5500
   990 N Main St Monroe (45050) *(G-11343)*
Litigation Management Inc 440 484-2000
   7976 Mayfield Rd Chesterland (44026) *(G-2038)*
Litter Distributing Co Inc 740 774-2831
   656 Hospital Rd Chillicothe (45601) *(G-2078)*

Little Bark View Limited (PA) 216 520-1250
   8111 Rockside Rd Ste 200 Cleveland (44125) *(G-4500)*
Little Drmers Big Blievers LLC 614 824-4666
   870 Michigan Ave Columbus (43215) *(G-6169)*
Little Leag Bsbal Englwood Inc 937 545-2670
   700 Arcadia Blvd Englewood (45322) *(G-8315)*
Little Scholars Inc 440 951-3596
   37912 3rd St Willoughby (44094) *(G-15206)*
Little Ssters of Poor Bltmore 513 281-8001
   476 Riddle Rd Cincinnati (45220) *(G-2982)*
Little Ssters of Poor Bltmore 419 698-4331
   860 Ansonia St Ste 13d Oregon (43616) *(G-12135)*
Little Ssters of Poor Bltmore 216 464-1222
   4291 Richmond Rd Warrensville Heights (44122) *(G-14584)*
Little Turtle Golf Club, Westerville *Also Called: Turtle Golf Management Ltd (G-15019)*
Live Media Group Holdings LLC 614 297-0001
   2091 Arlingate Ln Columbus (43228) *(G-6170)*
Live Technologies LLC 614 278-7777
   3445 Millennium Ct Columbus (43219) *(G-6171)*
Living Arrngmnts For Dvlpmntll 513 861-5233
   3603 Victory Pkwy Cincinnati (45229) *(G-2983)*
Living Assistance Services Inc 330 733-1532
   22 Northwest Ave Tallmadge (44278) *(G-13600)*
Living Care Altrntves of Utica 740 892-3414
   233 N Main St Utica (43080) *(G-14329)*
Lizzies Hse Senior HM Care LLC 216 816-4188
   48 Alpha Park Cleveland (44143) *(G-4501)*
Ljb Inc (PA) 937 259-5000
   2500 Newmark Dr Miamisburg (45342) *(G-11070)*
Ljb Incorporated 440 683-4504
   6480 Rockside Woods Blvd S Ste 290 Independence (44131) *(G-9446)*
Lkq Triplettasap Inc (HQ) 330 733-6333
   1435 Triplett Blvd Akron (44306) *(G-223)*
LL Bulding - Tmsich Pthlogy La, Cleveland *Also Called: Cleveland Clinic Foundation (G-4012)*
Llanfair Retirement Community, Cincinnati *Also Called: Ohio Living (G-3147)*
LLC, Cincinnati *Also Called: The Geiler Company (G-3466)*
LLC A Haystack Mssion Essntial 614 750-1908
   6525 W Campus Oval New Albany (43054) *(G-11573)*
LLC Moon Dye 440 623-9016
   6580 Glen Coe Dr Brecksville (44141) *(G-1358)*
Llk Greenhouse Solutions, Strongsville *Also Called: Greenhouse Sltons Acqsition LLC (G-13458)*
LLP Gallagher Sharp 216 241-5310
   1501 Euclid Ave Cleveland (44115) *(G-4502)*
LLP Ziegler Metzger 216 781-5470
   1111 Superior Ave E Ste 1000 Cleveland (44114) *(G-4503)*
Lm Constrction Trry Lvrini Inc 740 695-9604
   67682 Clark Rd Saint Clairsville (43950) *(G-12797)*
LMI Transports Inc 513 921-4564
   10300 Evendale Dr Ste 4 Cincinnati (45241) *(G-2984)*
Lmn Development LLC (PA) 419 433-7200
   7000 Kalahari Dr Sandusky (44870) *(G-12910)*
Lmsi LLC 800 838-0602
   2710 Centennial Rd Toledo (43617) *(G-13890)*
Lnb Bancorp Inc 440 244-6000
   457 Broadway Lorain (44052) *(G-10083)*
LNS America Inc (DH) 513 528-5674
   4621 E Tech Dr Cincinnati (45245) *(G-2110)*
Loan Protector Insurance Svcs, Solon *Also Called: LP Insurance Services LLC (G-13108)*
Lobby Shoppes Inc 937 324-0002
   200 N Murray St Springfield (45503) *(G-13263)*
Lobby Shoppes Inc-Springfield, Springfield *Also Called: Lobby Shoppes Inc (G-13263)*
Local 304, Cincinnati *Also Called: National Pstal Mail Hndlers Un (G-3096)*
Lochard Inc 937 492-8811
   903 Wapakoneta Ave Sidney (45365) *(G-13037)*
Lockhaven Apts, Lima *Also Called: The Lochhaven Company (G-9970)*
Locktooth Division, Cleveland *Also Called: Hodell-Natco Industries Inc (G-4372)*
Locum Medical Group LLC 216 464-2125
   6100 Oak Tree Blvd Ste 110 Independence (44131) *(G-9447)*
Locus AG Solutions LLC 440 248-8787
   30600 Aurora Rd Ste 180 Solon (44139) *(G-13105)*

ALPHABETIC SECTION — Loveland Hlth Care Nrsing Rhab

Locus Management LLC 888 510-0004
  30600 Aurora Rd Ste 180 Solon (44139) *(G-13106)*
Locus Performance Ingredients, Solon *Also Called: Locus Management LLC (G-13106)*
Locust Ridge Nursing Home Inc 937 444-2920
  12745 Elm Corner Rd Williamsburg (45176) *(G-15180)*
Lodge At Saw Mill Creek, The, Huron *Also Called: Saw Mill Creek Ltd (G-9392)*
Lodge Care Center Inc 513 683-9966
  9370 Union Cemetery Rd Loveland (45140) *(G-10147)*
LODGE NURSING & REHAB CENTER, Loveland *Also Called: Boy-Ko Management Inc (G-10128)*
Lodging Assoc St Clrsville Inc 740 695-5038
  51260 National Rd Saint Clairsville (43950) *(G-12798)*
Lodging First LLC 614 792-2770
  94 N High St Ste 250 Dublin (43017) *(G-8056)*
Lodging Industry Inc 419 625-7070
  5410 Milan Rd Sandusky (44870) *(G-12911)*
Lodi Community Hospital (HQ) 330 948-1222
  225 Elyria St Lodi (44254) *(G-10019)*
Loeb Electric Company (PA) 800 686-6351
  1800 E 5th Ave Ste A Columbus (43219) *(G-6172)*
Logan Acres, Bellefontaine *Also Called: County of Logan (G-1027)*
Logan Clutch Corporation 440 808-4258
  28855 Ranney Pkwy Cleveland (44145) *(G-4504)*
Logan Cnty Bd Mntal Rtardation, Bellefontaine *Also Called: County of Logan (G-1025)*
Logan Cnty Prbate Juvenile Crt, Bellefontaine *Also Called: County of Logan (G-1026)*
Logan County Childrens Svcs, Bellefontaine *Also Called: County of Logan (G-1028)*
Logan Elm Health Care Center 740 474-3121
  370 Tarlton Rd Circleville (43113) *(G-3712)*
Logan Healthcare Leasing LLC 216 367-1214
  300 Arlington Ave Logan (43138) *(G-10032)*
Logan Logistics, Canton *Also Called: W L Logan Trucking Company (G-1882)*
Logan View LLC 937 592-3902
  112 Dowell Ave Bellefontaine (43311) *(G-1031)*
Logan-Hocking School District 740 385-7844
  13483 Maysville Williams Rd Logan (43138) *(G-10033)*
Logic Soft Inc 614 884-5544
  5900 Sawmill Rd Ste 200 Dublin (43017) *(G-8057)*
Logik, Dayton *Also Called: Cycle-Logik LLC (G-7266)*
Logistical Resource Group Inc 330 283-3733
  573 Highland Rd E Ste 2 Macedonia (44056) *(G-10199)*
Logistics Inc 419 478-1514
  6010 Skyview Dr Toledo (43612) *(G-13891)*
Logistics Legacy LLC 513 244-3026
  1085 Summer St Cincinnati (45204) *(G-2985)*
Logos Communications Systems Inc 440 871-0777
  26100 1st St Westlake (44145) *(G-15076)*
Logtec Inc 937 878-8450
  1825 Commerce Center Blvd Fairborn (45324) *(G-8378)*
London Computer Systems Inc 513 583-0840
  9140 Waterstone Blvd Cincinnati (45249) *(G-2986)*
London Health & Rehab Ctr LLC 740 852-3100
  218 Elm St London (43140) *(G-10045)*
Long & Wilcox LLC 614 273-3100
  250 W Old Wilson Bridge Rd Ste 140 Worthington (43085) *(G-15433)*
Long Business Systems Inc 440 846-8500
  10749 Pearl Rd Ste 2a Strongsville (44136) *(G-13472)*
Long Term Care Ombudsman 216 696-2719
  8111 Rockside Rd Ste 250 Cleveland (44125) *(G-4505)*
Long-Stanton Mfg Company 513 874-8020
  9388 Sutton Pl West Chester (45011) *(G-14725)*
Longbow Research LLC (PA) 216 986-0700
  6100 Oak Tree Blvd Ste 440 Independence (44131) *(G-9448)*
Longmeadow Care Center Inc 330 297-5781
  565 Bryn Mawr St Ravenna (44266) *(G-12632)*
Longwood Family YMCA, Macedonia *Also Called: Young MNS Chrstn Assn of Akron (G-10210)*
Lonz Winery, Cleveland *Also Called: Paramount Distillers Inc (G-4718)*
Lorad LLC (PA) 800 504-4016
  24400 Sperry Dr Westlake (44145) *(G-15077)*
Lorain Cnty Alchol DRG Abuse S 440 323-6122
  1882 E 32nd St Lorain (44055) *(G-10084)*

Lorain Cnty Bd Dvlpmntal Dsblt 440 329-3734
  1091 Infirmary Rd Elyria (44035) *(G-8271)*
Lorain Cnty Bd Mntal Rtrdtion, Elyria *Also Called: County of Lorain (G-8238)*
Lorain Cnty Bys Girls CLB Inc 330 773-3375
  889 Jonathan Ave Akron (44306) *(G-224)*
Lorain Cnty Cmnty Action Agcy 440 246-0480
  1050 Reid Ave Lorain (44052) *(G-10085)*
Lorain County Alcohol and Drug 440 246-0109
  305 W 20th St Lorain (44052) *(G-10086)*
LORAIN COUNTY ALCOHOL AND DRUG, Lorain *Also Called: Lorain County Alcohol and Drug (G-10086)*
Lorain County Boys and Girls Club, Inc., Akron *Also Called: Lorain Cnty Bys Girls CLB Inc (G-224)*
Lorain County Childrens Svcs, Elyria *Also Called: County of Lorain (G-8240)*
Lorain County Senior Care Inc 440 353-3080
  35590 Center Ridge Rd Ste 101 North Ridgeville (44039) *(G-11931)*
Lorain Family Hlth & RES Ctrs, Lorain *Also Called: Cleveland Clinic Foundation (G-10065)*
Lorain Manor Inc 440 277-8173
  1882 E 32nd St Lorain (44055) *(G-10087)*
Lorain Manor Nursing Home, Lorain *Also Called: Lorain Manor Inc (G-10087)*
Lorain National Bank (HQ) 440 244-6000
  457 Broadway Lorain (44052) *(G-10088)*
Lorain National Bank 440 244-7242
  200 W 6th St Lorain (44052) *(G-10089)*
Lorantffy Care Center Inc 330 666-2631
  2631 Copley Rd Copley (44321) *(G-6960)*
Lord Corporation 440 542-0012
  33585 Bainbridge Rd Solon (44139) *(G-13107)*
Lorenz Corporation (PA) 937 228-6118
  501 E 3rd St Dayton (45402) *(G-7459)*
Lori Holding Co (PA) 740 342-3230
  1400 Commerce Dr New Lexington (43764) *(G-11628)*
Lormet Community Federal Cr Un (PA) 440 960-6600
  2051 Cooper Foster Park Rd Amherst (44001) *(G-431)*
Losant Iot Inc 513 381-2947
  1100 Sycamore St Fl 7 Cincinnati (45202) *(G-2987)*
Losantiville Country Club 513 631-4133
  3097 Losantiville Ave Cincinnati (45213) *(G-2988)*
Lost Creek Care Center, Lima *Also Called: Volunters Amer Care Facilities (G-9978)*
Lost Creek Hlth Care Rhbltion 419 225-9040
  804 S Mumaugh Rd Lima (45804) *(G-9929)*
Loth Inc (PA) 513 554-4900
  3574 E Kemper Rd Cincinnati (45241) *(G-2989)*
Loth Inc 614 487-4000
  855 Grandview Ave Ste 2 Columbus (43215) *(G-6173)*
Lott Industries, Maumee *Also Called: Lott Industries Incorporated (G-10741)*
Lott Industries Incorporated 419 891-5215
  1645 Holland Rd Maumee (43537) *(G-10741)*
Lou Ritenour Decorators Inc 330 425-3232
  2066 Case Pkwy S Twinsburg (44087) *(G-14202)*
Loudenville Training Center, Ashland *Also Called: Ashland Training Center (G-476)*
Louderback Fmly Invstments Inc 937 845-1762
  3545 Dayton Lakeview Rd New Carlisle (45344) *(G-11604)*
Louis Perry & Associates Inc 330 334-1585
  165 Smokerise Dr Wadsworth (44281) *(G-14441)*
Louis Stokes Cleveland Vamc, Cleveland *Also Called: Veterans Health Administration (G-5101)*
Louisana Vtrnary Rfrral Ctr LL, Worthington *Also Called: Medvet Louisiana LLC (G-15438)*
Louisville Title Agency, Toledo *Also Called: Louisvlle Title Agcy For NW OH (G-13892)*
Louisville YMCA, Louisville *Also Called: Young MNS Chrstn Assn Cntl STA (G-10124)*
Louisvlle Title Agcy For NW OH (PA) 419 248-4611
  626 Madison Ave Ste 100 Toledo (43604) *(G-13892)*
Love Insurance Agency, Chardon *Also Called: Insurnce Specialists Group Inc (G-2007)*
Loveland Excavating Inc 513 965-6600
  260 Osborne Dr Fairfield (45014) *(G-8427)*
Loveland Excavating and Paving, Fairfield *Also Called: Loveland Excavating Inc (G-8427)*
Loveland Health Care Center 513 605-6000
  501 N 2nd St Loveland (45140) *(G-10148)*
Loveland Hlth Care Nrsing Rhab, Loveland *Also Called: Loveland Health Care Center (G-10148)*

Loveman Steel Corporation 440 232-6200
5455 Perkins Rd Bedford (44146) *(G-969)*

Loving Care Day Care Ottawa LL 419 523-3133
360 N Locust St Ste A Ottawa (45875) *(G-12188)*

Loving Care Home Hlth Agcy LLC 216 322-9316
9545 Midwest Ave Ste I Garfield Heights (44125) *(G-8776)*

Loving Care Learning Center, Ottawa *Also Called: Loving Care Day Care Ottawa LL (G-12188)*

Loving Family Home Care Inc 888 469-2178
2600 N Reynolds Rd Ste 101a Toledo (43615) *(G-13893)*

Lowe's, Akron *Also Called: Lowes Home Centers LLC (G-225)*
Lowe's, Alliance *Also Called: Lowes Home Centers LLC (G-389)*
Lowe's, Ashtabula *Also Called: Lowes Home Centers LLC (G-540)*
Lowe's, Athens *Also Called: Lowes Home Centers LLC (G-582)*
Lowe's, Avon *Also Called: Lowes Home Centers LLC (G-660)*
Lowe's, Beavercreek *Also Called: Lowes Home Centers LLC (G-889)*
Lowe's, Bedford *Also Called: Lowes Home Centers LLC (G-970)*
Lowe's, Bellefontaine *Also Called: Lowes Home Centers LLC (G-1032)*
Lowe's, Canton *Also Called: Lowes Home Centers LLC (G-1797)*
Lowe's, Chillicothe *Also Called: Lowes Home Centers LLC (G-2079)*
Lowe's, Cincinnati *Also Called: Lowes Home Centers LLC (G-2990)*
Lowe's, Cleveland *Also Called: Lowes Home Centers LLC (G-4506)*
Lowe's, Columbus *Also Called: Lowes Home Centers LLC (G-6174)*
Lowe's, Dayton *Also Called: Lowes Home Centers LLC (G-7460)*
Lowe's, Dayton *Also Called: Lowes Home Centers LLC (G-7461)*
Lowe's, Dayton *Also Called: Lowes Home Centers LLC (G-7462)*
Lowe's, Defiance *Also Called: Lowes Home Centers LLC (G-7753)*
Lowe's, Dublin *Also Called: Lowes Home Centers LLC (G-8058)*
Lowe's, Elyria *Also Called: Lowes Home Centers LLC (G-8272)*
Lowe's, Findlay *Also Called: Lowes Home Centers LLC (G-8559)*
Lowe's, Fremont *Also Called: Lowes Home Centers LLC (G-8690)*
Lowe's, Greenville *Also Called: Lowes Home Centers LLC (G-8880)*
Lowe's, Hamilton *Also Called: Lowes Home Centers LLC (G-9061)*
Lowe's, Hilliard *Also Called: Lowes Home Centers LLC (G-9210)*
Lowe's, Lancaster *Also Called: Lowes Home Centers LLC (G-9733)*
Lowe's, Lima *Also Called: Lowes Home Centers LLC (G-9930)*
Lowe's, Lorain *Also Called: Lowes Home Centers LLC (G-10090)*
Lowe's, Marietta *Also Called: Lowes Home Centers LLC (G-10381)*
Lowe's, Marion *Also Called: Lowes Home Centers LLC (G-10433)*
Lowe's, Marysville *Also Called: Lowes Home Centers LLC (G-10492)*
Lowe's, Mason *Also Called: Lowes Home Centers LLC (G-10575)*
Lowe's, Massillon *Also Called: Lowes Home Centers LLC (G-10650)*
Lowe's, Mentor *Also Called: Lowes Home Centers LLC (G-10965)*
Lowe's, Middletown *Also Called: Lowes Home Centers LLC (G-11170)*
Lowe's, Milford *Also Called: Lowes Home Centers LLC (G-11237)*
Lowe's, Mount Vernon *Also Called: Lowes Home Centers LLC (G-11498)*
Lowe's, New Philadelphia *Also Called: Lowes Home Centers LLC (G-11657)*
Lowe's, Newark *Also Called: Lowes Home Centers LLC (G-11723)*
Lowe's, Northfield *Also Called: Lowes Home Centers LLC (G-11960)*
Lowe's, Ontario *Also Called: Lowes Home Centers LLC (G-12113)*
Lowe's, Perrysburg *Also Called: Lowes Home Centers LLC (G-12355)*
Lowe's, Reynoldsburg *Also Called: Lowes Home Centers LLC (G-12668)*
Lowe's, Rocky River *Also Called: Lowes Home Centers LLC (G-12748)*
Lowe's, Saint Clairsville *Also Called: Lowes Home Centers LLC (G-12799)*
Lowe's, Sandusky *Also Called: Lowes Home Centers LLC (G-12912)*
Lowe's, Sidney *Also Called: Lowes Home Centers LLC (G-13039)*
Lowe's, South Lebanon *Also Called: Lowes Home Centers LLC (G-13172)*
Lowe's, South Point *Also Called: Lowes Home Centers LLC (G-13177)*
Lowe's, Springfield *Also Called: Lowes Home Centers LLC (G-13264)*
Lowe's, Steubenville *Also Called: Lowes Home Centers LLC (G-13336)*
Lowe's, Stow *Also Called: Lowes Home Centers LLC (G-13380)*
Lowe's, Streetsboro *Also Called: Lowes Home Centers LLC (G-13420)*
Lowe's, Strongsville *Also Called: Lowes Home Centers LLC (G-13473)*
Lowe's, Toledo *Also Called: Lowes Home Centers LLC (G-13894)*
Lowe's, Troy *Also Called: Lowes Home Centers LLC (G-14145)*

Lowe's, Wadsworth *Also Called: Lowes Home Centers LLC (G-14442)*
Lowe's, Wapakoneta *Also Called: Lowes Home Centers LLC (G-14488)*
Lowe's, Warren *Also Called: Lowes Home Centers LLC (G-14536)*
Lowe's, West Chester *Also Called: Lowes Home Centers LLC (G-14726)*
Lowe's, Wheelersburg *Also Called: Lowes Home Centers LLC (G-15130)*
Lowe's, Willoughby *Also Called: Lowes Home Centers LLC (G-15207)*
Lowe's, Wilmington *Also Called: Lowes Home Centers LLC (G-15260)*
Lowe's, Wooster *Also Called: Lowes Home Centers LLC (G-15352)*
Lowe's, Wshngtn Ct Hs *Also Called: Lowes Home Centers LLC (G-15489)*
Lowe's, Xenia *Also Called: Lowes Home Centers LLC (G-15524)*
Lowe's, Youngstown *Also Called: Lowes Home Centers LLC (G-15653)*
Lowe's, Zanesville *Also Called: Lowes Home Centers LLC (G-15807)*

Lowe's Greenhouses & Gift Shop, Chagrin Falls *Also Called: Lowes Investments Inc (G-1984)*

Lowell Mackenzie 614 451-6669
1610 Wapakoneta Ave Sidney (45365) *(G-13038)*

Lower Great Lakes Kenworth Inc 419 874-3511
12650 Eckel Junction Rd Perrysburg (43551) *(G-12354)*

Lowes Home Centers LLC 330 665-9356
186 N Cleveland Massillon Rd Akron (44333) *(G-225)*

Lowes Home Centers LLC 330 829-2700
2595 W State St Alliance (44601) *(G-389)*

Lowes Home Centers LLC 440 998-6555
2416 Dillon Dr Ashtabula (44004) *(G-540)*

Lowes Home Centers LLC 740 589-3750
983 E State St Athens (45701) *(G-582)*

Lowes Home Centers LLC 440 937-3500
1445 Center Rd Avon (44011) *(G-660)*

Lowes Home Centers LLC 937 427-1110
2850 Centre Dr Ste I Beavercreek (45324) *(G-889)*

Lowes Home Centers LLC 216 831-2860
24500 Miles Rd Bedford (44146) *(G-970)*

Lowes Home Centers LLC 937 599-4000
2168 Us Highway 68 S Bellefontaine (43311) *(G-1032)*

Lowes Home Centers LLC 330 497-2720
6375 Strip Ave Nw Canton (44720) *(G-1797)*

Lowes Home Centers LLC 740 773-7777
867 N Bridge St Chillicothe (45601) *(G-2079)*

Lowes Home Centers LLC 513 598-7050
6150 Harrison Ave Cincinnati (45247) *(G-2990)*

Lowes Home Centers LLC 216 351-4723
7327 Northcliff Ave Cleveland (44144) *(G-4506)*

Lowes Home Centers LLC 614 853-6200
1675 Georgesville Square Dr Columbus (43228) *(G-6174)*

Lowes Home Centers LLC 937 235-2920
8421 Troy Pike Dayton (45424) *(G-7460)*

Lowes Home Centers LLC 937 438-4900
2900 Martins Dr Dayton (45449) *(G-7461)*

Lowes Home Centers LLC 937 854-8200
5252 Salem Ave Dayton (45426) *(G-7462)*

Lowes Home Centers LLC 419 782-9000
1831 N Clinton St Defiance (43512) *(G-7753)*

Lowes Home Centers LLC 614 659-0530
6555 Dublin Center Dr Dublin (43017) *(G-8058)*

Lowes Home Centers LLC 440 324-5004
646 Midway Blvd Elyria (44035) *(G-8272)*

Lowes Home Centers LLC 419 420-7531
1077 Bright Rd Findlay (45840) *(G-8559)*

Lowes Home Centers LLC 419 355-0221
1952 N State Route 53 Fremont (43420) *(G-8690)*

Lowes Home Centers LLC 937 547-2400
1550 Wagner Ave Greenville (45331) *(G-8880)*

Lowes Home Centers LLC 513 737-3700
1495 Main St Hamilton (45013) *(G-9061)*

Lowes Home Centers LLC 614 529-5900
3600 Park Mill Run Dr Hilliard (43026) *(G-9210)*

Lowes Home Centers LLC 740 681-3464
2240 Lowes Dr Lancaster (43130) *(G-9733)*

Lowes Home Centers LLC 419 331-3598
2411 N Eastown Rd Lima (45807) *(G-9930)*

ALPHABETIC SECTION — Luckey Farmers Inc

Lowes Home Centers LLC 440 985-5700
7500 Oak Point Rd Lorain (44053) *(G-10090)*

Lowes Home Centers LLC 740 374-2151
842 Pike St Marietta (45750) *(G-10381)*

Lowes Home Centers LLC 740 389-9737
1840 Marion Mount Gilead Rd Marion (43302) *(G-10433)*

Lowes Home Centers LLC 937 578-4440
15775 Us Highway 36 Marysville (43040) *(G-10492)*

Lowes Home Centers LLC 513 336-9741
9380 S Mason Montgomery Rd Mason (45040) *(G-10575)*

Lowes Home Centers LLC 330 832-1901
101 Massillon Marketplace Dr Sw Massillon (44646) *(G-10650)*

Lowes Home Centers LLC 440 392-0027
9600 Mentor Ave Mentor (44060) *(G-10965)*

Lowes Home Centers LLC 513 727-3900
3125 Towne Blvd Middletown (45044) *(G-11170)*

Lowes Home Centers LLC 513 965-3280
5694 Romar Dr Milford (45150) *(G-11237)*

Lowes Home Centers LLC 740 393-5350
1010 Coshocton Ave Mount Vernon (43050) *(G-11498)*

Lowes Home Centers LLC 330 339-1936
495 Mill Ave Se New Philadelphia (44663) *(G-11657)*

Lowes Home Centers LLC 740 522-0003
888 Hebron Rd Newark (43056) *(G-11723)*

Lowes Home Centers LLC 330 908-2750
8224 Golden Link Blvd Northfield (44067) *(G-11960)*

Lowes Home Centers LLC 419 747-1920
940 N Lexington Springmill Rd Ontario (44906) *(G-12113)*

Lowes Home Centers LLC 419 874-6758
10295 Fremont Pike Perrysburg (43551) *(G-12355)*

Lowes Home Centers LLC 614 769-9940
8231 E Broad St Reynoldsburg (43068) *(G-12668)*

Lowes Home Centers LLC 440 331-1027
20639 Center Ridge Rd Rocky River (44116) *(G-12748)*

Lowes Home Centers LLC 740 699-3000
50421 Valley Plaza Dr Saint Clairsville (43950) *(G-12799)*

Lowes Home Centers LLC 419 624-6000
5500 Milan Rd Ste 304 Sandusky (44870) *(G-12912)*

Lowes Home Centers LLC 937 498-8400
2700 Michigan St Sidney (45365) *(G-13039)*

Lowes Home Centers LLC 513 445-1000
575 Corwin Nixon Blvd South Lebanon (45065) *(G-13172)*

Lowes Home Centers LLC 740 894-7120
294 County Road 120 S South Point (45680) *(G-13177)*

Lowes Home Centers LLC 937 327-6000
1601 N Bechtle Ave Springfield (45504) *(G-13264)*

Lowes Home Centers LLC 740 266-3500
4115 Mall Dr Steubenville (43952) *(G-13336)*

Lowes Home Centers LLC 330 920-9280
3570 Hudson Dr Stow (44224) *(G-13380)*

Lowes Home Centers LLC 330 626-2980
1210 State Route 303 Streetsboro (44241) *(G-13420)*

Lowes Home Centers LLC 440 239-2630
9149 Pearl Rd Strongsville (44136) *(G-13473)*

Lowes Home Centers LLC 419 843-9758
7000 W Central Ave Toledo (43617) *(G-13894)*

Lowes Home Centers LLC 937 339-2544
2000 W Main St Troy (45373) *(G-14145)*

Lowes Home Centers LLC 330 335-1900
1065 Williams Reserve Blvd Wadsworth (44281) *(G-14442)*

Lowes Home Centers LLC 419 739-1300
1340 Bellefontaine St Wapakoneta (45895) *(G-14488)*

Lowes Home Centers LLC 330 609-8000
940 Niles Cortland Rd Se Warren (44484) *(G-14536)*

Lowes Home Centers LLC 513 755-4300
7975 Tylersville Square Dr West Chester (45069) *(G-14726)*

Lowes Home Centers LLC 740 574-6200
7915 Ohio River Rd Wheelersburg (45694) *(G-15130)*

Lowes Home Centers LLC 440 942-2759
36300 Euclid Ave Willoughby (44094) *(G-15207)*

Lowes Home Centers LLC 937 383-7000
1175 Rombach Ave Wilmington (45177) *(G-15260)*

Lowes Home Centers LLC 330 287-2261
3788 Burbank Rd Wooster (44691) *(G-15352)*

Lowes Home Centers LLC 740 636-2100
1895 Lowes Blvd Wshngtn Ct Hs (43160) *(G-15489)*

Lowes Home Centers LLC 937 347-4000
126 Hospitality Dr Xenia (45385) *(G-15524)*

Lowes Home Centers LLC 330 965-4500
1100 Doral Dr Youngstown (44514) *(G-15653)*

Lowes Home Centers LLC 740 450-5500
3755 Frazeysburg Rd Zanesville (43701) *(G-15807)*

Lowes Investments Inc 440 543-5123
16540 Chillicothe Rd Chagrin Falls (44023) *(G-1984)*

Loyal American Life Insur Co 800 633-6752
250 E 5th St 8th Fl Cincinnati (45202) *(G-2991)*

LP Coshocton LLC 470 622-1220
100 S Whitewoman St Coshocton (43812) *(G-6991)*

LP Insurance Services LLC 877 369-5121
6000 Cochran Rd Solon (44139) *(G-13108)*

LP Opco LLC 440 593-6266
22 Parrish Rd Conneaut (44030) *(G-6943)*

Lq Management LLC 513 771-0300
11029 Dowlin Dr Cincinnati (45241) *(G-2992)*

Lq Management LLC 216 447-1133
6161 Quarry Ln Cleveland (44131) *(G-4507)*

Lq Management LLC 419 774-0005
120 Stander Ave Mansfield (44903) *(G-10283)*

Lrt Restoration Technologies, Monroe *Also Called: Lithko Restoration Tech LLC (G-11343)*

LSI Adl Technology LLC 614 345-9040
2727 Scioto Pkwy Columbus (43221) *(G-6175)*

LSI Industries Inc 913 281-1100
10000 Alliance Rd Blue Ash (45242) *(G-1202)*

LSI Lightron Inc 845 562-5500
10000 Alliance Rd Blue Ash (45242) *(G-1203)*

LT Harnett Trucking Inc 440 997-5528
2440 State Rd Ashtabula (44004) *(G-541)*

Ltac Investors LLC 740 346-2600
200 School St Steubenville (43953) *(G-13337)*

Ltccorp Government Services-Oh Inc 419 794-3500
1480 Ford St Maumee (43537) *(G-10742)*

Lti Inc 614 278-7777
3445 Millennium Ct Columbus (43219) *(G-6176)*

LTV-Trico Inc 216 622-5000
25 W Prospect Ave Cleveland (44115) *(G-4508)*

Lu-Jean Feng Clinic LLC 216 831-7007
31200 Pinetree Rd Cleveland (44124) *(G-4509)*

Luburgh Inc (PA) 740 452-3668
4174 East Pike Zanesville (43701) *(G-15808)*

Lucas Cnty Bd Dvlpmntal Dsblti 419 380-4000
1154 Larc Ln Toledo (43614) *(G-13895)*

Lucas Cnty Brd of Mntl Rtrdtn, Toledo *Also Called: County of Lucas (G-13765)*

Lucas County Ohio 419 213-4808
1 Government Ctr Ste 600 Toledo (43604) *(G-13896)*

Lucas County Children Services 419 213-3247
705 Adams St Toledo (43604) *(G-13897)*

Lucas County Coroners Office, Toledo *Also Called: County of Lucas (G-13767)*

Lucas County Engineer, Holland *Also Called: County of Lucas (G-9283)*

Lucas County Home Training, Oregon *Also Called: Desoto Dialysis LLC (G-12132)*

Lucas County Prosecutors Off, Toledo *Also Called: County of Lucas (G-13764)*

Lucas County Regional Hlth Dst, Toledo *Also Called: County of Lucas (G-13766)*

Lucas Funeral Homes Inc (PA) 419 294-1985
476 S Sandusky Ave Upper Sandusky (43351) *(G-14291)*

Lucas Plumbing & Heating Inc 440 282-4567
2125 W Park Dr Lorain (44053) *(G-10091)*

Lucas Sumitomo Brakes Inc 513 934-0024
1650 Kingsview Dr Lebanon (45036) *(G-9776)*

Lucas-Batton Funeral Homes, Upper Sandusky *Also Called: Lucas Funeral Homes Inc (G-14291)*

Lucid Investments Inc 216 972-0058
4034 Skiff St Willoughby (44094) *(G-15208)*

Luckey Farmers Inc 419 665-2322
154 Dewey St Lindsey (43442) *(G-9995)*

Luckey Transfer LLC..800 435-4371
  401 E Robb Ave Lima (45801) *(G-9931)*

Lucrum Incorporated...513 241-5949
  7755 Montgomery Rd Ste 160 Cincinnati (45236) *(G-2993)*

Ludy Greenhouse Mfg Corp (PA)..........................800 255-5839
  122 Railroad St New Madison (45346) *(G-11634)*

Luk-Aftermarket Service Inc.................................330 273-4383
  5370 Wegman Dr Valley City (44280) *(G-14335)*

Lululemon USA Inc..614 418-9127
  4085 The Strand W Columbus (43219) *(G-6177)*

Lululemon USA Inc..440 250-0415
  201 Market St Westlake (44145) *(G-15078)*

Lumenomics Inc..614 798-3500
  8333 Green Meadows Dr N Ste B Lewis Center (43035) *(G-9827)*

Lument Real Estate Capital LLC (DH)..................614 586-9380
  10 W Broad St Ste 800 Columbus (43215) *(G-6178)*

Lumiere Detox Center..513 644-2275
  7593 Tylers Place Blvd West Chester (45069) *(G-14727)*

Luminance, Cuyahoga Falls Also Called: *American De Rosa Lamparts LLC (G-7038)*

Luminaut Inc...513 984-1070
  1100 Sycamore St Cincinnati (45202) *(G-2994)*

Luminex HD&f Company, Blue Ash Also Called: *Luminex HM Dcor Frgrnce Hldg C (G-1204)*

Luminex HM Dcor Frgrnce Hldg C (PA)................513 563-1113
  10521 Millington Ct Blue Ash (45242) *(G-1204)*

Lunar Cow Design Inc...330 836-0911
  120 E Mill St Ste 415 Akron (44308) *(G-226)*

Lunar Tool & Mold Inc...440 237-2141
  9860 York Alpha Dr North Royalton (44133) *(G-11944)*

Luper Neidental & Logan A Leg...........................614 221-7663
  1160 Dublin Rd Ste 400 Columbus (43215) *(G-6179)*

Luper Neidenthal & Logan, Columbus Also Called: *Luper Neidental & Logan A Leg (G-6179)*

Lupo & Koczkur PC..419 897-7931
  1690 Woodlands Dr Maumee (43537) *(G-10743)*

Lutheran Home..440 871-0090
  2116 Dover Center Rd Cleveland (44145) *(G-4510)*

Lutheran Home..419 724-1414
  131 N Wheeling St Ofc Toledo (43605) *(G-13898)*

Lutheran Homes Society Inc................................419 334-5500
  916 North St Fremont (43420) *(G-8691)*

Lutheran Homes Society Inc................................419 724-1525
  1905 Perrysburg Holland Rd Holland (43528) *(G-9294)*

Lutheran Homes Society Inc................................419 861-2233
  2001 Perrysburg Holland Rd Holland (43528) *(G-9295)*

Lutheran Homes Society Inc................................419 591-4060
  1036 S Perry St Napoleon (43545) *(G-11527)*

Lutheran Homes Society Inc (PA)........................419 861-4990
  2021 N Mccord Rd Toledo (43615) *(G-13899)*

Lutheran Medical Center Inc................................216 696-4300
  1730 W 25th St Cleveland (44113) *(G-4511)*

Lutheran Medical Center Inc (HQ)........................440 519-6800
  33001 Solon Rd Ste 112 Solon (44139) *(G-13109)*

Lutheran Memorial Home Inc...............................419 502-5700
  2021 N Mccord Rd Toledo (43615) *(G-13900)*

Lutheran Scial Svcs Centl Ohio............................419 289-3523
  622 Center St Ashland (44805) *(G-506)*

Lutheran Scial Svcs Centl Ohio (PA)....................419 289-3523
  500 W Wilson Bridge Rd Ste 245 Worthington (43085) *(G-15434)*

Lutheran Senior City Inc (HQ).............................614 228-5200
  935 N Cassady Ave Columbus (43219) *(G-6180)*

Lutheran Village At Wolf Creek............................419 861-2233
  2001 Perrysburg Holland Rd Ofc Holland (43528) *(G-9296)*

Lutheran Village Courtyard, Columbus Also Called: *Lutheran Senior City Inc (G-6180)*

Lutz Pto..419 332-0091
  1929 Buckland Ave Fremont (43420) *(G-8692)*

Luxe Omni Inc...937 929-0511
  2331 Far Hills Ave Ste 100 Oakwood (45419) *(G-12050)*

Luxfer Magtech Inc (HQ)....................................513 772-3066
  2940 Highland Ave Ste 210 Cincinnati (45212) *(G-2995)*

Luxury Heating Company...................................440 366-0971
  5327 Ford Rd Sheffield Village (44035) *(G-13001)*

Lvd Acquisition LLC (HQ)...................................614 861-1350
  222 E Campus View Blvd Columbus (43235) *(G-6181)*

Lw Equipment LLC...614 475-7376
  3430 Westerville Rd Columbus (43224) *(G-6182)*

Lyco Corporation...412 973-9176
  1089 N Hubbard Rd Lowellville (44436) *(G-10169)*

Lyden Oil Company..330 792-1100
  3711 Leharps Dr Youngstown (44515) *(G-15654)*

Lykins Companies Inc (PA).................................513 831-8820
  5163 Wolfpen Pleasant Hill Rd Milford (45150) *(G-11238)*

Lykins Energy Solutions, Milford Also Called: *Lykins Companies Inc (G-11238)*

Lykins Oil Company (HQ)...................................513 831-8820
  5163 Wolfpen Pleasant Hill Rd Milford (45150) *(G-11239)*

Lykins Transportation Inc...................................513 831-8820
  5163 Wolfpen Pleasant Hill Rd Milford (45150) *(G-11240)*

Lyman W Lggins Urban Affirs CT........................419 385-2532
  2155 Arlington Ave Toledo (43609) *(G-13901)*

Lynx Ems LLC..513 530-1600
  10123 Alliance Rd Blue Ash (45242) *(G-1205)*

Lyondell Chemical Company..............................513 530-4000
  11530 Northlake Dr Cincinnati (45249) *(G-2996)*

Lytle Park Inn LLC...513 621-4500
  311 Pike St Cincinnati (45202) *(G-2997)*

M & A Distributing Co Inc (PA)............................440 703-4580
  31031 Diamond Pkwy Solon (44139) *(G-13110)*

M & A Distribution, Solon Also Called: *M & A Distributing Co Inc (G-13110)*

M & D Blacktop Sealing, Grove City Also Called: *Pavement Protectors Inc (G-8944)*

M & M Wine Cellar Inc.......................................330 536-6450
  259 Bedford Rd Lowellville (44436) *(G-10170)*

M & W Construction Entps LLC..........................419 227-2000
  1201 Crestwood Dr Lima (45805) *(G-9932)*

M A C, Vandalia Also Called: *Nimers & Woody II Inc (G-14386)*

M A Folkes Company Inc...................................513 785-4200
  3095 Mcbride Ct Hamilton (45011) *(G-9062)*

M A M Inc..740 588-9882
  1926 Norwood Blvd Zanesville (43701) *(G-15809)*

M C C, Wadsworth Also Called: *Monitoring Ctrl Compliance Inc (G-14444)*

M Conley Company (PA)....................................330 456-8243
  1312 4th St Se Canton (44707) *(G-1798)*

M G Q Inc..419 992-4236
  1525 W County Road 42 Tiffin (44883) *(G-13631)*

M H Equipment, Medina Also Called: *MH Logistics Corp (G-10865)*

M J Baumann, Columbus Also Called: *Mj Baumann Co Inc (G-6252)*

M M Construction..513 553-0106
  1924 State Route 222 Bethel (45106) *(G-1093)*

M P Dory Co...614 444-2138
  2001 Integrity Dr S Columbus (43209) *(G-6183)*

M R S I, Cincinnati Also Called: *Marketing Research Services (G-3009)*

M Retail Engineering Inc....................................614 818-2323
  750 Brooksedge Blvd Westerville (43081) *(G-14997)*

M S G, Maumee Also Called: *Mannik & Smith Group Inc (G-10744)*

M S I Design, Columbus Also Called: *Myers/Schmalenberger Inc (G-6285)*

M T Golf Course Managment Inc (PA)................513 923-1188
  9799 Prechtel Rd Cincinnati (45252) *(G-2998)*

M-Pact Corporation...513 679-2023
  2323 Crowne Point Dr Cincinnati (45241) *(G-2999)*

M-V Rlty Mller Valentine Group, Dayton Also Called: *Miller-Valentine Partners Ltd (G-7506)*

M.O.M., Blue Ash Also Called: *Modern Office Methods Inc (G-1211)*

M.O.M., Cincinnati Also Called: *Modern Office Methods Inc (G-3076)*

M/I Financial LLC (HQ)......................................614 418-8661
  4131 Worth Ave Ste 340 Columbus (43219) *(G-6184)*

M/I Financial Corp...614 418-8700
  3 Easton Oval Ste 500 Columbus (43219) *(G-6185)*

M/I Homes Inc (PA)...614 418-8000
  4131 Worth Ave Ste 500 Columbus (43219) *(G-6186)*

M/I Homes Central Ohio LLC.............................614 418-8000
  3 Easton Oval Ste 500 Columbus (43219) *(G-6187)*

M/I Homes Service LLC....................................614 418-8300
  3 Easton Oval Ste 500 Columbus (43219) *(G-6188)*

M&C Hotel Interests Inc.....................................440 543-1331
  17021 Chillicothe Rd Chagrin Falls (44023) *(G-1985)*

M&C Hotel Interests Inc.....................................937 778-8100
  987 E Ash St Ste 171 Piqua (45356) *(G-12446)*

ALPHABETIC SECTION — Main Sequence Technology Inc

M3 Cleaning Services Inc.. 419 725-2100
  511 Phillips Ave Toledo (43612) *(G-13902)*
M3 Midstream LLC... 330 223-2220
  11543 State Route 644 Kensington (44427) *(G-9554)*
M3 Midstream LLC... 330 679-5580
  10 E Main St Salineville (43945) *(G-12860)*
M3 Midstream LLC... 740 945-1170
  37950 Crimm Rd Scio (43988) *(G-12942)*
MA Architects, Columbus *Also Called: Meacham & Apel Architects Inc (G-6220)*
Maaco Franchising Inc... 937 236-6700
  3474 Needmore Rd Dayton (45414) *(G-7463)*
Maag Automatik Inc... 330 677-2225
  235 Progress Blvd Kent (44240) *(G-9586)*
Maag Reduction Engineering, Kent *Also Called: Maag Automatik Inc (G-9586)*
Maass - Midwest Mfg Inc.. 419 485-6905
  14502 County Road 15 Pioneer (43554) *(G-12433)*
Mab Home Remodeling LLC.. 216 761-1360
  621 Eddy Rd Cleveland (44108) *(G-4512)*
Mac, Alliance *Also Called: Mac Manufacturing Inc (G-390)*
Mac Manufacturing Inc (HQ).. 330 823-9900
  14599 Commerce St Ne Alliance (44601) *(G-390)*
Mac Manufacturing Inc... 330 829-1680
  1453 Allen Rd Salem (44460) *(G-12846)*
Mac Trailer Manufacturing Inc (PA)................................... 800 795-8454
  14599 Commerce St Ne Alliance (44601) *(G-391)*
Macair, Xenia *Also Called: Macair Aviation LLC (G-15525)*
Macair Aviation LLC... 937 347-1302
  140 N Valley Rd Xenia (45385) *(G-15525)*
Macalogic, Dayton *Also Called: Tm Capture Services LLC (G-7671)*
Macaulay-Brown Inc... 937 426-3421
  2310 National Rd Beavercreek Township (45324) *(G-943)*
Macb, Beavercreek Township *Also Called: Macaulay-Brown Inc (G-943)*
Macdonald Hospital Resear.. 216 844-3888
  1110 Euclid Ave Cleveland (44115) *(G-4513)*
Mace Personal Def & SEC Inc (HQ)................................. 440 424-5321
  4400 Carnegie Ave Cleveland (44103) *(G-4514)*
Machine Drive Company.. 513 793-7077
  2513 Crescentville Rd Cincinnati (45241) *(G-3000)*
Machine Tool Division, Bluffton *Also Called: Grob Systems Inc (G-1281)*
Macys Cr & Customer Svcs Inc... 513 398-5221
  9111 Duke Blvd Mason (45040) *(G-10576)*
Mad Anthony's Lounge, Greenville *Also Called: Greenville Inn Inc (G-8875)*
Mad River, Zanesfield *Also Called: Mad River Mountain Resort (G-15764)*
Mad River Family Practice, West Liberty *Also Called: Mary Rutan Hospital (G-14860)*
Mad River Local School Dst... 937 237-4275
  1841 Harshman Rd Dayton (45424) *(G-7464)*
Mad River Mountain Resort... 937 303-3646
  1000 Snow Valley Rd Zanesfield (43360) *(G-15764)*
Made From Scratch Inc.. 614 873-3344
  7500 Montgomery Rd Plain City (43064) *(G-12484)*
Madeira Health Care Center, Cincinnati *Also Called: Euclid Health Care Inc (G-2638)*
Madeira Veterinary Hospital.. 513 561-7467
  7250 Miami Ave Cincinnati (45243) *(G-3001)*
Madison Avenue Mktg Group Inc..................................... 419 473-9000
  1600 Madison Ave Toledo (43604) *(G-13903)*
Madison Care Inc.. 440 428-1492
  7600 S Ridge Rd Madison (44057) *(G-10220)*
Madison Child Care Center, Mansfield *Also Called: Madison Local School District (G-10284)*
Madison County Community Hospital (PA)...................... 740 845-7000
  210 N Main St London (43140) *(G-10046)*
Madison County Hospital, London *Also Called: Madison County Community Hospital (G-10046)*
MADISON COUNTY HOSPITAL, London *Also Called: Madison Family Health Corp (G-10047)*
Madison Family Health Corp... 740 845-7000
  210 N Main St London (43140) *(G-10047)*
Madison Local School District.. 419 589-7851
  103 Bahl Ave Mansfield (44905) *(G-10284)*
Madison Medical Campus.. 440 428-6800
  6270 N Ridge Rd Madison (44057) *(G-10221)*
Madison Mine Supply Co, Jackson *Also Called: Waterloo Coal Company Inc (G-9529)*
Madison Square Apartments, Plain City *Also Called: Fairfield Homes Inc (G-12477)*
Madison Tree Care & Ldscpg Inc...................................... 513 576-6391
  636 Round Bottom Rd Milford (45150) *(G-11241)*
Madison Village Manor Inc.. 440 428-1519
  731 N Lake St Madison (44057) *(G-10222)*
Mae Holding Company (PA).. 513 751-2424
  7290 Deaconsbench Ct Cincinnati (45244) *(G-3002)*
Magic Fund, Cleveland *Also Called: Keybank Eb Mnged Grnteed Inv C (G-4459)*
MAGNET, Cleveland *Also Called: Manufacturing Advocacy & Growth Network Inc (G-4522)*
Magnetech, Massillon *Also Called: 3-D Service Ltd (G-10626)*
Magnetech Industrial Services, Massillon *Also Called: Magnetech Industrial Svcs Inc (G-10651)*
Magnetech Industrial Svcs Inc (DH).................................. 330 830-3500
  800 Nave Rd Se Massillon (44646) *(G-10651)*
Magnetic Springs Water Company (PA)............................ 614 421-1780
  1917 Joyce Ave Columbus (43219) *(G-6189)*
Magnit APC I LLC... 614 252-7300
  471 Morrison Rd Unit N Gahanna (43230) *(G-8721)*
Magnolia Clubhouse Inc... 216 721-3030
  11101 Magnolia Dr Cleveland (44106) *(G-4515)*
Magnum Management Corporation.................................. 419 627-2334
  1 Cedar Point Dr Sandusky (44870) *(G-12913)*
Maguire & Schneider LLP.. 614 224-1222
  1650 Lake Shore Dr Ste 150 Columbus (43204) *(G-6190)*
Mahle Behr Mt Sterling Inc.. 740 869-3333
  10500 Oday Harrison Rd Mount Sterling (43143) *(G-11474)*
Mahoning Clmbana Training Assn.................................... 330 420-9675
  7989 Dickey Dr Ste 4 Lisbon (44432) *(G-10004)*
Mahoning Country Club Inc... 330 545-2517
  710 E Liberty St Girard (44420) *(G-8819)*
Mahoning County.. 330 799-1581
  940 Bears Den Rd Youngstown (44511) *(G-15655)*
Mahoning County.. 330 793-5514
  761 Industrial Rd Youngstown (44509) *(G-15656)*
Mahoning County.. 330 797-2925
  130 Javit Ct Youngstown (44515) *(G-15657)*
Mahoning County Childrens Svcs..................................... 330 941-8888
  222 W Federal St Fl 4 Youngstown (44503) *(G-15658)*
Mahoning County Engineers, Youngstown *Also Called: Mahoning County (G-15655)*
MAHONING VALLEY HEMATOLOGY ONC, Warren *Also Called: Trumbull Mem Hosp Foundation (G-14567)*
Mahoning Valley Hospital, Youngstown *Also Called: Vibra Hosp Mahoning Vly LLC (G-15748)*
Mahoning Valley Sanitary Dst.. 330 799-6315
  1181 Ohltown Mcdonald Rd Mineral Ridge (44440) *(G-11303)*
Mahoning Valley Scrappers, Niles *Also Called: Palisdes Bsbal A Cal Ltd Prtnr (G-11795)*
Mahoning Vly Hmtlogy Oncology A................................... 330 318-1100
  500 Gypsy Ln Youngstown (44504) *(G-15659)*
Mahoning Vly Infusioncare Inc (PA).................................. 330 759-9487
  4891 Belmont Ave Youngstown (44505) *(G-15660)*
Mahoning Yngstown Cmnty Action (PA)........................... 330 747-7921
  1325 5th Ave Youngstown (44504) *(G-15661)*
Mahoning Youngstown Community................................... 330 747-0236
  1988 Mccartney Rd Youngstown (44505) *(G-15662)*
Mahoning Youngstown Community................................... 330 747-7921
  1350 5th Ave Youngstown (44504) *(G-15663)*
MAI Capital Management LLC (PA).................................. 216 920-4800
  6050 Oak Tree Blvd Ste 500 Independence (44131) *(G-9449)*
MAI Manufacturing, Marysville *Also Called: Straight 72 Inc (G-10511)*
MAI Wealth Advisors, Independence *Also Called: MAI Capital Management LLC (G-9449)*
Mail Contractors America Inc.. 513 769-5967
  3065 Cresecentville Rd Cincinnati (45262) *(G-3003)*
Mailender Inc... 513 942-5453
  9500 Glades Dr West Chester (45011) *(G-14728)*
Main Hospitality Holdings LLC.. 513 744-9900
  135 Joe Nuxhall Way Cincinnati (45202) *(G-3004)*
Main Lite Electric Co Inc.. 330 369-8333
  3000 Sferra Ave Nw Warren (44483) *(G-14537)*
Main Sail LLC.. 216 472-5100
  8279 Mayfield Rd Unit 12 Chesterland (44026) *(G-2039)*
Main Sequence Technology Inc (PA)................................. 440 946-5214
  5370 Pinehill Dr Mentor On The Lake (44060) *(G-11015)*

Main Sequence Technology Inc 440 946-5214
  4420 Sherwin Rd Ste 3 Willoughby (44094) *(G-15209)*

Main Street Photography, London *Also Called: Peters Main Street Photography (G-10049)*

Main Street Terrace Care Ctr 740 653-8767
  1318 E Main St Lancaster (43130) *(G-9734)*

Mainstreet Group Home, Barnesville *Also Called: Alternative Residences Two Inc (G-716)*

Maintenance Department, Logan *Also Called: Logan-Hocking School District (G-10033)*

Mainthia Technologies Inc 216 433-2198
  21000 Brookpark Rd Cleveland (44135) *(G-4516)*

Majestic Steel Service, Cleveland *Also Called: Majestic Steel Usa Inc (G-4517)*

Majestic Steel Usa Inc (PA) 440 786-2666
  31099 Chagrin Blvd Ste 150 Cleveland (44124) *(G-4517)*

Majidzadeh Enterprises Inc (PA) 614 823-4949
  6350 Presidential Gtwy Columbus (43231) *(G-6191)*

Major Legal Services, Independence *Also Called: Alliance Legal Solutions LLC (G-9401)*

Major Metals Company 419 886-4600
  844 Kochheiser Rd Mansfield (44904) *(G-10285)*

Mak Burtnett Inc 440 256-8080
  9183 Chillicothe Rd Ste A Willoughby (44094) *(G-15210)*

Make Believe, Parma *Also Called: Y & E Entertainment Group LLC (G-12268)*

Maketewah Country Club Company 513 242-9333
  5401 Reading Rd Cincinnati (45237) *(G-3005)*

Making Life Easy LLC 513 280-0422
  1731 Clayburn Cir Cincinnati (45240) *(G-3006)*

Makovich Pusti Architects Inc 440 891-8910
  111 Front St Berea (44017) *(G-1073)*

Malco Products, Barberton *Also Called: Malco Products Inc (G-700)*

Malco Products Inc (PA) 330 753-0361
  361 Fairview Ave Barberton (44203) *(G-700)*

Mallard Cove Senior Dev LLC 513 772-6655
  1410 Mallard Cove Dr Ofc Cincinnati (45246) *(G-3007)*

Mallard Cove Senior Living, Cincinnati *Also Called: Mallard Cove Senior Dev LLC (G-3007)*

Maloney & Associates Inc 330 477-7719
  4850 Southway St Sw Canton (44706) *(G-1799)*

Maloney + Novotny LLC (PA) 216 363-0100
  1111 Superior Ave E Ste 700 Cleveland (44114) *(G-4518)*

Mammoth Restoration and Clg, Worthington *Also Called: Farris Enterprises Inc (G-15416)*

Mammoth Tech Inc (PA) 419 782-3709
  1250 Geneva Blvd Defiance (43512) *(G-7754)*

Managed Care Advisory Group 800 355-0466
  3434 Granite Cir # 1 Toledo (43617) *(G-13904)*

Managed Cloud Service Provider, Westlake *Also Called: Calyx LLC (G-15043)*

Managed Marketing Solutions, Dayton *Also Called: Reynolds and Reynolds Holdings (G-7590)*

Management & Network Services, Dublin *Also Called: Management and Netwrk Svcs LLC (G-8059)*

Management and Netwrk Svcs LLC 800 949-2159
  6500 Emerald Pkwy Ste 310 Dublin (43016) *(G-8059)*

Manary Pool, Willowick *Also Called: City of Willowick (G-15235)*

Manatron Inc (DH) 937 431-4000
  4105 Executive Dr Beavercreek (45430) *(G-925)*

Manatron Sabre Systems and Svc (DH) 937 431-4000
  4105 Executive Dr Beavercreek (45430) *(G-926)*

Manav Enterprises Inc 513 563-4606
  11018 Reading Rd Sharonville (45241) *(G-12995)*

Mancan Inc 440 884-9675
  6341 Pearl Rd Cleveland (44130) *(G-4519)*

Mancan Inc 330 264-5375
  435 Beall Ave Wooster (44691) *(G-15353)*

Manco Real Estate MGT Inc 937 277-9551
  1905 Salem Ave Dayton (45406) *(G-7465)*

Mandel Jcc 781 934-5774
  26001 S Woodland Rd Beachwood (44122) *(G-808)*

Mandel Jcc, Beachwood *Also Called: Mandel Jwish Cmnty Ctr of Clvl (G-809)*

Mandel Jwish Cmnty Ctr of Clvl 216 831-0700
  26001 S Woodland Rd Beachwood (44122) *(G-809)*

Mangos Place 614 499-1711
  3967 Presidential Pkwy Ste I Powell (43065) *(G-12598)*

Manheim Auctions Inc 216 539-1701
  4720 Brookpark Rd Cleveland (44134) *(G-4520)*

Manifest Software, Upper Arlington *Also Called: Manifest Solutions Corp (G-14280)*

Manifest Solutions Corp 614 930-2800
  2035 Riverside Dr Upper Arlington (43221) *(G-14280)*

Manley Deas & Kochalski LLC (PA) 614 220-5611
  1555 Lake Shore Dr Columbus (43204) *(G-6192)*

Manleys Manor Nursing Home Inc 419 424-0402
  2820 Greenacre Dr Findlay (45840) *(G-8560)*

Mannik & Smith Group Inc (HQ) 419 891-2222
  1800 Indian Wood Cir Maumee (43537) *(G-10744)*

Mannys Cleaning Co 614 596-1919
  6605 Longshore St Dublin (43017) *(G-8060)*

Manor At Autumn Hills, Niles *Also Called: Niles Residential Care LLC (G-11794)*

Manor At Perrysburg, The, Perrysburg *Also Called: Hcf of Perrysburg Inc (G-12340)*

Manor At Whitehall, The, Columbus *Also Called: Shg Whitehall Holdings LLC (G-6671)*

Manor Care Inc (HQ) 419 252-5500
  333 N Summit St Toledo (43604) *(G-13905)*

Manor Care Barberton Oh LLC 330 753-5005
  85 3rd St Se Barberton (44203) *(G-701)*

Manor Care Wilmington De LLC 567 585-9600
  100 Madison Ave Toledo (43604) *(G-13906)*

Manor Cr-Pike Creek Wlmngton D 567 585-9600
  100 Madison Ave Toledo (43604) *(G-13907)*

Manorcare Health Services, Toledo *Also Called: Hcr Manorcare Med Svcs Fla LLC (G-13839)*

Manorcare Health Services LLC (DH) 419 252-5500
  333 N Summit St Ste 100 Toledo (43604) *(G-13908)*

Manorcare Health Svcs VA Inc 419 252-5500
  333 N Summit St Ste 100 Toledo (43604) *(G-13909)*

Manorcare Hlth Srvcs-Tica Rdge, Toledo *Also Called: Manorcare Health Services LLC (G-13908)*

Mansfeld Ohio Arie No 336 Frtn (PA) 419 636-7812
  221 S Walnut St Bryan (43506) *(G-1487)*

Mansfield Area Y, Mansfield *Also Called: Young MNS Chrstn Assn of Mnsfe (G-10327)*

Mansfield Cement Flooring Inc 419 884-3733
  11 N Mill St Mansfield (44904) *(G-10286)*

Mansfield Express, Ontario *Also Called: Mansfield Whsng & Dist Inc (G-12114)*

Mansfield Homecare & Staffing, Ontario *Also Called: Maxim Healthcare Services Inc (G-12116)*

Mansfield Hotel Partnership (PA) 419 529-1000
  500 N Trimble Rd Mansfield (44906) *(G-10287)*

Mansfield Memorial Homes 419 774-5100
  55 Wood St Mansfield (44903) *(G-10288)*

Mansfield Memorial Homes LLC (PA) 419 774-5100
  50 Blymyer Ave Mansfield (44903) *(G-10289)*

Mansfield Plumbing Pdts LLC (HQ) 419 938-5211
  150 E 1st St Perrysville (44864) *(G-12392)*

Mansfield Truck Sls & Svc Inc 419 522-9811
  85 Longview Ave E Mansfield (44903) *(G-10290)*

Mansfield Whsng & Dist Inc (HQ) 419 522-3510
  222 Tappan Dr N Ontario (44906) *(G-12114)*

Mansour Gavin Lpa 216 523-1501
  1001 Lakeside Ave E Ste 1400 Cleveland (44114) *(G-4521)*

Mansuetto Roofing Company, Martins Ferry *Also Called: N F Mansuetto & Sons Inc (G-10469)*

Manta Media Inc 888 875-5833
  8760 Orion Pl Ste 200 Columbus (43240) *(G-5268)*

Mantua Bed Frames, Solon *Also Called: Rize Home LLC (G-13138)*

Manufacturers Wholesale Lumber, Cleveland *Also Called: Flagship Trading Corporation (G-4263)*

Manufacturing Advocacy & Growth Network Inc (PA) 216 391-7002
  1768 E 25th St Cleveland (44114) *(G-4522)*

Map Systems and Solutions, Columbus *Also Called: Mapsys Inc (G-6193)*

Maple City Ice Company (PA) 419 668-2531
  371 Cleveland Rd Norwalk (44857) *(G-12016)*

Maple Crest, Bluffton *Also Called: Mennonite Memorial Home (G-1282)*

Maple Crest Senior Living Vlg, Bluffton *Also Called: Mennonite Memorial Home (G-1283)*

MAPLE GARDENS REHABILITATION A, Eaton *Also Called: Eaton Grdns Rhblttion Hlth Car (G-8213)*

Maple Grove Companies, Tiffin *Also Called: M G Q Inc (G-13631)*

Maple Grove Enterprises Inc 440 286-1342
  526 Water St Chardon (44024) *(G-2010)*

ALPHABETIC SECTION — Marriott

Maple House, Berea *Also Called: Northeast Care Center Inc (G-1075)*
Maple Knoll Communities Inc (PA).................... 513 782-2400
 11100 Springfield Pike Cincinnati (45246) *(G-3008)*
Maple Knoll Communities Inc.............................. 513 524-7990
 6727 Contreras Rd Oxford (45056) *(G-12209)*
Maple Knoll Village, Cincinnati *Also Called: Maple Knoll Communities Inc (G-3008)*
Maple Mountain Industries Inc............................ 330 948-2510
 312 Bank St Lodi (44254) *(G-10020)*
Maple Retail Ltd Partnership............................... 216 221-6600
 14600 Detroit Ave # 1500 Lakewood (44107) *(G-9678)*
Maplecrest Nursing HM For Aged, Struthers *Also Called: Cred-Kap Inc (G-13499)*
Mapleside Bakery, Brunswick *Also Called: Mapleside Valley LLC (G-1462)*
Mapleside Valley LLC (PA).................................. 330 225-5576
 294 Pearl Rd Brunswick (44212) *(G-1462)*
Mapleview Country Villa....................................... 440 286-8176
 775 South St Chardon (44024) *(G-2011)*
Mapother & Mapother Attorneys, Cincinnati *Also Called: Javitch Block LLC (G-2901)*
Mapsys Inc (PA)... 614 255-7258
 920 Michigan Ave Columbus (43215) *(G-6193)*
Marathon Canton Refinery, Canton *Also Called: Mplx Terminals LLC (G-1811)*
Marathon Oil, Edon *Also Called: Slattery Oil Company Inc (G-8229)*
Marathon Petroleum, Findlay *Also Called: Marathon Petroleum Corporation (G-8561)*
Marathon Petroleum Corporation (PA)................ 419 422-2121
 539 S Main St Findlay (45840) *(G-8561)*
Marathon Petroleum Supply LLC......................... 419 422-2121
 539 S Main St Findlay (45840) *(G-8562)*
Marathon Pipe Line LLC (HQ).............................. 419 422-2121
 539 S Main St Ste 7614 Findlay (45840) *(G-8563)*
Marc Glassman Inc.. 330 995-9246
 300 Aurora Commons Cir Aurora (44202) *(G-616)*
Marc's 45, Aurora *Also Called: Marc Glassman Inc (G-616)*
Marca Industries Inc.. 740 387-1035
 2387 Harding Hwy E Marion (43302) *(G-10434)*
March Investors Ltd... 740 373-5353
 508 Pike St Marietta (45750) *(G-10382)*
Marck & Associates, Toledo *Also Called: G G Marck & Associates Inc (G-15815)*
Marco Photo Service Inc..................................... 419 529-9010
 1655 Nussbaum Pkwy Ontario (44906) *(G-12115)*
Marco's Pizza, Toledo *Also Called: Marcos Inc (G-13910)*
Marcos Inc... 419 885-4844
 5252 Monroe St Toledo (43623) *(G-13910)*
Marcum Conference Center, Oxford *Also Called: Miami University (G-12211)*
Marcum LLP... 440 459-5700
 6685 Beta Dr Mayfield Village (44143) *(G-10794)*
Marcus Hotels Inc.. 614 228-3800
 310 S High St Columbus (43215) *(G-6194)*
Marcus MIlchap RE Inv Svcs Inc.......................... 614 360-9800
 230 West St Ste 100 Columbus (43215) *(G-6195)*
Marcus Theatres Corporation.............................. 614 436-9818
 200 Hutchinson Ave Columbus (43235) *(G-6196)*
Marcus Thomas Llc... 216 292-4700
 4781 Richmond Rd Cleveland (44128) *(G-4523)*
Marcus Thomas Llc (PA)..................................... 216 292-4700
 4781 Richmond Rd Cleveland (44128) *(G-4524)*
Marden Companies, The, Marietta *Also Called: Health Care Plus (G-10370)*
Marfo Company (PA)... 614 276-3352
 799 N Hague Ave Columbus (43204) *(G-6197)*
Margret Wagner House, Cleveland *Also Called: Benjamin Rose Institute (G-3868)*
Marhofer Development Co LLC........................... 330 686-2262
 1585 Commerce Dr Stow (44224) *(G-13381)*
Maria Gardens LLC (PA)...................................... 440 238-7637
 20465 Royalton Rd Strongsville (44149) *(G-13474)*
Marian Living Center, North Lima *Also Called: Assumption Village (G-11882)*
Marietta Coal Co (PA).. 740 695-2197
 67705 Friends Church Rd Saint Clairsville (43950) *(G-12800)*
Marietta Family YMCA, Marietta *Also Called: Young Mens Christian Assn (G-10415)*
Marietta Hlth Care Physicians............................. 740 376-5044
 400 Matthew St Ste 220 Marietta (45750) *(G-10383)*
Marietta Memorial Hospital................................. 740 401-0362
 809 Farson St Belpre (45714) *(G-1057)*
Marietta Memorial Hospital (PA)......................... 740 374-1400
 401 Matthew St Marietta (45750) *(G-10384)*
Marietta Occptnal Hlth Prtners............................ 740 374-9954
 401 Matthew St Marietta (45750) *(G-10385)*
Marietta Silos LLC... 740 373-2822
 2417 Waterford Rd Marietta (45750) *(G-10386)*
Marietta Surgery Center...................................... 740 373-7207
 611 2nd St Ste A Marietta (45750) *(G-10387)*
Marimor Industries Inc.. 419 221-1226
 2450 Ada Rd Lima (45801) *(G-9933)*
Marion Ancillary Services LLC............................. 740 383-7983
 1040 Delaware Ave Marion (43302) *(G-10435)*
Marion Area Health Center, Marion *Also Called: Frederick C Smith Clinic Inc (G-10427)*
Marion Care Leasing LLC.................................... 740 387-7537
 175 Community Dr Marion (43302) *(G-10436)*
Marion Cnty Bd Dev Dsabilities.......................... 740 387-1035
 2387 Harding Hwy E Marion (43302) *(G-10437)*
Marion County Board of Mr Dd, Marion *Also Called: Marion Cnty Bd Dev Dsabilities (G-10437)*
Marion District, Marion *Also Called: Ohio-American Water Co Inc (G-10449)*
Marion Family YMCA... 740 725-9622
 645 Barks Rd E Marion (43302) *(G-10438)*
Marion General Hospital Inc (HQ)....................... 740 383-8400
 1000 Mckinley Park Dr Marion (43302) *(G-10439)*
Marion Lodge... 740 389-4300
 1842 Marion Mount Gilead Rd Marion (43302) *(G-10440)*
Marion Manor.. 740 387-9545
 195 Executive Dr Marion (43302) *(G-10441)*
Maritain Health (PA).. 440 249-5750
 24651 Center Ridge Rd Ste 200 Westlake (44145) *(G-15079)*
Marjorie P Lee Rtirement Cmnty, Cincinnati *Also Called: Episcopal Retirement Homes Inc (G-2632)*
Mark Mlford Hcksvlle Jint Twn (PA).................... 419 542-6692
 208 Columbus St Hicksville (43526) *(G-9160)*
Mark D Sandridge Inc.. 330 764-6106
 133 Commerce Dr Medina (44256) *(G-10852)*
Mark Dura Inc.. 330 995-0883
 72 Emerald Ave Streetsboro (44241) *(G-13421)*
Mark H. Zangmeister Center, Columbus *Also Called: Mid-Ohio Oncology/Hematology Inc (G-6238)*
Mark Schaffer Excvtg Trckg Inc........................... 419 668-5990
 1623 Old State Rd N Norwalk (44857) *(G-12017)*
Mark Thomas Ford Inc.. 330 638-1010
 3098 State Route 5 Cortland (44410) *(G-6972)*
Mark-L Inc... 614 863-8832
 1180 Claycraft Rd Gahanna (43230) *(G-8722)*
Mark-L Construction, Gahanna *Also Called: Mark-L Inc (G-8722)*
Market Day Llc.. 513 860-1370
 5581 Spellmire Dr Bldg 6 West Chester (45246) *(G-14823)*
Market Day Distribution, West Chester *Also Called: Market Day Llc (G-14823)*
Marketing Essentials LLC.................................... 419 629-0080
 14 N Washington St New Bremen (45869) *(G-11599)*
Marketing Research Services (DH)..................... 513 579-1555
 310 Culvert St Fl 2 Cincinnati (45202) *(G-3009)*
MARKETING RESEARCH SERVICES, INC., Cincinnati *Also Called: Marketing Research Svcs Inc (G-3010)*
Marketing Research Svcs Inc.............................. 513 772-7580
 110 Boggs Ln Ste 380 Cincinnati (45246) *(G-3010)*
Marketing Support Services Inc (PA).................. 513 752-1200
 4921 Para Dr Cincinnati (45237) *(G-3011)*
Marketvision Research Inc (PA).......................... 513 791-3100
 5151 Pfeiffer Rd Ste 300 Blue Ash (45242) *(G-1206)*
Markwest Utica Emg LLC.................................... 740 942-4810
 46700 Giacobbi Rd Jewett (43986) *(G-9543)*
Marous Brothers Cnstr Inc.................................. 440 951-3904
 36933 Vine St Willoughby (44094) *(G-15211)*
Marquardt, Richard F Od, Mansfield *Also Called: Ohio Eye Associates Inc (G-10307)*
Marquee Broadcasting Ohio Inc.......................... 740 452-5431
 629 Downard Rd Zanesville (43701) *(G-15810)*
Marquette Group, Dayton *Also Called: Gypc Inc (G-7390)*
Marriott... 440 243-8785
 7345 Engle Rd Cleveland (44130) *(G-4525)*

Marriott — ALPHABETIC SECTION

Marriott.. 440 234-6688
  17525 Rosbough Blvd Cleveland (44130) *(G-4526)*
Marriott, Cleveland *Also Called: Cleveland East Hotel LLC (G-4042)*
Marriott, Cleveland *Also Called: Marriott Hotel Services Inc (G-4527)*
Marriott, Cleveland *Also Called: Marriott International Inc (G-4528)*
Marriott, Columbus *Also Called: Columbus Easton Hotel LLC (G-5631)*
Marriott, Columbus *Also Called: Courtyard Management Corp (G-5713)*
Marriott, Columbus *Also Called: Renaissance Hotel Operating Co (G-6577)*
Marriott, Mentor *Also Called: Residence Inn By Marriott LLC (G-10992)*
Marriott, Oregon *Also Called: TownePlace Management LLC (G-12145)*
Marriott, Westerville *Also Called: Renaissance Hotel MGT Co LLC (G-14934)*
Marriott Columbus Univ Area, Columbus *Also Called: Uph Holdings LLC (G-6826)*
Marriott Hotel Services Inc.. 216 252-5333
  4277 W 150th St Cleveland (44135) *(G-4527)*
MARRIOTT HOTELS, West Chester *Also Called: Union Centre Hotel LLC (G-14786)*
Marriott International Inc.. 216 696-9200
  127 Public Sq Fl 1 Cleveland (44114) *(G-4528)*
Mars Electric Company (PA).. 440 946-2250
  6655 Beta Dr Ste 200 Cleveland (44143) *(G-4529)*
Marsden Holding LLC... 440 973-7774
  6751 Engle Rd Ste H Middleburg Heights (44130) *(G-11119)*
Marsh, Cincinnati *Also Called: Marsh Inc (G-3012)*
Marsh, Dayton *Also Called: Marsh & McLennan Agency LLC (G-7466)*
Marsh Berry & Company LLC (PA)..................................... 440 637-8122
  28601 Chagrin Blvd Ste 400 Beachwood (44122) *(G-810)*
Marsh Inc... 513 421-1234
  333 E 8th St Cincinnati (45202) *(G-3012)*
Marsh & McLennan Agency LLC... 937 228-4135
  309 Webster St Dayton (45402) *(G-7466)*
Marsh Building Products, Columbus *Also Called: Installed Building Pdts LLC (G-6058)*
Marshall & Melhorn LLC.. 419 249-7100
  4 Seagate Ste 800 Toledo (43604) *(G-13911)*
Marshall County Coal Company.. 740 338-3100
  46226 National Rd Saint Clairsville (43950) *(G-12801)*
Marshall Ford Leasing, Cleveland *Also Called: Sorbir Inc (G-4919)*
Marshall Information Svcs LLC.. 614 430-0355
  2780 Airport Dr Ste 120 Columbus (43219) *(G-6198)*
Martel Lodging Ltd.. 740 373-7373
  329 S 7th St Marietta (45750) *(G-10388)*
Martin Wilson and Associates... 513 772-7284
  10385 Spartan Dr Cincinnati (45215) *(G-3013)*
Martin & Associates, Cincinnati *Also Called: Martin Wilson and Associates (G-3013)*
Martin + WD Apprisal Group Ltd.. 419 241-4998
  43 S Saint Clair St Toledo (43604) *(G-13912)*
Martin Carpet Cleaning Company....................................... 614 443-4655
  795 S Wall St Columbus (43206) *(G-6199)*
Martin Control Systems Inc.. 614 761-5600
  8460 Estates Ct Plain City (43064) *(G-12485)*
Martin Greg Excavating Inc.. 513 727-9300
  1501 S University Blvd Middletown (45044) *(G-11171)*
Martin Healthcare Group, The, Cleveland *Also Called: Physician Staffing Inc (G-4748)*
Martin Logistics Incorporated.. 330 456-8000
  4526 Louisville St Ne Canton (44705) *(G-1800)*
Martin-Brower Company LLC.. 513 773-2301
  4260 Port Union Rd West Chester (45011) *(G-14729)*
Martincsi, Plain City *Also Called: Martin Control Systems Inc (G-12485)*
Marvin W Mielke Inc.. 330 725-8845
  1040 Industrial Pkwy Medina (44256) *(G-10853)*
Marxent, Miamisburg *Also Called: Marxent Labs LLC (G-11071)*
Marxent Labs LLC (PA)... 727 851-9522
  10170 Penny Ln Ste 200 Miamisburg (45342) *(G-11071)*
Mary C Enterprises Inc (PA)... 937 253-6169
  2274 Patterson Rd Dayton (45420) *(G-7467)*
Mary Rtan Hlth Assn Logan Cnty (PA)................................ 937 592-4015
  205 E Palmer Rd Bellefontaine (43311) *(G-1033)*
Mary Rutan Hospital (HQ)... 937 592-4015
  205 E Palmer Rd Bellefontaine (43311) *(G-1034)*
Mary Rutan Hospital... 937 599-1411
  381 Township Road 191 West Liberty (43357) *(G-14860)*
Mary Rutan Hospital, Bellefontaine *Also Called: Mary Rtan Hlth Assn Logan Cnty (G-1033)*
MARY RUTAN HOSPITAL, Bellefontaine *Also Called: Mary Rutan Hospital (G-1034)*
Mary Scott Nursing Home Inc.. 937 278-0761
  3109 Campus Dr Dayton (45406) *(G-7468)*
Maryhaven, Columbus *Also Called: Maryhaven Inc (G-6200)*
Maryhaven Inc.. 419 562-1740
  137 Stetzer Rd Bucyrus (44820) *(G-1512)*
Maryhaven Inc (PA)... 614 449-1530
  1791 Alum Creek Dr Columbus (43207) *(G-6200)*
Maryhaven Inc.. 614 626-2432
  5560 Chantry Dr Columbus (43232) *(G-6201)*
Maryhaven Inc.. 740 203-3800
  88 N Sandusky St Delaware (43015) *(G-7816)*
Maryhaven Inc.. 740 375-5550
  333 E Center St Ste 102 Marion (43302) *(G-10442)*
Maryhaven Inc.. 937 644-9192
  715 S Plum St Marysville (43040) *(G-10493)*
Maryhaven Inc.. 419 946-6734
  245 Neal Ave Ste A Mount Gilead (43338) *(G-11462)*
Marymount Health Care Systems.. 216 332-1100
  13900 Mccracken Rd Cleveland (44125) *(G-4530)*
Marymount Hospital Inc (HQ)... 216 581-0500
  9500 Euclid Ave Cleveland (44195) *(G-4531)*
Marysville Steel Inc... 937 642-5971
  323 E 8th St Marysville (43040) *(G-10494)*
Marysvlle Exmpted Vlg Schl Dst... 937 645-6733
  1280 Charles Ln Marysville (43040) *(G-10495)*
Marysvlle Ohio Srgical Ctr LLC... 937 578-4200
  17853 State Route 31 Marysville (43040) *(G-10496)*
Marzetti Manufacturing Company (DH)............................... 856 205-1485
  380 Polaris Pkwy Ste 400 Westerville (43082) *(G-14908)*
Mas International Mktg LLC... 614 556-7083
  34 N High St Ste 208 Columbus (43215) *(G-6202)*
Maslyk Landscaping Inc... 440 748-3635
  12289 Eaton Commerce Pkwy Ste 2 Columbia Station (44028) *(G-5229)*
Mason Family Resorts LLC.. 608 237-5871
  2501 Great Wolf Dr Mason (45040) *(G-10577)*
Mason Health Care Center... 513 398-2881
  5640 Cox Smith Rd Mason (45040) *(G-10578)*
Mason Steel, Walton Hills *Also Called: Mssi Group Inc (G-14477)*
Mason Structural Steel LLC.. 440 439-1040
  7500 Northfield Rd Walton Hills (44146) *(G-14476)*
Mason Title Agency Ltd.. 614 446-1151
  2800 Delmar Dr Columbus (43209) *(G-6203)*
Massage Envy, Chagrin Falls *Also Called: Irish Envy LLC (G-1981)*
Massage Envy, Columbus *Also Called: 845 Yard Street LLC (G-5290)*
Massey's Pizza, Reynoldsburg *Also Called: Premier Broadcasting Co Inc (G-12672)*
Massillon Cable TV Inc (PA).. 330 833-4134
  814 Cable Ct Nw Massillon (44647) *(G-10652)*
Massillon Cmnty Hosp Hlth Plan, Massillon *Also Called: Health Plan of Ohio Inc (G-10643)*
Massillon Senior Living Ltd.. 330 833-7229
  2550 University Dr Se Massillon (44646) *(G-10653)*
Massmutual Ascend Lf Insur Co (HQ).................................. 800 854-3649
  191 Rosa Parks St Cincinnati (45202) *(G-3014)*
Mast Global Logistics, Columbus *Also Called: Bath Bdy Wrks Lgstics Svcs LLC (G-5421)*
Mast Global Logistics, Groveport *Also Called: Bath Bdy Wrks Lgstics Svcs LLC (G-8974)*
Mast Technology Services Inc (HQ).................................... 614 415-7000
  3 Limited Pkwy Columbus (43230) *(G-6204)*
Mast Trucking Inc.. 330 674-8913
  6471 County Road 625 Millersburg (44654) *(G-11285)*
Master Bldrs Sltons Cnstr Syst, Beachwood *Also Called: Sika Mbcc US LLC (G-838)*
Master Builders LLC (HQ)... 800 228-3318
  23700 Chagrin Blvd Beachwood (44122) *(G-811)*
Master Maintenance Co, Lima *Also Called: Nicholas D Starr Inc (G-9940)*
Masterbrand Cabinets LLC (HQ).. 812 482-2527
  3300 Enterprise Pkwy Ste 300 Beachwood (44122) *(G-812)*
Masters Drug Company Inc... 800 982-7922
  3600 Pharma Way Lebanon (45036) *(G-9777)*
Masters Pharmaceutical, Lebanon *Also Called: Masters Drug Company Inc (G-9777)*
Masters Pharmaceutical, Mason *Also Called: Masters Pharmaceutical LLC (G-10579)*

ALPHABETIC SECTION — Mc Knight Group

Masters Pharmaceutical LLC..800 982-7922
  3600 Pharma Way Mason (45036) *(G-10579)*

Mastic Home Exteriors Inc..937 497-7008
  2405 Campbell Rd Sidney (45365) *(G-13040)*

Matandy Steel & Metal Pdts LLC..513 844-2277
  1200 Central Ave Hamilton (45011) *(G-9063)*

Matandy Steel Sales, Hamilton Also Called: Matandy Steel & Metal Pdts LLC *(G-9063)*

Matco Tools, Stow Also Called: Matco Tools Corporation *(G-13382)*

Matco Tools Corporation (HQ)...330 929-4949
  4403 Allen Rd Stow (44224) *(G-13382)*

Materials MGT Microsystems...262 240-9900
  5960 Heisley Rd Mentor (44060) *(G-10966)*

Materion Brush Intl Inc..216 486-4200
  6070 Parkland Blvd Ste 3 Mayfield Heights (44124) *(G-10789)*

Materion Ceramics Inc...216 486-4200
  6070 Parkland Blvd Mayfield Heights (44124) *(G-10790)*

Maternohio Clinical Assoicates..614 457-7660
  1700 Lake Shore Dr Columbus (43204) *(G-6205)*

Matesich Distributing Co...740 349-8686
  1190 E Main St Newark (43055) *(G-11724)*

Mathews Auto Group, Marion Also Called: Mathews Kennedy Ford L-M Inc *(G-10444)*

Mathews Ddge Chrysler Jeep Inc..740 389-2341
  1866 Marion Waldo Rd Marion (43302) *(G-10443)*

Mathews Ford Sandusky Inc..419 626-4721
  610 E Perkins Ave Sandusky (44870) *(G-12914)*

Mathews Kennedy Ford L-M Inc (PA).......................................740 387-3673
  1155 Delaware Ave Marion (43302) *(G-10444)*

Matia Motors Inc..440 365-7311
  823 Leona St Elyria (44035) *(G-8273)*

Matic Insurance Services Inc...833 382-1304
  585 S Front St Ste 300 Columbus (43215) *(G-6206)*

Matlock Electric Co Inc...513 731-9600
  2780 Highland Ave Cincinnati (45212) *(G-3015)*

Mato Inc...440 729-9008
  8027 Mayfield Rd Chesterland (44026) *(G-2040)*

Matrix Claims Management LLC..513 351-1222
  644 Linn St Ste 900 Cincinnati (45203) *(G-3016)*

Matrix Invstgations Consulting, Cincinnati Also Called: Matrix Claims Management LLC *(G-3016)*

Matrix Media Services Inc...614 228-2200
  463 E Town St Ste 200 Columbus (43215) *(G-6207)*

Matrix Research Inc...937 427-8433
  3844 Research Blvd Beavercreek (45430) *(G-927)*

Matrix Sys Auto Finishes LLC..248 668-8135
  600 Nova Dr Se Massillon (44646) *(G-10654)*

Matrix Technologies Inc (PA)...419 897-7200
  1760 Indian Wood Cir Maumee (43537) *(G-10745)*

Matt Talbot Inn, Cleveland Also Called: Catholic Charities Corporation *(G-3932)*

Matthew T Hovanic Inc...330 898-3387
  579 Washington St Ne Warren (44483) *(G-14538)*

Matthews International Corp...513 679-7400
  5546 Fair Ln Cincinnati (45227) *(G-3017)*

Mattingly Foods, Zanesville Also Called: Mattingly Foods Inc *(G-15811)*

Mattingly Foods Inc..740 454-0136
  302 State St Zanesville (43701) *(G-15811)*

Maumee Bay Ldge Conference Ctr, Oregon Also Called: US Hotel Osp Ventures LLC *(G-12146)*

Maumee Eye Clinic Inc..419 893-4883
  5655 Monclova Rd Ste 2 Maumee (43537) *(G-10746)*

Maumee Valley Guidance Ctr Inc (PA).....................................419 782-8856
  211 Biede Ave Defiance (43512) *(G-7755)*

Maumee Youth Center, Liberty Center Also Called: Ohio Department Youth Services *(G-9846)*

Maupin Johnson & Schmidt Md's, Dayton Also Called: Plastic Srgery Inst Dayton Inc *(G-7556)*

Mauser, Mount Vernon Also Called: Mauser Usa LLC *(G-11499)*

Mauser Usa LLC..740 397-1762
  219 Commerce Dr Mount Vernon (43050) *(G-11499)*

Maval Industries LLC (PA)...330 405-1600
  1555 Enterprise Pkwy Twinsburg (44087) *(G-14203)*

Maval Manufacturing, Twinsburg Also Called: Maval Industries LLC *(G-14203)*

Maven LLC..614 353-3873
  620 E Broad St Ste 300 Columbus (43215) *(G-6208)*

Mavennext Inc..800 850-8708
  421 W State St Columbus (43215) *(G-6209)*

Maxi Automotive Toledo, Toledo Also Called: Auto-Wares Inc *(G-13695)*

Maxim Healthcare Services Inc...330 670-1054
  3737 Embassy Pkwy Ste 300 Akron (44333) *(G-227)*

Maxim Healthcare Services Inc...513 793-6444
  34 Triangle Park Dr Cincinnati (45246) *(G-3018)*

Maxim Healthcare Services Inc...614 880-1210
  445 Hutchinson Ave Ste 720 Columbus (43235) *(G-6210)*

Maxim Healthcare Services Inc...740 772-4100
  445 Hutchinson Ave Ste 720 Columbus (43235) *(G-6211)*

Maxim Healthcare Services Inc...614 986-3001
  735 Taylor Rd Gahanna (43230) *(G-8723)*

Maxim Healthcare Services Inc...740 526-2222
  96 Integrity Dr Ste A Hebron (43025) *(G-9146)*

Maxim Healthcare Services Inc...216 606-3000
  6155 Rockside Rd Independence (44131) *(G-9450)*

Maxim Healthcare Services Inc...419 747-8040
  2293 Village Park Ct Ontario (44906) *(G-12116)*

Maxwell Lightning Protection..937 228-7250
  621 Pond St Dayton (45402) *(G-7469)*

Maxx South Broadband, Toledo Also Called: BCI Mississippi Broadband LLC *(G-13702)*

May Dugan Center, Cleveland Also Called: Near W Side Multi-Service Corp *(G-4632)*

Mayer Laminates MA, Hudson Also Called: Meyer Decorative Surfaces USA Inc *(G-9364)*

Mayers Electric Co Inc..513 272-2900
  4004 Erie Ct Ste B Cincinnati (45227) *(G-3019)*

MAYERSON JCC, Cincinnati Also Called: Jewish Cmnty Ctr of Cincinnati *(G-2905)*

Mayfair Country Club, Uniontown Also Called: Mayfair Country Club Inc *(G-14258)*

Mayfair Country Club Inc..330 699-2209
  2229 Raber Rd Uniontown (44685) *(G-14258)*

Mayfair Nursing Care Centers..614 889-6320
  3000 Bethel Rd Columbus (43220) *(G-6212)*

Mayfair Village, Columbus Also Called: Mayfair Nursing Care Centers *(G-6212)*

Mayfare Village, Columbus Also Called: Life Care Centers America Inc *(G-6158)*

Mayfield Clinic Inc (PA)...513 221-1100
  3825 Edwards Rd Ste 300 Cincinnati (45209) *(G-3020)*

Mayfield Cntry CLB Schlrship F...216 381-0826
  1545 Sheridan Rd Cleveland (44121) *(G-4532)*

Mayfield Spine Surgery Ctr LLC...513 619-5899
  4020 Smith Rd Cincinnati (45209) *(G-3021)*

Mayflower Nursing Home Inc..330 492-7131
  836 34th St Nw Canton (44709) *(G-1801)*

Mayor's Office, Cleveland Also Called: City of Westlake *(G-3994)*

Maza Inc...614 760-0003
  7635 Commerce Pl Plain City (43064) *(G-12486)*

Mazanec Raskin & Ryder, Cleveland Also Called: Mazanec Raskin & Ryder Co Lpa *(G-4533)*

Mazanec Raskin & Ryder Co Lpa (PA).....................................440 248-7906
  34305 Solon Rd Ste 100 Cleveland (44139) *(G-4533)*

Mazda Saab of Bedford, Bedford Also Called: Partners Auto Group Bdford Inc *(G-980)*

Mazel Company, The, Solon Also Called: Aurora Wholesalers LLC *(G-13069)*

Mazella Companies, Cleveland Also Called: Mazzella Holding Company Inc *(G-4534)*

Mazzella Holding Company Inc (PA).......................................513 772-4466
  21000 Aerospace Pkwy Cleveland (44142) *(G-4534)*

MBC Holdings Inc (PA)...419 445-1015
  1613 S Defiance St Archbold (43502) *(G-462)*

Mbd Transport LLC...513 449-0777
  3906 Turnbridge Ct Unit 311 Brunswick (44212) *(G-1463)*

MBI Solutions Inc..937 619-4000
  332 Congress Park Dr Dayton (45459) *(G-7470)*

MBI Tree Service LLC..513 926-9857
  9447 Cold Springs Ln Waynesville (45068) *(G-14625)*

Mbp Holdings Inc
  2030 Winners Cir Dayton (45404) *(G-7471)*

Mbs Acquisition, Mason Also Called: Remtec Engineering *(G-10601)*

Mc Cabe Do-It-Center, Cincinnati Also Called: Robert McCabe Company Inc *(G-3314)*

Mc Cormack Advisors Intl..216 522-1200
  1360 E 9th St Ste 100 Cleveland (44114) *(G-4535)*

Mc Graw-Hill Educational Pubg, Ashland Also Called: McGraw-Hill Schl Edcatn Hldngs *(G-507)*

Mc Knight Group, Grove City Also Called: McKnight Development Corp *(G-8933)*

Mc Mahon Realestate Co (PA).. 740 344-2250
591 Country Club Dr Newark (43055) *(G-11725)*

McAfee Air Duct Cleaning, Dayton *Also Called: McAfee Heating & AC Co Inc (G-7472)*

McAfee Heating & AC Co Inc.. 937 438-1976
4750 Hempstead Station Dr Dayton (45429) *(G-7472)*

McBee Supply Corporation.. 216 881-0015
7440 Oak Leaf Rd Bedford (44146) *(G-971)*

McCabe Do It Center, Loveland *Also Called: The Robert McCabe Company Inc (G-10164)*

McCarthy Burgess & Wolff Inc (PA).. 440 735-5100
26000 Cannon Rd Bedford (44146) *(G-972)*

McCarthy, Burgess & Wolff, Bedford *Also Called: McCarthy Burgess & Wolff Inc (G-972)*

McClellan Management Inc.. 419 855-7755
300 Cherry St Genoa (43430) *(G-8795)*

McClintock Electric Inc.. 330 264-6380
402 E Henry St Wooster (44691) *(G-15354)*

McCloy Engineering LLC.. 513 984-4112
3701 Port Union Rd Fairfield (45014) *(G-8428)*

McCluskey Automotive, Loveland *Also Called: McCluskey Chevrolet Inc (G-10149)*

McCluskey Chevrolet Inc (PA).. 513 761-1111
179 Commerce Dr Loveland (45140) *(G-10149)*

McCo, Portsmouth *Also Called: Mechanical Construction Co (G-12563)*

McConnell Excavating Ltd.. 440 774-4578
15804 State Route 58 Oberlin (44074) *(G-12072)*

McCormick Equipment Co Inc (PA).. 513 677-8888
112 Northeast Dr Loveland (45140) *(G-10150)*

McCoy Center For The Arts, Columbus *Also Called: Jeanne B McCoy Cmnty Ctr For A (G-6085)*

McCracken Group Inc.. 513 697-2000
9145 Governors Way Cincinnati (45249) *(G-3022)*

McCrea Manor Nursing, Alliance *Also Called: Peregrine Health Services Inc (G-396)*

MCCREA MANOR NURSING & REHABIL, Alliance *Also Called: McCrea Operating Company LLC (G-392)*

McCrea Operating Company LLC.. 330 823-9055
2040 Mccrea St Alliance (44601) *(G-392)*

McCullough-Hyde Mem Hosp Inc.. 513 863-2215
1390 Eaton Ave Hamilton (45013) *(G-9064)*

McCullough-Hyde Mem Hosp Inc (PA).. 513 523-2111
110 N Poplar St Oxford (45056) *(G-12210)*

McDaniels Cnstr Corp Inc.. 614 252-5852
1069 Woodland Ave Columbus (43219) *(G-6213)*

McData Services Corporation.. 614 272-5529
265 S Westmoor Ave Columbus (43204) *(G-6214)*

McDonald Finanacial Group, Cleveland *Also Called: Keybanc Capital Markets Inc (G-4458)*

MCDONALD HOPKINS LLC (PA).. 216 348-5400
600 Superior Ave E Ste 2100 Cleveland (44114) *(G-4536)*

McDonald's, Mount Gilead *Also Called: Pam Johnsonident (G-11464)*

McDowell Homes LLC.. 440 205-2000
6272 Center St Mentor (44060) *(G-10967)*

McDowell Homes RE Svcs, Mentor *Also Called: McDowell Homes LLC (G-10967)*

McEp, Dayton *Also Called: The Medical Center At Elizabeth Place LLC (G-7668)*

McGill Airclean, Columbus *Also Called: McGill Airclean LLC (G-6215)*

McGill Airclean LLC.. 614 829-1200
1777 Refugee Rd Columbus (43207) *(G-6215)*

McGill Smith Punshon Inc.. 513 759-0004
3700 Park 42 Dr Ste 190b Cincinnati (45241) *(G-3023)*

McGinnis Inc (HQ).. 740 377-4391
502 2nd St E South Point (45680) *(G-13178)*

McGlinchey Stafford Pllc.. 216 378-9905
3401 Tuttle Rd Ste 200 Shaker Heights (44122) *(G-12981)*

McGohan Brabender, Moraine *Also Called: McGohan/Brabender Agency Inc (G-11421)*

McGohan/Brabender Agency Inc (PA).. 937 293-1600
3931 S Dixie Dr Moraine (45439) *(G-11421)*

McGowan & Company Inc (PA).. 800 545-1538
20595 Lorain Rd Ste 300 Cleveland (44126) *(G-4537)*

McGowan Program Administrators, Cleveland *Also Called: McGowan & Company Inc (G-4537)*

McGraw-Hill Schl Edcatn Hldngs.. 419 207-7400
1250 George Rd Ashland (44805) *(G-507)*

McGraw/Kokosing Inc.. 614 212-5700
101 Clark Blvd Monroe (45044) *(G-11344)*

McGregor Foundation.. 216 851-8200
14900 Private Dr Cleveland (44112) *(G-4538)*

McGregor Mtal Leffel Works LLC.. 937 325-5561
900 W Leffel Ln Springfield (45506) *(G-13265)*

McGregor Pace.. 216 361-0917
2390 E 79th St Cleveland (44104) *(G-4539)*

McGregor Pace.. 216 791-3580
26310 Emery Rd Cleveland (44128) *(G-4540)*

Mch Services Inc.. 260 432-9699
190 E Spring Valley Pike Dayton (45458) *(G-7473)*

MCI Communications Svcs LLC.. 440 635-0418
12956 Taylor Wells Rd Chardon (44024) *(G-2012)*

MCI Communications Svcs LLC.. 216 265-9953
21000 Brookpark Rd Cleveland (44135) *(G-4541)*

McJ Holdings Inc (PA).. 937 592-5025
1601 Pemberton Dr Columbus (43221) *(G-6216)*

McK Trucking Inc.. 419 622-1111
2952 Road 107 Haviland (45851) *(G-9132)*

McKeen Security Inc (PA).. 740 699-1301
69100 Bayberry Dr Ste 200 Saint Clairsville (43950) *(G-12802)*

McKeever & Niekamp Electric.. 937 431-9363
1834 Woods Dr Beavercreek (45432) *(G-890)*

McKesson, Urbancrest *Also Called: McKesson Medical-Surgical Inc (G-14321)*

McKesson Corporation.. 740 636-3500
3000 Kenskill Ave Wshngtn Ct Hs (43160) *(G-15490)*

McKesson Medical-Surgical Inc.. 614 539-2600
3500 Centerpoint Dr Ste A Urbancrest (43123) *(G-14321)*

McKesson Medmanagement, Dublin *Also Called: CPS Medmanagement LLC (G-7977)*

McKinley Air Transport Inc.. 330 497-6956
5430 Lauby Rd Bldg 4 Canton (44720) *(G-1802)*

McKinley Hall Inc.. 937 328-5300
2624 Lexington Ave Springfield (45505) *(G-13266)*

McKinley Health Care Ctr LLC.. 330 456-1014
800 Market Ave N Canton (44702) *(G-1803)*

McKnight Development Corp.. 614 875-1689
3351 Mcdowell Rd Grove City (43123) *(G-8933)*

McLane Foodservice Dist Inc.. 614 771-9660
4300 Diplomacy Dr Columbus (43228) *(G-6217)*

McLane Foodservice Dist Inc.. 614 662-7700
2240 Creekside Parkway Lockbourne (43137) *(G-10012)*

McLane Lockbourne, Lockbourne *Also Called: McLane Foodservice Dist Inc (G-10012)*

McM Capital Partners II LP (PA).. 216 514-1840
25201 Chagrin Blvd Ste 360 Beachwood (44122) *(G-813)*

McM Electronics Inc.. 888 235-4692
650 Congress Park Dr Centerville (45459) *(G-1947)*

McMahon Truck Center Columbus, Columbus *Also Called: Columbus Truck & Equipment Center LLC (G-5657)*

McMaster Farms LLC.. 330 482-2913
345 Old Fourteen Rd Columbiana (44408) *(G-5237)*

McMaster-Carr Supply Company.. 330 995-5500
200 Aurora Industrial Pkwy Aurora (44202) *(G-617)*

MCN Health LLC.. 740 788-6000
2000 Tamarack Rd Newark (43055) *(G-11726)*

McNational Inc (PA).. 740 377-4391
502 2nd St E South Point (45680) *(G-13179)*

McNaughton-Mckay Elc Ohio Inc (HQ).. 614 476-2800
2255 Citygate Dr Columbus (43219) *(G-6218)*

McNaughton-Mckay Elc Ohio Inc.. 419 784-0295
188 Fox Run Dr Defiance (43512) *(G-7756)*

McNaughton-Mckay Elc Ohio Inc.. 419 422-2984
1950 Industrial Dr Findlay (45840) *(G-8564)*

McNaughton-Mckay Elc Ohio Inc.. 740 929-2727
107 Capital Dr Hebron (43025) *(G-9147)*

McNaughton-Mckay Elc Ohio Inc.. 419 891-0262
355 Tomahawk Dr Unit 1 Maumee (43537) *(G-10747)*

McNaughton-Mckay Electric Co, Defiance *Also Called: McNaughton-Mckay Elc Ohio Inc (G-7756)*

McNaughton-Mckay Electric Ohio, Columbus *Also Called: McNaughton-Mckay Elc Ohio Inc (G-6218)*

McNeil Industries Inc.. 440 951-7756
835 Richmond Rd Ste 2 Painesville (44077) *(G-12236)*

ALPHABETIC SECTION — Medical Mutual of Ohio

McNerney & Associates LLC 513 241-9951
5443 Duff Dr West Chester (45246) *(G-14824)*

McOn Inds Inc (HQ) 937 294-2681
2221 Arbor Blvd Moraine (45439) *(G-11422)*

McPhillips Plbg Htg & AC Co 216 481-1400
16115 Waterloo Rd Cleveland (44110) *(G-4542)*

McR LLC 937 879-5055
2601 Mission Point Blvd Ste 320 Beavercreek (45431) *(G-891)*

MCR Services Inc 614 421-0860
340 Forest St Columbus (43206) *(G-6219)*

McSteen & Associates Inc 440 585-9800
1415 E 286th St Wickliffe (44092) *(G-15157)*

McTv Inc 330 833-4134
814 Cable Ct Nw Massillon (44647) *(G-10655)*

McV Health Care Facilities Inc 513 398-1486
411 Western Row Rd Mason (45040) *(G-10580)*

McWane Inc 740 622-6651
2266 S 6th St Coshocton (43812) *(G-6992)*

MD Omg Emp LLC (HQ) 513 489-7100
10123 Alliance Rd Blue Ash (45242) *(G-1207)*

Mdesign, Glenwillow *Also Called: Metro Decor LLC (G-8834)*

Meacham & Apel Architects Inc 614 764-0407
775 Yard St Ste 325 Columbus (43212) *(G-6220)*

Meade Construction Inc (PA) 740 694-5525
13 N Mill St Lexington (44904) *(G-9844)*

Meade Construction Company, Lexington *Also Called: Meade Construction Inc (G-9844)*

Meaden & Moore LLP (PA) 216 241-3272
1375 E 9th St Ste 1800 Cleveland (44114) *(G-4543)*

Meadow Wind Hlth Care Ctr Inc 330 833-2026
300 23rd St Ne Massillon (44646) *(G-10656)*

Meadowbrook Mall Company (PA) 330 747-2661
2445 Belmont Ave Youngstown (44505) *(G-15664)*

Meadowbrook Manor of Hartford 330 772-5253
3090 Five Points Hartford Rd Fowler (44418) *(G-8628)*

Meadowood Golf Course, Westlake *Also Called: City of Westlake (G-15049)*

Meadows Healthcare, West Chester *Also Called: Mkjb Inc (G-14733)*

MEALS ON WHEELS, Columbus *Also Called: Lifecare Alliance (G-6161)*

MEALS ON WHEELS, Dayton *Also Called: Senior Resource Connection (G-7615)*

MEALS ON WHEELS SOUTHWEST OHIO, Cincinnati *Also Called: Wesley Community Services LLC (G-3654)*

Meander Hspitality Group V LLC 740 948-9305
11349 Allen Rd Jeffersonville (43128) *(G-9540)*

Meander Hsptality Group II LLC 330 422-0500
800 Mondial Pkwy Streetsboro (44241) *(G-13422)*

Mechancal Optmzers Cncnnati Ht 513 467-1444
2145 Patterson St Cincinnati (45214) *(G-3024)*

Mechancal/Industrial Contg Inc 513 489-8282
11863 Solzman Rd Cincinnati (45249) *(G-3025)*

Mechanical Cnstr Managers LLC (PA) 937 274-1987
5245 Wadsworth Rd Dayton (45414) *(G-7474)*

Mechanical Construction Co 740 353-5668
2302 8th St Portsmouth (45662) *(G-12563)*

Mechanical Systems Dayton Inc 937 254-3235
4401 Springfield St Dayton (45431) *(G-7136)*

Mechanics Bank (HQ) 419 524-0831
2 S Main St Mansfield (44902) *(G-10291)*

Med America Hlth Systems Corp (PA) 937 223-6192
1 Wyoming St Dayton (45409) *(G-7475)*

Med Central HM Hlth & Hospice, Mansfield *Also Called: Medcentral Health System (G-10292)*

Med Vet Associates, Worthington *Also Called: Medvet Associates LLC (G-15436)*

Med-Pass Incorporated 937 438-8884
1 Reynolds Way Dayton (45430) *(G-7476)*

Med-Trans Inc (PA) 937 325-4926
714 W Columbia St Springfield (45504) *(G-13267)*

Med1care Ltd (PA) 419 866-0555
116 S Main St Findlay (45840) *(G-8565)*

Meda-Care Transportation Inc 513 521-4799
10490 Taconic Ter Cincinnati (45215) *(G-3026)*

Medallion Club (PA) 614 794-6999
5000 Club Dr Westerville (43082) *(G-14909)*

Medassist Incorporated 614 367-9416
735 Taylor Rd Ste 140 Gahanna (43230) *(G-8724)*

Medben Companies, Newark *Also Called: Medical Benefits Mutl Lf Insur (G-11728)*

Medcentral Health System 419 683-1040
291 Heiser Ct Crestline (44827) *(G-7025)*

Medcentral Health System 419 526-8442
335 Glessner Ave Mansfield (44903) *(G-10292)*

Medcentral Health System (HQ) 419 526-8000
335 Glessner Ave Mansfield (44903) *(G-10293)*

Medcentral Health System 419 526-8970
770 Balgreen Dr Ste 105 Mansfield (44906) *(G-10294)*

Medcentral Health System 419 526-8900
1750 W 4th St Ste 1 Ontario (44906) *(G-12117)*

Medcentral Health System 419 342-5015
199 W Main St Shelby (44875) *(G-13007)*

Medcentral Hlth Sys Spt Mdcine, Ontario *Also Called: Medcentral Health System (G-12117)*

Medco Health Solutions Inc 614 822-2000
5151 Blazer Pkwy Ste B Dublin (43017) *(G-8061)*

Medcor Safety LLC 740 876-4003
9076 Ohio River Rd Wheelersburg (45694) *(G-15131)*

Medcorp, Portsmouth *Also Called: American Ambulette & Ambulance Service Inc (G-12544)*

Medcorp Inc 419 425-9700
330 N Cory St Findlay (45840) *(G-8566)*

Meder Electronic Inc 508 295-0771
4150 Thunderbird Ln Fairfield (45014) *(G-8429)*

MEDFLIGHT OF OHIO, Columbus *Also Called: Cems of Ohio Inc (G-5526)*

MEDFLIGHT OF OHIO, Columbus *Also Called: Ohio Medical Trnsp Inc (G-6437)*

Medhurst Mason Contractors Inc 440 543-8885
17111 Munn Rd Ste 1 Chagrin Falls (44023) *(G-1986)*

Medi Home Health Agency Inc 740 441-1779
392 Silver Bridge Plz Gallipolis (45631) *(G-8763)*

Medi Home Health Agency Inc (HQ) 740 266-3977
105 Main St Steubenville (43953) *(G-13338)*

Medi-Home Care, Steubenville *Also Called: Medi Home Health Agency Inc (G-13338)*

Media & Marketing Associates, Zanesville *Also Called: M A M Inc (G-15809)*

Media Collections Inc 216 831-5626
8948 Canyon Falls Blvd Ste 200 Twinsburg (44087) *(G-14204)*

Media Group At Michael's, The, Dayton *Also Called: Mfh Inc (G-7484)*

Media Source Inc (PA) 614 873-7635
7858 Industrial Pkwy Plain City (43064) *(G-12487)*

Media Star Promotions, Cleveland *Also Called: Cosmic Concepts Ltd (G-4120)*

Medic Management Group LLC (PA) 330 670-5316
3201 Enterprise Pkwy Ste 370 Beachwood (44122) *(G-814)*

Medic Rspnse Ambulance Svc Inc (PA) 419 522-1998
98 S Diamond St Mansfield (44902) *(G-10295)*

Medical and Surgical Assoc 740 522-7600
1930 Tamarack Rd Newark (43055) *(G-11727)*

Medical Assessments LLC 216 397-0917
5035 Mayfield Rd Ste 210 Cleveland (44124) *(G-4544)*

Medical Assoc Cambridge Inc 740 439-3515
1515 Maple Dr Cambridge (43725) *(G-1575)*

Medical Assoc of Zanesville 740 454-8551
1210 Ashland Ave Zanesville (43701) *(G-15812)*

Medical Benefits Mutl Lf Insur (PA) 740 522-8425
1975 Tamarack Rd Newark (43055) *(G-11728)*

Medical Center, Columbus *Also Called: Ohio State University (G-6456)*

Medical Cllege Ohio Physcans L 419 383-7100
3355 Glendale Ave Fl 3 Toledo (43614) *(G-13913)*

Medical Diagnostic Lab Inc (PA) 440 333-1375
36711 American Way Ste 2a Avon (44011) *(G-661)*

Medical Group Associates Inc 740 283-4773
114 Brady Cir E Steubenville (43952) *(G-13339)*

Medical Housecalls LLC 513 699-9090
4850 Smith Rd Ste 250 Cincinnati (45212) *(G-3027)*

Medical Management Intl Inc 937 325-4509
361 E National Rd Vandalia (45377) *(G-14383)*

Medical Mutual of Ohio (PA) 216 687-7000
2060 E 9th St Cleveland (44115) *(G-4545)*

Medical Mutual of Ohio 216 292-0400
100 American Rd Cleveland (44144) *(G-4546)*

Medical Mutual of Ohio 614 621-4585
545 Metro Pl S Dublin (43017) *(G-8062)*

Medical Mutual of Ohio — ALPHABETIC SECTION

Medical Mutual of Ohio 419 473-7100
9848 Olde Us 20 Rossford (43460) *(G-12768)*

Medical Mutual Services LLC (HQ) 440 878-4800
17800 Royalton Rd Strongsville (44136) *(G-13475)*

Medical Radiation Physics, Milford *Also Called: Mrp Inc (G-11246)*

Medical Recovery Systems Inc 513 872-7000
3372 Central Pkwy Cincinnati (45225) *(G-3028)*

Medical Service Company (PA) 440 232-3000
24000 Broadway Ave Bedford (44146) *(G-973)*

Medical Transport Systems Inc 330 837-9818
909 Las Olas Blvd Nw North Canton (44720) *(G-11847)*

Medical Urgency Prep Svcs Inc 937 374-2420
36 N Detroit St Ste 102 Xenia (45385) *(G-15526)*

Medicine Midwest LLC 937 435-8786
979 Congress Park Dr Dayton (45459) *(G-7477)*

Medicount Management Inc 513 612-3144
10361 Spartan Dr Cincinnati (45215) *(G-3029)*

Medigistics Inc (PA) 614 430-5700
1111 Schrock Rd Ste 200 Columbus (43229) *(G-6221)*

Medin-Smmit Ambltory Srgery CT 330 952-0014
3780 Medina Rd Ste 120 Medina (44256) *(G-10854)*

Medina Cnty Sheltered Inds Inc 330 334-4491
150 Quadral Dr Ste D Wadsworth (44281) *(G-14443)*

Medina Community Recrtl Ctr, Medina *Also Called: Rec Center (G-10882)*

Medina Country Club LLC 330 725-6621
5588 Wedgewood Rd Medina (44256) *(G-10855)*

Medina County 330 723-9553
6144 Wedgewood Rd Medina (44256) *(G-10856)*

Medina County 330 722-9511
4800 Ledgewood Dr Medina (44256) *(G-10857)*

Medina County Health Dept, Medina *Also Called: Medina County (G-10857)*

Medina County Home, Medina *Also Called: Medina County (G-10856)*

Medina County Park District 330 722-9364
6364 Deerview Ln Medina (44256) *(G-10858)*

Medina Fiber LLC 330 366-2008
1671 Medina Rd Medina (44256) *(G-10859)*

Medina Hospital (PA) 330 725-1000
1000 E Washington St Medina (44256) *(G-10860)*

Medina Hospital 330 723-3117
1000 E Washington St Medina (44256) *(G-10861)*

Medina Meadows 330 725-1550
550 Miner Dr Medina (44256) *(G-10862)*

Medina Medical Investors Ltd 330 483-3131
2400 Columbia Rd Medina (44256) *(G-10863)*

Medina Medical Offices, Medina *Also Called: Kaiser Foundation Hospitals (G-10850)*

Medina Supply Company 330 364-4411
820 W Smith Rd Medina (44256) *(G-10864)*

Medina Surgery Center, The, Medina *Also Called: Medin-Smmit Ambltory Srgery CT (G-10854)*

Mediquant LLC (PA) 440 746-2300
6200 Oak Tree Blvd Independence (44131) *(G-9451)*

Medisync, Dayton *Also Called: Medisync Midwest Ltd Lblty Co (G-7478)*

Medisync Midwest Ltd Lblty Co 513 533-1199
3080 Ackerman Blvd Dayton (45429) *(G-7478)*

Mediu Inc 614 332-7410
106 Stover Dr Delaware (43015) *(G-7817)*

Medlink of Ohio Inc 330 773-9434
1225 E Waterloo Rd Akron (44306) *(G-228)*

Medlink of Ohio Inc (DH) 216 751-5900
20600 Chagrin Blvd Ste 290 Cleveland (44122) *(G-4547)*

Medone Health LLC 614 255-6900
3525 Olentangy River Rd Ste 4330 Columbus (43214) *(G-6222)*

Medone Healthcare Partners, Columbus *Also Called: Medone Health LLC (G-6222)*

Medone Hospital Physicians 314 255-6900
3525 Olentangy River Rd Ste 4330 Columbus (43214) *(G-6223)*

Medpace 513 254-1232
4820 Red Bank Rd Cincinnati (45227) *(G-3030)*

MEDPACE, Cincinnati *Also Called: Medpace Holdings Inc (G-3033)*

Medpace Inc (DH) 513 579-9711
5375 Medpace Way Cincinnati (45227) *(G-3031)*

Medpace Bioanalytical Labs LLC 513 366-3260
5365 Medpace Way Cincinnati (45227) *(G-3032)*

Medpace Holdings Inc (PA) 513 579-9911
5375 Medpace Way Cincinnati (45227) *(G-3033)*

Medplus Inc 513 229-5500
4690 Parkway Dr Mason (45040) *(G-10581)*

Medpro LLC 937 336-5586
251 W Lexington Rd Eaton (45320) *(G-8215)*

Medquest Health Center Inc 740 417-4567
840 Sunbury Rd Ste 506 Delaware (43015) *(G-7818)*

Medus Travelers 513 678-2179
4555 Lake Forest Dr Ste 540 Blue Ash (45242) *(G-1208)*

Medvet Akron, Copley *Also Called: Medvet Associates LLC (G-6961)*

Medvet Associates Inc 937 293-2714
2714 Springboro W Moraine (45439) *(G-11423)*

Medvet Associates LLC 614 829-5070
9696 Basil Western Rd Canal Winchester (43110) *(G-1612)*

Medvet Associates LLC 513 561-0069
3964 Red Bank Rd Cincinnati (45227) *(G-3034)*

Medvet Associates LLC 216 362-6000
14000 Keystone Pkwy Cleveland (44135) *(G-4548)*

Medvet Associates LLC 614 870-0480
5230 Renner Rd Columbus (43228) *(G-6224)*

Medvet Associates LLC 330 665-4996
1321 Centerview Cir Copley (44321) *(G-6961)*

Medvet Associates LLC 330 530-8387
2680 W Liberty St Girard (44420) *(G-8820)*

Medvet Associates LLC 937 293-2714
2714 Springboro W Moraine (45439) *(G-11424)*

Medvet Associates LLC 419 473-0328
2921 Douglas Rd Toledo (43606) *(G-13914)*

Medvet Associates LLC 614 486-5800
300 E Wilson Bridge Rd Ste 100 Worthington (43085) *(G-15435)*

Medvet Associates LLC (PA) 614 846-5800
350 E Wilson Bridge Rd Worthington (43085) *(G-15436)*

MEDVET ASSOCIATES, INC, Moraine *Also Called: Medvet Associates Inc (G-11423)*

Medvet California Inc (HQ) 614 846-5800
350 E Wilson Bridge Rd Worthington (43085) *(G-15437)*

Medvet Cincinnati, Cincinnati *Also Called: Medvet Associates LLC (G-3034)*

Medvet Cleveland West, Cleveland *Also Called: Medvet Associates LLC (G-4548)*

Medvet Columbus, Worthington *Also Called: Medvet Associates LLC (G-15435)*

Medvet Dayton, Moraine *Also Called: Medvet Associates LLC (G-11424)*

Medvet Diley Hill, Canal Winchester *Also Called: Medvet Associates LLC (G-1612)*

Medvet Hilliard, Columbus *Also Called: Medvet Associates LLC (G-6224)*

Medvet Louisiana LLC (HQ) 614 846-5800
300 E Wilson Bridge Rd Worthington (43085) *(G-15438)*

Medvet Mahoning Valley, Girard *Also Called: Medvet Associates LLC (G-8820)*

Medvet Texas LLC (HQ) 682 223-9770
350 E Wilson Bridge Rd Worthington (43085) *(G-15439)*

Medvet Toledo, Toledo *Also Called: Medvet Associates LLC (G-13914)*

Medx, Xenia *Also Called: Medical Urgency Prep Svcs Inc (G-15526)*

Meeder Asset Management Inc 614 760-2112
6125 Memorial Dr Dublin (43017) *(G-8063)*

Mees Distributors Inc (PA) 513 541-2311
1541 W Fork Rd Cincinnati (45223) *(G-3035)*

Megco Management Inc 330 874-9999
300 Yant St Bolivar (44612) *(G-1295)*

Megen Construction Company Inc (PA) 513 742-9191
11130 Ashburn Rd Cincinnati (45240) *(G-3036)*

Mehler & Hagestrom, Cleveland *Also Called: Edward Allen Company (G-4206)*

MEI Hotels Incorporated 216 589-0441
1375 E 9th St Ste 2800 Cleveland (44114) *(G-4549)*

Meigs Cnty Dept Jobs Fmly Svcs, Middleport *Also Called: County of Meigs (G-11147)*

Meigs County Care Center LLC 740 992-6472
333 Page St Middleport (45760) *(G-11148)*

Meigs County Coal Company 740 338-3100
46226 National Rd Saint Clairsville (43950) *(G-12803)*

Meigs County Emrgncy Med Svcs, Pomeroy *Also Called: County of Meigs (G-12513)*

Meijer Dist DC 804 Corp 616 791-5821
4240 S County Rd 25a Tipp City (45371) *(G-13662)*

Meinking's Service, Cincinnati *Also Called: Meinkings Service LLC (G-3037)*

Meinkings Service LLC 513 631-5198
1756 Sherman Ave Cincinnati (45212) *(G-3037)*

ALPHABETIC SECTION — Mercy Health Youngstown LLC

Mel Lanzer Co.. 419 592-2801
2266 Scott St Napoleon (43545) *(G-11528)*

Melink Corporation... 513 685-0958
5140 River Valley Rd Milford (45150) *(G-11242)*

Mellott & Mellott Pll... 513 241-2940
12 Walnut St Ste 2500 Cincinnati (45216) *(G-3038)*

Melrose Branch, Cincinnati *Also Called: Young MNS Chrstn Assn Grter CN (G-3691)*

Mels Auto Glass Inc.. 513 563-7771
11775 Reading Rd Cincinnati (45241) *(G-3039)*

Memorial Hall... 937 293-2841
125 E 1st St Dayton (45402) *(G-7479)*

Memorial Health, Marysville *Also Called: Memorial Hosp Aux Un Cnty Ohio (G-10497)*

Memorial Health System, Marietta *Also Called: Marietta Memorial Hospital (G-10384)*

Memorial Hosp Aux Un Cnty Ohio (PA)................. 937 644-6115
500 London Ave Marysville (43040) *(G-10497)*

Memorial Hospital... 419 547-6419
430 S Main St Clyde (43410) *(G-5206)*

Memorial Hospital (PA)...................................... 419 334-6657
715 S Taft Ave Fremont (43420) *(G-8693)*

MEMORIAL HOSPITAL HEALTHLINK, Fremont *Also Called: Memorial Hospital (G-8693)*

MEMORIAL HOSPITAL OF UNION COUNTY, Marysville *Also Called: Memorial Hospital Union County (G-10498)*

Memorial Hospital Union County.......................... 937 644-1001
660 London Ave Marysville (43040) *(G-10498)*

Memorial Tournament, The, Dublin *Also Called: Muirfield Village Golf Club (G-8066)*

Memphis House, Cleveland *Also Called: United Crbral Plsy Assn Grter (G-5059)*

Menard Inc.. 937 318-2831
1277 E Dayton Yellow Springs Rd Fairborn (45324) *(G-8379)*

Menard Inc.. 513 737-2204
2865 Princeton Rd Fairfield Township (45011) *(G-8463)*

Menard Inc.. 937 630-3550
8480 Springboro Pike Miamisburg (45342) *(G-11072)*

Menards Holiday City Dist Ctr, Pioneer *Also Called: Maass - Midwest Mfg Inc (G-12433)*

MENDED REEDS MENTAL HEALTH, Ironton *Also Called: Mended Reeds Services Inc (G-9511)*

Mended Reeds Services Inc................................. 740 532-6220
700 Park Ave Ironton (45638) *(G-9511)*

Mennel Milling Company.................................... 740 385-6824
1 W Front St Logan (43138) *(G-10034)*

Mennel Milling Logan, Logan *Also Called: Mennel Milling Company (G-10034)*

Mennonite Memorial Home................................. 419 358-7654
700 Maple Crest Ct Bluffton (45817) *(G-1282)*

Mennonite Memorial Home (PA)........................... 419 358-1015
410 W Elm St Bluffton (45817) *(G-1283)*

Mennonite Mutual Insurance Co........................... 330 682-2986
1000 S Main St Orrville (44667) *(G-12170)*

Menorah Pk Ctr For Snior Lving (PA)..................... 216 831-6500
27100 Cedar Rd Cleveland (44122) *(G-4550)*

Mental Health Service.. 937 399-9500
474 N Yellow Springs St Springfield (45504) *(G-13268)*

Mental Hlth Svcs For Clark CNT (PA)..................... 937 399-9500
474 N Yellow Springs St Springfield (45504) *(G-13269)*

Mental Hlth Svcs For Hmless PR (PA).................... 216 623-6555
1744 Payne Ave Cleveland (44114) *(G-4551)*

Mentor 67 LLC... 800 589-5842
300 W Mill St Curtice (43412) *(G-7031)*

Mentor Exempted Vlg Schl Dst............................. 440 974-5260
7060 Hopkins Rd Mentor (44060) *(G-10968)*

Mentor Hospitality LLC...................................... 440 951-7333
7701 Reynolds Rd Mentor (44060) *(G-10969)*

Mentor Hsley Rcquet Fitnes CLB, Mentor *Also Called: Jto Club Corp (G-10956)*

Mentor Lumber and Supply Co (PA)...................... 440 255-8814
7180 Center St Mentor (44060) *(G-10970)*

Mentor Medical Offices, Mentor *Also Called: Kaiser Foundation Hospitals (G-10958)*

Mentor REM... 216 642-5339
9775 Rockside Rd Ste 200 Cleveland (44125) *(G-4552)*

Mentor School Service Trnsp, Mentor *Also Called: Mentor Exempted Vlg Schl Dst (G-10968)*

Mentor Senior Living LLC................................... 440 701-4560
9150 Lake Shore Blvd Mentor (44060) *(G-10971)*

Mentor Surgery Center Ltd.................................. 440 205-5725
9485 Mentor Ave Ste 1 Mentor (44060) *(G-10972)*

Mentor Wholesale Lumber, Mentor *Also Called: Mentor Lumber and Supply Co (G-10970)*

MENTORING CENTER FOR CENTRAL O, Columbus *Also Called: Big Brthers Big Ssters Cntl OH (G-5437)*

Menzies Aviation (texas) Inc................................ 216 265-3777
5921 Cargo Rd Cleveland (44135) *(G-4553)*

Mep Health LLC.. 330 492-4559
4535 Dressler Rd Nw Canton (44718) *(G-1804)*

Merc Acquisitions Inc... 216 524-4141
1933 Highland Rd Twinsburg (44087) *(G-14205)*

Mercantile Title Agency Inc................................. 614 628-6880
191 W Nationwide Blvd Ste 300 Columbus (43215) *(G-6225)*

Mercer Cnty Jint Twnship Cmnty.......................... 419 586-1611
950 S Main St Celina (45822) *(G-1926)*

Mercer Cnty Joint Township Hosp......................... 419 584-0143
909 E Wayne St Ste 126oh Celina (45822) *(G-1927)*

Mercer Cnty Joint Township Hosp......................... 419 678-2341
800 W Main St Coldwater (45828) *(G-5217)*

Mercer Health... 419 678-4300
800 W Main St Coldwater (45828) *(G-5218)*

Mercer Hospitality Inc... 937 615-0140
950 E Ash St Piqua (45356) *(G-12447)*

Merchandise Inc.. 513 353-2200
5929 State Rte 128 Miamitown (45041) *(G-11107)*

Merchandising Services Co.................................. 866 479-8246
10999 Reed Hartman Hwy Ste 200 Blue Ash (45242) *(G-1209)*

Merchants National Bank (HQ)............................. 937 393-1134
100 N High St Hillsboro (45133) *(G-9263)*

Merchnts SEC Svc Dyton Ohio In........................... 937 256-9373
2015 Wayne Ave Dayton (45410) *(G-7480)*

Mercier's Tree Experts, South Point *Also Called: Merciers Incorporated (G-13180)*

Merciers Incorporated.. 410 590-4181
2393 County Road 1 South Point (45680) *(G-13180)*

Merco Group Inc... 937 890-5841
6528 Poe Ave Dayton (45414) *(G-7481)*

MERCY, Toledo *Also Called: St Anne Mercy Hospital (G-14025)*

Mercy Allen Hospital, Oberlin *Also Called: Bon Secours Mercy Health Inc (G-12064)*

Mercy Anderson Ambulatory Ctr, Cincinnati *Also Called: Bon Secours Mercy Health Inc (G-2272)*

Mercy Clinic, Toledo *Also Called: Mercy Hlth - St Vncent Med Ctr (G-13918)*

Mercy Franciscan Hosp Mt Airy (PA)...................... 513 853-5101
2446 Kipling Ave Cincinnati (45239) *(G-3040)*

Mercy Hamilton Hospital..................................... 513 603-8600
3000 Mack Rd Fairfield (45014) *(G-8430)*

Mercy Health (DH)... 513 639-2800
12621 Eckel Junction Rd Perrysburg (43551) *(G-12356)*

Mercy Health, Cincinnati *Also Called: Bon Secours Mercy Health Inc (G-2274)*

Mercy Health, Cincinnati *Also Called: Cranley Surgical Associates (G-2515)*

Mercy Health - Clermont Hosp, Batavia *Also Called: Mercy Hlth - Clermont Hosp LLC (G-743)*

Mercy Health - Tiffin Hosp LLC............................. 419 455-7000
45 St Lawrence Dr Tiffin (44883) *(G-13632)*

Mercy Health Anderson Hospital........................... 513 624-4500
7500 State Rd Cincinnati (45255) *(G-3041)*

Mercy Health Center Alliance, Alliance *Also Called: Cleveland Clinic Mercy Hosp (G-380)*

Mercy Health Cincinnati, Cincinnati *Also Called: Mercy Health Cincinnati LLC (G-3042)*

Mercy Health Cincinnati LLC (HQ)......................... 513 952-5000
1701 Mercy Health Pl Cincinnati (45237) *(G-3042)*

Mercy Health Dermatology.................................. 567 225-3407
3425 Executive Pkwy Toledo (43606) *(G-13915)*

Mercy Health Foundation.................................... 937 523-6670
100 W Mccreight Ave Ste 200 Springfield (45504) *(G-13270)*

MERCY HEALTH FOUNDATION, SPRIN, Springfield *Also Called: Community Mercy Hlth Partners (G-13239)*

Mercy Health North LLC..................................... 419 251-1359
2200 Jefferson Ave Toledo (43604) *(G-13916)*

Mercy Health Youngstown LLC............................. 440 960-4389
362 S Burnett Rd Springfield (45505) *(G-13271)*

Mercy Health Youngstown LLC............................. 330 841-4000
667 Eastland Ave Se Warren (44484) *(G-14539)*

Mercy Health Youngstown LLC (HQ)...................... 330 746-7211
1044 Belmont Ave Youngstown (44504) *(G-15665)*

Mercy Healthplex Anderson LLC.. 513 624-1871
201 E 5th St Ste 2500 Cincinnati (45202) *(G-3043)*

Mercy Hlth - Clermont Hosp LLC.. 513 732-8200
3000 Hospital Dr Batavia (45103) *(G-743)*

Mercy Hlth - Defiance Hosp LLC.. 419 782-8444
1404 E 2nd St Defiance (43512) *(G-7757)*

Mercy Hlth - Rgnal Med Ctr LLC.. 440 960-4000
3700 Kolbe Rd Lorain (44053) *(G-10092)*

Mercy Hlth - Sprngfeld Cncer C.. 937 323-5001
148 W North St Springfield (45504) *(G-13272)*

Mercy Hlth - St Anne Hosp LLC.. 419 407-2663
3404 W Sylvania Ave Toledo (43623) *(G-13917)*

Mercy Hlth - St Chrles Hosp LL.. 419 696-7200
2600 Navarre Ave Oregon (43616) *(G-12136)*

Mercy Hlth - St Rtas Med Ctr L (HQ).. 419 227-3361
730 W Market St Lima (45801) *(G-9934)*

Mercy Hlth - St Vncent Med Ctr.. 419 251-0580
2200 Jefferson Ave Toledo (43604) *(G-13918)*

Mercy Hlth - St Vncent Med Ctr (PA).. 419 251-3232
2213 Cherry St Toledo (43608) *(G-13919)*

Mercy Hlth - St Vncent Med Ctr.. 419 475-5433
2000 Regency Ct Ste 103 Toledo (43623) *(G-13920)*

Mercy Hlth - Willard Hosp LLC.. 419 964-5000
1100 Neal Zick Rd Willard (44890) *(G-15171)*

Mercy Hlth Fndtion Springfield, Springfield *Also Called: Community Mercy Health System* *(G-13238)*

Mercy Hlth-St Jseph Wrren Hosp, Warren *Also Called: Mercy Health Youngstown LLC* *(G-14539)*

Mercy Hospital.. 513 870-7767
11963 Lick Rd Cincinnati (45251) *(G-3044)*

Mercy Hospital.. 513 624-4590
7500 State Rd Cincinnati (45255) *(G-3045)*

Mercy Hospital Anderson, Cincinnati *Also Called: Mercy Health Anderson Hospital (G-3041)*

Mercy Hospital of Defiance, Defiance *Also Called: Mercy Hlth - Defiance Hosp LLC (G-7757)*

Mercy Hospital of Willard, Willard *Also Called: Mercy Hlth - Willard Hosp LLC (G-15171)*

Mercy House Partners, Cincinnati *Also Called: West Park Retirement Community (G-3656)*

Mercy Medical Center, Canton *Also Called: Cleveland Clinic Mercy Hosp (G-1715)*

Mercy Medical Center Hospice, Canton *Also Called: Cleveland Clinic Mercy Hosp (G-1714)*

Mercy Medical Center Hospice, Canton *Also Called: Cleveland Clinic Mercy Hosp (G-1716)*

Mercy Montessori Center.. 513 475-6700
2335 Grandview Ave Cincinnati (45206) *(G-3046)*

Mercy St Theresa Center Inc.. 513 271-7010
7010 Rowan Hill Dr Ste 200 Cincinnati (45227) *(G-3047)*

Meridian Condominiums Inc.. 216 228-4211
12550 Lake Ave Lakewood (44107) *(G-9679)*

Meridian Healthcare (PA).. 330 797-0070
527 N Meridian Rd Youngstown (44509) *(G-15666)*

Merieux Nutrisciences Corp.. 614 486-0150
2057 Builders Pl Columbus (43204) *(G-6226)*

Merit Brass, Cleveland *Also Called: Merit Brass Co (G-4554)*

Merit Brass Co (PA).. 216 261-9800
1 Merit Dr Cleveland (44143) *(G-4554)*

Merit House LLC.. 419 478-5131
4645 Lewis Ave Toledo (43612) *(G-13921)*

Merit Leasing Co LLC.. 216 261-9592
3 Merit Dr Cleveland (44143) *(G-4555)*

Meritech Inc (PA).. 216 459-8333
4577 Hinckley Industrial Pkwy Cleveland (44109) *(G-4556)*

Merkley Professionals Inc.. 419 447-9541
19 W Market St Ste A Tiffin (44883) *(G-13633)*

Merrill Lynch, Broadview Heights *Also Called: Merrill Lynch Prce Fnner Smith (G-1392)*

Merrill Lynch, Columbus *Also Called: Merrill Lynch Prce Fnner Smith (G-5269)*

Merrill Lynch Prce Fnner Smith.. 440 526-8880
6001 E Royalton Rd Broadview Heights (44147) *(G-1392)*

Merrill Lynch Prce Fnner Smith.. 614 225-3000
8890 Lyra Dr Ste 500 Columbus (43240) *(G-5269)*

Merrill Swanson DDS LLC.. 419 884-3411
355 W Main St Mansfield (44904) *(G-10296)*

Merry Maids, Columbus *Also Called: Merry Maids Ltd Partnership (G-6227)*

Merry Maids Ltd Partnership.. 614 430-8441
6185 Huntley Rd Ste O Columbus (43229) *(G-6227)*

Mes Painting and Graphics Ltd.. 614 496-1696
8298 Harlem Rd Westerville (43081) *(G-14998)*

Mesa Industries Inc (PA).. 513 321-2950
4027 Eastern Ave Cincinnati (45226) *(G-3048)*

Mesi, South Point *Also Called: Mike Enyart & Sons Inc (G-13181)*

Messer Construction Co.. 513 672-5000
2495 Langdon Farm Rd Cincinnati (45237) *(G-3049)*

Messer Construction Co (PA).. 513 242-1541
643 W Court St Cincinnati (45203) *(G-3050)*

Messer Construction Co.. 513 482-7402
1201 Glendale Milford Rd Cincinnati (45215) *(G-3051)*

Messer Construction Co.. 614 275-0141
3705 Business Park Dr Columbus (43204) *(G-6228)*

Messer Construction Co.. 937 291-1300
4801 Hempstead Station Dr Unit A Dayton (45429) *(G-7482)*

Messina Floor Covering LLC.. 216 595-0100
4300 Brookpark Rd Ste 1 Cleveland (44134) *(G-4557)*

Met-Ed, Akron *Also Called: Metropolitan Edison Company (G-231)*

Meta Manufacturing Corporation.. 513 793-6382
8901 Blue Ash Rd Ste 1 Blue Ash (45242) *(G-1210)*

Meta Solutions, Marion *Also Called: Metropltan Edctl Tchnical Assn (G-10445)*

Metal Framing Enterprises LLC.. 216 433-7080
9005 Bank St Cleveland (44125) *(G-4558)*

Metalcraft Solutions, Akron *Also Called: Acro Tool & Die Company (G-14)*

Metals USA, Wooster *Also Called: Metals USA Crbn Flat Rlled Inc (G-15355)*

Metals USA Crbn Flat Rlled Inc (DH).. 330 264-8416
1070 W Liberty St Wooster (44691) *(G-15355)*

Metalx LLC.. 260 232-3000
7300 State Route 109 Delta (43515) *(G-7852)*

Metcon Ltd (PA).. 937 447-9200
5150 Webster St Dayton (45414) *(G-7483)*

Metcut Research Associates Inc (PA).. 513 271-5100
3980 Rosslyn Dr Cincinnati (45209) *(G-3052)*

Metcut Research, Inc., Cincinnati *Also Called: Metcut Research Associates Inc (G-3052)*

METHODIST ELDER CARE SERVICES, Reynoldsburg *Also Called: Wesley Ridge Inc (G-12681)*

Methodist Eldercare Services, Columbus *Also Called: Methodist Rtrment Ctr of Cntl (G-6229)*

Methodist Rtrment Ctr of Cntl.. 614 888-7492
5156 Wesley Way Columbus (43214) *(G-6229)*

Metis Construction Svcs LLC.. 330 677-7333
175 E Erie St Ste 303 Kent (44240) *(G-9587)*

MetLife Legal Plans Inc.. 216 241-0022
1111 Superior Ave E Ste 800 Cleveland (44114) *(G-4559)*

Metro Air, Hilliard *Also Called: Metro Heating and AC Co (G-9212)*

Metro Decor LLC.. 855 498-5899
30320 Emerald Valley Pkwy Glenwillow (44139) *(G-8834)*

Metro Design Inc.. 440 458-4200
10740 Middle Ave Elyria (44035) *(G-8274)*

Metro Fiber & Cable Cnstr.. 419 724-9802
5566 Southwyck Blvd Toledo (43614) *(G-13922)*

Metro Fitness Hilliard.. 614 850-0070
3440 Heritage Club Dr Hilliard (43026) *(G-9211)*

Metro Health Dental Associates.. 216 778-4982
2500 Metrohealth Dr Cleveland (44109) *(G-4560)*

Metro Heating and AC Co.. 614 777-1237
4731 Northwest Pkwy Hilliard (43026) *(G-9212)*

Metro Parks, Westerville *Also Called: Columbus Frkln Cnty Pk (G-14970)*

Metro Regional Transit Auth (PA).. 330 762-0341
416 Kenmore Blvd Akron (44301) *(G-229)*

Metro Regional Transit Auth.. 330 762-0341
631 S Broadway St Akron (44311) *(G-230)*

Metro Staffing, Galena *Also Called: Midwest Investors Group Inc (G-8737)*

Metrohealth, Cleveland *Also Called: Metrohealth System (G-4563)*

Metrohealth, Cleveland *Also Called: Metrohealth System (G-4567)*

METROHEALTH, Cleveland *Also Called: Recovery Resources (G-4813)*

Metrohealth, Cleveland *Also Called: The Metrohealth System (G-5004)*

Metrohealth Beachwood Hlth Ctr, Beachwood *Also Called: Metrohealth System (G-815)*

Metrohealth Broadway Hlth Ctr, Cleveland *Also Called: Metrohealth System (G-4562)*

Metrohealth Buckeye Health Ctr, Cleveland *Also Called: Metrohealth System (G-4561)*

ALPHABETIC SECTION

Metrohealth System..216 765-0733
3609 Park East Dr Ste 300 Beachwood (44122) *(G-815)*

Metrohealth System..216 591-0523
3609 Park East Dr Ste 206 Beachwood (44122) *(G-816)*

Metrohealth System..216 957-9000
9200 Treeworth Blvd Brecksville (44141) *(G-1359)*

Metrohealth System..216 957-4000
2816 E 116th St Cleveland (44120) *(G-4561)*

Metrohealth System..216 957-1500
6835 Broadway Ave Cleveland (44105) *(G-4562)*

Metrohealth System..216 957-2100
4229 Pearl Rd Cleveland (44109) *(G-4563)*

Metrohealth System..216 957-5000
3838 W 150th St Cleveland (44111) *(G-4564)*

Metrohealth System..216 598-9908
2150 W 117th St Ste 1238 Cleveland (44111) *(G-4565)*

Metrohealth System..216 778-8446
2500 Metrohealth Dr Cleveland (44109) *(G-4566)*

Metrohealth System..216 778-3867
2500 Metrohealth Dr Cleveland (44109) *(G-4567)*

Metrohealth System..216 696-3876
10 Severance Cir Cleveland Heights (44118) *(G-5181)*

Metrohealth System..216 524-7377
12301 Snow Rd Parma (44130) *(G-12256)*

Metrohealth West Park Hlth Ctr, Cleveland *Also Called: Metrohealth System (G-4564)*

Metrohlth Brcksvlle Hlth Srger, Brecksville *Also Called: Metrohealth System (G-1359)*

Metrohlth Pepper Pike Hlth Ctr, Beachwood *Also Called: Metrohealth System (G-816)*

Metropltan Edctl Tchnical Assn...740 389-4798
100 Executive Dr Marion (43302) *(G-10445)*

Metropltan Swer Dst Grter Cncn...513 244-1300
1600 Gest St Cincinnati (45204) *(G-3053)*

Metropolitan Ceramics Div, Canton *Also Called: Ironrock Capital Incorporated (G-1782)*

Metropolitan Edison Company (HQ).....................................800 736-3402
76 S Main St Akron (44308) *(G-231)*

Metropolitan Envmtl Svcs Inc..614 771-1881
5055 Nike Dr Hilliard (43026) *(G-9213)*

Metropolitan Family Care, Reynoldsburg *Also Called: Metropolitian Family Care Inc (G-12669)*

Metropolitan Hotel LLC..216 239-1200
2017 E 9th St Cleveland (44115) *(G-4568)*

Metropolitan Pool Service Co..216 741-9451
3427 Brookpark Rd Parma (44134) *(G-12257)*

Metropolitan Pools, Parma *Also Called: Metropolitan Pool Service Co (G-12257)*

Metropolitan Security Svcs Inc..330 253-6459
2 S Main St Akron (44308) *(G-232)*

Metropolitan Security Svcs Inc..216 298-4076
801 W Superior Ave Cleveland (44113) *(G-4569)*

Metropolitan YMCA, Englewood *Also Called: Young MNS Chrstn Assn Grter Dy (G-8327)*

Metropolitian Family Care Inc...614 237-1067
7094 E Main St Reynoldsburg (43068) *(G-12669)*

Mettler-Toledo LLC (HQ)..614 438-4511
1900 Polaris Pkwy Columbus (43240) *(G-5270)*

Metzenbaum Sheltered Inds Inc..440 729-1919
8090 Cedar Rd Chesterland (44026) *(G-2041)*

Metzgers, Toledo *Also Called: Tj Metzgers Inc (G-14043)*

Meyer Decorative Surfaces USA Inc......................................800 776-3900
300 Executive Pkwy W Ste 100 Hudson (44236) *(G-9364)*

Meyer Hill Lynch Corporation...419 897-9797
1771 Indian Wood Cir Maumee (43537) *(G-10748)*

Meyerpt, Hudson *Also Called: Boxout LLC (G-9334)*

Meyers + Associates Arch LLC..614 221-9433
232 N 3rd St Ste 300 Columbus (43215) *(G-6230)*

Meyers Lake Sportsmans CLB Inc...330 456-1025
1672 N Park Ave Nw Canton (44708) *(G-1805)*

Meyers Ldscp Svcs & Nurs Inc...614 210-1194
6081 Columbus Pike Lewis Center (43035) *(G-9828)*

Mfbusiness Group..216 609-7297
3915 Carnegie Ave Cleveland (44115) *(G-4570)*

MFC, Cleveland *Also Called: Messina Floor Covering LLC (G-4557)*

Mff Somerset LLC...216 752-5600
3550 Northfield Rd Shaker Heights (44122) *(G-12982)*

Mfh Inc (PA)..937 435-4701
241 E Alex Bell Rd Dayton (45459) *(G-7484)*

Mfh Inc...937 435-4701
241 E Alex Bell Rd Dayton (45459) *(G-7485)*

Mfh Partners Inc (PA)...440 461-4100
6650 Beta Dr Cleveland (44143) *(G-4571)*

Mgj Enterprises Inc...740 364-1360
963 N 21st St Newark (43055) *(G-11729)*

MGM Hlth Care Wnchster Pl Nrsi, Canal Winchester *Also Called: Kindred Nursing Centers E LLC (G-1610)*

MGM Northfield Park, Northfield *Also Called: Northfield Park Associates LLC (G-11961)*

Mh Equipment, West Chester *Also Called: MH Logistics Corp (G-14825)*

MH Logistics Corp...330 425-2476
2575 Medina Rd Medina (44256) *(G-10865)*

MH Logistics Corp...513 681-2200
106 Circle Freeway Dr West Chester (45246) *(G-14825)*

Mhas, Columbus *Also Called: Ohio Department of Mental Health (G-6401)*

Mhrs Board of Stark County, Canton *Also Called: County of Stark (G-1727)*

MI, Miamitown *Also Called: Merchandise Inc (G-11107)*

MI - De - Con Inc..740 532-2277
3331 S 3rd St Ironton (45638) *(G-9512)*

Miami Cnty Cmnty Action Cuncil..937 335-7921
1695 Troy Sidney Rd Troy (45373) *(G-14146)*

Miami Co Highway Dept, Troy *Also Called: County of Miami (G-14132)*

Miami Co YMCA Child Care..937 778-5241
325 W Ash St Piqua (45356) *(G-12448)*

Miami Corporation (PA)...800 543-0448
720 Anderson Ferry Rd Cincinnati (45238) *(G-3054)*

Miami Fort Power Station, North Bend *Also Called: Vistra Energy Corp (G-11804)*

Miami Industrial Trucks, Moraine *Also Called: Miami Industrial Trucks Inc (G-11425)*

Miami Industrial Trucks Inc..419 424-0042
130 Stanford Pkwy Findlay (45840) *(G-8567)*

Miami Industrial Trucks Inc (PA)..937 293-4194
2830 E River Rd Moraine (45439) *(G-11425)*

Miami Metropolitan Hsing Auth, Troy *Also Called: Miami Cnty Cmnty Action Cuncil (G-14146)*

Miami University...513 727-3200
4200 E University Blvd Middletown (45042) *(G-11172)*

Miami University...513 529-6911
Fisher Dr Oxford (45056) *(G-12211)*

Miami University...513 529-1230
725 E Chestnut St Oxford (45056) *(G-12212)*

Miami University-Middletown, Middletown *Also Called: Miami University (G-11172)*

MIAMI VALLEY, Dayton *Also Called: Premier Health Partners (G-7560)*

MIAMI VALLEY, Troy *Also Called: Uvmc Management Corporation (G-14169)*

Miami Valley Broadcasting Corp (HQ)...................................937 259-2111
1611 S Main St Dayton (45409) *(G-7486)*

Miami Valley Family Care Ctr, Dayton *Also Called: Catholic Scial Svcs of Mami VI (G-7218)*

Miami Valley Gaming & Racg LLC..513 934-7070
6000 W State Route 63 Lebanon (45036) *(G-9778)*

Miami Valley Golf Club (PA)..937 278-7381
3311 Salem Ave Dayton (45406) *(G-7487)*

Miami Valley Hospital...937 208-7396
2451 Wayne Ave Dayton (45420) *(G-7488)*

Miami Valley Hospital...937 208-7450
1525 E Stroop Rd Dayton (45429) *(G-7489)*

Miami Valley Hospital...937 208-4076
5801 Clyo Rd Dayton (45459) *(G-7490)*

Miami Valley Hospital...937 438-2400
2400 Miami Valley Dr Dayton (45459) *(G-7491)*

Miami Valley Hospital (HQ)...937 208-8000
1 Wyoming St Dayton (45409) *(G-7492)*

Miami Valley Hospital...937 208-4673
122 S Patterson Blvd Ste 390 Dayton (45402) *(G-7493)*

Miami Valley Hospital...937 224-3916
1816 Harvard Blvd Dayton (45406) *(G-7494)*

Miami Valley Hospital...937 208-7065
211 Kenbrook Dr Vandalia (45377) *(G-14384)*

Miami Valley Hospital, Englewood *Also Called: Dayton Surgeons Inc (G-8305)*

Miami Valley Hospitalist Group..937 208-8394
30 E Apple St Ste 3300 Dayton (45409) *(G-7495)*

Miami Valley Hsing Assn I Inc — ALPHABETIC SECTION

Miami Valley Hsing Assn I Inc.. 937 263-4449
907 W 5th St Dayton (45402) *(G-7496)*

Miami Valley Intl Trcks Inc.. 513 733-8500
11775 Highway Dr Ste D Cincinnati (45241) *(G-3055)*

Miami Valley Intl Trcks Inc.. 937 324-5526
121 S Spring St Springfield (45502) *(G-13273)*

Miami Valley Memory Grdns Assn (DH).................................. 937 885-7779
1639 E Lytle 5 Points Rd Dayton (45458) *(G-7497)*

Miami Valley Regional Plg Comm... 937 223-6323
10 N Ludlow St Ste 700 Dayton (45402) *(G-7498)*

Miami Valley School.. 937 434-4444
5151 Denise Dr Dayton (45429) *(G-7499)*

Miami Valley South Campus, Dayton *Also Called: Miami Valley Hospital (G-7491)*

Miami Valley Steel Service Inc.. 937 773-7127
201 Fox Dr Piqua (45356) *(G-12449)*

Miami View Head Start, Dayton *Also Called: Miami Vly Child Dev Ctrs Inc (G-7501)*

Miami Vly Child Dev Ctrs Inc... 937 833-6600
75 June Pl Brookville (45309) *(G-1446)*

Miami Vly Child Dev Ctrs Inc (PA).. 937 226-5664
215 Horace St Dayton (45402) *(G-7500)*

Miami Vly Child Dev Ctrs Inc... 937 228-1644
215 Horace St Dayton (45402) *(G-7501)*

Miami Vly Child Dev Ctrs Inc... 937 258-2470
517 Noel Ct Dayton (45410) *(G-7502)*

Miami Vly Child Dev Ctrs Inc... 937 325-2559
1450 S Yellow Springs St Springfield (45506) *(G-13274)*

Miami Vly Cmnty Action Partnr (PA)...................................... 937 222-1009
719 S Main St Dayton (45402) *(G-7503)*

Miami Vly Jvnile Rhbltion Ctr.. 937 562-4000
2100 Greene Way Blvd Xenia (45385) *(G-15527)*

Miami Vly Regional Crime Lab, Dayton *Also Called: County of Montgomery (G-7252)*

Miba Bearings US LLC.. 740 962-4242
5037 N State Route 60 Nw Mcconnelsville (43756) *(G-10803)*

Miceli Dairy Products Co (PA).. 216 791-6222
2721 E 90th St Cleveland (44104) *(G-4572)*

Michael Baker Intl Inc.. 330 453-3110
101 Cleveland Ave Nw Ste 106 Canton (44702) *(G-1806)*

Michael Baker Intl Inc.. 412 269-6300
1111 Superior Ave E Ste 230 Cleveland (44114) *(G-4573)*

Michael Schuster Assoc Inc (PA).. 513 241-5666
316 W 4th St Ste 600 Cincinnati (45202) *(G-3056)*

Michaels Inc... 440 357-0384
5783 Heisley Rd Mentor (44060) *(G-10973)*

Michaels Finer Meats LLC... 614 527-4900
3775 Zane Trace Dr Columbus (43228) *(G-6231)*

Michaels For Hair, Dayton *Also Called: Mfh Inc (G-7485)*

Micnan Inc (PA).. 330 920-6200
3365 Cavalier Trl Cuyahoga Falls (44224) *(G-7088)*

Micro Center, Cincinnati *Also Called: Micro Electronics Inc (G-3057)*

Micro Center Inc (HQ)... 614 850-3000
4119 Leap Rd Hilliard (43026) *(G-9214)*

Micro Center Online, Columbus *Also Called: Micro Center Online Inc (G-6232)*

Micro Center Online Inc... 614 326-8500
747 Bethel Rd Columbus (43214) *(G-6232)*

Micro Electronics Inc.. 513 782-8500
11755 Mosteller Rd Rear Cincinnati (45241) *(G-3057)*

Micro Electronics Inc.. 614 334-1430
2701 Charter St Ste B Columbus (43228) *(G-6233)*

Micro Electronics Inc.. 614 850-3410
4055 Leap Rd Hilliard (43026) *(G-9215)*

Micro Industries Corporation (PA)... 740 548-7878
8399 Green Meadows Dr N Westerville (43081) *(G-14999)*

Micro Products Co Inc.. 440 943-0258
26653 Curtiss Wright Pkwy Willoughby Hills (44092) *(G-15233)*

Micro Thinner, Hilliard *Also Called: Micro Electronics Inc (G-9215)*

Microbac Laboratories Inc... 740 373-4071
158 Starlite Dr Marietta (45750) *(G-10389)*

Microcenter DC, Columbus *Also Called: Micro Electronics Inc (G-6233)*

Microman Inc (PA).. 614 923-8000
4393 Tuller Rd Ste A Dublin (43017) *(G-8064)*

Microplex Inc.. 330 498-0600
7568 Whipple Ave Nw North Canton (44720) *(G-11848)*

Micros Retail, Cleveland *Also Called: Datavantage Corporation (G-4150)*

Microsystems, Mentor *Also Called: Materials MGT Microsystems (G-10966)*

Microtek, Moraine *Also Called: Microtek Laboratories Inc (G-11426)*

Microtek Laboratories Inc.. 937 236-2213
2400 E River Rd Moraine (45439) *(G-11426)*

Microtel, Batavia *Also Called: Bansi & Pratima Inc (G-727)*

Microtel, Grove City *Also Called: Microtel Inn (G-8934)*

Microtel Inn... 614 277-0705
1800 Stringtown Rd Grove City (43123) *(G-8934)*

Mid America Glass Block, Cleveland *Also Called: Cleveland Glass Block Inc (G-4046)*

Mid Atlantic Stor Systems Inc.. 740 335-2019
1551 Robinson Rd Se Wshngtn Ct Hs (43160) *(G-15491)*

Mid Ohio Emergency Svcs LLC... 614 566-5070
3525 Olentangy River Rd Ste 4330 Columbus (43214) *(G-6234)*

Mid Ohio Vly Bulk Trnspt Inc.. 740 373-2481
16380 State Route 7 Marietta (45750) *(G-10390)*

Mid State Systems Inc... 740 928-1115
9455 Lancaster Rd Hebron (43025) *(G-9148)*

Mid-America Consulting Group Inc
3700 Euclid Ave 2 Cleveland (44115) *(G-4574)*

Mid-America Stainless, Cleveland *Also Called: Mid-America Steel Corp (G-4575)*

Mid-America Steel Corp... 800 282-3466
20900 Saint Clair Ave Rear Cleveland (44117) *(G-4575)*

Mid-America Store Fixtures, Obetz *Also Called: Lemon Group LLC (G-12081)*

Mid-American Clg Contrs Inc.. 614 291-7170
1046 King Ave Columbus (43212) *(G-6235)*

Mid-American Clg Contrs Inc.. 419 429-6222
1648 Tiffin Ave Findlay (45840) *(G-8568)*

Mid-American Clg Contrs Inc (PA)... 419 229-3899
447 N Elizabeth St Lima (45801) *(G-9935)*

Mid-East Truck & Tractor Service Inc..................................... 330 488-0398
831 Nassau St W East Canton (44730) *(G-8170)*

Mid-Ohio, Columbus *Also Called: Mid-Ohio Air Conditioning Corp (G-6236)*

Mid-Ohio Air Conditioning Corp... 614 291-4664
456 E 5th Ave Columbus (43201) *(G-6236)*

Mid-Ohio Contracting Inc... 330 343-2925
1817 Horns Ln Nw Dover (44622) *(G-7893)*

Mid-Ohio Energy Coop Inc.. 419 568-5321
1210 W Lima St Kenton (43326) *(G-9621)*

Mid-Ohio Foodbank.. 614 277-3663
3960 Brookham Dr Grove City (43123) *(G-8935)*

Mid-Ohio Heart Clinic Inc... 419 524-8151
335 Glessner Ave Mansfield (44903) *(G-10297)*

Mid-Ohio Onclgy/Hematology Inc... 614 383-6000
3100 Plaza Properties Blvd Columbus (43219) *(G-6237)*

Mid-Ohio Oncology/Hematology Inc (PA)............................. 614 383-6000
3100 Plaza Properties Blvd Columbus (43219) *(G-6238)*

Mid-Ohio Pipeline Company Inc.. 419 884-3772
2270 Eckert Rd Mansfield (44904) *(G-10298)*

Mid-Ohio Pipeline Services, Mansfield *Also Called: Mid-Ohio Pipeline Company Inc (G-10298)*

Mid-Ohio Pipeline Services LLC... 419 884-3772
4244 State Route 546 Mansfield (44904) *(G-10299)*

Mid-Ohio Psychological Svcs Inc (PA).................................. 740 687-0042
106 Starret St Ste 100 Lancaster (43130) *(G-9735)*

Mid-Ohio Regional Plg Comm.. 614 228-2663
111 Liberty St Ste 100 Columbus (43215) *(G-6239)*

Mid-State Industrial Pdts Inc (HQ).. 614 253-8631
1575 Alum Creek Dr Columbus (43209) *(G-6240)*

Mid-State Sales, Columbus *Also Called: Mid-State Sales Inc (G-6241)*

Mid-State Sales Inc (PA)... 614 864-1811
1101 Gahanna Pkwy Columbus (43230) *(G-6241)*

Mid-States Packaging, Lewistown *Also Called: Mid-States Packaging Inc (G-9843)*

Mid-States Packaging Inc.. 937 843-3243
12163 St Rt 274 Lewistown (43333) *(G-9843)*

Mid-West Direct, Cleveland *Also Called: Mid-West Presort Mailing Services Inc (G-4576)*

Mid-West Materials Inc.. 440 259-5200
3687 Shepard Rd Perry (44081) *(G-12309)*

Mid-West Presort Mailing Services Inc (PA)......................... 216 251-2500
2222 W 110th St Cleveland (44102) *(G-4576)*

Mid-Western Childrens Home.. 513 877-2141
4585 Long Spurling Rd Pleasant Plain (45162) *(G-12499)*

ALPHABETIC SECTION

Mid-Wood Inc.. 419 937-2233
6100 W Poplar St Bascom (44809) *(G-725)*

Midas Auto Systems Experts... 419 243-7281
1101 Monroe St Toledo (43604) *(G-13923)*

Middle Bass Ferry Company, The, Put In Bay *Also Called: Island Service Company (G-12617)*

Middlefield Banking Company.. 419 634-5015
118 S Main St Ada (45810) *(G-2)*

Middlefield Farm & Garden, Middlefield *Also Called: Old Meadow Farms Inc (G-11143)*

Middletown Innkeepers Inc.. 513 942-3440
430 Kolb Dr Fairfield (45014) *(G-8431)*

Middletown Tube Works Inc... 513 727-0080
2201 Trine St Middletown (45044) *(G-11173)*

Middltown Area Snior Ctzens In.. 513 423-1734
3907 Central Ave Middletown (45044) *(G-11174)*

Middough Inc (PA)... 216 367-6000
1901 E 13th St Ste 400 Cleveland (44114) *(G-4577)*

Midland Company... 513 947-5503
7000 Midland Blvd Amelia (45102) *(G-418)*

Midland Council Governments... 330 264-6047
2125 Eagle Pass Wooster (44691) *(G-15356)*

Midland Title Security Inc (DH)... 216 241-6045
1111 Superior Ave E Ste 700 Cleveland (44114) *(G-4578)*

Midland Title Security Inc... 513 863-7600
300 High St Ste 404 Hamilton (45011) *(G-9065)*

Midland-Guardian Co (HQ)... 513 943-7100
7000 Midland Blvd Amelia (45102) *(G-419)*

Midohio Crdiolgy Vascular Cons... 740 420-8174
600 N Pickaway St Circleville (43113) *(G-3713)*

Midohio Crdiolgy Vascular Cons (PA).. 614 262-6772
3705 Olentangy River Rd Ste 100 Columbus (43214) *(G-6242)*

MIDOHIO ENERGY COOPERATIVE, Kenton *Also Called: Mid-Ohio Energy Coop Inc (G-9621)*

Midtown Investment Co... 216 398-7210
5676 Broadview Rd Apt 127 Cleveland (44134) *(G-4579)*

Midtown Towers, Cleveland *Also Called: Midtown Investment Co (G-4579)*

Midusa Credit Union (PA)... 513 420-8640
1201 Crawford St Middletown (45044) *(G-11175)*

Midway Inc (PA)... 419 465-2551
220 Sandusky St Monroeville (44847) *(G-11357)*

Midway Truck Center, Monroeville *Also Called: Midway Inc (G-11357)*

Midwest, Canton *Also Called: Midwest Industrial Supply Inc (G-1807)*

Midwest Cmnty Federal Cr Un... 419 599-5522
1429 Scott St Napoleon (43545) *(G-11529)*

Midwest Cmnty Hlth Assoc Inc (HQ).. 419 633-4034
442 W High St Ste 3 Bryan (43506) *(G-1488)*

Midwest Communications LLC.. 419 420-8000
16380 E Us Route 224 Findlay (45840) *(G-8569)*

Midwest Contracting Inc.. 419 866-4560
1428 Albon Rd Holland (43528) *(G-9297)*

Midwest Curtainwalls Inc... 216 641-7900
5171 Grant Ave Cleveland (44125) *(G-4580)*

Midwest Cylinder, Harrison *Also Called: Kaplan Industries Inc (G-9111)*

Midwest Dairies Inc.. 419 678-8059
612 Plum Dr Coldwater (45828) *(G-5219)*

Midwest Digital Inc... 330 966-4744
4721 Eagle St Nw North Canton (44720) *(G-11849)*

Midwest Division - Brunswick, Brunswick *Also Called: W W Williams Company LLC (G-1473)*

Midwest East Division, Cincinnati *Also Called: Intren Inc (G-2885)*

Midwest Environmental Inc.. 419 382-9200
28757 Glenwood Rd Perrysburg (43551) *(G-12357)*

Midwest Express Inc (DH).. 937 642-0335
11590 Township Road 298 East Liberty (43319) *(G-8173)*

Midwest Fresh Foods Inc... 614 469-1492
38 N Glenwood Ave Columbus (43222) *(G-6243)*

Midwest Furniture & Mat Outl, Dublin *Also Called: Retail Service Systems Inc (G-8108)*

Midwest Health Services Inc (PA).. 330 828-0779
107 Tommy Henrich Dr Nw Massillon (44647) *(G-10657)*

Midwest Industrial Supply Inc (PA)... 330 456-3121
1101 3rd St Se Canton (44707) *(G-1807)*

Midwest Investors Group Inc... 270 887-8888
11619 Trenton Rd Galena (43021) *(G-8737)*

Midwest Laundry Inc... 513 563-5560
10110 Cincinnati Dayton Pike Cincinnati (45241) *(G-3058)*

Midwest Logistics Systems Ltd (HQ).. 419 584-1414
8779 State Route 703 Celina (45822) *(G-1928)*

Midwest Mfg Solutions LLC.. 513 381-7200
1 E 4th St Cincinnati (45202) *(G-3059)*

Midwest Motor Supply Co (PA).. 800 233-1294
4800 Roberts Rd Columbus (43228) *(G-6244)*

Midwest Painting, Dayton *Also Called: Muha Construction Inc (G-7517)*

Midwest Physcans Ansthsia Svcs... 614 884-0641
5151 Reed Rd Ste 225c Columbus (43220) *(G-6245)*

Midwest Protection Div LLC... 844 844-8200
2838 Fisher Rd Columbus (43204) *(G-6246)*

Midwest Reg Columbus, Columbus *Also Called: Sunbelt Rentals Inc (G-6729)*

Midwest Rehab Inc (PA).. 419 692-3405
118 E Highland Ave Ada (45810) *(G-3)*

Midwest Service Center, Grove City *Also Called: Safety Today Inc (G-8950)*

Midwest Springfield Dialysis, Springfield *Also Called: Storrie Dialysis LLC (G-13296)*

Midwest Transatlantic Lines Inc (PA).. 440 243-1993
1230 W Bagley Rd Berea (44017) *(G-1074)*

Midwest Trmnals Tledo Intl Inc... 419 897-6868
3518 Saint Lawrence Dr Toledo (43605) *(G-13924)*

Midwestern Auto Group, Dublin *Also Called: Brentlinger Enterprises (G-7947)*

Midwestern Plumbing Svc Inc... 513 753-0050
3984 Bach Buxton Rd Cincinnati (45202) *(G-3060)*

Mielke Holdings LLC... 330 725-8845
1040 Industrial Pkwy Medina (44256) *(G-10866)*

Mighty Mac Investments Inc (PA)... 937 335-2928
1494 Lytle Rd Troy (45373) *(G-14147)*

MII Brand Import LLC (HQ)... 614 256-7267
4 Limited Pkwy E Reynoldsburg (43068) *(G-12670)*

Mike Albert Fleet Solutions.. 800 985-3273
10340 Evendale Dr Cincinnati (45241) *(G-3061)*

Mike Castrucci Ford.. 513 831-7010
1020 Business 28 Milford (45150) *(G-11243)*

Mike Coates Cnstr Co Inc.. 330 652-0190
800 Summit Ave Niles (44446) *(G-11793)*

Mike Enyart & Sons Inc... 740 523-0235
77 Private Drive 615 South Point (45680) *(G-13181)*

Mike Ford Bass Inc... 440 934-3673
5050 Detroit Rd Sheffield Village (44035) *(G-13002)*

Mike Pusateri Excavating Inc... 330 385-5221
16363 Saint Clair Ave East Liverpool (43920) *(G-8186)*

Mike Ward Landscaping LLC.. 513 683-6436
424 E Us Highway 22 And 3 Maineville (45039) *(G-10228)*

Mike-Sells Potato Chip Co (HQ).. 937 228-9400
333 Leo St Dayton (45404) *(G-7504)*

Mike-Sells West Virginia Inc (PA).. 937 228-9400
333 Leo St Dayton (45404) *(G-7505)*

Mikes Carwash Inc (PA).. 513 677-4700
100 Northeast Dr Loveland (45140) *(G-10151)*

Mikes Trucking Ltd.. 614 879-8808
570 Plain City Georgesville Rd Se Galloway (43119) *(G-8773)*

Mikescar Wash.. 513 672-6440
100 Northeast Dr Loveland (45140) *(G-10152)*

Mikouis Enterprise Inc.. 330 424-1418
38655 Saltwell Rd Lisbon (44432) *(G-10005)*

Milan Skilled Nursing LLC... 216 727-3996
185 S Main St Milan (44846) *(G-11208)*

Milcrest Healthcare Inc... 937 642-0218
730 Millcrest Dr Marysville (43040) *(G-10499)*

Mile Inc.. 614 252-6724
1144 Alum Creek Dr Columbus (43209) *(G-6247)*

Mile Inc (PA)... 614 794-2203
110 E Wilson Bridge Rd Ste 100 Worthington (43085) *(G-15440)*

Miles Alloys Inc... 216 295-1000
13800 Miles Ave Cleveland (44105) *(G-4581)*

Miles Cleaning Services Inc... 216 626-0040
23580 Miles Rd Cleveland (44128) *(G-4582)*

Miles Farmers Market Inc... 440 248-5222
28560 Miles Rd Solon (44139) *(G-13111)*

Miles-Mcclellan Cnstr Co Inc (PA) 614 487-7744
2100 Builders Pl Columbus (43204) *(G-6248)*

Milestone Football League LLC 513 479-7602
11537 Norbourne Dr Cincinnati (45240) *(G-3062)*

Milestone Ventures LLC 317 908-2093
1776 Tamarack Rd Newark (43055) *(G-11730)*

Military Spec Packaging, Columbus *Also Called: Tri-W Group Inc (G-6786)*

Milky Acres LLC 419 561-1364
6348 Parks Rd Sycamore (44882) *(G-13532)*

Mill Creek Golf Club, Ostrander *Also Called: Mill Creek Golf Course Corp (G-12182)*

Mill Creek Golf Course, Youngstown *Also Called: Mill Creek Metropolitan Park (G-15667)*

Mill Creek Golf Course Corp 740 666-7711
7259 Penn Rd Ostrander (43061) *(G-12182)*

Mill Creek Metropolitan Park 330 740-7112
Boardman Canfield Rd Youngstown (44502) *(G-15667)*

Mill Creek Metropolitan Park 330 740-7116
123 Mckinley Ave Youngstown (44509) *(G-15668)*

Mill Distributors Inc 330 995-9200
45 Aurora Industrial Pkwy Aurora (44202) *(G-618)*

Mill Paper Packaging, Akron *Also Called: Rvc Inc (G-291)*

Mill Pond Family Physicians 330 928-3111
265 Portage Trail Ext W Ste 200 Cuyahoga Falls (44223) *(G-7089)*

Mill Rose Laboratories Inc 440 974-6730
7310 Corp Blvd Mentor (44060) *(G-10974)*

Mill Run Care Center LLC 614 527-3000
3399 Mill Run Dr Hilliard (43026) *(G-9216)*

MILL RUN GARDENS & CARE CENTER, Hilliard *Also Called: Mill Run Care Center LLC (G-9216)*

Mill Steel Co 216 464-4480
3550 Lander Rd Ste 200 Pepper Pike (44124) *(G-12301)*

Mill Supply Inc 216 518-5072
19801 Miles Rd Cleveland (44128) *(G-4583)*

Mill Tech LLC 614 496-9778
6355 Rutherford Dr Canal Winchester (43110) *(G-1613)*

Mill-Rose, Mentor *Also Called: Mill-Rose Company (G-10975)*

Mill-Rose Company (PA) 440 255-9171
7995 Tyler Blvd Mentor (44060) *(G-10975)*

Millcraft, Independence *Also Called: Millcraft Paper Company (G-9453)*

Millcraft Group LLC (PA) 216 441-5500
9000 Rio Nero Dr Independence (44131) *(G-9452)*

Millcraft Paper Company 614 675-4800
4311 Janitrol Rd Ste 600 Columbus (43228) *(G-6249)*

Millcraft Paper Company (HQ) 9010 Rio Nero Dr Independence (44131) *(G-9453)*

Millcreek Gardens LLC 740 666-7125
15088 Smart Cole Rd Ostrander (43061) *(G-12183)*

Millenium Control Systems LLC 440 510-0050
34525 Melinz Pkwy Ste 205 Eastlake (44095) *(G-8205)*

Millennia Commercial Group Ltd 216 520-1250
127 Public Sq Cleveland (44114) *(G-4584)*

Millennia Commercial Group Ltd, Beachwood *Also Called: Tower Real Estate Group LLC (G-845)*

Millennia Housing MGT Ltd (PA) 216 520-1250
4000 Key Tower 127 Public Sq Cleveland (44114) *(G-4585)*

Millennium Cpitl Recovery Corp 330 805-9063
388 S Main St Ste 320 Akron (44311) *(G-233)*

Millennium Operations LLC (HQ) 419 626-0830
1 Cedar Point Dr Sandusky (44870) *(G-12915)*

Miller & Co Portable Toil Svcs 330 453-9472
2400 Shepler Church Ave Sw Canton (44706) *(G-1808)*

Miller Bros Const Inc 419 445-1015
1613 S Defiance St Archbold (43502) *(G-463)*

Miller Bros Paint & Decorating, Cincinnati *Also Called: Miller Bros Wallpaper Company (G-3063)*

Miller Bros Wallpaper Company 513 231-4470
8460 Beechmont Ave Ste A Cincinnati (45255) *(G-3063)*

Miller Cable Company 419 639-2091
210 S Broadway St Green Springs (44836) *(G-8861)*

Miller Consolidated Inds Inc, Moraine *Also Called: McOn Inds Inc (G-11422)*

Miller Construction, Ottville *Also Called: Miller Contracting Group Inc (G-12198)*

Miller Contracting Group Inc 419 453-3825
17359 State Route 66 Ottville (45876) *(G-12198)*

Miller Fireworks Company Inc (PA) 419 865-7329
501 Glengary Rd Holland (43528) *(G-9298)*

Miller Fireworks Novelty, Holland *Also Called: Miller Fireworks Company Inc (G-9298)*

Miller Industrial Svc Team Inc 513 877-2708
8485 State Route 132 Pleasant Plain (45162) *(G-12500)*

Miller Landscape & Gardens, Norwalk *Also Called: Sand Road Enterprises Inc (G-12026)*

Miller Pipeline LLC 937 506-8837
11990 Peters Pike Tipp City (45371) *(G-13663)*

Miller Supply of WvA Inc (PA) 330 264-9146
1537 Blachleyville Rd Wooster (44691) *(G-15357)*

Miller Transfer, Rootstown *Also Called: Miller Transfer and Rigging Co (G-12762)*

Miller Transfer and Rigging Co (HQ) 330 325-2521
3833 State Route 183 Rootstown (44272) *(G-12762)*

Miller Trnsp Bus Svc Inc 614 915-7211
2510 Park Crescent Dr Columbus (43232) *(G-6250)*

Miller Valentin Construction, Cincinnati *Also Called: Mv Commercial Construction LLC (G-3092)*

Miller Valentine Group, Dayton *Also Called: Miller-Vlentine Operations Inc (G-7507)*

Miller Valentine Group, Dayton *Also Called: Miller-Vlentine Operations Inc (G-7508)*

Miller Yount Paving Inc 561 951-7416
2295 Hoagland Blackstub Rd Cortland (44410) *(G-6973)*

Miller- Valentine Group, Cincinnati *Also Called: Miller-Valentine Partners Ltd (G-3064)*

Miller-Valentine Partners Ltd (PA) 937 293-0900
9349 Waterstone Blvd Ste 200 Cincinnati (45249) *(G-3064)*

Miller-Valentine Partners Ltd. 513 588-1000
409 E Monument Ave Ste 200 Dayton (45402) *(G-7506)*

Miller-Vlentine Operations Inc (PA) 937 293-0900
409 E Monument Ave Ste 200 Dayton (45402) *(G-7507)*

Miller-Vlentine Operations Inc. 513 771-0900
9435 Waterstone Blvd Dayton (45409) *(G-7508)*

Millers Rental and Sls Co Inc (PA) 330 753-8600
2023 Romig Rd Akron (44320) *(G-234)*

Millersburg Tire Service Inc 330 674-1085
7375 State Route 39 Millersburg (44654) *(G-11286)*

Milliken's Dairy Cone, Frankfort *Also Called: David W Milliken (G-8629)*

Millikin & Fitton, Hamilton *Also Called: Millikin and Fitton Law Firm (G-9066)*

Millikin and Fitton Law Firm (PA) 513 863-6700
232 High St Hamilton (45011) *(G-9066)*

Millman National Land Services, Cleveland *Also Called: Millman Surveying Inc (G-4586)*

Millman Surveying Inc (HQ) 330 296-9017
950 Main Ave Cleveland (44113) *(G-4586)*

Millman Surveying Inc. 330 342-0723
3475 Forest Lake Dr Ste 175 Uniontown (44685) *(G-14259)*

Mills Corporation 513 671-2882
600 Cincinnati Mills Dr Cincinnati (45240) *(G-3065)*

Mills Fence Co LLC (PA) 513 631-0333
6315 Wiehe Rd Cincinnati (45237) *(G-3066)*

Mills James Productions, Hilliard *Also Called: Mills/James Inc (G-9217)*

Mills/James Inc 614 777-9933
3545 Fishinger Blvd Hilliard (43026) *(G-9217)*

Millstream Area Credit Un Inc 419 422-5626
1007 Western Ave Findlay (45840) *(G-8570)*

Milltown Family Physicians 330 345-8060
128 E Milltown Rd Ste 105 Wooster (44691) *(G-15358)*

Millwood, Vienna *Also Called: Millwood Inc (G-14422)*

Millwood Inc (PA) 330 393-4400
3708 International Blvd Vienna (44473) *(G-14422)*

Millwood Inc. 513 860-4567
4438 Muhlhauser Rd Ste 100 West Chester (45011) *(G-14730)*

Millwood Natural LLC 330 393-4400
3708 International Blvd Vienna (44473) *(G-14423)*

Mim Software Inc (PA) 216 455-0600
25800 Science Park Dr Ste 180 Beachwood (44122) *(G-817)*

Minamyer Rsdntial Care Svcs In 614 802-0190
967 Worthington Woods Loop Rd Columbus (43085) *(G-6251)*

Mindful, Akron *Also Called: Virtual Hold Tech Slutions LLC (G-353)*

Mindfully LLC 513 939-0300
1251 Nilles Rd Ste 5 Fairfield (45014) *(G-8432)*

Minerva Area YMCA, Minerva *Also Called: Young MNS Chrstn Assn Cntl STA (G-11311)*

Minerva Elder Care Inc. 330 868-4147
1035 E Lincolnway Minerva (44657) *(G-11309)*

ALPHABETIC SECTION

Minerva Elderly Care, Minerva *Also Called: Minerva Elder Care Inc (G-11309)*
Minerva Welding and Fabg Inc.. 330 868-7731
22133 Us Route 30 Minerva (44657) *(G-11310)*
Mini University Inc (PA)... 937 426-1414
115 Harbert Dr Ste A Dayton (45440) *(G-7509)*
Mini University Inc... 513 275-5184
401 Western College Dr Oxford (45056) *(G-12213)*
MINISTERIAL DARE CARE, Cleveland *Also Called: Ministerial Day Care Assn (G-4587)*
Ministerial Day Care Assn (PA).. 216 881-6924
7020 Superior Ave Cleveland (44103) *(G-4587)*
Ministerial Day Care-Headstart.. 216 707-0344
8409 Hough Ave Cleveland (44103) *(G-4588)*
MINISTERIAL DAY CARE-HEADSTART, Cleveland *Also Called: Ministerial Day Care-Headstart (G-4588)*
Minnesota Limited LLC... 330 343-4612
2198 Donald Dr Dover (44622) *(G-7894)*
Minster Bank (HQ).. 419 628-2351
95 W 4th St Minster (45865) *(G-11318)*
Minster Farmers Co-Op Exchange, Minster *Also Called: Minster Farmers Coop Exch (G-11319)*
Minster Farmers Coop Exch... 419 628-4705
292 W 4th St Minster (45865) *(G-11319)*
Minute Men Inc (PA)... 216 426-2225
3740 Carnegie Ave Ste 201 Cleveland (44115) *(G-4589)*
Minute Men of FL, Cleveland *Also Called: Minute Men Inc (G-4589)*
Minute Men Select Inc... 216 452-0100
3740 Carnegie Ave Ste 201 Cleveland (44115) *(G-4590)*
Miracle, Moraine *Also Called: Heading4ward Investment Co (G-11416)*
Miracle Motor Mart, Columbus *Also Called: Priced Right Cars Inc (G-6545)*
Miracle Path Staffing Agcy Inc... 234 205-3541
123 S Miller Rd Ste 225 Fairlawn (44333) *(G-8490)*
Miracle Plumbing & Heating Co... 330 477-2402
2121 Whipple Ave Nw Canton (44708) *(G-1809)*
Mirka USA Inc... 330 963-6421
2375 Edison Blvd Twinsburg (44087) *(G-14206)*
Misa Metals Inc.. 212 660-6000
9050 Centre Pointe Dr West Chester (45069) *(G-14731)*
Miscor Group Ltd.. 330 830-3500
800 Nave Rd Se Massillon (44646) *(G-10658)*
Mission Essential Group LLC (PA)... 614 416-2345
6525 W Campus Oval Ste 101 New Albany (43054) *(G-11574)*
Mission Essential Group Co, New Albany *Also Called: LLC A Haystack Mssion Essntial (G-11573)*
Mister Tire, Wooster *Also Called: Treadmaxx Tire Distrs Inc (G-15379)*
Mistras Group Inc... 740 788-9188
1480 James Pkwy Heath (43056) *(G-9136)*
MITCHELL'S SALON & DAY SPA INC, West Chester *Also Called: Mitchells Salon & Day Spa (G-14732)*
Mitchells Salon & Day Spa.. 513 793-0900
7795 University Ct Ste A West Chester (45069) *(G-14732)*
Mitchells Salon & Day Spa Inc (PA)... 513 793-0900
5901 E Galbraith Rd Ste 230 Cincinnati (45236) *(G-3067)*
Miter Masonry Contractors... 513 821-3334
421 Maple Ave Arlington Heights (45215) *(G-470)*
Mitsubshi Intl Fd Ingrdnts Inc (DH)... 614 652-1111
5475 Rings Rd Ste 450 Dublin (43017) *(G-8065)*
Mitsui Smitomo Mar MGT USA Inc.. 513 719-8480
312 Elm St Ste 1250 Cincinnati (45202) *(G-3068)*
Mix Talent LLC... 614 572-9452
1051 Evadell Dr Lewis Center (43035) *(G-9829)*
Mizar Motors Inc (HQ)... 419 729-2400
6003 Benore Rd Toledo (43612) *(G-13925)*
Mj Baumann Co Inc.. 614 759-7100
6400 Broughton Ave Columbus (43213) *(G-6252)*
MJM Management Corporation... 330 678-0761
1214 Anita Dr Apt 101 Kent (44240) *(G-9588)*
Mjo Industries Inc (PA)... 800 590-4055
8000 Technology Blvd Huber Heights (45424) *(G-9325)*
Mjr Sales, Plain City *Also Called: K Amalia Enterpriscs Inc (G-12483)*
Mjs Snow & Landscape LLC... 419 656-6724
6660 W Fritchie Rd Port Clinton (43452) *(G-12538)*

Mk Childcare Warsaw Ave LLC.. 513 922-6279
3711 Warsaw Ave Cincinnati (45205) *(G-3069)*
Mkc Associates Inc.. 740 657-3202
90 Hidden Ravines Dr Powell (43065) *(G-12599)*
Mke Holdings Inc (PA).. 440 238-2100
22350 Royalton Rd Strongsville (44149) *(G-13476)*
Mkjb Inc... 513 851-8400
4515 Guildford Dr West Chester (45069) *(G-14733)*
Mksk, Columbus *Also Called: Mksk Inc (G-6253)*
Mksk Inc (PA)... 614 621-2796
462 S Ludlow St Columbus (43215) *(G-6253)*
Mksk Inc... 614 621-2796
462 S Ludlow St Columbus (43215) *(G-6254)*
Mlm Childcare LLC... 513 623-8243
16 Beaufort Hunt Ln Cincinnati (45242) *(G-3070)*
Mm Ascend Life Inv Svcs LLC (DH)... 513 333-6030
301 E 4th St Fl 12 Cincinnati (45202) *(G-3071)*
Mmi of Kentucky, Cincinnati *Also Called: Contractors Materials Company (G-2502)*
Mmi-Cpr LLC (HQ)... 216 674-0645
7100 E Pleasant Valley Rd Ste 300 Independence (44131) *(G-9454)*
Mnm Hotels Inc.. 740 385-1700
12819 State Route 664 S Logan (43138) *(G-10035)*
Mobilcomm, Cincinnati *Also Called: Combined Technologies Inc (G-2478)*
Mobilcomm Inc... 513 742-5555
1211 W Sharon Rd Cincinnati (45240) *(G-3072)*
Mobile Air and Power Rentals, West Chester *Also Called: Resolute Industrial LLC (G-14831)*
Mobile Hyperbaric Centers LLC... 216 443-0430
1375 E 9th St Ste 1850 Cleveland (44114) *(G-4591)*
Mobile Hyperbaric Centers LLC... 216 443-0430
600 Superior Ave E Ste 2400 Cleveland (44114) *(G-4592)*
Mobile Meals (PA).. 330 376-7717
1357 Home Ave Ste 1 Akron (44310) *(G-235)*
Mobile Security Division, Cincinnati *Also Called: The OGara Group Inc (G-3467)*
Mobilexusa, Columbus *Also Called: Symphony Dagnstc Svcs No 1 LLC (G-6741)*
Mobilityworks, Bedford *Also Called: Wmk LLC (G-993)*
Mobilityworks, Richfield *Also Called: Wmk LLC (G-12714)*
MOCA CLEVELAND, Cleveland *Also Called: Museum Cntmprary Art Cleveland (G-4612)*
Mocha House Inc (PA)... 330 392-3020
467 High St Ne Warren (44481) *(G-14540)*
Mocho Ltd.. 330 832-8807
37 1st St Sw Massillon (44647) *(G-10659)*
Modal Shop Inc.. 513 351-9919
10310 Aerohub Blvd Cincinnati (45215) *(G-3073)*
Model Group Inc... 513 559-0048
1826 Race St Cincinnati (45202) *(G-3074)*
Modern Builders Supply, Akron *Also Called: Modern Builders Supply Inc (G-236)*
Modern Builders Supply Inc... 330 376-1031
809 E Exchange St Akron (44306) *(G-236)*
Modern Builders Supply Inc... 513 531-1000
6225 Wiehe Rd Cincinnati (45237) *(G-3075)*
Modern Builders Supply Inc... 216 273-3605
4549 Industrial Pkwy Cleveland (44135) *(G-4593)*
Modern Builders Supply Inc... 419 224-4627
1245 Neubrecht Rd Lima (45801) *(G-9936)*
Modern Builders Supply Inc (PA)... 419 241-3961
3500 Phillips Ave Toledo (43608) *(G-13926)*
Modern Business Associates Inc.. 727 563-1500
5801 Postal Rd Cleveland (44181) *(G-4594)*
Modern Day Concrete Cnstr Inc.. 513 738-1026
9773 Crosby Rd Harrison (45030) *(G-9112)*
Modern Finance Company... 614 351-7400
3449 Great Western Blvd Columbus (43204) *(G-6255)*
Modern Hire, Cleveland *Also Called: Modern Hire Inc (G-4595)*
Modern Hire Inc (DH)... 216 292-0202
3201 Enterprise Pkwy Ste 460 Cleveland (44122) *(G-4595)*
Modern Medical Inc.. 800 547-3330
250 Progressive Way Westerville (43082) *(G-14910)*
Modern Office Methods Inc.. 513 791-0909
11235 Williamson Rd Blue Ash (45241) *(G-1211)*
Modern Office Methods Inc (PA)... 513 791-0909
4747 Lake Forest Dr Ste 200 Cincinnati (45242) *(G-3076)*

Modern Office Methods Inc — ALPHABETIC SECTION

Modern Office Methods Inc 937 436-2295
  7485 Paragon Rd Dayton (45459) *(G-7510)*

Modern Office Methods Inc 614 891-3693
  929 Eastwind Dr Ste 220 Westerville (43081) *(G-15000)*

Modern Poured Walls Inc 440 647-6661
  41807 State Route 18 Wellington (44090) *(G-14634)*

Modern Welding Co Ohio Inc 740 344-9425
  1 Modern Way Newark (43055) *(G-11731)*

Modis, Dublin *Also Called: Akkodis Inc (G-7927)*

Modis, Independence *Also Called: Akkodis Inc (G-9400)*

Moeller Trucking Inc 419 925-4799
  8100 Industrial Dr Maria Stein (45860) *(G-10354)*

Mohammad Shoaib 513 831-7829
  301 Old Bank Rd Milford (45150) *(G-11244)*

Mohawk Golf Club 419 447-5876
  4399 S State Route 231 Tiffin (44883) *(G-13634)*

Mohun Health Care Center 614 416-6132
  2320 Airport Dr Columbus (43219) *(G-6256)*

MOHUN HEALTH CARE CENTER GIFT, Columbus *Also Called: Mohun Health Care Center (G-6256)*

Mole Constructors Inc 440 248-0616
  3201 Enterprise Pkwy Ste 220 Beachwood (44122) *(G-818)*

Molina Healthcare Inc 800 642-4168
  3000 Corporate Exchange Dr Ste 100 Columbus (43231) *(G-6257)*

Molina Healthcare Inc 216 606-1400
  6161 Oak Tree Blvd Independence (44131) *(G-9455)*

Molina Healthcare of Ohio, Columbus *Also Called: Molina Healthcare Inc (G-6257)*

Molina Healthcare of Ohio, Independence *Also Called: Molina Healthcare Inc (G-9455)*

Molloy Roofing Company 513 791-7400
  11099 Deerfield Rd Blue Ash (45242) *(G-1212)*

Mom, Dayton *Also Called: Modern Office Methods Inc (G-7510)*

Momentum Fleet MGT Group Inc 440 759-2219
  24481 Detroit Rd Westlake (44145) *(G-15080)*

Momentum Telecom, Westlake *Also Called: Dct Telecom Group LLC (G-15056)*

Mon Health Care Inc (HQ) 304 285-2700
  375 N West St Westerville (43082) *(G-14911)*

Mon Healthcare, Westerville *Also Called: Mon Health Care Inc (G-14911)*

Mon River Towing Inc 740 338-3100
  46226 National Rd Saint Clairsville (43950) *(G-12804)*

Mona Dermatology, Cincinnati *Also Called: Cincinnati Dermatology Ctr LLC (G-2409)*

Monarch, Cincinnati *Also Called: Monarch Construction Company (G-3077)*

Monarch, Cleveland *Also Called: Integrated Power Services LLC (G-4415)*

Monarch, Cleveland *Also Called: Monarch Steel Company Inc (G-4598)*

Monarch Construction Company 513 351-6900
  1654 Sherman Ave Cincinnati (45212) *(G-3077)*

Monarch Dental - Dayton, Miamisburg *Also Called: Monarch Dental Corp (G-11073)*

Monarch Dental Corp 440 324-2310
  435 Griswold Rd Elyria (44035) *(G-8275)*

Monarch Dental Corp 440 282-6677
  4785 Leavitt Rd Lorain (44053) *(G-10093)*

Monarch Dental Corp 937 684-4845
  36 Fiesta Ln Miamisburg (45342) *(G-11073)*

Monarch Dental Corp 937 778-0150
  987 E Ash St Ste 154 Piqua (45356) *(G-12450)*

Monarch Electric Service Co (HQ) 216 433-7800
  5325 W 130th St Cleveland (44130) *(G-4596)*

Monarch Inv & MGT Group LLC 216 453-3630
  2201 W 93rd St Cleveland (44102) *(G-4597)*

Monarch Skilled Nursing Rehab, Marysville *Also Called: Milcrest Healthcare Inc (G-10499)*

Monarch Steel Company Inc 216 587-8000
  4650 Johnston Pkwy Cleveland (44128) *(G-4598)*

Mondelez Global LLC 330 626-6500
  545 Mondial Pkwy Streetsboro (44241) *(G-13423)*

Mondelez Global LLC 419 691-5200
  2221 Front St Toledo (43605) *(G-13927)*

Mondelez Global LLC 513 714-0308
  8900 Global Way West Chester (45069) *(G-14734)*

Mondo Polymer Technologies Inc 740 376-9396
  27620 State Route 7 Marietta (45750) *(G-10391)*

Monesi Trucking & Eqp Repr Inc 614 921-9183
  1715 Atlas St Columbus (43228) *(G-6258)*

Monitoring Ctrl Compliance Inc 330 725-7766
  150 Smokerise Dr Wadsworth (44281) *(G-14444)*

Monode Marking Products Inc (PA) 440 975-8802
  9200 Tyler Blvd Mentor (44060) *(G-10976)*

Monroe County Care Center, Woodsfield *Also Called: County of Monroe (G-15301)*

Monroe Plumbing Inc 440 708-0006
  13745 Hale Rd Burton (44021) *(G-1531)*

Monsoon Lagoon Water Park, Port Clinton *Also Called: Goofy Golf II Inc (G-12528)*

Mont Granite Inc (PA) 440 287-0101
  6130 Cochran Rd Solon (44139) *(G-13112)*

Montaque Cleaning Services LLC 937 705-0429
  520 Liscum Dr Dayton (45417) *(G-7511)*

Montefiore Home 216 360-9080
  1 David Myers Pkwy Beachwood (44122) *(G-819)*

Montessori School Bowl Green 419 352-4203
  515 Sand Ridge Rd Bowling Green (43402) *(G-1327)*

Montford Heights, Cincinnati *Also Called: Duke Energy Ohio Inc (G-2581)*

Montgomery Family Medicine 513 891-2211
  11029 Montgomery Rd Cincinnati (45249) *(G-3078)*

Montgomery Home Training, Cincinnati *Also Called: Tenack Dialysis LLC (G-3452)*

Montgomery Jeep Eagle, Cincinnati *Also Called: Lincoln Mrcury Kings Auto Mall (G-2979)*

Montgomery Sanitary Engrg, Dayton *Also Called: County of Montgomery (G-7251)*

Montpelier Exempted Vlg Schl (PA) 419 485-3676
  1015 E Brown Rd Montpelier (43543) *(G-11385)*

Montpelier Hospital, Montpelier *Also Called: Community Hsptals Wllness Ctrs (G-11383)*

Montrose Ford Inc (PA) 330 666-0711
  3960 Medina Rd Fairlawn (44333) *(G-8491)*

Moody Nat Cy Dt Clumbus Mt LLC 614 228-3200
  35 W Spring St Columbus (43215) *(G-6259)*

Moody-Nolan Inc (PA) 614 461-4664
  300 Spruce St Ste 300 Columbus (43215) *(G-6260)*

Moody's, Miamisburg *Also Called: Moodys of Dayton Inc (G-11074)*

Moodys of Dayton Inc (PA) 614 443-3898
  4359 Infirmary Rd Miamisburg (45342) *(G-11074)*

Mooney and Moses, Mansfield *Also Called: Installed Building Pdts LLC (G-10272)*

Moonlight Security Inc 937 252-1600
  4977 Northcutt Pl Dayton (45414) *(G-7512)*

Moores Electric LLC 614 504-2909
  820 Mansfield Ave Columbus (43219) *(G-6261)*

Moores Fitness World Inc 513 424-0000
  413 S Breiel Blvd Middletown (45044) *(G-11176)*

Moores Rv Inc 800 523-1904
  35999 Lorain Rd North Ridgeville (44039) *(G-11932)*

Moraine Country Club 937 294-6200
  4075 Southern Blvd Dayton (45429) *(G-7513)*

Moraine Natatorium, Dayton *Also Called: City of Moraine (G-7234)*

More Than Gourmet Holdings Inc 330 762-6652
  929 Home Ave Akron (44310) *(G-237)*

Morelia Group LLC 513 469-1500
  8600 Governors Hill Dr Ste 160 Cincinnati (45249) *(G-3079)*

Moresteamcom LLC (PA) 614 602-8190
  9961 Brewster Ln Powell (43065) *(G-12600)*

Morgan Services Inc 216 241-3107
  2013 Columbus Rd Cleveland (44113) *(G-4599)*

Morgan Services Inc 937 223-5241
  817 Webster St Dayton (45404) *(G-7514)*

Morgan Services Inc 419 243-2214
  34 10th St Toledo (43604) *(G-13928)*

Morgan Stnley Smith Barney LLC 216 360-4900
  31099 Chagrin Blvd Fl 3 Cleveland (44124) *(G-4600)*

Morgan Stnley Smith Barney LLC 216 344-8700
  200 Public Sq Ste 2600 Cleveland (44114) *(G-4601)*

Morgan Tax Service 614 948-5296
  5495 Sierra Ridge Dr Columbus (43231) *(G-6262)*

Morgan Uniforms & Linen Rental, Cleveland *Also Called: Morgan Services Inc (G-4599)*

Moring View Care Center, New Philadelphia *Also Called: Dearth Management Company (G-11649)*

Morning View Delaware Inc 740 965-3984
  14961 N Old 3c Rd Sunbury (43074) *(G-13522)*

Morral Companies LLC (HQ) 740 465-3251
  132 Postle Ave Morral (43337) *(G-11454)*

Morris Kent Orthodontics Inc.. 513 226-0459
  9573 Montgomery Rd Montgomery (45242) *(G-11369)*
MORRIS NURSING HOME, Bethel *Also Called: H & G Nursery Home Inc (G-1091)*
Morris Technologies Inc... 513 733-1611
  11988 Tramway Dr Cincinnati (45241) *(G-3080)*
Morrison Inc... 740 373-5869
  410 Colegate Dr Marietta (45750) *(G-10392)*
Morrow Control and Supply Inc (PA)................................ 330 452-9791
  810 Marion Motley Ave Ne Canton (44705) *(G-1810)*
Morrow County Hospital... 419 949-3085
  651 W Marion Rd Mount Gilead (43338) *(G-11463)*
Morrow County Hospital MCH At, Mount Gilead *Also Called: Morrow County Hospital (G-11463)*
Mortgage Information Services (PA)............................... 216 514-7480
  4877 Galaxy Pkwy Ste I Cleveland (44128) *(G-4602)*
Mortgage Now Inc (PA)...800 245-1050
  9700 Rockside Rd Ste 295 Cleveland (44125) *(G-4603)*
Morton Salt Inc.. 440 354-9901
  570 Headlands Rd Painesville (44077) *(G-12237)*
Morton Salt Inc.. 330 925-3015
  151 Industrial Ave Rittman (44270) *(G-12731)*
Moss Affiliate Marketing, Solon *Also Called: Paul Moss LLC (G-13125)*
Moss Creek Golf Course.. 937 837-4653
  1 Club Dr Clayton (45315) *(G-3735)*
Mosser Construction Inc.. 419 861-5100
  1613 Henthorne Dr Maumee (43537) *(G-10749)*
Mosser Construction Inc (HQ)... 419 334-3801
  122 S Wilson Ave Fremont (43420) *(G-8694)*
Mosser Glass Inc.. 740 439-1827
  9279 Cadiz Rd Cambridge (43725) *(G-1576)*
Mosser Group, The, Fremont *Also Called: Wmog Inc (G-8709)*
Most Wrshpful Ereka Grnd Ldge...................................... 614 626-4076
  124 Stornoway Dr E Columbus (43213) *(G-6263)*
Mote and Associates Inc... 937 548-7511
  214 W 4th St Greenville (45331) *(G-8881)*
Motel 6, Troy *Also Called: R P L Corporation (G-14153)*
Motel Investments Marietta Inc....................................... 740 374-8190
  700 Pike St Marietta (45750) *(G-10393)*
Mother Teresa Elementary Sch, Middletown *Also Called: Archdiocese of Cincinnati (G-11152)*
Motion Controls Robotics Inc.. 419 334-5886
  1500 Walter Ave Fremont (43420) *(G-8695)*
Motion Industries, Dayton *Also Called: Motion Industries Inc (G-7515)*
Motion Industries Inc.. 937 236-7711
  7400 Webster St Dayton (45414) *(G-7515)*
Moto Franchise Corporation (PA)................................... 937 291-1900
  7086 Corporate Way Ste 2 Dayton (45459) *(G-7516)*
Motophoto, Dayton *Also Called: Moto Franchise Corporation (G-7516)*
Motor Carrier Service Inc.. 419 693-6207
  815 Lemoyne Rd Northwood (43619) *(G-11978)*
Motor Systems Incorporated... 513 576-1725
  460 Milford Pkwy Milford (45150) *(G-11245)*
Motorists Insurance Group, Columbus *Also Called: Motorists Mutual Insurance Co (G-6264)*
Motorists Mutual Insurance Co (HQ)...............................614 225-8211
  471 E Broad St Bsmt Columbus (43215) *(G-6264)*
Motz Group Inc (PA)... 513 533-6452
  1 Motz Way Cincinnati (45244) *(G-3081)*
Mougianis Industries Inc.. 740 264-6372
  1626 Cadiz Rd Steubenville (43953) *(G-13340)*
Mound Technologies Inc.. 937 748-2937
  25 Mound Park Dr Springboro (45066) *(G-13203)*
Moundbuilders Country Club Co.................................... 740 344-4500
  125 N 33rd St Newark (43055) *(G-11732)*
Mount Aloysius Corp.. 740 342-3343
  5375 Tile Plant Rd Se New Lexington (43764) *(G-11629)*
Mount Alverna Home, Cleveland *Also Called: Franciscan Sisters of Chicago (G-4283)*
Mount Carmel, Columbus *Also Called: Mount Carmel Health System (G-6274)*
Mount Carmel Behavioral Health, Columbus *Also Called: Mount Carmel Health System (G-6276)*
Mount Carmel East Hospital.. 614 234-6000
  6001 E Broad St Columbus (43213) *(G-6265)*

Mount Carmel Grove City, Grove City *Also Called: Mount Carmel Health System (G-8937)*
Mount Carmel Health.. 614 308-1803
  4171 Arlingate Plz Columbus (43228) *(G-6266)*
Mount Carmel Health.. 614 986-7752
  6599 E Broad St Columbus (43213) *(G-6267)*
Mount Carmel Health (DH)... 614 234-5000
  5300 N Meadows Dr Grove City (43123) *(G-8936)*
Mount Carmel Health.. 614 234-0034
  4473 Professional Pkwy Groveport (43125) *(G-8993)*
Mount Carmel Health.. 614 527-8674
  4674 Britton Pkwy Hilliard (43026) *(G-9218)*
Mount Carmel Health.. 614 855-4878
  55 N High St Ste A New Albany (43054) *(G-11575)*
Mount Carmel Health.. 614 234-4060
  444 N Cleveland Ave Ste 220 Westerville (43082) *(G-14912)*
Mount Carmel Health.. 614 776-5164
  955 Eastwind Dr Westerville (43081) *(G-15001)*
Mount Carmel Health.. 614 234-0100
  501 W Schrock Rd Ste 350 Westerville (43081) *(G-15002)*
Mount Carmel Health.. 614 234-9889
  81 E Wilson Bridge Rd Worthington (43085) *(G-15441)*
Mount Carmel Health Plan Inc.. 614 546-4300
  6150 E Broad St Columbus (43213) *(G-6268)*
Mount Carmel Health System.. 614 856-0700
  150 Taylor Station Rd Ste 350 Columbus (43213) *(G-6269)*
Mount Carmel Health System.. 734 343-4551
  6150 E Broad St Columbus (43213) *(G-6270)*
Mount Carmel Health System.. 614 860-0659
  5723 Westbourne Ave Columbus (43213) *(G-6271)*
Mount Carmel Health System.. 614 234-3355
  6400 E Broad St Columbus (43213) *(G-6272)*
Mount Carmel Health System.. 614 679-2184
  3721 Francine Ct Columbus (43232) *(G-6273)*
Mount Carmel Health System (HQ)................................. 614 234-6000
  1039 Kingsmill Pkwy Columbus (43229) *(G-6274)*
Mount Carmel Health System.. 614 221-1009
  750 Mount Carmel Mall Columbus (43222) *(G-6275)*
Mount Carmel Health System.. 614 636-6290
  4646 Hilton Corporate Dr Columbus (43232) *(G-6276)*
Mount Carmel Health System.. 614 866-3703
  5965 E Broad St Ste 390 Columbus (43213) *(G-6277)*
Mount Carmel Health System.. 614 445-6215
  946 Parsons Ave Columbus (43206) *(G-6278)*
Mount Carmel Health System.. 614 235-4039
  3480 Refugee Rd Columbus (43232) *(G-6279)*
Mount Carmel Health System.. 614 663-5300
  300 N Meadows Dr Grove City (43123) *(G-8937)*
Mount Carmel Health System.. 614 876-1260
  3617 Heritage Club Dr Hilliard (43026) *(G-9219)*
Mount Carmel Health System.. 614 775-6600
  7333 Smiths Mill Rd New Albany (43054) *(G-11576)*
Mount Carmel Health System.. 614 234-9889
  81 E Wilson Bridge Rd Worthington (43085) *(G-15442)*
Mount Carmel Home Care, Westerville *Also Called: Mount Carmel Health (G-15002)*
Mount Carmel Home Medical Eqp, Groveport *Also Called: Mount Carmel Health (G-8993)*
Mount Carmel St Anns Hospital, Toledo *Also Called: Digestive Hlth Cre Cnsltnts of (G-13779)*
Mount Crmel Cntl Ohio Nrlgcal.. 614 268-9561
  955 Eastwind Dr Ste B Westerville (43081) *(G-15003)*
Mount Notre Dame Health Center................................... 513 821-7448
  699 E Columbia Ave Cincinnati (45215) *(G-3082)*
Mount Orab Ems, Mount Orab *Also Called: Mt Orab Fire Department Inc (G-11472)*
Mount St Joseph Nursing Home, Euclid *Also Called: Sisters of St Jseph St Mark PR (G-8362)*
Mount Vernon Country Club Co..................................... 740 392-4216
  8927 Martinsburg Rd Mount Vernon (43050) *(G-11500)*
Mount Vernon Elderly Svcs LLC..................................... 740 397-2350
  1350 Yauger Rd Mount Vernon (43050) *(G-11501)*
Mount Vernon Plaza, Columbus *Also Called: Abel-Bishop & Clarke Realty Co (G-5295)*
Mount Washington Baptist Ch.. 513 231-4334
  2005 Sutton Ave Cincinnati (45230) *(G-3083)*
Mountain Crest OH Opco LLC... 419 882-1875
  5757 Whiteford Rd Sylvania (43560) *(G-13556)*

Mountain Laurel Assurance Co 440 461-5000
  6300 Wilson Mills Rd Cleveland (44143) *(G-4604)*
Mountain Supply and Svc LLC 304 547-1119
  66895 Executive Dr Saint Clairsville (43950) *(G-12805)*
Move Ez Inc 844 466-8339
  855 Grandview Ave Ste 140 Columbus (43215) *(G-6280)*
Moveeasy, Columbus Also Called: Move Ez Inc *(G-6280)*
Movement Fitness LLC 419 410-5733
  315 Gross St Marietta (45750) *(G-10394)*
Moving Ahead Services LLC 440 256-2224
  35160 Topps Industrial Pkwy Ste 5 Willoughby (44094) *(G-15212)*
Moving Solutions Inc 440 946-9300
  8001 Moving Way Mentor (44060) *(G-10977)*
Moxie Pest Control LP 513 216-1804
  7060 Fairfield Business Ctr Fairfield (45014) *(G-8433)*
Moyer Industries Inc 937 832-7283
  7555 Jacks Ln Clayton (45315) *(G-3736)*
Moyno Inc 937 327-3111
  1895 W Jefferson St Springfield (45506) *(G-13275)*
Mp Biomedicals LLC 440 337-1200
  29525 Fountain Pkwy Solon (44139) *(G-13113)*
Mpc Inc 440 835-1405
  5350 Tradex Pkwy Cleveland (44102) *(G-4605)*
Mpf Sales and Mktg Group LLC 513 793-6241
  11243 Cornell Park Dr Blue Ash (45242) *(G-1213)*
Mplx LP (HQ) 419 421-2121
  200 E Hardin St Findlay (45840) *(G-8571)*
Mplx Terminals LLC 330 479-5539
  2408 Gambrinus Ave Sw Canton (44706) *(G-1811)*
Mpower Inc 614 783-0478
  548 Chestnut Ave Westerville (43082) *(G-14913)*
MPW, Hebron Also Called: MPW Industrial Services Inc *(G-9149)*
MPW Industrial Services Inc (HQ) 800 827-8790
  9711 Lancaster Rd Hebron (43025) *(G-9149)*
MPW Industrial Svcs Group Inc 740 245-5393
  2860 State Route 850 Bidwell (45614) *(G-1105)*
MPW Industrial Svcs Group Inc (PA) 740 927-8790
  9711 Lancaster Rd Hebron (43025) *(G-9150)*
MPW Industrial Water Svcs Inc 800 827-8790
  9711 Lancaster Rd Hebron (43025) *(G-9151)*
Mr Box, Mansfield Also Called: Skybox Packaging LLC *(G-10317)*
Mr Direct, Toledo Also Called: Elkay Ohio Plumbing Pdts Co *(G-13788)*
Mr Excavator Inc 440 256-2008
  8616 Euclid Chardon Rd Kirtland (44094) *(G-9646)*
Mr. Beams, Mayfield Village Also Called: Wireless Environment LLC *(G-10797)*
MRDD, Sandusky Also Called: Ability Works Inc *(G-12861)*
Mreto, Cincinnati Also Called: Southwest Ohio Rgnal Trnst Aut *(G-3394)*
Mri Network, Akron Also Called: Global Exec Slutions Group LLC *(G-178)*
Mri Software LLC (PA) 800 321-8770
  28925 Fountain Pkwy Solon (44139) *(G-13114)*
Mrl, Xenia Also Called: Mrl Materials Resources LLC *(G-15528)*
Mrl Materials Resources LLC 937 531-6657
  123 Fairground Rd Xenia (45385) *(G-15528)*
Mrn, Cleveland Also Called: Mrn Limited Partnership *(G-4606)*
Mrn Limited Partnership 216 589-5631
  629 Euclid Ave Ste 1100 Cleveland (44114) *(G-4606)*
Mrn-Newgar Hotel Ltd 216 443-1000
  629 Euclid Ave Lbby 1 Cleveland (44114) *(G-4607)*
Mrp Inc 513 965-9700
  5632 Sugar Camp Rd Milford (45150) *(G-11246)*
Mrs Dennis Potato Farm Inc 419 335-2778
  15370 County Road K Wauseon (43567) *(G-14606)*
Mrsi, Cincinnati Also Called: Medical Recovery Systems Inc *(G-3028)*
Mrv Siding Supply, Millersburg Also Called: Holmes Siding Contractors Ltd *(G-11280)*
Ms Consultants Inc (PA) 330 744-5321
  333 E Federal St Youngstown (44503) *(G-15669)*
MSA Architects, Cincinnati Also Called: Michael Schuster Assoc Inc *(G-3056)*
MSA Family Medicine, Newark Also Called: Medical and Surgical Assoc *(G-11727)*
Msd, Dayton Also Called: Mechanical Systems Dayton Inc *(G-7136)*
MSDGC, Cincinnati Also Called: Metropltan Swer Dst Grter Cncn *(G-3053)*

MSI, Chesterland Also Called: Metzenbaum Sheltered Inds Inc *(G-2041)*
MSI, Milford Also Called: Motor Systems Incorporated *(G-11245)*
MSI Express Inc 740 498-4700
  301 Enterprise Dr Newcomerstown (43832) *(G-11770)*
Msr Legacy 216 381-0826
  1545 Sheridan Rd Cleveland (44121) *(G-4608)*
Mssi Group Inc 440 439-1040
  7500 Northfield Rd Walton Hills (44146) *(G-14477)*
Mssl Consolidated Inc 330 766-5510
  8640 E Market St Warren (44484) *(G-14541)*
Mt Airy Development LLC 855 537-2301
  2446 Kipling Ave Cincinnati (45239) *(G-3084)*
Mt Airy Grdns Rhblttion Care 513 591-0400
  2250 Banning Rd Cincinnati (45239) *(G-3085)*
Mt Business Technologies, Avon Lake Also Called: Mt Business Technologies Inc *(G-681)*
Mt Business Technologies Inc 440 933-7682
  33588 Pin Oak Pkwy Avon Lake (44012) *(G-681)*
Mt Business Technologies Inc (DH) 419 529-6100
  1150 National Pkwy Mansfield (44906) *(G-10300)*
Mt Carmel East Urgent Care 614 355-8150
  6435 E Broad St Columbus (43213) *(G-6281)*
Mt Healthy Christian Home Inc 513 931-5000
  8097 Hamilton Ave Cincinnati (45231) *(G-3086)*
Mt Hope Auction Inc (PA) 330 674-6188
  8076 State Rte 241 Mount Hope (44660) *(G-11467)*
Mt Orab Fire Department Inc 937 444-3945
  113 Spice St Mount Orab (45154) *(G-11472)*
Mt Royal Villa Care Center, Cleveland Also Called: Consulate Management Co LLC *(G-4110)*
Mt Vernon Star Properties Inc 740 392-1900
  11555 Upper Gilchrist Rd Mount Vernon (43050) *(G-11502)*
Mt View Terrace, Blue Ash Also Called: Sycamore Senior Center *(G-1251)*
Mt Washington Baptist Day Care, Cincinnati Also Called: Mount Washington Baptist Ch *(G-3083)*
Mt Washington Care Center Inc 513 231-4561
  6900 Beechmont Ave Cincinnati (45230) *(G-3087)*
MT. AIRY GARDENS REHABILITATIO, Cincinnati Also Called: Mt Airy Grdns Rhblttion Care *(G-3085)*
MTA Leasing, Fairlawn Also Called: Montrose Ford Inc *(G-8491)*
Mtd Holdings Inc (HQ) 330 225-2600
  5965 Grafton Rd Valley City (44280) *(G-14336)*
MTI, Cleveland Also Called: Mainthia Technologies Inc *(G-4516)*
MTI Engineering, Maumee Also Called: Matrix Technologies Inc *(G-10745)*
MTNA, Cincinnati Also Called: Music Teachers Nat Assn Inc *(G-3090)*
Mto Suncoke, Middletown Also Called: Suncoke Energy Inc *(G-11188)*
Muc Holdings LLC 513 417-8452
  2368 Victory Pkwy Ste 320 Cincinnati (45206) *(G-3088)*
Mud Made Logistics Corporation 614 284-2772
  3647 Douglas Rd Toledo (43613) *(G-13929)*
Mueller Art Cover & Binding Co 440 238-3303
  12005 Alameda Dr Strongsville (44149) *(G-13477)*
Muetzel Plumbing & Heating Co 614 299-7700
  1661 Kenny Rd Columbus (43212) *(G-6282)*
Muha Construction Inc 937 435-0678
  855 Congress Park Dr Ste 101 Dayton (45459) *(G-7517)*
Muhlenberg County Coal Co LLC 740 338-3100
  46226 National Rd Saint Clairsville (43950) *(G-12806)*
Muirfield Village Golf Club 614 889-6700
  5750 Memorial Dr Dublin (43017) *(G-8066)*
Mulch Masters of Ohio, Miamisburg Also Called: Gayston Corporation *(G-11057)*
Mull Iron, Rittman Also Called: Rittman Inc *(G-12732)*
Mullinax Ford North Canton Inc 330 238-3206
  5900 Whipple Ave Nw Canton (44720) *(G-1812)*
Multi Builders Supply Co 216 831-1121
  27800 Cedar Rd Cleveland (44122) *(G-4609)*
Multi Products Company 330 674-5981
  7188 State Route 39 Millersburg (44654) *(G-11287)*
Multi-Care Inc 440 352-0788
  60 Wood St Painesville (44077) *(G-12238)*
Multi-Care Inc 440 357-6181
  1515 Brookstone Blvd Painesville (44077) *(G-12239)*

ALPHABETIC SECTION — N Market Behavioral Hosp LLC

Multi-Cnty Jvnile Attntion Sys (PA)..330 484-6471
815 Faircrest St Sw Canton (44706) *(G-1813)*

Multi-Cnty Jvnile Attntion Sys...330 339-7775
241 University Dr Ne New Philadelphia (44663) *(G-11658)*

Multi-Flow Dispensers Ohio Inc (PA)..216 641-0200
4705 Van Epps Rd Brooklyn Heights (44131) *(G-1425)*

Multi-Fund Inc..216 750-2331
9700 Rockside Rd Ste 100 Cleveland (44125) *(G-4610)*

Multicare Hlth Eductl Svcs Inc...216 731-8900
27691 Euclid Ave Ste B-1 Euclid (44132) *(G-8358)*

Multicare Home Health Services, Euclid Also Called: Multicare Hlth Eductl Svcs Inc *(G-8358)*

Multicare Management Group Inc..513 868-6500
908 Symmes Rd Fairfield (45014) *(G-8434)*

Multicon Builders Inc..614 463-1142
503 S High St Columbus (43215) *(G-6283)*

Multicon Construction, Columbus Also Called: Multicon Builders Inc *(G-6283)*

Multifab, Elyria Also Called: Multilink Inc *(G-8276)*

Multilink Inc...440 366-6966
580 Ternes Ln Elyria (44035) *(G-8276)*

Munich RE America Services...609 480-6596
1308 Race St Ste 300 Cincinnati (45202) *(G-3089)*

Municipal Building Inspection..440 399-0850
24850 Aurora Rd Ste A Bedford Heights (44146) *(G-999)*

Municipal Government, Toledo Also Called: City of Toledo *(G-13741)*

Municipal Water Supply, Kent Also Called: City of Akron *(G-9563)*

Muransky Companies LLC..330 729-7400
7629 Market St Ste 200 Youngstown (44512) *(G-15670)*

Murfbooks LLC...937 260-3741
1825 Webster St Dayton (45404) *(G-7518)*

Murphy Contracting Co..330 743-8915
285 Andrews Ave Youngstown (44505) *(G-15671)*

Murphy Tractor & Eqp Co Inc...316 633-7215
9400 Bass Pro Blvd Rossford (43460) *(G-12769)*

Murray & Murray Co LPA (PA)...419 624-3000
111 E Shoreline Dr Ste 1 Sandusky (44870) *(G-12916)*

Murray American Energy Inc (DH)...740 338-3100
46226 National Rd Saint Clairsville (43950) *(G-12807)*

Murray Ridge Prod Ctr Inc..440 329-3734
1091 Infirmary Rd Elyria (44035) *(G-8277)*

Murtech Consulting LLC...216 328-8580
4700 Rockside Rd Ste 310 Cleveland (44131) *(G-4611)*

Murwood Real Estate Group LLC..216 839-5500
29225 Chagrin Blvd Beachwood (44122) *(G-820)*

Museum Cntmprary Art Cleveland..216 421-8671
11400 Euclid Ave Cleveland (44106) *(G-4612)*

Music Teachers Nat Assn Inc..513 421-1420
600 Vine St Ste 1710 Cincinnati (45202) *(G-3090)*

Musical Arts Association (PA)...216 231-7300
11001 Euclid Ave Cleveland (44106) *(G-4613)*

Musical Upcming Stars In Clssi...216 702-7047
3939 Lander Rd Chagrin Falls (44022) *(G-1963)*

Musicians Towers OH Tc LP...216 520-1250
2727 Lancashire Rd Cleveland Heights (44106) *(G-5182)*

Musillo Unkenholt LLC..513 744-4080
302 W 3rd St Cincinnati (45202) *(G-3091)*

Muskingum Behavioral Health, Zanesville Also Called: Muskingum Cnty DRG Alchol Sbst *(G-15813)*

Muskingum Cnty DRG Alchol Sbst..740 454-1266
1127 W Main St Zanesville (43701) *(G-15813)*

Muskingum County Engineers Off, Zanesville Also Called: Muskingum County Ohio *(G-15814)*

Muskingum County Ohio..740 453-0381
109 Graham St Zanesville (43701) *(G-15814)*

Muskingum Iron & Metal Co...740 452-9351
345 Arthur St Zanesville (43701) *(G-15815)*

Muskingum Starlight Industries (PA)..740 453-4622
1304 Newark Rd Zanesville (43701) *(G-15816)*

Muskingum Starlight Industries..740 453-4622
1330 Newark Rd Zanesville (43701) *(G-15817)*

Muskingum Wtrshed Cnsrvncy Dst...330 343-6780
4956 Shop Rd Ne Mineral City (44656) *(G-11301)*

Muskingum Wtrshed Cnsrvncy Dst (PA).......................................330 343-6647
1319 3rd St Nw New Philadelphia (44663) *(G-11659)*

Muskingum Wtrshed Cnsrvncy Dst...740 685-6013
22172 Park Rd Senecaville (43780) *(G-12950)*

Mustard Seed Health Fd Mkt Inc..440 519-3663
6025 Kruse Dr Ste 100 Solon (44139) *(G-13115)*

Mutual Electric Company..937 254-6211
3660 Dayton Park Dr Dayton (45414) *(G-7519)*

Mutual Health Services Company...216 687-7000
2060 E 9th St Cleveland (44115) *(G-4614)*

Mutual Holding Company, Cleveland Also Called: Mutual Health Services Company *(G-4614)*

Mv Commercial Construction LLC (PA)...513 774-8400
9349 Waterstone Blvd Ste 200 Cincinnati (45249) *(G-3092)*

Mv Residential Cnstr LLC..513 588-1000
9349 Waterstone Blvd Ste 200 Cincinnati (45249) *(G-3093)*

Mv Transportation Inc..740 681-5086
1801 Transpark Dr Cincinnati (45229) *(G-3094)*

Mv Transportation Inc..419 627-0740
1230 N Depot St Sandusky (44870) *(G-12917)*

Mvah Management LLC..513 964-1140
9100 Centre Pointe Dr West Chester (45069) *(G-14735)*

MVCAP, Dayton Also Called: Miami Vly Cmnty Action Partnr *(G-7503)*

MVCDC, Dayton Also Called: Miami Vly Child Dev Ctrs Inc *(G-7500)*

Mvd Communications LLC (PA)..513 683-4711
5188 Cox Smith Rd Mason (45040) *(G-10582)*

Mvd Connect, Mason Also Called: Mvd Communications LLC *(G-10582)*

Mvhe Inc (HQ)...937 499-8211
110 N Main St Ste 370 Dayton (45402) *(G-7520)*

Mvhe Inc..937 208-7575
111 Harbert Dr Dayton (45440) *(G-7521)*

Mvi Home Care, Youngstown Also Called: Mahoning Vly Infusioncare Inc *(G-15660)*

Mw Metals Group LLC..937 222-5992
461 Homestead Ave Dayton (45417) *(G-7522)*

Mw Mielke, Medina Also Called: Marvin W Mielke Inc *(G-10853)*

Mwd Logistics Inc...440 266-2500
7236 Justin Way Mentor (44060) *(G-10978)*

Mwe Investments LLC (HQ)...855 944-3571
777 Manor Park Dr Columbus (43228) *(G-6284)*

Mxd Group, New Albany Also Called: Ryder Last Mile Inc *(G-11586)*

Mxr Imaging, Mentor Also Called: Sourceone Healthcare Tech Inc *(G-10997)*

My Community Health Center..330 363-6242
2600 7th St Sw Canton (44710) *(G-1814)*

Mycafeteriaplan, Moraine Also Called: Businessplans Incorporated *(G-11393)*

Mycap, Youngstown Also Called: Mahoning Yngstown Cmnty Action *(G-15661)*

Myers Controlled Power LLC (HQ)..330 834-3200
219 E Maple St Ste 100-200 North Canton (44720) *(G-11850)*

Myers Equipment Corporation..330 533-5556
8860 Akron Canfield Rd Canfield (44406) *(G-1635)*

Myers Industries, Akron Also Called: Myers Industries Inc *(G-238)*

Myers Industries Inc (PA)...330 253-5592
1293 S Main St Akron (44301) *(G-238)*

Myers Machinery Movers Inc..614 871-5052
2210 Hardy Parkway St Grove City (43123) *(G-8938)*

Myers/Schmalenberger Inc (PA)...614 621-2796
462 S Ludlow St Columbus (43215) *(G-6285)*

Myteam1 LLC...877 698-3262
6450 Poe Ave Ste 500 Dayton (45414) *(G-7523)*

Mz-Russell Inc..216 675-2727
3185 E 79th St Cleveland (44104) *(G-4615)*

N & E Learning LLC...614 270-1559
1239 Lamplighter Dr Grove City (43123) *(G-8939)*

N A C S, Oberlin Also Called: National Assn Cllege Stres Inc *(G-12073)*

N C R Employees Benefit Assn...937 299-3571
4435 Dogwood Trl Dayton (45429) *(G-7524)*

N E C Columbus, Columbus Also Called: National Electric Coil Inc *(G-6296)*

N F Mansuetto & Sons Inc...740 633-7320
116 Wood St Martins Ferry (43935) *(G-10469)*

N L C, Independence Also Called: Nations Lending Corporation *(G-9457)*

N Market Behavioral Hosp LLC...513 530-1600
1223 Market Ave N Canton (44714) *(G-1815)*

N P I Audio Video Solutions, Cleveland Also Called: Northeast Projections Inc *(G-4663)*
N P Motel System Inc..330 492-5030
3950 Convenience Cir Nw Canton (44718) *(G-1816)*
N P Motel System Inc..330 339-7731
145 Bluebell Dr Sw New Philadelphia (44663) *(G-11660)*
N S International Ltd..248 251-1600
5910 Venture Dr Ste D Dublin (43017) *(G-8067)*
N W O, Northwood Also Called: Nwo Beverage Inc *(G-11980)*
N Wasserstrom & Sons Inc (HQ)..614 228-5550
2300 Lockbourne Rd Columbus (43207) *(G-6286)*
N. S. International, Ltd., Dublin Also Called: N S International Ltd *(G-8067)*
Nabisco, Streetsboro Also Called: Mondelez Global LLC *(G-13423)*
Nabisco, West Chester Also Called: Mondelez Global LLC *(G-14734)*
Nac, Columbus Also Called: Trinity Health Group Ltd *(G-6791)*
Nacco Industries Inc (PA)..440 229-5151
5875 Landerbrook Dr Ste 220 Cleveland (44124) *(G-4616)*
Nadine El Asmar MD - Uh Clvlan..216 844-3400
11100 Euclid Ave Ste 3400 Cleveland (44106) *(G-4617)*
Naffah South LLC..330 420-0111
40952 State Route 154 Lisbon (44432) *(G-10006)*
Nagle Line, Walbridge Also Called: Toledo Nagle Inc *(G-14467)*
Nagle Logistics Group Company..419 661-2500
4520 Moline Martin Rd Walbridge (43465) *(G-14462)*
Nai Ohio Equities, Columbus Also Called: Ohio Equities LLC *(G-6420)*
Nai Ohio Equities, Realtors, Columbus Also Called: Ohio Equities LLC *(G-6419)*
Naked Lime...855 653-5463
2405 County Line Rd Beavercreek (45430) *(G-928)*
Nami of Preble County Ohio..937 456-4947
800 E Saint Clair St Eaton (45320) *(G-8216)*
Namsa, Northwood Also Called: North Amercn Science Assoc LLC *(G-11979)*
Nannicola Wholesale Co..330 799-0888
2750 Salt Springs Rd Youngstown (44509) *(G-15672)*
Nanogate North America LLC..419 747-6639
1575 W Longview Ave Mansfield (44906) *(G-10301)*
Nanogate North America LLC (HQ)....................................419 524-3778
150 Longview Ave E Mansfield (44903) *(G-10302)*
NAPA, Steubenville Also Called: Fayette Parts Service Inc *(G-13324)*
NAPA, Wintersville Also Called: Fayette Parts Service Inc *(G-15294)*
NAPA Auto Parts, Cleveland Also Called: Chagrin Valley Auto Parts Co *(G-3960)*
Napoleon Machine LLC...419 591-7010
476 E Riverview Ave Napoleon (43545) *(G-11530)*
Napoleon Wash-N-Fill Inc..419 424-1726
1035 Croy Dr Findlay (45840) *(G-8572)*
Naragon Companies Inc..330 745-7700
2197 Wadsworth Rd Norton (44203) *(G-11995)*
Narrow Way Custom Tech Inc..937 743-1611
100 Industry Dr Carlisle (45005) *(G-1898)*
Nas Ventures..614 338-8501
4477 E 5th Ave Columbus (43219) *(G-6287)*
NASA, Sandusky Also Called: NASA/Glenn Research Center *(G-12918)*
NASA/Glenn Research Center..419 625-1123
6100 Columbus Ave Sandusky (44870) *(G-12918)*
Nassief Automotive Inc...440 997-5151
2920 Gh Dr Austinburg (44010) *(G-632)*
Nassief Honda, Austinburg Also Called: Nassief Automotive Inc *(G-632)*
National Affrdbl Hsing Tr Inc (PA)......................................614 451-9929
330 Rush Aly Ste 620 Columbus (43215) *(G-6288)*
National Alliance SEC Agcy Inc (PA)..................................866 636-3098
303 Corporate Center Dr Ste 322 Vandalia (45377) *(G-14385)*
National Assn Cllege Stres Inc (PA)....................................440 775-7777
500 E Lorain St Oberlin (44074) *(G-12073)*
National Associates Inc..440 333-0222
22720 Fairview Center Dr Ste 100 Cleveland (44126) *(G-4618)*
National At/Trckstops Hldngs C (DH).................................440 808-9100
24601 Center Ridge Rd Ste 200 Westlake (44145) *(G-15081)*
National Auto Care Corporation (HQ)................................800 548-1875
440 Polaris Pkwy Ste 250 Westerville (43082) *(G-14914)*
National Auto Experts LLC..440 274-5114
8370 Dow Cir Ste 100 Strongsville (44136) *(G-13478)*
National Bancshares Corporation......................................330 682-1010
112 W Market St Orrville (44667) *(G-12171)*

National Bd of Bler Prssure Vs (PA)...................................614 888-8320
1055 Crupper Ave Columbus (43229) *(G-6289)*
National Benefit Programs Inc..614 481-9000
1650 W 5th Ave Columbus (43212) *(G-6290)*
National Biochemicals LLC..330 425-2522
220 Lena Dr Aurora (44202) *(G-619)*
National Bronze Mtls Ohio Inc..440 277-1226
5311 W River Rd Lorain (44055) *(G-10094)*
National Car Rental, Strongsville Also Called: Clerac LLC *(G-13448)*
National Care Advisors LLC...937 748-9412
3982 Powell Rd Ste 231 Powell (43065) *(G-12601)*
National Ch Rsdnces Pmbroke GA.....................................614 451-2151
2335 Northbank Dr Columbus (43220) *(G-6291)*
National Ch Rsdnces Stygler Rd, Columbus Also Called: Traditions At Stygler Road *(G-6781)*
National Church, Cuyahoga Falls Also Called: Traditions At Bath Rd Inc *(G-7109)*
National Church Residences (PA)......................................614 451-2151
2335 N Bank Dr Columbus (43220) *(G-6292)*
National Church Residences Center For Senior Health, Columbus Also Called: Heritage Day Health Centers *(G-5987)*
National Church Residences First Community Village, Columbus Also Called: First Community Village *(G-5861)*
National Cinemedia LLC...614 297-8933
1410 Pennsylvania Ave Columbus (43201) *(G-6293)*
National City Capital Corp..216 222-2491
1965 E 6th St Fl 8 Cleveland (44114) *(G-4619)*
National City Cmnty Dev Corp..216 575-2000
1900 E 9th St Cleveland (44114) *(G-4620)*
National City Credit Corp...216 575-2000
1900 E 9th St Lowr Ll1 Cleveland (44114) *(G-4621)*
National City Mortgage Inc (HQ)......................................937 910-1200
3232 Newmark Dr Miamisburg (45342) *(G-11075)*
National Cngress Prnts Tachers, Mogadore Also Called: Ptao Sffeld Elem Ohio Congress *(G-11331)*
National Cnstr Rentals Inc..614 308-1100
2177 Mckinley Ave Columbus (43204) *(G-6294)*
National Commercial Warehouse, Cleveland Also Called: Revitalize Industries LLC *(G-4834)*
National Commercial Warehouse, Maple Heights Also Called: Revitalize Industries LLC *(G-10344)*
National Concession Company..216 881-9911
4582 Willow Pkwy Cleveland (44125) *(G-4622)*
National Continental Insur Co...631 320-2405
6300 Wilson Mills Rd Cleveland (44143) *(G-4623)*
National Ctr For Space Explrti, Cleveland Also Called: Universities Space Res Assn *(G-5070)*
National Dcp LLC...216 410-3215
8794 Independence Pkwy Ste 100 Twinsburg (44087) *(G-14207)*
National Dentex LLC...216 671-0577
2868 Westway Dr Ste G Brunswick (44212) *(G-1464)*
National Distribution Centers...419 422-3432
200 Mccormick Blvd Columbus (43213) *(G-6295)*
National Distributn Ctr 6, Columbus Also Called: National Freight Inc *(G-6298)*
National Electric Coil Inc (PA)..614 488-1151
800 King Ave Columbus (43212) *(G-6296)*
National Electro-Coatings Inc...216 898-0080
15655 Brookpark Rd Cleveland (44142) *(G-4624)*
National Engrg & Contg Co...440 238-3331
50 Public Sq Ste 2175 Cleveland (44113) *(G-4625)*
National Engrg Archtctral Svcs, Columbus Also Called: Barr Engineering Incorporated *(G-5420)*
National Entp Systems Inc (PA)..440 542-1360
29125 Solon Rd Solon (44139) *(G-13116)*
National Exch CLB Fndtion For...419 535-3232
3050 W Central Ave Toledo (43606) *(G-13930)*
National Federation Ind Bus...614 221-4107
10 W Broad St Ste 2450 Columbus (43215) *(G-6297)*
National Financial Svcs LLC..614 841-1790
1324 Polaris Pkwy Columbus (43240) *(G-5271)*
National Flight Services Inc..419 865-2311
10971 E Airport Service Rd Swanton (43558) *(G-13527)*
National Foods Packaging Inc...216 622-2740
8200 Madison Ave Cleveland (44102) *(G-4626)*
National Football Museum Inc..330 456-8207
2121 George Halas Dr Nw Canton (44708) *(G-1817)*

ALPHABETIC SECTION — Nationwide Asset MGT LLC

National Freight Inc 614 575-8490
200 Mccormick Blvd Columbus (43213) *(G-6298)*

National Gas & Oil Corporation (DH) 740 344-2102
1500 Granville Rd Newark (43055) *(G-11733)*

National Gas & Oil Corporation 740 454-7252
1423 Lake Dr Zanesville (43701) *(G-15818)*

National General Insurance Co 212 380-9462
800 Superior Ave E Cleveland (44114) *(G-4627)*

National Ground Water Assn Inc 614 898-7791
601 Dempsey Rd Westerville (43081) *(G-15004)*

National Heat Exch Clg Corp 330 482-0893
8397 Southern Blvd Youngstown (44512) *(G-15673)*

National Heating and AC Co 513 621-4620
4300 Creek Rd Blue Ash (45241) *(G-1214)*

National Heritg Academies Inc 937 223-2889
501 Hickory St Dayton (45410) *(G-7525)*

National Heritg Academies Inc 937 278-6671
3901 Turner Rd Dayton (45415) *(G-7526)*

National Heritg Academies Inc 330 792-4806
2420 Donald Ave Youngstown (44509) *(G-15674)*

National Hospice Cooperative 937 256-9507
7575 Paragon Rd Dayton (45459) *(G-7527)*

National Housing Corporation (PA) 614 481-8106
45 N 4th St Fl 2 Columbus (43215) *(G-6299)*

National Housing Tr Ltd Partnr 614 451-9929
2335 N Bank Dr Columbus (43220) *(G-6300)*

National Interstate Corp (HQ) 330 659-8900
3250 Interstate Dr Richfield (44286) *(G-12701)*

National Interstate Insur Co (DH) 330 659-8900
3250 Interstate Dr Richfield (44286) *(G-12702)*

National Lien Digest, Highland Heights *Also Called: C & S Associates Inc (G-9163)*

National Lime and Stone Co 419 562-0771
4580 Bethel Rd Bucyrus (44820) *(G-1513)*

National Lime and Stone Co 419 396-7671
370 N Patterson St Carey (43316) *(G-1894)*

National Lime and Stone Co 740 548-4206
2406 S Section Line Rd Delaware (43015) *(G-7819)*

National Lime and Stone Co 419 228-3434
1314 Findlay Rd Lima (45801) *(G-9937)*

National Lime and Stone Co 740 387-3485
700 Likens Rd Marion (43302) *(G-10446)*

National Lime Stone Clmbus Reg, Delaware *Also Called: National Lime and Stone Co (G-7819)*

National Liquidators, Cleveland *Also Called: G Robert Toney & Assoc Inc (G-4299)*

National Marketshare Group (PA) 513 921-0800
2155 W 8th St Cincinnati (45204) *(G-3095)*

National Mentor Holdings Inc 440 657-5658
1530 W River Rd N Ste 300 Elyria (44035) *(G-8278)*

National Mentor Holdings Inc 419 443-0867
526 Plaza Dr Fostoria (44830) *(G-8621)*

National Mentor Holdings Inc 234 806-5361
4451 Mahoning Ave Nw Warren (44483) *(G-14542)*

National Mentor Holdings Inc 330 491-4331
100 Debartolo Pl Ste 330 Youngstown (44512) *(G-15675)*

National Museum Usaf, Dayton *Also Called: The United States Dept A Force (G-7142)*

National Office Services, Cleveland *Also Called: National Electro-Coatings Inc (G-4624)*

National Pleasant Valley, Medina *Also Called: Pleasant Valley Corporation (G-10878)*

National Premier Protective (PA) 216 731-4000
1353 E 260th St Ste 1 Euclid (44132) *(G-8359)*

National Pstal Mail Hndlers Un 513 625-7192
6509 Montgomery Rd Cincinnati (45213) *(G-3096)*

NATIONAL REGISTRY-EMERGENCY, Columbus *Also Called: National Rgstry of Emrgncy Med (G-6301)*

National Rent A Fence, Columbus *Also Called: National Cnstr Rentals Inc (G-6294)*

National Rgstry of Emrgncy Med 614 888-4484
6610 Busch Blvd Columbus (43229) *(G-6301)*

NATIONAL SERVICE CLUB, Toledo *Also Called: National Exch CLB Fndtion For (G-13930)*

National Shunt Service LLC 978 637-7293
6375 Riverside Dr Ste 200 Dublin (43017) *(G-8068)*

National Smallwares, Columbus *Also Called: Wasserstrom Company (G-6867)*

National Tab LLC 513 860-2050
1329 E Kemper Rd Ste 4210 Cincinnati (45246) *(G-3097)*

National Testing Laboratories (PA) 440 449-2525
6571 Wilson Mills Rd Ste 3 Cleveland (44143) *(G-4628)*

National Tire Wholesale, Akron *Also Called: Carrolls LLC (G-81)*

National Tire Wholesale, West Chester *Also Called: Carrolls LLC (G-14659)*

National Tool Leasing Inc 866 952-8665
33801 Curtis Blvd Ste 114 Eastlake (44095) *(G-8206)*

National Undgrd RR Frdom Ctr I 513 333-7500
1301 Western Ave Ste 2253 Cincinnati (45203) *(G-3098)*

National Vtrans Mem Mseum Oper 614 362-2800
300 W Broad St Columbus (43215) *(G-6302)*

National Yuth Advcate Prgram I (PA) 614 487-8758
1801 Watermark Dr Ste 200 Columbus (43215) *(G-6303)*

NationaLease, Cleveland *Also Called: Aim Leasing Company (G-3777)*

NationaLease, Girard *Also Called: Aim Integrated Logistics Inc (G-8808)*

NationaLease, Girard *Also Called: Aim Leasing Company (G-8809)*

Nations Express Inc 440 234-4330
3931 Center Rd Brunswick (44212) *(G-1465)*

Nations Lending Corporation 877 816-1220
4 Summit Park Dr Ste 200 Independence (44131) *(G-9456)*

Nations Lending Corporation (PA) 216 363-6901
4 Summit Park Dr Ste 200 Independence (44131) *(G-9457)*

Nations Lending Corporation 440 785-0963
303 E Washington St Medina (44256) *(G-10867)*

Nations Lending Corporation 440 842-4817
30700 Center Ridge Rd Ste 3 Westlake (44145) *(G-15082)*

Nations Roof of Ohio LLC 937 439-4160
275 S Pioneer Blvd Springboro (45066) *(G-13204)*

Nationwide 800 421-3535
3101 Cleveland Ave Nw Canton (44709) *(G-1818)*

Nationwide, Canton *Also Called: Nationwide (G-1818)*

Nationwide, Canton *Also Called: Nationwide Mutual Insurance Co (G-1819)*

Nationwide, Canton *Also Called: Schauer Group Incorporated (G-1849)*

Nationwide, Cincinnati *Also Called: USI Insurance Services Nat Inc (G-3608)*

Nationwide, Cleveland *Also Called: Brooks & Stafford Co (G-3904)*

Nationwide, Cleveland *Also Called: National General Insurance Co (G-4627)*

Nationwide, Cleveland *Also Called: The James B Oswald Company (G-5002)*

Nationwide, Columbus *Also Called: Bazemore Insurance Group LLC (G-5424)*

Nationwide, Columbus *Also Called: Gardiner Allen Drbrts Insur LL (G-5913)*

Nationwide, Columbus *Also Called: Huntington Insurance Inc (G-6017)*

Nationwide, Columbus *Also Called: Insurance Intermediaries Inc (G-6060)*

Nationwide, Columbus *Also Called: Nationwide Corporation (G-6326)*

Nationwide, Columbus *Also Called: Nationwide General Insur Co (G-6331)*

Nationwide, Columbus *Also Called: Nationwide Insurance Co Fla (G-6332)*

Nationwide, Columbus *Also Called: Nationwide Life Insur Co Amer (G-6335)*

Nationwide, Columbus *Also Called: Nationwide Life Insurance Co (G-6336)*

Nationwide, Columbus *Also Called: Nationwide Mutl Fire Insur Co (G-6337)*

Nationwide, Columbus *Also Called: Nationwide Mutual Insurance Co (G-6338)*

Nationwide, Columbus *Also Called: Nationwide Mutual Insurance Co (G-6339)*

Nationwide, Columbus *Also Called: Nationwide Mutual Insurance Co (G-6340)*

Nationwide, Columbus *Also Called: Nationwide Prperty Cslty Insur (G-6341)*

Nationwide, Columbus *Also Called: USI Insurance Services Nat Inc (G-6839)*

Nationwide, Dublin *Also Called: Andrew Insurance Associates (G-7938)*

Nationwide, Dublin *Also Called: Firefly Agency LLC (G-8012)*

Nationwide, Dublin *Also Called: Nationwide Mutual Insurance Co (G-8071)*

Nationwide, Lewis Center *Also Called: Nationwide Mutual Insurance Co (G-9830)*

Nationwide, Lima *Also Called: Stolly Insurance Agency Inc (G-9966)*

Nationwide, London *Also Called: Nationwide Insrnce Spnning Ins (G-10048)*

Nationwide, Maumee *Also Called: Bridgepoint Risk MGT LLC (G-10704)*

Nationwide, Perrysburg *Also Called: Brown & Brown of Ohio LLC (G-12319)*

Nationwide, Strongsville *Also Called: Brooker Insurance Agency Inc (G-13446)*

Nationwide, Toledo *Also Called: Hylant Group Inc (G-13858)*

Nationwide, Toledo *Also Called: Knight Insurance Agency Inc (G-13880)*

Nationwide Affinity Insur Amer 614 249-2141
1 W Nationwide Blvd Ste 100 Columbus (43215) *(G-6304)*

Nationwide Arena LLC 614 232-8810
200 W Nationwide Blvd Columbus (43215) *(G-6305)*

Nationwide Asset MGT LLC 614 677-7300
1 Nationwide Plz Columbus (43215) *(G-6306)*

Nationwide Bank — ALPHABETIC SECTION

Nationwide Bank (DH) 800 882-2822
 1 Nationwide Plz Columbus (43215) *(G-6307)*

Nationwide Better Health Inc 614 249-7111
 1 Nationwide Plz Columbus (43215) *(G-6308)*

Nationwide Biweekly ADM Inc 937 376-5800
 855 Lower Bellbrook Rd Xenia (45385) *(G-15529)*

Nationwide Childrens 407 782-0053
 700 Childrens Dr Columbus (43205) *(G-6309)*

Nationwide Childrens Hospital 330 253-5200
 1 Canal Square Plz Ste 110 Akron (44308) *(G-239)*

Nationwide Childrens Hospital 513 636-6000
 796 Cincinnati Batavia Pike Ste 200 Cincinnati (45245) *(G-2111)*

Nationwide Childrens Hospital 614 722-5750
 555 S 18th St Ste 6g Columbus (43205) *(G-6310)*

Nationwide Childrens Hospital 614 355-1100
 255 E Main St Columbus (43215) *(G-6311)*

Nationwide Childrens Hospital 614 355-9300
 1390 Cleveland Ave Ste 202 Columbus (43211) *(G-6312)*

Nationwide Childrens Hospital (PA) 614 722-2000
 700 Childrens Dr Columbus (43205) *(G-6313)*

Nationwide Childrens Hospital 614 355-9900
 2857 W Broad St Columbus (43204) *(G-6314)*

Nationwide Childrens Hospital 614 722-5175
 479 Parsons Ave Columbus (43215) *(G-6315)*

Nationwide Childrens Hospital 614 355-8100
 6435 E Broad St Columbus (43213) *(G-6316)*

Nationwide Childrens Hospital 614 355-9200
 1125 E Main St Columbus (43205) *(G-6317)*

Nationwide Childrens Hospital 614 355-9400
 4560 Morse Centre Rd Columbus (43229) *(G-6318)*

Nationwide Childrens Hospital 614 355-6850
 575 Childrens Xrd Columbus (43215) *(G-6319)*

Nationwide Childrens Hospital 614 722-2000
 700 Childrens Dr Columbus (43205) *(G-6320)*

Nationwide Childrens Hospital 614 722-8200
 655 E Livingston Ave Columbus (43205) *(G-6321)*

Nationwide Childrens Hospital 614 355-0802
 3433 Agler Rd Ste 1400 Columbus (43219) *(G-6322)*

Nationwide Childrens Hospital 614 355-8000
 495 E Main St Columbus (43215) *(G-6323)*

Nationwide Childrens Hospital 614 355-8737
 5680 Venture Dr Dublin (43017) *(G-8069)*

Nationwide Childrens Hospital 614 355-7000
 7450 Hospital Dr Dublin (43016) *(G-8070)*

Nationwide Childrens Hospital 614 355-8200
 3955 Brown Park Dr Ste C Hilliard (43026) *(G-9220)*

Nationwide Childrens Hospital 419 221-3177
 830 W High St Lima (45801) *(G-9938)*

Nationwide Childrens Hospital 419 528-3140
 536 S Trimble Rd Mansfield (44906) *(G-10303)*

Nationwide Childrens Hospital 740 522-3221
 75 S Terrace Ave Newark (43055) *(G-11734)*

Nationwide Childrens Hospital 614 864-9216
 1310 Hill Rd N Pickerington (43147) *(G-12406)*

Nationwide Childrens Hospital 614 355-8300
 433 N Cleveland Ave Westerville (43082) *(G-14915)*

Nationwide Childrens Hospital 614 355-6100
 455 Executive Campus Dr Westerville (43082) *(G-14916)*

Nationwide Childrens Hospital 614 866-3473
 187 W Schrock Rd Westerville (43081) *(G-15005)*

Nationwide Childrens Hospital 614 355-8315
 275 W Schrock Rd Westerville (43081) *(G-15006)*

Nationwide Childrens Hospital 740 588-0237
 1166 Military Rd Zanesville (43701) *(G-15819)*

Nationwide Chld Hosp Fundation 614 355-5400
 700 Childrens Dr Columbus (43205) *(G-6324)*

Nationwide Chld Hosp Homecare 614 355-1100
 455 E Mound St Columbus (43215) *(G-6325)*

Nationwide Corporation (HQ) 614 249-7111
 1 Nationwide Plz Columbus (43215) *(G-6326)*

Nationwide Credit Union 614 249-6226
 1 Nationwide Plz Columbus (43215) *(G-6327)*

Nationwide Energy Partners LLC 614 918-2031
 230 West St Ste 150 Columbus (43215) *(G-6328)*

NATIONWIDE FINANCIAL, Columbus *Also Called: Nationwide Bank (G-6307)*

Nationwide Financial, Columbus *Also Called: Nationwide Financial Svcs Inc (G-6329)*

Nationwide Financial Svcs Inc (DH) 614 249-7111
 1 Nationwide Plz Columbus (43215) *(G-6329)*

Nationwide Fncl Instn Dstrs AG 614 249-6825
 1 Nationwide Plz 2-05-01 Columbus (43215) *(G-6330)*

Nationwide General Insur Co 614 249-7111
 1 W Nationwide Blvd Ste 100 Columbus (43215) *(G-6331)*

Nationwide Health MGT LLC 440 888-8888
 5700 Chevrolet Blvd Parma (44130) *(G-12258)*

Nationwide Insrnce Spnning Ins 408 520-6420
 11 S Union St London (43140) *(G-10048)*

Nationwide Insurance 513 341-7221
 633 High St Hamilton (45011) *(G-9067)*

Nationwide Insurance Co Fla 614 249-7111
 1 W Nationwide Blvd Columbus (43215) *(G-6332)*

Nationwide Inv Svcs Corp 614 249-7111
 2 Nationwide Plz Columbus (43215) *(G-6333)*

Nationwide Lf Annuity Insur Co 614 249-7111
 1 W Nationwide Blvd Ste 100 Columbus (43215) *(G-6334)*

Nationwide Life Insur Co Amer 800 688-5177
 1 Nationwide Plz Columbus (43215) *(G-6335)*

Nationwide Life Insurance Co (DH) 877 669-6877
 1 Nationwide Plz Columbus (43215) *(G-6336)*

Nationwide Mutl Fire Insur Co (HQ) 614 249-7111
 1 W Nationwide Blvd Ste 100 Columbus (43215) *(G-6337)*

Nationwide Mutual Insurance Co 330 489-5000
 1000 Market Ave N Canton (44702) *(G-1819)*

Nationwide Mutual Insurance Co (PA) 614 249-7111
 1 Nationwide Plz Columbus (43215) *(G-6338)*

Nationwide Mutual Insurance Co 614 249-7654
 275 Marconi Blvd Columbus (43215) *(G-6339)*

Nationwide Mutual Insurance Co 614 899-6300
 5017 Pine Creek Dr Columbus (43081) *(G-6340)*

Nationwide Mutual Insurance Co 614 734-1276
 5455 Rings Rd Dublin (43017) *(G-8071)*

Nationwide Mutual Insurance Co 614 430-3047
 9243 Columbus Pike Lewis Center (43035) *(G-9830)*

Nationwide Prperty Cslty Insur (HQ) 614 677-8166
 1 W Nationwide Blvd Ste 100 Columbus (43215) *(G-6341)*

Nationwide Rtrment Sltions Inc (DH) 614 854-8300
 5900 Parkwood Pl Dublin (43016) *(G-8072)*

Nationwide Truck Brokers Inc 937 335-9229
 3355 S County Road 25a Troy (45373) *(G-14148)*

Natraj Corporation 614 875-7770
 4026 Jackpot Rd Grove City (43123) *(G-8940)*

Nature Fresh Farms Usa Inc 419 330-5080
 7445 State Route 109 Delta (43515) *(G-7853)*

Natures Bin, Lakewood *Also Called: Cornucopia Inc (G-9662)*

Nautica Queen, Cleveland *Also Called: Paul A Ertel (G-4730)*

Navient Solutions LLC 513 605-7530
 4660 Duke Dr Ste 300 Mason (45040) *(G-10583)*

Navigate360, Richfield *Also Called: Navigate360 LLC (G-12703)*

Navigate360 LLC (PA) 330 661-0106
 3900 Kinross Lakes Pkwy Ste 200 Richfield (44286) *(G-12703)*

Navistone Inc 844 677-3667
 231 W 12th St Ste 200w Cincinnati (45202) *(G-3099)*

Nayak, Naresh K MD, Marietta *Also Called: First Settlement Orthopaedics (G-10368)*

NB&t Financial Group Inc 937 382-1441
 48 N South St Wilmington (45177) *(G-15261)*

Nba, Xenia *Also Called: Nationwide Biweekly ADM Inc (G-15529)*

NBBJ Construction Services, Columbus *Also Called: NBBJ LLC (G-6342)*

NBBJ LLC (HQ) 206 223-5026
 250 S High St Ste 300 Columbus (43215) *(G-6342)*

NBC 4, Columbus *Also Called: Outlet Broadcasting Inc (G-6493)*

NBD International Inc 330 296-0221
 100 Romito St Ste E Ravenna (44266) *(G-12633)*

Nbdc II LLC 513 681-5439
 2127 W North Bend Rd Cincinnati (45224) *(G-3100)*

ALPHABETIC SECTION

Nbw Inc...216 377-1700
  4556 Industrial Pkwy Cleveland (44135) *(G-4629)*

NC Hha Inc..216 593-7750
  1170 E Broad St Ste 101 Elyria (44035) *(G-8279)*

Ncbw Grter Clvland Chpter Wmen..216 232-2992
  12680 Rockside Rd Garfield Heights (44125) *(G-8777)*

Ncc Associates, Columbus *Also Called: North Cntl Mntal Hlth Svcs Inc (G-6366)*

Ncc Harvest Inc..440 582-3300
  13405 York Rd North Royalton (44133) *(G-11945)*

NCMF, Canton *Also Called: Aultman North Canton Med Group (G-1681)*

Ncp Holdings LP (PA)..937 228-5600
  205 Sugar Camp Cir Oakwood (45409) *(G-12051)*

NCR Country Club, Dayton *Also Called: N C R Employees Benefit Assn (G-7524)*

Ncs Healthcare LLC (DH)..513 719-2600
  201 E 4th St Ste 900 Cincinnati (45202) *(G-3101)*

Ncs Healthcare Inc..216 514-3350
  3201 Enterprise Pkwy Ste 220 Cleveland (44122) *(G-4630)*

Ncs Incorporated..440 684-9455
  729 Miner Rd Cleveland (44143) *(G-4631)*

Nct Retail...937 236-8000
  7 Dayton Wire Pkwy Dayton (45404) *(G-7528)*

NDC, Columbus *Also Called: National Distribution Centers (G-6295)*

Ndx Salem, Brunswick *Also Called: National Dentex LLC (G-1464)*

Neace Assoc Insur Agcy of Ohio..614 224-0772
  285 Cozzins St Columbus (43215) *(G-6343)*

Neace Lukens, Columbus *Also Called: Nl of Ky Inc (G-6361)*

Neals Construction Company..513 489-7700
  7770 E Kemper Rd Cincinnati (45249) *(G-3102)*

Neals Design Remodel, Cincinnati *Also Called: Neals Construction Company (G-3102)*

Near W Side Multi-Service Corp..216 631-5800
  4115 Bridge Ave Cleveland (44113) *(G-4632)*

Neatlysmart, Lima *Also Called: United States Plastic Corp (G-9976)*

Needmore Road Primary Care, Vandalia *Also Called: Primary Care Ntwrk Prmier Hlth (G-14387)*

Neesai Cad Designs LLC..614 822-7701
  68 N High St Bldg A New Albany (43054) *(G-11577)*

Neff & Associates, Cleveland *Also Called: T J Neff Holdings Inc (G-4975)*

Nehemiah Manufacturing Co LLC..513 351-5700
  1907 South St Cincinnati (45204) *(G-3103)*

Neidhardt, David MD, Lima *Also Called: West Market St Fmly Physicians (G-9983)*

Neighborcare Inc (DH)..513 719-2600
  201 E 4th St Ste 900 Cincinnati (45202) *(G-3104)*

Neighborhood Family Practice, Cleveland *Also Called: Neighborhood Health Care Inc (G-4633)*

Neighborhood Health Care Inc (PA)..216 281-8945
  4115 Bridge Ave # 300 Cleveland (44113) *(G-4633)*

Neighborhood Hospitality Inc..740 588-9244
  3181 Maple Ave Zanesville (43701) *(G-15820)*

Neighborhood Logistics Co Inc...440 466-0020
  5449 Bishop Rd Geneva (44041) *(G-8787)*

Neighborhood Properties Inc...419 473-2604
  2753 W Central Ave Toledo (43606) *(G-13931)*

Neighbrhood Hlth Assn Tledo In (PA)...419 720-7883
  313 Jefferson Ave Toledo (43604) *(G-13932)*

Nelbud Services Group Inc..317 202-0360
  2168 Cloverleaf St E Columbus (43232) *(G-6344)*

NELBUD SERVICES GROUP, INC., Columbus *Also Called: Nelbud Services Group Inc (G-6344)*

Nelsen Corporation (PA)..330 745-6000
  3250 Barber Rd Norton (44203) *(G-11996)*

Nelson..216 781-9144
  6000 Lombardo Ctr Ste 500 Seven Hills (44131) *(G-12955)*

Nelson, Dayton *Also Called: Nelson Tree Service Inc (G-7529)*

Nelson, Lima *Also Called: Nelson Packaging Company Inc (G-9939)*

Nelson Laboratories, Broadview Heights *Also Called: Sotera Health Holdings LLC (G-1397)*

Nelson Labs Fairfield Inc..973 227-6882
  9100 S Hills Blvd Broadview Heights (44147) *(G-1393)*

Nelson Manufacturing Company...419 523-5321
  6448 State Route 224 Ottawa (45875) *(G-12189)*

Nelson Packaging Company Inc...419 229-3471
  1801 Reservoir Rd Lima (45804) *(G-9939)*

Nelson Stark Company..513 489-0866
  7685 Fields Ertel Rd Ste D2 Cincinnati (45241) *(G-3105)*

Nelson Tree Service Inc (DH)..937 294-1313
  3300 Office Park Dr Dayton (45439) *(G-7529)*

Nemco Inc..419 542-7751
  301 Meuse Argonne St Hicksville (43526) *(G-9161)*

Nemco Food Equipment, Hicksville *Also Called: Nemco Inc (G-9161)*

Nentwick Convalescent Home...330 385-5001
  500 Selfridge St East Liverpool (43920) *(G-8187)*

Neo Administration Company...330 864-0690
  525 N Cleveland Massillon Rd Ste 204 Akron (44333) *(G-240)*

Neocap/Cbcf..330 675-2669
  411 Pine Ave Se Warren (44483) *(G-14543)*

Neoh Collinwood Health Center, Cleveland *Also Called: Northast Ohio Nghbrhood Hlth S (G-4656)*

Neptune Plumbing & Heating Co...216 475-9100
  23860 Miles Rd Cleveland (44128) *(G-4634)*

Nerone & Sons Inc...216 662-2235
  19501 S Miles Rd Ste 1 Cleveland (44128) *(G-4635)*

Nes, Solon *Also Called: National Entp Systems Inc (G-13116)*

Nesco Inc...513 772-5870
  11711 Princeton Pike Unit 301 Cincinnati (45246) *(G-3106)*

Nesco Inc...614 785-9675
  81 Mill St Ste 200 Gahanna (43230) *(G-8725)*

Nesco Inc...419 794-7452
  5425 Monroe St Toledo (43623) *(G-13933)*

Nest Tenders Limited...614 901-1570
  5083 Westerville Rd Columbus (43231) *(G-6345)*

Nestaway LLC...216 587-1500
  9100 Bank St Ste 1 Cleveland (44125) *(G-4636)*

Nestle Product Technology Ctr, Marysville *Also Called: R & D Nestle Center Inc (G-10503)*

Nestle Quality Assurance Ctr, Dublin *Also Called: Nestle Usa Inc (G-8073)*

Nestle Usa Inc...614 526-5300
  6625 Eiterman Rd Dublin (43016) *(G-8073)*

Nestle Usa Inc...440 349-5757
  30500 Bainbridge Rd Solon (44139) *(G-13117)*

Nestle Usa Inc...440 349-5757
  30003 Bainbridge Rd Solon (44139) *(G-13118)*

NETCARE ACCESS, Columbus *Also Called: Netcare Corporation (G-6346)*

Netcare Corporation (PA)..614 274-9500
  199 S Cent Ave Columbus (43223) *(G-6346)*

Netco, Cleveland *Also Called: National Engrg & Contg Co (G-4625)*

Netjets Assn Shred Arcft Plots..614 532-0555
  2740 Airport Dr Ste 330 Columbus (43219) *(G-6347)*

Netjets Aviation Inc (DH)..614 239-5500
  4111 Bridgeway Ave Columbus (43219) *(G-6348)*

Netjets International Inc (DH)..614 239-5500
  4111 Bridgeway Ave Columbus (43219) *(G-6349)*

Netjets Sales Inc..614 239-5500
  4111 Bridgeway Ave Columbus (43219) *(G-6350)*

Netsmart Technologies Inc..800 434-2642
  5455 Rings Rd Dublin (43017) *(G-8074)*

Nettleton Steel Treating Div, Wickliffe *Also Called: Thermal Treatment Center Inc (G-15164)*

Netwave, Dublin *Also Called: Netwave Corporation (G-8075)*

Netwave Corporation..614 850-6300
  8242 Inistork Ct Dublin (43017) *(G-8075)*

Network, Canton *Also Called: M Conley Company (G-1798)*

Network Polymers Inc..330 773-2700
  1353 Exeter Rd Akron (44306) *(G-241)*

Networking Partners Inc..727 417-7447
  185 Progress Pl Cincinnati (45246) *(G-3107)*

Neumeric Technologies Corp...614 610-4999
  590 Enterprise Dr Lewis Center (43035) *(G-9831)*

Neundorfer Inc..440 942-8990
  4590 Hamann Pkwy Willoughby (44094) *(G-15213)*

Neundorfer Engineering Service, Willoughby *Also Called: Neundorfer Inc (G-15213)*

Neurological Associates Inc..614 544-4455
  931 Chatham Ln Columbus (43221) *(G-6351)*

New Age Communications Cnstr, Cincinnati *Also Called: Davey Resource Group Inc (G-2541)*

New Albany Care Center LLC... 614 855-8866
5691 Thompson Rd Columbus (43230) *(G-6352)*

New Albany Cntry CLB Cmnty Ass.................................. 614 939-8500
1 Club Ln New Albany (43054) *(G-11578)*

New Albany Country Club LLC... 614 939-8500
1 Club Ln New Albany (43054) *(G-11579)*

New Albany Family Health, New Albany Also Called: Niagara Health Corporation *(G-11582)*

New Albany Links Dev Co Ltd... 614 939-5914
7100 New Albany Links Dr New Albany (43054) *(G-11580)*

New Albany Pre-School, New Albany Also Called: Leo Yssnoff Jwish Cmnty Ctr Gr *(G-11572)*

New Albany Surgery Center LLC....................................... 614 775-1616
5040 Forest Dr Ste 100 New Albany (43054) *(G-11581)*

New Avnues To Independence Inc (PA)............................. 216 481-1907
3615 Superior Ave E Ste 4404a Cleveland (44114) *(G-4637)*

New Avnues To Independence Inc..................................... 440 259-4300
5051 S Rdg Rd Perry (44081) *(G-12310)*

New Carlisle Cmnty Hlth Ctr, New Carlisle Also Called: Health Partners Western Ohio *(G-11601)*

New Cingular Wireless Svcs Inc... 614 847-5880
1495 Polaris Pkwy Columbus (43240) *(G-5272)*

New Cingular Wireless Svcs Inc... 440 324-7200
1547 W River Rd N Elyria (44035) *(G-8280)*

New Cingular Wireless Svcs Inc... 216 901-1296
6901 Rockside Rd Ste 10 Independence (44131) *(G-9458)*

New Cingular Wireless Svcs Inc... 440 975-8304
7701 Mentor Ave Mentor (44060) *(G-10979)*

New Cingular Wireless Svcs Inc... 419 473-9756
4906 Monroe St Toledo (43623) *(G-13934)*

New Concepts, Toledo Also Called: Philio Inc *(G-13963)*

New Dawn Child Care Center, Dover Also Called: Dover City Schools *(G-7881)*

New Dawn Health Care Inc... 330 343-5521
865 E Iron Ave Dover (44622) *(G-7895)*

New Dawn Retirement Community, Dover Also Called: New Dawn Health Care Inc *(G-7895)*

New Dimension Metals Corp... 937 299-2233
3050 Dryden Rd Moraine (45439) *(G-11427)*

New Directions Inc... 216 591-0324
30800 Chagrin Blvd Cleveland (44124) *(G-4638)*

New Flyer, Delaware Also Called: Aftermarket Parts Company LLC *(G-7777)*

New Hope Center, Mansfield Also Called: County of Richland *(G-10255)*

New Hope Christian Academy... 740 477-6467
2264 Walnut Creek Pike Circleville (43113) *(G-3714)*

New Horizons Surgery Ctr LLC... 740 375-5854
1167 Independence Ave Marion (43302) *(G-10447)*

New Hrzons Mntal Hlth Svcs Inc (PA)............................... 740 901-3150
230 N Columbus St Ste B Lancaster (43130) *(G-9736)*

New Innovations Inc... 330 899-9954
3540 Forest Lake Dr Uniontown (44685) *(G-14260)*

New Lebanon Center, New Lebanon Also Called: Harborside Dayton Ltd Partnr *(G-11619)*

New Lexington Head Start, New Lexington Also Called: Hockingthensperry Cmnty Action *(G-11625)*

New Life Hospice Inc... 440 934-1458
3500 Kolbe Rd Lorain (44053) *(G-10095)*

New Life Properties Inc... 513 221-3350
1501 Madison Rd Ste 2 Walnut Hills (45206) *(G-14475)*

New London Hills Club Inc... 513 868-9026
1400 Hamilton New London Rd Hamilton (45013) *(G-9068)*

New Mercy Outreach Inc.. 567 560-9021
1221 S Trimble Rd Mansfield (44907) *(G-10304)*

New Method Packaging LLC... 937 324-3838
1805 Commerce Rd Springfield (45504) *(G-13276)*

New Nghbors Rsdential Svcs Inc....................................... 937 717-5731
444 E Main St Saint Paris (43072) *(G-12838)*

New Republic Architecture... 513 800-8075
433 E 13th St Cincinnati (45202) *(G-3108)*

New River Electric, Westerville Also Called: New River Electrical Corp *(G-15007)*

New River Electrical Corp... 614 891-1142
6005 Westerville Rd Westerville (43081) *(G-15007)*

New Scotland Health Care LLC... 513 861-2044
1346 Lincoln Ave Cincinnati (45206) *(G-3109)*

New Tech West High School, Cleveland Also Called: Cleveland Municipal School Dst *(G-4061)*

New View Management Group Inc.................................... 513 733-4444
10680 Mcswain Dr Cincinnati (45241) *(G-3110)*

New World Communications of Ohio Inc........................... 216 432-4041
5800 S Marginal Rd Cleveland (44103) *(G-4639)*

New York Community Bancorp Inc.................................... 216 736-3480
1801 E 9th St Ste 200 Cleveland (44114) *(G-4640)*

New York Lf Insur Joe Stich RG.. 614 793-2121
5455 Rings Rd Ste 300 Dublin (43017) *(G-8076)*

NEWARK CARE AND REHABILITATION, Newark Also Called: Newark Leasing LLC *(G-11736)*

Newark Corporation.. 330 523-4457
4180 Highlander Pkwy Richfield (44286) *(G-12704)*

Newark Family Physicians Inc.. 740 348-1788
1272 W Main St Newark (43055) *(G-11735)*

Newark Leasing LLC... 740 344-0357
75 Mcmillen Dr Newark (43055) *(G-11736)*

Newark Metropolitan Hotel, Newark Also Called: Indus Newark Hotel LLC *(G-11709)*

Newark Parcel Service Company....................................... 614 253-3777
640 N Cassady Ave Columbus (43219) *(G-6353)*

Newcome Corp... 614 848-5688
9005 Antares Ave Columbus (43240) *(G-5273)*

Newcome Electronic Systems, Columbus Also Called: Newcome Corp *(G-5273)*

Newcomerstown Development Inc.................................... 740 498-5165
1100 E State Rd Newcomerstown (43832) *(G-11771)*

Newcomerstown Progress Corp.. 740 498-5165
1100 E State Rd Newcomerstown (43832) *(G-11772)*

Newfound Technologies, Columbus Also Called: Liberty Comm Sftwr Sltions Inc *(G-6156)*

Newmark & Company RE Inc... 216 861-3040
1300 E 9th St Ste 105 Cleveland (44114) *(G-4641)*

Newmark Grubb Knight Frank, Cleveland Also Called: Newmark & Company RE Inc *(G-4641)*

Newport, Westlake Also Called: Newport Tank Cntrs USA LLC *(G-15083)*

Newport Tank Cntrs USA LLC (PA).................................. 440 356-8866
2055 Crocker Rd Ste 300 Westlake (44145) *(G-15083)*

News Amer Mktg In-Store Svcs L..................................... 513 333-7373
221 E 4th St Ste 2410 Cincinnati (45202) *(G-3111)*

Newtown Nine Inc (PA).. 440 781-0623
8155 Roll And Hold Pkwy Macedonia (44056) *(G-10200)*

Nexgen Building Supply, Cincinnati Also Called: L & W Supply Corporation *(G-2960)*

Nexgen Building Supply, Cincinnati Also Called: Nexgen Enterprises Inc *(G-3112)*

Nexgen Enterprises Inc... 513 618-0300
3274 Spring Grove Ave Cincinnati (45225) *(G-3112)*

Nexstar Broadcasting Inc.. 614 263-4444
3165 Olentangy River Rd Columbus (43202) *(G-6354)*

Next Generation Bag Inc.. 419 884-1327
230 Industrial Dr Mansfield (44904) *(G-10305)*

Nextcable Corporation.. 330 576-3154
302 N Cleveland Massillon Rd Akron (44333) *(G-242)*

Nextchapter.. 888 861-7122
629 N High St Fl 400 Columbus (43215) *(G-6355)*

Nextgen Federal Systems LLC... 304 413-0208
4031 Colonel Glenn Hwy Ste T-101 Beavercreek Township (45431) *(G-944)*

Nextlink Wireless LLC... 216 619-3200
3 Summit Park Dr Ste 750 Independence (44131) *(G-9459)*

Nextmed Systems Inc (PA).. 216 674-0511
16 Triangle Park Dr Cincinnati (45246) *(G-3113)*

Nextrx LLC.. 317 532-6000
8990 Duke Blvd Mason (45040) *(G-10584)*

Nexus Engineering Group Inc (PA)................................... 216 404-7867
1422 Euclid Ave Ste 1400 Cleveland (44115) *(G-4642)*

Nexxtshow LLC
645 Linn St Cincinnati (45203) *(G-3114)*

Neyer Architects Engineers Inc... 513 271-6400
302 W 3rd St Ste 800 Cincinnati (45202) *(G-3115)*

Neyer Management, Cincinnati Also Called: Neyer Real Estate MGT LLC *(G-3116)*

Neyer Real Estate MGT LLC... 513 618-6000
1111 Meta Dr Cincinnati (45237) *(G-3116)*

Nf II Cleveland Op Co LLC... 216 443-9043
527 Prospect Ave E Cleveland (44115) *(G-4643)*

Nf Reinsurance Ltd... 614 249-7111
1 Nationwide Plz Columbus (43215) *(G-6356)*

Nfi Industries Inc... 740 527-9060
522 Milliken Dr Hebron (43025) *(G-9152)*

Ngo Development Corporation.. 740 622-9560
504 N 3rd St Coshocton (43812) *(G-6993)*

Ngts, Beavercreek Township *Also Called: Northrop Grmman Tchncal Svcs I (G-945)*

NGWA, Westerville *Also Called: National Ground Water Assn Inc (G-15004)*

Nht, Columbus *Also Called: National Housing Tr Ltd Partnr (G-6300)*

Niagara Health Corporation (HQ).. 614 898-4000
6150 E Broad St Columbus (43213) *(G-6357)*

Niagara Health Corporation.. 614 855-4878
55 N High St Ste A New Albany (43054) *(G-11582)*

Nichalex Inc.. 330 726-1422
801 Kentwood Dr Youngstown (44512) *(G-15676)*

Nicholas Auto Elec Rblding LLC.. 740 373-3861
202 Gibbons St Marietta (45750) *(G-10395)*

Nicholas Auto Electrical Rebuilding, LLC, Marietta *Also Called: Nicholas Auto Elec Rblding LLC (G-10395)*

Nicholas Carney-Mc Inc.. 330 792-5460
100 Victoria Rd Youngstown (44515) *(G-15677)*

Nicholas D Starr Inc (PA)... 419 229-3192
301 W Elm St Lima (45801) *(G-9940)*

Nicholas E Davis.. 937 228-2838
40 N Main St Ste 1700 Dayton (45423) *(G-7530)*

Nichols, Bowling Green *Also Called: Nichols Paper & Supply Co (G-1328)*

Nichols Paper & Supply Co.. 419 255-3022
475 W Woodland Cir Bowling Green (43402) *(G-1328)*

Nicholson Builders Inc.. 614 846-7388
6525 Busch Blvd Ste 101 Columbus (43229) *(G-6358)*

Nick Amster Inc (PA)... 330 264-9667
1700b Old Mansfield Rd Wooster (44691) *(G-15359)*

Nick Amster Inc... 330 264-9667
326 N Hillcrest Dr Ste C Wooster (44691) *(G-15360)*

Nick Mayer Lincoln-Mercury Inc... 877 836-5314
24400 Center Ridge Rd Westlake (44145) *(G-15084)*

Nick Strimbu Inc.. 330 448-4046
303 Oxford St Dover (44622) *(G-7896)*

Nickels Performance, Cleveland *Also Called: Transtar Industries LLC (G-5035)*

Nickles Bakery, Cleveland *Also Called: Alfred Nickles Bakery Inc (G-3786)*

Nicklas M Savko & Sons Inc.. 614 451-2242
4636 Shuster Rd Columbus (43214) *(G-6359)*

Nicola Gudbranson & Cooper LLC..................................... 216 621-7227
50 Public Sq # 2750 Cleveland (44113) *(G-4644)*

Nicoles Child Care Center.. 216 991-2416
12914 Union Ave Cleveland (44105) *(G-4645)*

Nicolozakes Trckg & Cnstr Inc... 740 432-5648
8555 Georgetown Rd Cambridge (43725) *(G-1577)*

Niederst Management Ltd (PA)... 440 331-8800
22730 Fairview Center Dr Ste 160 Cleveland (44126) *(G-4646)*

Niederst Management Ltd.. 440 331-8800
Rocky River (44116) *(G-12749)*

Nieman Plumbing Inc... 513 851-5588
2030 Stapleton Ct Cincinnati (45240) *(G-3117)*

Niese Leasing Inc.. 419 523-4400
12465 Road J Ottawa (45875) *(G-12190)*

Nightingale Holdings LLC.. 330 645-0200
670 Jarvis Rd Akron (44319) *(G-243)*

Nightingale Holdings LLC (PA)... 513 489-7100
4700 Ashwood Dr Ste 200 Blue Ash (45241) *(G-1215)*

Nightingale Montessori Inc.. 937 324-0336
2525 N Limestone St Springfield (45503) *(G-13277)*

NIGHTINGALE MONTESSORI SCHOOL, Springfield *Also Called: Nightingale Montessori Inc (G-13277)*

Nihon Kohden America Inc.. 330 935-0184
10700 Lair Rd Ne Alliance (44601) *(G-393)*

NIHON KOHDEN AMERICA, INC., Alliance *Also Called: Nihon Kohden America Inc (G-393)*

Niles Residential Care LLC.. 216 727-3996
2567 Niles Vienna Rd Niles (44446) *(G-11794)*

Nimers & Woody II Inc (PA).. 937 454-0722
1625 Fieldstone Way Vandalia (45377) *(G-14386)*

Nimishillen & Tuscarawas LLC... 330 438-5821
2633 8th St Ne Canton (44704) *(G-1820)*

Nippon Express USA Inc... 614 295-0030
3705 Urbancrest Industrial Dr Grove City (43123) *(G-8941)*

Nirvana Insurance.. 330 217-3079
100 E Campus View Blvd Ste 250 Columbus (43235) *(G-6360)*

Nissin International Transport, Marysville *Also Called: Nissin Intl Trnspt USA Inc (G-10500)*

Nissin Intl Trnspt USA Inc.. 937 644-2644
16940 Square Dr Marysville (43040) *(G-10500)*

Njasap, Columbus *Also Called: Netjets Assn Shred Arcft Plots (G-6347)*

Nk Parts Industries Inc (HQ).. 937 498-4651
777 S Kuther Rd Sidney (45365) *(G-13041)*

Nk Telco Inc... 419 753-5000
301 W South St New Knoxville (45871) *(G-11618)*

Nl of Ky Inc... 614 224-0772
285 Cozzins St Columbus (43215) *(G-6361)*

NM Residential, Cleveland *Also Called: Niederst Management Ltd (G-4646)*

Nmoble Hardwoods, Beverly *Also Called: Adkins Timber Products Inc (G-1099)*

Nms Wealth Management LLC.. 440 286-5222
121 South St Chardon (44024) *(G-2013)*

Noaca, Cleveland *Also Called: Northast Ohio Arwide Crdnting (G-4652)*

Noble's Pond Branch, Massillon *Also Called: Huntington National Bank (G-10646)*

Nobleinvestments LLC.. 216 856-6555
195 Columbus St Bedford (44146) *(G-974)*

Nobletek LLC.. 330 287-1500
1909 Old Mansfield Rd Ste B Wooster (44691) *(G-15361)*

Noco, Solon *Also Called: Noco Company (G-13119)*

Noco Company (PA)... 216 464-8131
30339 Diamond Pkwy Ste 102 Solon (44139) *(G-13119)*

Nofziger Door Sales Inc (PA).. 419 337-9900
320 Sycamore St Wauseon (43567) *(G-14607)*

Noic, Sylvania *Also Called: Northern Ohio Investment Co (G-13557)*

Nokia of America Corporation... 614 860-2000
5475 Rings Rd Ste 101 Dublin (43017) *(G-8077)*

Noland Company (HQ)... 937 396-7980
3110 Kettering Blvd Moraine (45439) *(G-11428)*

Noll - Fisher, Anna *Also Called: Noll Fisher Incorporated (G-443)*

Noll Fisher Incorporated.. 937 394-4181
214 W Main St Anna (45302) *(G-443)*

Nomac Drilling LLC... 330 476-7040
1258 Panda Rd Se Carrollton (44615) *(G-1910)*

Nomac Drilling LLC... 724 324-2205
67090 Executive Dr Saint Clairsville (43950) *(G-12808)*

Noms Internal Medicine... 419 626-6891
2500 W Strub Rd Ste 230 Sandusky (44870) *(G-12919)*

Noneman Real Estate Company... 419 531-4020
3519 Secor Rd Toledo (43606) *(G-13935)*

Nooney & Moses, Akron *Also Called: Installed Building Pdts LLC (G-202)*

Nor-Com LLC... 859 689-7451
1441 Western Ave Cincinnati (45214) *(G-3118)*

Norcare Enterprises Inc (PA).. 440 233-7232
6140 S Broadway Lorain (44053) *(G-10096)*

Nord Center.. 440 233-7232
6140 S Broadway Lorain (44053) *(G-10097)*

Nord Center Associates Inc (HQ)...................................... 440 233-7232
6140 S Broadway Lorain (44053) *(G-10098)*

Norfab, Elyria *Also Called: Northern Ohio Roofg Shtmtl Inc (G-8282)*

Norfolk Southern, Bedford *Also Called: Norfolk Southern Railway Co (G-975)*

Norfolk Southern, Columbus *Also Called: Norfolk Southern Railway Co (G-6362)*

Norfolk Southern Ashtabula, Ashtabula *Also Called: Norfolk Southern Corporation (G-542)*

Norfolk Southern Corporation.. 440 992-2238
Bridge Street Ashtabula (44004) *(G-542)*

Norfolk Southern Corporation.. 937 472-0067
6716 Crawfordsville Campbellstown Rd Eaton (45320) *(G-8217)*

Norfolk Southern Railway Co.. 440 439-1827
7847 Northfield Rd Bedford (44146) *(G-975)*

Norfolk Southern Railway Co.. 614 771-2183
4882 Trabue Rd Columbus (43228) *(G-6362)*

Norfolk Southern Railway Co.. 855 667-3655
248 N Market St East Palestine (44413) *(G-8197)*

Normandy Care Center, The, Rocky River *Also Called: Normandy II Ltd Partnership (G-12750)*

Normandy II Ltd Partnership.. 440 333-5401
22709 Lake Rd Rocky River (44116) *(G-12750)*

Normandy Swim & Tennis Club.. 513 683-0232
9595 Union Cemetery Rd Loveland (45140) *(G-10153)*

Noron Inc... 419 726-2677
    5465 Enterprise Blvd Toledo (43612) *(G-13936)*
Norplas Industries Inc... 419 666-6119
    232 J St Perrysburg (43551) *(G-12358)*
Norris Brothers Co Inc... 216 771-2233
    2138 Davenport Ave Cleveland (44114) *(G-4647)*
Norse Dairy Systems Inc... 614 294-4931
    1700 E 17th Ave Columbus (43219) *(G-6363)*
North Amer Sls & Svc Ret Div, Uniontown *Also Called: Diebold Nixdorf Incorporated*
(G-14248)
North Amercn Science Assoc LLC (PA)................................ 419 666-9455
    6750 Wales Rd Northwood (43619) *(G-11979)*
North America Hub-East, Troy *Also Called: Komyo America Co Inc (G-14143)*
North American Broadcasting.. 614 481-7800
    1458 Dublin Rd Columbus (43215) *(G-6364)*
North American Dental MGT LLC... 330 721-0606
    2736 Medina Rd Ste 114 Medina (44256) *(G-10868)*
North American Dental MGT LLC... 740 498-5155
    110 S River St Newcomerstown (43832) *(G-11773)*
North Amrcn Utlity Sltions LLC.. 513 313-2323
    9311 West Rd Cleves (45002) *(G-5191)*
North Bay Construction Inc... 440 835-1898
    25800 1st St Ste 1 Westlake (44145) *(G-15085)*
North Branch Nursery Inc... 419 287-4679
    3359 Kesson Rd Pemberville (43450) *(G-12290)*
North Broadway Childrens Ctr.. 614 262-6222
    48 E North Broadway St Columbus (43214) *(G-6365)*
North Canton Medical Offices, North Canton *Also Called: Kaiser Foundation Hospitals*
(G-11842)
NORTH CENTER, THE, Lorain *Also Called: Norcare Enterprises Inc (G-10096)*
NORTH CENTER, THE, Lorain *Also Called: Nord Center Associates Inc (G-10098)*
North Central Area Transit (PA)... 419 937-2428
    3446 S Township Road 151 Tiffin (44883) *(G-13635)*
North Central Elc Coop Inc... 800 426-3072
    350 Stump Pike Rd Attica (44807) *(G-600)*
North Central EMS, Milan *Also Called: Fisher - Titus Affiliated Svcs (G-11205)*
North Central Insulation, Lewis Center *Also Called: North Central Insulation Inc (G-9832)*
North Central Insulation Inc... 330 262-1998
    7538 E Lincoln Way Apple Creek (44606) *(G-451)*
North Central Insulation Inc... 740 548-8125
    5542 Columbus Pike Ste C Lewis Center (43035) *(G-9832)*
North Cntl Mntal Hlth Svcs Inc (PA)...................................... 614 227-6865
    1301 N High St Columbus (43201) *(G-6366)*
North Coast Bearings LLC... 440 930-7600
    1141 Jaycox Rd Avon (44011) *(G-662)*
North Coast Cancer Campus, Sandusky *Also Called: Cleveland Clinic Foundation (G-12882)*
North Coast Capital Funding (PA)... 330 923-5333
    1727 Portage Trl Cuyahoga Falls (44223) *(G-7090)*
NORTH COAST CENTER, Willoughby *Also Called: Signature Health Inc (G-15221)*
North Coast Commercial Roofing Systems Inc..................... 330 425-3359
    2440 Edison Blvd Twinsburg (44087) *(G-14208)*
North Coast Concrete Inc.. 216 642-1114
    6061 Carey Dr Cleveland (44125) *(G-4648)*
North Coast Logistics Inc (PA)... 216 362-7159
    18901 Snow Rd Frnt Brookpark (44142) *(G-1438)*
North Coast Prof Co LLC... 419 557-5541
    1912 Hayes Ave # 1 Sandusky (44870) *(G-12920)*
North Community Counseling Ctr, Columbus *Also Called: Franklin Cnty Bd Commissioners*
(G-5881)
North Dayton School Discovery, Dayton *Also Called: National Heritg Academies Inc (G-7526)*
North East Mechanical Inc... 440 871-7525
    26200 1st St Westlake (44145) *(G-15086)*
North East Ohio Health Svcs (PA).. 216 831-6466
    24200 Chagrin Blvd Beachwood (44122) *(G-821)*
North Gateway Tire Company Inc.. 330 725-8473
    4001 Pearl Rd Medina (44256) *(G-10869)*
North Hill YMCA, Akron *Also Called: Young MNS Chrstn Assn of Akron (G-372)*
North Jckson Specialty Stl LLC.. 330 538-9621
    2058 S Bailey Rd North Jackson (44451) *(G-11874)*
North Ohio Heart Center Inc (PA)... 440 204-4000
    125 E Broad St Ste 305 Elyria (44035) *(G-8281)*

North Ohio Regional Sewer.. 216 299-0312
    3900 Euclid Ave Cleveland (44115) *(G-4649)*
North Park Retirement Cmnty... 216 267-0555
    14801 Holland Rd Lbby Cleveland (44142) *(G-4650)*
North Randall Village (PA).. 216 663-1112
    21937 Miles Rd Cleveland (44128) *(G-4651)*
North Shore Gastroenterology.. 216 663-7064
    850 Columbia Rd Ste 200 Westlake (44145) *(G-15087)*
North Shore Gstrenterology Inc... 440 808-1212
    850 Columbia Rd Ste 200 Westlake (44145) *(G-15088)*
North Shore Gstrntrlogy Endsco, Westlake *Also Called: North Shore Gstrenterology Inc*
(G-15088)
North Side Bank and Trust Co (PA)...................................... 513 542-7800
    4125 Hamilton Ave Cincinnati (45223) *(G-3119)*
North Side Bank and Trust Co... 513 533-8000
    2739 Madison Rd Cincinnati (45209) *(G-3120)*
North South Delivery LLC.. 419 478-7400
    5272 Tractor Rd Ste H Toledo (43612) *(G-13937)*
North Star Bluescope Steel LLC... 419 822-2200
    6767 County Road 9 Delta (43515) *(G-7854)*
North Star Critical Care LLC.. 330 386-9110
    16356 State Route 267 East Liverpool (43920) *(G-8188)*
North Star Golf Club, Sunbury *Also Called: Championship Management Co Inc (G-13518)*
North Star Metals Mfg Co.. 740 254-4567
    6850 Edwards Ridge Rd Se Uhrichsville (44683) *(G-14235)*
North Star Painting Co Inc... 330 743-2333
    3526 Mccartney Rd Youngstown (44505) *(G-15678)*
North Wood Realty... 330 856-3915
    1985 Niles Cortland Rd Se Warren (44484) *(G-14544)*
Northeast Ohio Arwide Crdnting... 216 621-3055
    1299 Superior Ave E Cleveland (44114) *(G-4652)*
Northeast Ohio Crrctnal Fclty 1, Youngstown *Also Called: Corecivic Inc (G-15589)*
Northeast Ohio Nephrology Assoc....................................... 330 252-0600
    411 E Market St Akron (44304) *(G-244)*
Northeast Ohio Nghbrhood Hlth S (PA)................................ 216 231-7700
    4800 Payne Ave Cleveland (44103) *(G-4653)*
Northeast Ohio Nghbrhood Hlth S.. 216 851-2600
    12100 Superior Ave Cleveland (44106) *(G-4654)*
Northeast Ohio Nghbrhood Hlth S.. 216 541-5600
    15201 Euclid Ave Cleveland (44112) *(G-4655)*
Northeast Ohio Nghbrhood Hlth S.. 216 851-1500
    15322 Saint Clair Ave Cleveland (44110) *(G-4656)*
Northeast Ohio Rgonal Sewer Dst.. 216 641-6000
    4747 E 49th St Cleveland (44125) *(G-4657)*
Northeast Ohio Rgonal Sewer Dst.. 216 641-3200
    6000 Canal Rd Cleveland (44125) *(G-4658)*
Northeast Ohio Rgonal Sewer Dst (PA)................................ 216 881-6600
    3900 Euclid Ave Cleveland (44115) *(G-4659)*
Northeast Ohio Rgonal Sewer Dst.. 216 961-2187
    5800 Cleveland Memorial Sh Cleveland (44102) *(G-4660)*
Northeast Ohio Trnching Svc Inc... 216 663-6006
    17900 Miles Rd Ste 1 Cleveland (44128) *(G-4661)*
Northeast Srgcal Wound Care Inc (PA)................................ 216 643-2780
    6100 Rockside Woods Blvd N Ste 425 Independence (44131) *(G-9460)*
Northeastern Eductl TV Ohio Inc.. 330 677-4549
    1750 W Campus Center Dr Kent (44240) *(G-9589)*
Northbend Archtctural Pdts Inc.. 513 577-7988
    2080 Waycross Rd Cincinnati (45240) *(G-3121)*
Northeast Bhvral Halthcare Sys, Northfield *Also Called: Ohio Dept Mntal Hlth Addction*
(G-11962)
Northcoast Behavior Healthcare, Toledo *Also Called: Ohio Dept Mntal Hlth Addction*
(G-13945)
Northcoast Consult LLC.. 440 291-8987
    5715 Nathan Ave Ste B Ashtabula (44004) *(G-543)*
Northcoast Health Care Group... 330 856-2656
    3733 Park East Dr Ste 250 Beachwood (44122) *(G-822)*
Northcoast Moving Entps Inc... 440 943-3900
    1420 Lloyd Rd Wickliffe (44092) *(G-15158)*
Northcreek Family Practice, Cincinnati *Also Called: Trihealth G LLC (G-3523)*
Northcrest Nursing & Rehab.. 419 599-4070
    240 Northcrest Dr Napoleon (43545) *(G-11531)*

ALPHABETIC SECTION

Northeast Care Center Inc..440 234-9407
250 Maplelawn Dr Berea (44017) *(G-1075)*

Northeast Care Center Inc..440 888-9320
7001 W Sprague Rd North Royalton (44133) *(G-11946)*

Northeast Care Ctr Sprague, North Royalton Also Called: Northeast Care Center Inc *(G-11946)*

Northeast Obgyn..614 875-4191
2399 Old Stringtown Rd Grove City (43123) *(G-8942)*

Northeast Ohio Community Alter, Warren Also Called: Neocap/Cbcf *(G-14543)*

Northeast Ohio Electric LLC (PA)..216 587-9512
5069 Corbin Dr Cleveland (44128) *(G-4662)*

Northeast Ohio Heart Assoc LLC..440 352-9554
7580 Auburn Rd Ste 106 Concord Township (44077) *(G-6930)*

Northeast Ohio Nephrology, Akron Also Called: Northast Ohio Nephrology Assoc *(G-244)*

Northeast Professional Hm Care (PA)..330 966-2311
4580 Stephens Cir Nw Ste 301 Canton (44718) *(G-1821)*

Northeast Projections Inc..216 514-5023
8600 Sweet Valley Dr Cleveland (44125) *(G-4663)*

Northern Automotive Inc (PA)..614 436-2001
8600 N High St Columbus (43235) *(G-6367)*

Northern Bckeye Edcatn Council, Archbold Also Called: Northwest Ohio Computer Assn *(G-464)*

Northern Frozen Foods Inc..440 439-0600
21500 Alexander Rd Cleveland (44146) *(G-4664)*

Northern Haserot, Cleveland Also Called: Northern Frozen Foods Inc *(G-4664)*

Northern Kentucky..513 563-7555
2135 Dana Ave Ste 200 Cincinnati (45207) *(G-3122)*

Northern Ohio Animal Healthcar..419 499-4949
2502 State Route 113 E Milan (44846) *(G-11209)*

Northern Ohio Explosives, Forest Also Called: Wampum Hardware Co *(G-8602)*

Northern Ohio Investment Co..419 885-8300
6444 Monroe St Ste 6 Sylvania (43560) *(G-13557)*

Northern Ohio Roofg Shtmtl Inc..440 322-8262
880 Infirmary Rd Elyria (44035) *(G-8282)*

Northern Plumbing Systems..513 831-5111
1708 State Route 28 Goshen (45122) *(G-8837)*

Northern Tier Hospitality LLC..570 888-7711
1100 Crocker Rd Westlake (44145) *(G-15089)*

Northfield Park Associates LLC..330 908-7625
10777 Northfield Rd Northfield (44067) *(G-11961)*

Northfield Park Racetrack, Northfield Also Called: Park Northfield Associates LLC *(G-11964)*

Northgate Chrysler Ddge Jeep I..513 385-3900
8536 Colerain Ave Cincinnati (45251) *(G-3123)*

Northgate Ops LLC..812 945-4006
9500 Colerain Ave Cincinnati (45251) *(G-3124)*

Northgate Park, Cincinnati Also Called: Northgate Pk Retirement Cmnty *(G-3125)*

Northgate Pk Retirement Cmnty..513 923-3711
9191 Round Top Rd Ofc Cincinnati (45251) *(G-3125)*

Northland Hotel Inc..614 885-1601
1078 E Dublin Granville Rd Columbus (43229) *(G-6368)*

Northlich LLC..513 421-8840
720 E Pete Rose Way Cincinnati (45202) *(G-3126)*

Northlich Public Relations, Cincinnati Also Called: Northlich LLC *(G-3126)*

Northpointe Property MGT LLC..614 579-9712
3250 Henderson Rd Ste 103 Columbus (43220) *(G-6369)*

Northridge Health Center, North Ridgeville Also Called: Altercare Inc *(G-11922)*

Northrop Grmman Tchncal Svcs I..937 320-3100
4065 Colonel Glenn Hwy Beavercreek Township (44431) *(G-945)*

Northrop Grmmn Spce & Mssn Sys..937 259-4956
1900 Founders Dr Ste 202 Dayton (45420) *(G-7531)*

Northside Internal Medicine, Westerville Also Called: Central Ohio Prmry Care Physca *(G-14880)*

Northside Medical Center, Warren Also Called: Steward Northside Med Ctr Inc *(G-14560)*

Northstar Animal Care..614 846-5800
2447 North Star Rd Columbus (43221) *(G-6370)*

Northtowne Square Ltd Partnr..419 691-8911
2930 Navarre Ave Oregon (43616) *(G-12137)*

Northview Senior Living Center, Johnstown Also Called: Zandex Health Care Corporation *(G-9550)*

Northwest Bancshares Inc (PA)..800 859-1000
3 Easton Oval Ste 500 Columbus (43219) *(G-6371)*

Northwest Child Development An..937 559-9565
2823 Campus Dr Dayton (45406) *(G-7532)*

Northwest Country Place Inc..440 488-2700
7177 Industrial Park Blvd Mentor (44060) *(G-10980)*

Northwest Electrical Contg Inc..419 865-4757
3149 Centennial Rd Sylvania (43560) *(G-13558)*

Northwest Eye Surgeons Inc (PA)..614 451-7550
2250 N Bank Dr Columbus (43220) *(G-6372)*

Northwest Fmly Svcs Dda Fmly R, Lima Also Called: Family Rsource Ctr NW Ohio Inc *(G-9889)*

Northwest Local School Dst..513 923-1000
3308 Compton Rd Cincinnati (45251) *(G-3127)*

Northwest Ob Gyn, Hilliard Also Called: Northwest Obsttrics Gynclogy A *(G-9221)*

Northwest Obsttrics Gynclogy A..614 777-4801
3841 Trueman Ct Hilliard (43026) *(G-9221)*

Northwest Ohio Cardiology Cons (PA)..419 842-3000
2121 Hughes Dr Ste 850 Toledo (43606) *(G-13938)*

Northwest Ohio Chapter Cfma..419 891-1040
145 Chesterfield Ln Maumee (43537) *(G-10750)*

Northwest Ohio Computer Assn (PA)..419 267-5565
209 Nolan Pkwy Archbold (43502) *(G-464)*

Northwest Ohio Dvlopmental Ctr, Toledo Also Called: Ohio Dept Dvlpmntal Dsbilities *(G-13944)*

Northwest Ohio Gstrntrlgsts As..419 471-1350
4841 Monroe St Ste 111 Toledo (43623) *(G-13939)*

Northwest Ohio Orthpdics Spt M..419 427-1984
7595 County Road 236 Findlay (45840) *(G-8573)*

Northwest Ohio Prctice MGT Con, Maumee Also Called: William Vaughan Company *(G-10781)*

Northwest Ohio Srgcal Spcalist..419 998-8207
1003 Bellefontaine Ave Ste 150 Lima (45804) *(G-9941)*

Northwest Ohio Srgcal Spcalist, Lima Also Called: Northwest Ohio Srgcal Spcalist *(G-9941)*

NORTHWEST PRODUCTS, Stryker Also Called: Quadco Rehabilitation Ctr Inc *(G-13505)*

Northwest Products Div, Archbold Also Called: Quadco Rehabilitation Ctr Inc *(G-466)*

Northwesterly Ltd..216 228-2266
1341 Marlowe Ave Cleveland (44107) *(G-4665)*

Northwesterly Assisted Living, Cleveland Also Called: Northwesterly Ltd *(G-4665)*

NORTHWESTERN HEALTHCARE CENTER, Berea Also Called: Rocky River Leasing Co LLC *(G-1080)*

Northwestern Holding LLC..419 726-0850
805 Chicago St Toledo (43611) *(G-13940)*

Northwestern Ohio SEC Systems (PA)..419 227-1655
121 E High St Lima (45801) *(G-9942)*

Northwestern Water & Sewer Dst..419 354-9090
12560 Middleton Pike Bowling Green (43402) *(G-1329)*

Northwstern Ohio Cmnty Action (PA)..419 784-2150
1933 E 2nd St Defiance (43512) *(G-7758)*

Norwalk Custodial Service..419 668-1517
33 E Water St Norwalk (44857) *(G-12018)*

Norwalk Golf Properties Inc..419 668-8535
2406 New State Rd Norwalk (44857) *(G-12019)*

Norwood Dialysis, Cincinnati Also Called: Fields Dialysis LLC *(G-2661)*

Norwood Endoscopy Center..513 731-5600
4746 Montgomery Rd Ste 100 Cincinnati (45212) *(G-3128)*

Norwood Hardware and Supply Co..513 733-1175
2906 Glendale Milford Rd Cincinnati (45241) *(G-3129)*

Norwood Health Care Center LLC..513 351-0153
1578 Sherman Ave Cincinnati (45212) *(G-3130)*

Norwood Hghlnds Healthcare LLC..513 351-0153
1500 Sherman Ave Cincinnati (45212) *(G-3131)*

Norwood School, Marietta Also Called: Community Action Prgram Corp O *(G-10363)*

Norwood Towers Healthcare LLC..513 631-6800
1500 Sherman Ave Norwood (45212) *(G-12034)*

Norwood Towers Post Acute, Norwood Also Called: Norwood Towers Healthcare LLC *(G-12034)*

Nostress Inc..216 593-0226
4381 Renaissance Pkwy Cleveland (44128) *(G-4666)*

Notre Dame Pre-School, Chardon Also Called: Sisters of Ntre Dame of Chrdon *(G-2020)*

Nottingham Home, Cleveland Also Called: Help Foundation Inc *(G-4357)*

Nottinghm-Spirk Dsgn Assoc In..216 800-5782
2200 Overlook Rd Cleveland (44106) *(G-4667)*

Nouryon Chemicals LLC 419 229-0088
  1747 Fort Amanda Rd Lima (45804) *(G-9943)*
Nov Process & Flow Tech, Springfield *Also Called: Moyno Inc (G-13275)*
Nova Care 614 864-1089
  6465 E Broad St Ste B Columbus (43213) *(G-6373)*
Nova Engineering & Envmtl LLC 614 325-8092
  5400 N High St Columbus (43214) *(G-6374)*
Nova Passport Home Care Llc 419 531-9060
  242 S Reynolds Rd Ste A Toledo (43615) *(G-13941)*
Novagard Solutions Inc (PA) 216 881-8111
  5109 Hamilton Ave Cleveland (44114) *(G-4668)*
Novco, Ashville *Also Called: Noxious Vegetation Control Inc (G-553)*
Novel Writing Workshop, Blue Ash *Also Called: F+w Media Inc (G-1171)*
Novelart Manufacturing Company (PA) 513 351-7700
  2121 Section Rd Cincinnati (45237) *(G-3132)*
Novelis Alr Recycling Ohio LLC 740 922-2373
  7335 Newport Rd Se Uhrichsville (44683) *(G-14236)*
Novelty Advertising Co Inc 740 622-3113
  1148 Walnut St Coshocton (43812) *(G-6994)*
Novogradac & Company LLP 415 356-8000
  3025 N Wooster Ave Dover (44622) *(G-7897)*
Novotec Recycling LLC (PA) 614 231-8326
  3960 Groves Rd Columbus (43232) *(G-6375)*
Novus Clinic 330 630-9699
  518 West Ave Tallmadge (44278) *(G-13601)*
Novus Clinic, Tallmadge *Also Called: System Optics Csmt Srgcal Arts (G-13607)*
Now Security Group, Columbus *Also Called: US Protection Service LLC (G-6837)*
Noxious Vegetation Control Inc 614 486-8994
  14923 State Route 104 Ashville (43103) *(G-553)*
Npk Construction Equipment Inc (HQ) 440 232-7900
  7550 Independence Dr Bedford (44146) *(G-976)*
Nr Lee Restoration Ltd 419 692-2233
  7470 Grone Rd Delphos (45833) *(G-7842)*
Nrp Holdings LLC 216 475-8900
  5309 Transportation Blvd Cleveland (44125) *(G-4669)*
Nrp Management LLC 216 475-8900
  5309 Transportation Blvd Cleveland (44125) *(G-4670)*
Nsc Glbal Mnaged Resources LLC 646 499-9113
  4705 Duke Dr Ste 250 Mason (45040) *(G-10585)*
NSK Industries Inc (PA) 330 923-4112
  150 Ascot Pkwy Cuyahoga Falls (44223) *(G-7091)*
Nsl Analytical Services Inc (PA) 216 438-5200
  4450 Cranwood Pkwy Cleveland (44128) *(G-4671)*
Nssl, Dublin *Also Called: National Shunt Service LLC (G-8068)*
Ntb, Cleveland *Also Called: Tbc Retail Group Inc (G-4980)*
Ntk Hotel Group II LLC 614 559-2000
  501 N High St Columbus (43215) *(G-6376)*
Ntt Data Bus Solutions Inc (DH) 513 956-2000
  10856 Reed Hartman Hwy Cincinnati (45242) *(G-3133)*
Nu Waves Ltd 513 360-0800
  132 Edison Dr Middletown (45044) *(G-11177)*
Nu-Di, Cleveland *Also Called: Nu-Di Products Co Inc (G-4672)*
Nu-Di Products Co Inc 216 251-9070
  12730 Triskett Rd Cleveland (44111) *(G-4672)*
Nucentury Textile Services LLC (PA) 419 241-2267
  1 Southard Ave Toledo (43604) *(G-13942)*
Nucentury Textiles Linen Svcs, Toledo *Also Called: Nucentury Textile Services LLC (G-13942)*
Nucor Steel Marion Inc (HQ) 740 383-4011
  912 Cheney Ave Marion (43302) *(G-10448)*
Nuerological & Sleep Disorders 513 721-7533
  5240 E Galbraith Rd Cincinnati (45236) *(G-3134)*
Nueva Luz Urban Resource Ctr 216 651-8236
  2226 W 89th St Cleveland (44102) *(G-4673)*
Nuonosys Inc 888 666-7976
  5005 Rockside Rd Ste 1100 Independence (44131) *(G-9461)*
Nurenberg Pris Hller McCrthy L 440 423-0750
  600 Superior Ave E Ste 1200 Cleveland (44114) *(G-4674)*
Nurotoco Massachusetts Inc 513 762-6690
  255 E 5th St 2500 Chemed Ctr Cincinnati (45202) *(G-3135)*
Nurse Staffing Cincinnati LLC (PA) 513 984-8214
  9157 Montgomery Rd Ste 206 Cincinnati (45242) *(G-3136)*

Nursefinders, Akron *Also Called: Medlink of Ohio Inc (G-228)*
Nursenow LLC 812 868-7732
  644 Dussel Dr Maumee (43537) *(G-10751)*
Nurses Care Inc (PA) 513 424-1141
  9009 Springboro Pike Miamisburg (45342) *(G-11076)*
Nurses Care Inc 513 791-0233
  201 Mound Ave Milford (45150) *(G-11247)*
Nurses Heart Paramedics LLC 614 648-5111
  2056 Integrity Dr S Columbus (43209) *(G-6377)*
Nurtur Holdings LLC (PA) 614 487-3033
  6279 Tri Ridge Blvd Ste 250 Loveland (45140) *(G-10154)*
Nurtury 330 723-1800
  250 N Spring Grove St Medina (44256) *(G-10870)*
Nutis Press Inc (PA) 614 237-8626
  3540 E Fulton St Columbus (43227) *(G-6378)*
Nutrition Program, Toledo *Also Called: Lyman W Lggins Urban Affirs CT (G-13901)*
Nutrition Trnsp Svcs LLC 937 962-2661
  6531 State Route 503 N Lewisburg (45338) *(G-9841)*
Nutur Holdings LLC 513 576-9333
  6281 Tri Ridge Blvd Ste 140 Loveland (45140) *(G-10155)*
Nuwaves Engineering, Middletown *Also Called: Nu Waves Ltd (G-11177)*
Nvp Warranty 888 270-5835
  5755 Granger Rd Ste 777 Independence (44131) *(G-9462)*
Nvr Inc 440 232-5534
  6245 Sparrowhawk Way Bedford (44146) *(G-977)*
Nvr Inc 740 548-0136
  6407 Tournament Dr Westerville (43082) *(G-14917)*
NW Financial, Columbus *Also Called: Nationwide Lf Annuity Insur Co (G-6334)*
NW Financial, Columbus *Also Called: Pension Associates Inc (G-6514)*
Nwo Beverage Inc 419 725-2162
  6700 Wales Rd Northwood (43619) *(G-11980)*
Nwoca West 419 267-2544
  209 Nolan Pkwy Archbold (43502) *(G-465)*
Nx Autmotive Logistics USA Inc (DH) 937 642-8333
  13900 State Route 287 East Liberty (43319) *(G-8174)*
Nxstage Cincinnati LLC 513 712-1300
  12065 Montgomery Rd Cincinnati (45249) *(G-3137)*
Nxstage Kidney Care Cincinnati, Cincinnati *Also Called: Nxstage Cincinnati LLC (G-3137)*
Nyman Construction Co 216 475-7800
  23209 Miles Rd Fl 2 Cleveland (44128) *(G-4675)*
Nzr Retail of Toledo Inc 419 724-0005
  4820 Monroe St Toledo (43606) *(G-13943)*
O A I, Cleveland *Also Called: Ohio Aerospace Institute (G-4681)*
O A R D C, Wooster *Also Called: Ohio State University (G-15363)*
O B M, Cleveland *Also Called: Ohio Business Machines LLC (G-4683)*
O C I, Cincinnati *Also Called: Oncolgy/Hmatology Care Inc PSC (G-3163)*
O C I Construction Co Inc 440 338-3166
  8560 Pekin Rd Novelty (44072) *(G-12040)*
O D W, Columbus *Also Called: Odw Logistics Inc (G-6384)*
O E Meyer Co (PA) 419 625-1256
  3303 Tiffin Ave Sandusky (44870) *(G-12921)*
O F I C, Columbus *Also Called: Ohio Fundation of Ind Colleges (G-6422)*
O K I Bering, West Chester *Also Called: O K I Supply Co (G-14826)*
O K I Supply Co 513 341-4002
  9901 Princeton Glendale Rd Ste A West Chester (45246) *(G-14826)*
O S Walker Company Inc 614 492-1614
  2195 Wright Brothers Ave Columbus (43217) *(G-6379)*
O.C.S.E.A, Westerville *Also Called: Ohio Cvil Svc Emplyees Assn AF (G-14920)*
O'NEIL HEALTHCARE - NORTH OLMS, North Olmsted *Also Called: Wellington Place LLC (G-11920)*
O'Neill Group The, Wadsworth *Also Called: ONeill Insurance Agency Inc (G-14446)*
O'Rourke Wrecking Company, Cincinnati *Also Called: ORourke Wrecking Company (G-3169)*
OACB, Worthington *Also Called: Ohio Assn Cnty Brds Srving Ppl (G-15443)*
Oak Associates Ltd 330 666-5263
  3800 Embassy Pkwy Akron (44333) *(G-245)*
Oak Clinic 330 896-9625
  3838 Massillon Rd Ste 360 Uniontown (44685) *(G-14261)*
Oak Creek Terrace Inc 937 439-1454
  2316 Springmill Rd Dayton (45440) *(G-7533)*

ALPHABETIC SECTION — Ohio Addiction Recovery Center

Oak Grove Manor Inc..419 589-6222
  1670 Crider Rd Mansfield (44903) *(G-10306)*

Oak Harbor Lions Club Inc................................419 898-3828
  101 S Brookside Dr Oak Harbor (43449) *(G-12046)*

Oak Harbor Medical Center, Oak Harbor *Also Called: H B Magruder Memorial Hosp (G-12045)*

Oak Hill Financial Inc......................................740 286-3283
  14621 State Route 93 Jackson (45640) *(G-9523)*

Oak Hills Manor LLC..330 875-5060
  4466 Lynnhaven Ave Louisville (44641) *(G-10117)*

Oak Hlls Nrsing Rehabilitation, Cincinnati *Also Called: Oaktree LLC (G-3138)*

Oak Hlth Care Invstors Dfnce I (HQ).....................614 794-8800
  8181 Worthington Rd Westerville (43082) *(G-14918)*

Oak Hlth Care Invstors Mssllon (DH).....................614 794-8800
  8181 Worthington Rd Westerville (43082) *(G-14919)*

Oak Hlth Care Invstors of Mt V...........................740 397-3200
  13 Avalon Rd Mount Vernon (43050) *(G-11503)*

Oak Park Health Care Center, Cleveland *Also Called: Jma Healthcare LLC (G-4438)*

Oak Tree Physicians Inc....................................440 816-8000
  7255 Old Oak Blvd Cleveland (44130) *(G-4676)*

Oak Tree Woman Health, Cleveland *Also Called: Oak Tree Physicians Inc (G-4676)*

Oakdale Estates II Inv LLC................................216 520-1250
  310 Rice Dr West Union (45693) *(G-14871)*

Oakhill Manor Care Center................................330 875-5060
  4466 Lynnhaven Ave Louisville (44641) *(G-10118)*

Oakland Nursery Inc (PA)..................................614 268-3834
  1156 Oakland Park Ave Columbus (43224) *(G-6380)*

Oakland Pk Cnservation CLB Inc.........................614 989-8739
  3138 Strathaven Ct Dublin (43017) *(G-8078)*

OAKS OF BRECKSVILLE, THE, Brecksville *Also Called: Brecksvlle Halthcare Group Inc (G-1346)*

Oaktree LLC...513 598-8000
  4307 Bridgetown Rd Cincinnati (45211) *(G-3138)*

Oakwood Health Care Svcs Inc..........................440 439-7976
  24579 Broadway Ave Cleveland (44146) *(G-4677)*

Oakwood Hospitality Corp.................................440 786-1998
  23303 Oakwood Commons Dr Bedford (44146) *(G-978)*

Oakwood Management Company (PA)................614 866-8702
  6950 Americana Pkwy Ste A Reynoldsburg (43068) *(G-12671)*

Oakwood Optical, Oakwood *Also Called: Kunesh Eye Center Inc (G-12048)*

Oaoc Enterprise Inc...216 584-8677
  815 Superior Ave E Ste 1618 Cleveland (44114) *(G-4678)*

Oapse-Local 4, Columbus *Also Called: Ohio Assn Pub Schl Employees (G-6391)*

Oasis Golf Club, Loveland *Also Called: Creekside Ltd LLC (G-10133)*

Oasis International, Columbus *Also Called: Lvd Acquisition LLC (G-6181)*

Oatey, Cleveland *Also Called: Oatey Supply Chain Svcs Inc (G-4679)*

Oatey Supply Chain Svcs Inc (HQ)......................216 267-7100
  20600 Emerald Pkwy Cleveland (44135) *(G-4679)*

Ob-Gyn Specialists Lima Inc.............................419 227-0610
  830 W High St Ste 101 Lima (45801) *(G-9944)*

OBannon Creek Golf Club.................................513 683-5657
  6842 Oakland Rd Loveland (45140) *(G-10156)*

Oberer Companies, Miamisburg *Also Called: Oberer Development Co (G-11077)*

Oberer Development Co (PA)............................937 910-0851
  3445 Newmark Dr Miamisburg (45342) *(G-11077)*

Oberer Residential Cnstr Ltd.............................937 278-0851
  3445 Newmark Dr Miamisburg (45342) *(G-11078)*

Oberer Thompson Co, Beavercreek *Also Called: Greater Dayton Cnstr Ltd (G-923)*

Oberlin College...440 775-8665
  87 N Main St Oberlin (44074) *(G-12074)*

Oberlin Investments LLC..................................419 636-4001
  209 N Main St Bryan (43506) *(G-1489)*

Oberlin Municpl Light Pwr Sys, Oberlin *Also Called: City of Oberlin (G-12065)*

Obetz Animal Hospital.....................................614 491-5676
  3999 Alum Creek Dr Columbus (43207) *(G-6381)*

Obr Cooling Towers Inc....................................419 243-3443
  2845 Crane Way Northwood (43619) *(G-11981)*

Obstetric Anesthesia Assoc Inc.........................513 862-1400
  375 Dixmyth Ave Cincinnati (45220) *(G-3139)*

Ocali..614 410-0321
  470 Glenmont Ave Columbus (43214) *(G-6382)*

Occupational Health Link (PA)...........................614 885-0039
  557 Sunbury Rd Delaware (43015) *(G-7820)*

Occupational Health Services...........................937 492-7296
  915 Michigan St Sidney (45365) *(G-13042)*

Occupational Hlth Safety Dept, Independence *Also Called: Sterling Infosystems Inc (G-9487)*

Occupational Services.....................................419 891-8003
  5901 Monclova Rd Maumee (43537) *(G-10752)*

Occuptnal Mdcine Assoc Wyne CN....................330 263-7270
  2201 Benden Dr Ste 100 Wooster (44691) *(G-15362)*

Ocean Prime, Columbus *Also Called: Cameron Mitchell Rest LLC (G-5494)*

Oci LLC..513 713-3751
  8280 Montgomery Rd Ste 306 Cincinnati (45236) *(G-3140)*

Oclc, Dublin *Also Called: Oclc Inc (G-8079)*

Oclc Inc (PA)...614 764-6000
  6565 Kilgour Pl Dublin (43017) *(G-8079)*

Octavia Wealth Advisors LLC.............................513 762-7775
  9999 Carver Rd Ste 130 Blue Ash (45242) *(G-1216)*

October Enterprises Inc...................................937 456-9535
  501 W Lexington Rd Eaton (45320) *(G-8218)*

Odnr...614 338-4742
  2045 Morse Rd Columbus (43229) *(G-6383)*

Odnr Oil & Gas Resources MGT, Columbus *Also Called: Odnr (G-6383)*

Odw Logistics Inc...937 770-5602
  1 Collective Way Ste B Brookville (45309) *(G-1447)*

Odw Logistics Inc (PA)....................................614 549-5000
  400 W Nationwide Blvd Ste 200 Columbus (43215) *(G-6384)*

Odw Logistics Inc...614 549-5000
  301 Lau Pkwy Englewood (45315) *(G-8316)*

Odw Logistics Inc...513 785-4980
  345 High St Ste 600 Hamilton (45011) *(G-9069)*

Odw Logistics Inc...614 549-5000
  1533 Rohr Rd Lockbourne (43137) *(G-10013)*

Odw LTS, Hamilton *Also Called: Odw Lts LLC (G-9070)*

Odw Lts LLC..800 978-3168
  345 High St Hamilton (45011) *(G-9070)*

Oeconnection LLC (PA)...................................888 776-5792
  3600 Embassy Pkwy Ste 300 Akron (44333) *(G-246)*

Oesterlen - Svcs For Youth Inc...........................937 399-6101
  1918 Mechanicsburg Rd Springfield (45503) *(G-13278)*

Office For Children Fmly Svcs, Columbus *Also Called: Ohio Dept Job & Fmly Svcs (G-6407)*

Office of Divisional Support, Oxford *Also Called: Miami University (G-12212)*

Office World Inc (PA)......................................419 991-4694
  3820 S Dixie Hwy Lima (45806) *(G-9994)*

Offor Health Inc..877 789-8583
  1103 Schrock Rd Ste 201 Columbus (43229) *(G-6385)*

Ofori, Jason MD, Toledo *Also Called: Vision Associates Inc (G-14093)*

OGara Group Inc..513 275-8456
  4350 Port Union Rd West Chester (45011) *(G-14736)*

Oglebay Norton Mar Svcs Co LLC......................216 861-3300
  1001 Lakeside Ave E 15th Fl Cleveland (44114) *(G-4680)*

Oglethorpe Middlepoint LLC.............................419 968-2950
  17872 Lincoln Hwy Middle Point (45863) *(G-11110)*

Ogs Industries, Akron *Also Called: Ohio Gasket and Shim Co Inc (G-251)*

Oh-16 Clmbus Wrthngton Prprty.......................614 885-1557
  7272 Huntington Park Dr Columbus (43235) *(G-6386)*

Oh-16 Clvland Wstlake Prprty S........................440 892-4275
  25052 Sperry Dr Westlake (44145) *(G-15090)*

Oha Holdings Inc (DH)....................................614 221-7614
  155 E Broad St Ste 302 Columbus (43215) *(G-6387)*

Ohad Investment Group LLC............................513 426-5202
  11005 Reading Rd Ste 1 Cincinnati (45241) *(G-3141)*

Ohashi Technica USA Inc (HQ)..........................740 965-5115
  111 Burrer Dr Sunbury (43074) *(G-13523)*

Ohc Ohio Co-Manager LLC..............................513 751-2273
  4777 E Galbraith Rd Cincinnati (45236) *(G-3142)*

Oherbein Kpsic Rtirement Cmnty, Leipsic *Also Called: Otterbein Homes (G-9801)*

Ohic Insurance Company (HQ).........................614 221-7777
  300 E Broad St Ste 450 Columbus (43215) *(G-6388)*

Ohio Addiction Recovery Center.......................800 481-8457
  727 E Main St Columbus (43205) *(G-6389)*

Ohio Aerospace Institute   **ALPHABETIC SECTION**

Ohio Aerospace Institute (PA) 440 962-3000
22800 Cedar Point Rd Cleveland (44142) *(G-4681)*

Ohio Allergy Associates Inc (PA) 937 435-8999
8039 Washington Village Dr Ste 100 Centerville (45458) *(G-1948)*

Ohio and Indiana Roofing Co, Saint Henry *Also Called: Bruns Building & Dev Corp Inc* *(G-12824)*

Ohio Arson School Inc 740 881-4467
5600 Hughes Rd Galena (43021) *(G-8738)*

Ohio Assn Cmnty Hlth Ctrs Inc 614 884-3101
2109 Stella Ct Ste 100 Columbus (43215) *(G-6390)*

Ohio Assn Cnty Brds Srving Ppl 614 431-0616
73 E Wilson Bridge Rd Ste B1 Worthington (43085) *(G-15443)*

Ohio Assn Pub Schl Employees (PA) 614 890-4770
6805 Oak Creek Dr Ste 1 Columbus (43229) *(G-6391)*

Ohio Association of Foodbanks 614 221-4336
100 E Broad St Ste 450 Columbus (43215) *(G-6392)*

Ohio Auto Kolor Inc 614 272-2255
3211 W Broad St Columbus (43204) *(G-6393)*

Ohio Auto Loan Services, Ontario *Also Called: Ohio Auto Loan Services Inc* *(G-12118)*

Ohio Auto Loan Services, Zanesville *Also Called: Ohio Auto Loan Services Inc* *(G-15821)*

Ohio Auto Loan Services Inc 614 434-2397
3588 S High St Columbus (43207) *(G-6394)*

Ohio Auto Loan Services Inc 440 716-1710
27600 Lorain Rd North Olmsted (44070) *(G-11909)*

Ohio Auto Loan Services Inc 419 982-8013
695 N Lexington Springmill Rd Ontario (44906) *(G-12118)*

Ohio Auto Loan Services Inc 937 556-4687
2855 Progress Way Ste 300 Wilmington (45177) *(G-15262)*

Ohio Auto Loan Services Inc 330 272-9488
226 Boardman Canfield Rd Youngstown (44512) *(G-15679)*

Ohio Auto Loan Services Inc 740 624-8547
1834 Maple Ave Zanesville (43701) *(G-15821)*

Ohio Automobile Club 330 762-0631
100 Rosa Parks Dr Akron (44311) *(G-247)*

Ohio Automobile Club (PA) 614 431-7901
90 E Wilson Bridge Rd Fl 1 Worthington (43085) *(G-15444)*

Ohio Bar Title Insurance Co 614 310-8098
8740 Orion Pl Ste 310 Columbus (43240) *(G-5274)*

Ohio Bell Telephone Company (DH) 216 822-9700
6889 W Snowville Rd Brecksville (44141) *(G-1360)*

Ohio Bell Telephone Company 614 224-7424
96 Normandy Ave Columbus (43215) *(G-6395)*

Ohio Blow Pipe, Cleveland *Also Called: Ohio Blow Pipe Company* *(G-4682)*

Ohio Blow Pipe Company (PA) 216 681-7379
446 E 131st St Cleveland (44108) *(G-4682)*

Ohio Bridge Corporation 740 432-6334
201 Wheeling Ave Cambridge (43725) *(G-1578)*

Ohio Broach & Machine Company 440 946-1040
35264 Topps Industrial Pkwy Willoughby (44094) *(G-15214)*

Ohio Bulk Transfer Company Inc 216 883-7200
3203 Harvard Ave Newburgh Heights (44105) *(G-11758)*

Ohio Bureau Wkrs Compensation (DH) 800 644-6292
30 W Spring St Fl 25 Columbus (43215) *(G-6396)*

Ohio Bureau Wkrs Compensation 614 221-4064
77 S High St Columbus (43215) *(G-6397)*

Ohio Business Machines LLC 216 485-2000
1111 Superior Ave E Ste 105 Cleveland (44114) *(G-4683)*

Ohio Carts, Mentor *Also Called: Omni Cart Services Inc* *(G-10981)*

Ohio Casualty Insurance Co (DH) 800 843-6446
1876 Waycross Rd Cincinnati (45240) *(G-3143)*

Ohio Cat, Cadiz *Also Called: Ohio Machinery Co* *(G-1542)*

Ohio Cat, Troy *Also Called: Ohio Machinery Co* *(G-14149)*

Ohio Caverns, West Liberty *Also Called: Ohio Caverns Inc* *(G-14861)*

Ohio Caverns Inc 937 465-4017
2210 State Route 245 E West Liberty (43357) *(G-14861)*

Ohio Chest Physicians Ltd 216 267-5139
15805 Puritas Ave Cleveland (44135) *(G-4684)*

Ohio Citizen Action (PA) 216 861-5200
1511 Brookpark Rd Cleveland (44109) *(G-4685)*

Ohio Cllbrtive Lrng Sltons Inc (PA) 216 595-5289
17171 Golden Star Dr Strongsville (44136) *(G-13479)*

Ohio Community Dev Fin Fund 614 221-1114
175 S 3rd St Ste 1200 Columbus (43215) *(G-6398)*

Ohio Con Sawing & Drlg Inc (PA) 419 841-1330
8534 Central Ave Sylvania (43560) *(G-13559)*

Ohio County Coal Company 740 338-3100
46226 National Rd Saint Clairsville (43950) *(G-12809)*

Ohio Ctr For Atism Low Incdnce, Columbus *Also Called: Ocali* *(G-6382)*

Ohio Custodial Maintenance 614 443-1232
1291 S High St Columbus (43206) *(G-6399)*

Ohio Custodial Management, Columbus *Also Called: Ohio Custodial Maintenance* *(G-6399)*

Ohio Cvil Svc Emplyees Assn AF 614 865-4700
390 Worthington Rd Ste A Westerville (43082) *(G-14920)*

Ohio Democratic Party 614 221-6563
340 E Fulton St Columbus (43215) *(G-6400)*

Ohio Department of Mental Health 614 466-2337
30 E Broad St Fl 8 Columbus (43215) *(G-6401)*

Ohio Department Rehabilitat 614 877-4516
11271 State Route 762 Orient (43146) *(G-12152)*

Ohio Department Transportation 614 275-1300
1600 W Broad St Columbus (43223) *(G-6402)*

Ohio Department Youth Services 419 245-3040
615 W Superior Ave Cleveland (44113) *(G-4686)*

Ohio Department Youth Services 614 466-4314
51 N High St Fl 5 Columbus (43215) *(G-6403)*

Ohio Department Youth Services 419 875-6965
Township Rd 1 D U 469 Liberty Center (43532) *(G-9846)*

Ohio Dept Dvlpmntal Dsbilities 513 732-9200
4399 E Bauman Ln Batavia (45103) *(G-744)*

Ohio Dept Dvlpmntal Dsbilities 330 544-2231
30 E Broad St Fl 8 Columbus (43215) *(G-6404)*

Ohio Dept Dvlpmntal Dsbilities 614 272-0509
1601 W Broad St Columbus (43222) *(G-6405)*

Ohio Dept Dvlpmntal Dsbilities 740 446-1642
2500 Ohio Ave Gallipolis (45631) *(G-8764)*

Ohio Dept Dvlpmntal Dsbilities 419 385-0231
1101 S Detroit Ave Toledo (43614) *(G-13944)*

Ohio Dept Job & Fmly Svcs 330 484-5402
161 S High St Ste 300 Akron (44308) *(G-248)*

Ohio Dept Job & Fmly Svcs 614 752-9494
4300 Kimberly Pkwy N Columbus (43232) *(G-6406)*

Ohio Dept Job & Fmly Svcs 614 466-1213
255 E Main St Fl 3 Columbus (43215) *(G-6407)*

Ohio Dept Job & Fmly Svcs 740 295-7516
725 Pine St Coshocton (43812) *(G-6995)*

Ohio Dept Job & Fmly Svcs 419 334-3891
2511 Countryside Dr Fremont (43420) *(G-8696)*

Ohio Dept Job & Fmly Svcs 419 626-6781
221 W Parish St Sandusky (44870) *(G-12922)*

Ohio Dept Mntal Hlth Addction 740 594-5000
100 Hospital Dr Athens (45701) *(G-583)*

Ohio Dept Mntal Hlth Addction 740 773-2283
394 Chestnut St Chillicothe (45601) *(G-2080)*

Ohio Dept Mntal Hlth Addction 513 948-3600
1101 Summit Rd Cincinnati (45237) *(G-3144)*

Ohio Dept Mntal Hlth Addction 614 752-0333
2200 W Broad St Columbus (43223) *(G-6408)*

Ohio Dept Mntal Hlth Addction 614 752-0333
2200 W Broad St Columbus (43223) *(G-6409)*

Ohio Dept Mntal Hlth Addction 614 752-0333
2200 W Broad St Columbus (43223) *(G-6410)*

Ohio Dept Mntal Hlth Addction 330 467-7131
1756 Sagamore Rd Northfield (44067) *(G-11962)*

Ohio Dept Mntal Hlth Addction 419 381-1881
930 S Detroit Ave Toledo (43614) *(G-13945)*

Ohio Dept Mntal Hlth Addction 740 947-7581
111 N High St Waverly (45690) *(G-14614)*

Ohio Dept Rhbilitation Corectn 614 274-9000
770 W Broad St Columbus (43222) *(G-6411)*

Ohio Dept Rhbilitation Corectn 614 752-0800
1030 Alum Creek Dr Columbus (43209) *(G-6412)*

Ohio Dept Rhbilitation Corectn 419 782-3385
418 Auglaize St Defiance (43512) *(G-7759)*

ALPHABETIC SECTION — Ohio Living Holdings

Ohio Dept Rhbilitation Corectn.. 419 448-0004
111 N Washington St Tiffin (44883) *(G-13636)*

Ohio Desk, Cleveland *Also Called: The Ohio Desk Company (G-5005)*

Ohio Desk Company.. 216 623-0600
4851 Van Epps Rd Ste A Brooklyn Heights (44131) *(G-1426)*

Ohio Diversified Services Inc.. 440 356-7000
20226 Detroit Rd Cleveland (44116) *(G-4687)*

Ohio Domestic Violence Network.. 614 406-7274
174 E Long St Columbus (43215) *(G-6413)*

Ohio Dsblity Rghts Law Plicy C.. 614 466-7264
200 Civic Center Dr Columbus (43215) *(G-6414)*

Ohio Dst 5 Area Agcy On Aging.. 419 522-5612
2131 Park Ave W Ontario (44906) *(G-12119)*

Ohio Ecological Fd & Frm Assn.. 614 421-2022
41 Croswell Rd Ste D Columbus (43214) *(G-6415)*

Ohio Edison Company (HQ).. 800 736-3402
76 S Main St Bsmt Akron (44308) *(G-249)*

Ohio Edison Company.. 740 671-2900
57246 Ferry Landing Rd Shadyside (43947) *(G-12970)*

Ohio Edison Company.. 330 336-9880
9681 Silvercreek Rd Wadsworth (44281) *(G-14445)*

Ohio Edison Company.. 330 740-7754
730 South Ave Youngstown (44502) *(G-15680)*

Ohio Education Association (PA).. 614 228-4526
225 E Broad St Fl 2 Columbus (43215) *(G-6416)*

Ohio Educational Credit Un Inc (PA).. 216 621-6296
4141 Rockside Rd Ste 400 Seven Hills (44131) *(G-12956)*

Ohio Environmental Council.. 614 487-7506
1145 Chesapeake Ave Ste I Columbus (43212) *(G-6417)*

Ohio Equities LLC.. 614 207-1805
6210 Busch Blvd Columbus (43229) *(G-6418)*

Ohio Equities LLC.. 614 469-0058
17 S High St Ste 799 Columbus (43215) *(G-6419)*

Ohio Equities LLC (PA).. 614 224-2400
605 S Front St Ste 200 Columbus (43215) *(G-6420)*

Ohio Eye Alliance Inc (PA).. 330 823-1680
985 S Sawburg Ave Alliance (44601) *(G-394)*

Ohio Eye Associates Inc.. 800 423-0694
466 S Trimble Rd Mansfield (44906) *(G-10307)*

Ohio Eye Care Consultants LLC.. 330 722-8300
3583 Reserve Commons Dr Medina (44256) *(G-10871)*

Ohio Fabricators Inc.. 330 745-4406
1452 Kenmore Blvd Akron (44314) *(G-250)*

Ohio Fair Plan Undwrt Assn.. 614 839-6446
8800 Lyra Dr Columbus (43240) *(G-5275)*

Ohio Farm Bur Federation Inc (PA).. 614 249-2400
280 N High St Fl 6 Columbus (43215) *(G-6421)*

Ohio Farmers Food Service Dist, Cleveland *Also Called: Ohio Farmers Wholesale Dealers Inc (G-4688)*

Ohio Farmers Insurance Company (PA).. 800 243-0210
1 Park Cir Westfield Center (44251) *(G-15025)*

Ohio Farmers Wholesale Dealers Inc.. 216 391-9733
2700 E 55th St Cleveland (44104) *(G-4688)*

Ohio Ffa Camps Inc.. 330 627-2208
3266 Dyewood Rd Sw Carrollton (44615) *(G-1911)*

Ohio Fresh Eggs LLC.. 740 499-2352
2845 Larue Marseilles Rd La Rue (43332) *(G-9648)*

Ohio Fundation of Ind Colleges.. 614 469-1950
250 E Broad St Ste 1700 Columbus (43215) *(G-6422)*

Ohio Gas Company.. 419 636-3642
715 E Wilson St Bryan (43506) *(G-1490)*

Ohio Gas Company (HQ).. 419 636-1117
200 W High St Bryan (43506) *(G-1491)*

Ohio Gasket and Shim Co Inc (PA).. 330 630-0626
976 Evans Ave Akron (44305) *(G-251)*

Ohio Geothermal, Mansfield *Also Called: Jackson & Sons Drilling & Pump (G-10275)*

Ohio Gstroenterology Group Inc.. 614 754-5500
85 Mcnaughten Rd Ste 320 Columbus (43213) *(G-6423)*

Ohio Gstroenterology Group Inc (PA).. 614 754-5500
3400 Olentangy River Rd Columbus (43202) *(G-6424)*

Ohio Gstroenterology Group Inc.. 614 754-5500
6670 Perimeter Dr Ste 200 Dublin (43016) *(G-8080)*

Ohio Gypsum Supply, Springfield *Also Called: Robinson Insulation Co Inc (G-13286)*

Ohio Hckry Hrvest Brnd Pdts In.. 330 644-6266
90 Logan Pkwy Coventry Township (44319) *(G-7014)*

Ohio Head & Neck Surgeons Inc (PA).. 330 492-2844
4912 Higbee Ave Nw Ste 200 Canton (44718) *(G-1822)*

Ohio Health, Columbus *Also Called: Gerlach John J Ctr For Snior H (G-5930)*

Ohio Health, Nelsonville *Also Called: Doctors Hospital Cleveland Inc (G-11542)*

Ohio Health Center Inc.. 614 252-3636
1000 E Broad St Ste 101 Columbus (43205) *(G-6425)*

Ohio Health Choice Inc (DH).. 800 554-0027
400 E Market St Ste 400 Akron (44304) *(G-252)*

Ohio Health Group LLC.. 614 566-0010
3430 Ohio Health Pkwy Columbus (43202) *(G-6426)*

Ohio Health Info Partnr Inc.. 614 664-2600
3455 Mill Run Dr Ste 315 Hilliard (43026) *(G-9222)*

Ohio Heart and Vascular.. 513 206-1800
5885 Harrison Ave Ste 1900 Cincinnati (45248) *(G-3145)*

Ohio Heart Group Inc.. 740 348-0012
1311 W Main St Newark (43055) *(G-11737)*

Ohio Heart Health Center Inc (PA).. 513 351-9900
237 William Howard Taft Rd Cincinnati (45219) *(G-3146)*

Ohio Heart Health Center Inc.. 513 792-7800
10506 Montgomery Rd Ste 504 Montgomery (45242) *(G-11370)*

Ohio Heart Instit, Youngstown *Also Called: Cardiovascular Associates Inc (G-15571)*

Ohio Heart Institute Inc (PA).. 330 747-6446
1001 Belmont Ave Youngstown (44504) *(G-15681)*

Ohio Helping Hands Clg Svc LLC.. 937 402-0733
5356 Griffith Rd Hillsboro (45133) *(G-9264)*

Ohio Hills Health Services (PA).. 740 425-5165
101 E Main St Barnesville (43713) *(G-720)*

Ohio Historic Preservation Off.. 614 298-2000
1982 Velma Ave Columbus (43211) *(G-6427)*

Ohio Historical Society (PA).. 614 297-2300
800 E 17th Ave Columbus (43211) *(G-6428)*

OHIO HISTORY CONNECTION, Columbus *Also Called: Ohio Historical Society (G-6428)*

Ohio Hlth Hart Vsclar Physcans, Mansfield *Also Called: Ohiohealth Physician Group Inc (G-10309)*

Ohio Hlth Physcn Group Hritg C.. 740 594-8819
75 Hospital Dr Ste 216 Athens (45701) *(G-584)*

Ohio Hosp For Psychiatry LLC.. 614 449-9664
880 Greenlawn Ave Columbus (43223) *(G-6429)*

Ohio Hospital Association.. 614 221-7614
65 E State St Ste 500 Columbus (43215) *(G-6430)*

Ohio Hospital For Psychiatry, Columbus *Also Called: Ohio Hosp For Psychiatry LLC (G-6429)*

Ohio Living.. 330 867-2150
1150 W Market St Akron (44313) *(G-253)*

Ohio Living.. 513 681-4230
1701 Llanfair Ave Cincinnati (45224) *(G-3147)*

Ohio Living.. 614 228-8888
717 Neil Ave Columbus (43215) *(G-6431)*

Ohio Living.. 330 638-2420
303 N Mecca St Cortland (44410) *(G-6974)*

Ohio Living.. 513 539-7391
225 Britton Ln Monroe (45050) *(G-11345)*

Ohio Living.. 937 498-2391
3003 Cisco Rd Sidney (45365) *(G-13043)*

Ohio Living.. 419 865-4445
5916 Cresthaven Ln Ste 110 Toledo (43614) *(G-13946)*

Ohio Living (PA).. 614 888-7800
9200 Worthington Rd Ste 300 Westerville (43082) *(G-14921)*

Ohio Living.. 440 942-4342
36855 Ridge Rd Willoughby (44094) *(G-15215)*

Ohio Living.. 330 746-2944
1216 5th Ave Youngstown (44504) *(G-15682)*

Ohio Living, Westerville *Also Called: Ohio Prsbt Rtrment Svcs Dev Co (G-14922)*

Ohio Living Communities.. 614 888-7800
717 Neil Ave Columbus (43215) *(G-6432)*

Ohio Living Dorothy Love, Sidney *Also Called: Ohio Living (G-13043)*

Ohio Living Holdings.. 330 533-4350
6715 Tippecanoe Rd Ste E201 Canfield (44406) *(G-1636)*

Ohio Living Holdings.. 614 433-0031
2740 Airport Dr Ste 140 Columbus (43219) *(G-6433)*

(PA)=Parent Co (HQ)=Headquarters (DH)=Div Headquarters

Ohio Living Holdings — ALPHABETIC SECTION

Ohio Living Holdings 614 433-0031
 2740 Airport Dr Ste 140 Columbus (43219) *(G-6434)*

Ohio Living Holdings 937 415-5666
 3003 Cisco Rd Sidney (45365) *(G-13044)*

Ohio Living Holdings 419 865-1499
 1730 S Reynolds Rd Toledo (43614) *(G-13947)*

Ohio Living Holdings 440 953-1256
 36500 Euclid Ave Apt 152 Willoughby (44094) *(G-15216)*

Ohio Living Quaker Heights 937 897-6050
 514 High St Waynesville (45068) *(G-14626)*

Ohio Lving HM Hlth Grter Clmbu, Columbus *Also Called: Ohio Living Holdings (G-6434)*

Ohio Lving HM Hlth Grter Clvla, Willoughby *Also Called: Ohio Living Holdings (G-15216)*

Ohio Lving HM Hlth Grter Dyton, Sidney *Also Called: Ohio Living Holdings (G-13044)*

Ohio Lving HM Hlth Grter Tledo, Toledo *Also Called: Ohio Living Holdings (G-13947)*

Ohio Lving HM Hlth Grter Yngst, Canfield *Also Called: Ohio Living Holdings (G-1636)*

Ohio Lving Hspice Grter Clmbus, Columbus *Also Called: Ohio Living Holdings (G-6433)*

Ohio Lving Wstmeinster-Thurber, Columbus *Also Called: Ohio Living Communities (G-6432)*

Ohio Machinery Co 330 874-1003
 10955 Industrial Pkwy Nw Bolivar (44612) *(G-1296)*

Ohio Machinery Co (PA) 440 526-6200
 3993 E Royalton Rd Broadview Heights (44147) *(G-1394)*

Ohio Machinery Co 440 526-0520
 900 Ken Mar Industrial Pkwy Broadview Heights (44147) *(G-1395)*

Ohio Machinery Co 740 942-4626
 1016 E Market St Cadiz (43907) *(G-1542)*

Ohio Machinery Co 614 878-2287
 5252 Walcutt Ct Columbus (43228) *(G-6435)*

Ohio Machinery Co 614 878-2287
 5232 Walcutt Ct Columbus (43228) *(G-6436)*

Ohio Machinery Co 419 423-1447
 3541 Speedway Dr Findlay (45840) *(G-8574)*

Ohio Machinery Co 419 874-7975
 25970 Dixie Hwy Perrysburg (43551) *(G-12359)*

Ohio Machinery Co 937 335-7660
 1281 Brukner Dr Troy (45373) *(G-14149)*

Ohio Machinery Co 740 453-0563
 3415 East Pike Zanesville (43701) *(G-15822)*

Ohio Maint & Renovation Inc (PA) 330 315-3101
 124 Darrow Rd Akron (44305) *(G-254)*

Ohio Materials Handling, Macedonia *Also Called: Newtown Nine Inc (G-10200)*

Ohio Medical Group (PA) 440 414-9400
 29325 Health Campus Dr Ste 3 Westlake (44145) *(G-15091)*

Ohio Medical Trnsp Inc (PA) 614 791-4400
 2827 W Dublin Granville Rd Columbus (43235) *(G-6437)*

Ohio Mentor, Independence *Also Called: Ohio Mentor Inc (G-9463)*

Ohio Mentor Inc (DH) 216 525-1885
 6200 Rockside Woods Blvd N Ste 305 Independence (44131) *(G-9463)*

Ohio Minority Medical 513 400-5011
 517 Broadway St Ste 500 East Liverpool (43920) *(G-8189)*

Ohio Mutual Insurance Company (PA) 419 562-3011
 1725 Hopley Ave Bucyrus (44820) *(G-1514)*

Ohio Mutual Insurance Group, Bucyrus *Also Called: Ohio Mutual Insurance Company (G-1514)*

Ohio National Life Asrn Corp 513 794-6100
 1 Financial Way Ste 100 Montgomery (45242) *(G-11371)*

Ohio North E Hlth Systems Inc (PA) 330 747-9551
 726 Wick Ave Youngstown (44505) *(G-15683)*

Ohio Nursery Exchange, Franklin *Also Called: Sln Nursery LLC (G-8650)*

Ohio Nut & Bolt Company Div, Berea *Also Called: Fastener Industries Inc (G-1069)*

Ohio Orthopedic Ctr Excellence, Upper Arlington *Also Called: Orthopaedic & Trauma Surgeons Inc (G-14281)*

Ohio Orthpd Surgery Inst LLC 614 827-8777
 4605 Sawmill Rd Columbus (43220) *(G-6438)*

Ohio Packaging 330 833-2884
 777 3rd St Nw Massillon (44647) *(G-10660)*

Ohio Pediatric Care Alliance, Springfield *Also Called: Dayton Childrens Hospital (G-13246)*

Ohio Pediatrics Inc (PA) 937 299-2743
 1775 Delco Park Dr Dayton (45420) *(G-7534)*

Ohio Pizza Products LLC (DH) 937 294-6969
 201 Lawton Ave Monroe (45050) *(G-11346)*

Ohio Pools & Spas Inc (PA) 330 494-7755
 6815 Whipple Ave Nw Canton (44720) *(G-1823)*

Ohio Power Company (HQ) 614 716-1000
 1 Riverside Plz Columbus (43215) *(G-6439)*

Ohio Presbt Retirement Vlg, Monroe *Also Called: Ohio Living (G-11345)*

Ohio Prsbt Rtrment Svcs Dev Co 614 888-7800
 9200 Worthington Rd Ste 300 Westerville (43082) *(G-14922)*

Ohio Prsbt Rtrment Svcs Fndtio 614 888-7800
 9200 Worthington Rd Ste 300 Westerville (43082) *(G-14923)*

Ohio Pub Emplyees Rtrement Sys 614 228-8471
 277 E Town St Columbus (43215) *(G-6440)*

Ohio Real Title Agency LLC (PA) 216 373-9900
 1213 Prospect Ave E Ste 200 Cleveland (44115) *(G-4689)*

Ohio Renaissance Festival, Wilmington *Also Called: Brimstone & Fire LLC (G-15247)*

Ohio Renal Care Supply Co LLC 216 739-0500
 3280 W 25th St Cleveland (44109) *(G-4690)*

Ohio Reproductive Medicine 614 451-2280
 535 Reach Blvd # 200 Columbus (43215) *(G-6441)*

Ohio Republican Party, Columbus *Also Called: Replican State Cntl Exec Cmmt (G-6579)*

Ohio Restaurant Association 614 442-3535
 100 E Campus View Blvd Ste 150 Columbus (43235) *(G-6442)*

Ohio River Dialysis LLC 513 385-3580
 5520 Cheviot Rd Ste B Cincinnati (45247) *(G-3148)*

Ohio River Valley, Cincinnati *Also Called: Volunteers of America Inc (G-3633)*

OHIO RURAL ELECTRIC COOPERATIV, Columbus *Also Called: Buckeye Power Inc (G-5477)*

Ohio School Boards Association 614 540-4000
 8050 N High St Ste 100 Columbus (43235) *(G-6443)*

Ohio Sers 614 222-5853
 300 E Broad St Ste 100 Columbus (43215) *(G-6444)*

Ohio Shared Info Svcs Inc 513 677-5600
 7870 E Kemper Rd Cincinnati (45249) *(G-3149)*

Ohio Skate Inc (PA) 419 476-2808
 5735 Opportunity Dr Toledo (43612) *(G-13948)*

Ohio Ski Slopes Inc 419 774-9818
 3100 Possum Run Rd Mansfield (44903) *(G-10308)*

Ohio Soc of Crtif Pub Accntnts 614 764-2727
 4249 Easton Way Ste 150 Columbus (43219) *(G-6445)*

Ohio Soceity of Cpas, Columbus *Also Called: Ohio Soc of Crtif Pub Accntnts (G-6445)*

Ohio State Bar Association 614 487-2050
 1700 Lake Shore Dr Columbus (43204) *(G-6446)*

Ohio State Home Services Inc 614 850-5600
 4271 Weaver Ct N Hilliard (43026) *(G-9223)*

Ohio State Home Services Inc (PA) 330 467-1055
 365 Highland Rd E Macedonia (44056) *(G-10201)*

Ohio State Medical Association (PA) 614 527-6762
 4400 N High St Ste 402 Columbus (43214) *(G-6447)*

Ohio State Outpatient Care E, Columbus *Also Called: Osu Internal Medicine LLC (G-6484)*

Ohio State Parks Inc 513 664-3504
 5201 Lodge Rd College Corner (45003) *(G-5222)*

Ohio State Taxidermy Supply 330 674-8600
 20 Straits Ln Killbuck (44637) *(G-9639)*

Ohio State Univ Alumni Assn 614 292-2200
 2200 Olentangy River Rd Columbus (43210) *(G-6448)*

Ohio State Univ Physicians Inc (HQ) 614 947-3700
 700 Ackerman Rd Ste 600 Columbus (43202) *(G-6449)*

Ohio State Univ Vtrnarian Hosp, Columbus *Also Called: Ohio State University (G-6455)*

Ohio State Univ Wexner Med Ctr 614 293-6255
 410 W 10th Ave Columbus (43210) *(G-6450)*

Ohio State Univ Wexner Med Ctr (HQ) 614 293-8000
 410 W 10th Ave Columbus (43210) *(G-6451)*

Ohio State Univ Wexner Med Ctr 614 293-7521
 320 W 10th Ave Columbus (43210) *(G-6452)*

Ohio State University 614 257-3000
 181 Taylor Ave Columbus (43203) *(G-6453)*

Ohio State University 614 292-9678
 1800 N Pearl St Columbus (43201) *(G-6454)*

Ohio State University 614 292-6661
 601 Vernon L Tharp St Columbus (43210) *(G-6455)*

Ohio State University 614 293-3860
 1375 Perry St Columbus (43201) *(G-6456)*

Ohio State University 614 292-3416
 1224 Kinnear Rd Columbus (43212) *(G-6457)*

ALPHABETIC SECTION — Old Rpblic Ttle Nthrn Ohio LLC

Ohio State University 614 292-1284
1314 Kinnear Rd Columbus (43212) *(G-6458)*

Ohio State University 614 688-0857
1480 W Lane Ave Rm 255 Columbus (43221) *(G-6459)*

Ohio State University 330 263-3700
1680 Madison Ave Wooster (44691) *(G-15363)*

Ohio State Waterproofing, Macedonia Also Called: Ohio State Home Services Inc *(G-10201)*

Ohio Steel Sheet and Plate Inc 800 827-2401
7845 Chestnut Ridge Rd Hubbard (44425) *(G-9322)*

Ohio Support Services Corp (PA) 614 443-0291
1291 S High St Columbus (43206) *(G-6460)*

Ohio Surgery Center, Columbus Also Called: Ohio Surgery Center Ltd *(G-6461)*

Ohio Surgery Center Ltd. 614 451-0500
930 Bethel Rd Columbus (43214) *(G-6461)*

Ohio Tctcal Enfrcment Svcs LLC 614 989-9485
6100 Channingway Blvd Ste 4 Columbus (43232) *(G-6462)*

Ohio Tpk & Infrastructure Comm (DH) 440 234-2081
682 Prospect St Berea (44017) *(G-1076)*

Ohio Tpk & Infrastructure Comm 440 234-2081
682 Prospect St Berea (44017) *(G-1077)*

Ohio Tpk & Infrastructure Comm 440 234-2081
3245 Boston Mills Rd Richfield (44286) *(G-12705)*

Ohio Tpk & Infrastructure Comm 330 527-2169
9196 State Route 700 Windham (44288) *(G-15288)*

Ohio Transmission LLC (PA) 614 342-6247
1900 Jetway Blvd Columbus (43219) *(G-6463)*

Ohio Truck Sales LLC 419 582-8087
1801 George St Sandusky (44870) *(G-12923)*

Ohio United Agency Inc 419 562-3011
1725 Hopley Ave Bucyrus (44820) *(G-1515)*

Ohio Utilities Protection Svc 800 311-3692
12467 Mahoning Ave North Jackson (44451) *(G-11875)*

Ohio Valley Banc Corp (PA) 740 446-2631
420 3rd Ave Gallipolis (45631) *(G-8765)*

Ohio Valley Bank, Gallipolis Also Called: Ohio Valley Bank Company *(G-8766)*

Ohio Valley Bank Company (HQ) 740 446-2631
420 3rd Ave Gallipolis (45631) *(G-8766)*

Ohio Valley Coal Company 740 926-1351
46226 National Rd Saint Clairsville (43950) *(G-12810)*

Ohio Valley Elec Svcs LLC 513 771-2410
4585 Cornell Rd Blue Ash (45241) *(G-1217)*

Ohio Valley Electric Corp (HQ) 740 289-7200
3932 Us Rte 23 Piketon (45661) *(G-12425)*

Ohio Valley Flooring, Cincinnati Also Called: Ohio Valley Flooring Inc *(G-3150)*

Ohio Valley Flooring, Cleveland Also Called: Ohio Valley Flooring Inc *(G-4691)*

Ohio Valley Flooring Inc (PA) 513 271-3434
5555 Murray Ave Cincinnati (45227) *(G-3150)*

Ohio Valley Flooring Inc 216 328-9091
7620 Hub Pkwy Ste 4 Cleveland (44125) *(G-4691)*

Ohio Valley Home Health Inc 740 249-4219
2097 E State St Ste B1 Athens (45701) *(G-585)*

Ohio Valley Home Health Inc (PA) 740 441-1393
1480 Jackson Pike Gallipolis (45631) *(G-8767)*

Ohio Valley Mall Company 330 747-2661
2445 Belmont Ave Youngstown (44505) *(G-15684)*

Ohio Valley Manor Inc 937 392-4318
5280 Us Highway 62 And 68 Ripley (45167) *(G-12727)*

Ohio Valley Medical Center LLC 937 521-3900
100 E Main St Springfield (45502) *(G-13279)*

Ohio Valley Sports, Inc., Cincinnati Also Called: Cincinnati Bengals Inc *(G-2401)*

Ohio Valley Wine & Beer, Cincinnati Also Called: Ohio Valley Wine Company LLC *(G-3151)*

Ohio Valley Wine Company LLC 513 771-9370
1518 Dalton Ave Cincinnati (45214) *(G-3151)*

Ohio Vision of Toledo Inc Opt, Oregon Also Called: Optivue Inc *(G-12138)*

Ohio Vly Ambltory Srgery Ctr L 740 423-4684
608 Washington Blvd Belpre (45714) *(G-1058)*

Ohio Vly Athc Conference Inc 740 671-3269
64962 Breezy Point Ln Bellaire (43906) *(G-1014)*

Ohio Vly Integration Svcs Inc 937 492-0008
2005 Commerce Dr Sidney (45365) *(G-13045)*

Ohio-American Water Co Inc (HQ) 740 382-3993
365 E Center St Marion (43302) *(G-10449)*

Ohio-Kentucky Steel Corp 937 743-4600
2001 Commerce Center Dr Franklin (45005) *(G-8645)*

Ohio-Kentucky Steel LLC 937 743-4600
2001 Commerce Center Dr Franklin (45005) *(G-8646)*

Ohio-T-Home Hlth Care Agcy Ltd 614 947-0791
875 N High St Ste 300 Columbus (43215) *(G-6464)*

Ohio/Oklahoma Hearst TV Inc (DH) 513 412-5000
1700 Young St Cincinnati (45202) *(G-3152)*

Ohioans Home Healthcare Inc 419 843-4422
28315 Kensington Ln Perrysburg (43551) *(G-12360)*

Ohioguidestone 440 234-2006
343 W Bagley Rd Berea (44017) *(G-1078)*

Ohioguidestone (PA) 440 234-2006
434 Eastland Rd Berea (44017) *(G-1079)*

Ohioguidestone 440 234-2006
4579 Everhard Rd Nw Canton (44718) *(G-1824)*

Ohioguidestone 216 433-4136
17400 Holland Rd Cleveland (44142) *(G-4692)*

Ohioguidestone 440 260-8900
3500 Carnegie Ave Cleveland (44115) *(G-4693)*

Ohioguidestone 440 235-0918
24567 West Rd Olmsted Falls (44138) *(G-12088)*

Ohiohealth Corporation (PA) 614 788-8860
3430 Ohio Health Pkwy 5th Fl Columbus (43202) *(G-6465)*

Ohiohealth Corporation 614 566-5977
2601 Silver Dr Columbus (43211) *(G-6466)*

Ohiohealth Corporation 614 544-8000
7500 Hospital Dr Dublin (43016) *(G-8081)*

Ohiohealth Group Ltd 614 566-0056
445 Hutchinson Ave Columbus (43235) *(G-6467)*

Ohiohealth Mansfield Hospital, Mansfield Also Called: Medcentral Health System *(G-10293)*

Ohiohealth O'Bleness Hospital, Athens Also Called: Sheltring Arms Hosp Fndtion In *(G-589)*

Ohiohealth Physician Group Inc (HQ) 567 241-7000
335 Glessner Ave Mansfield (44903) *(G-10309)*

Ohiohlth Rverside Methdst Hosp 614 566-5000
3535 Olentangy River Rd Columbus (43214) *(G-6468)*

Ohios Hospice Inc 937 256-4490
7575 Paragon Rd Dayton (45459) *(G-7535)*

Ohios Hospice Foundation O 937 256-4490
324 Wilmington Ave Dayton (45420) *(G-7536)*

Ohlman Farm & Greenhouse Inc 419 535-5586
3901 Hill Ave Toledo (43607) *(G-13949)*

Ohman Family Living At Briar, Middlefield Also Called: Briar Hl Hlth Care Rsdence Inc *(G-11138)*

OIC, Springfield Also Called: Opportnties For Indvdual Chnge *(G-13280)*

Oil Distributing Co, Blue Ash Also Called: Four O Corporation *(G-1176)*

OK Interiors Corp 513 742-3278
11100 Ashburn Rd Cincinnati (45240) *(G-3153)*

Oki Auction LLC 513 679-7910
120 Citycentre Dr Cincinnati (45216) *(G-3154)*

Oki Auto Auction, Cincinnati Also Called: Oki Auction LLC *(G-3154)*

Oki Bering, West Chester Also Called: Oki Bering Management Co *(G-14827)*

Oki Bering Management Co 513 341-4002
9901 Princeton Glendale Rd Ste A West Chester (45246) *(G-14827)*

Oki Rgonal Council Governments, Cincinnati Also Called: Ride Share Information *(G-3298)*

OKL Can Line Inc
11235 Sebring Dr Cincinnati (45240) *(G-3155)*

Ol' Smokehaus, Clayton Also Called: Landes Fresh Meats Inc *(G-3734)*

Olberding Brand Family, Cincinnati Also Called: The Photo-Type Engraving Company *(G-3469)*

Old Forge Services Inc 330 733-5531
1490 Shanksdown Rd Windham (44288) *(G-15289)*

Old Meadow Farms Inc 440 632-5590
15980 Georgia Rd Middlefield (44062) *(G-11143)*

Old Republic, Columbus Also Called: Old Republic Nat Title Insur *(G-6469)*

Old Republic, Independence Also Called: Old Rpblic Ttle Nthrn Ohio LLC *(G-9464)*

Old Republic Nat Title Insur 614 341-1900
141 E Town St Ste 100 Columbus (43215) *(G-6469)*

Old Rpblic Ttle Nthrn Ohio LLC 216 524-5700
6480 Rockside Woods Blvd S Ste 170 Independence (44131) *(G-9464)*

Old Time Pottery LLC   **ALPHABETIC SECTION**

Old Time Pottery LLC 513 825-5211
   1191 Smiley Ave Cincinnati (45240) *(G-3156)*

Old Time Pottery LLC 440 842-1244
   7011 W 130th St Ste 1 Cleveland (44130) *(G-4694)*

Old Time Pottery LLC 614 337-1258
   2200 Morse Rd Columbus (43229) *(G-6470)*

Old Trail School 330 666-1118
   2315 Ira Rd Bath (44210) *(G-754)*

Oldies 95, Dayton *Also Called: Miami Valley Broadcasting Corp (G-7486)*

Oleco Inc 937 223-3000
   137 N Main St Ste 722 Dayton (45402) *(G-7537)*

Olin Brass, Alliance *Also Called: Wieland Rolled Pdts N Amer LLC (G-406)*

Oliver Steel Plate Co 330 425-7000
   7851 Bavaria Rd Twinsburg (44087) *(G-14209)*

Ollom Dental Group LLC 614 392-8090
   1245 S Sunbury Rd Ste 201 Westerville (43081) *(G-15008)*

Olmsted Falls City Bd Educatn 440 427-6350
   26894 Schady Rd Olmsted Twp (44138) *(G-12092)*

Olmsted Falls Cty SC Bus Gar, Olmsted Twp *Also Called: Olmsted Falls City Bd Educatn (G-12092)*

Olmsted Manor Ltd 440 777-8444
   27500 Mill Rd North Olmsted (44070) *(G-11910)*

Olmsted Parks and Recreation, North Olmsted *Also Called: City of North Olmsted (G-11896)*

Olmsted Residence Corporation 440 235-7100
   26376 John Rd Ofc Olmsted Twp (44138) *(G-12093)*

Ologie Inc 614 221-1107
   447 E Main St Ste 122 Columbus (43215) *(G-6471)*

Olon USA LLC 440 357-3300
   7528 Auburn Rd Concord Township (44077) *(G-6931)*

Olr America Inc 612 436-4970
   31300 Solon Rd Solon (44139) *(G-13120)*

Olympic Steel Inc 216 292-3800
   5080 Richmond Rd Bedford (44146) *(G-979)*

Olympic Steel Inc (PA) 216 292-3800
   22901 Millcreek Blvd Ste 650 Cleveland (44122) *(G-4695)*

Olympic Steel Inc 330 602-6279
   555 Commercial Pkwy Dover (44622) *(G-7898)*

Olympic Urogynecology LLC 330 953-3414
   3009 Smith Rd Ste 400 Fairlawn (44333) *(G-8492)*

Om Group, Westlake *Also Called: Borchers Americas Inc (G-15040)*

Om Partners LLC 216 861-7200
   1350 Euclid Ave Ste 700 Cleveland (44115) *(G-4696)*

Omdp Attorneys & Counselors, Sheffield Village *Also Called: OToole McLghlin Dley Pcora LP (G-13003)*

Omega Laboratories Inc 330 628-5748
   400 N Cleveland Ave Mogadore (44260) *(G-11330)*

Omega Title Agency LLC 330 436-0600
   495 Wolf Ledges Pkwy Ste 1 Akron (44311) *(G-255)*

Omegasea, Painesville *Also Called: Omegasea Ltd Liability Co (G-12240)*

Omegasea Ltd Liability Co 440 639-2372
   1000 Bacon Rd Painesville (44077) *(G-12240)*

Omni Cart Services Inc 440 205-8363
   7370 Production Dr Mentor (44060) *(G-10981)*

Omni Manor Inc (PA) 330 545-1550
   101 W Liberty St Girard (44420) *(G-8821)*

Omni Manor Inc 330 793-5648
   3245 Vestal Rd Youngstown (44509) *(G-15685)*

Omni Medical Center 330 492-5565
   4760 Belpar St Nw Canton (44718) *(G-1825)*

Omni Nursing Home, Youngstown *Also Called: Omni Manor Inc (G-15685)*

Omni Property Companies LLC 216 514-1950
   33095 Bainbridge Rd Solon (44139) *(G-13121)*

Omni Wellness Group LLC 937 540-9920
   1149 Experiment Farm Rd Troy (45373) *(G-14150)*

Omnicare LLC (DH) 513 719-2600
   900 Omnicare Ctr 201 E Fourth St Cincinnati (45202) *(G-3157)*

Omnicare Distribution Ctr LLC 419 720-8200
   201 E 4th St Ste 1 Cincinnati (45202) *(G-3158)*

Omnicare of Spartanburg, Cincinnati *Also Called: Pharmacy Consultants LLC (G-3205)*

Omnicare Pharmacies of The GP (DH) 513 719-2600
   201 E 4th St Ste 900 Cincinnati (45202) *(G-3159)*

Omnicare Phrm of Midwest LLC (DH) 513 719-2600
   201 E 4th St Ste 900 Cincinnati (45202) *(G-3160)*

Omnicare Purch Ltd Partner Inc 800 990-6664
   201 E 4th St Ste 900 Cincinnati (45202) *(G-3161)*

Omnisource LLC 419 537-1631
   2453 Hill Ave Toledo (43607) *(G-13950)*

Omsagar Hotels Ltd 703 675-7785
   11431 Allen Rd Jeffersonville (43128) *(G-9541)*

Omya, Mason *Also Called: Omya Industries Inc (G-10586)*

Omya Industries Inc (HQ) 513 387-4600
   4605 Duke Dr Mason (45040) *(G-10586)*

On Deck Services Inc 513 759-2854
   8263 Kyles Station Rd Ste 1 Liberty Township (45044) *(G-9855)*

On Search Partners LLC 440 318-1006
   102 1st St Ste 201 Hudson (44236) *(G-9365)*

Onbase, Westlake *Also Called: Hyland Software Inc (G-15068)*

Oncall LLC 513 381-4320
   8044 Montgomery Rd Ste 700 Cincinnati (45236) *(G-3162)*

Oncodiagnostic Laboratory Inc
   812 Huron Rd E Ste 520 Cleveland (44115) *(G-4697)*

Oncolgy/Hmatology Care Inc PSC (PA) 513 751-2145
   5053 Wooster Rd Cincinnati (45226) *(G-3163)*

Oncology Partners Network, Cincinnati *Also Called: Trihealth Oncology Inst LLC (G-3524)*

One Call Now, Dayton *Also Called: Myteam1 LLC (G-7523)*

ONE HEALTH OHIO AT YOUNGSTOWN, Youngstown *Also Called: Ohio North E Hlth Systems Inc (G-15683)*

One Lincoln Park 937 298-0594
   590 Isaac Prugh Way Dayton (45429) *(G-7538)*

One Nation Mortgages, Columbus *Also Called: Liberty Mortgage Company Inc (G-6157)*

One Sky Flight LLC (HQ) 877 703-2348
   26180 Curtiss Wright Pkwy Cleveland (44143) *(G-4698)*

One Stop Remodeling, Columbus *Also Called: Wingler Construction Corp (G-6898)*

One Way Express Incorporated 440 439-9182
   380 Solon Rd Ste 5 Cleveland (44146) *(G-4699)*

One80 Intermediaries Inc 617 330-5700
   3700 Park East Dr Ste 250 Beachwood (44122) *(G-823)*

Oneeighty Inc 330 263-6021
   104 Spink St Wooster (44691) *(G-15364)*

Onefifteen Recovery 937 223-5609
   601 S Edwin C Moses Blvd Dayton (45417) *(G-7539)*

Oneil, Miamisburg *Also Called: ONeil & Associates Inc (G-11079)*

ONeil & Associates Inc (PA) 937 865-0800
   495 Byers Rd Miamisburg (45342) *(G-11079)*

ONeil Tent Co Inc 614 837-6352
   895 W Walnut St Canal Winchester (43110) *(G-1614)*

Oneill Hlthcare - N Ridgeville, North Ridgeville *Also Called: Center Ridge Nursing Home Inc (G-11924)*

ONeill Insurance Agency Inc 330 334-1561
   111 High St Wadsworth (44281) *(G-14446)*

Onex Construction Inc 330 995-9015
   1430 Miller Pkwy Streetsboro (44241) *(G-13424)*

Online Imaging Solutions, Cleveland *Also Called: American Copy Equipment Inc (G-3801)*

Online Liquidation Auction LLC 440 596-8733
   8748 Ridge Rd North Royalton (44133) *(G-11947)*

Onosys, Independence *Also Called: Nuonosys Inc (G-9461)*

Onpoint Group LLC (PA) 567 336-9764
   3235 Levis Commons Blvd Perrysburg (43551) *(G-12361)*

Onpower Inc 513 228-2100
   3525 Grant Ave Ste A Lebanon (45036) *(G-9779)*

Onshift Inc (PA) 216 333-1353
   1621 Euclid Ave Ste 1500 Cleveland (44115) *(G-4700)*

Ontario Local School District 419 529-3814
   3644 Pearl St Ontario (44906) *(G-12120)*

Ontario Mechanical LLC 419 529-2578
   2880 Park Ave W Ontario (44906) *(G-12121)*

Onx Acquisition LLC 440 569-2300
   5910 Landerbrook Dr Ste 250 Mayfield Heights (44124) *(G-10791)*

Onx Enterprise Solutions, Cincinnati *Also Called: Onx Holdings LLC (G-3164)*

Onx Enterprise Solutions, Mayfield Heights *Also Called: Onx Acquisition LLC (G-10791)*

Onx Entrprise Solutions US Inc 440 569-2300
   5900 Landerbrook Dr Ste 100 Cleveland (44124) *(G-4701)*

ALPHABETIC SECTION — Orthopedic Cons Cincinnati

Onx Holdings LLC (DH).. 866 587-2287
  221 E 4th St Cincinnati (45202) *(G-3164)*

Onyx Creative Inc (PA).. 216 223-3200
  25001 Emery Rd Ste 400 Cleveland (44128) *(G-4702)*

Oodle, Cincinnati Also Called: Comcage LLC *(G-2479)*

Oovoo LLC... 917 515-2074
  1700 S Patterson Blvd Ste 300 Kettering (45409) *(G-9631)*

Open Arms Health Systems Llc................................. 614 385-8354
  868 Freeway Dr N Columbus (43229) *(G-6472)*

Open Door Christn Schools Inc.................................. 440 322-6386
  8287 W Ridge Rd Elyria (44035) *(G-8283)*

Open Practice Solutions Ltd....................................... 234 380-8345
  300 Executive Pkwy W Ste 300 Hudson (44236) *(G-9366)*

Open Road Distributing, Westlake Also Called: Ta Operating LLC *(G-15113)*

Open Text, Hilliard Also Called: Open Text Inc *(G-9224)*

Open Text Inc... 614 658-3588
  3671 Ridge Mill Dr Hilliard (43026) *(G-9224)*

Operating Tax Systems LLC....................................... 330 940-3967
  3924 Clock Pointe Trl Ste 105 Stow (44224) *(G-13383)*

Ophthlmic Srgons Cons Ohio Inc................................ 614 221-7464
  262 Neil Ave Ste 430 Columbus (43215) *(G-6473)*

Opocus... 800 724-8802
  300 W Wilson Bridge Rd Ste 300 Worthington (43085) *(G-15445)*

Opportnties For Indvdual Chnge.................................. 937 323-6461
  920 W Main St Springfield (45504) *(G-13280)*

Opportunities For Ohioans (DH).................................. 614 438-1200
  150 E Campus View Blvd Ste 150 Columbus (43235) *(G-6474)*

OPRS FOUNDATION, Westerville Also Called: Ohio Prsbt Rtrment Svcs Fndtio *(G-14923)*

Opti LLC... 212 651-7317
  5000 Willow Hills Ln Cincinnati (45243) *(G-3165)*

Optiem, Cleveland Also Called: Optiem LLC *(G-4703)*

Optiem LLC.. 216 574-9100
  1370 W 6th St 3rd Fl Cleveland (44113) *(G-4703)*

Optima 777 LLC... 216 771-7700
  777 Saint Clair Ave Ne Cleveland (44114) *(G-4704)*

Optima Rehabilitation Services, Tiffin Also Called: P T Svcs Rehabilitation Inc *(G-13638)*

Optimas Oe Solutions LLC.. 740 774-4553
  101 S Mcarthur St Chillicothe (45601) *(G-2081)*

Optimas Oe Solutions LLC.. 440 546-4400
  6565 Davis Industrial Pkwy Solon (44139) *(G-13122)*

Optimas Oe Solutions LLC.. 513 881-4600
  4440 Mulhauser Road West Chester (45011) *(G-14737)*

Optimum Graphics, Westerville Also Called: Optimum System Products Inc *(G-15009)*

Optimum System Products Inc (PA)........................... 614 885-4464
  921 Eastwind Dr Ste 133 Westerville (43081) *(G-15009)*

Optimum Technology Inc (PA).................................... 614 785-1110
  9922 Brewster Ln Powell (43065) *(G-12602)*

Optio-Vision By Kahn & Diehl, Oregon Also Called: Ottivue *(G-12141)*

Option Advisor, The, Blue Ash Also Called: Schaeffers Investment Research Inc *(G-1242)*

Option Care, Brecksville Also Called: Option Care Brecksville O *(G-1361)*

Option Care Brecksville O... 440 627-2031
  6955 Treeline Dr Brecksville (44141) *(G-1361)*

Options Flight Support Inc... 216 261-3500
  26180 Curtiss Wright Pkwy Cleveland (44143) *(G-4705)*

Options Home Services LLC...................................... 614 203-6340
  786 Northwest Blvd Columbus (43212) *(G-6475)*

Optivue Inc... 419 891-1391
  2740 Narvar Ave Oregon (43616) *(G-12138)*

Optum Infusion Svcs 550 Inc (DH).............................. 866 442-4679
  7167 E Kemper Rd Cincinnati (45249) *(G-3166)*

Optumrx Inc... 614 794-3300
  250 Progressive Way Westerville (43082) *(G-14924)*

Optumrx Home Delivery Ohio LLC.............................. 440 930-5520
  33381 Walker Rd Avon Lake (44012) *(G-682)*

Oracle Elevator Company.. 614 781-9731
  771 Dearborn Park Ln Columbus (43085) *(G-6476)*

Oracle Elevator Company, Columbus Also Called: Oracle Elevator Company *(G-6476)*

Oral & Facial Surgery Assoc....................................... 513 791-0550
  10506 Montgomery Rd Ste 203 Montgomery (45242) *(G-11372)*

Oral Fcial Srgons Ohio Rchard.................................... 614 764-9455
  5155 Bradenton Ave Ste 100 Dublin (43017) *(G-8082)*

Orange Barrel Media LLC.. 614 294-4898
  250 N Hartford Ave Columbus (43222) *(G-6477)*

Orange Early Childhood Center.................................. 216 831-4909
  32000 Chagrin Blvd Cleveland (44124) *(G-4706)*

Orbit Movers & Erectors Inc....................................... 937 277-8080
  1101 Negley Pl Dayton (45402) *(G-7540)*

Orchard, Cincinnati Also Called: Skylight Partners Inc *(G-3385)*

Orchard Hiltz & McCliment Inc.................................... 614 418-0600
  580 N 4th St Ste 610 Columbus (43215) *(G-6478)*

Orchard Villa Inc.. 419 697-4100
  2841 Munding Dr Oregon (43616) *(G-12139)*

Orchards of East Liverpool, East Liverpool Also Called: East Lverpool Convalescent Ctr *(G-8182)*

ORCHARDS OF WESTLAKE LIVING &, Westlake Also Called: Wlkop LLC *(G-15125)*

Order of Untd Coml Trvlers of (PA)............................. 614 487-9680
  1801 Watermark Dr Ste 100 Columbus (43215) *(G-6479)*

Oreco Inc... 724 349-7220
  110 Riverbend Ave Lewis Center (43035) *(G-9833)*

Oregon Clinic Inc... 419 691-8132
  3841 Navarre Ave Oregon (43616) *(G-12140)*

Organic Technologies, Coshocton Also Called: Wiley Companies *(G-7005)*

Organized Living, Cincinnati Also Called: Organized Living Inc *(G-3167)*

Organized Living Inc (PA)... 513 489-9300
  3100 E Kemper Rd Cincinnati (45241) *(G-3167)*

Oriana House Inc... 330 374-9610
  941 Sherman St Akron (44311) *(G-256)*

Oriana House Inc (PA).. 330 535-8116
  885 E Buchtel Ave Akron (44305) *(G-257)*

Oriana House Inc... 330 996-7730
  15 Frederick Ave Akron (44310) *(G-258)*

Oriana House Inc... 419 447-1444
  3055 S State Route 100 Tiffin (44883) *(G-13637)*

Oriana House Inc... 216 881-7882
  13820 Hale Rd Burton (44021) *(G-1532)*

Original Partners Ltd Partnr (PA)................................ 513 381-8696
  1055 Saint Paul Pl Cincinnati (45202) *(G-3168)*

Orion Care Services LLC.. 216 752-3600
  18810 Harvard Ave Cleveland (44122) *(G-4707)*

ORourke Wrecking Company...................................... 513 871-1400
  660 Lunken Park Dr Cincinnati (45226) *(G-3169)*

Orrville Trucking & Grading Co (PA)........................... 330 682-4010
  475 Orr St Orrville (44667) *(G-12172)*

Ortho Neuro, Westerville Also Called: Orthoneuro *(G-15010)*

Orthodontic Associates LLC.. 419 229-8771
  724 E Wayne St Celina (45822) *(G-1929)*

Ortholink Physicians, New Albany Also Called: Joint Implant Surgeons Inc *(G-11570)*

Orthoneuro (PA)... 614 890-6555
  70 S Cleveland Ave Westerville (43081) *(G-15010)*

Orthopaedic & Trauma Surgeons Inc.......................... 614 827-8700
  4605 Sawmill Rd Upper Arlington (43220) *(G-14281)*

Orthopaedic Associates Inc... 440 892-1440
  24723 Detroit Rd Westlake (44145) *(G-15092)*

Orthopaedic Institute Ohio Inc (PA)............................. 419 222-6622
  801 Medical Dr Ste A Lima (45804) *(G-9945)*

Orthopaedic Surgery Cente... 330 758-1065
  8551 Crossroad Dr Youngstown (44514) *(G-15686)*

Orthopdic Assoc Zanesville Inc................................... 740 454-3273
  2854 Bell St Zanesville (43701) *(G-15823)*

Orthopdic Spine Ctr At Plris L..................................... 937 707-4662
  4092 Gantz Rd Grove City (43123) *(G-8943)*

Orthopedic Assoc SW Ohio Inc (PA)........................... 937 415-9100
  7677 Yankee St Ste 110 Centerville (45459) *(G-1949)*

Orthopedic Associates... 800 824-9861
  7117 Dutchland Pkwy Liberty Township (45044) *(G-9856)*

Orthopedic Associates Dayton..................................... 937 280-4988
  7980 N Main St Dayton (45415) *(G-7541)*

Orthopedic Cons Cincinnati... 513 753-7488
  6620 Clough Pike Cincinnati (45244) *(G-3170)*

Orthopedic Cons Cincinnati... 513 232-6677
  6620 Clough Pike Cincinnati (45244) *(G-3171)*

Orthopedic Cons Cincinnati... 513 245-2500
  7663 5 Mile Rd Cincinnati (45230) *(G-3172)*

(PA)=Parent Co (HQ)=Headquarters (DH)=Div Headquarters

Orthopedic Cons Cincinnati

Orthopedic Cons Cincinnati.. 513 347-9999
　6909 Good Samaritan Dr Cincinnati (45247) *(G-3173)*

Orthopedic Cons Cincinnati.. 937 393-6169
　1275 N High St Hillsboro (45133) *(G-9265)*

Orthopedic Cons Cincinnati (PA).. 513 733-8894
　7798 Discovery Dr Ste A West Chester (45069) *(G-14738)*

Orthopedic One, Hilliard *Also Called: Orthopedic One Inc (G-9225)*

Orthopedic One Inc.. 614 827-8700
　4605 Sawmill Rd Columbus (43220) *(G-6480)*

Orthopedic One Inc (PA)... 614 545-7900
　170 Taylor Station Rd Columbus (43213) *(G-6481)*

Orthopedic One Inc.. 614 570-4419
　4945 Bradenton Ave Dublin (43017) *(G-8083)*

Orthopedic One Inc.. 614 488-1816
　3777 Trueman Ct Hilliard (43026) *(G-9225)*

Orthopedic One Inc.. 614 839-2300
　340 Polaris Pkwy Westerville (43082) *(G-14925)*

Orthorpdics Mltspcialty Netwrk (PA).................................... 330 493-1630
　4760 Belpar St Nw Canton (44718) *(G-1826)*

Orton Edward Jr Crmic Fndation... 614 895-2663
　6991 S Old 3c Hwy Westerville (43082) *(G-14926)*

Orum Stair Rsdntl Brkg OH.. 614 920-8100
　1217 Hill Rd N Pickerington (43147) *(G-12407)*

Orveon Global US LLC.. 614 348-4994
　343 N Front St Columbus (43215) *(G-6482)*

Orwell Tire Service Inc.. 440 437-6515
　431 E Main St Orwell (44076) *(G-12179)*

Osborn Engineering Company (PA)..................................... 216 861-2020
　1111 Superior Ave E Ste 2100 Cleveland (44114) *(G-4708)*

Osborn Engineering Company, Cleveland *Also Called: Osborn Engineering Company (G-4708)*

Osborne Trucking Company (PA).. 513 874-2090
　325 Osborne Dr Fairfield (45014) *(G-8435)*

Osgood State Bank Inc (HQ).. 419 582-2681
　275 W Main St Osgood (45351) *(G-12181)*

OSIS, Cincinnati *Also Called: Ohio Shared Info Svcs Inc (G-3149)*

OSMA, Columbus *Also Called: Ohio State Medical Association (G-6447)*

Osmans Pies Inc.. 330 607-9083
　3678 Elm Rd Stow (44224) *(G-13384)*

Ostendorf-Morris Company, Cleveland *Also Called: Om Partners LLC (G-4696)*

Oster Services LLC.. 440 596-8489
　17415 Northwood Ave Ste 100 Lakewood (44107) *(G-9680)*

Osterwisch, Cincinnati *Also Called: Osterwisch Company Inc (G-3174)*

Osterwisch Company Inc... 513 791-3282
　6755 Highland Ave Cincinnati (45236) *(G-3174)*

Osu, Columbus *Also Called: James Center (G-6083)*

Osu Harding Hospital.. 614 293-9600
　1670 Upham Dr Columbus (43210) *(G-6483)*

Osu Internal Medicine LLC... 614 688-6400
　543 Taylor Ave Columbus (43203) *(G-6484)*

Osu Internal Medicine LLC (PA)... 614 293-0080
　6700 University Blvd # 4c Dublin (43016) *(G-8084)*

Osu Nephrology Medical Ctr.. 614 293-8300
　410 W 10th Ave Columbus (43210) *(G-6485)*

OSu Spt Mdcine Physcians Inc.. 614 293-3600
　2835 Fred Taylor Dr Columbus (43202) *(G-6486)*

Osu Surgery LLC (PA)... 614 261-1141
　700 Ackerman Rd Ste 350 Columbus (43202) *(G-6487)*

Otherworld Inc.. 614 868-3631
　5819 Chantry Dr Columbus (43232) *(G-6488)*

Oti, Powell *Also Called: Optimum Technology Inc (G-12602)*

Otis Elevator Company.. 513 531-7888
　2463 Crowne Point Dr Cincinnati (45241) *(G-3175)*

Otis Elevator Company.. 216 573-2333
　9800 Rockside Rd Ste 1200 Cleveland (44125) *(G-4709)*

Otis Elevator Company.. 614 777-6500
　777 Dearborn Park Ln Ste L Columbus (43085) *(G-6489)*

Otis Elevator Company.. 740 282-1461
　1 Farm Spring Steubenville (43953) *(G-13341)*

OToole McLghlin Dley Pcora LP... 440 930-4001
　5455 Detroit Rd Sheffield Village (44054) *(G-13003)*

Otp Holding LLC (HQ).. 614 342-6123
　1900 Jetway Blvd Columbus (43219) *(G-6490)*

Otp Industrial Solutions, Columbus *Also Called: Ohio Transmission LLC (G-6463)*

Ottawa Cnty Rvrview Hlthcare C, Oak Harbor *Also Called: County of Ottawa (G-12044)*

Ottawa House, Toledo *Also Called: Zepf Housing Corp One Inc (G-14120)*

Otterbein Cridersville, Cridersville *Also Called: Otterbein Homes (G-7029)*

Otterbein Homes... 419 645-5114
　100 Red Oak Dr Cridersville (45806) *(G-7029)*

Otterbein Homes... 513 696-8565
　585 N State Route 741 Lebanon (45036) *(G-9780)*

Otterbein Homes (PA)... 513 933-5400
　3855 Lower Market St Ste 300 Lebanon (45036) *(G-9781)*

Otterbein Homes... 419 943-4376
　901 E Main St Leipsic (45856) *(G-9801)*

Otterbein Homes... 513 260-7690
　105 Atrium Dr Middletown (45005) *(G-11200)*

Otterbein Homes... 419 394-1622
　11300 Yost Cir Saint Marys (45885) *(G-12833)*

Otterbein Homes... 419 394-2366
　11230 State Route 364 Saint Marys (45885) *(G-12834)*

Otterbein Portage Valley Inc... 888 749-4950
　20311 Pemberville Rd Ofc Pemberville (43450) *(G-12291)*

Otterbein Prtage Vly Rtrment C, Pemberville *Also Called: Otterbein Portage Valley Inc (G-12291)*

OTTERBEIN SENIOR LIFESTYLE CHO, Lebanon *Also Called: Otterbein Homes (G-9781)*

OTTERBEIN SENIOR LIFESTYLE CHOICES, Dayton *Also Called: Otterbein Snior Lfstyle Chices (G-7542)*

OTTERBEIN SENIOR LIFESTYLE CHOICES, Pemberville *Also Called: Otterbein Snior Lfstyle Chices (G-12292)*

Otterbein Snior Lfstyle Chices.. 937 885-5426
　9320 Avalon Cir Dayton (45458) *(G-7542)*

Otterbein Snior Lfstyle Chices.. 419 833-7000
　20311 Pemberville Rd Pemberville (43450) *(G-12292)*

Otterbein St Mrys Rtrment Cmnt, Saint Marys *Also Called: Otterbein Homes (G-12834)*

Ottivue (PA)... 419 693-4444
　2740 Navarre Ave Oregon (43616) *(G-12141)*

Otto Insurance Group LLC.. 740 278-7888
　5855 Chandler Ct Westerville (43082) *(G-14927)*

Ouicare Rcrtment Stffing Svcs... 440 536-4829
　1110 Lake Ave Ashtabula (44004) *(G-544)*

Our House Inc... 440 835-2110
　27633 Bassett Rd Westlake (44145) *(G-15093)*

Our Lady Bellefonte Hosp Inc (HQ)...................................... 606 833-3333
　1701 Mercy Health Pl Cincinnati (45237) *(G-3176)*

Our Lady Bellefonte Hospital, Cincinnati *Also Called: Our Lady Bellefonte Hosp Inc (G-3176)*

Our Lady Bethlehem Schools Inc.. 614 459-8285
　4567 Olentangy River Rd Columbus (43214) *(G-6491)*

Our Ohio Communications, Columbus *Also Called: Ohio Farm Bur Federation Inc (G-6421)*

Our Town Studios Inc... 614 832-2121
　781 Northwest Blvd Columbus (43212) *(G-6492)*

Out Patient, Sandusky *Also Called: Firelands Regional Health Sys (G-12898)*

Outdoor Family Center, Perry *Also Called: Lake County YMCA (G-12307)*

Outlet Broadcasting Inc.. 614 263-4444
　3165 Olentangy River Rd Columbus (43202) *(G-6493)*

Outlook Pointe, Northfield *Also Called: Balanced Care Corporation (G-11952)*

Outlook Pointe At Ravenna, Ravenna *Also Called: Balanced Care Corporation (G-12619)*

Outpatient Anderson, Cincinnati *Also Called: Childrens Hospital Medical Ctr (G-2367)*

Outreach Professional Svcs Inc.. 216 472-4094
　2351 E 22nd St Cleveland (44115) *(G-4710)*

Ovatient, Cleveland *Also Called: Metrohealth System (G-4565)*

Ovec, Piketon *Also Called: Ohio Valley Electric Corp (G-12425)*

Over Rainbow Adult Daycare.. 330 638-9599
　110 Windsor Dr Cortland (44410) *(G-6975)*

Overbrook Center, Middleport *Also Called: Meigs County Care Center LLC (G-11148)*

Overdrive Inc (HQ).. 216 573-6886
　1 Overdrive Way Cleveland (44125) *(G-4711)*

Overfeld Erly Chldhood Program.. 937 339-5111
　172 S Ridge Ave Troy (45373) *(G-14151)*

Overhead Door Co of Dayton, Dayton *Also Called: Dayton Door Sales Inc (G-7280)*

ALPHABETIC SECTION

Overhead Door Co of Toledo, Toledo Also Called: Overhead Inc *(G-13951)*
Overhead Door Co- Cincinnati.. 513 346-4000
  9345 Princeton Glendale Rd West Chester (45011) *(G-14739)*
Overhead Door Corporation.. 330 674-7015
  One Door Dr Mount Hope (44660) *(G-11468)*
Overhead Doors, West Chester Also Called: Overhead Door Co- Cincinnati *(G-14739)*
Overhead Inc (PA)... 419 476-7811
  340 New Towne Square Dr Toledo (43612) *(G-13951)*
Overland Xpress LLC (PA)... 513 528-1158
  431 Ohio Pike Ste 311 Cincinnati (45255) *(G-3177)*
Overmyer Hall Associates.. 614 453-4400
  1600 W Lane Ave Ste 200 Columbus (43221) *(G-6494)*
Ovm Investment Group LLC.. 937 392-0145
  5280 Us Highway 62 And 68 Ripley (45167) *(G-12728)*
Owens & Minor Distribution Inc... 614 491-8465
  2820 Global Dr Groveport (43125) *(G-8994)*
Owens Corning Sales LLC (HQ).. 419 248-8000
  1 Owens Corning Pkwy Toledo (43659) *(G-13952)*
Owens Crning Inslting Systm (HQ)....................................... 419 248-8000
  1 Owens Corning Pkwy Toledo (43659) *(G-13953)*
Owens Intermodal LLC... 419 365-2704
  1415 Holland Rd Ste A Maumee (43537) *(G-10753)*
Owens-Corning Fiberglas Corp (HQ).................................... 419 248-8000
  1 Owens Corning Pkwy Toledo (43659) *(G-13954)*
Owners Management Company... 440 232-6093
  25400 Rockside Rd Bedford Heights (44146) *(G-1000)*
Owners Management Company... 440 439-3800
  5555 Powers Blvd Parma (44129) *(G-12259)*
Owv Exc, Shadyside Also Called: Virginia Ohio-West Excvtg Co *(G-12971)*
Oxcyon Inc.. 440 239-3345
  127 N Cleveland Massillon Rd Akron (44333) *(G-259)*
Oxford Harriman & Co AM LLC.. 216 755-7150
  3201 Enterprise Pkwy Ste 400 Beachwood (44122) *(G-824)*
OXFORD HEALTHCARE, Maineville Also Called: Prime Home Care LLC *(G-10230)*
Oxford Hospitality Group Inc.. 513 524-0114
  5056 College Corner Pike Oxford (45056) *(G-12214)*
Oxford Mining Company Inc... 330 878-5120
  7551 Reed Rd Nw Strasburg (44680) *(G-13404)*
Oxford Mining Company Inc... 740 588-0190
  1855 Kemper Ct Zanesville (43701) *(G-15824)*
Oxford Mining Company - KY LLC.. 740 622-6302
  544 Chestnut St Coshocton (43812) *(G-6996)*
Oxford Motel & LP.. 513 523-0000
  6 E Sycamore St Oxford (45056) *(G-12215)*
Oxford Physcl Thrapy Rhblttion.. 513 549-1927
  5988 S State Route 48 Maineville (45039) *(G-10229)*
Oxford Physcl Thrapy Rhblttion.. 513 229-7560
  7567 Central Parke Blvd Ste B Mason (45040) *(G-10587)*
Oxford Physical Therapy Inc... 513 745-9877
  9395 Kenwood Rd Ste 101 Blue Ash (45242) *(G-1218)*
Oxford Physical Therapy Inc... 513 469-1444
  11003 Montgomery Rd Cincinnati (45249) *(G-3178)*
Oxford Physical Therapy Inc... 513 229-7560
  7567 Central Parke Blvd Mason (45040) *(G-10588)*
OXFORD PHYSICAL THERAPY INC, Blue Ash Also Called: Oxford Physical Therapy Inc *(G-1218)*
OXFORD PHYSICAL THERAPY INC, Cincinnati Also Called: Oxford Physical Therapy Inc *(G-3178)*
OXFORD PHYSICAL THERAPY INC, Mason Also Called: Oxford Physical Therapy Inc *(G-10588)*
Oxymed Inc (PA)... 513 705-4250
  4765 Emerald Way Middletown (45044) *(G-11178)*
Ozanne Construction Co Inc.. 216 696-2876
  1635 E 25th St Cleveland (44114) *(G-4712)*
P & D Transportation Inc (PA)... 740 454-1221
  1705 Moxahala Ave Zanesville (43701) *(G-15825)*
P & M Exhaust Systems Whse Inc....................................... 513 825-2660
  11843 Kemper Springs Dr Cincinnati (45240) *(G-3179)*
P & R Communications Svc Inc (PA)................................... 937 512-8100
  731 E 1st St Dayton (45402) *(G-7543)*
P & S Bakery Inc.. 330 707-4141
  2720 Intertech Dr Youngstown (44509) *(G-15687)*

P A I, Cleveland Also Called: Delta Corporate Holdings LLC *(G-4161)*
P B S Animal Health, Massillon Also Called: Robert J Matthews Company *(G-10664)*
P C G Computers, Cleveland Also Called: P C Guru Inc *(G-4713)*
P C Guru Inc... 216 292-4878
  23250 Chagrin Blvd Ste 200 Cleveland (44122) *(G-4713)*
P C Vpa.. 513 841-0777
  4623 Wesley Ave Ste P Cincinnati (45212) *(G-3180)*
P C Vpa.. 440 826-0500
  16600 W Sprague Rd Ste 80 Cleveland (44130) *(G-4714)*
P C Vpa.. 614 840-1688
  355 E Campus View Blvd Ste 180 Columbus (43235) *(G-6495)*
P D I, Springboro Also Called: Pdi Communication Systems Inc *(G-13206)*
P Dakota Inc (PA)... 833 325-6827
  154 E Aurora Rd Northfield (44067) *(G-11963)*
P E I, Akron Also Called: Power Engineers Incorporated *(G-271)*
P E Systems Inc.. 937 258-0141
  5100 Springfield St Ste 510 Dayton (45431) *(G-7137)*
P I & I Motor Express Inc (PA).. 330 448-4035
  908 Broadway St Masury (44438) *(G-10679)*
P I C C A, Circleville Also Called: Pickaway Cnty Cmnty Action Org *(G-3716)*
P J & R J Connection Inc.. 513 398-2777
  754 Reading Rd Mason (45040) *(G-10589)*
P J McNerney & Associates, West Chester Also Called: McNerney & Associates LLC *(G-14824)*
P K Wadsworth Heating & Coolg... 440 248-4821
  34280 Solon Rd Frnt Solon (44139) *(G-13123)*
P N P Inc.. 330 386-1231
  48444 Bell School Rd East Liverpool (43920) *(G-8190)*
P P M C, Dublin Also Called: Physicians Professional Mgt *(G-8091)*
P R Machine Works Inc.. 419 529-5748
  1825 Nussbaum Pkwy Ontario (44906) *(G-12122)*
P T I, Walbridge Also Called: Professional Transportation *(G-14463)*
P T Svcs Rehabilitation Inc.. 419 455-8600
  27 St Lawrence Dr Ste 104 Tiffin (44883) *(G-13638)*
Pac Associates Inc... 330 869-9000
  3150 W Market St Fairlawn (44333) *(G-8493)*
Pac Manufacturing, Monroe Also Called: Pac Worldwide Corporation *(G-11347)*
Pac Worldwide Corporation.. 800 535-0039
  575 Gateway Blvd Monroe (45050) *(G-11347)*
Pac Worldwide Corporation.. 800 535-0039
  575 Gateway Blvd Monroe (45050) *(G-11348)*
Pac Worldwide Holding Company....................................... 513 217-3200
  3131 Cincinnati Dayton Rd Middletown (45044) *(G-11179)*
Pace America, Batavia Also Called: Trendco Supply Inc *(G-750)*
Pace Drivers Inc... 216 377-6831
  35104 Euclid Ave Ste 101 Willoughby (44094) *(G-15217)*
Pace Plus Corp... 419 754-1897
  7850 W Central Ave Toledo (43617) *(G-13955)*
Pacer, Dublin Also Called: Pacer Transport Inc *(G-8085)*
Pacer Stacktrain, Dublin Also Called: Stg Stacktrain LLC *(G-8131)*
Pacer Transport Inc... 614 923-1400
  5165 Emerald Pkwy Dublin (43017) *(G-8085)*
Pacific Heritg Inn Polaris LLC.. 614 880-9080
  9090 Lyra Dr Columbus (43240) *(G-5276)*
Pacific Life Insurance Company.. 513 241-5000
  9078 Union Centre Blvd West Chester (45069) *(G-14740)*
Pacific MGT Holdings LLC.. 440 324-3339
  250 Warden Ave Elyria (44035) *(G-8284)*
Pacific Valve, Piqua Also Called: Crane Pumps & Systems Inc *(G-12440)*
Packaging & Pads R Us LLC (PA)....................................... 419 499-2905
  12406 Us Highway 250 N Milan (44846) *(G-11210)*
PacLease, Cincinnati Also Called: Kenworth of Cincinnati Inc *(G-2937)*
Pactiv LLC.. 614 771-5400
  2120 Westbelt Dr Columbus (43228) *(G-6496)*
Pae & Associates Inc... 937 833-0013
  7925 Paragon Rd Dayton (45459) *(G-7544)*
Pag Mentor A1 Inc... 440 951-1040
  8599 Market St Mentor (44060) *(G-10982)*
Pagan, Fremont Also Called: Flex-Temp Employment Svcs Inc *(G-8677)*
Page Plus Cellular.. 800 550-2436
  1615 Timber Wolf Dr Holland (43528) *(G-9299)*

Pain Care Specialists LLC 614 865-2120
  6397 Emerald Pkwy Ste 100 Dublin (43016) *(G-8086)*

Pain Evaluation & MGT Ctr O, Dayton *Also Called: Pain Evlation MGT Ctr Ohio Inc (G-7545)*

Pain Evlation MGT Ctr Ohio Inc 937 439-4949
  1550 Yankee Park Pl Ste A Dayton (45458) *(G-7545)*

Pain Management, Sandusky *Also Called: Firelands Regional Health Sys (G-12894)*

Pain Management Associates Inc 937 252-2000
  1010 Woodman Dr Ste 100 Dayton (45432) *(G-7138)*

Pain Management Group LLC 419 462-4547
  269 Portland Way S Galion (44833) *(G-8750)*

Pain Spcialists Cincinnati LLC 513 922-2204
  3328 Westbourne Dr Cincinnati (45248) *(G-3181)*

Paint Creek Youth Center, Bainbridge *Also Called: Lighthouse Youth Services Inc (G-685)*

Paint Vly Alchol DRG Addction, Chillicothe *Also Called: Ohio Dept Mntal Hlth Addction (G-2080)*

Painting Company 614 873 1334
  6969 Industrial Pkwy Plain City (43064) *(G-12488)*

Pajka Eye Center Inc 419 228-7432
  855 W Market St Ste A Lima (45805) *(G-9946)*

Paklab, Batavia *Also Called: Universal Packg Systems Inc (G-751)*

Paklab, Cincinnati *Also Called: Universal Packg Systems Inc (G-3563)*

Paladina Health LLC 440 368-0900
  7695 Mentor Ave Mentor (44060) *(G-10983)*

Paladina Health LLC 440 368-0930
  5700 Lombardo Ctr Seven Hills (44131) *(G-12957)*

PALADINA HEALTH, LLC, Mentor *Also Called: Paladina Health LLC (G-10983)*

PALADINA HEALTH, LLC, Seven Hills *Also Called: Paladina Health LLC (G-12957)*

Palazzo Brothers Electric Inc 419 668-1100
  2811 State Route 18 Norwalk (44857) *(G-12020)*

Palestine Chld Relief Fund 330 678-2645
  1340 Morris Rd Kent (44240) *(G-9590)*

Palisdes Bsbal A Cal Ltd Prtnr 330 505-0000
  111 Eastwood Mall Blvd Niles (44446) *(G-11795)*

Pallet Distributors Inc (PA) 888 805-9670
  14701 Detroit Ave Ste 750 Lakewood (44107) *(G-9681)*

PALLIATIVE CARE OF OHIO, Newark *Also Called: Hospice of Central Ohio (G-11707)*

Pallotta Ford Inc 330 345-5051
  4141 Cleveland Rd Wooster (44691) *(G-15365)*

Pallotta Ford Lincoln Mercury, Wooster *Also Called: Pallotta Ford Inc (G-15365)*

Palmer Holland Inc 440 686-2300
  191 American Blvd Ste 300 Westlake (44145) *(G-15094)*

Palmer-Donavin Mfg Co 419 692-5000
  911 Spencerville Rd Delphos (45833) *(G-7843)*

Palmer-Donavin Mfg Co (PA) 800 652-1234
  3210 Centerpoint Dr Urbancrest (43123) *(G-14322)*

Pam Johnsonident 419 946-4551
  535 W Marion Rd Mount Gilead (43338) *(G-11464)*

Pam Specialty Hosp Dayton LLC 937 384-8300
  4000 Miamisburg Centerville Rd Miamisburg (45342) *(G-11080)*

Pam Specialty Hospital Dayton, Miamisburg *Also Called: Pam Specialty Hosp Dayton LLC (G-11080)*

PAm Transportation Svcs Inc 419 935-9501
  2501 Miller Rd Willard (44890) *(G-15172)*

Pamee LLC 216 232-9255
  18500 Lake Rd Rocky River (44116) *(G-12751)*

Panacea Products Corporation (PA) 614 850-7000
  2711 International St Columbus (43228) *(G-6497)*

Pandora Manufacturing Llc (PA) 419 384-3241
  157 W Main St Ottawa (45875) *(G-12191)*

Panelmatic Inc 330 782-8007
  1125 Meadowbrook Ave Youngstown (44512) *(G-15688)*

Panelmatic Youngstown, Youngstown *Also Called: Panelmatic Inc (G-15688)*

Panini North America Inc 937 291-2195
  1229 Byers Rd Miamisburg (45342) *(G-11081)*

Pannu Petroleum Inc 937 599-5454
  1504 S Main St Bellefontaine (43311) *(G-1035)*

Pantek Incorporated 216 344-1614
  4401 Rockside Rd Ste 205 Independence (44131) *(G-9465)*

Panther, Medina *Also Called: Panther II Transportation Inc (G-10872)*

Panther II Transportation Inc (DH) 800 685-0657
  84 Medina Rd Medina (44256) *(G-10872)*

Panther Premium Logistics Inc (HQ) 800 685-0657
  84 Medina Rd Medina (44256) *(G-10873)*

Pantherx Specialty LLC 855 726-8479
  6715 Tippecanoe Rd Ste C1 Canfield (44406) *(G-1637)*

Panzica, Cleveland *Also Called: Panzica Construction Co (G-4715)*

Panzica Construction Co 440 442-4300
  739 Beta Drive Mayfield Village Cleveland (44143) *(G-4715)*

Paper Mill and Converting, Circleville *Also Called: Sofidel America Corp (G-3724)*

Papyrus-Recycled Greetings Inc 773 348-6410
  1 American Blvd Westlake (44145) *(G-15095)*

Par International Inc 614 529-1300
  2160 Mcgaw Rd Obetz (43207) *(G-12082)*

Paradigm Industrial, Dayton *Also Called: Paradigm Industrial LLC (G-7546)*

Paradigm Industrial LLC 937 224-4415
  730 Lorain Ave Dayton (45410) *(G-7546)*

Paradise Hotels LLC 937 836-8339
  9325 N Main St Englewood (45415) *(G-8317)*

Paragon Consulting Inc 440 684-3101
  5900 Landerbrook Dr Ste 205 Cleveland (44124) *(G-4716)*

Paragon Obstetrics & Gyne Asso 330 665-8270
  1 Park West Blvd Ste 200 Akron (44320) *(G-260)*

Paragon Salons Inc (PA) 513 574-7610
  6775 Harrison Ave Cincinnati (45247) *(G-3182)*

Paragon Tec Inc 216 361-5555
  3740 Carnegie Ave Ste 302 Cleveland (44115) *(G-4717)*

Parallax Advanced RES Corp 937 775-2620
  3640 Colonel Glenn Hwy Dayton (45435) *(G-7139)*

Parallel Technologies Inc 614 798-9700
  4868 Blazer Pkwy Dublin (43017) *(G-8087)*

Paramont Care of Michigan 419 887-2728
  1901 Indian Wood Cir Maumee (43537) *(G-10754)*

Paramount Care Inc (DH) 419 887-2500
  1901 Indian Wood Cir Maumee (43537) *(G-10755)*

Paramount Distillers Inc 216 671-6300
  3116 Berea Rd Cleveland (44111) *(G-4718)*

Paramount Health Care, Maumee *Also Called: Paramount Care Inc (G-10755)*

Paramount Lawn Service Inc 513 984-5200
  8900 Glendale Milford Rd Unit A1 Loveland (45140) *(G-10157)*

Paramounts Kings Island 513 754-5700
  6300 Kings Island Dr Mason (45040) *(G-10590)*

Paramunt Spport Svc of St Clrs 740 526-0540
  252 W Main St Ste H Saint Clairsville (43950) *(G-12811)*

Paran Management Company Ltd 216 921-5663
  2720 Van Aken Blvd Ste 200 Cleveland (44120) *(G-4719)*

Paris Home Health Care LLC 888 416-9889
  4630 Richmond Rd Ste 270c Warrensville Heights (44128) *(G-14585)*

Park & Spruce Acquisitions LLC 614 227-6100
  150 E Broad St Columbus (43215) *(G-6498)*

Park Corporation (PA) 216 267-4870
  3555 Reserve Commons Dr Medina (44256) *(G-10874)*

Park Creek Rtirement Cmnty Inc 440 842-5100
  10064 N Church Dr Cleveland (44130) *(G-4720)*

Park Health Center, Saint Clairsville *Also Called: Belmont County Home (G-12775)*

Park Hospitality LLC 419 525-6000
  116 Park Ave W Mansfield (44902) *(G-10310)*

Park Hotels & Resorts Inc 513 421-9100
  35 W 5th St Cincinnati (45202) *(G-3183)*

Park Inn 419 241-3000
  101 N Summit St Toledo (43604) *(G-13956)*

Park Inn, Toledo *Also Called: Park Inn (G-13956)*

Park Lane Manor Akron Inc 330 724-3315
  744 Colette Dr Akron (44306) *(G-261)*

Park n Fly Llc 404 264-1000
  19000 Snow Rd Cleveland (44142) *(G-4721)*

Park National Bank (HQ) 740 349-8451
  50 N 3rd St Newark (43055) *(G-11738)*

Park National Bank, Newark *Also Called: Park National Corporation (G-11739)*

Park National Corporation (PA) 740 349-8451
  50 N 3rd St Newark (43055) *(G-11739)*

Park Northfield Associates LLC (HQ) 330 467-4101
  10705 Northfield Rd Northfield (44067) *(G-11964)*

ALPHABETIC SECTION — Patrician Skilled Nursing Ctr

Park Place, Cleveland *Also Called: Park Place Technologies LLC (G-4723)*

Park Place Nursery, Cleveland *Also Called: TLC Landscaping LLC (G-5021)*

Park Place Operations Inc 513 241-0415
250 W Court St Ste 200e Cincinnati (45202) *(G-3184)*

Park Place Operations Inc 513 381-2179
250 W Court St Ste 100e Cincinnati (45202) *(G-3185)*

Park Place Operations Inc 216 265-0500
18899 Snow Rd Cleveland (44142) *(G-4722)*

Park Place Operations Inc 614 224-3827
333 S Front St Columbus (43215) *(G-6499)*

Park Place Operations Inc (PA) 513 241-0415
250 W Court St Ste 200e Cincinnati (45202) *(G-3186)*

Park Place Technologies LLC 603 617-7123
5910 Landerbrook Dr Ste 300 Cleveland (44124) *(G-4723)*

Park Place Technologies LLC (PA) 877 778-8707
5910 Landerbrook Dr Ste 300 Cleveland (44124) *(G-4724)*

Park Place Technologies LLC 610 544-0571
5910 Landerbrook Dr Ste 300 Mayfield Heights (44124) *(G-10792)*

Park View Federal Savings Bank 440 248-7171
30000 Aurora Rd Solon (44139) *(G-13124)*

Park View Manor Inc (PA) 937 296-1550
425 Lauricella Ct Englewood (45322) *(G-8318)*

Park Village Health Care Ctr, Dover *Also Called: Dover Nursing Center Llc (G-7883)*

Park Vista Retirement Cmnty, Youngstown *Also Called: Ohio Living (G-15682)*

Park Vlg Assisted Living LLC 330 364-4436
1525 N Crater Ave Dover (44622) *(G-7899)*

Parker-Hannifin Corporation 614 279-7070
3885 Gateway Blvd Columbus (43228) *(G-6500)*

Parker-Hannifin Corporation 937 456-5571
725 N Beech St Eaton (45320) *(G-8219)*

Parker-Hannifin Corporation 440 366-5100
520 Ternes Ln Elyria (44035) *(G-8285)*

Parker-Hannifin Corporation 937 644-3915
14249 Industrial Pkwy Marysville (43040) *(G-10501)*

Parker-Hannifin Corporation 330 296-2871
1300 N Freedom St Ravenna (44266) *(G-12634)*

Parker-Hannifin Corporation 610 926-1115
30242 Lakeland Blvd Wickliffe (44092) *(G-15159)*

Parker-Hannifin Intl Corp (HQ) 216 896-3000
6035 Parkland Blvd Cleveland (44124) *(G-4725)*

Parking Sltions For Healthcare, Columbus *Also Called: Parking Solutions Inc (G-6501)*

Parking Solutions Inc (DH) 614 469-7000
353 W Nationwide Blvd Columbus (43215) *(G-6501)*

Parkins Incorporated 614 334-1800
3950 Lyman Dr Hilliard (43026) *(G-9226)*

Parkman Automotive LLC 234 223-2806
2625 Parkman Rd Nw Warren (44485) *(G-14545)*

Parks Maintenance, Dayton *Also Called: City of Kettering (G-7233)*

Parks Ob Gyn Assoc, Chillicothe *Also Called: Adena Health System (G-2046)*

Parks Recreation & Prpts Dept, Cleveland *Also Called: City of Cleveland (G-3979)*

Parkside Care Corporation 440 286-2273
11250 Thwing Rd Chardon (44024) *(G-2014)*

PARKSIDE MANOR, Maumee *Also Called: Consulate Healthcare Inc (G-10711)*

Parkside Nrsing Rehabilitation, Fairfield *Also Called: Embassy Healthcare Inc (G-8411)*

Parkside Nrsing Rhbltation Ctr, Fairfield *Also Called: Multicare Management Group Inc (G-8434)*

Parkside Village, Westerville *Also Called: Westerville Senior Dev Ltd (G-14954)*

PARKVIEW CARE CENTER, Fremont *Also Called: Caritas Inc (G-8668)*

Parkview Health Care, Sandusky *Also Called: United Church Homes Inc (G-12938)*

Parkview Manor Inc 419 243-5191
2051 Collingwood Blvd Toledo (43620) *(G-13957)*

Parkview Physicians Group, Bryan *Also Called: Midwest Cmnty Hlth Assoc Inc (G-1488)*

Parkway Operating Co LLC 513 530-1600
955 Garden Lake Pkwy Toledo (43614) *(G-13958)*

Parkway Pizza Incorporated 937 303-8800
968 Columbus Ave Marysville (43040) *(G-10502)*

Parkway Surgery Center Inc
2120 W Central Ave Toledo (43606) *(G-13959)*

Parkwood LLC 216 875-6500
1000 Lakeside Ave E Cleveland (44114) *(G-4726)*

Parkwood Corporation (PA) 216 875-6500
1000 Lakeside Ave E Cleveland (44114) *(G-4727)*

Parma Care Center Inc 216 661-6800
5553 Broadview Rd Cleveland (44134) *(G-4728)*

Parma Care Nrsing Rhblttion Ct, Cleveland *Also Called: Parma Care Center Inc (G-4728)*

Parma Community General Hosp (PA) 440 743-3000
7007 Powers Blvd Parma (44129) *(G-12260)*

Parma Medical Center, Brooklyn Heights *Also Called: Kaiser Foundation Hospitals (G-1424)*

Parma Medical Center, Parma *Also Called: Metrohealth System (G-12256)*

Parman Group Inc (PA) 513 673-0077
4501 Hilton Corporate Dr Columbus (43232) *(G-6502)*

Parole & Community Services, Columbus *Also Called: Ohio Dept Rhbilitation Corectn (G-6411)*

Parole & Community Services, Defiance *Also Called: Ohio Dept Rhbilitation Corectn (G-7759)*

Parta, Kent *Also Called: Portage Area Rgonal Trnsp Auth (G-9591)*

Partitions Plus Incorporated 419 422-2600
12517 County Road 99 Findlay (45840) *(G-8575)*

Partners Auto Group Bdford Inc 440 439-2323
22501 Rockside Rd Bedford (44146) *(G-980)*

Partners For Incentives, Cleveland *Also Called: Schaffer Partners Inc (G-4882)*

Partners In Prime (PA) 513 867-1998
230 Ludlow St Hamilton (45011) *(G-9071)*

Partners Mrion Care Rhblttion, Marion *Also Called: Sunbridge Marion Hlth Care LLC (G-10456)*

Partnership, Oberlin *Also Called: Partnership LLC (G-12075)*

Partnership LLC 440 471-8310
528 E Lorain St Oberlin (44074) *(G-12075)*

Parts Express International Inc (PA) 800 338-0531
725 Pleasant Valley Dr Springboro (45066) *(G-13205)*

Parts Pro Automotive Warehouse, Wickliffe *Also Called: GTM Service Inc (G-15151)*

Partssource Inc 330 562-9900
777 Lena Dr Aurora (44202) *(G-620)*

Pas Technologies Inc 937 840-1053
214 Hobart Dr Hillsboro (45133) *(G-9266)*

Pasco Inc 330 650-0613
5600 Hudson Industrial Pkwy Ste 200 Hudson (44236) *(G-9367)*

Passport, Cleveland *Also Called: Western Rsrve Area Agcy On Agi (G-5139)*

PASSPORT, Columbus *Also Called: Central Ohio Area Agcy On Agin (G-5535)*

Passport Health LLC 614 453-3920
5650 Blazer Pkwy Ste 174 Dublin (43017) *(G-8088)*

Pastoral Cnsling Svc Smmit CNT 330 996-4600
611 W Market St Akron (44303) *(G-262)*

Pat Young Service Co Inc (PA) 216 447-8550
6100 Hillcrest Dr Cleveland (44125) *(G-4729)*

Patel LLC 330 759-3180
4055 Belmont Ave Youngstown (44505) *(G-15689)*

Patented Acquisition Corp (PA) 937 353-2299
2490 Cross Pointe Dr Miamisburg (45342) *(G-11082)*

Pathlabs, Toledo *Also Called: Pathology Laboratories Inc (G-13960)*

Pathology Laboratories Inc (DH) 419 255-4600
1946 N 13th St Ste 301 Toledo (43604) *(G-13960)*

Pathway, Toledo *Also Called: Pathway Inc (G-13961)*

Pathway Inc 419 242-7304
505 Hamilton St Toledo (43604) *(G-13961)*

Pathway Caring For Children (PA) 330 493-0083
4895 Dressler Rd Nw Ste A Canton (44718) *(G-1827)*

Pathways Financial Cr Un Inc (PA) 614 416-7588
5665 N Hamilton Rd Columbus (43230) *(G-6503)*

Pathways of Central Ohio 740 345-6166
1627 Bryn Mawr Dr Newark (43055) *(G-11740)*

Patient Financial Services, Rocky River *Also Called: JP Recovery Services Inc (G-12745)*

Patientpint Hosp Solutions LLC 513 936-6800
8230 Montgomery Rd Ste 300 Cincinnati (45236) *(G-3187)*

Patientpoint LLC (PA) 513 936-6800
5901 E Galbraith Rd Ste R1000 Cincinnati (45236) *(G-3188)*

Patricia A Dickerson MD 937 436-1117
1299 E Alex Bell Rd Dayton (45459) *(G-7547)*

Patrician Inc 440 237-3104
1026 Pearl Rd Ste 5 Brunswick (44212) *(G-1466)*

Patrician Skilled Nursing Ctr, Brunswick *Also Called: Patrician Inc (G-1466)*

Patrick J Burke & Co 513 455-8200
  901 Adams Crossing Fl 1 Cincinnati (45202) *(G-3189)*

Patrick's, Leipsic *Also Called: Pretium Packaging LLC (G-9802)*

Patriot Homecare Inc 330 306-9651
  986 Tibbetts Wick Rd Girard (44420) *(G-8822)*

Patriot Protection Svcs LLC 614 379-1333
  433 Industry Dr Columbus (43204) *(G-6504)*

Patriot Software LLC 877 968-7147
  4883 Dressler Rd Nw Ste 301 Canton (44718) *(G-1828)*

Patrol Urban Services LLC 614 620-4672
  4563 E Walnut St Westerville (43081) *(G-15011)*

Patterson Dental 632, Middleburg Heights *Also Called: Patterson Dental Supply Inc (G-11120)*

Patterson Dental Supply Inc 440 891-1050
  6920 Engle Rd Ste Bb Middleburg Heights (44130) *(G-11120)*

Patterson Pools, Plain City *Also Called: Patterson Pools LLC (G-12489)*

Patterson Pools LLC 614 334-2629
  8155 Memorial Dr Plain City (43064) *(G-12489)*

Patterson Pope, Cincinnati *Also Called: Central Business Equipment Co (G-2333)*

Patterson-Erie Corporation 440 593-6161
  183 Gateway Ave Conneaut (44030) *(G-6944)*

Pattie Group Inc (PA) 440 338-1288
  15533 Chillicothe Rd Novelty (44072) *(G-12041)*

Pattie's Landscaping, Novelty *Also Called: Pattie Group Inc (G-12041)*

Patton Pest Control Co 440 338-3101
  15526 Chillicothe Rd Novelty (44072) *(G-12042)*

Paul A Ertel 216 696-8888
  1153 Main Ave Cleveland (44113) *(G-4730)*

Paul G. Toys, Plain City *Also Called: Regal-Elite Inc (G-12492)*

Paul Hrnchar Ford-Mercury Inc 330 533-3673
  366 W Main St Canfield (44406) *(G-1638)*

Paul Moss LLC 216 765-1580
  5895 Harper Rd Solon (44139) *(G-13125)*

Paul Peterson Safety Div Inc 614 486-4735
  950 Dublin Rd Columbus (43215) *(G-6505)*

Paulding Area Visiting Nurses, Paulding *Also Called: Community Hlth Prfssionals Inc (G-12281)*

Paulding County Hospital 419 399-4080
  1035 W Wayne St Paulding (45879) *(G-12285)*

Paulding County Hospital, Paulding *Also Called: Paulding County Hospital (G-12285)*

Paulding Exempted Vlg Schl Dst (PA) 419 594-3309
  405 N Water St Paulding (45879) *(G-12286)*

PAULDING PUTNAM ELECTRIC COOPE, Paulding *Also Called: Paulding-Putnam Electric Coop (G-12287)*

Paulding-Putnam Electric Coop (PA) 419 399-5015
  401 Mc Donald Pike Paulding (45879) *(G-12287)*

Paulo Products Company 440 942-0153
  4428 Hamann Pkwy Willoughby (44094) *(G-15218)*

Pavement Protectors Inc 614 875-9989
  2020 Longwood Ave Grove City (43123) *(G-8944)*

Pavement Prtners Cncinnati LLC 513 367-0250
  6000 Madden Way Harrison (45030) *(G-9113)*

Pavement Technology Inc 440 892-1895
  24144 Detroit Rd Westlake (44145) *(G-15096)*

PAVILION AT PIKETON, THE, Piketon *Also Called: Pavilion At Pkton For Nrsing R (G-12426)*

Pavilion At Pkton For Nrsing R 740 289-2394
  7143 Us Highway 23 Piketon (45661) *(G-12426)*

Payal Development LLC 937 429-2222
  3971 Colonel Glenn Hwy Beavercreek (45324) *(G-892)*

Paychex Inc 800 939-2462
  675 W Market St Lima (45801) *(G-9947)*

Paychex Advance LLC 216 831-8900
  23000 Millcreek Blvd Fl 2 Cleveland (44122) *(G-4731)*

Paycom Software Inc 888 678-0796
  255 E 5th St Ste 1420 Cincinnati (45202) *(G-3190)*

Paycor, Cincinnati *Also Called: Paycor Inc (G-3191)*

Paycor Inc (PA) 513 381-0505
  4811 Montgomery Rd Cincinnati (45212) *(G-3191)*

Payliance, Columbus *Also Called: Collections Acquisition Co LLC (G-5595)*

Payne Trucking Co 440 998-5538
  1635 E 6th St Ashtabula (44004) *(G-545)*

Payrix Solutions LLC (HQ) 718 506-9250
  8500 Governors Hill Dr Symmes Township (45249) *(G-13580)*

Pbsi, Cincinnati *Also Called: Positive Bus Solutions Inc (G-3222)*

PC Connection Inc 937 382-4800
  3336 Progress Way Bldg 11 Wilmington (45177) *(G-15263)*

PC Connection Sales Corp 937 382-4800
  2870 Old State Route 73 Ste 1 Wilmington (45177) *(G-15264)*

PC Recorder, Willoughby *Also Called: Main Sequence Technology Inc (G-15209)*

PCC, Columbus *Also Called: Producers Credit Corporation (G-6548)*

PCC Air Fils Llc-Cramics Group, Wickliffe *Also Called: PCC Airfoils LLC (G-15160)*

PCC Airfoils LLC 216 692-7900
  16601 Euclid Ave Cleveland (44112) *(G-4732)*

PCC Airfoils LLC 440 944-1880
  1470 E 289th St Wickliffe (44092) *(G-15160)*

PCC Metals Group, Warrensville Heights *Also Called: Special Metals Corporation (G-14588)*

PCI Services, Cincinnati *Also Called: Process Construction Inc (G-3238)*

Pcms, Blue Ash *Also Called: Pcms Datafit Inc (G-1219)*

Pcms Datafit Inc 513 587-3100
  4270 Glendale Milford Rd Blue Ash (45242) *(G-1219)*

Pcms International Inc 513 587-3100
  25 Merchant St Ste 135 Cincinnati (45246) *(G-3192)*

Pcrf, The, Kent *Also Called: Palestine Chld Relief Fund (G-9590)*

PDG, Bowling Green *Also Called: Poggemeyer Design Group Inc (G-1331)*

PDHC ADMINISTRATIVE OFFICE, Columbus *Also Called: Pregnancy Decision Health Ctr (G-6541)*

Pdi Communication Systems Inc (PA) 937 743-6010
  40 Greenwood Ln Springboro (45066) *(G-13206)*

Pdk Construction Inc 740 992-6451
  34070 Crew Rd Pomeroy (45769) *(G-12514)*

Pdmi 330 757-0724
  8530 Crossroad Dr Youngstown (44514) *(G-15690)*

Pdsi, Groveport *Also Called: Pinnacle Data Systems Inc (G-8995)*

Pe, Westlake *Also Called: North Bay Construction Inc (G-15085)*

Peabody Coal Company 740 450-2420
  2810 East Pike Apt 3 Zanesville (43701) *(G-15826)*

Peabody Landscape Cnstr Inc 614 488-2877
  2253 Dublin Rd Columbus (43228) *(G-6506)*

Peabody Landscape Group, Columbus *Also Called: Peabody Landscape Cnstr Inc (G-6506)*

Peace Foundation, Medina *Also Called: Intervention For Peace Inc (G-10848)*

Peacock Hotels LLC 330 725-1395
  5021 Eastpointe Dr Medina (44256) *(G-10875)*

Peak Nano, Cleveland *Also Called: Peak Nanosystems LLC (G-4733)*

Peak Nanosystems LLC 216 264-4818
  7700 Hub Pkwy Ste 8 Cleveland (44125) *(G-4733)*

Peak Performance Solutions Inc 614 344-4640
  10639 Welch Rd Orient (43146) *(G-12153)*

Pearl Interactive Network Inc 614 556-4470
  1103 Schrock Rd Ste 109 Columbus (43229) *(G-6507)*

Pearl Leasing Co LLC 513 530-1600
  6455 Pearl Rd Parma (44130) *(G-12261)*

Pease Bell Cpas LLC (PA) 216 348-9600
  1422 Euclid Ave Ste 400 Cleveland (44115) *(G-4734)*

Pebble Creek, Akron *Also Called: Nightingale Holdings LLC (G-243)*

Pebble Creek Golf Course, Cincinnati *Also Called: M T Golf Course Managment Inc (G-2998)*

Peck Distributors Inc 216 587-6814
  17000 Rockside Rd Maple Heights (44137) *(G-10343)*

Peck Food Service, Maple Heights *Also Called: Peck Distributors Inc (G-10343)*

Peck Hannaford Briggs Service, Cincinnati *Also Called: Peck-Hannaford Briggs Svc Corp (G-3193)*

Peck-Hannaford Briggs Svc Corp 513 681-1200
  4673 Spring Grove Ave Cincinnati (45232) *(G-3193)*

Pedco E & A Services Inc 513 782-4920
  10300 Alliance Rd Blue Ash (45242) *(G-1220)*

Pedersen Insulation Company 614 471-3788
  2901 Johnstown Rd Columbus (43219) *(G-6508)*

Pedianet, Dayton *Also Called: Home Care Network Inc (G-7134)*

Pediatric Adlscent Mdicine Inc 614 326-1600
  5072 Reed Rd Columbus (43220) *(G-6509)*

Pediatric Assoc Youngstown 330 965-7454
  4308 Belmont Ave Ste 1 Youngstown (44505) *(G-15691)*

ALPHABETIC SECTION — Perk Company of Ohio, Inc.

Pediatric Associates, Youngstown *Also Called: Pediatric Assoc Youngstown (G-15691)*

Pediatric Associates Inc (PA)... 614 501-7337
  1021 Country Club Rd Unit A Columbus (43213) *(G-6510)*

Pediatric Ophthlmlogy Assoc In... 614 224-6222
  555 S 18th St Ste 4c Columbus (43205) *(G-6511)*

Pediatric Physicians of Newark, Dublin *Also Called: American Hlth Netwrk Ohio LLC (G-7934)*

Pediatric Physicians of Newark, Newark *Also Called: American Hlth Netwrk Ohio LLC (G-11686)*

Pediatric Services Inc (PA).. 440 845-1500
  6707 Powers Blvd Ste 203 Cleveland (44129) *(G-4735)*

PEEBLES FAMILY HEALTH & DENTAL, Loveland *Also Called: Healthsource of Ohio Inc (G-10141)*

Peerless Pump Clveland Svc Ctr, Cleveland *Also Called: Wm Plotz Machine and Forge Co (G-5156)*

Peerless Technologies Corp... 937 490-5000
  2300 National Rd Beavercreek Township (45324) *(G-946)*

Pegasus Technical Services Inc... 513 793-0094
  46 E Hollister St Cincinnati (45219) *(G-3194)*

Peitro Properties Ltd Partnr... 216 328-7777
  6191 Quarry Ln Cleveland (44131) *(G-4736)*

Pel LLC.. 216 267-5775
  4666 Manufacturing Ave Cleveland (44135) *(G-4737)*

Pella Window & Door, Cleveland *Also Called: Gunton Corporation (G-4342)*

Pembroke Pl Sklled Nrsing Rhbl, Columbus *Also Called: Vrable IV Inc (G-6860)*

Pemco North Canton Division, North Canton *Also Called: Powell Electrical Systems Inc (G-11853)*

Penelec, Akron *Also Called: Pennsylvania Electric Company (G-263)*

Penn National Gaming Inc.. 614 308-3333
  200 Georgesville Rd Columbus (43228) *(G-6512)*

Penn National Holding Company... 419 661-5200
  1968 Miami St Toledo (43605) *(G-13962)*

PENN NATIONAL HOLDING COMPANY, Toledo *Also Called: Penn National Holding Company (G-13962)*

Penn Ohio Electrical Contrs, Masury *Also Called: Penn-Ohio Electrical Company (G-10680)*

Penn Power, Akron *Also Called: Pennsylvania Power Company (G-264)*

Penn Tool, Youngstown *Also Called: Pennsylvania Tl Sls & Svc Inc (G-15692)*

Penn-Ohio Electrical Company.. 330 448-1234
  1370 Sharon Hogue Rd Masury (44438) *(G-10680)*

Penney Opco LLC... 614 863-7043
  5555 Scarborough Blvd Unit 1 Columbus (43232) *(G-6513)*

Pennsylvania Electric Company (HQ).. 800 545-7741
  2800 Pottsville Pike Akron (44308) *(G-263)*

Pennsylvania Power Company (DH).. 800 720-3600
  76 S Main St Bsmt Akron (44308) *(G-264)*

Pennsylvania Steel Co Ohio, Cleveland *Also Called: Pennsylvania Steel Company Inc (G-4738)*

Pennsylvania Steel Company Inc.. 330 823-7383
  432 Keystone St Alliance (44601) *(G-395)*

Pennsylvania Steel Company Inc.. 440 243-9800
  4521 Willow Pkwy Cleveland (44125) *(G-4738)*

Pennsylvania Tl Sls & Svc Inc (PA)... 330 758-0845
  625 Bev Rd Youngstown (44512) *(G-15692)*

Pension Associates Inc.. 614 249-7111
  1 W Nationwide Blvd Ste 100 Columbus (43215) *(G-6514)*

Pension Corporation America.. 513 281-3366
  2133 Luray Ave Cincinnati (45206) *(G-3195)*

Penske Logistics, Beachwood *Also Called: Penske Logistics LLC (G-825)*

Penske Logistics LLC... 216 765-5475
  3000 Auburn Dr Ste 100 Beachwood (44122) *(G-825)*

Pentaflex Inc.. 937 325-5551
  4981 Gateway Blvd Springfield (45502) *(G-13281)*

People Developed Systems Inc.. 330 479-7823
  4914 Hills And Dales Rd Nw Canton (44708) *(G-1829)*

Peoples Bancorp Inc (PA).. 740 373-3155
  138 Putnam St Marietta (45750) *(G-10396)*

Peoples Bank (HQ)... 740 373-3155
  138 Putnam St Marietta (45750) *(G-10397)*

Peoples Bank.. 740 354-3177
  503 Chillicothe St Portsmouth (45662) *(G-12564)*

Peoples Cartage Inc... 330 833-8571
  8045 Navarre Rd Sw Massillon (44648) *(G-10661)*

Peoples Community Bancorp Inc (PA).. 513 870-3530
  6100 W Chester Rd West Chester (45069) *(G-14741)*

Peoples Hospital, Ashland *Also Called: Samaritan Regional Health Sys (G-510)*

Peoples Nat Bnk of New Lxngton (HQ)... 740 342-5111
  110 N Main St New Lexington (43764) *(G-11630)*

Peoples National Bank, New Lexington *Also Called: Peoples Nat Bnk of New Lxngton (G-11630)*

Peoples Savings and Loan Co (PA).. 419 562-6896
  300 S Walnut St Bucyrus (44820) *(G-1516)*

Peoplfrst Hmcare Hspice Ohio L (DH).. 937 433-2400
  7887 Washington Village Dr Ste 135 Dayton (45459) *(G-7548)*

Pep, Cincinnati *Also Called: Promotion Exction Partners LLC (G-3253)*

Pep Boys, Columbus *Also Called: Pep Boys - Mnny Moe Jack Del L (G-6515)*

Pep Boys - Mnny Moe Jack Del L.. 614 864-2092
  2830 S Hamilton Rd Columbus (43232) *(G-6515)*

Pepco, Akron *Also Called: Professional Electric Pdts Co (G-272)*

Pepco, Eastlake *Also Called: Professional Electric Products Co Inc (G-8207)*

Pepco, Elyria *Also Called: Professional Electric Pdts Co (G-8288)*

Pepco, Toledo *Also Called: Professional Electric Pdts Co (G-13967)*

Pepper Cnstr Co Ohio LLC... 513 563-7700
  4350 Glendale Milford Rd Ste 160 Blue Ash (45242) *(G-1221)*

Pepper Pike Club Company Inc.. 216 831-9400
  2800 Som Center Rd Cleveland (44124) *(G-4739)*

PEPPER PIKE GOLF CLUB, Cleveland *Also Called: Pepper Pike Club Company Inc (G-4739)*

Pepperl + Fuchs Inc (DH).. 330 425-3555
  1600 Enterprise Pkwy Twinsburg (44087) *(G-14210)*

Pepperl+fuchs Americas Inc... 330 425-3555
  1600 Enterprise Pkwy Twinsburg (44087) *(G-14211)*

Pepperl+fuchs Mfg Inc.. 330 425-3555
  1600 Enterprise Pkwy Twinsburg (44087) *(G-14212)*

Pepsi-Cola, Athens *Also Called: G & J Pepsi-Cola Bottlers Inc (G-568)*

Pepsi-Cola, Dayton *Also Called: Pepsi-Cola Metro Btlg Co Inc (G-7549)*

Pepsi-Cola, Twinsburg *Also Called: Pepsi-Cola Metro Btlg Co Inc (G-14213)*

Pepsi-Cola Metro Btlg Co Inc... 937 461-4664
  526 Milburn Ave Dayton (45404) *(G-7549)*

Pepsi-Cola Metro Btlg Co Inc... 330 425-8236
  1999 Enterprise Pkwy Twinsburg (44087) *(G-14213)*

Pepsico, Franklin Furnace *Also Called: G & J Pepsi-Cola Bottlers Inc (G-8654)*

Pepsico, Zanesville *Also Called: G & J Pepsi-Cola Bottlers Inc (G-15788)*

Peq Services + Solutions Inc (HQ).. 937 610-4800
  1 Prestige Pl Ste 900 Miamisburg (45342) *(G-11083)*

Perduco Group Inc... 937 401-0268
  2647 Commons Blvd Beavercreek (45431) *(G-893)*

Peregrine Health Services Inc... 330 823-9005
  2040 Mccrea St Alliance (44601) *(G-396)*

Perfect Cut-Off Inc.. 440 943-0000
  29201 Anderson Rd Wickliffe (44092) *(G-15161)*

Perfect Power Wash... 330 697-0131
  3443 Summit Rd Norton (44203) *(G-11997)*

Perfection Group Inc (PA).. 513 772-7545
  2649 Commerce Blvd Cincinnati (45241) *(G-3196)*

Perfection Services Inc.. 513 772-7545
  2649 Commerce Blvd Cincinnati (45241) *(G-3197)*

Performance Health, Avon Lake *Also Called: Phoenix Administrators LLC (G-683)*

Performance Site Company.. 614 445-7161
  2323 Performance Way Columbus (43207) *(G-6516)*

Performance Technologies LLC... 330 875-1216
  3690 Tulane Ave Louisville (44641) *(G-10119)*

Performnce Fodservice - Presto, Monroe *Also Called: Ohio Pizza Products LLC (G-11346)*

Peri Natal Partners LLC... 937 208-6970
  7707 Paragon Rd Ste 103 Dayton (45459) *(G-7550)*

Perinatal Partners, Dayton *Also Called: Primary Care Ntwrk Prmier Hlth (G-7562)*

Periodontal Associates Inc.. 440 461-3400
  29001 Cedar Rd Ste 450 Cleveland (44124) *(G-4740)*

Perishable Shipg Solutions LLC... 724 944-9024
  1701 Henn Pkwy Sw Warren (44481) *(G-14546)*

Perk Company Inc (PA).. 216 391-1444
  3740 Carnegie Ave Ste 301 Bldg A Cleveland (44115) *(G-4741)*

Perk Company of Ohio, Inc., Cleveland *Also Called: Perk Company Inc (G-4741)*

Perkins Family Restaurant   ALPHABETIC SECTION

Perkins Family Restaurant, Alliance *Also Called: Dino Persichetti* *(G-381)*

Permanent Gen Asrn Corp Ohio.. 216 986-3000
  9700 Rockside Rd Cleveland (44125) *(G-4742)*

Permedion Inc.. 614 895-9900
  5475 Rings Rd Ste 200 Dublin (43017) *(G-8089)*

Permian Oil & Gas Division, Newark *Also Called: National Gas & Oil Corporation* *(G-11733)*

Perram Electric Inc.. 330 239-2661
  6882 Ridge Rd Wadsworth (44281) *(G-14447)*

Perrin Asphalt Co Inc... 330 253-1020
  525 Dan St Akron (44310) *(G-265)*

Perry County Engineer, New Lexington *Also Called: County of Perry* *(G-11623)*

Perry County Fmly Practice Inc..................................... 740 342-3435
  1625 Airport Rd New Lexington (43764) *(G-11631)*

Perry County Home, New Lexington *Also Called: County of Perry* *(G-11621)*

Perry County Senior Center, New Lexington *Also Called: County of Perry* *(G-11622)*

Perry Fitness Center... 440 259-9499
  1 Success Blvd Perry (44081) *(G-12311)*

Perry Interiors Inc.. 513 761-9333
  4054 Clough Woods Dr Batavia (45103) *(G-745)*

Perry Pro Tech Inc (PA)... 419 228-1360
  265 Commerce Pkwy Lima (45804) *(G-9948)*

Perrysburg Board of Education..................................... 419 874-3127
  25715 Fort Meigs Rd Perrysburg (43551) *(G-12362)*

Perrysburg Bus Garage, Perrysburg *Also Called: Perrysburg Board of Education* *(G-12362)*

Persistent Systems Inc.. 614 763-6500
  5080 Tuttle Crossing Blvd Ste 150 Dublin (43016) *(G-8090)*

Person Centered Services Inc...................................... 419 782-7274
  197 A Park Island Ave Defiance (43512) *(G-7760)*

Person Centered Services Inc...................................... 419 874-4900
  741 Commerce Dr Perrysburg (43551) *(G-12363)*

Personacare of Ohio Inc.. 440 357-1311
  70 Normandy Dr Painesville (44077) *(G-12241)*

Personal & Family Counseling, New Philadelphia *Also Called: Personal Fmly Cnsling Svcs of* *(G-11661)*

Personal Fmly Cnsling Svcs of...................................... 330 343-8171
  1433 5th St Nw New Philadelphia (44663) *(G-11661)*

Personal Touch HM Care IPA Inc................................... 513 984-9600
  8260 Northcreek Dr Ste 140 Cincinnati (45236) *(G-3198)*

Personal Touch HM Care IPA Inc................................... 614 227-6952
  454 E Main St Ste 227 Columbus (43215) *(G-6517)*

Personal Touch HM Care IPA Inc................................... 513 868-2272
  7924 Jessies Way Ste C Hamilton (45011) *(G-9072)*

Personal Touch HM Care IPA Inc................................... 330 263-1112
  543 Riffel Rd Ste F Wooster (44691) *(G-15366)*

Personalized Data Corporation..................................... 216 289-2200
  26155 Euclid Ave Uppr Cleveland (44132) *(G-4743)*

Personalized Data Entry & Word, Cleveland *Also Called: Personalized Data Corporation* *(G-4743)*

Perspectus Architecture LLC (PA)................................. 216 752-1800
  1300 E 9th St Ste 910 Cleveland (44114) *(G-4744)*

Pete Baur Buick GMC Inc (PA)..................................... 440 238-5600
  14000 Pearl Rd Cleveland (44136) *(G-4745)*

Peter A Wimberg Company Inc.................................... 513 271-2332
  1354 Us Route 50 Milford (45150) *(G-11248)*

Peterbilt of Cincinnati.. 513 772-1740
  2550 Annuity Dr Cincinnati (45241) *(G-3199)*

Petermann, Cincinnati *Also Called: Petermann Ltd* *(G-3200)*

Petermann Ltd... 330 773-4222
  860 S Arlington St Akron (44306) *(G-266)*

Petermann Ltd (HQ)... 513 351-7383
  1861 Section Rd Cincinnati (45237) *(G-3200)*

Petermann Ltd... 740 967-7533
  6097 Johnstown Utica Rd Johnstown (43031) *(G-9548)*

Petermann Ltd... 513 539-0324
  505 Yankee Rd Monroe (45050) *(G-11349)*

Petermann Northeast LLC... 513 351-7383
  8041 Hosbrook Rd Ste 330 Cincinnati (45236) *(G-3201)*

Peters Main Street Photography (PA)............................ 740 852-2731
  314 N Main St London (43140) *(G-10049)*

Peterson Construction Company................................... 419 941-2233
  18817 State Route 501 Wapakoneta (45895) *(G-14489)*

Petland Inc (PA).. 740 775-2464
  250 Riverside St Chillicothe (45601) *(G-2082)*

Petro Cells, Cincinnati *Also Called: Petro Environmental Tech* *(G-3202)*

Petro Environmental Tech (PA).................................... 513 489-6789
  8160 Corporate Park Dr Ste 300 Cincinnati (45242) *(G-3202)*

Petro-Com Corp (PA)... 440 327-6900
  32523 Lorain Rd North Ridgeville (44039) *(G-11933)*

Petrolube, Napoleon *Also Called: Trep Ltd* *(G-11533)*

Petsmart, Columbus *Also Called: Petsmart LLC* *(G-6518)*

Petsmart, Mason *Also Called: Petsmart Inc* *(G-10591)*

Petsmart Inc.. 513 336-0365
  8175 Arbor Square Dr Mason (45040) *(G-10591)*

Petsmart LLC... 614 418-9389
  3713 Easton Market Columbus (43219) *(G-6518)*

Pfb Manufacturing LLC... 513 836-3232
  2725 Henkle Dr Lebanon (45036) *(G-9782)*

Pffa Acquisition LLC (PA).. 859 835-6088
  1216 Central Pkwy Cincinnati (45202) *(G-3203)*

Pfg Ventures LP (PA)... 216 520-8400
  8800 E Pleasant Valley Rd Ste 1 Independence (44131) *(G-9466)*

Pfp Columbus LLC... 614 456-0123
  1500 Polaris Pkwy Ste 2034 Columbus (43240) *(G-5277)*

Pfp Holdings LLC... 419 647-4191
  220 S Elizabeth St Spencerville (45887) *(G-13190)*

Pfsc Inc.. 513 221-5080
  2813 Gilbert Ave Cincinnati (45206) *(G-3204)*

Pg.. 513 698-6901
  3900 Aero Dr Mason (45040) *(G-10592)*

Pg One Commerce, Cincinnati *Also Called: Saatchi & Saatchi X Inc* *(G-3336)*

Pgn Op Summit LLC... 614 252-4987
  935 N Cassady Ave Columbus (43219) *(G-6519)*

PH B, Cincinnati *Also Called: The Peck-Hannaford Briggs Co* *(G-3468)*

PH Fairborn Ht Owner 2800 LLC................................... 937 426-7800
  2800 Presidential Dr Beavercreek (45324) *(G-894)*

Phantom Fireworks Inc... 330 746-1064
  555 Mrtin Lther King Blvd Youngstown (44502) *(G-15693)*

Phantom Technical Services Inc................................... 614 868-9920
  111 Outerbelt St Columbus (43213) *(G-6520)*

Pharmacy Benefit Direct, Youngstown *Also Called: Pharmacy Data Management Inc* *(G-15694)*

Pharmacy Consultants LLC (DH).................................. 864 578-8788
  201 E 4th St Ste 900 Cincinnati (45202) *(G-3205)*

Pharmacy Data Management...................................... 330 757-0724
  8530 Crossroad Dr Poland (44514) *(G-12506)*

Pharmacy Data Management Inc................................. 330 757-1500
  1170 E Western Reserve Rd Youngstown (44514) *(G-15694)*

Pharmacy-Lite Packaging, Elyria *Also Called: Pacific MGT Holdings LLC* *(G-8284)*

Pharmed Corporation... 440 250-5400
  24340 Sperry Dr Westlake (44145) *(G-15097)*

Pharmed Institutional Pharmacy, Westlake *Also Called: Pharmed Corporation* *(G-15097)*

Pharmscript LLC.. 908 389-1818
  1685 Westbelt Dr Columbus (43228) *(G-6521)*

PHD Manufacturing Inc... 330 482-9256
  44018 Columbiana Waterford Rd Columbiana (44408) *(G-5238)*

Phil Giessler.. 614 888-0307
  882 High St Ste A Worthington (43085) *(G-15446)*

Philio Inc.. 419 531-5544
  111 S Byrne Rd Toledo (43615) *(G-13963)*

Philips Healthcare, Cleveland *Also Called: Philips Med Systems Clvland In* *(G-4746)*

Philips Healthcare Cleveland....................................... 440 483-3235
  595 Miner Rd Highland Heights (44143) *(G-9169)*

Philips Med Systems Clvland In (HQ)............................ 440 483-3000
  595 Miner Rd Cleveland (44143) *(G-4746)*

Phillips Edison - ARC Shopping, Cincinnati *Also Called: Phillips Edison Institutional* *(G-3207)*

Phillips Edison & Company, Cincinnati *Also Called: Phillips Edison & Company LLC* *(G-3206)*

Phillips Edison & Company LLC (HQ)............................. 513 554-1110
  11501 Northlake Dr Fl 1 Cincinnati (45249) *(G-3206)*

Phillips Edison Institutional... 513 554-1110
  11501 Northlake Dr Cincinnati (45249) *(G-3207)*

Phillips Hthcare LLC DBA Cring.................................... 330 531-6110
  1577 Woodland St Ne Warren (44483) *(G-14547)*

ALPHABETIC SECTION — Piqua Materials Inc

Phillips Mfg and Tower Co (PA) 419 347-1720
5578 State Route 61 N Shelby (44875) *(G-13008)*

Phillips Supply Company (PA) 513 579-1762
1230 Findlay Street (1 Crosley Field Lane) Cincinnati (45214) *(G-3208)*

Philo Band Boosters 740 221-3023
1359 Wheeling Ave Zanesville (43701) *(G-15827)*

Phinney Industrial Roofing 614 308-9000
700 Hadley Dr Columbus (43228) *(G-6522)*

Phoenix Administrators LLC 440 628-4235
33479 Lake Rd Avon Lake (44012) *(G-683)*

Phoenix Cargo LLC 614 407-3322
1679 Gateway Cir Grove City (43123) *(G-8945)*

Phoenix Corporation 513 727-4763
1401 Made Dr Middletown (45044) *(G-11180)*

Phoenix Group Holding Co 937 704-9850
509 Windsor Park Dr Dayton (45459) *(G-7551)*

Phoenix Masonry Ltd 740 344-5787
645 W Church St Newark (43055) *(G-11741)*

Phoenix Metals, Middletown *Also Called: Phoenix Corporation (G-11180)*

Phoenix Residential Ctrs Inc 440 887-6097
6465 Pearl Rd Ste 1 Cleveland (44130) *(G-4747)*

Phoenix Technologies Intl LLC (HQ) 419 353-7738
1098 Fairview Ave Bowling Green (43402) *(G-1330)*

Phoenix Technology Services 740 325-1138
4 Commerce Pkwy Bellaire (43906) *(G-1015)*

Photo Art, Cincinnati *Also Called: Photo-Type Engraving Company (G-3209)*

Photo-Type Engraving Company 513 281-0999
2150 Florence Ave Cincinnati (45206) *(G-3209)*

Photo-Type Engraving Company 513 475-5638
2141 Gilbert Ave Cincinnati (45206) *(G-3210)*

Physical Therapy Dept, Dennison *Also Called: Twin City Hospital (G-7860)*

Physicans Dlysis Cntr-Yngstown, Youngstown *Also Called: Fersenius Medical Center (G-15611)*

Physicans Srgons For Women Inc 937 323-7340
1821 E High St Springfield (45505) *(G-13282)*

Physician Staffing Inc 440 542-5000
30575 Bainbridge Rd Ste 200 Cleveland (44139) *(G-4748)*

Physicians Ambulance Svc Inc (PA) 216 454-4911
6670 W Snowville Rd Ste 2 Brecksville (44141) *(G-1362)*

Physicians Care of Marietta (PA) 740 373-2519
800 Pike St Ste 2 Marietta (45750) *(G-10398)*

Physicians Care of Marrita, Marietta *Also Called: Physicians Care of Marietta (G-10398)*

Physicians Medical Trnspt Team, Brecksville *Also Called: Physicians Ambulance Svc Inc (G-1362)*

Physicians Professional Mgt 207 782-7494
5475 Rings Rd Dublin (43017) *(G-8091)*

Physicians Urology Centre, Akron *Also Called: Center For Urologic Health LLC (G-85)*

Physna Inc 844 474-9762
250 West St Ste 100 Columbus (43215) *(G-6523)*

Piada Group LLC 614 397-1339
1423 Goodale Blvd Columbus (43212) *(G-6524)*

Picasso For Nail LLC 440 308-4470
35494 Spatterdock Ln Solon (44139) *(G-13126)*

Pick Pull Auto Dismantling Inc 614 497-8858
2716 Groveport Rd Columbus (43207) *(G-6525)*

Pickaway Area Rcovery Svcs Inc 740 477-1745
110 Highland Ave Circleville (43113) *(G-3715)*

Pickaway Cnty Cmnty Action Org (PA) 740 477-1655
469 E Ohio St Circleville (43113) *(G-3716)*

Pickaway Growers LLC 614 344-4956
12061 Federal Rd Orient (43146) *(G-12154)*

PICKAWAY MANOR CARE CENTER, Columbus *Also Called: West Park Care Center LLC (G-6880)*

Pickaway Manor Inc 740 474-5400
391 Clark Dr Circleville (43113) *(G-3717)*

Pickerngton Area Cunseling Ctr, Lancaster *Also Called: New Hrzons Mntal Hlth Svcs Inc (G-9736)*

Pickrel Bros Inc 937 461-5960
901 S Perry St Dayton (45402) *(G-7552)*

Pickrel Brothers, Dayton *Also Called: Pickrel Bros Inc (G-7552)*

Pickrel Schaeffer Ebeling Lpa 937 223-1130
40 N Main St Ste 2700 Dayton (45423) *(G-7553)*

Picoma Industries Inc 740 432-2146
9208 Jeffrey Dr Cambridge (43725) *(G-1579)*

Piedmont Airlines Inc 330 499-3260
5400 Lauby Rd North Canton (44720) *(G-11851)*

Pike County 740 947-9339
502 Pike St Waverly (45690) *(G-14615)*

Pike County Recovery Council (PA) 740 835-8437
218 E North St Waverly (45690) *(G-14616)*

Pike Natural Gas Company 937 393-4602
144 Bowers Ave Hillsboro (45133) *(G-9267)*

Pikes Inc 440 275-2000
2900 Gh Dr # H Austinburg (44010) *(G-633)*

Piketon Nursing Center Inc 740 289-4074
300 Overlook Dr Piketon (45661) *(G-12427)*

Pillar of Fire 513 542-1212
6275 Collegevue Pl Cincinnati (45224) *(G-3211)*

Pilorusso Construction Div, Lowellville *Also Called: Lyco Corporation (G-10169)*

Pine Hills Golf Club Inc 330 225-4477
433 W 130th St Hinckley (44233) *(G-9271)*

Pine Lake Trout Club, Chagrin Falls *Also Called: M&C Hotel Interests Inc (G-1985)*

Pine Valley Care Center, Richfield *Also Called: Brecksville Leasing Co LLC (G-12689)*

Pine Valley Care Center, Richfield *Also Called: Communicare Health Svcs Inc (G-12692)*

Pines Alf Inc 330 856-4232
18144 Claridon Troy Rd Hiram (44234) *(G-9275)*

Pines Healthcare Center, The, Canton *Also Called: Communicare Health Svcs Inc (G-1719)*

Pines Manufacturing Inc (PA) 440 835-5553
29100 Lakeland Blvd Westlake (44145) *(G-15098)*

Pines Technology, Westlake *Also Called: Pines Manufacturing Inc (G-15098)*

Pinnacle Data Systems Inc 614 748-1150
6600 Port Rd Groveport (43125) *(G-8995)*

Pinnacle Paving & Sealing LLC 513 474-4900
793 Round Bottom Rd Milford (45150) *(G-11249)*

Pinnacle Realty Management Co 614 430-3678
402 E Wilson Bridge Rd Worthington (43085) *(G-15447)*

Pinnacle Trtmnt Ctrs Oh-I LLC 330 577-5881
6847 N Chestnut St Ravenna (44266) *(G-12635)*

Pinney Dock & Transport LLC 440 964-7186
1149 E 5th St Ashtabula (44004) *(G-546)*

Pioneer Athletics, Cleveland *Also Called: Pioneer Manufacturing Inc (G-4750)*

Pioneer Automotive Tech Inc (DH) 937 746-2293
10100 Innovation Dr Miamisburg (45342) *(G-11084)*

Pioneer Cldding Glzing Systems 216 816-4242
2550 Brookpark Rd Cleveland (44134) *(G-4749)*

Pioneer Cldding Glzing Systems (PA) 513 583-5925
4074 Bethany Rd Mason (45040) *(G-10593)*

Pioneer Group, Marietta *Also Called: Pioneer Pipe Inc (G-10399)*

Pioneer Manufacturing Inc (PA) 216 671-5500
4529 Industrial Pkwy Cleveland (44135) *(G-4750)*

Pioneer Pipe Inc 740 376-2400
2021 Hanna Rd Marietta (45750) *(G-10399)*

Pioneer Quick Lubes Inc 419 782-2213
1166 S Clinton St Defiance (43512) *(G-7761)*

Pioneer Rural Electric Coop (PA) 800 762-0997
344 W Us Route 36 Piqua (45356) *(G-12451)*

Pioneer Trails Inc 330 674-1234
7572 State Route 241 Millersburg (44654) *(G-11288)*

Pipe Products Inc 513 587-7532
5122 Rialto Rd West Chester (45069) *(G-14742)*

Pipe-Valves Inc 614 294-4971
1200 E 5th Ave Columbus (43219) *(G-6526)*

Pipeline Packaging Corporation (HQ) 440 349-3200
100 Executive Pkwy Hudson (44236) *(G-9368)*

Pipino, Youngstown *Also Called: Donald P Pipino Company Ltd (G-15601)*

Piqua Country Club Holding Co 937 773-7744
9812 Country Club Rd Piqua (45356) *(G-12452)*

Piqua Country Club Pool, Piqua *Also Called: Piqua Country Club Holding Co (G-12452)*

Piqua Family Practice 937 773-6314
110 N Main St Ste 350 Dayton (45402) *(G-7554)*

Piqua Materials Inc 937 773-4824
1750 W Statler Rd Piqua (45356) *(G-12453)*

Piqua Mineral Division — ALPHABETIC SECTION

Piqua Mineral Division, Piqua *Also Called: Piqua Materials Inc (G-12453)*

Piqua Steel Co (PA) 937 773-3632
4243 W Us Route 36 Piqua (45356) *(G-12454)*

Piqua Transfer & Storage Co 937 773-3743
9782 Looney Rd Piqua (45356) *(G-12455)*

Pirhl Contractors LLC 216 378-9690
800 W Saint Clair Ave # 4 Cleveland (44113) *(G-4751)*

Pitt-Ohio Express LLC 216 433-9000
5570 Chevrolet Blvd Cleveland (44130) *(G-4752)*

Pitt-Ohio Express LLC 614 801-1064
2101 Hardy Parkway St Grove City (43123) *(G-8946)*

Pitt-Ohio Express LLC 419 726-6523
5200 Stickney Ave Toledo (43612) *(G-13964)*

Pitt-Ohio Express LLC 513 860-3424
5000 Duff Dr West Chester (45246) *(G-14828)*

Pittsburgh & Conneaut Dock, Conneaut *Also Called: Bessemer and Lake Erie RR Co (G-6940)*

Pivotal HP Management, West Chester *Also Called: Mvah Management LLC (G-14735)*

Pivotek LLC 513 372-6205
910 Lila Ave Rear Milford (45150) *(G-11250)*

Pixel Technologies, Cincinnati *Also Called: Nor-Com LLC (G-3118)*

Pizzuti Inc (PA) 614 280-4000
29 W 3rd Ave Columbus (43201) *(G-6527)*

Pk Management LLC (PA) 216 472-1870
26301 Curtiss Wright Pkwy Ste 300 Cleveland (44143) *(G-4753)*

Plain City Molding, Plain City *Also Called: GK Packaging Inc (G-12478)*

Plain Dealer Federal Cr Un Inc 216 999-4270
5341 Pearl Rd Cleveland (44129) *(G-4754)*

Plane Detail LLC 614 734-1201
2720 S 3 Bs And K Rd Galena (43021) *(G-8739)*

Planes Companies, West Chester *Also Called: Planes Moving & Storage Inc (G-14743)*

Planes Moving & Storage Inc (PA) 513 759-6000
9823 Cincinnati Dayton Rd West Chester (45069) *(G-14743)*

Planes Mvg & Stor Co Columbus 614 777-9090
2000 Dividend Dr Columbus (43228) *(G-6528)*

Planet Aid Inc 440 542-1171
30901c Carter St Solon (44139) *(G-13127)*

Planet Healthcare LLC 888 845-2539
24651 Center Ridge Rd Ste 475 Westlake (44145) *(G-15099)*

Planned Parenthood Association (PA) 937 226-0780
224 N Wilkinson St Dayton (45402) *(G-7555)*

Planned Prenthood Greater Ohio (PA) 614 224-2235
206 E State St Columbus (43215) *(G-6529)*

Planned Prnthood of Grter Mami, Dayton *Also Called: Planned Parenthood Association (G-7555)*

Planned Prnthood Sthwest Ohio (PA) 513 721-7635
2314 Auburn Ave Cincinnati (45219) *(G-3212)*

Plante & Moran Pllc 614 849-3000
250 S High St Ste 100 Columbus (43215) *(G-6530)*

Plasco Safety Products, Gahanna *Also Called: Benchmark Industrial Inc (G-8711)*

Plasmacare Inc 614 231-5722
3840 E Main St Columbus (43213) *(G-6531)*

Plasti-Fab Eps PDT Solutions, Lebanon *Also Called: Pfb Manufacturing LLC (G-9782)*

Plastic Recycling Tech Inc (PA) 937 615-9286
9054 N County Road 25a Piqua (45356) *(G-12456)*

Plastic Recycling Tech Inc 419 238-9395
7600 Us Route 127 Van Wert (45891) *(G-14349)*

Plastic Safety Systems Inc 216 231-8590
2444 Baldwin Rd Cleveland (44104) *(G-4755)*

Plastic Srgery Inst Dayton Inc 937 886-2980
9985 Dayton Lebanon Pike Dayton (45458) *(G-7556)*

Plastic Technologies Inc (PA) 419 867-5400
1440 Timber Wolf Dr Holland (43528) *(G-9300)*

Plastics Family Holdings Inc 330 733-9595
4700 Hudson Dr Stow (44224) *(G-13385)*

PLASTICS FAMILY HOLDINGS INC, Stow *Also Called: Plastics Family Holdings Inc (G-13385)*

Plastics R Unique Inc 330 334-4820
330 Grandview Ave Wadsworth (44281) *(G-14448)*

Plastipak Packaging Inc 937 596-5166
300 Washington St Jackson Center (45334) *(G-9532)*

Plastipak Packaging Inc 330 725-0205
850 W Smith Rd Medina (44256) *(G-10876)*

Platform Cement Inc 440 602-9750
7503 Tyler Blvd Mentor (44060) *(G-10984)*

Platform Contracting, Mentor *Also Called: Platform Cement Inc (G-10984)*

Platinum Carriers LLC 877 318-9607
12325 Broadway Ave Garfield Heights (44125) *(G-8778)*

Platinum Couriers Inc 216 370-8972
4615 W Streetsboro Rd Richfield (44286) *(G-12706)*

Platinum Express Inc 937 235-9540
2549 Stanley Ave Dayton (45404) *(G-7557)*

Platinum Recovery LLC 740 373-8811
2019 State Route 821 Marietta (45750) *(G-10400)*

Platinum Restoration Inc 440 327-0699
104 Reaser Ct Elyria (44035) *(G-8286)*

Platinum Rstoration Contrs Inc 440 327-0699
104 Reaser Ct Elyria (44035) *(G-8287)*

Platinumtele Solutions LLC 216 609-5804
7415 Broadway Ave Cleveland (44105) *(G-4756)*

Play & Learn Express, Chillicothe *Also Called: Chillcth-Ross Child Care Ctr I (G-2054)*

Play & Learn School, Malta *Also Called: Community Action Prgram Corp O (G-10231)*

Playaway Products LLC 440 893-0808
31999 Aurora Rd Ste 1 Solon (44139) *(G-13128)*

PLAYHOUSE SQUARE, Cleveland *Also Called: Playhouse Square Foundation (G-4757)*

Playhouse Square Foundation (PA) 216 771-4444
1501 Euclid Ave Ste 200 Cleveland (44115) *(G-4757)*

Playhouse Square Foundation 216 615-7500
1260 Euclid Ave Cleveland (44115) *(G-4758)*

Playhouse Square Holdg Co LLC (PA) 216 771-4444
1501 Euclid Ave Ste 200 Cleveland (44115) *(G-4759)*

Playland Day Care Ltd 419 625-8200
314 Lucas St E Castalia (44824) *(G-1915)*

Plaza Inn Foods Inc 937 354-2181
491 S Main St Mount Victory (43340) *(G-11512)*

Plaza Inn Restaurant, Mount Victory *Also Called: Plaza Inn Foods Inc (G-11512)*

Plaza Properties Inc (PA) 614 237-3726
3016 Maryland Ave Columbus (43209) *(G-6532)*

Pleasant Hill Leasing LLC 740 289-2394
7143 Us Rte 23 S Piketon (45661) *(G-12428)*

Pleasant Hill Manor, Piketon *Also Called: Pleasant Hill Leasing LLC (G-12428)*

Pleasant Hl Otptent Thrapy Ctr, Piketon *Also Called: H C F Inc (G-12421)*

Pleasant Ridge Care Center, Cincinnati *Also Called: Pleasant Ridge Care Center Inc (G-3213)*

Pleasant Ridge Care Center Inc (PA) 513 631-1310
5501 Verulam Ave Cincinnati (45213) *(G-3213)*

Pleasant Valley Cnstr Co 330 239-0176
1093 Medina Rd Ste 100 Medina (44256) *(G-10877)*

Pleasant Valley Corporation 330 239-0176
1093 Medina Rd Ste 100 Medina (44256) *(G-10878)*

Pleasant View Health Care Ctr, Barberton *Also Called: Pleasant View Nursing Home Inc (G-703)*

Pleasant View N Retirement Ctr, Salem *Also Called: West Branch Nursing Home Ltd (G-12857)*

Pleasant View Nursing Home Inc 330 848-5028
220 3rd St Se Barberton (44203) *(G-702)*

Pleasant View Nursing Home Inc (PA) 330 745-6028
401 Snyder Ave Barberton (44203) *(G-703)*

Pleasantview Nursing Home, Cleveland *Also Called: Ridge-Pleasant Valley Inc (G-4840)*

Plebees, Zanesville *Also Called: Neighborhood Hospitality Inc (G-15820)*

Plevniak Construction, Youngstown *Also Called: Plevniak Construction Inc (G-15695)*

Plevniak Construction Inc 330 718-1600
1235 Townsend Ave Youngstown (44505) *(G-15695)*

Plezall Wipers Inc 216 535-4300
26301 Curtiss Wright Pkwy Ste 200 Richmond Heights (44143) *(G-12721)*

Plk Communities LLC (PA) 513 561-5080
5905 E Galbraith Rd Ste 4100 Cincinnati (45236) *(G-3214)*

Ploger Transportation LLC 419 465-2100
149 Sandusky St Monroeville (44847) *(G-11358)*

Ploger Transportation LLC (PA) 419 465-2100
300 Cleveland Rd Norwalk (44857) *(G-12021)*

Pls Financial Services Inc 513 421-4200
702 Reading Rd Cincinnati (45202) *(G-3215)*

Plug Smart, Worthington *Also Called: Juice Technologies Inc (G-15424)*

ALPHABETIC SECTION — Post-Up Stand

Plumbers Lcal 55 Federal Cr Un.. 216 459-0099
  980 Keynote Cir Independence (44131) *(G-9467)*
Plumbing & Heating, Massillon Also Called: Whisler Plumbing & Heating Inc *(G-10673)*
Plumbing Mechanical, Pataskala Also Called: Crawford Mechanical Svcs Inc *(G-12272)*
Plumbline Consulting LLC.. 419 581-2973
  2498 Bluestone Dr Findlay (45840) *(G-8576)*
Plumbline Solutions Inc... 419 581-2963
  1219 W Main Cross St Ste 101 Findlay (45840) *(G-8577)*
Plunketts Pest Control Inc.. 614 794-8169
  1001 Checkrein Ave Columbus (43229) *(G-6533)*
Plus Group, Cincinnati Also Called: Process Plus LLC *(G-3239)*
Plus Management Services Inc.. 419 331-2273
  2440 Baton Rouge Ofc Lima (45805) *(G-9949)*
Plus Management Services Inc (PA)... 419 225-9018
  2905 Oak Hill Ct Lima (45805) *(G-9950)*
Plus One Communications LLC.. 330 255-4500
  1115 S Main St Akron (44301) *(G-267)*
PMC Systems Limited... 330 538-2268
  12155 Commissioner Dr North Jackson (44451) *(G-11876)*
PMI Supply Inc... 760 598-1128
  5000 Tuttle Crossing Blvd Dublin (43016) *(G-8092)*
PNC, Miamisburg Also Called: PNC Mortgage Company *(G-11085)*
PNC Banc Corp Ohio... 513 981-2420
  7355 N Liberty Dr Liberty Township (45044) *(G-9857)*
PNC Banc Corp Ohio (HQ)... 513 651-8738
  201 E 5th St Cincinnati (45202) *(G-3216)*
PNC Bank, Cincinnati Also Called: PNC Banc Corp Ohio *(G-3216)*
PNC Mortgage Company (DH)... 412 762-2000
  3232 Newmark Dr Bldg 2 Miamisburg (45342) *(G-11085)*
Pncef LLC... 513 421-9191
  995 Dalton Ave Cincinnati (45203) *(G-3217)*
Png Telecommunications Inc (PA).. 513 942-7900
  8805 Governors Hill Dr Ste 250 Cincinnati (45249) *(G-3218)*
Pnk (ohio) LLC.. 513 232-8000
  6301 Kellogg Rd Cincinnati (45230) *(G-3219)*
Poggemeyer Design Group Inc (HQ)... 419 244-8074
  1168 N Main St Bowling Green (43402) *(G-1331)*
Pohl Transportation Inc... 800 837-2122
  9297 Mcgreevey Rd Versailles (45380) *(G-14416)*
Point Place, Toledo Also Called: Harborside Pointe Place LLC *(G-13835)*
Point Recognition Ltd.. 330 220-6777
  1015 Industrial Pkwy N Brunswick (44212) *(G-1467)*
Poison & Toxic Control Center, Amherst Also Called: Bon Secours Mercy Health Inc *(G-425)*
Poison Information Center.. 513 636-5111
  3333 Burnet Ave 3rd Fl Cincinnati (45229) *(G-3220)*
Polaris Automation Inc.. 614 431-0170
  6956 E Broad St Pmb 321 Columbus (43213) *(G-6534)*
Polaris Fashion Place, Columbus Also Called: Pfp Columbus LLC *(G-5277)*
Polaris Innkeepers LLC.. 614 568-0770
  9000 Worthington Rd Westerville (43082) *(G-14928)*
Polaris Pkwy Intrnal Mdcine Pd.. 614 865-4800
  110 Polaris Pkwy Ste 230 Westerville (43082) *(G-14929)*
Polaris Technologies, Toledo Also Called: Modern Builders Supply Inc *(G-13926)*
Polaris Towne Center LLC.. 614 456-0123
  1500 Polaris Pkwy Ste 3000 Columbus (43240) *(G-5278)*
Polivka International Co Inc.. 704 321-0802
  8256 E Market St Ste 114 Warren (44484) *(G-14548)*
Pollock Research & Design Inc.. 330 332-3300
  1134 Salem Pkwy Salem (44460) *(G-12847)*
Poly Flex, Baltic Also Called: Flex Technologies Inc *(G-688)*
Polychem LLC... 419 547-1400
  202 Watertower Dr Clyde (43410) *(G-5207)*
Polymer Additives Inc (HQ).. 216 875-7200
  7500 E Pleasant Valley Rd Independence (44131) *(G-9468)*
Polymer Additives Holdings Inc (PA)... 216 875-7200
  7500 E Pleasant Valley Rd Independence (44131) *(G-9469)*
Polymer Packaging Inc (PA).. 330 832-2000
  7755 Freedom Ave Nw North Canton (44720) *(G-11852)*
Polymer Solutions Group LLC... 229 435-8394
  12819 Coit Rd Cleveland (44108) *(G-4760)*

Pomegranate Development Ltd.. 614 223-1650
  765 Pierce Dr Columbus (43223) *(G-6535)*
Pomerene Hospital (PA)... 330 674-1015
  981 Wooster Rd Millersburg (44654) *(G-11289)*
Pomeroy It Solutions Sls Inc.. 440 717-1364
  6670 W Snowville Rd Ste 3 Brecksville (44141) *(G-1363)*
Pomeroy It Solutions Sls Inc.. 614 876-6521
  2339 Westbrooke Dr Columbus (43228) *(G-6536)*
Pomeroy Opco LLC.. 740 992-6606
  36759 Rocksprings Rd Pomeroy (45769) *(G-12515)*
Pontiac Bill Delord Autocenter, Maineville Also Called: Bill Delord Autocenter Inc *(G-10225)*
Pontoon Solutions Inc... 855 881-1533
  1695 Indian Wood Cir Ste 200 Maumee (43537) *(G-10756)*
Pop A Lock of Ohio, Grafton Also Called: Kelco Enterprises Inc *(G-8840)*
Pope & Associates Inc... 513 671-1277
  9277 Centre Pointe Dr Ste 150 West Chester (45069) *(G-14744)*
Pope Consulting, West Chester Also Called: Pope & Associates Inc *(G-14744)*
Pork Champ LLC... 740 493-2164
  1136 Coldicott Hill Rd Lucasville (45648) *(G-10179)*
Port Control, Cleveland Also Called: City of Cleveland *(G-3980)*
Port Lawrence Title and Tr Co (DH)... 419 244-4605
  4 Seagate Ste 101 Toledo (43604) *(G-13965)*
Portage Animal Clinic, Kent Also Called: Stow-Kent Animal Hospital Inc *(G-9599)*
Portage Area Rgonal Trnsp Auth.. 330 678-1287
  2000 Summit Rd Kent (44240) *(G-9591)*
Portage Cnty Bd Dvlpmntal Dsbl.. 330 678-2400
  2500 Brady Lake Rd Ravenna (44266) *(G-12636)*
Portage Community Bank (HQ).. 330 296-8090
  1311 E Main St Ravenna (44266) *(G-12637)*
PORTAGE COMMUNITY BANK, Ravenna Also Called: Portage Community Bank *(G-12637)*
Portage Country Club Company.. 330 836-8565
  240 N Portage Path Akron (44303) *(G-268)*
Portage County Board (PA).. 330 297-6209
  2606 Brady Lake Rd Ravenna (44266) *(G-12638)*
PORTAGE LEARNING CENTERS, Ravenna Also Called: Portage Prvate Indust Cncil In *(G-12639)*
Portage Path Behavioral Health (PA)... 330 253-3100
  340 S Broadway St Akron (44308) *(G-269)*
Portage Path Behavioral Health, Cuyahoga Falls Also Called: Portage Path Behavorial Health *(G-7092)*
Portage Path Behavorial Health... 330 762-6110
  10 Penfield Ave Akron (44310) *(G-270)*
Portage Path Behavorial Health... 330 928-2324
  792 Graham Rd Ste C Cuyahoga Falls (44221) *(G-7092)*
Portage Prvate Indust Cncil In... 330 297-7795
  145 N Chestnut St Lowr Ravenna (44266) *(G-12639)*
Porter Wrght Morris Arthur LLP.. 513 381-4700
  250 E 5th St Ste 2200 Cincinnati (45202) *(G-3221)*
Porter Wrght Morris Arthur LLP.. 216 443-2506
  950 Main Ave Ste 500 Cleveland (44113) *(G-4761)*
Porter Wrght Morris Arthur LLP.. 937 449-6810
  1 S Main St Ste 1600 Dayton (45402) *(G-7558)*
Porter Wright, Columbus Also Called: Porter Wright Morris & Arthur LLP *(G-6537)*
Porter Wright Morris & Arthur LLP (PA)..................................... 614 227-2000
  41 S High St Ste 2900 Columbus (43215) *(G-6537)*
Ports Petroleum Company Inc (PA).. 330 264-1885
  1337 Blachleyville Rd Wooster (44691) *(G-15367)*
Portsmouth Hospital Corp.. 740 991-4000
  1901 Argonne Rd Portsmouth (45662) *(G-12565)*
Positive Bus Solutions Inc... 513 772-2255
  200 Northland Blvd # 100 Cincinnati (45246) *(G-3222)*
Positive Education Program.. 216 227-2730
  11500 Franklin Blvd Cleveland (44102) *(G-4762)*
Positive Education Program.. 440 471-8200
  4320 W 220th St Cleveland (44126) *(G-4763)*
Possible Worldwide LLC (HQ)... 513 381-1380
  302 W 3rd St Ste 900 Cincinnati (45202) *(G-3223)*
Post Browning, Cincinnati Also Called: Convergint Technologies LLC *(G-2505)*
Post-Browning Inc... 513 771-1717
  7812 Redsky Dr Cincinnati (45249) *(G-3224)*
Post-Up Stand, Maple Heights Also Called: Suntwist Corp *(G-10350)*

Postal Family Credit Union Inc 513 381-8600
   1243 W 8th St Cincinnati (45203) *(G-3225)*

Potential Development Program 330 746-7641
   2405 Market St Youngstown (44507) *(G-15696)*

Potter, Bryan Also Called: Potter Inc *(G-1492)*

Potter Inc (PA) 419 636-5624
   630 Commerce Dr Bryan (43506) *(G-1492)*

Poured LLC 614 432-0804
   1443 Giles Ct Columbus (43228) *(G-6538)*

Powel Crosley Jr Branch, Cincinnati Also Called: Young MNS Chrstn Assn Grter CN *(G-3690)*

Powell Company Inc 419 228-3552
   3255 Saint Johns Rd Lima (45804) *(G-9951)*

Powell Electrical Systems Inc 330 966-1750
   8967 Pleasantwood Ave Nw North Canton (44720) *(G-11853)*

Powell Enterprises Inc 614 882-0111
   8750 Olde Worthington Rd Westerville (43082) *(G-14930)*

Power Acquisition LLC (HQ) 614 228-5000
   5025 Bradenton Ave Ste 130 Dublin (43017) *(G-8093)*

Power Direct, Cleveland Also Called: R D D Inc *(G-4804)*

Power Distributors LLC (PA) 614 876-3533
   3700 Paragon Dr Columbus (43228) *(G-6539)*

Power Engineers Incorporated 234 678-9875
   1 S Main St Ste 501 Akron (44308) *(G-271)*

Power Engineers Incorporated 513 326-1500
   11733 Chesterdale Rd Cincinnati (45246) *(G-3226)*

Power System Engineering Inc 740 568-9220
   2349a State Route 821 Marietta (45750) *(G-10401)*

Power Train Components Inc 419 636-4430
   509 E Edgerton St Bryan (43506) *(G-1493)*

Powerbilt Mtl Hdlg Sltions LLC 937 592-5660
   230 Reynolds Ave Bellefontaine (43311) *(G-1036)*

Powernet Global Communications, Cincinnati Also Called: Png Telecommunications Inc *(G-3218)*

Powers Agency, Cincinnati Also Called: Charles W Powers & Assoc Inc *(G-2347)*

Powersteps, Wadsworth Also Called: Stable Step LLC *(G-14452)*

Ppc Flexible Packaging LLC 614 876-1204
   4041 Roberts Rd Columbus (43228) *(G-6540)*

Ppi Technical Communications, Solon Also Called: Advancement LLC *(G-13062)*

Ppmc, Columbus Also Called: Engage Healthcare Svcs Corp *(G-5818)*

Practical Solution, Dayton Also Called: Centric Consulting LLC *(G-7220)*

Practice Bldrs Wster Orthpdic, Wooster Also Called: Wooster Orthpdics Sprtsmdcine *(G-15398)*

Praetorian Holdings Group LLC 440 665-4246
   127 Public Sq Ste 4120 Cleveland (44114) *(G-4764)*

Prater Engineering Assoc Inc 614 766-4896
   6130 Wilcox Rd Dublin (43016) *(G-8094)*

Pratt Paper (oh) LLC 567 320-3353
   602 Leon Pratt Dr Wapakoneta (45895) *(G-14490)*

Praxair, Akron Also Called: Linde Gas & Equipment Inc *(G-222)*

PRC Medical LLC (PA) 330 493-9004
   111 Stow Ave Ste 200 Cuyahoga Falls (44221) *(G-7093)*

Pre-Clinical Services, Spencerville Also Called: Charles River Laboratories Inc *(G-13187)*

Pre-Fore Inc 740 467-2206
   410 Blacklick Eastern Rd Ne Millersport (43046) *(G-11298)*

Preble Cnty Bd Dvlpmntal Dsblt (PA) 937 456-5891
   200 Eaton Lewisburg Rd Eaton (45320) *(G-8220)*

Preble County Board of Dd, Eaton Also Called: Preble Cnty Bd Dvlpmntal Dsblt *(G-8220)*

Preble County Head Start 937 456-2800
   304 Eaton Lewisburg Rd Eaton (45320) *(G-8221)*

Precious Cargo Trnsp Inc 440 543-9272
   15050 Cross Creek Pkwy Newbury (44065) *(G-11763)*

Precision Brdband Instlltons I 614 523-2917
   7642 Red Bank Rd Westerville (43081) *(G-15012)*

Precision Diagnostic Imaging 216 360-8300
   3609 Park East Dr Ste 101 Beachwood (44122) *(G-826)*

Precision Duct Systems LLC 937 335-2626
   2331 W State Route 55 Troy (45373) *(G-14152)*

Precision Electrical Svcs Inc 740 474-4490
   201 W Main St Circleville (43113) *(G-3718)*

Precision Endoscopy Amer Inc (PA) 410 527-9598
   4575 Hudson Dr Stow (44224) *(G-13386)*

Precision Engrg & Contg Inc 440 349-1204
   31340 Solon Rd Ste 25 Solon (44139) *(G-13129)*

Precision Environmental Co (HQ) 216 642-6040
   5500 Old Brecksville Rd Independence (44131) *(G-9470)*

Precision Geophysical Inc (PA) 330 674-2198
   2695 State Route 83 Millersburg (44654) *(G-11290)*

Precision Impacts LLC 937 530-8254
   721 Richard St Miamisburg (45342) *(G-11086)*

Precision Metalforming Assn 216 901-8800
   6363 Oak Tree Blvd Independence (44131) *(G-9471)*

Precision Mtal Fabrication Inc (PA) 937 235-9261
   191 Heid Ave Dayton (45404) *(G-7559)*

Precision Paving Inc 419 499-7283
   3414 State Route 113 E Milan (44846) *(G-11211)*

Precision Products Group Inc 330 698-4711
   339 Mill St Apple Creek (44606) *(G-452)*

Precision Rebuilding Division, Wickliffe Also Called: Parker-Hannifin Corporation *(G-15159)*

Precision Strip Inc 419 674-4186
   190 Bales Rd Kenton (43326) *(G-9622)*

Precision Strip Inc 513 423-4166
   4400 Oxford State Rd Middletown (45044) *(G-11181)*

Precision Strip Inc (HQ) 419 628-2343
   86 S Ohio St Minster (45865) *(G-11320)*

Precision Strip Inc 419 661-1100
   7401 Ponderosa Rd Perrysburg (43551) *(G-12364)*

Precision Strip Inc 937 667-6255
   315 Park Ave Tipp City (45371) *(G-13664)*

Precision Strip Transport Inc (HQ) 419 628-2343
   86 S Ohio St Minster (45865) *(G-11321)*

Precision Supply Company Inc 330 225-5530
   2845 Interstate Pkwy Brunswick (44212) *(G-1468)*

Precision Tools Service Inc 614 873-8000
   8205 Estates Pkwy Ste I Plain City (43064) *(G-12490)*

Precision Welding Corporation 216 524-6110
   7900 Exchange St Cleveland (44125) *(G-4765)*

Predator Trucking Company (PA) 330 530-0712
   3181 Trumbull Ave Mc Donald (44437) *(G-10801)*

Predictive Service LLC (PA) 866 772-6770
   25200 Chagrin Blvd Ste 300 Cleveland (44122) *(G-4766)*

Preferred Acquisition Co LLC (PA) 216 587-0957
   4871 Neo Pkwy Cleveland (44128) *(G-4767)*

Preferred Airparts, Kidron Also Called: Jilco Industries Inc *(G-9636)*

Preferred Medical Group Inc 404 403-8310
   23600 Commerce Park Beachwood (44122) *(G-827)*

Preferred Temporary Svcs Inc 330 494-5502
   4791 Munson St Nw Canton (44718) *(G-1830)*

Pregnancy Decision Health Ctr 614 888-8774
   665 E Dublin Granville Rd Ste 120 Columbus (43229) *(G-6541)*

Premier, Defiance Also Called: Premier Financial Corp *(G-7762)*

Premier Bank (HQ) 330 742-0500
   275 W Federal St Youngstown (44503) *(G-15697)*

Premier Broadcasting Co Inc 614 866-0700
   177 Cypress St Sw Reynoldsburg (43068) *(G-12672)*

Premier Estates 525 LLC 513 631-6800
   1578 Sherman Ave Cincinnati (45212) *(G-3227)*

Premier Estates 526 LLC 513 922-1440
   5999 Bender Rd Cincinnati (45233) *(G-3228)*

Premier Esttes Cncnnt-Rverside, Cincinnati Also Called: Pristine Senior Living *(G-3231)*

Premier Esttes Cncnnt-Rverview, Cincinnati Also Called: Premier Estates 526 LLC *(G-3228)*

Premier Financial Corp (PA) 419 782-5015
   601 Clinton St Defiance (43512) *(G-7762)*

Premier Groupe LLC 937 272-1520
   6045 Manning Rd Miamisburg (45342) *(G-11087)*

Premier Health, Dayton Also Called: Miami Valley Hospital *(G-7492)*

Premier Health Partners (PA) 937 499-9596
   110 N Main St Ste 450 Dayton (45402) *(G-7560)*

Premier Health Pharmacy Fidelity, Moraine Also Called: Fidelity Health Care *(G-11409)*

Premier Home Health LLC 740 403-6806
   35 S Park Pl Ste 350 Newark (43055) *(G-11742)*

Premier Hotel Group LLC 937 754-9109
   730 E Xenia Dr Fairborn (45324) *(G-8380)*

ALPHABETIC SECTION

Premier Hotels Inc.. 419 747-2227
2069 Walker Lake Rd Ontario (44906) *(G-12123)*

Premier Integrated Med Assoc (PA)................. 937 291-6813
6551 Centerville Business Pkwy Ste 110 Dayton (45459) *(G-7561)*

Premier Nursing Network LLC........................... 440 563-1586
15561 W High St Ste 3 Middlefield (44062) *(G-11144)*

Premier Physican Centers, Avon *Also Called: Medical Diagnostic Lab Inc (G-661)*

Premier Physicians, Cleveland *Also Called: Gloria Gadmack Do (G-4316)*

Premier Protective Security, Euclid *Also Called: Deacon 10 LLC (G-8340)*

Premier Security, Euclid *Also Called: National Premier Protective (G-8359)*

Premier Senior Living, West Chester *Also Called: Provision Living LLC (G-14749)*

Premier Sports Medicine..................................... 937 312-1661
2350 Miami Valley Dr Ste 320 Centerville (45459) *(G-1950)*

Premier Truck Sls & Rentl Inc............................. 800 825-1255
7700 Wall St Cleveland (44125) *(G-4768)*

Premiere Medical Resources Inc........................ 330 923-5899
2750 Front St Cuyahoga Falls (44221) *(G-7094)*

Premiere Produce, Cleveland *Also Called: Anselmo Rssis Premier Prod Ltd (G-3818)*

Premiere Service Mortgage Corp (PA).............. 513 546-9895
6266 Centre Park Dr West Chester (45069) *(G-14745)*

Premise Solutions LLC.. 440 703-8200
7105 Krick Rd Walton Hills (44146) *(G-14478)*

Premium Beverage Supply Ltd.......................... 614 777-1007
3701 Lacon Rd Hilliard (43026) *(G-9227)*

Premium Outlet Partners LP............................... 330 562-2000
549 S Chillicothe Rd Ste 185 Aurora (44202) *(G-621)*

Premium Utility Contractor Inc........................... 951 313-0808
50263 State Route 14 East Palestine (44413) *(G-8198)*

Prescribe Fit Inc.. 614 598-8788
401 W Town St Ste 232 Columbus (43215) *(G-6542)*

Prescription Supply Inc....................................... 419 661-6600
2233 Tracy Rd Northwood (43619) *(G-11982)*

Preserve Operating Co LLC............................... 513 471-8667
315 Lilienthal St Cincinnati (45204) *(G-3229)*

Presidio Infrstrcture Sltons L.............................. 614 381-1400
5025 Bradenton Ave Ste B Dublin (43017) *(G-8095)*

Presidio Infrstrcture Sltons L.............................. 419 241-8303
20 N Saint Clair St Toledo (43604) *(G-13966)*

Pressco Technology Inc...................................... 440 715-2559
29200 Aurora Rd Solon (44139) *(G-13130)*

Pressley Ridge Foundation................................. 513 752-4548
4355 Ferguson Dr Ste 125 Cincinnati (45245) *(G-2112)*

Pressley Ridge Foundation................................. 216 763-0800
23701 Miles Rd Cleveland (44128) *(G-4769)*

Pressley Ridge Foundation................................. 513 737-0400
734 Dayton St Hamilton (45011) *(G-9073)*

Pressure Connections Corp................................ 614 863-6930
610 Claycraft Rd Columbus (43230) *(G-6543)*

Pressworks, Plain City *Also Called: Bindery & Spc Pressworks Inc (G-12470)*

Prestan Products LLC... 440 229-5100
5101 Naiman Pkwy Solon (44139) *(G-13131)*

Prestige Technical Svcs Inc (PA)....................... 513 779-6800
7908 Cincinnati Dayton Rd Ste T West Chester (45069) *(G-14746)*

Preterm Foundation.. 216 991-4577
12000 Shaker Blvd Cleveland (44120) *(G-4770)*

Pretium Packaging LLC...................................... 419 943-3733
150 S Werner St Leipsic (45856) *(G-9802)*

Prevention Action Alliance.................................. 614 540-9985
6171 Huntley Rd Ste G Columbus (43229) *(G-6544)*

PRI, Blue Ash *Also Called: Professional Radiology Inc (G-1225)*

Price For Profit LLC... 440 646-9490
6140 Parkland Blvd Ste 250 Cleveland (44124) *(G-4771)*

Price Thrice Supply, Columbus *Also Called: Valley Interior Systems Inc (G-6840)*

Priced Right Cars Inc.. 614 337-0037
5100 E Main St Columbus (43213) *(G-6545)*

Pride Care Ambulance, Huntsville *Also Called: Coloma Emergency Ambulance Inc (G-9383)*

Pride Dlvry & Installation LLC............................ 216 749-7481
8730 Brookpark Rd Parma (44129) *(G-12362)*

Pridecraft Enterprises, Cincinnati *Also Called: Standard Textile Co Inc (G-3409)*

Primary Care Ntwrk Prmier Hlth......................... 937 424-9800
2350 Miami Valley Dr Ste 410 Dayton (45459) *(G-7562)*

Primary Care Ntwrk Prmier Hlth......................... 937 836-5170
9000 N Main St Ste 202 Englewood (45415) *(G-8319)*

Primary Care Ntwrk Prmier Hlth......................... 937 743-5965
8401 Claude Thomas Rd Franklin (45005) *(G-8647)*

Primary Care Ntwrk Prmier Hlth......................... 937 237-9575
6251 Good Samaritan Way Ste 210a Huber Heights (45424) *(G-9326)*

Primary Care Ntwrk Prmier Hlth......................... 513 988-6369
3590 Busenbark Rd Ste 400 Trenton (45067) *(G-14124)*

Primary Care Ntwrk Prmier Hlth......................... 937 278-5854
600 Aviator Ct Vandalia (45377) *(G-14387)*

Primary Care Nursing Services.......................... 614 764-0960
3140 Lilly Mar Ct Dublin (43017) *(G-8096)*

Primary Colors Design Corp., Ashland *Also Called: Bendon Inc (G-481)*

Primary Cr Ntwrk Prmr Hlth Prt.......................... 937 208-7000
722 N Fairfield Rd Beavercreek (45434) *(G-895)*

Primary Cr Ntwrk Prmr Hlth Prt (PA)................. 937 226-7085
110 N Main St Ste 350 Dayton (45402) *(G-7563)*

Primary Cr Ntwrk Prmr Hlth Prt.......................... 937 208-9090
1222 S Patterson Blvd Ste 120 Dayton (45402) *(G-7564)*

Primary Cr Ntwrk Prmr Hlth Prt.......................... 513 204-5785
7450 S Mason Montgomery Rd Mason (45040) *(G-10594)*

Primary Cr Ntwrk Prmr Hlth Prt.......................... 513 492-5940
4859 Nixon Park Dr Ste A Mason (45040) *(G-10595)*

Primary Cr Ntwrk Prmr Hlth Prt.......................... 513 420-5233
1 Medical Center Dr Middletown (45005) *(G-11201)*

Primary Cr Ntwrk Prmr Hlth Prt.......................... 937 890-6644
900 S Dixie Dr Ste 40 Vandalia (45377) *(G-14388)*

Primary Dayton Innkeepers LLC........................ 937 938-9550
7701 Washington Village Dr Dayton (45459) *(G-7565)*

Primary Health Care Clinic, New Lexington *Also Called: Hopewell Health Centers Inc (G-11626)*

PRIMARY HEALTH SOLUTIONS, Hamilton *Also Called: Butler Cnty Cmnty Hlth Cnsrtiu (G-9023)*

Primary Packaging Incorporated........................ 330 874-3131
10810 Industrial Pkwy Nw Bolivar (44612) *(G-1297)*

Primary Solutions, Columbus *Also Called: Marshall Information Svcs LLC (G-6198)*

Primaryone Health, Columbus *Also Called: Columbus Nghbrhood Hlth Ctr In (G-5649)*

Prime Ae Group Inc... 614 839-0250
8415 Pulsar Pl Ste 300 Columbus (43240) *(G-5279)*

Prime Care, Zanesville *Also Called: Medical Assoc of Zanesville (G-15812)*

Prime Club, Hamilton *Also Called: Partners In Prime (G-9071)*

Prime Healthcare Foundation............................. 740 623-4178
1460 Orange St Coshocton (43812) *(G-6997)*

Prime Hlthcare Fndtn-Cshcton L........................ 740 623-4013
1397 Walnut St Coshocton (43812) *(G-6998)*

Prime Hlthcare Fndton- E Lvrpo (DH)................ 330 385-7200
425 W 5th St East Liverpool (43920) *(G-8191)*

Prime Home Care LLC (HQ).............................. 513 340-4183
2775 W Us Highway 22 And 3 Ste 1b Maineville (45039) *(G-10230)*

Prime NDT Services Inc..................................... 330 878-4202
10119 Oh-21 Strasburg (44680) *(G-13405)*

Prime Otlets At Jffrsonville I, Jeffersonville *Also Called: Prime Outlets Acquisition LLC (G-9542)*

Prime Outlets Acquisition LLC............................ 740 948-9090
8000 Factory Shops Blvd Jeffersonville (43128) *(G-9542)*

Prime Time Pty Event Rentl LLC........................ 937 296-9262
5225 Springboro Pike Moraine (45439) *(G-11429)*

Prime Valet Cleaners Inc.................................... 513 860-9595
8204 Princeton Glendale Rd West Chester (45069) *(G-14747)*

Primed At Congress Park, Dayton *Also Called: Medicine Midwest LLC (G-7477)*

Primed Kettering Pediatrics................................ 937 433-7991
5250 Far Hills Ave Ste 110 Dayton (45429) *(G-7566)*

Primed Physicians... 937 237-4945
8501 Troy Pike # 1 Dayton (45424) *(G-7567)*

Primed Physicians... 937 298-8058
6551 Centerville Business Pkwy Ste 110 Dayton (45459) *(G-7568)*

Primed Physicians, Dayton *Also Called: Premier Integrated Med Assoc (G-7561)*

Primehealth Perry Hlth & Welln, Perry *Also Called: Lake Hospital System Inc (G-12308)*

Primetals Technologies USA LLC...................... 419 929-1554
81 E Washburn St New London (44851) *(G-11633)*

Primetech Communications Inc.......................... 513 942-6000
4505 Mulhauser Rd Hamilton (45011) *(G-9074)*

Primrose Rtrment Cmmnities LLC 419 422-6200
  8580 Township Road 237 Findlay (45840) *(G-8578)*
Primrose Rtrment Cmmnities LLC 740 653-3900
  1481 Wesley Way Lancaster (43130) *(G-9737)*
Primrose Rtrment Cmmnities LLC 419 224-1200
  3500 W Elm St Lima (45807) *(G-9952)*
Primrose Rtrment Cmnty Findlay, Findlay *Also Called: Primrose Senior Holdings LLC (G-8579)*
Primrose Rtrment Cmnty Znsvlle, Zanesville *Also Called: Tsmm Management LLC (G-15834)*
Primrose School, Powell *Also Called: Primrose School Lewis Cente (G-12603)*
Primrose School Lewis Cente 740 548-5808
  8273 Owenfield Dr Powell (43065) *(G-12603)*
Primrose Senior Holdings LLC 605 226-3300
  8580 Township Road 237 Findlay (45840) *(G-8579)*
Princeton Precision Group, Mentor *Also Called: Princeton Tool Inc (G-10985)*
Princeton Tool Inc (PA) 440 290-8666
  7830 Division Dr Mentor (44060) *(G-10985)*
Print Management Partners Inc 513 942-9202
  6285 Schumacher Park Dr West Chester (45069) *(G-14748)*
Printed Resources, Columbus *Also Called: Nutis Press Inc (G-6378)*
Printers Devil Inc 330 650-1218
  77 Maple Dr Hudson (44236) *(G-9369)*
Printing Concepts, Stow *Also Called: Traxium LLC (G-13398)*
Priority Designs Inc 614 337-9979
  100 S Hamilton Rd Columbus (43213) *(G-6546)*
Priority Dispatch Inc (PA) 513 791-3900
  4665 Malsbary Rd Blue Ash (45242) *(G-1222)*
Priority Equipment Rental Ltd 724 227-3070
  581 Country Club Dr Ste D Newark (43055) *(G-11743)*
Priority III Contracting Inc 513 922-0203
  5178 Crookshank Rd Cincinnati (45238) *(G-3230)*
Priority Mortgage Corp 614 431-1141
  150 E Wilson Bridge Rd Ste 350 Worthington (43085) *(G-15448)*
Prisma Integration Corp 330 545-8690
  50 Harry St Girard (44420) *(G-8823)*
Pristine Senior Living 513 471-8667
  315 Lilienthal St Cincinnati (45204) *(G-3231)*
Pristine Senior Living, Cincinnati *Also Called: Premier Estates 525 LLC (G-3227)*
Pristine Senior Living and, Willard *Also Called: Pristine Senior Living of (G-15173)*
Pristine Senior Living of 419 935-0148
  370 E Howard St Willard (44890) *(G-15173)*
Pristine Snior Lving Englewood 937 836-5143
  425 Lauricella Ct Englewood (45322) *(G-8320)*
Private Duty & Visiting Nurses, Celina *Also Called: Community Hlth Prfssionals Inc (G-1921)*
Private Duty Services Inc 419 238-3714
  1157 Westwood Dr Van Wert (45891) *(G-14350)*
Private School Aid Service, Westlake *Also Called: Facts Management Company (G-15059)*
Priya Pvt Ltd 740 389-1998
  2117 Marion Mount Gilead Rd Marion (43302) *(G-10450)*
Prn Health Services Inc 513 792-2217
  8044 Montgomery Rd Ste 700 Cincinnati (45236) *(G-3232)*
Prn Nurse Inc 614 864-9292
  6161 Radekin Rd Columbus (43232) *(G-6547)*
Pro Audio Video Inc 330 494-2100
  1620 30th St Ne Canton (44714) *(G-1831)*
Pro Century, Westerville *Also Called: CSC Insurance Agency Inc (G-14886)*
Pro Football Fcs 513 381-3404
  1216 Central Pkwy Cincinnati (45202) *(G-3233)*
Pro Health Care Services Ltd 614 856-9111
  270 Main St Ste A Groveport (43125) *(G-8996)*
Pro Kids & Families Program, Cleveland *Also Called: Ohioguidestone (G-4693)*
Pro Oncall Technologies LLC (PA) 513 489-7660
  6902 E Kemper Rd Cincinnati (45249) *(G-3234)*
Pro Quip Inc 330 468-1850
  850 Highland Rd E Macedonia (44056) *(G-10202)*
Pro Seniors Inc 513 345-4160
  7162 Reading Rd Ste 1150 Cincinnati (45237) *(G-3235)*
Pro Tire, Rossford *Also Called: Capital Tire Inc (G-12765)*
Pro-Lam, Milford *Also Called: Professional Laminate Mllwk Inc (G-11251)*
Pro-Model & Talent Mgmt Inc 330 665-0723
  3421 Ridgewood Rd Fairlawn (44333) *(G-8494)*

Pro-Pet LLC 419 394-3374
  1601 Mckinley Rd Saint Marys (45885) *(G-12835)*
Pro-Touch, Columbus *Also Called: T&L Global Management LLC (G-6744)*
Proampac, Cincinnati *Also Called: Ampac Holdings LLC (G-2194)*
Proampac Holdings Inc (PA) 513 671-1777
  12025 Tricon Rd Cincinnati (45246) *(G-3236)*
Proampac Intermediate, Cincinnati *Also Called: Proampac Holdings Inc (G-3236)*
Probation Department, Newark *Also Called: Licking County Adult Crt Svcs (G-11714)*
Procamps Inc 513 745-5855
  10001 Alliance Rd Blue Ash (45242) *(G-1223)*
Process Construction Inc 513 251-2211
  2128 State Ave Cincinnati (45214) *(G-3237)*
Process Construction Inc (PA) 513 251-2211
  1421 Queen City Ave Cincinnati (45214) *(G-3238)*
Process Plus LLC (HQ) 513 742-7590
  135 Merchant St Ste 300 Cincinnati (45246) *(G-3239)*
Process Plus Design Build LLC 513 262-2261
  135 Merchant St Ste 300 Cincinnati (45246) *(G-3240)*
Process Plus Holdings Inc 513 742-7590
  135 Merchant St Ste 300 Cincinnati (45246) *(G-3241)*
Process Pump & Seal Inc 513 988-7000
  4317 Kugler Mill Rd Cincinnati (45236) *(G-3242)*
Procon Prof Cnstr Svcs Inc 740 474-5455
  2530 Kingston Pike Circleville (43113) *(G-3719)*
Procter & Gamble, Blue Ash *Also Called: Procter & Gamble Distrg LLC (G-1224)*
Procter & Gamble, Cincinnati *Also Called: Procter & Gamble Distrg LLC (G-3243)*
Procter & Gamble Distrg LLC 513 626-2500
  11510 Reed Hartman Hwy Blue Ash (45241) *(G-1224)*
Procter & Gamble Distrg LLC 513 945-7960
  2 Procter And Gamble Plz Cincinnati (45202) *(G-3243)*
Procter Gamble US Bus Svcs Co 513 983-7777
  1 Procter And Gamble Plz Cincinnati (45202) *(G-3244)*
Prodigal Media Company Inc 330 707-2088
  42 Mcclurg Rd Youngstown (44512) *(G-15698)*
Produce One Inc 931 253-4749
  904 Woodley Rd Dayton (45403) *(G-7569)*
Produce Packaging Inc 216 391-6129
  27853 Chardon Rd Willoughby Hills (44092) *(G-15234)*
Producers Credit Corporation 800 641-7522
  8351 N High St Ste 250 Columbus (43235) *(G-6548)*
Producers Service LLC 740 454-6253
  109 Graham St Zanesville (43701) *(G-15828)*
Producers Service Corporation 740 454-6253
  109 Graham St Zanesville (43701) *(G-15829)*
Product Fulfillment Solutions, Cincinnati *Also Called: Networking Partners Inc (G-3107)*
Production Svcs Unlimited Inc 513 695-1658
  575 Columbus Ave Lebanon (45036) *(G-9783)*
Production Tool Supply Ohio 216 265-0000
  10801 Brookpark Rd Cleveland (44130) *(G-4772)*
Products Chemical Company LLC 216 281-1155
  4005 Clark Ave Cleveland (44109) *(G-4773)*
Professional Bldg Maint Inc 440 666-8509
  26851 Miles Rd Ste 206 Warrensville Heights (44128) *(G-14586)*
Professional Building Maint, Moraine *Also Called: Space Management Inc (G-11440)*
Professional Electric Pdts Co 330 896-3790
  1140 E Waterloo Rd Akron (44306) *(G-272)*
Professional Electric Pdts Co 614 563-2504
  5193 Sinclair Rd Columbus (43229) *(G-6549)*
Professional Electric Pdts Co 800 379-3790
  1190 E Broad St Elyria (44035) *(G-8288)*
Professional Electric Pdts Co 330 896-3790
  3729 Boettler Oaks Drive Green (44232) *(G-8857)*
Professional Electric Pdts Co 419 269-3790
  501 Phillips Ave Toledo (43612) *(G-13967)*
Professional Electric Products Co Inc (DH) 800 872-7000
  33210 Lakeland Blvd Eastlake (44095) *(G-8207)*
Professional Maint of Columbus 513 579-1762
  1 Crosley Field Ln Cincinnati (45214) *(G-3245)*
Professional Pavement Svcs LLC 740 726-2222
  152 Troutman Rd Delaware (43015) *(G-7821)*
Professional Plumbing Svcs Inc 740 454-1066
  3570 Old Wheeling Rd Zanesville (43701) *(G-15830)*

ALPHABETIC SECTION

Professional Property Maint, New Carlisle *Also Called: Louderback Fmly Invstments Inc* *(G-11604)*

Professional Radiology Inc.. 513 872-4500
9825 Kenwood Rd Ste 105 Blue Ash (45242) *(G-1225)*

Professional Restoration Svc.. 330 825-1803
1170 Industrial Pkwy Medina (44256) *(G-10879)*

Professional Review Netwrk Inc.. 614 791-2700
5126 Blazer Pkwy Dublin (43017) *(G-8097)*

Professional Rfrgn & AC, Millersport *Also Called: Pre-Fore Inc* *(G-11298)*

Professional Security Bur Inc... 330 438-6800
318 Cleveland Ave Nw Canton (44702) *(G-1832)*

Professional Service Inds Inc... 216 447-1335
5555 Canal Rd Cleveland (44125) *(G-4774)*

Professional Services, Beachwood *Also Called: Jewish Fmly Svc Assn Clvland O* *(G-805)*

Professional Transportation... 419 661-0576
30801 Drouillard Rd Walbridge (43465) *(G-14463)*

Professional Travel Inc (PA)... 440 734-8800
25000 Country Club Blvd Ste 170 North Olmsted (44070) *(G-11911)*

Professionals For Womens Hlth (PA)..................................... 614 268-8800
921 Jasonway Ave Ste B Columbus (43214) *(G-6550)*

Professionals Group, Akron *Also Called: Professionals Group LLC* *(G-273)*

Professionals Group LLC... 330 957-5114
2022 Adelaide Blvd Akron (44305) *(G-273)*

Professnal Cbling Slutions LLC.. 513 733-9473
11711 Chesterdale Rd Cincinnati (45246) *(G-3246)*

Professnal Glfers Assn of Amer.. 419 882-3197
5201 Corey Rd Sylvania (43560) *(G-13560)*

Professnal Mint Lttle Ohio Div, Cincinnati *Also Called: Professional Maint of Columbus* *(G-3245)*

Professnal Psychiatric Svcs LLC.. 513 229-7585
6402 Thornberry Ct Mason (45040) *(G-10596)*

Professional Football Hall Fame, Canton *Also Called: National Football Museum Inc* *(G-1817)*

Professional Laminate Mllwk Inc.. 513 891-7858
1003 Tech Dr Milford (45150) *(G-11251)*

Profill Holdings LLC.. 513 742-4000
255 W Crescentville Rd Cincinnati (45246) *(G-3247)*

Profiol, Canton *Also Called: Graco Ohio Inc* *(G-1766)*

Profit Track Ltd... 330 848-2730
588 W Tuscarawas Ave Barberton (44203) *(G-704)*

Proforma, Independence *Also Called: Pfg Ventures LP* *(G-9466)*

Proforma (PA).. 800 825-1525
8800 E Pleasant Valley Rd Ste 1 Independence (44131) *(G-9472)*

Proforma Worldwide Support Ctr, Independence *Also Called: Proforma Inc* *(G-9472)*

Profunds.. 888 776-5717
3435 Stelzer Rd Ste 1000 Columbus (43219) *(G-6551)*

Program Transportation Inc... 440 772-4134
815 Crocker Rd Ste 6 Westlake (44145) *(G-15100)*

Progress Sup A Gstave A Larson, Cincinnati *Also Called: Gustave A Larson Company* *(G-2785)*

Progressive Adjusting Co Inc... 440 461-5000
6300 Wilson Mills Rd Cleveland (44143) *(G-4775)*

Progressive Advanced Insur Co.. 440 461-5000
6300 Wilson Mills Rd Cleveland (44143) *(G-4776)*

Progressive Aurora LLC... 330 995-0094
425 S Chillicothe Rd Aurora (44202) *(G-622)*

Progressive Bayside Insur Co (DH)....................................... 440 395-4460
6300 Wilson Mills Rd Cleveland (44143) *(G-4777)*

Progressive Casualty Insur Co... 440 603-4033
747 Alpha Dr Ste A21 Cleveland (44143) *(G-4778)*

Progressive Casualty Insur Co (DH)..................................... 855 347-3939
6300 Wilson Mills Rd Mayfield Village (44143) *(G-10795)*

Progressive Choice Insur Co.. 440 461-5000
6300 Wilson Mills Rd Cleveland (44143) *(G-4779)*

Progressive Classic Insur Co... 440 661-5000
6300 Wilson Mills Rd Cleveland (44143) *(G-4780)*

Progressive Coml Cslty Co.. 440 461-5000
6300 Wilson Mills Rd Cleveland (44143) *(G-4781)*

Progressive Express Insur Co.. 440 461-5000
6300 Wilson Mills Rd Cleveland (44143) *(G-4782)*

Progressive Flooring Svcs Inc.. 614 868-9005
100 Heritage Dr Etna (43062) *(G-8334)*

Progressive Freedom Insur Co... 440 461-5000
6300 Wilson Mills Rd Cleveland (44143) *(G-4783)*

Progressive Grdn State Insur.. 440 461-5000
6300 Wilson Mills Rd Cleveland (44143) *(G-4784)*

Progressive Green Meadows LLC....................................... 330 875-1456
7770 Columbus Rd Ne Louisville (44641) *(G-10120)*

Progressive Hawaii Insur Corp... 440 461-5000
6300 Wilson Mills Rd Cleveland (44143) *(G-4785)*

Progressive Insurance, Cleveland *Also Called: Progressive Adjusting Co Inc* *(G-4775)*
Progressive Insurance, Cleveland *Also Called: Progressive Advanced Insur Co* *(G-4776)*
Progressive Insurance, Cleveland *Also Called: Progressive Bayside Insur Co* *(G-4777)*
Progressive Insurance, Cleveland *Also Called: Progressive Choice Insur Co* *(G-4779)*
Progressive Insurance, Cleveland *Also Called: Progressive Classic Insur Co* *(G-4780)*
Progressive Insurance, Cleveland *Also Called: Progressive Coml Cslty Co* *(G-4781)*
Progressive Insurance, Cleveland *Also Called: Progressive Express Insur Co* *(G-4782)*
Progressive Insurance, Cleveland *Also Called: Progressive Freedom Insur Co* *(G-4783)*
Progressive Insurance, Cleveland *Also Called: Progressive Grdn State Insur* *(G-4784)*
Progressive Insurance, Cleveland *Also Called: Progressive Hawaii Insur Corp* *(G-4785)*
Progressive Insurance, Cleveland *Also Called: Progressive Paloverde Insur Co* *(G-4786)*
Progressive Insurance, Cleveland *Also Called: Progressive Premier Insur Ill* *(G-4787)*
Progressive Insurance, Cleveland *Also Called: Progressive Rsc Inc* *(G-4788)*
Progressive Insurance, Cleveland *Also Called: Progressive Select Insur Co* *(G-4789)*
Progressive Insurance, Cleveland *Also Called: Progressive Specialty Insur Co* *(G-4790)*
Progressive Insurance, Cleveland *Also Called: Progressive Universal Insur Co* *(G-4791)*
Progressive Insurance, Cleveland *Also Called: Progrssive Coml Advntage Agcy* *(G-4792)*
Progressive Insurance, Cleveland *Also Called: Progrssive Spclty Insur Agcy I* *(G-4793)*
Progressive Insurance, Mayfield Village *Also Called: Progressive Casualty Insur Co* *(G-10795)*

Progressive Macedonia LLC.. 330 748-8800
9730 Valley View Rd Macedonia (44056) *(G-10203)*

Progressive Medical Intl, Dublin *Also Called: PMI Supply Inc* *(G-8092)*
Progressive Medical Intl, Dublin *Also Called: Progressive Medical Intl Inc* *(G-8098)*

Progressive Medical Intl Inc.. 760 957-5500
5000 Tuttle Crossing Blvd Dublin (43016) *(G-8098)*

Progressive Medical LLC... 614 794-3300
250 Progressive Way Westerville (43082) *(G-14931)*

Progressive Paloverde Insur Co.. 440 461-5000
6300 Wilson Mills Rd Cleveland (44143) *(G-4786)*

Progressive Premier Insur Ill.. 440 461-5000
6300 Wilson Mills Rd W33 Cleveland (44143) *(G-4787)*

Progressive Quality Care Inc... 330 875-7866
7770 Columbus Rd Ne Louisville (44641) *(G-10121)*

Progressive Quality Care Inc (PA).. 216 661-6800
5553 Broadview Rd Parma (44134) *(G-12263)*

Progressive Rsc Inc.. 440 461-5000
6300 Wilson Mills Rd Cleveland (44143) *(G-4788)*

Progressive Select Insur Co.. 440 461-5000
6300 Wilson Mills Rd Cleveland (44143) *(G-4789)*

Progressive Specialty Insur Co.. 440 461-5000
6300 Wilson Mills Rd Cleveland (44143) *(G-4790)*

Progressive Universal Insur Co.. 440 461-5000
6300 Wilson Mills Rd Cleveland (44143) *(G-4791)*

Progressive West Insurance Co, Cleveland *Also Called: Drive Insurance Company* *(G-4185)*

Progrssive Coml Advntage Agcy.. 440 461-5000
6300 Wilson Mills Rd Cleveland (44143) *(G-4792)*

Progrssive Fghting Systems LLC... 216 520-0271
6900 Granger Rd Independence (44131) *(G-9473)*

Progrssive Spclty Insur Agcy I.. 440 461-5000
6300 Wilson Mills Rd Cleveland (44143) *(G-4793)*

Prohealth Partners Inc.. 419 491-7150
12661 Eckil Junction Perrysburg (43551) *(G-12365)*

Project CURE Inc... 937 262-3500
200 Daruma Pkwy Dayton (45439) *(G-7570)*

PROJECT HOPE, Painesville *Also Called: Ecumenical Shlter Ntwrk Lk Cnty* *(G-12228)*

Projects Unlimited Inc (PA)... 937 918-2200
6300 Sand Lake Rd Dayton (45414) *(G-7571)*

Projetech, Cincinnati *Also Called: Projetech Inc* *(G-3248)*

Projetech Inc.. 513 481-4900
3815 Harrison Ave Cincinnati (45211) *(G-3248)*

Prokids 513 281-2000
222 W 7th St Cincinnati (45202) *(G-3249)*

Prolift Industrial Equipment, Dayton *Also Called: Toyota Industries N Amer Inc (G-7675)*

Prolink, Cincinnati *Also Called: Prolink Resources LLC (G-3250)*

Prolink Healthcare Staffing 513 489-5300
10700 Montgomery Rd Ste 1 Montgomery (45242) *(G-11373)*

Prolink Resources LLC 866 777-3704
4600 Montgomery Rd Ste 300 Cincinnati (45212) *(G-3250)*

Prolink Staffing Services LLC (PA) 513 489-5300
4600 Montgomery Rd Ste 300 Cincinnati (45212) *(G-3251)*

Prolink Staffing Services LLC 614 405-9810
4700 Lakehurst Ct Ste 200 Dublin (43016) *(G-8099)*

Prologue Research Intl Inc 614 324-1500
580 N 4th St Ste 270 Columbus (43215) *(G-6552)*

PROMEDICA, Fostoria *Also Called: Fostoria Hospital Association (G-8616)*

PROMEDICA, Sylvania *Also Called: Promedica Cntning Care Svcs Co (G-13561)*

PROMEDICA, Sylvania *Also Called: Promedica Physcn Cntinuum Svcs (G-13565)*

Promedica, Toledo *Also Called: Bay Park Community Hospital (G-13701)*

Promedica, Toledo *Also Called: Promedica Health System Inc (G-13972)*

PROMEDICA, Toledo *Also Called: Promedica Toledo Hospital (G-13976)*

Promedica, Toledo *Also Called: Promedica Toledo Hospital (G-13978)*

Promedica Bay Park Hospital, Oregon *Also Called: Bay Park Community Hospital (G-12129)*

Promedica Cntning Care Svcs Co 419 885-1715
5855 Monroe St Ste 200 Sylvania (43560) *(G-13561)*

Promedica Employment Svcs LLC 419 824-7529
100 Madison Ave Toledo (43604) *(G-13968)*

Promedica Gnt-Urinary Surgeons (PA) 419 531-8558
2100 W Central Ave Toledo (43606) *(G-13969)*

Promedica Grlich Mmory Care Ct, Sylvania *Also Called: Promedica of Sylvania Oh LLC (G-13564)*

Promedica Health Care, Sylvania *Also Called: Promedica Health Systems Inc (G-13563)*

Promedica Health System Inc 513 831-5800
3960 Red Bank Rd Ste 140 Cincinnati (45227) *(G-3252)*

Promedica Health System Inc 419 783-6802
1200 Ralston Ave Defiance (43512) *(G-7763)*

Promedica Health System Inc 419 355-9209
907 W State St Ste A Fremont (43420) *(G-8697)*

Promedica Health System Inc 419 891-6201
660 Beaver Creek Cir Ste 200 Maumee (43537) *(G-10757)*

Promedica Health System Inc 419 291-6720
5700 Monroe St Unit 209 Sylvania (43560) *(G-13562)*

Promedica Health System Inc 419 291-2121
3922 Woodley Rd Ste 100 Toledo (43606) *(G-13970)*

Promedica Health System Inc 419 534-6600
3170 W Central Ave Ste C Toledo (43606) *(G-13971)*

Promedica Health System Inc (PA) 567 585-9600
100 Madison Ave Toledo (43604) *(G-13972)*

Promedica Health Systems Inc 419 690-7700
2801 Bay Park Dr Oregon (43616) *(G-12142)*

Promedica Health Systems Inc 419 824-1444
5200 Harroun Rd Sylvania (43560) *(G-13563)*

Promedica Health Systems Inc 419 578-7036
2865 N Reynolds Rd Ste 130 Toledo (43615) *(G-13973)*

Promedica Health Systems Inc 419 291-4000
2142 N Cove Blvd Toledo (43606) *(G-13974)*

Promedica Health Systems Inc 800 477-4035
300 N Summit St Ste 100 Toledo (43604) *(G-13975)*

PROMEDICA HEALTH SYSTEMS, INC., Oregon *Also Called: Promedica Health Systems Inc (G-12142)*

PROMEDICA HEALTH SYSTEMS, INC., Toledo *Also Called: Promedica Health Systems Inc (G-13974)*

Promedica Medicare Plan, Maumee *Also Called: Paramount Care of Michigan (G-10754)*

Promedica of Sylvania Oh LLC 844 247-5337
5320 Harroun Rd Sylvania (43560) *(G-13564)*

Promedica Physcn Cntinuum Svcs 419 824-7200
5855 Monroe St Fl 1 Sylvania (43560) *(G-13565)*

Promedica Senior Care, Toledo *Also Called: Hcr Manorcare Inc (G-13838)*

Promedica Sklled Nrsing Rhbltt, Barberton *Also Called: Manor Care Barberton Oh LLC (G-701)*

Promedica Sklled Nrsing Rhbltt, Miamisburg *Also Called: Heartland Miamisburg Oh LLC (G-11060)*

Promedica Sklled Nrsing Rhbltt, Perrysburg *Also Called: Heartland Perrysburg Oh LLC (G-12341)*

Promedica Sklled Nrsing Rhbltt, Sylvania *Also Called: Hcrmc-Promedica LLC (G-13549)*

Promedica Sklled Nrsing Rhbltt, Toledo *Also Called: Manor Care Wilmington De LLC (G-13906)*

Promedica Sklled Nrsing Rhbltt, Toledo *Also Called: Manor Cr-Pike Creek Wlmngton D (G-13907)*

Promedica Sklled Nrsing Rhbltt, Westerville *Also Called: Heartland Vlg Wstrvlle OH RC L (G-14983)*

Promedica Toledo Hospital 419 291-2273
5520 Monroe St Sylvania (43560) *(G-13566)*

Promedica Toledo Hospital (HQ) 419 291-4000
2142 N Cove Blvd Toledo (43606) *(G-13976)*

Promedica Toledo Hospital 419 291-2051
2051 W Central Ave Toledo (43606) *(G-13977)*

Promedica Toledo Hospital 419 291-8701
2150 W Central Ave Ste A Toledo (43606) *(G-13978)*

Promedica Wldwood Orthpdic SPI 419 578-7107
2901 N Reynolds Rd Toledo (43615) *(G-13979)*

Promedidcal Heath Syytem, Maumee *Also Called: Promedica Health System Inc (G-10757)*

Promotion Exction Partners LLC (DH) 513 826-0101
302 W 3rd St Cincinnati (45202) *(G-3253)*

Prompt Prvate Nursing Care Inc 614 834-1105
26 W Waterloo St Canal Winchester (43110) *(G-1615)*

Prop Shop, Cleveland *Also Called: Playhouse Square Holdg Co LLC (G-4759)*

Property 3, Cleveland *Also Called: Weston Inc (G-5143)*

Pros Freight Corporation 440 543-7555
16687 Hilltop Park Pl Chagrin Falls (44023) *(G-1987)*

Proscan Imaging LLC (PA) 513 281-3400
5400 Kennedy Ave Cincinnati (45213) *(G-3254)*

Protection One, Columbus *Also Called: ADT LLC (G-5317)*

Protective Coatings Inc 937 275-7711
4321 Webster St Dayton (45414) *(G-7572)*

Protective Packg Solutions LLC 513 769-5777
10345 S Medallion Dr Cincinnati (45241) *(G-3255)*

Protegis LLC (DH) 216 377-3044
6155 Rockside Rd Ste 400 Independence (44131) *(G-9474)*

Protegis Fire & Safety, Independence *Also Called: Protegis LLC (G-9474)*

Prout Boiler Htg & Wldg Inc 330 744-0293
3124 Temple St Youngstown (44510) *(G-15699)*

Provantage LLC 330 494-3781
7576 Freedom Ave Nw North Canton (44720) *(G-11854)*

Provia - Heritage Stone, Sugarcreek *Also Called: Provia Holdings Inc (G-13512)*

Provia Holdings Inc (PA) 330 852-4711
2150 State Route 39 Sugarcreek (44681) *(G-13512)*

Provia LLC (HQ) 330 852-4711
2150 State Route 39 Sugarcreek (44681) *(G-13513)*

Provide-A-Care Inc 330 828-2278
15028 Old Lincoln Way Dalton (44618) *(G-7121)*

Providence Care Center 419 627-2273
2025 Hayes Ave Sandusky (44870) *(G-12924)*

Providence Healthcare MGT Inc 216 200-5917
29225 Chagrin Blvd Ste 230 Cleveland (44122) *(G-4794)*

Providence House Inc 216 651-5982
2050 W 32nd St Cleveland (44113) *(G-4795)*

Providence Medical Group Inc 937 297-8999
2912 Springboro W Ste 201 Moraine (45439) *(G-11430)*

Providence Medical Group LLC 513 897-0085
4353 E State Route 73 Waynesville (45068) *(G-14627)*

Provider Services Inc 614 888-2021
111 Lazelle Rd Columbus (43235) *(G-6553)*

Providers For Healthy Living 614 664-3595
8351 N High St Ste 155 Columbus (43235) *(G-6554)*

Provimi North America Inc (HQ) 937 770-2400
6571 State Route 503 N Lewisburg (45338) *(G-9842)*

Provision Living LLC 513 970-9201
4299 Bach Buxton Rd Batavia (45103) *(G-746)*

Provision Living LLC 513 847-9050
5531 Chappell Crossing Blvd West Chester (45069) *(G-14749)*

Proware, Cincinnati *Also Called: Sadler-Necamp Financial Svcs (G-3337)*

Prt, Piqua *Also Called: Plastic Recycling Tech Inc (G-12456)*

ALPHABETIC SECTION — Quail Hollow Resort

Prudential, Columbus *Also Called: Residential One Realty Inc (G-6585)*
Prudential Dehoff Realtors, Canton *Also Called: Dehoff Agency Inc (G-1733)*
Prudential Select Properties (PA) 440 255-1111
  7395 Center St Mentor (44060) *(G-10986)*
Prus Construction Company 513 321-7774
  5325 Wooster Pike Cincinnati (45226) *(G-3256)*
Prusaks Precision Cnstr Inc 440 655-8564
  10701 Royalton Rd Ste A North Royalton (44133) *(G-11948)*
Pry Professional Group, Findlay *Also Called: Gilmore Jasion Mahler Ltd (G-8538)*
PS Lifestyle LLC 440 600-1595
  55 Public Sq Ste 2075 Cleveland (44113) *(G-4796)*
Psa Airlines Inc 330 490-2939
  5430 N Hangar Ln Bldg 3 North Canton (44720) *(G-11855)*
Psa Airlines Inc (HQ) 937 454-1116
  3400 Terminal Rd Vandalia (45377) *(G-14389)*
PSC Crane & Rigging, Piqua *Also Called: Piqua Steel Co (G-12454)*
PSC Metals LLC 330 484-7610
  3101 Varley Ave Sw Canton (44706) *(G-1833)*
PSC Metals LLC 614 299-4175
  1283 Joyce Ave Columbus (43219) *(G-6555)*
Pse, Marietta *Also Called: Power System Engineering Inc (G-10401)*
Pse Credit Union Inc 330 661-0160
  3845 Pearl Rd Medina (44256) *(G-10880)*
Pse Credit Union Inc 440 572-3830
  12700 Prospect Rd Strongsville (44149) *(G-13480)*
PSI, Twinsburg *Also Called: PSI Associates LLC (G-14214)*
PSI Associates LLC 330 425-8474
  2112 Case Pkwy Ste 10 Twinsburg (44087) *(G-14214)*
PSI Supply Chain Solutions LLC 614 389-4717
  5050 Bradenton Ave Dublin (43017) *(G-8100)*
PSI Testing and Engineering, Cleveland *Also Called: Professional Service Inds Inc (G-4774)*
Psp Operations Inc 614 888-5700
  7440 Pingue Dr Worthington (43085) *(G-15449)*
Pss, Cleveland *Also Called: Plastic Safety Systems Inc (G-4755)*
Psycare Inc 330 856-6663
  8577 E Market St Warren (44484) *(G-14549)*
Psycare Inc 330 318-3078
  520 Youngstown Poland Rd Struthers (44471) *(G-13502)*
Psycare Inc (PA) 330 759-2310
  2980 Belmont Ave Youngstown (44505) *(G-15700)*
Psycare Struthers, Struthers *Also Called: Psycare Inc (G-13502)*
Psychpros Inc 513 651-9500
  2404 Auburn Ave Cincinnati (45219) *(G-3257)*
Pta Engineering Inc 330 666-3702
  275 Springside Dr Ste 300 Akron (44333) *(G-274)*
Ptao Sffeld Elem Ohio Congress 330 628-3430
  1128 Waterloo Rd Mogadore (44260) *(G-11331)*
Ptc Transport Ltd 513 738-0900
  1849 Sky Meadow Dr Hamilton (45013) *(G-9075)*
Ptech, Beavercreek Township *Also Called: Peerless Technologies Corp (G-946)*
Pti, Bowling Green *Also Called: Phoenix Technologies Intl LLC (G-1330)*
Pti, Holland *Also Called: Plastic Technologies Inc (G-9300)*
Ptmj Enterprises Inc 440 543-8000
  32000 Aurora Rd Solon (44139) *(G-13132)*
Pubco Corporation (PA) 216 881-5300
  3830 Kelley Ave Cleveland (44114) *(G-4797)*
Public Brdcstg Fndtion of NW O (PA) 419 380-4600
  1270 S Detroit Ave Toledo (43614) *(G-13980)*
Public Safety, Cleveland *Also Called: City of Cleveland (G-3981)*
Public Service Company Okla 888 216-3523
  301 Cleveland Ave Canton (44702) *(G-1834)*
Pull-A-Part LLC 330 456-8349
  1551 Belden Ave Se Canton (44707) *(G-1835)*
Pull-A-Part LLC 330 631-6280
  4433 W 130th St Cleveland (44135) *(G-4798)*
Pulmonary Critical Care and SL 513 893-5864
  25 Office Park Dr Hamilton (45013) *(G-9076)*
Pulmonary Crtcal Care Cons Inc 937 461-5815
  1520 S Main St Ste 2 Dayton (45409) *(G-7573)*
Pulmonary Rehabilitation 330 758-7575
  925 Trailwood Dr Youngstown (44512) *(G-15701)*

Pulmonary Solutions Inc 937 393-0991
  4701 Creek Rd Ste 100 Blue Ash (45242) *(G-1226)*
Pulse Ltd LLC 216 570-7732
  12628 Chillicothe Rd Chesterland (44026) *(G-2042)*
Pumpserve, Columbus *Also Called: Corrosion Fluid Products Corp (G-5704)*
Punderson Mnor Ldge Cnfrnce Ct, Newbury *Also Called: US Hotel Osp Ventures LLC (G-11765)*
Pure Concept Ecosalon & Spa, Mason *Also Called: Pure Concept Salon Inc (G-10597)*
Pure Concept Salon Inc 513 770-2120
  5625 Deerfield Cir Mason (45040) *(G-10597)*
Pure Health Care Llc 937 668-7873
  2200 Miami Valley Dr Centerville (45459) *(G-1951)*
Pure Healthcare 937 668-7873
  324 Wilmington Ave Dayton (45420) *(G-7574)*
Purple Land Management LLC 740 238-4259
  5590 Lauby Rd Ste 5 North Canton (44720) *(G-11856)*
Putnam Cnty Amblatory Care Ctr, Lima *Also Called: Mercy Hlth - St Rtas Med Ctr L (G-9934)*
Putnam Cnty Commissioners Off 419 523-6832
  304 E 2nd St Ottawa (45875) *(G-12192)*
Putnam Cnty Homecare & Hospice 419 523-4449
  575 Ottawa Glandorf Rd Ste 3 Ottawa (45875) *(G-12193)*
Putnam County Public Hlth Dept 419 523-5608
  256 E Williamstown Rd Ottawa (45875) *(G-12194)*
Putnam County Y M C A, Ottawa *Also Called: Young MNS Chrstn Assn of Akron (G-12196)*
Putnam Truck Load Direct, Zanesville *Also Called: P & D Transportation Inc (G-15825)*
Pve Sheffler LLC 330 332-5200
  1156 E State St Salem (44460) *(G-12848)*
PVE SHEFFLER, LLC, Salem *Also Called: Pve Sheffler LLC (G-12848)*
Pvf Capital Corp 440 248-7171
  30000 Aurora Rd Solon (44139) *(G-13133)*
PWC International, Independence *Also Called: IHS Enterprise LLC (G-9436)*
Pxp Ohio 614 575-4242
  6800 Tussing Rd Reynoldsburg (43068) *(G-12673)*
Pyramid Controls, Cincinnati *Also Called: Matthews International Corp (G-3017)*
Pyxis Data Systems, Dublin *Also Called: Cardinal Health 301 LLC (G-7955)*
Q C M, West Chester *Also Called: Quality Construction MGT Inc (G-14750)*
Q Laboratories, Cincinnati *Also Called: Q Labs LLC (G-3258)*
Q Labs LLC (PA) 513 471-1300
  1911 Radcliff Dr Cincinnati (45204) *(G-3258)*
Q Medical LLC 440 903-1827
  30100 Chagrin Blvd Ste 201 Pepper Pike (44124) *(G-12302)*
Q, The, Cleveland *Also Called: Cavaliers Operating Co LLC (G-3938)*
Q4-2 Inc 440 256-3870
  9250 Amber Wood Dr Willoughby (44094) *(G-15219)*
Qc Software LLC 513 469-1424
  50 E Business Way Cincinnati (45241) *(G-3259)*
Qh Management Company LLC 440 497-1100
  11080 Concord Hambden Rd Concord Township (44077) *(G-6932)*
QT Equipment Company (PA) 330 724-3055
  151 W Dartmore Ave Akron (44301) *(G-275)*
Qtg Marketing, Columbus *Also Called: Quality Too Good Mktg Group LL (G-6557)*
Quadax Inc 216 765-1144
  25201 Chagrin Blvd Ste 290 Beachwood (44122) *(G-828)*
Quadax Inc (PA) 440 777-6300
  7500 Old Oak Blvd Middleburg Heights (44130) *(G-11121)*
Quadax Inc 330 759-4600
  17 Colonial Dr Ste 101 Youngstown (44505) *(G-15702)*
Quadco Rehabilitation Center 419 782-0389
  1838 E 2nd St Defiance (43512) *(G-7764)*
QUADCO REHABILITATION CENTER INC, Defiance *Also Called: Quadco Rehabilitation Center (G-7764)*
Quadco Rehabilitation Ctr Inc 419 445-1950
  600 Oak St Archbold (43502) *(G-466)*
Quadco Rehabilitation Ctr Inc (PA) 419 682-1011
  427 N Defiance St Stryker (43557) *(G-13505)*
Quadra Tooling and Automation, Pepper Pike *Also Called: Q Medical LLC (G-12302)*
Quail Hollow Management Inc 440 639-4000
  11295 Quail Hollow Dr Concord Township (44077) *(G-6933)*
Quail Hollow Resort, Concord Township *Also Called: Qh Management Company LLC (G-6932)*

Quail Hollow Resort Cntry CLB, Concord Township Also Called: Quail Hollow Management Inc *(G-6933)*

Quaker Sales & Dist Inc 914 767-7010
2155 Rohr Rd Lockbourne (43137) *(G-10014)*

Qualchoice Health Plan Inc (HQ) 440 544-2800
24701 Euclid Ave Euclid (44117) *(G-8360)*

Qualitor Subsidiary H Inc 419 562-7987
1232 Whetstone St Bucyrus (44820) *(G-1517)*

Quality Associates Inc 513 242-4477
9842 International Blvd West Chester (45246) *(G-14829)*

Quality Assured Cleaning Inc 614 798-1505
6407 Nicholas Dr Columbus (43235) *(G-6556)*

Quality Block & Supply Inc (DH) 330 364-4411
Rte 250 Mount Eaton (44659) *(G-11458)*

Quality Care Nursing Svc Inc 740 377-9095
501 Washington St Ste 13 South Point (45680) *(G-13182)*

Quality Carrier, Cincinnati Also Called: LMI Transports Inc *(G-2984)*

Quality Cmfort Living Svcs LLC 330 280-7659
4117 Whipple Ave Nw Canton (44718) *(G-1836)*

Quality Construction MGT Inc 513 779-8425
7395 Kingsgate Way West Chester (45069) *(G-14750)*

Quality Control Inspection (PA) 440 359-1900
9500 Midwest Ave Cleveland (44125) *(G-4799)*

Quality Control Services LLC (PA) 216 862-9264
3214 Saint Clair Ave Ne Cleveland (44114) *(G-4800)*

Quality Fabricated Metals Inc 330 332-7008
14000 W Middletown Rd Salem (44460) *(G-12849)*

Quality Inn, Holland Also Called: Quality Inn Toledo Airport *(G-9301)*

Quality Inn, Mansfield Also Called: Mansfield Hotel Partnership *(G-10287)*

Quality Inn, Marietta Also Called: Motel Investments Marietta Inc *(G-10393)*

Quality Inn, Miamisburg Also Called: Rhea Aryan Inc *(G-11090)*

Quality Inn, Montpelier Also Called: Bob-Mor Inc *(G-11381)*

Quality Inn, Richfield Also Called: Richfield Bnquet Cnfrnce Ctr LL *(G-12708)*

Quality Inn, Upper Sandusky Also Called: Sk Hospitality LLC *(G-14293)*

Quality Inn Toledo Airport 419 867-1144
1401 E Mall Dr Holland (43528) *(G-9301)*

Quality Ip LLC 330 931-4141
145 River St Ste 101 Kent (44240) *(G-9592)*

Quality Lines Inc 740 815-1165
2440 Bright Rd Findlay (45840) *(G-8580)*

Quality Plus, Concord Township Also Called: Emily Management Inc *(G-6926)*

Quality Restaurant Supply, Cincinnati Also Called: Quality Supply Co *(G-3260)*

Quality Solutions Inc 440 933-9946
Cleveland (44140) *(G-4801)*

QUALITY SOLUTIONS INC, Cleveland Also Called: Quality Solutions Inc *(G-4801)*

Quality Supply Chain Co-Op Inc 614 764-3124
1 Dave Thomas Blvd Dublin (43017) *(G-8101)*

Quality Supply Co (PA) 937 890-6114
4020 Rev Dr Cincinnati (45232) *(G-3260)*

Quality Team Management Inc 937 490-2000
4430 Stratford Dr Middletown (45042) *(G-11182)*

Quality Too Good Mktg Group LL 877 202-6245
470 W Broad St Ste 21 Columbus (43215) *(G-6557)*

Quality Towing, West Chester Also Called: Sprandel Enterprises Inc *(G-14768)*

Qualstl Corp 937 294-4133
2221 Arbor Blvd Moraine (45439) *(G-11431)*

Qualtech NP, Cincinnati Also Called: Curtiss-Wright Flow Ctrl Corp *(G-2101)*

Qualus Corp (PA) 800 434-0415
4040 Rev Dr Cincinnati (45232) *(G-3261)*

Quantech Services Inc 937 490-8461
4141 Colonel Glenn Hwy Ste 273 Beavercreek Township (45431) *(G-947)*

Quantum Health Inc 800 257-2038
5240 Blazer Pkwy Dublin (43017) *(G-8102)*

Quantum Metals Inc 513 573-0144
3675 Taft Rd Lebanon (45036) *(G-9784)*

Quantum Services, Columbus Also Called: Accurate Invntory Clclting Svc *(G-5304)*

Quarry Pines, Poland Also Called: Reserve Run Golf Club LLC *(G-12508)*

Quarry Pool, Cleveland Also Called: City of South Euclid *(G-3993)*

Quasonix, West Chester Also Called: Quasonix Inc *(G-14751)*

Quasonix Inc (PA) 513 942-1287
6025 Schumacher Park Dr West Chester (45069) *(G-14751)*

Quebe Holdings Inc (HQ) 937 222-2290
1985 Founders Dr Dayton (45420) *(G-7575)*

Queen City Hospice LLC 513 510-4406
4605 Duke Dr Ste 220 Mason (45040) *(G-10598)*

Queen City Mechanicals Inc 513 353-1430
1950 Waycross Rd Cincinnati (45240) *(G-3262)*

Queen City of Physicians, Cincinnati Also Called: Queen City Physicians *(G-3263)*

Queen City Physicians 513 872-2061
2475 W Galbraith Rd Ste 3 Cincinnati (45239) *(G-3263)*

Queen City Polymers Inc (PA) 513 779-0990
6101 Schumacher Park Dr West Chester (45069) *(G-14752)*

Queen City Racquet Club LLC 513 771-2835
11275 Chester Rd Cincinnati (45246) *(G-3264)*

Queen City Reprographics 513 326-2300
2863 E Sharon Rd Cincinnati (45241) *(G-3265)*

Queen City Reprographics Inc 513 326-2300
2863 E Sharon Rd Cincinnati (45241) *(G-3266)*

Queen City Skilled Care LLC 513 802-5010
7265 Kenwood Rd Ste 370 Cincinnati (45236) *(G-3267)*

Queen City Transportation LLC 513 941-8700
211 Township Ave # C Cincinnati (45216) *(G-3268)*

Queen Cy Physcans Wstn Rdge In, Cincinnati Also Called: Trihealth Inc *(G-3507)*

Queens Beauty Bar LLC 216 804-0533
4321 Storer Ave Cleveland (44109) *(G-4802)*

Queensgate Food Group LLC 513 721-5503
619 Linn St Cincinnati (45203) *(G-3269)*

Queensgate Foodservice, Cincinnati Also Called: Queensgate Food Group LLC *(G-3269)*

Quest Def Systems Slutions Inc 513 628-4521
10300 Alliance Rd Ste 500 Blue Ash (45242) *(G-1227)*

Quest Diagnostics, Beavercreek Also Called: Wright State University *(G-916)*

Quest Gymnstics Extreme Spt CT 937 426-3547
3820 Kemp Rd Beavercreek (45431) *(G-896)*

Quest Recovery Prevention Svcs (PA) 330 453-8252
1341 Market Ave N Canton (44714) *(G-1837)*

Quest Software Inc 614 336-9223
6500 Emerald Pkwy Ste 400 Dublin (43016) *(G-8103)*

Questar Solutions LLC 330 966-2070
7948 Freedom Ave Nw North Canton (44720) *(G-11857)*

Questmark, Stow Also Called: Centimark Corporation *(G-13357)*

Quick Delivery Service Inc (HQ) 330 453-3709
2207 Kimball Rd Se Canton (44707) *(G-1838)*

Quick Lane, Cincinnati Also Called: Walt Ford Sweeney Inc *(G-3639)*

Quick Lane, Columbus Also Called: Dick Masheter Ford Inc *(G-5764)*

Quick Lane, Columbus Also Called: Germain Ford LLC *(G-5931)*

Quick Lane, Cuyahoga Falls Also Called: Al Spitzer Ford Inc *(G-7034)*

Quick Lane, London Also Called: Buckeye Ford Inc *(G-10038)*

Quick Lane, Miamisburg Also Called: Interstate Ford Inc *(G-11065)*

Quick Lane, Sandusky Also Called: Mathews Ford Sandusky Inc *(G-12914)*

Quick Lane, Westlake Also Called: Nick Mayer Lincoln-Mercury Inc *(G-15084)*

Quick Med Urgent Care LLC 234 320-7770
120 N Lincoln Ave Salem (44460) *(G-12850)*

Quick Solutions Inc 614 825-8000
8940 Lyra Dr # 220 Columbus (43240) *(G-5280)*

Quick Tab II Inc (PA) 419 448-6622
241 Heritage Dr Tiffin (44883) *(G-13639)*

Quicken Loans Arena, Cleveland Also Called: Cavaliers Holdings LLC *(G-3937)*

Quickinsured Brkg A Ritter Co, Medina Also Called: Quickinsured Brokerage *(G-10881)*

Quickinsured Brokerage 330 722-7070
1684 Medina Rd Medina (44256) *(G-10881)*

Quickslide, Springboro Also Called: Hardy Diagnostics *(G-13200)*

Quilter Cvlian Cnsrvation Camp, Green Springs Also Called: Great Lkes Cmnty Action Partnr *(G-8859)*

Quintus Technologies LLC 614 891-2732
8270 Green Meadows Dr N Lewis Center (43035) *(G-9834)*

Quirk Cultural Center, Cuyahoga Falls Also Called: City of Cuyahoga Falls *(G-7057)*

Qwaide Enterprises LLC 614 209-0551
6044 Phar Lap Dr New Albany (43054) *(G-11583)*

ALPHABETIC SECTION

Qwest, Dublin Also Called: Qwest Corporation (G-8104)
- Qwest Corporation 614 793-9258
  4650 Lakehurst Ct Dublin (43016) (G-8104)
- R & D Nestle Center Inc (HQ) 937 642-7015
  809 Collins Ave Marysville (43040) (G-10503)
- R & D Nestle Center Inc 440 264-2200
  29300 Cannon Rd Solon (44139) (G-13134)
- R & G Nursing Care Inc 330 562-3120
  849 N Aurora Rd Aurora (44202) (G-623)
- R & H Service Inc 330 626-2888
  9420 State Route 14 Streetsboro (44241) (G-13425)
- R & J Investment Co Inc 440 934-5204
  37800 French Creek Rd Avon (44011) (G-663)

R & J Trucking, Youngstown Also Called: American Bulk Commodities Inc (G-15549)
- R & J Trucking Inc 440 960-1508
  5250 Baumhart Rd Lorain (44053) (G-10099)
- R & J Trucking Inc 740 374-3050
  14530 State Route 7 Marietta (45750) (G-10402)
- R & J Trucking Inc 330 758-0841
  147 Curtis Dr Shelby (44875) (G-13009)
- R & J Trucking Inc (HQ) 800 262-9365
  8063 Southern Blvd Youngstown (44512) (G-15703)
- R & K Gorby LLC 419 222-0004
  1920 Roschman Ave Lima (45804) (G-9953)

R & L Carriers, Norwalk Also Called: R & L Transfer Inc (G-12022)
R & L Carriers, Wilmington Also Called: Greenwood Motor Lines Inc (G-15255)
- R & L Carriers Inc (PA) 800 543-5589
  600 Gilliam Rd Wilmington (45177) (G-15265)
- R & L Transfer Inc 330 482-5800
  1320 Springfield Rd Columbiana (44408) (G-5239)
- R & L Transfer Inc 216 531-3324
  1403 State Route 18 Norwalk (44857) (G-12022)
- R & L Transfer Inc 937 305-9287
  1221 Warren Dr Wilmington (45177) (G-15266)
- R & L Transfer Inc 614 871-3813
  2483 W Us Highway 22 3 Wilmington (45177) (G-15267)
- R & L Transfer Inc 330 743-3609
  5550 Dunlap Rd Youngstown (44515) (G-15704)
- R & L Transfer Inc (HQ) 937 382-1494
  600 Gilliam Rd Wilmington (45177) (G-15268)

R & M, Springfield Also Called: R&M Materials Handling Inc (G-13283)
- R & M Leasing Inc 937 382-6800
  600 Gilliam Rd Wilmington (45177) (G-15269)
- R & R Inc (PA) 330 799-1536
  44 Victoria Rd Youngstown (44515) (G-15705)

R & R Auto Body, Cleveland Also Called: Roemer Unlimited Inc (G-4852)
- R & R Chiropractic 419 425-2225
  26 N Main St Attica (44807) (G-601)

R & R Cleveland Mack Sales, Youngstown Also Called: R & R Inc (G-15705)
- R & R Pipeline Inc (PA) 740 345-3692
  155 Dayton Rd Ne Newark (43055) (G-11744)
- R & R Truck Sales Inc 330 784-5881
  1650 E Waterloo Rd Akron (44306) (G-276)

R & S Data Products, Hillsboro Also Called: Highland Computer Forms Inc (G-9257)
- R & S Halley and Company Inc 614 771-0388
  9050 Amity Pike Plain City (43064) (G-12491)

R A I, Cleveland Also Called: Research Associates Inc (G-4828)
- R A Mueller Inc 513 489-5200
  11270 Cornell Park Dr Blue Ash (45242) (G-1228)
- R and J Corporation 440 871-6009
  24142 Detroit Rd Westlake (44145) (G-15101)
- R B C Apollo Equity Partners (DH) 216 875-2626
  600 Superior Ave E Ste 2300 Cleveland (44114) (G-4803)
- R B Jergens Contractors Inc 937 669-9799
  11418 N Dixie Dr Vandalia (45377) (G-14390)
- R C Hemm Glass Shops Inc (PA) 937 773-5591
  514 S Main St Piqua (45356) (G-12457)

R C M, Akron Also Called: Rubber City Machinery Corp (G-288)
- R D D Inc (PA) 216 781-5858
  4719 Blythin Rd Cleveland (44125) (G-4804)
- R D Jergens Contractors Inc (PA) 937 669-9799
  11418 N Dixie Dr Vandalia (45377) (G-14391)
- R D Jones Excavating Inc 419 648-5870
  10225 Alger Rd Harrod (45850) (G-9122)
- R D Thompson Paper Pdts Co Inc 419 994-3614
  1 Madison St Loudonville (44842) (G-10110)
- R Dorsey & Company Inc 614 486-8900
  1250 Arthur E Adams Dr Columbus (43221) (G-6558)
- R E Kramig & Co Inc 513 761-4010
  323 S Wayne Ave Cincinnati (45215) (G-3270)
- R E Warner & Associates Inc 440 835-9400
  25777 Detroit Rd Ste 200 Westlake (44145) (G-15102)
- R E Whitney Insur Agcy LLC 877 652-7765
  250 E 5th St Fl 15 Cincinnati (45202) (G-3271)
- R G Barry Corporation (HQ) 614 864-6400
  13405 Yarmouth Dr Pickerington (43147) (G-12408)

R G Seller Co, Moraine Also Called: R G Sellers Company (G-11432)
- R G Sellers Company (PA) 937 299-1545
  3185 Elbee Rd Moraine (45439) (G-11432)
- R G Smith Company (PA) 330 456-3415
  1249 Dueber Ave Sw Canton (44706) (G-1839)
- R K Industries Inc 419 523-5001
  725 N Locust St Ottawa (45875) (G-12195)
- R L A Utilities 513 554-1453
  389 S Wayne Ave Cincinnati (45215) (G-3272)
- R L Bondy Insulation LLC 419 843-6283
  2830 Crane Way Northwood (43619) (G-11983)
- R L Fender Construction Co 937 258-9604
  362 Huffman Ave Dayton (45403) (G-7576)
- R L Fortney Management Inc (PA) 440 716-4000
  31269 Bradley Rd North Olmsted (44070) (G-11912)
- R L Lipton Distributing Co 216 475-4150
  9797 Sweet Valley Dr Cleveland (44125) (G-4805)
- R L Morrissey & Assoc Inc (PA) 440 498-3730
  30450 Bruce Industrial Pkwy Solon (44139) (G-13135)
- R L O Inc (PA) 937 620-9998
  466 Windsor Park Dr Dayton (45459) (G-7577)
- R P L Corporation 937 335-0021
  1375 W Market St Troy (45373) (G-14153)
- R R Donnelley & Sons Company 614 539-5527
  3801 Gantz Rd Ste A Grove City (43123) (G-8947)
- R Robnsons Twing Recovery LLC 937 458-3666
  1859 N Central Dr Beavercreek (45432) (G-897)
- R S Hanline and Co Inc (PA) 419 347-8077
  17 Republic Ave Shelby (44875) (G-13010)
- R S Stoll and Company 937 434-7800
  1801 S Metro Pkwy Dayton (45459) (G-7578)

R T A, Cleveland Also Called: Greater Cleveland Regional Transit Authority (G-4334)
R T A, Dayton Also Called: Greater Dyton Rgnal Trnst Auth (G-7386)
- R W Sauder Inc 330 359-5440
  2648 Us Rt 62 Winesburg (44690) (G-15290)
- R W Sidley Incorporated (PA) 440 352-9343
  436 Casement Ave Painesville (44077) (G-12242)
- R W Sidley Incorporated 440 298-3232
  6900 Madison Rd Thompson (44086) (G-13618)

R. W. Sidley, Painesville Also Called: R W Sidley Incorporated (G-12242)
R.dorsey & Company, Columbus Also Called: R Dorsey & Company Inc (G-6558)
R.S.i, North Olmsted Also Called: Relational Solutions Inc (G-11913)
- R&L Hero Delivery LLC 937 824-0291
  3830 Linden Ave Dayton (45432) (G-7140)
- R&M Materials Handling Inc 937 328-5100
  4400 Gateway Blvd Springfield (45502) (G-13283)
- R3 Safety LLC (DH) 800 421-7081
  6021 Union Centre Blvd West Chester (45014) (G-14753)
- Ra Consultants LLC 513 469-6600
  10856 Kenwood Rd Blue Ash (45242) (G-1229)
- RA Staff Company 440 891-9900
  16500 W Sprague Rd, Middlebourough Heights Cleveland (44130) (G-4806)

Racar Engineering, Dublin Also Called: Toogann Technologies LLC (G-8142)
Rack & Ballauer Excavating, Hamilton Also Called: Rack & Ballauer Excvtg Co Inc (G-9077)
- Rack & Ballauer Excvtg Co Inc 513 738-7000
  11321 Paddys Run Rd Hamilton (45013) (G-9077)

Racquet Club At Harper's Point, Cincinnati *Also Called: Towne Properties Assoc Inc (G-3494)*
Racquet Club Columbus Ltd.. 614 457-5671
   1100 Bethel Rd Columbus (43220) *(G-6559)*
Radebaugh-Fetzer Company... 440 878-4700
   22400 Ascoa Ct Strongsville (44149) *(G-13481)*
Radha Corporation... 614 851-5599
   5625 Trabue Rd Columbus (43228) *(G-6560)*
Radial South LP... 678 584-4047
   6360 Port Rd 6440 Groveport (43125) *(G-8997)*
Radian Guaranty Inc... 614 847-8300
   250 E Wilson Bridge Rd Ste 175 Worthington (43085) *(G-15450)*
Radiance Technologies Inc... 937 425-0747
   3715 Pentagon Blvd Beavercreek (45431) *(G-898)*
Radiology Assoc Canton Inc... 330 363-2842
   2600 6th St Sw Canton (44710) *(G-1840)*
Radiology Associates, Athens *Also Called: Radiology Associates Athens (G-586)*
Radiology Associates Athens... 740 593-5551
   55 Hospital Dr Athens (45701) *(G-586)*
Radiology Physicians Inc.. 614 717-9840
   3769 Kingman Hill Dr Ste 220 Delaware (43015) *(G-7822)*
Radiometer America Inc... 440 871-8900
   810 Sharon Dr Westlake (44145) *(G-15103)*
Radisson Eastlake, Eastlake *Also Called: Eastlake Lodging LLC (G-8202)*
Radisson Inn, Cincinnati *Also Called: Winegrdner Hmmons Ht Group LLC (G-3674)*
Radisson Inn, Cleveland *Also Called: Cleveland Cbd Hotel LLC (G-4004)*
Radisson Inn 550, Copley *Also Called: Shree Hospitality Corporation (G-6963)*
Radix Wire Co (PA)... 216 731-9191
   30333 Emerald Valley Pkwy Solon (44139) *(G-13136)*
Radix Wire Company, The, Solon *Also Called: Radix Wire Co (G-13136)*
Rae-Ann Center Inc.. 440 466-5733
   839 W Main St Geneva (44041) *(G-8788)*
Rae-Ann Enterprises Inc... 440 249-5092
   27310 W Oviatt Rd Cleveland (44140) *(G-4807)*
Rae-Ann Gneva Sklled Nrsing Rh, Geneva *Also Called: Rae-Ann Center Inc (G-8788)*
Rae-Ann Suburban, Cleveland *Also Called: Rae-Ann Enterprises Inc (G-4807)*
Raf Automation, Solon *Also Called: Fak Group Inc (G-13085)*
Rags Brooms & Mops Inc.. 440 969-0164
   790 State Route 307 E Jefferson (44047) *(G-9539)*
Rahal Land and Racing, Hilliard *Also Called: Team Rahal Inc (G-9236)*
Rahn Dental Group Inc... 937 435-0324
   5660 Far Hills Ave Dayton (45429) *(G-7579)*
Railway Equipment Lsg & Maint, Solon *Also Called: RELAM Inc (G-13137)*
Railworks Track Services Llc... 330 538-2261
   1550 N Bailey Rd North Jackson (44451) *(G-11877)*
Railworks Track Services, Inc., North Jackson *Also Called: Railworks Track Services Llc (G-11877)*
Rainbow Babies & Children, Cleveland *Also Called: University Hsptals Clvland Med (G-5080)*
Rainbow Child - Officeview, Pickerington *Also Called: Rainbow Station Day Care Inc (G-12410)*
Rainbow Child - Reynoldsburg, Reynoldsburg *Also Called: Rainbow Station Day Care Inc (G-12674)*
Rainbow Child Development Ctr, Blue Ash *Also Called: Rainbow Rascals Lrng Ctr Inc (G-1230)*
Rainbow Data Systems Inc.. 937 431-8000
   2358 Lakeview Dr Ste A Beavercreek (45431) *(G-899)*
Rainbow Pharmacy, Cleveland *Also Called: University Hsptals Clvland Med (G-5077)*
Rainbow Rascals Lrng Ctr Inc.. 513 769-7529
   10631 Techwoods Cir Blue Ash (45242) *(G-1230)*
Rainbow Station, Pickerington *Also Called: Rainbow Station Day Care Inc (G-12409)*
Rainbow Station Day Care Inc.. 614 759-8667
   1829 Winderly Ln Pickerington (43147) *(G-12409)*
Rainbow Station Day Care Inc (PA).................................... 614 759-8667
   226 Durand St Pickerington (43147) *(G-12410)*
Rainbow Station Day Care Inc.. 614 575-5040
   8315 Taylor Rd Sw Reynoldsburg (43068) *(G-12674)*
Rainstar Capital Group... 419 801-4113
   7630 Reitz Rd Lot 138 Perrysburg (43551) *(G-12366)*
Raintree Country Club Inc.. 330 699-3232
   4350 Mayfair Rd Uniontown (44685) *(G-14262)*
Rakesh Ranjan MD & Assoc Inc.. 440 324-5555
   347 Midway Blvd Ste 210 Elyria (44035) *(G-8289)*

Ram Cnstrction Svcs Cncnnati L....................................... 513 297-1857
   4710 Ashley Dr West Chester (45011) *(G-14754)*
Ram Construction Services, West Chester *Also Called: Ram Cnstrction Svcs Cncnnati L (G-14754)*
Ram Resources, Dayton *Also Called: Ram Restoration LLC (G-7580)*
Ram Restoration LLC... 937 347-7418
   11125 Yankee St Dayton (45458) *(G-7580)*
Rama Inc.. 614 473-9888
   2890 Airport Dr Columbus (43219) *(G-6561)*
Ramada By Wyndham, Elyria *Also Called: Ramada Elyria Rsrvtons Wrld WI (G-8290)*
Ramada Elyria Rsrvtons Wrld WI....................................... 440 324-5411
   1825 Lorain Blvd Elyria (44035) *(G-8290)*
Ramada Inn, Dublin *Also Called: Sb Hotel LLC (G-8115)*
Ramada Inn, Mason *Also Called: Cobb Motel Company LLC (G-10541)*
Ramada Inn, Middletown *Also Called: Quality Team Management Inc (G-11182)*
Ramada Inn, Wadsworth *Also Called: Akron Inn Limited Partnership (G-14426)*
Ramada Inn, Wickliffe *Also Called: Inn At Wickliffe LLC (G-15154)*
Ramada Inn Cumberland Hotel, Cincinnati *Also Called: Cumberland Gap LLC (G-2522)*
Ramada Inn East - Airport, Columbus *Also Called: Broad Street Hotel Assoc LP (G-5467)*
Ramada Xenia, Xenia *Also Called: AK Group Hotels Inc (G-15498)*
Ramar-Genesis, Akron *Also Called: Community Drug Board Inc (G-117)*
Randall Mortgage Services (PA).. 614 336-7948
   655 Metro Pl S Ste 600 Dublin (43017) *(G-8105)*
Randall R Leab.. 330 689-6263
   1895 Township Road 1215 Ashland (44805) *(G-508)*
Rands Trucking Inc.. 740 397-1144
   1201 Gambier Rd Mount Vernon (43050) *(G-11504)*
Randstad Professionals Us LLC.. 513 791-8600
   4600 Mcauley Pl Ste 140 Blue Ash (45242) *(G-1231)*
Rankin Wiesenburger and Otto.. 419 539-2160
   5532 W Central Ave Ste 101 Toledo (43615) *(G-13981)*
Ranpak Corp (HQ)... 440 354-4445
   7990 Auburn Rd Concord Township (44077) *(G-6934)*
Rapid Aerial Imaging, Cincinnati *Also Called: Rapid Mortgage Company (G-3273)*
Rapid Mortgage Company (PA)... 937 748-8888
   7466 Beechmont Ave Unit 420 Cincinnati (45255) *(G-3273)*
Rapid Transit Line.. 216 621-9500
   1240 W 6th St Cleveland (44113) *(G-4808)*
Rapids Nursing Homes Inc... 216 292-5706
   24201 W 3rd St Grand Rapids (43522) *(G-8846)*
Rapps Enterprises Inc.. 330 542-2362
   10201 Main St New Middletown (44442) *(G-11636)*
Rathbone Group LLC (PA).. 800 870-5521
   1250 E Granger Rd Cleveland (44131) *(G-4809)*
Rattlesnake Ridge Golf Club, Sunbury *Also Called: Diamondback Golf LLC (G-13520)*
Rave - Rlable Audio Video Elec, Dayton *Also Called: Reliable Contractors Inc (G-7583)*
Ravenna City Schools Warehouse, Ravenna *Also Called: Ravenna School District (G-12640)*
Ravenna School District.. 330 297-4138
   315 N Walnut St Ravenna (44266) *(G-12640)*
Ravenwood Health, Chardon *Also Called: Ravenwood Mental Hlth Ctr Inc (G-2015)*
Ravenwood Mental Hlth Ctr Inc (PA)................................. 440 285-3568
   12557 Ravenwood Dr Chardon (44024) *(G-2015)*
Ravenwood Mental Hlth Ctr Inc... 440 632-5355
   16030 E High St Middlefield (44062) *(G-11145)*
Rawiga Country Club Inc... 330 336-2220
   10353 Rawiga Rd Seville (44273) *(G-12964)*
Rax Restaurant, Lancaster *Also Called: Carpediem Management Company (G-9699)*
Ray Hamilton Companies... 513 641-5400
   4817 Section Ave Cincinnati (45212) *(G-3274)*
Ray Hamilton Company, Cincinnati *Also Called: Ray Hamilton Companies (G-3274)*
Ray Hamilton Company, Cincinnati *Also Called: Wnb Group LLC (G-3677)*
Ray St Clair Roofing Inc... 513 874-1234
   3810 Port Union Rd Fairfield (45014) *(G-8436)*
Raymond A Greiner DDS Inc.. 440 951-6688
   7553 Center St Mentor (44060) *(G-10987)*
Raymond H Vecchio... 440 365-9580
   1288 Abbe Rd N Ste C Elyria (44035) *(G-8291)*
Raymond Storage Concepts Inc (PA)................................. 513 891-7290
   5480 Creek Rd Unit 1 Blue Ash (45242) *(G-1232)*

ALPHABETIC SECTION — Red Roof Inns Inc

Raymond Storage Concepts Inc 614 275-3494
  4333 Directors Blvd Groveport (43125) *(G-8998)*
RB Knoxville LLC 865 523-2300
  4100 Regent St Ste G Columbus (43219) *(G-6562)*
RB Sigma LLC 440 290-0577
  6111 Heisley Rd Mentor (44060) *(G-10988)*
RB Watkins An Alstom Company, Stow *Also Called: RB Watkins Inc (G-13387)*
RB Watkins Inc 330 688-4061
  778 Mccauley Rd Unit 140 Stow (44224) *(G-13387)*
Rbg Inc 513 247-0175
  6043 Interstate Cir Blue Ash (45242) *(G-1233)*
Rcf Group, The, West Chester *Also Called: River City Furniture LLC (G-14756)*
RCT Engineering Inc (PA) 561 684-7534
  24880 Shaker Blvd Beachwood (44122) *(G-829)*
RDF Logistics, Lorain *Also Called: RDF Trucking Corporation (G-10101)*
RDF Logistics Inc 440 282-9060
  7425 Industrial Parkway Dr Lorain (44053) *(G-10100)*
RDF Trucking Corporation 440 282-9060
  7425 Industrial Parkway Dr Lorain (44053) *(G-10101)*
Rdh Ohio LLC 419 475-8621
  1255 Corporate Dr Holland (43528) *(G-9302)*
Rdi Corporation 513 524-3320
  110 S Locust St Ste A Oxford (45056) *(G-12216)*
Rdp Foodservice Ltd 614 261-5661
  4200 Parkway Ct Hilliard (43026) *(G-9228)*
Rdsi Banking Systems, Defiance *Also Called: Rurbanc Data Services Inc (G-7767)*
Re/Max 614 694-0255
  1131 Hill Rd N Pickerington (43147) *(G-12411)*
Re/Max, Columbus *Also Called: Re/Max Premiere Choice (G-6563)*
Re/Max, Pickerington *Also Called: Re/Max (G-12411)*
Re/Max, Westerville *Also Called: Re/Max Affiliates Inc (G-14932)*
Re/Max Affiliates Inc 614 891-1661
  570 N State St Ste 110 Westerville (43082) *(G-14932)*
Re/Max Premiere Choice 614 436-0330
  1214 Middlefield Ct Columbus (43235) *(G-6563)*
REA & Associates Inc (PA) 330 339-6651
  419 W High Ave New Philadelphia (44663) *(G-11662)*
Reach Livery Taxi LLC 330 278-8080
  814 Marshall St Youngstown (44502) *(G-15706)*
Reach24, Poland *Also Called: Vantage Solutions Inc (G-12511)*
Reader Tinning & Roofing Co 216 451-1355
  676 E 152nd St Cleveland (44110) *(G-4810)*
Reader Tinning Roofg & Frnc Co, Cleveland *Also Called: Reader Tinning & Roofing Co (G-4810)*
Ready Set Grow LLC 513 445-2939
  9863 Mistymorn Ln Cincinnati (45242) *(G-3275)*
Reagan Elementary School, Ashland *Also Called: Ashland City School District (G-473)*
Real Art Design Group Inc (PA) 937 223-9955
  520 E 1st St Dayton (45402) *(G-7581)*
Real Estate Mortgage Corp 440 356-5373
  200 Jackson Dr Chagrin Falls (44022) *(G-1964)*
Real Estate Vltion Prtners LLC 281 313-1571
  300 Madison Ave Ste 900 Toledo (43604) *(G-13982)*
Real Property Management Inc (PA) 614 766-6500
  5550 Blazer Pkwy Ste 175 Dublin (43017) *(G-8106)*
Realmark Property Investors 937 434-7242
  2095 Valley Greene Dr Dayton (45440) *(G-7582)*
Reardon Smith Whittaker, Cincinnati *Also Called: Rsw/Us GP (G-3328)*
Rebiz LLC 844 467-3249
  1925 Saint Clair Ave Ne Cleveland (44114) *(G-4811)*
Rec Center 330 721-6900
  855 Weymouth Rd Medina (44256) *(G-10882)*
Recker & Boerger Appliances, West Chester *Also Called: Recker and Boerger Inc (G-14830)*
Recker and Boerger Inc 513 942-9663
  10115 Transportation Way West Chester (45246) *(G-14830)*
Recmv2 Inc 330 367-5461
  7997 Market St Youngstown (44512) *(G-15707)*
Reco LLC ....
  6860 Ashfield Dr Blue Ash (45242) *(G-1234)*
Recon 740 609-3050
  54382 National Rd Bridgeport (43912) *(G-1377)*

Recovery Center 740 687-4500
  201 S Columbus St Lancaster (43130) *(G-9738)*
Recovery Council, The, Waverly *Also Called: Ohio Dept Mntal Hlth Addction (G-14614)*
Recovery One LLC 614 336-4207
  3250 Henderson Rd Ste 203 Columbus (43220) *(G-6564)*
Recovery Prevention Resources 740 369-6811
  118 Stover Dr Delaware (43015) *(G-7823)*
Recovery Resources 216 431-4131
  4269 Pearl Rd Ste 300 Cleveland (44109) *(G-4812)*
Recovery Resources (HQ) 216 431-4131
  3950 Chester Ave Cleveland (44114) *(G-4813)*
Recovery Works Portage, Ravenna *Also Called: Pinnacle Trtmnt Ctrs Oh-I LLC (G-12635)*
Recreation Center, Westlake *Also Called: City of Westlake (G-15050)*
Recruiting Department, Dayton *Also Called: Greater Dyton Rgnal Trnst Auth (G-7387)*
Recycle Waste Services Inc 419 517-1323
  3793 Silica Rd # B Sylvania (43560) *(G-13567)*
Recycling Services Inc (PA) 419 381-7762
  3940 Technology Dr Maumee (43537) *(G-10758)*
Red Architecture LLC 614 487-8770
  589 W Nationwide Blvd Ste B Columbus (43215) *(G-6565)*
Red Bank Hetzel LP 513 834-9191
  5311 Hetzell St Cincinnati (45227) *(G-3276)*
Red Barn Group Inc 419 625-7838
  2110 Caldwell St Sandusky (44870) *(G-12925)*
Red Bull Media Hse N Amer Inc 614 801-5193
  2101 Southwest Blvd Grove City (43123) *(G-8948)*
Red Capital Markets LLC 614 857-1400
  10 W Broad St Ste 900 Columbus (43215) *(G-6566)*
Red Carpet Health Care Center 740 439-4401
  8420 Georgetown Rd Cambridge (43725) *(G-1580)*
Red Carpet Inn, Middletown *Also Called: Days Inn Middletown (G-11194)*
Red Carpet Janitorial Service (PA) 513 242-7575
  3478 Hauck Rd Ste D Cincinnati (45241) *(G-3277)*
Red Cross, Canton *Also Called: American National Red Cross (G-1665)*
Red Cross, Toledo *Also Called: American National Red Cross (G-13686)*
Red Group Limited 440 256-1268
  7314 Lake Shore Blvd Mentor (44060) *(G-10989)*
Red Oak Behavioral Health, Akron *Also Called: Pastoral Cnsling Svc Smmit CNT (G-262)*
Red Robin, Canton *Also Called: Red Robin Gourmet Burgers Inc (G-1841)*
Red Robin Gourmet Burgers Inc 330 305-1080
  6522 Strip Ave Nw Canton (44720) *(G-1841)*
Red Roof Inn, Akron *Also Called: Red Roof Inns Inc (G-277)*
Red Roof Inn, Canton *Also Called: Red Roof Inns Inc (G-1842)*
Red Roof Inn, Cleveland *Also Called: Red Roof Inns Inc (G-4814)*
Red Roof Inn, Cleveland *Also Called: Red Roof Inns Inc (G-4815)*
Red Roof Inn, Cleveland *Also Called: Red Roof Inns Inc (G-4816)*
Red Roof Inn, Clyde *Also Called: Lake Erie Hospitality LLC (G-5205)*
Red Roof Inn, Columbus *Also Called: Red Roof Inns Inc (G-6567)*
Red Roof Inn, Columbus *Also Called: Red Roof Inns Inc (G-6568)*
Red Roof Inn, Englewood *Also Called: Paradise Hotels LLC (G-8317)*
Red Roof Inn, Grove City *Also Called: Dhanlaxmi LLC (G-8916)*
Red Roof Inn, Jackson *Also Called: Red Roof Inns Inc (G-9524)*
Red Roof Inn, Medina *Also Called: Peacock Hotels LLC (G-10875)*
Red Roof Inn, Miamisburg *Also Called: Red Roof Inns Inc (G-11088)*
Red Roof Inn, New Albany *Also Called: Red Roof Inns Inc (G-11584)*
Red Roof Inn, Poland *Also Called: Red Roof Inns Inc (G-12507)*
Red Roof Inn, Saint Clairsville *Also Called: Red Roof Inns Inc (G-12812)*
Red Roof Inn, Springfield *Also Called: Welcome Hospitality Corp (G-13311)*
Red Roof Inn, Toledo *Also Called: Red Roof Inns Inc (G-13983)*
Red Roof Inn, Willoughby *Also Called: Red Roof Inns Inc (G-15220)*
Red Roof Inns Inc 330 644-7748
  2939 S Arlington Rd Akron (44312) *(G-277)*
Red Roof Inns Inc 330 499-1970
  5353 Inn Cir Nw Canton (44720) *(G-1842)*
Red Roof Inns Inc 216 447-0030
  6020 Quarry Ln Cleveland (44131) *(G-4814)*
Red Roof Inns Inc 440 892-7920
  29595 Clemens Rd Cleveland (44145) *(G-4815)*

Red Roof Inns Inc   **ALPHABETIC SECTION**

Red Roof Inns Inc 440 202-1521
  17555 Bagley Rd Cleveland (44130) *(G-4816)*
Red Roof Inns Inc 614 267-9941
  441 Ackerman Rd Columbus (43202) *(G-6567)*
Red Roof Inns Inc 614 224-6539
  111 Nationwide Plz Columbus (43215) *(G-6568)*
Red Roof Inns Inc 740 288-1200
  1000 Acy Ave Jackson (45640) *(G-9524)*
Red Roof Inns Inc 937 866-0705
  222 Byers Rd Miamisburg (45342) *(G-11088)*
Red Roof Inns Inc (HQ) 614 744-2600
  7815 Walton Pkwy New Albany (43054) *(G-11584)*
Red Roof Inns Inc 330 758-1999
  1051 Tiffany S Poland (44514) *(G-12507)*
Red Roof Inns Inc 740 695-4057
  68301 Red Roof Ln Saint Clairsville (43950) *(G-12812)*
Red Roof Inns Inc 419 536-0118
  3530 Executive Pkwy Toledo (43606) *(G-13983)*
Red Roof Inns Inc 440 946-9872
  4166 State Route 306 Willoughby (44094) *(G-15220)*
Red Rover LLC (DH) 330 262-6501
  3000 Old Airport Rd Wooster (44691) *(G-15368)*
Red Squirrel, Fairfield Township *Also Called: Robiden Inc (G-8464)*
Reddy Electric Co 937 372-8205
  1145 Bellbrook Ave Xenia (45385) *(G-15530)*
Redefine Enterprises LLC 330 952-2024
  3839 Pearl Rd Medina (44256) *(G-10883)*
Redhawk Global LLC 614 487-8505
  2642 Fisher Rd Ste B Columbus (43204) *(G-6569)*
Redhawk Logistics, Columbus *Also Called: Redhawk Global LLC (G-6569)*
Redi Cincinnati LLC 513 562-8474
  3 E 4th St Cincinnati (45202) *(G-3278)*
Redkey Express LLC 859 393-3221
  123 E Main St Mason (45040) *(G-10599)*
Reduction Engineering Inc 330 677-2225
  235 Progress Blvd Kent (44240) *(G-9593)*
Redwood, Maumee *Also Called: Redwood Living Inc (G-10759)*
Redwood Living Inc 216 360-9441
  1520 Market Place Dr W8 Maumee (43537) *(G-10759)*
Reece-Campbell Inc 513 542-4600
  10839 Chester Rd Cincinnati (45246) *(G-3279)*
Reed Air Products, Bradner *Also Called: American Warming and Vent (G-1341)*
Reed Funeral Home Inc 330 477-6721
  705 Raff Rd Sw Canton (44710) *(G-1843)*
Reed Park Golf Course, Springfield *Also Called: City of Springfield (G-13228)*
Reed Westlake Leskosky Ltd 216 522-0449
  1422 Euclid Ave Ste 300 Cleveland (44115) *(G-4817)*
Reese Pyle Drake & Meyer (PA) 740 345-3431
  36 N 2nd St Newark (43055) *(G-11745)*
Refectory, Columbus *Also Called: Refectory Restaurant Inc (G-6570)*
Refectory Restaurant Inc 614 451-9774
  1092 Bethel Rd Columbus (43220) *(G-6570)*
Reference Laboratory, Columbus *Also Called: Childrens Hosp Reference Lab (G-5562)*
Reflexis Systems Inc 614 948-1931
  579 Executive Campus Dr Ste 310 Westerville (43082) *(G-14933)*
Refrigeration Sales Company LLC (DH) 216 525-8200
  9450 Allen Dr Ste A Cleveland (44125) *(G-4818)*
Refrigeration Systems Company (HQ) 614 263-0913
  1770 Genessee Ave Columbus (43211) *(G-6571)*
Refrigrtion Sls Corp Cleveland, Cleveland *Also Called: Refrigeration Sales Company LLC (G-4818)*
Regal Hospitality LLC 614 436-0004
  201 Hutchinson Ave Columbus (43235) *(G-6572)*
Regal Plumbing & Heating Co 937 492-2894
  9303 State Route 29 W Sidney (45365) *(G-13046)*
Regal-Elite Inc 614 873-3800
  8140 Business Way Plain City (43064) *(G-12492)*
Regard Recovery Florida LLC 330 866-0700
  2650 Lodge Rd Sw Sherrodsville (44675) *(G-13012)*
Regency Hospital - Cleveland E, Warrensville Heights *Also Called: Regency Hospital Company LLC (G-14587)*

Regency Hospital Company LLC 614 456-0300
  1430 S High St Columbus (43207) *(G-6573)*
Regency Hospital Company LLC 440 202-4200
  6990 Engle Rd Middleburg Heights (44130) *(G-11122)*
Regency Hospital Company LLC 216 910-3800
  4200 Interchange Corporate Center Rd Warrensville Heights (44128) *(G-14587)*
Regency Hospital Toledo LLC 419 318-5700
  5220 Alexis Rd Sylvania (43560) *(G-13568)*
Regency Leasing Co LLC 614 542-3100
  2000 Regency Manor Cir Columbus (43207) *(G-6574)*
Regency Manor Rehab, Columbus *Also Called: Regency Leasing Co LLC (G-6574)*
Regency Mnor Rhbltton Sbcute, Columbus *Also Called: Communicare Health Svcs Inc (G-5668)*
Regency Park Surgery Ctr LLC 419 882-0003
  2000 Regency Ct Ste 101 Toledo (43623) *(G-13984)*
Regency Technologies, Solon *Also Called: RSR Partners LLC (G-13140)*
Regency Technologies, Stow *Also Called: RSR Partners LLC (G-13389)*
Regent, Toledo *Also Called: Regent Electric Inc (G-13985)*
Regent Electric Inc 419 476-8333
  5235 Tractor Rd Toledo (43612) *(G-13985)*
Regional Acceptance Corp 513 398-2106
  8044 Montgomery Rd Ste 340 Cincinnati (45236) *(G-3280)*
Regional Collection Services, Marietta *Also Called: Platinum Recovery LLC (G-10400)*
Regional Express Inc 516 458-3514
  4615 W Streetsboro Rd Ste 203 Richfield (44286) *(G-12707)*
Regional Finance, Cincinnati *Also Called: Regional Acceptance Corp (G-3280)*
Regional Income Tax Agency (PA) 800 860-7482
  10107 Brecksville Rd Brecksville (44141) *(G-1364)*
Registered Contractors Inc 440 205-0873
  8425 Station St Mentor (44060) *(G-10990)*
Rehab At The Nat, Cuyahoga Falls *Also Called: Summa Western Reserve Hosp LLC (G-7103)*
Rehab Center 330 297-2770
  6847 N Chestnut St Ravenna (44266) *(G-12641)*
Rehab Continuum, The, Blue Ash *Also Called: Counseling Source Inc (G-1160)*
Rehab Medical LLC 513 381-3740
  2860 Cooper Rd Cincinnati (45241) *(G-3281)*
Rehab Nursing Ctr At Firelands, New London *Also Called: 204 W Main Street Oper Co LLC (G-11632)*
Rehab Resources Inc 513 474-4123
  8595 Beechmont Ave Ste 204 Cincinnati (45255) *(G-3282)*
Rehabcare Group East Inc 330 220-8950
  3151 Mayfield Rd Cleveland (44118) *(G-4819)*
Rehabcenter, Ravenna *Also Called: Rehab Center (G-12641)*
Rehabilitation Inst Bus Indust, Columbus *Also Called: Doctors Ohiohealth Corporation (G-5780)*
Rehabilitation Support Svcs 330 252-9012
  594 W Market St Akron (44303) *(G-278)*
Rehablttion Ctr At Mrietta Mem 740 374-1407
  401 Matthew St Marietta (45750) *(G-10403)*
Rehablttion Ctr At Mrtta Mmori, Marietta *Also Called: Rehablttion Ctr At Mrietta Mem (G-10403)*
Rehmann, Independence *Also Called: Rehmann Robson LLC (G-9475)*
Rehmann Robson LLC 248 952-5000
  6060 Rockside Woods Blvd N Ste 125 Independence (44131) *(G-9475)*
Reichart Leasing Co LLC 513 530-1600
  135 Reichart Ave Wintersville (43953) *(G-15296)*
Reichle Klein Group Inc 419 861-1100
  1 Seagate Fl 26 Toledo (43604) *(G-13986)*
Reid Physician Associates Inc 937 456-4400
  109 E Washington Jackson Rd Ste B Eaton (45320) *(G-8222)*
Reid Physicians Associates, Eaton *Also Called: Reid Physician Associates Inc (G-8222)*
Reidy Medical Supply Inc 800 398-2723
  1397 Commerce Dr Stow (44224) *(G-13388)*
Reilly Painting & Contg Inc 216 371-8160
  1899 S Taylor Rd Cleveland Heights (44118) *(G-5183)*
Reily Township, Oxford *Also Called: Butler County of Ohio (G-12202)*
Reineke Ford Inc 888 691-8175
  1303 Perrysburg Rd Fostoria (44830) *(G-8622)*
Reino Cleaners, Gibsonburg *Also Called: Reino Linen Service Inc (G-8806)*
Reino Linen Service Inc (HQ) 419 637-2151
  119 S Main St Gibsonburg (43431) *(G-8806)*

ALPHABETIC SECTION — RES-Care Inc

Reis Trucking Inc 513 353-1960
10080 Valley Junction Rd Cleves (45002) *(G-5192)*

Reisenfeld & Assoc Lpa LLC (PA) 513 322-7000
3962 Red Bank Rd Cincinnati (45227) *(G-3283)*

Reitter Stucco Inc 614 291-2212
1100 King Ave Columbus (43212) *(G-6575)*

Reladyne Florida LLC 904 354-8411
8280 Montgomery Rd Ste 101 Cincinnati (45236) *(G-3284)*

Reladyne Inc (PA) 513 941-2800
8280 Montgomery Rd Ste 101 Cincinnati (45236) *(G-3285)*

RELAM Inc (PA) 440 232-3354
7695 Bond St Solon (44139) *(G-13137)*

Relational Solutions Inc 440 899-3296
25050 Country Club Blvd Ste 105 North Olmsted (44070) *(G-11913)*

Relentless Recovery Inc 216 621-8333
1898 Scranton Rd Uppr Cleveland (44113) *(G-4820)*

Reliability First Corporation 216 503-0600
3 Summit Park Dr Ste 600 Cleveland (44131) *(G-4821)*

Reliable Appl Installation Inc 614 246-6840
3736 Paragon Dr Columbus (43228) *(G-6576)*

Reliable Contractors Inc 937 433-0262
94 Compark Rd Ste 200 Dayton (45459) *(G-7583)*

Reliable Home Healthcare LLC 937 274-2900
50 Chestnut St Ste 224 Dayton (45440) *(G-7584)*

Reliable Rnners Curier Svc Inc 440 578-1011
8624 Station St Mentor (44060) *(G-10991)*

Reliance Financial Services NA 419 783-8007
401 Clinton St Defiance (43512) *(G-7765)*

Reliance Medical Products, Mason *Also Called: Haag-Streit Usa Inc (G-10559)*

Reliant Capital Solutions LLC (PA) 614 452-6100
670 Cross Pointe Rd Gahanna (43230) *(G-8726)*

Reliant Mechanical Inc 937 644-0074
3271 County Rd 154 East Liberty (43319) *(G-8175)*

Reliant Recovery Solutions, Gahanna *Also Called: Reliant Capital Solutions LLC (G-8726)*

Reliant Technology LLC 404 551-4534
5910 Landerbrook Dr Ste 100 Cleveland (44124) *(G-4822)*

Relink Medical LLC (PA) 330 954-1199
1755 Enterprise Pkwy Ste 400 Twinsburg (44087) *(G-14215)*

Relmec Mechanical LLC 216 391-1030
4975 Hamilton Ave Cleveland (44114) *(G-4823)*

Relx Inc 937 865-1012
9393 Springboro Pike Dayton (45432) *(G-7141)*

REM Corp 740 828-2601
26 E 3rd St Frazeysburg (43822) *(G-8656)*

REM Ohio Waivered Services, Reynoldsburg *Also Called: REM-Ohio Inc (G-12675)*

REM-Ohio Inc 937 335-8267
721 Lincoln Ave Troy (45373) *(G-14154)*

REM-Ohio Inc 330 644-9730
470 Portage Lakes Dr Ste 207 Coventry Township (44319) *(G-7015)*

REM-Ohio Inc 614 367-1370
6402 E Main St Ste 103 Reynoldsburg (43068) *(G-12675)*

Remax Preferred Associates LLC 419 720-5600
3306 Executive Pkwy Ste 101 Toledo (43606) *(G-13987)*

Remedi Seniorcare of Ohio LLC (DH) 800 232-4239
962 S Dorset Rd Troy (45373) *(G-14155)*

Remel Products, Oakwood Village *Also Called: Thermo Fisher Scientific Inc (G-12059)*

Remesh Inc 561 809-9885
6815 Euclid Ave Cleveland (44103) *(G-4824)*

Reminger Co LPA (PA) 216 687-1311
200 Public Sq Ste 1200 Cleveland (44114) *(G-4825)*

Remington Steel, Springfield *Also Called: Westfield Steel Inc (G-13312)*

Remington Steel Inc 937 322-2414
1120 S Burnett Rd Springfield (45505) *(G-13284)*

Remote Support Services, Green Springs *Also Called: Wynn-Reeth Inc (G-8862)*

Remtec Automation LLC 877 759-8151
6049 Hi Tek Ct Mason (45040) *(G-10600)*

Remtec Engineering 513 860-4299
6049 Hi Tek Ct Mason (45040) *(G-10601)*

Renaissance Cleveland Hotel, Cleveland *Also Called: Skyline Clvland Rnaissance LLC (G-4913)*

Renaissance Home Health Care 216 662-8702
5311 Northfield Rd Bedford (44146) *(G-981)*

Renaissance Hotel, Cleveland *Also Called: Renaissance Hotel Operating Co (G-4826)*

Renaissance Hotel MGT Co LLC 614 882-6800
409 Altair Pkwy Westerville (43082) *(G-14934)*

Renaissance Hotel Operating Co 216 696-5600
24 Public Sq Fl 1 Cleveland (44113) *(G-4826)*

Renaissance Hotel Operating Co 614 228-5050
50 N 3rd St Columbus (43215) *(G-6577)*

Renaissance House Inc 419 425-0633
1665 Tiffin Ave Ste E Findlay (45840) *(G-8581)*

Renaissance House Inc 419 663-1316
48 Executive Dr Ste 1 Norwalk (44857) *(G-12023)*

Renaissance House Inc 419 626-1110
158 E Market St Ste 805 Sandusky (44870) *(G-12926)*

Renaissance Toledo, Toledo *Also Called: First Tdt LLC (G-13809)*

Renaissance, The, Olmsted Twp *Also Called: Olmsted Residence Corporation (G-12093)*

Renaissancetech 419 569-3999
5880 Venture Dr Ste B Dublin (43017) *(G-8107)*

Renascence Ottawa LLC 614 863-4640
6880 Tussing Rd Reynoldsburg (43068) *(G-12676)*

Renascent Salvage Holdings LLC 216 539-1033
6910 Carriage Hill Dr Brecksville (44141) *(G-1365)*

Rendigs Fry Kiely & Dennis LLP (PA) 513 381-9200
600 Vine St Ste 2602 Cincinnati (45202) *(G-3286)*

Renier Construction Corp 614 866-4580
2164 Citygate Dr Columbus (43219) *(G-6578)*

Renner Kenner, Akron *Also Called: Renner Knner Greve Bbak Tylor (G-279)*

Renner Knner Greve Bbak Tylor (PA) 330 376-1242
106 S Main St Akron (44308) *(G-279)*

Renner Otto Boiselle & Sklar 216 621-1113
1621 Euclid Ave Ste 1900 Cleveland (44115) *(G-4827)*

Rental Concepts Inc (PA) 216 525-3870
695 Boston Mills Rd Hudson (44236) *(G-9370)*

Rental Tools Online, Eastlake *Also Called: National Tool Leasing Inc (G-8206)*

Renthotel Dayton LLC 937 461-4700
11 S Ludlow St Dayton (45402) *(G-7585)*

Rentokil North America Inc 440 964-5641
1618 W 7th St Ashtabula (44004) *(G-547)*

Rentokil North America Inc 513 247-9300
3253 E Kemper Rd Cincinnati (45241) *(G-3287)*

Rentokil North America Inc 614 837-0099
6300 Commerce Center Dr Ste G Groveport (43125) *(G-8999)*

Repros Inc (PA) 330 247-3747
1518 Copley Rd Akron (44320) *(G-280)*

Republcan State Cntl Exec Cmmt 614 228-2481
211 S 5th St Columbus (43215) *(G-6579)*

Republic Bank & Trust Company 513 651-3000
8050 Hosbrook Rd Ste 220 Cincinnati (45236) *(G-3288)*

Republic N&T Railroad Inc 330 438-5826
2633 8th St Ne Canton (44704) *(G-1844)*

Republic Services, Massillon *Also Called: Republic Services Inc (G-10662)*

Republic Services, Williamsburg *Also Called: Republic Services Kentucky LLC (G-15181)*

Republic Services Inc 330 830-9050
2800 Erie St S Massillon (44646) *(G-10662)*

Republic Services Kentucky LLC 859 824-5466
5092 Aber Rd Williamsburg (45176) *(G-15181)*

Republic Services Ohio Hlg LLC 513 771-4200
11563 Mosteller Rd Cincinnati (45241) *(G-3289)*

Republic Telcom Worldwide LLC (HQ) 330 966-4586
3939 Everhard Rd Nw Canton (44709) *(G-1845)*

Republic Telcom Worldwide LLC 330 244-8285
8000 Freedom Ave Nw North Canton (44720) *(G-11858)*

Req/Jqh Holdings Inc 513 891-1066
4243 Hunt Rd Ste 2 Blue Ash (45242) *(G-1235)*

Requarth Lumber Co., Dayton *Also Called: The F A Requarth Company (G-7665)*

RES Care, Waverly *Also Called: RES-Care Inc (G-14617)*

Res Care Home Care 937 436-3966
8265 Mcewen Rd Dayton (45458) *(G-7586)*

RES Care OH, Carrollton *Also Called: RES-Care Inc (G-1912)*

RES-Care Inc 740 782-1476
39555 National Rd Bethesda (43719) *(G-1097)*

RES-Care Inc 330 452-2913
   2424 Market Ave N Canton (44714) *(G-1846)*

RES-Care Inc 330 627-7552
   520 S Lisbon St Carrollton (44615) *(G-1912)*

RES-Care Inc 513 271-0708
   5535 Fair Ln Ste A Cincinnati (45227) *(G-3290)*

RES-Care Inc 740 968-0181
   41743 Mount Hope Rd Flushing (43977) *(G-8601)*

RES-Care Inc 419 435-6620
   1016 Dillon Cir Fostoria (44830) *(G-8623)*

RES-Care Inc 740 446-7549
   240 3rd Ave Gallipolis (45631) *(G-8768)*

RES-Care Inc 937 298-6276
   2012 Springboro W Moraine (45439) *(G-11433)*

RES-Care Inc 419 523-4981
   3033 Kettering Blvd Ste 325 Moraine (45439) *(G-11434)*

RES-Care Inc 740 526-0285
   66387 Airport Rd Saint Clairsville (43950) *(G-12813)*

RES-Care Inc 740 695-4931
   67051 Executive Dr Saint Clairsville (43950) *(G-12814)*

RES-Care Inc 740 941-1178
   212 Saint Anns Ln Waverly (45690) *(G-14617)*

RES-Care Inc 513 858-4550
   7908 Cincinnati Dayton Rd West Chester (45069) *(G-14755)*

Rescare, Moraine *Also Called: RES-Care Inc (G-11433)*

Rescare Ohio Inc (DH) 513 724-1177
   613 W Main St Mount Orab (45154) *(G-11473)*

Rescare Workforce Services, Cincinnati *Also Called: RES-Care Inc (G-3290)*

Rescue Incorporated 419 255-9585
   3350 Collingwood Blvd Ste 2 Toledo (43610) *(G-13988)*

RESCUE MENTAL HEALTH & ADDICTI, Toledo *Also Called: Rescue Incorporated (G-13988)*

Rescue91 Healthcare Svcs LLC 937 500-5371
   1715 Springfield St Ste 4 Dayton (45403) *(G-7587)*

Research & Development, Maumee *Also Called: Bprex Closures LLC (G-10703)*

Research Associates Inc (PA) 440 892-1000
   27999 Clemens Rd Cleveland (44145) *(G-4828)*

Research Inst At Ntnwide Chld 614 722-2700
   700 Childrens Dr Columbus (43205) *(G-6580)*

Research Institute, Dayton *Also Called: University of Dayton (G-7693)*

Research Institute Univ Hosp, Cleveland *Also Called: University Hospitals Cleveland (G-5073)*

Reserve Run Golf Club LLC 330 758-1017
   625 E Western Reserve Rd Poland (44514) *(G-12508)*

Reserve Square Apartments, Cleveland *Also Called: K&D Management LLC (G-4447)*

Reserves Network Inc (PA) 440 779-1400
   22021 Brookpark Rd Cleveland (44126) *(G-4829)*

Residence At Huntington Court, Hamilton *Also Called: Residence At Kensington Place (G-9078)*

Residence At Kensington Place 513 863-4218
   350 Hancock Ave Hamilton (45011) *(G-9078)*

Residence Inn 614 222-2610
   36 E Gay St Columbus (43215) *(G-6581)*

Residence Inn By Marriott 513 771-2525
   11689 Chester Rd Cincinnati (45246) *(G-3291)*

Residence Inn By Marriott, Blue Ash *Also Called: Residence Inn By Marriott LLC (G-1236)*

Residence Inn By Marriott, Cincinnati *Also Called: 506 Phelps Holdings LLC (G-2124)*

Residence Inn By Marriott, Cincinnati *Also Called: Residence Inn By Marriott (G-3291)*

Residence Inn By Marriott, Cleveland *Also Called: Chester Ave Hotel LLC (G-3967)*

Residence Inn By Marriott, Cleveland *Also Called: Nf II Cleveland Op Co LLC (G-4643)*

Residence Inn By Marriott, Cleveland *Also Called: Summit Hotel Trs 144 LLC (G-4958)*

Residence Inn By Marriott, Columbus *Also Called: 5 Star Hotel Management IV LP (G-5288)*

Residence Inn By Marriott, Columbus *Also Called: Columbus Easton Hotel LLC (G-5630)*

Residence Inn By Marriott, Columbus *Also Called: Residence Inn (G-6581)*

Residence Inn By Marriott, Columbus *Also Called: Residence Inn By Marriott LLC (G-6582)*

Residence Inn By Marriott, Columbus *Also Called: Residence Inn By Marriott LLC (G-6583)*

Residence Inn By Marriott, Middleburg Heights *Also Called: Residence Inn By Marriott LLC (G-11123)*

Residence Inn By Marriott LLC 513 530-5060
   11401 Reed Hartman Hwy Blue Ash (45241) *(G-1236)*

Residence Inn By Marriott LLC 614 222-2610
   36 E Gay St Columbus (43215) *(G-6582)*

Residence Inn By Marriott LLC 614 885-0799
   7300 Huntington Park Dr Columbus (43235) *(G-6583)*

Residence Inn By Marriott LLC 440 392-0800
   5660 Emerald Ct Mentor (44060) *(G-10992)*

Residence Inn By Marriott LLC 440 638-5856
   19149 Bagley Rd Middleburg Heights (44130) *(G-11123)*

Residence Inn Cleveland Airpor, Cleveland *Also Called: Marriott (G-4526)*

Residence Inn Toledo Maumee 419 891-2233
   1370 Arrowhead Dr Maumee (43537) *(G-10760)*

Residence of Chardon 440 286-2277
   501 Chardon Windsor Rd Chardon (44024) *(G-2016)*

Resident HM Assn Grter Dyton I 937 278-0791
   3661 Salem Ave Dayton (45406) *(G-7588)*

RESIDENT HOME, THE, Cincinnati *Also Called: Rhc Inc (G-3294)*

Residential Care Inc 937 299-8090
   1250 W Dorothy Ln Ste 304 Dayton (45409) *(G-7589)*

Residential Finance Corp 614 324-4700
   1 Easton Oval Ste 400 Columbus (43219) *(G-6584)*

Residential HM Assn Marion Inc (PA) 740 387-9999
   205 Center St Ste 100 Marion (43302) *(G-10451)*

Residential MGT Systems Inc (PA) 614 880-6009
   250 E Wilson Bridge Rd Ste 205 Worthington (43085) *(G-15451)*

Residential One Realty Inc (PA) 614 436-9830
   8351 N High St Ste 150 Columbus (43235) *(G-6585)*

Residents of Chardon, Chardon *Also Called: Residence of Chardon (G-2016)*

Residntl HM For Dvlpmntlly D (PA) 740 622-9778
   925 Chestnut St Coshocton (43812) *(G-6999)*

Residntl HM For Dvlpmntlly D 740 677-0500
   49 Connett Rd The Plains (45780) *(G-13616)*

Resilience Fund III LP (PA) 216 292-0200
   25101 Chagrin Blvd Ste 350 Cleveland (44122) *(G-4830)*

Resolute Bank 419 868-1750
   3425 Briarfield Blvd Ste 100 Maumee (43537) *(G-10761)*

Resolute Industrial LLC 513 779-7909
   9950 Commerce Park Dr West Chester (45246) *(G-14831)*

Resolvit, Cincinnati *Also Called: Resolvit Resources LLC (G-3292)*

Resolvit Resources LLC (HQ) 513 619-5900
   1308 Race St Ste 200 Cincinnati (45202) *(G-3292)*

Resonant Sciences LLC 937 431-8180
   3975 Research Blvd Beavercreek (45430) *(G-929)*

Resource, Columbus *Also Called: Resource Interactive (G-6586)*

Resource Alliance Homecare LLC 216 465-9977
   2000 Lee Rd Ste 24 Cleveland Heights (44118) *(G-5184)*

Resource Imaging Supply, Cincinnati *Also Called: Queen City Reprographics Inc (G-3266)*

Resource Interactive 614 621-2888
   250 S High St Ste 400 Columbus (43215) *(G-6586)*

Resource International, Columbus *Also Called: Majidzadeh Enterprises Inc (G-6191)*

Resource International Inc 614 823-4949
   6350 Presidential Gtwy Columbus (43231) *(G-6587)*

Resource One, Blue Ash *Also Called: Rbg Inc (G-1233)*

Resource One Cmpt Systems Inc 614 485-4800
   651 Lakeview Plaza Blvd Ste E Worthington (43085) *(G-15452)*

Resource One Solutions LLC 614 485-8500
   651 Lakeview Plaza Blvd Ste E Worthington (43085) *(G-15453)*

Resource Systems, New Concord *Also Called: Cerner Corporation (G-11609)*

Resource Title Agency Inc (PA) 216 520-0050
   7100 E Pleasant Valley Rd Ste 100 Cleveland (44131) *(G-4831)*

Resource Title Nat Agcy Inc 216 520-0050
   7100 E Pleasant Valley Rd Ste 100 Independence (44131) *(G-9476)*

Resource-One, An SES Company, Bellefontaine *Also Called: Superior Envmtl Solutions LLC (G-1038)*

Resources Technology, Westlake *Also Called: Pavement Technology Inc (G-15096)*

Rest Care, Dayton *Also Called: Res Care Home Care (G-7586)*

REST HAVEN NURSING HOME, Mc Dermott *Also Called: Voiers Enterprises Inc (G-10800)*

Rest Haven Nursing Home Inc 937 548-1138
   1096 N Ohio St Greenville (45331) *(G-8882)*

Restaurant Refreshment Service, Cincinnati *Also Called: Coffee Break Corporation (G-2468)*

Restaurant Specialties Inc 614 885-9707
   801 W Cherry St Ste 200 Sunbury (43074) *(G-13524)*

Restoration Resources Inc 330 650-4486
   1546 Georgetown Rd Hudson (44236) *(G-9371)*

ALPHABETIC SECTION

Retail Distribution Center, Maumee *Also Called: Andersons Inc (G-10693)*
Retail Renovations Inc (PA)..330 334-4501
   7530 State Rd Wadsworth (44281) *(G-14449)*
Retail Service Systems Inc...614 203-6126
   6221 Riverside Dr Ste 2n Dublin (43017) *(G-8108)*
Retalix Inc..937 384-2277
   2490 Technical Dr Miamisburg (45342) *(G-11089)*
Retina Associate of Cleveland (PA)...216 831-5700
   3401 Enterprise Pkwy Ste 300 Beachwood (44122) *(G-830)*
Retirement Corp of America...513 769-4040
   10300 Alliance Rd Ste 100 Blue Ash (45242) *(G-1237)*
Reuben Co (PA)...419 241-3400
   24 S Huron St Toledo (43604) *(G-13989)*
Reuben Group, The, Brooklyn *Also Called: Trg Studios Inc (G-1411)*
Reupert Heating and AC Co Inc..513 922-5050
   5137 Crookshank Rd Cincinnati (45238) *(G-3293)*
Reve Salon and Spa Inc...419 885-1140
   5633 Main St Sylvania (43560) *(G-13569)*
Revel It Inc..614 336-1122
   4900 Blazer Pkwy Dublin (43017) *(G-8109)*
Revenue Assistance Corporation..216 763-2100
   3711 Chester Ave Cleveland (44114) *(G-4832)*
Revenue Group, Cleveland *Also Called: Revenue Assistance Corporation (G-4832)*
Revere Title Agency Inc..216 447-4070
   6480 Rockside Woods Blvd S Ste 280 Cleveland (44131) *(G-4833)*
Reville Tire Co (PA)..330 468-1900
   8044 Olde 8 Rd Northfield (44067) *(G-11965)*
Reville Wholesale Distributing, Northfield *Also Called: Reville Tire Co (G-11965)*
Revitalize Industries LLC..440 570-3473
   4444 Lee Rd Cleveland (44128) *(G-4834)*
Revitalize Industries LLC..440 570-3473
   17000 Rockside Rd Maple Heights (44137) *(G-10344)*
Revlocal (PA)...800 456-7470
   4009 Columbus Rd Granville (43023) *(G-8854)*
Revol Communications, Independence *Also Called: Cleveland Unlimited Inc (G-9422)*
Revolution Group Inc..614 212-1111
   670 Meridian Way Westerville (43082) *(G-14935)*
Revolution Mortgage, Westerville *Also Called: T2 Financial LLC (G-14941)*
Revolution Trucking LLC..330 975-4145
   257 Main St Ste 103 Wadsworth (44281) *(G-14450)*
Revvity Health Sciences Inc...330 825-4525
   520 S Main St Ste 2423 Akron (44311) *(G-281)*
Rexel Usa Inc..216 778-6400
   5605 Granger Rd Cleveland (44131) *(G-4835)*
Rexel Usa Inc..419 625-6761
   140 Lane St Sandusky (44870) *(G-12927)*
Reynolds & Co Inc..740 353-1040
   839 Gallia St Portsmouth (45662) *(G-12566)*
Reynolds & Company Cpa's, Portsmouth *Also Called: Reynolds & Co Inc (G-12566)*
Reynolds and Reynolds, Kettering *Also Called: Reynolds and Reynolds Company (G-9632)*
Reynolds and Reynolds Company (HQ)..................................937 485-2000
   1 Reynolds Way Kettering (45430) *(G-9632)*
Reynolds and Reynolds Holdings..937 485-8125
   1 Reynolds Way Dayton (45430) *(G-7590)*
Reynolds Road Surgical Ctr LLC...419 578-7500
   2865 N Reynolds Rd Ste 190 Toledo (43615) *(G-13990)*
Rez Stone, Toledo *Also Called: Hoover & Wells Inc (G-13850)*
RG Barry Brands, Pickerington *Also Called: R G Barry Corporation (G-12408)*
Rgbsi A&D, Beavercreek *Also Called: RGBSI Aerospace & Defense LLC (G-900)*
RGBSI Aerospace & Defense LLC...248 761-0412
   2850 Presidential Dr Ste 120 Beavercreek (45324) *(G-900)*
Rgh Enterprises LLC (HQ)..330 963-6996
   1810 Summit Commerce Park Twinsburg (44087) *(G-14216)*
Rgs, Canton *Also Called: R G Smith Company (G-1839)*
RGT Management Inc..513 715-4640
   10554 Harrison Ave Harrison (45030) *(G-9114)*
Rgt Services LLC...440 786-9777
   26185 Broadway Ave Oakwood Village (44146) *(G-12056)*
RHAM, Marion *Also Called: Residential HM Assn Marion Inc (G-10451)*
Rhc Inc (PA)..513 389-7501
   3030 W Fork Rd Cincinnati (45211) *(G-3294)*

Rhdd, Coshocton *Also Called: Residntial HM For Dvlpmntlly D (G-6999)*
Rhea Aryan Inc..937 865-0077
   250 Byers Rd Miamisburg (45342) *(G-11090)*
Rhein Chemie Corporation...440 279-2367
   145 Parker Ct Chardon (44024) *(G-2017)*
Rhenium Alloys, North Ridgeville *Also Called: Rhenium Alloys Inc (G-11934)*
Rhenium Alloys Inc (PA)...440 365-7388
   38683 Taylor Pkwy North Ridgeville (44035) *(G-11934)*
Rhiel Supply Co (PA)..330 799-7777
   3735 Oakwood Ave Austintown (44515) *(G-636)*
Rhiel Supply Co, The, Austintown *Also Called: Rhiel Supply Co (G-636)*
Rhinegeist LLC..513 381-1367
   1910 Elm St Cincinnati (45202) *(G-3295)*
Rhinegeist Brewery, Cincinnati *Also Called: Rhinegeist LLC (G-3295)*
Rhl Logistics, Springfield *Also Called: Tri-State Forest Logistics LLC (G-13303)*
Rhm Real Estate Inc..216 360-8333
   5845 Landerbrook Dr Cleveland (44124) *(G-4836)*
Rhoads Farm Inc...740 404-5696
   1357 Hitler Road 1 Circleville (43113) *(G-3720)*
Rhodes Hs-Sch of Leadership, Cleveland *Also Called: Cleveland Municipal School Dst (G-4059)*
Rhyme Software Corporation...888 213-3728
   102 W Main St New Albany (43054) *(G-11585)*
Ribbit, Oxford *Also Called: Cash Flow Solutions Inc (G-12205)*
Ricart Automotive, Groveport *Also Called: Ricart Ford Inc (G-9000)*
Ricart Ford Inc..614 836-5321
   4255 S Hamilton Rd Groveport (43125) *(G-9000)*
Ricco Enterprises Incorporated..216 883-7775
   6010 Fleet Ave Ste Frnt Cleveland (44105) *(G-4837)*
Richard Equipment Co, Blue Ash *Also Called: Reco LLC (G-1234)*
Richard Goettle Inc..513 825-8100
   12071 Hamilton Ave Cincinnati (45231) *(G-3296)*
Richard Health Systems LLC...419 534-2371
   5237 Renwyck Dr Ste A Toledo (43615) *(G-13991)*
Richard L Bowen & Assoc Inc (PA)...216 491-9300
   13000 Shaker Blvd Ste 1 Cleveland (44120) *(G-4838)*
Richard Lawrence Teaberry Inc (PA)   1900 Hubbard Rd Youngstown (44505) *(G-15708)*
Richard Wolfe Trucking Inc..740 392-2445
   7203 Newark Rd Mount Vernon (43050) *(G-11505)*
Richard's Fence Company, Akron *Also Called: Richards Whl Fence Co Inc (G-282)*
Richards Electric Sup Co LLC (DH)...513 242-8800
   4620 Reading Rd Cincinnati (45229) *(G-3297)*
Richards Whl Fence Co Inc..330 773-0423
   1600 Firestone Pkwy Akron (44301) *(G-282)*
Richardson Glass Service Inc (PA)...740 366-5090
   1165 Mount Vernon Rd Newark (43055) *(G-11746)*
RICHARDSON GLASS SERVICE INC DBA LEE'S GLASS SERVICE, Newark *Also Called: Richardson Glass Service Inc (G-11746)*
Richardson Printing Corp (PA)..800 848-9752
   201 Acme St Marietta (45750) *(G-10404)*
Richfeld Bnquet Cnfrnce Ctr LL..330 659-6151
   4742 Brecksville Rd Richfield (44286) *(G-12708)*
Richfield Inn Inc...248 946-5838
   415 W Dussel Dr Maumee (43537) *(G-10762)*
Richland Co & Associates Inc (PA)...419 782-0141
   101 Clinton St Ste 2200 Defiance (43512) *(G-7766)*
Richland Manor, Delphos *Also Called: Jwj Investments Inc (G-7841)*
Richland Newhope, Mansfield *Also Called: Richland Newhope Inds Inc (G-10311)*
Richland Newhope Inds Inc..419 774-4200
   314 Cleveland Ave Mansfield (44902) *(G-10311)*
Richland Newhope Inds Inc..419 774-4496
   985 W Longview Ave Mansfield (44906) *(G-10312)*
Richland Newhope Inds Inc (PA)...419 774-4400
   150 E 4th St Mansfield (44902) *(G-10313)*
Richland Trust Company..419 525-8700
   3 N Main St Ste 1 Mansfield (44902) *(G-10314)*
Richmond Medical Center (PA)...440 585-6500
   27100 Chardon Rd Richmond Heights (44143) *(G-12722)*
Richs Towing & Service Inc (PA)..440 234-3435
   20531 1st Ave Middleburg Heights (44130) *(G-11124)*

Richter & Associates Inc 216 593-7140
   8948 Canyon Falls Blvd Ste 400 Twinsburg (44087) *(G-14217)*
Richwood Banking Company (HQ) 740 943-2317
   28 N Franklin St Richwood (43344) *(G-12724)*
Richwood Banking Company 937 390-0470
   2454 N Limestone St Springfield (45503) *(G-13285)*
Ricking Holding Co 513 825-3551
   5800 Grant Ave Cleveland (44105) *(G-4839)*
Riddell All American Sport, North Ridgeville *Also Called: All American Sports Corp (G-11921)*
Ride Share Information 513 621-6300
   720 E Pete Rose Way Ste 420 Cincinnati (45202) *(G-3298)*
Riders Inn, Willoughby *Also Called: East End Ro Burton Inc (G-15190)*
Ridge & Associates Inc 419 423-3641
   9747 W Us Route 224 Findlay (45840) *(G-8582)*
Ridge Corporation 740 513-9880
   5777 Raiders Rd Frazeysburg (43822) *(G-8657)*
Ridge Ohio 513 804-2204
   25 Whitney Dr Ste 120 Milford (45150) *(G-11252)*
Ridge Park Dialysis, Cleveland *Also Called: Garrett Dialysis LLC (G-4303)*
Ridge Road Depot, Cleveland *Also Called: Cleveland Municipal School Dst (G-4062)*
Ridge-Pleasant Valley Inc (PA) 440 845-0200
   7377 Ridge Rd Cleveland (44129) *(G-4840)*
Ridgecrest Healthcare Group In 216 292-5706
   26691 Richmond Rd Bedford (44146) *(G-982)*
Ridgehills Hotel Ltd Partnr 440 585-0600
   28600 Ridgehills Dr Wickliffe (44092) *(G-15162)*
Ridgeview Hospital, Middle Point *Also Called: Oglethorpe Middlepoint LLC (G-11110)*
Ridgewood Government Svcs LLC 740 294-7261
   21190 County Road 151 West Lafayette (43845) *(G-14858)*
Rieck Services, Dayton *Also Called: Mechanical Cnstr Managers LLC (G-7474)*
Rieman Arszman Cstm Distrs Inc 513 874-5444
   9190 Seward Rd Fairfield (45014) *(G-8437)*
Rife's Autobody, Columbus *Also Called: Grandview Fifth Auto Svc Inc (G-5945)*
Right Drction Bhvral Hlth Svcs 216 260-9022
   5 Severance Cir Ste 510 Cleveland Heights (44118) *(G-5185)*
Righter Co Inc 614 272-9700
   2424 Harrison Rd Columbus (43204) *(G-6588)*
Rightthing LLC (HQ) 419 420-1830
   3401 Technology Dr Findlay (45840) *(G-8583)*
Rightthing, The, Findlay *Also Called: Rightthing LLC (G-8583)*
Rightway Food Service, Lima *Also Called: Powell Company Inc (G-9951)*
Rii, Columbus *Also Called: Resource International Inc (G-6587)*
Riley Hotel Group LLC 330 590-8040
   387 Medina Rd Ste 400 Medina (44256) *(G-10884)*
Rinaldi Orthodontics Inc 513 831-6160
   5987 Meijer Dr Milford (45150) *(G-11253)*
Ringside Search Partners LLC 614 643-0700
   266 N 4th St Ste 100 Columbus (43215) *(G-6589)*
Ringside Talent, Columbus *Also Called: Ringside Search Partners LLC (G-6589)*
Ripcho Studio Inc 216 631-0664
   7630 Lorain Ave Cleveland (44102) *(G-4841)*
Rippe & Kingston Systems Inc (PA) 513 977-4578
   4850 Smith Rd Ste 100 Cincinnati (45212) *(G-3299)*
Rise Brands 614 754-7522
   134 E Long St Columbus (43215) *(G-6590)*
Rise Fitness, Medina *Also Called: Redefine Enterprises LLC (G-10883)*
Riser Foods Company (HQ) 216 292-7000
   5300 Richmond Rd Bedford Heights (44146) *(G-1001)*
Rising Sun Express LLC 937 596-6167
   1003 S Main St Jackson Center (45334) *(G-9533)*
Risque Soles LLC 216 965-5261
   854 Storer Ave Akron (44320) *(G-283)*
Ritchies Food Distributors Inc 740 443-6303
   527 S West St Piketon (45661) *(G-12429)*
Rite Aid, Barberton *Also Called: Rite Aid of Ohio Inc (G-705)*
Rite Aid, Brookville *Also Called: Rite Aid of Ohio Inc (G-1448)*
Rite Aid, Cadiz *Also Called: Rite Aid of Ohio Inc (G-1543)*
Rite Aid, Cuyahoga Falls *Also Called: Rite Aid of Ohio Inc (G-7095)*
Rite Aid, Dayton *Also Called: Rite Aid of Ohio Inc (G-7591)*
Rite Aid, Dayton *Also Called: Rite Aid of Ohio Inc (G-7592)*
Rite Aid, Dayton *Also Called: Rite Aid of Ohio Inc (G-7593)*
Rite Aid, Englewood *Also Called: Rite Aid of Ohio Inc (G-8321)*
Rite Aid, Garrettsville *Also Called: Rite Aid of Ohio Inc (G-8779)*
Rite Aid, New Lebanon *Also Called: Rite Aid of Ohio Inc (G-11620)*
Rite Aid of Ohio Inc 330 706-1004
   1403 Wooster Rd W Barberton (44203) *(G-705)*
Rite Aid of Ohio Inc 937 833-2174
   437 N Wolf Creek St Brookville (45309) *(G-1448)*
Rite Aid of Ohio Inc 740 942-3101
   651 Lincoln Ave Cadiz (43907) *(G-1543)*
Rite Aid of Ohio Inc 330 922-4466
   1914 Bailey Rd Cuyahoga Falls (44221) *(G-7095)*
Rite Aid of Ohio Inc 937 277-1611
   3875 Salem Ave Dayton (45406) *(G-7591)*
Rite Aid of Ohio Inc 937 258-8101
   2532 E 3rd St Dayton (45403) *(G-7592)*
Rite Aid of Ohio Inc 937 256-3111
   2916 Linden Ave Dayton (45410) *(G-7593)*
Rite Aid of Ohio Inc 937 836-5204
   900 Union Blvd Englewood (45322) *(G-8321)*
Rite Aid of Ohio Inc 330 527-2828
   10764 North St Garrettsville (44231) *(G-8779)*
Rite Aid of Ohio Inc 937 687-3456
   590 W Main St New Lebanon (45345) *(G-11620)*
Rite Rug Co 614 478-3365
   5465 N Hamilton Rd Columbus (43230) *(G-6591)*
Ritenour Industrial, Twinsburg *Also Called: Lou Ritenour Decorators Inc (G-14202)*
Rittal Corporation 937 399-0500
   1000 S Edgewood Ave Urbana (43078) *(G-14310)*
Rittal North America LLC 937 399-0500
   1 Rittal Pl Urbana (43078) *(G-14311)*
Rittenhouse 513 423-2322
   3000 Mcgee Ave Middletown (45044) *(G-11183)*
Ritter & Associates, Inc., Maumee *Also Called: Alta360 Research Inc (G-10688)*
Ritter & Hagee Optometrists, Blue Ash *Also Called: Thomas Ritter Od Inc (G-1254)*
Rittman Inc 330 927-6855
   10 Mull Dr Rittman (44270) *(G-12732)*
Ritz-Carlton, Cleveland *Also Called: Ritz-Carlton Hotel Company LLC (G-4842)*
Ritz-Carlton Hotel Company LLC 216 623-1300
   1515 W 3rd St 6th Fl Cleveland (44113) *(G-4842)*
Rivals Sports Grille LLC 216 267-0005
   6710 Smith Rd Middleburg Heights (44130) *(G-11125)*
River Centre Clinic 419 885-8800
   5465 Main St Sylvania (43560) *(G-13570)*
River City Furniture LLC (PA) 513 612-7303
   6454 Centre Park Dr West Chester (45069) *(G-14756)*
River City Mortgage LLC 513 631-6400
   4555 Lake Forest Dr Ste 450 Blue Ash (45242) *(G-1238)*
River Consulting LLC (DH) 614 797-2480
   445 Hutchinson Ave Ste 740 Columbus (43235) *(G-6592)*
River Downs, Cincinnati *Also Called: Pnk (ohio) LLC (G-3219)*
River Financial Inc 415 878-3375
   80 E Rich St Apt 706 Columbus (43215) *(G-6593)*
River Oaks Rcquet CLB Assoc In 440 331-4980
   21220 Center Ridge Rd Ste B Rocky River (44116) *(G-12752)*
River Rose Obstetrics & Gyneco, Athens *Also Called: Ohio Hlth Physcn Group Hrltg C (G-584)*
River Services Inc 612 588-8141
   559 Liberty Hl Ste 1 Cincinnati (45202) *(G-3300)*
River Valley Dialysis LLC 513 922-5900
   5040 Delhi Rd Cincinnati (45238) *(G-3301)*
River Valley Dialysis LLC 513 793-0555
   6929 Silverton Ave Cincinnati (45236) *(G-3302)*
River Valley Dialysis LLC 513 741-1062
   5520 Cheviot Rd Ste B Cincinnati (45247) *(G-3303)*
River Valley Dialysis LLC 513 934-0272
   918b Columbus Ave Lebanon (45036) *(G-9785)*
River Valley Health Partners, East Liverpool *Also Called: Prime Hlthcare Fndton- E Lvrpo (G-8191)*

ALPHABETIC SECTION — Robeck Fluid Power Co

River Valley Physicians LLC.. 330 386-3610
  15655 State Route 170 Ste H East Liverpool (43920) *(G-8192)*
River View Surgery Center, Lancaster *Also Called: Riverview Surgery Center (G-9739)*
River Vista Hlth Wellness LLC.. 614 643-5454
  1599 Alum Creek Dr Columbus (43209) *(G-6594)*
Riverain Medical, Miamisburg *Also Called: Riverain Technologies Inc (G-11091)*
Riverain Technologies Inc... 937 425-6811
  3130 S Tech Blvd Miamisburg (45342) *(G-11091)*
RIVERBEND MUSIC CENTER, Cincinnati *Also Called: Cincinnati Symphony Orchestra (G-2425)*
Riverbend Music Center, Cincinnati *Also Called: Cincinnati Symphony Orchestra (G-2426)*
Riverfront Antique Mall Inc... 330 339-4448
  1203 Front Ave Sw New Philadelphia (44663) *(G-11663)*
Riverfront Diversified Inc... 513 874-7200
  9814 Harwood Ct West Chester (45014) *(G-14757)*
Riverfront Steel Inc... 513 769-9999
  10310 S Medallion Dr Cincinnati (45241) *(G-3304)*
Riverfront Stffing Sltions Inc... 330 929-3002
  2121 Front St Ste A Cuyahoga Falls (44221) *(G-7096)*
Riverfront YMCA Schl Age - Ech... 330 733-2551
  544 Broad Blvd Cuyahoga Falls (44221) *(G-7097)*
Riverhills Healthcare Inc... 513 624-6031
  8000 5 Mile Rd Ste 330 Cincinnati (45230) *(G-3305)*
Riverhills Healthcare Inc (PA).. 513 241-2370
  111 Wellington Pl Lowr Cincinnati (45219) *(G-3306)*
Rivers Bend Health Care LLC.. 740 894-3476
  335 Township Road 1026 South Point (45680) *(G-13183)*
Riverscape Counseling, Dayton *Also Called: Darcie R Clark Lpcc LLC (G-7267)*
Riverside Cnstr Svcs Inc.. 513 723-0900
  218 W Mcmicken Ave Cincinnati (45214) *(G-3307)*
Riverside Company... 216 344-1040
  127 Public Sq Cleveland (44114) *(G-4843)*
Riverside Company, The, Cleveland *Also Called: Riverside Partners LLC (G-4845)*
Riverside Computing Inc.. 937 440-9199
  8613 N Dixie Dr Dayton (45414) *(G-7594)*
Riverside Drives, Cleveland *Also Called: Riverside Drives Inc (G-4844)*
Riverside Drives Inc.. 216 362-1211
  4509 W 160th St Cleveland (44135) *(G-4844)*
Riverside Hospital.. 614 566-5000
  3535 Olentangy River Rd Columbus (43214) *(G-6595)*
Riverside Manor, Newcomerstown *Also Called: Newcomerstown Progress Corp (G-11772)*
RIVERSIDE MANOR NURSING & REHA, Newcomerstown *Also Called: Newcomerstown Development Inc (G-11771)*
Riverside Methodist Hospital, Columbus *Also Called: Ohiohlth Rverside Methdst Hosp (G-6468)*
Riverside Nephrology Assoc Inc... 614 538-2250
  929 Jasonway Ave Ste A Columbus (43214) *(G-6596)*
Riverside of Miami County, Troy *Also Called: RT Industries Inc (G-14157)*
Riverside Partners LLC.. 216 344-1040
  127 Public Sq Cleveland (44114) *(G-4845)*
Riverside Pulmonary Assoc Inc.. 614 267-8585
  1679 Old Henderson Rd Columbus (43220) *(G-6597)*
Riverside Rdlgy Intrvntnal Ass (DH).. 614 340-7747
  100 E Campus View Blvd Ste 100 Columbus (43235) *(G-6598)*
Riverside Research Institute... 937 431-3810
  2640 Hibiscus Way Beavercreek (45431) *(G-901)*
Riverside Surgical Associates.. 614 261-1900
  3545 Olentangy River Rd Ste 525 Columbus (43214) *(G-6599)*
Rivertreechristian.com, Massillon *Also Called: Christian Rivertree School (G-10635)*
Riverview Health Institute... 937 222-5390
  1 Elizabeth Pl Dayton (45417) *(G-7595)*
Riverview Hospitality Corp... 330 339-7000
  1299 W High Ave New Philadelphia (44663) *(G-11664)*
Riverview Hotel LLC... 614 268-8700
  3160 Olentangy River Rd Columbus (43202) *(G-6600)*
Riverview Industries Inc... 419 898-5250
  8380 W State Route 163 Oak Harbor (43449) *(G-12047)*
Riverview Surgery Center... 740 681-2700
  2401 N Columbus St Lancaster (43130) *(G-9739)*
Rize Home LLC (PA).. 800 333-8333
  31050 Diamond Pkwy Solon (44139) *(G-13138)*

Rj Matthews Company... 330 834-3000
  2780 Richville Dr Se Massillon (44646) *(G-10663)*
RJ Runge Company Inc... 419 740-5781
  3539 Ne Catawba Rd Port Clinton (43452) *(G-12539)*
Rk Family Inc... 740 474-3874
  23625 Us Highway 23 S Lot 3a Circleville (43113) *(G-3721)*
Rk Family Inc... 419 355-8230
  1800 E State St Fremont (43420) *(G-8698)*
Rk Family Inc... 513 737-0436
  1416 Main St Hamilton (45013) *(G-9079)*
Rk Family Inc... 513 934-0015
  1879 Deerfield Rd Lebanon (45036) *(G-9786)*
Rk Family Inc... 740 389-2674
  233 America Blvd Marion (43302) *(G-10452)*
Rk Family Inc... 330 308-5075
  1203 Front Ave Sw New Philadelphia (44663) *(G-11665)*
Rk Family Inc... 419 660-0363
  1600 Us Highway 20 W Norwalk (44857) *(G-12024)*
Rk Family Inc... 419 443-1663
  2300 W Market St Tiffin (44883) *(G-13640)*
Rk Family Inc... 330 264-5475
  3541 E Lincoln Way Wooster (44691) *(G-15369)*
RL Best Company... 330 758-8601
  723 Bev Rd Boardman (44512) *(G-1290)*
Rl Carriers, Wilmington *Also Called: R & L Carriers Inc (G-15265)*
RL Trucking Inc... 419 732-4177
  58 Grande Lake Dr Port Clinton (43452) *(G-12540)*
Rla Utilities LLC... 513 554-1470
  389 Wade St Cincinnati (45214) *(G-3308)*
Rlj III - Em Clmbus Lessee LLC.. 614 890-8600
  2700 Corporate Exchange Dr Columbus (43231) *(G-6601)*
Rlj Management Co Inc (PA)... 614 942-2020
  3021 E Dublin Granville Rd Columbus (43231) *(G-6602)*
RLR Investments LLC... 937 382-1494
  600 Gilliam Rd Wilmington (45177) *(G-15270)*
Rls & Associates Inc.. 937 299-5007
  3131 S Dixie Dr Ste 545 Moraine (45439) *(G-11435)*
Rm Advisory Group Inc... 513 242-2100
  5300 Vine St Cincinnati (45217) *(G-3309)*
Rmf Nooter LLC.. 419 727-1970
  915 Matzinger Rd Toledo (43612) *(G-13992)*
Rmi International Inc... 937 642-5032
  24500 Honda Pkwy Marysville (43040) *(G-10504)*
RMS, Cincinnati *Also Called: RMS of Ohio Inc (G-3310)*
RMS Management, Westlake *Also Called: RMS of Ohio Inc (G-15104)*
RMS of Ohio Inc... 513 841-0990
  2824 E Kemper Rd Cincinnati (45241) *(G-3310)*
RMS of Ohio Inc... 440 617-6605
  24651 Center Ridge Rd Ste 300 Westlake (44145) *(G-15104)*
Rmt Acquisition Inc... 513 241-5566
  3111 Spring Grove Ave Cincinnati (45225) *(G-3311)*
Rnr Tire Express, Fairfield *Also Called: Big Oki LLC (G-8394)*
Rnw Holdings Inc.. 330 792-0600
  200 Division Street Ext Youngstown (44510) *(G-15709)*
Road & Rail Services Inc.. 502 365-5361
  3101 N Township Road 47 Fostoria (44830) *(G-8624)*
Road & Rail Services Inc.. 937 578-0089
  24500 Honda Pkwy Marysville (43040) *(G-10505)*
Road Runner Holdco, Westerville *Also Called: Holdco LLC (G-14985)*
Roadlink USA Midwest LLC (DH).. 419 686-2113
  29180 Glenwood Rd Perrysburg (43551) *(G-12367)*
Rob Lynn Inc.. 330 773-6470
  330 Kennedy Rd Akron (44305) *(G-284)*
Rob Richter Landscaping Inc.. 513 539-0300
  240 Senate Dr Monroe (45050) *(G-11350)*
Robbie L Sarles and Associates, Moraine *Also Called: Rls & Associates Inc (G-11435)*
Robbins Kelly Patterson Tucker.. 513 721-3330
  312 Elm St Ste 2200 Cincinnati (45202) *(G-3312)*
Robeck, Aurora *Also Called: Robeck Fluid Power Co (G-624)*
Robeck Fluid Power Co... 330 562-1140
  350 Lena Dr Aurora (44202) *(G-624)*

Robert Kelly & Bucio LLP 937 332-9300
10 N Market St Troy (45373) *(G-14156)*

Robert Bettinger Inc 419 832-6033
21211 W State Route 65 Grand Rapids (43522) *(G-8847)*

Robert C Barney Dvm Inc 216 221-5380
14587 Madison Ave Lakewood (44107) *(G-9682)*

Robert E Davis DDS Ms Inc 614 878-7887
5249 W Broad St Columbus (43228) *(G-6603)*

Robert F Lindsay Co (PA) 419 476-6221
4268 Rose Garden Dr Toledo (43623) *(G-13993)*

Robert G Owen Trucking Inc (PA) 330 756-1013
9260 Erie Ave Sw Navarre (44662) *(G-11539)*

Robert J Matthews Company (PA) 330 834-3000
2780 Richville Dr Se Massillon (44646) *(G-10664)*

ROBERT K FOX FAMILY WIDE, Lancaster *Also Called: Family YMCA Lncster Frfeld CNT (G-9722)*

Robert L Dawson M.D., James, Galion *Also Called: Avita Health System (G-8742)*

Robert L Stark Enterprises Inc 216 292-0240
629 Euclid Ave Ste 1300 Cleveland (44114) *(G-4846)*

Robert Lucke Homes Inc 513 683-3300
8825 Chapelsquare Ln Ste B Cincinnati (45249) *(G-3313)*

Robert M Neff Inc 614 444-1562
711 Stimmel Rd Columbus (43223) *(G-6604)*

Robert McCabe Company Inc 513 469-2500
10821 Montgomery Rd Cincinnati (45242) *(G-3314)*

Robert Sturges Memorial Homes, Mansfield *Also Called: Mansfield Memorial Homes (G-10288)*

Robert Wiley MD Inc 216 621-3211
2740 Carnegie Ave Cleveland (44115) *(G-4847)*

Roberts Truck Parts, Wilmington *Also Called: R & M Leasing Inc (G-15269)*

Robertson, Alliance *Also Called: Robertson Heating Sup Co Ohio (G-397)*

Robertson Bereavement Center, Medina *Also Called: Hospice of Medina County (G-10840)*

Robertson Cnstr Svcs Inc 740 929-1000
1801 Thornwood Dr Heath (43056) *(G-9137)*

Robertson Heating Sup Co Ohio (PA) 800 433-9532
2155 W Main St Alliance (44601) *(G-397)*

Robertson Heating Supply, Alliance *Also Called: Robertson Htg Sup Clumbus Ohio (G-399)*

Robertson Htg Sup Aliance Ohio (HQ) 330 821-9180
2155 W Main St Alliance (44601) *(G-398)*

Robertson Htg Sup Clumbus Ohio (PA) 330 821-9180
2155 W Main St Alliance (44601) *(G-399)*

Robertson Plumbing & Heating 330 863-0611
7389 Canton Rd Nw Malvern (44644) *(G-10235)*

Robertson's Building Center, Malvern *Also Called: Robertson Plumbing & Heating (G-10235)*

Robex LLC (PA) 419 270-0770
1745 Indian Wood Cir Maumee (43537) *(G-10763)*

Robiden Inc 513 421-0000
6059 Creekside Way Fairfield Township (45011) *(G-8464)*

Robinair Leasing Co LLC 513 530-1600
924 Charlies Way Montpelier (43543) *(G-11386)*

Robins & Morton Corporation 419 660-2980
285 Benedict Ave Norwalk (44857) *(G-12025)*

Robinson Cleaners, Cincinnati *Also Called: Wilkers Inc (G-3671)*

Robinson Health Affiliates, Aurora *Also Called: Robinson Health System Inc (G-625)*

Robinson Health System Inc 330 562-3169
700 Walden Pl Aurora (44202) *(G-625)*

Robinson Health System Inc 330 677-3434
408 Devon Pl Ste B Kent (44240) *(G-9594)*

Robinson Health System Inc 330 678-0900
401 Devon Pl Ste 115 Kent (44240) *(G-9595)*

Robinson Health System Inc 330 297-0811
1993 State Route 59 Kent (44240) *(G-9596)*

Robinson Health System Inc 330 678-4100
411 Devon Pl Kent (44240) *(G-9597)*

Robinson Health System Inc 330 297-8844
6847 N Chestnut St Ste 100 Ravenna (44266) *(G-12642)*

Robinson Health System Inc (HQ) 330 297-0811
6847 N Chestnut St Ravenna (44266) *(G-12643)*

Robinson Health System Inc 330 626-3455
9424 State Route 14 Streetsboro (44241) *(G-13426)*

Robinson Hlth Affl Med Ctr One, Streetsboro *Also Called: Robinson Health System Inc (G-13426)*

Robinson Htg Air-Conditioning 513 422-6812
1208 2nd Ave Middletown (45044) *(G-11184)*

Robinson Insulation Co Inc 937 323-9599
4715 Urbana Rd Springfield (45502) *(G-13286)*

Robinson Investments Ltd 937 593-1849
811 N Main St Bellefontaine (43311) *(G-1037)*

Robinson Memorial Training Ctr, Kent *Also Called: Robinson Health System Inc (G-9594)*

Robinson Surgery Center, Kent *Also Called: Robinson Health System Inc (G-9597)*

Robots and Pencils LP 866 515-9897
7 1/2 N Franklin St Chagrin Falls (44022) *(G-1965)*

Robotworx, Marion *Also Called: Ka Wanner Inc (G-10432)*

Rock Creek Medical Center, Rock Creek *Also Called: Glenbeigh (G-12733)*

Rock Homes Inc 330 497-5200
7630 Freedom Ave Nw North Canton (44720) *(G-11859)*

Rock Hotel Ltd LLC 216 520-2020
6020 Jefferson Dr Cleveland (44131) *(G-4848)*

Rock House Entrmt Group Inc 440 232-7625
7809 First Pl Oakwood Village (44146) *(G-12057)*

Rock Medical Orthopedics Inc 216 496-3168
571 Boston Mills Rd Ste 100 Hudson (44236) *(G-9372)*

Rock Pile Inc 440 937-5100
900 Nagel Rd Avon (44011) *(G-664)*

Rock Roll Hall of Fame Mseum I 216 781-7625
1100 Rock And Roll Blvd Cleveland (44114) *(G-4849)*

Rockbridge Capital LLC (PA) 614 246-2400
4124 Worth Ave Columbus (43219) *(G-6605)*

Rocket Mortgage LLC 216 586-8900
100 Public Sq Ste 400 Cleveland (44113) *(G-4850)*

Rockfish Interactive LLC 513 381-1583
659 Van Meter St Ste 520 Cincinnati (45202) *(G-3315)*

Rockford Homes Inc (PA) 614 785-0015
999 Polaris Pkwy Ste 200 Columbus (43240) *(G-5281)*

Rockhill Holding Company (DH) 816 412-2800
518 E Broad St Columbus (43215) *(G-6606)*

Rockhill Insurance Company, Columbus *Also Called: Rockhill Holding Company (G-6606)*

Rockhold Bank 740 634-2331
101 E Main St Bainbridge (45612) *(G-686)*

Rockin Jump Holdings LLC 513 373-4260
8350 Colerain Ave Cincinnati (45239) *(G-3316)*

Rockin' Jump, Cincinnati *Also Called: Rockin Jump Holdings LLC (G-3316)*

Rockside Family Dental Care, Cleveland *Also Called: Dean A Carmichael (G-4156)*

Rockside Hospitality LLC 216 524-0700
5300 Rockside Rd Independence (44131) *(G-9477)*

Rockside Park Towers, Bedford Heights *Also Called: Owners Management Company (G-1000)*

Rockwell Automation Ohio LLC (HQ) 513 576-6151
1700 Edison Dr Milford (45150) *(G-11254)*

Rockwell Springs Trout Club 419 684-7971
1581 County Road 310 Clyde (43410) *(G-5208)*

Rockwood Door & Millwork, Millersburg *Also Called: Rockwood Products Ltd (G-11291)*

Rockwood Equity Partners LLC (PA) 216 342-1760
3201 Enterprise Pkwy Ste 370 Cleveland (44122) *(G-4851)*

Rockwood Products Ltd 330 893-2392
5264 Township Road 401 Millersburg (44654) *(G-11291)*

Rocky Fork Country Club, Gahanna *Also Called: Rocky Fork Hunt and Cntry CLB (G-8727)*

Rocky Fork Hunt and Cntry CLB 614 471-7828
5189 Clark State Rd Gahanna (43230) *(G-8727)*

Rocky River Leasing Co LLC 440 243-5688
570 N Rocky River Dr Berea (44017) *(G-1080)*

Rockynol Retirement Community, Akron *Also Called: Ohio Living (G-253)*

Rod Lightning Mutual Insur Co (PA) 330 262-9060
2845 Benden Dr Wooster (44691) *(G-15370)*

Rodbat Security Services, Marysville *Also Called: Rmi International Inc (G-10504)*

Roddy Group Inc 216 763-0088
24500 Chagrin Blvd Ste 200 Beachwood (44122) *(G-831)*

Rodem Inc (PA) 513 922-6140
10001 Martins Way Harrison (45030) *(G-9115)*

Rodem Process Equipment, Harrison *Also Called: Rodem Inc (G-9115)*

Roderick Linton Belfance LLP 330 434-3000
50 S Main St Fl 10 Akron (44308) *(G-285)*

ALPHABETIC SECTION — Rosewind Limited Partnership

Rodeway Inn, Dublin Also Called: Jackson I-94 Ltd Partnership *(G-8042)*
Rodeway Inn Nort, Sandusky Also Called: S & S Realty Ltd *(G-12928)*
Roe Dental Laboratory Inc 216 663-2233
  7165 E Pleasant Valley Rd Independence (44131) *(G-9478)*
Roeder Cartage Company Inc (PA) 419 221-1600
  1979 N Dixie Hwy Lima (45801) *(G-9954)*
Roehrenbeck Electric Inc 614 443-9709
  2525 English Rd Columbus (43207) *(G-6607)*
Roemer Unlimited Inc 216 267-5454
  15620 Brookpark Rd Cleveland (44135) *(G-4852)*
Roetzel Andress A Lgal Prof As (PA) 330 376-2700
  222 S Main St Ste 400 Akron (44308) *(G-286)*
Roetzel Andress A Lgal Prof As 216 623-0150
  1375 E 9th St Fl 10 Cleveland (44114) *(G-4853)*
Roger Bettis Trucking Inc 330 863-2111
  7089 Alliance Rd Nw Malvern (44644) *(G-10236)*
Roger D Fields Associates Inc 614 451-2248
  4588 Kenny Rd Ste 201d Columbus (43220) *(G-6608)*
Roger Storer & Son Inc 937 325-9873
  315 S Center St Ste 1 Springfield (45506) *(G-13287)*
Rogers Family Dental Practice, Cincinnati Also Called: Rogers Family Dentistry Inc *(G-3317)*
Rogers Family Dentistry Inc 513 231-1012
  8284 Beechmont Ave Cincinnati (45255) *(G-3317)*
Rogue Fitness, Columbus Also Called: Coulter Ventures Llc *(G-5708)*
Roholt Vision Institute Inc 330 702-8755
  25 Manor Hill Dr Ste 300 Canfield (44406) *(G-1639)*
Rohrbchers Light Crone Trimble 419 471-1160
  405 Madison Ave Fl 8 Toledo (43604) *(G-13994)*
Rohrs Farms 419 757-0110
  810 Courtright St Mc Guffey (45859) *(G-10802)*
Rolfes Henry Co LPA (PA) 513 579-0080
  18 W 9th St Cincinnati (45202) *(G-3318)*
Rollhouse Entertainment S 440 248-4080
  33185 Bainbridge Rd Solon (44139) *(G-13139)*
Rolling Acres Care Center, North Lima Also Called: Guardian Hlthcare HM Off I LLC *(G-11888)*
Rolling Hlls Rhab Wellness Ctr 330 225-9121
  4426 Homestead Dr Brunswick (44212) *(G-1469)*
Rollins Moving and Storage Inc 937 525-4013
  1050 Wheel St Springfield (45503) *(G-13288)*
Rolls-Royce Energy Systems Inc 703 834-1700
  105 N Sandusky St Mount Vernon (43050) *(G-11506)*
Roman Catholic Church, Newark Also Called: St Francis De Sales Church *(G-11749)*
Roman Catholic Diocese Toledo 419 243-7255
  1601 Jefferson Ave Toledo (43604) *(G-13995)*
Roman Catholic Diocese Toledo 419 531-5747
  5725 Hill Ave Toledo (43615) *(G-13996)*
Roman Cthlic Docese Youngstown 330 875-5562
  2308 Reno Dr Louisville (44641) *(G-10122)*
Roman Cthlic Docese Youngstown 330 792-4721
  248 S Belle Vista Ave Youngstown (44509) *(G-15710)*
Romanelli & Hughes Building Co 614 891-2042
  148 W Schrock Rd Westerville (43081) *(G-15013)*
Romanelli & Hughes Contractors, Westerville Also Called: Romanelli & Hughes Building Co *(G-15013)*
Romanoff Elc Residential LLC 614 755-4500
  1288 Research Rd Gahanna (43230) *(G-8728)*
Romanoff Electric Inc (PA) 614 755-4500
  1288 Research Rd Gahanna (43230) *(G-8729)*
Romanoff Electric Co LLC 937 640-7925
  5570 Enterprise Blvd Toledo (43612) *(G-13997)*
Romanoff Group LLC (PA) 614 755-4500
  1288 Research Rd Gahanna (43230) *(G-8730)*
Romeo's Pizza, Medina Also Called: Romeos Pizza Franchise LLC *(G-10885)*
Romeos Pizza Franchise LLC 234 248-4549
  1113 Medina Rd Ste 200 Medina (44256) *(G-10885)*
Romitech Inc (HQ) 937 297-9529
  321 Conover Dr Franklin (45005) *(G-8648)*
Ron Burge Trucking Inc 330 624-5373
  1876 W Britton Rd Burbank (44214) *(G-1522)*
Ron Carrocce Trucking Co Inc 330 758-0841
  8063 Southern Blvd Youngstown (44512) *(G-15711)*

Ron Marhofer Auto Family 330 940-4422
  257 Huddleston Ave Cuyahoga Falls (44221) *(G-7098)*
Ron Marhofer Automall Inc 330 835-6707
  1260 Main St Cuyahoga Falls (44221) *(G-7099)*
Ron Marhofer Automall Inc (PA) 330 923-5059
  1350 Main St Cuyahoga Falls (44221) *(G-7100)*
Ron Mrhfer Lncoln Mrcury Hynda, Cuyahoga Falls Also Called: Ron Marhofer Automall Inc *(G-7100)*
Ron Neff Her Realtors, Chillicothe Also Called: Ron Neff Real Estate *(G-2083)*
Ron Neff Real Estate (PA) 740 773-4670
  75 W 2nd St Chillicothe (45601) *(G-2083)*
Ron-Joy Nursing Home Inc 330 286-9122
  7246 Ronjoy Pl Youngstown (44512) *(G-15712)*
Ron's Truck Trlr & Auto Repr, Fremont Also Called: Garner Trucking Inc *(G-8681)*
Ronald McDnald Hse Chrties CNT 614 227-3700
  711 E Livingston Ave Columbus (43205) *(G-6609)*
Ronald McDnald Hse Chrties Grt 513 636-7642
  341 Erkenbrecher Ave Cincinnati (45229) *(G-3319)*
Ronald McDnald Hse Chrties NW 419 471-4663
  3883 Monroe St Toledo (43606) *(G-13998)*
Rondy & Co., Barberton Also Called: Tahoma Rubber & Plastics Inc *(G-715)*
Rondy Fleet Services Inc 330 745-9016
  255 Wooster Rd N Barberton (44203) *(G-706)*
Ronyak Paving Inc 440 279-0616
  12063 Fowlers Mill Rd Chardon (44024) *(G-2018)*
Rood Trucking Company Inc (PA) 330 652-3519
  3505 Union St Mineral Ridge (44440) *(G-11304)*
Roofsmith Restoration Inc 330 812-4245
  122 Western Ave Akron (44313) *(G-287)*
Roosevelt Surgical Associates 513 424-0941
  4040 Roosevelt Blvd Middletown (45044) *(G-11185)*
Root, Columbus Also Called: Root Inc *(G-6610)*
Root Inc (PA) 866 980-9431
  80 E Rich St Ste 500 Columbus (43215) *(G-6610)*
Root LLC (DH) 419 874-0077
  5470 Main St Ste 100 Sylvania (43560) *(G-13571)*
Roschmans Restaurant ADM 419 225-8300
  1933 Roschman Ave Lima (45804) *(G-9955)*
Roscoe Medical Inc (HQ) 440 572-1962
  6753 Engle Rd Ste A Middleburg Heights (44130) *(G-11126)*
Roscoe Village Foundation 740 622-2222
  200 N Whitewoman St Coshocton (43812) *(G-7000)*
Rose & Dobyns, Wilmington Also Called: Rose & Dobyns An Ohio Partnr *(G-15271)*
Rose & Dobyns An Ohio Partnr (PA) 937 382-2838
  97 N South St Wilmington (45177) *(G-15271)*
Rose & Dobyns An Ohio Partnr 740 335-4700
  298 N Fayette St Wshngtn Ct Hs (43160) *(G-15492)*
Rose Community Management LLC (PA) 917 542-3600
  6000 Freedom Square Dr Ste 500 Independence (44131) *(G-9479)*
Rose Health Care Services Ltd 937 277-7518
  419 Grafton Ave Dayton (45406) *(G-7596)*
Rose Lane Health Center, Massillon Also Called: Rose Ln Hlth Rhabilitation Inc *(G-10665)*
Rose Ln Hlth Rhabilitation Inc 330 833-3174
  5425 High Mill Ave Nw Massillon (44646) *(G-10665)*
Rose Mary Johanna Grassell (PA) 216 481-4823
  2346 W 14th St Cleveland (44113) *(G-4854)*
Rose Transport Inc 614 864-4004
  6747 Taylor Rd Sw Reynoldsburg (43068) *(G-12677)*
Rosebud Mining Company 740 768-2275
  9076 County Road 53 Bergholz (43908) *(G-1088)*
Rosebud Mining Company 740 658-4217
  28490 Birmingham Rd Freeport (43973) *(G-8663)*
Roseland Lanes Inc 440 439-0097
  26383 Broadway Ave Bedford (44146) *(G-983)*
Roseland Lanes I, Bedford Also Called: Roseland Lanes Inc *(G-983)*
Rosens Inc 419 225-7382
  1132 E Hanthorn Rd Lima (45804) *(G-9956)*
Rosens, Inc, Lima Also Called: Rosens Inc *(G-9956)*
Rosenthal Collins Group, Columbus Also Called: Bakkt Clearing LLC *(G-5415)*
Rosewind Limited Partnership 614 421-6000
  960 E 5th Ave Columbus (43201) *(G-6611)*

ALPHABETIC SECTION

Rosmansearch Inc..216 256-9020
30799 Pinetree Rd Cleveland (44124) *(G-4855)*

Ross Sinclaire & Assoc LLC (PA)..............................513 381-3939
700 Walnut St Ste 600 Cincinnati (45202) *(G-3320)*

Ross Brittain Schonberg Lpa..................................216 447-1551
6480 Rockside Woods Blvd S Ste 350 Independence (44131) *(G-9480)*

Ross Cnty Cmnty Action Comm In (PA).......................740 702-7222
250 N Woodbridge Ave Chillicothe (45601) *(G-2084)*

Ross Cnty Job Fmly Svcs Chldre, Chillicothe *Also Called: Ross County Children Svcs Ctr* *(G-2085)*

Ross Consolidated Corp (PA)..................................440 748-5800
36790 Giles Rd Grafton (44044) *(G-8841)*

Ross County Children Svcs Ctr (PA)..........................740 773-2651
150 E 2nd St Chillicothe (45601) *(G-2085)*

Ross County Health District..................................740 775-1114
150 E 2nd St Chillicothe (45601) *(G-2086)*

Ross County Home Health LLC................................740 775-1114
1550 Western Ave # A Chillicothe (45601) *(G-2087)*

Ross County Water Company Inc.............................740 774-4117
663 Fairgrounds Rd Chillicothe (45601) *(G-2088)*

Ross Incineration Services Inc................................440 366-2000
36790 Giles Rd Grafton (44044) *(G-8842)*

Ross Medical Education Center, Dayton *Also Called: Imdt Acquisition LLC (G-7418)*

Ross Transportation Svcs Inc..................................440 748-5900
36790 Giles Rd Grafton (44044) *(G-8843)*

Rossford Grtric Care Ltd Prtnr.................................614 459-0445
1496 Old Henderson Rd Columbus (43220) *(G-6612)*

Rotary International Inc.......................................740 385-8575
11153 Walnut Dowler Rd Logan (43138) *(G-10036)*

Roth Bros Inc (DH)...330 793-5571
3847 Crum Rd Youngstown (44515) *(G-15713)*

Roth Produce Co..614 337-2825
3882 Agler Rd Columbus (43219) *(G-6613)*

Roth Roofing Products LLC..................................800 872-7684
3847 Crum Rd Youngstown (44515) *(G-15714)*

Roto, Dublin *Also Called: Roto Group LLC (G-8110)*

Roto Group LLC (PA)...614 760-8690
7001 Discovery Blvd Fl 2 Dublin (43017) *(G-8110)*

Roto Rt Inc (DH)..513 762-6690
255 E 5th St Ste 2500 Cincinnati (45202) *(G-3321)*

Roto-Rooter, Cincinnati *Also Called: Nurotoco Massachusetts Inc (G-3135)*

Roto-Rooter, Cincinnati *Also Called: Roto Rt Inc (G-3321)*

Roto-Rooter, Cincinnati *Also Called: Roto-Rooter Development Co (G-3322)*

Roto-Rooter, Cincinnati *Also Called: Roto-Rooter Group Inc (G-3323)*

Roto-Rooter, Cincinnati *Also Called: Roto-Rooter Services Company (G-3324)*

Roto-Rooter, North Canton *Also Called: Canton-Stark Cnty Swer Clg Inc (G-11814)*

Roto-Rooter Development Co (HQ)..........................513 762-6690
255 E 5th St Ste 2500 Cincinnati (45202) *(G-3322)*

Roto-Rooter Group Inc (HQ)..................................513 762-6690
255 E 5th St Ste 2500 Cincinnati (45202) *(G-3323)*

Roto-Rooter Services Company (DH)........................513 762-6690
255 E 5th St Cincinnati (45202) *(G-3324)*

Rouen Chrysler Plymouth Dodge..............................419 837-6228
1091 Fremont Pike Woodville (43469) *(G-15306)*

Rouen Dodge, Woodville *Also Called: Rouen Chrysler Plymouth Dodge (G-15306)*

Rough Brothers Mfg Inc......................................513 242-0310
5513 Vine St Cincinnati (45217) *(G-3325)*

Roulan Enterprises Inc.......................................440 543-2070
4900 Countryside Rd Cleveland (44124) *(G-4856)*

Roulston & Company Inc (PA).................................216 431-3000
1350 Euclid Ave Ste 400 Cleveland (44115) *(G-4857)*

Round Lk Christn Assembly Inc...............................419 827-2018
114 State Route 3 Lakeville (44638) *(G-9656)*

Round Room LLC..937 429-2230
3301 Dayton Xenia Rd Beavercreek (45432) *(G-902)*

Round Room LLC..330 880-6500
3 Massillon Marketplace Dr Sw Massillon (44646) *(G-10666)*

Roundstone Management Ltd................................440 617-0333
15422 Detroit Ave Lakewood (44107) *(G-9683)*

Roundtable Learning LLC...................................440 220-5252
8401 Chagrin Rd Ste 6 Chagrin Falls (44023) *(G-1988)*

Roundtower Technologies LLC (DH).........................513 247-7900
5905 E Galbraith Rd Fl 3 Cincinnati (45236) *(G-3326)*

Roush Equipment Inc (PA)...................................614 882-1535
100 W Schrock Rd Westerville (43081) *(G-15014)*

Roush Honda, Westerville *Also Called: Roush Equipment Inc (G-15014)*

Rovisys Company (PA).......................................330 562-8600
1455 Danner Dr Aurora (44202) *(G-626)*

Rownd Metal Sales Inc
432 Keystone St Alliance (44601) *(G-400)*

Royal Electric Cnstr Corp....................................614 253-6600
1250 Memory Ln N Ste B Columbus (43209) *(G-6614)*

Royal F & S Holdings LLC....................................614 402-8422
190 S High St Apt 475 Columbus (43215) *(G-6615)*

Royal Landscape Gardening Inc..............................216 883-7000
7801 Old Granger Rd Cleveland (44125) *(G-4858)*

Royal Manor Health Care Inc (PA)............................216 752-3600
18810 Harvard Ave Cleveland (44122) *(G-4859)*

ROYAL MANOR HOMES, Cleveland *Also Called: Royal Oak Nrsing Rhblttion Ctr (G-4860)*

Royal Oak Nrsing Rhblttion Ctr...............................440 884-9191
6973 Pearl Rd Cleveland (44130) *(G-4860)*

Royal Paper Stock Company Inc (PA)........................614 851-4714
1300 Norton Rd Columbus (43228) *(G-6616)*

Royal Rdeemer Lutheran Ch Schl, North Royalton *Also Called: Royal Rdmer Lthran Ch N Rylton (G-11949)*

Royal Rdmer Lthran Ch N Rylton............................440 237-7958
11680 Royalton Rd North Royalton (44133) *(G-11949)*

Royalmont Academy...513 754-0555
200 Northcrest Dr Mason (45040) *(G-10602)*

Royalty Care Nursing LLC....................................216 386-8762
2490 Lee Blvd Ste 200 Cleveland (44118) *(G-4861)*

Royalty Trucking Inc..513 771-1860
4836 Tylersville Rd Mason (45040) *(G-10603)*

Royce Security Services, Cleveland *Also Called: Sam-Tom Inc (G-4874)*

RP Gatta Inc..330 562-2288
435 Gentry Dr Aurora (44202) *(G-627)*

RPC Electronics Inc (PA).....................................440 461-4700
749 Miner Rd Highland Heights (44143) *(G-9170)*

RPC Mechanical Services (HQ)...............................513 733-1641
5301 Lester Rd Cincinnati (45213) *(G-3327)*

Rrr Express LLC..800 723-3424
6432 Centre Park Dr West Chester (45069) *(G-14758)*

Rrr Logistics, West Chester *Also Called: Rrr Express LLC (G-14758)*

RSI Construction, Sunbury *Also Called: Restaurant Specialties Inc (G-13524)*

RSM US LLP..216 523-1900
1001 Lakeside Ave E Ste 200 Cleveland (44114) *(G-4862)*

RSR Partners LLC..440 248-3991
6111 Cochran Rd Solon (44139) *(G-13140)*

RSR Partners LLC (PA).......................................440 519-1768
4550 Darrow Rd Stow (44224) *(G-13389)*

Rss, Cleveland *Also Called: Dwellworks LLC (G-4190)*

Rsw/Us GP...513 898-0940
6725 Miami Ave Cincinnati (45243) *(G-3328)*

RT Industries Inc...937 339-8313
1625 Troy Sidney Rd Troy (45373) *(G-14157)*

Rt80 Express Inc...330 706-0900
4409 S Cleveland Massillon Rd Barberton (44203) *(G-707)*

Rthrford B Hayes Prsdntial Ctr................................419 332-2081
Spiegel Grove Fremont (43420) *(G-8699)*

Rti, Akron *Also Called: Park Lane Manor Akron Inc (G-261)*

Rttw Ltd..614 291-7944
939 N High St Unit 202 Columbus (43201) *(G-6617)*

Rtw Inc (DH)...952 893-0403
518 E Broad St Columbus (43215) *(G-6618)*

Ruan Transport Corporation.................................330 484-1450
3800 Commerce St Sw Canton (44706) *(G-1847)*

Rubber & Plastics News, Cuyahoga Falls *Also Called: Crain Communications Inc (G-7065)*

Rubber City Machinery Corp.................................330 434-3500
One Thousand Sweitzer Avenue Akron (44311) *(G-288)*

Rubber City Radio Group Inc (PA)............................330 869-9800
1795 W Market St Akron (44313) *(G-289)*

Rubber Seal Products, Dayton *Also Called: Teknol Inc (G-7661)*

ALPHABETIC SECTION

Rubbermaid, Akron *Also Called: Rubbermaid Incorporated (G-290)*

Rubbermaid Incorporated..330 733-7771
3009 Gilchrist Rd Akron (44305) *(G-290)*

Rucker & Sill, Cincinnati *Also Called: Tile Shop LLC (G-3480)*

Rudd Equipment Company Inc..513 321-7833
11807 Enterprise Dr Cincinnati (45241) *(G-3329)*

Rudemiller Family Medicine, Cincinnati *Also Called: Trihealth Inc (G-3506)*

Rudolph Libbe Inc...216 369-0198
4937 Mills Industrial Pkwy North Ridgeville (44039) *(G-11935)*

Rudolph Libbe Inc (HQ)..419 241-5000
6494 Latcha Rd Walbridge (43465) *(G-14464)*

Rudolph/Libbe, Walbridge *Also Called: Rudolph/Libbe Companies Inc (G-14465)*

Rudolph/Libbe Companies Inc (PA)......................................419 241-5000
6494 Latcha Rd Walbridge (43465) *(G-14465)*

Rudzik Excavating Inc..330 755-1540
401 Lowellville Rd Struthers (44471) *(G-13503)*

RUFFING MONTESSORI SCHOOL, Cleveland *Also Called: Fairmount Montessori Assn (G-4235)*

Ruhlin Company (PA)..330 239-2800
6931 Ridge Rd Sharon Center (44274) *(G-12989)*

Rukh-Jagi Holdings LLC..330 494-2770
4520 Everhard Rd Nw Canton (44718) *(G-1848)*

Rummell Dvid G Schmcher Mike R.......................................614 451-1110
3600 Olentangy River Rd Columbus (43214) *(G-6619)*

Rumpf Corporation (PA)...419 255-5005
701 Jefferson Ave Toledo (43604) *(G-13999)*

Rumpke, Cincinnati *Also Called: Rumpke Waste Inc (G-3332)*

Rumpke Cnsld Companies Inc (PA).....................................800 828-8171
3990 Generation Dr Cincinnati (45251) *(G-3330)*

Rumpke Container Service, Cincinnati *Also Called: Rumpke Transportation Co LLC (G-3331)*

Rumpke Container Service, Dayton *Also Called: Rumpke Transportation Co LLC (G-7597)*

Rumpke of Ohio Inc..740 947-7082
11775 State Route 220 Waverly (45690) *(G-14618)*

Rumpke Recycling, Cincinnati *Also Called: Rumpke Waste Inc (G-3333)*

Rumpke Recycling, Circleville *Also Called: Rumpke Waste Inc (G-3722)*

Rumpke Transportation Co LLC..513 242-4600
553 Vine St Cincinnati (45202) *(G-3331)*

Rumpke Transportation Co LLC..937 461-0004
1932 E Monument Ave Dayton (45402) *(G-7597)*

Rumpke Waste Inc (HQ)...513 851-0122
10795 Hughes Rd Cincinnati (45251) *(G-3332)*

Rumpke Waste Inc..513 242-4401
5535 Vine St Cincinnati (45217) *(G-3333)*

Rumpke Waste Inc..740 474-9790
819 Island Rd Circleville (43113) *(G-3722)*

Rumpke Waste Inc..513 851-0122
1191 Fields Ave Columbus (43201) *(G-6620)*

Rumpke Waste Inc..937 378-4126
9427 Beyers Rd Georgetown (45121) *(G-8801)*

Rumpke Waste Inc..937 548-1939
5474 Jaysville Saint Johns Rd Greenville (45331) *(G-8883)*

Rumpke Waste Inc..419 895-0058
170 Noble Rd E Shiloh (44878) *(G-13014)*

Rumpke Waste Inc..740 384-4400
28 A W Long Rd Wellston (45692) *(G-14641)*

Rumpke Waste and Recycl Svcs, Cincinnati *Also Called: Rumpke Cnsld Companies Inc (G-3330)*

Rumpke/Kenworth Contract..740 774-5111
65 Kenworth Dr Chillicothe (45601) *(G-2089)*

Runyon & Sons Roofing Inc..440 974-6810
8745 Munson Rd Mentor (44060) *(G-10993)*

Rural Lorain County Water Auth..440 355-5121
42401 State Route 303 Lagrange (44050) *(G-9650)*

Rural Water Utility, Chillicothe *Also Called: Ross County Water Company Inc (G-2088)*

Rurbanc Data Services Inc..419 782-2530
7622 N State Route 66 Defiance (43512) *(G-7767)*

Ruscilli Construction Co Inc (PA)...614 876-9484
5815 Wall St Ste 1 Dublin (43017) *(G-8111)*

Rush Expediting Inc...937 885-0894
2619 Needmore Rd Dayton (45414) *(G-7598)*

Rush Package Delivery Inc...937 297-6182
1733 Mckinley Ave Columbus (43222) *(G-6621)*

Rush Trnsp & Logistics, Columbus *Also Called: Rush Package Delivery Inc (G-6621)*

Rush Truck Center, Cincinnati, Cincinnati *Also Called: Rush Truck Centers Ohio Inc (G-3334)*

Rush Truck Centers Ohio Inc (HQ).......................................513 733-8500
11775 Highway Dr Cincinnati (45241) *(G-3334)*

Rush Truck Leasing Inc..937 264-2365
7655 Poe Ave Dayton (45414) *(G-7599)*

Rush Truck Leasing Inc..419 224-6045
2655 Saint Johns Rd Lima (45804) *(G-9957)*

Rush Truck Leasing Inc..330 798-0600
7307 Young Dr Ste E Walton Hills (44146) *(G-14479)*

Rushcard, Blue Ash *Also Called: Unifund Corporation (G-1263)*

Rusk Industries Inc...419 841-6055
2930 Centennial Rd Toledo (43617) *(G-14000)*

Russell Real Estate Service...440 835-8300
27121 Center Ridge Rd Cleveland (44145) *(G-4863)*

Russell T Bundy Associates Inc (PA).................................937 652-2151
417 E Water St Urbana (43078) *(G-14312)*

Russell Weisman Jr MD..216 844-3127
11100 Euclid Ave Cleveland (44106) *(G-4864)*

Rustic Pathways LLC...440 497-4166
6082 Pinecone Dr Mentor (44060) *(G-10994)*

Rustys Towing Service Inc..614 491-6288
4845 Obetz Reese Rd Columbus (43207) *(G-6622)*

RUTHERFORD B HAYES PRESIDENTIA, Fremont *Also Called: Rthrford B Hayes Prsdntial Ctr (G-8699)*

Rutherford House, Fremont *Also Called: Assisted Living Concepts LLC (G-8667)*

Rvc Architects Inc..740 592-5615
131 W State St Athens (45701) *(G-587)*

Rvc Inc...330 535-2211
131 N Summit St Akron (44304) *(G-291)*

Rvsharecom..330 907-9479
155 Montrose West Ave Copley (44321) *(G-6962)*

Rwam Bros Inc..419 826-3671
420 N Hallett Avenue Swanton (43558) *(G-13528)*

Rwk Services Inc (PA)..440 526-2144
4700 Rockside Rd Ste 330 Cleveland (44131) *(G-4865)*

Rwk Services Inc CCI...216 387-3754
4700 Rockside Rd Ste 330 Independence (44131) *(G-9481)*

Rwlp Company..216 883-2424
5260 Commerce Pkwy W Cleveland (44130) *(G-4866)*

Rxcrossroads 3pl LLC...866 447-9758
4200 Binion Way Ste 200 Mason (45036) *(G-10604)*

Rxp Ohio LLC..614 937-2844
630 E Broad St Columbus (43215) *(G-6623)*

Ryan G Harris DMD...937 426-5411
1205 Meadow Bridge Dr Beavercreek (45434) *(G-903)*

Ryan Homes, Bedford *Also Called: Nvr Inc (G-977)*

Ryan Logistics Inc..937 642-4158
648 Clymer Rd Marysville (43040) *(G-10506)*

Ryan Partnership, Westerville *Also Called: D L Ryan Companies LLC (G-14887)*

Ryan Senior Care LLC...419 389-0800
5020 Ryan Rd Toledo (43614) *(G-14001)*

Ryan, Charles R MD Facog, Lima *Also Called: Ob-Gyn Specialists Lima Inc (G-9944)*

Ryans All-Glass Incorporated (PA).....................................513 771-4440
9401 Le Saint Dr West Chester (45014) *(G-14759)*

Rycon Construction Inc..440 481-3770
7661 W Ridgewood Dr Parma (44129) *(G-12264)*

Ryder, Grove City *Also Called: Ryder Integrated Logistics Inc (G-8949)*

Ryder Integrated Logistics Inc..614 801-0224
3750 Brookham Dr Ste A Grove City (43123) *(G-8949)*

Ryder Last Mile Inc (HQ)..866 711-3129
7795 Walton Pkwy New Albany (43054) *(G-11586)*

Ryerson, Streetsboro *Also Called: Singer Steel Company (G-13427)*

S & G 3 LLC..937 988-0050
5161 Cornerstone North Blvd Dayton (45440) *(G-7600)*

S & S Aggregates Inc...419 938-5604
4540 State Route 39 Perrysville (44864) *(G-12393)*

S & S Haltcare Strategies Ltd...513 772-8866
1385 Kemper Meadow Dr Cincinnati (45240) *(G-3335)*

S & S Management Inc.. 937 235-2000
   5612 Merily Way Dayton (45424) *(G-7601)*

S & S Management Inc.. 567 356-4151
   1510 Saturn Dr Wapakoneta (45895) *(G-14491)*

S & S Management Inc.. 937 382-5858
   155 Holiday Dr Wilmington (45177) *(G-15272)*

S & S Realty Ltd.. 419 625-0362
   1021 Cleveland Rd Sandusky (44870) *(G-12928)*

S & T Truck and Auto Svc Inc... 614 272-8163
   3150 Valleyview Dr Rm 8 Columbus (43204) *(G-6624)*

S A, Columbus Also Called: Safe Auto Insurance Company *(G-6626)*

S A Comunale Co Inc... 419 334-3841
   1524 Oak Harbor Rd Fremont (43420) *(G-8700)*

S A Comunale Co Inc... 440 684-9325
   135 Alpha Park Highland Heights (44143) *(G-9171)*

S A Comunale Co Inc (DH)... 330 706-3040
   2900 Newpark Dr Barberton (44203) *(G-708)*

S A F Y, Delphos Also Called: Specilzed Altrntves For Fmlies *(G-7845)*

S A I, New Albany Also Called: Shremshock Architects Inc *(G-11587)*

S A W - Rcky Rver Adult Trning, Rocky River Also Called: A W S Inc *(G-12738)*

S A W Adult Training Center, Cleveland Also Called: A W S Inc *(G-3751)*

S and S Gilardi Inc... 740 397-2751
   1033 Newark Rd Mount Vernon (43050) *(G-11507)*

S B Morabito Trucking Inc... 216 441-3070
   7353 Dunham Rd Bedford (44146) *(G-984)*

S B S Transit Inc... 440 288-2222
   42242 Albrecht Rd Elyria (44035) *(G-8292)*

S C A T, Tiffin Also Called: North Central Area Transit *(G-13635)*

S C E, Brookpark Also Called: Standard Contg & Engrg Inc *(G-1440)*

S C S, Cleveland Also Called: Specialty Chemical Sales Inc *(G-4928)*

S D Myers Inc... 330 630-7000
   180 South Ave Tallmadge (44278) *(G-13602)*

S E S, West Chester Also Called: Superior Envmtl Sltons SES Inc *(G-14835)*

S E T Inc... 330 536-6724
   235 E Water St Ste C Lowellville (44436) *(G-10171)*

S F S, Clyde Also Called: Spader Freight Services Inc *(G-5210)*

S G I, Cincinnati Also Called: The Sheakley Group Inc *(G-3471)*

S Gary Shmker Rgging Trnspt L.. 330 899-9090
   3385 Miller Park Rd Akron (44312) *(G-292)*

S M C, Upper Sandusky Also Called: Schmidt Machine Company *(G-14292)*

S M E, Columbus Also Called: Settle Muter Electric Ltd *(G-6667)*

S Meridian Leasing Co LLC... 513 530-1600
   650 S Meridian Rd Youngstown (44509) *(G-15715)*

S O M C Urgent Care, Wheelersburg Also Called: Southern Ohio Medical Center *(G-15132)*

S O R T A, Cincinnati Also Called: Southwest Ohio Rgnal Trnst Aut *(G-3393)*

S O S Shades, Lewis Center Also Called: Inside Outfitters Inc *(G-9824)*

S P A, Milford Also Called: Spa LLC *(G-11258)*

S P C A CINCINNATI, Cincinnati Also Called: Hamilton Cnty Soc For The Prvn *(G-2794)*

S P Richards Company.. 614 497-2270
   1815 Beggrow St Lockbourne (43137) *(G-10015)*

S R Door Inc (PA)... 740 927-3558
   1120 O Neill Dr Hebron (43025) *(G-9153)*

S-P Company Inc (PA).. 330 782-5651
   400 W Railroad St Ste 1 Columbiana (44408) *(G-5240)*

S-T Acquisition Company LLC... 440 735-1505
   7589 First Pl Cleveland (44146) *(G-4868)*

S. B. Stone & Company, Brecksville Also Called: Level Seven *(G-1357)*

S.A. Comunale Co., Highland Heights Also Called: S A Comunale Co Inc *(G-9171)*

S.E.I., New Philadelphia Also Called: Starlight Enterprises Inc *(G-11668)*

S.E.S. Engineering, Alliance Also Called: Steel Eqp Specialists Inc *(G-401)*

S.E.T. Inc.of Ohio, Lowellville Also Called: S E T Inc *(G-10171)*

S&D/Osterfeld Mech Contrs Inc.. 937 277-1700
   1101 Negley Pl Dayton (45402) *(G-7602)*

S&P Data Ohio LLC.. 216 965-0018
   1500 W 3rd St Ste 400 Cleveland (44113) *(G-4867)*

S&S / Superior Coach Co Inc... 888 324-7895
   2550 Central Point Pkwy Lima (45804) *(G-9958)*

S&S Management.. 937 332-1700
   60 Troy Town Dr Troy (45373) *(G-14158)*

S&V Industries Inc (PA)... 330 666-1986
   5054 Paramount Dr Medina (44256) *(G-10886)*

Saama Technologies Inc.. 614 652-6100
   100 W Old Wilson Bridge Rd Ste 201 Worthington (43085) *(G-15454)*

Saatchi & Saatchi X Inc.. 479 575-0200
   231 W 12th St Ste 600 Cincinnati (45202) *(G-3336)*

Sabco Industries Inc... 419 531-5347
   5242 Angola Rd Ste 150 Toledo (43615) *(G-14002)*

Saber Healthcare Group LLC.. 216 464-4300
   25825 Science Park Dr Beachwood (44122) *(G-832)*

Saber Healthcare Group LLC (PA)... 216 292-5706
   23700 Commerce Park Beachwood (44122) *(G-833)*

Saber Healthcare Group LLC.. 740 852-3100
   218 Elm St London (43140) *(G-10050)*

Saber Healthcare Holdings LLC... 216 292-5706
   26691 Richmond Rd Frnt Bedford Heights (44146) *(G-1002)*

Sabin Robbins LLC.. 513 874-5270
   9365 Allen Rd West Chester (45069) *(G-14760)*

Sabo Inc... 937 222-7939
   1137 Brown St Dayton (45409) *(G-7603)*

Sachs Management Corp.. 740 282-0901
   1401 University Blvd Steubenville (43952) *(G-13342)*

Sack n Save Inc.. 740 382-2464
   725 Richmond Ave Marion (43302) *(G-10453)*

Sacred Hour Inc.. 216 228-9750
   17917 Detroit Ave Lakewood (44107) *(G-9684)*

Sacred Hour Wellness Spas, Lakewood Also Called: Sacred Hour Inc *(G-9684)*

Sacs Cnslting Invstigative Svc, Akron Also Called: Sacs Cnslting Training Ctr Inc *(G-293)*

Sacs Cnslting Training Ctr Inc.. 330 255-1101
   520 S Main St Ste 2516 Akron (44311) *(G-293)*

Sadler-Necamp Financial Svcs... 513 489-5477
   7621 E Kemper Rd Cincinnati (45249) *(G-3337)*

Saec/Kinetic Vision Inc... 513 793-4959
   10651 Aerohub Blvd Cincinnati (45215) *(G-3338)*

Safe and Secure Homecare Corp.. 614 808-0164
   1945 North Star Rd Columbus (43212) *(G-6625)*

Safe Auto Insurance Company (DH)... 614 231-0200
   4 Easton Oval Columbus (43219) *(G-6626)*

Safe Auto Insurance Company... 740 472-1900
   47060 Black Walnut Pkwy Woodsfield (43793) *(G-15302)*

Safe Auto Insurance Group Inc (HQ).. 614 231-0200
   4 Easton Oval Columbus (43219) *(G-6627)*

Safe Dig, Youngstown Also Called: Ground Tech Inc *(G-15625)*

Safe-N-Sound Security Inc... 330 491-1148
   5555 County Road 203 Unit B2 Millersburg (44654) *(G-11292)*

Safegard Bckgrund Screening LLC... 877 700-7345
   2000 Auburn Dr Ste 200 Beachwood (44122) *(G-834)*

Safegate, Columbus Also Called: Safegate Airport Systems Inc *(G-6628)*

Safegate Airport Systems Inc.. 763 535-9299
   700 Science Blvd Columbus (43230) *(G-6628)*

Safeguard, Cleveland Also Called: Safeguard Properties MGT LLC *(G-4870)*

Safeguard Properties LLC (HQ)... 216 739-2900
   7887 Safeguard Cir Cleveland (44125) *(G-4869)*

Safeguard Properties MGT LLC (PA).. 216 739-2900
   7887 Hub Pkwy Cleveland (44125) *(G-4870)*

Safelite Autoglass, Columbus Also Called: Safelite Glass Corp *(G-6631)*

Safelite Autoglass, Columbus Also Called: Safelite Group Inc *(G-6632)*

Safelite Autoglass Foundation.. 614 210-9000
   7400 Safelite Way Columbus (43235) *(G-6629)*

Safelite Billing Services Corp... 614 210-9000
   7400 Safelite Way Columbus (43235) *(G-6630)*

Safelite Glass Corp (DH).. 614 210-9000
   7400 Safelite Way Columbus (43235) *(G-6631)*

Safelite Glass Corp... 614 431-4936
   600 Lakeview Plaza Blvd Ste A Worthington (43085) *(G-15455)*

Safelite Group Inc (DH)... 614 210-9000
   7400 Safelite Way Columbus (43235) *(G-6632)*

Safelite Solutions LLC.. 614 210-9000
   7400 Safelite Way Columbus (43235) *(G-6633)*

Safety and Hygiene, Columbus Also Called: Bureau Workers Compensation *(G-5484)*

Safety Grooving & Grinding LP
   13226 County Road R Napoleon (43545) *(G-11532)*

ALPHABETIC SECTION

Safety Solutions Inc (HQ) 614 799-9900
6999 Huntley Rd Ste L Columbus (43229) *(G-6634)*

Safety Today Inc (HQ) 614 409-7200
3287 Southwest Blvd Grove City (43123) *(G-8950)*

Safran, Twinsburg *Also Called: Safran Power Usa LLC (G-14218)*

Safran Humn Rsrces Support Inc (HQ) 513 552-3230
111 Merchant St Cincinnati (45246) *(G-3339)*

Safran Power Usa LLC (DH) 330 487-2000
8380 Darrow Rd Twinsburg (44087) *(G-14218)*

SAFY, Delphos *Also Called: Specilzed Altrntves For Fmlies (G-7844)*

Safy Behavioral Health of Lima, Lima *Also Called: Specialized Alternatives For F (G-9963)*

Safy of Cincinnati, Cincinnati *Also Called: Specialized Alternatives For F (G-3395)*

Safy of Cleveland, Shaker Heights *Also Called: Specialized Alternatives For F (G-12985)*

Sagamore Hills Medical Center, Northfield *Also Called: Cleveland Clnic Hlth Systm-AST (G-11954)*

Sage Hospitality Resources LLC 513 771-2080
11320 Chester Rd Cincinnati (45246) *(G-3340)*

Sahaj Hospitality Ltd 740 593-5565
997 E State St Athens (45701) *(G-588)*

Sahara Global Security LLC 614 448-7940
601 S High St Columbus (43215) *(G-6635)*

Saia, Dayton *Also Called: Saia Motor Freight Line LLC (G-7604)*

Saia Motor Freight Line LLC 614 870-8778
1717 Krieger St Columbus (43228) *(G-6636)*

Saia Motor Freight Line LLC 937 237-0140
3154 Transportation Rd Dayton (45404) *(G-7604)*

Saia Motor Freight Line LLC 330 659-4277
2920 Brecksville Rd Ste B Richfield (44286) *(G-12709)*

Saia Motor Freight Line LLC 419 726-9761
1919 E Manhattan Blvd Toledo (43608) *(G-14003)*

Saint Cecilia Church 614 878-5353
440 Norton Rd Columbus (43228) *(G-6637)*

Saint Joseph Orphanage (PA) 513 741-3100
5400 Edalbert Dr Cincinnati (45239) *(G-3341)*

Saint Joseph Orphanage 513 231-5010
274 Sutton Rd Cincinnati (45230) *(G-3342)*

Saint Joseph Orphanage 937 643-0398
6680 Poe Ave Ste 450 Dayton (45414) *(G-7605)*

Saint Moritz Security Services, Youngstown *Also Called: St Moritz Security Svcs Inc (G-15729)*

Saint-Gobain Glass Corporation 614 777-5867
2779 Westbelt Dr Columbus (43228) *(G-6638)*

Sajovie Brothers Ldscpg Inc 216 662-4983
7991 Pennsylvania Ave Maple Heights (44137) *(G-10345)*

Sakrete Inc 513 242-3644
5155 Fischer Ave Cincinnati (45217) *(G-3343)*

Salem City Schools 330 332-2321
1150 Pennsylvania Ave Salem (44460) *(G-12851)*

Salem Community Center Inc 330 332-5885
1098 N Ellsworth Ave Salem (44460) *(G-12852)*

Salem Community Hospital 330 482-2265
116 Carriage Dr Columbiana (44408) *(G-5241)*

Salem Community Hospital 330 337-9922
2235 E Pershing St Ste G Salem (44460) *(G-12853)*

Salem Community Hospital (PA) 330 332-1551
1995 E State St Salem (44460) *(G-12854)*

Salem Healthcare MGT LLC 330 332-1588
1985 E Pershing St Salem (44460) *(G-12855)*

Salem Home Health Care Center, Salem *Also Called: Salem Community Hospital (G-12853)*

SALEM REGIONAL MEDICAL CENTER, Salem *Also Called: Salem Community Hospital (G-12854)*

SALEM WEST HEALTHCARE CENTER, Salem *Also Called: Bentley Leasing Co LLC (G-12839)*

Salesfuel Inc 614 794-0500
600 N Cleveland Ave Ste 260 Westerville (43082) *(G-14936)*

Salidawoods, Mentor *Also Called: Lifeservices Management Corp (G-10964)*

Salineville Office, Salineville *Also Called: M3 Midstream LLC (G-12860)*

Salini Impregilo/Healy 216 539-2050
786 E 140th St Cleveland (44110) *(G-4871)*

Salix Ltd 513 381-2679
5712 Carthage Ave Cincinnati (45212) *(G-3344)*

Salo Inc 419 419-0038
1216 W Wooster St Bowling Green (43402) *(G-1332)*

Salo Inc 740 432-2966
2146 Southgate Pkwy Ste 7 Cambridge (43725) *(G-1581)*

Salo Inc 513 984-1110
8035 Hosbrook Rd Cincinnati (45236) *(G-3345)*

Salo Inc (PA) 614 436-9404
300 W Wilson Bridge Rd Ste 250 Columbus (43085) *(G-6639)*

Salo Inc 740 623-2331
232 Chestnut St Coshocton (43812) *(G-7001)*

Salo Inc 877 759-2106
450 N 3rd St Coshocton (43812) *(G-7002)*

Salo Inc 330 836-5571
3040 W Market St Ste 1 Fairlawn (44333) *(G-8495)*

Salo Inc 740 653-5990
2680 N Columbus St Ste A Lancaster (43130) *(G-9740)*

Salo Inc 740 651-5209
109 E Main St Mcconnelsville (43756) *(G-10804)*

Salo Inc 740 964-2904
350 S Main St # B Pataskala (43062) *(G-12276)*

Salon Lofts 440 356-1062
3141 Westgate Cleveland (44126) *(G-4872)*

Salon PS, Cleveland *Also Called: PS Lifestyle LLC (G-4796)*

Salt Fork Lodge Conference Ctr, Cambridge *Also Called: US Hotel Osp Ventures LLC (G-1586)*

Salt Fork Resort Club Inc 740 498-8116
74978 Broadhead Rd Kimbolton (43749) *(G-9641)*

Salutary Providers Inc 440 964-8446
2217 West Ave Ashtabula (44004) *(G-548)*

Salvagnini America Inc (DH) 513 874-8284
27 Bicentennial Ct Hamilton (45015) *(G-9080)*

Salvanalle Inc 419 529-4700
2760 Crider Rd Mansfield (44903) *(G-10315)*

Salvation Army 937 461-2769
2250 Park Ave Cincinnati (45212) *(G-3346)*

Salvation Army 330 773-3331
5005 Euclid Ave Cleveland (44103) *(G-4873)*

Salvation Army 614 252-7171
966 E Main St Columbus (43205) *(G-6640)*

Salvation Army 800 728-7825
1675 S High St Columbus (43207) *(G-6641)*

Salvation Army 937 528-5100
1000 N Keowee St Dayton (45404) *(G-7606)*

Salvation Army 419 447-2252
505 E Market St Tiffin (44883) *(G-13641)*

Salvation Army, Cincinnati *Also Called: Salvation Army (G-3346)*

Salvation Army, Cleveland *Also Called: Salvation Army (G-4873)*

Salvation Army, Columbus *Also Called: Salvation Army (G-6640)*

Salvation Army, Columbus *Also Called: Salvation Army (G-6641)*

Salvation Army, Dayton *Also Called: Salvation Army (G-7606)*

Salvation Army, Tiffin *Also Called: Salvation Army (G-13641)*

Sam-Tom Inc 216 426-7752
4600 Euclid Ave Ste 400 Cleveland (44103) *(G-4874)*

Samanritan Family Care, Dayton *Also Called: Primary Cr Ntwrk Prmr Hlth Prt (G-7563)*

Samaritan Behavioral Hlth Inc (DH) 937 734-8333
601 S Edwin C Moses Blvd Dayton (45417) *(G-7607)*

Samaritan Behavioral Hlth Inc 937 456-1915
2172 Us Route 127 N Eaton (45320) *(G-8223)*

Samaritan Care Center, Medina *Also Called: Samaritan Care Center Inc (G-10887)*

Samaritan Care Center Inc 330 725-4123
806 E Washington St Medina (44256) *(G-10887)*

Samaritan Care Center & Villa, Medina *Also Called: Ahf Ohio Inc (G-10805)*

Samaritan Family Care, Huber Heights *Also Called: Primary Care Ntwrk Prmier Hlth (G-9326)*

Samaritan Health & Rehab Ctr, Ashland *Also Called: Samaritan Regional Health Sys (G-511)*

Samaritan Health Partners (HQ) 937 208-8400
2222 Philadelphia Dr Dayton (45406) *(G-7608)*

Samaritan N Fmly Physicians, Englewood *Also Called: Primary Care Ntwrk Prmier Hlth (G-8319)*

Samaritan N Surgery Ctr Ltd 937 567-6100
9000 N Main St Englewood (45415) *(G-8322)*

Samaritan Professional Corp   **ALPHABETIC SECTION**

Samaritan Professional Corp 419 289-0491
   1025 Center St Ashland (44805) *(G-509)*

Samaritan Regional Health Sys (PA) 419 289-0491
   1025 Center St Ashland (44805) *(G-510)*

Samaritan Regional Health Sys 419 281-1330
   2163 Claremont Ave Ashland (44805) *(G-511)*

Samaritan Regional Health Sys 419 289-0491
   1941 S Baney Rd Ashland (44805) *(G-512)*

Sammy's, Cleveland *Also Called: City Life Inc (G-3975)*

Sample Machining Inc 937 258-3338
   220 N Jersey St Dayton (45403) *(G-7609)*

Samsel Rope & Marine Supply Co (PA) 216 241-0333
   1285 Old River Rd Uppr Cleveland (44113) *(G-4875)*

Samsel Supply Company, Cleveland *Also Called: Samsel Rope & Marine Supply Co (G-4875)*

Samuel Son & Co (usa) Inc 740 522-2500
   1455 James Pkwy Heath (43056) *(G-9138)*

Samuel Son & Co (usa) Inc 419 470-7070
   1500 Coining Dr Toledo (43612) *(G-14004)*

Samuel Joseph Corp 330 983-6557
   675 Cuyahoga St Akron (44310) *(G-294)*

Samuel Steel Pickling Company, Twinsburg *Also Called: Worthngton Smuel Coil Proc LLC (G-14231)*

Samuels Products Inc 513 891-4456
   9851 Redhill Dr Blue Ash (45242) *(G-1239)*

Sanctary Grnde Snior Lving LLC 330 470-4411
   (Even Range 850 - 898) Applegrove St Nw North Canton (44720) *(G-11860)*

Sanctuary At The Ohio Valley, Ironton *Also Called: Ahf Ohio Inc (G-9501)*

Sanctuary At Tuttle Crossing 614 408-0182
   4880 Tuttle Rd Ofc Dublin (43017) *(G-8112)*

Sanctuary Medina LLC 330 725-3393
   555 Springbrook Dr Medina (44256) *(G-10888)*

Sanctuary of The Ohio Valley, Ironton *Also Called: Bryant Health Center Inc (G-9504)*

Sanctuary Software Studio Inc 330 666-9690
   3090 W Market St Ste 300 Fairlawn (44333) *(G-8496)*

Sanctuary, The, Canton *Also Called: Brookwood Management Co LLC (G-1690)*

Sand Ridge Golf Club 440 285-8088
   12150 Mayfield Rd Chardon (44024) *(G-2019)*

Sand Road Enterprises Inc 419 668-3670
   4352 Sand Rd Norwalk (44857) *(G-12026)*

Sandco Industries 419 547-3273
   567 Premier Dr Clyde (43410) *(G-5209)*

Sandoval 2 Gc Joint Venture, Cincinnati *Also Called: Mv Residential Cnstr LLC (G-3093)*

Sandusky Cnty Job & Fmly Svcs, Fremont *Also Called: Ohio Dept Job & Fmly Svcs (G-8696)*

Sandusky Mall, Sandusky *Also Called: Cafaro Northwest Partnership (G-12867)*

Sandusky Newspaper Group, Sandusky *Also Called: Isaac Foster Mack Co (G-12905)*

Sandusky Orthopedic Surgeons 419 625-4900
   1401 Bone Creek Dr Sandusky (44870) *(G-12929)*

Sandusky Yacht Club Inc 419 625-6567
   529 E Water St Sandusky (44870) *(G-12930)*

Sandy Shores Partners Inc 513 469-6130
   11275 Deerfield Rd Blue Ash (45242) *(G-1240)*

Sandys Auto & Truck Svc Inc 937 461-4980
   3053 Springboro W Moraine (45439) *(G-11436)*

Sandys Towing 937 228-6832
   1541 S Broadway St Dayton (45417) *(G-7610)*

Sanese Services, Warren *Also Called: Sanese Services Inc (G-14550)*

Sanese Services Inc 614 436-1234
   2590 Elm Rd Ne Warren (44483) *(G-14550)*

Sanfillipo Produce Co Inc 614 237-3300
   4561 E 5th Ave Ste 1 Columbus (43219) *(G-6642)*

Sanfillipo Produce Company, Columbus *Also Called: Sanfillipo Produce Co Inc (G-6642)*

Sanfrey Freight Services Inc 330 372-1883
   695 Summit St Nw Ste 1 Warren (44485) *(G-14551)*

Sanson Produce Company, Cleveland *Also Called: The Sanson Company (G-5006)*

Santmyer Coml Fling Netwrk LLC, Wooster *Also Called: Red Rover LLC (G-15368)*

Santmyer Logistics Inc 330 262-6501
   3000 Old Airport Rd Wooster (44691) *(G-15371)*

Santmyer Transportation, Inc., Wooster *Also Called: Santmyer Logistics Inc (G-15371)*

Santo Salon & Spa, Pepper Pike *Also Called: Frank Santo LLC (G-12299)*

Santon Electric Company, Youngstown *Also Called: Santon Electric Inc (G-15716)*

Santon Electric Inc 330 758-0082
   7870 Southern Blvd Youngstown (44512) *(G-15716)*

Sar Enterprises LLC 419 472-8181
   2631 W Central Ave Toledo (43606) *(G-14005)*

SAR Warehouse Staffing LLC 740 963-6235
   1425 E Dublin Granville Rd Ste 109b Columbus (43229) *(G-6643)*

Sarah Moore Community, Delaware *Also Called: Sarah Moore Hlth Care Ctr Inc (G-7824)*

Sarah Moore Hlth Care Ctr Inc 740 362-9641
   26 N Union St Delaware (43015) *(G-7824)*

Sarap, Michael D MD, Cambridge *Also Called: Southstern Ohio Physicians Inc (G-1583)*

Saras Garden 419 335-7272
   620 W Leggett St Wauseon (43567) *(G-14608)*

Sarcom Inc 614 854-1300
   8337a Green Meadows Dr N Lewis Center (43035) *(G-9835)*

Sarnova Inc (HQ) 614 760-5000
   5000 Tuttle Crossing Blvd Dublin (43016) *(G-8113)*

Sarnova Holdings Inc 614 760-5000
   5000 Tuttle Crossing Blvd Dublin (43016) *(G-8114)*

Sarta, Canton *Also Called: Stark Area Regional Trnst Auth (G-1857)*

Sasi, Toledo *Also Called: Compass Corp For Recovery Svcs (G-13753)*

Sateri Home Inc (PA) 330 758-8106
   7246 Ronjoy Pl Youngstown (44512) *(G-15717)*

Saturn Electric Inc 937 278-2580
   2628 Nordic Rd Dayton (45414) *(G-7611)*

Saturn-West, Columbus *Also Called: Northern Automotive Inc (G-6367)*

Satyam Computer Services Ltd 216 654-1800
   6000 Fredom Sq Dr Ste 250 Cleveland (44131) *(G-4876)*

Sauder, Archbold *Also Called: Sauder Woodworking Co (G-467)*

Sauder Woodworking Co (PA) 419 446-2711
   502 Middle St Archbold (43502) *(G-467)*

Sauder's Quality Eggs, Winesburg *Also Called: R W Sauder Inc (G-15290)*

Sauer Construction LLC 614 853-2500
   1105 Schrock Rd Columbus (43229) *(G-6644)*

Sauer Group LLC 614 853-2500
   1105 Schrock Rd Columbus (43229) *(G-6645)*

Savage and Associates Inc (PA) 419 475-8665
   655 Beaver Creek Cir Maumee (43537) *(G-10764)*

Savage Companies 216 642-1311
   4600 Brookpark Rd Cleveland (44134) *(G-4877)*

Savage Services Corporation 216 268-7290
   610 E 152nd St Cleveland (44110) *(G-4878)*

Savings Bank (PA) 740 474-3191
   118 N Court St # 120 Circleville (43113) *(G-3723)*

Savino Del Bene USA Inc 347 960-5568
   7043 Pearl Rd Ste 230 Middleburg Heights (44130) *(G-11127)*

Savour Hospitality LLC 216 308-0018
   4000 Key Tower 127 Public Sq Fl 40 Cleveland (44114) *(G-4879)*

Saw Mill Creek Ltd 419 433-3800
   400 Sawmill Creek Dr W Huron (44839) *(G-9392)*

Saw Service and Supply Company 216 252-5600
   11925 Zelis Rd Cleveland (44135) *(G-4880)*

Sawdey Solution Services Inc (PA) 937 490-4060
   1430 Oak Ct Ste 304 Beavercreek (45430) *(G-930)*

Sawmill Creek Resort, Ltd., Huron *Also Called: SC Resort Ltd (G-9393)*

Sawmill Road Management Co LLC (PA) 937 342-9071
   370 S 5th St Columbus (43215) *(G-6646)*

Saxton Real Estate Co (PA) 614 875-2327
   3703 Broadway Grove City (43123) *(G-8951)*

Say Yes Cleveland, Cleveland *Also Called: Say Yes Clvland Schlarship Inc (G-4881)*

Say Yes Clvland Schlarship Inc 216 273-6350
   325 Superior Ave E Rm 38 Cleveland (44114) *(G-4881)*

Sb Capital Acquisitions LLC 614 443-4080
   4010 E 5th Ave Columbus (43219) *(G-6647)*

Sb Financial Group Inc (PA) 419 783-8950
   401 Clinton St Defiance (43512) *(G-7768)*

Sb Hotel LLC (PA) 614 793-2244
   5775 Perimeter Dr Ste 290 Dublin (43017) *(G-8115)*

SBC, East Liverpool *Also Called: AT&T Teleholdings Inc (G-8178)*

SBC Advertising Ltd 614 891-7070
   4030 Easton Sta Ste 300 Columbus (43219) *(G-6648)*

ALPHABETIC SECTION — SCI Shared Resources LLC

SBC Recycling, Centerburg *Also Called: Shredded Bedding Corporation (G-1936)*

SC Chippewa Preschool, Doylestown *Also Called: Chippewa School District (G-7914)*

SC Resort Ltd.. 419 433-3800
400 Sawmill Creek Dr W Huron (44839) *(G-9393)*

SC Strategic Solutions LLC... 567 424-6054
600 Industrial Pkwy Norwalk (44857) *(G-12027)*

Sca of Ca LLC (DH).. 216 777-2750
4141 Rockside Rd Ste 100 Seven Hills (44131) *(G-12958)*

Sca of Mi LLC (DH)... 216 777-2750
4141 Rockside Rd Ste 100 Seven Hills (44131) *(G-12959)*

Sca of Sc LLC... 216 777-2750
4141 Rockside Rd Ste 100 Seven Hills (44131) *(G-12960)*

Scana Energy Marketing LLC... 803 217-1322
6100 Emerald Pkwy Dublin (43016) *(G-8116)*

Scandinavian Tob Group Ln Ltd... 770 934-4594
1424 Diagonal Rd Akron (44320) *(G-295)*

Scar Holdings LLC... 419 214-0890
505 E Alexis Rd Toledo (43612) *(G-14006)*

Scared Heart Nursing Home, Oregon *Also Called: Little Ssters of Poor Bltmore (G-12135)*

Scenic View Transportation, Canton *Also Called: A Blessed Path Inc (G-1651)*

Scg Fields LLC... 440 546-1200
10303 Brecksville Rd Brecksville (44141) *(G-1366)*

Schaefer, Cincinnati *Also Called: Steven Schaefer Associates Inc (G-3420)*

Schaefer & Company... 937 339-2638
3205 S County Road 25a Troy (45373) *(G-14159)*

Schaefer Group, Blue Ash *Also Called: Schaefer Group Inc (G-1241)*

Schaefer Group Inc... 513 489-2420
11310 Tamarco Dr Blue Ash (45242) *(G-1241)*

Schaeffers Investment Research Inc.. 513 589-3800
5151 Pfeiffer Rd Ste 450 Blue Ash (45242) *(G-1242)*

Schaeffler Group US, Wooster *Also Called: Schaeffler Group USA Inc (G-15372)*

Schaeffler Group USA Inc.. 330 202-6215
3401 Old Airport Rd Wooster (44691) *(G-15372)*

Schaffer Partners Inc.. 216 881-3000
6545 Carnegie Ave Cleveland (44103) *(G-4882)*

Schauer Group Incorporated (PA).. 330 453-7721
200 Market Ave N Ste 100 Canton (44702) *(G-1849)*

Schawk, Cincinnati *Also Called: Sgk LLC (G-3365)*

Schechter, Gross Day School, Pepper Pike *Also Called: Jewish Day Schl Assn Grter Clv (G-12300)*

Scheeser Buckley Mayfield LLC... 330 896-4664
1540 Corporate Woods Pkwy Uniontown (44685) *(G-14263)*

Scheiderer Transport Inc.. 614 873-5103
8520 State Route 161 E Plain City (43064) *(G-12493)*

Scherzinger Corporation.. 513 531-7848
10557 Medallion Dr Cincinnati (45241) *(G-3347)*

Scherzinger Trmt & Pest Ctrl, Cincinnati *Also Called: Scherzinger Corporation (G-3347)*

Schiff Agency, Fairfield *Also Called: Schiff John J & Thomas R & Co (G-8438)*

Schiff John J & Thomas R & Co... 513 870-2580
6200 S Gilmore Rd Fairfield (45014) *(G-8438)*

Schill Grounds Management, North Ridgeville *Also Called: Schill Ldscpg Lawn Care Svcs L (G-11936)*

Schill Ldscpg Lawn Care Svcs L.. 513 271-5296
8915 Blue Ash Rd Ste 1 Blue Ash (45242) *(G-1243)*

Schill Ldscpg Lawn Care Svcs L (PA).. 440 327-3030
5000 Mills Industrial Pkwy North Ridgeville (44039) *(G-11936)*

Schindewolf Express Inc.. 937 585-5919
200 S Boggs St De Graff (43318) *(G-7739)*

Schindler Elevator Corporation... 419 867-5100
1530 Timber Wolf Dr Holland (43528) *(G-9303)*

Schindler Logistics Center, Holland *Also Called: Adams Elevator Equipment Co (G-9276)*

Schirmer Construction Co.. 440 716-4900
31350 Industrial Pkwy North Olmsted (44070) *(G-11914)*

Schlabach Wood Design Inc.. 330 897-2600
52567 State Route 651 Baltic (43804) *(G-691)*

Schlosser, David W DDS, Stow *Also Called: Stow Dental Group Inc (G-13393)*

Schmid Mechanical Inc.. 330 264-3633
207 N Hillcrest Dr Wooster (44691) *(G-15373)*

Schmids Service Now Inc.. 330 499-0157
258 S Columbus Ave Wooster (44691) *(G-15374)*

Schmidt Builders Inc.. 513 779-9300
9679 Cincinnati Columbus Rd Cincinnati (45241) *(G-3348)*

Schmidt Hsptality Concepts Inc... 614 878-4527
240 E Kossuth St Columbus (43206) *(G-6649)*

Schmidt Machine Company... 419 294-3814
7013 State Highway 199 Upper Sandusky (43351) *(G-14292)*

Schmidt SEC & Investigations, Mansfield *Also Called: W William Schmidt & Associates (G-10323)*

Schmidt-Vogel Consulting, Cincinnati *Also Called: Itelligence Outsourcing Inc (G-2890)*

Schneder Smltz Spieth Bell LLP.. 216 535-1001
1375 E 9th St Ste 900 Cleveland (44114) *(G-4883)*

Schneider Downs & Co Inc... 614 621-4060
65 E State St Ste 2000 Columbus (43215) *(G-6650)*

Schneider Electric, Oxford *Also Called: Schneider Electric Usa Inc (G-12217)*

Schneider Electric, West Chester *Also Called: Schneider Electric Usa Inc (G-14761)*

Schneider Electric Usa Inc... 513 523-4171
5735 College Corner Pike Oxford (45056) *(G-12217)*

Schneider Electric Usa Inc... 513 777-4445
9870 Crescent Park Dr West Chester (45069) *(G-14761)*

Schneider Home Equipment Co (PA)... 513 522-1200
7948 Pippin Rd Cincinnati (45239) *(G-3349)*

Schneider Nat Carriers Inc... 740 362-6910
600 London Rd Delaware (43015) *(G-7825)*

Schneider Saddlery LLC... 440 543-2700
8255 Washington St Chagrin Falls (44023) *(G-1989)*

Schnippel Construction Inc.. 937 693-3831
302 N Main St Botkins (45306) *(G-1300)*

Schoch Tile, Cincinnati *Also Called: Schoch Tile & Carpet Inc (G-3350)*

Schoch Tile & Carpet Inc... 513 922-3466
5282 Crookshank Rd Cincinnati (45238) *(G-3350)*

Schoedinger Fnrl & Cremation, Columbus *Also Called: SCI Shared Resources LLC (G-6654)*

Schoednger Fnrl HM - Nrris Gro, Grove City *Also Called: SCI Shared Resources LLC (G-8952)*

Schoenbrunn Healthcare.. 330 339-3595
2594 E High Ave New Philadelphia (44663) *(G-11666)*

Schoner Chevrolet Inc.. 330 877-6731
720 W Maple St Hartville (44632) *(G-9129)*

School Age Child Care, Columbus *Also Called: Upper Arlington City Schl Dst (G-6827)*

School Emplyees Lrain Cnty Cr.. 440 324-3400
340 Griswold Rd Elyria (44035) *(G-8293)*

School Emplyees Rtrment Sys OH... 614 222-5853
300 E Broad St Ste 100 Columbus (43215) *(G-6651)*

SCHOOL OF FINE ARTS, THE, Willoughby *Also Called: The Fine Arts Association (G-15223)*

School of Hope, Fremont *Also Called: County of Sandusky (G-8672)*

School Transportation.. 937 855-3897
59 Peffley St Germantown (45327) *(G-8804)*

Schooley Caldwell Assoc Inc.. 614 628-0300
300 Marconi Blvd Ste 100 Columbus (43215) *(G-6652)*

Schottenstein RE Group LLC.. 614 418-8900
2 Easton Oval Ste 510 Columbus (43219) *(G-6653)*

Schroedel Scullin & Bestic LLC.. 330 533-1131
196 N Broad St Ste A Canfield (44406) *(G-1640)*

Schroeder Associates Inc (PA)... 419 258-5075
5554 County Road 424 Antwerp (45813) *(G-448)*

Schroeder Company (PA)... 419 473-3139
27024 W River Rd Perrysburg (43551) *(G-12368)*

Schroer Properties Navarre Inc (PA).. 330 498-8200
339 E Maple St North Canton (44720) *(G-11861)*

Schuerger Law Group, Wilmington *Also Called: Law Offces Rbert A Schrger Lpa (G-15256)*

Schumacher Development Inc... 513 777-9800
6355 Centre Park Dr West Chester (45069) *(G-14762)*

Schumacher Homes, Belmont *Also Called: 50 X 20 Holding Company Inc (G-1053)*

Schumacher Homes, Canton *Also Called: 50 X 20 Holding Company Inc (G-1650)*

Schweizer Dipple Inc.. 440 786-8090
7227 Division St Cleveland (44146) *(G-4884)*

Schwerman Trucking Co.. 419 666-0818
6626 State Route 795 Walbridge (43465) *(G-14466)*

SCI, Fremont *Also Called: Keller Ochs Koch Inc (G-8689)*

SCI, Miamisburg *Also Called: Shawntech Communications Inc (G-11093)*

SCI Shared Resources LLC.. 614 224-6105
229 E State St Columbus (43215) *(G-6654)*

(PA)=Parent Co (HQ)=Headquarters (DH)=Div Headquarters

SCI Shared Resources LLC — ALPHABETIC SECTION

SCI Shared Resources LLC 614 875-6333
   4242 Hoover Rd Grove City (43123) *(G-8952)*

Sciot-Pint Vly Mental Hlth Ctr (PA) 740 775-1260
   4449 State Route 159 Chillicothe (45601) *(G-2090)*

Scioto LLC (HQ) 937 644-0888
   405 S Oak St Marysville (43040) *(G-10507)*

Scioto Cnty Counseling Ctr Inc (PA) 740 354-6685
   411 Court St Portsmouth (45662) *(G-12567)*

Scioto County Region Wtr Dst 1 .... 740 259-2301
   326 Robert Lucas Rd Lucasville (45648) *(G-10180)*

Scioto Darby Concrete Inc 614 876-3114
   4540 Edgewyn Ave Hilliard (43026) *(G-9229)*

Scioto Downs Inc 614 295-4700
   6000 S High St Columbus (43207) *(G-6655)*

Scioto Lodging Inc 740 851-6140
   547 Plyleys Ln Apt 18 Chillicothe (45601) *(G-2091)*

Scioto Memorial Hosp Campus, Portsmouth *Also Called: Southern Ohio Medical Center (G-12571)*

Scioto Pnt Vly Mental Hlth Ctr 740 335-6935
   1300 E Paint St Wshngtn Ct Hs (43160) *(G-15493)*

Scioto Pnt Vly Mental Hlth Ctr, Wshngtn Ct Hs *Also Called: Scioto Pnt Vly Mental Hlth Ctr (G-15493)*

Scioto Reserve Inc (PA) 740 881-9082
   7383 Scioto Pkwy Powell (43065) *(G-12604)*

Scioto Reserve Inc 740 881-6500
   3982 Powell Rd Ste 332 Powell (43065) *(G-12605)*

Scioto Reserve Inc 740 881-3903
   7743 Riverside Dr Powell (43065) *(G-12606)*

Scioto Reserve Country Club, Powell *Also Called: Scioto Reserve Inc (G-12605)*

Scioto Reserve Golf & Athc CLB, Powell *Also Called: Scioto Reserve Inc (G-12604)*

Scioto Residential Services 740 353-0288
   2333 Vinton Ave Portsmouth (45662) *(G-12568)*

Scioto Services, Marysville *Also Called: Scioto LLC (G-10507)*

Scot Burton Contractors LLC 440 564-1011
   11330 Kinsman Rd Newbury (44065) *(G-11764)*

Scot Industries Inc 330 262-7585
   6578 Ashland Rd Wooster (44691) *(G-15375)*

Scott Fetzer Company 216 267-9000
   4801 W 150th St Cleveland (44135) *(G-4885)*

Scott Fetzer Company (PA) 440 892-3000
   28800 Clemens Rd Westlake (44145) *(G-15105)*

Scott Industrial Systems Inc (PA) 937 233-8146
   4433 Interpoint Blvd Dayton (45424) *(G-7612)*

Scott S Duko Attorney At Law 800 593-6676
   3560 W Market St Fairlawn (44333) *(G-8497)*

Scott Steel LLC 937 552-9670
   125 Clark Ave Ste A Piqua (45356) *(G-12458)*

Scottcare Crdvscular Solutions 216 362-0550
   4791 W 150th St Cleveland (44135) *(G-4886)*

Scotts Company LLC (HQ) 937 644-0011
   14111 Scottslawn Rd Marysville (43040) *(G-10508)*

Scotts Miracle-Gro, Marysville *Also Called: Scotts Miracle-Gro Company (G-10509)*

Scotts Miracle-Gro Company (PA) 937 644-0011
   14111 Scottslawn Rd Marysville (43040) *(G-10509)*

Scotts Miracle-Gro Products, Marysville *Also Called: Scotts Company LLC (G-10508)*

Screen Works Inc (PA) 937 264-9111
   3970 Image Dr Dayton (45414) *(G-7613)*

Scripps Media Inc (HQ) 513 977-3000
   312 Walnut St Ste 2800 Cincinnati (45202) *(G-3351)*

Scriptdrop Inc 614 641-0648
   855 Grandview Ave Ste 110 Columbus (43215) *(G-6656)*

Scrogginsgrear Inc 513 672-4281
   200 Northland Blvd Cincinnati (45246) *(G-3352)*

SD Myers LLC 330 630-7000
   180 South Ave Tallmadge (44278) *(G-13603)*

Sdx Home Care Operations LLC 937 322-6288
   101 N Fountain Ave Springfield (45502) *(G-13289)*

Sea Ltd (PA) 614 888-4160
   7001 Buffalo Pkwy Columbus (43229) *(G-6657)*

Sea Ltd., Columbus *Also Called: Sea Ltd (G-6657)*

Sea-Land Chemical Co (PA) 440 871-7887
   18013 Cleveland Pkwy Dr Ste 100 Cleveland (44135) *(G-4887)*

Seagate Roofg & Waterproofing, Toledo *Also Called: Burbank Inc (G-13723)*

Seal Aftermarket Products LLC 419 355-1200
   1110 Napoleon St Fremont (43420) *(G-8701)*

Seal-Rite Door, Hebron *Also Called: S R Door Inc (G-9153)*

Sealing Resource Div, Sylvania *Also Called: Thermodyn Corporation (G-13577)*

Seals Construction Inc 614 836-7200
   10283 Busey Rd Nw Canal Winchester (43110) *(G-1616)*

Search Masters Inc 216 532-8660
   2 Summit Park Dr Independence (44131) *(G-9482)*

Sears Dental Center, Independence *Also Called: Dentalcare Partners Inc (G-9428)*

Seaway Building Services, Toledo *Also Called: Seaway Sponge & Chamois Co (G-14007)*

Seaway Gas & Petroleum Inc 216 566-9070
   1690 Columbus Rd Cleveland (44113) *(G-4888)*

Seaway Sponge & Chamois Co (PA) 419 691-4694
   458 2nd St Toledo (43605) *(G-14007)*

Sebaly Shllito Dyer A Lgal Pro (PA) 937 222-2500
   1900 Kettering Tower 40 N Main St Lbby 11 Dayton (45423) *(G-7614)*

Sebastiani Trucking Inc 330 286-0059
   61 Railroad St Canfield (44406) *(G-1641)*

Second Hrvest Fdbank of Mhning 330 792-5522
   2805 Salt Springs Rd Youngstown (44509) *(G-15718)*

Second National Bank (HQ) 937 548-2122
   499 S Broadway St Greenville (45331) *(G-8884)*

Second National Bank 937 548-5068
   1302 Wagner Ave Greenville (45331) *(G-8885)*

Second Wind Vitamins Inc (PA) 330 336-9260
   516 Corporate Pkwy Wadsworth (44281) *(G-14451)*

Secura Fact, Lakewood *Also Called: Security Hut Inc (G-9685)*

Securedata LLC 323 944-0822
   700 Beta Dr Ste 100 Mayfield Village (44143) *(G-10796)*

Securestate LLC 216 927-0115
   9330 Fairmount Rd Novelty (44072) *(G-12043)*

Securitas Electronic, Uniontown *Also Called: Securitas Technology Corp (G-14264)*

Securitas SEC Svcs USA Inc 440 887-6800
   12000 Snow Rd Ste 5 Cleveland (44130) *(G-4889)*

Securitas SEC Svcs USA Inc 614 871-6051
   2180 Southwest Blvd Grove City (43123) *(G-8953)*

Securitas Technology Corp 800 548-4478
   3800 Tabs Dr Uniontown (44685) *(G-14264)*

Security, Columbus *Also Called: Sahara Global Security LLC (G-6635)*

Security Check, Columbus *Also Called: Security Check LLC (G-6658)*

Security Check LLC (PA) 614 944-5788
   2 Easton Oval Ste 350 Columbus (43219) *(G-6658)*

Security Fence Group Inc (PA) 513 681-3700
   4260 Dane Ave Cincinnati (45223) *(G-3353)*

Security Hut Inc (PA) 216 226-0461
   18614 Detroit Ave Lakewood (44107) *(G-9685)*

Security Nat Auto Accptnce LLC 513 459-8118
   6951 Cintas Blvd Mason (45040) *(G-10605)*

Security National Bank, Newark *Also Called: Security National Bank & Tr Co (G-11747)*

Security National Bank & Tr Co 937 845-3811
   201 N Main St New Carlisle (45344) *(G-11605)*

Security National Bank & Tr Co (HQ) 740 426-6384
   50 N 3rd St Newark (43055) *(G-11747)*

Security National Bank & Tr Co 937 325-0351
   2730 E Main St Springfield (45503) *(G-13290)*

Sedgwick CMS, Hilliard *Also Called: Sedgwick CMS Holdings Inc (G-9230)*

Sedgwick CMS Holdings Inc 800 825-6755
   6377 Emerald Pkwy Dublin (43016) *(G-8117)*

Sedgwick CMS Holdings Inc 614 658-0900
   3455 Mill Run Dr Hilliard (43026) *(G-9230)*

Sedlak Management Consultants 216 206-4700
   22901 Millcreek Blvd Ste 600 Cleveland (44122) *(G-4890)*

Seed Consultants Inc (DH) 740 333-8644
   648 Miami Trace Rd Sw Wshngtn Ct Hs (43160) *(G-15494)*

Seeley Enterprises Company (PA) 440 293-6600
   104 Parker Dr Andover (44003) *(G-440)*

Seeley Medical, Andover *Also Called: Seeley Enterprises Company (G-440)*

Seeley Medical Oxygen Co (HQ) 440 255-7163
   104 Parker Dr Andover (44003) *(G-441)*

ALPHABETIC SECTION — ServiceMaster Elite Janitorial

Seeley Svdge Ebert Gourash Lpa..216 566-8200
    26600 Detroit Rd Westlake (44145) *(G-15106)*
Seg of Ohio Inc (PA)...614 414-7300
    4016 Townsfair Way Ste 201 Columbus (43219) *(G-6659)*
Sehlhorst Equipment Svcs Inc...513 353-9300
    8073 Furlong Dr Cleves (45002) *(G-5193)*
Sehlhorst Equipment Svcs LLC..513 353-9300
    8073 Furlong Dr Cleves (45002) *(G-5194)*
SEI - Cincinnati LLC..513 459-1992
    7870 E Kemper Rd Ste 400 Cincinnati (45249) *(G-3354)*
SEI Engineers Inc...740 657-1860
    65 Hidden Ravines Dr Ste 200 Powell (43065) *(G-12607)*
Seibert-Keck Insurance Agency (PA)...330 867-3140
    2950 W Market St Ste A Fairlawn (44333) *(G-8498)*
Seifert Technologies Inc (PA)...330 833-2700
    2323 Nave Rd Se Massillon (44646) *(G-10667)*
Seikel, Daniel D DDS, Dublin *Also Called: Smiley Samuel E DDS PC (G-8122)*
Seilers Landscaping Inc..513 791-2824
    7011 Plainfield Rd Cincinnati (45236) *(G-3355)*
Seilkop Industries Inc (PA)..513 761-1035
    425 W North Bend Rd Cincinnati (45216) *(G-3356)*
Selby General Hospital (PA)...740 568-2000
    1106 Colegate Dr Marietta (45750) *(G-10405)*
Select Hotels Group LLC..513 754-0003
    5070 Natorp Blvd Mason (45040) *(G-10606)*
Select Medical Corporation..216 983-8030
    11900 Fairhill Rd Ste 100 Cleveland (44120) *(G-4891)*
SELECT PHYSICAL THEREPAHY AND, Cincinnati *Also Called: Trihealth Rehabilitation Hosp (G-3526)*
SELECT PHYSICAL THEREPAHY AND, Sylvania *Also Called: Regency Hospital Toledo LLC (G-13568)*
Select Sires Inc (PA)..614 873-4683
    11740 Us Highway 42 N Plain City (43064) *(G-12494)*
Select Spcalty Hosp - Boardman...330 729-1750
    8401 Market St Fl 7 Youngstown (44512) *(G-15719)*
Select Spclty Hosp - Clmbs/AST..614 293-6931
    181 Taylor Ave Fl 6 Columbus (43203) *(G-6660)*
Select Spclty Hosp - Clmbus In...614 291-8467
    1087 Dennison Ave Columbus (43201) *(G-6661)*
Select Spclty Hosp - Clvland F, Cleveland *Also Called: Select Medical Corporation (G-4891)*
Select Spclty Hosp - Yngstown..330 480-3488
    1044 Belmont Ave Fl 4 Youngstown (44504) *(G-15720)*
Select Spclty Hsptal-Akron LLC..330 761-7500
    200 E Market St Akron (44308) *(G-296)*
Select Spclty Hsptl-Columbus S, Columbus *Also Called: Regency Hospital Company LLC (G-6573)*
Select Steel Inc..330 652-1756
    1825 Hunter Ave Niles (44446) *(G-11796)*
Self Mployed..216 408-3280
    6157 Creekhaven Dr Apt 5 Cleveland (44130) *(G-4892)*
Self Reliance Inc..937 525-0809
    3674 E National Rd Ste 3 Springfield (45505) *(G-13291)*
Self-Funded Plans Inc (PA)..216 566-1455
    6000 Lombardo Ctr Seven Hills (44131) *(G-12961)*
Selinsky Force LLC..330 477-4527
    4015 23rd St Sw Canton (44706) *(G-1850)*
Selling Precision, Stow *Also Called: Hydraulic Manifolds USA LLC (G-13376)*
Selman & Company (DH)...440 646-9336
    1 Integrity Pkwy Cleveland (44143) *(G-4893)*
Selmanco, Cleveland *Also Called: Selman & Company (G-4893)*
Seneca County..419 435-0729
    602 S Corporate Dr W Fostoria (44830) *(G-8625)*
Seneca County..419 447-5011
    3362 S Township Rd Tiffin (44883) *(G-13642)*
Seneca County Board Mr/Dd -...419 447-7521
    780 E County Road 20 Tiffin (44883) *(G-13643)*
Seneca County Human Services, Tiffin *Also Called: Seneca County (G-13642)*
Seneca Lake Park, Senecaville *Also Called: Muskingum Wtrshed Cnsrvncy Dst (G-12950)*
Seneca Medical, Tiffin *Also Called: Concordnce Hlthcare Sltons LLC (G-13625)*
Seneca Medical LLC (HQ)...800 447-0225
    85 Shaffer Park Dr Tiffin (44883) *(G-13644)*

Senior Behaviroal Health, Cincinnati *Also Called: Trihealth Inc (G-3512)*
Senior Center West, Lakewood *Also Called: City of Lakewood (G-9660)*
SENIOR CITIZENS CENTER, Portsmouth *Also Called: United Scoto Senior Activities (G-12579)*
Senior Citizens Resources Inc...216 459-2870
    3100 Devonshire Rd Cleveland (44109) *(G-4894)*
Senior Employment Center, Cincinnati *Also Called: Vantage Aging (G-3615)*
Senior Lifestyle Evergreen Ltd...513 948-2308
    230 W Galbraith Rd Cincinnati (45215) *(G-3357)*
Senior Resource Connection (PA)..937 223-8246
    222 Salem Ave Dayton (45406) *(G-7615)*
Senior Services, Maple Heights *Also Called: City of Maple Heights (G-10334)*
Senior Star Management Company..513 271-1747
    5435 Kenwood Rd Cincinnati (45227) *(G-3358)*
Senior Touch Solution..216 862-4841
    6659 Pearl Rd Cleveland (44130) *(G-4895)*
Sensor Technology Systems, Miamisburg *Also Called: Steiner Eoptics Inc (G-11095)*
Sensource Global Sourcing, Milford *Also Called: Si Liquidating Inc (G-11255)*
Sentient Studios Ltd..330 204-8636
    2894 Chamberlain Rd Apt 6 Fairlawn (44333) *(G-8499)*
Sentinel Fluid Controls LLC (DH)...419 478-9086
    5702 Opportunity Dr Toledo (43612) *(G-14008)*
Sentry Life Insurance Company..513 733-0100
    4015 Executive Park Dr Ste 218 Cincinnati (45241) *(G-3359)*
Seovec, Athens *Also Called: Southstern Ohio Vlntary Edcatn (G-591)*
Sequent Inc (PA)..614 436-5880
    570 Polaris Pkwy Ste 125 Westerville (43082) *(G-14937)*
Sequent Information Solutions, Westerville *Also Called: Sequent Inc (G-14937)*
Sequoia Financial Group LLC (PA)...330 375-9480
    3500 Embassy Pkwy Ste 100 Akron (44333) *(G-297)*
Sequoia Insurance Company (DH)...831 655-9612
    800 Superior Ave E Ste 2100 # 21 Cleveland (44114) *(G-4896)*
Sequoia Pro Bowl Inc...614 885-7043
    5501 Sandalwood Blvd Columbus (43229) *(G-6662)*
Serco Inc..502 364-8157
    2661 Commons Blvd Beavercreek (45431) *(G-904)*
Serco Services Inc...937 369-4066
    2217 Acorn Dr Dayton (45419) *(G-7616)*
Serenity Center Inc..614 891-1111
    2841 E Dublin Granville Rd Columbus (43231) *(G-6663)*
Serex Corporation (PA)..330 726-6062
    55 Victoria Rd Youngstown (44515) *(G-15721)*
Serv Pro of Barberton/Norton, Medina *Also Called: Professional Restoration Svc (G-10879)*
Serv-A-Lite Products Inc (DH)...309 762-7741
    10590 Hamilton Ave Cincinnati (45231) *(G-3360)*
Servall Electric Company Inc...513 771-5584
    11697 Lebanon Rd Cincinnati (45241) *(G-3361)*
Servatii Inc (PA)...513 271-5040
    3888 Virginia Ave Cincinnati (45227) *(G-3362)*
Servatii Pastry and Dealey, Cincinnati *Also Called: Servatii Inc (G-3362)*
Server Suites Llc...513 831-5528
    6281 Tri Ridge Blvd Ste 10 Loveland (45140) *(G-10158)*
Service and Support ADM, Lisbon *Also Called: Columbana Cnty For Dvlpmntal D (G-9998)*
Service Experts LLC..614 334-3192
    4247 Diplomacy Dr Columbus (43228) *(G-6664)*
Service Master By Allen Keith, Canton *Also Called: Allen-Keith Construction Co (G-1659)*
Service Master Co..330 864-7300
    33851 Curtis Blvd Ste 202 Eastlake (44095) *(G-8208)*
Service Mstr By Disaster Recon, Eastlake *Also Called: Service Master Co (G-8208)*
Service Pronet LLC..614 874-4300
    1535 Georgesville Rd Ste A Columbus (43228) *(G-6665)*
Service Tech Company, Cleveland *Also Called: S-T Acquisition Company LLC (G-4868)*
Service-Tech, Cleveland *Also Called: A Bee C Service Inc (G-3747)*
Servicelink Field Services LLC..440 424-0058
    30825 Aurora Rd Ste 140 Solon (44139) *(G-13141)*
ServiceMaster, Berea *Also Called: T & L Enterprises Inc (G-1083)*
ServiceMaster, Lima *Also Called: Kleman Services LLC (G-9916)*
ServiceMaster By Angler, Dayton *Also Called: G7 Services Inc (G-7372)*
ServiceMaster Elite Janitorial, Columbus *Also Called: Integrity Concepts Llc Inc (G-6062)*

Servicmster Coml Clg Advantage, Lancaster *Also Called: CMS Business Services LLC (G-9703)*

Servisair LLC (DH) 216 267-9910
5851 Cargo Rd Cleveland (44135) *(G-4897)*

SERVPRO, Elyria *Also Called: I E R Inc (G-8261)*

SERVPRO, Hudson *Also Called: Restoration Resources Inc (G-9371)*

SERVPRO, North Canton *Also Called: Caveney Inc (G-11815)*

SERVPRO, Worthington *Also Called: Heco Operations Inc (G-15420)*

SERVPRO of Northeast Columbus, Worthington *Also Called: Psp Operations Inc (G-15449)*

Servus LLC 844 737-8871
2000 Auburn Dr Ste 200 Beachwood (44122) *(G-835)*

SES, West Chester *Also Called: Superior Envmtl Solutions LLC (G-14836)*

Setech Incorporated 937 425-9482
3100 Dryden Rd Moraine (45439) *(G-11437)*

Setech Dayton OH, Moraine *Also Called: Setech Incorporated (G-11437)*

Seton Catholic School Hudson 330 342-4200
6923 Stow Rd Hudson (44236) *(G-9373)*

Setterlin, Columbus *Also Called: Setterlin Building Company (G-6666)*

Setterlin Building Company 614 459-7077
560 Harmon Ave Columbus (43223) *(G-6666)*

Settle Muter Electric Ltd (PA) 614 866-7554
711 Claycraft Rd Columbus (43230) *(G-6667)*

Seven Hill Anesthesia LLC 513 865-5204
10191 Evendale Commons Dr Cincinnati (45241) *(G-3363)*

Seven Hlls Neighborhood Houses (PA) 513 407-5362
901 Findlay St Cincinnati (45214) *(G-3364)*

Seven Seventeen Credit Un Inc (PA) 330 372-8100
3181 Larchmont Ave Ne Warren (44483) *(G-14552)*

Sewage Department, Cuyahoga Falls *Also Called: City of Cuyahoga Falls (G-7058)*

Sewell Leasing Corporation 937 382-3847
370 Davids Dr Wilmington (45177) *(G-15273)*

Sewell Motor Express, Wilmington *Also Called: Sewell Leasing Corporation (G-15273)*

Sewer & Drainage Services, Toledo *Also Called: City of Toledo (G-13744)*

Sewer Rodding Equipment Co 419 991-2065
3434 S Dixie Hwy Lima (45804) *(G-9959)*

Sexton Industrial Inc 513 530-5555
366 Circle Freeway Dr West Chester (45246) *(G-14832)*

Sfa Architects, Inc., Cincinnati *Also Called: Elevar Design Group Inc (G-2611)*

Sfn Group Inc 419 727-4104
1212 E Alexis Rd Toledo (43612) *(G-14009)*

SGB Management Inc 614 539-1177
4017 Jackpot Rd Grove City (43123) *(G-8954)*

Sgi Matrix LLC (PA) 937 438-9033
1041 Byers Rd Miamisburg (45342) *(G-11092)*

Sgk LLC 513 569-9900
537 E Pete Rose Way Ste 100 Cincinnati (45202) *(G-3365)*

SGS North America Inc 513 674-7048
650 Northland Blvd Ste 600 Cincinnati (45240) *(G-3366)*

Sgt Clans Wstlake Holdings LLC 440 653-5146
25247 Detroit Rd Westlake (44145) *(G-15107)*

SH Bell Company 412 963-9910
2217 Michigan Ave East Liverpool (43920) *(G-8193)*

Shadoart Productions Inc 614 416-7625
503 S Front St Ste 260 Columbus (43215) *(G-6668)*

SHADOWBOX, Columbus *Also Called: Shadoart Productions Inc (G-6668)*

Shady Hollow Cntry CLB Co Inc 330 832-1581
4865 Wales Ave Nw Massillon (44646) *(G-10668)*

Shady Lawn Nursing Home, Dalton *Also Called: Provide-A-Care Inc (G-7121)*

Shaker Grdns Nursing Rehab Ctr, Shaker Heights *Also Called: Mff Somerset LLC (G-12982)*

Shaker Heights Country Club Co 216 991-3660
3300 Courtland Blvd Shaker Heights (44122) *(G-12983)*

Shaker House 216 991-6000
3700 Northfield Rd Ste 3 Cleveland (44122) *(G-4898)*

Shaker Hts High Schl Crew Prnt 216 991-6138
15911 Aldersyde Dr Shaker Heights (44120) *(G-12984)*

Shalom House Inc (HQ) 614 239-1999
1135 College Ave Columbus (43209) *(G-6669)*

Shama Express LLC 216 925-6530
1014 Commerce Dr Grafton (44044) *(G-8844)*

Shamrock Acquisition Company, Westlake *Also Called: Shamrock Companies Inc (G-15108)*

Shamrock Companies Inc (PA) 440 899-9510
24090 Detroit Rd Westlake (44145) *(G-15108)*

Shamrock Golf Club, Delaware *Also Called: Ganzfair Investment Inc (G-7800)*

Shannon Electric LLC 216 378-3620
1400 E 34th St Cleveland (44114) *(G-4899)*

Shaq Inc 770 427-0402
22901 Millcreek Blvd Ste 650 Beachwood (44122) *(G-836)*

Share and Kare Inc 330 493-6600
110 15th St Ne Canton (44714) *(G-1851)*

Sharon Gay Phlps - Hward Hnna 216 539-2696
1903 W 25th St Cleveland (44113) *(G-4900)*

Sharpnack Chevrolet Co (PA) 800 752-7513
5401 Portage Dr Vermilion (44089) *(G-14408)*

Shaw Jewish Community Center 330 867-7850
750 White Pond Dr Akron (44320) *(G-298)*

Shaw Stainless, Beachwood *Also Called: Shaq Inc (G-836)*

Shawcor Pipe Protection LLC 513 683-7800
173 Commerce Dr Loveland (45140) *(G-10159)*

Shawnee Country Club 419 227-7177
1700 Shawnee Rd Lima (45805) *(G-9960)*

SHAWNEE MANOR, Lima *Also Called: Hcf of Shawnee Inc (G-9901)*

Shawnee Manor Nursing Home, Lima *Also Called: Hcf Management Inc (G-9897)*

Shawnee Mental Health, Coal Grove *Also Called: Shawnee Mental Health Ctr Inc (G-5211)*

Shawnee Mental Health Ctr Inc 740 533-6280
225 Carlton Davidson Ln Coal Grove (45638) *(G-5211)*

Shawnee Mental Health Ctr Inc 937 544-5581
192 Chestnut Ridge Rd West Union (45693) *(G-14872)*

Shawnee Optical Inc 440 997-2020
3705 State Rd Ashtabula (44004) *(G-549)*

Shawnee Trophies & Sptg Gds, Chillicothe *Also Called: Chillicothe Bowling Lanes Inc (G-2055)*

Shawneespring Hlth Cre Cntr Rl 513 943-4000
390 Wards Corner Rd Loveland (45140) *(G-10160)*

Shawntech Communications Inc (PA) 937 898-4900
8521 Gander Creek Dr Miamisburg (45342) *(G-11093)*

She Is US 863 315-1233
10310 Saint Clair Ave Cleveland (44108) *(G-4901)*

Sheakley, Cincinnati *Also Called: Comprehensive Hr Solutions LLC (G-2488)*

Sheakley-Uniservice Inc (PA) 513 771-2277
1 Sheakley Way Cincinnati (45246) *(G-3367)*

Shearer Farm Inc 330 345-9023
7762 Cleveland Rd Wooster (44691) *(G-15376)*

Shearer's Snacks, Massillon *Also Called: Shearers Foods LLC (G-10669)*

Shearers Foods LLC (HQ) 800 428-6843
100 Lincoln Way E Massillon (44646) *(G-10669)*

Shearers Foods Phoenix LLC 330 834-4330
100 Lincoln Way E Massillon (44646) *(G-10670)*

Sheckler Excavating Inc 330 866-1999
6203 Alliance Rd Nw Malvern (44644) *(G-10237)*

Sheconna L Daniels 216 370-0256
24370 Garden Dr Apt 1206 Euclid (44123) *(G-8361)*

Sheedy Paving Inc 614 252-2111
730 N Rose Ave Columbus (43219) *(G-6670)*

Sheffield Steel Products Company 330 468-0091
355 Ledge Rd Macedonia (44056) *(G-10204)*

Shelby County Child Care, Sidney *Also Called: Council On Rur Svc Prgrams Inc (G-13025)*

Shelby County Highway Dept, Sidney *Also Called: County of Shelby (G-13026)*

Shelby County Mem Hosp Assn 937 492-9591
705 Fulton St Sidney (45365) *(G-13047)*

Shelby County Mem Hosp Assn (PA) 937 498-2311
915 Michigan St Sidney (45365) *(G-13048)*

Shelby Golf Course Inc 937 492-2883
9900 Sidney Freyburg Rd Sidney (45365) *(G-13049)*

Shelby Health & Wellness Ctr 419 525-6795
31 E Main St Shelby (44875) *(G-13011)*

Shelby Oaks Golf Course, Sidney *Also Called: Shelby Golf Course Inc (G-13049)*

Shelby Welded Tube Div, Shelby *Also Called: Phillips Mfg and Tower Co (G-13008)*

Shell, Cleveland *Also Called: West Park Shell (G-5132)*

Shelley Company, Maumee *Also Called: Stoneco Inc (G-10771)*

Shelly & Sands Zanesville OH, Perrysville *Also Called: S & S Aggregates Inc (G-12393)*

ALPHABETIC SECTION

Shumsky Promotional

Shelly Company (DH)..740 246-6315
80 Park Dr Thornville (43076) *(G-13621)*

Shelly Company, The, Thornville *Also Called: Shelly Materials Inc (G-13622)*

Shelly Materials, Thornville *Also Called: Shelly Company (G-13621)*

Shelly Materials Inc..740 666-5841
8328 Watkins Rd Ostrander (43061) *(G-12184)*

Shelly Materials Inc (DH)..740 246-6315
80 Park Dr Thornville (43076) *(G-13622)*

Shelter Moving & Storage, West Chester *Also Called: Shetler Moving & Stor of Ohio (G-14763)*

Shelterhouse Vlntr Group Inc (PA)...............................513 721-0643
411 Gest St Cincinnati (45203) *(G-3368)*

Sheltring Arms Hosp Fndtion In....................................740 592-9300
55 Hospital Dr Athens (45701) *(G-589)*

Shepards Meadows, Poland *Also Called: Shepherd of Vly Lthran Rtrment (G-12509)*

Shepards Wood Nursing, Youngstown *Also Called: Shepherd of Vly Lthran Rtrment (G-15723)*

Shepherd Excavating Inc...614 889-1115
6295 Cosgray Rd Dublin (43016) *(G-8118)*

Shepherd of Vly Lthran Rtrment...................................330 544-0771
1501 Tibbetts Wick Rd Girard (44420) *(G-8824)*

Shepherd of Vly Lthran Rtrment...................................330 726-7110
301 W Western Reserve Rd Poland (44514) *(G-12509)*

Shepherd of Vly Lthran Rtrment...................................330 856-9232
4100 N River Rd Ne Warren (44484) *(G-14553)*

Shepherd of Vly Lthran Rtrment (PA)..........................330 530-4038
5525 Silica Rd Youngstown (44515) *(G-15722)*

Shepherd of Vly Lthran Rtrment...................................330 726-9061
7148 West Blvd Youngstown (44512) *(G-15723)*

SHEPHERDS WOODS, Youngstown *Also Called: Shepherd of Vly Lthran Rtrment (G-15722)*

Sheraton, Cleveland *Also Called: Hopkins Partners (G-4377)*

Sheraton, Columbus *Also Called: Grill Rest At Sheraton Suites (G-5957)*

Sheraton, Columbus *Also Called: Regal Hospitality LLC (G-6572)*

Sheraton Columbus, Columbus *Also Called: Hotel 75 E State Opco L P (G-6012)*

Shereton Hotel Independance, Cleveland *Also Called: Independent Hotel Partners LLC (G-4406)*

Sheriff's Office, Dayton *Also Called: County of Montgomery (G-7255)*

Sherman Financial Group LLC......................................513 707-3000
8600 Governors Hill Dr Ste 201 Cincinnati (45249) *(G-3369)*

Sherman Thompson Oh Tc LP......................................216 520-1250
275 N 3rd St Ironton (45638) *(G-9513)*

Sherwood Fd Dstrs Clveland Div, Maple Heights *Also Called: Sherwood Food Distributors LLC (G-10346)*

Sherwood Food Distributors LLC.................................216 662-8000
16625 Granite Rd Maple Heights (44137) *(G-10346)*

Shetler Moving & Stor of Ohio......................................513 755-0700
9917 Charter Park Dr West Chester (45069) *(G-14763)*

Shg Whitehall Holdings LLC...614 501-8271
4805 Langley Ave Columbus (43213) *(G-6671)*

Shields Capital Corporation..216 767-1340
20600 Chagrin Blvd Ste 800 Beachwood (44122) *(G-837)*

Shiftwise...513 476-1532
1263 Ashburnham Dr Columbus (43230) *(G-6672)*

Shihasi Starwind Ne Llp..513 683-9700
9011 Fields Ertel Rd Cincinnati (45249) *(G-3370)*

Shilling AC Heating & Plumbing, Port Clinton *Also Called: Gundlach Sheet Metal Works Inc (G-12531)*

Shiloh Springs Care Center, Dayton *Also Called: Carriage Inn Trotwood Inc (G-7214)*

Shiloh Springs Care Center, Miamisburg *Also Called: Carriage Inn of Trotwood Inc (G-11034)*

Shin-Etsu Silicones of America Inc (HQ)....................330 630-9460
1150 Damar Dr Akron (44305) *(G-299)*

Shining Star Rsdntial Svcs LLC....................................419 318-0932
360 S Reynolds Rd Ste A Toledo (43615) *(G-14010)*

Ship-Paq, Fairfield *Also Called: Ship-Paq Inc (G-8439)*

Ship-Paq Inc...513 860-0700
3845 Port Union Rd Fairfield (45014) *(G-8439)*

Shippers Automotive Group LLC..................................937 484-7780
1155 Phoenix Dr Urbana (43078) *(G-14313)*

Shipping Pilot LLC...505 744-7669
13000 Darice Pkwy Strongsville (44149) *(G-13482)*

Shir-Sath Inc..330 759-9820
1615 E Liberty St Girard (44420) *(G-8825)*

Shirk Odnvan Cnslting Engneers..................................614 436-6465
370 E Wilson Bridge Rd Worthington (43085) *(G-15456)*

Shive-Hattery Inc...216 532-7143
2515 Jay Ave Cleveland (44113) *(G-4902)*

Shively Brothers Inc..419 626-5091
2509 Hayes Ave Sandusky (44870) *(G-12931)*

Shiver Security Systems LLC.......................................513 719-4000
6404 Thornberry Ct Ste 410 Mason (45040) *(G-10607)*

Shoemaker Electric Company.......................................614 294-5626
831 Bonham Ave Columbus (43211) *(G-6673)*

Shoemaker Industrial Solutions, Columbus *Also Called: Shoemaker Electric Company (G-6673)*

Shoemaker Masonry Cnstr LLC....................................989 948-2377
8856 Harrison Pike Cleves (45002) *(G-5195)*

Shoemaker Rigging, Akron *Also Called: S Gary Shmker Rgging Trnspt L (G-292)*

Shoemetro, Columbus *Also Called: Ebuys Inc (G-5803)*

Shook Construction, Dayton *Also Called: Shook National Corporation (G-7617)*

Shook Construction Co (PA)...937 276-6666
2000 W Dorothy Ln Moraine (45439) *(G-11438)*

Shook National Corporation...937 276-6666
4977 Northcutt Pl Dayton (45414) *(G-7617)*

Shoptech Industrial Sftwr Corp....................................513 985-9900
400 E Business Way Ste 300 Cincinnati (45241) *(G-3371)*

Shoreby Club Inc...216 851-2587
40 Shoreby Dr Cleveland (44108) *(G-4903)*

Shoreline Company, Strongsville *Also Called: Shoreline Transportation Inc (G-13483)*

Shoreline Transportation Inc..440 878-2000
20137 Progress Dr Strongsville (44149) *(G-13483)*

Short Freight Lines Inc...419 729-1691
6180 Benore Rd Toledo (43612) *(G-14011)*

Show What You Know, Dayton *Also Called: Lorenz Corporation (G-7459)*

Showe Management Corporation..................................614 492-8111
14 Oak Rd Columbus (43217) *(G-6674)*

Shp, Cincinnati *Also Called: Steed Hammond Paul Inc (G-3415)*

Shrader Tire & Oil Inc..614 445-6601
2021 Harmon Ave Columbus (43223) *(G-6675)*

Shrader Tire & Oil Inc..740 788-8032
433 Hopewell Dr Heath (43056) *(G-9139)*

Shrader Tire & Oil Inc (PA)...419 472-2128
2045 W Sylvania Ave Ste 51 Toledo (43613) *(G-14012)*

Shred-It, Dayton *Also Called: Shred-It US JV LLC (G-7618)*

Shred-It US JV LLC...937 401-4224
903 Brandt St Dayton (45404) *(G-7618)*

Shredded Bedding Corporation (PA)............................740 893-3567
6328 Bennington Chapel Rd Centerburg (43011) *(G-1936)*

Shree Hospitality Corporation.......................................330 666-9300
200 Montrose West Ave Copley (44321) *(G-6963)*

Shree Sava Ltd..440 324-7676
739 Leona St Elyria (44035) *(G-8294)*

Shree Shiv LLC..419 897-5555
1702 Toll Gate Dr Maumee (43537) *(G-10765)*

Shremshock Architects Inc (PA)..................................614 545-4550
7775 Walton Pkwy Ste 250 New Albany (43054) *(G-11587)*

Shri Guru Inc..614 552-2071
4320 Groves Rd Columbus (43232) *(G-6676)*

Shri Mahalaxmi Inc..614 860-9804
1899 Winderly Ln Pickerington (43147) *(G-12412)*

SHRINER'S INTERNATIONAL HEADQUARTERS INC, Cincinnati *Also Called: Shriners International Hdqtr (G-3373)*

Shriners Children's Ohio, Dayton *Also Called: Shriners International (G-7619)*

Shriners Hspitals For Children......................................513 872-6000
3229 Burnet Ave Cincinnati (45229) *(G-3372)*

Shriners International...855 206-2096
1 Childrens Plz 2 Dayton (45404) *(G-7619)*

Shriners International Hdqtr...800 875-8580
3229 Burnet Ave Cincinnati (45229) *(G-3373)*

Shumaker Loop & Kendrick LLP..................................614 463-9441
41 S High St Ste 2400 Columbus (43215) *(G-6677)*

Shumaker Loop & Kendrick LLP (PA).........................419 241-9000
1000 Jackson St Toledo (43604) *(G-14013)*

Shumsky Promotional, Dayton *Also Called: Boost Engagement LLC (G-7197)*

(PA)=Parent Co (HQ)=Headquarters (DH)=Div Headquarters

Shur-Green Farms LLC 937 547-9633
  9159 State Route 118 Ansonia (45303) *(G-446)*

Shurmer Place At Altenheim 440 238-9001
  18821 Shurmer Rd Strongsville (44136) *(G-13484)*

Si Liquidating Inc 513 388-2076
  5405 Dupont Cir Ste A Milford (45150) *(G-11255)*

Si-MO Remodeling Inc 419 609-9036
  1802 Knupke St Sandusky (44870) *(G-12932)*

Sibcy Cline Inc 513 793-2121
  8040 Montgomery Rd Cincinnati (45236) *(G-3374)*

Sibcy Cline Inc (PA) 513 984-4100
  8044 Montgomery Rd Ste 300 Cincinnati (45236) *(G-3375)*

Sibcy Cline Inc 513 931-7700
  9250 Winton Rd Cincinnati (45231) *(G-3376)*

Sibcy Cline Inc 937 610-3404
  8353 Yankee St Dayton (45458) *(G-7620)*

Sibcy Cline Inc 513 385-3330
  600 Wessel Dr Fairfield (45014) *(G-8440)*

Sibcy Cline Inc 513 932-6334
  103 Oregonia Rd Lebanon (45036) *(G-9787)*

Sibcy Cline Inc 513 793-2700
  9979 Montgomery Rd Montgomery (45242) *(G-11374)*

Sibcy Cline Inc 513 777-8100
  7677 Voice Of America Centre Dr West Chester (45069) *(G-14764)*

Sibcy Cline Inc 513 677-1830
  7677 Voice Of America Centre Dr West Chester (45069) *(G-14765)*

Sibcy Cline Realtors, Cincinnati *Also Called: Sibcy Cline Inc (G-3375)*

Sibcy Cline Realtors, Cincinnati *Also Called: Sibcy Cline Inc (G-3376)*

Sibcy Cline Realtors, West Chester *Also Called: Sibcy Cline Inc (G-14764)*

Sibcy Cline Realtors, West Chester *Also Called: Sibcy Cline Inc (G-14765)*

Sibcy, Cline Realtors, Lebanon *Also Called: Sibcy Cline Inc (G-9787)*

Sibley Inc 440 233-5836
  41530 Schadden Rd Elyria (44035) *(G-8295)*

Sibley Door Company, Elyria *Also Called: Sibley Inc (G-8295)*

Sidney Electric, Sidney *Also Called: Sidney Electric Company (G-13050)*

Sidney Electric Company (PA) 419 222-1109
  840 S Vandemark Rd Sidney (45365) *(G-13050)*

Sidney Host LLC 937 498-8888
  1600 Hampton Ct Sidney (45365) *(G-13051)*

Sidney Lodges 937 492-3001
  1959 Michigan St Sidney (45365) *(G-13052)*

Sidney-Shelby County YMCA (PA) 937 492-9134
  300 E Parkwood St Sidney (45365) *(G-13053)*

Siebenthaler Company (PA) 937 274-1154
  2074 Beaver Valley Rd Beavercreek (45434) *(G-905)*

Siebenthaler's Garden Center, Beavercreek *Also Called: Siebenthaler Company (G-905)*

Siemens Energy Inc 740 393-8897
  105 N Sandusky St Mount Vernon (43050) *(G-11508)*

Siemens Government Tech Inc 513 492-7759
  8114 Indian Summer Way Mason (45040) *(G-10608)*

Siemens Industry Inc 800 879-8079
  4170 Columbia Rd Lebanon (45036) *(G-9788)*

Siemens Industry Software Inc 513 576-2400
  2000 Eastman Dr Milford (45150) *(G-11256)*

Siemens Med Solutions USA Inc 937 859-5413
  651 Skyview Dr Dayton (45449) *(G-7621)*

Siemer Distributing, New Lexington *Also Called: Lori Holding Co (G-11628)*

Sierra Lobo, Fremont *Also Called: Sierra Lobo Inc (G-8702)*

Sierra Lobo Inc 419 621-3367
  21000 Brookpark Rd Cleveland (44135) *(G-4904)*

Sierra Lobo Inc (PA) 419 332-7101
  102 Pinnacle Dr Fremont (43420) *(G-8702)*

Sierra Lobo Inc 301 345-1386
  11401 Hoover Rd Milan (44846) *(G-11212)*

Sierra Nevada Corporation 937 431-2800
  2611 Commons Blvd Beavercreek (45431) *(G-906)*

Siertek Ltd (PA) 937 623-2466
  4141 Colonel Glenn Hwy Ste 250 Beavercreek Township (45431) *(G-948)*

Sievers Security Inc (PA) 216 291-2222
  9775 Rockside Rd Ste 200 Cleveland (44125) *(G-4905)*

Sievers Security Systems Inc 216 383-1234
  9775 Rockside Rd Ste 200 Cleveland (44125) *(G-4906)*

Siffrin Residential Assn 330 799-8932
  136 Westchester Dr Ste 1 Youngstown (44515) *(G-15724)*

Siffron, Twinsburg *Also Called: Fasteners For Retail Inc (G-14191)*

SIGHT CENTER OF NORTHWEST OHIO, Toledo *Also Called: Toledo Society For The Blind (G-14066)*

Sightless Children Club Inc 937 671-9162
  1028 E 4th St Franklin (45005) *(G-8649)*

SIGHTLESS CHILDREN CLUB INC, Franklin *Also Called: Sightless Children Club Inc (G-8649)*

Sigma T E K, Cincinnati *Also Called: Sigmatek Systems LLC (G-3377)*

Sigma Technologies Ltd 419 874-9252
  27096 Oakmead Dr Perrysburg (43551) *(G-12369)*

Sigma-Aldrich, Miamisburg *Also Called: Aldrich Chemical (G-11023)*

Sigma-Aldrich Corporation 216 206-5424
  4353 E 49th St Cleveland (44125) *(G-4907)*

Sigmatek Systems LLC (HQ) 513 674-0005
  1445 Kemper Meadow Dr Cincinnati (45240) *(G-3377)*

Signal Terminal, The, Lisbon *Also Called: Buckeye Transfer LLC (G-9997)*

Signature Inc (PA) 614 766-5101
  7689 Birch Ln Dublin (43016) *(G-8119)*

Signature Inc 614 766-5101
  7689 Birch Ln Dublin (43016) *(G-8120)*

Signature Closers LLC 614 448-7750
  3136 Kingsdale Ctr Ste 117 Columbus (43221) *(G-6678)*

Signature Control Systems LLC 614 864-2222
  2228 Citygate Dr Columbus (43219) *(G-6679)*

Signature Controls, Columbus *Also Called: Signature Control Systems LLC (G-6679)*

Signature Dermatology LLC 614 777-1200
  3853 Trueman Ct Hilliard (43026) *(G-9231)*

Signature Health Inc 440 578-8200
  7232 Justin Way Mentor (44060) *(G-10995)*

Signature Health Inc 440 953-9999
  38882 Mentor Ave Willoughby (44094) *(G-15221)*

Signature Healthcare Coshocton, Coshocton *Also Called: LP Coshocton LLC (G-6991)*

Signature Solon Golf Course, Solon *Also Called: Weymouth Valley Inc (G-13163)*

Signature Worldwide, Dublin *Also Called: Signature Inc (G-8120)*

Signet Management Co Ltd 330 762-9102
  19 N High St Akron (44308) *(G-300)*

Signum LLC (PA) 440 248-2233
  32000 Aurora Rd Ste C Solon (44139) *(G-13142)*

Sika Mbcc US LLC 216 839-7500
  23700 Chagrin Blvd Beachwood (44122) *(G-838)*

Sikich LLP 513 482-1127
  665 Balbriggan Ct Cincinnati (45255) *(G-3378)*

Silco Fire Protection Company 330 535-4343
  451 Kennedy Rd Akron (44305) *(G-301)*

Silco Fire Protection Company, Beavercreek *Also Called: Brakefire Incorporated (G-919)*

Silco Fire Protection Company, Cincinnati *Also Called: Brakefire Incorporated (G-2276)*

Siler Excavation Services 513 400-8628
  6025 Catherine Dr Milford (45150) *(G-11257)*

Sill Public Adjusters, Cleveland *Also Called: Alex N Sill Company LLC (G-3783)*

Silliker Laboratories Ohio Inc 614 486-0150
  2057 Builders Pl Columbus (43204) *(G-6680)*

Silvan Trucking Company Ohio, Columbus *Also Called: S & T Truck and Auto Svc Inc (G-6624)*

Silver Lake Country Club 330 688-6066
  1325 Graham Rd Silver Lake (44224) *(G-13060)*

Silver Meadows, Kent *Also Called: MJM Management Corporation (G-9588)*

Silver Platter Catering, Columbus *Also Called: Schmidt Hsptality Concepts Inc (G-6649)*

Silver Spruce Holding LLC 937 259-1200
  3123 Research Blvd Ste 250 Dayton (45420) *(G-7622)*

Silverspot Cinema, Beachwood *Also Called: Beachwood Cinema LLC (G-767)*

Silverton Dialysis, Cincinnati *Also Called: River Valley Dialysis LLC (G-3302)*

Simmons Brothers Corporation 330 722-1415
  780 W Smith Rd Ste A Medina (44256) *(G-10889)*

Simo Creations Unlimited, Sandusky *Also Called: Si-MO Remodeling Inc (G-12932)*

Simon Knton Cncil Byscuts Amer (PA) 614 436-7200
  807 Kinnear Rd Columbus (43212) *(G-6681)*

ALPHABETIC SECTION
Skyline Cem Holdings LLC

Simon Property Group... 614 798-3015
   5043 Tuttle Crossing Blvd Ste 200 Dublin (43016) *(G-8121)*
Simon Roofing, Youngstown *Also Called: Simon Roofing and Shtmtl Corp (G-15725)*
Simon Roofing and Shtmtl Corp (PA)................................ 330 629-7392
   70 Karago Ave Youngstown (44512) *(G-15725)*
Simon, Richard E MD, Newark *Also Called: Licking Memorial Hospital (G-11718)*
Simonton Windows, Columbus *Also Called: Fortune Brands Windows Inc (G-5879)*
Simos Insourcing Solutions LLC....................................... 614 470-6088
   1356 Cherry Bottom Rd Columbus (43230) *(G-6682)*
Simple Bath Ltd.. 614 888-2284
   4235 Leap Rd Hilliard (43026) *(G-9232)*
Simple Journey Inc... 513 360-2678
   913 Lebanon St Monroe (45050) *(G-11351)*
Simplified Logistics LLC... 440 250-8912
   28915 Clemens Rd Ste 220 Westlake (44145) *(G-15109)*
Simply EZ HM Dlvred Mals Nrtha..................................... 330 633-7490
   1130 Damar Dr Akron (44305) *(G-302)*
Simpson Strong-Tie Company Inc.................................... 614 876-8060
   2600 International St Columbus (43228) *(G-6683)*
Sims Bros Inc (PA)...740 387-9041
   1011 S Prospect St Marion (43302) *(G-10454)*
Sims Brothers Recycling, Marion *Also Called: Sims Bros Inc (G-10454)*
Sims Buick-GMC Truck Inc... 330 372-3500
   3100 Elm Rd Ne Warren (44483) *(G-14554)*
Sims GMC Trucks, Warren *Also Called: Sims Buick-GMC Truck Inc (G-14554)*
Sims-Lohman Inc (PA)..513 651-3510
   6325 Este Ave Cincinnati (45232) *(G-3379)*
Sims-Lohman Fine Kitchens Gran, Cincinnati *Also Called: Sims-Lohman Inc (G-3379)*
Sinclair Media II Inc.. 614 481-6666
   1261 Dublin Rd Columbus (43215) *(G-6684)*
Singer Steel Company.. 330 562-7200
   10100 Singer Dr Streetsboro (44241) *(G-13427)*
Singerman Mlls Dsberg Kntz Lpa..................................... 216 292-5807
   3333 Richmond Rd Ste 370 Cleveland (44122) *(G-4908)*
Singleton Construction LLC... 740 756-7331
   4730 Wilson Rd Nw Lancaster (43130) *(G-9741)*
Singleton Health Care Ctr Inc... 216 231-0076
   1867 E 82nd St Cleveland (44103) *(G-4909)*
Sirak Financial Companies, Canton *Also Called: Sirak Financial Services Inc (G-1852)*
Sirak Financial Services Inc (PA)..................................... 330 493-0642
   4700 Dressler Rd Nw Canton (44718) *(G-1852)*
Sirak Insurance Partners, Canton *Also Called: Insurance Partners Agency LLC (G-1781)*
Sirna & Sons Produce, Norwalk *Also Called: Stv Holdings Inc (G-12028)*
Sirna & Sons Produce, Ravenna *Also Called: Freshedge LLC (G-12626)*
Sirpilla Recrtl Vhcl Ctr Inc... 330 494-2525
   1005 Interstate Pkwy Akron (44312) *(G-303)*
Sirva Mortgage Inc... 800 531-3837
   6200 Oak Tree Blvd Ste 300 Independence (44131) *(G-9483)*
Sirva Relocation LLC (DH)... 216 606-4000
   6200 Oak Tree Blvd Ste 300 Independence (44131) *(G-9484)*
Sirva Worldwide Relocation Mvg, Independence *Also Called: Sirva Relocation LLC (G-9484)*
Sisler Heating & Cooling Inc... 330 722-7101
   249 S State Rd Medina (44256) *(G-10890)*
Sister Sister Cleaning, Cleveland *Also Called: Alexis Eppinger (G-3785)*
Sisters of Charity.. 216 696-5560
   2475 E 22nd St Cleveland (44115) *(G-4910)*
SISTERS OF CHARITY OF ST. AUGU, Cleveland *Also Called: St Vincent Charity Med Ctr (G-4940)*
Sisters of Chrity Cncnnati Ohi (HQ).................................. 513 347-5200
   5900 Delhi Rd Cincinnati (45233) *(G-3380)*
Sisters of Mercy Fremont, Ohio, Fremont *Also Called: Sisters of Mrcy of The Amrcas (G-8703)*
Sisters of Mrcy of The Amrcas.. 419 332-8208
   1220 Tiffin St Fremont (43420) *(G-8703)*
Sisters of Ntre Dame of Chrdon.. 440 279-0575
   13000 Auburn Rd Chardon (44024) *(G-2020)*
Sisters of St Jseph St Mark PR... 216 531-7426
   21800 Chardon Rd Euclid (44117) *(G-8362)*
Sisters of The Transfiguration, Cincinnati *Also Called: Society of The Transfiguration (G-3391)*

Site Centers Corp (PA)... 216 755-5500
   3300 Enterprise Pkwy Beachwood (44122) *(G-839)*
Site Group Inc.. 937 845-7305
   2484 Addison New Carlisle Rd New Carlisle (45344) *(G-11606)*
Site K62, Williamsburg *Also Called: Cecos International Inc (G-15178)*
Site Worx LLC.. 513 229-0295
   3800 Turtlecreek Rd Lebanon (45036) *(G-9789)*
Siteworx, Lebanon *Also Called: Site Worx LLC (G-9789)*
Sive/Young & Rubicam, Cincinnati *Also Called: Young & Rubicam LLC (G-3687)*
Six Continents Hotels Inc... 216 707-4100
   9801 Carnegie Ave Cleveland (44106) *(G-4911)*
Six Sigma Logistics Inc.. 440 666-6026
   6745 Cliffside Dr Vermilion (44089) *(G-14409)*
Siya Motel LLC... 330 264-6211
   969 Timken Rd Wooster (44691) *(G-15377)*
Sjn Data Center LLC (PA).. 513 386-7871
   4620 Wesley Ave Cincinnati (45212) *(G-3381)*
Sk Food Group Inc... 614 409-0666
   3301 Toy Rd Groveport (43125) *(G-9001)*
Sk Hospitality LLC.. 419 294-3891
   105 Comfort Dr Upper Sandusky (43351) *(G-14293)*
Skally's Restaurant, Cincinnati *Also Called: Skallys Old World Bakery Inc (G-3382)*
Skallys Old World Bakery Inc... 513 931-1411
   1933 W Galbraith Rd Cincinnati (45239) *(G-3382)*
Skanska USA Building Inc.. 513 421-0082
   201 E 5th St Ste 2020 Cincinnati (45202) *(G-3383)*
Skateworld Inc.. 937 890-6550
   333 S Brown School Rd Vandalia (45377) *(G-14392)*
Skateworld of Vandalia, Vandalia *Also Called: Skateworld Inc (G-14392)*
Skeye Wholesale, Maumee *Also Called: Skeye Wholesale Inc (G-10766)*
Skeye Wholesale Inc.. 419 720-4440
   6630 Maumee Western Rd Maumee (43537) *(G-10766)*
Skgai Holdings Inc... 330 493-1480
   4665 Belpar St Nw Canton (44718) *(G-1853)*
Skidmore Sales, West Chester *Also Called: Skidmore Sales & Distrg Co Inc (G-14766)*
Skidmore Sales & Distrg Co Inc (PA)............................... 513 755-4200
   9889 Cincinnati Dayton Rd West Chester (45069) *(G-14766)*
Skilken, Columbus *Also Called: Skilkengold Development LLC (G-6685)*
Skilkengold Development LLC... 614 418-3100
   4270 Morse Rd Columbus (43230) *(G-6685)*
Skilled In Management Co LLC....................................... 513 489-7100
   10123 Alliance Rd Blue Ash (45242) *(G-1244)*
Skinner Diesel Services Inc (PA)..................................... 614 491-8785
   2440 Lockbourne Rd Columbus (43207) *(G-6686)*
Skipco, Canal Fulton *Also Called: Skipco Financial Adjusters Inc (G-1594)*
Skipco Financial Adjusters Inc (PA)................................. 330 854-4800
   700 Elm Ridge Ave Canal Fulton (44614) *(G-1594)*
SKW Management LLC... 937 382-7938
   3841 Panhandle Rd Lynchburg (45142) *(G-10186)*
Sky Climber Telecom, Delaware *Also Called: Sky Climber Twr Solutions LLC (G-7826)*
Sky Climber Twr Solutions LLC.. 740 203-3900
   1800 Pittsburgh Dr Delaware (43015) *(G-7826)*
Sky Lane Drive-Thru, Garrettsville *Also Called: Skylane LLC (G-8780)*
Sky Quest LLC... 216 362-9904
   6200 Riverside Dr Cleveland (44135) *(G-4912)*
Sky Zone Boston Heights, Hudson *Also Called: Wonderworker Inc (G-9379)*
Skybox Investments Inc... 419 525-6013
   1275 Pollock Pkwy Mansfield (44905) *(G-10316)*
Skybox Packaging LLC.. 419 525-7209
   1275 Pollock Pkwy Mansfield (44905) *(G-10317)*
Skylane LLC... 330 527-9999
   8311 Windham St Garrettsville (44231) *(G-8780)*
Skylight Financial Group LLC.. 513 579-8555
   3825 Edwards Rd Ste 210 Cincinnati (45209) *(G-3384)*
Skylight Financial Group LLC.. 419 885-0011
   1 Maritime Plz Fl 4 Toledo (43604) *(G-14014)*
Skylight Partners Inc.. 513 381-5555
   708 Walnut St Cincinnati (45202) *(G-3385)*
Skyline Cem Holdings LLC (PA)...................................... 513 874-1188
   4180 Thunderbird Ln Fairfield (45014) *(G-8441)*

Skyline Chili   **ALPHABETIC SECTION**

Skyline Chili, Fairfield *Also Called: Skyline Cem Holdings LLC* **(G-8441)**

Skyline Clvland Rnaissance LLC 216 696-5600
   24 Public Sq Cleveland (44113) **(G-4913)**

Skyways Logistics LLC 614 333-0333
   2122 Lockbourne Rd Columbus (43207) **(G-6687)**

Skyworks LLC 419 662-8630
   26501 Baker Dr Perrysburg (43551) **(G-12370)**

SL Seasons LLC 513 984-9400
   7300 Dearwester Dr Cincinnati (45236) **(G-3386)**

SL Wellspring LLC 513 948-2339
   8000 Evergreen Ridge Dr Cincinnati (45215) **(G-3387)**

Slagle Mechanical Contractors 937 492-4151
   877 W Russell Rd Sidney (45365) **(G-13054)**

Slattery Oil Company Inc 419 272-3305
   107 W Indiana St Edon (43518) **(G-8229)**

SLC Custom Packaging, Macedonia *Also Called: Specialty Lubricants Corp* **(G-10205)**

Sleep Care Inc 614 901-8989
   985 Schrock Rd Ste 204 Columbus (43229) **(G-6688)**

Sleep Network Inc (PA) 419 535-9282
   3450 W Central Ave Ste 118 Toledo (43606) **(G-14015)**

Sleepmed, North Olmsted *Also Called: Sleepmed Incorporated* **(G-11915)**

Sleepmed Incorporated 440 716-8139
   25000 Country Club Blvd Ste 120 North Olmsted (44070) **(G-11915)**

Slesnick Iron & Metal Co 330 453-8475
   927 Warner Rd Se Canton (44707) **(G-1854)**

Sliddy Ent LLC 419 376-1797
   417 Bronson Ave Toledo (43608) **(G-14016)**

Sliddy Entertainment, Toledo *Also Called: Sliddy Ent LLC* **(G-14016)**

Slimans Chrysler Plymouth Dodge, Amherst *Also Called: Slimans Sales & Service Inc* **(G-432)**

Slimans Sales & Service Inc 440 988-4484
   7498 Leavitt Rd Amherst (44001) **(G-432)**

Slipgrips, Nelsonville *Also Called: Lehigh Outfitters LLC* **(G-11549)**

Slmg Brand LLC 216 333-6468
   1637 Pleasantdale Rd Apt 2 Cleveland (44109) **(G-4914)**

Slmg Brand Management Firm, Cleveland *Also Called: Slmg Brand LLC* **(G-4914)**

Sln Nursery LLC 937 845-3130
   2969 Beal Rd Franklin (45005) **(G-8650)**

Slovene Home For The Aged 216 486-0268
   18621 Neff Rd Cleveland (44119) **(G-4915)**

Small Hnds Big Drams Lrng Ctrs 440 708-0559
   8505 Tanglewood Sq Ste T26 Chagrin Falls (44023) **(G-1990)**

Small World Childrens Center 513 867-9963
   3100 Hamilton Princeton Rd Hamilton (45011) **(G-9081)**

SMART - TRANSPORTATION DIVISIO, Independence *Also Called: United Trnsp Un Insur Assn* **(G-9493)**

Smart Harbor, Columbus *Also Called: Insurance Technologies Corp* **(G-6061)**

Smart Solutions, Strongsville *Also Called: Ohio Cllbrtive Lrng Sltons Inc* **(G-13479)**

Smarter Mortgages, Powell *Also Called: Keller Mortgage LLC* **(G-12596)**

Smartpay, Cincinnati *Also Called: Tempoe LLC* **(G-3451)**

Smartpay Leasing LLC 800 374-5587
   7755 Montgomery Rd Ste 400 Cincinnati (45236) **(G-3388)**

Smb Construction Co Inc (PA) 419 269-1473
   5120 Jackman Rd Toledo (43613) **(G-14017)**

Smg Holdings LLC 614 827-2500
   400 N High St Ofc Columbus (43215) **(G-6689)**

Smgoa, Columbus *Also Called: Sports Medicine Grant Inc* **(G-6705)**

Smilemd, Columbus *Also Called: Offor Health Inc* **(G-6385)**

Smiley Samuel E DDS PC 614 889-0726
   5156 Blazer Pkwy Ste 200 Dublin (43017) **(G-8122)**

Smith & Associates Excavating 740 362-3355
   2765 Drake Rd Columbus (43219) **(G-6690)**

Smith & Oby Company 440 735-5333
   7676 Northfield Rd Walton Hills (44146) **(G-14480)**

Smith & Oby Service Co 440 735-5322
   7676 Northfield Rd Bedford (44146) **(G-985)**

Smith & Schaefer, Bethel *Also Called: Smith & Schaefer Inc* **(G-1094)**

Smith & Schaefer Inc 216 226-6700
   202 E Plane St # 400 Bethel (45106) **(G-1094)**

Smith Ambulance Service Inc 330 825-0205
   594 Hudson Run Rd Barberton (44203) **(G-709)**

Smith Ambulance Service Inc (PA) 330 602-0050
   214 W 3rd St Dover (44622) **(G-7900)**

Smith Concrete Co (PA) 740 373-7441
   2301 Progress St Dover (44622) **(G-7901)**

Smith Trucking Inc 419 841-8676
   3775 Centennial Rd Sylvania (43560) **(G-13572)**

Smith-Boughan Inc 419 991-8040
   777 S Copus Rd Lima (45805) **(G-9961)**

Smith-Boughan Mechanical Svcs, Lima *Also Called: Smith-Boughan Inc* **(G-9961)**

Smithers Group Inc (PA) 330 762-7441
   121 S Main St Ste 300 Akron (44308) **(G-304)**

Smithers Group Inc 330 833-8548
   1845 Harsh Ave Se Massillon (44646) **(G-10671)**

Smithers MSE Inc (HQ) 330 762-7441
   425 W Market St Akron (44303) **(G-305)**

Smithers MSE Inc 330 297-1495
   1150 N Freedom St Ravenna (44266) **(G-12644)**

Smithers Rapra, Akron *Also Called: Smithers MSE Inc* **(G-305)**

Smithers Tire Auto Tstg of Txa 330 762-7441
   425 W Market St Akron (44303) **(G-306)**

Smithers Trnsp Test Ctrs, Akron *Also Called: Smithers Tire Auto Tstg of Txa* **(G-306)**

Smithfield Direct LLC 216 267-6196
   15751 Commerce Park Dr Brookpark (44142) **(G-1439)**

Smithfield Direct LLC 419 422-2233
   1124 E Lincoln St Findlay (45840) **(G-8584)**

Smithfield Direct LLC 614 539-9600
   6130 Enterprise Pkwy Grove City (43123) **(G-8955)**

Smoot Construction, Columbus *Also Called: Smoot Construction Co Ohio* **(G-6691)**

Smoot Construction Co Ohio (HQ) 614 253-9000
   1907 Leonard Ave Columbus (43219) **(G-6691)**

SMS, Alliance *Also Called: Rownd Metal Sales Inc* **(G-400)**

Smylie One Heating & Cooling 440 449-4328
   5108 Richmond Rd Bedford (44146) **(G-986)**

Smyrna Ready Mix Concrete LLC 937 855-0410
   9151 Township Park Dr Germantown (45327) **(G-8805)**

Smyth Automotive Inc (PA) 513 528-2800
   4275 Mount Carmel Tobasco Rd Cincinnati (45244) **(G-3389)**

Snap Gourmet Foods, Cleveland *Also Called: Symba & Snap Gourmet Foods Inc* **(G-4972)**

Snap-On Business Solutions Inc (HQ) 330 659-1600
   4025 Kinross Lakes Pkwy Richfield (44286) **(G-12710)**

Snapblox Hosted Solutions LLC 866 524-7707
   131 Eight Mile Rd Cincinnati (45255) **(G-3390)**

Snavely Building Company (PA) 440 585-9091
   7139 Pine St Ste 110 Chagrin Falls (44022) **(G-1966)**

Snavely Development Company (PA) 440 585-9091
   7139 Pine St Chagrin Falls (44022) **(G-1967)**

Snf Wadsworth LLC 330 336-3472
   5625 Emerald Ridge Pkwy Solon (44139) **(G-13143)**

Snow Trails Ski Resort, Mansfield *Also Called: Ohio Ski Slopes Inc* **(G-10308)**

Snow Transport & Brokerage 937 474-8058
   308 Fernwood Ave Dayton (45405) **(G-7623)**

Sns Hospitality LLC 740 522-8499
   773 Hebron Rd Heath (43056) **(G-9140)**

Snyder's Service Now, Wooster *Also Called: Schmids Service Now Inc* **(G-15374)**

Snyders Antique Auto Parts Inc 330 549-5313
   12925 Woodworth Rd New Springfield (44443) **(G-11679)**

SOCIAL MINISTRY ORGANIZATION, Springfield *Also Called: Oesterlen - Svcs For Youth Inc* **(G-13278)**

SOCIETY FOR HANDICAPPED CITIZENS OF MEDINA COUNTY, Medina *Also Called: Society Handicapped Citz Medin* **(G-10891)**

Society For Hndcpped Ctzens of (PA) 330 722-1900
   4283 Paradise Rd Seville (44273) **(G-12965)**

Society Handicapped Citz Medin 330 722-1710
   5810 Deerview Ln Medina (44256) **(G-10891)**

Society of The Transfiguration (PA) 513 771-7462
   555 Albion Ave Cincinnati (45246) **(G-3391)**

Socius, Dublin *Also Called: Socius1 LLC* **(G-8123)**

Socius1 LLC 614 280-9880
   5747 Perimeter Dr Ste 200 Dublin (43017) **(G-8123)**

Sodexo Roth, Youngstown *Also Called: Roth Roofing Products LLC* **(G-15714)**

ALPHABETIC SECTION

Sofco Erectors Inc (PA)..513 771-1600
10360 Wayne Ave Cincinnati (45215) *(G-3392)*

Sofidel America Corp..740 500-1965
25910 Us Highway 23 S Circleville (43113) *(G-3724)*

Sofo Importing Company, Toledo *Also Called: Antonio Sofo Son Importing Co* *(G-13690)*

Soft Touch Wood LLC..330 545-4204
1560 S State St Girard (44420) *(G-8826)*

Soft Tuch Furn Repr Rfinishing, Girard *Also Called: Soft Touch Wood LLC* *(G-8826)*

Soft-Lite LLC (HQ)..330 528-3400
10250 Philipp Pkwy Streetsboro (44241) *(G-13428)*

Soft-Lite Windows, Streetsboro *Also Called: Soft-Lite LLC* *(G-13428)*

Software Craftsmanship Guild....................................330 888-8519
526 S Main St Akron (44311) *(G-307)*

Sogeti, Miamisburg *Also Called: Capgemini America Inc* *(G-11032)*

Sogeti, Westerville *Also Called: Sogeti USA LLC* *(G-15015)*

Sogeti USA LLC..513 824-3000
4445 Lake Forest Dr Ste 550 Blue Ash (45242) *(G-1245)*

Sogeti USA LLC..216 654-2230
6055 Rockside Woods Blvd N Ste 170 Cleveland (44131) *(G-4916)*

Sogeti USA LLC..937 433-3334
6494 Centerville Business Pkwy Dayton (45459) *(G-7624)*

Sogeti USA LLC (DH)...937 291-8100
10100 Innovation Dr Ste 200 Miamisburg (45342) *(G-11094)*

Sogeti USA LLC..937 291-8142
9050 Centre Pointe Dr West Chester (45069) *(G-14767)*

Sogeti USA LLC..614 847-4477
240 S State St Westerville (43081) *(G-15015)*

Soh Trumbul Co Help ME Grow.....................................330 675-6610
3688 Nelson Mosier Rd Leavittsburg (44430) *(G-9751)*

Sojourner Recovery Services, Hamilton *Also Called: Sojourner Recovery Svcs LLC* *(G-9082)*

Sojourner Recovery Svcs LLC (PA)................................513 868-7654
515 Dayton St Hamilton (45011) *(G-9082)*

Solar Flexrack LLC..888 380-8138
3207 Innovation Pl Youngstown (44509) *(G-15726)*

Solar Is Freedom, Amelia *Also Called: American Dream Solar & Win Inc* *(G-410)*

Solar Testing Laboratories Inc (PA).............................216 741-7007
1125 Valley Belt Rd Brooklyn Heights (44131) *(G-1427)*

Solid Waste Auth Centl Ohio.....................................614 871-5100
4239 London Groveport Rd Grove City (43123) *(G-8956)*

Solidarity Health Network Inc...................................216 831-1220
4853 Galaxy Pkwy Ste K Cleveland (44128) *(G-4917)*

Solivita of Summit's Trace, Columbus *Also Called: Pgn Op Summit LLC* *(G-6519)*

Sollmann Electric Co..937 492-0346
310 E Russell Rd Sidney (45365) *(G-13055)*

Solman Inc..330 580-5188
2716 Shepler Church Ave Sw Canton (44706) *(G-1855)*

Solomon Cloud Solutions, Findlay *Also Called: Plumbline Solutions Inc* *(G-8577)*

Solomon Lei & Associates Inc....................................419 246-6931
947 Belmont Ave Toledo (43607) *(G-14018)*

Solomon, Lei & Associates, Toledo *Also Called: Solomon Lei & Associates Inc* *(G-14018)*

Solon Creative Playroom Center, Solon *Also Called: Creative Playroom* *(G-13079)*

Solon Crtive Plyroom Mntessori, Cleveland *Also Called: Creative Playroom* *(G-4135)*

Solon Janitorial Services, Solon *Also Called: C & S Cleaning Services Inc* *(G-13071)*

Solon Lodging Associates LLC....................................440 248-9600
30100 Aurora Rd Solon (44139) *(G-13144)*

Solon Pnte At Emerald Ridge LLC.................................440 498-3000
5625 Emerald Ridge Pkwy Solon (44139) *(G-13145)*

Solon VFW Post 1863, Solon *Also Called: Veterans of Foreign Wars of US* *(G-13160)*

Solution Industries Inc...440 816-9500
21555 Drake Rd Strongsville (44149) *(G-13485)*

Solutons Thrugh Innvtive Tech (PA)..............................937 320-9994
3152 Presidential Dr Beavercreek (45324) *(G-907)*

Solv-All LLC..888 765-8255
9142 Tyler Blvd Mentor (44060) *(G-10996)*

Solvita, Kettering *Also Called: Community Blood Center* *(G-9627)*

Somc, Portsmouth *Also Called: Southern Ohio Medical Center* *(G-12569)*

Somc Minford Family Practice, Minford *Also Called: Southern Ohio Medical Center* *(G-11312)*

Somc Urgent Care Ctr Prtsmouth, Portsmouth *Also Called: Southern Ohio Medical Center* *(G-12573)*

Something Special Lrng Ctr Inc (PA).............................419 878-4190
8251 Waterville Swanton Rd Waterville (43566) *(G-14594)*

Sommers Market LLC (PA)...330 352-7470
214 Market Ave Sw Hartville (44632) *(G-9130)*

Somnus Corporation..740 695-3961
51130 National Rd Saint Clairsville (43950) *(G-12815)*

Sonesta Columbus, Columbus *Also Called: Hpt Trs Ihg-2 Inc* *(G-6014)*

Sonesta Es Cincinnati, Sharonville *Also Called: Cambridge Trs Inc* *(G-12992)*

Sonesta Es Cncnnati Shrnvlle W, Cincinnati *Also Called: 11689 Sharon West Inc* *(G-2118)*

Sonesta Es Stes Clvland Wstlak, Westlake *Also Called: Cambridge Trs Inc* *(G-15044)*

Sonic Automotive..614 870-8200
1500 Auto Mall Dr Columbus (43228) *(G-6692)*

Sonitrol of South West Ohio, Mason *Also Called: Shiver Security Systems LLC* *(G-10607)*

Sonkin & Koberna Co Lpa...216 514-8300
3401 Enterprise Pkwy Ste 400 Cleveland (44112) *(G-4918)*

Sonkin & Koberna Co, Lpa, Cleveland *Also Called: Sonkin & Koberna Co Lpa* *(G-4918)*

Sonoco Products Company...937 429-0040
761 Space Dr Beavercreek Township (45434) *(G-949)*

Sorbir Inc..440 449-1000
6200 Mayfield Rd Cleveland (44124) *(G-4919)*

Sortino Management & Dev Co.....................................419 627-8884
4315 Milan Rd Sandusky (44870) *(G-12933)*

SOS Group, The, Westlake *Also Called: Head Mercantile Co Inc* *(G-15065)*

Sotera Health Company (PA)......................................440 262-1410
9100 S Hills Blvd Ste 300 Broadview Heights (44147) *(G-1396)*

Sotera Health Holdings LLC......................................440 262-1410
9100 S Hills Blvd Ste 300 Broadview Heights (44147) *(G-1397)*

Sotera Health LLC (HQ)..440 262-1410
9100 S Hills Blvd Ste 300 Broadview Heights (44147) *(G-1398)*

Sotera Health Services LLC......................................440 262-1410
9100 S Hills Blvd Ste 300 Broadview Heights (44147) *(G-1399)*

Sotera Health Topco Parent LP...................................440 262-1410
9100 S Hills Blvd Ste 300 Broadview Heights (44147) *(G-1400)*

Sottile & Barile LLC..513 345-0592
394 Wards Corner Rd Ste 180 Loveland (45140) *(G-10161)*

Sound Com Corporation...440 234-2604
227 Depot St Berea (44017) *(G-1081)*

Sound Com System, Berea *Also Called: Sound Com Corporation* *(G-1081)*

Source Diagnostics LLC (PA).....................................440 542-9481
5275 Naiman Pkwy Ste E Solon (44139) *(G-13146)*

Sourceone Healthcare Tech Inc (HQ)..............................440 701-1200
8020 Tyler Blvd Mentor (44060) *(G-10997)*

Sourcepoint...740 363-6677
800 Cheshire Rd Delaware (43015) *(G-7827)*

South Brdway Hlthcare Group In..................................330 339-2151
245 S Broadway St # 251 New Philadelphia (44663) *(G-11667)*

South Central Ohio Eductl Ctr (PA)..............................740 456-0517
522 Glenwood Ave New Boston (45662) *(G-11595)*

South Central Power Company.....................................740 425-4018
37801 Barnesville Bethesda Rd Barnesville (43713) *(G-721)*

South Central Power Company (PA)................................740 653-4422
720 Mill Park Dr Lancaster (43130) *(G-9742)*

South Central Power Company.....................................614 837-4351
720 Mill Park Dr Lancaster (43130) *(G-9743)*

South Cmty Family YMCA Cdc, Dayton *Also Called: Young MNS Chrstn Assn Grter Dy* *(G-7733)*

South Cntl Ohio Rgnal Jvnile D, Chillicothe *Also Called: County of Ross* *(G-2062)*

South Community Inc...937 252-0100
2745 S Smithville Rd Ste 14 Dayton (45420) *(G-7625)*

South Community Inc...937 293-1115
1349 E Stroop Rd Dayton (45429) *(G-7626)*

South Community Inc (PA)..937 293-8300
3095 Kettering Blvd Ste 1 Moraine (45439) *(G-11439)*

South Dayton Family Physicians..................................937 208-7400
1525 E Stroop Rd Ste 200 Dayton (45429) *(G-7627)*

South Dyton Acute Care Cons In..................................937 433-8990
33 W Rahn Rd Dayton (45429) *(G-7628)*

South Dyton Urlgcal Asscations (PA).............................937 294-1489
10 Southmoor Cir Nw Ste 1 Dayton (45429) *(G-7629)*

South E Harley Davidson Sls Co (PA).............................440 439-5300
23105 Aurora Rd Cleveland (44146) *(G-4920)*

South Eastern Ohio Legal Svcs   **ALPHABETIC SECTION**

South Eastern Ohio Legal Svcs, Portsmouth *Also Called: Legal Aid Southeast Centl Ohio* *(G-12561)*

South Franklin Circle.. 440 247-1300
16575 S Franklin St Chagrin Falls (44023) *(G-1991)*

South I Leasing Co LLC.. 513 530-1600
8064 South Ave Boardman (44512) *(G-1291)*

South Lrrain Cnty Amblance Dst, Wellington *Also Called: County of Lorain* *(G-14630)*

South Pointe Hospital, Warrensville Heights *Also Called: Cleveland Clnic Hlth Systm-Wst* *(G-14579)*

South River Healthcare Center, Blue Ash *Also Called: Washington MD Leasing Co LLC* *(G-1273)*

South Shore Cable Cnstr Inc....................................... 440 816-0033
6400 Kolthoff Dr Cleveland (44142) *(G-4921)*

South Shore Controls Inc.. 440 259-2500
9395 Pinecone Dr Mentor (44060) *(G-10998)*

South Shore Electric, Elyria *Also Called: South Shore Electric Inc* *(G-8296)*

South Shore Electric Inc... 440 366-6289
589 Ternes Ln Elyria (44035) *(G-8296)*

South Side Learning & Dev Ctr.................................. 614 212-4696
1621 W 1st Ave Ste 2 Columbus (43212) *(G-6693)*

South Suburban Montessori Assn............................. 440 526-1966
4450 Oakes Rd Bldg 7 Brecksville (44141) *(G-1367)*

Southast Cmnty Mental Hlth Ctr (PA)........................ 614 225-0980
16 W Long St Columbus (43215) *(G-6694)*

Southast Ohio Srgcal Sites LLC................................. 740 856-9044
20 University Estates Blvd Ste 110 Athens (45701) *(G-590)*

Southeast, New Philadelphia *Also Called: Cornerstone Support Services* *(G-11644)*

Southeast Golf Cars, Cleveland *Also Called: South E Harley Davidson Sls Co* *(G-4920)*

Southeast Inc.. 614 225-0990
16 W Long St Columbus (43215) *(G-6695)*

Southeast Security Corporation................................ 330 239-4600
1385 Wolf Creek Trail Sharon Center (44274) *(G-12990)*

Southeastern Equipment Co Inc (PA)........................ 740 432-6303
10874 E Pike Rd Cambridge (43725) *(G-1582)*

Southeastern Health Care Ctr................................... 740 425-3648
400 Carrie Ave Barnesville (43713) *(G-722)*

Southeastern Med, Cambridge *Also Called: Southstern Ohio Rgonal Med Ctr* *(G-1584)*

Southerland Lumber and Home, Circleville *Also Called: Sutherland Building Pdts Inc* *(G-3725)*

Southern Care Inc.. 419 774-0555
2291 W 4th St Ste G Ontario (44906) *(G-12124)*

Southern Care Inc.. 330 797-8940
970 Windham Ct Ste 9 Youngstown (44512) *(G-15727)*

Southern Express Lubes Inc..................................... 937 278-5807
3781 Salem Ave Dayton (45406) *(G-7630)*

Southern Glzers Dstrs Ohio LLC (DH)....................... 614 552-7900
4800 Poth Rd Columbus (43213) *(G-6696)*

Southern Glzers Dstrs Ohio LLC............................... 440 542-7000
7800 Cochran Rd Solon (44139) *(G-13147)*

Southern Glzers Wine Sprits TX................................ 513 755-7082
4305 Mulhauser Rd Ste 4 Fairfield (45014) *(G-8442)*

Southern Hlls Hlth Rhblttion C................................... 614 545-5502
3248 Henderson Rd Columbus (43220) *(G-6697)*

Southern Ohio Bhvoral Hlth LLC............................... 740 533-0055
2113 S 7th St Ironton (45638) *(G-9514)*

Southern Ohio Cardiology Assoc, Chillicothe *Also Called: Adena Health System* *(G-2045)*

Southern Ohio Medical Center.................................. 740 259-5699
10 Thomas Hollow Rd Lucasville (45648) *(G-10181)*

Southern Ohio Medical Center.................................. 740 820-2141
8792 State Route 335 Minford (45653) *(G-11312)*

Southern Ohio Medical Center.................................. 740 354-5000
1805 27th St Portsmouth (45662) *(G-12569)*

Southern Ohio Medical Center.................................. 740 356-8171
1025 Robinson Ave Portsmouth (45662) *(G-12570)*

Southern Ohio Medical Center (PA)......................... 740 354-5000
1805 27th St Portsmouth (45662) *(G-12571)*

Southern Ohio Medical Center.................................. 740 356-5600
724 8th St Portsmouth (45662) *(G-12572)*

Southern Ohio Medical Center.................................. 740 356-5000
1248 Kinneys Ln Portsmouth (45662) *(G-12573)*

Southern Ohio Medical Center.................................. 740 356-6160
1202 18th St Ste 4 Portsmouth (45662) *(G-12574)*

Southern Ohio Medical Center.................................. 740 947-7662
300 E 2nd St Waverly (45690) *(G-14619)*

Southern Ohio Medical Center.................................. 937 544-8989
90 Cic Blvd West Union (45693) *(G-14873)*

Southern Ohio Medical Center.................................. 740 574-9090
8770 Ohio River Rd Wheelersburg (45694) *(G-15132)*

Southern Ohio Medical Center.................................. 740 574-4022
8430 Hayport Rd Wheelersburg (45694) *(G-15133)*

Southern Ohio Women's Health, Seaman *Also Called: Healthsource of Ohio Inc* *(G-12944)*

Southerntier Telecom Inc (PA).................................. 330 550-2733
5555 Sampson Dr Girard (44420) *(G-8827)*

Southrly Wstwater Trtmnt Plant, Cleveland *Also Called: Northast Ohio Rgonal Sewer Dst* *(G-4658)*

Southstern Ohio Cnsling Ctr LL................................. 740 260-9440
239a Old National Rd Old Washington (43768) *(G-12087)*

Southstern Ohio Physicians Inc................................ 740 432-5685
1230 Clark St Apt B Cambridge (43725) *(G-1583)*

Southstern Ohio Rgonal Med Ctr (PA)..................... 740 439-3561
1341 Clark St Cambridge (43725) *(G-1584)*

Southstern Ohio Vlntary Edcatn................................ 740 594-7663
221 Columbus Rd Athens (45701) *(G-591)*

Southview Hosp & Fmly Hlth Ctr, Dayton *Also Called: Dayton Osteopathic Hospital* *(G-7295)*

Southwest Anesthesia Svcs Inc................................ 419 897-8370
5901 Monclova Rd Maumee (43537) *(G-10767)*

Southwest Community Health Sys............................ 440 816-8000
18697 Bagley Rd Middleburg Heights (44130) *(G-11128)*

Southwest Fmly Physicians Inc................................. 440 816-2750
7225 Old Oak Blvd Ste D210 Cleveland (44130) *(G-4922)*

Southwest General Health Ctr (PA).......................... 440 816-8000
18697 Bagley Rd Cleveland (44130) *(G-4923)*

Southwest General Hospital, Middleburg Heights *Also Called: Southwest Community Health Sys (G-11128)*

Southwest General Med Group................................. 440 816-8000
18697 Bagley Rd Middleburg Heights (44130) *(G-11129)*

Southwest Hlthcare Brown Cnty................................ 937 378-7800
425 Home St Georgetown (45121) *(G-8802)*

Southwest Lcking Kndrgrten Ctr............................... 740 927-1130
927 South St Unit B Pataskala (43062) *(G-12277)*

Southwest Lithotripsy.. 614 447-0281
100 W 3rd Ave Ste 350 Columbus (43201) *(G-6698)*

Southwest Ohio Ambltory Srgery.............................. 513 425-0930
295 N Breiel Blvd Middletown (45042) *(G-11186)*

Southwest Ohio Computer Assn, Fairfield Township *Also Called: Butler Tech* *(G-8458)*

Southwest Ohio Dvlopmental Ctr, Batavia *Also Called: Ohio Dept Dvlpmntal Dsbilities* *(G-744)*

Southwest Ohio Rgnal Trnst Aut (PA)....................... 513 621-4455
525 Vine St Ste 500 Cincinnati (45202) *(G-3393)*

Southwest Ohio Rgnal Trnst Aut............................... 513 632-7511
1401 Bank St Cincinnati (45214) *(G-3394)*

Southwest Regional Medical Ctr, Georgetown *Also Called: Southwest Hlthcare Brown Cnty* *(G-8802)*

Southwest Sports Center Inc.................................... 440 234-6448
1005 W Bagley Rd Berea (44017) *(G-1082)*

Southwest Urlogy Wmen Cnnctons, Cleveland *Also Called: Southwest Urology LLC* *(G-4924)*

Southwest Urology LLC (PA).................................... 440 845-0900
6900 Pearl Rd Ste 200 Cleveland (44130) *(G-4924)*

Southwestern Electric Power Co (HQ)..................... 614 716-1000
1 Riverside Plz Columbus (43215) *(G-6699)*

Southwestern Tile and MBL Co................................. 614 464-1257
1030 Cable Ave Columbus (43222) *(G-6700)*

Southwood Pallet LLC... 330 682-3747
8849 Lincoln Way E Orrville (44667) *(G-12173)*

Sovereign Healthcare, Cleveland *Also Called: North Park Retirement Cmnty* *(G-4650)*

Spa Fitness Centers Inc (PA).................................... 419 476-6018
343 New Towne Square Dr Toledo (43612) *(G-14019)*

Spa LLC (DH)... 513 733-8800
401 Milford Pkwy Milford (45150) *(G-11258)*

Spa Performance Inc... 216 455-1540
2701 Park Dr Cleveland (44120) *(G-4925)*

Space & Asset Management Inc (PA)...................... 937 918-1000
3680 Wyse Rd Dayton (45414) *(G-7631)*

Space Management Inc... 937 254-6622
2601 W Dorothy Ln Moraine (45439) *(G-11440)*

ALPHABETIC SECTION — Spr Therapeutics Inc

Spacepointe Inc.. 937 886-7995
   1231 Lyons Rd Dayton (45458) *(G-7632)*

Spader Freight Services Inc (PA)... 419 547-1117
   1134 E Mcpherson Hwy Clyde (43410) *(G-5210)*

Spallinger Millwright Svc Co.. 419 225-5830
   1155 E Hanthorn Rd Lima (45804) *(G-9962)*

Spallnger Atclave Systms/US MI, Lima *Also Called: Spallinger Millwright Svc Co (G-9962)*

Spangenberg Law Firm, Cleveland *Also Called: Spangenberg Shibley Liber LLP (G-4926)*

Spangenberg Shibley Liber LLP.. 216 215-7445
   1001 Lakeside Ave E Ste 1700 Cleveland (44114) *(G-4926)*

Sparkbase Inc.. 216 867-0877
   3615 Superior Ave E Ste 4403c Cleveland (44114) *(G-4927)*

Sparkbox, Bellbrook *Also Called: Forge LLC (G-1016)*

Spartan, Maumee *Also Called: Spartan Chemical Company Inc (G-10768)*

Spartan Chemical Company Inc... 419 897-5551
   1110 Spartan Dr Maumee (43537) *(G-10768)*

Spartan Logistics, Columbus *Also Called: Spartan Whse & Dist Co Inc (G-6701)*

Spartan Supply Co.. 513 932-6954
   942 Old 122 Rd Lebanon (45036) *(G-9790)*

Spartan Whse & Dist Co Inc (PA)... 614 497-1777
   4140 Lockbourne Rd Columbus (43207) *(G-6701)*

Spears Transfer & Expediting.. 937 275-2443
   2637 Nordic Rd Dayton (45414) *(G-7633)*

SPEARS TRANSFER & EXPEDITING, Dayton *Also Called: Spears Transfer & Expediting (G-7633)*

Special Metals Corporation (DH)... 216 755-3030
   4832 Richmond Rd Ste 100 Warrensville Heights (44128) *(G-14588)*

Special Service Transportation Inc.. 330 273-0755
   1529 Substation Rd Brunswick (44212) *(G-1470)*

Specialized Alternatives For F... 513 771-7239
   11590 Century Blvd Ste 116 Cincinnati (45246) *(G-3395)*

Specialized Alternatives For F... 419 222-1527
   658 W Market St Ste 101 Lima (45801) *(G-9963)*

Specialized Alternatives For F... 216 295-7239
   20600 Chagrin Blvd Ste 900 Shaker Heights (44122) *(G-12985)*

Specialized Medical Billing, Worthington *Also Called: Specilzed Med Blling Rvnue Rcv (G-15457)*

Specialized Pharmacy Svcs - N, Cincinnati *Also Called: Specialized Pharmacy Svcs LLC (G-3396)*

Specialized Pharmacy Svcs LLC (DH).. 513 719-2600
   201 E 4th St Ste 900 Cincinnati (45202) *(G-3396)*

Specialized Senior Care, Youngstown *Also Called: Specilzed HM Care Prviders LLC (G-15728)*

Specialty Chemical Sales Inc (HQ)... 216 267-4248
   4561 W 160th St Cleveland (44135) *(G-4928)*

Specialty Hosp Cleveland LLC.. 216 592-2830
   2351 E 22nd St Fl 7 Cleveland (44115) *(G-4929)*

Specialty Hospital of Lorain... 440 988-6088
   254 Cleveland Ave Amherst (44001) *(G-433)*

Specialty Lubricants Corp... 330 425-2567
   8300 Corporate Park Dr Macedonia (44056) *(G-10205)*

Specialty Pumps Group Inc (DH).. 216 589-0198
   127 Public Sq Ste 5110 Cleveland (44114) *(G-4930)*

Specilzed Altrntves For Fmlies (PA).. 419 695-8010
   10100 Elida Rd Delphos (45833) *(G-7844)*

Specilzed Altrntves For Fmlies (PA).. 419 695-8010
   10100 Elida Rd Delphos (45833) *(G-7845)*

Specilzed HM Care Prviders LLC.. 330 758-8740
   6006 Market St Youngstown (44512) *(G-15728)*

Specilzed Med Blling Rvnue Rcv (PA).. 614 461-8154
   330 E Wilson Bridge Rd Ste 100 Worthington (43085) *(G-15457)*

Specilzed Med Blling Rvnue Rcv.. 614 461-8154
   330 E Wilson Bridge Rd Ste 100 Worthington (43085) *(G-15458)*

Spectra Contract Flooring, Columbus *Also Called: Spectra Holdings Inc (G-6702)*

Spectra Holdings Inc... 614 921-8493
   3031 International St Columbus (43228) *(G-6702)*

Spectra Photopolymers, Millbury *Also Called: Formlabs Ohio Inc (G-11268)*

Spectrum Eye Care, Inc.. 419 423-8665
   15840 Medical Dr S Ste A Findlay (45840) *(G-8585)*

Spectrum MGT Holdg Co LLC.. 614 344-4159
   1015 Olentangy River Rd Columbus (43212) *(G-6703)*

Spectrum Orthpedics Inc Canton... 330 455-5367
   7442 Frank Ave Nw North Canton (44720) *(G-11862)*

Spectrum Rehabilitation, Cincinnati *Also Called: Christ Hospital (G-2379)*

Spectrum Rtrment Cmmnities LLC.. 440 892-9777
   27569 Detroit Rd Apt 251 Westlake (44145) *(G-15110)*

Spectrum Supportive Services.. 216 875-0460
   4269 Pearl Rd Ste 300 Cleveland (44109) *(G-4931)*

Spectrum Supportive Services, Cleveland *Also Called: Spectrum Supportive Services (G-4931)*

Spectrum Surgical Instruments Corp.. 800 783-9251
   4575 Hudson Dr Stow (44224) *(G-13390)*

Speech Center, Saint Marys *Also Called: Jtd Health Systems Inc (G-12832)*

Speedeon Data LLC... 440 264-2100
   5875 Landerbrook Dr Ste 130 Cleveland (44124) *(G-4932)*

Speelman Electric Inc.. 330 633-1410
   235 Northeast Ave Tallmadge (44278) *(G-13604)*

Speer Industries Incorporated (PA).. 614 261-6331
   5255 Sinclair Rd Columbus (43229) *(G-6704)*

Speer Mechanical, Columbus *Also Called: Julian Speer Co (G-6100)*

Speer Mechanical, Columbus *Also Called: Speer Industries Incorporated (G-6704)*

Spencer Half-Way House Inc.. 740 345-5074
   69 Granville St Newark (43055) *(G-11748)*

Spencer Halfway Hse, Newark *Also Called: Spencer Half-Way House Inc (G-11748)*

Spencer Products Co (HQ)... 330 487-5200
   1859 Summit Commerce Park Twinsburg (44087) *(G-14219)*

SPENCERVILLE FIRE DEPARTMENT, Spencerville *Also Called: Invincible Fire Co Inc (G-13189)*

Spend and Send... 216 381-5459
   4852 Foxwynde Trl Cleveland (44143) *(G-4933)*

Spengler Nathanson PLL.. 419 241-2201
   4 Seagate Ste 400 Toledo (43604) *(G-14020)*

Spherion of Lima Inc... 567 208-5471
   7746 County Road 140 Findlay (45840) *(G-8586)*

Spherion of Lima Inc (PA).. 419 224-8367
   216 N Elizabeth St Lima (45801) *(G-9964)*

Spherion Outsourcing Group, Toledo *Also Called: Sfn Group Inc (G-14009)*

SPI LLC... 440 914-1122
   6810 Cochran Rd Solon (44139) *(G-13148)*

Spires Motors Inc... 614 771-2345
   3820 Parkway Ln Hilliard (43026) *(G-9233)*

Spirit, Cambridge *Also Called: Van Dyne-Crotty Co (G-1587)*

Spirit Medical Transport LLC... 937 548-2800
   5484 S State Route 49 Greenville (45331) *(G-8886)*

Spirit Rent-A-Car Inc... 440 715-1000
   29100 Aurora Rd Ste 400 Cleveland (44139) *(G-4934)*

Spirit Services, Solon *Also Called: Van Dyne-Crotty Co (G-13158)*

Spitz Law Firm LLC... 216 291-4744
   25825 Science Park Dr Ste 200 Beachwood (44122) *(G-840)*

Spitzer Chevrolet Inc... 330 467-4141
   333 E Aurora Rd Northfield (44067) *(G-11966)*

Spitzer Lakewood, Brookpark *Also Called: Lakewood Chrysler-Plymouth (G-1437)*

Splash Financial Inc.. 216 452-0113
   812 Huron Rd E Ste 350 Cleveland (44115) *(G-4935)*

Splish Splash Auto Bath, Springfield *Also Called: JKL Development Company (G-13261)*

Split Rail Nursery, Circleville *Also Called: Rhoads Farm Inc (G-3720)*

Sponseller Group Inc (PA).. 419 861-3000
   1600 Timber Wolf Dr Holland (43528) *(G-9304)*

Sportclinic, Ravenna *Also Called: Robinson Health System Inc (G-12642)*

Sports Construction Group, Brecksville *Also Called: Sports Surfaces Cnstr LLC (G-1368)*

Sports Medicine Center, Dayton *Also Called: Miami Valley Hospital (G-7489)*

Sports Medicine Grant Inc (PA)... 614 461-8174
   323 E Town St Ste 100 Columbus (43215) *(G-6705)*

Sports Surfaces Cnstr LLC.. 440 546-1200
   10303 Brecksville Rd Brecksville (44141) *(G-1368)*

Sportsmans Market Inc... 513 735-9100
   2001 Sportys Dr Batavia (45103) *(G-747)*

Sportsmens Alliance Foundation, Columbus *Also Called: United Sttes Sprtsmens Alnce F (G-6818)*

Sportys Pilot Shop, Batavia *Also Called: Sportsmans Market Inc (G-747)*

Spr Therapeutics Inc... 216 378-2658
   22901 Millcreek Blvd Ste 500 Cleveland (44122) *(G-4936)*

Sprandel Enterprises Inc 513 777-6622
  6467 Gano Rd West Chester (45069) *(G-14768)*

Spray Products Corporation 610 277-1010
  1000 Lake Rd Medina (44256) *(G-10892)*

Spray Repair Services Div, Toledo *Also Called: Chas F Mann Painting Co (G-13730)*

Spread Eagle Tavern Inc 330 223-1583
  10150 Plymouth St Hanoverton (44423) *(G-9095)*

Sprenger Enterprises Inc (PA) 630 529-0700
  3905 Oberlin Ave Ste 1 Lorain (44053) *(G-10102)*

SPRENGER HEALTH CARE SYSTEMS, Lorain *Also Called: Anchor Lodge Nursing Home Inc (G-10054)*

Sprenger Health Care Systems, Lorain *Also Called: Bluesky Healthcare Inc (G-10061)*

Sprenger Retirement Centers, Lorain *Also Called: CMS & Co Management Svcs Inc (G-10067)*

Spring Creek Nursing Center, Dayton *Also Called: Care One LLC (G-7210)*

Spring Grove Center, Cincinnati *Also Called: Talbert House (G-3437)*

Spring Grove Cmtry & Arboretum (PA) 513 681-7526
  4521 Spring Grove Ave Cincinnati (45232) *(G-3397)*

Spring Grove Rsrce Rcovery Inc 513 681-6242
  4879 Spring Grove Ave Cincinnati (45232) *(G-3398)*

Spring Hill Suites 513 381-8300
  610 Eden Park Dr Cincinnati (45202) *(G-3399)*

Spring Hills At Middletown, Middletown *Also Called: Spring Hills Health Care LLC (G-11202)*

Spring Hills At Singing Woods, Dayton *Also Called: Spring Hills Health Care LLC (G-7634)*

Spring Hills Health Care LLC 937 274-1400
  140 E Woodbury Dr Dayton (45415) *(G-7634)*

Spring Hills Health Care LLC 513 424-9999
  3851 Towne Blvd Middletown (45005) *(G-11202)*

Spring Mdow Extnded Care Ctr F (PA) 419 866-6124
  1125 Clarion Ave Holland (43528) *(G-9305)*

Spring Meadow Extended Care Ce 419 866-6124
  105 S Main St Mansfield (44902) *(G-10318)*

SPRING MEADOWS CARE CENTER, Woodstock *Also Called: Woodstock Healthcare Group Inc (G-15305)*

Springboro Family Health Care 937 748-4211
  630 N Main St Ste 210 Springboro (45066) *(G-13207)*

Springboro Family Medicine, Springboro *Also Called: Springboro Family Health Care (G-13207)*

Springdale Family Medicine PC 513 771-7213
  212 W Sharon Rd Cincinnati (45246) *(G-3400)*

Springdot, Cincinnati *Also Called: Springdot Inc (G-3401)*

Springdot Inc (PA) 513 542-4000
  2611 Colerain Ave Cincinnati (45214) *(G-3401)*

Springfeld Ctr For Fmly Mdcine 937 399-7777
  3250 Middle Urbana Rd Springfield (45502) *(G-13292)*

Springfeld Halthcare Group Inc 937 399-8311
  404 E Mccreight Ave Springfield (45503) *(G-13293)*

Springfield Business Eqp Co (PA) 937 322-3828
  3783 W National Rd Springfield (45504) *(G-13294)*

Springfield Cartage LLC 937 222-2120
  1615 Springfield St Dayton (45403) *(G-7635)*

Springfield Home and Hardware, Tipp City *Also Called: Bruns Construction Enterprises Inc (G-13653)*

Springfield Masonic Community 937 325-1531
  2655 W National Rd Springfield (45504) *(G-13295)*

Springfield Nursing And Rehabilitation Center, Springfield *Also Called: Springfeld Halthcare Group Inc (G-13293)*

SPRINGFIELD, CITY OF (INC), Springfield *Also Called: City of Springfield (G-13227)*

Springhill Construction, Dundee *Also Called: Cbtk Group Inc (G-8168)*

Springhill Suites, Cincinnati *Also Called: Spring Hill Suites (G-3399)*

Springhill Suites, Columbus *Also Called: Black Spphire C Clmbus Univ 20 (G-5443)*

Springhill Suites, Solon *Also Called: Solon Lodging Associates LLC (G-13144)*

Springhill Suites Independence, Independence *Also Called: Jagi Springhill LLC (G-9438)*

Springhills LLC 937 705-5002
  51 Plum St Dayton (45440) *(G-7636)*

SPRINGHILLS LLC, Dayton *Also Called: Springhills LLC (G-7636)*

Springleaf Financial Svc., Toledo *Also Called: Springleaf Fincl Holdings LLC (G-14021)*

Springleaf Fincl Holdings LLC 419 334-9748
  2200 Sean Dr Ste 10 Fremont (43420) *(G-8704)*

Springleaf Fincl Holdings LLC 419 841-0785
  5950 Airport Hwy Ste 1 Toledo (43615) *(G-14021)*

Springmeade, Tipp City *Also Called: Uvmc Nursing Care Inc (G-13668)*

Springs Window Fashions LLC 614 492-6770
  6295 Commerce Center Dr Groveport (43125) *(G-9002)*

Springvale Golf Crse Ballroom, North Olmsted *Also Called: City of North Olmsted (G-11895)*

Springvale Health Centers Inc (PA) 330 343-6631
  201 Hospital Dr Dover (44622) *(G-7902)*

SPRINGVIEW MANOR, Lima *Also Called: Springview Manor Nursing Home (G-9965)*

Springview Manor Nursing Home 419 227-3661
  883 W Spring St Lima (45805) *(G-9965)*

Sprinkfab, Barberton *Also Called: S A Comunale Co Inc (G-708)*

Sprint, Cleveland *Also Called: Sprint Corporation (G-4937)*

Sprint Communications Co LP 419 725-2444
  1708 W Alexis Rd Toledo (43613) *(G-14022)*

Sprint Corporation 216 661-2977
  3340 Steelyard Dr Cleveland (44109) *(G-4937)*

Spritle Software, Hilliard *Also Called: Balaji D Loganathan (G-9182)*

SPROUTFIVE, Columbus *Also Called: South Side Learning & Dev Ctr (G-6693)*

Sps Inc 937 339-7801
  45 Troy Town Dr Troy (45373) *(G-14160)*

Spunfab, Cuyahoga Falls *Also Called: Keuchel & Associates Inc (G-7085)*

Squeaky Banana Inc 614 492-1208
  4852 Frusta Dr Ste D Obetz (43207) *(G-12083)*

Squire Patton Boggs (us) LLP 513 361-1200
  201 E 4th St Ste 324 Cincinnati (45202) *(G-3402)*

Squire Patton Boggs (us) LLP (PA) 216 479-8500
  1000 Key Tower 127 Public Sq Cleveland (44114) *(G-4938)*

Src Inc 937 431-0717
  2900 Presidential Dr Ste 240 Beavercreek (45324) *(G-908)*

Sreco Flexible, Lima *Also Called: Sewer Rodding Equipment Co (G-9959)*

Sree SAI Hotels LLC 630 440-0765
  35000 Curtis Blvd Eastlake (44095) *(G-8209)*

Sroka Inc 440 572-2811
  21265 Westwood Dr Strongsville (44149) *(G-13486)*

SS Kemp & Co LLC (HQ) 216 271-7700
  4567 Willow Pkwy Cleveland (44125) *(G-4939)*

Ssb Community Bank 330 878-5555
  152 N Wooster Ave Strasburg (44680) *(G-13406)*

Ssb Cpas, Canfield *Also Called: Schroedel Scullin & Bestic LLC (G-1640)*

SSE&g, Westlake *Also Called: Seeley Svdge Ebert Gourash Lpa (G-15106)*

Ssi Fabricated Inc 513 217-3535
  2860 Cincinnati Dayton Rd Middletown (45044) *(G-11187)*

Ssoe Group, Toledo *Also Called: Ssoe Inc (G-14023)*

Ssoe Group, Toledo *Also Called: Ssoe Systems Inc (G-14024)*

Ssoe Inc (PA) 419 255-3830
  1001 Madison Ave Toledo (43604) *(G-14023)*

Ssoe Systems Inc 419 255-3830
  1001 Madison Ave Toledo (43604) *(G-14024)*

SSP, Twinsburg *Also Called: SSP Fittings Corp (G-14220)*

SSP Fittings Corp (PA) 330 425-4250
  8250 Boyle Pkwy Twinsburg (44087) *(G-14220)*

Sst, Loveland *Also Called: Sst Bearing Corporation (G-10162)*

Sst Bearing Corporation (HQ) 513 583-5500
  154 Commerce Dr Loveland (45140) *(G-10162)*

St Anne Mercy Hospital 419 407-2663
  3404 W Sylvania Ave Toledo (43623) *(G-14025)*

St Anne Mercy Hospital, Dublin *Also Called: Pain Care Specialists LLC (G-8086)*

St Anthony Feed Mill, Fort Recovery *Also Called: Fort Recovery Equity Inc (G-8608)*

St Augustine Manor 440 888-7722
  6707 State Rd Parma (44134) *(G-12265)*

St Bartholomew Cons School, Cincinnati *Also Called: Archdiocese of Cincinnati (G-2212)*

St Benedict School, Cambridge *Also Called: Catholic Chrties Sthstern Ohio (G-1563)*

St Catherine's Manor, Fostoria *Also Called: St Cthrnes Care Ctrs Fstria I (G-8626)*

St Catherines Care Ctr Findlay 419 422-3978
  8455 County Road 140 Findlay (45840) *(G-8587)*

St Cecilia School, Columbus *Also Called: Saint Cecilia Church (G-6637)*

St Clare Commons 419 931-0050
  12469 Five Point Rd Perrysburg (43551) *(G-12371)*

St Cthrnes Care Ctrs Fstria I 419 435-8112
  25 Christopher Dr Fostoria (44830) *(G-8626)*

ALPHABETIC SECTION — Stanley Steemer Intl Inc

St Edward Elementary School, Ashland *Also Called: Catholic Charities Corporation (G-487)*

St Edward Home.. 330 668-2828
3131 Smith Rd Fairlawn (44333) *(G-8500)*

St Elizabeth Boardman Hospital, Youngstown *Also Called: Bon Secours Mercy Health Inc (G-15563)*

St Elizabeth Health Center, Youngstown *Also Called: Mercy Health Youngstown LLC (G-15665)*

St Elzabeth Boardman Hlth Ctr... 330 729-4580
8401 Market St Boardman (44512) *(G-1292)*

St Francis De Sales Church... 740 345-9874
40 Granville St Newark (43055) *(G-11749)*

ST FRANCIS SENIOR MINISTRIES, Tiffin *Also Called: Csji-Tiffin Inc (G-13626)*

St Jhns Evang Lthran Ch Mrysv... 937 644-5540
12809 State Route 736 Marysville (43040) *(G-10510)*

St John Central High School, Steubenville *Also Called: Catholic Chrties Sthstern Ohio (G-13319)*

St John's Lutheran School, Marysville *Also Called: St Jhns Evang Lthran Ch Mrysv (G-10510)*

St Johns Villa.. 330 627-4662
701 Crest St Nw Carrollton (44615) *(G-1913)*

St Johns West Shore Hosp Phrm... 440 835-8000
29000 Center Ridge Rd Westlake (44145) *(G-15111)*

St Joseph Care Center, Louisville *Also Called: Roman Cthlic Docese Youngstown (G-10122)*

St Joseph Infant Maternity HM.. 513 563-2520
10722 Wyscarver Rd Cincinnati (45241) *(G-3403)*

St Joseph Riverside Hospital... 330 841-4000
667 Eastland Ave Se Warren (44484) *(G-4555)*

St Joseph S Home, Cincinnati *Also Called: St Joseph Infant Maternity HM (G-3403)*

St Lawrence Holdings LLC... 330 562-9000
16500 Rockside Rd Maple Heights (44137) *(G-10347)*

St Lawrence Steel Corporation.. 330 562-9000
16500 Rockside Rd Maple Heights (44137) *(G-10348)*

St Luke Lutheran Community.. 330 644-3914
615 Latham Ln New Franklin (44319) *(G-11616)*

St Lukes Gift Shop, Maumee *Also Called: Auxiliary St Lukes Hospital (G-10697)*

St Lukes Hospital (DH).. 419 893-5911
5901 Monclova Rd Maumee (43537) *(G-10769)*

St Lukes Hospital... 419 441-1002
900 Waterville Monclova Rd Waterville (43566) *(G-14595)*

St Lukes Wtrvlle Physcl Thrapy, Waterville *Also Called: St Lukes Hospital (G-14595)*

St Mary & Joseph Home, Warrensville Heights *Also Called: Little Ssters of Poor Bltmore (G-14584)*

St Mary's Central, Saint Clairsville *Also Called: Catholic Chrties Sthstern Ohio (G-12784)*

St Marys City Board Education.. 419 394-2616
650 Armstrong St Saint Marys (45885) *(G-12836)*

St Moritz Security Svcs Inc.. 614 351-8798
705 Lakeview Plaza Blvd Ste G Worthington (43085) *(G-15459)*

St Moritz Security Svcs Inc.. 330 270-5922
32 N Four Mile Run Rd Youngstown (44515) *(G-15729)*

St Pauls Catholic Church (PA)... 330 724-1263
433 Mission Dr Akron (44301) *(G-308)*

St Pauls Community Center... 419 255-5520
230 13th St Toledo (43604) *(G-14026)*

St Performing Arts LLC.. 419 381-8851
4645 Heatherdowns Blvd Toledo (43614) *(G-14027)*

ST STEPHENS COMMUNITY SERVICE, Columbus *Also Called: St Stphens Cmnty Hmes Ltd Prt (G-6706)*

St Stphens Cmnty Hmes Ltd Prt.. 614 294-6347
1500 E 17th Ave Columbus (43219) *(G-6706)*

St Thomas Episcopal Church... 513 831-6908
100 Miami Ave Terrace Park (45174) *(G-13614)*

St Thomas Nursery School, Terrace Park *Also Called: St Thomas Episcopal Church (G-13614)*

St Vincent Charity Med Ctr (HQ)... 216 861-6200
2351 E 22nd St Cleveland (44115) *(G-4940)*

St Vincent Family Services (PA)... 614 252-0731
1490 E Main St Columbus (43205) *(G-6707)*

ST VINCENT MEDICAL CENTER, Toledo *Also Called: Ambulatory Care Pharmacy (G-13680)*

St. Cthrnes Manor Wash Crt Hse, Wshngtn Ct Hs *Also Called: Hcf of Washington Inc (G-15488)*

St. Elizabeth Youngstown Hosp, Youngstown *Also Called: Bon Secours Mercy Health Inc (G-15562)*

St. John's Medical Center, Westlake *Also Called: University Hospital (G-15120)*

St. Vincent Medical Group, Cleveland *Also Called: Outreach Professional Svcs Inc (G-4710)*

St. Vncent Hosp Mdial Ctr Tled, Toledo *Also Called: Mercy Hlth - St Vncent Med Ctr (G-13919)*

Stable Step LLC... 800 491-1571
961 Seville Rd Wadsworth (44281) *(G-14452)*

Stack Constructyion Technology, Mason *Also Called: To Scale Software LLC (G-10616)*

Stack Heating and Cooling LLC.. 440 937-9134
37520 Colorado Ave Avon (44011) *(G-665)*

Stack Heating Cooling & Elc, Avon *Also Called: Stack Heating and Cooling LLC (G-665)*

Stafast Products Inc (PA)... 440 357-5546
505 Lakeshore Blvd Painesville (44077) *(G-12243)*

Stafast West, Painesville *Also Called: Stafast Products Inc (G-12243)*

Staffco-Campisano, Cleveland *Also Called: RA Staff Company (G-4806)*

Staffing Studio LLC... 614 934-1860
4449 Easton Way Fl 2 Columbus (43219) *(G-6708)*

Staffmark, Cincinnati *Also Called: CBS Personnel Services LLC (G-2325)*

Staffmark, Cincinnati *Also Called: Staffmark Investment LLC (G-3405)*

Staffmark Group LLC (HQ).. 513 651-1111
191 Rosa Parks St Pmb 10 Cincinnati (45202) *(G-3404)*

Staffmark Investment LLC (DH).. 513 651-3600
201 E 4th St Cincinnati (45202) *(G-3405)*

Stafftech Inc... 937 228-2667
8534 Yankee St Ste 1c Dayton (45458) *(G-7637)*

Staffworks Group 2 Inc.. 419 515-0655
1244 Broadway St Ste 8 Toledo (43609) *(G-14028)*

Stagnaro Saba Patterson Co Lpa... 513 533-2700
7373 Beechmont Ave Cincinnati (45230) *(G-3406)*

Stahl Vision Laser Surgery Ctr.. 937 643-2020
4235 Indian Ripple Rd Ste 100 Dayton (45440) *(G-7638)*

Stallion Oilfield Cnstr LLC... 330 868-2083
3361 Baird Ave Se Paris (44669) *(G-12247)*

Stambaugh Charter Academy, Youngstown *Also Called: National Heritg Academies Inc (G-15674)*

Stamper Staffing LLC.. 937 938-7010
2812 Purdue Dr Kettering (45420) *(G-9633)*

Stan Hywet Hall and Grdns Inc... 330 836-5533
714 N Portage Path Akron (44303) *(G-309)*

Stan-Kell LLC.. 440 998-1116
2621 West Ave Ashtabula (44004) *(G-550)*

Stand Energy Corporation... 513 621-1113
1077 Celestial St Ste 110 Cincinnati (45202) *(G-3407)*

Standard Contg & Engrg Inc... 440 243-1001
6356 Eastland Rd Brookpark (44142) *(G-1440)*

Standard Insurance Company... 513 241-7275
312 Elm St Ste 1400 Cincinnati (45202) *(G-3408)*

Standard Plumbing & Heating Co (HQ)............................. 330 453-5150
435 Walnut Ave Se Canton (44702) *(G-1856)*

Standard Textile Co Inc (PA)... 513 761-9255
1 Knollcrest Dr Cincinnati (45237) *(G-3409)*

Standard Wellness Company LLC..................................... 330 931-1037
425 Literary Rd Apt 100 Cleveland (44113) *(G-4941)*

Standardaero, Cincinnati *Also Called: Standrdaero Component Svcs Inc (G-3410)*

Standardaero, Hillsboro *Also Called: Pas Technologies Inc (G-9266)*

Standex Electronics Inc (HQ).. 513 871-3777
4150 Thunderbird Ln Fairfield (45014) *(G-8443)*

Standex-Meder Electronics, Fairfield *Also Called: Standex Electronics Inc (G-8443)*

Standing Stone National Bank (PA)................................... 740 653-5115
137 W Wheeling St Lancaster (43130) *(G-9744)*

Standrdaero Component Svcs Inc (DH)............................. 513 618-9588
11550 Mosteller Rd Cincinnati (45241) *(G-3410)*

Stanley Engineered Fastening, Lakewood *Also Called: Ferry Cap & Set Screw Company (G-9666)*

Stanley Steemer, Wickliffe *Also Called: Lazar Brothers Inc (G-15156)*

Stanley Steemer Carpet Cleaner, Dublin *Also Called: Stanley Steemer Intl Inc (G-8124)*

Stanley Steemer Intl Inc.. 614 764-2007
824 Space Dr Beavercreek Township (45434) *(G-950)*

Stanley Steemer Intl Inc.. 513 771-0213
637 Redna Ter Cincinnati (45215) *(G-3411)*

Stanley Steemer Intl Inc.. 614 767-8017
4621 Hinckley Industrial Pkwy Unit 12 Cleveland (44109) *(G-4942)*

Stanley Steemer Intl Inc (PA).. 614 764-2007
5800 Innovation Dr Dublin (43016) *(G-8124)*

Stansley Mineral Resources Inc (PA).................................... 419 843-2813
3793 Silica Rd # B Sylvania (43560) *(G-13573)*

Stantec Consulting Svcs Inc.. 216 621-2407
1001 Lakeside Ave E Ste 1600 Cleveland (44114) *(G-4943)*

Stanwade Metal Products Inc.. 330 772-2421
6868 State Rt 305 Hartford (44424) *(G-9123)*

Stanwade Tanks and Equipment, Hartford Also Called: Stanwade Metal Products Inc *(G-9123)*

Staples Contract & Coml LLC.. 740 845-5600
500 E High St London (43140) *(G-10051)*

Star, Marion Also Called: Steam Trbine Altmtive Rsrces *(G-10455)*

Star 93.3 FM, Cincinnati Also Called: Pillar of Fire *(G-3211)*

Star Builders Inc.. 440 986-5951
46405 Telegraph Rd Amherst (44001) *(G-434)*

Star Distribution and Mfg LLC.. 513 860-3573
10179 Commerce Park Dr West Chester (45246) *(G-14833)*

Star House.. 614 826-5868
1220 Corrugated Way Columbus (43201) *(G-6709)*

Star Inc... 740 354-1517
2625 Gallia St Portsmouth (45662) *(G-12575)*

Star Leasing Company LLC (PA)... 614 278-9999
4080 Business Park Dr Columbus (43204) *(G-6710)*

Star Manufacturring, West Chester Also Called: Star Distribution and Mfg LLC *(G-14833)*

Star Packaging Inc.. 614 564-9936
1796 Frebis Ave Columbus (43206) *(G-6711)*

Star Seven Six Ltd... 800 669-9623
2550 Corporate Exchange Dr Ste 109 Columbus (43231) *(G-6712)*

Starbucks Licensed Store, Cincinnati Also Called: Hard Rock Csino Cincinnati LLC *(G-2800)*

Starbucks Licensed Store, Cleveland Also Called: Cleveland Westin Downtown *(G-4073)*

Starbucks Licensed Store, Columbus Also Called: Greater Clmbus Cnvntion Ctr Fo *(G-5953)*

Starforce National Corporation.. 513 979-3600
455 Delta Ave Ste 410 Cincinnati (45226) *(G-3412)*

Stark Area Regional Trnst Auth (PA)....................................... 330 477-2782
1600 Gateway Blvd Se Canton (44707) *(G-1857)*

Stark County Board of Developm.. 330 477-5200
4065 Bradley Cir Nw Canton (44718) *(G-1858)*

Stark County Engineer, Canton Also Called: County of Stark *(G-1724)*

Stark County Neurologists Inc.. 330 494-2097
4105 Holiday St Nw Canton (44718) *(G-1859)*

Stark County Park District... 330 477-3552
5300 Tyner Ave Nw Canton (44708) *(G-1860)*

Stark County Sewer Dept, Canton Also Called: County of Stark *(G-1725)*

Stark Enterprises, Cleveland Also Called: Robert L Stark Enterprises Inc *(G-4846)*

Stark Sandblasting & Pntg Co, Canton Also Called: Flamos Enterprises Inc *(G-1755)*

Stark Summit Ambulance, North Canton Also Called: Medical Transport Systems Inc *(G-11847)*

Starlight Enterprises Inc... 330 339-2020
400 E High Ave New Philadelphia (44663) *(G-11668)*

Starlight Special School, Zanesville Also Called: Muskingum Starlight Industries *(G-15817)*

Starr Construction & Demo LLC... 330 538-7214
2887 N Salem Warren Rd Warren (44481) *(G-14556)*

Stars Yuth Enrchment Prgram In... 513 978-7735
4972 Maplecreek Dr Trotwood (45426) *(G-14128)*

Starship Technologies Inc... 440 251-7096
707 N College Dr Bowling Green (43403) *(G-1333)*

Startech.com USA, Groveport Also Called: Startechcom USA LLP *(G-9003)*

Startechcom USA LLP... 800 265-1844
4490 S Hamilton Rd Groveport (43125) *(G-9003)*

Startek Inc.. 419 528-7801
850 W 4th St Ontario (44906) *(G-12125)*

Starting Point, Cleveland Also Called: Child Care Resource Center *(G-3969)*

Startupscom LLC.. 800 799-6998
7691 Perry Rd Delaware (43015) *(G-7828)*

Starwin Industries LLC... 937 293-8568
3387 Woodman Dr Dayton (45429) *(G-7639)*

Starwood Hotels & Resorts, Cincinnati Also Called: Host Cincinnati Hotel LLC *(G-2850)*

Stat Communications, Columbus Also Called: Universal Recovery Systems Inc *(G-6821)*

Stat Integrated Tech Inc (PA)... 440 286-7663
10779 Mayfield Rd Chardon (44024) *(G-2021)*

State 8 Motorcycle & Atv, Peninsula Also Called: Wholecycle Inc *(G-12296)*

State Alarm Inc (PA)... 888 726-8111
5956 Market St Youngstown (44512) *(G-15730)*

State Alarm Systems, Youngstown Also Called: State Alarm Inc *(G-15730)*

State Auto Financial Corp (HQ)... 614 464-5000
518 E Broad St Columbus (43215) *(G-6713)*

State Auto Insurance Companies, Columbus Also Called: State Automobile Mutl Insur Co *(G-6714)*

State Automobile Mutl Insur Co (DH)..................................... 833 724-3577
518 E Broad St Columbus (43215) *(G-6714)*

State Bank, Defiance Also Called: State Bank and Trust Company *(G-7769)*

State Bank and Trust Company (HQ)..................................... 419 783-8950
401 Clinton St Defiance (43512) *(G-7769)*

State Chemical, Cleveland Also Called: Zucker Building Company *(G-5176)*

State Chemical Manufacturing, Cleveland Also Called: State Industrial Products Corp *(G-4944)*

State Chemical Manufacturing, Hebron Also Called: State Industrial Products Corp *(G-9154)*

State Crest Carpet & Flooring (PA).. 440 232-3980
5400 Perkins Rd Bedford (44146) *(G-987)*

State Farm General Insur Co.. 513 662-7283
6323 Glenway Ave Cincinnati (45211) *(G-3413)*

State Farm General Insur Co.. 513 231-4975
2063 Beechmont Ave Ste 2 Cincinnati (45230) *(G-3414)*

State Farm General Insur Co.. 740 364-5000
1440 Granville Rd Newark (43055) *(G-11750)*

State Farm General Insur Co.. 440 268-0600
11220 Pearl Rd Strongsville (44136) *(G-13487)*

State Farm General Insur Co.. 513 870-0285
4837 Realtor Road Ste B West Chester (45069) *(G-14769)*

State Farm Insurance, Cincinnati Also Called: State Farm General Insur Co *(G-3413)*

State Farm Insurance, Cincinnati Also Called: State Farm General Insur Co *(G-3414)*

State Farm Insurance, Dayton Also Called: State Farm Life Insurance Co *(G-7640)*

State Farm Insurance, Newark Also Called: State Farm General Insur Co *(G-11750)*

State Farm Insurance, Strongsville Also Called: State Farm General Insur Co *(G-13487)*

State Farm Insurance, West Chester Also Called: State Farm General Insur Co *(G-14769)*

State Farm Life Insurance Co... 937 276-1900
1436 Needmore Rd Dayton (45414) *(G-7640)*

State Industrial Products Corp (PA)...................................... 877 747-6986
5915 Landerbrook Dr Ste 300 Cleveland (44124) *(G-4944)*

State Industrial Products Corp... 740 929-6370
383 N High St Hebron (43025) *(G-9154)*

STATE OF THE HEART HOSPICE, Greenville Also Called: Hospice of Darke County Inc *(G-8878)*

State Tchers Rtrement Sys Ohio (HQ)................................... 614 227-4090
275 E Broad St Columbus (43215) *(G-6715)*

Stateco Financial Services Inc.. 614 464-5000
518 E Broad St Columbus (43215) *(G-6716)*

Stateside Undwrt Agcy Inc... 440 893-9917
13 1/2 N Franklin St Ste 1 Chagrin Falls (44022) *(G-1968)*

Stationers Inc.. 740 423-1400
214 Stone Rd Belpre (45714) *(G-1059)*

Status Solutions, Westerville Also Called: Status Solutions LLC *(G-14938)*

Status Solutions LLC... 434 296-1789
999 County Line Rd W # A Westerville (43082) *(G-14938)*

Staybrdge Sites Columbus Arprt, Columbus Also Called: Rama Inc *(G-6561)*

Staybridge Suites... 330 945-4180
4351 Steels Pointe Stow (44224) *(G-13391)*

Staymobile Franchising LLC... 614 601-3345
1598 N High St Columbus (43201) *(G-6717)*

Steady Care Behavioral LLC... 330 956-1190
723 E Tallmadge Ave Rear Akron (44310) *(G-310)*

Steak Escape, Columbus Also Called: Escape Enterprises Inc *(G-5828)*

Stealth Auto Recovery, Columbus Also Called: Lw Equipment LLC *(G-6182)*

Steam Trbine Altrntive Rsrces.. 740 387-5535
370 W Fairground St Marion (43302) *(G-10455)*

Stecu, Columbus Also Called: Struthers CU A Div Brdge Cr Un *(G-6723)*

Steed Hammond Paul Inc (PA).. 513 381-2112
312 Plum St Ste 700 Cincinnati (45202) *(G-3415)*

Steel Eqp Specialists Inc (PA).. 330 823-8260
1507 Beeson St Ne Alliance (44601) *(G-401)*

ALPHABETIC SECTION

Steel Warehouse Cleveland LLC (DH) 888 225-3760
3193 Independence Rd Cleveland (44105) *(G-4945)*

Steel Warehouse Company LLC 216 206-2800
4700 Heidtman Pkwy Cleveland (44105) *(G-4946)*

Steel Warehouse of Ohio LLC 888 225-3760
4700 Heidtman Pkwy Cleveland (44105) *(G-4947)*

Steel Warehouse Ohio, Cleveland *Also Called: Steel Warehouse Company LLC (G-4946)*

Steelcase Authorized Dealer, Dayton *Also Called: Business Furniture LLC (G-7207)*

Steelial Cnstr Met Fabrication, Vinton *Also Called: Steelial Wldg Met Fbrction Inc (G-14425)*

Steelial Wldg Met Fbrction Inc 740 669-5300
70764 State Route 124 Vinton (45686) *(G-14425)*

Stein Hospice Service Inc (PA) 800 625-5269
1200 Sycamore Line Sandusky (44870) *(G-12934)*

Stein Hospice Services Inc 419 502-0019
126 Columbus Ave Sandusky (44870) *(G-12935)*

STEIN HOSPICE SERVICES, INC., Sandusky *Also Called: Stein Hospice Services Inc (G-12935)*

Stein Steel Mill Services LLC 440 526-9301
4000 Mahoning Ave Nw Warren (44483) *(G-14557)*

Steiner Associates, Columbus *Also Called: Easton Town Center II LLC (G-5799)*

Steiner Associates, Columbus *Also Called: Seg of Ohio Inc (G-6659)*

Steiner Eoptics Inc (PA) 937 426-2341
3475 Newmark Dr Miamisburg (45342) *(G-11095)*

Steingass Mechanical Contg LLC 330 725-6090
754 S Progress Dr Medina (44256) *(G-10893)*

Steinke Tractor Sales Inc 937 456-4271
707 S Barron St Eaton (45320) *(G-8224)*

Stella Maris Inc 216 781-0550
1320 Washington Ave Cleveland (44113) *(G-4948)*

Stella Mris Detoxification Ctr, Cleveland *Also Called: Stella Maris Inc (G-4948)*

Stellar Automotive Group, Seville *Also Called: Stellar Srkg Acquisition LLC (G-12966)*

Stellar Srkg Acquisition LLC 330 769-8484
4935 Enterprise Pkwy Seville (44273) *(G-12966)*

Stellar Technology, Solon *Also Called: Lord Corporation (G-13107)*

Stemcor USA Inc 330 373-1885
8700 E Market St Ste 11 Warren (44484) *(G-14558)*

Step Forward (PA) 216 696-9077
1801 Superior Ave E Ste 400 Cleveland (44114) *(G-4949)*

Step Forward 216 692-4010
1883 Torbenson Dr Cleveland (44112) *(G-4950)*

Stepforward 216 541-7878
14209 Euclid Ave Cleveland (44112) *(G-4951)*

Stepforward 216 476-3201
14402 Puritas Ave Cleveland (44135) *(G-4952)*

Stepforward 216 736-2934
2421 Community College Ave Cleveland (44115) *(G-4953)*

STEPFORWARD, Cleveland *Also Called: Stepforward (G-4951)*

STEPFORWARD, Cleveland *Also Called: Stepforward (G-4952)*

Stephen M Trudick 440 834-1891
13813 Station Road Burton (44021) *(G-1533)*

Stephens Investments LLC 937 299-4993
417 E Stroop Rd Dayton (45429) *(G-7641)*

Stephens Pipe & Steel LLC 740 869-2257
10732 Schadel Ln Mount Sterling (43143) *(G-11475)*

Stephens-Matthews Mktg LLC 740 984-8011
605 Center St Beverly (45715) *(G-1102)*

Steps At Liberty Center, Wooster *Also Called: Oneeighty Inc (G-15364)*

Stepstone Group Real Estate LP 216 522-0330
127 Public Sq Ste 5050 Cleveland (44114) *(G-4954)*

Steriltek Inc (PA) 615 627-0241
11910 Briarwyck Woods Dr Concord Township (44077) *(G-6935)*

Steris Isomedix, Groveport *Also Called: Isomedix Operations Inc (G-8992)*

Steris Isomedix, Mentor *Also Called: Steris Isomedix Services Inc (G-10999)*

Steris Isomedix Services Inc 440 354-2600
5960 Heisley Rd Mentor (44060) *(G-10999)*

Sterling Buying Group LLC 513 564-9000
4540 Cooper Rd Ste 200 Cincinnati (45242) *(G-3416)*

Sterling Check Corp (PA) 212 736-5100
6150 Oak Tree Blvd Ste 490 Independence (44131) *(G-9485)*

Sterling Commerce (america) LLC 614 793-7000
4600 Lakehurst Ct Dublin (43016) *(G-8125)*

Sterling Commerce Group, Dublin *Also Called: Sterling Commerce (america) LLC (G-8125)*

Sterling Commerce LLC 614 798-2192
4600 Lakehurst Ct Dublin (43016) *(G-8126)*

Sterling Infosystems Inc (DH) 212 736-5100
6150 Oak Tree Blvd Ste 490 Independence (44131) *(G-9486)*

Sterling Infosystems Inc 216 685-7600
4511 Rockside Rd Fl 4 Independence (44131) *(G-9487)*

Sterling Med Staffing Group, Cincinnati *Also Called: Sterling Medical Corporation (G-3418)*

Sterling Medical Associates 513 984-1800
411 Oak St Cincinnati (45219) *(G-3417)*

Sterling Medical Corporation (PA) 513 984-1800
411 Oak St Cincinnati (45219) *(G-3418)*

Sterling Medical Corporation 513 984-1800
411 Oak St Cincinnati (45219) *(G-3419)*

Sterling Paper Co (HQ) 614 443-0303
1845 Progress Ave Columbus (43207) *(G-6718)*

Sterlingbackcheck, Independence *Also Called: Sterling Infosystems Inc (G-9486)*

Steubenville Country Club Inc 740 264-0521
413 Lovers Ln Steubenville (43953) *(G-13343)*

Steubnvlle Cntry CLB Manor Inc 740 266-6118
575 Lovers Ln Steubenville (43953) *(G-13344)*

Steve Brown 937 436-2700
1353 Lyons Rd Dayton (45458) *(G-7642)*

Steve Cndy Rsmssen Inst For Gn, Columbus *Also Called: Nationwide Childrens Hospital (G-6319)*

Steve Crawford Trucking Inc 866 748-9505
59965 Olive St Byesville (43723) *(G-1536)*

Steve Crwford Trucking-Se Ohio, Byesville *Also Called: Steve Crawford Trucking Inc (G-1536)*

Steven Schaefer Associates Inc (PA) 513 542-3300
537 E Pete Rose Way Ste 400 Cincinnati (45202) *(G-3420)*

Stevens Arospc Def Systems LLC 937 454-3400
3500 Hangar Dr Vandalia (45377) *(G-14393)*

Steward Hllside Rhblttion Hosp 330 841-3700
8747 Squires Ln Ne Warren (44484) *(G-14559)*

Steward Northside Med Ctr Inc 330 884-1000
1350 E Market St Warren (44483) *(G-14560)*

Steward Trumbull Mem Hosp Inc 330 841-9011
1350 E Market St Warren (44482) *(G-14561)*

Stewart & Calhoun Fnrl HM Inc 330 535-1543
529 W Thornton St Akron (44307) *(G-311)*

Stewart Advnced Land Title Ltd (PA) 513 753-2800
792 Eastgate South Dr Cincinnati (45245) *(G-2113)*

Stfc, Columbus *Also Called: State Auto Financial Corp (G-6713)*

Stg Cartage LLC 614 923-1400
5165 Emerald Pkwy Ste 300 Dublin (43017) *(G-8127)*

Stg Cartage LLC 614 923-1400
5165 Emerald Pkwy Ste 300 Dublin (43017) *(G-8128)*

Stg Electric Services LLC 330 650-0513
360 Highland Rd E Macedonia (44056) *(G-10206)*

Stg Intermodal Inc (DH) 614 923-1400
5165 Emerald Pkwy Ste 300 Dublin (43017) *(G-8129)*

Stg Intermodal Inc 440 833-0924
29115 Anderson Rd Wickliffe (44092) *(G-15163)*

STG Intermodal Solutions, Dublin *Also Called: STG Intermodal Solutions Inc (G-8130)*

STG Intermodal Solutions Inc (DH) 614 923-1400
5165 Emerald Pkwy Dublin (43017) *(G-8130)*

Stg Lane, Akron *Also Called: Scandinavian Tob Group Ln Ltd (G-295)*

Stg Stacktrain LLC (DH) 614 923-1400
5165 Emerald Pkwy Ste 300 Dublin (43017) *(G-8131)*

STI-TEC, Beavercreek *Also Called: Solutons Through Innvtive Tech (G-907)*

Stifel Ind Advisors LLC 937 293-1220
1250 W Dorothy Ln Ste 307 Dayton (45409) *(G-7643)*

Stifel Ind Advisors LLC 937 312-0111
28 E Rahn Rd Ste 112 Dayton (45429) *(G-7644)*

Stifel Ind Advisors LLC 740 653-9222
109 E Main St Lancaster (43130) *(G-9745)*

Stillwater Center, Dayton *Also Called: County of Montgomery (G-7257)*

Stiner and Sons Cnstr Inc 440 775-2345
13728 Hale Rd Oberlin (44074) *(G-12076)*

Stingray Pressure Pumping LLC (PA) 405 648-4177
42739 National Rd Belmont (43718) *(G-1055)*

Stlukes Medical Imagery 419 893-4856
5757 Monclova Rd Maumee (43537) *(G-10770)*

Stock Equipment Company, Solon *Also Called: Stock Fairfield Corporation (G-13149)*

Stock Fairfield Corporation 440 543-6000
30825 Aurora Rd # 150 Solon (44139) *(G-13149)*

Stockmeister Enterprises Inc 740 286-1619
700 E Main St Jackson (45640) *(G-9525)*

Stockton Mortgage Corporation 513 486-4140
5155 Financial Way Ste 8 Mason (45040) *(G-10609)*

Stofcheck Ambulance Svc Inc (PA) 740 499-2200
220 S High St La Rue (43332) *(G-9649)*

Stoll & Co, Dayton *Also Called: R S Stoll and Company (G-7578)*

Stolle Canton, North Canton *Also Called: Stolle Machinery Company LLC (G-11863)*

Stolle Machinery Company LLC 330 493-0444
4150 Belden Village St Nw Ste 504 Canton (44718) *(G-1861)*

Stolle Machinery Company LLC 330 494-6382
4337 Excel St North Canton (44720) *(G-11863)*

Stolly Insurance Agency Inc 419 227-2570
1730 Allentown Rd Lima (45805) *(G-9966)*

Stone Creek Alliance Inc 330 856-4232
1280 S Sawburg Ave Alliance (44601) *(G-402)*

Stone Crssing Asssted Lving LL 330 492-7131
820 34th St Nw Canton (44709) *(G-1862)*

Stone Oak Country Club 419 867-0969
100 Stone Oak Blvd Holland (43528) *(G-9306)*

Stone Ridge Golf Club, Bowling Green *Also Called: Wryneck Development LLC (G-1339)*

Stoneco Inc (DH) 419 422-8854
1700 Fostoria Ave Ste 200 Findlay (45840) *(G-8588)*

Stoneco Inc 419 893-7645
1360 Ford St Maumee (43537) *(G-10771)*

Stoneco Inc 419 393-2555
13762 Road 179 Oakwood (45873) *(G-12054)*

Stonecreek Dental, Pickerington *Also Called: J Clarke Sanders DDS Inc (G-12404)*

Stonegate Construction Inc 740 423-9170
1378 Way Rd Belpre (45714) *(G-1060)*

Stonehenge Capital Company LLC 614 246-2456
191 W Nationwide Blvd Ste 600 Columbus (43215) *(G-6719)*

Stonehenge Fincl Holdings Inc (PA) 614 246-2500
191 W Nationwide Blvd Ste 600 Columbus (43215) *(G-6720)*

Stonespring Trnstnal Care Ctr 937 415-8000
4000 Singing Hills Blvd Dayton (45414) *(G-7645)*

Stoney Hollow Tire Inc 740 635-5200
7 N 1st St Martins Ferry (43935) *(G-10470)*

Stoops of Lima Inc 419 228-4334
598 E Hanthorn Rd Lima (45804) *(G-9967)*

Store & Haul Inc 419 238-4284
1001 Vision Dr Van Wert (45891) *(G-14351)*

Store & Haul Trucking, Van Wert *Also Called: Store & Haul Inc (G-14351)*

Store N, Middletown *Also Called: Moores Fitness World Inc (G-11176)*

Stores Consulting Group LLC 717 309-5302
783 Mitchell Rd Wilmington (45177) *(G-15274)*

Storopack Inc (DH) 513 874-0314
4758 Devitt Dr West Chester (45246) *(G-14834)*

Storrie Dialysis LLC 937 390-3125
2200 N Limestone St Ste 104 Springfield (45503) *(G-13296)*

Stouffer Realty Inc (PA) 330 835-4900
130 N Miller Rd Ste A Fairlawn (44333) *(G-8501)*

Stouffer Realty Inc 330 564-0711
4936 Darrow Rd Stow (44224) *(G-13392)*

Stouffer Realty LLC 440 247-4210
68 Olive St Chagrin Falls (44022) *(G-1969)*

Stow Dental Group Inc 330 688-6456
3506 Darrow Rd Stow (44224) *(G-13393)*

Stow Opco LLC 502 429-8062
2910 Lermitage Pl Stow (44224) *(G-13394)*

Stow-Kent Animal Hospital Inc (PA) 330 673-0049
4559 Kent Rd Kent (44240) *(G-9598)*

Stow-Kent Animal Hospital Inc 330 673-1002
4148 State Route 43 Kent (44240) *(G-9599)*

Strader's Green House, Columbus *Also Called: Straders Garden Centers Inc (G-6721)*

Straders Garden Centers Inc (PA) 614 889-1314
5350 Riverside Dr Columbus (43220) *(G-6721)*

Straight 72 Inc 740 943-5730
20078 State Route 4 Marysville (43040) *(G-10511)*

Stranahan Theater & Great Hall, Toledo *Also Called: St Performing Arts LLC (G-14027)*

Strang Corporation (PA) 216 961-6767
8905 Lake Ave Fl 1 Cleveland (44102) *(G-4955)*

Stratacache Inc (PA) 937 224-0485
40 N Main St Ste 2600 Dayton (45423) *(G-7646)*

Stratacache Products, Dayton *Also Called: Stratacache Inc (G-7646)*

Strategic Comp 770 225-3532
301 E 4th St Fl 24 Cincinnati (45202) *(G-3421)*

Strategic Data Systems Inc 513 772-7374
11260 Chester Rd Ste 425 Cincinnati (45246) *(G-3422)*

Strategic Systems Inc 614 717-4774
475 Metro Pl S Ste 450 Dublin (43017) *(G-8132)*

Strategic Wealth Partners 216 800-9000
5005 Rockside Rd Ste 1200 Independence (44131) *(G-9488)*

Strategy Group For Media Inc 740 201-5500
7669 Stagers Loop Delaware (43015) *(G-7829)*

Strategy Network LLC (PA) 614 595-0688
1349 E Broad St Columbus (43205) *(G-6722)*

Stratford Commons Inc 440 914-0900
7000 Cochran Rd Solon (44139) *(G-13150)*

Stratos Wealth Partners 330 666-8131
291 N Cleveland Massillon Rd Ste 100 Akron (44333) *(G-312)*

Stratos Wealth Partners Ltd 440 519-2500
3750 Park East Dr Beachwood (44122) *(G-841)*

Strauss Gerald DDS Inc 937 642-8500
123 N Court St Marysville (43040) *(G-10512)*

Strawser Construction Inc 513 874-6192
8600 Bilstein Blvd Hamilton (45015) *(G-9083)*

STRAWSER CONSTRUCTION INC, Hamilton *Also Called: Strawser Construction Inc (G-9083)*

Streacker Tractor Sales Inc 419 422-6973
1218 Trenton Ave Findlay (45840) *(G-8589)*

Streamline Technical Svcs LLC 614 441-7448
4555 Creekside Pkwy Lockbourne (43137) *(G-10016)*

Streamlinemd LLC 330 564-2627
111 Stow Ave Ste 200 Cuyahoga Falls (44221) *(G-7101)*

Streem-Rsnick Ttelman Young PC 440 461-8200
29001 Cedar Rd Ste 660 Cleveland (44124) *(G-4956)*

Street Department, Cuyahoga Falls *Also Called: City of Cuyahoga Falls (G-7060)*

Streetsboro Board Education 330 626-4909
1901 Annalane Dr Streetsboro (44241) *(G-13429)*

Streetsboro Bus Garage, Streetsboro *Also Called: Streetsboro Board Education (G-13429)*

Streetsboro Opco LLC 502 429-8062
1645 Maplewood Dr Streetsboro (44241) *(G-13430)*

Streetsboro Operations, Twinsburg *Also Called: Facil North America Inc (G-14190)*

Stress Care/Bridges 937 723-3200
405 W Grand Ave Dayton (45405) *(G-7647)*

Stress Engineering Svcs Inc 513 336-6701
7030 Stress Engineering Way Mason (45040) *(G-10610)*

Stricker Auto Sales, Batavia *Also Called: Stricker Bros Inc (G-748)*

Stricker Bros Inc 513 732-1152
4955 Benton Rd Batavia (45103) *(G-748)*

Stridas LLC 513 725-4626
8259 Beechmont Ave Cincinnati (45255) *(G-3423)*

Strike Logistics, Toledo *Also Called: Bolt Express LLC (G-13711)*

Strike Zone Inc 440 235-4420
8501 Stearns Rd Olmsted Twp (44138) *(G-12094)*

Strive Enterprises Inc (PA) 614 593-2840
6555 Longshore St Ste 220 Dublin (43017) *(G-8133)*

Strivetogether Inc 513 929-1150
125 E 9th St Fl 2 Cincinnati (45202) *(G-3424)*

Strollo Architects Inc 330 743-1177
201 W Federal St Youngstown (44503) *(G-15731)*

Strong Style Mma Training Ctr, Independence *Also Called: Progrssive Fghting Systems LLC (G-9473)*

Strongsville Medical Offices, Strongsville *Also Called: Kaiser Foundation Hospitals (G-13467)*

STRONGSVILLE RECREATION CENTER, Cleveland *Also Called: Strongville Recreation Complex (G-4957)*

Strongsvlle Ldging Assoc I Ltd 440 238-8800
15471 Royalton Rd Strongsville (44136) *(G-13488)*

ALPHABETIC SECTION — Summit County

Strongville Recreation Complex (PA)..........440 878-6000
18100 Royalton Rd Cleveland (44136) *(G-4957)*

Strongville Recreation Complex..........440 580-3230
18688 Royalton Rd Strongsville (44136) *(G-13489)*

STRS Ohio, Columbus Also Called: State Tchers Rtrement Sys Ohio *(G-6715)*

Struktol, Stow Also Called: Struktol Company America LLC *(G-13395)*

Struktol Company America LLC (DH)..........330 928-5188
201 E Steels Corners Rd Stow (44224) *(G-13395)*

Struthers CU A Div Brdge Cr Un..........800 434-7300
1980 W Broad St Columbus (43223) *(G-6723)*

Stud Welding, Strongsville Also Called: Stud Welding Associates Inc *(G-13490)*

Stud Welding Associates Inc..........440 783-3160
12200 Alameda Dr Strongsville (44149) *(G-13490)*

Studebaker Electric Company..........937 890-9510
8459 N Main St Ste 106 Dayton (45415) *(G-7648)*

Studebaker Nurseries Inc..........800 845-0584
11140 Milton Carlisle Rd New Carlisle (45344) *(G-11607)*

Studebaker Wholesale Nurseries, New Carlisle Also Called: Studebaker Nurseries Inc *(G-11607)*

Student Computer Center, Columbus Also Called: Ohio State University *(G-6457)*

Student Ln Fnding Rsources LLC..........513 763-4300
1 W 4th St Ste 200 Cincinnati (45202) *(G-3425)*

Student Loan Funding, Cincinnati Also Called: Student Ln Fnding Rsources LLC *(G-3425)*

Student Vol Opt Serv To Humnty..........614 292-9086
338 W 10th Ave Columbus (43210) *(G-6724)*

Studer-Obringer Inc..........419 492-2121
525 S Kibler St New Washington (44854) *(G-11683)*

Stuertz Machinery Inc..........330 405-0444
1624 Highland Rd Twinsburg (44087) *(G-14221)*

Sturtz Machinery, Twinsburg Also Called: Stuertz Machinery Inc *(G-14221)*

Stv Holdings Inc..........419 668-4857
650 Us Highway 20 E Norwalk (44857) *(G-12028)*

Stykemain-Buick-Gmc Ltd (PA)..........419 784-5252
25124 Elliott Rd Defiance (43512) *(G-7770)*

Style Crest Enterprises Inc (PA)..........419 355-8586
2450 Enterprise St Fremont (43420) *(G-8705)*

Style-Line Incorporated (PA)..........614 291-0600
901 W 3rd Ave Ste A Columbus (43212) *(G-6725)*

Styx Acquisition LLC..........330 264-9900
3540 Burbank Rd Wooster (44691) *(G-15378)*

Submarine House, Dayton Also Called: Sabo Inc *(G-7603)*

Subtropolis Mine, Petersburg Also Called: Subtropolis Mining Co *(G-12395)*

Subtropolis Mining Co..........330 549-2165
5455 E Garfield Rd Petersburg (44454) *(G-12395)*

Suburban Collision Centers..........440 777-1717
26618 Brookpark Road Ext North Olmsted (44070) *(G-11916)*

Suburban Maint & Cnstr Inc..........440 237-7765
16330 York Rd Ste 2 North Royalton (44133) *(G-11950)*

Suburban Oil Company..........513 459-8100
4291 State Route 741 S Mason (45040) *(G-10611)*

SUBURBAN PAVILION NURSING AND, Cleveland Also Called: Emery Leasing Co LLC *(G-4212)*

Suburban Veterinarian Clinic..........937 433-2160
102 E Spring Valley Pike Dayton (45458) *(G-7649)*

Sudhi Infomatics Inc..........855 200-6650
590 Enterprise Dr Lewis Center (43035) *(G-9836)*

Sugar & Spice Spa llc..........513 319-0112
4635 Court Yard Dr Mason (45040) *(G-10612)*

Sugar Creek Vly Frm & Game CLB..........330 492-3071
2505 Grove St Ne Canton (44721) *(G-1863)*

Sugar Valley Country Club..........937 372-4820
1250 Mead Rd Xenia (45385) *(G-15531)*

Sugarcreek Health Center, Dayton Also Called: Dayton Osteopathic Hospital *(G-7294)*

Suite224 and Cablesuite541, Conneaut Also Called: Conneaut Telephone Company *(G-6942)*

Suitelife, Columbus Also Called: Royal F & S Holdings LLC *(G-6615)*

Sullivan Bruck Architects Inc..........614 464-9800
8 S Grant Ave Columbus (43215) *(G-6726)*

Sumaria Systems LLC..........937 429-6070
3164 Presidential Dr Beavercreek (45324) *(G-909)*

Summa Akron Cy St Thmas Hsptal..........330 375-3159
525 E Market St Akron (44304) *(G-313)*

Summa Barberton Citizens Hospital..........330 615-3000
155 5th St Ne Barberton (44203) *(G-710)*

Summa Barberton Hospital, Barberton Also Called: Summa Barberton Citizens Hospital *(G-710)*

Summa Barberton Hospital, Barberton Also Called: Summa Health System *(G-713)*

Summa Care, Akron Also Called: Summa Health System *(G-318)*

Summa Health..........330 375-3315
55 Arch St Ste 1b Akron (44304) *(G-314)*

Summa Health..........330 864-8060
1 Park West Blvd Ste 130 Akron (44320) *(G-315)*

Summa Health..........330 615-5200
155 5th St Ne Barberton (44203) *(G-711)*

Summa Health..........330 753-3649
165 5th St Se Ste A Barberton (44203) *(G-712)*

Summa Health..........330 926-0384
2345 4th St Cuyahoga Falls (44221) *(G-7102)*

Summa Health..........330 836-9023
3378 W Market St # B Fairlawn (44333) *(G-8502)*

Summa Health..........330 688-4531
3869 Darrow Rd Ste 208 Stow (44224) *(G-13396)*

Summa Health..........330 899-5599
3838 Massillon Rd Ste 320 Uniontown (44685) *(G-14265)*

SUMMA HEALTH, Cuyahoga Falls Also Called: Summa Health *(G-7102)*

SUMMA HEALTH, Uniontown Also Called: Summa Health *(G-14265)*

Summa Health Center Lk Medina..........330 952-0014
3780 Medina Rd Ste 220 Medina (44256) *(G-10894)*

Summa Health System (PA)..........330 375-3000
141 N Forge St Akron (44304) *(G-316)*

Summa Health System..........330 375-3000
141 N Forge St Akron (44304) *(G-317)*

Summa Health System..........330 535-7319
1200 E Market St Ste 400 Akron (44305) *(G-318)*

Summa Health System..........330 798-5026
820 W Wilbeth Rd Akron (44314) *(G-319)*

Summa Health System..........330 928-8700
1260 Independence Ave Akron (44310) *(G-320)*

Summa Health System..........330 615-3000
155 5th St Ne Barberton (44203) *(G-713)*

Summa Health System..........330 334-1504
195 Wadsworth Rd Wadsworth (44281) *(G-14453)*

Summa Health System Corp (HQ)..........330 375-4848
95 Arch St Ste G50 Akron (44304) *(G-321)*

Summa Hlth Sys Breast Imaging, Akron Also Called: Summa Health System Corp *(G-321)*

Summa Insurance Company Inc (DH)..........800 996-8411
10 N Main St Akron (44308) *(G-322)*

Summa Park West, Akron Also Called: Summa Health *(G-315)*

Summa Purchasing Department, Akron Also Called: Summa Health System *(G-319)*

SUMMA REHAB HOSPITAL, Akron Also Called: Summa Rehab Hospital LLC *(G-323)*

Summa Rehab Hospital LLC..........330 572-7300
29 N Adams St Akron (44304) *(G-323)*

Summa Rehabilitation Services, Fairlawn Also Called: Summa Health *(G-8502)*

Summa Western Reserve Hosp LLC..........330 926-0384
2345 4th St Cuyahoga Falls (44221) *(G-7103)*

Summa Western Reserve Hosp LLC..........330 650-5110
5655 Hudson Dr Hudson (44236) *(G-9374)*

Summa Western Reserve Hosp LLC..........330 926-3337
307 W Main St Ste B Kent (44240) *(G-9600)*

Summa Western Reserve Hosp LLC..........330 633-7782
116 East Ave Ste 3 Tallmadge (44278) *(G-13605)*

Summacare, Akron Also Called: Summa Insurance Company Inc *(G-322)*

Summerville At Mentor, Mentor Also Called: Summerville Senior Living Inc *(G-11000)*

Summerville Senior Living Inc..........440 354-5499
5700 Emerald Ct Mentor (44060) *(G-11000)*

Summit Acres Inc (PA)..........740 732-2364
44565 Sunset Rd Caldwell (43724) *(G-1551)*

Summit Acres Nursing Home, Caldwell Also Called: Summit Acres Inc *(G-1551)*

Summit Bhvioral Healthcare Ctr, Cincinnati Also Called: Ohio Dept Mntal Hlth Addction *(G-3144)*

Summit County..........330 762-3500
1867 W Market St Ste B2 Akron (44313) *(G-324)*

Summit County — ALPHABETIC SECTION

Summit County 330 643-2101
85 N Summit St Akron (44308) *(G-325)*

Summit County 330 643-2850
538 E South St Akron (44311) *(G-326)*

Summit County Developmental, Tallmadge *Also Called: County of Summit (G-13590)*

Summit Enterprises Contg Corp 513 426-1623
640 N Broadway St Lebanon (45036) *(G-9791)*

Summit Facility Operations LLC 330 633-0555
330 Southwest Ave Tallmadge (44278) *(G-13606)*

Summit Financial Strategies, Columbus *Also Called: Summit Fincl Strategies Inc (G-6727)*

Summit Fincl Strategies Inc 614 885-1115
4111 Worth Ave Ste 510 Columbus (43219) *(G-6727)*

Summit Funding Group Inc (HQ) 513 489-1222
4680 Parkway Dr Ste 300 Mason (45040) *(G-10613)*

Summit Homes, Canton *Also Called: K Hovnanian Summit Homes LLC (G-1788)*

Summit Hotel Trs 144 LLC 216 443-9043
527 Prospect Ave E Cleveland (44115) *(G-4958)*

Summit Management Services Inc 330 723-0864
201 Northland Dr Ofc Medina (44256) *(G-10895)*

Summit NW, Dublin *Also Called: Summit NW Corporation (G-8134)*

Summit NW Corporation (DH) 503 255-3826
5165 Emerald Pkwy Dublin (43017) *(G-8134)*

Summit Ophthalmology Inc 330 899-9641
3838 Massillon Rd Ste 370 Uniontown (44685) *(G-14266)*

Summit Ortho Home Care 513 898-3375
4600 Mcauley Pl Ste 150 Blue Ash (45242) *(G-1246)*

Summit Quest, Dayton *Also Called: Summit Solutions Inc (G-7650)*

Summit Quest Academy, Dublin *Also Called: Viaquest Behavioral Health LLC (G-8153)*

Summit Solutions Inc 937 291-4333
446 Windsor Park Dr Dayton (45459) *(G-7650)*

Summitt Ohio Leasing Co LLC 937 436-2273
3800 Summit Glen Dr Dayton (45449) *(G-7651)*

Sumner Home For The Aged Inc (PA) 330 666-2952
4327 Cobblestone Dr Copley (44321) *(G-6964)*

Sumner On Merriman, Copley *Also Called: Sumner Home For The Aged Inc (G-6964)*

Sumser Health Care Center, Canton *Also Called: Mayflower Nursing Home Inc (G-1801)*

Sumtotal Systems LLC 352 264-2800
100 E Campus View Blvd Ste 250 Columbus (43235) *(G-6728)*

Sun Coke Energy, Franklin Furnace *Also Called: Haverhill Coke Company LLC (G-8655)*

Sun Development & Mgt Corp 614 801-9000
3951 Jackpot Rd Grove City (43123) *(G-8957)*

Sun Federal Credit Union (PA) 800 786-0945
1625 Holland Rd Maumee (43537) *(G-10772)*

Sun Lodging LLC 330 670-0888
160 Montrose West Ave Copley (44321) *(G-6965)*

Sun Pharmacy, Toledo *Also Called: Heartland Healthcare Svcs LLC (G-13842)*

Sun Yer Bunz LLC 937 222-3474
235 W Grand Ave Dayton (45405) *(G-7652)*

Sunbelt Rentals Inc 614 848-4075
1461 Polaris Pkwy Columbus (43240) *(G-5282)*

Sunbelt Rentals Inc 614 341-9770
1275 W Mound St Columbus (43223) *(G-6729)*

Sunbridge Marion Hlth Care LLC 740 389-6306
524 James Way Marion (43302) *(G-10456)*

Suncoke Energy Inc 513 727-5571
3353 Yankee Rd Middletown (45044) *(G-11188)*

Suncrest Gardens Inc 330 650-4969
5157 Akron Cleveland Rd Peninsula (44264) *(G-12294)*

Sundance Property MGT LLC (PA) 513 489-3363
9918 Carver Rd Ste 110 Blue Ash (45242) *(G-1247)*

Sundance Real Estate Holdings, Blue Ash *Also Called: Sundance Property MGT LLC (G-1247)*

Sunesis Construction Co 513 326-6000
2610 Crescentville Rd West Chester (45069) *(G-14770)*

Sunesis Environmental LLC 513 326-6000
325 Commercial Dr Fairfield (45014) *(G-8444)*

Sunny Slope Nursing Home, Bowerston *Also Called: Carriage Inn Bowerston Inc (G-1301)*

Sunny View Nursing Home, Zanesville *Also Called: Careserve (G-15776)*

Sunnyside Cars Inc 440 777-9911
27000 Lorain Rd North Olmsted (44070) *(G-11917)*

Sunohio Inc 330 477-6769
1515 Bank Pl Sw Canton (44706) *(G-1864)*

Sunpower Inc 740 594-2221
2005 E State St Ste 104 Athens (45701) *(G-592)*

Sunrise At Parma, Cleveland *Also Called: Sunrise Senior Living LLC (G-4961)*

Sunrise At Shaker Heights, Cleveland *Also Called: Sunrise Senior Living LLC (G-4962)*

Sunrise Connecticut Ave Assn 614 451-6766
4590 Knightsbridge Blvd Columbus (43214) *(G-6730)*

Sunrise Cooperative Inc 419 683-7340
3000 W Bucyrus St Crestline (44827) *(G-7026)*

Sunrise Development Co (DH) 216 621-6060
1200 Terminal Tower Cleveland (44113) *(G-4959)*

Sunrise Healthcare Group LLC 216 662-3343
19900 Clare Ave Maple Heights (44137) *(G-10349)*

Sunrise Homes, Lisbon *Also Called: Mikouis Enterprise Inc (G-10005)*

Sunrise Hospitality Inc 567 331-8900
27355 Carronade Dr Perrysburg (43551) *(G-12372)*

Sunrise Hospitality Inc 567 331-8613
27355 Carronade Dr Perrysburg (43551) *(G-12373)*

Sunrise Hospitality Inc 937 492-6010
450 Folkerth Ave Sidney (45365) *(G-13056)*

Sunrise Industries Harps Jantr, Warren *Also Called: Turn Around Group Inc (G-14568)*

Sunrise Land Co (DH) 216 621-6060
1250 Terminal Tower 50 Public Sq Cleveland (44113) *(G-4960)*

Sunrise Nursing Healthcare LLC 513 797-5144
3434 State Route 132 Amelia (45102) *(G-420)*

Sunrise of Cuyahoga Falls, Cuyahoga Falls *Also Called: Sunrise Senior Living LLC (G-7104)*

Sunrise of Dublin, Dublin *Also Called: Sunrise Senior Living LLC (G-8135)*

Sunrise of Findlay, Findlay *Also Called: Sunrise Senior Living LLC (G-8590)*

Sunrise of Gahanna, Gahanna *Also Called: Sunrise Senior Living LLC (G-8731)*

Sunrise of Hamilton, Hamilton *Also Called: Sunrise Senior Living LLC (G-9084)*

Sunrise of Poland, Poland *Also Called: Sunrise Senior Living LLC (G-12510)*

Sunrise of Rocky River, Rocky River *Also Called: Sunrise Senior Living LLC (G-12753)*

Sunrise On The Scioto, Upper Arlington *Also Called: Sunrise Senior Living LLC (G-14282)*

Sunrise Pnte Care Rhblttion Ct, Maple Heights *Also Called: Sunrise Healthcare Group LLC (G-10349)*

Sunrise Senior Living LLC 216 447-8909
7766 Broadview Rd Cleveland (44134) *(G-4961)*

Sunrise Senior Living LLC 216 751-0930
16333 Chagrin Blvd Cleveland (44120) *(G-4962)*

Sunrise Senior Living LLC 330 929-8500
1500 State Rd Cuyahoga Falls (44223) *(G-7104)*

Sunrise Senior Living LLC 937 438-0054
6800 Paragon Rd Ofc Dayton (45459) *(G-7653)*

Sunrise Senior Living LLC 614 718-2062
4175 Stoneridge Ln Dublin (43017) *(G-8135)*

Sunrise Senior Living LLC 937 836-9617
95 W Wenger Rd Englewood (45322) *(G-8323)*

Sunrise Senior Living LLC 419 425-3440
401 Lake Cascade Pkwy Findlay (45840) *(G-8590)*

Sunrise Senior Living LLC 614 418-9775
775 E Johnstown Rd Gahanna (43230) *(G-8731)*

Sunrise Senior Living LLC 513 893-9000
896 Nw Washington Blvd Hamilton (45013) *(G-9084)*

Sunrise Senior Living LLC 330 707-1313
335 W Mckinley Way Poland (44514) *(G-12510)*

Sunrise Senior Living LLC 440 895-2383
21600 Detroit Rd Rocky River (44116) *(G-12753)*

Sunrise Senior Living LLC 614 457-3500
3500 Riverside Dr Upper Arlington (43221) *(G-14282)*

Sunrise Senior Living LLC 440 808-0074
27819 Center Ridge Rd Ofc Westlake (44145) *(G-15112)*

Sunrise Senior Living MGT Inc 614 235-3900
2600 E Main St Columbus (43209) *(G-6731)*

Sunrise Treatment Center LLC (PA) 513 941-4999
6460 Harrison Ave Ste 100 Cincinnati (45247) *(G-3426)*

Sunrise Treatment Center LLC 513 595-5340
680 Northland Blvd Cincinnati (45240) *(G-3427)*

Sunrise Treatment Center LLC 513 217-4676
160 N Breiel Blvd Middletown (45042) *(G-11189)*

ALPHABETIC SECTION — Swaco

Sunrise Vista Hlth & Wellnesss, Canton *Also Called: N Market Behavioral Hosp LLC (G-1815)*

Sunset Hills Cemetery Corp 330 494-2051
5001 Everhard Rd Nw Canton (44718) *(G-1865)*

Sunset House Inc 419 536-4645
4020 Indian Rd Toledo (43606) *(G-14029)*

Sunset Mnor Hlthcare Group Inc 216 795-5710
1802 Crawford Rd Cleveland (44106) *(G-4963)*

Sunset Nursing Center, Ironton *Also Called: Coal Grove Long Term Care Inc (G-9506)*

Sunshine Communities (PA) 419 865-0251
7223 Maumee Western Rd Maumee (43537) *(G-10773)*

Sunshine Inc. Northwest Ohio, Maumee *Also Called: Sunshine Communities (G-10773)*

Sunshine Nursery School, Columbus *Also Called: Christian Missionary Alliance (G-5570)*

Sunsong North America Inc 919 365-3825
3535 Kettering Blvd Moraine (45439) *(G-11441)*

Suntan Supply, Avon *Also Called: JLW - TW Corp (G-657)*

Suntan Supply, Cleveland *Also Called: J L Wilson Co (G-4426)*

Suntwist Corp 800 935-3534
5461 Dunham Rd Maple Heights (44137) *(G-10350)*

Super 8 .... 419 529-0444
736 Us Highway 250 E Ashland (44805) *(G-513)*

Super 8 Motel, Ashland *Also Called: Super 8 (G-513)*

Super 8 Motel, Marion *Also Called: Priya Pvt Ltd (G-10450)*

Super 8 Motel, Saint Clairsville *Also Called: Doro Inc (G-12790)*

Super 8 Motel, Sandusky *Also Called: Lodging Industry Inc (G-12911)*

Super 8 Motel Columbus North, Columbus *Also Called: Northland Hotel Inc (G-6368)*

Super Shine Inc 513 423-8999
1549 S Breiel Blvd Ste A Middletown (45044) *(G-11190)*

Super Systems Inc (PA) 513 772-0060
7205 Edington Dr Cincinnati (45249) *(G-3428)*

Superior Ar-Grund Amblnce Svc 630 832-2000
2160 Southwest Blvd Grove City (43123) *(G-8958)*

Superior Bev Group Centl Ohio, Lewis Center *Also Called: Central Beverage Group Ltd (G-9813)*

Superior Beverage Group Ltd 419 529-0702
32 Eagle Dr Unit A Lexington (44904) *(G-9845)*

Superior Dental Care Inc 937 438-0283
6683 Centerville Business Pkwy Dayton (45459) *(G-7654)*

Superior Envmtl Sltons SES Inc 513 874-6910
9976 Joseph James Dr West Chester (45246) *(G-14835)*

Superior Envmtl Solutions LLC 937 593-0425
471 County Road 32 N Bellefontaine (43311) *(G-1038)*

Superior Envmtl Solutions LLC (PA) 513 874-8355
9996 Joseph James Dr West Chester (45246) *(G-14836)*

Superior Health Center, Cleveland *Also Called: Northast Ohio Nghbrhood Hlth S (G-4654)*

Superior Holding LLC (DH) 216 651-9400
3786 Ridge Rd Cleveland (44144) *(G-4964)*

Superior Marine Ways Inc 740 894-6224
5852 County Rd 1 Suoth Pt Proctorville (45669) *(G-12613)*

Superior Med LLC (PA) 740 439-8839
1251 Clark St Cambridge (43725) *(G-1585)*

Superior Paving & Materials 330 499-5849
5947 Whipple Ave Nw Canton (44720) *(G-1866)*

Superior Products LLC 216 651-9400
3786 Ridge Rd Cleveland (44144) *(G-4965)*

Superior Walls of Ohio Inc 330 393-4101
1401 Pine Ave Se Warren (44483) *(G-14562)*

Superior Water Conditioning Co, Moraine *Also Called: Enting Water Conditioning Inc (G-11407)*

Superior Wholesale Distrs, Lima *Also Called: Swd Corporation (G-9968)*

Superior's Brand Meats, Massillon *Also Called: Fresh Mark Inc (G-10641)*

Superkids Reading Program, Columbus *Also Called: Zaner-Bloser Inc (G-6918)*

Supernova Lgstic Solutions LLC 937 369-8618
5850 Shady Cove Ln Dayton (45426) *(G-7655)*

Supershuttle, Cleveland *Also Called: Ace Taxi Service Inc (G-3762)*

Supplemental Healthcare 937 247-0169
10050 Innovation Dr Ste 320 Miamisburg (45342) *(G-11096)*

Supply Technologies LLC (HQ) 440 947-2100
6065 Parkland Blvd Ste 1 Cleveland (44124) *(G-4966)*

Supply Technologies LLC 937 898-5795
6675 Homestretch Rd Dayton (45414) *(G-7656)*

Supply Technologies LLC 440 248-8170
5370 Naiman Pkwy Solon (44139) *(G-13151)*

Supplyone Retail, Cleveland *Also Called: Cleveland Supplyone Inc (G-4068)*

Supportcare Ohio, Dublin *Also Called: Viaquest Residential Svcs LLC (G-8154)*

Supportive Healthcare, Cincinnati *Also Called: Medical Housecalls LLC (G-3027)*

Supreme Acquisition Holdg LLC 330 906-2509
6545 Market Ave N Ste 100 Canton (44721) *(G-1867)*

Supreme Touch Home Health Svcs 614 783-1115
2547 W Broad St Columbus (43204) *(G-6732)*

Supreme Ventures LLC 614 372-0355
3034 Lamb Ave Columbus (43219) *(G-6733)*

Supreme Xpress Trnsp Inc 234 738-4047
810 S Main St Ste 159 Akron (44311) *(G-327)*

Sure Home Improvements LLC 614 975-7727
6031 E Main St Columbus (43213) *(G-6734)*

Surepoint Technologies, Cincinnati *Also Called: Rippe & Kingston Systems Inc (G-3299)*

Sureshot Communications LLC 216 496-6100
3500 Payne Ave Ste Mb Cleveland (44114) *(G-4967)*

Surfside Motors Inc (PA) 419 419-4776
7459 State Route 309 Galion (44833) *(G-8751)*

Surge Management LLC 614 431-5100
4 Easton Oval Columbus (43219) *(G-6735)*

Surgeforce LLC 614 431-4991
4 Easton Oval Columbus (43219) *(G-6736)*

Surgere LLC 330 966-3746
3500 Massillon Rd Ste 100 Uniontown (44685) *(G-14267)*

Surgery Alliance Ltd 330 821-7997
975 S Sawburg Ave Alliance (44601) *(G-403)*

Surgery Center, Cincinnati *Also Called: Christ Hospital (G-2382)*

Surgery Center Canfield LLC 330 449-0030
4147 Westford Pl Canfield (44406) *(G-1642)*

Surgery Center, The, Cleveland *Also Called: Surgery Ctr An Ohio Ltd Partnr (G-4968)*

Surgery Ctr An Ohio Ltd Partnr 440 826-3240
19250 Bagley Rd Cleveland (44130) *(G-4968)*

Surgery Ctr At Southwoods LLC 330 729-8000
7630 Southern Blvd Youngstown (44512) *(G-15732)*

Surgical Assoc Springfield Inc 937 521-1111
30 Warder St Ste 220 Springfield (45504) *(G-13297)*

Surgical Associates Inc 740 453-0661
2916 Vangader Dr Zanesville (43701) *(G-15831)*

Surgical Assocs of Zanesville, Zanesville *Also Called: Surgical Associates Inc (G-15831)*

Surgical Hosp At Southwoods, Youngstown *Also Called: Surgery Ctr At Southwoods LLC (G-15732)*

Surgical Partners Inc 419 841-6600
4235 Secor Rd Toledo (43623) *(G-14030)*

Surveying and Mapping LLC 512 447-0575
929 Eastwind Dr Ste 201 Westerville (43081) *(G-15016)*

Sustain LLC 888 525-0029
4547 Bentwood Rd New Waterford (44445) *(G-11684)*

Sutherland Building Pdts Inc 740 477-2244
460 Lancaster Pike Circleville (43113) *(G-3725)*

Sutphen, Dublin *Also Called: Sutphen Corporation (G-8136)*

Sutphen Corporation (PA) 800 726-7030
6450 Eiterman Rd Dublin (43016) *(G-8136)*

Sutphen Towers Inc 614 876-1262
4500 Sutphen Ct Hilliard (43026) *(G-9234)*

Sutter OConnell Co 216 928-4504
1301 E 9th St Ste 36 Cleveland (44114) *(G-4969)*

Sutton & Associates Inc 614 487-9096
2250 Mckinley Ave Columbus (43204) *(G-6737)*

Svats Inc 614 214-4115
589 Carle Ave Lewis Center (43035) *(G-9837)*

SW Griffin Co LLC 513 601-3894
4910 Hunt Rd Unit 2328 Blue Ash (45242) *(G-1248)*

SW Griffin Co Llc 513 678-4741
4910 Hunt Rd Blue Ash (45242) *(G-1249)*

SW Squared LLC 614 300-5304
1410 Williams Rd Columbus (43207) *(G-6738)*

Swa Inc 440 243-7888
7250 Old Oak Blvd Cleveland (44130) *(G-4970)*

Swaco, Grove City *Also Called: Solid Waste Auth Centl Ohio (G-8956)*

Swagelok Company — ALPHABETIC SECTION

Swagelok Company 440 349-5962
29495 F A Lennon Dr Solon (44139) *(G-13152)*

Swagelok Company 440 542-1250
32550 Old South Miles Rd Solon (44139) *(G-13153)*

Swagelok Company 440 349-5934
29495 F A Lennon Dr Solon (44139) *(G-13154)*

Swan Creek Retirement Village, Toledo *Also Called: Ohio Living (G-13946)*

Swan Point Care Center, Maumee *Also Called: Consulate Management Co LLC (G-10712)*

Swanton Hlth Care Rtrment Ctr 419 825-1145
214 S Munson Rd Swanton (43558) *(G-13529)*

Swanton Vly Care Rhblttion Ctr, Swanton *Also Called: Harborside Healthcare LLC (G-13526)*

Swapalease Inc 513 381-0100
11224 Cornell Park Dr Blue Ash (45242) *(G-1250)*

Swapalease.com, Blue Ash *Also Called: Swapalease Inc (G-1250)*

Swd Corporation 419 227-2436
435 N Main St Lima (45801) *(G-9968)*

Swift Filters Inc (PA) 440 735-0995
24040 Forbes Rd Oakwood Village (44146) *(G-12058)*

Swiminc Incorporated 614 885-1619
400 W Dublin Granville Rd Worthington (43085) *(G-15460)*

Swingle J and P Plumbing & Htg 330 723-4840
645 Lafayette Rd Medina (44256) *(G-10896)*

Swingle Mechanical Contractors, Medina *Also Called: Swingle J and P Plumbing & Htg (G-10896)*

Swings N Things Family Fun Pk, Olmsted Twp *Also Called: Strike Zone Inc (G-12094)*

Swiss Tech Products, Solon *Also Called: Interdesign Inc (G-13101)*

Switchbox Inc 614 334-9517
4500 Mobile Dr Columbus (43220) *(G-6739)*

Swrh Physicians Inc 330 923-5899
3913 Darrow Rd Stow (44224) *(G-13397)*

Sws Environmental Service Inc 513 793-7417
5770 Park Rd Cincinnati (45243) *(G-3429)*

Swx Enterprises Inc 216 676-4600
5231 Engle Rd Brookpark (44142) *(G-1441)*

Sycamore Board of Education 513 489-3937
9609 Montgomery Rd Montgomery (45242) *(G-11375)*

Sycamore Creek Country Club 937 748-0791
8300 Country Club Ln Springboro (45066) *(G-13208)*

Sycamore Lake Inc 440 729-9775
10620 Mayfield Rd Chesterland (44026) *(G-2043)*

Sycamore Medical Center, Miamisburg *Also Called: Kettering Medical Center (G-11066)*

Sycamore Senior Center (PA) 513 984-1234
4455 Carver Woods Dr Blue Ash (45242) *(G-1251)*

Sygma, Columbus *Also Called: Sygma Network Inc (G-6740)*

Sygma, Dublin *Also Called: Sygma Network Inc (G-8137)*

Sygma Network Inc (HQ) 614 734-2500
5550 Blazer Pkwy Ste 300 Dublin (43017) *(G-8137)*

Sygma Network Inc 614 771-3801
2400 Harrison Rd Columbus (43204) *(G-6740)*

Sylvania Center, Sylvania *Also Called: Harborside Sylvania LLC (G-13548)*

Sylvania Cmnty Svcs Ctr Inc 419 885-2451
4747 N Holland Sylvania Rd Sylvania (43560) *(G-13574)*

Sylvania Country Club 419 392-0530
5201 Corey Rd Sylvania (43560) *(G-13575)*

Sylvania Franciscan Health 419 824-3674
5942 Renaissance Pl Ste A Toledo (43623) *(G-14031)*

Sylvania Veterinary Hospital (PA) 419 885-4421
4801 N Holland Sylvania Rd Sylvania (43560) *(G-13576)*

Sylvester Highland Holding Inc 440 473-1640
699 Miner Rd Cleveland (44143) *(G-4971)*

Symba & Snap Gourmet Foods Inc 407 252-9581
2275 E 55th St Cleveland (44103) *(G-4972)*

Symphony Dagnstc Svcs No 1 LLC 614 888-2226
6185 Huntley Rd Ste Q Columbus (43229) *(G-6741)*

Synapse Tech Services Inc 337 592-3205
4449 Easton Way Ste 200 Columbus (43219) *(G-6742)*

Syncreon America Inc 419 727-4593
1515 Matzinger Rd Toledo (43612) *(G-14032)*

SYNCREON AMERICA INC., Toledo *Also Called: Syncreon America Inc (G-14032)*

Syneos Health Communications Inc (DH) 614 543-6650
500 Olde Worthington Rd Westerville (43082) *(G-14939)*

Synerfac Inc 614 416-6010
440 Polaris Pkwy Ste 130 Westerville (43082) *(G-14940)*

Synergy Health North America Inc 813 891-9550
5960 Heisley Rd Mentor (44060) *(G-11001)*

Synergy Homecare 937 610-0555
501 Windsor Park Dr Dayton (45459) *(G-7657)*

Synergy Homecare of Westlake, Lakewood *Also Called: Jmo & Dsl Llc (G-9670)*

Synergy Homecare South Dayton, Dayton *Also Called: Synergy Homecare (G-7657)*

Synergy Hotels LLC 614 492-9000
4870 Old Rathmell Ct Obetz (43207) *(G-12084)*

Synthomer Inc 330 794-6300
2990 Gilchrist Rd Akron (44305) *(G-328)*

Synthomer LLC 678 400-6655
25435 Harvard Rd Beachwood (44122) *(G-842)*

Sysco, Cincinnati *Also Called: Sysco Cincinnati LLC (G-3430)*

Sysco, Cleveland *Also Called: Sysco Cleveland Inc (G-4973)*

Sysco, Columbus *Also Called: Sysco Central Ohio Inc (G-6743)*

Sysco Central Ohio Inc
2400 Harrison Rd Columbus (43204) *(G-6743)*

Sysco Cincinnati LLC 513 563-6300
10510 Evendale Dr Cincinnati (45241) *(G-3430)*

Sysco Cleveland Inc (HQ) 216 201-3000
4747 Grayton Rd Cleveland (44135) *(G-4973)*

Sysco Guest Supply LLC 614 539-9348
3330 Urbancrest Industrial Dr Urbancrest (43123) *(G-14323)*

System EDM of Ohio, Mason *Also Called: Hi-Tek Manufacturing Inc (G-10562)*

System Optics Csmt Srgcal Arts 330 630-9699
518 West Ave Tallmadge (44278) *(G-13607)*

System Seals Inc 216 220-1800
6600 W Snowville Rd Brecksville (44141) *(G-1369)*

Systemax Manufacturing Inc 937 368-2300
6450 Poe Ave Ste 200 Dayton (45414) *(G-7658)*

Systems Evolution Inc (PA) 513 459-1992
11500 Northlake Dr Ste 450 Cincinnati (45249) *(G-3431)*

Systems Pack Inc 330 467-5729
649 Highland Rd E Macedonia (44056) *(G-10207)*

Sytronics Inc 937 431-6100
4433 Dayton Xenia Rd Bldg 1 Beavercreek (45432) *(G-910)*

T & F Systems Inc
1599 E 40th St Cleveland (44103) *(G-4974)*

T & L Enterprises Inc 440 234-5900
1060 W Bagley Rd Ste 101 Berea (44017) *(G-1083)*

T & R Properties (PA) 614 923-4000
3895 Stoneridge Ln Dublin (43017) *(G-8138)*

T & R Property Management, Dublin *Also Called: T & R Properties (G-8138)*

T Allen Inc 440 234-2366
200 Depot St Berea (44017) *(G-1084)*

T and D Interiors Incorporated 419 331-4372
3626 Allentown Rd Lima (45807) *(G-9969)*

T C P, Aurora *Also Called: Technical Consumer Pdts Inc (G-628)*

T E S - East, Versailles *Also Called: Bnsf Logistics LLC (G-14413)*

T I G Fleet Service Inc 419 250-6333
7401 Fremont Pike Perrysburg (43551) *(G-12374)*

T J Automation Inc 419 267-5687
U075 State Route 66 Archbold (43502) *(G-468)*

T J Neff Holdings Inc 440 884-3100
6405 York Rd Cleveland (44130) *(G-4975)*

T L C Packaging Inc 330 722-7622
1077 Ty Dr Medina (44256) *(G-10897)*

T M I, Cincinnati *Also Called: TMI Electrical Contractors Inc (G-3482)*

T M S, Cincinnati *Also Called: Modal Shop Inc (G-3073)*

T O J Inc (PA) 440 352-1900
6011 Heisley Rd Mentor (44060) *(G-11002)*

T P McHncal Cntrs Svc Fbrction, Columbus *Also Called: TP Mechanical Contractors Inc (G-6777)*

T S Expediting Services Inc (PA) 419 837-2401
27681 Cummings Rd Millbury (43447) *(G-11271)*

T S G, Dublin *Also Called: Empire Food Brokers Inc (G-8003)*

T W I International Inc (DH) 440 439-1830
24460 Aurora Rd Cleveland (44146) *(G-4976)*

T W Ruff, Columbus Also Called: Loth Inc (G-6173)
T-Cetra LLC 877 956-2359
  7240 Muirfield Dr Ste 200 Dublin (43017) (G-8139)
T-Mobile 740 500-4250
  511 E Main St Circleville (43113) (G-3726)
T-Mobile Central LLC 513 855-3170
  8234 Princeton Glendale Rd West Chester (45069) (G-14771)
T-Shirt City, Cincinnati Also Called: TSC Apparel LLC (G-3534)
T&B Manufacturing, Miamiville Also Called: Aim Mro Holdings LLC (G-11108)
T&L Global Management LLC 614 586-0303
  1572 Lafayette Dr Columbus (43220) (G-6744)
T&T Enterprises of Ohio Inc 513 942-1141
  5100 Duff Dr West Chester (45246) (G-14837)
T2 Financial LLC 614 697-2021
  579 Executive Campus Dr Westerville (43082) (G-14941)
Ta Operating LLC (DH) 440 808-9100
  24601 Center Ridge Rd Ste 200 Westlake (44145) (G-15113)
Tab Construction Company Inc 330 454-5228
  530 Walnut Ave Ne Canton (44702) (G-1868)
Tabco Consulting Services LLC 740 217-0010
  700 Morse Rd Ste 210 Columbus (43214) (G-6745)
Table Rock Golf Club Inc 740 625-6859
  3005 Wilson Rd Centerburg (43011) (G-1937)
TAC Industries Inc 937 328-5200
  2160 Old Selma Rd Springfield (45505) (G-13298)
TAC Industries Inc (PA) 937 328-5200
  2160 Old Selma Rd Springfield (45505) (G-13299)
TAC Worldwide Companies, Cincinnati Also Called: Technical Aid Corporation (G-3448)
Tacg, Beavercreek Also Called: Tacg LLC (G-931)
Tacg LLC (PA) 937 203-8201
  1430 Oak Ct Ste 100 Beavercreek (45430) (G-931)
Taft Law, Dayton Also Called: Nicholas E Davis (G-7530)
Taft Museum of Art 513 241-0343
  316 Pike St Cincinnati (45202) (G-3432)
Taft Stettinius Hollister LLP (PA) 513 381-2838
  425 Walnut St Ste 1800 Cincinnati (45202) (G-3433)
Tahoma Enterprises Inc (PA) 330 745-9016
  255 Wooster Rd N Barberton (44203) (G-714)
Tahoma Rubber & Plastics Inc (HQ) 330 745-9016
  255 Wooster Rd N Barberton (44203) (G-715)
Tailored Healthcare Staffing, Cincinnati Also Called: Health Carousel LLC (G-2808)
Tailored Management, Columbus Also Called: Tailored Management Services (G-6746)
Tailored Management Services (PA) 614 859-1500
  1165 Dublin Rd Columbus (43215) (G-6746)
Taitech Inc 937 255-4141
  Wright Patterson Afb Fairborn (45324) (G-8381)
Takkt Foodservices LLC (PA) 513 367-8600
  9555 Dry Fork Rd Harrison (45030) (G-9116)
Talawanda City School District 513 273-3200
  5301 University Park Blvd Oxford (45056) (G-12218)
Talawanda H S, Oxford Also Called: Talawanda City School District (G-12218)
Talbert House 513 872-8870
  3009 Burnet Ave Cincinnati (45219) (G-3434)
Talbert House 513 541-1184
  1611 Emerson Ave Cincinnati (45239) (G-3435)
Talbert House 513 751-7747
  5837 Hamilton Ave Cincinnati (45224) (G-3436)
Talbert House 513 541-0127
  1817 Logan St Apt 508 Cincinnati (45202) (G-3437)
Talbert House 513 221-2398
  2880 Central Pkwy Cincinnati (45225) (G-3438)
Talbert House (PA) 513 872-5863
  2600 Victory Pkwy Cincinnati (45206) (G-3439)
Talbert House 513 629-2303
  1617 Reading Rd Cincinnati (45202) (G-3440)
Talbert House 513 684-7968
  328 Mcgregor Ave Ste 106 Cincinnati (45219) (G-3441)
Talbert House 513 933-9304
  5234 W State Route 63 Lebanon (45036) (G-9792)
Talbert House, Cincinnati Also Called: Talbert House (G-3441)

Talbert House Health (HQ) 513 541-7577
  4868 Glenway Ave Cincinnati (45238) (G-3442)
Talemed, Loveland Also Called: Triage LLC (G-10165)
Talentlaunch, Independence Also Called: Alliance Solutions Group LLC (G-9402)
Taleris Credit Union Inc 216 739-2300
  6111 Oak Tree Blvd Ste 110 Independence (44131) (G-9489)
Talis Clinical LLC 234 284-2399
  650 Mondial Pkwy Streetsboro (44241) (G-13431)
Tallmadge Asphalt and Paving Company Inc 330 677-0000
  741 Tallmadge Rd Kent (44240) (G-9601)
Tallmadge Collision Center (PA) 330 630-2188
  195 Northeast Ave Tallmadge (44278) (G-13608)
Tallmadge Reacreation Center, Tallmadge Also Called: City of Tallmadge (G-13588)
Talx Corporation 614 527-9404
  3455 Mill Run Dr Hilliard (43026) (G-9235)
Tam-O-Shanter Sports Complex, Sylvania Also Called: City of Sylvania (G-13539)
Tameran, Solon Also Called: Tameran Graphic Systems Inc (G-13155)
Tameran Graphic Systems Inc 440 349-7100
  30300 Solon Industrial Pkwy Ste F Solon (44139) (G-13155)
Tangoe Us Inc 614 842-9918
  200 E Campus View Blvd Columbus (43235) (G-6747)
Tangram Flex Inc 937 985-3199
  607 E 3rd St Ste 500 Dayton (45402) (G-7659)
Tanner Heating & AC Inc 937 299-2500
  2238 E River Rd Moraine (45439) (G-11442)
Tansky Motors Inc (PA) 650 322-7069
  11973 Dalton Rd Rockbridge (43149) (G-12736)
Tansky Sales Inc 614 793-2080
  2475 W Dublin Granville Rd Columbus (43235) (G-6748)
Tanskys Auto Body & Paint Ctr, Columbus Also Called: Tansky Sales Inc (G-6748)
Tanyas Image & Wellness Salon, Cincinnati Also Called: Tanyas Image LLC (G-3443)
Tanyas Image LLC (PA) 513 386-9981
  2716 Erie Ave Ste 3 Cincinnati (45208) (G-3443)
Tapco Tube Co Inc 330 576-1750
  6600 Ridge Rd Wadsworth (44281) (G-14454)
Tappan Lake Marina Inc 740 269-2031
  33315 Cadiz Dennison Rd Scio (43988) (G-12943)
Tappan Marina, Scio Also Called: Tappan Lake Marina Inc (G-12943)
Target Systems Inc 440 239-1600
  7819 Freeway Cir Cleveland (44130) (G-4977)
Tarrier, Columbus Also Called: Tarrier Foods Corp (G-6749)
Tarrier Foods Corp 614 876-8594
  2700 International St Columbus (43228) (G-6749)
Tarta, Toledo Also Called: Toledo Area Rgional Trnst Auth (G-14050)
Tartan Fields Golf Club Ltd 614 792-0900
  8070 Tartan Fields Dr Dublin (43017) (G-8140)
TAS Aviation Defiance Inc 419 658-4444
  20399 Airport Rd Defiance (43512) (G-7771)
TAS Inc 419 693-3353
  433 Dearborn Ave Toledo (43605) (G-14033)
Tasty Pure Food Company (PA) 330 434-8141
  1557 Industrial Pkwy Akron (44310) (G-329)
Tata America Intl Corp 513 677-6500
  1000 Summit Dr Unit 1 Milford (45150) (G-11259)
Tata Consultancy Services, Milford Also Called: Tata America Intl Corp (G-11259)
Tata Consultancy Services Ltd 515 553-8300
  4270 Ivy Pointe Blvd Ste 400 Cincinnati (45245) (G-2114)
Taylor Chevrolet Inc 740 653-2091
  1164 Stone Run Ct Lancaster (43130) (G-9746)
Taylor CJ Development Inc 330 628-5501
  3470 Gilchrist Rd Mogadore (44260) (G-11332)
Taylor Coil Processing, Warren Also Called: Taylor Steel Inc (G-14563)
Taylor Companies Ohio Inc 330 677-8380
  4200 Mogadore Rd Kent (44240) (G-9602)
Taylor Dealership, Lancaster Also Called: Taylor Chevrolet Inc (G-9746)
Taylor Distributing Company 513 771-1850
  9756 International Blvd West Chester (45246) (G-14838)
Taylor Logistics Inc (PA) 513 771-1850
  9756 International Blvd West Chester (45246) (G-14839)
Taylor Murtis Human Svcs Sys (PA) 216 283-4400
  13422 Kinsman Rd Cleveland (44120) (G-4978)

Taylor Murtis Human Svcs Sys 216 283-4400
  12395 Mccracken Rd Cleveland (44125) (G-4979)
Taylor Station Surgical Center, Columbus Also Called: Taylor Stn Surgical Ctr Ltd (G-6750)
Taylor Steel Inc 330 824-8600
  2260 Industrial Trce Sw Warren (44481) (G-14563)
Taylor Stn Surgical Ctr Ltd 614 751-4466
  275 Taylor Station Rd Unit A Columbus (43213) (G-6750)
Taylor Warehouse Corporation 513 771-1850
  9287 Meridian Way West Chester (45069) (G-14772)
Taylor Warehouse Corporation (PA) 513 771-1850
  9756 International Blvd West Chester (45246) (G-14840)
Taylor Warehouse Corporation, West Chester Also Called: Taylor Warehouse Corporation (G-14772)
Tazmanian Freight Fwdg Inc (PA) 216 265-7881
  6640 Engle Rd Ste H Middleburg Heights (44130) (G-11130)
Tazmanian Freight Systems, Middleburg Heights Also Called: Tazmanian Freight Fwdg Inc (G-11130)
Tbc Retail Group Inc 216 267-8040
  5370 W 130th St Cleveland (44142) (G-4980)
Tc Architects Inc 330 867-1093
  430 Grant St Akron (44311) (G-330)
Tccc Inc (PA) 513 779-1111
  9624 Cincinnati Columbus Rd West Chester (45241) (G-14841)
TCI 513 557-3200
  415 Greenwell Ave Cincinnati (45238) (G-3444)
Tcn Behavioral Health Svcs Inc (PA) 937 376-8700
  452 W Market St Xenia (45385) (G-15532)
TCS, Cincinnati Also Called: Trans-Continental Systems Inc (G-3500)
Tdg Facilities LLC 513 834-6105
  11400 Rockfield Ct Cincinnati (45241) (G-3445)
Tdk Refrigeration Leasing, Delphos Also Called: All Temp Refrigeration Inc (G-7836)
Team Fishel, Columbus Also Called: Fishel Company (G-5868)
Team Green Lawn LLC 937 673-4315
  1070 Union Rd Xenia (45385) (G-15533)
Team Health Holdings Inc 937 252-2000
  6229 Troy Pike Dayton (45424) (G-7660)
Team Lubrication Inc 614 231-9909
  921 Robinwood Ave Ste C Columbus (43213) (G-6751)
Team Rahal Inc 614 529-7000
  4601 Lyman Dr Hilliard (43026) (G-9236)
Team Special, West Chester Also Called: Fishel Company (G-14812)
Teamdynamix, Columbus Also Called: Teamdynamix Solutions LLC (G-6752)
Teamdynamix Solutions LLC 877 752-6196
  1600 Dublin Rd Ste 200 Columbus (43215) (G-6752)
Teasdale Fnton Crpt Clg Rstrti 513 797-0900
  12145 Centron Pl Cincinnati (45246) (G-3446)
Teater Orthopedic Surgeons 330 343-3335
  515 Union Ave Ste 167 Dover (44622) (G-7903)
Teater, Thomas L MD, Dover Also Called: Teater Orthopedic Surgeons (G-7903)
Teating Mueting & Klekamp Pll 513 579-6462
  1 E 4th St Ste 1400 Cincinnati (45202) (G-3447)
Tebo Financial Services Inc 234 207-2500
  4740 Belpar St Nw Ste A Canton (44718) (G-1869)
Tech Elevator Inc 216 310-3497
  7100 Euclid Ave Ste 140 Cleveland (44103) (G-4981)
Tech International, Johnstown Also Called: Technical Rubber Company Inc (G-9549)
Technical Aid Corporation (DH) 781 251-8000
  201 E 4th St Ste 800 Cincinnati (45202) (G-3448)
Technical Assurance Inc 440 953-3147
  38112 2nd St Willoughby (44094) (G-15222)
Technical Consumer Pdts Inc 330 995-6111
  325 Campus Dr Aurora (44202) (G-628)
Technical Rubber Company Inc (PA) 740 967-9015
  200 E Coshocton St Johnstown (43031) (G-9549)
Technical Youth, Cincinnati Also Called: Eight Eleven Group LLC (G-2607)
Technique Roofing Systems LLC 419 680-2025
  290 Main St Helena (43435) (G-9157)
Technology Hub, Columbus Also Called: Km2 Solutions LLC (G-6122)
Technology Recovery Group Ltd (PA) 440 250-9970
  31390 Viking Pkwy Westlake (44145) (G-15114)

TECHSOLVE, Cincinnati Also Called: Techsolve Inc (G-3449)
Techsolve Inc 513 948-2000
  6705 Steger Dr Cincinnati (45237) (G-3449)
Tecoglas Inc 419 537-9750
  3400 Executive Pkwy Ste 4 Toledo (43606) (G-14034)
Tecta America Kentucky, Cincinnati Also Called: Tecta America Zero Company LLC (G-3450)
Tecta America Zero Company LLC (HQ) 513 541-1848
  6225 Wiehe Rd Cincinnati (45237) (G-3450)
Tegam, Geneva Also Called: Tegam Inc (G-8789)
Tegam Inc (HQ) 440 466-6100
  10 Tegam Way Geneva (44041) (G-8789)
Tegna Inc 419 248-1111
  730 N Summit St Toledo (43604) (G-14035)
Tek Logistics LLC 614 260-9250
  4557 Belvedere Park Columbus (43228) (G-6753)
Tek-Collect Incorporated 614 299-2766
  871 Park St Columbus (43215) (G-6754)
Tekni-Plex Inc 419 491-2399
  1445 Timber Wolf Dr Holland (43528) (G-9307)
Teknobility LLC 216 255-9433
  3013 Gary Kyle Ct Medina (44256) (G-10898)
Teknol Inc (PA) 937 264-0190
  5751 Webster St Dayton (45414) (G-7661)
Telarc International Corp 216 464-2313
  23412 Commerce Park Beachwood (44122) (G-843)
Telco Pros Inc 877 244-0182
  2019 Center St Ste 320 Cleveland (44113) (G-4982)
Telcom Construction Svcs Inc 330 239-6900
  5067 Paramount Dr Medina (44256) (G-10899)
Tele-Solutions Inc (PA) 330 782-2888
  6001 Southern Blvd Ste 102 Youngstown (44512) (G-15733)
Telecommunications Contractor, Mount Vernon Also Called: Ewers Utility Service LLC (G-11487)
Teledyne Brown Engineering Inc 419 470-3000
  1330 W Laskey Rd Toledo (43612) (G-14036)
Teledyne Instruments Inc 513 229-7000
  4736 Socialville Foster Rd Mason (45040) (G-10614)
Teledyne Tekmar, Mason Also Called: Teledyne Instruments Inc (G-10614)
Teleperformance USA, Columbus Also Called: Tpusa Inc (G-6778)
Telephone Service Company, Wapakoneta Also Called: TSC Communications Inc (G-14492)
TELEPHONY & DATA SOLUTIONS, Dublin Also Called: DOT Net Factory LLC (G-7988)
Telephony & Data Solutions, Dublin Also Called: Microman Inc (G-8064)
Teletronics Communications, Strongsville Also Called: Teletronics Services Inc (G-13491)
Teletronics Services Inc (PA) 216 778-6500
  22550 Ascoa Ct Strongsville (44149) (G-13491)
Telhio Credit Union Inc (PA) 614 221-3233
  330 Rush Aly Columbus (43215) (G-6755)
Tembec Btlsr Inc 419 244-5856
  2112 Sylvan Ave Toledo (43606) (G-14037)
Temenos 513 791-7022
  4156 Crossgate Ln Blue Ash (45236) (G-1252)
Temp Tech, Cleveland Also Called: Temp Tech LLC (G-4983)
Temp Tech LLC 440 805-6037
  1536 Saint Clair Ave Ne Ste 103 Cleveland (44114) (G-4983)
Tempoe LLC 415 390-2620
  7755 Montgomery Rd Ste 400 Cincinnati (45236) (G-3451)
Temporary Health Care Service, Dayton Also Called: Residential Care Inc (G-7589)
Ten Pin Alley 614 876-2475
  5499 Ten Pin Aly Hilliard (43026) (G-9237)
Tenable Protective Svcs Inc (PA) 216 361-0002
  2423 Payne Ave Cleveland (44114) (G-4984)
Tenack Dialysis LLC 513 810-4369
  11135 Montgomery Rd Cincinnati (45249) (G-3452)
Tender Hrts At HM Snior Care I 513 234-0805
  9435 Waterstone Blvd Ste 140 Cincinnati (45249) (G-3453)
TENDER MERCIES, Cincinnati Also Called: Tender Mercies Inc (G-3455)
Tender Mercies Inc 513 721-8666
  15 W 12th St Cincinnati (45202) (G-3454)
Tender Mercies Inc (PA) 513 721-8666
  27 W 12th St Cincinnati (45202) (G-3455)

ALPHABETIC SECTION — The D S Brown Company

Tennessee Centerstone Inc 740 779-4888
455 Shawnee Ln Chillicothe (45601) *(G-2092)*

Tennessee Rand, Fort Loramie *Also Called: Lincoln Electric Automtn Inc (G-8605)*

Tennfreight Inc 615 977-2125
4240 Airport Rd Ste 213 Cincinnati (45226) *(G-3456)*

Tennis Unlimited Inc 330 928-8763
2108 Akron Peninsula Rd Akron (44313) *(G-331)*

Tensile Tstg A Div J T Adams I 216 641-3290
4520 Willow Pkwy Cleveland (44125) *(G-4985)*

Tensile Tsting Mtllurgical Lab, Cleveland *Also Called: Tensile Tstg A Div J T Adams I (G-4985)*

Tensure Consulting LLC 513 428-4493
5325 Deerfield Blvd Ste 144 Mason (45040) *(G-10615)*

Teradata International Inc (HQ) 866 548-8348
10000 Innovation Dr Dayton (45449) *(G-7662)*

Terex Services, Miamisburg *Also Called: Crane America Services Inc (G-11041)*

Terik Roofing Inc 330 785-0060
72 Hanna Pkwy Coventry Township (44319) *(G-7016)*

Terillium Inc 513 621-9500
201 E 5th St Ste 2700 Cincinnati (45202) *(G-3457)*

Terminal Ready-Mix Inc 440 288-0181
524 Colorado Ave Lorain (44052) *(G-10103)*

Terminal Warehouse Inc 330 773-2056
2207 Kimball Rd Se Canton (44707) *(G-1870)*

Terrace Construction Co Inc 216 739-3170
3965 Pearl Rd Cleveland (44109) *(G-4986)*

Terrace Park Country Club Inc 513 965-4061
5341 S Milford Rd Milford (45150) *(G-11260)*

Terrace View Gardens, Cincinnati *Also Called: Carefor Place Nursing Home Inc (G-2312)*

Terracon Consultants Inc 513 321-5816
611 Lunken Park Dr Cincinnati (45226) *(G-3458)*

Terracon Consultants Inc 614 863-3113
800 Morrison Rd Gahanna (43230) *(G-8732)*

Terracon Consultants Inc 513 321-5816
611 Lunken Park Dr Cincinnati (45226) *(G-3459)*

Terracon Consultants N1, Cincinnati *Also Called: Terracon Consultants Inc (G-3458)*

Terracon Consultants N4, Gahanna *Also Called: Terracon Consultants Inc (G-8732)*

Terrafirm Construction LLC 913 433-2998
3458 Lewis Centre Way Urbancrest (43123) *(G-14324)*

Tesar Industrial Contrs Inc (PA) 216 741-8008
3920 Jennings Rd Cleveland (44109) *(G-4987)*

Tesoro Refining & Mktg Co LLC 419 421-2159
539 S Main St Findlay (45840) *(G-8591)*

Testa Enterprises Inc 330 926-9060
2335 2nd St Ste A Cuyahoga Falls (44221) *(G-7105)*

Testech Inc 937 435-8584
10051 Beaufort Run Dayton (45458) *(G-7663)*

Testerman Dental 513 932-4806
767 Columbus Ave Ste 1 Lebanon (45036) *(G-9793)*

Testoil, Inc., Strongsville *Also Called: Eurofins Testoil Inc (G-13453)*

Tetra Tech, Richfield *Also Called: American Envmtl Group Ltd (G-12685)*

Teva Womens Health LLC (DH) 513 731-9900
5040 Duramed Rd Cincinnati (45213) *(G-3460)*

Texas Infusion Partners, Cincinnati *Also Called: Infusion Partners Inc (G-2871)*

Texas Migrant Council Inc 937 846-0699
476 N Dayton Lakeview Rd New Carlisle (45344) *(G-11608)*

Tforce Freight Inc 513 771-7555
3250 E Kemper Rd Cincinnati (45241) *(G-3461)*

Tforce Freight Inc 216 676-4560
15775 Industrial Pkwy Cleveland (44135) *(G-4988)*

Tforce Freight Inc 614 238-2355
3400 Refugee Rd Columbus (43232) *(G-6756)*

Tforce Freight Inc 937 236-4700
3730 Valley St Dayton (45424) *(G-7664)*

Tforce Freight Inc 330 448-0440
7945 3rd St Masury (44438) *(G-10681)*

Tforce Freight Inc 330 659-6693
3495 Brecksville Rd Richfield (44286) *(G-12711)*

Tforce Freight Inc 419 537-1445
3235 Nebraska Ave Toledo (43607) *(G-14038)*

Tforce Logistics East LLC 614 276-6000
2735 Westbelt Dr Columbus (43228) *(G-6757)*

Tfs, Perrysburg *Also Called: Tfs Ltd (G-12375)*

Tfs Ltd (HQ) 419 868-8853
3235 Levis Commons Blvd Perrysburg (43551) *(G-12375)*

Tfs Financial Corporation 216 441-6000
7007 Broadway Ave Cleveland (44105) *(G-4989)*

Tg of Toledo LLC (PA) 419 241-3151
103 Avondale Ave Toledo (43604) *(G-14039)*

TGI Friday's, Cleveland *Also Called: Cleveland Rest Oper Ltd Partnr (G-4064)*

TGI Friday's, Ontario *Also Called: CFC Mansfield LLC (G-12101)*

Tglcc, Hinckley *Also Called: The Great Lakes Construction Co (G-9272)*

Tgm Associates LP 513 829-8383
1400 Sherwood Dr Fairfield (45014) *(G-8445)*

Tgs International Inc 330 893-4828
4464 State Route 39 Millersburg (44654) *(G-11293)*

TH Martin Inc 216 741-2020
8500 Brookpark Rd Cleveland (44129) *(G-4990)*

Thakore, Gnan N MD, Dayton *Also Called: Pulmonary Crtcal Care Cons Inc (G-7573)*

Tharaldson Hospitality MGT 513 947-9402
4521 Eastgate Blvd Cincinnati (45245) *(G-2115)*

Thayer Power & Comm Line, Pataskala *Also Called: Thayer Pwr Comm Line Cnstr LLC (G-12278)*

Thayer Pwr Comm Line Cnstr LLC 330 922-4950
3432 State Rd Ste A Cuyahoga Falls (44223) *(G-7106)*

Thayer Pwr Comm Line Cnstr LLC (HQ) 740 927-0021
12345 Worthington Rd Nw Pataskala (43062) *(G-12278)*

The Abbewood, Elyria *Also Called: Abbewood Limited Partnership (G-8231)*

THE AMERICAN NATIONAL RED CROSS, Youngstown *Also Called: American National Red Cross (G-15550)*

The Andersons Marathon Ethanol LLC 937 316-3700
5728 Sebring Warner Rd N Greenville (45331) *(G-8887)*

The Andrews Moving and Storage Company (PA) 330 656-8700
10235 Philipp Pkwy Streetsboro (44241) *(G-13432)*

The Apostolos Group Inc 330 670-9900
1 Thomarios Rd Copley (44321) *(G-6966)*

The Arras Group Inc 216 621-1601
1151 N Marginal Rd Cleveland (44114) *(G-4991)*

The Beaver Excavating Co (PA) 330 478-2151
2000 Beaver Place Ave Sw Canton (44706) *(G-1871)*

The Berger Hospital (HQ) 740 474-2126
600 N Pickaway St Circleville (43113) *(G-3727)*

The Blonder Company 216 431-3560
3950 Prospect Ave E Cleveland (44115) *(G-4992)*

The Bluff, Sherrodsville *Also Called: Regard Recovery Florida LLC (G-13012)*

The Boston Company Inc., Urbana *Also Called: Boston Company Inc (G-14298)*

The Cadle Company (PA) 330 872-0918
100 N Center St Newton Falls (44444) *(G-11778)*

The Chas E Phipps Company (PA) 216 641-2150
4560 Willow Pkwy Cleveland (44125) *(G-4993)*

The Chas G Buchy Packing Company
10510 Evendale Dr Cincinnati (45241) *(G-3462)*

The Cincinnati Playhouse In The Park Inc 513 345-2242
962 Mount Adams Cir Cincinnati (45202) *(G-3463)*

The Cleveland Museum of Art 216 421-7340
11150 East Blvd Cleveland (44106) *(G-4994)*

The Cleveland Plant and Flower Company (PA) 216 898-3500
12920 Corporate Dr Cleveland (44130) *(G-4995)*

The Cleveland Vicon Co Inc (PA) 216 341-3300
4550 Willow Pkwy Cleveland (44125) *(G-4996)*

The Cleveland-Cliffs Iron Co 216 694-5700
1100 Superior Ave E Ste 1500 Cleveland (44114) *(G-4997)*

THE COMMERCIAL TRAFFIC COMPANY 216 267-2000
12487 Plaza Dr Cleveland (44130) *(G-4998)*

The Community Hospital of Springfield and Clark County 937 325-0531
100 Medical Center Dr Springfield (45504) *(G-13300)*

The Community Mercy Foundation 937 328-7000
1 S Limestone St Ste 700 Springfield (45502) *(G-13301)*

The Cornwell Quality Tools Company (PA) 330 336-3506
667 Seville Rd Wadsworth (44281) *(G-14455)*

The Cottingham Paper Co 614 294-6444
324 E 2nd Ave Columbus (43201) *(G-6758)*

The D S Brown Company (HQ) 419 257-3561
300 E Cherry St North Baltimore (45872) *(G-11802)*

The Daimler Group Inc..614 488-4424
   1533 Lake Shore Dr Columbus (43204) *(G-6759)*

The David J Joseph Company (HQ)...513 419-6200
   300 Pike St Fl 3 Cincinnati (45202) *(G-3464)*

The Dean Supply Co...216 771-3300
   3500 Woodland Ave Cleveland (44115) *(G-4999)*

The Delaware County Bank Inc..740 657-7000
   110 Riverbend Ave Lewis Center (43035) *(G-9838)*

The E and R Trailer Sales and Services Inc (PA).......................419 968-2115
   20186 Lincoln Hwy Middle Point (45863) *(G-11111)*

The East Toledo Family Ctr Inc (PA)..419 691-1429
   1020 Varland Ave Toledo (43605) *(G-14040)*

The Elder-Beerman Stores Corp..937 296-2700
   3155 Elbee Rd Moraine (45439) *(G-11443)*

The Ellenbee-Leggett Company Inc...513 874-3200
   3765 Port Union Rd Fairfield (45014) *(G-8446)*

The Expediting Co (PA)...937 890-1524
   1295 S Brown School Rd Vandalia (45377) *(G-14394)*

The F A Requarth Company...937 224-1141
   447 E Monument Ave Dayton (45402) *(G-7665)*

The F D Lawrence Electric Company (PA)..................................513 542-1100
   3450 Beekman St Cincinnati (45223) *(G-3465)*

The Famous Manufacturing Co..330 762-9621
   2620 Ridgewood Rd Ste 200 Akron (44313) *(G-332)*

The Fine Arts Association..440 951-7500
   38660 Mentor Ave Willoughby (44094) *(G-15223)*

The Fountain On The Greens, Cleveland *Also Called: Greens of Lyndhurst The Inc (G-4340)*

The Galehouse Companies Inc..330 658-2023
   12667 Portage St Doylestown (44230) *(G-7916)*

The Garretson Firm Resolution Group Inc..................................513 794-0400
   6281 Tri Ridge Blvd Ste 300 Loveland (45140) *(G-10163)*

The Geiler Company...513 574-1200
   6561 Glenway Ave Cincinnati (45211) *(G-3466)*

The Glockner Chevrolet Company (PA)......................................740 353-2161
   4368 Us Highway 23 Portsmouth (45662) *(G-12576)*

The Good Shepherd, Ashland *Also Called: Good Shepherd Home For Aged (G-499)*

The Great Lakes Construction Co..330 220-3900
   2608 Great Lakes Way Hinckley (44233) *(G-9272)*

The Great Lakes Towing Company (PA).....................................216 621-4854
   4500 Division Ave Cleveland (44102) *(G-5000)*

The H T Hackney Co..614 751-5100
   875 Taylor Station Rd Gahanna (43230) *(G-8733)*

The Hattenbach Company...216 881-5200
   5309 Hamilton Ave Cleveland (44114) *(G-5001)*

The Hc Companies Inc...440 313-4712
   1400 Lowell St Elyria (44035) *(G-8297)*

The Hercules Tire & Rubber Company (DH)..............................800 677-9535
   1995 Tiffin Ave Ste 205 Findlay (45840) *(G-8592)*

The Home Savings and Loan Company of Youngstown Ohio.....330 742-0500
   275 W Federal St Youngstown (44503) *(G-15734)*

The Huntington Investment Co (HQ)..614 480-3600
   41 S High St Fl 7 Columbus (43215) *(G-6760)*

The Interlake Steamship Co...440 260-6900
   7300 Engle Rd Middleburg Heights (44130) *(G-11131)*

The James B Oswald Company (PA)..216 367-8787
   1100 Superior Ave E Ste 1500 Cleveland (44114) *(G-5002)*

The John A Becker Co..937 226-1341
   1341 E 4th St Dayton (45402) *(G-7666)*

The Kindt-Collins Company LLC...216 252-4122
   12651 Elmwood Ave Cleveland (44111) *(G-5003)*

The Lochhaven Company...419 227-5450
   1640 Allentown Rd Ofc Lima (45805) *(G-9970)*

The Lodge of Montgomery, Cincinnati *Also Called: Emeritus Corporation (G-2615)*

The Maple City Ice Company..419 747-4777
   1245 W Longview Ave Mansfield (44906) *(G-10319)*

The Maria-Joseph Center...937 278-2692
   4830 Salem Ave Dayton (45416) *(G-7667)*

The Medical Center At Elizabeth Place LLC..............................937 223-6237
   7970 N Main St Dayton (45415) *(G-7668)*

The Metrohealth System (PA)...216 778-7800
   2500 Metrohealth Dr Cleveland (44109) *(G-5004)*

The National Lime and Stone Company (PA).............................419 422-4341
   551 Lake Cascade Pkwy Findlay (45840) *(G-8593)*

The Oaks Lodge...330 769-2601
   5878 Longacre Ln Chippewa Lake (44215) *(G-2094)*

The OGara Group Inc (PA)..513 881-9800
   7870 E Kemper Rd Ste 460 Cincinnati (45249) *(G-3467)*

The Ohio Desk Company (PA)..216 623-0600
   1122 Prospect Ave E Cleveland (44115) *(G-5005)*

The Olen Corporation (PA)..614 491-1515
   4755 S High St Columbus (43207) *(G-6761)*

The Pavilion, Sidney *Also Called: Shelby County Mem Hosp Assn (G-13047)*

The Payne Firm Inc..513 489-2255
   11231 Cornell Park Dr Blue Ash (45242) *(G-1253)*

The Peck-Hannaford Briggs Co (PA)..513 681-4600
   4670 Chester Ave Cincinnati (45232) *(G-3468)*

The Peoples Bank Co Inc (PA)..419 678-2385
   112 W Main St 114 Coldwater (45828) *(G-5220)*

The Photo-Type Engraving Company (PA).................................513 281-0999
   2141 Gilbert Ave Cincinnati (45206) *(G-3469)*

The Rdi Corporation (PA)...513 984-5927
   4350 Glendale Milford Rd Ste 250 Cincinnati (45242) *(G-3470)*

The Robert McCabe Company Inc (PA)......................................513 683-2662
   118 Northeast Dr Loveland (45140) *(G-10164)*

The Sanson Company (PA)...216 431-8560
   3716 Croton Ave Frnt Cleveland (44115) *(G-5006)*

The Schaefer Group Inc (PA)..937 253-3342
   1300 Grange Hall Rd Beavercreek (45430) *(G-932)*

The Selinsky Force LLC (PA)..330 477-4527
   5365 E Center Dr Ne Ste C Canton (44721) *(G-1872)*

The Sheakley Group Inc (PA)..513 771-2277
   1 Sheakley Way Cincinnati (45246) *(G-3471)*

The Sisters of Charity of St Augustine Health System Inc (PA)....216 696-5560
   2475 E 22nd St Cleveland (44115) *(G-5007)*

The Union Central Life Insurance Company...............................866 696-7478
   1876 Waycross Rd Cincinnati (45240) *(G-3472)*

The United States Dept A Force..937 255-3286
   1100 Spaatz St Dayton (45433) *(G-7142)*

The Voto Manufacturers Sales Company (PA)...........................740 282-3621
   500 N 3rd St Steubenville (43952) *(G-13345)*

The W L Tucker Supply Company (PA).....................................330 928-2155
   2800 2nd St Cuyahoga Falls (44221) *(G-7107)*

The Wadsworth-Rittman Area Hospital Association..................330 334-1504
   195 Wadsworth Rd Wadsworth (44281) *(G-14456)*

The Wagner-Smith Company..866 338-0398
   3201 Encrete Ln Moraine (45439) *(G-11444)*

The Young Mens Christian Association of Central Ohio (PA)....614 389-4409
   1907 Leonard Ave Ste 150 Columbus (43219) *(G-6762)*

Theken Spine LLC..330 733-7600
   1800 Triplett Blvd Akron (44306) *(G-333)*

Therapy Advantage Group LLC..614 784-0400
   965 High St Worthington (43085) *(G-15461)*

Thermal Solutions Inc..513 742-2836
   9491 Seward Rd Fairfield (45014) *(G-8447)*

Thermal Solutions Inc (PA)...740 886-2861
   9329 County Road 107 Proctorville (45669) *(G-12614)*

Thermal Treatment Center Inc (HQ)...216 881-8100
   28910 Lakeland Blvd Wickliffe (44092) *(G-15164)*

Thermaltech Engineering, Cincinnati *Also Called: Thermaltech Engineering Inc (G-3473)*

Thermaltech Engineering Inc (PA)..513 561-2271
   3960 Red Bank Rd Ste 250 Cincinnati (45227) *(G-3473)*

Thermedx LLC..440 542-0883
   31200 Solon Rd Ste 1 Solon (44139) *(G-13156)*

Thermo Fisher Scientific Inc...800 871-8909
   1 Thermo Fisher Way Oakwood Village (44146) *(G-12059)*

Thermodyn Corporation (PA)..419 841-7782
   3550 Silica Rd Sylvania (43560) *(G-13577)*

Thiel's Home Solutions, Hudson *Also Called: Leaf Home LLC (G-9362)*

Things Remembered, Highland Heights *Also Called: Things Remembered Inc (G-9172)*

Things Remembered Inc...440 473-2000
   5500 Avion Park Dr Highland Heights (44143) *(G-9172)*

Think Patented, Miamisburg *Also Called: Patented Acquisition Corp (G-11082)*

ALPHABETIC SECTION — Tiffin Paper Company

THINK TV, Dayton *Also Called: Greater Dayton Public TV Inc (G-7384)*

Thinkpath Engineering Svcs LLC (PA) 937 291-8374
9080 Springboro Pike Ste 300 Miamisburg (45342) *(G-11097)*

Third Dimension Inc (HQ) 440 466-4040
633 Pleasant Ave Geneva (44041) *(G-8790)*

Third Fdral Sav Ln Assn Clvlan (HQ) 800 844-7333
7007 Broadway Ave Cleveland (44105) *(G-5008)*

Third Fdral Sav Ln Assn Clvlan 440 885-4900
5950 Ridge Rd Cleveland (44129) *(G-5009)*

Third Fdral Sav Ln Assn Clvlan 216 581-0881
12594 Rockside Rd Cleveland (44125) *(G-5010)*

Third Fdral Sav Ln Assn Clvlan 440 526-3001
8943 Brecksville Rd Cleveland (44141) *(G-5011)*

Third Fdral Sav Ln Assn Clvlan 440 238-4333
18380 Royalton Rd Cleveland (44136) *(G-5012)*

Third Fdral Sav Ln Assn Clvlan 440 946-9040
7339 Mentor Ave Mentor (44060) *(G-11003)*

Third Fdral Sav Ln Assn Clvlan 330 963-3130
9057 Darrow Rd Twinsburg (44087) *(G-14222)*

Third Federal, Cleveland *Also Called: Third Fdral Sav Ln Assn Clvlan (G-5008)*

Third Federal, Mentor *Also Called: Third Fdral Sav Ln Assn Clvlan (G-11003)*

Third Federal Savings, Twinsburg *Also Called: Third Fdral Sav Ln Assn Clvlan (G-14222)*

Third Savings, Piqua *Also Called: Unity National Bank (G-12460)*

Thirty One Gifts, New Albany *Also Called: Thirty-One Gifts LLC (G-11588)*

Thirty-One Gifts LLC (PA) 614 414-4300
8131 Smiths Mill Rd New Albany (43054) *(G-11588)*

Thomarios, Copley *Also Called: The Apostolos Group Inc (G-6966)*

Thomas & Thomas, Cincinnati *Also Called: Ernest V Thomas Jr (G-2635)*

Thomas A Wildey School, Owensville *Also Called: Clermont Cnty Bd Dvlpmntal DSB (G-12199)*

Thomas Do-It Center Inc (PA) 740 446-2002
176 Mccormick Rd Gallipolis (45631) *(G-8769)*

Thomas E Keller Trucking Inc 419 784-4805
24862 Elliott Rd Defiance (43512) *(G-7772)*

Thomas Edson Erly Chldhood Ctr 419 238-1514
813 N Franklin St Van Wert (45891) *(G-14352)*

Thomas Glass Company Inc (PA) 614 268-8611
400 E Wilson Bridge Rd Ste A Worthington (43085) *(G-15462)*

Thomas Glbraith Htg Coolg Plbg, Fairfield *Also Called: Wca Group LLC (G-8453)*

Thomas J Dyer Company (PA) 513 321-8100
5240 Lester Rd Cincinnati (45213) *(G-3474)*

Thomas J Dyer Company, Cincinnati *Also Called: Thomas J Dyer Company (G-3474)*

Thomas Packer & Co (PA) 330 533-9777
6601 Westford Pl Ste 101 Canfield (44406) *(G-1643)*

Thomas Rental, Gallipolis *Also Called: Thomas Do-It Center Inc (G-8769)*

Thomas Ritter Od Inc 513 984-0202
9912 Carver Rd Ste 101 Blue Ash (45242) *(G-1254)*

Thomas Trucking Inc 513 731-8411
2558 Apple Ridge Ln Cincinnati (45236) *(G-3475)*

Thomasville Limosine Service, Akron *Also Called: Rob Lynn Inc (G-284)*

Thompkins Child Adlescent Svcs 740 622-4470
1199 S 2nd St Coshocton (43812) *(G-7003)*

Thompson Dunlap Heydinger Ltd 937 593-6065
1111 Rush Ave Bellefontaine (43311) *(G-1039)*

Thompson Electric Inc 330 686-2300
49 Northmoreland Ave Munroe Falls (44262) *(G-11514)*

Thompson Heating & Cooling Co, Warren *Also Called: G H A T Inc (G-14522)*

Thompson Hine LLP (PA) 216 566-5500
127 Public Sq Ste 3900 Cleveland (44114) *(G-5013)*

Thompson Hine LLP 614 469-3200
10 W Broad St Ste 700 Columbus (43215) *(G-6763)*

Thompson Hine LLP 614 469-3200
41 S High St Ste 1700 Columbus (43215) *(G-6764)*

Thompson Hine LLP 937 443-6859
10050 Innovation Dr Ste 400 Miamisburg (45342) *(G-11098)*

Thor Construction, Columbus *Also Called: Central Ohio Building Co Inc (G-5536)*

Thornhill Financial Inc 440 238-0445
18400 Pearl Rd Ste A Cleveland (44136) *(G-5014)*

Thornville Family Med Ctr Inc 740 246-6361
41 Foster Dr Thornville (43076) *(G-13623)*

Thorsens Greenhouse LLC 740 363-5069
2069 Hyatts Rd Delaware (43015) *(G-7830)*

Thorson Baker & Assoc Inc 513 579-8200
2055 Reading Rd Ste 280 Cincinnati (45202) *(G-3476)*

Thorson Baker & Assoc Inc 614 389-3144
525 Metro Pl N Ste 440 Dublin (43017) *(G-8141)*

THORSON BAKER & ASSOC, INC, Cincinnati *Also Called: Thorson Baker & Assoc Inc (G-3476)*

THORSON BAKER & ASSOC, INC, Dublin *Also Called: Thorson Baker & Assoc Inc (G-8141)*

Thorson Baker & Associates Inc (PA) 330 659-6688
3030 W Streetsboro Rd Richfield (44286) *(G-12712)*

Thorsport Inc 419 621-8800
2520 Campbell St Sandusky (44870) *(G-12936)*

Thp Limited Inc 513 241-3222
100 E 8th St Ste 3 Cincinnati (45202) *(G-3477)*

Thrasher Group Inc 330 620-4790
400 3rd St Se Ste 309 Canton (44702) *(G-1873)*

Thread Information Design Inc 419 887-6801
4635 W Alexis Rd Toledo (43623) *(G-14041)*

Thread Marketing Group, Toledo *Also Called: Thread Information Design Inc (G-14041)*

Three C Body Shop Inc (PA) 614 274-9700
2300 Briggs Rd Columbus (43223) *(G-6765)*

Three C Body Shop Inc 614 885-0900
8321 N High St Columbus (43235) *(G-6766)*

Three D Metals, Valley City *Also Called: Three D Metals Inc (G-14337)*

Three D Metals Inc (PA) 330 220-0451
5462 Innovation Dr Valley City (44280) *(G-14337)*

Three Gables Surgery Ctr LLC 740 886-9911
5897 County Road 107 Proctorville (45669) *(G-12615)*

Three Village Condominium 440 461-1483
5150 Three Village Dr Cleveland (44124) *(G-5015)*

Three-D Transport Inc 419 924-5368
14237 Us Highway 127 West Unity (43570) *(G-14875)*

Threebond International 513 759-8771
6184 Schumacher Park Dr West Chester (45069) *(G-14773)*

Thrifty LLC 614 237-1500
2980 Switzer Ave Columbus (43219) *(G-6767)*

Thrive Childcare, Perrysburg *Also Called: Thrive Ministries Inc (G-12376)*

Thrive Lgbt 440 319-5906
568 E 101st St Apt 4 Cleveland (44108) *(G-5016)*

Thrive Ministries Inc 419 873-0870
1134 Professional Dr Perrysburg (43551) *(G-12376)*

Thunder Tech Inc 216 391-2255
3635 Perkins Ave Ste 5ne Cleveland (44114) *(G-5017)*

Thunderyard Solutions LLC 281 222-3644
1382 W Melrose Dr Westlake (44145) *(G-15115)*

Thurman Scale Company 614 221-9077
4025 Lakeview Xing Groveport (43125) *(G-9004)*

Thyssenkrupp Bilstein Amer Inc 513 881-7600
3033 Symmes Rd Hamilton (45015) *(G-9085)*

Thyssenkrupp Bilstein Amer Inc (HQ) 513 881-7600
8685 Bilstein Blvd Hamilton (45015) *(G-9086)*

Thyssenkrupp Logistics Inc (DH) 419 662-1800
8001 Thyssenkrupp Pkwy Northwood (43619) *(G-11984)*

Thyssenkrupp Materials NA Inc 440 234-7500
17901 Englewood Dr Cleveland (44130) *(G-5018)*

Thyssenkrupp Materials NA Inc 216 883-8100
6050 Oak Tree Blvd Ste 110 Independence (44131) *(G-9490)*

Thyssenkrupp Materials NA Inc 419 662-1845
1212 E Alexis Rd Toledo (43612) *(G-14042)*

TI Resort LLC 216 464-5130
4832 Richmond Rd Ste 200 Cleveland (44128) *(G-5019)*

Tiaa-Cref Indvdual Instnl Svcs 614 659-1000
625 Eden Park Dr Ste 500 Cincinnati (45202) *(G-3478)*

Tiffin Cmnty YMCA Rcration Ctr (PA) 419 447-8711
180 Summit St Tiffin (44883) *(G-13645)*

Tiffin Developmental Center, Tiffin *Also Called: Department of Health Ohio (G-13627)*

Tiffin Loader Crane Company 419 448-8156
4151 W State Route 18 Tiffin (44883) *(G-13646)*

Tiffin Paper Company (PA) 419 447-2121
401 Wall St Tiffin (44883) *(G-13647)*

Tiger 2010 LLC (PA) 330 236-5100
6929 Portage St Nw North Canton (44720) *(G-11864)*

Tigerspike Inc 646 330-4636
201 E 4th St Ste 400 Cincinnati (45202) *(G-3479)*

Tiki Bowling Lanes Inc 740 654-4513
1521 Tiki Ln Lancaster (43130) *(G-9747)*

Tiki Lounge & Restaurant, Lancaster Also Called: Tiki Bowling Lanes Inc *(G-9747)*

Tilden Mining Company LC (HQ) 216 694-5700
200 Public Sq Ste 3300 Cleveland (44114) *(G-5020)*

Tile Shop LLC 513 554-4435
11973 Lebanon Rd Cincinnati (45241) *(G-3480)*

Tim Lally Chevrolet Inc 440 232-2000
19000 Rockside Rd Bedford (44146) *(G-988)*

Timbuk Farms Inc 740 587-2178
2030 Timbuk Rd Granville (43023) *(G-8855)*

Time Warner, Blue Ash Also Called: Time Warner Cable Entps LLC *(G-1255)*

Time Warner, Columbus Also Called: Spectrum MGT Holdg Co LLC *(G-6703)*

Time Warner, Columbus Also Called: Time Warner Cable Entps LLC *(G-6768)*

Time Warner, Columbus Also Called: Time Warner Cable Entps LLC *(G-6769)*

Time Warner Cable Entps LLC 513 489-5000
11325 Reed Hartman Hwy Ste 100 Blue Ash (45241) *(G-1255)*

Time Warner Cable Entps LLC 614 255-6289
1600 Dublin Rd Fl 2 Columbus (43215) *(G-6768)*

Time Warner Cable Entps LLC 614 481-5072
1125 Chambers Rd Columbus (43212) *(G-6769)*

Timeless By Design, Seville Also Called: Wholesale Decor LLC *(G-12967)*

Timeline Construction LLC 330 595-4462
80 Cole Ave Akron (44301) *(G-334)*

Times Reporter/Midwest Offset, New Philadelphia Also Called: Copley Ohio Newspapers Inc *(G-11643)*

Timet, Warrensville Heights Also Called: Titanium Metals Corporation *(G-14589)*

TIMKEN, North Canton Also Called: Timken Company *(G-11865)*

Timken Company 419 563-2200
2325 E Mansfield St Bucyrus (44820) *(G-1518)*

Timken Company 234 262-3000
1819 N Main St Niles (44446) *(G-11797)*

Timken Company (PA) 234 262-3000
4500 Mount Pleasant St Nw North Canton (44720) *(G-11865)*

Timken Corporation (DH) 330 471-3378
4500 Mount Pleasant St Nw North Canton (44720) *(G-11866)*

Timken Mercy Health Center, Carrollton Also Called: Cleveland Clinic Mercy Hosp *(G-1904)*

Tipp City Veterinary Hosp Inc 937 667-8489
4900 S County Road 25a Tipp City (45371) *(G-13665)*

Tipp Machine & Tool Inc 937 890-8428
4201 Little York Rd Dayton (45414) *(G-7669)*

Tippecanoe Country Club Inc 330 758-7518
5870 Tippecanoe Rd Canfield (44406) *(G-1644)*

Tippecanoe Pro Shop, Canfield Also Called: Tippecanoe Country Club Inc *(G-1644)*

Tipton Group Inc 937 885-6300
10554 Success Ln Ste D Dayton (45458) *(G-7670)*

Tire Dealers Warehouse, Findlay Also Called: The Hercules Tire & Rubber Company *(G-8592)*

Titan Electric, Dublin Also Called: Ke Gutridge LLC *(G-8048)*

Titan Logistics Ltd 614 901-4212
861 Taylor Rd Columbus (43230) *(G-6770)*

Titan Mechanical Solutions LLC 513 738-5800
11003 State Route 128 Harrison (45030) *(G-9117)*

Titan Propane LLC 419 332-9832
2145 Napoleon Rd Fremont (43420) *(G-8706)*

Titan Reinforcing LLC 513 539-4000
990 N Garver Rd Monroe (45050) *(G-11352)*

Titanium Metals Corporation (DH) 740 537-5600
4832 Richmond Rd Ste 100 Warrensville Heights (44128) *(G-14589)*

Title First Agency Inc (HQ) 614 347-8383
495 Executive Campus Dr Ste 110 Westerville (43082) *(G-14942)*

Tj Metzgers Inc 419 861-8611
207 Arco Dr Toledo (43607) *(G-14043)*

Tjm Clmbus LLC Tjm Clumbus LLC 614 885-1885
6500 Doubletree Ave Columbus (43229) *(G-6771)*

Tjm Express Inc 216 385-4164
212 Sandstone Ridge Way Berea (44017) *(G-1085)*

Tk Elevator Corporation 440 717-0080
9200 Market Pl Broadview Heights (44147) *(G-1401)*

Tk Elevator Corporation 513 241-6000
934 Dalton Ave Cincinnati (45203) *(G-3481)*

Tk Elevator Corporation 614 895-8930
929 Eastwind Dr Ste 218 Westerville (43081) *(G-15017)*

Tk Gas Services Inc 740 826-0303
2303 John Glenn Hwy New Concord (43762) *(G-11612)*

Tk Homecare Llc 419 517-7000
7110 W Central Ave Ste A Toledo (43617) *(G-14044)*

Tky Associates LLC 419 535-7777
2451 N Reynolds Rd Toledo (43615) *(G-14045)*

TL Industries Inc (PA) 419 666-8144
28271 Cedar Park Blvd Ste 8 Perrysburg (43551) *(G-12377)*

TLC Landscaping LLC 440 248-4852
38000 Aurora Rd Cleveland (44139) *(G-5021)*

Tlevay Inc 419 385-3958
1621 S Byrne Rd Toledo (43614) *(G-14046)*

Tlx, Mantua Also Called: Awl Transport Inc *(G-10328)*

Tm Capture Services LLC 937 728-1781
4380 Buckeye Ln Ste 222 Dayton (45440) *(G-7671)*

Tm Final Ltd 419 724-8473
1549 Campbell St Toledo (43607) *(G-14047)*

TMC Micrographic Services Inc 614 761-1033
2709 Sawbury Blvd Columbus (43235) *(G-6772)*

TMI Electrical Contractors Inc 513 821-9900
423 W Wyoming Ave Cincinnati (45215) *(G-3482)*

TMR Inc 330 220-8564
2945 Carquest Dr Brunswick (44212) *(G-1471)*

Tmt Consolidated Inc 216 781-7016
3040 Quigley Rd Cleveland (44113) *(G-5022)*

Tmt Warehousing LLC 419 662-3146
655 D St Perrysburg (43551) *(G-12378)*

To Scale Software LLC 513 253-0053
6398 Thornberry Ct Mason (45040) *(G-10616)*

TOA Technologies Inc (PA) 216 925-5950
3333 Richmond Rd Ste 420 Beachwood (44122) *(G-844)*

Toagosei America Inc 614 718-3855
1450 W Main St West Jefferson (43162) *(G-14853)*

Toast.net Internet Service, Toledo Also Called: End-User Computing Inc *(G-13793)*

Tobal Products, Columbus Also Called: Abbott Laboratories *(G-5294)*

Todds Enviroscapes Inc 330 875-0768
7727 Paris Ave Louisville (44641) *(G-10123)*

Toga-Pak Inc 937 294-7311
2208 Sandridge Dr Dayton (45439) *(G-7672)*

Tolco, Toledo Also Called: Tolco Corporation *(G-14048)*

Tolco Corporation (PA) 419 241-1113
1920 Linwood Ave Toledo (43604) *(G-14048)*

Toledo Area Insulator Wkrs Jac 419 531-5911
4535 Hill Ave Toledo (43615) *(G-14049)*

Toledo Area Rgional Trnst Auth (PA) 419 243-7433
1127 W Central Ave Toledo (43610) *(G-14050)*

Toledo Bar Association Inc 419 242-9363
311 N Superior St Toledo (43604) *(G-14051)*

Toledo Building Services Co 419 241-3101
2121 Adams St Toledo (43604) *(G-14052)*

Toledo Cardiology Cons Inc (PA) 419 251-6183
2409 Cherry St Ste 100 Toledo (43608) *(G-14053)*

Toledo City Parks, Toledo Also Called: City of Toledo *(G-13738)*

Toledo Clinic Inc 419 865-3111
6135 Trust Dr Ste 230 Holland (43528) *(G-9308)*

Toledo Clinic Inc (PA) 419 473-3561
4235 Secor Rd Toledo (43623) *(G-14054)*

Toledo Clinic Inc 419 841-1600
3909 Woodley Rd Ste 800 Toledo (43606) *(G-14055)*

Toledo Clinic Inc 419 381-9977
1414 S Byrne Rd Toledo (43614) *(G-14056)*

Toledo Clinic Inc 419 479-5960
4235 Secor Rd Toledo (43623) *(G-14057)*

Toledo Clinic Inc 419 330-5288
1080 N Shoop Ave Wauseon (43567) *(G-14609)*

ALPHABETIC SECTION

Toledo Clinic Cancer Centers..419 691-4235
  2751 Bay Park Dr Ste 206 Oregon (43616) *(G-12143)*
Toledo Clinic Physical Therapy, Toledo *Also Called: Toledo Clinic Inc (G-14057)*
Toledo Club..419 243-2200
  709 Madison Ave Ste 305 Toledo (43604) *(G-14058)*
Toledo Cntre For Eting Dsrders, Sylvania *Also Called: River Centre Clinic (G-13570)*
Toledo Cutting Tools, Perrysburg *Also Called: Imco Carbide Tool Inc (G-12346)*
Toledo Edison Company (HQ)..800 447-3333
  76 S Main St Bsmt Akron (44308) *(G-335)*
Toledo Express Airport, Swanton *Also Called: Toledo-Lucas County Port Auth (G-13530)*
Toledo Family Health Center, Toledo *Also Called: Neighbrhood Hlth Assn Tledo In (G-13932)*
Toledo Inn North LLC..419 476-0170
  445 E Alexis Rd Toledo (43612) *(G-14059)*
Toledo Inns Inc..440 243-4040
  7230 Engle Rd Cleveland (44130) *(G-5023)*
Toledo Innvtion Ctr Lndlord LL...419 585-3684
  100 Madison Ave Toledo (43604) *(G-14060)*
Toledo Medical Equipment Co (PA)..419 866-7120
  4060 Technology Dr Maumee (43537) *(G-10774)*
Toledo Mirror & Glass, Toledo *Also Called: Tg of Toledo LLC (G-14039)*
Toledo Molding & Die LLC...419 692-6022
  24086 State Route 697 Delphos (45833) *(G-7846)*
Toledo Mtro Area Cncil Gvrnmnt..419 241-9155
  300 Martin Luther King Jr Dr Ste 300 Toledo (43604) *(G-14061)*
Toledo Mud Hens, Toledo *Also Called: Toledo Mud Hens Basbal CLB Inc (G-14062)*
Toledo Mud Hens Basbal CLB Inc..419 725-4367
  406 Washington St Fl 5 Toledo (43604) *(G-14062)*
Toledo Museum of Art...419 255-8000
  2445 Monroe St Toledo (43620) *(G-14063)*
Toledo Nagle Inc...419 661-2500
  4520 Moline Martin Rd Walbridge (43465) *(G-14467)*
Toledo North Assembly Plant, Toledo *Also Called: FCA US LLC (G-13804)*
Toledo Police Dept, Toledo *Also Called: City of Toledo (G-13742)*
Toledo Refining Company LLC (DH)..419 698-6600
  1819 Woodville Rd Oregon (43616) *(G-12144)*
Toledo Regional Office, Cleveland *Also Called: Ohio Department Youth Services (G-4686)*
Toledo Rgonal Chamber Commerce..419 243-8191
  300 Madison Ave Ste 200 Toledo (43604) *(G-14064)*
Toledo Science Center..419 244-2674
  1 Discovery Way Toledo (43604) *(G-14065)*
Toledo Society For The Blind...419 720-3937
  1002 Garden Lake Pkwy Toledo (43614) *(G-14066)*
Toledo Walleye Hockey, Toledo *Also Called: Toledo Walleye Prof Hockey CLB (G-14067)*
Toledo Walleye Prof Hockey CLB...419 725-4350
  500 Jefferson Ave Toledo (43604) *(G-14067)*
Toledo Zoo..419 385-5721
  2700 Broadway St Toledo (43609) *(G-14068)*
Toledo Zoological Society (PA)..419 385-4040
  2 Hippo Way Toledo (43609) *(G-14069)*
Toledo Zoological Society...419 385-4040
  749 Spencer St Toledo (43609) *(G-14070)*
Toledo-Lucas County Port Auth...419 865-2351
  11013 Airport Hwy Ste 11 Swanton (43558) *(G-13530)*
Toltest, Maumee *Also Called: Ltccorp Government Services-Oh Inc (G-10742)*
Tom Ahl Chryslr-Plymouth-Dodge..419 227-0202
  617 King Ave Lima (45805) *(G-9971)*
Tom Paige Catering Company...216 431-4236
  2275 E 55th St Cleveland (44103) *(G-5024)*
Tony Packo's Food Company, Maumee *Also Called: Tony Packos Toledo LLC (G-10775)*
Tony Packos Toledo LLC (PA)...419 691-6054
  1412 Arrowhead Dr Maumee (43537) *(G-10775)*
Toogann Technologies LLC...614 973-9266
  555 Metro Pl N Ste 500 Dublin (43017) *(G-8142)*
Tool Testing Lab Inc..937 898-5696
  11601 N Dixie Dr Tipp City (45371) *(G-13666)*
Tooling Components Division, Cleveland *Also Called: Jergens Inc (G-4437)*
Top Line Express Inc...419 221-1705
  1805 N Dixie Hwy Lima (45801) *(G-9972)*
Top Network, Columbus *Also Called: Essilor Laboratories Amer Inc (G-5831)*
Top Notch Truckers Inc...540 787-7777
  113 Portage Trl Ste E Cuyahoga Falls (44221) *(G-7108)*

Topicz, Cincinnati *Also Called: Novelart Manufacturing Company (G-3132)*
Topre America Corporation...256 339-8407
  1100 Reaper Ave Springfield (45503) *(G-13302)*
Tops Roofing Inc...937 228-6074
  1116 W Stewart St Dayton (45417) *(G-7673)*
Torq, Bedford *Also Called: Torq Corporation (G-989)*
Torq Corporation...440 232-4100
  32 W Monroe Ave Bedford (44146) *(G-989)*
Torrence Sound Equipment Company..419 661-0678
  29050 Glenwood Rd Perrysburg (43551) *(G-12379)*
Tosoh America Inc (HQ)..614 539-8622
  3600 Gantz Rd Grove City (43123) *(G-8959)*
Total Fleet Solutions LLC..419 868-8853
  7050 Spring Meadows Dr W Ste A Holland (43528) *(G-9309)*
Total Homecare Solutions LLC..513 277-0915
  4010 Executive Park Dr Ste 200 Cincinnati (45241) *(G-3483)*
Total Loan Services LLC...937 228-5600
  205 Sugar Camp Cir Oakwood (45409) *(G-12052)*
Total Loop Inc...888 614-5667
  1790 Town Park Blvd Ste A Uniontown (44685) *(G-14268)*
Total Maintenance Solution Inc...513 770-0925
  155 Tri County Pkwy Ste 105 Cincinnati (45246) *(G-3484)*
Total Quality Logistics LLC..513 831-2600
  50 S Main St Ste 900 Akron (44308) *(G-336)*
Total Quality Logistics LLC..800 580-3101
  6525 Centerville Business Pkwy Centerville (45459) *(G-1952)*
Total Quality Logistics LLC..513 831-2600
  4270 Ivy Pointe Blvd Cincinnati (45245) *(G-2116)*
Total Quality Logistics LLC..513 831-2600
  5130 Glencrossing Way Ste 3 Cincinnati (45238) *(G-3485)*
Total Quality Logistics LLC..513 831-2600
  1701 Edison Dr Milford (45150) *(G-11261)*
Total Quality Logistics LLC..800 580-3101
  8488 Shepherd Farm Dr West Chester (45069) *(G-14774)*
Total Solutions, Northwood *Also Called: Campbell Inc (G-11971)*
Total System Services...614 385-9221
  1500 Boltonfield St Columbus (43228) *(G-6773)*
Total Wireless...419 724-2363
  2005 Glendale Ave Toledo (43614) *(G-14071)*
Touchmark, Dublin *Also Called: Advanced Prgrm Resources Inc (G-7920)*
Touchstone Advisors Inc...800 638-8194
  221 E 4th St Ste 300 Cincinnati (45202) *(G-3486)*
Touchstone Mdse Group LLC (PA)..513 741-0400
  7200 Industrial Row Dr Mason (45040) *(G-10617)*
Toward Independence Inc...513 531-0804
  5021 Oaklawn Dr Cincinnati (45227) *(G-3487)*
Towards Employment Inc..216 696-5750
  1255 Euclid Ave Ste 300 Cleveland (44115) *(G-5025)*
Tower City Center Management, Cleveland *Also Called: Forest City Commercial MGT Inc (G-4270)*
Tower Real Estate Group LLC..216 520-1250
  1000 Eaton Blvd Beachwood (44122) *(G-845)*
Towlift Inc (HQ)...216 749-6800
  1395 Valley Belt Rd Brooklyn Heights (44131) *(G-1428)*
Towlift Inc...614 851-1001
  1200 Milepost Dr Columbus (43228) *(G-6774)*
Towlift Inc...440 951-9519
  7520 Clover Ave Ste A Mentor (44060) *(G-11004)*
Towlift Inc...419 666-1333
  2860 Crane Way Northwood (43619) *(G-11985)*
Towlift Inc...419 531-6110
  140 N Byrne Rd Toledo (43607) *(G-14072)*
Town & Country Adult Services, Springfield *Also Called: TAC Industries Inc (G-13298)*
Town & Country Plbg & Htg Inc...330 726-5755
  6400 Southern Blvd Youngstown (44512) *(G-15735)*
Town & Country School, Springfield *Also Called: Clark County Board of Developm (G-13232)*
Town and Country City, Columbus *Also Called: Casto Communities Cnstr Ltd (G-5519)*
Town Inn Co LLC...614 221-3281
  175 E Town St Columbus (43215) *(G-6775)*
Towne & Country Vet Clinic, Warren *Also Called: Howland Crners Twne Cntry Vtrn (G-14526)*
Towne Building Group Inc (PA)...513 381-8696
  1055 Saint Paul Pl Cincinnati (45202) *(G-3488)*

Towne Construction Svcs LLC 513 561-3700
500 Kent Rd Ste A Batavia (45103) *(G-749)*

Towne Development Group Ltd 513 381-8696
1055 Saint Paul Pl Ste 300 Cincinnati (45202) *(G-3489)*

Towne Mall, Middletown *Also Called: Ermc II LP (G-11197)*

Towne Management Realty, Cincinnati *Also Called: Towne Properties Assoc Inc (G-3492)*

Towne Place Suites Worthington 614 885-1557
7272 Huntington Park Dr Columbus (43235) *(G-6776)*

Towne Properties, Cincinnati *Also Called: Original Partners Ltd Partnr (G-3168)*

Towne Properties Asset MGT (PA) 513 381-8696
1055 Saint Paul Pl Ste 100 Cincinnati (45202) *(G-3490)*

Towne Properties Asset MGT, Cincinnati *Also Called: Towne Properties Asset MGT (G-3490)*

Towne Properties Assoc Inc 513 793-6976
5701 Kugler Mill Rd Cincinnati (45236) *(G-3491)*

Towne Properties Assoc Inc 513 489-4059
11340 Montgomery Rd Ste 202 Cincinnati (45249) *(G-3492)*

Towne Properties Assoc Inc 513 874-3737
11840 Kemper Springs Dr Ste C Cincinnati (45240) *(G-3493)*

Towne Properties Assoc Inc 513 489-9700
8675 E Kemper Rd Cincinnati (45249) *(G-3494)*

Towne Properties Associates Inc (PA) 513 381-8696
1055 Saint Paul Pl Cincinnati (45202) *(G-3495)*

Towne Properties Machine Group, Batavia *Also Called: Towne Construction Svcs LLC (G-749)*

TownePlace Management LLC 419 724-0044
2851 Navarre Ave Oregon (43616) *(G-12145)*

TownePlace Stes Clmbus Wrthngt, Columbus *Also Called: Oh-16 Clmbus Wrthngton Prprty (G-6386)*

TownePlace Stes Clvland Wstlak, Westlake *Also Called: Oh-16 Clvland Wstlake Prprty S (G-15090)*

TownePlace Suites By Marriott 513 774-0610
9369 Waterstone Blvd Cincinnati (45249) *(G-3496)*

TownePlace Suites By Marriott 419 425-9545
2501 Tiffin Ave Findlay (45840) *(G-8594)*

TownePlace Suites By Marriott 440 871-3756
25052 Sperry Dr Westlake (44145) *(G-15116)*

TownePlace Suites By Marriott, Cincinnati *Also Called: TownePlace Suites By Marriott (G-3496)*

TownePlace Suites By Marriott, Cleveland *Also Called: Townplace Suites By Marriott (G-5026)*

TownePlace Suites By Marriott, Columbus *Also Called: Towne Place Suites Worthington (G-6776)*

TownePlace Suites By Marriott, Dayton *Also Called: TownePlace Suites Dayton North (G-7674)*

TownePlace Suites By Marriott, Findlay *Also Called: TownePlace Suites By Marriott (G-8594)*

TownePlace Suites By Marriott, Streetsboro *Also Called: CER Hotels LLC (G-13411)*

TownePlace Suites By Marriott, Westlake *Also Called: TownePlace Suites By Marriott (G-15116)*

TownePlace Suites Columbus N, Upper Arlington *Also Called: Lane Avenue Hotel Holdings LLC (G-14279)*

TownePlace Suites Dayton North 937 898-5700
3642 Maxton Rd Dayton (45414) *(G-7674)*

Townhall 2 .... 330 678-3006
155 N Water St Kent (44240) *(G-9603)*

Townhall 2 24 Hour Helpline, Kent *Also Called: Townhall 2 (G-9603)*

Townplace Suites By Marriott 440 816-9300
7325 Engle Rd Cleveland (44130) *(G-5026)*

Township of Colerain 513 741-7551
3360 W Galbraith Rd Cincinnati (45239) *(G-3497)*

Township of Copley 330 666-1853
1540 S Cleveland Massillon Rd Copley (44321) *(G-6967)*

Towpath Racquet Club, Akron *Also Called: Tennis Unlimited Inc (G-331)*

Toyota Industries N Amer Inc 937 237-0976
6254 Executive Blvd Dayton (45424) *(G-7675)*

Toyota Material Hdlg Ohio Inc (HQ) 216 328-0970
5667 E Schaaf Rd Cleveland (44131) *(G-5027)*

Toyota of Logan, Rockbridge *Also Called: Tansky Motors Inc (G-12736)*

Toyota West, Columbus *Also Called: Sonic Automotive (G-6692)*

TP Mechanical Contractors LLC (HQ) 513 851-8881
1500 Kemper Meadow Dr Cincinnati (45240) *(G-3498)*

TP Mechanical Contractors Inc 614 253-8556
2130 Franklin Rd Columbus (43209) *(G-6777)*

TPC and Thomas LLC 614 354-0717
371 County Line Rd W Ste 100b Westerville (43082) *(G-14943)*

TPC Food Service, Tiffin *Also Called: Tiffin Paper Company (G-13647)*

TPC Packaging Solutions, Cincinnati *Also Called: TPC Packaging Solutions Inc (G-3499)*

TPC Packaging Solutions Inc (PA) 513 489-8840
11630 Deerfield Rd Cincinnati (45242) *(G-3499)*

TPC Wire & Cable Corp (HQ) 800 211-4520
9600 Valley View Rd Macedonia (44056) *(G-10208)*

Tpi Effiency, Cleveland *Also Called: Telco Pros Inc (G-4982)*

Tpusa Inc 614 621-5512
4335 Equity Dr Columbus (43228) *(G-6778)*

Tql, Milford *Also Called: Total Quality Logistics LLC (G-11261)*

TRAC, Athens *Also Called: Tri County Mental Health Svcs (G-593)*

Tractor Supply, Columbus *Also Called: Tractor Supply Company (G-6779)*

Tractor Supply, Wilmington *Also Called: Tractor Supply Company (G-15275)*

Tractor Supply 492, Beavercreek Township *Also Called: Tractor Supply Company (G-951)*

Tractor Supply 673, Jackson *Also Called: Tractor Supply Company (G-9526)*

Tractor Supply Co., Portsmouth *Also Called: Tractor Supply Company (G-12577)*

Tractor Supply Company 937 320-1855
610 Orchard Ln Beavercreek Township (45434) *(G-951)*

Tractor Supply Company 614 878-7170
5525 W Broad St Columbus (43228) *(G-6779)*

Tractor Supply Company 740 288-1079
780 E Main St Jackson (45640) *(G-9526)*

Tractor Supply Company 419 673-8900
948 E Columbus St Kenton (43326) *(G-9623)*

Tractor Supply Company 740 456-0000
4000 Rhodes Ave Ste A Portsmouth (45662) *(G-12577)*

Tractor Supply Company 937 446-9425
7110 Bachman Rd Sardinia (45171) *(G-12941)*

Tractor Supply Company 937 382-2595
1627 Rombach Ave Ste B Wilmington (45177) *(G-15275)*

Tradefull LLC 888 203-0826
2100 International Pkwy North Canton (44720) *(G-11867)*

Tradeglobal, West Chester *Also Called: Tradeglobal LLC (G-14775)*

Tradeglobal LLC 866 345-5835
9271 Meridian Way West Chester (45069) *(G-14775)*

Trademark Exteriors LLC 330 893-0000
1504 Us Route 62 Wilmot (44689) *(G-15282)*

Trademark Games, Lorain *Also Called: Trademark Global LLC (G-10104)*

Trademark Global LLC (HQ) 440 960-6200
7951 W Erie Ave Lorain (44053) *(G-10104)*

Tradeone Marketing Inc 512 343-2002
1500 W 3rd St Ste 325 Cleveland (44113) *(G-5028)*

Trades Cnstr Staffing Inc 833 668-0444
9604 Lackawana Ct West Chester (45069) *(G-14776)*

Trades Equipment LLC 419 625-4444
8200 E Pleasant Valley Rd Independence (44131) *(G-9491)*

Tradesmen Group Inc (PA) 614 799-0889
8465 Rausch Dr Plain City (43064) *(G-12495)*

Tradesource Inc 614 824-3883
1550 Old Henderson Rd Columbus (43220) *(G-6780)*

Tradesource Inc 216 801-4944
5504 State Rd Parma (44134) *(G-12266)*

Trading Corp of America, Columbus *Also Called: Marfo Company (G-6197)*

Traditions At Bath Rd Inc 330 929-6272
300 E Bath Rd Cuyahoga Falls (44223) *(G-7109)*

Traditions At Stygler Road 614 475-8778
167 N Stygler Rd Columbus (43230) *(G-6781)*

Traffic Safety Solutions LLC 216 214-3735
572 Scenic Valley Way Cuyahoga Falls (44223) *(G-7110)*

Trafftech Inc 216 361-8808
7000 Hubbard Ave Cleveland (44127) *(G-5029)*

Trailines Incorporated 513 755-7900
10045 Windisch Rd West Chester (45069) *(G-14777)*

Traincroft Inc 513 792-0291
10901 Reed Hartman Hwy Ste 305 Blue Ash (45242) *(G-1256)*

Traincroft Staffing Associates, Blue Ash *Also Called: Traincroft Inc (G-1256)*

Training Center, The, Columbus *Also Called: Vertical Adventures Inc (G-6845)*

Training Services Group, Solon *Also Called: Swagelok Company (G-13152)*

ALPHABETIC SECTION

Trane Technologies Company LLC.. 419 633-6800
 209 N Main St Bryan (43506) *(G-1494)*
Trane, The, Uniontown *Also Called: Gardiner Service Company LLC (G-14253)*
Trans-Continental Systems Inc (PA)... 513 769-4774
 1718 Ralston Ave Cincinnati (45223) *(G-3500)*
Trans-States Express Inc... 513 679-7100
 7750 Reinhold Dr Cincinnati (45237) *(G-3501)*
Transamerica Agency Netwrk Inc... 614 824-4964
 1650 Watermark Dr Ste 120 Columbus (43215) *(G-6782)*
Transamerica Building Co.. 614 457-8322
 2000 Henderson Rd Ste 500 Columbus (43220) *(G-6783)*
Transcon Builders Inc (PA)... 440 439-3400
 25250 Rockside Rd Ste 2 Cleveland (44146) *(G-5030)*
Transdigm, Cleveland *Also Called: Transdigm Group Incorporated (G-5031)*
Transdigm Group Incorporated (PA)... 216 706-2960
 1301 E 9th St Ste 3000 Cleveland (44114) *(G-5031)*
Transfreight LLC.. 937 865-9270
 98 Quality Ln Dayton (45449) *(G-7676)*
Transfreight LLC.. 937 576-2800
 1351 Blauser Dr Tipp City (45371) *(G-13667)*
Transinternational System Inc (DH)... 614 891-4942
 130 E Wilson Bridge Rd Ste 150 Worthington (43085) *(G-15463)*
Transitional Living LLC (HQ).. 513 863-6383
 2052 Princeton Rd Fairfield Township (45011) *(G-8465)*
Transitional Living Inc, Fairfield Township *Also Called: Transitional Living LLC (G-8465)*
Transoft Inc... 937 427-6200
 7333 Paragon Rd Ste 250 Dayton (45459) *(G-7677)*
Transport Service Co., North Canton *Also Called: Kenan Advantage Group Inc (G-11844)*
Transport Services Inc (PA)... 440 582-4900
 10499 Royalton Rd Cleveland (44133) *(G-5032)*
Transportation Center, Warren *Also Called: Warren City Board Education (G-14574)*
Transportation Department, Ashtabula *Also Called: Ashtabula Area City School Dst (G-517)*
Transportation Department, Ontario *Also Called: Ontario Local School District (G-12120)*
Transportation Dept, Dayton *Also Called: Kettering City School District (G-7437)*
Transportation Improvement Dst, Dayton *Also Called: County of Montgomery (G-7250)*
Transportation Research Center Inc... 937 666-2011
 10820 State Route 347 East Liberty (43319) *(G-8176)*
Transportation Resources Inc.. 614 253-7948
 1120 Rarig Ave Columbus (43219) *(G-6784)*
Transportation Unlimited Inc (PA).. 216 426-0088
 3740 Carnegie Ave Ste 101 Cleveland (44115) *(G-5033)*
Transtar Electric Inc... 419 385-7573
 767 Warehouse Rd Toledo (43615) *(G-14073)*
Transtar Electric SEC & Tech, Toledo *Also Called: Transtar Electric Inc (G-14073)*
Transtar Industries Inc.. 855 872-6782
 7350 Young Dr Cleveland (44146) *(G-5034)*
Transtar Industries LLC (DH).. 440 232-5100
 7350 Young Dr Cleveland (44146) *(G-5035)*
Transtech Consulting Inc.. 614 751-0575
 600 N Cleveland Ave Ste 190 Westerville (43082) *(G-14944)*
Transworld News, Cleveland *Also Called: Windy Hill Ltd Inc (G-5150)*
Travelcenters of America Inc (DH)... 440 808-9100
 24601 Center Ridge Rd Ste 200 Westlake (44145) *(G-15117)*
Travelers Insurance, Cincinnati *Also Called: Travelers Property Cslty Corp (G-3502)*
Travelers Insurance, Columbus *Also Called: Freedom Specialty Insurance Co (G-5893)*
Travelers Property Cslty Corp.. 513 639-5300
 615 Elsinore Pl Bldg B Cincinnati (45202) *(G-3502)*
Travelodge, Zanesville *Also Called: Travelodge Zanesville (G-15832)*
Travelodge Zanesville... 740 453-0611
 58 N 6th St Zanesville (43701) *(G-15832)*
Traxium LLC.. 330 572-8200
 4246 Hudson Dr Stow (44224) *(G-13398)*
Trayak Inc.. 513 252-8089
 7577 Central Parke Blvd Ste 317 Mason (45040) *(G-10618)*
Treadmaxx Tire Distrs Inc... 404 762-4944
 519 Madison Ave Wooster (44691) *(G-15379)*
Treasurers Office, Dayton *Also Called: County of Montgomery (G-7254)*
Treatment Technologies LLC.. 937 802-4883
 313 Smith Dr Clayton (45315) *(G-3737)*
Treetree, Columbus *Also Called: Rttw Ltd (G-6617)*

Tremco Cpg Inc (HQ)... 216 292-5000
 3735 Green Rd Beachwood (44122) *(G-846)*
Tremco Incorporated (HQ) 3735 Green Rd Beachwood (44122) *(G-847)*
Trend Construction, Cincinnati *Also Called: Ford Development Corp (G-2693)*
Trendco Supply Inc (PA)... 513 752-1871
 1236 Clough Pike Ste B Batavia (45103) *(G-750)*
Trep Ltd... 419 717-5624
 900 American Rd Napoleon (43545) *(G-11533)*
Treu House of Munch Inc.. 419 666-7770
 8000 Arbor Dr Northwood (43619) *(G-11986)*
Trew LLC (PA).. 800 571-8739
 10045 International Blvd Fairfield (45014) *(G-8448)*
Trewbric III Inc... 614 444-2184
 1701 Moler Rd Columbus (43207) *(G-6785)*
Trg Maintenance LLC... 614 891-4850
 514 N State St Ste B Westerville (43082) *(G-14945)*
Trg Repair, Westlake *Also Called: Technology Recovery Group Ltd (G-15114)*
Trg Studios Inc.. 216 781-8644
 1 American Rd Brooklyn (44144) *(G-1411)*
Tri Advertising Inc... 614 548-0913
 371 County Line Rd W Ste 150 Westerville (43082) *(G-14946)*
Tri Area Electric, Youngstown *Also Called: Tri Area Electric Co Inc (G-15736)*
Tri Area Electric, Youngstown *Also Called: W T Leones Tri-Area Elc Inc (G-15750)*
Tri Area Electric Co Inc... 330 744-0151
 37 Wayne Ave Youngstown (44502) *(G-15736)*
Tri County Eggs, Versailles *Also Called: Weaver Bros Inc (G-14417)*
Tri County Extended Care Ctr.. 513 829-3555
 5200 Camelot Dr Fairfield (45014) *(G-8449)*
Tri County Family Physicians.. 614 837-6363
 11925 Lithopolis Rd Nw Canal Winchester (43110) *(G-1617)*
Tri County Mental Health, Mc Arthur *Also Called: Hopewell Health Centers Inc (G-10798)*
Tri County Mental Health Svcs (PA).. 740 592-3091
 90 Hospital Dr Athens (45701) *(G-593)*
Tri County Mental Health Svcs.. 740 594-5045
 90 Hospital Dr Athens (45701) *(G-594)*
Tri County Tower LLC.. 330 538-9874
 8900 Mahoning Ave North Jackson (44451) *(G-11878)*
Tri County Veterinary Service.. 937 693-2131
 16200 County Road 25a Anna (45302) *(G-444)*
Tri Health Facility, Cincinnati *Also Called: Hospice Cincinnati Inc (G-2846)*
Tri State Urlogic Svcs PSC Inc (PA).. 513 841-7400
 2000 Joseph E Sanker Blvd Cincinnati (45212) *(G-3503)*
Tri State Urologic Svcs PSC... 513 681-2700
 2450 Kipling Ave Ste G11 Cincinnati (45239) *(G-3504)*
Tri Zob Inc.. 216 252-4500
 4117 Rocky River Dr Cleveland (44135) *(G-5036)*
Tri-America Contractors Inc (PA).. 740 574-0148
 1664 State Route 522 Wheelersburg (45694) *(G-15134)*
Tri-Anim Health Services Inc (DH)... 614 760-5000
 5000 Tuttle Crossing Blvd Dublin (43016) *(G-8143)*
Tri-C Construction Company Inc... 330 836-2722
 1765 Merriman Rd Akron (44313) *(G-337)*
Tri-County Ambulance Svc Inc... 440 951-4600
 7000 Spinach Dr Mentor (44060) *(G-11005)*
Tri-County Computer Svcs Assn, Wooster *Also Called: Midland Council Governments (G-15356)*
Tri-County Heating & Cooling, Barberton *Also Called: Blind & Son LLC (G-695)*
Tri-County Help Center Inc (PA).. 740 695-5441
 104 1/2 N Marietta St Saint Clairsville (43950) *(G-12816)*
Tri-Mor Corp (PA).. 330 963-3101
 8530 N Boyle Pkwy Twinsburg (44087) *(G-14223)*
Tri-State Expedited Service, Millbury *Also Called: T S Expediting Services Inc (G-11271)*
Tri-State Forest Logistics LLC... 937 323-6325
 2105 Sheridan Ave Springfield (45505) *(G-13303)*
Tri-State Forest Products Inc (PA).. 937 323-6325
 2105 Sheridan Ave Springfield (45505) *(G-13304)*
Tri-State Wholesale Building Supplies Inc................................. 513 381-1231
 651 Evans St Cincinnati (45204) *(G-3505)*
Tri-Tech Medical Inc.. 800 253-8692
 35401 Avon Commerce Pkwy Avon (44011) *(G-666)*

Tri-Tech Pipeline   ALPHABETIC SECTION

Tri-Tech Pipeline, Avon Also Called: Tri-Tech Medical Inc *(G-666)*

Tri-Valley Equipment Sales Inc 740 695-5895
Main St W Barnesville (43713) *(G-723)*

Tri-W Group Inc 614 228-5000
835 Goodale Blvd Columbus (43212) *(G-6786)*

Triad Architects Ltd 614 942-1050
172 E State St Ste 600 Columbus (43215) *(G-6787)*

Triad Communications Inc 330 237-3531
1701 Front St Cuyahoga Falls (44221) *(G-7111)*

Triad Engineering & Contg Co (PA) 440 786-1000
9715 Clinton Rd Cleveland (44144) *(G-5037)*

Triad Marketing & Media, Westerville Also Called: Tri Advertising Inc *(G-14946)*

Triad Technologies LLC (PA) 937 832-2861
985 Falls Creek Dr Vandalia (45377) *(G-14395)*

Triad Transport Inc 614 491-9497
1484 Williams Rd Columbus (43207) *(G-6788)*

Triage LLC 513 774-7300
6279 Tri Ridge Blvd Ste 110 Loveland (45140) *(G-10165)*

Triangle Commercial Properties, Westerville Also Called: Donald R Kenney & Co Rlty LLC *(G-14891)*

Triangle Label, West Chester Also Called: Bgr Inc *(G-14651)*

Triangle Leasing Corp 419 729-3868
6041 Benore Rd Toledo (43612) *(G-14074)*

Triangle Precision Industries 937 299-6776
1650 Delco Park Dr Dayton (45420) *(G-7678)*

Trico, Cleveland Also Called: Trico Products Corporation *(G-5038)*

Trico Products Corporation (DH) 248 371-1700
127 Public Sq Cleveland (44114) *(G-5038)*

Tricont Trucking Company 614 527-7398
2200 Westbelt Dr Columbus (43228) *(G-6789)*

Tricor Industrial Inc (PA) 330 264-3299
3225 W Old Lincoln Way Wooster (44691) *(G-15380)*

Tricor Metals, Wooster Also Called: Tricor Industrial Inc *(G-15380)*

TRIDIA HOSPICE & PALLIATIVE CA, Westerville Also Called: Tridia Hospice Care Inc *(G-14947)*

Tridia Hospice Care Inc 614 915-8882
110 Polaris Pkwy Ste 302 Westerville (43082) *(G-14947)*

Triec Electrical Services Inc 937 323-3721
1630 Progress Rd Springfield (45505) *(G-13305)*

Trihealth, Cincinnati Also Called: Trihealth Inc *(G-3517)*

Trihealth Inc 513 734-9050
210 N Union St Bethel (45106) *(G-1095)*

Trihealth Inc 513 891-1627
4665 Cornell Rd Ste 350 Blue Ash (45241) *(G-1257)*

Trihealth Inc 513 481-9700
6350 Glenway Ave Ste 300 Cincinnati (45211) *(G-3506)*

Trihealth Inc 513 931-2400
6949 Good Samaritan Dr Ste 210 Cincinnati (45247) *(G-3507)*

Trihealth Inc 513 389-1400
3260 Westbourne Dr Cincinnati (45248) *(G-3508)*

Trihealth Inc 513 985-3700
8311 Montgomery Rd Cincinnati (45236) *(G-3509)*

Trihealth Inc 513 246-7000
6909 Good Samaritan Dr Ste A Cincinnati (45247) *(G-3510)*

Trihealth Inc 513 241-4135
1150 W 8th St Ste 120 Cincinnati (45203) *(G-3511)*

Trihealth Inc 513 569-6777
375 Dixmyth Ave Cincinnati (45220) *(G-3512)*

Trihealth Inc 513 871-2340
2753 Erie Ave Cincinnati (45208) *(G-3513)*

Trihealth Inc 513 624-5558
7810 5 Mile Rd Cincinnati (45230) *(G-3514)*

Trihealth Inc 513 853-4900
3425 North Bend Rd Ste A Cincinnati (45239) *(G-3515)*

Trihealth Inc 513 751-5900
400 Martin Luther King Dr Cincinnati (45229) *(G-3516)*

Trihealth Inc (HQ) 513 569-5400
625 Eden Park Dr Cincinnati (45202) *(G-3517)*

Trihealth Inc 513 221-4848
4030 Smith Rd Cincinnati (45209) *(G-3518)*

Trihealth Inc 513 867-0015
3145 Hamilton Mason Rd Ste 300 Fairfield Township (45011) *(G-8466)*

Trihealth Inc 513 874-3990
8500 Bilstein Blvd Ste 100 Hamilton (45015) *(G-9087)*

Trihealth Inc 513 282-7300
100 Arrow Springs Blvd Ste 2800 Lebanon (45036) *(G-9794)*

Trihealth Inc 513 794-5600
10600 Montgomery Rd Ste 300 Montgomery (45242) *(G-11376)*

Trihealth Inc 513 865-1111
10506 Montgomery Rd Montgomery (45242) *(G-11377)*

Trihealth Inc 513 985-0900
6200 Pfeiffer Rd Ste 330 Montgomery (45242) *(G-11378)*

Trihealth Inc 513 860-6820
4900 Wunnenberg Way West Chester (45069) *(G-14778)*

Trihealth Evendale Hospital (DH) 513 454-2222
3155 Glendale Milford Rd Cincinnati (45241) *(G-3519)*

Trihealth Fitnes Hlth Pavilion, Montgomery Also Called: Trihealth Inc *(G-11378)*

Trihealth G LLC (DH) 513 732-0700
4600 Wesley Ave Ste N Cincinnati (45212) *(G-3520)*

Trihealth G LLC 513 862-1888
3219 Clifton Ave Ste 100 Cincinnati (45220) *(G-3521)*

Trihealth G LLC 513 922-1200
2001 Anderson Ferry Rd Cincinnati (45238) *(G-3522)*

Trihealth G LLC 513 792-4700
8240 Northcreek Dr Cincinnati (45236) *(G-3523)*

Trihealth G LLC 513 398-3445
7423 S Mason Montgomery Rd Mason (45040) *(G-10619)*

Trihealth Hf LLC 513 398-3445
7423 S Mason Montgomery Rd Ste B Mason (45040) *(G-10620)*

Trihealth Oncology Inst LLC 513 451-4033
5520 Cheviot Rd Cincinnati (45247) *(G-3524)*

Trihealth Orthpd & Spine Inst, Cincinnati Also Called: Trihealth Os LLC *(G-3525)*

Trihealth Orthpd & Spine Inst, Montgomery Also Called: Trihealth Os LLC *(G-11379)*

Trihealth Os LLC (DH) 513 985-3700
8311 Montgomery Rd Cincinnati (45236) *(G-3525)*

Trihealth Os LLC 513 791-6611
10547 Montgomery Rd Ste 400a Montgomery (45242) *(G-11379)*

Trihealth Rehabilitation Hosp 513 601-0600
2155 Dana Ave Cincinnati (45207) *(G-3526)*

Trihelth Orthpaedic Spine Inst, Cincinnati Also Called: Trihealth Inc *(G-3509)*

Trihelth Orthpaedic Spine Inst, West Chester Also Called: Trihealth Inc *(G-14778)*

Trihelth Wns Svcs Advnced Gync, Cincinnati Also Called: Trihealth G LLC *(G-3521)*

Trilegiant Corporation 614 823-5215
300 W Schrock Rd Westerville (43081) *(G-15018)*

Trillium Family Solutions Inc 330 454-7066
111 Stow Ave Ste 100 Cuyahoga Falls (44221) *(G-7112)*

Trilogy, Zanesville Also Called: Trilogy Rehab Services LLC *(G-15833)*

Trilogy Fulfillment LLC 614 491-0553
6600 Alum Creek Dr Groveport (43125) *(G-9005)*

Trilogy Health Services LLC 419 935-6511
1050 Neal Zick Rd Willard (44890) *(G-15174)*

Trilogy Healthcare Putnam LLC 419 532-2961
755 Ottawa St Kalida (45853) *(G-9551)*

Trilogy Rehab Services LLC 740 452-3000
2991 Maple Ave Zanesville (43701) *(G-15833)*

Trimark Ss Kemp, Cleveland Also Called: SS Kemp & Co LLC *(G-4939)*

Trimat Construction Inc 740 388-9515
13621 State Route 554 Bidwell (45614) *(G-1106)*

Trimble & Julian, Westerville Also Called: Julian & Grube Inc *(G-14902)*

Trimble Trnsp Entp Sltions Inc (HQ) 216 831-6606
6085 Parkland Blvd Mayfield Heights (44124) *(G-10793)*

Trimor, Twinsburg Also Called: Tri-Mor Corp *(G-14223)*

Trinity Community At Fairborn, Fairborn Also Called: United Church Homes Inc *(G-8382)*

Trinity Community Beavercreek, Dayton Also Called: United Church Homes Inc *(G-7682)*

Trinity Health 614 227-0197
120 S Green St Columbus (43222) *(G-6790)*

Trinity Health Group Ltd 614 899-4830
827 Yard St Columbus (43212) *(G-6791)*

Trinity Health System (DH) 740 283-7000
380 Summit Ave Steubenville (43952) *(G-13346)*

Trinity Home Builders LLC 614 898-7200
14099 Sunladen Dr Sw Etna (43068) *(G-8331)*

ALPHABETIC SECTION — Tsm Logistics LLC

Trinity Hospital Holding Co (DH) 740 264-8000
380 Summit Ave Steubenville (43952) *(G-13347)*

Trinity Hospital Twin City 740 922-2800
819 N 1st St Dennison (44621) *(G-7858)*

Trinity Medical Center East, Steubenville *Also Called: Trinity Health System (G-13346)*

Trinity Medical Center East, Steubenville *Also Called: Trinity Hospital Holding Co (G-13347)*

Trinity Rhabilitation Svcs LLC 740 695-0069
72640 Fairpoint New Athens Rd Saint Clairsville (43950) *(G-12817)*

Trinity School of Nursing 740 283-7525
380 Summit Ave Steubenville (43952) *(G-13348)*

Trinity United Methodist Ch 614 488-3659
1581 Cambridge Blvd Columbus (43212) *(G-6792)*

Trinity West 740 264-8000
4000 Johnson Rd Steubenville (43952) *(G-13349)*

Trio Orthodontics 614 889-7613
7420 State Route 161 E Plain City (43064) *(G-12496)*

Trio Trucking Inc 513 679-7100
7750 Reinhold Dr Cincinnati (45237) *(G-3527)*

Tripack LLC 513 248-1255
401 Milford Pkwy Ste C Milford (45150) *(G-11262)*

Triple Crown Services Company 419 625-0672
3811 Old Railroad Rd Sandusky (44870) *(G-12937)*

Triple Q Foundations Co Inc 513 932-3121
139 Harmon Ave Lebanon (45036) *(G-9795)*

Triple T Transport Inc (PA) 740 657-3244
433 Lewis Center Rd Lewis Center (43035) *(G-9839)*

Triplefin LLC (HQ) 855 877-5346
8990 Duke Blvd Mason (45040) *(G-10621)*

Triplett ASAP, Akron *Also Called: Lkq Triplettasap Inc (G-223)*

Tripoint Medical Center 440 375-8100
7590 Auburn Rd Concord Township (44077) *(G-6936)*

Tripoint Medical Center, Concord Township *Also Called: Lake Hospital System Inc (G-6927)*

Trips, Fremont *Also Called: Great Lkes Cmnty Action Partnr (G-8686)*

Trisco Systems Incorporated 419 339-3906
2000 Baty Rd Lima (45807) *(G-9973)*

Triumph Energy Corporation 513 367-9900
9171 Dry Fork Rd Harrison (45030) *(G-9118)*

Triversity Construction, Cincinnati *Also Called: Triversity Construction Co LLC (G-3528)*

Triversity Construction Co LLC 513 733-0046
921 Curtis St Cincinnati (45206) *(G-3528)*

Trk Investments Montgomery LLC 513 388-0186
3045 Williams Creek Dr Cincinnati (45244) *(G-3529)*

Troilo & Associates, New Albany *Also Called: Allstars Travel Group Inc (G-11556)*

Tropical Nut & Fruit, Urbancrest *Also Called: Hayden Valley Foods Inc (G-14320)*

Trowbridge Mvg Relocation Svcs, Groveport *Also Called: Trowbridge Storage Company (G-9006)*

Trowbridge Storage Company 614 766-0116
5825 Green Pointe Dr S Groveport (43125) *(G-9006)*

Troy Center, Troy *Also Called: Genesis Healthcare (G-14136)*

Troy Christian Schools Inc 937 339-5692
1586 Mckaig Rd Troy (45373) *(G-14161)*

Troy City School District 937 339-0457
301 W Main St Troy (45373) *(G-14162)*

Troy Country Club 937 335-5691
1830 Peters Rd Troy (45373) *(G-14163)*

Troy Hayner Cultural Center, Troy *Also Called: Troy City School District (G-14162)*

Troy Hotel II LLC 937 332-1446
83 Troy Town Dr Troy (45373) *(G-14164)*

Troy Motel Assn Inc 614 299-4300
1690 Clara St Columbus (43211) *(G-6793)*

Troy Nursing & Rehab, Troy *Also Called: Troy Rhblttion Hlthcare Ctr LL (G-14165)*

Troy Rhblttion Hlthcare Ctr LL 937 335-7161
512 Crescent Dr Troy (45373) *(G-14165)*

Troy Strauss Co Lpa 513 621-2120
150 E 4th St Cincinnati (45202) *(G-3530)*

Troyer Cheese, Inc., Millersburg *Also Called: Cheese Holdings Inc (G-11275)*

Troyer Manufacturing, Millersburg *Also Called: Lipari Foods Operating Co LLC (G-11284)*

TRT Management Corporation (PA) 419 661-1233
487 J St Perrysburg (43551) *(G-12380)*

Trucare Provider Services LLC 513 201-5611
3600 Park 42 Dr Ste 3670 Cincinnati (45241) *(G-3531)*

Trucco Construction Co Inc 740 417-9010
3531 Airport Rd Delaware (43015) *(G-7831)*

Trucent Renewable Chem LLC 877 280-7212
1202 Industrial Dr Van Wert (45891) *(G-14353)*

Truckmen, Geneva *Also Called: Neighborhood Logistics Co Inc (G-8787)*

Truckomat Corporation 740 467-2818
10707 Lancaster Rd Ste 37 Hebron (43025) *(G-9155)*

Truckway Leasing, Cincinnati *Also Called: Interstate Truckway Inc (G-2883)*

Trucraft Roofing LLC 513 965-9200
807 Round Bottom Rd Milford (45150) *(G-11263)*

True Core Federal Credit Union 740 345-6608
215 Deo Dr Newark (43055) *(G-11751)*

True North Energy LLC (PA) 877 245-9336
10346 Brecksville Rd Brecksville (44141) *(G-1370)*

True North Energy LLC 330 722-2031
241 S State Rd Medina (44256) *(G-10900)*

True Torq, Blanchester *Also Called: Fulflo Specialties Company (G-1117)*

True Value, Hartville *Also Called: Hrm Enterprises Inc (G-9127)*

True Wing Aviation LLC 937 657-3990
2061 Tumbleweed Ln Lebanon (45036) *(G-9796)*

Truepoint Inc 513 792-6648
4901 Hunt Rd Ste 200 Blue Ash (45242) *(G-1258)*

Truepoint Wealth Counsel LLC (PA) 513 792-6648
9999 Carver Rd Ste 200 Blue Ash (45242) *(G-1259)*

Trulite GL Alum Solutions LLC 740 929-2443
160 N High St Hebron (43025) *(G-9156)*

Trumbll-Mahoning Med Group Inc 330 372-8800
2600 State Route 5 Cortland (44410) *(G-6976)*

Trumbll-Mhoning Med Group Phrm, Cortland *Also Called: Trumbll-Mahoning Med Group Inc (G-6976)*

Trumbull Cmnty Action Program (PA) 330 393-2507
1230 Palmyra Rd Sw Warren (44485) *(G-14564)*

Trumbull County Engineering (PA) 330 675-2640
650 N River Rd Nw Warren (44483) *(G-14565)*

Trumbull County Engineers, Warren *Also Called: County of Trumbull (G-14514)*

Trumbull Industries, Warren *Also Called: Trumbull Industries Inc (G-14566)*

Trumbull Industries Inc 330 270-7800
1040 N Meridian Rd Youngstown (44509) *(G-15737)*

Trumbull Industries Inc (PA) 800 477-1799
400 Dietz Rd Ne Warren (44483) *(G-14566)*

Trumbull Mem Hosp Foundation 330 841-9376
1350 E Market St Warren (44483) *(G-14567)*

Trumbull Memorial Hospital, Warren *Also Called: Steward Trumbull Mem Hosp Inc (G-14561)*

Trupartner Credit Union Inc (PA) 513 241-2050
1717 Western Ave Cincinnati (45214) *(G-3532)*

Trupointe Cooperative Inc 937 575-6780
215 Looney Rd Piqua (45356) *(G-12459)*

Trust Processing 513 774-8805
11804 Conrey Rd Cincinnati (45249) *(G-3533)*

Trustaff Management LLC 513 272-3999
4675 Cornell Rd Ste 100 Blue Ash (45241) *(G-1260)*

Trustaff Travel Nurses, Blue Ash *Also Called: Trustaff Management LLC (G-1260)*

Trx Great Plains, Inc., Cleveland *Also Called: Horizon Mid Atlantic Inc (G-4379)*

Trz Holdings Inc 419 931-0072
28350 Kensington Ln Perrysburg (43551) *(G-12381)*

TS Tech Americas Inc 740 593-5958
10 Kenny Dr Athens (45701) *(G-595)*

TS Tech Americas Inc (HQ) 614 575-4100
8458 E Broad St Reynoldsburg (43068) *(G-12678)*

TS Trim Industries Inc (DH) 614 837-4114
6380 Canal St Canal Winchester (43110) *(G-1618)*

TSC Apparel LLC (HQ) 800 289-5400
10856 Reed Hartman Hwy Ste 150 Cincinnati (45242) *(G-3534)*

TSC Communications Inc 419 739-2200
2 Willipie St Wapakoneta (45895) *(G-14492)*

Tsk Assisted Living Svcs Inc 330 297-2000
240 W Riddle Ave Ravenna (44266) *(G-12645)*

Tsl Ltd (PA) 419 843-3200
5217 Monroe St Ste A1 Toledo (43623) *(G-14075)*

Tsm Logistics LLC 419 234-6074
4567 Old Town Run Rd Rockford (45882) *(G-12737)*

Tsmm Management LLC 740 450-1100
4212 Northpointe Dr Zanesville (43701) *(G-15834)*

TSS Technologies, West Chester *Also Called: Cbn Westside Technologies Inc (G-14660)*

Tsys, Columbus *Also Called: Total System Services (G-6773)*

Ttl Associates Inc (HQ) 419 241-4556
1915 N 12th St Toledo (43604) *(G-14076)*

Ttx 216 778-6500
22550 Ascoa Ct Strongsville (44149) *(G-13492)*

Tube Fittings Division, Columbus *Also Called: Parker-Hannifin Corporation (G-6500)*

Tucker Ellis LLP (PA) 216 592-5000
950 Main Ave Ste 1100 Cleveland (44113) *(G-5039)*

Tucker Landscaping Inc 440 786-9840
1000 Broadway Ave Bedford (44146) *(G-990)*

Tucker Landscaping Company, Bedford *Also Called: Tucker Landscaping Inc (G-990)*

Tucson Inc 330 339-4935
3497 University Dr Ne New Philadelphia (44663) *(G-11669)*

Tudor Arms Mstr Subtenant LLC 216 696-6611
10660 Carnegie Ave Cleveland (44106) *(G-5040)*

Tuffy Associates Corp (PA) 419 865-6900
7150 Granite Cir Ste 100 Toledo (43617) *(G-14077)*

Tuffy Auto Service Centers, Toledo *Also Called: Tuffy Associates Corp (G-14077)*

Turbo Parts LLC 740 223-1695
1676 Cascade Dr Marion (43302) *(G-10457)*

Turf Care Supply Corp 740 633-8247
100 Picoma Rd Martins Ferry (43935) *(G-10471)*

TURF CARE SUPPLY CORP., Martins Ferry *Also Called: Turf Care Supply Corp (G-10471)*

Turfscape LLC 330 405-7979
8490 Tower Dr Twinsburg (44087) *(G-14224)*

Turn Around Group Inc 330 372-0064
1512 Phoenix Rd Ne Warren (44483) *(G-14568)*

Turn-Key Industrial Svcs LLC 614 274-1128
4512 Harrisburg Pike Grove City (43123) *(G-8960)*

Turnbull-Wahlert Construction Inc 513 731-7300
5533 Fair Ln Cincinnati (45227) *(G-3535)*

Turner Construction Company 513 721-4224
250 W Court St Ste 300w Cincinnati (45202) *(G-3536)*

Turner Construction Company 216 522-1180
1422 Euclid Ave Ste 200 Cleveland (44115) *(G-5041)*

Turner Construction Company 614 984-3000
262 Hanover St Columbus (43215) *(G-6794)*

Turner Property Svcs Group Inc 937 461-7474
3199 Klepinger Rd # 200 Dayton (45406) *(G-7679)*

TURNING POINT, Marion *Also Called: Concerned Ctzens Agnst Vlnce A (G-10423)*

Turning Point Residential Inc 330 788-0669
357 E Midlothian Blvd Youngstown (44507) *(G-15738)*

Turning Pt Counseling Svcs Inc (PA) 330 744-2991
611 Belmont Ave Youngstown (44502) *(G-15739)*

Turning Technologies LLC (PA) 330 746-3015
6000 Mahoning Ave Youngstown (44515) *(G-15740)*

Turnkey Technology LLC 513 725-2177
6813 Harrison Ave Cincinnati (45247) *(G-3537)*

Turnserv LLC 216 600-8876
231 Springside Dr Ste 150 Akron (44333) *(G-338)*

Turocy & Watson LLP 216 696-8730
127 Public Sq Fl 57 Cleveland (44114) *(G-5042)*

Turtle Golf Management Ltd (HQ) 614 882-5920
5400 Little Turtle Way W Westerville (43081) *(G-15019)*

Tuscarawas Cnty Job Fmly Svcs, New Philadelphia *Also Called: County of Tuscarawas (G-11646)*

Tuscarwas Ambltory Srgery Ctr 330 365-2101
320 Oxford St Dover (44622) *(G-7904)*

Tuscarwas Oral Mxllfcial Srger 330 364-8665
1456 Kaderly St Nw New Philadelphia (44663) *(G-11670)*

Tusco Grocers Inc 740 922-8721
30 S 4th St Dennison (44621) *(G-7859)*

Tusing Builders Ltd 419 465-3100
2596 Us Highway 20 E Monroeville (44847) *(G-11359)*

Tutor Time Learning Ctrs LLC 513 755-6690
7218 Liberty Way West Chester (45069) *(G-14779)*

Tuttle Construction Inc 419 228-6262
880 Shawnee Rd Lima (45805) *(G-9974)*

Tuttle Crossing Associates, Dublin *Also Called: Simon Property Group (G-8121)*

Tuttle Inn Developers LLC 614 793-5500
5500 Tuttle Crossing Blvd Dublin (43016) *(G-8144)*

TV Minority Company Inc 937 832-9350
30 Lau Pkwy Englewood (45315) *(G-8324)*

TVC Group LLC 919 241-7830
2802 London Groveport Rd Grove City (43123) *(G-8961)*

TWC Enterprises, Millersport *Also Called: TWC Entrprises Elec Contrs LLC (G-11299)*

TWC Entrprises Elec Contrs LLC 740 467-9004
2438 Blacklick Eastern Rd Ne Millersport (43046) *(G-11299)*

Twenty First Century Communications Inc 614 442-1215
760 Communications Pkwy Columbus (43214) *(G-6795)*

Twg Staffing LLC 877 293-3670
8280 Montgomery Rd Ste 205 Cincinnati (45236) *(G-3538)*

Twh, Hicksville *Also Called: Wholesale House Inc (G-9162)*

Twilight Gardens Home, Norwalk *Also Called: Twilight Grdns Hlthcare Group (G-12029)*

Twilight Grdns Hlthcare Group 419 668-2086
196 W Main St Norwalk (44857) *(G-12029)*

Twin City Hospital 740 922-6675
6408 Mckee Rd Dennison (44621) *(G-7860)*

Twin Lakes Senior Living Cmnty 360 933-0741
9840 Montgomery Rd Montgomery (45242) *(G-11380)*

Twin Sisters Productions LLC 330 631-0361
4710 Hudson Dr Stow (44224) *(G-13399)*

Twin Towers Head Start, Dayton *Also Called: Miami Vly Child Dev Ctrs Inc (G-7502)*

Twin Valley, Columbus *Also Called: Ohio Dept Mntal Hlth Addction (G-6410)*

Twin Vly Behavioral Healthcare, Columbus *Also Called: Ohio Dept Mntal Hlth Addction (G-6408)*

Twin Vly Behavioral Hlth Care, Columbus *Also Called: Ohio Dept Mntal Hlth Addction (G-6409)*

Twinsburg Medical Offices, Twinsburg *Also Called: Kaiser Foundation Hospitals (G-14198)*

Twism Enterprises LLC 513 800-1098
12110 Regency Run Ct Apt 9 Cincinnati (45240) *(G-3539)*

Twist Aero LLC 937 675-9581
5100 Waynesville Jamestown Rd Jamestown (45335) *(G-9536)*

Two Men & A Truck, Columbus *Also Called: Nest Tenders Limited (G-6345)*

Two Men & A Vacuum LLC 614 300-7970
2025 S High St Columbus (43207) *(G-6796)*

Two Men and A Truck, Akron *Also Called: E & V Ventures Inc (G-143)*

Two Men and A Truck/Cleveland, Wickliffe *Also Called: Northcoast Moving Entps Inc (G-15158)*

Tyrone Townhouses PA Inv LLC 216 520-1250
8111 Rockside Rd Cleveland (44125) *(G-5043)*

Tyson Group 800 659-1080
5650 Blazer Pkwy Dublin (43017) *(G-8145)*

Tyto Government Solutions Inc 937 306-3030
2940 Presidential Dr Ste 390 Beavercreek (45324) *(G-911)*

Tzangas Plakas Mannos Recupero (PA) 330 453-5466
200 Market Ave N Ste 300 Canton (44702) *(G-1874)*

U C Health Dermatology, West Chester *Also Called: Uc Health Llc (G-14784)*

U D F, Cincinnati *Also Called: United Dairy Farmers Inc (G-3553)*

U Haul Co of Northwestern Ohio (DH) 419 478-1101
50 W Alexis Rd Toledo (43612) *(G-14078)*

U Hcmc 216 721-3405
11100 Euclid Ave Cleveland (44106) *(G-5044)*

U S C, Miamisburg *Also Called: Ulliman Schutte Cnstr LLC (G-11099)*

U S Development Corp 330 673-6900
900 W Main St Kent (44240) *(G-9604)*

U S Diagnostics, Dayton *Also Called: Dayton Medical Imaging (G-7290)*

U S Molding Machinery Co Inc 440 918-1701
38294 Pelton Rd Willoughby (44094) *(G-15224)*

U S Protective Services, Independence *Also Called: United Sttes Prtctive Svcs Cor (G-9492)*

U S Rail Corporation of Ohio 419 720-7588
7846 W Central Ave Toledo (43617) *(G-14079)*

U S Rail Holdings, Toledo *Also Called: U S Rail Corporation of Ohio (G-14079)*

U S Weatherford L P 330 746-2502
1100 Performance Pl Youngstown (44502) *(G-15741)*

U S Xpress Inc 440 743-7177
7177 W 130th St Cleveland (44130) *(G-5045)*

U S Xpress Inc 740 363-0700
2000 Nutter Farms Ln Delaware (43015) *(G-7832)*

ALPHABETIC SECTION

U S Xpress Inc.. 937 328-4100
  825 W Leffel Ln Springfield (45506) *(G-13306)*

U S Xpress Inc.. 419 244-6384
  401 Adams St Toledo (43604) *(G-14080)*

U S Xpress Inc.. 740 452-4153
  2705 E Pointe Dr Zanesville (43701) *(G-15835)*

U-Co Industries Inc.. 937 644-3021
  16900 Square Dr Ste 110 Marysville (43040) *(G-10513)*

U-Haul, Toledo *Also Called: U Haul Co of Northwestern Ohio (G-14078)*

U.S. Bridge, Cambridge *Also Called: Ohio Bridge Corporation (G-1578)*

Uai Agency, Cleveland *Also Called: United Agencies Inc (G-5052)*

Uasi, Cincinnati *Also Called: United Audit Systems Inc (G-3552)*

Uber Greenlight Hub... 800 593-7069
  4803 Montgomery Rd Bldg D Norwood (45212) *(G-12035)*

UBS Americas Inc... 440 356-5237
  18500 Lake Rd Ste 400 Rocky River (44116) *(G-12754)*

UBS Financial Services, Rocky River *Also Called: UBS Americas Inc (G-12754)*

UBS Financial Services Inc... 513 576-5000
  312 Walnut St Ste 3300 Cincinnati (45202) *(G-3540)*

Uc Health, Cincinnati *Also Called: University Ear Nose Throat Spc (G-3567)*

Uc Health, Cincinnati *Also Called: University Radiology Assoc (G-3596)*

Uc Health Llc... 513 585-7600
  3200 Burnet Ave Cincinnati (45229) *(G-3541)*

Uc Health Llc... 513 475-7880
  222 Piedmont Ave Ste 6000 Cincinnati (45219) *(G-3542)*

Uc Health Llc... 513 271-5111
  3590 Lucille Dr Ste 1000 Cincinnati (45213) *(G-3543)*

Uc Health Llc... 513 648-9077
  11590 Century Blvd Ste 102 Cincinnati (45246) *(G-3544)*

Uc Health Llc... 513 584-8600
  3120 Burnet Ave Ste 203 Cincinnati (45229) *(G-3545)*

Uc Health Llc (PA).. 513 585-6000
  3200 Burnet Ave Cincinnati (45229) *(G-3546)*

Uc Health Llc... 513 584-6999
  9313 S Mason Montgomery Rd Ste 200 Mason (45040) *(G-10622)*

Uc Health Llc... 513 475-8050
  300 Chamber Dr Milford (45150) *(G-11264)*

Uc Health Llc... 513 475-8282
  7759 University Dr West Chester (45069) *(G-14780)*

Uc Health Llc... 513 475-7777
  7710 University Ct West Chester (45069) *(G-14781)*

Uc Health Llc... 513 475-8300
  7750 Discovery Dr West Chester (45069) *(G-14782)*

Uc Health Llc... 513 475-7458
  7700 University Ct Ste 1800 West Chester (45069) *(G-14783)*

Uc Health Llc... 513 475-7630
  7690 Discovery Dr Unit 3100 West Chester (45069) *(G-14784)*

Uc Health Llc... 513 298-3000
  7798 Discovery Dr Ste F West Chester (45069) *(G-14785)*

Uc Health Dermatology, Cincinnati *Also Called: Univ Dermatology (G-3559)*

Uc Health Partners LLC.. 513 475-8524
  222 Piedmont Ave Cincinnati (45219) *(G-3547)*

Uc Health Primary Care Mason, Mason *Also Called: Uc Health Llc (G-10622)*

Uc Health Varsity Vlg Imaging, Cincinnati *Also Called: Uc Health Partners LLC (G-3547)*

Uc Helth Cncnnati Arthrtis Ass, Cincinnati *Also Called: Uc Health Llc (G-3543)*

Uc Helth W Chster Surgical Ctr, West Chester *Also Called: Uc Health Llc (G-14782)*

Uc Physicians, Cincinnati *Also Called: University Cncnnati Physcans I (G-3565)*

Uc Physicians At Univ Pointe, West Chester *Also Called: University of Cincinnati Phys (G-14788)*

Ucb, Toledo *Also Called: United Collection Bureau Inc (G-14082)*

Ucc Ix DBA Barrington Square.. 740 382-4885
  170 E Center St Marion (43302) *(G-10458)*

UCI, Cleveland *Also Called: University Circle Incorporated (G-5071)*

UCP OF GREATER CLEVELAND, Cleveland *Also Called: United Crbral Plsy Assn Grter (G-5057)*

Ucvp For Research, Cincinnati *Also Called: University of Cincinnati (G-3591)*

UFCW LOCAL 1059, Columbus *Also Called: United Fd Coml Wkrs Un Lcal 10 (G-6805)*

UFCW LOCAL 880, Broadview Heights *Also Called: United Fd Coml Wkrs Un Lcal 88 (G-1402)*

Uh Geauga Medical Center, Chardon *Also Called: Uh Regional Hospitals (G-2022)*

Uh Landerbrook Health Center, Beachwood *Also Called: University Hospitals Cleveland (G-848)*

Uh Regional Hospitals... 440 735-3900
  44 Blaine Ave Bedford (44146) *(G-991)*

Uh Regional Hospitals... 440 285-6000
  13207 Ravenna Rd Chardon (44024) *(G-2022)*

Uh Regional Hospitals (HQ).. 440 585-6439
  27100 Chardon Rd Richmond Heights (44143) *(G-12723)*

Uh Urgent Care Broadview Hts, Broadview Heights *Also Called: University Hsptals Clvland Med (G-1403)*

Uhc Construction Services, Northfield *Also Called: Uhc United Heating & Coolg LLC (G-11967)*

Uhc United Heating & Coolg LLC................................... 866 931-0118
  41 Leonard Ave Northfield (44067) *(G-11967)*

Uhhs Westlake Medical Center....................................... 440 250-2070
  960 Clague Rd Ste 3201 Westlake (44145) *(G-15118)*

Uhhs-Memorial Hosp of Geneva..................................... 440 466-1141
  870 W Main St Geneva (44041) *(G-8791)*

Uhhs/Csahs - Cuyahoga Inc... 440 746-3401
  2351 E 22nd St Cleveland (44115) *(G-5046)*

Uhmg Department of Urologist.. 216 844-3009
  1611 S Green Rd Ste 106 Cleveland (44121) *(G-5047)*

Uhrichsville Hlth Care Ctr Inc.. 740 922-2208
  5166 Spanson Dr Se Uhrichsville (44683) *(G-14237)*

Uima, Cincinnati *Also Called: University of Cincinnati (G-3583)*

Ull Inc.. 440 543-5195
  9812 Washington St Chagrin Falls (44023) *(G-1992)*

Ulliman Schutte Cnstr LLC (PA)..................................... 937 247-0375
  9111 Springboro Pike Miamisburg (45342) *(G-11099)*

Ullman Electric & Technologies Company...................... 216 432-5777
  3901 Chester Ave Ste B Cleveland (44114) *(G-5048)*

Ulmer, Cleveland *Also Called: Ulmer & Berne LLP (G-5049)*

Ulmer & Berne LLP... 513 698-5000
  600 Vine St Ste 2800 Cincinnati (45202) *(G-3548)*

Ulmer & Berne LLP (PA)... 216 583-7000
  1660 W 2nd St Ste 1100 Cleveland (44113) *(G-5049)*

Ulmer & Berne LLP... 614 229-0000
  65 E State St Ste 1100 Columbus (43215) *(G-6797)*

Ultimate Health Care, South Point *Also Called: Quality Care Nursing Svc Inc (G-13182)*

Ultimate Home Services LLC... 614 888-8698
  7340 Sancus Blvd Worthington (43085) *(G-15464)*

Ultimate Rehab Ltd.. 513 563-8777
  9403 Kenwood Rd Blue Ash (45242) *(G-1261)*

Ultimus Fund Solutions LLC (PA)................................... 513 587-3400
  225 Pictoria Dr Ste 450 Cincinnati (45246) *(G-3549)*

Ultra Tech Machinery Inc.. 330 929-5544
  297 Ascot Pkwy Cuyahoga Falls (44223) *(G-7113)*

Ultraedit Inc.. 216 464-7465
  5559 Eureka Dr Ste B Hamilton (45011) *(G-9088)*

Underground Services Inc.. 330 323-0166
  3223 Rockingham St Nw Uniontown (44685) *(G-14269)*

Underground Utilities Inc.. 419 465-2587
  416 Monroe St Monroeville (44847) *(G-11360)*

Unfors Raysafe Inc... 508 435-5600
  6045 Cochran Rd Solon (44139) *(G-13157)*

Unibilt Inds Hlth & Welfare Tr.. 937 890-7570
  4671 Poplar Creek Rd Vandalia (45377) *(G-14396)*

Unico Alloys & Metals Inc... 614 299-0545
  1177 Joyce Ave Columbus (43219) *(G-6798)*

Unicon International Inc (PA).. 614 861-7070
  241 Outerbelt St Columbus (43213) *(G-6799)*

Unified Bank (HQ)... 740 633-0445
  201 S 4th St Martins Ferry (43935) *(G-10472)*

Unifirst, Blacklick *Also Called: Unifirst Corporation (G-1114)*

Unifirst, Franklin *Also Called: Unifirst Corporation (G-8651)*

Unifirst Corporation.. 614 575-9999
  211 Reynoldsburg New Albany Rd Blacklick (43004) *(G-1114)*

Unifirst Corporation.. 937 746-0531
  265 Industrial Dr Franklin (45005) *(G-8651)*

Unifund Ccr LLC... 513 489-8877
  10625 Techwoods Cir Blue Ash (45242) *(G-1262)*

Unifund Corporation — ALPHABETIC SECTION

Unifund Corporation 513 489-8877
  10625 Techwoods Cir Blue Ash (45242) *(G-1263)*
Uniglobe Travel Designers, Columbus *Also Called: West Enterprises Inc (G-6879)*
Union Centre Hotel LLC 513 874-7335
  6189 Muhlhauser Rd West Chester (45069) *(G-14786)*
Union Club Company 216 621-4230
  1211 Euclid Ave Cleveland (44115) *(G-5050)*
Union Country Club 330 343-5544
  1000 N Bellevue Ave Dover (44622) *(G-7905)*
Union County Physician Corp 800 686-4677
  500 London Ave Marysville (43040) *(G-10514)*
Union First Care Inc 614 396-6192
  6555 Busch Blvd Ste 104 Columbus (43229) *(G-6800)*
Union Healthcare Services Inc 614 686-2322
  2021 E Dublin Granville Rd Columbus (43229) *(G-6801)*
Union Home Mortgage Corp (PA) 800 767-4684
  8241 Dow Cir Strongsville (44136) *(G-13493)*
Union Hospital, Dover *Also Called: Union Hospital Association (G-7907)*
Union Hospital Association 330 602-0719
  500 Medical Park Dr Dover (44622) *(G-7906)*
Union Hospital Association (HQ) 330 343-3311
  659 Boulevard St Dover (44622) *(G-7907)*
Union Mortgage Services Inc (PA) 614 457-4815
  1080 Fishinger Rd Columbus (43221) *(G-6802)*
Union Process Inc 330 929-3333
  1925 Akron Peninsula Rd Akron (44313) *(G-339)*
Union Rural Electric Coop Inc (PA) 937 642-1826
  15461 Us Highway 36 Marysville (43040) *(G-10515)*
Union Savings Bank (PA) 513 247-0300
  8534 E Kemper Rd Fl 1 Cincinnati (45249) *(G-3550)*
Unique Lawn Care, West Chester *Also Called: Tccc Inc (G-14841)*
Unique Paving Materials Corp 216 341-7711
  3993 E 93rd St Cleveland (44105) *(G-5051)*
Uniserv, Brookfield *Also Called: United Steel Service LLC (G-1407)*
Unison Bhvioral Hlth Group Inc (PA) 419 214-4673
  1425 Starr Ave Toledo (43605) *(G-14081)*
Unison Industries LLC 904 667-9904
  2455 Dayton Xenia Rd Dayton (45434) *(G-7143)*
Unistrut-Columbus, Columbus *Also Called: Loeb Electric Company (G-6172)*
United, Dayton *Also Called: United Building Materials Inc (G-7681)*
United - Maier Signs Inc 513 681-6600
  1030 Straight St Cincinnati (45214) *(G-3551)*
United Agencies Inc 216 696-8044
  1422 Euclid Ave Ste 510 Cleveland (44115) *(G-5052)*
United Airlines Inc 216 501-4700
  5970 Cargo Rd Cleveland (44135) *(G-5053)*
United Airlines Inc 216 501-5644
  6090 Cargo Rd Cleveland (44135) *(G-5054)*
United Airlines Inc 216 501-5169
  5300 Riverside Dr Cleveland (44135) *(G-5055)*
United Airlines Inc 937 454-2009
  3600 Terminal Rd Vandalia (45377) *(G-14397)*
United Alloys & Metals Inc 614 299-0545
  1177 Joyce Ave Columbus (43219) *(G-6803)*
United Alloys and Metals, Columbus *Also Called: Unico Alloys & Metals Inc (G-6798)*
United Amblnce Svc of Cmbridge 740 685-2277
  217 Watson Ave Byesville (43723) *(G-1537)*
United American Sales, West Chester *Also Called: R3 Safety LLC (G-14753)*
United Architectural Mtls Inc 330 433-9220
  7830 Cleveland Ave Nw North Canton (44720) *(G-11868)*
United Armored Services, Columbus *Also Called: Garda CL Great Lakes Inc (G-5911)*
United Art and Education Inc 800 322-3247
  799 Lyons Rd Dayton (45459) *(G-7680)*
United Audit Systems Inc 513 723-1122
  1924 Dana Ave Cincinnati (45207) *(G-3552)*
United Bank National Assn 419 683-1010
  245 N Seltzer St Crestline (44827) *(G-7027)*
United Building Materials Inc 937 222-4444
  1509 Stanley Ave Dayton (45404) *(G-7681)*
United Ch Residences Goshen 740 382-4885
  170 E Center St Marion (43302) *(G-10459)*

United Ch Rsdnces Immklee Cypr 740 382-4885
  170 E Center St Marion (43302) *(G-10460)*
United Ch Rsdnces Immklee Fla 740 382-4885
  170 E Center St Marion (43302) *(G-10461)*
United Ch Rsdnces Knton Ohio I 740 382-4885
  900 E Columbus St Kenton (43326) *(G-9624)*
United Church Homes Inc 937 426-8481
  3218 Indian Ripple Rd Dayton (45440) *(G-7682)*
United Church Homes Inc 937 878-0262
  789 Stoneybrook Trl Fairborn (45324) *(G-8382)*
United Church Homes Inc 740 286-7551
  215 Seth Ave Jackson (45640) *(G-9527)*
United Church Homes Inc 800 837-2211
  170 E Center St Marion (43302) *(G-10462)*
United Church Homes Inc 419 621-1900
  3800 Boardwalk Blvd Sandusky (44870) *(G-12938)*
United Church Homes Inc 419 294-4973
  850 Marseilles Ave Upper Sandusky (43351) *(G-14294)*
United Church Homes Inc 740 376-5600
  401 Harmar St Marietta (45750) *(G-10406)*
United Collection Bureau Inc 614 732-5000
  4100 Horizons Dr Ste 101 Columbus (43220) *(G-6804)*
United Collection Bureau Inc 419 866-6227
  1345 Ford St Maumee (43537) *(G-10776)*
United Collection Bureau Inc (PA) 419 866-6227
  5620 Southwyck Blvd Toledo (43614) *(G-14082)*
United Community, Youngstown *Also Called: United Community Financial Corp (G-15742)*
United Community Financial Corp 330 742-0500
  275 W Federal St Youngstown (44503) *(G-15742)*
United Consumer Fincl Svcs Co 440 835-3230
  865 Bassett Rd Cleveland (44145) *(G-5056)*
United Crbral Plsy Assn Grter (PA) 216 791-8363
  10011 Euclid Ave Cleveland (44106) *(G-5057)*
United Crbral Plsy Assn Grter 216 381-9993
  1374 Edendale St Cleveland (44121) *(G-5058)*
United Crbral Plsy Assn Grter 216 351-4888
  9401 Memphis Ave Cleveland (44144) *(G-5059)*
United Crbral Plsy Assn Grter 440 835-5511
  28687 Center Ridge Rd Westlake (44145) *(G-15119)*
United Dairy Farmers Inc (PA) 513 396-8700
  3955 Montgomery Rd Cincinnati (45212) *(G-3553)*
United Dental Laboratories (PA) 330 253-1810
  261 South Ave Tallmadge (44278) *(G-13609)*
United Disability Services Inc 330 379-3337
  1275 Sweitzer Ave Akron (44301) *(G-340)*
United Disability Services Inc (PA) 330 374-1169
  701 S Main St Akron (44311) *(G-341)*
United Discount, Cleveland *Also Called: Dollar Paradise (G-4174)*
United Engraving, Cincinnati *Also Called: Wood Graphics Inc (G-3680)*
United Fd Coml Wkrs Un Lcal 10 .... 614 235-3635
  4150 E Main St Fl 2 Columbus (43213) *(G-6805)*
United Fd Coml Wkrs Un Lcal 88 (PA) 216 241-5930
  9199 Market Pl Ste 2 Broadview Heights (44147) *(G-1402)*
United Financial Casualty Co 440 461-5000
  6300 Wilson Mills Rd Cleveland (44143) *(G-5060)*
United GL & Panl Systems Inc 330 244-9745
  8040 Whipple Ave Nw North Canton (44720) *(G-11869)*
United Grinding North Amer Inc (DH) 937 859-1975
  2100 United Grinding Blvd Miamisburg (45342) *(G-11100)*
United Group Services Inc (PA) 800 633-9690
  9740 Near Dr West Chester (45246) *(G-14842)*
United Healthcare, Cincinnati *Also Called: United Healthcare Ohio Inc (G-3554)*
United Healthcare, Cleveland *Also Called: United Healthcare Ohio Inc (G-5061)*
UNITED HEALTHCARE, Columbus *Also Called: United Healthcare Ohio Inc (G-6806)*
United Healthcare, Lorain *Also Called: Unitedhealthcare Insurance Co (G-10106)*
United Healthcare Ohio Inc 513 603-6200
  400 E Business Way Ste 100 Cincinnati (45241) *(G-3554)*
United Healthcare Ohio Inc 216 694-4080
  1001 Lakeside Ave E Ste 1000 Cleveland (44114) *(G-5061)*
United Healthcare Ohio Inc (DH) 614 410-7000
  9200 Worthington Rd Columbus (43085) *(G-6806)*

ALPHABETIC SECTION — United Way

United Hsptality Solutions LLC 800 238-0487
11998 Clay Pike Rd Buffalo (43722) *(G-1521)*

United Labor Agency Inc 216 664-3446
737 Bolivar Rd Ste 3000 Cleveland (44115) *(G-5062)*

United Management Inc (PA) 614 228-5331
250 Civic Center Dr Columbus (43215) *(G-6807)*

United McGill Corporation (HQ) 614 829-1200
1 Mission Park Groveport (43125) *(G-9007)*

United Media Solutions, Cincinnati Also Called: Info-Hold Inc *(G-2870)*

United Methodist Camps, Worthington Also Called: West Ohio Cnfrnce of Untd Mthd *(G-15468)*

UNITED METHODIST CHILDREN'S HO, Columbus Also Called: United Mthdst Chld HM W Ohio C *(G-6808)*

United Methodist Church, Columbus Also Called: Trinity United Methodist Ch *(G-6792)*

United Mthdst Chld HM W Ohio C (PA) 614 885-5020
431 E Broad St Columbus (43215) *(G-6808)*

United Parcel Service Inc 740 592-4570
1 Kenny Dr Athens (45701) *(G-596)*

United Parcel Service Inc 440 275-3301
1553 State Route 45 Austinburg (44010) *(G-634)*

United Parcel Service Inc 740 598-4293
500 Labelle St Brilliant (43913) *(G-1381)*

United Parcel Service Inc 419 586-8556
1851 Industrial Dr Celina (45822) *(G-1930)*

United Parcel Service Inc 513 852-6135
500 Gest St Cincinnati (45203) *(G-3555)*

United Parcel Service Inc 513 241-5289
640 W 3rd St Cincinnati (45202) *(G-3556)*

United Parcel Service Inc 513 782-4000
11141 Canal Rd Cincinnati (45241) *(G-3557)*

United Parcel Service Inc 800 742-5877
4300 E 68th St Cleveland (44105) *(G-5063)*

United Parcel Service Inc 216 676-4560
18685 Sheldon Rd Cleveland (44130) *(G-5064)*

United Parcel Service Inc 440 826-2591
17940 Englewood Dr Cleveland (44130) *(G-5065)*

United Parcel Service Inc 440 826-2508
947 Englewood Dr Cleveland (44134) *(G-5066)*

United Parcel Service Inc 614 841-7159
100 E Campus View Blvd Ste 300 Columbus (43235) *(G-6809)*

United Parcel Service Inc 614 870-4111
5101 Trabue Rd Columbus (43228) *(G-6810)*

United Parcel Service Inc 614 237-9171
3400 Refugee Rd Columbus (43232) *(G-6811)*

United Parcel Service Inc 614 385-9100
1711 Georgesville Rd Columbus (43228) *(G-6812)*

United Parcel Service Inc 419 782-3552
820 Carpenter Rd Defiance (43512) *(G-7773)*

United Parcel Service Inc 419 424-9494
1301 Commerce Pkwy Findlay (45840) *(G-8595)*

United Parcel Service Inc 330 545-0177
800 Trumbull Ave Girard (44420) *(G-8828)*

United Parcel Service Inc 800 742-5877
2250 Spiegel Dr Groveport (43125) *(G-9008)*

United Parcel Service Inc 513 863-1681
1951 Logan Ave Hamilton (45015) *(G-9089)*

United Parcel Service Inc 419 222-7399
801 Industry Ave Lima (45804) *(G-9975)*

United Parcel Service Inc 419 747-3080
875 W Longview Ave Mansfield (44906) *(G-10320)*

United Parcel Service Inc 740 373-0772
105 Industry Rd Marietta (45750) *(G-10407)*

United Parcel Service Inc 614 383-4580
1476 Likens Rd Marion (43302) *(G-10463)*

United Parcel Service Inc 419 891-6776
1550 Holland Rd Maumee (43537) *(G-10777)*

United Parcel Service Inc 216 676-1570
18401 Sheldon Rd Middleburg Heights (44130) *(G-11432)*

United Parcel Service Inc 330 339-6281
241 8th Street Ext Sw New Philadelphia (44663) *(G-11671)*

United Parcel Service Inc 614 272-8500
2450 Rathmell Rd Obetz (43207) *(G-12085)*

United Parcel Service Inc 419 872-0211
12171 Eckel Rd Perrysburg (43551) *(G-12382)*

United Parcel Service Inc 740 962-7971
21 Gingersnap Rd Portsmouth (45662) *(G-12578)*

United Parcel Service Inc 740 968-3508
44191 Lafferty Rd Saint Clairsville (43950) *(G-12818)*

United Parcel Service Inc 419 891-6841
1212 E Alexis Rd Toledo (43612) *(G-14083)*

United Parcel Service Inc 614 277-3300
3500 Centerpoint Dr Urbancrest (43123) *(G-14325)*

United Parcel Service Inc 937 382-0658
2500 S Us Highway 68 Wilmington (45177) *(G-15276)*

United Parcel Service Inc 800 742-5877
95 Karago Ave Ste 4 Youngstown (44512) *(G-15743)*

United Parcel Service Inc 800 742-5877
1507 Augusta St Zanesville (43701) *(G-15836)*

United Performance Metals, Hamilton Also Called: United Performance Metals LLC *(G-9090)*

United Performance Metals LLC (HQ) 513 860-6500
3475 Symmes Rd Hamilton (45015) *(G-9090)*

United Producers Inc (PA) 614 433-2150
8351 N High St Ste 250 Columbus (43235) *(G-6813)*

United Rentals, Columbus Also Called: United Rentals North Amer Inc *(G-6814)*

United Rentals, Perrysburg Also Called: United Rentals North Amer Inc *(G-12383)*

United Rentals North Amer Inc 614 276-5444
580 Phillipi Rd Columbus (43228) *(G-6814)*

United Rentals North Amer Inc 800 877-3687
620 Eckel Rd Perrysburg (43551) *(G-12383)*

United Rhblttion Svcs Grter Dy 937 233-1230
4710 Troy Pike Dayton (45424) *(G-7683)*

United Roofing & Sheet Metal 419 865-5576
7255 Progress St Holland (43528) *(G-9310)*

United Scoto Senior Activities (PA) 740 354-6672
117 Market St 119 Portsmouth (45662) *(G-12579)*

UNITED SENIOR SERVICES, Springfield Also Called: Untd Elderly Clark C Sprngfeld *(G-13307)*

United Skates America Inc 614 431-2751
4900 Evanswood Dr Columbus (43229) *(G-6815)*

United Skates of America Inc (PA) 614 802-2440
3362 Refugee Rd Columbus (43232) *(G-6816)*

United States Plastic Corp 419 228-2242
1390 Neubrecht Rd Lima (45801) *(G-9976)*

United States Steel Corp 440 240-2500
2199 E 28th St Lorain (44055) *(G-10105)*

United States Trotting Assn 614 224-2291
800 Michigan Ave Columbus (43215) *(G-6817)*

United States Trotting Assn (PA) 614 224-2291
6130 S Sunbury Rd Westerville (43081) *(G-15020)*

United Steel Service LLC (HQ) 330 448-4057
4500 Parkway Dr Brookfield (44403) *(G-1407)*

United Sttes Dept of Hmland SE 937 821-5543
2748 Symphony Way Dayton (45449) *(G-7684)*

United Sttes Prtctive Svcs Cor (PA) 216 475-8550
750 W Resource Dr Ste 200 Independence (44131) *(G-9492)*

United Sttes Sprtsmens Alnce F 614 888-4868
801 Kingsmill Pkwy Columbus (43229) *(G-6818)*

United Sttes Trining Tstg Ctrs, Hamilton Also Called: Hhd Aviation LLC *(G-9052)*

United Technical Support Svcs 330 562-3330
10325 State Route 43 Ste F Streetsboro (44241) *(G-13433)*

United Telemanagement Corp 937 454-1888
6640 Poe Ave Dayton (45414) *(G-7685)*

United Telephone Company Ohio 419 227-1660
122 S Elizabeth St Lima (45801) *(G-9977)*

United Trnsp Un Insur Assn (PA) 216 228-9400
6060 Rockside Woods Blvd N Independence (44131) *(G-9493)*

United Van Lines, Streetsboro Also Called: The Andrews Moving and Storage Company *(G-13432)*

United Way, Akron Also Called: United Way Summit and Medina *(G-342)*

UNITED WAY, Canton Also Called: United Way Grter Stark Cnty In *(G-1875)*

United Way, Cincinnati Also Called: Family Service *(G-2648)*

UNITED WAY, Cincinnati Also Called: United Way Greater Cincinnati *(G-3558)*

United Way, Cleveland Also Called: United Way Greater Cleveland *(G-5067)*

United Way — ALPHABETIC SECTION

United Way, Columbus *Also Called: United Way Central Ohio Inc (G-6819)*
UNITED WAY, Dayton *Also Called: United Way of The Grter Dyton (G-7686)*
UNITED WAY, Mentor *Also Called: United Way of Lake County Inc (G-11006)*
UNITED WAY, Toledo *Also Called: United Way of Greater Toledo (G-14084)*

United Way Central Ohio Inc 614 227-2700
  360 S 3rd St Columbus (43215) *(G-6819)*

United Way Greater Cincinnati (PA) 513 762-7100
  2400 Reading Rd Cincinnati (45202) *(G-3558)*

United Way Greater Cleveland (PA) 216 436-2100
  1331 Euclid Ave Cleveland (44115) *(G-5067)*

United Way Grter Stark Cnty In 330 491-0445
  401 Market Ave N Ste 300 Canton (44702) *(G-1875)*

United Way of Greater Toledo (PA) 419 254-4742
  1001 Madison Ave # 100 Toledo (43604) *(G-14084)*

United Way of Lake County Inc 440 639-4420
  9285 Progress Pkwy Mentor (44060) *(G-11006)*

United Way of The Grter Dyton (PA) 937 225-3060
  409 E Monument Ave Dayton (45402) *(G-7686)*

United Way of Yngstown The Mhn 330 746-8494
  255 Watt St Youngstown (44505) *(G-15744)*

United Way Summit and Medina (PA) 330 762-7601
  37 N High St Ste A Akron (44308) *(G-342)*

United Wheels Inc 937 865-2813
  8877 Gander Creek Dr Miamisburg (45342) *(G-11101)*

UNITED-WAY, Youngstown *Also Called: United Way of Yngstown The Mhn (G-15744)*

Unitedhealthcare Insurance Co 440 282-1357
  2022 W 29th St Lorain (44052) *(G-10106)*

Unity Health Network, Tallmadge *Also Called: Unity Health Network LLC (G-13610)*

Unity Health Network LLC 330 655-3820
  5655 Hudson Dr Ste 110 Hudson (44236) *(G-9375)*

Unity Health Network LLC 330 678-7782
  307 W Main St Kent (44240) *(G-9605)*

Unity Health Network LLC 330 626-0549
  9330 Market Square Dr Ste 100 Streetsboro (44241) *(G-13434)*

Unity Health Network LLC 330 633-7782
  116 East Ave Tallmadge (44278) *(G-13610)*

Unity I Home Healthcare LLC 740 351-0500
  221 Market St Portsmouth (45662) *(G-12580)*

Unity National Bank (HQ) 937 773-0752
  215 N Wayne St Piqua (45356) *(G-12460)*

Univ Dermatology 513 475-7630
  5575 Cheviot Rd Ste 1 Cincinnati (45247) *(G-3559)*

Univ Hospital, The, Cincinnati *Also Called: University of Cincinnati (G-3580)*

Univenture Inc (PA) 937 645-4600
  4266 Tuller Rd Dublin (43017) *(G-8146)*

Univenture Inc 877 831-9428
  16710 Square Dr Marysville (43040) *(G-10516)*

Univenture CD Packg & Systems, Dublin *Also Called: Univenture Inc (G-8146)*
Univenture CD Packg & Systems, Marysville *Also Called: Univenture Inc (G-10516)*
Univerrsal 1 Credit Union, Beavercreek *Also Called: Universal One Inc (G-912)*

Universal 1 Credit Union Inc (PA) 800 762-9555
  1 River Park Dr Dayton (45409) *(G-7687)*

Universal Advg Assoc Inc 513 522-5000
  2530 Civic Center Dr Cincinnati (45231) *(G-3560)*

Universal Contracting Corp 513 482-2700
  5151 Fishwick Dr Cincinnati (45216) *(G-3561)*

Universal Development MGT Inc (PA) 330 759-7017
  1607 Motor Inn Dr Ste 1 Girard (44420) *(G-8829)*

Universal Disposal Inc 440 286-3153
  9954 Old State Rd Chardon (44024) *(G-2023)*

Universal Enterprises Inc (PA) 419 529-3500
  545 Beer Rd Ontario (44906) *(G-12126)*

Universal Express LLC 404 642-4747
  129 Mcclure St Dayton (45403) *(G-7688)*

Universal Lawncare LLC 513 289-9391
  1452 Waycross Rd Cincinnati (45240) *(G-3562)*

Universal Marketing Group LLC 419 720-6581
  5454 Airport Hwy Toledo (43615) *(G-14085)*

Universal Nursing Services (PA) 330 434-7318
  483 Augusta Dr Akron (44333) *(G-343)*

Universal Oil Inc 216 771-4300
  265 Jefferson Ave Cleveland (44113) *(G-5068)*

Universal One Inc 937 431-3100
  2450 Esquire Dr Beavercreek (45431) *(G-912)*

Universal Packg Systems Inc 513 732-2000
  5055 State Route 276 Batavia (45103) *(G-751)*

Universal Packg Systems Inc 513 735-4777
  5069 State Route 276 Batavia (45103) *(G-752)*

Universal Packg Systems Inc 513 674-9400
  470 Northland Blvd Cincinnati (45240) *(G-3563)*

Universal Pallets Inc 614 444-1095
  611 Marion Rd Columbus (43207) *(G-6820)*

Universal Recovery Systems Inc 614 299-0184
  850 Harmon Ave Columbus (43223) *(G-6821)*

Universal Refrigeration Div, Ontario *Also Called: Universal Enterprises Inc (G-12126)*

Universal Services America LP 937 454-9035
  407 Corporate Center Dr Ste D Vandalia (45377) *(G-14398)*

Universal Stainless, North Jackson *Also Called: North Jckson Specialty Stl LLC (G-11874)*

Universal Steel Company 216 883-4972
  6600 Grant Ave Cleveland (44105) *(G-5069)*

Universal Transportation Syste (PA) 513 829-1287
  5284 Winton Rd Fairfield (45014) *(G-8450)*

Universal Well Services Inc 814 333-2656
  11 S Washington St Millersburg (44654) *(G-11294)*

Universal Windows Direct 440 232-9060
  24801 Rockside Rd Bedford Heights (44146) *(G-1003)*

Universal Windows Direct Inc 614 418-5232
  3563 Interchange Rd Columbus (43204) *(G-6822)*

Universities Space Res Assn 216 368-0750
  10900 Euclid Ave Cleveland (44106) *(G-5070)*

University Cincinnati Book Str, Cincinnati *Also Called: University of Cincinnati (G-3582)*

University Circle Incorporated (PA) 216 791-3900
  10831 Magnolia Dr Cleveland (44106) *(G-5071)*

University Cncnnati Med Ctr LL (HQ) 513 584-1000
  234 Goodman St Cincinnati (45219) *(G-3564)*

University Cncnnati Med Ctr LL 513 475-8300
  7690 Discovery Dr Unit 3000 West Chester (45069) *(G-14787)*

University Cncnnati Physcans I (HQ) 513 475-8521
  222 Piedmont Ave Ste 2200 Cincinnati (45219) *(G-3565)*

University Cncnnati Purch Dept, Cincinnati *Also Called: University of Cincinnati (G-3576)*
University Dayton RES Inst, Dayton *Also Called: University of Dayton (G-7691)*

University Ear Nose Throat Spc 513 475-8403
  222 Piedmont Ave Ste 5200 Cincinnati (45219) *(G-3566)*

University Ear Nose Throat Spc 513 558-4158
  231 Albert Sabin Way 6411 Cincinnati (45267) *(G-3567)*

University Family Physicians 513 929-0104
  2123 Auburn Ave Cincinnati (45219) *(G-3568)*

University Family Physicians 513 475-7505
  175 W Galbraith Rd Cincinnati (45216) *(G-3569)*

University GYN&ob Cnsltnts Inc (PA) 614 293-8697
  1654 Upham Dr Rm N500 Columbus (43210) *(G-6823)*

University Hosp A & MBL Care, Cincinnati *Also Called: University of Cincinnati (G-3579)*

University Hosp Geneva Med Ctr 440 415-0159
  870 W Main St Geneva (44041) *(G-8792)*

University Hosp Prtage Med Ctr, Ravenna *Also Called: Robinson Health System Inc (G-12643)*
University Hosp Rdilology Dept, Cincinnati *Also Called: University of Cincinnati (G-3581)*

University Hospital 513 584-1000
  2264 Westwood Northern Blvd Cincinnati (45225) *(G-3570)*

University Hospital 330 486-9610
  8819 Commons Blvd Twinsburg (44087) *(G-14225)*

University Hospital 440 835-8922
  29101 Health Campus Dr Ste 200 Westlake (44145) *(G-15120)*

University Hospital, Cincinnati *Also Called: University of Cincinnati (G-3578)*

University Hospitals 216 536-3020
  2915 Ludlow Rd Cleveland (44120) *(G-5072)*

UNIVERSITY HOSPITALS, Richmond Heights *Also Called: Uh Regional Hospitals (G-12723)*
University Hospitals, Shaker Heights *Also Called: University Hsptals Hlth Sys In (G-12987)*

University Hospitals Cleveland 440 646-2626
  26001 S Woodland Rd Beachwood (44122) *(G-848)*

ALPHABETIC SECTION

University Hospitals Cleveland 216 844-1000
11100 Euclid Ave Cleveland (44106) *(G-5073)*

University Hospitals Cleveland 216 983-3066
10524 Euclid Avenue, W.O. Walker Center, Suite 3200 Suite 3200 Cleveland (44106) *(G-5074)*

University Hospitals Hlth Sys, Cleveland *Also Called: University Hsptals Clvland Med* *(G-5078)*

University Hospitals Hlth Sys, Euclid *Also Called: Qualchoice Health Plan Inc (G-8360)*

UNIVERSITY HOSPITALS OF CLEVELAND, Cleveland *Also Called: University Hospitals Cleveland (G-5074)*

University Hsptals Bdford Med, Bedford *Also Called: Uh Regional Hospitals (G-991)*

University Hsptals Clvland Med 216 378-6240
26001 S Woodland Rd Beachwood (44122) *(G-849)*

University Hsptals Clvland Med 216 342-5556
23215 Commerce Park Ste 300 Beachwood (44122) *(G-850)*

University Hsptals Clvland Med 440 499-5900
5901 E Royalton Rd Broadview Heights (44147) *(G-1403)*

University Hsptals Clvland Med 216 844-1369
11100 Euclid Ave Stop Rvc5041 Cleveland (44106) *(G-5075)*

University Hsptals Clvland Med 216 358-2346
20800 Harvard Rd Cleveland (44122) *(G-5076)*

University Hsptals Clvland Med 216 675-6640
5805 Euclid Ave Cleveland (44103) *(G-5077)*

University Hsptals Clvland Med (HQ) 216 844-1000
11100 Euclid Ave Cleveland (44106) *(G-5078)*

University Hsptals Clvland Med 216 844-4663
4510 Richmond Rd Cleveland (44128) *(G-5079)*

University Hsptals Clvland Med 216 844-1767
11100 Euclid Ave Rm 737 Cleveland (44106) *(G-5080)*

University Hsptals Clvland Med 216 844-3528
2101 Adelbert Rd Cleveland (44106) *(G-5081)*

University Hsptals Clvland Med 440 205-5755
9485 Mentor Ave Ste 102 Mentor (44060) *(G-11007)*

University Hsptals Clvland Med 216 844-4323
3605 Warrensville Center Rd Shaker Heights (44122) *(G-12986)*

University Hsptals Cnnaut Med 440 593-1131
158 W Main Rd Conneaut (44030) *(G-6945)*

University Hsptals Hlth Sys In (PA) 216 767-8900
3605 Warrensville Center Rd Shaker Heights (44122) *(G-12987)*

University Hsptals Hlth Systm- (PA) 440 285-4040
12340 Bass Lake Rd Chardon (44024) *(G-2024)*

University Hsptals St John Med 440 835-8000
29000 Center Ridge Rd Westlake (44145) *(G-15121)*

University Hsptl-Uc Physicians, Cincinnati *Also Called: University of Cincinnati (G-3575)*

University Manor Health Care Center, Cleveland *Also Called: University Mnor Hlthcare Group (G-5083)*

University Manor Hlth Care Ctr 216 721-1400
2186 Ambleside Dr Cleveland (44106) *(G-5082)*

University Medical Assoc Inc 740 593-0753
350 Parks Hall Athens (45701) *(G-597)*

University Mednet 440 285-9079
22750 Rockside Rd Ste 210 Bedford (44146) *(G-992)*

University Mednet (PA) 216 383-0100
18599 Lake Shore Blvd Euclid (44119) *(G-8363)*

University Mednet 440 255-0800
9000 Mentor Ave Ste 101 Mentor (44060) *(G-11008)*

University Mnor Hlthcare Group 216 721-1400
2186 Ambleside Dr Cleveland (44106) *(G-5083)*

University Neurology Inc 513 475-8730
222 Piedmont Ave Ste 3200 Cincinnati (45219) *(G-3571)*

University of Cincinnati 513 556-6932
4450 Carver Woods Dr Ste 3 Blue Ash (45242) *(G-1264)*

University of Cincinnati 513 558-4194
231 Albert Sabin Way Cincinnati (45267) *(G-3572)*

University of Cincinnati 513 558-1200
3130 Highland Ave Fl 3 Cincinnati (45219) *(G-3573)*

University of Cincinnati 513 584-0618
200 Albert Sabin Way Cincinnati (45267) *(G-3574)*

University of Cincinnati 513 475-8771
222 Piedmont Ave Ste 7000 Cincinnati (45219) *(G-3575)*

University of Cincinnati 513 556-2389
51 Goodman St Ste 320 Cincinnati (45219) *(G-3576)*

University of Cincinnati 513 556-2700
290 Ccm Blvd Cincinnati (45221) *(G-3577)*

University of Cincinnati 513 584-1000
234 Goodman St Cincinnati (45219) *(G-3578)*

University of Cincinnati 513 584-7522
3200 Burnet Ave Cincinnati (45229) *(G-3579)*

University of Cincinnati 513 584-1000
331 Albert Sabin Way Cincinnati (45229) *(G-3580)*

University of Cincinnati 513 584-4396
234 Goodman St Cincinnati (45219) *(G-3581)*

University of Cincinnati 513 556-4200
51 W Goodman Dr Cincinnati (45221) *(G-3582)*

University of Cincinnati 513 558-4231
231 Albert Sabin Way Ste 6065 Cincinnati (45267) *(G-3583)*

University of Cincinnati 513 556-2263
147 Corry Blvd Ste 2100 Cincinnati (45221) *(G-3584)*

University of Cincinnati 513 558-4110
170 Panzeca Way Cincinnati (45267) *(G-3585)*

University of Cincinnati 513 556-4603
2751 O'varsity Way Ste 880 Cincinnati (45221) *(G-3586)*

University of Cincinnati 513 558-4444
3125 Eden Ave Cincinnati (45219) *(G-3587)*

University of Cincinnati 513 584-5331
234 Goodman St Cincinnati (45219) *(G-3588)*

University of Cincinnati 513 558-1243
3130 Highland Ave Fl 3 Cincinnati (45219) *(G-3589)*

University of Cincinnati 513 556-6381
51 Goodman Dr Cincinnati (45219) *(G-3590)*

University of Cincinnati 513 556-4054
2614 Mecken Cir Cincinnati (45221) *(G-3591)*

University of Cincinnati 513 556-3732
500 Geo Physics Bldg 5th Fl Cincinnati (45221) *(G-3592)*

University of Cincinnati 513 556-3803
1 Bldg Cincinnati (45221) *(G-3593)*

University of Cincinnati 513 584-3200
234 Goodman St Cincinnati (45219) *(G-3594)*

University of Cincinnati Phys 513 475-7934
2830 Victory Pkwy Ste 320 Cincinnati (45206) *(G-3595)*

University of Cincinnati Phys 513 475-8000
7700 University Ct Ste 1800 West Chester (45069) *(G-14788)*

University of Dayton (PA) 937 229-1000
300 College Park Ave Dayton (45469) *(G-7689)*

University of Dayton 937 229-2113
300 College St Dayton (45402) *(G-7690)*

University of Dayton 937 229-3822
711 E Monument Ave Ste 101 Dayton (45469) *(G-7691)*

University of Dayton 937 255-3141
300 College Park Dr Dayton (45469) *(G-7692)*

University of Dayton 937 229-3913
1529 Brown St Dayton (45469) *(G-7693)*

University of Dyton Schl Engrg, Dayton *Also Called: University of Dayton (G-7690)*

University of Toledo 419 383-4000
3000 Arlington Ave Toledo (43614) *(G-14086)*

University of Toledo 419 383-5322
3000 Arlington Ave Toledo (43614) *(G-14087)*

University of Toledo Med Ctr, Toledo *Also Called: University of Toledo (G-14086)*

UNIVERSITY OF TOLEDO PHYSICIAN, Toledo *Also Called: Medical Cllege Ohio Physcans L (G-13913)*

University Ophthalmologist, Beachwood *Also Called: University Hsptals Clvland Med (G-849)*

University Ophthlmlogy Assoc I 216 382-8022
29001 Cedar Rd Ste 110 Cleveland (44124) *(G-5084)*

University Otlryngologists Inc (PA) 614 273-2241
810 Mackenzie Dr Columbus (43220) *(G-6824)*

University Primary Care Prac 216 844-1000
11100 Euclid Ave Cleveland (44106) *(G-5085)*

University Primary Care Practices, Westlake *Also Called: University Prmry Care Prctices (G-15122)*

University Prmry Care Prctices 440 808-1283
26908 Detroit Rd Ste 201 Westlake (44145) *(G-15122)*

University Radiology Assoc 513 475-8760
222 Piedmont Ave Ste 2100 Cincinnati (45219) *(G-3596)*

University Settlement Inc   **ALPHABETIC SECTION**

University Settlement Inc (PA) 216 641-8948
   4800 Broadway Ave Cleveland (44127) *(G-5086)*

University Suburban Health Ctr (PA) 216 382-8920
   1611 S Green Rd Cleveland (44121) *(G-5087)*

University Tledo Physcians LLC 419 931-0030
   4510 Dorr St Toledo (43615) *(G-14088)*

Universty of Cincinnti Medcl C 513 475-8000
   222 Piedmont Ave Ste 1200 Cincinnati (45219) *(G-3597)*

Untapped Potentials LLC 888 811-1469
   175 S 3rd St Ste 200 Columbus (43215) *(G-6825)*

Untd Elderly Clark C Sprngfeld (PA) 937 323-4948
   125 W Main St Springfield (45502) *(G-13307)*

Uph Holdings LLC 614 447-9777
   3100 Olentangy River Rd Columbus (43202) *(G-6826)*

Upper Arlington City Schl Dst 614 487-5133
   4770 Burbank Dr Columbus (43220) *(G-6827)*

Upper Arlington Lutheran Ch 614 451-3736
   3500 Mill Run Dr Hilliard (43026) *(G-9238)*

Upper Valley Medical Center 937 440-7107
   110 N Main St Ste 450 Dayton (45402) *(G-7694)*

Upper Valley Medical Center (HQ) 937 440-4000
   3130 N County Road 25a Troy (45373) *(G-14166)*

Upper Valley Medical Center 937 440-4820
   3130 N County Road 25a Troy (45373) *(G-14167)*

UPPER VALLEY MEDICAL CENTER, Tipp City *Also Called: After Hours Family Care Inc (G-13651)*

Uppervalley Professional Corp 937 440-4000
   3130 N County Road 25a Troy (45373) *(G-14168)*

Upreach LLC 614 442-7702
   4488 Mobile Dr Columbus (43220) *(G-6828)*

UPS, Athens *Also Called: United Parcel Service Inc (G-596)*

UPS, Austinburg *Also Called: United Parcel Service Inc (G-634)*

UPS, Brilliant *Also Called: United Parcel Service Inc (G-1381)*

UPS, Celina *Also Called: United Parcel Service Inc (G-1930)*

UPS, Cincinnati *Also Called: United Parcel Service Inc (G-3555)*

UPS, Cincinnati *Also Called: United Parcel Service Inc (G-3556)*

UPS, Cincinnati *Also Called: United Parcel Service Inc (G-3557)*

UPS, Cleveland *Also Called: United Parcel Service Inc (G-5063)*

UPS, Cleveland *Also Called: United Parcel Service Inc (G-5064)*

UPS, Cleveland *Also Called: United Parcel Service Inc (G-5065)*

UPS, Cleveland *Also Called: United Parcel Service Inc (G-5066)*

UPS, Cleveland *Also Called: UPS Supply Chain Solutions Inc (G-5088)*

UPS, Columbus *Also Called: United Parcel Service Inc (G-6809)*

UPS, Columbus *Also Called: United Parcel Service Inc (G-6810)*

UPS, Columbus *Also Called: United Parcel Service Inc (G-6811)*

UPS, Columbus *Also Called: United Parcel Service Inc (G-6812)*

UPS, Defiance *Also Called: United Parcel Service Inc (G-7773)*

UPS, Findlay *Also Called: United Parcel Service Inc (G-8595)*

UPS, Girard *Also Called: United Parcel Service Inc (G-8828)*

UPS, Groveport *Also Called: United Parcel Service Inc (G-9008)*

UPS, Hamilton *Also Called: United Parcel Service Inc (G-9089)*

UPS, Lima *Also Called: United Parcel Service Inc (G-9975)*

UPS, Mansfield *Also Called: United Parcel Service Inc (G-10320)*

UPS, Marietta *Also Called: United Parcel Service Inc (G-10407)*

UPS, Marion *Also Called: United Parcel Service Inc (G-10463)*

UPS, Maumee *Also Called: United Parcel Service Inc (G-10777)*

UPS, Middleburg Heights *Also Called: United Parcel Service Inc (G-11132)*

UPS, New Philadelphia *Also Called: United Parcel Service Inc (G-11671)*

UPS, Obetz *Also Called: United Parcel Service Inc (G-12085)*

UPS, Perrysburg *Also Called: United Parcel Service Inc (G-12382)*

UPS, Portsmouth *Also Called: United Parcel Service Inc (G-12578)*

UPS, Saint Clairsville *Also Called: United Parcel Service Inc (G-12818)*

UPS, Toledo *Also Called: United Parcel Service Inc (G-14083)*

UPS, Urbancrest *Also Called: United Parcel Service Inc (G-14325)*

UPS, Wilmington *Also Called: United Parcel Service Inc (G-15276)*

UPS, Youngstown *Also Called: United Parcel Service Inc (G-15743)*

UPS, Zanesville *Also Called: United Parcel Service Inc (G-15836)*

UPS Family Health Center North 330 364-8038
   110 Dublin Dr Dover (44622) *(G-7908)*

UPS Supply Chain Solutions Inc 360 332-5222
   18401 Sheldon Rd Ste C Cleveland (44130) *(G-5088)*

UPS Supply Chain Solutions Inc 614 208-0396
   700 Manor Park Dr Ste 100 Columbus (43228) *(G-6829)*

Upshift, Cincinnati *Also Called: Upshift Work LLC (G-3598)*

Upshift Work LLC 513 813-5695
   2300 Montana Ave Ste 301 Cincinnati (45211) *(G-3598)*

Uptown Rental Properties LLC 513 861-9394
   2718 Short Vine St Cincinnati (45219) *(G-3599)*

Uranium Disposition Svcs LLC 740 289-3620
   3930 Us Highway 23 Anx Piketon (45661) *(G-12430)*

Urban Five Construction 614 241-2070
   495 S High St Ste 150 Columbus (43215) *(G-6830)*

Urban Leag Grter Cleveland Inc 216 622-0999
   2930 Prospect Ave E Cleveland (44115) *(G-5089)*

Urban Leag Grter Sthwstern Ohi 513 281-9955
   3458 Reading Rd Cincinnati (45229) *(G-3600)*

Urban Minority Alcoholism, Akron *Also Called: Akron-Rban Mnrity Alchlism DRG (G-41)*

Urban Retail Properties LLC 937 433-0957
   2700 Miamisburg Centerville Rd Dayton (45459) *(G-7695)*

Urbana Country Club 937 653-1690
   4761 E Us Highway 36 Urbana (43078) *(G-14314)*

Urbana Health & Rehab Center, Urbana *Also Called: Urbana Healthcare Group LLC (G-14315)*

Urbana Healthcare Group LLC 937 652-1381
   741 E Water St Urbana (43078) *(G-14315)*

Urgent Care, Coshocton *Also Called: Doctors Office (G-6983)*

Urgent Care Specialists LLC 614 472-2880
   2880 Stelzer Rd Columbus (43219) *(G-6831)*

Urgent Care Specialists LLC 614 272-1100
   4300 Clime Rd Ste 110 Columbus (43228) *(G-6832)*

Urgent Care Specialists LLC 614 263-4400
   4400 N High St Ste 101 Columbus (43214) *(G-6833)*

Urgent Care Specialists LLC 614 505-7601
   2400 Corporate Exchange Dr Ste 102 Columbus (43231) *(G-6834)*

Urgent Care Specialists LLC 937 236-8630
   6210 Brandt Pike Dayton (45424) *(G-7696)*

Urgent Care Specialists LLC 614 835-0400
   3813 S Hamilton Rd Groveport (43125) *(G-9009)*

Urgent Care Specialists LLC 937 322-6222
   1301 W 1st St Springfield (45504) *(G-13308)*

Urgent Care Specialists LLC 330 505-9400
   1997 Niles Cortland Rd Se Warren (44484) *(G-14569)*

Urgent Care-Hillsboro, Hillsboro *Also Called: Adena Health System (G-9248)*

Urology Center LLC 513 841-7500
   2000 Joseph E Sanker Blvd Cincinnati (45212) *(G-3601)*

Urology Group, Cincinnati *Also Called: Tri State Urlogic Svcs PSC Inc (G-3503)*

Urology Group, Cincinnati *Also Called: Tri State Urologic Svcs PSC (G-3504)*

Urology Group Inc 513 662-0222
   3301 Mercy Health Blvd Ste 525 Cincinnati (45211) *(G-3602)*

URS, Akron *Also Called: URS Group Inc (G-344)*

URS, Cincinnati *Also Called: URS Group Inc (G-3603)*

URS, Cleveland *Also Called: URS Group Inc (G-5090)*

URS, Columbus *Also Called: URS Group Inc (G-6835)*

URS Group Inc 330 836-9111
   564 White Pond Dr Akron (44320) *(G-344)*

URS Group Inc 513 651-3440
   525 Vine St Ste 1900 Cincinnati (45202) *(G-3603)*

URS Group Inc 216 622-2300
   1300 E 9th St Ste 500 Cleveland (44114) *(G-5090)*

URS Group Inc 614 464-4500
   277 W Nationwide Blvd Columbus (43215) *(G-6835)*

US Acute Care Solutions LLC 800 828-0898
   4535 Dressler Rd Nw Canton (44718) *(G-1876)*

US Advanced Systems LLC 330 425-0020
   1900 Case Pkwy S Twinsburg (44087) *(G-14226)*

US Airways Express, Vandalia *Also Called: Psa Airlines Inc (G-14389)*

US Bank, Cincinnati *Also Called: US Bank National Association (G-3604)*

ALPHABETIC SECTION

US Bank, Columbus *Also Called: Huntington National Bank (G-6025)*
US Bank, Euclid *Also Called: Huntington National Bank (G-8348)*
US Bank National Association (HQ)..513 632-4234
  425 Walnut St Fl 14 Cincinnati (45202) *(G-3604)*
US Capital Inc..330 867-4525
  423 S Rose Blvd Akron (44320) *(G-345)*
US Communications and Elc Inc..440 519-0880
  4933 Neo Pkwy Cleveland (44128) *(G-5091)*
US Expediting Logistics LLC..937 235-1014
  4311 Old Springfield Rd Vandalia (45377) *(G-14399)*
US Foods Inc..216 475-7400
  16645 Granite Rd Cleveland (44137) *(G-5092)*
US Foods Inc..513 874-3900
  4487 Le Saint Ct Fairfield (45014) *(G-8451)*
US Foods Inc..330 963-6789
  8000 Bavaria Rd Twinsburg (44087) *(G-14227)*
US Foods Inc..614 539-7993
  5445 Spellmire Dr West Chester (45246) *(G-14843)*
US Footwear Holdings LLC..740 753-9100
  39 E Canal St Nelsonville (45764) *(G-11550)*
US Healthcare System..513 585-1821
  3200 Burnet Ave Cincinnati (45229) *(G-3605)*
US Hotel Osp Ventures LLC..740 435-9000
  Us Route 22 E Cambridge (43725) *(G-1586)*
US Hotel Osp Ventures LLC..740 767-2112
  10660 Burr Oak Lodge Rd Glouster (45732) *(G-8836)*
US Hotel Osp Ventures LLC..440 564-9144
  11755 Kinsman Rd Newbury (44065) *(G-11765)*
US Hotel Osp Ventures LLC..419 836-9009
  1750 State Park Rd Ste 2 Oregon (43616) *(G-12146)*
US Inspection Services Inc..513 671-7073
  502 W Crescentville Rd Cincinnati (45246) *(G-3606)*
US Inspection Services Inc (DH)..937 660-9879
  7333 Paragon Rd Ste 240 Dayton (45459) *(G-7697)*
US Lumber Group LLC..330 538-3386
  489 Rosemont Rd North Jackson (44451) *(G-11879)*
US Postal Service..614 600-5544
  374 E 16th Ave Columbus (43201) *(G-6836)*
US Protection Service LLC (PA)..614 794-4950
  5785 Emporium Sq Columbus (43231) *(G-6837)*
US Radius Services Inc..929 505-1063
  5498 Alan B Shepherd St Trenton (45067) *(G-14125)*
US Safetygear, Warren *Also Called: US Safetygear Inc (G-14570)*
US Safetygear Inc (PA)..330 898-1344
  5001 Enterprise Dr Nw Warren (44481) *(G-14570)*
US Security Associates Inc..937 454-9035
  230 Northland Blvd Ste 307 Cincinnati (45246) *(G-3607)*
US Security Associates Inc..937 454-9035
  69 N Dixie Dr Ste F Vandalia (45377) *(G-14400)*
US Tank Alliance Inc..440 238-7705
  19511 Progress Dr Ste 3 Strongsville (44149) *(G-13494)*
US Teleradiology LLC (HQ)..678 904-2599
  5655 Hudson Dr Ste 210 Hudson (44236) *(G-9376)*
US Together Inc..614 437-9941
  1415 E Dublin Granville Rd Ste 100 Columbus (43229) *(G-6838)*
US Tsubaki Power Transm LLC..419 626-4560
  1010 Edgewater Ave Sandusky (44870) *(G-12939)*
US Tubular Products Inc..330 832-1734
  14852 Lincoln Way W North Lawrence (44666) *(G-11880)*
US Utility Electrical Svcs..419 837-9753
  3592 Genoa Rd Perrysburg (43551) *(G-12384)*
US Xpress, Cleveland *Also Called: U S Xpress Inc (G-5045)*
USA, Columbus *Also Called: United Skates America Inc (G-6815)*
USA Parking Systems..216 621-9255
  1124 Bolivar Rd Cleveland (44115) *(G-5093)*
USA Precast Concrete Limited..330 854-9600
  801 Elm Ridge Ave Canal Fulton (44614) *(G-1595)*
Usacs Management Group Ltd..330 493-4443
  4535 Dressler Rd Nw Canton (44718) *(G-1877)*
Usacs Medical Group Ltd..330 493-4443
  4535 Dressler Rd Nw Canton (44718) *(G-1878)*

Usavinyl LLC..614 771-4805
  5795 Green Pointe Dr S Groveport (43125) *(G-9010)*
Uscg Station Cleveland Harbor..216 937-0141
  1055 E 9th St Cleveland (44114) *(G-5094)*
Usdhsa, Dayton *Also Called: United Sttes Dept of Hmland SE (G-7684)*
Usher Transport, Grove City *Also Called: Usher Transport Inc (G-8962)*
Usher Transport Inc..614 875-0528
  2040 Hendrix Dr Grove City (43123) *(G-8962)*
USI, Cincinnati *Also Called: USI Midwest LLC (G-3610)*
USI Insurance Services Nat Inc..513 657-3116
  720 E Pete Rose Way Ste 400 Cincinnati (45202) *(G-3608)*
USI Insurance Services Nat Inc..513 852-6300
  312 Elm St Fl 24 Cincinnati (45202) *(G-3609)*
USI Insurance Services Nat Inc..614 228-5565
  580 N 4th St Ste 400 Columbus (43215) *(G-6839)*
USI Midwest LLC (DH)..513 852-6300
  312 Elm St Ste 24 Cincinnati (45202) *(G-3610)*
Usic Locating Services LLC..330 733-9393
  441 Munroe Falls Rd Akron (44312) *(G-346)*
Usic Locating Services LLC..513 554-0456
  3478 Hauck Rd Ste D Cincinnati (45241) *(G-3611)*
Usradius, Trenton *Also Called: Utilities Services Radius LLC (G-14126)*
Utah Spas, Toledo *Also Called: Spa Fitness Centers Inc (G-14019)*
Utahamerican Energy Inc..435 888-4000
  153 Highway 7 S Powhatan Point (43942) *(G-12611)*
Uti, Groveport *Also Called: Utility Technologies Intl Corp (G-9011)*
Uti Corp..614 879-7316
  2685 Plain City Georgesville Rd Ne West Jefferson (43162) *(G-14854)*
Utica East Ohio Midstream LLC..740 431-4168
  8349 Azalea Rd Sw Dennison (44621) *(G-7861)*
Utica Nursing Home, Utica *Also Called: Living Care Altrntves of Utica (G-14329)*
Utilicon Corporation..216 391-8500
  6140 Parkland Blvd Cleveland (44124) *(G-5095)*
Utilities Business Office, The, Akron *Also Called: City of Akron (G-101)*
Utilities Department, Toledo *Also Called: City of Toledo (G-13743)*
Utilities Services Radius LLC..800 515-7650
  5498 Alan B Shepherd St Trenton (45067) *(G-14126)*
Utility Technologies Intl, West Jefferson *Also Called: Uti Corp (G-14854)*
Utility Technologies Intl Corp..614 879-7624
  4700 Homer Ohio Ln Groveport (43125) *(G-9011)*
UTILITY TRAILER MANUFACTURING COMPANY, Batavia *Also Called: Utility Trailer Mfg Co (G-753)*
Utility Trailer Mfg Co..513 436-2600
  4225 Curliss Ln Batavia (45103) *(G-753)*
Utility Truck & Equipment Inc..740 474-5151
  23893 Us Highway 23 S Circleville (43113) *(G-3728)*
Uts, Fairfield *Also Called: Universal Transportation Syste (G-8450)*
Utter Construction Inc..513 876-2246
  1302 State Route 133 Bethel (45106) *(G-1096)*
Uvmc Management Corporation (HQ)..937 440-4000
  3130 N County Road 25a Troy (45373) *(G-14169)*
Uvmc Nursing Care Inc..937 473-2075
  75 Mote Dr Covington (45318) *(G-7019)*
Uvmc Nursing Care Inc..937 667-7500
  4375 S County Road 25a Tipp City (45371) *(G-13668)*
Uvmc Nursing Care Inc..937 440-7663
  3232 N County Road 25a Troy (45373) *(G-14170)*
V & P Hydraulic Products LLC..740 203-3600
  1700 Pittsburgh Dr Delaware (43015) *(G-7833)*
V and V Appliance Parts Inc (PA)..330 743-5144
  27 W Myrtle Ave Youngstown (44507) *(G-15745)*
V H Cooper & Co Inc (HQ)..419 375-4116
  2321 State Route 49 Fort Recovery (45846) *(G-8611)*
V Metro, Fairborn *Also Called: Vmetro Inc (G-8386)*
Vaco Cincinnati LLC..513 239-5674
  9987 Carver Rd Ste 440 Blue Ash (45242) *(G-1265)*
Vaco LLC..513 239-5674
  4500 Cooper Rd Ste 101 Blue Ash (45242) *(G-1266)*
Vadakin Inc..740 373-7518
  110 Industry Rd Marietta (45750) *(G-10408)*

Vadakin Industrial Services, Marietta Also Called: Vadakin Inc *(G-10408)*

Valam Hospitality Inc.. 419 232-6040
 840 N Washington St Van Wert (45891) *(G-14354)*

Valassis, Independence Also Called: Valassis Direct Mail Inc *(G-9494)*

Valassis Direct Mail Inc... 859 283-2386
 7722 Reinhold Dr Cincinnati (45237) *(G-3612)*

Valassis Direct Mail Inc... 216 573-1400
 3 Summit Park Dr Ste 430 Independence (44131) *(G-9494)*

Valassis Direct Mail Inc... 614 987-2200
 100 W Old Wilson Bridge Rd Ste 106 Worthington (43085) *(G-15465)*

Valeo North America Inc... 248 550-6054
 12979 County Road 153 East Liberty (43319) *(G-8177)*

Valic Financial Advisor... 216 643-6340
 2 Summit Park Dr Independence (44131) *(G-9495)*

Valicor, Monroe Also Called: Valicor Environmental Svcs LLC *(G-11353)*

Valicor Environmental Svcs LLC............................ 937 268-6501
 300 Cherokee Dr Dayton (45417) *(G-7698)*

Valicor Environmental Svcs LLC (HQ)..................513 733-4666
 1045 Reed Dr Monroe (45050) *(G-11353)*

Valicor Federal Services LLC................................. 313 724-8600
 11140 Deerfield Rd Blue Ash (45242) *(G-1267)*

Validex, Cincinnati Also Called: DE Foxx & Associates Inc *(G-2547)*

Vallejo Company.. 216 741-3933
 4000 Brookpark Rd Cleveland (44134) *(G-5096)*

Vallen Distribution Inc
 673 Gateway Blvd Monroe (45050) *(G-11354)*

Valley Care Health System, Warren Also Called: Community Health Systems Inc *(G-14511)*

Valley Fleet, Ashland Also Called: Valley Transportation Inc *(G-514)*

Valley Ford Truck Inc (PA)......................................216 524-2400
 5715 Canal Rd Cleveland (44125) *(G-5097)*

Valley Hospice Inc (PA)... 740 859-5041
 10686 State Route 150 Rayland (43943) *(G-12648)*

Valley Hospitality Inc... 740 374-9660
 701 Pike St Marietta (45750) *(G-10409)*

Valley Industrial Trucks Inc (PA)........................... 330 788-4081
 1152 Meadowbrook Ave Youngstown (44512) *(G-15746)*

Valley Interior Systems Inc (PA)............................ 513 961-0400
 2203 Fowler St Cincinnati (45206) *(G-3613)*

Valley Interior Systems Inc.................................... 614 351-8440
 3840 Fisher Rd Columbus (43228) *(G-6840)*

Valley Interior Systems Inc.................................... 937 890-7319
 2760 Thunderhawk Ct Dayton (45414) *(G-7699)*

Valley Machine Tool Inc... 513 899-2737
 9773 Morrow Cozaddale Rd Morrow (45152) *(G-11456)*

Valley Mining Inc... 740 922-3942
 4412 Pleasant Valley Rd Se Dennison (44621) *(G-7862)*

Valley Sterling of Cleveland, Cleveland Also Called: Valley Ford Truck Inc *(G-5097)*

Valley Transportation Inc....................................... 419 289-6200
 1 Valley Dr Ashland (44805) *(G-514)*

VALLEY VIEW ALZHEIMER'S CARE C, Frankfort Also Called: Valley View Mnor Nrsing HM Inc *(G-8630)*

Valley View Management Co Inc........................... 419 886-4000
 855 Comfort Plaza Dr Bellville (44813) *(G-1052)*

Valley View Mnor Nrsing HM Inc........................... 740 998-2948
 3363 Ragged Ridge Rd Frankfort (45628) *(G-8630)*

Valley Wholesale Foods Inc (PA)..........................740 354-5216
 415 Market St Portsmouth (45662) *(G-12581)*

Valleywood Golf Club Inc.. 419 826-3991
 13501 Airport Hwy Swanton (43558) *(G-13531)*

Valmark Financial Group LLC................................ 330 576-1234
 130 Springside Dr Ste 300 Akron (44333) *(G-347)*

Valtris, Independence Also Called: Polymer Additives Holdings Inc *(G-9469)*

Valtris Specialty Chemicals, Independence Also Called: Polymer Additives Inc *(G-9468)*

Valuation Partners, Toledo Also Called: Real Estate Vltion Prtners LLC *(G-13982)*

Valucadd Solutions, Cincinnati Also Called: Twism Enterprises LLC *(G-3539)*

Valucentric LLC.. 410 912-2085
 300 Madison Ave Toledo (43604) *(G-14089)*

Value Add Management LLC.................................. 614 291-2600
 222 E 11th Ave Columbus (43201) *(G-6841)*

Value Inn Inc... 888 315-2378
 1947 Stringtown Rd Grove City (43123) *(G-8963)*

Valvoline Instant Oil Change.................................. 937 548-0123
 661 Wagner Ave Greenville (45331) *(G-8888)*

Valvoline Instant Oil Change, Canton Also Called: Valvoline Instant Oil Chnge Fr *(G-1879)*

Valvoline Instant Oil Change, Greenville Also Called: Valvoline Instant Oil Change *(G-8888)*

Valvoline Instant Oil Change, Mansfield Also Called: Valvoline Instant Oil Chnge Fr *(G-10321)*

Valvoline Instant Oil Change, Piqua Also Called: Valvoline Instant Oil Chnge Fr *(G-12461)*

Valvoline Instant Oil Change, Reynoldsburg Also Called: Valvoline Instant Oil Chnge Fr *(G-12679)*

Valvoline Instant Oil Change, Warren Also Called: Valvoline Instant Oil Chnge Fr *(G-14571)*

Valvoline Instant Oil Change, Youngstown Also Called: Valvoline Instant Oil Chnge Fr *(G-15747)*

Valvoline Instant Oil Chnge Fr............................... 330 453-4549
 2203 Columbus Rd Ne Canton (44705) *(G-1879)*

Valvoline Instant Oil Chnge Fr............................... 419 589-5396
 1439 Ashland Rd Mansfield (44905) *(G-10321)*

Valvoline Instant Oil Chnge Fr............................... 513 422-4980
 1321 S Breiel Blvd Middletown (45044) *(G-11191)*

Valvoline Instant Oil Chnge Fr............................... 937 773-0112
 1275 E Ash St Piqua (45356) *(G-12461)*

Valvoline Instant Oil Chnge Fr............................... 614 452-4682
 8217 E Broad St Reynoldsburg (43068) *(G-12679)*

Valvoline Instant Oil Chnge Fr............................... 330 372-4416
 2769 Elm Rd Ne Warren (44483) *(G-14571)*

Valvoline Instant Oil Chnge Fr............................... 330 726-5676
 7210 South Ave Youngstown (44512) *(G-15747)*

Valvoline LLC.. 513 557-3100
 3901 River Rd Cincinnati (45204) *(G-3614)*

Van Boxel Stor Solutions LLC................................ 440 721-1504
 13770 Gar Hwy Chardon (44024) *(G-2025)*

Van Devere Inc (PA).. 330 253-6137
 300 W Market St Akron (44303) *(G-348)*

Van Devere Buick, Akron Also Called: Van Devere Inc *(G-348)*

Van Dyk Mortgage Corporation.............................. 419 720-4384
 111 N Reynolds Rd Toledo (43615) *(G-14090)*

Van Dyne-Crotty Co... 740 432-7503
 1305 Marquand Ave Cambridge (43725) *(G-1587)*

Van Dyne-Crotty Co... 440 248-6935
 30400 Bruce Industrial Pkwy Solon (44139) *(G-13158)*

Van Mayberrys & Storage Inc................................. 937 298-8800
 1850 Cardington Rd Moraine (45409) *(G-11445)*

Van Rue Incorporated.. 419 238-0715
 10357 Van Wert Decatur Rd Van Wert (45891) *(G-14355)*

Van Wert Cnty Day Care Ctr Inc............................. 419 238-9918
 10485 Van Wert Decatur Rd Van Wert (45891) *(G-14356)*

Van Wert County Hospital Assn (PA).....................419 238-2390
 1250 S Washington St Van Wert (45891) *(G-14357)*

Van Wert Family Physicians LLC........................... 419 238-6251
 1178 Professional Dr Van Wert (45891) *(G-14358)*

Van Wert Federal Sav Bnk Inc................................ 419 238-9662
 976 S Shannon St Van Wert (45891) *(G-14359)*

VAN WERT HEALTH, Van Wert Also Called: Van Wert County Hospital Assn *(G-14357)*

Van Wert Medical Services Ltd............................... 419 238-7727
 140 Fox Rd Ste 105 Van Wert (45891) *(G-14360)*

Vana Solutions LLC.. 937 242-6399
 3610 Pentagon Blvd Ste 110 Beavercreek (45431) *(G-913)*

Vancare Inc.. 937 898-4202
 208 N Cassel Rd Vandalia (45377) *(G-14401)*

Vancrest Ltd.. 419 695-2871
 1425 E 5th St Delphos (45833) *(G-7847)*

Vancrest Ltd.. 937 456-3010
 1600 Park Ave Eaton (45320) *(G-8225)*

VANCREST HEALTH CARE CENTER, Van Wert Also Called: Van Rue Incorporated *(G-14355)*

Vancrest Healthcare Cntr, Delphos Also Called: Vancrest Ltd *(G-7847)*

Vancrest Healthcare Cntr Eaton, Eaton Also Called: Vancrest Ltd *(G-8225)*

Vancrest Management Corp................................... 419 238-0715
 120 W Main St Ste 200 Van Wert (45891) *(G-14361)*

Vandalia Blcktop Slcoating Inc............................... 937 454-0571
 6740 Webster St Dayton (45414) *(G-7700)*

Vandalia Butler Emrgncy Fd Ctr............................. 937 898-4202
 208 N Cassel Rd Vandalia (45377) *(G-14402)*

ALPHABETIC SECTION — Verizon New York Inc

Vandalia Park, Vandalia *Also Called: Vancare Inc (G-14401)*
Vandalia Rental, Vandalia *Also Called: Bnd Rentals Inc (G-14367)*
Vangard Labs, Cincinnati *Also Called: Ncs Healthcare LLC (G-3101)*
Vanguard Property Management..216 521-8222
   18900 Detroit Ext Unit 800 Lakewood (44107) *(G-9686)*
Vanguard Wines LLC (PA)...614 291-3493
   1020 W 5th Ave Columbus (43212) *(G-6842)*
Vanner Inc..614 771-2718
   4282 Reynolds Dr Hilliard (43026) *(G-9239)*
Vantage Aging (PA)...330 253-4597
   388 S Main St Ste 325 Akron (44311) *(G-349)*
Vantage Aging..330 785-9770
   1155 E Tallmadge Ave Akron (44310) *(G-350)*
Vantage Aging..513 924-9100
   644 Linn St Ste 1200 Cincinnati (45203) *(G-3615)*
Vantage Aging..440 324-3588
   42495 N Ridge Rd Elyria (44035) *(G-8298)*
Vantage Solutions Inc...330 757-4864
   207 S Main St Poland (44514) *(G-12511)*
Vargo LLC (PA)..614 876-1163
   5555 Frantz Rd Dublin (43017) *(G-8147)*
Vargo Solutions, Dublin *Also Called: Vargo Solutions Inc (G-8148)*
Vargo Solutions Inc...614 876-1163
   5555 Frantz Rd Dublin (43017) *(G-8148)*
Vargo Whse Exction Systems LLC, Dublin *Also Called: Vargo LLC (G-8147)*
Various Views Research Inc..513 489-9000
   11353 Reed Hartman Hwy Ste 200 Blue Ash (45241) *(G-1268)*
Varment Guard Wildlife, Columbus *Also Called: Plunketts Pest Control Inc (G-6533)*
Varney Dispatch Inc..513 682-4200
   4 Triangle Park Dr Ste 404 Cincinnati (45246) *(G-3616)*
Varo Engineers Inc..740 587-2228
   2790 Columbus Rd Granville (43023) *(G-8856)*
Varo Engineers Inc..513 729-9313
   9078 Union Centre Blvd Ste 350 West Chester (45069) *(G-14789)*
Varo Engineers A Salas Obrien, Dublin *Also Called: Varo Engineers Inc (G-8149)*
Varo Engineers Inc (HQ)..614 459-0424
   2751 Tuller Pkwy Dublin (43017) *(G-8149)*
Vartek, Donnelsville *Also Called: Vartek Services Inc (G-7870)*
Vartek Services Inc...937 438-3550
   17 S Hampton Rd Donnelsville (45319) *(G-7870)*
Vaughn, Carey *Also Called: Vaughn Industries LLC (G-1895)*
Vaughn Industries LLC (PA)...419 396-3900
   1201 E Findlay St Carey (43316) *(G-1895)*
Vaughn Industries LLC..419 396-3900
   21934 Twp Rd 218 Fostoria (44830) *(G-8627)*
Vaughn Industries LLC..740 548-7100
   7749 Green Meadows Dr Lewis Center (43035) *(G-9840)*
VCA Animal Hospitals Inc..419 423-7232
   2141 Bright Rd Findlay (45840) *(G-8596)*
VCA Animal Hospitals Inc..419 841-3323
   6705 W Bancroft St Toledo (43615) *(G-14091)*
VCA Findlay Animal Hospital, Findlay *Also Called: VCA Animal Hospitals Inc (G-8596)*
VCA Holly Farms, Toledo *Also Called: VCA Animal Hospitals Inc (G-14091)*
Vds, Columbus *Also Called: Video Duplication Services Inc (G-6850)*
Vec Inc..330 539-4044
   977 Tibbetts Wick Rd Girard (44420) *(G-8830)*
Vecmar Computer Solutions, Mentor *Also Called: Vecmar Corporation (G-11009)*
Vecmar Corporation..440 953-1119
   7595 Jenther Dr Mentor (44060) *(G-11009)*
Vector Technical Inc (PA)...440 946-8800
   4860 Robinhood Dr Willoughby (44094) *(G-15225)*
Vectra Inc..614 351-6868
   3950 Business Park Dr Columbus (43204) *(G-6843)*
Vectra Visual, Columbus *Also Called: Vectra Inc (G-6843)*
Vectren Energy Dlvry Ohio LLC..937 331-3080
   175 W Wenger Rd Englewood (45322) *(G-8325)*
Vectren Energy Dlvry Ohio LLC..937 259-7400
   1335 E Dayton Yellow Springs Rd Fairborn (45324) *(G-8383)*
Veeam Software Corporation (PA)...614 339-8200
   8800 Lyra Dr Ste 350 Columbus (43240) *(G-5283)*

Vega Americas Inc..513 272-0524
   3877 Mason Research Pkwy Lebanon (45036) *(G-9797)*
Vein Clinics of America Inc (HQ)..630 725-2700
   8044 Montgomery Rd Ste 525 Cincinnati (45236) *(G-3617)*
Vela Investment Management LLC..614 653-8352
   220 Market St Ste 208 New Albany (43054) *(G-11589)*
Velco Inc..513 772-4226
   10280 Chester Rd Cincinnati (45215) *(G-3618)*
Velocity A Managed Svcs Co Inc (PA).......................................419 868-9983
   6936 Spring Valley Dr Holland (43528) *(G-9311)*
Velocity A Managed Svcs Co Inc..281 221-4444
   7130 Spring Meadows Dr W Holland (43528) *(G-9312)*
Velocys Inc..614 733-3300
   8520 Warner Rd Plain City (43064) *(G-12497)*
Velosio LLC (PA)..614 280-9880
   5747 Perimeter Dr Ste 200 Dublin (43017) *(G-8150)*
Velotta Company..330 239-1211
   6740 Ridge Road Sharon Center (44274) *(G-12991)*
Velvet Blue Transport Co Inc...330 478-1426
   4821 Corporate St Sw Canton (44706) *(G-1880)*
Velvet Ice Cream Company...419 562-2009
   1233 Whetstone St Bucyrus (44820) *(G-1519)*
Velvet Ice Cream Company (PA)..740 892-3921
   11324 Mount Vernon Rd Utica (43080) *(G-14330)*
Venco Venturo Industries LLC (PA)...513 772-8448
   12110 Best Pl Cincinnati (45241) *(G-3619)*
Venco/Venturo Div, Cincinnati *Also Called: Venco Venturo Industries LLC (G-3619)*
Vendor Supply of Ohio, West Chester *Also Called: Vendors Supply Inc (G-14790)*
Vendorinsight..800 997-2674
   9987 Carver Rd Ste 130 Blue Ash (45242) *(G-1269)*
Vendors Exchange International Inc..216 432-1800
   8700 Brookpark Rd Cleveland (44129) *(G-5098)*
Vendors Supply Inc...513 755-2111
   6448 Gano Rd West Chester (45069) *(G-14790)*
Ventech Solutions Inc (PA)...614 757-1167
   8425 Pulsar Pl Ste 300 Columbus (43240) *(G-5284)*
Ventra Salem LLC (HQ)...330 337-8002
   800 Pennsylvania Ave Salem (44460) *(G-12856)*
Ventrac...330 682-0159
   500 Venture Dr Orrville (44667) *(G-12174)*
Venture Lighting Intl Inc (HQ)...800 451-2606
   7905 Cochran Rd Ste 300 Solon (44139) *(G-13159)*
Veolia Es Tchncal Slutions LLC...937 859-6101
   4301 Infirmary Rd Miamisburg (45342) *(G-11102)*
Veolia Nuclear Solutions, Piketon *Also Called: Vns Federal Services LLC (G-12431)*
Veolia Wts Usa Inc..330 339-2292
   2118 Reiser Ave Se New Philadelphia (44663) *(G-11672)*
Ver-A-Fast Corp..440 331-0250
   20545 Center Ridge Rd Ste 300 Rocky River (44116) *(G-12755)*
Verantis Corporation (PA)..440 243-0700
   7251 Engle Rd Ste 300 Middleburg Heights (44130) *(G-11133)*
Verdant Commercial Capital LLC...513 769-2033
   9987 Carver Rd Ste 110 Blue Ash (45242) *(G-1270)*
Verdantas LLC (PA)..614 793-8777
   6397 Emerald Pkwy Ste 200 Dublin (43016) *(G-8151)*
Veritext Holding Company..216 664-0799
   1100 Superior Ave E Cleveland (44114) *(G-5099)*
Veritiv Operating Company...513 285-0999
   6120 S Gilmore Rd Ste 400 Fairfield (45014) *(G-8452)*
Veritiv Pubg & Print MGT Inc (DH)..614 288-0911
   4852 Gray Ln Stow (44224) *(G-13400)*
Verizon, Columbus *Also Called: Rxp Ohio LLC (G-6623)*
Verizon, Hilliard *Also Called: Verizon New York Inc (G-9240)*
Verizon, Medina *Also Called: Cellco Partnership (G-10818)*
Verizon Bus Netwrk Svcs LLC..513 897-1501
   9073 Lytle Ferry Rd Waynesville (45068) *(G-14628)*
Verizon Business, Chardon *Also Called: MCI Communications Svcs LLC (G-2012)*
Verizon Business, Cleveland *Also Called: MCI Communications Svcs LLC (G-4541)*
Verizon Business, Waynesville *Also Called: Verizon Bus Netwrk Svcs LLC (G-14628)*
Verizon New York Inc..614 301-2498
   5000 Britton Pkwy Hilliard (43026) *(G-9240)*

(PA)=Parent Co (HQ)=Headquarters (DH)=Div Headquarters

Verizon Wireless 330 963-1300
2000 Highland Rd Twinsburg (44087) *(G-14228)*

Verizon Wireless, Ashland *Also Called: Cellco Partnership (G-489)*

Verizon Wireless, Chagrin Falls *Also Called: Cellco Partnership (G-1954)*

Verizon Wireless, Dayton *Also Called: Verizon Wireless Inc (G-7701)*

Verizon Wireless, Fairlawn *Also Called: Cellco Partnership (G-8469)*

Verizon Wireless, Parma *Also Called: Cellco Partnership (G-12251)*

Verizon Wireless Inc 937 434-2355
2340 Miamisburg Centerville Rd Dayton (45459) *(G-7701)*

Vermeer Heartland Inc (PA) 740 335-8571
2574 Us Highway 22 Nw Wshngtn Ct Hs (43160) *(G-15495)*

Vermilion Family YMCA 440 967-4208
1230 Beechview Dr Vermilion (44089) *(G-14410)*

Vermilion Local Schools 440 204-1700
1065 Decatur St Vermilion (44089) *(G-14411)*

Vermilion School Bus Garage, Vermilion *Also Called: Vermilion Local Schools (G-14411)*

Vernon Funeral Homes Inc 937 653-8888
235 Miami St Urbana (43078) *(G-14316)*

Vernon Nagel Inc 419 592-3861
0154 County Road 11c Napoleon (43545) *(G-11534)*

Vernovis Ltd 513 234-7201
4770 Duke Dr Ste 180 Mason (45040) *(G-10623)*

Vero Rn, Cincinnati *Also Called: Twg Staffing LLC (G-3538)*

Versa-Pak Ltd 419 586-5466
500 Staeger Rd Celina (45822) *(G-1931)*

Versailles Health Care Center, Versailles *Also Called: Covenant Care Ohio Inc (G-14415)*

Versapay Corporation 216 535-9016
1900 Enterprise Pkwy Ste A Twinsburg (44087) *(G-14229)*

Versatex LLC 513 639-3119
324 W 9th St Cincinnati (45202) *(G-3620)*

Verst Group Logistics Inc 513 772-2494
11880 Enterprise Dr Cincinnati (45241) *(G-3621)*

Verst Group Logistics Inc 859 379-1207
11700 Enterprise Dr Ste 101 Cincinnati (45241) *(G-3622)*

Verst Group Logistics Inc 513 782-1725
98 Glendale Milford Rd Cincinnati (45215) *(G-3623)*

Verst Group Logistics Inc 859 379-1230
9696 International Blvd West Chester (45246) *(G-14844)*

Vertex Computer Systems Inc 513 662-6888
11260 Chester Rd Ste 300 Cincinnati (45246) *(G-3624)*

Verti Insurance Company 844 448-3784
3590 Twin Creeks Dr Columbus (43204) *(G-6844)*

Vertical Adventures Inc 614 888-8393
6513 Kingsmill Ct Columbus (43229) *(G-6845)*

Vertical Knowledge LLC (HQ) 216 920-7790
8 E Washington St Ste 200 Chagrin Falls (44022) *(G-1970)*

Vertiv, Dayton *Also Called: High Voltage Maintenance Corp (G-7406)*

Vertiv, Lorain *Also Called: Vertiv Energy Systems Inc (G-10107)*

Vertiv, Westerville *Also Called: Vertiv Services Inc (G-14950)*

Vertiv Corporation 614 841-6400
610 Executive Campus Dr Westerville (43082) *(G-14948)*

Vertiv Corporation (DH) 614 888-0246
505 N Cleveland Ave Westerville (43082) *(G-14949)*

Vertiv Energy Systems Inc 440 288-1122
1510 Kansas Ave Lorain (44052) *(G-10107)*

Vertiv JV Holdings LLC 614 888-0246
1050 Dearborn Dr Columbus (43085) *(G-6846)*

Vertiv Services Inc 614 841-6400
610 Executive Campus Dr Westerville (43082) *(G-14950)*

Vertneys LLC 937 272-0585
70 Birch Aly Ste 240-7347 Dayton (45440) *(G-7702)*

Vestis Corporation 513 533-1000
Cincinnati (45212) *(G-3625)*

Vestis Corporation 216 341-7400
3600 E 93rd St Cleveland (44105) *(G-5100)*

Vestis Corporation 614 445-8341
1900 Progress Ave Columbus (43207) *(G-6847)*

Vestis Corporation 937 223-6667
1200 Webster St Dayton (45404) *(G-7703)*

Vestis Corporation 419 729-5454
5120 Advantage Dr Toledo (43612) *(G-14092)*

Vet Path Services Inc 513 469-0777
6450 Castle Dr Mason (45040) *(G-10624)*

Veteran Security Patrol Co 513 381-4482
36 E 7th St Ste 2201 Cincinnati (45202) *(G-3626)*

Veteran Security Patrol Co 937 222-7333
601 S Edwin C Moses Blvd Ste 170 Dayton (45417) *(G-7704)*

Veterans Health Administration 740 773-1141
17273 State Route 104 Chillicothe (45601) *(G-2093)*

Veterans Health Administration 513 861-3100
3200 Vine St Cincinnati (45220) *(G-3627)*

Veterans Health Administration 216 791-3800
10701 East Blvd Cleveland (44106) *(G-5101)*

Veterans Health Administration 614 257-5200
420 N James Rd Columbus (43219) *(G-6848)*

Veterans Health Administration 614 257-5524
420 N James Rd Columbus (43219) *(G-6849)*

Veterans Health Administration 937 268-6511
4100 W 3rd St Dayton (45428) *(G-7705)*

Veterans of Foreign Wars, Piqua *Also Called: Veterans of Foreign Wars of US (G-12462)*

Veterans of Foreign Wars of US 740 698-8841
3025 Dickson Rd Albany (45710) *(G-373)*

Veterans of Foreign Wars of US 513 563-6830
3318 E Sharon Rd Cincinnati (45241) *(G-3628)*

Veterans of Foreign Wars of US 937 864-2361
5075 Enon Xenia Rd Ste B Fairborn (45324) *(G-8384)*

Veterans of Foreign Wars of US 740 653-1516
116 Perry St Lancaster (43130) *(G-9748)*

Veterans of Foreign Wars of US 937 773-9122
8756 N County Road 25a Piqua (45356) *(G-12462)*

Veterans of Foreign Wars of US 419 899-2775
115 Cedar St Sherwood (43556) *(G-13013)*

Veterans of Foreign Wars of US 440 349-1863
6340 Melbury Ave Solon (44139) *(G-13160)*

Veterans of Foreign Wars of US 330 532-1423
359 Main St Wellsville (43968) *(G-14642)*

Veterans of Foreign Wars of US 740 472-1199
112 N Sycamore St Woodsfield (43793) *(G-15303)*

Vetrad, Worthington *Also Called: Vetrad LLC (G-15466)*

Vetrad LLC 888 483-8723
300 E Wilson Bridge Rd Worthington (43085) *(G-15466)*

Vf Valley, Portsmouth *Also Called: Valley Wholesale Foods Inc (G-12581)*

Vgp Holdings LLC 513 557-3100
3901 River Rd Cincinnati (45204) *(G-3629)*

Vgs Inc 216 431-7800
2239 E 55th St Cleveland (44103) *(G-5102)*

Via Quest, Dublin *Also Called: Alexson Services Inc (G-7928)*

Viaquest LLC (PA) 614 889-5837
525 Metro Pl N Ste 300 Dublin (43017) *(G-8152)*

Viaquest Behavioral Health LLC (HQ) 614 339-0868
525 Metro Pl N Ste 450 Dublin (43017) *(G-8153)*

Viaquest Residential Svcs LLC (PA) 614 889-5837
525 Metro Pl N Ste 350 Dublin (43017) *(G-8154)*

Viaquest Residential Svcs LLC 216 446-2650
4700 Rockside Rd Ste 100 Independence (44131) *(G-9496)*

Vibo Construction Inc 614 210-6780
4140 Tuller Rd Ste 112 Dublin (43017) *(G-8155)*

Vibra Hosp Mahoning Vly LLC 330 726-5000
8049 South Ave Youngstown (44512) *(G-15748)*

Victim Assistance Program Inc 330 376-7022
137 S Main St Ste 300 Akron (44308) *(G-351)*

Victor J Cassano Health Center, Dayton *Also Called: Dayton Osteopathic Hospital (G-7292)*

Victoria Fire & Casualty Co 513 648-9888
5915 Landerbrook Dr Cleveland (44124) *(G-5103)*

Victoria Theatre Association 937 461-8190
138 N Main St Dayton (45402) *(G-7706)*

VICTORY, Brooklyn *Also Called: Victory Capital Holdings Inc (G-1412)*

Victory Capital Holdings Inc (PA) 216 898-2400
4900 Tiedeman Rd Fl 4 Brooklyn (44144) *(G-1412)*

Victory Packaging LP 216 898-9130
18300 Snow Rd Brookpark (44142) *(G-1442)*

Victory White Metal Company (PA) 216 271-1400
6100 Roland Ave Cleveland (44127) *(G-5104)*

ALPHABETIC SECTION — Vitalsolution

Victory Wholesale Groceries, Springboro Also Called: Brothers Trading Co Inc *(G-13195)*
Victory Wholesale Group, Springboro Also Called: Brothers Trading Co Inc *(G-13194)*
Video Duplication Services Inc (PA) 614 871-3827
   3777 Busineoh Pk Dr Ste A Columbus (43204) *(G-6850)*
Viewray Inc (PA) 440 703-3210
   2 Thermo Fisher Way Oakwood Village (44146) *(G-12060)*
Viewray Systems Inc 303 339-0500
   2 Thermo Fisher Way Oakwood Village (44146) *(G-12061)*
Vigilant Defense 513 309-0672
   7570 Bales St Ste 250 Liberty Township (45069) *(G-9858)*
Vigilant Global Trade Svcs LLC (PA) 260 417-1825
   3140 Courtland Blvd Ste 3400 Shaker Heights (44122) *(G-12988)*
Vigilant LLC 513 300-1460
   7570 Bales St Ste 250 Liberty Township (45069) *(G-9859)*
Vigilant Technology Solutions, Liberty Township Also Called: Vigilant Defense *(G-9858)*
Villa Angela Care Center, Columbus Also Called: Karl Hc LLC *(G-6102)*
Villa At Baton Rouge, The, Lima Also Called: Plus Management Services Inc *(G-9949)*
Villa Georgetown, Georgetown Also Called: Covenant Care Ohio Inc *(G-8800)*
Villa Milano Inc 614 882-2058
   1630 Schrock Rd Columbus (43229) *(G-6851)*
Villa Mlano Bnquet Cnfrnce Ctr, Columbus Also Called: Villa Milano Inc *(G-6851)*
Villa Restaurant, Carrollton Also Called: St Johns Villa *(G-1913)*
Villa Springfield, Springfield Also Called: Covenant Care Ohio Inc *(G-13244)*
Villa Vista Royale LLC 740 264-7301
   1800 Sinclair Ave Steubenville (43953) *(G-13350)*
VILLAGE AT SAINT EDWARD, Fairlawn Also Called: St Edward Home *(G-8500)*
Village At The Greene, Beavercreek Also Called: Hcf of Crestview Inc *(G-924)*
VILLAGE CHRISTIAN SCHOOLS, Pleasant Plain Also Called: Mid-Western Childrens Home *(G-12499)*
Village Chrysler-Dodge, Millersburg Also Called: Village Motors Inc *(G-11295)*
Village Communities LLC 614 540-2400
   470 Olde Worthington Rd Ste 100 Westerville (43082) *(G-14951)*
Village Green Healthcare Ctr 937 548-1993
   405 Chestnut St Greenville (45331) *(G-8889)*
Village Inn Restaurant, Columbus Also Called: Arpita LLC *(G-5386)*
Village Inn Restaurant, Coshocton Also Called: Roscoe Village Foundation *(G-7000)*
Village Motors Inc 330 674-2055
   784 Wooster Rd Millersburg (44654) *(G-11295)*
Village Network (PA) 330 264-3232
   2000 Noble Dr Wooster (44691) *(G-15381)*
Village of Cuyahoga Heights (PA) 216 641-7020
   4863 E 71st St Frnt Cleveland (44125) *(G-5105)*
Village of Sycamore 419 927-4262
   132 North Sycamore Avenue Sycamore (44882) *(G-13533)*
Village of Sycamore 419 927-2357
   Sycamore (44882) *(G-13534)*
Village of Sycamore, Sycamore Also Called: Village of Sycamore *(G-13533)*
Village of Valley View 216 524-6511
   6848 Hathaway Rd Cleveland (44125) *(G-5106)*
Village Party Center, Brookfield Also Called: Yankee Lake Inc *(G-1408)*
Village Veterinary Clinic 440 461-2226
   6529 Wilson Mills Rd Cleveland (44143) *(G-5107)*
Village Veterinary Clinic, Cleveland Also Called: Keith E Huston DVM Llc *(G-4453)*
Vin Devers Inc (PA) 888 847-9535
   5570 Monroe St Sylvania (43560) *(G-13578)*
Vincent & Vincent 513 617-2089
   3237 Stanhope Ave Cincinnati (45211) *(G-3630)*
Vincent Lighting Systems Co (PA) 216 475-7600
   6161 Cochran Rd Ste D Solon (44139) *(G-13161)*
Vinebrook Homes LLC 855 513-5678
   3500 Park Center Dr Ste 100 Dayton (45414) *(G-7707)*
Vinebrook II LLC 614 783-5573
   5550 Huber Rd Dayton (45424) *(G-7708)*
Vinson Group LLC 440 283-8832
   283 E Waterloo Rd Akron (44319) *(G-352)*
Vintage Wine Distributor Inc (PA) 440 248-1750
   6555 Davis Industrial Pkwy Solon (44139) *(G-13162)*
Vintek, Wilmington Also Called: Vintek Inc *(G-15277)*
Vintek Inc 937 382-8986
   3268 Progress Way Wilmington (45177) *(G-15277)*

VINTON CO NATIONAL BANK, Mc Arthur Also Called: Vinton County National Bank *(G-10799)*
Vinton County National Bank (HQ) 800 223-4031
   112 W Main St Mc Arthur (45651) *(G-10799)*
Vinyl Design Corporation 419 283-4009
   7856 Hill Ave Holland (43528) *(G-9313)*
Vio Med Spa Strongsville LLC 440 268-6100
   16738 Pearl Rd Strongsville (44136) *(G-13495)*
VIOLA STARTZMAN CLINIC, Wooster Also Called: Healthcare 2000 Cmnty Clnic In *(G-15343)*
Viox Services, Cincinnati Also Called: Emcor Facilities Services Inc *(G-2613)*
Virginia Ohio-West Excvtg Co 740 676-7464
   56461 Ferry Landing Rd Shadyside (43947) *(G-12971)*
Virtual Hold Tech Slutions LLC (DH) 330 670-2200
   3875 Embassy Pkwy Ste 350 Akron (44333) *(G-353)*
Virtual Pc's, Lima Also Called: Office World Inc *(G-9994)*
Visconsi Companies Ltd 216 464-5550
   30050 Chagrin Blvd Ste 360 Cleveland (44124) *(G-5108)*
Visible Logistics, West Chester Also Called: Visible Supply Chain MGT LLC *(G-14791)*
Visible Supply Chain MGT LLC 801 859-3082
   9271 Meridian Way West Chester (45069) *(G-14791)*
Visicon Inc 937 879-2696
   Bldg 823 Area A Fairborn (45324) *(G-8385)*
Vision Associates Inc (PA) 419 578-7598
   2865 N Reynolds Rd Ste 170 Toledo (43615) *(G-14093)*
Vision Development Inc 614 487-1804
   3300 Riverside Dr Ste 100 Upper Arlington (43221) *(G-14283)*
Vision Home Health Care LLC 614 338-8100
   14057 Broad St Sw Pataskala (43062) *(G-12279)*
Visiting Angels, Ravenna Also Called: Tsk Assisted Living Svcs Inc *(G-12645)*
Visiting Angels, Tallmadge Also Called: Living Assistance Services Inc *(G-13600)*
Visiting Angels, Toledo Also Called: Tk Homecare Llc *(G-14044)*
Visiting Angels, Westerville Also Called: Graves Care Services LLC *(G-14982)*
Visiting Angels Lving Assstnce, West Chester Also Called: Dillon Holdings LLC *(G-14685)*
Visiting Angels of NW Ohio, Edgerton Also Called: Adams Hlping Hands HM Care LLC *(G-8226)*
Visiting Angels Toledo, Toledo Also Called: Liberty Provider LLC *(G-13888)*
Visiting Nrse Assn Hlthcare PR 216 931-1300
   925 Keynote Cir Ste 300 Independence (44131) *(G-9497)*
Visiting Nrse Assn Hspice Nrth 330 841-5440
   8747 Squires Ln Ne Warren (44484) *(G-14572)*
Visiting Nrse Assn of Clveland 419 281-2480
   1165 E Main St Ashland (44805) *(G-515)*
Visiting Nrse Assn of Clveland 419 522-4969
   40 W 4th St Mansfield (44902) *(G-10322)*
Visiting Nrse Assn of Grter CN (PA) 513 345-8000
   2400 Reading Rd Ste 207 Cincinnati (45202) *(G-3631)*
Visiting Nrse Assn of Mid-Ohio 216 931-1300
   2500 E 22nd St Cleveland (44115) *(G-5109)*
Visiting Nurse, Independence Also Called: Visiting Nrse Assn Hlthcare PR *(G-9497)*
Visiting Nurse Assn Ashland, Ashland Also Called: Visiting Nrse Assn of Clveland *(G-515)*
Visiting Physicians Assn, Columbus Also Called: P C Vpa *(G-6495)*
VISON SUPPORT SERVICES, Akron Also Called: Akron Blind Center & Workshop *(G-21)*
Vista Centre 330 424-5852
   100 Vista Dr Lisbon (44432) *(G-10007)*
Visteon Corporation 419 627-3600
   3020 Tiffin Ave Sandusky (44870) *(G-12940)*
Vistra Corp 513 467-5289
   1781 Us Highway 52 Moscow (45153) *(G-11457)*
Vistra Energy Corp 513 467-4900
   11021 Brower Rd North Bend (45052) *(G-11804)*
Vistula Management Company 419 242-2300
   1931 Scottwood Ave Ste 700 Toledo (43620) *(G-14094)*
Visual Edge It Inc (PA) 800 828-4801
   3874 Highland Park Nw North Canton (44720) *(G-11870)*
Visual Edge Technology Inc (PA) 330 494-9694
   3874 Highland Park Nw Canton (44720) *(G-1881)*
Vita Pup, Hudson Also Called: JE Carsten Company *(G-9359)*
Vitalant 440 322-8720
   333 E Bridge St Elyria (44035) *(G-8299)*
Vitalsolution, Blue Ash Also Called: Cardiosolution LLC *(G-1141)*

(PA)=Parent Co (HQ)=Headquarters (DH)=Div Headquarters

Vitalyst LLC 216 201-9070
   3615 Superior Ave E Ste 4406a Cleveland (44114) *(G-5110)*
Vitas Healthcare Corp Midwest 614 822-2700
   655 Metro Pl S Dublin (43017) *(G-8156)*
Vitas Healthcare Corporation 513 742-6310
   11500 Northlake Dr Ste 400 Cincinnati (45249) *(G-3632)*
Vitas Healthcare Corporation 937 299-5379
   3055 Kettering Blvd Ste 218 Moraine (45439) *(G-11446)*
Vitran, Columbus *Also Called: Vitran Express Inc (G-6852)*
Vitran Express Inc 216 426-8584
   5300 Crayton Ave Cleveland (44104) *(G-5111)*
Vitran Express Inc 614 870-2255
   5075 Krieger Ct Columbus (43228) *(G-6852)*
Vitran Express Inc 513 771-4894
   2789 Crescentville Rd West Chester (45069) *(G-14792)*
Vjp Hospitality Ltd 614 475-8383
   3030 Plaza Properties Blvd Columbus (43219) *(G-6853)*
Vloan, Strongsville *Also Called: Union Home Mortgage Corp (G-13493)*
Vmetro Inc (DH) 281 584-0728
   2600 Paramount Pl Ste 200 Fairborn (45324) *(G-8386)*
Vmi Group Inc 330 405-4146
   8413 Tower Dr Twinsburg (44087) *(G-14230)*
Vna, Cleveland *Also Called: Visiting Nrse Assn of Mid-Ohio (G-5109)*
Vna Comprehensive Services Inc 419 695-8101
   602 E 5th St Delphos (45833) *(G-7848)*
Vna of Mid Ohio, Mansfield *Also Called: Visiting Nrse Assn of Clveland (G-10322)*
Vndly LLC 513 572-2500
   4900 Parkway Dr Ste 125 Mason (45040) *(G-10625)*
Vns Federal Services LLC (PA) 740 443-7005
   1571 Shyville Rd Piketon (45661) *(G-12431)*
Voa Rehabilitation Centers Inc 419 447-7151
   48 St Lawrence Dr Tiffin (44883) *(G-13648)*
Vocalink Inc 937 223-1415
   405 W 1st St Ste A Dayton (45402) *(G-7709)*
Vocational Guidance Services (PA) 216 431-7800
   2239 E 55th St Cleveland (44103) *(G-5112)*
Vocational Guidance Services 614 222-2899
   200 N High St Columbus (43215) *(G-6854)*
Vocational Guidance Services 440 322-1123
   359 Lowell St Elyria (44035) *(G-8300)*
Vocational Services, Elyria *Also Called: Vocational Guidance Services (G-8300)*
Vocational Services Inc 216 431-8085
   2239 E 55th St Cleveland (44103) *(G-5113)*
Vocon Design Inc (PA) 216 588-0800
   3142 Prospect Ave E Cleveland (44115) *(G-5114)*
Vocworks, Dublin *Also Called: Careworks of Ohio Inc (G-7958)*
Voestlpine Precision Strip LLC (HQ) 330 220-7800
   3052 Interstate Pkwy Brunswick (44212) *(G-1472)*
Vogt Santer Insights Ltd 614 224-4300
   1310 Dublin Rd Columbus (43215) *(G-6855)*
Vogt Strategic Insights, Columbus *Also Called: Vogt Santer Insights Ltd (G-6855)*
Voiers Enterprises Inc 740 259-2838
   2274 Mc Dermott Pond Creek Rd Mc Dermott (45652) *(G-10800)*
Volk Optical, Mentor *Also Called: Volk Optical Inc (G-11010)*
Volk Optical Inc 440 942-6161
   7893 Enterprise Dr Mentor (44060) *(G-11010)*
Volpenhein Brothers Electric Inc 513 385-9355
   474 W Crescentville Rd West Chester (45246) *(G-14845)*
Volpini Law LLC 216 956-4133
   15300 Pearl Rd Ste 201 Strongsville (44136) *(G-13496)*
Volunteer Amer Atmwood Care Ct, Tiffin *Also Called: Volunters Amer Care Facilities (G-13649)*
Volunteer Energy, Pickerington *Also Called: Volunteer Energy Services Inc (G-12413)*
Volunteer Energy Services Inc (PA) 614 856-3128
   790 Windmiller Dr Ste A Pickerington (43147) *(G-12413)*
Volunteers America Ohio & Ind (PA) 614 253-6100
   1780 E Broad St Columbus (43203) *(G-6856)*
Volunteers of America, Columbus *Also Called: Volunteers of America NW Ohio (G-6857)*
Volunteers of America Inc 513 381-1954
   644 Linn St Ste 105 Cincinnati (45203) *(G-3633)*

Volunteers of America Inc 513 420-1887
   2101 S Main St Apt 312 Middletown (45044) *(G-11192)*
Volunteers of America NW Ohio 419 248-3733
   1780 E Broad St Columbus (43203) *(G-6857)*
Volunters Amer Care Facilities 419 334-9521
   600 N Brush St Fremont (43420) *(G-8707)*
Volunters Amer Care Facilities 419 225-9040
   804 S Mumaugh Rd Lima (45804) *(G-9978)*
Volunters Amer Care Facilities 419 447-7151
   670 E State Route 18 Tiffin (44883) *(G-13649)*
Volvo BMW Dyton Evans Volkswag 937 890-6200
   7124 Poe Ave Dayton (45414) *(G-7710)*
Vonlehman & Company Inc 513 891-5911
   9987 Carver Rd Ste 120 Blue Ash (45242) *(G-1271)*
Vooks Inc 503 694-9217
   4584 Bunker Ln Stow (44224) *(G-13401)*
Vora Solution Center LLC 513 867-7277
   100 Tri County Pkwy Cincinnati (45246) *(G-3634)*
Vora Ventures LLC (PA) 513 792-5100
   10290 Alliance Rd Blue Ash (45242) *(G-1272)*
Vorys Sater Seymour and Pease LLP (PA) 614 464-6400
   52 E Gay St Columbus (43215) *(G-6858)*
Vorys Sater Seymour Pease LLP 513 723-4000
   301 E 4th St Ste 3500 Cincinnati (45202) *(G-3635)*
Vorys Sater Seymour Pease LLP 216 479-6100
   200 Public Sq Ste 1400 Cleveland (44114) *(G-5115)*
Voss Auto Network Inc (PA) 937 428-2447
   766 Miamisburg Centerville Rd Dayton (45459) *(G-7711)*
Voss Auto Network Inc 937 433-1444
   100 Loop Rd Dayton (45459) *(G-7712)*
Voss Chevrolet Inc 937 428-2500
   100 Loop Rd Dayton (45459) *(G-7713)*
Voss Dodge (PA) 937 435-7800
   90 Loop Rd Dayton (45459) *(G-7714)*
Voss Honda, Tipp City *Also Called: Hoss II Inc (G-13660)*
Voss Hyundai, Dayton *Also Called: Hoss Value Cars & Trucks Inc (G-7415)*
Votem Corp (PA) 216 930-4300
   2515 Jay Ave Fl 1 Cleveland (44113) *(G-5116)*
Voto Sales, Steubenville *Also Called: The Voto Manufacturers Sales Company (G-13345)*
Vps, Mason *Also Called: Vet Path Services Inc (G-10624)*
Vrable Healthcare Inc (PA) 614 545-5500
   3248 Henderson Rd Columbus (43220) *(G-6859)*
Vrable Healthcare Inc 614 889-8585
   4500 John Shields Pkwy Dublin (43017) *(G-8157)*
Vrable II, Inc., Columbus *Also Called: Southern Hlls Hlth Rhblttion C (G-6697)*
Vrable IV Inc (HQ) 614 545-5502
   3248 Henderson Rd Columbus (43220) *(G-6860)*
Vrc Companies LLC 614 299-2122
   3827 Brookham Dr Grove City (43123) *(G-8964)*
Vrc Companies LLC 419 381-7762
   3940 Technology Dr Maumee (43537) *(G-10778)*
VSI Global LLC 216 642-8778
   9090 Bank St Cleveland (44125) *(G-5117)*
VSI International, Cleveland *Also Called: VSI Global LLC (G-5117)*
Vsp Vision Care 614 471-1372
   3400 Morse Xing Columbus (43219) *(G-6861)*
Vulcan Enterprises Inc 419 396-3535
   2600 State Highway 568 Ste A Carey (43316) *(G-1896)*
Vulcan Fire Protection, Carey *Also Called: Vulcan Enterprises Inc (G-1896)*
Vwc Liquidation Company LLC 330 372-6776
   1701 Henn Pkwy Sw Warren (44481) *(G-14573)*
W & H Realty Inc (DH) 513 891-1066
   8044 Montgomery Rd Ste 385 Cincinnati (45236) *(G-3636)*
W B Mason Co Inc 216 267-5000
   31387 Industrial Pkwy North Olmsted (44070) *(G-11918)*
W C P O - T V, Cincinnati *Also Called: Wfts (G-3667)*
W D Tire Warehouse Inc (PA) 614 461-8944
   3805 E Livingston Ave Columbus (43227) *(G-6862)*
W Design Interiors, Chagrin Falls *Also Called: W Home Collection LLC (G-1971)*
W G U C-FM RADIO, Cincinnati *Also Called: Cincinnati Public Radio Inc (G-2419)*

ALPHABETIC SECTION

W G T E TV 30 FM 91 Pub Brdcstg.. 419 380-4600
1270 S Detroit Ave Toledo (43614) *(G-14095)*

W H O T Inc (PA).. 330 783-1000
4040 Simon Rd Ste 1 Youngstown (44512) *(G-15749)*

W Home Collection LLC.. 440 247-4474
86 West St Chagrin Falls (44022) *(G-1971)*

W J Alarm Service, Warren Also Called: Wj Service Co Inc *(G-14576)*

W K S, Cleves Also Called: Wm Kramer and Son Inc *(G-5196)*

W K Y C Channel 3, Cleveland Also Called: Wkyc-Tv Inc *(G-5155)*

W L Logan Trucking Company.. 330 478-1404
3224 Navarre Rd Sw Canton (44706) *(G-1882)*

W N W O, Toledo Also Called: Barrington Toledo LLC *(G-13699)*

W Nail Bar LLC.. 614 299-9587
3697 Corporate Dr Columbus (43231) *(G-6863)*

W O I O, Cleveland Also Called: Gray Media Group Inc *(G-4327)*

W P T V - T V, Cincinnati Also Called: Scripps Media Inc *(G-3351)*

W R Shepherd Inc (PA).. 614 889-2896
390 W Olentangy St Powell (43065) *(G-12608)*

W S E M, Cleveland Also Called: West Side Ecumenical Ministry *(G-5134)*

W T Leones Tri-Area Elc Inc.. 330 744-0151
37 Wayne Ave Youngstown (44502) *(G-15750)*

W Team Company (PA).. 440 942-7939
7433 Clover Ave Mentor (44060) *(G-11011)*

W Tov Tv9.. 740 282-9999
9 Red Donley Plz Steubenville (43952) *(G-13351)*

W W Grainger Inc.. 330 425-8388
8211 Bavaria Dr E Macedonia (44056) *(G-10209)*

W W Williams Company LLC.. 330 225-7751
1176 Industrial Pkwy N Brunswick (44212) *(G-1473)*

W W Williams Company LLC (DH).. 614 228-5000
400 Metro Pl N Dublin (43017) *(G-8158)*

W W Williams Company LLC.. 614 527-9400
3535 Parkway Ln Hilliard (43026) *(G-9241)*

W W Williams Midwest Inc.. 330 225-7751
1176 Industrial Pkwy N Brunswick (44212) *(G-1474)*

W William Schmidt & Associates.. 419 526-4747
514 Airport Rd Hanger 6 Mansfield (44903) *(G-10323)*

W X I X, Cincinnati Also Called: Gray Media Group Inc *(G-2752)*

W.F. Hann & Sons, Warrensville Heights Also Called: WF Hann & Sons LLC *(G-14590)*

WA Butler Company (DH).. 614 761-9095
400 Metro Pl N Ste 100 Dublin (43017) *(G-8159)*

Wabash National Trlr Ctrs Inc.. 614 878-6088
5825 Green Pointe Dr S Groveport (43125) *(G-9012)*

Wabe Maquaw Holdings Inc.. 419 243-1191
17 Corey Creek Rd Toledo (43623) *(G-14096)*

Wabush Mnes Clffs Min Mnging A.. 216 694-5700
200 Public Sq Ste 3300 Cleveland (44114) *(G-5118)*

Waco Scaffolding & Equipment Inc.. 216 749-8900
4545 Spring Rd Cleveland (44131) *(G-5119)*

Wad Investments Oh Inc (PA).. 513 891-4477
11755 Lebanon Rd Cincinnati (45241) *(G-3637)*

Wade Trim.. 216 363-0300
1621 Euclid Ave Cleveland (44115) *(G-5120)*

Wadsworth Hie Management Inc.. 330 334-7666
231 Park Centre Dr Wadsworth (44281) *(G-14457)*

Wadsworth Service Inc.. 419 861-8181
7851 Freeway Cir Middleburg Heights (44130) *(G-11134)*

Wadsworth Solutions Northeast, Perrysburg Also Called: Wadsworth-Slawson Inc *(G-12385)*

Wadsworth-Rittman Hospital, Wadsworth Also Called: The Wadsworth-Rittman Area Hospital Association *(G-14456)*

Wadsworth-Slawson Inc.. 216 391-7263
1500 Michael Owens Way Perrysburg (43551) *(G-12385)*

Wagner Industrial Electric, West Chester Also Called: E S I Inc *(G-14808)*

Wagner Metals LLC.. 419 594-7445
1340 W High St Ste E Defiance (43512) *(G-7774)*

Wagner Roofg & Cnstr Solutions, Defiance Also Called: Wagner Metals LLC *(G-7774)*

Wahl Refractory Solutions, Fremont Also Called: Fosbel Wahl Holdings LLC *(G-8678)*

Waibel Energy Systems Inc.. 937 264-4343
815 Falls Creek Dr Vandalia (45377) *(G-14403)*

Waite Schnder Byless Chsley LP (PA).. 513 621-0267
810 Sycamore St Fl 6 Cincinnati (45202) *(G-3638)*

Walden Club.. 330 995-7162
1119 Aurora Hudson Rd Aurora (44202) *(G-629)*

Walden Ponds Golf Club, Fairfield Township Also Called: Creekside Golf Ltd *(G-8459)*

Walden Security, Akron Also Called: Metropolitan Security Svcs Inc *(G-232)*

Walden Security, Cleveland Also Called: Metropolitan Security Svcs Inc *(G-4569)*

Waldon Management Corp (PA).. 330 792-7688
111 Westchester Dr Youngstown (44515) *(G-15751)*

Walker Auto Group Inc.. 937 433-4950
8457 Springboro Pike Miamisburg (45342) *(G-11103)*

Walker Mitsubishi, Miamisburg Also Called: Walker Auto Group Inc *(G-11103)*

Walker National Inc.. 614 492-1614
2195 Wright Brothers Ave Columbus (43217) *(G-6864)*

Wallace, Grove City Also Called: R R Donnelley & Sons Company *(G-8947)*

Walleye Power LLC.. 567 298-7400
4701 Bay Shore Rd Oregon (43616) *(G-12147)*

Wallick, Reynoldsburg Also Called: Wallick Construction Co *(G-12680)*

Wallick Company, The, New Albany Also Called: Brodhead Village Ltd *(G-11557)*

Wallick Construction Co (PA).. 614 863-4640
6880 Tussing Rd Reynoldsburg (43068) *(G-12680)*

Wallick Construction Co.. 937 399-7009
3001 Middle Urbana Rd Springfield (45502) *(G-13309)*

Wallick Construction LLC.. 614 863-4640
160 W Main St Ste 200 New Albany (43054) *(G-11590)*

Wallick Properties Midwest LLC (PA).. 419 381-7477
160 W Main St # 200 New Albany (43054) *(G-11591)*

Wallover Enterprises Inc (DH).. 440 238-9250
21845 Drake Rd Strongsville (44149) *(G-13497)*

Walmart, Jackson Also Called: Walmart Inc *(G-9528)*

Walmart, Lockbourne Also Called: Walmart Inc *(G-10017)*

Walmart, Springfield Also Called: Walmart Inc *(G-13310)*

Walmart, Wintersville Also Called: Walmart Inc *(G-15297)*

Walmart Inc.. 740 286-8203
100 Walmart Dr Jackson (45640) *(G-9528)*

Walmart Inc.. 614 409-5500
2525 Rohr Rd Ste A Lockbourne (43137) *(G-10017)*

Walmart Inc.. 937 399-0370
2100 N Bechtle Ave Springfield (45504) *(G-13310)*

Walmart Inc.. 740 765-5700
843 State Route 43 Wintersville (43952) *(G-15297)*

Walnut Creek Foods, Millersburg Also Called: Coblentz Distributing Inc *(G-11277)*

Walnut Creek Nursing Facility, Moraine Also Called: April Enterprises Inc *(G-11389)*

Walnut Creek Snior Lving Cmpus.. 937 293-7703
5070 Lamme Rd Moraine (45439) *(G-11447)*

Walnut Hills Inc.. 330 852-2457
4748 Olde Pump St Walnut Creek (44687) *(G-14472)*

Walnut Hlls Rtrment Cmmnties I.. 330 893-3200
4748 Olde Pump St Walnut Creek (44687) *(G-14473)*

Walnut Ridge Strgc MGT Co LLC.. 234 678-3900
100 Park Ave Ste 400 Beachwood (44122) *(G-851)*

Walt Ford Sweeney Inc (PA).. 513 347-2600
5400 Glenway Ave Cincinnati (45238) *(G-3639)*

Walter F Stephens Jr Inc.. 937 746-0521
415 South Ave Franklin (45005) *(G-8652)*

Walter Haverfield LLP (PA).. 216 781-1212
1500 W 3rd St Cleveland (44113) *(G-5121)*

Walthall LLP (PA).. 216 573-2330
6300 Rockside Rd Ste 100 Cleveland (44131) *(G-5122)*

Walton Home Health Care LLC.. 513 270-0555
7225 Colerain Ave Ste 205 Cincinnati (45239) *(G-3640)*

Walton Manor Health Care Center, Cleveland Also Called: Healthcare Walton Group LLC *(G-4355)*

Walton Retirement Home.. 740 425-2344
1254 E Main St Barnesville (43713) *(G-724)*

Walts Cleaning Contrs Inc.. 330 899-0040
515 E Turkeyfoot Lake Rd Ste E Akron (44319) *(G-354)*

Wampum Hardware Co.. 419 273-2542
17507 Township Road 50 Forest (45843) *(G-8602)*

Wannemacher Enterprises Inc (PA).. 419 225-9060
400 E Hanthorn Rd Lima (45804) *(G-9979)*

Wannemacher Total Logistics, Lima Also Called: Wannemacher Enterprises Inc *(G-9979)*

Wapakneta Fmly Yung MNS Chrstn.. 419 739-9622
1100 Defiance St Wapakoneta (45895) *(G-14493)*

Wapakoneta Manor, Wapakoneta *Also Called: Hcf of Wapakoneta Inc (G-14485)*

Wappoo Wood Products Inc.. 937 492-1166
12877 Kirkwood Rd Sidney (45365) *(G-13057)*

Ward Financial Group Inc... 513 791-0303
11500 Northlake Dr Ste 305 Cincinnati (45249) *(G-3641)*

Wardjet LLC.. 330 677-9100
180 South Ave Tallmadge (44278) *(G-13611)*

Warehouse, Cleveland *Also Called: Basista Furniture Inc (G-3854)*

Warehouse Facility, West Chester *Also Called: Deanhouston Creative Group Inc (G-14684)*

Warehouse Svcs Group Ltd Lblty.. 419 868-6400
6145 Merger Dr Holland (43528) *(G-9314)*

Warm 98, Cincinnati *Also Called: Cumulus Media Inc (G-2523)*

Warner Buick-Nissan Inc... 419 423-7161
1060 County Road 95 Findlay (45840) *(G-8597)*

Warner Mechanical Corporation... 419 332-7116
1609 Dickinson St Fremont (43420) *(G-8708)*

Warner Nissan, Findlay *Also Called: Warner Buick-Nissan Inc (G-8597)*

Warren Bros & Sons Inc (PA)... 740 373-1430
108 S 7th St B Marietta (45750) *(G-10410)*

Warren City Board Education... 330 841-2265
600 Roanoke Ave Sw Warren (44483) *(G-14574)*

Warren Cnty Bd Dvlpmntal Dsblt....................................... 513 925-1813
42 Kings Way Lebanon (45036) *(G-9798)*

Warren County Cmnty Svcs Inc (PA)................................. 513 695-2100
645 Oak St Ste A Lebanon (45036) *(G-9799)*

WARREN COUNTY OF PRODUCTION SE, Lebanon *Also Called: Production Svcs Unlimited Inc (G-9783)*

Warren County Wtr & Sewer Dept, Lebanon *Also Called: County of Warren (G-9762)*

Warren Dialysis Center LLC.. 330 609-5502
8720 E Market St Ste 1a Warren (44484) *(G-14575)*

Warren Drilling Co Inc.. 740 783-2775
305 Smithson St Dexter City (45727) *(G-7868)*

Warren Trucking, Dexter City *Also Called: Warren Drilling Co Inc (G-7868)*

Warrens IGA, Marietta *Also Called: Warren Bros & Sons Inc (G-10410)*

Warsteiner Importers Agency... 513 942-9872
9359 Allen Rd West Chester (45069) *(G-14793)*

Warsteiner USA, West Chester *Also Called: Warsteiner Importers Agency (G-14793)*

Warstler Bros Landscaping Inc.. 330 492-9500
4125 Salway Ave Nw Canton (44718) *(G-1883)*

Warwick Communications Inc (PA).................................... 216 787-0300
405 Ken Mar Industrial Pkwy Broadview Heights (44147) *(G-1404)*

Wasco Inc (PA)... 740 373-3418
340 Muskingum Dr Marietta (45750) *(G-10411)*

Washing Systems LLC (HQ).. 800 272-1974
167 Commerce Dr Loveland (45140) *(G-10166)*

Washington Cnty Engineers Off, Marietta *Also Called: County of Washington (G-10364)*

Washington County Coal Company.................................... 740 338-3100
46226 National Rd Saint Clairsville (43950) *(G-12819)*

Washington Group, Cleveland *Also Called: Aecom Energy & Cnstr Inc (G-3771)*

Washington Local Schools.. 419 473-8356
5201 Douglas Rd Toledo (43613) *(G-14097)*

Washington MD Leasing Co LLC (HQ).............................. 513 489-7100
10123 Alliance Rd Blue Ash (45242) *(G-1273)*

Washington Prime Acqsition LLC....................................... 614 621-9000
180 E Broad St Columbus (43215) *(G-6865)*

Washington Prime Group Inc (PA)..................................... 614 621-9000
4900 E Dublin Granville Rd Columbus (43215) *(G-6866)*

Washington Square Nursing Ctr, Warren *Also Called: Harbor Operator LLC (G-14525)*

Washington Twnship Mntgmery CN................................... 937 433-0130
895 Miamisburg Centerville Rd Dayton (45459) *(G-7715)*

Washington Twnship Rcrtion Ctr, Dayton *Also Called: Washington Twnship Mntgmery CN (G-7715)*

Wasiniak Construction Inc.. 419 668-8624
2519 State Route 61 Norwalk (44857) *(G-12030)*

Wasserstrom Company (PA).. 614 228-6525
4500 E Broad St Columbus (43213) *(G-6867)*

Wasserstrom Holdings Inc.. 614 228-6525
477 S Front St Columbus (43215) *(G-6868)*

Wasserstrom Marketing Division, Columbus *Also Called: N Wasserstrom & Sons Inc (G-6286)*

Waste Management, Fairborn *Also Called: Waste Management Ohio Inc (G-8387)*

Waste Management, Glenford *Also Called: Waste Management Michigan Inc (G-8832)*

Waste Management, Glenford *Also Called: Waste Management Ohio Inc (G-8833)*

Waste Management, Newark *Also Called: Waste Management Ohio Inc (G-11752)*

Waste Management, Waynesburg *Also Called: American Landfill Inc (G-14621)*

Waste Management Michigan Inc...................................... 740 787-2327
3415 Township Rd Ste 447 Glenford (43739) *(G-8832)*

Waste Management Ohio Inc (HQ)................................... 800 343-6047
1700 N Broad St Fairborn (45324) *(G-8387)*

Waste Management Ohio Inc.. 740 787-2327
3415 Township Road 447 Glenford (43739) *(G-8833)*

Waste Management Ohio Inc.. 419 221-2029
1550 E 4th St Lima (45804) *(G-9980)*

Waste Management Ohio Inc.. 740 345-1212
100 Ecology Row Newark (43055) *(G-11752)*

Waste Water Treatment Plant, Zanesville *Also Called: City of Zanesville (G-15781)*

Waste-Away Systems LLC.. 740 349-2783
995 Keller Dr Newark (43056) *(G-11753)*

Wastewater Treatment Plant, Alliance *Also Called: City of Alliance (G-379)*

Wastren - Enrgx Mssion Spport.. 740 897-3724
1571 Shyville Rd Piketon (45661) *(G-12432)*

Water & Sewer Department, Avon Lake *Also Called: City of Avon Lake (G-676)*

Water 1, Lucasville *Also Called: Scioto County Region Wtr Dst 1 (G-10180)*

Water Department, Cuyahoga Falls *Also Called: City of Cuyahoga Falls (G-7056)*

Water Department, Dayton *Also Called: City of Dayton (G-7232)*

Water Leasing Co LLC.. 440 285-9400
620 Water St Chardon (44024) *(G-2026)*

Water Treatment, Middletown *Also Called: City of Middletown (G-11157)*

Waterbeds n Stuff Inc (PA)... 614 871-1171
3933 Brookham Dr Grove City (43123) *(G-8965)*

Waterloo Coal Company Inc (PA)..................................... 740 286-0004
235 E Main St Jackson (45640) *(G-9529)*

Watermark Rtrment Cmmnties Inc.................................... 405 751-3600
4500 Dorr St Toledo (43615) *(G-14098)*

Watershed Distillery LLC.. 614 357-1936
1145 Chesapeake Ave Ste D Columbus (43212) *(G-6869)*

Waterville Fmly Physicians Inc... 419 878-2026
900 Waterville Monclova Rd Ste A Waterville (43566) *(G-14596)*

Waterway Gas & Wash Company..................................... 330 995-2900
7010 N Aurora Rd Aurora (44202) *(G-630)*

Waterway Gas & Wash Company..................................... 636 537-1111
5611 Darrow Rd Hudson (44236) *(G-9377)*

Waterworks LLC... 614 253-7246
550 Schrock Rd Columbus (43229) *(G-6870)*

Waterworks, The, Columbus *Also Called: Waterworks LLC (G-6870)*

Watkins and Shepard Trckg Inc... 614 832-0440
3430 Urbancrest Industrial Dr Urbancrest (43123) *(G-14326)*

Watson Gravel Inc (PA).. 513 863-0070
2728 Hamilton Cleves Rd Hamilton (45013) *(G-9091)*

Watteredge, Avon Lake *Also Called: Watteredge LLC (G-684)*

Watteredge LLC (DH).. 440 933-6110
567 Miller Rd Avon Lake (44012) *(G-684)*

Wauseon Machine & Mfg Inc, Wauseon *Also Called: Cornerstone Wauseon Inc (G-14598)*

Waxman Consumer Pdts Group Inc (HQ)......................... 440 439-1830
24460 Aurora Rd Bedford Heights (44146) *(G-1004)*

Waxman Consumer Pdts Group Inc.................................. 614 491-0500
5920 Green Pointe Dr S Ste A Groveport (43125) *(G-9013)*

Waxman Consumer Products Group, Bedford Heights *Also Called: Waxman Consumer Pdts Group Inc (G-1004)*

Waxman Industries Inc (PA)... 440 439-1830
24460 Aurora Rd Bedford Heights (44146) *(G-1005)*

Waxxpot, Columbus *Also Called: Waxxpot Group Franchise LLC (G-6871)*

Waxxpot Group Franchise LLC... 614 622-3018
629 N High St Fl 4 Columbus (43215) *(G-6871)*

Waycraft Inc... 419 563-0550
118 River St Bucyrus (44820) *(G-1520)*

Waymaker Medstaff LLC.. 330 526-8594
5458 Fulton Dr Nw Ste B Canton (44718) *(G-1884)*

Wayne County Childrens Svcs, Wooster *Also Called: County of Wayne* ***(G-15329)***

Wayne County Engineers Wooster, Wooster *Also Called: County of Wayne* ***(G-15330)***

Wayne Gar Door Sls & Svc Inc (PA)........330 343-6679
2150 State Route 39 Nw Dover (44622) ***(G-7909)***

Wayne Garage Door Sales & Svc, Dover *Also Called: Wayne Gar Door Sls & Svc Inc* ***(G-7909)***

Wayne Health Corporation (PA)........919 736-1110
835 Sweitzer St Greenville (45331) ***(G-8890)***

Wayne Healthcare (PA)........937 548-1141
835 Sweitzer St Greenville (45331) ***(G-8891)***

WAYNE HEALTHCARE, Greenville *Also Called: Wayne Healthcare* ***(G-8891)***

Wayne Homes, Uniontown *Also Called: Wh Midwest LLC* ***(G-14270)***

Wayne Manor II Inc........330 345-2835
4138 Swanson Blvd Wooster (44691) ***(G-15382)***

Wayne Savings Bancshares Inc (PA)........330 264-5767
151 N Market St Wooster (44691) ***(G-15383)***

Wayne Savings Community Bank (HQ)........330 264-5767
151 N Market St Wooster (44691) ***(G-15384)***

Wayne Signer Enterprises Inc........513 841-1351
6545 Wiehe Rd Cincinnati (45237) ***(G-3642)***

Wayne Street Development LLC........740 373-5455
424 2nd St Marietta (45750) ***(G-10412)***

Wayne Water Systems, Harrison *Also Called: Wayne/Scott Fetzer Company* ***(G-9119)***

Wayne/Scott Fetzer Company........800 237-0987
101 Production Dr Harrison (45030) ***(G-9119)***

Waynesville Pharmacy, Waynesville *Also Called: Fields Family Enterprises Inc* ***(G-14622)***

Wayside Farm Inc........330 666-7716
4557 Quick Rd Peninsula (44264) ***(G-12295)***

Wayside Frms Nrsing Rhblttion, Peninsula *Also Called: Wayside Farm Inc* ***(G-12295)***

Wbns TV Inc........614 460-3700
770 Twin Rivers Dr Columbus (43215) ***(G-6872)***

Wbnx TV 55, Cuyahoga Falls *Also Called: Winston Brdcstg Netwrk Inc* ***(G-7118)***

Wca Group LLC........513 540-2761
9520 Le Saint Dr Fairfield (45014) ***(G-8453)***

WCCS, Lebanon *Also Called: Warren County Cmnty Svcs Inc* ***(G-9799)***

Wch, Bowling Green *Also Called: Wood County Hospital* ***(G-1336)***

Wcm Holdings Inc........513 705-2100
11500 Canal Rd Cincinnati (45241) ***(G-3643)***

Wcmh, Columbus *Also Called: Nexstar Broadcasting Inc* ***(G-6354)***

WD Bpi LLC........440 717-4112
6055 W Snowville Rd Brecksville (44141) ***(G-1371)***

WD Partners Inc (PA)........614 634-7000
7007 Discovery Blvd Dublin (43017) ***(G-8160)***

Wdg, Lagrange *Also Called: West Development Group LLC* ***(G-9651)***

Wdht Enterprises Inc........440 846-0200
14675 Foltz Pkwy Strongsville (44149) ***(G-13498)***

We Fresh N Refresh LLC........216 937-9798
1011 Spring Rd Cleveland (44109) ***(G-5123)***

Wealth Bartlett Management........513 345-6217
600 Vine St Ste 2100 Cincinnati (45202) ***(G-3644)***

Weastec Incorporated........614 734-9645
6195 Enterprise Ct Dublin (43016) ***(G-8161)***

Weatherables, Groveport *Also Called: Usavinyl LLC* ***(G-9010)***

Weaver Appliance Sls & Svc LLC........330 852-4555
2613 N Wooster Ave Dover (44622) ***(G-7910)***

Weaver Bros Inc (PA)........937 526-3907
895 E Main St Versailles (45380) ***(G-14417)***

Weaver Custom Homes Inc........330 264-5444
124 E Liberty St Ste A Wooster (44691) ***(G-15385)***

Weaver Fab & Finishing, Akron *Also Called: Bogie Industries Inc Ltd* ***(G-72)***

Weaver Industries Inc........330 379-3606
636 W Exchange St Akron (44302) ***(G-355)***

Weaver Industries Inc (PA)........330 379-3660
520 S Main St Ste 2441 Akron (44311) ***(G-356)***

Weaver Industries Inc........330 666-5114
340 N Cleveland Massillon Rd Akron (44333) ***(G-357)***

Weaver Industries Inc........330 745-2400
2337 Romig Rd Ste 2 Akron (44320) ***(G-358)***

Weaver Industries Inc........330 379-3660
66 Osceola Ave Tallmadge (44278) ***(G-13612)***

Weaver Leather LLC (HQ)........330 674-7548
7540 County Road 201 Millersburg (44654) ***(G-11296)***

Weaver Secure Shred, Akron *Also Called: Weaver Industries Inc* ***(G-358)***

Webb, Barry W, Cincinnati *Also Called: Springdale Family Medicine PC* ***(G-3400)***

Webmd Health Corp........419 324-8000
100 N Byrne Rd Toledo (43607) ***(G-14099)***

Wedgewood Estates........419 756-7400
600 S Trimble Rd Mansfield (44906) ***(G-10324)***

Wedgewood Golf & Country Club........614 793-9600
9600 Wedgewood Blvd Powell (43065) ***(G-12609)***

Wedgewood Urgent Care, Westerville *Also Called: Immediate Health Associates* ***(G-14989)***

Wednesday Auto Auction, Obetz *Also Called: Aaj Enterprises Inc* ***(G-12078)***

Wedron Silica LLC........815 433-2449
3 Summit Park Dr Ste 700 Independence (44131) ***(G-9498)***

Wee Care Day Care Lrng Centre, Youngstown *Also Called: Nichalex Inc* ***(G-15676)***

WEE CARE LEARNING CENTER, Van Wert *Also Called: Van Wert Cnty Day Care Ctr Inc* ***(G-14356)***

Weekleys Mailing Service Inc........440 234-4325
1420 W Bagley Rd Berea (44017) ***(G-1086)***

Wegman Hessler Vanderburg........216 642-3342
6055 Rockside Woods Blvd N Ste 200 Cleveland (44131) ***(G-5124)***

Wegman Company........513 381-1111
1531 Western Ave Cincinnati (45214) ***(G-3645)***

Wegman Company, Cincinnati *Also Called: Wegman Construction Company* ***(G-3646)***

Wegman Construction Company........513 381-1111
1531 Western Ave Cincinnati (45214) ***(G-3646)***

Weiffenbach Marble & Tile Co........937 832-7055
150 Lau Pkwy Englewood (45315) ***(G-8326)***

Weiland's Gourmet Market, Columbus *Also Called: Weilands Fine Meats Inc* ***(G-6873)***

Weilands Fine Meats Inc........614 267-9910
3600 Indianola Ave Columbus (43214) ***(G-6873)***

Weiler Welding Company Inc........937 222-8312
2400 Sandridge Dr Moraine (45439) ***(G-11448)***

Weinberg Capital Group Inc (PA)........216 503-8307
30195 Chagrin Blvd Ste 222 Cleveland (44124) ***(G-5125)***

Weiner Keith D Co L P A Inc........216 771-6500
75 Public Sq Ste 600 Cleveland (44113) ***(G-5126)***

Welch Holdings Inc........513 353-3220
8953 E Miami River Rd Cincinnati (45247) ***(G-3647)***

Welch Packaging, Toledo *Also Called: Welch Packaging Group Inc* ***(G-14100)***

Welch Packaging Columbus, Columbus *Also Called: Welch Packaging Group Inc* ***(G-6874)***

Welch Packaging Group Inc........614 870-2000
4700 Alkire Rd Columbus (43228) ***(G-6874)***

Welch Packaging Group Inc........419 726-3491
1240 Matzinger Rd Toledo (43612) ***(G-14100)***

Welcome Hospitality Corp........937 325-5356
155 W Leffel Ln Springfield (45506) ***(G-13311)***

Welcome House Inc........440 471-7601
29756 Lorain Rd North Olmsted (44070) ***(G-11919)***

WELCOME NURSING HOME, Oberlin *Also Called: Wessell Generations Inc* ***(G-12077)***

Weld Plus Inc........513 941-4411
4790 River Rd Cincinnati (45233) ***(G-3648)***

Weldco Inc........513 744-9353
2121 Spring Grove Ave Cincinnati (45214) ***(G-3649)***

Welded Construction LP........419 874-3548
26933 Eckel Rd Perrysburg (43551) ***(G-12386)***

Welded Ring Properties Co........216 961-3800
2180 W 114th St Cleveland (44102) ***(G-5127)***

Welders Supply Inc........216 267-4470
5575 Engle Rd Brookpark (44142) ***(G-1443)***

Welding Cutting Tls & ACC LLC (HQ)........216 481-8100
22801 Saint Clair Ave Cleveland (44117) ***(G-5128)***

Wellcare Physicians Group LLC........419 891-8541
5901 Monclova Rd Maumee (43537) ***(G-10779)***

Wellert Corporation........330 239-2699
5136 Beach Rd Medina (44256) ***(G-10901)***

Welles-Bowen Realty Inc........419 535-0011
2460 N Reynolds Rd Toledo (43615) ***(G-14101)***

Wellington Orthopedics, Cincinnati *Also Called: Orthopedic Cons Cincinnati* ***(G-3171)***

Wellington Orthpd Spt Medicine, Cincinnati *Also Called: Orthopedic Cons Cincinnati* ***(G-3172)***

Wellington Orthpd Spt Medicine, Cincinnati *Also Called: Orthopedic Cons Cincinnati* ***(G-3173)***

Wellington Orthpd Spt Medicine, West Chester *Also Called: Orthopedic Cons Cincinnati* ***(G-14738)***

ALPHABETIC

(PA)=Parent Co (HQ)=Headquarters (DH)=Div Headquarters
2024 Harris Ohio
Services Directory
1253

Wellington Place LLC..440 734-9933
4800 Clague Rd Apt 108 North Olmsted (44070) *(G-11920)*

Wellington Technologies Inc................................440 238-4377
802 Sharon Dr Westlake (44145) *(G-15123)*

Wellness Grove LLC..330 244-1566
4200 Munson St Nw Canton (44718) *(G-1885)*

Wellness Iq Inc...216 264-2727
6450 Rockside Woods Blvd S Ste 220 Independence (44131) *(G-9499)*

Wellness Residential Svc LLC...............................513 969-4160
260 Northland Blvd Ste 216 Cincinnati (45246) *(G-3650)*

Wellnow Urgent Care PC.......................................937 236-8630
6210 Brandt Pike Ste 102 Dayton (45424) *(G-7716)*

Wellnow Urgent Care and RES, Dayton *Also Called: Wellnow Urgent Care PC (G-7716)*

Wellpoint Health Networks, Mason *Also Called: Nextrx LLC (G-10584)*

Wells Brothers Inc..937 394-7559
105 Shue Dr Anna (45302) *(G-445)*

Wells Fargo, Cincinnati *Also Called: Wells Fargo Fincl SEC Svcs Inc (G-3651)*

Wells Fargo Fincl SEC Svcs Inc.............................513 530-0333
8170 Corporate Park Dr Cincinnati (45242) *(G-3651)*

Wells Fargo Insurance Services of Ohio LLC.......614 324-2820
580 N 4th St Ste 400 Columbus (43215) *(G-6875)*

Wells Township...740 598-9602
409 Prospect St Brilliant (43913) *(G-1382)*

Wellspring Health Care, Cincinnati *Also Called: SL Wellspring LLC (G-3387)*

Wellston Auditor's Office, Wellston *Also Called: City of Wellston (G-14636)*

Welltower Inc (PA)...419 247-2800
4500 Dorr St Toledo (43615) *(G-14102)*

Welltower Inc., Toledo *Also Called: Welltower Op LLC (G-14103)*

Welltower Op LLC (HQ)..419 247-2800
4500 Dorr St Toledo (43615) *(G-14103)*

WELSH HOME FOR THE AGED, Rocky River *Also Called: Womens Welsh Clubs of America (G-12757)*

Welspun Usa Inc...614 945-5100
3901 Gantz Rd Ste A Grove City (43123) *(G-8966)*

Weltman Weinberg & Reis Co Lpa.........................513 723-2200
312 Elm St Ste 1200 Cincinnati (45202) *(G-3652)*

Weltman Weinberg & Reis Co Lpa.........................216 459-8633
981 Keynote Cir Cleveland (44131) *(G-5129)*

Weltman Weinberg & Reis Co Lpa.........................614 801-2600
5000 Bradenton Ave Ste 100 Dublin (43017) *(G-8162)*

Weltman Weinberg & Reis Co Lpa (PA).................216 685-1000
965 Keynote Cir Independence (44131) *(G-9500)*

Weltman, Weinberg & Reis Co.,, Cleveland *Also Called: Weltman Weinberg & Reis Co Lpa (G-5129)*

Welty Building Company Ltd.................................216 931-2400
1400 W 10th St Cleveland (44113) *(G-5130)*

Welty Building Company Ltd (PA).........................330 867-2400
3421 Ridgewood Rd Ste 200 Fairlawn (44333) *(G-8503)*

Wems, Piketon *Also Called: Wastren - Enrgx Mssion Spport (G-12432)*

Wendt-Bristol Health Services...............................614 403-9966
921 Jasonway Ave Ste B Columbus (43214) *(G-6876)*

Wendy's, Dublin *Also Called: Wendys Company (G-8163)*

Wendy's, Dublin *Also Called: Wendys Restaurants LLC (G-8164)*

Wendys Company (PA)...614 764-3100
1 Dave Thomas Blvd Dublin (43017) *(G-8163)*

Wendys Restaurants LLC (HQ)..............................614 764-3100
1 Dave Thomas Blvd Dublin (43017) *(G-8164)*

Wenger Excavating Inc..330 837-4767
26 N Cochran St Dalton (44618) *(G-7122)*

Wensminger Holdings Inc......................................513 563-8822
3330 E Kemper Rd Cincinnati (45241) *(G-3653)*

Wentz Hc Holdings Inc...614 294-4966
6969 Worthington Galena Rd Ste A Worthington (43085) *(G-15467)*

Wenzler Day Learning Ctr Inc................................937 435-8200
4535 Presidential Way Dayton (45429) *(G-7717)*

Wenzler Daycare & Learning Ctr, Dayton *Also Called: Wenzler Day Learning Ctr Inc (G-7717)*

Werks Kraft Engineering LLC.................................330 721-7374
935 Heritage Dr Medina (44256) *(G-10902)*

Werlor Inc..419 784-4285
1420 Ralston Ave Defiance (43512) *(G-7775)*

Werlor Waste Control, Defiance *Also Called: Werlor Inc (G-7775)*

Wesbanco Title Agency LLC..................................866 295-1714
1160 Dublin Rd Ste 500 Columbus (43215) *(G-6877)*

Weschler Instruments, Strongsville *Also Called: Hughes Corporation (G-13463)*

Wesco Distribution Inc..216 741-0441
17909 Cleveland Pkwy Dr Rear Cleveland (44135) *(G-5131)*

Wesley Community Services LLC.........................513 661-2777
2091 Radcliff Dr Cincinnati (45204) *(G-3654)*

Wesley Glen Rtrement Cmnty LLC........................614 888-7492
5155 N High St Columbus (43214) *(G-6878)*

Wesley Ridge, Columbus *Also Called: Glen Wesley Inc (G-5937)*

Wesley Ridge Inc..614 759-0023
2225 Taylor Park Dr Reynoldsburg (43068) *(G-12681)*

Wessell Generations Inc..440 775-1491
417 S Main St Oberlin (44074) *(G-12077)*

West After School Center......................................740 653-5678
625 Garfield Ave Lancaster (43130) *(G-9749)*

West Bay Care Rhbilitation Ctr, Westlake *Also Called: Harborside Clveland Ltd Partnr (G-15064)*

West Bay Center, Westlake *Also Called: Harborside Clveland Ltd Partnr (G-15063)*

West Branch Local School Dst..............................330 938-1122
2900 Knox School Rd Alliance (44601) *(G-404)*

West Branch Nursing Home Ltd............................330 537-4621
451 Valley Rd Salem (44460) *(G-12857)*

West Branch Preschool, Alliance *Also Called: West Branch Local School Dst (G-404)*

West Central Ohio Group Ltd................................419 224-7586
801 Medical Dr Ste B Lima (45804) *(G-9981)*

West Chester Holdings LLC...................................513 705-2100
11500 Canal Rd Cincinnati (45241) *(G-3655)*

West Chester Hospital, West Chester *Also Called: Chester West Medical Center (G-14663)*

West Chester Protective Gear, Cincinnati *Also Called: West Chester Holdings LLC (G-3655)*

West Chster Dntstry Dr Jffrey................................330 753-7734
1575 Vernon Odom Blvd Akron (44320) *(G-359)*

West Cntl Ohio Srgery Endscopy..........................419 226-8700
770 W High St Ste 100 Lima (45801) *(G-9982)*

West Development Group LLC (DH).....................440 355-4682
300 Commerce Dr Lagrange (44050) *(G-9651)*

West End Branch, Willoughby *Also Called: Lake County YMCA (G-15198)*

West End YMCA, Cincinnati *Also Called: Young MNS Chrstn Assn Grter CN (G-3694)*

West Enterprises Inc..614 237-4488
480 S 3rd St Columbus (43215) *(G-6879)*

West Entitlement Operations, Columbus *Also Called: Defense Fin & Accounting Svc (G-5750)*

West Hamilton Dialysis, Hamilton *Also Called: Borrego Dialysis LLC (G-9018)*

West Haven IV, North Olmsted *Also Called: Welcome House Inc (G-11919)*

West Market St Fmly Physicians...........................419 229-4747
915 W Market St Ste E Lima (45805) *(G-9983)*

West Ohio Cmnty Action Partnr (PA)....................419 227-2586
540 S Central Ave Lima (45804) *(G-9984)*

West Ohio Cmnty Action Partnr...........................419 227-2586
540 S Central Ave Lima (45804) *(G-9985)*

West Ohio Cnfrnce of Untd Mthd (PA).................614 844-6200
32 Wesley Blvd Worthington (43085) *(G-15468)*

West Park Animal Hospital, Cleveland *Also Called: Tri Zob Inc (G-5036)*

West Park Care Center LLC...................................614 274-4222
1700 Heinzerling Dr Columbus (43223) *(G-6880)*

West Park Retirement Community.......................513 451-8900
2950 W Park Dr Ofc Cincinnati (45238) *(G-3656)*

West Park Shell..216 252-5086
13960 Lorain Ave Cleveland (44111) *(G-5132)*

West Roofing Systems Inc (PA)............................800 356-5748
121 Commerce Dr Lagrange (44050) *(G-9652)*

West Shell Commercial Inc....................................513 721-4200
425 Walnut St Ste 1200 Cincinnati (45202) *(G-3657)*

West Shore Day Treatment Ctr, Cleveland *Also Called: Positive Education Program (G-4763)*

West Side Community House...............................216 771-7297
9300 Lorain Ave Cleveland (44102) *(G-5133)*

West Side Dtscher Fruen Verein............................440 238-3361
520 Abbyshire Dr Berea (44017) *(G-1087)*

West Side Ecumenical Ministry (PA)....................216 325-9369
5209 Detroit Ave Cleveland (44102) *(G-5134)*

ALPHABETIC SECTION

West Side Montessori 419 866-1931
   7115 W Bancroft St Toledo (43615) *(G-14104)*

West Side Pediatrics Inc (PA) 513 922-8200
   663 Anderson Ferry Rd Ste 1 Cincinnati (45238) *(G-3658)*

West Toledo Animal Hosp Ltd 419 475-1527
   4404 Secor Rd Toledo (43623) *(G-14105)*

West View Manor Inc 330 264-8640
   1715 Mechanicsburg Rd Wooster (44691) *(G-15386)*

WEST VIEW MANOR RETIREMENT CEN, Wooster Also Called: West View Manor Inc *(G-15386)*

Westainer Lines, Middleburg Heights Also Called: World Ex Shipg Trnsp Fwdg Svcs *(G-11135)*

Westar Construction Inc 937 667-8402
   4225 Gibson Dr Tipp City (45371) *(G-13669)*

Westcare Ohio Inc 937 259-1898
   624 Xenia Ave Dayton (45410) *(G-7718)*

Westerly Wstwater Trtmnt Plant, Cleveland Also Called: Northast Ohio Rgonal Sewer Dst *(G-4660)*

Westerman Inc (PA) 800 338-8265
   245 N Broad St Bremen (43107) *(G-1372)*

Western & Southern, Cincinnati Also Called: Western Sthern Fincl Group Inc *(G-3665)*

Western & Southern Lf Insur Co (DH) 513 629-1800
   400 Broadway St Stop G Cincinnati (45202) *(G-3659)*

Western Bowl Inc 513 574-2200
   6383 Glenway Ave Cincinnati (45211) *(G-3660)*

Western Branch Diesel LLC 740 695-6301
   67755 Friends Church Rd Saint Clairsville (43950) *(G-12820)*

Western Family Physicians, Cincinnati Also Called: Trihealth Inc *(G-3515)*

Western Hills Care Center 513 941-0099
   6210 Cleves Warsaw Pike Cincinnati (45233) *(G-3661)*

Western Hills Country Club 513 922-0011
   5780 Cleves Warsaw Pike Cincinnati (45233) *(G-3662)*

Western Hills Dialysis, Cincinnati Also Called: Dva Hlthcare - Sthwest Ohio LL *(G-2588)*

Western Hills Retirement Vlg, Cincinnati Also Called: Ebenezer Road Corporation *(G-2601)*

Western Hills Sportsplex Inc 513 451-4900
   2323 Ferguson Rd Ste 1 Cincinnati (45238) *(G-3663)*

Western Inventory Service Inc 419 756-7071
   1251 Lexington Ave Ste 4 Mansfield (44907) *(G-10325)*

Western Kentucky Coal Co LLC 740 338-3334
   46226 National Rd Saint Clairsville (43950) *(G-12821)*

Western KY Coal Resources LLC (DH) 740 338-3100
   46226 National Rd Saint Clairsville (43950) *(G-12822)*

Western Management Inc (PA) 216 941-3333
   14577 Lorain Ave Rear Cleveland (44111) *(G-5135)*

Western Ohio Mortgage Corp 937 497-9662
   733 Fair Rd Sidney (45365) *(G-13058)*

Western Reserve Farm Cooperative Inc 440 632-0271
   16003 E High St Middlefield (44062) *(G-11146)*

Western Reserve Group (PA) 330 262-9060
   2865 Benden Dr Wooster (44691) *(G-15387)*

Western Reserve Health Sys LLC 330 923-8660
   2750 Front St Cuyahoga Falls (44221) *(G-7114)*

Western Reserve Historical Soc 330 666-3711
   2686 Oak Hill Dr Bath (44210) *(G-755)*

Western Reserve Historical Soc (PA) 216 721-5722
   10825 East Blvd Cleveland (44106) *(G-5136)*

Western Reserve Hospital LLC (HQ) 330 971-7000
   1900 23rd St Cuyahoga Falls (44223) *(G-7115)*

Western Reserve Interiors Inc 216 447-1081
   7777 Exchange St Ste 7 Cleveland (44125) *(G-5137)*

Western Reserve Mechanical Inc 330 652-3888
   3041 S Main St Niles (44446) *(G-11798)*

Western Reserve Public Media, Kent Also Called: Northeastern Eductl TV Ohio Inc *(G-9589)*

Western Reserve Transit Auth (PA) 330 744-8431
   604 Mahoning Ave Youngstown (44502) *(G-15752)*

Western Rsrve Area Agcy On Agi (PA) 216 621-0303
   1700 E 13th St Ste 114 Cleveland (44114) *(G-5138)*

Western Rsrve Area Agcy On Agi 216 621-0303
   1700 E 13th St Ste 114 Cleveland (44114) *(G-5139)*

Western Rsrve Hosp Prtners LLC (PA) 330 971-7000
   1900 23rd St Cuyahoga Falls (44223) *(G-7116)*

Western Rsrve Msonic Cmnty Inc 330 721-3000
   4931 Nettleton Rd Apt 4318 Medina (44256) *(G-10903)*

Western Rsrve Racquet CLB Corp 330 653-3103
   11013 Aurora Hudson Rd Streetsboro (44241) *(G-13435)*

Western Southern Mutl Holdg Co (PA) 866 832-7719
   400 Broadway St Cincinnati (45202) *(G-3664)*

Western Sports Mall, Cincinnati Also Called: Western Hills Sportsplex Inc *(G-3663)*

Western States Envelope Co 419 666-7480
   6859 Commodore Dr Walbridge (43465) *(G-14468)*

Western States Envelope Label, Walbridge Also Called: Western States Envelope Co *(G-14468)*

Western Sthern Fincl Group Inc (HQ) 877 367-9734
   400 Broadway St Cincinnati (45202) *(G-3665)*

Western-Southern Life, Cincinnati Also Called: Western & Southern Lf Insur Co *(G-3659)*

Western-Southern Life Asrn Co 513 629-1800
   400 Broadway St Cincinnati (45202) *(G-3666)*

Westerville Family Physicians 614 899-2700
   400 Altair Pkwy Westerville (43082) *(G-14952)*

Westerville Internal Medicine 614 891-8080
   484 County Line Rd W Ste 200 Westerville (43082) *(G-14953)*

Westerville Senior Dev Ltd 614 794-9300
   730 N Spring Rd Westerville (43082) *(G-14954)*

Westfall Towing LLC 740 371-5185
   1024 Pike St Marietta (45750) *(G-10413)*

Westfield Bank, Westfield Center Also Called: Westfield Bank Fsb *(G-15026)*

Westfield Bank Fsb (DH) 800 368-8930
   2 Park Cir Westfield Center (44251) *(G-15026)*

Westfield Electric Inc 419 862-0078
   2995 State Route 51 Gibsonburg (43431) *(G-8807)*

Westfield Group, Westfield Center Also Called: Ohio Farmers Insurance Company *(G-15025)*

Westfield Insurance Company (HQ) 800 243-0210
   1 Park Cir Westfield Center (44251) *(G-15027)*

Westfield National Insur Co (HQ) 330 887-0101
   1 Park Cir Westfield Center (44251) *(G-15028)*

Westfield Steel Inc 937 322-2414
   1120 S Burnett Rd Springfield (45505) *(G-13312)*

Westgate Lanes Incorporated 419 229-3845
   721 N Cable Rd Lima (45805) *(G-9986)*

Westin Cincinnati, The, Cincinnati Also Called: Hst Lessee Cincinnati LLC *(G-2853)*

Westin Cleveland, Cleveland Also Called: Optima 777 LLC *(G-4704)*

Westin Columbus, Columbus Also Called: Marcus Hotels Inc *(G-6194)*

Westin Columbus, Columbus Also Called: Wm Columbus Hotel LLC *(G-6899)*

Westin Hotel, Columbus Also Called: First Hotel Associates LP *(G-5862)*

Westinghouse, Columbus Also Called: Mwe Investments LLC *(G-6284)*

Westlake Dimex LLC 740 374-3100
   28305 State Route 7 Marietta (45750) *(G-10414)*

Westlake Reed Leskosky, Cleveland Also Called: Dlr Group Inc *(G-4169)*

Westlake Ten Inc 440 250-9804
   25777 Detroit Rd Westlake (44145) *(G-15124)*

Westlake Village Inc 440 892-4200
   28550 Westlake Village Dr Cleveland (44145) *(G-5140)*

Westland Heating & AC, Westlake Also Called: North East Mechanical Inc *(G-15086)*

Westminster Fincl Companies, Dayton Also Called: Westmnster Fncl Securities Inc *(G-7719)*

Westminster Thurber Community, Columbus Also Called: Ohio Living *(G-6431)*

Westmnster Fncl Securities Inc 937 898-5010
   50 Chestnut St Dayton (45440) *(G-7719)*

Westmoreland Place, Chillicothe Also Called: Chillicothe Long-Term Care Inc *(G-2057)*

Westmoreland Place, Cincinnati Also Called: Chillicothe Long-Term Care Inc *(G-2372)*

Westmoreland Resources Gp LLC 740 622-6302
   544 Chestnut St Coshocton (43812) *(G-7004)*

Weston and Associates LLC 330 791-7118
   295 Wetmore Ave Se Massillon (44646) *(G-10672)*

Weston Development Company LLC 440 914-8427
   4832 Richmond Rd Ste 100 Cleveland (44128) *(G-5141)*

Weston Hurd LLP (PA) 216 241-6602
   1301 E 9th St Ste 1900 Cleveland (44114) *(G-5142)*

Weston Inc (PA) 440 349-9000
   4760 Richmond Rd Ste 200 Cleveland (44128) *(G-5143)*

Weston Management Co, Cleveland Also Called: Legacy Properties Inc *(G-4484)*

Westover Preparatory School

ALPHABETIC SECTION

Westover Preparatory School, Hamilton *Also Called: Colonial Senior Services Inc* *(G-9031)*

Westover Retirement Communitry, Hamilton *Also Called: Colonial Senior Services Inc* *(G-9032)*

Westpatrick Corp.. 614 875-8200
3458 Lewis Centre Way Urbancrest (43123) *(G-14327)*

Westpost Columbus LLC...................................... 614 885-1885
6500 Doubletree Ave Columbus (43229) *(G-6881)*

Westrock Commercial LLC................................... 419 476-9101
1635 Coining Dr Toledo (43612) *(G-14106)*

Westshore Prmry Care Assoc Inc, Westlake *Also Called: University Hsptals St John Med* *(G-15121)*

Westshore Ymca/Westlake Chrn, Westlake *Also Called: Young MNS Chrstn Assn Grter CL* *(G-15126)*

Westwood Country Club Company......................... 440 331-3016
22625 Detroit Rd Rocky River (44116) *(G-12756)*

Wetherngton Golf Cntry CLB Inc (PA).................... 513 755-2582
7337 Country Club Ln West Chester (45069) *(G-14794)*

Wexner Heritage Village (PA)................................ 614 231-4900
1151 College Ave Columbus (43209) *(G-6882)*

Wexner Research Institute, Columbus *Also Called: Nationwide Childrens Hospital* *(G-6320)*

Weymouth Valley Inc... 440 498-8888
39000 Signature Dr Solon (44139) *(G-13163)*

WF Hann & Sons LLC (PA).................................. 216 831-4200
26401 Miles Rd Warrensville Heights (44128) *(G-14590)*

Wfmj Television Inc.. 330 744-8611
101 W Boardman St Youngstown (44503) *(G-15753)*

Wfts.. 513 721-9900
1720 Gilbert Ave Cincinnati (45202) *(G-3667)*

Wfts.. 216 431-5555
3001 Euclid Ave Cleveland (44115) *(G-5144)*

Wgte-Tv-Fm, Toledo *Also Called: Public Brdcstg Fndtion of NW O* *(G-13980)*

Wh Midwest LLC (PA).. 330 896-7611
3777 Boettler Oaks Dr Uniontown (44685) *(G-14270)*

Whalen & Co CPA, Worthington *Also Called: Whalen and Company Cpas Inc* *(G-15469)*

Whalen and Company Cpas Inc........................... 614 396-4200
250 W Old Wilson Bridge Rd Worthington (43085) *(G-15469)*

Whbc-FM, Canton *Also Called: Alpha Media LLC* *(G-1662)*

Wheatland Tube LLC... 724 342-6851
1800 Hunter Ave Niles (44446) *(G-11799)*

Wheatland Tube Company, Cambridge *Also Called: Zekelman Industries Inc* *(G-1588)*

Wheatland Tube Company, Niles *Also Called: Wheatland Tube LLC* *(G-11799)*

Wheeling & Lake Erie Rlwy Co............................ 330 767-3401
100 East First St Brewster (44613) *(G-1374)*

Wheeling Hospital Inc....................................... 740 942-4631
951 E Market St Cadiz (43907) *(G-1544)*

Whelco Industrial Ltd....................................... 419 385-4627
28210 Cedar Park Blvd Perrysburg (43551) *(G-12387)*

Whetstone Medical Clinic Inc............................. 740 467-2787
12135 Lancaster St Millersport (43046) *(G-11300)*

Whirlpool Corporation...................................... 740 383-7122
1300 Marion Agosta Rd Marion (43302) *(G-10464)*

Whisler Plumbing & Heating Inc......................... 330 833-2875
2521 Lincoln Way E Massillon (44646) *(G-10673)*

Whitaker-Myers Insur Agcy Inc........................... 330 345-5000
3524 Commerce Pkwy Wooster (44691) *(G-15388)*

White Allen Chevrolet, Dayton *Also Called: White Family Companies Inc* *(G-7720)*

White Castle, Columbus *Also Called: White Castle System Inc* *(G-6883)*

White Castle System Inc (PA)............................ 614 228-5781
555 Edgar Waldo Way Columbus (43215) *(G-6883)*

White Family Companies Inc.............................. 937 222-3701
442 N Main St Dayton (45405) *(G-7720)*

White Fnce Surgical Suites LLC......................... 614 289-6282
7277 Smiths Mill Rd Ste 300 New Albany (43054) *(G-11592)*

White Gorilla Corporation................................. 202 384-6486
6218 Lampton Pond Dr Hilliard (43026) *(G-9242)*

White Lght Bhvral Hlth Clmbus........................... 614 350-4010
4040 E Broad St Columbus (43213) *(G-6884)*

White Oak Dialysis, Cincinnati *Also Called: River Valley Dialysis LLC* *(G-3303)*

White Oak Home Training, Cincinnati *Also Called: Ohio River Dialysis LLC* *(G-3148)*

White Oak Investments Inc................................ 614 491-1000
3730 Lockbourne Rd Columbus (43207) *(G-6885)*

White Oak Partners Inc..................................... 614 855-1155
5150 E Dublin Granville Rd Ste 130 Westerville (43081) *(G-15021)*

White Swan Inc.. 707 615-5005
100 E Campus Blvd Ste 250, Columbus (43215) *(G-6886)*

White' S Ford, Urbana *Also Called: Whites Service Center Inc* *(G-14317)*

Whiteboard Marketing...................................... 614 562-1912
5950 Venture Dr Ste D Dublin (43017) *(G-8165)*

Whiteford Kenworth, Perrysburg *Also Called: Lower Great Lakes Kenworth Inc* *(G-12354)*

Whitehall City Schools..................................... 614 417-5680
4738 Kae Ave Columbus (43213) *(G-6887)*

Whitehall Family Health, Columbus *Also Called: Mount Carmel Health System* *(G-6269)*

Whitehead Falana.. 513 742-1766
2538 Hansford Pl Cincinnati (45214) *(G-3668)*

Whitehouse Country Manor, Whitehouse *Also Called: Whitehouse Operator LLC* *(G-15144)*

Whitehouse Inn, Whitehouse *Also Called: Frog and Toad Inc* *(G-15142)*

Whitehouse Operator LLC................................ 419 877-5338
11239 Waterville St Whitehouse (43571) *(G-15144)*

Whitehurst Company (PA)................................ 419 534-6022
6325 Garden Rd Maumee (43537) *(G-10780)*

Whites Service Center Inc................................ 937 653-5279
1246 N Main St Urbana (43078) *(G-14317)*

Whitespace Creative, Akron *Also Called: Whitespace Design Group Inc* *(G-360)*

Whitespace Design Group Inc........................... 330 762-9320
243 Furnace St Akron (44304) *(G-360)*

Whitestone Group Inc..................................... 614 501-7007
6422 E Main St Ste 101 Reynoldsburg (43068) *(G-12682)*

Whitey's Booze & Burgers, Richfield *Also Called: Whiteys Restaurant Inc* *(G-12713)*

Whiteys Restaurant Inc................................... 330 659-3600
3600 Brecksville Rd Frnt Frnt Richfield (44286) *(G-12713)*

Whiting-Turner Contracting Co......................... 440 449-9200
1001 Lakeside Ave E Ste 100 Cleveland (44114) *(G-5145)*

Whiting-Turner Contracting Co......................... 614 459-6515
445 Hutchinson Ave Ste 142 Columbus (43235) *(G-6888)*

Whitney Home Care LLC.................................. 440 647-2200
508 Dickson St Ste 3 Wellington (44090) *(G-14635)*

Whitney Insurance Group The, Cincinnati *Also Called: R E Whitney Insur Agcy LLC* *(G-3271)*

Whittguard Security Svcs Inc........................... 440 288-7233
37435 Colorado Ave Avon (44011) *(G-667)*

Whiz - TV & Radio, Zanesville *Also Called: Marquee Broadcasting Ohio Inc* *(G-15810)*

Whole Health Dentistry, Lima *Also Called: Eric W Warnock* *(G-9887)*

Whole Health Management Inc (DH).................. 216 921-8601
1375 E 9th St Ste 2500 Cleveland (44114) *(G-5146)*

Wholecycle Inc.. 330 929-8123
100 Cuyahoga Falls Industrial Pkwy Peninsula (44264) *(G-12296)*

Wholesale Decor LLC....................................... 330 587-7100
650 S Prospect Ave Ste 200 Hartville (44632) *(G-9131)*

Wholesale Decor LLC (PA)................................ 877 745-5050
286 W Greenwich Rd Seville (44273) *(G-12967)*

Wholesale House Inc (PA)................................ 419 542-1315
503 W High St Hicksville (43526) *(G-9162)*

Wholesome Pet Co Inc.................................... 877 345-7297
1630 Commerce Dr Orrville (44667) *(G-12175)*

Whs Engineering Inc....................................... 216 227-8505
2012 W 25th St Ste 200 Cleveland (44113) *(G-5147)*

Wic Program, Athens *Also Called: Hopewell Health Centers Inc* *(G-577)*

Wichman Co.. 419 385-6438
7 N Westwood Ave Toledo (43607) *(G-14107)*

Wickens Herzer Panza Co................................. 440 695-8000
35765 Chester Rd Avon (44011) *(G-668)*

Wickliffe Country Place Ltd.............................. 440 944-9400
1919 Bishop Rd Wickliffe (44092) *(G-15165)*

Wickshire Deer Park, Cincinnati *Also Called: Wickshire Deer Park Opco LLC* *(G-3669)*

Wickshire Deer Park Opco LLC......................... 513 745-7600
3801 E Galbraith Rd Ofc Cincinnati (45236) *(G-3669)*

Wide Open West, Columbus *Also Called: Wideopenwest Networks LLC* *(G-6889)*

Wideopenwest Networks LLC........................... 614 948-4600
3675 Corporate Dr Columbus (43231) *(G-6889)*

Widepint Intgrted Sltions Corp......................... 614 410-1587
8351 N High St Ste 200 Columbus (43235) *(G-6890)*

Widewaters Edr Solon Ht Co LLC...................... 440 542-0400
6035 Enterprise Pkwy Solon (44139) *(G-13164)*

ALPHABETIC SECTION — WILSON HEALTH

Widmer's, Cincinnati *Also Called: C&C Clean Team Enterprises LLC (G-2299)*

Widmer's Drycleaners, Cincinnati *Also Called: Widmers LLC (G-3670)*

Widmers LLC (HQ) 513 321-5100
 2016 Madison Rd Cincinnati (45208) *(G-3670)*

Widows Home of Dayton Ohio 937 252-1661
 50 S Findlay St Dayton (45403) *(G-7721)*

Wiechart Enterprises Inc 419 227-0027
 4511 Elida Rd Lima (45807) *(G-9987)*

Wieland Chase LLC (HQ) 419 485-3193
 14212 Selwyn Dr Montpelier (43543) *(G-11387)*

Wieland Metal Svcs Foils LLC 330 823-1700
 2081 Mccrea St Alliance (44601) *(G-405)*

Wieland Rolled Pdts N Amer LLC 330 823-1700
 2081 Mccrea St Alliance (44601) *(G-406)*

Wiers Farm Incorporated (PA) 419 935-0131
 4465 State Route 103 S Willard (44890) *(G-15175)*

Wiggins Clg & Crpt Svc Inc (PA) 937 279-9080
 4699 Salem Ave Ste 2 Dayton (45416) *(G-7722)*

Wil-Sites Truck Lines LLC 614 444-8873
 1250 Walcutt Rd Columbus (43228) *(G-6891)*

Wilbur Realty Inc 330 673-5883
 548 S Water St Kent (44240) *(G-9606)*

Wilcoxon, James H Jr, Columbus *Also Called: Johnsons Real Ice Cream LLC (G-6095)*

Wild Republic, Independence *Also Called: K & M International Inc (G-9439)*

Wildwood Family Practice, Toledo *Also Called: Promedica Health Systems Inc (G-13973)*

Wildwood Surgical Center, Toledo *Also Called: Reynolds Road Surgical Ctr LLC (G-13990)*

Wiles Boyle Burkholder & 614 221-5216
 2 Miranova Pl Columbus (43215) *(G-6892)*

Wiles Doucher, Columbus *Also Called: Wiles Boyle Burkholder & (G-6892)*

Wiley Avenue Group Home, Saint Clairsville *Also Called: Alternative Residences Two Inc (G-12773)*

Wiley Companies (PA) 740 622-0755
 545 Walnut St Coshocton (43812) *(G-7005)*

Wilkers Inc 513 851-4000
 11 Wyoming Ave Cincinnati (45215) *(G-3671)*

Will-Burt Company (PA) 330 682-7015
 401 Collins Blvd Orrville (44667) *(G-12176)*

Willard Head Start Center, Willard *Also Called: Community Action Comm Erie Hro (G-15166)*

Willard Kelsey Solar Group LLC 419 931-2001
 1775 Progress Dr Perrysburg (43551) *(G-12388)*

Willcare Inc 216 289-5300
 6150 Parkland Blvd Ste 250 Cleveland (44124) *(G-5148)*

Willglo Services Inc 614 443-3020
 995 Thurman Ave Columbus (43206) *(G-6893)*

William & Clippard YMCA, Cincinnati *Also Called: Young MNS Chrstn Assn Grter CN (G-3695)*

William H Zimmer Power Station, Moscow *Also Called: Vistra Corp (G-11457)*

William Henry Harrison Jr Hs 513 367-4831
 9830 West Rd Harrison (45030) *(G-9120)*

William J Hagerty DDS Inc 937 434-3987
 7058 Corporate Way Ste 2 Dayton (45459) *(G-7723)*

William Morris Endeavor Entrmt, Cleveland *Also Called: Interntnal MGT Group Ovrseas L (G-4419)*

William O Cleverley & Assoc 614 543-7777
 438 E Wilson Bridge Rd Ste 200 Worthington (43085) *(G-15470)*

William Patrick Day, Cleveland *Also Called: Stepforward (G-4953)*

William R Hague Inc 614 836-2115
 4343 S Hamilton Rd Groveport (43125) *(G-9014)*

William Thomas Group Inc 800 582-3107
 10795 Hughes Rd Cincinnati (45251) *(G-3672)*

William Vaughan Company 419 891-1040
 145 Chesterfield Ln Maumee (43537) *(G-10781)*

William X Greene Bus Advisor, Cincinnati *Also Called: Scrogginsgrear Inc (G-3352)*

Williamfall Group Inc 419 418-5252
 300 Madison Ave Toledo (43604) *(G-14108)*

Williams Bros Builders Inc 440 365-3261
 686 Sugar Ln Elyria (44035) *(G-8301)*

Williams Concrete Cnstr Co Inc 330 745-6388
 753 W Waterloo Rd Akron (44314) *(G-361)*

Williams Dtroit Diesel-Allison, Hilliard *Also Called: W W Williams Company LLC (G-9241)*

Williams Last Mile HM Lgstics 937 313-9096
 6510 Semmes Ln Dayton (45424) *(G-7724)*

Williams Scotsman Inc 614 449-8675
 871 Buckeye Park Rd Columbus (43207) *(G-6894)*

Williams Scotsman Inc 978 228-0305
 4444 Dixie Hwy Fairfield (45014) *(G-8454)*

Williams Scotsman Inc 513 874-1280
 125 Distribution Dr Hamilton (45014) *(G-9092)*

Williams Scotsman Inc 216 399-6285
 2643 Great Lakes Way Hinckley (44233) *(G-9273)*

Williams Scotsman - Cincinnati, Hamilton *Also Called: Williams Scotsman Inc (G-9092)*

Williams Street Apartments, Columbus *Also Called: Buckeye Cmnty Eighty One LP (G-5473)*

Williams Super Service Inc 330 733-7750
 9462 Main Ave Se East Sparta (44626) *(G-8199)*

Williams Toyota Lift, East Sparta *Also Called: Williams Super Service Inc (G-8199)*

Williamsburg of Cincinnati Mgt 513 948-2308
 230 W Galbraith Rd Cincinnati (45215) *(G-3673)*

Willimsburg Rsdntial Altrntves, Mount Orab *Also Called: Rescare Ohio Inc (G-11473)*

Willis Spangler Starling 614 586-7900
 4635 Trueman Blvd Hilliard (43026) *(G-9243)*

Willis Towers Watson, Cleveland *Also Called: Wtw Delaware Holdings LLC (G-5161)*

Willo Putt-Putt Course Inc 440 951-7888
 38886 Mentor Ave Willoughby (44094) *(G-15226)*

Willo Security Inc 614 481-9456
 1989 W 5th Ave Ste 3 Columbus (43212) *(G-6895)*

WILLO SECURITY, INC., Columbus *Also Called: Willo Security Inc (G-6895)*

Willodell Nurs Grdn & Lawn Ctr, Ashland *Also Called: Dell Willo Nursery Inc (G-496)*

Willory LLC 330 576-5486
 1970 N Cleveland Massillon Rd Unit 50 Bath (44210) *(G-756)*

Willoughby Ir & Waste Mtls LLC 440 946-8990
 3884 Church St Willoughby (44094) *(G-15227)*

Willoughby Physical Therapy, Willoughby *Also Called: Lake Hospital System Inc (G-15200)*

Willoughby Services Inc (PA) 440 953-9191
 38230 Glenn Ave Willoughby (44094) *(G-15228)*

Willoughby Supply, Mentor *Also Called: W Team Company (G-11011)*

Willow Brook Christian Home, Columbus *Also Called: Brook Willow Chrstn Cmmunities (G-5468)*

Willow Brook Christian Svcs 740 201-5640
 100 Delaware Xing W Delaware (43015) *(G-7834)*

WILLOW BROOK CHRISTIAN VILLAGE, Delaware *Also Called: Willow Brook Chrstn Cmmunities (G-7835)*

Willow Brook Chrstn Cmmunities (PA) 740 369-0048
 100 Willow Brook Way S Delaware (43015) *(G-7835)*

Willow Haven Nursing Home, Zanesville *Also Called: Zandex Health Care Corporation (G-15837)*

Willow Knoll Nursing Center, Middletown *Also Called: Church of God Retirement Cmnty (G-11156)*

Willoway Nurseries Inc (PA) 440 934-4435
 4534 Center Rd Avon (44011) *(G-669)*

Willowbend Nurseries LLC 440 259-3121
 4654 Davis Rd Perry (44081) *(G-12312)*

Willowood Care Center 330 225-3156
 1186 Hadcock Rd Brunswick (44212) *(G-1475)*

WILLOWOOD NURSING, Brunswick *Also Called: Willowood Care Center (G-1475)*

Willows At Willard, The, Willard *Also Called: Trilogy Health Services LLC (G-15174)*

Willows Health & Rehab Center, The, Euclid *Also Called: Indian Hlls Hlthcare Group Inc (G-8350)*

Wilmer 419 678-6000
 515 W Sycamore St Coldwater (45828) *(G-5221)*

Wilmington Hlthcare Group Inc 937 382-1621
 75 Hale St Wilmington (45177) *(G-15278)*

Wilmington Medical Associates 937 382-1616
 1184 W Locust St Wilmington (45177) *(G-15279)*

WILMINGTON NURSING & REHABILIT, Wilmington *Also Called: Wilmington Hlthcare Group Inc (G-15278)*

Wilmington Savings Bank 937 382-1659
 184 N South St Wilmington (45177) *(G-15280)*

Wilson Shannon & Snow Inc 740 345-6611
 10 W Locust St Uppr Newark (43055) *(G-11754)*

Wilson Enterprises Inc 614 444-8873
 900 Buckeye Park Rd Columbus (43207) *(G-6896)*

WILSON HEALTH, Sidney *Also Called: Shelby County Mem Hosp Assn (G-13048)*

Wilson Insulation Company LLC
495 S High St Ste 50 Columbus (43215) *(G-6897)* ... 626 812-6070

Wilson Mem Hosp Occptnal Clnic, Sidney *Also Called: Occupational Health Services (G-13042)*

Wilson's Garden Center, Newark *Also Called: Wilsons Hillview Farm Inc (G-11755)*

Wilson's Turf, Columbus *Also Called: Wilson Enterprises Inc (G-6896)*

Wilsons Hillview Farm Inc ... 740 763-2873
10923 Lambs Ln Newark (43055) *(G-11755)*

Wimberg Lansdscaping, Milford *Also Called: Peter A Wimberg Company Inc (G-11248)*

Winchester Care Rehabilitation, Canal Winchester *Also Called: Embassy Winchester LLC (G-1605)*

Winchester Care Rehabilitation, Canal Winchester *Also Called: Winchester Place Leasing LLC (G-1619)*

Winchester Place Leasing LLC ... 614 834-2273
36 Lehman Dr Canal Winchester (43110) *(G-1619)*

Winchester Wholesale, Winchester *Also Called: Cantrell Oil Company (G-15286)*

WINDFALL INDUSTRIES, Wadsworth *Also Called: Medina Cnty Sheltered Inds Inc (G-14443)*

Windgate Inn, The, Toledo *Also Called: Allen County Property LLC (G-13678)*

Windsong Care Center, Akron *Also Called: Windsong Healthcare Group LLC (G-362)*

Windsong Healthcare Group LLC ... 216 292-5706
120 Brookmont Rd Akron (44333) *(G-362)*

Windsor Companies (PA) ... 740 653-8822
1430 Collins Rd Nw Lancaster (43130) *(G-9750)*

Windsor Medical Center Inc ... 330 499-8300
1454 E Maple St Canton (44720) *(G-1886)*

Windstream Services LLC ... 216 394-0065
1625 Rockwell Ave Cleveland (44114) *(G-5149)*

Windstream Services LLC ... 216 242-6315
25900 Lakeland Blvd Euclid (44132) *(G-8364)*

Windstream Services LLC ... 330 650-7044
4574 Chatwood Dr Stow (44224) *(G-13402)*

WINDSTREAM SERVICES, LLC, Cleveland *Also Called: Windstream Services LLC (G-5149)*

WINDSTREAM SERVICES, LLC, Euclid *Also Called: Windstream Services LLC (G-8364)*

WINDSTREAM SERVICES, LLC, Stow *Also Called: Windstream Services LLC (G-13402)*

Windy Hill Ltd Inc (PA) ... 216 391-4800
3700 Kelley Ave Cleveland (44114) *(G-5150)*

Wine Trends ... 937 222-8692
3601 Dryden Rd Moraine (45439) *(G-11449)*

Wine-Art of Ohio Inc ... 330 678-7733
463 Portage Blvd Kent (44240) *(G-9607)*

Winegrdner Hmmons Ht Group LLC (HQ) ... 513 891-1066
8044 Montgomery Rd Cincinnati (45236) *(G-3674)*

Winelco Inc ... 513 755-8050
6141 Centre Park Dr West Chester (45069) *(G-14795)*

Wing-FM, Dayton *Also Called: Alpha Media LLC (G-7166)*

Wingate Inc ... 216 591-1061
23775 Commerce Park Cleveland (44122) *(G-5151)*

Wingate By Wyndham, Beavercreek *Also Called: Wingate By Wyndham Dyton Frbor (G-914)*

Wingate By Wyndham Dyton Frbor ... 937 912-9350
3055 Presidential Dr Beavercreek (45324) *(G-914)*

Wingate Inn ... 614 844-5888
8505 Pulsar Pl Columbus (43240) *(G-5285)*

Wingate Inn ... 330 422-9900
9705 State Route 14 Streetsboro (44241) *(G-13436)*

Wingate Packaging Inc (PA) ... 513 745-8600
4347 Indeco Ct Cincinnati (45241) *(G-3675)*

Wingate Packaging South, Cincinnati *Also Called: Wingate Packaging Inc (G-3675)*

Wingler Construction Corp ... 614 626-8546
771 S Hamilton Rd Columbus (43213) *(G-6898)*

Wings of Change Therapy Inc ... 330 715-6046
1909 3rd St Cuyahoga Falls (44221) *(G-7117)*

Wings of Love Services LLC ... 937 789-8192
4130 Linden Ave Ste 180 Dayton (45432) *(G-7144)*

Wingspan Care Group (PA) ... 216 932-2800
463 Lowell Dr Highland Heights (44143) *(G-9173)*

Winking Lizard Inc ... 330 220-9944
3634 Center Rd Brunswick (44212) *(G-1476)*

Winkle Industries Inc ... 330 823-9730
2080 W Main St Alliance (44601) *(G-407)*

Winn-Scapes Inc ... 614 866-9466
6079 Taylor Rd Gahanna (43230) *(G-8734)*

Winncom Technologies Corp ... 440 498-9510
28900 Fountain Pkwy Unit B Solon (44139) *(G-13165)*

Winner Aviation Corporation ... 330 856-5000
1453 Youngstown Kingsville Rd Ne Vienna (44473) *(G-14424)*

Winner Corporation (PA) ... 419 582-4321
8544 State Route 705 Yorkshire (45388) *(G-15538)*

Winner's Meat Service, Yorkshire *Also Called: Winner Corporation (G-15538)*

Winnscapes Inc/Schmidt Nurs Co, Gahanna *Also Called: Winn-Scapes Inc (G-8734)*

Winston Brdcstg Netwrk Inc ... 330 928-5711
2690 State Rd Cuyahoga Falls (44223) *(G-7118)*

Winston Products LLC ... 440 945-6912
30339 Diamond Pkwy Ste 105 Solon (44139) *(G-13166)*

Winsupply Inc (PA) ... 937 294-5331
3110 Kettering Blvd Moraine (45439) *(G-11450)*

Winsupply St Petersburg FL Co., Moraine *Also Called: Noland Company (G-11428)*

Winton Road Dialysis, Cincinnati *Also Called: Dva Hlthcare - Sthwest Ohio LL (G-2589)*

Wireless Center Inc (PA) ... 216 503-3777
1925 Saint Clair Ave Ne Cleveland (44114) *(G-5152)*

Wireless Connections, Norwalk *Also Called: Advanced Cmpt Connections LLC (G-11999)*

Wireless Environment LLC ... 216 455-0192
600 Beta Dr Ste 100 Mayfield Village (44143) *(G-10797)*

Wireless Master LLC ... 877 995-5888
4340 Lyman Dr Hilliard (43026) *(G-9244)*

Wireless Masters, Hilliard *Also Called: Wireless Master LLC (G-9244)*

Wireless Partners LLC ... 614 850-0040
4485 Cemetery Rd Hilliard (43026) *(G-9245)*

Wisewel LLC ... 440 591-4896
32350 S Woodland Rd Cleveland (44124) *(G-5153)*

Wishing Well Acquisition Ltd (PA) ... 440 237-5000
14574 Ridge Rd Cleveland (44133) *(G-5154)*

Wishing Well Preschool, Cleveland *Also Called: Wishing Well Acquisition Ltd (G-5154)*

Within3 Inc (PA) ... 855 948-4463
17415 Northwood Ave Ste 300 Lakewood (44107) *(G-9687)*

Witmers Inc ... 330 427-2147
39821 Salem Unity Rd Salem (44460) *(G-12858)*

Wittenberg University, Springfield *Also Called: Board of Dirs of Wttnberg Clle (G-13222)*

Wj Service Co Inc (PA) ... 330 372-5040
2592 Elm Rd Ne Warren (44483) *(G-14576)*

Wjw TV, Cleveland *Also Called: New World Communications of Ohio Inc (G-4639)*

Wkhr Radio Inc ... 440 708-0915
17425 Snyder Rd Bainbridge (45612) *(G-687)*

Wkyc-Tv Inc ... 216 344-3300
1333 Lakeside Ave E Cleveland (44114) *(G-5155)*

Wl Electric Inc ... 614 882-2160
6155 Westerville Rd Westerville (43081) *(G-15022)*

Wlio Television-Channel 35, Lima *Also Called: Lima Communications Corp (G-9921)*

Wlkop LLC ... 440 892-2100
4000 Crocker Rd Westlake (44145) *(G-15125)*

Wlwt, Cincinnati *Also Called: Ohio/Oklahoma Hearst TV Inc (G-3152)*

Wm Ccp Solutions LLC ... 513 871-9733
4228 Airport Rd Cincinnati (45226) *(G-3676)*

Wm Columbus Hotel LLC ... 614 228-3800
310 S High St Columbus (43215) *(G-6899)*

Wm Kramer and Son Inc ... 513 353-1142
9171 Harrison Pike Unit 12 Cleves (45002) *(G-5196)*

Wm Plotz Machine and Forge Co ... 216 861-0441
2514 Center St Cleveland (44113) *(G-5156)*

Wmk LLC ... 440 951-4335
5040 Richmond Rd Bedford (44146) *(G-993)*

Wmk LLC (PA) ... 234 312-2000
4199 Kinross Lakes Pkwy Ste 300 Richfield (44286) *(G-12714)*

Wmog Inc (PA) ... 419 334-3801
122 S Wilson Ave Fremont (43420) *(G-8709)*

Wnb Group LLC ... 513 641-5400
4817 Section Ave Cincinnati (45212) *(G-3677)*

Wnbs Channel 10 Weatherline, Columbus *Also Called: Wbns TV Inc (G-6872)*

Woda Construction Inc ... 614 396-3200
500 S Front St Fl 10 Columbus (43215) *(G-6900)*

Woda Group Inc ... 614 396-3200
500 S Front St Fl 10 Columbus (43215) *(G-6901)*

ALPHABETIC SECTION

Wojos Heating & AC Inc... 419 693-3220
   5523 Woodville Rd Northwood (43619) *(G-11987)*

Wolcott Group, Akron *Also Called: Wolcott Systems Group LLC (G-363)*

Wolcott Systems Group LLC... 330 666-5900
   3700 Embassy Pkwy Ste 430 Akron (44333) *(G-363)*

Wolf and Woof LLC.. 614 527-2267
   5100 Nike Dr Ste B Hilliard (43026) *(G-9246)*

Wolf Creek Federal Svcs Inc... 216 433-5609
   21000 Brookpark Rd Bldg 107-1 Cleveland (44135) *(G-5157)*

Wolf Machine Company (PA)... 513 791-5194
   5570 Creek Rd Blue Ash (45242) *(G-1274)*

Wolfes Roofing Inc.. 419 666-6233
   6568 State Route 795 Walbridge (43465) *(G-14469)*

Wolff Bros Supply Inc (PA).. 330 725-3451
   6078 Wolff Rd Medina (44256) *(G-10904)*

Wolseley Industrial Group... 513 587-7532
   5122 Rialto Rd West Chester (45069) *(G-14796)*

Wolters Kluwer Clinical Drug Information Inc........................... 330 650-6506
   1100 Terex Rd Hudson (44236) *(G-9378)*

Womans Health Center, Wooster *Also Called: Cleveland Clinic Foundation (G-15323)*

Women's Residential, Bowling Green *Also Called: Behavral Cnnctions WD Cnty Inc (G-1305)*

Womens Care Inc.. 419 756-6000
   500 S Trimble Rd Mansfield (44906) *(G-10326)*

Womens Welsh Clubs of America... 440 331-0420
   22199 Center Ridge Rd Rocky River (44116) *(G-12757)*

Wonderworker Inc... 234 249-3030
   6217 Chittenden Rd Hudson (44236) *(G-9379)*

Wong Margaret W Assoc Co Lpa (PA)..................................... 313 527-9989
   3150 Chester Ave Cleveland (44114) *(G-5158)*

Wonnell, Dirk M, Cincinnati *Also Called: Urology Group Inc (G-3602)*

Wood Herron & Evans LLP (PA).. 513 241-2324
   600 Vine St Ste 2800 Cincinnati (45202) *(G-3678)*

Wood & Lamping, Cincinnati *Also Called: Wood & Lamping LLP (G-3679)*

Wood & Lamping LLP.. 513 852-6000
   600 Vine St Ste 2500 Cincinnati (45202) *(G-3679)*

Wood Cnty Cmmttee On Aging Inc (PA)................................... 419 353-5661
   140 S Grove St Bowling Green (43402) *(G-1334)*

Wood County Chld Svcs Assn.. 419 352-7588
   1045 Klotz Rd Bowling Green (43402) *(G-1335)*

Wood County Health Department, Bowling Green *Also Called: County of Wood (G-1315)*

Wood County Hospital (PA).. 419 354-8900
   950 W Wooster St Bowling Green (43402) *(G-1336)*

Wood Electric Inc.. 330 339-7002
   210 11th St Nw New Philadelphia (44663) *(G-11673)*

Wood Graphics Inc (PA)... 513 771-6300
   8075 Reading Rd Ste 301 Cincinnati (45237) *(G-3680)*

Wood Haven Health Care, Bowling Green *Also Called: County of Wood (G-1314)*

Wood Health Company LLC... 419 353-7069
   745 Haskins Rd Ste B Bowling Green (43402) *(G-1337)*

Wood Investment Property LLC... 330 644-5100
   1011 Lake Rd Medina (44256) *(G-10905)*

Wood Lane Residential Svcs Inc.. 419 353-9577
   545 Pearl St Ste A Bowling Green (43402) *(G-1338)*

Woodard Photographic, Inc., Bellevue *Also Called: Wp7pro Inc (G-1046)*

Woodhill Supply Inc (PA).. 440 269-1100
   4665 Beidler Rd Willoughby (44094) *(G-15229)*

Woodhull LLC (PA).. 937 294-5311
   125 Commercial Way Springboro (45066) *(G-13209)*

Woodland Centers (PA)... 740 446-5500
   3086 State Route 160 Gallipolis (45631) *(G-8770)*

Woodland Country Manor Inc.. 513 523-4449
   4166 Somerville Rd Somerville (45064) *(G-13167)*

Woodlands, Middletown *Also Called: Volunteers of America Inc (G-11192)*

Woodlands At Sunset House, Toledo *Also Called: Sunset House Inc (G-14029)*

Woodlands Healthcare Group LLC.. 330 297-4564
   6831 N Chestnut St Ravenna (44266) *(G-12646)*

Woodley Park Internal Med, Sylvania *Also Called: Promedica Health System Inc (G-13562)*

Woodlnds Hlth Rhbilitation Ctr, Ravenna *Also Called: Woodlands Healthcare Group LLC (G-12646)*

Woodrow Manufacturing Co.. 937 399-9333
   4300 River Rd Springfield (45502) *(G-13313)*

Woodruff Enterprises Inc... 937 399-9300
   4951 Gateway Blvd Springfield (45502) *(G-13314)*

Woods Edge Point, Cincinnati *Also Called: CHS Norwood Inc (G-2387)*

Woods Hardware, Cincinnati *Also Called: AWH Holdings Inc (G-2230)*

Woodsage Corporation.. 419 866-8000
   7400 Airport Hwy Holland (43528) *(G-9315)*

Woodsfield Opco LLC.. 740 472-1678
   37930 Airport Rd Woodsfield (43793) *(G-15304)*

Woodside Properties I Ltd... 419 396-7287
   821 E Findlay St Carey (43316) *(G-1897)*

Woodside Village Care Center... 419 947-2015
   841 W Marion Rd Mount Gilead (43338) *(G-11465)*

Woodson Operations One Ltd.. 419 420-1776
   941 Interstate Dr Findlay (45840) *(G-8598)*

Woodspring Hotels Holdings LLC.. 614 272-2170
   2305 Wilson Rd Columbus (43228) *(G-6902)*

Woodstock Healthcare Group Inc.. 937 826-3351
   1649 Park Rd Woodstock (43084) *(G-15305)*

Woodward Excavating Co... 614 866-4384
   7340 Tussing Rd Reynoldsburg (43068) *(G-12683)*

Woody Sander Ford Inc (PA).. 513 541-5586
   235 W Mitchell Ave Cincinnati (45232) *(G-3681)*

Woolace Electric Corp.. 419 428-3161
   1978 County Road 22a Stryker (43557) *(G-13506)*

Woolpert Inc (PA).. 937 461-5660
   4454 Idea Center Blvd Dayton (45430) *(G-7725)*

Wooster Ambltory Srgery Ctr LL.. 330 804-2000
   3373 Commerce Pkwy Ste 1 Wooster (44691) *(G-15389)*

Wooster Christian School Inc.. 330 345-6436
   4599 Burbank Rd Ste B Wooster (44691) *(G-15390)*

Wooster City Schools... 330 262-9616
   318 Branstetter St Wooster (44691) *(G-15391)*

Wooster Cmnty Hosp Blmngton ME.. 330 263-8100
   1761 Beall Ave Wooster (44691) *(G-15392)*

Wooster Community Hosp Aux Inc (PA).................................. 330 263-8389
   1761 Beall Ave Wooster (44691) *(G-15393)*

Wooster Community Hospital, Wooster *Also Called: City of Wooster (G-15321)*

Wooster Community Hospital, Wooster *Also Called: Wooster Cmnty Hosp Blmngton ME (G-15392)*

Wooster Cy Schols Mntnace Cmpl, Wooster *Also Called: Wooster City Schools (G-15391)*

Wooster Ent Associates Inc.. 330 264-9699
   1749 Cleveland Rd Wooster (44691) *(G-15394)*

Wooster Hydrostatics Inc.. 330 263-6555
   4570 W Old Lincoln Way Wooster (44691) *(G-15395)*

Wooster Inn, The, Wooster *Also Called: Kmb Management Services Corp (G-15349)*

Wooster Motor Ways Inc (PA).. 330 264-9557
   3501 W Old Lincoln Way Wooster (44691) *(G-15396)*

Wooster Ophthalmologists Inc.. 330 345-7800
   3519 Friendsville Rd Wooster (44691) *(G-15397)*

Wooster Orthpdics Sprtsmdcine.. 330 804-9712
   3373 Commerce Pkwy Ste 2 Wooster (44691) *(G-15398)*

Wooster Radio, Wooster *Also Called: Wqkt 1045 FM (G-15399)*

Workflowone LLC.. 877 735-4966
   220 E Monument Ave Dayton (45402) *(G-7726)*

Working Community Services, Columbus *Also Called: Goodwill Inds Centl Ohio Inc (G-5942)*

Workshops Inc... 330 479-3958
   4065 Bradley Cir Nw Canton (44718) *(G-1887)*

Workshops, The, Canton *Also Called: Stark County Board of Developm (G-1858)*

Workstate Consulting LLC... 614 559-3904
   30 Spruce St Ste 300 Columbus (43215) *(G-6903)*

World Equestrian Center, Wilmington *Also Called: Arena Horse Shows Ocala LLC (G-15246)*

World Equestrian Center, The, Wilmington *Also Called: Arena Horse Shows LLC (G-15245)*

World Ex Shipg Trnsp Fwdg Svcs (PA).................................... 440 826-5055
   17851 Jefferson Park Rd Ste 101 Middleburg Heights (44130) *(G-11135)*

World Group Securities Inc... 513 367-5900
   1010 Harrison Ave Harrison (45030) *(G-9121)*

World Harvest Church Inc (PA).. 614 837-1990
   4595 Gender Rd Canal Winchester (43110) *(G-1620)*

World Shipping Inc (PA)... 440 356-7676
   1340 Depot St Ste 200 Cleveland (44116) *(G-5159)*

ALPHABETIC SECTION

World Synergy Enterprises Inc 440 349-4940
   3700 Park East Dr Ste 350 Beachwood (44122) *(G-852)*

World Trck Towing Recovery Inc 330 723-1116
   4970 Park Ave W Seville (44273) *(G-12968)*

Worldpay Inc (PA) 866 622-2390
   8500 Governors Hill Dr Symmes Township (45249) *(G-13581)*

Worldpay LLC (DH) 8500 Governors Hill Dr Symmes Twp (45249) *(G-13583)*

Worldpay Holding LLC (HQ) 513 358-6192
   8500 Governors Hill Dr Symmes Twp (45249) *(G-13584)*

Worldpay Iso Inc (HQ) 502 961-5200
   8500 Governors Hill Dr Symmes Twp (45249) *(G-13585)*

Worldwide Equipment Inc 614 876-0336
   5440 Renner Rd Columbus (43228) *(G-6904)*

Worldwide Sfety Prfssonals LLC, Wheelersburg Also Called: Medcor Safety LLC *(G-15131)*

Worly Plumbing Supply, Columbus Also Called: Worly Plumbing Supply Inc *(G-6905)*

Worly Plumbing Supply Inc (PA) 614 445-1000
   400 Greenlawn Ave Columbus (43223) *(G-6905)*

Worner Roofing, Ontario Also Called: Jackson Corporation *(G-12108)*

Worthington Analytical Svcs 614 599-5254
   2657 Pleasant Valley Rd Lucas (44843) *(G-10172)*

Worthington Enterprises Inc 513 539-9291
   350 Lawton Ave Monroe (45050) *(G-11355)*

Worthington Industries Inc 216 641-6995
   4600 Heidtman Pkwy Cleveland (44105) *(G-5160)*

Worthington Industries Inc 614 438-3028
   1055 Dearborn Dr Columbus (43085) *(G-6906)*

Worthington Industries Inc 909 594-7777
   200 W Old Wilson Bridge Rd Worthington (43085) *(G-15471)*

Worthington Industries, Inc., Cleveland Also Called: Worthington Industries Inc *(G-5160)*

Worthington Inn, The, Worthington Also Called: Epiqurian Inns *(G-15414)*

Worthington Public Library 614 807-2626
   820 High St Worthington (43085) *(G-15472)*

WORTHINGTON SWIMMING POOL, Worthington Also Called: Swiminc Incorporated *(G-15460)*

Worthngton Chrstn Vlg Cngrgate 614 846-6076
   165 Highbluffs Blvd Columbus (43235) *(G-6907)*

Worthngton Smuel Coil Proc LLC (HQ) 330 963-3777
   1400 Enterprise Pkwy Twinsburg (44087) *(G-14231)*

Worthngton Stelpac Systems LLC (HQ) 614 438-3205
   1205 Dearborn Dr Columbus (43085) *(G-6908)*

Wosu Public Media, Columbus Also Called: Ohio State University *(G-6454)*

Wow Family Fun Center, Columbus Also Called: United Skates of America Inc *(G-6816)*

Wp7pro Inc (DH) 419 483-3364
   550 Goodrich Rd Bellevue (44811) *(G-1046)*

Wpafb Medical Center 937 522-2778
   4881 Sugar Maple Dr Wright Patterson Afb (45433) *(G-15475)*

Wpmi Inc 440 392-2171
   9325 Progress Pkwy Mentor (44060) *(G-11012)*

Wqkt 1045 FM 330 264-5122
   186 S Hillcrest Dr Wooster (44691) *(G-15399)*

Wqkt/Wkvx, Wooster Also Called: Wwst Corporation LLC *(G-15400)*

Wqmx 94.9 FM, Akron Also Called: Rubber City Radio Group Inc *(G-289)*

WRAAA, Cleveland Also Called: Western Rsrve Area Agcy On Agi *(G-5138)*

Wrap-Tite, Solon Also Called: B D G Wrap-Tite Inc *(G-13070)*

Wrencare, Middletown Also Called: Oxymed Inc *(G-11178)*

Wrhpi Cardiovascular Tstg Ctr, Tallmadge Also Called: Summa Western Reserve Hosp LLC *(G-13605)*

Wright Executive Ht Ltd Partnr (PA) 937 426-7800
   2800 Presidential Dr Beavercreek (45324) *(G-915)*

Wright Mulch Inc 419 228-1173
   1227 E Hanthorn Rd Lima (45804) *(G-9988)*

Wright State Physcans Drmtlogy 937 401-1100
   2350 Miami Valley Dr Ste 210 Dayton (45459) *(G-7727)*

Wright State Physicians Inc 937 208-3999
   30 E Apple St Ste 6257 Dayton (45409) *(G-7728)*

Wright State University 937 775-3333
   3640 Colonel Glenn Hwy Beavercreek (45324) *(G-916)*

Wright State University 937 208-2177
   1 Wyoming St 128 E Apple St 7th Fl Dayton (45409) *(G-7729)*

Wright State University 937 298-4331
   3525 Southern Blvd Kettering (45429) *(G-9634)*

Wright-Patt Credit Union Inc (PA) 937 912-7000
   3560 Pentagon Blvd Beavercreek (45431) *(G-917)*

Wrkz, Columbus Also Called: North American Broadcasting *(G-6364)*

Wryneck Development LLC 419 354-2535
   1553 Muirfield Dr Bowling Green (43402) *(G-1339)*

Ws One Investment Usa LLC (PA) 855 895-3728
   1263 S Chillicothe Rd Aurora (44202) *(G-631)*

Ws1, Aurora Also Called: Ws One Investment Usa LLC *(G-631)*

Wsa Studio 614 824-1633
   982 S Front St Columbus (43206) *(G-6909)*

Wsb Rehabilitation Svcs Inc (PA) 330 533-1338
   510 W Main St Canfield (44406) *(G-1645)*

Wsb Rehabilitation Svcs Inc 330 847-7819
   4329 Mahoning Ave Nw Ste B Warren (44483) *(G-14577)*

Wsny FM, Columbus Also Called: Franklin Communications Inc *(G-5886)*

Wss-Dayton, Moraine Also Called: Winsupply Inc *(G-11450)*

Wsyx and ABC 6, Columbus Also Called: Sinclair Media II Inc *(G-6684)*

Wtol, Toledo Also Called: Tegna Inc *(G-14035)*

Wtvg 13 ABC, Toledo Also Called: Wtvg Inc *(G-14109)*

Wtvg Inc 419 531-1313
   4247 Dorr St Toledo (43607) *(G-14109)*

Wtvg-TV, Toledo Also Called: Gray Media Group Inc *(G-13824)*

Wtw Delaware Holdings LLC 216 937-4000
   1001 Lakeside Ave E Ste 1500 Cleveland (44114) *(G-5161)*

Wulco Inc (PA) 513 679-2600
   6899 Steger Dr Ste A Cincinnati (45237) *(G-3682)*

Wulco Inc 513 379-6115
   1010 Eaton Ave Ste B # B Hamilton (45013) *(G-9093)*

Wurtec Incorporated (PA) 419 726-1066
   6200 Brent Dr Toledo (43611) *(G-14110)*

Wurth Elecktronik, Miamisburg Also Called: Wurth Electronics Ics Inc *(G-11104)*

Wurth Electronics Ics Inc 937 415-7700
   1982 Byers Rd Miamisburg (45342) *(G-11104)*

WVIZ/PBS HD, Cleveland Also Called: Ideastream *(G-4401)*

Wvno-FM, Ontario Also Called: Johnny Appleseed Brdcstg Co *(G-12109)*

Wvxu Radio, Cincinnati Also Called: Xavier University *(G-3683)*

WW&r, Independence Also Called: Weltman Weinberg & Reis Co Lpa *(G-9500)*

Wwcd Ltd 614 221-9923
   1036 S Front St Columbus (43206) *(G-6910)*

Wwst Corporation LLC 330 264-5122
   186 S Hillcrest Dr Wooster (44691) *(G-15400)*

Www.logicsoftusa.com, Dublin Also Called: Logic Soft Inc *(G-8057)*

Wxkr, Toledo Also Called: Cumulus Media Inc *(G-13771)*

Wyandot Cnty Cncil On Aging In 419 294-5733
   127 S Sandusky Ave Upper Sandusky (43351) *(G-14295)*

Wyandot County Home, Upper Sandusky Also Called: County of Wyandot *(G-14286)*

Wyant Leasing Co LLC 330 836-7953
   200 Wyant Rd Akron (44313) *(G-364)*

Wyant Woods Care Center, Akron Also Called: Wyant Leasing Co LLC *(G-364)*

Wynn-Reeth Inc 419 639-2094
   137 S Broadway St Green Springs (44836) *(G-8862)*

Wyoming Casing Service Inc 330 479-8785
   1414 Raff Rd Sw Canton (44710) *(G-1888)*

Wyoming Family Practice Center, Cincinnati Also Called: University Family Physicians *(G-3569)*

Wyse Advertising Inc 216 696-2424
   668 Euclid Ave Ste 100 Cleveland (44114) *(G-5162)*

Wz Management Inc 330 628-4881
   3417 E Waterloo Rd Akron (44312) *(G-365)*

X F Construction Svcs Inc 614 575-2700
   1120 Claycraft Rd Columbus (43230) *(G-6911)*

X F Petroleum Equipment, Columbus Also Called: X F Construction Svcs Inc *(G-6911)*

X-Ray Industries Inc 216 642-0100
   5403 E Schaaf Rd Cleveland (44131) *(G-5163)*

Xaloy LLC (PA) 330 726-4000
   375 Victoria Rd Ste 1 Austintown (44515) *(G-637)*

Xavier University 513 745-3335
   3800 Victory Pkwy Cincinnati (45207) *(G-3683)*

Xcess Limited 330 347-4901
   1605 Sylvan Rd Wooster (44691) *(G-15401)*

ALPHABETIC SECTION — Yorktown Automotive Center Inc

Xenia Waster Water, Xenia Also Called: City of Xenia *(G-15501)*
Xlc Services, Cincinnati Also Called: Xlc Srvces Cincinnati Ohio Inc *(G-3684)*
Xlc Srvces Cincinnati Ohio Inc (HQ) 513 621-3912
  324 W 9th St Fl 5 Cincinnati (45202) *(G-3684)*
Xngage LLC 440 990-5767
  16900 Bagley Rd Middleburg Heights (44130) *(G-11136)*
Xpert Staffing LLC 330 969-9949
  692 Virginia Ave Akron (44306) *(G-366)*
Xpo Cartage Inc 614 766-6111
  5165 Emerald Pkwy Ste 300 Dublin (43017) *(G-8166)*
Xpo Logistics, Milan Also Called: Xpo Logistics Freight Inc *(G-11213)*
Xpo Logistics, South Point Also Called: Xpo Logistics Freight Inc *(G-13184)*
Xpo Logistics Cartage, LLC, Dublin Also Called: Stg Cartage LLC *(G-8127)*
Xpo Logistics Freight Inc 614 876-7100
  2625 Westbelt Dr Columbus (43228) *(G-6912)*
Xpo Logistics Freight Inc 937 898-9808
  3410 Stop 8 Rd Dayton (45414) *(G-7730)*
Xpo Logistics Freight Inc 937 364-2361
  5215 Us Highway 50 Hillsboro (45133) *(G-9268)*
Xpo Logistics Freight Inc 419 499-8888
  12518 Us Highway 250 N Milan (44846) *(G-11213)*
Xpo Logistics Freight Inc 216 433-1000
  12901 Snow Rd Parma (44130) *(G-12267)*
Xpo Logistics Freight Inc 419 666-3022
  28291 Glenwood Rd Perrysburg (43551) *(G-12389)*
Xpo Logistics Freight Inc 937 492-3899
  2021 Campbell Rd Sidney (45365) *(G-13059)*
Xpo Logistics Freight Inc 740 894-3859
  96 Private Drive 339 South Point (45680) *(G-13184)*
Xpo Logistics Freight Inc 740 922-5614
  2401 N Water Street Ext Uhrichsville (44683) *(G-14238)*
Xpo Logistics Freight Inc 330 896-7300
  3733 Massillon Rd Uniontown (44685) *(G-14271)*
Xpo Logistics Freight Inc 419 294-5728
  1850 E Wyandot Ave Upper Sandusky (43351) *(G-14296)*
Xpo Logistics Freight Inc 330 824-2242
  6700 Muth Rd Sw Warren (44481) *(G-14578)*
Xpo Logistics Freight Inc 513 870-0044
  5289 Duff Dr West Chester (45246) *(G-14846)*
Xri Testing, Cleveland Also Called: X-Ray Industries Inc *(G-5163)*
Xscape Theaters, Cincinnati Also Called: Northgate Ops LLC *(G-3124)*
Xtek Partners, Columbus Also Called: Xtek Partners Inc *(G-6913)*
Xtek Partners Inc 614 973-7400
  1721 Westbelt Dr Columbus (43228) *(G-6913)*
Xtreme Elements LLC 330 612-0075
  1016 Morse St Akron (44320) *(G-367)*
Xtreme Express, Columbus Also Called: Xtreme Express LLC *(G-6914)*
Xtreme Express LLC 614 735-0291
  6611 Broughton Ave Columbus (43213) *(G-6914)*
Y & E Entertainment Group LLC 440 385-5500
  8303 Day Dr Parma (44129) *(G-12268)*
Y M C A, Cincinnati Also Called: Young MNS Chrstn Assn Grter CN *(G-3692)*
Y M C A Hilltop Educare Inc 614 752-8877
  1952 W Broad St Ste A Columbus (43223) *(G-6915)*
Y M C A of Ashland Ohio Inc 419 289-0626
  207 Miller St Ashland (44805) *(G-516)*
Y. M. C. A., Toledo Also Called: Young MNS Chrstn Assn of Grter *(G-14115)*
Y. M. C. A. of Lima, Lima Also Called: Lima Family YMCA *(G-9923)*
Yanfeng US Auto Intr Systems I 419 662-4905
  7560 Arbor Dr Northwood (43619) *(G-11988)*
Yankee Lake Inc 330 448-8866
  1800 State Route 7 Ne Brookfield (44403) *(G-1408)*
Yardi Systems 805 699-2056
  6001 E Royalton Rd Ste 150 Cleveland (44147) *(G-5164)*
Yardmaster Inc (PA) 440 357-8400
  1447 N Ridge Rd Painesville (44077) *(G-12244)*
Yardmaster of Columbus Inc 614 863-4510
  570 Reynoldsburg New Albany Rd Blacklick (43004) *(G-1115)*
Yark Automotive Group Inc (PA) 419 841-7771
  3335 Meijer Dr Ste 400 Toledo (43617) *(G-14111)*

Yark Subaru, Toledo Also Called: Yark Automotive Group Inc *(G-14111)*
Yashco Systems Inc 614 467-4600
  3974 Brown Park Dr Hilliard (43026) *(G-9247)*
Yaskawa America Inc 937 847-6200
  100 Automation Way Miamisburg (45342) *(G-11105)*
Yaskawa America Inc 614 733-3200
  8628 Industrial Pkwy Ste A Plain City (43064) *(G-12498)*
Ye Olde Mille Shoppe, Utica Also Called: Velvet Ice Cream Company *(G-14330)*
Yeater Alene K MD 740 348-4694
  15 Messimer Dr Newark (43055) *(G-11756)*
Yellow Cabs, Columbus Also Called: Columbus Green Cabs Inc *(G-5634)*
Yellow Springs Primary Care 937 767-1088
  888 Dayton St Unit 102 Yellow Springs (45387) *(G-15536)*
Yes Management Inc 330 747-8593
  44612 State Route 14 Columbiana (44408) *(G-5242)*
YMCA 330 823-1930
  205 S Union Ave Alliance (44601) *(G-408)*
YMCA, Akron Also Called: Young MNS Chrstn Assn of Akron *(G-371)*
YMCA, Ashland Also Called: Y M C A of Ashland Ohio Inc *(G-516)*
YMCA, Chardon Also Called: Young MNS Chrstn Assn Grter CL *(G-2027)*
YMCA, Cincinnati Also Called: Young Mens Christian Association of Greater Cincinnati *(G-3689)*
YMCA, Cleveland Also Called: Young MNS Chrstn Assn Grter CL *(G-5166)*
YMCA, East Liverpool Also Called: Young MNS Chrstn Assn of E Lvr *(G-8194)*
YMCA, Lebanon Also Called: Young MNS Chrstn Assn Grter CN *(G-9800)*
YMCA, Maineville Also Called: Countryside Yung MNS Chrstn As *(G-10227)*
YMCA, Marion Also Called: Marion Family YMCA *(G-10438)*
YMCA, Maumee Also Called: Young MNS Chrstn Assn of Grter *(G-10782)*
YMCA, Maumee Also Called: Young MNS Chrstn Assn of Grter *(G-10783)*
YMCA, Mount Vernon Also Called: Young MNS Chrstn Assn of Mt Vr *(G-11510)*
YMCA, Piqua Also Called: Miami Co YMCA Child Care *(G-12448)*
YMCA, Tiffin Also Called: Tiffin Cmnty YMCA Rcration Ctr *(G-13645)*
YMCA, Toledo Also Called: Young MNS Chrstn Assn of Grter *(G-14112)*
YMCA, Toledo Also Called: Young MNS Chrstn Assn of Grter *(G-14113)*
YMCA, Uniontown Also Called: Young MNS Chrstn Assn of Akron *(G-14272)*
YMCA, Van Wert Also Called: Young MNS Chrstn Assn of Van W *(G-14362)*
YMCA, Wapakoneta Also Called: Wapakneta Fmly Yung MNS Chrstn *(G-14493)*
YMCA Camp Campbell Gard, Hamilton Also Called: Great Miami Valley YMCA *(G-9047)*
YMCA Child Care, Canton Also Called: Young MNS Chrstn Assn Cntl STA *(G-1889)*
YMCA Child Care Center West, Cincinnati Also Called: Young MNS Chrstn Assn Grter CN *(G-3696)*
YMCA Crayon Club Chld Care, Dayton Also Called: Young MNS Chrstn Assn Grter Dy *(G-7732)*
YMCA Cuyahoga Falls Branch, Cuyahoga Falls Also Called: Young MNS Chrstn Assn of Akron *(G-7119)*
YMCA of Central Ohio, Columbus Also Called: The Young Mens Christian Association of Central Ohio *(G-6762)*
YMCA OF FINDLAY, Findlay Also Called: Young MNS Chrstn Assn Findlay *(G-8599)*
YMCA of Greater Toledo, Perrysburg Also Called: Young MNS Chrstn Assn of Grter *(G-12390)*
YMCA of Greater Toledo, Sylvania Also Called: Young MNS Chrstn Assn of Grter *(G-13579)*
YMCA of Massillon (PA) 330 837-5116
  131 Tremont Ave Se Massillon (44646) *(G-10674)*
YMCA OF THE USA, Wooster Also Called: Young MNS Chrstn Assn Wster OH *(G-15402)*
YMCA OF WESTERN STARK COUNTY, Massillon Also Called: YMCA of Massillon *(G-10674)*
YMCA OF YOUNGSTOWN, Youngstown Also Called: Young MNS Chrstn Assn Yngstown *(G-15755)*
Ymca/M.e.lions, Cincinnati Also Called: Young MNS Chrstn Assn Grter CN *(G-3693)*
YNDC, Youngstown Also Called: Youngstown Nghborhood Dev Corp *(G-15759)*
Yoder Industries Inc (PA) 937 278-5769
  2520 Needmore Rd Dayton (45414) *(G-7731)*
Yoder Trading Company, Barberton Also Called: Aris Horticulture Inc *(G-693)*
YORK GOLF CLUB, Columbus Also Called: York Temple Country Club *(G-6916)*
York Street Fresh Foods LLC 201 868-9088
  3465 Hauck Rd Cincinnati (45241) *(G-3685)*
York Temple Country Club 614 885-5459
  7459 N High St Columbus (43235) *(G-6916)*
Yorktown Automotive Center Inc 440 885-2803
  6177 Pearl Rd Cleveland (44130) *(G-5165)*

Young & Alexander Co LPA 513 326-5555
1 Sheakley Way Ste 125 Cincinnati (45246) *(G-3686)*

Young & Bertke Air Systems Co., Cincinnati Also Called: Rmt Acquisition Inc *(G-3311)*

Young & Rubicam LLC 513 345-3400
36 E 7th St Ste 2500 Cincinnati (45202) *(G-3687)*

Young & Rubicam LLC 513 419-2300
110 Shillito Pl Cincinnati (45202) *(G-3688)*

Young and Associates Inc 330 678-0524
121 E Main St Kent (44240) *(G-9608)*

Young Chemical Co LLC (HQ) 330 486-4210
1755 Enterprise Pkwy Ste 400 Twinsburg (44087) *(G-14232)*

Young Medical Services, Maumee Also Called: Toledo Medical Equipment Co *(G-10774)*

YOUNG MEN'S CHRISTIAN ASSOCIAT, Sidney Also Called: Sidney-Shelby County YMCA *(G-13053)*

Young Mens Christian Assn 740 373-2250
1303 Colegate Dr Ste B Marietta (45750) *(G-10415)*

Young Mens Christian Assn 330 480-5656
45 Mcclurg Rd Youngstown (44512) *(G-15754)*

Young Mens Christian Assn, Mount Vernon Also Called: Young MNS Chrstn Assn Grter NY *(G-11509)*

Young Mens Christian Association of Greater Cincinnati (PA) 513 651-2100
1105 Elm St Cincinnati (45202) *(G-3689)*

Young MNS Chrstn Assn Findlay (PA) 419 422-4424
300 E Lincoln St Findlay (45840) *(G-8599)*

Young MNS Chrstn Assn Cntl STA 330 305-5437
200 Charlotte St Nw Canton (44720) *(G-1889)*

Young MNS Chrstn Assn Cntl STA 330 498-4082
7241 Whipple Ave Nw Canton (44720) *(G-1890)*

Young MNS Chrstn Assn Cntl STA 330 875-1611
1421 S Nickelplate St Louisville (44641) *(G-10124)*

Young MNS Chrstn Assn Cntl STA 330 830-6275
7389 Caritas Cir Nw Massillon (44646) *(G-10675)*

Young MNS Chrstn Assn Cntl STA 330 868-5988
687 Lynnwood Dr Minerva (44657) *(G-11311)*

Young MNS Chrstn Assn Grter CL 440 285-7543
12460 Bass Lake Rd Chardon (44024) *(G-2027)*

Young MNS Chrstn Assn Grter CL 216 344-7700
1801 E 12th St Fl 1 Cleveland (44114) *(G-5166)*

Young MNS Chrstn Assn Grter CL 216 521-8400
16915 Detroit Ave Lakewood (44107) *(G-9688)*

Young MNS Chrstn Assn Grter CL 440 808-8150
1575 Columbia Rd Westlake (44145) *(G-15126)*

Young MNS Chrstn Assn Grter CN 513 791-5000
5000 Ymca Dr Blue Ash (45242) *(G-1275)*

Young MNS Chrstn Assn Grter CN 513 521-7112
9601 Winton Rd Cincinnati (45231) *(G-3690)*

Young MNS Chrstn Assn Grter CN 513 961-3510
2840 Melrose Ave Cincinnati (45206) *(G-3691)*

Young MNS Chrstn Assn Grter CN 513 731-0115
2039 Sherman Ave Cincinnati (45212) *(G-3692)*

Young MNS Chrstn Assn Grter CN 513 474-1400
8108 Clough Pike Fl 1 Cincinnati (45244) *(G-3693)*

Young MNS Chrstn Assn Grter CN 513 241-9622
1425b Linn St Cincinnati (45214) *(G-3694)*

Young MNS Chrstn Assn Grter CN 513 923-4466
8920 Cheviot Rd Cincinnati (45251) *(G-3695)*

Young MNS Chrstn Assn Grter CN 513 921-0911
112 Findlay St Cincinnati (45202) *(G-3696)*

Young MNS Chrstn Assn Grter CN 513 932-1424
1699 Deerfield Rd Lebanon (45036) *(G-9800)*

Young MNS Chrstn Assn Grter Dy 937 228-9622
316 N Wilkinson St Dayton (45402) *(G-7732)*

Young MNS Chrstn Assn Grter Dy 937 312-1810
4545 Marshall Rd Dayton (45429) *(G-7733)*

Young MNS Chrstn Assn Grter Dy 937 426-9622
111 W 1st St Ste 207 Dayton (45402) *(G-7734)*

Young MNS Chrstn Assn Grter Dy 937 836-9622
1200 W National Rd Englewood (45315) *(G-8327)*

Young MNS Chrstn Assn Grter Dy 513 932-3756
5291 State Route 350 Oregonia (45054) *(G-12150)*

Young MNS Chrstn Assn Grter Dy 937 223-5201
88 Remick Blvd Springboro (45066) *(G-13210)*

Young MNS Chrstn Assn Grter NY 740 392-9622
103 N Main St Mount Vernon (43050) *(G-11509)*

Young MNS Chrstn Assn Mtro Los 740 286-7008
594 E Main St Jackson (45640) *(G-9530)*

Young MNS Chrstn Assn of Akron 330 376-1335
1 Canal Square Plz Akron (44308) *(G-368)*

Young MNS Chrstn Assn of Akron 330 434-5900
475 Ohio St Akron (44304) *(G-369)*

Young MNS Chrstn Assn of Akron 330 376-1335
50 S Main St Ste Ll100 Akron (44308) *(G-370)*

Young MNS Chrstn Assn of Akron 330 724-1255
350 E Wilbeth Rd Akron (44301) *(G-371)*

Young MNS Chrstn Assn of Akron 330 983-5573
210 E North St Akron (44304) *(G-372)*

Young MNS Chrstn Assn of Akron 330 376-1335
815 Mount Pleasant Rd Clinton (44216) *(G-5197)*

Young MNS Chrstn Assn of Akron 330 923-5223
544 Broad Blvd Cuyahoga Falls (44221) *(G-7119)*

Young MNS Chrstn Assn of Akron 330 467-8366
8761 Shepard Rd Macedonia (44056) *(G-10210)*

Young MNS Chrstn Assn of Akron 419 523-5233
101 Putnam Pkwy Ottawa (45875) *(G-12196)*

Young MNS Chrstn Assn of Akron 330 899-9622
3800 Massillon Rd Uniontown (44685) *(G-14272)*

Young MNS Chrstn Assn of E Lvr 330 385-0663
500 E 4th St East Liverpool (43920) *(G-8194)*

Young MNS Chrstn Assn of Grter 419 866-9622
2100 S Holland Sylvania Rd Maumee (43537) *(G-10782)*

Young MNS Chrstn Assn of Grter 419 794-7304
716 Askin St Maumee (43537) *(G-10783)*

Young MNS Chrstn Assn of Grter 419 691-3523
2960 Pickle Rd Oregon (43616) *(G-12148)*

Young MNS Chrstn Assn of Grter 419 251-9622
13415 Eckel Junction Rd Perrysburg (43551) *(G-12390)*

Young MNS Chrstn Assn of Grter (PA) 419 729-8135
6465 Sylvania Ave Sylvania (43560) *(G-13579)*

Young MNS Chrstn Assn of Grter 419 474-3995
1500 N Superior St Fl 2 Toledo (43604) *(G-14112)*

Young MNS Chrstn Assn of Grter 419 475-3496
2110 Tremainsville Rd Toledo (43613) *(G-14113)*

Young MNS Chrstn Assn of Grter 419 381-7980
5025 Glendale Ave Toledo (43614) *(G-14114)*

Young MNS Chrstn Assn of Grter 419 241-7218
2053 N 14th St Toledo (43620) *(G-14115)*

Young MNS Chrstn Assn of Mnsfe 419 522-3511
750 Scholl Rd Mansfield (44907) *(G-10327)*

Young MNS Chrstn Assn of Mt Vr 740 392-9622
103 N Main St Mount Vernon (43050) *(G-11510)*

Young MNS Chrstn Assn of Van W 419 238-0443
241 W Main St Van Wert (45891) *(G-14362)*

Young MNS Chrstn Assn Wster OH 330 264-3131
680 Woodland Ave Wooster (44691) *(G-15402)*

Young MNS Chrstn Assn Yngstown (PA) 330 744-8411
17 N Champion St Youngstown (44503) *(G-15755)*

Young Truck Sales Inc (PA) 330 477-6271
4970 Southway St Sw Canton (44706) *(G-1891)*

Young Wns Chrstn Assn Clvland (PA) 216 881-6878
4019 Prospect Ave Cleveland (44103) *(G-5167)*

Young Wns Chrstn Assn of Cnton 330 453-0789
1700 Gateway Blvd Se Canton (44707) *(G-1892)*

Young Wns Chrstn Assn of Lima 419 241-3230
1018 Jefferson Ave Toledo (43604) *(G-14116)*

Young Womens Christian Assn (PA) 614 224-9121
65 S 4th St Columbus (43215) *(G-6917)*

Younglearnersworld 937 426-5437
2308 Lakeview Dr Beavercreek (45431) *(G-918)*

Youngs Jersey Dairy Inc 937 325-0629
6880 Springfield Xenia Rd Yellow Springs (45387) *(G-15537)*

Youngstown Area Jwish Fdration (PA) 330 746-3251
505 Gypsy Ln Youngstown (44504) *(G-15756)*

Youngstown Country Club 330 759-1040
1402 Country Club Dr Youngstown (44505) *(G-15757)*

ALPHABETIC SECTION — Zipscene

Youngstown Developmental Ctr, Columbus *Also Called: Ohio Dept Dvlpmntal Dsbilities* *(G-6404)*

Youngstown Electric Supply, Columbiana *Also Called: Yes Management Inc (G-5242)*

Youngstown Hospitality LLC 330 759-9555
4400 Belmont Ave Youngstown (44505) *(G-15758)*

Youngstown Nghborhood Dev Corp 330 480-0423
820 Canfield Rd Youngstown (44511) *(G-15759)*

Youngstown Orthpedic Assoc Ltd 330 726-1466
6470 Tippecanoe Rd Ste A Canfield (44406) *(G-1646)*

Youngstown Pipe & Steel LLC 330 783-2700
4111 Simon Rd Youngstown (44512) *(G-15760)*

Youngstown Wlcome Hsptlity LLC 330 759-6600
1620 Motor Inn Dr Girard (44420) *(G-8831)*

Youngstown YMCA Association, Youngstown *Also Called: Young Mens Christian Assn (G-15754)*

Your Agency Inc 937 550-9596
664 N Main St Springboro (45066) *(G-13211)*

Your Home Court Advantage LLC 330 364-6602
122 W High Ave New Philadelphia (44663) *(G-11674)*

Youth For Christ/Usa Inc 216 252-9883
709 Brookpark Rd Ste 1 Cleveland (44109) *(G-5168)*

Youth Intensive Services Inc 330 318-3436
238 S Meridian Rd Youngstown (44509) *(G-15761)*

Youth Partial Hospitalization, Dayton *Also Called: South Community Inc (G-7625)*

Youth To Youth, Columbus *Also Called: Compdrug (G-5675)*

Yowell Transportation Svc Inc 937 294-5933
1840 Cardington Rd Moraine (45409) *(G-11451)*

Yp LLC 216 642-4000
9445 Rockside Rd Cleveland (44125) *(G-5169)*

Yp LLC 330 896-6000
1530 Corporate Woods Pkwy Ste 100 Uniontown (44685) *(G-14273)*

Ysi Management LLC 440 891-4100
6745 Engle Rd Ste 300 Cleveland (44130) *(G-5170)*

YWCA, Canton *Also Called: Young Wns Chrstn Assn of Cnton (G-1892)*

YWCA, Columbus *Also Called: Young Womens Christian Assn (G-6917)*

YWCA, Toledo *Also Called: Young Wns Chrstn Assn of Lima (G-14116)*

YWCA, Toledo *Also Called: YWCA of Northwest Ohio (G-14117)*

YWCA, Youngstown *Also Called: YWCA Mahoning Valley (G-15762)*

YWCA Mahoning Valley 330 746-6361
25 W Rayen Ave Youngstown (44503) *(G-15762)*

YWCA of Cleveland, Cleveland *Also Called: Young Wns Chrstn Assn Clvland (G-5167)*

YWCA of Greater Cincinnati (PA) 513 241-7090
898 Walnut St Fl 1 Cincinnati (45202) *(G-3697)*

YWCA of Northwest Ohio 419 241-3235
1018 Jefferson Ave Toledo (43604) *(G-14117)*

Z & Sons Limited Partnership 440 249-5164
7100 E Pleasant Valley Rd # 300 Cleveland (44131) *(G-5171)*

Zaaz, Cincinnati *Also Called: Possible Worldwide LLC (G-3223)*

Zandex Health Care Corporation 740 454-1400
267 N Main St Johnstown (43031) *(G-9550)*

Zandex Health Care Corporation 740 392-1099
1133 Gambier Rd # 1139 Mount Vernon (43050) *(G-11511)*

Zandex Health Care Corporation 740 454-1400
1280 Friendship Dr New Concord (43762) *(G-11613)*

Zandex Health Care Corporation 740 695-7233
100 Reservoir Rd Saint Clairsville (43950) *(G-12823)*

Zandex Health Care Corporation 740 454-9747
1020 Taylor St Zanesville (43701) *(G-15837)*

Zandex Health Care Corporation 740 452-4636
1136 Adair Ave Zanesville (43701) *(G-15838)*

Zandex Health Care Corporation 740 454-9769
1856 Adams Ln Zanesville (43701) *(G-15839)*

Zaner-Bloser Inc (HQ) 614 486-0221
1400 Goodale Blvd Ste 200 Columbus (43212) *(G-6918)*

Zanesville, Zanesville *Also Called: Cambridge Counseling Center (G-15775)*

Zanesville Country Club 740 452-2726
1300 Country Club Dr Zanesville (43701) *(G-15840)*

Zanesville Metro Hsing Auth. 740 454-9714
407 Pershing Rd Zanesville (43701) *(G-15841)*

Zanesville Surgery Center LLC 740 453-5713
2907 Bell St Zanesville (43701) *(G-15842)*

Zanesvlle Wlfare Orgnztion Gdw (PA) 740 450-6060
3610 West Pike Zanesville (43701) *(G-15843)*

Zappia Enterprises LLC 937 277-3010
3210 Early Rd Dayton (45415) *(G-7735)*

Zappys Auto Washes 844 927-9274
8806 Mentor Ave Mentor (44060) *(G-11013)*

Zaps Technocrats Inc 614 664-3199
545 Metro Pl S Ste 100 Dublin (43017) *(G-8167)*

Zara Construction Inc 419 525-3613
3240 Park Ave W Ontario (44906) *(G-12127)*

Zaremba Group LLC 216 221-6600
14600 Detroit Ave Lakewood (44107) *(G-9689)*

Zartran LLC 513 870-4800
3035 Symmes Rd Hamilton (45015) *(G-9094)*

Zashin & Rich Co LPA (PA) 216 696-4441
950 Main Ave Fl 4 Cleveland (44113) *(G-5172)*

Zavarella Brothers Cnstr Co 440 232-2243
5381 Erie St Ste B Cleveland (44146) *(G-5173)*

Zebec of North America Inc 513 829-5533
210 Donald Dr Fairfield (45014) *(G-8455)*

Zeigler Habilitation Homes Inc 419 973-7629
540 Independence Rd Toledo (43607) *(G-14118)*

Zeiter Leasing, Norwalk *Also Called: Zeiter Trucking Inc (G-12031)*

Zeiter Trucking Inc 419 668-2229
2590 State Route 18 Norwalk (44857) *(G-12031)*

Zekelman Industries Inc 740 432-2146
9208 Jeffrey Dr Cambridge (43725) *(G-1588)*

Zemba Bros Inc 740 452-1880
3401 East Pike Zanesville (43701) *(G-15844)*

Zenith Systems LLC 216 406-7916
9627 Price St Ne Atwater (44201) *(G-602)*

Zenith Systems LLC (PA) 216 587-9510
5055 Corbin Dr Cleveland (44128) *(G-5174)*

Zepf Center (PA) 419 841-7701
6605 W Central Ave Ste 100 Toledo (43617) *(G-14119)*

Zepf Housing Corp One Inc 419 531-0019
5310 Hill Ave Toledo (43615) *(G-14120)*

Ziebart, Cleveland *Also Called: Ziebart of Ohio Inc (G-5175)*

Ziebart, Fairborn *Also Called: Dave Marshall Inc (G-8372)*

Ziebart of Ohio Inc 440 845-6031
6754 Pearl Rd Cleveland (44130) *(G-5175)*

Ziegler Bolt & Nut House, Canton *Also Called: Ziegler Bolt & Parts Co (G-1893)*

Ziegler Bolt & Parts Co (PA) 330 478-2542
4848 Corporate St Sw Canton (44706) *(G-1893)*

Ziegler Oil Co, Dover *Also Called: Ziegler Tire and Supply Co (G-7911)*

Ziegler Tire, Massillon *Also Called: Ziegler Tire and Supply Co (G-10676)*

Ziegler Tire and Supply Co 330 343-7739
411 Commercial Pkwy Dover (44622) *(G-7911)*

Ziegler Tire and Supply Co (PA) 330 834-3332
4150 Millennium Blvd Se Massillon (44646) *(G-10676)*

Ziehler Landscaping 937 312-9575
1045 E Centerville Station Rd Dayton (45459) *(G-7736)*

Ziks Family Pharmacy 100 .... 937 225-9350
1130 W 3rd St Dayton (45402) *(G-7737)*

Ziks Home Healthcare LLC 937 225-9350
1130 W 3rd St Dayton (45402) *(G-7738)*

Zimohana LLC 330 922-4721
1213 Medina Rd Medina (44256) *(G-10906)*

Zin Technologies Inc (HQ) 440 625-2200
6745 Engle Rd Ste 105 Middleburg Heights (44130) *(G-11137)*

Zink Commercial, Columbus *Also Called: Zink Foodservice Group Inc (G-6919)*

Zink Foodservice Group Inc 800 492-7400
655 Dearborn Park Ln Ste C Columbus (43085) *(G-6919)*

Zinner & Co 216 831-0733
3201 Enterprise Pkwy Ste 410 Beachwood (44122) *(G-853)*

Zinz Cnstr & Restoration Inc 330 332-7939
6487 Mahoning Ave Youngstown (44515) *(G-15763)*

Zip Center, The-Division, Marietta *Also Called: Richardson Printing Corp (G-10404)*

Zipline Logistics LLC (PA) 888 469-4754
1600 Dublin Rd Fl 2 Columbus (43215) *(G-6920)*

Zipscene, Cincinnati *Also Called: Zipscene LLC (G-3698)*

Zipscene LLC 513 201-5174
615 Main St Fl 5 Cincinnati (45202) *(G-3698)*

Zone Safety 365, Columbia Station *Also Called: Zone Safety LLC (G-5230)*

Zone Safety LLC 440 752-9545
27100 Royalton Rd Unit 2 Columbia Station (44028) *(G-5230)*

Zoo Cincinnati 513 961-0041
3400 Vine St Cincinnati (45220) *(G-3699)*

Zoological Society Cincinnati 513 281-4700
3400 Vine St Cincinnati (45220) *(G-3700)*

Zucker Building Company 216 861-7114
5915 Landerbrook Dr Ste 300 Cleveland (44124) *(G-5176)*

Zullix LLC 440 536-9300
18500 Lake Rd Rocky River (44116) *(G-12758)*

Zumstein Inc (PA) 419 375-4132
2200 State Route 119 Fort Recovery (45846) *(G-8612)*

Zvn Properties, Canal Fulton *Also Called: Zvn Properties Inc (G-1596)*

Zvn Properties Inc 330 854-5890
957 Cherry St E Canal Fulton (44614) *(G-1596)*

SERVICES INDEX

- Service categories are listed in alphabetical order.

A

ABRASIVES
ACCIDENT INSURANCE CARRIERS
ACOUSTICAL BOARD & TILE
ADHESIVES
ADHESIVES & SEALANTS
ADHESIVES & SEALANTS WHOLESALERS
ADULT DAYCARE CENTERS
ADVERTISING AGENCIES
ADVERTISING AGENCIES: Consultants
ADVERTISING MATERIAL DISTRIBUTION
ADVERTISING REPRESENTATIVES: Electronic Media
ADVERTISING REPRESENTATIVES: Newspaper
ADVERTISING REPRESENTATIVES: Printed Media
ADVERTISING SPECIALTIES, WHOLESALE
ADVERTISING SVCS: Direct Mail
ADVERTISING SVCS: Display
ADVERTISING SVCS: Outdoor
ADVERTISING SVCS: Sample Distribution
AGENTS, BROKERS & BUREAUS: Personal Service
AGRICULTURAL CREDIT INSTITUTIONS
AGRICULTURAL EQPT: Elevators, Farm
AGRICULTURAL EQPT: Fertilizing Machinery
AGRICULTURAL MACHINERY & EQPT: Wholesalers
AIR CONDITIONING & VENTILATION EQPT & SPLYS: Wholesales
AIR CONDITIONING EQPT
AIR CONDITIONING EQPT, WHOLE HOUSE: Wholesalers
AIR CONDITIONING REPAIR SVCS
AIR CONDITIONING UNITS: Complete, Domestic Or Indl
AIR DUCT CLEANING SVCS
AIR POLLUTION MEASURING SVCS
AIRCRAFT & AEROSPACE FLIGHT INSTRUMENTS & GUIDANCE SYSTEMS
AIRCRAFT & HEAVY EQPT REPAIR SVCS
AIRCRAFT DEALERS
AIRCRAFT ELECTRICAL EQPT REPAIR SVCS
AIRCRAFT ENGINES & ENGINE PARTS: Nonelectric Starters
AIRCRAFT ENGINES & ENGINE PARTS: Pumps
AIRCRAFT ENGINES & PARTS
AIRCRAFT EQPT & SPLYS WHOLESALERS
AIRCRAFT MAINTENANCE & REPAIR SVCS
AIRCRAFT PARTS & EQPT, NEC
AIRCRAFT PARTS WHOLESALERS
AIRCRAFT SERVICING & REPAIRING
AIRLINE TRAINING
AIRPORT TERMINAL SVCS
AIRPORTS & FLYING FIELDS
AIRPORTS, FLYING FIELDS & SVCS
ALKALIES & CHLORINE
ALLOYS: Additive, Exc Copper Or Made In Blast Furnaces
ALUMINUM: Coil & Sheet
AMBULANCE SVCS
AMUSEMENT & RECREATION SVCS: Arcades
AMUSEMENT & RECREATION SVCS: Exhibition Operation
AMUSEMENT & RECREATION SVCS: Exposition Operation
AMUSEMENT & RECREATION SVCS: Gambling & Lottery Svcs
AMUSEMENT & RECREATION SVCS: Golf Club, Membership
AMUSEMENT & RECREATION SVCS: Pool Parlor
AMUSEMENT & RECREATION SVCS: Recreation Center
AMUSEMENT & RECREATION SVCS: Recreation SVCS
AMUSEMENT ARCADES
AMUSEMENT PARKS
ANIMAL FEED & SUPPLEMENTS: Livestock & Poultry
ANIMAL FEED: Wholesalers
ANIMAL FOOD & SUPPLEMENTS: Bird Food, Prepared
ANIMAL FOOD & SUPPLEMENTS: Cat
ANIMAL FOOD & SUPPLEMENTS: Dog
ANIMAL FOOD & SUPPLEMENTS: Livestock
ANIMAL FOOD & SUPPLEMENTS: Poultry
ANTENNAS: Radar Or Communications
ANTIQUE REPAIR & RESTORATION SVCS, EXC FURNITURE & AUTOS
APPAREL DESIGNERS: Commercial
APPLIANCES, HOUSEHOLD OR COIN OPERATED: Laundry Dryers
APPLIANCES, HOUSEHOLD: Kitchen, Major, Exc Refrigs & Stoves
APPLIANCES: Household, Refrigerators & Freezers
APPLIANCES: Major, Cooking
APPLIANCES: Small, Electric
APPLICATIONS SOFTWARE PROGRAMMING
APPRAISAL SVCS, EXC REAL ESTATE
ARCHITECTURAL SVCS
ARCHITECTURAL SVCS: Engineering
ARMATURE REPAIRING & REWINDING SVC
ART GOODS & SPLYS WHOLESALERS
ART SPLY STORES
ARTS & CRAFTS SCHOOL
ASPHALT & ASPHALT PRDTS
ASPHALT COATINGS & SEALERS
ASPHALT MIXTURES WHOLESALERS
ASSOCIATION FOR THE HANDICAPPED
ASSOCIATIONS: Bar
ASSOCIATIONS: Business
ASSOCIATIONS: Engineering
ASSOCIATIONS: Real Estate Management
ASSOCIATIONS: Scientists'
ASSOCIATIONS: Trade
ATOMIZERS
AUCTIONEERS: Fee Basis
AUDIO & VIDEO EQPT, EXC COMMERCIAL
AUDIO-VISUAL PROGRAM PRODUCTION SVCS
AUTO & HOME SUPPLY STORES: Auto & Truck Eqpt & Parts
AUTO & HOME SUPPLY STORES: Automotive parts
AUTO & HOME SUPPLY STORES: Trailer Hitches, Automotive
AUTO & HOME SUPPLY STORES: Truck Eqpt & Parts
AUTO SPLYS & PARTS, NEW, WHSLE: Exhaust Sys, Mufflers, Etc
AUTOMATIC REGULATING CONTROL: Building Svcs Monitoring, Auto
AUTOMATIC REGULATING CONTROLS: Appliance, Exc AirCond/Refr
AUTOMOBILE FINANCE LEASING
AUTOMOBILES & OTHER MOTOR VEHICLES WHOLESALERS
AUTOMOBILES: Wholesalers
AUTOMOTIVE & TRUCK GENERAL REPAIR SVC
AUTOMOTIVE BODY SHOP
AUTOMOTIVE BODY, PAINT & INTERIOR REPAIR & MAINTENANCE SVC
AUTOMOTIVE CUSTOMIZING SVCS, NONFACTORY BASIS
AUTOMOTIVE GLASS REPLACEMENT SHOPS
AUTOMOTIVE PAINT SHOP
AUTOMOTIVE PARTS, ACCESS & SPLYS
AUTOMOTIVE PARTS: Plastic
AUTOMOTIVE PRDTS: Rubber
AUTOMOTIVE REPAIR SHOPS: Diesel Engine Repair
AUTOMOTIVE REPAIR SHOPS: Electrical Svcs
AUTOMOTIVE REPAIR SHOPS: Machine Shop
AUTOMOTIVE REPAIR SHOPS: Muffler Shop, Sale/Rpr/Installation
AUTOMOTIVE REPAIR SHOPS: Rebuilding & Retreading Tires
AUTOMOTIVE REPAIR SHOPS: Tire Recapping
AUTOMOTIVE REPAIR SHOPS: Tire Repair Shop
AUTOMOTIVE REPAIR SHOPS: Trailer Repair
AUTOMOTIVE REPAIR SHOPS: Truck Engine Repair, Exc Indl
AUTOMOTIVE REPAIR SVC
AUTOMOTIVE SPLYS & PARTS, NEW, WHOL: Auto Servicing Eqpt
AUTOMOTIVE SPLYS & PARTS, NEW, WHOLESALE: Engines/Eng Parts
AUTOMOTIVE SPLYS & PARTS, NEW, WHOLESALE: Splys
AUTOMOTIVE SPLYS & PARTS, NEW, WHOLESALE: Tools & Eqpt
AUTOMOTIVE SPLYS & PARTS, NEW, WHOLESALE: Trailer Parts
AUTOMOTIVE SPLYS & PARTS, WHOLESALE, NEC
AUTOMOTIVE SPLYS/PART, NEW, WHOL: Spring, Shock Absorb/Strut
AUTOMOTIVE SVCS, EXC REPAIR & CARWASHES: Insp & Diagnostic
AUTOMOTIVE SVCS, EXC REPAIR & CARWASHES: Lubrication
AUTOMOTIVE TOWING SVCS
AUTOMOTIVE TRANSMISSION REPAIR SVC
AUTOMOTIVE WELDING SVCS
AUTOMOTIVE: Seating
AVIATION PROPELLER & BLADE REPAIR SVCS
AVIATION SCHOOL

B

BAGS: Paper
BAGS: Plastic, Made From Purchased Materials
BAGS: Shopping, Made From Purchased Materials
BAKERIES, COMMERCIAL: On Premises Baking Only
BAKERIES: On Premises Baking & Consumption
BAKERY PRDTS: Cookies & crackers
BAKERY PRDTS: Pretzels
BAKERY PRDTS: Wholesalers
BALLET PRODUCTION SVCS
BANKS: Mortgage & Loan
BANQUET HALL FACILITIES
BAR
BAR FIXTURES: Wood
BARGES BUILDING & REPAIR
BARRICADES: Metal
BARS: Concrete Reinforcing, Fabricated Steel
BATTERY CHARGERS
BEARINGS: Ball & Roller
BEAUTY & BARBER SHOP EQPT
BEAUTY SALONS
BEER & ALE WHOLESALERS
BEER & ALE, WHOLESALE: Beer & Other Fermented Malt Liquors
BEER, WINE & LIQUOR STORES: Beer, Packaged
BEVERAGE STORES
BEVERAGES, ALCOHOLIC: Distilled Liquors
BEVERAGES, ALCOHOLIC: Wines
BEVERAGES, NONALCOHOLIC: Bottled & canned soft drinks
BEVERAGES, NONALCOHOLIC: Carbonated
BEVERAGES, NONALCOHOLIC: Flavoring extracts & syrups, nec
BEVERAGES, NONALCOHOLIC: Soft Drinks, Canned & Bottled, Etc
BEVERAGES, WINE & DISTILLED ALCOHOLIC, WHOLESALE: Wine
BILLIARD & POOL TABLES & SPLYS
BILLIARD TABLE REPAIR SVCS
BILLING & BOOKKEEPING SVCS
BINDING SVC: Books & Manuals
BIOLOGICAL PRDTS: Exc Diagnostic
BLINDS : Window
BLOCKS: Landscape Or Retaining Wall, Concrete
BLOCKS: Standard, Concrete Or Cinder
BLOOD BANK
BLOOD RELATED HEALTH SVCS
BLOWERS & FANS
BLOWERS & FANS
BLUEPRINTING SVCS
BOAT BUILDING & REPAIR
BOAT DEALERS
BOAT DEALERS: Motor
BOAT REPAIR SVCS
BODIES: Truck & Bus
BOILER & HEATING REPAIR SVCS
BOILER REPAIR SHOP
BOOK STORES
BOOKS, WHOLESALE
BOTTLED GAS DEALERS: Propane
BOTTLES: Plastic
BOWLING CENTERS
BOXES & SHOOK: Nailed Wood
BOXES: Corrugated
BOXES: Paperboard, Folding

SERVICES INDEX

BOXES: Paperboard, Set-Up
BOXES: Wooden
BRAKES & BRAKE PARTS
BRASS & BRONZE PRDTS: Die-casted
BRAZING SVCS
BRICK, STONE & RELATED PRDTS WHOLESALERS
BROACHING MACHINES
BROADCASTING STATIONS, TELEVISION: Translator Station
BROKERS & DEALERS: Securities
BROKERS & DEALERS: Security
BROKERS' SVCS
BROKERS: Business
BROKERS: Food
BROKERS: Loan
BROKERS: Log & Lumber
BROKERS: Mortgage, Arranging For Loans
BROKERS: Printing
BROOMS & BRUSHES
BROOMS & BRUSHES: Household Or Indl
BUCKETS: Plastic
BUILDING & OFFICE CLEANING SVCS
BUILDING & STRUCTURAL WOOD MEMBERS
BUILDING CLEANING & MAINTENANCE SVCS
BUILDING COMPONENTS: Structural Steel
BUILDING MAINTENANCE SVCS, EXC REPAIRS
BUILDING PRDTS & MATERIALS DEALERS
BUILDINGS & COMPONENTS: Prefabricated Metal
BUILDINGS: Portable
BUILDINGS: Prefabricated, Metal
BUILDINGS: Prefabricated, Wood
BURIAL VAULTS: Concrete Or Precast Terrazzo
BUS BARS: Electrical
BUSHINGS & BEARINGS
BUSINESS ACTIVITIES: Non-Commercial Site
BUSINESS FORMS WHOLESALERS
BUSINESS FORMS: Printed, Manifold
BUSINESS MACHINE REPAIR, ELECTRIC

C

CABINETS: Entertainment
CABINETS: Kitchen, Wood
CABINETS: Office, Wood
CABINETS: Show, Display, Etc, Wood, Exc Refrigerated
CABLE & PAY TELEVISION DISTRIBUTION
CABLE & PAY TELEVISION SVCS: Direct Broadcast Satellite
CABLE TELEVISION
CABLE: Fiber Optic
CABLE: Noninsulated
CABLE: Ropes & Fiber
CAFETERIAS
CALIBRATING SVCS, NEC
CAMERAS & RELATED EQPT: Photographic
CANDLES
CANDLES: Wholesalers
CANDY & CONFECTIONS: Popcorn Balls/Other Trtd Popcorn Prdts
CANDY MAKING GOODS & SPLYS, WHOLESALE
CANDY, NUT & CONFECTIONERY STORES: Candy
CANNED SPECIALTIES
CANS: Metal
CANVAS PRDTS
CAR WASH EQPT
CARBON & GRAPHITE PRDTS, NEC
CARBON PAPER & INKED RIBBONS
CARDS: Beveled
CARDS: Greeting
CARPET & UPHOLSTERY CLEANING SVCS
CARPET & UPHOLSTERY CLEANING SVCS: Carpet/Furniture, On Loc
CARPETS, RUGS & FLOOR COVERING
CARTONS: Egg, Molded Pulp, Made From Purchased Materials
CASH REGISTER REPAIR SVCS
CASH REGISTERS WHOLESALERS
CASTINGS: Commercial Investment, Ferrous
CASTINGS: Die, Aluminum
CASTINGS: Die, Nonferrous
CASTINGS: Precision
CATALOG & MAIL-ORDER HOUSES
CATALOG SALES
CATALYSTS: Chemical
CATERERS

CEMENT & CONCRETE RELATED PRDTS & EQPT: Bituminous
CEMENT: Hydraulic
CHARGE ACCOUNT SVCS
CHASSIS: Motor Vehicle
CHEESE WHOLESALERS
CHEMICAL CLEANING SVCS
CHEMICAL PROCESSING MACHINERY & EQPT
CHEMICALS & ALLIED PRDTS WHOLESALERS, NEC
CHEMICALS & ALLIED PRDTS, WHOL: Chemicals, Swimming Pool/Spa
CHEMICALS & ALLIED PRDTS, WHOLESALE: Alkalines & Chlorine
CHEMICALS & ALLIED PRDTS, WHOLESALE: Chemicals, Indl
CHEMICALS & ALLIED PRDTS, WHOLESALE: Chemicals, Indl & Heavy
CHEMICALS & ALLIED PRDTS, WHOLESALE: Detergent/Soap
CHEMICALS & ALLIED PRDTS, WHOLESALE: Detergents
CHEMICALS & ALLIED PRDTS, WHOLESALE: Oxygen
CHEMICALS & ALLIED PRDTS, WHOLESALE: Plastics Film
CHEMICALS & ALLIED PRDTS, WHOLESALE: Plastics Materials, NEC
CHEMICALS & ALLIED PRDTS, WHOLESALE: Plastics Prdts, NEC
CHEMICALS & ALLIED PRDTS, WHOLESALE: Plastics Sheets & Rods
CHEMICALS & ALLIED PRDTS, WHOLESALE: Resins
CHEMICALS & ALLIED PRDTS, WHOLESALE: Resins, Plastics
CHEMICALS & ALLIED PRDTS, WHOLESALE: Spec Clean/Sanitation
CHEMICALS & ALLIED PRDTS, WHOLESALE: Syn Resin, Rub/Plastic
CHEMICALS, AGRICULTURE: Wholesalers
CHEMICALS: Aluminum Compounds
CHEMICALS: High Purity, Refined From Technical Grade
CHEMICALS: Inorganic, NEC
CHEMICALS: NEC
CHEMICALS: Organic, NEC
CHEMICALS: Water Treatment
CHICKEN SLAUGHTERING & PROCESSING
CHILD DAY CARE SVCS
CHILD RESTRAINT SEATS, AUTOMOTIVE, WHOLESALE
CHILDBIRTH PREPARATION CLINIC
CHILDREN'S & INFANTS' CLOTHING STORES
CHOCOLATE, EXC CANDY FROM BEANS: Chips, Powder, Block, Syrup
CHURCHES
CIRCUITS: Electronic
CLEANING EQPT: Commercial
CLEANING OR POLISHING PREPARATIONS, NEC
CLEANING SVCS: Industrial Or Commercial
CLIPS & FASTENERS, MADE FROM PURCHASED WIRE
CLOTHING & ACCESS, WOMEN, CHILD & INFANT, WHOL: Diapers
CLOTHING & ACCESS, WOMEN, CHILDREN & INFANT, WHOL: Handbags
CLOTHING & ACCESS, WOMEN, CHILDREN & INFANT, WHOL: Uniforms
CLOTHING & ACCESS, WOMEN, CHILDREN/INFANT, WHOL: Baby Goods
CLOTHING & ACCESS: Costumes, Theatrical
CLOTHING & FURNISHINGS, MEN'S & BOYS', WHOLESALE: Uniforms
CLOTHING & FURNISHINGS, MENS & BOYS, WHOLESALE: Apprl Belts
CLOTHING STORES: Designer Apparel
CLOTHING STORES: T-Shirts, Printed, Custom
CLOTHING STORES: Work
CLOTHING/ACCESS, WOMEN, CHILDREN/INFANT, WHOL: Hosp Gowns
CLOTHING: Caps, Baseball
CLOTHING: T-Shirts & Tops, Knit
CLOTHING: Uniforms & Vestments
CLOTHING: Uniforms, Ex Athletic, Women's, Misses' & Juniors'
CLOTHING: Uniforms, Firemen's, From Purchased Materials
CLOTHING: Uniforms, Military, Men/Youth, Purchased Materials
CLOTHING: Uniforms, Work
CLUTCHES, EXC VEHICULAR

COAL & OTHER MINERALS & ORES WHOLESALERS
COAL MINING SERVICES
COAL MINING: Anthracite
COAL MINING: Bituminous & Lignite Surface
COAL MINING: Bituminous Coal & Lignite-Surface Mining
COAL MINING: Bituminous, Strip
COAL MINING: Bituminous, Surface, NEC
COAL MINING: Lignite, Surface, NEC
COAL PREPARATION PLANT: Bituminous or Lignite
COAL, MINERALS & ORES, WHOLESALE: Coal
COATING SVC: Metals, With Plastic Or Resins
COATINGS: Epoxy
COFFEE SVCS
COILS & TRANSFORMERS
COILS: Pipe
COLLEGE, EXC JUNIOR
COLLEGES, UNIVERSITIES & PROFESSIONAL SCHOOLS
COMBINATION UTILITIES, NEC
COMBINED ELEMENTARY & SECONDARY SCHOOLS, PRIVATE
COMBINED ELEMENTARY & SECONDARY SCHOOLS, PUBLIC
COMMERCIAL & OFFICE BUILDINGS RENOVATION & REPAIR
COMMERCIAL ART & GRAPHIC DESIGN SVCS
COMMERCIAL ART & ILLUSTRATION SVCS
COMMERCIAL CONTAINERS WHOLESALERS
COMMERCIAL EQPT WHOLESALERS, NEC
COMMERCIAL EQPT, WHOLESALE: Bakery Eqpt & Splys
COMMERCIAL EQPT, WHOLESALE: Restaurant, NEC
COMMERCIAL EQPT, WHOLESALE: Scales, Exc Laboratory
COMMERCIAL EQPT, WHOLESALE: Store Fixtures & Display Eqpt
COMMERCIAL EQPT, WHOLESALE: Vending Machines, Coin-Operated
COMMERCIAL PHOTOGRAPHIC STUDIO
COMMERCIAL PRINTING & NEWSPAPER PUBLISHING
COMMON SAND MINING
COMMUNICATIONS EQPT WHOLESALERS
COMMUNICATIONS SVCS
COMMUNICATIONS SVCS: Data
COMMUNICATIONS SVCS: Internet Connectivity Svcs
COMMUNICATIONS SVCS: Internet Host Svcs
COMMUNICATIONS SVCS: Online Svc Providers
COMMUNICATIONS SVCS: Proprietary Online Svcs Networks
COMMUNICATIONS SVCS: Signal Enhancement Network Svcs
COMMUNICATIONS SVCS: Telephone, Broker
COMMUNICATIONS SVCS: Telephone, Local
COMMUNICATIONS SVCS: Telephone, Local & Long Distance
COMMUNICATIONS SVCS: Telephone, Long Distance
COMMUNICATIONS SVCS: Telephone, Voice
COMMUNITY SVCS EMPLOYMENT TRAINING PROGRAM
COMMUTATORS: Electronic
COMPOST
COMPRESSORS: Air & Gas, Including Vacuum Pumps
COMPUTER & COMPUTER SOFTWARE STORES
COMPUTER & COMPUTER SOFTWARE STORES: Peripheral Eqpt
COMPUTER & COMPUTER SOFTWARE STORES: Personal Computers
COMPUTER & COMPUTER SOFTWARE STORES: Software & Access
COMPUTER & COMPUTER SOFTWARE STORES: Software, Bus/Non-Game
COMPUTER & DATA PROCESSING EQPT REPAIR & MAINTENANCE
COMPUTER & OFFICE MACHINE MAINTENANCE & REPAIR
COMPUTER CODE AUTHORS
COMPUTER DATA ESCROW SVCS
COMPUTER FACILITIES MANAGEMENT SVCS
COMPUTER GRAPHICS SVCS
COMPUTER PERIPHERAL EQPT REPAIR & MAINTENANCE
COMPUTER PERIPHERAL EQPT, NEC
COMPUTER PERIPHERAL EQPT, WHOLESALE
COMPUTER PROCESSING SVCS
COMPUTER PROGRAMMING SVCS: Custom
COMPUTER RELATED MAINTENANCE SVCS
COMPUTER SOFTWARE DEVELOPMENT

SERVICES INDEX

COMPUTER SOFTWARE DEVELOPMENT & APPLICATIONS
COMPUTER SOFTWARE SYSTEMS ANALYSIS & DESIGN: Custom
COMPUTER STORAGE DEVICES, NEC
COMPUTER STORAGE UNITS: Auxiliary
COMPUTER SYSTEM SELLING SVCS
COMPUTER SYSTEMS ANALYSIS & DESIGN
COMPUTER TERMINALS
COMPUTER TIME-SHARING
COMPUTERS, NEC
COMPUTERS, NEC, WHOLESALE
COMPUTERS, PERIPHERALS & SOFTWARE, WHOLESALE: Printers
COMPUTERS, PERIPHERALS & SOFTWARE, WHOLESALE: Software
CONCENTRATES, FLAVORING, EXC DRINK
CONCRETE CURING & HARDENING COMPOUNDS
CONCRETE PRDTS
CONCRETE PRDTS, PRECAST, NEC
CONCRETE: Asphaltic, Not From Refineries
CONCRETE: Dry Mixture
CONCRETE: Ready-Mixed
CONDENSERS: Heat Transfer Eqpt, Evaporative
CONFINEMENT SURVEILLANCE SYS MAINTENANCE & MONITORING SVCS
CONNECTORS: Electronic
CONSTRUCTION & MINING MACHINERY WHOLESALERS
CONSTRUCTION EQPT REPAIR SVCS
CONSTRUCTION EQPT: Cranes
CONSTRUCTION EQPT: Roofing Eqpt
CONSTRUCTION MATERIALS, WHOLESALE: Air Ducts, Sheet Metal
CONSTRUCTION MATERIALS, WHOLESALE: Asphalt Felts & coating
CONSTRUCTION MATERIALS, WHOLESALE: Building Stone, Marble
CONSTRUCTION MATERIALS, WHOLESALE: Building, Exterior
CONSTRUCTION MATERIALS, WHOLESALE: Building, Interior
CONSTRUCTION MATERIALS, WHOLESALE: Cement
CONSTRUCTION MATERIALS, WHOLESALE: Door Frames
CONSTRUCTION MATERIALS, WHOLESALE: Doors, Garage
CONSTRUCTION MATERIALS, WHOLESALE: Glass
CONSTRUCTION MATERIALS, WHOLESALE: Limestone
CONSTRUCTION MATERIALS, WHOLESALE: Masons' Materials
CONSTRUCTION MATERIALS, WHOLESALE: Millwork
CONSTRUCTION MATERIALS, WHOLESALE: Molding, All Materials
CONSTRUCTION MATERIALS, WHOLESALE: Pallets, Wood
CONSTRUCTION MATERIALS, WHOLESALE: Particleboard
CONSTRUCTION MATERIALS, WHOLESALE: Paving Materials
CONSTRUCTION MATERIALS, WHOLESALE: Prefabricated Structures
CONSTRUCTION MATERIALS, WHOLESALE: Roofing & Siding Material
CONSTRUCTION MATERIALS, WHOLESALE: Sand
CONSTRUCTION MATERIALS, WHOLESALE: Sewer Pipe, Clay
CONSTRUCTION MATERIALS, WHOLESALE: Siding, Exc Wood
CONSTRUCTION MATERIALS, WHOLESALE: Stone, Crushed Or Broken
CONSTRUCTION MATERIALS, WHOLESALE: Veneer
CONSTRUCTION MATERIALS, WHOLESALE: Windows
CONSTRUCTION SAND MINING
CONSTRUCTION: Agricultural Building
CONSTRUCTION: Airport Runway
CONSTRUCTION: Apartment Building
CONSTRUCTION: Athletic & Recreation Facilities
CONSTRUCTION: Bridge
CONSTRUCTION: Commercial & Office Building, New
CONSTRUCTION: Dams, Waterways, Docks & Other Marine
CONSTRUCTION: Elevated Highway
CONSTRUCTION: Food Prdts Manufacturing or Packing Plant
CONSTRUCTION: Gas Main
CONSTRUCTION: Heavy Highway & Street
CONSTRUCTION: Indl Buildings, New, NEC
CONSTRUCTION: Indl Plant
CONSTRUCTION: Institutional Building
CONSTRUCTION: Land Preparation
CONSTRUCTION: Oil & Gas Pipeline Construction
CONSTRUCTION: Pharmaceutical Manufacturing Plant
CONSTRUCTION: Pipeline, NEC
CONSTRUCTION: Power & Communication Transmission Tower
CONSTRUCTION: Power Plant
CONSTRUCTION: Railroad & Subway
CONSTRUCTION: Residential, Nec
CONSTRUCTION: Scaffolding
CONSTRUCTION: Sewer Line
CONSTRUCTION: Single-Family Housing
CONSTRUCTION: Single-family Housing, New
CONSTRUCTION: Street Sign Installation & Mntnce
CONSTRUCTION: Swimming Pools
CONSTRUCTION: Transmitting Tower, Telecommunication
CONSTRUCTION: Warehouse
CONSTRUCTION: Waste Water & Sewage Treatment Plant
CONSTRUCTION: Water & Sewer Line
CONSULTING SVC: Business, NEC
CONSULTING SVC: Educational
CONSULTING SVC: Financial Management
CONSULTING SVC: Human Resource
CONSULTING SVC: Management
CONSULTING SVCS, BUSINESS: Energy Conservation
CONSULTING SVCS, BUSINESS: Environmental
CONSULTING SVCS, BUSINESS: Indl Development Planning
CONSULTING SVCS, BUSINESS: Safety Training Svcs
CONSULTING SVCS, BUSINESS: Sys Engnrg, Exc Computer/ Prof
CONSULTING SVCS, BUSINESS: Systems Analysis & Engineering
CONSULTING SVCS, BUSINESS: Testing, Educational Or Personnel
CONSULTING SVCS: Scientific
CONTACT LENSES
CONTAINERS: Food, Liquid Tight, Including Milk
CONTAINERS: Plastic
CONTAINERS: Shipping, Bombs, Metal Plate
CONTAINERS: Wood
CONTRACTOR: Dredging
CONTRACTOR: Framing
CONTRACTOR: Rigging & Scaffolding
CONTRACTORS: Acoustical & Ceiling Work
CONTRACTORS: Acoustical & Insulation Work
CONTRACTORS: Artificial Turf Installation
CONTRACTORS: Asbestos Removal & Encapsulation
CONTRACTORS: Boiler Maintenance Contractor
CONTRACTORS: Building Site Preparation
CONTRACTORS: Cable Laying
CONTRACTORS: Carpentry Work
CONTRACTORS: Carpentry, Cabinet & Finish Work
CONTRACTORS: Closet Organizers, Installation & Design
CONTRACTORS: Coating, Caulking & Weather, Water & Fire
CONTRACTORS: Commercial & Office Building
CONTRACTORS: Communications Svcs
CONTRACTORS: Concrete Reinforcement Placing
CONTRACTORS: Core Drilling & Cutting
CONTRACTORS: Corrosion Control Installation
CONTRACTORS: Directional Oil & Gas Well Drilling Svc
CONTRACTORS: Drywall
CONTRACTORS: Electric Power Systems
CONTRACTORS: Electronic Controls Installation
CONTRACTORS: Energy Management Control
CONTRACTORS: Erection & Dismantling, Poured Concrete Forms
CONTRACTORS: Fence Construction
CONTRACTORS: Fiber Optic Cable Installation
CONTRACTORS: Fire Detection & Burglar Alarm Systems
CONTRACTORS: Floor Laying & Other Floor Work
CONTRACTORS: Foundation & Footing
CONTRACTORS: Gas Field Svcs, NEC
CONTRACTORS: General Electric
CONTRACTORS: Glass Tinting, Architectural & Automotive
CONTRACTORS: Heating & Air Conditioning
CONTRACTORS: Heating Systems Repair & Maintenance Svc
CONTRACTORS: Highway & Street Construction, General
CONTRACTORS: Highway & Street Paving
CONTRACTORS: Hydraulic Eqpt Installation & Svcs
CONTRACTORS: Machine Rigging & Moving
CONTRACTORS: Machinery Installation
CONTRACTORS: Marble Installation, Interior
CONTRACTORS: Masonry & Stonework
CONTRACTORS: Office Furniture Installation
CONTRACTORS: Oil & Gas Field Geophysical Exploration Svcs
CONTRACTORS: Oil & Gas Field Tools Fishing Svcs
CONTRACTORS: Oil & Gas Wells Pumping Svcs
CONTRACTORS: Oil Field Mud Drilling Svcs
CONTRACTORS: Painting, Commercial
CONTRACTORS: Painting, Commercial, Exterior
CONTRACTORS: Painting, Indl
CONTRACTORS: Pile Driving
CONTRACTORS: Plumbing
CONTRACTORS: Pollution Control Eqpt Installation
CONTRACTORS: Power Generating Eqpt Installation
CONTRACTORS: Prefabricated Window & Door Installation
CONTRACTORS: Process Piping
CONTRACTORS: Refractory or Acid Brick Masonry
CONTRACTORS: Septic System
CONTRACTORS: Sheet Metal Work, NEC
CONTRACTORS: Siding
CONTRACTORS: Structural Iron Work, Structural
CONTRACTORS: Structural Steel Erection
CONTRACTORS: Tile Installation, Ceramic
CONTRACTORS: Underground Utilities
CONTRACTORS: Ventilation & Duct Work
CONTRACTORS: Warm Air Heating & Air Conditioning
CONTRACTORS: Water Well Drilling
CONTRACTORS: Windows & Doors
CONTRACTORS: Wood Floor Installation & Refinishing
CONTRACTORS: Wrecking & Demolition
CONTROL EQPT: Electric
CONTROL EQPT: Noise
CONTROLS & ACCESS: Indl, Electric
CONTROLS & ACCESS: Motor
CONTROLS: Environmental
CONVENIENCE STORES
CONVEYOR SYSTEMS: Belt, General Indl Use
CONVEYOR SYSTEMS: Bulk Handling
CONVEYOR SYSTEMS: Robotic
CONVEYORS & CONVEYING EQPT
COOKING & FOODWARMING EQPT: Commercial
CORRECTIONAL INSTITUTIONS, GOVERNMENT: Prison, government
COSMETIC PREPARATIONS
COSMETICS & TOILETRIES
COSMETICS WHOLESALERS
COSMETOLOGY & PERSONAL HYGIENE SALONS
COSMETOLOGY SCHOOL
COUNTRY CLUBS
CRANE & AERIAL LIFT SVCS
CRANES: Indl Plant
CREDIT CARD SVCS
CREDIT UNIONS: Federally Chartered
CRUDE PETROLEUM & NATURAL GAS PRODUCTION
CRUDE PETROLEUM PRODUCTION
CUPS: Paper, Made From Purchased Materials
CURTAIN WALLS: Building, Steel
CURTAINS: Window, From Purchased Materials
CUT STONE & STONE PRODUCTS
CUTLERY
CYLINDER & ACTUATORS: Fluid Power
CYLINDERS: Pressure

D

DAIRY PRDTS STORE: Cheese
DAIRY PRDTS STORE: Ice Cream, Packaged
DAIRY PRDTS STORES
DAIRY PRDTS: Cheese
DAIRY PRDTS: Dietary Supplements, Dairy & Non-Dairy Based
DAIRY PRDTS: Ice Cream & Ice Milk
DAIRY PRDTS: Ice Cream, Bulk
DAIRY PRDTS: Milk, Condensed & Evaporated
DAIRY PRDTS: Natural Cheese
DAIRY PRDTS: Whipped Topping, Exc Frozen Or Dry Mix
DATA ENTRY SVCS
DATA PROCESSING & PREPARATION SVCS
DATA PROCESSING SVCS
DEFENSE SYSTEMS & EQPT
DENTAL EQPT & SPLYS
DENTAL EQPT & SPLYS WHOLESALERS
DENTAL EQPT & SPLYS: Orthodontic Appliances

SERVICES INDEX

DENTISTS' OFFICES & CLINICS
DEPARTMENT STORES
DEPARTMENT STORES: Non-Discount
DEPARTMENT STORES: Surplus & Salvage
DESIGN SVCS, NEC
DESIGN SVCS: Commercial & Indl
DESIGN SVCS: Computer Integrated Systems
DETECTIVE & ARMORED CAR SERVICES
DIAGNOSTIC SUBSTANCES
DIAGNOSTIC SUBSTANCES OR AGENTS: Radioactive
DIAMONDS, GEMS, WHOLESALE
DIES & TOOLS: Special
DIODES: Light Emitting
DISASTER SVCS
DISCOUNT DEPARTMENT STORES
DISINFECTING & PEST CONTROL SERVICES
DISINFECTING SVCS
DISKETTE DUPLICATING SVCS
DISPLAY FIXTURES: Wood
DISTRIBUTORS: Motor Vehicle Engine
DOORS & WINDOWS: Storm, Metal
DOORS: Garage, Overhead, Metal
DOORS: Garage, Overhead, Wood
DRAPERIES & CURTAINS
DRAPERY & UPHOLSTERY STORES: Draperies
DRINKING FOUNTAINS: Metal, Nonrefrigerated
DRINKING PLACES: Bars & Lounges
DRINKING WATER COOLERS WHOLESALERS: Mechanical
DRUG STORES
DRUGS & DRUG PROPRIETARIES, WHOLESALE
DRUGS & DRUG PROPRIETARIES, WHOLESALE: Medicinals/ Botanicals
DRUGS & DRUG PROPRIETARIES, WHOLESALE: Patent Medicines
DRUGS & DRUG PROPRIETARIES, WHOLESALE: Pharmaceuticals
DRUGS & DRUG PROPRIETARIES, WHOLESALE: Vitamins & Minerals
DUCTS: Sheet Metal
DYES & PIGMENTS: Organic

E

EATING PLACES
EDUCATIONAL SVCS
ELECTRIC & OTHER SERVICES COMBINED
ELECTRIC MOTOR REPAIR SVCS
ELECTRIC POWER DISTRIBUTION TO CONSUMERS
ELECTRIC POWER GENERATION: Fossil Fuel
ELECTRIC SERVICES
ELECTRIC SVCS, NEC: Power Generation
ELECTRICAL APPARATUS & EQPT WHOLESALERS
ELECTRICAL DISCHARGE MACHINING, EDM
ELECTRICAL EQPT REPAIR SVCS
ELECTRICAL EQPT: Automotive, NEC
ELECTRICAL GOODS, WHOLESALE: Boxes & Fittings
ELECTRICAL GOODS, WHOLESALE: Cable Conduit
ELECTRICAL GOODS, WHOLESALE: Electrical Appliances, Major
ELECTRICAL GOODS, WHOLESALE: Electronic Parts
ELECTRICAL GOODS, WHOLESALE: Fittings & Construction Mat
ELECTRICAL GOODS, WHOLESALE: Generators
ELECTRICAL GOODS, WHOLESALE: Household Appliances, NEC
ELECTRICAL GOODS, WHOLESALE: Light Bulbs & Related Splys
ELECTRICAL GOODS, WHOLESALE: Lighting Fittings & Access
ELECTRICAL GOODS, WHOLESALE: Modems, Computer
ELECTRICAL GOODS, WHOLESALE: Security Control Eqpt & Systems
ELECTRICAL GOODS, WHOLESALE: Switchgear
ELECTRICAL GOODS, WHOLESALE: Telephone & Telegraphic Eqpt
ELECTRICAL GOODS, WHOLESALE: Telephone Eqpt
ELECTRICAL GOODS, WHOLESALE: Wire & Cable
ELECTRICAL GOODS, WHOLESALE: Wire & Cable, Electronic
ELECTRICAL MEASURING INSTRUMENT REPAIR & CALIBRATION SVCS
ELECTRICAL SPLYS
ELECTRICAL SUPPLIES: Porcelain
ELECTRODES: Thermal & Electrolytic

ELECTROMEDICAL EQPT
ELECTROMETALLURGICAL PRDTS
ELECTRONIC EQPT REPAIR SVCS
ELECTRONIC PARTS & EQPT WHOLESALERS
ELECTRONIC SHOPPING
ELEMENTARY & SECONDARY SCHOOLS, PUBLIC
ELEMENTARY & SECONDARY SCHOOLS, SPECIAL EDUCATION
ELEVATORS & EQPT
ELEVATORS WHOLESALERS
ELEVATORS: Installation & Conversion
EMBROIDERY ADVERTISING SVCS
EMERGENCY ALARMS
EMERGENCY SHELTERS
EMPLOYMENT SVCS: Labor Contractors
ENGINEERING HELP SVCS
ENGINEERING SVCS
ENGINEERING SVCS: Acoustical
ENGINEERING SVCS: Building Construction
ENGINEERING SVCS: Chemical
ENGINEERING SVCS: Civil
ENGINEERING SVCS: Construction & Civil
ENGINEERING SVCS: Electrical Or Electronic
ENGINEERING SVCS: Machine Tool Design
ENGINEERING SVCS: Mechanical
ENGINEERING SVCS: Structural
ENGINES: Diesel & Semi-Diesel Or Duel Fuel
ENGINES: Gasoline, NEC
ENGINES: Jet Propulsion
ENGRAVING SVCS
ENVELOPES
ENVELOPES WHOLESALERS
ENZYMES
EPOXY RESINS
EQUIPMENT & VEHICLE FINANCE LEASING COMPANIES
EQUIPMENT: Rental & Leasing, NEC
EXHAUST HOOD OR FAN CLEANING SVCS

F

FABRIC STORES
FABRICS: Nonwoven
FACILITIES SUPPORT SVCS
FARM & GARDEN MACHINERY WHOLESALERS
FARM MACHINERY REPAIR SVCS
FARM MORTGAGE COMPANIES
FARM SPLYS WHOLESALERS
FARM SPLYS, WHOLESALE: Feed
FARM SPLYS, WHOLESALE: Fertilizers & Agricultural Chemicals
FARM SPLYS, WHOLESALE: Garden Splys
FASTENERS WHOLESALERS
FASTENERS: Metal
FENCING: Chain Link
FERTILIZER, AGRICULTURAL: Wholesalers
FERTILIZERS: Nitrogenous
FERTILIZERS: Phosphatic
FILTERS
FILTERS & SOFTENERS: Water, Household
FILTERS: Air
FINANCIAL SVCS
FINISHING SVCS
FIRE ALARM MAINTENANCE & MONITORING SVCS
FIRE CONTROL EQPT REPAIR SVCS, MILITARY
FIREARMS & AMMUNITION, EXC SPORTING, WHOLESALE
FIREWORKS
FIREWORKS
FISH & SEAFOOD WHOLESALERS
FITTINGS & ASSEMBLIES: Hose & Tube, Hydraulic Or Pneumatic
FITTINGS: Pipe
FITTINGS: Pipe, Fabricated
FLAT GLASS: Construction
FLOOR COVERING STORES
FLOOR COVERING STORES: Carpets
FLOOR COVERINGS WHOLESALERS
FLORIST: Flowers, Fresh
FLOWERS, FRESH, WHOLESALE
FLUID POWER PUMPS & MOTORS
FLUID POWER VALVES & HOSE FITTINGS
FOAM RUBBER
FOAMS & RUBBER, WHOLESALE
FOIL & LEAF: Metal
FOOD PRDTS, CANNED: Fruits

FOOD PRDTS, CANNED: Puddings, Exc Meat
FOOD PRDTS, CANNED: Vegetables
FOOD PRDTS, CONFECTIONERY, WHOLESALE: Candy
FOOD PRDTS, CONFECTIONERY, WHOLESALE: Pretzels
FOOD PRDTS, CONFECTIONERY, WHOLESALE: Snack Foods
FOOD PRDTS, FRUITS & VEGETABLES, FRESH, WHOLESALE: Fruits
FOOD PRDTS, POULTRY, WHOLESALE: Poultry Prdts, NEC
FOOD PRDTS, WHOLESALE: Baking Splys
FOOD PRDTS, WHOLESALE: Beverages, Exc Coffee & Tea
FOOD PRDTS, WHOLESALE: Coffee & Tea
FOOD PRDTS, WHOLESALE: Coffee, Green Or Roasted
FOOD PRDTS, WHOLESALE: Condiments
FOOD PRDTS, WHOLESALE: Cookies
FOOD PRDTS, WHOLESALE: Dog Food
FOOD PRDTS, WHOLESALE: Dried or Canned Foods
FOOD PRDTS, WHOLESALE: Grain Elevators
FOOD PRDTS, WHOLESALE: Grains
FOOD PRDTS, WHOLESALE: Juices
FOOD PRDTS, WHOLESALE: Pizza Splys
FOOD PRDTS, WHOLESALE: Salt, Edible
FOOD PRDTS, WHOLESALE: Soybeans
FOOD PRDTS, WHOLESALE: Specialty
FOOD PRDTS, WHOLESALE: Water, Distilled
FOOD PRDTS: Dried & Dehydrated Fruits, Vegetables & Soup Mix
FOOD PRDTS: Flour & Other Grain Mill Products
FOOD PRDTS: Flour, Blended From Purchased Flour
FOOD PRDTS: Pizza Doughs From Purchased Flour
FOOD PRDTS: Potato Chips & Other Potato-Based Snacks
FOOD PRDTS: Poultry, Processed, Frozen
FOOD PRDTS: Seasonings & Spices
FOOD PRDTS: Sugar
FOOD PRODUCTS MACHINERY
FOOD STORES: Convenience, Chain
FOOD STORES: Delicatessen
FOOD STORES: Grocery, Chain
FOOD STORES: Grocery, Independent
FOOD STORES: Supermarkets, Chain
FOOD STORES: Supermarkets, Independent
FOOTWEAR, WHOLESALE: Shoes
FORGINGS: Construction Or Mining Eqpt, Ferrous
FORGINGS: Iron & Steel
FORGINGS: Plumbing Fixture, Nonferrous
FOUNDRIES: Aluminum
FOUNDRIES: Nonferrous
FOUNDRIES: Steel
FOUNDRY MACHINERY & EQPT
FRAMES & FRAMING WHOLESALE
FRANCHISES, SELLING OR LICENSING
FREIGHT CAR LOADING & UNLOADING SVCS
FREIGHT FORWARDING ARRANGEMENTS
FREIGHT FORWARDING ARRANGEMENTS: Domestic
FRUIT & VEGETABLE MARKETS
FRUIT STANDS OR MARKETS
FRUITS & VEGETABLES WHOLESALERS: Fresh
FUEL DEALERS: Coal
FUEL OIL DEALERS
FUND RAISING ORGANIZATION, NON-FEE BASIS
FUNGICIDES OR HERBICIDES
FURNACES & OVENS: Indl
FURNACES: Indl, Electric
FURNACES: Indl, Electric
FURNACES: Warm Air, Electric
FURNITURE REFINISHING SVCS
FURNITURE REPAIR & MAINTENANCE SVCS
FURNITURE STORES
FURNITURE WHOLESALERS
FURNITURE, HOUSEHOLD: Wholesalers
FURNITURE, OFFICE: Wholesalers
FURNITURE, WHOLESALE: Chairs
FURNITURE, WHOLESALE: Racks
FURNITURE, WHOLESALE: Shelving
FURNITURE: Cabinets & Filing Drawers, Office, Exc Wood
FURNITURE: Chairs, Household Wood
FURNITURE: Mattresses & Foundations
FURNITURE: Office, Exc Wood
FURNITURE: Play Pens, Children's, Wood
FURNITURE: Restaurant
FURNITURE: Upholstered

G

SERVICES INDEX

GAS & OIL FIELD EXPLORATION SVCS
GAS FIELD MACHINERY & EQPT
GASES: Acetylene
GASES: Indl
GASKETS
GASOLINE FILLING STATIONS
GASOLINE WHOLESALERS
GEARS: Power Transmission, Exc Auto
GENERAL & INDUSTRIAL LOAN INSTITUTIONS
GENERAL COUNSELING SVCS
GENERATOR REPAIR SVCS
GIFT SHOP
GIFTS & NOVELTIES: Wholesalers
GLASS PRDTS, FROM PURCHASED GLASS: Glassware
GLASS PRDTS, FROM PURCHASED GLASS: Windshields
GLASS PRDTS, PRESSED OR BLOWN: Glass Fibers, Textile
GLASS PRDTS, PRESSED OR BLOWN: Yarn, Fiberglass
GLASS: Fiber
GLASS: Tempered
GLOVES: Work
GOLF CARTS: Wholesalers
GOLF COURSES: Public
GOLF EQPT
GOLF GOODS & EQPT
GOURMET FOOD STORES
GOVERNMENT, GENERAL: Administration
GRADING SVCS
GRANITE: Crushed & Broken
GRANITE: Cut & Shaped
GRAPHIC ARTS & RELATED DESIGN SVCS
GRAPHITE MINING SVCS
GRAVEL MINING
GREENHOUSES: Prefabricated Metal
GREETING CARDS WHOLESALERS
GRINDING SVC: Precision, Commercial Or Indl
GROCERIES, GENERAL LINE WHOLESALERS
GUARD PROTECTIVE SVCS
GUARD SVCS

H

HAND TOOLS, NEC: Wholesalers
HARDWARE
HARDWARE & BUILDING PRDTS: Plastic
HARDWARE & EQPT: Stage, Exc Lighting
HARDWARE STORES
HARDWARE STORES: Pumps & Pumping Eqpt
HARDWARE STORES: Tools
HARDWARE STORES: Tools, Hand
HARDWARE WHOLESALERS
HARDWARE, WHOLESALE: Bolts
HARDWARE, WHOLESALE: Builders', NEC
HARDWARE, WHOLESALE: Casters & Glides
HARDWARE, WHOLESALE: Nuts
HARDWARE, WHOLESALE: Power Tools & Access
HARNESS ASSEMBLIES: Cable & Wire
HEALTH & WELFARE COUNCIL
HEALTH INSURANCE CARRIERS
HEAT TREATING: Metal
HELP SUPPLY SERVICES
HIGHWAY & STREET MAINTENANCE SVCS
HOBBY, TOY & GAME STORES: Arts & Crafts & Splys
HOLDING COMPANIES: Investment, Exc Banks
HOLDING COMPANIES: Personal, Exc Banks
HOME FOR THE MENTALLY HANDICAPPED
HOME FOR THE MENTALLY RETARDED
HOME HEALTH CARE SVCS
HOMEFURNISHING STORES: Fireplaces & Wood Burning Stoves
HOMEFURNISHING STORES: Lighting Fixtures
HOMEFURNISHINGS, WHOLESALE: Carpets
HOMEFURNISHINGS, WHOLESALE: Draperies
HOMEFURNISHINGS, WHOLESALE: Kitchenware
HOMEFURNISHINGS, WHOLESALE: Wood Flooring
HOSE: Automobile, Rubber
HOSPITALS: Medical & Surgical
HOSPITALS: Specialty, NEC
HOTELS & MOTELS
HOUSEHOLD APPLIANCE STORES: Appliance Parts
HOUSEHOLD APPLIANCE STORES: Gas Appliances
HOUSEHOLD FURNISHINGS, NEC
HOUSEWARES, ELECTRIC: Cooking Appliances
HYDRAULIC EQPT REPAIR SVC

I

ICE
ICE CREAM & ICES WHOLESALERS
INCINERATORS
INCUBATORS & BROODERS: Farm
INDL & PERSONAL SVC PAPER WHOLESALERS
INDL & PERSONAL SVC PAPER, WHOLESALE: Shipping Splys
INDL CONTRACTORS: Exhibit Construction
INDL DIAMONDS WHOLESALERS
INDL EQPT SVCS
INDL MACHINERY & EQPT WHOLESALERS
INDL SPLYS WHOLESALERS
INDL SPLYS, WHOLESALE: Abrasives
INDL SPLYS, WHOLESALE: Adhesives, Tape & Plasters
INDL SPLYS, WHOLESALE: Bearings
INDL SPLYS, WHOLESALE: Bins & Containers, Storage
INDL SPLYS, WHOLESALE: Fasteners & Fastening Eqpt
INDL SPLYS, WHOLESALE: Gaskets
INDL SPLYS, WHOLESALE: Gaskets & Seals
INDL SPLYS, WHOLESALE: Glass Bottles
INDL SPLYS, WHOLESALE: Mill Splys
INDL SPLYS, WHOLESALE: Power Transmission, Eqpt & Apparatus
INDL SPLYS, WHOLESALE: Rubber Goods, Mechanical
INDL SPLYS, WHOLESALE: Seals
INDL SPLYS, WHOLESALE: Tools
INDL SPLYS, WHOLESALE: Valves & Fittings
INDL TRUCK REPAIR SVCS
INDUSTRIAL & COMMERCIAL EQPT INSPECTION SVCS
INFORMATION RETRIEVAL SERVICES
INFORMATION SVCS: Consumer
INSECTICIDES
INSECTICIDES & PESTICIDES
INSPECTION & TESTING SVCS
INSTRUMENTS, MEASURING & CONTROLLING: Cable Testing
INSTRUMENTS: Analytical
INSTRUMENTS: Measurement, Indl Process
INSTRUMENTS: Measuring & Controlling
INSTRUMENTS: Measuring, Electrical Energy
INSTRUMENTS: Medical & Surgical
INSTRUMENTS: Radio Frequency Measuring
INSTRUMENTS: Signal Generators & Averagers
INSTRUMENTS: Test, Electrical, Engine
INSTRUMENTS: Test, Electronic & Electric Measurement
INSULATION MATERIALS WHOLESALERS
INSULATION: Fiberglass
INSULATORS & INSULATION MATERIALS: Electrical
INSURANCE AGENTS, NEC
INSURANCE BROKERS, NEC
INSURANCE CARRIERS: Automobile
INSURANCE CARRIERS: Life
INSURANCE CARRIERS: Property & Casualty
INSURANCE CARRIERS: Title
INSURANCE CLAIM PROCESSING, EXC MEDICAL
INSURANCE INFORMATION & CONSULTING SVCS
INSURANCE: Agents, Brokers & Service
INTEGRATED CIRCUITS, SEMICONDUCTOR NETWORKS, ETC
INTERIOR DECORATING SVCS
INTERIOR DESIGN SVCS, NEC
INVENTORY COMPUTING SVCS
INVESTMENT ADVISORY SVCS
INVESTMENT FIRM: General Brokerage
INVESTMENT OFFICES: Management, Closed-End
INVESTMENT RESEARCH SVCS
INVESTORS, NEC
INVESTORS: Real Estate, Exc Property Operators
IRON & STEEL PRDTS: Hot-Rolled
IRON ORE MINING
IRON ORES

J

JEWELRY REPAIR SVCS
JEWELRY STORES
JEWELRY, WHOLESALE
JEWELRY: Precious Metal
JIGS & FIXTURES
JOB TRAINING SVCS

K

KEY DUPLICATING SHOP

KIDNEY DIALYSIS CENTERS
KITCHEN CABINETS WHOLESALERS
KITCHENWARE STORES
KNIVES: Agricultural Or indl

L

LABELS: Paper, Made From Purchased Materials
LABELS: Woven
LABORATORIES, TESTING: Automobile Proving & Testing Ground
LABORATORIES, TESTING: Food
LABORATORIES, TESTING: Forensic
LABORATORIES, TESTING: Metallurgical
LABORATORIES, TESTING: Product Testing
LABORATORIES, TESTING: Product Testing, Safety/Performance
LABORATORIES, TESTING: Radiation
LABORATORIES: Biological Research
LABORATORIES: Biotechnology
LABORATORIES: Commercial Nonphysical Research
LABORATORIES: Dental, Crown & Bridge Production
LABORATORIES: Electronic Research
LABORATORIES: Medical
LABORATORIES: Noncommercial Research
LABORATORIES: Physical Research, Commercial
LABORATORIES: Testing
LABORATORIES: Testing
LABORATORY APPARATUS & FURNITURE
LABORATORY APPARATUS: Pipettes, Hemocytometer
LABORATORY EQPT, EXC MEDICAL: Wholesalers
LABORATORY EQPT: Clinical Instruments Exc Medical
LABORATORY EQPT: Incubators
LABORATORY INSTRUMENT REPAIR SVCS
LADDERS: Metal
LAMINATED PLASTICS: Plate, Sheet, Rod & Tubes
LAMINATING SVCS
LAMP SHADES: Glass
LAND SUBDIVIDERS & DEVELOPERS: Commercial
LAND SUBDIVIDERS & DEVELOPERS: Residential
LAND SUBDIVISION & DEVELOPMENT
LAUNDRY SVC: Work Clothing Sply
LAUNDRY SVCS: Indl
LAWN & GARDEN EQPT
LEASING & RENTAL SVCS: Cranes & Aerial Lift Eqpt
LEASING & RENTAL SVCS: Oil Field Eqpt
LEASING & RENTAL: Construction & Mining Eqpt
LEASING & RENTAL: Medical Machinery & Eqpt
LEASING & RENTAL: Trucks, Indl
LEASING & RENTAL: Trucks, Without Drivers
LEASING & RENTAL: Utility Trailers & RV's
LEASING: Passenger Car
LEATHER & CUT STOCK WHOLESALERS
LEATHER GOODS, EXC FOOTWEAR, GLOVES, LUGGAGE/ BELTING, WHOL
LEATHER GOODS: Personal
LEGAL AID SVCS
LEGAL OFFICES & SVCS
LEGAL SVCS: General Practice Attorney or Lawyer
LIFE INSURANCE CARRIERS
LIGHTING FIXTURES WHOLESALERS
LIGHTING FIXTURES, NEC
LIGHTING FIXTURES: Airport
LIGHTING FIXTURES: Indl & Commercial
LIGHTING FIXTURES: Motor Vehicle
LIME
LIME ROCK: Ground
LIMESTONE: Crushed & Broken
LIMESTONE: Dimension
LIMESTONE: Ground
LINEN SPLY SVC: Uniform
LINENS & TOWELS WHOLESALERS
LIQUEFIED PETROLEUM GAS DEALERS
LIQUEFIED PETROLEUM GAS WHOLESALERS
LIVESTOCK WHOLESALERS, NEC
LOADS: Electronic
LOCKSMITHS
LOTIONS OR CREAMS: Face
LUBRICATING OIL & GREASE WHOLESALERS
LUGGAGE & BRIEFCASES
LUMBER & BLDG MATLS DEALER, RET: Garage Doors, Sell/Install
LUMBER & BLDG MATLS DEALERS, RET: Energy Conservation Prdts

SERVICES INDEX

LUMBER & BLDG MATRLS DEALERS, RETAIL: Doors, Wood/Metal
LUMBER & BLDG MTRLS DEALERS, RET: Planing Mill Prdts/Lumber
LUMBER & BUILDING MATERIALS DEALER, RET: Door & Window Prdts
LUMBER & BUILDING MATERIALS DEALER, RET: Masonry Matls/Splys
LUMBER & BUILDING MATERIALS DEALERS, RETAIL: Brick
LUMBER & BUILDING MATERIALS DEALERS, RETAIL: Cement
LUMBER & BUILDING MATERIALS DEALERS, RETAIL: Siding
LUMBER & BUILDING MATERIALS RET DEALERS: Millwork & Lumber
LUMBER & BUILDING MATLS DEALERS, RET: Concrete/Cinder Block
LUMBER: Dimension, Hardwood
LUMBER: Hardwood Dimension & Flooring Mills
LUMBER: Plywood, Hardwood
LUMBER: Treated

M

MACHINE PARTS: Stamped Or Pressed Metal
MACHINE TOOL ACCESS: Drill Bushings, Drilling Jig
MACHINE TOOL ACCESS: Tools & Access
MACHINE TOOLS & ACCESS
MACHINE TOOLS, METAL CUTTING: Home Workshop
MACHINE TOOLS, METAL CUTTING: Tool Replacement & Rpr Parts
MACHINE TOOLS, METAL FORMING: Bending
MACHINE TOOLS, METAL FORMING: Marking
MACHINE TOOLS, METAL FORMING: Mechanical, Pneumatic Or Hyd
MACHINE TOOLS: Metal Cutting
MACHINE TOOLS: Metal Forming
MACHINERY & EQPT FINANCE LEASING
MACHINERY & EQPT, AGRICULTURAL, WHOLESALE: Agricultural, NEC
MACHINERY & EQPT, AGRICULTURAL, WHOLESALE: Landscaping Eqpt
MACHINERY & EQPT, AGRICULTURAL, WHOLESALE: Lawn
MACHINERY & EQPT, AGRICULTURAL, WHOLESALE: Lawn & Garden
MACHINERY & EQPT, INDL, WHOLESALE: Chemical Process
MACHINERY & EQPT, INDL, WHOLESALE: Conveyor Systems
MACHINERY & EQPT, INDL, WHOLESALE: Cranes
MACHINERY & EQPT, INDL, WHOLESALE: Engines & Parts, Diesel
MACHINERY & EQPT, INDL, WHOLESALE: Engs & Parts, Air-Cooled
MACHINERY & EQPT, INDL, WHOLESALE: Food Product Manufacturng
MACHINERY & EQPT, INDL, WHOLESALE: Hydraulic Systems
MACHINERY & EQPT, INDL, WHOLESALE: Indl Machine Parts
MACHINERY & EQPT, INDL, WHOLESALE: Instruments & Cntrl Eqpt
MACHINERY & EQPT, INDL, WHOLESALE: Lift Trucks & Parts
MACHINERY & EQPT, INDL, WHOLESALE: Machine Tools & Access
MACHINERY & EQPT, INDL, WHOLESALE: Measure/Test, Electric
MACHINERY & EQPT, INDL, WHOLESALE: Packaging
MACHINERY & EQPT, INDL, WHOLESALE: Petroleum Industry
MACHINERY & EQPT, INDL, WHOLESALE: Processing & Packaging
MACHINERY & EQPT, INDL, WHOLESALE: Recycling
MACHINERY & EQPT, INDL, WHOLESALE: Safety Eqpt
MACHINERY & EQPT, INDL, WHOLESALE: Tanks, Storage
MACHINERY & EQPT, WHOLESALE: Construction, General
MACHINERY & EQPT, WHOLESALE: Oil Field Eqpt
MACHINERY & EQPT: Electroplating
MACHINERY & EQPT: Farm
MACHINERY, FOOD PRDTS: Food Processing, Smokers
MACHINERY, SEWING: Sewing & Hat & Zipper Making
MACHINERY: Automotive Related
MACHINERY: Construction
MACHINERY: Custom
MACHINERY: Metalworking
MACHINERY: Mining
MACHINERY: Packaging
MACHINERY: Plastic Working
MACHINERY: Printing Presses
MACHINERY: Road Construction & Maintenance
MACHINERY: Rubber Working
MACHINERY: Textile
MAGAZINES, WHOLESALE
MAGNETS: Permanent
MAIL-ORDER HOUSE, NEC
MAIL-ORDER HOUSES: Computer Software
MAIL-ORDER HOUSES: Educational Splys & Eqpt
MAIL-ORDER HOUSES: Food
MAILBOX RENTAL & RELATED SVCS
MAILING & MESSENGER SVCS
MAILING SVCS, NEC
MANAGEMENT CONSULTING SVCS: Administrative
MANAGEMENT CONSULTING SVCS: Automation & Robotics
MANAGEMENT CONSULTING SVCS: Business
MANAGEMENT CONSULTING SVCS: Business Planning & Organizing
MANAGEMENT CONSULTING SVCS: Construction Project
MANAGEMENT CONSULTING SVCS: Corporation Organizing
MANAGEMENT CONSULTING SVCS: Distribution Channels
MANAGEMENT CONSULTING SVCS: Food & Beverage
MANAGEMENT CONSULTING SVCS: General
MANAGEMENT CONSULTING SVCS: Hospital & Health
MANAGEMENT CONSULTING SVCS: Industrial
MANAGEMENT CONSULTING SVCS: Industrial & Labor
MANAGEMENT CONSULTING SVCS: Industry Specialist
MANAGEMENT CONSULTING SVCS: Information Systems
MANAGEMENT CONSULTING SVCS: Manufacturing
MANAGEMENT CONSULTING SVCS: Quality Assurance
MANAGEMENT CONSULTING SVCS: Real Estate
MANAGEMENT CONSULTING SVCS: Training & Development
MANAGEMENT CONSULTING SVCS: Transportation
MANAGEMENT SERVICES
MANAGEMENT SVCS: Administrative
MANAGEMENT SVCS: Business
MANAGEMENT SVCS: Construction
MANAGEMENT SVCS: Hotel Or Motel
MANAGEMENT SVCS: Nursing & Personal Care Facility
MANAGEMENT SVCS: Restaurant
MANPOWER POOLS
MANPOWER TRAINING
MARINAS
MARINE CARGO HANDLING SVCS
MARINE CARGO HANDLING SVCS: Marine Terminal
MARINE SPLYS WHOLESALERS
MARKETS: Meat & fish
MARKING DEVICES: Embossing Seals & Hand Stamps
MATS OR MATTING, NEC: Rubber
MATS, MATTING & PADS: Nonwoven
MEAT MARKETS
MEAT PRDTS: Cooked Meats, From Purchased Meat
MEAT PRDTS: Frozen
MEAT PRDTS: Prepared Beef Prdts From Purchased Beef
MEDICAL & HOSPITAL EQPT WHOLESALERS
MEDICAL & SURGICAL SPLYS: Bandages & Dressings
MEDICAL & SURGICAL SPLYS: Clothing, Fire Resistant & Protect
MEDICAL & SURGICAL SPLYS: Foot Appliances, Orthopedic
MEDICAL & SURGICAL SPLYS: Prosthetic Appliances
MEDICAL & SURGICAL SPLYS: Splints, Pneumatic & Wood
MEDICAL CENTERS
MEDICAL EQPT REPAIR SVCS, NON-ELECTRIC
MEDICAL HELP SVCS
MEDICAL INSURANCE CLAIM PROCESSING: Contract Or Fee Basis
MEDICAL SVCS ORGANIZATION
MEDICAL, DENTAL & HOSP EQPT, WHOLESALE: X-ray Film & Splys
MEDICAL, DENTAL & HOSPITAL EQPT, WHOL: Hospital Eqpt & Splys
MEDICAL, DENTAL & HOSPITAL EQPT, WHOL: Surgical Eqpt & Splys
MEDICAL, DENTAL & HOSPITAL EQPT, WHOLESALE: Artificial Limbs
MEMBERSHIP ORGANIZATIONS, BUSINESS: Contractors' Association
MEMBERSHIP ORGANIZATIONS, NEC: Charitable
MEMBERSHIP ORGANIZATIONS, NEC: Personal Interest
MEMBERSHIP ORGANIZATIONS, PROFESSIONAL: Accounting Assoc
MEMBERSHIP ORGANIZATIONS, PROFESSIONAL: Health Association
MEMBERSHIP ORGANIZATIONS, REL: Churches, Temples & Shrines
MEMBERSHIP ORGANIZATIONS, RELIGIOUS: Catholic Church
MEMBERSHIP ORGANIZATIONS, RELIGIOUS: Lutheran Church
MEMBERSHIP ORGANIZATIONS, RELIGIOUS: Methodist Church
MEMBERSHIP ORGS, RELIGIOUS: Non-Denominational Church
MEMBERSHIP SPORTS & RECREATION CLUBS
MEN'S & BOYS' CLOTHING STORES
MEN'S & BOYS' CLOTHING WHOLESALERS, NEC
MERCHANDISING MACHINE OPERATORS: Vending
METAL & STEEL PRDTS: Abrasive
METAL COMPONENTS: Prefabricated
METAL FABRICATORS: Plate
METAL MINING SVCS
METAL SERVICE CENTERS & OFFICES
METAL STAMPING, FOR THE TRADE
METALS SVC CENTERS & WHOLESALERS: Cable, Wire
METALS SVC CENTERS & WHOLESALERS: Flat Prdts, Iron Or Steel
METALS SVC CENTERS & WHOLESALERS: Foundry Prdts
METALS SVC CENTERS & WHOLESALERS: Pipe & Tubing, Steel
METALS SVC CENTERS & WHOLESALERS: Steel
METALS SVC CENTERS & WHOLESALERS: Tubing, Metal
METALS: Primary Nonferrous, NEC
METALWORK: Miscellaneous
METALWORK: Ornamental
METALWORKING MACHINERY WHOLESALERS
MILITARY INSIGNIA
MILK, FLUID: Wholesalers
MILLWORK
MINE & QUARRY SVCS: Nonmetallic Minerals
MINERAL WOOL
MINERALS: Ground or Treated
MIXTURES & BLOCKS: Asphalt Paving
MOLDED RUBBER PRDTS
MOLDING COMPOUNDS
MOLDINGS OR TRIM: Automobile, Stamped Metal
MOLDS: Indl
MOPS: Floor & Dust
MORTGAGE BANKERS
MOTION PICTURE & VIDEO DISTRIBUTION
MOTION PICTURE & VIDEO PRODUCTION SVCS: Commercials, TV
MOTION PICTURE & VIDEO PRODUCTION SVCS: Educational
MOTION PICTURE PRODUCTION & DISTRIBUTION
MOTION PICTURE PRODUCTION ALLIED SVCS
MOTOR SCOOTERS & PARTS
MOTOR VEHICLE ASSEMBLY, COMPLETE: Fire Department Vehicles
MOTOR VEHICLE DEALERS: Automobiles, New & Used
MOTOR VEHICLE PARTS & ACCESS: Body Components & Frames
MOTOR VEHICLE PARTS & ACCESS: Clutches
MOTOR VEHICLE PARTS & ACCESS: Engines & Parts
MOTOR VEHICLE PARTS & ACCESS: Fuel Systems & Parts
MOTOR VEHICLE PARTS & ACCESS: Mufflers, Exhaust
MOTOR VEHICLE PARTS & ACCESS: Power Steering Eqpt
MOTOR VEHICLE PARTS & ACCESS: Sanders, Safety
MOTOR VEHICLE RACING & DRIVER SVCS
MOTOR VEHICLE SPLYS & PARTS WHOLESALERS: New
MOTOR VEHICLE SPLYS & PARTS WHOLESALERS: Used
MOTOR VEHICLE: Shock Absorbers
MOTOR VEHICLES & CAR BODIES
MOTOR VEHICLES, WHOLESALE: Truck tractors
MOTOR VEHICLES, WHOLESALE: Trucks, commercial
MOTORCYCLE DEALERS
MOTORCYCLE DEALERS: All-Terrain Vehicle Parts & Access
MOTORCYCLE PARTS: Wholesalers
MOTORS: Electric

SERVICES INDEX

MOTORS: Generators
MULTIPLEXERS: Telephone & Telegraph
MUSEUMS & ART GALLERIES
MUSICAL INSTRUMENTS & ACCESS: NEC
MUSICAL INSTRUMENTS WHOLESALERS

N

NATURAL GAS DISTRIBUTION TO CONSUMERS
NATURAL GAS LIQUIDS PRODUCTION
NATURAL GAS PRODUCTION
NATURAL GAS TRANSMISSION
NATURAL GAS TRANSMISSION & DISTRIBUTION
NATURAL GASOLINE PRODUCTION
NAVIGATIONAL SYSTEMS & INSTRUMENTS
NEIGHBORHOOD DEVELOPMENT GROUP
NETS: Launderers & Dyers
NEW & USED CAR DEALERS
NONCURRENT CARRYING WIRING DEVICES
NOVELTIES, PAPER, WHOLESALE
NURSERIES & LAWN & GARDEN SPLY STORES, RETAIL: Fertilizer
NURSERY STOCK, WHOLESALE
NURSING CARE FACILITIES: Skilled
NUTRITION SVCS
NUTS: Metal

O

OFFICE EQPT WHOLESALERS
OFFICE EQPT, WHOLESALE: Photocopy Machines
OFFICE FURNITURE REPAIR & MAINTENANCE SVCS
OFFICE SPLY & STATIONERY STORES: Office Forms & Splys
OFFICE SPLYS, NEC, WHOLESALE
OFFICES & CLINICS OF DOCTORS OF MEDICINE: Radiologist
OFFICES & CLINICS OF DRS OF MEDICINE: Physician, Orthopedic
OFFICES & CLINICS OF OPTOMETRISTS: Specialist, Contact Lens
OIL & GAS FIELD EQPT: Drill Rigs
OIL FIELD MACHINERY & EQPT
OIL FIELD SVCS, NEC
OILS: Mineral, Natural
OLEFINS
OPHTHALMIC GOODS
OPHTHALMIC GOODS WHOLESALERS
OPHTHALMIC GOODS: Lenses, Ophthalmic
OPTICAL GOODS STORES
OPTICAL GOODS STORES: Contact Lenses, Prescription
OPTICAL INSTRUMENTS & LENSES
ORGANIZATIONS: Civic & Social
ORGANIZATIONS: Educational Research Agency
ORGANIZATIONS: Medical Research
ORGANIZATIONS: Noncommercial Social Research
ORGANIZATIONS: Physical Research, Noncommercial
ORGANIZATIONS: Professional
ORGANIZATIONS: Religious
ORGANIZATIONS: Research Institute

P

PACKAGE DESIGN SVCS
PACKAGING & LABELING SVCS
PACKAGING MATERIALS, WHOLESALE
PACKAGING MATERIALS: Paper
PACKAGING MATERIALS: Plastic Film, Coated Or Laminated
PACKING & CRATING SVC
PAINTS & ADDITIVES
PAINTS & ALLIED PRODUCTS
PAINTS, VARNISHES & SPLYS WHOLESALERS
PAINTS, VARNISHES & SPLYS, WHOLESALE: Paints
PALLET REPAIR SVCS
PALLETIZERS & DEPALLETIZERS
PALLETS & SKIDS: Wood
PALLETS: Plastic
PAPER & BOARD: Die-cut
PAPER PRDTS: Sanitary
PAPER, WHOLESALE: Fine
PAPER, WHOLESALE: Printing
PAPER: Adhesive
PAPER: Cloth, Lined, Made From Purchased Materials
PAPER: Wrapping & Packaging
PARTITIONS & FIXTURES: Except Wood
PARTITIONS: Wood & Fixtures

PARTS: Metal
PATENT OWNERS & LESSORS
PATIENT MONITORING EQPT WHOLESALERS
PATTERNS: Indl
PAYROLL SVCS
PENSION FUNDS
PERSONAL CARE FACILITY
PERSONAL CREDIT INSTITUTIONS: Consumer Finance Companies
PERSONAL DOCUMENT & INFORMATION SVCS
PERSONAL SVCS
PEST CONTROL IN STRUCTURES SVCS
PEST CONTROL SVCS
PET FOOD WHOLESALERS
PET SPLYS
PETROLEUM & PETROLEUM PRDTS, WHOLESALE: Bulk Stations
PETROLEUM BULK STATIONS & TERMINALS
PHARMACEUTICALS
PHARMACEUTICALS: Mail-Order Svc
PHOSPHATES
PHOTOCOPYING & DUPLICATING SVCS
PHOTOGRAPHIC EQPT & SPLYS WHOLESALERS
PHOTOGRAPHY SVCS: Commercial
PHYSICAL EXAMINATION & TESTING SVCS
PHYSICIANS' OFFICES & CLINICS: Medical doctors
PICTURE FRAMING SVCS, CUSTOM
PIECE GOODS, NOTIONS & DRY GOODS, WHOL: Textiles, Woven
PIECE GOODS, NOTIONS & OTHER DRY GOODS, WHOLESALE: Fabrics
PILOT SVCS: Aviation
PIPE & FITTINGS: Cast Iron
PIPE FITTINGS: Plastic
PIPE SECTIONS, FABRICATED FROM PURCHASED PIPE
PIPELINE & POWER LINE INSPECTION SVCS
PIPELINE TERMINAL FACILITIES: Independent
PIPELINES, EXC NATURAL GAS: Gasoline, Common Carriers
PIPELINES: Crude Petroleum
PIPELINES: Refined Petroleum
PIPES & TUBES: Steel
PIPES: Steel & Iron
PLASTICS FILM & SHEET
PLASTICS FILM & SHEET: Vinyl
PLASTICS MATERIAL & RESINS
PLASTICS MATERIALS, BASIC FORMS & SHAPES WHOLESALERS
PLASTICS PROCESSING
PLASTICS: Molded
PLASTICS: Polystyrene Foam
PLASTICS: Thermoformed
PLATING & POLISHING SVC
PLEATING & STITCHING SVC
PLUMBING FIXTURES
PLUMBING FIXTURES: Plastic
PLUMBING FIXTURES: Vitreous
POLYSTYRENE RESINS
POULTRY & POULTRY PRDTS WHOLESALERS
POULTRY & SMALL GAME SLAUGHTERING & PROCESSING
POWDER: Metal
POWER SUPPLIES: All Types, Static
PRECIPITATORS: Electrostatic
PRINTED CIRCUIT BOARDS
PRINTERS' SVCS: Folding, Collating, Etc
PRINTING MACHINERY
PRINTING, COMMERCIAL: Labels & Seals, NEC
PRINTING, COMMERCIAL: Literature, Advertising, NEC
PRINTING, COMMERCIAL: Periodicals, NEC
PRINTING, COMMERCIAL: Promotional
PRINTING, COMMERCIAL: Screen
PRINTING, LITHOGRAPHIC: Calendars
PRINTING, LITHOGRAPHIC: Forms, Business
PRINTING: Books
PRINTING: Commercial, NEC
PRINTING: Flexographic
PRINTING: Gravure, Forms, Business
PRINTING: Gravure, Rotogravure
PRINTING: Letterpress
PRINTING: Lithographic
PRINTING: Offset
PRINTING: Photolithographic

PROFESSIONAL EQPT & SPLYS, WHOLESALE: Analytical Instruments
PROFESSIONAL EQPT & SPLYS, WHOLESALE: Engineers', NEC
PROFESSIONAL EQPT & SPLYS, WHOLESALE: Optical Goods
PROFESSIONAL INSTRUMENT REPAIR SVCS
PROFESSIONAL SCHOOLS
PROFILE SHAPES: Unsupported Plastics
PROMOTION SVCS
PROPERTY DAMAGE INSURANCE
PUBLIC LIBRARY
PUBLIC RELATIONS & PUBLICITY SVCS
PUBLIC RELATIONS SVCS
PUBLISHERS: Music, Sheet
PUBLISHERS: Telephone & Other Directory
PUBLISHING & BROADCASTING: Internet Only
PUBLISHING & PRINTING: Books
PUBLISHING & PRINTING: Magazines: publishing & printing
PUBLISHING & PRINTING: Newsletters, Business Svc
PUBLISHING & PRINTING: Newspapers
PULP MILLS
PUMPS & PUMPING EQPT REPAIR SVCS
PUMPS & PUMPING EQPT WHOLESALERS
PUMPS: Domestic, Water Or Sump
PUMPS: Measuring & Dispensing
PURCHASING SVCS
PURIFICATION & DUST COLLECTION EQPT

R

RADIO BROADCASTING & COMMUNICATIONS EQPT
RADIO BROADCASTING STATIONS
RADIO COMMUNICATIONS: Airborne Eqpt
RADIO COMMUNICATIONS: Carrier Eqpt
RADIO REPAIR & INSTALLATION SVCS
RAILROAD CAR REPAIR SVCS
RAILROAD EQPT
RAILROAD EQPT & SPLYS WHOLESALERS
RAILROAD MAINTENANCE & REPAIR SVCS
REAL ESTATE AGENCIES & BROKERS
REAL ESTATE AGENCIES: Rental
REAL ESTATE AGENTS & MANAGERS
REAL ESTATE ESCROW AGENCIES
REAL ESTATE INVESTMENT TRUSTS
RECREATIONAL VEHICLE DEALERS
REFINING: Petroleum
REFRACTORY MATERIALS WHOLESALERS
REFRIGERATION EQPT & SPLYS WHOLESALERS
REFRIGERATION REPAIR SVCS
REFRIGERATION SVC & REPAIR
REFUSE SYSTEMS
REGULATORS: Power
REHABILITATION CENTER, OUTPATIENT TREATMENT
REHABILITATION CTR, RESIDENTIAL WITH HEALTH CARE INCIDENTAL
REHABILITATION SVCS
REINSURANCE CARRIERS: Accident & Health
RELOCATION SVCS
RENTAL SVCS: Aircraft
RENTAL SVCS: Audio-Visual Eqpt & Sply
RENTAL SVCS: Business Machine & Electronic Eqpt
RENTAL SVCS: Costume
RENTAL SVCS: Electronic Eqpt, Exc Computers
RENTAL SVCS: Live Plant
RENTAL SVCS: Vending Machine
RENTAL SVCS: Video Disk/Tape, To The General Public
RENTAL SVCS: Work Zone Traffic Eqpt, Flags, Cones, Etc
RENTAL: Portable Toilet
RENTAL: Video Tape & Disc
RESEARCH & DEVELOPMENT SVCS, COMMERCIAL: Engineering Lab
RESEARCH, DEVELOPMENT & TESTING SVCS, COMM: Agricultural
RESEARCH, DEVELOPMENT & TESTING SVCS, COMMERCIAL: Medical
RESEARCH, DEVELOPMENT & TESTING SVCS, COMMERCIAL: Physical
RESIDENTIAL CARE FOR THE HANDICAPPED
RESINS: Custom Compound Purchased
RESTAURANTS: Fast Food
RESTAURANTS:Full Svc, American
RETAIL BAKERY: Bagels
RETAIL BAKERY: Bread

SVCS INDEX

SERVICES INDEX

RETAIL BAKERY: Pretzels
RETAIL STORES: Audio-Visual Eqpt & Splys
RETAIL STORES: Business Machines & Eqpt
RETAIL STORES: Cleaning Eqpt & Splys
RETAIL STORES: Communication Eqpt
RETAIL STORES: Cosmetics
RETAIL STORES: Educational Aids & Electronic Training Mat
RETAIL STORES: Electronic Parts & Eqpt
RETAIL STORES: Hearing Aids
RETAIL STORES: Medical Apparatus & Splys
RETAIL STORES: Orthopedic & Prosthesis Applications
RETAIL STORES: Pet Food
RETAIL STORES: Pet Splys
RETAIL STORES: Religious Goods
RETAIL STORES: Safety Splys & Eqpt
RETAIL STORES: Swimming Pools, Above Ground
RETAIL STORES: Telephone & Communication Eqpt
RETAIL STORES: Water Purification Eqpt
RETAIL STORES: Welding Splys
ROBOTS: Assembly Line
RODS: Steel & Iron, Made In Steel Mills
ROLLING MILL MACHINERY
ROOFING MATERIALS: Asphalt
RUBBER PRDTS: Silicone

S

SAFETY EQPT & SPLYS WHOLESALERS
SAFETY INSPECTION SVCS
SALES PROMOTION SVCS
SAND & GRAVEL
SAND MINING
SANITARY SVC, NEC
SANITARY SVCS: Hazardous Waste, Collection & Disposal
SANITARY SVCS: Oil Spill Cleanup
SANITARY SVCS: Refuse Collection & Disposal Svcs
SANITARY SVCS: Toxic Or Hazardous Waste Cleanup
SANITARY SVCS: Waste Materials, Recycling
SATELLITES: Communications
SCAFFOLDS: Mobile Or Stationary, Metal
SCALE REPAIR SVCS
SCALES: Indl
SCHOOLS: Vocational, NEC
SCRAP & WASTE MATERIALS, WHOLESALE: Ferrous Metal
SCRAP & WASTE MATERIALS, WHOLESALE: Metal
SCRAP & WASTE MATERIALS, WHOLESALE: Nonferrous Metals Scrap
SCRAP & WASTE MATERIALS, WHOLESALE: Paper
SCRAP STEEL CUTTING
SCREW MACHINE PRDTS
SEALANTS
SEALING COMPOUNDS: Sealing, synthetic rubber or plastic
SEALS: Hermetic
SEARCH & NAVIGATION SYSTEMS
SECURE STORAGE SVC: Household & Furniture
SECURITY GUARD SVCS
SECURITY SYSTEMS SERVICES
SELF-PROPELLED AIRCRAFT DEALER
SEMICONDUCTOR CIRCUIT NETWORKS
SEMICONDUCTORS & RELATED DEVICES
SEPTIC TANK CLEANING SVCS
SEPTIC TANKS: Concrete
SERVICE STATION EQPT REPAIR SVCS
SEWAGE & WATER TREATMENT EQPT
SHAPES & PILINGS, STRUCTURAL: Steel
SHEET METAL SPECIALTIES, EXC STAMPED
SHIMS: Metal
SHOE STORES
SHOE STORES: Men's
SHOES: Men's
SHOES: Plastic Or Rubber
SHOES: Women's
SHOPPING CART REPAIR SVCS
SIDING: Plastic
SIGN PAINTING & LETTERING SHOP
SIGNALS: Traffic Control, Electric
SIGNS & ADVERTISING SPECIALTIES
SIGNS, EXC ELECTRIC, WHOLESALE
SIGNS: Electrical
SILICA MINING
SILICONES
SILK SCREEN DESIGN SVCS
SKILL TRAINING CENTER
SLIPPERS: House

SOCIAL SVCS CENTER
SOFTWARE PUBLISHERS: Home Entertainment
SOFTWARE TRAINING, COMPUTER
SOUND EFFECTS & MUSIC PRODUCTION: Motion Picture
SPAS
SPECIALIZED LEGAL SVCS
SPECIALIZED LIBRARIES
SPECIALTY FOOD STORES: Juices, Fruit Or Vegetable
SPECIALTY FOOD STORES: Vitamin
SPECIALTY OUTPATIENT CLINICS, NEC
SPORTING & ATHLETIC GOODS: Water Sports Eqpt
SPORTING & RECREATIONAL GOODS, WHOLESALE: Boat Access & Part
SPORTING CAMPS
SPORTING FIREARMS WHOLESALERS
SPORTING GOODS
SPORTING GOODS STORES: Hunting Eqpt
SPORTING GOODS STORES: Specialty Sport Splys, NEC
SPORTS APPAREL STORES
SPORTS CLUBS, MANAGERS & PROMOTERS
SPRINGS: Steel
SPRINGS: Wire
STAINLESS STEEL
STAMPINGS: Automotive
STAMPINGS: Metal
STATIONERY & OFFICE SPLYS WHOLESALERS
STEEL, COLD-ROLLED: Flat Bright, From Purchased HotRolled
STEEL, HOT-ROLLED: Sheet Or Strip
STONE: Quarrying & Processing, Own Stone Prdts
STONEWARE PRDTS: Pottery
STORE FIXTURES: Wood
STORES: Auto & Home Supply
STUDS & JOISTS: Sheet Metal
SUBSCRIPTION FULFILLMENT SVCS: Magazine, Newspaper, Etc
SUBSTANCE ABUSE COUNSELING
SUMMER CAMPS, EXC DAY & SPORTS INSTRUCTIONAL
SURGICAL APPLIANCES & SPLYS
SURGICAL INSTRUMENT REPAIR SVCS
SUSPENSION SYSTEMS: Acoustical, Metal
SVC ESTABLISHMENT EQPT, WHOLESALE: Firefighting Eqpt
SVC ESTABLISHMENT EQPT, WHOLESALE: Laundry Eqpt & Splys
SVC ESTABLISHMENT EQPT, WHOLESALE: Restaurant Splys
SVC ESTABLISHMENT EQPT, WHOLESALE: Vending Machines & Splys
SWIMMING POOL & HOT TUB CLEANING & MAINTENANCE SVCS
SWIMMING POOLS, EQPT & SPLYS: Wholesalers
SWITCHGEAR & SWITCHBOARD APPARATUS
SYRUPS, DRINK
SYSTEMS ENGINEERING: Computer Related
SYSTEMS INTEGRATION SVCS
SYSTEMS INTEGRATION SVCS: Local Area Network
SYSTEMS SOFTWARE DEVELOPMENT SVCS

T

TABULATING SVCS
TANK REPAIR & CLEANING SVCS
TANK REPAIR SVCS
TANK TOWERS: Metal Plate
TANKS & OTHER TRACKED VEHICLE CMPNTS
TANKS: Cryogenic, Metal
TANKS: Fuel, Including Oil & Gas, Metal Plate
TANKS: Lined, Metal
TANKS: Standard Or Custom Fabricated, Metal Plate
TAPES: Pressure Sensitive
TAPES: Pressure Sensitive, Rubber
TARPAULINS, WHOLESALE
TECHNICAL MANUAL PREPARATION SVCS
TELECOMMUNICATION EQPT REPAIR SVCS, EXC TELEPHONES
TELECONFERENCING SVCS
TELEPHONE ANSWERING SVCS
TELEPHONE EQPT: NEC
TELEPHONE SVCS
TELEVISION BROADCASTING STATIONS
TEMPORARY HELP SVCS
TEN PIN CENTERS
TESTING SVCS

TEXTILE DESIGNERS
TEXTILES: Linen Fabrics
THEATRICAL PRODUCERS & SVCS
THEATRICAL PRODUCTION SVCS
THERMOPLASTIC MATERIALS
THERMOSETTING MATERIALS
TIRE & TUBE REPAIR MATERIALS, WHOLESALE
TIRE CORD & FABRIC
TIRE SUNDRIES OR REPAIR MATERIALS: Rubber
TIRES & TUBES WHOLESALERS
TIRES & TUBES, WHOLESALE: Automotive
TOBACCO & PRDTS, WHOLESALE: Cigarettes
TOBACCO & TOBACCO PRDTS WHOLESALERS
TOBACCO: Smoking
TOILETRIES, WHOLESALE: Hair Preparations
TOILETRIES, WHOLESALE: Perfumes
TOILETRIES, WHOLESALE: Toilet Soap
TOILETRIES, WHOLESALE: Toiletries
TOOLS: Hand, Mechanics
TOWING & TUGBOAT SVC
TOWING SVCS: Marine
TOYS & HOBBY GOODS & SPLYS, WHOLESALE: Bingo Games & Splys
TOYS & HOBBY GOODS & SPLYS, WHOLESALE: Toys & Games
TOYS & HOBBY GOODS & SPLYS, WHOLESALE: Toys, NEC
TRADE SHOW ARRANGEMENT SVCS
TRADERS: Commodity, Contracts
TRAILERS: Semitrailers, Truck Tractors
TRANSPORTATION AGENTS & BROKERS
TRANSPORTATION BROKERS: Truck
TRANSPORTATION EQPT & SPLYS WHOLESALERS, NEC
TRANSPORTATION SVCS, AIR, NONSCHEDULED: Air Cargo Carriers
TRANSPORTATION SVCS, WATER: Cleaning
TRANSPORTATION SVCS: Railroad Switching
TRANSPORTATION: Deep Sea Foreign Freight
TRANSPORTATION: Great Lakes Domestic Freight
TRAVEL AGENCIES
TRAVEL TRAILERS & CAMPERS
TRUCK & BUS BODIES: Utility Truck
TRUCK BODIES: Body Parts
TRUCK BODY SHOP
TRUCK GENERAL REPAIR SVC
TRUCK PARTS & ACCESSORIES: Wholesalers
TRUCKING & HAULING SVCS: Building Materials
TRUCKING & HAULING SVCS: Contract Basis
TRUCKING & HAULING SVCS: Hazardous Waste
TRUCKING & HAULING SVCS: Heavy Machinery, Local
TRUCKING & HAULING SVCS: Heavy, NEC
TRUCKING & HAULING SVCS: Liquid Petroleum, Exc Local
TRUCKING & HAULING SVCS: Machinery, Heavy
TRUCKING & HAULING SVCS: Petroleum, Local
TRUCKING: Except Local
TRUCKING: Local, With Storage
TRUCKING: Local, Without Storage
TRUCKS & TRACTORS: Industrial
TRUSSES: Wood, Floor
TRUST MANAGEMENT SVCS: Charitable
TRUST MANAGEMENT SVCS: Personal Investment
TUBES: Paper
TUBES: Steel & Iron
TUBING: Flexible, Metallic
TUBING: Rubber
TUGBOAT SVCS
TURBINES & TURBINE GENERATOR SETS
TURBINES: Gas, Mechanical Drive
TURBINES: Steam
TURNKEY VENDORS: Computer Systems
TYPESETTING SVC
TYPESETTING SVC: Computer

U

UNIFORM SPLY SVCS: Indl
UNISEX HAIR SALONS
UNIVERSITY
UPHOLSTERY WORK SVCS
USED CAR DEALERS
USED MERCHANDISE STORES
UTILITY TRAILER DEALERS

V

SERVICES INDEX

VALUE-ADDED RESELLERS: Computer Systems
VALVES & PIPE FITTINGS
VALVES: Aerosol, Metal
VALVES: Aircraft, Hydraulic
VALVES: Fluid Power, Control, Hydraulic & pneumatic
VALVES: Gas Cylinder, Compressed
VALVES: Indl
VAN CONVERSIONS
VARIETY STORES
VENDING MACHINE OPERATORS: Sandwich & Hot Food
VENDING MACHINE REPAIR SVCS
VENDING MACHINES & PARTS
VENTILATING EQPT: Metal
VENTURE CAPITAL COMPANIES
VIDEO & AUDIO EQPT, WHOLESALE
VIDEO PRODUCTION SVCS
VIDEO TAPE PRODUCTION SVCS
VISUAL COMMUNICATIONS SYSTEMS
VOCATIONAL REHABILITATION AGENCY
VOCATIONAL TRAINING AGENCY

W

WALL COVERINGS WHOLESALERS
WALLPAPER STORE
WALLPAPER: Made From Purchased Paper
WALLS: Curtain, Metal
WAREHOUSING & STORAGE FACILITIES, NEC
WAREHOUSING & STORAGE, REFRIGERATED: Cold Storage Or Refrig
WAREHOUSING & STORAGE: General
WAREHOUSING & STORAGE: Miniwarehouse
WAREHOUSING & STORAGE: Refrigerated
WAREHOUSING & STORAGE: Self Storage
WARM AIR HEATING/AC EQPT/SPLYS, WHOL Warm Air Htg Eqpt/Splys
WASHERS: Metal
WATCH REPAIR SVCS
WATER SUPPLY
WATER TREATMENT EQPT: Indl
WAXES: Petroleum, Not Produced In Petroleum Refineries
WELDING EQPT & SPLYS WHOLESALERS
WELDING EQPT REPAIR SVCS
WELDING REPAIR SVC
WELDING SPLYS, EXC GASES: Wholesalers
WELDMENTS
WINDOW & DOOR FRAMES
WINDOW FRAMES & SASHES: Plastic
WINDOW FRAMES, MOLDING & TRIM: Vinyl
WINDSHIELD WIPER SYSTEMS
WINE & DISTILLED ALCOHOLIC BEVERAGES WHOLESALERS
WIRE & WIRE PRDTS
WIRE MATERIALS: Steel
WIRE: Nonferrous
WOMEN'S & CHILDREN'S CLOTHING WHOLESALERS, NEC
WOMEN'S & GIRLS' SPORTSWEAR WHOLESALERS
WOMEN'S CLOTHING STORES
WOOD FENCING WHOLESALERS
WOOD PRDTS: Mulch, Wood & Bark
WOOD TREATING: Structural Lumber & Timber
WOODWORK & TRIM: Interior & Ornamental
WORK EXPERIENCE CENTER

X

X-RAY EQPT & TUBES
X-RAY EQPT REPAIR SVCS

SERVICES SECTION

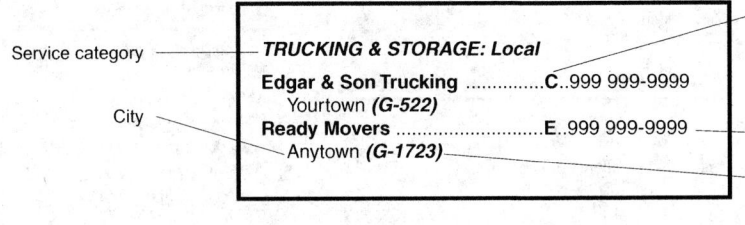

See footnotes for symbols and codes identification.
- Refer to the Industrial Product Index preceding this section to locate product headings.

ABRASIVES

Lawrence Industries Inc .... E 216 518-7000
　Cleveland *(G-4483)*

Mill-Rose Company .... C 440 255-9171
　Mentor *(G-10975)*

National Lime and Stone Co .... E 419 396-7671
　Carey *(G-1894)*

ACCIDENT INSURANCE CARRIERS

Nationwide Corporation .... E 614 249-7111
　Columbus *(G-6326)*

Nationwide Mutual Insurance Co .... A 614 249-7111
　Columbus *(G-6338)*

Paramount Care Inc .... B 419 887-2500
　Maumee *(G-10755)*

Progressive Casualty Insur Co .... E 440 603-4033
　Cleveland *(G-4778)*

ACOUSTICAL BOARD & TILE

Mpc Inc .... E 440 835-1405
　Cleveland *(G-4605)*

ADHESIVES

Chemspec Usa Inc .... D 330 669-8512
　Orrville *(G-12158)*

Conversion Tech Intl Inc .... E 419 924-5566
　West Unity *(G-14874)*

Evans Adhesive Corporation .... E 614 451-2665
　Columbus *(G-5833)*

Toagosei America Inc .... D 614 718-3855
　West Jefferson *(G-14853)*

ADHESIVES & SEALANTS

Cincinnati Assn For The Blind .... C 513 221-8558
　Cincinnati *(G-2395)*

Consolidated Coatings Corp .... A 216 514-7596
　Cleveland *(G-4106)*

Hexpol Compounding LLC .... C 440 834-4644
　Burton *(G-1528)*

Hoover & Wells Inc .... C 419 691-9220
　Toledo *(G-13850)*

Sonoco Products Company .... D 937 429-0040
　Beavercreek Township *(G-949)*

United McGill Corporation .... E 614 829-1200
　Groveport *(G-9007)*

ADHESIVES & SEALANTS WHOLESALERS

Consolidated Coatings Corp .... A 216 514-7596
　Cleveland *(G-4106)*

Novagard Solutions Inc .... C 216 881-8111
　Cleveland *(G-4668)*

Synthomer LLC .... D 678 400-6655
　Beachwood *(G-842)*

ADULT DAYCARE CENTERS

Active Day Inc .... E 513 984-8000
　Cincinnati *(G-2143)*

Antonine Ssters Adult Day Care .... E 330 538-9822
　North Jackson *(G-11871)*

Brookwood Management Company .... E 330 497-8718
　Canton *(G-1691)*

Creative Options LLC .... E 614 868-1231
　Columbus *(G-5722)*

DMD Management Inc .... C 216 371-3600
　Cleveland *(G-4172)*

Gardens Western Reserve Inc .... E 330 342-9100
　Streetsboro *(G-13412)*

Goods Hands Supported Living .... E 740 474-2646
　Circleville *(G-3709)*

Lark Residential Support Inc .... E 614 582-9721
　Columbus *(G-6141)*

Maxim Healthcare Services Inc .... C 614 880-1210
　Columbus *(G-6210)*

Over Rainbow Adult Daycare .... E 330 638-9599
　Cortland *(G-6975)*

Person Centered Services Inc .... E 419 874-4900
　Perrysburg *(G-12363)*

United Disability Services Inc .... D 330 379-3337
　Akron *(G-340)*

Wings of Love Services LLC .... E 937 789-8192
　Dayton *(G-7144)*

ADVERTISING AGENCIES

Advent Media Group LLC .... E 513 421-2267
　Cincinnati *(G-2152)*

Bbs & Associates Inc .... E 330 665-5227
　Akron *(G-63)*

Berry Network .... D 513 702-3373
　Dayton *(G-7191)*

Black River Group Inc .... E 419 524-6699
　Mansfield *(G-10245)*

Brandience LLC .... E 513 333-4100
　Cincinnati *(G-2277)*

Clum Media Inc .... E 216 239-1525
　Cleveland *(G-4085)*

Comcage LLC .... E 513 549-4003
　Cincinnati *(G-2479)*

Comcast Spotlight LP .... E 216 575-8016
　Cleveland *(G-4091)*

Deanhouston Creative Group Inc .... E 513 659-5051
　West Chester *(G-14684)*

Distributor Marketing MGT Inc .... E 440 236-5534
　Columbia Station *(G-5227)*

Dix & Eaton Incorporated .... E 216 241-0405
　Cleveland *(G-4168)*

Engauge Holdings LLC .... E 614 573-1010
　Columbus *(G-5819)*

Epipheo Inc .... E 888 687-7620
　Cincinnati *(G-2631)*

Gerbig Snell/Weisheimer Adv .... B 614 848-4848
　Westerville *(G-14896)*

ICC Lowe Pace LLC .... E 330 823-7223
　Alliance *(G-384)*

Inquiry Systems Inc .... E 614 464-3800
　Columbus *(G-6055)*

JWT Action .... E 513 578-6721
　Cincinnati *(G-2924)*

JWT Action .... D 330 376-6148
　Akron *(G-214)*

Lind Outdoor Advertising Co .... E 419 522-2600
　Mansfield *(G-10282)*

M A M Inc .... E 740 588-9882
　Zanesville *(G-15809)*

Madison Avenue Mktg Group Inc ...... E 419 473-9000
　Toledo *(G-13903)*

Marketing Support Services Inc .... E 513 752-1200
　Cincinnati *(G-3011)*

Nct Retail .... E 937 236-8000
　Dayton *(G-7528)*

Northlich LLC .... C 513 421-8840
　Cincinnati *(G-3126)*

Opti LLC .... E 212 651-7317
　Cincinnati *(G-3165)*

Prodigal Media Company Inc .... E 330 707-2088
　Youngstown *(G-15698)*

Rockfish Interactive LLC .... E 513 381-1583
　Cincinnati *(G-3315)*

Saatchi & Saatchi X Inc .... E 479 575-0200
　Cincinnati *(G-3336)*

Sgk LLC .... C 513 569-9900
　Cincinnati *(G-3365)*

Skylight Partners Inc .... E 513 381-5555
　Cincinnati *(G-3385)*

The Arras Group Inc .... E 216 621-1601
　Cleveland *(G-4991)*

Thread Information Design Inc .... E 419 887-6801
　Toledo *(G-14041)*

Tigerspike Inc .... E 646 330-4636
　Cincinnati *(G-3479)*

Whitespace Design Group Inc .... E 330 762-9320
　Akron *(G-360)*

Young & Rubicam LLC .... D 513 345-3400
　Cincinnati *(G-3687)*

ADVERTISING AGENCIES: Consultants

Airmate Co Inc .... D 419 636-3184
　Bryan *(G-1478)*

BBDO Worldwide Inc .... E 513 861-3668
　Cincinnati *(G-2241)*

Brokaw Inc .... E 216 241-8003
　Cleveland *(G-3900)*

Employee Codes: A=Over 500 employees, B=251-500
C=101-250, D=51-100, E=20-50, F=10-19, G=1-9

ADVERTISING AGENCIES: Consultants

Charles W Powers & Assoc Inc............... E 513 721-5353
  Cincinnati *(G-2347)*
Cooper-Smith Advertising LLC............... D 419 470-5900
  Toledo *(G-13761)*
Curiosity LLC.. D 513 744-6000
  Cincinnati *(G-2525)*
Fahlgren Inc... E 614 383-1500
  Columbus *(G-5843)*
Fruchtman Advertising Inc..................... E 419 539-2770
  Toledo *(G-13814)*
Guardian Enterprise Group Inc.............. E 614 416-6080
  Columbus *(G-5959)*
Gypc Inc... C 309 677-0405
  Dayton *(G-7390)*
Hart Associates Inc................................ D 419 893-9600
  Toledo *(G-13836)*
Hitchcock Fleming & Assoc Inc............. D 330 376-2111
  Akron *(G-193)*
Kreber Graphics Inc................................ D 614 529-5701
  Columbus *(G-6128)*
Marcus Thomas Llc................................ D 216 292-4700
  Cleveland *(G-4524)*
Matrix Media Services Inc...................... E 614 228-2200
  Columbus *(G-6207)*
National Cinemedia LLC......................... C 614 297-8933
  Columbus *(G-6293)*
Real Art Design Group Inc..................... D 937 223-9955
  Dayton *(G-7581)*
Rttw Ltd... E 614 291-7944
  Columbus *(G-6617)*
SBC Advertising Ltd............................... C 614 891-7070
  Columbus *(G-6648)*
Syneos Health Communications Inc..... D 614 543-6650
  Westerville *(G-14939)*
Tri Advertising Inc.................................. E 614 548-0913
  Westerville *(G-14946)*
Triad Communications Inc..................... D 330 237-3531
  Cuyahoga Falls *(G-7111)*
Universal Advg Assoc Inc...................... E 513 522-5000
  Cincinnati *(G-3560)*
Wyse Advertising Inc............................. E 216 696-2424
  Cleveland *(G-5162)*
Young & Rubicam LLC............................ C 513 419-2300
  Cincinnati *(G-3688)*

ADVERTISING MATERIAL DISTRIBUTION

Berry Network LLC................................ C 800 366-1264
  Moraine *(G-11391)*
Dispatch Consumer Services............... E 740 548-5555
  Columbus *(G-5771)*
Yp LLC... C 216 642-4000
  Cleveland *(G-5169)*

ADVERTISING REPRESENTATIVES: Electronic Media

Ctv Media Inc... E 614 848-5800
  Powell *(G-12590)*
Madison Avenue Mktg Group Inc........ E 419 473-9000
  Toledo *(G-13903)*

ADVERTISING REPRESENTATIVES: Newspaper

American City Bus Journals Inc............ B 937 528-4400
  Dayton *(G-7170)*
Copley Ohio Newspapers Inc............... C 330 364-5577
  New Philadelphia *(G-11643)*
Gazette Publishing Company............... D 419 335-2010
  Napoleon *(G-11523)*

ADVERTISING REPRESENTATIVES: Printed Media

Manta Media Inc.................................... E 888 875-5833
  Columbus *(G-5268)*

ADVERTISING SPECIALTIES, WHOLESALE

American Business Forms Inc.............. E 513 312-2522
  West Chester *(G-14798)*
Associated Premium Corporation........ E 513 679-4444
  Cincinnati *(G-2219)*
Boost Engagement LLC........................ E 937 223-2203
  Dayton *(G-7197)*
Bottomline Ink Corporation................. E 419 897-8000
  Perrysburg *(G-12318)*
D & D Advertising Entps Inc................ E 513 921-6827
  Cincinnati *(G-2529)*
General Commercial Corporation........ E 330 938-1000
  Sebring *(G-12949)*
Halo Branded Solutions Inc.................. E 855 425-6266
  Cincinnati *(G-2793)*
Halo Branded Solutions Inc.................. E 614 434-6275
  Columbus *(G-5965)*
Kaeser and Blair Incorporated............. D 513 732-6400
  Batavia *(G-742)*
Leader Promotions Inc......................... D 614 416-6565
  Columbus *(G-6150)*
Novelty Advertising Co Inc................... E 740 622-3113
  Coshocton *(G-6994)*
Nutis Press Inc...................................... C 614 237-8626
  Columbus *(G-6378)*
Profill Holdings LLC............................... A 513 742-4000
  Cincinnati *(G-3247)*
Rdh Ohio LLC.. E 419 475-8621
  Holland *(G-9302)*
Screen Works Inc.................................. E 937 264-9111
  Dayton *(G-7613)*
Shamrock Companies Inc..................... D 440 899-9510
  Westlake *(G-15108)*
Touchstone Mdse Group LLC............... E 513 741-0400
  Mason *(G-10617)*

ADVERTISING SVCS: Direct Mail

A W S Inc... B 216 749-0356
  Cleveland *(G-3751)*
A W S Inc... A 440 333-1791
  Rocky River *(G-12738)*
Amerimark Holdings LLC...................... B 440 325-2000
  Cleveland *(G-3809)*
Amsive OH LLC....................................... D 937 885-8000
  Miamisburg *(G-11024)*
Angstrom Graphics Inc Midwest.......... C 216 271-5300
  Cleveland *(G-3817)*
Baesman Group Inc.............................. D 614 771-2300
  Hilliard *(G-9181)*
Clipper Magazine LLC........................... D 513 794-4100
  Blue Ash *(G-1151)*
Consolidated Graphics Group Inc........ C 216 881-9191
  Cleveland *(G-4104)*
Deepwood Industries Inc..................... C 440 350-5231
  Mentor *(G-10933)*
Harte-Hanks Trnsp Svcs....................... D 513 458-7600
  Cincinnati *(G-2803)*
Northlich LLC... C 513 421-8840
  Cincinnati *(G-3126)*
Promotion Exction Partners LLC......... E 513 826-0101
  Cincinnati *(G-3253)*
Resource Interactive............................ E 614 621-2888
  Columbus *(G-6586)*
TMR Inc... E 330 220-8564
  Brunswick *(G-1471)*

Traxium LLC... E 330 572-8200
  Stow *(G-13398)*

ADVERTISING SVCS: Display

Downing Displays Inc........................... D 513 248-9800
  Milford *(G-11225)*
IMG College LLC.................................... E 513 556-4532
  Cincinnati *(G-2866)*
Innomark Communications LLC........... D 513 379-7800
  West Chester *(G-14713)*
News Amer Mktg In-Store Svcs L........ A 513 333-7373
  Cincinnati *(G-3111)*
Promotion Exction Partners LLC......... E 513 826-0101
  Cincinnati *(G-3253)*

ADVERTISING SVCS: Outdoor

Kessler Sign Company.......................... E 740 453-0668
  Zanesville *(G-15805)*
Matrix Media Services Inc.................... E 614 228-2200
  Columbus *(G-6207)*
Orange Barrel Media LLC..................... D 614 294-4898
  Columbus *(G-6477)*

ADVERTISING SVCS: Sample Distribution

Dismas Distribution Services............... E 614 861-2525
  Columbus *(G-5770)*
Signum LLC.. D 440 248-2233
  Solon *(G-13142)*

AGENTS, BROKERS & BUREAUS: Personal Service

500 Degrees LLC................................... D 786 615-8265
  Columbus *(G-5289)*
A L D Precast Corp................................ E 614 449-3366
  Columbus *(G-5291)*
Abraham Ford LLC................................ E 440 233-7402
  Elyria *(G-8232)*
Aghapy Plus Inc..................................... D 216 820-3996
  Euclid *(G-8336)*
Barklyn Heights LLC.............................. E 216 577-5960
  Cleveland *(G-3850)*
Dqr 4 Ted.. E 740 264-4323
  Steubenville *(G-13322)*
Essilor of America Inc.......................... E 614 492-0888
  Groveport *(G-8986)*
Five Cfc Inc.. E 937 578-3271
  Lewis Center *(G-9821)*
Franklin Works Inc................................ E 361 215-2300
  Columbus *(G-5890)*
Great Lkes Cmnty Action Partnr......... E 419 332-8089
  Fremont *(G-8686)*
Illuminate USA LLC............................... A 614 598-9742
  Pataskala *(G-12275)*
Invincible Fire Co Inc............................ E 419 647-4615
  Spencerville *(G-13189)*
Iten Defense LLC.................................. D 440 990-2440
  Ashtabula *(G-539)*
Mak Burtnett Inc................................... E 440 256-8080
  Willoughby *(G-15210)*
Manav Enterprises Inc......................... E 513 563-4606
  Sharonville *(G-12995)*
Marysvlle Exmpted Vlg Schl Dst......... E 937 645-6733
  Marysville *(G-10495)*
Nestle Usa Inc....................................... C 440 349-5757
  Solon *(G-13118)*
Oak Hill Financial Inc............................ B 740 286-3283
  Jackson *(G-9523)*
Persistent Systems Inc........................ E 614 763-6500
  Dublin *(G-8090)*
Progressive Quality Care Inc............... E 330 875-7866
  Louisville *(G-10121)*

SERVICES SECTION

AIRCRAFT SERVICING & REPAIRING

Progressive Quality Care Inc.............. D 216 661-6800
Parma *(G-12263)*

Soh Trumbul Co Help ME Grow............ E 330 675-6610
Leavittsburg *(G-9751)*

Spa LLC .... E 513 733-8800
Milford *(G-11258)*

Specialty Pumps Group Inc................. E 216 589-0198
Cleveland *(G-4930)*

Woody Sander Ford Inc........................ D 513 541-5586
Cincinnati *(G-3681)*

Xcess Limited.. E 330 347-4901
Wooster *(G-15401)*

AGRICULTURAL CREDIT INSTITUTIONS

Agri Business Finance Inc................... E 937 663-0186
Saint Paris *(G-12837)*

AGRICULTURAL EQPT: Elevators, Farm

Gerald Grain Center Inc........................ E 419 445-2451
Archbold *(G-459)*

AGRICULTURAL EQPT: Fertilizing Machinery

Shearer Farm Inc.................................. C 330 345-9023
Wooster *(G-15376)*

AGRICULTURAL MACHINERY & EQPT: Wholesalers

Ag-Pro Ohio LLC................................... E 740 389-5458
Marion *(G-10416)*

Ag-Pro Ohio LLC................................... E 937 486-5211
Wilmington *(G-15238)*

Buckeye Companies.............................. E 740 452-3641
Zanesville *(G-15772)*

Deerfield AG Services Inc.................... E 330 584-4715
Massillon *(G-10637)*

Deerfield Farms Service Inc................. D 330 584-4715
Deerfield *(G-7741)*

JD Equipment Inc................................. C 614 879-6620
London *(G-10044)*

Liechty Inc... E 419 592-3075
Napoleon *(G-11526)*

Liechty Inc... E 419 445-1565
Archbold *(G-461)*

Steinke Tractor Sales Inc..................... E 937 456-4271
Eaton *(G-8224)*

AIR CONDITIONING & VENTILATION EQPT & SPLYS: Wholesales

Brock Air Products Inc......................... D 937 335-2626
Troy *(G-14130)*

G D Supply Inc...................................... E 614 258-1111
Columbus *(G-5904)*

Gardiner Service Company LLC........... C 440 248-3400
Solon *(G-13091)*

Refrigeration Sales Company LLC....... E 216 525-8200
Cleveland *(G-4818)*

Wolff Bros Supply Inc........................... C 330 725-3451
Medina *(G-10904)*

AIR CONDITIONING EQPT

Vertiv Corporation................................ A 614 888-0246
Westerville *(G-14949)*

AIR CONDITIONING EQPT, WHOLE HOUSE: Wholesalers

Habegger Corporation.......................... D 513 612-4700
Cincinnati *(G-2787)*

Noland Company................................... C 937 396-7980
Moraine *(G-11428)*

AIR CONDITIONING REPAIR SVCS

Columbs/Worthington Htg AC Inc........ E 614 771-5381
Columbus *(G-5605)*

Cov-Ro Inc.. E 330 856-3176
Warren *(G-14515)*

Smith & Oby Service Co....................... E 440 735-5322
Bedford *(G-985)*

AIR CONDITIONING UNITS: Complete, Domestic Or Indl

Vertiv JV Holdings LLC......................... A 614 888-0246
Columbus *(G-6846)*

AIR DUCT CLEANING SVCS

Miles Cleaning Services Inc................. E 216 626-0040
Cleveland *(G-4582)*

AIR POLLUTION MEASURING SVCS

Siertek Ltd... E 937 623-2466
Beavercreek Township *(G-948)*

AIRCRAFT & AEROSPACE FLIGHT INSTRUMENTS & GUIDANCE SYSTEMS

General Electric Company.................... A 617 443-3000
Cincinnati *(G-2725)*

AIRCRAFT & HEAVY EQPT REPAIR SVCS

Airborne Maint Engrg Svcs Inc............ C 937 366-2559
Wilmington *(G-15242)*

Airborne Maint Engrg Svcs Inc............ C 937 382-5591
Wilmington *(G-15243)*

Apph Wichita Inc.................................. E 316 943-5752
Strongsville *(G-13442)*

Component Repair Technologies Inc... B 440 255-1793
Mentor *(G-10925)*

Equipment Maintenance Inc................ E 513 353-3518
Cleves *(G-5188)*

GE Engine Services LLC....................... C 513 243-2000
Cincinnati *(G-2721)*

Grimes Aerospace Company................ D 937 484-2001
Urbana *(G-14308)*

McNational Inc...................................... D 740 377-4391
South Point *(G-13179)*

Ohio Machinery Co............................... C 440 526-6200
Broadview Heights *(G-1394)*

Pas Technologies Inc............................ D 937 840-1053
Hillsboro *(G-9266)*

AIRCRAFT DEALERS

IAC Wauseon LLC................................. E 419 335-1000
Wauseon *(G-14605)*

Options Flight Support Inc................... A 216 261-3500
Cleveland *(G-4705)*

AIRCRAFT ELECTRICAL EQPT REPAIR SVCS

General Electric Company.................... E 513 977-1500
Cincinnati *(G-2723)*

Winner Aviation Corporation................ C 330 856-5000
Vienna *(G-14424)*

AIRCRAFT ENGINES & ENGINE PARTS: Nonelectric Starters

Dreison International Inc..................... C 216 362-0755
Cleveland *(G-4184)*

AIRCRAFT ENGINES & ENGINE PARTS: Pumps

At Holdings Corporation....................... A 216 692-6000
Cleveland *(G-3837)*

AIRCRAFT ENGINES & PARTS

Hi-Tek Manufacturing Inc..................... C 513 459-1094
Mason *(G-10562)*

Miba Bearings US LLC.......................... B 740 962-4242
Mcconnelsville *(G-10803)*

Pas Technologies Inc............................ D 937 840-1053
Hillsboro *(G-9266)*

AIRCRAFT EQPT & SPLYS WHOLESALERS

PCC Airfoils LLC................................... B 440 944-1880
Wickliffe *(G-15160)*

Sportsmans Market Inc........................ C 513 735-9100
Batavia *(G-747)*

Transdigm Group Incorporated............ B 216 706-2960
Cleveland *(G-5031)*

AIRCRAFT MAINTENANCE & REPAIR SVCS

Aero Propulsion Support Inc................ E 513 367-9452
Harrison *(G-9096)*

Constant Aviation LLC.......................... C 800 440-9004
Cleveland *(G-4108)*

General Electric Company.................... A 617 443-3000
Cincinnati *(G-2725)*

Jet East Inc.. C 215 937-9020
Solon *(G-13102)*

Winner Aviation Corporation................ C 330 856-5000
Vienna *(G-14424)*

AIRCRAFT PARTS & EQPT, NEC

Apph Wichita Inc.................................. E 316 943-5752
Strongsville *(G-13442)*

Arctos Mission Solutions LLC.............. E 813 609-5591
Beavercreek *(G-858)*

At Holdings Corporation....................... A 216 692-6000
Cleveland *(G-3837)*

Drt Holdings Inc................................... D 937 298-7391
Dayton *(G-7317)*

Eaton Industrial Corporation................ C 216 692-5456
Cleveland *(G-4204)*

General Electric Company.................... E 513 977-1500
Cincinnati *(G-2723)*

Lincoln Electric Automtn Inc................ B 937 295-2120
Fort Loramie *(G-8605)*

Starwin Industries LLC......................... E 937 293-8568
Dayton *(G-7639)*

Transdigm Group Incorporated............ B 216 706-2960
Cleveland *(G-5031)*

Unison Industries LLC.......................... B 904 667-9904
Dayton *(G-7143)*

AIRCRAFT PARTS WHOLESALERS

Abx Air Inc.. B 937 382-5591
Wilmington *(G-15237)*

Airborne Maint Engrg Svcs Inc............ C 937 366-2559
Wilmington *(G-15242)*

Airborne Maint Engrg Svcs Inc............ C 937 382-5591
Wilmington *(G-15243)*

Grimes Aerospace Company................ D 937 484-2001
Urbana *(G-14308)*

Jilco Industries Inc............................... E 330 698-0280
Kidron *(G-9636)*

Netjets Sales Inc.................................. C 614 239-5500
Columbus *(G-6350)*

AIRCRAFT SERVICING & REPAIRING

Abx Air Inc.. B 937 382-5591
Wilmington *(G-15237)*

Lane Aviation Corporation................... C 614 237-3747
Columbus *(G-6138)*

AIRCRAFT SERVICING & REPAIRING

National Flight Services Inc.................. C 419 865-2311
  Swanton *(G-13527)*
Stevens Arospc Def Systems LLC......... D 937 454-3400
  Vandalia *(G-14393)*
Unison Industries LLC........................ B 904 667-9904
  Dayton *(G-7143)*

AIRLINE TRAINING

Macair Aviation LLC.......................... E 937 347-1302
  Xenia *(G-15525)*

AIRPORT TERMINAL SVCS

Air General Inc................................. E 216 501-5643
  Cleveland *(G-3778)*
Servisair LLC..................................... C 216 267-9910
  Cleveland *(G-4897)*

AIRPORTS & FLYING FIELDS

Macair Aviation LLC.......................... E 937 347-1302
  Xenia *(G-15525)*

AIRPORTS, FLYING FIELDS & SVCS

Capital City Aviation Inc..................... E 614 459-2541
  Columbus *(G-5497)*
Executive Jet Management Inc............. B 513 979-6600
  Cincinnati *(G-2644)*
Flexjet Inc.. E 866 309-2214
  Richmond Heights *(G-12718)*
Hhd Aviation LLC............................... D 513 426-8378
  Hamilton *(G-9052)*
Menzies Aviation (texas) Inc................ D 216 265-3777
  Cleveland *(G-4553)*
Sky Quest LLC.................................. D 216 362-9904
  Cleveland *(G-4912)*
True Wing Aviation LLC...................... E 937 657-3990
  Lebanon *(G-9796)*

ALKALIES & CHLORINE

National Lime and Stone Co................ E 419 396-7671
  Carey *(G-1894)*

ALLOYS: Additive, Exc Copper Or Made In Blast Furnaces

Morris Technologies Inc...................... E 513 733-1611
  Cincinnati *(G-3080)*

ALUMINUM: Coil & Sheet

Monarch Steel Company Inc................ E 216 587-8000
  Cleveland *(G-4598)*

AMBULANCE SVCS

American Ambulette & Ambula............. A 937 237-1105
  Portsmouth *(G-12544)*
Apex Transit Solutions LLC.................. E 216 938-5606
  Cleveland *(G-3819)*
Bkp Ambulance District...................... E 419 674-4574
  Kenton *(G-9610)*
Cems of Ohio Inc............................... B 614 751-6651
  Columbus *(G-5526)*
City of Cleveland................................ E 216 664-2555
  Cleveland *(G-3981)*
City of Cleveland................................ E 216 664-2555
  Cleveland *(G-3982)*
Coloma Emergency Ambulance Inc....... D 269 343-2224
  Huntsville *(G-9383)*
Community Ambulance Service............ C 740 454-6800
  Zanesville *(G-15784)*
Community Care Amblance Netwrk...... D 440 992-1401
  Ashtabula *(G-527)*
Coshocton Cnty Emrgncy Med Svc....... C 740 622-4294
  Coshocton *(G-6980)*

County of Lorain................................. E 440 647-5803
  Wellington *(G-14630)*
County of Meigs................................. E 740 992-6617
  Pomeroy *(G-12513)*
Courtesy Ambulance Inc..................... D 740 522-8588
  Newark *(G-11697)*
Donald Mrtens Sons Amblnce Svc........ D 216 265-4211
  Cleveland *(G-4176)*
East Inc... E 330 609-1339
  Vienna *(G-14419)*
Ems Team LLC................................. E 800 735-8190
  Dayton *(G-7335)*
First Care Ohio LLC........................... D 513 563-8811
  Cincinnati *(G-2670)*
Fisher - Titus Affiliated Svcs................. B 419 663-1367
  Milan *(G-11205)*
Hanco Ambulance Inc......................... E 419 423-2912
  Findlay *(G-8540)*
Life Ambulance Service Inc.................. A 740 354-6169
  Portsmouth *(G-12562)*
Lifecare Ambulance Inc...................... E 440 323-2527
  Elyria *(G-8269)*
Lifefleet LLC..................................... E 330 549-9716
  North Lima *(G-11892)*
Lifestar Ambulance Inc....................... E 419 245-6210
  Toledo *(G-13889)*
Med-Trans Inc................................... D 937 325-4926
  Springfield *(G-13267)*
Meda-Care Transportation Inc............. E 513 521-4799
  Cincinnati *(G-3026)*
Medcorp Inc...................................... C 419 425-9700
  Findlay *(G-8566)*
Medic Rspnse Ambulance Svc Inc........ E 419 522-1998
  Mansfield *(G-10295)*
Medical Transport Systems Inc............. E 330 837-9818
  North Canton *(G-11847)*
Medpro LLC..................................... D 937 336-5586
  Eaton *(G-8215)*
Metrohealth System........................... B 216 957-4000
  Cleveland *(G-4561)*
Metrohealth System........................... C 216 778-3867
  Cleveland *(G-4567)*
Mt Orab Fire Department Inc............... E 937 444-3945
  Mount Orab *(G-11472)*
North Star Critical Care LLC................ E 330 386-9110
  East Liverpool *(G-8188)*
Ohio Medical Trnsp Inc....................... D 614 791-4400
  Columbus *(G-6437)*
Physicians Ambulance Svc Inc............. E 216 454-4911
  Brecksville *(G-1362)*
Portage Path Behavorial Health............ E 330 762-6110
  Akron *(G-270)*
Smith Ambulance Service Inc.............. E 330 825-0205
  Barberton *(G-709)*
Smith Ambulance Service Inc.............. E 330 602-0050
  Dover *(G-7900)*
Spirit Medical Transport LLC................ D 937 548-2800
  Greenville *(G-8886)*
Stofcheck Ambulance Svc Inc.............. E 740 499-2200
  La Rue *(G-9649)*
Superior Ar-Grund Amblnce Svc.......... C 630 832-2000
  Grove City *(G-8958)*
Tri-County Ambulance Svc Inc............. E 440 951-4600
  Mentor *(G-11005)*
United Amblnce Svc of Cmbridge......... E 740 685-2277
  Byesville *(G-1537)*

AMUSEMENT & RECREATION SVCS: Arcades

Beach At Mason Ltd Partnership........... E 513 398-7946
  Lebanon *(G-9756)*

SERVICES SECTION

Cedar Fair LP.................................... A 419 627-2344
  Sandusky *(G-12871)*
Cedar Point Park LLC......................... E 419 627-2350
  Sandusky *(G-12874)*
Cedar Point Park LLC......................... D 419 627-2500
  Sandusky *(G-12875)*
Kings Dominion LLC.......................... E 419 626-0830
  Sandusky *(G-12908)*
Kings Island Company........................ C 513 754-5700
  Kings Mills *(G-9642)*
Kings Island Park LLC........................ C 513 754-5901
  Kings Mills *(G-9643)*
Kings Island Park LLC........................ E 419 626-0830
  Sandusky *(G-12909)*
Millennium Operations LLC.................. E 419 626-0830
  Sandusky *(G-12915)*
Paramounts Kings Island.................... C 513 754-5700
  Mason *(G-10590)*
Strongville Recreation Complex........... C 440 580-3230
  Strongsville *(G-13489)*

AMUSEMENT & RECREATION SVCS: Exhibition Operation

Asm International.............................. D 440 338-5151
  Novelty *(G-12037)*
Roto Group LLC................................ D 614 760-8690
  Dublin *(G-8110)*

AMUSEMENT & RECREATION SVCS: Exposition Operation

Nexxtshow LLC.................................. E
  Cincinnati *(G-3114)*
Park Corporation................................ B 216 267-4870
  Medina *(G-10874)*

AMUSEMENT & RECREATION SVCS: Gambling & Lottery Svcs

Miami Valley Gaming & Racg LLC......... C 513 934-7070
  Lebanon *(G-9778)*

AMUSEMENT & RECREATION SVCS: Golf Club, Membership

Akron Management Corp..................... B 330 644-8441
  Akron *(G-34)*
Canterbury Golf Club Inc..................... D 216 561-1914
  Cleveland *(G-3923)*
Congress Lake Club Company............. E 330 877-9318
  Hartville *(G-9124)*
Jefferson Golf & Country Club.............. D 614 759-7500
  Blacklick *(G-1112)*
Lake Club... C 330 549-3996
  Poland *(G-12505)*
Mill Creek Golf Course Corp................ E 740 666-7711
  Ostrander *(G-12182)*
Mohawk Golf Club.............................. E 419 447-5876
  Tiffin *(G-13634)*
Muirfield Village Golf Club.................... E 614 889-6700
  Dublin *(G-8066)*
OBannon Creek Golf Club................... E 513 683-5657
  Loveland *(G-10156)*
Pepper Pike Club Company Inc............ D 216 831-9400
  Cleveland *(G-4739)*
Quail Hollow Management Inc............. C 440 639-4000
  Concord Township *(G-6933)*
Sand Ridge Golf Club......................... E 440 285-8088
  Chardon *(G-2019)*
Shelby Golf Course Inc....................... E 937 492-2883
  Sidney *(G-13049)*
Stone Oak Country Club..................... D 419 867-0969
  Holland *(G-9306)*

SERVICES SECTION

Tartan Fields Golf Club Ltd.................. D 614 792-0900
  Dublin (G-8140)
Walden Club.. E 330 995-7162
  Aurora (G-629)

AMUSEMENT & RECREATION SVCS: Pool Parlor

S & S Management Inc............................ D 567 356-4151
  Wapakoneta (G-14491)

AMUSEMENT & RECREATION SVCS: Recreation Center

Allwell Behavioral Health Svcs............... E 740 432-7155
  Cambridge (G-1553)
City of North Olmsted................................ D 440 734-8200
  North Olmsted (G-11896)
City of Seven Hills..................................... D 216 524-6262
  Seven Hills (G-12952)
City of Westlake... D 440 808-5700
  Westlake (G-15050)
Rec Center... E 330 721-6900
  Medina (G-10882)
Society of The Transfiguration................ D 513 771-7462
  Cincinnati (G-3391)
Strongville Recreation Complex.............. E 440 878-6000
  Cleveland (G-4957)
Troy City School District........................... E 937 339-0457
  Troy (G-14162)
Washington Twnship Mntgmery CN....... E 937 433-0130
  Dayton (G-7715)
Willo Putt-Putt Course Inc....................... E 440 951-7888
  Willoughby (G-15226)
Young MNS Chrstn Assn Grter Dy......... C 937 228-9622
  Dayton (G-7732)
Young MNS Chrstn Assn Wster OH....... E 330 264-3131
  Wooster (G-15402)

AMUSEMENT & RECREATION SVCS: Recreation SVCS

Anderson Township Park Dst.................. E 513 474-0003
  Cincinnati (G-2201)
Cleveland Metroparks............................... B 216 635-3200
  Cleveland (G-4056)
Columbus Frkln Cnty Pk........................... E 614 891-0700
  Westerville (G-14970)
Columbus Frnklin Cnty Mtro Pk............... E 614 891-0700
  Reynoldsburg (G-12659)
Columbus Frnklin Cnty Mtro Pk............... E 614 895-6219
  Westerville (G-14971)
Erie Metroparks General Info................... E 419 621-4220
  Huron (G-9387)
Five Rivers Metroparks............................. E 937 278-2601
  Dayton (G-7357)
Five Rivers Metroparks............................. E 937 228-2088
  Dayton (G-7358)
Friends Five Rivers Metroparks.............. C 937 275-7275
  Dayton (G-7369)
Goodrich Gnnett Nghborhood Ctr.......... E 216 432-1717
  Cleveland (G-4320)
Jack Entertainment LLC........................... D 313 309-5225
  Cleveland (G-4430)
Lake Metroparks....................................... E 440 256-2122
  Kirtland (G-9645)
Lake Metroparks....................................... E 440 639-7275
  Painesville (G-12233)
Mill Creek Metropolitan Park................... E 330 740-7116
  Youngstown (G-15668)
Stark County Park District........................ C 330 477-3552
  Canton (G-1860)

Strike Zone Inc... D 440 235-4420
  Olmsted Twp (G-12094)
Village of Sycamore.................................. D 419 927-2357
  Sycamore (G-13534)

AMUSEMENT ARCADES

Edwards Realty & Inv Corp..................... C 330 253-9171
  Copley (G-6957)
Good Inc... D 740 592-9667
  Athens (G-569)
Pnk (ohio) LLC... A 513 232-8000
  Cincinnati (G-3219)

AMUSEMENT PARKS

Cedar Point Park LLC............................... D 419 626-0830
  Sandusky (G-12873)
Lmn Development LLC............................ C 419 433-7200
  Sandusky (G-12910)
Magnum Management Corporation........ C 419 627-2334
  Sandusky (G-12913)
Muskingum Wtrshed Cnsrvncy Dst........ C 330 343-6780
  Mineral City (G-11301)
Sugar & Spice Spa llc............................... D 513 319-0112
  Mason (G-10612)
Willo Putt-Putt Course Inc....................... E 440 951-7888
  Willoughby (G-15226)

ANIMAL FEED & SUPPLEMENTS: Livestock & Poultry

Cooper Hatchery Inc................................. C 419 594-3325
  Oakwood (G-12053)
Pro-Pet LLC.. D 419 394-3374
  Saint Marys (G-12835)
Provimi North America Inc...................... B 937 770-2400
  Lewisburg (G-9842)

ANIMAL FEED: Wholesalers

Gerald Grain Center Inc........................... E 419 445-2451
  Archbold (G-459)
Griffin Industries LLC................................ E 419 257-3560
  North Baltimore (G-11800)
Provimi North America Inc...................... B 937 770-2400
  Lewisburg (G-9842)

ANIMAL FOOD & SUPPLEMENTS: Bird Food, Prepared

Centerra Co-Op... E 419 281-2153
  Ashland (G-490)

ANIMAL FOOD & SUPPLEMENTS: Cat

Pro-Pet LLC.. D 419 394-3374
  Saint Marys (G-12835)

ANIMAL FOOD & SUPPLEMENTS: Dog

JM Smucker LLC....................................... D 330 682-3000
  Orrville (G-12169)

ANIMAL FOOD & SUPPLEMENTS: Livestock

Hanby Farms Inc....................................... E 740 763-3554
  Nashport (G-11535)

ANIMAL FOOD & SUPPLEMENTS: Poultry

Cooper Farms Inc..................................... D 419 375-4116
  Fort Recovery (G-8606)

ANTENNAS: Radar Or Communications

Circle Prime Manufacturing..................... E 330 923-0019
  Cuyahoga Falls (G-7054)
Quasonix Inc... E 513 942-1287
  West Chester (G-14751)

ARCHITECTURAL SVCS

ANTIQUE REPAIR & RESTORATION SVCS, EXC FURNITURE & AUTOS

Ag-Pro Ohio LLC.. E 937 486-5211
  Wilmington (G-15238)

APPAREL DESIGNERS: Commercial

Atrium Apparel Corporation..................... D 740 966-8200
  Johnstown (G-9544)

APPLIANCES, HOUSEHOLD OR COIN OPERATED: Laundry Dryers

Whirlpool Corporation............................... E 740 383-7122
  Marion (G-10464)

APPLIANCES, HOUSEHOLD: Kitchen, Major, Exc Refrigs & Stoves

Sandco Industries..................................... E 419 547-3273
  Clyde (G-5209)

APPLIANCES: Household, Refrigerators & Freezers

Whirlpool Corporation............................... E 740 383-7122
  Marion (G-10464)

APPLIANCES: Major, Cooking

Nacco Industries Inc................................. E 440 229-5151
  Cleveland (G-4616)

APPLIANCES: Small, Electric

Johnson Bros Rubber Co Inc.................. E 419 752-4814
  Greenwich (G-8892)

APPLICATIONS SOFTWARE PROGRAMMING

B-Tek Scales LLC..................................... E 330 471-8900
  Canton (G-1684)
Balaji D Loganathan.................................. C 614 918-0411
  Hilliard (G-9182)
Campuseai Inc... C 216 589-9626
  Cleveland (G-3921)
Cerkl Incorporated.................................... D 513 813-8425
  Blue Ash (G-1147)
Data Systems Intgrtion Group I.............. C 614 344-4600
  Dublin (G-7982)
Epicor Edi Source Inc.............................. D 440 519-7800
  Solon (G-13084)
Foundation Software LLC........................ B 330 220-8383
  Strongsville (G-13457)
Icr Inc.. C 513 900-7007
  Mason (G-10563)
Iotco LLC.. E 877 464-6826
  Cincinnati (G-2887)
Jenne Inc.. C 440 835-0040
  Avon (G-656)
Overdrive Inc... D 216 573-6886
  Cleveland (G-4711)
Playaway Products LLC........................... D 440 893-0808
  Solon (G-13128)
Rhyme Software Corporation.................. D 888 213-3728
  New Albany (G-11585)

APPRAISAL SVCS, EXC REAL ESTATE

Amos Media Company.............................. C 937 638-0967
  Sidney (G-13018)
Real Estate Vltion Prtners LLC............... E 281 313-1571
  Toledo (G-13982)

ARCHITECTURAL SVCS

Arcadis A California Partnr...................... E 614 818-4900
  Columbus (G-5382)

Employee Codes: A=Over 500 employees, B=251-500
C=101-250, D=51-100, E=20-50, F=10-19, G=1-9

ARCHITECTURAL SVCS

ASC Group Inc .... E 614 268-2514
  Columbus *(G-5391)*
Big Red Rooster .... E 614 255-0200
  Columbus *(G-5440)*
Burgess & Niple Inc .... D 703 631-6041
  Columbus *(G-5486)*
Burgess & Niple/Heapy LLC .... D 614 459-2050
  Columbus *(G-5487)*
Ceso Inc .... E 937 435-8584
  Miamisburg *(G-11035)*
Chemstress Consultant Company .... C 330 535-5591
  Akron *(G-87)*
Chute Gerdeman Inc .... D 614 469-1001
  Westerville *(G-14966)*
Continental Office Furn Corp .... C 614 262-5010
  Columbus *(G-5693)*
Csa America Inc .... D 513 791-6918
  Cincinnati *(G-2520)*
CT Consultants Inc .... C 440 951-9000
  Mentor *(G-10930)*
Davis-Mcmackin Inc .... E 614 824-1587
  Columbus *(G-5742)*
Dlr Group Inc .... D 216 522-1350
  Cleveland *(G-4169)*
Dlz Ohio Inc .... C 614 888-0040
  Columbus *(G-5778)*
Emersion Design LLC .... E 513 841-9100
  Cincinnati *(G-2616)*
Garland/Dbs Inc .... C 216 641-7500
  Cleveland *(G-4302)*
Gbc Design Inc .... E 330 836-0228
  Akron *(G-171)*
Glaus Pyle Schmer Brns Dhven I .... E 216 518-5544
  Cleveland *(G-4314)*
Glaus Pyle Schmer Brns Dhven I .... D 614 210-0751
  Columbus *(G-5936)*
Glaus Pyle Schmer Brns Dhven I .... B 330 572-2100
  Akron *(G-176)*
Gpd Services Company Inc .... C 330 572-2100
  Akron *(G-180)*
HWH Archtcts-Ngnrs-Plnners Inc .... D 216 875-4000
  Cleveland *(G-4394)*
Karlsberger Companies .... C 614 461-9500
  Columbus *(G-6104)*
Ljb Incorporated .... E 440 683-4504
  Independence *(G-9446)*
Loth Inc .... D 513 554-4900
  Cincinnati *(G-2989)*
Louis Perry & Associates Inc .... C 330 334-1585
  Wadsworth *(G-14441)*
Ms Consultants Inc .... C 330 744-5321
  Youngstown *(G-15669)*
Onyx Creative Inc .... D 216 223-3200
  Cleveland *(G-4702)*
Poggemeyer Design Group Inc .... C 419 244-8074
  Bowling Green *(G-1331)*
Reed Westlake Leskosky Ltd .... C 216 522-0449
  Cleveland *(G-4817)*
Trinity Health Group Ltd .... E 614 899-4830
  Columbus *(G-6791)*
United Architectural Mtls Inc .... E 330 433-9220
  North Canton *(G-11868)*
URS Group Inc .... B 614 464-4500
  Columbus *(G-6835)*
WD Partners Inc .... B 614 634-7000
  Dublin *(G-8160)*

ARCHITECTURAL SVCS: Engineering

A D A Architects Inc .... E 216 521-5134
  Cleveland *(G-3749)*
Abbot Stdios Archtcts + Plnner .... E 614 461-0101
  Columbus *(G-5293)*
Andrews Architects Inc .... E 614 766-1117
  Worthington *(G-15404)*
Austin Building and Design Inc .... C 440 544-2600
  Cleveland *(G-3839)*
Baxter Hdell Dnnlly Prston Inc .... C 513 271-1634
  Cincinnati *(G-2240)*
Bostwick Design Partnr Inc .... E 216 621-7900
  Cleveland *(G-3882)*
Buehrer Group Arch & Engrg .... E 419 893-9021
  Maumee *(G-10706)*
Burgess & Niple Inc .... B 614 459-2050
  Columbus *(G-5485)*
Champlin Haupt Architects Inc .... E 513 241-4474
  Cincinnati *(G-2346)*
City Architecture Inc .... E 216 881-2444
  Cleveland *(G-3974)*
Collaborative Inc .... E 419 242-7405
  Toledo *(G-13748)*
Cornelia C Hodgson - Architec .... E 216 593-0057
  Beachwood *(G-784)*
David A Levy Inc .... E 330 352-1289
  Akron *(G-132)*
Dorsky Hodgson + Partners Inc .... D 216 464-8600
  Cleveland *(G-4179)*
Elevar Design Group Inc .... E 513 721-0600
  Cincinnati *(G-2611)*
Fanning/Howey Associates Inc .... D 614 764-4661
  Dublin *(G-8010)*
Fanning/Howey Associates Inc .... E 419 586-2292
  Celina *(G-1922)*
Garmann/Miller & Assoc Inc .... E 419 628-4240
  Minster *(G-11316)*
Harris Day Architects Inc .... E 330 493-3722
  North Canton *(G-11838)*
Hasenstab Architects Inc .... E 330 434-4464
  Akron *(G-187)*
Hixson Incorporated .... C 513 241-1230
  Cincinnati *(G-2829)*
Jdi Group Inc .... D 419 725-7161
  Maumee *(G-10733)*
K4 Architecture LLC .... D 513 455-5005
  Cincinnati *(G-2928)*
Karlsberger Architecture Inc .... E 614 471-1812
  Columbus *(G-6103)*
KZF Design Inc .... D 513 621-6211
  Cincinnati *(G-2959)*
Ljb Inc .... C 937 259-5000
  Miamisburg *(G-11070)*
Luminaut Inc .... E 513 984-1070
  Cincinnati *(G-2994)*
Makovich Pusti Architects Inc .... E 440 891-8910
  Berea *(G-1073)*
McGill Smith Punshon Inc .... E 513 759-0004
  Cincinnati *(G-3023)*
Meacham & Apel Architects Inc .... D 614 764-0407
  Columbus *(G-6220)*
Meyers + Associates Arch LLC .... E 614 221-9433
  Columbus *(G-6230)*
Michael Schuster Assoc Inc .... E 513 241-5666
  Cincinnati *(G-3056)*
Middough Inc .... B 216 367-6000
  Cleveland *(G-4577)*
Mkc Associates Inc .... E 740 657-3202
  Powell *(G-12599)*
Moody-Nolan Inc .... C 614 461-4664
  Columbus *(G-6260)*
NBBJ LLC .... C 206 223-5026
  Columbus *(G-6342)*
Nelson .... C 216 781-9144
  Seven Hills *(G-12955)*
New Republic Architecture .... E 513 800-8075
  Cincinnati *(G-3108)*
Neyer Architects Engineers Inc .... E 513 271-6400
  Cincinnati *(G-3115)*
Osborn Engineering Company .... D 216 861-2020
  Cleveland *(G-4708)*
Perspectus Architecture LLC .... E 216 752-1800
  Cleveland *(G-4744)*
R E Warner & Associates Inc .... D 440 835-9400
  Westlake *(G-15102)*
Red Architecture LLC .... D 614 487-8770
  Columbus *(G-6565)*
Richard L Bowen & Assoc Inc .... D 216 491-9300
  Cleveland *(G-4838)*
Rvc Architects Inc .... E 740 592-5615
  Athens *(G-587)*
Schooley Caldwell Assoc Inc .... D 614 628-0300
  Columbus *(G-6652)*
Shremshock Architects Inc .... D 614 545-4550
  New Albany *(G-11587)*
Ssoe Inc .... B 419 255-3830
  Toledo *(G-14023)*
Strollo Architects Inc .... E 330 743-1177
  Youngstown *(G-15731)*
Sullivan Bruck Architects Inc .... E 614 464-9800
  Columbus *(G-6726)*
Tc Architects Inc .... E 330 867-1093
  Akron *(G-330)*
Triad Architects Ltd .... E 614 942-1050
  Columbus *(G-6787)*
URS Group Inc .... B 330 836-9111
  Akron *(G-344)*

ARMATURE REPAIRING & REWINDING SVC

Yaskawa America Inc .... C 937 847-6200
  Miamisburg *(G-11105)*

ART GOODS & SPLYS WHOLESALERS

Checker Notions Company Inc .... C 419 893-3636
  Maumee *(G-10710)*
Distribution Data Incorporated .... D 216 362-3009
  Brookpark *(G-1433)*

ART SPLY STORES

United Art and Education Inc .... E 800 322-3247
  Dayton *(G-7680)*

ARTS & CRAFTS SCHOOL

South Central Ohio Eductl Ctr .... D 740 456-0517
  New Boston *(G-11595)*

ASPHALT & ASPHALT PRDTS

Central Allied Enterprises Inc .... E 330 477-6751
  Canton *(G-1706)*
Gerken Materials Inc .... E 419 533-2421
  Napoleon *(G-11524)*
Shelly Materials Inc .... E 740 666-5841
  Ostrander *(G-12184)*
Stoneco Inc .... E 419 422-8854
  Findlay *(G-8588)*

ASPHALT COATINGS & SEALERS

Hy-Grade Corporation .... E 216 341-7711
  Cleveland *(G-4395)*
Owens Corning Sales LLC .... A 419 248-8000
  Toledo *(G-13952)*
Pioneer Manufacturing Inc .... D 216 671-5500
  Cleveland *(G-4750)*
Simon Roofing and Shtmtl Corp .... C 330 629-7392
  Youngstown *(G-15725)*
State Industrial Products Corp .... B 877 747-6986
  Cleveland *(G-4944)*

SERVICES SECTION

AUDIO & VIDEO EQPT, EXC COMMERCIAL

ASPHALT MIXTURES WHOLESALERS

Hy-Grade Corporation.................................. E 216 341-7711
  Cleveland (G-4395)

ASSOCIATION FOR THE HANDICAPPED

Cincinnati Assn For The Blind..................... C 513 221-8558
  Cincinnati (G-2395)
Cleveland Soc For The Blind....................... C 216 791-8118
  Cleveland (G-4067)
Hattie Larlham Community Svcs.................. E 330 274-2272
  Mantua (G-10330)
Spectrum Supportive Services..................... E 216 875-0460
  Cleveland (G-4931)

ASSOCIATIONS: Bar

Action Bar LLC... E 419 250-1938
  Bowling Green (G-1302)
Columbus Bar Association........................... E 614 221-4112
  Columbus (G-5615)
Ohio State Bar Association......................... D 614 487-2050
  Columbus (G-6446)
Toledo Bar Association Inc......................... E 419 242-9363
  Toledo (G-14051)

ASSOCIATIONS: Business

Archdiocese of Cincinnati............................ E 513 779-6585
  Middletown (G-11152)
Blue Chip Pavement Maintenance Inc....... D 513 321-9595
  Cincinnati (G-2268)
Certified Angus Beef LLC........................... D 330 345-2333
  Wooster (G-15318)
City of Kenton.. E 419 674-4850
  Kenton (G-9612)
City of Louisville.. E 330 875-3321
  Louisville (G-10114)
City of Oberlin... E 440 775-1531
  Oberlin (G-12065)
City of Toledo.. E 419 245-1400
  Toledo (G-13739)
City of Toledo.. E 419 245-1001
  Toledo (G-13741)
Consolidated Cooperative........................... D 419 947-3055
  Mount Gilead (G-11459)
County of Montgomery................................ C 937 225-4010
  Dayton (G-7254)
Department of Commerce Ohio................. D 614 728-8400
  Columbus (G-5756)
Interstate Contractors LLC......................... E 513 372-5393
  Mason (G-10568)
Lucas County Ohio..................................... D 419 213-4808
  Toledo (G-13896)
Mid-Ohio Regional Plg Comm................... D 614 228-2663
  Columbus (G-6239)
Ohio Cvil Svc Emplyees Assn AF.............. D 614 865-4700
  Westerville (G-14920)
Prime Outlets Acquisition LLC................... E 740 948-9090
  Jeffersonville (G-9542)
Redi Cincinnati LLC.................................... E 513 562-8474
  Cincinnati (G-3278)
Union Rural Electric Coop Inc.................... E 937 642-1826
  Marysville (G-10515)
Universal Advg Assoc Inc........................... E 513 522-5000
  Cincinnati (G-3560)

ASSOCIATIONS: Engineering

CCI Engineering... E 614 485-0670
  Columbus (G-5524)

ASSOCIATIONS: Real Estate Management

Al Neyer LLC... D 513 271-6400
  Cincinnati (G-2157)

Alpha PHI Alpha Homes Inc....................... E 330 376-9956
  Akron (G-44)
American Bulk Commodities Inc................ C 330 758-0841
  Youngstown (G-15549)
Bock & Clark Corporation........................... E 330 665-4821
  Canton (G-1688)
Community Management Corp.................. D 513 761-6339
  Cincinnati (G-2484)
Eagle Realty Group LLC............................. E 513 361-7700
  Cincinnati (G-2595)
Fairfield Homes Inc..................................... E 740 653-3583
  Lancaster (G-9714)
Forest City Commercial MGT Inc.............. C 216 696-7701
  Cleveland (G-4268)
Forest City Commercial MGT Inc.............. E 216 621-6060
  Cleveland (G-4269)
Forest Cy Residential MGT Inc.................. C 216 621-6060
  Cleveland (G-4276)
G J Goudreau & Co.................................... E 216 351-5233
  Cleveland (G-4297)
Ihs Services Inc.. D 419 224-8811
  Lima (G-9909)
Irg Realty Advisors LLC.............................. E 330 659-4060
  Richfield (G-12699)
John Stewart Company............................... E 513 703-5412
  Cincinnati (G-2914)
Klingbeil Management Group Co............... E 614 220-8900
  Columbus (G-6120)
Manco Real Estate MGT Inc...................... E 937 277-9551
  Dayton (G-7465)
Miller-Vlentine Operations Inc.................... B 513 771-0900
  Dayton (G-7508)
Miller-Vlentine Operations Inc.................... E 937 293-0900
  Dayton (G-7507)
MJM Management Corporation.................. E 330 678-0761
  Kent (G-9588)
Model Group Inc... E 513 559-0048
  Cincinnati (G-3074)
Monarch Inv & MGT Group LLC................ A 216 453-3630
  Cleveland (G-4597)
Neyer Real Estate MGT LLC...................... C 513 618-6000
  Cincinnati (G-3116)
Oakwood Management Company.............. E 614 866-8702
  Reynoldsburg (G-12671)
Olmsted Residence Corporation................ C 440 235-7100
  Olmsted Twp (G-12093)
Paran Management Company Ltd............. E 216 921-5663
  Cleveland (G-4719)
Pizzuti Inc.. E 614 280-4000
  Columbus (G-6527)
Plaza Properties Inc.................................... E 614 237-3726
  Columbus (G-6532)
Plk Communities LLC................................ D 513 561-5080
  Cincinnati (G-3214)
Real Property Management Inc................. E 614 766-6500
  Dublin (G-8106)
Reuben Co... E 419 241-3400
  Toledo (G-13989)
Rlj Management Co Inc.............................. C 614 942-2020
  Columbus (G-6602)
Rose Community Management LLC......... C 917 542-3600
  Independence (G-9479)
Schottenstein RE Group LLC..................... E 614 418-8900
  Columbus (G-6653)
Schroeder Company................................... E 419 473-3139
  Perrysburg (G-12368)
Sundance Property MGT LLC.................... E 513 489-3363
  Blue Ash (G-1247)
T & R Properties... E 614 923-4000
  Dublin (G-8138)
Tipton Group Inc... E 937 885-6300
  Dayton (G-7670)

Turnserv LLC.. E 216 600-8876
  Akron (G-338)
Vistula Management Company.................. D 419 242-2300
  Toledo (G-14094)
Wallick Properties Midwest LLC................ A 419 381-7477
  New Albany (G-11591)
Whitehurst Company................................... E 419 534-6022
  Maumee (G-10780)
Zaremba Group LLC................................... D 216 221-6600
  Lakewood (G-9689)

ASSOCIATIONS: Scientists'

American Ceramic Society.......................... E 614 890-4700
  Westerville (G-14877)

ASSOCIATIONS: Trade

Allied Construction Industries..................... D 513 221-8020
  Cincinnati (G-2167)
American Jersey Cattle Assn...................... E 614 861-3636
  Reynoldsburg (G-12652)
Buckeye Power Inc..................................... E 614 781-0573
  Columbus (G-5477)
Council Dev Fin Agencies.......................... E 614 705-1300
  Columbus (G-5709)
County Commissioners Assn Ohio............ E 614 220-0636
  Columbus (G-5710)
Gs1 Us Inc... C 609 620-0200
  Dayton (G-7389)
Hospital Council of NW Ohio..................... E 419 842-0800
  Toledo (G-13852)
National Assn Cllege Stres Inc................... D 440 775-7777
  Oberlin (G-12073)
National Federation Ind Bus...................... D 614 221-4107
  Columbus (G-6297)
National Ground Water Assn Inc............... E 614 898-7791
  Westerville (G-15004)
Ohio Hospital Association........................... D 614 221-7614
  Columbus (G-6430)
Ohio Restaurant Association...................... E 614 442-3535
  Columbus (G-6442)
Precision Metalforming Assn...................... E 216 901-8800
  Independence (G-9471)
United States Trotting Assn........................ D 614 224-2291
  Westerville (G-15020)
Vigilant Global Trade Svcs LLC................. E 260 417-1825
  Shaker Heights (G-12988)

ATOMIZERS

Automtve Rfnish Clor Sltons I..................... E 330 461-6067
  Medina (G-10810)

AUCTIONEERS: Fee Basis

2mc Management LLC............................... E 513 771-1700
  Cincinnati (G-2122)
Cowans LLC.. D 513 871-1670
  Cincinnati (G-2513)
Kaufman Realty & Auctions LLC................ E 330 852-4111
  Sugarcreek (G-13511)
Mt Hope Auction Inc................................... E 330 674-6188
  Mount Hope (G-11467)
Oki Auction LLC.. D 513 679-7910
  Cincinnati (G-3154)
Online Liquidation Auction LLC................. E 440 596-8733
  North Royalton (G-11947)
Skipco Financial Adjusters Inc................... D 330 854-4800
  Canal Fulton (G-1594)

AUDIO & VIDEO EQPT, EXC COMMERCIAL

Fellhauer Mechanical Systems................... E 419 734-3674
  Port Clinton (G-12525)
Floyd Bell Inc.. D 614 294-4000
  Columbus (G-5874)

Pioneer Automotive Tech Inc................... C 937 746-2293
  Miamisburg *(G-11084)*

AUDIO-VISUAL PROGRAM PRODUCTION SVCS

Arctos Tech Solutions LLC.................... D 937 426-2808
  Beavercreek *(G-859)*
Bkg Holdings LLC.............................. E 614 252-7455
  Columbus *(G-5442)*
Strategy Group For Media Inc............... E 740 201-5500
  Delaware *(G-7829)*

AUTO & HOME SUPPLY STORES: Auto & Truck Eqpt & Parts

Allstate Trck Sls Estrn Ohio L................ E 330 339-5555
  New Philadelphia *(G-11639)*
Dutro Ford Lincoln-Mercury Inc............. D 740 452-6334
  Zanesville *(G-15786)*
Pete Baur Buick GMC Inc..................... E 440 238-5600
  Cleveland *(G-4745)*
Stricker Bros Inc................................. E 513 732-1152
  Batavia *(G-748)*

AUTO & HOME SUPPLY STORES: Automotive parts

Auto Parts Center-Cuyahoga FLS........... E 330 928-2149
  Cuyahoga Falls *(G-7045)*
Autozone Inc..................................... E 216 751-0571
  Cleveland *(G-3842)*
Autozone Inc..................................... E 216 267-6586
  Cleveland *(G-3843)*
Autozone Inc..................................... E 440 593-6934
  Conneaut *(G-6939)*
Autozone Inc..................................... E 440 639-2247
  Painesville *(G-12221)*
Autozone Inc..................................... E 419 872-2813
  Perrysburg *(G-12315)*
Bridgeport Auto Parts Inc.................... E 740 635-0441
  Bridgeport *(G-1375)*
Car Parts Warehouse Inc..................... E 216 281-4500
  Brookpark *(G-1429)*
Chagrin Valley Auto Parts Co................ E 216 398-9800
  Cleveland *(G-3960)*
Cole Valley Motor Company Ltd............ D 330 372-1665
  Warren *(G-14509)*
Dave Dennis Inc................................. D 937 429-5566
  Beavercreek Township *(G-935)*
Fayette Parts Service Inc..................... E 724 880-3616
  Wintersville *(G-15294)*
Four Wheel Drive Hardware LLC........... C 330 482-4733
  Columbiana *(G-5235)*
Haasz Automall LLC............................ E 330 296-2866
  Ravenna *(G-12627)*
Jegs Automotive LLC.......................... C 614 294-5050
  Delaware *(G-7808)*
KOI Enterprises Inc............................. C 513 648-3020
  Cincinnati *(G-2947)*
Pat Young Service Co Inc..................... E 216 447-8550
  Cleveland *(G-4729)*
Pep Boys - Mnny Moe Jack Del L........... E 614 864-2092
  Columbus *(G-6515)*
Smyth Automotive Inc......................... D 513 528-2800
  Cincinnati *(G-3389)*
Snyders Antique Auto Parts Inc............ E 330 549-5313
  New Springfield *(G-11679)*
Weastec Incorporated......................... E 614 734-9645
  Dublin *(G-8161)*

AUTO & HOME SUPPLY STORES: Trailer Hitches, Automotive

Ziebart of Ohio Inc.............................. E 440 845-6031
  Cleveland *(G-5175)*

AUTO & HOME SUPPLY STORES: Truck Eqpt & Parts

Bulldawg Holdings LLC........................ E 419 423-3131
  Findlay *(G-8519)*
Esec Corporation............................... E 614 875-3732
  Grove City *(G-8918)*
Helton Enterprises Inc......................... E 419 423-4180
  Findlay *(G-8546)*
Hill Intl Trcks NA LLC........................... D 330 386-6440
  East Liverpool *(G-8185)*
Miami Valley Intl Trcks Inc.................... E 937 324-5526
  Springfield *(G-13273)*
R & M Leasing Inc............................... C 937 382-6800
  Wilmington *(G-15269)*
Tractor Supply Company...................... E 937 382-2595
  Wilmington *(G-15275)*
Valley Ford Truck Inc........................... D 216 524-2400
  Cleveland *(G-5097)*
Wabash National Trlr Ctrs Inc................ D 614 878-6088
  Groveport *(G-9012)*
Wz Management Inc........................... E 330 628-4881
  Akron *(G-365)*

AUTO SPLYS & PARTS, NEW, WHSLE: Exhaust Sys, Mufflers, Etc

Dreison International Inc..................... C 216 362-0755
  Cleveland *(G-4184)*
P & M Exhaust Systems Whse Inc......... E 513 825-2660
  Cincinnati *(G-3179)*

AUTOMATIC REGULATING CONTROL: Building Svcs Monitoring, Auto

Evokes LLC....................................... E 513 947-8433
  Mason *(G-10545)*

AUTOMATIC REGULATING CONTROLS: Appliance, Exc AirCond/Refr

Melink Corporation............................. D 513 685-0958
  Milford *(G-11242)*

AUTOMOBILE FINANCE LEASING

BMW Financial Services Na LLC........... D 614 718-6900
  Dublin *(G-7945)*
BMW Financial Services Na LLC........... E 614 718-6900
  Hilliard *(G-9184)*
Ford Motor Company.......................... E 513 573-1101
  Mason *(G-10549)*
Keybank National Association............... B 800 539-2968
  Cleveland *(G-4461)*
Momentum Fleet MGT Group Inc.......... D 440 759-2219
  Westlake *(G-15080)*
Security Nat Auto Accptnce LLC........... C 513 459-8118
  Mason *(G-10605)*

AUTOMOBILES & OTHER MOTOR VEHICLES WHOLESALERS

Abers Garage Inc............................... E 419 281-5500
  Ashland *(G-471)*
Bobb Automotive Inc.......................... E 614 853-3000
  Columbus *(G-5452)*
Cerni Leasing LLC.............................. B 515 967-3300
  Youngstown *(G-15574)*
Coughlin Chevrolet Inc........................ D 740 964-9191
  Pataskala *(G-12271)*
Cronin Auto Inc.................................. C 419 874-4331
  Perrysburg *(G-12327)*
Dave Knapp Ford Lincoln Inc................ E 937 547-3000
  Greenville *(G-8869)*
Donley Ford-Lincoln Inc....................... E 419 281-3673
  Ashland *(G-497)*
Dons Automotive Group Llc................. E 419 337-3010
  Wauseon *(G-14599)*
Doug Bigelow Chevrolet Inc................. D 330 644-7500
  Akron *(G-136)*
Downtown Ford Lincoln Inc.................. D 330 456-2781
  Canton *(G-1738)*
Dutro Ford Lincoln-Mercury Inc............. D 740 452-6334
  Zanesville *(G-15786)*
Ed Tomko Chrysler Jeep Ddge In.......... E 440 835-5900
  Avon Lake *(G-677)*
George P Ballas Buick GMC Trck........... E 419 535-1000
  Toledo *(G-13820)*
Graham Chevrolet-Cadillac Co.............. C 419 989-4012
  Ontario *(G-12105)*
Haydocy Automotive Inc...................... D 614 279-8880
  Columbus *(G-5973)*
Hidy Motors Inc.................................. D 937 426-9564
  Dayton *(G-7133)*
Klaben Lincoln Ford Inc....................... D 330 593-6800
  Kent *(G-9585)*
Laria Chevrolet-Buick Inc..................... E 330 925-2015
  Rittman *(G-12730)*
McCluskey Chevrolet Inc..................... C 513 761-1111
  Loveland *(G-10149)*
Recmv2 Inc....................................... D 330 367-5461
  Youngstown *(G-15707)*
Rush Truck Leasing Inc........................ E 937 264-2365
  Dayton *(G-7599)*
Rush Truck Leasing Inc........................ E 419 224-6045
  Lima *(G-9957)*
Rush Truck Leasing Inc........................ E 330 798-0600
  Walton Hills *(G-14479)*
Sharpnack Chevrolet Co...................... E 800 752-7513
  Vermilion *(G-14408)*
Sims Buick-GMC Truck Inc................... E 330 372-3500
  Warren *(G-14554)*
Slimans Sales & Service Inc................. E 440 988-4484
  Amherst *(G-432)*
Valley Ford Truck Inc........................... D 216 524-2400
  Cleveland *(G-5097)*
Village Motors Inc............................... D 330 674-2055
  Millersburg *(G-11295)*
Voss Auto Network Inc........................ E 937 428-2447
  Dayton *(G-7711)*
Voss Chevrolet Inc.............................. C 937 428-2500
  Dayton *(G-7713)*
Voss Dodge....................................... E 937 435-7800
  Dayton *(G-7714)*
Wabash National Trlr Ctrs Inc................ D 614 878-6088
  Groveport *(G-9012)*
Warner Buick-Nissan Inc...................... E 419 423-7161
  Findlay *(G-8597)*
White Family Companies Inc................ E 937 222-3701
  Dayton *(G-7720)*

AUTOMOBILES: Wholesalers

Albert Mike Leasing............................ C 513 563-1400
  Cincinnati *(G-2158)*
Beechmont Chevrolet Inc.................... D 513 624-1100
  Cincinnati *(G-2247)*
Beechmont Motors Inc........................ E 513 388-3883
  Cincinnati *(G-2248)*
Beechmont Motors T Inc..................... D 513 388-3800
  Cincinnati *(G-2249)*

SERVICES SECTION

AUTOMOTIVE & TRUCK GENERAL REPAIR SVC

Broadvue Motors Inc..................................D 440 845-6000
  Cleveland *(G-3899)*

Stykemain-Buick-Gmc Ltd......................D 419 784-5252
  Defiance *(G-7770)*

AUTOMOTIVE & TRUCK GENERAL REPAIR SVC

Abraham Ford LLC...................................E 440 233-7402
  Elyria *(G-8232)*

Advantage Ford Lincoln Mercury...........E 419 334-9751
  Fremont *(G-8664)*

Al Spitzer Ford Inc....................................E 330 929-6546
  Cuyahoga Falls *(G-7034)*

Ashtabula Area City School Dst.............E 440 992-1221
  Ashtabula *(G-517)*

Automtive Rfnish Clor Sltons I................E 330 461-6067
  Medina *(G-10810)*

Beechmont Ford Inc.................................C 513 752-6611
  Cincinnati *(G-2098)*

Belle Tire Distributors Inc.......................E 419 535-3033
  Toledo *(G-13704)*

Bill Delord Autocenter Inc.......................D 513 932-3000
  Maineville *(G-10225)*

Bob Ford Chapman Inc............................E 937 642-0015
  Marysville *(G-10475)*

Bob-Boyd Ford Inc...................................D 614 860-0606
  Lancaster *(G-9697)*

Bowling Green Lincoln Inc......................E 419 352-2553
  Bowling Green *(G-1312)*

Brentlinger Enterprises............................C 614 889-2571
  Dublin *(G-7947)*

Broadvue Motors Inc................................D 440 845-6000
  Cleveland *(G-3899)*

Brondes Ford..E 419 473-1411
  Toledo *(G-13719)*

Brown Motor Sales Co..............................E 419 531-0151
  Toledo *(G-13720)*

Buckeye Ford Inc......................................E 740 852-7842
  London *(G-10038)*

Cain Motors Inc...E 330 494-5588
  Canton *(G-1695)*

Central Cadillac Limited..........................D 216 861-5800
  Cleveland *(G-3954)*

City of Athens..E 740 592-3343
  Athens *(G-561)*

Classic Automotive Group Inc................E 440 255-5511
  Mentor *(G-10922)*

Cole Valley Motor Company Ltd............D 330 372-1665
  Warren *(G-14509)*

Columbus SAI Motors LLC.....................E 614 851-3273
  Columbus *(G-5653)*

Conrads Tire Service Inc.........................E 216 941-3333
  Cleveland *(G-4103)*

Coughlin Chevrolet Inc............................D 740 964-9191
  Pataskala *(G-12271)*

Cronin Auto Inc...C 419 874-4331
  Perrysburg *(G-12327)*

Cronin Automotive Co LLC....................E 513 202-5812
  Harrison *(G-9100)*

D & S Custom Van Inc.............................E 440 946-2178
  Mentor *(G-10931)*

D + S Distribution Inc..............................D 330 804-5590
  Orrville *(G-12160)*

Dave Dennis Inc..D 937 429-5566
  Beavercreek Township *(G-935)*

Dcr Systems LLC......................................E 440 205-9900
  Mentor *(G-10932)*

Decosky Motor Holdings Inc...................E 740 397-9122
  Mount Vernon *(G-11483)*

Delaware City School District.................D 740 363-5901
  Delaware *(G-7794)*

Detroit Tire & Auto Supply Inc...............E 937 426-0949
  Xenia *(G-15503)*

Dick Masheter Ford Inc...........................D 614 861-7150
  Columbus *(G-5764)*

Don Wood Inc..E 740 593-6641
  Athens *(G-566)*

Doug Bigelow Chevrolet Inc...................D 330 644-7500
  Akron *(G-136)*

Downtown Ford Lincoln Inc....................D 330 456-2781
  Canton *(G-1738)*

Dunning Motor Sales Inc........................E 740 439-4465
  Cambridge *(G-1568)*

Dutro Ford Lincoln-Mercury Inc............D 740 452-6334
  Zanesville *(G-15786)*

Duvall Automotive LLC...........................E 513 836-6447
  Blanchester *(G-1116)*

Ed Mullinax Ford LLC..............................C 440 984-2431
  Amherst *(G-427)*

Ed Tomko Chrysler Jeep Ddge In..........E 440 835-5900
  Avon Lake *(G-677)*

Fairborn Buick-GMC Truck Inc...............D 937 878-7371
  Fairborn *(G-8374)*

FCA US LLC...E 419 727-7285
  Toledo *(G-13804)*

Germain of Beavercreek II LLC............D 937 429-2400
  Beavercreek *(G-880)*

Germain of Sidney III LLC......................E 937 498-4014
  Sidney *(G-13035)*

Goodyear Tire & Rubber Company........A 330 796-2121
  Akron *(G-179)*

Greenwood Chevrolet Inc.......................C 330 270-1299
  Youngstown *(G-15624)*

Grismer Tire Company.............................E 937 643-2526
  Centerville *(G-1945)*

Grogans Towne Chrysler Inc..................D 419 476-0761
  Toledo *(G-13830)*

Guess Motors Inc......................................E 866 890-0522
  Carrollton *(G-1908)*

Harry Humphries Auto City Inc.............E 330 343-6681
  Dover *(G-7888)*

Haydocy Automotive Inc.........................D 614 279-8880
  Columbus *(G-5973)*

Highway Auto Center LLC......................E 440 543-9569
  Chagrin Falls *(G-1979)*

Hill Intl Trcks NA LLC...............................D 330 386-6440
  East Liverpool *(G-8185)*

Hoss Value Cars & Trucks Inc................E 937 428-2400
  Dayton *(G-7415)*

I-75 Pierson Automotive Inc...................E 513 424-1881
  Franklin *(G-8642)*

IAC Wauseon LLC....................................E 419 335-1000
  Wauseon *(G-14605)*

Interstate Ford Inc....................................C 937 866-0781
  Miamisburg *(G-11065)*

Irace Inc..E 330 836-7247
  Akron *(G-204)*

Jake Sweeney Automotive Inc...............D 513 782-2800
  Cincinnati *(G-2896)*

Jerry Haag Motors Inc.............................E 937 402-2090
  Hillsboro *(G-9261)*

Jim Keim Ford..D 614 888-3333
  Columbus *(G-6091)*

Kempthorn Motors Inc............................D 800 451-3877
  Canton *(G-1790)*

Kenworth of Cincinnati Inc.....................E 513 771-5831
  Cincinnati *(G-2937)*

Kerry Ford Inc...D 513 671-6400
  Cincinnati *(G-2939)*

Kings Toyota Inc.......................................D 513 583-4333
  Cincinnati *(G-2941)*

Klaben Lincoln Ford Inc..........................D 330 593-6800
  Kent *(G-9585)*

Knox Auto LLC..E 330 701-5266
  Mount Vernon *(G-11490)*

Krieger Ford Inc..C 614 888-3320
  Columbus *(G-6129)*

Lakewood Chrysler-Plymouth.................E 216 521-1000
  Brookpark *(G-1437)*

Lariche Chevrolet-Cadillac Inc...............D 419 422-1855
  Findlay *(G-8556)*

Lavery Chevrolet-Buick Inc.....................E 330 823-1100
  Alliance *(G-388)*

Lebanon Ford Inc......................................D 513 932-1010
  Lebanon *(G-9775)*

Lima Auto Mall Inc...................................D 419 993-6000
  Lima *(G-9918)*

Lima City School District........................E 419 996-3400
  Lima *(G-9919)*

Lincoln Mrcury Kings Auto Mall............E 513 683-3800
  Cincinnati *(G-2979)*

Lower Great Lakes Kenworth Inc..........E 419 874-3511
  Perrysburg *(G-12354)*

Mark Thomas Ford Inc............................E 330 638-1010
  Cortland *(G-6972)*

Mathews Ddge Chrysler Jeep Inc.........E 740 389-2341
  Marion *(G-10443)*

Mathews Ford Sandusky Inc..................E 419 626-4721
  Sandusky *(G-12914)*

Mathews Kennedy Ford L-M Inc............D 740 387-3673
  Marion *(G-10444)*

Matia Motors Inc......................................E 440 365-7311
  Elyria *(G-8273)*

Meinkings Service LLC..........................E 513 631-5198
  Cincinnati *(G-3037)*

Midway Inc...D 419 465-2551
  Monroeville *(G-11357)*

Mike Castrucci Ford..................................C 513 831-7010
  Milford *(G-11243)*

Mike Ford Bass Inc...................................D 440 934-3673
  Sheffield Village *(G-13002)*

Montrose Ford Inc.....................................C 330 666-0711
  Fairlawn *(G-8491)*

Nassief Automotive Inc...........................E 440 997-5151
  Austinburg *(G-632)*

National Auto Experts LLC.....................C 440 274-5114
  Strongsville *(G-13478)*

Nicholas Auto Elec Rblding LLC...........D 740 373-3861
  Marietta *(G-10395)*

Nick Mayer Lincoln-Mercury Inc............D 877 836-5314
  Westlake *(G-15084)*

Northern Automotive Inc........................E 614 436-2001
  Columbus *(G-6367)*

Northgate Chrysler Ddge Jeep I...........D 513 385-3900
  Cincinnati *(G-3123)*

Nvp Warranty...D 888 270-5835
  Independence *(G-9462)*

Orwell Tire Service Inc............................D 440 437-6515
  Orwell *(G-12179)*

Pallotta Ford Inc..D 330 345-5051
  Wooster *(G-15365)*

Parkman Automotive LLC.......................E 234 223-2806
  Warren *(G-14545)*

Pep Boys - Mnny Moe Jack Del L.........E 614 864-2092
  Columbus *(G-6515)*

Priced Right Cars Inc..............................E 614 337-0037
  Columbus *(G-6545)*

Putnam Cnty Commissioners Off..........E 419 523-6832
  Ottawa *(G-12192)*

Ricart Ford Inc..B 614 836-5321
  Groveport *(G-9000)*

Ron Marhofer Auto Family......................E 330 940-4422
  Cuyahoga Falls *(G-7098)*

Ron Marhofer Automall Inc....................E 330 923-5059
  Cuyahoga Falls *(G-7100)*

Employee Codes: A=Over 500 employees, B=251-500
C=101-250, D=51-100, E=20-50, F=10-19, G=1-9

AUTOMOTIVE & TRUCK GENERAL REPAIR SVC

Company	Col	Phone
Rondy Fleet Services Inc	E	330 745-9016
Barberton (G-706)		
Roush Equipment Inc	C	614 882-1535
Westerville (G-15014)		
Rush Truck Centers Ohio Inc	E	513 733-8500
Cincinnati (G-3334)		
Rush Truck Leasing Inc	E	937 264-2365
Dayton (G-7599)		
Rush Truck Leasing Inc	E	419 224-6045
Lima (G-9957)		
Rush Truck Leasing Inc	E	330 798-0600
Walton Hills (G-14479)		
Salem City Schools	E	330 332-2321
Salem (G-12851)		
Schoner Chevrolet Inc	E	330 877-6731
Hartville (G-9129)		
Seaway Gas & Petroleum Inc	E	216 566-9070
Cleveland (G-4888)		
Sharpnack Chevrolet Co	E	800 752-7513
Vermilion (G-14408)		
Sonic Automotive	D	614 870-8200
Columbus (G-6692)		
Spires Motors Inc	E	614 771-2345
Hilliard (G-9233)		
Spitzer Chevrolet Inc	E	330 467-4141
Northfield (G-11966)		
Sunnyside Cars Inc	E	440 777-9911
North Olmsted (G-11917)		
Surfside Motors Inc	E	419 419-4776
Galion (G-8751)		
T I G Fleet Service Inc	E	419 250-6333
Perrysburg (G-12374)		
Tansky Motors Inc	E	650 322-7069
Rockbridge (G-12736)		
Taylor Chevrolet Inc	E	740 653-2091
Lancaster (G-9746)		
Tim Lally Chevrolet Inc	D	440 232-2000
Bedford (G-988)		
Tm Final Ltd	B	419 724-8473
Toledo (G-14047)		
United Parcel Service Inc	D	419 872-0211
Perrysburg (G-12382)		
Valley Ford Truck Inc	D	216 524-2400
Cleveland (G-5097)		
Vin Devers Inc	C	888 847-9535
Sylvania (G-13578)		
Volvo BMW Dyton Evans Volkswag	E	937 890-6200
Dayton (G-7710)		
Voss Auto Network Inc	E	937 428-2447
Dayton (G-7711)		
Walker Auto Group Inc	E	937 433-4950
Miamisburg (G-11103)		
Walt Ford Sweeney Inc	D	513 347-2600
Cincinnati (G-3639)		
Warner Buick-Nissan Inc	E	419 423-7161
Findlay (G-8597)		
Yorktown Automotive Center Inc	E	440 885-2803
Cleveland (G-5165)		
Young Truck Sales Inc	E	330 477-6271
Canton (G-1891)		

AUTOMOTIVE BODY SHOP

Company	Col	Phone
American Nat Fleet Svc Inc	D	216 447-6060
Cleveland (G-3805)		
Buckeye Collision Service Inc	E	740 387-5313
Marion (G-10420)		
Coughlin Chevrolet Inc	E	740 852-1122
London (G-10040)		
Dave Dennis Inc	D	937 429-5566
Beavercreek Township (G-935)		
Highway Auto Center LLC	E	440 543-9569
Chagrin Falls (G-1979)		
Jake Sweeney Body Shop	D	513 782-1100
Cincinnati (G-2897)		
Joyce Buick Inc	E	419 529-3211
Ontario (G-12110)		
Kumler Collision Inc	E	740 653-4301
Lancaster (G-9728)		
Meinkings Service LLC	E	513 631-5198
Cincinnati (G-3037)		
Northgate Chrysler Ddge Jeep I	D	513 385-3900
Cincinnati (G-3123)		
Paul Hrnchar Ford-Mercury Inc	E	330 533-3673
Canfield (G-1638)		
Roemer Unlimited Inc	E	216 267-5454
Cleveland (G-4852)		
Ron Marhofer Automall Inc	C	330 835-6707
Cuyahoga Falls (G-7099)		
S&S / Superior Coach Co Inc	E	888 324-7895
Lima (G-9958)		
Suburban Collision Centers	E	440 777-1717
North Olmsted (G-11916)		
Tallmadge Collision Center	E	330 630-2188
Tallmadge (G-13608)		
Three C Body Shop Inc	E	614 885-0900
Columbus (G-6766)		
Three C Body Shop Inc	D	614 274-9700
Columbus (G-6765)		
Voss Auto Network Inc	B	937 433-1444
Dayton (G-7712)		

AUTOMOTIVE BODY, PAINT & INTERIOR REPAIR & MAINTENANCE SVC

Company	Col	Phone
Advantage Ford Lincoln Mercury	E	419 334-9751
Fremont (G-8664)		
Aero Industries Inc	D	330 626-3246
Kent (G-9555)		
Brondes Ford	E	419 473-1411
Toledo (G-13719)		
Brown Motor Sales Co	E	419 531-0151
Toledo (G-13720)		
Chesrown Oldsmobile GMC Inc	E	614 846-3040
Columbus (G-5554)		
Coughlin Chevrolet Inc	D	740 964-9191
Pataskala (G-12271)		
Coughlin Chevrolet Toyota Inc	D	740 366-1381
Newark (G-11696)		
Cronin Auto Inc	C	419 874-4331
Perrysburg (G-12327)		
Doug Bigelow Chevrolet Inc	D	330 644-7500
Akron (G-136)		
Dutro Ford Lincoln-Mercury Inc	D	740 452-6334
Zanesville (G-15786)		
Ed Mullinax Ford LLC	C	440 984-2431
Amherst (G-427)		
Fairborn Buick-GMC Truck Inc	D	937 878-7371
Fairborn (G-8374)		
George P Ballas Buick GMC Trck	E	419 535-1000
Toledo (G-13820)		
Grogans Towne Chrysler Inc	D	419 476-0761
Toledo (G-13830)		
Haydocy Automotive Inc	D	614 279-8880
Columbus (G-5973)		
I-75 Pierson Automotive Inc	E	513 424-1881
Franklin (G-8642)		
Jake Sweeney Automotive Inc	D	513 782-2800
Cincinnati (G-2896)		
Kerry Ford Inc	D	513 671-6400
Cincinnati (G-2939)		
Lavery Chevrolet-Buick Inc	E	330 823-1100
Alliance (G-388)		
Leikin Motor Companies Inc	D	440 946-6900
Willoughby (G-15204)		
Lima Auto Mall Inc	D	419 993-6000
Lima (G-9918)		
Mark Thomas Ford Inc	E	330 638-1010
Cortland (G-6972)		
Mathews Kennedy Ford L-M Inc	D	740 387-3673
Marion (G-10444)		
Matia Motors Inc	E	440 365-7311
Elyria (G-8273)		
Mike Castrucci Ford	C	513 831-7010
Milford (G-11243)		
Montrose Ford Inc	C	330 666-0711
Fairlawn (G-8491)		
Ron Marhofer Automall Inc	E	330 923-5059
Cuyahoga Falls (G-7100)		
Roush Equipment Inc	C	614 882-1535
Westerville (G-15014)		
Sharpnack Chevrolet Co	E	800 752-7513
Vermilion (G-14408)		
Sunnyside Cars Inc	E	440 777-9911
North Olmsted (G-11917)		
Surfside Motors Inc	E	419 419-4776
Galion (G-8751)		
Tansky Motors Inc	E	650 322-7069
Rockbridge (G-12736)		
Tansky Sales Inc	E	614 793-2080
Columbus (G-6748)		
Walker Auto Group Inc	D	937 433-4950
Miamisburg (G-11103)		
Warner Buick-Nissan Inc	E	419 423-7161
Findlay (G-8597)		

AUTOMOTIVE CUSTOMIZING SVCS, NONFACTORY BASIS

Company	Col	Phone
Afg Industries Inc	D	614 322-4580
Grove City (G-8893)		
Ground Effects LLC	E	440 565-5925
Westlake (G-15062)		

AUTOMOTIVE GLASS REPLACEMENT SHOPS

Company	Col	Phone
Advanced Auto Glass Inc	E	412 373-6675
Akron (G-17)		
Belletech Corp	C	937 599-3774
Bellefontaine (G-1021)		
Keystone Auto Glass Inc	D	419 509-0497
Maumee (G-10736)		
Mels Auto Glass Inc	E	513 563-7771
Cincinnati (G-3039)		
Ryans All-Glass Incorporated	E	513 771-4440
West Chester (G-14759)		
Safelite Autoglass Foundation	C	614 210-9000
Columbus (G-6629)		
Safelite Billing Services Corp	C	614 210-9000
Columbus (G-6630)		
Safelite Glass Corp	E	614 431-4936
Worthington (G-15455)		
Safelite Glass Corp	A	614 210-9000
Columbus (G-6631)		
Safelite Group Inc	A	614 210-9000
Columbus (G-6632)		
Wiechart Enterprises Inc	E	419 227-0027
Lima (G-9987)		

AUTOMOTIVE PAINT SHOP

Company	Col	Phone
American Bulk Commodities Inc	C	330 758-0841
Youngstown (G-15549)		
Decorative Paint Incorporated	D	419 485-0632
Montpelier (G-11384)		
Maaco Franchising Inc	E	937 236-6700
Dayton (G-7463)		

SERVICES SECTION

AUTOMOTIVE SPLYS & PARTS, NEW, WHOLESALE: Trailer Parts

AUTOMOTIVE PARTS, ACCESS & SPLYS

Accel Performance Group LLC............ C 216 658-6413
  Independence *(G-9394)*

Amsted Industries Incorporated............ D 614 836-2323
  Groveport *(G-8969)*

Buyers Products Company..................... C 440 974-8888
  Mentor *(G-10915)*

Falls Stamping & Welding Co................ C 330 928-1191
  Cuyahoga Falls *(G-7075)*

Hendrickson International Corp............ D 740 929-5600
  Hebron *(G-9143)*

Hi-Tek Manufacturing Inc..................... C 513 459-1094
  Mason *(G-10562)*

Industry Products Co............................. B 937 778-0585
  Piqua *(G-12445)*

Joseph Industries Inc........................... D 330 528-0091
  Streetsboro *(G-13419)*

Keystone Auto Glass Inc..................... D 419 509-0497
  Maumee *(G-10736)*

Leadec Corp... E 513 731-3590
  Blue Ash *(G-1200)*

Pioneer Automotive Tech Inc................ C 937 746-2293
  Miamisburg *(G-11084)*

Toledo Molding & Die LLC.................... E 419 692-6022
  Delphos *(G-7846)*

TS Trim Industries Inc........................... B 614 837-4114
  Canal Winchester *(G-1618)*

Unison Industries LLC........................... B 904 667-9904
  Dayton *(G-7143)*

US Tsubaki Power Transm LLC............ C 419 626-4560
  Sandusky *(G-12939)*

Venco Venturo Industries LLC.............. E 513 772-8448
  Cincinnati *(G-3619)*

AUTOMOTIVE PARTS: Plastic

Cpp Group Holdings LLC....................... E 216 453-4800
  Cleveland *(G-4134)*

Xaloy LLC.. C 330 726-4000
  Austintown *(G-637)*

AUTOMOTIVE PRDTS: Rubber

Myers Industries Inc............................. E 330 253-5592
  Akron *(G-238)*

AUTOMOTIVE REPAIR SHOPS: Diesel Engine Repair

Ohio Machinery Co................................ E 419 423-1447
  Findlay *(G-8574)*

Power Acquisition LLC.......................... D 614 228-5000
  Dublin *(G-8093)*

Skinner Diesel Services Inc.................. E 614 491-8785
  Columbus *(G-6686)*

Tri-W Group Inc..................................... A 614 228-5000
  Columbus *(G-6786)*

W W Williams Company LLC................ E 330 225-7751
  Brunswick *(G-1473)*

W W Williams Company LLC................ D 614 228-5000
  Dublin *(G-8158)*

W W Williams Midwest Inc................... E 330 225-7751
  Brunswick *(G-1474)*

AUTOMOTIVE REPAIR SHOPS: Electrical Svcs

Miscor Group Ltd................................... B 330 830-3500
  Massillon *(G-10658)*

AUTOMOTIVE REPAIR SHOPS: Machine Shop

RL Best Company.................................. E 330 758-8601
  Boardman *(G-1290)*

AUTOMOTIVE REPAIR SHOPS: Muffler Shop, Sale/Rpr/Installation

Midas Auto Systems Experts................ A 419 243-7281
  Toledo *(G-13923)*

Tuffy Associates Corp........................... E 419 865-6900
  Toledo *(G-14077)*

AUTOMOTIVE REPAIR SHOPS: Rebuilding & Retreading Tires

Grismer Tire Company.......................... E 937 643-2526
  Centerville *(G-1945)*

Ziegler Tire and Supply Co.................... E 330 343-7739
  Dover *(G-7911)*

AUTOMOTIVE REPAIR SHOPS: Tire Recapping

Best One Tire & Svc Lima Inc............... E 419 229-2380
  Lima *(G-9868)*

AUTOMOTIVE REPAIR SHOPS: Tire Repair Shop

Big Oki LLC... E 513 874-1111
  Fairfield *(G-8394)*

AUTOMOTIVE REPAIR SHOPS: Trailer Repair

Double A Trailer Sales Inc.................... E 419 692-7626
  Delphos *(G-7840)*

Girard Equipment Co............................. E 330 545-2575
  Girard *(G-8814)*

Hans Truck and Trlr Repr Inc................ D 216 581-0046
  Cleveland *(G-4349)*

Mac Trailer Manufacturing Inc.............. A 800 795-8454
  Alliance *(G-391)*

Nelson Manufacturing Company........... D 419 523-5321
  Ottawa *(G-12189)*

Trailines Incorporated........................... E 513 755-7900
  West Chester *(G-14777)*

Transport Services Inc.......................... E 440 582-4900
  Cleveland *(G-5032)*

AUTOMOTIVE REPAIR SHOPS: Truck Engine Repair, Exc Indl

Aim Leasing Company.......................... E 216 883-6300
  Cleveland *(G-3777)*

Fleetpride Inc.. E 740 282-2711
  Steubenville *(G-13326)*

Hartwig Transit Inc................................ C 513 563-1765
  Cincinnati *(G-2804)*

Hy-Tek Material Handling LLC.............. D 614 497-2500
  Columbus *(G-6030)*

Kirk NationaLease Co........................... E 937 498-1151
  Sidney *(G-13036)*

Mizar Motors Inc.................................... E 419 729-2400
  Toledo *(G-13925)*

Ohio Machinery Co................................ E 614 878-2287
  Columbus *(G-6436)*

Sutphen Towers Inc............................... D 614 876-1262
  Hilliard *(G-9234)*

AUTOMOTIVE REPAIR SVC

Beechmont Chevrolet Inc..................... D 513 624-1100
  Cincinnati *(G-2247)*

Beechmont Motors Inc.......................... E 513 388-3883
  Cincinnati *(G-2248)*

Beechmont Motors T Inc...................... D 513 388-3800
  Cincinnati *(G-2249)*

Bobby Layman Cadillac GMC Inc........... E 740 654-9590
  Carroll *(G-1899)*

Coates Car Care Inc............................. E 330 652-4180
  Niles *(G-11785)*

East Manufacturing Corporation........... B 330 325-9921
  Randolph *(G-12618)*

First Services Inc.................................. A 513 241-2200
  Cincinnati *(G-2675)*

First Transit Inc..................................... D 513 241-2200
  Cincinnati *(G-2682)*

Fred Martin Nissan LLC........................ E 330 644-8888
  Akron *(G-168)*

Germain Ford LLC................................. C 614 889-7777
  Columbus *(G-5931)*

Goodyear Tire & Rubber Company........ A 330 796-2121
  Akron *(G-179)*

Haasz Automall LLC.............................. E 330 296-2866
  Ravenna *(G-12627)*

Hoss II Inc... E 937 669-4300
  Tipp City *(G-13660)*

Irace Inc... E 330 836-7247
  Akron *(G-204)*

Paul Hrnchar Ford-Mercury Inc............. E 330 533-3673
  Canfield *(G-1638)*

Spitzer Chevrolet Inc............................. E 330 467-4141
  Northfield *(G-11966)*

Wabash National Trlr Ctrs Inc.............. D 614 878-6088
  Groveport *(G-9012)*

AUTOMOTIVE SPLYS & PARTS, NEW, WHOL: Auto Servicing Eqpt

Columbus City School District............... E 614 365-5263
  Columbus *(G-5622)*

AUTOMOTIVE SPLYS & PARTS, NEW, WHOLESALE: Engines/Eng Parts

Cadna Rubber Company Inc.................. E 901 566-9090
  Fairlawn *(G-8468)*

Interstate Diesel Service Inc................. C 216 881-0015
  Cleveland *(G-4420)*

Mahle Behr Mt Sterling Inc.................... B 740 869-3333
  Mount Sterling *(G-11474)*

Vgp Holdings LLC.................................. B 513 557-3100
  Cincinnati *(G-3629)*

AUTOMOTIVE SPLYS & PARTS, NEW, WHOLESALE: Splys

Autobody Supply Company Inc............. D 614 228-4328
  Columbus *(G-5407)*

Car Parts Warehouse Inc...................... E 216 281-4500
  Brookpark *(G-1429)*

AUTOMOTIVE SPLYS & PARTS, NEW, WHOLESALE: Tools & Eqpt

Cedar Elec Holdings Corp..................... D 773 804-6288
  West Chester *(G-14662)*

Cornwell Quality Tools Company.......... E 330 335-2933
  Wadsworth *(G-14434)*

Matco Tools Corporation....................... B 330 929-4949
  Stow *(G-13382)*

Myers Industries Inc............................. E 330 253-5592
  Akron *(G-238)*

AUTOMOTIVE SPLYS & PARTS, NEW, WHOLESALE: Trailer Parts

Knox Auto LLC...................................... E 330 701-5266
  Mount Vernon *(G-11490)*

Trailines Incorporated........................... E 513 755-7900
  West Chester *(G-14777)*

AUTOMOTIVE SPLYS & PARTS, WHOLESALE, NEC

Transport Services Inc .... E 440 582-4900
Cleveland *(G-5032)*

AUTOMOTIVE SPLYS & PARTS, WHOLESALE, NEC

Accel Performance Group LLC .... C 216 658-6413
Independence *(G-9394)*

Auto Parts Center-Cuyahoga FLS .... E 330 928-2149
Cuyahoga Falls *(G-7045)*

Auto-Wares Inc .... D 419 867-1927
Toledo *(G-13695)*

Automotive Distributors Co Inc .... E 216 398-2014
Cleveland *(G-3841)*

Automotive Distributors Co Inc .... D 614 476-1515
Columbus *(G-5408)*

Autosales Incorporated .... E 330 630-0888
Tallmadge *(G-13586)*

Bendix Coml Vhcl Systems LLC .... B 440 329-9000
Avon *(G-640)*

Borgers Ohio Inc .... B 419 663-3700
Norwalk *(G-12002)*

Bridgeport Auto Parts Inc .... E 740 635-0441
Bridgeport *(G-1375)*

Building 8 Inc .... E 513 771-8000
Cincinnati *(G-2289)*

Car Parts Warehouse Inc .... E 216 581-4800
Cleveland *(G-3925)*

Car Parts Warehouse Inc .... E 216 496-6540
Perry *(G-12304)*

Fayette Parts Service Inc .... E 740 282-4547
Steubenville *(G-13324)*

Four Wheel Drive Hardware LLC .... C 330 482-4733
Columbiana *(G-5235)*

Freudenberg-Nok General Partnr .... C 419 499-2502
Milan *(G-11206)*

G-Cor Automotive Corp .... E 614 443-6735
Columbus *(G-5907)*

Great Lakes-Ramco Inc .... E 586 759-5500
Mentor *(G-10944)*

Ieh Auto Parts LLC .... E 740 732-2395
Caldwell *(G-1550)*

Ieh Auto Parts LLC .... E 740 373-8327
Marietta *(G-10373)*

Ieh Auto Parts LLC .... D 740 373-8151
Marietta *(G-10374)*

Interstate-Mcbee LLC .... C 216 881-0015
Bedford *(G-967)*

Jegs Automotive Inc .... B 614 294-5451
Columbus *(G-6086)*

Jegs Automotive LLC .... C 614 294-5050
Delaware *(G-7808)*

Jobbers Automotive LLC .... E 216 524-2229
Eastlake *(G-8203)*

KOI Enterprises Inc .... C 513 648-3020
Cincinnati *(G-2947)*

KOI Enterprises Inc .... D 513 357-2400
Cincinnati *(G-2948)*

Lake County Parts Warehouse Inc .... E 440 259-2991
Perry *(G-12306)*

McBee Supply Corporation .... D 216 881-0015
Bedford *(G-971)*

Midway Inc .... D 419 465-2551
Monroeville *(G-11357)*

Mill Supply Inc .... E 216 518-5072
Cleveland *(G-4583)*

Myers Equipment Corporation .... E 330 533-5556
Canfield *(G-1635)*

National Marketshare Group .... E 513 921-0800
Cincinnati *(G-3095)*

Ohashi Technica USA Inc .... E 740 965-5115
Sunbury *(G-13523)*

Pag Mentor A1 Inc .... E 440 951-1040
Mentor *(G-10982)*

Par International Inc .... E 614 529-1300
Obetz *(G-12082)*

Pat Young Service Co Inc .... E 216 447-8550
Cleveland *(G-4729)*

Pioneer Automotive Tech Inc .... C 937 746-2293
Miamisburg *(G-11084)*

Qualitor Subsidiary H Inc .... C 419 562-7987
Bucyrus *(G-1517)*

R L Morrissey & Assoc Inc .... E 440 498-3730
Solon *(G-13135)*

Sims Bros Inc .... D 740 387-9041
Marion *(G-10454)*

Smyth Automotive Inc .... D 513 528-2800
Cincinnati *(G-3389)*

Snyders Antique Auto Parts Inc .... E 330 549-5313
New Springfield *(G-11679)*

The Glockner Chevrolet Company .... C 740 353-2161
Portsmouth *(G-12576)*

Transtar Industries LLC .... C 440 232-5100
Cleveland *(G-5035)*

TS Trim Industries Inc .... B 614 837-4114
Canal Winchester *(G-1618)*

Turbo Parts LLC .... D 740 223-1695
Marion *(G-10457)*

Ventra Salem LLC .... A 330 337-8002
Salem *(G-12856)*

Whites Service Center Inc .... E 937 653-5279
Urbana *(G-14317)*

AUTOMOTIVE SPLYS/PART, NEW, WHOL: Spring, Shock Absorb/Strut

Thyssenkrupp Bilstein Amer Inc .... C 513 881-7600
Hamilton *(G-9086)*

AUTOMOTIVE SVCS, EXC REPAIR & CARWASHES: Insp & Diagnostic

SGS North America Inc .... E 513 674-7048
Cincinnati *(G-3366)*

AUTOMOTIVE SVCS, EXC REPAIR & CARWASHES: Lubrication

Coates Car Care Inc .... E 330 652-4180
Niles *(G-11785)*

Pioneer Quick Lubes Inc .... E 419 782-2213
Defiance *(G-7761)*

Southern Express Lubes Inc .... E 937 278-5807
Dayton *(G-7630)*

Team Lubrication Inc .... D 614 231-9909
Columbus *(G-6751)*

Valvoline Instant Oil Change .... C 937 548-0123
Greenville *(G-8888)*

Valvoline Instant Oil Chnge Fr .... E 513 422-4980
Middletown *(G-11191)*

Valvoline Instant Oil Chnge Fr .... E 330 372-4416
Warren *(G-14571)*

Valvoline LLC .... C 513 557-3100
Cincinnati *(G-3614)*

Ziebart of Ohio Inc .... E 440 845-6031
Cleveland *(G-5175)*

AUTOMOTIVE TOWING SVCS

Abers Garage Inc .... E 419 281-5500
Ashland *(G-471)*

Charlie Towing Service Inc .... E 440 234-5300
Berea *(G-1064)*

Eitel Towing Service Inc .... E 614 877-4139
Orient *(G-12151)*

Englewood Truck Inc .... E 937 836-5109
Clayton *(G-3732)*

R Robnsons Twing Recovery LLC .... E 937 458-3666
Beavercreek *(G-897)*

Richs Towing & Service Inc .... E 440 234-3435
Middleburg Heights *(G-11124)*

Rustys Towing Service Inc .... D 614 491-6288
Columbus *(G-6622)*

Sandys Auto & Truck Svc Inc .... D 937 461-4980
Moraine *(G-11436)*

Sandys Towing .... E 937 228-6832
Dayton *(G-7610)*

Sprandel Enterprises Inc .... E 513 777-6622
West Chester *(G-14768)*

World Trck Towing Recovery Inc .... E 330 723-1116
Seville *(G-12968)*

AUTOMOTIVE TRANSMISSION REPAIR SVC

Power Acquisition LLC .... D 614 228-5000
Dublin *(G-8093)*

Tri-W Group Inc .... A 614 228-5000
Columbus *(G-6786)*

W W Williams Company LLC .... E 330 225-7751
Brunswick *(G-1473)*

W W Williams Company LLC .... D 614 228-5000
Dublin *(G-8158)*

W W Williams Midwest Inc .... E 330 225-7751
Brunswick *(G-1474)*

AUTOMOTIVE WELDING SVCS

Brown Industrial Inc .... E 937 693-3838
Botkins *(G-1299)*

Industry Products Co .... B 937 778-0585
Piqua *(G-12445)*

McGregor Mtal Leffel Works LLC .... D 937 325-5561
Springfield *(G-13265)*

R K Industries Inc .... D 419 523-5001
Ottawa *(G-12195)*

Turn-Key Industrial Svcs LLC .... D 614 274-1128
Grove City *(G-8960)*

AUTOMOTIVE: Seating

Evenflo Company Inc .... E 937 415-3300
Miamisburg *(G-11053)*

AVIATION PROPELLER & BLADE REPAIR SVCS

Standrdaero Component Svcs Inc .... D 513 618-9588
Cincinnati *(G-3410)*

AVIATION SCHOOL

Griffings Flying Service Inc .... E 419 734-5400
Port Clinton *(G-12530)*

BAGS: Paper

Berk Enterprises Inc .... D 330 369-1192
Warren *(G-14506)*

Dazpak Flexible Packaging Corp .... C 614 252-2121
Columbus *(G-5746)*

Ricking Holding Co .... E 513 825-3551
Cleveland *(G-4839)*

BAGS: Plastic, Made From Purchased Materials

Ampac Holdings LLC .... A 513 671-1777
Cincinnati *(G-2194)*

Dazpak Flexible Packaging Corp .... C 614 252-2121
Columbus *(G-5746)*

SERVICES SECTION

BARRICADES: Metal

BAGS: Shopping, Made From Purchased Materials
Ampac Holdings LLC................................ A 513 671-1777
  Cincinnati (G-2194)

BAKERIES, COMMERCIAL: On Premises Baking Only
Amish Door Inc.. C 330 359-5464
  Wilmot (G-15281)
Buns of Delaware Inc............................... E 740 363-2867
  Delaware (G-7781)
Klosterman Baking Co LLC..................... D 513 242-5667
  Cincinnati (G-2944)
Mustard Seed Health Fd Mkt Inc............ E 440 519-3663
  Solon (G-13115)
Osmans Pies Inc...................................... E 330 607-9083
  Stow (G-13384)
White Castle System Inc......................... B 614 228-5781
  Columbus (G-6883)

BAKERIES: On Premises Baking & Consumption
Buns of Delaware Inc............................... E 740 363-2867
  Delaware (G-7781)
Mapleside Valley LLC............................. D 330 225-5576
  Brunswick (G-1462)
Mocha House Inc..................................... E 330 392-3020
  Warren (G-14540)
Osmans Pies Inc...................................... E 330 607-9083
  Stow (G-13384)
Servatii Inc.. D 513 271-5040
  Cincinnati (G-3362)

BAKERY PRDTS: Cookies & crackers
Osmans Pies Inc...................................... E 330 607-9083
  Stow (G-13384)

BAKERY PRDTS: Pretzels
Ditsch Usa LLC....................................... E 513 782-8888
  Cincinnati (G-2568)

BAKERY PRDTS: Wholesalers
Alfred Nickles Bakery Inc...................... E 216 267-8055
  Cleveland (G-3786)
Bagel Place Inc....................................... E 419 537-9377
  Toledo (G-13698)
Busken Bakery Inc.................................. D 513 871-2114
  Cincinnati (G-2294)
Ditsch Usa LLC....................................... E 513 782-8888
  Cincinnati (G-2568)
Dutchman Hospitality Group Inc............ C 614 873-3414
  Plain City (G-12474)
Flowers Baking Co Ohio LLC................ E 419 661-2586
  Northwood (G-11974)
Griffin Industries LLC............................ E 419 257-3560
  North Baltimore (G-11800)
Interbake Foods LLC.............................. C 614 294-4931
  Columbus (G-6064)
Klosterman Baking Co LLC................... D 513 242-5667
  Cincinnati (G-2944)
Made From Scratch Inc........................... E 614 873-3344
  Plain City (G-12484)
Marzetti Manufacturing Company........... C 856 205-1485
  Westerville (G-14908)
Osmans Pies Inc...................................... E 330 607-9083
  Stow (G-13384)
P & S Bakery Inc..................................... E 330 707-4141
  Youngstown (G-15687)

Skallys Old World Bakery Inc................. E 513 931-1411
  Cincinnati (G-3382)

BALLET PRODUCTION SVCS
Ballet Metropolitan Inc............................ C 614 229-4860
  Columbus (G-5417)

BANKS: Mortgage & Loan
Amerifirst Financial Corp....................... D 216 452-5120
  Lakewood (G-9657)
Apex Mortgage Services LLC................. D 614 839-2739
  Columbus (G-5373)
C O Howard Hanna Mortgage.................. D 412 967-9000
  Cleveland (G-3917)
Crosscountry Mortgage Inc.................... E 440 845-3700
  Cleveland (G-4139)
Crosscountry Mortgage LLC.................. D 216 314-0107
  Beachwood (G-785)
Crosscountry Mortgage LLC.................. E 513 373-4240
  Blue Ash (G-1162)
Crosscountry Mortgage LLC.................. E 419 636-4663
  Bryan (G-1483)
Crosscountry Mortgage LLC.................. D 440 262-3528
  Cleveland (G-4140)
Crosscountry Mortgage LLC.................. D 614 779-0316
  Columbus (G-5731)
Crosscountry Mortgage LLC.................. D 440 413-0867
  Mentor (G-10928)
Crosscountry Mortgage LLC.................. D 440 354-5206
  Painesville (G-12225)
Crosscountry Mortgage LLC.................. D 330 655-5626
  Stow (G-13360)
Crosscountry Mortgage LLC.................. D 330 715-4878
  Stow (G-13361)
Crosscountry Mortgage LLC.................. B 440 845-3700
  Brecksville (G-1352)
Equity Resources Inc.............................. E 740 363-7300
  Delaware (G-7795)
Equity Resources Inc.............................. E 614 389-4462
  Dublin (G-8006)
Fifth Third Bnk of Sthern OH I................ E 937 840-5353
  Hillsboro (G-9253)
First Day Fincl Federal Cr Un................. E 937 222-4546
  Dayton (G-7352)
First Ohio Banc & Lending Inc................ D 216 642-8900
  Cleveland (G-4259)
Guaranteed Rate Inc................................ C 513 609-4477
  Cincinnati (G-2779)
Guardian Savings Bank............................ E 513 842-8900
  Cincinnati (G-2781)
Jpmorgan Chase & Co............................. C 614 248-5800
  Columbus (G-5263)
M/I Homes Inc... B 614 418-8000
  Columbus (G-6186)
National City Mortgage Inc..................... A 937 910-1200
  Miamisburg (G-11075)
Nations Lending Corporation.................. D 440 842-4817
  Westlake (G-15082)
PNC Mortgage Company......................... E 412 762-2000
  Miamisburg (G-11085)
Priority Mortgage Corp........................... E 614 431-1141
  Worthington (G-15448)
Real Estate Mortgage Corp..................... D 440 356-5373
  Chagrin Falls (G-1964)
Stockton Mortgage Corporation............... E 513 486-4140
  Mason (G-10609)
Van Dyk Mortgage Corporation............... E 419 720-4384
  Toledo (G-14090)
Vinton County National Bank.................. E 800 223-4031
  Mc Arthur (G-10799)
Western Ohio Mortgage Corp.................. E 937 497-9662
  Sidney (G-13058)

BANQUET HALL FACILITIES
Brown Derby Roadhouse......................... E 330 528-3227
  Hudson (G-9335)
Buns of Delaware Inc............................... E 740 363-2867
  Delaware (G-7781)
Castaway Bay Resort............................... E 419 627-2500
  Sandusky (G-12870)
City Life Inc... E 216 523-5899
  Cleveland (G-3975)
City of Centerville.................................. D 937 438-3585
  Dayton (G-7227)
Cleveland Metroparks.............................. E 216 661-6500
  Cleveland (G-4057)
Connor Concepts Inc.............................. E 937 291-1661
  Dayton (G-7246)
Findlay Inn & Conference Ctr................. E 419 422-5682
  Findlay (G-8529)
German Family Society Inc..................... E 330 678-8229
  Kent (G-9576)
Kohler Foods Inc..................................... E 937 291-3600
  Dayton (G-7445)
Mason Family Resorts LLC.................... B 608 237-5871
  Mason (G-10577)
Memorial Hall... D 937 293-2841
  Dayton (G-7479)
Michaels Inc.. D 440 357-0384
  Mentor (G-10973)
Mocha House Inc..................................... E 330 392-3020
  Warren (G-14540)
Mocho Ltd.. E 330 832-8807
  Massillon (G-10659)
Mustard Seed Health Fd Mkt Inc............ E 440 519-3663
  Solon (G-13115)
Refectory Restaurant Inc........................ E 614 451-9774
  Columbus (G-6570)
Robert Bettinger Inc............................... E 419 832-6033
  Grand Rapids (G-8847)
Roscoe Village Foundation..................... D 740 622-2222
  Coshocton (G-7000)
Schmidt Hsptality Concepts Inc.............. E 614 878-4527
  Columbus (G-6649)
The Oaks Lodge...................................... D 330 769-2601
  Chippewa Lake (G-2094)
Valley Hospitality Inc............................. D 740 374-9660
  Marietta (G-10409)
Villa Milano Inc...................................... E 614 882-2058
  Columbus (G-6851)
Winking Lizard Inc................................. E 330 220-9944
  Brunswick (G-1476)

BAR
Big Bang Bar Cleveland LLC................. E 615 264-5650
  Cleveland (G-3873)
Hyatt Corporation................................... D 614 463-1234
  Columbus (G-6031)
Mohawk Golf Club................................... E 419 447-5876
  Tiffin (G-13634)
OBannon Creek Golf Club....................... E 513 683-5657
  Loveland (G-10156)

BAR FIXTURES: Wood
Ingle-Barr Inc... D 740 702-6117
  Chillicothe (G-2072)

BARGES BUILDING & REPAIR
McGinnis Inc... C 740 377-4391
  South Point (G-13178)
McNational Inc.. D 740 377-4391
  South Point (G-13179)
Superior Marine Ways Inc...................... C 740 894-6224
  Proctorville (G-12613)

BARRICADES: Metal
Df Supply Inc.. E 330 650-9226
　Twinsburg *(G-14181)*

BARS: Concrete Reinforcing, Fabricated Steel
Gateway Con Forming Svcs Inc.............. D 513 353-2000
　Miamitown *(G-11106)*
Industrial Millwright Svcs LLC................. E 419 523-9147
　Ottawa *(G-12187)*
Ohio Bridge Corporation......................... C 740 432-6334
　Cambridge *(G-1578)*

BATTERY CHARGERS
Noco Company....................................... D 216 464-8131
　Solon *(G-13119)*
TL Industries Inc.................................... C 419 666-8144
　Perrysburg *(G-12377)*

BEARINGS: Ball & Roller
Timken Company.................................... A 234 262-3000
　North Canton *(G-11865)*

BEAUTY & BARBER SHOP EQPT
Aluminum Line Products Company........ D 440 835-8880
　Westlake *(G-15032)*
Clarity Retail Services LLC.................... D 513 800-9369
　West Chester *(G-14668)*
Downing Enterprises Inc........................ D 330 666-3888
　Copley *(G-6956)*
RB Sigma LLC....................................... D 440 290-0577
　Mentor *(G-10988)*

BEAUTY SALONS
American Salon Group LLC................... D 330 975-0085
　Medina *(G-10806)*
Ihs Services Inc..................................... D 614 396-9980
　Worthington *(G-15422)*
New View Management Group Inc........ D 513 733-4444
　Cincinnati *(G-3110)*
Queens Beauty Bar LLC........................ E 216 804-0533
　Cleveland *(G-4802)*

BEER & ALE WHOLESALERS
Arrow Wine Stores Inc.......................... E 937 433-6778
　Dayton *(G-7180)*
Southern Glzers Dstrs Ohio LLC............ D 440 542-7000
　Solon *(G-13147)*
Southern Glzers Dstrs Ohio LLC............ D 614 552-7900
　Columbus *(G-6696)*

BEER & ALE, WHOLESALE: Beer & Other Fermented Malt Liquors
Anheuser-Busch LLC............................. E 513 381-3927
　Cincinnati *(G-2205)*
Anheuser-Busch LLC............................. E 419 221-2337
　Lima *(G-9865)*
Beverage Distributors Inc..................... C 216 431-1600
　Cleveland *(G-3872)*
Bonbright Distributors Inc.................... E 937 222-1001
　Springfield *(G-13223)*
Bonbright Distributors Inc.................... D 937 222-1001
　Dayton *(G-7196)*
Cavalier Distributing Company.............. D 513 247-9222
　Blue Ash *(G-1143)*
Central Beverage Group Ltd................. C 614 294-3555
　Lewis Center *(G-9813)*
Columbus Distributing Company........... D 740 726-2211
　Waldo *(G-14470)*
Columbus Distributing Company........... C 614 846-1000
　Columbus *(G-5628)*
Dayton Heidelberg Distrg Co................. B 513 421-5000
　Cincinnati *(G-2544)*
Dayton Heidelberg Distrg Co................. C 216 520-2626
　Cleveland *(G-4153)*
Dayton Heidelberg Distrg Co................. B 614 308-0400
　Columbus *(G-5745)*
Dayton Heidelberg Distrg Co................. B 937 220-6450
　Moraine *(G-11401)*
Dayton Heidelberg Distrg Co................. C 419 666-9783
　Perrysburg *(G-12330)*
Dayton Heidelberg Distrg LLC............... B 937 222-8692
　Moraine *(G-11402)*
Heidelberg Distributing C...................... D 513 771-9370
　Cincinnati *(G-2816)*
House of La Rose Cleveland.................. C 440 746-7500
　Brecksville *(G-1354)*
Litter Distributing Co Inc....................... D 740 774-2831
　Chillicothe *(G-2078)*
M & A Distributing Co Inc..................... E 440 703-4580
　Solon *(G-13110)*
Maple City Ice Company....................... E 419 668-2531
　Norwalk *(G-12016)*
Matesich Distributing Co....................... D 740 349-8686
　Newark *(G-11724)*
Nwo Beverage Inc................................. E 419 725-2162
　Northwood *(G-11980)*
Ohio Valley Wine Company LLC............ C 513 771-9370
　Cincinnati *(G-3151)*
R L Lipton Distributing Co..................... D 216 475-4150
　Cleveland *(G-4805)*
Rhinegeist LLC...................................... D 513 381-1367
　Cincinnati *(G-3295)*
The Maple City Ice Company................ E 419 747-4777
　Mansfield *(G-10319)*
Treu House of Munch Inc...................... D 419 666-7770
　Northwood *(G-11986)*
Warsteiner Importers Agency................ E 513 942-9872
　West Chester *(G-14793)*

BEER, WINE & LIQUOR STORES: Beer, Packaged
Dayton Heidelberg Distrg Co................. B 937 220-6450
　Moraine *(G-11401)*
G J Shue Inc... E 330 722-0082
　Medina *(G-10837)*
Premium Beverage Supply Ltd.............. D 614 777-1007
　Hilliard *(G-9227)*
Yankee Lake Inc................................... E 330 448-8866
　Brookfield *(G-1408)*

BEVERAGE STORES
Superior Beverage Group Ltd................ C 419 529-0702
　Lexington *(G-9845)*

BEVERAGES, ALCOHOLIC: Distilled Liquors
Paramount Distillers Inc........................ B 216 671-6300
　Cleveland *(G-4718)*
Watershed Distillery LLC....................... E 614 357-1936
　Columbus *(G-6869)*

BEVERAGES, ALCOHOLIC: Wines
Paramount Distillers Inc........................ B 216 671-6300
　Cleveland *(G-4718)*

BEVERAGES, NONALCOHOLIC: Bottled & canned soft drinks
Borden Dairy Co Cincinnati LLC............. E 513 948-8811
　Cleveland *(G-3881)*
Central Coca-Cola Btlg Co Inc............... E 330 875-1487
　Akron *(G-86)*
Central Coca-Cola Btlg Co Inc............... E 740 474-2180
　Circleville *(G-3705)*
Central Coca-Cola Btlg Co Inc............... C 419 476-6622
　Toledo *(G-13727)*
Pepsi-Cola Metro Btlg Co Inc................ C 330 425-8236
　Twinsburg *(G-14213)*

BEVERAGES, NONALCOHOLIC: Carbonated
G & J Pepsi-Cola Bottlers Inc................ E 740 593-3366
　Athens *(G-568)*
G & J Pepsi-Cola Bottlers Inc................ B 740 354-9191
　Franklin Furnace *(G-8654)*
G & J Pepsi-Cola Bottlers Inc................ E 740 354-9191
　Zanesville *(G-15788)*

BEVERAGES, NONALCOHOLIC: Flavoring extracts & syrups, nec
Agrana Fruit Us Inc............................... C 937 693-3821
　Anna *(G-442)*

BEVERAGES, NONALCOHOLIC: Soft Drinks, Canned & Bottled, Etc
American Bottling Company................... C 614 237-4201
　Columbus *(G-5346)*
Pepsi-Cola Metro Btlg Co Inc................ E 937 461-4664
　Dayton *(G-7549)*

BEVERAGES, WINE & DISTILLED ALCOHOLIC, WHOLESALE: Wine
Dayton Heidelberg Distrg Co................. B 937 220-6450
　Moraine *(G-11401)*
Gervasi Vinyrd Itln Bistro LLC............... D 330 497-1000
　Canton *(G-1762)*
M & M Wine Cellar Inc.......................... E 330 536-6450
　Lowellville *(G-10170)*
Ohio Valley Wine Company LLC............ C 513 771-9370
　Cincinnati *(G-3151)*
Paramount Distillers Inc........................ B 216 671-6300
　Cleveland *(G-4718)*
R L Lipton Distributing Co..................... D 216 475-4150
　Cleveland *(G-4805)*
Southern Glzers Dstrs Ohio LLC............ D 614 552-7900
　Columbus *(G-6696)*
Southern Glzers Wine Sprits TX............ D 513 755-7082
　Fairfield *(G-8442)*
Vanguard Wines LLC............................. E 614 291-3493
　Columbus *(G-6842)*
Vintage Wine Distributor Inc................. E 440 248-1750
　Solon *(G-13162)*
Watershed Distillery LLC....................... E 614 357-1936
　Columbus *(G-6869)*
Wine Trends.. E 937 222-8692
　Moraine *(G-11449)*

BILLIARD & POOL TABLES & SPLYS
Burnett Pools Inc................................... E 330 372-1725
　Cortland *(G-6968)*

BILLIARD TABLE REPAIR SVCS
Dtv Inc... E 216 226-5465
　Cleveland *(G-4187)*

BILLING & BOOKKEEPING SVCS
Advocate Rcm LLC................................ D 614 210-1885
　Dublin *(G-7921)*
APS Medical Billing............................... D 419 866-1804
　Toledo *(G-13692)*

SERVICES SECTION

BOILER REPAIR SHOP

Chicago Mso Inc..................................... E 513 624-8300
  Cincinnati *(G-2354)*

E T Financial Service Inc........................ E 937 716-1726
  Trotwood *(G-14127)*

Healthpro Medical Billing Inc................. D 419 223-2717
  Lima *(G-9904)*

Lbk Health Care Inc............................... E 937 296-1550
  Bellbrook *(G-1018)*

MBI Solutions Inc.................................. A 937 619-4000
  Dayton *(G-7470)*

Medic Management Group LLC............ D 330 670-5316
  Beachwood *(G-814)*

Medicount Management Inc.................. E 513 612-3144
  Cincinnati *(G-3029)*

Nationwide Childrens Hospital................ C 330 253-5200
  Akron *(G-239)*

Ohio Bell Telephone Company............... A 216 822-9700
  Brecksville *(G-1360)*

Physicians Professional Mgt................... E 207 782-7494
  Dublin *(G-8091)*

Promedica Health Systems Inc.............. B 800 477-4035
  Toledo *(G-13975)*

Quadax Inc... C 216 765-1144
  Beachwood *(G-828)*

Quadax Inc... C 330 759-4600
  Youngstown *(G-15702)*

Quadax Inc... E 440 777-6300
  Middleburg Heights *(G-11121)*

Radiology Assoc Canton Inc.................. E 330 363-2842
  Canton *(G-1840)*

Real Property Management Inc............. E 614 766-6500
  Dublin *(G-8106)*

Specilzed Med Blling Rvnue Rcv............ E 614 461-8154
  Worthington *(G-15458)*

Specilzed Med Blling Rvnue Rcv............ E 614 461-8154
  Worthington *(G-15457)*

BINDING SVC: Books & Manuals

A-A Blueprint Co Inc............................. E 330 794-8803
  Akron *(G-11)*

AGS Custom Graphics Inc..................... D 330 963-7770
  Macedonia *(G-10188)*

Baesman Group Inc................................ D 614 771-2300
  Hilliard *(G-9181)*

Bindery & Spc Presswrks Inc................. D 614 873-4623
  Plain City *(G-12470)*

Black River Group Inc........................... E 419 524-6699
  Mansfield *(G-10245)*

Boundless Cmnty Pathways Inc............. A 937 461-0034
  West Carrollton *(G-14644)*

Consolsdated Graphics Group Inc......... C 216 881-9191
  Cleveland *(G-4104)*

Copley Ohio Newspapers Inc................. C 330 364-5577
  New Philadelphia *(G-11643)*

Quick Tab II Inc..................................... D 419 448-6622
  Tiffin *(G-13639)*

Tj Metzgers Inc...................................... D 419 861-8611
  Toledo *(G-14043)*

Traxium LLC.. E 330 572-8200
  Stow *(G-13398)*

BIOLOGICAL PRDTS: Exc Diagnostic

Bio-Blood Components Inc.................... C 614 294-3183
  Columbus *(G-5441)*

EMD Millipore Corporation.................... C 513 631-0445
  Norwood *(G-12032)*

Revvity Health Sciences Inc.................. C 330 825-4525
  Akron *(G-281)*

BLINDS : Window

Golden Drapery Supply Inc.................... E 216 351-3283
  Cleveland *(G-4318)*

BLOCKS: Landscape Or Retaining Wall, Concrete

Green Impressions LLC.......................... D 440 240-8508
  Sheffield Village *(G-12998)*

BLOCKS: Standard, Concrete Or Cinder

Quality Block & Supply Inc.................... E 330 364-4411
  Mount Eaton *(G-11458)*

BLOOD BANK

Bio-Blood Components Inc.................... C 614 294-3183
  Columbus *(G-5441)*

Biotest Pharmaceuticals Corp................ E 419 819-3068
  Bowling Green *(G-1309)*

Contining Hlthcare Sltions Inc............... D 419 529-7272
  Brunswick *(G-1454)*

Foundtion For Cmnty Blood Cntr........... C 937 461-3450
  Dayton *(G-7363)*

Lifeshare Cmnty Blood Svcs Inc............ E 440 322-5700
  Elyria *(G-8270)*

Plasmacare Inc....................................... D 614 231-5322
  Columbus *(G-6531)*

Vitalant... E 440 322-8720
  Elyria *(G-8299)*

BLOOD RELATED HEALTH SVCS

Blood Services Centl Ohio Reg.............. C 614 253-7981
  Columbus *(G-5447)*

Carespring Health Care MGT LLC......... E 513 943-4000
  Loveland *(G-10130)*

Catholic Health Initiatives...................... A 614 871-3047
  Grove City *(G-8906)*

Cleveland Clinic Foundation.................. E 614 358-4223
  Columbus *(G-5583)*

Crn Healthcare Inc................................. D 937 250-1412
  Dayton *(G-7261)*

Dayton Childrens Hospital..................... D 937 641-3000
  Miamisburg *(G-11046)*

Engage Healthcare Svcs Corp............... E 614 457-8180
  Columbus *(G-5818)*

Health Data MGT Solutions Inc............. D 216 595-1232
  Beachwood *(G-797)*

Health Partners Western Ohio............... E 419 679-5994
  Kenton *(G-9617)*

Health Partners Western Ohio............... E 937 667-1122
  New Carlisle *(G-11601)*

Maxim Healthcare Services Inc............. C 740 772-4100
  Columbus *(G-6211)*

Molina Healthcare Inc............................ E 216 606-1400
  Independence *(G-9455)*

Paladina Health LLC.............................. E 440 368-0930
  Seven Hills *(G-12957)*

Paramont Care of Michigan................... D 419 887-2728
  Maumee *(G-10754)*

Providence Healthcare MGT Inc............ B 216 200-5917
  Cleveland *(G-4794)*

Providence Medical Group LLC............ E 513 897-0085
  Waynesville *(G-14627)*

Rehab Medical LLC............................... D 513 381-3740
  Cincinnati *(G-3281)*

Toledo Clinic Inc.................................... D 419 865-3111
  Holland *(G-9308)*

Unity Health Network LLC..................... E 330 655-3820
  Hudson *(G-9375)*

Unity Health Network LLC..................... E 330 633-7782
  Tallmadge *(G-13610)*

University of Cincinnati.......................... C 513 558-1243
  Cincinnati *(G-3589)*

Western Reserve Health Sys LLC......... E 330 923-8660
  Cuyahoga Falls *(G-7114)*

BLOWERS & FANS

Atmos360 Inc... E 513 772-4777
  West Chester *(G-14799)*

Kirk Williams Company Inc.................... D 614 875-9023
  Grove City *(G-8931)*

Langdon Inc... E 513 733-5955
  Cincinnati *(G-2965)*

Ohio Blow Pipe Company...................... E 216 681-7379
  Cleveland *(G-4682)*

Rmt Acquisition Inc............................... E 513 241-5566
  Cincinnati *(G-3311)*

Tosoh America Inc................................. B 614 539-8622
  Grove City *(G-8959)*

Verantis Corporation.............................. E 440 243-0700
  Middleburg Heights *(G-11133)*

BLUEPRINTING SVCS

ARC Document Solutions Inc................ D 216 281-1234
  Cleveland *(G-3830)*

Ers Digital Inc.. D 216 281-1234
  Cleveland *(G-4221)*

Key Blue Prints Inc................................ D 614 228-3285
  Columbus *(G-6113)*

Queen City Reprographics..................... C 513 326-2300
  Cincinnati *(G-3265)*

Repros Inc.. E 330 247-3747
  Akron *(G-280)*

BOAT BUILDING & REPAIR

Don Wartko Construction Co................. D 330 673-5252
  Kent *(G-9572)*

BOAT DEALERS

Bob Pulte Chevrolet Inc........................ E 513 932-0303
  Lebanon *(G-9757)*

S B S Transit Inc.................................... E 440 288-2222
  Elyria *(G-8292)*

BOAT DEALERS: Motor

Beaver Park Marina Inc......................... E 440 282-6308
  Lorain *(G-10059)*

Lakeside Marine Inc.............................. E 419 732-7160
  Port Clinton *(G-12537)*

BOAT REPAIR SVCS

Superior Marine Ways Inc..................... C 740 894-6224
  Proctorville *(G-12613)*

BODIES: Truck & Bus

Hendrickson International Corp............. D 740 929-5600
  Hebron *(G-9143)*

Joseph Industries Inc............................ D 330 528-0091
  Streetsboro *(G-13419)*

BOILER & HEATING REPAIR SVCS

Babcock & Wilcox Company.................. A 330 753-4511
  Akron *(G-59)*

Columbs/Worthington Htg AC Inc......... E 614 771-5381
  Columbus *(G-5605)*

Nbw Inc.. E 216 377-1700
  Cleveland *(G-4629)*

Rmf Nooter LLC..................................... D 419 727-1970
  Toledo *(G-13992)*

Smith & Oby Service Co........................ E 440 735-5322
  Bedford *(G-985)*

BOILER REPAIR SHOP

Norris Brothers Co Inc........................... C 216 771-2233
  Cleveland *(G-4647)*

Schaefer Group Inc................................ E 513 489-2420
  Blue Ash *(G-1241)*

Employee Codes: A=Over 500 employees, B=251-500
C=101-250, D=51-100, E=20-50, F=10-19, G=1-9

BOOK STORES

Daedalus Books Inc	C	800 395-2665	
Hudson *(G-9342)*			
Grail	E	513 683-2340	
Loveland *(G-10139)*			
Mile Inc	D	614 794-2203	
Worthington *(G-15440)*			
University of Cincinnati	C	513 556-4200	
Cincinnati *(G-3582)*			

BOOKS, WHOLESALE

Alliance Medical Inc .... E 800 890-3092
  Dublin *(G-7930)*
Daedalus Books Inc .... C 800 395-2665
  Hudson *(G-9342)*
Ed Map Inc .... D 740 753-3439
  Nelsonville *(G-11543)*
Hubbard Company .... E 419 784-4455
  Defiance *(G-7750)*
Media Source Inc .... D 614 873-7635
  Plain City *(G-12487)*
Murfbooks LLC .... E 937 260-3741
  Dayton *(G-7518)*
Zaner-Bloser Inc .... C 614 486-0221
  Columbus *(G-6918)*

BOTTLED GAS DEALERS: Propane

Ngo Development Corporation .... B 740 622-9560
  Coshocton *(G-6993)*
Titan Propane LLC .... C 419 332-9832
  Fremont *(G-8706)*
Welders Supply Inc .... E 216 267-4470
  Brookpark *(G-1443)*

BOTTLES: Plastic

Phoenix Technologies Intl LLC .... E 419 353-7738
  Bowling Green *(G-1330)*

BOWLING CENTERS

Skylane LLC .... E 330 527-9999
  Garrettsville *(G-8760)*
Westgate Lanes Incorporated .... E 419 229-3845
  Lima *(G-9986)*

BOXES & SHOOK: Nailed Wood

Quadco Rehabilitation Ctr Inc .... B 419 682-1011
  Stryker *(G-13505)*

BOXES: Corrugated

Adapt-A-Pak Inc .... E 937 845-0386
  Fairborn *(G-8365)*
Brimar Packaging Inc .... E 440 934-3080
  Avon *(G-641)*
Cambridge Packaging Inc .... E 740 432-3351
  Cambridge *(G-1560)*
Protective Packg Solutions LLC .... E 513 769-5777
  Cincinnati *(G-3255)*
Skybox Packaging LLC .... C 419 525-7209
  Mansfield *(G-10317)*

BOXES: Paperboard, Folding

Brimar Packaging Inc .... E 440 934-3080
  Avon *(G-641)*

BOXES: Paperboard, Set-Up

Brimar Packaging Inc .... E 440 934-3080
  Avon *(G-641)*

BOXES: Wooden

Lalac One LLC .... E 216 432-4422
  Cleveland *(G-4482)*

BRAKES & BRAKE PARTS

Bendix Coml Vhcl Systems LLC .... B 440 329-9000
  Avon *(G-640)*
Lucas Sumitomo Brakes Inc .... E 513 934-0024
  Lebanon *(G-9776)*
Qualitor Subsidiary H Inc .... C 419 562-7987
  Bucyrus *(G-1517)*

BRASS & BRONZE PRDTS: Die-casted

American De Rosa Lamparts LLC .... D
  Cuyahoga Falls *(G-7038)*
The Kindt-Collins Company LLC .... D 216 252-4122
  Cleveland *(G-5003)*

BRAZING SVCS

Paulo Products Company .... E 440 942-0153
  Willoughby *(G-15218)*

BRICK, STONE & RELATED PRDTS WHOLESALERS

Collinwood Shale Brick Sup Co .... E 216 587-2700
  Cleveland *(G-4088)*
Empire Enterprises Inc .... E 330 665-7800
  Akron *(G-147)*
Exhibit Concepts Inc .... D 937 890-7000
  Vandalia *(G-14376)*
Grafton Ready Mix Concret Inc .... C 440 926-2911
  Grafton *(G-8839)*
Hamilton-Parker Company .... D 614 358-7800
  Columbus *(G-5968)*
Kuhlman Corporation .... E 419 897-6000
  Maumee *(G-10737)*
Modern Builders Supply Inc .... C 419 241-3961
  Toledo *(G-13926)*
Nexgen Enterprises Inc .... B 513 618-0300
  Cincinnati *(G-3112)*
Tremco Cpg Inc .... D 216 292-5000
  Beachwood *(G-846)*
Van Boxel Stor Solutions LLC .... E 440 721-1504
  Chardon *(G-2025)*

BROACHING MACHINES

Ohio Broach & Machine Company ...... E 440 946-1040
  Willoughby *(G-15214)*

BROADCASTING STATIONS, TELEVISION: Translator Station

Gray Media Group Inc .... D 419 534-3886
  Toledo *(G-13824)*
Ohio State University .... D 614 292-9678
  Columbus *(G-6454)*

BROKERS & DEALERS: Securities

Capital Securities of America .... E 419 609-9489
  Sandusky *(G-12869)*
Cincinnati Insurance Company .... A 513 870-2000
  Fairfield *(G-8404)*
Corporate Fin Assoc Clmbus Inc .... D 614 457-9219
  Columbus *(G-5703)*
Department of Commerce Ohio .... D 614 644-7381
  Columbus *(G-5757)*
Fifth Third Securities Inc .... E 513 346-2775
  Cincinnati *(G-2667)*
Ifs Financial Services Inc .... E 513 362-8000
  Westerville *(G-14988)*
Keybanc Capital Markets Inc .... B 800 553-2240
  Cleveland *(G-4458)*
National Associates Inc .... D 440 333-0222
  Cleveland *(G-4618)*
Nationwide Inv Svcs Corp .... B 614 249-7111
  Columbus *(G-6333)*
Stifel Ind Advisors LLC .... E 937 293-1220
  Dayton *(G-7643)*
Valmark Financial Group LLC .... C 330 576-1234
  Akron *(G-347)*
World Group Securities Inc .... D 513 367-5900
  Harrison *(G-9121)*

BROKERS & DEALERS: Security

Merrill Lynch Prce Fnner Smith .... D 440 526-8880
  Broadview Heights *(G-1392)*
Merrill Lynch Prce Fnner Smith .... C 614 225-3000
  Columbus *(G-5269)*

BROKERS' SVCS

Culinary Metz Management LLC .... C 330 684-3368
  Orrville *(G-12159)*
Shamrock Companies Inc .... D 440 899-9510
  Westlake *(G-15108)*
Shredded Bedding Corporation .... D 740 893-3567
  Centerburg *(G-1936)*
Stifel Ind Advisors LLC .... E 937 312-0111
  Dayton *(G-7644)*
Wad Investments Oh Inc .... E 513 891-4477
  Cincinnati *(G-3637)*

BROKERS: Business

Corporate Fin Assoc Clmbus Inc .... D 614 457-9219
  Columbus *(G-5703)*

BROKERS: Food

Atlantic Fish & Distrg Co .... E 330 454-1307
  Canton *(G-1673)*
Brothers Trading Co Inc .... E 937 746-1010
  Springboro *(G-13195)*
Brothers Trading Co Inc .... C 937 746-1010
  Springboro *(G-13194)*
Cantrell Oil Company .... E 937 695-8003
  Winchester *(G-15286)*
Comber Holdings Inc .... E 216 961-8600
  Cleveland *(G-4090)*
Empire Food Brokers Inc .... E 614 889-2322
  Dublin *(G-8003)*
Euclid Fish Company .... D 440 951-6448
  Mentor *(G-10938)*
Impact Sales Inc .... D 937 274-1905
  Dayton *(G-7419)*
J M Sealts Company .... E 419 224-8075
  Blue Ash *(G-1188)*
McLane Foodservice Dist Inc .... C 614 771-9660
  Columbus *(G-6217)*
McLane Foodservice Dist Inc .... E 614 662-7700
  Lockbourne *(G-10012)*
Mpf Sales and Mktg Group LLC .... C 513 793-6241
  Blue Ash *(G-1213)*
Novelart Manufacturing Company .... D 513 351-7700
  Cincinnati *(G-3132)*
Queensgate Food Group LLC .... D 513 721-5503
  Cincinnati *(G-3269)*
R G Sellers Company .... E 937 299-1545
  Moraine *(G-11432)*
Sygma Network Inc .... C 614 734-2500
  Dublin *(G-8137)*
Sygma Network Inc .... B 614 771-3801
  Columbus *(G-6740)*
Sysco Cleveland Inc .... A 216 201-3000
  Cleveland *(G-4973)*
The Chas G Buchy Packing Company ... E
  Cincinnati *(G-3462)*
The H T Hackney Co .... E 614 751-5100
  Gahanna *(G-8733)*

SERVICES SECTION

US Foods Inc... E 330 963-6789
  Twinsburg *(G-14227)*
US Foods Inc... E 614 539-7993
  West Chester *(G-14843)*
Valley Wholesale Foods Inc................ E 740 354-5216
  Portsmouth *(G-12581)*
Vendors Supply Inc............................. E 513 755-2111
  West Chester *(G-14790)*

BROKERS: Loan

Board of Dirs of Wttnberg Clle............ D 937 327-6310
  Springfield *(G-13222)*
Civista Bank.. E 419 599-1065
  Napoleon *(G-11518)*
Firefighters Cmnty Cr Un Inc.............. E 216 621-4644
  Cleveland *(G-4252)*
Firelands Federal Credit Union........... E 419 483-4180
  Bellevue *(G-1044)*
First Merchants Bank........................... E 614 486-9000
  Upper Arlington *(G-14278)*
Guardian Savings Bank........................ E 513 842-8900
  Cincinnati *(G-2781)*
Guardian Savings Bank........................ E 513 528-8787
  Cincinnati *(G-2782)*
Guardian Savings Bank........................ E 513 942-3535
  West Chester *(G-14702)*
Impact Credit Union Inc....................... E 419 547-7781
  Clyde *(G-5203)*
Millstream Area Credit Un Inc............. E 419 422-5626
  Findlay *(G-8570)*
Osgood State Bank Inc........................ E 419 582-2681
  Osgood *(G-12181)*
Second National Bank......................... E 937 548-2122
  Greenville *(G-8884)*
State Bank and Trust Company.......... E 419 783-8950
  Defiance *(G-7769)*
Struthers CU A Div Brdge Cr Un......... E 800 434-7300
  Columbus *(G-6723)*
Student Ln Fnding Rsources LLC........ E 513 763-4300
  Cincinnati *(G-3425)*
The Home Savings and Loan C........... C 330 742-0500
  Youngstown *(G-15734)*

BROKERS: Log & Lumber

Southwood Pallet LLC......................... D 330 682-3747
  Orrville *(G-12173)*

BROKERS: Mortgage, Arranging For Loans

BP Financial Group Inc......................... E 513 851-8525
  Cincinnati *(G-2275)*
Crosscountry Mortgage LLC................ B 440 845-3700
  Brecksville *(G-1352)*
Forest City Residential Dev................. E 216 621-6060
  Cleveland *(G-4275)*
Multi-Fund Inc...................................... E 216 750-2331
  Cleveland *(G-4610)*
Nations Lending Corporation............... C 216 363-6901
  Independence *(G-9457)*
North Coast Capital Funding................ D 330 923-5333
  Cuyahoga Falls *(G-7090)*
Premiere Service Mortgage Corp........ E 513 546-9895
  West Chester *(G-14745)*
Randall Mortgage Services.................. C 614 336-7948
  Dublin *(G-8105)*
Union Mortgage Services Inc............... E 614 457-4815
  Columbus *(G-6802)*
Welles-Bowen Realty Inc..................... C 419 535-0011
  Toledo *(G-14101)*

BROKERS: Printing

Depot Direct Inc.................................... E 419 661-1233
  Perrysburg *(G-12332)*

Pxp Ohio.. E 614 575-4242
  Reynoldsburg *(G-12673)*
Veritiv Pubg & Print MGT Inc............... E 614 288-0911
  Stow *(G-13400)*

BROOMS & BRUSHES

Mill Rose Laboratories Inc.................... E 440 974-6730
  Mentor *(G-10974)*
Stephen M Trudick.............................. E 440 834-1891
  Burton *(G-1533)*

BROOMS & BRUSHES: Household Or Indl

Ekco Cleaning Inc................................ C 513 733-8882
  Cincinnati *(G-2608)*
Mill-Rose Company.............................. C 440 255-9171
  Mentor *(G-10975)*

BUCKETS: Plastic

Impact Products LLC........................... D 419 841-2891
  Toledo *(G-13860)*

BUILDING & OFFICE CLEANING SVCS

August Groh & Sons Inc...................... E 513 821-0090
  Cincinnati *(G-2229)*
Corporate Cleaning Inc....................... E 614 203-6051
  Columbus *(G-5702)*
High-TEC Industrial Services............... D 937 667-1772
  Tipp City *(G-13659)*

BUILDING & STRUCTURAL WOOD MEMBERS

Holmes Lumber & Bldg Ctr Inc............ E 330 479-8314
  Canton *(G-1775)*
Holmes Lumber & Bldg Ctr Inc............ C 330 674-9060
  Millersburg *(G-11279)*

BUILDING CLEANING & MAINTENANCE SVCS

Allen-Keith Construction Co................. D 330 266-2220
  Canton *(G-1659)*
C & K Industrial Services Inc............... D 216 642-0055
  Independence *(G-9414)*
Caveney Inc.. E 330 497-4600
  North Canton *(G-11815)*
County of Cuyahoga............................ B 216 443-6954
  Cleveland *(G-4131)*
Divisions Inc... C 859 448-9730
  Cincinnati *(G-2571)*
G7 Services Inc.................................... E 937 256-3473
  Dayton *(G-7372)*
Green Impressions LLC....................... D 440 240-8508
  Sheffield Village *(G-12998)*
Heco Operations Inc............................ C 614 888-5700
  Worthington *(G-15420)*
I E R Inc.. E 440 324-2620
  Elyria *(G-8261)*
Integrity Concepts Llc Inc.................... D 614 529-8332
  Columbus *(G-6062)*
Kettering City School District................ E 937 297-1990
  Dayton *(G-7438)*
Kleman Services LLC.......................... D 419 339-0871
  Lima *(G-9916)*
Northpointe Property MGT LLC........... C 614 579-9712
  Columbus *(G-6369)*
Professional Restoration Svc................ E 330 825-1803
  Medina *(G-10879)*
Psp Operations Inc.............................. C 614 888-5700
  Worthington *(G-15449)*
Restoration Resources Inc................... E 330 650-4486
  Hudson *(G-9371)*

BUILDING PRDTS & MATERIALS DEALERS

Richland Newhope Inds Inc.................. C 419 774-4400
  Mansfield *(G-10313)*
Service Master Co................................ E 330 864-7300
  Eastlake *(G-8208)*
Solv-All LLC.. D 888 765-8255
  Mentor *(G-10996)*
Star Inc.. C 740 354-1517
  Portsmouth *(G-12575)*
T & L Enterprises Inc............................ E 440 234-5900
  Berea *(G-1083)*
Trg Maintenance LLC........................... A 614 891-4850
  Westerville *(G-14945)*
Trk Investments Montgomery LLC....... E 513 388-0186
  Cincinnati *(G-3529)*
United Scoto Senior Activities.............. E 740 354-6672
  Portsmouth *(G-12579)*
Universal Services America LP............ A 937 454-9035
  Vandalia *(G-14398)*
University of Cincinnati........................ D 513 556-6381
  Cincinnati *(G-3590)*

BUILDING COMPONENTS: Structural Steel

Frederick Steel Company LLC.............. D 513 821-6400
  Cincinnati *(G-2703)*
JJ&pl Services-Consulting LLC............ E 330 923-5783
  Cuyahoga Falls *(G-7082)*
Mound Technologies Inc...................... E 937 748-2937
  Springboro *(G-13203)*
Turn-Key Industrial Svcs LLC............... D 614 274-1128
  Grove City *(G-8960)*

BUILDING MAINTENANCE SVCS, EXC REPAIRS

Blanchard Valley Health System........... A 419 423-4500
  Findlay *(G-8514)*
G J Goudreau & Co............................. E 216 351-5233
  Cleveland *(G-4297)*
Lima Sheet Metal Machine & Mfg........ E 419 229-1161
  Lima *(G-9927)*
Louderback Fmly Invstments Inc......... E 937 845-1762
  New Carlisle *(G-11604)*
Maass - Midwest Mfg Inc..................... A 419 485-6905
  Pioneer *(G-12433)*

BUILDING PRDTS & MATERIALS DEALERS

Clays Heritage Carpet Inc.................... E 330 497-1280
  Canton *(G-1711)*
Contract Lumber Inc............................ C 740 964-3147
  Pataskala *(G-12270)*
Contractors Materials Company........... E 513 733-3000
  Cincinnati *(G-2502)*
Do It Best Corp..................................... B 330 725-3859
  Medina *(G-10831)*
Graves Lumber Co............................... C 330 666-1115
  Copley *(G-6958)*
Holmes Lumber & Bldg Ctr Inc............ E 330 479-8314
  Canton *(G-1775)*
Holmes Lumber & Bldg Ctr Inc............ C 330 674-9060
  Millersburg *(G-11279)*
Keim Lumber Company........................ D 330 893-2251
  Millersburg *(G-11282)*
Khempco Bldg Sup Co Ltd Partnr....... D 740 549-0465
  Delaware *(G-7811)*
Kurtz Bros Inc....................................... E 216 986-7000
  Independence *(G-9442)*
Lang Stone Company Inc..................... E 614 235-4099
  Columbus *(G-6139)*
Mentor Lumber and Supply Co............ C 440 255-8814
  Mentor *(G-10970)*
Modern Builders Supply Inc................. E 330 376-1031
  Akron *(G-236)*

BUILDING PRDTS & MATERIALS DEALERS — SERVICES SECTION

Modern Builders Supply Inc .... E 216 273-3605
 Cleveland *(G-4593)*

The F A Requarth Company .... E 937 224-1141
 Dayton *(G-7665)*

Western Reserve Farm Cooperative Inc D 440 632-0271
 Middlefield *(G-11146)*

BUILDINGS & COMPONENTS: Prefabricated Metal

Hoge Lumber Company .... E 419 753-2263
 New Knoxville *(G-11617)*

BUILDINGS: Portable

Williams Scotsman Inc .... D 614 449-8675
 Columbus *(G-6894)*

BUILDINGS: Prefabricated, Metal

Enclosure Suppliers LLC .... E 513 782-3900
 Cincinnati *(G-2619)*

BUILDINGS: Prefabricated, Wood

Cooper Enterprises Inc .... D 419 347-5232
 Shelby *(G-13006)*

Vinyl Design Corporation .... E 419 283-4009
 Holland *(G-9213)*

BURIAL VAULTS: Concrete Or Precast Terrazzo

Bell Vault and Monu Works Inc .... E 937 866-2444
 Miamisburg *(G-11025)*

BUS BARS: Electrical

Schneider Electric Usa Inc .... D 513 777-4445
 West Chester *(G-14761)*

BUSHINGS & BEARINGS

McNeil Industries Inc .... E 440 951-7756
 Painesville *(G-12236)*

BUSINESS ACTIVITIES: Non-Commercial Site

Ability Works Inc .... C 419 626-1048
 Sandusky *(G-12861)*

Alexis Eppinger .... E 216 509-0475
 Cleveland *(G-3785)*

Alexzander Angels LLC .... E 678 984-3093
 Cincinnati *(G-2160)*

Alterntive Rsrces Homecare Inc .... D 216 256-3049
 Shaker Heights *(G-12973)*

Andydandy Center LLC .... E 513 272-6141
 Cincinnati *(G-2203)*

Arrc One LLC .... E 440 754-0855
 Oberlin *(G-12063)*

Ashland Aqualon Functional .... E 614 790-3333
 Dublin *(G-7940)*

Balaji D Loganathan .... C 614 918-0411
 Hilliard *(G-9182)*

Blessing Home Health Care Inc .... E 614 329-2086
 Hilliard *(G-9183)*

Buckeye Mechanical Contg Inc .... E 740 282-0089
 Toronto *(G-14121)*

Burrilla LLC .... E 513 615-9350
 West Chester *(G-14656)*

Cardio Partners Inc .... E 614 760-5000
 Dublin *(G-7957)*

Catalyst Recovery La LLC .... E 513 354-3640
 Cincinnati *(G-2320)*

Chief Delivery LLC .... E 419 277-6190
 Toledo *(G-13732)*

Cleary Company .... E 614 459-4000
 Columbus *(G-5582)*

Dan & Maria Davis Inc .... E 937 669-2271
 Tipp City *(G-13657)*

Dehart Works LLC .... D 440 600-8003
 Cleveland *(G-4159)*

DJ Roofing & Imprvs LLC .... E 419 307-5712
 Fremont *(G-8675)*

Euclidean Support Services Inc .... E 330 405-8501
 Euclid *(G-8342)*

Findaway World LLC .... E 330 794-7758
 Akron *(G-158)*

Flexsys Inc .... B 212 605-6000
 Akron *(G-165)*

Flying Pig Logistics Inc .... E 513 300-9331
 West Chester *(G-14692)*

Grays Trnsp & Logistics LLC .... E 614 656-3460
 Columbus *(G-5949)*

Holloway Ventures LLC .... E 740 641-3592
 Newark *(G-11705)*

Industrial Insul Coatings LLC .... E 800 506-1399
 Girard *(G-8816)*

Ineos ABS (usa) LLC .... C 513 467-2400
 Addyston *(G-4)*

Jumbo Logistics LLC .... E 216 662-5420
 Macedonia *(G-10195)*

Koinonia Partners Holdings LLC .... E 216 588-8777
 Maple Heights *(G-10342)*

Lions Gate SEC Solutions Inc .... E 440 539-8382
 Euclid *(G-8357)*

Making Life Easy LLC .... D 513 280-0422
 Cincinnati *(G-3006)*

Matic Insurance Services Inc .... C 833 382-1304
 Columbus *(G-6206)*

Montaque Cleaning Services LLC .... E 937 705-0429
 Dayton *(G-7511)*

Mt Washington Care Center Inc .... E 513 231-4561
 Cincinnati *(G-3087)*

Ohio-T-Home Hlth Care Agcy Ltd .... D 614 947-0791
 Columbus *(G-6464)*

Sacred Hour Inc .... D 216 228-9750
 Lakewood *(G-9684)*

SAR Warehouse Staffing LLC .... D 740 963-6235
 Columbus *(G-6643)*

Self Mployed .... E 216 408-3280
 Cleveland *(G-4892)*

Service Pronet LLC .... E 614 874-4300
 Columbus *(G-6665)*

Spend and Send .... E 216 381-5459
 Cleveland *(G-4933)*

Standard Wellness Company LLC ...... C 330 931-1037
 Cleveland *(G-4941)*

Tm Capture Services LLC .... D 937 728-1781
 Dayton *(G-7671)*

Vigilant Global Trade Svcs LLC .... E 260 417-1825
 Shaker Heights *(G-12988)*

Vincent & Vincent .... E 513 617-2089
 Cincinnati *(G-3630)*

Wolseley Industrial Group .... E 513 587-7532
 West Chester *(G-14796)*

BUSINESS FORMS WHOLESALERS

American Business Forms Inc .... E 513 312-2522
 West Chester *(G-14798)*

American Business Forms Inc .... E 614 664-0202
 Westerville *(G-14958)*

GBS Corp .... C 330 494-5330
 North Canton *(G-11833)*

Highland Computer Forms Inc .... D 937 393-4215
 Hillsboro *(G-9257)*

Optimum System Products Inc .... E 614 885-4464
 Westerville *(G-15009)*

Reynolds and Reynolds Holdings .... E 937 485-8125
 Dayton *(G-7590)*

Shamrock Companies Inc .... D 440 899-9510
 Westlake *(G-15108)*

Wilmer .... E 419 678-6000
 Coldwater *(G-5221)*

BUSINESS FORMS: Printed, Manifold

Custom Products Corporation .... D 440 528-7100
 Solon *(G-13080)*

Eleet Cryogenics Inc .... E 330 874-4009
 Bolivar *(G-1294)*

GBS Corp .... C 330 494-5330
 North Canton *(G-11833)*

BUSINESS MACHINE REPAIR, ELECTRIC

Leppo Inc .... E 330 633-3999
 Tallmadge *(G-13599)*

Modern Office Methods Inc .... E 513 791-0909
 Blue Ash *(G-1211)*

Modern Office Methods Inc .... E 614 891-3693
 Westerville *(G-15000)*

Modern Office Methods Inc .... D 513 791-0909
 Cincinnati *(G-3076)*

Ohio Business Machines LLC .... E 216 485-2000
 Cleveland *(G-4683)*

CABINETS: Entertainment

Kraftmaid Trucking Inc .... D 440 632-2531
 Middlefield *(G-11142)*

CABINETS: Kitchen, Wood

Climate Pros LLC .... D 216 881-5200
 Cleveland *(G-4083)*

Climate Pros LLC .... D 330 744-2732
 Youngstown *(G-15579)*

Holmes Lumber & Bldg Ctr Inc .... E 330 479-8314
 Canton *(G-1775)*

Holmes Lumber & Bldg Ctr Inc .... C 330 674-9060
 Millersburg *(G-11279)*

Knapke Cabinets Inc .... E 937 335-8383
 Troy *(G-14142)*

Masterbrand Cabinets LLC .... B 812 482-2527
 Beachwood *(G-812)*

Riverside Cnstr Svcs Inc .... E 513 723-0900
 Cincinnati *(G-3307)*

The Hattenbach Company .... D 216 881-5200
 Cleveland *(G-5001)*

CABINETS: Office, Wood

Hoge Lumber Company .... E 419 753-2263
 New Knoxville *(G-11617)*

CABINETS: Show, Display, Etc, Wood, Exc Refrigerated

Climate Pros LLC .... D 216 881-5200
 Cleveland *(G-4083)*

Climate Pros LLC .... D 330 744-2732
 Youngstown *(G-15579)*

The Hattenbach Company .... D 216 881-5200
 Cleveland *(G-5001)*

CABLE & OTHER PAY TELEVISION DISTRIBUTION

ASC of Cincinnati Inc .... E 513 886-7100
 Lebanon *(G-9755)*

CABLE & PAY TELEVISION SVCS: Direct Broadcast Satellite

SERVICES SECTION

CATERERS

Sun Yer Bunz LLC..................................D..... 937 222-3474
Dayton (G-7652)

CABLE TELEVISION

Armstrong Utilities Inc........................D..... 330 723-3536
Medina (G-10808)

Armstrong Utilities Inc........................D..... 330 758-6411
North Lima (G-11881)

Block Communications Inc..................D..... 419 724-2539
Northwood (G-11969)

Charter Communications.....................E..... 614 588-5036
Columbus (G-5551)

Chillicothe Telephone Company............C..... 740 772-8200
Chillicothe (G-2060)

Coaxial Cmmnctons of Sthern OH.........D..... 513 797-4400
Columbus (G-5589)

Erie County Cablevision Inc.................C..... 419 627-0800
Sandusky (G-12891)

Massillon Cable TV Inc........................D..... 330 833-4134
Massillon (G-10652)

McTv Inc..D..... 330 833-4134
Massillon (G-10655)

Spectrum MGT Holdg Co LLC...............E..... 614 344-4159
Columbus (G-6703)

Time Warner Cable Entps LLC...............E..... 513 489-5000
Blue Ash (G-1255)

Time Warner Cable Entps LLC...............E..... 614 255-6289
Columbus (G-6768)

Time Warner Cable Entps LLC...............E..... 614 481-5072
Columbus (G-6769)

CABLE: Fiber Optic

Cbst Acquisition LLC...........................D..... 513 361-9600
Cincinnati (G-2326)

CABLE: Noninsulated

Microplex Inc......................................E..... 330 498-0600
North Canton (G-11848)

CABLE: Ropes & Fiber

Atwood Rope Manufacturing Inc............E..... 614 920-0534
Canal Winchester (G-1598)

CAFETERIAS

Westgate Lanes Incorporated................E..... 419 229-3845
Lima (G-9986)

CALIBRATING SVCS, NEC

Cincinnati Prcision Instrs Inc................E..... 513 874-2122
West Chester (G-14805)

CAMERAS & RELATED EQPT: Photographic

Dodd Camera Holdings Inc....................E..... 216 361-6811
Cleveland (G-4173)

CANDLES

Gorant Chocolatier LLC........................C..... 330 726-8821
Boardman (G-1288)

CANDLES: Wholesalers

Alene Candles LLC..............................C..... 614 933-4005
New Albany (G-11555)

CANDY & CONFECTIONS: Popcorn Balls/ Other Trtd Popcorn Prdts

Jml Holdings Inc.................................E..... 419 866-7500
Holland (G-9291)

CANDY MAKING GOODS & SPLYS, WHOLESALE

Just Candy LLC...................................E..... 201 805-8562
Fairfield (G-8424)

CANDY, NUT & CONFECTIONERY STORES: Candy

Gorant Chocolatier LLC........................C..... 330 726-8821
Boardman (G-1288)

CANNED SPECIALTIES

Bittersweet Inc...................................D..... 419 875-6986
Whitehouse (G-15138)

Hayden Valley Foods Inc.......................D..... 614 539-7233
Urbancrest (G-14320)

Skyline Cem Holdings LLC....................C..... 513 874-1188
Fairfield (G-8441)

CANS: Metal

Organized Living Inc............................E..... 513 489-9300
Cincinnati (G-3167)

CANVAS PRDTS

Samsel Rope & Marine Supply Co..........E..... 216 241-0333
Cleveland (G-4875)

CAR WASH EQPT

Giant Industries Inc............................E..... 419 531-4600
Toledo (G-13821)

CARBON & GRAPHITE PRDTS, NEC

Ges Graphite Inc.................................E..... 216 658-6660
Parma (G-12254)

Graftech Holdings Inc..........................D..... 216 676-2000
Independence (G-9434)

Mill-Rose Company..............................C..... 440 255-9171
Mentor (G-10975)

CARBON PAPER & INKED RIBBONS

Pubco Corporation...............................D..... 216 881-5300
Cleveland (G-4797)

CARDS: Beveled

Cott Systems Inc.................................D..... 614 847-4405
Columbus (G-5707)

CARDS: Greeting

Papyrus-Recycled Greetings Inc............D..... 773 348-6410
Westlake (G-15095)

CARPET & UPHOLSTERY CLEANING SVCS

Allen-Keith Construction Co..................D..... 330 266-2220
Canton (G-1659)

B&L Acquisition Group LLC..................E..... 216 626-0040
Bedford Heights (G-994)

Best Karpet Klean Ohio LLC..................E..... 440 942-2481
Cleveland (G-3871)

C&C Clean Team Enterprises LLC..........C..... 513 321-5100
Cincinnati (G-2299)

Interfinish LLC....................................E..... 216 662-6550
Cleveland (G-4418)

Teasdale Fnton Crpt Clg Rstrti..............D..... 513 797-0900
Cincinnati (G-3446)

Widmers LLC......................................C..... 513 321-5100
Cincinnati (G-3670)

CARPET & UPHOLSTERY CLEANING SVCS: Carpet/Furniture, On Loc

Lazar Brothers Inc..............................E..... 440 585-9333
Wickliffe (G-15156)

Miles Cleaning Services Inc..................E..... 216 626-0040
Cleveland (G-4582)

Stanley Steemer Intl Inc......................E..... 614 764-2007
Beavercreek Township (G-950)

Stanley Steemer Intl Inc......................E..... 513 771-0213
Cincinnati (G-3411)

Stanley Steemer Intl Inc......................E..... 614 767-8017
Cleveland (G-4942)

Stanley Steemer Intl Inc......................C..... 614 764-2007
Dublin (G-8124)

Velco Inc..E..... 513 772-4226
Cincinnati (G-3618)

Wiggins Clg & Crpt Svc Inc...................D..... 937 279-9080
Dayton (G-7722)

CARPETS, RUGS & FLOOR COVERING

Ccp Industries Inc...............................B..... 216 535-4227
Richmond Heights (G-12716)

CARTONS: Egg, Molded Pulp, Made From Purchased Materials

Tekni-Plex Inc.....................................E..... 419 491-2399
Holland (G-9307)

CASH REGISTER REPAIR SVCS

Aptos LLC...D..... 614 840-1400
Lewis Center (G-9806)

CASH REGISTERS WHOLESALERS

Aptos LLC...D..... 614 840-1400
Lewis Center (G-9806)

CASTINGS: Commercial Investment, Ferrous

B W Grinding Co..................................E..... 419 923-1376
Lyons (G-10187)

CASTINGS: Die, Aluminum

Akron Foundry Co................................C..... 330 745-3101
Akron (G-28)

Seilkop Industries Inc..........................E..... 513 761-1035
Cincinnati (G-3356)

The Kindt-Collins Company LLC............D..... 216 252-4122
Cleveland (G-5003)

Yoder Industries Inc............................C..... 937 278-5769
Dayton (G-7731)

CASTINGS: Die, Nonferrous

Yoder Industries Inc............................C..... 937 278-5769
Dayton (G-7731)

CASTINGS: Precision

Akron Foundry Co................................C..... 330 745-3101
Akron (G-28)

CATALOG & MAIL-ORDER HOUSES

Cornerstone Brands Group Inc..............A..... 513 603-1000
West Chester (G-14677)

Cornerstone Consolidated Se................A..... 513 603-1100
West Chester (G-14678)

Franchise Group Inc............................B..... 740 363-2222
Delaware (G-7799)

CATALOG SALES

Amerimark Holdings LLC.....................B..... 440 325-2000
Cleveland (G-3809)

CATALYSTS: Chemical

BASF Catalysts LLC.............................C..... 216 360-5005
Cleveland (G-3853)

Chemspec Usa Inc..............................D..... 330 669-8512
Orrville (G-12158)

CATERERS

CATERERS

AVI Food Systems Inc .... B 330 372-6000
   Warren *(G-14505)*

Bagel Place Inc .... E 419 537-9377
   Toledo *(G-13698)*

Kohler Foods Inc .... E 937 291-3600
   Dayton *(G-7445)*

Made From Scratch Inc .... E 614 873-3344
   Plain City *(G-12484)*

Mustard Seed Health Fd Mkt Inc .... E 440 519-3663
   Solon *(G-13115)*

Plaza Inn Foods Inc .... E 937 354-2181
   Mount Victory *(G-11512)*

Schmidt Hsptality Concepts Inc .... E 614 878-4527
   Columbus *(G-6649)*

Sycamore Lake Inc .... E 440 729-9775
   Chesterland *(G-2043)*

Yankee Lake Inc .... E 330 448-8866
   Brookfield *(G-1408)*

CEMENT & CONCRETE RELATED PRDTS & EQPT: Bituminous

Mesa Industries Inc .... E 513 321-2950
   Cincinnati *(G-3048)*

CEMENT: Hydraulic

Huron Cement Products Company ...... E 419 433-4161
   Huron *(G-9390)*

CHARGE ACCOUNT SVCS

Medigistics Inc .... D 614 430-5700
   Columbus *(G-6221)*

CHASSIS: Motor Vehicle

Falls Stamping & Welding Co .... C 330 928-1191
   Cuyahoga Falls *(G-7075)*

CHEESE WHOLESALERS

Coblentz Distributing Inc .... C 330 893-3895
   Millersburg *(G-11277)*

CHEMICAL CLEANING SVCS

Chemical Solvents Inc .... E 216 741-9310
   Cleveland *(G-3965)*

CHEMICAL PROCESSING MACHINERY & EQPT

Chemineer Inc .... C 937 454-3200
   Dayton *(G-7222)*

Guild Associates Inc .... D 614 798-8215
   Dublin *(G-8023)*

CHEMICALS & ALLIED PRDTS WHOLESALERS, NEC

Applied Industrial Tech Inc .... B 216 426-4000
   Cleveland *(G-3827)*

Ashland Chemco Inc .... C 614 790-3333
   Columbus *(G-5394)*

Avalon Foodservice Inc .... C 330 854-4551
   Canal Fulton *(G-1592)*

Calvary Industries Inc .... E 513 874-1113
   Fairfield *(G-8398)*

Chemical Associates of Illinois Inc ...... E 330 666-7200
   Copley *(G-6949)*

Cimcool Industrial Pdts LLC .... E 513 458-8100
   Cincinnati *(G-2389)*

Cleveland FP Inc .... D 216 249-4900
   Cleveland *(G-4045)*

Detrex Corporation .... E 440 997-6131
   Ashtabula *(G-533)*

Dover Chemical Corporation .... C 330 343-7711
   Dover *(G-7880)*

Dubois Chemicals Inc .... E 513 868-9662
   Hamilton *(G-9037)*

Dubois Chemicals Inc .... E 800 438-2647
   Sharonville *(G-12993)*

Emerald Hilton Davis LLC .... D 513 841-0057
   Cincinnati *(G-2614)*

Formlabs Ohio Inc .... E 419 837-9783
   Millbury *(G-11268)*

Imcd Us LLC .... E 216 228-8900
   Westlake *(G-15069)*

Kellermeyer Company .... D 419 255-3022
   Bowling Green *(G-1326)*

Knight Material Tech LLC .... D 330 488-1651
   East Canton *(G-8169)*

Morton Salt Inc .... C 440 354-9901
   Painesville *(G-12237)*

National Biochemicals LLC .... E 330 425-2522
   Aurora *(G-619)*

Polymer Additives Inc .... D 216 875-7200
   Independence *(G-9468)*

Polymer Additives Holdings Inc .... C 216 875-7200
   Independence *(G-9469)*

Polymer Solutions Group LLC .... E 229 435-8394
   Cleveland *(G-4760)*

Red Rover LLC .... E 330 262-6501
   Wooster *(G-15368)*

Santmyer Logistics Inc .... E 330 262-6501
   Wooster *(G-15371)*

Sigma-Aldrich Corporation .... D 216 206-5424
   Cleveland *(G-4907)*

Skidmore Sales & Distrg Co Inc .... E 513 755-4200
   West Chester *(G-14766)*

Spartan Chemical Company Inc .... C 419 897-5551
   Maumee *(G-10768)*

Specialty Chemical Sales Inc .... E 216 267-4248
   Cleveland *(G-4928)*

Struktol Company America LLC .... E 330 928-5188
   Stow *(G-13395)*

T&L Global Management LLC .... D 614 586-0303
   Columbus *(G-6744)*

Toagosei America Inc .... D 614 718-3855
   West Jefferson *(G-14853)*

Tricor Industrial Inc .... D 330 264-3299
   Wooster *(G-15380)*

Veolia Wts Usa Inc .... E 330 339-2292
   New Philadelphia *(G-11672)*

CHEMICALS & ALLIED PRDTS, WHOL: Chemicals, Swimming Pool/Spa

Rhiel Supply Co .... E 330 799-7777
   Austintown *(G-636)*

CHEMICALS & ALLIED PRDTS, WHOLESALE: Alkalines & Chlorine

Ashland Chemco Inc .... D 614 232-8510
   Columbus *(G-5393)*

CHEMICALS & ALLIED PRDTS, WHOLESALE: Chemicals, Indl

Chemical Solvents Inc .... D 216 741-9310
   Cleveland *(G-3966)*

CL Zimmerman Delaware LLC .... E 513 860-9300
   West Chester *(G-14667)*

Custom Chemical Solutions LLC .... E 800 291-1057
   Loveland *(G-10134)*

FBC Chemical Corporation .... E 330 723-7780
   Medina *(G-10833)*

SERVICES SECTION

Fisk Kinne Holdings Inc .... E 937 461-9906
   Dayton *(G-7356)*

Fort Amanda Specialties LLC .... D 419 229-0088
   Lima *(G-9890)*

Galaxy Associates Inc .... C 513 731-6350
   Cincinnati *(G-2714)*

Gem City Chemicals Inc .... D 937 224-0711
   Dayton *(G-7373)*

Palmer Holland Inc .... C 440 686-2300
   Westlake *(G-15094)*

Products Chemical Company LLC ...... D 216 281-1155
   Cleveland *(G-4773)*

Rhein Chemie Corporation .... C 440 279-2367
   Chardon *(G-2017)*

Sea-Land Chemical Co .... E 440 871-7887
   Cleveland *(G-4887)*

Tembec Btlsr Inc .... E 419 244-5856
   Toledo *(G-14037)*

Tosoh America Inc .... B 614 539-8622
   Grove City *(G-8959)*

Young Chemical Co LLC .... E 330 486-4210
   Twinsburg *(G-14232)*

CHEMICALS & ALLIED PRDTS, WHOLESALE: Chemicals, Indl & Heavy

Harwick Standard Dist Corp .... D 330 798-9300
   Akron *(G-186)*

Hexion Inc .... C 888 443-9466
   Columbus *(G-5989)*

Industrial Chemical Corp .... E 330 725-0800
   Medina *(G-10846)*

CHEMICALS & ALLIED PRDTS, WHOLESALE: Detergent/Soap

Anatrace Products LLC .... E 800 252-1280
   Maumee *(G-10691)*

Chemical Solvents Inc .... E 216 741-9310
   Cleveland *(G-3965)*

CHEMICALS & ALLIED PRDTS, WHOLESALE: Detergents

Procter & Gamble Distrg LLC .... B 513 626-2500
   Blue Ash *(G-1224)*

Procter & Gamble Distrg LLC .... C 513 945-7960
   Cincinnati *(G-3243)*

Washing Systems LLC .... C 800 272-1974
   Loveland *(G-10166)*

CHEMICALS & ALLIED PRDTS, WHOLESALE: Oxygen

Braden Med Services Inc .... E 740 732-2356
   Caldwell *(G-1547)*

Lincare Inc .... E 216 581-9649
   Cleveland *(G-4497)*

Medi Home Health Agency Inc .... E 740 266-3977
   Steubenville *(G-13338)*

CHEMICALS & ALLIED PRDTS, WHOLESALE: Plastics Film

Cleveland Supplyone Inc .... E 216 514-7000
   Cleveland *(G-4068)*

CHEMICALS & ALLIED PRDTS, WHOLESALE: Plastics Materials, NEC

Alro Steel Corporation .... E 614 878-7271
   Columbus *(G-5340)*

Alro Steel Corporation .... D 419 720-5300
   Toledo *(G-13679)*

SERVICES SECTION

CHEMICALS & ALLIED PRDTS, WHOLESALE: Plastics Prdts, NEC

American Plastics Inc .... D 330 945-4100
  Akron *(G-48)*
Plastics R Unique Inc .... E 330 334-4820
  Wadsworth *(G-14448)*

CHEMICALS & ALLIED PRDTS, WHOLESALE: Plastics Prdts, NEC

Curbell Plastics Inc .... E 513 742-9898
  Cincinnati *(G-2524)*
Plastics Family Holdings Inc .... E 330 733-9595
  Stow *(G-13385)*
Polymer Packaging Inc .... D 330 832-2000
  North Canton *(G-11852)*
Queen City Polymers Inc .... E 513 779-0990
  West Chester *(G-14752)*
Tahoma Enterprises Inc .... D 330 745-9016
  Barberton *(G-714)*
Tahoma Rubber & Plastics Inc .... D 330 745-9016
  Barberton *(G-715)*

CHEMICALS & ALLIED PRDTS, WHOLESALE: Plastics Sheets & Rods

HP Manufacturing Company Inc .... D 216 361-6500
  Cleveland *(G-4386)*

CHEMICALS & ALLIED PRDTS, WHOLESALE: Resins

Avient Corporation .... D 440 930-1000
  Avon Lake *(G-672)*
Epsilyte Holdings LLC .... D 937 778-9500
  Piqua *(G-12441)*
Hexpol Compounding LLC .... C 440 834-4644
  Burton *(G-1528)*

CHEMICALS & ALLIED PRDTS, WHOLESALE: Resins, Plastics

Network Polymers Inc .... E 330 773-2700
  Akron *(G-241)*

CHEMICALS & ALLIED PRDTS, WHOLESALE: Spec Clean/Sanitation

Ccp Industries Inc .... B 216 535-4227
  Richmond Heights *(G-12716)*
Gergelys Mint King Sups Svc In .... E 440 244-4446
  Lorain *(G-10076)*

CHEMICALS & ALLIED PRDTS, WHOLESALE: Syn Resin, Rub/Plastic

Akrochem Corporation .... D 330 535-2100
  Akron *(G-19)*
Flex Technologies Inc .... D 330 897-6311
  Baltic *(G-688)*
Kraton Polymers US LLC .... B 740 423-7571
  Belpre *(G-1056)*
Phoenix Technologies Intl LLC .... E 419 353-7738
  Bowling Green *(G-1330)*

CHEMICALS, AGRICULTURE: Wholesalers

Imcd Us LLC .... E 216 228-8900
  Westlake *(G-15069)*

CHEMICALS: Aluminum Compounds

Gayston Corporation .... C 937 743-6050
  Miamisburg *(G-11057)*

CHEMICALS: High Purity, Refined From Technical Grade

Heraeus Epurio LLC .... E 937 264-1000
  Vandalia *(G-14380)*

CHEMICALS: Inorganic, NEC

Borchers Americas Inc .... D 440 899-2950
  Westlake *(G-15040)*
Calvary Industries Inc .... E 513 874-1113
  Fairfield *(G-8398)*
Cirba Solutions Us Inc .... E 740 653-6290
  Lancaster *(G-9700)*
Dover Chemical Corporation .... C 330 343-7711
  Dover *(G-7880)*
Flexsys Inc .... B 212 605-6000
  Akron *(G-165)*
Malco Products Inc .... C 330 753-0361
  Barberton *(G-700)*

CHEMICALS: NEC

Aldrich Chemical .... D 937 859-1808
  Miamisburg *(G-11023)*
Ashland Chemco Inc .... C 614 790-3333
  Columbus *(G-5394)*
Borchers Americas Inc .... D 440 899-2950
  Westlake *(G-15040)*
Chemstation International Inc .... E 937 294-8265
  Moraine *(G-11397)*
Cincinnati - Vulcan Company .... D 513 242-5300
  Cincinnati *(G-2391)*
Dover Chemical Corporation .... C 330 343-7711
  Dover *(G-7880)*
EMD Millipore Corporation .... C 513 631-0445
  Norwood *(G-12032)*
Flexsys America LP .... D 330 666-4111
  Akron *(G-164)*
Formlabs Ohio Inc .... E 419 837-9783
  Millbury *(G-11268)*
Hexpol Compounding LLC .... C 440 834-4644
  Burton *(G-1528)*
Malco Products Inc .... C 330 753-0361
  Barberton *(G-700)*
Morton Salt Inc .... C 330 925-3015
  Rittman *(G-12731)*
Noco Company .... D 216 464-8131
  Solon *(G-13119)*
Polymer Additives Holdings Inc .... C 216 875-7200
  Independence *(G-9469)*
Rhenium Alloys Inc .... E 440 365-7388
  North Ridgeville *(G-11934)*
Sigma-Aldrich Corporation .... D 216 206-5424
  Cleveland *(G-4907)*
State Industrial Products Corp .... B 877 747-6986
  Cleveland *(G-4944)*
Teknol Inc .... D 937 264-0190
  Dayton *(G-7661)*

CHEMICALS: Organic, NEC

Nouryon Chemicals LLC .... E 419 229-0088
  Lima *(G-9943)*

CHEMICALS: Water Treatment

Applied Specialties Inc .... E 440 933-9442
  Avon Lake *(G-671)*

CHICKEN SLAUGHTERING & PROCESSING

V H Cooper & Co Inc .... C 419 375-4116
  Fort Recovery *(G-8611)*

CHILD DAY CARE SVCS

A Childs Hope Intl Inc .... E 513 771-2244
  Cincinnati *(G-2129)*
Abilities First Foundation Inc .... D 513 423-9496
  Middletown *(G-11149)*
Action For Children Inc .... E 614 224-0222
  Columbus *(G-5310)*
Advanced Solutions For Educatn .... E 224 518-3111
  Mentor *(G-10908)*
Bay Village City School Dst .... D 440 617-7330
  Cleveland *(G-3857)*
Canton Country Day School .... E 330 453-8279
  Canton *(G-1700)*
Catholic Scial Svcs of Mami VI .... E 937 223-7217
  Dayton *(G-7218)*
Child Care Resource Center .... E 216 575-0061
  Cleveland *(G-3969)*
Child Focus Inc .... E 937 444-1613
  Mount Orab *(G-11469)*
Childrens Hosp Med Ctr Akron .... D 330 543-8503
  Akron *(G-92)*
City of Lakewood .... E 216 226-0080
  Cleveland *(G-3989)*
Columbus Christian Center Inc .... E 614 416-9673
  Columbus *(G-5619)*
Community Action Comm Erie Hro .... E 419 935-6481
  Willard *(G-15166)*
Community Action Prgram Corp O .... C 740 962-3792
  Malta *(G-10231)*
Council On Rur Svc Prgrams Inc .... D 937 773-0773
  Piqua *(G-12439)*
Countryside Yung MNS Chrstn As .... E 513 677-3702
  Maineville *(G-10227)*
County of Guernsey .... E 740 439-5555
  Cambridge *(G-1567)*
Creative Connections LLC .... E 513 389-0213
  Cincinnati *(G-2516)*
David Evangelical Lutheran Ch .... E 614 920-3517
  Canal Winchester *(G-1603)*
Dover City Schools .... E 330 343-8880
  Dover *(G-7881)*
Family YMCA of LANcstr&fairfld .... D 740 277-7373
  Lancaster *(G-9723)*
First Assembly Child Care .... E 419 529-6501
  Mansfield *(G-10263)*
First Community Church .... E 614 488-0681
  Columbus *(G-5860)*
Gateway To Grace Foundation Inc .... E 513 869-4645
  Fairfield *(G-8416)*
Geary Fmly Yung MNS Chrstn Ass .... E 419 435-6608
  Fostoria *(G-8617)*
Grace Brthren Ch Columbus Ohio .... E 614 888-7733
  Westerville *(G-14897)*
Great Mami Vly Yung MNS Chrstn .... D 513 887-0001
  Hamilton *(G-9046)*
Great Miami Valley YMCA .... D 513 829-3091
  Fairfield *(G-8417)*
Great Miami Valley YMCA .... D 513 892-9622
  Fairfield Township *(G-8461)*
Great Miami Valley YMCA .... D 513 887-0014
  Hamilton *(G-9048)*
Great Miami Valley YMCA .... D 513 868-9622
  Hamilton *(G-9049)*
Horizon Education Centers .... E 440 277-5437
  Lorain *(G-10077)*
Hunt Tiffani .... E 216 258-1923
  Cleveland *(G-4389)*
Ladan Learning Center LLC .... E 614 426-4306
  Columbus *(G-6133)*
Lake Cnty Yung MNS Chrstn Assn .... C 440 352-3303
  Painesville *(G-12231)*
Lake County YMCA .... C 440 428-5125
  Madison *(G-10219)*
Lake County YMCA .... C 440 259-2724
  Perry *(G-12307)*
Lake County YMCA .... C 440 946-1160
  Willoughby *(G-15198)*

Employee Codes: A=Over 500 employees, B=251-500
C=101-250, D=51-100, E=20-50, F=10-19, G=1-9

CHILD DAY CARE SVCS

Lakewood Catholic Academy.................. E 216 521-4352
  Lakewood *(G-9672)*
Lawrence Cnty Bd Dev Dsblities............ E 740 377-2356
  South Point *(G-13176)*
Learning Spectrum Ltd......................... E 614 316-1160
  Lewis Center *(G-9825)*
Learning Spectrum Ltd......................... E 614 844-5433
  Columbus *(G-6151)*
Lima Family YMCA................................ D 419 223-6055
  Lima *(G-9923)*
Lima Family YMCA................................ D 419 223-6045
  Lima *(G-9922)*
Madison Local School District............... E 419 589-7851
  Mansfield *(G-10284)*
Mahoning Youngstown Community........ E 330 747-0236
  Youngstown *(G-15662)*
Mk Childcare Warsaw Ave LLC.............. E 513 922-6279
  Cincinnati *(G-3069)*
Mlm Childcare LLC................................ E 513 623-8243
  Cincinnati *(G-3070)*
Mount Washington Baptist Ch................ E 513 231-4334
  Cincinnati *(G-3083)*
N & E Learning LLC.............................. E 614 270-1559
  Grove City *(G-8939)*
Nbdc II LLC... E 513 681-5439
  Cincinnati *(G-3100)*
New Dawn Health Care Inc................... C 330 343-5521
  Dover *(G-7895)*
Nicoles Child Care Center..................... E 216 991-2416
  Cleveland *(G-4645)*
Northwest Child Development An.......... E 937 559-9565
  Dayton *(G-7532)*
Ohio Dept Job & Fmly Svcs.................. E 614 466-1213
  Columbus *(G-6407)*
Ohioguidestone..................................... C 216 433-4136
  Cleveland *(G-4692)*
Ohioguidestone..................................... E 440 234-2006
  Berea *(G-1079)*
Our Lady Bethlehem Schools Inc.......... E 614 459-8285
  Columbus *(G-6491)*
Professional Maint of Columbus............ E 513 579-1762
  Cincinnati *(G-3245)*
Promedica Health System Inc............... A 567 585-9600
  Toledo *(G-13972)*
R & J Investment Co Inc....................... C 440 934-5204
  Avon *(G-663)*
Roman Catholic Diocese Toledo............ D 419 243-7255
  Toledo *(G-13995)*
Seton Catholic School Hudson.............. D 330 342-4200
  Hudson *(G-9373)*
St Johns Villa...................................... C 330 627-4662
  Carrollton *(G-1913)*
St Marys City Board Education.............. C 419 394-2616
  Saint Marys *(G-12836)*
St Stphens Cmnty Hmes Ltd Prt............ D 614 294-6347
  Columbus *(G-6706)*
St Thomas Episcopal Church................ E 513 831-6908
  Terrace Park *(G-13614)*
Step Forward.. D 216 696-9077
  Cleveland *(G-4949)*
Sycamore Board of Education............... C 513 489-3937
  Montgomery *(G-11375)*
Sylvania Cmnty Svcs Ctr Inc................. E 419 885-2451
  Sylvania *(G-13574)*
Texas Migrant Council Inc.................... E 937 846-0699
  New Carlisle *(G-11608)*
Trinity United Methodist Ch.................. E 614 488-3659
  Columbus *(G-6792)*
Troy Christian Schools Inc................... E 937 339-5692
  Troy *(G-14161)*
United Rhbltton Svcs Grter Dy............. D 937 233-1230
  Dayton *(G-7683)*

Upper Arlington City Schl Dst................ E 614 487-5133
  Columbus *(G-6827)*
Vermilion Family YMCA......................... E 440 967-4208
  Vermilion *(G-14410)*
West Ohio Cmnty Action Partnr............ C 419 227-2586
  Lima *(G-9984)*
Whitehead Falana................................. E 513 742-1766
  Cincinnati *(G-3668)*
Y M C A of Ashland Ohio Inc................ D 419 289-0626
  Ashland *(G-516)*
YMCA.. E 330 823-1930
  Alliance *(G-408)*
Young Mens Christian Assn................... D 740 373-2250
  Marietta *(G-10415)*
Young Mens Christian Assn................... D 330 480-5656
  Youngstown *(G-15754)*
Young MNS Chrstn Assn Cntl STA........ D 330 305-5437
  Canton *(G-1889)*
Young MNS Chrstn Assn Cntl STA........ D 330 498-4082
  Canton *(G-1890)*
Young MNS Chrstn Assn Cntl STA........ D 330 875-1611
  Louisville *(G-10124)*
Young MNS Chrstn Assn Cntl STA........ C 330 830-6275
  Massillon *(G-10675)*
Young MNS Chrstn Assn Grter CL......... E 440 285-7543
  Chardon *(G-2027)*
Young MNS Chrstn Assn Grter CL......... D 216 521-8400
  Lakewood *(G-9688)*
Young MNS Chrstn Assn Grter CN........ B 513 791-5000
  Blue Ash *(G-1275)*
Young MNS Chrstn Assn Grter CN........ C 513 731-0115
  Cincinnati *(G-3692)*
Young MNS Chrstn Assn Grter CN........ B 513 474-1400
  Cincinnati *(G-3693)*
Young MNS Chrstn Assn Grter CN........ D 513 241-9622
  Cincinnati *(G-3694)*
Young MNS Chrstn Assn Grter CN........ C 513 923-4466
  Cincinnati *(G-3695)*
Young MNS Chrstn Assn Grter CN........ C 513 921-0911
  Cincinnati *(G-3696)*
Young MNS Chrstn Assn Grter CN........ A 513 932-1424
  Lebanon *(G-9800)*
Young MNS Chrstn Assn Grter Dy......... C 937 228-9622
  Dayton *(G-7732)*
Young MNS Chrstn Assn Grter Dy......... C 937 312-1810
  Dayton *(G-7733)*
Young MNS Chrstn Assn Grter Dy......... C 937 223-5201
  Springboro *(G-13210)*
Young MNS Chrstn Assn Grter NY........ C 740 392-9622
  Mount Vernon *(G-11509)*
Young MNS Chrstn Assn of Akron........ E 330 376-1335
  Akron *(G-368)*
Young MNS Chrstn Assn of Akron........ E 330 724-1255
  Akron *(G-371)*
Young MNS Chrstn Assn of Akron........ E 330 983-5573
  Akron *(G-372)*
Young MNS Chrstn Assn of Akron........ D 330 923-5223
  Cuyahoga Falls *(G-7119)*
Young MNS Chrstn Assn of Akron........ E 330 467-8366
  Macedonia *(G-10210)*
Young MNS Chrstn Assn of Akron........ D 419 523-5233
  Ottawa *(G-12196)*
Young MNS Chrstn Assn of Akron........ E 330 899-9622
  Uniontown *(G-14272)*
Young MNS Chrstn Assn of Grter......... C 419 866-9622
  Maumee *(G-10782)*
Young MNS Chrstn Assn of Grter......... C 419 691-3523
  Oregon *(G-12148)*
Young MNS Chrstn Assn of Grter......... E 419 474-3995
  Toledo *(G-14112)*
Young MNS Chrstn Assn of Grter......... D 419 241-7218
  Toledo *(G-14115)*

Young MNS Chrstn Assn of Grter......... E 419 729-8135
  Sylvania *(G-13579)*
Young MNS Chrstn Assn of Mt Vr......... D 740 392-9622
  Mount Vernon *(G-11510)*
Young MNS Chrstn Assn of Van W....... E 419 238-0443
  Van Wert *(G-14362)*
Young Wns Chrstn Assn Clvland........... E 216 881-6878
  Cleveland *(G-5167)*
Young Wns Chrstn Assn of Cnton........ D 330 453-0789
  Canton *(G-1892)*
Young Womens Christian Assn............. D 614 224-9121
  Columbus *(G-6917)*
YWCA Mahoning Valley.......................... E 330 746-6361
  Youngstown *(G-15762)*
YWCA of Greater Cincinnati.................. D 513 241-7090
  Cincinnati *(G-3697)*
YWCA of Northwest Ohio...................... D 419 241-3235
  Toledo *(G-14117)*

CHILD RESTRAINT SEATS, AUTOMOTIVE, WHOLESALE

TS Tech Americas Inc............................ C 740 593-5958
  Athens *(G-595)*
TS Tech Americas Inc............................ B 614 575-4100
  Reynoldsburg *(G-12678)*

CHILDBIRTH PREPARATION CLINIC

Akron General Health System................ A 330 945-9300
  Stow *(G-13353)*
Cleveland Clinic Foundation................... D 216 839-3000
  Beachwood *(G-778)*
Everside Health LLC............................. E 216 672-0211
  Beachwood *(G-790)*
Heritage Valley Health Sys Inc.............. E 724 773-1995
  East Liverpool *(G-8184)*
High Point Home Health Ltd.................. E 419 674-4090
  Kenton *(G-9618)*
Mount Carmel Health............................ D 614 776-5164
  Westerville *(G-15001)*
Mount Carmel Health System................ C 614 235-4039
  Columbus *(G-6279)*
Omni Wellness Group LLC.................... E 937 540-9920
  Troy *(G-14150)*
Paladina Health LLC............................ E 440 368-0900
  Mentor *(G-10983)*
Primary Cr Ntwrk Prmr Hlth Prt............ E 513 204-5785
  Mason *(G-10594)*
River Valley Physicians LLC.................. D 330 386-3610
  East Liverpool *(G-8192)*
Riverhills Healthcare Inc....................... E 513 624-6031
  Cincinnati *(G-3305)*
St Elzabeth Boardman Hlth Ctr.............. E 330 729-4580
  Boardman *(G-1292)*
Toledo Clinic Cancer Centers................ D 419 691-4235
  Oregon *(G-12143)*
Trihealth Inc.. C 513 734-9050
  Bethel *(G-1095)*
Trihealth Inc.. C 513 221-4848
  Cincinnati *(G-3518)*
Uc Health Llc....................................... D 513 475-8050
  Milford *(G-11264)*
Uc Health Llc....................................... D 513 475-8282
  West Chester *(G-14780)*

CHILDREN'S & INFANTS' CLOTHING STORES

Abercrombie & Fitch Trading Co............ D 614 283-6500
  New Albany *(G-11551)*

SERVICES SECTION

COAL & OTHER MINERALS & ORES WHOLESALERS

CHOCOLATE, EXC CANDY FROM BEANS: Chips, Powder, Block, Syrup

Gorant Chocolatier LLC.................... C 330 726-8821
   Boardman (G-1288)

CHURCHES

First Christian Church...................... E 330 445-2700
   Canton (G-1753)
Salvation Army................................. E 937 528-5100
   Dayton (G-7606)

CIRCUITS: Electronic

Channel Products Inc...................... D 440 423-0113
   Solon (G-13075)
Mjo Industries Inc............................ D 800 590-4055
   Huber Heights (G-9325)

CLEANING EQPT: Commercial

High-TEC Industrial Services........... D 937 667-1772
   Tipp City (G-13659)
MPW Industrial Svcs Group Inc....... B 740 927-8790
   Hebron (G-9150)

CLEANING OR POLISHING PREPARATIONS, NEC

Chemstation International Inc.......... E 937 294-8265
   Moraine (G-11397)

CLEANING SVCS: Industrial Or Commercial

A B M Inc... A 419 421-2292
   Findlay (G-8505)
Ajax Commercial Cleaning Inc........ D 330 928-4543
   Cuyahoga Falls (G-7033)
Alexis Eppinger................................ E 216 509-0475
   Cleveland (G-3785)
Blast-All Inc..................................... E 606 393-5786
   Ironton (G-9503)
Blue Chip 2000 Coml Clg Inc........... A 513 561-2999
   Cincinnati (G-2267)
Cardinal Group Inc.......................... C 330 252-1047
   Akron (G-80)
Center Cleaning Services Inc.......... D 440 327-5099
   Avon (G-642)
Champion Clg Specialists Inc.......... E 513 871-2333
   Cincinnati (G-2344)
Flawless Janitorial LLC.................... E 216 266-1425
   Maple Heights (G-10338)
Galaxie Industrial Svcs LLC............. E 330 503-2334
   Youngstown (G-15616)
Gergelys Mint King Sups Svc In...... E 440 244-4446
   Lorain (G-10076)
Metropolitan Envmtl Svcs Inc.......... D 614 771-1881
   Hilliard (G-9213)
MPW Industrial Services Inc........... A 800 827-8790
   Hebron (G-9149)
MPW Industrial Svcs Group Inc....... E 740 245-5393
   Bidwell (G-1105)
MPW Industrial Svcs Group Inc....... B 740 927-8790
   Hebron (G-9150)
Nelbud Services Group Inc............. E 317 202-0360
   Columbus (G-6344)
Ohio Helping Hands Clg Svc LLC... E 937 402-0733
   Hillsboro (G-9264)
Professional Bldg Maint Inc............. D 440 666-8509
   Warrensville Heights (G-14586)
Professional Pavement Svcs LLC.... E 740 726-2222
   Delaware (G-7821)
Rags Brooms & Mops Inc............... D 440 969-0164
   Jefferson (G-9539)

Total Maintenance Solution Inc........ E 513 770-0925
   Cincinnati (G-3484)
Two Men & A Vacuum LLC.............. D 614 300-7970
   Columbus (G-6796)
Vadakin Inc...................................... E 740 373-7518
   Marietta (G-10408)
Wiggins Clg & Crpt Svc Inc............. D 937 279-9080
   Dayton (G-7722)

CLIPS & FASTENERS, MADE FROM PURCHASED WIRE

Stud Welding Associates Inc........... D 440 783-3160
   Strongsville (G-13490)

CLOTHING & ACCESS, WOMEN, CHILD & INFANT, WHOL: Diapers

Procter & Gamble Distrg LLC.......... B 513 626-2500
   Blue Ash (G-1224)

CLOTHING & ACCESS, WOMEN, CHILDREN & INFANT, WHOL: Handbags

Atrium Buying Corporation............... D 740 966-8200
   Blacklick (G-1110)
R G Barry Corporation..................... A 614 864-6400
   Pickerington (G-12408)

CLOTHING & ACCESS, WOMEN, CHILDREN & INFANT, WHOL: Uniforms

Cintas Corporation No 1.................. A 513 459-1200
   Mason (G-10533)
Cintas Corporation No 2.................. D 800 444-2687
   Vandalia (G-14370)
Cintas Sales Corporation................. B 513 459-1200
   Cincinnati (G-2445)
Lion-Vallen Ltd Partnership............. C 937 898-1949
   Dayton (G-7458)

CLOTHING & ACCESS, WOMEN, CHILDREN/ INFANT, WHOL: Baby Goods

1 Natural Way LLC.......................... E 888 977-2229
   Maumee (G-10682)

CLOTHING & ACCESS: Costumes, Theatrical

Costume Specialists Inc.................. E 614 464-2115
   Columbus (G-5706)

CLOTHING & FURNISHINGS, MEN'S & BOYS', WHOLESALE: Uniforms

Cintas Corporation No 1.................. A 513 459-1200
   Mason (G-10533)
Cintas Sales Corporation................. B 513 459-1200
   Cincinnati (G-2445)
Lion-Vallen Ltd Partnership............. C 937 898-1949
   Dayton (G-7458)
Walter F Stephens Jr Inc................. E 937 746-0521
   Franklin (G-8652)

CLOTHING & FURNISHINGS, MENS & BOYS, WHOLESALE: Apprl Belts

J Peterman Company LLC............... E 888 647-2555
   Blue Ash (G-1189)
JP Outfitters LLC............................. E 513 745-1137
   Blue Ash (G-1192)

CLOTHING STORES: Designer Apparel

K Amalia Enterprises Inc................. E 614 733-3800
   Plain City (G-12483)

CLOTHING STORES: T-Shirts, Printed, Custom

TSC Apparel LLC............................. D 800 289-5400
   Cincinnati (G-3534)

CLOTHING STORES: Work

Tractor Supply Company................. E 937 382-2595
   Wilmington (G-15275)

CLOTHING/ACCESS, WOMEN, CHILDREN/ INFANT, WHOL: Hosp Gowns

Philips Med Systems Clvland In....... B 440 483-3000
   Cleveland (G-4746)

CLOTHING: Caps, Baseball

Barbs Graffiti Inc............................. E 216 881-5550
   Cleveland (G-3849)

CLOTHING: T-Shirts & Tops, Knit

E Retailing Associates LLC.............. D 614 300-5785
   Columbus (G-5798)

CLOTHING: Uniforms & Vestments

Walter F Stephens Jr Inc................. E 937 746-0521
   Franklin (G-8652)

CLOTHING: Uniforms, Ex Athletic, Women's, Misses' & Juniors'

Cintas Corporation.......................... D 513 631-5750
   Cincinnati (G-2443)
Cintas Corporation.......................... A 513 459-1200
   Cincinnati (G-2442)
Cintas Corporation No 2.................. D 330 966-7800
   Canton (G-1709)

CLOTHING: Uniforms, Firemen's, From Purchased Materials

Lion First Responder Ppe Inc.......... D 937 898-1949
   Dayton (G-7456)
Lion Group Inc................................. D 937 898-1949
   Dayton (G-7457)

CLOTHING: Uniforms, Military, Men/Youth, Purchased Materials

Vgs Inc.. C 216 431-7800
   Cleveland (G-5102)

CLOTHING: Uniforms, Work

Cintas Corporation.......................... D 513 631-5750
   Cincinnati (G-2443)
Cintas Corporation.......................... A 513 459-1200
   Cincinnati (G-2442)
Cintas Corporation No 2.................. D 330 966-7800
   Canton (G-1709)
Cintas Sales Corporation................. B 513 459-1200
   Cincinnati (G-2445)
Vgs Inc.. C 216 431-7800
   Cleveland (G-5102)

CLUTCHES, EXC VEHICULAR

Logan Clutch Corporation............... E 440 808-4258
   Cleveland (G-4504)

COAL & OTHER MINERALS & ORES WHOLESALERS

Graphel Corporation........................ C 513 779-6166
   West Chester (G-14700)

COAL MINING SERVICES

Tosoh America Inc.................................. B 614 539-8622
  Grove City *(G-8959)*

COAL MINING SERVICES

Appalachian Fuels LLC............................ C 606 928-0460
  Dublin *(G-7939)*
Coal Services Inc................................... B 740 795-5220
  Powhatan Point *(G-12610)*
Ohio Valley Coal Company....................... B 740 926-1351
  Saint Clairsville *(G-12810)*
Peabody Coal Company........................... E 740 450-2420
  Zanesville *(G-15826)*
Rosebud Mining Company........................ D 740 658-4217
  Freeport *(G-8663)*
Suncoke Energy Inc................................ E 513 727-5571
  Middletown *(G-11188)*

COAL MINING: Anthracite

Coal Services Inc.................................... B 740 795-5220
  Powhatan Point *(G-12610)*

COAL MINING: Bituminous & Lignite Surface

Murray American Energy Inc..................... C 740 338-3100
  Saint Clairsville *(G-12807)*
Washington County Coal Company............. B 740 338-3100
  Saint Clairsville *(G-12819)*

COAL MINING: Bituminous Coal & Lignite-Surface Mining

Buckingham Coal Company LLC................ D
  Zanesville *(G-15774)*
Coal Resources Inc................................. E 216 765-1240
  Saint Clairsville *(G-12785)*
Coal Services Inc.................................... B 740 795-5220
  Powhatan Point *(G-12610)*
Franklin County Coal Company.................. B 740 338-3100
  Saint Clairsville *(G-12793)*
Kimble Company.................................... C 330 343-1226
  Dover *(G-7891)*
Meigs County Coal Company.................... B 740 338-3100
  Saint Clairsville *(G-12803)*
Muhlenberg County Coal Co LLC............... D 740 338-3100
  Saint Clairsville *(G-12806)*
Oxford Mining Company Inc..................... C 740 588-0190
  Zanesville *(G-15824)*
Rosebud Mining Company........................ D 740 768-2275
  Bergholz *(G-1088)*
Subtropolis Mining Co............................. E 330 549-2165
  Petersburg *(G-12395)*
Westmoreland Resources Gp LLC.............. D 740 622-6302
  Coshocton *(G-7004)*

COAL MINING: Bituminous, Strip

B&N Coal Inc... E 740 783-3575
  Dexter City *(G-7867)*
Oxford Mining Company - KY LLC.............. E 740 622-6302
  Coshocton *(G-6996)*
Waterloo Coal Company Inc..................... D 740 286-0004
  Jackson *(G-9529)*

COAL MINING: Bituminous, Surface, NEC

Marietta Coal Co.................................... E 740 695-2197
  Saint Clairsville *(G-12800)*

COAL MINING: Lignite, Surface, NEC

Nacco Industries Inc............................... E 440 229-5151
  Cleveland *(G-4616)*

COAL PREPARATION PLANT: Bituminous or Lignite

Cliffs Logan County Coal LLC.................... C 216 694-5700
  Cleveland *(G-4077)*

COAL, MINERALS & ORES, WHOLESALE: Coal

Marshall County Coal Company................. B 740 338-3100
  Saint Clairsville *(G-12801)*
Ohio County Coal Company...................... D 740 338-3100
  Saint Clairsville *(G-12809)*
Oxford Mining Company Inc..................... C 330 878-5120
  Strasburg *(G-13404)*

COATING SVC: Metals, With Plastic Or Resins

Corrotec Inc.. E 937 325-3585
  Springfield *(G-13242)*
Godfrey & Wing Inc................................ E 330 562-1440
  Aurora *(G-615)*

COATINGS: Epoxy

Master Builders LLC............................... E 800 228-3318
  Beachwood *(G-811)*

COFFEE SVCS

Filterfresh Coffee Service Inc.................... D 513 681-8911
  West Chester *(G-14811)*
Sanese Services Inc............................... A 614 436-1234
  Warren *(G-14550)*

COILS & TRANSFORMERS

Schneider Electric Usa Inc....................... B 513 523-4171
  Oxford *(G-12217)*

COILS: Pipe

Industrial Power Systems Inc.................... B 419 531-3121
  Rossford *(G-12767)*

COLLEGE, EXC JUNIOR

Hebrew Un Cllg-Jwish Inst Rlgi.................. E 513 221-1875
  Cincinnati *(G-2815)*
Kenyon College...................................... E 740 427-2202
  Gambier *(G-8774)*
Oberlin College...................................... E 440 775-8665
  Oberlin *(G-12074)*
University of Toledo................................ A 419 383-4000
  Toledo *(G-14086)*

COLLEGES, UNIVERSITIES & PROFESSIONAL SCHOOLS

Antioch University.................................. C 937 769-1366
  Yellow Springs *(G-15534)*
Aultman Hospital.................................... A 330 452-9911
  Canton *(G-1679)*
Cleveland Clinic Lrner Cllege M................. C 216 445-3853
  Cleveland *(G-4039)*
Ohio State University.............................. D 614 292-3416
  Columbus *(G-6457)*
University Hospital................................. D 440 835-8922
  Westlake *(G-15120)*
University of Cincinnati........................... E 513 556-2263
  Cincinnati *(G-3584)*

COMBINATION UTILITIES, NEC

City of Lorain.. D 440 204-2500
  Lorain *(G-10064)*
Ohio Edison Company............................. E 740 671-2900
  Shadyside *(G-12970)*

COMBINED ELEMENTARY & SECONDARY SCHOOLS, PRIVATE

Christian Schools Inc.............................. D 330 857-7311
  Kidron *(G-9635)*
East Dayton Christian School.................... E 937 252-5400
  Dayton *(G-7132)*
Laurel School.. C 216 464-1441
  Shaker Heights *(G-12980)*
Open Door Christn Schools Inc.................. D 440 322-6386
  Elyria *(G-8283)*

COMBINED ELEMENTARY & SECONDARY SCHOOLS, PUBLIC

Butler Tech... E 513 867-1028
  Fairfield Township *(G-8458)*

COMMERCIAL & OFFICE BUILDINGS RENOVATION & REPAIR

3d Building Systems LLC......................... E 614 351-9695
  Columbus *(G-5287)*
Apex Restoration Contrs Ltd..................... E 513 489-1795
  Cincinnati *(G-2209)*
Brackett Builders Inc.............................. E 937 339-7505
  Dayton *(G-7200)*
Canton Floors Inc.................................. E 330 492-1121
  Canton *(G-1701)*
Drake Construction Company.................... E 216 664-6500
  Cleveland *(G-4183)*
Fryman-Kuck General Contrs Inc............... E 937 274-2892
  Dayton *(G-7371)*
James Hunt Construction Co Inc................ E 513 721-0559
  Cincinnati *(G-2898)*
Plevniak Construction Inc........................ E 330 718-1600
  Youngstown *(G-15695)*
Ram Cnstrction Svcs Cncnnati L................ E 513 297-1857
  West Chester *(G-14754)*
Smb Construction Co Inc......................... E 419 269-1473
  Toledo *(G-14017)*
Trisco Systems Incorporated.................... C 419 339-3906
  Lima *(G-9973)*
Valicor Federal Services LLC.................... E 313 724-8600
  Blue Ash *(G-1267)*
Wingler Construction Corp....................... E 614 626-8546
  Columbus *(G-6898)*

COMMERCIAL ART & GRAPHIC DESIGN SVCS

Clarity Retail Services LLC....................... D 513 800-9369
  West Chester *(G-14668)*
Concept Imaging Group Inc...................... E 888 466-6627
  Miamisburg *(G-11037)*
Dr Alxander C Nnabue Assoc PA............... E 614 499-7687
  Columbus *(G-5785)*
Exhibitpro Inc.. E 614 885-9541
  New Albany *(G-11564)*
General Theming Contrs LLC.................... C 614 252-6342
  Columbus *(G-5925)*
The Photo-Type Engraving Company.......... D 513 281-0999
  Cincinnati *(G-3469)*
Whitespace Design Group Inc................... E 330 762-9320
  Akron *(G-360)*
Young MNS Chrstn Assn Grter CN............. B 513 791-5000
  Blue Ash *(G-1275)*

COMMERCIAL ART & ILLUSTRATION SVCS

ONeil & Associates Inc............................ C 937 865-0800
  Miamisburg *(G-11079)*

COMMERCIAL CONTAINERS WHOLESALERS

Brimar Packaging Inc................................ E 440 934-3080
  Avon (G-641)
Kaufman Container Company.................. C 216 898-2000
  Cleveland (G-4450)

COMMERCIAL EQPT WHOLESALERS, NEC

Acorn Distributors Inc............................. E 614 294-6444
  Columbus (G-5307)
AVI Food Systems Inc............................. E 740 452-9363
  Zanesville (G-15768)
Bakemark USA LLC................................. D 513 870-0880
  Fairfield (G-8391)
Buckeye Body and Equipment.................. E 614 299-1136
  Columbus (G-5472)
General Data Company Inc...................... B 513 752-7978
  Cincinnati (G-2105)
The Dean Supply Co............................... E 216 771-3300
  Cleveland (G-4999)
Utility Truck & Equipment Inc.................. E 740 474-5151
  Circleville (G-3728)
Ventrac... D 330 682-0159
  Orrville (G-12174)

COMMERCIAL EQPT, WHOLESALE: Bakery Eqpt & Splys

Cmbb LLC.. C 937 652-2151
  Urbana (G-14304)
Russell T Bundy Associates Inc.............. D 937 652-2151
  Urbana (G-14312)

COMMERCIAL EQPT, WHOLESALE: Restaurant, NEC

Best Restaurant Equipment & Design..... D 614 488-2378
  Columbus (G-5433)
Burkett and Sons Inc.............................. E 419 242-7377
  Perrysburg (G-12321)
Gen III Inc... D 614 228-5550
  Columbus (G-5924)
Globe Food Equipment Company............ E 937 299-5493
  Moraine (G-11413)
Harry C Lobalzo & Sons Inc.................... E 330 666-6758
  Akron (G-184)
Hobart International Holdings................. C 937 332-3000
  Troy (G-14138)
ITW Food Equipment Group LLC............. C 937 393-4271
  Hillsboro (G-9260)
ITW Food Equipment Group LLC............. A 937 332-2396
  Troy (G-14141)
John H Kappus Co.................................. E 216 367-6677
  Cleveland (G-4441)
N Wasserstrom & Sons Inc..................... C 614 228-5550
  Columbus (G-6286)
Nemco Inc... D 419 542-7751
  Hicksville (G-9161)
SS Kemp & Co LLC................................. D 216 271-7700
  Cleveland (G-4939)
The Cottingham Paper Co....................... E 614 294-6444
  Columbus (G-6758)
Trendco Supply Inc................................. E 513 752-1871
  Batavia (G-750)
Wasserstrom Holdings Inc..................... C 614 228-6525
  Columbus (G-6868)

COMMERCIAL EQPT, WHOLESALE: Scales, Exc Laboratory

B-Tek Scales LLC.................................... E 330 471-8900
  Canton (G-1684)
Brechbuhler Scales Inc........................... E 330 458-3060
  Canton (G-1689)
Thurman Scale Company......................... C 614 221-9077
  Groveport (G-9004)

COMMERCIAL EQPT, WHOLESALE: Store Fixtures & Display Eqpt

Fasteners For Retail Inc......................... B 330 998-7800
  Twinsburg (G-14191)

COMMERCIAL EQPT, WHOLESALE: Vending Machines, Coin-Operated

Dtv Inc... E 216 226-5465
  Cleveland (G-4187)

COMMERCIAL PHOTOGRAPHIC STUDIO

Eclipse 3d/Pi LLC................................... E 614 626-8536
  Columbus (G-5804)
Trg Studios Inc....................................... E 216 781-8644
  Brooklyn (G-1411)

COMMERCIAL PRINTING & NEWSPAPER PUBLISHING

Copley Ohio Newspapers Inc.................. C 330 364-5577
  New Philadelphia (G-11643)

COMMON SAND MINING

Welch Holdings Inc................................. E 513 353-3220
  Cincinnati (G-3647)

COMMUNICATIONS EQPT WHOLESALERS

Bear Communications Inc....................... D 216 642-1670
  Independence (G-9410)
Communications III Inc........................... E 614 901-7720
  Westerville (G-14973)
Midwest Digital Inc................................. D 330 966-4744
  North Canton (G-11849)
Quasonix Inc... E 513 942-1287
  West Chester (G-14751)
Sound Com Corporation......................... D 440 234-2604
  Berea (G-1081)
Winncom Technologies Corp................... C 440 498-9510
  Solon (G-13165)

COMMUNICATIONS SVCS

Drips Holdings LLC................................. D 512 643-7477
  Akron (G-140)

COMMUNICATIONS SVCS: Data

A M Communications Ltd........................ D 419 528-3051
  Galion (G-8741)
Calvert Wire & Cable Corp...................... E 216 433-7600
  Cleveland (G-3919)
Oovoo LLC... D 917 515-2074
  Kettering (G-9631)
Springdot Inc.. D 513 542-4000
  Cincinnati (G-3401)
Twenty First Century Commun................ D 614 442-1215
  Columbus (G-6795)
Velocity A Managed Svcs Co Inc............ C 419 868-9983
  Holland (G-9311)
Wireless Master LLC............................... D 877 995-5888
  Hilliard (G-9244)

COMMUNICATIONS SVCS: Internet Connectivity Svcs

Bluespring Software Inc......................... E 513 794-1764
  Blue Ash (G-1138)
Buckeye Telesystem Inc......................... D 419 724-9898
  Northwood (G-11970)
Com Net Inc.. D 419 739-3100
  Wapakoneta (G-14481)
Community Isp Inc.................................. E 419 867-6060
  Toledo (G-13752)
County of Lorain..................................... D 440 324-5777
  Elyria (G-8239)
Dct Telecom Group LLC.......................... E 440 892-0300
  Westlake (G-15056)
Great Lakes Telcom Ltd.......................... E 330 629-8848
  Youngstown (G-15622)
Imagine Networks LLC............................ E 937 552-2340
  Troy (G-14140)
Intellinet Corporation.............................. D 216 289-4100
  Chardon (G-2008)
Medina Fiber LLC................................... E 330 366-2008
  Medina (G-10859)
Mgj Enterprises Inc................................. E 740 364-1360
  Newark (G-11729)
Revolution Group Inc.............................. D 614 212-1111
  Westerville (G-14935)
Southstern Ohio Vlntary Edcatn.............. E 740 594-7663
  Athens (G-591)
TSC Communications Inc........................ D 419 739-2200
  Wapakoneta (G-14492)

COMMUNICATIONS SVCS: Internet Host Svcs

Advanced Cmpt Connections LLC........... E 419 668-4080
  Norwalk (G-11999)
Massillon Cable TV Inc........................... D 330 833-4134
  Massillon (G-10652)
Oxcyon Inc.. E 440 239-3345
  Akron (G-259)
Roundtable Learning LLC....................... E 440 220-5252
  Chagrin Falls (G-1988)

COMMUNICATIONS SVCS: Online Svc Providers

Altoria Solutions LLC.............................. E 513 612-2007
  Cincinnati (G-2174)
Cardinal Commercecom Inc.................... E 440 352-8444
  Mentor (G-10917)
F+w Media Inc... A 513 531-2690
  Blue Ash (G-1171)
Holdco LLC... E 614 255-7285
  Westerville (G-14985)
Midwest Communications LLC............... E 419 420-8000
  Findlay (G-8569)
Pantek Incorporated................................ E 216 344-1614
  Independence (G-9465)

COMMUNICATIONS SVCS: Proprietary Online Svcs Networks

End-User Computing Inc......................... D 419 292-2200
  Toledo (G-13793)

COMMUNICATIONS SVCS: Signal Enhancement Network Svcs

Logos Communications Systems Inc...... D 440 871-0777
  Westlake (G-15076)
Telcom Construction Svcs Inc................ D 330 239-6900
  Medina (G-10899)

COMMUNICATIONS SVCS: Telephone, Broker

Rxp Ohio LLC.. D 614 937-2844
  Columbus (G-6623)

COMMUNICATIONS SVCS: Telephone, Local

COMMUNICATIONS SVCS: Telephone, Local

Chillicothe Telephone Company............ C 740 772-8100
  Chillicothe *(G-2060)*
Cincinnati Bell Tele Co LLC................... B 513 397-9900
  Cincinnati *(G-2399)*
Conneaut Telephone Company.............. E 440 593-7140
  Conneaut *(G-6942)*
Doylestown Telephone Company........... E 330 658-2121
  Doylestown *(G-7915)*
Ohio Bell Telephone Company............... A 614 224-7424
  Columbus *(G-6395)*

COMMUNICATIONS SVCS: Telephone, Local & Long Distance

AT&T Corp.. D 419 547-0578
  Vickery *(G-14418)*
Block Communications Inc..................... D 419 724-2539
  Northwood *(G-11969)*
Cincinnati Bell Inc.................................... B 513 397-9900
  Cincinnati *(G-2398)*
Communication Options Inc.................... E 614 901-7095
  New Albany *(G-11560)*
Ohio Bell Telephone Company............... A 216 822-9700
  Brecksville *(G-1360)*
Round Room LLC................................. E 937 429-2230
  Beavercreek *(G-902)*
Round Room LLC................................. E 330 880-0660
  Massillon *(G-10666)*
Windstream Services LLC..................... E 216 394-0065
  Cleveland *(G-5149)*
Yp LLC.. C 216 642-4000
  Cleveland *(G-5169)*

COMMUNICATIONS SVCS: Telephone, Long Distance

Cavalier Tele Mid-Atlantic LLC............... A 614 884-0000
  Columbus *(G-5521)*
MCI Communications Svcs LLC............. D 440 635-0418
  Chardon *(G-2012)*
MCI Communications Svcs LLC............. E 216 265-9953
  Cleveland *(G-4541)*
Png Telecommunications Inc.................. D 513 942-7900
  Cincinnati *(G-3218)*

COMMUNICATIONS SVCS: Telephone, Voice

Brcom Inc... D 513 397-9900
  Cincinnati *(G-2278)*
Pearl Interactive Network Inc.................. B 614 556-4470
  Columbus *(G-6507)*

COMMUNITY SVCS EMPLOYMENT TRAINING PROGRAM

Community Action Orgnztion Sco........... C 740 354-7541
  Portsmouth *(G-12548)*
Goodwill Inds Rhbilitation Ctr................. C 330 454-9461
  Canton *(G-1764)*
Goodwill Inds S Centl Ohio..................... D 740 702-4000
  Chillicothe *(G-2067)*
Gw Business Solutions LLC................... C 740 345-9861
  Newark *(G-11703)*
Licking-Knox Goodwill Inds Inc............... D 740 345-9861
  Newark *(G-11721)*
Ohio Dept Job & Fmly Svcs.................... E 614 752-9494
  Columbus *(G-6406)*
Vocational Guidance Services................ A 216 431-7800
  Cleveland *(G-5112)*
Workshops Inc....................................... D 330 479-3958
  Canton *(G-1887)*

COMMUTATORS: Electronic

Ra Consultants LLC............................... E 513 469-6600
  Blue Ash *(G-1229)*

COMPOST

Werlor Inc... E 419 784-4285
  Defiance *(G-7775)*

COMPRESSORS: Air & Gas, Including Vacuum Pumps

Autobody Supply Company Inc.............. D 614 228-4328
  Columbus *(G-5407)*

COMPUTER & COMPUTER SOFTWARE STORES

Datavantage Corporation........................ B 440 498-4414
  Cleveland *(G-4150)*
Great Lakes Computer Corp................... D 440 937-1100
  Avon *(G-652)*
Harley-Dvidson Dlr Systems Inc.............. D 216 573-1393
  Cleveland *(G-4350)*
Micro Center Inc..................................... E 614 850-3000
  Hilliard *(G-9214)*
Micro Electronics Inc.............................. B 614 334-1430
  Columbus *(G-6233)*
Office World Inc...................................... E 419 991-4694
  Lima *(G-9994)*
Ohio Business Machines LLC................ E 216 485-2000
  Cleveland *(G-4683)*
Resource One Cmpt Systems Inc........... E 614 485-4800
  Worthington *(G-15452)*
Xtek Partners Inc................................... E 614 973-7400
  Columbus *(G-6913)*

COMPUTER & COMPUTER SOFTWARE STORES: Peripheral Eqpt

Cbts Technology Solutions LLC.............. B 513 841-2287
  Cincinnati *(G-2328)*
Microman Inc.. E 614 923-8000
  Dublin *(G-8064)*
Personalized Data Corporation............... E 216 289-2200
  Cleveland *(G-4743)*

COMPUTER & COMPUTER SOFTWARE STORES: Personal Computers

Micro Center Online Inc.......................... D 614 326-8500
  Columbus *(G-6232)*
Micro Electronics Inc.............................. C 513 782-8500
  Cincinnati *(G-3057)*
Micro Electronics Inc.............................. D 614 850-3410
  Hilliard *(G-9215)*

COMPUTER & COMPUTER SOFTWARE STORES: Software & Access

Provantage LLC...................................... D 330 494-3781
  North Canton *(G-11854)*

COMPUTER & COMPUTER SOFTWARE STORES: Software, Bus/Non-Game

Autozone Inc.. E 216 751-0571
  Cleveland *(G-3842)*
Autozone Inc.. E 216 267-6586
  Cleveland *(G-3843)*
Autozone Inc.. E 440 593-6934
  Conneaut *(G-6939)*
Autozone Inc.. E 440 639-2247
  Painesville *(G-12221)*
Autozone Inc.. E 419 872-2813
  Perrysburg *(G-12315)*

Nuonosys Inc.. E 888 666-7976
  Independence *(G-9461)*
RB Sigma LLC....................................... D 440 290-0577
  Mentor *(G-10988)*
Retalix LLC.. E 937 384-2277
  Miamisburg *(G-11089)*
Stratacache Inc...................................... C 937 224-0485
  Dayton *(G-7646)*

COMPUTER & DATA PROCESSING EQPT REPAIR & MAINTENANCE

Aptos LLC.. D 614 840-1400
  Lewis Center *(G-9806)*
Custom Hdwr Engrg Cnslting LLC......... C 636 305-9669
  Cleveland *(G-4145)*
Datatech Depot (east) Inc....................... E 513 860-5651
  West Chester *(G-14682)*
Efix It Solutions LLC............................... E 937 476-7533
  Dayton *(G-7330)*
Geeks On Call.. D 800 905-4335
  Independence *(G-9433)*
Positive Bus Solutions Inc...................... D 513 772-2255
  Cincinnati *(G-3222)*
Projetech Inc.. E 513 481-4900
  Cincinnati *(G-3248)*

COMPUTER & OFFICE MACHINE MAINTENANCE & REPAIR

Avnet Integrated Inc............................... E 614 851-8700
  Groveport *(G-8972)*
Bpi Infrmtion Systems Ohio Inc............... E 440 717-4112
  Brecksville *(G-1345)*
Bsl - Applied Laser Tech LLC................. E 216 663-8181
  Independence *(G-9413)*
Career Cnnctons Stffing Svcs I............... E 440 471-8210
  Westlake *(G-15045)*
CTS Construction Inc............................. D 513 489-8290
  Cincinnati *(G-2521)*
DMC Technology Group Inc................... E 419 535-2900
  Toledo *(G-13782)*
Evanhoe & Associates Inc...................... E 937 235-2995
  Xenia *(G-15505)*
Government Acquisitions Inc.................. E 513 721-8700
  Cincinnati *(G-2744)*
Park Place Technologies LLC................. E 603 617-7123
  Cleveland *(G-4723)*
Park Place Technologies LLC................. B 610 544-0571
  Mayfield Heights *(G-10792)*
Perry Pro Tech Inc.................................. D 419 228-1360
  Lima *(G-9948)*
Pinnacle Data Systems Inc..................... C 614 748-1150
  Groveport *(G-8995)*
Pomeroy It Solutions Sls Inc................... E 440 717-1364
  Brecksville *(G-1363)*
Resource One Cmpt Systems Inc........... E 614 485-4800
  Worthington *(G-15452)*
Sjn Data Center LLC.............................. E 513 386-7871
  Cincinnati *(G-3381)*
Vertiv Corporation.................................. C 614 841-6400
  Westerville *(G-14948)*
Vertiv Services Inc.................................. A 614 841-6400
  Westerville *(G-14950)*
WD Bpi LLC... E 440 717-4112
  Brecksville *(G-1371)*
Wellington Technologies Inc................... E 440 238-4377
  Westlake *(G-15123)*
Xtek Partners Inc................................... E 614 973-7400
  Columbus *(G-6913)*

COMPUTER CODE AUTHORS

SERVICES SECTION

COMPUTER SOFTWARE DEVELOPMENT

Envisionware Inc.. E 678 382-6530
  Columbus (G-5822)

COMPUTER DATA ESCROW SVCS

Speedeon Data LLC... E 440 264-2100
  Cleveland (G-4932)

COMPUTER FACILITIES MANAGEMENT SVCS

ARC Healthcare LLC....................................... E 888 552-0677
  Worthington (G-15405)
Career Cnnctons Stffing Svcs I....................... E 440 471-8210
  Westlake (G-15045)
City of Cleveland... E 216 664-2941
  Cleveland (G-3986)
Dedicated Tech Services Inc.......................... E 614 309-0059
  Dublin (G-7986)
Evanhoe & Associates Inc.............................. E 937 235-2995
  Xenia (G-15505)
General Electric Company.............................. C 513 583-3500
  Cincinnati (G-2724)
Interactive Payer Network LLC....................... E
  Cleveland (G-4417)
Jjr Solutions LLC... E 937 912-0288
  Dayton (G-7429)
Jyg Innovations LLC....................................... D 937 630-3858
  Dayton (G-7431)
K&R Network Solutions.................................. E 858 292-5766
  Dublin (G-8044)
Park Place Technologies LLC......................... C 877 778-8707
  Cleveland (G-4724)
Reliant Technology LLC................................. E 404 551-4534
  Cleveland (G-4822)
Siertek Ltd.. E 937 623-2466
  Beavercreek Township (G-948)
Technical Assurance Inc................................. E 440 953-3147
  Willoughby (G-15222)

COMPUTER GRAPHICS SVCS

Alt Media Studios LLC.................................... E 440 777-6666
  Novelty (G-12036)
Clubessential LLC.. E 800 448-1475
  Blue Ash (G-1153)
Comcage LLC... E 513 549-4003
  Cincinnati (G-2479)
Continental Broadband PA............................. D 877 570-7827
  Columbus (G-5691)
Great Lakes Publishing Company.................. D 216 771-2833
  Cleveland (G-4330)
Hyperquake LLC... E 513 563-6555
  Cincinnati (G-2862)
Interact One Inc.. E 513 469-7042
  Blue Ash (G-1185)
Karcher Group Inc.. E 330 493-6141
  North Canton (G-11843)
Lunar Cow Design Inc.................................... D 330 836-0911
  Akron (G-226)
Service Pronet LLC.. E 614 874-4300
  Columbus (G-6665)
Skylight Partners Inc...................................... E 513 381-5555
  Cincinnati (G-3385)
Thunder Tech Inc.. E 216 391-2255
  Cleveland (G-5017)
Universal Enterprises Inc................................ C 419 529-3500
  Ontario (G-12126)

COMPUTER PERIPHERAL EQPT REPAIR & MAINTENANCE

Great Lakes Computer Corp........................... D 440 937-1100
  Avon (G-652)

Mt Business Technologies Inc........................ C 419 529-6100
  Mansfield (G-10300)
Park Place Technologies LLC......................... C 877 778-8707
  Cleveland (G-4724)

COMPUTER PERIPHERAL EQPT, NEC

Data Processing Sciences Corporation.......... D 513 791-7100
  Cincinnati (G-2539)
Government Acquisitions Inc......................... E 513 721-8700
  Cincinnati (G-2744)
Sierra Nevada Corporation............................. C 937 431-2800
  Beavercreek (G-906)
Systemax Manufacturing Inc.......................... D 937 368-2300
  Dayton (G-7658)
Vmetro Inc.. D 281 584-0728
  Fairborn (G-8386)

COMPUTER PERIPHERAL EQPT, WHOLESALE

Advanced Cmpt Connections LLC.................. E 419 668-4080
  Norwalk (G-11999)
Advantech Corporation.................................. D 513 742-8895
  Blue Ash (G-1124)
Alignement Engine Inc................................... E 330 401-8251
  North Canton (G-11810)
Cranel Incorporated....................................... D 614 431-8000
  Columbus (G-5255)
Legrand North America LLC.......................... B 937 224-0639
  Dayton (G-7451)
Manatron Inc... E 937 431-4000
  Beavercreek (G-925)
Micro Center Online Inc.................................. D 614 326-8500
  Columbus (G-6232)
Micro Electronics Inc..................................... C 513 782-8500
  Cincinnati (G-3057)
Micro Electronics Inc..................................... B 614 334-1430
  Columbus (G-6233)
Micro Electronics Inc..................................... D 614 850-3410
  Hilliard (G-9215)
Microplex Inc.. E 330 498-0600
  North Canton (G-11848)
Pomeroy It Solutions Sls Inc.......................... E 440 717-1364
  Brecksville (G-1363)
Startechcom USA LLP.................................... B 800 265-1844
  Groveport (G-9003)
Systemax Manufacturing Inc.......................... D 937 368-2300
  Dayton (G-7658)
Target Systems Inc.. E 440 239-1600
  Cleveland (G-4977)

COMPUTER PROCESSING SVCS

Cash Flow Solutions Inc................................ D 513 524-2320
  Oxford (G-12205)

COMPUTER PROGRAMMING SVCS: Custom

Critical Business Analysis Inc........................ E 419 874-0800
  Perrysburg (G-12326)
Csg Cleveland Enterprises Inc....................... E 440 918-9341
  Richmond Heights (G-12717)
Evanhoe & Associates Inc.............................. E 937 235-2995
  Xenia (G-15505)
Horizon Payroll Services Inc.......................... B 937 434-8244
  Dayton (G-7414)
Netsmart Technologies Inc............................ B 800 434-2642
  Dublin (G-8074)
Strategic Data Systems Inc........................... C 513 772-7374
  Cincinnati (G-3422)

COMPUTER RELATED MAINTENANCE SVCS

Atos It Solutions and Svcs Inc....................... B 513 336-1000
  Mason (G-10521)

Career Cnnctons Stffing Svcs I....................... E 440 471-8210
  Westlake (G-15045)
Contingent Network Services LLC.................. C 513 616-5773
  West Chester (G-14674)
Creek Technologies Company........................ C 937 272-4581
  Beavercreek (G-876)
Dedicated Tech Services Inc.......................... E 614 309-0059
  Dublin (G-7986)
Freedom Usa Inc... E 216 503-6374
  Twinsburg (G-14192)
Greentree Group Inc...................................... D 937 490-5500
  Dayton (G-7388)
Jjr Solutions LLC... E 937 912-0288
  Dayton (G-7429)
Jyg Innovations LLC....................................... D 937 630-3858
  Dayton (G-7431)
Plus One Communications LLC..................... B 330 255-4500
  Akron (G-267)
Premiere Medical Resources Inc.................... E 330 923-5899
  Cuyahoga Falls (G-7094)
Securedata LLC.. E 323 944-0822
  Mayfield Village (G-10796)
Siertek Ltd.. E 937 623-2466
  Beavercreek Township (G-948)
Thunderyard Solutions LLC........................... E 281 222-3644
  Westlake (G-15115)
Vana Solutions LLC.. E 937 242-6399
  Beavercreek (G-913)
Ventech Solutions Inc.................................... D 614 757-1167
  Columbus (G-5284)
Wolters Kluwer Clinical Dru............................ D 330 650-6506
  Hudson (G-9378)

COMPUTER SOFTWARE DEVELOPMENT

121ecommerce LLC.. E 216 586-6656
  University Heights (G-14274)
1worldsync Inc.. D 866 280-4013
  Dayton (G-7146)
3d Systems Inc... E 216 229-2040
  Cleveland (G-3746)
Agility Partners LLC....................................... D 740 819-2712
  Columbus (G-5330)
Analex Corporation.. E 703 721-6001
  Brook Park (G-1405)
Arcos LLC... C 614 396-5500
  Columbus (G-5384)
Assurecare LLC... E 513 618-2150
  Cincinnati (G-2220)
Bennett Adelson Prof Svcs LLC..................... E 216 369-0140
  Cleveland (G-3870)
Bluespring Software Inc................................. E 513 794-1764
  Blue Ash (G-1138)
Briteskies LLC.. E 216 369-3600
  Cleveland (G-3895)
Business Equipment Co Inc........................... E 513 948-1500
  Cincinnati (G-2293)
Cincom Systems Inc...................................... B 513 612-2300
  Cincinnati (G-2438)
Cintech LLC.. E 513 731-6000
  Cincinnati (G-2446)
Clubessential LLC.. E 800 448-1475
  Blue Ash (G-1153)
Cochin Technologies LLC.............................. E 440 941-4856
  Avon (G-648)
Commercial Time Sharing Inc........................ E 330 644-3059
  Akron (G-115)
Computer Aided Technology LLC.................. D 513 745-2700
  Cincinnati (G-2491)
Constructconnect Inc..................................... C 800 364-2059
  Cincinnati (G-2498)
Crosschx Inc... D 800 501-3161
  Columbus (G-5730)

COMPUTER SOFTWARE DEVELOPMENT

CT Logistics Inc .... C 216 267-1636
  Cleveland *(G-4143)*

Dedicated Tech Services Inc .... E 614 309-0059
  Dublin *(G-7986)*

Differential Dev Shop LLC .... E 513 205-8930
  Cincinnati *(G-2564)*

Digitek Software Inc .... E 614 764-8875
  Lewis Center *(G-9819)*

Dizer Corp .... C 440 368-0201
  Painesville *(G-12227)*

DOT Net Factory LLC .... D 614 792-0645
  Dublin *(G-7988)*

Dotloop LLC .... E 513 257-0550
  Cincinnati *(G-2575)*

Double A Solutions LLC .... D 256 489-6458
  Toledo *(G-13783)*

E2 Infosystems Ltd .... E 833 832-4637
  New Albany *(G-11562)*

Echo 360 Inc .... D 877 324-6360
  Youngstown *(G-15606)*

Eci Macola/Max LLC .... C 978 539-6186
  Dublin *(G-8000)*

Edaptive Computing Inc .... D 937 433-0477
  Dayton *(G-7329)*

Emplifi Inc .... E 614 508-6100
  Columbus *(G-5815)*

Emprise Technologies LLC .... E 419 720-6982
  Toledo *(G-13791)*

Engineering Cons Group Inc .... D 330 869-9949
  Fairlawn *(G-8477)*

Epsilon .... C 513 248-2882
  Milford *(G-11226)*

Evolv LLC .... E 440 994-9115
  Hudson *(G-9346)*

Expesite LLC .... E 614 917-1100
  Columbus *(G-5839)*

Fastems LLC .... E 513 779-4614
  West Chester *(G-14690)*

Fenetech LLC .... C 330 995-2830
  Solon *(G-13088)*

First Mobile Trust LLC .... E 855 270-3592
  Miamisburg *(G-11055)*

Flairsoft Ltd .... E 614 888-0700
  Columbus *(G-5872)*

Foresight Corporation .... E 614 791-1600
  Dublin *(G-8013)*

Formfire LLC .... E 866 448-2302
  Cleveland *(G-4277)*

Framework Mi Inc .... E 513 444-2165
  Cincinnati *(G-2700)*

Fscreations Corporation .... D 330 746-3015
  Youngstown *(G-15614)*

Fusion Alliance LLC .... C 513 563-8444
  Blue Ash *(G-1177)*

Fusion Alliance LLC .... C 614 852-8000
  Columbus *(G-5259)*

Geoamps LLC .... E 614 389-4872
  Delaware *(G-7801)*

Henry Call Inc .... C 216 433-5609
  Cleveland *(G-4358)*

Ils Technology LLC .... E 800 695-8650
  Cleveland *(G-4404)*

Imflux Inc .... D 513 488-1017
  Cincinnati *(G-2865)*

Infinite Tiers Inc .... B 513 769-1900
  Cincinnati *(G-2869)*

Infovision21 Inc .... E 614 761-8844
  Dublin *(G-8038)*

Intelligrated Systems Inc .... A 866 936-7500
  Mason *(G-10565)*

Intelligrated Systems LLC .... A 513 701-7300
  Mason *(G-10566)*

International Technegroup Inc .... D 513 576-3900
  Milford *(G-11233)*

Irth Solutions Inc .... E 614 459-2328
  Columbus *(G-6071)*

Itcube LLC .... E 513 891-7300
  Blue Ash *(G-1186)*

J Becker Solutions Inc .... D 888 421-1155
  Westlake *(G-15072)*

Jifiticom Inc .... C 914 339-5376
  Columbus *(G-6090)*

Keithley Instruments LLC .... C 440 248-0400
  Solon *(G-13103)*

Keyfactor Inc .... C 216 785-2986
  Independence *(G-9440)*

Knowledge MGT Interactive Inc .... E 614 224-0664
  Columbus *(G-6124)*

Knowledge Support Systems Inc .... E 973 408-9157
  Independence *(G-9441)*

Kognetics LLC .... E 614 591-4416
  Gahanna *(G-8720)*

Krish Services Group Inc .... E 813 784-0039
  Brecksville *(G-1356)*

Leidos Inc .... D 937 656-8433
  Beavercreek *(G-886)*

Liberty Comm Sftwr Sltions Inc .... E 614 318-5000
  Columbus *(G-6156)*

Lisnr Inc .... E 513 322-8400
  Cincinnati *(G-2981)*

Logic Soft Inc .... D 614 884-5544
  Dublin *(G-8057)*

London Computer Systems Inc .... D 513 583-0840
  Cincinnati *(G-2986)*

Losant Iot Inc .... E 513 381-2947
  Cincinnati *(G-2987)*

Main Sequence Technology Inc .... E 440 946-5214
  Willoughby *(G-15209)*

Main Sequence Technology Inc .... E 440 946-5214
  Mentor On The Lake *(G-11015)*

Marshall Information Svcs LLC .... E 614 430-0355
  Columbus *(G-6198)*

Masterbrand Cabinets LLC .... B 812 482-2527
  Beachwood *(G-812)*

Materials MGT Microsystems .... D 262 240-9900
  Mentor *(G-10966)*

Mediu Inc .... E 614 332-7410
  Delaware *(G-7817)*

Mri Software LLC .... B 800 321-8770
  Solon *(G-13114)*

Muc Holdings LLC .... E 513 417-8452
  Cincinnati *(G-3088)*

Navistone Inc .... E 844 677-3667
  Cincinnati *(G-3099)*

Neumeric Technologies Corp .... D 614 610-4999
  Lewis Center *(G-9831)*

New Innovations Inc .... E 330 899-9954
  Uniontown *(G-14260)*

Oeconnection LLC .... D 888 776-5792
  Akron *(G-246)*

Onshift Inc .... C 216 333-1353
  Cleveland *(G-4700)*

Open Practice Solutions Ltd .... E 234 380-8345
  Hudson *(G-9366)*

Operating Tax Systems LLC .... A 330 940-3967
  Stow *(G-13383)*

Pcms International Inc .... D 513 587-3100
  Cincinnati *(G-3192)*

Physna Inc .... D 844 474-9762
  Columbus *(G-6523)*

Plumbline Solutions Inc .... E 419 581-2963
  Findlay *(G-8577)*

Positive Bus Solutions Inc .... D 513 772-2555
  Cincinnati *(G-3222)*

Qc Software LLC .... E 513 469-1424
  Cincinnati *(G-3259)*

Quick Solutions Inc .... C 614 825-8000
  Columbus *(G-5280)*

Ready Set Grow LLC .... E 513 445-2939
  Cincinnati *(G-3275)*

Reflexis Systems Inc .... C 614 948-1931
  Westerville *(G-14933)*

Renaissancetech .... E 419 569-3999
  Dublin *(G-8107)*

Rippe & Kingston Systems Inc .... D 513 977-4578
  Cincinnati *(G-3299)*

Robots and Pencils LP .... C 866 515-9897
  Chagrin Falls *(G-1965)*

Saama Technologies Inc .... D 614 652-6100
  Worthington *(G-15454)*

Sadler-Necamp Financial Svcs .... E 513 489-5477
  Cincinnati *(G-3337)*

Sanctuary Software Studio Inc .... E 330 666-9690
  Fairlawn *(G-8496)*

Shiftwise .... E 513 476-1532
  Columbus *(G-6672)*

Shoptech Industrial Sftwr Corp .... E 513 985-9900
  Cincinnati *(G-3371)*

Siemens Industry Software Inc .... E 513 576-2400
  Milford *(G-11256)*

Sumtotal Systems LLC .... E 352 264-2800
  Columbus *(G-6728)*

Switchbox Inc .... E 614 334-9517
  Columbus *(G-6739)*

Systems Evolution Inc .... E 513 459-1992
  Cincinnati *(G-3431)*

T-Cetra LLC .... C 877 956-2359
  Dublin *(G-8139)*

Talis Clinical LLC .... D 234 284-2399
  Streetsboro *(G-13431)*

Teamdynamix Solutions LLC .... D 877 752-6196
  Columbus *(G-6752)*

Tensure Consulting LLC .... D 513 428-4493
  Mason *(G-10615)*

Tradeglobal LLC .... C 866 345-5835
  West Chester *(G-14775)*

Trz Holdings Inc .... E 419 931-0072
  Perrysburg *(G-12381)*

Vendorinsight .... E 800 997-2674
  Blue Ash *(G-1269)*

Ventech Solutions Inc .... D 614 757-1167
  Columbus *(G-5284)*

Vertex Computer Systems Inc .... C 513 662-6888
  Cincinnati *(G-3624)*

Virtual Hold Tech Slutions LLC .... E 330 670-2200
  Akron *(G-353)*

Votem Corp .... D 216 930-4300
  Cleveland *(G-5116)*

Widepint Intgrted Sltions Corp .... D 614 410-1587
  Columbus *(G-6890)*

Xngage LLC .... E 440 990-5767
  Middleburg Heights *(G-11136)*

Yardi Systems .... E 805 699-2056
  Cleveland *(G-5164)*

COMPUTER SOFTWARE DEVELOPMENT & APPLICATIONS

1848 Ventures LLC .... C 330 887-0187
  Westfield Center *(G-15023)*

2immersive4u Corporation .... E 440 570-4055
  North Royalton *(G-11937)*

Amcs Group Inc .... D 419 891-1100
  Toledo *(G-13681)*

Avertest LLC .... E 330 591-7219
  Medina *(G-10812)*

Batterii LLC.. E 513 379-3595
  Cincinnati (G-2239)
Camgen Ltd... D 330 204-8636
  Cleveland (G-3920)
Cengage Learning Inc................................. B 513 229-1000
  Mason (G-10527)
Chesterfield Services Inc............................ E 330 896-9777
  Uniontown (G-14245)
Convention Vstors Bur of Grter................. E 216 875-6600
  Cleveland (G-4114)
Cott Systems Inc... D 614 847-4405
  Columbus (G-5707)
Darcie R Clark Lpcc LLC............................ E 937 319-4448
  Dayton (G-7267)
Deemsys Inc.. D 614 322-9928
  Gahanna (G-8715)
Deep Mind Music LLC................................ D 440 829-6401
  Lakewood (G-9664)
Digital Forensics Corp LLC........................ E 888 210-1296
  Warrensville Heights (G-14580)
Drund Ltd... D 330 402-5944
  Boardman (G-1287)
Dynamite Technologies LLC...................... E 614 538-0095
  Columbus (G-5797)
Empora Title Inc.. E 937 360-8876
  Columbus (G-5816)
Frontier Technology Inc.............................. E 937 429-3302
  Beavercreek Township (G-939)
Fund Evaluation Group LLC...................... E 513 977-4400
  Cincinnati (G-2711)
Fundable LLC.. E 614 364-4523
  Powell (G-12591)
Fusian Inc.. E 937 361-7146
  Columbus (G-5902)
Insurance Technologies Corp.................... E 866 683-6915
  Columbus (G-6061)
Jjr Solutions LLC... E 937 912-0288
  Dayton (G-7429)
Kk Associates LLC..................................... E 614 783-7966
  Dublin (G-8050)
Lakeland Foundation.................................. E 440 525-7094
  Willoughby (G-15202)
Liberty Home Mortgage Corp.................... C 440 644-0001
  Independence (G-9443)
Mansfeld Ohio Arie No 336 Frtn................ E 419 636-7812
  Bryan (G-1487)
Marxent Labs LLC...................................... E 727 851-9522
  Miamisburg (G-11071)
Montpelier Exempted Vlg Schl................... E 419 485-3676
  Montpelier (G-11385)
New Albany Country Club LLC.................. C 614 939-8500
  New Albany (G-11579)
Nuonosys Inc... E 888 666-7976
  Independence (G-9461)
Premier Nursing Network LLC................... D 440 563-1586
  Middlefield (G-11144)
Projetech Inc... E 513 481-4900
  Cincinnati (G-3248)
Pulse Ltd LLC... E 216 570-7732
  Chesterland (G-2042)
Sacred Hour Inc.. D 216 228-9750
  Lakewood (G-9684)
Saec/Kinetic Vision Inc.............................. C 513 793-4959
  Cincinnati (G-3338)
Scriptdrop Inc... D 614 641-0648
  Columbus (G-6656)
Service Pronet LLC.................................... E 614 874-4300
  Columbus (G-6665)
Solutons Thrugh Innvtive Tech.................. D 937 320-9994
  Beavercreek (G-907)
Starship Technologies Inc.......................... C 440 251-7096
  Bowling Green (G-1333)
Trayak Inc.. E 513 252-8089
  Mason (G-10618)
Vantage Solutions Inc................................ D 330 757-4864
  Poland (G-12511)
Vooks Inc... D 503 694-9217
  Stow (G-13401)
Zaps Technocrats Inc................................ D 614 664-3199
  Dublin (G-8167)

COMPUTER SOFTWARE SYSTEMS ANALYSIS & DESIGN: Custom

22nd Century Technologies Inc................ B 866 537-9191
  Beavercreek (G-854)
Akkodis Inc.. C 513 769-9797
  Blue Ash (G-1126)
ARC Healthcare LLC.................................. E 888 552-0677
  Worthington (G-15405)
Autoway Investors Ltd............................... E 419 841-6691
  Toledo (G-13696)
Benchmark Digital Partners LLC............... D 513 774-1000
  Mason (G-10523)
Big Red Rooster.. E 614 255-0200
  Columbus (G-5440)
Blue Creek Enterprises Inc....................... E 937 364-2920
  Lynchburg (G-10183)
Cdo Technologies Inc................................ D 937 258-0022
  Dayton (G-7128)
Click4care Inc... E 614 431-3700
  Powell (G-12588)
Commsys Inc... E 937 220-4990
  Dayton (G-7241)
Diversified Systems Inc.............................. E 614 476-9939
  Westerville (G-14976)
Genomoncology LLC.................................. E 440 617-6087
  Mentor (G-10942)
Info-Hold Inc... E 513 248-5600
  Cincinnati (G-2870)
Manifest Solutions Corp............................. D 614 930-2800
  Upper Arlington (G-14280)
Nextgen Federal Systems LLC................. C 304 413-0208
  Beavercreek Township (G-944)
Tangram Flex Inc.. E 937 985-3199
  Dayton (G-7659)
Unicon International Inc............................ D 614 861-7070
  Columbus (G-6799)
Wtw Delaware Holdings LLC..................... D 216 937-4000
  Cleveland (G-5161)

COMPUTER STORAGE DEVICES, NEC

Freedom Usa Inc... E 216 503-6374
  Twinsburg (G-14192)
Park Place Technologies LLC................... C 877 778-8707
  Cleveland (G-4724)

COMPUTER STORAGE UNITS: Auxiliary

Pinnacle Data Systems Inc........................ C 614 748-1150
  Groveport (G-8995)

COMPUTER SYSTEM SELLING SVCS

Velocity A Managed Svcs Co Inc.............. C 419 868-9983
  Holland (G-9311)

COMPUTER SYSTEMS ANALYSIS & DESIGN

3c Technology Solutions LLC.................... E 614 319-4681
  Hilliard (G-9174)
Caci Mtl Systems Inc................................. D 937 429-2771
  Beavercreek (G-868)
Career Cnnctons Stffing Svcs I................. E 440 471-8210
  Westlake (G-15045)
Contingent Network Services LLC............ C 513 616-5773
  West Chester (G-14674)
Sytronics Inc... E 937 431-6100
  Beavercreek (G-910)
Teknobility LLC... E 216 255-9433
  Medina (G-10898)

COMPUTER TERMINALS

Freedom Usa Inc... E 216 503-6374
  Twinsburg (G-14192)
Pinnacle Data Systems Inc........................ C 614 748-1150
  Groveport (G-8995)

COMPUTER TIME-SHARING

Ohio State University................................. D 614 292-3416
  Columbus (G-6457)

COMPUTERS, NEC

Park Place Technologies LLC................... C 877 778-8707
  Cleveland (G-4724)
Systemax Manufacturing Inc..................... D 937 368-2300
  Dayton (G-7658)

COMPUTERS, NEC, WHOLESALE

Office World Inc.. E 419 991-4694
  Lima (G-9994)
Vecmar Corporation.................................... E 440 953-1119
  Mentor (G-11009)

COMPUTERS, PERIPHERALS & SOFTWARE, WHOLESALE: Printers

Bsl - Applied Laser Tech LLC.................... E 216 663-8181
  Independence (G-9413)

COMPUTERS, PERIPHERALS & SOFTWARE, WHOLESALE: Software

Autozone Inc.. E 216 751-0571
  Cleveland (G-3842)
Autozone Inc.. E 216 267-6586
  Cleveland (G-3843)
Autozone Inc.. E 440 593-6934
  Conneaut (G-6939)
Autozone Inc.. E 440 639-2247
  Painesville (G-12221)
Autozone Inc.. E 419 872-2813
  Perrysburg (G-12315)
Avid Technologies Inc................................ E 330 487-0770
  Twinsburg (G-14173)
Brightedge Technologies Inc..................... D 800 578-8023
  Cleveland (G-3893)
Canon Solutions America Inc.................... E 937 260-4495
  Miamisburg (G-11031)
Commercial Time Sharing Inc................... E 330 644-3059
  Akron (G-115)
Constructconnect Inc................................. C 800 364-2059
  Cincinnati (G-2498)
Eci Macola/Max LLC................................... C 978 539-6186
  Dublin (G-8000)
Envirnmntal Systems RES Inst I................ E 614 933-8698
  Columbus (G-5820)
Fundriver LLC... E 513 618-8718
  Cincinnati (G-2712)
GBS Corp... C 330 494-5330
  North Canton (G-11833)
Government Acquisitions Inc.................... E 513 721-8700
  Cincinnati (G-2744)
Manatron Sabre Systems and Svc........... D 937 431-4000
  Beavercreek (G-926)
Mediquant LLC.. C 440 746-2300
  Independence (G-9451)
Positive Bus Solutions Inc......................... D 513 772-2255
  Cincinnati (G-3222)

CONCENTRATES, FLAVORING, EXC DRINK

Total Loop Inc.. D 888 614-5667
Uniontown *(G-14268)*

CONCENTRATES, FLAVORING, EXC DRINK

Wiley Companies................................... C 740 622-0755
Coshocton *(G-7005)*

CONCRETE CURING & HARDENING COMPOUNDS

Master Builders LLC............................. E 800 228-3318
Beachwood *(G-811)*

CONCRETE PRDTS

Hilltop Basic Resources Inc................... D 513 621-1500
Cincinnati *(G-2826)*

Huron Cement Products Company......... E 419 433-4161
Huron *(G-9390)*

Lang Stone Company Inc....................... E 614 235-4099
Columbus *(G-6139)*

Orrville Trucking & Grading Co............... E 330 682-4010
Orrville *(G-12172)*

R W Sidley Incorporated........................ C 440 298-3232
Thompson *(G-13618)*

CONCRETE PRDTS, PRECAST, NEC

Eldorado Stone LLC.............................. E 330 698-3931
Apple Creek *(G-449)*

CONCRETE: Asphaltic, Not From Refineries

Shelly Materials Inc............................... D 740 246-6315
Thornville *(G-13622)*

CONCRETE: Dry Mixture

Smith Concrete Co................................ E 740 373-7441
Dover *(G-7901)*

CONCRETE: Ready-Mixed

Beazer East Inc..................................... E 937 364-2311
Hillsboro *(G-9249)*

Central Ready Mix LLC.......................... E 513 402-5001
Cincinnati *(G-2337)*

Collinwood Shale Brick Sup Co............... E 216 587-2700
Cleveland *(G-4088)*

D W Dickey and Son Inc........................ C 330 424-1441
Lisbon *(G-10001)*

Grafton Ready Mix Concret Inc............... C 440 926-2911
Grafton *(G-8839)*

Hilltop Basic Resources Inc................... D 513 621-1500
Cincinnati *(G-2826)*

Huron Cement Products Company......... E 419 433-4161
Huron *(G-9390)*

Integrated Resources Inc....................... E 419 885-7122
Sylvania *(G-13552)*

Kuhlman Corporation............................. E 419 897-6000
Maumee *(G-10737)*

Orrville Trucking & Grading Co............... E 330 682-4010
Orrville *(G-12172)*

Quality Block & Supply Inc.................... E 330 364-4411
Mount Eaton *(G-11458)*

Sakrete Inc... E 513 242-3644
Cincinnati *(G-3343)*

Smith Concrete Co................................ E 740 373-7441
Dover *(G-7901)*

Smyrna Ready Mix Concrete LLC........... E 937 855-0410
Germantown *(G-8805)*

Terminal Ready-Mix Inc......................... E 440 288-0181
Lorain *(G-10103)*

The National Lime and Stone Company.. E 419 422-4341
Findlay *(G-8593)*

CONDENSERS: Heat Transfer Eqpt, Evaporative

Hydro-Dyne Inc..................................... E 330 832-5076
Massillon *(G-10647)*

CONFINEMENT SURVEILLANCE SYS MAINTENANCE & MONITORING SVCS

Macair Aviation LLC.............................. E 937 347-1302
Xenia *(G-15525)*

CONNECTORS: Electronic

Ladd Distribution LLC............................ D 937 438-2646
Kettering *(G-9630)*

Mjo Industries Inc................................. D 800 590-4055
Huber Heights *(G-9325)*

CONSTRUCTION & MINING MACHINERY WHOLESALERS

Ag-Pro Ohio LLC................................... E 740 653-6951
Lancaster *(G-9691)*

Ag-Pro Ohio LLC................................... E 740 450-7446
Zanesville *(G-15765)*

Caterpllar Trmble Ctrl Tech LL................ D 937 233-8921
Dayton *(G-7217)*

Ebony Construction Co.......................... E 419 841-3455
Sylvania *(G-13542)*

Equipment Maintenance Inc.................. E 513 353-3518
Cleves *(G-5188)*

Lefeld Implement Inc............................ E 419 678-2375
Coldwater *(G-5215)*

Liechty Inc... E 419 298-2302
Edgerton *(G-8228)*

Mesa Industries Inc.............................. E 513 321-2950
Cincinnati *(G-3048)*

Ohio Machinery Co................................ E 330 874-1003
Bolivar *(G-1296)*

Ohio Machinery Co................................ E 614 878-2287
Columbus *(G-6436)*

Seal Aftermarket Products LLC.............. E 419 355-1200
Fremont *(G-8701)*

Shearer Farm Inc.................................. C 330 345-9023
Wooster *(G-15376)*

Simpson Strong-Tie Company Inc........... C 614 876-8060
Columbus *(G-6683)*

The Wagner-Smith Company.................. B 866 338-0398
Moraine *(G-11444)*

United Rentals North Amer Inc............... E 614 276-5444
Columbus *(G-6814)*

Zink Foodservice Group Inc................... C 800 492-7400
Columbus *(G-6919)*

CONSTRUCTION EQPT REPAIR SVCS

Hans Truck and Trlr Repr Inc.................. D 216 581-0046
Cleveland *(G-4349)*

CONSTRUCTION EQPT: Cranes

American Crane Inc............................... E 614 496-2268
Reynoldsburg *(G-12651)*

CONSTRUCTION EQPT: Roofing Eqpt

Dimensional Metals Inc......................... E 740 927-3633
Reynoldsburg *(G-12660)*

CONSTRUCTION MATERIALS, WHOLESALE: Air Ducts, Sheet Metal

American Warming and Vent.................. D 419 288-2703
Bradner *(G-1341)*

CONSTRUCTION MATERIALS, WHOLESALE: Asphalt Felts & coating

Famous Distribution Inc........................ E 740 282-0951
Steubenville *(G-13323)*

CONSTRUCTION MATERIALS, WHOLESALE: Building Stone, Marble

Maza Inc... D 614 760-0003
Plain City *(G-12486)*

CONSTRUCTION MATERIALS, WHOLESALE: Building, Exterior

Boise Cascade Company........................ C 740 382-6766
Marion *(G-10419)*

Francis-Schulze Co................................ E 937 295-3941
Russia *(G-12770)*

Lowes Home Centers LLC..................... C 330 665-9356
Akron *(G-225)*

Lowes Home Centers LLC..................... C 330 829-2700
Alliance *(G-389)*

Lowes Home Centers LLC..................... C 440 998-6555
Ashtabula *(G-540)*

Lowes Home Centers LLC..................... C 740 589-3750
Athens *(G-582)*

Lowes Home Centers LLC..................... C 440 937-3500
Avon *(G-660)*

Lowes Home Centers LLC..................... C 937 427-1110
Beavercreek *(G-889)*

Lowes Home Centers LLC..................... C 216 831-2860
Bedford *(G-970)*

Lowes Home Centers LLC..................... D 937 599-4000
Bellefontaine *(G-1032)*

Lowes Home Centers LLC..................... C 330 497-2720
Canton *(G-1797)*

Lowes Home Centers LLC..................... C 740 773-7777
Chillicothe *(G-2079)*

Lowes Home Centers LLC..................... C 513 598-7050
Cincinnati *(G-2990)*

Lowes Home Centers LLC..................... C 216 351-4723
Cleveland *(G-4506)*

Lowes Home Centers LLC..................... C 614 853-6200
Columbus *(G-6174)*

Lowes Home Centers LLC..................... C 937 235-2920
Dayton *(G-7460)*

Lowes Home Centers LLC..................... C 937 438-4900
Dayton *(G-7461)*

Lowes Home Centers LLC..................... C 937 854-8200
Dayton *(G-7462)*

Lowes Home Centers LLC..................... C 419 782-9000
Defiance *(G-7753)*

Lowes Home Centers LLC..................... C 614 659-0530
Dublin *(G-8058)*

Lowes Home Centers LLC..................... C 440 324-5004
Elyria *(G-8272)*

Lowes Home Centers LLC..................... C 419 420-7531
Findlay *(G-8559)*

Lowes Home Centers LLC..................... C 419 355-0221
Fremont *(G-8690)*

Lowes Home Centers LLC..................... C 937 547-2400
Greenville *(G-8880)*

Lowes Home Centers LLC..................... C 513 737-3700
Hamilton *(G-9061)*

Lowes Home Centers LLC..................... C 614 529-5900
Hilliard *(G-9210)*

Lowes Home Centers LLC..................... C 740 681-3464
Lancaster *(G-9733)*

Lowes Home Centers LLC..................... C 419 331-3598
Lima *(G-9930)*

Lowes Home Centers LLC.................... C 440 985-5700
Lorain (G-10090)

Lowes Home Centers LLC.................... C 740 374-2151
Marietta (G-10381)

Lowes Home Centers LLC.................... C 740 389-9737
Marion (G-10433)

Lowes Home Centers LLC.................... C 937 578-4440
Marysville (G-10492)

Lowes Home Centers LLC.................... C 513 336-9741
Mason (G-10575)

Lowes Home Centers LLC.................... C 330 832-1901
Massillon (G-10650)

Lowes Home Centers LLC.................... C 440 392-0027
Mentor (G-10965)

Lowes Home Centers LLC.................... C 513 727-3900
Middletown (G-11170)

Lowes Home Centers LLC.................... C 513 965-3280
Milford (G-11237)

Lowes Home Centers LLC.................... C 740 393-5350
Mount Vernon (G-11498)

Lowes Home Centers LLC.................... D 330 339-1936
New Philadelphia (G-11657)

Lowes Home Centers LLC.................... C 740 522-0003
Newark (G-11723)

Lowes Home Centers LLC.................... D 330 908-2750
Northfield (G-11960)

Lowes Home Centers LLC.................... C 419 747-1920
Ontario (G-12113)

Lowes Home Centers LLC.................... C 419 874-6758
Perrysburg (G-12355)

Lowes Home Centers LLC.................... D 614 769-9940
Reynoldsburg (G-12668)

Lowes Home Centers LLC.................... C 440 331-1027
Rocky River (G-12748)

Lowes Home Centers LLC.................... D 740 699-3000
Saint Clairsville (G-12799)

Lowes Home Centers LLC.................... C 419 624-6000
Sandusky (G-12912)

Lowes Home Centers LLC.................... C 937 498-8400
Sidney (G-13039)

Lowes Home Centers LLC.................... C 513 445-1000
South Lebanon (G-13172)

Lowes Home Centers LLC.................... C 740 894-7120
South Point (G-13177)

Lowes Home Centers LLC.................... C 937 327-6000
Springfield (G-13264)

Lowes Home Centers LLC.................... C 740 266-3500
Steubenville (G-13336)

Lowes Home Centers LLC.................... C 330 920-9280
Stow (G-13380)

Lowes Home Centers LLC.................... C 330 626-2980
Streetsboro (G-13420)

Lowes Home Centers LLC.................... C 440 239-2630
Strongsville (G-13473)

Lowes Home Centers LLC.................... C 419 843-9758
Toledo (G-13894)

Lowes Home Centers LLC.................... C 937 339-2544
Troy (G-14145)

Lowes Home Centers LLC.................... C 330 335-1900
Wadsworth (G-14442)

Lowes Home Centers LLC.................... C 419 739-1300
Wapakoneta (G-14488)

Lowes Home Centers LLC.................... C 330 609-8000
Warren (G-14536)

Lowes Home Centers LLC.................... C 513 755-4300
West Chester (G-14726)

Lowes Home Centers LLC.................... C 740 574-6200
Wheelersburg (G-15130)

Lowes Home Centers LLC.................... C 440 942-2759
Willoughby (G-15207)

Lowes Home Centers LLC.................... C 937 383-7000
Wilmington (G-15260)

Lowes Home Centers LLC.................... C 330 287-2261
Wooster (G-15352)

Lowes Home Centers LLC.................... C 937 347-4000
Xenia (G-15524)

Lowes Home Centers LLC.................... C 330 965-4500
Youngstown (G-15653)

Lowes Home Centers LLC.................... C 740 450-5500
Zanesville (G-15807)

Orrville Trucking & Grading Co............... E 330 682-4010
Orrville (G-12172)

Robertson Plumbing & Heating............... E 330 863-0611
Malvern (G-10235)

Schneider Home Equipment Co.............. E 513 522-1200
Cincinnati (G-3349)

Usavinyl LLC.. D 614 771-4805
Groveport (G-9010)

CONSTRUCTION MATERIALS, WHOLESALE: Building, Interior

Meyer Decorative Surfaces USA Inc....... C 800 776-3900
Hudson (G-9364)

SPI LLC... E 440 914-1122
Solon (G-13148)

CONSTRUCTION MATERIALS, WHOLESALE: Cement

Huron Cement Products Company.......... E 419 433-4161
Huron (G-9390)

CONSTRUCTION MATERIALS, WHOLESALE: Door Frames

Mae Holding Company............................ E 513 751-2424
Cincinnati (G-3002)

Provia Holdings Inc................................. C 330 852-4711
Sugarcreek (G-13512)

CONSTRUCTION MATERIALS, WHOLESALE: Doors, Garage

A-E Door Sales and Service Inc.............. E 513 742-1984
Cincinnati (G-2132)

Dayton Door Sales Inc............................ E 937 253-9181
Dayton (G-7280)

CONSTRUCTION MATERIALS, WHOLESALE: Glass

Cleveland Glass Block Inc...................... E 614 252-5888
Columbus (G-5584)

Cleveland Glass Block Inc...................... E 216 531-6363
Cleveland (G-4046)

Harmon Inc... D 513 645-1550
West Chester (G-14704)

Harmon Inc... E 513 645-1550
West Chester (G-14705)

Multi Builders Supply Co........................ E 216 831-1121
Cleveland (G-4609)

CONSTRUCTION MATERIALS, WHOLESALE: Limestone

Pinney Dock & Transport LLC................ D 440 964-7186
Ashtabula (G-546)

R W Sidley Incorporated......................... C 440 298-3232
Thompson (G-13618)

CONSTRUCTION MATERIALS, WHOLESALE: Masons' Materials

Most Wrshpful Ereka Grnd Ldge............. E 614 626-4076
Columbus (G-6263)

CONSTRUCTION MATERIALS, WHOLESALE: Millwork

Jeld-Wen Inc... C 513 874-6771
West Chester (G-14821)

CONSTRUCTION MATERIALS, WHOLESALE: Molding, All Materials

Toledo Molding & Die LLC...................... B 419 692-6022
Delphos (G-7846)

CONSTRUCTION MATERIALS, WHOLESALE: Pallets, Wood

Jackpot Pallets LLC................................ E 877 770-0005
Brooklyn Heights (G-1421)

Pallet Distributors Inc............................. E 888 805-9670
Lakewood (G-9681)

Universal Pallets Inc............................... E 614 444-1095
Columbus (G-6820)

CONSTRUCTION MATERIALS, WHOLESALE: Particleboard

Litco International Inc............................. D 330 539-5433
Vienna (G-14421)

CONSTRUCTION MATERIALS, WHOLESALE: Paving Materials

The D S Brown Company........................ C 419 257-3561
North Baltimore (G-11802)

CONSTRUCTION MATERIALS, WHOLESALE: Prefabricated Structures

Modern Builders Supply Inc.................... E 330 376-1031
Akron (G-236)

Palmer-Donavin Mfg Co.......................... E 419 692-5000
Delphos (G-7843)

The Chas E Phipps Company................. E 216 641-2150
Cleveland (G-4993)

Will-Burt Company.................................. C 330 682-7015
Orrville (G-12176)

CONSTRUCTION MATERIALS, WHOLESALE: Roofing & Siding Material

Associated Materials LLC....................... A 330 929-1811
Cuyahoga Falls (G-7041)

Associated Materials Group Inc.............. C 330 929-1811
Cuyahoga Falls (G-7043)

Associated Mtls Holdings LLC................ A 330 929-1811
Cuyahoga Falls (G-7044)

Installed Building Pdts LLC.................... C 614 272-5577
Columbus (G-6058)

Modern Builders Supply Inc.................... E 419 224-4627
Lima (G-9936)

North Coast Commercial Roof................ C 330 425-3359
Twinsburg (G-14208)

Palmer-Donavin Mfg Co.......................... D 800 652-1234
Urbancrest (G-14322)

W Team Company................................... E 440 942-7939
Mentor (G-11011)

CONSTRUCTION MATERIALS, WHOLESALE: Sand

Columbus Coal & Lime Co...................... E 614 224-9241
Columbus (G-5624)

Kenmore Construction Co Inc................. C 330 762-8936
Akron (G-215)

CONSTRUCTION MATERIALS, WHOLESALE: Sewer Pipe, Clay

CONSTRUCTION MATERIALS, WHOLESALE: Sewer Pipe, Clay

Sewer Rodding Equipment Co............... C 419 991-2065
  Lima *(G-9959)*

CONSTRUCTION MATERIALS, WHOLESALE: Siding, Exc Wood

Alside Inc... D 419 865-0934
  Maumee *(G-10687)*

Apco Industries Inc............................. D 614 224-2345
  Columbus *(G-5371)*

Modern Builders Supply Inc................ E 216 273-3605
  Cleveland *(G-4593)*

Vinyl Design Corporation..................... E 419 283-4009
  Holland *(G-9313)*

CONSTRUCTION MATERIALS, WHOLESALE: Stone, Crushed Or Broken

Stoneco Inc... E 419 893-7645
  Maumee *(G-10771)*

CONSTRUCTION MATERIALS, WHOLESALE: Veneer

Milestone Ventures LLC...................... E 317 908-2093
  Newark *(G-11730)*

CONSTRUCTION MATERIALS, WHOLESALE: Windows

Allied Window Inc................................ E 513 559-1212
  Cincinnati *(G-2169)*

Alside Inc... E 330 929-1811
  Cuyahoga Falls *(G-7036)*

Associated Materials LLC.................... A 330 929-1811
  Cuyahoga Falls *(G-7041)*

Associated Materials Group Inc........... C 330 929-1811
  Cuyahoga Falls *(G-7043)*

Associated Mtls Holdings LLC............. A 330 929-1811
  Cuyahoga Falls *(G-7044)*

Champion Opco LLC........................... E 440 249-6768
  Macedonia *(G-10190)*

Enterprise Door & Supply Inc.............. E 440 942-3478
  Mentor *(G-10937)*

Gunton Corporation.............................. C 216 831-2420
  Cleveland *(G-4342)*

Mastic Home Exteriors Inc................... C 937 497-7008
  Sidney *(G-13040)*

Provia LLC... E 330 852-4711
  Sugarcreek *(G-13513)*

Soft-Lite LLC....................................... C 330 528-3400
  Streetsboro *(G-13428)*

Universal Windows Direct.................... D 440 232-9060
  Bedford Heights *(G-1003)*

CONSTRUCTION SAND MINING

S & S Aggregates Inc.......................... B 419 938-5604
  Perrysville *(G-12393)*

CONSTRUCTION: Agricultural Building

Witmers Inc... E 330 427-2147
  Salem *(G-12858)*

CONSTRUCTION: Airport Runway

Crp Contracting................................... D 614 338-8501
  Columbus *(G-5732)*

Nas Ventures...................................... D 614 338-8501
  Columbus *(G-6287)*

CONSTRUCTION: Apartment Building

Ackermann Enterprises Inc.................. D 513 842-3100
  Cincinnati *(G-2141)*

Appalachian Inc................................... E 937 444-3043
  Williamsburg *(G-15176)*

Donald R Kenney & Co Rlty LLC......... E 614 540-2404
  Westerville *(G-14891)*

Forest City Residential Dev.................. E 216 621-6060
  Cleveland *(G-4275)*

G J Goudreau & Co............................. E 216 351-5233
  Cleveland *(G-4297)*

Joint Development & Hsing Corp......... D 513 381-8696
  Cincinnati *(G-2919)*

National Housing Corporation.............. E 614 481-8106
  Columbus *(G-6299)*

Schroeder Company............................ E 419 473-3139
  Perrysburg *(G-12368)*

Snavely Building Company.................. E 440 585-9091
  Chagrin Falls *(G-1966)*

Titan Reinforcing LLC......................... E 513 539-4000
  Monroe *(G-11352)*

Towne Building Group Inc.................... D 513 381-8696
  Cincinnati *(G-3488)*

Woda Construction Inc........................ E 614 396-3200
  Columbus *(G-6900)*

CONSTRUCTION: Athletic & Recreation Facilities

Welty Building Company Ltd................ D 216 931-2400
  Cleveland *(G-5130)*

CONSTRUCTION: Bridge

A P OHoro Company............................ D 330 759-9317
  Youngstown *(G-15539)*

Aecom Energy & Cnstr Inc................... E 216 622-2300
  Cleveland *(G-3771)*

Armstrong Steel Erectors Inc............... E 740 345-4503
  Newark *(G-11689)*

Brumbaugh Construction Inc................ E 937 692-5107
  Arcanum *(G-453)*

Clayton Railroad Cnstr LLC................. E 937 549-2952
  West Union *(G-14867)*

Colas Solutions LLC............................ B 513 272-5648
  Cincinnati *(G-2472)*

Complete General Cnstr Co................. C 614 258-9515
  Columbus *(G-5677)*

Eagle Bridge Co................................... D 937 492-5654
  Sidney *(G-13030)*

ESwagner Company Inc....................... D 419 691-8651
  Oregon *(G-12133)*

J & J Schlaegel Inc.............................. E 937 652-2045
  Urbana *(G-14309)*

Kokosing Construction Co Inc.............. D 740 694-6315
  Fredericktown *(G-8662)*

Kokosing Construction Co Inc.............. C 614 228-1029
  Westerville *(G-14993)*

MBC Holdings Inc................................ E 419 445-1015
  Archbold *(G-462)*

National Engrg & Contg Co.................. E 440 238-3331
  Cleveland *(G-4625)*

Ohio Bridge Corporation...................... C 740 432-6334
  Cambridge *(G-1578)*

Prus Construction Company................ C 513 321-7774
  Cincinnati *(G-3256)*

Righter Co Inc..................................... E 614 272-9700
  Columbus *(G-6588)*

Ruhlin Company................................... C 330 239-2800
  Sharon Center *(G-12989)*

Sunesis Construction Co...................... C 513 326-6000
  West Chester *(G-14770)*

Velotta Company.................................. E 330 239-1211
  Sharon Center *(G-12991)*

Vernon Nagel Inc.................................. D 419 592-3861
  Napoleon *(G-11534)*

Westpatrick Corp.................................. E 614 875-8200
  Urbancrest *(G-14327)*

CONSTRUCTION: Commercial & Office Building, New

A P & P Dev & Cnstr Co....................... E 330 833-8886
  Massillon *(G-10628)*

Adams-Robinson Enterprises Inc......... E 937 274-5318
  Dayton *(G-7155)*

Alvada Const Inc.................................. C 419 595-4224
  Findlay *(G-8508)*

American Prservation Bldrs LLC.......... D 216 236-2007
  Cleveland *(G-3806)*

Armcorp Construction Inc.................... D 419 778-7024
  Celina *(G-1916)*

Austin Building and Design Inc............ C 440 544-2600
  Cleveland *(G-3839)*

B & B Contrs & Developers Inc............ D 330 270-5020
  Youngstown *(G-15554)*

Bogner Construction Company............ D 330 262-6730
  Wooster *(G-15312)*

Bogner Corporation............................. D 330 262-6393
  Wooster *(G-15313)*

Bostleman Corp.................................... E
  Holland *(G-9281)*

Brexton Construction LLC................... E 614 441-4110
  Columbus *(G-5464)*

Brumbaugh Construction Inc................ E 937 692-5107
  Arcanum *(G-453)*

Bruns Construction Enterprises Inc...... E 937 339-2300
  Tipp City *(G-13653)*

Calvary Contracting Inc....................... E 937 754-0300
  Tipp City *(G-13654)*

Campbell Construction Inc................... D 330 262-5186
  Wooster *(G-15316)*

Canaan Companies Inc....................... E 419 842-8373
  Toledo *(G-13724)*

Cavanaugh Building Corporation......... D 330 753-6658
  Akron *(G-83)*

Chaney Roofing Maintenance Inc........ E 419 639-2761
  Clyde *(G-5199)*

Cintech Construction Inc..................... E 513 563-1991
  Cincinnati *(G-2447)*

Cleveland Construction Inc.................. C 440 255-8000
  Mason *(G-10539)*

Colaianni Construction Inc................... E 740 769-2362
  Dillonvale *(G-7869)*

Conger Construction Group Inc........... E 513 932-1206
  Lebanon *(G-9760)*

Corporate Cleaning Inc....................... E 614 203-6051
  Columbus *(G-5702)*

D & G Focht Construction Co.............. E 419 732-2412
  Port Clinton *(G-12522)*

DAG Construction Co Inc.................... E 513 542-8597
  Cincinnati *(G-2534)*

Dan Marchetta Cnstr Co Inc................ E 330 668-4800
  Akron *(G-131)*

Danis Building Construction Co........... E 513 984-9696
  Cincinnati *(G-2537)*

Danis Building Construction Co........... C 614 761-8385
  Columbus *(G-5739)*

Danis Building Construction Co........... E 937 228-1225
  Miamisburg *(G-11042)*

Davis Construction Management......... E 440 248-7770
  Cleveland *(G-4151)*

Ddw Consulting Inc............................. D 937 299-9920
  Moraine *(G-11403)*

Desalvo Construction Company........... E 330 759-8145
  Hubbard *(G-9321)*

SERVICES SECTION

CONSTRUCTION: Dams, Waterways, Docks & Other Marine

DKM Construction Inc .... E 740 289-3006
  Piketon *(G-12418)*

Donleys Inc .... D 216 524-6800
  Cleveland *(G-4178)*

DSV Builders Inc .... D 330 652-3784
  Niles *(G-11788)*

Dugan & Meyers Cnstr Svcs Ltd .... E 614 257-7430
  Columbus *(G-5258)*

Dugan & Meyers Industrial LLC .... D 513 539-4000
  Monroe *(G-11338)*

Dunlop and Johnston Inc .... E 330 220-2700
  Valley City *(G-14333)*

Dynamic Construction Inc .... D 740 927-8898
  Pataskala *(G-12273)*

Eckinger Construction Company .... E 330 453-2566
  Canton *(G-1744)*

Elford Inc .... C 614 488-4000
  Columbus *(G-5811)*

Equity Cnstr Solutions LLC .... E 614 802-2900
  Hilliard *(G-9195)*

Equity LLC .... D 614 802-2900
  Hilliard *(G-9196)*

Exxcel Project Management LLC .... E 614 621-4500
  Columbus *(G-5840)*

Feick Contractors Inc .... E 419 625-3241
  Sandusky *(G-12893)*

Ferguson Construction Company .... C 937 498-2381
  Sidney *(G-13032)*

Fiorilli Construction Co Inc .... E 216 696-5845
  Medina *(G-10836)*

Ford Development Corp .... D 513 772-1521
  Cincinnati *(G-2693)*

Fortney & Weygandt Inc .... E 440 716-4000
  North Olmsted *(G-11901)*

Fred Olivieri Construction Co .... C 330 494-1007
  North Canton *(G-11832)*

G J Goudreau & Co .... E 216 351-5233
  Cleveland *(G-4297)*

Geis Companies LLC .... C 330 528-3500
  Streetsboro *(G-13413)*

Grae-Con Construction Inc .... E 740 282-6830
  Steubenville *(G-13328)*

Greater Dayton Cnstr Ltd .... D 937 426-3577
  Beavercreek *(G-923)*

Gutknecht Construction Company .... E 614 532-5410
  Columbus *(G-5962)*

H A Dorsten Inc .... E 419 628-2327
  Minster *(G-11317)*

Hanlin-Rainaldi Construction .... E 614 436-4204
  Columbus *(G-5970)*

Hi-Five Development Svcs Inc .... E 513 336-9280
  Mason *(G-10561)*

Hummel Construction Company .... E 330 274-8584
  Ravenna *(G-12628)*

Ideal Company Inc .... E 937 836-8683
  Clayton *(G-3733)*

Ingle-Barr Inc .... D 740 702-6117
  Chillicothe *(G-2072)*

J & F Construction and Dev Inc .... E 419 562-6662
  Bucyrus *(G-1510)*

J D Williamson Cnstr Co Inc .... D 330 633-1258
  Tallmadge *(G-13596)*

Jhi Group Inc .... C 419 465-4611
  Monroeville *(G-11356)*

JJO Construction Inc .... E 216 347-7802
  Wickliffe *(G-15155)*

JLJI Enterprises Inc .... C 216 481-2175
  Euclid *(G-8351)*

John G Johnson Construction Co .... D 216 938-5050
  Cleveland *(G-4440)*

Kapp Construction Inc .... E 937 324-0134
  Springfield *(G-13262)*

Knoch Corporation .... D 330 244-1440
  Solon *(G-13104)*

Kokosing Construction Co Inc .... C 614 228-1029
  Westerville *(G-14993)*

Kokosing Mosser Joint Venture .... C 740 848-4955
  Westerville *(G-14996)*

Krumroy-Cozad Cnstr Corp .... E 330 376-4136
  Akron *(G-217)*

L Brands Store Dsign Cnstr Inc .... C 614 415-7000
  Columbus *(G-6131)*

L R G Inc .... D 937 890-0510
  Dayton *(G-7447)*

Lathrop Company Inc .... E 419 893-7000
  Toledo *(G-13882)*

Lincoln Construction Inc .... E 614 457-6015
  Columbus *(G-6166)*

Lm Constrction Trry Lvrini Inc .... E 740 695-9604
  Saint Clairsville *(G-12797)*

Long & Wilcox LLC .... E 614 273-3100
  Worthington *(G-15433)*

Mark-L Inc .... E 614 863-8832
  Gahanna *(G-8722)*

McKnight Development Corp .... E 614 875-1689
  Grove City *(G-8933)*

MCR Services Inc .... E 614 421-0860
  Columbus *(G-6219)*

Megen Construction Company Inc .... E 513 742-9191
  Cincinnati *(G-3036)*

Messer Construction Co .... C 513 672-5000
  Cincinnati *(G-3049)*

Messer Construction Co .... C 614 275-0141
  Columbus *(G-6228)*

Messer Construction Co .... E 937 291-1300
  Dayton *(G-7482)*

Midwest Contracting Inc .... E 419 866-4560
  Holland *(G-9297)*

Miles-Mcclellan Cnstr Co Inc .... E 614 487-7744
  Columbus *(G-6248)*

Miller Contracting Group Inc .... E 419 453-3825
  Ottoville *(G-12198)*

Miller Industrial Svc Team Inc .... D 513 877-2708
  Pleasant Plain *(G-12500)*

Monarch Construction Company .... C 513 351-6900
  Cincinnati *(G-3077)*

Mosser Construction Inc .... E 419 861-5100
  Maumee *(G-10749)*

Mosser Construction Inc .... C 419 334-3801
  Fremont *(G-8694)*

Murphy Contracting Co .... E 330 743-8915
  Youngstown *(G-15671)*

National Housing Corporation .... E 614 481-8106
  Columbus *(G-6299)*

Ozanne Construction Co Inc .... E 216 696-2876
  Cleveland *(G-4712)*

Pepper Cnstr Co Ohio LLC .... E 513 563-7700
  Blue Ash *(G-1221)*

Peterson Construction Company .... C 419 941-2233
  Wapakoneta *(G-14489)*

R L Fender Construction Co .... E 937 258-9604
  Dayton *(G-7576)*

R L Fortney Management Inc .... D 440 716-4000
  North Olmsted *(G-11912)*

Reece-Campbell Inc .... D 513 542-4600
  Cincinnati *(G-3279)*

Renier Construction Corp .... E 614 866-4580
  Columbus *(G-6578)*

Restaurant Specialties Inc .... E 614 885-9707
  Sunbury *(G-13524)*

Robertson Cnstr Svcs Inc .... D 740 929-1000
  Heath *(G-9137)*

Robins & Morton Corporation .... E 419 660-2980
  Norwalk *(G-12025)*

Romanelli & Hughes Building Co .... E 614 891-1042
  Westerville *(G-15013)*

Ruhlin Company .... C 330 239-2800
  Sharon Center *(G-12989)*

Ruscilli Construction Co Inc .... D 614 876-9484
  Dublin *(G-8111)*

Rycon Construction Inc .... C 440 481-3770
  Parma *(G-12264)*

Schirmer Construction Co .... E 440 716-4900
  North Olmsted *(G-11914)*

Schnippel Construction Inc .... E 937 693-3831
  Botkins *(G-1300)*

Schumacher Development Inc .... D 513 777-9800
  West Chester *(G-14762)*

Setterlin Building Company .... E 614 459-7077
  Columbus *(G-6666)*

Shook Construction Co .... D 937 276-6666
  Moraine *(G-11438)*

Shook National Corporation .... C 937 276-6666
  Dayton *(G-7617)*

Site Worx LLC .... D 513 229-0295
  Lebanon *(G-9789)*

Smoot Construction Co Ohio .... E 614 253-9000
  Columbus *(G-6691)*

Snavely Building Company .... E 440 585-9091
  Chagrin Falls *(G-1966)*

Star Builders Inc .... E 440 986-5951
  Amherst *(G-434)*

Stockmeister Enterprises Inc .... E 740 286-1619
  Jackson *(G-9525)*

Studer-Obringer Inc .... E 419 492-2121
  New Washington *(G-11683)*

T O J Inc .... E 440 352-1900
  Mentor *(G-11002)*

The Apostolos Group Inc .... C 330 670-9900
  Copley *(G-6966)*

The Galehouse Companies Inc .... E 330 658-2023
  Doylestown *(G-7916)*

Transamerica Building Co .... E 614 457-8322
  Columbus *(G-6783)*

Turner Construction Company .... C 513 721-4224
  Cincinnati *(G-3536)*

Turner Construction Company .... E 216 522-1180
  Cleveland *(G-5041)*

Turner Construction Company .... D 614 984-3000
  Columbus *(G-6794)*

Tusing Builders Ltd .... E 419 465-3100
  Monroeville *(G-11359)*

Tuttle Construction Inc .... C 419 228-6262
  Lima *(G-9974)*

Ulliman Schutte Cnstr LLC .... E 937 247-0375
  Miamisburg *(G-11099)*

Universal Contracting Corp .... E 513 482-2700
  Cincinnati *(G-3561)*

Wallick Construction Co .... E 614 863-4640
  Reynoldsburg *(G-12680)*

Wallick Construction LLC .... E 614 863-4640
  New Albany *(G-11590)*

Weaver Custom Homes Inc .... E 330 264-5444
  Wooster *(G-15385)*

Welty Building Company Ltd .... E 330 867-2400
  Fairlawn *(G-8503)*

West Roofing Systems Inc .... E 800 356-5748
  Lagrange *(G-9652)*

Whiting-Turner Contracting Co .... D 614 459-6515
  Columbus *(G-6888)*

CONSTRUCTION: Dams, Waterways, Docks & Other Marine

Aecom Energy & Cnstr Inc .... E 216 622-2300
  Cleveland *(G-3771)*

CONSTRUCTION: Dams, Waterways, Docks & Other Marine

Kokosing Industrial Inc .... D 614 212-5700
　Westerville *(G-14995)*
Sunesis Environmental LLC .... D 513 326-6000
　Fairfield *(G-8444)*

CONSTRUCTION: Elevated Highway

Fryman-Kuck General Contrs Inc .... E 937 274-2892
　Dayton *(G-7371)*

CONSTRUCTION: Food Prdts Manufacturing or Packing Plant

Refrigeration Systems Company .... D 614 263-0913
　Columbus *(G-6571)*
Symba & Snap Gourmet Foods Inc .... E 407 252-9581
　Cleveland *(G-4972)*
York Street Fresh Foods LLC .... E 201 868-9088
　Cincinnati *(G-3685)*

CONSTRUCTION: Gas Main

Fishel Company .... E 937 233-2268
　Dayton *(G-7355)*
KS Energy Services LLC .... C 513 271-0276
　Cincinnati *(G-2955)*

CONSTRUCTION: Heavy Highway & Street

A P OHoro Company .... D 330 759-9317
　Youngstown *(G-15539)*
Central Allied Enterprises Inc .... E 330 477-6751
　Canton *(G-1706)*
City of Cuyahoga Falls .... E 330 971-8030
　Cuyahoga Falls *(G-7060)*
Colas Solutions LLC .... B 513 272-5648
　Cincinnati *(G-2472)*
Cook Paving and Cnstr Co .... E 216 267-7705
　Independence *(G-9424)*
County of Delaware .... C 740 833-2400
　Delaware *(G-7788)*
County of Shelby .... D 937 498-7244
　Sidney *(G-13026)*
Fabrizi Trucking & Pav Co Inc .... D 440 234-1284
　Cleveland *(G-4233)*
Nickolas M Savko & Sons Inc .... C 614 451-2242
　Columbus *(G-6359)*
Pavement Prtners Cncinnati LLC .... E 513 367-0250
　Harrison *(G-9113)*
Pike County .... E 740 947-9339
　Waverly *(G-14615)*
R D Jergens Contractors Inc .... D 937 669-9799
　Vandalia *(G-14391)*
Tab Construction Company Inc .... E 330 454-5228
　Canton *(G-1868)*
The Beaver Excavating Co .... A 330 478-2151
　Canton *(G-1871)*
Township of Copley .... E 330 666-1853
　Copley *(G-6967)*
Trucco Construction Co Inc .... C 740 417-9010
　Delaware *(G-7831)*
Wmog Inc .... E 419 334-3801
　Fremont *(G-8709)*

CONSTRUCTION: Indl Buildings, New, NEC

Adena Corporation .... C 419 529-4456
　Ontario *(G-12096)*
Aecom Energy & Cnstr Inc .... E 216 622-2300
　Cleveland *(G-3771)*
Austin Building and Design Inc .... C 440 544-2600
　Cleveland *(G-3839)*
Ayrshire Inc .... E 440 286-9507
　Chardon *(G-1994)*
B & B Contrs & Developers Inc .... D 330 270-5020
　Youngstown *(G-15554)*

Beem Construction Inc .... E 937 693-3176
　Botkins *(G-1298)*
Bruns Construction Enterprises Inc .... E 937 339-2300
　Tipp City *(G-13653)*
Burkshire Construction Company .... E 440 885-9700
　Cleveland *(G-3911)*
Butt Construction Company Inc .... E 937 426-1313
　Dayton *(G-7127)*
Canaan Companies Inc .... E 419 842-8373
　Toledo *(G-13724)*
Cavanaugh Building Corporation .... D 330 753-6658
　Akron *(G-83)*
Central Ohio Building Co Inc .... E 614 475-6392
　Columbus *(G-5536)*
D & G Focht Construction Co .... E 419 732-2412
　Port Clinton *(G-12522)*
Davis Construction Management .... E 440 248-7770
　Cleveland *(G-4151)*
Ddw Consulting Inc .... D 937 299-9920
　Moraine *(G-11403)*
Delventhal Company .... E 419 244-5570
　Millbury *(G-11267)*
Desalvo Construction Company .... E 330 759-8145
　Hubbard *(G-9321)*
Diaz Construction Inc .... E 740 289-4898
　Piketon *(G-12417)*
Dugan & Meyers Cnstr Svcs Ltd .... E 614 257-7430
　Columbus *(G-5258)*
Dugan & Meyers LLC .... D 513 891-4300
　Blue Ash *(G-1164)*
Elford Inc .... C 614 488-4000
　Columbus *(G-5811)*
Equity Cnstr Solutions LLC .... E 614 802-2900
　Hilliard *(G-9195)*
Equity LLC .... D 614 802-2900
　Hilliard *(G-9196)*
Exxcel Project Management LLC .... E 614 621-4500
　Columbus *(G-5840)*
Ferguson Construction Company .... E 937 274-1173
　Dayton *(G-7350)*
Ferguson Construction Company .... C 937 498-2381
　Sidney *(G-13032)*
Fortney & Weygandt Inc .... E 440 716-4000
　North Olmsted *(G-11901)*
Geiger Brothers Inc .... B 740 286-0800
　Jackson *(G-9518)*
H A Dorsten Inc .... E 419 628-2327
　Minster *(G-11317)*
Head Inc .... E 614 338-8501
　Columbus *(G-5975)*
Hume Supply Inc .... E 419 991-5751
　Lima *(G-9992)*
Imhoff Construction Svcs Inc .... E 330 683-4498
　Orrville *(G-12166)*
Knoch Corporation .... D 330 244-1440
　Solon *(G-13104)*
Kokosing Construction Co Inc .... C 614 228-1029
　Westerville *(G-14993)*
McKnight Development Corp .... E 614 875-1689
　Grove City *(G-8933)*
Mel Lanzer Co .... E 419 592-2801
　Napoleon *(G-11528)*
Miles-Mcclellan Cnstr Co Inc .... E 614 487-7744
　Columbus *(G-6248)*
Mosser Construction Inc .... E 419 861-5100
　Maumee *(G-10749)*
Mosser Construction Inc .... C 419 334-3801
　Fremont *(G-8694)*
Murphy Contracting Co .... E 330 743-2915
　Youngstown *(G-15671)*
Nicolozakes Trckg & Cnstr Inc .... E 740 432-5648
　Cambridge *(G-1577)*

Norris Brothers Co Inc .... C 216 771-2233
　Cleveland *(G-4647)*
R L Fender Construction Co .... E 937 258-9604
　Dayton *(G-7576)*
Rudolph Libbe Inc .... C 419 241-5000
　Walbridge *(G-14464)*
Ruhlin Company .... C 330 239-2800
　Sharon Center *(G-12989)*
Ruscilli Construction Co Inc .... D 614 876-9484
　Dublin *(G-8111)*
Schirmer Construction Co .... E 440 716-4900
　North Olmsted *(G-11914)*
Schnippel Construction Inc .... C 937 693-3831
　Botkins *(G-1300)*
Shook National Corporation .... C 937 276-6666
　Dayton *(G-7617)*
Simmons Brothers Corporation .... E 330 722-1415
　Medina *(G-10889)*
Ssoe Systems Inc .... D 419 255-3830
　Toledo *(G-14024)*
Standard Contg & Engrg Inc .... D 440 243-1001
　Brookpark *(G-1440)*
Testa Enterprises Inc .... E 330 926-9060
　Cuyahoga Falls *(G-7105)*
The Apostolos Group Inc .... C 330 670-9900
　Copley *(G-6966)*
Turner Construction Company .... C 513 721-4224
　Cincinnati *(G-3536)*
Tuttle Construction Inc .... C 419 228-6262
　Lima *(G-9974)*
Universal Contracting Corp .... E 513 482-2700
　Cincinnati *(G-3561)*
Williams Bros Builders Inc .... E 440 365-3261
　Elyria *(G-8301)*
Wmog Inc .... E 419 334-3801
　Fremont *(G-8709)*

CONSTRUCTION: Indl Plant

Babcock & Wilcox Company .... A 330 753-4511
　Akron *(G-59)*
Danis Companies .... B 937 228-1225
　Miamisburg *(G-11043)*
ISI Systems Inc .... E 740 942-0050
　Cadiz *(G-1541)*
Jack Gibson Construction Co .... D 330 394-5280
　Warren *(G-14530)*
KHD Company LLC .... E 614 935-9939
　Worthington *(G-15426)*
Pae & Associates Inc .... D 937 833-0013
　Dayton *(G-7544)*
Tri-America Contractors Inc .... E 740 574-0148
　Wheelersburg *(G-15134)*
Whiting-Turner Contracting Co .... B 440 449-9200
　Cleveland *(G-5145)*

CONSTRUCTION: Institutional Building

Aecom Energy & Cnstr Inc .... E 216 622-2300
　Cleveland *(G-3771)*
Butt Construction Company Inc .... E 937 426-1313
　Dayton *(G-7127)*
Central Ohio Building Co Inc .... E 614 475-6392
　Columbus *(G-5536)*
Head Inc .... E 614 338-8501
　Columbus *(G-5975)*
Imhoff Construction Svcs Inc .... E 330 683-4498
　Orrville *(G-12166)*
Mike Coates Cnstr Co Inc .... C 330 652-0190
　Niles *(G-11793)*

CONSTRUCTION: Land Preparation

Independence Excavating Inc .... E 216 524-1700
　Independence *(G-9437)*

SERVICES SECTION

CONSTRUCTION: Single-Family Housing

Petro Environmental Tech.................... E 513 489-6789
  Cincinnati *(G-3202)*
Royal Landscape Gardening Inc............ E 216 883-7000
  Cleveland *(G-4858)*
The Great Lakes Construction Co.......... C 330 220-3900
  Hinckley *(G-9272)*
Valley Mining Inc................................... C 740 922-3942
  Dennison *(G-7862)*

CONSTRUCTION: Oil & Gas Pipeline Construction

Buckeye Pipeline Cnstr Inc................... E 330 804-0101
  Wooster *(G-15315)*
J B Express Inc.................................... D 740 702-9830
  Chillicothe *(G-2075)*
Mid-Ohio Pipeline Company Inc............ E 419 884-3772
  Mansfield *(G-10298)*
Minnesota Limited LLC........................ C 330 343-4612
  Dover *(G-7894)*
US Tank Alliance Inc............................ D 440 238-7705
  Strongsville *(G-13494)*
Vallejo Company.................................. E 216 741-3933
  Cleveland *(G-5096)*
Welded Construction LP....................... E 419 874-3548
  Perrysburg *(G-12386)*

CONSTRUCTION: Pharmaceutical Manufacturing Plant

Liebel-Flarsheim Company LLC............ C 513 761-2700
  Cincinnati *(G-2975)*

CONSTRUCTION: Pipeline, NEC

AAA Flexible Pipe Clg Corp................... E 216 341-2900
  Cleveland *(G-3755)*
Aecom Energy & Cnstr Inc................... E 216 622-2300
  Cleveland *(G-3771)*
Bolt Construction Inc........................... D 330 549-0349
  Youngstown *(G-15561)*
Kirk Williams Piping & Plbg Co.............. E 614 875-9023
  Grove City *(G-8932)*
Mid-Ohio Contracting Inc..................... E 330 343-2925
  Dover *(G-7893)*
Miller Pipeline LLC.............................. B 937 506-8837
  Tipp City *(G-13663)*
Quality Lines Inc.................................. C 740 815-1165
  Findlay *(G-8580)*
R & R Pipeline Inc............................... E 740 345-3692
  Newark *(G-11744)*

CONSTRUCTION: Power & Communication Transmission Tower

Broadband Express LLC....................... D 419 536-9127
  Toledo *(G-13718)*
J Daniel & Company Inc....................... D 513 575-3100
  Loveland *(G-10143)*
Thayer Pwr Comm Line Cnstr LLC........ D 330 922-4950
  Cuyahoga Falls *(G-7106)*
Thayer Pwr Comm Line Cnstr LLC........ E 740 927-0021
  Pataskala *(G-12278)*

CONSTRUCTION: Power Plant

Babcock & Wilcox Cnstr Co LLC............ D 330 753-9750
  Akron *(G-58)*
Enerfab LLC.. B 513 641-0500
  Cincinnati *(G-2620)*
Siemens Energy Inc............................. E 740 393-8897
  Mount Vernon *(G-11508)*

CONSTRUCTION: Railroad & Subway

ESwagner Company Inc........................ D 419 691-8651
  Oregon *(G-12133)*

CONSTRUCTION: Residential, Nec

Cbtk Group Inc.................................... E 330 359-9111
  Dundee *(G-8168)*
Central Ohio Contractors Inc................ D 740 369-7700
  Delaware *(G-7784)*
Cristo Homes...................................... E 513 755-0570
  West Chester *(G-14680)*
Danis Industrial Cnstr Co..................... D 937 228-1225
  Miamisburg *(G-11044)*
Fabrizi Trucking & Pav Co Inc............... D 440 277-0127
  Lorain *(G-10074)*
Fairfield Homes Inc.............................. C 614 873-3533
  Plain City *(G-12477)*
Forest City Residential Dev.................. E 440 888-8664
  Cleveland *(G-4274)*
Greater Dayton Cnstr Ltd..................... D 937 426-3577
  Beavercreek *(G-923)*
Installed Building Pdts Inc................... C 614 221-3399
  Columbus *(G-6057)*
L R G Inc.. D 937 890-0510
  Dayton *(G-7447)*
Long & Wilcox LLC.............................. E 614 273-3100
  Worthington *(G-15433)*
Mv Residential Cnstr LLC..................... A 513 588-1000
  Cincinnati *(G-3093)*
Oberer Development Co....................... E 937 910-0851
  Miamisburg *(G-11077)*
Oberer Residential Cnstr Ltd................ D 937 278-0851
  Miamisburg *(G-11078)*
Otterbein Homes.................................. B 513 933-5400
  Lebanon *(G-9781)*
Pivotek LLC.. E 513 372-6205
  Milford *(G-11250)*
Rockford Homes Inc............................ D 614 785-0015
  Columbus *(G-5281)*
Taylor Companies Ohio Inc................... E 330 677-8380
  Kent *(G-9602)*
Transcon Builders Inc.......................... E 440 439-3400
  Cleveland *(G-5030)*

CONSTRUCTION: Scaffolding

Waco Scaffolding & Equipment Inc........ A 216 749-8900
  Cleveland *(G-5119)*

CONSTRUCTION: Sewer Line

A P OHoro Company............................ D 330 759-9317
  Youngstown *(G-15539)*
Adleta Inc... E 513 554-1469
  Cincinnati *(G-2145)*
Cook Paving and Cnstr Co.................... E 216 267-7705
  Independence *(G-9424)*
Darby Creek Excavating Inc................. D 740 477-8600
  Circleville *(G-3706)*
Degen Excavating Inc.......................... D 419 225-6871
  Lima *(G-9884)*
ESwagner Company Inc........................ D 419 691-8651
  Oregon *(G-12133)*
George J Igel & Co Inc......................... A 614 445-8421
  Columbus *(G-5928)*
H M Miller Construction Co.................. D 330 628-4811
  Mogadore *(G-11327)*
Jack Conie & Sons Corp....................... E 614 291-5931
  Columbus *(G-6080)*
Kokosing Construction Co Inc............... C 614 228-1029
  Westerville *(G-14993)*
Mike Enyart & Sons Inc........................ D 740 523-0235
  South Point *(G-13181)*
National Engrg & Contg Co................... E 440 238-3331
  Cleveland *(G-4625)*

Nerone & Sons Inc.............................. E 216 662-2235
  Cleveland *(G-4635)*
Rla Utilities LLC.................................. E 513 554-1470
  Cincinnati *(G-3308)*
Sunesis Environmental LLC.................. D 513 326-6000
  Fairfield *(G-8444)*
The Beaver Excavating Co.................... A 330 478-2151
  Canton *(G-1871)*
Wenger Excavating Inc........................ E 330 837-4767
  Dalton *(G-7122)*
Zemba Bros Inc................................... E 740 452-1880
  Zanesville *(G-15844)*

CONSTRUCTION: Single-Family Housing

50 X 20 Holding Company Inc.............. E 330 865-4663
  Akron *(G-7)*
Buckeye Cmnty Hope Foundation......... D 614 942-2014
  Columbus *(G-5474)*
Cahill Cnstr Inc Cahill Cnstr................ E 614 442-8570
  Columbus *(G-5492)*
Cbtk Group Inc.................................... E 330 359-9111
  Dundee *(G-8168)*
Cleveland Construction Inc.................. C 440 255-8000
  Mason *(G-10539)*
Combs Interior Specialties Inc.............. D 937 879-2047
  Fairborn *(G-8369)*
Construction Mechanics Inc................. C 330 630-9239
  Akron *(G-122)*
Construction One Inc........................... D 614 235-0057
  Columbus *(G-5685)*
Cricket Construction Ltd...................... E 330 536-8773
  Lowellville *(G-10167)*
Danessa Construction Llc.................... D 330 219-1212
  Niles *(G-11787)*
Design Homes & Development Co......... E 937 438-3667
  Dayton *(G-7311)*
Double Z Construction Company........... D 614 274-9334
  Columbus *(G-5783)*
Dublin Building Systems Co.................. E 614 760-5831
  Dublin *(G-7989)*
Einheit Electric Co............................... E 216 661-6000
  Independence *(G-9429)*
Evans Construction.............................. E 330 305-9355
  North Canton *(G-11829)*
Ferguson Construction Company........... E 614 876-8496
  Columbus *(G-5855)*
Fms Construction Company.................. E 330 225-9320
  North Royalton *(G-11940)*
G & G Concrete Cnstr LLC.................... E 614 475-4151
  Columbus *(G-5903)*
GCI Construction LLC.......................... E 216 831-6100
  Beachwood *(G-794)*
Gentlebrook Inc................................... C 740 545-7487
  West Lafayette *(G-14856)*
Goettle Co.. D 513 825-8100
  Cincinnati *(G-2737)*
Great Lakes Companies Inc.................. D 513 554-0720
  Cincinnati *(G-2762)*
Home Green Home Inc......................... E 513 900-1702
  Cincinnati *(G-2838)*
Hoppes Construction LLC..................... D 580 310-0090
  Malvern *(G-10234)*
Knose Concrete Constructn Inc............ E 513 738-8200
  Hamilton *(G-9058)*
Lei Cbus LLC...................................... E 614 302-8830
  Worthington *(G-15432)*
Level Up Custom Cnstr Inc................... E 888 505-9676
  Cleveland *(G-4491)*
M M Construction................................. E 513 553-0106
  Bethel *(G-1093)*
Miller Contracting Group Inc................ E 419 453-3825
  Ottoville *(G-12198)*

Employee Codes: A=Over 500 employees, B=251-500
C=101-250, D=51-100, E=20-50, F=10-19, G=1-9

CONSTRUCTION: Single-Family Housing

Moyer Industries Inc..................................D 937 832-7283
  Clayton *(G-3736)*
North Bay Construction Inc...................E 440 835-1898
  Westlake *(G-15085)*
O C I Construction Co Inc.....................E 440 338-3166
  Novelty *(G-12040)*
Oberer Development Co.........................E 937 910-0851
  Miamisburg *(G-11077)*
Pirhl Contractors LLC............................E 216 378-9690
  Cleveland *(G-4751)*
Registered Contractors Inc...................E 440 205-0873
  Mentor *(G-10990)*
Retail Renovations Inc..........................E 330 334-4501
  Wadsworth *(G-14449)*
Schmidt Builders Inc.............................E 513 779-9300
  Cincinnati *(G-3348)*
Shoemaker Masonry Cnstr LLC..........E 989 948-2377
  Cleves *(G-5195)*
Skilkengold Development LLC............E 614 418-3100
  Columbus *(G-6685)*
Stiner and Sons Cnstr Inc.....................E 440 775-2345
  Oberlin *(G-12076)*
Strawser Construction Inc....................C 513 874-6192
  Hamilton *(G-9083)*
Tusing Builders Ltd...............................E 419 465-3100
  Monroeville *(G-11359)*
Vibo Construction Inc...........................E 614 210-6780
  Dublin *(G-8155)*
Wegman Company.................................D 513 381-1111
  Cincinnati *(G-3645)*
Zeigler Habilitation Homes Inc............E 419 973-7629
  Toledo *(G-14118)*

CONSTRUCTION: Single-family Housing, New

50 X 20 Holding Company Inc............E 740 238-4262
  Belmont *(G-1053)*
50 X 20 Holding Company Inc............D 330 478-4500
  Canton *(G-1650)*
Ackermann Enterprises Inc.................D 513 842-3100
  Cincinnati *(G-2141)*
Alexander and Bebout Inc....................E 419 238-9567
  Van Wert *(G-14339)*
American Suncraft Co Inc.....................E 937 849-9475
  Medway *(G-10907)*
Bruns Construction Entps LLC...........E 419 586-9367
  Celina *(G-1917)*
C V Perry & Co......................................E 614 221-4131
  Columbus *(G-5490)*
Cavalear Corporation............................E 419 882-7125
  Sylvania *(G-13538)*
Dan Marchetta Cnstr Co Inc................E 330 668-4800
  Akron *(G-131)*
David W Milliken....................................E 740 998-5023
  Frankfort *(G-8629)*
Dold Homes Inc.....................................E 419 874-2535
  Perrysburg *(G-12334)*
Doyle Ja Corporation............................E 419 705-1091
  Whitehouse *(G-15141)*
Dutch Valley Home Inc.........................C 330 273-8322
  Hinckley *(G-9269)*
Greater Dayton Cnstr Ltd.....................D 937 426-3577
  Beavercreek *(G-923)*
H & H Custom Homes LLC..................E 419 994-4070
  Loudonville *(G-10109)*
Hoge Lumber Company........................E 419 753-2263
  New Knoxville *(G-11617)*
Homes America Inc...............................E 614 848-8551
  Columbus *(G-6004)*
Homewood Corporation.......................C 614 898-7200
  Columbus *(G-6007)*

J & W Enterprises Inc..........................E 740 774-4500
  Chillicothe *(G-2074)*
Justin Doyle Homes..............................E 513 623-1418
  Mason *(G-10570)*
K Hovnanian Summit Homes LLC.......E 330 454-4048
  Canton *(G-1788)*
Kopf Construction Corporation...........D 440 933-6908
  Avon Lake *(G-680)*
M/I Financial Corp.................................E 614 418-8700
  Columbus *(G-6185)*
M/I Homes Central Ohio LLC...............E 614 418-8000
  Columbus *(G-6187)*
M/I Homes Service LLC........................E 614 418-8300
  Columbus *(G-6188)*
Marous Brothers Cnstr Inc..................B 440 951-3904
  Willoughby *(G-15211)*
Nicholson Builders Inc.........................E 614 846-7388
  Columbus *(G-6358)*
Nvr Inc..E 440 232-5534
  Bedford *(G-977)*
Nvr Inc..E 740 548-0136
  Westerville *(G-14917)*
Oberer Residential Cnstr Ltd...............D 937 278-0851
  Miamisburg *(G-11078)*
Oster Services LLC..............................E 440 596-8489
  Lakewood *(G-9680)*
Robert Lucke Homes Inc......................E 513 683-3300
  Cincinnati *(G-3313)*
Rockford Homes Inc.............................D 614 785-0015
  Columbus *(G-5281)*
Romanelli & Hughes Building Co.......E 614 891-2042
  Westerville *(G-15013)*
Snavely Building Company..................E 440 585-9091
  Chagrin Falls *(G-1966)*
Snavely Development Company.........E 440 585-9091
  Chagrin Falls *(G-1967)*
Society Handicapped Citz Medin........C 330 722-1710
  Medina *(G-10891)*
The Galehouse Companies Inc...........E 330 658-2023
  Doylestown *(G-7916)*
Towne Development Group Ltd..........E 513 381-8696
  Cincinnati *(G-3489)*
Trimat Construction Inc.......................E 740 388-9515
  Bidwell *(G-1106)*
Trinity Home Builders LLC..................E 614 898-7200
  Etna *(G-8331)*
Weaver Custom Homes Inc.................E 330 264-5444
  Wooster *(G-15385)*
Wh Midwest LLC...................................D 330 896-7611
  Uniontown *(G-14270)*
Woda Construction Inc........................E 614 396-3200
  Columbus *(G-6900)*

CONSTRUCTION: Street Sign Installation & Mntnce

A & A Safety Inc...................................E 513 943-6100
  Amelia *(G-409)*

CONSTRUCTION: Swimming Pools

Buckeye Pools Inc................................E 937 434-7916
  Dayton *(G-7203)*
Burnett Pools Inc..................................E 330 372-1725
  Cortland *(G-6968)*
High-Tech Pools Inc.............................E 440 979-5070
  North Olmsted *(G-11905)*
Metropolitan Pool Service Co..............E 216 741-9451
  Parma *(G-12257)*
Ohio Pools & Spas Inc.........................E 330 494-7755
  Canton *(G-1823)*
Patterson Pools LLC............................E 614 334-2629
  Plain City *(G-12489)*

CONSTRUCTION: Transmitting Tower, Telecommunication

American Power Tower LLC.................E 440 261-2245
  Jefferson *(G-9537)*
Custom Cable Construction Inc..........D 330 351-1207
  Canton *(G-1729)*
Sky Climber Twr Solutions LLC..........E 740 203-3900
  Delaware *(G-7826)*
Tri County Tower LLC..........................E 330 538-9874
  North Jackson *(G-11878)*

CONSTRUCTION: Warehouse

Koroseal Interior Products LLC..........C 855 753-5474
  Marietta *(G-10379)*

CONSTRUCTION: Waste Water & Sewage Treatment Plant

A P OHoro Company.............................D 330 759-9317
  Youngstown *(G-15539)*
Fryman-Kuck General Contrs Inc.......E 937 274-2892
  Dayton *(G-7371)*
Kokosing Construction Co Inc............C 614 228-1029
  Westerville *(G-14993)*
Peterson Construction Company........C 419 941-2233
  Wapakoneta *(G-14489)*
Platinum Restoration Inc.....................E 440 327-0699
  Elyria *(G-8286)*
Shook Construction Co........................D 937 276-6666
  Moraine *(G-11438)*
Shook National Corporation................C 937 276-6666
  Dayton *(G-7617)*

CONSTRUCTION: Water & Sewer Line

Fields Excavating Inc...........................D 740 532-1780
  Kitts Hill *(G-9647)*
Foill Inc..E 740 947-1117
  Waverly *(G-14613)*
J & J General Maintenance Inc...........D 740 533-9729
  Ironton *(G-9509)*

CONSULTING SVC: Business, NEC

Abdouni Enterprises LLC.....................E 419 345-6773
  Ottawa Hills *(G-12197)*
ABS Transitions LLC............................E 513 832-2884
  Cincinnati *(G-2136)*
Accenture LLP......................................C 216 685-1435
  Cleveland *(G-3760)*
Accenture LLP......................................C 614 629-2000
  Columbus *(G-5301)*
Actionlink LLC.......................................A 888 737-8757
  Akron *(G-15)*
Allendevaux & Company LLC..............E 937 657-1270
  Englewood *(G-8302)*
Altix Corporation...................................E 513 216-8386
  Mason *(G-10519)*
Apex Control Systems Inc...................D 330 938-2588
  Sebring *(G-12945)*
Apple Growth Partners Inc..................D 330 867-7350
  Akron *(G-53)*
Ardent Technologies Inc......................D 937 312-1345
  Dayton *(G-7178)*
Ashtabula Cnty Eductl Svc Ctr...........E 440 576-4085
  Ashtabula *(G-520)*
Avantia Inc...E 216 901-9366
  Cleveland *(G-3845)*
Bbs & Associates Inc...........................E 330 665-5227
  Akron *(G-63)*
Bechtold Enterprises Inc.....................E 440 791-7177
  Grafton *(G-8838)*

SERVICES SECTION
CONSULTING SVC: Human Resource

Benchmark National Corporation........... E 419 843-6691
  Bellevue (G-1043)
Blue Chip Consulting Group................... E 216 503-6000
  Independence (G-9411)
Boundless Strgc Resources Inc............. E 614 844-3800
  Worthington (G-15406)
Bowser-Morner Inc.................................. C 937 236-8805
  Dayton (G-7198)
Business Volunteers Unlimited............... E 216 736-7711
  Cleveland (G-3913)
Cardiosolution LLC................................. E 513 618-2394
  Blue Ash (G-1141)
Cash Flow Solutions Inc........................ D 513 524-2320
  Oxford (G-12205)
Cavu Group... E 937 429-2114
  Moraine (G-11396)
Cgh-Global Technologies LLC............... E 800 376-0655
  Cincinnati (G-2341)
Cmbf Products Inc................................ C 330 725-4941
  Medina (G-10824)
Colia Group LLC..................................... E 614 270-4545
  Columbus (G-5594)
Commcapp America Inc......................... E 678 780-0937
  Cleveland (G-4093)
Compass Clinical Consulting Co............ E 513 241-0142
  Cincinnati (G-2485)
Compmanagement Inc........................... E 440 546-7100
  Seven Hills (G-12954)
Corbus LLC... A 937 226-7724
  Dayton (G-7248)
Dancor Inc.. E 614 340-2155
  Columbus (G-5738)
Datavantage Corporation....................... B 440 498-4414
  Cleveland (G-4150)
Db Consulting Group Inc....................... D 216 433-5132
  Cleveland (G-4154)
Dedicated Technologies Inc.................. D 614 460-3200
  Columbus (G-5748)
Deemsys Inc... D 614 322-9928
  Gahanna (G-8715)
Deloitte & Touche LLP........................... B 513 784-7100
  Cincinnati (G-2556)
Deloitte Consulting LLP......................... E 937 223-8821
  Dayton (G-7309)
E Retailing Associates LLC.................... D 614 300-5785
  Columbus (G-5798)
Emprise Technologies LLC.................... E 419 720-6982
  Toledo (G-13791)
Enviroscience Inc.................................. D 330 688-0111
  Stow (G-13366)
Evergreen Cooperative Corp.................. B 216 268-5399
  Cleveland (G-4226)
Excellence In Motivation Inc................. C 763 445-3000
  Dayton (G-7341)
Fanning/Howey Associates Inc.............. E 419 586-2292
  Celina (G-1922)
Fass Management & Consulting L.......... E 330 405-0545
  Cleveland (G-4242)
First Choice Sourcing Solution............... E 419 359-4002
  Findlay (G-8532)
First Hospital Labs LLC.......................... C 215 396-5500
  Independence (G-9432)
For Impact Suddes Gro........................... E 614 352-2505
  Columbus (G-5877)
Geo Global Partners LLC....................... E 561 598-6000
  Aurora (G-613)
High Score Mentor LLC.......................... E 513 485-2848
  Cincinnati (G-2820)
Hinge Consulting LLC............................ E 513 404-1547
  Cincinnati (G-2827)
HPM America LLC................................. D 419 946-0222
  Mount Gilead (G-11461)

Humantics Innvtive Sltions Inc.............. C 567 265-5200
  Huron (G-9389)
Idillnire Cnslting Sltions LLC................. D 305 413-8522
  Cleveland (G-4402)
Illumination Works LLC......................... E 937 938-1321
  Beavercreek (G-884)
Impact Sales Solutions Inc................... E 419 466-0131
  Toledo (G-13861)
Informtion Applied Lrng Evltio............... C 214 329-9100
  Rootstown (G-12759)
Infoverity LLC... E 614 327-5173
  Dublin (G-8037)
Interex Inc.. E 646 905-0091
  Beachwood (G-803)
J V Enviroserve Limited Partnership....... E 216 642-1311
  Cleveland (G-4427)
Jubilee Limited Partnership.................... A 614 221-9200
  Columbus (G-6099)
Juice Technologies Inc.......................... E 800 518-5576
  Worthington (G-15424)
Kalogerou Enterprises Inc..................... D 330 544-9696
  Niles (G-11792)
Kemper Company................................... D 440 846-1100
  Strongsville (G-13468)
Landrum & Brown Incorporated............. E 513 530-5333
  Blue Ash (G-1198)
Leadfirstai LLC....................................... E 419 424-6647
  Findlay (G-8557)
Lifetime Value LLC................................. E 216 544-3215
  Cleveland (G-4493)
Logtec Inc.. C 937 878-8450
  Fairborn (G-8378)
Long Business Systems Inc................... E 440 846-8500
  Strongsville (G-13472)
Mannik & Smith Group Inc.................... E 419 891-2222
  Maumee (G-10744)
Modern Hire Inc..................................... E 216 292-0202
  Cleveland (G-4595)
Municipal Building Inspection................ C 440 399-0850
  Bedford Heights (G-999)
National Premier Protective.................... D 216 731-4000
  Euclid (G-8359)
Nor-Com LLC.. E 859 689-7451
  Cincinnati (G-3118)
Northcoast Consult LLC......................... E 440 291-8987
  Ashtabula (G-543)
Occupational Health Services................ E 937 492-7296
  Sidney (G-13042)
Ohio Utilities Protection Svc.................. D 800 311-3692
  North Jackson (G-11875)
Opocus... C 800 724-8802
  Worthington (G-15445)
Optum Infusion Svcs 550 LLC................ D 866 442-4679
  Cincinnati (G-3166)
Oxford Harriman & Co AM LLC.............. E 216 755-7150
  Beachwood (G-824)
P C Guru Inc.. E 216 292-4878
  Cleveland (G-4713)
Pdmi... D 330 757-0724
  Youngstown (G-15690)
Peq Services + Solutions Inc................ D 937 610-4800
  Miamisburg (G-11083)
Pg.. D 513 698-6901
  Mason (G-10592)
Price For Profit LLC............................... D 440 646-9490
  Cleveland (G-4771)
Profit Track Ltd..................................... E 330 848-2730
  Barberton (G-704)
Q4-2 Inc... E 440 256-3870
  Willoughby (G-15219)
Qwaide Enterprises LLC......................... E 614 209-0551
  New Albany (G-11583)

RJ Runge Company Inc.......................... E 419 740-5781
  Port Clinton (G-12539)
Romitech Inc... E 937 297-9529
  Franklin (G-8648)
Rsw/Us GP... E 513 898-0940
  Cincinnati (G-3328)
Setech Incorporated.............................. C 937 425-9482
  Moraine (G-11437)
Sk Food Group Inc................................ B 614 409-0666
  Groveport (G-9001)
Staffworks Group 2 Inc......................... E 419 515-0655
  Toledo (G-14028)
Stores Consulting Group LLC................ E 717 309-5302
  Wilmington (G-15274)
Strategy Network LLC........................... E 614 595-0688
  Columbus (G-6722)
Summit Solutions Inc............................ E 937 291-4333
  Dayton (G-7650)
Tata Consultancy Services Ltd.............. D 515 553-8300
  Cincinnati (G-2114)
Techsolve Inc.. D 513 948-2000
  Cincinnati (G-3449)
Uc Health Llc.. E 513 475-7630
  West Chester (G-14784)
Velosio LLC... E 614 280-9880
  Dublin (G-8150)
Workstate Consulting LLC..................... E 614 559-3904
  Columbus (G-6903)
Yashco Systems Inc.............................. D 614 467-4600
  Hilliard (G-9247)
Zappia Enterprises LLC......................... E 937 277-3010
  Dayton (G-7735)
Zone Safety LLC.................................... D 440 752-9545
  Columbia Station (G-5230)

CONSULTING SVC: Educational

Advanced Solutions For Educatn........... E 224 518-3111
  Mentor (G-10908)
Eastwood Local Schools........................ E 419 833-1196
  Bowling Green (G-1318)
Learning Spectrum Ltd.......................... E 614 844-5433
  Columbus (G-6151)
Metropltan Edctl Tchnical Assn............. C 740 389-4798
  Marion (G-10445)
Rainbow Station Day Care Inc............... E 614 759-8667
  Pickerington (G-12409)
Rainbow Station Day Care Inc............... E 614 575-5040
  Reynoldsburg (G-12674)

CONSULTING SVC: Financial Management

Critical Business Analysis Inc............... E 419 874-0800
  Perrysburg (G-12326)
Dco LLC... E 419 931-9086
  Perrysburg (G-12331)
Ensemble RCM LLC............................... A 704 765-3715
  Cincinnati (G-2624)
Hill Barth & King LLC............................ E 330 758-8613
  Canfield (G-1631)
J & P Asset Management Inc................. D 216 408-7693
  Akron (G-205)
Jmac Inc.. E 614 436-2418
  Columbus (G-6092)
Nms Wealth Management LLC............... E 440 286-5222
  Chardon (G-2013)
Richter & Associates Inc....................... D 216 593-7140
  Twinsburg (G-14217)
Walnut Ridge Strgc MGT Co LLC.......... D 234 678-3900
  Beachwood (G-851)
Westlake Ten Inc................................... E 440 250-9804
  Westlake (G-15124)

CONSULTING SVC: Human Resource

Company	Loc	Phone
4mybenefits Inc	E	513 891-6726
Blue Ash (G-1119)		
Acloche LLC	E	888 608-0889
Columbus (G-5306)		
Booz Allen Hamilton Inc	E	937 912-6400
Beavercreek (G-864)		
Careercurve LLC	D	800 314-8230
Cleveland (G-3928)		
Comprehensive Hr Solutions LLC	C	513 771-2277
Cincinnati (G-2488)		
Delphia Consulting LLC	E	614 421-2000
Columbus (G-5754)		
Devry University Inc	D	614 251-6969
Columbus (G-5759)		
Hr Butler LLC	E	614 923-2900
Dublin (G-8032)		
Modern Business Associates Inc	D	727 563-1500
Cleveland (G-4594)		
Safegard Bckgrund Screning LLC	E	877 700-7345
Beachwood (G-834)		
Sterling Check Corp	D	212 736-5100
Independence (G-9485)		
Sterling Infosystems Inc	B	212 736-5100
Independence (G-9486)		

CONSULTING SVC: Management

Company	Loc	Phone
Accelerant Technologies LLC	D	419 236-8768
Maumee (G-10684)		
Adroit Assoc Cnslting Svcs LLC	D	614 966-6925
Columbus (G-5315)		
Advanced Prgrm Resources Inc	E	614 761-9994
Dublin (G-7920)		
All In Staffing	E	330 315-1530
Parma (G-12248)		
ARC Healthcare LLC	E	888 552-0677
Worthington (G-15405)		
Armada Ltd	D	614 505-7256
Powell (G-12585)		
Austin Building and Design Inc	C	440 544-2600
Cleveland (G-3839)		
Avaap USA LLC	E	732 710-3425
Columbus (G-5409)		
Azimuth Corporation	D	937 256-8571
Beavercreek (G-861)		
Barium Holdings Company Inc	E	740 282-9776
Steubenville (G-13317)		
Baxter Hdell Dnnlly Prston Inc	C	513 271-1634
Cincinnati (G-2240)		
Belcap Inc	E	330 456-0031
Canton (G-1685)		
Burke Inc	C	513 241-5663
Cincinnati (G-2290)		
C H Dean LLC	D	937 222-9531
Beavercreek (G-867)		
Cbiz Inc	A	216 447-9000
Cleveland (G-3942)		
Cbiz Accnting Tax Advsory Wash	E	216 447-9000
Cleveland (G-3943)		
Cbiz Mhm Northern Cal LLC	E	216 447-9000
Cleveland (G-3944)		
Cha - Community Health Affairs	D	800 362-2628
Cleveland (G-3959)		
Clearsulting LLC	D	440 488-4274
Cleveland (G-4000)		
Clgt Solutions LLC	E	740 920-4795
Granville (G-8852)		
Commquest Services Inc	C	330 455-0374
Canton (G-1718)		
Cooper Adel Vu & Assoc Lpa	D	740 625-4220
Centerburg (G-1934)		
CPS Solutions LLC	C	901 748-0470
Dublin (G-7978)		
Crown Associates LLC	D	419 629-2220
New Bremen (G-11597)		
Dedicated Tech Services Inc	E	614 309-0059
Dublin (G-7986)		
Deloitte & Touche LLP	B	513 784-7100
Cincinnati (G-2556)		
Deloitte & Touche LLP	A	216 589-1300
Cleveland (G-4160)		
Deloitte & Touche LLP	E	937 223-8821
Dayton (G-7308)		
Deloitte Consulting LLP	E	937 223-8821
Dayton (G-7309)		
Diversified Systems Inc	E	614 476-9939
Westerville (G-14976)		
Djd Express Inc	D	740 676-7464
Shadyside (G-12969)		
Dms Inc	C	440 951-9838
Willoughby (G-15189)		
Engauge Holdings LLC	D	614 573-1010
Columbus (G-5819)		
EP Ferris & Associates Inc	E	614 299-2999
Columbus (G-5823)		
Fortune Brnds Wtr Innvtons LLC	D	440 962-2782
North Olmsted (G-11902)		
Gbq Consulting LLC	E	614 221-1120
Columbus (G-5919)		
Goken America LLC	D	614 495-8104
Dublin (G-8021)		
GP Strategies Corporation	E	513 583-8810
Cincinnati (G-2745)		
Grants Plus LLC	E	216 916-7376
Cleveland (G-4326)		
Greentree Group Inc	D	937 490-5500
Dayton (G-7388)		
H T V Industries Inc	D	216 514-0060
Cleveland (G-4345)		
Health and Safety Sciences LLC	E	513 488-1952
Fairfield Township (G-8462)		
Healthlinx Inc	E	614 542-2228
Columbus (G-5976)		
Henry Call Inc	C	216 433-5609
Cleveland (G-4358)		
Humanit Solutions LLC	D	937 901-7576
Beavercreek Township (G-941)		
Hyperion Companies Inc	B	949 309-2409
Columbus (G-6034)		
Innovative Technologies Corp	D	937 252-2145
Dayton (G-7135)		
Iotco LLC	E	877 464-6826
Cincinnati (G-2887)		
Island Hospitality MGT LLC	E	614 864-8844
Columbus (G-6075)		
Jyg Innovations LLC	D	937 630-3858
Dayton (G-7431)		
Kaleidoscope Prototyping LLC	E	513 206-9137
Blue Ash (G-1194)		
Knowledgeworks Foundation	E	513 929-4777
Cincinnati (G-2945)		
Level Seven	D	216 524-9055
Brecksville (G-1357)		
Levitan Enterprise LLC	D	628 208-7016
Toledo (G-13885)		
LLC A Haystack Mssion Essntial	D	614 750-1908
New Albany (G-11573)		
Manufacturing Advocacy & Gr	E	216 391-7002
Cleveland (G-4522)		
Marcus Thomas Llc	D	216 292-4900
Cleveland (G-4523)		
Matrix Claims Management LLC	D	513 351-1222
Cincinnati (G-3016)		
Med-Pass Incorporated	E	937 438-8884
Dayton (G-7476)		
Medco Health Solutions Inc	C	614 822-2000
Dublin (G-8061)		
Medpace	D	513 254-1232
Cincinnati (G-3030)		
Menard Inc	D	937 318-2831
Fairborn (G-8379)		
Mid-America Consulting Group Inc	D	
Cleveland (G-4574)		
Miracle Path Staffing Agcy Inc	E	234 205-3541
Fairlawn (G-8490)		
Nationwide Rtrment Sltions Inc	C	614 854-8300
Dublin (G-8072)		
Netsmart Technologies Inc	B	800 434-2642
Dublin (G-8074)		
Northwest Country Place Inc	C	440 488-2700
Mentor (G-10980)		
Ohio Custodial Maintenance	C	614 443-1232
Columbus (G-6399)		
Perduco Group Inc	E	937 401-0268
Beavercreek (G-893)		
Plus Management Services Inc	E	419 331-2273
Lima (G-9949)		
Quality Solutions Inc	E	440 933-9946
Cleveland (G-4801)		
Redwood Living Inc	C	216 360-9441
Maumee (G-10759)		
Remesh Inc	D	561 809-9885
Cleveland (G-4824)		
Residential HM Assn Marion Inc	C	740 387-9999
Marion (G-10451)		
Ringside Search Partners LLC	E	614 643-0700
Columbus (G-6589)		
RMS of Ohio Inc	C	440 617-6605
Westlake (G-15104)		
Safelite Solutions LLC	A	614 210-9000
Columbus (G-6633)		
Salesfuel Inc	D	614 794-0500
Westerville (G-14936)		
SEI - Cincinnati LLC	D	513 459-1992
Cincinnati (G-3354)		
Setech Incorporated	C	937 425-9482
Moraine (G-11437)		
Silver Spruce Holding LLC	E	937 259-1200
Dayton (G-7622)		
Skylight Financial Group LLC	D	513 579-8555
Cincinnati (G-3384)		
Ssoe Inc	B	419 255-3830
Toledo (G-14023)		
Tabco Consulting Services LLC	E	740 217-0010
Columbus (G-6745)		
Topre America Corporation	C	256 339-8407
Springfield (G-13302)		
Tower Real Estate Group LLC	A	216 520-1250
Beachwood (G-845)		
TPC and Thomas LLC	D	614 354-0717
Westerville (G-14943)		
Tyto Government Solutions Inc	E	937 306-3030
Beavercreek (G-911)		
University of Dayton	D	937 255-3141
Dayton (G-7692)		
University of Dayton	B	937 229-3913
Dayton (G-7693)		
William Thomas Group Inc	D	800 582-3107
Cincinnati (G-3672)		
Willowood Care Center	C	330 225-3156
Brunswick (G-1475)		
Worthington Public Library	C	614 807-2626
Worthington (G-15472)		

CONSULTING SVCS, BUSINESS: Energy Conservation

Aeroseal LLC... E 937 428-9300
Dayton *(G-7158)*

Aeroseal LLC... E 937 428-9300
Miamisburg *(G-11021)*

BHP Energy LLC.. B 866 720-2700
Walbridge *(G-14460)*

Eco Engineering Inc................................. D 513 985-8300
Cincinnati *(G-2604)*

Go Sustainable Energy LLC..................... E 614 268-4263
Worthington *(G-15417)*

Hercules Led LLC..................................... E 844 437-2533
Boardman *(G-1289)*

Melink Corporation................................... D 513 685-0958
Milford *(G-11242)*

Nationwide Energy Partners LLC............. E 614 918-2031
Columbus *(G-6328)*

Telco Pros Inc... E 877 244-0182
Cleveland *(G-4982)*

CONSULTING SVCS, BUSINESS: Environmental

3e Company Environmental Ecolo............ C 330 451-4900
Canton *(G-1647)*

Acrt Inc... E 800 622-2562
Stow *(G-13352)*

Aecom.. D 513 651-3440
Cincinnati *(G-2153)*

Allied Environmental Svcs Inc.................. E 419 227-4004
Lima *(G-9864)*

American Envmtl Group Ltd..................... B 330 659-5930
Richfield *(G-12685)*

Aptim Corp.. B 419 423-3526
Findlay *(G-8510)*

August Mack Environmental Inc.............. C 740 548-1500
Lewis Center *(G-9809)*

Bhe Environmental Inc............................. C
Cincinnati *(G-2260)*

Bjaam Environmental Inc......................... E 330 854-5300
Canal Fulton *(G-1593)*

Brownflynn Ltd... E 216 303-6000
Cleveland *(G-3906)*

Bureau Veritas North Amer Inc................ E 330 252-5100
Akron *(G-78)*

C & W Tank Cleaning Company.............. D 419 691-1995
Oregon *(G-12131)*

Coact Associates Ltd............................... E 866 646-4400
Toledo *(G-13747)*

Cwm Envronmental Cleveland LLC......... E 216 663-0808
Cleveland *(G-4147)*

Eagle Certification Group........................ D 937 293-2000
Dayton *(G-7321)*

Emergncy Rspnse Trning Sltons.............. E 440 349-2700
Solon *(G-13083)*

Envirnmntal Sltons Innvtons In................ E 513 451-1777
Cincinnati *(G-2626)*

Environmental Quality MGT..................... D 513 825-7500
Cincinnati *(G-2628)*

Gray & Pape Inc....................................... E 513 287-7700
Cincinnati *(G-2751)*

Guardian Environmental Inc.................... E 304 224-2011
North Olmsted *(G-11904)*

Haley & Aldrich Inc.................................. D 216 739-0555
Independence *(G-9435)*

Hzw Environmental Cons LLC................. E 800 804-8484
Mentor *(G-10950)*

Kemron Environmental Svcs Inc............. E 740 373-4071
Marietta *(G-10378)*

Lawhon and Associates Inc..................... E 614 481-8600
Columbus *(G-6145)*

Ohio State University................................ E 614 292-1284
Columbus *(G-6458)*

Superior Envmtl Solutions LLC................ D 937 593-0425
Bellefontaine *(G-1038)*

The Payne Firm Inc.................................. E 513 489-2255
Blue Ash *(G-1253)*

Ttl Associates Inc.................................... D 419 241-4556
Toledo *(G-14076)*

Valicor Environmental Svcs LLC.............. E 513 733-4666
Monroe *(G-11353)*

Verdantas LLC.. C 614 793-8777
Dublin *(G-8151)*

Wellert Corporation.................................. E 330 239-2699
Medina *(G-10901)*

CONSULTING SVCS, BUSINESS: Indl Development Planning

Big Red Rooster....................................... E 614 255-0200
Columbus *(G-5440)*

CONSULTING SVCS, BUSINESS: Safety Training Svcs

Life Safety Enterprises Inc...................... E 440 918-1641
Willoughby *(G-15205)*

Mission Essential Group LLC.................. D 614 416-2345
New Albany *(G-11574)*

Navigate360 LLC...................................... C 330 661-0106
Richfield *(G-12703)*

CONSULTING SVCS, BUSINESS: Sys Engnrg, Exc Computer/ Prof

Akkodis Inc... C 614 781-6070
Dublin *(G-7927)*

Centric Consulting LLC........................... D 888 781-7567
Dayton *(G-7220)*

Cohesion Consulting LLC........................ D 513 587-7700
Blue Ash *(G-1155)*

Controlsoft Inc... E 440 443-3900
Cleveland *(G-4113)*

Devcare Solutions Ltd............................. E 614 221-2277
Westerville *(G-14888)*

Ellipse Solutions LLC............................... E 937 312-1547
Dayton *(G-7334)*

Flexential Corp... E 513 645-2900
Hamilton *(G-9040)*

Jyg Innovations LLC................................ D 937 630-3858
Dayton *(G-7431)*

Sadler-Necamp Financial Svcs................ E 513 489-5477
Cincinnati *(G-3337)*

Sawdey Solution Services Inc................. E 937 490-4060
Beavercreek *(G-930)*

Sjn Data Center LLC................................ E 513 386-7871
Cincinnati *(G-3381)*

Wolcott Systems Group LLC................... E 330 666-5900
Akron *(G-363)*

CONSULTING SVCS, BUSINESS: Systems Analysis & Engineering

Humanit Solutions LLC............................ D 937 901-7576
Beavercreek Township *(G-941)*

Premise Solutions LLC............................. E 440 703-8200
Walton Hills *(G-14478)*

Solutons Thrugh Innvtive Tech................. D 937 320-9994
Beavercreek *(G-907)*

CONSULTING SVCS, BUSINESS: Testing, Educational Or Personnel

Clgt Solutions LLC................................... E 740 920-4795
Granville *(G-8852)*

Envision Corporation............................... D 513 772-5437
Cincinnati *(G-2630)*

Hhd Aviation LLC..................................... D 513 426-8378
Hamilton *(G-9052)*

CONSULTING SVCS: Scientific

Clinical Management Cons Inc................ D 440 638-5000
Cleveland *(G-4084)*

Mrl Materials Resources LLC................... E 937 531-6657
Xenia *(G-15528)*

Solutons Thrugh Innvtive Tech................. D 937 320-9994
Beavercreek *(G-907)*

CONTACT LENSES

Diversified Ophthalmics Inc..................... E 803 783-3454
Cincinnati *(G-2570)*

CONTAINERS: Food, Liquid Tight, Including Milk

Kerry Inc... E 760 685-2548
Byesville *(G-1535)*

CONTAINERS: Plastic

Hendrickson International Corp............... D 740 929-5600
Hebron *(G-9143)*

Plastics R Unique Inc.............................. E 330 334-4820
Wadsworth *(G-14448)*

CONTAINERS: Shipping, Bombs, Metal Plate

Industrial Repair and Mfg......................... E 419 822-4232
Delta *(G-7851)*

CONTAINERS: Wood

Brimar Packaging Inc.............................. E 440 934-3080
Avon *(G-641)*

CONTRACTOR: Dredging

Metropolitan Envmtl Svcs Inc.................. D 614 771-1881
Hilliard *(G-9213)*

CONTRACTOR: Framing

Contract Lumber Inc................................ C 740 964-3147
Pataskala *(G-12270)*

Metal Framing Enterprises LLC............... E 216 433-7080
Cleveland *(G-4558)*

CONTRACTOR: Rigging & Scaffolding

Janson Industries..................................... D 330 455-7029
Canton *(G-1783)*

CONTRACTORS: Acoustical & Ceiling Work

Fairfield Insul & Drywall LLC................... E 740 654-8811
Lancaster *(G-9715)*

Frank Novak & Sons Inc.......................... D 216 475-2495
Cleveland *(G-4285)*

J & B Acoustical Inc................................ D 419 884-1155
Mansfield *(G-10273)*

OK Interiors Corp..................................... C 513 742-3278
Cincinnati *(G-3153)*

T and D Interiors Incorporated................ E 419 331-4372
Lima *(G-9969)*

CONTRACTORS: Acoustical & Insulation Work

R E Kramig & Co Inc................................ C 513 761-4010
Cincinnati *(G-3270)*

CONTRACTORS: Artificial Turf Installation

CONTRACTORS: Asbestos Removal & Encapsulation

Motz Group Inc... E 513 533-6452
Cincinnati *(G-3081)*

CONTRACTORS: Asbestos Removal & Encapsulation

Allied Environmental Svcs Inc................... E 419 227-4004
Lima *(G-9864)*

Central Insulation Systems Inc................... E 513 242-0600
Cincinnati *(G-2336)*

Daniel A Terreri & Sons Inc...................... E 330 538-2950
Youngstown *(G-15591)*

Environmental Quality MGT....................... D 513 825-7500
Cincinnati *(G-2628)*

Lepi Enterprises Inc................................. D 740 453-2980
Zanesville *(G-15806)*

Pedersen Insulation Company................... E 614 471-3788
Columbus *(G-6508)*

Precision Environmental Co....................... B 216 642-6040
Independence *(G-9470)*

CONTRACTORS: Boiler Maintenance Contractor

Arise Incorporated.................................... E 440 746-8860
Brecksville *(G-1244)*

McPhillips Plbg Htg & AC Co..................... E 216 481-1400
Cleveland *(G-4542)*

Prout Boiler Htg & Wldg Inc...................... E 330 744-0293
Youngstown *(G-15699)*

CONTRACTORS: Building Site Preparation

Fortuna Construction Co Inc...................... E 440 892-3834
Cleveland *(G-4278)*

Rudzik Excavating Inc............................... E 330 755-1540
Struthers *(G-13503)*

CONTRACTORS: Cable Laying

Edgar Trent Cnstr Co LLC......................... D 419 683-4939
Crestline *(G-7022)*

South Shore Cable Cnstr Inc..................... D 440 816-0033
Cleveland *(G-4921)*

Universal Recovery Systems Inc............... D 614 299-0184
Columbus *(G-6821)*

CONTRACTORS: Carpentry Work

Combs Interior Specialties Inc................... D 937 879-2047
Fairborn *(G-8369)*

Command Roofing Co................................ C 937 298-1155
Moraine *(G-11398)*

Competitive Interiors Inc........................... C 330 297-1281
Ravenna *(G-12623)*

Finelli Ornamental Iron Co........................ E 440 248-0050
Cleveland *(G-4251)*

Hgc Construction Co................................. D 513 861-8866
Cincinnati *(G-2818)*

Lakeside Interior Contractors Inc............... C 419 867-1300
Perrysburg *(G-12351)*

Marous Brothers Cnstr Inc........................ B 440 951-3904
Willoughby *(G-15211)*

Overhead Door Co- Cincinnati................... C 513 346-4000
West Chester *(G-14739)*

Riverside Cnstr Svcs Inc........................... E 513 723-0900
Cincinnati *(G-3307)*

Rock Homes Inc....................................... E 330 497-5200
North Canton *(G-11859)*

T Allen Inc... C 440 234-2366
Berea *(G-1084)*

CONTRACTORS: Carpentry, Cabinet & Finish Work

Prusaks Precision Cnstr Inc...................... E 440 655-8564
North Royalton *(G-11948)*

Schlabach Wood Design Inc...................... E 330 897-2600
Baltic *(G-691)*

CONTRACTORS: Closet Organizers, Installation & Design

Closets By Design.................................... E 513 469-6130
Blue Ash *(G-1152)*

Ptmj Enterprises Inc................................ D 440 543-8000
Solon *(G-13132)*

CONTRACTORS: Coating, Caulking & Weather, Water & Fire

Canaan Companies Inc............................. E 419 842-8373
Toledo *(G-13724)*

Capital Fire Protection Co......................... E 614 279-9448
Columbus *(G-5500)*

Central Fire Protection Co Inc................... E 937 322-0713
Springfield *(G-13225)*

M T Golf Course Managment Inc............... E 513 923-1188
Cincinnati *(G-2998)*

Sika Mbcc US LLC.................................... A 216 839-7500
Beachwood *(G-838)*

CONTRACTORS: Commercial & Office Building

Beck Suppliers Inc................................... E 419 426-3051
Attica *(G-598)*

Boyas Enterprises I Inc............................ E 216 524-3620
Cleveland *(G-3886)*

Brenmar Construction Inc......................... D 740 286-2151
Jackson *(G-9516)*

Capital Land Services Inc.......................... E 330 338-4709
Norton *(G-11991)*

Cathedral Holdings Inc.............................. D 513 271-6400
Cincinnati *(G-2322)*

Cattrell Companies Inc............................. D 740 537-2481
Toronto *(G-14122)*

Cleveland Construction Inc....................... E 440 255-8000
Mentor *(G-10923)*

Delventhal Company................................ E 419 244-5570
Millbury *(G-11267)*

Design Homes & Development Co............. E 937 438-3667
Dayton *(G-7311)*

Hammond Construction Inc....................... D 330 455-7039
Uniontown *(G-14254)*

J&H Rnfrcing Strl Erectors Inc................... C 740 355-0141
Portsmouth *(G-12558)*

Kramer & Feldman Inc............................. E 513 821-7444
Cincinnati *(G-2950)*

Link Construction Group Inc..................... E 937 292-7774
Bellefontaine *(G-1030)*

Mel Lanzer Co... E 419 592-2801
Napoleon *(G-11528)*

Metis Construction Svcs LLC..................... D 330 677-7333
Kent *(G-9587)*

Muha Construction Inc............................. E 937 435-0678
Dayton *(G-7517)*

Multicon Builders Inc............................... E 614 463-1142
Columbus *(G-6283)*

Ohio Diversified Services Inc.................... E 440 356-7000
Cleveland *(G-4687)*

Ohio Maint & Renovation Inc.................... E 330 315-3101
Akron *(G-254)*

Pivotek LLC... E 513 372-6205
Milford *(G-11250)*

Pleasant Valley Cnstr Co.......................... D 330 239-0176
Medina *(G-10877)*

Procon Prof Cnstr Svcs Inc....................... E 740 474-5455
Circleville *(G-3719)*

Registered Contractors Inc....................... E 440 205-0873
Mentor *(G-10990)*

Rudolph/Libbe Companies Inc.................. D 419 241-5000
Walbridge *(G-14465)*

Runyon & Sons Roofing Inc...................... D 440 974-6810
Mentor *(G-10993)*

Singleton Construction LLC....................... D 740 756-7331
Lancaster *(G-9741)*

Tri-C Construction Company Inc............... E 330 836-2722
Akron *(G-337)*

Williams Bros Builders Inc........................ E 440 365-3261
Elyria *(G-8301)*

Winsupply Inc.. D 937 294-5331
Moraine *(G-11450)*

CONTRACTORS: Communications Svcs

Broadband Express LLC............................ D 216 712-7505
Cleveland *(G-3898)*

Combined Technologies Inc...................... E 513 595-5900
Cincinnati *(G-2478)*

Gatesair Inc.. D 513 459-3400
Mason *(G-10553)*

Legrand North America LLC..................... B 937 224-0639
Dayton *(G-7451)*

Zenith Systems LLC................................. B 216 406-7916
Atwater *(G-602)*

Zenith Systems LLC................................. C 216 587-9510
Cleveland *(G-5174)*

CONTRACTORS: Concrete Reinforcement Placing

Armeton US Co.. E 419 660-9296
Norwalk *(G-12001)*

CONTRACTORS: Core Drilling & Cutting

Barr Engineering Incorporated.................. E 614 714-0299
Columbus *(G-5420)*

CONTRACTORS: Corrosion Control Installation

Columbus Dnv Inc.................................... C 614 761-1214
Dublin *(G-7966)*

CONTRACTORS: Directional Oil & Gas Well Drilling Svc

Warren Drilling Co Inc............................. C 740 783-2775
Dexter City *(G-7868)*

CONTRACTORS: Drywall

A & A Wall Systems Inc........................... E 513 489-0086
Cincinnati *(G-2128)*

Architctral Intr Rstrtions Inc..................... E 216 241-2255
Cleveland *(G-3831)*

Brocon Construction Inc........................... E 614 871-7300
Grove City *(G-8900)*

Compass Construction Inc........................ D 614 761-7800
Dublin *(G-7969)*

Competitive Interiors Inc.......................... C 330 297-1281
Ravenna *(G-12623)*

Construction Systems Inc......................... D 614 252-0708
Columbus *(G-5686)*

Danessa Construction Llc......................... D 330 219-1212
Niles *(G-11787)*

Dayton Walls & Ceilings Inc..................... D 937 277-0531
Dayton *(G-7305)*

Valley Interior Systems Inc...................... D 614 351-8440
Columbus *(G-6840)*

SERVICES SECTION

CONTRACTORS: General Electric

Valley Interior Systems Inc.................... D 937 890-7319
  Dayton *(G-7699)*
Valley Interior Systems Inc.................... B 513 961-0400
  Cincinnati *(G-3613)*

CONTRACTORS: Electric Power Systems

Dovetail Construction Co Inc................. E 740 592-1800
  Cleveland *(G-4181)*
Geiger Brothers Inc............................... B 740 286-0800
  Jackson *(G-9518)*
Generator One LLC.............................. E 440 942-8449
  Mentor *(G-10941)*
Vaughn Industries LLC......................... D 419 396-3900
  Fostoria *(G-8627)*

CONTRACTORS: Electronic Controls Installation

Industrial Comm & Sound Inc................ E 614 276-8123
  Cincinnati *(G-2868)*

CONTRACTORS: Energy Management Control

McPhillips Plbg Htg & AC Co................. E 216 481-1400
  Cleveland *(G-4542)*
Rittal North America LLC...................... C 937 399-0500
  Urbana *(G-14311)*
Siemens Energy Inc............................. E 740 393-8897
  Mount Vernon *(G-11508)*

CONTRACTORS: Erection & Dismantling, Poured Concrete Forms

Ceco Concrete Construction LLC.......... C 513 874-6953
  West Chester *(G-14661)*
R W Sidley Incorporated....................... C 440 298-3232
  Thompson *(G-13618)*

CONTRACTORS: Fence Construction

Allied Builders Inc................................ E 937 226-0311
  Dayton *(G-7163)*
Deerfield Farms................................... E 330 584-4715
  Deerfield *(G-7740)*
Mills Fence Co LLC.............................. E 513 631-0333
  Cincinnati *(G-3066)*
National Cnstr Rentals Inc.................... E 614 308-1100
  Columbus *(G-6294)*
Security Fence Group Inc..................... E 513 681-3700
  Cincinnati *(G-3353)*

CONTRACTORS: Fiber Optic Cable Installation

Neesai Cad Designs LLC...................... E 614 822-7701
  New Albany *(G-11577)*
Newcome Corp..................................... E 614 848-5688
  Columbus *(G-5273)*
Professnl Cbling Slutions LLC............... D 513 733-9473
  Cincinnati *(G-3246)*
Taylor CJ Development Inc................... D 330 628-5501
  Mogadore *(G-11332)*
Universal Recovery Systems Inc........... D 614 299-0184
  Columbus *(G-6821)*

CONTRACTORS: Fire Detection & Burglar Alarm Systems

Acree-Daily Corporation........................ E 614 452-7300
  Columbus *(G-5308)*
GA Business Purchaser LLC................. E 419 255-8400
  Toledo *(G-13816)*
Gillmore Security Systems Inc.............. E 440 232-1000
  Cleveland *(G-4313)*

Guardian Protection Svcs Inc................ E 330 797-1570
  Bedford *(G-962)*
Sievers Security Inc............................. E 216 291-2222
  Cleveland *(G-4905)*
Southeast Security Corporation............. E 330 239-4600
  Sharon Center *(G-12990)*
State Alarm Inc.................................... E 888 726-8111
  Youngstown *(G-15730)*

CONTRACTORS: Floor Laying & Other Floor Work

Centimark Corporation.......................... C 330 920-3560
  Stow *(G-13357)*
Clays Heritage Carpet Inc..................... E 330 497-1280
  Canton *(G-1711)*
Cleveland Construction Inc................... E 440 255-8000
  Mentor *(G-10923)*
Lakeside Interior Contractors Inc........... C 419 867-1300
  Perrysburg *(G-12351)*
Messina Floor Covering LLC................. D 216 595-0100
  Cleveland *(G-4557)*
Preferred Acquisition Co LLC................ D 216 587-0957
  Cleveland *(G-4767)*
Protective Coatings Inc........................ E 937 275-7711
  Dayton *(G-7572)*
Spectra Holdings Inc........................... E 614 921-8493
  Columbus *(G-6702)*
T and D Interiors Incorporated.............. E 419 331-4372
  Lima *(G-9969)*
Tremco Incorporated............................ B
  Beachwood *(G-847)*
W R Shepherd Inc................................ E 614 889-2896
  Powell *(G-12608)*

CONTRACTORS: Foundation & Footing

Arledge Construction Inc...................... E 614 732-4258
  Columbus *(G-5385)*
Cleveland Concrete Cnstr Inc................ D 216 741-3954
  Brooklyn Heights *(G-1415)*
Gateway Con Forming Svcs Inc............ D 513 353-2000
  Miamitown *(G-11106)*
Goettle Holding Company Inc............... C 513 825-8100
  Cincinnati *(G-2738)*
J & D Home Improvement Inc.............. D 800 288-0831
  Columbus *(G-6076)*
Metcon Ltd.. E 937 447-9200
  Dayton *(G-7483)*
Modern Poured Walls Inc..................... E 440 647-6661
  Wellington *(G-14634)*
Shepherd Excavating Inc...................... E 614 889-1115
  Dublin *(G-8118)*
The Beaver Excavating Co.................... A 330 478-2151
  Canton *(G-1871)*
Triple Q Foundations Co Inc................. E 513 932-3121
  Lebanon *(G-9795)*

CONTRACTORS: Gas Field Svcs, NEC

Stingray Pressure Pumping LLC............ D 405 648-4177
  Belmont *(G-1055)*

CONTRACTORS: General Electric

A J Goulder Electric Co........................ E 440 942-4026
  Willoughby *(G-15182)*
A T Emmett LLC.................................. E 419 734-2520
  Port Clinton *(G-12516)*
Abbott Electric Inc............................... D 330 343-8941
  Dover *(G-7871)*
Abbott Electric Inc............................... D 330 452-6601
  Canton *(G-1652)*
Accurate Electric Cnstr Inc................... E 614 863-1844
  Reynoldsburg *(G-12650)*

Aey Electric Inc................................... E 330 792-5745
  Youngstown *(G-15543)*
All Phase Power and Ltg Inc................. E 419 624-9640
  Sandusky *(G-12862)*
Archiable Electric Company.................. D 513 621-1307
  Cincinnati *(G-2214)*
Area Energy & Electric Inc.................... C 937 498-4784
  Sidney *(G-13019)*
Atkins & Stang Inc............................... D 513 242-8300
  Cincinnati *(G-2226)*
B & J Electrical Company Inc............... E 513 351-7100
  Cincinnati *(G-2234)*
Bansal Construction Inc....................... E 513 874-5410
  Fairfield *(G-8392)*
Banta Electrical Contrs Inc................... E 513 353-4446
  Cleves *(G-5187)*
BCU Electric Inc.................................. D 419 281-8944
  Ashland *(G-480)*
Beacon Electric Company..................... D 513 851-0711
  Cincinnati *(G-2242)*
Bechtel Jacobs Company LLC.............. C 740 897-2700
  Piketon *(G-12415)*
Biz Com Electric LLC........................... E 513 961-7200
  Cincinnati *(G-2263)*
Bodie Electric Inc................................. E 419 435-3672
  Fostoria *(G-8613)*
Calvin Electric LLC............................... E 937 670-2558
  Clayton *(G-3731)*
Capital City Electric Inc........................ E 614 933-8700
  New Albany *(G-11558)*
Carey Electric Co................................. D 937 669-3399
  Vandalia *(G-14368)*
Cattrell Companies Inc......................... D 740 537-2481
  Toronto *(G-14122)*
Chapel Electric Co LLC........................ B 937 222-2290
  Dayton *(G-7221)*
Claypool Electric Inc............................ C 740 653-5683
  Lancaster *(G-9702)*
Contemporary Electric Inc.................... E 440 975-9965
  Willoughby *(G-15188)*
Converse Electric Inc........................... D 614 808-4377
  Grove City *(G-8912)*
Craftsman Electric Inc.......................... D 513 891-4426
  Cincinnati *(G-2514)*
D E Williams Electric Inc...................... E 440 543-1222
  Chagrin Falls *(G-1957)*
Darana Hybrid Inc................................ D 513 860-4490
  Hamilton *(G-9036)*
Davis H Elliot Cnstr Co Inc................... E 937 847-8025
  Miamisburg *(G-11045)*
Davis Pickering & Company Inc............ D 740 373-5896
  Marietta *(G-10365)*
Delta Electrical Contrs Ltd.................... E 513 421-7744
  Cincinnati *(G-2557)*
Denier Electric Co Inc.......................... D 614 338-4664
  Grove City *(G-8915)*
Denier Electric Co Inc.......................... C 513 738-2641
  Harrison *(G-9101)*
E S I Inc... D 513 454-3741
  West Chester *(G-14808)*
Electric Connection Inc........................ D 614 436-1121
  Columbus *(G-5810)*
Electrical Accents LLC......................... E 440 988-2852
  South Amherst *(G-13169)*
Electrical Corp America Inc.................. C 440 245-3007
  Lorain *(G-10072)*
Emcor Facilities Services Inc................ D 513 948-8469
  Cincinnati *(G-2612)*
Enertech Electrical Inc......................... E 330 536-2131
  Lowellville *(G-10168)*
Erb Electric Co..................................... C 740 633-5055
  Bridgeport *(G-1376)*

CONTRACTORS: General Electric

Ferenc/Lakeside Electric Inc .... D 216 426-1880
  Cleveland (G-4248)
Fishel Company .... D 614 274-8100
  Columbus (G-5869)
Fowler Electric Co .... E 440 735-2385
  Bedford (G-960)
Frey Electric Inc .... D 513 385-0700
  Cincinnati (G-2708)
Garber Electrical Contrs Inc .... D 937 771-5202
  Englewood (G-8306)
Gateway Electric LLC .... C 216 518-5500
  Cleveland (G-4304)
Gem Electric .... E 440 286-6200
  Chardon (G-2003)
Gem Industrial Inc .... D 419 666-6554
  Walbridge (G-14461)
Great Lakes Indus Contg Ltd .... E 419 945-4542
  Toledo (G-13826)
Harrington Electric Company .... D 216 361-5101
  Cleveland (G-4351)
Hatzel and Buehler Inc .... E 216 777-6000
  Cleveland (G-4352)
Herbst Electric LLC .... D 216 621-5890
  Cleveland (G-4359)
Hilscher-Clarke Electric Co .... C 740 622-5557
  Coshocton (G-6986)
Hilscher-Clarke Electric Co .... E 330 452-9806
  Canton (G-1772)
Industrial Power Systems Inc .... B 419 531-3121
  Rossford (G-12767)
Instrmntation Ctrl Systems Inc .... E 513 662-2600
  Cincinnati (G-2873)
J & J General Maintenance Inc .... D 740 533-9729
  Ironton (G-9509)
J W Didado Electric Inc .... C 330 374-0070
  Akron (G-207)
Jess Howard Electric Company .... C 614 864-2167
  Blacklick (G-1113)
Jims Electric Inc .... E 440 327-8800
  North Ridgeville (G-11930)
Joe Dickey Electric Inc .... D 330 549-3976
  North Lima (G-11889)
JW Didado Electric LLC .... D 330 374-0070
  Akron (G-213)
Kastle Electric Company .... C 937 254-2681
  Moraine (G-11419)
Kathman Electric Co Inc .... E 513 353-3365
  Cleves (G-5189)
Kidron Electric Inc .... C 330 857-2871
  Kidron (G-9637)
Kraft Electrical Contg Inc .... E 513 467-0500
  Cincinnati (G-2949)
Kween Industries Inc .... D 513 932-2293
  Lebanon (G-9772)
Lake Erie Electric Inc .... C 330 724-1241
  Akron (G-218)
Lake Erie Electric Inc .... C 937 743-1220
  Franklin (G-8644)
Lake Erie Electric Inc .... C 419 529-4611
  Ontario (G-12111)
LAKE ERIE ELECTRIC INC .... D 440 835-5565
  Westlake (G-15074)
Lake Horry Electric .... D 440 808-8791
  Chagrin Falls (G-1961)
M-Pact Corporation .... E 513 679-2023
  Cincinnati (G-2999)
Main Lite Electric Co Inc .... E 330 369-8333
  Warren (G-14537)
Maxwell Lightning Protection .... E 937 228-7250
  Dayton (G-7469)
Mayers Electric Co Inc .... C 513 272-2900
  Cincinnati (G-3019)

McClintock Electric Inc .... E 330 264-6380
  Wooster (G-15354)
McKeever & Niekamp Electric .... E 937 431-9363
  Beavercreek (G-890)
Miller Cable Company .... D 419 639-2091
  Green Springs (G-8861)
Mutual Electric Company .... E 937 254-6211
  Dayton (G-7519)
New River Electrical Corp .... A 614 891-1142
  Westerville (G-15007)
Noll Fisher Incorporated .... E 937 394-4181
  Anna (G-443)
Northeast Ohio Electric LLC .... B 216 587-9512
  Cleveland (G-4662)
Northwest Electrical Contg Inc .... E 419 865-4757
  Sylvania (G-13558)
Ohio Valley Elec Svcs LLC .... D 513 771-2410
  Blue Ash (G-1217)
Osterwisch Company Inc .... D 513 791-3282
  Cincinnati (G-3174)
Palazzo Brothers Electric Inc .... E 419 668-1100
  Norwalk (G-12020)
Penn-Ohio Electrical Company .... E 330 448-1234
  Masury (G-10680)
Perram Electric Inc .... E 330 239-2661
  Wadsworth (G-14447)
Precision Electrical Svcs Inc .... E 740 474-4490
  Circleville (G-3718)
Reddy Electric Co .... C 937 372-8205
  Xenia (G-15530)
Regent Electric Inc .... D 419 476-8333
  Toledo (G-13985)
Reliable Contractors Inc .... D 937 433-0262
  Dayton (G-7583)
Rgt Services LLC .... E 440 786-9777
  Oakwood Village (G-12056)
Roehrenbeck Electric Inc .... E 614 443-9709
  Columbus (G-6607)
Romanoff Elc Residential LLC .... D 614 755-4500
  Gahanna (G-8728)
Romanoff Electric Inc .... C 614 755-4500
  Gahanna (G-8729)
Romanoff Electric Co LLC .... B 937 640-7925
  Toledo (G-13997)
Romanoff Group LLC .... E 614 755-4500
  Gahanna (G-8730)
Royal Electric Cnstr Corp .... E 614 253-6600
  Columbus (G-6614)
Santon Electric Inc .... D 330 758-0082
  Youngstown (G-15716)
Saturn Electric Inc .... E 937 278-2580
  Dayton (G-7611)
Security Fence Group Inc .... E 513 681-3700
  Cincinnati (G-3353)
Servall Electric Company Inc .... E 513 771-5584
  Cincinnati (G-3361)
Settle Muter Electric Ltd .... C 614 866-7554
  Columbus (G-6667)
Shannon Electric LLC .... E 216 378-3620
  Cleveland (G-4899)
Sidney Electric Company .... D 419 222-1109
  Sidney (G-13050)
Sollmann Electric Co .... E 937 492-0346
  Sidney (G-13055)
South Shore Electric Inc .... E 440 366-6289
  Elyria (G-8296)
Speelman Electric Inc .... C 330 633-1410
  Tallmadge (G-13604)
Studebaker Electric Company .... D 937 890-9510
  Dayton (G-7648)
TAS Inc .... E 419 693-3353
  Toledo (G-14033)

The Wagner-Smith Company .... B 866 338-0398
  Moraine (G-11444)
Thompson Electric Inc .... C 330 686-2300
  Munroe Falls (G-11514)
TMI Electrical Contractors Inc .... E 513 821-9900
  Cincinnati (G-3482)
Transtar Electric Inc .... D 419 385-7573
  Toledo (G-14073)
Tri Area Electric Co Inc .... E 330 744-0151
  Youngstown (G-15736)
Triec Electrical Services Inc .... E 937 323-3721
  Springfield (G-13305)
TWC Entrprises Elec Contrs LLC .... E 740 467-9004
  Millersport (G-11299)
Ullman Electric & Technolog .... C 216 432-5777
  Cleveland (G-5048)
US Utility Electrical Svcs .... E 419 837-9753
  Perrysburg (G-12384)
Vaughn Industries LLC .... D 740 548-7100
  Lewis Center (G-9840)
Vaughn Industries LLC .... B 419 396-3900
  Carey (G-1895)
Vec Inc .... D 330 539-4044
  Girard (G-8830)
Volpenhein Brothers Electric Inc .... D 513 385-9355
  West Chester (G-14845)
Wells Brothers Inc .... D 937 394-7559
  Anna (G-445)
Westfield Electric Inc .... E 419 862-0078
  Gibsonburg (G-8807)
WI Electric Inc .... E 614 882-2160
  Westerville (G-15022)
Wood Electric Inc .... E 330 339-7002
  New Philadelphia (G-11673)
Woolace Electric Corp .... E 419 428-3161
  Stryker (G-13506)
X F Construction Svcs Inc .... E 614 575-2700
  Columbus (G-6911)

CONTRACTORS: Glass Tinting, Architectural & Automotive

Afg Industries Inc .... D 614 322-4580
  Grove City (G-8893)
Ziebart of Ohio Inc .... E 440 845-6031
  Cleveland (G-5175)

CONTRACTORS: Heating & Air Conditioning

A Bee C Service Inc .... E 440 735-1505
  Cleveland (G-3747)
Area Energy & Electric Inc .... C 937 498-4784
  Sidney (G-13019)
Enginring Exclince Nat Accnts .... D 844 969-3923
  Blue Ash (G-1168)
Ohio Fabricators Inc .... D 330 745-4406
  Akron (G-250)
Reader Tinning & Roofing Co .... E 216 451-1355
  Cleveland (G-4810)
Town & Country Plbg & Htg Inc .... E 330 726-5755
  Youngstown (G-15735)
Waibel Energy Systems Inc .... D 937 264-4343
  Vandalia (G-14403)

CONTRACTORS: Heating Systems Repair & Maintenance Svc

Integra Svcs Intermediate LLC .... B 317 409-2130
  Mentor (G-10952)

CONTRACTORS: Highway & Street Construction, General

SERVICES SECTION   **CONTRACTORS: Painting, Commercial**

Aecom Energy & Cnstr Inc.................................. E 216 622-2300
  Cleveland *(G-3771)*
Altruism Society Inc.............................. D 877 283-4001
  Beachwood *(G-765)*
Brock & Sons Inc...................................... E 513 874-4555
  Fairfield *(G-8395)*
Colas Construction USA Inc.................. C 513 272-5648
  Cincinnati *(G-2471)*
Erie Construction Group Inc................. D 419 625-7374
  Sandusky *(G-12890)*
Ferrous Metal Transfer Co..................... E 216 671-8500
  Brooklyn *(G-1409)*
Fred A Nemann Co................................. E 513 467-9400
  Cincinnati *(G-2702)*
Freedom Construction Entps Inc........ E 740 255-5818
  New Concord *(G-11610)*
Fryman-Kuck General Contrs Inc.......... E 937 274-2892
  Dayton *(G-7371)*
Hazama Ando Corporation..................... E 614 985-4906
  Worthington *(G-15418)*
Independence Excavating Inc................ E 216 524-1700
  Independence *(G-9437)*
J&B Steel Erectors Inc............................ E 513 874-1722
  West Chester *(G-14714)*
John R Jurgensen Co.............................. B 513 771-0820
  Cincinnati *(G-2913)*
Kenmore Construction Co Inc................ D 330 832-8888
  Massillon *(G-10649)*
Kenmore Construction Co Inc............... C 330 762-8936
  Akron *(G-215)*
Kokosing Inc... D 614 212-5700
  Westerville *(G-14992)*
Kokosing Construction Inc.................... D 330 263-4168
  Wooster *(G-15350)*
Kokosing Construction Co Inc................ D 740 694-6315
  Fredericktown *(G-8662)*
Kokosing Construction Co Inc................ C 419 524-5656
  Mansfield *(G-10279)*
Kokosing Construction Co Inc............... C 614 228-1029
  Westerville *(G-14994)*
Kokosing Construction Co Inc............... C 614 228-1029
  Westerville *(G-14993)*
McDaniels Cnstr Corp Inc....................... D 614 252-5852
  Columbus *(G-6213)*
Nerone & Sons Inc.................................. E 216 662-2235
  Cleveland *(G-4635)*
Perk Company Inc................................... E 216 391-1444
  Cleveland *(G-4741)*
R B Jergens Contractors Inc.................. D 937 669-9799
  Vandalia *(G-14390)*
Ruhlin Company...................................... C 330 239-2800
  Sharon Center *(G-12989)*
Stonegate Construction Inc.................... E 740 423-9170
  Belpre *(G-1060)*
Sunesis Construction Co........................ C 513 326-6000
  West Chester *(G-14770)*
The Great Lakes Construction Co.......... C 330 220-3900
  Hinckley *(G-9272)*
Trafftech Inc... E 216 361-8808
  Cleveland *(G-5029)*
Tucson Inc.. E 330 339-4935
  New Philadelphia *(G-11669)*
Velotta Company..................................... E 330 239-1211
  Sharon Center *(G-12991)*
Westpatrick Corp.................................... E 614 875-8200
  Urbancrest *(G-14327)*

CONTRACTORS: Highway & Street Paving

Ambrose Asphalt Inc.............................. E 419 774-1780
  Mansfield *(G-10243)*
American Pavements Inc........................ E 614 873-2191
  Plain City *(G-12467)*
Columbus Asphalt Paving Inc................ E 614 759-9800
  Columbus *(G-5611)*
Ebony Construction Co.......................... E 419 841-3455
  Sylvania *(G-13542)*
Erie Blacktop Inc.................................... E 419 625-7374
  Sandusky *(G-12889)*
Gerken Materials Inc............................... E 419 533-2421
  Napoleon *(G-11524)*
Hicon Inc... E 513 242-3612
  Cincinnati *(G-2819)*
Kelly Paving Inc...................................... E 740 373-6495
  Marietta *(G-10377)*
MBC Holdings Inc................................... E 419 445-1015
  Archbold *(G-462)*
Miller Bros Const Inc.............................. A 419 445-1015
  Archbold *(G-463)*
Ronyak Paving Inc.................................. E 440 279-0616
  Chardon *(G-2018)*
Scot Burton Contractors LLC................ E 440 564-1011
  Newbury *(G-11764)*
Superior Paving & Materials.................. E 330 499-5849
  Canton *(G-1866)*
Terminal Ready-Mix Inc.......................... E 440 288-0181
  Lorain *(G-10103)*
Vandalia Blcktop Slcoating Inc.............. E 937 454-0571
  Dayton *(G-7700)*

CONTRACTORS: Hydraulic Eqpt Installation & Svcs

North Bay Construction Inc.................... E 440 835-1898
  Westlake *(G-15085)*

CONTRACTORS: Machine Rigging & Moving

Atlas Industrial Contrs LLC................... B 614 841-4500
  Columbus *(G-5403)*
Canton Erectors Inc................................ E 330 453-7363
  Massillon *(G-10634)*
Fenton Rigging & Contg Inc................... C 513 631-5500
  Cincinnati *(G-2657)*
Hensley Industries Inc........................... E 513 769-6666
  Cincinnati *(G-2817)*
Myers Machinery Movers Inc................. E 614 871-5052
  Grove City *(G-8938)*
Nk Parts Industries Inc.......................... C 937 498-4651
  Sidney *(G-13041)*
Piqua Steel Co.. D 937 773-3632
  Piqua *(G-12454)*
S Gary Shmker Rggng Trnspt L............ E 330 899-9090
  Akron *(G-292)*
Standard Contg & Engrg Inc.................. D 440 243-1001
  Brookpark *(G-1440)*

CONTRACTORS: Machinery Installation

Expert Crane Inc..................................... E 216 451-9900
  Wellington *(G-14632)*
Gem Industrial Inc.................................. D 419 666-6554
  Walbridge *(G-14461)*
Hy-Tek Material Handling LLC............... D 614 497-2500
  Columbus *(G-6030)*
Norris Brothers Co Inc........................... C 216 771-2233
  Cleveland *(G-4647)*
Spallinger Millwright Svc Co.................. E 419 225-5830
  Lima *(G-9962)*
Tesar Industrial Contrs Inc.................... D 216 741-8008
  Cleveland *(G-4987)*
United Technical Support Svcs.............. C 330 562-3330
  Streetsboro *(G-13433)*

CONTRACTORS: Marble Installation, Interior

Cleveland Marble Mosaic Co.................. C 216 749-2840
  Cleveland *(G-4054)*
Cutting Edge Countertops Inc................ E 419 873-9500
  Perrysburg *(G-12328)*
Legacy Ntral Stone Srfaces LLC............ E 419 420-7440
  Findlay *(G-8558)*

CONTRACTORS: Masonry & Stonework

Appelgren Ltd... E 330 945-6402
  Cuyahoga Falls *(G-7040)*
Canaan Companies Inc........................... E 419 842-8373
  Toledo *(G-13724)*
Carlisle Msnry/Cnstruction Inc.............. E 740 966-5045
  Johnstown *(G-9545)*
Design Built Construction Inc................ E 419 563-0185
  Bucyrus *(G-1507)*
Hicon Inc... E 513 242-3612
  Cincinnati *(G-2819)*
Industrial First Inc................................. C 216 991-8605
  Bedford *(G-966)*
Miter Masonry Contractors................... E 513 821-3334
  Arlington Heights *(G-470)*
Phoenix Masonry Ltd.............................. D 740 344-5787
  Newark *(G-11741)*
Pioneer Cldding Glzing Systems............ E 216 816-4242
  Cleveland *(G-4749)*
Wasiniak Construction Inc..................... D 419 668-8624
  Norwalk *(G-12030)*

CONTRACTORS: Office Furniture Installation

Jtc Contracting Inc................................. E 216 635-0745
  Cleveland *(G-4443)*
Lincoln Moving & Storage Co................. E 216 741-5500
  Strongsville *(G-13470)*
National Electro-Coatings Inc................ D 216 898-0080
  Cleveland *(G-4624)*
Wegman Construction Company........... E 513 381-1111
  Cincinnati *(G-3646)*

CONTRACTORS: Oil & Gas Field Geophysical Exploration Svcs

Dlz Ohio Inc... C 614 888-0040
  Columbus *(G-5778)*

CONTRACTORS: Oil & Gas Field Tools Fishing Svcs

Klx Energy Services LLC........................ E 740 922-1155
  Midvale *(G-11204)*

CONTRACTORS: Oil & Gas Wells Pumping Svcs

Performance Technologies LLC.............. D 330 875-1216
  Louisville *(G-10119)*

CONTRACTORS: Oil Field Mud Drilling Svcs

Kelchner Inc.. C 937 704-9890
  Springboro *(G-13202)*

CONTRACTORS: Painting, Commercial

August Groh & Sons Inc......................... E 513 821-0090
  Cincinnati *(G-2229)*
Chas F Mann Painting Co....................... E 419 385-7151
  Toledo *(G-13730)*
E B Miller Contracting Inc...................... E 513 531-7030
  Cincinnati *(G-2592)*
Johnson & Fischer Incorporated............ E 614 276-8868
  Columbus *(G-6094)*
Mes Painting and Graphics Ltd.............. E 614 496-1696
  Westerville *(G-14998)*
Muha Construction Inc........................... E 937 435-0678
  Dayton *(G-7517)*

CONTRACTORS: Painting, Commercial

Napoleon Machine LLC................................ E 419 591-7010
  Napoleon (G-11530)
Painting Company................................ C 614 873-1334
  Plain City (G-12488)
Preferred Acquisition Co LLC................ D 216 587-0957
  Cleveland (G-4767)

CONTRACTORS: Painting, Commercial, Exterior

Dependable Painting Co........................ E 216 431-4470
  Cleveland (G-4162)
Francis C Skinner Painting Svc............ E 937 773-3858
  Piqua (G-12442)
Howard Painting Inc................................ E 419 782-7786
  Defiance (G-7749)

CONTRACTORS: Painting, Indl

A1 Industrial Painting Inc...................... E 330 750-9441
  Youngstown (G-15540)
Cartruck Packaging Inc.......................... E 216 631-7225
  Cleveland (G-3931)
Eagle Industrial Painting LLC.............. E 330 866-5965
  Canton (G-1739)
Flamos Enterprises Inc.......................... E 330 478-0009
  Canton (G-1755)

CONTRACTORS: Pile Driving

Goettle Holding Company Inc................ C 513 825-8100
  Cincinnati (G-2738)

CONTRACTORS: Plumbing

1 Tom Plumber LLC................................ E 866 758-6237
  Milford (G-11214)
A-1 Advanced Plumbing Inc................ E 614 873-0548
  Plain City (G-12463)
Aggressive Mechanical Inc.................. E 614 443-3280
  Columbus (G-5329)
Allegiant Plumbing LLC........................ E 614 824-5002
  Columbus (G-5335)
American Plumbing................................ E 440 871-8293
  Bay Village (G-757)
Applied Mechanical Systems Inc........ C 937 854-3073
  Dayton (G-7176)
B B & E Inc.. E 740 354-5469
  Portsmouth (G-12545)
Bay Mechanical & Elec Corp................ D 440 282-6816
  Lorain (G-10058)
Bruner Corporation................................ C 614 334-9000
  Hilliard (G-9185)
Christopher Burkey.............................. E 330 770-9607
  North Lima (G-11886)
Crawford Mechanical Svcs Inc............ D 614 478-9424
  Pataskala (G-12272)
Ecoplumbers LLC................................ E 614 299-9903
  Hilliard (G-9194)
Freeland Contracting Co...................... E 614 443-2718
  Columbus (G-5894)
GM Mechanical Inc................................ D 937 473-3006
  Covington (G-7018)
Grabill Plumbing & Heating.................. E 330 756-2075
  Beach City (G-761)
Gross Plumbing Incorporated.............. E 440 324-9999
  Elyria (G-8253)
Haslett Heating & Cooling Inc............ E 614 299-2133
  Dublin (G-8027)
Houston Dick Plbg & Htg Inc................ E 740 763-3961
  Newark (G-11708)
J & D Home Improvement Inc............ D 800 288-0831
  Columbus (G-6076)
Ke Gutridge LLC................................ D 614 299-2133
  Dublin (G-8047)

Ken Neyer Plumbing Inc........................ C 513 353-3311
  Cleves (G-5190)
Kinn Bros Plbg Htg & AC Inc................ E 419 562-1484
  Bucyrus (G-1511)
Kirk Williams Piping & Plbg Co............ E 614 875-9023
  Grove City (G-8932)
Lippincott Plmbng-Hting AC Inc......... E 419 222-0856
  Lima (G-9928)
Lucas Plumbing & Heating Inc............ E 440 282-4567
  Lorain (G-10091)
Marvin W Mielke Inc.............................. D 330 725-8845
  Medina (G-10853)
Mechanical Construction Co................ E 740 353-5668
  Portsmouth (G-12563)
Midwestern Plumbing Svc Inc............ E 513 753-0050
  Cincinnati (G-3060)
Mj Baumann Co Inc............................ D 614 759-7100
  Columbus (G-6252)
Monroe Plumbing Inc.......................... E 440 708-0006
  Burton (G-1531)
Muetzel Plumbing & Heating Co........ D 614 299-7700
  Columbus (G-6282)
Nelson Stark Company........................ C 513 489-0866
  Cincinnati (G-3105)
Neptune Plumbing & Heating Co........ D 216 475-9100
  Cleveland (G-4634)
Northern Plumbing Systems................ E 513 831-5111
  Goshen (G-8837)
Pioneer Pipe Inc................................ A 740 376-2400
  Marietta (G-10399)
Pleasant Valley Corporation................ D 330 239-0176
  Medina (G-10878)
Professional Plumbing Svcs Inc........ E 740 454-1066
  Zanesville (G-15830)
Queen City Mechanicals Inc................ E 513 353-1430
  Cincinnati (G-3262)
Reliant Mechanical Inc........................ D 937 644-0074
  East Liberty (G-8175)
Robertson Plumbing & Heating............ E 330 863-0611
  Malvern (G-10235)
Roger Storer & Son Inc...................... E 937 325-9873
  Springfield (G-13287)
Roto-Rooter Development Co............ D 513 762-6690
  Cincinnati (G-3322)
Roto-Rooter Services Company.......... D 513 762-6690
  Cincinnati (G-3324)
Slagle Mechanical Contractors............ E 937 492-4151
  Sidney (G-13054)
Standard Plumbing & Heating Co........ D 330 453-5150
  Canton (G-1856)
Steingass Mechanical Contg LLC........ E 330 725-6090
  Medina (G-10893)
The Geiler Company............................ C 513 574-1200
  Cincinnati (G-3466)
Thomas J Dyer Company.................... C 513 321-8100
  Cincinnati (G-3474)
Trades Equipment LLC........................ E 419 625-4444
  Independence (G-9491)
Wells Brothers Inc.............................. D 937 394-7559
  Anna (G-445)
WF Hann & Sons LLC........................ E 216 831-4200
  Warrensville Heights (G-14590)
Whisler Plumbing & Heating Inc......... D 330 833-2875
  Massillon (G-10673)

CONTRACTORS: Pollution Control Eqpt Installation

McGill Airclean LLC.............................. D 614 829-1200
  Columbus (G-6215)

CONTRACTORS: Power Generating Eqpt Installation

Clopay Corporation................................ C 800 282-2260
  Mason (G-10540)

CONTRACTORS: Prefabricated Window & Door Installation

Alside Inc.. D 419 865-0934
  Maumee (G-10687)
Burbank Inc.. E 419 698-3434
  Toledo (G-13723)
Cabinet Restylers Inc.......................... D 419 281-8449
  Ashland (G-486)
Midwest Curtainwalls Inc.................... D 216 641-7900
  Cleveland (G-4580)
OK Interiors Corp................................ C 513 742-3278
  Cincinnati (G-3153)
Ray St Clair Roofing Inc...................... E 513 874-1234
  Fairfield (G-8436)
Rwlp Company.................................... E 216 883-2424
  Cleveland (G-4866)
Ryans All-Glass Incorporated............ E 513 771-4440
  West Chester (G-14759)
Schaefer & Company........................ E 937 339-2638
  Troy (G-14159)

CONTRACTORS: Process Piping

United Group Services Inc.................. C 800 633-9690
  West Chester (G-14842)

CONTRACTORS: Refractory or Acid Brick Masonry

Allen Refractories Company................ C 740 927-8000
  Pataskala (G-12269)
Onex Construction Inc........................ E 330 995-9015
  Streetsboro (G-13424)
The Schaefer Group Inc...................... E 937 253-3342
  Beavercreek (G-932)

CONTRACTORS: Septic System

Accurate Mechanical Inc.................... D 740 681-1332
  Lancaster (G-9690)
Cac Group LLC.................................. E 740 369-4328
  Delaware (G-7782)
Nieman Plumbing Inc.......................... D 513 851-5588
  Cincinnati (G-3117)
Swingle J and P Plumbing & Htg........ E 330 723-4840
  Medina (G-10896)
Zemba Bros Inc.................................. E 740 452-1880
  Zanesville (G-15844)

CONTRACTORS: Sheet Metal Work, NEC

All-Type Welding & Fabrication............ E 440 439-3990
  Cleveland (G-3792)
Anchor Metal Processing Inc.............. E 216 362-1850
  Cleveland (G-3814)
Avon Lake Sheet Metal Co.................. E 440 933-3505
  Avon Lake (G-673)
Defabco Inc.. D 614 231-2700
  Columbus (G-5749)
Dimensional Metals Inc...................... E 740 927-3633
  Reynoldsburg (G-12660)
Eckstein Roofing Company................ E 513 941-1511
  Cincinnati (G-2603)
Franck and Fric Incorporated............ D 216 524-4451
  Cleveland (G-4284)
Geauga Mechanical Company............ D 440 285-2000
  Chardon (G-2000)

Global Insulation Inc .... E 330 479-3100
  Canton *(G-1763)*
Hickey Metal Fabrication Roofg .... E 330 337-9329
  Salem *(G-12843)*
Kirk & Blum Manufacturing Co .... C 513 458-2600
  Cincinnati *(G-2942)*
Mechanical Cnstr Managers LLC .... C 937 274-1987
  Dayton *(G-7474)*
Mechanical Construction Co .... E 740 353-5668
  Portsmouth *(G-12563)*
Ohio Fabricators Inc .... D 330 745-4406
  Akron *(G-250)*
Ontario Mechanical LLC .... E 419 529-2578
  Ontario *(G-12121)*
Precision Impacts LLC .... D 937 530-8254
  Miamisburg *(G-11086)*
Rmt Acquisition Inc .... E 513 241-5566
  Cincinnati *(G-3311)*
Slagle Mechanical Contractors .... E 937 492-4151
  Sidney *(G-13054)*

CONTRACTORS: Siding

Cardinal Builders Inc .... E 614 237-1000
  Columbus *(G-5507)*
Champion Opco LLC .... B 513 327-7338
  Cincinnati *(G-2345)*
Erie Construction Mid-West Inc .... D 937 898-4688
  Dayton *(G-7339)*
Erie Construction Mid-West Inc .... B 419 472-4200
  Toledo *(G-13794)*
Erie Construction Mid-West Inc .... B 419 472-4200
  Toledo *(G-13795)*
Holmes Siding Contractors Ltd .... E 330 674-3382
  Millersburg *(G-11280)*
Industrial First Inc .... C 216 991-8605
  Bedford *(G-966)*
Summit Enterprises Contg Corp .... E 513 426-1623
  Lebanon *(G-9791)*
Trademark Exteriors LLC .... D 330 893-0000
  Wilmot *(G-15282)*

CONTRACTORS: Structural Iron Work, Structural

APA Solar LLC .... D 419 267-5280
  Ridgeville Corners *(G-12725)*
Foundation Steel LLC .... C 419 402-4241
  Swanton *(G-13525)*
J&H Rnfrcing Strl Erectors Inc .... C 740 355-0141
  Portsmouth *(G-12558)*
Orbit Movers & Erectors Inc .... E 937 277-8080
  Dayton *(G-7540)*
Sofco Erectors Inc .... C 513 771-1600
  Cincinnati *(G-3392)*

CONTRACTORS: Structural Steel Erection

Black Swamp Steel Inc .... E 419 867-8050
  Holland *(G-9280)*
Chc Fabricating Corp .... D 513 821-7757
  Cincinnati *(G-2348)*
CK Construction Group Inc .... B 614 901-8844
  Westerville *(G-14967)*
Diamond Steel Construction .... E 330 549-5500
  Youngstown *(G-15596)*
Dublin Building Systems Co .... E 614 760-5831
  Dublin *(G-7989)*
Frederick Steel Company LLC .... D 513 821-6400
  Cincinnati *(G-2703)*
G & P Construction LLC .... E 855 494-4830
  North Royalton *(G-11941)*
Industrial First Inc .... C 216 991-8605
  Bedford *(G-966)*

Kelley Steel Erectors Inc .... D 440 232-1573
  Cleveland *(G-4455)*
Lakeside Interior Contractors Inc .... C 419 867-1300
  Perrysburg *(G-12351)*
Marysville Steel Inc .... E 937 642-5971
  Marysville *(G-10494)*
Mound Technologies Inc .... E 937 748-2937
  Springboro *(G-13203)*
Northbend Archtctural Pdts Inc .... E 513 577-7988
  Cincinnati *(G-3121)*
Ontario Mechanical LLC .... E 419 529-2578
  Ontario *(G-12121)*
Rittman .... D 330 927-6855
  Rittman *(G-12732)*

CONTRACTORS: Tile Installation, Ceramic

Ironrock Capital Incorporated .... D 330 484-4887
  Canton *(G-1782)*
Southwestern Tile and MBL Co .... E 614 464-1257
  Columbus *(G-6700)*
Tile Shop LLC .... E 513 554-4435
  Cincinnati *(G-3480)*
Weiffenbach Marble & Tile Co .... E 937 832-7055
  Englewood *(G-8326)*

CONTRACTORS: Underground Utilities

Anderzack-Pitzen Cnstr Inc .... D 419 644-2111
  Metamora *(G-11016)*
Bmu77 LLC .... E 740 652-1679
  Lancaster *(G-9696)*
Buckeye Excavating & Cnstr Inc .... E 419 663-3113
  Norwalk *(G-12003)*
Capitol Tunneling Inc .... E 614 444-0255
  Columbus *(G-5505)*
CST Utilities L L C .... D 614 801-9600
  Grove City *(G-8913)*
Ewers Utility Service LLC .... E 740 326-4451
  Mount Vernon *(G-11487)*
Fishel Company .... D 614 921-8504
  Columbus *(G-5868)*
Geotex Construction Svcs Inc .... E 614 444-5690
  Columbus *(G-5929)*
Gleason Construction Co Inc .... E 419 865-7480
  Holland *(G-9285)*
Great Lakes Crushing Ltd .... D 440 944-5500
  Wickliffe *(G-15150)*
JS Bova Excavating LLC .... E 234 254-4040
  Struthers *(G-13501)*
Kenneth G Myers Cnstr Co Inc .... D 419 639-2051
  Green Springs *(G-8860)*
Nickolas M Savko & Sons Inc .... C 614 451-2242
  Columbus *(G-6359)*
Ohio Utilities Protection Svc .... D 800 311-3692
  North Jackson *(G-11875)*
Precision Engrg & Contg Inc .... D 440 349-1204
  Solon *(G-13129)*
R D Jergens Contractors Inc .... D 937 669-9799
  Vandalia *(G-14391)*
R L A Utilities .... E 513 554-1453
  Cincinnati *(G-3272)*
Terrace Construction Co Inc .... D 216 739-3170
  Cleveland *(G-4986)*
Trucco Construction Co Inc .... C 740 417-9010
  Delaware *(G-7831)*
Underground Utilities Inc .... D 419 465-2587
  Monroeville *(G-11360)*
US Radius Services Inc .... E 929 505-1063
  Trenton *(G-14125)*
Usic Locating Services LLC .... E 513 554-0456
  Cincinnati *(G-3611)*
Utilicon Corporation .... E 216 391-8500
  Cleveland *(G-5095)*

Vernon Nagel Inc .... D 419 592-3861
  Napoleon *(G-11534)*
Woodward Excavating Co .... E 614 866-4384
  Reynoldsburg *(G-12683)*

CONTRACTORS: Ventilation & Duct Work

Franck and Fric Incorporated .... D 216 524-4451
  Cleveland *(G-4284)*
Hartley Company .... E 740 439-6668
  Zanesville *(G-15798)*
Jacobs Mechanical Co .... C 513 681-6800
  Cincinnati *(G-2895)*
Sisler Heating & Cooling Inc .... E 330 722-7101
  Medina *(G-10890)*
TH Martin Inc .... D 216 741-2020
  Cleveland *(G-4990)*

CONTRACTORS: Warm Air Heating & Air Conditioning

Airtron Inc .... D 614 274-2345
  Columbus *(G-5333)*
Breeze 33 Products LLC .... D 833 273-3950
  Akron *(G-74)*
Buckeye Heating and AC Sup Inc .... E 216 831-0066
  Bedford Heights *(G-996)*
Hamilton-Parker Company .... D 614 358-7800
  Columbus *(G-5968)*
Luxury Heating Company .... D 440 366-0971
  Sheffield Village *(G-13001)*
Robertson Heating Sup Co Ohio .... C 800 433-9532
  Alliance *(G-397)*
Robertson Htg Sup Clumbus Ohio .... C 330 821-9180
  Alliance *(G-399)*
Style Crest Enterprises Inc .... D 419 355-8586
  Fremont *(G-8705)*
Wadsworth-Slawson Inc .... E 216 391-7263
  Perrysburg *(G-12385)*
Waibel Energy Systems Inc .... D 937 264-4343
  Vandalia *(G-14403)*
Yanfeng US Auto Intr Systems I .... E 419 662-4905
  Northwood *(G-11988)*

CONTRACTORS: Water Well Drilling

Collector Wells Intl Inc .... D 614 888-6263
  Columbus *(G-5596)*
Moodys of Dayton Inc .... E 614 443-3898
  Miamisburg *(G-11074)*

CONTRACTORS: Windows & Doors

Fortune Brands Windows Inc .... C 614 532-3500
  Columbus *(G-5879)*

CONTRACTORS: Wood Floor Installation & Refinishing

Frank Novak & Sons Inc .... D 216 475-2495
  Cleveland *(G-4285)*
Hoover & Wells Inc .... C 419 691-9220
  Toledo *(G-13850)*
Jackson Bluford and Son Inc .... D 513 831-6231
  Milford *(G-11234)*

CONTRACTORS: Wrecking & Demolition

Aztec Services Group Inc .... D 513 541-2002
  Cincinnati *(G-2233)*
Boyas Enterprises I Inc .... E 216 524-3620
  Cleveland *(G-3886)*
Brunk Excavating Inc .... E 513 360-0308
  Monroe *(G-11335)*
Cook Paving and Cnstr Co .... E 216 267-7705
  Independence *(G-9424)*

CONTRACTORS: Wrecking & Demolition

Dave Sugar Excavating LLC............................. E 330 542-1100
   Petersburg *(G-12394)*

Fluor-Bwxt Portsmouth LLC............................ A 866 706-6992
   Piketon *(G-12419)*

Fortuna Construction Co Inc........................... E 440 892-3834
   Cleveland *(G-4278)*

Fox Services Inc... E 513 858-2022
   Fairfield *(G-8414)*

Mark Schaffer Excvtg Trckg Inc...................... D 419 668-5990
   Norwalk *(G-12017)*

Rnw Holdings Inc.. E 330 792-0600
   Youngstown *(G-15709)*

Sunesis Environmental LLC............................. D 513 326-6000
   Fairfield *(G-8444)*

SW Griffin Co LLC... E 513 601-3894
   Blue Ash *(G-1248)*

SW Griffin Co Llc... E 513 678-4741
   Blue Ash *(G-1249)*

CONTROL EQPT: Electric

Machine Drive Company................................ D 513 793-7077
   Cincinnati *(G-3000)*

CONTROL EQPT: Noise

Kinetics Noise Control Inc............................... C 614 889-0480
   Dublin *(G-8049)*

CONTROLS & ACCESS: Indl, Electric

Apex Control Systems Inc.............................. D 330 938-2588
   Sebring *(G-12945)*

Corrotec Inc... E 937 325-3585
   Springfield *(G-13242)*

PMC Systems Limited..................................... E 330 538-2268
   North Jackson *(G-11876)*

CONTROLS & ACCESS: Motor

Standex Electronics Inc.................................. D 513 871-3777
   Fairfield *(G-8443)*

CONTROLS: Environmental

Alan Manufacturing Inc.................................. E 330 262-1555
   Wooster *(G-15308)*

Babcock & Wilcox Company........................... A 330 753-4511
   Akron *(G-59)*

Cincinnati Air Conditioning Co....................... D 513 721-5622
   Cincinnati *(G-2392)*

Hunter Defense Tech Inc................................ E 216 438-6111
   Solon *(G-13096)*

Pepperl + Fuchs Inc....................................... C 330 425-3555
   Twinsburg *(G-14210)*

CONVENIENCE STORES

Beck Suppliers Inc.. E 419 426-3051
   Attica *(G-598)*

Duncan Oil Co.. E 937 426-5945
   Dayton *(G-7131)*

Holland Oil Company..................................... D 330 835-1815
   Akron *(G-194)*

National At/Trckstops Hldngs C..................... A 440 808-9100
   Westlake *(G-15081)*

Ta Operating LLC... B 440 808-9100
   Westlake *(G-15113)*

CONVEYOR SYSTEMS: Belt, General Indl Use

Mfh Partners Inc... B 440 461-4100
   Cleveland *(G-4571)*

CONVEYOR SYSTEMS: Bulk Handling

Air Technical Industries Inc............................. E 440 951-5191
   Mentor *(G-10909)*

CONVEYOR SYSTEMS: Robotic

Grob Systems Inc... A 419 358-9015
   Bluffton *(G-1281)*

CONVEYORS & CONVEYING EQPT

Alba Manufacturing Inc.................................. D 513 874-0551
   Fairfield *(G-8388)*

Allied Fabricating & Wldg Co......................... E 614 751-6664
   Columbus *(G-5338)*

Defabco Inc.. D 614 231-2700
   Columbus *(G-5749)*

Dillin Engineered Systems Corp..................... E 419 666-6789
   Perrysburg *(G-12333)*

Innovative Controls Corp................................ E 419 691-6684
   Toledo *(G-13863)*

Intelligrated Inc.. A 513 874-0788
   West Chester *(G-14820)*

Intelligrated Systems Inc................................ A 866 936-7300
   Mason *(G-10565)*

Intelligrated Systems LLC............................... A 513 701-7300
   Mason *(G-10566)*

Intelligrated Systems Ohio LLC...................... A 513 701-7300
   Mason *(G-10567)*

Stock Fairfield Corporation............................ C 440 543-6000
   Solon *(G-13149)*

Werks Kraft Engineering LLC.......................... E 330 721-7374
   Medina *(G-10902)*

COOKING & FOODWARMING EQPT: Commercial

Lima Sheet Metal Machine & Mfg................... E 419 229-1161
   Lima *(G-9927)*

CORRECTIONAL INSTITUTIONS, GOVERNMENT: Prison, government

Ohio Department Youth Services................... C 419 245-3040
   Cleveland *(G-4686)*

Ohio Department Youth Services................... C 419 875-6965
   Liberty Center *(G-9846)*

COSMETIC PREPARATIONS

Universal Packg Systems Inc.......................... C 513 732-2000
   Batavia *(G-751)*

Universal Packg Systems Inc.......................... C 513 735-4777
   Batavia *(G-752)*

Universal Packg Systems Inc.......................... C 513 674-9400
   Cincinnati *(G-3563)*

COSMETICS & TOILETRIES

Luminex HM Dcor Frgrnce Hldg C.................. B 513 563-1113
   Blue Ash *(G-1204)*

Nehemiah Manufacturing Co LLC.................. C 513 351-5700
   Cincinnati *(G-3103)*

COSMETICS WHOLESALERS

Orveon Global US LLC................................... B 614 348-4994
   Columbus *(G-6482)*

COSMETOLOGY & PERSONAL HYGIENE SALONS

Face Forward Aesthetics LLC......................... E 844 307-5929
   Columbus *(G-5841)*

Sugar & Spice Spa llc..................................... D 513 319-0112
   Mason *(G-10612)*

Waxxpot Group Franchise LLC...................... C 614 622-3018
   Columbus *(G-6871)*

COSMETOLOGY SCHOOL

AFA Beauty Inc... E 740 331-1655
   Athens *(G-554)*

Nurtur Holdings LLC....................................... E 614 487-3033
   Loveland *(G-10154)*

Nutur Holdings LLC.. C 513 576-9333
   Loveland *(G-10155)*

COUNTRY CLUBS

Athens Golf & Country Club.......................... E 740 592-1655
   Athens *(G-558)*

Avalon Golf and Cntry CLB Inc...................... C 330 856-8898
   Warren *(G-14500)*

Avon-Oaks Country Club................................ D 440 892-0660
   Avon *(G-639)*

Barrington Golf Club Inc................................ D 330 995-0821
   Aurora *(G-609)*

Barrington Golf Club Inc................................ D 330 995-0600
   Aurora *(G-608)*

Belmont Country Club.................................... D 419 666-1472
   Perrysburg *(G-12316)*

Belmont Hills Country Club............................ D 740 695-2181
   Saint Clairsville *(G-12779)*

Bowling Green Country Club Inc................... E 419 352-5546
   Bowling Green *(G-1311)*

Brook Plum Country Club............................... D 419 625-5394
   Sandusky *(G-12866)*

Brookside Golf & Cntry CLB Co..................... C 614 889-2581
   Columbus *(G-5469)*

Browns Run Country Club.............................. E 513 423-6291
   Middletown *(G-11154)*

Camargo Club.. C 513 561-9292
   Cincinnati *(G-2302)*

Catawba-Cleveland Dev Corp....................... D 419 797-4424
   Port Clinton *(G-12518)*

Chagrin Valley Country Club Co.................... D 440 248-4310
   Chagrin Falls *(G-1955)*

Chagrin Valley Hunt Club............................... E 440 423-4414
   Gates Mills *(G-8782)*

Cincinnati Country Club................................ C 513 533-5200
   Cincinnati *(G-2405)*

Cleveland Skating Club.................................. D 216 791-2800
   Cleveland *(G-4066)*

Clovernook Country Club............................... D 513 521-0333
   Cincinnati *(G-2463)*

Coldstream Country Club............................... D 513 231-3900
   Cincinnati *(G-2473)*

Columbia Hills Country CLB Inc.................... D 440 236-5051
   Columbia Station *(G-5225)*

Country Club Inc.. C 216 831-9200
   Cleveland *(G-4121)*

Country Club At Muirfield Vlg........................ E 614 764-1714
   Dublin *(G-7974)*

Country Club of Hudson................................ D 330 650-1188
   Hudson *(G-9341)*

County of Perry.. E 740 342-0416
   New Lexington *(G-11624)*

Dayton Country Club Company.................... D 937 294-3352
   Dayton *(G-7278)*

Dry Run Limited Partnership.......................... E 513 561-9119
   Cincinnati *(G-2577)*

East Liverpool Country Club.......................... E 330 385-7197
   East Liverpool *(G-8181)*

Elyria Country Club Company....................... D 440 322-6391
   Elyria *(G-8245)*

Escalante - Cntry CLB of N LLC..................... E 937 374-5000
   Xenia *(G-15504)*

Findlay Country Club..................................... E 419 422-9263
   Findlay *(G-8528)*

Four Bridges Country Club Ltd...................... D 513 759-4620
   Liberty Township *(G-9852)*

Golf Club Co.. D 614 855-7326
   New Albany *(G-11567)*

SERVICES SECTION — CUTLERY

Heritage Club .... D 513 459-7711
  Mason *(G-10560)*

Highland Meadows Golf Club .... E 419 882-7153
  Sylvania *(G-13550)*

Hillbrook Club Inc .... E 440 247-4940
  Cleveland *(G-4362)*

Hyde Park Golf & Country Club .... D 513 871-3111
  Cincinnati *(G-2858)*

Inverness Club .... D 419 578-9000
  Toledo *(G-13864)*

Kirtland Country Club Company .... D 440 942-4400
  Willoughby *(G-15196)*

Lakes Golf & Country Club Inc .... E 614 882-2582
  Westerville *(G-14904)*

Lakewood Country Club Company .... D 440 871-0400
  Cleveland *(G-4479)*

Lenau Park .... E 440 235-2646
  Olmsted Twp *(G-12091)*

Losantiville Country Club .... D 513 631-4133
  Cincinnati *(G-2988)*

Maketewah Country Club Company .... D 513 242-9333
  Cincinnati *(G-3005)*

Mayfield Cntry CLB Schlrship F .... E 216 381-0826
  Cleveland *(G-4532)*

Medallion Club .... C 614 794-6999
  Westerville *(G-14909)*

Medina Country Club LLC .... D 330 725-6621
  Medina *(G-10855)*

Moraine Country Club .... E 937 294-6200
  Dayton *(G-7513)*

Moundbuilders Country Club Co .... D 740 344-4500
  Newark *(G-11732)*

Mount Vernon Country Club Co .... D 740 392-4216
  Mount Vernon *(G-11500)*

Msr Legacy .... D 216 381-0826
  Cleveland *(G-4608)*

N C R Employees Benefit Assn .... C 937 299-3571
  Dayton *(G-7524)*

New Albany Cntry CLB Cmnty Ass .... C 614 939-8500
  New Albany *(G-11578)*

New Albany Country Club LLC .... C 614 939-8500
  New Albany *(G-11579)*

New London Hills Club Inc .... E 513 868-9026
  Hamilton *(G-9068)*

Piqua Country Club Holding Co .... E 937 773-7744
  Piqua *(G-12452)*

Portage Country Club Company .... D 330 836-8565
  Akron *(G-268)*

Raintree Country Club Inc .... E 330 699-3232
  Uniontown *(G-14262)*

Rawiga Country Club Inc .... E 330 336-2220
  Seville *(G-12964)*

Rocky Fork Hunt and Cntry CLB .... D 614 471-7828
  Gahanna *(G-8727)*

Scioto Reserve Inc .... D 740 881-3903
  Powell *(G-12606)*

Shady Hollow Cntry CLB Co Inc .... D 330 832-1581
  Massillon *(G-10668)*

Shaker Heights Country Club Co .... C 216 991-3660
  Shaker Heights *(G-12983)*

Shawnee Country Club .... D 419 227-7177
  Lima *(G-9960)*

Silver Lake Country Club .... E 330 688-6066
  Silver Lake *(G-13060)*

Steubenville Country Club Inc .... E 740 264-0521
  Steubenville *(G-13343)*

Sycamore Creek Country Club .... C 937 748-0791
  Springboro *(G-13208)*

Sylvania Country Club .... D 419 392-0530
  Sylvania *(G-13575)*

Terrace Park Country Club Inc .... D 513 965-4061
  Milford *(G-11260)*

Tippecanoe Country Club Inc .... E 330 758-7518
  Canfield *(G-1644)*

Toledo Club .... D 419 243-2200
  Toledo *(G-14058)*

Troy Country Club .... E 937 335-5691
  Troy *(G-14163)*

Turtle Golf Management Ltd .... D 614 882-5920
  Westerville *(G-15019)*

Union Country Club .... E 330 343-5544
  Dover *(G-7905)*

Urbana Country Club .... E 937 653-1690
  Urbana *(G-14314)*

Wedgewood Golf & Country Club .... C 614 793-9600
  Powell *(G-12609)*

Western Hills Country Club .... D 513 922-0011
  Cincinnati *(G-3662)*

Westwood Country Club Company .... D 440 331-3016
  Rocky River *(G-12756)*

Wetherngton Golf Cntry CLB Inc .... E 513 755-2582
  West Chester *(G-14794)*

Weymouth Valley Inc .... D 440 498-8888
  Solon *(G-13163)*

York Temple Country Club .... D 614 885-5459
  Columbus *(G-6916)*

Youngstown Country Club .... D 330 759-1040
  Youngstown *(G-15757)*

Zanesville Country Club .... D 740 452-2726
  Zanesville *(G-15840)*

CRANE & AERIAL LIFT SVCS

American Crane Inc .... E 614 496-2268
  Reynoldsburg *(G-12651)*

Bay Mechanical & Elec Corp .... D 440 282-6816
  Lorain *(G-10058)*

In Terminal Services Corp .... C 216 518-8407
  Maple Heights *(G-10341)*

Jeffers Crane Service Inc .... E 419 223-9010
  Lima *(G-9912)*

Pollock Research & Design Inc .... E 330 332-3300
  Salem *(G-12847)*

CRANES: Indl Plant

Hiab USA Inc .... D 419 482-6000
  Perrysburg *(G-12343)*

CREDIT CARD SVCS

Advanced Financial Services .... E 800 320-0000
  Copley *(G-6946)*

Best Payment Solutions Inc .... E 630 321-0117
  Symmes Twp *(G-13582)*

Bread Financial Holdings Inc .... C 614 729-3000
  Columbus *(G-5460)*

Bread Financial Holdings Inc .... C 614 729-5800
  Reynoldsburg *(G-12655)*

Bread Financial Holdings Inc .... C 614 729-5000
  Westerville *(G-14963)*

Bread Financial Holdings Inc .... C 614 729-4000
  Columbus *(G-5461)*

Citicorp Credit Services Inc .... B 212 559-1000
  Columbus *(G-5575)*

Collections Acquisition Co LLC .... C 614 944-5788
  Columbus *(G-5595)*

Dfs Corporate Services LLC .... E 614 777-7020
  Hilliard *(G-9192)*

Dfs Corporate Services LLC .... B 614 283-2499
  New Albany *(G-11561)*

Federal Card Services LLC .... E 513 429-4459
  Cincinnati *(G-2653)*

Jpmorgan Chase Bank Nat Assn .... A 614 436-3055
  Columbus *(G-5264)*

Macys Cr & Customer Svcs Inc .... A 513 398-5221
  Mason *(G-10576)*

Payrix Solutions LLC .... E 718 506-9250
  Symmes Township *(G-13580)*

The Elder-Beerman Stores Corp .... A 937 296-2700
  Moraine *(G-11443)*

Versapay Corporation .... D 216 535-9016
  Twinsburg *(G-14229)*

Worldpay Inc .... A 866 622-2390
  Symmes Township *(G-13581)*

Worldpay Holding LLC .... C 513 358-6192
  Symmes Twp *(G-13584)*

Worldpay Iso Inc .... C 502 961-5200
  Symmes Twp *(G-13585)*

CREDIT UNIONS: Federally Chartered

Buckeye State Credit Union Inc .... E 330 823-7930
  Alliance *(G-376)*

Firefighters Cmnty Cr Un Inc .... E 216 621-4644
  Cleveland *(G-4252)*

Homeland Credit Union Inc .... E 740 775-3024
  Chillicothe *(G-2069)*

Kemba Financial Credit Un Inc .... D 614 235-2395
  Columbus *(G-6110)*

Kemba Financial Credit Union .... E 614 235-2395
  Columbus *(G-6111)*

Struthers CU A Div Brdge Cr Un .... E 800 434-7300
  Columbus *(G-6723)*

Wright-Patt Credit Union Inc .... B 937 912-7000
  Beavercreek *(G-917)*

CRUDE PETROLEUM & NATURAL GAS PRODUCTION

Bijoe Development Inc .... E 330 674-5981
  Millersburg *(G-11274)*

CRUDE PETROLEUM PRODUCTION

Knight Material Tech LLC .... D 330 488-1651
  East Canton *(G-8169)*

CUPS: Paper, Made From Purchased Materials

Ricking Holding Co .... E 513 825-3551
  Cleveland *(G-4839)*

CURTAIN WALLS: Building, Steel

Clouse Construction Corp .... E 419 448-1365
  New Riegel *(G-11678)*

Ferrous Metal Transfer Co .... E 216 671-8500
  Brooklyn *(G-1409)*

J & J General Maintenance Inc .... D 740 533-9729
  Ironton *(G-9509)*

CURTAINS: Window, From Purchased Materials

Style-Line Incorporated .... E 614 291-0600
  Columbus *(G-6725)*

CUT STONE & STONE PRODUCTS

Bell Vault and Monu Works Inc .... E 937 866-2444
  Miamisburg *(G-11025)*

Kellstone Inc .... E 419 746-2396
  Kelleys Island *(G-9553)*

Lang Stone Company Inc .... E 614 235-4099
  Columbus *(G-6139)*

National Lime and Stone Co .... E 419 562-0771
  Bucyrus *(G-1513)*

National Lime and Stone Co .... E 419 396-7671
  Carey *(G-1894)*

CUTLERY

CUTLERY

G & S Metal Products Co Inc.................... C 216 441-0700
Cleveland (G-4295)

Npk Construction Equipment Inc............ D 440 232-7900
Bedford (G-976)

CYLINDER & ACTUATORS: Fluid Power

Eaton Leasing Corporation...................... B 216 382-2292
Beachwood (G-788)

Hydraulic Parts Store Inc....................... E 330 364-6667
New Philadelphia (G-11656)

Robeck Fluid Power Co.......................... D 330 562-1140
Aurora (G-624)

Steel Eqp Specialists Inc....................... D 330 823-8260
Alliance (G-401)

Swagelok Company................................. D 440 349-5934
Solon (G-13154)

CYLINDERS: Pressure

Gayston Corporation............................... C 937 743-6050
Miamisburg (G-11057)

DAIRY PRDTS STORE: Cheese

Cheese Holdings Inc............................... E 330 893-2479
Millersburg (G-11275)

Coblentz Distributing Inc........................ C 330 893-3895
Millersburg (G-11277)

Great Lakes Cheese Co Inc.................... B 440 834-2500
Hiram (G-9274)

Lori Holding Co...................................... E 740 342-3230
New Lexington (G-11628)

DAIRY PRDTS STORE: Ice Cream, Packaged

Austintown Dairy Inc.............................. E 330 629-6170
Youngstown (G-15553)

DAIRY PRDTS STORES

Discount Drug Mart Inc........................... C 330 725-2340
Medina (G-10829)

Hans Rothenbuhler & Son Inc................ E 440 632-6000
Middlefield (G-11140)

S and S Gilardi Inc................................. D 740 397-2751
Mount Vernon (G-11507)

United Dairy Farmers Inc....................... C 513 396-8700
Cincinnati (G-3553)

Youngs Jersey Dairy Inc........................ B 937 325-0629
Yellow Springs (G-15537)

DAIRY PRDTS: Cheese

Lipari Foods Operating Co LLC............. E 330 893-2479
Millersburg (G-11284)

DAIRY PRDTS: Dietary Supplements, Dairy & Non-Dairy Based

Instantwhip-Columbus Inc...................... E 614 871-9447
Grove City (G-8928)

DAIRY PRDTS: Ice Cream & Ice Milk

United Dairy Farmers Inc....................... C 513 396-8700
Cincinnati (G-3553)

DAIRY PRDTS: Ice Cream, Bulk

Velvet Ice Cream Company.................... D 740 892-3921
Utica (G-14330)

DAIRY PRDTS: Milk, Condensed & Evaporated

Hans Rothenbuhler & Son Inc................ D 440 632-6000
Middlefield (G-11140)

DAIRY PRDTS: Natural Cheese

Great Lakes Cheese Co Inc.................... B 440 834-2500
Hiram (G-9274)

Hans Rothenbuhler & Son Inc................ E 440 632-6000
Middlefield (G-11140)

Miceli Dairy Products Co....................... D 216 791-6222
Cleveland (G-4572)

DAIRY PRDTS: Whipped Topping, Exc Frozen Or Dry Mix

Instantwhip-Columbus Inc...................... E 614 871-9447
Grove City (G-8928)

DATA ENTRY SVCS

ACS Computer Services Corp................ D 614 351-8298
Columbus (G-5209)

Coleman Professional Svcs Inc............. C 330 673-1347
Kent (G-9565)

DATA PROCESSING & PREPARATION SVCS

Bold Penguin Company LLC.................. C 614 344-1029
Columbus (G-5454)

Btas Inc... D 937 431-9431
Beavercreek (G-866)

City of Cleveland.................................... E 216 664-2430
Cleveland (G-3985)

Datatrak International Inc...................... E 440 443-0082
Beachwood (G-786)

Gracie Plum Investments Inc................. E 740 355-9029
Portsmouth (G-12552)

Illumination Works LLC......................... D 937 938-1321
Beavercreek (G-884)

Infovision21 Inc..................................... E 614 761-8844
Dublin (G-8038)

ITM Marketing Inc.................................. C 740 295-3575
Coshocton (G-6988)

Mast Technology Services Inc.............. E 614 415-7000
Columbus (G-6204)

Medical Mutual Services LLC................ C 440 878-4800
Strongsville (G-13475)

Midland Council Governments............... E 330 264-6047
Wooster (G-15356)

Mri Software LLC................................... B 800 321-8770
Solon (G-13114)

Northrop Grmmn Spce & Mssn Sys....... D 937 259-4956
Dayton (G-7531)

Prisma Integration Corp......................... E 330 545-8690
Girard (G-8823)

Sarcom Inc.. A 614 854-1300
Lewis Center (G-9835)

SC Strategic Solutions LLC................... C 567 424-6054
Norwalk (G-12027)

Sedlak Management Consultants........... E 216 206-4700
Cleveland (G-4890)

Southstern Ohio Vlntary Edcatn............. E 740 594-7663
Athens (G-591)

Sumaria Systems LLC............................ C 937 429-6070
Beavercreek (G-909)

DATA PROCESSING SVCS

1st All File Recovery Usa...................... E 800 399-7150
Cleveland (G-3742)

ADP Rpo.. E 419 420-1830
Findlay (G-8507)

Aero Fulfillment Services Corp.............. D 800 225-7145
Mason (G-10517)

Amsive OH LLC....................................... D 937 885-8000
Miamisburg (G-11024)

Cincinnati Bell Inc.................................. B 513 397-9900
Cincinnati (G-2398)

Concentrix Cvg Corporation.................. A 800 747-0583
Cincinnati (G-2492)

Concentrix Solutions Corp..................... E 480 968-2496
Cincinnati (G-2494)

County of Stark...................................... E 330 451-7232
Canton (G-1726)

Csi Complete Inc.................................... E 800 343-0641
Plain City (G-12472)

Ctrac Inc... E 440 572-1000
Cleveland (G-4144)

Early Express Services Inc................... E 937 223-5801
Dayton (G-7322)

Integrated Data Services Inc................. E 937 656-5496
Dayton (G-7422)

Integrated Marketing Tech Inc.............. D 330 225-3550
Brunswick (G-1460)

Isaac Instruments LLC........................... E 888 658-7520
Cleveland (G-4424)

Northwest Ohio Computer Assn............. E 419 267-5565
Archbold (G-464)

Office World Inc..................................... E 419 991-4694
Lima (G-9994)

Ohio United Agency Inc......................... E 419 562-3011
Bucyrus (G-1515)

Relational Solutions Inc......................... E 440 899-3296
North Olmsted (G-11913)

Rurbanc Data Services Inc.................... D 419 782-2530
Defiance (G-7767)

Spa Performance Inc............................. E 216 455-1540
Cleveland (G-4925)

Speedeon Data LLC................................ E 440 264-2100
Cleveland (G-4932)

Vndly LLC.. E 513 572-2500
Mason (G-10625)

Worldpay LLC... B
Symmes Twp (G-13583)

DEFENSE SYSTEMS & EQPT

Mrl Materials Resources LLC................ E 937 531-6657
Xenia (G-15528)

DENTAL EQPT & SPLYS

Boxout LLC... C 833 462-7746
Hudson (G-9334)

Dental Ceramics Inc............................... E 330 523-5240
Richfield (G-12694)

United Dental Laboratories.................... E 330 253-1810
Tallmadge (G-13609)

DENTAL EQPT & SPLYS WHOLESALERS

Coltene/Whaledent Inc........................... C 330 916-8800
Cuyahoga Falls (G-7063)

Dentronix Inc.. D 330 916-7300
Cuyahoga Falls (G-7070)

Patterson Dental Supply Inc.................. E 440 891-1050
Middleburg Heights (G-11120)

DENTAL EQPT & SPLYS: Orthodontic Appliances

Dentronix Inc.. D 330 916-7300
Cuyahoga Falls (G-7070)

DENTISTS' OFFICES & CLINICS

Concorde Therapy Group Inc................. C 330 493-4210
Canton (G-1721)

Dental Support Specialties LLC............. E 330 639-1333
Canton (G-1734)

Hani Ashqar DDS & Partners LLC......... E 203 560-3131
Euclid (G-8344)

Healthsource of Ohio Inc....................... E 937 386-0049
Seaman (G-12944)

Merkley Professionals Inc..................... E 419 447-9541
Tiffin (G-13633)

SERVICES SECTION

DISTRIBUTORS: Motor Vehicle Engine

Metro Health Dental Associates.............C.....216 778-4982
  Cleveland (G-4560)
Metrohealth System...............................A.....216 957-1500
  Cleveland (G-4562)

DEPARTMENT STORES

Centro Properties Group LLC................E.....440 324-6610
  Elyria (G-8235)

DEPARTMENT STORES: Non-Discount

JC Penney Corporation Inc....................D.....419 394-7610
  Saint Marys (G-12827)
The Elder-Beerman Stores Corp............A.....937 296-2700
  Moraine (G-11443)

DEPARTMENT STORES: Surplus & Salvage

Goodwill Inds Cent'l Ohio Inc..................B.....614 294-5181
  Columbus (G-5941)

DESIGN SVCS, NEC

ADS Manufacturing Ohio LLC................D.....513 217-4502
  Middletown (G-11150)
Ambers Design Studio LLC...................E.....614 221-1237
  Columbus (G-5344)
Bollin & Sons Inc...................................E.....419 693-6573
  Toledo (G-13710)
Dollries Group LLC...............................E.....513 834-6105
  North Bend (G-11803)
Elevar Design Group Inc.......................E.....513 721-0600
  Cincinnati (G-2611)
Emersion Design LLC...........................E.....513 841-9100
  Cincinnati (G-2616)
Gencraft Designs LLC...........................E.....330 359-6251
  Navarre (G-11537)
Loth Inc..D.....513 554-4900
  Cincinnati (G-2989)
Process Plus Design Build LLC............C.....513 262-2261
  Cincinnati (G-3240)
Rise Brands..E.....614 754-7522
  Columbus (G-6590)
Rustic Pathways LLC............................D.....440 497-4166
  Mentor (G-10994)
Samuel Joseph Corp.............................E.....330 983-6557
  Akron (G-294)
Total System Services...........................E.....614 385-9221
  Columbus (G-6773)

DESIGN SVCS: Commercial & Indl

Design Central Inc.................................E.....614 890-0202
  Columbus (G-5758)
Ies Systems Inc.....................................E.....330 533-6683
  Canfield (G-1632)
North Bay Construction Inc...................E.....440 835-1898
  Westlake (G-15085)
Polaris Automation Inc..........................E.....614 431-0170
  Columbus (G-6534)
Priority Designs Inc...............................D.....614 337-9979
  Columbus (G-6546)
R and J Corporation..............................E.....440 871-6009
  Westlake (G-15101)
Ultra Tech Machinery Inc......................E.....330 929-5544
  Cuyahoga Falls (G-7113)

DESIGN SVCS: Computer Integrated Systems

Aclara Technologies LLC......................C.....440 528-7200
  Solon (G-13061)
Afidence Inc..E.....513 234-5822
  Mason (G-10518)
Baxter Hdell Dnnlly Prston Inc...............C.....513 271-1634
  Cincinnati (G-2240)

Bpi Infrmtion Systems Ohio Inc.............E.....440 717-4112
  Brecksville (G-1345)
Caci Mtl Systems Inc............................D.....937 426-3111
  Beavercreek (G-869)
Caci-CMS Info Systems LLC................C.....937 986-3600
  Fairborn (G-8368)
Cdo Technologies Inc...........................D.....937 258-0022
  Dayton (G-7128)
Cincinnati Trning Trml Svcs In..............D.....513 563-4474
  Cincinnati (G-2429)
Concentrix Cvg Corporation..................A.....800 747-0583
  Cincinnati (G-2492)
Cott Systems Inc...................................D.....614 847-4405
  Columbus (G-5707)
Jackson Control Co Inc.........................E.....513 824-9850
  Cincinnati (G-2893)
Logos Communications Systems Inc....D.....440 871-0777
  Westlake (G-15076)
Mapsys Inc..E.....614 255-7258
  Columbus (G-6193)
Marcus Thomas Llc..............................D.....216 292-4700
  Cleveland (G-4523)
Microman Inc...E.....614 923-8000
  Dublin (G-8064)
Northrop Grmman Tchncal Svcs I........D.....937 320-3100
  Beavercreek Township (G-945)
Pantek Incorporated.............................E.....216 344-1614
  Independence (G-9465)
Pcms Datafit Inc....................................D.....513 587-3100
  Blue Ash (G-1219)
Pomeroy It Solutions Sls Inc.................E.....440 717-1364
  Brecksville (G-1363)
Possible Worldwide LLC.......................E.....513 381-1380
  Cincinnati (G-3223)
Presidio Infrstrcture Sltons L.................E.....614 381-1400
  Dublin (G-8095)
Rainbow Data Systems Inc...................E.....937 431-8000
  Beavercreek (G-899)
Reynolds and Reynolds Company.........A.....937 485-2000
  Kettering (G-9632)
Rovisys Company..................................D.....330 562-8600
  Aurora (G-626)
Sarcom Inc..A.....614 854-1300
  Lewis Center (G-9835)
Sentient Studios Ltd..............................E.....330 204-8636
  Fairlawn (G-8499)
Sgi Matrix LLC......................................D.....937 438-9033
  Miamisburg (G-11092)
Siertek Ltd...E.....937 623-2466
  Beavercreek Township (G-948)
Sogeti USA LLC....................................C.....614 847-4477
  Westerville (G-15015)
Streamline Technical Svcs LLC............D.....614 441-7448
  Lockbourne (G-10016)
Sumaria Systems LLC..........................C.....937 429-6070
  Beavercreek (G-909)
Tata America Intl Corp..........................B.....513 677-6500
  Milford (G-11259)

DETECTIVE & ARMORED CAR SERVICES

Hereford Security Group.......................D.....330 644-1371
  Uniontown (G-14257)
Safeguard Properties LLC....................A.....216 739-2900
  Cleveland (G-4869)
United Sttes Dept of Hmland SE..........D.....937 821-5543
  Dayton (G-7684)
Universal Services America LP.............A.....937 454-9035
  Vandalia (G-14398)

DIAGNOSTIC SUBSTANCES

Revvity Health Sciences Inc.................E.....330 825-4525
  Akron (G-281)

Thermo Fisher Scientific Inc.................E.....800 871-8909
  Oakwood Village (G-12059)

DIAGNOSTIC SUBSTANCES OR AGENTS: Radioactive

Cardinal Health 414 LLC......................C.....614 757-5000
  Dublin (G-7956)

DIAMONDS, GEMS, WHOLESALE

Gottlieb & Sons Inc...............................E.....216 771-4785
  Beachwood (G-795)

DIES & TOOLS: Special

Acro Tool & Die Company.....................E.....330 773-5173
  Akron (G-14)
Athens Mold and Machine Inc..............D.....740 593-6613
  Athens (G-559)
General Tool Company..........................C.....513 733-5500
  Cincinnati (G-2728)
Lunar Tool & Mold Inc..........................E.....440 237-2141
  North Royalton (G-11944)
Mtd Holdings Inc...................................B.....330 225-2600
  Valley City (G-14336)
Seilkop Industries Inc............................E.....513 761-1035
  Cincinnati (G-3356)
Tipp Machine & Tool Inc.......................C.....937 890-8428
  Dayton (G-7669)
Worthington Industries Inc....................E.....614 438-3028
  Columbus (G-6906)

DIODES: Light Emitting

Ceso Inc..E.....937 435-8584
  Miamisburg (G-11035)

DISASTER SVCS

Christian Aid Ministries.........................E.....330 893-2428
  Millersburg (G-11276)
Custom Clg Svcs Disaster LLC............E.....440 774-1222
  Oberlin (G-12067)

DISCOUNT DEPARTMENT STORES

Walmart Inc...E.....740 286-8203
  Jackson (G-9528)
Walmart Inc...C.....937 399-0370
  Springfield (G-13310)

DISINFECTING & PEST CONTROL SERVICES

Duncan Sales Inc..................................E.....614 755-6580
  Columbus (G-5793)
Innovative Cleaning Svcs & Sup...........D.....513 981-1287
  Cincinnati (G-2872)

DISINFECTING SVCS

DCS Sanitation Management Inc..........A.....513 891-4980
  Cincinnati (G-2545)

DISKETTE DUPLICATING SVCS

Evanhoe & Associates Inc....................E.....937 235-2995
  Xenia (G-15505)
McData Services Corporation...............E.....614 272-5529
  Columbus (G-6214)

DISPLAY FIXTURES: Wood

Ptmj Enterprises Inc..............................D.....440 543-8000
  Solon (G-13132)

DISTRIBUTORS: Motor Vehicle Engine

Power Acquisition LLC..........................D.....614 228-5000
  Dublin (G-8093)
Tri-W Group Inc.....................................A.....614 228-5000
  Columbus (G-6786)

Employee Codes: A=Over 500 employees, B=251-500
C=101-250, D=51-100, E=20-50, F=10-19, G=1-9

2024 Harris Ohio
Services Directory

DOORS & WINDOWS: Storm, Metal

W W Williams Company LLC.............. D..... 614 228-5000
 Dublin *(G-8158)*

DOORS & WINDOWS: Storm, Metal

Champion Opco LLC.......................... B..... 513 327-7338
 Cincinnati *(G-2345)*

DOORS: Garage, Overhead, Metal

Clopay Corporation............................. C..... 800 282-2260
 Mason *(G-10540)*

DOORS: Garage, Overhead, Wood

Clopay Corporation............................. C..... 800 282-2260
 Mason *(G-10540)*

DRAPERIES & CURTAINS

Accent Drapery Co Inc...................... E..... 614 488-0741
 Columbus *(G-5300)*

Janson Industries................................ D..... 330 455-7029
 Canton *(G-1783)*

Vocational Services Inc..................... E..... 216 431-8085
 Cleveland *(G-5113)*

DRAPERY & UPHOLSTERY STORES: Draperies

Accent Drapery Co Inc...................... E..... 614 488-0741
 Columbus *(G-5300)*

DRINKING FOUNTAINS: Metal, Nonrefrigerated

Lvd Acquisition LLC........................... D..... 614 861-1350
 Columbus *(G-6181)*

DRINKING PLACES: Bars & Lounges

Brewdog Franchising LLC.................. E..... 614 908-3051
 Canal Winchester *(G-1599)*

Rhinegeist LLC..................................... D..... 513 381-1367
 Cincinnati *(G-3295)*

Valley Hospitality Inc......................... D..... 740 374-9660
 Marietta *(G-10409)*

DRINKING WATER COOLERS WHOLESALERS: Mechanical

Lvd Acquisition LLC........................... D..... 614 861-1350
 Columbus *(G-6181)*

DRUG STORES

City of Wooster................................... A..... 330 263-8100
 Wooster *(G-15321)*

Columbus Prescr Phrms Inc............... E..... 614 294-1600
 Westerville *(G-14972)*

Compass Community Health............. E..... 740 355-7102
 Portsmouth *(G-12549)*

CVS Revco DS Inc.............................. D..... 740 593-8501
 Athens *(G-563)*

CVS Revco DS Inc.............................. D..... 440 729-9070
 Chesterland *(G-2034)*

CVS Revco DS Inc.............................. C..... 937 393-4218
 Hillsboro *(G-9252)*

CVS Revco DS Inc.............................. E..... 740 389-1122
 Marion *(G-10424)*

CVS Revco DS Inc.............................. E..... 740 383-6244
 Marion *(G-10425)*

CVS Revco DS Inc.............................. D..... 513 523-6378
 Oxford *(G-12206)*

Dayton Osteopathic Hospital............. E..... 937 439-6000
 Dayton *(G-7295)*

Discount Drug Mart Inc..................... E..... 330 343-7700
 Dover *(G-7879)*

Discount Drug Mart Inc..................... C..... 330 725-2340
 Medina *(G-10829)*

Fields Family Enterprises Inc.............. E..... 513 897-1000
 Waynesville *(G-14622)*

Giant Eagle Inc.................................... D..... 330 364-5301
 Dover *(G-7885)*

Hursh Drugs Inc................................... E..... 419 524-0521
 Mansfield *(G-10271)*

Medical Service Company................. D..... 440 232-3000
 Bedford *(G-973)*

Omnicare Phrm of Midwest LLC....... D..... 513 719-2600
 Cincinnati *(G-3160)*

Promedica Health System Inc........... A..... 567 585-9600
 Toledo *(G-13972)*

Rite Aid of Ohio Inc........................... E..... 330 706-1004
 Barberton *(G-705)*

Rite Aid of Ohio Inc........................... E..... 937 833-2174
 Brookville *(G-1448)*

Rite Aid of Ohio Inc........................... E..... 740 942-3101
 Cadiz *(G-1543)*

Rite Aid of Ohio Inc........................... E..... 330 922-4466
 Cuyahoga Falls *(G-7095)*

Rite Aid of Ohio Inc........................... E..... 937 277-1611
 Dayton *(G-7591)*

Rite Aid of Ohio Inc........................... E..... 937 258-8101
 Dayton *(G-7592)*

Rite Aid of Ohio Inc........................... E..... 937 256-3111
 Dayton *(G-7593)*

Rite Aid of Ohio Inc........................... E..... 937 836-5204
 Englewood *(G-8321)*

Rite Aid of Ohio Inc........................... E..... 330 527-2828
 Garrettsville *(G-8779)*

Rite Aid of Ohio Inc........................... E..... 937 687-3456
 New Lebanon *(G-11620)*

St Lukes Hospital................................ B..... 419 893-5911
 Maumee *(G-10769)*

Trumbll-Mahoning Med Group Inc... E..... 330 372-8800
 Cortland *(G-6976)*

Ziks Family Pharmacy 100................. E..... 937 225-9350
 Dayton *(G-7737)*

DRUGS & DRUG PROPRIETARIES, WHOLESALE

Ncs Healthcare Inc.............................. A..... 216 514-3350
 Cleveland *(G-4630)*

Omnicare Phrm of Midwest LLC....... D..... 513 719-2600
 Cincinnati *(G-3160)*

Pharmed Corporation......................... D..... 440 250-5400
 Westlake *(G-15097)*

DRUGS & DRUG PROPRIETARIES, WHOLESALE: Medicinals/ Botanicals

Gem Edwards Inc................................. D..... 330 342-8300
 Hudson *(G-9352)*

DRUGS & DRUG PROPRIETARIES, WHOLESALE: Patent Medicines

ICP Inc.. D..... 419 447-6216
 Tiffin *(G-13628)*

Teva Womens Health LLC................. C..... 513 731-9900
 Cincinnati *(G-3460)*

DRUGS & DRUG PROPRIETARIES, WHOLESALE: Pharmaceuticals

Absolute Pharmacy Inc....................... E..... 330 498-8200
 Canton *(G-1653)*

American Regent Inc.......................... D..... 614 436-2222
 Hilliard *(G-9178)*

Braden Med Services Inc................... E..... 740 732-2356
 Caldwell *(G-1547)*

Capital Wholesale Drug Company.... D..... 614 297-8225
 Columbus *(G-5502)*

Cardinal Health Inc............................. D..... 614 409-6770
 Groveport *(G-8976)*

Cardinal Health Inc............................. E..... 614 497-9552
 Obetz *(G-12079)*

Cardinal Health Inc............................. A..... 614 757-5000
 Dublin *(G-7950)*

Cardinal Health 200 LLC................... E..... 614 757-5000
 Dublin *(G-7953)*

Cardinal Health 201 Inc..................... E..... 614 757-5000
 Dublin *(G-7954)*

Cardinal Health 301 LLC................... A..... 614 757-5000
 Dublin *(G-7955)*

Cardinal Health Systems Inc............. A..... 513 874-5940
 West Chester *(G-14802)*

Cencora Inc.. E..... 610 727-7000
 Columbus *(G-5527)*

Discount Drug Mart Inc..................... C..... 330 725-2340
 Medina *(G-10829)*

Elixir Pharmacy LLC........................... C..... 330 491-4200
 North Canton *(G-11827)*

Evergreen Pharmaceutical LLC.......... B..... 513 719-2600
 Cincinnati *(G-2641)*

Evergreen Phrm Cal LLC.................... E..... 513 719-2600
 Cincinnati *(G-2642)*

Greenfield Hts Oper Group LLC........ E..... 312 877-1153
 Lima *(G-9894)*

Heartland Healthcare Svcs LLC......... C..... 419 535-8435
 Toledo *(G-13842)*

Masters Drug Company Inc............... B..... 800 982-7922
 Lebanon *(G-9777)*

Masters Pharmaceutical LLC............. C..... 800 982-7922
 Mason *(G-10579)*

McKesson Corporation....................... E..... 740 636-3500
 Wshngtn Ct Hs *(G-15490)*

McKesson Medical-Surgical Inc........ C..... 614 539-2600
 Urbancrest *(G-14321)*

Medpace Inc... A..... 513 579-9911
 Cincinnati *(G-3031)*

Ncs Healthcare LLC............................ E..... 513 719-2600
 Cincinnati *(G-3101)*

Neighborcare Inc................................. A..... 513 719-2600
 Cincinnati *(G-3104)*

Omnicare LLC...................................... C..... 513 719-2600
 Cincinnati *(G-3157)*

Omnicare Distribution Ctr LLC........ D..... 419 720-8200
 Cincinnati *(G-3158)*

Optum Infusion Svcs 550 LLC.......... D..... 866 442-4679
 Cincinnati *(G-3166)*

Pharmscript LLC.................................. D..... 908 389-1818
 Columbus *(G-6521)*

Prescription Supply Inc...................... D..... 419 661-6600
 Northwood *(G-11982)*

Remedi Seniorcare of Ohio LLC........ E..... 800 232-4239
 Troy *(G-14155)*

Robert J Matthews Company........... D..... 330 834-3000
 Massillon *(G-10664)*

Rxcrossroads 3pl LLC......................... C..... 866 447-9758
 Mason *(G-10604)*

Specialized Pharmacy Svcs LLC........ E..... 513 719-2600
 Cincinnati *(G-3396)*

Triplefin LLC.. D..... 855 877-5346
 Mason *(G-10621)*

DRUGS & DRUG PROPRIETARIES, WHOLESALE: Vitamins & Minerals

Basic Drugs Inc.................................... E..... 937 898-4010
 Vandalia *(G-14366)*

Boxout LLC... C..... 833 462-7746
 Hudson *(G-9334)*

SERVICES SECTION

Firelands Tech Ventures LLC.............. E 419 616-5115
  Huron *(G-9388)*
Mitsubshi Intl Fd Ingrdnts Inc.............. E 614 652-1111
  Dublin *(G-8065)*
Second Wind Vitamins Inc.............. E 330 336-9260
  Wadsworth *(G-14451)*

DUCTS: Sheet Metal

Langdon Inc.............. E 513 733-5955
  Cincinnati *(G-2965)*
R G Smith Company.............. D 330 456-3415
  Canton *(G-1839)*
United McGill Corporation.............. E 614 829-1200
  Groveport *(G-9007)*

DYES & PIGMENTS: Organic

Hexpol Compounding LLC.............. C 440 834-4644
  Burton *(G-1528)*

EATING PLACES

5901 Pfffer Rd Htels Sites LLC.............. E 513 793-4500
  Blue Ash *(G-1120)*
A C Management Inc.............. E 440 461-9200
  Cleveland *(G-3748)*
Akron Management Corp.............. B 330 644-8441
  Akron *(G-34)*
Avalon Foodservice Inc.............. C 330 854-4551
  Canal Fulton *(G-1592)*
AVI Food Systems Inc.............. E 740 452-9363
  Zanesville *(G-15768)*
B & I Hotel Management LLC.............. C 330 995-0200
  Aurora *(G-607)*
Bob-Mor Inc.............. C 419 485-5555
  Montpelier *(G-11381)*
Broad Street Hotel Assoc LP.............. D 614 861-0321
  Columbus *(G-5467)*
Buehler Food Markets Inc.............. C 330 364-3079
  Dover *(G-7874)*
Buns of Delaware Inc.............. E 740 363-2867
  Delaware *(G-7781)*
Buxton Inn Inc.............. E 740 587-0001
  Granville *(G-8849)*
Cameron Mitchell Rest LLC.............. E 614 621-3663
  Columbus *(G-5494)*
Canterbury Golf Club Inc.............. D 216 561-1914
  Cleveland *(G-3923)*
Ch Relty Iv/Clmbus Partners LP.............. D 614 885-3334
  Columbus *(G-5550)*
Charter Hotel Group Ltd Partnr.............. E 216 772-4538
  Mentor *(G-10920)*
Cherry Jack Ltd Partnership.............. C 740 788-1200
  Newark *(G-11691)*
Chgc Inc.............. E 330 225-6122
  Valley City *(G-14332)*
City of Centerville.............. D 937 438-3585
  Dayton *(G-7227)*
Cleveland Arprt Hspitality LLC.............. D 440 871-6000
  Westlake *(G-15051)*
Cleveland Rest Oper Ltd Partnr.............. E 216 328-1421
  Cleveland *(G-4064)*
Columbus Airport Ltd Partnr.............. C 614 475-7551
  Columbus *(G-5606)*
Columbus Museum of Art.............. D 614 221-6801
  Columbus *(G-5647)*
Commodore Prry Inns Suites LLC.............. E 419 732-2645
  Port Clinton *(G-12520)*
Country Club of Hudson.............. D 330 650-1188
  Hudson *(G-9341)*
Davis Construction Management.............. E 440 248-7770
  Cleveland *(G-4151)*
Emmett Dan House Ltd Partnr.............. E 740 392-6886
  Mount Vernon *(G-11485)*

Findlay Country Club.............. E 419 422-9263
  Findlay *(G-8528)*
Findlay Inn & Conference Ctr.............. E 419 422-5682
  Findlay *(G-8529)*
First Hotel Associates LP.............. E 614 228-3800
  Columbus *(G-5862)*
Fred W Albrecht Grocery Co.............. C 330 645-6222
  Coventry Township *(G-7008)*
Gallipolis Hospitality Inc.............. C 740 446-0090
  Gallipolis *(G-8756)*
Glenlaurel Inc.............. E 740 385-4070
  Rockbridge *(G-12735)*
Green Township Hospitality LLC.............. E 513 574-6000
  Cincinnati *(G-2774)*
Greenville Inn Inc.............. E 937 548-3613
  Greenville *(G-8875)*
Grill Rest At Sheraton Suites.............. E 614 436-0004
  Columbus *(G-5957)*
Grizzly Golf Center Inc.............. B 513 398-5200
  Mason *(G-10557)*
Hauck Hospitality LLC.............. D 513 563-8330
  Cincinnati *(G-2805)*
Hotel 50 S Front Opco L P.............. D 614 885-3334
  Columbus *(G-6010)*
Hyatt Corporation.............. C 216 575-1234
  Cleveland *(G-4396)*
Hyatt Corporation.............. E 614 228-1234
  Columbus *(G-6032)*
I-X Center Corporation.............. C 216 265-2675
  Cleveland *(G-4398)*
Island Service Company.............. E 419 285-3695
  Put In Bay *(G-12617)*
Jackson I-94 Ltd Partnership.............. D 614 793-2244
  Dublin *(G-8042)*
Lancaster Country Club.............. D 740 654-3535
  Lancaster *(G-9730)*
Mahoning Country Club Inc.............. E 330 545-2517
  Girard *(G-8819)*
Mapleside Valley LLC.............. D 330 225-5576
  Brunswick *(G-1462)*
Marriott Hotel Services Inc.............. C 216 252-5333
  Cleveland *(G-4527)*
Medallion Club.............. C 614 794-6999
  Westerville *(G-14909)*
Mohawk Golf Club.............. E 419 447-5876
  Tiffin *(G-13634)*
Mount Vernon Country Club Co.............. D 740 392-4216
  Mount Vernon *(G-11500)*
Msr Legacy.............. D 216 381-0826
  Cleveland *(G-4608)*
N C R Employees Benefit Assn.............. C 937 299-3571
  Dayton *(G-7524)*
National At/Trckstops Hldngs C.............. A 440 808-9100
  Westlake *(G-15081)*
Ohio Ski Slopes Inc.............. D 419 774-9818
  Mansfield *(G-10308)*
Ohio State Parks Inc.............. D 513 664-3504
  College Corner *(G-5222)*
Paramount Distillers Inc.............. B 216 671-6300
  Cleveland *(G-4718)*
Piqua Country Club Holding Co.............. E 937 773-7744
  Piqua *(G-12452)*
Playhouse Square Foundation.............. C 216 615-7500
  Cleveland *(G-4758)*
Quail Hollow Management Inc.............. C 440 639-4000
  Concord Township *(G-6933)*
Ridgehills Hotel Ltd Partnr.............. D 440 585-0600
  Wickliffe *(G-15162)*
Rockwell Springs Trout Club.............. E 419 684-7971
  Clyde *(G-5208)*
Rocky Fork Hunt and Cntry CLB.............. D 614 471-7828
  Gahanna *(G-8727)*

EDUCATIONAL SVCS

S & S Management Inc.............. D 567 356-4151
  Wapakoneta *(G-14491)*
S & S Realty Ltd.............. E 419 625-0362
  Sandusky *(G-12928)*
Sachs Management Corp.............. D 740 282-0901
  Steubenville *(G-13342)*
Sanese Services Inc.............. A 614 436-1234
  Warren *(G-14550)*
Savour Hospitality LLC.............. C 216 308-0018
  Cleveland *(G-4879)*
Saw Mill Creek Ltd.............. E 419 433-3800
  Huron *(G-9392)*
SC Resort Ltd.............. E 419 433-3800
  Huron *(G-9393)*
Shady Hollow Cntry CLB Co Inc.............. D 330 832-1581
  Massillon *(G-10668)*
Shawnee Country Club.............. E 419 227-7177
  Lima *(G-9960)*
Silver Lake Country Club.............. E 330 688-6066
  Silver Lake *(G-13060)*
Skallys Old World Bakery Inc.............. E 513 931-1411
  Cincinnati *(G-3382)*
Spread Eagle Tavern Inc.............. C 330 223-1583
  Hanoverton *(G-9095)*
St Johns Villa.............. E 330 627-4662
  Carrollton *(G-1913)*
Sugar Valley Country Club.............. E 937 372-4820
  Xenia *(G-15531)*
Ta Operating LLC.............. B 440 808-9100
  Westlake *(G-15113)*
Tartan Fields Golf Club Ltd.............. D 614 792-0900
  Dublin *(G-8140)*
Tiki Bowling Lanes Inc.............. E 740 654-4513
  Lancaster *(G-9747)*
Tippecanoe Country Club Inc.............. E 330 758-7518
  Canfield *(G-1644)*
Travelcenters of America Inc.............. A 440 808-9100
  Westlake *(G-15117)*
Union Club Company.............. D 216 621-4230
  Cleveland *(G-5050)*
United Scoto Senior Activities.............. E 740 354-6672
  Portsmouth *(G-12579)*
University of Cincinnati.............. D 513 556-6381
  Cincinnati *(G-3590)*
Walden Club.............. E 330 995-7162
  Aurora *(G-629)*
Western Bowl Inc.............. E 513 574-2200
  Cincinnati *(G-3660)*
Weymouth Valley Inc.............. D 440 498-8888
  Solon *(G-13163)*
York Temple Country Club.............. E 614 885-5459
  Columbus *(G-6916)*
Youngstown Country Club.............. D 330 759-1040
  Youngstown *(G-15757)*

EDUCATIONAL SVCS

Allen County Eductl Svc Ctr.............. E 419 222-1836
  Lima *(G-9863)*
County of Lorain.............. D 440 324-5777
  Elyria *(G-8239)*
Grail.............. E 513 683-2340
  Loveland *(G-10139)*
Jo-Ann Stores LLC.............. E 419 621-8101
  Sandusky *(G-12906)*
Knowledgeworks Foundation.............. E 513 929-4777
  Cincinnati *(G-2945)*
Lakeland Foundation.............. E 440 525-7094
  Willoughby *(G-15202)*
Osu Nephrology Medical Ctr.............. A 614 293-8300
  Columbus *(G-6485)*
Roundtable Learning LLC.............. E 440 220-5252
  Chagrin Falls *(G-1988)*

Employee Codes: A=Over 500 employees, B=251-500
C=101-250, D=51-100, E=20-50, F=10-19, G=1-9

ELECTRIC & OTHER SERVICES COMBINED | SERVICES SECTION

ELECTRIC & OTHER SERVICES COMBINED

Consumers Energy Company Cincinnati *(G-2499)*	E	800 477-5050
Dayton Power and Light Company Manchester *(G-10240)*	D	937 549-2641
Dayton Power and Light Company Miamisburg *(G-11047)*	E	937 331-3032
Dayton Power and Light Company Dayton *(G-7129)*	C	937 331-3900
Duke Energy Kentucky Inc Cincinnati *(G-2580)*	C	704 594-6200
Duke Energy Ohio Inc Cincinnati *(G-2583)*	D	704 382-3853
RB Watkins Inc Stow *(G-13387)*	E	330 688-4061

ELECTRIC MOTOR REPAIR SVCS

3-D Service Ltd Massillon *(G-10626)*	C	330 830-3500
E-Z Electric Motor Svc Corp Cleveland *(G-4195)*	E	216 581-8820
Fenton Bros Electric Co New Philadelphia *(G-11651)*	E	330 343-0093
Integrated Power Services LLC Cleveland *(G-4415)*	D	216 433-7808
Integrated Power Services LLC Hamilton *(G-9055)*	E	513 863-8816
Kiemle-Hankins Company Perrysburg *(G-12349)*	E	419 661-2430
Magnetech Industrial Svcs Inc Massillon *(G-10651)*	D	330 830-3500
Matlock Electric Co Inc Cincinnati *(G-3015)*	E	513 731-9600
National Electric Coil Inc Columbus *(G-6296)*	B	614 488-1151
Shoemaker Electric Company Columbus *(G-6673)*	E	614 294-5626
Whelco Industrial Ltd Perrysburg *(G-12387)*	D	419 385-4627

ELECTRIC POWER DISTRIBUTION TO CONSUMERS

AEP Power Marketing Inc Columbus *(G-5324)*	A	614 716-1000
AEP Texas Central Company Columbus *(G-5325)*	A	614 716-1000
American Electric Pwr Svc Corp Columbus *(G-5349)*	D	614 582-1742
American Electric Pwr Svc Corp Columbus *(G-5348)*	B	614 716-1000
American Municipal Power Inc Columbus *(G-5354)*	C	614 540-1111
Appalachian Power Company Canton *(G-1669)*	C	330 438-7102
Appalachian Power Company Columbus *(G-5374)*	C	614 716-1000
Buckeye Rural Elc Coop Inc Patriot *(G-12280)*	E	740 379-2025
Butler Rural Electric Coop Oxford *(G-12203)*	E	513 867-4400
Carroll Electric Coop Inc Carrollton *(G-1903)*	E	330 627-2116
Cinergy Corp Cincinnati *(G-2440)*	A	513 421-9500
City of Cleveland Cleveland *(G-3983)*	D	216 664-4277
City of Cuyahoga Falls Cuyahoga Falls *(G-7055)*	E	330 971-8000
Consolidated Cooperative Mount Gilead *(G-11459)*	D	419 947-3055
Duke Energy Ohio Inc Cincinnati *(G-2581)*	A	800 544-6900
Duke Energy Ohio Inc Cincinnati *(G-2582)*	A	513 287-1120
Duke Energy Ohio Inc New Richmond *(G-11676)*	A	513 467-5000
Duke Energy Ohio Inc Cincinnati *(G-2583)*	D	704 382-3853
Duke Energy One Inc Cincinnati *(G-2584)*	A	980 373-3931
Energy Harbor LLC Akron *(G-150)*	A	888 254-6356
Firstenergy Corp Akron *(G-161)*	A	800 736-3402
Frontier Power Company Coshocton *(G-6985)*	E	740 622-6755
Guernsy-Muskingum Elc Coop Inc New Concord *(G-11611)*	E	740 826-7661
Hancock-Wood Electric Coop Inc North Baltimore *(G-11801)*	E	419 257-3241
Holmes-Wayne Electric Coop Millersburg *(G-11281)*	E	330 674-1055
Indiana Michigan Power Company Columbus *(G-6045)*	D	614 716-1000
Licking Rur Elctrification Inc Utica *(G-14328)*	D	740 892-2071
Metropolitan Edison Company Akron *(G-231)*	C	800 736-3402
Mid-Ohio Energy Coop Inc Kenton *(G-9621)*	E	419 568-5321
North Central Elc Coop Inc Attica *(G-600)*	E	800 426-3072
Ohio Edison Company Youngstown *(G-15680)*	C	330 740-7754
Paulding-Putnam Electric Coop Paulding *(G-12287)*	E	419 399-5015
Pennsylvania Power Company Akron *(G-264)*	C	800 720-3600
Pioneer Rural Electric Coop Piqua *(G-12451)*	E	800 762-0997
Public Service Company Okla Canton *(G-1834)*	D	888 216-3523
South Central Power Company Barnesville *(G-721)*	D	740 425-4018
South Central Power Company Lancaster *(G-9743)*	E	614 837-4351
South Central Power Company Lancaster *(G-9742)*	C	740 653-4422
Toledo Edison Company Akron *(G-335)*	C	800 447-3333
Union Rural Electric Coop Inc Marysville *(G-10515)*	E	937 642-1826
Vectren Energy Dlvry Ohio LLC Fairborn *(G-8383)*	E	937 259-7400
Vistra Corp Moscow *(G-11457)*	C	513 467-5289

ELECTRIC POWER GENERATION: Fossil Fuel

Dayton Power and Light Company Manchester *(G-10239)*	C	937 549-2641
Dayton Power and Light Company Manchester *(G-10240)*	D	937 549-2641
Vistra Energy Corp North Bend *(G-11804)*	C	513 467-4900
Walleye Power LLC Oregon *(G-12147)*	D	567 298-7400

ELECTRIC SERVICES

AEP Investments Holding Co Inc Columbus *(G-5323)*	B	614 583-2900
AEP Texas Inc Columbus *(G-5326)*	D	614 716-1000
AEP Texas North Company Columbus *(G-5327)*	B	614 716-1000
Andrew Casey Electric LLC Dayton *(G-7174)*	E	937 765-4210
City of Dublin Dublin *(G-7964)*	D	614 410-4750
City of Lebanon Lebanon *(G-9759)*	E	513 228-3200
City of Toledo Toledo *(G-13743)*	D	419 245-1800
Consumers Energy Company Cincinnati *(G-2499)*	E	800 477-5050
Duke Energy Beckjord LLC Cincinnati *(G-2578)*	A	513 287-2561
Duke Energy Ohio Inc Monroe *(G-11340)*	A	513 287-4622
Energy Cooperative Inc Newark *(G-11699)*	E	740 348-1206
Energy Harbor Corp Akron *(G-149)*	E	888 254-6359
Jersey Central Pwr & Light Co Stratton *(G-13407)*	C	740 537-6391
Moores Electric LLC Columbus *(G-6261)*	E	614 504-2909
National Gas & Oil Corporation Newark *(G-11733)*	E	740 344-2102
Ohio Edison Company Wadsworth *(G-14445)*	E	330 336-9880
Ohio Power Company Columbus *(G-6439)*	C	614 716-1000
Pennsylvania Electric Company Akron *(G-263)*	D	800 545-7741
Scana Energy Marketing LLC Dublin *(G-8116)*	D	803 217-1322
Stg Electric Services LLC Macedonia *(G-10206)*	E	330 650-0513
Village of Sycamore Sycamore *(G-13533)*	D	419 927-4262
W T Leones Tri-Area Elc Inc Youngstown *(G-15750)*	E	330 744-0151

ELECTRIC SVCS, NEC: Power Generation

AEP Energy Partners Inc Columbus *(G-5321)*	C	614 716-1000
AEP Generating Company Columbus *(G-5322)*	A	614 223-1000
Buckeye Power Inc Brilliant *(G-1378)*	C	740 598-6534
Buckeye Power Inc Columbus *(G-5477)*	E	614 781-0573
Cardinal Operating Company Brilliant *(G-1379)*	B	740 598-4164
Cleveland Elc Illuminating Co Akron *(G-109)*	D	800 589-3101
Dayton Power and Light Company Marysville *(G-10482)*	D	937 642-9100
Dayton Power and Light Company Miamisburg *(G-11047)*	E	937 331-3032
Dayton Power and Light Company Dayton *(G-7129)*	C	937 331-3900
DPL Inc Dayton *(G-7130)*	C	937 259-7215
Dynegy Coml Asset MGT LLC Cincinnati *(G-2590)*	C	513 287-5033
Gavin AEP Plant Cheshire *(G-2030)*	E	740 925-3166
Gavin Power LLC Cheshire *(G-2031)*	D	740 925-3140
Jersey Central Pwr & Light Co Akron *(G-211)*	B	800 736-3402

SERVICES SECTION

ELECTRICAL GOODS, WHOLESALE: Telephone Eqpt

Ohio Edison Company .... E 740 671-2900
  Shadyside *(G-12970)*
Ohio Edison Company .... C 800 736-3402
  Akron *(G-249)*
Ohio Valley Electric Corp .... D 740 289-7200
  Piketon *(G-12425)*
Southwestern Electric Power Co .... D 614 716-1000
  Columbus *(G-6699)*

ELECTRICAL APPARATUS & EQPT WHOLESALERS

Abb Inc .... E 440 725-2968
  Chardon *(G-1993)*
Adalet Enclosure Systems .... E 216 201-2710
  Cleveland *(G-3767)*
Allen Fields Assoc Inc .... E 513 228-1010
  Lebanon *(G-9753)*
Belting Company of Cincinnati .... D 937 498-2104
  Sidney *(G-13021)*
Best Lighting Products Inc .... D 740 964-1198
  Etna *(G-8332)*
Bostwick-Braun Company .... D 419 259-3600
  Toledo *(G-13713)*
Brohl & Appell Inc .... E 419 625-6761
  Sandusky *(G-12865)*
Connector Manufacturing Co .... C 513 860-4455
  Hamilton *(G-9035)*
Dickman Supply Inc .... D 937 492-6166
  Sidney *(G-13029)*
Dkmp Consulting Inc .... C 614 733-0979
  Plain City *(G-12473)*
Eaton Aerospace LLC .... B 216 523-5000
  Cleveland *(G-4201)*
Eaton Corporation .... D 216 265-2799
  Cleveland *(G-4203)*
Eaton Corporation .... D 614 839-4387
  Columbus *(G-5802)*
Eaton Corporation .... E 419 891-7627
  Maumee *(G-10719)*
Eis Intermediate Holdings LLC .... D 800 228-2790
  Miamisburg *(G-11049)*
FDL Automation and Supply Co .... E 937 498-2104
  Sidney *(G-13031)*
Hubbell Power Systems Inc .... C 330 335-2361
  Wadsworth *(G-14436)*
Hughes Corporation .... E 440 238-2550
  Strongsville *(G-13463)*
Industrial Power Systems Inc .... B 419 531-3121
  Rossford *(G-12767)*
Ke Gutridge LLC .... C 614 885-5200
  Dublin *(G-8048)*
Kirk Key Interlock Company LLC .... E 330 833-8223
  North Canton *(G-11846)*
Laughlin Music & Vending Svc .... E 740 593-7778
  Athens *(G-580)*
LSI Lightron Inc .... A 845 562-5500
  Blue Ash *(G-1203)*
Machine Drive Company .... D 513 793-7077
  Cincinnati *(G-3000)*
Monarch Electric Service Co .... D 216 433-7800
  Cleveland *(G-4596)*
Motor Systems Incorporated .... E 513 576-1725
  Milford *(G-11245)*
Myers Controlled Power LLC .... C 330 834-3200
  North Canton *(G-11850)*
Optimas Oe Solutions LLC .... E 440 546-4400
  Solon *(G-13122)*
Optimas Oe Solutions LLC .... E 513 881-4600
  West Chester *(G-14737)*
Powell Electrical Systems Inc .... D 330 966-1750
  North Canton *(G-11853)*
Schneider Electric Usa Inc .... D 513 777-4445
  West Chester *(G-14761)*
The F D Lawrence Electric Company ..... D 513 542-1100
  Cincinnati *(G-3465)*
Torq Corporation .... E 440 232-4100
  Bedford *(G-989)*
Wolff Bros Supply Inc .... C 330 725-3451
  Medina *(G-10904)*
Wright State University .... E 937 775-3333
  Beavercreek *(G-916)*

ELECTRICAL DISCHARGE MACHINING, EDM

Morris Technologies Inc .... E 513 733-1611
  Cincinnati *(G-3080)*

ELECTRICAL EQPT REPAIR SVCS

Electrical Appl Repr Svc Inc .... E 216 459-8700
  Brooklyn Heights *(G-1417)*
Fak Group Inc .... E 440 498-8465
  Solon *(G-13085)*
Kiemle-Hankins Company .... E 419 661-2430
  Perrysburg *(G-12349)*
Miscor Group Ltd .... B 330 830-3500
  Massillon *(G-10658)*
S D Myers Inc .... C 330 630-7000
  Tallmadge *(G-13602)*

ELECTRICAL EQPT: Automotive, NEC

Electra Sound Inc .... D 216 433-9600
  Avon Lake *(G-678)*

ELECTRICAL GOODS, WHOLESALE: Boxes & Fittings

Akron Electric Inc .... E 330 745-8891
  Akron *(G-25)*
Akron Foundry Co .... C 330 745-3101
  Akron *(G-28)*

ELECTRICAL GOODS, WHOLESALE: Cable Conduit

Legrand North America LLC .... B 937 224-0639
  Dayton *(G-7451)*

ELECTRICAL GOODS, WHOLESALE: Electrical Appliances, Major

C C Mitchell Supply Co Inc .... E 440 526-2040
  Cleveland *(G-3915)*
Don Walter Kitchen Distrs Inc .... E 330 793-9338
  Youngstown *(G-15600)*
Rieman Arszman Cstm Distrs Inc .... E 513 874-5444
  Fairfield *(G-8437)*

ELECTRICAL GOODS, WHOLESALE: Electronic Parts

Arrow Electronics Inc .... D 440 349-1300
  Solon *(G-13068)*
FAI Electronics Corp .... E 937 426-0090
  Dayton *(G-7345)*
Koehlke Components Inc .... E 937 435-5435
  Franklin *(G-8643)*
Newark Corporation .... B 330 523-4457
  Richfield *(G-12704)*
Parts Express International Inc .... D 800 338-0531
  Springboro *(G-13205)*
Pepperl+fuchs Americas Inc .... D 330 425-3555
  Twinsburg *(G-14211)*
RPC Electronics Inc .... E 440 461-4700
  Highland Heights *(G-9170)*
Wurth Electronics Ics Inc .... E 937 415-7700
  Miamisburg *(G-11104)*

ELECTRICAL GOODS, WHOLESALE: Fittings & Construction Mat

C & E Sales LLC .... D 937 434-8830
  Miamisburg *(G-11029)*
Schneider Electric Usa Inc .... B 513 523-4171
  Oxford *(G-12217)*

ELECTRICAL GOODS, WHOLESALE: Generators

Generator One LLC .... E 440 942-8449
  Mentor *(G-10941)*
Mwe Investments LLC .... E 855 944-3571
  Columbus *(G-6284)*

ELECTRICAL GOODS, WHOLESALE: Household Appliances, NEC

G D Supply Inc .... E 614 258-1111
  Columbus *(G-5904)*

ELECTRICAL GOODS, WHOLESALE: Light Bulbs & Related Splys

Handl-It Inc .... E 440 439-9400
  Bedford *(G-964)*

ELECTRICAL GOODS, WHOLESALE: Lighting Fittings & Access

Technical Consumer Pdts Inc .... B 330 995-6111
  Aurora *(G-628)*

ELECTRICAL GOODS, WHOLESALE: Modems, Computer

Enviro It LLC .... E 614 453-0709
  Columbus *(G-5821)*

ELECTRICAL GOODS, WHOLESALE: Security Control Eqpt & Systems

Convergint Technologies LLC .... C 513 771-1717
  Cincinnati *(G-2505)*
Mace Personal Def & SEC Inc .... E 440 424-5321
  Cleveland *(G-4514)*
Post-Browning Inc .... C 513 771-1717
  Cincinnati *(G-3224)*

ELECTRICAL GOODS, WHOLESALE: Switchgear

ABB Inc .... E 513 860-1749
  West Chester *(G-14797)*

ELECTRICAL GOODS, WHOLESALE: Telephone & Telegraphic Eqpt

Acuative Corporation .... D 440 202-4500
  Strongsville *(G-13439)*
Wurtec Incorporated .... D 419 726-1066
  Toledo *(G-14110)*

ELECTRICAL GOODS, WHOLESALE: Telephone Eqpt

Cbst Acquisition LLC .... D 513 361-9600
  Cincinnati *(G-2326)*
Famous Industries Inc .... E 330 535-1811
  Akron *(G-157)*
Floyd Bell Inc .... D 614 294-4000
  Columbus *(G-5874)*
Pro Oncall Technologies LLC .... E 513 489-7660
  Cincinnati *(G-3234)*
Tele-Solutions Inc .... E 330 782-2888
  Youngstown *(G-15733)*

ELECTRICAL GOODS, WHOLESALE: Telephone Eqpt

Teletronics Services Inc............................ E 216 778-6500
  Strongsville (G-13491)
Warwick Communications Inc.................. E 216 787-0300
  Broadview Heights (G-1404)

ELECTRICAL GOODS, WHOLESALE: Wire & Cable

Afc Cable Systems Inc............................. E 740 435-3340
  Cambridge (G-1552)
Associated Mtls Holdings LLC.................. A 330 929-1811
  Cuyahoga Falls (G-7044)
Calvert Wire & Cable Corp........................ E 216 433-7600
  Cleveland (G-3919)
Mjo Industries Inc.................................... D 800 590-4055
  Huber Heights (G-9325)
Multilink Inc... C 440 366-6966
  Elyria (G-8276)
Noco Company.. D 216 464-8131
  Solon (G-13119)
Scott Fetzer Company............................. C 216 267-9000
  Cleveland (G-4885)

ELECTRICAL GOODS, WHOLESALE: Wire & Cable, Electronic

TPC Wire & Cable Corp........................... C 800 211-4520
  Macedonia (G-10208)

ELECTRICAL MEASURING INSTRUMENT REPAIR & CALIBRATION SVCS

Instrmntation Ctrl Systems Inc................. E 513 662-2600
  Cincinnati (G-2873)
Tegam Inc... E 440 466-6100
  Geneva (G-8789)

ELECTRICAL SPLYS

Accurate Mechanical Inc......................... D 740 681-1332
  Lancaster (G-9690)
Consolidated Elec Distrs Inc.................... E 614 445-8871
  Columbus (G-5682)
Control System Mfg Inc........................... E 330 542-0000
  New Middletown (G-11635)
Fenton Bros Electric Co........................... E 330 343-0093
  New Philadelphia (G-11651)
Furbay Electric Supply Co....................... E 330 454-3033
  Canton (G-1758)
Gatto Electric Supply Co......................... E 216 641-8400
  Cleveland (G-4307)
Graybar Electric Company Inc................. E 216 573-0456
  Cleveland (G-4328)
Graybar Electric Company Inc................. E 419 228-7441
  Lima (G-9893)
Graybar Electric Company Inc................. E 330 526-2800
  North Canton (G-11837)
Graybar Electric Company Inc................. E 419 729-1641
  Toledo (G-13825)
Gross Electric Inc.................................... E 419 537-1818
  Toledo (G-13831)
Hle Company.. C 216 325-0941
  Cleveland (G-4368)
Kirby Risk Corporation............................ D 419 221-0123
  Lima (G-9915)
Loeb Electric Company........................... D 800 686-6351
  Columbus (G-6172)
Mars Electric Company............................ D 440 946-2250
  Cleveland (G-4529)
McNaughton-Mckay Elc Ohio Inc............. E 419 784-0295
  Defiance (G-7756)
McNaughton-Mckay Elc Ohio Inc............. E 419 422-2984
  Findlay (G-8564)
McNaughton-Mckay Elc Ohio Inc............. E 740 929-2727
  Hebron (G-9147)
McNaughton-Mckay Elc Ohio Inc............. E 419 891-0262
  Maumee (G-10747)
McNaughton-Mckay Elc Ohio Inc............. D 614 476-2800
  Columbus (G-6218)
Noland Company..................................... C 937 396-7980
  Moraine (G-11428)
Professional Electric Pdts Co................... E 330 896-3790
  Akron (G-272)
Professional Electric Pdts Co................... E 614 563-2504
  Columbus (G-6549)
Professional Electric Pdts Co................... E 800 379-3790
  Elyria (G-8288)
Professional Electric Pdts Co................... E 330 896-3790
  Green (G-8857)
Professional Electric Pdts Co................... E 419 269-3790
  Toledo (G-13967)
Professional Electric Products Co Inc....... D 800 872-7000
  Eastlake (G-8207)
Rexel Usa Inc... E 216 778-6400
  Cleveland (G-4835)
Rexel Usa Inc... E 419 625-6761
  Sandusky (G-12927)
Richard Lawrence Teaberry Inc............... E
  Youngstown (G-15708)
Richards Electric Sup Co LLC.................. E 513 242-8800
  Cincinnati (G-3297)
Wesco Distribution Inc............................. D 216 741-0441
  Cleveland (G-5131)
Yes Management Inc............................... E 330 747-8593
  Columbiana (G-5242)

ELECTRICAL SUPPLIES: Porcelain

Channel Products Inc............................. D 440 423-0113
  Solon (G-13075)
Weldco Inc.. E 513 744-9353
  Cincinnati (G-3649)

ELECTRODES: Thermal & Electrolytic

De Nora Tech LLC.................................. D 440 710-5334
  Concord Township (G-6924)
Graphel Corporation................................ C 513 779-6166
  West Chester (G-14700)

ELECTROMEDICAL EQPT

Viewray Inc... D 440 703-3210
  Oakwood Village (G-12060)

ELECTROMETALLURGICAL PRDTS

Rhenium Alloys Inc................................. E 440 365-7388
  North Ridgeville (G-11934)

ELECTRONIC EQPT REPAIR SVCS

Automation & Control Tech Ltd................ E 419 661-6400
  Perrysburg (G-12314)
CP Redi LLC... C 866 682-7462
  Columbus (G-5717)
Electric Service Co Inc............................ E 513 271-6387
  Cincinnati (G-2610)
Vertiv Corporation................................... A 614 888-0246
  Westerville (G-14949)

ELECTRONIC PARTS & EQPT WHOLESALERS

Access Catalog Company LLC................ C 440 572-5377
  Strongsville (G-13438)
Cornerstone Controls Inc......................... E 513 489-2500
  Cincinnati (G-2509)
DSI Systems Inc...................................... E 614 871-1456
  Grove City (G-8917)
Fox International Limited Inc.................... C 216 454-1001
  Beachwood (G-793)
Geep USA Inc.. E 919 544-1443
  Stow (G-13369)
Graybar Electric Company Inc................. E 216 573-0456
  Cleveland (G-4328)
Graybar Electric Company Inc................. E 419 729-1641
  Toledo (G-13825)
Kyocera Precision Tools Inc.................... D 419 738-6652
  Wapakoneta (G-14486)
McM Electronics Inc................................ C 888 235-4692
  Centerville (G-1947)
Meder Electronic Inc............................... D 508 295-0771
  Fairfield (G-8429)
Mobilcomm Inc.. D 513 742-5555
  Cincinnati (G-3072)
Pepperl + Fuchs Inc................................ C 330 425-3555
  Twinsburg (G-14210)
Pepperl+fuchs Mfg Inc............................ C 330 425-3555
  Twinsburg (G-14212)
Projects Unlimited Inc.............................. C 937 918-2200
  Dayton (G-7571)
Standex Electronics Inc........................... D 513 871-3777
  Fairfield (G-8443)
Vmetro Inc.. D 281 584-0728
  Fairborn (G-8386)
Wholesale House Inc.............................. D 419 542-1315
  Hicksville (G-9162)

ELECTRONIC SHOPPING

Ampersand Group LLC........................... E 330 379-0044
  Akron (G-49)
E Retailing Associates LLC..................... D 614 300-5785
  Columbus (G-5798)
Perishable Shipg Solutions LLC............... E 724 944-9024
  Warren (G-14546)
Trademark Global LLC............................ E 440 960-6200
  Lorain (G-10104)

ELEMENTARY & SECONDARY SCHOOLS, PUBLIC

Boardman Local Schools........................ D 330 726-3409
  Youngstown (G-15560)
Cleveland Municipal School Dst............... E 216 838-8700
  Cleveland (G-4061)
Dover City Schools................................. E 330 343-8880
  Dover (G-7881)
Franklin City Schools.............................. E 937 743-8670
  Franklin (G-8637)
Kettering City School District................... E 937 499-1770
  Dayton (G-7437)
Montpelier Exempted Vlg Schl................. E 419 485-3676
  Montpelier (G-11385)
Northwest Local School Dst..................... E 513 923-1000
  Cincinnati (G-3127)
St Marys City Board Education................ C 419 394-2616
  Saint Marys (G-12836)
Sycamore Board of Education................. C 513 489-3937
  Montgomery (G-11375)
Talawanda City School District................ D 513 273-3200
  Oxford (G-12218)

ELEMENTARY & SECONDARY SCHOOLS, SPECIAL EDUCATION

Catholic Chrties Ststhern Ohio................. B 740 676-4932
  Steubenville (G-13319)
Childrens Lab Schools Inc....................... E 937 274-7195
  Dayton (G-7224)
Educatonal Svc Ctr Lorain Cnty............... C 440 244-1659
  Elyria (G-8244)

SERVICES SECTION

ENGINEERING SVCS

Harrison Avenue Assembly God........... E 513 367-6109
  Harrison *(G-9107)*
Interval Brotherhood Homes Inc............ D 330 644-4095
  Coventry Township *(G-7011)*
Miami Valley School............................... D 937 434-4444
  Dayton *(G-7499)*
Midland Council Governments................. E 330 264-6047
  Wooster *(G-15356)*
Northwest Ohio Computer Assn............... E 419 267-5565
  Archbold *(G-464)*
Ohio Arson School Inc............................ E 740 881-4467
  Galena *(G-8738)*
Paulding Exempted Vlg Schl Dst............. E 419 594-3309
  Paulding *(G-12286)*
St Jhns Evang Lthran Ch Mrysv................. E 937 644-5540
  Marysville *(G-10510)*

ELEVATORS & EQPT

Adams Elevator Equipment Co.............. D 847 581-2900
  Holland *(G-9276)*
Otis Elevator Company............................ E 216 573-2333
  Cleveland *(G-4709)*

ELEVATORS WHOLESALERS

Fujitec America Inc................................. C 513 755-6100
  Mason *(G-10551)*
Oracle Elevator Company........................ E 614 781-9731
  Columbus *(G-6476)*
Otis Elevator Company........................... C 513 531-7888
  Cincinnati *(G-3175)*
Otis Elevator Company............................ E 216 573-2333
  Cleveland *(G-4709)*
Otis Elevator Company........................... C 614 777-6500
  Columbus *(G-6489)*
Otis Elevator Company............................ E 740 282-1461
  Steubenville *(G-13341)*
Tech Elevator Inc.................................... D 216 310-3497
  Cleveland *(G-4981)*
Tk Elevator Corporation......................... C 440 717-0080
  Broadview Heights *(G-1401)*
Tk Elevator Corporation......................... D 614 895-8930
  Westerville *(G-15017)*
Wurtec Incorporated............................... D 419 726-1066
  Toledo *(G-14110)*

ELEVATORS: Installation & Conversion

Otis Elevator Company............................ E 216 573-2333
  Cleveland *(G-4709)*
Tk Elevator Corporation......................... C 513 241-6000
  Cincinnati *(G-3481)*
Tk Elevator Corporation......................... D 614 895-8930
  Westerville *(G-15017)*

EMBROIDERY ADVERTISING SVCS

Screen Works Inc.................................... E 937 264-9111
  Dayton *(G-7613)*

EMERGENCY ALARMS

Floyd Bell Inc.. D 614 294-4000
  Columbus *(G-5874)*
Status Solutions LLC............................... D 434 296-1789
  Westerville *(G-14938)*

EMERGENCY SHELTERS

Compass Family and Cmnty Svcs........... E 330 782-5664
  Youngstown *(G-15584)*
Homefull.. D 937 293-1945
  Moraine *(G-11418)*
Light of Hearts Villa Inc.......................... D 440 232-1991
  Cleveland *(G-4495)*
Tender Mercies Inc................................. E 513 721-8666
  Cincinnati *(G-3455)*

Tri-County Help Center Inc..................... E 740 695-5441
  Saint Clairsville *(G-12816)*
YWCA of Northwest Ohio........................ D 419 241-3235
  Toledo *(G-14117)*

EMPLOYMENT SVCS: Labor Contractors

Advantage Resourcing Amer Inc............. E 781 472-8900
  Cincinnati *(G-2149)*
Alliance Legal Solutions LLC.................. D 216 525-0100
  Independence *(G-9401)*
Belflex Staffing Network LLC.................. C 513 488-8588
  Cincinnati *(G-2255)*
Cavalry Staffing LLC............................... E 440 663-9990
  Cleveland *(G-3939)*
CBS Personnel Services LLC.................. A 513 651-3600
  Cincinnati *(G-2325)*
Compassnate Hnds Stffing Sltion............ E 216 710-6736
  Highland Heights *(G-9164)*
Construction Labor Contrs LLC............... C 216 741-3351
  Cleveland *(G-4109)*
Construction Labor Contrs LLC............... C 614 932-9937
  Columbus *(G-5684)*
Construction Labor Contrs LLC............... C 513 539-2904
  Monroe *(G-11337)*
Construction Labor Contrs LLC............... C 330 724-1906
  Uniontown *(G-14246)*
Staffmark Group LLC............................. D 513 651-1111
  Cincinnati *(G-3404)*
Staffmark Investment LLC....................... C 513 651-3600
  Cincinnati *(G-3405)*
Tradesource Inc..................................... D 614 824-3883
  Columbus *(G-6780)*

ENGINEERING HELP SVCS

Belcan LLC... A 513 891-0972
  Blue Ash *(G-1132)*
Belcan Svcs Group Ltd Partnr................. C 513 891-0972
  Blue Ash *(G-1136)*
Nobletek LLC.. E 330 287-1500
  Wooster *(G-15361)*
Prestige Technical Svcs Inc.................... D 513 779-6800
  West Chester *(G-14746)*

ENGINEERING SVCS

Actalent Services LLC............................ C 614 328-4900
  New Albany *(G-11553)*
Aerospace Corporation.......................... E 937 657-9634
  Dayton *(G-7125)*
Alfons Haar Inc....................................... E 937 560-2031
  Springboro *(G-13192)*
American Electric Pwr Svc Corp............. B 614 716-1000
  Columbus *(G-5348)*
Arcadis A California Partnr..................... E 614 818-4900
  Columbus *(G-5382)*
Arctos Tech Solutions LLC..................... D 937 426-2808
  Beavercreek *(G-859)*
Austin Building and Design Inc.............. C 440 544-2600
  Cleveland *(G-3839)*
B&N Coal Inc... E 740 783-3575
  Dexter City *(G-7867)*
Babcock & Wilcox Holdings Inc.............. A 704 625-4900
  Akron *(G-60)*
Bae Systems Science & Technology Inc A
  Beavercreek *(G-862)*
Belcan LLC... E 513 985-7777
  Blue Ash *(G-1133)*
Belcan LLC... C 513 277-3100
  Cincinnati *(G-2253)*
Belcan LLC... A 513 891-0972
  Blue Ash *(G-1132)*
Belcan Engineering Group LLC............. A 513 891-0972
  Blue Ash *(G-1135)*

Bowser-Morner Inc.................................. C 937 236-8805
  Dayton *(G-7198)*
Brewer-Garrett Company......................... C 440 243-3535
  Middleburg Heights *(G-11113)*
Buehrer Group Arch & Engrg................... E 419 893-9021
  Maumee *(G-10706)*
Capablity Anlis Msrment Orgnzt............... E 937 260-9373
  Beavercreek Township *(G-933)*
Circle Prime Manufacturing..................... E 330 923-0019
  Cuyahoga Falls *(G-7054)*
City of Akron... C 330 375-2355
  Akron *(G-103)*
City of Cuyahoga Falls............................ E 330 971-8230
  Cuyahoga Falls *(G-7059)*
City of Toledo... D 419 936-2275
  Toledo *(G-13740)*
Clarkwstern Dtrich Bldg System............... C 513 870-1100
  West Chester *(G-14671)*
Coal Services Inc.................................... B 740 795-5220
  Powhatan Point *(G-12610)*
Colas Construction USA Inc.................... C 513 272-5648
  Cincinnati *(G-2471)*
County of Cuyahoga............................... B 216 348-3800
  Cleveland *(G-4125)*
County of Delaware................................. E 740 833-2400
  Delaware *(G-7788)*
County of Erie.. E 419 627-7710
  Sandusky *(G-12886)*
County of Gallia...................................... E 740 446-4009
  Gallipolis *(G-8754)*
County of Logan..................................... E 937 592-2791
  Bellefontaine *(G-1024)*
County of Lucas...................................... C 419 213-2892
  Holland *(G-9283)*
County of Montgomery............................ D 937 854-4576
  Dayton *(G-7253)*
County of Perry....................................... E 740 342-2191
  New Lexington *(G-11623)*
County of Stark....................................... C 330 477-6781
  Canton *(G-1724)*
County of Washington............................. E 740 376-7430
  Marietta *(G-10364)*
Custom Materials Inc.............................. D 440 543-8284
  Chagrin Falls *(G-1976)*
Dctech Ltd.. E 330 687-3977
  Twinsburg *(G-14180)*
Dizer Corp.. C 440 368-0201
  Painesville *(G-12227)*
Dlr Group Inc.. D 216 522-1350
  Cleveland *(G-4169)*
Dms Inc.. C 440 951-9838
  Willoughby *(G-15189)*
Eco Engineering Inc............................... D 513 985-8300
  Cincinnati *(G-2604)*
Edison Welding Institute Inc................... C 614 688-5000
  Columbus *(G-5807)*
Elevar Design Group Inc........................ E 513 721-0600
  Cincinnati *(G-2611)*
Fishel Company...................................... C 614 850-4400
  Columbus *(G-5867)*
Fishel Company...................................... D 614 274-8100
  Columbus *(G-5869)*
Frost Engineering Inc............................. E 513 541-6330
  Cincinnati *(G-2710)*
Garmann/Miller & Assoc Inc................... E 419 628-4240
  Minster *(G-11316)*
Gohypersonic Incorporated..................... E 937 331-9460
  Dayton *(G-7377)*
Greene County....................................... D 937 562-7500
  Xenia *(G-15514)*
Gus Perdikakis Associates..................... D 513 583-0900
  Cincinnati *(G-2784)*

ENGINEERING SVCS

Hdr Inc .... E 614 839-5770
  Columbus *(G-5260)*

Hdt Global Inc .... A 216 438-6111
  Solon *(G-13095)*

Hill Technical Services Inc .... E 330 494-3656
  Canton *(G-1771)*

Hokuto USA Inc .... E 614 782-6200
  Grove City *(G-8927)*

Hunter Defense Tech Inc .... E 216 438-6111
  Solon *(G-13096)*

Hydro-Dyne Inc .... E 330 832-5076
  Massillon *(G-10647)*

Icr Inc .... C 513 900-7007
  Mason *(G-10563)*

Imeg Consultants Corp .... E 614 443-1178
  Columbus *(G-6041)*

Innovative Controls Corp .... E 419 691-6684
  Toledo *(G-13863)*

Integris Composites Inc .... D 740 928-0326
  Hebron *(G-9144)*

Interbrand Design Forum LLC .... C 513 421-2210
  Cincinnati *(G-2880)*

Jdi Group Inc .... D 419 725-7161
  Maumee *(G-10733)*

Jjr Solutions LLC .... E 937 912-0288
  Dayton *(G-7429)*

Koehlke Components Inc .... D 937 435-5435
  Franklin *(G-8643)*

Kudu Dynamics LLC .... D 973 209-0305
  Worthington *(G-15428)*

KZF Design Inc .... D 513 621-6211
  Cincinnati *(G-2959)*

Linquest Corporation .... D 937 306-6040
  Beavercreek *(G-888)*

Mahoning County .... E 330 799-1581
  Youngstown *(G-15655)*

Matrix Research Inc .... D 937 427-8433
  Beavercreek *(G-927)*

Micro Industries Corporation .... D 740 548-7878
  Westerville *(G-14999)*

Mkc Associates Inc .... E 740 657-3202
  Powell *(G-12599)*

Modal Shop Inc .... D 513 351-9919
  Cincinnati *(G-3073)*

Moody-Nolan Inc .... C 614 461-4664
  Columbus *(G-6260)*

Mrl Materials Resources LLC .... E 937 531-6657
  Xenia *(G-15528)*

Muskingum County Ohio .... E 740 453-0381
  Zanesville *(G-15814)*

Neesai Cad Designs LLC .... E 614 822-7701
  New Albany *(G-11577)*

Northrop Grmman Tchncal Svcs I ...... D 937 320-3100
  Beavercreek Township *(G-945)*

Ohio Blow Pipe Company .... E 216 681-7379
  Cleveland *(G-4682)*

Onyx Creative Inc .... D 216 223-3200
  Cleveland *(G-4702)*

Pike County .... E 740 947-9339
  Waverly *(G-14615)*

Plastic Safety Systems Inc .... E 216 231-8590
  Cleveland *(G-4755)*

Polaris Automation Inc .... E 614 431-0170
  Columbus *(G-6534)*

Quality Control Services LLC .... E 216 862-9264
  Cleveland *(G-4800)*

Qualus Corp .... D 800 434-0415
  Cincinnati *(G-3261)*

Reed Westlake Leskosky Ltd .... C 216 522-0449
  Cleveland *(G-4817)*

Rolls-Royce Energy Systems Inc .... A 703 834-1700
  Mount Vernon *(G-11506)*

Safran Power Usa LLC .... D 330 487-2000
  Twinsburg *(G-14218)*

Sgi Matrix LLC .... D 937 438-9033
  Miamisburg *(G-11092)*

Shive-Hattery Inc .... E 216 532-7143
  Cleveland *(G-4902)*

Si Liquidating Inc .... E 513 388-2076
  Milford *(G-11255)*

Sierra Lobo Inc .... C 419 621-3367
  Cleveland *(G-4904)*

Siertek Ltd .... E 937 623-2466
  Beavercreek Township *(G-948)*

Solutons Thrugh Innvtive Tech .... D 937 320-9994
  Beavercreek *(G-907)*

Star Distribution and Mfg LLC .... E 513 860-3573
  West Chester *(G-14833)*

Summit County .... C 330 643-2850
  Akron *(G-326)*

Sunpower Inc .... D 740 594-2221
  Athens *(G-592)*

Sutton & Associates Inc .... E 614 487-9096
  Columbus *(G-6737)*

Technical Assurance Inc .... E 440 953-3147
  Willoughby *(G-15222)*

Tecoglas Inc .... D 419 537-9750
  Toledo *(G-14034)*

Terracon Consultants Inc .... B 513 321-5816
  Cincinnati *(G-3459)*

Testech Inc .... D 937 435-8584
  Dayton *(G-7663)*

Thermal Treatment Center Inc .... E 216 881-8100
  Wickliffe *(G-15164)*

Toogann Technologies LLC .... D 614 973-9266
  Dublin *(G-8142)*

Triad Engineering & Contg Co .... E 440 786-1000
  Cleveland *(G-5037)*

Trumbull County Engineering .... D 330 675-2640
  Warren *(G-14565)*

Underground Services Inc .... E 330 323-0166
  Uniontown *(G-14269)*

University of Cincinnati .... D 513 556-3732
  Cincinnati *(G-3592)*

URS Group Inc .... B 614 464-4500
  Columbus *(G-6835)*

Vns Federal Services LLC .... E 740 443-7005
  Piketon *(G-12431)*

Weastec Incorporated .... E 614 734-9645
  Dublin *(G-8161)*

Werks Kraft Engineering LLC .... E 330 721-7374
  Medina *(G-10902)*

Winncom Technologies Corp .... C 440 498-9510
  Solon *(G-13165)*

Xaloy LLC .... C 330 726-4000
  Austintown *(G-637)*

ENGINEERING SVCS: Acoustical

L&T Technology Services Ltd .... B 732 688-4402
  Dublin *(G-8052)*

Straight 72 Inc .... D 740 943-5730
  Marysville *(G-10511)*

ENGINEERING SVCS: Building Construction

Jumporg LLC .... E 216 250-4678
  Cleveland *(G-4446)*

ENGINEERING SVCS: Chemical

Hexion Inc .... C 888 443-9466
  Columbus *(G-5989)*

ENGINEERING SVCS: Civil

Bair Goodie and Assoc Inc .... E 330 343-3499
  New Philadelphia *(G-11641)*

Barr Engineering Incorporated .... E 614 714-0299
  Columbus *(G-5420)*

Bayer & Becker Inc .... E 513 492-7401
  Mason *(G-10522)*

Ceso Inc .... E 937 435-8584
  Miamisburg *(G-11035)*

Chagrin Valley Engineering Ltd .... E 440 439-1999
  Cleveland *(G-3961)*

Civil & Environmental Cons Inc .... E 513 985-0226
  Blue Ash *(G-1150)*

County of Crawford .... D 419 562-7731
  Bucyrus *(G-1505)*

CT Consultants Inc .... C 440 951-9000
  Mentor *(G-10930)*

Design Homes & Development Co ..... E 937 438-3667
  Dayton *(G-7311)*

Engineering Associates Inc .... D 330 345-6556
  Wooster *(G-15337)*

Euthenics Inc .... E 440 260-1555
  Strongsville *(G-13454)*

Feller Finch & Associates Inc .... E 419 893-3680
  Maumee *(G-10724)*

Glaus Pyle Schmer Brns Dhven I .... E 216 518-5544
  Cleveland *(G-4314)*

Jones & Henry Engineers Ltd .... E 419 473-9611
  Toledo *(G-13870)*

Kleingers Group Inc .... D 614 882-4311
  Westerville *(G-14903)*

Kokosing Construction Co Inc .... D 440 322-2685
  Elyria *(G-8265)*

KS Associates Inc .... D 440 365-4730
  Elyria *(G-8266)*

Michael Baker Intl Inc .... E 330 453-3110
  Canton *(G-1806)*

Michael Baker Intl Inc .... E 412 269-6300
  Cleveland *(G-4573)*

Mote and Associates Inc .... E 937 548-7511
  Greenville *(G-8881)*

Northast Ohio Rgonal Sewer Dst .... C 216 961-2187
  Cleveland *(G-4660)*

Nova Engineering & Envmtl LLC .... D 614 325-8092
  Columbus *(G-6374)*

Pollock Research & Design Inc .... E 330 332-3300
  Salem *(G-12847)*

Prime Ae Group Inc .... D 614 839-0250
  Columbus *(G-5279)*

Ra Consultants LLC .... E 513 469-6600
  Blue Ash *(G-1229)*

Red Barn Group Inc .... E 419 625-7838
  Sandusky *(G-12925)*

Richard L Bowen & Assoc Inc .... E 216 491-9300
  Cleveland *(G-4838)*

T J Neff Holdings Inc .... E 440 884-3100
  Cleveland *(G-4975)*

Thrasher Group Inc .... D 330 620-4790
  Canton *(G-1873)*

Wade Trim .... E 216 363-0300
  Cleveland *(G-5120)*

Wellert Corporation .... E 330 239-2699
  Medina *(G-10901)*

ENGINEERING SVCS: Construction & Civil

EP Ferris & Associates Inc .... E 614 299-2999
  Columbus *(G-5823)*

Geiger Brothers Inc .... B 740 286-0800
  Jackson *(G-9518)*

Intren Inc .... E 815 482-0651
  Cincinnati *(G-2885)*

Mole Constructors Inc .... A 440 248-0616
  Beachwood *(G-818)*

Precision Engrg & Contg Inc .... D 440 349-1204
  Solon *(G-13129)*

SERVICES SECTION

ENGINEERING SVCS: Electrical Or Electronic

Acpi Systems Inc..................................E 513 738-3840
Hamilton *(G-9016)*

Apec Engineering Inc..........................E 440 708-2303
Chagrin Falls *(G-1973)*

Awp Inc..A 330 677-7401
North Canton *(G-11813)*

High Voltage Maintenance Corp..........E 937 278-0811
Dayton *(G-7406)*

L-3 Cmmncations Nova Engrg Inc......C 877 282-1168
Mason *(G-10571)*

Matthews International Corp...............E 513 679-7400
Cincinnati *(G-3017)*

Nu Waves Ltd......................................E 513 360-0800
Middletown *(G-11177)*

Phantom Technical Services Inc.........E 614 868-9920
Columbus *(G-6520)*

PMC Systems Limited.........................E 330 538-2268
North Jackson *(G-11876)*

Stock Fairfield Corporation................C 440 543-6000
Solon *(G-13149)*

TL Industries Inc................................C 419 666-8144
Perrysburg *(G-12377)*

Vanner Inc...D 614 771-2718
Hilliard *(G-9239)*

ENGINEERING SVCS: Machine Tool Design

Hahn Automation Group Us Inc..........D 937 886-3232
Miamisburg *(G-11058)*

Shively Brothers Inc...........................E 419 626-5091
Sandusky *(G-12931)*

ENGINEERING SVCS: Mechanical

Cbn Westside Technologies Inc..........B 513 772-7000
West Chester *(G-14660)*

Dillin Engineered Systems Corp........E 419 666-6789
Perrysburg *(G-12333)*

Genius Solutions Engrg Co................E 419 794-9914
Maumee *(G-10727)*

Genpact LLC.......................................E 513 763-7660
Cincinnati *(G-2729)*

Houston Interests LLC.......................A 614 890-3456
Columbus *(G-6013)*

Jdrm Engineering Inc.........................E 419 824-2400
Sylvania *(G-13553)*

Juice Technologies Inc.......................E 800 518-5576
Worthington *(G-15424)*

Morris Technologies Inc.....................E 513 733-1611
Cincinnati *(G-3080)*

R E Warner & Associates Inc.............D 440 835-9400
Westlake *(G-15102)*

Roger D Fields Associates Inc...........E 614 451-2248
Columbus *(G-6608)*

Saec/Kinetic Vision Inc......................C 513 793-4959
Cincinnati *(G-3338)*

Techsolve Inc.....................................D 513 948-2000
Cincinnati *(G-3449)*

Thinkpath Engineering Svcs LLC.......E 937 291-8374
Miamisburg *(G-11097)*

Twism Enterprises LLC......................E 513 800-1098
Cincinnati *(G-3539)*

ENGINEERING SVCS: Structural

Emersion Design LLC........................E 513 841-9100
Cincinnati *(G-2616)*

RCT Engineering Inc..........................E 561 684-7534
Beachwood *(G-829)*

Ssoe Inc..B 419 255-3830
Toledo *(G-14023)*

Steven Schaefer Associates Inc.........D 513 542-3300
Cincinnati *(G-3420)*

ENGINES: Diesel & Semi-Diesel Or Duel Fuel

Miscor Group Ltd................................B 330 830-3500
Massillon *(G-10658)*

ENGINES: Gasoline, NEC

Miba Bearings US LLC.......................B 740 962-4242
Mcconnelsville *(G-10803)*

ENGINES: Jet Propulsion

General Electric Company..................A 617 443-3000
Cincinnati *(G-2725)*

ENGRAVING SVCS

Genius Solutions Engrg Co................E 419 794-9914
Maumee *(G-10727)*

Point Recognition Ltd........................E 330 220-6777
Brunswick *(G-1467)*

Things Remembered Inc....................A 440 473-2000
Highland Heights *(G-9172)*

ENVELOPES

American Paper Group Inc.................B 330 758-4545
Youngstown *(G-15551)*

Ampac Holdings LLC.........................A 513 671-1777
Cincinnati *(G-2194)*

Jbm Packaging Company...................C 513 933-8333
Lebanon *(G-9770)*

Pac Worldwide Corporation...............E 800 535-0039
Monroe *(G-11347)*

Western States Envelope Co..............E 419 666-7480
Walbridge *(G-14468)*

ENVELOPES WHOLESALERS

EMI Enterprises Inc...........................E 419 666-0012
Northwood *(G-11973)*

Jbm Packaging Company...................C 513 933-8333
Lebanon *(G-9770)*

Pac Worldwide Corporation...............E 800 535-0039
Monroe *(G-11347)*

Pac Worldwide Holding Company......E 513 217-3200
Middletown *(G-11179)*

Western States Envelope Co..............E 419 666-7480
Walbridge *(G-14468)*

ENZYMES

Mp Biomedicals LLC..........................C 440 337-1200
Solon *(G-13113)*

EPOXY RESINS

Hexion Inc..C 888 443-9466
Columbus *(G-5989)*

EQUIPMENT & VEHICLE FINANCE LEASING COMPANIES

Summit Funding Group Inc................E 513 489-1222
Mason *(G-10613)*

EQUIPMENT: Rental & Leasing, NEC

All Erection & Crane Rental..............E 216 524-6550
Cleveland *(G-3789)*

All Erection & Crane Rental..............C 216 524-6550
Cleveland *(G-3788)*

All Temp Refrigeration Inc.................E 419 692-5016
Delphos *(G-7836)*

Auto Mall Rental & Leasing LLC........D 419 874-4331
Perrysburg *(G-12313)*

Brandsafway Services LLC................E 614 443-1314
Columbus *(G-5459)*

Budget Dumpster LLC........................E 866 284-6164
Westlake *(G-15041)*

CFC Investment Company..................E 513 870-2203
Fairfield *(G-8399)*

De Nora Tech LLC..............................D 440 710-5334
Concord Township *(G-6924)*

Dearing Compressor and Pump.........E 330 783-2258
Youngstown *(G-15595)*

Eaton Leasing Corporation................B 216 382-2292
Beachwood *(G-788)*

Elliott Tool Technologies Ltd.............D 937 253-6133
Dayton *(G-7333)*

Enerstar Rentals and Svcs Ltd..........E 570 360-3271
Bellaire *(G-1011)*

Fifth Third Equipment Fin Co............E 800 972-3030
Cincinnati *(G-2665)*

Fleming Leasing LLC........................C 703 842-1358
Girard *(G-8812)*

Franklin Equipment LLC...................E 614 389-2161
Dublin *(G-8015)*

Franklin Equipment LLC...................E 513 893-9105
West Chester *(G-14694)*

Franklin Equipment LLC...................E 614 948-3409
Westerville *(G-14980)*

Garda CL Great Lakes Inc.................B 561 939-7000
Columbus *(G-5911)*

Gordon Brothers Inc..........................E 800 331-7611
Salem *(G-12842)*

Great Lakes Crushing Ltd.................D 440 944-5500
Wickliffe *(G-15150)*

Hogan Truck Leasing Inc...................E 314 802-5995
Obetz *(G-12080)*

Kmh Systems Inc..............................E 800 962-3178
Dayton *(G-7444)*

Leading Families Home.....................E 419 244-2175
Toledo *(G-13883)*

MH Logistics Corp..............................D 330 425-2476
Medina *(G-10865)*

Miami Industrial Trucks Inc...............D 937 293-4194
Moraine *(G-11425)*

Ohio Machinery Co............................D 419 874-7975
Perrysburg *(G-12359)*

Piqua Steel Co...................................D 937 773-3632
Piqua *(G-12454)*

Pncef LLC..D 513 421-9191
Cincinnati *(G-3217)*

Priority Equipment Rental Ltd...........E 724 227-3070
Newark *(G-11743)*

Resolute Industrial LLC....................E 513 779-7909
West Chester *(G-14831)*

Robinair Leasing Co LLC..................E 513 530-1600
Montpelier *(G-11386)*

Rumpke Waste Inc............................C 937 548-1939
Greenville *(G-8883)*

Smartpay Leasing LLC......................E 800 374-5587
Cincinnati *(G-3388)*

South I Leasing Co LLC....................E 513 530-1600
Boardman *(G-1291)*

Sunbelt Rentals Inc...........................E 614 341-9770
Columbus *(G-6729)*

Tempoe LLC.......................................E 415 390-2620
Cincinnati *(G-3451)*

Thomas Do-It Center Inc...................E 740 446-2002
Gallipolis *(G-8769)*

Towlift Inc..C 216 749-6800
Brooklyn Heights *(G-1428)*

U Haul Co of Northwestern Ohio......E 419 478-1101
Toledo *(G-14078)*

United Rentals North Amer Inc.........E 614 276-5444
Columbus *(G-6814)*

United Rentals North Amer Inc.........E 800 877-3687
Perrysburg *(G-12383)*

EQUIPMENT: Rental & Leasing, NEC

Valley Industrial Trucks Inc .... E 330 788-4081
  Youngstown (G-15746)
Vincent Lighting Systems Co .... E 216 475-7600
  Solon (G-13161)
Waco Scaffolding & Equipment Inc ..... A 216 749-8900
  Cleveland (G-5119)
Williams Scotsman Inc .... D 614 449-8675
  Columbus (G-6894)
Wmog Inc .... E 419 334-3801
  Fremont (G-8709)

EXHAUST HOOD OR FAN CLEANING SVCS

Ecobryt LLC .... E 877 326-2798
  Cincinnati (G-2605)

FABRIC STORES

Everfast Inc .... E 614 789-0900
  Dublin (G-8008)

FABRICS: Nonwoven

Ccp Industries Inc .... B 216 535-4227
  Richmond Heights (G-12716)

FACILITIES SUPPORT SVCS

Aetna Building Maintenance Inc .... C 937 324-5711
  Springfield (G-13214)
Alcyon Tchncal Svcs Ats JV LLC .... B 216 433-2488
  Cleveland (G-3782)
Aramark Facility Services LLC .... C 216 687-5000
  Cleveland (G-3828)
Disinfection MGT Tech LLC .... E 440 212-1061
  Copley (G-6955)
Firstgroup America Inc .... D 513 241-2200
  Cincinnati (G-2684)
Franklin Cnty Bd Commissioners .... C 614 462-3800
  Columbus (G-5880)
Green Clean Ohio LLC .... E 866 853-6337
  Cleveland (G-4337)
Katmai Government Services LLC ...... B 740 314-5432
  Steubenville (G-13333)
L B & B Associates Inc .... E 216 451-2672
  Cleveland (G-4471)
Ltccorp Government Services-Oh Inc ... B 419 794-3500
  Maumee (G-10742)
MPW Industrial Svcs Group Inc .... B 740 927-8790
  Hebron (G-9150)
Serco Inc .... D 502 364-8157
  Beavercreek (G-904)
Servus LLC .... A 844 737-8871
  Beachwood (G-835)
Sunohio Inc .... D 330 477-6769
  Canton (G-1864)
Technical Assurance Inc .... E 440 953-3147
  Willoughby (G-15222)
Uscg Station Cleveland Harbor .... E 216 937-0141
  Cleveland (G-5094)
Vns Federal Services LLC .... E 740 443-7005
  Piketon (G-12431)
Wastren - Enrgx Mssion Spport .... C 740 897-3724
  Piketon (G-12432)

FARM & GARDEN MACHINERY WHOLESALERS

Bryan Equipment Sales Inc .... D 513 248-2000
  Loveland (G-10129)
Clarke Power Services Inc .... D 513 771-2200
  Cincinnati (G-2456)
Gardner-Connell LLC .... E 614 456-4000
  Columbus (G-5915)
Hull Bros Inc .... E 419 375-2827
  Fort Recovery (G-8610)
Leslie Equipment Co .... E 740 373-5255
  Marietta (G-10380)
Old Meadow Farms Inc .... E 440 632-5590
  Middlefield (G-11143)
Streacker Tractor Sales Inc .... E 419 422-6973
  Findlay (G-8589)
United Rentals North Amer Inc .... E 614 276-5444
  Columbus (G-6814)

FARM MACHINERY REPAIR SVCS

Apple Farm Service Inc .... E 937 526-4851
  Covington (G-7017)
Liechty Inc .... E 419 298-2302
  Edgerton (G-8228)
Steinke Tractor Sales Inc .... E 937 456-4271
  Eaton (G-8224)
Witmers Inc .... E 330 427-2147
  Salem (G-12858)

FARM MORTGAGE COMPANIES

Farm Credit Svcs Mid-America .... A 740 373-8211
  Marietta (G-10367)

FARM SPLYS WHOLESALERS

A M Leonard Inc .... D 937 773-2694
  Piqua (G-12434)
Andersons Inc .... C 419 893-5050
  Maumee (G-10692)
Custom Agri Systems Inc .... E 419 599-5180
  Napoleon (G-11521)
Evans Landscaping Inc .... E 513 271-1119
  Cincinnati (G-2639)
Family Farm & Home Inc .... E 440 307-1030
  Madison (G-10216)
Fort Recovery Equity Inc .... C 419 942-1148
  Fort Recovery (G-8608)
Gardner-Connell LLC .... E 614 456-4000
  Columbus (G-5915)
Green Valley Co-Op Inc .... D 740 374-7741
  Marietta (G-10369)
Jiffy Products America Inc .... D 440 282-2818
  Lorain (G-10078)
Minster Farmers Coop Exch .... D 419 628-4705
  Minster (G-11319)
Rk Family Inc .... C 740 474-3874
  Circleville (G-3721)
Rk Family Inc .... C 419 355-8230
  Fremont (G-8698)
Rk Family Inc .... C 513 737-0436
  Hamilton (G-9079)
Rk Family Inc .... C 513 934-0015
  Lebanon (G-9786)
Rk Family Inc .... C 740 389-2674
  Marion (G-10452)
Rk Family Inc .... C 330 308-5075
  New Philadelphia (G-11665)
Rk Family Inc .... C 419 660-0363
  Norwalk (G-12024)
Rk Family Inc .... B 419 443-1663
  Tiffin (G-13640)
Rk Family Inc .... C 330 264-5475
  Wooster (G-15369)
Sunrise Cooperative Inc .... E 419 683-7340
  Crestline (G-7026)
Tractor Supply Company .... E 937 320-1855
  Beavercreek Township (G-951)
Tractor Supply Company .... E 614 878-7170
  Columbus (G-6779)
Tractor Supply Company .... E 740 288-1079
  Jackson (G-9526)
Tractor Supply Company .... E 419 673-8900
  Kenton (G-9623)
Tractor Supply Company .... E 740 456-0000
  Portsmouth (G-12577)
Tractor Supply Company .... E 937 446-9425
  Sardinia (G-12941)
Trupointe Cooperative Inc .... B 937 575-6780
  Piqua (G-12459)
Western Reserve Farm Cooperative Inc D 440 632-0271
  Middlefield (G-11146)

FARM SPLYS, WHOLESALE: Feed

Cooper Farms Inc .... D 419 375-4116
  Fort Recovery (G-8606)
Gerber Feed Service Inc .... E 330 857-4421
  Dalton (G-7120)
Keynes Bros Inc .... D 740 385-6824
  Logan (G-10030)
Mennel Milling Company .... E 740 385-6824
  Logan (G-10034)
Rj Matthews Company .... E 330 834-3000
  Massillon (G-10663)

FARM SPLYS, WHOLESALE: Fertilizers & Agricultural Chemicals

Rosens Inc .... D 419 225-7382
  Lima (G-9956)

FARM SPLYS, WHOLESALE: Garden Splys

Bfg Supply Co LLC .... E 800 883-0234
  Burton (G-1526)
Geoglobal Partners LLC .... D 561 598-6000
  Aurora (G-614)

FASTENERS WHOLESALERS

Midwest Motor Supply Co .... C 800 233-1294
  Columbus (G-6244)

FASTENERS: Metal

Contitech Usa Inc .... D 937 644-8900
  Marysville (G-10481)
Midwest Motor Supply Co .... C 800 233-1294
  Columbus (G-6244)

FENCING: Chain Link

Richards Whl Fence Co Inc .... E 330 773-0423
  Akron (G-282)

FERTILIZER, AGRICULTURAL: Wholesalers

Deerfield AG Services Inc .... E 330 584-4715
  Massillon (G-10637)
Deerfield Farms Service Inc .... D 330 584-4715
  Deerfield (G-7741)
Hanby Farms Inc .... E 740 763-3554
  Nashport (G-11535)
Morral Companies LLC .... E 740 465-3251
  Morral (G-11454)

FERTILIZERS: Nitrogenous

Scotts Miracle-Gro Company .... B 937 644-0011
  Marysville (G-10509)

FERTILIZERS: Phosphatic

Andersons Inc .... C 419 893-5050
  Maumee (G-10692)

FILTERS

Hunter Defense Tech Inc .... E 216 438-6111
  Solon (G-13096)
Swift Filters Inc .... E 440 735-0995
  Oakwood Village (G-12058)

FILTERS & SOFTENERS: Water, Household

SERVICES SECTION

FLUID POWER VALVES & HOSE FITTINGS

Enting Water Conditioning Inc............... E 937 294-5100
  Moraine *(G-11407)*

William R Hague Inc............................ D 614 836-2115
  Groveport *(G-9014)*

FILTERS: Air

Swift Filters Inc................................... E 440 735-0995
  Oakwood Village *(G-12058)*

FINANCIAL SVCS

Allstate Insurance Company................. E 330 650-2917
  Hudson *(G-9330)*

Aml Rightsource LLC........................... D 216 771-1250
  Cleveland *(G-3810)*

Ampersand Group LLC........................ E 330 379-0044
  Akron *(G-49)*

Banc One Services Corporation............ A 614 248-5800
  Columbus *(G-5247)*

Byrider Finance Inc............................. D 513 407-4140
  Cincinnati *(G-2297)*

Cbiz Inc... A 216 447-9000
  Cleveland *(G-3942)*

Cbiz Accnting Tax Advsory Wash.......... E 216 447-9000
  Cleveland *(G-3943)*

Cincinnati Financial Corp..................... A 513 870-2000
  Fairfield *(G-8402)*

Cleveland Clinic Foundation................. D 216 444-5000
  Cleveland *(G-4030)*

Credit First National Assn..................... E 216 362-5300
  Cleveland *(G-4136)*

E T Financial Service Inc...................... E 937 716-1726
  Trotwood *(G-14127)*

Facts Management Company.............. D 440 892-4272
  Westlake *(G-15059)*

Fiducius... E 513 645-5400
  Cincinnati *(G-2660)*

Fis Investor Services LLC..................... E 904 438-6000
  Columbus *(G-5866)*

Gabriel Partners LLC.......................... E 216 771-1250
  Cleveland *(G-4300)*

Hamilton Capital LLC......................... D 614 273-1000
  Columbus *(G-5966)*

Hd Davis Cpas LLC............................ D 330 759-8522
  Youngstown *(G-15626)*

Lendly LLC... E 844 453-6359
  Oakwood *(G-12049)*

Lowell Mackenzie................................ E 614 451-6669
  Sidney *(G-13038)*

Nationwide General Insur Co............... A 614 249-7111
  Columbus *(G-6331)*

Ncp Holdings LP................................. E 937 228-5600
  Oakwood *(G-12051)*

Producers Credit Corporation.............. C 800 641-7522
  Columbus *(G-6548)*

Reliance Financial Services NA............ E 419 783-8007
  Defiance *(G-7765)*

River Financial Inc.............................. E 415 878-3375
  Columbus *(G-6593)*

Ryder Last Mile Inc............................. D 866 711-3129
  New Albany *(G-11586)*

Sequoia Financial Group LLC.............. E 330 375-9480
  Akron *(G-297)*

Signature Closers LLC........................ E 614 448-7750
  Columbus *(G-6678)*

Sparkbase Inc..................................... E 216 867-0877
  Cleveland *(G-4927)*

Springleaf Fincl Holdings LLC.............. B 419 334-9748
  Fremont *(G-8704)*

Sterling Buying Group LLC.................. E 513 564-9000
  Cincinnati *(G-3416)*

Strive Enterprises Inc......................... E 614 593-2840
  Dublin *(G-8133)*

T2 Financial LLC................................. B 614 697-2021
  Westerville *(G-14941)*

Tebo Financial Services Inc................. E 234 207-2500
  Canton *(G-1869)*

Uhhs/Csahs - Cuyahoga Inc................ D 440 746-3401
  Cleveland *(G-5046)*

Wesbanco Title Agency LLC................ E 866 295-1714
  Columbus *(G-6877)*

Wisewel LLC....................................... E 440 591-4896
  Cleveland *(G-5153)*

FINISHING SVCS

Springleaf Fincl Holdings LLC.............. B 419 841-0785
  Toledo *(G-14021)*

FIRE ALARM MAINTENANCE & MONITORING SVCS

Gillmore Security Systems Inc............. E 440 232-1000
  Cleveland *(G-4313)*

FIRE CONTROL EQPT REPAIR SVCS, MILITARY

Brakefire Incorporated........................ D 513 733-5655
  Cincinnati *(G-2276)*

Fire Foe Corp...................................... E 330 759-9834
  Girard *(G-8811)*

FIREARMS & AMMUNITION, EXC SPORTING, WHOLESALE

Animal Supply Company LLC.............. E 330 642-6037
  Orrville *(G-12155)*

Keidel Sup LLC Fka Kdel Sup In.......... E 513 351-1600
  Cincinnati *(G-2933)*

Merco Group Inc................................ D 937 890-5841
  Dayton *(G-7481)*

Red Bull Media Hse N Amer Inc........... C 614 801-5193
  Grove City *(G-8948)*

FIREWORKS

Miller Fireworks Company Inc............. E 419 865-7329
  Holland *(G-9298)*

Phantom Fireworks Inc....................... B 330 746-1064
  Youngstown *(G-15693)*

Miller Fireworks Company Inc............. E 419 865-7329
  Holland *(G-9298)*

FISH & SEAFOOD WHOLESALERS

101 River Inc...................................... E 440 352-6343
  Grand River *(G-8848)*

Ohio Farmers Wholesale Dealers Inc.... D 216 391-9733
  Cleveland *(G-4688)*

Omegasea Ltd Liability Co................... E 440 639-2372
  Painesville *(G-12240)*

FITTINGS & ASSEMBLIES: Hose & Tube, Hydraulic Or Pneumatic

Mid-State Sales Inc............................ D 614 864-1811
  Columbus *(G-6241)*

FITTINGS: Pipe

Mid-State Sales Inc............................ D 614 864-1811
  Columbus *(G-6241)*

Parker-Hannifin Corporation................ C 614 279-7070
  Columbus *(G-6500)*

Parker-Hannifin Corporation................ D 937 456-5571
  Eaton *(G-8219)*

SSP Fittings Corp............................... D 330 425-4250
  Twinsburg *(G-14220)*

FITTINGS: Pipe, Fabricated

Pipe Products Inc............................... C 513 587-7532
  West Chester *(G-14742)*

FLAT GLASS: Construction

S R Door Inc....................................... D 740 927-3558
  Hebron *(G-9153)*

FLOOR COVERING STORES

Rite Rug Co.. E 614 478-3365
  Columbus *(G-6591)*

Schoch Tile & Carpet Inc..................... E 513 922-3466
  Cincinnati *(G-3350)*

FLOOR COVERING STORES: Carpets

Americas Floor Source LLC................. D 614 808-3915
  Columbus *(G-5363)*

Clays Heritage Carpet Inc.................... E 330 497-1280
  Canton *(G-1711)*

J L G Co Inc....................................... E 513 248-1755
  Loveland *(G-10144)*

Stanley Steemer Intl Inc...................... C 614 764-2007
  Dublin *(G-8124)*

FLOOR COVERINGS WHOLESALERS

Americas Floor Source LLC................. D 614 808-3915
  Columbus *(G-5363)*

Black River Group Inc......................... E 419 524-4312
  Mansfield *(G-10246)*

Cdc Distributors Inc............................ D 513 771-3100
  Cincinnati *(G-2329)*

Messina Floor Covering LLC............... D 216 595-0100
  Cleveland *(G-4557)*

FLORIST: Flowers, Fresh

Deans Greenhouse Inc........................ E 440 871-2050
  Cleveland *(G-4158)*

HJ Benken Flor & Greenhouses............ E 513 891-1040
  Cincinnati *(G-2830)*

Lowes Investments Inc........................ E 440 543-5123
  Chagrin Falls *(G-1984)*

Pickaway Growers LLC....................... E 614 344-4956
  Orient *(G-12154)*

FLOWERS, FRESH, WHOLESALE

Claprood Roman J Co......................... E 614 221-5515
  Columbus *(G-5579)*

Flowers Baking Co Ohio LLC............... E 419 661-2586
  Northwood *(G-11974)*

The Cleveland Plant and Flo................. E 216 898-3500
  Cleveland *(G-4995)*

FLUID POWER PUMPS & MOTORS

Aerocontrolex Group Inc..................... D 216 291-6025
  South Euclid *(G-13170)*

Anchor Flange Company...................... D 513 527-3512
  Cincinnati *(G-2196)*

Apph Wichita Inc................................. E 316 943-5752
  Strongsville *(G-13442)*

Eaton Leasing Corporation.................. B 216 382-2292
  Beachwood *(G-788)*

Giant Industries Inc............................. E 419 531-4600
  Toledo *(G-13821)*

Hydraulic Parts Store Inc..................... E 330 364-6667
  New Philadelphia *(G-11656)*

Robeck Fluid Power Co....................... D 330 562-1140
  Aurora *(G-624)*

Trane Technologies Company LLC....... E 419 633-6800
  Bryan *(G-1494)*

FLUID POWER VALVES & HOSE FITTINGS

Alkon Corporation.................................. D 419 355-9111
  Fremont *(G-8665)*
Hydraulic Parts Store Inc..................... E 330 364-6667
  New Philadelphia *(G-11656)*
Kirtland Capital Partners LP................. E 216 593-0100
  Beachwood *(G-806)*
Parker-Hannifin Corporation................. D 937 456-5571
  Eaton *(G-8219)*
Pressure Connections Corp................... D 614 863-6930
  Columbus *(G-6543)*
SSP Fittings Corp.................................. D 330 425-4250
  Twinsburg *(G-14220)*
Superior Holding LLC........................... E 216 651-9400
  Cleveland *(G-4964)*
Superior Products LLC......................... D 216 651-9400
  Cleveland *(G-4965)*

FOAM RUBBER

Pfp Holdings LLC.................................. A 419 647-4191
  Spencerville *(G-13190)*

FOAMS & RUBBER, WHOLESALE

Acor Orthopaedic LLC.......................... E 216 662-4500
  Cleveland *(G-3764)*
Johnson Bros Rubber Co Inc................ E 419 752-4814
  Greenwich *(G-8892)*
Johnson Bros Rubber Co...................... D 419 853-4122
  West Salem *(G-14863)*
Tahoma Enterprises Inc........................ D 330 745-9016
  Barberton *(G-714)*
Tahoma Rubber & Plastics Inc.............. D 330 745-9016
  Barberton *(G-715)*

FOIL & LEAF: Metal

Wieland Metal Svcs Foils LLC............... D 330 823-1700
  Alliance *(G-405)*

FOOD PRDTS, CANNED: Fruits

Clovervale Farms LLC.......................... D 440 960-0146
  Amherst *(G-426)*

FOOD PRDTS, CANNED: Puddings, Exc Meat

Clovervale Farms LLC.......................... D 440 960-0146
  Amherst *(G-426)*

FOOD PRDTS, CANNED: Vegetables

Bfc Inc.. E 330 364-6645
  Dover *(G-7873)*

FOOD PRDTS, CONFECTIONERY, WHOLESALE: Candy

Bendon Inc... D 419 207-3600
  Ashland *(G-482)*
Gorant Chocolatier LLC........................ C 330 726-8821
  Boardman *(G-1288)*
Gummer Wholesale Inc......................... D 740 928-0415
  Heath *(G-9133)*

FOOD PRDTS, CONFECTIONERY, WHOLESALE: Pretzels

Mike-Sells West Virginia Inc.................. D 937 228-9400
  Dayton *(G-7505)*

FOOD PRDTS, CONFECTIONERY, WHOLESALE: Snack Foods

Frito-Lay North America Inc.................. E 216 491-4000
  Cleveland *(G-4292)*

Frito-Lay North America Inc.................. E 614 508-3004
  Columbus *(G-5899)*
Gold Medal Products Co....................... E 614 228-1155
  Columbus *(G-5939)*
Mike-Sells Potato Chip Co.................... E 937 228-9400
  Dayton *(G-7504)*
Shearers Foods LLC............................. A 800 428-6843
  Massillon *(G-10669)*
Shearers Foods Phoenix LLC............... E 330 834-4330
  Massillon *(G-10670)*

FOOD PRDTS, FRUITS & VEGETABLES, FRESH, WHOLESALE: Fruits

Cecil T Brinager.................................... D 740 843-5280
  Portland *(G-12542)*

FOOD PRDTS, POULTRY, WHOLESALE: Poultry Prdts, NEC

Michaels Finer Meats LLC..................... C 614 527-4900
  Columbus *(G-6231)*
Ohio Farmers Wholesale Dealers Inc..... D 216 391-9733
  Cleveland *(G-4688)*

FOOD PRDTS, WHOLESALE: Baking Splys

Bakemark USA LLC............................... D 513 870-0880
  Fairfield *(G-8391)*
Cassanos Inc... E 937 294-8400
  Dayton *(G-7215)*

FOOD PRDTS, WHOLESALE: Beverages, Exc Coffee & Tea

Esber Beverage Company..................... E 330 456-4361
  Canton *(G-1750)*
G & J Pepsi-Cola Bottlers Inc................ E 740 593-3366
  Athens *(G-568)*
Superior Beverage Group Ltd............... C 419 529-0702
  Lexington *(G-9845)*

FOOD PRDTS, WHOLESALE: Coffee & Tea

Boston Company Inc............................. A 937 652-0410
  Urbana *(G-14298)*

FOOD PRDTS, WHOLESALE: Coffee, Green Or Roasted

Coffee Break Corporation...................... E 513 841-1100
  Cincinnati *(G-2468)*

FOOD PRDTS, WHOLESALE: Condiments

Kerry Inc.. E 760 685-2548
  Byesville *(G-1535)*

FOOD PRDTS, WHOLESALE: Cookies

Bendon Inc... D 419 207-3600
  Ashland *(G-482)*

FOOD PRDTS, WHOLESALE: Dog Food

Kinetic Nutrition Group LLC.................. E 513 279-8966
  Cincinnati *(G-2940)*

FOOD PRDTS, WHOLESALE: Dried or Canned Foods

Tarrier Foods Corp................................ E 614 876-8594
  Columbus *(G-6749)*
US Foods Inc... C 216 475-7400
  Cleveland *(G-5092)*
US Foods Inc... C 513 874-3900
  Fairfield *(G-8451)*

FOOD PRDTS, WHOLESALE: Grain Elevators

Deerfield AG Services Inc..................... E 330 584-4715
  Massillon *(G-10637)*
Deerfield Farms Service Inc.................. D 330 584-4715
  Deerfield *(G-7741)*
Fort Recovery Equity Inc....................... C 419 942-1148
  Fort Recovery *(G-8608)*
Fort Recovery Equity Inc....................... E 419 375-4119
  Fort Recovery *(G-8609)*
Minster Farmers Coop Exch.................. D 419 628-4705
  Minster *(G-11319)*

FOOD PRDTS, WHOLESALE: Grains

Andersons Inc....................................... C 419 893-5050
  Maumee *(G-10692)*
Andersons Agriculture Group LP........... E 419 893-5050
  Maumee *(G-10694)*
Bunge North America East LLC............ A 419 692-6010
  Delphos *(G-7837)*
Champion Feed and Pet Sup LLC......... E 740 369-3020
  Granville *(G-8851)*
Consolidated Grain & Barge Co............ E 513 244-7400
  Cincinnati *(G-2495)*
Cooper Hatchery Inc............................. C 419 594-3325
  Oakwood *(G-12053)*
Heritage Cooperative Inc...................... E 330 533-5551
  Canfield *(G-1630)*
Heritage Cooperative Inc...................... D 877 240-4393
  Delaware *(G-7804)*
Mid-Wood Inc.. E 419 937-2233
  Bascom *(G-725)*
The Andersons Marathon Ethanol LLC.. E 937 316-3700
  Greenville *(G-8887)*
Trupointe Cooperative Inc..................... B 937 575-6780
  Piqua *(G-12459)*

FOOD PRDTS, WHOLESALE: Juices

M & M Wine Cellar Inc........................... E 330 536-6450
  Lowellville *(G-10170)*

FOOD PRDTS, WHOLESALE: Pizza Splys

Ohio Pizza Products LLC...................... D 937 294-6969
  Monroe *(G-11346)*
Rdp Foodservice Ltd............................. D 614 261-5661
  Hilliard *(G-9228)*

FOOD PRDTS, WHOLESALE: Salt, Edible

Morton Salt Inc...................................... C 330 925-3015
  Rittman *(G-12731)*

FOOD PRDTS, WHOLESALE: Soybeans

Milky Acres LLC.................................... E 419 561-1364
  Sycamore *(G-13532)*

FOOD PRDTS, WHOLESALE: Specialty

Antonio Sofo Son Importing Co............. C 419 476-4211
  Toledo *(G-13690)*
Atlantic Foods Corp.............................. D 513 772-3535
  Cincinnati *(G-2227)*
Cheese Holdings Inc............................. E 330 893-2479
  Millersburg *(G-11275)*
Euro Usa Inc... D 216 714-0500
  Cleveland *(G-4224)*
JM Smucker LLC................................... D 330 682-3000
  Orrville *(G-12169)*
Lajd Warehousing & Leasing Inc........... D 330 452-5010
  Canton *(G-1793)*
National Marketshare Group................. E 513 921-0800
  Cincinnati *(G-3095)*

FOOD PRDTS, WHOLESALE: Water, Distilled

Distillata Company................................. D 216 771-2900
  Cleveland *(G-4167)*

SERVICES SECTION

FRANCHISES, SELLING OR LICENSING

FOOD PRDTS: Dried & Dehydrated Fruits, Vegetables & Soup Mix

Hayden Valley Foods Inc .... D 614 539-7233
　Urbancrest *(G-14320)*

FOOD PRDTS: Flour & Other Grain Mill Products

Minster Farmers Coop Exch .... D 419 628-4705
　Minster *(G-11319)*

FOOD PRDTS: Flour, Blended From Purchased Flour

Busken Bakery Inc .... D 513 871-2114
　Cincinnati *(G-2294)*

FOOD PRDTS: Pizza Doughs From Purchased Flour

Cassanos Inc .... E 937 294-8400
　Dayton *(G-7215)*

FOOD PRDTS: Potato Chips & Other Potato-Based Snacks

Ballreich Bros Inc .... C 419 447-1814
　Tiffin *(G-13624)*
Jones Potato Chip Co .... E 419 529-9424
　Mansfield *(G-10276)*
Mike-Sells Potato Chip Co .... E 937 228-9400
　Dayton *(G-7504)*
Mike-Sells West Virginia Inc .... D 937 228-9400
　Dayton *(G-7505)*

FOOD PRDTS: Poultry, Processed, Frozen

Martin-Brower Company LLC .... C 513 773-2301
　West Chester *(G-14729)*

FOOD PRDTS: Seasonings & Spices

National Foods Packaging Inc .... E 216 622-2740
　Cleveland *(G-4626)*

FOOD PRDTS: Sugar

Domino Foods Inc .... C 216 432-3222
　Cleveland *(G-4175)*

FOOD PRODUCTS MACHINERY

Chemineer Inc .... C 937 454-3200
　Dayton *(G-7222)*
G & S Metal Products Co Inc .... C 216 441-0700
　Cleveland *(G-4295)*
Gold Medal Products Co .... B 513 769-7676
　Cincinnati *(G-2739)*
Harry C Lobalzo & Sons Inc .... E 330 666-6758
　Akron *(G-184)*
Innovative Controls Corp .... E 419 691-6684
　Toledo *(G-13863)*
ITW Food Equipment Group LLC .... A 937 332-2396
　Troy *(G-14141)*
Lima Sheet Metal Machine & Mfg .... E 419 229-1161
　Lima *(G-9927)*
N Wasserstrom & Sons Inc .... C 614 228-5550
　Columbus *(G-6286)*
Norse Dairy Systems Inc .... C 614 294-4931
　Columbus *(G-6363)*
R and J Corporation .... E 440 871-6009
　Westlake *(G-15101)*
Wolf Machine Company .... E 513 791-5194
　Blue Ash *(G-1274)*

FOOD STORES: Convenience, Chain

Convenient Food Mart Inc .... E 800 860-4844
　Mentor *(G-10926)*
Lykins Companies Inc .... E 513 831-8820
　Milford *(G-11238)*
United Dairy Farmers Inc .... C 513 396-8700
　Cincinnati *(G-3553)*

FOOD STORES: Delicatessen

Bagel Place Inc .... E 419 537-9377
　Toledo *(G-13698)*
Weilands Fine Meats Inc .... E 614 267-9910
　Columbus *(G-6873)*

FOOD STORES: Grocery, Chain

Fred W Albrecht Grocery Co .... C 330 666-6781
　Akron *(G-169)*
Sack n Save Inc .... E 740 382-2464
　Marion *(G-10453)*

FOOD STORES: Grocery, Independent

Buehler Food Markets Inc .... C 330 364-3079
　Dover *(G-7874)*
Carfagnas Incorporated .... E 614 846-6340
　Columbus *(G-5248)*
Sommers Market LLC .... D 330 352-7470
　Hartville *(G-9130)*

FOOD STORES: Supermarkets, Chain

Giant Eagle Inc .... C 412 968-5300
　Columbus *(G-5933)*
Giant Eagle Inc .... D 330 364-5301
　Dover *(G-7885)*
Krlp Inc .... A 513 762-4000
　Cincinnati *(G-2953)*
Riser Foods Company .... D 216 292-7000
　Bedford Heights *(G-1001)*

FOOD STORES: Supermarkets, Independent

Fisher Foods Marketing Inc .... C 330 497-3000
　North Canton *(G-11830)*
Mary C Enterprises Inc .... D 937 253-6169
　Dayton *(G-7467)*

FOOTWEAR, WHOLESALE: Shoes

Drew Ventures Inc .... E 740 653-4271
　Lancaster *(G-9708)*
Ebuys Inc .... E 858 831-0839
　Columbus *(G-5803)*
Georgia-Boot Inc .... D 740 753-1951
　Nelsonville *(G-11545)*
Lehigh Outfitters LLC .... C 740 753-1951
　Nelsonville *(G-11549)*
Safety Solutions Inc .... D 614 799-9900
　Columbus *(G-6634)*

FORGINGS: Construction Or Mining Eqpt, Ferrous

Rudd Equipment Company Inc .... D 513 321-7833
　Cincinnati *(G-3329)*

FORGINGS: Iron & Steel

S&V Industries Inc .... E 330 666-1986
　Medina *(G-10886)*

FORGINGS: Plumbing Fixture, Nonferrous

Mansfield Plumbing Pdts LLC .... A 419 938-5211
　Perrysville *(G-12392)*

FOUNDRIES: Aluminum

Akron Foundry Co .... C 330 745-3101
　Akron *(G-28)*

Aluminum Line Products Company ..... D 440 835-8880
　Westlake *(G-15032)*
Miba Bearings US LLC .... B 740 962-4242
　Mcconnelsville *(G-10803)*
Yoder Industries Inc .... C 937 278-5769
　Dayton *(G-7731)*

FOUNDRIES: Nonferrous

Yoder Industries Inc .... C 937 278-5769
　Dayton *(G-7731)*

FOUNDRIES: Steel

Jmac Inc .... E 614 436-2418
　Columbus *(G-6092)*
Worthington Enterprises Inc .... D 513 539-9291
　Monroe *(G-11355)*
Worthngton Stelpac Systems LLC .... C 614 438-3205
　Columbus *(G-6908)*

FOUNDRY MACHINERY & EQPT

Equipment Mfrs Intl Inc .... E 216 651-6700
　Cleveland *(G-4217)*

FRAMES & FRAMING WHOLESALE

Hobby Lobby Stores Inc .... E 330 686-1508
　Stow *(G-13373)*

FRANCHISES, SELLING OR LICENSING

Bagel Place Inc .... E 419 537-9377
　Toledo *(G-13698)*
Brewdog Franchising LLC .... E 614 908-3051
　Canal Winchester *(G-1599)*
Cassanos Inc .... E 937 294-8400
　Dayton *(G-7215)*
Chemstation International Inc .... E 937 294-8265
　Moraine *(G-11397)*
Clark Brands LLC .... A 330 723-9886
　Medina *(G-10821)*
Convenient Food Mart Inc .... E 800 860-4844
　Mentor *(G-10926)*
East of Chicago Pizza Inc .... D 419 225-7116
　Lima *(G-9885)*
Epcon Cmmnties Franchising Inc .... D 614 761-1010
　Dublin *(G-8005)*
Escape Enterprises Inc .... D 614 224-0300
　Columbus *(G-5828)*
Frickers USA LLC .... E 937 865-9242
　Miamisburg *(G-11056)*
Giant Eagle Inc .... C 412 968-5300
　Columbus *(G-5933)*
Gioninos Pizzeria Inc .... E 330 630-2010
　Tallmadge *(G-13592)*
Gold Star Chili Inc .... E 513 231-4541
　Cincinnati *(G-2740)*
Gosh Enterprises Inc .... E 614 923-4700
　Columbus *(G-5943)*
Hometeam Inspection Service .... C 513 831-1300
　Milford *(G-11230)*
Larosas Inc .... A 513 347-5660
　Cincinnati *(G-2966)*
Lei Home Enhancements .... C 513 738-4663
　Cincinnati *(G-2970)*
Marcos Inc .... D 419 885-4844
　Toledo *(G-13910)*
Moto Franchise Corporation .... E 937 291-1900
　Dayton *(G-7516)*
Parkway Pizza Incorporated .... D 937 303-8800
　Marysville *(G-10502)*
Petland Inc .... E 740 775-2464
　Chillicothe *(G-2082)*
Pfg Ventures LP .... D 216 520-8400
　Independence *(G-9466)*

FRANCHISES, SELLING OR LICENSING

Premier Broadcasting Co Inc.............. E 614 866-0700
  Reynoldsburg (G-12672)
Red Robin Gourmet Burgers Inc.......... C 330 305-1080
  Canton (G-1841)
Red Roof Inns Inc................................ A 614 744-2600
  New Albany (G-11584)
Romeos Pizza Franchise LLC............... C 234 248-4549
  Medina (G-10885)
Sabo Inc... E 937 222-7939
  Dayton (G-7603)
Skyline Cem Holdings LLC.................. C 513 874-1188
  Fairfield (G-8441)
Stanley Steemer Intl Inc..................... C 614 764-2007
  Dublin (G-8124)
Staymobile Franchising LLC................ D 614 601-3345
  Columbus (G-6717)
Ta Operating LLC................................ B 440 808-9100
  Westlake (G-15113)
The Cornwell Quality Tools Company... D 330 336-3506
  Wadsworth (G-14455)
Tuffy Associates Corp......................... E 419 865-6900
  Toledo (G-14077)
Waxxpot Group Franchise LLC............ C 614 622-3018
  Columbus (G-6871)
Wendys Company................................ B 614 764-3100
  Dublin (G-8163)
Wendys Restaurants LLC.................... E 614 764-3100
  Dublin (G-8164)

FREIGHT CAR LOADING & UNLOADING SVCS

Contrlled Chaos Enrgy Svcs LLC........... E 740 257-0724
  Belmont (G-1054)
Dayton Synchrnous Spport Ctr I........... E 937 226-1559
  Dayton (G-7302)

FREIGHT FORWARDING ARRANGEMENTS

A Plus Expediting & Logistics.............. E 937 424-0220
  Dayton (G-7149)
Alliance Customs Clearance................ E 513 794-9400
  Cincinnati (G-2162)
Ascent Global Logistics LLC............... C 330 342-8700
  Hudson (G-9332)
Ascent Globl Lgstics Hldngs In............ E 603 881-3450
  Hudson (G-9333)
Bolt Express LLC................................ D 419 729-6698
  Toledo (G-13711)
Buckeye Transfer LLC......................... D 330 719-0375
  Lisbon (G-9997)
Ceva Logistics LLC............................ C 614 482-5000
  Groveport (G-8977)
Contech Trckg & Logistics LLC............ D 513 645-7000
  West Chester (G-14673)
Dayton Synchrnous Spport Ctr I........... E 937 226-1559
  Dayton (G-7302)
Dhl Express (usa) Inc......................... E 614 865-8325
  Westerville (G-14889)
Diamond W LLC.................................. D 970 434-9435
  Clarington (G-3729)
Distribution Data Incorporated............. D 216 362-3009
  Brookpark (G-1433)
DSV Solutions LLC............................ C 740 989-1200
  Little Hocking (G-10008)
Exel Global Logistics Inc.................... C 440 243-5900
  Cleveland (G-4231)
Exel Inc... D 614 836-1265
  Groveport (G-8977)
Exel Inc... E 614 865-8294
  Westerville (G-14894)
Exel N Amercn Logistics Inc................ C 800 272-1052
  Westerville (G-14978)

Fedex Custom Critical Inc................... B 234 310-4090
  Richfield (G-12698)
Gateway Freight Forwarding Inc........... D 513 248-1514
  Cincinnati (G-2718)
Gxo Logistics Supply Chain Inc........... E 614 305-1705
  Grove City (G-8923)
Innovative Logistics Svcs Inc............... D 330 468-6422
  Northfield (G-11958)
Komyo America Co Inc....................... E 937 339-0157
  Troy (G-14143)
Kuehne + Nagel Inc............................ C 440 243-6070
  Berea (G-1072)
Kw International Inc........................... D 513 942-8999
  Cincinnati (G-2957)
Martin Logistics Incorporated.............. D 330 456-8000
  Canton (G-1800)
Nations Express Inc........................... E 440 234-4330
  Brunswick (G-1465)
Nissin Intl Trnspt USA Inc.................. D 937 644-2644
  Marysville (G-10500)
North South Delivery LLC................... E 419 478-7400
  Toledo (G-13937)
Nutrition Trnsp Svcs LLC.................... D 937 962-2661
  Lewisburg (G-9841)
Overland Xpress LLC.......................... E 513 528-1158
  Cincinnati (G-3177)
Pacer Transport Inc........................... D 614 923-1400
  Dublin (G-8085)
R&L Hero Delivery LLC....................... D 937 824-0291
  Dayton (G-7140)
Redhawk Global LLC.......................... E 614 487-8505
  Columbus (G-6569)
Ryan Logistics Inc.............................. D 937 642-4158
  Marysville (G-10506)
Ryder Integrated Logistics Inc............. E 614 801-0224
  Grove City (G-8949)
Stg Cartage LLC................................. A 614 923-1400
  Dublin (G-8127)
Stg Cartage LLC................................. E 614 923-1400
  Dublin (G-8128)
Stg Intermodal Inc............................. E 440 833-0924
  Wickliffe (G-15163)
T S Expediting Services Inc................. D 419 837-2401
  Millbury (G-11271)
Tazmanian Freight Fwdg Inc................ E 216 265-7881
  Middleburg Heights (G-11130)
Tforce Freight Inc............................... E 216 676-4560
  Cleveland (G-4988)
Tgs International Inc.......................... E 330 893-4828
  Millersburg (G-11293)
Tjm Express Inc................................. E 216 385-4164
  Berea (G-1085)
Transfreight LLC................................ B 937 576-2800
  Tipp City (G-13667)
TV Minority Company Inc.................... E 937 832-9350
  Englewood (G-8324)
UPS Supply Chain Solutions Inc........... E 360 332-5222
  Cleveland (G-5088)
US Expediting Logistics LLC................ E 937 235-1014
  Vandalia (G-14399)
World Ex Shipg Trnsp Fwdg Svcs......... E 440 826-5055
  Middleburg Heights (G-11135)

FREIGHT FORWARDING ARRANGEMENTS: Domestic

Ardmore Power Logistics LLC.............. E 216 502-0640
  Westlake (G-15034)
Exel Global Logistics Inc.................... C 614 409-4500
  Columbus (G-5838)
IHS Enterprise LLC............................ C 216 588-9078
  Independence (G-9436)

SERVICES SECTION

Integrity Ex Logistics LLC................... B 888 374-5138
  Cincinnati (G-2877)
Nippon Express USA Inc..................... E 614 295-0030
  Grove City (G-8941)

FRUIT & VEGETABLE MARKETS

Euclid Fish Company.......................... D 440 951-6448
  Mentor (G-10938)

FRUIT STANDS OR MARKETS

Mapleside Valley LLC......................... D 330 225-5576
  Brunswick (G-1462)
Miles Farmers Market Inc................... C 440 248-5222
  Solon (G-13111)

FRUITS & VEGETABLES WHOLESALERS: Fresh

Chefs Garden Inc............................... C 419 433-4947
  Huron (G-9385)
Giant Eagle Inc.................................. C 412 968-5300
  Columbus (G-5933)
Kaleel Bros Inc.................................. D 330 758-0861
  Youngstown (G-15644)
Produce Packaging Inc........................ C 216 391-6129
  Willoughby Hills (G-15234)
US Foods Inc..................................... E 614 539-7993
  West Chester (G-14843)

FUEL DEALERS: Coal

Cliffs Logan County Coal LLC.............. C 216 694-5700
  Cleveland (G-4077)

FUEL OIL DEALERS

Aim Leasing Company......................... D 330 759-0438
  Girard (G-8809)
Bazell Oil Co Inc................................ E 740 385-5420
  Logan (G-10021)
Centerra Co-Op.................................. E 419 281-2153
  Ashland (G-490)
Cincinnati - Vulcan Company............... D 513 242-5300
  Cincinnati (G-2391)
Duncan Oil Co.................................... E 937 426-5945
  Dayton (G-7131)
Energy Cooperative Inc....................... E 740 348-1206
  Newark (G-11699)
Lykins Oil Company............................ E 513 831-8820
  Milford (G-11239)
Mighty Mac Investments Inc................ E 937 335-2928
  Troy (G-14147)
Ports Petroleum Company Inc.............. E 330 264-1885
  Wooster (G-15367)
Red Rover LLC................................... E 330 262-6501
  Wooster (G-15368)
Santmyer Logistics Inc....................... D 330 262-6501
  Wooster (G-15371)
Suburban Oil Company....................... E 513 459-8100
  Mason (G-10611)
Ull Inc.. E 440 543-5195
  Chagrin Falls (G-1992)
Western Reserve Farm Cooperative Inc D 440 632-0271
  Middlefield (G-11146)

FUND RAISING ORGANIZATION, NON-FEE BASIS

Catholic Charities Corporation............. D 419 289-7456
  Ashland (G-487)
Catholic Charities Corporation............. D 419 289-1903
  Ashland (G-488)
Catholic Charities Corporation............. D 216 432-0680
  Cleveland (G-3932)

SERVICES SECTION

Catholic Charities Corporation............... D 216 939-3713
  Cleveland *(G-3933)*

Catholic Charities Corporation............... D 216 268-4006
  Cleveland *(G-3934)*

Catholic Charities Corporation............... D 330 262-7836
  Wooster *(G-15317)*

Colonial Senior Services Inc.................. D 513 856-8600
  Hamilton *(G-9030)*

Columbus Jewish Federation................. E 614 237-7686
  Columbus *(G-5641)*

Interact For Health................................ E 513 458-6600
  Cincinnati *(G-2878)*

Planet Aid Inc..................................... E 440 542-1171
  Solon *(G-13127)*

Playhouse Square Holdg Co LLC........... C 216 771-4444
  Cleveland *(G-4759)*

FUNGICIDES OR HERBICIDES

Scotts Company LLC............................ C 937 644-0011
  Marysville *(G-10508)*

FURNACES & OVENS: Indl

Hannon Company................................. D 330 456-4728
  Canton *(G-1770)*

Resilience Fund III LP.......................... E 216 292-0200
  Cleveland *(G-4830)*

United McGill Corporation..................... E 614 829-1200
  Groveport *(G-9007)*

FURNACES: Indl, Electric

Ajax Tocco Magnethermic Corp............ C 800 547-1527
  Warren *(G-14496)*

The Schaefer Group Inc....................... E 937 253-3342
  Beavercreek *(G-932)*

Ajax Tocco Magnethermic Corp............ C 800 547-1527
  Warren *(G-14496)*

FURNACES: Warm Air, Electric

Columbus Heating & Vent Co................ C 614 274-1177
  Columbus *(G-5635)*

FURNITURE REFINISHING SVCS

Soft Touch Wood LLC.......................... E 330 545-4204
  Girard *(G-8826)*

FURNITURE REPAIR & MAINTENANCE SVCS

Business Furniture LLC........................ E 937 293-1010
  Dayton *(G-7207)*

Dayton Ews Inc.................................. E 937 293-1010
  Moraine *(G-11400)*

FURNITURE STORES

Big Sandy Furniture Inc....................... D 740 894-4242
  Chesapeake *(G-2028)*

Big Sandy Furniture Inc....................... D 740 775-4244
  Chillicothe *(G-2052)*

Big Sandy Furniture Inc....................... D 740 354-3193
  Portsmouth *(G-12546)*

Big Sandy Furniture Inc....................... D 740 574-2113
  Franklin Furnace *(G-8653)*

Dtv Inc.. E 216 226-5465
  Cleveland *(G-4187)*

Globe Furniture Rentals Inc.................. D 513 771-8287
  Cincinnati *(G-2734)*

Indepndence Office Bus Sup Inc........... D 216 398-8880
  Cleveland *(G-4408)*

W Home Collection LLC....................... E 440 247-4474
  Chagrin Falls *(G-1971)*

FURNITURE WHOLESALERS

Big Lots Stores LLC............................ A 614 278-6800
  Columbus *(G-5439)*

Cornerstone Brands Inc....................... A 513 603-1000
  West Chester *(G-14676)*

D Yoder Hardwoods LLC...................... D 330 852-8105
  Sugarcreek *(G-13508)*

Friends Service Co Inc........................ D 419 427-1704
  Findlay *(G-8534)*

Mill Distributors Inc............................. D 330 995-9200
  Aurora *(G-618)*

Retail Service Systems Inc................... D 614 203-6126
  Dublin *(G-8108)*

Space & Asset Management Inc........... E 937 918-1000
  Dayton *(G-7631)*

FURNITURE, HOUSEHOLD: Wholesalers

Sauder Woodworking Co...................... A 419 446-2711
  Archbold *(G-467)*

FURNITURE, OFFICE: Wholesalers

12985 Snow Holdings Inc..................... E 216 267-5000
  Cleveland *(G-3739)*

American Interiors Inc......................... E 419 535-1808
  Toledo *(G-13683)*

Business Furniture LLC....................... E 937 293-1010
  Dayton *(G-7207)*

Commercial Works Inc......................... D 614 870-2342
  Columbus *(G-5667)*

Dayton Ews Inc.................................. E 937 293-1010
  Moraine *(G-11400)*

Loth Inc... E 614 487-4000
  Columbus *(G-6173)*

S P Richards Company........................ E 614 497-2270
  Lockbourne *(G-10015)*

Springfield Business Eqp Co................ E 937 322-3828
  Springfield *(G-13294)*

The Ohio Desk Company...................... E 216 623-0600
  Cleveland *(G-5005)*

W B Mason Co Inc.............................. E 216 267-5000
  North Olmsted *(G-11918)*

Wasserstrom Company........................ B 614 228-6525
  Columbus *(G-6867)*

FURNITURE, WHOLESALE: Chairs

Gasser Chair Co Inc........................... D 330 742-2234
  Youngstown *(G-15617)*

FURNITURE, WHOLESALE: Racks

KMC Holdings LLC.............................. C 419 238-2442
  Van Wert *(G-14347)*

Partitions Plus Incorporated................. E 419 422-2600
  Findlay *(G-8575)*

FURNITURE, WHOLESALE: Shelving

G & P Construction LLC....................... E 855 494-4830
  North Royalton *(G-11941)*

FURNITURE: Cabinets & Filing Drawers, Office, Exc Wood

Jsc Employee Leasing Corp.................. D 330 773-8971
  Akron *(G-212)*

FURNITURE: Chairs, Household Wood

Gencraft Designs LLC......................... E 330 359-6251
  Navarre *(G-11537)*

Vocational Services Inc....................... E 216 431-8085
  Cleveland *(G-5113)*

FURNITURE: Mattresses & Foundations

Walter F Stephens Jr Inc..................... E 937 746-0521
  Franklin *(G-8652)*

FURNITURE: Office, Exc Wood

GASOLINE FILLING STATIONS

Casco Mfg Solutions Inc...................... D 513 681-0003
  Cincinnati *(G-2318)*

National Electro-Coatings Inc................ D 216 898-0080
  Cleveland *(G-4624)*

FURNITURE: Play Pens, Children's, Wood

Western & Southern Lf Insur Co............ A 513 629-1800
  Cincinnati *(G-3659)*

FURNITURE: Restaurant

Best Restaurant Equipment & Design.... D 614 488-2378
  Columbus *(G-5433)*

FURNITURE: Upholstered

Sauder Woodworking Co...................... A 419 446-2711
  Archbold *(G-467)*

GAS & OIL FIELD EXPLORATION SVCS

Antero Resources Corporation.............. E 303 357-7310
  Caldwell *(G-1545)*

Antero Resources Corporation.............. D 740 760-1000
  Marietta *(G-10356)*

BD Oil Gathering Corp......................... E 740 374-9355
  Marietta *(G-10357)*

Blue Racer Midstream LLC.................. D 740 630-7556
  Cambridge *(G-1556)*

Diversified Production LLC................... C 740 373-8771
  Marietta *(G-10366)*

Husky Marketing and Supply Co........... E 614 210-2300
  Dublin *(G-8033)*

M3 Midstream LLC.............................. E 330 223-2220
  Kensington *(G-9554)*

M3 Midstream LLC.............................. E 330 679-5580
  Salineville *(G-12860)*

M3 Midstream LLC.............................. E 740 945-1170
  Scio *(G-12942)*

Ngo Development Corporation.............. B 740 622-9560
  Coshocton *(G-6993)*

Precision Geophysical Inc.................... E 330 674-2198
  Millersburg *(G-11290)*

Utica East Ohio Midstream LLC............ B 740 431-4168
  Dennison *(G-7861)*

GAS FIELD MACHINERY & EQPT

Jet Rubber Company........................... E 330 325-1821
  Rootstown *(G-12760)*

GASES: Acetylene

Delille Oxygen Company...................... E 614 444-1177
  Columbus *(G-5752)*

GASES: Indl

National Gas & Oil Corporation............. E 740 344-2102
  Newark *(G-11733)*

GASKETS

Industry Products Co.......................... B 937 778-0585
  Piqua *(G-12445)*

Ohio Gasket and Shim Co Inc.............. E 330 630-0626
  Akron *(G-251)*

GASOLINE FILLING STATIONS

1st Stop Inc....................................... E 937 695-0318
  Winchester *(G-15283)*

Beck Suppliers Inc............................. E 419 426-3051
  Attica *(G-598)*

Convenient Food Mart Inc.................... E 800 860-4844
  Mentor *(G-10926)*

G J Shue Inc..................................... E 330 722-0082
  Medina *(G-10837)*

Holland Oil Company........................... D 330 835-1815
  Akron *(G-194)*

GASOLINE FILLING STATIONS

Mighty Mac Investments Inc................ E 937 335-2928
  Troy *(G-14147)*
National At/Trckstops Hldngs C.......... A 440 808-9100
  Westlake *(G-15081)*
Ports Petroleum Company Inc............. E 330 264-1885
  Wooster *(G-15367)*
Santmyer Logistics Inc....................... D 330 262-6501
  Wooster *(G-15371)*
Seaway Gas & Petroleum Inc.............. E 216 566-9070
  Cleveland *(G-4888)*
Ta Operating LLC................................ B 440 808-9100
  Westlake *(G-15113)*
True North Energy LLC....................... E 877 245-9336
  Brecksville *(G-1370)*
United Dairy Farmers Inc.................... C 513 396-8700
  Cincinnati *(G-3553)*
Yorktown Automotive Center Inc......... E 440 885-2803
  Cleveland *(G-5165)*

GASOLINE WHOLESALERS

Duncan Oil Co..................................... E 937 426-5945
  Dayton *(G-7131)*
Holland Oil Company........................... D 330 835-1815
  Akron *(G-194)*
Lykins Companies Inc......................... E 513 831-8820
  Milford *(G-11238)*
Lykins Oil Company............................ E 513 831-8820
  Milford *(G-11239)*
Marathon Petroleum Corporation......... A 419 422-2121
  Findlay *(G-8561)*
Mplx Terminals LLC............................. D 330 479-5539
  Canton *(G-1811)*
Nzr Retail of Toledo Inc....................... D 419 724-0005
  Toledo *(G-13943)*
Ports Petroleum Company Inc............. E 330 264-1885
  Wooster *(G-15367)*
True North Energy LLC....................... D 330 722-2031
  Medina *(G-10900)*
True North Energy LLC....................... E 877 245-9336
  Brecksville *(G-1370)*

GEARS: Power Transmission, Exc Auto

Forge Industries Inc............................ A 330 960-2468
  Youngstown *(G-15613)*

GENERAL & INDUSTRIAL LOAN INSTITUTIONS

Pfsc Inc.. E 513 221-5080
  Cincinnati *(G-3204)*

GENERAL COUNSELING SVCS

Abuse Refuge Inc............................... D 614 686-2121
  Lewis Center *(G-9803)*
ADS Alliance Data Systems Inc........... D 513 707-6800
  Columbus *(G-5316)*
Akron Family Institute Inc................... E 330 644-3469
  Akron *(G-27)*
Bluestone Counseling LLC.................. E 614 406-0299
  Columbus *(G-5450)*
Bobby Tripodi Foundation Inc............. E 216 524-3787
  Independence *(G-9412)*
Cambridge Counseling Center............. C 740 450-7790
  Zanesville *(G-15775)*
Catholic Charities Corporation............. D 216 939-3713
  Cleveland *(G-3933)*
Clermont Counseling Center............... D 513 345-8555
  Cincinnati *(G-2457)*
Clermont Counseling Center............... E 513 947-7000
  Amelia *(G-416)*
College Now Grter Clveland Inc........... E 216 241-5587
  Cleveland *(G-4087)*
Community Cnsling Wllness Ctrs......... E 740 387-5210
  Marion *(G-10422)*
Counsling Ctr of Wyne Hlmes CN........ D 330 264-9029
  Wooster *(G-15327)*
County of Lorain................................. E 440 233-2020
  Lorain *(G-10069)*
Darcie R Clark Lpcc LLC..................... E 937 319-4448
  Dayton *(G-7267)*
Emerge Ministries Inc......................... E 330 865-8351
  Akron *(G-146)*
Freedom Recovery LLC....................... E 614 754-8051
  Columbus *(G-5892)*
Greenleaf Family Center..................... E 330 376-9494
  Akron *(G-181)*
Grow Well Cleveland Corp................... E 216 282-3838
  Cleveland *(G-4341)*
Healing Hrts Cunseling Ctr Inc............ E 419 528-5993
  Mansfield *(G-10268)*
Hopewell Health Centers Inc............... E 740 596-4809
  Mc Arthur *(G-10798)*
Lighthuse Bhvral Hlth Sltons L............ D 614 334-6903
  Columbus *(G-6163)*
Mid-Ohio Psychological Svcs Inc......... E 740 687-0042
  Lancaster *(G-9735)*
New Hrzons Mntal Hlth Svcs Inc.......... D 740 901-3150
  Lancaster *(G-9736)*
North East Ohio Health Svcs............... D 216 831-6466
  Beachwood *(G-821)*
Ohio Addiction Recovery Center.......... E 800 481-8457
  Columbus *(G-6389)*
Ohio Mentor Inc.................................. C 216 525-1885
  Independence *(G-9463)*
Oneeighty Inc..................................... D 330 263-6021
  Wooster *(G-15364)*
Pastoral Cnsling Svc Smmit CNT........ E 330 996-4600
  Akron *(G-262)*
Sciot-Pint Vly Mental Hlth Ctr.............. C 740 775-1260
  Chillicothe *(G-2090)*
Southstern Ohio Cnsling Ctr LL........... E 740 260-9440
  Old Washington *(G-12087)*
Talbert House Health.......................... E 513 541-7577
  Cincinnati *(G-3442)*
Tcn Behavioral Health Svcs Inc........... C 937 376-8700
  Xenia *(G-15532)*
Tennessee Centerstone Inc................ E 740 779-4888
  Chillicothe *(G-2092)*
Trillium Family Solutions Inc.............. E 330 454-7066
  Cuyahoga Falls *(G-7112)*
Turning Pt Counseling Svcs Inc.......... D 330 744-2991
  Youngstown *(G-15739)*
Wellness Grove LLC........................... E 330 244-1566
  Canton *(G-1885)*

GENERATOR REPAIR SVCS

Generator One LLC.............................. E 440 942-8449
  Mentor *(G-10941)*

GIFT SHOP

Amish Door Inc................................... C 330 359-5464
  Wilmot *(G-15281)*
Auxiliary St Lukes Hospital................. D 419 893-5911
  Maumee *(G-10697)*
Civic Grdn Ctr Grter Cncinnati............. E 513 221-0981
  Cincinnati *(G-2454)*
Columbus Zoological Park Assn.......... C 614 645-3400
  Powell *(G-12589)*
Dutchman Hospitality Group Inc.......... C 614 873-3414
  Plain City *(G-12474)*
Golden Lamb....................................... D 513 932-5065
  Lebanon *(G-9767)*
Hrm Enterprises Inc............................ C 330 877-9353
  Hartville *(G-9127)*
Lowes Investments Inc....................... E 440 543-5123
  Chagrin Falls *(G-1984)*
Mapleside Valley LLC.......................... D 330 225-5576
  Brunswick *(G-1462)*
S-P Company Inc................................ D 330 782-5651
  Columbiana *(G-5240)*
Things Remembered Inc..................... A 440 473-2000
  Highland Heights *(G-9172)*
Thirty-One Gifts LLC........................... C 614 414-4300
  New Albany *(G-11588)*
Velvet Ice Cream Company................. D 740 892-3921
  Utica *(G-14330)*
Waterbeds n Stuff Inc........................ E 614 871-1171
  Grove City *(G-8965)*
Youngs Jersey Dairy Inc..................... B 937 325-0629
  Yellow Springs *(G-15537)*

GIFTS & NOVELTIES: Wholesalers

Artwall LLC... E 216 476-0635
  Cleveland *(G-3836)*
Dollar Paradise................................... E 216 432-0421
  Cleveland *(G-4174)*
Flower Factory Inc.............................. B 330 494-7978
  North Canton *(G-11831)*
K & M International Inc....................... D 330 425-2550
  Independence *(G-9439)*
Nannicola Wholesale Co...................... D 330 799-0888
  Youngstown *(G-15672)*
Papyrus-Recycled Greetings Inc......... D 773 348-6410
  Westlake *(G-15095)*
Par International Inc........................... E 614 529-1300
  Obetz *(G-12082)*
Regal-Elite Inc.................................... E 614 873-3800
  Plain City *(G-12492)*
Waterbeds n Stuff Inc........................ E 614 871-1171
  Grove City *(G-8965)*

GLASS PRDTS, FROM PURCHASED GLASS: Glassware

Mosser Glass Inc................................ E 740 439-1827
  Cambridge *(G-1576)*

GLASS PRDTS, FROM PURCHASED GLASS: Windshields

Safelite Group Inc.............................. A 614 210-9000
  Columbus *(G-6632)*

GLASS PRDTS, PRESSED OR BLOWN: Glass Fibers, Textile

Owens Corning Sales LLC................... A 419 248-8000
  Toledo *(G-13952)*

GLASS PRDTS, PRESSED OR BLOWN: Yarn, Fiberglass

Integris Composites Inc...................... D 740 928-0326
  Hebron *(G-9144)*

GLASS: Fiber

Industrial Fiberglass Spc Inc.............. E 937 222-9000
  Dayton *(G-7421)*

GLASS: Tempered

Trulite GL Alum Solutions LLC............. D 740 929-2443
  Hebron *(G-9156)*

GLOVES: Work

Wcm Holdings Inc............................... C 513 705-2100
  Cincinnati *(G-3643)*
West Chester Holdings LLC................ C 513 705-2100
  Cincinnati *(G-3655)*

SERVICES SECTION — GROCERIES, GENERAL LINE WHOLESALERS

GOLF CARTS: Wholesalers

- Century Equipment Inc ..... E 419 865-7400
  Toledo (G-13728)

GOLF COURSES: Public

- Aboutgolf Limited ..... E 419 482-9095
  Maumee (G-10683)
- American Golf Corporation ..... E 419 726-9353
  Toledo (G-13682)
- Arrowhead Park Golf Club Inc ..... E 419 628-2444
  Minster (G-11315)
- Avalon Lakes Golf Inc ..... E 330 856-8898
  Warren (G-14503)
- Boulder Creek Golf Club ..... E 330 626-2828
  Streetsboro (G-13410)
- Bowling Green Country Club Inc ..... E 419 352-5546
  Bowling Green (G-1311)
- Brassboys Enterprises Inc ..... E 740 545-7796
  West Lafayette (G-14855)
- Brookwood Management Co LLC ..... E 330 499-7721
  Canton (G-1690)
- Championship Management Co Inc ..... E 740 524-4653
  Sunbury (G-13518)
- Chardon Lakes Golf Course Inc ..... E 440 285-4653
  Chardon (G-1996)
- Chgc Inc ..... E 330 225-6122
  Valley City (G-14332)
- Chippewa Golf Corp ..... E 330 658-2566
  Doylestown (G-7913)
- City of Cuyahoga Falls ..... E 330 971-8416
  Cuyahoga Falls (G-7061)
- City of Springfield ..... E 937 324-7725
  Springfield (G-13228)
- City of Westlake ..... E 440 835-6442
  Westlake (G-15049)
- Columbus Zoological Park Assn ..... C 614 645-3400
  Powell (G-12589)
- Creekside Golf Ltd ..... E 513 785-2999
  Fairfield Township (G-8459)
- Creekside Ltd LLC ..... D 513 583-4977
  Loveland (G-10133)
- Diamondback Golf LLC ..... D 614 410-1313
  Sunbury (G-13520)
- Edgewater Golf Inc ..... E 330 862-2630
  Minerva (G-11306)
- Ganzfair Investment Inc ..... E 614 792-6630
  Delaware (G-7800)
- Grizzly Golf Center Inc ..... B 513 398-5200
  Mason (G-10557)
- Hawthorne Hills Cntry CLB Inc ..... E 419 221-1891
  Lima (G-9895)
- Heather Downs Cntry CLB Assoc ..... E 419 385-0248
  Toledo (G-13844)
- Hickory Woods Golf Course Inc ..... E 513 575-3900
  Loveland (G-10142)
- Kinsale Golf & Fitnes CLB LLC ..... C 740 881-6500
  Powell (G-12597)
- Mahoning Country Club Inc ..... E 330 545-2517
  Girard (G-8819)
- Mayfair Country Club Inc ..... D 330 699-2209
  Uniontown (G-14258)
- Miami Valley Golf Club ..... D 937 278-7381
  Dayton (G-7487)
- Mill Creek Golf Course Corp ..... E 740 666-7711
  Ostrander (G-12182)
- Mill Creek Metropolitan Park ..... E 330 740-7112
  Youngstown (G-15667)
- Moss Creek Golf Course ..... E 937 837-4653
  Clayton (G-3735)
- Moundbuilders Country Club Co ..... D 740 344-4500
  Newark (G-11732)
- Mount Vernon Country Club Co ..... D 740 392-4216
  Mount Vernon (G-11500)
- New Albany Links Dev Co Ltd ..... E 614 939-5914
  New Albany (G-11580)
- Norwalk Golf Properties Inc ..... E 419 668-8535
  Norwalk (G-12019)
- Ohio State Parks Inc ..... D 513 664-3504
  College Corner (G-5222)
- Pine Hills Golf Club Inc ..... E 330 225-4477
  Hinckley (G-9271)
- Quail Hollow Management Inc ..... C 440 639-4000
  Concord Township (G-6933)
- Reserve Run Golf Club LLC ..... D 330 758-1017
  Poland (G-12508)
- Scioto Reserve Inc ..... E 740 881-6500
  Powell (G-12605)
- Scioto Reserve Inc ..... D 740 881-9082
  Powell (G-12604)
- Shady Hollow Cntry CLB Co Inc ..... D 330 832-1581
  Massillon (G-10668)
- Silver Lake Country Club ..... E 330 688-6066
  Silver Lake (G-13060)
- Sugar Valley Country Club ..... E 937 372-4820
  Xenia (G-15531)
- Table Rock Golf Club Inc ..... E 740 625-6859
  Centerburg (G-1937)
- Valleywood Golf Club Inc ..... E 419 826-3991
  Swanton (G-13531)
- Wryneck Development LLC ..... E 419 354-2535
  Bowling Green (G-1339)

GOLF EQPT

- Golf Galaxy Golfworks Inc ..... C 740 328-4193
  Newark (G-11702)

GOLF GOODS & EQPT

- Akron Management Corp ..... B 330 644-8441
  Akron (G-34)
- Arrowhead Park Golf Club Inc ..... E 419 628-2444
  Minster (G-11315)
- Grizzly Golf Center Inc ..... B 513 398-5200
  Mason (G-10557)
- Lakewood Country Club Pro Shop ..... E 440 871-0400
  Cleveland (G-4480)
- Lancaster Country Club ..... D 740 654-3535
  Lancaster (G-9730)
- OBannon Creek Golf Club ..... E 513 683-5657
  Loveland (G-10156)
- Tippecanoe Country Club Inc ..... E 330 758-7518
  Canfield (G-1644)
- Walden Club ..... E 330 995-7162
  Aurora (G-629)

GOURMET FOOD STORES

- Antonio Sofo Son Importing Co ..... C 419 476-4211
  Toledo (G-13690)
- Mustard Seed Health Fd Mkt Inc ..... E 440 519-3663
  Solon (G-13115)

GOVERNMENT, GENERAL: Administration

- City of Cleveland ..... E 216 664-2430
  Cleveland (G-3985)
- Ohio Bureau Wkrs Compensation ..... A 800 644-6292
  Columbus (G-6396)

GRADING SVCS

- Carter Site Development LLC ..... E 513 831-8843
  Miamiville (G-11109)
- Fox Services Inc ..... E 513 858-2022
  Fairfield (G-8414)
- Great Lakes Crushing Ltd ..... D 440 944-5500
  Wickliffe (G-15150)

GRANITE: Crushed & Broken

- The National Lime and Stone Company ..... E 419 422-4341
  Findlay (G-8593)

GRANITE: Cut & Shaped

- Cutting Edge Countertops Inc ..... E 419 873-9500
  Perrysburg (G-12328)

GRAPHIC ARTS & RELATED DESIGN SVCS

- Adcom Group Inc ..... C 216 574-9100
  Cleveland (G-3769)
- Container Graphics Corp ..... E 419 531-5133
  Toledo (G-13760)
- Coyne Graphic Finishing Inc ..... E 740 397-6232
  Mount Vernon (G-11481)
- Edward Howard & Co ..... E 216 781-2400
  Cleveland (G-4207)
- Fitch Inc ..... D 614 885-3453
  Columbus (G-5870)
- Haney Inc ..... D 513 561-1441
  Cincinnati (G-2799)
- Hofrichter Brothers Inc ..... E 740 314-5669
  Steubenville (G-13331)
- Interbrand Hulefeld Inc ..... E 513 421-2210
  Cincinnati (G-2881)
- Libby Prszyk Kthman Hldngs Inc ..... D 513 241-6401
  Cincinnati (G-2973)
- Mueller Art Cover & Binding Co ..... E 440 238-3303
  Strongsville (G-13477)
- Real Art Design Group Inc ..... D 937 223-9955
  Dayton (G-7581)
- Suntwist Corp ..... D 800 935-3534
  Maple Heights (G-10350)
- Third Dimension Inc ..... E 440 466-4040
  Geneva (G-8790)

GRAPHITE MINING SVCS

- Graftech Holdings Inc ..... D 216 676-2000
  Independence (G-9434)

GRAVEL MINING

- Stansley Mineral Resources Inc ..... E 419 843-2813
  Sylvania (G-13573)
- Watson Gravel Inc ..... E 513 863-0070
  Hamilton (G-9091)

GREENHOUSES: Prefabricated Metal

- Ludy Greenhouse Mfg Corp ..... D 800 255-5839
  New Madison (G-11634)
- Rough Brothers Mfg Inc ..... D 513 242-0310
  Cincinnati (G-3325)

GREETING CARDS WHOLESALERS

- Large & Loving Cards Inc ..... E 440 877-0261
  North Royalton (G-11943)

GRINDING SVC: Precision, Commercial Or Indl

- Micro Products Co Inc ..... E 440 943-0258
  Willoughby Hills (G-15233)
- Tipp Machine & Tool Inc ..... C 937 890-8428
  Dayton (G-7669)

GROCERIES, GENERAL LINE WHOLESALERS

- Albert Guarnieri & Co ..... D 330 794-9834
  Hudson (G-9328)
- Anderson and Dubose Inc ..... D 440 248-8800
  Warren (G-14499)
- Artwall LLC ..... E 216 476-0635
  Cleveland (G-3836)

GROCERIES, GENERAL LINE WHOLESALERS

Food Sample Express LLc .... D 330 225-3550
  Brunswick *(G-1456)*
Foxtail Foods LLC .... A 973 582-4613
  Fairfield *(G-8415)*
Generative Growth II LLC .... B 419 422-8090
  Findlay *(G-8537)*
Giant Eagle Inc .... C 412 968-5300
  Columbus *(G-5933)*
Gummer Wholesale Inc .... D 740 928-0415
  Heath *(G-9133)*
John Zidian Co Inc .... E 330 743-6050
  Youngstown *(G-15642)*
Krlp Inc .... A 513 762-4000
  Cincinnati *(G-2953)*
Larosas Inc .... A 513 347-5660
  Cincinnati *(G-2966)*
Mattingly Foods Inc .... C 740 454-0136
  Zanesville *(G-15811)*
Mondelez Global LLC .... E 513 714-0308
  West Chester *(G-14734)*
R S Hanline and Co Inc .... C 419 347-8077
  Shelby *(G-13010)*
Ricking Holding Co .... E 513 825-3551
  Cleveland *(G-4839)*
Riser Foods Company .... D 216 292-7000
  Bedford Heights *(G-1001)*
Sommers Market LLC .... D 330 352-7470
  Hartville *(G-9130)*
Sysco Central Ohio Inc .... B
  Columbus *(G-6743)*
Tasty Pure Food Company .... E 330 434-8141
  Akron *(G-329)*
The Ellenbee-Leggett Company Inc .... C 513 874-3200
  Fairfield *(G-8446)*
Tusco Grocers Inc .... D 740 922-8721
  Dennison *(G-7859)*

GUARD PROTECTIVE SVCS

Community Crime Patrol .... E 614 247-1765
  Columbus *(G-5669)*
Darke County Sheriffs Patrol .... E 937 548-3399
  Greenville *(G-8868)*

GUARD SVCS

City of Cleveland .... D 216 664-2625
  Cleveland *(G-3987)*
Ohio Tctcal Enfrcment Svcs LLC ... D 614 989-9485
  Columbus *(G-6462)*
Stifel Ind Advisors LLC .... E 740 653-9222
  Lancaster *(G-9745)*

HAND TOOLS, NEC: Wholesalers

Elliott Tool Technologies Ltd .... D 937 253-6133
  Dayton *(G-7333)*

HARDWARE

Action Coupling & Eqp Inc .... D 330 279-4242
  Holmesville *(G-9316)*
Gateway Con Forming Svcs Inc .... D 513 353-2000
  Miamitown *(G-11106)*
Qualitor Subsidiary H Inc .... C 419 562-7987
  Bucyrus *(G-1517)*
Samsel Rope & Marine Supply Co ...... E 216 241-0333
  Cleveland *(G-4875)*

HARDWARE & BUILDING PRDTS: Plastic

Associated Materials LLC .... A 330 929-1811
  Cuyahoga Falls *(G-7041)*
Associated Materials Group Inc .... C 330 929-1811
  Cuyahoga Falls *(G-7043)*
Gorell Enterprises Inc .... B 724 465-1800
  Streetsboro *(G-13414)*

Style Crest Enterprises Inc .... D 419 355-8586
  Fremont *(G-8705)*
Westlake Dimex LLC .... C 740 374-3100
  Marietta *(G-10414)*

HARDWARE & EQPT: Stage, Exc Lighting

Janson Industries .... D 330 455-7029
  Canton *(G-1783)*

HARDWARE STORES

Carter-Jones Companies Inc .... E 330 673-6100
  Kent *(G-9560)*
Carter-Jones Lumber Company .... E 330 784-5441
  Akron *(G-82)*
De Haven Home and Garden Ce ... E 419 227-7003
  Lima *(G-9883)*
Do It Best Corp .... B 330 725-3859
  Medina *(G-10831)*
E&H Hardware Group LLC .... C 330 683-2060
  Orrville *(G-12164)*
Lochard Inc .... D 937 492-8811
  Sidney *(G-13037)*
Matco Tools Corporation .... B 330 929-4949
  Stow *(G-13382)*
Robert McCabe Company Inc .... E 513 469-2500
  Cincinnati *(G-3314)*
Robertson Plumbing & Heating .... E 330 863-0611
  Malvern *(G-10235)*
The Robert McCabe Company Inc .... D 513 683-2662
  Loveland *(G-10164)*
Thomas Do-It Center Inc .... E 740 446-2002
  Gallipolis *(G-8769)*

HARDWARE STORES: Pumps & Pumping Eqpt

Best Aire Compressor Service ...... D 419 726-0055
  Millbury *(G-11266)*

HARDWARE STORES: Tools

National Tool Leasing Inc .... E 866 952-8665
  Eastlake *(G-8206)*
Tool Testing Lab Inc .... E 937 898-5696
  Tipp City *(G-13666)*
Tractor Supply Company .... E 937 382-2595
  Wilmington *(G-15275)*

HARDWARE STORES: Tools, Hand

Cdc Distributors Inc .... D 513 771-3100
  Cincinnati *(G-2329)*

HARDWARE WHOLESALERS

Ackerman Chacco Company Inc .... E 513 791-4252
  Blue Ash *(G-1121)*
Atlas Bolt & Screw Company LLC ..... C 419 289-6171
  Ashland *(G-478)*
B B I T Inc .... C 419 259-3600
  Toledo *(G-13697)*
Babin Building Solutions LLC .... E 216 292-2500
  Broadview Heights *(G-1383)*
Barnes Group Inc .... C 419 891-9292
  Maumee *(G-10698)*
E&H Hardware Group LLC .... C 330 683-2060
  Orrville *(G-12164)*
F & M Mafco Inc .... C 513 367-2151
  Harrison *(G-9104)*
G & S Metal Products Co Inc .... C 216 441-0700
  Cleveland *(G-4295)*
Hd Supply Facilities Maint Ltd ...... D 440 542-9188
  Solon *(G-13094)*
Hillman Companies Inc .... B 513 851-4900
  Cincinnati *(G-2822)*

SERVICES SECTION

Hillman Group Inc .... C 513 851-4900
  Cincinnati *(G-2823)*
Hillman Solutions Corp .... E 513 851-4900
  Cincinnati *(G-2824)*
Khempco Bldg Sup Co Ltd Partnr ...... D 740 549-0465
  Delaware *(G-7811)*
Mae Holding Company .... E 513 751-2424
  Cincinnati *(G-3002)*
Matco Tools Corporation .... B 330 929-4949
  Stow *(G-13382)*
Multi Builders Supply Co .... E 216 831-1121
  Cleveland *(G-4609)*
Norwood Hardware and Supply Co ..... D 513 733-1175
  Cincinnati *(G-3129)*
Ohashi Technica USA Inc .... E 740 965-5115
  Sunbury *(G-13523)*
Production Tool Supply Ohio .... D 216 265-0000
  Cleveland *(G-4772)*
Reitter Stucco Inc .... E 614 291-2212
  Columbus *(G-6575)*
Robert McCabe Company Inc .... E 513 469-2500
  Cincinnati *(G-3314)*
Serv-A-Lite Products Inc .... C 309 762-7741
  Cincinnati *(G-3360)*
The Robert McCabe Company Inc .... D 513 683-2662
  Loveland *(G-10164)*
Waxman Industries Inc .... C 440 439-1830
  Bedford Heights *(G-1005)*
Ziegler Bolt & Parts Co .... E 330 478-2542
  Canton *(G-1893)*

HARDWARE, WHOLESALE: Bolts

Hodell-Natco Industries Inc .... E 216 447-0165
  Cleveland *(G-4372)*
Mid-State Industrial Pdts Inc .... E 614 253-8631
  Columbus *(G-6240)*

HARDWARE, WHOLESALE: Builders', NEC

Akron Hardware Consultants Inc .... E 330 644-7167
  Akron *(G-33)*
Bostwick-Braun Company .... D 419 259-3600
  Toledo *(G-13713)*
Buckeye Parts Services Inc .... E 614 274-1888
  Columbus *(G-5476)*
Do It Best Corp .... B 330 725-3859
  Medina *(G-10831)*
Hardware Suppliers of America Inc ..... D 330 644-7167
  Akron *(G-183)*
L E Smith Company .... D 419 636-4555
  Bryan *(G-1486)*
Mazzella Holding Company Inc .... D 513 772-4466
  Cleveland *(G-4534)*
The Cleveland Vicon Co Inc .... E 216 341-3300
  Cleveland *(G-4996)*

HARDWARE, WHOLESALE: Casters & Glides

Waxman Consumer Pdts Group Inc ..... E 614 491-0500
  Groveport *(G-9013)*
Waxman Consumer Pdts Group Inc ..... D 440 439-1830
  Bedford Heights *(G-1004)*

HARDWARE, WHOLESALE: Nuts

Facil North America Inc .... C 330 487-2500
  Twinsburg *(G-14190)*

HARDWARE, WHOLESALE: Power Tools & Access

Noco Company .... D 216 464-8131
  Solon *(G-13119)*
Saw Service and Supply Company ..... E 216 252-5600
  Cleveland *(G-4880)*

HARNESS ASSEMBLIES: Cable & Wire

Microplex Inc .... E 330 498-0600
North Canton *(G-11848)*

Nimers & Woody II Inc .... C 937 454-0722
Vandalia *(G-14386)*

Projects Unlimited Inc .... C 937 918-2200
Dayton *(G-7571)*

HEALTH & WELFARE COUNCIL

Concord Counseling Services .... E 614 882-9338
Westerville *(G-14974)*

County of Tuscarawas .... D 330 343-5555
Dover *(G-7877)*

HEALTH INSURANCE CARRIERS

Aultcare Insurance Company .... B 330 363-6360
Canton *(G-1676)*

Caresource .... A 937 224-3300
Dayton *(G-7211)*

Caresource Management Group Co ...... E 614 221-3370
Hilliard *(G-9188)*

Medical Benefits Mutl Lf Insur .... C 740 522-8425
Newark *(G-11728)*

Sentry Life Insurance Company .... C 513 733-0100
Cincinnati *(G-3359)*

State Farm General Insur Co .... D 513 662-7283
Cincinnati *(G-3413)*

Summa Insurance Company Inc .... B 800 996-8411
Akron *(G-322)*

Superior Dental Care Inc .... D 937 438-0283
Dayton *(G-7654)*

HEAT TREATING: Metal

Carpe Diem Industries LLC .... D 419 358-0129
Bluffton *(G-1280)*

Carpe Diem Industries LLC .... D 419 659-5639
Columbus Grove *(G-6921)*

Clifton Steel Company .... D 216 662-6111
Maple Heights *(G-10336)*

Gerdau McSteel Atmsphere Annli .... E 330 478-0314
Canton *(G-1761)*

Lapham-Hickey Steel Corp .... E 614 443-4881
Columbus *(G-6140)*

McOn Inds Inc .... E 937 294-2681
Moraine *(G-11422)*

Oliver Steel Plate Co .... D 330 425-7000
Twinsburg *(G-14209)*

Thermal Treatment Center Inc .... E 216 881-8100
Wickliffe *(G-15164)*

Worthngton Smuel Coil Proc LLC .... E 330 963-3777
Twinsburg *(G-14231)*

HELP SUPPLY SERVICES

Amerimed LLC .... A 513 942-3670
West Chester *(G-14650)*

Belflex Staffing Network LLC .... C 513 488-8588
Cincinnati *(G-2255)*

Edge Plastics Inc .... E 419 522-6696
Mansfield *(G-10260)*

Falcon Partners LLC .... E 216 896-1010
Cleveland *(G-4239)*

Hogan Truck Leasing Inc .... E 937 293-0033
Moraine *(G-11417)*

Innovtive Sltons Unlimited LLC .... C 740 289-3282
Piketon *(G-12423)*

Interim Hlthcare Cambridge Inc .... E 740 432-2966
Worthington *(G-15423)*

Ohio Dept Job & Fmly Svcs .... E 419 334-3891
Fremont *(G-8696)*

Professional Transportation .... B 419 661-0576
Walbridge *(G-14463)*

Residential Care Inc .... B 937 299-8090
Dayton *(G-7589)*

Ringside Search Partners LLC .... E 614 643-0700
Columbus *(G-6589)*

Salo Inc .... C 419 419-0038
Bowling Green *(G-1332)*

Salo Inc .... C 740 653-5990
Lancaster *(G-9740)*

Technical Aid Corporation .... E 781 251-8000
Cincinnati *(G-3448)*

Vernovis Ltd .... D 513 234-7201
Mason *(G-10623)*

Youth Intensive Services Inc .... E 330 318-3436
Youngstown *(G-15761)*

HIGHWAY & STREET MAINTENANCE SVCS

Belmont County of Ohio .... D 740 695-1580
Saint Clairsville *(G-12777)*

City of Aurora .... E 330 562-8662
Aurora *(G-611)*

City of Brecksville .... C 440 526-1384
Brecksville *(G-1350)*

County of Ashtabula .... C 440 576-2816
Jefferson *(G-9538)*

County of Trumbull .... E 330 675-2640
Warren *(G-14514)*

Eaton Construction Co Inc .... D 740 474-3414
Circleville *(G-3707)*

Ohio Tpk & Infrastructure Comm .... D 440 234-2081
Berea *(G-1077)*

Ohio Tpk & Infrastructure Comm .... E 440 234-2081
Richfield *(G-12705)*

Ohio Tpk & Infrastructure Comm .... D 330 527-2169
Windham *(G-15288)*

HOBBY, TOY & GAME STORES: Arts & Crafts & Splys

Hobby Lobby Stores Inc .... E 330 686-1508
Stow *(G-13373)*

HOLDING COMPANIES: Investment, Exc Banks

2023 Ventures Inc .... D
Archbold *(G-454)*

Akron Brass Holding Corp .... E 330 264-5678
Wooster *(G-15307)*

Ampac Holdings LLC .... A 513 671-1777
Cincinnati *(G-2194)*

Armor Consolidated Inc .... A 513 923-5260
Mason *(G-10520)*

Brake Parts Holdings Inc .... B 216 589-0198
Cleveland *(G-3889)*

Cai Holdings LLC .... D 419 656-3568
Sandusky *(G-12868)*

Cauffiel Industries Corp .... E
Toledo *(G-13725)*

CNG Holdings Inc .... A 513 336-7735
Cincinnati *(G-2466)*

Cpp Group Holdings LLC .... E 216 453-4800
Cleveland *(G-4134)*

Crane Carrier Holdings LLC .... C 918 286-2889
New Philadelphia *(G-11648)*

Drt Holdings Inc .... D 937 298-7391
Dayton *(G-7317)*

Elyria Foundry Holdings LLC .... B 440 322-4657
Elyria *(G-8247)*

Entelco Corporation .... D 419 872-4620
Maumee *(G-10721)*

Exochem Corporation .... D 440 277-1246
Lorain *(G-10073)*

Fosbel Holding Inc .... E 216 362-3900
Cleveland *(G-4279)*

Hexion Topco LLC .... D 614 225-4000
Columbus *(G-5990)*

IBP Corporation Holdings Inc .... A 614 692-6360
Columbus *(G-6038)*

Lion Group Inc .... D 937 898-1949
Dayton *(G-7457)*

LTV-Trico Inc .... B 216 622-5000
Cleveland *(G-4508)*

Mbp Holdings Inc .... D
Dayton *(G-7471)*

Midwest Dairies Inc .... D 419 678-8059
Coldwater *(G-5219)*

Mssl Consolidated Inc .... B 330 766-5510
Warren *(G-14541)*

Nationwide Life Insur Co Amer .... A 800 688-5177
Columbus *(G-6335)*

Norse Dairy Systems Inc .... C 614 294-4931
Columbus *(G-6363)*

Sarnova Holdings Inc .... B 614 760-5000
Dublin *(G-8114)*

Vertiv JV Holdings LLC .... A 614 888-0246
Columbus *(G-6846)*

Wensminger Holdings Inc .... D 513 563-8822
Cincinnati *(G-3653)*

HOLDING COMPANIES: Personal, Exc Banks

Eci Macola/Max Holding LLC .... E 614 410-2712
Dublin *(G-8001)*

Hopkins Acquisition Inc .... A 248 371-1700
Cleveland *(G-4375)*

Qualus Corp .... D 800 434-0415
Cincinnati *(G-3261)*

HOME FOR THE MENTALLY HANDICAPPED

Abilities First Foundation Inc .... D 513 423-9496
Middletown *(G-11149)*

Alternative Residences Two Inc .... D 740 425-1565
Barnesville *(G-716)*

Alternative Residences Two Inc .... D 330 627-7552
Carrollton *(G-1902)*

Alternative Residences Two Inc .... D 330 833-5564
Massillon *(G-10630)*

Alternative Residences Two Inc .... C 740 526-0514
Saint Clairsville *(G-12773)*

Ashtabula Cnty Rsdntial Svcs C .... E 440 593-6404
Conneaut *(G-6938)*

Assoction For Dvlpmntlly Dsble .... C 614 447-0606
Columbus *(G-5397)*

Assoction For Dvlpmntlly Dsble .... E 614 486-4361
Westerville *(G-14961)*

Bittersweet Inc .... D 419 875-6986
Whitehouse *(G-15138)*

Brittany Residential Inc .... E 216 692-3212
Cleveland *(G-3896)*

Cincinntis Optmum Rsdntial Env .... C 513 771-2673
Cincinnati *(G-2436)*

Community Living Experiences .... E 614 588-0320
Columbus *(G-5671)*

County of Auglaize .... D 419 629-2419
New Bremen *(G-11596)*

County of Lorain .... D 440 329-3734
Elyria *(G-8238)*

Dag-Dell Inc .... E 740 754-2600
Dresden *(G-7917)*

Department of Health Ohio .... E 419 447-1450
Tiffin *(G-13627)*

Evant .... E 330 920-1517
Stow *(G-13367)*

Fairhaven Industries .... E 330 652-6168
Niles *(G-11789)*

HOME FOR THE MENTALLY HANDICAPPED

Flat Rock Care Center...................... D 419 483-7330
Flat Rock *(G-8600)*

Hattie Lrlham Ctr For Chldren.............. E 330 274-2272
Akron *(G-189)*

Hattie Lrlham Ctr For Chldren.............. E 440 232-9320
Bedford Heights *(G-998)*

Hattie Lrlham Ctr For Chldren.............. E 330 274-2272
Uniontown *(G-14256)*

Hopewell... E 440 426-2000
Middlefield *(G-11141)*

Horizons Tuscarawas/Carroll.............. C 330 262-4183
Wooster *(G-15346)*

I AM Boundless Inc.............................. B 614 844-3800
Worthington *(G-15421)*

Josina Lott Foundation........................ E 419 866-9013
Toledo *(G-13871)*

Koinonia Homes Inc............................. B 216 588-8777
Cleveland *(G-4469)*

Ladd Inc.. E 513 861-4089
Cincinnati *(G-2962)*

Living Arrngmnts For Dvlpmntll........... C 513 861-5233
Cincinnati *(G-2983)*

National Mentor Holdings Inc............. B 419 443-0867
Fostoria *(G-8621)*

New Nghbors Rsdential Svcs Inc........ E 937 717-7531
Saint Paris *(G-12838)*

Northeast Care Center Inc.................. D 440 234-9407
Berea *(G-1075)*

Northeast Care Center Inc.................. D 440 888-9320
North Royalton *(G-11946)*

Portage County Board......................... E 330 297-6209
Ravenna *(G-12638)*

Regard Recovery Florida LLC............. D 330 866-0900
Sherrodsville *(G-13012)*

Renaissance House Inc....................... D 419 425-0633
Findlay *(G-8581)*

Resident HM Assn Grter Dyton I......... D 937 278-0791
Dayton *(G-7588)*

Residential MGT Systems Inc............. E 614 880-6009
Worthington *(G-15451)*

Residntial HM For Dvlpmntlly D........... E 740 677-0500
The Plains *(G-13616)*

Residntial HM For Dvlpmntlly D........... C 740 622-9778
Coshocton *(G-6999)*

Rhc Inc... D 513 389-7501
Cincinnati *(G-3294)*

Society For Hndcpped Ctzens of........ E 330 722-1900
Seville *(G-12965)*

St Johns Villa....................................... C 330 627-4662
Carrollton *(G-1913)*

Thomas Edson Erly Chldhood Ctr....... D 419 238-1514
Van Wert *(G-14352)*

Tri County Mental Health Svcs............ D 740 592-3091
Athens *(G-593)*

United Crbral Plsy Assn Grter............. E 440 835-5511
Westlake *(G-15119)*

Welcome House Inc............................. D 440 471-7601
North Olmsted *(G-11919)*

Wynn-Reeth Inc.................................... E 419 639-2094
Green Springs *(G-8862)*

HOME FOR THE MENTALLY RETARDED

Alexson Services Inc.......................... D 513 874-0423
Fairfield *(G-8389)*

Anne Grady Corporation...................... C 419 380-8985
Holland *(G-9278)*

Ardmore Inc... D 330 535-2601
Akron *(G-55)*

Buckeye Community Services Inc...... D 740 797-4166
The Plains *(G-13615)*

Butler Cnty Bd Dvlpmntal Dsblt........... D 513 867-5913
Fairfield *(G-8396)*

Butler Cnty Bd Dvlpmntal Dsblt........... D 513 785-2870
Fairfield Township *(G-8457)*

Butler Cnty Bd Dvlpmntal Dsblt........... D 513 785-2815
Hamilton *(G-9022)*

Champaign Residential Svcs Inc......... A 740 852-3850
London *(G-10039)*

Champaign Residential Svcs Inc......... D 937 653-1320
Urbana *(G-14301)*

Choices In Community Living.............. D 937 325-0344
Springfield *(G-13226)*

Choices In Community Living.............. C 937 898-3655
Dayton *(G-7225)*

Clark Cnty Bd Dvlpmntal Dsblti........... E 937 328-5200
Springfield *(G-13230)*

County of Cuyahoga............................. A 216 241-8230
Cleveland *(G-4126)*

Friends of Good Shepherd Manor....... E 740 289-2861
Lucasville *(G-10178)*

Gateways To Better Living Inc............. E 330 792-2854
Youngstown *(G-15618)*

Gentlebrook Inc.................................... D 330 877-3694
Hartville *(G-9125)*

Hattie Lrlham Ctr For Chldren.............. C 330 274-2272
Mantua *(G-10331)*

Mount Aloysius Corp............................ D 740 342-3343
New Lexington *(G-11629)*

New Avnues To Independence Inc...... D 440 259-4300
Perry *(G-12310)*

New Avnues To Independence Inc...... D 216 481-1907
Cleveland *(G-4637)*

Ohio Dept Dvlpmntal Dsbilities............ C 330 544-2231
Columbus *(G-6404)*

Ohio Dept Dvlpmntal Dsbilities............ C 419 385-0231
Toledo *(G-13944)*

REM-Ohio Inc....................................... E 937 335-8267
Troy *(G-14154)*

REM-Ohio Inc....................................... E 330 644-9730
Coventry Township *(G-7015)*

REM-Ohio Inc....................................... E 614 367-1370
Reynoldsburg *(G-12675)*

Renaissance House Inc....................... E 419 663-1316
Norwalk *(G-12023)*

Residential HM Assn Marion Inc......... C 740 387-9999
Marion *(G-10451)*

Scioto Residential Services................ E 740 353-0288
Portsmouth *(G-12568)*

Simple Journey Inc.............................. D 513 360-2678
Monroe *(G-11351)*

Sunshine Communities........................ B 419 865-0251
Maumee *(G-10773)*

Toward Independence Inc................... C 513 531-0804
Cincinnati *(G-3487)*

HOME HEALTH CARE SVCS

1-888-Ohiocomp Inc............................. D 888 644-6266
Mansfield *(G-10241)*

17322 Euclid Avenue Co LLC.............. E 216 486-2280
Cleveland *(G-3741)*

A Loving Hart HM Hlth Care LLC........ D 937 549-4484
Manchester *(G-10238)*

A Touch of Grace Inc........................... E 567 560-2350
Mansfield *(G-10242)*

Abcap Foundation................................ E 937 378-6041
Georgetown *(G-8796)*

Academic Bhvral Lrng Enrchment...... E 513 544-4991
Columbus *(G-5298)*

Adams Hlping Hands HM Care LLC.... E 419 298-0034
Edgerton *(G-8226)*

Addus Healthcare Inc........................... D 614 407-0977
Columbus *(G-5312)*

Addus Healthcare Inc........................... D 630 296-3400
Steubenville *(G-13315)*

Addus Homecare Corporation............. C 440 219-0245
Perry *(G-12303)*

Addus Homecare Corporation............. C 866 684-0385
Wintersville *(G-15291)*

Adult Comfort Care Inc........................ E 440 320-3335
Vermilion *(G-14404)*

Advance Home Care LLC.................... D 937 723-6335
Dayton *(G-7157)*

Advance Home Care LLC.................... D 614 436-3611
Columbus *(G-5318)*

Advantage Home Health Svcs Inc...... E 330 491-8161
North Canton *(G-11807)*

Aide For You LLC................................. E 419 214-0111
Toledo *(G-13676)*

Aims Supported Living LLC................ E 614 805-1507
Westerville *(G-14957)*

Alexson Services Inc........................... D 614 889-5837
Dublin *(G-7928)*

Alexzander Angels LLC....................... E 678 984-3093
Cincinnati *(G-2160)*

All About Home Care Svcs LLC.......... E 937 222-2980
Dayton *(G-7162)*

All Gods Graces Inc............................. D 419 222-8109
Lima *(G-9862)*

All Heart Home Care LLC................... E 419 298-0034
Wauseon *(G-14597)*

All Hearts Home Health Care.............. E 440 342-2026
Cleveland *(G-3790)*

Alliance HM Hlth Care Svcs LLC........ D 614 928-3053
Columbus *(G-5336)*

Alpine Nursing Care Inc....................... D 216 662-7096
Cleveland *(G-3796)*

Alternate Solutions First LLC............. C 937 298-1111
Dayton *(G-7169)*

Amara Homecare Bedford Tel No....... D 440 353-0600
North Ridgeville *(G-11923)*

Amazing Grace HM Hlth Care LLC..... D 937 825-4862
Huber Heights *(G-9323)*

Amber Home Care LLC....................... E 614 523-0668
Columbus *(G-5343)*

American Cmpassionate Care LLC.... E 513 443-8156
Cincinnati *(G-2177)*

American Nursing Care Inc................. B 513 731-4600
Cincinnati *(G-2184)*

American Nursing Care Inc................. B 937 438-3844
Dayton *(G-7172)*

Amorso At HM Snior Dsblity Car........ E 513 761-6500
Cincinnati *(G-2193)*

Angels In Waiting Home Care............. E 440 946-0349
Mentor *(G-10911)*

Answercare LLC................................... D 855 213-1511
Canton *(G-1667)*

Arcadia Services Inc............................ E 330 869-9520
Akron *(G-54)*

Arcadia Services Inc............................ E 937 912-5800
Beavercreek *(G-857)*

Area Agcy On Aging Plg Svc Are........ C 800 258-7277
Dayton *(G-7179)*

Area Office On Aging Nrthwster......... D 419 382-0624
Toledo *(G-13693)*

Ash Brothers Home Health Care........ E 614 882-3600
Westerville *(G-14960)*

Assurecare LLC................................... E 513 618-2150
Cincinnati *(G-2220)*

Avita Home Health and Hospice......... E 419 468-7985
Galion *(G-8744)*

Benjamin Rose Institute....................... D 216 791-8000
Cleveland *(G-3867)*

Bethesda Hospital Association........... B 740 454-4000
Zanesville *(G-15770)*

Beyond Homecare LLC........................ E 937 704-4002
Urbana *(G-14297)*

SERVICES SECTION — HOME HEALTH CARE SVCS

Black Stone Cincinnati LLC.................. D 513 924-1370
Cincinnati (G-2264)

Blessing Home Health Care Inc............ E 614 329-2086
Hilliard (G-9183)

Blu Diamond Home Care LLC................ E 937 723-7836
Kettering (G-9626)

Braden Med Services Inc..................... E 740 732-2356
Caldwell (G-1547)

Bradley Bay Assisted Living.................. E 440 871-4509
Bay Village (G-758)

Briarfield of Boardman LLC................... E 330 259-9393
Youngstown (G-15566)

Bridgeshome Health Care Inc................ B 330 764-1000
Medina (G-10815)

Buckeye Home Health Care.................. C 513 791-6446
Blue Ash (G-1139)

Buckeye Homecare Services Inc........... D 216 321-9300
Cleveland (G-3908)

Buckeye Rsdntial Solutions LLC............ D 330 235-9183
Ravenna (G-12620)

C K Franchising Inc............................... D 937 264-1933
Dayton (G-7209)

Cambridge Home Health Care............... A 419 775-1253
Mansfield (G-10250)

Cambridge Home Health Care............... A 330 725-1968
Medina (G-10816)

Capital City Hospice.............................. D 614 441-9300
Columbus (G-5499)

Caprice Health Care Inc........................ E 330 965-9200
North Lima (G-11885)

Carestar Inc... C 513 618-8300
Cincinnati (G-2313)

Caring Hearts HM Hlth Care Inc............ C 513 339-1237
Mason (G-10526)

Centerwell Health Services Inc.............. D 419 482-6519
Maumee (G-10709)

Central Star... B 419 756-9449
Ontario (G-12100)

Cherished Companions Home Care....... D 440 273-7230
Chagrin Falls (G-1975)

Chesterfield Services Inc....................... E 330 896-9777
Uniontown (G-14245)

CHI National Home Care........................ D 513 576-0262
Loveland (G-10131)

Childrens Home Care Dayton................ D 937 641-4663
Dayton (G-7223)

Childrens Home Care Group.................. B 330 543-5000
Akron (G-88)

Christian Home Care LLC...................... E 419 254-2840
Toledo (G-13734)

Cincinnati Aml Refl Emer C LLC............ E 937 610-0414
Dayton (G-7226)

Cincinnati Home Care Inc...................... D 513 771-2760
Cincinnati (G-2412)

Circle J Home Health Care Inc.............. D 330 482-0877
Salineville (G-12859)

Columbus Home Health Svcs LLC......... E 614 985-1464
Columbus (G-5637)

Community Caregivers.......................... D 330 725-9800
Wadsworth (G-14433)

Community Concepts Inc....................... C 513 398-8181
Mason (G-10542)

Companion Care Services Inc............... E 440 257-0075
Mentor On The Lake (G-11014)

Companions of Ashland LLC................. E 419 281-2273
Ashland (G-494)

Comprhnsive Halthcare Svcs Inc........... C 513 245-0100
Cincinnati (G-2490)

Connections In Ohio Inc........................ D 216 228-9760
Cleveland (G-4102)

Consumer Support Services Inc............ D 330 652-8800
Niles (G-11786)

Continental Home Health Care.............. E 937 323-4499
Springfield (G-13241)

Counting Blessings HM Care LLC......... E 440 850-1050
Ashtabula (G-529)

Crawford Cnty Shared Hlth Svcs........... E 419 468-7985
Galion (G-8746)

D&J Quality Care Entps Inc................... D 440 638-7001
Strongsville (G-13451)

Daynas Homecare LLC......................... E 216 323-0323
Maple Heights (G-10337)

Ddc Group Inc....................................... C 937 619-3111
Dayton (G-7307)

Decahealth Inc....................................... D 866 908-3514
Toledo (G-13773)

Detox Health Care Corp Ohio................ D 513 742-6310
Cincinnati (G-2560)

Diamonds Pearls Hlth Svcs LLC............ D 216 752-8500
Beachwood (G-787)

Dillon Holdings LLC............................... C 513 942-5600
West Chester (G-14685)

Discount Drug Mart Inc......................... C 330 725-2340
Medina (G-10829)

Diversified Health MGT Inc.................... D 614 338-8888
Columbus (G-5774)

Ecumencal Shlter Ntwrk Lk Cnty........... E 440 354-6417
Painesville (G-12228)

Ember Complete Care........................... D 740 922-6968
Uhrichsville (G-14233)

Every Child Succeeds Inc..................... E 513 636-2830
Cincinnati (G-2643)

Everyday Homecare LLC...................... E 937 444-1672
Mount Orab (G-11470)

Excellence Home Healthcare LLC......... E 614 755-6502
Columbus (G-5836)

Fairfield Community Health Ctr............. E 740 277-6043
Lancaster (G-9710)

Fairhope Hspice Plltive Care I............... D 740 654-7077
Lancaster (G-9721)

Family Service of NW Ohio................... D 419 321-6455
Toledo (G-13803)

Fidelity Health Care............................... A 937 208-6400
Moraine (G-11409)

First Assist Health Care LLC................. E 440 421-9256
Cleveland (G-4255)

First Choice Medical Staffing................. D 419 861-2722
Toledo (G-13807)

First Community Village........................ B 614 324-4455
Columbus (G-5861)

Firsticare Inc.. E 614 721-2273
Columbus (G-5865)

Freedom Caregivers.............................. E 567 560-8277
Mansfield (G-10265)

Friends In Deed Inc............................... E 330 345-9222
Wooster (G-15339)

Gaash Home Health Care LLC.............. D 419 775-4823
Mansfield (G-10266)

Good Samaritan Hosp Cincinnati........... E 513 569-6251
Cincinnati (G-2742)

Goods Hands Supported Living............. E 740 773-4170
Chillicothe (G-2066)

Graves Care Services LLC.................... E 614 392-2820
Westerville (G-14982)

Great Home Healthcare LLC................. E 614 475-4026
Columbus (G-5950)

Greater Clvland HM Hlth Care I............. D 440 232-4995
Beachwood (G-796)

Greenville Nursing Services.................. E 937 736-2272
Xenia (G-15519)

Guardian Angels HM Hlth Care I........... D 419 517-7797
Sylvania (G-13547)

Healing Touch Agency LLC................... E 937 813-8333
Dayton (G-7400)

Health Care Rtrment Corp Amer............ C 304 925-4771
Toledo (G-13841)

Health With Hart Snior Svcs LL............. E 513 229-8888
West Chester (G-14706)

Hearty Hearts Home Health LLC........... E 216 898-5533
Cleveland (G-4356)

Heavenly Home Health LLC.................. E 740 859-4735
Rayland (G-12647)

Helping Hands Healthcare Inc............... C 513 755-4181
West Chester (G-14816)

Helping U Home Health Care LLC......... E 440 724-3754
Beachwood (G-798)

Heritage Health Care Services.............. C 614 848-6550
Columbus (G-5988)

Heritage Health Care Services.............. C 419 867-2002
Lima (G-9905)

HH Franchising Systems Inc................. D 513 563-8339
Blue Ash (G-1181)

Holistic Hlpers HM Hlth Care L............. D 216 331-5014
Shaker Heights (G-12978)

Holzer Home Care Services.................. D 740 288-4287
Jackson (G-9519)

Home Care Network Inc........................ C 937 258-1111
Dayton (G-7134)

Home Care Network Inc........................ C 740 353-2329
Portsmouth (G-12555)

Home Instead Senior Care.................... D 440 914-1400
Bedford (G-965)

Home Instead Senior Care.................... E 614 432-8524
Canal Winchester (G-1608)

Home Instead Senior Care.................... E 330 334-4664
Wadsworth (G-14435)

Home Is Where Hart Is HM Care........... E 740 457-5240
Wintersville (G-15295)

Homecare With Heart LLC.................... C 330 726-0700
Youngstown (G-15632)

Hometown Care LLC............................. E 330 926-1118
Cuyahoga Falls (G-7079)

Honorworth Homecare LLC................... E 513 557-0093
Cincinnati (G-2841)

Hope Homes Inc.................................... E 330 688-4935
Stow (G-13374)

Horizon HM Hlth Care Agcy LLC........... E 614 279-2933
Columbus (G-6008)

Horizon Home Health Care LLC............ C 937 410-3838
Vandalia (G-14381)

Hospice Cincinnati Inc........................... D 513 891-7700
Cincinnati (G-2848)

Hospice North Central Ohio Inc............. E 419 281-7107
Ashland (G-501)

Hospice of Genesis Health.................... E 740 454-5381
Zanesville (G-15801)

Hospice of Knox County........................ E 740 397-5188
Mount Vernon (G-11489)

Hospice of Medina County.................... D 330 725-1900
Medina (G-10840)

Hospice of Memorial Hospita L............. E 419 334-6626
Clyde (G-5202)

Hospice of The Western Reserve.......... E 330 800-2240
Medina (G-10841)

Hospice Southwest Ohio Inc................. D 513 770-0820
Cincinnati (G-2849)

Hospital HM Hlth Svcs Hghland............. E 937 393-6371
Hillsboro (G-9259)

In Home Health Inc................................ C 419 252-5500
Toledo (G-13862)

Infinity Health Services Inc.................... D 440 614-0145
Westlake (G-15070)

Infusion Partners Inc............................. E 419 843-2100
Sylvania (G-13551)

Infusion Partners Inc............................. E 513 396-6060
Cincinnati (G-2871)

HOME HEALTH CARE SVCS — SERVICES SECTION

Company	Col	Phone
Interim Halthcare Columbus Inc, Heath *(G-9134)*	B	740 349-8700
Interim Halthcare Columbus Inc, Marion *(G-10431)*	C	740 387-0301
Interim Halthcare Columbus Inc, Gahanna *(G-8719)*	E	614 888-3130
Interim Healthcare, Portsmouth *(G-12557)*	D	740 354-5550
Interim Healthcare Inc, Columbus *(G-6065)*	D	614 552-3400
Interim Healthcare Inc, Kent *(G-9581)*	D	330 677-8010
Interim Healthcare of Dayton, Dayton *(G-7423)*	A	937 291-5330
Interim Hlth Care of Nrthwster, Findlay *(G-8550)*	D	419 422-5328
Interim Hlth Care of Nrthwster, Lima *(G-9993)*	D	419 228-9345
Interim Hlth Care of Nrthwster, New Lexington *(G-11627)*	D	740 343-4112
Interim Hlth Care of Nrthwster, Zanesville *(G-15804)*	D	740 453-5130
Interim Hlthcare Cambridge Inc, Coshocton *(G-6987)*	D	740 623-2949
Interim Hlthcare Cambridge Inc, Worthington *(G-15423)*	E	740 432-2966
International Healthcare Corp, Cincinnati *(G-2882)*	D	513 731-3338
Interntnal Qlty Healthcare Corp, Dayton *(G-7425)*	E	513 731-3338
Jag Healthcare Inc, Rocky River *(G-12744)*	A	440 385-4370
Jmo & Dsl Llc, Lakewood *(G-9670)*	E	216 785-9375
Joint Township Dst Mem Hosp, Saint Marys *(G-12828)*	E	419 394-3335
Kentix Developmental Hlth Inc, Cuyahoga Falls *(G-7084)*	E	330 949-0131
Khc Inc, Chillicothe *(G-2076)*	D	740 775-5463
Knox County, Mount Vernon *(G-11494)*	E	740 392-2200
L JC Home Care LLC, Worthington *(G-15429)*	D	614 495-0276
Labelle Hmhealth Care Svcs LLC, Mount Vernon *(G-11497)*	D	740 392-1405
Ladneir Healthcare Service LLC, South Euclid *(G-13171)*	E	216 744-7296
Lake Hospital Sys HM Hlth Svcs, Painesville *(G-12232)*	E	440 639-0900
Liberty Provider LLC, Toledo *(G-13888)*	D	419 517-7000
Lifecare Alliance, Columbus *(G-6161)*	C	614 278-3130
Lincare Inc, Middletown *(G-11169)*	E	513 705-4250
Living Assistance Services Inc, Tallmadge *(G-13600)*	E	330 733-1532
Lizzies Hse Senior HM Care LLC, Cleveland *(G-4501)*	E	216 816-4188
Lorain County Senior Care Inc, North Ridgeville *(G-11931)*	E	440 353-3080
Mahoning Vly Infusioncare Inc, Youngstown *(G-15660)*	C	330 759-9487
Manor Care Inc, Toledo *(G-13905)*	D	419 252-5500
Maple Grove Enterprises Inc, Chardon *(G-2010)*	D	440 286-1342
Maple Knoll Communities Inc, Cincinnati *(G-3008)*	B	513 782-2400
Marymount Hospital Inc, Cleveland *(G-4531)*	B	216 581-0500
Maxim Healthcare Services Inc, Cincinnati *(G-3018)*	C	513 793-6444
Maxim Healthcare Services Inc, Gahanna *(G-8723)*	C	614 986-3001
Maxim Healthcare Services Inc, Hebron *(G-9146)*	C	740 526-2222
Maxim Healthcare Services Inc, Ontario *(G-12116)*	C	419 747-8040
McGregor Pace, Cleveland *(G-4539)*	E	216 361-0917
McGregor Pace, Cleveland *(G-4540)*	E	216 791-3580
Mch Services Inc, Dayton *(G-7473)*	C	260 432-9699
Med America Hlth Systems Corp, Dayton *(G-7475)*	A	937 223-6192
Medcentral Health System, Mansfield *(G-10292)*	C	419 526-8442
Medcorp Inc, Findlay *(G-8566)*	C	419 425-9700
Medi Home Health Agency Inc, Gallipolis *(G-8763)*	E	740 441-1779
Medi Home Health Agency Inc, Steubenville *(G-13338)*	E	740 266-3977
Medical Housecalls LLC, Cincinnati *(G-3027)*	E	513 699-9090
Medlink of Ohio Inc, Cleveland *(G-4547)*	B	216 751-5900
Memorial Hospital, Clyde *(G-5206)*	C	419 547-6419
Mercer Cnty Joint Townshp Hosp, Celina *(G-1927)*	D	419 584-0143
Mobile Hyperbaric Centers LLC, Cleveland *(G-4591)*	E	216 443-0430
Multicare Hlth Eductl Svcs Inc, Euclid *(G-8358)*	E	216 731-8900
National Mentor Holdings Inc, Fostoria *(G-8621)*	B	419 443-0867
National Mentor Holdings Inc, Warren *(G-14542)*	B	234 806-5361
Nationwide Childrens Hospital, Newark *(G-11734)*	C	740 522-3221
Nationwide Childrens Hospital, Westerville *(G-14915)*	C	614 355-8300
Nationwide Chld Hosp Homecare, Columbus *(G-6325)*	A	614 355-1100
Nationwide Health MGT LLC, Parma *(G-12258)*	D	440 888-8888
NC Hha Inc, Elyria *(G-8279)*	C	216 593-7750
New Life Hospice Inc, Lorain *(G-10095)*	C	440 934-1458
Northcoast Health Care Group, Beachwood *(G-822)*	E	330 856-2656
Nurses Care Inc, Miamisburg *(G-11076)*	D	513 424-1141
Ohio North E Hlth Systems Inc, Youngstown *(G-15683)*	E	330 747-9551
Ohio Valley Home Health Inc, Athens *(G-585)*	E	740 249-4219
Ohio Valley Home Health Inc, Gallipolis *(G-8767)*	E	740 441-1393
Ohiohealth Corporation, Columbus *(G-6465)*	A	614 788-8860
Open Arms Health Systems Llc, Columbus *(G-6472)*	D	614 385-8354
Option Care Brecksville O, Brecksville *(G-1361)*	E	440 627-2031
Options Home Services LLC, Columbus *(G-6475)*	E	614 203-6340
Our Lady Bellefonte Hosp Inc, Cincinnati *(G-3176)*	A	606 833-3333
P C Vpa, Cincinnati *(G-3180)*	D	513 841-0777
Pace Plus Corp, Toledo *(G-13955)*	D	419 754-1897
Paramount Spport Svc of St Clrs, Saint Clairsville *(G-12811)*	E	740 526-0540
Paris Home Health Care LLC, Warrensville Heights *(G-14585)*	E	888 416-9889
Parkside Care Corporation, Chardon *(G-2014)*	D	440 286-2273
Peoplfrst Hmcare Hspice Ohio L, Dayton *(G-7548)*	E	937 433-2400
Personal Touch HM Care IPA Inc, Cincinnati *(G-3198)*	C	513 984-9600
Personal Touch HM Care IPA Inc, Columbus *(G-6517)*	C	614 227-6952
Personal Touch HM Care IPA Inc, Hamilton *(G-9072)*	C	513 868-2272
Personal Touch HM Care IPA Inc, Wooster *(G-15366)*	C	330 263-1112
Phillips Hthcare LLC DBA Cring, Warren *(G-14547)*	E	330 531-6110
Preferred Medical Group Inc, Beachwood *(G-827)*	C	404 403-8310
Premier Health Partners, Dayton *(G-7560)*	A	937 499-9596
Promedica Toledo Hospital, Sylvania *(G-13566)*	D	419 291-2273
Prompt Prvate Nursing Care Inc, Canal Winchester *(G-1615)*	D	614 834-1105
Pulmonary Solutions Inc, Blue Ash *(G-1226)*	E	937 393-0991
Pure Health Care Llc, Centerville *(G-1951)*	E	937 668-7873
Pure Healthcare, Dayton *(G-7574)*	E	937 668-7873
Putnam Cnty Homecare & Hospice, Ottawa *(G-12193)*	D	419 523-4449
Quality Care Nursing Svc Inc, South Point *(G-13182)*	C	740 377-9095
Quality Cmfort Living Svcs LLC, Canton *(G-1836)*	D	330 280-7659
Quantum Health Inc, Dublin *(G-8102)*	A	800 257-2038
Queen City Hospice LLC, Mason *(G-10598)*	A	513 510-4406
Queen City Skilled Care LLC, Cincinnati *(G-3267)*	D	513 802-5010
Reliable Home Healthcare LLC, Dayton *(G-7584)*	E	937 274-2900
REM Corp, Frazeysburg *(G-8656)*	C	740 828-2601
Res Care Home Care, Dayton *(G-7586)*	D	937 436-3966
RES-Care Inc, Bethesda *(G-1097)*	D	740 782-1476
RES-Care Inc, Canton *(G-1846)*	D	330 452-2913
RES-Care Inc, Gallipolis *(G-8768)*	D	740 446-7549
RES-Care Inc, Saint Clairsville *(G-12813)*	D	740 526-0285
RES-Care Inc, Saint Clairsville *(G-12814)*	C	740 695-4931
RES-Care Inc, West Chester *(G-14755)*	D	513 858-4550
Rescue91 Healthcare Svcs LLC, Dayton *(G-7587)*	E	937 500-5371
Resource Alliance Homecare LLC, Cleveland Heights *(G-5184)*	D	216 465-9977
Rose Health Care Services Ltd, Dayton *(G-7596)*	E	937 277-7518

SERVICES SECTION

HOSPITALS: Medical & Surgical

Rosmansearch Inc............................... E 216 256-9020
  Cleveland *(G-4855)*

Ross County Health District................ E 740 775-1114
  Chillicothe *(G-2086)*

Ross County Home Health LLC........ D 740 775-1114
  Chillicothe *(G-2087)*

Royalty Care Nursing LLC.................. D 216 386-8762
  Cleveland *(G-4861)*

Safe and Secure Homecare Corp....... D 614 808-0164
  Columbus *(G-6625)*

Salo Inc... C 419 419-0038
  Bowling Green *(G-1332)*

Salo Inc... B 740 432-2966
  Cambridge *(G-1581)*

Salo Inc... C 513 984-1110
  Cincinnati *(G-3345)*

Salo Inc... C 740 623-2331
  Coshocton *(G-7001)*

Salo Inc... C 330 836-5571
  Fairlawn *(G-8495)*

Salo Inc... C 740 653-5990
  Lancaster *(G-9740)*

Salo Inc... C 740 651-5209
  Mcconnelsville *(G-10804)*

Salo Inc... C 740 964-2904
  Pataskala *(G-12276)*

Salo Inc... D 614 436-9404
  Columbus *(G-6639)*

Sar Enterprises LLC............................ E 419 472-8181
  Toledo *(G-14005)*

Schroer Properties Navarre Inc.......... D 330 498-8200
  North Canton *(G-11861)*

Scriptdrop Inc....................................... D 614 641-0648
  Columbus *(G-6656)*

Sdx Home Care Operations LLC........ D 937 322-6288
  Springfield *(G-13289)*

Senior Touch Solution......................... E 216 862-4841
  Cleveland *(G-4895)*

Source Diagnostics LLC...................... E 440 542-9481
  Solon *(G-13146)*

Southern Care Inc............................... D 330 797-8940
  Youngstown *(G-15727)*

Specilzed HM Care Prviders LLC....... D 330 758-8740
  Youngstown *(G-15728)*

St Augustine Manor.............................. C 440 888-7722
  Parma *(G-12265)*

Summit Acres Inc................................. C 740 732-2364
  Caldwell *(G-1551)*

Summit Ortho Home Care.................... D 513 898-3375
  Blue Ash *(G-1246)*

Sunrise Nursing Healthcare LLC........ D 513 797-5144
  Amelia *(G-420)*

Supreme Touch Home Health Svcs.... E 614 783-1115
  Columbus *(G-6732)*

Synergy Homecare................................ D 937 610-0555
  Dayton *(G-7657)*

Tender Hrts At HM Snior Care I........... D 513 234-0805
  Cincinnati *(G-3453)*

Tk Homecare Llc.................................. C 419 517-7000
  Toledo *(G-14044)*

Tky Associates LLC............................. E 419 535-7777
  Toledo *(G-14045)*

Toledo Society For The Blind.............. E 419 720-3937
  Toledo *(G-14066)*

Total Homecare Solutions LLC.......... D 513 277-0915
  Cincinnati *(G-3483)*

Trucare Provider Services LLC.......... C 513 201-5611
  Cincinnati *(G-3531)*

Tsk Assisted Living Svcs Inc.............. D 330 297-2000
  Ravenna *(G-12645)*

Turning Point Residential Inc............. E 330 788-0669
  Youngstown *(G-15738)*

Ultimate Home Services LLC.............. E 614 888-8698
  Worthington *(G-15464)*

Union Healthcare Services Inc........... E 614 686-2322
  Columbus *(G-6801)*

Unity I Home Healthcare LLC............. E 740 351-0500
  Portsmouth *(G-12580)*

Universal Nursing Services................. E 330 434-7318
  Akron *(G-343)*

University Hsptals Clvland Med.......... A 216 844-4663
  Cleveland *(G-5079)*

University Mednet................................ B 216 383-0100
  Euclid *(G-8363)*

Vandalia Butler Emrgncy Fd Ctr......... D 937 898-4202
  Vandalia *(G-14402)*

Viaquest Behavioral Health LLC........ E 614 339-0868
  Dublin *(G-8153)*

Viaquest Residential Svcs LLC.......... C 216 446-2650
  Independence *(G-9496)*

Viaquest Residential Svcs LLC.......... E 614 889-5837
  Dublin *(G-8154)*

Vision Home Health Care LLC............ E 614 338-8100
  Pataskala *(G-12279)*

Visiting Nrse Assn Hspice Nrth.......... D 330 841-5440
  Warren *(G-14572)*

Walton Home Health Care LLC........... E 513 270-0555
  Cincinnati *(G-3640)*

West Branch Nursing Home Ltd........ D 330 537-4621
  Salem *(G-12857)*

Western Rsrve Area Agcy On Agi...... C 216 621-0303
  Cleveland *(G-5138)*

Whitney Home Care LLC...................... E 440 647-2200
  Wellington *(G-14635)*

Willcare Inc... E 216 289-5300
  Cleveland *(G-5148)*

Willglo Services Inc............................. E 614 443-3020
  Columbus *(G-6893)*

Ziks Family Pharmacy 100................. E 937 225-9350
  Dayton *(G-7737)*

Ziks Home Healthcare LLC................ D 937 225-9350
  Dayton *(G-7738)*

Zimohana LLC...................................... D 330 922-4721
  Medina *(G-10906)*

HOMEFURNISHING STORES: Fireplaces & Wood Burning Stoves

Overhead Inc.. E 419 476-7811
  Toledo *(G-13951)*

HOMEFURNISHING STORES: Lighting Fixtures

Gross Electric Inc............................... E 419 537-1818
  Toledo *(G-13831)*

Mars Electric Company....................... D 440 946-2250
  Cleveland *(G-4529)*

HOMEFURNISHINGS, WHOLESALE: Carpets

Business Furniture LLC...................... E 937 293-1010
  Dayton *(G-7207)*

Certified Carpet Distrs Inc.................. E 216 573-1422
  Cleveland *(G-3957)*

Dayton Ews Inc.................................... E 937 293-1010
  Moraine *(G-11400)*

Dealers Supply North Inc.................... E 614 274-6285
  Lockbourne *(G-10011)*

Ohio Valley Flooring Inc..................... D 216 328-9091
  Cleveland *(G-4691)*

Ohio Valley Flooring Inc..................... D 513 271-3434
  Cincinnati *(G-3150)*

State Crest Carpet & Flooring............ E 440 232-3980
  Bedford *(G-987)*

HOMEFURNISHINGS, WHOLESALE: Draperies

Accent Drapery Co Inc........................ E 614 488-0741
  Columbus *(G-5300)*

Inside Outfitters Inc............................ E 614 798-3500
  Lewis Center *(G-9824)*

Lumenomics Inc.................................. E 614 798-3500
  Lewis Center *(G-9827)*

HOMEFURNISHINGS, WHOLESALE: Kitchenware

Famous Distribution Inc..................... D 330 762-9621
  Akron *(G-154)*

G & S Metal Products Co Inc.............. C 216 441-0700
  Cleveland *(G-4295)*

G G Marck & Associates Inc............... E 419 478-0900
  Toledo *(G-13815)*

Walter F Stephens Jr Inc.................... E 937 746-0521
  Franklin *(G-8652)*

HOMEFURNISHINGS, WHOLESALE: Wood Flooring

JP Flooring Systems Inc..................... E 513 346-4300
  West Chester *(G-14715)*

Van Boxel Stor Solutions LLC............ E 440 721-1504
  Chardon *(G-2025)*

HOSE: Automobile, Rubber

Myers Industries Inc........................... E 330 253-5592
  Akron *(G-238)*

HOSPITALS: Medical & Surgical

Acute Care Specialty Hospital............ E 330 363-4860
  Canton *(G-1654)*

Adams County Regional Med Ctr....... C 937 900-2316
  West Union *(G-14865)*

Adena Health System........................... E 740 947-2186
  Waverly *(G-14610)*

Adena Health System........................... E 740 779-7500
  Wshngtn Ct Hs *(G-15476)*

Adena Regional Medical Center......... E 740 779-4050
  Chillicothe *(G-2049)*

After Hours Family Care Inc............... E 937 667-2614
  Tipp City *(G-13651)*

Akron Children S Hospital.................. D 330 310-0157
  Doylestown *(G-7912)*

Akron City Hospital Inc....................... A 330 253-5046
  Akron *(G-23)*

Akron General Health System............. A 330 896-5070
  Uniontown *(G-14240)*

Akron General Medical Center........... A 330 344-6000
  Akron *(G-32)*

Akron Radiology Inc............................ E 330 375-3043
  Akron *(G-35)*

Alliance Citizens Health Assn............ D 330 596-6000
  Alliance *(G-374)*

Alliance Community Hospital............. D 330 596-6000
  Alliance *(G-375)*

Ambulatory Care Pharmacy................ D 419 251-2545
  Toledo *(G-13680)*

Amherst Hospital Association............ D 440 988-6000
  Amherst *(G-421)*

Appalachian Cmnty Vsting Nrse A..... E 740 594-8226
  Athens *(G-555)*

Arthur G Jmes Cncer Hosp RES I...... E 614 293-3300
  Columbus *(G-5389)*

Ashland Hospital Corporation............ D 740 894-2080
  South Point *(G-13173)*

HOSPITALS: Medical & Surgical — SERVICES SECTION

Ashtabula County Medical Ctr............... B 440 997-6960
  Ashtabula (G-523)
Ashtabula County Medical Ctr............... B 440 997-6680
  Ashtabula (G-524)
Ashtabula County Medical Ctr............... A 440 997-2262
  Ashtabula (G-522)
Atrium Medical Center.......................... A 513 424-2111
  Middletown (G-11153)
Aultman Health Foundation.................. B 330 305-6999
  Canton (G-1677)
Aultman Health Foundation.................. C 330 875-6050
  Louisville (G-10113)
Aultman Health Foundation.................. A 330 682-3010
  Orrville (G-12157)
Aultman Health Foundation.................. E 330 452-9911
  Canton (G-1678)
Aultman Hospital.................................... A 330 452-9911
  Canton (G-1679)
Aultman Mso Inc................................... E 330 479-8705
  Canton (G-1680)
Aultman North Canton Med Group........ C 330 433-1200
  Canton (G-1681)
Aultman North Inc................................. D 330 305-6999
  Canton (G-1683)
Auxiliary Bd Fairview Gen Hosp............ A 216 476-7000
  Cleveland (G-3844)
Baptist Health Hardin........................... C 419 673-0761
  Kenton (G-9609)
Bay Park Community Hospital............... E 419 690-7900
  Oregon (G-12129)
Bay Park Community Hospital............... E 419 690-8725
  Toledo (G-13700)
Bay Park Community Hospital............... B 567 585-9600
  Toledo (G-13701)
Beavercreek Medical Center.................. C 937 702-4000
  Beavercreek (G-863)
Bellevue Hospital................................... B 419 483-4040
  Bellevue (G-1042)
Belmont Bhc Pines Hospital Inc............. D 330 759-2700
  Youngstown (G-15558)
Belmont Community Hospital................ B 740 671-1200
  Bellaire (G-1007)
Bethesda Hospital Inc........................... D 513 563-1505
  Cincinnati (G-2259)
Bethesda Hospital Inc........................... C 513 894-8888
  Fairfield Township (G-8456)
Bethesda Hospital Inc........................... B 513 745-1111
  Montgomery (G-11363)
Bethesda Hospital Inc........................... A 513 569-6100
  Cincinnati (G-2258)
Bethesda Hospital Association.............. B 740 454-4000
  Zanesville (G-15770)
Blanchard Vly Rgional Hlth Ctr.............. C 419 358-9010
  Bluffton (G-1277)
Bluffton Community Hospital................ C 419 358-9010
  Bluffton (G-1278)
Bon Scurs Mrcy Hlth Foundation........... D 513 952-4019
  Cincinnati (G-2270)
Bon Secours Mercy Health Inc.............. A 440 233-1000
  Amherst (G-425)
Bon Secours Mercy Health Inc.............. E 513 639-2800
  Cincinnati (G-2271)
Bon Secours Mercy Health Inc.............. E 513 624-1950
  Cincinnati (G-2272)
Bon Secours Mercy Health Inc.............. E 513 639-2800
  Cincinnati (G-2273)
Bon Secours Mercy Health Inc.............. E 419 991-7805
  Lima (G-9870)
Bon Secours Mercy Health Inc.............. D 440 774-6800
  Oberlin (G-12064)
Bon Secours Mercy Health Inc.............. E 419 251-2659
  Toledo (G-13712)

Bon Secours Mercy Health Inc.............. E 330 746-7211
  Youngstown (G-15562)
Bon Secours Mercy Health Inc.............. D 513 956-3729
  Cincinnati (G-2274)
Bowling Green Clinic Inc....................... E 419 352-1121
  Bowling Green (G-1310)
Bridgeshome Health Care Inc................ B 330 764-1000
  Medina (G-10815)
Bucyrus Community Hospital LLC......... D 419 562-4677
  Bucyrus (G-1498)
C C F Vsclar Srgery At Mrymunt........... C 216 475-1551
  Cleveland (G-3914)
Canton Altman Emrgncy Physcans....... E 330 456-2695
  Canton (G-1696)
Catholic Hlthcare Prtners Fndt.............. D 513 639-2800
  Cincinnati (G-2324)
Cha - Community Health Affairs........... D 800 362-2628
  Cleveland (G-3959)
Chester West Medical Center................ A 513 298-3000
  West Chester (G-14663)
Childrens H Cincinnati.......................... C 513 803-2707
  Cincinnati (G-2356)
Childrens Hosp Med Ctr Akron............. D 330 543-8521
  Akron (G-93)
Childrens Hosp Med Ctr Akron............. D 330 375-3528
  Akron (G-94)
Childrens Hosp Med Ctr Akron............. D 330 865-1252
  Akron (G-95)
Childrens Hosp Med Ctr Akron............. D 330 543-1000
  Akron (G-96)
Childrens Hosp Med Ctr Akron............. D 330 543-8260
  Akron (G-97)
Childrens Hosp Med Ctr Akron............. D 330 543-8530
  Akron (G-99)
Childrens Hosp Med Ctr Akron............. D 330 823-7311
  Alliance (G-378)
Childrens Hosp Med Ctr Akron............. D 419 281-3077
  Ashland (G-493)
Childrens Hosp Med Ctr Akron............. D 330 746-8040
  Boardman (G-1286)
Childrens Hosp Med Ctr Akron............. D 440 526-4543
  Brecksville (G-1348)
Childrens Hosp Med Ctr Akron............. D 330 676-1020
  Kent (G-9562)
Childrens Hosp Med Ctr Akron............. D 419 521-2900
  Mansfield (G-10253)
Childrens Hosp Med Ctr Akron............. D 330 308-5432
  New Philadelphia (G-11642)
Childrens Hosp Med Ctr Akron............. D 419 529-6285
  Ontario (G-12102)
Childrens Hosp Med Ctr Akron............. D 330 425-3344
  Twinsburg (G-14176)
Childrens Hosp Med Ctr Akron............. A 330 543-1000
  Akron (G-98)
Childrens Hospital................................. C 513 636-9900
  Cincinnati (G-2358)
Childrens Hospital................................. D 513 636-4051
  Cincinnati (G-2359)
Childrens Hospital Medical Ctr.............. B 513 636-6036
  Cincinnati (G-2099)
Childrens Hospital Medical Ctr.............. A 513 541-4500
  Cincinnati (G-2360)
Childrens Hospital Medical Ctr.............. A 513 636-4200
  Cincinnati (G-2361)
Childrens Hospital Medical Ctr.............. A 513 803-1751
  Cincinnati (G-2362)
Childrens Hospital Medical Ctr.............. A 513 636-4200
  Cincinnati (G-2363)
Childrens Hospital Medical Ctr.............. A 513 636-4366
  Cincinnati (G-2364)
Childrens Hospital Medical Ctr.............. A 513 636-4288
  Cincinnati (G-2365)

Childrens Hospital Medical Ctr.............. B 513 636-8778
  Cincinnati (G-2366)
Childrens Hospital Medical Ctr.............. A 513 803-9600
  Liberty Township (G-9848)
Chirst Hospital Surgery Center.............. E 513 272-3448
  Cincinnati (G-2374)
Chmc Cmnty Hlth Svcs Netwrk............. A 513 636-8778
  Cincinnati (G-2375)
Christ Hospital...................................... D 513 631-3300
  Cincinnati (G-2376)
Christ Hospital...................................... D 513 351-0800
  Cincinnati (G-2377)
Christ Hospital...................................... E 513 585-2000
  Cincinnati (G-2378)
Christ Hospital...................................... D 513 651-0094
  Cincinnati (G-2381)
Christ Hospital...................................... D 513 272-3448
  Cincinnati (G-2382)
Christ Hospital...................................... D 513 347-2300
  Cincinnati (G-2383)
Christ Hospital...................................... D 513 561-7809
  Cincinnati (G-2384)
Christ Hospital...................................... D 513 648-7950
  Liberty Township (G-9849)
Christ Hospital...................................... D 513 648-7800
  Liberty Township (G-9850)
Christ Hospital...................................... D 513 755-4700
  West Chester (G-14665)
Christus Hlth Southeast Texas.............. C 330 726-0771
  Youngstown (G-15577)
City Hospital Association...................... A 330 385-7200
  East Liverpool (G-8179)
City of Wooster..................................... A 330 263-8100
  Wooster (G-15321)
Cleveland Anesthesia Group................. E 216 901-5706
  Independence (G-9419)
Cleveland Clinic Avon Hospital.............. D 440 695-5000
  Avon (G-645)
Cleveland Clinic Cole Eye Inst.............. E 216 444-4508
  Cleveland (G-4009)
Cleveland Clinic Foundation.................. E 330 864-8060
  Akron (G-107)
Cleveland Clinic Foundation.................. E 440 937-9099
  Avon (G-647)
Cleveland Clinic Foundation.................. D 216 831-0120
  Beachwood (G-780)
Cleveland Clinic Foundation.................. E 216 448-0116
  Beachwood (G-781)
Cleveland Clinic Foundation.................. D 800 223-2273
  Beachwood (G-782)
Cleveland Clinic Foundation.................. E 216 455-6400
  Beachwood (G-783)
Cleveland Clinic Foundation.................. E 440 986-4000
  Broadview Heights (G-1384)
Cleveland Clinic Foundation.................. E 440 717-1370
  Broadview Heights (G-1385)
Cleveland Clinic Foundation.................. E 330 533-8350
  Canfield (G-1626)
Cleveland Clinic Foundation.................. E 440 729-9000
  Chesterland (G-2033)
Cleveland Clinic Foundation.................. B 800 223-2273
  Cleveland (G-4010)
Cleveland Clinic Foundation.................. D 800 223-2273
  Cleveland (G-4011)
Cleveland Clinic Foundation.................. D 216 444-5755
  Cleveland (G-4012)
Cleveland Clinic Foundation.................. B 216 444-5715
  Cleveland (G-4013)
Cleveland Clinic Foundation.................. B 216 448-4325
  Cleveland (G-4014)
Cleveland Clinic Foundation.................. E 866 223-8100
  Cleveland (G-4015)

SERVICES SECTION

HOSPITALS: Medical & Surgical

Cleveland Clinic Foundation................. D 216 444-1764
  Cleveland *(G-4016)*
Cleveland Clinic Foundation................. D 216 442-6700
  Cleveland *(G-4017)*
Cleveland Clinic Foundation................. E 216 444-5600
  Cleveland *(G-4018)*
Cleveland Clinic Foundation................. E 216 445-4500
  Cleveland *(G-4019)*
Cleveland Clinic Foundation................. E 216 445-6888
  Cleveland *(G-4021)*
Cleveland Clinic Foundation................. D 216 986-4000
  Cleveland *(G-4022)*
Cleveland Clinic Foundation................. B 216 444-2200
  Cleveland *(G-4023)*
Cleveland Clinic Foundation................. E 216 444-6618
  Cleveland *(G-4026)*
Cleveland Clinic Foundation................. E 234 815-5100
  Copley *(G-6950)*
Cleveland Clinic Foundation................. E 330 923-9585
  Cuyahoga Falls *(G-7062)*
Cleveland Clinic Foundation................. E 833 427-5634
  Fairlawn *(G-8471)*
Cleveland Clinic Foundation................. E 330 948-5523
  Lodi *(G-10018)*
Cleveland Clinic Foundation................. E 440 988-5651
  Lorain *(G-10065)*
Cleveland Clinic Foundation................. E 440 282-7420
  Lorain *(G-10066)*
Cleveland Clinic Foundation................. E 440 428-1111
  Madison *(G-10212)*
Cleveland Clinic Foundation................. D 440 250-5737
  North Olmsted *(G-11897)*
Cleveland Clinic Foundation................. E 440 327-1050
  North Ridgeville *(G-11925)*
Cleveland Clinic Foundation................. E 419 660-6946
  Norwalk *(G-12006)*
Cleveland Clinic Foundation................. D 419 609-2812
  Sandusky *(G-12882)*
Cleveland Clinic Foundation................. D 216 444-2200
  Solon *(G-13076)*
Cleveland Clinic Foundation................. A 440 878-2500
  Strongsville *(G-13449)*
Cleveland Clinic Foundation................. E 330 334-4620
  Wadsworth *(G-14432)*
Cleveland Clinic Foundation................. E 440 647-0004
  Wellington *(G-14629)*
Cleveland Clinic Foundation................. E 440 516-8896
  Willoughby Hills *(G-15231)*
Cleveland Clinic Foundation................. B 330 287-4500
  Wooster *(G-15322)*
Cleveland Clinic Foundation................. E 330 287-4930
  Wooster *(G-15323)*
Cleveland Clinic Foundation................. A 216 636-8335
  Cleveland *(G-4020)*
Cleveland Clinic Mercy Hosp................. B 330 823-3856
  Alliance *(G-380)*
Cleveland Clinic Mercy Hosp................. B 330 966-8884
  Canton *(G-1712)*
Cleveland Clinic Mercy Hosp................. B 330 588-4892
  Canton *(G-1713)*
Cleveland Clinic Mercy Hosp................. B 330 649-4380
  Canton *(G-1714)*
Cleveland Clinic Mercy Hosp................. B 330 489-1329
  Canton *(G-1715)*
Cleveland Clinic Mercy Hosp................. B 330 492-8803
  Canton *(G-1716)*
Cleveland Clinic Mercy Hosp................. E 330 489-1000
  Canton *(G-1717)*
Cleveland Clnic Chld Hosp For................. C 216 721-5400
  Cleveland *(G-4033)*
Cleveland Clnic Hlth Systm-AST................. E 440 449-4500
  Cleveland *(G-4035)*

Cleveland Clnic Hlth Systm-AST................. D 216 692-7555
  Cleveland *(G-4036)*
Cleveland Clnic Hlth Systm-AST................. E 330 468-0190
  Northfield *(G-11954)*
Cleveland Clnic Hlth Systm-AST................. D 330 287-4830
  Wooster *(G-15324)*
Cleveland Clnic Hlth Systm-Wst................. D 216 518-3444
  Cleveland *(G-4037)*
Cleveland Clnic Hlth Systm-Wst................. C 216 491-6000
  Warrensville Heights *(G-14579)*
Clinton Memorial Hospital................. B 937 382-6611
  Wilmington *(G-15249)*
Columbus Cardiology Cons Inc................. C 614 224-2281
  Grove City *(G-8910)*
Community Health Systems Inc................. D 330 841-9011
  Warren *(G-14511)*
Community Hlth Prtners Rgnal F................. A 440 960-4000
  Lorain *(G-10068)*
Community Hospitals................. B 419 636-1131
  Bryan *(G-1480)*
Community Hospitals Wellness................. D 419 636-1131
  Bryan *(G-1481)*
Community Hsptals Wllness Ctrs................. E 419 445-2015
  Archbold *(G-456)*
Community Hsptals Wllness Ctrs................. E 419 485-3154
  Montpelier *(G-11383)*
Community Hsptals Wllness Ctrs................. C 419 636-1131
  Bryan *(G-1482)*
Community Mercy Health System................. D 937 523-5500
  Springfield *(G-13238)*
Community Mercy Hlth Partners................. C 937 523-6670
  Springfield *(G-13239)*
Convalescent Hospital For Chil................. E 513 636-4415
  Cincinnati *(G-2504)*
Copc Hospitals................. C 614 268-8164
  Columbus *(G-5701)*
Dayton Childrens Cardiology................. E 937 641-3418
  Dayton *(G-7273)*
Dayton Childrens Hospital................. D 937 641-5760
  Dayton *(G-7274)*
Dayton Childrens Hospital................. D 937 641-3500
  Dayton *(G-7275)*
Dayton Childrens Hospital................. D 513 424-2850
  Middletown *(G-11195)*
Dayton Osteopathic Hospital................. E 937 401-6400
  Centerville *(G-1944)*
Dayton Osteopathic Hospital................. E 937 558-0200
  Dayton *(G-7292)*
Dayton Osteopathic Hospital................. E 937 558-3800
  Dayton *(G-7294)*
Dayton Osteopathic Hospital................. E 937 439-6000
  Dayton *(G-7295)*
Dayton Osteopathic Hospital................. E 937 401-6503
  Dayton *(G-7296)*
Dayton Osteopathic Hospital................. E 937 456-8300
  Eaton *(G-8212)*
Dayton Osteopathic Hospital................. E 513 696-1200
  Lebanon *(G-9763)*
Dayton Osteopathic Hospital................. E 937 898-9729
  Vandalia *(G-14374)*
Dayton Osteopathic Hospital................. A 937 762-1629
  Dayton *(G-7293)*
Deaconess Hospital of Cincinna................. C 513 559-2100
  Cincinnati *(G-2549)*
Defiance Hospital Inc................. B 419 783-6955
  Toledo *(G-13774)*
Doctors Hospital Cleveland Inc................. C 740 753-7300
  Nelsonville *(G-11542)*
Doctors Ohiohealth Corporation................. A 614 297-4000
  Columbus *(G-5780)*
East Ohio Hospital LLC................. C 740 633-1100
  Martins Ferry *(G-10467)*

East Ohio Hospital LLC................. C 740 695-5955
  Saint Clairsville *(G-12791)*
East Ohio Hospital LLC................. E 740 633-1100
  Martins Ferry *(G-10468)*
Emh Regional Medical Center................. A 440 329-7500
  Elyria *(G-8249)*
Equitas Health Inc................. E 937 424-1440
  Dayton *(G-7338)*
Euclid Hospital................. B 216 531-9000
  Euclid *(G-8341)*
Fairfield Diagnstc Imaging LLC................. E 740 654-6312
  Lancaster *(G-9711)*
Fairfield Medical Associates................. E 740 687-8377
  Lancaster *(G-9717)*
Fairfield Medical Center................. A 740 687-8000
  Lancaster *(G-9718)*
Fairview Hospital................. A 216 476-7000
  Cleveland *(G-4238)*
Falls Family Practice Inc................. E 330 923-9585
  Cuyahoga Falls *(G-7072)*
Family Birth Center Lima Mem................. E 419 998-4570
  Lima *(G-9888)*
Family Physicians of Coshocton................. D 740 622-0332
  Coshocton *(G-6984)*
Far Oaks Orthopedists Inc................. E 937 433-5309
  Dayton *(G-7348)*
Fayette County Memorial Hosp................. C 740 335-1210
  Wshngtn Ct Hs *(G-15482)*
Findlay Surgery Center Ltd................. E 419 421-4845
  Findlay *(G-8530)*
Firelands Regional Health Sys................. E 419 557-6161
  Sandusky *(G-12894)*
Firelands Regional Health Sys................. D 419 557-7455
  Sandusky *(G-12895)*
Firelands Regional Health Sys................. E 419 557-7485
  Sandusky *(G-12896)*
Fisher - Titus Health................. A 419 668-8101
  Norwalk *(G-12010)*
Fisher-Titus Medical Center................. D 419 663-6464
  Norwalk *(G-12011)*
Fisher-Titus Medical Center................. A 419 668-8101
  Norwalk *(G-12013)*
Flower Hospital................. A 419 824-1444
  Sylvania *(G-13544)*
Fort Hamilton Hospital................. C 513 867-2382
  Hamilton *(G-9042)*
Fort Hamilton Hospital................. B 513 867-2280
  Hamilton *(G-9043)*
Fort Hamilton Hospital................. D 513 867-2000
  Hamilton *(G-9041)*
Foundtion Srgery Afflate Mddlb................. E 440 743-8400
  Middleburg Heights *(G-11115)*
Frederick C Smith Clinic Inc................. B 740 383-7000
  Marion *(G-10427)*
Fulton County Health Center................. C 419 335-2017
  Wauseon *(G-14601)*
Fulton County Health Center................. B 419 335-2015
  Wauseon *(G-14602)*
Garden II Leasing Co LLC................. D 419 381-0037
  Toledo *(G-13817)*
Geauga Regional Hosp HM Care................. E 440 285-6834
  Chardon *(G-2002)*
Genesis Healthcare System................. D 740 454-5922
  Zanesville *(G-15790)*
Genesis Healthcare System................. D 740 454-5913
  Zanesville *(G-15792)*
Genesis Healthcare System................. D 740 454-4585
  Zanesville *(G-15793)*
Genesis Healthcare System................. E 740 586-6732
  Zanesville *(G-15794)*
Genesis Healthcare System................. E 740 454-4566
  Zanesville *(G-15795)*

HOSPITALS: Medical & Surgical — SERVICES SECTION

Genesis Healthcare System................... A 740 454-5000
Zanesville (G-15791)

Gerlach John J Ctr For Snior H............... E 614 566-5858
Columbus (G-5930)

Good Samaritan Hosp Cincinnati........... E 513 569-6251
Cincinnati (G-2742)

Grace Hospital.................................... D 216 687-4013
Amherst (G-429)

Grace Hospital.................................... D 216 687-1500
Bedford (G-961)

Grace Hospital.................................... D 216 476-2704
Cleveland (G-4325)

Grady Memorial Hospital..................... B 740 615-1000
Delaware (G-7802)

Greene Oaks...................................... D 937 352-2800
Xenia (G-15518)

Greenfield Area Medical Ctr................. B 937 981-9400
Greenfield (G-8864)

Guernsey Health Systems................... A 740 439-3561
Cambridge (G-1573)

H B Magruder Memorial Hosp.............. C 419 734-3131
Oak Harbor (G-12045)

H B Magruder Memorial Hosp.............. C 419 732-6520
Port Clinton (G-12532)

H B Magruder Memorial Hosp.............. C 419 734-4539
Port Clinton (G-12533)

Hcl of Dayton Inc................................. C 937 384-8300
Miamisburg (G-11059)

Health Care Specialists........................ E 740 454-4530
Zanesville (G-15799)

Heart Care.. E 614 533-5000
Gahanna (G-8718)

Henry County Hospital Inc................... B 419 592-4015
Napoleon (G-11525)

Hillcrest Hospital Auxiliary................... D 440 449-4500
Cleveland (G-4364)

Holzer Clinic LLC................................. E 740 589-3100
Athens (G-574)

Holzer Clinic LLC................................. E 304 746-3701
Gallipolis (G-8760)

Holzer Health System.......................... A 740 446-5000
Gallipolis (G-8761)

Holzer Hospital Foundation.................. A 740 446-5000
Gallipolis (G-8762)

Holzer Medical Ctr - Jackson................ D 740 288-4625
Jackson (G-9520)

Hometown Urgent Care....................... D 937 342-9520
Springfield (G-13254)

Hospice of Genesis Health................... E 740 454-5381
Zanesville (G-15801)

Internists of Fairfield Inc...................... E 513 896-9595
Fairfield (G-8420)

Jewish Hospital................................... E 513 569-2434
Cincinnati (G-2907)

Jewish Hospital LLC............................ B 513 686-5970
Cincinnati (G-2908)

Jewish Hospital LLC............................ B 513 585-2668
Cincinnati (G-2909)

Jewish Hospital LLC............................ B 513 988-6067
Trenton (G-14123)

Jewish Hospital LLC............................ A 513 686-3000
Cincinnati (G-2910)

Jewish Hospital Cincinnati Inc.............. A 513 686-3303
Cincinnati (G-2911)

Joint Township Dst Mem Hosp............. E 419 394-3335
Saint Marys (G-12828)

Joint Township Dst Mem Hosp............. E 419 394-9959
Saint Marys (G-12830)

Joint Township Dst Mem Hosp............. B 419 394-3335
Saint Marys (G-12829)

Joint Township Home Health............... D 419 394-3335
Saint Marys (G-12831)

Jtd Health Systems Inc........................ D 419 394-3335
Saint Marys (G-12832)

Junior Coop Soc Chldren S Hosp........... E 513 636-4310
Cincinnati (G-2923)

Kettering Adventist Healthcare............. A 937 298-4331
Dayton (G-7435)

Kettering Health Hamilton.................... A 513 867-2000
Hamilton (G-9056)

Kettering Medical Center..................... B 937 866-0551
Miamisburg (G-11066)

Kettering Pathology Assoc Inc.............. D 937 298-4331
Dayton (G-7440)

Khn Pharmacy Huber........................... C 937 558-3333
Huber Heights (G-9324)

Kindred Healthcare LLC....................... E 937 222-5963
Dayton (G-7442)

Kindred Healthcare LLC....................... E 937 222-5963
Dayton (G-7443)

Kindred Healthcare LLC....................... E 419 224-1888
Lima (G-9914)

Knox Cardiology Associates................. E 740 397-0108
Mount Vernon (G-11491)

Knox Community Hospital.................... A 740 393-9000
Mount Vernon (G-11492)

Lake Health Inc................................... D 440 279-1500
Chardon (G-2009)

Lake Hospital System Inc..................... C 216 545-4800
Beachwood (G-807)

Lake Hospital System Inc..................... C 440 205-8818
Mentor (G-10962)

Lake Hospital System Inc..................... C 440 953-9600
Willoughby (G-15199)

Lake Hospital System Inc..................... C 440 975-0027
Willoughby (G-15200)

Lake Hospital System Inc..................... C 440 942-4226
Willoughby (G-15201)

Lake Hospital System Inc..................... C 440 833-2095
Willowick (G-15236)

Lakewood Hospital Association............ C 216 228-5437
Cleveland (G-4481)

Lakewood Hospital Association............ A 216 529-7201
Lakewood (G-9674)

Licking Memorial Hospital.................... B 740 348-7915
Heath (G-9135)

Licking Memorial Hospital.................... B 740 348-1750
Newark (G-11718)

Licking Memorial Hospital.................... B 740 348-4870
Newark (G-11719)

Licking Memorial Hospital.................... E 740 348-4137
Newark (G-11720)

Lima Memorial Hospital....................... A 419 228-3335
Lima (G-9925)

Lima Memorial Hospital La................... B 419 738-5151
Wapakoneta (G-14487)

Lima Memorial Joint Oper Co............... A 419 228-5165
Lima (G-9926)

Lodi Community Hospital..................... D 330 948-1222
Lodi (G-10019)

Ltac Investors LLC.............................. C 740 346-2600
Steubenville (G-13337)

Lutheran Medical Center Inc................ C 216 696-4300
Cleveland (G-4511)

Lutheran Medical Center Inc................ B 440 519-6800
Solon (G-13109)

Macdonald Hospital Resear.................. E 216 844-3888
Cleveland (G-4513)

Madison County Community Hospital... B 740 845-7000
London (G-10046)

Madison Family Health Corp................ E 740 845-7000
London (G-10047)

Madison Medical Campus..................... D 440 428-6800
Madison (G-10221)

Manor Care Inc................................... D 419 252-5500
Toledo (G-13905)

Marietta Memorial Hospital.................. D 740 401-0362
Belpre (G-1057)

Marietta Memorial Hospital.................. A 740 374-1400
Marietta (G-10384)

Mary Rutan Hospital............................ E 937 599-1411
West Liberty (G-14860)

Mary Rutan Hospital............................ A 937 592-4015
Bellefontaine (G-1034)

Marymount Hospital Inc....................... B 216 581-0500
Cleveland (G-4531)

Mayfield Spine Surgery Ctr LLC............ D 513 619-5899
Cincinnati (G-3021)

McCullough-Hyde Mem Hosp Inc.......... E 513 863-2215
Hamilton (G-9064)

McCullough-Hyde Mem Hosp Inc.......... B 513 523-2111
Oxford (G-12210)

MCN Health LLC................................. C 740 788-6000
Newark (G-11726)

Med America Hlth Systems Corp.......... A 937 223-6192
Dayton (G-7475)

Medcentral Health System................... B 419 683-1040
Crestline (G-7025)

Medcentral Health System................... C 419 526-8442
Mansfield (G-10292)

Medcentral Health System................... C 419 526-8970
Mansfield (G-10294)

Medcentral Health System................... B 419 526-8900
Ontario (G-12117)

Medcentral Health System................... C 419 342-5015
Shelby (G-13007)

Medcentral Health System................... A 419 526-8000
Mansfield (G-10293)

Medical Assoc of Zanesville.................. D 740 454-8551
Zanesville (G-15812)

Medina Hospital.................................. E 330 723-3117
Medina (G-10861)

Medina Hospital.................................. A 330 725-1000
Medina (G-10860)

Medone Hospital Physicians................. C 314 255-6900
Columbus (G-6223)

Memorial Hospital............................... C 419 547-6419
Clyde (G-5206)

Memorial Hospital............................... B 419 334-6657
Fremont (G-8693)

Memorial Hospital Union County.......... C 937 644-1001
Marysville (G-10498)

Mep Health LLC.................................. E 330 492-4559
Canton (G-1804)

Mercer Cnty Jint Twnship Cmnty.......... D 419 586-1611
Celina (G-1926)

Mercer Cnty Joint Townshp Hosp......... C 419 678-2341
Coldwater (G-5217)

Mercer Health.................................... D 419 678-4300
Coldwater (G-5218)

Mercy Franciscan Hosp Mt Airy............ A 513 853-5101
Cincinnati (G-3040)

Mercy Hamilton Hospital..................... E 513 603-8600
Fairfield (G-8430)

Mercy Health - Tiffin Hosp LLC............. B 419 455-7000
Tiffin (G-13632)

Mercy Health...................................... B 513 639-2800
Perrysburg (G-12356)

Mercy Health Anderson Hospital.......... A 513 624-4500
Cincinnati (G-3041)

Mercy Health Cincinnati LLC................ D 513 952-5000
Cincinnati (G-3042)

Mercy Health Dermatology.................. E 567 225-3407
Toledo (G-13915)

Mercy Health North LLC...................... A 419 251-1359
Toledo (G-13916)

SERVICES SECTION

HOSPITALS: Medical & Surgical

Mercy Hlth - Clermont Hosp LLC........... A 513 732-8200
  Batavia (G-743)
Mercy Hlth - Defiance Hosp LLC........... C 419 782-8444
  Defiance (G-7757)
Mercy Hlth - Sprngfeld Cncer C............ A 937 323-5001
  Springfield (G-13272)
Mercy Hlth - St Anne Hosp LLC............ D 419 407-2663
  Toledo (G-13917)
Mercy Hlth - St Chrles Hosp LL............ A 419 696-7200
  Oregon (G-12136)
Mercy Hlth - St Rtas Med Ctr L............ A 419 227-3361
  Lima (G-9934)
Mercy Hlth - St Vncent Med Ctr............ A 419 251-0580
  Toledo (G-13918)
Mercy Hlth - St Vncent Med Ctr............ A 419 251-3232
  Toledo (G-13919)
Mercy Hlth - Willard Hosp LLC............. C 419 964-5000
  Willard (G-15171)
Mercy Hospital.................................. C 513 870-7767
  Cincinnati (G-3044)
Mercy Hospital.................................. D 513 624-4590
  Cincinnati (G-3045)
Metrohealth System.......................... B 216 765-0733
  Beachwood (G-815)
Metrohealth System.......................... C 216 591-0523
  Beachwood (G-816)
Metrohealth System.......................... A 216 957-1500
  Cleveland (G-4562)
Metrohealth System.......................... C 216 696-3876
  Cleveland Heights (G-5181)
Miami Valley Hospital......................... B 937 208-7396
  Dayton (G-7488)
Miami Valley Hospital......................... B 937 208-4076
  Dayton (G-7490)
Miami Valley Hospital......................... A 937 438-2400
  Dayton (G-7491)
Miami Valley Hospital......................... B 937 208-4673
  Dayton (G-7493)
Miami Valley Hospital......................... B 937 208-7065
  Vandalia (G-14384)
Miami Valley Hospital......................... A 937 208-8000
  Dayton (G-7492)
Mid-Ohio Heart Clinic Inc................. E 419 524-8151
  Mansfield (G-10297)
Midohio Crdiolgy Vascular Cons........ E 740 420-8174
  Circleville (G-3713)
Midohio Crdiolgy Vascular Cons........ D 614 262-6772
  Columbus (G-6242)
Midwest Cmnty Hlth Assoc Inc........... C 419 633-4034
  Bryan (G-1488)
Mill Pond Family Physicians............... E 330 928-3111
  Cuyahoga Falls (G-7089)
Morrow County Hospital..................... B 419 949-3085
  Mount Gilead (G-11463)
Mount Carmel East Hospital............... A 614 234-6000
  Columbus (G-6265)
Mount Carmel Health.......................... C 614 308-1803
  Columbus (G-6266)
Mount Carmel Health.......................... D 614 986-7752
  Columbus (G-6267)
Mount Carmel Health.......................... C 614 234-0034
  Groveport (G-8993)
Mount Carmel Health.......................... C 614 527-8674
  Hilliard (G-9218)
Mount Carmel Health.......................... A 614 855-4878
  New Albany (G-11575)
Mount Carmel Health.......................... C 614 234-0100
  Westerville (G-15002)
Mount Carmel Health.......................... A 614 234-9889
  Worthington (G-15441)
Mount Carmel Health Plan Inc........... D 614 546-4300
  Columbus (G-6268)

Mount Carmel Health System............ A 614 856-0700
  Columbus (G-6269)
Mount Carmel Health System............ E 734 343-4551
  Columbus (G-6270)
Mount Carmel Health System............ B 614 860-0659
  Columbus (G-6271)
Mount Carmel Health System............ A 614 234-3355
  Columbus (G-6272)
Mount Carmel Health System............ A 614 679-2184
  Columbus (G-6273)
Mount Carmel Health System............ A 614 221-1009
  Columbus (G-6275)
Mount Carmel Health System............ E 614 663-5300
  Grove City (G-8937)
Mount Carmel Health System............ A 614 775-6600
  New Albany (G-11576)
Mount Carmel Health System............ A 614 234-9889
  Worthington (G-15442)
Mount Carmel Health System............ A 614 234-6000
  Columbus (G-6274)
Mt Carmel East Urgent Care.............. D 614 355-8150
  Columbus (G-6281)
Nationwide Childrens......................... E 407 782-0053
  Columbus (G-6309)
Nationwide Childrens Hospital........... C 513 636-6000
  Cincinnati (G-2111)
Nationwide Childrens Hospital........... B 614 722-5750
  Columbus (G-6310)
Nationwide Childrens Hospital........... B 614 355-1100
  Columbus (G-6311)
Nationwide Childrens Hospital........... C 614 355-9300
  Columbus (G-6312)
Nationwide Childrens Hospital........... C 614 355-9900
  Columbus (G-6314)
Nationwide Childrens Hospital........... A 614 722-5175
  Columbus (G-6315)
Nationwide Childrens Hospital........... C 614 355-8100
  Columbus (G-6316)
Nationwide Childrens Hospital........... C 614 355-9200
  Columbus (G-6317)
Nationwide Childrens Hospital........... C 614 355-9400
  Columbus (G-6318)
Nationwide Childrens Hospital........... C 614 355-6850
  Columbus (G-6319)
Nationwide Childrens Hospital........... E 614 355-8737
  Dublin (G-8069)
Nationwide Childrens Hospital........... D 419 221-3177
  Lima (G-9938)
Nationwide Childrens Hospital........... D 419 528-3140
  Mansfield (G-10303)
Nationwide Childrens Hospital........... C 614 355-6100
  Westerville (G-14916)
Nationwide Childrens Hospital........... B 614 866-3473
  Westerville (G-15005)
Nationwide Childrens Hospital........... D 614 355-8315
  Westerville (G-15006)
Nationwide Childrens Hospital........... C 740 588-0237
  Zanesville (G-15819)
Nationwide Childrens Hospital........... A 614 722-2000
  Columbus (G-6313)
Nationwide Chld Hosp Fundation....... E 614 355-5400
  Columbus (G-6324)
New Albany Surgery Center LLC....... C 614 775-1616
  New Albany (G-11581)
Newark Family Physicians Inc........... E 740 348-1788
  Newark (G-11735)
Niagara Health Corporation................ C 614 898-4000
  Columbus (G-6357)
Northeast Ohio Heart Assoc LLC....... D 440 352-9554
  Concord Township (G-6930)
Northwest Ohio Srgcal Spcalist.......... E 419 998-8207
  Lima (G-9941)

Oak Tree Physicians Inc..................... E 440 816-8000
  Cleveland (G-4676)
Ohio Dept Mntal Hlth Addction........... C 614 752-0333
  Columbus (G-6409)
Ohio Heart and Vascular..................... E 513 206-1800
  Cincinnati (G-3145)
Ohio Hlth Physcn Group Hritg C......... E 740 594-8819
  Athens (G-584)
Ohio Medical Group............................ E 440 414-9400
  Westlake (G-15091)
Ohio State Univ Wexner Med Ctr....... A 614 293-8000
  Columbus (G-6451)
Ohio State University......................... C 614 257-3000
  Columbus (G-6453)
Ohio Valley Medical Center LLC........ D 937 521-3900
  Springfield (G-13279)
Ohiohealth Corporation...................... D 614 566-5977
  Columbus (G-6466)
Ohiohealth Corporation...................... B 614 544-8000
  Dublin (G-8081)
Ohiohealth Corporation...................... A 614 788-8860
  Columbus (G-6465)
Ohiohealth Group Ltd........................ E 614 566-0056
  Columbus (G-6467)
Ohiohealth Physician Group Inc........ E 567 241-7000
  Mansfield (G-10309)
Ohiohlth Rverside Methdst Hosp....... A 614 566-5000
  Columbus (G-6468)
Osu Nephrology Medical Ctr.............. A 614 293-8300
  Columbus (G-6485)
Pam Specialty Hosp Dayton LLC....... B 937 384-8300
  Miamisburg (G-11080)
Parma Community General Hosp...... A 440 743-3000
  Parma (G-12260)
Patientpoint LLC................................ D 513 936-6800
  Cincinnati (G-3188)
Poison Information Center................. E 513 636-5111
  Cincinnati (G-3220)
Pomerene Hospital............................. B 330 674-1015
  Millersburg (G-11289)
Primary Care Ntwrk Prmier Hlth......... D 937 237-9575
  Huber Heights (G-9326)
Prime Healthcare Foundation............ B 740 623-4178
  Coshocton (G-6997)
Prime Hlthcare Fndtn-Cshcton L....... C 740 623-4013
  Coshocton (G-6998)
Promedica Cntning Care Svcs Co..... A 419 885-1715
  Sylvania (G-13561)
Promedica Gnt-Urinary Surgeons..... E 419 531-8558
  Toledo (G-13969)
Promedica Health System Inc.......... C 419 783-6250
  Defiance (G-7763)
Promedica Health System Inc.......... C 419 891-6201
  Maumee (G-10757)
Promedica Health System Inc.......... B 419 291-6720
  Sylvania (G-13562)
Promedica Health System Inc.......... C 419 291-2121
  Toledo (G-13970)
Promedica Health Systems Inc........ D 419 690-7700
  Oregon (G-12142)
Promedica Health Systems Inc........ A 419 824-1444
  Sylvania (G-13563)
Promedica Health Systems Inc........ B 419 578-7036
  Toledo (G-13973)
Promedica Health Systems Inc........ A 419 291-4000
  Toledo (G-13974)
Promedica of Sylvania Oh LLC.......... A 844 247-5337
  Sylvania (G-13564)
Promedica Toledo Hospital................ D 419 291-2051
  Toledo (G-13977)
Promedica Toledo Hospital................ E 419 291-8701
  Toledo (G-13978)

HOSPITALS: Medical & Surgical

Promedica Wldwood Orthpdic SPI......... C 419 578-7107
  Toledo *(G-13979)*
Regency Hospital Company LLC............ C 614 456-0300
  Columbus *(G-6573)*
Regency Hospital Company LLC............ D 440 202-4200
  Middleburg Heights *(G-11122)*
Regency Hospital Company LLC............ C 216 910-3800
  Warrensville Heights *(G-14587)*
Research Inst At Ntnwide Chld................ C 614 722-2700
  Columbus *(G-6580)*
Richmond Medical Center.......................... B 440 585-6500
  Richmond Heights *(G-12722)*
Riverside Hospital....................................... E 614 566-5000
  Columbus *(G-6595)*
Riverview Surgery Center.......................... E 740 681-2700
  Lancaster *(G-9739)*
Robinson Health System Inc..................... A 330 562-3169
  Aurora *(G-625)*
Robinson Health System Inc..................... A 330 677-3434
  Kent *(G-9594)*
Robinson Health System Inc..................... A 330 678-0900
  Kent *(G-9595)*
Robinson Health System Inc..................... A 330 297-0811
  Kent *(G-9596)*
Robinson Health System Inc..................... A 330 678-4100
  Kent *(G-9597)*
Robinson Health System Inc..................... A 330 297-8844
  Ravenna *(G-12642)*
Robinson Health System Inc..................... A 330 626-3455
  Streetsboro *(G-13426)*
Robinson Health System Inc..................... A 330 297-0811
  Ravenna *(G-12643)*
Salem Community Hospital....................... E 330 337-9922
  Salem *(G-12853)*
Salem Community Hospital....................... A 330 332-1551
  Salem *(G-12854)*
Samaritan Health Partners........................ A 937 208-8400
  Dayton *(G-7608)*
Samaritan N Surgery Ctr Ltd..................... E 937 567-6100
  Englewood *(G-8322)*
Samaritan Professional Corp.................... E 419 289-0491
  Ashland *(G-509)*
Samaritan Regional Health Sys................ D 419 281-1330
  Ashland *(G-511)*
Samaritan Regional Health Sys................ D 419 289-0491
  Ashland *(G-512)*
Samaritan Regional Health Sys................ B 419 289-0491
  Ashland *(G-510)*
Select Medical Corporation....................... E 216 983-8030
  Cleveland *(G-4891)*
Select Spcalty Hosp - Boardman.............. E 330 729-1750
  Youngstown *(G-15719)*
Select Spclty Hosp - Clmbs/AST............... B 614 293-6931
  Columbus *(G-6660)*
Select Spclty Hosp - Clmbus In................. A 614 291-8467
  Columbus *(G-6661)*
Shelby County Mem Hosp Assn................. E 937 492-9591
  Sidney *(G-13047)*
Shelby County Mem Hosp Assn................. A 937 498-2311
  Sidney *(G-13048)*
Sheltring Arms Hosp Fndtion In................ B 740 592-9300
  Athens *(G-589)*
Shriners Hspitals For Children.................. B 513 872-6000
  Cincinnati *(G-3372)*
Southast Ohio Srgcal Sites LLC................ E 740 856-9044
  Athens *(G-590)*
Southern Ohio Medical Center.................. D 740 259-5699
  Lucasville *(G-10181)*
Southern Ohio Medical Center.................. D 740 820-2141
  Minford *(G-11312)*
Southern Ohio Medical Center.................. A 740 354-5000
  Portsmouth *(G-12569)*
Southern Ohio Medical Center.................. D 740 356-8171
  Portsmouth *(G-12570)*
Southern Ohio Medical Center.................. D 740 356-5600
  Portsmouth *(G-12572)*
Southern Ohio Medical Center.................. E 740 356-5000
  Portsmouth *(G-12573)*
Southern Ohio Medical Center.................. C 937 544-8989
  West Union *(G-14873)*
Southern Ohio Medical Center.................. C 740 574-9090
  Wheelersburg *(G-15132)*
Southern Ohio Medical Center.................. C 740 574-4022
  Wheelersburg *(G-15133)*
Southern Ohio Medical Center.................. C 740 354-5000
  Portsmouth *(G-12571)*
Southstern Ohio Rgonal Med Ctr.............. E 740 439-3561
  Cambridge *(G-1584)*
Southwest Community Health Sys........... A 440 816-8000
  Middleburg Heights *(G-11128)*
Southwest General Health Ctr.................. A 440 816-8000
  Cleveland *(G-4923)*
Southwest General Med Group................ A 440 816-8000
  Middleburg Heights *(G-11129)*
Southwest Hlthcare Brown Cnty................ C 937 378-7800
  Georgetown *(G-8802)*
Specialty Hosp Cleveland LLC.................. E 216 592-2830
  Cleveland *(G-4929)*
Specialty Hospital of Lorain...................... E 440 988-6088
  Amherst *(G-433)*
Springboro Family Health Care................ E 937 748-4211
  Springboro *(G-13207)*
St Anne Mercy Hospital.............................. C 419 407-2663
  Toledo *(G-14025)*
St Elzabeth Boardman Hlth Ctr................. E 330 729-4580
  Boardman *(G-1292)*
St Johns West Shore Hosp Phrm.............. E 440 835-8000
  Westlake *(G-15111)*
St Joseph Riverside Hospital.................... A 330 841-4000
  Warren *(G-14555)*
St Vincent Charity Med Ctr........................ D 216 861-6200
  Cleveland *(G-4940)*
Steward Hllside Rhblttion Hosp................ D 330 841-3700
  Warren *(G-14559)*
Steward Northside Med Ctr Inc................ C 330 884-1000
  Warren *(G-14560)*
Steward Trumbull Mem Hosp Inc............. A 330 841-9011
  Warren *(G-14561)*
Stlukes Medical Imagery............................ E 419 893-4856
  Maumee *(G-10770)*
Stress Care/Bridges.................................. D 937 723-3200
  Dayton *(G-7647)*
Summa Akron Cy St Thmas Hsptal........... A 330 375-3159
  Akron *(G-313)*
Summa Barberton Citizens Hospital....... A 330 615-3000
  Barberton *(G-710)*
Summa Health.. C 330 375-3315
  Akron *(G-314)*
Summa Health.. D 330 864-8060
  Akron *(G-315)*
Summa Health.. A 330 615-5200
  Barberton *(G-711)*
Summa Health.. D 330 753-3649
  Barberton *(G-712)*
Summa Health.. D 330 926-0384
  Cuyahoga Falls *(G-7102)*
Summa Health.. D 330 836-9023
  Fairlawn *(G-8502)*
Summa Health.. D 330 688-4531
  Stow *(G-13396)*
Summa Health.. D 330 899-5500
  Uniontown *(G-14265)*
Summa Health Center Lk Medina............ D 330 952-0014
  Medina *(G-10894)*
Summa Health System............................... C 330 375-3000
  Akron *(G-317)*
Summa Health System............................... B 330 535-7319
  Akron *(G-318)*
Summa Health System............................... C 330 798-5026
  Akron *(G-319)*
Summa Health System............................... D 330 928-8700
  Akron *(G-320)*
Summa Health System............................... A 330 615-3000
  Barberton *(G-713)*
Summa Health System............................... A 330 334-1504
  Wadsworth *(G-14453)*
Summa Health System............................... D 330 375-3000
  Akron *(G-316)*
Superior Med LLC...................................... E 740 439-8839
  Cambridge *(G-1585)*
Surgery Alliance Ltd.................................. E 330 821-7997
  Alliance *(G-403)*
Surgical Associates Inc............................ D 740 453-0661
  Zanesville *(G-15831)*
Teater Orthopedic Surgeons..................... E 330 343-3335
  Dover *(G-7903)*
The Community Hospital of S.................... A 937 325-0531
  Springfield *(G-13300)*
The Medical Center At Eliza...................... C 937 223-6237
  Dayton *(G-7668)*
The Wadsworth-Rittman Area................... A 330 334-1504
  Wadsworth *(G-14456)*
Thornville Family Med Ctr Inc.................. E 740 246-6361
  Thornville *(G-13623)*
Trihealth Inc... B 513 624-5558
  Cincinnati *(G-3514)*
Trihealth Inc... B 513 794-5600
  Montgomery *(G-11376)*
Trihealth Inc... E 513 569-5400
  Cincinnati *(G-3517)*
Trihealth Evendale Hospital..................... C 513 454-2222
  Cincinnati *(G-3519)*
Trinity Health System............................... B 740 283-7000
  Steubenville *(G-13346)*
Trinity Hospital Holding Co...................... A 740 264-8000
  Steubenville *(G-13347)*
Trinity West... A 740 264-8000
  Steubenville *(G-13349)*
Tripoint Medical Center............................ A 440 375-8100
  Concord Township *(G-6936)*
Trumbull Mem Hosp Foundation............. D 330 841-9376
  Warren *(G-14567)*
Twin City Hospital..................................... E 740 922-6675
  Dennison *(G-7860)*
U Hcmc... D 216 721-3405
  Cleveland *(G-5044)*
Uc Health Llc... C 513 584-8600
  Cincinnati *(G-3545)*
Uc Health Llc... D 513 475-8300
  West Chester *(G-14782)*
Uc Health Llc... C 513 475-7458
  West Chester *(G-14783)*
Uh Regional Hospitals.............................. D 440 735-3900
  Bedford *(G-991)*
Uh Regional Hospitals.............................. A 440 285-6000
  Chardon *(G-2022)*
Uh Regional Hospitals.............................. D 440 585-6439
  Richmond Heights *(G-12723)*
Uhhs Westlake Medical Center................ E 440 250-2070
  Westlake *(G-15118)*
Uhhs-Memorial Hosp of Geneva.............. B 440 466-1141
  Geneva *(G-8791)*
Union Hospital Association..................... E 330 602-0719
  Dover *(G-7906)*
Union Hospital Association..................... A 330 343-3311
  Dover *(G-7907)*

SERVICES SECTION — HOTELS & MOTELS

University Cncnnati Med Ctr LL............... A 513 475-8300
  West Chester (G-14787)
University Cncnnati Med Ctr LL............... B 513 584-1000
  Cincinnati (G-3564)
University Hosp Geneva Med Ctr.............. D 440 415-0159
  Geneva (G-8792)
University Hospital................................. D 513 584-1000
  Cincinnati (G-3570)
University Hospital................................. D 440 835-8922
  Westlake (G-15120)
University Hospitals................................ D 216 536-3020
  Cleveland (G-5072)
University Hospitals Cleveland................. A 440 646-2626
  Beachwood (G-848)
University Hospitals Cleveland................. A 216 844-1000
  Cleveland (G-5073)
University Hsptals Clvland Med................ A 216 378-6240
  Beachwood (G-849)
University Hsptals Clvland Med................ A 216 342-5556
  Beachwood (G-850)
University Hsptals Clvland Med................ A 216 844-1369
  Cleveland (G-5075)
University Hsptals Clvland Med................ A 216 358-2346
  Cleveland (G-5076)
University Hsptals Clvland Med................ A 216 675-6640
  Cleveland (G-5077)
University Hsptals Clvland Med................ A 216 844-4663
  Cleveland (G-5079)
University Hsptals Clvland Med................ A 216 844-1767
  Cleveland (G-5080)
University Hsptals Clvland Med................ A 216 844-3528
  Cleveland (G-5081)
University Hsptals Clvland Med................ A 440 205-5755
  Mentor (G-11007)
University Hsptals Clvland Med................ A 216 844-3323
  Shaker Heights (G-12986)
University Hsptals Clvland Med................ A 216 844-1000
  Cleveland (G-5078)
University Hsptals Cnnaut Med................. D 440 593-1131
  Conneaut (G-6945)
University Hsptals St John Med................ A 440 835-8000
  Westlake (G-15121)
University Medical Assoc Inc.................... D 740 593-0753
  Athens (G-597)
University of Cincinnati............................ B 513 584-1000
  Cincinnati (G-3578)
University of Cincinnati............................ B 513 584-4396
  Cincinnati (G-3581)
University Primary Care Prac................... D 216 844-1000
  Cleveland (G-5085)
Upper Valley Medical Center.................... A 937 440-4000
  Troy (G-14166)
Uvmc Management Corporation............... C 937 440-4000
  Troy (G-14169)
Van Wert County Hospital Assn................ B 419 238-2390
  Van Wert (G-14357)
Van Wert Medical Services Ltd................. C 419 238-7727
  Van Wert (G-14360)
Vibra Hosp Mahoning Vly LLC.................. D 330 726-5000
  Youngstown (G-15748)
Wayne Health Corporation....................... A 919 736-1110
  Greenville (G-8890)
Wayne Healthcare................................... B 937 548-1141
  Greenville (G-8891)
Whetstone Medical Clinic Inc................... E 740 467-2787
  Millersport (G-11300)
Wilmington Medical Associates................ D 937 382-1616
  Wilmington (G-15279)
Wood County Hospital............................. A 419 354-8900
  Bowling Green (G-1336)

HOSPITALS: Specialty, NEC

Anderson Healthcare Ltd........................ E 513 474-6200
  Cincinnati (G-2197)
Arthur G Jmes Cncer Hosp Rchar............ B 614 293-4878
  Columbus (G-5388)
Aultman Hospital.................................... A 330 452-9911
  Canton (G-1679)
Covenant Care Ohio Inc......................... D 937 878-7046
  Fairborn (G-8370)
Edwin Shaw Rehab LLC.......................... D 330 436-0910
  Cuyahoga Falls (G-7071)
Greenbrier Senior Living Cmnty............... C 440 888-5900
  Cleveland (G-4339)
Hospice of The Western Reserve............. E 330 800-2240
  Medina (G-10841)
Hospice of Valley Inc............................. D 330 788-1992
  Girard (G-8815)
Liberty Nrsing Ctr Rvrside LLC................ E 513 557-3621
  Cincinnati (G-2974)
Lutheran Medical Center Inc................... C 216 696-4300
  Cleveland (G-4511)
Lutheran Medical Center Inc................... B 440 519-6800
  Solon (G-13109)
Salvation Army....................................... E 330 773-3331
  Cleveland (G-4873)
Select Spclty Hosp - Yngstown................ C 330 480-3488
  Youngstown (G-15720)
Sleepmed Incorporated........................... E 440 716-8139
  North Olmsted (G-11915)
Southeast Inc... B 614 225-0990
  Columbus (G-6695)
Stein Hospice Services Inc..................... C 419 502-0019
  Sandusky (G-12935)
University Hsptals Clvland Med............... A 216 844-1000
  Cleveland (G-5078)
University Hsptals Hlth Systm-................ B 440 285-4040
  Chardon (G-2024)
University Mednet................................... B 216 383-0100
  Euclid (G-8363)
Uvmc Nursing Care Inc.......................... C 937 473-2075
  Covington (G-7019)

HOTELS & MOTELS

1460 Ninth St Assoc Ltd Partnr................ E 216 241-6600
  Cleveland (G-3740)
16644 Snow Rd LLC................................ E 216 676-5200
  Beachwood (G-762)
5 Star Hotel Management IV LP................ E 614 431-1819
  Columbus (G-5288)
5145 Corporation.................................... D 330 659-6662
  Richfield (G-12684)
6300 Sharonville Assoc LLC.................... E 513 489-3636
  Cincinnati (G-2126)
A C Management Inc.............................. E 440 461-9200
  Cleveland (G-3748)
Aashna Corporation................................ E 614 871-0065
  Urbancrest (G-14318)
Aatish Hospitality LLC............................ E 937 437-8009
  New Paris (G-11637)
AFP 116 Corp... C 614 536-0500
  Columbus (G-5328)
Ahip OH Columbus Entps LLC................. D 614 790-9000
  Dublin (G-7925)
Akron Inn Limited Partnership................. D 330 336-7692
  Wadsworth (G-14426)
All Star Mgmt Inc................................... E 330 792-9740
  Austintown (G-635)
Alliance Hospitality Inc.......................... E 614 885-4334
  Columbus (G-5337)
Amish Door Inc...................................... C 330 359-5464
  Wilmot (G-15281)
Anishiv Inc... E 513 932-3034
  Lebanon (G-9754)
Ap/Aim Indpndnce Sites Trs LLC............. D 216 986-9900
  Independence (G-9405)
Apple Hospitality Five Inc....................... E 440 519-9500
  Solon (G-13066)
Apple Sven Hospitality MGT Inc............... E 513 248-4663
  Milford (G-11216)
Arbys.. E 740 369-0317
  Sunbury (G-13517)
Arvind Sagar Inc.................................... D 614 428-8800
  Columbus (G-5390)
Ashford Trs Clumbus Easton LLC............ E 614 473-9911
  Columbus (G-5392)
Athens OH State 405 LLC....................... E 740 593-5600
  Athens (G-556)
Avalon Resort and Spa LLC.................... C 330 856-1900
  Warren (G-14504)
Awe Hospitality Group LLC.................... E 330 888-8836
  Macedonia (G-10189)
Bansi & Pratima Inc............................... D 513 735-0453
  Batavia (G-727)
Beachwood Lodging LLC........................ E 216 831-3735
  Beachwood (G-768)
Bellefontaine Lodging Inc...................... D 937 599-6666
  Bellefontaine (G-1020)
Bennett Enterprises Inc.......................... C 419 893-1004
  Maumee (G-10699)
Best Western Adena Inn......................... E 877 722-3422
  Chillicothe (G-2051)
Best Western Caldwell Inn Inc................ E 740 732-7599
  Caldwell (G-1546)
Best Western Executive Inn.................... E 330 794-1050
  Akron (G-67)
Best Western Suites............................... D 614 870-2378
  Columbus (G-5435)
Bindu Associates LLC Elyria................... E 440 324-0099
  Amherst (G-424)
Black Sphire C Clmbus Univ 20.............. D 614 297-9912
  Columbus (G-5443)
Blissful Corporation............................... D 614 539-3500
  Grove City (G-8897)
Bob-Mor Inc.. C 419 485-5555
  Montpelier (G-11381)
Boulevard Motel Corp............................. C 440 234-3131
  Cleveland (G-3884)
Brighton Manor Company........................ B 216 241-3123
  Cleveland (G-3894)
Buckeye Hospitality Inc......................... E 614 586-1001
  Columbus (G-5475)
Buffalo-6305 Eb Associates LLC............. E 614 322-8000
  Columbus (G-5482)
Burton Carol Management....................... E 216 464-5130
  Cleveland (G-3912)
Ca-Mj Hotel Associates Ltd.................... D 330 494-6494
  Canton (G-1694)
Cambrdge Prperty Investors Ltd............. E 740 432-7313
  Cambridge (G-1557)
Cambria Green Management LLC............ E 330 899-1263
  Uniontown (G-14244)
Cambridge Associates Ltd...................... E 740 432-7313
  Cambridge (G-1558)
Carol Ruta... D 419 663-3501
  Norwalk (G-12004)
Ch Relty Iv/Clmbus Partners LP.............. D 614 885-3334
  Columbus (G-5550)
Chandni Inc... E 419 228-4251
  Lima (G-9873)
Charter Hotel Group Ltd Partnr................ E 216 772-4538
  Mentor (G-10920)
Chester Ave Hotel LLC........................... E 216 249-9090
  Cleveland (G-3967)

Employee Codes: A=Over 500 employees, B=251-500
C=101-250, D=51-100, E=20-50, F=10-19, G=1-9

HOTELS & MOTELS — SERVICES SECTION

Chillicothe Motel LLC .... D 740 773-3903
　Chillicothe *(G-2058)*

Cinci Hospitalities Inc .... E 513 398-8075
　Mason *(G-10531)*

Clermont Hills Co LLC .... D 513 752-4400
　Cincinnati *(G-2100)*

Cleveland Bchwood Hsptlity LLC .... D 216 464-5950
　Beachwood *(G-777)*

Cleveland Cbd Hotel LLC .... E 216 377-9000
　Cleveland *(G-4004)*

Cleveland East Hotel LLC .... D 216 378-9191
　Cleveland *(G-4042)*

Cleveland S Hospitality LLC .... D 216 447-1300
　Cleveland *(G-4065)*

Cmp I Blue Ash Owner LLC .... D 513 733-4334
　Blue Ash *(G-1154)*

Cni Thl Ops LLC .... E 937 890-6112
　Dayton *(G-7237)*

Cobb Motel Company LLC .... E 513 336-8871
　Mason *(G-10541)*

Columbia Properties Lima LLC .... C 419 222-0004
　Lima *(G-9875)*

Columbia Sussex Corporation .... E 937 898-4946
　Dayton *(G-7239)*

Columbus Arprt N Cssady Ht LLC .... D 614 475-7551
　Columbus *(G-5609)*

Columbus Concord Ltd Partnr .... D 614 228-3200
　Columbus *(G-5625)*

Columbus Easton Hotel LLC .... D 614 414-1000
　Columbus *(G-5630)*

Columbus Hospitality LLC .... E 614 461-2648
　Columbus *(G-5638)*

Columbus Hotel Partnership LLC .... D 614 890-8600
　Columbus *(G-5639)*

Columbus Lintel Inc .... E 614 871-0440
　Grove City *(G-8911)*

Columbus OH 0617 LLC .... E 614 855-9766
　Columbus *(G-5651)*

Comfort Inn .... D 740 454-4144
　Zanesville *(G-15783)*

Concord Dayton Hotel II LLC .... E 937 223-1000
　Dayton *(G-7245)*

Concord Hmltnian Rvrfront Ht L .... E 513 896-6200
　Hamilton *(G-9034)*

Concord Testa Hotel Assoc LLC .... D 330 252-9228
　Akron *(G-119)*

Continental RE Companies .... C 614 221-1800
　Columbus *(G-5695)*

Continental/Olentangy Ht LLC .... E 614 297-9912
　Columbus *(G-5698)*

Courtyard By Marriott .... E 937 429-5203
　Beavercreek *(G-874)*

Courtyard By Marriott .... E 216 765-1900
　Cleveland *(G-4132)*

Courtyard By Marriott .... E 937 433-3131
　Miamisburg *(G-11040)*

Courtyard By Marriott .... E 740 344-1800
　Newark *(G-11698)*

Courtyard By Marriott Rossford .... D 419 872-5636
　Rossford *(G-12766)*

Courtyard By Mrrott Columbus W .... E 614 771-8999
　Columbus *(G-5712)*

Courtyard By Mrrott Dytn-Nvrsi .... E 937 220-9060
　Dayton *(G-7258)*

Courtyard Management Corp .... E 216 901-9988
　Cleveland *(G-4133)*

Courtyard Management Corp .... E 614 436-7070
　Columbus *(G-5713)*

Courtyard Management Corp .... E 614 475-8530
　Columbus *(G-5714)*

Courtyard Management Corp .... E 419 866-1001
　Holland *(G-9284)*

Courtyard Management Corp .... E 419 897-2255
　Maumee *(G-10713)*

CPX Canton Airport LLC .... E 330 305-0500
　North Canton *(G-11819)*

Crossroads Hospitality Co LLC .... D 216 241-6600
　Cleveland *(G-4141)*

Cumberland Gap LLC .... E 513 681-9300
　Cincinnati *(G-2522)*

Days Inn .... D 740 695-0100
　Saint Clairsville *(G-12789)*

Days Inn Htels Athens Clmbus R .... E 740 593-6655
　Athens *(G-565)*

Days Inn Middletown .... D 513 420-9378
　Middletown *(G-11194)*

Days Inns of America .... E 330 345-1500
　Wooster *(G-15334)*

Dbp Enterprises LLC .... D 740 513-2399
　Sunbury *(G-13519)*

Dchm Inc .... D 330 874-3435
　Bolivar *(G-1293)*

Detroit Westfield LLC .... D 330 666-4131
　Akron *(G-133)*

Dhanlaxmi LLC .... D 614 871-9617
　Grove City *(G-8916)*

Donlen Inc .... D 216 961-6767
　Cleveland *(G-4177)*

Doro Inc .... E 740 695-1994
　Saint Clairsville *(G-12790)*

Doubletree By Hilton .... E 330 333-8284
　Youngstown *(G-15602)*

Dublin Hotel Ltd Liability Co .... E 513 891-1066
　Dublin *(G-7994)*

Econo Lodge .... D 216 475-4070
　Cleveland *(G-4205)*

Econo Lodge .... E 419 627-8000
　Sandusky *(G-12888)*

Equity Lodging LLC .... E 740 435-0427
　Cambridge *(G-1570)*

Fairfield Inn Stes Clmbus Arprt .... E 614 237-2100
　Columbus *(G-5844)*

Fairfield Inn .... E 614 267-1111
　Columbus *(G-5845)*

Fairlawn Associates Ltd .... C 330 867-5000
　Fairlawn *(G-8478)*

First Group America .... E 908 281-4589
　Cincinnati *(G-2673)*

First Hospitality Company LLC .... D 614 864-4555
　Reynoldsburg *(G-12663)*

First Management Company .... D 614 885-9696
　Columbus *(G-5864)*

First Tdt LLC .... D 419 244-2444
　Toledo *(G-13809)*

Future Lodging Northwood LLC .... E 419 666-2600
　Northwood *(G-11975)*

Gallipolis Hospitality Inc .... C 740 446-0090
　Gallipolis *(G-8756)*

Ganga Hospitality Ohio LLC .... E 614 870-3700
　Columbus *(G-5909)*

Gateway Hotel Ltd .... E 513 772-2837
　Sharonville *(G-12994)*

Good Venture Enterprises LLC .... E 740 282-0901
　Steubenville *(G-13327)*

Goodnight Inn Inc .... E 419 334-9551
　Fremont *(G-8682)*

Goodnight Inn Inc .... E 419 734-2274
　Port Clinton *(G-12527)*

Green Township Hospitality LLC .... D 513 574-6000
　Cincinnati *(G-2774)*

Hampton Inn .... E 513 752-8584
　Cincinnati *(G-2106)*

Hampton Inn .... E 937 387-0598
　Dayton *(G-7392)*

Hampton Inn .... E 740 282-9800
　Steubenville *(G-13329)*

Hampton Inn & Suite Inc .... E 440 234-0206
　Middleburg Heights *(G-11116)*

Hampton Inn Columbus East .... D 614 864-8383
　Pickerington *(G-12402)*

Hampton Inn Dry Ridge .... E 859 823-7111
　Cincinnati *(G-2797)*

Hampton Inn of Huber Heights .... E 937 233-4300
　Dayton *(G-7393)*

Hampton Inn Stow .... E 330 945-4160
　Stow *(G-13372)*

Hampton Inn Wooster .... D 330 345-4424
　Wooster *(G-15342)*

Hariom Associates Medina LLC .... D 330 723-4994
　Medina *(G-10839)*

Hauck Hospitality LLC .... D 513 563-8330
　Cincinnati *(G-2805)*

He Hari Inc .... D 614 436-0700
　Worthington *(G-15419)*

Hilton Garden Inn .... D 614 263-7200
　Columbus *(G-5994)*

Hilton Garden Inn .... D 614 539-8944
　Grove City *(G-8925)*

Hilton Garden Inns MGT LLC .... B 937 247-5850
　Miamisburg *(G-11061)*

Hilton Grdn Inn - Cleveland E .... E 440 646-1777
　Cleveland *(G-4365)*

Holiday Inn .... E 440 951-7333
　Mentor *(G-10947)*

Holiday Inn Ex Ht & Suites .... E 330 821-6700
　Alliance *(G-383)*

Holiday Inn Ex Ht Stes Lamalfa .... E 440 357-0384
　Mentor *(G-10948)*

Holiday Inn Express .... E 614 447-1212
　Columbus *(G-5998)*

Holiday Inn Express .... E 937 424-5757
　Dayton *(G-7407)*

Holiday Inn Express .... E 513 860-2900
　Fairfield *(G-8419)*

Hopkins Partners .... C 216 267-1500
　Cleveland *(G-4377)*

Hospitality Inc .... D 419 227-0112
　Lima *(G-9906)*

Host Cincinnati Hotel LLC .... C 513 621-7700
　Cincinnati *(G-2850)*

Hotel 1100 Carnegie Opco L P .... C 216 658-6400
　Cleveland *(G-4383)*

Hotel 50 S Front Opco L P .... D 614 885-3334
　Columbus *(G-6010)*

Hotel Dayton Opco L P .... D 937 432-9161
　Miamisburg *(G-11062)*

Hotel Stow LP .... E 330 945-9722
　Stow *(G-13375)*

Hyatt Corporation .... C 216 575-1234
　Cleveland *(G-4396)*

Hyatt Corporation .... D 614 463-1234
　Columbus *(G-6031)*

Hyatt Regency Columbus .... B 614 463-1234
　Columbus *(G-6033)*

IA Urban Htels Bchwood Trs LLC .... D 216 765-8066
　Beachwood *(G-801)*

Impac Hotel Group LLC .... E 440 238-8800
　Strongsville *(G-13465)*

Indiana Hospitality Group .... D 937 505-1670
　Springfield *(G-13258)*

Indus Airport Hotels II LLC .... D 614 235-0717
　Columbus *(G-6047)*

Inn At Wickliffe LLC .... E 440 585-0600
　Wickliffe *(G-15154)*

Inn Hampton and Suites .... E 614 473-9911
　Columbus *(G-6053)*

SERVICES SECTION
HOTELS & MOTELS

Inn Hampton and Suites .... E 440 324-7755
  Elyria (G-8262)
Jackson I-94 Ltd Partnership .... D 614 793-2244
  Dublin (G-8042)
Jag Guru Inc .... D 614 552-2400
  Columbus (G-6081)
Jagi Clvland - Indpendence LLC .... C 216 524-8050
  Cleveland (G-4431)
Jagi Springhill LLC .... E 216 264-4190
  Independence (G-9438)
Jai Bapa Swami LLC .... E 513 791-2822
  Blue Ash (G-1190)
Jai Guru II Inc .... D 614 920-2400
  Columbus (G-6082)
Janessa Inc .... D 740 687-4823
  Lancaster (G-9726)
Jay Ganesh LLC .... E 740 344-2136
  Newark (G-11710)
Kaival Corporation .... E 330 467-1981
  Macedonia (G-10196)
Kay Surati .... E 419 727-8725
  Toledo (G-13875)
Kenyon College .... E 740 427-2202
  Gambier (G-8774)
Khodiyar Inc .... E 419 589-2200
  Mansfield (G-10278)
Kishan Inc .... D 330 821-5688
  Alliance (G-386)
Kribha LLC .... E 740 788-8991
  Newark (G-11711)
Krish Hospitality LLC .... D 859 351-1060
  Dayton (G-7446)
Lake Erie Hospitality LLC .... D 419 547-6660
  Clyde (G-5205)
Lancaster Host LLC .... E 740 654-4445
  Lancaster (G-9731)
Landmark Star Properties Inc .... E 937 316-5252
  Greenville (G-8879)
Lane Avenue Hotel Holdings LLC ..... E 614 486-5433
  Upper Arlington (G-14279)
Lawnfield Mentor LLC .... E 440 205-7378
  Mentor (G-10963)
Liberty Ashtabula Holdings .... E 330 872-6000
  Newton Falls (G-11777)
Liberty Hospitality Inc .... E 330 759-3180
  Youngstown (G-15649)
Liberty Mahoning LLC .... E 330 549-0070
  North Lima (G-11891)
LLC Moon Dye .... E 440 623-9016
  Brecksville (G-1358)
Lodging Industry Inc .... E 419 625-7070
  Sandusky (G-12911)
Lq Management LLC .... E 513 771-0300
  Cincinnati (G-2992)
Lq Management LLC .... E 216 447-1133
  Cleveland (G-4507)
Lq Management LLC .... E 419 774-0005
  Mansfield (G-10283)
Mansfield Hotel Partnership .... E 419 529-1000
  Mansfield (G-10287)
March Investors Ltd .... E 740 373-5353
  Marietta (G-10382)
Marion Lodge .... E 740 389-4300
  Marion (G-10440)
Marriott .... E 440 243-8785
  Cleveland (G-4525)
Marriott .... E 440 234-6688
  Cleveland (G-4526)
Marriott Hotel Services Inc .... C 216 252-5333
  Cleveland (G-4527)
Marriott International Inc .... E 216 696-9200
  Cleveland (G-4528)

Mason Family Resorts LLC .... B 608 237-5871
  Mason (G-10577)
Meander Hsptality Group V LLC ..... E 740 948-9305
  Jeffersonville (G-9540)
Meander Hsptality Group II LLC ..... E 330 422-0500
  Streetsboro (G-13422)
Mentor Hospitality LLC .... E 440 951-7333
  Mentor (G-10969)
Mercer Hospitality Inc .... E 937 615-0140
  Piqua (G-12447)
Microtel Inn .... D 614 277-0705
  Grove City (G-8934)
Middletown Innkeepers Inc .... E 513 942-3440
  Fairfield (G-8431)
Mohammad Shoaib .... E 513 831-7829
  Milford (G-11244)
Moody Nat Cy Dt Clumbus Mt LLC ... E 614 228-3200
  Columbus (G-6259)
Motel Investments Marietta Inc ..... E 740 374-8190
  Marietta (G-10393)
Mrn-Newgar Hotel Ltd .... E 216 443-1000
  Cleveland (G-4607)
Mt Vernon Star Properties Inc .... E 740 392-1900
  Mount Vernon (G-11502)
N P Motel System Inc .... E 330 339-7731
  New Philadelphia (G-11660)
Naffah South LLC .... E 330 420-0111
  Lisbon (G-10006)
Natraj Corporation .... E 614 875-7770
  Grove City (G-8940)
Neighborhood Hospitality Inc .... E 740 588-9244
  Zanesville (G-15820)
Nf II Cleveland Op Co LLC .... E 216 443-9043
  Cleveland (G-4643)
Northern Tier Hospitality LLC .... E 570 888-7711
  Westlake (G-15089)
Northtowne Square Ltd Partnr .... E 419 691-8911
  Oregon (G-12137)
Ntk Hotel Group II LLC .... D 614 559-2000
  Columbus (G-6376)
Oakwood Hospitality Corp .... E 440 786-1998
  Bedford (G-978)
Oxford Hospitality Group Inc .... E 513 524-0114
  Oxford (G-12214)
Paradise Hotels LLC .... E 937 836-8339
  Englewood (G-8317)
Park & Spruce Acquisitions LLC ..... D 614 227-6100
  Columbus (G-6498)
Park Hospitality LLC .... E 419 525-6000
  Mansfield (G-10310)
Park Inn .... D 419 241-3000
  Toledo (G-13956)
Parkins Incorporated .... E 614 334-1800
  Hilliard (G-9226)
Patel LLC .... E 330 759-3180
  Youngstown (G-15689)
Payal Development LLC .... E 937 429-2222
  Beavercreek (G-892)
Peacock Hotels LLC .... E 330 725-1395
  Medina (G-10875)
Peitro Properties Ltd Partnr .... E 216 328-7777
  Cleveland (G-4736)
PH Fairborn Ht Owner 2800 LLC .... D 937 426-7800
  Beavercreek (G-894)
Pikes Inc .... E 440 275-2000
  Austinburg (G-633)
Playhouse Square Foundation .... C 216 615-7500
  Cleveland (G-4758)
Polaris Innkeepers LLC .... E 614 568-0770
  Westerville (G-14928)
Premier Hotels Inc .... E 419 747-2227
  Ontario (G-12123)

Priya Pvt Ltd .... D 740 389-1998
  Marion (G-10450)
Quail Hollow Management Inc .... C 440 639-4000
  Concord Township (G-6933)
Quality Inn Toledo Airport .... E 419 867-1144
  Holland (G-9301)
Quality Team Management Inc ...... E 937 490-2000
  Middletown (G-11182)
R & K Gorby LLC .... E 419 222-0004
  Lima (G-9953)
R P L Corporation .... E 937 335-0021
  Troy (G-14153)
Radha Corporation .... D 614 851-5599
  Columbus (G-6560)
Rama Inc .... D 614 473-9888
  Columbus (G-6561)
RB Knoxville LLC .... D 865 523-2300
  Columbus (G-6562)
Red Bank Hetzel LP .... E 513 834-9191
  Cincinnati (G-3276)
Red Roof Inns Inc .... E 330 644-7748
  Akron (G-277)
Red Roof Inns Inc .... E 330 499-1970
  Canton (G-1842)
Red Roof Inns Inc .... E 216 447-0030
  Cleveland (G-4814)
Red Roof Inns Inc .... E 440 892-7920
  Cleveland (G-4815)
Red Roof Inns Inc .... E 440 202-1521
  Cleveland (G-4816)
Red Roof Inns Inc .... E 614 267-9941
  Columbus (G-6567)
Red Roof Inns Inc .... D 614 224-6539
  Columbus (G-6568)
Red Roof Inns Inc .... E 740 288-1200
  Jackson (G-9524)
Red Roof Inns Inc .... E 937 866-0705
  Miamisburg (G-11088)
Red Roof Inns Inc .... E 330 758-1999
  Poland (G-12507)
Red Roof Inns Inc .... E 740 695-4057
  Saint Clairsville (G-12812)
Red Roof Inns Inc .... E 419 536-0118
  Toledo (G-13983)
Red Roof Inns Inc .... E 440 946-9872
  Willoughby (G-15220)
Red Roof Inns Inc .... A 614 744-2600
  New Albany (G-11584)
Renaissance Hotel MGT Co LLC ..... D 614 882-6800
  Westerville (G-14934)
Renaissance Hotel Operating Co .... A 216 696-5600
  Cleveland (G-4826)
Renaissance Hotel Operating Co .... B 614 228-5050
  Columbus (G-6577)
Req/Jqh Holdings Inc .... B 513 891-1066
  Blue Ash (G-1235)
Residence Inn .... E 614 222-2610
  Columbus (G-6581)
Residence Inn By Marriott .... E 513 771-2525
  Cincinnati (G-3291)
Residence Inn By Marriott LLC .... E 513 530-5060
  Blue Ash (G-1236)
Residence Inn By Marriott LLC .... E 614 222-2610
  Columbus (G-6582)
Residence Inn By Marriott LLC .... E 614 885-0799
  Columbus (G-6583)
Residence Inn By Marriott LLC .... E 440 392-0800
  Mentor (G-10992)
Residence Inn By Marriott LLC .... E 440 638-5856
  Middleburg Heights (G-11123)
Rhea Aryan Inc .... C 937 865-0077
  Miamisburg (G-11090)

HOTELS & MOTELS

Richfeld Bnquet Cnfrnce Ctr LL............. E 330 659-6151
  Richfield (G-12708)
Richfield Inn Inc.................................... E 248 946-5838
  Maumee (G-10762)
Ridgehills Hotel Ltd Partnr.................... D 440 585-0600
  Wickliffe (G-15162)
Riverview Hospitality Corp.................... D 330 339-7000
  New Philadelphia (G-11664)
Rlj III - Em Clmbus Lessee LLC............ D 614 890-8600
  Columbus (G-6601)
Rock Hotel Ltd LLC................................ E 216 520-2020
  Cleveland (G-4848)
Rockbridge Capital LLC........................ D 614 246-2400
  Columbus (G-6605)
Roschmans Restaurant ADM.................. E 419 225-8300
  Lima (G-9955)
Rukh-Jagi Holdings LLC....................... D 330 494-2770
  Canton (G-1848)
S & S Management Inc........................... D 937 235-2000
  Dayton (G-7601)
S & S Management Inc........................... D 567 356-4151
  Wapakoneta (G-14491)
S & S Management Inc........................... D 937 382-5858
  Wilmington (G-15272)
S & S Realty Ltd..................................... E 419 625-0362
  Sandusky (G-12928)
S&S Management.................................... E 937 332-1700
  Troy (G-14158)
Sachs Management Corp........................ D 740 282-0901
  Steubenville (G-13342)
Sahaj Hospitality Ltd.............................. D 740 593-5565
  Athens (G-588)
Saw Mill Creek Ltd................................ D 419 433-3800
  Huron (G-9392)
Sb Hotel LLC.. E 614 793-2244
  Dublin (G-8115)
Scioto Lodging Inc................................. D 740 851-6140
  Chillicothe (G-2091)
Select Hotels Group LLC....................... D 513 754-0003
  Mason (G-10606)
SGB Management Inc............................ E 614 539-1177
  Grove City (G-8954)
Shir-Sath Inc.. D 330 759-9820
  Girard (G-8825)
Shree Hospitality Corporation................ E 330 666-9300
  Copley (G-6963)
Shree Sava Ltd....................................... E 440 324-7676
  Elyria (G-8294)
Shree Shiv LLC...................................... E 419 897-5555
  Maumee (G-10765)
Shri Guru Inc... E 614 552-2071
  Columbus (G-6676)
Sidney Host LLC.................................... E 937 498-8888
  Sidney (G-13051)
Sk Hospitality LLC................................. C 419 294-3891
  Upper Sandusky (G-14293)
Sns Hospitality LLC................................ E 740 522-8499
  Heath (G-9140)
Solon Lodging Associates LLC............. C 440 248-9600
  Solon (G-13144)
Somnus Corporation............................... E 740 695-3961
  Saint Clairsville (G-12815)
Sortino Management & Dev Co............. E 419 627-8884
  Sandusky (G-12933)
Spring Hill Suites................................... E 513 381-8300
  Cincinnati (G-3399)
Sps Inc.. E 937 339-7801
  Troy (G-14160)
Staybridge Suites.................................... E 330 945-4180
  Stow (G-13391)
Strang Corporation................................. E 216 961-6767
  Cleveland (G-4955)

Strongsvlle Ldging Assoc I Ltd.............. D 440 238-8800
  Strongsville (G-13488)
Summit Hotel Trs 144 LLC.................... E 216 443-9043
  Cleveland (G-4958)
Sun Development & Mgt Corp............... C 614 801-9000
  Grove City (G-8957)
Sun Lodging LLC................................... E 330 670-0888
  Copley (G-6965)
Sunrise Hospitality Inc.......................... E 937 492-6010
  Sidney (G-13056)
Super 8.. E 419 529-0444
  Ashland (G-513)
Toledo Inn North LLC............................ E 419 476-0170
  Toledo (G-14059)
Town Inn Co LLC................................... D 614 221-3281
  Columbus (G-6775)
TownePlace Management LLC.............. D 419 724-0044
  Oregon (G-12145)
Travelodge Zanesville............................ E 740 453-0611
  Zanesville (G-15832)
Troy Hotel II LLC................................... E 937 332-1446
  Troy (G-14164)
Tudor Arms Mstr Subtenant LLC.......... D 216 696-6611
  Cleveland (G-5040)
Tuttle Inn Developers LLC.................... E 614 793-5500
  Dublin (G-8144)
Union Centre Hotel LLC........................ C 513 874-7335
  West Chester (G-14786)
United Hsptality Solutions LLC............. E 800 238-0487
  Buffalo (G-1521)
Universal Development MGT Inc.......... E 330 759-7017
  Girard (G-8829)
Uph Holdings LLC................................. D 614 447-9777
  Columbus (G-6826)
Valam Hospitality Inc............................ E 419 232-6040
  Van Wert (G-14354)
Valley Hospitality Inc............................ D 740 374-9660
  Marietta (G-10409)
Valley View Management Co Inc.......... E 419 886-4000
  Bellville (G-1052)
Velocity A Managed Svcs Co Inc.......... D 281 221-4444
  Holland (G-9312)
W & H Realty Inc.................................. E 513 891-1066
  Cincinnati (G-3636)
Wadsworth Hie Management Inc.......... D 330 334-7666
  Wadsworth (G-14457)
Welcome Hospitality Corp..................... E 937 325-5356
  Springfield (G-13311)
Westpost Columbus LLC....................... E 614 885-1885
  Columbus (G-6881)
Widewaters Edr Solon Ht Co LLC......... E 440 542-0400
  Solon (G-13164)
Winegrdner Hmmons Ht Group LLC..... C 513 891-1066
  Cincinnati (G-3674)
Wingate Inc... E 216 591-1061
  Cleveland (G-5151)
Wingate Inn.. E 614 844-5888
  Columbus (G-5285)
Wingate Inn.. D 330 422-9900
  Streetsboro (G-13436)
Woodson Operations One Ltd................ E 419 420-1776
  Findlay (G-8598)
Wright Executive Ht Ltd Partnr.............. D 937 426-7800
  Beavercreek (G-915)
Youngstown Hospitality LLC................. E 330 759-9555
  Youngstown (G-15758)
Youngstown Wlcome Hsptlity LLC........ C 330 759-6000
  Girard (G-8831)

HOUSEHOLD APPLIANCE STORES: Appliance Parts

Dayton Appliance Parts LLC................. E 937 224-0487
  Dayton (G-7270)
Merc Acquisitions Inc............................ C 216 524-4141
  Twinsburg (G-14205)
Trumbull Industries Inc.......................... D 800 477-1799
  Warren (G-14566)
V and V Appliance Parts Inc................. E 330 743-5144
  Youngstown (G-15745)

HOUSEHOLD APPLIANCE STORES: Gas Appliances

Big Sandy Furniture Inc........................ D 740 354-3193
  Portsmouth (G-12546)
Big Sandy Furniture Inc........................ D 740 574-2113
  Franklin Furnace (G-8653)

HOUSEHOLD FURNISHINGS, NEC

Casco Mfg Solutions Inc........................ D 513 681-0003
  Cincinnati (G-2318)
Ccp Industries Inc.................................. B 216 535-4227
  Richmond Heights (G-12716)
Nestaway LLC.. D 216 587-1500
  Cleveland (G-4636)

HOUSEWARES, ELECTRIC: Cooking Appliances

Nacco Industries Inc.............................. E 440 229-5151
  Cleveland (G-4616)

HYDRAULIC EQPT REPAIR SVC

American Hydraulic Svcs Inc................. E 606 739-8680
  Ironton (G-9502)
Dover Hydraulics Inc............................. D 330 364-1617
  Dover (G-7882)
Ohio Machinery Co................................ E 330 874-1003
  Bolivar (G-1296)

ICE

Lori Holding Co..................................... E 740 342-3230
  New Lexington (G-11628)
Velvet Ice Cream Company................... E 419 562-2009
  Bucyrus (G-1519)

ICE CREAM & ICES WHOLESALERS

United Dairy Farmers Inc...................... C 513 396-8700
  Cincinnati (G-3553)
Velvet Ice Cream Company................... E 419 562-2009
  Bucyrus (G-1519)

INCINERATORS

Novagard Solutions Inc......................... C 216 881-8111
  Cleveland (G-4668)

INCUBATORS & BROODERS: Farm

Chick Master Incubator Company.......... D 330 722-5591
  Medina (G-10819)

INDL & PERSONAL SVC PAPER WHOLESALERS

Aetna Building Maintenance Inc............ C 937 324-5711
  Springfield (G-13214)
Apex Environmental Services L............. C 513 772-2739
  Cincinnati (G-2208)
Avalon Foodservice Inc......................... C 330 854-4551
  Canal Fulton (G-1592)
Buckeye Paper Co Inc........................... E 330 477-5925
  Canton (G-1692)
Cleveland Supplyone Inc....................... E 216 514-7000
  Cleveland (G-4068)

SERVICES SECTION

INDL MACHINERY & EQPT WHOLESALERS

Commerce Paper Company.................. E 419 241-9101
  Toledo *(G-13750)*
Friendly Wholesale Co...................... E 724 224-6580
  Wooster *(G-15338)*
Gergelys Mint King Sups Svc In........... E 440 244-4446
  Lorain *(G-10076)*
I Supply Co....................................... C 937 878-5240
  Fairborn *(G-8377)*
Kaleel Bros Inc................................... D 330 758-0861
  Youngstown *(G-15644)*
Kellermeyer Company......................... D 419 255-3022
  Bowling Green *(G-1326)*
Millcraft Group LLC............................. D 216 441-5500
  Independence *(G-9452)*
Millcraft Paper Company..................... E 614 675-4800
  Columbus *(G-6249)*
Millcraft Paper Company..................... D
  Independence *(G-9453)*
Peck Distributors Inc.......................... E 216 587-6814
  Maple Heights *(G-10343)*
Ranpak Corp..................................... C 440 354-4445
  Concord Township *(G-6934)*
Rvc Inc... E 330 535-2211
  Akron *(G-291)*
Sofidel America Corp.......................... C 740 500-1965
  Circleville *(G-3724)*
Sysco Cincinnati LLC.......................... B 513 563-6300
  Cincinnati *(G-3430)*
The Cottingham Paper Co.................... E 614 294-6444
  Columbus *(G-6758)*
The Dean Supply Co........................... E 216 771-3300
  Cleveland *(G-4999)*
Trendco Supply Inc............................. E 513 752-1871
  Batavia *(G-750)*
Veritiv Operating Company................... E 513 285-0999
  Fairfield *(G-8452)*

INDL & PERSONAL SVC PAPER, WHOLESALE: Shipping Splys

Adapt-A-Pak Inc................................. E 937 845-0386
  Fairborn *(G-8365)*
Bath Bdy Wrks Lgstics Svcs LLC........... E 513 435-1643
  Groveport *(G-8974)*
Bath Bdy Wrks Lgstics Svcs LLC........... C 614 415-7500
  Columbus *(G-5421)*
Systems Pack Inc............................... E 330 467-5729
  Macedonia *(G-10207)*

INDL CONTRACTORS: Exhibit Construction

Benchmark Craftsman Inc.................... E 866 313-4700
  Seville *(G-12963)*
Boss Display Corporation..................... D 614 443-9495
  Columbus *(G-5456)*
Exhibit Concepts Inc........................... D 937 890-7000
  Vandalia *(G-14376)*
Greenheart Companies LLC.................. E 330 259-3070
  Youngstown *(G-15623)*

INDL DIAMONDS WHOLESALERS

Chardon Tool & Supply Co Inc.............. E 440 286-6440
  Chardon *(G-1997)*

INDL EQPT SVCS

3-D Service Ltd................................. C 330 830-3500
  Massillon *(G-10626)*
Commercial Electric Pdts Corp.............. E 216 241-2886
  Cleveland *(G-4094)*
Eagleburgmann Ke Inc........................ E 859 746-0091
  Cincinnati *(G-2596)*
Famous Enterprises Inc....................... E 330 762-9621
  Akron *(G-156)*

Forge Industries Inc........................... A 330 960-2468
  Youngstown *(G-15613)*
Graphic Systems Services Inc............... E 937 746-0708
  Springboro *(G-13199)*
Grob Systems Inc.............................. A 419 358-9015
  Bluffton *(G-1281)*
Interstate Lift Trucks Inc..................... E 216 328-0970
  Cleveland *(G-4421)*
Miami Industrial Trucks Inc.................. D 937 293-4194
  Moraine *(G-11425)*
Moyno Inc.. C 937 327-3111
  Springfield *(G-13275)*
Obr Cooling Towers Inc....................... E 419 243-3443
  Northwood *(G-11981)*
Primetals Technologies USA LLC........... E 419 929-1554
  New London *(G-11633)*
Quintus Technologies LLC.................... E 614 891-2732
  Lewis Center *(G-9834)*
Raymond Storage Concepts Inc............. E 614 275-3494
  Groveport *(G-8998)*
Raymond Storage Concepts Inc............. D 513 891-7290
  Blue Ash *(G-1232)*
Scott Fetzer Company......................... E 440 892-3000
  Westlake *(G-15105)*
Siemens Industry Inc.......................... E 800 879-8079
  Lebanon *(G-9788)*
Ssi Fabricated Inc.............................. E 513 217-3535
  Middletown *(G-11187)*
Towlift Inc.. E 614 851-1001
  Columbus *(G-6774)*
Towlift Inc.. E 419 666-1333
  Northwood *(G-11985)*
U S Molding Machinery Co Inc.............. E 440 918-1701
  Willoughby *(G-15224)*
Walker National Inc............................ E 614 492-1614
  Columbus *(G-6864)*
Winelco Inc....................................... E 513 755-8050
  West Chester *(G-14795)*

INDL MACHINERY & EQPT WHOLESALERS

Access Drywall Supply Co Inc............... E 614 890-2111
  Westerville *(G-14955)*
Addition Manufacturing Tech................. C 513 228-7000
  Lebanon *(G-9752)*
Aerocontrolex Group Inc...................... D 216 291-6025
  South Euclid *(G-13170)*
Alkon Corporation.............................. D 419 355-9111
  Fremont *(G-8665)*
Ats Systems Oregon Inc...................... C 541 738-0932
  Lewis Center *(G-9808)*
Automatic Feed Co............................. D 419 592-0050
  Napoleon *(G-11517)*
Automation Tooling Systems................ C 614 781-8063
  Lewis Center *(G-9810)*
Bevcorp LLC..................................... D 440 954-3500
  Eastlake *(G-8200)*
Bionix Safety Technologies Ltd............. E 419 727-0552
  Maumee *(G-10702)*
Blastmaster Holdings Usa LLC.............. D 877 725-2781
  Columbus *(G-5445)*
Bohl Crane Inc.................................. D 419 214-3940
  Toledo *(G-13708)*
Bostwick-Braun Company..................... D 419 259-3600
  Toledo *(G-13713)*
Brown Industrial Inc........................... E 937 693-3838
  Botkins *(G-1299)*
Cangen Holdings Inc........................... B 770 458-4882
  Blue Ash *(G-1140)*
Cbg Biotech Ltd Co............................ D 800 941-9484
  Solon *(G-13074)*
Cho Bedford Inc................................ E 330 433-2270
  North Canton *(G-11816)*

Cold Jet LLC..................................... C 513 831-3211
  Loveland *(G-10132)*
Combined Tech Group Inc.................... E 937 274-4866
  Dayton *(G-7240)*
Contitech Usa Inc.............................. D 937 644-8900
  Marysville *(G-10481)*
Ctm Integration Incorporated................ E 330 332-1800
  Salem *(G-12840)*
EMI Corp.. D 937 596-5511
  Jackson Center *(G-9531)*
Equipment Mfrs Intl Inc....................... E 216 651-6700
  Cleveland *(G-4217)*
Esec Corporation............................... E 614 875-3732
  Grove City *(G-8918)*
Feintool Equipment Corporation............ E 513 791-1118
  Blue Ash *(G-1172)*
Franklin Equipment LLC...................... E 937 951-3819
  Dayton *(G-7366)*
Freeman Manufacturing & Sup Co.......... E 440 934-1902
  Avon *(G-651)*
Freeman Schwabe Machinery LLC.......... E 513 947-2888
  Batavia *(G-740)*
G & P Construction LLC....................... E 855 494-4830
  North Royalton *(G-11941)*
Gei Wide Format Solutions.................. E 330 494-8189
  North Canton *(G-11834)*
Global EDM Inc................................. D 513 701-0468
  Mason *(G-10555)*
Gnco Inc.. E 216 706-2349
  Brooklyn Heights *(G-1419)*
Hannon Company............................... D 330 456-4728
  Canton *(G-1770)*
Hendrickson International Corp............. D 740 929-5600
  Hebron *(G-9143)*
Hydrotech Inc................................... D 888 651-5712
  West Chester *(G-14819)*
Intelligrated Inc................................ A 513 874-0788
  West Chester *(G-14820)*
Intelligrated Systems Inc..................... A 866 936-7300
  Mason *(G-10565)*
Intelligrated Systems Ohio LLC............. A 513 701-7300
  Mason *(G-10567)*
Jackson International Inc..................... E 866 379-2009
  Mineral Ridge *(G-11302)*
Ka Wanner Inc.................................. E 740 251-4636
  Marion *(G-10432)*
Kinetics Noise Control Inc.................... C 614 889-0480
  Dublin *(G-8049)*
Kraft Fluid Systems Inc....................... E 440 238-5545
  Strongsville *(G-13469)*
Kyocera SGS Precision Tls Inc.............. E 330 688-6667
  Cuyahoga Falls *(G-7086)*
Linden-Two Inc.................................. E 330 928-4064
  Cuyahoga Falls *(G-7087)*
Maple Mountain Industries Inc.............. E 330 948-2510
  Lodi *(G-10020)*
Mfh Partners Inc............................... B 440 461-4100
  Cleveland *(G-4571)*
Midwest Industrial Supply Inc............... E 330 456-3121
  Canton *(G-1807)*
Minerva Welding and Fabg Inc.............. E 330 868-7731
  Minerva *(G-11310)*
Multi Products Company...................... E 330 674-5981
  Millersburg *(G-11287)*
O S Walker Company Inc..................... E 614 492-1614
  Columbus *(G-6379)*
Oci LLC... D 513 713-3751
  Cincinnati *(G-3140)*
Park Corporation............................... B 216 267-4870
  Medina *(G-10874)*
Pines Manufacturing Inc...................... E 440 835-5553
  Westlake *(G-15098)*

Employee Codes: A=Over 500 employees, B=251-500
C=101-250, D=51-100, E=20-50, F=10-19, G=1-9

INDL MACHINERY & EQPT WHOLESALERS

Precision Tools Service Inc .... D 614 873-8000
  Plain City *(G-12490)*
Primetals Technologies USA LLC .... E 419 929-1554
  New London *(G-11633)*
Pro Quip Inc .... D 330 468-1850
  Macedonia *(G-10202)*
Reduction Engineering Inc .... E 330 677-2225
  Kent *(G-9593)*
Ridge Corporation .... E 740 513-9880
  Frazeysburg *(G-8657)*
RP Gatta Inc .... D 330 562-2288
  Aurora *(G-627)*
Rubber City Machinery Corp .... E 330 434-3500
  Akron *(G-288)*
Samuel Son & Co (usa) Inc .... D 740 522-2500
  Heath *(G-9138)*
Shawcor Pipe Protection LLC .... E 513 683-7800
  Loveland *(G-10159)*
Stolle Machinery Company LLC .... D 330 493-0444
  Canton *(G-1861)*
Stolle Machinery Company LLC .... D 330 494-6382
  North Canton *(G-11863)*
Stuertz Machinery Inc .... E 330 405-0444
  Twinsburg *(G-14221)*
Super Systems Inc .... E 513 772-0060
  Cincinnati *(G-3428)*
T J Automation Inc .... E 419 267-5687
  Archbold *(G-468)*
Transtar Industries Inc .... D 855 872-6782
  Cleveland *(G-5034)*
Union Process Inc .... E 330 929-3333
  Akron *(G-339)*
United Grinding North Amer Inc .... D 937 859-1975
  Miamisburg *(G-11100)*
US Advanced Systems LLC .... E 330 425-0020
  Twinsburg *(G-14226)*
W W Williams Midwest Inc .... E 330 225-7751
  Brunswick *(G-1474)*
Wardjet LLC .... D 330 677-9100
  Tallmadge *(G-13611)*
Winelco Inc .... E 513 755-8050
  West Chester *(G-14795)*
Yaskawa America Inc .... E 614 733-3200
  Plain City *(G-12498)*

INDL SPLYS WHOLESALERS

3b Holdings Inc .... E 800 791-7124
  Cleveland *(G-3745)*
All Ohio Threaded Rod Co Inc .... E 216 426-1800
  Cleveland *(G-3791)*
Alro Steel Corporation .... E 614 878-7271
  Columbus *(G-5340)*
Alro Steel Corporation .... D 419 720-5300
  Toledo *(G-13679)*
American Ring .... E 414 355-9206
  Solon *(G-13065)*
Anchor Flange Company .... D 513 527-3512
  Cincinnati *(G-2196)*
Applied Industrial Tech Inc .... B 216 426-4000
  Cleveland *(G-3827)*
Applied Mint Sups Slutions LLC .... E 216 456-3600
  Strongsville *(G-13443)*
Benchmark Industrial Inc .... D 614 695-6500
  Gahanna *(G-8711)*
Blackhawk Industrial Dist Inc .... E 918 610-4719
  Brunswick *(G-1451)*
Bonnie Plants LLC .... C 937 642-7764
  Marysville *(G-10476)*
Ci Disposition Co .... D 216 587-5200
  Brooklyn Heights *(G-1414)*
Continental .... E 937 644-8940
  Marysville *(G-10480)*

Cornerstone Controls Inc .... E 513 489-2500
  Cincinnati *(G-2509)*
Cornwell Quality Tools Company .... D 330 628-2627
  Mogadore *(G-11325)*
Cornwell Quality Tools Company .... E 330 335-2933
  Wadsworth *(G-14434)*
Dearing Compressor and Pump .... E 330 783-2258
  Youngstown *(G-15595)*
Fcx Performance Inc .... E 614 253-1996
  Columbus *(G-5853)*
Festo Corporation .... E 513 486-1050
  Mason *(G-10548)*
G M Industrial LLC .... C 440 786-1177
  Cleveland *(G-4298)*
General Factory Sups Co Inc .... E 513 681-6300
  Cincinnati *(G-2727)*
Ges Graphite Inc .... E 216 658-6660
  Parma *(G-12254)*
H3d Tool Corporation .... E 740 498-5181
  Newcomerstown *(G-11768)*
Hd Supply Facilities Maint Ltd .... D 440 542-9188
  Solon *(G-13094)*
Indelco Custom Products Inc .... E 216 797-7300
  Euclid *(G-8349)*
Industrial Cont Svcs - CA LLC .... B 614 864-1900
  Blacklick *(G-1111)*
Japo Inc .... E 614 263-2850
  Columbus *(G-6084)*
Kellermeyer Company .... D 419 255-3022
  Bowling Green *(G-1326)*
Lawrence Industries Inc .... E 216 518-7000
  Cleveland *(G-4483)*
Logan Clutch Corporation .... E 440 808-4258
  Cleveland *(G-4504)*
Mazzella Holding Company Inc .... D 513 772-4466
  Cleveland *(G-4534)*
McMaster-Carr Supply Company .... A 330 995-5500
  Aurora *(G-617)*
McWane Inc .... B 740 622-6651
  Coshocton *(G-6992)*
Merchandise Inc .... D 937 353-2200
  Miamitown *(G-11107)*
Mill-Rose Company .... C 440 255-9171
  Mentor *(G-10975)*
Motion Industries Inc .... E 937 236-7711
  Dayton *(G-7515)*
Noland Company .... C 937 396-7980
  Moraine *(G-11428)*
O K I Supply Co .... C 513 341-4002
  West Chester *(G-14826)*
Optimas Oe Solutions LLC .... E 740 774-4553
  Chillicothe *(G-2081)*
Precision Supply Company Inc .... D 330 225-5530
  Brunswick *(G-1468)*
Pressure Connections Corp .... D 614 863-6930
  Columbus *(G-6543)*
Samsel Rope & Marine Supply Co .... E 216 241-0333
  Cleveland *(G-4875)*
Samuel Son & Co (usa) Inc .... D 740 522-2500
  Heath *(G-9138)*
Scioto LLC .... B 937 644-0888
  Marysville *(G-10507)*
Setech Incorporated .... C 937 425-9482
  Moraine *(G-11437)*
SSP Fittings Corp .... D 330 425-4250
  Twinsburg *(G-14220)*
Steam Trbine Altrntive Rsrces .... E 740 387-5535
  Marion *(G-10455)*
Sunsong North America Inc .... E 919 365-3825
  Moraine *(G-11441)*
Superior Holding LLC .... E 216 651-9400
  Cleveland *(G-4964)*

SERVICES SECTION

The Cornwell Quality Tools Company .... D 330 336-3506
  Wadsworth *(G-14455)*
The Kindt-Collins Company LLC .... D 216 252-4122
  Cleveland *(G-5003)*
The Voto Manufacturers Sale .... E 740 282-3621
  Steubenville *(G-13345)*
Trumbull Industries Inc .... D 800 477-1799
  Warren *(G-14566)*
Vallen Distribution Inc .... E
  Monroe *(G-11354)*
W W Grainger Inc .... E 330 425-8388
  Macedonia *(G-10209)*
Watteredge LLC .... D 440 933-6110
  Avon Lake *(G-684)*
Wesco Distribution Inc .... D 216 741-0441
  Cleveland *(G-5131)*
Winsupply Inc .... E 937 294-5331
  Moraine *(G-11450)*
Wulco Inc .... E 513 379-6115
  Hamilton *(G-9093)*
Wulco Inc .... E 513 679-2600
  Cincinnati *(G-3682)*

INDL SPLYS, WHOLESALE: Abrasives

American Producers Sup Co Inc .... D 740 373-5050
  Marietta *(G-10355)*
Lake Erie Abrasive & Tool Inc .... E 216 692-2778
  Euclid *(G-8353)*
Mirka USA Inc .... D 330 963-6421
  Twinsburg *(G-14206)*

INDL SPLYS, WHOLESALE: Adhesives, Tape & Plasters

Gorilla Glue Company LLC .... B 513 271-3300
  Cincinnati *(G-2743)*

INDL SPLYS, WHOLESALE: Bearings

Applied Indus Tech - CA LLC .... B 216 426-4000
  Cleveland *(G-3825)*
Bdi Inc .... C 216 642-9100
  Cleveland *(G-3858)*
Bearing & Drive Systems Inc .... D 440 846-4272
  Strongsville *(G-13445)*
Bearing Distributors Inc .... C 216 642-9100
  Cleveland *(G-3860)*
Bearing Technologies Ltd .... D 800 597-3486
  Avon Lake *(G-675)*
Belting Company of Cincinnati .... D 937 498-2104
  Sidney *(G-13022)*
Belting Company of Cincinnati .... C 513 621-9050
  Cincinnati *(G-2256)*
Catensys US Inc .... B 330 273-4383
  Strongsville *(G-13447)*
Forge Industries Inc .... A 330 960-2468
  Youngstown *(G-15613)*
Miba Bearings US LLC .... B 740 962-4242
  Mcconnelsville *(G-10803)*
North Coast Bearings LLC .... E 440 930-7600
  Avon *(G-662)*
Timken Company .... D 419 563-2200
  Bucyrus *(G-1518)*
Timken Company .... E 234 262-3000
  Niles *(G-11797)*
Timken Corporation .... E 330 471-3378
  North Canton *(G-11866)*

INDL SPLYS, WHOLESALE: Bins & Containers, Storage

Williams Scotsman Inc .... E 216 399-6285
  Hinckley *(G-9273)*

SERVICES SECTION

INDL SPLYS, WHOLESALE: Fasteners & Fastening Eqpt

Ackerman Chacco Company Inc............ E 513 791-4252
  Blue Ash *(G-1121)*
Supply Technologies LLC....................... E 440 248-8170
  Solon *(G-13151)*

INDL SPLYS, WHOLESALE: Gaskets

Thermodyn Corporation.......................... E 419 841-7782
  Sylvania *(G-13577)*

INDL SPLYS, WHOLESALE: Gaskets & Seals

Buckeye Rubber & Packing Co................ E 216 464-8900
  Beachwood *(G-771)*

INDL SPLYS, WHOLESALE: Glass Bottles

Bottle Solutions LLC............................... E 216 889-3330
  Cleveland *(G-3883)*
Cincinnati Container Company................ E 513 874-6874
  West Chester *(G-14804)*
Cleveland Supplyone Inc........................ E 216 514-7000
  Cleveland *(G-4068)*

INDL SPLYS, WHOLESALE: Mill Splys

Allied Supply Company Inc..................... E 937 224-9833
  Dayton *(G-7164)*
Kirby Risk Corporation........................... D 419 221-0123
  Lima *(G-9915)*

INDL SPLYS, WHOLESALE: Power Transmission, Eqpt & Apparatus

Allied Power Transmission Co................ E 440 708-1006
  Chagrin Falls *(G-1972)*
Binkelman Corporation........................... E 419 537-9333
  Bowling Green *(G-1308)*
Commercial Electric Pdts Corp............... E 216 241-2886
  Cleveland *(G-4094)*
Great Lakes Power Products Inc............ D 440 951-5111
  Mentor *(G-10943)*
Ohio Transmission LLC.......................... C 614 342-6247
  Columbus *(G-6463)*

INDL SPLYS, WHOLESALE: Rubber Goods, Mechanical

Datwyler Sling Sltions USA Inc............... D 937 387-2800
  Vandalia *(G-14373)*
Johnson Bros Rubber Co....................... D 419 853-4122
  West Salem *(G-14863)*
The D S Brown Company....................... C 419 257-3561
  North Baltimore *(G-11802)*

INDL SPLYS, WHOLESALE: Seals

Datwyler Sling Sltions USA Inc............... D 937 387-2800
  Vandalia *(G-14373)*
McNeil Industries Inc............................. E 440 951-7756
  Painesville *(G-12236)*

INDL SPLYS, WHOLESALE: Tools

B W Grinding Co.................................... E 419 923-1376
  Lyons *(G-10187)*
H & D Steel Service Inc......................... E 800 666-3390
  North Royalton *(G-11942)*
Pennsylvania Tl Sls & Svc Inc................ D 330 758-0845
  Youngstown *(G-15692)*

INDL SPLYS, WHOLESALE: Valves & Fittings

Crane Pumps & Systems Inc.................. C 937 773-2442
  Piqua *(G-12440)*

Dayton Windustrial Co........................... E 937 461-2603
  Dayton *(G-7306)*
Famous Distribution Inc......................... D 330 762-9621
  Akron *(G-154)*
Ferguson Enterprises LLC..................... E 513 771-6000
  Cincinnati *(G-2658)*
Fulflo Specialties Company.................... E 937 783-2411
  Blanchester *(G-1117)*
Lakeside Supply Co............................... E 216 941-6800
  Cleveland *(G-4478)*
PHD Manufacturing Inc.......................... C 330 482-9256
  Columbiana *(G-5238)*
Pipe Products Inc.................................. C 513 587-7532
  West Chester *(G-14742)*
Pipe-Valves Inc..................................... E 614 294-4971
  Columbus *(G-6526)*
Shaq Inc... D 770 427-0402
  Beachwood *(G-836)*
Swagelok Company................................ D 440 349-5962
  Solon *(G-13152)*
Swagelok Company................................ E 440 542-1250
  Solon *(G-13153)*
Victory White Metal Company................. D 216 271-1400
  Cleveland *(G-5104)*

INDL TRUCK REPAIR SVCS

Aim Integrated Logistics Inc................... B 330 759-0438
  Girard *(G-8808)*
All Lift Service Company Inc.................. E 440 585-1542
  Willoughby *(G-15183)*
Fallsway Equipment Co Inc.................... C 330 633-6000
  Akron *(G-152)*
Great Lakes-Ramco Inc......................... E 586 759-5500
  Mentor *(G-10944)*
Toyota Industries N Amer Inc................. D 937 237-0976
  Dayton *(G-7675)*

INDUSTRIAL & COMMERCIAL EQPT INSPECTION SVCS

Cec Combustion Safety LLC................... E 216 749-2992
  Brookpark *(G-1430)*
Ohio Fabricators Inc.............................. D 330 745-4406
  Akron *(G-250)*
Predictive Service LLC........................... D 866 772-6770
  Cleveland *(G-4766)*
Quintus Technologies LLC..................... E 614 891-2732
  Lewis Center *(G-9834)*

INFORMATION RETRIEVAL SERVICES

AGS Custom Graphics Inc..................... D 330 963-7770
  Macedonia *(G-10188)*
Armstrong Utilities Inc.......................... D 330 723-3536
  Medina *(G-10808)*
Atlas Partners LLC................................ C 937 439-7970
  Dayton *(G-7183)*
Bluespring Software Inc........................ E 513 794-1764
  Blue Ash *(G-1138)*
Com Net Inc.. D 419 739-3100
  Wapakoneta *(G-14481)*
Community Isp Inc................................. E 419 867-6060
  Toledo *(G-13752)*
End-User Computing Inc........................ D 419 292-2200
  Toledo *(G-13793)*
Hkm Drect Mkt Cmmnications Inc.......... C 800 860-4456
  Cleveland *(G-4367)*
Innovative Technologies Corp................ D 937 252-2145
  Dayton *(G-7135)*
Medical Mutual Services LLC................. C 440 878-4800
  Strongsville *(G-13475)*
Png Telecommunications Inc.................. D 513 942-7900
  Cincinnati *(G-3218)*

INSTRUMENTS: Medical & Surgical

Relx Inc.. C 937 865-1012
  Dayton *(G-7141)*
Security Hut Inc.................................... D 216 226-0461
  Lakewood *(G-9685)*
TSC Communications Inc....................... D 419 739-2200
  Wapakoneta *(G-14492)*

INFORMATION SVCS: Consumer

Action For Children Inc.......................... E 614 224-0222
  Columbus *(G-5310)*
Research Associates Inc....................... D 440 892-1000
  Cleveland *(G-4828)*

INSECTICIDES

Abbott Laboratories............................... D 847 937-6100
  Columbus *(G-5294)*

INSECTICIDES & PESTICIDES

Scotts Miracle-Gro Company.................. B 937 644-0011
  Marysville *(G-10509)*

INSPECTION & TESTING SVCS

Acuren Inspection Inc............................ C 513 671-7073
  West Chester *(G-14646)*
Benchmark National Corporation............ E 419 843-6691
  Bellevue *(G-1043)*
Benchmark National Corporation............ E 419 424-0900
  Findlay *(G-8511)*
Contrlled Envmt Crtfction Svcs.............. E 513 870-0293
  Cincinnati *(G-2503)*
Csa Amrica Tstg Crtfcation LLC............. B 216 524-4990
  Independence *(G-9427)*
National Bd of Bler Prssure Vs.............. D 614 888-8320
  Columbus *(G-6289)*
Servicelink Field Services LLC............... A 440 424-0058
  Solon *(G-13141)*
US Inspection Services Inc.................... D 513 671-7073
  Cincinnati *(G-3606)*

INSTRUMENTS, MEASURING & CONTROLLING: Cable Testing

Multilink Inc.. C 440 366-6966
  Elyria *(G-8276)*

INSTRUMENTS: Analytical

Bionix Safety Technologies Ltd............... E 419 727-0552
  Maumee *(G-10702)*
Dentronix Inc.. D 330 916-7300
  Cuyahoga Falls *(G-7070)*
Orton Edward Jr Crmic Fndation............. E 614 895-2663
  Westerville *(G-14926)*
Teledyne Instruments Inc...................... E 513 229-7000
  Mason *(G-10614)*

INSTRUMENTS: Measurement, Indl Process

Command Alkon Incorporated................. E 614 799-0600
  Dublin *(G-7967)*

INSTRUMENTS: Measuring & Controlling

Interstop Corporation............................ E 513 272-1133
  Cincinnati *(G-2884)*
Modal Shop Inc..................................... D 513 351-9919
  Cincinnati *(G-3073)*

INSTRUMENTS: Measuring, Electrical Energy

Drs Signal Technologies Inc................... E 937 429-7470
  Beavercreek *(G-878)*
Westerman Inc...................................... C 800 338-8265
  Bremen *(G-1372)*

INSTRUMENTS: Medical & Surgical

INSTRUMENTS: Medical & Surgical

Abbott Laboratories................................. D 847 937-6100
Columbus *(G-5294)*

Applied Medical Technology Inc............ E 440 717-4000
Brecksville *(G-1343)*

Beam Technologies Inc........................... B 800 648-1179
Columbus *(G-5428)*

Casco Mfg Solutions Inc......................... D 513 681-0003
Cincinnati *(G-2318)*

Dentronix Inc... D 330 916-7300
Cuyahoga Falls *(G-7070)*

General Data Company Inc..................... B 513 752-7978
Cincinnati *(G-2105)*

Haag-Streit Usa Inc................................. D 513 398-3937
Mason *(G-10559)*

KMC Holdings LLC................................... C 419 238-2442
Van Wert *(G-14347)*

Morris Technologies Inc.......................... E 513 733-1611
Cincinnati *(G-3080)*

Thermo Fisher Scientific Inc.................... E 800 871-8909
Oakwood Village *(G-12059)*

INSTRUMENTS: Radio Frequency Measuring

Resonant Sciences LLC........................... E 937 431-8180
Beavercreek *(G-929)*

INSTRUMENTS: Signal Generators & Averagers

Adams Elevator Equipment Co................ D 847 581-2900
Holland *(G-9276)*

INSTRUMENTS: Test, Electrical, Engine

Nu-Di Products Co Inc............................. D 216 251-9070
Cleveland *(G-4672)*

INSTRUMENTS: Test, Electronic & Electric Measurement

Bionix Safety Technologies Ltd............... E 419 727-0552
Maumee *(G-10702)*

Keithley Instruments LLC....................... C 440 248-0400
Solon *(G-13103)*

Vmetro Inc.. D 281 584-0728
Fairborn *(G-8386)*

INSULATION MATERIALS WHOLESALERS

Alpine Insulation I LLC............................ D 614 221-3399
Columbus *(G-5339)*

Installed Building Pdts Inc...................... C 614 221-3399
Columbus *(G-6057)*

Owens-Corning Fiberglas Corp............... E 419 248-8000
Toledo *(G-13954)*

Pfb Manufacturing LLC........................... E 513 836-3232
Lebanon *(G-9782)*

R E Kramig & Co Inc................................ C 513 761-4010
Cincinnati *(G-3270)*

INSULATION: Fiberglass

Owens Corning Sales LLC....................... A 419 248-8000
Toledo *(G-13952)*

INSULATORS & INSULATION MATERIALS: Electrical

Koebbe Products Inc............................... D 513 753-4200
Amelia *(G-417)*

INSURANCE AGENTS, NEC

A A Hammersmith Insurance Inc............ E 330 832-7411
Massillon *(G-10627)*

A-1 General Insurance Agency................ D 216 986-3000
Cleveland *(G-3752)*

Aba Insurance Services Inc.................... D 800 274-5222
Shaker Heights *(G-12972)*

All America Insurance Company............. B 419 238-1010
Van Wert *(G-14340)*

American Family Home Insur Co............ E 513 943-7100
Amelia *(G-411)*

American Fidelity Assurance Co............. E 800 437-1011
Columbus *(G-5350)*

American Highways Insur Agcy.............. E 330 659-8900
Richfield *(G-12686)*

American Modrn Select Insur Co............ C 513 943-7100
Amelia *(G-414)*

American Mutl Share Insur Corp............ E 614 764-1900
Dublin *(G-7936)*

Andrew Insurance Associates................. D 614 336-8030
Dublin *(G-7938)*

Auto-Owners Life Insurance Co.............. E 419 227-1452
Lima *(G-9866)*

Auto-Owners Life Insurance Co.............. E 419 887-1218
Maumee *(G-10696)*

Bazemore Insurance Group LLC............. E 614 559-8585
Columbus *(G-5424)*

Beecher Carlson Insur Svcs LLC............. D 330 726-8177
Youngstown *(G-15556)*

Benefit Services Inc................................ D 330 666-0337
Copley *(G-6948)*

Brands Insurance Agency Inc................. E 513 777-7775
West Chester *(G-14654)*

Brooker Insurance Agency Inc................ E 440 238-5454
Strongsville *(G-13446)*

Brooks & Stafford Co............................... E 216 696-3000
Cleveland *(G-3904)*

Brown & Brown of Ohio LLC.................. E 419 874-1974
Perrysburg *(G-12319)*

Brunswick Insurance Agency.................. E 330 864-8800
Cleveland *(G-3907)*

Cincinnati Casualty Company................. C 513 870-2000
Fairfield *(G-8401)*

Cincinnati Indeminty Co.......................... D 513 870-2000
Fairfield *(G-8403)*

Cincinnati Life Insurance Co................... A 513 870-2000
Fairfield *(G-8405)*

Clark Theders Insurance Agency............ E 513 779-2800
West Chester *(G-14669)*

Cornerstone Brk Insur Svcs AGC............ E 513 241-7675
Cincinnati *(G-2508)*

Donald P Pipino Company Ltd................ D 330 726-8177
Youngstown *(G-15601)*

Erie Indemnity Company......................... C 330 433-6300
Canton *(G-1748)*

Erie Insur Exch Actvties Assn................. E 330 433-1925
Canton *(G-1749)*

Erie Insur Exch Actvties Assn................. E 614 430-8530
Columbus *(G-5826)*

Evarts-Tremaine-Flicker Co..................... E 216 621-7183
Cleveland *(G-4225)*

Explorer Rv Insurance Agcy Inc.............. E 330 659-8900
Richfield *(G-12697)*

Fedeli Group LLC..................................... D 216 328-8080
Cleveland *(G-4244)*

Galt Enterprises Inc................................. E 216 464-6744
Moreland Hills *(G-11452)*

Gardiner Allen Drbrts Insur LL................ E 614 221-1500
Columbus *(G-5913)*

Geico General Insurance Co................... B 513 794-3426
Cincinnati *(G-2722)*

Grange Life Insurance Company............. E 800 445-3030
Columbus *(G-5948)*

Hagerty Insurance Agency LLC.............. D 877 922-9701
Dublin *(G-8025)*

Hauser Inc.. D 513 745-9200
Cincinnati *(G-2806)*

SERVICES SECTION

Health Management Solutions................ E 419 536-5690
Maumee *(G-10730)*

Holtz Agency Ltd...................................... E 513 671-7220
Cincinnati *(G-2832)*

Huntington Insurance Inc........................ C 419 720-7900
Columbus *(G-6017)*

Hylant Administrative Services............... E 419 255-1020
Toledo *(G-13857)*

Hylant Group Inc...................................... D 419 255-1020
Toledo *(G-13858)*

Insurance Intermediaries Inc.................. A 614 846-1111
Columbus *(G-6060)*

Insurance Partners Agency LLC............. E 330 493-3211
Canton *(G-1781)*

Insurancecom Inc.................................... D 440 498-0001
Solon *(G-13100)*

Insurnce Office Centl Ohio Inc................ E 614 939-5471
New Albany *(G-11569)*

Insurnce Specialists Group Inc.............. E 440 975-0309
Chardon *(G-2007)*

Integrity Mutual Insurance Co................. D 920 734-4511
Columbus *(G-6063)*

Knight Insurance Agency Inc.................. E 419 241-5133
Toledo *(G-13880)*

Lang Financial Group Inc........................ E 513 699-2966
Blue Ash *(G-1199)*

Lighthouse Insurance Group LLC........... E 216 503-2439
Independence *(G-9445)*

McGohan/Brabender Agency Inc........... E 937 293-1600
Moraine *(G-11421)*

McGowan & Company Inc...................... D 800 545-1538
Cleveland *(G-4537)*

Medical Mutual of Ohio........................... C 216 292-0400
Cleveland *(G-4546)*

Medical Mutual of Ohio........................... C 419 473-7100
Rossford *(G-12768)*

Medical Mutual of Ohio........................... A 216 687-7000
Cleveland *(G-4545)*

Mennonite Mutual Insurance Co............. D 330 682-2986
Orrville *(G-12170)*

Mutual Health Services Company.......... B 216 687-7000
Cleveland *(G-4614)*

National Auto Care Corporation............. E 800 548-1875
Westerville *(G-14914)*

National General Insurance Co............... E 212 380-9462
Cleveland *(G-4627)*

Nationwide... E 800 421-3535
Canton *(G-1818)*

Nationwide Affinity Insur Amer............... B 614 249-2141
Columbus *(G-6304)*

Nationwide Bank...................................... C 800 882-2822
Columbus *(G-6307)*

Nationwide Corporation........................... E 614 249-7111
Columbus *(G-6326)*

Nationwide Fncl Instn Dstrs AG.............. D 614 249-6825
Columbus *(G-6330)*

Nationwide Insrnce Spnning Ins............. E 408 520-6420
London *(G-10048)*

Nationwide Lf Annuity Insur Co.............. A 614 249-7111
Columbus *(G-6334)*

Nationwide Life Insur Co Amer............... A 800 688-5177
Columbus *(G-6335)*

Nationwide Mutl Fire Insur Co................ E 614 249-7111
Columbus *(G-6337)*

Nationwide Mutual Insurance Co........... E 330 489-5000
Canton *(G-1819)*

Nationwide Mutual Insurance Co........... E 614 249-7654
Columbus *(G-6339)*

Nationwide Mutual Insurance Co........... E 614 899-6300
Columbus *(G-6340)*

Nationwide Mutual Insurance Co........... E 614 734-1276
Dublin *(G-8071)*

SERVICES SECTION

INSURANCE CLAIM PROCESSING, EXC MEDICAL

Nationwide Mutual Insurance Co............ D 614 430-3047
   Lewis Center *(G-9830)*

Nationwide Prperty Cslty Insur................ D 614 677-8166
   Columbus *(G-6341)*

Neace Assoc Insur Agcy of Ohio............ E 614 224-0772
   Columbus *(G-6343)*

Nirvana Insurance...................................... E 330 217-3079
   Columbus *(G-6360)*

NI of Ky Inc.. E 614 224-0772
   Columbus *(G-6361)*

Ohio United Agency Inc............................ E 419 562-3011
   Bucyrus *(G-1515)*

ONeill Insurance Agency Inc.................... E 330 334-1561
   Wadsworth *(G-14446)*

Otto Insurance Group LLC....................... E 740 278-7888
   Westerville *(G-14927)*

Progressive Advanced Insur Co.............. B 440 461-5000
   Cleveland *(G-4776)*

Progressive Express Insur Co................. C 440 461-5000
   Cleveland *(G-4782)*

Progressive Select Insur Co..................... A 440 461-5000
   Cleveland *(G-4789)*

Progrssive Coml Advntage Agcy............. E 440 461-5000
   Cleveland *(G-4792)*

Progrssive Spclty Insur Agcy I................. C 440 461-5000
   Cleveland *(G-4793)*

R E Whitney Insur Agcy LLC................... D 877 652-7765
   Cincinnati *(G-3271)*

Safe Auto Insurance Company................ B 740 472-1900
   Woodsfield *(G-15302)*

Safe Auto Insurance Company................ B 614 231-0200
   Columbus *(G-6626)*

Schauer Group Incorporated................... E 330 453-7721
   Canton *(G-1849)*

Sedgwick CMS Holdings Inc.................... B 800 825-6755
   Dublin *(G-8117)*

Seibert-Keck Insurance Agency.............. E 330 867-3140
   Fairlawn *(G-8498)*

Self-Funded Plans Inc.............................. E 216 566-1455
   Seven Hills *(G-12961)*

Selman & Company.................................. D 440 646-9336
   Cleveland *(G-4893)*

Stephens-Matthews Mktg LLC................ E 740 984-8011
   Beverly *(G-1102)*

Stolly Insurance Agency Inc.................... E 419 227-2570
   Lima *(G-9966)*

The James B Oswald Company............... D 216 367-8787
   Cleveland *(G-5002)*

Travelers Property Cslty Corp.................. C 513 639-5300
   Cincinnati *(G-3502)*

United Agencies Inc.................................. E 216 696-8044
   Cleveland *(G-5052)*

United Financial Casualty Co................... D 440 461-5000
   Cleveland *(G-5060)*

USI Insurance Services Nat Inc............... E 513 657-3116
   Cincinnati *(G-3608)*

USI Insurance Services Nat Inc............... E 513 852-6300
   Cincinnati *(G-3609)*

USI Insurance Services Nat Inc............... E 614 228-5565
   Columbus *(G-6839)*

USI Midwest LLC....................................... C 513 852-6300
   Cincinnati *(G-3610)*

Wabe Maquaw Holdings Inc.................... D 419 243-1191
   Toledo *(G-14096)*

Whitaker-Myers Insur Agcy Inc................ E 330 345-5000
   Wooster *(G-15388)*

Your Agency Inc.. E 937 550-9596
   Springboro *(G-13211)*

INSURANCE BROKERS, NEC

A J Amer Agency Inc................................ E 330 665-9966
   Akron *(G-10)*

A J Amer Agency Inc................................ E 330 665-9966
   Akron *(G-9)*

American Risk Services LLC.................... E 513 772-3712
   Cincinnati *(G-2187)*

Britton-Gallagher & Assoc Inc................. D 216 658-7100
   Cleveland *(G-3897)*

CSC Insurance Agency Inc...................... C 614 895-2000
   Westerville *(G-14886)*

Dawson Companies................................. D 440 333-9000
   Richfield *(G-12693)*

Fairlawn Partners LLC.............................. E 330 576-1100
   Akron *(G-151)*

Forge Industries Inc.................................. A 330 960-2468
   Youngstown *(G-15613)*

Kellison & Co... E 216 464-5160
   Cleveland *(G-4456)*

Marsh & McLennan Agency LLC............. C 937 228-4135
   Dayton *(G-7466)*

MetLife Legal Plans Inc............................ D 216 241-0022
   Cleveland *(G-4559)*

National Benefit Programs Inc................. E 614 481-9000
   Columbus *(G-6290)*

Ohio Mutual Insurance Company............ C 419 562-3011
   Bucyrus *(G-1514)*

One80 Intermediaries Inc......................... E 617 330-5700
   Beachwood *(G-823)*

Overmyer Hall Associates........................ E 614 453-4400
   Columbus *(G-6494)*

Stateside Undwrt Agcy Inc....................... E 440 893-9917
   Chagrin Falls *(G-1968)*

INSURANCE CARRIERS: Automobile

Artisan and Truckers Cslty Co................. D 440 461-5000
   Cleveland *(G-3835)*

Drive Insurance Company........................ D 440 446-5100
   Cleveland *(G-4185)*

Freedom Specialty Insurance Co............ C 614 249-1545
   Columbus *(G-5893)*

Grange Insurance Company.................... A 800 422-0550
   Columbus *(G-5947)*

Mountain Laurel Assurance Co............... B 440 461-5000
   Cleveland *(G-4604)*

Progressive Casualty Insur Co................. E 440 603-4033
   Cleveland *(G-4778)*

Rod Lightning Mutual Insur Co................ B 330 262-9060
   Wooster *(G-15370)*

Safe Auto Insurance Group Inc............... C 614 231-0200
   Columbus *(G-6627)*

Verti Insurance Company......................... D 844 448-3784
   Columbus *(G-6844)*

INSURANCE CARRIERS: Life

21st Century Financial Inc........................ D 330 668-9065
   Akron *(G-5)*

Afc Holding Company Inc......................... D 513 579-2121
   Cincinnati *(G-2154)*

Allstate Insurance Company.................... E 330 650-2917
   Hudson *(G-9330)*

Alpha Investment Partnership.................. D 513 621-1826
   Cincinnati *(G-2170)*

American Security Insurance Co............. C 937 327-7700
   Springfield *(G-13216)*

Ameritas Life Insurance Corp.................. C 513 595-2334
   Cincinnati *(G-2191)*

Buckeye State Mutual Insur Co............... D 937 778-5000
   Piqua *(G-12436)*

Family Heritg Lf Insur Co Amer............... D 440 922-5222
   Broadview Heights *(G-1389)*

Gerber Life Agency LLC.......................... E 917 765-3572
   Cincinnati *(G-2731)*

Grange Indemnity Insurance Co.............. C 614 445-2900
   Columbus *(G-5946)*

Great American Insurance Co................. A 513 369-5000
   Cincinnati *(G-2757)*

Guardian Life Insur Co Amer................... E 513 579-1114
   Cincinnati *(G-2780)*

Hancock Cnty Bd Dvlpmntal Dsbl........... D 419 422-6387
   Findlay *(G-8541)*

J P Farley Corporation............................. E 440 250-4300
   Westlake *(G-15073)*

Nationwide Financial Svcs Inc................. C 614 249-7111
   Columbus *(G-6329)*

Nationwide General Insur Co................... A 614 249-7111
   Columbus *(G-6331)*

Nationwide Insurance............................... E 513 341-7221
   Hamilton *(G-9067)*

Nf Reinsurance Ltd................................... C 614 249-7111
   Columbus *(G-6356)*

Peak Performance Solutions Inc............. E 614 344-4640
   Orient *(G-12153)*

Premier Financial Corp............................. D 419 782-5015
   Defiance *(G-7762)*

Summa Insurance Company Inc............. B 800 996-8411
   Akron *(G-322)*

Transamerica Agency Netwrk Inc........... B 614 824-4964
   Columbus *(G-6782)*

Valic Financial Advisor............................. E 216 643-6340
   Independence *(G-9495)*

Western & Southern Lf Insur Co............. A 513 629-1800
   Cincinnati *(G-3659)*

Western-Southern Life Asrn Co.............. D 513 629-1800
   Cincinnati *(G-3666)*

INSURANCE CARRIERS: Property & Casualty

American Financial Group Inc.................. A 513 579-2121
   Cincinnati *(G-2180)*

Cincinnati Financial Corp......................... A 513 870-2000
   Fairfield *(G-8402)*

National Interstate Corp........................... B 330 659-8900
   Richfield *(G-12701)*

Nationwide Life Insurance Co.................. C 877 669-6877
   Columbus *(G-6336)*

Ohio Farmers Insurance Company......... A 800 243-0210
   Westfield Center *(G-15025)*

Progressive Grdn State Insur................... B 440 461-5000
   Cleveland *(G-4784)*

Rod Lightning Mutual Insur Co................ B 330 262-9060
   Wooster *(G-15370)*

Schiff John J & Thomas R & Co............. E 513 870-2580
   Fairfield *(G-8438)*

Westfield Insurance Company................. C 800 243-0210
   Westfield Center *(G-15027)*

Westfield National Insur Co...................... D 330 887-0101
   Westfield Center *(G-15028)*

INSURANCE CARRIERS: Title

Mercantile Title Agency Inc...................... E 614 628-6880
   Columbus *(G-6225)*

Mortgage Information Services................ D 216 514-7480
   Cleveland *(G-4602)*

Omega Title Agency LLC......................... D 330 436-0600
   Akron *(G-255)*

Stewart Advnced Land Title Ltd.............. E 513 753-2800
   Cincinnati *(G-2113)*

INSURANCE CLAIM PROCESSING, EXC MEDICAL

Amtrust North America Inc...................... C 216 328-6100
   Cleveland *(G-3813)*

Gates McDonald of Ohio LLC................. A 614 677-3700
   Columbus *(G-5917)*

INSURANCE INFORMATION & CONSULTING SVCS — SERVICES SECTION

Safelite Group Inc .... A 614 210-9000
  Columbus *(G-6632)*

INSURANCE INFORMATION & CONSULTING SVCS

4mybenefits Inc .... E 513 891-6726
  Blue Ash *(G-1119)*
Business Admnstrators Cons Inc .... E 614 863-8780
  Reynoldsburg *(G-12656)*
C GI Voluntary .... E 216 401-0081
  Cleveland *(G-3916)*
Pasco Inc .... E 330 650-0613
  Hudson *(G-9367)*
Paul Moss LLC .... E 216 765-1580
  Solon *(G-13125)*

INSURANCE: Agents, Brokers & Service

Allstate Insurance Company .... E 330 650-2917
  Hudson *(G-9330)*
American Insurance Strategies .... E 937 221-8896
  Dayton *(G-7171)*
Beam Technologies Inc .... B 800 648-1179
  Columbus *(G-5428)*
Bold Penguin Inc .... D 614 344-1029
  Columbus *(G-5453)*
Bridgepoint Risk MGT LLC .... E 419 794-1075
  Maumee *(G-10704)*
Cannasure Insurance Svcs LLC .... E 800 420-5757
  Cleveland *(G-3922)*
Careworks of Ohio Inc .... A 614 792-1085
  Dublin *(G-7958)*
Columbus Life Insurance Co .... C 513 361-6700
  Cincinnati *(G-2477)*
Compmanagement Inc .... E 614 376-5300
  Dublin *(G-7970)*
Corporate Plans Inc .... E 440 542-7800
  Solon *(G-13078)*
Farmers Insurance Columbus Inc .... B 614 799-3200
  Columbus *(G-5851)*
Firefly Agency LLC .... E 614 507-7847
  Dublin *(G-8012)*
International Healthcare Corp .... D 513 731-3338
  Cincinnati *(G-2882)*
Investment Pdts Ffl Inv Svcs .... E 216 529-2700
  Lakewood *(G-9669)*
Licking Memorial Hlth Systems .... A 220 564-4000
  Newark *(G-11717)*
Mm Ascend Life Inv Svcs LLC .... E 513 333-6030
  Cincinnati *(G-3071)*
Move Ez Inc .... D 844 466-8339
  Columbus *(G-6280)*
Nationwide Rtrment Sltions Inc .... C 614 854-8300
  Dublin *(G-8072)*
New York Lf Insur Joe Stich RG .... E 614 793-2121
  Dublin *(G-8076)*
Ohio Bureau Wkrs Compensation .... E 614 221-4064
  Columbus *(G-6397)*
Old Republic Nat Title Insur .... E 614 341-1900
  Columbus *(G-6469)*
Old Rpblic Ttle Nthrn Ohio LLC .... C 216 524-5700
  Independence *(G-9464)*
Order of Untd Coml Trvlers of .... D 614 487-9680
  Columbus *(G-6479)*
Progressive Casualty Insur Co .... A 855 347-3939
  Mayfield Village *(G-10795)*
Safe Auto Insurance Group Inc .... C 614 231-0200
  Columbus *(G-6627)*
Schaeffler Group USA Inc .... A 330 202-6215
  Wooster *(G-15372)*
Sentry Life Insurance Company .... C 513 733-0100
  Cincinnati *(G-3359)*

State Automobile Mutl Insur Co .... A 833 724-3577
  Columbus *(G-6714)*
The Sheakley Group Inc .... E 513 771-2277
  Cincinnati *(G-3471)*
United Trnsp Un Insur Assn .... C 216 228-9400
  Independence *(G-9493)*
Valmark Financial Group LLC .... C 330 576-1234
  Akron *(G-347)*
Wells Fargo Insurance Servi .... D 614 324-2820
  Columbus *(G-6875)*

INTEGRATED CIRCUITS, SEMICONDUCTOR NETWORKS, ETC

Leidos Inc .... D 937 656-8433
  Beavercreek *(G-886)*

INTERIOR DECORATING SVCS

Decorate With Style Inc .... E 419 621-5577
  Sandusky *(G-12887)*
Flamos Enterprises Inc .... E 330 478-0009
  Canton *(G-1755)*
Karlsberger Architecture Inc .... D 614 471-1812
  Columbus *(G-6103)*
Karlsberger Companies .... C 614 461-9500
  Columbus *(G-6104)*

INTERIOR DESIGN SVCS, NEC

Commercial Works Inc .... D 614 870-2342
  Columbus *(G-5667)*
Continental Office Furn Corp .... C 614 262-5010
  Columbus *(G-5693)*
Interbrand Design Forum LLC .... E 513 421-2210
  Cincinnati *(G-2880)*
Interior Supply Cincinnati LLC .... E 614 424-6611
  Columbus *(G-6066)*
Rite Rug Co .... E 614 478-3365
  Columbus *(G-6591)*
River City Furniture LLC .... E 513 612-7303
  West Chester *(G-14756)*
Space & Asset Management Inc .... E 937 918-1000
  Dayton *(G-7631)*
Vocon Design Inc .... E 216 588-0800
  Cleveland *(G-5114)*

INVENTORY COMPUTING SVCS

Accurate Invntory Clclting Svc .... B 800 777-9414
  Columbus *(G-5304)*
Western Inventory Service Inc .... C 419 756-7071
  Mansfield *(G-10325)*

INVESTMENT ADVISORY SVCS

Allworth Financial LP .... E 513 469-7500
  Blue Ash *(G-1128)*
Ancora Group LLC .... D 216 825-4000
  Cleveland *(G-3815)*
Bartlett & Co LLC .... D 513 621-4612
  Cincinnati *(G-2238)*
Beacon Capital Management Inc .... A 937 203-4025
  Dayton *(G-7188)*
Buckingham & Company .... E 937 435-2742
  Dayton *(G-7205)*
Carnegie Capital Asset MGT LLC .... E 216 595-1349
  Cleveland *(G-3930)*
Cmt II Advisors LLC .... E 937 434-3095
  Centerville *(G-1942)*
Diamond Hill Capital MGT Inc .... E 614 255-3333
  Columbus *(G-5761)*
Diamond Hill Funds .... E 614 255-3333
  Columbus *(G-5762)*
Eubel Brady Sttman Asset MGT I .... E 937 291-1223
  Miamisburg *(G-11052)*

Everhart Advisors .... D 614 717-9705
  Dublin *(G-8009)*
Fort Wash Inv Advisors Inc .... D 513 361-7600
  Cincinnati *(G-2695)*
Foster & Motley Inc .... D 513 561-6640
  Cincinnati *(G-2697)*
Fund Evaluation Group LLC .... E 513 977-4400
  Cincinnati *(G-2711)*
Hamilton Capital MGT Inc .... D 614 273-1000
  Columbus *(G-5967)*
Horter Investment MGT LLC .... E 513 984-9933
  Cincinnati *(G-2844)*
Jpmorgan Inv Advisors Inc .... A 614 248-5800
  Columbus *(G-5265)*
Lancaster Pollard Mrtg Co LLC .... D 614 224-8800
  Columbus *(G-6134)*
MAI Capital Management LLC .... D 216 920-4800
  Independence *(G-9449)*
Morgan Stnley Smith Barney LLC .... C 216 344-8700
  Cleveland *(G-4601)*
Oak Associates Ltd .... E 330 666-5263
  Akron *(G-245)*
Octavia Wealth Advisors LLC .... E 513 762-7775
  Blue Ash *(G-1216)*
Parkwood LLC .... E 216 875-6500
  Cleveland *(G-4726)*
Parkwood Corporation .... E 216 875-6500
  Cleveland *(G-4727)*
Quickinsured Brokerage .... E 330 722-7070
  Medina *(G-10881)*
Roulston & Company Inc .... E 216 431-3000
  Cleveland *(G-4857)*
Strategic Wealth Partners .... E 216 800-9000
  Independence *(G-9488)*
Truepoint Wealth Counsel LLC .... E 513 792-6648
  Blue Ash *(G-1259)*
UBS Americas Inc .... D 440 356-5237
  Rocky River *(G-12754)*
Vela Investment Management LLC .... E 614 653-8352
  New Albany *(G-11589)*
Victory Capital Holdings Inc .... E 216 898-2400
  Brooklyn *(G-1412)*
Wealth Bartlett Management .... D 513 345-6217
  Cincinnati *(G-3644)*

INVESTMENT FIRM: General Brokerage

Cincinnati Financial Corp .... A 513 870-2000
  Fairfield *(G-8402)*
Red Capital Markets LLC .... C 614 857-1400
  Columbus *(G-6566)*
Skilkengold Development LLC .... E 614 418-3100
  Columbus *(G-6685)*
Stateco Financial Services Inc .... C 614 464-5000
  Columbus *(G-6716)*
Western & Southern Lf Insur Co .... A 513 629-1800
  Cincinnati *(G-3659)*
Western Southern Mutl Holdg Co .... A 866 832-7719
  Cincinnati *(G-3664)*
Western Sthern Fincl Group Inc .... A 877 367-9734
  Cincinnati *(G-3665)*

INVESTMENT OFFICES: Management, Closed-End

National Housing Tr Ltd Partnr .... E 614 451-9929
  Columbus *(G-6300)*

INVESTMENT RESEARCH SVCS

Cleveland Research Company LLC .... E 216 649-7250
  Cleveland *(G-4063)*
Longbow Research LLC .... D 216 986-0700
  Independence *(G-9448)*

SERVICES SECTION

INVESTORS, NEC

BAIN CAPITAL PRIVATE EQUITY............ E 614 751-5315
  Columbus *(G-5413)*

Bit Mining Limited................................. D 346 204-8537
  Akron *(G-69)*

Camelot Realty Investments.................. E 740 357-5291
  Lucasville *(G-10173)*

Capital Investment Group Llc................ E 513 241-5090
  Cincinnati *(G-2306)*

Cke Acquisition Co LLC........................ E 614 205-0242
  Columbus *(G-5577)*

Ctd Investments LLC........................... E 614 570-9949
  Columbus *(G-5735)*

Dg3 Topco Holdings LLC....................... D 216 292-0200
  Cleveland *(G-4163)*

Drive Capital.. E 614 284-9436
  Columbus *(G-5786)*

Elite Investments LLC......................... D 419 350-8949
  Maumee *(G-10720)*

Golden Reserve LLC............................ E 614 563-2818
  Dublin *(G-8022)*

Greenhuse Sltons Acqsition LLC........... E 440 236-8332
  Strongsville *(G-13458)*

Horan Capital Advisors LLC.................. D 513 745-0707
  Cincinnati *(G-2842)*

Imdt Acquisition LLC........................... D 937 235-0510
  Dayton *(G-7418)*

Kassel Equity Group LLC..................... E 614 310-4060
  Dublin *(G-8046)*

Kaulig Capital LLC............................... C 330 968-1110
  Hudson *(G-9360)*

Kinetico Incorporated........................... B 440 564-9111
  Newbury *(G-11761)*

Lazear Capital Partners Ltd................. E 614 221-1616
  Columbus *(G-6148)*

Lucid Investments Inc.......................... D 216 972-0058
  Willoughby *(G-15208)*

Lument Real Estate Capital LLC............ E 614 586-9380
  Columbus *(G-6178)*

McM Capital Partners II LP................... B 216 514-1840
  Beachwood *(G-813)*

National Financial Svcs LLC.................. A 614 841-1790
  Columbus *(G-5271)*

Newmark & Company RE Inc................ E 216 861-3040
  Cleveland *(G-4641)*

Oakdale Estates II Inv LLC................... D 216 520-1250
  West Union *(G-14871)*

Praetorian Holdings Group LLC............. E 440 665-4246
  Cleveland *(G-4764)*

Rainstar Capital Group........................ E 419 801-4113
  Perrysburg *(G-12366)*

Resilience Fund III LP.......................... E 216 292-0200
  Cleveland *(G-4830)*

Riverside Company.............................. D 216 344-1040
  Cleveland *(G-4843)*

Riverside Partners LLC........................ A 216 344-1040
  Cleveland *(G-4845)*

Shields Capital Corporation................... D 216 767-1340
  Beachwood *(G-837)*

Sotera Health Holdings LLC.................. B 440 262-1410
  Broadview Heights *(G-1397)*

Stephens Investments LLC................... E 937 299-4993
  Dayton *(G-7641)*

Styx Acquisition LLC........................... A 330 264-9900
  Wooster *(G-15378)*

Ultimus Fund Solutions LLC.................. E 513 587-3400
  Cincinnati *(G-3549)*

Weinberg Capital Group Inc.................. D 216 503-8307
  Cleveland *(G-5125)*

White Oak Partners Inc........................ D 614 855-1155
  Westerville *(G-15021)*

Ws One Investment Usa LLC................ D 855 895-3728
  Aurora *(G-631)*

INVESTORS: Real Estate, Exc Property Operators

Jpmorgan Chase Bank Nat Assn............ A 614 436-3055
  Columbus *(G-5264)*

Klingbeil Capital MGT Ltd..................... D 415 398-0106
  Worthington *(G-15427)*

Producers Service LLC........................ E 740 454-6253
  Zanesville *(G-15828)*

IRON & STEEL PRDTS: Hot-Rolled

Nucor Steel Marion Inc........................ B 740 383-4011
  Marion *(G-10448)*

IRON ORE MINING

Cliffs Natural Resources Explo............. C 216 694-5700
  Cleveland *(G-4079)*

The Cleveland-Cliffs Iron Co................. C 216 694-5700
  Cleveland *(G-4997)*

Tilden Mining Company LC.................. A 216 694-5700
  Cleveland *(G-5020)*

Wabush Mnes Clffs Min Mnging A......... B 216 694-5700
  Cleveland *(G-5118)*

IRON ORES

Cleveland-Cliffs Intl Holdg Co................ D 216 694-5700
  Cleveland *(G-4075)*

Cliffs Mining Services Company............ C 218 262-5913
  Cleveland *(G-4078)*

JEWELRY REPAIR SVCS

Sunrise Senior Living MGT Inc.............. C 614 235-3900
  Columbus *(G-6731)*

JEWELRY STORES

Equity Diamond Brokers Inc................. E 513 793-4760
  Montgomery *(G-11367)*

Gottlieb & Sons Inc............................ E 216 771-4785
  Beachwood *(G-795)*

JEWELRY, WHOLESALE

Cas-Ker Company Inc......................... E 513 674-7700
  Cincinnati *(G-2317)*

Equity Diamond Brokers Inc................. E 513 793-4760
  Montgomery *(G-11367)*

Marfo Company.................................. D 614 276-3352
  Columbus *(G-6197)*

JEWELRY: Precious Metal

Associated Premium Corporation........... E 513 679-4444
  Cincinnati *(G-2219)*

JIGS & FIXTURES

Jergens Inc....................................... C 216 486-5540
  Cleveland *(G-4437)*

JOB TRAINING SVCS

Akron Blind Center & Workshop............ E 330 253-2555
  Akron *(G-21)*

Butler Cnty Bd Dvlpmntal Dsblt.............. D 513 785-2870
  Fairfield Township *(G-8457)*

Cincinnati Works Corp......................... C 513 744-9675
  Cincinnati *(G-2431)*

County of Crawford............................. E 419 562-0015
  Bucyrus *(G-1502)*

Goodwill Inds Centl Ohio Inc................ D 614 274-5296
  Columbus *(G-5942)*

Goodwill Inds Centl Ohio Inc................ B 614 294-5181
  Columbus *(G-5941)*

KIDNEY DIALYSIS CENTERS

GP Strategies Corporation.................... E 513 583-8810
  Cincinnati *(G-2745)*

Great Lkes Cmnty Action Partnr............ E 419 334-8511
  Fremont *(G-8685)*

Great Lkes Cmnty Action Partnr............ E 419 332-8089
  Fremont *(G-8686)*

Great Lkes Cmnty Action Partnr............ E 419 732-7007
  Port Clinton *(G-12529)*

Great Lkes Cmnty Action Partnr............ D 419 333-6068
  Fremont *(G-8684)*

Miami University................................. B 513 727-3200
  Middletown *(G-11172)*

Portage Prvate Indust Cncil In.............. D 330 297-7795
  Ravenna *(G-12639)*

Star Inc... C 740 354-1517
  Portsmouth *(G-12575)*

KEY DUPLICATING SHOP

Hillman Companies Inc........................ B 513 851-4900
  Cincinnati *(G-2822)*

KIDNEY DIALYSIS CENTERS

022808 Kenwood LLC.......................... E 513 745-0800
  Cincinnati *(G-2117)*

Bio-Mdcal Applcations Ohio Inc............. E 330 376-4905
  Akron *(G-68)*

Borrego Dialysis LLC.......................... E 513 737-0158
  Hamilton *(G-9018)*

Columbus-Rna-Davita LLC................... E 614 501-7224
  Columbus *(G-5660)*

Columbus-Rna-Davita LLC................... E 614 228-1773
  Columbus *(G-5661)*

Columbus-Rna-Davita LLC................... E 614 985-1732
  Columbus *(G-5662)*

Community Dialysis Center................... C 216 295-7000
  Cleveland *(G-4098)*

Community Dialysis Center................... C 216 229-6170
  Cleveland *(G-4099)*

Community Dialysis Center................... C 330 609-0370
  Warren *(G-14510)*

Court Dialysis LLC.............................. E 740 773-3733
  Chillicothe *(G-2063)*

Desoto Dialysis LLC............................ E 419 691-1514
  Oregon *(G-12132)*

Dialysis Centers Dayton LLC................ D 937 208-7900
  Dayton *(G-7312)*

Dialysis Centers Dayton LLC................ D 937 548-7019
  Greenville *(G-8871)*

Dialysis Clinic Inc............................... D 513 281-0091
  Cincinnati *(G-2562)*

Dialysis Clinic Inc............................... E 740 351-0596
  Portsmouth *(G-12551)*

Dva Hlthcare - Sthwest Ohio LL............ E 513 733-8215
  Blue Ash *(G-1165)*

Dva Hlthcare - Sthwest Ohio LL............ D 513 347-0444
  Cincinnati *(G-2588)*

Dva Hlthcare - Sthwest Ohio LL............ D 513 591-2900
  Cincinnati *(G-2589)*

Dva Hlthcare - Sthwest Ohio LL............ E 513 939-1110
  Fairfield *(G-8408)*

Dva Hlthcare - Sthwest Ohio LL............ E 513 422-1467
  Middletown *(G-11196)*

Fields Dialysis LLC............................. E 513 531-2111
  Cincinnati *(G-2661)*

Fresenius Med Care Butler Cty............. E 513 737-1415
  Hamilton *(G-9044)*

Fresenius Med Care Milford LLC........... E 513 248-1690
  Milford *(G-11228)*

Fresenius Med Care S Grove Cy........... E 614 801-2505
  Grove City *(G-8920)*

Fresenius Med Care Wlmngton HM....... E 937 382-3379
  Wilmington *(G-15254)*

Employee Codes: A=Over 500 employees, B=251-500
C=101-250, D=51-100, E=20-50, F=10-19, G=1-9

KIDNEY DIALYSIS CENTERS

Garrett Dialysis LLC......................... D 216 398-6029
　Cleveland *(G-4303)*
Greenfield Health Systems Corp............. E 419 389-9681
　Toledo *(G-13829)*
Kidney Center of Bexley LLC................ D 614 231-2200
　Columbus *(G-6115)*
Kidney Group Inc........................... E 330 746-1488
　Youngstown *(G-15646)*
Kidney Services W Centl Ohio............... E 419 227-0918
　Lima *(G-9913)*
Nxstage Cincinnati LLC..................... E 513 712-1300
　Cincinnati *(G-3137)*
Ohio Renal Care Supply Co LLC.............. E 216 739-0500
　Cleveland *(G-4690)*
Ohio River Dialysis LLC.................... E 513 385-3580
　Cincinnati *(G-3148)*
River Valley Dialysis LLC.................. E 513 922-5900
　Cincinnati *(G-3301)*
River Valley Dialysis LLC.................. E 513 793-0555
　Cincinnati *(G-3302)*
River Valley Dialysis LLC.................. E 513 741-1062
　Cincinnati *(G-3303)*
River Valley Dialysis LLC.................. E 513 934-0272
　Lebanon *(G-9785)*
Storrie Dialysis LLC....................... E 937 390-3125
　Springfield *(G-13296)*
Tenack Dialysis LLC........................ E 513 810-4369
　Cincinnati *(G-3452)*
Warren Dialysis Center LLC................. E 330 609-5502
　Warren *(G-14575)*

KITCHEN CABINETS WHOLESALERS

Babin Building Solutions LLC............... E 216 292-2500
　Broadview Heights *(G-1383)*
Direct Import Home Decor Inc............... E 216 898-9758
　Cleveland *(G-4166)*
Don Walter Kitchen Distrs Inc.............. E 330 793-9338
　Youngstown *(G-15600)*
Famous Distribution Inc.................... E 740 282-0951
　Steubenville *(G-13323)*
Keidel Sup LLC Fka Kdel Sup In............. E 513 351-1600
　Cincinnati *(G-2933)*
Professional Laminate Mllwk Inc............ E 513 891-7858
　Milford *(G-11251)*
Sims-Lohman Inc............................ E 513 651-3510
　Cincinnati *(G-3379)*

KITCHENWARE STORES

Nacco Industries Inc....................... E 440 229-5151
　Cleveland *(G-4616)*
Wasserstrom Company........................ B 614 228-6525
　Columbus *(G-6867)*

KNIVES: Agricultural Or indl

C B Mfg & Sls Co Inc....................... D 937 866-5986
　Miamisburg *(G-11030)*

LABELS: Paper, Made From Purchased Materials

General Data Company Inc................... B 513 752-7978
　Cincinnati *(G-2105)*

LABELS: Woven

Crane Consumables Inc...................... E 513 539-9980
　Middletown *(G-11160)*

LABORATORIES, TESTING: Automobile Proving & Testing Ground

Ohio Department Transportation............. E 614 275-1300
　Columbus *(G-6402)*

Transportation Research Center Inc......... A 937 666-2011
　East Liberty *(G-8176)*

LABORATORIES, TESTING: Food

Agrana Fruit Us Inc........................ C 937 693-3821
　Anna *(G-442)*
Food Safety Net Services Ltd............... E 614 274-2070
　Columbus *(G-5876)*
Nestle Usa Inc............................. B 614 526-5300
　Dublin *(G-8073)*
Silliker Laboratories Ohio Inc............. E 614 486-0150
　Columbus *(G-6680)*

LABORATORIES, TESTING: Forensic

County of Lake............................. E 440 350-2793
　Painesville *(G-12224)*

LABORATORIES, TESTING: Metallurgical

Bowser-Morner Inc.......................... E 419 691-4800
　Toledo *(G-13714)*
Ctl Engineering Inc........................ C 614 276-8123
　Columbus *(G-5736)*
Metcut Research Associates Inc............. D 513 271-5100
　Cincinnati *(G-3052)*
Mrl Materials Resources LLC................ E 937 531-6657
　Xenia *(G-15528)*
Tensile Tstg A Div J T Adams I............. E 216 641-3290
　Cleveland *(G-4985)*

LABORATORIES, TESTING: Product Testing

Bwi North America Inc...................... E 937 212-2892
　Moraine *(G-11395)*
Ics Laboratories Inc....................... E 330 220-0515
　Brunswick *(G-1458)*
McCloy Engineering LLC..................... E 513 984-4112
　Fairfield *(G-8428)*
Smithers MSE Inc........................... E 330 297-1495
　Ravenna *(G-12644)*
Smithers MSE Inc........................... D 330 762-7441
　Akron *(G-305)*
Smithers Tire Auto Tstg of Txa............. C 330 762-7441
　Akron *(G-306)*
Wallover Enterprises Inc................... E 440 238-9250
　Strongsville *(G-13497)*

LABORATORIES, TESTING: Product Testing, Safety/Performance

Cincinnati Testing Laboratories Inc........ E 513 851-3313
　Cincinnati *(G-2427)*
Plastic Technologies Inc................... D 419 867-5400
　Holland *(G-9300)*
Smithers Group Inc......................... D 330 833-8548
　Massillon *(G-10671)*

LABORATORIES, TESTING: Radiation

University of Cincinnati................... E 513 558-4110
　Cincinnati *(G-3585)*

LABORATORIES: Biological Research

Infinity Labs LLC.......................... E 937 317-0030
　Xenia *(G-15522)*
Innovest Global Inc........................ D 216 815-1122
　Chesterland *(G-2036)*
Mp Biomedicals LLC......................... C 440 337-1200
　Solon *(G-13113)*

LABORATORIES: Biotechnology

Amplifybio LLC............................. D 833 641-2006
　West Jefferson *(G-14847)*
Caterpllar Trmble Ctrl Tech LL............. D 937 233-8921
　Dayton *(G-7217)*

Charles River Laboratories Inc............. E 419 647-4196
　Spencerville *(G-13187)*
Charles River Labs Ashland LLC............. A 419 282-8700
　Ashland *(G-492)*
Charles Rver Labs Clveland Inc............. D 216 332-1665
　Cleveland *(G-3962)*
Childrens Hospital Medical Ctr............. A 513 636-4200
　Cincinnati *(G-2369)*
Childrens Hospital Medical Ctr............. A 513 636-4200
　Cincinnati *(G-2368)*
Concord Biosciences LLC.................... D 440 357-3200
　Concord Township *(G-6923)*
EMD Millipore Corporation.................. C 513 631-0445
　Norwood *(G-12032)*
Medpace Inc................................ A 513 579-9911
　Cincinnati *(G-3031)*
Olon USA LLC............................... D 440 357-3300
　Concord Township *(G-6931)*
R & D Nestle Center Inc.................... D 937 642-7015
　Marysville *(G-10503)*
Solutons Through Innvtive Tech............. D 937 320-9994
　Beavercreek *(G-907)*
Spr Therapeutics Inc....................... E 216 378-2658
　Cleveland *(G-4936)*

LABORATORIES: Commercial Nonphysical Research

Icon Government............................ B 330 278-2343
　Hinckley *(G-9270)*
Impact Sales Solutions Inc................. E 419 466-0131
　Toledo *(G-13861)*
Infocision Management Corp................. C 330 544-1400
　Youngstown *(G-15640)*
Sytronics Inc.............................. E 937 431-6100
　Beavercreek *(G-910)*

LABORATORIES: Dental, Crown & Bridge Production

Dental Ceramics Inc........................ E 330 523-5240
　Richfield *(G-12694)*
Lantz Dental Prosthetics Inc............... E 419 866-1515
　Maumee *(G-10738)*
National Dentex LLC........................ D 216 671-0577
　Brunswick *(G-1464)*
Roe Dental Laboratory Inc.................. D 216 663-2233
　Independence *(G-9478)*

LABORATORIES: Electronic Research

Oleco Inc.................................. E 937 223-3000
　Dayton *(G-7537)*
Sierra Nevada Corporation.................. C 937 431-2800
　Beavercreek *(G-906)*
Steiner Eoptics Inc........................ D 937 426-2341
　Miamisburg *(G-11095)*

LABORATORIES: Medical

Amerathon LLC.............................. E 419 230-9108
　Euclid *(G-8337)*
American Health Imaging S LLC.............. A 513 752-7300
　Cincinnati *(G-2097)*
Arbor View Family Medicine Inc............. E 740 687-3386
　Lancaster *(G-9695)*
Belmont Manor Inc.......................... E 740 695-4404
　Saint Clairsville *(G-12780)*
Bon Secours Mercy Health Inc............... C 330 729-1420
　Youngstown *(G-15563)*
Cellular Technology Limited................ E 216 791-5084
　Shaker Heights *(G-12975)*
Center For Dialysis Care................... E 440 286-4103
　Chardon *(G-1995)*

SERVICES SECTION

LABORATORIES: Testing

Childrens Hosp Reference Lab............ E 614 722-5477
  Columbus (G-5562)
Childrens Hospital Medical Ctr............ B 513 636-6400
  Fairfield (G-8400)
Cleveland Clinic Foundation................ E 216 445-6636
  Cleveland (G-4029)
Cleveland Clnic Hlth Systm-Wst........... D 440 716-9810
  North Olmsted (G-11898)
Cleveland Heartlab Inc....................... D 866 358-9828
  Cleveland (G-4049)
Community Blood Center.................... D 800 684-7783
  Kettering (G-9627)
Compunet Clinical Labs LLC................ E 937 912-9017
  Beavercreek (G-873)
Compunet Clinical Labs LLC................ E 937 427-2655
  Beavercreek (G-921)
Compunet Clinical Labs LLC................ E 937 208-3555
  Dayton (G-7244)
Compunet Clinical Labs LLC................ E 937 342-0015
  Springfield (G-13240)
Compunet Clinical Labs LLC................ E 937 372-9681
  Xenia (G-15502)
Compunet Clinical Labs LLC................ C 937 296-0844
  Moraine (G-11399)
County of Lake.................................. E 440 350-2793
  Painesville (G-12224)
Drew Medical Inc............................... E 407 363-6700
  Hudson (G-9343)
Kettering Pathology Assoc Inc............. D 937 298-4331
  Dayton (G-7440)
Mp Biomedicals LLC........................... C 440 337-1200
  Solon (G-13113)
Nationwide Childrens Hospital............. C 614 355-8200
  Hilliard (G-9220)
Nationwide Childrens Hospital............. D 419 528-3140
  Mansfield (G-10303)
Northast Ohio Nghbrhood Hlth S......... C 216 231-7700
  Cleveland (G-4653)
P C Vpa... E 614 840-1688
  Columbus (G-6495)
Perry County Fmly Practice Inc............ D 740 342-3435
  New Lexington (G-11631)
Smithers Group Inc............................ D 330 833-8548
  Massillon (G-10671)
Sotera Health Topco Parent LP............ A 440 262-1410
  Broadview Heights (G-1400)
Southwest Urology LLC...................... E 440 845-0900
  Cleveland (G-4924)
St Lukes Hospital............................... A 419 441-1002
  Waterville (G-14595)
Summa Health.................................... D 330 753-3649
  Barberton (G-712)
Summa Health.................................... D 330 688-4531
  Stow (G-13396)
Summit County................................... D 330 643-2101
  Akron (G-325)
Symphony Dagnstc Svcs No 1 LLC....... A 614 888-2226
  Columbus (G-6741)
University Hsptals Clvland Med............ A 216 844-1369
  Cleveland (G-5075)
University of Cincinnati....................... C 513 558-4444
  Cincinnati (G-3587)

LABORATORIES: Noncommercial Research

Benjamin Rose Institute...................... E 216 791-8000
  Cleveland (G-3869)
The Sisters of Charity of S.................. E 216 696-5560
  Cleveland (G-5007)
Trihealth Inc..................................... C 513 985-3700
  Cincinnati (G-3509)
Trihealth Inc..................................... C 513 246-7000
  Cincinnati (G-3510)
Trihealth Inc..................................... C 513 860-6820
  West Chester (G-14778)
University of Dayton........................... A 937 229-1000
  Dayton (G-7689)

LABORATORIES: Physical Research, Commercial

Aerospace Corporation........................ E 937 657-9634
  Dayton (G-7125)
Alliance Imaging Inc........................... D 330 493-5100
  Canton (G-1660)
Antioch University............................. C 937 769-1366
  Yellow Springs (G-15534)
Apex Software Technologies Inc........... E 614 932-2167
  Powell (G-12584)
Arthur G Jmes Cncer Hosp Rchar.......... B 614 293-4878
  Columbus (G-5388)
Azimuth Corporation.......................... C 937 256-8571
  Beavercreek (G-861)
BASF Catalysts LLC............................ C 216 360-5005
  Cleveland (G-3853)
Berriehill Research Corp..................... E 937 435-1016
  Dayton (G-7190)
Borchers Americas Inc....................... D 440 899-2950
  Westlake (G-15040)
Brilligent Solutions LLC...................... E 937 879-4148
  Fairborn (G-8367)
Chemimage Filter Tech LLC................ E 330 686-2726
  Stow (G-13358)
Childrens Hosp Reference Lab............ E 614 722-5477
  Columbus (G-5562)
Circle Prime Manufacturing................. E 330 923-0019
  Cuyahoga Falls (G-7054)
Columbus Dnv Inc.............................. C 614 761-1214
  Dublin (G-7966)
Ctl Engineering Inc............................ C 614 276-8123
  Columbus (G-5736)
Curtiss-Wright Controls...................... E 937 252-5601
  Fairborn (G-8371)
Edison Welding Institute Inc............... C 614 688-5000
  Columbus (G-5807)
Flexsys America LP............................ D 330 666-4111
  Akron (G-164)
Hii Mission Technologies Corp............. C 937 426-3421
  Beavercreek Township (G-940)
Imarc Research Inc........................... D 440 801-1540
  Strongsville (G-13464)
Kbr Wyle Services LLC...................... C 937 320-2713
  Dayton (G-7433)
Kemron Environmental Svcs Inc........... E 740 373-4071
  Marietta (G-10378)
Kenmore Research Company............... D 330 297-1407
  Ravenna (G-12631)
Lyondell Chemical Company................ C 513 530-4000
  Cincinnati (G-2996)
Medpace Holdings Inc......................... C 513 579-9911
  Cincinnati (G-3033)
Muskingum Starlight Industries............ D 740 453-4622
  Zanesville (G-15817)
Nokia of America Corporation............. D 614 860-2000
  Dublin (G-8077)
Phoenix Technology Services............... E 740 325-1138
  Bellaire (G-1015)
Plastic Technologies Inc..................... D 419 867-5400
  Holland (G-9300)
Q Labs LLC....................................... C 513 471-1300
  Cincinnati (G-3258)
Quality Construction MGT Inc............. D 513 779-8425
  West Chester (G-14750)
Radiance Technologies Inc.................. C 937 425-0747
  Beavercreek (G-898)
RGBSI Aerospace & Defense LLC......... D 248 761-0412
  Beavercreek (G-900)
Sunpower Inc.................................... D 740 594-2221
  Athens (G-592)
Synthomer Inc.................................. D 330 794-6300
  Akron (G-328)
Sytronics Inc.................................... E 937 431-6100
  Beavercreek (G-910)
Taitech Inc....................................... E 937 255-4141
  Fairborn (G-8381)
Terracon Consultants Inc.................... B 513 321-5816
  Cincinnati (G-3459)
Trico Products Corporation................. C 248 371-1700
  Cleveland (G-5038)
Wiley Companies............................... C 740 622-0755
  Coshocton (G-7005)

LABORATORIES: Testing

Advanced Testing Lab Inc.................... C 513 489-8447
  Blue Ash (G-1122)
Advanced Testing MGT Group Inc......... D 513 489-8447
  Blue Ash (G-1123)
Akron Rubber Dev Lab Inc.................. E 330 794-6600
  Barberton (G-692)
Akron Rubber Dev Lab Inc.................. D 330 794-6600
  Akron (G-36)
Als Group Usa Corp............................ D 281 530-5656
  Cleveland (G-3797)
Andritz Inc....................................... C 937 390-3400
  Springfield (G-13217)
Balancing Company Inc...................... E 937 898-9111
  Vandalia (G-14365)
Barr Engineering Incorporated............. E 614 714-0299
  Columbus (G-5420)
Bowser-Morner Inc............................ E 937 236-8805
  Dayton (G-7198)
Bwi Chassis Dynamics NA Inc.............. E 937 455-5230
  Moraine (G-11394)
Cincinnati Testing Labs Inc.................. E 513 851-3313
  Cincinnati (G-2428)
Columbus Dnv Inc.............................. C 614 761-1214
  Dublin (G-7966)
Csa America Standards Inc.................. C 216 524-4990
  Cleveland (G-4142)
Curtiss-Wright Flow Ctrl Corp.............. D 513 528-7900
  Cincinnati (G-2101)
Dna Diagnostics Center Inc................. D 513 881-7800
  Fairfield (G-8407)
Electro-Analytical Inc......................... E 440 951-3514
  Mentor (G-10935)
Element Materials Technolog............... E 216 524-1450
  Cleveland (G-4210)
Element Mtls Tech Cncnnati Inc........... E 513 984-4112
  Fairfield (G-8410)
Energy Harbor Nuclear Corp................ D 440 604-9836
  Cleveland (G-4214)
Eurofins Testoil Inc............................ D 216 251-2510
  Strongsville (G-13453)
General Electric Company................... C 937 587-2631
  Peebles (G-12288)
Genthrm Medical LLC........................ D 513 326-5252
  Cincinnati (G-2730)
Godfrey & Wing Inc........................... E 330 562-1440
  Aurora (G-615)
Headwinds LP................................... E 724 209-5543
  Steubenville (G-13330)
High Voltage Maintenance Corp........... E 937 278-0811
  Dayton (G-7406)
Intertek Testing Svcs NA Inc............... E 614 279-8090
  Columbus (G-6070)
Isomedix Operations Inc..................... D 877 783-7497
  Mentor (G-10953)

LABORATORIES: Testing

Kbr Wyle Services LLC .... E 937 912-3470
  Beavercreek *(G-885)*
Kemron Environmental Svcs Inc .... E 740 373-4071
  Marietta *(G-10378)*
Kenmore Research Company .... D 330 297-1407
  Ravenna *(G-12631)*
Lexamed Ltd .... E 419 693-5307
  Toledo *(G-13886)*
Lmsi LLC .... E 800 838-0602
  Toledo *(G-13890)*
Merieux Nutrisciences Corp .... D 614 486-0150
  Columbus *(G-6226)*
Microtek Laboratories Inc .... E 937 236-2213
  Moraine *(G-11426)*
Mistras Group Inc .... C 740 788-9188
  Heath *(G-9136)*
Nelson Labs Fairfield Inc .... E 973 227-6882
  Broadview Heights *(G-1393)*
North Amercn Science Assoc LLC .... C 419 666-9455
  Northwood *(G-11979)*
Northast Ohio Rgonal Sewer Dst .... C 216 641-6000
  Cleveland *(G-4657)*
Nsl Analytical Services Inc .... D 216 438-5200
  Cleveland *(G-4671)*
Omega Laboratories Inc .... D 330 628-5748
  Mogadore *(G-11330)*
Prime NDT Services Inc .... D 330 878-4202
  Strasburg *(G-13405)*
Q Labs LLC .... C 513 471-1300
  Cincinnati *(G-3258)*
Resource International Inc .... C 614 823-4949
  Columbus *(G-6587)*
S D Myers Inc .... C 330 630-7000
  Tallmadge *(G-13602)*
Sample Machining Inc .... E 937 258-3338
  Dayton *(G-7609)*
SD Myers LLC .... C 330 630-7000
  Tallmadge *(G-13603)*
Sotera Health Company .... E 440 262-1410
  Broadview Heights *(G-1396)*
Sotera Health Holdings LLC .... B 440 262-1410
  Broadview Heights *(G-1397)*
Sotera Health Services LLC .... D 440 262-1410
  Broadview Heights *(G-1399)*
Technology Recovery Group Ltd .... D 440 250-9970
  Westlake *(G-15114)*
Teledyne Brown Engineering Inc .... D 419 470-3000
  Toledo *(G-14036)*
Terracon Consultants Inc .... B 513 321-5816
  Cincinnati *(G-3459)*
Trico Products Corporation .... C 248 371-1700
  Cleveland *(G-5038)*
US Inspection Services Inc .... E 937 660-9879
  Dayton *(G-7697)*
X-Ray Industries Inc .... D 216 642-0100
  Cleveland *(G-5163)*
Yoder Industries Inc .... C 937 278-5769
  Dayton *(G-7731)*
Amerathon LLC .... E 216 409-7201
  Uniontown *(G-14241)*
Avertest LLC .... E 330 591-7219
  Medina *(G-10812)*
Cadx Systems Inc .... D 937 431-1464
  Beavercreek *(G-870)*
Connie Parks .... E 330 759-8334
  Hubbard *(G-9320)*
Laboratory of Dermatopathology .... E 937 434-2351
  Dayton *(G-7448)*
Medical Diagnostic Lab Inc .... E 440 333-1475
  Avon *(G-661)*
Medpace Bioanalytical Labs LLC .... E 513 366-3260
  Cincinnati *(G-3032)*

Q Medical LLC .... B 440 903-1827
  Pepper Pike *(G-12302)*
Senior Touch Solution .... E 216 862-4841
  Cleveland *(G-4895)*
University of Cincinnati .... C 513 584-5331
  Cincinnati *(G-3588)*

LABORATORY APPARATUS & FURNITURE

Dentronix Inc .... D 330 916-7300
  Cuyahoga Falls *(G-7070)*
Gilson Company Inc .... E 740 548-7298
  Lewis Center *(G-9823)*
Ies Systems Inc .... E 330 533-6683
  Canfield *(G-1632)*
Philips Med Systems Clvland In .... B 440 483-3000
  Cleveland *(G-4746)*
Teledyne Instruments Inc .... E 513 229-7000
  Mason *(G-10614)*

LABORATORY APPARATUS: Pipettes, Hemocytometer

Mettler-Toledo LLC .... A 614 438-4511
  Columbus *(G-5270)*

LABORATORY EQPT, EXC MEDICAL: Wholesalers

Revvity Health Sciences Inc .... E 330 825-4525
  Akron *(G-281)*
Smith & Schaefer Inc .... E 216 226-6700
  Bethel *(G-1094)*
Teledyne Instruments Inc .... E 513 229-7000
  Mason *(G-10614)*

LABORATORY EQPT: Clinical Instruments Exc Medical

Cellular Technology Limited .... E 216 791-5084
  Shaker Heights *(G-12975)*

LABORATORY EQPT: Incubators

Health Aid of Ohio Inc .... E 216 252-3900
  Cleveland *(G-4353)*

LABORATORY INSTRUMENT REPAIR SVCS

Worthington Analytical Svcs .... D 614 599-5254
  Lucas *(G-10172)*

LADDERS: Metal

Bauer Corporation .... E 800 321-4760
  Wooster *(G-15310)*

LAMINATED PLASTICS: Plate, Sheet, Rod & Tubes

Applied Medical Technology Inc .... E 440 717-4000
  Brecksville *(G-1343)*
Organized Living Inc .... E 513 489-9300
  Cincinnati *(G-3167)*
TS Trim Industries Inc .... B 614 837-4114
  Canal Winchester *(G-1618)*

LAMINATING SVCS

Conversion Tech Intl Inc .... E 419 924-5566
  West Unity *(G-14874)*
Kent Adhesive Products Co .... D 330 678-1626
  Kent *(G-9583)*
United Art and Education Inc .... E 800 322-3247
  Dayton *(G-7680)*

LAMP SHADES: Glass

Cleveland Glass Block Inc .... E 614 252-5888
  Columbus *(G-5584)*

Cleveland Glass Block Inc .... E 216 531-6363
  Cleveland *(G-4046)*
R C Hemm Glass Shops Inc .... E 937 773-5591
  Piqua *(G-12457)*

LAND SUBDIVIDERS & DEVELOPERS: Commercial

C V Perry & Co .... E 614 221-4131
  Columbus *(G-5490)*
Cardida Corporation .... D 740 439-4359
  Kimbolton *(G-9640)*
Cathedral Holdings Inc .... D 513 271-6400
  Cincinnati *(G-2322)*
Coral Company .... E 216 932-8822
  Independence *(G-9425)*
Dehoff Agency Inc .... E 330 499-8153
  Canton *(G-1733)*
Eagle Realty Group LLC .... E 513 361-7700
  Cincinnati *(G-2595)*
Highland Som Development .... E 330 528-3500
  Streetsboro *(G-13415)*
Multicon Builders Inc .... E 614 463-1142
  Columbus *(G-6283)*
Oberer Development Co .... E 937 910-0851
  Miamisburg *(G-11077)*
Phillips Edison & Company LLC .... E 513 554-1110
  Cincinnati *(G-3206)*
Req/Jqh Holdings Inc .... B 513 891-1066
  Blue Ash *(G-1235)*
Robert L Stark Enterprises Inc .... E 216 292-0240
  Cleveland *(G-4846)*
Sunrise Land Co .... E 216 621-6060
  Cleveland *(G-4960)*
T O J Inc .... E 440 352-1900
  Mentor *(G-11002)*
The Daimler Group Inc .... E 614 488-4424
  Columbus *(G-6759)*
Visconsi Companies Ltd .... E 216 464-5550
  Cleveland *(G-5108)*
Zaremba Group LLC .... D 216 221-6600
  Lakewood *(G-9689)*

LAND SUBDIVIDERS & DEVELOPERS: Residential

Columbus Housing Partnr Inc .... D 614 221-8889
  Columbus *(G-5640)*
Towne Development Group Ltd .... E 513 381-8696
  Cincinnati *(G-3489)*

LAND SUBDIVISION & DEVELOPMENT

Bostleman Corp .... E
  Holland *(G-9281)*
Carnegie Management & Dev Corp .... E 440 892-6800
  Westlake *(G-15046)*
Carter-Jones Companies Inc .... E 330 673-6100
  Kent *(G-9560)*
Cavalear Corporation .... E 419 882-7125
  Sylvania *(G-13538)*
Equity Cnstr Solutions LLC .... E 614 802-2900
  Hilliard *(G-9195)*
Equity LLC .... D 614 802-2900
  Hilliard *(G-9196)*
Ford Development Corp .... E 513 207-9118
  Cincinnati *(G-2694)*
Forest City Enterprises LP .... B 216 621-6060
  Cleveland *(G-4271)*
Forest Cy Residential MGT Inc .... C 216 621-6060
  Cleveland *(G-4276)*
George J Igel & Co Inc .... A 614 445-8421
  Columbus *(G-5928)*

Jack Gray.. D..... 216 688-0466
 Cincinnati *(G-2892)*

Magnum Management Corporation......... C..... 419 627-2334
 Sandusky *(G-12913)*

Midwestern Plumbing Svc Inc................... E..... 513 753-0050
 Cincinnati *(G-3060)*

Miller-Vlentine Operations Inc.................. B..... 513 771-0900
 Dayton *(G-7508)*

Miller-Vlentine Operations Inc.................. E..... 937 293-0900
 Dayton *(G-7507)*

Pizzuti Inc... E..... 614 280-4000
 Columbus *(G-6527)*

Rockford Homes Inc................................. D..... 614 785-0015
 Columbus *(G-5281)*

Seg of Ohio Inc.. E..... 614 414-7300
 Columbus *(G-6659)*

Sunrise Development Co.......................... B..... 216 621-6060
 Cleveland *(G-4959)*

Vision Development Inc........................... E..... 614 487-1804
 Upper Arlington *(G-14283)*

Windsor Companies.................................. E..... 740 653-8822
 Lancaster *(G-9750)*

LAUNDRY SVC: Work Clothing Sply

Unifirst Corporation................................. E..... 614 575-9999
 Blacklick *(G-1114)*

LAUNDRY SVCS: Indl

Cintas Corporation No 2........................... D..... 614 878-7313
 Columbus *(G-5572)*

Midwest Laundry Inc................................ D..... 513 563-5560
 Cincinnati *(G-3058)*

Morgan Services Inc................................. D..... 419 243-2214
 Toledo *(G-13928)*

Vestis Corporation.................................... E..... 216 341-7400
 Cleveland *(G-5100)*

Vestis Corporation.................................... E..... 614 445-8341
 Columbus *(G-6847)*

LAWN & GARDEN EQPT

Franklin Equipment LLC........................... D..... 614 228-2014
 Groveport *(G-8990)*

Mtd Holdings Inc...................................... B..... 330 225-2600
 Valley City *(G-14336)*

Power Distributors LLC............................ D..... 614 876-3533
 Columbus *(G-6539)*

Scotts Company LLC................................ C..... 937 644-0011
 Marysville *(G-10508)*

LEASING & RENTAL SVCS: Cranes & Aerial Lift Eqpt

All Crane Rental Corp............................... D..... 614 261-1800
 Columbus *(G-5334)*

All Erection & Crane Rental..................... E..... 216 524-6550
 Cleveland *(G-3789)*

All Erection & Crane Rental..................... C..... 216 524-6550
 Cleveland *(G-3788)*

American Crane Inc.................................. E..... 614 496-2268
 Reynoldsburg *(G-12651)*

Canton Erectors Inc.................................. E..... 330 453-7363
 Massillon *(G-10634)*

Capital City Group Inc.............................. E..... 614 278-2120
 Columbus *(G-5498)*

General Crane Rental LLC........................ E..... 330 908-0001
 Macedonia *(G-10192)*

Interstate Lift Trucks Inc.......................... E..... 216 328-0970
 Cleveland *(G-4421)*

Jeffers Crane Service Inc......................... E..... 419 223-9010
 Lima *(G-9912)*

Kelley Steel Erectors Inc.......................... D..... 440 232-1573
 Cleveland *(G-4455)*

Piqua Steel Co.. D..... 937 773-3632
 Piqua *(G-12454)*

Skyworks LLC... E..... 419 662-8630
 Perrysburg *(G-12370)*

United Rentals North Amer Inc................ E..... 800 877-3687
 Perrysburg *(G-12383)*

LEASING & RENTAL SVCS: Oil Field Eqpt

Eleet Cryogenics Inc................................ E..... 330 874-4009
 Bolivar *(G-1294)*

LEASING & RENTAL: Construction & Mining Eqpt

Bobcat Enterprises Inc............................. D..... 513 874-8945
 West Chester *(G-14652)*

Columbus Equipment Company............... E..... 614 437-0352
 Columbus *(G-5633)*

F & M Mafco Inc....................................... C..... 513 367-2151
 Harrison *(G-9104)*

H M Miller Construction Co..................... D..... 330 628-4811
 Mogadore *(G-11327)*

Henry Jergens Contractor Inc.................. E..... 937 233-1830
 Dayton *(G-7405)*

Lefeld Welding & Stl Sups Inc................. E..... 419 678-2397
 Coldwater *(G-5216)*

Leppo Inc.. E..... 330 633-3999
 Tallmadge *(G-13599)*

Messer Construction Co........................... C..... 513 482-7402
 Cincinnati *(G-3051)*

National Tool Leasing Inc......................... E..... 866 952-8665
 Eastlake *(G-8206)*

Ohio Machinery Co................................... C..... 440 526-6200
 Broadview Heights *(G-1394)*

Pollock Research & Design Inc................ E..... 330 332-3300
 Salem *(G-12847)*

RELAM Inc.. E..... 440 232-3354
 Solon *(G-13137)*

Selinsky Force LLC................................... C..... 330 477-4527
 Canton *(G-1850)*

Sunbelt Rentals Inc................................... D..... 614 848-4075
 Columbus *(G-5282)*

Sunbelt Rentals Inc................................... E..... 614 341-9770
 Columbus *(G-6729)*

The Selinsky Force LLC............................ D..... 330 477-4527
 Canton *(G-1872)*

The Wagner-Smith Company.................... B..... 866 338-0398
 Moraine *(G-11444)*

Towlift Inc... E..... 440 951-9519
 Mentor *(G-11004)*

Towlift Inc... E..... 419 666-1333
 Northwood *(G-11985)*

United Rentals North Amer Inc................ E..... 614 276-5444
 Columbus *(G-6814)*

LEASING & RENTAL: Medical Machinery & Eqpt

Boardman Medical Supply Co.................. C..... 330 545-6700
 Girard *(G-8810)*

Braden Med Services Inc......................... E..... 740 732-2356
 Caldwell *(G-1547)*

Care Medical Inc...................................... E..... 513 821-7272
 Cincinnati *(G-2309)*

Cornerstone Med Svcs - Mdwest............. E..... 330 374-0229
 Akron *(G-123)*

Fairfield Medical Center.......................... A..... 740 687-8000
 Lancaster *(G-9718)*

First Choice Homecare Inc....................... E..... 440 717-1984
 Broadview Heights *(G-1390)*

Health Aid of Ohio Inc............................. E..... 216 252-3900
 Cleveland *(G-4353)*

Hill-Rom Inc... E..... 513 769-6343
 Cincinnati *(G-2821)*

Integrated Medical Inc............................. E..... 216 332-1550
 Cleveland *(G-4414)*

Lincare Inc... E..... 330 928-0884
 Akron *(G-221)*

Lincare Inc... E..... 304 243-9605
 Barnesville *(G-719)*

Lincare Inc... E..... 513 272-6050
 Cincinnati *(G-2978)*

Lincare Inc... E..... 216 581-9649
 Cleveland *(G-4497)*

Lincare Inc... E..... 419 499-1188
 Milan *(G-11207)*

Lincare Inc... E..... 937 299-1141
 Moraine *(G-11420)*

Lincare Inc... E..... 740 349-8236
 Newark *(G-11722)*

Medical Service Company........................ D..... 440 232-3000
 Bedford *(G-973)*

Mercy Hlth - St Rtas Med Ctr L............... A..... 419 227-3361
 Lima *(G-9934)*

Millers Rental and Sls Co Inc.................. D..... 330 753-8600
 Akron *(G-234)*

Sateri Home Inc....................................... D..... 330 758-8106
 Youngstown *(G-15717)*

Seeley Enterprises Company................... E..... 440 293-6600
 Andover *(G-440)*

Seeley Medical Oxygen Co...................... E..... 440 255-7163
 Andover *(G-441)*

Toledo Medical Equipment Co................. E..... 419 866-7120
 Maumee *(G-10774)*

LEASING & RENTAL: Trucks, Indl

All Lift Service Company Inc................... E..... 440 585-1542
 Willoughby *(G-15183)*

Brennan Equipment Services Co.............. E..... 419 867-6000
 Holland *(G-9282)*

Fallsway Equipment Co Inc..................... C..... 330 633-6000
 Akron *(G-152)*

LEASING & RENTAL: Trucks, Without Drivers

Graham Chevrolet-Cadillac Co................. C..... 419 989-4012
 Ontario *(G-12105)*

Hogan Truck Leasing Inc......................... E..... 513 454-3500
 Fairfield *(G-8418)*

Hogan Truck Leasing Inc......................... E..... 937 293-0033
 Moraine *(G-11417)*

Interstate Truckway Inc........................... D..... 513 542-5500
 Cincinnati *(G-2883)*

Kempthorn Motors Inc............................. D..... 800 451-3877
 Canton *(G-1790)*

Krieger Ford Inc....................................... C..... 614 888-3320
 Columbus *(G-6129)*

McCluskey Chevrolet Inc......................... C..... 513 761-1111
 Loveland *(G-10149)*

Miami Valley Intl Trcks Inc...................... E..... 513 733-8500
 Cincinnati *(G-3055)*

Miami Valley Intl Trcks Inc...................... E..... 937 324-5526
 Springfield *(G-13273)*

Montrose Ford Inc.................................... C..... 330 666-0711
 Fairlawn *(G-8491)*

Penske Logistics LLC............................... D..... 216 765-5475
 Beachwood *(G-825)*

Premier Truck Sls & Rentl Inc................. E..... 800 825-1255
 Cleveland *(G-4768)*

Reineke Ford Inc...................................... E..... 888 691-8175
 Fostoria *(G-8622)*

Rouen Chrysler Plymouth Dodge............. E..... 419 837-6228
 Woodville *(G-15306)*

Roush Equipment Inc............................... C..... 614 882-1535
 Westerville *(G-15014)*

LEASING & RENTAL: Trucks, Without Drivers

Rush Truck Centers Ohio Inc............... E 513 733-8500
  Cincinnati *(G-3334)*
Rush Truck Leasing Inc...................... E 937 264-2365
  Dayton *(G-7599)*
Rush Truck Leasing Inc...................... E 419 224-6045
  Lima *(G-9957)*
Rush Truck Leasing Inc...................... E 330 798-0600
  Walton Hills *(G-14479)*
Schoner Chevrolet Inc......................... E 330 877-6731
  Hartville *(G-9129)*
Triangle Leasing Corp......................... E 419 729-3868
  Toledo *(G-14074)*
U Haul Co of Northwestern Ohio........... E 419 478-1101
  Toledo *(G-14078)*
Vin Devers Inc.................................... C 888 847-9535
  Sylvania *(G-13578)*
Voss Auto Network Inc........................ E 937 428-2447
  Dayton *(G-7711)*
White Family Companies Inc................ E 937 222-3701
  Dayton *(G-7720)*

LEASING & RENTAL: Utility Trailers & RV's

Brown Gibbons Lang Ltd Ptrship........... E 216 241-2800
  Cleveland *(G-3905)*

LEASING: Passenger Car

Albert Mike Leasing............................. C 513 563-1400
  Cincinnati *(G-2158)*
Beechmont Ford Inc............................ C 513 752-6611
  Cincinnati *(G-2098)*
Bob Pulte Chevrolet Inc....................... E 513 932-0303
  Lebanon *(G-9757)*
Bobb Automotive Inc........................... E 614 853-3000
  Columbus *(G-5452)*
Brondes All Makes Auto Leasing........... D 419 887-1511
  Maumee *(G-10705)*
Brown Motor Sales Co......................... E 419 531-0151
  Toledo *(G-13720)*
Carcorp Inc.. C 877 857-2801
  Columbus *(G-5506)*
Chesrown Oldsmobile GMC Inc............. E 614 846-3040
  Columbus *(G-5554)*
Classic Automotive Group Inc............... E 440 255-5511
  Mentor *(G-10922)*
Classic Bick Oldsmbile Cdliac............... E 440 639-4500
  Painesville *(G-12222)*
Clerac LLC.. E 440 345-3999
  Strongsville *(G-13448)*
Columbus SAI Motors LLC................... E 614 851-3273
  Columbus *(G-5653)*
Dunning Motor Sales Inc..................... E 740 439-4465
  Cambridge *(G-1568)*
Ed Tomko Chrysler Jeep Ddge In.......... E 440 835-5900
  Avon Lake *(G-677)*
Enterprise Holdings Inc....................... E 513 538-6200
  Blue Ash *(G-1169)*
Graham Chevrolet-Cadillac Co.............. C 419 989-4012
  Ontario *(G-12105)*
Grogans Towne Chrysler Inc................ D 419 476-0761
  Toledo *(G-13830)*
Hidy Motors Inc.................................. D 937 426-9564
  Dayton *(G-7133)*
Jake Sweeney Automotive Inc............... E 513 782-2800
  Cincinnati *(G-2896)*
Jim Brown Chevrolet Inc...................... C 440 255-5511
  Mentor *(G-10955)*
Kempthorn Motors Inc......................... D 800 451-3877
  Canton *(G-1790)*
Kerry Ford Inc.................................... D 513 671-6400
  Cincinnati *(G-2939)*
Kings Toyota Inc................................. D 513 583-4333
  Cincinnati *(G-2941)*

Klaben Lincoln Ford Inc....................... D 330 593-6800
  Kent *(G-9585)*
Krieger Ford Inc.................................. C 614 888-3320
  Columbus *(G-6129)*
Lakewood Chrysler-Plymouth................ E 216 521-1000
  Brookpark *(G-1437)*
Lariche Chevrolet-Cadillac Inc.............. D 419 422-1855
  Findlay *(G-8556)*
Lavery Chevrolet-Buick Inc.................. E 330 823-1100
  Alliance *(G-388)*
Lima Auto Mall Inc.............................. D 419 993-6000
  Lima *(G-9918)*
Lincoln Mrcury Kings Auto Mall............ E 513 683-3800
  Cincinnati *(G-2979)*
Mathews Ddge Chrysler Jeep Inc.......... E 740 389-2341
  Marion *(G-10443)*
Mathews Kennedy Ford L-M Inc........... D 740 387-3673
  Marion *(G-10444)*
McCluskey Chevrolet Inc..................... C 513 761-1111
  Loveland *(G-10149)*
Mike Albert Fleet Solutions.................. C 800 985-3273
  Cincinnati *(G-3061)*
Montrose Ford Inc.............................. C 330 666-0711
  Fairlawn *(G-8491)*
Mullinax Ford North Canton Inc............ C 330 238-3206
  Canton *(G-1812)*
Nick Mayer Lincoln-Mercury Inc........... D 877 836-5314
  Westlake *(G-15084)*
Northgate Chrysler Ddge Jeep I............ E 513 385-3900
  Cincinnati *(G-3123)*
Partners Auto Group Bdford Inc............ D 440 439-2323
  Bedford *(G-980)*
Reineke Ford Inc................................ E 888 691-8175
  Fostoria *(G-8622)*
Ron Marhofer Automall Inc.................. E 330 923-5059
  Cuyahoga Falls *(G-7100)*
Rouen Chrysler Plymouth Dodge........... E 419 837-6228
  Woodville *(G-15306)*
Roush Equipment Inc.......................... C 614 882-1535
  Westerville *(G-15014)*
Schoner Chevrolet Inc......................... E 330 877-6731
  Hartville *(G-9129)*
Sharpnack Chevrolet Co...................... E 800 752-7513
  Vermilion *(G-14408)*
Sonic Automotive................................ D 614 870-8200
  Columbus *(G-6692)*
Sorbir Inc.. D 440 449-1000
  Cleveland *(G-4919)*
Sunnyside Cars Inc............................. E 440 777-9911
  North Olmsted *(G-11917)*
Swapalease Inc.................................. D 513 381-0100
  Blue Ash *(G-1250)*
Tansky Motors Inc.............................. E 650 322-7069
  Rockbridge *(G-12736)*
Tom Ahl Chryslr-Plymouth-Dodge......... C 419 227-0202
  Lima *(G-9971)*
Van Devere Inc................................... D 330 253-6137
  Akron *(G-348)*
Vin Devers Inc.................................... C 888 847-9535
  Sylvania *(G-13578)*
Yark Automotive Group Inc.................. B 419 841-7771
  Toledo *(G-14111)*

LEATHER & CUT STOCK WHOLESALERS

Weaver Leather LLC............................ D 330 674-7548
  Millersburg *(G-11296)*

LEATHER GOODS, EXC FOOTWEAR, GLOVES, LUGGAGE/ BELTING, WHOL

B D G Wrap-Tite Inc............................ E 440 349-5400
  Solon *(G-13070)*

LEATHER GOODS: Personal

Weaver Leather LLC............................ D 330 674-7548
  Millersburg *(G-11296)*

LEGAL AID SVCS

Advoctes For Bsic Lgal Eqlity................ E 419 255-0814
  Toledo *(G-13675)*
Legal Aid Society Cincinnati................. D 513 241-9400
  Cincinnati *(G-2969)*
Legal Aid Society of Cleveland.............. E 440 324-1121
  Elyria *(G-8267)*
Legal Aid Society of Cleveland.............. D 216 861-5500
  Cleveland *(G-4486)*
Legal Aid Society of Columbus.............. E 614 737-0139
  Columbus *(G-6153)*
Legal Aid Southeast Centl Ohio............. D 740 354-7563
  Portsmouth *(G-12561)*
Legal Aid Western Ohio Inc.................. E 419 724-0030
  Toledo *(G-13884)*
Litigation Management Inc................... C 440 484-2000
  Chesterland *(G-2038)*

LEGAL OFFICES & SVCS

Arthur Mddlton Cpitl Hldngs In.............. D 330 966-9000
  North Canton *(G-11812)*
City of Lakewood................................ E 216 529-6170
  Cleveland *(G-3991)*
City of Pepper Pike.............................. E 216 831-9604
  Pepper Pike *(G-12298)*
Cleveland Metro Bar Assn.................... E 216 696-3525
  Cleveland *(G-4055)*
Cleveland Teachers Union Inc.............. E 216 861-7676
  Cleveland *(G-4070)*
County of Portage............................... E 330 297-3850
  Ravenna *(G-12625)*
Criminal Jstice Crdnting Cncil............... E 567 200-6850
  Toledo *(G-13770)*
Deedscom Inc..................................... E 330 606-0119
  Fairlawn *(G-8473)*
Fairfield Federal Sav Ln Assn............... E 740 653-3863
  Lancaster *(G-9712)*
Gbd Legacy LLC................................. E 330 441-0785
  Akron *(G-172)*
General Audit Corporation.................... D 419 993-2900
  Lima *(G-9891)*
Legal Dfnders Off Smmit Cnty O........... D 330 434-3461
  Akron *(G-220)*
Legal Support Simplified LLC................ E 440 546-3368
  Cleveland *(G-4487)*
Ohio Dsblity Rghts Law Plicy C............. E 614 466-7264
  Columbus *(G-6414)*
Recovery One LLC.............................. D 614 336-4207
  Columbus *(G-6564)*
Toledo Bar Association Inc................... E 419 242-9363
  Toledo *(G-14051)*
Turocy & Watson LLP.......................... E 216 696-8730
  Cleveland *(G-5042)*
United Scoto Senior Activities............... E 740 354-6672
  Portsmouth *(G-12579)*
Zaremba Group LLC............................ D 216 221-6600
  Lakewood *(G-9689)*

LEGAL SVCS: General Practice Attorney or Lawyer

Anspach Meeks Ellenberger LLP........... E 419 447-6181
  Toledo *(G-13689)*
Bailey Cavalieri LLC............................ D 614 221-3258
  Columbus *(G-5412)*
Baker & Hostetler LLP......................... D 513 929-3400
  Cincinnati *(G-2236)*

SERVICES SECTION

LEGAL SVCS: General Practice Attorney or Lawyer

Baker & Hostetler LLP........................... E 216 430-2960
 Cleveland (G-3848)
Baker & Hostetler LLP........................... D 614 228-1541
 Columbus (G-5414)
Baker & Hostetler LLP........................... B 216 621-0200
 Cleveland (G-3847)
Benesch Frdlnder Cplan Arnoff............. E 216 363-4686
 Cleveland (G-3865)
Benesch Frdlnder Cplan Arnoff............. E 614 223-9300
 Columbus (G-5432)
Benesch Friedlander Coplan.................. C 216 363-4500
 Cleveland (G-3866)
Bieser Greer & Landis LLP..................... D 937 223-3277
 Dayton (G-7192)
Bordas & Bordas Pllc............................. D 740 695-8141
 Saint Clairsville (G-12782)
Buckingham Dlttle Brroughs LLC........... E 330 492-8717
 Canton (G-1693)
Buckingham Dlttle Brroughs LLC........... E 216 621-5300
 Cleveland (G-3909)
Buckingham Dlttle Brroughs LLC........... C 330 376-5300
 Akron (G-77)
Burke Manley Lpa.................................... E 513 721-5525
 Cincinnati (G-2291)
Calfee Halter & Griswold LLP................. E 513 693-4880
 Cincinnati (G-2301)
Calfee Halter & Griswold LLP................. E 614 621-1500
 Columbus (G-5493)
Calfee Halter & Griswold LLP................. B 216 622-8200
 Cleveland (G-3918)
Carlile Patchen & Murphy LLP............... D 614 228-6135
 Columbus (G-5512)
Carlisle McNlllie Rini Krmer Ul............... E 216 360-7200
 Beachwood (G-772)
Carpenter Lipps LLP............................... D 614 365-4100
 Columbus (G-5514)
Chambrlain Hrdlcka White Wllam........... D 216 589-9280
 Avon (G-643)
Clunk Hoose Co Lpa.............................. E 330 922-5492
 Akron (G-110)
Coolidge Wall Co LPA............................ D 937 223-8177
 Dayton (G-7247)
Cors & Bassett LLC................................. D 513 852-8200
 Cincinnati (G-2510)
County of Ottawa................................... C 567 262-3600
 Oak Harbor (G-12044)
Dagger Jhnston Mller Oglvie HM.......... E 740 653-6464
 Lancaster (G-9707)
David L Barth Lwyr................................. D 513 852-8228
 Cincinnati (G-2543)
Dinsmore & Shohl LLP............................ D 614 628-6880
 Columbus (G-5766)
Dinsmore & Shohl LLP............................ E 937 449-6400
 Dayton (G-7315)
Dinsmore & Shohl LLP............................ B 513 977-8200
 Cincinnati (G-2565)
Dungan & Lefevre Co LPA..................... E 937 339-0511
 Troy (G-14134)
Dworken & Bernstein Co Lpa................. E 216 230-5170
 Cleveland (G-4191)
Eastman & Smith Ltd.............................. C 419 241-6000
 Toledo (G-13785)
Ernest V Thomas Jr................................ E 513 961-5311
 Cincinnati (G-2635)
Faust Hrrlson Flker McCrthy SC........... E 937 335-8324
 Troy (G-14135)
Finney Law Firm LLC............................. E 513 943-6650
 Cincinnati (G-2104)
Flanagan Lberman Hoffman Swaim...... E 937 223-5200
 Dayton (G-7359)
Flannery Georgalis LLC.......................... E 216 367-2095
 Cleveland (G-4264)

Frantz Ward LLP..................................... C 216 515-1660
 Cleveland (G-4286)
Freking Myers & Reul LLC..................... E 513 721-1975
 Cincinnati (G-2707)
Freund Freze Arnold A Lgal Pro........... D 937 222-2424
 Dayton (G-7368)
Friedman Domiano Smith Co Lpa......... E 216 621-0070
 Cleveland (G-4289)
Frost Brown Todd LLC........................... B 513 651-6800
 Cincinnati (G-2709)
Gallagher Sharp..................................... C 216 241-5310
 Cleveland (G-4301)
Gallon Tkacs Bssnult Schffer L............ D 419 843-2001
 Maumee (G-10726)
Gottlieb Jhnson Beam Dal Pnte............ E 740 452-7555
 Zanesville (G-15797)
Hahn Loeser & Parks LLP...................... C 216 621-0150
 Cleveland (G-4346)
Hoover Kacyon LLC................................ E 330 922-4491
 Cuyahoga Falls (G-7080)
Kademenos Wisehart Hines................. E 419 524-6011
 Mansfield (G-10277)
Kademnos Wshart Hnes Dlyk Zher..... E 440 967-6136
 Vermilion (G-14406)
Katz Teller Brant Hild Co Lpa................ D 513 721-4532
 Cincinnati (G-2931)
Keating Muething & Klekamp Pll........... B 513 579-6400
 Cincinnati (G-2932)
Kegler Brown Hl Ritter Co Lpa.............. C 614 462-5400
 Columbus (G-6107)
Keis George LLP.................................... E 216 241-4100
 Cleveland (G-4452)
Kelley Ferraro LLC.................................. E 216 575-0777
 Cleveland (G-4454)
Kohrman Jackson & Krantz LLP............ D 216 696-8700
 Cleveland (G-4468)
Krugliak Wlkins Grffths Dghrty............. D 330 497-0700
 Canton (G-1792)
Law Offces Rbert A Schrger Lpa........ E 614 824-5731
 Wilmington (G-15256)
Levy & Associates LLC.......................... E 614 898-5200
 Columbus (G-6155)
Lindhorst & Dreidame Co Lpa............... E 513 421-6630
 Cincinnati (G-2980)
LLP Gallagher Sharp............................... E 216 241-5310
 Cleveland (G-4502)
LLP Ziegler Metzger............................... E 216 781-5470
 Cleveland (G-4503)
Lupo & Koczkur PC............................... E 419 897-7931
 Maumee (G-10743)
Maguire & Schneider LLP...................... E 614 224-1222
 Columbus (G-6190)
Mansour Gavin Lpa................................ D 216 523-1501
 Cleveland (G-4521)
Marshall & Melhorn LLC........................ D 419 249-7100
 Toledo (G-13911)
Mazanec Raskin & Ryder Co Lpa......... D 440 248-7906
 Cleveland (G-4533)
McGlinchey Stafford Pllc....................... E 216 378-9905
 Shaker Heights (G-12981)
Millikin and Fitton Law Firm................... E 513 863-6700
 Hamilton (G-9066)
Murray & Murray Co LPA...................... E 419 624-3000
 Sandusky (G-12916)
Nicola Gudbranson & Cooper LLC........ E 216 621-7227
 Cleveland (G-4644)
OGara Group Inc................................... A 513 275-8456
 West Chester (G-14736)
Porter Wrght Morris Arthur LLP............. E 513 381-4700
 Cincinnati (G-3221)
Reese Pyle Drake & Meyer.................... E 740 345-3431
 Newark (G-11745)

Reminger Co LPA................................... C 216 687-1311
 Cleveland (G-4825)
Rendigs Fry Kiely & Dennis LLP............ D 513 381-9200
 Cincinnati (G-3286)
Renner Knner Greve Bbak Tylor........... E 330 376-1242
 Akron (G-279)
Robbins Kelly Patterson Tucker............. E 513 721-3330
 Cincinnati (G-3312)
Robert Kelly & Bucio LLP....................... E 937 332-9300
 Troy (G-14156)
Roetzel Andress A Lgal Prof As............ E 216 623-0150
 Cleveland (G-4853)
Roetzel Andress A Lgal Prof As............ C 330 376-2700
 Akron (G-286)
Rohrbchers Light Crone Trimble........... E 419 471-1160
 Toledo (G-13994)
Rolfes Henry Co LPA............................. E 513 579-0080
 Cincinnati (G-3318)
Rose & Dobyns An Ohio Partnr............ E 740 335-4700
 Wshngtn Ct Hs (G-15492)
Rose & Dobyns An Ohio Partnr............ E 937 382-2838
 Wilmington (G-15271)
Scott S Duko Attorney At Law............... E 800 593-6676
 Fairlawn (G-8497)
Sebaly Shllito Dyer A Lgal Pro.............. D 937 222-2500
 Dayton (G-7614)
Seeley Svdge Ebert Gourash Lpa........ E 216 566-8200
 Westlake (G-15106)
Shumaker Loop & Kendrick LLP.......... D 614 463-9441
 Columbus (G-6677)
Shumaker Loop & Kendrick LLP.......... C 419 241-9000
 Toledo (G-14013)
Singerman Mlls Dsberg Kntz Lpa........ E 216 292-5807
 Cleveland (G-4908)
Sottile & Barile LLC................................ E 513 345-0592
 Loveland (G-10161)
Spengler Nathanson PLL....................... E 419 241-2201
 Toledo (G-14020)
Sutter OConnell Co................................ E 216 928-4504
 Cleveland (G-4969)
Teating Mueting & Klekamp Pll............. E 513 579-6462
 Cincinnati (G-3447)
Thompson Hine LLP............................... D 614 469-3200
 Columbus (G-6763)
Thompson Hine LLP............................... D 614 469-3200
 Columbus (G-6764)
Thompson Hine LLP............................... D 937 443-6859
 Miamisburg (G-11098)
Thompson Hine LLP............................... B 216 566-5500
 Cleveland (G-5013)
Tucker Ellis LLP...................................... C 216 592-5000
 Cleveland (G-5039)
Tzangas Plakas Mannos Recupero...... E 330 453-5466
 Canton (G-1874)
Ulmer & Berne LLP................................ D 614 229-0000
 Columbus (G-6797)
Ulmer & Berne LLP................................ B 216 583-7000
 Cleveland (G-5049)
Vorys Sater Seymour and Pease LLP.... B 614 464-6400
 Columbus (G-6858)
Vorys Sater Seymour Pease LLP.......... E 513 723-4000
 Cincinnati (G-3635)
Vorys Sater Seymour Pease LLP.......... D 216 479-6100
 Cleveland (G-5115)
Waite Schnder Byless Chsley LP........ D 513 621-0267
 Cincinnati (G-3638)
Walter Haverfield LLP............................. D 216 781-1212
 Cleveland (G-5121)
Wegman Hessler Vanderburg................ D 216 642-3342
 Cleveland (G-5124)
Weiner Keith D Co L P A Inc.................. E 216 771-6500
 Cleveland (G-5126)

Employee Codes: A=Over 500 employees, B=251-500
C=101-250, D=51-100, E=20-50, F=10-19, G=1-9

2024 Harris Ohio Services Directory

Wiles Boyle Burkholder &............... D..... 614 221-5216
  Columbus (G-6892)
Willis Spangler Starling.................... D..... 614 586-7900
  Hilliard (G-9243)
Wood & Lamping LLP...................... D..... 513 852-6000
  Cincinnati (G-3679)
Young & Alexander Co LPA............ E..... 513 326-5555
  Cincinnati (G-3686)
Zashin & Rich Co LPA..................... E..... 216 696-4441
  Cleveland (G-5172)

LIFE INSURANCE CARRIERS

Andrew Insurance Associates........... D..... 614 336-8030
  Dublin (G-7938)
Cincinnati Financial Corp.................. A..... 513 870-2000
  Fairfield (G-8402)
Cincinnati Insurance Company......... A..... 513 870-2000
  Fairfield (G-8404)
Columbus Life Insurance Co............. C..... 513 361-6700
  Cincinnati (G-2477)
Lafayette Life Insurance Co.............. C..... 800 443-8793
  Cincinnati (G-2963)
Midland-Guardian Co......................... A..... 513 943-7100
  Amelia (G-419)
Modern Finance Company................ E..... 614 351-7400
  Columbus (G-6255)
Nationwide Mutual Insurance Co..... A..... 614 249-7111
  Columbus (G-6338)
Ohio Casualty Insurance Co.............. A..... 800 843-6446
  Cincinnati (G-3143)
Pacific Life Insurance Company........ E..... 513 241-5000
  West Chester (G-14740)
Standard Insurance Company........... C..... 513 241-7275
  Cincinnati (G-3408)
State Farm General Insur Co............ D..... 513 662-7283
  Cincinnati (G-3413)

LIGHTING FIXTURES WHOLESALERS

American De Rosa Lamparts LLC..... D
  Cuyahoga Falls (G-7038)
D & L Lighting Inc............................. D..... 614 841-1200
  Columbus (G-5256)
Eye Lighting Intl N Amer Inc............. C..... 440 350-7000
  Mentor (G-10939)
Lighting Services Inc......................... D..... 330 405-4879
  Twinsburg (G-14201)
LSI Industries Inc............................... C..... 913 281-1100
  Blue Ash (G-1202)
Venture Lighting Intl Inc.................... D..... 800 451-2606
  Solon (G-13159)
Vincent Lighting Systems Co............ E..... 216 475-7600
  Solon (G-13161)

LIGHTING FIXTURES, NEC

Will-Burt Company............................. C..... 330 682-7015
  Orrville (G-12176)

LIGHTING FIXTURES: Airport

Akron-Canton Regional Airport......... E..... 330 499-4059
  North Canton (G-11809)
City of Cleveland................................ A..... 216 265-6000
  Cleveland (G-3980)
City of Dayton..................................... C..... 937 454-8200
  Vandalia (G-14371)
Cleveland Hopkins Intl Arprt.............. E..... 216 265-6000
  Cleveland (G-4051)
Columbus Regional Airport Auth....... B..... 614 239-4000
  Columbus (G-5652)
Griffings Flying Service Inc................ E..... 419 734-5400
  Port Clinton (G-12530)
Safegate Airport Systems Inc............ E..... 763 535-9299
  Columbus (G-6628)

TAS Aviation Defiance Inc................. E..... 419 658-4444
  Defiance (G-7771)
Toledo-Lucas County Port Auth........ D..... 419 865-2351
  Swanton (G-13530)

LIGHTING FIXTURES: Indl & Commercial

Best Lighting Products Inc................. D..... 740 964-1198
  Etna (G-8332)
LSI Industries Inc............................... C..... 913 281-1100
  Blue Ash (G-1202)
LSI Lightron Inc.................................. A..... 845 562-5500
  Blue Ash (G-1203)

LIGHTING FIXTURES: Motor Vehicle

Akron Brass Holding Corp................. E..... 330 264-5678
  Wooster (G-15307)
Grimes Aerospace Company............ D..... 937 484-2001
  Urbana (G-14308)

LIME

Bluffton Stone Co............................... E..... 419 358-6941
  Bluffton (G-1279)
National Lime and Stone Co.............. E..... 419 396-7671
  Carey (G-1894)
Piqua Materials Inc............................ D..... 937 773-4824
  Piqua (G-12453)
Shelly Materials Inc........................... E..... 740 666-5841
  Ostrander (G-12184)

LIME ROCK: Ground

National Lime and Stone Co.............. E..... 419 396-7671
  Carey (G-1894)

LIMESTONE: Crushed & Broken

Beazer East Inc.................................. E..... 937 364-2311
  Hillsboro (G-9249)
Bluffton Stone Co............................... E..... 419 358-6941
  Bluffton (G-1279)
Carmeuse Lime Inc........................... E..... 419 986-5200
  Bettsville (G-1098)
Custar Stone Co................................. E..... 419 669-4327
  Napoleon (G-11520)
Kellstone Inc....................................... E..... 419 746-2396
  Kelleys Island (G-9553)
Lang Stone Company Inc.................. E..... 614 235-4099
  Columbus (G-6139)
National Lime and Stone Co.............. E..... 419 562-0771
  Bucyrus (G-1513)
National Lime and Stone Co.............. E..... 740 548-4206
  Delaware (G-7819)
National Lime and Stone Co.............. E..... 419 228-3434
  Lima (G-9937)
Oglebay Norton Mar Svcs Co LLC.... A..... 216 861-3300
  Cleveland (G-4680)
Omya Industries Inc........................... D..... 513 387-4600
  Mason (G-10586)
Shelly Materials Inc............................ E..... 740 666-5841
  Ostrander (G-12184)
Shelly Materials Inc............................ D..... 740 246-6315
  Thornville (G-13622)
Stoneco Inc... E..... 419 893-7645
  Maumee (G-10771)
Stoneco Inc... E..... 419 393-2555
  Oakwood (G-12054)
The National Lime and Stone Company.E..... 419 422-4341
  Findlay (G-8593)

LIMESTONE: Dimension

National Lime and Stone Co.............. E..... 419 562-0771
  Bucyrus (G-1513)
Stoneco Inc... E..... 419 422-8854
  Findlay (G-8588)

Waterloo Coal Company Inc............. D..... 740 286-0004
  Jackson (G-9529)

LIMESTONE: Ground

National Lime and Stone Co.............. E..... 740 387-3485
  Marion (G-10446)
Piqua Materials Inc............................ D..... 937 773-4824
  Piqua (G-12453)

LINEN SPLY SVC: Uniform

Ameripride Services Inc.................... D..... 859 371-4037
  Cincinnati (G-2189)
Barberton Laundry and Clg Inc......... D..... 330 825-6911
  Barberton (G-694)
Cintas Corporation No 1.................... A..... 513 459-1200
  Mason (G-10533)
Cintas Corporation No 2.................... C..... 513 965-0800
  Milford (G-11223)
Cintas Corporation No 2.................... D..... 800 444-2687
  Vandalia (G-14370)
Kramer Enterprises Inc...................... E..... 419 422-7924
  Findlay (G-8555)
Unifirst Corporation............................ E..... 614 575-9999
  Blacklick (G-1114)
Unifirst Corporation............................ E..... 937 746-0531
  Franklin (G-8651)
Vestis Corporation.............................. C..... 513 533-1000
  Cincinnati (G-3625)
Vestis Corporation.............................. E..... 614 445-8341
  Columbus (G-6847)
Vestis Corporation.............................. E..... 937 223-6667
  Dayton (G-7703)
Vestis Corporation.............................. C..... 419 729-5454
  Toledo (G-14092)

LINENS & TOWELS WHOLESALERS

Standard Textile Co Inc..................... B..... 513 761-9255
  Cincinnati (G-3409)

LIQUEFIED PETROLEUM GAS DEALERS

Beck Suppliers Inc............................. E..... 419 426-3051
  Attica (G-598)

LIQUEFIED PETROLEUM GAS WHOLESALERS

Centerra Co-Op.................................. E..... 419 281-2153
  Ashland (G-490)

LIVESTOCK WHOLESALERS, NEC

Hord Livestock Company Inc............ E..... 419 562-0277
  Bucyrus (G-1509)

LOADS: Electronic

TL Industries Inc................................ C..... 419 666-8144
  Perrysburg (G-12377)

LOCKSMITHS

Kirk Key Interlock Company LLC...... E..... 330 833-8223
  North Canton (G-11846)

LOTIONS OR CREAMS: Face

Beautyavenues LLC........................... C..... 614 856-6000
  Reynoldsburg (G-12654)
Beiersdorf Inc..................................... C..... 513 682-7300
  West Chester (G-14800)

LUBRICATING OIL & GREASE WHOLESALERS

Applied Indus Tech - Dixie Inc.......... D..... 216 426-4546
  Cleveland (G-3826)

SERVICES SECTION

MACHINERY & EQPT, AGRICULTURAL, WHOLESALE: Lawn

Fisk Kinne Holdings Inc .... E 937 461-9906
  Dayton *(G-7356)*
Reladyne Inc .... C 513 941-2800
  Cincinnati *(G-3285)*
Specialty Lubricants Corp .... E 330 425-2567
  Macedonia *(G-10205)*
Suburban Oil Company .... E 513 459-8100
  Mason *(G-10611)*

LUGGAGE & BRIEFCASES

Weaver Leather LLC .... D 330 674-7548
  Millersburg *(G-11296)*

LUMBER & BLDG MATLS DEALER, RET: Garage Doors, Sell/Install

Installed Building Products LLC .... C 614 221-3399
  Columbus *(G-6059)*
Overhead Door Co- Cincinnati .... C 513 346-4000
  West Chester *(G-14739)*
Overhead Inc .... E 419 476-7811
  Toledo *(G-13951)*
Sievers Security Inc .... E 216 291-2222
  Cleveland *(G-4905)*

LUMBER & BLDG MATLS DEALERS, RET: Energy Conservation Prdts

Hercules Led LLC .... E 844 437-2533
  Boardman *(G-1289)*

LUMBER & BLDG MATRLS DEALERS, RETAIL: Doors, Wood/Metal

Nofziger Door Sales Inc .... C 419 337-9900
  Wauseon *(G-14607)*

LUMBER & BLDG MTRLS DEALERS, RET: Planing Mill Prdts/Lumber

Keim Lumber Company .... D 330 893-2251
  Baltic *(G-690)*

LUMBER & BUILDING MATERIALS DEALER, RET: Door & Window Prdts

Dun Rite Home Improvement Inc .... E 330 650-5322
  Macedonia *(G-10191)*
Erie Construction Mid-West Inc .... D 937 898-4688
  Dayton *(G-7339)*
Erie Construction Mid-West Inc .... B 419 472-4200
  Toledo *(G-13795)*
Fortune Brands Windows Inc .... C 614 532-3500
  Columbus *(G-5879)*
Rockwood Products Ltd .... E 330 893-2392
  Millersburg *(G-11291)*
Schneider Home Equipment Co .... E 513 522-1200
  Cincinnati *(G-3349)*

LUMBER & BUILDING MATERIALS DEALER, RET: Masonry Matls/Splys

BG Trucking & Cnstr Inc .... E 234 759-3440
  North Lima *(G-11884)*
Grafton Ready Mix Concret Inc .... C 440 926-2911
  Grafton *(G-8839)*
Maza Inc .... D 614 760-0003
  Plain City *(G-12486)*
The W L Tucker Supply Company .... E 330 928-2155
  Cuyahoga Falls *(G-7107)*

LUMBER & BUILDING MATERIALS DEALERS, RETAIL: Brick

Columbus Coal & Lime Co .... E 614 224-9241
  Columbus *(G-5624)*
Hamilton-Parker Company .... D 614 358-7800
  Columbus *(G-5968)*

LUMBER & BUILDING MATERIALS DEALERS, RETAIL: Cement

Smyrna Ready Mix Concrete LLC .... E 937 855-0410
  Germantown *(G-8805)*

LUMBER & BUILDING MATERIALS DEALERS, RETAIL: Siding

Erie Construction Mid-West Inc .... D 419 472-4200
  Toledo *(G-13794)*

LUMBER & BUILDING MATERIALS RET DEALERS: Millwork & Lumber

Carter-Jones Companies Inc .... E 330 673-6100
  Kent *(G-9560)*
The Galehouse Companies Inc .... E 330 658-2023
  Doylestown *(G-7916)*

LUMBER & BUILDING MATLS DEALERS, RET: Concrete/Cinder Block

Encore Precast LLC .... E 513 726-5678
  Seven Mile *(G-12962)*

LUMBER: Dimension, Hardwood

Stephen M Trudick .... E 440 834-1891
  Burton *(G-1533)*

LUMBER: Hardwood Dimension & Flooring Mills

Baillie Lumber Co LP .... E 419 462-2000
  Galion *(G-8745)*
Hartzell Hardwoods Inc .... D 937 773-7054
  Piqua *(G-12443)*
Holmes Lumber & Bldg Ctr Inc .... E 330 479-8314
  Canton *(G-1775)*
Holmes Lumber & Bldg Ctr Inc .... C 330 674-9060
  Millersburg *(G-11279)*
Wappoo Wood Products Inc .... E 937 492-1166
  Sidney *(G-13057)*

LUMBER: Plywood, Hardwood

Exhibit Concepts Inc .... D 937 890-7000
  Vandalia *(G-14376)*
Sims-Lohman Inc .... E 513 651-3510
  Cincinnati *(G-3379)*
Wappoo Wood Products Inc .... E 937 492-1166
  Sidney *(G-13057)*

LUMBER: Treated

The F A Requarth Company .... E 937 224-1141
  Dayton *(G-7665)*

MACHINE PARTS: Stamped Or Pressed Metal

Abbott Tool Inc .... E 419 476-6742
  Toledo *(G-13673)*

MACHINE TOOL ACCESS: Drill Bushings, Drilling Jig

Jergens Inc .... C 216 486-5540
  Cleveland *(G-4437)*

MACHINE TOOL ACCESS: Tools & Access

Imco Carbide Tool Inc .... D 419 661-6313
  Perrysburg *(G-12346)*

MACHINE TOOLS & ACCESS

Johnson Bros Rubber Co Inc .... E 419 752-4814
  Greenwich *(G-8892)*
Ohio Broach & Machine Company .... E 440 946-1040
  Willoughby *(G-15214)*

MACHINE TOOLS, METAL CUTTING: Home Workshop

H & D Steel Service Inc .... E 800 666-3390
  North Royalton *(G-11942)*

MACHINE TOOLS, METAL CUTTING: Tool Replacement & Rpr Parts

Cardinal Builders Inc .... E 614 237-1000
  Columbus *(G-5507)*

MACHINE TOOLS, METAL FORMING: Bending

Addition Manufacturing Tech .... C 513 228-7000
  Lebanon *(G-9752)*
Pines Manufacturing Inc .... E 440 835-5553
  Westlake *(G-15098)*

MACHINE TOOLS, METAL FORMING: Marking

Monode Marking Products Inc .... E 440 975-8802
  Mentor *(G-10976)*

MACHINE TOOLS, METAL FORMING: Mechanical, Pneumatic Or Hyd

Compass Systems & Sales LLC .... D 330 733-2111
  Norton *(G-11993)*

MACHINE TOOLS: Metal Cutting

Acro Tool & Die Company .... E 330 773-5173
  Akron *(G-14)*
Channel Products Inc .... D 440 423-0113
  Solon *(G-13075)*
Elliott Tool Technologies Ltd .... D 937 253-6133
  Dayton *(G-7333)*

MACHINE TOOLS: Metal Forming

Anderson & Vreeland Inc .... D 419 636-5002
  Bryan *(G-1479)*
Elliott Tool Technologies Ltd .... D 937 253-6133
  Dayton *(G-7333)*

MACHINERY & EQPT FINANCE LEASING

Dana Credit Corporation .... B 419 887-3000
  Maumee *(G-10715)*
Ohio Machinery Co .... C 440 526-6200
  Broadview Heights *(G-1394)*
Reynolds and Reynolds Company .... A 937 485-2000
  Kettering *(G-9632)*

MACHINERY & EQPT, AGRICULTURAL, WHOLESALE: Agricultural, NEC

Apple Farm Service Inc .... E 937 526-4851
  Covington *(G-7017)*

MACHINERY & EQPT, AGRICULTURAL, WHOLESALE: Landscaping Eqpt

Rock Pile Inc .... E 440 937-5100
  Avon *(G-664)*

MACHINERY & EQPT, AGRICULTURAL, WHOLESALE: Lawn

Lesco Inc .... C 216 706-9250
Cleveland *(G-4490)*

MACHINERY & EQPT, AGRICULTURAL, WHOLESALE: Lawn & Garden

Arnold Corporation .... C 330 225-2600
Valley City *(G-14331)*

Bostwick-Braun Company .... D 419 259-3600
Toledo *(G-13713)*

Buckeye Supply Company .... E 740 452-3641
Zanesville *(G-15773)*

Hayward Distributing Co .... E 614 272-5953
Columbus *(G-5974)*

MACHINERY & EQPT, INDL, WHOLESALE: Chemical Process

Aldrich Chemical .... D 937 859-1808
Miamisburg *(G-11023)*

R A Mueller Inc .... E 513 489-5200
Blue Ash *(G-1228)*

MACHINERY & EQPT, INDL, WHOLESALE: Conveyor Systems

Alba Manufacturing Inc .... D 513 874-0551
Fairfield *(G-8388)*

Vargo LLC .... E 614 876-1163
Dublin *(G-8147)*

Vargo Solutions Inc .... D 614 876-1163
Dublin *(G-8148)*

MACHINERY & EQPT, INDL, WHOLESALE: Cranes

Expert Crane Inc .... E 216 451-9900
Wellington *(G-14632)*

Hiab USA Inc .... D 419 482-6000
Perrysburg *(G-12343)*

Tiffin Loader Crane Company .... D 419 448-8156
Tiffin *(G-13646)*

Venco Venturo Industries LLC .... E 513 772-8448
Cincinnati *(G-3619)*

MACHINERY & EQPT, INDL, WHOLESALE: Engines & Parts, Diesel

Clarke Fire Prtection Pdts Inc .... E 513 771-2200
Cincinnati *(G-2455)*

Cummins Inc .... E 513 563-6670
West Chester *(G-14681)*

Detroit Diesel Corporation .... B 330 430-4300
Canton *(G-1735)*

Interstate-Mcbee LLC .... C 216 881-0015
Bedford *(G-967)*

Ohio Machinery Co .... E 419 423-1447
Findlay *(G-8574)*

W W Williams Company LLC .... E 330 225-7751
Brunswick *(G-1473)*

Western Branch Diesel LLC .... E 740 695-6301
Saint Clairsville *(G-12820)*

MACHINERY & EQPT, INDL, WHOLESALE: Engs & Parts, Air-Cooled

Power Distributors LLC .... D 614 876-3533
Columbus *(G-6539)*

MACHINERY & EQPT, INDL, WHOLESALE: Food Product Manufacturng

Bettcher Industries Inc .... C 440 965-4422
Birmingham *(G-1107)*

Chemineer Inc .... C 937 454-3200
Dayton *(G-7222)*

MACHINERY & EQPT, INDL, WHOLESALE: Hydraulic Systems

Air-Way Manufacturing Company .... C 419 298-2366
Edgerton *(G-8227)*

Argo-Hytos Inc .... A 419 353-6070
Bowling Green *(G-1303)*

Bay Advanced Technologies LLC .... E 510 857-0900
Cleveland *(G-3856)*

Bosch Rexroth Corporation .... E 614 527-7400
Grove City *(G-8898)*

Clippard Instrument Lab Inc .... C 513 521-4261
Cincinnati *(G-2460)*

Depot Direct Inc .... E 419 661-1233
Perrysburg *(G-12332)*

Eagle Equipment Corporation .... E 937 746-0510
Franklin *(G-8635)*

Fluid Line Products Inc .... C 440 946-9470
Willoughby *(G-15193)*

Hagglunds Drives Inc .... D 614 527-7400
Columbus *(G-5964)*

Hydraulic Manifolds USA LLC .... E 973 728-1214
Stow *(G-13376)*

Hydraulic Parts Store Inc .... E 330 364-6667
New Philadelphia *(G-11656)*

Mid-State Sales Inc .... D 614 864-1811
Columbus *(G-6241)*

Parker-Hannifin Corporation .... D 440 366-5100
Elyria *(G-8285)*

Parker-Hannifin Corporation .... E 937 644-3915
Marysville *(G-10501)*

Parker-Hannifin Corporation .... C 330 296-2871
Ravenna *(G-12634)*

Parker-Hannifin Corporation .... E 610 926-1115
Wickliffe *(G-15159)*

Robeck Fluid Power Co .... D 330 562-1140
Aurora *(G-624)*

Scott Industrial Systems Inc .... D 937 233-8146
Dayton *(G-7612)*

Sentinel Fluid Controls LLC .... E 419 478-9086
Toledo *(G-14008)*

Sylvester Highland Holding Inc .... D 440 473-1640
Cleveland *(G-4971)*

System Seals Inc .... E 216 220-1800
Brecksville *(G-1369)*

Triad Technologies LLC .... E 937 832-2861
Vandalia *(G-14395)*

V & P Hydraulic Products LLC .... D 740 203-3600
Delaware *(G-7833)*

MACHINERY & EQPT, INDL, WHOLESALE: Indl Machine Parts

Double A Trailer Sales Inc .... E 419 692-7626
Delphos *(G-7840)*

MACHINERY & EQPT, INDL, WHOLESALE: Instruments & Cntrl Eqpt

Columbus Dnv Inc .... C 614 761-1214
Dublin *(G-7966)*

Fcx Performance Inc .... E 614 253-1996
Columbus *(G-5853)*

Lord Corporation .... E 440 542-0012
Solon *(G-13107)*

South Shore Controls Inc .... E 440 259-2500
Mentor *(G-10998)*

MACHINERY & EQPT, INDL, WHOLESALE: Lift Trucks & Parts

Fastener Industries Inc .... E 440 891-2031
Berea *(G-1069)*

Interstate Lift Trucks Inc .... E 216 328-0970
Cleveland *(G-4421)*

Joseph Industries Inc .... D 330 528-0091
Streetsboro *(G-13419)*

Newtown Nine Inc .... D 440 781-0623
Macedonia *(G-10200)*

Towlift Inc .... E 614 851-1001
Columbus *(G-6774)*

Williams Super Service Inc .... E 330 733-7750
East Sparta *(G-8199)*

MACHINERY & EQPT, INDL, WHOLESALE: Machine Tools & Access

Absolute Machine Tools Inc .... E 440 960-6911
Lorain *(G-10052)*

Ellison Technologies Inc .... E 513 874-2736
Hamilton *(G-9038)*

Eurolink Inc .... E 740 392-1549
Mount Vernon *(G-11486)*

Gosiger Holdings Inc .... E 734 582-2100
Solon *(G-13093)*

Gosiger Holdings Inc .... C 937 228-5174
Dayton *(G-7381)*

Gosiger Inc .... B 937 228-5174
Dayton *(G-7382)*

Imco Carbide Tool Inc .... D 419 661-6313
Perrysburg *(G-12346)*

Jergens Inc .... C 216 486-5540
Cleveland *(G-4437)*

LNS America Inc .... E 513 528-5674
Cincinnati *(G-2110)*

Precision Supply Company Inc .... D 330 225-5530
Brunswick *(G-1468)*

Salvagnini America Inc .... E 513 874-8284
Hamilton *(G-9080)*

Wolf Machine Company .... E 513 791-5194
Blue Ash *(G-1274)*

MACHINERY & EQPT, INDL, WHOLESALE: Measure/Test, Electric

Dreier & Maller Inc .... E 614 575-0065
Reynoldsburg *(G-12661)*

MACHINERY & EQPT, INDL, WHOLESALE: Packaging

Alfons Haar Inc .... E 937 560-2031
Springboro *(G-13192)*

Bollin & Sons Inc .... E 419 693-6573
Toledo *(G-13710)*

Millwood Inc .... E 513 860-4567
West Chester *(G-14730)*

Toga-Pak Inc .... E 937 294-7311
Dayton *(G-7672)*

TPC Packaging Solutions Inc .... D 513 489-8840
Cincinnati *(G-3499)*

Tripack LLC .... E 513 248-1255
Milford *(G-11262)*

MACHINERY & EQPT, INDL, WHOLESALE: Petroleum Industry

C H Bradshaw Co .... E 614 871-2087
Grove City *(G-8904)*

SERVICES SECTION

MACHINERY: Textile

Stanwade Metal Products Inc..................E..... 330 772-2421
  Hartford *(G-9123)*

MACHINERY & EQPT, INDL, WHOLESALE: Processing & Packaging

Ampac Packaging LLC......................C..... 513 671-1777
  Cincinnati *(G-2195)*

Equipment Depot Ohio Inc.................E..... 513 934-2121
  Lebanon *(G-9765)*

Tractor Supply Company....................E..... 937 382-2595
  Wilmington *(G-15275)*

MACHINERY & EQPT, INDL, WHOLESALE: Recycling

Gateway Products Recycling Inc..........E..... 216 341-8777
  Cleveland *(G-4306)*

RSR Partners LLC................................D..... 440 519-1768
  Stow *(G-13389)*

MACHINERY & EQPT, INDL, WHOLESALE: Safety Eqpt

A & A Safety Inc..................................E..... 513 943-6100
  Amelia *(G-409)*

Cintas Corporation...............................D..... 513 631-5750
  Cincinnati *(G-2443)*

Cintas Corporation...............................A..... 513 459-1200
  Cincinnati *(G-2442)*

Cintas Corporation No 2......................D..... 330 966-7800
  Canton *(G-1709)*

Cintas Corporation No 2......................D..... 614 878-7313
  Columbus *(G-5572)*

Cintas Corporation No 2......................A..... 513 459-1200
  Mason *(G-10534)*

Cintas Corporation No 2......................C..... 513 965-0800
  Milford *(G-11223)*

Cintas Corporation No 2......................A..... 513 459-1200
  Mason *(G-10535)*

Impact Products LLC...........................D..... 419 841-2891
  Toledo *(G-13860)*

Lorad LLC..E..... 800 504-4016
  Westlake *(G-15077)*

M Conley Company..............................D..... 330 456-8243
  Canton *(G-1798)*

Safety Solutions Inc............................D..... 614 799-9900
  Columbus *(G-6634)*

Safety Today Inc.................................E..... 614 409-7200
  Grove City *(G-8950)*

US Safetygear Inc...............................D..... 330 898-1344
  Warren *(G-14570)*

MACHINERY & EQPT, INDL, WHOLESALE: Tanks, Storage

Cleveland Tank & Supply Inc..............E..... 216 771-8265
  Cleveland *(G-4069)*

MACHINERY & EQPT, WHOLESALE: Construction, General

Ackerman Chacco Company Inc.........E..... 513 791-4252
  Blue Ash *(G-1121)*

All Make Solutions LLC......................D..... 800 255-6253
  Middletown *(G-11151)*

CCC Contractors LLC..........................E..... 937 579-5100
  Lynchburg *(G-10184)*

Columbus Equipment Company..........E..... 614 437-0352
  Columbus *(G-5633)*

Company Wrench Ltd..........................D..... 740 654-5304
  Carroll *(G-1900)*

F & M Mafco Inc..................................C..... 513 367-2151
  Harrison *(G-9104)*

Gibson 2021 LLC.................................E..... 440 439-4000
  Cleveland *(G-4312)*

Leppo Inc..E..... 330 633-3999
  Tallmadge *(G-13599)*

Murphy Tractor & Eqp Co Inc..............E..... 316 633-7215
  Rossford *(G-12769)*

Npk Construction Equipment Inc..........D..... 440 232-7900
  Bedford *(G-976)*

Ohio Machinery Co..............................D..... 440 526-0520
  Broadview Heights *(G-1395)*

Ohio Machinery Co..............................D..... 740 942-4626
  Cadiz *(G-1542)*

Ohio Machinery Co..............................B..... 614 878-2287
  Columbus *(G-6435)*

Ohio Machinery Co..............................D..... 419 874-7975
  Perrysburg *(G-12359)*

Ohio Machinery Co..............................D..... 937 335-7660
  Troy *(G-14149)*

Ohio Machinery Co..............................D..... 740 453-0563
  Zanesville *(G-15822)*

Ohio Machinery Co..............................C..... 440 526-6200
  Broadview Heights *(G-1394)*

Reco LLC..E
  Blue Ash *(G-1234)*

Southeastern Equipment Co Inc..........E..... 740 432-6303
  Cambridge *(G-1582)*

Vermeer Heartland Inc........................E..... 740 335-8571
  Wshngtn Ct Hs *(G-15495)*

MACHINERY & EQPT, WHOLESALE: Oil Field Eqpt

Global Energy Partners LLC...............E..... 419 756-8027
  Mansfield *(G-10267)*

Mountain Supply and Svc LLC............E..... 304 547-1119
  Saint Clairsville *(G-12805)*

MACHINERY & EQPT: Electroplating

Corrotec Inc..E..... 937 325-3585
  Springfield *(G-13242)*

MACHINERY & EQPT: Farm

Ohio Machinery Co..............................C..... 440 526-6200
  Broadview Heights *(G-1394)*

Stephens Pipe & Steel LLC.................C..... 740 869-2257
  Mount Sterling *(G-11475)*

MACHINERY, FOOD PRDTS: Food Processing, Smokers

Frost Engineering Inc..........................E..... 513 541-6330
  Cincinnati *(G-2710)*

MACHINERY, SEWING: Sewing & Hat & Zipper Making

Velocys Inc...D..... 614 733-3300
  Plain City *(G-12497)*

MACHINERY: Automotive Related

Cornerstone Wauseon Inc...................C..... 419 337-0940
  Wauseon *(G-14598)*

MACHINERY: Construction

Chemineer Inc.....................................C..... 937 454-3200
  Dayton *(G-7222)*

Npk Construction Equipment Inc..........D..... 440 232-7900
  Bedford *(G-976)*

Pubco Corporation..............................D..... 216 881-5300
  Cleveland *(G-4797)*

The Wagner-Smith Company..............B..... 866 338-0398
  Moraine *(G-11444)*

MACHINERY: Custom

Alfons Haar Inc....................................E..... 937 560-2031
  Springboro *(G-13192)*

East End Welding LLC.........................C..... 330 677-6000
  Kent *(G-9573)*

Hahn Automation Group Us Inc..........D..... 937 886-3232
  Miamisburg *(G-11058)*

Interscope Manufacturing Inc..............E..... 513 423-8866
  Middletown *(G-11166)*

Metro Design Inc.................................E..... 440 458-4200
  Elyria *(G-8274)*

Narrow Way Custom Tech Inc.............E..... 937 743-1611
  Carlisle *(G-1898)*

S-P Company Inc................................D..... 330 782-5651
  Columbiana *(G-5240)*

Sample Machining Inc.........................E..... 937 258-3338
  Dayton *(G-7609)*

Steel Eqp Specialists Inc.....................D..... 330 823-8260
  Alliance *(G-401)*

MACHINERY: Metalworking

Addition Manufacturing Tech...............C..... 513 228-7000
  Lebanon *(G-9752)*

Ctm Integration Incorporated..............E..... 330 332-1800
  Salem *(G-12840)*

Pines Manufacturing Inc.....................E..... 440 835-5553
  Westlake *(G-15098)*

South Shore Controls Inc....................E..... 440 259-2500
  Mentor *(G-10998)*

MACHINERY: Mining

Npk Construction Equipment Inc.........D..... 440 232-7900
  Bedford *(G-976)*

MACHINERY: Packaging

Advanced Poly-Packaging Inc.............C..... 330 785-4000
  Akron *(G-18)*

Atmos360 Inc......................................E..... 513 772-4777
  West Chester *(G-14799)*

Ctm Integration Incorporated..............E..... 330 332-1800
  Salem *(G-12840)*

G and J Automatic Systems Inc..........E..... 216 741-6070
  Cleveland *(G-4296)*

Millwood Inc..E..... 513 860-4567
  West Chester *(G-14730)*

Millwood Natural LLC..........................E..... 330 393-4400
  Vienna *(G-14423)*

Norse Dairy Systems Inc....................C..... 614 294-4931
  Columbus *(G-6363)*

MACHINERY: Plastic Working

Linden-Two Inc...................................E..... 330 928-4064
  Cuyahoga Falls *(G-7087)*

MACHINERY: Printing Presses

Graphic Systems Services Inc............E..... 937 746-0708
  Springboro *(G-13199)*

MACHINERY: Road Construction & Maintenance

Forge Industries Inc............................A..... 330 960-2468
  Youngstown *(G-15613)*

Lake Township Trustees.....................E..... 419 836-1143
  Millbury *(G-11270)*

MACHINERY: Rubber Working

Rubber City Machinery Corp...............E..... 330 434-3500
  Akron *(G-288)*

MACHINERY: Textile

MAGAZINES, WHOLESALE

Wolf Machine Company..............................E 513 791-5194
  Blue Ash *(G-1274)*

MAGAZINES, WHOLESALE

Kable News Company Inc......................C 815 734-4151
  West Chester *(G-14716)*
Windy Hill Ltd Inc....................................D 216 391-4800
  Cleveland *(G-5150)*

MAGNETS: Permanent

Walker National Inc................................E 614 492-1614
  Columbus *(G-6864)*
Winkle Industries Inc.............................D 330 823-9730
  Alliance *(G-407)*

MAIL-ORDER HOUSE, NEC

American Frame Corporation...................D 419 893-5595
  Maumee *(G-10690)*
Schneider Saddlery LLC........................E 440 543-2700
  Chagrin Falls *(G-1989)*

MAIL-ORDER HOUSES: Computer Software

Provantage LLC......................................D 330 494-3781
  North Canton *(G-11854)*

MAIL-ORDER HOUSES: Educational Splys & Eqpt

Bendon Inc..D 419 207-3600
  Ashland *(G-482)*
Twin Sisters Productions LLC.................E 330 631-0361
  Stow *(G-13399)*

MAIL-ORDER HOUSES: Food

Gem Edwards Inc...................................D 330 342-8300
  Hudson *(G-9352)*

MAILBOX RENTAL & RELATED SVCS

US Postal Service...................................E 614 600-5544
  Columbus *(G-6836)*

MAILING & MESSENGER SVCS

Richardson Printing Corp........................D 800 848-9752
  Marietta *(G-10404)*

MAILING SVCS, NEC

Aero Fulfillment Services Corp................D 800 225-7145
  Mason *(G-10517)*
American Paper Group Inc.....................B 330 758-4545
  Youngstown *(G-15551)*
Bindery & Spc Pressworks Inc................D 614 873-4623
  Plain City *(G-12470)*
Ctrac Inc..E 440 572-1000
  Cleveland *(G-4144)*
Ddm-Dgtal Imging Data Proc Mli.............D 740 928-1110
  Hebron *(G-9142)*
Early Express Services Inc.....................E 937 223-5801
  Dayton *(G-7322)*
Fine Line Graphics Corp.........................C 614 486-0276
  Columbus *(G-5857)*
Hkm Drect Mkt Cmmnications Inc..........D 800 860-4456
  Cleveland *(G-4367)*
Mid-West Presort Mailing Services Inc....C 216 251-2500
  Cleveland *(G-4576)*
Patented Acquisition Corp......................D 937 353-2299
  Miamisburg *(G-11082)*
Valassis Direct Mail Inc..........................D 859 283-2386
  Cincinnati *(G-3612)*
Valassis Direct Mail Inc..........................D 216 573-1400
  Independence *(G-9494)*
Valassis Direct Mail Inc..........................E 614 987-2200
  Worthington *(G-15465)*

Weekleys Mailing Service Inc..................D 440 234-4325
  Berea *(G-1086)*

MANAGEMENT CONSULTING SVCS: Administrative

Consoliplex Holding LLC........................E 216 202-3499
  Cleveland *(G-4107)*
Klingbeil Management Group Co............E 614 220-8900
  Columbus *(G-6120)*
Ride Share Information..........................E 513 621-6300
  Cincinnati *(G-3298)*

MANAGEMENT CONSULTING SVCS: Automation & Robotics

Motion Controls Robotics Inc..................D 419 334-5886
  Fremont *(G-8695)*
Remtec Automation LLC........................E 877 759-8151
  Mason *(G-10600)*
Robex LLC...E 419 270-0770
  Maumee *(G-10763)*

MANAGEMENT CONSULTING SVCS: Business

5me LLC..E 513 719-1600
  Cincinnati *(G-2095)*
Accenture LLP.......................................C 513 455-1000
  Cincinnati *(G-2137)*
Accenture LLP.......................................E 513 651-2444
  Cincinnati *(G-2138)*
Accenture LLP.......................................C 216 685-1435
  Cleveland *(G-3760)*
Accenture LLP.......................................C 614 629-2000
  Columbus *(G-5301)*
Accurate Invntory Clclting Svc................B 800 777-9414
  Columbus *(G-5304)*
Advocate Solutions LLC........................E 614 444-5144
  Columbus *(G-5320)*
Aileron...E 937 669-6500
  Tipp City *(G-13652)*
Barrett & Associates Inc........................E 330 928-2323
  Cuyahoga Falls *(G-7047)*
Booz Allen Hamilton Inc.........................E 937 429-5580
  Beavercreek *(G-865)*
Btas Inc...D 937 431-9431
  Beavercreek *(G-866)*
Cass Information Systems Inc................D 614 839-4500
  Columbus *(G-5516)*
Cincinnati Cnslting Consortium..............E 513 233-0011
  Cincinnati *(G-2404)*
Corporate Fin Assoc Clmbus Inc............D 614 457-9219
  Columbus *(G-5703)*
Dayton Aerospace Inc............................E 937 426-4300
  Beavercreek Township *(G-936)*
DE Foxx & Associates Inc......................B 513 621-5522
  Cincinnati *(G-2547)*
Engage Healthcare Svcs Corp................E 614 457-8180
  Columbus *(G-5818)*
Ernst & Young LLP................................C 513 612-1400
  Cincinnati *(G-2637)*
Ernst & Young LLP................................C 614 224-5678
  Columbus *(G-5827)*
Everstream Holding Company LLC........C 216 923-2260
  Cleveland *(G-4228)*
Finit Group LLC.....................................D 513 793-4648
  Cincinnati *(G-2669)*
Gardner Insurance Partners LLC............E 614 221-1900
  Columbus *(G-5914)*
Ignite Philanthropy.................................E 513 381-1848
  Cincinnati *(G-2864)*

Keene Inc..D 440 605-1020
  Cleveland *(G-4451)*
Marsh Berry & Company LLC................E 440 637-8122
  Beachwood *(G-810)*
Medcor Safety LLC................................E 740 876-4003
  Wheelersburg *(G-15131)*
Omni Property Companies LLC..............E 216 514-1950
  Solon *(G-13121)*
Onefifteen Recovery..............................E 937 223-5609
  Dayton *(G-7539)*
Piada Group LLC...................................D 614 397-1339
  Columbus *(G-6524)*
Plante & Moran Pllc...............................A 614 849-3000
  Columbus *(G-6530)*
Promedica Health System Inc................B 419 534-6600
  Toledo *(G-13971)*
Root LLC...D 419 874-0077
  Sylvania *(G-13571)*
Scrogginsgrear Inc.................................C 513 672-4281
  Cincinnati *(G-3352)*
Signet Management Co Ltd....................C 330 762-9102
  Akron *(G-300)*
Smithers Group Inc................................D 330 762-7441
  Akron *(G-304)*
Smithers MSE Inc..................................D 330 762-7441
  Akron *(G-305)*
Socius1 LLC..D 614 280-9880
  Dublin *(G-8123)*
Sureshot Communications LLC..............D 216 496-6100
  Cleveland *(G-4967)*
Surgere LLC..D 330 966-3746
  Uniontown *(G-14267)*
Tacg LLC...E 937 203-8201
  Beavercreek *(G-931)*
Teradata International Inc......................C 866 548-8348
  Dayton *(G-7662)*
Transtech Consulting Inc.......................C 614 751-0575
  Westerville *(G-14944)*
Untapped Potentials LLC.......................E 888 811-1469
  Columbus *(G-6825)*
Versatex LLC...E 513 639-3119
  Cincinnati *(G-3620)*
Visteon Corporation...............................E 419 627-3600
  Sandusky *(G-12940)*

MANAGEMENT CONSULTING SVCS: Business Planning & Organizing

Dayton Dev Coalition Inc.......................E 937 222-4422
  Dayton *(G-7279)*
Goering Ctr For Fmly/Prvate Bu.............D 513 556-7185
  Cincinnati *(G-2736)*
Integrated Prj Resources LLC................E 330 272-0998
  Salem *(G-12844)*
Logistical Resource Group Inc...............D 330 283-3733
  Macedonia *(G-10199)*
NBD International Inc.............................E 330 296-0221
  Ravenna *(G-12633)*
Nesco Inc..C 513 772-5870
  Cincinnati *(G-3106)*
Nesco Inc..C 419 794-7452
  Toledo *(G-13933)*

MANAGEMENT CONSULTING SVCS: Construction Project

Buckeye Elm Contracting LLC................E 888 315-8663
  Gahanna *(G-8712)*
Critical Business Analysis Inc................E 419 874-0800
  Perrysburg *(G-12326)*
Ohio Diversified Services Inc.................E 440 356-7000
  Cleveland *(G-4687)*

SERVICES SECTION

MANAGEMENT SERVICES

Uhc United Heating & Coolg LLC............ E 866 931-0118
  Northfield *(G-11967)*

MANAGEMENT CONSULTING SVCS: Corporation Organizing

Comex North America Inc...................... D 303 307-2100
  Cleveland *(G-4092)*

MANAGEMENT CONSULTING SVCS: Distribution Channels

The Arras Group Inc.............................. E 216 621-1601
  Cleveland *(G-4991)*
Trilogy Fulfillment LLC............................ D 614 491-0553
  Groveport *(G-9005)*

MANAGEMENT CONSULTING SVCS: Food & Beverage

AVI Food Systems Inc........................... B 330 372-6000
  Warren *(G-14505)*

MANAGEMENT CONSULTING SVCS: General

Astoria Place Cincinnati LLC................. C 513 961-8881
  Cincinnati *(G-2221)*
Career Partners Intl LLC........................ E 919 401-4260
  Columbus *(G-5509)*
Kaleidoscope Project Inc....................... D 330 702-1822
  Canfield *(G-1633)*
Midwest Investors Group Inc................. C 270 887-8888
  Galena *(G-8737)*
Murtech Consulting LLC......................... D 216 328-8580
  Cleveland *(G-4611)*
Oncall LLC.. D 513 381-4320
  Cincinnati *(G-3162)*
Paragon Consulting Inc.......................... E 440 684-3101
  Cleveland *(G-4716)*
Paragon Tec Inc..................................... E 216 361-5555
  Cleveland *(G-4717)*
Turtle Golf Management Ltd.................. D 614 882-5920
  Westerville *(G-15019)*
Xlc Srvces Cincinnati Ohio Inc............... E 513 621-3912
  Cincinnati *(G-3684)*

MANAGEMENT CONSULTING SVCS: Hospital & Health

Caff LLC.. E 440 918-4570
  Westlake *(G-15042)*
Clinlogix LLC... E 215 855-9054
  Northwood *(G-11972)*
East Way Behavioral Hlth Care............. D 937 222-4900
  Dayton *(G-7323)*
Emerald Health Network Inc................. D 216 479-2030
  Fairlawn *(G-8476)*
First Chice Med Stffing Ohio I................ E 419 626-9740
  Sandusky *(G-12899)*
Human ARC Corporation....................... B 216 431-5200
  Cleveland *(G-4388)*
Imarc Research Inc............................... D 440 801-1540
  Strongsville *(G-13464)*
Intellihartx LLC...................................... E 419 949-5040
  Findlay *(G-8549)*
Medical Recovery Systems Inc............. E 513 872-7000
  Cincinnati *(G-3028)*
Medisync Midwest Ltd Lblty Co............ D 513 533-1199
  Dayton *(G-7478)*
Ncs Healthcare Inc................................ A 216 514-3350
  Cleveland *(G-4630)*
Nova Passport Home Care Llc.............. E 419 531-9060
  Toledo *(G-13941)*
Ohic Insurance Company...................... D 614 221-7777
  Columbus *(G-6388)*

Ohio Health Info Partnr Inc.................... E 614 664-2600
  Hilliard *(G-9222)*
Plus Management Services Inc............. C 419 225-9018
  Lima *(G-9950)*
Premiere Medical Resources Inc........... E 330 923-5899
  Cuyahoga Falls *(G-7094)*
Prime Hlthcare Fndton- E Lvrpo............ D 330 385-7200
  East Liverpool *(G-8191)*
Professional Review Netwrk Inc............ E 614 791-2700
  Dublin *(G-8097)*
PSI Supply Chain Solutions LLC............ B 614 389-4717
  Dublin *(G-8100)*
United Audit Systems Inc..................... C 513 723-1122
  Cincinnati *(G-3552)*

MANAGEMENT CONSULTING SVCS: Industrial

E-Volve Systems LLC............................ E 765 543-8123
  Blue Ash *(G-1166)*

MANAGEMENT CONSULTING SVCS: Industrial & Labor

Mancan Inc.. A 440 884-9675
  Cleveland *(G-4519)*

MANAGEMENT CONSULTING SVCS: Industry Specialist

A-1 Hlthcare Stffing Plcements............. C 216 329-3500
  Cleveland *(G-3753)*
Applied Specialties Inc.......................... E 440 933-9442
  Avon Lake *(G-671)*
Dedicated Technologies Inc.................. D 614 460-3200
  Columbus *(G-5748)*
Pharmacy Consultants LLC................... E 864 578-8788
  Cincinnati *(G-3205)*
Steris Isomedix Services Inc................. B 440 354-2600
  Mentor *(G-10999)*
Vintek Inc.. D 937 382-8986
  Wilmington *(G-15277)*

MANAGEMENT CONSULTING SVCS: Information Systems

3sg Plus LLC... E 614 652-0019
  Columbus *(G-5243)*
Alta It Services LLC.............................. C 813 999-3101
  Cincinnati *(G-2173)*
Calyx LLC.. E 216 916-0639
  Westlake *(G-15043)*
Cohesion Corporation........................... C 813 999-3101
  Cincinnati *(G-2469)*
Dataeconomy Inc.................................. E 614 356-8153
  Dublin *(G-7983)*
Emprise Technologies LLC.................... E 419 720-6982
  Toledo *(G-13791)*
Isaac Fair Consulting Inc...................... E 216 643-6790
  Cleveland *(G-4423)*
Jjr Solutions LLC................................... E 937 912-0288
  Dayton *(G-7429)*
Kreller Consulting Group Inc................. E 513 723-8900
  Cincinnati *(G-2952)*
Vartek Services Inc............................... E 937 438-3550
  Donnelsville *(G-7870)*

MANAGEMENT CONSULTING SVCS: Manufacturing

Midwest Mfg Solutions LLC.................. E 513 381-7200
  Cincinnati *(G-3059)*
Techsolve Inc.. D 513 948-2000
  Cincinnati *(G-3449)*

MANAGEMENT CONSULTING SVCS: Quality Assurance

Benchmark National Corporation........... E 419 843-6691
  Bellevue *(G-1043)*

MANAGEMENT CONSULTING SVCS: Real Estate

Colliers International............................. E 614 436-9800
  Columbus *(G-5597)*
Cushman Wakefield Holdings Inc.......... E 513 241-4880
  Cincinnati *(G-2526)*
Muransky Companies LLC..................... E 330 729-7400
  Youngstown *(G-15670)*
Ohio Equities LLC................................. D 614 207-1805
  Columbus *(G-6418)*
Signature Closers LLC.......................... E 614 448-7750
  Columbus *(G-6678)*
Stepstone Group Real Estate LP........... E 216 522-0330
  Cleveland *(G-4954)*

MANAGEMENT CONSULTING SVCS: Training & Development

1st Advnce SEC Invstgtions Inc............ E 937 317-4433
  Dayton *(G-7145)*
Honda Dev & Mfg Amer LLC................. C 937 644-0724
  Marysville *(G-10488)*
Leidos Inc.. D 937 656-8433
  Beavercreek *(G-886)*
Miami University.................................... B 513 727-3200
  Middletown *(G-11172)*
Pope & Associates Inc.......................... E 513 671-1277
  West Chester *(G-14744)*
Sacs Cnslting Training Ctr Inc............... E 330 255-1101
  Akron *(G-293)*

MANAGEMENT CONSULTING SVCS: Transportation

Agar LLC.. E 513 549-4576
  Cincinnati *(G-2155)*
Aldelano Corporation............................. E 909 861-3970
  Lima *(G-9861)*
Ardmore Power Logistics LLC............... E 216 502-0640
  Westlake *(G-15034)*
Distribution Data Incorporated.............. D 216 362-3009
  Brookpark *(G-1433)*
Fedex Supplychain Systems Inc........... A
  Hudson *(G-9348)*
First Transit Inc..................................... D 513 241-2200
  Cincinnati *(G-2682)*
Interchez Lgistics Systems Inc.............. E 330 923-5080
  Stow *(G-13378)*
Jarrett Logistics Systems Inc................ C 330 682-0099
  Orrville *(G-12168)*
Landrum & Brown Incorporated............ E 513 530-5333
  Blue Ash *(G-1198)*
Rls & Associates Inc............................. E 937 299-5007
  Moraine *(G-11435)*
Senior Touch Solution........................... E 216 862-4841
  Cleveland *(G-4895)*
TV Minority Company Inc...................... E 937 832-9350
  Englewood *(G-8324)*
Universal Transportation Syste............. C 513 829-1287
  Fairfield *(G-8450)*

MANAGEMENT SERVICES

Acme Dynamite...................................... E 313 867-5309
  Toledo *(G-13674)*
Adaptive Development Corp.................. E 937 890-3388
  Dayton *(G-7156)*

MANAGEMENT SERVICES

Agile Pursuits Inc .... D 513 945-9908
Cincinnati *(G-2156)*

Aim Integrated Logistics Inc .... B 330 759-0438
Girard *(G-8808)*

Babcock & Wilcox Company .... A 330 753-4511
Akron *(G-59)*

Benjamin Rose Institute .... C 216 791-3580
Cleveland *(G-3868)*

Bionix Development Corporation ...... E 800 551-7096
Toledo *(G-13706)*

Bridgepoint Risk MGT LLC .... E 419 794-1075
Maumee *(G-10704)*

Brown Co Ed Service Center .... E 937 378-6118
Georgetown *(G-8799)*

Cameron Mitchell Rest LLC .... D 724 824-7558
Dublin *(G-7949)*

Cardinal Health Inc .... E 614 497-9552
Obetz *(G-12079)*

Cardinal Health Inc .... A 614 757-5000
Dublin *(G-7950)*

Careworks of Ohio Inc .... A 614 792-1085
Dublin *(G-7958)*

Cargotec Services USA Inc .... E 419 482-6000
Perrysburg *(G-12322)*

Catastrophe MGT Solutions Inc .... D 800 959-2630
Hudson *(G-9337)*

Central Coca-Cola Btlg Co Inc .... E 330 875-1487
Akron *(G-86)*

Central Coca-Cola Btlg Co Inc .... E 740 474-2180
Circleville *(G-3705)*

CFC Mansfield LLC .... E 216 328-1121
Ontario *(G-12101)*

CFM Religion Pubg Group LLC .... D 513 931-4050
Cincinnati *(G-2339)*

Cks & Associates MGT LLC .... E 614 621-9710
Columbus *(G-5578)*

Cleveland Clinic Foundation .... D 419 609-2812
Sandusky *(G-12882)*

Coal Services Inc .... B 740 795-5220
Powhatan Point *(G-12610)*

Colonial Senior Services Inc .... D 513 856-8600
Hamilton *(G-9030)*

Colonial Senior Services Inc .... E 513 867-4006
Hamilton *(G-9031)*

Colonial Senior Services Inc .... D 513 844-8004
Hamilton *(G-9032)*

Communications Buying Group .... D 216 377-3000
Cleveland *(G-4095)*

Corvel Corporation .... E 800 275-6463
Cleveland *(G-4119)*

County of Lucas .... C 419 248-3585
Toledo *(G-13765)*

Cpca Manufacturing LLC .... D 937 723-9031
Dayton *(G-7260)*

CPS Medmanagement LLC .... D 901 748-0470
Dublin *(G-7977)*

CPS Solutions LLC .... C 901 748-0470
Dublin *(G-7978)*

Crane Group Co .... E 614 754-3000
Columbus *(G-5719)*

Crescent Park Corporation .... C 513 759-7000
West Chester *(G-14679)*

Crown Group Incorporated .... E 586 558-5311
Lima *(G-9882)*

Distribution Data Incorporated .... D 216 362-3009
Brookpark *(G-1433)*

DMD Management Inc .... C 216 749-4010
Cleveland *(G-4170)*

Eleet Cryogenics Inc .... E 330 874-4009
Bolivar *(G-1294)*

Ensemble Health Partners Inc .... A 704 765-3715
Cincinnati *(G-2623)*

Erie Indemnity Company .... C 330 433-6300
Canton *(G-1748)*

Excellence In Motivation Inc .... C 763 445-3000
Dayton *(G-7341)*

Executive Jet Management Inc .... B 513 979-6600
Cincinnati *(G-2644)*

Fedex Supplychain Systems Inc .... A
Hudson *(G-9348)*

First Hospital Labs LLC .... C 215 396-5500
Independence *(G-9432)*

First Services Inc .... A 513 241-2200
Cincinnati *(G-2675)*

First Transit Inc .... D 513 241-2200
Cincinnati *(G-2682)*

Fisher Foods Marketing Inc .... C 330 497-3000
North Canton *(G-11830)*

Flat Rock Care Center .... D 419 483-7330
Flat Rock *(G-8600)*

French Company LLC .... D 330 963-4344
Twinsburg *(G-14193)*

Genesis .... E 740 453-3122
Zanesville *(G-15789)*

Gentlebrook Inc .... D 330 877-3694
Hartville *(G-9125)*

Grace Management Inc .... B 763 971-9271
Cincinnati *(G-2747)*

Hanger Prsthtics Orthtics E In .... E 330 633-9807
Tallmadge *(G-13593)*

Holzer Clinic LLC .... A 740 446-5411
Gallipolis *(G-8759)*

Imflux Inc .... D 513 488-1017
Cincinnati *(G-2865)*

Instantwhip-Columbus Inc .... E 614 871-9447
Grove City *(G-8928)*

Integrated Resources Inc .... E 419 885-7122
Sylvania *(G-13552)*

Interservice Corporation .... C 216 272-3519
Novelty *(G-12039)*

Ironwood Development Corp .... C 440 895-1200
Cleveland *(G-4422)*

Island Service Company .... E 419 285-3695
Put In Bay *(G-12617)*

ITW Air Management .... E 513 891-7474
Blue Ash *(G-1187)*

Jake Sweeney Automotive Inc .... D 513 782-2800
Cincinnati *(G-2896)*

Juice Technologies Inc .... E 800 518-5576
Worthington *(G-15424)*

Kaleidoscope Innovation .... C 513 791-3009
Blue Ash *(G-1193)*

Klingbeil Capital MGT Ltd .... D 415 398-0106
Worthington *(G-15427)*

Knowlton Development Corp .... E 614 656-1130
Johnstown *(G-9547)*

Leadec Corp .... E 513 731-3590
Blue Ash *(G-1200)*

Leatherman Nursing Ctrs Corp .... B 330 336-6684
Wadsworth *(G-14439)*

Legacy Village Management LLC ...... D 216 382-3871
Cleveland *(G-4485)*

Lendkey Technologies Inc .... C 646 626-7396
Blue Ash *(G-1201)*

Liberty Technology Company LLC .... E 740 363-1941
Delaware *(G-7815)*

Licking-Knox Goodwill Inds Inc .... D 740 345-9861
Newark *(G-11721)*

Lincolnview Local Schools .... C 419 968-2226
Van Wert *(G-14348)*

Locus Management LLC .... D 888 510-0004
Solon *(G-13106)*

M A Folkes Company Inc .... E 513 785-4200
Hamilton *(G-9062)*

Marsh Berry & Company LLC .... E 440 637-8122
Beachwood *(G-810)*

Med America Hlth Systems Corp ...... A 937 223-6192
Dayton *(G-7475)*

Michael Baker Intl Inc .... E 330 453-3110
Canton *(G-1806)*

Michael Baker Intl Inc .... E 412 269-6300
Cleveland *(G-4573)*

Ministerial Day Care Assn .... E 216 881-6924
Cleveland *(G-4587)*

Momentum Fleet MGT Group Inc ...... D 440 759-2219
Westlake *(G-15080)*

Munich RE America Services .... E 609 480-6596
Cincinnati *(G-3089)*

Mvah Management LLC .... E 513 964-1140
West Chester *(G-14735)*

National Dcp LLC .... D 216 410-3215
Twinsburg *(G-14207)*

National Heritg Academies Inc .... E 937 223-2889
Dayton *(G-7525)*

National Heritg Academies Inc .... E 937 278-6671
Dayton *(G-7526)*

National Heritg Academies Inc .... E 330 792-4806
Youngstown *(G-15674)*

Niederst Management Ltd .... E 440 331-8800
Cleveland *(G-4646)*

Novotec Recycling LLC .... C 614 231-8326
Columbus *(G-6375)*

Nrp Management LLC .... E 216 475-8900
Cleveland *(G-4670)*

Ohc Ohio Co-Manager LLC .... E 513 751-2273
Cincinnati *(G-3142)*

Ohio Shared Info Svcs Inc .... D 513 677-5600
Cincinnati *(G-3149)*

Oki Bering Management Co .... D 513 341-4002
West Chester *(G-14827)*

P I & I Motor Express Inc .... C 330 448-4035
Masury *(G-10679)*

Perduco Group Inc .... E 937 401-0268
Beavercreek *(G-893)*

Pharmacy Data Management .... D 330 757-0724
Poland *(G-12506)*

Plus Management Services Inc .... E 419 331-2273
Lima *(G-9949)*

Plus Management Services Inc .... C 419 225-9018
Lima *(G-9950)*

Pro-Model & Talent Mgmt Inc .... E 330 665-0723
Fairlawn *(G-8494)*

Promedica Health System Inc .... A 567 585-9600
Toledo *(G-13972)*

Promedica Physcn Cntinuum Svcs ... C 419 824-7200
Sylvania *(G-13565)*

Purple Land Management LLC .... D 740 238-4259
North Canton *(G-11856)*

RB Sigma LLC .... D 440 290-0577
Mentor *(G-10988)*

Resource International Inc .... C 614 823-4949
Columbus *(G-6587)*

Revolution Group Inc .... D 614 212-1111
Westerville *(G-14935)*

Ricco Enterprises Incorporated .... E 216 883-7775
Cleveland *(G-4837)*

Ridgewood Government Svcs LLC ..... E 740 294-7261
West Lafayette *(G-14858)*

Ross Consolidated Corp .... D 440 748-5800
Grafton *(G-8841)*

Safeguard Properties LLC .... A 216 739-2900
Cleveland *(G-4869)*

Salvation Army .... E 419 447-2252
Tiffin *(G-13641)*

Serco Services Inc .... C 937 369-4066
Dayton *(G-7616)*

SERVICES SECTION

MANAGEMENT SVCS: Construction

Signature Inc .... E 614 766-5101
  Dublin *(G-8119)*

Skanska USA Building Inc .... D 513 421-0082
  Cincinnati *(G-3383)*

Sleep Network Inc .... E 419 535-9282
  Toledo *(G-14015)*

Smg Holdings LLC .... E 614 827-2500
  Columbus *(G-6689)*

Stat Integrated Tech Inc .... E 440 286-7663
  Chardon *(G-2021)*

Surge Management LLC .... E 614 431-5100
  Columbus *(G-6735)*

TAC Industries Inc .... B 937 328-5200
  Springfield *(G-13299)*

Talawanda City School District .... D 513 273-3200
  Oxford *(G-12218)*

The Sheakley Group Inc .... E 513 771-2277
  Cincinnati *(G-3471)*

Toledo Innvtion Ctr Lndlord LL .... C 419 585-3684
  Toledo *(G-14060)*

Transinternational System Inc .... E 614 891-4942
  Worthington *(G-15463)*

Trihealth Inc .... D 513 241-4135
  Cincinnati *(G-3511)*

Trinity Hospital Holding Co .... A 740 264-8000
  Steubenville *(G-13347)*

Uc Health Llc .... C 513 584-8600
  Cincinnati *(G-3545)*

United Telemanagement Corp .... E 937 454-1888
  Dayton *(G-7685)*

University Hsptals Clvland Med .... A 216 844-3528
  Cleveland *(G-5081)*

University of Cincinnati .... E 513 556-6932
  Blue Ash *(G-1264)*

Urban Retail Properties LLC .... E 937 433-0957
  Dayton *(G-7695)*

Vein Clinics of America Inc .... E 630 725-2700
  Cincinnati *(G-3617)*

Verst Group Logistics Inc .... E 513 772-2494
  Cincinnati *(G-3621)*

Verst Group Logistics Inc .... D 859 379-1230
  West Chester *(G-14844)*

Vrc Companies LLC .... D 614 299-2122
  Grove City *(G-8964)*

Vrc Companies LLC .... E 419 381-7762
  Maumee *(G-10778)*

Wayne Street Development LLC .... E 740 373-5455
  Marietta *(G-10412)*

Western Management Inc .... E 216 941-3333
  Cleveland *(G-5135)*

Weston and Associates LLC .... C 330 791-7118
  Massillon *(G-10672)*

Wolf Creek Federal Svcs Inc .... A 216 433-5609
  Cleveland *(G-5157)*

MANAGEMENT SVCS: Administrative

Arthur Mddlton Cpitl Hldngs In .... D 330 966-9000
  North Canton *(G-11812)*

Bethesda Hospital Inc .... E 513 247-0224
  Montgomery *(G-11362)*

Bravo Wellness LLC .... E 216 658-9500
  Cleveland *(G-3891)*

City of Youngstown .... B 330 742-8700
  Youngstown *(G-15578)*

Educatonal Svc Ctr Lorain Cnty .... C 440 244-1659
  Elyria *(G-8244)*

Help Foundation Inc .... E 216 432-4810
  Euclid *(G-8346)*

McR LLC .... E 937 879-5055
  Beavercreek *(G-891)*

Nationwide General Insur Co .... A 614 249-7111
  Columbus *(G-6331)*

Parker-Hannifin Intl Corp .... B 216 896-3000
  Cleveland *(G-4725)*

Phoenix Administrators LLC .... E 440 628-4235
  Avon Lake *(G-683)*

Providence Medical Group Inc .... E 937 297-8999
  Moraine *(G-11430)*

Salvation Army .... E 330 773-3331
  Cleveland *(G-4873)*

Sterling Medical Corporation .... C 513 984-1800
  Cincinnati *(G-3418)*

Tm Capture Services LLC .... D 937 728-1781
  Dayton *(G-7671)*

University of Cincinnati .... C 513 556-4200
  Cincinnati *(G-3582)*

University of Cincinnati .... C 513 558-4231
  Cincinnati *(G-3583)*

Village of Valley View .... E 216 524-6511
  Cleveland *(G-5106)*

MANAGEMENT SVCS: Business

Act For Health Inc .... B 740 443-5000
  Piketon *(G-12414)*

Amend Consulting LLC .... D 513 399-6300
  Cincinnati *(G-2176)*

Ashland Home Towne Phrm Inc .... E 419 281-4040
  Ashland *(G-475)*

Chronic Care Management Inc .... C 440 248-6500
  Independence *(G-9418)*

Clinical Management Cons Inc .... D 440 638-5000
  Cleveland *(G-4084)*

Consoldted Fndries Hldngs Corp .... A 216 772-1041
  Cleveland *(G-4105)*

EDM Management Inc .... E 330 726-5790
  Youngstown *(G-15607)*

Hat White Management LLC .... C 800 525-7967
  Akron *(G-188)*

Kaiser Logistics LLC .... D 937 534-0213
  Monroe *(G-11342)*

Mfbusiness Group .... E 216 609-7297
  Cleveland *(G-4570)*

Niederst Management Ltd .... C 440 331-8800
  Rocky River *(G-12749)*

Ohio Cllbrtive Lrng Sltons Inc .... E 216 595-5289
  Strongsville *(G-13479)*

Omnicare Purch Ltd Partner Inc .... A 800 990-6664
  Cincinnati *(G-3161)*

Osu Internal Medicine LLC .... D 614 293-0080
  Dublin *(G-8084)*

Quality Supply Chain Co-Op Inc .... E 614 764-3124
  Dublin *(G-8101)*

RGT Management Inc .... E 513 715-4640
  Harrison *(G-9114)*

RMS of Ohio Inc .... C 440 617-6605
  Westlake *(G-15104)*

Roth Roofing Products LLC .... D 800 872-7684
  Youngstown *(G-15714)*

Roundstone Management Ltd .... C 440 617-0333
  Lakewood *(G-9683)*

Safran Power Usa LLC .... D 330 487-2000
  Twinsburg *(G-14218)*

Value Add Management LLC .... E 614 291-2600
  Columbus *(G-6841)*

Vanguard Property Management .... E 216 521-8222
  Lakewood *(G-9686)*

Viaquest LLC .... E 614 889-5837
  Dublin *(G-8152)*

Vora Ventures LLC .... B 513 792-5100
  Blue Ash *(G-1272)*

MANAGEMENT SVCS: Construction

Baxter Hdell Dnnlly Prston Inc .... C 513 271-1634
  Cincinnati *(G-2240)*

Bostleman Corp .... E
  Holland *(G-9281)*

C M M Inc .... E 216 789-7480
  Hudson *(G-9336)*

Chemstress Consultant Company .... C 330 535-5591
  Akron *(G-87)*

CK Construction Group Inc .... B 614 901-8844
  Westerville *(G-14967)*

Collins Assoc Tchncal Svcs Inc .... C 740 574-2320
  Wheelersburg *(G-15128)*

Complete General Cnstr Co .... D 614 258-9515
  Columbus *(G-5678)*

Cook Paving and Cnstr Co .... E 216 267-7705
  Independence *(G-9424)*

Core Resources Inc .... D 513 731-1771
  Cincinnati *(G-2507)*

Danis Building Construction Co .... E 513 984-9696
  Cincinnati *(G-2537)*

Danis Building Construction Co .... D 614 761-8385
  Columbus *(G-5739)*

DE Foxx & Associates Inc .... B 513 621-5522
  Cincinnati *(G-2547)*

Elford Inc .... C 614 488-4000
  Columbus *(G-5811)*

G Stephens Inc .... D 614 227-0304
  Columbus *(G-5906)*

Gilbane Building Company .... E 614 948-4000
  Columbus *(G-5934)*

Hammond Construction Inc .... D 330 455-7039
  Uniontown *(G-14254)*

Hills Developers Inc .... C 513 984-0300
  Blue Ash *(G-1182)*

Ingle-Barr Inc .... D 740 702-6117
  Chillicothe *(G-2072)*

Jack Gibson Construction Co .... D 330 394-5280
  Warren *(G-14530)*

Jance & Company Incorporated .... E 440 255-5800
  Mentor *(G-10954)*

JP Compass Cnsulting Cnstr Inc .... E 440 635-0500
  Chesterland *(G-2037)*

KHD Company LLC .... E 614 935-9939
  Worthington *(G-15426)*

Lathrop Company Inc .... E 419 893-7000
  Toledo *(G-13882)*

Majidzadeh Enterprises Inc .... E 614 823-4949
  Columbus *(G-6191)*

McDaniels Cnstr Corp Inc .... D 614 252-5852
  Columbus *(G-6213)*

Quality Construction MGT Inc .... D 513 779-8425
  West Chester *(G-14750)*

Quality Control Inspection .... D 440 359-1900
  Cleveland *(G-4799)*

Renier Construction Corp .... E 614 866-4580
  Columbus *(G-6578)*

Richard L Bowen & Assoc Inc .... D 216 491-9300
  Cleveland *(G-4838)*

RJ Runge Company Inc .... E 419 740-5781
  Port Clinton *(G-12539)*

Ruscilli Construction Co Inc .... D 614 876-9484
  Dublin *(G-8111)*

SEI Engineers Inc .... E 740 657-1860
  Powell *(G-12607)*

Shook Construction Co .... D 937 276-6666
  Moraine *(G-11438)*

Shook National Corporation .... C 937 276-6666
  Dayton *(G-7617)*

Tri-C Construction Company Inc .... E 330 836-2722
  Akron *(G-337)*

Triversity Construction Co LLC .... D 513 733-0046
  Cincinnati *(G-3528)*

Ttl Associates Inc .... D 419 241-4556
  Toledo *(G-14076)*

MANAGEMENT SVCS: Construction

Turnbull-Wahlert Construction Inc........... D 513 731-7300
   Cincinnati *(G-3535)*
Turnserv LLC.. E 216 600-8876
   Akron *(G-338)*
Welty Building Company Ltd.................... E 330 867-2400
   Fairlawn *(G-8503)*

MANAGEMENT SVCS: Hotel Or Motel

American Hospitality Group Inc............... B 330 336-6684
   Wadsworth *(G-14428)*
Chu Management Co Inc.......................... E 330 725-4571
   Medina *(G-10820)*
M&C Hotel Interests Inc........................... C 440 543-1331
   Chagrin Falls *(G-1985)*
MEI Hotels Incorporated........................... C 216 589-0441
   Cleveland *(G-4549)*
Savour Hospitality LLC............................. C 216 308-0018
   Cleveland *(G-4879)*
Select Hotels Group LLC......................... D 513 754-0003
   Mason *(G-10606)*
Tjm Clmbus LLC Tjm Clumbus LLC........ D 614 885-1885
   Columbus *(G-6771)*

MANAGEMENT SVCS: Nursing & Personal Care Facility

Atrium Living Centers of Ea.................... E 614 416-2662
   Columbus *(G-5405)*
Balanced Care Corporation..................... E 330 908-1166
   Northfield *(G-11952)*
Balanced Care Corporation..................... D 330 296-4545
   Ravenna *(G-12619)*
Canton Rhbltion Nrsing Ctr LL................ E 330 456-2842
   Canton *(G-1704)*
Christian Benevolent Assn....................... C 513 931-5000
   Cincinnati *(G-2385)*
Connecting Dots Cnncting To SL............ E 216 356-2362
   Cleveland *(G-4101)*
DMD Management Inc............................. C 440 944-9400
   Wickliffe *(G-15147)*
DMD Management Inc............................. E 216 898-8399
   Cleveland *(G-4171)*
Holzer Senior Care Center...................... E 740 446-5001
   Bidwell *(G-1104)*
Kingston Healthcare Company................ E 419 247-2880
   Toledo *(G-13879)*
Management and Netwrk Svcs LLC....... D 800 949-2159
   Dublin *(G-8059)*
Saber Healthcare Group LLC.................. E 216 292-5706
   Beachwood *(G-833)*
Sprenger Enterprises Inc......................... D 630 529-0700
   Lorain *(G-10102)*
Stonespring Trnstnal Care Ctr................. E 937 415-8000
   Dayton *(G-7645)*

MANAGEMENT SVCS: Restaurant

Bon Appetit Management Co................... C 614 823-1880
   Westerville *(G-14962)*
Cameron Mitchell Rest LLC..................... E 614 621-3663
   Columbus *(G-5494)*
Carpediem Management Company......... E 740 687-1563
   Lancaster *(G-9699)*
Jordan Hospitality Group LLC................. E 614 406-5139
   New Albany *(G-11571)*
Piada Group LLC...................................... D 614 397-1339
   Columbus *(G-6524)*

MANPOWER POOLS

Channel Products Inc............................... D 440 423-0110
   Solon *(G-13075)*

MANPOWER TRAINING

Esc of Cuyahoga County........................... E 216 524-3000
   Independence *(G-9431)*
Midwest Investors Group Inc................... C 270 887-8888
   Galena *(G-8737)*
Opportnties For Indvdual Chnge............. E 937 323-6461
   Springfield *(G-13280)*
Riverview Industries Inc.......................... D 419 898-5250
   Oak Harbor *(G-12047)*

MARINAS

Beaver Park Marina Inc........................... E 440 282-6308
   Lorain *(G-10059)*
Catawba-Cleveland Dev Corp.................. D 419 797-4424
   Port Clinton *(G-12518)*
Island Service Company.......................... E 419 285-3695
   Put In Bay *(G-12617)*
S B S Transit Inc...................................... E 440 288-2222
   Elyria *(G-8292)*
Saw Mill Creek Ltd................................... D 419 433-3800
   Huron *(G-9392)*
Tappan Lake Marina Inc......................... E 740 269-2031
   Scio *(G-12943)*

MARINE CARGO HANDLING SVCS

McGinnis Inc... C 740 377-4391
   South Point *(G-13178)*
McNational Inc.. D 740 377-4391
   South Point *(G-13179)*

MARINE CARGO HANDLING SVCS: Marine Terminal

Cincinnati Bulk Terminals LLC................ E 513 621-4800
   Cincinnati *(G-2402)*
River Services Inc.................................... C 612 588-8141
   Cincinnati *(G-3300)*

MARINE SPLYS WHOLESALERS

Mazzella Holding Company Inc............... D 513 772-4466
   Cleveland *(G-4534)*

MARKETS: Meat & fish

Euclid Fish Company............................... D 440 951-6448
   Mentor *(G-10938)*
Weilands Fine Meats Inc......................... E 614 267-9910
   Columbus *(G-6873)*

MARKING DEVICES: Embossing Seals & Hand Stamps

System Seals Inc...................................... E 216 220-1800
   Brecksville *(G-1369)*

MATS OR MATTING, NEC: Rubber

Durable Corporation................................. D 800 537-1603
   Norwalk *(G-12008)*
Westlake Dimex LLC................................ C 740 374-3100
   Marietta *(G-10414)*

MATS, MATTING & PADS: Nonwoven

Durable Corporation................................. D 800 537-1603
   Norwalk *(G-12008)*

MEAT MARKETS

Landes Fresh Meats Inc.......................... E 937 836-3613
   Clayton *(G-3734)*
Mary C Enterprises Inc........................... D 937 253-6169
   Dayton *(G-7467)*
S and S Gilardi Inc................................... D 740 397-2751
   Mount Vernon *(G-11507)*

MEAT PRDTS: Cooked Meats, From Purchased Meat

King Kold Inc.. E 937 836-2731
   Englewood *(G-8311)*

MEAT PRDTS: Frozen

A To Z Portion Ctrl Meats Inc.................. E 419 358-2926
   Bluffton *(G-1276)*
Blue Ribbon Meats Inc............................ D 216 631-8850
   Cleveland *(G-3875)*
The Ellenbee-Leggett Company Inc....... C 513 874-3200
   Fairfield *(G-8446)*
White Castle System Inc......................... B 614 228-5781
   Columbus *(G-6883)*

MEAT PRDTS: Prepared Beef Prdts From Purchased Beef

Fresh Mark Inc.. B 330 832-7491
   Massillon *(G-10641)*

MEDICAL & HOSPITAL EQPT WHOLESALERS

Amerimed LLC.. A 513 942-3670
   West Chester *(G-14650)*
Assuramed Inc.. C 330 963-6998
   Twinsburg *(G-14171)*
Boxout LLC.. C 833 462-7746
   Hudson *(G-9334)*
Cardinal Health 100 Inc.......................... B 614 757-5000
   Dublin *(G-7951)*
Concordnce Hlthcare Sltons LLC........... D 419 447-0222
   Tiffin *(G-13625)*
Dermamed Coatings Company LLC....... E 330 634-9449
   Tallmadge *(G-13591)*
Espt Liquidation Inc................................. D 330 698-4711
   Apple Creek *(G-450)*
ICP Inc... D 419 447-6216
   Tiffin *(G-13628)*
JLW - TW Corp... E 440 937-7775
   Avon *(G-657)*
Modern Medical Inc................................. C 800 547-3330
   Westerville *(G-14910)*
O E Meyer Co.. D 419 625-1256
   Sandusky *(G-12921)*
Optum Infusion Svcs 550 LLC................. D 866 442-4679
   Cincinnati *(G-3166)*
Pharmed Corporation............................... D 440 250-5400
   Westlake *(G-15097)*
Precision Products Group Inc................. D 330 698-4711
   Apple Creek *(G-452)*
Prestan Products LLC.............................. E 440 229-5100
   Solon *(G-13131)*
Viewray Systems Inc............................... E 303 339-0500
   Oakwood Village *(G-12061)*
Ziks Family Pharmacy 100...................... E 937 225-9350
   Dayton *(G-7737)*

MEDICAL & SURGICAL SPLYS: Bandages & Dressings

Beiersdorf Inc.. C 513 682-7300
   West Chester *(G-14800)*

MEDICAL & SURGICAL SPLYS: Clothing, Fire Resistant & Protect

Lion First Responder Ppe Inc.................. D 937 898-1949
   Dayton *(G-7456)*
Wcm Holdings Inc.................................... C 513 705-2100
   Cincinnati *(G-3643)*

SERVICES SECTION

MEDICAL SVCS ORGANIZATION

West Chester Holdings LLC................C.....513 705-2100
  Cincinnati (G-3655)

MEDICAL & SURGICAL SPLYS: Foot Appliances, Orthopedic

Stable Step LLC...............................C.....800 491-1571
  Wadsworth (G-14452)

MEDICAL & SURGICAL SPLYS: Prosthetic Appliances

Acor Orthopaedic LLC........................E.....216 662-4500
  Cleveland (G-3764)

MEDICAL & SURGICAL SPLYS: Splints, Pneumatic & Wood

Ferno-Washington Inc.......................C.....877 733-0911
  Wilmington (G-15252)

MEDICAL CENTERS

Ashland Hospital Corporation..............D.....740 894-2080
  South Point (G-13173)
Atrium Medical Center.......................E.....513 424-2111
  Dayton (G-7184)
Childrens Hosp Med Ctr Akron............D.....330 543-8503
  Akron (G-92)
Childrens Hospital Medical Ctr............A.....513 803-9600
  Liberty Township (G-9848)
Cleveland Clinic Foundation................E.....216 444-5540
  Cleveland (G-4025)
Cleveland Clinic Foundation................D.....419 609-2812
  Sandusky (G-12882)
Columbus Nghbrhood Hlth Ctr In........E.....614 859-1947
  Columbus (G-5649)
Fauster-Cameron Inc........................B.....419 784-1414
  Defiance (G-7746)
Fayette Medical Center......................E.....740 335-1210
  Wshngtn Ct Hs (G-15484)
Heritage Valley Health Sys Inc............D.....724 773-8209
  East Liverpool (G-8183)
Hometown Urgent Care......................E.....513 831-5900
  Milford (G-11231)
Hometown Urgent Care......................D.....937 342-9520
  Springfield (G-13254)
Hometown Urgent Care......................E.....937 252-2000
  Wooster (G-15345)
Hometown Urgent Care......................E.....330 629-2300
  Youngstown (G-15633)
Hometown Urgent Care of Ken...........E.....614 505-7601
  Columbus (G-6006)
James Center..................................C.....614 410-5615
  Columbus (G-6083)
Kaiser Foundation Hospitals...............E.....216 524-7377
  Avon (G-658)
Kaiser Foundation Hospitals...............E.....800 524-7377
  Brooklyn Heights (G-1424)
Kaiser Foundation Hospitals...............E.....216 524-7377
  Strongsville (G-13467)
Kaiser Foundation Hospitals...............E.....330 486-2800
  Twinsburg (G-14198)
Mercy Hlth - Rgnal Med Ctr LLC..........A.....440 960-4000
  Lorain (G-10092)
Metrohealth System..........................C.....216 524-7377
  Parma (G-12256)
Nadine El Asmar MD - Uh Clvlan.........E.....216 844-3400
  Cleveland (G-4617)
Nationwide Childrens Hospital.............C.....740 522-3221
  Newark (G-11734)
Ohio State University........................D.....614 293-3860
  Columbus (G-6456)

Our Lady Bellefonte Hosp Inc..............A.....606 833-3333
  Cincinnati (G-3176)
Portsmouth Hospital Corp..................A.....740 991-4000
  Portsmouth (G-12565)
Promedica Toledo Hospital.................A.....419 291-4000
  Toledo (G-13976)
Rgh Enterprises LLC.........................A.....330 963-6996
  Twinsburg (G-14216)
Richmond Medical Center...................B.....440 585-6500
  Richmond Heights (G-12722)
Riverview Health Institute...................D.....937 222-5390
  Dayton (G-7595)
Salem Community Hospital.................E.....330 482-2265
  Columbiana (G-5241)
Saras Garden..................................D.....419 335-7272
  Wauseon (G-14608)
Shriners International Hdqtr................D.....800 875-8580
  Cincinnati (G-3373)
Tri State Urlogic Svcs PSC Inc............D.....513 841-7400
  Cincinnati (G-3503)
Trinity Hospital Twin City....................B.....740 922-2800
  Dennison (G-7858)
Trumbll-Mahoning Med Group Inc.......E.....330 372-8800
  Cortland (G-6976)
Uc Health Llc...................................D.....513 475-7777
  West Chester (G-14781)
Uc Health Llc...................................A.....513 585-6000
  Cincinnati (G-3546)
University Hsptals Clvland Med...........A.....440 499-5900
  Broadview Heights (G-1403)
University Suburban Health Ctr..........C.....216 382-8920
  Cleveland (G-5087)
Universty of Cincinnti Medcl C............A.....513 475-8000
  Cincinnati (G-3597)
Veterans Health Administration...........A.....740 773-1141
  Chillicothe (G-2093)
Veterans Health Administration...........A.....513 861-3100
  Cincinnati (G-3627)
Veterans Health Administration...........A.....216 791-3800
  Cleveland (G-5101)
Veterans Health Administration...........A.....937 268-6511
  Dayton (G-7705)
Wood Health Company LLC................D.....419 353-7069
  Bowling Green (G-1337)
Wpafb Medical Center........................E.....937 522-2778
  Wright Patterson Afb (G-15475)

MEDICAL EQPT REPAIR SVCS, NON-ELECTRIC

Equipment MGT Svc & Repr Inc..........E.....937 383-1052
  Wilmington (G-15250)
Precision Endoscopy Amer Inc...........E.....410 527-9598
  Stow (G-13386)

MEDICAL HELP SVCS

Arcadia Services Inc.........................E.....330 869-9520
  Akron (G-54)
Arcadia Services Inc.........................E.....937 912-5800
  Beavercreek (G-857)
Central Ohio Hospitalists...................E.....614 255-6900
  Columbus (G-5539)
CHI Health At Home..........................E.....513 576-0262
  Milford (G-11221)
Classic Medical Staffing LLC..............D.....216 688-0900
  Cleveland (G-3998)
Dedicated Nursing Assoc Inc.............C.....888 465-6929
  Beavercreek (G-922)
Dedicated Nursing Assoc Inc.............C.....866 450-5550
  Hilliard (G-9191)
Emp Holdings Ltd............................E.....330 493-4443
  Canton (G-1746)

Frontline National LLC......................D.....513 528-7823
  Milford (G-11229)
Locum Medical Group LLC.................D.....216 464-2125
  Independence (G-9447)
Maxim Healthcare Services Inc..........D.....330 670-1054
  Akron (G-227)
Maxim Healthcare Services Inc..........D.....216 606-3000
  Independence (G-9450)
Med1care Ltd..................................D.....419 866-0555
  Findlay (G-8565)
Physician Staffing Inc......................B.....440 542-5000
  Cleveland (G-4748)
Prn Nurse Inc..................................B.....614 864-9292
  Columbus (G-6547)
Promedica Employment Svcs LLC......A.....419 824-7529
  Toledo (G-13968)
Quadax Inc.....................................D.....330 759-4600
  Youngstown (G-15702)
Salo Inc...E.....877 759-2106
  Coshocton (G-7002)

MEDICAL INSURANCE CLAIM PROCESSING: Contract Or Fee Basis

Acu-Serve Corp...............................C.....330 923-5258
  Akron (G-16)
Compmed Analysis LLC.....................E.....330 650-0888
  Hudson (G-9340)
Conduent Care Solutions LLC............E.....330 644-0927
  Akron (G-120)
Optumrx Inc....................................A.....614 794-3300
  Westerville (G-14924)
Progressive Medical LLC...................A.....614 794-3300
  Westerville (G-14931)

MEDICAL SVCS ORGANIZATION

Bon Secours Mercy Health Inc..........D.....513 956-3729
  Cincinnati (G-2274)
Bucyrus Community Physicians.........D.....419 563-9801
  Bucyrus (G-1499)
Cleveland Clinic Foundation..............D.....216 448-0770
  Beachwood (G-779)
Cleveland Clnic Edctl Fndtion............E.....216 444-1157
  Cleveland (G-4034)
Clinix Healthcare LLC........................E.....614 792-5422
  Dublin (G-7965)
Cornerstone Hlthcare Sltons LL.........D.....937 985-4011
  Lebanon (G-9761)
Excelas LLC....................................E.....440 442-7310
  Cleveland (G-4229)
First Chice Med Stffing Ohio I............D.....330 867-1409
  Fairlawn (G-8480)
Larlham Care Hattie Group................D.....330 274-2272
  Mantua (G-10332)
Lifecenter Organ Donor Network........E.....513 558-5555
  Cincinnati (G-2976)
Lifestges Smrtan Ctrs For Wmen.......E.....937 277-8988
  Dayton (G-7454)
Mvhe Inc..E.....937 499-8211
  Dayton (G-7520)
Northast Ohio Nghbrhood Hlth S........E.....216 851-2600
  Cleveland (G-4654)
Northast Ohio Nghbrhood Hlth S........E.....216 541-5600
  Cleveland (G-4655)
Northast Ohio Nghbrhood Hlth S........E.....216 851-1500
  Cleveland (G-4656)
Northast Ohio Nghbrhood Hlth S........C.....216 231-7700
  Cleveland (G-4653)
P C Vpa..E.....440 826-0500
  Cleveland (G-4714)
Palestine Chld Relief Fund................D.....330 678-2645
  Kent (G-9590)

MEDICAL SVCS ORGANIZATION

Sterling Medical Associates.................... D 513 984-1800
   Cincinnati *(G-3417)*
Trihealth Os LLC................................. E 513 985-3700
   Cincinnati *(G-3525)*
University Tledo Physcians LLC............ E 419 931-0030
   Toledo *(G-14088)*
Vincent & Vincent............................... E 513 617-2089
   Cincinnati *(G-3630)*

MEDICAL, DENTAL & HOSP EQPT, WHOLESALE: X-ray Film & Splys

Philips Med Systems Clvland In............ B 440 483-3000
   Cleveland *(G-4746)*

MEDICAL, DENTAL & HOSPITAL EQPT, WHOL: Hospital Eqpt & Splys

Boardman Medical Supply Co............. C 330 545-6700
   Girard *(G-8810)*
Health Services Inc........................... E 330 837-7678
   Massillon *(G-10644)*
Millers Rental and Sls Co Inc................ D 330 753-8600
   Akron *(G-234)*

MEDICAL, DENTAL & HOSPITAL EQPT, WHOL: Surgical Eqpt & Splys

Cardinal Health Inc........................... E 614 497-9552
   Obetz *(G-12079)*
Cardinal Health Inc........................... A 614 757-5000
   Dublin *(G-7950)*
Columbus Prescr Phrms Inc................ E 614 294-1600
   Westerville *(G-14972)*
Haag-Sreit Usa Inc............................ C 513 336-7255
   Mason *(G-10558)*
Rgh Enterprises LLC.......................... A 330 963-6996
   Twinsburg *(G-14216)*
Synergy Health North America Inc........ A 813 891-9550
   Mentor *(G-11001)*

MEDICAL, DENTAL & HOSPITAL EQPT, WHOLESALE: Artificial Limbs

Pel LLC.. E 216 267-5775
   Cleveland *(G-4737)*

MEMBERSHIP ORGANIZATIONS, BUSINESS: Contractors' Association

Builders Exchange Inc........................ E 216 393-6300
   Cleveland *(G-3910)*
Home Bldrs Assn Grter Cncnnati.......... D 513 851-6300
   Cincinnati *(G-2834)*

MEMBERSHIP ORGANIZATIONS, NEC: Charitable

Irish Youth Sports Inc........................ E 859 257-7910
   Bellaire *(G-1013)*
Nwoca West..................................... E 419 267-2544
   Archbold *(G-465)*

MEMBERSHIP ORGANIZATIONS, NEC: Personal Interest

Affinion Group LLC........................... A 614 895-1803
   Westerville *(G-14956)*
People Developed Systems Inc............ D 330 479-7823
   Canton *(G-1829)*
Shoreby Club Inc.............................. D 216 851-2587
   Cleveland *(G-4903)*
Volunteers of America NW Ohio........... E 419 248-3733
   Columbus *(G-6857)*

MEMBERSHIP ORGANIZATIONS, PROFESSIONAL: Accounting Assoc

Ohio Soc of Crtif Pub Accntnts............. D 614 764-2727
   Columbus *(G-6445)*

MEMBERSHIP ORGANIZATIONS, PROFESSIONAL: Health Association

Caresource Ohio Inc.......................... C 937 224-3300
   Dayton *(G-7212)*
Clark County Combined Hlth Dst.......... D 937 390-5600
   Springfield *(G-13233)*
Columbus Medical Association............. D 614 240-7410
   Columbus *(G-5644)*
County of Crawford........................... E 419 562-5871
   Bucyrus *(G-1504)*
Healthspot Inc.................................. D 614 361-1193
   Dublin *(G-8028)*
Jefferson Behavioral Hlth Sys............... D 740 535-1314
   Mingo Junction *(G-11313)*
Lake County General Health Dst........... D 440 350-2543
   Mentor *(G-10960)*

MEMBERSHIP ORGANIZATIONS, REL: Churches, Temples & Shrines

Harrison Avenue Assembly God............ E 513 367-6109
   Harrison *(G-9107)*

MEMBERSHIP ORGANIZATIONS, RELIGIOUS: Catholic Church

Catholic Charities Corporation.............. D 419 289-7456
   Ashland *(G-487)*
Christ King Catholic Church................. E 614 236-8838
   Columbus *(G-5569)*
Our Lady Bethlehem Schools Inc.......... E 614 459-8285
   Columbus *(G-6491)*
Society of The Transfiguration............. D 513 771-7462
   Cincinnati *(G-3391)*
St Francis De Sales Church................. D 740 345-9874
   Newark *(G-11749)*
St Pauls Catholic Church..................... E 330 724-1263
   Akron *(G-308)*

MEMBERSHIP ORGANIZATIONS, RELIGIOUS: Lutheran Church

Royal Rdmer Lthran Ch N Rylton.......... E 440 237-7958
   North Royalton *(G-11949)*
St Jhns Evang Lthran Ch Mrysv............ E 937 644-5540
   Marysville *(G-10510)*
Upper Arlington Lutheran Ch............... E 614 451-3736
   Hilliard *(G-9238)*

MEMBERSHIP ORGANIZATIONS, RELIGIOUS: Methodist Church

Trinity United Methodist Ch................. E 614 488-3659
   Columbus *(G-6792)*
West Ohio Cnfrnce of Untd Mthd.......... E 614 844-6200
   Worthington *(G-15468)*

MEMBERSHIP ORGS, RELIGIOUS: Non-Denominational Church

Church On North Coast....................... E 440 960-1100
   Lorain *(G-10063)*
Columbus Christian Center Inc............. E 614 416-9673
   Columbus *(G-5619)*
Haven Rest Ministries Inc.................... D 330 535-1563
   Akron *(G-190)*

MEMBERSHIP SPORTS & RECREATION CLUBS

Boys and Girls CLB Wooster Inc........... D 330 988-1616
   Wooster *(G-15314)*
Chagrin Valley Athc CLB Inc................ D 440 543-5141
   Chagrin Falls *(G-1974)*
Chiller LLC....................................... E 614 246-3380
   Columbus *(G-5566)*
Cincinnati Sports Mall Inc................... C 513 527-4000
   Cincinnati *(G-2423)*
City of Sylvania................................ E 419 885-1167
   Sylvania *(G-13539)*
City of Tallmadge.............................. E 330 634-2349
   Tallmadge *(G-13588)*
Dayton Classics Basbal CLB Inc........... E 937 974-6722
   West Carrollton *(G-14645)*
Eastern Ohio Conservation Club........... D 330 799-7393
   Salem *(G-12841)*
Family YMCA Lncster Frfeld CNT.......... E 740 654-0616
   Lancaster *(G-9722)*
Fitworks Holding LLC......................... E 440 333-4141
   Rocky River *(G-12741)*
Futbol Club Cincinnati LLC.................. C 513 977-5425
   Cincinnati *(G-2713)*
Game Haus LLC................................ E 513 490-1799
   Franklin *(G-8638)*
Ganzfair Investment Inc..................... E 614 792-6630
   Delaware *(G-7800)*
Geneva Area Rcrtl Edctl Athc T............ E 440 466-1002
   Geneva *(G-8785)*
German Family Society Inc.................. E 330 678-8229
   Kent *(G-9576)*
Hof Fitness Center Inc....................... D 330 455-0555
   Canton *(G-1773)*
M&C Hotel Interests Inc..................... C 440 543-1331
   Chagrin Falls *(G-1985)*
Oakland Pk Cnservation CLB Inc.......... D 614 989-8739
   Dublin *(G-8078)*
River Oaks Rcquet CLB Assoc In.......... E 440 331-4980
   Rocky River *(G-12752)*
Salt Fork Resort Club Inc................... E 740 498-8116
   Kimbolton *(G-9641)*
Scioto Reserve Inc............................ D 740 881-9082
   Powell *(G-12604)*
Sightless Children Club Inc................. E 937 671-9162
   Franklin *(G-8649)*
Sugar Valley Country Club.................. E 937 372-4820
   Xenia *(G-15531)*
Tiffin Cmnty YMCA Rcration Ctr........... D 419 447-8711
   Tiffin *(G-13645)*
Toledo Walleye Prof Hockey CLB.......... D 419 725-4350
   Toledo *(G-14067)*
Vermilion Family YMCA...................... E 440 967-4208
   Vermilion *(G-14410)*
Vertical Adventures Inc...................... D 614 888-8393
   Columbus *(G-6845)*
William Henry Harrison Jr Hs............... E 513 367-4831
   Harrison *(G-9120)*
Young MNS Christn Assn Findlay.......... D 419 422-4424
   Findlay *(G-8599)*
Young MNS Chrstn Assn Grter CN........ B 513 791-5000
   Blue Ash *(G-1275)*
Young MNS Chrstn Assn Grter CN........ B 513 521-7112
   Cincinnati *(G-3690)*
Young MNS Chrstn Assn Grter CN........ E 513 961-3510
   Cincinnati *(G-3691)*
Young MNS Chrstn Assn Grter CN........ C 513 731-0115
   Cincinnati *(G-3692)*
Young MNS Chrstn Assn Grter CN........ B 513 474-1400
   Cincinnati *(G-3693)*

SERVICES SECTION

METALS SVC CENTERS & WHOLESALERS: Steel

Young MNS Chrstn Assn Grter Dy............. C 937 228-9622
  Dayton *(G-7732)*
Young MNS Chrstn Assn Grter Dy............. D 937 426-9622
  Dayton *(G-7734)*
Young MNS Chrstn Assn Grter Dy............. C 937 836-9622
  Englewood *(G-8327)*
Young MNS Chrstn Assn Grter Dy............. C 937 223-5201
  Springboro *(G-13210)*
Young MNS Chrstn Assn Mtro Los............. D 740 286-7008
  Jackson *(G-9530)*
Young MNS Chrstn Assn Wster OH............. E 330 264-3131
  Wooster *(G-15402)*
Young MNS Chrstn Assn Yngstown............. D 330 744-8411
  Youngstown *(G-15755)*

MEN'S & BOYS' CLOTHING STORES

Abercrombie & Fitch Trading Co............. D 614 283-6500
  New Albany *(G-11551)*
For Women Like Me Inc............. E 407 848-7339
  Chagrin Falls *(G-1958)*
J Peterman Company LLC............. E 888 647-2555
  Blue Ash *(G-1189)*

MEN'S & BOYS' CLOTHING WHOLESALERS, NEC

Abercrombie & Fitch Trading Co............. D 614 283-6500
  New Albany *(G-11551)*
Alsico Usa Inc............. D 330 673-7413
  Kent *(G-9557)*
For Women Like Me Inc............. E 407 848-7339
  Chagrin Falls *(G-1958)*
K Amalia Enterprises Inc............. E 614 733-3800
  Plain City *(G-12483)*
Legend............. D 216 534-1541
  Cleveland *(G-4488)*
Mll Brand Import LLC............. C 614 256-7267
  Reynoldsburg *(G-12670)*
Profill Holdings LLC............. A 513 742-4000
  Cincinnati *(G-3247)*
West Chester Holdings LLC............. C 513 705-2100
  Cincinnati *(G-3655)*

MERCHANDISING MACHINE OPERATORS: Vending

AVI Food Systems Inc............. E 740 452-9363
  Zanesville *(G-15768)*
AVI Food Systems Inc............. B 330 372-6000
  Warren *(G-14505)*
Dtv Inc............. E 216 226-5465
  Cleveland *(G-4187)*

METAL & STEEL PRDTS: Abrasive

Cleveland Granite & Marble LLC............. E 216 291-7637
  Cleveland *(G-4047)*

METAL COMPONENTS: Prefabricated

Pioneer Cldding Glzing Systems............. E 216 816-4242
  Cleveland *(G-4749)*

METAL FABRICATORS: Plate

Loveman Steel Corporation............. D 440 232-6200
  Bedford *(G-969)*

METAL MINING SVCS

Cliffs UTAC Holding LLC............. D 216 694-5700
  Cleveland *(G-4081)*
Western Kentucky Coal Co LLC............. E 740 338-3334
  Saint Clairsville *(G-12821)*

METAL SERVICE CENTERS & OFFICES

American Tank & Fabricating Co............. D 216 252-1500
  Cleveland *(G-3808)*
Atlas Bolt & Screw Company LLC............. C 419 289-6171
  Ashland *(G-478)*
Boston Retail Products Inc............. E 330 744-8100
  Youngstown *(G-15564)*
Canfield Metal Coating Corp............. D 330 702-3876
  Canfield *(G-1623)*
Clinton Aluminum Acquisition LLC............. B 330 882-6743
  New Franklin *(G-11614)*
Concast Birmingham LLC............. D 440 965-4455
  Wakeman *(G-14458)*
Kirtland Capital Partners LP............. E 216 593-0100
  Beachwood *(G-806)*
Matandy Steel & Metal Pdts LLC............. D 513 844-2277
  Hamilton *(G-9063)*
Materion Brush Intl Inc............. D 216 486-4200
  Mayfield Heights *(G-10789)*
Materion Ceramics Inc............. B 216 486-4200
  Mayfield Heights *(G-10790)*
Merit Brass Co............. C 216 261-9800
  Cleveland *(G-4554)*
Modern Welding Co Ohio Inc............. E 740 344-9425
  Newark *(G-11731)*
Northwestern Holding LLC............. D 419 726-0850
  Toledo *(G-13940)*
Ohio Steel Sheet and Plate Inc............. E 800 827-2401
  Hubbard *(G-9322)*
Oliver Steel Plate Co............. D 330 425-7000
  Twinsburg *(G-14209)*
Panacea Products Corporation............. E 614 850-7000
  Columbus *(G-6497)*
SL Wellspring LLC............. D 513 948-2339
  Cincinnati *(G-3387)*
Tricor Industrial Inc............. D 330 264-3299
  Wooster *(G-15380)*
Watteredge LLC............. D 440 933-6110
  Avon Lake *(G-684)*
Wieland Chase LLC............. D 419 485-3193
  Montpelier *(G-11387)*
Wieland Metal Svcs Foils LLC............. D 330 823-1700
  Alliance *(G-405)*
Wieland Rolled Pdts N Amer LLC............. B 330 823-1700
  Alliance *(G-406)*
Worthington Enterprises Inc............. D 513 539-9291
  Monroe *(G-11355)*
Worthngton Smuel Coil Proc LLC............. E 330 963-3777
  Twinsburg *(G-14231)*
Worthngton Stelpac Systems LLC............. C 614 438-3205
  Columbus *(G-6908)*

METAL STAMPING, FOR THE TRADE

Acro Tool & Die Company............. E 330 773-5173
  Akron *(G-14)*
Bayloff Stmped Pdts Knsman Inc............. D 330 876-4511
  Kinsman *(G-9644)*
Falls Stamping & Welding Co............. C 330 928-1191
  Cuyahoga Falls *(G-7075)*
Ohio Gasket and Shim Co Inc............. E 330 630-0626
  Akron *(G-251)*
Pentaflex Inc............. C 937 325-5551
  Springfield *(G-13281)*
Quality Fabricated Metals Inc............. E 330 332-7008
  Salem *(G-12849)*
Supply Technologies LLC............. C 440 947-2100
  Cleveland *(G-4966)*

METALS SVC CENTERS & WHOLESALERS: Cable, Wire

Nimers & Woody II Inc............. C 937 454-0722
  Vandalia *(G-14386)*
Radix Wire Co............. D 216 731-9191
  Solon *(G-13136)*

METALS SVC CENTERS & WHOLESALERS: Flat Prdts, Iron Or Steel

H & D Steel Service Inc............. E 800 666-3390
  North Royalton *(G-11942)*
Major Metals Company............. E 419 886-4600
  Mansfield *(G-10285)*

METALS SVC CENTERS & WHOLESALERS: Foundry Prdts

Founders Service & Mfg Inc............. D 330 584-7759
  North Benton *(G-11805)*

METALS SVC CENTERS & WHOLESALERS: Pipe & Tubing, Steel

Industrial Pping Spcalists Inc............. E 330 750-2800
  Struthers *(G-13500)*
McWane Inc............. B 740 622-6651
  Coshocton *(G-6992)*
Pipe Products Inc............. C 513 587-7532
  West Chester *(G-14742)*
Shaq Inc............. D 770 427-0402
  Beachwood *(G-836)*
Youngstown Pipe & Steel LLC............. E 330 783-2700
  Youngstown *(G-15760)*

METALS SVC CENTERS & WHOLESALERS: Steel

Act Acquisition Inc............. E 216 292-3800
  Cleveland *(G-3765)*
Albco Sales Inc............. E 330 424-9446
  Lisbon *(G-9996)*
All Foils Inc............. D 440 572-3645
  Strongsville *(G-13440)*
Alro Steel Corporation............. D 513 769-9999
  Cincinnati *(G-2172)*
Alro Steel Corporation............. E 614 878-7271
  Columbus *(G-5340)*
Alro Steel Corporation............. E 330 929-4660
  Cuyahoga Falls *(G-7035)*
Alro Steel Corporation............. E 937 253-6121
  Dayton *(G-7167)*
Alro Steel Corporation............. D 419 720-5300
  Toledo *(G-13679)*
Alumalloy Metalcasting Company............. D 440 930-2222
  Avon Lake *(G-670)*
Aluminum Line Products Company............. D 440 835-8880
  Westlake *(G-15032)*
American Consolidated Inds Inc............. E 216 587-8000
  Cleveland *(G-3800)*
American Posts LLC............. E 419 720-0652
  Toledo *(G-13687)*
Arcelrmttal Tblar Pdts Mrion I............. D 740 382-3979
  Marion *(G-10418)*
Atlas Steel Products Co............. C 330 425-1600
  Twinsburg *(G-14172)*
Aviva Metals Inc............. D 440 277-1226
  Lorain *(G-10057)*
Bertin Steel Processing Inc............. E 440 943-0094
  Wickliffe *(G-15146)*
Bico Akron Inc............. D 330 794-1716
  Mogadore *(G-11324)*
Byer Steel Inc............. E 513 821-6400
  Cincinnati *(G-2295)*
Byer Steel Service Center Inc............. E 513 821-6400
  Cincinnati *(G-2296)*
Central Steel and Wire Co LLC............. E 513 242-2233
  Cincinnati *(G-2338)*

METALS SVC CENTERS & WHOLESALERS: Steel

Chillicothe Steel Company .... E 740 772-2481
  Chillicothe *(G-2059)*
Cincinnati Steel Products Co .... E 513 871-4444
  Cincinnati *(G-2424)*
Ciralsky & Associates Inc .... E 419 470-1328
  Toledo *(G-13735)*
Clifton Steel Company .... E 216 662-6111
  Maple Heights *(G-10335)*
Clifton Steel Company .... D 216 662-6111
  Maple Heights *(G-10336)*
Clinton Aluminum Dist Inc .... E 866 636-7640
  Jamestown *(G-9534)*
Clinton Aluminum Dist Inc .... D 330 882-6743
  Norton *(G-11992)*
Coilplus Inc .... D 937 778-8884
  Piqua *(G-12437)*
Coilplus Inc .... D 614 866-1338
  Springfield *(G-13236)*
Coilplus Inc .... E 937 322-4455
  Springfield *(G-13237)*
Conley Group Inc .... E 330 372-2030
  Warren *(G-14513)*
Contractors Steel Company .... D 330 425-3050
  Twinsburg *(G-14178)*
Diamond Metals Dist Inc .... E 216 898-7900
  Cleveland *(G-4165)*
Earle M Jorgensen Company .... E 513 771-3223
  Cincinnati *(G-2597)*
Earle M Jorgensen Company .... D 330 425-1500
  Twinsburg *(G-14183)*
Earle M Jorgensen Company .... D 330 425-1500
  Twinsburg *(G-14184)*
Fedmet International Corp .... D 440 248-9500
  Solon *(G-13087)*
Ferragon Corporation .... D 216 671-6161
  Cleveland *(G-4249)*
Fisher Cast Steel Products Inc .... E 614 879-8325
  West Jefferson *(G-14851)*
Greer Steel Company .... C 330 343-8811
  Dover *(G-7886)*
Haverhill Coke Company LLC .... D 740 355-9819
  Franklin Furnace *(G-8655)*
Heartland Valley Metals LLC .... D 419 886-0220
  Bellville *(G-1050)*
Industrial Tube and Steel Corp .... E 513 777-5512
  West Chester *(G-14712)*
Industrial Tube and Steel Corp .... E 330 474-5530
  Kent *(G-9580)*
Infra-Metals Co .... D 740 353-1350
  Portsmouth *(G-12556)*
Is Acquisition Inc .... E 440 287-0150
  Streetsboro *(G-13418)*
Jade-Sterling Steel Co Inc .... E 330 425-3141
  Bedford *(G-968)*
JSW Steel USA Ohio Inc .... B 740 535-8172
  Mingo Junction *(G-11314)*
Kenilworth Steel Co .... E 330 373-1885
  Warren *(G-14532)*
Kloeckner Metals Corporation .... E 513 769-4000
  Cincinnati *(G-2943)*
Lapham-Hickey Steel Corp .... E 614 443-4881
  Columbus *(G-6140)*
Lapham-Hickey Steel Corp .... D 937 236-6940
  Dayton *(G-7450)*
Latrobe Spcialty Mtls Dist Inc .... D 330 609-5137
  Vienna *(G-14420)*
Liberty Steel Industries Inc .... C 330 372-6363
  Warren *(G-14535)*
Liberty Steel Products Inc .... E 330 538-2236
  North Jackson *(G-11873)*
Majestic Steel Usa Inc .... C 440 786-2666
  Cleveland *(G-4517)*

McOn Inds Inc .... E 937 294-2681
  Moraine *(G-11422)*
Metals USA Crbn Flat Rlled Inc .... D 330 264-8416
  Wooster *(G-15355)*
Miami Valley Steel Service Inc .... C 937 773-7127
  Piqua *(G-12449)*
Mid-America Steel Corp .... E 800 282-3466
  Cleveland *(G-4575)*
Mid-West Materials Inc .... E 440 259-5200
  Perry *(G-12309)*
Middletown Tube Works Inc .... D 513 727-0080
  Middletown *(G-11173)*
Mill Steel Co .... E 216 464-4480
  Pepper Pike *(G-12301)*
Misa Metals Inc .... B 212 660-6000
  West Chester *(G-14731)*
Monarch Steel Company Inc .... E 216 587-8000
  Cleveland *(G-4598)*
New Dimension Metals Corp .... E 937 299-2233
  Moraine *(G-11427)*
North Jckson Specialty Stl LLC .... E 330 538-9621
  North Jackson *(G-11874)*
North Star Bluescope Steel LLC .... B 419 822-2200
  Delta *(G-7854)*
Ohio-Kentucky Steel Corp .... E 937 743-4600
  Franklin *(G-8645)*
Ohio-Kentucky Steel LLC .... E 937 743-4600
  Franklin *(G-8646)*
Olympic Steel Inc .... C 216 292-3800
  Bedford *(G-979)*
Olympic Steel Inc .... D 330 602-6279
  Dover *(G-7898)*
Olympic Steel Inc .... D 216 292-3800
  Cleveland *(G-4695)*
Pennsylvania Steel Company Inc .... E 330 823-7383
  Alliance *(G-395)*
Pennsylvania Steel Company Inc .... D 440 243-9800
  Cleveland *(G-4738)*
Phoenix Corporation .... E 513 727-4763
  Middletown *(G-11180)*
Precision Strip Inc .... D 513 423-4166
  Middletown *(G-11181)*
Precision Strip Inc .... D 419 661-1100
  Perrysburg *(G-12364)*
Precision Strip Inc .... C 419 628-2343
  Minster *(G-11320)*
Qualstl Corp .... E 937 294-4133
  Moraine *(G-11431)*
Remington Steel Inc .... D 937 322-2414
  Springfield *(G-13284)*
Riverfront Steel Inc .... D 513 769-9999
  Cincinnati *(G-3304)*
Rownd Metal Sales Inc .... E
  Alliance *(G-400)*
Samuel Son & Co (usa) Inc .... D 740 522-2500
  Heath *(G-9138)*
Samuel Son & Co (usa) Inc .... D 419 470-7070
  Toledo *(G-14004)*
Scot Industries Inc .... D 330 262-7585
  Wooster *(G-15375)*
Scott Steel LLC .... E 937 552-9670
  Piqua *(G-12458)*
Select Steel Inc .... E 330 652-1756
  Niles *(G-11796)*
Sheffield Steel Products Company .... E 330 468-0091
  Macedonia *(G-10204)*
Singer Steel Company .... E 330 562-7200
  Streetsboro *(G-13427)*
Solman Inc .... E 330 580-5188
  Canton *(G-1855)*
Special Metals Corporation .... B 216 755-3030
  Warrensville Heights *(G-14588)*

St Lawrence Holdings LLC .... E 330 562-9000
  Maple Heights *(G-10347)*
St Lawrence Steel Corporation .... E 330 562-9000
  Maple Heights *(G-10348)*
Steel Warehouse Cleveland LLC .... E 888 225-3760
  Cleveland *(G-4945)*
Steel Warehouse Company LLC .... E 216 206-2800
  Cleveland *(G-4946)*
Steel Warehouse of Ohio LLC .... D 888 225-3760
  Cleveland *(G-4947)*
Stein Steel Mill Services LLC .... D 440 526-9301
  Warren *(G-14557)*
Stemcor USA Inc .... E 330 373-1885
  Warren *(G-14558)*
Tapco Tube Co Inc .... D 330 576-1750
  Wadsworth *(G-14454)*
Taylor Steel Inc .... D 330 824-8600
  Warren *(G-14563)*
Three D Metals Inc .... D 330 220-0451
  Valley City *(G-14337)*
Thyssenkrupp Materials NA Inc .... C 440 234-7500
  Cleveland *(G-5018)*
Thyssenkrupp Materials NA Inc .... D 216 883-8100
  Independence *(G-9490)*
Thyssenkrupp Materials NA Inc .... E 419 662-1845
  Toledo *(G-14042)*
United Performance Metals LLC .... B 513 860-6500
  Hamilton *(G-9090)*
United States Steel Corp .... A 440 240-2500
  Lorain *(G-10105)*
United Steel Service LLC .... C 330 448-4057
  Brookfield *(G-1407)*
Universal Steel Company .... D 216 883-4972
  Cleveland *(G-5069)*
Westfield Steel Inc .... D 937 322-2414
  Springfield *(G-13312)*
Worthington Industries Inc .... D 216 641-6995
  Cleveland *(G-5160)*

METALS SVC CENTERS & WHOLESALERS: Tubing, Metal

Swagelok Company .... D 440 349-5934
  Solon *(G-13154)*

METALS: Primary Nonferrous, NEC

Aci Industries Ltd .... E 740 368-4160
  Delaware *(G-7776)*
Rhenium Alloys Inc .... E 440 365-7388
  North Ridgeville *(G-11934)*

METALWORK: Miscellaneous

Precision Impacts LLC .... D 937 530-8254
  Miamisburg *(G-11086)*
Watteredge LLC .... D 440 933-6110
  Avon Lake *(G-684)*
Will-Burt Company .... C 330 682-7015
  Orrville *(G-12176)*

METALWORK: Ornamental

Finelli Ornamental Iron Co .... E 440 248-0050
  Cleveland *(G-4251)*

METALWORKING MACHINERY WHOLESALERS

Hemly Tool Supply Inc .... E 800 445-1068
  Thompson *(G-13617)*
Production Tool Supply Ohio .... D 216 265-0000
  Cleveland *(G-4772)*

MILITARY INSIGNIA

Gayston Corporation.................................. C 937 743-6050
Miamisburg (G-11057)

MILK, FLUID: Wholesalers

Austintown Dairy Inc............................. E 330 629-6170
Youngstown (G-15553)

MILLWORK

Holmes Lumber & Bldg Ctr Inc................ E 330 479-8314
Canton (G-1775)

Holmes Lumber & Bldg Ctr Inc................ C 330 674-9060
Millersburg (G-11279)

Riverside Cnstr Svcs Inc......................... E 513 723-0900
Cincinnati (G-3307)

Stephen M Trudick.................................. E 440 834-1891
Burton (G-1533)

The F A Requarth Company..................... E 937 224-1141
Dayton (G-7665)

The Galehouse Companies Inc................. E 330 658-2023
Doylestown (G-7916)

MINE & QUARRY SVCS: Nonmetallic Minerals

M G Q Inc... E 419 992-4236
Tiffin (G-13631)

MINERAL WOOL

Kinetics Noise Control Inc...................... C 614 889-0480
Dublin (G-8049)

MINERALS: Ground or Treated

EMD Millipore Corporation..................... C 513 631-0445
Norwood (G-12032)

MIXTURES & BLOCKS: Asphalt Paving

Bluffton Stone Co................................... E 419 358-6941
Bluffton (G-1279)

Hy-Grade Corporation............................. E 216 341-7711
Cleveland (G-4395)

Mplx Terminals LLC................................ D 330 479-5539
Canton (G-1811)

Stoneco Inc.. E 419 393-2555
Oakwood (G-12054)

MOLDED RUBBER PRDTS

Datwyler Sling Sltions USA Inc............... D 937 387-2800
Vandalia (G-14373)

Jet Rubber Company.............................. E 330 325-1821
Rootstown (G-12760)

MOLDING COMPOUNDS

Flex Technologies Inc............................. D 330 897-6311
Baltic (G-688)

MOLDINGS OR TRIM: Automobile, Stamped Metal

TS Trim Industries Inc........................... B 614 837-4114
Canal Winchester (G-1618)

MOLDS: Indl

Stan-Kell LLC.. E 440 998-1116
Ashtabula (G-550)

MOPS: Floor & Dust

Ekco Cleaning Inc.................................. C 513 733-8882
Cincinnati (G-2608)

Impact Products LLC.............................. E 419 841-2891
Toledo (G-13860)

MORTGAGE BANKERS

American Midwest Mortgage Corp........... E 440 882-5210
Cleveland (G-3804)

Amerifirst Financial Corp........................ D 614 766-5709
Dublin (G-7937)

Chase Manhattan Mortgage Corp............ C 614 422-7982
Columbus (G-5552)

Fairway Independent Mrtg Corp.............. E 614 930-6552
Columbus (G-5847)

Fairway Independent Mrtg Corp.............. E 513 833-1973
Milford (G-11227)

Fairway Independent Mrtg Corp.............. E 937 304-1443
Springboro (G-13198)

Fairway Independent Mrtg Corp.............. E 330 587-9152
Uniontown (G-14250)

Firstmerit Mortgage Corp....................... D 330 478-3400
Canton (G-1754)

Huntington National Bank...................... D 513 762-1860
Cincinnati (G-2857)

Huntington National Bank...................... E 419 226-8200
Lima (G-9908)

Huntington National Bank...................... E 740 852-1234
London (G-10043)

Huntington National Bank...................... E 419 734-2157
Port Clinton (G-12534)

Huntington National Bank...................... E 419 249-3340
Toledo (G-13856)

Jpmorgan Chase Bank Nat Assn.............. A 614 436-3055
Columbus (G-5264)

Keller Mortgage LLC.............................. D 614 310-3100
Powell (G-12596)

Lancaster Pollard Mrtg Co LLC................ D 614 224-8800
Columbus (G-6134)

Liberty Mortgage Company Inc............... E 614 224-4000
Columbus (G-6157)

Mortgage Now Inc.................................. E 800 245-1050
Cleveland (G-4603)

Nations Lending Corporation.................. D 877 816-1220
Independence (G-9456)

Nations Lending Corporation.................. D 440 785-0963
Medina (G-10867)

Nations Lending Corporation.................. C 216 363-6901
Independence (G-9457)

Northern Ohio Investment Co................. D 419 885-8300
Sylvania (G-13557)

Old Rpblic Ttle Nthrn Ohio LLC............... C 216 524-5700
Independence (G-9464)

River City Mortgage LLC......................... C 513 631-6400
Blue Ash (G-1238)

Rocket Mortgage LLC............................. E 216 586-8900
Cleveland (G-4850)

Sibcy Cline Inc....................................... C 513 777-8100
West Chester (G-14764)

Sirva Mortgage Inc................................. D 800 531-3837
Independence (G-9483)

Union Home Mortgage Corp.................... E 800 767-4684
Strongsville (G-13493)

MOTION PICTURE & VIDEO DISTRIBUTION

Arconic Wheel Wheel Forge..................... E 479 750-6359
Cleveland (G-3832)

Billie Lawless.. E 714 851-6372
Cleveland (G-3874)

Enterprise Pdts Partners LP.................... D 513 423-2122
Middletown (G-11162)

Spray Products Corporation.................... D 610 277-1010
Medina (G-10892)

Vooks Inc.. D 503 694-9217
Stow (G-13401)

MOTION PICTURE & VIDEO PRODUCTION SVCS: Commercials, TV

P Dakota Inc.. B 833 325-6827
Northfield (G-11963)

MOTION PICTURE & VIDEO PRODUCTION SVCS: Educational

Lakewood Rngers Edcatn Fndtion............ E 216 521-2100
Lakewood (G-9676)

MOTION PICTURE PRODUCTION & DISTRIBUTION

Mills/James Inc...................................... C 614 777-9933
Hilliard (G-9217)

MOTION PICTURE PRODUCTION ALLIED SVCS

Mills/James Inc...................................... C 614 777-9933
Hilliard (G-9217)

MOTOR SCOOTERS & PARTS

Dco LLC.. E 419 931-9086
Perrysburg (G-12331)

MOTOR VEHICLE ASSEMBLY, COMPLETE: Fire Department Vehicles

Sutphen Corporation.............................. C 800 726-7030
Dublin (G-8136)

MOTOR VEHICLE DEALERS: Automobiles, New & Used

Advantage Ford Lincoln Mercury............. E 419 334-9751
Fremont (G-8664)

Al Spitzer Ford Inc................................. E 330 929-6546
Cuyahoga Falls (G-7034)

Allstate Trck Sls Estrn Ohio L................. E 330 339-5555
New Philadelphia (G-11639)

Beechmont Chevrolet Inc....................... D 513 624-1100
Cincinnati (G-2247)

Beechmont Ford Inc............................... C 513 752-6611
Cincinnati (G-2098)

Beechmont Motors Inc........................... E 513 388-3883
Cincinnati (G-2248)

Beechmont Motors T Inc........................ D 513 388-3800
Cincinnati (G-2249)

Bill Delord Autocenter Inc...................... D 513 932-3000
Maineville (G-10225)

Bob Ford Chapman Inc........................... E 937 642-0015
Marysville (G-10475)

Bob Pulte Chevrolet Inc.......................... E 513 932-0303
Lebanon (G-9757)

Bob-Boyd Ford Inc................................. D 614 860-0606
Lancaster (G-9697)

Bobb Automotive Inc.............................. E 614 853-3000
Columbus (G-5452)

Bobby Layman Cadillac GMC Inc............. E 740 654-9590
Carroll (G-1899)

Bowling Green Lincoln Inc..................... E 419 352-2553
Bowling Green (G-1312)

Brentlinger Enterprises.......................... C 614 889-2571
Dublin (G-7947)

Broadvue Motors Inc.............................. D 440 845-6000
Cleveland (G-3899)

Brondes Ford... E 419 473-1411
Toledo (G-13719)

Buckeye Ford Inc................................... E 740 852-7842
London (G-10038)

Cain Motors Inc..................................... E 330 494-5588
Canton (G-1695)

Carcorp Inc... C 877 857-2801
Columbus (G-5506)

MOTOR VEHICLE DEALERS: Automobiles, New & Used — SERVICES SECTION

Central Cadillac Limited .... D 216 861-5800
  Cleveland *(G-3954)*

Chesrown Oldsmobile GMC Inc .... E 614 846-3040
  Columbus *(G-5554)*

Classic Automotive Group Inc .... E 440 255-5511
  Mentor *(G-10922)*

Classic Bick Oldsmbile Cdliac .... E 440 639-4500
  Painesville *(G-12222)*

Cole Valley Motor Company Ltd .... D 330 372-1665
  Warren *(G-14509)*

Columbus SAI Motors LLC .... E 614 851-3273
  Columbus *(G-5653)*

Coughlin Chevrolet Inc .... E 740 852-1122
  London *(G-10040)*

Coughlin Chevrolet Inc .... D 740 964-9191
  Pataskala *(G-12271)*

Coughlin Chevrolet Toyota Inc .... D 740 366-1381
  Newark *(G-11696)*

Cronin Auto Inc .... C 419 874-4331
  Perrysburg *(G-12327)*

Dave Dennis Inc .... D 937 429-5566
  Beavercreek Township *(G-935)*

Dave Knapp Ford Lincoln Inc .... E 937 547-3000
  Greenville *(G-8869)*

Decosky Motor Holdings Inc .... D 740 397-9122
  Mount Vernon *(G-11483)*

Diane Sauer Chevrolet Inc .... E 330 373-1600
  Warren *(G-14518)*

Dick Masheter Ford Inc .... D 614 861-7150
  Columbus *(G-5764)*

Don Wood Inc .... E 740 593-6641
  Athens *(G-566)*

Donley Ford-Lincoln Inc .... E 419 281-3673
  Ashland *(G-497)*

Dons Automotive Group Llc .... E 419 337-3010
  Wauseon *(G-14599)*

Doug Bigelow Chevrolet Inc .... D 330 644-7500
  Akron *(G-136)*

Downtown Ford Lincoln Inc .... D 330 456-2781
  Canton *(G-1738)*

Driverge Vhcl Innovations LLC .... E 330 861-1118
  Akron *(G-141)*

Dunning Motor Sales Inc .... E 740 439-4465
  Cambridge *(G-1568)*

Dutro Ford Lincoln-Mercury Inc .... D 740 452-6334
  Zanesville *(G-15786)*

Ed Mullinax Ford LLC .... C 440 984-2431
  Amherst *(G-427)*

Ed Tomko Chrysler Jeep Ddge In .... E 440 835-5900
  Avon Lake *(G-677)*

Fairborn Buick-GMC Truck Inc .... D 937 878-7371
  Fairborn *(G-8374)*

Falls Motor City Inc .... E 330 929-3066
  Cuyahoga Falls *(G-7074)*

Fred Martin Nissan LLC .... E 330 644-8888
  Akron *(G-168)*

George P Ballas Buick GMC Trck .... E 419 535-1000
  Toledo *(G-13820)*

Germain Ford LLC .... C 614 889-7777
  Columbus *(G-5931)*

Germain of Beavercreek II LLC .... D 937 429-2400
  Beavercreek *(G-880)*

Germain of Sidney III LLC .... E 937 498-4014
  Sidney *(G-13035)*

Graham Chevrolet-Cadillac Co .... E 419 989-4012
  Ontario *(G-12105)*

Greenwood Chevrolet Inc .... C 330 270-1299
  Youngstown *(G-15624)*

Grogans Towne Chrysler Inc .... E 419 476-0761
  Toledo *(G-13830)*

Guess Motors Inc .... E 866 890-0522
  Carrollton *(G-1908)*

Harry Humphries Auto City Inc .... E 330 343-6681
  Dover *(G-7888)*

Haydocy Automotive Inc .... D 614 279-8880
  Columbus *(G-5973)*

Herrnstein Chrysler Inc .... C 740 773-2203
  Chillicothe *(G-2068)*

Hidy Motors Inc .... D 937 426-9564
  Dayton *(G-7133)*

Honda Dev & Mfg Amer LLC .... C 937 644-0724
  Marysville *(G-10488)*

Hoss II Inc .... E 937 669-4300
  Tipp City *(G-13660)*

Hoss Value Cars & Trucks Inc .... E 937 428-2400
  Dayton *(G-7415)*

I-75 Pierson Automotive Inc .... E 513 424-1881
  Franklin *(G-8642)*

Interstate Ford Inc .... C 937 866-0781
  Miamisburg *(G-11065)*

Jerry Haag Motors Inc .... E 937 402-2090
  Hillsboro *(G-9261)*

Jim Brown Chevrolet Inc .... C 440 255-5511
  Mentor *(G-10955)*

Jim Keim Ford .... D 614 888-3333
  Columbus *(G-6091)*

Jmac Inc .... E 614 436-2418
  Columbus *(G-6092)*

Joyce Buick Inc .... E 419 529-3211
  Ontario *(G-12110)*

Kempthorn Motors Inc .... D 800 451-3877
  Canton *(G-1790)*

Kerry Ford Inc .... D 513 671-6400
  Cincinnati *(G-2939)*

Kings Toyota Inc .... D 513 583-4333
  Cincinnati *(G-2941)*

Klaben Lincoln Ford Inc .... D 330 593-6800
  Kent *(G-9585)*

Knox Auto LLC .... E 330 701-5266
  Mount Vernon *(G-11490)*

Krieger Ford Inc .... C 614 888-3320
  Columbus *(G-6129)*

Lakewood Chrysler-Plymouth .... E 216 521-1000
  Brookpark *(G-1437)*

Laria Chevrolet-Buick Inc .... E 330 925-2015
  Rittman *(G-12730)*

Lariche Chevrolet-Cadillac Inc .... D 419 422-1855
  Findlay *(G-8556)*

Lavery Chevrolet-Buick Inc .... E 330 823-1100
  Alliance *(G-388)*

Lebanon Ford Inc .... D 513 932-1010
  Lebanon *(G-9775)*

Leikin Motor Companies Inc .... D 440 946-6900
  Willoughby *(G-15204)*

Lima Auto Mall Inc .... D 419 993-6000
  Lima *(G-9918)*

Lincoln Mrcury Kings Auto Mall .... E 513 683-3800
  Cincinnati *(G-2979)*

Mark Thomas Ford Inc .... E 330 638-1010
  Cortland *(G-6972)*

Mathews Ddge Chrysler Jeep Inc .... E 740 389-2341
  Marion *(G-10443)*

Mathews Ford Sandusky Inc .... E 419 626-4721
  Sandusky *(G-12914)*

Mathews Kennedy Ford L-M Inc .... D 740 387-3673
  Marion *(G-10444)*

Matia Motors Inc .... E 440 365-7311
  Elyria *(G-8273)*

McCluskey Chevrolet Inc .... E 513 761-1111
  Loveland *(G-10149)*

Mike Castrucci Ford .... C 513 831-7010
  Milford *(G-11243)*

Mike Ford Bass Inc .... D 440 934-3673
  Sheffield Village *(G-13002)*

Montrose Ford Inc .... C 330 666-0711
  Fairlawn *(G-8491)*

Mullinax Ford North Canton Inc .... C 330 238-3206
  Canton *(G-1812)*

Nassief Automotive Inc .... E 440 997-5151
  Austinburg *(G-632)*

Nick Mayer Lincoln-Mercury Inc .... D 877 836-5314
  Westlake *(G-15084)*

Northern Automotive Inc .... E 614 436-2001
  Columbus *(G-6367)*

Northgate Chrysler Ddge Jeep I .... D 513 385-3900
  Cincinnati *(G-3123)*

Pag Mentor A1 Inc .... E 440 951-1040
  Mentor *(G-10982)*

Pallotta Ford Inc .... D 330 345-5051
  Wooster *(G-15365)*

Partners Auto Group Bdford Inc .... D 440 439-2323
  Bedford *(G-980)*

Paul Hrnchar Ford-Mercury Inc .... E 330 533-3673
  Canfield *(G-1638)*

Pete Baur Buick GMC Inc .... E 440 238-5600
  Cleveland *(G-4745)*

Reineke Ford Inc .... E 888 691-8175
  Fostoria *(G-8622)*

Ricart Ford Inc .... B 614 836-5321
  Groveport *(G-9000)*

Ron Marhofer Automall Inc .... C 330 835-6707
  Cuyahoga Falls *(G-7099)*

Ron Marhofer Automall Inc .... E 330 923-5059
  Cuyahoga Falls *(G-7100)*

Rouen Chrysler Plymouth Dodge .... E 419 837-6228
  Woodville *(G-15306)*

Roush Equipment Inc .... C 614 882-1535
  Westerville *(G-15014)*

Rush Truck Centers Ohio Inc .... E 513 733-8500
  Cincinnati *(G-3334)*

Schoner Chevrolet Inc .... E 330 877-6731
  Hartville *(G-9129)*

Sharpnack Chevrolet Co .... E 800 752-7513
  Vermilion *(G-14408)*

Sims Buick-GMC Truck Inc .... E 330 372-3500
  Warren *(G-14554)*

Slimans Sales & Service Inc .... E 440 988-4484
  Amherst *(G-432)*

Sonic Automotive .... D 614 870-8200
  Columbus *(G-6692)*

Sorbir Inc .... D 440 449-1000
  Cleveland *(G-4919)*

Spires Motors Inc .... E 614 771-2345
  Hilliard *(G-9233)*

Spitzer Chevrolet Inc .... E 330 467-4141
  Northfield *(G-11966)*

Stykemain-Buick-Gmc Ltd .... D 419 784-5252
  Defiance *(G-7770)*

Sunnyside Cars Inc .... E 440 777-9911
  North Olmsted *(G-11917)*

Surfside Motors Inc .... E 419 419-4776
  Galion *(G-8751)*

Tansky Motors Inc .... E 650 322-7069
  Rockbridge *(G-12736)*

Taylor Chevrolet Inc .... E 740 653-2091
  Lancaster *(G-9746)*

The Glockner Chevrolet Company .... C 740 353-2161
  Portsmouth *(G-12576)*

Tim Lally Chevrolet Inc .... D 440 232-2000
  Bedford *(G-988)*

Tom Ahl Chryslr-Plymouth-Dodge .... C 419 227-0202
  Lima *(G-9971)*

Toyota Industries N Amer Inc .... D 937 237-0976
  Dayton *(G-7675)*

Valley Ford Truck Inc .... D 216 524-2200
  Cleveland *(G-5097)*

SERVICES SECTION

MULTIPLEXERS: Telephone & Telegraph

Van Devere Inc .... D 330 253-6137
Akron (G-348)

Village Motors Inc .... D 330 674-2055
Millersburg (G-11295)

Vin Devers Inc .... C 888 847-9535
Sylvania (G-13578)

Volvo BMW Dyton Evans Volkswag .... E 937 890-6200
Dayton (G-7710)

Voss Auto Network Inc .... E 937 428-2447
Dayton (G-7711)

Voss Chevrolet Inc .... C 937 428-2500
Dayton (G-7713)

Voss Dodge .... E 937 435-7800
Dayton (G-7714)

Walker Auto Group Inc .... D 937 433-4950
Miamisburg (G-11103)

Walt Ford Sweeney Inc .... D 513 347-2600
Cincinnati (G-3639)

Warner Buick-Nissan Inc .... E 419 423-7161
Findlay (G-8597)

White Family Companies Inc .... E 937 222-3701
Dayton (G-7720)

Whites Service Center Inc .... E 937 653-5279
Urbana (G-14317)

Wmk LLC .... E 234 312-2000
Richfield (G-12714)

Yark Automotive Group Inc .... B 419 841-7771
Toledo (G-14111)

Young Truck Sales Inc .... E 330 477-6271
Canton (G-1891)

MOTOR VEHICLE PARTS & ACCESS: Body Components & Frames

ARE Inc .... A 330 830-7800
Massillon (G-10631)

MOTOR VEHICLE PARTS & ACCESS: Clutches

Remington Steel Inc .... D 937 322-2414
Springfield (G-13284)

Westfield Steel Inc .... D 937 322-2414
Springfield (G-13312)

MOTOR VEHICLE PARTS & ACCESS: Engines & Parts

Mahle Behr Mt Sterling Inc .... B 740 869-3333
Mount Sterling (G-11474)

MOTOR VEHICLE PARTS & ACCESS: Fuel Systems & Parts

Interstate Diesel Service Inc .... C 216 881-0015
Cleveland (G-4420)

MOTOR VEHICLE PARTS & ACCESS: Mufflers, Exhaust

Emssons Faurecia Ctrl Systems .... C 812 341-2000
Toledo (G-13792)

MOTOR VEHICLE PARTS & ACCESS: Power Steering Eqpt

Maval Industries LLC .... C 330 405-1600
Twinsburg (G-14203)

MOTOR VEHICLE PARTS & ACCESS: Sanders, Safety

Doran Mfg LLC .... D 866 816-7233
Blue Ash (G-1163)

MOTOR VEHICLE RACING & DRIVER SVCS

Team Rahal Inc .... D 614 529-7000
Hilliard (G-9236)

Thorsport Inc .... E 419 621-8800
Sandusky (G-12936)

MOTOR VEHICLE SPLYS & PARTS WHOLESALERS: New

ARE Inc .... A 330 830-7800
Massillon (G-10631)

Axiom Automotive Tech Inc .... A 800 321-8830
Bedford (G-954)

Beechmont Chevrolet Inc .... D 513 624-1100
Cincinnati (G-2247)

Beechmont Ford Inc .... C 513 752-6611
Cincinnati (G-2098)

Beechmont Motors Inc .... E 513 388-3883
Cincinnati (G-2248)

Beechmont Motors T Inc .... D 513 388-3800
Cincinnati (G-2249)

Chagrin Valley Auto Parts Co .... E 216 398-9800
Cleveland (G-3960)

Chemspec Usa Inc .... D 330 669-8512
Orrville (G-12158)

Ctek Inc .... D 330 963-0981
Twinsburg (G-14179)

Doran Mfg LLC .... D 866 816-7233
Blue Ash (G-1163)

Emssons Faurecia Ctrl Systems .... C 812 341-2000
Toledo (G-13792)

Goodyear Tire & Rubber Company .... A 330 796-2121
Akron (G-179)

International Brake Inds Inc .... E 419 227-4421
Lima (G-9911)

Keystone Auto Glass Inc .... D 419 509-0497
Maumee (G-10736)

Kyocera Precision Tools Inc .... D 419 738-6652
Wapakoneta (G-14486)

Lower Great Lakes Kenworth Inc .... E 419 874-3511
Perrysburg (G-12354)

Luk-Aftermarket Service Inc .... D 330 273-4383
Valley City (G-14335)

Mac Trailer Manufacturing Inc .... A 800 795-8454
Alliance (G-391)

N S International Ltd .... D 248 251-1600
Dublin (G-8067)

Nk Parts Industries Inc .... C 937 498-4651
Sidney (G-13041)

Ohio Auto Kolor Inc .... E 614 272-2255
Columbus (G-6393)

Shrader Tire & Oil Inc .... E 419 472-2128
Toledo (G-14012)

Truckomat Corporation .... E 740 467-2818
Hebron (G-9155)

Wabash National Trlr Ctrs Inc .... D 614 878-6088
Groveport (G-9012)

MOTOR VEHICLE SPLYS & PARTS WHOLESALERS: Used

Lucas Sumitomo Brakes Inc .... E 513 934-0024
Lebanon (G-9776)

Mac Trailer Manufacturing Inc .... A 800 795-8454
Alliance (G-391)

MOTOR VEHICLE: Shock Absorbers

Thyssenkrupp Bilstein Amer Inc .... C 513 881-7600
Hamilton (G-9086)

MOTOR VEHICLES & CAR BODIES

Honda Dev & Mfg Amer LLC .... C 937 644-0724
Marysville (G-10488)

MOTOR VEHICLES, WHOLESALE: Truck tractors

Bulldawg Holdings LLC .... E 419 423-3131
Findlay (G-8519)

Helton Enterprises Inc .... E 419 423-4180
Findlay (G-8546)

Peterbilt of Cincinnati .... B 513 772-1740
Cincinnati (G-3199)

MOTOR VEHICLES, WHOLESALE: Trucks, commercial

Cerni Motor Sales Inc .... D 330 652-9917
Youngstown (G-15575)

Columbus Truck & Equipment .... D 614 252-3111
Columbus (G-5657)

Esec Corporation .... E 614 875-3732
Grove City (G-8918)

Fyda Frghtliner Youngstown Inc .... D 330 797-0224
Youngstown (G-15615)

Kenworth of Cincinnati Inc .... E 513 771-5831
Cincinnati (G-2937)

Lower Great Lakes Kenworth Inc .... E 419 874-3511
Perrysburg (G-12354)

Mansfield Truck Sls & Svc Inc .... D 419 522-9811
Mansfield (G-10290)

Midway Inc .... D 419 465-2551
Monroeville (G-11357)

Ohio Truck Sales LLC .... D 419 582-8087
Sandusky (G-12923)

R & R Inc .... E 330 799-1536
Youngstown (G-15705)

R & R Truck Sales Inc .... E 330 784-5881
Akron (G-276)

Stoops of Lima Inc .... D 419 228-4334
Lima (G-9967)

Whites Service Center Inc .... E 937 653-5279
Urbana (G-14317)

Worldwide Equipment Inc .... E 614 876-0336
Columbus (G-6904)

MOTORCYCLE DEALERS

Carcorp Inc .... C 877 857-2801
Columbus (G-5506)

South E Harley Davidson Sls Co .... E 440 439-5300
Cleveland (G-4920)

MOTORCYCLE DEALERS: All-Terrain Vehicle Parts & Access

Old Meadow Farms Inc .... E 440 632-5590
Middlefield (G-11143)

MOTORCYCLE PARTS: Wholesalers

Dixie Distributing Company .... E 937 322-0033
Springfield (G-13247)

MOTORS: Electric

Ametek Tchnical Indus Pdts Inc .... D 330 673-3451
Kent (G-9559)

Dreison International Inc .... C 216 362-0755
Cleveland (G-4184)

Hannon Company .... D 330 456-4728
Canton (G-1770)

MOTORS: Generators

General Electric Company .... E 216 883-1000
Cleveland (G-4310)

MULTIPLEXERS: Telephone & Telegraph
- DTE Inc .... E 419 522-3428
  Mansfield (G-10259)
- Floyd Bell Inc .... D 614 294-4000
  Columbus (G-5874)
- Vertiv Energy Systems Inc .... A 440 288-1122
  Lorain (G-10107)

MUSEUMS & ART GALLERIES
- Cincinnati Museum Center .... B 513 287-7000
  Cincinnati (G-2416)

MUSICAL INSTRUMENTS & ACCESS: NEC
- Belco Works Inc .... D 740 695-0500
  Saint Clairsville (G-12774)
- Jatiga Inc .... D 859 817-7100
  Blue Ash (G-1191)

MUSICAL INSTRUMENTS WHOLESALERS
- Jatiga Inc .... D 859 817-7100
  Blue Ash (G-1191)

NATURAL GAS DISTRIBUTION TO CONSUMERS
- Bay State Gas Company .... D 614 460-4292
  Columbus (G-5423)
- Cinergy Corp .... A 513 421-9500
  Cincinnati (G-2440)
- City of Lancaster .... E 740 687-6670
  Lancaster (G-9701)
- City of Toledo .... D 419 245-1800
  Toledo (G-13743)
- Columbia Gas of Ohio Inc .... D 419 562-4003
  Bucyrus (G-1500)
- Columbia Gas of Ohio Inc .... D 559 683-1567
  Cambridge (G-1564)
- Columbia Gas of Ohio Inc .... C 440 891-2458
  Cleveland (G-4089)
- Columbia Gas of Ohio Inc .... D 614 878-6015
  Columbus (G-5599)
- Columbia Gas of Ohio Inc .... C 614 481-1000
  Columbus (G-5600)
- Columbia Gas of Ohio Inc .... C 614 460-6000
  Columbus (G-5601)
- Columbia Gas of Ohio Inc .... D 614 818-2101
  Columbus (G-5602)
- Columbia Gas of Ohio Inc .... C 419 435-7725
  Findlay (G-8523)
- Columbia Gas of Ohio Inc .... D 419 332-9951
  Fremont (G-8670)
- Columbia Gas of Ohio Inc .... D 740 264-5577
  Steubenville (G-13320)
- Columbia Gas of Ohio Inc .... D 419 539-6046
  Toledo (G-13749)
- Columbia Gas of Ohio Inc .... D 740 450-1215
  Zanesville (G-15782)
- Columbia Gas of Ohio Inc .... E 614 460-6000
  Columbus (G-5598)
- Columbia Gas Transmission LLC .... E 614 460-4704
  Columbus (G-5603)
- Columbia Gulf Transmission LLC .... D 614 460-6991
  Columbus (G-5604)
- Columbia Gulf Transmission LLC .... D 740 746-9105
  Sugar Grove (G-13507)
- Consumers Energy Company .... E 800 477-5050
  Cincinnati (G-2499)
- Duke Energy Ohio Inc .... D 704 382-3853
  Cincinnati (G-2583)
- Dynegy Coml Asset MGT LLC .... C 513 287-5033
  Cincinnati (G-2590)
- East Ohio Gas Company .... D 800 362-7557
  Akron (G-145)
- East Ohio Gas Company .... D 216 736-6120
  Ashtabula (G-534)
- East Ohio Gas Company .... D 740 439-2721
  Byesville (G-1534)
- East Ohio Gas Company .... D 330 266-2161
  Canton (G-1741)
- East Ohio Gas Company .... D 330 477-9411
  Canton (G-1742)
- East Ohio Gas Company .... D 330 499-2501
  Canton (G-1743)
- East Ohio Gas Company .... D 216 736-6959
  Cleveland (G-4198)
- East Ohio Gas Company .... D 330 266-2169
  New Franklin (G-11615)
- East Ohio Gas Company .... E 216 736-6917
  Wickliffe (G-15148)
- East Ohio Gas Company .... D 330 478-3114
  Wooster (G-15335)
- East Ohio Gas Company .... A 800 362-7557
  Cleveland (G-4197)
- Energy Cooperative Inc .... E 740 348-1206
  Newark (G-11699)
- National Gas & Oil Corporation .... E 740 454-7252
  Zanesville (G-15818)
- National Gas & Oil Corporation .... E 740 344-2102
  Newark (G-11733)
- Ohio Gas Company .... E 419 636-1117
  Bryan (G-1491)
- Pike Natural Gas Company .... D 937 393-4602
  Hillsboro (G-9267)
- Scana Energy Marketing LLC .... D 803 217-1322
  Dublin (G-8116)
- Stand Energy Corporation .... E 513 621-1113
  Cincinnati (G-3407)
- Vectren Energy Dlvry Ohio LLC .... E 937 331-3080
  Englewood (G-8325)
- Volunteer Energy Services Inc .... E 614 856-3128
  Pickerington (G-12413)

NATURAL GAS LIQUIDS PRODUCTION
- Markwest Utica Emg LLC .... C 740 942-4810
  Jewett (G-9543)

NATURAL GAS PRODUCTION
- D & L Energy Inc .... E 330 270-1201
  Canton (G-1730)
- Interstate Gas Supply LLC .... B 877 995-4447
  Dublin (G-8041)

NATURAL GAS TRANSMISSION
- Duke Energy Ohio Inc .... D 704 382-3853
  Cincinnati (G-2583)
- Knight Material Tech LLC .... D 330 488-1651
  East Canton (G-8169)
- Ko Transmission Company .... E 513 287-3553
  Cincinnati (G-2946)
- National Gas & Oil Corporation .... E 740 454-7252
  Zanesville (G-15818)
- National Gas & Oil Corporation .... E 740 344-2102
  Newark (G-11733)
- Ohio Gas Company .... E 419 636-3642
  Bryan (G-1490)

NATURAL GAS TRANSMISSION & DISTRIBUTION
- Aspire Energy of Ohio LLC .... E 330 682-7726
  Orrville (G-12156)
- National Gas & Oil Corporation .... E 740 454-7252
  Zanesville (G-15818)
- Ngo Development Corporation .... B 740 622-9560
  Coshocton (G-6993)

NATURAL GASOLINE PRODUCTION
- Husky Marketing and Supply Co ..... E 614 210-2300
  Dublin (G-8033)

NAVIGATIONAL SYSTEMS & INSTRUMENTS
- Cedar Elec Holdings Corp .... D 773 804-6288
  West Chester (G-14662)

NEIGHBORHOOD DEVELOPMENT GROUP
- Ohio Community Dev Fin Fund .... E 614 221-1114
  Columbus (G-6398)

NETS: Launderers & Dyers
- TAC Industries Inc .... B 937 328-5200
  Springfield (G-13299)

NEW & USED CAR DEALERS
- Albert Mike Leasing .... C 513 563-1400
  Cincinnati (G-2158)
- Allegiance Administrators LLC .... E 877 895-1414
  Dublin (G-7929)
- Jake Sweeney Automotive Inc .... D 513 782-2800
  Cincinnati (G-2896)
- Miami Valley Intl Trcks Inc .... E 937 324-5526
  Springfield (G-13273)
- Ron Marhofer Auto Family .... E 330 940-4422
  Cuyahoga Falls (G-7098)

NONCURRENT CARRYING WIRING DEVICES
- Vertiv Energy Systems Inc .... A 440 288-1122
  Lorain (G-10107)
- Zekelman Industries Inc .... C 740 432-2146
  Cambridge (G-1588)

NOVELTIES, PAPER, WHOLESALE
- Gummer Wholesale Inc .... D 740 928-0415
  Heath (G-9133)

NURSERIES & LAWN & GARDEN SPLY STORES, RETAIL: Fertilizer
- Centerra Co-Op .... E 419 281-2153
  Ashland (G-490)
- Heritage Cooperative Inc .... D 877 240-4393
  Delaware (G-7804)

NURSERY STOCK, WHOLESALE
- Dennis Top Soil & Ldscpg Inc .... E 419 865-5656
  Toledo (G-13775)
- Millcreek Gardens LLC .... E 740 666-7125
  Ostrander (G-12183)
- Siebenthaler Company .... D 937 274-1154
  Beavercreek (G-905)
- Thorsens Greenhouse LLC .... E 740 363-5069
  Delaware (G-7830)

NURSING CARE FACILITIES: Skilled
- Ahf Ohio Inc .... D 937 256-4663
  Dayton (G-7160)
- Ahf Ohio Inc .... D 614 760-8870
  Dublin (G-7923)
- Ahf Ohio Inc .... D 740 532-6188
  Ironton (G-9501)
- Ahf Ohio Inc .... D 330 725-4123
  Medina (G-10805)
- Ahf/Central States Inc .... C 724 941-7150
  Dublin (G-7924)
- Alexson Services Inc .... D 513 874-0423
  Fairfield (G-8389)

SERVICES SECTION

NURSING CARE FACILITIES: Skilled

Altercare Inc... E 330 929-4231
   Cuyahoga Falls *(G-7037)*

Altercare Nobles Pond Inc...................... E 330 834-4800
   Canton *(G-1663)*

American Nursing Care Inc...................... B 513 731-4600
   Cincinnati *(G-2184)*

American Nursing Care Inc...................... C 513 245-1500
   Cincinnati *(G-2185)*

American Nursing Care Inc...................... B 937 438-3844
   Dayton *(G-7172)*

American Nursing Care Inc...................... B 614 847-0555
   Zanesville *(G-15767)*

American Retirement Corp........................ C 216 291-6140
   Cleveland *(G-3807)*

Amherst Manor Inc.................................... B 440 988-4415
   Amherst *(G-422)*

Anchor Lodge Nursing Home Inc............ E 440 244-2019
   Lorain *(G-10054)*

Anna Maria of Aurora Inc......................... D 330 562-3120
   Aurora *(G-604)*

Anna Maria of Aurora Inc......................... C 330 562-6171
   Aurora *(G-603)*

Apostolic Christian Home Inc.................. D 330 927-1010
   Rittman *(G-12729)*

April Enterprises Inc................................. C 937 293-7703
   Moraine *(G-11389)*

Arbors East LLC.. E 614 575-9003
   Columbus *(G-5377)*

Arbors West LLC....................................... E 614 879-7661
   West Jefferson *(G-14848)*

Ashley Enterprises LLC............................. D 330 726-5790
   Boardman *(G-1284)*

Assisted Living Concepts LLC................. E 419 334-6962
   Fremont *(G-8667)*

Astoria Place of Clyde LLC..................... D 419 547-9595
   Clyde *(G-5198)*

Atrium Centers Inc.................................... E 614 416-0600
   Columbus *(G-5404)*

Atrium Living Centers of Ea..................... E 614 416-2662
   Columbus *(G-5405)*

Autumn Court Operating Co LLC............ D 419 523-4370
   Ottawa *(G-12185)*

Balanced Care Corporation...................... E 330 908-1166
   Northfield *(G-11952)*

Beaver Dam Health Care Center............ E 330 762-6486
   Akron *(G-64)*

Beaver Dam Health Care Center............ E 440 247-4200
   Chagrin Falls *(G-1953)*

Beaver Dam Health Care Center............ E 614 861-6666
   Columbus *(G-5429)*

Beaver Dam Health Care Center............ E 330 335-1558
   Wadsworth *(G-14429)*

Beeghly Nursing LLC................................ D 330 884-2300
   Boardman *(G-1285)*

Belmont County Home.............................. D 740 695-4925
   Saint Clairsville *(G-12775)*

Bentley Leasing Co LLC........................... A 330 337-9503
   Salem *(G-12839)*

Birchaven Village....................................... D 419 424-3000
   Findlay *(G-8512)*

Blue Ash Healthcare Group Inc.............. E 513 793-3362
   Cincinnati *(G-2266)*

Blue Creek Healthcare LLC...................... D 419 877-5338
   Whitehouse *(G-15139)*

Bluesky Healthcare Inc............................. E 440 989-5200
   Lorain *(G-10061)*

Brethren Care Inc..................................... C 419 289-0803
   Ashland *(G-484)*

Brethren Care Village LLC...................... D 419 289-1585
   Ashland *(G-485)*

Brewster Parke Inc................................... D 330 767-4179
   Brewster *(G-1373)*

Briarfield Manor LLC................................ C 330 270-3468
   Youngstown *(G-15565)*

Brook Willow Chrstn Cmmunities............ C 614 885-3300
   Columbus *(G-5468)*

Brookdale Lving Cmmunities Inc............ E 330 666-4545
   Akron *(G-76)*

Brookview Healthcare Ctr........................ D 419 784-1014
   Defiance *(G-7742)*

Brookville Enterprises Inc....................... C 937 833-2133
   Brookville *(G-1445)*

Brookwood Realty Company................... D 513 530-9555
   Cincinnati *(G-2283)*

Bryant Health Center Inc........................ D 740 532-6188
   Ironton *(G-9504)*

Buckeye Frest Rsmount Pavilion............ C 740 354-4505
   Portsmouth *(G-12547)*

Butler County of Ohio.............................. D 513 887-3728
   Hamilton *(G-9020)*

Canterbury Vlla Oprations Corp............. E 330 821-4000
   Alliance *(G-377)*

Canton Christian Home Inc..................... D 330 456-0004
   Canton *(G-1698)*

Capital Health Services Inc..................... E 937 277-0505
   Miamisburg *(G-11033)*

Carington Health Systems....................... E 513 682-2700
   Hamilton *(G-9025)*

Carriage Inn of Steubenville.................... C 740 264-7161
   Steubenville *(G-13318)*

Cedar Hill Opco LLC................................. D 740 454-6823
   Zanesville *(G-15777)*

Center Ridge Nursing Home Inc............. C 440 808-5500
   North Ridgeville *(G-11924)*

CHI Living Communities........................... C 419 627-2273
   Sandusky *(G-12879)*

Clovernook Inc... D 513 605-4000
   Cincinnati *(G-2462)*

CMS & Co Management Svcs Inc........... D 440 989-5200
   Lorain *(G-10067)*

Columbus Alzheimers Care Ctr............... D 614 459-7050
   Columbus *(G-5607)*

Community Hlth Prfssionals Inc.............. E 419 634-7443
   Ada *(G-1)*

Concord Care Ctr Cortland Inc............... E 330 637-7906
   Cortland *(G-6969)*

Concordia of Ohio..................................... E 330 664-1000
   Copley *(G-6952)*

Congregate Living of America................ D 937 393-6700
   Hillsboro *(G-9251)*

Congregate Living of America................ D 513 899-2801
   Morrow *(G-11455)*

Consulate Healthcare Inc........................ E 419 865-1248
   Maumee *(G-10711)*

Consulate Management Co LLC.............. C 419 886-3922
   Bellville *(G-1047)*

Consulate Management Co LLC.............. B 440 237-7966
   Cleveland *(G-4110)*

Consulate Management Co LLC.............. B 740 259-2351
   Lucasville *(G-10174)*

Consulate Management Co LLC.............. B 330 837-1001
   Massillon *(G-10636)*

Consulate Management Co LLC.............. C 419 867-7926
   Maumee *(G-10712)*

Contining Hlthcare Sltions Inc................. B 440 466-1181
   Geneva *(G-8784)*

Cottingham Rtirement Cmnty Inc........... D 513 563-3600
   Cincinnati *(G-2511)*

Country CLB Retirement Ctr LLC........... D 440 992-0022
   Ashtabula *(G-530)*

Country CLB Retirement Ctr LLC........... D 740 671-9330
   Bellaire *(G-1010)*

County of Allen... E 419 221-1103
   Lima *(G-9881)*

County of Logan....................................... C 937 592-2901
   Bellefontaine *(G-1027)*

County of Monroe..................................... D 740 472-0144
   Woodsfield *(G-15301)*

County of Shelby...................................... D 937 492-6900
   Sidney *(G-13027)*

Covenant Care Ohio Inc.......................... D 937 878-7046
   Fairborn *(G-8370)*

Cridersville Health Care Ctr.................... D 419 645-4468
   Cridersville *(G-7028)*

Csji-Tiffin Inc... D 419 447-2723
   Tiffin *(G-13626)*

Daniel Drake Ctr For PST-Cute............... A 513 418-2500
   Cincinnati *(G-2536)*

Dayspring Health Care Center................ E 937 864-5800
   Fairborn *(G-8373)*

Deaconess Long Term Care of MI......... A 513 487-3600
   Cincinnati *(G-2551)*

Dearth Management Company............... D 419 253-0144
   Marengo *(G-10352)*

Dearth Management Company............... D 330 339-3595
   New Philadelphia *(G-11649)*

Debmar Inc... D 419 728-7010
   Bowling Green *(G-1317)*

Dedicated Nursing Assoc Inc.................. C 888 465-6929
   Beavercreek *(G-922)*

Dedicated Nursing Assoc Inc.................. C 866 450-5550
   Hilliard *(G-9191)*

Diversicare St Theresa LLC.................... D 513 271-7010
   Cincinnati *(G-2569)*

DMD Management Inc.............................. C 216 371-3600
   Cleveland *(G-4172)*

Doctors Hospital Cleveland Inc.............. C 740 753-7300
   Nelsonville *(G-11542)*

Dover Nursing Center Llc....................... D 330 364-4436
   Dover *(G-7883)*

Dublin Geriatric Care Co LP.................... E 614 761-1188
   Dublin *(G-7993)*

Eagle Creek Hlthcare Group Inc............ B 937 544-5531
   West Union *(G-14869)*

Eastgate Health Care Center.................. D 513 752-3710
   Cincinnati *(G-2103)*

Ebenezer Road Corporation.................... C 513 941-0099
   Cincinnati *(G-2601)*

Echoing Hills Village Inc.......................... D 937 854-5151
   Dayton *(G-7326)*

Echoing Hills Village Inc.......................... D 440 989-1400
   Lorain *(G-10071)*

Edgewood Mnor Rhblttion Hlthca......... 732 730-7360
   Port Clinton *(G-12524)*

Eliza Jnnngs Snior Care Netwrk............. C 216 226-5000
   Olmsted Twp *(G-12090)*

Elms Retirement Village Inc.................... B 440 647-2414
   Wellington *(G-14631)*

Elmwood Centers Inc............................... D 419 332-3378
   Green Springs *(G-8858)*

Embassy Healthcare MGT Inc................. E 216 378-2050
   Beachwood *(G-789)*

Embassy Winchester LLC........................ D 614 834-2273
   Canal Winchester *(G-1605)*

Emeritus Corporation................................ E 330 477-5727
   Canton *(G-1745)*

Emeritus Corporation................................ D 440 201-9200
   Cleveland *(G-4211)*

Emeritus Corporation................................ C 614 836-5990
   Groveport *(G-8985)*

Emeritus Corporation................................ D 330 342-0934
   Stow *(G-13365)*

Emeritus Corporation................................ C 440 269-8600
   Willoughby *(G-15191)*

Esop Realty Inc.. C 216 361-0718
   Cleveland *(G-4223)*

NURSING CARE FACILITIES: Skilled — SERVICES SECTION

Euclid Health Care Inc .... C 513 561-6400
Cincinnati (G-2638)

Evanglcal Lthran Good Smrtan S .... C 419 365-5115
Arlington (G-469)

Fairchild MD Leasing Co LLC .... C 330 678-4912
Kent (G-9574)

Fairhope Hspice Plltive Care I .... D 740 654-7077
Lancaster (G-9721)

Fairmount Nursing Home Inc .... D 440 338-8220
Newbury (G-11760)

First Community Village .... B 614 324-4455
Columbus (G-5861)

Fisher - Titus Health .... A 419 668-8101
Norwalk (G-12010)

Five Star Senior Living Inc .... E 614 451-6793
Columbus (G-5871)

Fountains At Canterbury .... E 405 751-3600
Toledo (G-13810)

Franciscan Sisters of Chicago .... B 440 843-7800
Cleveland (G-4283)

Friends Health Care Assn .... C 937 767-7363
Yellow Springs (G-15535)

Friendship Vlg of Clumbus Ohio .... C 614 890-8282
Columbus (G-5898)

Friendship Vlg of Dublin Ohio .... C 614 764-1600
Dublin (G-8016)

Fulton County Health Center .... C 419 335-2017
Wauseon (G-14601)

Gateway Health Care Center .... D 216 486-4949
Cleveland (G-4305)

Generation Health Corp .... E 614 337-1066
Columbus (G-5926)

Genertion Hlth Rhblttion Ctr L .... D 740 348-1300
Newark (G-11701)

Gillette Nursing Home Inc .... D 330 372-1960
Warren (G-14524)

Glen Wesley Inc .... D 614 888-7492
Columbus (G-5937)

Glenward Inc .... E 513 863-3100
Fairfield Township (G-8460)

Good Samaritan Health Group Inc C
Cleveland (G-4319)

Good Shepherd Home .... C 419 937-1801
Fostoria (G-8618)

Graceworks Lutheran Services .... A 937 433-2140
Dayton (G-7383)

Greenbrier Senior Living Cmnty .... D 440 888-0400
Cleveland (G-4338)

H & G Nursery Home Inc .... E 513 734-7401
Bethel (G-1091)

H & G Nursing Homes Inc .... D 937 544-2205
West Union (G-14870)

Hackensack Meridian Health Inc .... D 513 792-9697
Cincinnati (G-2791)

Harborside Clveland Ltd Partnr .... D 440 871-5900
Westlake (G-15064)

Harborside Healthcare LLC .... C 937 436-6155
Dayton (G-7397)

Harborside Sylvania LLC .... D 419 882-1875
Sylvania (G-13548)

Hcf Management Inc .... D 419 999-2055
Lima (G-9897)

Hcf Management Inc .... E 740 289-2394
Piketon (G-12422)

Health Care Opportunities Inc .... E 513 932-0300
Lebanon (G-9768)

Heath Nursing Care Center .... D 740 522-1171
Newark (G-11704)

Heatherdowns Operating Co LLC .... D 419 382-5050
Toledo (G-13845)

Heritage Corner Nursing HM LLC .... E 419 728-7010
Bowling Green (G-1324)

Hickory Creek Hlthcare Fndtion .... E 419 542-7795
Hicksville (G-9158)

Hillandale Health Care Inc .... E 513 777-1400
West Chester (G-14708)

Holzer Senior Care Center .... E 740 446-5001
Bidwell (G-1104)

Home Echo Club Inc .... D 614 864-1718
Pickerington (G-12403)

Home The Friends Inc .... D 513 897-6050
Waynesville (G-14624)

Homefront Nursing LLC .... E 513 404-1189
Cincinnati (G-2840)

Horizon Health Management LLC .... E 513 793-5220
Cincinnati (G-2843)

Hospice Cincinnati Inc .... D 513 891-7700
Cincinnati (G-2848)

Hospice North Central Ohio Inc .... E 419 281-7107
Ashland (G-501)

Hospice of Genesis Health .... E 740 454-5381
Zanesville (G-15801)

Hosser Assisted Living .... E 740 286-8785
Jackson (G-9521)

Humility House .... D 330 505-0144
Youngstown (G-15634)

Hyde Park Health Center .... E 513 272-0600
Cincinnati (G-2859)

Independence Care Community .... E 419 435-8505
Fostoria (G-8620)

Indian Hlls Hlthcare Group Inc .... A 216 486-8880
Euclid (G-8350)

Inner City Nursing Home Inc .... C 216 795-1363
Cleveland (G-4413)

Jackson Cnty Hlth Fclities Inc .... D 740 384-0722
Wellston (G-14639)

Jewish Fdrtion Grter Dyton Inc .... D 937 837-2651
Dayton (G-7428)

Jewish Home Cincinnati Inc .... B 513 754-3100
Mason (G-10569)

Jo-Lin Health Center Inc .... E 740 532-0860
Ironton (G-9510)

Joint Township Dst Mem Hosp .... B 419 394-3335
Saint Marys (G-12829)

Judson Care Center Inc .... A 513 662-5880
Cincinnati (G-2922)

Jwj Investments Inc .... C 419 643-3161
Delphos (G-7841)

Karl Hc LLC .... B 614 846-5420
Columbus (G-6102)

Karrington Operating Co Inc .... B 614 875-0514
Grove City (G-8929)

Kendal At Oberlin .... C 440 775-0094
Oberlin (G-12071)

Kindred Healthcare LLC .... E 937 222-5963
Dayton (G-7443)

Kingston Healthcare Company .... E 440 967-1800
Vermilion (G-14407)

Kingston of Miamisburg LLC .... D 937 866-9089
Miamisburg (G-11067)

Kingston Rsdnce Perrysburg LLC .... C 419 872-6200
Perrysburg (G-12350)

Lakewood Senior Campus LLC .... E 216 228-7650
Lakewood (G-9677)

Laurel Health Care Company .... D 740 264-5042
Steubenville (G-13335)

Laurel Health Care Company .... D 614 794-8800
Westerville (G-14905)

Laurel Hlth Care Battle Creek .... E 614 794-8800
Westerville (G-14906)

Lexington Court Care Center .... E 419 884-2000
Mansfield (G-10281)

Liberty Retirement Cmnty Lima .... E 419 331-2273
Lima (G-9917)

Lima Cnvlscent HM Fndation Inc .... D 419 227-5450
Lima (G-9920)

Little Ssters of Poor Bltmore .... D 419 698-4331
Oregon (G-12135)

Little Ssters of Poor Bltmore .... D 216 464-1222
Warrensville Heights (G-14584)

Longmeadow Care Center Inc .... E 330 297-5781
Ravenna (G-12632)

Lorain Manor Inc .... D 440 277-8173
Lorain (G-10087)

Lost Creek Hlth Care Rhblttion .... C 419 225-9040
Lima (G-9929)

LP Coshocton LLC .... E 470 622-1220
Coshocton (G-6991)

LP Opco LLC .... D 440 593-6266
Conneaut (G-6943)

Lutheran Home .... B 440 871-0090
Cleveland (G-4510)

Lutheran Homes Society Inc .... C 419 861-2233
Holland (G-9295)

Lutheran Scial Svcs Centl Ohio .... E 419 289-3523
Ashland (G-506)

Lutheran Village At Wolf Creek .... E 419 861-2233
Holland (G-9296)

Main Street Terrace Care Ctr .... D 740 653-8767
Lancaster (G-9734)

Mallard Cove Senior Dev LLC .... C 513 772-6655
Cincinnati (G-3007)

Manor Care Barberton Oh LLC .... E 330 753-5005
Barberton (G-701)

Mapleview Country Villa .... D 440 286-8176
Chardon (G-2011)

Marion Manor .... E 740 387-9545
Marion (G-10441)

Mary Scott Nursing Home Inc .... D 937 278-0761
Dayton (G-7468)

Marymount Hospital Inc .... B 216 581-0500
Cleveland (G-4531)

McGregor Foundation .... B 216 851-8200
Cleveland (G-4538)

McKinley Hall Inc .... E 937 328-5300
Springfield (G-13266)

MD Omg Emp LLC .... D 513 489-7100
Blue Ash (G-1207)

Mennonite Memorial Home .... D 419 358-7654
Bluffton (G-1282)

Mennonite Memorial Home .... C 419 358-1015
Bluffton (G-1283)

Menorah Pk Ctr For Snior Lving .... A 216 831-6500
Cleveland (G-4550)

Mercy St Theresa Center Inc .... E 513 271-7010
Cincinnati (G-3047)

Merit House LLC .... C 419 478-5131
Toledo (G-13921)

Mill Run Care Center LLC .... E 614 527-3000
Hilliard (G-9216)

Mkjb Inc .... D 513 851-8400
West Chester (G-14733)

Mon Health Care Inc .... E 304 285-2700
Westerville (G-14911)

Montefiore Home .... B 216 360-9080
Beachwood (G-819)

Mount Vernon Elderly Svcs LLC .... D 740 397-2350
Mount Vernon (G-11501)

Mountain Crest OH Opco LLC .... D 419 882-1875
Sylvania (G-13556)

Mt Airy Grdns Rhblttion Care .... E 513 591-0400
Cincinnati (G-3085)

Multi-Care Inc .... D 440 357-6181
Painesville (G-12239)

National Ch Rsdnces Pmbroke GA .... D 614 451-2151
Columbus (G-6291)

SERVICES SECTION

NURSING CARE FACILITIES: Skilled

National Church Residences..............C..... 614 451-2151
  Columbus *(G-6292)*
Nentwick Convalescent Home.............E..... 330 385-5001
  East Liverpool *(G-8187)*
New Dawn Health Care Inc...................C..... 330 343-5521
  Dover *(G-7895)*
New Life Hospice Inc..............................C..... 440 934-1458
  Lorain *(G-10095)*
Newcomerstown Development Inc.........E..... 740 498-5165
  Newcomerstown *(G-11771)*
Nightingale Holdings LLC.......................A..... 513 489-7100
  Blue Ash *(G-1215)*
North Park Retirement Cmnty.................E..... 216 267-0555
  Cleveland *(G-4650)*
Northwesterly Ltd..................................E..... 216 228-2266
  Cleveland *(G-4665)*
Norwood Hghlnds Healthcare LLC..........D..... 513 351-0153
  Cincinnati *(G-3131)*
Norwood Towers Healthcare LLC..........D..... 513 631-6800
  Norwood *(G-12034)*
Oak Hlth Care Invstors Dfnce I...............E..... 614 794-8800
  Westerville *(G-14918)*
Oakhill Manor Care Center....................E..... 330 875-5060
  Louisville *(G-10118)*
Ohio Living..B..... 330 867-2150
  Akron *(G-253)*
Ohio Living..B..... 513 681-4230
  Cincinnati *(G-3147)*
Ohio Living..B..... 513 539-7391
  Monroe *(G-11345)*
Ohio Living..B..... 937 498-2391
  Sidney *(G-13043)*
Ohio Living..B..... 330 746-2944
  Youngstown *(G-15682)*
Ohio Living Communities........................D..... 614 888-7800
  Columbus *(G-6432)*
Ohio Living Holdings...............................E..... 330 533-4350
  Canfield *(G-1636)*
Ohio Living Holdings...............................D..... 614 433-0031
  Columbus *(G-6433)*
Ohio Living Holdings...............................D..... 937 415-5666
  Sidney *(G-13044)*
Ohio Living Holdings...............................D..... 419 865-1499
  Toledo *(G-13947)*
Ohio Valley Manor Inc............................C..... 937 392-4318
  Ripley *(G-12727)*
Ohioguidestone.......................................B..... 440 234-2006
  Berea *(G-1078)*
Ohioguidestone.......................................E..... 440 234-2006
  Berea *(G-1079)*
Olmsted Manor Ltd.................................D..... 440 777-8444
  North Olmsted *(G-11910)*
Optum Infusion Svcs 550 LLC................D..... 866 442-4679
  Cincinnati *(G-3166)*
Orchard Villa Inc.....................................D..... 419 697-4100
  Oregon *(G-12139)*
Orion Care Services LLC........................E..... 216 752-3600
  Cleveland *(G-4707)*
Otterbein Homes.....................................D..... 419 645-5114
  Cridersville *(G-7029)*
Otterbein Homes.....................................E..... 513 696-8565
  Lebanon *(G-9780)*
Otterbein Homes.....................................E..... 419 943-4376
  Leipsic *(G-9801)*
Otterbein Homes.....................................E..... 513 260-7690
  Middletown *(G-11200)*
Otterbein Homes.....................................E..... 419 394-1622
  Saint Marys *(G-12833)*
Otterbein Homes.....................................E..... 419 394-2366
  Saint Marys *(G-12834)*
Otterbein Homes.....................................B..... 513 933-5400
  Lebanon *(G-9781)*

Otterbein Portage Valley Inc..................C..... 888 749-4950
  Pemberville *(G-12291)*
Otterbein Snior Lfstyle Chices................E..... 937 885-5426
  Dayton *(G-7542)*
Ovm Investment Group LLC..................C..... 937 392-0145
  Ripley *(G-12728)*
Park View Manor Inc..............................D..... 937 296-1550
  Englewood *(G-8318)*
Park Vlg Assisted Living LLC.................E..... 330 364-4436
  Dover *(G-7899)*
Parma Care Center Inc..........................C..... 216 661-6800
  Cleveland *(G-4728)*
Patrician Inc...C..... 440 237-3104
  Brunswick *(G-1466)*
Pearl Leasing Co LLC...........................E..... 513 530-1600
  Parma *(G-12261)*
Peregrine Health Services Inc...............D..... 330 823-9005
  Alliance *(G-396)*
Personacare of Ohio Inc.........................C..... 440 357-1311
  Painesville *(G-12241)*
Pgn Op Summit LLC..............................E..... 614 252-4987
  Columbus *(G-6519)*
Pomeroy Opco LLC................................D..... 740 992-6606
  Pomeroy *(G-12515)*
Progressive Aurora LLC.........................E..... 330 995-0094
  Aurora *(G-622)*
Progressive Macedonia LLC..................E..... 330 748-8800
  Macedonia *(G-10203)*
Provide-A-Care Inc................................C..... 330 828-2278
  Dalton *(G-7121)*
Quality Care Nursing Svc Inc.................C..... 740 377-9095
  South Point *(G-13182)*
Rae-Ann Center Inc...............................E..... 440 466-5733
  Geneva *(G-8788)*
Red Carpet Health Care Center.............E..... 740 439-4401
  Cambridge *(G-1580)*
Regency Leasing Co LLC.....................B..... 614 542-3100
  Columbus *(G-6574)*
Rest Haven Nursing Home Inc..............D..... 937 548-1138
  Greenville *(G-8882)*
River Vista Hlth Wellness LLC...............D..... 614 643-5454
  Columbus *(G-6594)*
Roman Cthlic Docese Youngstown.......C..... 330 875-5562
  Louisville *(G-10122)*
Rossford Grtric Care Ltd Prtnr..............E..... 614 459-0445
  Columbus *(G-6612)*
Royal Manor Health Care Inc................E..... 216 752-3600
  Cleveland *(G-4859)*
Saber Healthcare Holdings LLC............E..... 216 292-5706
  Bedford Heights *(G-1002)*
Salem Community Hospital....................A..... 330 332-1551
  Salem *(G-12854)*
Salem Healthcare MGT LLC..................E..... 330 332-1588
  Salem *(G-12855)*
Salutary Providers Inc...........................C..... 440 964-8446
  Ashtabula *(G-548)*
Samaritan Care Center Inc....................D..... 330 725-4123
  Medina *(G-10887)*
Sanctuary At Tuttle Crossing.................D..... 614 408-0182
  Dublin *(G-8112)*
Sateri Home Inc.....................................D..... 330 758-8106
  Youngstown *(G-15717)*
Schoenbrunn Healthcare.......................A..... 330 339-3595
  New Philadelphia *(G-11666)*
Select Spclty Hosp - Yngstown.............C..... 330 480-3488
  Youngstown *(G-15720)*
Select Spclty Hsptal-Akron LLC............D..... 330 761-7500
  Akron *(G-296)*
Senior Lifestyle Evergreen Ltd...............E..... 513 948-2308
  Cincinnati *(G-3357)*
Shelby County Mem Hosp Assn............E..... 937 492-9591
  Sidney *(G-13047)*

Shepherd of Vly Lthran Rtrment.............E..... 330 726-9061
  Youngstown *(G-15723)*
Singleton Health Care Ctr Inc.................D..... 216 231-0076
  Cleveland *(G-4909)*
Sisters of Chrity Cncnnati Ohi................C..... 513 347-5200
  Cincinnati *(G-3380)*
Slovene Home For The Aged.................C..... 216 486-0268
  Cleveland *(G-4915)*
Snf Wadsworth LLC................................E..... 330 336-3472
  Solon *(G-13143)*
Southeastern Health Care Ctr................D..... 740 425-3648
  Barnesville *(G-722)*
Spring Hills Health Care LLC.................D..... 513 424-9999
  Middletown *(G-11202)*
Spring Mdow Extnded Care Ctr F..........D..... 419 866-6124
  Holland *(G-9305)*
Springfeld Halthcare Group Inc..............C..... 937 399-8311
  Springfield *(G-13293)*
St Clare Commons..................................E..... 419 931-0050
  Perrysburg *(G-12371)*
St Edward Home.....................................C..... 330 668-2828
  Fairlawn *(G-8500)*
Stone Crssing Asssted Lving LL............C..... 330 492-7131
  Canton *(G-1862)*
Summerville Senior Living Inc................E..... 440 354-5499
  Mentor *(G-11000)*
Summit Facility Operations LLC.............A..... 330 633-0555
  Tallmadge *(G-13606)*
Sumner Home For The Aged Inc............C..... 330 666-2952
  Copley *(G-6964)*
Sunbridge Marion Hlth Care LLC............D..... 740 389-6306
  Marion *(G-10456)*
Sunrise Connecticut Ave Assn................A..... 614 451-6766
  Columbus *(G-6730)*
Sunrise Senior Living LLC......................E..... 216 447-8909
  Cleveland *(G-4961)*
Sunrise Senior Living LLC......................E..... 216 751-0930
  Cleveland *(G-4962)*
Sunrise Senior Living LLC......................E..... 330 929-8500
  Cuyahoga Falls *(G-7104)*
Sunrise Senior Living LLC......................E..... 937 438-0054
  Dayton *(G-7653)*
Sunrise Senior Living LLC......................E..... 614 718-2062
  Dublin *(G-8135)*
Sunrise Senior Living LLC......................E..... 937 836-9617
  Englewood *(G-8323)*
Sunrise Senior Living LLC......................E..... 419 425-3440
  Findlay *(G-8590)*
Sunrise Senior Living LLC......................E..... 614 418-9775
  Gahanna *(G-8731)*
Sunrise Senior Living LLC......................E..... 513 893-9000
  Hamilton *(G-9084)*
Sunrise Senior Living LLC......................E..... 330 707-1313
  Poland *(G-12510)*
Sunrise Senior Living LLC......................E..... 440 895-2383
  Rocky River *(G-12753)*
Sunrise Senior Living LLC......................E..... 614 457-3500
  Upper Arlington *(G-14282)*
Sunrise Senior Living LLC......................E..... 440 808-0074
  Westlake *(G-15112)*
Sunrise Senior Living MGT Inc...............C..... 614 235-3900
  Columbus *(G-6731)*
The Community Hospital of S.................A..... 937 325-0531
  Springfield *(G-13300)*
The Maria-Joseph Center........................B..... 937 278-2692
  Dayton *(G-7667)*
Tlevay Inc...C..... 419 385-3958
  Toledo *(G-14046)*
Traditions At Bath Rd Inc........................D..... 330 929-6272
  Cuyahoga Falls *(G-7109)*
Traditions At Stygler Road......................E..... 614 475-8778
  Columbus *(G-6781)*

NURSING CARE FACILITIES: Skilled

Trilogy Health Services LLC.................. D 419 935-6511
  Willard *(G-15174)*
Trilogy Healthcare Putnam LLC.............. A 419 532-2961
  Kalida *(G-9551)*
Trilogy Rehab Services LLC................... C 740 452-3000
  Zanesville *(G-15833)*
Troy Rhbltion Hlthcare Ctr LL................. D 937 335-7161
  Troy *(G-14165)*
United Church Homes Inc........................ D 937 878-0262
  Fairborn *(G-8382)*
United Church Homes Inc........................ E 740 286-7551
  Jackson *(G-9527)*
United Church Homes Inc........................ E 740 376-5600
  Marietta *(G-10406)*
University Hsptals Hlth Systm-................. B 440 285-4040
  Chardon *(G-2024)*
University Manor Hlth Care Ctr................ E 216 721-1400
  Cleveland *(G-5082)*
Uvmc Management Corporation................ C 937 440-4000
  Troy *(G-14169)*
Uvmc Nursing Care Inc........................... C 937 473-2075
  Covington *(G-7019)*
Uvmc Nursing Care Inc........................... C 937 667-7500
  Tipp City *(G-13668)*
Valley View Mnor Nrsing HM Inc.............. E 740 998-2948
  Frankfort *(G-8630)*
Vancare Inc... D 937 898-4202
  Vandalia *(G-14401)*
Vancrest Management Corp..................... D 419 238-0715
  Van Wert *(G-14361)*
Vista Centre....................................... E 330 424-5852
  Lisbon *(G-10007)*
Voa Rehabilitation Centers Inc................. E 419 447-7151
  Tiffin *(G-13648)*
Volunters Amer Care Facilities................. C 419 225-9040
  Lima *(G-9978)*
Walnut Creek Snior Lving Cmpus.............. E 937 293-7703
  Moraine *(G-11447)*
Walnut Hills Inc.................................. E 330 852-2457
  Walnut Creek *(G-14472)*
Watermark Rtrment Cmmnties Inc............ D 405 751-3600
  Toledo *(G-14098)*
Wayside Farm Inc................................ D 330 666-7716
  Peninsula *(G-12295)*
Wellington Place LLC........................... D 440 734-9933
  North Olmsted *(G-11920)*
West Side Dtscher Fruen Verein............... B 440 238-3361
  Berea *(G-1087)*
Western Rsrve Msonic Cmnty Inc.............. C 330 721-3000
  Medina *(G-10903)*
Wexner Heritage Village........................ B 614 231-4900
  Columbus *(G-6882)*
Whitehouse Operator LLC....................... D 419 877-5338
  Whitehouse *(G-15144)*
Willow Brook Christian Svcs.................... E 740 201-5640
  Delaware *(G-7834)*
Willow Brook Chrstn Cmmunities............... D 740 369-0048
  Delaware *(G-7835)*
Windsong Healthcare Group LLC.............. D 216 292-5706
  Akron *(G-362)*
Windsor Medical Center Inc................... D 330 499-8300
  Canton *(G-1886)*
Wlkop LLC... C 440 892-2100
  Westlake *(G-15125)*
Woodside Properties I Ltd..................... E 419 396-7287
  Carey *(G-1897)*
Woodside Village Care Center................. D 419 947-2015
  Mount Gilead *(G-11465)*
Wyant Leasing Co LLC........................... E 330 836-7953
  Akron *(G-364)*
Zandex Health Care Corporation.............. C 740 454-1400
  New Concord *(G-11613)*
Zandex Health Care Corporation.............. C 740 695-7233
  Saint Clairsville *(G-12823)*
Zandex Health Care Corporation.............. C 740 452-4636
  Zanesville *(G-15838)*
Zandex Health Care Corporation.............. C 740 454-9769
  Zanesville *(G-15839)*

NUTRITION SVCS

County of Cuyahoga............................. E 216 941-8800
  Cleveland *(G-4128)*
Ironton Lwrnce Cnty Area Cmnty.............. B 740 532-3534
  Ironton *(G-9508)*

NUTS: Metal

Facil North America Inc........................ C 330 487-2500
  Twinsburg *(G-14190)*

OFFICE EQPT WHOLESALERS

12985 Snow Holdings Inc....................... E 216 267-5000
  Cleveland *(G-3739)*
American Copy Equipment Inc.................. C 330 722-9555
  Cleveland *(G-3801)*
Big Lots Stores LLC............................. A 614 278-6800
  Columbus *(G-5439)*
Canon Solutions America Inc................... E 216 446-3830
  Independence *(G-9415)*
Canon Solutions America Inc................... E 216 750-2980
  Independence *(G-9416)*
Canon Solutions America Inc................... E 419 897-9244
  Maumee *(G-10707)*
Collaborative Inc................................. E 419 242-7405
  Toledo *(G-13748)*
Comdoc Inc.. C 330 896-2346
  North Canton *(G-11818)*
Dolbey Systems Inc.............................. E 440 392-9900
  Concord Township *(G-6925)*
Electronic Merch Systems LLC................. C 216 524-0900
  Cleveland *(G-4209)*
Essendant Co..................................... C 614 876-7774
  Columbus *(G-5829)*
Essendant Co..................................... C 800 733-4091
  Twinsburg *(G-14188)*
Friends Service Co Inc......................... D 419 427-1704
  Findlay *(G-8534)*
Modern Office Methods Inc.................... E 513 791-0909
  Blue Ash *(G-1211)*
Modern Office Methods Inc.................... D 513 791-0909
  Cincinnati *(G-3076)*
Mpc Inc... E 440 835-1405
  Cleveland *(G-4605)*
Mt Business Technologies Inc................. C 440 933-7682
  Avon Lake *(G-681)*
Office World Inc................................. E 419 991-4694
  Lima *(G-9994)*
Ohio Business Machines LLC................... E 216 485-2000
  Cleveland *(G-4683)*
Perry Pro Tech Inc.............................. D 419 228-1360
  Lima *(G-9948)*
Springfield Business Eqp Co................... E 937 322-3828
  Springfield *(G-13294)*
Tameran Graphic Systems Inc.................. E 440 349-7100
  Solon *(G-13155)*
Visual Edge It Inc............................... A 800 828-4801
  North Canton *(G-11870)*
W B Mason Co Inc................................ E 216 267-5000
  North Olmsted *(G-11918)*

OFFICE EQPT, WHOLESALE: Photocopy Machines

Donnellon McCarthy Inc......................... E 513 769-7800
  Cincinnati *(G-2574)*
Graphic Enterprises Inc......................... D 800 553-6616
  North Canton *(G-11835)*

OFFICE FURNITURE REPAIR & MAINTENANCE SVCS

National Electro-Coatings Inc.................. D 216 898-0080
  Cleveland *(G-4624)*

OFFICE SPLY & STATIONERY STORES: Office Forms & Splys

Hubbard Company................................ E 419 784-4455
  Defiance *(G-7750)*
Stationers Inc................................... E 740 423-1400
  Belpre *(G-1059)*

OFFICE SPLYS, NEC, WHOLESALE

Essendant Co..................................... C 614 876-7774
  Columbus *(G-5829)*
Essendant Co..................................... E 330 650-9361
  Hudson *(G-9345)*
Essendant Co..................................... C 800 733-4091
  Twinsburg *(G-14188)*
Essendant Co..................................... E 330 425-7343
  Twinsburg *(G-14189)*
Essendant Co..................................... D 513 942-1354
  West Chester *(G-14810)*
Indepndence Office Bus Sup Inc............... D 216 398-8880
  Cleveland *(G-4408)*
Powell Company Inc............................. D 419 228-3552
  Lima *(G-9951)*
S P Richards Company........................... E 614 497-2270
  Lockbourne *(G-10015)*
Wasserstrom Company........................... B 614 228-6525
  Columbus *(G-6867)*

OFFICES & CLINICS OF DOCTORS OF MEDICINE: Radiologist

Childrens Rdiological Inst Inc................. A 614 722-2363
  Columbus *(G-5565)*
Dayton Medical Imaging........................ E 937 439-0390
  Dayton *(G-7290)*
Far Hills Open Mri Inc......................... D 937 435-6674
  Dayton *(G-7346)*
Lancaster Radiation Oncology.................. E 740 687-8554
  Lancaster *(G-9732)*
Mrp Inc... E 513 965-9700
  Milford *(G-11246)*
Professional Radiology Inc..................... E 513 872-4500
  Blue Ash *(G-1225)*
Proscan Imaging LLC............................. D 513 281-3400
  Cincinnati *(G-3254)*
Radiology Associates Athens................... E 740 593-5551
  Athens *(G-586)*
Radiology Physicians Inc....................... E 614 717-9840
  Delaware *(G-7822)*
Riverside Rdlgy Intrvntnal Ass................. E 614 340-7747
  Columbus *(G-6598)*
University of Toledo............................ E 419 383-5322
  Toledo *(G-14087)*
University Radiology Assoc..................... D 513 475-8760
  Cincinnati *(G-3596)*
US Teleradiology LLC............................ E 678 904-2599
  Hudson *(G-9376)*

OFFICES & CLINICS OF DRS OF MEDICINE: Physician, Orthopedic

Beacon Orthpaedcs & Sprts Med................ B 513 354-3700
  Cincinnati *(G-2243)*
Beacon Orthpdics Spt Mdcine Lt............... A 513 985-2252
  Cincinnati *(G-2244)*

SERVICES SECTION

ORGANIZATIONS: Medical Research

Beacon Orthpdics Spt Mdcine Lt............ D 513 354-3700
 Cincinnati *(G-2245)*
Cardinal Orthopaedic Group Inc............. E 614 759-1186
 Columbus *(G-5508)*
Cardinal Orthopedic Institute.................. E 614 488-1816
 Hilliard *(G-9187)*
Crystal Clinic Inc................................... E 330 644-7436
 Akron *(G-126)*
Crystal Clinic Inc................................... E 330 929-9136
 Cuyahoga Falls *(G-7066)*
Crystal Clinic Surgery Ctr LLC................ E 330 668-4040
 Akron *(G-127)*
Crystal Clnic Orthpdic Ctr LLC............... D 330 535-3396
 Akron *(G-128)*
Dayton Orthpdic Srgery Spt Mdc............ E 937 436-5763
 Dayton *(G-7291)*
Joint Implant Surgeons Inc..................... E 614 221-6331
 New Albany *(G-11570)*
Joint Implant Surgeons Inc A.................. E 740 566-4640
 Athens *(G-578)*
Kolczun Klczun Orthpd Assoc In............. A 440 985-3113
 Lorain *(G-10080)*
Marysvlle Ohio Srgical Ctr LLC............... C 937 578-4200
 Marysville *(G-10496)*
Northwest Ohio Orthpdics Spt M............. C 419 427-1984
 Findlay *(G-8573)*
Ohio Orthpd Surgery Inst LLC................. E 614 827-8777
 Columbus *(G-6438)*
Omni Medical Center.............................. E 330 492-5565
 Canton *(G-1825)*
Orthoneuro... E 614 890-6555
 Westerville *(G-15010)*
Orthopaedic & Trauma Surgeons Inc...... D 614 827-8700
 Upper Arlington *(G-14281)*
Orthopaedic Associates Inc..................... E 440 892-1440
 Westlake *(G-15092)*
Orthopaedic Institute Ohio Inc................. D 419 222-6622
 Lima *(G-9945)*
Orthopaedic Surgery Cente..................... E 330 758-1065
 Youngstown *(G-15686)*
Orthopedic Assoc Zanesville Inc............. D 740 454-3273
 Zanesville *(G-15823)*
Orthopdic Spine Ctr At Plris L.................. E 937 707-4662
 Grove City *(G-8943)*
Orthopedic Assoc SW Ohio Inc............... E 937 415-9100
 Centerville *(G-1949)*
Orthopedic Associates............................ D 800 824-9861
 Liberty Township *(G-9856)*
Orthopedic Associates Dayton................ E 937 280-4988
 Dayton *(G-7541)*
Orthopedic Cons Cincinnati..................... E 513 753-7488
 Cincinnati *(G-3170)*
Orthopedic Cons Cincinnati..................... E 513 232-6677
 Cincinnati *(G-3171)*
Orthopedic Cons Cincinnati..................... E 513 245-2500
 Cincinnati *(G-3172)*
Orthopedic Cons Cincinnati..................... E 513 347-9999
 Cincinnati *(G-3173)*
Orthopedic Cons Cincinnati..................... E 937 393-6169
 Hillsboro *(G-9265)*
Orthopedic Cons Cincinnati..................... E 513 733-8894
 West Chester *(G-14738)*
Orthopedic One Inc................................ D 614 827-8700
 Columbus *(G-6480)*
Orthopedic One Inc................................ E 614 570-4419
 Dublin *(G-8083)*
Orthopedic One Inc................................ E 614 488-1816
 Hilliard *(G-9225)*
Orthopedic One Inc................................ E 614 839-2300
 Westerville *(G-14925)*
Orthopedic One Inc................................ E 614 545-7900
 Columbus *(G-6481)*

Orthorpdics Mltspcialty Netwrk................ E 330 493-1630
 Canton *(G-1826)*
OSu Spt Mdcine Physcians Inc............... E 614 293-3600
 Columbus *(G-6486)*
Pain Care Specialists LLC...................... E 614 865-2120
 Dublin *(G-8086)*
Pain Evlation MGT Ctr Ohio Inc.............. E 937 439-4949
 Dayton *(G-7545)*
Premier Sports Medicine........................ E 937 312-1661
 Centerville *(G-1950)*
Sandusky Orthopedic Surgeons.............. E 419 625-4900
 Sandusky *(G-12929)*
Spectrum Orthpedics Inc Canton............ D 330 455-5367
 North Canton *(G-11862)*
Unity Health Network LLC...................... E 330 626-0549
 Streetsboro *(G-13434)*
West Central Ohio Group Ltd................. D 419 224-7586
 Lima *(G-9981)*
Wooster Orthpdics Sprtsmdcine............. E 330 804-9712
 Wooster *(G-15398)*
Youngstown Orthpedic Assoc Ltd............ E 330 726-1466
 Canfield *(G-1646)*

OFFICES & CLINICS OF OPTOMETRISTS: Specialist, Contact Lens

Dickman Kettler & Bruner Ltd................. E 419 678-3016
 Coldwater *(G-5212)*
Shawnee Optical Inc.............................. E 440 997-2020
 Ashtabula *(G-549)*

OIL & GAS FIELD EQPT: Drill Rigs

Buckeye Companies............................... E 740 452-3641
 Zanesville *(G-15772)*

OIL FIELD MACHINERY & EQPT

Multi Products Company......................... E 330 674-5981
 Millersburg *(G-11287)*

OIL FIELD SVCS, NEC

Bijoe Development Inc........................... E 330 674-5981
 Millersburg *(G-11274)*
CDK Perforating LLC............................. D 817 862-9834
 Marietta *(G-10361)*
Global Energy Partners LLC.................. E 419 756-8027
 Mansfield *(G-10267)*
Recon.. D 740 609-3050
 Bridgeport *(G-1377)*
Stallion Oilfield Cnstr LLC....................... D 330 868-2083
 Paris *(G-12247)*
Tk Gas Services Inc............................... E 740 826-0303
 New Concord *(G-11612)*
U S Weatherford L P............................... C 330 746-2502
 Youngstown *(G-15741)*
Universal Well Services Inc.................... D 814 333-2656
 Millersburg *(G-11294)*
Westerman Inc....................................... C 800 338-8265
 Bremen *(G-1372)*
Wyoming Casing Service Inc.................. D 330 479-8785
 Canton *(G-1888)*

OILS: Mineral, Natural

Gfl Environmental Svcs USA Inc............. E 614 441-4001
 Columbus *(G-5932)*

OLEFINS

Lyondell Chemical Company................... C 513 530-4000
 Cincinnati *(G-2996)*

OPHTHALMIC GOODS

Steiner Eoptics Inc................................. D 937 426-2341
 Miamisburg *(G-11095)*

OPHTHALMIC GOODS WHOLESALERS

Haag-Sreit Usa Inc................................. C 513 336-7255
 Mason *(G-10558)*
Haag-Streit Usa Inc................................ D 513 398-3937
 Mason *(G-10559)*
Walmart Inc... E 740 286-8203
 Jackson *(G-9528)*

OPHTHALMIC GOODS: Lenses, Ophthalmic

Volk Optical Inc...................................... D 440 942-6161
 Mentor *(G-11010)*

OPTICAL GOODS STORES

Big Sandy Furniture Inc.......................... D 740 574-2113
 Franklin Furnace *(G-8653)*
Shawnee Optical Inc.............................. E 440 997-2020
 Ashtabula *(G-549)*

OPTICAL GOODS STORES: Contact Lenses, Prescription

Cambridge Eye Associates Inc............... C 513 527-9700
 West Chester *(G-14657)*

OPTICAL INSTRUMENTS & LENSES

Volk Optical Inc...................................... D 440 942-6161
 Mentor *(G-11010)*

ORGANIZATIONS: Civic & Social

Fred Crdnal Athc Schlrship Fun.............. E 812 801-7641
 Barberton *(G-697)*
Guiding Fndtons Spport Svcs LL............ D 440 485-3772
 Bedford *(G-963)*
Help Foundation Inc............................... E 216 289-7710
 Euclid *(G-8345)*
Independence Foundation Inc................. C 330 296-2851
 Ravenna *(G-12630)*
International Dev Assn Africa.................. E 314 629-2431
 Columbus *(G-6068)*
Jack Jseph Mrton Mndel Fndtio.............. E 216 875-6511
 Cleveland *(G-4428)*
Jobsohio... D 614 224-6446
 Columbus *(G-6093)*
Lenau Park... E 440 235-2646
 Olmsted Twp *(G-12091)*
Licking Area Computer Assn................... D 740 345-3400
 Newark *(G-11713)*
Salvation Army....................................... E 419 447-2252
 Tiffin *(G-13641)*
Say Yes Clvland Schlarship Inc.............. E 216 273-6350
 Cleveland *(G-4881)*
Star House... E 614 826-5868
 Columbus *(G-6709)*
The Community Mercy Foundation......... A 937 328-7000
 Springfield *(G-13301)*
University of Cincinnati........................... E 513 556-2263
 Cincinnati *(G-3584)*
Village of Cuyahoga Heights................... D 216 641-7020
 Cleveland *(G-5105)*
Young MNS Chrstn Assn of Akron.......... D 330 376-1335
 Clinton *(G-5197)*
Youth For Christ/Usa Inc........................ E 216 252-9883
 Cleveland *(G-5168)*

ORGANIZATIONS: Educational Research Agency

Within3 Inc... B 855 948-4463
 Lakewood *(G-9687)*

ORGANIZATIONS: Medical Research

ORGANIZATIONS: Medical Research

Aramark .... D 614 921-7495
   Hilliard *(G-9179)*
Arthur G Jmes Cncer Hosp Rchar .... B 614 293-4878
   Columbus *(G-5388)*
Aventiv Research Inc .... E 614 495-8970
   Columbus *(G-5410)*
Childrens Hosp Med Ctr Akron .... D 330 633-2055
   Tallmadge *(G-13587)*
Childrens Hospital Medical Ctr .... B 513 636-6100
   Cincinnati *(G-2367)*
Childrens Hospital Medical Ctr .... A 513 636-4200
   Cincinnati *(G-2369)*
Childrens Hospital Medical Ctr .... B 513 636-6400
   Fairfield *(G-8400)*
Childrens Hospital Medical Ctr .... B 513 636-6800
   Mason *(G-10529)*
Childrens Hospital Medical Ctr .... A 513 636-4200
   Cincinnati *(G-2368)*
Lazurite Inc .... E 216 334-3127
   Warrensville Heights *(G-14583)*
Mp Biomedicals LLC .... C 440 337-1200
   Solon *(G-13113)*
Prologue Research Intl Inc .... C 614 324-1500
   Columbus *(G-6552)*
Research Inst At Ntnwide Chld .... C 614 722-2700
   Columbus *(G-6580)*
Uc Health Llc .... A 513 585-6000
   Cincinnati *(G-3546)*
Wright State University .... D 937 298-4331
   Kettering *(G-9634)*

ORGANIZATIONS: Noncommercial Social Research

Help Foundation Inc .... E 216 432-4810
   Northfield *(G-11956)*

ORGANIZATIONS: Physical Research, Noncommercial

Air Force Research Laboratory .... D 937 255-9209
   Wright Patterson Afb *(G-15474)*
Jjr Solutions LLC .... E 937 912-0288
   Dayton *(G-7429)*
Quasonix Inc .... E 513 942-1287
   West Chester *(G-14751)*
Sunpower Inc .... D 740 594-2221
   Athens *(G-592)*

ORGANIZATIONS: Professional

Almo Distributing PA Inc .... A 267 350-2726
   Groveport *(G-8968)*
American Heart Association Inc .... E 614 848-6676
   Columbus *(G-5351)*
Balanced Care Corporation .... E 330 908-1166
   Northfield *(G-11952)*
Central Ohio Diabetes Assn .... E 614 884-4400
   Columbus *(G-5537)*
Community Tissue Services .... E 937 222-0228
   Kettering *(G-9628)*
Egp 2022 Vehicle Inc .... E 866 538-1909
   Cincinnati *(G-2606)*
Health Collaborative .... D 513 618-3600
   Cincinnati *(G-2809)*
Lakeside Association .... E 419 798-4461
   Lakeside *(G-9654)*
Ohio Domestic Violence Network .... E 614 406-7274
   Columbus *(G-6413)*

ORGANIZATIONS: Religious

Catholic Charities Corporation .... D 216 432-0680
   Cleveland *(G-3932)*
Comfort Inn .... D 740 454-4144
   Zanesville *(G-15783)*
Community Ambulance Service .... C 740 454-6800
   Zanesville *(G-15784)*
Cyo & Community Services Inc .... E 330 762-2961
   Akron *(G-130)*
First Assembly Child Care .... E 419 529-6501
   Mansfield *(G-10263)*
Heartbeat International Inc .... E 614 885-7577
   Columbus *(G-5977)*
Ohio State Univ Alumni Assn .... D 614 292-2200
   Columbus *(G-6448)*
Pillar of Fire .... E 513 542-1212
   Cincinnati *(G-3211)*
Saint Cecilia Church .... E 614 878-5353
   Columbus *(G-6637)*
Sidney-Shelby County YMCA .... E 937 492-9134
   Sidney *(G-13053)*
United Church Homes Inc .... E 419 294-4973
   Upper Sandusky *(G-14294)*
Wapakneta Fmly Yung MNS Chrstn ...... D 419 739-9622
   Wapakoneta *(G-14493)*
West Side Ecumenical Ministry .... C 216 325-9369
   Cleveland *(G-5134)*
Windsor Medical Center Inc .... D 330 499-8300
   Canton *(G-1886)*
Young MNS Chrstn Assn Grter CL .... E 440 808-8150
   Westlake *(G-15126)*
Young MNS Chrstn Assn Grter Dy .... C 937 836-9622
   Englewood *(G-8327)*
Youth For Christ/Usa Inc .... E 216 252-9883
   Cleveland *(G-5168)*

ORGANIZATIONS: Research Institute

Applied Research Solutions Inc .... D 937 912-6100
   Dayton *(G-7177)*
Hebrew Un Cllg-Jwish Inst Rlgi .... E 513 221-1875
   Cincinnati *(G-2815)*
Kumho Tire Co Inc .... E 330 666-4030
   Fairlawn *(G-8489)*
Lerner RES Inst Clvland Clinic .... D 216 444-3900
   Cleveland *(G-4489)*
Macaulay-Brown Inc .... A 937 426-3421
   Beavercreek Township *(G-943)*
Nationwide Childrens Hospital .... C 614 722-2000
   Columbus *(G-6320)*
Ohio Aerospace Institute .... E 440 962-3000
   Cleveland *(G-4681)*
Ohio State University .... C 614 688-0857
   Columbus *(G-6459)*
Phillips Edison Institutional .... E 513 554-1110
   Cincinnati *(G-3207)*
Riverside Research Institute .... C 937 431-3810
   Beavercreek *(G-901)*
University of Dayton .... C 937 229-2113
   Dayton *(G-7690)*
University of Dayton .... B 937 229-3822
   Dayton *(G-7691)*

PACKAGE DESIGN SVCS

Bottle Solutions LLC .... E 216 889-3330
   Cleveland *(G-3883)*
Marsh Inc .... D 513 421-1234
   Cincinnati *(G-3012)*
Nottinghm-Spirk Dsign Assoc In .... E 216 800-5782
   Cleveland *(G-4667)*
Photo-Type Engraving Company .... E 513 475-5638
   Cincinnati *(G-3210)*
Univenture Inc .... D 877 831-9428
   Marysville *(G-10516)*
Univenture Inc .... D 937 645-4600
   Dublin *(G-8146)*

PACKAGING & LABELING SVCS

365 Holdings LLC .... D 800 403-8182
   Akron *(G-6)*
Accel Inc .... C 614 656-1100
   New Albany *(G-11552)*
Aim Integrated Logistics Inc .... B 330 759-0438
   Girard *(G-8808)*
Aldelano Corporation .... E 909 861-3970
   Lima *(G-9861)*
Amros Industries Inc .... E 216 433-0010
   Cleveland *(G-3812)*
Baumfolder Corporation .... E 937 492-1281
   Sidney *(G-13020)*
Bgr Inc .... D 800 628-9195
   West Chester *(G-14651)*
Cartruck Packaging Inc .... E 216 631-7225
   Cleveland *(G-3931)*
Corporate Support Inc .... E 419 221-3838
   Lima *(G-9877)*
Crane Consumables Inc .... E 513 539-9980
   Middletown *(G-11160)*
Crescent Park Corporation .... C 513 759-7000
   West Chester *(G-14679)*
Custom Products Corporation .... D 440 528-7100
   Solon *(G-13080)*
Custom-Pak Inc .... D 330 725-0800
   Medina *(G-10827)*
Domino Foods Inc .... C 216 432-3222
   Cleveland *(G-4175)*
First Choice Packaging Inc .... C 419 333-4100
   Fremont *(G-8676)*
Freudenberg-Nok General Partnr .... C 419 499-2502
   Milan *(G-11206)*
G and J Automatic Systems Inc .... E 216 741-6070
   Cleveland *(G-4296)*
Garda CL Great Lakes Inc .... B 561 939-7000
   Columbus *(G-5911)*
Gem City Chemicals Inc .... D 937 224-0711
   Dayton *(G-7373)*
Grand Encore Cincinnati LLC .... E 513 482-7500
   West Chester *(G-14699)*
Industrial Chemical Corp .... E 330 725-0800
   Medina *(G-10846)*
Keller Logistics Group Inc .... E 866 276-9486
   Defiance *(G-7751)*
King Tut Logistics LLC .... E 614 538-0509
   Columbus *(G-6117)*
M A Folkes Company Inc .... E 513 785-4200
   Hamilton *(G-9062)*
Metzenbaum Sheltered Inds Inc .... D 440 729-1919
   Chesterland *(G-2041)*
MSI Express Inc .... D 740 498-4700
   Newcomerstown *(G-11770)*
Nelson Packaging Company Inc .... D 419 229-3471
   Lima *(G-9939)*
Ohio Gasket and Shim Co Inc .... E 330 630-0626
   Akron *(G-251)*
Pactiv LLC .... D 614 771-5400
   Columbus *(G-6496)*
Pandora Manufacturing Llc .... D 419 384-3241
   Ottawa *(G-12191)*
Pro-Pet LLC .... D 419 394-3374
   Saint Marys *(G-12835)*
Proampac Holdings Inc .... D 513 671-1777
   Cincinnati *(G-3236)*
Quality Associates Inc .... B 513 242-4477
   West Chester *(G-14829)*
Richland Newhope Inds Inc .... C 419 774-4400
   Mansfield *(G-10313)*
Specialty Lubricants Corp .... E 330 425-2567
   Macedonia *(G-10205)*

SERVICES SECTION

PAINTS, VARNISHES & SPLYS, WHOLESALE: Paints

Systems Pack Inc.................................. E 330 467-5729
  Macedonia *(G-10207)*

T W I International Inc........................ C 440 439-1830
  Cleveland *(G-4976)*

Tekni-Plex Inc..................................... E 419 491-2399
  Holland *(G-9307)*

Teva Womens Health LLC................... C 513 731-9900
  Cincinnati *(G-3460)*

Third Dimension Inc........................... E 440 466-4040
  Geneva *(G-8790)*

Univenture Inc..................................... D 937 645-4600
  Dublin *(G-8146)*

Universal Packg Systems Inc.............. C 513 732-2000
  Batavia *(G-751)*

Universal Packg Systems Inc.............. C 513 735-4777
  Batavia *(G-752)*

Universal Packg Systems Inc.............. C 513 674-9400
  Cincinnati *(G-3563)*

Weaver Industries Inc......................... D 330 379-3606
  Akron *(G-355)*

Weaver Industries Inc......................... C 330 666-5114
  Akron *(G-357)*

Weaver Industries Inc......................... D 330 379-3660
  Tallmadge *(G-13612)*

Weaver Industries Inc......................... E 330 379-3660
  Akron *(G-356)*

Welch Packaging Group Inc................ C 614 870-2000
  Columbus *(G-6874)*

PACKAGING MATERIALS, WHOLESALE

A-Roo Company LLC........................... D 440 238-8850
  Strongsville *(G-13437)*

Advanced Poly-Packaging Inc............. C 330 785-4000
  Akron *(G-18)*

Amcor Flexibles North Amer Inc........ D 419 334-9465
  Fremont *(G-8666)*

Ample Industries Inc........................... C 937 746-9700
  Franklin *(G-8631)*

Bgr Inc.. D 800 628-9195
  West Chester *(G-14651)*

BP 10 Inc.. E 513 346-3900
  West Chester *(G-14653)*

Bprex Closures LLC............................. D 812 424-2904
  Maumee *(G-10703)*

Buckhorn Inc....................................... E 513 831-4402
  Milford *(G-11219)*

Cambridge Packaging Inc................... E 740 432-3351
  Cambridge *(G-1560)*

Compass Packaging LLC...................... E 330 274-2001
  Mantua *(G-10329)*

Crown Packaging Corporation........... C 937 294-6580
  Dayton *(G-7263)*

Custom Products Corporation........... D 440 528-7100
  Solon *(G-13080)*

Dayton Corrugated Packaging Corp... E 937 254-8422
  Dayton *(G-7277)*

Eastgate Group Ltd............................. E 513 228-5522
  Lebanon *(G-9764)*

GK Packaging Inc................................ D 614 873-3900
  Plain City *(G-12478)*

Gpax Inc... E 614 501-7622
  Reynoldsburg *(G-12664)*

Graham Packg Plastic Pdts LLC.......... E 419 423-3271
  Findlay *(G-8539)*

Graphic Packaging Intl LLC................ D 630 584-2900
  Cincinnati *(G-2750)*

Greif Inc... D 740 549-6000
  Cincinnati *(G-2775)*

Huhtamaki Inc..................................... C 937 987-3078
  New Vienna *(G-11680)*

Inno-Pak LLC....................................... D 740 363-0090
  Delaware *(G-7807)*

Jlt Packaging Cincinnati Inc............... E 513 933-0250
  Lebanon *(G-9771)*

Kopco Graphics Inc............................. E 513 874-7230
  West Chester *(G-14721)*

Lineage Logistics LLC......................... E 330 559-4860
  Youngstown *(G-15652)*

Mid-States Packaging Inc................... E 937 843-3243
  Lewistown *(G-9843)*

New Method Packaging LLC............... E 937 324-3838
  Springfield *(G-13276)*

Next Generation Bag Inc.................... E 419 884-1327
  Mansfield *(G-10305)*

Ohio Packaging.................................... D 330 833-2884
  Massillon *(G-10660)*

Old Forge Services Inc........................ E 330 733-5531
  Windham *(G-15289)*

Pac Worldwide Corporation............... D 800 535-0039
  Monroe *(G-11348)*

Pacific MGT Holdings LLC.................. E 440 324-3339
  Elyria *(G-8284)*

Packaging & Pads R Us LLC................ E 419 499-2905
  Milan *(G-11210)*

Pipeline Packaging Corporation......... E 440 349-3200
  Hudson *(G-9368)*

Plastipak Packaging Inc...................... D 937 596-5166
  Jackson Center *(G-9532)*

Plastipak Packaging Inc...................... C 330 725-0205
  Medina *(G-10876)*

Ppc Flexible Packaging LLC................ C 614 876-1204
  Columbus *(G-6540)*

Pretium Packaging LLC....................... C 419 943-3733
  Leipsic *(G-9802)*

Primary Packaging Incorporated........ D 330 874-3131
  Bolivar *(G-1297)*

Proampac Holdings Inc....................... D 513 671-1777
  Cincinnati *(G-3236)*

Protective Packg Solutions LLC......... E 513 769-5777
  Cincinnati *(G-3255)*

Questar Solutions LLC........................ E 330 966-2070
  North Canton *(G-11857)*

R D Thompson Paper Pdts Co Inc...... E 419 994-3614
  Loudonville *(G-10110)*

Samuel Son & Co (usa) Inc.................. D 740 522-2500
  Heath *(G-9138)*

Ship-Paq Inc.. E 513 860-0700
  Fairfield *(G-8439)*

Skybox Investments Inc...................... E 419 525-6013
  Mansfield *(G-10316)*

Skybox Packaging LLC........................ C 419 525-7209
  Mansfield *(G-10317)*

Star Packaging Inc.............................. E 614 564-9936
  Columbus *(G-6711)*

Sterling Paper Co................................ E 614 443-0303
  Columbus *(G-6718)*

Storopack Inc...................................... E 513 874-0314
  West Chester *(G-14834)*

Systems Pack Inc................................. E 330 467-5729
  Macedonia *(G-10207)*

Third Dimension Inc........................... E 440 466-4040
  Geneva *(G-8790)*

Toga-Pak Inc.. E 937 294-7311
  Dayton *(G-7672)*

Versa-Pak Ltd..................................... E 419 586-5466
  Celina *(G-1931)*

Victory Packaging LP.......................... D 216 898-9130
  Brookpark *(G-1442)*

Wayne Signer Enterprises Inc............ E 513 841-1351
  Cincinnati *(G-3642)*

Welch Packaging Group Inc................ C 419 726-3491
  Toledo *(G-14100)*

Wingate Packaging Inc....................... E 513 745-8600
  Cincinnati *(G-3675)*

PACKAGING MATERIALS: Paper

Bollin & Sons Inc................................ E 419 693-6573
  Toledo *(G-13710)*

Custom Products Corporation........... D 440 528-7100
  Solon *(G-13080)*

Norse Dairy Systems Inc.................... C 614 294-4931
  Columbus *(G-6363)*

Springdot Inc....................................... D 513 542-4000
  Cincinnati *(G-3401)*

Storopack Inc...................................... E 513 874-0314
  West Chester *(G-14834)*

PACKAGING MATERIALS: Plastic Film, Coated Or Laminated

Universal Packg Systems Inc.............. C 513 732-2000
  Batavia *(G-751)*

Universal Packg Systems Inc.............. C 513 735-4777
  Batavia *(G-752)*

Universal Packg Systems Inc.............. C 513 674-9400
  Cincinnati *(G-3563)*

Versa-Pak Ltd..................................... E 419 586-5466
  Celina *(G-1931)*

PACKING & CRATING SVC

Bates Metal Products Inc................... D 740 498-8371
  Port Washington *(G-12541)*

Crescent Park Corporation................. C 513 759-7000
  West Chester *(G-14679)*

Impact Fulfillment Svcs LLC.............. C 614 262-8911
  Columbus *(G-6043)*

Lalac One LLC..................................... E 216 432-4422
  Cleveland *(G-4482)*

Morral Companies LLC....................... E 740 465-3251
  Morral *(G-11454)*

PAINTS & ADDITIVES

Akrochem Corporation....................... D 330 535-2100
  Akron *(G-19)*

Comex North America Inc.................. D 303 307-2100
  Cleveland *(G-4092)*

PAINTS & ALLIED PRODUCTS

Bollin & Sons Inc................................ E 419 693-6573
  Toledo *(G-13710)*

Consolidated Coatings Corp............... A 216 514-7596
  Cleveland *(G-4106)*

Hexpol Compounding LLC.................. C 440 834-4644
  Burton *(G-1528)*

Hoover & Wells Inc............................. C 419 691-9220
  Toledo *(G-13850)*

Matrix Sys Auto Finishes LLC............ B 248 668-8135
  Massillon *(G-10654)*

Teknol Inc.. D 937 264-0190
  Dayton *(G-7661)*

Tremco Incorporated.......................... B
  Beachwood *(G-847)*

PAINTS, VARNISHES & SPLYS WHOLESALERS

Autobody Supply Company Inc.......... D 614 228-4328
  Columbus *(G-5407)*

Teknol Inc.. D 937 264-0190
  Dayton *(G-7661)*

PAINTS, VARNISHES & SPLYS, WHOLESALE: Paints

Comex North America Inc.................. D 303 307-2100
  Cleveland *(G-4092)*

Dutch Boy Group................................. E 800 828-5669
  Cleveland *(G-4189)*

PAINTS, VARNISHES & SPLYS, WHOLESALE: Paints

Jmac Inc .... E 614 436-2418
 Columbus *(G-6092)*

Matrix Sys Auto Finishes LLC .... B 248 668-8135
 Massillon *(G-10654)*

Miller Bros Wallpaper Company .... E 513 231-4470
 Cincinnati *(G-3063)*

Nanogate North America LLC .... B 419 747-6639
 Mansfield *(G-10301)*

Ohio Auto Kolor Inc .... E 614 272-2255
 Columbus *(G-6393)*

Synthomer LLC .... D 678 400-6655
 Beachwood *(G-842)*

PALLET REPAIR SVCS

Spartan Supply Co .... E 513 932-6954
 Lebanon *(G-9790)*

PALLETIZERS & DEPALLETIZERS

Intelligrated Systems Ohio LLC .... A 513 701-7300
 Mason *(G-10567)*

PALLETS & SKIDS: Wood

Belco Works Inc .... D 740 695-0500
 Saint Clairsville *(G-12774)*

Quadco Rehabilitation Ctr Inc .... E 419 445-1950
 Archbold *(G-466)*

Quadco Rehabilitation Ctr Inc .... B 419 682-1011
 Stryker *(G-13505)*

Richland Newhope Inds Inc .... C 419 774-4400
 Mansfield *(G-10313)*

Southwood Pallet LLC .... D 330 682-3747
 Orrville *(G-12173)*

PALLETS: Plastic

Myers Industries Inc .... E 330 253-5592
 Akron *(G-238)*

PAPER & BOARD: Die-cut

Kent Adhesive Products Co .... D 330 678-1626
 Kent *(G-9583)*

Springdot Inc .... D 513 542-4000
 Cincinnati *(G-3401)*

PAPER PRDTS: Sanitary

Giant Industries Inc .... E 419 531-4600
 Toledo *(G-13821)*

PAPER, WHOLESALE: Fine

Catalyst Paper (usa) Inc .... E 937 528-3800
 Dayton *(G-7216)*

Sabin Robbins LLC .... C 513 874-5270
 West Chester *(G-14760)*

Veritiv Pubg & Print MGT Inc .... E 614 288-0911
 Stow *(G-13400)*

PAPER, WHOLESALE: Printing

Millcraft Group LLC .... D 216 441-5500
 Independence *(G-9452)*

Millcraft Paper Company .... E 614 675-4800
 Columbus *(G-6249)*

Millcraft Paper Company .... D
 Independence *(G-9453)*

Sterling Paper Co .... E 614 443-0303
 Columbus *(G-6718)*

PAPER: Adhesive

Bollin & Sons Inc .... E 419 693-6573
 Toledo *(G-13710)*

Kent Adhesive Products Co .... D 330 678-1626
 Kent *(G-9583)*

PAPER: Cloth, Lined, Made From Purchased Materials

Tekni-Plex Inc .... E 419 491-2399
 Holland *(G-9307)*

PAPER: Wrapping & Packaging

Polymer Packaging Inc .... D 330 832-2000
 North Canton *(G-11852)*

Welch Packaging Group Inc .... C 614 870-2000
 Columbus *(G-6874)*

PARTITIONS & FIXTURES: Except Wood

HP Manufacturing Company Inc .... D 216 361-6500
 Cleveland *(G-4386)*

Organized Living Inc .... E 513 489-9300
 Cincinnati *(G-3167)*

Panacea Products Corporation .... E 614 850-7000
 Columbus *(G-6497)*

PARTITIONS: Wood & Fixtures

L E Smith Company .... D 419 636-4555
 Bryan *(G-1486)*

Lemon Group LLC .... E 614 409-9850
 Obetz *(G-12081)*

Partitions Plus Incorporated .... E 419 422-2600
 Findlay *(G-8575)*

PARTS: Metal

Clifton Steel Company .... D 216 662-6111
 Maple Heights *(G-10336)*

PATENT OWNERS & LESSORS

Cleveland Rest Oper Ltd Partnr .... E 216 328-1121
 Cleveland *(G-4064)*

Franchise Group Inc .... B 740 363-2222
 Delaware *(G-7799)*

Hobby Lobby Stores Inc .... E 419 861-1862
 Holland *(G-9288)*

Ohio/Oklahoma Hearst TV Inc .... D 513 412-5000
 Cincinnati *(G-3152)*

PATIENT MONITORING EQPT WHOLESALERS

Clinical Technology Inc .... E 440 526-0160
 Brecksville *(G-1351)*

PATTERNS: Indl

Freeman Manufacturing & Sup Co .... E 440 934-1902
 Avon *(G-651)*

PAYROLL SVCS

Ahola Corporation .... D 440 717-7620
 Brecksville *(G-1342)*

Cavcapital Ltd .... C 216 831-8900
 Cleveland *(G-3940)*

Chard Snyder & Associates LLC .... C 513 459-9997
 Mason *(G-10528)*

Doyle Hcm Inc .... E 614 322-9310
 Columbus *(G-5784)*

Hr Butler LLC .... E 614 923-2900
 Dublin *(G-8032)*

Paychex Inc .... D 800 939-2462
 Lima *(G-9947)*

Paychex Advance LLC .... D 216 831-8900
 Cleveland *(G-4731)*

Paycom Software Inc .... C 888 678-0796
 Cincinnati *(G-3190)*

Paycor Inc .... C 513 381-0505
 Cincinnati *(G-3191)*

SERVICES SECTION

Sheakley-Uniservice Inc .... E 513 771-2277
 Cincinnati *(G-3367)*

PENSION FUNDS

Diocese Tledo Prest Retirement .... E 419 244-6711
 Toledo *(G-13781)*

Nationwide Rtrment Sltions Inc .... C 614 854-8300
 Dublin *(G-8072)*

Ohio Pub Emplyees Rtrement Sys .... B 614 228-8471
 Columbus *(G-6440)*

State Tchers Rtrement Sys Ohio .... C 614 227-4090
 Columbus *(G-6715)*

PERSONAL CARE FACILITY

Asana Hospice Cleveland LLC .... E 419 903-0300
 Berea *(G-1061)*

Blossom Hill Inc .... E 440 652-6749
 North Royalton *(G-11938)*

Brown Memorial Home Inc .... D 740 474-6238
 Circleville *(G-3703)*

Compassus .... D 440 249-6036
 Seven Hills *(G-12953)*

Connecting Dots Cnncting To SL .... E 216 356-2362
 Cleveland *(G-4101)*

Continuum Care Home Health LLC .... E 216 898-8399
 Parma *(G-12252)*

Crossrads Sleep Dsrders Ctr LL .... E 330 965-0220
 Youngstown *(G-15590)*

Dayton Hospice Incorporated .... C 513 422-0300
 Franklin *(G-8633)*

Dayton Hospice Incorporated .... B 937 256-4490
 Dayton *(G-7288)*

Dearth Management Company .... D 330 339-3595
 New Philadelphia *(G-11649)*

Fayette Hospice County Inc .... E 740 335-0149
 Wshngtn Ct Hs *(G-15483)*

Fc Compassus LLC .... E 380 207-1526
 West Jefferson *(G-14850)*

Grace Hospice LLC .... C 513 458-5545
 Cincinnati *(G-2746)*

Grace Hospice LLC .... D 216 288-7413
 Cleveland *(G-4323)*

Grace Hospice LLC .... C 440 826-0350
 Cleveland *(G-4324)*

Grace Hospice LLC .... C 937 293-1381
 Moraine *(G-11414)*

H & G Nursing Homes Inc .... D 937 544-2205
 West Union *(G-14870)*

Heritage Professional Services .... E 740 456-8245
 New Boston *(G-11594)*

Holzer Clinic LLC .... E 740 446-5074
 Gallipolis *(G-8758)*

Hospice Cincinnati Inc .... D 513 389-5528
 Cincinnati *(G-2845)*

Hospice Cincinnati Inc .... D 513 598-5093
 Cincinnati *(G-2846)*

Hospice Cincinnati Inc .... E 513 386-6000
 Cincinnati *(G-2847)*

Hospice of Central Ohio .... D 740 344-0311
 Newark *(G-11707)*

Hospice of Darke County Inc .... E 937 548-2999
 Greenville *(G-8878)*

Hospice of Hope Inc .... D 937 444-4900
 Mount Orab *(G-11471)*

Hospice of Miami County Inc .... E 937 335-5191
 Troy *(G-14139)*

Hospice of Miami Valley LLC .... E 937 458-6028
 Beavercreek *(G-883)*

Hospice of Northwest Ohio .... D 419 661-4001
 Toledo *(G-13851)*

Hospice of Northwest Ohio .... B 419 661-4001
 Perrysburg *(G-12344)*

SERVICES SECTION — PHYSICAL EXAMINATION & TESTING SVCS

Hospice of The Western Reserve............ C 216 227-9048
 Cleveland *(G-4381)*

Hospice of The Western Reserve............ E 440 414-7349
 Westlake *(G-15066)*

Hospice of Western Reserve Inc............. C 216 383-2222
 Cleveland *(G-4382)*

Hospice Tuscarawas County Inc............. E 330 627-4796
 Carrollton *(G-1909)*

Hospice Tuscarawas County Inc............. D 330 343-7605
 New Philadelphia *(G-11654)*

Judson Care Center Inc.......................... A 513 662-5880
 Cincinnati *(G-2922)*

Lifecare Hospice..................................... E 330 674-8448
 Millersburg *(G-11283)*

Lifecare Hospice..................................... E 330 264-4899
 Wooster *(G-15351)*

Living Care Altrntves of Utica................. E 740 892-3414
 Utica *(G-14329)*

Lutheran Memorial Home Inc.................. D 419 502-5700
 Toledo *(G-13900)*

Meigs County Care Center LLC............. C 740 992-6472
 Middleport *(G-11148)*

Northcrest Nursing & Rehab................... E 419 599-4070
 Napoleon *(G-11531)*

Ohio Living Holdings............................... D 614 433-0031
 Columbus *(G-6434)*

Ohios Hospice Inc.................................. D 937 256-4490
 Dayton *(G-7535)*

Ohios Hospice Foundation 0.................. E 937 256-4490
 Dayton *(G-7536)*

Pleasant View Nursing Home Inc............ D 330 848-5028
 Barberton *(G-702)*

Promedica Health System Inc................. B 513 831-5800
 Cincinnati *(G-3252)*

Singleton Health Care Ctr Inc.................. D 216 231-0076
 Cleveland *(G-4909)*

Southern Care Inc................................... D 419 774-0555
 Ontario *(G-12124)*

St Luke Lutheran Community.................. E 330 644-3914
 New Franklin *(G-11616)*

Stein Hospice Service Inc....................... E 800 625-5269
 Sandusky *(G-12934)*

Tridia Hospice Care Inc.......................... D 614 915-8882
 Westerville *(G-14947)*

Valley Hospice Inc.................................. E 740 859-5041
 Rayland *(G-12648)*

Vitas Healthcare Corp Midwest............... C 614 822-2700
 Dublin *(G-8156)*

Vitas Healthcare Corporation.................. C 513 742-6310
 Cincinnati *(G-3632)*

Vitas Healthcare Corporation.................. D 937 299-5379
 Moraine *(G-11446)*

Voiers Enterprises Inc............................. E 740 259-2838
 Mc Dermott *(G-10800)*

West Park Retirement Community........... E 513 451-8900
 Cincinnati *(G-3656)*

Zandex Health Care Corporation............. C 740 695-7233
 Saint Clairsville *(G-12823)*

PERSONAL CREDIT INSTITUTIONS: Consumer Finance Companies

Farm Credit Svcs Mid-America............... E 740 335-3306
 Wshngtn Ct Hs *(G-15480)*

Modern Finance Company....................... E 614 351-7400
 Columbus *(G-6255)*

Splash Financial Inc................................ D 216 452-0113
 Cleveland *(G-4935)*

United Consumer Fincl Svcs Co............. C 440 835-3230
 Cleveland *(G-5056)*

PERSONAL DOCUMENT & INFORMATION SVCS

3sg Plus LLC.. E 614 652-0019
 Columbus *(G-5243)*

Cintas Document Management LLC........ E 800 914-1960
 Mason *(G-10537)*

Continntal Mssage Solution Inc............... D 614 224-4534
 Columbus *(G-5699)*

PERSONAL SVCS

Nobleinvestments LLC............................ E 216 856-6555
 Bedford *(G-974)*

PEST CONTROL IN STRUCTURES SVCS

Aabel Exterminating Co.......................... E 937 434-4343
 Dayton *(G-7151)*

Apex Pest Control Service Inc................ E 440 461-6530
 Bedford *(G-953)*

Extermital Chemicals Inc........................ E 937 253-6144
 Dayton *(G-7342)*

Greenix Holdings LLC............................ D 614 961-7378
 Hilliard *(G-9197)*

Moxie Pest Control LP........................... E 513 216-1804
 Fairfield *(G-8433)*

Patton Pest Control Co........................... E 440 338-3101
 Novelty *(G-12042)*

PEST CONTROL SVCS

J T Eaton & Co Inc................................. E 330 425-7801
 Twinsburg *(G-14197)*

Rentokil North America Inc..................... E 440 964-5641
 Ashtabula *(G-547)*

Scotts Miracle-Gro Company.................. B 937 644-0011
 Marysville *(G-10509)*

PET FOOD WHOLESALERS

Jo-Ann Stores LLC................................. E 419 621-8101
 Sandusky *(G-12906)*

WA Butler Company................................ E 614 761-9095
 Dublin *(G-8159)*

PET SPLYS

Heading4ward Investment Co.................. D 937 293-9994
 Moraine *(G-11416)*

PETROLEUM & PETROLEUM PRDTS, WHOLESALE: Bulk Stations

Beck Suppliers Inc................................. E 419 426-3051
 Attica *(G-598)*

Cincinnati - Vulcan Company.................. D 513 242-5300
 Cincinnati *(G-2391)*

Slattery Oil Company Inc........................ E 419 272-3305
 Edon *(G-8229)*

Universal Oil Inc..................................... E 216 771-4300
 Cleveland *(G-5068)*

PETROLEUM BULK STATIONS & TERMINALS

Four O Corporation................................. E 513 941-2800
 Blue Ash *(G-1176)*

Red Rover LLC....................................... E 330 262-6501
 Wooster *(G-15368)*

Santmyer Logistics Inc........................... E 330 262-6501
 Wooster *(G-15371)*

PHARMACEUTICALS

Abbott Laboratories................................. D 847 937-6100
 Columbus *(G-5294)*

American Regent Inc.............................. D 614 436-2222
 Hilliard *(G-9178)*

Cardinal Health 414 LLC........................ C 614 757-5000
 Dublin *(G-7956)*

Imcd Us LLC.. E 216 228-8900
 Westlake *(G-15069)*

Medpace Holdings Inc............................ C 513 579-9911
 Cincinnati *(G-3033)*

Mp Biomedicals LLC.............................. C 440 337-1200
 Solon *(G-13113)*

Omnicare Phrm of Midwest LLC............ D 513 719-2600
 Cincinnati *(G-3160)*

Optum Infusion Svcs 550 LLC................ D 866 442-4679
 Cincinnati *(G-3166)*

Teva Womens Health LLC...................... C 513 731-9900
 Cincinnati *(G-3460)*

PHARMACEUTICALS: Mail-Order Svc

Medco Health Solutions Inc.................... C 614 822-2000
 Dublin *(G-8061)*

Nextrx LLC... A 317 532-6000
 Mason *(G-10584)*

Optumrx Home Delivery Ohio LLC......... D 440 930-5520
 Avon Lake *(G-682)*

PHOSPHATES

Scotts Company LLC............................. C 937 644-0011
 Marysville *(G-10508)*

PHOTOCOPYING & DUPLICATING SVCS

A-A Blueprint Co Inc.............................. E 330 794-8803
 Akron *(G-11)*

Comdoc Inc... D 330 920-3900
 Cuyahoga Falls *(G-7064)*

Printers Devil Inc.................................... E 330 650-1218
 Hudson *(G-9369)*

Queen City Reprographics Inc................ E 513 326-2300
 Cincinnati *(G-3266)*

TMR Inc.. E 330 220-8564
 Brunswick *(G-1471)*

PHOTOGRAPHIC EQPT & SPLYS WHOLESALERS

KAO Collins Inc...................................... E 513 948-9000
 Cincinnati *(G-2929)*

PHOTOGRAPHY SVCS: Commercial

AG Interactive Inc.................................. C 216 889-5000
 Cleveland *(G-3774)*

Jackson & Sons Drilling & Pump............ E 419 756-2758
 Mansfield *(G-10275)*

Marsh Inc.. D 513 421-1234
 Cincinnati *(G-3012)*

Photo-Type Engraving Company............ E 513 281-0999
 Cincinnati *(G-3209)*

Queen City Reprographics...................... C 513 326-2300
 Cincinnati *(G-3265)*

Rapid Mortgage Company...................... E 937 748-8888
 Cincinnati *(G-3273)*

The Photo-Type Engraving Company...... D 513 281-0999
 Cincinnati *(G-3469)*

Wp7pro Inc... E 419 483-3364
 Bellevue *(G-1046)*

PHYSICAL EXAMINATION & TESTING SVCS

Akron General Health System................. A 330 344-3030
 Hudson *(G-9327)*

Brecksvlle Hlthcare Group Inc................ E 440 546-0643
 Brecksville *(G-1346)*

Ohio North E Hlth Systems Inc............... E 330 747-9551
 Youngstown *(G-15683)*

PHYSICIANS' OFFICES & CLINICS: Medical doctors

Putnam County Public Hlth Dept............ E 419 523-5608
Ottawa *(G-12194)*

PHYSICIANS' OFFICES & CLINICS: Medical doctors

A-1 Hlthcare Stffing Plcements............... C 216 329-3500
Cleveland *(G-3753)*

Advanced Surgical Associates................ E 937 578-2650
Marysville *(G-10473)*

American Health Network Inc................ E 614 794-4500
Dublin *(G-7933)*

American Hlth Netwrk Ohio LLC............ D 614 794-4500
Dublin *(G-7934)*

Ameriwound.. D 216 273-9800
Mayfield Heights *(G-10784)*

Ashtabula County Medical Ctr................ B 440 997-6960
Ashtabula *(G-523)*

Belmont Bhc Pines Hospital Inc............. D 330 759-2700
Youngstown *(G-15558)*

Brigids Path Inc...................................... E 937 350-1785
Moraine *(G-11392)*

Cei Vision Partners LLC......................... D 513 569-3114
Blue Ash *(G-1145)*

Central Ohio Prmry Care Physca............ D 614 442-7550
Columbus *(G-5542)*

Childrens Hosp Med Ctr Akron............... D 330 543-8004
Akron *(G-90)*

Childrens Hosp Med Ctr Akron............... D 330 746-8040
Boardman *(G-1286)*

Childrens Hospital.................................. C 513 636-9900
Cincinnati *(G-2358)*

Childrens Hospital Medical Ctr............... B 513 636-6800
Mason *(G-10529)*

Christ Hospital....................................... D 513 561-7809
Cincinnati *(G-2384)*

Christian Hlthcare Mnstries In................ E 330 848-1511
Barberton *(G-696)*

Cleveland Clinic Foundation................... E 216 442-3412
Cleveland *(G-4024)*

Cleveland Clinic Foundation................... E 614 358-4223
Columbus *(G-5583)*

Coleman Professional Svcs Inc.............. C 330 673-1437
Kent *(G-9565)*

Compass Community Health.................. E 740 355-7102
Portsmouth *(G-12549)*

County of Lucas..................................... C 419 248-3585
Toledo *(G-13765)*

Covenant Care Ohio Inc........................ A 937 526-5570
Versailles *(G-14415)*

Crossroads Health.................................. D 440 255-1700
Mentor *(G-10929)*

Davis Eye Center Inc............................. D 330 923-5676
Cuyahoga Falls *(G-7069)*

Dayton Childrens Hospital...................... D 513 424-2850
Middletown *(G-11195)*

Emergency Services Inc........................ D 614 224-6420
Columbus *(G-5814)*

Fairview Hospital.................................... A 216 476-7000
Cleveland *(G-4238)*

Far Oaks Orthopedists Inc..................... E 937 298-0452
Vandalia *(G-14377)*

Good Samaritan Hosp Cincinnati............ E 513 569-6251
Cincinnati *(G-2742)*

H B Magruder Memorial Hosp................ C 419 734-3131
Oak Harbor *(G-12045)*

H B Magruder Memorial Hosp................ C 419 732-6520
Port Clinton *(G-12532)*

Healthsource of Ohio Inc....................... E 513 575-1444
Loveland *(G-10140)*

Healthsource of Ohio Inc....................... E 937 386-0049
Seaman *(G-12944)*

Hearinglife Usa Inc................................ D 513 759-2999
West Chester *(G-14707)*

Home Health Connection Inc................. E 614 839-4545
Lancaster *(G-9725)*

Hudson L Surgcenter L C....................... E 330 655-5460
Akron *(G-196)*

Kaiser Foundation Hospitals................... E 216 524-7377
Brooklyn Heights *(G-1423)*

Kaiser Foundation Hospitals................... E 800 524-7377
Fairlawn *(G-8488)*

Kaiser Foundation Hospitals................... E 800 524-7377
Kent *(G-9582)*

Kaiser Foundation Hospitals................... E 800 524-7377
Medina *(G-10850)*

Kaiser Foundation Hospitals................... E 800 524-7377
Mentor *(G-10958)*

Kaiser Foundation Hospitals................... E 800 524-7377
North Canton *(G-11842)*

Lake Health... E 440 816-2225
Cleveland *(G-4476)*

Lakewood Hospital Association.............. C 216 228-5437
Cleveland *(G-4481)*

Libbey Inc.. C 419 671-6000
Toledo *(G-13887)*

Lifestages Boutique For Women............ D 937 274-5420
Englewood *(G-8314)*

Lifestges Smrtan Ctrs For Wmen............ E 937 277-8988
Dayton *(G-7454)*

Lutheran Medical Center Inc.................. C 216 696-4300
Cleveland *(G-4511)*

Lutheran Medical Center Inc.................. B 440 519-6800
Solon *(G-13109)*

Manheim Auctions Inc........................... D 216 539-1701
Cleveland *(G-4520)*

Medplus Inc... B 513 229-5500
Mason *(G-10581)*

Mercer Cnty Jint Twnship Cmnty............ D 419 586-1611
Celina *(G-1926)*

Metrohealth System............................... C 216 957-9000
Brecksville *(G-1359)*

Miami Valley Hospital............................. B 937 208-7396
Dayton *(G-7488)*

Mid-Ohio Oncology/Hematology Inc....... E 614 383-6000
Columbus *(G-6238)*

Mount Carmel Health System................ B 614 866-3703
Columbus *(G-6277)*

Mount Carmel Health System................ B 614 445-6215
Columbus *(G-6278)*

Mount Carmel Health System................ C 614 876-1260
Hilliard *(G-9219)*

Mount Notre Dame Health Center.......... E 513 821-7448
Cincinnati *(G-3082)*

Mvhe Inc.. E 937 499-8211
Dayton *(G-7520)*

National Rgstry of Emrgncy Med............ E 614 888-4484
Columbus *(G-6301)*

Nationwide Childrens Hospital................ C 614 355-7000
Dublin *(G-8070)*

Niagara Health Corporation.................... A 614 855-4878
New Albany *(G-11582)*

Northast Ohio Nghbrhood Hlth S............ C 216 231-7700
Cleveland *(G-4653)*

Occupational Services........................... E 419 891-8003
Maumee *(G-10752)*

Ohio Heart Group Inc............................ E 740 348-0012
Newark *(G-11737)*

Ohio Minority Medical............................ E 513 400-5011
East Liverpool *(G-8189)*

Ohio State Univ Wexner Med Ctr........... C 614 293-7521
Columbus *(G-6452)*

Osu Internal Medicine LLC.................... D 614 688-6400
Columbus *(G-6484)*

Peri Natal Partners LLC......................... D 937 208-6970
Dayton *(G-7550)*

Preterm Foundation................................ E 216 991-4577
Cleveland *(G-4770)*

Primary Care Nursing Services.............. E 614 764-0960
Dublin *(G-8096)*

Promedica Health System Inc............... B 419 534-6600
Toledo *(G-13971)*

Robinson Health System Inc................. A 330 297-0811
Ravenna *(G-12643)*

Shawneespring Hlth Cre Cntr Rl............ D 513 943-4000
Loveland *(G-10160)*

Southast Cmnty Mental Hlth Ctr............. C 614 225-0980
Columbus *(G-6694)*

Southern Ohio Medical Center............... D 740 947-7662
Waverly *(G-14619)*

Tri County Mental Health Svcs.............. D 740 592-3091
Athens *(G-593)*

Trihealth Inc... C 513 891-1627
Blue Ash *(G-1257)*

Trihealth Inc... C 513 389-1400
Cincinnati *(G-3508)*

Trihealth Inc... A 513 985-0900
Montgomery *(G-11378)*

Trihealth G LLC..................................... E 513 922-1200
Cincinnati *(G-3522)*

Trihealth Os LLC................................... E 513 985-3700
Cincinnati *(G-3525)*

Trinity Health System............................ B 740 283-7000
Steubenville *(G-13346)*

Uc Health Llc.. D 513 475-8050
Milford *(G-11264)*

Uc Health Partners LLC........................ E 513 475-8524
Cincinnati *(G-3547)*

Union County Physician Corp................ C 800 686-4677
Marysville *(G-10514)*

Union Hospital Association.................... A 330 343-3311
Dover *(G-7907)*

University Cncnnati Physcans I............. E 513 475-8521
Cincinnati *(G-3565)*

University Hsptals Clvland Med............. A 216 378-6240
Beachwood *(G-849)*

University Hsptals Clvland Med............. A 216 342-5556
Beachwood *(G-850)*

University of Cincinnati.......................... E 513 558-4194
Cincinnati *(G-3572)*

University of Cincinnati.......................... B 513 558-1200
Cincinnati *(G-3573)*

University of Cincinnati Phys................. C 513 475-7934
Cincinnati *(G-3595)*

University of Cincinnati Phys................. D 513 475-8000
West Chester *(G-14788)*

Upper Valley Medical Center................. A 937 440-4000
Troy *(G-14166)*

US Healthcare System........................... D 513 585-1821
Cincinnati *(G-3605)*

Usacs Management Group Ltd.............. D 330 493-4443
Canton *(G-1877)*

Usacs Medical Group Ltd...................... D 330 493-4443
Canton *(G-1878)*

Vein Clinics of America Inc................... E 630 725-2700
Cincinnati *(G-3617)*

Volk Optical Inc..................................... D 440 942-6161
Mentor *(G-11010)*

West Chster Dntstry Dr Jffrey................ E 330 753-7734
Akron *(G-359)*

Wooster Cmnty Hosp Blmngton ME...... D 330 263-8100
Wooster *(G-15392)*

Wooster Community Hosp Aux Inc........ D 330 263-8389
Wooster *(G-15393)*

Yeater Alene K MD................................ E 740 348-4694
Newark *(G-11756)*

PICTURE FRAMING SVCS, CUSTOM

American Frame Corporation............... D 419 893-5595
Maumee (G-10690)

PIECE GOODS, NOTIONS & DRY GOODS, WHOL: Textiles, Woven

Welspun Usa Inc.............................. E 614 945-5100
Grove City (G-8966)

PIECE GOODS, NOTIONS & OTHER DRY GOODS, WHOLESALE: Fabrics

Everfast Inc.................................... E 614 789-0900
Dublin (G-8008)

PILOT SVCS: Aviation

Constant Aviation LLC...................... C 800 440-9004
Cleveland (G-4108)

Corporate Aviation Svcs Inc................ D 740 338-3100
Saint Clairsville (G-12788)

Macair Aviation LLC......................... E 937 347-1302
Xenia (G-15525)

Netjets Assn Shred Arcft Plots............ E 614 532-0555
Columbus (G-6347)

Twist Aero LLC................................ E 937 675-9581
Jamestown (G-9536)

PIPE & FITTINGS: Cast Iron

McWane Inc.................................... B 740 622-6651
Coshocton (G-6992)

PIPE FITTINGS: Plastic

Indelco Custom Products Inc.............. E 216 797-7300
Euclid (G-8349)

Lenz Inc.. E 937 277-9364
Dayton (G-7452)

PIPE SECTIONS, FABRICATED FROM PURCHASED PIPE

Pioneer Pipe Inc.............................. A 740 376-2400
Marietta (G-10399)

PIPELINE & POWER LINE INSPECTION SVCS

Dreier & Maller Inc........................... E 614 575-0065
Reynoldsburg (G-12661)

Mid-Ohio Pipeline Services LLC........... E 419 884-3772
Mansfield (G-10299)

PIPELINE TERMINAL FACILITIES: Independent

Air Transport Intl Inc......................... C 937 382-5591
Wilmington (G-15239)

Brothers Auto Transport LLC.............. E 330 824-0082
Warren (G-14508)

CT Logistics Inc............................... C 216 267-1636
Cleveland (G-4143)

Haggerty Logistics Inc...................... D 734 713-9800
Cincinnati (G-2792)

Hansen Adkins Auto Trnspt Inc........... E 562 430-4100
West Chester (G-14815)

Health Care Logistics Inc.................. D 800 848-1633
Galloway (G-8771)

Hogan Services Inc.......................... E 614 491-8402
Columbus (G-5997)

Schroeder Associates Inc.................. E 419 258-5075
Antwerp (G-448)

Snow Transport & Brokerage.............. E 937 474-8058
Dayton (G-7623)

Tforce Freight Inc............................ E 216 676-4560
Cleveland (G-4988)

Transfreight LLC.............................. B 937 865-9270
Dayton (G-7676)

United Parcel Service Inc.................. E 800 742-5877
Groveport (G-9008)

Woodruff Enterprises Inc................... E 937 399-9300
Springfield (G-13314)

PIPELINES, EXC NATURAL GAS: Gasoline, Common Carriers

Integrity Kksing Ppline Svcs L............ C 740 694-6315
Fredericktown (G-8660)

PIPELINES: Crude Petroleum

BP Oil Pipeline Company.................... A 216 398-8685
Cleveland (G-3887)

Buckeye Pipe Line Services Co........... B 419 698-8770
Oregon (G-12130)

Hardin Street Marine LLC.................. D 419 672-6500
Findlay (G-8544)

Marathon Pipe Line LLC.................... C 419 422-2121
Findlay (G-8563)

Mplx LP.. E 419 421-2121
Findlay (G-8571)

PIPELINES: Refined Petroleum

Marathon Pipe Line LLC.................... C 419 422-2121
Findlay (G-8563)

Mplx LP.. E 419 421-2121
Findlay (G-8571)

PIPES & TUBES: Steel

Alro Steel Corporation...................... E 937 253-6121
Dayton (G-7167)

Crest Bending Inc............................ E 419 492-2108
New Washington (G-11682)

Kirtland Capital Partners LP............... E 216 593-0100
Beachwood (G-806)

Major Metals Company...................... E 419 886-4600
Mansfield (G-10285)

Phillips Mfg and Tower Co................. D 419 347-1720
Shelby (G-13008)

Unison Industries LLC...................... B 904 667-9904
Dayton (G-7143)

Wheatland Tube LLC........................ C 724 342-6851
Niles (G-11799)

PIPES: Steel & Iron

JSW Steel USA Ohio Inc.................... B 740 535-8172
Mingo Junction (G-11314)

PLASTICS FILM & SHEET

Clopay Corporation........................... C 800 282-2260
Mason (G-10540)

PLASTICS FILM & SHEET: Vinyl

Clarkwstern Dtrich Bldg System.......... C 513 870-1100
West Chester (G-14671)

PLASTICS MATERIAL & RESINS

Flexsys America LP.......................... D 330 666-4111
Akron (G-164)

Freeman Manufacturing & Sup Co....... E 440 934-1902
Avon (G-651)

Ineos ABS (usa) LLC........................ C 513 467-2400
Addyston (G-4)

Kraton Polymers US LLC................... B 740 423-7571
Belpre (G-1056)

Network Polymers Inc....................... E 330 773-2700
Akron (G-241)

Polymer Packaging Inc..................... D 330 832-2000
North Canton (G-11852)

Tembec Btlsr Inc.............................. E 419 244-5856
Toledo (G-14037)

PLASTICS MATERIALS, BASIC FORMS & SHAPES WHOLESALERS

Skybox Packaging LLC...................... C 419 525-7209
Mansfield (G-10317)

United States Plastic Corp................. D 419 228-2242
Lima (G-9976)

PLASTICS PROCESSING

Samuel Son & Co (usa) Inc................ D 740 522-2500
Heath (G-9138)

Tahoma Enterprises Inc..................... D 330 745-9016
Barberton (G-714)

Tahoma Rubber & Plastics Inc........... D 330 745-9016
Barberton (G-715)

United States Plastic Corp................. D 419 228-2242
Lima (G-9976)

PLASTICS: Molded

U S Development Corp...................... D 330 673-6900
Kent (G-9604)

PLASTICS: Polystyrene Foam

Acor Orthopaedic LLC....................... E 216 662-4500
Cleveland (G-3764)

Armaly LLC..................................... E 740 852-3621
London (G-10037)

Myers Industries Inc......................... E 330 253-5592
Akron (G-238)

PLASTICS: Thermoformed

First Choice Packaging Inc................ C 419 333-4100
Fremont (G-8676)

PLATING & POLISHING SVC

Conley Group Inc............................. E 330 372-2030
Warren (G-14513)

Electro Prime Group LLC................... D 419 476-0100
Toledo (G-13786)

Miba Bearings US LLC...................... B 740 962-4242
Mcconnelsville (G-10803)

Scot Industries Inc.......................... D 330 262-7585
Wooster (G-15375)

Wieland Metal Svcs Foils LLC............. D 330 823-1700
Alliance (G-405)

Worthington Enterprises Inc.............. D 513 539-9291
Monroe (G-11355)

Worthngton Smuel Coil Proc LLC........ E 330 963-3777
Twinsburg (G-14231)

Yoder Industries Inc......................... C 937 278-5769
Dayton (G-7731)

PLEATING & STITCHING SVC

Barbs Graffiti Inc............................. E 216 881-5550
Cleveland (G-3849)

Shamrock Companies Inc.................. D 440 899-9510
Westlake (G-15108)

PLUMBING FIXTURES

Mansfield Plumbing Pdts LLC............. A 419 938-5211
Perrysville (G-12392)

Merit Brass Co................................. C 216 261-9800
Cleveland (G-4554)

Waxman Industries Inc..................... C 440 439-1830
Bedford Heights (G-1005)

Zekelman Industries Inc.................... C 740 432-2146
Cambridge (G-1588)

PLUMBING FIXTURES: Plastic

PLUMBING FIXTURES: Vitreous

Mansfield Plumbing Pdts LLC .... A 419 938-5211
Perrysville *(G-12392)*

PLUMBING FIXTURES: Vitreous

Mansfield Plumbing Pdts LLC .... A 419 938-5211
Perrysville *(G-12392)*

POLYSTYRENE RESINS

Epsilyte Holdings LLC .... D 937 778-9500
Piqua *(G-12441)*

POULTRY & POULTRY PRDTS WHOLESALERS

Borden Dairy Co Cincinnati LLC .... E 513 948-8811
Cleveland *(G-3881)*

Euclid Fish Company .... D 440 951-6448
Mentor *(G-10938)*

Sysco Cincinnati LLC .... B 513 563-6300
Cincinnati *(G-3430)*

POULTRY & SMALL GAME SLAUGHTERING & PROCESSING

Cal-Maine Foods Inc .... D 937 337-9576
Rossburg *(G-12764)*

Daylay Egg Farm Inc .... D 937 355-6531
West Mansfield *(G-14862)*

The Ellenbee-Leggett Company Inc ..... C 513 874-3200
Fairfield *(G-8446)*

Weaver Bros Inc .... D 937 526-3907
Versailles *(G-14417)*

POWDER: Metal

Bogie Industries Inc Ltd .... E 330 745-3105
Akron *(G-72)*

POWER SUPPLIES: All Types, Static

Vertiv JV Holdings LLC .... A 614 888-0246
Columbus *(G-6846)*

PRECIPITATORS: Electrostatic

McGill Airclean LLC .... D 614 829-1200
Columbus *(G-6215)*

Neundorfer Inc .... E 440 942-8990
Willoughby *(G-15213)*

United McGill Corporation .... E 614 829-1200
Groveport *(G-9007)*

PRINTED CIRCUIT BOARDS

Circle Prime Manufacturing .... E 330 923-0019
Cuyahoga Falls *(G-7054)*

Metzenbaum Sheltered Inds Inc .... D 440 729-1919
Chesterland *(G-2041)*

Projects Unlimited Inc .... C 937 918-2200
Dayton *(G-7571)*

Vmetro Inc .... D 281 584-0728
Fairborn *(G-8386)*

Wurth Electronics Ics Inc .... E 937 415-7700
Miamisburg *(G-11104)*

PRINTERS' SVCS: Folding, Collating, Etc

Bookmasters Inc .... C 419 281-1802
Ashland *(G-483)*

Patented Acquisition Corp .... D 937 353-2299
Miamisburg *(G-11082)*

PRINTING MACHINERY

Anderson & Vreeland Inc .... D 419 636-5002
Bryan *(G-1479)*

Wood Graphics Inc .... E 513 771-6300
Cincinnati *(G-3680)*

PRINTING, COMMERCIAL: Labels & Seals, NEC

CMC Group Inc .... D 419 354-2591
Bowling Green *(G-1313)*

PRINTING, COMMERCIAL: Literature, Advertising, NEC

Bottomline Ink Corporation .... E 419 897-8000
Perrysburg *(G-12318)*

PRINTING, COMMERCIAL: Periodicals, NEC

AGS Custom Graphics Inc .... D 330 963-7770
Macedonia *(G-10188)*

Crain Communications Inc .... E 330 836-9180
Cuyahoga Falls *(G-7065)*

Schaeffers Investment Research Inc .... D 513 589-3800
Blue Ash *(G-1242)*

PRINTING, COMMERCIAL: Promotional

American Business Forms Inc .... E 513 312-2522
West Chester *(G-14798)*

PRINTING, COMMERCIAL: Screen

Kaufman Container Company .... C 216 898-2000
Cleveland *(G-4450)*

PRINTING, LITHOGRAPHIC: Calendars

Novelty Advertising Co Inc .... E 740 622-3113
Coshocton *(G-6994)*

PRINTING, LITHOGRAPHIC: Forms, Business

Quick Tab II Inc .... D 419 448-6622
Tiffin *(G-13639)*

PRINTING: Books

Hubbard Company .... E 419 784-4455
Defiance *(G-7750)*

PRINTING: Commercial, NEC

Aero Fulfillment Services Corp .... D 800 225-7145
Mason *(G-10517)*

AGS Custom Graphics Inc .... D 330 963-7770
Macedonia *(G-10188)*

Bindery & Spc Pressworks Inc .... D 614 873-4623
Plain City *(G-12470)*

Bollin & Sons Inc .... E 419 693-6573
Toledo *(G-13710)*

Consolidated Graphics Group Inc .... C 216 881-9191
Cleveland *(G-4104)*

Custom Products Corporation .... D 440 528-7100
Solon *(G-13080)*

GBS Corp .... C 330 494-5330
North Canton *(G-11833)*

General Data Company Inc .... B 513 752-7978
Cincinnati *(G-2105)*

General Theming Contrs LLC .... C 614 252-6342
Columbus *(G-5925)*

Hkm Drect Mkt Cmmnications Inc .... C 800 860-4456
Cleveland *(G-4367)*

Springdot Inc .... D 513 542-4000
Cincinnati *(G-3401)*

Tj Metzgers Inc .... D 419 861-8611
Toledo *(G-14043)*

Workflowone LLC .... A 877 735-4966
Dayton *(G-7726)*

PRINTING: Flexographic

Kopco Graphics Inc .... E 513 874-7230
West Chester *(G-14721)*

Samuels Products Inc .... E 513 891-4456
Blue Ash *(G-1239)*

PRINTING: Gravure, Forms, Business

Workflowone LLC .... A 877 735-4966
Dayton *(G-7726)*

PRINTING: Gravure, Rotogravure

Shamrock Companies Inc .... D 440 899-9510
Westlake *(G-15108)*

The Photo-Type Engraving Company ... D 513 281-0999
Cincinnati *(G-3469)*

PRINTING: Letterpress

A-A Blueprint Co Inc .... E 330 794-8803
Akron *(G-11)*

Eci Macola/Max LLC .... C 978 539-6186
Dublin *(G-8000)*

Traxium LLC .... E 330 572-8200
Stow *(G-13398)*

PRINTING: Lithographic

Amsive OH LLC .... D 937 885-8000
Miamisburg *(G-11024)*

Baesman Group Inc .... D 614 771-2300
Hilliard *(G-9181)*

Black River Group Inc .... E 419 524-6699
Mansfield *(G-10245)*

Bookmasters Inc .... C 419 281-1802
Ashland *(G-483)*

BP 10 Inc .... E 513 346-3900
West Chester *(G-14653)*

Coyne Graphic Finishing Inc .... E 740 397-6232
Mount Vernon *(G-11481)*

Highland Computer Forms Inc .... D 937 393-4215
Hillsboro *(G-9257)*

Hkm Drect Mkt Cmmnications Inc .... C 800 860-4456
Cleveland *(G-4367)*

Isaac Foster Mack Co .... C 419 625-5500
Sandusky *(G-12905)*

Vectra Inc .... C 614 351-6868
Columbus *(G-6843)*

Westrock Commercial LLC .... D 419 476-9101
Toledo *(G-14106)*

Woodrow Manufacturing Co .... E 937 399-9333
Springfield *(G-13313)*

Workflowone LLC .... A 877 735-4966
Dayton *(G-7726)*

PRINTING: Offset

A-A Blueprint Co Inc .... E 330 794-8803
Akron *(G-11)*

AGS Custom Graphics Inc .... D 330 963-7770
Macedonia *(G-10188)*

Angstrom Graphics Inc Midwest .... C 216 271-5300
Cleveland *(G-3817)*

Bindery & Spc Pressworks Inc .... D 614 873-4623
Plain City *(G-12470)*

Consolidated Graphics Group Inc .... C 216 881-9191
Cleveland *(G-4104)*

Copley Ohio Newspapers Inc .... C 330 364-5577
New Philadelphia *(G-11643)*

Fine Line Graphics Corp .... C 614 486-0276
Columbus *(G-5857)*

Hubbard Company .... E 419 784-4455
Defiance *(G-7750)*

McNerney & Associates LLC .... E 513 241-9951
West Chester *(G-14824)*

Printers Devil Inc .... E 330 650-1218
Hudson *(G-9369)*

SERVICES SECTION

Richardson Printing Corp.................... D 800 848-9752
Marietta *(G-10404)*

Springdot Inc.................................... D 513 542-4000
Cincinnati *(G-3401)*

Tj Metzgers Inc................................. D 419 861-8611
Toledo *(G-14043)*

Traxium LLC..................................... E 330 572-8200
Stow *(G-13398)*

PRINTING: Photolithographic

Friends Service Co Inc....................... D 419 427-1704
Findlay *(G-8534)*

PROFESSIONAL EQPT & SPLYS, WHOLESALE: Analytical Instruments

Gilson Company Inc.......................... E 740 548-7298
Lewis Center *(G-9823)*

Mettler-Toledo LLC............................ A 614 438-4511
Columbus *(G-5270)*

PROFESSIONAL EQPT & SPLYS, WHOLESALE: Engineers', NEC

S&V Industries Inc............................ E 330 666-1986
Medina *(G-10886)*

US Tsubaki Power Transm LLC........... C 419 626-4560
Sandusky *(G-12939)*

PROFESSIONAL EQPT & SPLYS, WHOLESALE: Optical Goods

Approved Networks LLC..................... E 216 831-1800
Independence *(G-9406)*

Diversified Ophthalmics Inc................ E 803 783-3454
Cincinnati *(G-2570)*

Essilor Laboratories Amer Inc............. E 614 274-0840
Columbus *(G-5831)*

Shawnee Optical Inc......................... E 440 997-2020
Ashtabula *(G-549)*

PROFESSIONAL INSTRUMENT REPAIR SVCS

Cleveland Electric Labs Co.................. E 800 447-2207
Twinsburg *(G-14177)*

Mettler-Toledo LLC............................ A 614 438-4511
Columbus *(G-5270)*

Modern Office Methods Inc................ E 937 436-2295
Dayton *(G-7510)*

PROFESSIONAL SCHOOLS

Cleveland Municipal School Dst.......... D 216 459-4200
Cleveland *(G-4059)*

PROFILE SHAPES: Unsupported Plastics

HP Manufacturing Company Inc.......... D 216 361-6500
Cleveland *(G-4386)*

PROMOTION SVCS

Marsh Inc... D 513 421-1234
Cincinnati *(G-3012)*

PROPERTY DAMAGE INSURANCE

Afc Holding Company Inc................... D 513 579-2121
Cincinnati *(G-2154)*

Central Mutual Insurance Co.............. B 419 238-1010
Van Wert *(G-14341)*

Crestbrook Insurance Company.......... A 614 249-7111
Columbus *(G-5725)*

Matic Insurance Services Inc.............. C 833 382-1304
Columbus *(G-6206)*

Midland Company............................. A 513 947-5503
Amelia *(G-418)*

Nationwide Insurance Co Fla.............. A 614 249-7111
Columbus *(G-6332)*

Ohio Fair Plan Undwrt Assn............... E 614 839-6446
Columbus *(G-5275)*

Platinum Rstoration Contrs Inc........... E 440 327-0699
Elyria *(G-8287)*

Westfield National Insur Co................ D 330 887-0101
Westfield Center *(G-15028)*

PUBLIC LIBRARY

Worthington Public Library................. C 614 807-2626
Worthington *(G-15472)*

PUBLIC RELATIONS & PUBLICITY SVCS

City of Kettering................................ E 937 296-2486
Dayton *(G-7233)*

Dix & Eaton Incorporated................... E 216 241-0405
Cleveland *(G-4168)*

Domestic Relations............................ E 937 225-4063
Dayton *(G-7316)*

Edward Howard & Co........................ E 216 781-2400
Cleveland *(G-4207)*

Marketing Essentials LLC................... E 419 629-0080
New Bremen *(G-11599)*

SBC Advertising Ltd.......................... C 614 891-7070
Columbus *(G-6648)*

United States Trotting Assn............... E 614 224-2291
Columbus *(G-6817)*

Ver-A-Fast Corp................................ E 440 331-0250
Rocky River *(G-12755)*

PUBLIC RELATIONS SVCS

Cosmic Concepts Ltd........................ D 216 696-4230
Cleveland *(G-4120)*

County of Logan............................... E 937 599-7252
Bellefontaine *(G-1026)*

L Brands Service Company LLC......... D 614 415-7000
Columbus *(G-6130)*

Northlich LLC................................... C 513 421-8840
Cincinnati *(G-3126)*

Whitespace Design Group Inc............ E 330 762-9320
Akron *(G-360)*

PUBLISHERS: Music, Sheet

Lorenz Corporation............................ D 937 228-6118
Dayton *(G-7459)*

PUBLISHERS: Telephone & Other Directory

ITM Marketing Inc............................. C 740 295-3575
Coshocton *(G-6988)*

PUBLISHING & BROADCASTING: Internet Only

Cerkl Incorporated............................ D 513 813-8425
Blue Ash *(G-1147)*

Deemsys Inc..................................... D 614 322-9928
Gahanna *(G-8715)*

Marketing Essentials LLC................... E 419 629-0080
New Bremen *(G-11599)*

PUBLISHING & PRINTING: Books

McGraw-Hill Schl Edcatn Hldngs......... A 419 207-7400
Ashland *(G-507)*

World Harvest Church Inc.................. C 614 837-1990
Canal Winchester *(G-1620)*

PUBLISHING & PRINTING: Magazines: publishing & printing

Family Motor Coach Assn Inc............. E 513 474-3622
Cincinnati *(G-2647)*

RADIO BROADCASTING STATIONS

PUBLISHING & PRINTING: Newsletters, Business Svc

Quality Solutions Inc......................... E 440 933-9946
Cleveland *(G-4801)*

PUBLISHING & PRINTING: Newspapers

Amos Media Company....................... C 937 638-0967
Sidney *(G-13018)*

PULP MILLS

Rumpke Transportation Co LLC.......... B 513 242-4600
Cincinnati *(G-3331)*

PUMPS & PUMPING EQPT REPAIR SVCS

Eaton Industrial Corporation............... C 216 692-5456
Cleveland *(G-4204)*

Wm Plotz Machine and Forge Co........ E 216 861-0441
Cleveland *(G-5156)*

Wooster Hydrostatics Inc................... E 330 263-6555
Wooster *(G-15395)*

PUMPS & PUMPING EQPT WHOLESALERS

Dreison International Inc.................... C 216 362-0755
Cleveland *(G-4184)*

General Electric Company.................. E 216 883-1000
Cleveland *(G-4310)*

Giant Industries Inc.......................... E 419 531-4600
Toledo *(G-13821)*

Indelco Custom Products Inc............. E 216 797-7300
Euclid *(G-8349)*

Tolco Corporation............................. D 419 241-1113
Toledo *(G-14048)*

Trane Technologies Company LLC...... E 419 633-6800
Bryan *(G-1494)*

PUMPS: Domestic, Water Or Sump

Wayne/Scott Fetzer Company............. C 800 237-0987
Harrison *(G-9119)*

PUMPS: Measuring & Dispensing

Tolco Corporation............................. D 419 241-1113
Toledo *(G-14048)*

PURCHASING SVCS

Aim Leasing Company....................... E 216 883-6300
Cleveland *(G-3777)*

Neighborcare Inc............................... A 513 719-2600
Cincinnati *(G-3104)*

University of Cincinnati...................... D 513 556-2389
Cincinnati *(G-3576)*

PURIFICATION & DUST COLLECTION EQPT

Dreison International Inc.................... C 216 362-0755
Cleveland *(G-4184)*

RADIO BROADCASTING & COMMUNICATIONS EQPT

Circle Prime Manufacturing................ E 330 923-0019
Cuyahoga Falls *(G-7054)*

Gatesair Inc...................................... D 513 459-3400
Mason *(G-10553)*

RADIO BROADCASTING STATIONS

Alpha Media LLC............................... E 330 456-7166
Canton *(G-1662)*

Alpha Media LLC............................... E 937 294-5858
Dayton *(G-7166)*

Bucyrus Radio Group........................ E 614 451-2191
Columbus *(G-5480)*

Employee Codes: A=Over 500 employees, B=251-500
C=101-250, D=51-100, E=20-50, F=10-19, G=1-9

RADIO BROADCASTING STATIONS

Cumulus Media Inc................................. E 513 241-9898
  Cincinnati (G-2523)
Cumulus Media Inc................................. D 419 725-5700
  Toledo (G-13771)
Elyria-Lorain Broadcasting Co.............. E 440 322-3761
  Elyria (G-8248)
Franklin Communications Inc................ E 614 459-9769
  Columbus (G-5886)
Ideastream... C 216 916-6100
  Cleveland (G-4401)
Isaac Foster Mack Co............................ C 419 625-5500
  Sandusky (G-12905)
Johnny Appleseed Brdcstg Co............... E 419 529-5900
  Ontario (G-12109)
Marquee Broadcasting Ohio Inc............. E 740 452-5431
  Zanesville (G-15810)
North American Broadcasting................. D 614 481-7800
  Columbus (G-6364)
Ohio State University.............................. D 614 292-9678
  Columbus (G-6454)
Pillar of Fire.. E 513 542-1212
  Cincinnati (G-3211)
Public Brdcstg Fndtion of NW O............ D 419 380-4600
  Toledo (G-13980)
Rubber City Radio Group Inc................. D 330 869-9800
  Akron (G-289)
TCI.. E 513 557-3200
  Cincinnati (G-3444)
Wkhr Radio Inc..................................... E 440 708-0915
  Bainbridge (G-687)
Wqkt 1045 FM...................................... B 330 264-5122
  Wooster (G-15399)
Wwcd Ltd... E 614 221-9923
  Columbus (G-6910)
Wwst Corporation LLC......................... B 330 264-5122
  Wooster (G-15400)
Xavier University.................................. E 513 745-3335
  Cincinnati (G-3683)

RADIO COMMUNICATIONS: Airborne Eqpt

Quasonix Inc.. E 513 942-1287
  West Chester (G-14751)

RADIO COMMUNICATIONS: Carrier Eqpt

L-3 Cmmncations Nova Engrg Inc.......... C 877 282-1168
  Mason (G-10571)

RADIO REPAIR & INSTALLATION SVCS

Comproducts Inc................................... E 614 276-5552
  Columbus (G-5679)

RAILROAD CAR REPAIR SVCS

Andersons Inc....................................... C 419 893-5050
  Maumee (G-10692)
Cathcart Rail LLC.................................. E 380 390-2058
  Columbus (G-5249)
Cathcart Repair Facilities LLC................ E
  Columbus (G-5250)
Jk-Co LLC... E 419 422-5240
  Findlay (G-8552)

RAILROAD EQPT

Amsted Industries Incorporated.............. D 614 836-2323
  Groveport (G-8969)
Buck Equipment Inc.............................. E 614 539-3039
  Grove City (G-8901)
Johnson Bros Rubber Co Inc................. E 419 752-4814
  Greenwich (G-8892)

RAILROAD EQPT & SPLYS WHOLESALERS

Amsted Industries Incorporated.............. D 614 836-2323
  Groveport (G-8969)

Buck Equipment Inc.............................. E 614 539-3039
  Grove City (G-8901)
Djj Holding Corporation......................... C 513 419-6200
  Cincinnati (G-2572)

RAILROAD MAINTENANCE & REPAIR SVCS

Cincinnati & Ohio Rlwy Svc LLC............ E 513 371-3277
  Hamilton (G-9027)
Road & Rail Services Inc....................... D 502 365-5361
  Fostoria (G-8624)
Road & Rail Services Inc....................... D 937 578-0089
  Marysville (G-10505)

REAL ESTATE AGENCIES & BROKERS

Bellwether.. D 949 247-8912
  Cleveland (G-3862)
C V Perry & Co.................................... E 614 221-4131
  Columbus (G-5490)
Coastal Ridge Management LLC............ B 614 339-4608
  Columbus (G-5588)
E-Merge Real Estate............................. D 614 804-5600
  Pickerington (G-12401)
Essex Healthcare Corporation................ E 614 416-0600
  Columbus (G-5830)
Garland Group Inc................................. E 614 294-4411
  Columbus (G-5916)
Lenz Inc... E 937 277-9364
  Dayton (G-7452)
Link Real Estate Group LLC.................. D 614 686-7775
  Columbus (G-6168)
Luxe Omni Inc...................................... E 937 929-0511
  Oakwood (G-12050)
Newmark & Company RE Inc................. E 216 861-3040
  Cleveland (G-4641)
Noneman Real Estate Company............. E 419 531-4020
  Toledo (G-13935)
Ohio Equities LLC................................. D 614 224-2400
  Columbus (G-6420)
Om Partners LLC.................................. E 216 861-7200
  Cleveland (G-4696)
Phil Giessler... E 614 888-0307
  Worthington (G-15446)
Phillips Edison & Company LLC............. E 513 554-1110
  Cincinnati (G-3206)
Pinnacle Realty Management Co............ D 614 430-3678
  Worthington (G-15447)
Rhm Real Estate Inc............................. E 216 360-8333
  Cleveland (G-4836)
Ron Neff Real Estate............................. E 740 773-4670
  Chillicothe (G-2083)
Sgt Clans Wstlake Holdings LLC............ E 440 653-5146
  Westlake (G-15107)
Stouffer Realty LLC............................... E 440 247-4210
  Chagrin Falls (G-1969)
Tyson Group... E 800 659-1080
  Dublin (G-8145)
Vinebrook II LLC................................... D 614 783-5573
  Dayton (G-7708)

REAL ESTATE AGENCIES: Rental

Millennia Housing MGT Ltd.................... C 216 520-1250
  Cleveland (G-4585)
Village Communities LLC....................... C 614 540-2400
  Westerville (G-14951)

REAL ESTATE AGENTS & MANAGERS

Ackermann Group.................................. D 513 480-5204
  Cincinnati (G-2142)
American Homes 4 Rent........................ E 513 429-7174
  Cincinnati (G-2182)
Arena Management Holdings LLC.......... A 513 421-4111
  Cincinnati (G-2215)

SERVICES SECTION

Brunswick Senior Living LLC................. E 330 460-4244
  Brunswick (G-1452)
Cavalear Corporation............................. E 419 882-7125
  Sylvania (G-13538)
Connor Group A RE Inv Firm LLC.......... B 937 434-3095
  Miamisburg (G-11038)
Crawford Hoying Ltd.............................. C 614 335-2020
  Dublin (G-7979)
Danbury Wods At Grnfeld Crssin........... D 330 264-0355
  Wooster (G-15333)
Dari Pizza Enterprises II Inc.................. C 419 534-3000
  Maumee (G-10717)
Dayton Realtors..................................... E 937 223-0900
  Dayton (G-7301)
Design Homes & Development Co........ E 937 438-3667
  Dayton (G-7311)
Echoing Hills Village Inc....................... E 740 327-2311
  Warsaw (G-14591)
Fairfield Homes Inc............................... C 614 873-3533
  Plain City (G-12477)
Fay Limited Partnership........................ E 513 241-1911
  Cincinnati (G-2651)
Flashhouse Inc..................................... E 216 600-0504
  Beachwood (G-792)
Globe Furniture Rentals Inc................... D 513 771-8287
  Cincinnati (G-2734)
Her Majesty Management Group............ D 614 680-7461
  Columbus (G-5986)
Industrial Coml Prpts LLC..................... D 440 539-1046
  Solon (G-13099)
Integra Cncinnati/Columbus Inc............. E 614 764-8040
  Dublin (G-8040)
Johnson Rose LLC................................ E 440 785-9892
  North Olmsted (G-11907)
Meadowbrook Mall Company................. E 330 747-2661
  Youngstown (G-15664)
Miller-Valentine Partners Ltd................. E 513 588-1000
  Dayton (G-7506)
Mri Software LLC.................................. B 800 321-8770
  Solon (G-13114)
National Church Residences.................. C 614 451-2151
  Columbus (G-6292)
Nationwide Mutual Insurance Co........... A 614 249-7111
  Columbus (G-6338)
Neighborhood Properties Inc.................. E 419 473-2604
  Toledo (G-13931)
Oberer Residential Cnstr Ltd.................. D 937 278-0851
  Miamisburg (G-11078)
One Lincoln Park................................... E 937 298-0594
  Dayton (G-7538)
Orum Stair Rsdntl Brkg OH................... E 614 920-8100
  Pickerington (G-12407)
Owners Management Company.............. E 440 439-3800
  Parma (G-12259)
Pk Management LLC............................. C 216 472-1870
  Cleveland (G-4753)
Port Lawrence Title and Tr Co............... E 419 244-4605
  Toledo (G-13965)
Residential HM Assn Marion Inc............ C 740 387-9999
  Marion (G-10451)
Towne Properties Assoc Inc.................. D 513 874-3737
  Cincinnati (G-3493)
University Circle Incorporated................ E 216 791-3900
  Cleveland (G-5071)
Visconsi Companies Ltd........................ E 216 464-5550
  Cleveland (G-5108)
Your Home Court Advantage LLC.......... E 330 364-6602
  New Philadelphia (G-11674)

REAL ESTATE ESCROW AGENCIES

Resource Title Agency Inc..................... D 216 520-0050
  Cleveland (G-4831)

SERVICES SECTION

REHABILITATION SVCS

Resource Title Nat Agcy Inc..................D..... 216 520-0050
Independence *(G-9476)*

REAL ESTATE INVESTMENT TRUSTS

American Cmpus Communities Inc.........E..... 216 687-5196
Cleveland *(G-3799)*

Associated Estates Realty Corporation. B..... 216 261-5000
Richmond Heights *(G-12715)*

Divine Strings Investment LLC................D..... 937 241-0782
Canton *(G-1737)*

Forest City Realty Trust Inc....................A..... 216 621-6060
Cleveland *(G-4273)*

Ohad Investment Group LLC..................E..... 513 426-5202
Cincinnati *(G-3141)*

Profill Holdings LLC................................A..... 513 742-4000
Cincinnati *(G-3247)*

Site Centers Corp..................................C..... 216 755-5500
Beachwood *(G-839)*

Washington Prime Acqsition LLC............C..... 614 621-9000
Columbus *(G-6865)*

Welltower Inc..D..... 419 247-2800
Toledo *(G-14102)*

Welltower Op LLC.................................D..... 419 247-2800
Toledo *(G-14103)*

RECREATIONAL VEHICLE DEALERS

L B Brunk & Sons Inc...........................E..... 330 332-0359
Salem *(G-12845)*

Surfside Motors Inc..............................E..... 419 419-4776
Galion *(G-8751)*

REFINING: Petroleum

Knight Material Tech LLC......................D..... 330 488-1651
East Canton *(G-8169)*

Marathon Petroleum Corporation..........A..... 419 422-2121
Findlay *(G-8561)*

REFRACTORY MATERIALS WHOLESALERS

Allen Refractories Company..................C..... 740 927-8000
Pataskala *(G-12269)*

Fosbel Wahl Holdings LLC....................D..... 419 334-2650
Fremont *(G-8678)*

REFRIGERATION EQPT & SPLYS WHOLESALERS

Allied Supply Company Inc....................E..... 937 224-9833
Dayton *(G-7164)*

Buckeye Heating and AC Sup Inc..........E..... 216 831-0066
Bedford Heights *(G-996)*

Gordon Brothers Inc.............................E..... 800 331-7611
Salem *(G-12842)*

Gustave A Larson Company..................E..... 513 681-4089
Cincinnati *(G-2785)*

Refrigeration Sales Company LLC.........E..... 216 525-8200
Cleveland *(G-4818)*

REFRIGERATION REPAIR SVCS

Refrigeration Systems Company...........D..... 614 263-0913
Columbus *(G-6571)*

The Geiler Company.............................C..... 513 574-1200
Cincinnati *(G-3466)*

REFRIGERATION SVC & REPAIR

Cac Group LLC.....................................E..... 740 369-4328
Delaware *(G-7782)*

Electrical Appl Repr Svc Inc..................E..... 216 459-8700
Brooklyn Heights *(G-1417)*

Gardiner Service Company LLC............C..... 440 248-3400
Solon *(G-13091)*

McPhillips Plbg Htg & AC Co.................E..... 216 481-1400
Cleveland *(G-4542)*

REFUSE SYSTEMS

City of Dayton......................................D..... 937 333-4860
Dayton *(G-7230)*

City of Lakewood..................................E..... 216 252-4322
Cleveland *(G-3990)*

City of Perrysburg................................E..... 419 872-8020
Perrysburg *(G-12324)*

Waste Management Ohio Inc................E..... 419 221-2029
Lima *(G-9980)*

Waste Management Ohio Inc................D..... 740 345-1212
Newark *(G-11752)*

REGULATORS: Power

Vertiv Corporation................................A..... 614 888-0246
Westerville *(G-14949)*

REHABILITATION CENTER, OUTPATIENT TREATMENT

Aurora Manor Ltd Partnership...............B..... 330 562-5000
Aurora *(G-606)*

Brecksville Halthcare Group Inc............E..... 440 546-0643
Brecksville *(G-1346)*

Cleveland Clnic Rhbltion Physc.............C..... 440 516-5400
Willoughby Hills *(G-15232)*

Concept Rehab Inc..............................D..... 419 843-6002
Toledo *(G-13756)*

Country Meadow Care Center LLC........E..... 419 886-3922
Bellville *(G-1048)*

County of Carroll..................................D..... 330 627-7651
Carrollton *(G-1906)*

De Coach Team LLC............................D..... 513 942-4673
Cincinnati *(G-2546)*

Easter Seal Society of..........................D..... 330 743-1168
Youngstown *(G-15603)*

Education Alternatives..........................D..... 216 332-9360
Brookpark *(G-1434)*

Encore Rehabilitation Services..............E..... 614 459-6901
Dublin *(G-8004)*

Hcf of Roselawn Inc.............................C..... 419 647-4115
Spencerville *(G-13188)*

Heartland Rhbltation Svcs Inc...............D..... 419 537-0764
Toledo *(G-13843)*

Medcentral Health System....................B..... 419 683-1040
Crestline *(G-7025)*

Meigs County Care Center LLC............C..... 740 992-6472
Middleport *(G-11148)*

Metrohealth System..............................C..... 216 778-8446
Cleveland *(G-4566)*

Ohio Dept Mntal Hlth Addction...............C..... 740 947-7581
Waverly *(G-14614)*

Ohio State University............................C..... 614 257-3000
Columbus *(G-6453)*

P T Svcs Rehabilitation Inc...................B..... 419 455-8600
Tiffin *(G-13638)*

Peregrine Health Services Inc...............D..... 330 823-9005
Alliance *(G-396)*

Preserve Operating Co LLC..................E..... 513 471-8667
Cincinnati *(G-3229)*

Quadco Rehabilitation Center................E..... 419 782-0389
Defiance *(G-7764)*

Recovery Center...................................E..... 740 687-4500
Lancaster *(G-9738)*

Rehab Center.......................................C..... 330 297-2770
Ravenna *(G-12641)*

Rehabcare Group East Inc...................C..... 330 220-8950
Cleveland *(G-4819)*

Rehabilitation Support Svcs..................E..... 330 252-9012
Akron *(G-278)*

Rehabltion Ctr At Mrietta Mem..............E..... 740 374-1407
Marietta *(G-10403)*

Select Spclty Hosp - Yngstown..............C..... 330 480-3488
Youngstown *(G-15720)*

Summa Rehab Hospital LLC.................D..... 330 572-7300
Akron *(G-323)*

Summit Acres Inc.................................C..... 740 732-2364
Caldwell *(G-1551)*

Sunbridge Marion Hlth Care LLC...........D..... 740 389-6306
Marion *(G-10456)*

Therapy Advantage Group LLC............D..... 614 784-0400
Worthington *(G-15461)*

Trinity Rhabilitation Svcs LLC................D..... 740 695-0069
Saint Clairsville *(G-12817)*

Ultimate Rehab Ltd..............................D..... 513 563-8777
Blue Ash *(G-1261)*

United Disability Services Inc................D..... 330 374-1169
Akron *(G-341)*

United Rhbltion Svcs Grter Dy...............D..... 937 233-1230
Dayton *(G-7683)*

Urbana Healthcare Group LLC..............C..... 937 652-1381
Urbana *(G-14315)*

Wsb Rehabilitation Svcs Inc..................A..... 330 847-7819
Warren *(G-14577)*

Wsb Rehabilitation Svcs Inc..................D..... 330 533-1338
Canfield *(G-1645)*

REHABILITATION CTR, RESIDENTIAL WITH HEALTH CARE INCIDENTAL

Atrium Living Centers of Ea...................E..... 614 416-2662
Columbus *(G-5405)*

Blue Stream LLC..................................D..... 330 659-6166
Richfield *(G-12688)*

Butterfield Recovery Group LLC............E..... 513 932-4673
Oregonia *(G-12149)*

Cherry St Mission Ministries..................E..... 419 242-5141
Toledo *(G-13731)*

City Mission..E..... 216 431-3510
Cleveland *(G-3976)*

Compass Family and Cmnty Svcs.........E..... 330 782-5664
Youngstown *(G-15582)*

Compdrug...D..... 614 224-4506
Columbus *(G-5675)*

Comprhnsive Addction Svc Syste..........D..... 419 241-8827
Toledo *(G-13755)*

Health Recovery Services Inc...............C..... 740 592-6720
Athens *(G-571)*

Hitchcock Center For Women Inc..........E..... 216 421-0662
Cleveland *(G-4366)*

Interval Brotherhood Homes Inc.............D..... 330 644-4095
Coventry Township *(G-7011)*

Jefferson Rehab & Wellness LLC..........E..... 440 576-0043
Andover *(G-439)*

Jo-Lin Health Center Inc.......................E..... 740 532-0860
Ironton *(G-9510)*

New Directions Inc...............................D..... 216 591-0324
Cleveland *(G-4638)*

Promedica Toledo Hospital...................D..... 419 291-2273
Sylvania *(G-13566)*

Rose Mary Johanna Grassell................D..... 216 481-4823
Cleveland *(G-4854)*

Shining Star Rsdntial Svcs LLC............D..... 419 318-0932
Toledo *(G-14010)*

United Crbral Plsy Assn Grter...............E..... 216 381-9993
Cleveland *(G-5058)*

United Crbral Plsy Assn Grter...............D..... 216 791-8363
Cleveland *(G-5057)*

REHABILITATION SVCS

A W S Inc...E..... 216 486-0600
Euclid *(G-8335)*

Altercare Inc...E..... 330 929-4231
Cuyahoga Falls *(G-7037)*

REHABILITATION SVCS

Altercare Inc... E 330 677-4550
  Kent *(G-9558)*

Altercare of Ohio Inc............................. E 330 498-8110
  Canton *(G-1664)*

Arbor Rehabilitation & Healtcr............ B 440 423-0206
  Gates Mills *(G-8781)*

Carriage Inn of Cadiz Inc..................... D 740 942-8084
  Cadiz *(G-1538)*

City Mission.. E 216 431-3510
  Cleveland *(G-3976)*

Clark County Board of Developm....... E 937 328-2675
  Springfield *(G-13232)*

Clovernook Ctr For Blind Vslly............. C 513 522-3860
  Cincinnati *(G-2464)*

Eastern Ohio Correction Center........... E 740 765-4324
  Wintersville *(G-15293)*

Friends For Lf Rhblttion Svcs................ E 440 558-2859
  Cleveland *(G-4291)*

Goodwill Inds Rhbilitation Ctr............... C 330 454-9461
  Canton *(G-1764)*

Harrison Pavilion..................................... E 513 662-5800
  Cincinnati *(G-2802)*

Hcf Management Inc............................. E 740 289-2394
  Piketon *(G-12422)*

Hcf of Roselawn Inc.............................. C 419 647-4115
  Spencerville *(G-13188)*

Hearing Spech Deaf Ctr Grter C.......... E 513 221-0527
  Cincinnati *(G-2814)*

Landmark Recovery Ohio LLC............ B 855 950-5035
  Willard *(G-15169)*

Lifeline Partners Inc............................... E 330 501-6316
  Girard *(G-8818)*

Miami Vly Jvnile Rhblttion Ctr............. E 937 562-4000
  Xenia *(G-15527)*

Mount Carmel Health............................ E 614 234-4060
  Westerville *(G-14912)*

Ohio Department Rehabilitat................ E 614 877-4516
  Orient *(G-12152)*

Ohio Dept Mntal Hlth Addction............ D 740 773-2283
  Chillicothe *(G-2080)*

Rehab Resources Inc............................ E 513 474-4123
  Cincinnati *(G-3282)*

Talbert House.. E 513 541-0127
  Cincinnati *(G-3437)*

Talbert House.. E 513 221-2398
  Cincinnati *(G-3438)*

Talbert House.. D 513 872-5863
  Cincinnati *(G-3439)*

Trihealth Rehabilitation Hosp................ C 513 601-0600
  Cincinnati *(G-3526)*

REINSURANCE CARRIERS: Accident & Health

American Modern Home Svc Co........... E 513 943-7100
  Amelia *(G-412)*

RELOCATION SVCS

Dwellworks LLC..................................... D 216 682-4200
  Cleveland *(G-4190)*

Sirva Relocation LLC............................. B 216 606-4000
  Independence *(G-9484)*

Wegman Construction Company......... E 513 381-1111
  Cincinnati *(G-3646)*

RENTAL SVCS: Aircraft

Flexjet LLC... C 216 261-3880
  Cleveland *(G-4265)*

Flight Options Inc................................... B 216 261-3880
  Richmond Heights *(G-12719)*

Flight Options LLC................................. C 216 261-3500
  Cleveland *(G-4266)*

Flight Options Intl Inc............................. E 216 261-3500
  Richmond Heights *(G-12720)*

One Sky Flight LLC............................... E 877 703-2348
  Cleveland *(G-4698)*

RENTAL SVCS: Audio-Visual Eqpt & Sply

Bkg Holdings LLC.................................. E 614 252-7455
  Columbus *(G-5442)*

ITA INC.. E 513 631-7000
  Cincinnati *(G-2889)*

Live Technologies LLC.......................... D 614 278-7777
  Columbus *(G-6171)*

Northeast Projections Inc...................... E 216 514-5023
  Cleveland *(G-4663)*

RENTAL SVCS: Business Machine & Electronic Eqpt

Comdoc Inc.. C 330 896-2346
  North Canton *(G-11818)*

Diane Sauer Chevrolet Inc.................... E 330 373-1600
  Warren *(G-14518)*

Electronic Merch Systems LLC............. C 216 524-0900
  Cleveland *(G-4209)*

RENTAL SVCS: Costume

Costume Specialists Inc......................... E 614 464-2115
  Columbus *(G-5706)*

RENTAL SVCS: Electronic Eqpt, Exc Computers

Fern Exposition Services LLC............... E 888 621-3376
  Cincinnati *(G-2659)*

Modal Shop Inc...................................... D 513 351-9919
  Cincinnati *(G-3073)*

Warwick Communications Inc.............. E 216 787-0300
  Broadview Heights *(G-1404)*

RENTAL SVCS: Live Plant

Rentokil North America Inc................... E 513 247-9300
  Cincinnati *(G-3287)*

RENTAL SVCS: Vending Machine

Cuyahoga Vending Co Inc.................... C 440 353-9595
  North Ridgeville *(G-11926)*

Multi-Flow Dispensers Ohio Inc............ D 216 641-0200
  Brooklyn Heights *(G-1425)*

RENTAL SVCS: Video Disk/Tape, To The General Public

Emerge Ministries Inc............................. E 330 865-8351
  Akron *(G-146)*

Mile Inc.. C 614 252-6724
  Columbus *(G-6247)*

RENTAL SVCS: Work Zone Traffic Eqpt, Flags, Cones, Etc

A & A Safety Inc..................................... E 513 943-6100
  Amelia *(G-409)*

American Roadway Logistics Inc......... E 330 659-2003
  Norton *(G-11989)*

Paul Peterson Safety Div Inc................ E 614 486-4375
  Columbus *(G-6505)*

RENTAL: Portable Toilet

Miller & Co Portable Toil Svcs.............. E 330 453-9472
  Canton *(G-1808)*

Rumpke Transportation Co LLC........... B 937 461-0004
  Dayton *(G-7597)*

RENTAL: Video Tape & Disc

Mile Inc.. D 614 794-2203
  Worthington *(G-15440)*

RESEARCH & DEVELOPMENT SVCS, COMMERCIAL: Engineering Lab

Morris Technologies Inc......................... E 513 733-1611
  Cincinnati *(G-3080)*

Zin Technologies Inc.............................. E 440 625-2200
  Middleburg Heights *(G-11137)*

RESEARCH, DEVELOPMENT & TESTING SVCS, COMM: Agricultural

Ohio State University.............................. D 330 263-3700
  Wooster *(G-15363)*

RESEARCH, DEVELOPMENT & TESTING SVCS, COMMERCIAL: Medical

Applied Medical Technology Inc........... E 440 717-4000
  Brecksville *(G-1343)*

Center For Eating Disorders................. E 614 896-8222
  Columbus *(G-5531)*

Icon Government................................... B 330 278-2343
  Hinckley *(G-9270)*

Lazurite Inc.. E 216 334-3127
  Warrensville Heights *(G-14583)*

North Amercn Science Assoc LLC....... C 419 666-9455
  Northwood *(G-11979)*

RESEARCH, DEVELOPMENT & TESTING SVCS, COMMERCIAL: Physical

Battelle Memorial Institute...................... A 614 424-6424
  Columbus *(G-5422)*

Leidos Inc.. D 937 656-8433
  Beavercreek *(G-886)*

Leidos Inc.. E 614 575-4900
  Columbus *(G-6154)*

Velocys Inc.. D 614 733-3300
  Plain City *(G-12497)*

RESIDENTIAL CARE FOR THE HANDICAPPED

Ability Ctr of Greater Toledo................. E 419 517-7123
  Sylvania *(G-13535)*

Basinger Lfe Enhncmnt Sprt Svc.......... D 614 557-5461
  Marysville *(G-10474)*

Echos Haven LLC.................................. E 513 715-1189
  Harrison *(G-9103)*

RMS of Ohio Inc..................................... C 513 841-0990
  Cincinnati *(G-3310)*

St Vincent Family Services.................... C 614 252-0731
  Columbus *(G-6707)*

RESINS: Custom Compound Purchased

Avient Corporation................................. D 440 930-1000
  Avon Lake *(G-672)*

Flex Technologies Inc............................ D 330 897-6311
  Baltic *(G-688)*

Freeman Manufacturing & Sup Co....... E 440 934-1902
  Avon *(G-651)*

Hexpol Compounding LLC.................... C 440 834-4644
  Burton *(G-1528)*

RESTAURANTS: Fast Food

Marcus Theatres Corporation............... D 614 436-9818
  Columbus *(G-6196)*

Winking Lizard Inc.................................. E 330 220-9944
  Brunswick *(G-1476)*

SERVICES SECTION

RESTAURANTS: Full Svc, American

Aurora Hotel Partners LLC............... E 330 562-0767
  Aurora *(G-605)*
City Life Inc........................ E 216 523-5899
  Cleveland *(G-3975)*
Concord Dayton Hotel II LLC........... E 937 223-1000
  Dayton *(G-7245)*
Connor Concepts Inc.................. E 937 291-1661
  Dayton *(G-7246)*
Crefiii Wrmaug Sprngfeld Lssee......... E 937 322-3600
  Springfield *(G-13245)*
Durga Llc............................ E 513 771-2080
  Cincinnati *(G-2587)*
Epiqurian Inns....................... D 614 885-2600
  Worthington *(G-15414)*
Frickers USA LLC.................... E 937 865-9242
  Miamisburg *(G-11056)*
Golden Lamb......................... D 513 932-5065
  Lebanon *(G-9767)*
Henderson Rd Rest Systems Inc........ E 614 442-3310
  Columbus *(G-5984)*
Hillbrook Club Inc.................... E 440 247-4940
  Cleveland *(G-4362)*
Hrm Enterprises Inc.................. C 330 877-9353
  Hartville *(G-9127)*
Paul A Ertel......................... E 216 696-8888
  Cleveland *(G-4730)*
Shelby Golf Course Inc............... E 937 492-2883
  Sidney *(G-13049)*
Velvet Ice Cream Company............. D 740 892-3921
  Utica *(G-14330)*
Whiteys Restaurant Inc............... E 330 659-3600
  Richfield *(G-12713)*

RETAIL BAKERY: Bagels

Bagel Place Inc....................... E 419 537-9377
  Toledo *(G-13698)*

RETAIL BAKERY: Bread

Alfred Nickles Bakery Inc............. E 216 267-8055
  Cleveland *(G-3786)*
Busken Bakery Inc................... D 513 871-2114
  Cincinnati *(G-2294)*

RETAIL BAKERY: Pretzels

Cedar Fair LP........................ A 419 627-2344
  Sandusky *(G-12871)*

RETAIL STORES: Audio-Visual Eqpt & Splys

Findaway World LLC.................. E 440 893-0808
  Solon *(G-13089)*

RETAIL STORES: Business Machines & Eqpt

Modern Office Methods Inc............ E 614 891-3693
  Westerville *(G-15000)*

RETAIL STORES: Cleaning Eqpt & Splys

Jani-Source LLC..................... E 740 374-6298
  Marietta *(G-10376)*

RETAIL STORES: Communication Eqpt

Combined Technologies Inc........... E 513 595-5900
  Cincinnati *(G-2478)*
Mobilcomm Inc....................... D 513 742-5555
  Cincinnati *(G-3072)*
Shawntech Communications Inc........ E 937 898-4900
  Miamisburg *(G-11093)*

RETAIL STORES: Cosmetics

Boxout LLC........................... C 833 462-7746
  Hudson *(G-9334)*

RETAIL STORES: Educational Aids & Electronic Training Mat

Bendon Inc........................... D 419 207-3600
  Ashland *(G-482)*
Hhd Aviation LLC.................... D 513 426-8378
  Hamilton *(G-9052)*

RETAIL STORES: Electronic Parts & Eqpt

Ctd Investments LLC................. E 614 570-9949
  Columbus *(G-5735)*
Parts Express International Inc....... D 800 338-0531
  Springboro *(G-13205)*

RETAIL STORES: Hearing Aids

Hearinglife Usa Inc.................. D 513 759-2999
  West Chester *(G-14707)*
United Rhblttion Svcs Grter Dy........ D 937 233-1230
  Dayton *(G-7683)*
University Otlryngologists Inc........ E 614 273-2241
  Columbus *(G-6824)*

RETAIL STORES: Medical Apparatus & Splys

Advanced Medical Equipment Inc...... E 937 534-1080
  Miamisburg *(G-11020)*
Amerimed LLC....................... A 513 942-3670
  West Chester *(G-14650)*
Care Medical Inc..................... E 513 821-7272
  Cincinnati *(G-2309)*
Fairfield Medical Center.............. A 740 687-8000
  Lancaster *(G-9718)*
Health Aid of Ohio Inc................ E 216 252-3900
  Cleveland *(G-4353)*
Modern Medical Inc.................. C 800 547-3330
  Westerville *(G-14910)*
Our Lady Bellefonte Hosp Inc......... A 606 833-3333
  Cincinnati *(G-3176)*
Rgh Enterprises LLC................. A 330 963-6996
  Twinsburg *(G-14216)*
Sarnova Inc.......................... D 614 760-5000
  Dublin *(G-8113)*
Sateri Home Inc...................... D 330 758-8106
  Youngstown *(G-15717)*
Seeley Enterprises Company.......... E 440 293-6600
  Andover *(G-440)*
Toledo Medical Equipment Co......... E 419 866-7120
  Maumee *(G-10774)*
University Mednet.................... B 216 383-0100
  Euclid *(G-8363)*

RETAIL STORES: Orthopedic & Prosthesis Applications

Hanger Prsthtics Orthtics E In........ E 330 633-9807
  Tallmadge *(G-13593)*
Stable Step LLC...................... C 800 491-1571
  Wadsworth *(G-14452)*
Unity Health Network LLC............ E 330 626-0549
  Streetsboro *(G-13434)*

RETAIL STORES: Pet Food

Petsmart LLC........................ E 614 418-9389
  Columbus *(G-6518)*

RETAIL STORES: Pet Splys

Heading4ward Investment Co.......... D 937 293-9994
  Moraine *(G-11416)*
Petsmart Inc......................... E 513 336-0365
  Mason *(G-10591)*

RETAIL STORES: Religious Goods

Christian Aid Ministries.............. E 330 893-2428
  Millersburg *(G-11276)*

RETAIL STORES: Safety Splys & Eqpt

Paul Peterson Safety Div Inc.......... E 614 486-4375
  Columbus *(G-6505)*
US Safetygear Inc.................... E 330 898-1344
  Warren *(G-14570)*

RETAIL STORES: Swimming Pools, Above Ground

Litehouse Products LLC............... E 440 638-2350
  Strongsville *(G-13471)*

RETAIL STORES: Telephone & Communication Eqpt

High Line Corporation................ E 330 848-8800
  Akron *(G-192)*

RETAIL STORES: Water Purification Eqpt

Enting Water Conditioning Inc........ E 937 294-5100
  Moraine *(G-11407)*
Gordon Brothers Inc................. E 800 331-7611
  Salem *(G-12842)*
William R Hague Inc................. D 614 836-2115
  Groveport *(G-9014)*

RETAIL STORES: Welding Splys

Albright Welding Supply Co Inc....... E 330 264-2021
  Wooster *(G-15309)*
Welders Supply Inc.................. E 216 267-4470
  Brookpark *(G-1443)*

ROBOTS: Assembly Line

Advanced Design Industries Inc....... E 440 277-4141
  Sheffield Village *(G-12997)*
Air Technical Industries Inc.......... E 440 951-5191
  Mentor *(G-10909)*
Ats Systems Oregon Inc.............. C 541 738-0932
  Lewis Center *(G-9808)*
Kc Robotics Inc...................... E 513 860-4442
  West Chester *(G-14717)*
Sentient Studios Ltd................. E 330 204-8636
  Fairlawn *(G-8499)*

RODS: Steel & Iron, Made In Steel Mills

American Posts LLC.................. E 419 720-0652
  Toledo *(G-13687)*

ROLLING MILL MACHINERY

Addition Manufacturing Tech.......... C 513 228-7000
  Lebanon *(G-9752)*
Cornerstone Wauseon Inc............ C 419 337-0940
  Wauseon *(G-14598)*
Park Corporation..................... B 216 267-4870
  Medina *(G-10874)*
Pines Manufacturing Inc............. E 440 835-5553
  Westlake *(G-15098)*
Steel Eqp Specialists Inc............ D 330 823-8260
  Alliance *(G-401)*

ROOFING MATERIALS: Asphalt

West Development Group LLC........ D 440 355-4682
  Lagrange *(G-9651)*

RUBBER PRDTS: Silicone

Novagard Solutions Inc.............. C 216 881-8111
  Cleveland *(G-4668)*
Shin-Etsu Silicones of America Inc... C 330 630-9460
  Akron *(G-299)*

SAFETY EQPT & SPLYS WHOLESALERS

Abco Holdings LLC.................. C 216 433-7200
  Cleveland *(G-3757)*

SAFETY EQPT & SPLYS WHOLESALERS

Safety Today Inc .... E 614 409-7200
  Grove City (G-8950)
Wcm Holdings Inc .... C 513 705-2100
  Cincinnati (G-3643)
West Chester Holdings LLC .... C 513 705-2100
  Cincinnati (G-3655)

SAFETY INSPECTION SVCS

Industrial Power Systems Inc .... B 419 531-3121
  Rossford (G-12767)

SALES PROMOTION SVCS

Campbell Sales Company .... B 513 697-2900
  Cincinnati (G-2304)
Consolidus LLC .... E 330 319-7200
  Akron (G-121)
County of Montgomery .... C 937 225-4990
  Dayton (G-7252)
D L Ryan Companies LLC .... D 614 436-6558
  Westerville (G-14887)
Distributor Marketing MGT Inc .... E 440 236-5534
  Columbia Station (G-5227)
RA Staff Company .... E 440 891-9900
  Cleveland (G-4806)

SAND & GRAVEL

Central Allied Enterprises Inc .... E 330 477-6751
  Canton (G-1706)
Hilltop Basic Resources Inc .... D 513 621-1500
  Cincinnati (G-2826)
Kenmore Construction Co Inc .... D 330 832-8888
  Massillon (G-10649)
National Lime and Stone Co .... E 419 396-7671
  Carey (G-1894)
Shelly Materials Inc .... D 740 246-6315
  Thornville (G-13622)
Smith Concrete Co .... E 740 373-7441
  Dover (G-7901)
The Olen Corporation .... D 614 491-1515
  Columbus (G-6761)

SAND MINING

Central Ready Mix LLC .... E 513 402-5001
  Cincinnati (G-2337)
John R Jurgensen Co .... B 513 771-0820
  Cincinnati (G-2913)
The National Lime and Stone Company . E 419 422-4341
  Findlay (G-8593)

SANITARY SVC, NEC

American Beauty Landscaping .... E 330 788-1501
  Youngstown (G-15548)
City of Lima .... E 419 221-5294
  Lima (G-9874)
City of Toledo .... D 419 936-2924
  Toledo (G-13744)
Cuyahoga County Sani Engrg Svc .... E 216 443-8211
  Cleveland (G-4146)
Northast Ohio Rgonal Sewer Dst .... C 216 641-3200
  Cleveland (G-4658)
Vns Federal Services LLC .... E 740 443-7005
  Piketon (G-12431)

SANITARY SVCS: Hazardous Waste, Collection & Disposal

Avalon Holdings Corporation .... D 330 856-8800
  Warren (G-14501)
Clean Hrbors Es Indus Svcs Inc .... D 937 425-0512
  Dayton (G-7235)
Enviroserve Inc .... C 330 361-7764
  North Canton (G-11828)

Sustain LLC .... E 888 525-0029
  New Waterford (G-11684)
Triad Transport Inc .... E 614 491-9497
  Columbus (G-6788)
Wm Ccp Solutions LLC .... D 513 871-9733
  Cincinnati (G-3676)

SANITARY SVCS: Oil Spill Cleanup

Cousins Waste Control LLC .... D 419 726-1500
  Toledo (G-13768)

SANITARY SVCS: Refuse Collection & Disposal Svcs

Cecos International Inc .... E 513 724-6114
  Williamsburg (G-15178)
Central Ohio Contractors Inc .... D 740 369-7700
  Delaware (G-7784)
Industrial Waste Control Inc .... D 330 270-9900
  Youngstown (G-15638)
Republic Services Inc .... E 330 830-9050
  Massillon (G-10662)
Republic Services Kentucky LLC .... C 859 824-5466
  Williamsburg (G-15181)
Rumpke of Ohio Inc .... C 740 947-7082
  Waverly (G-14618)
Rumpke Transportation Co LLC .... B 937 461-0004
  Dayton (G-7597)
Rumpke Waste Inc .... C 937 378-4126
  Georgetown (G-8801)
Waste-Away Systems LLC .... E 740 349-2783
  Newark (G-11753)

SANITARY SVCS: Toxic Or Hazardous Waste Cleanup

Environmental Enterprises Inc .... C 513 772-2818
  Cincinnati (G-2627)
Petro Environmental Tech .... E 513 489-6789
  Cincinnati (G-3202)

SANITARY SVCS: Waste Materials, Recycling

Ace Iron & Metal Company .... E 614 443-5196
  Columbus (G-5305)
Adams - Brown Counties .... E 937 544-2650
  West Union (G-14864)
Adams Brown Cnties Ecnmic Oppr .... E 937 378-3431
  Georgetown (G-8797)
American Landfill Inc .... D 330 866-3265
  Waynesburg (G-14621)
B & B Plastics Recyclers Inc .... C 614 409-2880
  Columbus (G-5411)
Bluescope Recycling & Mtls LLC .... D 419 747-6522
  Mansfield (G-10247)
Chemtron Corporation .... E 440 937-6348
  Avon (G-644)
Cirba Solutions Us Inc .... E 740 653-6290
  Lancaster (G-9700)
City of Akron .... E 330 375-2650
  Akron (G-101)
Clm Pallet Recycling Inc .... D 614 272-5761
  Columbus (G-5586)
Cross-Roads Asphalt Recycling Inc ...... E 440 236-5066
  Columbia Station (G-5226)
DMS Recycling LLC .... E 740 397-0790
  Mount Vernon (G-11484)
Envirite of Ohio Inc .... E 330 456-6238
  Canton (G-1747)
Fpt Cleveland LLC .... C 216 441-3800
  Cleveland (G-4282)
Fultz & Son Inc .... E 419 547-9365
  Clyde (G-5201)

SERVICES SECTION

Garden Street Iron & Metal Inc .... E 513 721-4660
  Cincinnati (G-2715)
Gateway Products Recycling Inc .... E 216 341-8777
  Cleveland (G-4306)
Global Scrap Management Inc .... E 513 576-6600
  Batavia (G-741)
H Hafner & Sons Inc .... E 513 321-1895
  Cincinnati (G-2786)
Hope Timber Pallet Recycl LLC .... E 740 344-1788
  Newark (G-11706)
Hpj Industries Inc .... E 419 278-1000
  Bowling Green (G-1325)
Interstate Shredding LLC .... E 330 545-5477
  Girard (G-8817)
Jasar Recycling Inc .... D 864 233-5421
  East Palestine (G-8196)
Kimble Recycl & Disposal Inc .... E 330 963-5493
  Twinsburg (G-14200)
Liberty Tire Services LLC .... E 330 868-0097
  Minerva (G-11308)
Miles Alloys Inc .... E 216 295-1000
  Cleveland (G-4581)
Mondo Polymer Technologies Inc .... E 740 376-9396
  Marietta (G-10391)
Muskingum Iron & Metal Co .... E 740 452-9351
  Zanesville (G-15815)
Novelis Alr Recycling Ohio LLC .... C 740 922-2373
  Uhrichsville (G-14236)
Novotec Recycling LLC .... E 614 231-8326
  Columbus (G-6375)
Plastic Recycling Tech Inc .... E 419 238-9395
  Van Wert (G-14349)
Plastic Recycling Tech Inc .... E 937 615-9286
  Piqua (G-12456)
Polychem LLC .... D 419 547-1400
  Clyde (G-5207)
Pratt Paper (oh) LLC .... E 567 320-3353
  Wapakoneta (G-14490)
PSC Metals LLC .... D 330 484-7610
  Canton (G-1833)
PSC Metals LLC .... E 614 299-4175
  Columbus (G-6555)
Rbg Inc .... E 513 247-0175
  Blue Ash (G-1233)
Recycle Waste Services Inc .... D 419 517-1323
  Sylvania (G-13567)
Royal Paper Stock Company Inc .... D 614 851-4714
  Columbus (G-6616)
RSR Partners LLC .... C 440 248-3991
  Solon (G-13140)
Rumpke Cnsld Companies Inc .... C 800 828-8171
  Cincinnati (G-3330)
Rumpke Transportation Co LLC .... B 513 242-4600
  Cincinnati (G-3331)
Rumpke Waste Inc .... C 513 242-4401
  Cincinnati (G-3333)
Rumpke Waste Inc .... C 513 851-0122
  Columbus (G-6620)
Rumpke Waste Inc .... C 937 548-1939
  Greenville (G-8883)
Rumpke Waste Inc .... C 419 895-0058
  Shiloh (G-13014)
Rumpke Waste Inc .... C 740 384-4400
  Wellston (G-14641)
Rumpke Waste Inc .... D 513 851-0122
  Cincinnati (G-3332)
Shredded Bedding Corporation .... D 740 893-3567
  Centerburg (G-1936)
Shur-Green Farms LLC .... D 937 547-9633
  Ansonia (G-446)
Valicor Environmental Svcs LLC .... D 937 268-6501
  Dayton (G-7698)

SERVICES SECTION

SECURITY GUARD SVCS

Veolia Es Tchncal Slutions LLC............... E 937 859-6101
  Miamisburg *(G-11102)*
Waste Management Ohio Inc.................. E 740 787-2327
  Glenford *(G-8833)*
Werlor Inc... E 419 784-4285
  Defiance *(G-7775)*

SATELLITES: Communications

Great Lakes Telcom Ltd........................... E 330 629-8848
  Youngstown *(G-15622)*

SCAFFOLDS: Mobile Or Stationary, Metal

Waco Scaffolding & Equipment Inc......... A 216 749-8900
  Cleveland *(G-5119)*

SCALE REPAIR SVCS

Brechbuhler Scales Inc............................ E 330 458-3060
  Canton *(G-1689)*

SCALES: Indl

Mettler-Toledo LLC.................................. A 614 438-4511
  Columbus *(G-5270)*

SCHOOLS: Vocational, NEC

Great Oaks Inst Tech Creer Dev............. E 513 771-8840
  Cincinnati *(G-2763)*
Great Oaks Inst Tech Creer Dev............. D 513 613-3657
  Cincinnati *(G-2764)*
New View Management Group Inc.......... D 513 733-4444
  Cincinnati *(G-3110)*

SCRAP & WASTE MATERIALS, WHOLESALE: Ferrous Metal

Agmet LLC... E 440 439-7400
  Cleveland *(G-3775)*
Cohen Brothers Inc................................. E 513 422-3696
  Middletown *(G-11158)*
Cohen Electronics Inc.............................. D 513 425-6911
  Middletown *(G-11159)*
Daniel Cohen Enterprises Inc.................. C 513 896-4547
  Oxford *(G-12207)*
David J Joseph Company........................ E 513 419-6016
  Cincinnati *(G-2542)*
Djj Holding Corporation............................ C 513 419-6200
  Cincinnati *(G-2572)*
Fpt Cleveland LLC................................... C 216 441-3800
  Cleveland *(G-4282)*
Franklin Iron & Metal Corp....................... C 937 253-8184
  Dayton *(G-7367)*
Lakeside Scrap Metals Inc....................... E 216 458-7150
  Cleveland *(G-4477)*
Omnisource LLC...................................... D 419 537-1631
  Toledo *(G-13950)*
Quantum Metals Inc................................. E 513 573-0144
  Lebanon *(G-9784)*
Rm Advisory Group Inc........................... E 513 242-2100
  Cincinnati *(G-3309)*
Slesnick Iron & Metal Co......................... E 330 453-8475
  Canton *(G-1854)*
The David J Joseph Company................. C 513 419-6200
  Cincinnati *(G-3464)*
Unico Alloys & Metals Inc........................ D 614 299-0545
  Columbus *(G-6798)*
United Alloys & Metals Inc....................... E 614 299-0545
  Columbus *(G-6803)*
Willoughby Ir & Waste Mtls LLC.............. B 440 946-8990
  Willoughby *(G-15227)*

SCRAP & WASTE MATERIALS, WHOLESALE: Metal

Diproinduca (usa) Limited LLC................ D 330 722-4442
  Medina *(G-10828)*
G-Cor Automotive Corp........................... E 614 443-6735
  Columbus *(G-5907)*
Geep USA Inc.. E 919 544-1443
  Stow *(G-13369)*
Metalx LLC... D 260 232-3000
  Delta *(G-7852)*

SCRAP & WASTE MATERIALS, WHOLESALE: Nonferrous Metals Scrap

Legend Smelting and Recycl Inc............. D 740 928-0139
  Hebron *(G-9145)*

SCRAP & WASTE MATERIALS, WHOLESALE: Paper

Sims Bros Inc.. D 740 387-9041
  Marion *(G-10454)*

SCRAP STEEL CUTTING

Geneva Liberty Steel Ltd........................ E 330 740-0103
  Youngstown *(G-15620)*
Jck Recycling LLC................................... E 419 698-1153
  Fairlawn *(G-8487)*

SCREW MACHINE PRDTS

NSK Industries Inc................................... D 330 923-4112
  Cuyahoga Falls *(G-7091)*
Qualitor Subsidiary H Inc......................... C 419 562-7987
  Bucyrus *(G-1517)*

SEALANTS

Sika Mbcc US LLC................................... A 216 839-7500
  Beachwood *(G-838)*
Teknol Inc.. D 937 264-0190
  Dayton *(G-7661)*
Tremco Incorporated................................ B
  Beachwood *(G-847)*

SEALING COMPOUNDS: Sealing, synthetic rubber or plastic

Technical Rubber Company Inc.............. C 740 967-9015
  Johnstown *(G-9549)*

SEALS: Hermetic

Aeroseal LLC.. E 937 428-9300
  Dayton *(G-7158)*
Aeroseal LLC.. E 937 428-9300
  Miamisburg *(G-11021)*

SEARCH & NAVIGATION SYSTEMS

Grimes Aerospace Company................... D 937 484-2001
  Urbana *(G-14308)*
Northrop Grmman Tchncal Svcs I........... D 937 320-3100
  Beavercreek Township *(G-945)*

SECURE STORAGE SVC: Household & Furniture

Fox... E 419 352-1673
  Bowling Green *(G-1320)*

SECURITY GUARD SVCS

1st Advnce SEC Invstgtions Inc.............. D 937 210-9010
  Dayton *(G-7123)*
1st Advnce SEC Invstgtions Inc.............. E 937 317-4433
  Dayton *(G-7145)*
1st Choice Security Inc............................ C 513 381-6789
  Cincinnati *(G-2120)*
Allied Security LLC.................................. D 513 771-3776
  Cincinnati *(G-2168)*
American Svcs & Protection LLC............ D 614 884-0177
  Columbus *(G-5362)*
Danson Inc... D 513 948-0066
  Cincinnati *(G-2538)*
Deacon 10 LLC....................................... D 216 731-4000
  Euclid *(G-8340)*
Dunbar Armored Inc................................ E 513 381-8000
  Cincinnati *(G-2585)*
Dunbar Armored Inc................................ D 614 475-1969
  Columbus *(G-5791)*
Extract LLC.. D 937 732-9495
  Dayton *(G-7343)*
Falu Corporation...................................... E 502 641-8106
  Cincinnati *(G-2646)*
Gardaworld Security Corp....................... D 614 963-2098
  Columbus *(G-5912)*
Genric Inc.. B 937 553-9250
  Marysville *(G-10486)*
Home State Protective Svcs LLC............ E 513 253-3095
  Cincinnati *(G-2839)*
Industrial Security Svc Inc....................... E 614 785-7046
  Columbus *(G-6051)*
Industrial Security Svc Inc....................... D 216 898-9970
  Cleveland *(G-4410)*
Job1usa Inc... E 419 255-5005
  Toledo *(G-13868)*
McKeen Security Inc............................... D 740 699-1301
  Saint Clairsville *(G-12802)*
Merchnts SEC Svc Dyton Ohio In........... C 937 256-9373
  Dayton *(G-7480)*
Metropolitan Security Svcs Inc................ C 330 253-6459
  Akron *(G-232)*
Metropolitan Security Svcs Inc................ E 216 298-4076
  Cleveland *(G-4569)*
Midwest Protection Div LLC.................... D 844 844-8200
  Columbus *(G-6246)*
Moonlight Security Inc............................. D 937 252-1600
  Dayton *(G-7512)*
National Alliance SEC Agcy Inc.............. E 866 636-3098
  Vandalia *(G-14385)*
Ohio Support Services Corp.................... E 614 443-0291
  Columbus *(G-6460)*
Patriot Protection Svcs LLC..................... D 614 379-1333
  Columbus *(G-6504)*
Patrol Urban Services LLC...................... E 614 620-4672
  Westerville *(G-15011)*
Professional Security Bur Inc.................. D 330 438-6800
  Canton *(G-1832)*
Rmi International Inc............................... E 937 642-5032
  Marysville *(G-10504)*
Rumpf Corporation.................................. E 419 255-5005
  Toledo *(G-13999)*
Sahara Global Security LLC.................... D 614 448-7940
  Columbus *(G-6635)*
Sam-Tom Inc... E 216 426-7752
  Cleveland *(G-4874)*
Securitas SEC Svcs USA Inc.................. E 440 887-6800
  Cleveland *(G-4889)*
Securitas SEC Svcs USA Inc.................. E 614 871-6051
  Grove City *(G-8953)*
St Moritz Security Svcs Inc..................... D 614 351-8798
  Worthington *(G-15459)*
St Moritz Security Svcs Inc..................... D 330 270-5922
  Youngstown *(G-15729)*
SW Squared LLC..................................... D 614 300-5304
  Columbus *(G-6738)*
Tenable Protective Svcs Inc.................... A 216 361-0002
  Cleveland *(G-4984)*
US Protection Service LLC...................... E 614 794-4950
  Columbus *(G-6837)*
US Security Associates Inc..................... B 937 454-9035
  Cincinnati *(G-3607)*

Employee Codes: A=Over 500 employees, B=251-500
C=101-250, D=51-100, E=20-50, F=10-19, G=1-9

SECURITY GUARD SVCS — SERVICES SECTION

US Security Associates Inc .... A 937 454-9035
 Vandalia *(G-14400)*

Veteran Security Patrol Co .... C 513 381-4482
 Cincinnati *(G-3626)*

Veteran Security Patrol Co .... C 937 222-7333
 Dayton *(G-7704)*

W William Schmidt & Associates .... C 419 526-4747
 Mansfield *(G-10323)*

Whitestone Group Inc .... B 614 501-7007
 Reynoldsburg *(G-12682)*

Whittguard Security Svcs Inc .... C 440 288-7233
 Avon *(G-667)*

Willo Security Inc .... C 614 481-9456
 Columbus *(G-6895)*

Willoughby Services Inc .... D 440 953-9191
 Willoughby *(G-15228)*

SECURITY SYSTEMS SERVICES

Bass Family LLC C
 Bedford Heights *(G-995)*

Bureau Workers Compensation .... D 614 466-5109
 Columbus *(G-5484)*

Electra Sound Inc .... C 216 433-1050
 Cleveland *(G-4208)*

Fe Moran SEC Solutions LLC .... E 217 403-6444
 Uniontown *(G-14251)*

Fellhauer Mechanical Systems .... E 419 734-3674
 Port Clinton *(G-12525)*

Finite State Inc .... D 614 639-5107
 Columbus *(G-5858)*

GA Business Purchaser LLC .... E 419 255-8400
 Toledo *(G-13816)*

Genric Inc .... B 937 553-9250
 Marysville *(G-10486)*

Guardian Protection Svcs Inc .... E 330 797-1570
 Bedford *(G-962)*

Habitec Security Inc .... D 419 537-6768
 Holland *(G-9286)*

Jenne Inc .... C 440 835-0040
 Avon *(G-656)*

Koorsen Fire & Security Inc .... E 513 398-4300
 Blue Ash *(G-1196)*

Koorsen Fire & Security Inc .... E 614 878-2228
 Columbus *(G-6126)*

Northwestern Ohio SEC Systems .... E 419 227-1655
 Lima *(G-9942)*

Ohio Tctcal Enfrcment Svcs LLC .... D 614 989-9485
 Columbus *(G-6462)*

Protegis LLC .... E 216 377-3044
 Independence *(G-9474)*

Safeguard Properties LLC .... A 216 739-2900
 Cleveland *(G-4869)*

Sahara Global Security LLC .... D 614 448-7940
 Columbus *(G-6635)*

Securestate LLC .... E 216 927-0115
 Novelty *(G-12043)*

Sievers Security Systems Inc .... E 216 383-1234
 Cleveland *(G-4906)*

Tacg LLC .... E 937 203-8201
 Beavercreek *(G-931)*

The OGara Group Inc .... D 513 881-9800
 Cincinnati *(G-3467)*

Turnkey Technology LLC .... E 513 725-2177
 Cincinnati *(G-3537)*

Vigilant Defense .... E 513 309-0672
 Liberty Township *(G-9858)*

Wj Service Co Inc .... E 330 372-5040
 Warren *(G-14576)*

Yp LLC .... C 330 896-6000
 Uniontown *(G-14273)*

SELF-PROPELLED AIRCRAFT DEALER

Lane Aviation Corporation .... C 614 237-3747
 Columbus *(G-6138)*

McKinley Air Transport Inc .... E 330 497-6956
 Canton *(G-1802)*

SEMICONDUCTOR CIRCUIT NETWORKS

Micro Industries Corporation .... D 740 548-7878
 Westerville *(G-14999)*

SEMICONDUCTORS & RELATED DEVICES

Pepperl + Fuchs Inc .... C 330 425-3555
 Twinsburg *(G-14210)*

SEPTIC TANK CLEANING SVCS

Wood Investment Property LLC .... E 330 644-5100
 Medina *(G-10905)*

SEPTIC TANKS: Concrete

Encore Precast LLC .... E 513 726-5678
 Seven Mile *(G-12962)*

SERVICE STATION EQPT REPAIR SVCS

Dp Medina Holdings Inc .... E 216 254-7883
 Medina *(G-10832)*

Petro-Com Corp .... E 440 327-6900
 North Ridgeville *(G-11933)*

SEWAGE & WATER TREATMENT EQPT

De Nora Tech LLC .... D 440 710-5334
 Concord Township *(G-6924)*

SHAPES & PILINGS, STRUCTURAL: Steel

Brenmar Construction Inc .... D 740 286-2151
 Jackson *(G-9516)*

SHEET METAL SPECIALTIES, EXC STAMPED

Allied Fabricating & Wldg Co .... E 614 751-6664
 Columbus *(G-5338)*

C & R Inc .... E 614 497-1130
 Groveport *(G-8975)*

Kirk & Blum Manufacturing Co .... C 513 458-2600
 Cincinnati *(G-2942)*

SHIMS: Metal

Ohio Gasket and Shim Co Inc .... E 330 630-0626
 Akron *(G-251)*

SHOE STORES

The Elder-Beerman Stores Corp .... A 937 296-2700
 Moraine *(G-11443)*

SHOE STORES: Men's

Cov-Ro Inc .... E 330 856-3176
 Warren *(G-14515)*

Lehigh Outfitters LLC .... C 740 753-1951
 Nelsonville *(G-11549)*

SHOES: Men's

Acor Orthopaedic LLC .... E 216 662-4500
 Cleveland *(G-3764)*

Georgia-Boot Inc .... D 740 753-1951
 Nelsonville *(G-11545)*

SHOES: Plastic Or Rubber

Georgia-Boot Inc .... D 740 753-1951
 Nelsonville *(G-11545)*

US Footwear Holdings LLC .... C 740 753-9100
 Nelsonville *(G-11550)*

SHOES: Women's

Acor Orthopaedic LLC .... E 216 662-4500
 Cleveland *(G-3764)*

Georgia-Boot Inc .... D 740 753-1951
 Nelsonville *(G-11545)*

SHOPPING CART REPAIR SVCS

Omni Cart Services Inc .... E 440 205-8363
 Mentor *(G-10981)*

SIDING: Plastic

Alside Inc .... D 419 865-0934
 Maumee *(G-10687)*

SIGN PAINTING & LETTERING SHOP

General Theming Contrs LLC .... C 614 252-6342
 Columbus *(G-5925)*

SIGNALS: Traffic Control, Electric

Security Fence Group Inc .... E 513 681-3700
 Cincinnati *(G-3353)*

SIGNS & ADVERTISING SPECIALTIES

A & A Safety Inc .... E 513 943-6100
 Amelia *(G-409)*

Archer Corporation .... E 330 455-9995
 Canton *(G-1670)*

Associated Premium Corporation .... E 513 679-4444
 Cincinnati *(G-2219)*

Bates Metal Products Inc .... D 740 498-8371
 Port Washington *(G-12541)*

Belco Works Inc .... D 740 695-0500
 Saint Clairsville *(G-12774)*

Brown Cnty Bd Mntal Rtardation .... E 937 378-4891
 Georgetown *(G-8798)*

HP Manufacturing Company Inc .... E 216 361-6500
 Cleveland *(G-4386)*

Identitek Systems Inc .... D 330 832-9844
 Massillon *(G-10648)*

Mes Painting and Graphics Ltd .... E 614 496-1696
 Westerville *(G-14998)*

Orange Barrel Media LLC .... D 614 294-4898
 Columbus *(G-6477)*

Sabco Industries Inc .... E 419 531-5347
 Toledo *(G-14002)*

Screen Works Inc .... E 937 264-9111
 Dayton *(G-7613)*

SIGNS, EXC ELECTRIC, WHOLESALE

Dualite Sales & Service Inc .... C 513 724-7100
 Williamsburg *(G-15179)*

SIGNS: Electrical

Brilliant Electric Sign Co Ltd .... D 216 741-3800
 Brooklyn Heights *(G-1413)*

Danite Holdings Ltd .... E 614 444-3333
 Columbus *(G-5740)*

Gus Holthaus Signs Inc .... E 513 861-0060
 Cincinnati *(G-2783)*

United - Maier Signs Inc .... D 513 681-6600
 Cincinnati *(G-3551)*

SILICA MINING

Covia Holdings LLC .... D 800 255-7263
 Independence *(G-9426)*

SILICONES

Hexion Topco LLC .... D 614 225-4000
 Columbus *(G-5990)*

Novagard Solutions Inc .... C 216 881-8111
 Cleveland *(G-4668)*

SERVICES SECTION

SILK SCREEN DESIGN SVCS

Screen Works Inc .... E 937 264-9111
Dayton *(G-7613)*

Woodrow Manufacturing Co .... E 937 399-9333
Springfield *(G-13313)*

SKILL TRAINING CENTER

Ohio Arson School Inc .... E 740 881-4467
Galena *(G-8738)*

SLIPPERS: House

R G Barry Corporation .... A 614 864-6400
Pickerington *(G-12408)*

SOCIAL SVCS CENTER

Access Inc .... E 330 535-2999
Akron *(G-13)*

Achievement Ctrs For Children .... D 440 250-2520
Westlake *(G-15029)*

Aids Tskfrce Grter Clvland Inc .... D 216 357-3131
Cleveland *(G-3776)*

Akron Cmnty Svc Ctr Urban Leag .... E 234 542-4141
Akron *(G-24)*

Akron-Canton Regional Foodbank .... E 330 535-6900
Akron *(G-40)*

Always With US Chrties Awu CHR .... E 800 675-4710
Columbus *(G-5341)*

American National Red Cross .... D 330 535-6131
Akron *(G-46)*

American National Red Cross .... E 330 535-6131
Akron *(G-47)*

American National Red Cross .... E 330 452-1111
Canton *(G-1665)*

American National Red Cross .... E 614 253-2740
Columbus *(G-5355)*

American National Red Cross .... E 614 326-2337
Columbus *(G-5356)*

American National Red Cross .... E 800 448-3543
Columbus *(G-5357)*

American National Red Cross .... E 614 334-0425
Columbus *(G-5358)*

American National Red Cross .... E 614 473-3783
Gahanna *(G-8710)*

American National Red Cross .... E 614 436-3862
Lewis Center *(G-9805)*

American National Red Cross .... E 740 344-2510
Newark *(G-11687)*

American National Red Cross .... E 216 303-5476
Parma *(G-12249)*

American National Red Cross .... C 419 382-2707
Toledo *(G-13684)*

American National Red Cross .... E 800 733-2767
Toledo *(G-13685)*

American National Red Cross .... D 419 329-2900
Toledo *(G-13686)*

American National Red Cross .... E 330 469-6403
Warren *(G-14498)*

American National Red Cross .... E 330 726-6063
Youngstown *(G-15550)*

American Red Cross .... A 513 579-3000
Cincinnati *(G-2186)*

American Red Cross of Grtr Col .... E 614 253-7981
Columbus *(G-5360)*

Ashtabula Cnty Cmnty Action AG .... E 440 997-1721
Ashtabula *(G-519)*

Battered Womens Shelter .... E 330 723-3900
Medina *(G-10814)*

Bridges To Independence Inc .... C 740 362-1996
Delaware *(G-7780)*

Bridgeway Inc .... C 216 688-4114
Cleveland *(G-3892)*

Cancer Family Care Inc .... E 513 731-3346
Cincinnati *(G-2305)*

Catholic Charities Corporation .... D 330 723-9615
Medina *(G-10817)*

Catholic Charities Corporation .... E 216 334-2900
Cleveland *(G-3935)*

Catholic Charities of Southwst .... D 937 325-8715
Springfield *(G-13224)*

Catholic Chrties of Sthwstern .... D 513 241-7745
Cincinnati *(G-2323)*

Catholic Chrties Regional Agcy .... E 330 744-3320
Youngstown *(G-15572)*

Catholic Social Services Inc .... E 614 221-5891
Columbus *(G-5520)*

Central Community Hse Columbus .... E 614 252-3157
Columbus *(G-5534)*

Childrens Hunger Alliance .... E 614 341-7700
Columbus *(G-5564)*

Cincinn-Hmlton Cnty Cmnty Act .... E 513 354-3900
Cincinnati *(G-2435)*

Cincinnt-Hmlton Cnty Cmnty Act .... C 513 569-1840
Cincinnati *(G-2434)*

City of Maple Heights .... E 216 587-5451
Maple Heights *(G-10334)*

Clark Cnty Bd Dvlpmntal Dsblti .... D 937 328-5240
Springfield *(G-13231)*

Cleveland Christian Home Inc .... E 216 671-0977
Cleveland *(G-4006)*

Columbus Urban League .... E 614 257-6300
Columbus *(G-5658)*

Community Action - Wyne/Medina .... D 330 264-8677
Wooster *(G-15325)*

Community Action Comm Blmont C ..... D 740 676-0800
Bellaire *(G-1009)*

Community Action Comm Blmont C ..... E 740 695-0293
Saint Clairsville *(G-12786)*

Community Action Comm Fytte CN ...... D 740 335-7282
Wshngtn Ct Hs *(G-15478)*

Community Action Orgnztion Sco .... C 740 354-7541
Portsmouth *(G-12548)*

Community Action Prgram Comm O ..... D 740 345-8750
Newark *(G-11693)*

Community Action Prgram Comm O ..... D 740 653-1711
Lancaster *(G-9704)*

Community For New Drction Incr .... E 614 272-1464
Columbus *(G-5670)*

Compass Family and Cmnty Svcs .... E 330 743-9275
Youngstown *(G-15583)*

Compdrug .... D 614 224-4506
Columbus *(G-5675)*

Concerned Ctzens Agnst Vlnce A .... E 740 382-8988
Marion *(G-10423)*

Consumer Support Services Inc .... D 216 447-1521
Independence *(G-9423)*

Consumer Support Services Inc .... D 740 522-5464
Newark *(G-11694)*

Consumer Support Services Inc .... D 740 344-3600
Newark *(G-11695)*

Consumer Support Services Inc .... D 440 354-7082
Painesville *(G-12223)*

Corportion For Ohio Applchian .... E 740 594-8499
Athens *(G-562)*

County of Allen .... E 419 228-2120
Lima *(G-9879)*

County of Lorain .... D 440 329-5340
Elyria *(G-8238)*

County of Meigs .... E 740 992-2117
Middleport *(G-11147)*

Creative Foundations Inc .... E 877 345-6793
Delaware *(G-7790)*

Dan Sechkar Sech Kar C .... E 740 753-9955
Nelsonville *(G-11541)*

SOCIAL SVCS CENTER

Daybreak Inc .... E 937 395-4600
Dayton *(G-7269)*

Directions For Youth Families .... E 614 694-0203
Columbus *(G-5768)*

Directions For Youth Families .... E 614 294-2661
Columbus *(G-5769)*

Easter Seals Tristate LLC .... D 513 281-2316
Cincinnati *(G-2600)*

Eastersals Cntl Southeast Ohio .... C 614 228-5523
Hilliard *(G-9193)*

Epilepsy Ctr of Nrthwstern Ohi .... E 419 867-5950
Maumee *(G-10722)*

Faith Mission Inc .... D 614 224-6617
Columbus *(G-5848)*

Family Service Association .... E 937 222-9481
Moraine *(G-11408)*

Family Service of NW Ohio .... D 419 321-6455
Toledo *(G-13803)*

Family Vlnce Prvntion Ctr Gren .... E 937 372-4552
Xenia *(G-15506)*

Foodbank Inc .... E 937 461-0265
Dayton *(G-7360)*

Free Store/Food Bank Inc .... E 513 482-4526
Cincinnati *(G-2704)*

Freestore Foodbank Inc .... E 513 482-4500
Cincinnati *(G-2706)*

Friendly Inn Settlement Inc .... E 216 431-7656
Cleveland *(G-4290)*

Front Steps Housing & Svcs Inc .... E 216 781-2250
Cleveland *(G-4293)*

G M N Tri Cnty Cmnty Action CM .... E 740 732-2388
Caldwell *(G-1549)*

Goodwill Ester Seals Miami Vly .... C 937 461-4800
Dayton *(G-7379)*

Great Lkes Cmnty Action Partnr .... E 419 729-8035
Toledo *(G-13828)*

Greene County Council On Aging .... E 937 374-5600
Xenia *(G-15516)*

Handson Central Ohio Inc .... E 614 221-2255
Columbus *(G-5969)*

Harcatus Tr-Cnty Cmnty Action .... E 740 922-3600
Dennison *(G-7857)*

Harcatus Tr-Cnty Cmnty Action .... E 740 922-0933
Dover *(G-7887)*

Helpline Del Mrrow Cunties Inc .... E 740 369-3316
Delaware *(G-7803)*

Highland Cnty Cmnty Action Org .... E 937 393-3060
Hillsboro *(G-9255)*

Hockingthensperry Cmnty Action .... E 740 385-6813
Logan *(G-10024)*

Hockins Athens Prry Cmnty Acti .... C 740 753-3062
Nelsonville *(G-11547)*

Hockins Athens Prry Cmnty Acti .... E 740 385-3644
Athens *(G-573)*

Homeless Families Foundation .... D 614 461-9247
Columbus *(G-6002)*

Impact Community Action .... D 614 252-2799
Columbus *(G-6042)*

Inside Out .... E 937 525-7880
Springfield *(G-13259)*

Jewish Family Service .... C 614 231-1890
Columbus *(G-6089)*

Jewish Fmly Svc Assn Clvland O .... B 216 292-3999
Beachwood *(G-805)*

Jewish Fmly Svc Assn Clvland O .... E 216 292-3999
Beachwood *(G-804)*

Jewish Fmly Svc of Cncnnati AR .... E 513 469-1188
Cincinnati *(G-2906)*

Leeda Services Inc .... C 330 325-1560
Rootstown *(G-12761)*

Long Term Care Ombudsman .... E 216 696-2719
Cleveland *(G-4505)*

Employee Codes: A=Over 500 employees, B=251-500
C=101-250, D=51-100, E=20-50, F=10-19, G=1-9

SOCIAL SVCS CENTER

Lutheran Scial Svcs Centl Ohio............... E 419 289-3523
  Worthington *(G-15434)*
Marion Cnty Bd Dev Dsabilities............... D 740 387-1035
  Marion *(G-10437)*
Mentor REM... A 216 642-5339
  Cleveland *(G-4552)*
Near W Side Multi-Service Corp............. D 216 631-5800
  Cleveland *(G-4632)*
Nick Amster Inc.................................... D 330 264-9667
  Wooster *(G-15360)*
Nueva Luz Urban Resource Ctr............. E 216 651-8236
  Cleveland *(G-4673)*
Ocali... E 614 410-0321
  Columbus *(G-6382)*
Ohio Assn Cnty Brds Srving Ppl............. E 614 431-0616
  Worthington *(G-15443)*
Ohio Association of Foodbanks............. D 614 221-4336
  Columbus *(G-6392)*
Ohio Dept Job & Fmly Svcs................... E 740 295-7516
  Coshocton *(G-6995)*
Ohio Dept Rhbilitation Corectn.............. E 419 782-3385
  Defiance *(G-7759)*
Ohioguidestone..................................... B 440 260-8900
  Cleveland *(G-4693)*
Pathway Inc.. E 419 242-7304
  Toledo *(G-13961)*
Pathways of Central Ohio...................... E 740 345-6166
  Newark *(G-11740)*
Personal Fmly Cnsling Svcs of.............. E 330 343-8171
  New Philadelphia *(G-11661)*
Pickaway Cnty Cmnty Action Org........... E 740 477-1655
  Circleville *(G-3716)*
Prokids... E 513 281-2000
  Cincinnati *(G-3249)*
Ronald McDnald Hse Chrties CNT......... E 614 227-3700
  Columbus *(G-6609)*
Ronald McDnald Hse Chrties Grt........... E 513 636-7642
  Cincinnati *(G-3319)*
Ronald McDnald Hse Chrties NW.......... E 419 471-4663
  Toledo *(G-13998)*
Royal Rdmer Lthran Ch N Rylton........... E 440 237-7958
  North Royalton *(G-11949)*
Second Hrvest Fdbank of Mhning......... E 330 792-5522
  Youngstown *(G-15718)*
St Vincent Family Services................... C 614 252-0731
  Columbus *(G-6707)*
The East Toledo Family Ctr Inc............. E 419 691-1429
  Toledo *(G-14040)*
Towards Employment Inc...................... E 216 696-5750
  Cleveland *(G-5025)*
Townhall 2... E 330 678-3006
  Kent *(G-9603)*
United Crbral Plsy Assn Grter............... E 216 351-4888
  Cleveland *(G-5059)*
United Way Central Ohio Inc................. D 614 227-2700
  Columbus *(G-6819)*
United Way Greater Cincinnati............... D 513 762-7100
  Cincinnati *(G-3558)*
United Way Grter Stark Cnty In.............. E 330 491-0445
  Canton *(G-1875)*
United Way of Greater Toledo................ E 419 254-4742
  Toledo *(G-14084)*
United Way of Lake County Inc............. E 440 639-4420
  Mentor *(G-11006)*
United Way of Yngstown The Mhn.......... E 330 746-8494
  Youngstown *(G-15744)*
United Way Summit and Medina............ D 330 762-7601
  Akron *(G-342)*
University Settlement Inc...................... E 216 641-8948
  Cleveland *(G-5086)*
Urban Leag Grter Sthwstern Ohi........... D 513 281-9955
  Cincinnati *(G-3600)*

Victim Assistance Program Inc.............. E 330 376-7022
  Akron *(G-351)*
Volunteers America Ohio & Ind.............. C 614 253-6100
  Columbus *(G-6856)*
Volunteers of America Inc..................... C 513 420-1887
  Middletown *(G-11192)*
Volunters Amer Care Facilities.............. C 419 334-9521
  Fremont *(G-8707)*
West Ohio Cmnty Action Partnr............. E 419 227-2586
  Lima *(G-9985)*
West Side Community House................ E 216 771-7297
  Cleveland *(G-5133)*
Westcare Ohio Inc................................ E 937 259-1898
  Dayton *(G-7718)*
Youngstown Area Jwish Fdration........... C 330 746-3251
  Youngstown *(G-15756)*
Youngstown Nghborhood Dev Corp...... E 330 480-0423
  Youngstown *(G-15759)*

SOFTWARE PUBLISHERS: Home Entertainment

Cerner Corporation............................... D 740 826-7678
  New Concord *(G-11609)*

SOFTWARE TRAINING, COMPUTER

Critical Business Analysis Inc.............. E 419 874-0800
  Perrysburg *(G-12326)*

SOUND EFFECTS & MUSIC PRODUCTION: Motion Picture

Live Technologies LLC......................... D 614 278-7777
  Columbus *(G-6171)*

SPAS

Jbentley Studio & Spa LLC................... D 614 790-8828
  Powell *(G-12593)*
Mitchells Salon & Day Spa Inc.............. D 513 793-0900
  Cincinnati *(G-3067)*
Paragon Salons Inc.............................. E 513 574-7610
  Cincinnati *(G-3182)*
Sacred Hour Inc................................... D 216 228-9750
  Lakewood *(G-9684)*
Spa Fitness Centers Inc....................... E 419 476-6018
  Toledo *(G-14019)*
Vio Med Spa Strongsville LLC............... D 440 268-6100
  Strongsville *(G-13495)*

SPECIALIZED LEGAL SVCS

Garden City Group LLC....................... C 631 470-5000
  Dublin *(G-8019)*

SPECIALIZED LIBRARIES

Western Reserve Historical Soc............ D 216 721-5722
  Cleveland *(G-5136)*

SPECIALTY FOOD STORES: Juices, Fruit Or Vegetable

M & M Wine Cellar Inc.......................... E 330 536-6450
  Lowellville *(G-10170)*

SPECIALTY FOOD STORES: Vitamin

Second Wind Vitamins Inc.................... E 330 336-9260
  Wadsworth *(G-14451)*

SPECIALTY OUTPATIENT CLINICS, NEC

American Kidney Stone MGT Ltd........... E 800 637-5188
  Columbus *(G-5352)*
Appleseed Cmnty Mntal Hlth Ctr........... D 419 281-3716
  Ashland *(G-472)*

SERVICES SECTION

Aultman North Canton Med Group........ E 330 363-6333
  Canton *(G-1682)*
Best Care Nrsing Rhblttion Ctr............. A 740 574-2558
  Wheelersburg *(G-15127)*
Bridgeway Inc....................................... C 216 688-4114
  Cleveland *(G-3892)*
Caprice Health Care Inc....................... E 330 965-9200
  North Lima *(G-11885)*
Center For Addiction Treatment............ D 513 381-6672
  Cincinnati *(G-2332)*
Central Cmnty Hlth Bd Hmlton C........... E 513 559-2000
  Cincinnati *(G-2335)*
CHI Health At Home.............................. E 513 576-0262
  Milford *(G-11221)*
Childrens Hospital Medical Ctr............. B 513 636-6100
  Cincinnati *(G-2367)*
Childrens Hospital Medical Ctr............. B 513 636-6800
  Mason *(G-10529)*
Cleveland Clinic Foundation................. E 440 988-5651
  Lorain *(G-10065)*
Cleveland Clinic Mercy Hosp................ B 330 627-7641
  Carrollton *(G-1904)*
Cleveland Clnic Hlth Systm-AST........... E 330 468-0190
  Northfield *(G-11954)*
Cleveland Clnic Hlth Systm-AST........... D 330 287-4830
  Wooster *(G-15324)*
Community Cnsling Wllness Ctrs.......... E 740 387-5210
  Marion *(G-10422)*
Community Mental Health Svc.............. D 740 695-9344
  Saint Clairsville *(G-12787)*
Comprhnsive Addction Svc Syste........ D 419 241-8827
  Toledo *(G-13755)*
Crossroads Center............................... C 513 475-5300
  Cincinnati *(G-2517)*
Fort Hamilton Hospital.......................... B 513 867-2280
  Hamilton *(G-9043)*
Healthsource of Ohio Inc..................... E 513 753-2820
  Cincinnati *(G-2812)*
Healthsource of Ohio Inc..................... E 513 575-1444
  Loveland *(G-10140)*
Healthsource of Ohio Inc..................... E 937 386-0049
  Seaman *(G-12944)*
Healthsource of Ohio Inc..................... E 513 576-7700
  Loveland *(G-10141)*
Mahoning Vly Hmtlogy Onclogy A........ E 330 318-1100
  Youngstown *(G-15659)*
Mayfield Spine Surgery Ctr LLC........... D 513 619-5899
  Cincinnati *(G-3021)*
McKinley Hall Inc.................................. E 937 328-5300
  Springfield *(G-13266)*
Medcentral Health System.................... C 419 526-8442
  Mansfield *(G-10292)*
Metrohealth System.............................. C 216 957-5000
  Cleveland *(G-4564)*
Nationwide Childrens Hospital............. C 614 355-7000
  Dublin *(G-8070)*
Ncs Healthcare Inc............................... A 216 514-3350
  Cleveland *(G-4630)*
Neighbrhood Hlth Assn Tledo In........... E 419 720-7883
  Toledo *(G-13932)*
North East Ohio Health Svcs................ D 216 831-6466
  Beachwood *(G-821)*
Oak Clinic... E 330 896-9625
  Uniontown *(G-14261)*
Ohio Heart Institute Inc........................ E 330 747-6446
  Youngstown *(G-15681)*
Osu Harding Hospital........................... A 614 293-9600
  Columbus *(G-6483)*
Pain Management Associates Inc........ B 937 252-2000
  Dayton *(G-7138)*
Positive Education Program................. E 440 471-8200
  Cleveland *(G-4763)*

SERVICES SECTION — SUBSTANCE ABUSE COUNSELING

Rescue Incorporated.................................C..... 419 255-9585
  Toledo (G-13988)
Robinson Health System Inc....................A..... 330 678-4100
  Kent (G-9597)
St Vincent Family Services......................C..... 614 252-0731
  Columbus (G-6707)
Tcn Behavioral Health Svcs Inc...............C..... 937 376-8700
  Xenia (G-15532)
Tuscarwas Ambltory Srgery Ctr...............D..... 330 365-2101
  Dover (G-7904)
Univ Dermatology......................................E..... 513 475-7630
  Cincinnati (G-3559)
University Mednet.....................................C..... 440 255-0800
  Mentor (G-11008)
University of Cincinnati............................E..... 513 584-3200
  Cincinnati (G-3594)
University Radiology Assoc.....................D..... 513 475-8760
  Cincinnati (G-3596)
Wendt-Bristol Health Services................C..... 614 403-9966
  Columbus (G-6876)
Wood County Chld Svcs Assn.................E..... 419 352-7588
  Bowling Green (G-1335)

SPORTING & ATHLETIC GOODS: Water Sports Eqpt

Litehouse Products LLC...........................E..... 440 638-2350
  Strongsville (G-13471)

SPORTING & RECREATIONAL GOODS, WHOLESALE: Boat Access & Part

Atwood Rope Manufacturing Inc.............E..... 614 920-0534
  Canal Winchester (G-1598)
Miami Corporation.....................................E..... 800 543-0448
  Cincinnati (G-3054)

SPORTING CAMPS

Stars Yuth Enrchment Prgram In............E..... 513 978-7735
  Trotwood (G-14128)

SPORTING FIREARMS WHOLESALERS

Aspc Corp..C..... 937 593-7010
  Bellefontaine (G-1019)

SPORTING GOODS

Jack Entertainment LLC...........................D..... 313 309-5225
  Cleveland (G-4430)

SPORTING GOODS STORES: Hunting Eqpt

Kames Inc..E..... 330 499-4558
  Canton (G-1789)

SPORTING GOODS STORES: Specialty Sport Splys, NEC

Capitol Varsity Sports Inc........................E..... 513 523-4126
  Oxford (G-12204)
Hof Fitness Center Inc.............................D..... 330 455-0555
  Canton (G-1773)

SPORTS APPAREL STORES

Gymnastics World Inc..............................E..... 440 526-2970
  Cleveland (G-4343)
Lululemon USA Inc...................................C..... 614 418-9127
  Columbus (G-6177)

SPORTS CLUBS, MANAGERS & PROMOTERS

Brimstone & Fire LLC..............................E..... 937 776-5182
  Wilmington (G-15247)
Cincinnati Cyclones LLC.........................E..... 513 421-7825
  Cincinnati (G-2407)

Crew SC Team Company LLC................D..... 614 447-2739
  Columbus (G-5727)

SPRINGS: Steel

Hendrickson International Corp...............D..... 740 929-5600
  Hebron (G-9143)

SPRINGS: Wire

Barnes Group Inc.....................................C..... 419 891-9292
  Maumee (G-10698)

STAINLESS STEEL

Latrobe Spcialty Mtls Dist Inc..................D..... 330 609-5137
  Vienna (G-14420)
Shaq Inc..D..... 770 427-0402
  Beachwood (G-836)

STAMPINGS: Automotive

Falls Stamping & Welding Co..................C..... 330 928-1191
  Cuyahoga Falls (G-7075)
Honda Dev & Mfg Amer LLC....................C..... 937 644-0724
  Marysville (G-10488)
R K Industries Inc.....................................D..... 419 523-5001
  Ottawa (G-12195)

STAMPINGS: Metal

R L Morrissey & Assoc Inc......................E..... 440 498-3730
  Solon (G-13135)

STATIONERY & OFFICE SPLYS WHOLESALERS

12985 Snow Holdings Inc.........................E..... 216 267-5000
  Cleveland (G-3739)
AW Faber-Castell Usa Inc........................D..... 216 643-4660
  Independence (G-9408)
Friends Service Co Inc............................D..... 419 427-1704
  Findlay (G-8534)
Lake Business Products Inc....................C..... 440 953-1199
  Highland Heights (G-9168)
Pfg Ventures LP..D..... 216 520-8400
  Independence (G-9466)
Proforma Inc..C..... 800 825-1525
  Independence (G-9472)
Queen City Reprographics Inc................E..... 513 326-2300
  Cincinnati (G-3266)
Quick Tab II Inc...D..... 419 448-6622
  Tiffin (G-13639)
Staples Contract & Coml LLC..................E..... 740 845-5600
  London (G-10051)
W B Mason Co Inc....................................E..... 216 267-5000
  North Olmsted (G-11918)
Westrock Commercial LLC......................D..... 419 476-9101
  Toledo (G-14106)

STEEL, COLD-ROLLED: Flat Bright, From Purchased HotRolled

Geneva Liberty Steel Ltd.........................E..... 330 740-0103
  Youngstown (G-15620)

STEEL, HOT-ROLLED: Sheet Or Strip

Ohio Steel Sheet and Plate Inc...............E..... 800 827-2401
  Hubbard (G-9322)

STONE: Quarrying & Processing, Own Stone Prdts

Beazer East Inc..E..... 937 364-2311
  Hillsboro (G-9249)

STONEWARE PRDTS: Pottery

Clay Burley Products Co..........................E..... 740 452-3633
  Roseville (G-12763)

STORE FIXTURES: Wood

CIP International Inc.................................D..... 513 874-9925
  West Chester (G-14666)

STORES: Auto & Home Supply

Abraham Ford LLC....................................E..... 440 233-7402
  Elyria (G-8232)
Albert Mike Leasing..................................C..... 513 563-1400
  Cincinnati (G-2158)
Beechmont Ford Inc.................................C..... 513 752-6611
  Cincinnati (G-2098)
Brown Motor Sales Co..............................E..... 419 531-0151
  Toledo (G-13720)
Chesrown Oldsmobile GMC Inc..............E..... 614 846-3040
  Columbus (G-5554)
Coughlin Chevrolet Inc.............................D..... 740 964-9191
  Pataskala (G-12271)
Coughlin Chevrolet Toyota Inc................D..... 740 366-1381
  Newark (G-11696)
Cronin Auto Inc...C..... 419 874-4331
  Perrysburg (G-12327)
Dave Knapp Ford Lincoln Inc..................E..... 937 547-3000
  Greenville (G-8869)
Haydocy Automotive Inc..........................D..... 614 279-8880
  Columbus (G-5973)
Jerry Haag Motors Inc..............................E..... 937 402-2090
  Hillsboro (G-9261)
Kerry Ford Inc...D..... 513 671-6400
  Cincinnati (G-2939)
Keystone Auto Glass Inc.........................D..... 419 509-0497
  Maumee (G-10736)
KOI Enterprises Inc..................................D..... 513 357-2400
  Cincinnati (G-2948)
Leikin Motor Companies Inc...................D..... 440 946-6900
  Willoughby (G-15204)
Matia Motors Inc.......................................E..... 440 365-7311
  Elyria (G-8273)
Ron Marhofer Auto Family.......................E..... 330 940-4422
  Cuyahoga Falls (G-7098)
Rush Truck Centers Ohio Inc..................E..... 513 733-8500
  Cincinnati (G-3334)
Rush Truck Leasing Inc...........................E..... 937 264-2365
  Dayton (G-7599)
Rush Truck Leasing Inc...........................E..... 419 224-6045
  Lima (G-9957)
Rush Truck Leasing Inc...........................E..... 330 798-0600
  Walton Hills (G-14479)
Sonic Automotive.....................................D..... 614 870-8200
  Columbus (G-6692)
Sunnyside Cars Inc..................................E..... 440 777-9911
  North Olmsted (G-11917)
Tansky Motors Inc....................................E..... 650 322-7069
  Rockbridge (G-12736)
Walker Auto Group Inc............................D..... 937 433-4950
  Miamisburg (G-11103)

STUDS & JOISTS: Sheet Metal

Clarkwstern Dtrich Bldg System.............C..... 513 870-1100
  West Chester (G-14671)

SUBSCRIPTION FULFILLMENT SVCS: Magazine, Newspaper, Etc

Inquiry Systems Inc..................................E..... 614 464-3800
  Columbus (G-6055)
Kable News Company Inc.......................C..... 815 734-4151
  West Chester (G-14716)

SUBSTANCE ABUSE COUNSELING

SUBSTANCE ABUSE COUNSELING

Alterntive Rsrces Homecare Inc............ D 216 256-3049
  Shaker Heights *(G-12973)*

Community Drug Board Inc................. D 330 315-5590
  Akron *(G-116)*

Oriana House Inc............................... B 330 374-9610
  Akron *(G-256)*

Oriana House Inc............................... E 216 881-7882
  Burton *(G-1532)*

Quest Recovery Prevention Svcs........... C 330 453-8252
  Canton *(G-1837)*

Talbert House..................................... E 513 541-1184
  Cincinnati *(G-3435)*

Talbert House..................................... D 513 933-9304
  Lebanon *(G-9792)*

SUMMER CAMPS, EXC DAY & SPORTS INSTRUCTIONAL

Ashland Training Center..................... E 419 281-2767
  Ashland *(G-476)*

Camp Patmos Inc............................... E 419 746-2214
  Kelleys Island *(G-9552)*

Young MNS Chrstn Assn Grter Dy........ C 513 932-3756
  Oregonia *(G-12150)*

SURGICAL APPLIANCES & SPLYS

Cardinal Health Inc............................. A 614 757-5000
  Dublin *(G-7950)*

Dentronix Inc..................................... D 330 916-7300
  Cuyahoga Falls *(G-7070)*

Jones Metal Products Company............ E 740 545-6341
  West Lafayette *(G-14857)*

Philips Med Systems Clvland In............ B 440 483-3000
  Cleveland *(G-4746)*

SURGICAL INSTRUMENT REPAIR SVCS

McJ Holdings Inc................................ C 937 592-5025
  Columbus *(G-6216)*

SUSPENSION SYSTEMS: Acoustical, Metal

Kinetics Noise Control Inc.................... C 614 889-0480
  Dublin *(G-8049)*

SVC ESTABLISHMENT EQPT, WHOLESALE: Firefighting Eqpt

A-1 Sprinkler Company Inc.................. D 937 859-6198
  Miamisburg *(G-11019)*

Action Coupling & Eqp Inc................... D 330 279-4242
  Holmesville *(G-9316)*

Brakefire Incorporated......................... E 330 535-4343
  Akron *(G-73)*

Brakefire Incorporated......................... D 513 733-5655
  Cincinnati *(G-2276)*

Fox International Limited Inc............... C 216 454-1001
  Beachwood *(G-793)*

Sutphen Corporation........................... C 800 726-7030
  Dublin *(G-8136)*

SVC ESTABLISHMENT EQPT, WHOLESALE: Laundry Eqpt & Splys

Laughlin Music & Vending Svc.............. E 740 593-7778
  Athens *(G-580)*

SVC ESTABLISHMENT EQPT, WHOLESALE: Restaurant Splys

Commercial Parts & Ser....................... D 614 221-0057
  Columbus *(G-5666)*

Martin-Brower Company LLC.............. C 513 773-2301
  West Chester *(G-14729)*

Rdp Foodservice Ltd........................... D 614 261-5661
  Hilliard *(G-9228)*

Wasserstrom Company........................ B 614 228-6525
  Columbus *(G-6867)*

SVC ESTABLISHMENT EQPT, WHOLESALE: Vending Machines & Splys

Vendors Exchange International Inc....... D 216 432-1800
  Cleveland *(G-5098)*

SWIMMING POOL & HOT TUB CLEANING & MAINTENANCE SVCS

Buckeye Pools Inc............................... E 937 434-7916
  Dayton *(G-7203)*

Hastings Water Works Inc.................... E 440 832-7700
  Brecksville *(G-1353)*

Metropolitan Pool Service Co................ E 216 741-9451
  Parma *(G-12257)*

SWIMMING POOLS, EQPT & SPLYS: Wholesalers

Competitor Swim Products Inc.............. D 800 888-7946
  Columbus *(G-5676)*

Heritage Pool Supply Group Inc............ D 440 238-2100
  Strongsville *(G-13460)*

Litehouse Products LLC........................ E 440 638-2350
  Strongsville *(G-13471)*

Metropolitan Pool Service Co................ E 216 741-9451
  Parma *(G-12257)*

Mke Holdings Inc................................ E 440 238-2100
  Strongsville *(G-13476)*

SWITCHGEAR & SWITCHBOARD APPARATUS

General Electric Company.................... E 216 883-1000
  Cleveland *(G-4310)*

Schneider Electric Usa Inc.................... D 513 777-4445
  West Chester *(G-14761)*

SYRUPS, DRINK

Central Coca-Cola Btlg Co Inc............... C 419 476-6622
  Toledo *(G-13727)*

SYSTEMS ENGINEERING: Computer Related

Belcan Corporation............................. E 513 891-0972
  Blue Ash *(G-1134)*

Devcare Solutions Ltd......................... E 614 221-2277
  Westerville *(G-14888)*

Freedom Usa Inc................................. E 216 503-6374
  Twinsburg *(G-14192)*

Leidos Inc.. D 937 656-8433
  Beavercreek *(G-886)*

Tangram Flex Inc................................ E 937 985-3199
  Dayton *(G-7659)*

Ventech Solutions Inc.......................... D 614 757-1167
  Columbus *(G-5284)*

SYSTEMS INTEGRATION SVCS

Advanced Prgrm Resources Inc............. E 614 761-9994
  Dublin *(G-7920)*

Alta It Services LLC............................ C 813 999-3101
  Cincinnati *(G-2173)*

Altamira Technologies Corp.................. C 937 490-4804
  Beavercreek *(G-856)*

Ats Carolina Inc.................................. C 803 324-9300
  Lewis Center *(G-9807)*

Carolinas It LLC................................. D 919 856-2300
  Dublin *(G-7959)*

Cohesion Corporation.......................... C 813 999-3101
  Cincinnati *(G-2469)*

Commercial Time Sharing Inc............... E 330 644-3059
  Akron *(G-115)*

SERVICES SECTION

Commsys Inc...................................... E 937 220-4990
  Dayton *(G-7241)*

Creative Microsystems Inc.................... D 937 836-4499
  Englewood *(G-8304)*

Data Processing Sciences Corporation... D 513 791-7100
  Cincinnati *(G-2539)*

E-Merging Technologies Group Inc........ D 440 779-5680
  Cleveland *(G-4194)*

Eosys Group Inc.................................. E 513 217-7294
  Middletown *(G-11163)*

Kc Robotics Inc................................... E 513 860-4442
  West Chester *(G-14717)*

Lucrum Incorporated........................... E 513 241-5949
  Cincinnati *(G-2993)*

Millenium Control Systems LLC........... E 440 510-0050
  Eastlake *(G-8205)*

Sterling Buying Group LLC.................. E 513 564-9000
  Cincinnati *(G-3416)*

Systemax Manufacturing Inc................. D 937 368-2300
  Dayton *(G-7658)*

SYSTEMS INTEGRATION SVCS: Local Area Network

Dedicated Tech Services Inc................. E 614 309-0059
  Dublin *(G-7986)*

K&R Network Solutions........................ E 858 292-5766
  Dublin *(G-8044)*

Manifest Solutions Corp....................... D 614 930-2800
  Upper Arlington *(G-14280)*

United Technical Support Svcs.............. C 330 562-3330
  Streetsboro *(G-13433)*

SYSTEMS SOFTWARE DEVELOPMENT SVCS

Blue Creek Enterprises Inc.................... E 937 364-2920
  Lynchburg *(G-10183)*

Brandmuscle Inc.................................. C 216 464-4342
  Cleveland *(G-3890)*

Cincinnati Bell Inc............................... B 513 397-9900
  Cincinnati *(G-2398)*

Deemsys Inc....................................... D 614 322-9928
  Gahanna *(G-8715)*

Dewesoft LLC..................................... D 855 339-3669
  Whitehouse *(G-15140)*

Drb Holdings LLC............................... B 330 645-3299
  Akron *(G-138)*

Drb Systems LLC................................ B 330 645-3299
  Akron *(G-139)*

Easy2 Technologies Inc........................ E 216 479-0482
  Cleveland *(G-4200)*

Humanit Solutions LLC........................ D 937 901-7576
  Beavercreek Township *(G-941)*

ID Networks Inc.................................. E 440 992-0062
  Ashtabula *(G-538)*

Mid-America Consulting Group Inc........ D
  Cleveland *(G-4574)*

Pinnacle Data Systems Inc.................... C 614 748-1150
  Groveport *(G-8995)*

Rockwell Automation Ohio LLC............ D 513 576-6151
  Milford *(G-11254)*

Sterling Commerce (america) LLC......... A 614 793-7000
  Dublin *(G-8125)*

Talx Corporation................................. D 614 527-9404
  Hilliard *(G-9235)*

TABULATING SVCS

Personalized Data Corporation.............. E 216 289-2200
  Cleveland *(G-4743)*

TANK REPAIR & CLEANING SVCS

SERVICES SECTION

TEMPORARY HELP SVCS

American Suncraft Co Inc...................... E 937 849-9475
  Medway (G-10907)

Amko Service Company....................... E 330 364-8857
  Midvale (G-11203)

Sabco Industries Inc.............................. E 419 531-5347
  Toledo (G-14002)

TANK REPAIR SVCS

C H Bradshaw Co.................................. E 614 871-2087
  Grove City (G-8904)

Corrotec Inc.. E 937 325-3585
  Springfield (G-13242)

TANK TOWERS: Metal Plate

Complete Mechanical Svcs LLC............ D 513 489-3080
  Blue Ash (G-1158)

TANKS & OTHER TRACKED VEHICLE CMPNTS

Integris Composites Inc......................... D 740 928-0326
  Hebron (G-9144)

TANKS: Cryogenic, Metal

Amko Service Company....................... E 330 364-8857
  Midvale (G-11203)

Eleet Cryogenics Inc............................. E 330 874-4009
  Bolivar (G-1294)

TANKS: Fuel, Including Oil & Gas, Metal Plate

Stanwade Metal Products Inc................ E 330 772-2421
  Hartford (G-9123)

TANKS: Lined, Metal

Modern Welding Co Ohio Inc................. E 740 344-9425
  Newark (G-11731)

TANKS: Standard Or Custom Fabricated, Metal Plate

Enerfab LLC... B 513 641-0500
  Cincinnati (G-2620)

Gaspar Inc.. D 330 477-2222
  Canton (G-1759)

S-P Company Inc................................... D 330 782-5651
  Columbiana (G-5240)

TAPES: Pressure Sensitive

TPC Packaging Solutions Inc................ D 513 489-8840
  Cincinnati (G-3499)

TAPES: Pressure Sensitive, Rubber

Beiersdorf Inc... C 513 682-7300
  West Chester (G-14800)

TARPAULINS, WHOLESALE

Aero Industries Inc................................. D 330 626-3246
  Kent (G-9555)

TECHNICAL MANUAL PREPARATION SVCS

ONeil & Associates Inc.......................... C 937 865-0800
  Miamisburg (G-11079)

TELECOMMUNICATION EQPT REPAIR SVCS, EXC TELEPHONES

Cbst Acquisition LLC............................. D 513 361-9600
  Cincinnati (G-2326)

Vertiv Energy Systems Inc..................... A 440 288-1122
  Lorain (G-10107)

TELECONFERENCING SVCS

Brand Protect Plus LLC......................... E 216 539-1880
  Beachwood (G-770)

TELEPHONE ANSWERING SVCS

Accucall LLC.. E 440 522-8681
  Elyria (G-8233)

Answernet Inc... E 978 710-5856
  Akron (G-51)

Answernet Inc... E 877 864-2251
  Akron (G-52)

C M R Inc.. E 614 447-7100
  Columbus (G-5489)

TELEPHONE EQPT: NEC

Commercial Electric Pdts Corp.............. E 216 241-2886
  Cleveland (G-4094)

TELEPHONE SVCS

Continntal Mssage Solution Inc.............. D 614 224-4534
  Columbus (G-5699)

Infotelecom LLC.................................... B 216 373-4600
  Cleveland (G-4412)

McCracken Group Inc............................ E 513 697-2000
  Cincinnati (G-3022)

Republic Telcom Worldwide LLC........... D 330 244-8285
  North Canton (G-11858)

Republic Telcom Worldwide LLC........... C 330 966-4586
  Canton (G-1845)

TELEVISION BROADCASTING STATIONS

Ai-Media Inc... E 213 337-8552
  Youngstown (G-15544)

Barrington Toledo LLC........................... E 419 535-0024
  Toledo (G-13699)

Fox Sports Net Ohio LLC...................... D 216 415-3300
  Cleveland (G-4280)

Fox Television Stations Inc.................... C 216 431-8888
  Cleveland (G-4281)

Gray Media Group Inc........................... D 513 421-1919
  Cincinnati (G-2752)

Gray Media Group Inc........................... D 216 367-7300
  Cleveland (G-4327)

Greater Cncnnati TV Edctl Fndt............. D 513 381-4033
  Cincinnati (G-2773)

Greater Dayton Public TV Inc................ D 937 220-1600
  Dayton (G-7384)

Ion Media Stations Inc........................... B 561 659-4122
  Cincinnati (G-2886)

Johnny Appleseed Brdcstg Co.............. E 419 529-5900
  Ontario (G-12109)

Lima Communications Corp.................. D 419 228-8835
  Lima (G-9921)

Marquee Broadcasting Ohio Inc............ E 740 452-5431
  Zanesville (G-15810)

Miami Valley Broadcasting Corp............ C 937 259-2111
  Dayton (G-7486)

New World Communications of............. C 216 432-4041
  Cleveland (G-4639)

Nexstar Broadcasting Inc....................... C 614 263-4444
  Columbus (G-6354)

Northastern Eductl TV Ohio Inc............. E 330 677-4549
  Kent (G-9589)

Ohio/Oklahoma Hearst TV Inc............... D 513 412-5000
  Cincinnati (G-3152)

Outlet Broadcasting Inc......................... C 614 263-4444
  Columbus (G-6493)

Public Brdcstg Fndtion of NW O............ D 419 380-4600
  Toledo (G-13980)

Scripps Media Inc.................................. D 513 977-3000
  Cincinnati (G-3351)

Sinclair Media II Inc............................... C 614 481-6666
  Columbus (G-6684)

Tegna Inc.. C 419 248-1111
  Toledo (G-14035)

W GTE TV 30 FM 91 Pub Brdcstg......... D 419 380-4600
  Toledo (G-14095)

W Tov Tv9... E 740 282-9999
  Steubenville (G-13351)

Wbns TV Inc... C 614 460-3700
  Columbus (G-6872)

Wfmj Television Inc................................ C 330 744-8611
  Youngstown (G-15753)

Wfts... D 513 721-9900
  Cincinnati (G-3667)

Wfts... D 216 431-5555
  Cleveland (G-5144)

Winston Brdcstg Netwrk Inc................... C 330 928-5711
  Cuyahoga Falls (G-7118)

Wkyc-Tv Inc.. C 216 344-3300
  Cleveland (G-5155)

Wtvg Inc.. D 419 531-1313
  Toledo (G-14109)

TEMPORARY HELP SVCS

Acloche LLC... E 888 608-0889
  Columbus (G-5306)

Act I Temporaries Findlay Inc................ E 419 423-0713
  Findlay (G-8506)

Ado Staffing Inc..................................... B 330 922-2077
  Cuyahoga Falls (G-7032)

Alliance Solutions Group LLC................ E 216 503-1690
  Independence (G-9402)

Alternate Sltons Hlth Ntwrk LL.............. D 937 681-9269
  Dayton (G-7168)

Alternate Sltons Hmcare Dyton.............. A 937 298-1111
  Kettering (G-9625)

Amotec Inc.. E 440 250-4600
  Cleveland (G-3811)

Area Temps Inc...................................... A 440 842-2100
  Cleveland (G-3833)

Area Temps Inc...................................... A 216 227-8200
  Lakewood (G-9658)

Area Temps Inc...................................... A 216 518-2000
  Maple Heights (G-10333)

Area Temps Inc...................................... A 440 975-4400
  Mentor (G-10913)

Area Temps Inc...................................... E 216 781-5350
  Independence (G-9407)

Belflex Staffing Network LLC................. A 513 939-3444
  Fairfield (G-8393)

Callos Resource LLC............................. E 330 788-3033
  Youngstown (G-15569)

Cavalry Staffing LLC.............................. E 440 663-9990
  Cleveland (G-3939)

Creative Fincl Staffing LLC.................... E 614 343-7800
  Worthington (G-15410)

Decapua Enterprises Inc....................... E 614 255-1400
  Columbus (G-5747)

Emily Management Inc.......................... D 440 354-6713
  Concord Township (G-6926)

Extras Support Staffing.......................... C 740 671-3996
  Bellaire (G-1012)

Flex-Temp Employment Svcs Inc.......... C 419 355-9675
  Fremont (G-8677)

Health Carousel LLC.............................. C 855 665-4544
  Cincinnati (G-2808)

Heiser Staffing Services LLC................ E 614 800-4188
  Columbus (G-5983)

Horizon Personnel Resources............... D 440 585-0031
  Wickliffe (G-15152)

Interim Halthcare Columbus Inc............ B 330 836-5571
  Fairlawn (G-8486)

Employee Codes: A=Over 500 employees, B=251-500 C=101-250, D=51-100, E=20-50, F=10-19, G=1-9

2024 Harris Ohio Services Directory

TEMPORARY HELP SVCS

Its Technologies Inc........................... D 419 842-2100
  Holland *(G-9290)*
Job1usa Inc.. C 419 255-5005
  Toledo *(G-13868)*
Labor Ready Midwest Inc................. D 419 382-6565
  Toledo *(G-13881)*
Medlink of Ohio Inc........................... B 330 773-9434
  Akron *(G-228)*
Minute Men Inc.................................. D 216 426-2225
  Cleveland *(G-4589)*
Minute Men Select Inc...................... E 216 452-0100
  Cleveland *(G-4590)*
Nursenow LLC.................................... D 812 868-7732
  Maumee *(G-10751)*
Planet Healthcare LLC....................... D 888 845-2539
  Westlake *(G-15099)*
Pontoon Solutions Inc........................ A 855 881-1533
  Maumee *(G-10756)*
Preferred Temporary Svcs Inc........... E 330 494-5502
  Canton *(G-1830)*
Prolink Healthcare Staffing............... D 513 489-5300
  Montgomery *(G-11373)*
Prolink Staffing Services LLC............ A 614 405-9810
  Dublin *(G-8099)*
Prolink Staffing Services LLC............ D 513 489-5300
  Cincinnati *(G-3251)*
Reserves Network Inc........................ E 440 779-1400
  Cleveland *(G-4829)*
Rumpf Corporation............................. E 419 255-5005
  Toledo *(G-13999)*
Sfn Group Inc..................................... A 419 727-4104
  Toledo *(G-14009)*
Spherion of Lima Inc.......................... A 567 208-5471
  Findlay *(G-8586)*
Spherion of Lima Inc.......................... E 419 224-8367
  Lima *(G-9964)*
Stafftech Inc....................................... D 937 228-2667
  Dayton *(G-7637)*
Supplemental Healthcare................... E 937 247-0169
  Miamisburg *(G-11096)*
Upshift Work LLC................................ C 513 813-5695
  Cincinnati *(G-3598)*

TEN PIN CENTERS

AMF Bowling Centers Inc.................. E 614 889-0880
  Columbus *(G-5365)*
AMF Bowling Centers Inc.................. E 330 725-4548
  Medina *(G-10807)*
Chillicothe Bowling Lanes Inc........... E 740 773-3300
  Chillicothe *(G-2055)*
Columbus Sq Bowl Palace Inc.......... E 614 895-1122
  Columbus *(G-5655)*
Roseland Lanes Inc........................... D 440 439-0097
  Bedford *(G-983)*
Sequoia Pro Bowl Inc........................ E 614 885-7043
  Columbus *(G-6662)*
Ten Pin Alley...................................... E 614 876-2475
  Hilliard *(G-9237)*
Tiki Bowling Lanes Inc...................... E 740 654-4513
  Lancaster *(G-9747)*
Western Bowl Inc............................... E 513 574-2200
  Cincinnati *(G-3660)*

TESTING SVCS

Alpha Technologies Svcs LLC.......... D 330 745-1641
  Hudson *(G-9331)*
Cleveland Clnic Hlth Systm-Wst....... D 440 716-9810
  North Olmsted *(G-11898)*
Orton Edward Jr Crmic Fndation...... E 614 895-2663
  Westerville *(G-14926)*
Solar Testing Laboratories Inc......... D 216 741-7007
  Brooklyn Heights *(G-1427)*

South Central Ohio Eductl Ctr........... D 740 456-0517
  New Boston *(G-11595)*

TEXTILE DESIGNERS

Standard Textile Co Inc.................... B 513 761-9255
  Cincinnati *(G-3409)*

TEXTILES: Linen Fabrics

Standard Textile Co Inc.................... B 513 761-9255
  Cincinnati *(G-3409)*

THEATRICAL PRODUCERS & SVCS

Cleveland Ballet................................. E 216 320-9000
  Bedford Heights *(G-997)*
Hob Entertainment LLC..................... D 216 523-2583
  Cleveland *(G-4370)*
Interntnal MGT Group Ovrseas L..... B 216 522-1200
  Cleveland *(G-4419)*
Rock Roll Hall of Fame Mseum I....... D 216 781-7625
  Cleveland *(G-4849)*

THEATRICAL PRODUCTION SVCS

The Cincinnati Playhouse In............. C 513 345-2242
  Cincinnati *(G-3463)*

THERMOPLASTIC MATERIALS

Amros Industries Inc......................... E 216 433-0010
  Cleveland *(G-3812)*
Avient Corporation............................. D 440 930-1000
  Avon Lake *(G-672)*
Genius Solutions Engrg Co.............. E 419 794-9914
  Maumee *(G-10727)*

THERMOSETTING MATERIALS

Hexion Topco LLC.............................. D 614 225-4000
  Columbus *(G-5990)*

TIRE & TUBE REPAIR MATERIALS, WHOLESALE

Myers Industries Inc.......................... E 330 253-5592
  Akron *(G-238)*
Technical Rubber Company Inc....... C 740 967-9015
  Johnstown *(G-9549)*

TIRE CORD & FABRIC

Mfh Partners Inc................................ B 440 461-4100
  Cleveland *(G-4571)*

TIRE SUNDRIES OR REPAIR MATERIALS: Rubber

Technical Rubber Company Inc....... C 740 967-9015
  Johnstown *(G-9549)*

TIRES & TUBES WHOLESALERS

Bestdrive LLC..................................... A 614 284-7549
  Urbancrest *(G-14319)*
Gateway Tire of Texas Inc................ E 513 874-2500
  West Chester *(G-14813)*
Rush Truck Centers Ohio Inc........... E 513 733-8500
  Cincinnati *(G-3334)*
Rush Truck Leasing Inc.................... E 937 264-2365
  Dayton *(G-7599)*
Rush Truck Leasing Inc.................... E 419 224-6045
  Lima *(G-9957)*
Rush Truck Leasing Inc.................... E 330 798-0600
  Walton Hills *(G-14479)*
Shrader Tire & Oil Inc........................ E 614 445-6601
  Columbus *(G-6675)*
Shrader Tire & Oil Inc........................ E 740 788-8032
  Heath *(G-9139)*

Shrader Tire & Oil Inc........................ E 419 472-2128
  Toledo *(G-14012)*
The Hercules Tire & Rubber Company... E 800 677-9535
  Findlay *(G-8592)*
Treadmaxx Tire Distrs Inc................ D 404 762-4944
  Wooster *(G-15379)*

TIRES & TUBES, WHOLESALE: Automotive

Belle Tire Distributors Inc................. E 419 535-3033
  Toledo *(G-13704)*
Best One Tire & Svc Lima Inc........... E 419 229-2380
  Lima *(G-9868)*
Conrads Tire Service Inc................... E 216 941-3333
  Cleveland *(G-4103)*
Dealer Tire LLC.................................. B 216 432-0088
  Cleveland *(G-4155)*
Detroit Tire & Auto Supply Inc......... E 937 426-0949
  Xenia *(G-15503)*
Goodyear Tire & Rubber Company... A 330 796-2121
  Akron *(G-179)*
Grismer Tire Company....................... E 937 643-2526
  Centerville *(G-1945)*
Millersburg Tire Service Inc............. E 330 674-1085
  Millersburg *(G-11286)*
North Gateway Tire Company Inc.... E 330 725-8473
  Medina *(G-10869)*
Orwell Tire Service Inc..................... D 440 437-6515
  Orwell *(G-12179)*
QT Equipment Company.................... E 330 724-3055
  Akron *(G-275)*
Tbc Retail Group Inc......................... E 216 267-8040
  Cleveland *(G-4980)*
Tm Final Ltd....................................... B 419 724-8473
  Toledo *(G-14047)*
Treadmaxx Tire Distrs Inc................ D 404 762-4944
  Wooster *(G-15379)*
Ziegler Tire and Supply Co............... E 330 343-7739
  Dover *(G-7911)*
Ziegler Tire and Supply Co............... E 330 834-3332
  Massillon *(G-10676)*

TOBACCO & PRDTS, WHOLESALE: Cigarettes

Cju Enterprises Inc............................ D 330 493-1800
  Canton *(G-1710)*
Core-Mark Holding Company Inc..... C 650 589-9445
  Solon *(G-13077)*
Dittman-Adams Company.................. E 513 870-7530
  Harrison *(G-9102)*
Gummer Wholesale Inc...................... D 740 928-0415
  Heath *(G-9133)*
JE Carsten Company......................... E 330 794-4440
  Hudson *(G-9359)*

TOBACCO & TOBACCO PRDTS WHOLESALERS

Albert Guarnieri & Co........................ D 330 794-9834
  Hudson *(G-9328)*
Arrow Wine Stores Inc...................... E 937 433-6778
  Dayton *(G-7180)*
Friendly Wholesale Co...................... E 724 224-6580
  Wooster *(G-15338)*
Novelart Manufacturing Company... D 513 351-7700
  Cincinnati *(G-3132)*
Scandinavian Tob Group Ln Ltd...... C 770 934-4594
  Akron *(G-295)*
Swd Corporation................................ E 419 227-2436
  Lima *(G-9968)*

TOBACCO: Smoking

SERVICES SECTION

Scandinavian Tob Group Ln Ltd............ C 770 934-4594
Akron *(G-295)*

TOILETRIES, WHOLESALE: Hair Preparations

ICM Distributing Company Inc................ E 234 212-3030
Twinsburg *(G-14196)*

TOILETRIES, WHOLESALE: Perfumes

Beautyavenues LLC............................ C 614 856-6000
Reynoldsburg *(G-12654)*

TOILETRIES, WHOLESALE: Toilet Soap

Sysco Guest Supply LLC...................... E 614 539-9348
Urbancrest *(G-14323)*

TOILETRIES, WHOLESALE: Toiletries

Nehemiah Manufacturing Co LLC............ D 513 351-5700
Cincinnati *(G-3103)*

Walter F Stephens Jr Inc...................... E 937 746-0521
Franklin *(G-8652)*

TOOLS: Hand, Mechanics

The Cornwell Quality Tools Company.... D 330 336-3506
Wadsworth *(G-14455)*

TOWING & TUGBOAT SVC

A M & O Towing Inc........................... E 330 385-0639
Negley *(G-11540)*

TOWING SVCS: Marine

Bellaire Harbor Service LLC................. E 740 676-4305
Bellaire *(G-1006)*

Great Lakes Group............................. C 216 621-4854
Cleveland *(G-4329)*

TOYS & HOBBY GOODS & SPLYS, WHOLESALE: Bingo Games & Splys

Lancaster Bingo Company LLC............. C 800 866-5001
Lancaster *(G-9729)*

Nannicola Wholesale Co...................... D 330 799-0888
Youngstown *(G-15672)*

TOYS & HOBBY GOODS & SPLYS, WHOLESALE: Toys & Games

Closeout Distribution LLC................... A 614 278-6800
Westerville *(G-14968)*

CSC Distribution LLC......................... A 614 278-6800
Columbus *(G-5734)*

TOYS & HOBBY GOODS & SPLYS, WHOLESALE: Toys, NEC

ICM Distributing Company Inc................ E 234 212-3030
Twinsburg *(G-14196)*

K & M International Inc...................... D 330 425-2550
Independence *(G-9439)*

National Marketshare Group................ E 513 921-0800
Cincinnati *(G-3095)*

TRADE SHOW ARRANGEMENT SVCS

Downing Enterprises Inc..................... D 330 666-3888
Copley *(G-6956)*

Exhibitpro Inc................................... E 614 885-9541
New Albany *(G-11564)*

TRADERS: Commodity, Contracts

Wisewel LLC.................................... E 440 591-4896
Cleveland *(G-5153)*

TRAILERS: Semitrailers, Truck Tractors

Nelson Manufacturing Company............ D 419 523-5321
Ottawa *(G-12189)*

TRANSPORTATION AGENTS & BROKERS

Berkshire Local School Dst.................. E 440 834-4123
Burton *(G-1525)*

Complete Care Providers Inc................ E 937 825-4698
Cincinnati *(G-2487)*

Con-Way Multimodal Inc..................... D 614 923-1400
Dublin *(G-7971)*

Geist Logistics LLC........................... E 954 463-6910
Columbus *(G-5923)*

Grays Trnsp & Logistics LLC................ E 614 656-3460
Columbus *(G-5949)*

J B Express Inc................................. D 740 702-9830
Chillicothe *(G-2075)*

Nagle Logistics Group Company............ D 419 661-2500
Walbridge *(G-14462)*

Odw Lts LLC.................................... C 800 978-3168
Hamilton *(G-9070)*

Shoreline Transportation Inc................ C 440 878-2000
Strongsville *(G-13483)*

Taylor Logistics Inc........................... E 513 771-1850
West Chester *(G-14839)*

Total Quality Logistics LLC.................. D 513 831-2600
Cincinnati *(G-2116)*

Xtreme Express LLC.......................... C 614 735-0291
Columbus *(G-6914)*

TRANSPORTATION BROKERS: Truck

Aim Leasing Company......................... D 330 759-0438
Girard *(G-8809)*

Ameri-Line Inc.................................. E 440 316-4500
Columbia Station *(G-5223)*

American Marine Express Inc............... E 216 268-3005
Cleveland *(G-3803)*

Bnsf Logistics LLC............................ E 937 526-3141
Versailles *(G-14413)*

Claust LLC...................................... E 440 783-2847
Columbia Station *(G-5224)*

DATA Den Inc................................... E 216 622-0900
Cleveland *(G-4149)*

Esj Carrier Corporation...................... E 513 728-7388
Fairfield *(G-8413)*

Garner Trucking Inc........................... D 419 422-5742
Findlay *(G-8536)*

J Rayl Transport Inc.......................... D 330 784-1134
Akron *(G-206)*

Kag Specialty Products Group LLC....... E 330 409-1124
North Canton *(G-11841)*

Kgbo Holdings Inc............................. D 513 831-2600
Cincinnati *(G-2107)*

Ptc Transport Ltd.............................. E 513 738-0900
Hamilton *(G-9075)*

Schneider Nat Carriers Inc.................. A 740 362-6910
Delaware *(G-7825)*

Total Quality Logistics LLC.................. D 513 831-2600
Akron *(G-336)*

Total Quality Logistics LLC.................. C 800 580-3101
Centerville *(G-1952)*

Total Quality Logistics LLC.................. D 513 831-2600
Cincinnati *(G-3485)*

Total Quality Logistics LLC.................. E 513 831-2600
Milford *(G-11261)*

Total Quality Logistics LLC.................. D 800 580-3101
West Chester *(G-14774)*

TRANSPORTATION EQPT & SPLYS WHOLESALERS, NEC

Greenfield Products Inc...................... D 937 981-2696
Greenfield *(G-8865)*

Lippert Enterprises Inc....................... E 419 281-8084
Ashland *(G-505)*

TRANSPORTATION SVCS, AIR, NONSCHEDULED: Air Cargo Carriers

Air Tahoma Inc.................................. D 614 774-0728
Powell *(G-12583)*

Airnet Systems Inc............................ E 614 409-4900
Columbus *(G-5331)*

TRANSPORTATION SVCS, WATER: Cleaning

MPW Industrial Water Svcs Inc............. C 800 827-8790
Hebron *(G-9151)*

TRANSPORTATION SVCS: Railroad Switching

Road & Rail Services Inc..................... D 502 365-5361
Fostoria *(G-8624)*

TRANSPORTATION: Deep Sea Foreign Freight

Midwest Transatlantic Lines Inc............ E 440 243-1993
Berea *(G-1074)*

TRANSPORTATION: Great Lakes Domestic Freight

The Interlake Steamship Co................. B ,..... 440 260-6900
Middleburg Heights *(G-11131)*

TRAVEL AGENCIES

AAA Club Alliance Inc......................... E 513 984-3553
Cincinnati *(G-2133)*

AAA Club Alliance Inc......................... A 513 762-3301
Cincinnati *(G-2134)*

AAA East Central.............................. E 330 652-6466
Niles *(G-11779)*

AAA Miami Valley.............................. D 937 224-2896
Dayton *(G-7150)*

American Ex Trvl Rlted Svcs In............ E 330 922-5700
Cuyahoga Falls *(G-7039)*

Avalon Holdings Corporation................ D 330 856-8800
Warren *(G-14501)*

Medus Travelers............................... D 513 678-2179
Blue Ash *(G-1208)*

TRAVEL TRAILERS & CAMPERS

ARE Inc... A 330 830-7800
Massillon *(G-10631)*

TRUCK & BUS BODIES: Utility Truck

QT Equipment Company...................... E 330 724-3055
Akron *(G-275)*

TRUCK BODIES: Body Parts

ARE Inc... A 330 830-7800
Massillon *(G-10631)*

Crane Carrier Company LLC................ C 918 286-2889
New Philadelphia *(G-11647)*

Crane Carrier Holdings LLC................. C 918 286-2889
New Philadelphia *(G-11648)*

Sutphen Towers Inc........................... D 614 876-1262
Hilliard *(G-9234)*

TRUCK BODY SHOP

QT Equipment Company...................... E 330 724-3055
Akron *(G-275)*

Skinner Diesel Services Inc................. E 614 491-8785
Columbus *(G-6686)*

TRUCK GENERAL REPAIR SVC

TRUCK GENERAL REPAIR SVC

Abers Garage Inc	E	419 281-5500	
Ashland (G-471)			
Aim Leasing Company	D	330 759-0438	
Girard (G-8809)			
Allstate Trck Sls Estrn Ohio L	E	330 339-5555	
New Philadelphia (G-11639)			
American Nat Fleet Svc Inc	D	216 447-6060	
Cleveland (G-3805)			
Benedict Enterprises Inc	E	513 539-9216	
Monroe (G-11334)			
City of Toledo	D	419 936-2507	
Toledo (G-13737)			
Fyda Frghtliner Youngstown Inc	D	330 797-0224	
Youngstown (G-15615)			
Garner Trucking Inc	E	419 334-4040	
Fremont (G-8681)			
Jones Truck & Spring Repr Inc	D	614 443-4619	
Columbus (G-6097)			
Mansfield Truck Sls & Svc Inc	D	419 522-9811	
Mansfield (G-10290)			
National At/Trckstops Hldngs C	A	440 808-9100	
Westlake (G-15081)			
Peterbilt of Cincinnati	B	513 772-1740	
Cincinnati (G-3199)			
R & M Leasing Inc	C	937 382-6800	
Wilmington (G-15269)			
R & R Inc	E	330 799-1536	
Youngstown (G-15705)			
Ta Operating LLC	B	440 808-9100	
Westlake (G-15113)			
Travelcenters of America Inc	A	440 808-9100	
Westlake (G-15117)			
W W Williams Company LLC	E	614 527-9400	
Hilliard (G-9241)			

TRUCK PARTS & ACCESSORIES: Wholesalers

Adelmans Truck Parts Corp	E	330 456-0206	
Canton (G-1655)			
All Lift Service Company Inc	E	440 585-1542	
Willoughby (G-15183)			
BTMC Corporation	E	614 891-1454	
Thornville (G-13619)			
Buyers Products Company	C	440 974-8888	
Mentor (G-10916)			
Buyers Products Company	C	440 974-8888	
Mentor (G-10915)			
Columbus Truck & Equipment	D	614 252-3111	
Columbus (G-5657)			
Crane Carrier Company LLC	C	918 286-2889	
New Philadelphia (G-11647)			
Crane Carrier Holdings LLC	C	918 286-2889	
New Philadelphia (G-11648)			
Cross Truck Equipment Co Inc	E	330 477-8151	
Canton (G-1728)			
Dp Medina Holdings Inc	E	216 254-7883	
Medina (G-10832)			
East Manufacturing Corporation	B	330 325-9921	
Randolph (G-12618)			
GTM Service Inc	E	440 944-5099	
Wickliffe (G-15151)			
Hy-Tek Material Handling LLC	D	614 497-2500	
Columbus (G-6030)			
Kaffenbarger Truck Eqp Co	C	937 845-3804	
New Carlisle (G-11602)			
Kenworth of Cincinnati Inc	D	513 771-5831	
Cincinnati (G-2937)			
Lippert Enterprises Inc	E	419 281-8084	
Ashland (G-505)			
Peterbilt of Cincinnati	B	513 772-1740	
Cincinnati (G-3199)			
Power Train Components Inc	D	419 636-4430	
Bryan (G-1493)			
R & R Inc	E	330 799-1536	
Youngstown (G-15705)			
Stellar Srkg Acquisition LLC	E	330 769-8484	
Seville (G-12966)			
The E and R Trailer Sales a	E	419 968-2115	
Middle Point (G-11111)			
Valley Ford Truck Inc	D	216 524-2400	
Cleveland (G-5097)			
Worldwide Equipment Inc	E	614 876-0336	
Columbus (G-6904)			
Wz Management Inc	E	330 628-4881	
Akron (G-365)			
Young Truck Sales Inc	E	330 477-6271	
Canton (G-1891)			

TRUCKING & HAULING SVCS: Building Materials

Home Run Inc	E	800 543-9198	
Xenia (G-15520)			

TRUCKING & HAULING SVCS: Contract Basis

A L Smith Trucking Inc	E	937 526-3651	
Versailles (G-14412)			
AG Trucking Inc	E	937 497-7770	
Sidney (G-13017)			
Ameri-Line Inc	E	440 316-4500	
Columbia Station (G-5223)			
Arctic Express Inc	C	614 876-4008	
Hilliard (G-9180)			
Arms Trucking Co Inc	E	800 362-1343	
Huntsburg (G-9380)			
Awl Transport Inc	D	330 899-3444	
Mantua (G-10328)			
B D Transportation Inc	E	937 773-9280	
Piqua (G-12435)			
Berlin Transportation LLC	E	330 674-3395	
Millersburg (G-11273)			
Bowling Transportation Inc	D	419 436-9590	
Fostoria (G-8614)			
Bulk Transit Corporation	E	614 873-4632	
Plain City (G-12471)			
Burd Brothers Inc	E	800 538-2873	
Batavia (G-729)			
By-Line Transit Inc	E	937 642-2500	
Marysville (G-10477)			
Cavins Trucking & Garage LLC	E	419 661-9447	
Perrysburg (G-12323)			
Chambers Leasing Systems Corp	E	937 547-9777	
Greenville (G-8867)			
Chambers Leasing Systems Corp	E	937 642-4260	
Marysville (G-10479)			
Cimarron Express Inc	D	419 855-7713	
Genoa (G-8793)			
Clark Trucking Inc	C	937 642-0335	
East Liberty (G-8171)			
Classic Carriers Inc	E	937 604-8118	
Versailles (G-14414)			
Cliff Viessman Inc	D	937 454-6490	
Dayton (G-7236)			
Covenant Transport Inc	A	423 821-1212	
Columbus (G-5715)			
Cowen Truck Line Inc	D	419 938-3401	
Perrysville (G-12391)			
Crete Carrier Corporation	C	614 853-4500	
Columbus (G-5726)			
Crw Inc	E	330 264-3785	
Shreve (G-13016)			
Dayton Freight Lines Inc	D	330 346-0750	
Kent (G-9571)			
Dedicated Transport LLC	C	216 641-2500	
Brooklyn Heights (G-1416)			
DLC Transport Inc	E	740 282-1763	
Steubenville (G-13321)			
Drew Ag-Transport Inc	D	937 548-3200	
Greenville (G-8872)			
Dworkin Inc	E	216 271-5318	
Cleveland (G-4192)			
Eastern Express Inc	C	513 267-1212	
Middletown (G-11161)			
Eastern Express Logistics Inc	C	800 348-6514	
Cleveland (G-4199)			
Erie Trucking Inc	E	419 625-7374	
Sandusky (G-12892)			
Estes Express Lines	D	614 275-6000	
Columbus (G-5832)			
Estes Express Lines	E	419 531-1500	
Toledo (G-13799)			
Estes Express Lines	E	513 779-9581	
West Chester (G-14688)			
Fedex Ground Package Sys Inc	D	800 463-3339	
Grove City (G-8919)			
Fetter Son Farms Ltd Lblty Co	E	740 465-2961	
Morral (G-11453)			
Fleetmaster Express Inc	D	419 420-1835	
Findlay (G-8533)			
Foodliner Inc	D	937 898-0075	
Dayton (G-7361)			
Fraley & Schilling Inc	E	740 598-4118	
Brilliant (G-1380)			
Garner Trucking Inc	D	419 422-5742	
Findlay (G-8536)			
Green Lines Transportation Inc	E	330 863-2111	
Malvern (G-10233)			
Harris Distributing Co	E	513 541-4222	
Cincinnati (G-2801)			
Hillsboro Transportation Co	E	513 772-9223	
Cincinnati (G-2825)			
Hilltrux Tank Lines Inc	E	330 538-3700	
North Jackson (G-11872)			
Hyway Trucking Company	D	419 423-7145	
Findlay (G-8548)			
J P Jenks Inc	D	440 428-4500	
Madison (G-10218)			
J P Transportation Co Inc	E	513 424-6978	
Middletown (G-11167)			
Jmt Cartage Inc	E	330 478-2430	
Canton (G-1784)			
K-Limited Carrier Ltd	D	419 269-0002	
Toledo (G-13874)			
Kag Specialty Products Group LLC	E	330 409-1124	
North Canton (G-11841)			
Kaplan Trucking Company	D	216 341-3322	
Cleveland (G-4448)			
Klingshirn & Sons Trucking	E	937 338-5000	
Burkettsville (G-1524)			
Kuntzman Trucking Inc	E	330 821-9160	
Alliance (G-387)			
L V Trucking Inc	E	614 275-4994	
Columbus (G-6132)			
Luckey Transfer LLC	D	800 435-4371	
Lima (G-9931)			
Mast Trucking Inc	D	330 674-8913	
Millersburg (G-11285)			
Mjs Snow & Landscape LLC	D	419 656-6724	
Port Clinton (G-12538)			
Moeller Trucking Inc	D	419 925-4799	
Maria Stein (G-10354)			

SERVICES SECTION

TRUCKING: Except Local

Motor Carrier Service Inc.................................C..... 419 693-6207
  Northwood *(G-11978)*
Nationwide Truck Brokers Inc.......................C..... 937 335-9229
  Troy *(G-14148)*
P & D Transportation Inc..............................E..... 740 454-1221
  Zanesville *(G-15825)*
Piqua Transfer & Storage Co.........................D..... 937 773-3743
  Piqua *(G-12455)*
Pitt-Ohio Express LLC..................................C..... 614 801-1064
  Grove City *(G-8946)*
Pitt-Ohio Express LLC..................................B..... 419 726-6523
  Toledo *(G-13964)*
Pitt-Ohio Express LLC..................................B..... 513 860-3424
  West Chester *(G-14828)*
Pros Freight Corporation.............................E..... 440 543-7555
  Chagrin Falls *(G-1987)*
Richard Wolfe Trucking Inc..........................E..... 740 392-2445
  Mount Vernon *(G-11505)*
Robert G Owen Trucking Inc........................E..... 330 756-1013
  Navarre *(G-11539)*
Robert M Neff Inc..E..... 614 444-1562
  Columbus *(G-6604)*
Roeder Cartage Company Inc.......................D..... 419 221-1600
  Lima *(G-9954)*
Ron Burge Trucking Inc..............................E..... 330 624-5373
  Burbank *(G-1522)*
Ross Transportation Svcs Inc.......................C..... 440 748-5900
  Grafton *(G-8843)*
Ruan Transport Corporation........................E..... 330 484-1450
  Canton *(G-1847)*
Saia Motor Freight Line LLC.......................D..... 614 870-8778
  Columbus *(G-6636)*
Saia Motor Freight Line LLC.......................D..... 937 237-0140
  Dayton *(G-7604)*
Saia Motor Freight Line LLC.......................D..... 330 659-4277
  Richfield *(G-12709)*
Saia Motor Freight Line LLC.......................D..... 419 726-9761
  Toledo *(G-14003)*
Sanfrey Freight Services Inc........................E..... 330 372-1883
  Warren *(G-14551)*
Scheiderer Transport Inc.............................D..... 614 873-5103
  Plain City *(G-12493)*
Schindewolf Express Inc..............................D..... 937 585-5919
  De Graff *(G-7739)*
Schwerman Trucking Co..............................D..... 419 666-0818
  Walbridge *(G-14466)*
Sewell Leasing Corporation.........................D..... 937 382-3847
  Wilmington *(G-15273)*
Short Freight Lines Inc................................E..... 419 729-1691
  Toledo *(G-14011)*
Spader Freight Services Inc.........................D..... 419 547-1117
  Clyde *(G-5210)*
Special Service Transportation Inc..............E..... 330 273-0755
  Brunswick *(G-1470)*
Tforce Freight Inc..E..... 513 771-7555
  Cincinnati *(G-3461)*
Tforce Freight Inc..D..... 614 238-2355
  Columbus *(G-6756)*
Tforce Freight Inc..E..... 937 236-4700
  Dayton *(G-7664)*
Tforce Freight Inc..E..... 330 448-0440
  Masury *(G-10681)*
Tforce Freight Inc..E..... 330 659-6693
  Richfield *(G-12711)*
Tforce Freight Inc..D..... 419 537-1445
  Toledo *(G-14038)*
Thomas E Keller Trucking Inc.....................B..... 419 784-4805
  Defiance *(G-7772)*
Thomas Trucking Inc..................................E..... 513 731-8411
  Cincinnati *(G-3475)*
Trans-States Express Inc.............................D..... 513 679-7100
  Cincinnati *(G-3501)*

U S Xpress Inc..B..... 440 743-7177
  Cleveland *(G-5045)*
U S Xpress Inc..B..... 740 363-0700
  Delaware *(G-7832)*
U S Xpress Inc..A..... 937 328-4100
  Springfield *(G-13306)*
U S Xpress Inc..B..... 740 452-4153
  Zanesville *(G-15835)*
Usher Transport Inc....................................D..... 614 875-0528
  Grove City *(G-8962)*
Vitran Express Inc......................................B..... 216 426-8584
  Cleveland *(G-5111)*
W L Logan Trucking Company..................C..... 330 478-1404
  Canton *(G-1882)*
Xpo Logistics Freight Inc...........................D..... 937 898-9808
  Dayton *(G-7730)*
Xpo Logistics Freight Inc...........................E..... 937 364-2361
  Hillsboro *(G-9268)*
Xpo Logistics Freight Inc...........................D..... 216 433-1000
  Parma *(G-12267)*
Xpo Logistics Freight Inc...........................D..... 937 492-3899
  Sidney *(G-13059)*
Xpo Logistics Freight Inc...........................E..... 740 894-3859
  South Point *(G-13184)*
Xpo Logistics Freight Inc...........................D..... 740 922-5614
  Uhrichsville *(G-14238)*
Xpo Logistics Freight Inc...........................D..... 330 896-7300
  Uniontown *(G-14271)*
Xpo Logistics Freight Inc...........................E..... 419 294-5728
  Upper Sandusky *(G-14296)*
Xpo Logistics Freight Inc...........................D..... 330 824-2242
  Warren *(G-14578)*
Xpo Logistics Freight Inc...........................D..... 513 870-0044
  West Chester *(G-14846)*
Yowell Transportation Svc Inc....................D..... 937 294-5933
  Moraine *(G-11451)*

TRUCKING & HAULING SVCS: Hazardous Waste

Cousins Waste Control LLC......................D..... 419 726-1500
  Toledo *(G-13768)*
Environmental Enterprises Inc...................C..... 513 772-2818
  Cincinnati *(G-2627)*
J V Enviroserve Limited Partnership.........E..... 216 642-1311
  Cleveland *(G-4427)*
Sustain LLC..E..... 888 525-0029
  New Waterford *(G-11684)*
Waterworks LLC...C..... 614 253-7246
  Columbus *(G-6870)*

TRUCKING & HAULING SVCS: Heavy Machinery, Local

Bob Miller Rigging Inc..............................E..... 419 422-7477
  Findlay *(G-8518)*
Mid-East Truck & Tractor Service Inc......D..... 330 488-0398
  East Canton *(G-8170)*
Tesar Industrial Contrs Inc........................D..... 216 741-8008
  Cleveland *(G-4987)*

TRUCKING & HAULING SVCS: Heavy, NEC

B & T Express Inc......................................B..... 330 549-0000
  North Lima *(G-11883)*
Energy Trucking LLC.................................D..... 740 240-2204
  Pataskala *(G-12274)*
Falcon Transport Co..................................A..... 330 793-1345
  Youngstown *(G-15609)*
Ferrous Metal Transfer Co........................E..... 216 671-8500
  Brooklyn *(G-1409)*
Golden Hawk Transportation Co..............D..... 419 683-3304
  Crestline *(G-7024)*

Iddings Trucking Inc..................................C..... 740 568-1780
  Marietta *(G-10372)*
Mizar Motors Inc..D..... 419 729-2400
  Toledo *(G-13925)*
R & J Trucking Inc.....................................E..... 740 374-3050
  Marietta *(G-10402)*

TRUCKING & HAULING SVCS: Liquid Petroleum, Exc Local

Disttech Inc..A..... 800 969-5419
  North Canton *(G-11825)*
Kenan Advantage Group Inc.....................C..... 800 969-5419
  North Canton *(G-11844)*
Lykins Transportation Inc.........................D..... 513 831-8820
  Milford *(G-11240)*

TRUCKING & HAULING SVCS: Machinery, Heavy

B M Machine..E..... 419 595-2898
  New Riegel *(G-11677)*
Hodges Trucking Company LLC..............E..... 405 947-7764
  Navarre *(G-11538)*
Miller Transfer and Rigging Co................E..... 330 325-2521
  Rootstown *(G-12762)*
Myers Machinery Movers Inc...................E..... 614 871-5052
  Grove City *(G-8938)*
Nicolozakes Trckg & Cnstr Inc................E..... 740 432-5648
  Cambridge *(G-1577)*
Tesar Industrial Contrs Inc........................D..... 216 741-8008
  Cleveland *(G-4987)*

TRUCKING & HAULING SVCS: Petroleum, Local

Howland Logistics LLC..............................E..... 513 469-5263
  Cincinnati *(G-2851)*

TRUCKING: Except Local

1st Carrier Corp..E..... 740 477-2587
  Circleville *(G-3701)*
Ace Doran Hauling & Rigging Co............D..... 513 681-7900
  Cincinnati *(G-2140)*
Advance Trnsp Systems Inc......................D..... 513 818-4311
  Cincinnati *(G-2147)*
Advantage Tank Lines Inc.........................E..... 330 491-0474
  North Canton *(G-11808)*
AG Container Transport LLC....................D..... 740 862-8866
  Lockbourne *(G-10009)*
All Pro Freight Systems Inc......................D..... 440 934-2222
  Westlake *(G-15030)*
Artemis Fine Arts Inc................................E..... 214 357-2577
  Akron *(G-56)*
As Logistics Inc..D..... 513 863-4627
  Liberty Township *(G-9847)*
Atlas Transportation LLC..........................E..... 202 963-4241
  Medina *(G-10809)*
B & L Transport Inc..................................E..... 866 848-2888
  Millersburg *(G-11272)*
Badilad LLC..E..... 330 805-3173
  Cuyahoga Falls *(G-7046)*
Balanced Logistics Brkg LLC....................D..... 216 296-4817
  Twinsburg *(G-14174)*
Bestway Transport Co...............................E..... 419 687-2000
  Plymouth *(G-12501)*
Black Horse Brothers Inc..........................E..... 267 265-0013
  Cuyahoga Falls *(G-7050)*
Brendamour Moving & Stor Inc..............D..... 800 354-9715
  Cincinnati *(G-2279)*
Bridge Logistics Inc...................................E..... 513 874-7444
  West Chester *(G-14801)*

Employee Codes: A=Over 500 employees, B=251-500
C=101-250, D=51-100, E=20-50, F=10-19, G=1-9

TRUCKING: Except Local — SERVICES SECTION

Brookside Holdings LLC .... E 419 925-4457
  Maria Stein *(G-10353)*

Brown Logistics Solutions Inc .... E 614 866-9111
  Columbus *(G-5471)*

Bryan Truck Line Inc .... D 419 485-8373
  Montpelier *(G-11382)*

Burd Brothers Inc .... E 513 708-7787
  Dayton *(G-7206)*

BWC Trucking Company Inc .... E 740 532-5188
  Ironton *(G-9505)*

Cargo Solution Express Inc .... E 614 980-0351
  Columbus *(G-5511)*

Chambers Leasing Systems Corp .... E 419 726-9747
  Toledo *(G-13729)*

CJ Logstics Holdings Amer Corp .... D 614 879-9659
  West Jefferson *(G-14849)*

Cle Transportation Company .... D 567 805-4008
  Norwalk *(G-12005)*

Clopay Transportation Company .... D 937 440-6790
  Troy *(G-14131)*

Containerport Group Inc .... E 440 333-1330
  Columbus *(G-5689)*

Cotter Moving & Storage Co .... E 330 535-5115
  Akron *(G-125)*

Coy Bros Inc .... E 330 533-6864
  Canfield *(G-1627)*

Craig Transportation Co .... E 419 874-7981
  Maumee *(G-10714)*

Dayton Freight Lines Inc .... C 614 860-1080
  Columbus *(G-5744)*

Dayton Freight Lines Inc .... D 419 589-0350
  Mansfield *(G-10257)*

Dayton Freight Lines Inc .... C 419 661-8600
  Perrysburg *(G-12329)*

Dayton Freight Lines Inc .... C 937 264-4060
  Dayton *(G-7284)*

Diamond Logistics Inc .... C 614 274-9750
  Columbus *(G-5763)*

Dill-Elam Inc .... E 513 575-0017
  Loveland *(G-10135)*

Dist-Trans Inc .... C 614 497-1660
  Columbus *(G-5773)*

Dutch Maid Logistics Inc .... C 419 935-0136
  Willard *(G-15167)*

Enterprise Hill Farm Inc .... E 419 668-0242
  Norwalk *(G-12009)*

Exel Inc .... B 614 865-5819
  Westerville *(G-14893)*

Fabrizi Trucking & Pav Co Inc .... D 440 277-0127
  Lorain *(G-10074)*

FANTON Logistics Inc .... D 216 341-2400
  Cleveland *(G-4241)*

Fedex Supplychain Systems Inc .... A
  Hudson *(G-9348)*

First Group Investment Partnr .... D 513 241-2200
  Cincinnati *(G-2674)*

Firstenterprises Inc .... B 740 369-5100
  Delaware *(G-7797)*

Firstgroup Usa Inc .... B 513 241-2200
  Cincinnati *(G-2687)*

Garner Trnsp Group Inc .... C 419 422-5742
  Findlay *(G-8535)*

General Transport & Cons Inc .... E 330 645-6055
  Akron *(G-173)*

General Transport Incorporated .... E 330 786-3400
  Akron *(G-174)*

Gillson Solutions Inc .... E 937 751-0119
  Dayton *(G-7375)*

Glm Transport Inc .... E 419 363-2041
  Van Wert *(G-14345)*

Global Workplace Solutions LLC .... E 513 759-6000
  West Chester *(G-14697)*

Greenwood Motor Lines Inc .... B 800 543-5589
  Wilmington *(G-15255)*

Horizon Freight System Inc .... E 216 341-7410
  Cleveland *(G-4378)*

Horizon Mid Atlantic Inc .... D 800 480-6829
  Cleveland *(G-4379)*

Huntley Trucking Co .... E 740 385-7615
  New Plymouth *(G-11675)*

Imperial Express Inc .... E 937 399-9400
  Springfield *(G-13257)*

Integres Global Logistics Inc .... D 866 347-2101
  Medina *(G-10847)*

J B Hunt Transport Inc .... D 419 547-2777
  Clyde *(G-5204)*

J Rayl Transport Inc .... D 330 784-1134
  Akron *(G-206)*

J-Trac Inc .... E 419 524-3456
  Mansfield *(G-10274)*

Jaro Transportation Svcs Inc .... C 330 393-5659
  Warren *(G-14531)*

Keroam Transportation Inc .... D 937 274-7033
  Dayton *(G-7434)*

Kroger Dedicated Logistics Co .... E 309 691-9670
  Cincinnati *(G-2954)*

Kuhnle Brothers Inc .... C 440 564-7168
  Newbury *(G-11762)*

Landstar Global Logistics Inc .... D 740 575-4700
  Coshocton *(G-6990)*

Lh Trucking Inc .... E 513 398-1682
  Mason *(G-10573)*

Lincoln Moving & Storage Co .... D 216 741-5500
  Strongsville *(G-13470)*

LT Harnett Trucking Inc .... E 440 997-5528
  Ashtabula *(G-541)*

Lykins Companies Inc .... E 513 831-8820
  Milford *(G-11238)*

Mansfield Whsng & Dist Inc .... C 419 522-3510
  Ontario *(G-12114)*

Mark D Sandridge Inc .... E 330 764-6106
  Medina *(G-10852)*

Nick Strimbu Inc .... C 330 448-4046
  Dover *(G-7896)*

Niese Leasing Inc .... E 419 523-4400
  Ottawa *(G-12190)*

One Way Express Incorporated .... E 440 439-9182
  Cleveland *(G-4699)*

Osborne Trucking Company .... E 513 874-2090
  Fairfield *(G-8435)*

P I & I Motor Express Inc .... C 330 448-4035
  Masury *(G-10679)*

Pacer Transport Inc .... D 614 923-1400
  Dublin *(G-8085)*

PAm Transportation Svcs Inc .... E 419 935-9501
  Willard *(G-15172)*

Panther II Transportation Inc .... C 800 685-0657
  Medina *(G-10872)*

Panther Premium Logistics Inc .... B 800 685-0657
  Medina *(G-10873)*

Phoenix Cargo LLC .... C 614 407-3322
  Grove City *(G-8945)*

Pitt-Ohio Express LLC .... C 216 433-9000
  Cleveland *(G-4752)*

Planes Moving & Storage Inc .... C 513 759-6000
  West Chester *(G-14743)*

Platinum Carriers LLC .... D 877 318-9607
  Garfield Heights *(G-8778)*

Platinum Express Inc .... E 937 235-9540
  Dayton *(G-7557)*

Ploger Transportation LLC .... E 419 465-2100
  Norwalk *(G-12021)*

Pohl Transportation Inc .... D 800 837-2122
  Versailles *(G-14416)*

Predator Trucking Company .... E 330 530-0712
  Mc Donald *(G-10801)*

R & L Carriers Inc .... A 800 543-5589
  Wilmington *(G-15265)*

R & L Transfer Inc .... B 330 482-5800
  Columbiana *(G-5239)*

R & L Transfer Inc .... B 216 531-3324
  Norwalk *(G-12022)*

R & L Transfer Inc .... B 937 305-9287
  Wilmington *(G-15266)*

R & L Transfer Inc .... B 614 871-3813
  Wilmington *(G-15267)*

Rands Trucking Inc .... E 740 397-1144
  Mount Vernon *(G-11504)*

RDF Logistics Inc .... C 440 282-9060
  Lorain *(G-10100)*

RDF Trucking Corporation .... D 440 282-9060
  Lorain *(G-10101)*

Rising Sun Express LLC .... D 937 596-6167
  Jackson Center *(G-9533)*

RL Trucking Inc .... C 419 732-4177
  Port Clinton *(G-12540)*

Roadlink USA Midwest LLC .... E 419 686-2113
  Perrysburg *(G-12367)*

Roger Bettis Trucking Inc .... E 330 863-2111
  Malvern *(G-10236)*

Rood Trucking Company Inc .... C 330 652-3519
  Mineral Ridge *(G-11304)*

Rrr Express LLC .... E 800 723-3424
  West Chester *(G-14758)*

Rt80 Express Inc .... E 330 706-0900
  Barberton *(G-707)*

Ryder Last Mile Inc .... D 866 711-3129
  New Albany *(G-11586)*

Schneider Nat Carriers Inc .... A 740 362-6910
  Delaware *(G-7825)*

Schroeder Associates Inc .... E 419 258-5075
  Antwerp *(G-448)*

Shama Express LLC .... D 216 925-6530
  Grafton *(G-8844)*

Shoreline Transportation Inc .... C 440 878-2000
  Strongsville *(G-13483)*

Smith Trucking Inc .... E 419 841-8676
  Sylvania *(G-13572)*

Store & Haul Inc .... E 419 238-4284
  Van Wert *(G-14351)*

Swx Enterprises Inc .... E 216 676-4600
  Brookpark *(G-1441)*

Taylor Distributing Company .... D 513 771-1850
  West Chester *(G-14838)*

Tennfreight Inc .... E 615 977-2125
  Cincinnati *(G-3456)*

The Expediting Co .... D 937 890-1524
  Vandalia *(G-14394)*

Three-D Transport Inc .... E 419 924-5368
  West Unity *(G-14875)*

Thyssenkrupp Logistics Inc .... E 419 662-1800
  Northwood *(G-11984)*

Tk Gas Services Inc .... E 740 826-0303
  New Concord *(G-11612)*

Toledo Nagle Inc .... D 419 661-2500
  Walbridge *(G-14467)*

Top Line Express Inc .... E 419 221-1705
  Lima *(G-9972)*

Top Notch Truckers Inc .... D 540 787-7777
  Cuyahoga Falls *(G-7108)*

Trans-Continental Systems Inc .... E 513 769-4774
  Cincinnati *(G-3500)*

Transportation Unlimited Inc .... A 216 426-0088
  Cleveland *(G-5033)*

Triad Transport Inc .... E 614 491-9497
  Columbus *(G-6788)*

SERVICES SECTION

TRUCKING: Local, Without Storage

Triangle Leasing Corp............................ E 419 729-3868
 Toledo *(G-14074)*

Trio Trucking Inc.................................... D 513 679-7100
 Cincinnati *(G-3527)*

Triple Crown Services Company............ E 419 625-0672
 Sandusky *(G-12937)*

Triple T Transport Inc........................... C 740 657-3244
 Lewis Center *(G-9839)*

U S Xpress Inc....................................... B 419 244-6384
 Toledo *(G-14080)*

Vitran Express Inc.................................. E 614 870-2255
 Columbus *(G-6852)*

Wannemacher Enterprises Inc................ E 419 225-9060
 Lima *(G-9979)*

Watkins and Shepard Trckg Inc.............. D 614 832-0440
 Urbancrest *(G-14326)*

World Shipping Inc................................. E 440 356-7676
 Cleveland *(G-5159)*

Xpo Logistics Freight Inc...................... C 614 876-7100
 Columbus *(G-6912)*

Zipline Logistics LLC............................. E 888 469-4754
 Columbus *(G-6920)*

Zumstein Inc... D 419 375-4132
 Fort Recovery *(G-8612)*

TRUCKING: Local, With Storage

All Pro Freight Systems Inc................... D 440 934-2222
 Westlake *(G-15030)*

Arms Trucking Co Inc............................ E 800 362-1343
 Huntsburg *(G-9380)*

Aviation Auto Trnsp Spclsts In............... E 502 785-4657
 Fort Loramie *(G-8603)*

Bls Trucking Inc..................................... B 937 224-0494
 New Carlisle *(G-11600)*

Clark Trucking Inc.................................. C 937 642-0335
 East Liberty *(G-8171)*

Cordell Transportation Co LLC.............. C 937 277-7271
 Dayton *(G-7249)*

Dawson Logistics LLC........................... E 217 689-2610
 West Chester *(G-14683)*

Getgo Transportation Co LLC................ E 419 666-6850
 Millbury *(G-11269)*

J-Trac Inc... E 419 524-3456
 Mansfield *(G-10274)*

King Tut Logistics LLC.......................... E 614 538-0509
 Columbus *(G-6117)*

Landstar Global Logistics Inc................. D 740 575-4700
 Coshocton *(G-6990)*

Lincoln Moving & Storage Co................. C 216 741-5500
 Strongsville *(G-13470)*

M G Q Inc... E 419 992-4236
 Tiffin *(G-13631)*

Moving Solutions Inc.............................. D 440 946-9300
 Mentor *(G-10977)*

National Shunt Service LLC................... B 978 637-2293
 Dublin *(G-8068)*

Neighborhood Logistics Co Inc............... E 440 466-0020
 Geneva *(G-8787)*

Piqua Transfer & Storage Co.................. D 937 773-3743
 Piqua *(G-12455)*

Planes Mvg & Stor Co Columbus........... D 614 777-9090
 Columbus *(G-6528)*

Roadlink USA Midwest LLC................... E 419 686-2113
 Perrysburg *(G-12367)*

Royalty Trucking Inc............................... C 513 771-1860
 Mason *(G-10603)*

Spears Transfer & Expediting................. D 937 275-2443
 Dayton *(G-7633)*

Van Mayberrys & Storage Inc................. D 937 298-8800
 Moraine *(G-11445)*

Wnb Group LLC..................................... E 513 641-5400
 Cincinnati *(G-3677)*

Wooster Motor Ways Inc........................ C 330 264-9557
 Wooster *(G-15396)*

Yowell Transportation Svc Inc................ D 937 294-5933
 Moraine *(G-11451)*

TRUCKING: Local, Without Storage

1st Carrier Corp..................................... E 740 477-2587
 Circleville *(G-3701)*

A L Smith Trucking Inc.......................... E 937 526-3651
 Versailles *(G-14412)*

AG Trucking Inc..................................... E 937 497-7770
 Sidney *(G-13017)*

All Trucks Inc... E 614 800-4595
 Hilliard *(G-9176)*

B D Transportation Inc........................... E 937 773-9280
 Piqua *(G-12435)*

Big Blue Trucking Inc............................. E 330 372-1421
 Warren *(G-14507)*

Bowling Transportation Inc..................... D 419 436-9590
 Fostoria *(G-8614)*

Brookside Holdings LLC........................ E 419 925-4457
 Maria Stein *(G-10353)*

Bryan Truck Line Inc.............................. D 419 485-8373
 Montpelier *(G-11382)*

C & G Transportation Inc....................... E 419 288-2653
 Wayne *(G-14620)*

City Dash LLC.. C 513 562-2000
 Cincinnati *(G-2450)*

City of Dayton.. D 937 333-4860
 Dayton *(G-7230)*

CJ Logstics Holdings Amer Corp............ D 614 879-9659
 West Jefferson *(G-14849)*

Continental Express Inc......................... A 937 497-2100
 Sidney *(G-13024)*

Cotter Moving & Storage Co................... E 330 535-5115
 Akron *(G-125)*

Cowen Truck Line Inc............................ D 419 938-3401
 Perrysville *(G-12391)*

Cs Trucking LLC..................................... C 330 878-1990
 Dover *(G-7878)*

Dayton Freight Lines Inc........................ E 937 264-4060
 Dayton *(G-7284)*

Dayton Synchrnous Spport Ctr I............ E 937 226-1559
 Dayton *(G-7302)*

Dedicated Transport LLC....................... C 216 641-2500
 Brooklyn Heights *(G-1416)*

Dill-Elam Inc.. E 513 575-0017
 Loveland *(G-10135)*

Dr Transportation Inc............................. E 216 588-6110
 Cleveland *(G-4182)*

Dutch Maid Logistics Inc........................ C 419 935-0136
 Willard *(G-15167)*

Edora Logistics Inc................................ E 937 573-9090
 Vandalia *(G-14375)*

Energy Power Services Inc.................... E 330 343-2312
 New Philadelphia *(G-11650)*

Fabrizi Trucking & Pav Co Inc................ D 440 234-1284
 Cleveland *(G-4233)*

Fedex Ground Package Sys Inc.............. D 800 463-3339
 Grove City *(G-8919)*

Findlay Truck Line Inc........................... D 419 422-1945
 Findlay *(G-8531)*

First Group Investment Partnr................ D 513 241-2200
 Cincinnati *(G-2674)*

Firstgroup Usa Inc................................. B 513 241-2200
 Cincinnati *(G-2687)*

Fraley & Schilling Inc............................. E 740 598-4118
 Brilliant *(G-1380)*

Fst Brokerage Services Inc.................... D 614 529-7900
 Dublin *(G-8017)*

Garner Trucking Inc................................ D 419 422-5742
 Findlay *(G-8536)*

Glm Transport Inc.................................. E 419 363-2041
 Van Wert *(G-14345)*

Golden Hawk Inc.................................... D 419 683-3304
 Crestline *(G-7023)*

Greenwood Motor Lines Inc................... B 800 543-5589
 Wilmington *(G-15255)*

Henderson Turf Farm Inc....................... E 937 748-1559
 Franklin *(G-8640)*

Home Run Inc.. E 800 543-9198
 Xenia *(G-15520)*

Hyway Trucking Company..................... D 419 423-7145
 Findlay *(G-8548)*

International Truck & Eng Corp.............. A 937 390-4045
 Springfield *(G-13260)*

J P Jenks Inc... D 440 428-4500
 Madison *(G-10218)*

J P Transportation Co Inc...................... E 513 424-6978
 Middletown *(G-11167)*

J-Trac Inc... E 419 524-3456
 Mansfield *(G-10274)*

Kenan Advantage Group Inc.................. C 800 969-5419
 North Canton *(G-11844)*

Keroam Transportation Inc.................... D 937 274-7033
 Dayton *(G-7434)*

Klingshirn & Sons Trucking.................... E 937 338-5000
 Burkettsville *(G-1524)*

KMu Trucking & Excvtg LLC.................. E 440 934-1008
 Avon *(G-659)*

Kuhnle Brothers Inc............................... C 440 564-7168
 Newbury *(G-11762)*

Kuntzman Trucking Inc.......................... E 330 821-9160
 Alliance *(G-387)*

L V Trucking Inc..................................... E 614 275-4994
 Columbus *(G-6132)*

Lesaint Logistics Inc.............................. C 513 874-3900
 West Chester *(G-14722)*

LT Harnett Trucking Inc......................... E 440 997-5528
 Ashtabula *(G-541)*

Mail Contractors America Inc................ D 513 769-5967
 Cincinnati *(G-3003)*

McK Trucking Inc................................... E 419 622-1111
 Haviland *(G-9132)*

Midwest Logistics Systems Ltd.............. D 419 584-1414
 Celina *(G-1928)*

Moeller Trucking Inc.............................. D 419 925-4799
 Maria Stein *(G-10354)*

Myers Machinery Movers Inc................. E 614 871-5052
 Grove City *(G-8938)*

Neighborhood Logistics Co Inc............... E 440 466-0020
 Geneva *(G-8787)*

Nicholas Carney-Mc Inc........................ D 330 792-5460
 Youngstown *(G-15677)*

Ohio Bulk Transfer Company Inc............ D 216 883-7200
 Newburgh Heights *(G-11758)*

Old Forge Services Inc.......................... E 330 733-5531
 Windham *(G-15289)*

One Way Express Incorporated.............. E 440 439-9182
 Cleveland *(G-4699)*

P I & I Motor Express Inc...................... C 330 448-4035
 Masury *(G-10679)*

Panther II Transportation Inc................. C 800 685-0657
 Medina *(G-10872)*

Panther Premium Logistics Inc............... B 800 685-0657
 Medina *(G-10873)*

Payne Trucking Co................................. E 440 998-5538
 Ashtabula *(G-545)*

Pitt-Ohio Express LLC........................... C 216 433-9000
 Cleveland *(G-4752)*

Pitt-Ohio Express LLC........................... B 513 860-3424
 West Chester *(G-14828)*

Precision Strip Transport Inc................. E 419 628-2343
 Minster *(G-11321)*

TRUCKING: Local, Without Storage

R & L Transfer Inc................................. B 330 482-5800
　Columbiana (G-5239)
R & L Transfer Inc................................. B 216 531-3324
　Norwalk (G-12022)
Red Rover LLC..................................... E 330 262-6501
　Wooster (G-15368)
Reis Trucking Inc.................................. E 513 353-1960
　Cleves (G-5192)
Republic Services Ohio Hlg LLC............ E 513 771-4200
　Cincinnati (G-3289)
Revolution Trucking LLC........................ E 330 975-4145
　Wadsworth (G-14450)
Rising Sun Express LLC........................ D 937 596-6167
　Jackson Center (G-9533)
Rose Transport Inc................................ D 614 864-4004
　Reynoldsburg (G-12677)
Ross Consolidated Corp........................ D 440 748-5800
　Grafton (G-8841)
Rt80 Express Inc................................... E 330 706-0900
　Barberton (G-707)
Rumpke Waste Inc................................ C 513 242-4401
　Cincinnati (G-3333)
Rumpke Waste Inc................................ C 937 378-4126
　Georgetown (G-8801)
Rumpke Waste Inc................................ C 937 548-1939
　Greenville (G-8883)
Rush Package Delivery Inc.................... D 937 297-6182
　Columbus (G-6621)
S & T Truck and Auto Svc Inc................. E 614 272-8163
　Columbus (G-6624)
S B Morabito Trucking Inc..................... D 216 441-3070
　Bedford (G-984)
Sanfrey Freight Services Inc.................. E 330 372-1883
　Warren (G-14551)
Santmyer Logistics Inc.......................... D 330 262-6501
　Wooster (G-15371)
Savage Companies................................ E 216 642-1311
　Cleveland (G-4877)
Schindewolf Express Inc....................... D 937 585-5919
　De Graff (G-7739)
Sewell Leasing Corporation................... D 937 382-3847
　Wilmington (G-15273)
Shoreline Transportation Inc.................. C 440 878-2000
　Strongsville (G-13483)
Spears Transfer & Expediting................. D 937 275-2443
　Dayton (G-7633)
Special Service Transportation Inc......... E 330 273-0755
　Brunswick (G-1470)
Spring Grove Rsrce Rcovery Inc............ E 513 681-6242
　Cincinnati (G-3398)
Steve Crawford Trucking Inc.................. E 866 748-9505
　Byesville (G-1536)
Tforce Freight Inc.................................. E 937 236-4700
　Dayton (G-7664)
Tforce Freight Inc.................................. E 330 659-6693
　Richfield (G-12711)
The Andrews Moving and Stor............... E 330 656-8700
　Streetsboro (G-13432)
Tk Gas Services Inc.............................. E 740 826-0303
　New Concord (G-11612)
Trans-States Express Inc...................... D 513 679-7100
　Cincinnati (G-3501)
Transportation Unlimited Inc.................. A 216 426-0088
　Cleveland (G-5033)
Tri-State Forest Logistics LLC............... E 937 323-6325
　Springfield (G-13303)
Triangle Leasing Corp........................... E 419 729-3868
　Toledo (G-14074)
Tricont Trucking Company..................... C 614 527-7398
　Columbus (G-6789)
Trio Trucking Inc................................... D 513 679-7100
　Cincinnati (G-3527)

Tsm Logistics LLC................................ E 419 234-6074
　Rockford (G-12737)
Vallejo Company................................... E 216 741-3933
　Cleveland (G-5096)
Valley Transportation Inc....................... E 419 289-6200
　Ashland (G-514)
Vin Devers Inc...................................... C 888 847-9535
　Sylvania (G-13578)
W L Logan Trucking Company............... C 330 478-1404
　Canton (G-1882)
White Swan Inc..................................... E 707 615-5005
　Columbus (G-6886)
Wil-Sites Truck Lines LLC...................... E 614 444-8873
　Columbus (G-6891)
Wooster Motor Ways Inc....................... C 330 264-9557
　Wooster (G-15396)
Xpo Logistics Freight Inc....................... C 614 876-7100
　Columbus (G-6912)
Xpo Logistics Freight Inc....................... E 216 433-1000
　Parma (G-12267)
Xpo Logistics Freight Inc....................... D 330 896-7300
　Uniontown (G-14271)
Xpo Logistics Freight Inc....................... D 513 870-0044
　West Chester (G-14846)
Zemba Bros Inc.................................... E 740 452-1880
　Zanesville (G-15844)

TRUCKS & TRACTORS: Industrial

Forte Industrial Equipment Systems Inc E 513 398-2800
　Mason (G-10550)
General Electric Company...................... E 513 977-1500
　Cincinnati (G-2723)
Pollock Research & Design Inc.............. E 330 332-3300
　Salem (G-12847)
Stock Fairfield Corporation.................... C 440 543-6000
　Solon (G-13149)

TRUSSES: Wood, Floor

Khempco Bldg Sup Co Ltd Partnr.......... D 740 549-0465
　Delaware (G-7811)

TRUST MANAGEMENT SVCS: Charitable

Cleveland Foundation............................. D 216 861-3810
　Cleveland (G-4044)
Mercy Health Foundation....................... B 937 523-6670
　Springfield (G-13270)

TRUST MANAGEMENT SVCS: Personal Investment

Equity Trust Company........................... B 440 323-5491
　Westlake (G-15057)

TUBES: Paper

Espt Liquidation Inc.............................. D 330 698-4711
　Apple Creek (G-450)
Precision Products Group Inc................ D 330 698-4711
　Apple Creek (G-452)
Sonoco Products Company................... D 937 429-0040
　Beavercreek Township (G-949)

TUBES: Steel & Iron

Crest Bending Inc................................. E 419 492-2108
　New Washington (G-11682)
Kirtland Capital Partners LP................... E 216 593-0100
　Beachwood (G-806)
Phillips Mfg and Tower Co..................... D 419 347-1720
　Shelby (G-13008)

TUBING: Flexible, Metallic

Lincoln Electric Automtn Inc.................. B 937 295-2120
　Fort Loramie (G-8605)

TUBING: Rubber

Trico Products Corporation.................... C 248 371-1700
　Cleveland (G-5038)

TUGBOAT SVCS

Shelly Materials Inc............................... D 740 246-6315
　Thornville (G-13622)
The Great Lakes Towing Company........ D 216 621-4854
　Cleveland (G-5000)

TURBINES & TURBINE GENERATOR SETS

Babcock & Wilcox Holdings Inc............. A 704 625-4900
　Akron (G-60)
Eaton Leasing Corporation.................... B 216 382-2292
　Beachwood (G-788)
Miba Bearings US LLC......................... B 740 962-4242
　Mcconnelsville (G-10803)
Rolls-Royce Energy Systems Inc........... A 703 834-1700
　Mount Vernon (G-11506)
Siemens Energy Inc.............................. E 740 393-8897
　Mount Vernon (G-11508)

TURBINES: Gas, Mechanical Drive

Onpower Inc... E 513 228-2100
　Lebanon (G-9779)

TURBINES: Steam

Steam Trbine Altrntive Rsrces................ E 740 387-5535
　Marion (G-10455)

TURNKEY VENDORS: Computer Systems

Manatron Inc.. E 937 431-4000
　Beavercreek (G-925)

TYPESETTING SVC

A-A Blueprint Co Inc............................. E 330 794-8803
　Akron (G-11)
AGS Custom Graphics Inc.................... D 330 963-7770
　Macedonia (G-10188)
Baesman Group Inc.............................. D 614 771-2300
　Hilliard (G-9181)
Bindery & Spc Pressworks Inc.............. E 614 873-4623
　Plain City (G-12470)
Black River Group Inc.......................... E 419 524-6699
　Mansfield (G-10245)
Bookmasters Inc................................... C 419 281-1802
　Ashland (G-483)
Consolidated Graphics Group Inc........... C 216 881-9191
　Cleveland (G-4104)
Copley Ohio Newspapers Inc................. C 330 364-5577
　New Philadelphia (G-11643)
Hkm Drect Mkt Cmmnications Inc......... C 800 860-4456
　Cleveland (G-4367)
Quick Tab II Inc.................................... D 419 448-6622
　Tiffin (G-13639)
The Photo-Type Engraving Company..... D 513 281-0999
　Cincinnati (G-3469)
Workflowone LLC.................................. A 877 735-4966
　Dayton (G-7726)

TYPESETTING SVC: Computer

Wolters Kluwer Clinical Dru................... D 330 650-6506
　Hudson (G-9378)

UNIFORM SPLY SVCS: Indl

Cintas Corporation................................ D 513 631-5750
　Cincinnati (G-2443)
Cintas Corporation................................ A 513 459-1200
　Cincinnati (G-2442)
Cintas Corporation No 3........................ D 513 459-1200
　Mason (G-10536)

SERVICES SECTION

USED CAR DEALERS

Cintas R US Inc.. D 513 459-1200
  Cincinnati (G-2444)
Cintas Sales Corporation....................... B 513 459-1200
  Cincinnati (G-2445)
Cintas-Rus LP... E 513 459-1200
  Mason (G-10538)
G&K Services LLC................................. B 513 459-1200
  Mason (G-10552)
Leef Bros Inc.. E 952 912-5500
  Mason (G-10572)
Morgan Services Inc.............................. C 216 241-3107
  Cleveland (G-4599)
Unifirst Corporation............................... E 937 746-0531
  Franklin (G-8651)
Van Dyne-Crotty Co............................... D 740 432-7503
  Cambridge (G-1587)
Van Dyne-Crotty Co............................... D 440 248-6935
  Solon (G-13158)
Vestis Corporation................................. E 937 223-6667
  Dayton (G-7703)
Vestis Corporation................................. C 419 729-5454
  Toledo (G-14092)

UNISEX HAIR SALONS

Jbentley Studio & Spa LLC................... D 614 790-8828
  Powell (G-12593)
PS Lifestyle LLC..................................... A 440 600-1595
  Cleveland (G-4796)
R L O Inc... E 937 620-9998
  Dayton (G-7577)

UNIVERSITY

Board of Dirs of Wttnberg Clle.............. D 937 327-6310
  Springfield (G-13222)
Devry University Inc.............................. D 614 251-6969
  Columbus (G-5759)
Miami University..................................... B 513 727-3200
  Middletown (G-11172)
Miami University..................................... C 513 529-6911
  Oxford (G-12211)
Miami University..................................... D 513 529-1230
  Oxford (G-12212)
Ohio State Univ Wexner Med Ctr.......... C 614 293-6255
  Columbus (G-6450)
Ohio State Univ Wexner Med Ctr.......... C 614 293-7521
  Columbus (G-6452)
Ohio State University............................. E 614 292-6661
  Columbus (G-6455)
Ohio State University............................. D 614 293-3860
  Columbus (G-6456)
Ohio State University............................. E 614 292-1284
  Columbus (G-6458)
Ohio State University............................. C 614 688-0857
  Columbus (G-6459)
Ohio State University............................. D 330 263-3700
  Wooster (G-15363)
University Ear Nose Throat Spc........... C 513 475-8403
  Cincinnati (G-3566)
University Hospital................................. D 330 486-9610
  Twinsburg (G-14225)
University of Cincinnati......................... E 513 556-6932
  Blue Ash (G-1264)
University of Cincinnati......................... E 513 558-4194
  Cincinnati (G-3572)
University of Cincinnati......................... B 513 558-1200
  Cincinnati (G-3573)
University of Cincinnati......................... C 513 475-8771
  Cincinnati (G-3575)
University of Cincinnati......................... D 513 556-2389
  Cincinnati (G-3576)
University of Cincinnati......................... D 513 556-2700
  Cincinnati (G-3577)

University of Cincinnati......................... B 513 584-1000
  Cincinnati (G-3578)
University of Cincinnati......................... A 513 584-7522
  Cincinnati (G-3579)
University of Cincinnati......................... C 513 584-1000
  Cincinnati (G-3580)
University of Cincinnati......................... B 513 584-4396
  Cincinnati (G-3581)
University of Cincinnati......................... C 513 558-4231
  Cincinnati (G-3583)
University of Cincinnati......................... E 513 558-4110
  Cincinnati (G-3585)
University of Cincinnati......................... C 513 556-4603
  Cincinnati (G-3586)
University of Cincinnati......................... C 513 558-4444
  Cincinnati (G-3587)
University of Cincinnati......................... C 513 584-5331
  Cincinnati (G-3588)
University of Cincinnati......................... D 513 556-6381
  Cincinnati (G-3590)
University of Cincinnati......................... D 513 556-4054
  Cincinnati (G-3591)
University of Cincinnati......................... D 513 556-3732
  Cincinnati (G-3592)
University of Cincinnati......................... E 513 556-3803
  Cincinnati (G-3593)
University of Cincinnati......................... E 513 584-3200
  Cincinnati (G-3594)
University of Dayton............................... C 937 229-2113
  Dayton (G-7690)
University of Dayton............................... B 937 229-3822
  Dayton (G-7691)
University of Dayton............................... D 937 255-3141
  Dayton (G-7692)
University of Dayton............................... B 937 229-3913
  Dayton (G-7693)
University of Dayton............................... A 937 229-1000
  Dayton (G-7689)
University of Toledo.............................. E 419 383-5322
  Toledo (G-14087)
Wright State University......................... E 937 775-3333
  Beavercreek (G-916)
Wright State University......................... D 937 208-2177
  Dayton (G-7729)
Wright State University......................... D 937 298-4331
  Kettering (G-9634)
Xavier University.................................... E 513 745-3335
  Cincinnati (G-3683)

UPHOLSTERY WORK SVCS

Casco Mfg Solutions Inc....................... D 513 681-0003
  Cincinnati (G-2318)

USED CAR DEALERS

Aaj Enterprises Inc................................ A 614 497-2000
  Obetz (G-12078)
Abraham Ford LLC................................ E 440 233-7402
  Elyria (G-8232)
Brown Motor Sales Co........................... E 419 531-0151
  Toledo (G-13720)
Cain Motors Inc..................................... E 330 494-5588
  Canton (G-1695)
Carcorp Inc... C 877 857-2801
  Columbus (G-5506)
Central Cadillac Limited........................ D 216 861-5800
  Cleveland (G-3954)
Chesrown Oldsmobile GMC Inc........... E 614 846-3040
  Columbus (G-5554)
Columbus SAI Motors LLC.................... E 614 851-3273
  Columbus (G-5653)
Coughlin Chevrolet Toyota Inc............. D 740 366-1381
  Newark (G-11696)

Cronin Auto Inc...................................... C 419 874-4331
  Perrysburg (G-12327)
Dons Automotive Group Llc................. E 419 337-3010
  Wauseon (G-14599)
Doug Bigelow Chevrolet Inc................. D 330 644-7500
  Akron (G-136)
Ed Mullinax Ford LLC............................ C 440 984-2431
  Amherst (G-427)
George P Ballas Buick GMC Trck......... E 419 535-1000
  Toledo (G-13820)
Graham Chevrolet-Cadillac Co............. C 419 989-4012
  Ontario (G-12105)
Greenwood Chevrolet Inc..................... C 330 270-1299
  Youngstown (G-15624)
Grogans Towne Chrysler Inc................ D 419 476-0761
  Toledo (G-13830)
Interstate Ford Inc................................. C 937 866-0781
  Miamisburg (G-11065)
Jake Sweeney Automotive Inc............. D 513 782-2800
  Cincinnati (G-2896)
Jim Keim Ford.. D 614 888-3333
  Columbus (G-6091)
Kempthorn Motors Inc.......................... D 800 451-3877
  Canton (G-1790)
Laria Chevrolet-Buick Inc..................... E 330 925-2015
  Rittman (G-12730)
Lariche Chevrolet-Cadillac Inc............. D 419 422-1855
  Findlay (G-8556)
Lavery Chevrolet-Buick Inc.................. E 330 823-1100
  Alliance (G-388)
Lebanon Ford Inc.................................. D 513 932-1010
  Lebanon (G-9775)
Leikin Motor Companies Inc................ D 440 946-6900
  Willoughby (G-15204)
Lincoln Mrcury Kings Auto Mall............ E 513 683-3800
  Cincinnati (G-2979)
Lkq Triplettasap Inc.............................. C 330 733-6333
  Akron (G-223)
Mark Thomas Ford Inc.......................... E 330 638-1010
  Cortland (G-6972)
McCluskey Chevrolet Inc...................... C 513 761-1111
  Loveland (G-10149)
Mike Castrucci Ford............................... C 513 831-7010
  Milford (G-11243)
Montrose Ford Inc................................. C 330 666-0711
  Fairlawn (G-8491)
Mullinax Ford North Canton Inc........... C 330 238-3206
  Canton (G-1812)
Northern Automotive Inc....................... E 614 436-2001
  Columbus (G-6367)
Reineke Ford Inc................................... E 888 691-8175
  Fostoria (G-8622)
Rouen Chrysler Plymouth Dodge.......... E 419 837-6228
  Woodville (G-15306)
Roush Equipment Inc............................ C 614 882-1535
  Westerville (G-15014)
Schoner Chevrolet Inc.......................... E 330 877-6731
  Hartville (G-9129)
Sharpnack Chevrolet Co....................... E 800 752-7513
  Vermilion (G-14408)
Skipco Financial Adjusters Inc............. D 330 854-4800
  Canal Fulton (G-1594)
Sonic Automotive................................... D 614 870-8200
  Columbus (G-6692)
Spitzer Chevrolet Inc............................ E 330 467-4141
  Northfield (G-11966)
Sunnyside Cars Inc............................... E 440 777-9911
  North Olmsted (G-11917)
Surfside Motors Inc............................... E 419 419-4776
  Galion (G-8751)
Tansky Motors Inc................................. E 650 322-7069
  Rockbridge (G-12736)

Village Motors Inc.................................. D 330 674-2055
  Millersburg (G-11295)
Vin Devers Inc....................................... C 888 847-9535
  Sylvania (G-13578)
Voss Auto Network Inc......................... E 937 428-2447
  Dayton (G-7711)
Voss Chevrolet Inc................................ C 937 428-2500
  Dayton (G-7713)
Voss Dodge... E 937 435-7800
  Dayton (G-7714)
Walker Auto Group Inc......................... E 937 433-4950
  Miamisburg (G-11103)
Warner Buick-Nissan Inc...................... E 419 423-7161
  Findlay (G-8597)

USED MERCHANDISE STORES

Goodwill Inds Ashtabula Inc.................. D 440 964-3565
  Ashtabula (G-536)
Goodwill Inds Centl Ohio Inc.................. E 740 439-7000
  Cambridge (G-1572)
Goodwill Inds Wyne Hlmes Cntie........... E 330 264-1300
  Wooster (G-15341)
Gw Business Solutions LLC................... C 740 345-9861
  Newark (G-11703)
Licking-Knox Goodwill Inds Inc.............. D 740 345-9861
  Newark (G-11721)
Salvation Army....................................... E 330 773-3331
  Cleveland (G-4873)
Salvation Army....................................... E 419 447-2252
  Tiffin (G-13641)
Student Ln Fnding Rsources LLC........... E 513 763-4300
  Cincinnati (G-3425)
Zanesvlle Wlfare Orgnztion Gdw............ E 740 450-6060
  Zanesville (G-15843)

UTILITY TRAILER DEALERS

Wabash National Trlr Ctrs Inc................ D 614 878-6088
  Groveport (G-9012)

VALUE-ADDED RESELLERS: Computer Systems

Advizex Technologies LLC..................... E 513 229-8400
  Blue Ash (G-1125)
Advizex Technologies LLC..................... D 614 318-0386
  Columbus (G-5319)
Advizex Technologies LLC..................... E 216 901-1818
  Independence (G-9397)
Cameo Solutions Inc.............................. E 513 645-4220
  West Chester (G-14658)
Evanhoe & Associates Inc..................... E 937 235-2995
  Xenia (G-15505)
Netsmart Technologies Inc..................... B 800 434-2642
  Dublin (G-8074)
Vintek Inc... D 937 382-8986
  Wilmington (G-15277)

VALVES & PIPE FITTINGS

Anchor Flange Company........................ D 513 527-3512
  Cincinnati (G-2196)
Crane Pumps & Systems Inc.................. C 937 773-2442
  Piqua (G-12240)
Fcx Performance Inc.............................. E 614 253-1996
  Columbus (G-5853)
Kirtland Capital Partners LP.................... E 216 593-0100
  Beachwood (G-806)
Pressure Connections Corp.................... D 614 863-6930
  Columbus (G-6543)
Robeck Fluid Power Co.......................... D 330 562-1140
  Aurora (G-624)
Stephens Pipe & Steel LLC.................... C 740 869-2257
  Mount Sterling (G-11475)

Superior Holding LLC............................. E 216 651-9400
  Cleveland (G-4964)
Superior Products LLC........................... D 216 651-9400
  Cleveland (G-4965)
Swagelok Company................................ D 440 349-5934
  Solon (G-13154)
Waxman Industries Inc........................... C 440 439-1830
  Bedford Heights (G-1005)

VALVES: Aerosol, Metal

Accurate Mechanical Inc........................ D 740 681-1332
  Lancaster (G-9690)
B M Machine.. E 419 595-2898
  New Riegel (G-11677)
Jfdb Ltd... C 513 870-0601
  Cincinnati (G-2912)

VALVES: Aircraft, Hydraulic

Aerocontrolex Group Inc........................ D 216 291-6025
  South Euclid (G-13170)
Hydraulic Manifolds USA LLC................ E 973 728-1214
  Stow (G-13376)

VALVES: Fluid Power, Control, Hydraulic & pneumatic

Hydrotech Inc... D 888 651-5712
  West Chester (G-14819)

VALVES: Gas Cylinder, Compressed

Kaplan Industries Inc............................. D 856 779-8181
  Harrison (G-9111)

VALVES: Indl

Waxman Industries Inc........................... C 440 439-1830
  Bedford Heights (G-1005)

VAN CONVERSIONS

Wmk LLC.. E 440 951-4335
  Bedford (G-993)

VARIETY STORES

Big Lots Stores LLC............................... A 614 278-6800
  Columbus (G-5439)
Discount Drug Mart Inc.......................... C 330 725-2340
  Medina (G-10829)
Dollar Paradise...................................... E 216 432-0421
  Cleveland (G-4174)
Glow Industries Inc................................ D 419 872-4772
  Perrysburg (G-12339)
Lululemon USA Inc................................. E 440 250-0415
  Westlake (G-15078)
Marc Glassman Inc................................ C 330 995-9246
  Aurora (G-616)

VENDING MACHINE OPERATORS: Sandwich & Hot Food

Laughlin Music & Vending Svc............... E 740 593-7778
  Athens (G-580)

VENDING MACHINE REPAIR SVCS

Serex Corporation.................................. E 330 726-6062
  Youngstown (G-15721)
Vendors Exchange International Inc....... D 216 432-1800
  Cleveland (G-5098)

VENDING MACHINES & PARTS

Giant Industries Inc................................ E 419 531-4600
  Toledo (G-13821)
Gold Medal Products Co........................ B 513 769-7676
  Cincinnati (G-2739)

VENTILATING EQPT: Metal

Famous Industries Inc........................... E 330 535-1811
  Akron (G-157)

VENTURE CAPITAL COMPANIES

Igs Ventures Inc.................................... C 614 659-5000
  Dublin (G-8035)
Linsalata Capital Partners Inc................ B 440 684-1400
  Mayfield Heights (G-10788)
National City Capital Corp...................... B 216 222-2491
  Cleveland (G-4619)
Stonehenge Capital Company LLC........ E 614 246-2456
  Columbus (G-6719)
Stonehenge Fincl Holdings Inc............... E 614 246-2500
  Columbus (G-6720)
Verdant Commercial Capital LLC........... E 513 769-2033
  Blue Ash (G-1270)

VIDEO & AUDIO EQPT, WHOLESALE

Live Technologies LLC........................... D 614 278-7777
  Columbus (G-6171)
Merchandise Inc..................................... D 513 353-2200
  Miamitown (G-11107)

VIDEO PRODUCTION SVCS

Boxcast Inc.. E 888 392-2278
  Cleveland (G-3885)
Live Media Group Holdings LLC............. D 614 297-0001
  Columbus (G-6170)
Madison Avenue Mktg Group Inc........... E 419 473-9000
  Toledo (G-13903)

VIDEO TAPE PRODUCTION SVCS

Video Duplication Services Inc............... E 614 871-3827
  Columbus (G-6850)
World Harvest Church Inc...................... C 614 837-1990
  Canal Winchester (G-1620)

VISUAL COMMUNICATIONS SYSTEMS

Findaway World LLC.............................. E 440 893-0808
  Solon (G-13089)

VOCATIONAL REHABILITATION AGENCY

A W S Inc.. E 216 486-0600
  Euclid (G-8335)
Center of Voctnl Altrntvs Mntl................. D 614 294-7117
  Columbus (G-5533)
Community Support Services Inc........... C 330 253-9388
  Akron (G-118)
Cornucopia Inc....................................... E 216 521-4600
  Lakewood (G-9662)
Creative Learning Workshop LLC........... E 330 393-5929
  Warren (G-14516)
Easter Seals Tristate............................. C 513 985-0515
  Cincinnati (G-2599)
Goodwill Inds Ashtabula Inc.................. D 440 964-3565
  Ashtabula (G-536)
Goodwill Inds Centl Ohio Inc.................. E 740 439-7000
  Cambridge (G-1572)
Goodwill Inds NW Ohio Inc.................... D 419 255-0070
  Toledo (G-13822)
In Youngstown Area Gdwill Inds............ C 330 759-7921
  Youngstown (G-15637)
Jewish Family Service............................ C 614 231-1890
  Columbus (G-6089)
L & M Products Inc................................ E 937 456-7141
  Eaton (G-8214)
Marimor Industries Inc........................... D 419 221-1226
  Lima (G-9933)
Murray Ridge Prod Ctr Inc..................... C 440 329-3734
  Elyria (G-8277)

SERVICES SECTION

WAREHOUSING & STORAGE: General

Quadco Rehabilitation Ctr Inc.................. E 419 445-1950
   Archbold *(G-466)*

Quadco Rehabilitation Ctr Inc.................. B 419 682-1011
   Stryker *(G-13505)*

Spectrum Supportive Services................. E 216 875-0460
   Cleveland *(G-4931)*

United Crbral Plsy Assn Grter................... D 216 791-8363
   Cleveland *(G-5057)*

Waycraft Inc... C 419 563-0550
   Bucyrus *(G-1520)*

VOCATIONAL TRAINING AGENCY

A W S Inc.. B 216 749-0356
   Cleveland *(G-3751)*

A W S Inc.. A 440 333-1791
   Rocky River *(G-12738)*

County of Hardin.................................... E 419 674-4158
   Kenton *(G-9613)*

Software Craftsmanship Guild................. E 330 888-8519
   Akron *(G-307)*

Vocational Guidance Services................. B 440 322-1123
   Elyria *(G-8300)*

WALL COVERINGS WHOLESALERS

The Blonder Company............................ C 216 431-3560
   Cleveland *(G-4992)*

WALLPAPER STORE

Decorate With Style Inc.......................... E 419 621-5577
   Sandusky *(G-12887)*

WALLPAPER: Made From Purchased Paper

The Blonder Company............................ C 216 431-3560
   Cleveland *(G-4992)*

WALLS: Curtain, Metal

Midwest Curtainwalls Inc........................ D 216 641-7900
   Cleveland *(G-4580)*

WAREHOUSING & STORAGE FACILITIES, NEC

Abbott Laboratories................................ D 847 937-6100
   Columbus *(G-5294)*

American Excelsior Company.................. D 419 663-3241
   Norwalk *(G-12000)*

ARC Healthcare LLC.............................. E 888 552-0677
   Worthington *(G-15405)*

Ballreich Bros Inc................................... C 419 447-1814
   Tiffin *(G-13624)*

Cornerstone Consolidated Se.................. A 513 603-1100
   West Chester *(G-14678)*

Exel Holdings (usa) Inc........................... C 614 865-8500
   Westerville *(G-14892)*

Honda Logistics North Amer Inc.............. A 937 642-0335
   East Liberty *(G-8172)*

Kuhlman Corporation.............................. E 419 897-6000
   Maumee *(G-10737)*

Lalac One LLC....................................... E 216 432-4422
   Cleveland *(G-4482)*

Midwest Express Inc............................... A 937 642-0335
   East Liberty *(G-8173)*

Nx Autmotive Logistics USA Inc............... C 937 642-8333
   East Liberty *(G-8174)*

PC Connection Inc.................................. E 937 382-4800
   Wilmington *(G-15263)*

Radial South LP..................................... B 678 584-4047
   Groveport *(G-8997)*

SH Bell Company................................... E 412 963-9910
   East Liverpool *(G-8193)*

Warren City Board Education.................. E 330 841-2265
   Warren *(G-14574)*

Wooster Motor Ways Inc......................... C 330 264-9557
   Wooster *(G-15396)*

WAREHOUSING & STORAGE, REFRIGERATED: Cold Storage Or Refrig

Americold Logistics LLC......................... D 419 599-5015
   Napoleon *(G-11515)*

Americold Logistics LLC......................... E 419 599-5015
   Napoleon *(G-11516)*

Fresh Mark Inc....................................... B 330 833-9870
   Massillon *(G-10640)*

Perishable Shipp Solutions LLC............... E 724 944-9024
   Warren *(G-14546)*

RLR Investments LLC............................. D 937 382-1494
   Wilmington *(G-15270)*

WAREHOUSING & STORAGE: General

Aldelano Corporation.............................. E 909 861-3970
   Lima *(G-9861)*

AM Industrial Group LLC........................ E 216 267-6783
   Cleveland *(G-3798)*

Amazon... E 951 733-5325
   Columbus *(G-5342)*

B D S Inc... E 513 921-8441
   Cincinnati *(G-2235)*

Backyard Storage Solutions LLC............. D 330 723-4412
   Medina *(G-10813)*

Basista Furniture Inc.............................. E 216 398-5900
   Cleveland *(G-3854)*

Bendon Inc.. D 419 903-0403
   Ashland *(G-481)*

Big Sandy Furniture Inc.......................... D 740 894-4242
   Chesapeake *(G-2028)*

Big Sandy Furniture Inc.......................... D 740 775-4244
   Chillicothe *(G-2052)*

Big Sandy Furniture Inc.......................... D 740 354-3193
   Portsmouth *(G-12546)*

Big Sandy Furniture Inc.......................... D 740 574-2113
   Franklin Furnace *(G-8653)*

Cartcom Inc... D 740 644-0912
   Hebron *(G-9141)*

Caruso Inc... E 513 860-9200
   Cincinnati *(G-2316)*

CFS Family Holdings Inc........................ E 740 492-0595
   Newcomerstown *(G-11766)*

Chewy Inc.. B 937 669-4839
   Vandalia *(G-14369)*

CJ Logistics America LLC...................... D 847 390-6800
   Toledo *(G-13745)*

CJ Logstics Holdings Amer Corp............. D 614 879-9659
   West Jefferson *(G-14849)*

Compak Inc... E 330 345-5666
   Wooster *(G-15326)*

Contanda Terminals LLC........................ E 513 921-8441
   Cincinnati *(G-2500)*

Cotter Moving & Storage Co................... E 330 535-5115
   Akron *(G-125)*

D + S Distribution Inc............................ D 800 752-5993
   Orrville *(G-12161)*

Eddie Bauer LLC.................................... E 614 497-8200
   Groveport *(G-8983)*

Eddie Buer Flfillment Svcs Inc................ A 614 497-8200
   Groveport *(G-8984)*

Elyria Foundry Company LLC................. D 440 322-4657
   Elyria *(G-8246)*

Essilor of America Inc............................ E 614 492-0888
   Groveport *(G-8986)*

Ferry Cap & Set Screw Company............ D 440 315-9291
   Lakewood *(G-9665)*

Fremont Logistics LLC........................... E 419 333-0669
   Fremont *(G-8680)*

G & S Metal Products Co Inc.................. D 216 831-2388
   Cleveland *(G-4294)*

Goodwill Ester Seals Miami Vly............... B 937 461-4800
   Dayton *(G-7380)*

Graham Investment Co........................... D 740 382-0902
   Marion *(G-10429)*

Home Depot USA Inc.............................. D 419 299-2000
   Van Buren *(G-14338)*

Ieh Auto Parts LLC................................. E 216 351-2560
   Cleveland *(G-4403)*

J B Express Inc...................................... D 740 702-9830
   Chillicothe *(G-2075)*

Kandel Cold Storage Inc......................... D 330 798-4111
   Tallmadge *(G-13597)*

Keller Logistics Group Inc....................... E 866 276-9486
   Defiance *(G-7751)*

King Tut Logistics LLC........................... E 614 538-0509
   Columbus *(G-6117)*

Kohls Department Stores Inc.................. E 419 421-5301
   Findlay *(G-8554)*

Kroger Co... D 859 630-6959
   Milford *(G-11235)*

Kroger Company.................................... A 740 657-2124
   Delaware *(G-7813)*

Lakota Local School District................... E 513 777-2150
   Liberty Township *(G-9853)*

Lesaint Logistics Inc.............................. C 513 874-3900
   West Chester *(G-14722)*

Lowes Home Centers LLC...................... D 740 636-2100
   Wshngtn Ct Hs *(G-15489)*

M A Folkes Company Inc........................ E 513 785-4200
   Hamilton *(G-9062)*

Micro Electronics Inc.............................. B 614 334-1430
   Columbus *(G-6233)*

Mid State Systems Inc............................ E 740 928-1115
   Hebron *(G-9148)*

Millwood Inc.. E 330 393-4400
   Vienna *(G-14422)*

Neighborhood Logistics Co Inc................ E 440 466-0020
   Geneva *(G-8787)*

Norplas Industries Inc............................ B 419 666-6119
   Perrysburg *(G-12358)*

Odw Logistics Inc................................... E 614 549-5000
   Lockbourne *(G-10013)*

Ohio Desk Company............................... E 216 623-0600
   Brooklyn Heights *(G-1426)*

PC Connection Sales Corp...................... D 937 382-4800
   Wilmington *(G-15264)*

Penney Opco LLC.................................. B 614 863-7043
   Columbus *(G-6513)*

Precision Strip Inc.................................. D 419 674-4186
   Kenton *(G-9622)*

Precision Strip Inc.................................. D 937 667-6255
   Tipp City *(G-13664)*

R R Donnelley & Sons Company............. E 614 539-5527
   Grove City *(G-8947)*

Ravenna School District......................... E 330 297-4138
   Ravenna *(G-12640)*

Reliable Rnners Curier Svc Inc............... E 440 578-1011
   Mentor *(G-10991)*

SH Bell Company................................... E 412 963-9910
   East Liverpool *(G-8193)*

Shippers Automotive Group LLC............. C 937 484-7780
   Urbana *(G-14313)*

Specialty Chemical Sales Inc.................. E 216 267-4248
   Cleveland *(G-4928)*

Springs Window Fashions LLC............... E 614 492-6770
   Groveport *(G-9002)*

Stationers Inc.. E 740 423-1400
   Belpre *(G-1059)*

Summit NW Corporation......................... D 503 255-3826
   Dublin *(G-8134)*

WAREHOUSING & STORAGE: General

Taylor Warehouse Corporation............... E 513 771-1850
   West Chester *(G-14772)*
Tmt Warehousing LLC........................... C 419 662-3146
   Perrysburg *(G-12378)*
Trane Technologies Company LLC........ E 419 633-6800
   Bryan *(G-1494)*
Utility Trailer Mfg Co............................... B 513 436-2600
   Batavia *(G-753)*
Van Boxel Stor Solutions LLC................ E 440 721-1504
   Chardon *(G-2025)*
Vectra Inc... C 614 351-6868
   Columbus *(G-6843)*
Verst Group Logistics Inc...................... E 513 772-2494
   Cincinnati *(G-3621)*
Verst Group Logistics Inc...................... C 859 379-1207
   Cincinnati *(G-3622)*
W W Grainger Inc................................... E 330 425-8388
   Macedonia *(G-10209)*
Wad Investments Oh Inc........................ E 513 891-4477
   Cincinnati *(G-3637)*
Walmart Inc... E 614 409-5500
   Lockbourne *(G-10017)*
Walmart Inc... C 740 765-5700
   Wintersville *(G-15297)*
Wannemacher Enterprises Inc............... E 419 225-9060
   Lima *(G-9979)*
Warehouse Svcs Group Ltd Lblty........... E 419 868-6400
   Holland *(G-9314)*
Williams Scotsman Inc........................... E 978 228-0305
   Fairfield *(G-8454)*
Workflowone LLC................................... A 877 735-4966
   Dayton *(G-7726)*
Xtreme Express LLC.............................. C 614 735-0291
   Columbus *(G-6914)*

WAREHOUSING & STORAGE: Miniwarehouse

Durant Dc LLC.. B 614 278-6800
   Columbus *(G-5795)*
Quaker Sales & Dist Inc......................... A 914 767-7010
   Lockbourne *(G-10014)*
Revitalize Industries LLC....................... E 440 570-3473
   Maple Heights *(G-10344)*

WAREHOUSING & STORAGE: Refrigerated

Crescent Park Corporation..................... C 513 759-7000
   West Chester *(G-14679)*
Produce Packaging Inc........................... C 216 391-6129
   Willoughby Hills *(G-15234)*
Woodruff Enterprises Inc........................ E 937 399-9300
   Springfield *(G-13314)*

WAREHOUSING & STORAGE: Self Storage

151 W 4th Cincinnati LLC....................... D 312 283-3683
   Cincinnati *(G-2119)*
Imcd Us LLC... C 216 228-8900
   Akron *(G-200)*
Ysi Management LLC............................. E 440 891-4100
   Cleveland *(G-5170)*

WARM AIR HEATING/AC EQPT/SPLYS, WHOL Warm Air Htg Eqpt/Splys

2 J Supply Llc... E 937 223-0811
   Dayton *(G-7147)*
Allied Supply Company Inc.................... E 937 224-9833
   Dayton *(G-7164)*
Famous Enterprises Inc.......................... E 330 762-9621
   Akron *(G-156)*
Habegger Corporation............................ E 513 853-6644
   Cincinnati *(G-2788)*

Lakeside Supply Co................................ E 216 941-6800
   Cleveland *(G-4478)*
Resolute Industrial LLC.......................... E 513 779-7909
   West Chester *(G-14831)*

WASHERS: Metal

Atlas Bolt & Screw Company LLC.......... C 419 289-6171
   Ashland *(G-478)*

WATCH REPAIR SVCS

Family Liquidation Company Inc............ D 937 780-3075
   Wshngtn Ct Hs *(G-15479)*
R S Stoll and Company........................... E 937 434-7800
   Dayton *(G-7578)*

WATER SUPPLY

Aqua Ohio Inc... D 440 255-3984
   Mentor *(G-10912)*
Belmont County of Ohio......................... E 740 695-3144
   Saint Clairsville *(G-12778)*
City of Akron... D 330 678-0077
   Kent *(G-9563)*
City of Avon Lake................................... E 440 933-6226
   Avon Lake *(G-676)*
City of Cleveland.................................... E 216 348-7277
   Newburgh Heights *(G-11757)*
City of Columbus.................................... E 614 645-7490
   Columbus *(G-5576)*
City of Cuyahoga Falls........................... E 330 971-8130
   Cuyahoga Falls *(G-7056)*
City of Dayton... D 937 333-6070
   Dayton *(G-7228)*
City of Dayton... E 937 333-3725
   Dayton *(G-7232)*
City of Lorain.. D 440 204-2500
   Lorain *(G-10064)*
City of Middletown.................................. D 513 425-7781
   Middletown *(G-11157)*
City of Toledo... D 419 245-1800
   Toledo *(G-13743)*
Clearwater Services Inc......................... E 330 836-4946
   Akron *(G-106)*
Cleveland Water Department................. E 216 664-3168
   Cleveland *(G-4072)*
County of Guernsey............................... E 740 439-1269
   Cambridge *(G-1565)*
County of Portage.................................. D 330 297-3670
   Ravenna *(G-12624)*
County of Warren................................... D 513 925-1377
   Lebanon *(G-9762)*
Del-Co Water Company Inc.................... D 740 548-7746
   Delaware *(G-7793)*
Hecla Water Association........................ E 740 533-0526
   Ironton *(G-9507)*
Knox County... D 740 397-7041
   Mount Vernon *(G-11493)*
Mahoning Valley Sanitary Dst................ D 330 799-6315
   Mineral Ridge *(G-11303)*
Northast Ohio Rgonal Sewer Dst........... C 216 881-6600
   Cleveland *(G-4659)*
Northwestern Water & Sewer Dst.......... E 419 354-9090
   Bowling Green *(G-1329)*
Ohio-American Water Co Inc.................. E 740 382-3993
   Marion *(G-10449)*
Ross County Water Company Inc.......... E 740 774-4117
   Chillicothe *(G-2088)*
Rural Lorain County Water Auth............ D 440 355-5121
   Lagrange *(G-9650)*
Scioto County Region Wtr Dst 1............ E 740 259-2301
   Lucasville *(G-10180)*

WATER TREATMENT EQPT: Indl

City of Middletown.................................. D 513 425-7781
   Middletown *(G-11157)*
Crown Solutions Co LLC........................ C 937 890-4075
   Vandalia *(G-14372)*
Kinetico Incorporated............................. B 440 564-9111
   Newbury *(G-11761)*

WAXES: Petroleum, Not Produced In Petroleum Refineries

The Kindt-Collins Company LLC............ D 216 252-4122
   Cleveland *(G-5003)*

WELDING EQPT & SPLYS WHOLESALERS

Airgas Inc.. D 937 222-8312
   Moraine *(G-11388)*
Airgas Merchant Gases LLC.................. E 800 242-0105
   Cleveland *(G-3780)*
Airgas Usa LLC...................................... B 216 642-6600
   Independence *(G-9399)*
Albright Welding Supply Co Inc............. E 330 264-2021
   Wooster *(G-15309)*
American Welding & Gas Inc................. E 859 519-8772
   Cincinnati *(G-2188)*
Daihen Inc... E 937 667-0800
   Tipp City *(G-13656)*
Forney Industries Inc............................. D 937 494-6102
   Dayton *(G-7362)*
Lefeld Welding & Stl Sups Inc................ E 419 678-2397
   Coldwater *(G-5216)*
Linde Gas & Equipment Inc.................... E 330 376-2242
   Akron *(G-222)*
O E Meyer Co... D 419 625-1256
   Sandusky *(G-12921)*
R3 Safety LLC.. E 800 421-7081
   West Chester *(G-14753)*
Weiler Welding Company Inc................. D 937 222-8312
   Moraine *(G-11448)*
Weld Plus Inc.. E 513 941-4411
   Cincinnati *(G-3648)*
Weldco Inc... E 513 744-9353
   Cincinnati *(G-3649)*

WELDING EQPT REPAIR SVCS

Lyco Corporation.................................... E 412 973-9176
   Lowellville *(G-10169)*

WELDING REPAIR SVC

A & G Manufacturing Co Inc................... E 419 468-7433
   Galion *(G-8740)*
Abbott Tool Inc....................................... E 419 476-6742
   Toledo *(G-13673)*
All-Type Welding & Fabrication.............. E 440 439-3990
   Cleveland *(G-3792)*
Allied Fabricating & Wldg Co................. E 614 751-6664
   Columbus *(G-5338)*
Arctech Fabricating Inc......................... E 937 525-9353
   Springfield *(G-13219)*
Athens Mold and Machine Inc................ D 740 593-6613
   Athens *(G-559)*
Bayloff Stmped Pdts Knsman Inc........... D 330 876-4511
   Kinsman *(G-9644)*
Breitinger Company................................ C 419 526-4255
   Mansfield *(G-10248)*
Byron Products Inc................................. D 513 870-9111
   Fairfield *(G-8397)*
C & R Inc... E 614 497-1130
   Groveport *(G-8975)*
C-N-D Industries Inc.............................. E 330 478-8811
   Massillon *(G-10633)*

SERVICES SECTION

Ceramic Holdings Inc.............................. C 216 362-3900
  Brookpark *(G-1431)*

Combs Manufacturing Inc....................... D 330 784-3151
  Akron *(G-114)*

Crest Bending Inc................................... E 419 492-2108
  New Washington *(G-11682)*

Dynamic Weld Corporation..................... E 419 582-2900
  Osgood *(G-12180)*

East End Welding LLC............................ C 330 677-6000
  Kent *(G-9573)*

Falls Stamping & Welding Co.................. C 330 928-1191
  Cuyahoga Falls *(G-7075)*

Fleetpride Inc... E 740 282-2711
  Steubenville *(G-13326)*

Gaspar Inc... D 330 477-2222
  Canton *(G-1759)*

General Tool Company............................ C 513 733-5500
  Cincinnati *(G-2728)*

George Steel Fabricating Inc................... E 513 932-2887
  Lebanon *(G-9766)*

Glenridge Machine Co............................. E 440 975-1055
  Solon *(G-13092)*

Hi-Tek Manufacturing Inc........................ C 513 459-1094
  Mason *(G-10562)*

J & S Industrial Mch Pdts Inc................... D 419 691-1380
  Toledo *(G-13865)*

Jerl Machine Inc...................................... E 419 873-0270
  Perrysburg *(G-12348)*

JMw Welding and Mfg Inc........................ E 330 484-2428
  Canton *(G-1785)*

Kinninger Prod Wldg Co Inc.................... D 419 629-3491
  New Bremen *(G-11598)*

Laserflex Corporation.............................. D 614 850-9600
  Hilliard *(G-9209)*

Lima Sheet Metal Machine & Mfg............ E 419 229-1161
  Lima *(G-9927)*

Lincoln Electric Automtn Inc.................... B 937 295-2120
  Fort Loramie *(G-8605)*

Long-Stanton Mfg Company.................... E 513 874-8020
  West Chester *(G-14725)*

Lunar Tool & Mold Inc............................. E 440 237-2141
  North Royalton *(G-11944)*

Meta Manufacturing Corporation............. E 513 793-6382
  Blue Ash *(G-1210)*

Pentaflex Inc.. C 937 325-5551
  Springfield *(G-13281)*

Phillips Mfg and Tower Co....................... D 419 347-1720
  Shelby *(G-13008)*

Precision Mtal Fabrication Inc................. D 937 235-9261
  Dayton *(G-7559)*

Precision Welding Corporation................ E 216 524-6110
  Cleveland *(G-4765)*

Prout Boiler Htg & Wldg Inc..................... E 330 744-0293
  Youngstown *(G-15699)*

Schmidt Machine Company..................... E 419 294-3814
  Upper Sandusky *(G-14292)*

Stan-Kell LLC.. E 440 998-1116
  Ashtabula *(G-550)*

Triangle Precision Industries................... D 937 299-6776
  Dayton *(G-7678)*

Valley Machine Tool Inc.......................... E 513 899-2737
  Morrow *(G-11456)*

Welders Supply Inc................................. E 216 267-4470
  Brookpark *(G-1443)*

Worthington Industries Inc...................... E 614 438-3028
  Columbus *(G-6906)*

WELDING SPLYS, EXC GASES: Wholesalers

Albright Welding Supply Co Inc............... E 330 264-2021
  Wooster *(G-15309)*

Delille Oxygen Company......................... E 614 444-1177
  Columbus *(G-5752)*

F & M Mafco Inc...................................... E 513 367-2151
  Harrison *(G-9105)*

F & M Mafco Inc...................................... C 513 367-2151
  Harrison *(G-9104)*

Lincoln Electric Company........................ E 216 481-8100
  Euclid *(G-8355)*

Lincoln Electric Intl Holdg Co................... D 216 481-8100
  Euclid *(G-8356)*

Welding Cutting Tls & ACC LLC.............. E 216 481-8100
  Cleveland *(G-5128)*

WELDMENTS

American Tank & Fabricating Co............. D 216 252-1500
  Cleveland *(G-3808)*

Loveman Steel Corporation..................... D 440 232-6200
  Bedford *(G-969)*

WINDOW & DOOR FRAMES

Midwest Curtainwalls Inc......................... D 216 641-7900
  Cleveland *(G-4580)*

WINDOW FRAMES & SASHES: Plastic

Champion Opco LLC............................... B 513 327-7338
  Cincinnati *(G-2345)*

WINDOW FRAMES, MOLDING & TRIM: Vinyl

Modern Builders Supply Inc.................... C 419 241-3961
  Toledo *(G-13926)*

Owens Corning Sales LLC...................... A 419 248-8000
  Toledo *(G-13952)*

Vinyl Design Corporation......................... E 419 283-4009
  Holland *(G-9313)*

WINDSHIELD WIPER SYSTEMS

Trico Products Corporation..................... C 248 371-1700
  Cleveland *(G-5038)*

WINE & DISTILLED ALCOHOLIC BEVERAGES WHOLESALERS

Arrow Wine Stores Inc............................ E 937 433-6778
  Dayton *(G-7180)*

Esber Beverage Company....................... E 330 456-4361
  Canton *(G-1750)*

M & A Distributing Co Inc........................ E 440 703-4580
  Solon *(G-13110)*

Premium Beverage Supply Ltd................ D 614 777-1007
  Hilliard *(G-9227)*

Southern Glzers Dstrs Ohio LLC............. D 440 542-7000
  Solon *(G-13147)*

WIRE & WIRE PRDTS

Gateway Con Forming Svcs Inc............... D 513 353-2000
  Miamitown *(G-11106)*

Panacea Products Corporation................ E 614 850-7000
  Columbus *(G-6497)*

R G Smith Company................................ D 330 456-3415
  Canton *(G-1839)*

Schweizer Dipple Inc............................... D 440 786-8090
  Cleveland *(G-4884)*

Stephens Pipe & Steel LLC..................... C 740 869-2257
  Mount Sterling *(G-11475)*

WIRE MATERIALS: Steel

Bayloff Stmped Pdts Knsman Inc............ D 330 876-4511
  Kinsman *(G-9644)*

WIRE: Nonferrous

Legrand North America LLC................... B 937 224-0639
  Dayton *(G-7451)*

Projects Unlimited Inc............................. C 937 918-2200
  Dayton *(G-7571)*

X-RAY EQPT & TUBES

Radix Wire Co... D 216 731-9191
  Solon *(G-13136)*

Schneider Electric Usa Inc...................... B 513 523-4171
  Oxford *(G-12217)*

Scott Fetzer Company............................. E 216 267-9000
  Cleveland *(G-4885)*

WOMEN'S & CHILDREN'S CLOTHING WHOLESALERS, NEC

Abercrombie & Fitch Trading Co.............. D 614 283-6500
  New Albany *(G-11551)*

For Women Like Me Inc.......................... E 407 848-7339
  Chagrin Falls *(G-1958)*

J Peterman Company LLC...................... E 888 647-2555
  Blue Ash *(G-1189)*

MII Brand Import LLC.............................. C 614 256-7267
  Reynoldsburg *(G-12670)*

Profill Holdings LLC................................ A 513 742-4000
  Cincinnati *(G-3247)*

West Chester Holdings LLC.................... C 513 705-2100
  Cincinnati *(G-3655)*

WOMEN'S & GIRLS' SPORTSWEAR WHOLESALERS

Barbs Graffiti Inc..................................... E 216 881-5550
  Cleveland *(G-3849)*

Gymnastics World Inc............................. E 440 526-2970
  Cleveland *(G-4343)*

TSC Apparel LLC.................................... D 800 289-5400
  Cincinnati *(G-3534)*

WOMEN'S CLOTHING STORES

Abercrombie & Fitch Trading Co.............. D 614 283-6500
  New Albany *(G-11551)*

For Women Like Me Inc.......................... E 407 848-7339
  Chagrin Falls *(G-1958)*

J Peterman Company LLC...................... E 888 647-2555
  Blue Ash *(G-1189)*

Jcherie LLC... E 216 453-1051
  Shaker Heights *(G-12979)*

WOOD FENCING WHOLESALERS

Df Supply Inc... E 330 650-9226
  Twinsburg *(G-14181)*

WOOD PRDTS: Mulch, Wood & Bark

Gayston Corporation................................ C 937 743-6050
  Miamisburg *(G-11057)*

H Hafner & Sons Inc................................ E 513 321-1895
  Cincinnati *(G-2786)*

Scotts Company LLC.............................. C 937 644-0011
  Marysville *(G-10508)*

WOOD TREATING: Structural Lumber & Timber

Flagship Trading Corporation.................. E
  Cleveland *(G-4263)*

WOODWORK & TRIM: Interior & Ornamental

L E Smith Company................................ D 419 636-4555
  Bryan *(G-1486)*

WORK EXPERIENCE CENTER

TAC Industries Inc................................... B 937 328-5200
  Springfield *(G-13299)*

X-RAY EQPT & TUBES

Metro Design Inc..................................... E 440 458-4200
  Elyria *(G-8274)*

Employee Codes: A=Over 500 employees, B=251-500
C=101-250, D=51-100, E=20-50, F=10-19, G=1-9

X-RAY EQPT REPAIR SVCS

Philips Med Systems Clvland In............. B 440 483-3000
 Cleveland *(G-4746)*

X-RAY EQPT REPAIR SVCS

Alpha Imaging LLC......................................D 440 953-3800
 Willoughby *(G-15185)*
Metro Design Inc...................................... E 440 458-4200
 Elyria *(G-8274)*

Siemens Med Solutions USA Inc............ B 937 859-5413
 Dayton *(G-7621)*